The

EUROPA WORLD OF LEARNING

2015

65th Edition

VOLUME II

NAMIBIA–ZIMBABWE

INDEX

Routledge
Taylor & Francis Group

LONDON AND NEW YORK

Sixty-fifth edition published 2014
by Routledge
2 Park Square, Milton Park, Abingdon, Oxfordshire, OX14 4RN, United Kingdom

and by Routledge
711 Third Avenue, New York, NY 10017

www.worldoflearning.com

Routledge is an imprint of the Taylor & Francis Group, an Informa business

First published 1947

Library of Congress Catalog Card Number 47-30172

ISBN: 978-1-85743-723-2 (The Set)
ISBN: 978-1-85743-725-6 (Vol. II)
ISSN: 0084-2117

Typeset in New Century Schoolbook
by Data Standards Limited, Frome, Somerset

Senior Editor: Anthony Gladman

Editorial Researchers: Denize Rodricks (*Editorial Research Team Leader*), Nimisha Chaurasia, Shikha Garg, Anindita Mondal, Robinson Raju, Minkushree Saikia

Editorial Assistant: Lydia de Cruz

Editorial Director: Paul Kelly

FSC
www.fsc.org
MIX
Paper from
responsible sources
FSC® C020872

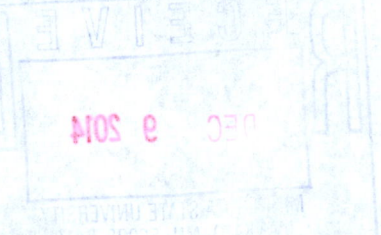

The

EUROPA WORLD
OF LEARNING

2015

FOREWORD

It gives us great pleasure to introduce the 2015 edition of THE EUROPA WORLD OF LEARNING. First published in 1947, it has since become established as an authoritative reference work on academic institutions all over the world.

THE EUROPA WORLD OF LEARNING is unique in offering information over the entire spectrum of academic activity. Our listings cover not only universities and colleges, but also research institutes, libraries and archives, museums and art galleries and learned societies. Further to this, regulatory and representative bodies are covered in a section which also has details of relevant ministries, accrediting bodies and funding organizations. Each chapter has an introductory survey outlining the country's higher education system.

Each year we invite entrants to review and update their entries. Entrants may do so by email to wol@routledge.co.uk or online at updates.worldoflearning.com. We are, as ever, grateful to those who help bring our information up to date with their prompt replies. Continuous research on the internet and in the world's press, as well as contact with official sources worldwide, supplements this method of revision.

In addition to the regular updating of our entries, this edition has expanded coverage of institutions in a number of areas. Special projects to update and expand our listings were undertaken in chapters covering South and Central America (Argentina, Belize, Bolivia, Brazil, Chile, Colombia, Costa Rica, Ecuador, El Salvador, French Guiana, Guatemala, Guyana, Honduras, Mexico, Nicaragua, Panama, Paraguay, Peru, Puerto Rico, Suriname, Uruguay, and Venezuela), and chapters covering Ireland, New Zealand, South Africa, and the United Kingdom.

This edition of THE EUROPA WORLD OF LEARNING features essays commissioned by its editorial board. For each edition the board chooses a theme pertinent to international higher education, and guides the commissioning of about five essays to address it. The board's remit is to approve essays that are lively, panoramic, and engaging; that argue a proposition rather than summarize an issue. The theme for this edition is academic freedom. The board also appoints guest editors to oversee each set of thematically linked essays and to write an accompanying introduction to the issue. For details of the editorial board members, and the guest editors and authors contributing to this edition, please see page 3.

In the sections on Universities and Colleges, our classification follows the practice of the country concerned. This in no way implies any official evaluation on our part. Readers who are interested in the matter of the equivalence of institutions, degrees or diplomas should correspond directly with the institutions concerned, or with the national or international bodies set up for this purpose. Further information on these can be found in the Regulatory and Representative Bodies section of each chapter under the subheading Accreditation.

An online version of THE EUROPA WORLD OF LEARNING offers regular updates of content and an unprecedented level of access to institutions of higher education and learning worldwide, and to the people who work within them. Please see page vi or visit www.worldoflearning.com for further details.

August 2014

CONTENTS

ABBREVIATIONS

AB	Aktiebolag, Aktiebolaget (stock company); Alberta	CO	Colorado	GA	Georgia
Abog.	Abogado (lawyer)	Co	Company; County	Gdns	Gardens
Acad.	Academician; Academy	COAH	Coahuila	Gen.	general
ACT	Australian Capital Territory	COL	Colima	GmbH	Gesellschaft mit beschränkter Haftung (limited liability company)
Admin.	Administration; Administrative	Col	Colonel		
AGS	Aguascalientes	Col.	Colonia (district)		
AIDS	acquired immunodeficiency syndrome	colln	collection	Gov.	Governor
		Comm.	Commission	Govt	Government
AK	Alaska	Commr	Commissioner	GPOB	Government Post Office Box
AL	Alabama	Conf.	Conference	GRO	Guerrero
Apdo	Apartado (post box)	Corp.	Corporation	GTO	Guanajuato
approx.	approximately	Corresp.	Correspondent; Corresponding		
AR	Arkansas	CP	Caixa postal, Case postale, Casella postale (post box)	HE	His (Her) Excellency; His Eminence
Arq.	Arquitecto; Arquiteto	Cr	Contador	HEI	Higher Education Institution
AS	Aksjeselskap (stock company)	CRC	Cooperative Research Centre	HGO	Hidalgo
AS CR	Academcy of Sciences of the Czech Republic	CT	Connecticut	HI	Hawaii
		Ctra	carretera (highway)	HIV	human immunodeficiency virus
Asscn	Association; Associate	Cttee	Committee	HM	His (Her) Majesty
Asst	Assistant	cu	cubic	HND	Higher National Diploma
Atty	Attorney			Hon.	Honorary; Honourable
AV ČR	Akademie věd České republiky (Academcy of Sciences of the Czech Republic)	DC	District of Colombia	HQ	Headquarters
		DE	Delaware	HRH	His (Her) Royal Highness
		Del.	Delegación (borough); Delegate; Delegation		
Av.	Avenida (avenue)			IA	Iowa
Avda	Avenida (avenue)	Dept	Department	ID	Idaho
Ave	Avenue	Deptl	Departmental	IL	Illinois
Avv.	Avvocato (Advocate)	devt	development	ILO	International Labour Organization
AZ	Arizona	DF	Distrito Federal		
		DGO	Durango	IN	Indiana
BA	Bachelor of Arts	Dipl.	Diploma	Inc.	Incorporated
BC	Baja California; British Columbia	Dir	Director	incl.	include; includes; including
		Dist.	District	Ind.	Independent
BCS	Baja California Sur	Div.	Division	Ing.	Ingénieur (Engineer)
Bd	Bulevard (boulevard)	Divs	Divisions	Instn	Institution
Bdul	Bulevardul (boulevard)	Doc.	Docent	Int.	International
Beng	Bachelor of Engineering	Dott.	Dottore; Dottoressa	Ir	Insinyur (Engineer)
BiH	Bosne i Hercegovine (Bosnia and Herzegovina)	Doz.	Dozent (lecturer)	IT	information technology
		Dr Hab.	Doktor Habilitowany (Assistant Professor)		
Bldg	Building			JAL	Jalisco
Blvd	Boulevard	Dr	Doctor	Jl	Jalan (street)
Blvr	Bulevar (boulevard)	Dr.	Drive	Jr	Junior
BP	Boîte postale (post box)	Dra	Doctora	Jr.	Jirón (street)
Br.	Branch	Drs	Doctorandus	JSC	joint Stock Company
Brig.	Brigadier	DVD	digital versatile disc	jt	joint
Bro.	Brother			jtly	jointly
Brs	Branches				
BSc	Bachelor of Science	E.	East, Eastern	Kft	korlátolt felelösségû társaság (limited liability company)
Bul.	Bulvar (boulevard)	e.g.	exempli gratia		
bulv.	bulvāris (boulevard)	Edif.	Edificio (building)	km	kilometre; kilometres
		edn	edition	korp.	korpus (building)
		Eng.	Engineer	KS	Kansas
c.	circa (approximately)	EngD	Doctor of Engineering	küç.	küçasi (street)
c/o	care of	esp.	especially	kv.	kvartal (apartment block); kvartira (apartment)
CA	California	Esq.	Esquina (corner)		
CAM	Campeche	Est.	Established	KY	Kentucky
Capt.	Captain	etc.	et cetera		
CAR	Central African Republic	EU	European Union	LA	Louisiana
Ccl	Council	eV	Eingetragener Verein (non-profit society/association)	Lic.	Licenciado
Cdra	cuadra (block)			Licda	Licenciada
CD-ROM	compact disc read-only memory	Exec.	Executive	Lt	Lieutenant
CEA	Commissariat à l'Energie Atomique			Ltd.	Limited
CEO	Chief Executive Officer	f.	founded	m	metre; metres
Chair.	Chairman; Chairperson; Chairwoman	f.t.e.	Full-time equivalent	m.	million
		FAO	Food and Agriculture Organization	MA	Massachusetts; Master of Arts
CHIH	Chihuahua			Mag.	Magister (Masters degree)
CHIS	Chiapas	Fed.	Federal; Federation	Man.	Manager; Managing
Cmdr	Commander	FL	Florida	MB	Manitoba
CNR	Consiglio Nazionale delle Ricerche	Fl.	Floor	MBA	Master of Business Administration
		fmr	former		
cnr	corner	fmrly	formerly	MD	Maryland
CNRS	Centre National de la Recherche Scientifique	Fr	Father	ME	Maine
		ft	feet		

viii

Mem.	Member
Mems	Members
MEng	Master of Engineering
MEX	Mexico
Mgr	Monseigneur; Monsignor
MI	Michigan
MICH	Michoacan
Min.	Minister; Ministry
misc.	miscellaneous
mm	millimetre; millimetres
MN	Minnesota
MO	Missouri
MOR	Morelos
MRC	Medical Research Council
MS	Mississippi
MSc	Master of Science
MSS	Manuscripts
MT	Montana
N	North, Northern
N°	Número (number)
nám.	náměstí (square)
NASA	National Aeronautics and Space Administration
Nat.	National
NAY	Nayarit
NB	New Brunswick
NC	North Carolina
ND	North Dakota
NE	Nebraska; Northeast; Northeastern
NGO	Non-Governmental Organization
NH	New Hampshire
NJ	New Jersey
NL	Newfoundland and Labrador; Nuevo Leon
NM	New Mexico
No	Número (number)
NS	Nova Scotia
NSW	New South Wales
NT	Northern Territory; Northwest Territories
NU	Nunavut Territory
NV	Nevada
NW	Northwest, Northwestern
NY	New York
NZ	New Zealand
OAX	Oaxaca
obl.	oblast
Of.	Oficina
OH	Ohio
OK	Oklahoma
ON	Ontario
OR	Oregon
Org.	Organization
PA	Pennsylvania

PAN	Polska Akademia Nauk (Polish Academy of Sciences)
PE	Prince Edward Island
PEN	Poets, Playwrights, Essayists, Editors and Novelists (Club)
PhD	Doctor of Philosophy
pl.	place, platz, ploshchad (square)
PMB	private Mail Bag
POB	Post Office Box
pr.	prospekt (avenue)
Pres.	President
Prin.	Principal
Prof.	Professor
Profa	Professora
Psje	Pasaje (passage)
Publ.	publication
Publs	publications
PUE	Puebla
Q ROO	Quintana Roo
QC	Québec
QLD	Queensland
QRO	Queretaro
q.v.	quod vide (to which refer)
Rd	Road
Rep.	Representative
retd	retired
Rev.	Reverend
RI	Rhode Island
RP	Révérend Père
Rr.	Rruga
Rt Hon.	Right Honourable
Rt Rev.	Right Reverend
ry	rekisteröity yhdistys (registered association)
S	South, Southern
s/n	sin número (without number)
SA	South Africa(n); South Australia
SAR	Special Administrative Region
SC	South Carolina
SD	South Dakota
SDI	Selective Dissemination of Information
SE	Southeast, Southeastern
Sec.	Secretary
SIN	Sinaloa
Sis.	Sister
SK	Saskatchewan
SLP	San Luis Potosi
Soc.	Society
SON	Sonora
spec.	special
Sq.	Square
Sr	Senior
St	Saint, Sint; Street
Sta	Santa

Ste	Sainte
str.	stradă, strada, Strasse (street)
SW	Southwest; Southwestern
TAB	Tabasco
TAMPS	Tamaulipas
TAS	Tasmania
tel.	telephone
TLAX	Tlaxcala
TN	Tennessee
Treas.	Treasurer
TX	Texas
u.	utca (street)
UK	United Kingdom
ul.	ulica, ulitsa (street)
UN	United Nations
UNESCO	United Nations Educational, Scientific and Cultural Organization
Univ.	Universidad, Universidade, Università, Universität, Université, Universitas, Universitat, Universitatea, Universiteit, Universitet, Universiteti, Universiti, University, Univerza, Univerzita, Univerzitet, Uniwersytet (University)
Urb.	Urbanización (neighbourhood)
USA	United States of America
UT	Utah
VA	Virginia
VER	Veracruz
VIC	Victoria
Vols	Volumes
VT	Vermont
vul.	vulitsa, vulytsa (street)
W	West, Western
WA	Washington (State); Western Australia
WI	Wisconsin
WV	West Virginia
WY	Wyoming
YT	Yukon Territory
YUC	Yucatan
ZAC	Zacatecas
ZRC SAZU	Znanstvenoraziskovalni center Slovenske akademije znanosti in umetnosti (Research Centre of the Slovenian Academy of Sciences and Arts)

INTERNATIONAL TELEPHONE CODES

To make international calls to telephone and fax numbers listed in *The Europa World of Learning*, dial the international access code of the country from which you are calling, followed by the appropriate country code for the organization you wish to call (listed below), followed by the area code (if applicable) and telephone or fax number listed in the entry.

	Country code	+ or − GMT*
Afghanistan	93	+4½
Åland Islands	358	+2
Albania	355	+1
Algeria	213	+1
Andorra	376	+1
Angola	244	+1
Antigua and Barbuda	1 268	−4
Argentina	54	−3
Armenia	374	+4
Aruba	297	−4
Australia	61	+8 to +10
Austria	43	+1
Azerbaijan	994	+5
Bahamas	1 242	−5
Bahrain	973	+3
Bangladesh	880	+6
Barbados	1 246	−4
Belarus	375	+2
Belgium	32	+1
Belize	501	−6
Benin	229	+1
Bermuda	1 441	−4
Bhutan	975	+6
Bolivia	591	−4
Bonaire	599	−4
Bosnia and Herzegovina	387	+1
Botswana	267	+2
Brazil	55	−3 to −4
Brunei	673	+8
Bulgaria	359	+2
Burkina Faso	226	0
Burundi	257	+2
Cambodia	855	+7
Cameroon	237	+1
Canada	1	−3 to −8
Cabo Verde	238	−1
Cayman Islands	1 345	−5
Central African Republic	236	+1
Chad	235	+1
Chile	56	−4
China, People's Republic	86	+8
Christmas Island	61	+7
Cocos (Keeling) Islands	61	+6½
Colombia	57	−5
Comoros	269	+3
Congo, Democratic Republic	243	+1
Congo, Republic	242	+1
Cook Islands	682	−10
Costa Rica	506	−6
Côte d'Ivoire	225	0
Croatia	385	+1
Cuba	53	−5
Curaçao	599	−4
Cyprus	357	+2
Czech Republic	420	+1
Denmark	45	+1

	Country code	+ or − GMT*
Djibouti	253	+3
Dominica	1 767	−4
Dominican Republic	1 809	−4
Ecuador	593	−5
Egypt	20	+2
El Salvador	503	−6
Equatorial Guinea	240	+1
Eritrea	291	+3
Estonia	372	+2
Ethiopia	251	+3
Faroe Islands	298	0
Fiji	679	+12
Finland	358	+2
France	33	+1
French Guiana	594	−3
French Polynesia	689	−9 to −10
Gabon	241	+1
Gambia	220	0
Georgia	995	+4
Germany	49	+1
Ghana	233	0
Gibraltar	350	+1
Greece	30	+2
Greenland	299	−1 to −4
Grenada	1 473	−4
Guadeloupe	590	−4
Guam	1 671	+10
Guatemala	502	−6
Guernsey	44	0
Guinea	224	0
Guinea-Bissau	245	0
Guyana	592	−4
Haiti	509	−5
Honduras	504	−6
Hong Kong	852	+8
Hungary	36	+1
Iceland	354	0
India	91	+5½
Indonesia	62	+7 to +9
Iran	98	+3½
Iraq	964	+3
Ireland	353	0
Isle of Man	44	0
Israel	972	+2
Italy	39	+1
Jamaica	1 876	−5
Japan	81	+9
Jersey	44	0
Jordan	962	+2
Kazakhstan	7	+6
Kenya	254	+3
Kiribati	686	+12 to +13
Korea, Democratic People's Republic (North Korea)	850	+9
Korea, Republic (South Korea)	82	+9
Kosovo	381†	+3

	Country code	+ or – GMT*
Kuwait	965	+3
Kyrgyzstan	996	+5
Laos	856	+7
Latvia	371	+2
Lebanon	961	+2
Lesotho	266	+2
Liberia	231	0
Libya	218	+1
Liechtenstein	423	+1
Lithuania	370	+2
Luxembourg	352	+1
Macao	853	+8
Macedonia, former Yugoslav republic	389	+1
Madagascar	261	+3
Malawi	265	+2
Malaysia	60	+8
Maldives	960	+5
Mali	223	0
Malta	356	+1
Marshall Islands	692	+12
Martinique	596	−4
Mauritania	222	0
Mauritius	230	+4
Mayotte	262	+3
Mexico	52	−6 to −7
Micronesia, Federated States	691	+10 to +11
Moldova	373	+2
Monaco	377	+1
Mongolia	976	+7 to +9
Montenegro	382	+1
Morocco	212	0
Mozambique	258	+2
Myanmar	95	+6½
Namibia	264	+2
Nauru	674	+12
Nepal	977	+5¾
Netherlands	31	+1
New Caledonia	687	+11
New Zealand	64	+12
Nicaragua	505	−6
Niger	227	+1
Nigeria	234	+1
Norway	47	+1
Oman	968	+4
Pakistan	92	+5
Palau	680	+9
Palestinian Territories	970 or 972	+2
Panama	507	−5
Papua New Guinea	675	+10
Paraguay	595	−4
Peru	51	−5
Philippines	63	+8
Poland	48	+1
Portugal	351	0
Puerto Rico	1 787	−4
Qatar	974	+3
Réunion	262	+4
Romania	40	+2
Russia	7	+3 to +12
Rwanda	250	+2
Saba	599	−4
Saint Christopher and Nevis	1 869	−4
Saint Lucia	1 758	−4
Saint Vincent and the Grenadines	1 784	−4
Samoa	685	+13

	Country code	+ or – GMT*
San Marino	378	+1
São Tomé and Príncipe	239	0
Saudi Arabia	966	+3
Senegal	221	0
Serbia	381	+1
Seychelles	248	+4
Sierra Leone	232	0
Singapore	65	+8
Sint Eustatius	1721	−4
Sint Maarten	1721	−4
Slovakia	421	+1
Slovenia	386	+1
Solomon Islands	677	+11
Somalia	252	+3
South Africa	27	+2
South Sudan	211	+2
Spain	34	+1
Sri Lanka	94	+5½
Sudan	249	+2
Suriname	597	−3
Swaziland	268	+2
Sweden	46	+1
Switzerland	41	+1
Syria	963	+2
Taiwan	886	+8
Tajikistan	992	+5
Tanzania	255	+3
Thailand	66	+7
Timor-Leste	670	+9
Togo	228	0
Tonga	676	+13
Trinidad and Tobago	1 868	−4
Tunisia	216	+1
Turkey	90	+2
'Turkish Republic of Northern Cyprus' 90	392	+2
Turkmenistan	993	+5
Turks and Caicos Islands	1 649	−5
Tuvalu	688	+12
Uganda	256	+3
Ukraine	380	+2
United Arab Emirates	971	+4
United Kingdom	44	0
United States of America	1	−5 to −10
United States Virgin Islands	1 340	−4
Uruguay	598	−3
Uzbekistan	998	+5
Vanuatu	678	+11
Vatican City	39	+1
Venezuela	58	−4½
Viet Nam	84	+7
Yemen	967	+3
Zambia	260	+2
Zimbabwe	263	+2

* The times listed compare the standard (winter) times in the various countries. Some countries adopt Summer (Daylight Saving) Time—i.e. +1 hour—for part of the year.

† Mobile telephone numbers for Kosovo use either the country code for Monaco (377) or the country code for Slovenia (386).

Note: Telephone and fax numbers using the Inmarsat ocean region code 870 are listed in full. No country or area code is required, but it is necessary to precede the number with the international access code of the country from which the call is made.

PART FOUR
Namibia–Zimbabwe

NAMIBIA

The Higher Education System

From 1925 Namibia was under South African control, first as a League of Nations protectorate and then as a de facto province. Independence was finally achieved in 1990. The University of Namibia was founded in 1992, based on the former Windhoek Academy of Education, following a report by a presidential commission into the state of higher education in Namibia. The International University of Management (IUM—formerly the Institute of Higher Education, founded in 1994) was accorded university status in 2002. Higher education is also provided by the Polytechnic of Namibia (founded in 1980), six vocational colleges and four teacher-training colleges. The Ministry of Basic Education, Sport and Culture and the Ministry of Higher Education, Training and Employment Creation were combined in 2005 to form the Ministry of Education, which is responsible for higher education and vocational training. In 2007/08 there were 19,970 students enrolled in tertiary education.

Since 1996 the Namibia Qualifications Authority (NQA) is responsible for quality assurance, accreditation, evaluation and standards setting procedures. The National Council of Higher Education (NCHE), established by the Higher Education Act No. 26/2003, advises the Minister of Education on coordination, accreditation and quality assurance in higher education; however, the Council's advice is non-binding, with the Minister retaining the right to ignore any suggestions. Proposed legislative amendments put forward in late 2010 would, if approved, clarify the role of the council and enable it to build capacity. Some observers noted that the NCHE would eventually need to become a fully independent body in order to strengthen its authority and effectiveness.

Undergraduate admission is based upon results in the International General Certificate of Secondary Education examinations; however, Higher International General Certificate of Secondary Education passes are given more weight when applicants are being evaluated. Non-degree university-level qualifications include two- or three-year Certificate courses and three- or four-year Diploma courses. Undergraduate Bachelors degree programmes last four years and are offered in most subject fields. The two foremost postgraduate degrees offered by the University of Namibia are the Masters and the Doctorate; the former is a one-year (full-time) or three-year (part-time) course, and the latter requires a minimum of two years of study following the Masters (or, in the case of administration and nursing science, a minimum of four years' part-time study). A joint cooperation agreement signed between the University of Namibia and the IUM in October 2010 aimed to enhance and expand collaboration between the two institutions, particularly within the fields of research, teaching, community service, and the exchange of students, staff and information materials.

Post-secondary technical and vocational education is offered by the Polytechnic of Namibia, and qualifications include Certificate (one year), Diploma (three years) and Bachelor of Technology. There are also a number of agricultural colleges, which offer Certificate and Diploma courses. The Namibia Training Authority was established by the Vocational Education and Training Act of 2008 to regulate provision, provide funding, appoint quality system auditors, and, in collaboration with the NQA, to develop occupational standards.

The Ministry of Education has developed the Education and Training Sector Improvement Programme (ETSIP), a 15-year strategic plan for 2006–20, the aim of which is to reform comprehensively the education and training sectors. The total cost of the first phase of the project (2006–11) was estimated at N $2,400m., which was to be jointly financed by the Namibian Government and a consortium of international development partners.

Regulatory Bodies

GOVERNMENT

Ministry of Education: Government Office Park, Luther St, Private Bag 13186, Windhoek; tel. (61) 2933358; e-mail info@moe.gov.na; internet www.moe.gov.na; Minister Hon. Dr DAVID NAMWANDI.

Ministry of Youth, National Service, Sport and Culture: NDC Bldg, Goethe St, Private Bag 13391, Windhoek; tel. (61) 2706111; Minister IMMANUEL NGATJIZEKO.

Learned Societies

GENERAL

UNESCO Office Windhoek: POB 24519, Windhoek; 38–44 Stein St, Klein, Windhoek; tel. (61) 2917220; e-mail windhoek@unesco.org; designated Cluster Office for Angola, Lesotho, Namibia, S Africa and Swaziland; Dir Prof. ALAPHIA WRIGHT.

ARCHITECTURE AND TOWN PLANNING

Namibia Institute of Architects: Love St, POB 1478, Windhoek; tel. (61) 231559; e-mail nia@mweb.com.na; f. 1952; 98 mems; Pres. ANDRE CHRISTENSEN.

LANGUAGE AND LITERATURE

British Council: 116 Robert Mugabe Ave, Private Bag 13392, Windhoek; tel. (61) 274800; e-mail ssa.enquiries@britishcouncil.org; internet www.britishcouncil.org/namibia; the office in Pretoria, South Africa, is responsible for all British Council work in Namibia (see chapter on South Africa); Officer in Charge PATIENCE MAHLALELA.

Goethe-Zentrum/Namibisch-Deutsche Stiftung für Kulturelle Zusammenarbeit (Goethe-Centre/Namibian-German Institute for Cultural Cooperation): POB 1208, 1–5 Fidel Castro St, Windhoek; tel. (61) 225700; e-mail reception@nads.org.na; internet www.goethe.de/ins/na/win/deindex.htm; f. 1988; affiliated to Goethe-Institut (see chapter on Germany); promotes use of the German language in Namibia and cultural exchange between Namibia and Germany; Dir SABINE AQUILINI.

Research Institutes

NATURAL SCIENCES

Biological Sciences

Gobabeb Training and Research Centre: POB 953, Walvis Bay; e-mail gobabeb@gobabeb.org; internet www.gobabeb.org; f. 1963; research in Namib Desert and semi-arid Namibia, emphasizing basic and applied research, conservation biology, community applications, training and environmental education; library of 18,700 off-print colln, 1,600 bibliographic entries; Dir Dr GILLIAN MAGGS-KOLLING; Librarian SYLKE LUBBERT.

National Botanical Research Institute: Private Bag 13184, 8 Orban St, Windhoek; tel. (61) 2029111; e-mail info@nbri.org.na; internet www.nbri.org.na; f. 1953; herbarium colln of 74,000 plant specimens; gene bank colln of 2,500 seed accessions; botanical reference library; incorporates National Botanic Garden; library of 3,053 books, 320 periodicals; Head BEN STROBACH.

Libraries and Archives

Swakopmund

Sam Cohen Library: POB 361, Swakopmund; tel. (64) 402695; e-mail office@swakopmund-museum.de; internet www.swakopmund-museum.de; f. 1977; attached to Museum Swakopmund; 10,000 vols on SW Africa and Africana, 20,000 historical pics, old Namibian maps; Chair. Prof. E. MERCKER; publs *Der Wahrheit eine Gasse, Pre-colonial times in South West Africa, Swakopmund— eine kleine Chronik*.

Windhoek

Namibian Agriculture and Water Information Centre: c/o Ministry of Agriculture,

Water and Forestry, Govt Park Office, Private Bag 13184, Windhoek 9000; tel. (61) 2087111; e-mail info@nbri.org.na; internet www.mawf.gov.na; f. 1966; 30,555 books, 600 periodical titles; 284 theses, 69 video cassettes, 4,200 pamphlets, 1,960 govt reports, 3,065 audiovisual items; depository for FAO publs; Librarian (vacant).

National Library of Namibia: 1–7 Eugene Marais St, Private Bag 13349, Windhoek; tel. (61) 2935300; e-mail natlib@mec.gov.na; internet www.nln.gov.na; f. 1994; legal deposit and general reference library; deposit library for UN, WTO and World Bank publications; Head JOHAN LOUBSER; Chief Librarian CHARLES MLAMBO; publ. *National Bibliography of Namibia* (every 3 years).

Museums and Art Galleries

Swakopmund

Museum Swakopmund: POB 361, Strand St, Swakopmund; tel. (64) 402046; e-mail museum@swakopmund-museum.de; internet www.swakopmund-museum.de; f. 1951; natural history, mineralogy, marine life, history, archaeology, ethnology, technology; Chair. Prof. E. FÖRTSCH.

Windhoek

National Museum of Namibia: POB 1203, Windhoek; tel. (61) 276822; e-mail willa@iway.na; f. 1907; natural history, history, anthropology, archaeology, education;

library of 6,000 vols, 600 journal titles; publ. *Cimbebasia*.

Universities

INTERNATIONAL UNIVERSITY OF MANAGEMENT

21–31 Hercules St, POB 14005, Bachbrecht, Windhoek

Telephone: (61) 4336000
E-mail: ium@ium.edu.na
Internet: www.ium.edu.na

Founded 2002
Private control
Academic year: January to December

Faculties of humanities, HIV, AIDS and sustainable development; information technology and systems management; small business and entrepreneurship development; strategic management and business administration; tourism, travel, hospitality and events management

Chancellor: Dr BISHOP K. DUMENI
Vice-Chancellor: V. W. NAMWANDI
Deputy Vice-Chancellor: Prof. EARLE TAYLOR
Pro-Vice-Chancellor for Academic Affairs and Research: Prof. FRED OPALI
Pro-Vice-Chancellor for Admin. and Management: USKO SHIVUTE
Number of students: 6,500

UNIVERSITY OF NAMIBIA

Private Bag 13301, 340 Mandume Ndemufayo Ave, Pioneerspark, Windhoek

Telephone: (61) 2063111
E-mail: registrar@unam.na
Internet: www.unam.na

Founded 1992 upon the dissolution of the Academy, Windhoek
State control
Language of instruction: English
Academic year: January to November

Chancellor: Dr HIFIKEPUNYE POHAMBA
Vice-Chancellor: Prof. LAZARUS HANGULA
Pro-Vice-Chancellor for Academic Affairs and Research: Prof. OSMUND MWANDEMELE
Pro-Vice-Chancellor for Admin. and Finance: Dr BONIFACE MUTUMBA
Registrar: ALOIS FLEDERSBACHER
Librarian: ELLEN NDESHI NAMHILA

Library of 132,334 vols, 40,000 UNIN books and documents, 498 periodicals
Number of teachers: 343
Number of students: 13,000 (incl. distance learning)

DEANS

Faculty of Agriculture and Natural Resources: Dr M. B. SCHNEIDER
Faculty of Economics and Management Science: (vacant)
Faculty of Education: Dr C. VILLET
Faculty of Humanities and Social Science: Prof. KINGO JOTHAM MCHOMBU
Faculty of Law: FRITZ NGHIISHILILWA (acting)
Faculty of Medical and Health Sciences: Prof. P. NYARANGO
Faculty of Science: Prof. E. M. R. KIREMIRE

NAURU

The Higher Education System

During 1947–68 Nauru was a UN Trusteeship, administered by Australia on behalf of Australia, New Zealand and the United Kingdom. Independence was declared in 1968. There is a branch campus of the University of the South Pacific on the island but most Nauruans receive tertiary-level education overseas.

The Nauru Vocational Training Centre (NVTC) was the major technical and vocational education training (TVET) provider on the island before its partial destruction by fire in 2002. The NVTC no longer operates. The focus of formal vocational and technical training has shifted to the TVET training facility at the secondary school. In its Education and Training Strategic Plan for 2008–13 (Footpath II) the government made one of its priorities the putting in place of a functioning TVET system as a means of encouraging students to continue in the education system. Absenteeism from secondary school is one of the country's main problems.

Australia's annual performance report on Nauru for 2007–08 stated that a great deal of external support was still required. In February 2012 the Australian and New Zealand Governments were to launch a joint programme intended to develop further Nauru's education sector. Under the arrangement, Australia and New Zealand were to provide funding and undertake annual joint planning exercises, which it was hoped would help to enhance the efficiency and effectiveness of the island's education services.

Regulatory Body

GOVERNMENT

Ministry of Education: Yaren; tel. 444-3130; e-mail minister.education@naurugov.nr; Minister Hon. CHARMAINE SCOTTY.

Museums and Art Galleries

Aiwo

Arts and Crafts Centre: Aiwo, Nauru; tel. 444-3292; f. 1993; baskets, stone tools, fishing nets, a pandanus grater, *ingurig* (grass skirts made from hibiscus), paintings, photographs; spec. collns shells, written materials; organizes craft classes; access by arrangement with Ministry of Internal Affairs.

Nauru Phosphate Corporation Museum: Aiwo, Nauru; tel. 444-3382; f. 1995 by Nauru Phosphate foundation; photographs and items from 20th century, particularly the Second World War incl. Japanese weapons and ammunition, colonial-era cannons, Japanese pottery; access by arrangement with Ministry of Internal Affairs; reported to be closed pending settlement of island-wide land disputes.

University

UNIVERSITY OF THE SOUTH PACIFIC, NAURU CAMPUS

PMB, Nauru Post Office, Aiwo, Nauru 00674
Telephone: 444-3774
E-mail: lauti_a@usp.ac.fj
Internet: www.usp.ac.fj/index.php?id=usp_nauru_home
Founded 1987

Areas of study: accounting, management, education, early childhood education, English and library and informational studies; regional univ. serving 12 mem. countries: Cook Islands, Fiji Islands, Kiribati, Marshall Islands, Nauru, Niue, Samoa, Solomon Islands, Tokelau, Tonga, Tuvalu and Vanuatu

Pres. and Vice-Chancellor: Prof. RAJESH CHANDRA
Dir of Campus: ALAMANDA LAUTI
Library Officer: DALYS DANNANG

Library: periodicals, video cassettes and reference books; all documents in English

Publications: *Directions: Journal of Educational Studies*, *Journal of Pacific Studies*, *The South Pacific Journal of Natural and Applied Sciences* (online)

The Higher Education System

There are six state universities in Nepal, all of which are autonomous, and the oldest of which is Tribhuvan University (founded in 1959). University-level programmes are also offered by the B. P. Koirala Institute of Health Sciences and the National Academy of Medical Sciences. In 2010 there were 376,869 students enrolled in tertiary education. While the Ministry of Education administers the education system at the primary and secondary levels, Tribhuvan University is responsible for developing curriculums at college and Bachelors degree level. In 2012/13 there were 373,846 students enrolled in the university and its affiliated colleges.

Plans were mooted in the late 2000s for the creation of an open university, which would require parliamentary approval of the Higher Education Bill. This legislation was drafted in 2010 but is still awaiting approval. Assuming enactment of the necessary legislation, a limited number of courses—in distance education, information technology and rural information management—was initially to be offered by the open university, with a significant expansion envisaged subsequently. In 2012 the Ministry of Education, Government of Nepal, Non-Resident Nepali Association, Canada Foundation for Nepal, and Athabasca University Canada launched a joint appeal for all interested parties to join them with a view to launching the open university in 2015.

Admission to higher education is on the basis of successful completion of the School Leaving Certificate or the Higher Secondary Certificate. Students with the Higher Secondary Certificate may directly enter Bachelors degree courses (although, owing to the limited number of places and the high number of applicants, some students may also be required to pass an entrance examination in their chosen discipline), whereas students with the School Leaving Certificate must obtain the Proficiency Certificate, a university-level course lasting two years, which is regarded as the first cycle of university education. The second cycle of university-level education is the Bachelors degree, which lasts four years in most disciplines but slightly longer (five-and-a-half years) in disciplines such as medicine, veterinary medicine and animal husbandry. Following the Bachelors degree students may undertake a Postgraduate Diploma, which lasts for one year and enables students to submit a dissertation or complete a further year of study prior to enrolling in a Masters degree course. The latter is a two-year course, and requires the submission of a dissertation in all subjects. Subsequent to a Masters degree, a Master of Philosophy course, lasting between 18 months and three years, is offered in commerce, education, humanities and science disciplines. The highest university-level degree is the Doctor of Philosophy, awarded after a minimum of a further two years of study following the Masters.

Recently the University Grants Commission launched the Quality Assurance and Accreditation (QAA) programme as part of the higher education reform. A Quality Assurance and Accreditation Committee has been established to prepare the way for a national system of quality assurance and accreditation under a National Board of QAA that was expected to be fully operational by 2014.

The Council for Technical Education and Vocational Training, chaired by the Minister of Education, is responsible for the provision of technical and vocational education, which is offered at various secondary and post-secondary levels.

Regulatory and Representative Bodies

GOVERNMENT

Ministry for Science, Technology and Environment: Singha Durbar, Kathmandu; tel. (1) 4211641; e-mail info@moste.gov.np; internet www.moste.gov.np; Minister UMA KANT JHA.

Ministry of Culture, Tourism and Civil Aviation: Singha Durbar, Kathmandu; tel. (1) 4211847; e-mail info@tourism.gov.np; internet www.tourism.gov.np; Minister RAM KUMAR SHRESTHA.

Ministry of Education: Singhadurbar, Kathmandu; tel. (1) 4200340; e-mail infomoe@moe.gov.np; internet www.moe.gov.np; Minister MADHAV PRASAD PAUDEL.

FUNDING

University Grants Commission: Sanothimi, Bhaktapur, POB 10796, Kathmandu; tel. (1) 6638548; e-mail ugc@ugcnepal.edu.np; internet www.ugcnepal.edu.np; f. 1994; advises govt of Nepal on establishment of new universities; formulates policy for allocation of govt grants to univs and higher education instns; maintains standard and quality of higher education; 11 mems; Chair. Prof. Dr GANESH MAN GURUNG.

Learned Societies

GENERAL

Nepal Academy/Nepal Pragya Pratisthan: GPOB 23058, Kamaladi, Kathmandu; tel. (1) 4221283; e-mail office@nepalacademy.org.np; internet www.nepalacademy.org.np; f. 1957 as Nepal Sahitya Kala Academy, present name 2007; promotes language, literature, culture, philosophy, social science of Nepal; awards prizes annually; 178 mems; library of 10,562 vols, 4,697 periodicals; Chancellor BAIRAGI KAINLA; Vice-Chancellor GANGA PRASAD UPRETY; publs *Angan* (1 a year, in Maithili), *Journal of Nepalese Literature, Art and Culture* (2 a year), *Kavita* (on Nepalese poetry, 4 a year), *Pragyā* (2 a year), *Samakalin Sahitya* (4 a year), *Sayapatri* (2 a year), *Thayabhu* (1 a year, in Newari).

Nepal Academy of Science and Technology: GPOB 3323, Khumaltar, Lalitpur; tel. (1) 5547715; e-mail info@nast.org.np; internet www.nast.org.np; f. 1982 as Royal Nepal Academy of Science and Technology; preserves and furthers modernization of indigenous technologies; promotes research; facilitates technology transfer; 157 mems; library of 13,000 vols, 150 periodicals; Chancellor Rt Hon. PRIME MIN. OF NEPAL; Vice-Chancellor Prof. Dr SURENDRA RAJ KAFLE; Sec. Prof. Dr PRAKASH CHANDRA ADHIKARI; publs *Nepal Journal of Science and Technology* (1 a year), *Vigyan Lekhmala* (1 a year).

UNESCO Office Kathmandu: POB 14391, Sanepa-2, Lalitpur; Ring Rd, Bansbari, Kathmandu; tel. (1) 5554396; e-mail kathmandu@unesco.org; internet www.unesco.org/kathmandu; f. 1998; promotes peace; fosters sustainable devt and intercultural dialogue in Nepal through education, science, culture, communication, information; library of 4,500 vols, periodicals, reports, audiovisual materials; Head of Office and UNESCO Rep. AXEL PLATHE.

FINE AND PERFORMING ARTS

Indigenous Film Archive: POB 10487, Anamnagar, Kathmandu; tel. (1) 4102577; e-mail ifanepal@yahoo.com; internet ifanepal.org.np; f. 2006; provides a forum for film makers, film journalists, artists, actors, sociologists, activists; promotes and screens nat. and int. films, film related information on indigenous issues and topics; Chair. NABIN CHANDRA LIMBU; Vice-Chair. DIPENDRA LAMA.

LANGUAGE AND LITERATURE

Alliance Française de Katmandou (Alliance française in Kathmandu): Tripureshwor, Ganeshman Singh Path, POB 452 Kathmandu; tel. (1) 4241163; internet www.alliancefrancaise.org.np; offers courses and exams in French language and culture and promotes cultural exchange with France; Dir ANNE-LISE HEYNEN; Deputy Dir PRABIN BIKRAM RANA; Course Dir BENOÎT GILLET.

British Council: POB 640, Lainchaur, Kathmandu; tel. (1) 4410798; e-mail general.enquiry@britishcouncil.org.np; internet www.britishcouncil.org/nepal; f. 1959; teaching centre; offers courses and exams in

English language and British culture and promotes cultural exchange with the UK; 6,774 mems; library of 15,036 vols, 30 periodicals, 54 video cassettes, 219 audio items, DVDs and CD-ROMs; Dir ROBERT MONRO.

RELIGION, SOCIOLOGY AND ANTHROPOLOGY

Nepal Institute of Peace: Kathmandu; tel. (1) 5526680; e-mail nageshbadu@gmail.com; internet www.idps-nepal.org; f. 2002; Pres. SHIVA KUMAR DHUNGANA.

TECHNOLOGY

Biotechnology Society of Nepal: POB 8973, Kathmandu; Second Fl., 16 Gurju Marg, Dillibazar Height, Ward 32, Kathmandu; e-mail info@bsn.org.np; internet www.bsn.org.np; Pres. SAROJ RAJ GHIMIRE; Vice-Pres. RAVI BHANDARI.

Research Institutes

GENERAL

International Centre for Integrated Mountain Development (ICIMOD): GPOB 3226, Khumaltar, Kathmandu, Lalitpur; tel. (1) 5003222; e-mail info@icimod.org; internet www.icimod.org; f. 1983; regional intergovernmental learning and knowledge sharing centre serving the 8 regional mem. countries of the Hindu Kush Himalayan (HKH) region—Afghanistan, Bangladesh, Bhutan, China, India, Myanmar, Nepal and Pakistan; builds awareness and takes action to preserve the unique role that the HKH mountain system plays; Dir-Gen. DAVID JAMES MOLDEN; Deputy Dir-Gen. MADHAV KARKI.

Nepal Development Research Institute: GPOB 8975, EPC 2201, Kathmandu; Shree Durbar Tole, Pulchowk, Lalitpur; tel. (1) 5554975; e-mail info@ndri.org.np; internet www.ndri.org.np; f. 2004; provides analytical inputs for policy making on contemporary issues through research and dissemination of findings; research areas incl. policy analysis on nat. economy, infrastructure policy and planning, poverty reduction and sustainable livelihoods, climate change, agriculture and natural resources; Pres. Dr BASU DEV PANDEY; Exec. Dir and Vice-Pres. Dr DIVAS BAHADUR BASNYAT.

Nepal Institute of Development Studies: House 23, Madhur Marg, Chun Devi, Maharajgunj POB 7647, Kathmandu; tel. (1) 4721277; e-mail nids@mail.com.np; internet www.nids.org.np; f. 1998; Exec. Dir Dr GANESH GURUNG.

AGRICULTURE, FISHERIES AND VETERINARY SCIENCE

Nepal Agricultural Research Council: POB 5459, Kathmandu; Singhadurbar Pl., Kathmandu; tel. (1) 4256837; e-mail ednarc@ntc.net.np; internet narc.gov.np; f. 1991; Exec. Dir Dr DIL BAHADUR GURUNG; publ. *Nepal Agriculture Research Journal* (1 a year).

ECONOMICS, LAW AND POLITICS

Institute for Policy Research and Development: GPOB 8975, Kathmandu; Kalimati, Kathmandu; tel. (1) 6212276; e-mail iprad@ntc.net.np; internet www.iprad.org.np; f. 1995; research on economic, social, management, institutional, legal, environmental issues; Chair. Dr PUSHPA RAJ RAJKARNIKAR; Vice-Chair. Dr BHIM PRASAD NEUPANE.

Institute of Integrated Development Studies: POB 2254, Mandikhatar, Kathmandu; tel. (1) 4371006; e-mail info@iids.org.np; internet www.iids.org.np; f. 1990; conducts policy-oriented research on Nepal's economic, social devt in nat., regional, int. contexts; Chair. Dr MOHAN MAN SAINJU; Exec. Dir Dr BISHNU DEV PANT.

Nepal Institute for Policy Studies: POB 14352, Kathmandu; 90 Mahadevsthan Marga, Baneshwor, Kathmandu; tel. (1) 4482530; e-mail nips@nipsnepal.org; internet www.nipsnepal.org; f. 2008; library of 300 vols; Chair. RAJAN BHATTARAI.

RELIGION, SOCIOLOGY AND ANTHROPOLOGY

Center for Nepal and Asian Studies: POB 3757, Kathmandu; tel. (1) 4332078; e-mail info@cnastu.org.np; internet www.cnastu.org.np; f. 1969 as Institute of Nepal Studies, fmrly Institute of Nepal and Asian Studies, present name and status 1977; attached to Tribhuvan Univ.; research on issues and studies in social sciences incl. ethnic diversity, tradition and change in political values, cultural studies within Nepal and across other Asian countries; Exec. Dir Assoc. Prof. NANIRAM KHATRI; Deputy Dir Prof. DILLIRAJ SHARMA.

Institute for Social and Environmental Research—Nepal: POB 57, Bharatpur, Chitwan; Fulbari 1, Chitwan; tel. (56) 591054; e-mail iser@wlink.com.np; internet isernepal.org.np; f. 2001; research areas incl. population dynamics, population and environmental dynamics, education and empowerment; br. in Kathmandu; Dir Dr DIRGHA JIBI GHIMIRE.

Lotus Research Centre: Khwayabahil, POB 59, Lalitpur; tel. (1) 5549343; e-mail info@lrcnepal.org; internet www.lrcnepal.org; f. 1988; research on cultural heritage and Buddhism of Nepal Mandala; Chair. Dr BHADRA RATNA BAJRACHARYA; Vice-Chair. INDRASIDDHI BAJRACHARYA; publ. *Paleswan*.

Lumbini International Research Institute: POB 39, Bhairahawa, Rupandehi; tel. (71) 580175; e-mail liri@mos.com.np; internet www.lumbiniresearch.com; f. 1995; conducts research in Buddhism and other religions; library of 35,000 vols.

Libraries and Archives

Banke

Mahendra Library: Tribhuwan Chowk, Nepalgunj, Banke; tel. (81) 525492; e-mail info@nnl.org.np; f. 1947; attached to Nepal Nat. Library; 10,000 vols.

Kailali

Kailali Public Library: Dhangadi, Kailali; tel. (91) 521535; e-mail info@nnl.org.np; f. 1957; attached to Nepal Nat. Library; organizes monthly discussions, talks with a literary theme; 7,000 vols, 82 journals.

Kathmandu

Dilliraman—Kalyani Regmi Memorial Library: Ward 2, Lazimpat, Kathmandu; GPOB 20865, Kathmandu; tel. (1) 4417835; e-mail dkrmlibrary@htp.com.np; internet www.drkrmlibrary.org; f. 1980; museum colln incl. archeological objects made of stone and other metals; 30,000 vols; Chief Librarian PASHUPATI NATH ADHIKARI.

Indian Cultural Centre: POB 6967, Bal Mandir, Naxal, Kathmandu; tel. (1) 4412715; internet www.indianembassy.org.np/indian-culture-center.php; f. 2007; promotes cultural ties between India and Nepal; Dir Dr GEETI SEN.

Kaiser Library: Kaiser Mahal, Kathmandu; tel. (1) 4411318; e-mail info@klib.gov.np; internet www.klib.gov.np; f. 1969; 50,000 vols, 43 journals; Chief Librarian JANAKI KARMACHARYA.

Kathmandu University Central Library: POB 6250, Kathmandu; Dhulikhel; tel. (11) 661399; e-mail librarian@ku.edu.np; internet www.ku.edu.np/library; f. 1991; 45,000 vols, 160 journals and newsletters; Library Officer DEV RAJ ADHIKARY; Man. RUDRA P. ARYAL; publs *Bodhi* (1 a year), *KUSET: Kathmandu University Journal of Science, Engineering & Technology* (2 a year).

National Archives: Ramshahpath, Kathmandu; tel. (1) 4264353; e-mail mail@nationalarchives.gov.np; internet www.nationalarchives.gov.np; f. 1967; public records management office for govt of Nepal; 12,000 vols, 30,000 MSS, 151,000 microfilm copies of MSS in private colln, 20,000 historical documents; Chief Archivist UTTAM KHANAL; publ. *Abhilekh* (1 a year).

Nepal Bharat Library: Nepal Airlines Bldg, New Rd Gate, Kathmandu; tel. (1) 4243497; e-mail librarian@eoiktm.com; internet www.indianembassy.org.np/nepal-bharat-library.php; f. 1956; colln on Indian culture, economy, engineering, entertainment, history, int. relations, literature, mass communication, medicine, politics, science and technology, society; 62,000 vols; Sr Librarian K. C. MEENA.

Tribhuvan University Central Library: Kirtipur, Kathmandu; tel. (1) 4330834; e-mail tucl@tucl.org.np; internet www.tucl.org.np; f. 1959; depository for the UN; 350,000 vols, 450 periodicals; Chief Librarian JANARDAN DHUNGANA (acting); publs *Education Quarterly*, *Journal of Tribhuvan University*, *Nepalese National Bibliography*.

Lalitpur

Madan Puraskar Pustakalaya: POB 42, Patan Dhoka, Lalitpur; tel. (1) 5005515; e-mail info@mpp.org.np; internet www.mpp.org.np; f. 1955; collects and preserves resources in Nepali language; manages Nepal's literary prizes: Madan Puraskar, Jagadamba Shree; 23,700 vols, 5,247 periodical titles, 28,765 monographs, 13,000 ephemera in Nepali language, 710 MSS; Chair. KAMAL MANI DIXIT.

Nepal National Library: Harihar Bhawan, Pulchowk, POB 182, Lalitpur; tel. (1) 5521132; e-mail nnl@nnl.wlink.com.np; internet www.nnl.gov.np; f. 1957; 90,000 vols, 96 periodicals, 1,000 rare books and MSS, 7,000 children's books, 400 other items; Chief Librarian DASHARATH THAPA.

Pokhara

Pokhara Public Library: Mahendrapool, Pokhara; tel. (61) 521855; e-mail info@nnl.org.np; attached to Nepal Nat. Library; 4,000 vols.

Sunsari

Sarbajanik Vidyabhawan Library: Dharan, Sunsari; tel. (25) 526115; e-mail info@nnl.org.np; f. 1947; attached to Nepal Nat. Library.

Museums and Art Galleries

Kathmandu

Music Museum of Nepal: Tripureshwor, Kathmandu; tel. (1) 4242741; e-mail info@musicmuseumnepal.org; internet www.musicmuseumnepal.org; f. 2002 as Nepali

Folk Musical Instrument Museum; Dir RAM PRASAD KADEL.

Natural History Museum: Manjushree Bajaar, Swayambhu, Kathmandu; tel. (1) 4271899; e-mail info@nhmnepal.org; internet nhmnepal.org; attached to Tribhuvan Univ.; collects and preserves floral, fauna, geological and other natural specimens of Nepal; publ. *Journal of Natural History Museum.*

National Museum of Nepal: Museum Rd, Chhauni, Kathmandu; tel. (1) 4271478; e-mail info@nationalmuseum.gov.np; internet www.nationalmuseum.gov.np; f. 1928; art, history, culture, ethnology, philately, natural history; library of 10,000 vols; Chief SANU NANI KANSAKAR; publ. *Nepal Museum.*

Nepal Olympic Museum: c/o Nat. Sports Ccl, Tripureshwor, Kathmandu; tel. (1) 4256560; e-mail info@sportsnepal.org; internet www.sportsnepal.org; f. 1999; preserves and collects sport-related material of historic value; promotes sports; organizes symposium, workshop, contests on sport; Pres. CHHITIJ ARUN SHRESTHA.

Patan Museum: Patan Darbar, Kathmandu; tel. (1) 5521492; e-mail info@patanmuseum.gov.np; internet www.patanmuseum.gov.np; f. 1997; 18th century fmr royal palace housing Hindu and Buddhist sacred art of Nepal, Nepalese metalwork, photographs of Nepal taken in 1899, and a Hindu Tantric MS; Exec. Dir DEWENDRA NATH TIWAREE.

Pokhara

Gurkha Memorial Museum: Pokhara; tel. (61) 441762; e-mail gmtmuseum@wlink.com.np; internet www.gurkhamuseum.org.np; f. 1994; displays knives, medals, photographs, uniforms, items used by Gurkha soldiers; Chair. YAMBAHADUR GURUNG.

Universities
KATHMANDU UNIVERSITY

POB 6250, Dhulikhel
Telephone: (11) 661399
E-mail: admission@ku.edu.np
Internet: www.ku.edu.np
Founded 1991
State control
Academic year: August to June
Language of instruction: English
Chancellor: Rt Hon. PRIME MIN. OF NEPAL
Pro-Chancellor: Hon. MIN. OF EDUCATION
Vice-Chancellor: Prof. Dr SURESH RAJ SHARMA
Registrar: Prof. Dr BHADRA MAN TULADHAR
Library Officer: Dr DEV RAJ ADHIKARY
Library: see under Libraries and Archives
Number of teachers: 344
Number of students: 8,266 (incl. 4,897 enrolled in affiliated colleges)

DEANS

School of Arts: Dr MAHESH BANSKOTA
School of Education: Prof. Dr MANA PRASAD WAGLEY
School of Engineering: Prof. Dr BHOLA THAPA
School of Management: Prof. SUBAS K. C.
School of Medical Sciences: Dr NARENDRA BAHADUR RANA
School of Science: Prof. Dr PANNA THAPA

LUMBINI BUDDHIST UNIVERSITY

Bhrikuti Mandap, Exhibition Rd, Kathmandu
Siddharthanagar, Municipality–8, Rupandehi, Lumbini
Telephone: (1) 4246032

E-mail: info@lbu.edu.np
Internet: www.lbu.edu.np
Founded 2004
State control
Origin and devt of Buddhism, religion and philosophy, Pali and Sanskrit Buddhist literature
Chancellor: Rt Hon. PRIME MIN. OF NEPAL
Pro-Chancellor: Hon. MIN. OF EDUCATION
Vice-Chancellor: Prof. TRI RATNA MANANDHAR
Registrar: Prof. KHADGA MAN SHRESTHA
Dean: Prof. SHANKER THAPA

NEPAL SANSKRIT UNIVERSITY

POB 5003, Kathmandu
Beljhundi, Dang
Telephone: (1) 4221510
E-mail: registraroffice@nsu.edu.np
Internet: www.nsu.edu.np
Founded 1986, fmrly Mahendra Sanskrit Univ.
State control
Languages of instruction: English, Nepali, Sanskrit
Academic year: July to May
Depts of ayurveda, Buddhist philosophy and tantra, darshna, dernashast, economics, English, Hindi and Maithali, itihasa purana, karmakanda, mathematics, Nepali, nyaya, political science, purva mamamsa, veda, vedanta, vyakarana, yoga
Chancellor: Rt Hon. PRIME MIN. OF NEPAL
Pro-Chancellor: Hon. MIN. OF EDUCATION
Vice-Chancellor: Prof. SHIVA HARI MARAHATHA
Rector: Prof. NARAYAN KUMAR ACHARYA
Registrar: Dr JAGAT PRASAD UPADHYAYA
Librarian: KHEM RAJ GYNAWALI
Number of teachers: 315
Number of students: 2,400
Publications: *Maryada* (1 a year), *Ritumbara* (4 a year)

POKHARA UNIVERSITY

POB 427, Dhungepatan, Lekhnath Municipality, Kaski
Telephone: (61) 561046
E-mail: info@pu.edu.np
Internet: www.pu.edu.np
Founded 1997
State control
Languages of instruction: English, Nepali
Academic year: August to June
Chancellor: Rt Hon. PRIME MIN. OF NEPAL
Pro-Chancellor: Hon. MIN. OF EDUCATION
Vice-Chancellor: Prof. KHAGENDRA PRASAD BHATTARAI
Registrar: Dr MAN BAHADUR K. C.
Library of 22,000 vols
Number of teachers: 1,550
Number of students: 32,000
Publications: *Journal of Health and Allied Sciences, PACE: The Journal of Business and Management*

DEANS

Faculty of Humanities and Social Science: Prof. Dr INDRA PRASAD TIWARI
Faculty of Management: Dr KARNA BIR POUDYAL
Faculty of Science and Technology: Dr SURESH PRASAD BANSTOLA

PURBANCHAL UNIVERSITY

POB 142, Biratnagar, Morang
Telephone: (21) 22165
E-mail: info@puniv.edu.np
Internet: www.purbuniv.edu.np
Founded 1995

State control
Academic year: August to June
Languages of instruction: English, Nepali
Faculties of arts, education, management, science and technology; 65 affiliated colleges
Chancellor: Rt Hon. PRIME MIN. OF NEPAL
Pro-Chancellor: Hon. MIN. OF EDUCATION
Vice-Chancellor: Prof. Dr MAHESHWOR MAN SHRESTHA
Publications: *Business Horizon, Expressions*

TRIBHUVAN UNIVERSITY

POB 8212, Kirtipur, Kathmandu
Telephone: (1) 4330433
E-mail: vcoffice@tribhuvan-university.edu.np
Internet: www.tribhuvan-university.edu.np
Founded 1959
State control
Languages of instruction: English, Nepali
Academic year: July to June
Chancellor: Rt Hon. PRIME MIN. OF NEPAL
Pro-Chancellor: DINA NATH SHARMA
Vice-Chancellor: Prof. Dr HIRA BAHADUR MAHARJAN
Rector: Prof. GUNA NIDHI NYAUPANE
Registrar: Dr CHANDRA MANI PAUDEL
Chief Librarian: JANARDAN DHUNGANA
Library: see under Libraries and Archives
Number of teachers: 7,841
Number of students: 389,460 (incl. 2,30,066 enrolled in affiliated colleges)
Publications: *Contributions to Nepalese Studies, Economic Journal of Development Issues* (2 a year), *Education and Development* (CERID, 1 a year), *Journal of Development and Administrative Studies* (CEDA, 1 a year), *Nepalese Journal of Development and Rural Studies* (Central Department of Rural Development (Kirtipur), 2 a year), *Tribhuvan University Today* (1 a year), *TU Journal* (Research Division, 2 a year)

DEANS

Faculty of Education: Prof. Dr PRAKASH MAN SHRESTHA (acting)
Faculty of Humanities and Social Sciences: Dr TARA KANT PANDEY (acting)
Faculty of Law: Prof. Dr VIDYA KISHOR ROY
Faculty of Management: Prof. Dr PURUSOTTAM SHARMA (acting)
Institute of Agriculture and Animal Science: Prof. Dr SUNDAR MAN SHRESTHA
Institute of Engineering: Dr BHARAT RAJ PAHARI (acting)
Institute of Forestry: Prof. CHIRANJIBI PRASAD UPADHYAYA (acting)
Institute of Medicine: Prof. Dr ARUN SAYAMI
Institute of Science and Technology: Prof. Dr SUMAN LAL SHRESTHA (acting)

Deemed Universities

B. P. Koirala Institute of Health Science: POB 7053, Dharan, Kathmandu; tel. (25) 525555; e-mail registrar@bpkihs.edu; internet www.bpkihs.edu; f. 1993, present status 1998; colleges of dental surgery, nursing; medical college; school of public health and community medicine; Vice-Chancellor Prof. Dr BALBHADRA PRASAD DAS; Rector Prof. Dr RUPA RAJBHANDARI SINGH; Registrar NAND KUMAR THAPA; publ. *Parikrama*.

National Academy of Medical Sciences: Bir Hospital, POB 13606, Kathmandu; tel. (1) 4247032; internet www.nams.org.np; Chancellor Rt Hon. PRIME MIN. OF NEPAL.

NETHERLANDS

The Higher Education System

Universiteit Leiden (Leiden University—founded in 1575, when the Low Countries or Netherlands were under Spanish rule) is the oldest existing university in the Netherlands. The seven northernmost provinces of the Netherlands formed the Treaty of Utrecht in 1579, declared their independence from Spain in 1581 and in 1648 were recognized as the independent United Provinces or Dutch Republic under the terms of the Treaty of Westphalia. Institutions established during 1579–1648 include Rijksuniversiteit Groningen (the University of Groningen—founded in 1614), Universiteit van Amsterdam (the University of Amsterdam—founded in 1632) and Universiteit Utrecht (Utrecht University—founded in 1636).

The modern higher education system is subject to a number of different legislative acts, including the Higher Professional Education Act, the University Education Act (both 1986) and the Higher Education and Research Act (1993, amended in 2009). The last of these granted greater autonomy to institutions and introduced a 'credit'-based system for the award of degrees. The Netherlands participates in the Bologna Process to establish a European Higher Education Area, the first phase of which was to adopt a credit-based system of comparable degrees with two main cycles (undergraduate and graduate). The country operates a binary system of 14 research universities which combine teaching with academic research (Wetenschappelijk Onderwijs—academic education) and 41 universities of applied sciences which are geared towards the acquisition of vocational qualifications and training in arts and sciences (Hoger Beroepsonderwijs—higher professional education). The Open University (founded in 1984) offers both academic and professional qualifications. A third, smaller branch of higher education includes the institutes for international education, which offer programmes especially designed for international students, such as the Berlage Institute, which specializes in architecture and urban design, and which in 2012 launched a new postgraduate programme. The main focus of the universities of applied sciences (Hogescholen) is on professional degrees and titles in several subject areas, including economics and management, engineering and technology, health care, behavioural science and social studies, agriculture and the environment, fine arts, performing arts and education. Since 2002 the universities of applied sciences have also offered Masters degrees. A short cycle programme within the first cycle was introduced as a pilot programme from 2006 and was implemented as a permanent part of the education system in 2011. This short-cycle degree is called an Associate degree and comprises a minimum of 120 ECTS points. The Association of Universities of Applied Sciences (HBO-Raad) is responsible for quality assurance and accreditation. The Minister of Education, Culture and Science, advised by an Education Council, is responsible for educational legislation and its enforcement. A system of accreditation was introduced in 2002, responsibility for which was accorded to the newly created Accreditation Organization of The Netherlands and Flanders. Plans mooted in 2011 to bolster cooperation among, and perhaps ultimately to merge, three of the country's universities—Universiteit Leiden, Technische Universiteit Delft and Erasmus Universiteit Rotterdam—provoked vociferous opposition in 2011; critics of a possible merger argued that such a move would inevitably lead to a marked decline in standards at each of the constituent institutions. In 2011/12 some 243,686 students were enrolled in research universities, while it was estimated that 416,000 were enrolled in professional programmes at the universities of applied sciences. It was also estimated that there were 81,700 international students studying in the Netherlands.

Traditionally, the Netherlands has maintained subsidized fees for all students. However, from 2008 the Government ended subsidies for students from non-European Union (EU) countries. Moreover, new legislation enacted in April 2010 granted universities the right to set their own tuition fees for all students taking a second Bachelors or Masters degree, with effect from the beginning of the 2011/12 academic year. Tuition fees are higher for students coming from outside the EU than for Dutch and EU students.

Admission to degree-level education requires students to hold the Voorbereidend Wetenschappelijk Onderwijs (VWO—Preparatory Scientific Education), the Hoger Algemeen Voortgezet Onderwijs (HAVO—Higher General Continued Education) or the Hoger Beroepsonderwijs (HBO—Higher Applied Education). The two-tier system of undergraduate Bachelors and postgraduate Masters degrees was first introduced in 2002 and was to have been adopted by all university-level institutions by 2010. The undergraduate Bachelors degree is a three-year programme of study, starting with one year of general studies. The first postgraduate degree is the Masters, a one- to three-year course of study involving research, a written thesis or final test. A Masters in medicine lasts three years and students are required to study for a further three to six years to qualify for independent practice. Following completion of the Masters, the Doctorate is awarded after a minimum of four years of research and public defence of a thesis. Quotas are in place for admission to the most popular fields of study, such as medicine or dentistry, and the university may choose half of its intake, the other half .

Post-secondary technical and vocational education (Middelbaar Beroepsonderwijs—MBO) is administered according to the Adult and Vocational Education Act (1996). The MBO is divided into four levels of qualifications (in ascending order): assistant training (six months to one year), basic vocational training (two to three years), vocational training (two to four years) and management training (three to four years). Alternatively, school-leavers with 10 years of primary and secondary education may undertake apprenticeships based in the workplace. The Netherlands Association of Vocational and Educational Training (VET) Colleges (MBO-Raad) oversees the sector and in 2012 it estimated that 485,000 students were taking part in regular VET courses while a further 145,000 were in adult education programmes.

Regulatory and Representative Bodies

GOVERNMENT

Ministry of Education, Culture and Science: POB 16375, 2500 BJ The Hague; Rijnstraat 50, 2515 XP The Hague; tel. (70) 4123456; e-mail ocwinfo@postbus51.nl; internet www.rijksoverheid.nl/ministeries/ocw; Minister JET BUSSEMAKER.

ACCREDITATION

ENIC/NARIC Netherlands: Int. Recognition Dept, POB 29777, 2502 LT The Hague; Kortenaerkade 11, 2518 AX The Hague; tel. (70) 4260260; e-mail info@nuffic.nl; internet www.nuffic.nl; f. 1952; provides information on postgraduate int. courses; advises various educational and govt bodies on matters of academic equivalence and the recognition of professional credentials; promotes int. cooperation in several European and nat. exchange programmes; offers educational and scientific help to developing countries; Dir-Gen. Drs SANDER VAN DEN EIJNDEN; publs Nieuwsbrief (4 a year), Study in the Netherlands: Your Gateway to Europe (1 a year).

Nederlands-Vlaamse Accreditatieorganisatie (Accreditation Organisation of the Netherlands and Flanders): POB 85498, 2508 CD The Hague; Parkstraat 28, 2514 JK The Hague; tel. (70) 3122300; e-mail info@nvao.net; internet www.nvao.net; independently ensures the quality of higher education in the Netherlands and Flanders by assessing and accrediting programmes; Chair. K. L. L. M. (KARL) DITTRICH; Vice-Chair. GUIDO LANGOUCHE; Man. Dir RUDY DERDELINCKX.

NATIONAL BODIES

HBO-raad (Netherlands Association of Universities of Applied Sciences): POB 123, 2501 CC The Hague; Prinsessegracht 21, 2514 AP The Hague; tel. (70) 3122121; e-mail post@hbo-raad.nl; internet www.hbo-raad.nl; works to strengthen the social position of the univs of applied sciences; Pres. (vacant); Sec. Drs A. DE GRAAF.

Nederlandse Vereniging van Pedagogen en Onderwijskundigen (NVO) (Dutch Society of Educational Psychologists): St Jacobsstraat 331, 3511 BP Utrecht; tel. (30) 2322407; e-mail secretariaat@nvo.nl; internet www.nvo.nl; f. 1962; maintenance of standards in univ. education; Chair. Dr XAVIER MOONEN; Vice-Chair. Drs MARJOLIJN WILSCHUT; Treas. Drs ROBBERT VAN KAMPEN; Dir Drs HANS BOSMAN; publs *Nederlands Tijdschrift voor Opvoeding, Vorming en Onderwijs* (6 a year).

Rectoren College (Rectors' Conference of the Netherlands): POB 19270, 3501 DG Utrecht; tel. (71) 5273130; e-mail hj.graafland@bb.leidenuniv.nl; Chair. D. F. J. BOSSCHER; Sec. F. VAN STEIJN.

Vereniging van Universiteiten (VSNU) (Association of Universities in the Netherlands): POB 13739, 2501 ES The Hague; Lange Houtstraat 2, 2511 CW The Hague; tel. (70) 3021400; e-mail post@vsnu.nl; internet www.vsnu.nl; f. 1985; promotes common interests of univs vis-à-vis Dutch and European politicians, govt and civil soc. orgs to create a forum for discussion; Pres. Dr KARL DITTRICH; Dir JOSEPHINE SCHOLTEN.

Learned Societies
GENERAL

Koninklijke Hollandsche Maatschappij der Wetenschappen (Royal Holland Society of Sciences and Humanities): POB 9698, 2003 LR Haarlem; Spaarne 17, 2011 CD Haarlem; tel. (23) 5321773; e-mail hollmij@wxs.nl; internet www.hollmij.nl; f. 1752; present bldg 1841; furthers contact between scientists and laymen by arranging lectures, confs, symposia on scientific subjects; awards annual prizes and subsidies for research and publ. of scientific work; 350 mems, 350 dirs, 30 foreign mems; Chair. Dr A. H. G. RINNOOY KAN; Vice-Chair. M. E. BIERMAN-BEUKEMA TOE WATER; Treas. R. E. ROGAAR; publ. *Haarlem Presentations* (1 a year).

Koninklijke Nederlandse Akademie van Wetenschappen (Royal Netherlands Academy of Arts and Sciences): POB 19121, 1000 GC Amsterdam; Kloveniersburgwal 29, 1011 JV Amsterdam; tel. (20) 5510700; e-mail knaw@knaw.nl; internet www.knaw.nl; f. 1808, current name adopted 1938; advises govt on matters related to scientific research; assesses the quality of scientific research (peer review); provides a forum for the scientific world and promotes int. scientific cooperation; acts as an umbrella org. for the institutes primarily engaged in basic and strategic scientific research and disseminates information; 300 mems (200 ordinary, 40 corresp., 60 foreign); Pres. Prof. Dr HANS CLEVERS; Vice-Pres. Prof. P. A. DYKSTRA; Vice-Pres. Prof. B. L. FERINGA; Sec. Gen. Prof. J. W. GUNNING; Dir for Gen. Affairs, Finance and Operations Dr K. HANS CHANG;

Dir for Research Prof. Dr THEO W. MULDER; publs *Akademienieuws*, *Mededelingen der Afdeling Letterkunde*, *Verhandelingen der Afdeling Letterkunde*, *Verhandelingen Eerste en Tweede Reeks der Afdeling Natuurkunde*, *Verslag van de Gewone Vergaderingen der Afdeling Natuurkunde*.

Zuid-Afrikahuis (South Africa House): Keizersgracht 141, 1015 CK Amsterdam; tel. (20) 6249318; e-mail info@zuidafrikahuis.nl; internet www.zuidafrikahuis.nl; f. 1939; study of Afrikaans language and literature, history and culture of S Africa; attached institutes: Netherlands-S African Soc., S African Institute; library of 46,000 vols; Librarian CORINE DE MAIJER; publ. *Maandblad Zuid-Afrika* (10 a year).

AGRICULTURE, FISHERIES AND VETERINARY SCIENCE

Groei & Bloei (Growth and Bloom): POB 485, 2700 AL Zoetermeer; Louis Pasteurlaan 6, 2719 EE Zoetermeer; tel. (79) 3681215; e-mail info@groei.nl; internet www.groei.nl; f. 1873 as Royal Soc. of Horticulture and Botany; 146 brs; 60,000 mems; Gen. Sec. J. P. VAN LEEUWEN; publ. *Groei & Bloei* (11 a year).

KLV Wageningen Alumni Netwerk (KLV Wageningen Alumni Network): POB 79, 6700 AB Wageningen; Stippeneng 2, 6708 WE Wageningen; tel. (317) 485191; e-mail secretariaat.klv@wur.nl; internet www.klv.nl; f. 1886, present name 2009; network for Wageningen Univ. graduates and for other professionals with links to Wageningen; organizes workshops, debates, lectures related to entrepreneurship, career and networking in life sciences; 8,000 mems; Pres. TINY VAN BOEKEL; Vice-Pres. HAN SWINKELS; Sec. MARJOLEIN HELDER.

Koninklijke Nederlandse Bosbouw Vereniging (Royal Dutch Forestry Association): Parkweg 27, 2585 JH The Hague; tel. (70) 3688222; e-mail secretaris@knbv.nl; internet www.knbv.nl; f. 1910; promotes forestry, landscape management, nature conservation; advocates functions and values of forests, such as carbon sequestration, historical monuments, nature, recreation, timber production, water, etc.; organizes thematic meetings, symposia, excursions and study tours abroad; 600 mems; Chair. Dr Ir HANK H. BARTELINK; Vice-Chair. Ir ERWIN J. AL; Sec. Ing. MARLEEN VAN DEN HAM; publ. *Vakblad Natuur Bos Landschap* (10 a year).

Nederlandse Tuinbouwraad (Netherlands Horticultural Council): POB 1000, 1430 BA Aalsmeer; Legmeerdijk 313, 1431 GB Aalsmeer; tel. (29) 7395005; e-mail informatie@tuinbouwraad.nl; internet www.tuinbouwraad.nl; f. 1908; organizes int. horticultural exhibition 'Floriade'; 14 mem. nat. orgs of cooperatives and producers of edible and non-edible horticultural products; Chair. Dr NICO KOOMEN; Sec. Dr GEORGE TH. FRANKE.

ARCHITECTURE AND TOWN PLANNING

Erfgoedvereniging Heemschut: Nieuwezijds Kolk 28, 1012 PV Amsterdam; tel. (20) 6225292; e-mail info@heemschut.nl; internet www.heemschut.nl; f. 1911; asscn for safeguarding the architectural heritage of the Netherlands; 12 provincial sub-cttees; 6,500 mems; Chair. P. BREUKINK; Dir KAREL LOEFF; Sec. K. LOEFF; publ. *Heemschut* (6 a year).

Genootschap Architectura et Amicitia: Duke Ellingtonstraat 34, 2324 LA Leiden; e-mail mail@aeta.nl; internet www.aeta.nl; f. 1855; asscn of architects and individuals from related disciplines; 380 mems; Chair. RENS SCHULZE; Sec. FRANCISCA BENTHEM; publ. *FORUM* (1 a year).

Koninklijke Maatschappij tot Bevordering der Bouwkunst Bond van Nederlandse Architekten (BNA) (Royal Institute of Dutch Architects): POB 19606, 1000 GP Amsterdam; Jollemanhof 14, 1019 GW Amsterdam; tel. (20) 5553666; e-mail bna@bna.nl; internet www.bna.nl; f. 1919 by merger of Soc. for the Advancement of Architecture (f. 1842) and Asscn of Dutch Architects (f. 1908), present status 1957; promotes cultural, economic, skills, social profile of architect and architecture; 3,000 mems; Chair. BJARNE MASTENBROEK; Vice-Chair. FREERK HOEKSTRA; Exec. Sec MARIJKE ZANDHUIS; publ. *BNABlad* (12 a year).

Nederlands Architectuur Instituut (Netherlands Architecture Institute): POB 237, 3000 AE Rotterdam; Museum Park 25, 3015 CB Rotterdam; tel. (10) 4401358; e-mail info@nai.nl; internet www.nai.nl; f. 1988, present location 1993; museum, archives, collns; 100 mems; library of 35,000 vols; Dir OLE BOUMAN; Man. Dir PETER HAASBROEK; publs *Delft Architectural Studies on Housing Design (DASH)* (2 a year), *Hunch* (2 a year), *OASE* (3 a year), *Open* (2 a year), *Positions* (irregular).

Raad voor Cultuur (Council for Culture): POB 61243, 2506 AE The Hague; Prins Willem Alexanderhof 20, 2595 BE The Hague; tel. (70) 3106686; e-mail info@cultuur.nl; internet www.cultuur.nl; f. 1995; statutory advisory body to the govt and both Chambers of Parliament for cultural and media policy; 7 mems; Chair. JOOP DAALMEIJER; Gen. Sec. JEROEN BARTELSE.

Rijksdienst voor het Cultureel Erfgoed (National Heritage Board): POB 1600, 3800 BP Amersfoort; Smallepad 5, 3811 MG Amersfoort; tel. (33) 4217421; e-mail info@cultureelerfgoed.nl; internet www.cultureelerfgoed.nl; f. 1918, present name and status 2009; attached to Min. of Education, Culture and Science; conservation of nat. heritage; Dir Drs CEES VAN 'T VEEN; publ. *Tijdschrift van de Rijksdienst voor het Cultureel Erfgoed* (4 a year).

BIBLIOGRAPHY, LIBRARY SCIENCE AND MUSEOLOGY

FOBID Netherlands Library Forum: POB 90407, 2509 LK The Hague; tel. (70) 3140511; e-mail info@fobid.nl; internet www.fobid.nl; f. 1974; library umbrella org. for advocacy and devt in the field of legal matters, professional education, classification standards, int. affairs; promotion of cooperation and integration among public, research and spec. libraries in the Netherlands; mems: Netherlands Public Library Asscn (VOB), Netherlands Asscn for Library, Information and Knowledge Professionals (NVB), Nat. Library of the Netherlands (KB) and UKB, the cooperative Asscn of 13 univ. libraries, the Nat. Library and the Library of the Royal Dutch Acad. of Science; serves as int. office for library matters; seat for the network The Hague—World Library Capital; Dir Dr MARIAN KOREN; Sec. MONIQUE BAARDMAN.

Nederlandse Museumvereniging (Netherlands Museums Association): POB 2975, 1000 CZ Amsterdam; Rapenburgerstraat 123, 1011 VL Amsterdam; tel. (20) 5512900; e-mail info@museumvereniging.nl; internet www.museumvereniging.nl; f. 1926; devt of museums in terms of professionalism and quality; 450 mems; Chair. ERIC FISCHER; Vice-Chair. and Sec. WILLEM BIJLEVELD; Treas. PETER VERHOEVEN; publ. *Museumvisie* (4 a year).

Nederlandse Vereniging voor Beroepsbeoefenaren in de bibliotheek-, informatie- en kennissector (NVB) (Netherlands

Association for Library, Information and Knowledge Professionals): Mariaplaats 3, 3511 LH Utrecht; tel. (30) 2330050; e-mail info@nvbonline.nl; internet www.nvbonline.nl; f. 1912; maintenance of lawful regulation of library system; arrangement of meetings and int. cooperation; professional education; 1,300 individual and 500 institutional mems; Pres. Drs BART VAN DER MEIJ; Chair. M. G. WESSELING; Man. Dir Drs JAN VAN DER BURG; Sec. C. KORLVINKE; Treas. HUIB VERHOEFF; publs *NVB—Nieuwsbrief, Informatie Professional*.

Vereniging Openbare Bibliotheken (Netherlands Public Library Association): POB 16146, 2500 BC The Hague; Grote Marktstraat 43, 2511 BH The Hague; tel. (70) 3090500; e-mail vereniging@debibliotheken.nl; internet www.debibliotheken.nl; f. 1908; defends common interests of the public library sector; 160 mem. instns; Chair. KARS VELING; Vice-Chair. and Treas. CHARLES NOORDAM; Dir AP DE VRIES; Sec. MARION MERTENS; publ. *Bibliotheekblad* (26 a year).

ECONOMICS, LAW AND POLITICS

Internationaal Juridisch Instituut (International Legal Institute): Spui 186, 2511 BW The Hague; tel. (70) 3460974; e-mail info@iji.nl; internet www.iji.nl; f. 1918; supplies legal opinions regarding private int. law and foreign (also mostly private) law to the Netherlands judiciary, the Netherlands Bar and to other mems of the legal profession, such as civil law notaries; also gives information to judges and lawyers outside the Netherlands; Chair. Prof. A. V. M. STRUYCKEN; Vice-Chair. L. STRIKWERDA; Dir Prof. W. G. HUIJGEN; Deputy Dir E. N. FROHN; Sec. A.C. OLLAND; Treas. G. J. C. VAN ENGELEN.

Koninklijke Vereniging voor de Staathuishoudkunde (Royal Netherlands Economic Association): c/o De Nederlandsche Bank NV, POB 98, 1000 AB Amsterdam; tel. (20) 5242280; e-mail info@kvsweb.nl; internet www.kvsweb.nl; f. 1849; promotes economic knowledge; 1,500 mems; and Chair. Prof. Dr A. W. A. BOOT; Sec. and Treas. Prof. Dr J. SWANK; publs *Jaarboek* (4 a year), *Preadviezen* (1 a year).

Nederlandse Vereniging voor Internationaal Recht (Netherlands Branch of International Law Association): POB 9520, 2300 RA Leiden; Steenschuur 25, 2311 ES Leiden; tel. (71) 5277748; e-mail info@nvir.org; internet www.nvir.org; f. 1910; practises and promotes int. public and private law; 475 mems; Pres. Prof. W. J. M. VAN GENUGTEN; Hon. Sec. Prof. Dr M. M. T. A. BRUS; publ. *Mededelingen* (1 a year).

Vereniging voor Agrarisch Recht (Agrarian Law Society): Maliesingel 20, 3581 BE Utrecht; tel. (30) 2320826; e-mail hvanbasten@verenigingagrarischrecht.nl; internet www.verenigingagrarischrecht.nl; f. 1959; promotes practice of agricultural law; organizes seminars, discussion meetings and excursions; 300 mems; Chair. Prof. G. M. F. SNIJDERS; Sec. and Treas. H. A. VAN BASTEN; publ. *Agrarisch Recht* (Agrarian Law).

Vereniging voor Arbeidsrecht (Labour Law Society): De Eem 15, 3448 DS Woerden; e-mail info@verenigingvoorarbeidsrecht.nl; internet www.verenigingvoorarbeidsrecht.nl; f. 1946; acts as a forum for those who practise labour law; 940 mems; Chair. Prof. WILLEM H. A. C. M. BOUWENS; Sec. P. DE CASPARIS; Treas. R. J. KOOIJ.

FINE AND PERFORMING ARTS

Arti et Amicitiae: Rokin 112, 1012 LB Amsterdam; tel. (20) 6245134; e-mail arti@arti.nl; internet www.arti.nl; f. 1839; nat. soc. of painters, sculptors and graphic artists; exhibition gallery; 1,550 mems (incl. 550 artist mems); Chair. ARIE VAN DEN BERG; Vice-Chair. ROBERT SAMKALDEN; Sec DIRK JAN JAGER; publ. *De Nieuwe* (6 a year).

Koninklijke Nederlandse Toonkunstenaars Vereniging (Royal Dutch Musician's Union): Grote Bickersstraat 50A, 1013 KS Amsterdam; tel. (20) 5221020; e-mail office@kntv.nl; internet www.kntv.nl; f. 1875; promotes the interests of professional musicians working in the field of performing arts and education; 3,400 mems; Dir GUSTA KORTEWEG; publ. *KNTV-Magazine* (6 a year).

Rijksbureau voor Kunsthistorische Documentatie (Netherlands Institute for Art History): POB 90418, 2509 LK The Hague; Prins Willem-Alexanderhof 5, 2595 BE The Hague; tel. (70) 3339777; e-mail info@rkd.nl; internet www.rkd.nl; f. 1932, present status 1995; art-historical information centre; administers colln of documentary, library and archive material on W art from late Middle Ages to present; library of 450,000 vols, periodicals and catalogues, and press-cuttings, archives, 7m. photos and reproductions; Chair. Prof. P. SCHNABEL; Dir Prof. Dr RUDI E.O. EKKART; publ. *Oud-Holland* (4 a year).

Vereniging Toonkunst Nederland (Society for the Advancement of Music): Atlantisplein 1, Room 2.04, 1093 NE Amsterdam; tel. (20) 6713091; e-mail info@toonkunstnederland.nl; internet www.toonkunstnederland.nl; f. 1829, present status 2007; asscn of amateur choirs and orchestras; 5,000 mems; Chair. GERARD BROEKMANS; Sec. RIA ROELANDS.

Wagnergenootschap Nederland (Wagner Society Netherlands): De Helling 79, 1502 GE, Zaandam; tel. (75) 6157793; e-mail bestuur@wagnergenootschap.nl; internet www.wagnergenootschap.nl; f. 1961; promotes and studies works and life of composer Richard Wagner; 300 mems; Chair. TON HOGENES; Sec. JACK VAN DONGEN; Treas. JAN BURGER; publ. *Wagner After All* (5 a year).

HISTORY, GEOGRAPHY AND ARCHAEOLOGY

Centraal Bureau voor Genealogie (Central Bureau for Genealogy): POB 11755, 2502 AT The Hague; Prins Willem-Alexanderhof 22, 2595 BE The Hague; tel. (70) 3150570; e-mail info@cbg.nl; internet www.cbg.nl; f. 1945; large genealogical and heraldic collns; 14,350 mems; library of 100,000 vols; Chair. Dr PIETER WINSEMIUS; Deputy Chair. Dr ELS M. KLOEK; Dir Dr A. J. LEVER; publs *Genealogie* (4 a year), *Jaarboek* (yearbook).

Internationaal Instituut voor Sociale Geschiedenis (International Institute of Social History): POB 2169, 1000 CD Amsterdam; Cruquiusweg 31, 1019 AT Amsterdam; tel. (20) 6685866; e-mail info@iisg.nl; internet www.iisg.nl; f. 1935; attached to Royal Netherlands Acad. of Arts and Sciences; documentation and research centre in the field of social history; colln, preservation and availability of heritage of social movements worldwide; library of 1,000,000 vols, archives, esp. on the labour movement, 60,000 periodicals; Gen. Dir Prof. Dr ERIK-JAN ZÜRCHER; Dir for Collns and Digital Infrastructure TITIA VAN DER WERF-DAVELAAR; Dir for Research MARCEL VAN DER LINDEN; Exec. Sec. MONIQUE KRUITHOF; publ. *International Review of Social History* (3 a year, plus supplement).

Koninklijk Fries Genootschap voor Geschiedenis en Cultuur/Keninklik Frysk Genoatskip foar Skiednis en Kultuer (Royal Frisian Society for History and Culture): Turfmarkt 11, 8911 KS Leeuwarden; tel. (58) 2555500; e-mail fries.genootschap@friesmuseum.nl; internet www.friesgenootschap.nl; f. 1827, current name adopted 2003; promotes history and culture of Friesland; supports research in that field; 1,800 mems; Chair. Dr PIET HEMMINGA; Sec. LOURENS OLDERSMA; Treas. Drs DIRK VAN DER BIJ; publs *De Vrije Fries* (yearbook), *Fryslân* (4 a year).

Koninklijk Nederlands Aardrijkskundig Genootschap (Royal Dutch Geographical Society): POB 805, 3500 AV Utrecht; Ganzenmarkt 6, 3512 GD Utrecht; tel. (30) 2361202; e-mail info@knag.nl; internet www.knag.nl; f. 1873; promotes geography as subject and profession; organizes confs, workshops, lectures, seminars; publishes scientific journals and books; 3,500 mems; Dir Drs EELKO POSTMA; Chair. HENK OTTENS; Treas. LEON BUSSCHOPS; publs *Geografie* (9 a year), *Tijdschrift voor Economische en Sociale Geografie (TESG)* (Journal of Economic and Social Geography, 5 a year).

Koninklijk Nederlands Historisch Genootschap (Royal Netherlands Historical Society): POB 90406, 2509 LK The Hague; Prins Willem-Alexanderhof 5, 2595 BE The Hague; tel. (70) 3140363; e-mail info@knhg.nl; internet www.knhg.nl; f. 1845; promotes historical studies and dissemination of historical research with spec. regard to history of low countries; 1,250 mems; Chair. Prof. Dr SUSAN LEGÊNE; Dir Dr LEONIE DE GOEI; Treas. Dr JOOST DANKERS; publs *Bijdragen en Mededelingen Betreffende de Geschiedenis der Nederlanden* (Low Countries' Historical Review, 4 a year), *HG-Nieuwsbrief* (4 a year, online).

Koninklijk Oudheidkundig Genootschap (Royal Dutch Antiquarian Society): POB 74888, 1070 DN Amsterdam; Hobbemastraat 25, 1071 XZ Amsterdam; tel. (20) 6747380; e-mail kog@rijksmuseum.nl; internet www.kog.nu; f. 1858; colln of applied art (furniture, silver, sculpture, etc.), paintings, objects of historical value, prints and drawings concerning the topography of Amsterdam, manners and customs of the Netherlands; coins, medals, books; 585 mems; library of 6,100 vols; Pres. CHRIS P. VAN EEGHEN; Sec. HESTER H. MANGER CATS VAN DEN BERG; Treas. Dr J. KAMP.

Nederlandsch Economisch-Historisch Archief (NEHA) (Netherlands Economic-Historical Archives Society): Cruquiusweg 31, 1019 AT Amsterdam; tel. (20) 6685866; e-mail info@neha.nl; internet www.neha.nl; f. 1914; attached to Royal Netherlands Acad. of Arts and Sciences; specializes in economic history and business studies; 400 mems; library: see Libraries and Archives; Pres. Prof. Dr J. L. VAN ZANDEN; Sec. Dr E. A. G. VAN DEN BENT; Archivist JACK HOFMAN; Treas. Drs J. A. DE JONGH; publ. *Tijdschrift voor Sociale en Economische Geschiedenis* (4 a year).

Vereniging Gelre: Markt 1, 6811 CG Arnhem; tel. (26) 3521600; e-mail info@geldersarchief.nl; internet www.geldersarchief.nl; f. 1897; promotes practice of archeology, history and law of Gelderland; organizes seminars and symposia; Pres. Dr J. A. H. Bots; Sec. Dr F. J. W. VAN KAN; Treas. DE HEER M. GRAS; publs *Bijdragen en Mededelingen* (1 a year), *Werken*.

LANGUAGE AND LITERATURE

Alliance Française: POB 75736, 1070 AS Amsterdam; tel. (35) 6237667; e-mail info@alliance-francaise.nl; internet www.alliance-francaise.nl; f. 1888; offers courses and exams in French language and culture and promotes cultural exchange with France;

attached offices in Alkmaar, Amersfoort, Apeldoorn, Arnhem, Baarland, Bergen-op-Zoom, Betuwe, Boskoop, Brakel, Breda, Den Haag, Den Helder, Deventer, Dordrecht, Eindhoven, Enschede, Friesland, Hart van Zeeland, Hoorn, Kennemerland, Maastricht, Meppel, Nijmegen, Ommen, Roermond, Roosendaal, Rotterdam, Twente, Utrecht, Vorden, Walcheren, Zutphen and Zwolle; Pres. E. J. A. VAN TINTEREN-AMERICA; publs *En France* (4 a year), *En Route* (1 a year).

British Council: Weteringschans 85A, 1017 RZ Amsterdam; tel. (20) 5506060; e-mail exams@britishcouncil.nl; internet www .britishcouncil.org/netherlands; offers exams in English language and British culture; promotes cultural exchange with the UK; not open to gen. public; Dir MARTIN HOPE.

Goethe-Institut: Herengracht 470, 1017 CA Amsterdam; tel. (20) 5312900; e-mail amsterdam.goethe.org; internet www.goethe .de/ins/nl/ams/deindex.htm; offers courses and exams in German language and culture; promotes cultural exchange with Germany; attached centre in Rotterdam; Dir Dr BARBARA HONRATH.

Instituto Cervantes: Domplein 3, 3512 JC Utrecht; tel. (30) 2428477; e-mail cenutr@ cervantes.es; internet utrecht.cervantes.es; f. 1992; offers courses and exams in Spanish language and culture; promotes cultural exchange with Spain and Spanish-speaking Latin and Central America; library of 14,000 vols; Dir ISABEL LORDA.

Maatschappij der Nederlandse Letterkunde (Society of Netherlands Literature): POB 9501, 2300 RA Leiden; Witte Singel 27, 2300 RA Leiden; tel. (71) 5272109; e-mail mnl@library.leidenuniv.nl; internet www .maatschappijdernederlandseletterkunde.nl; f. 1766; library administered by the library of Leiden Univ.; 1,700 mems; Chair. PETER SIGMOND; Vice-Chair. KRIS HUMBEECK; Sec. BERRY DONGELMANS; publs *Jaarboek der Maatschappij* (1 a year), *Nieuw Letterkundig Magazijn* (2 a year), *Tijdschrift voor Nederlandse Taal- en Letterkunde* (4 a year).

Netherlands Centre of the International PEN: Emmalaan 29, 3051 JC Rotterdam; tel. (10) 4229805; e-mail secretariat@ pencentrum.nl; f. 1923; 350 mems; Pres. HESTER KNIBBE; Sec. RENÉ APPEL; publ. *PEN Nieuwsbrief* (2 a year).

MEDICINE

Genootschap ter bevordering van Natuur-, Genees- en Heelkunde (Association for Advancement of Natural, Medical and Surgical Sciences): POB 94248, 1090 GE Amsterdam; tel. (20) 5255055; e-mail b.e .fabius@uva.nl; internet www.science.uva.nl/ ngh; f. 1790; encourages physics, medicine, surgery; awards individuals who contribute original research of great interest; Pres. Prof. Dr C. J. F. VAN NOORDEN; Sec. Prof. Dr J. J. O. O. WIEGERINCK; Treas. Prof. Dr D. ROOS.

Koninklijke Nederlandsche Maatschappij tot bevordering der Geneeskunst (Royal Dutch Medical Association): POB 20051, 3502 LB Utrecht; Domus Medica, Mercatorlaan 1200, 3528 BL Utrecht; tel. (30) 2823800; e-mail info@fed.knmg.nl; internet knmg.artsennet.nl; f. 1849; professional org. for physicians of the Netherlands; improves quality of medical care and healthcare; library on history of medicine in the Netherlands; 49,000 mems; Chair. Prof. Dr ARIE C. NIEUWENHUIJZEN KRUSEMAN; publs *Arts in Spe* (4 a year), *Medisch Contact* (52 a year).

Koninklijke Nederlandse Maatschappij ter Bevordering der Pharmacie (Royal Dutch Association for the Advancement of

Pharmacy): POB 30460, 2500 GL The Hague; Alexanderstraat 11, 2514 JL The Hague; tel. (70) 3737373; e-mail communicatie@knmp .nl; internet www.knmp.nl; f. 1842; promotes the interests of professional and industrial pharmacists; 3,500 mems; Pres. JAN SMITS; Vice-Pres. MAAYKE FLUITMAN; Dir-Gen. LÉON TINKE; Sec. JARD BALJET; Treas. BART SMALS; publ. *Pharmaceutisch Weekblad*.

Koninklijke Nederlandse Vereniging voor Microbiologie (KNVM) (Royal Netherlands Society for Microbiology): Touwbaan 40, 3142 BV Maassluis; tel. (10) 7509766; e-mail secretariaat@nvvm-online.nl; internet www.knvm.org; f. 1911; attached to Fed. of European Microbiological Socs; promotes microbiology in the Netherlands and Flanders; organizes symposia; 1,405 mems; Chair. Prof. Dr. H. A. B. (HAN) WÖSTEN; Vice-Chair. Prof. Dr J. A. G. (JOS) VAN STRIJP; Sec. Dr B. (BIRGITTA) DUIM; Sec. J. J. E. BIJLSMA; Treas. Dr J. W. (JAN WILLEM) SANDERS.

Nederlandse Vereniging voor Heelkunde (Association of Surgeons of the Netherlands): POB 20061, 3502 LB Utrecht; Domus Medica, Mercatorlaan 1200, 3528 BL Utrecht; tel. (30) 2823327; e-mail nvvh@ nvvh.knmg.nl; internet www.heelkunde.nl; f. 1902; promotes surgery and interests of gen. surgeons; 1,330 mems (incl. 15 hon. mems, 200 assoc. mems, 490 asst mems); Chair. Dr P. J. VAN DEN AKKER; Dir Drs B. X. OUDE ELBERINK; Vice-Chair. Prof. Dr R. A. E. M. TOLLENAAR; Sec.-Gen. Dr G. A. P. NIEUWENHUIJZEN; Treas. Dr M. H. A. BEMELMANS; publ. *Nederlands Tijdschrift voor Heelkunde* (12 a year); publ. *The European Journal of Surgery* (English, 12 a year).

Nederlandse Vereniging voor Neurologie (Netherlands Society for Neurology): POB 20050, 3502 LB Utrecht; Mercatorlaan 1200, 3528 BL Utrecht; tel. (30) 2823343; e-mail bureau@neurologie.nl; internet www .neurologie.nl; f. 1871, reorganized 1974; monitors, promotes and optimizes professional quality of care for people with diseases of the nervous system or muscles; 800 mems; Pres. Prof. Dr M. DE VISSER; Sec. Prof. Dr C. H. POLMAN; publ. *Clinical Neurology and Neurosurgery*.

Nederlandse Vereniging voor Orthodontische Studie (Netherlands Orthodontics Society): Mahatma Gandhistraat 10, 3066 VA Rotterdam; tel. (10) 2020006; e-mail info@nvos.info; internet www.nvos.info; f. 1946; offers guidance, training and information on changing insight and new methods; 700 mems; Chair. HERMAN VAN BEEK; Vice-Chair. CARINE CARELS; Sec. MANFRED LEUNISSE; publ. *Chain Nieuwsbrief* (2 a year).

Nederlandse Vereniging voor Psychiatrie (Netherlands Psychiatric Association): POB 20062, 3502 LB Utrecht; Mercatorlaan 1200, 3528 BL Utrecht; tel. (30) 2823303; e-mail info@nvvp.net; internet www.nvvp .net; f. 1871, reorganized 1973; 3,498 mems; Pres. Prof. Dr A. T. F. BEEKMAN; Vice-Pres. Dr W. CAHN; Dir NOORTJE SAX; Treas. J. A. VAN WAARDE; publ. *Tijdschrift voor Psychiatrie*.

Nederlandse Vereniging voor Tropische Geneeskunde en Internationale Gezondheidszorg (Netherlands Society for Tropical Medicine and International Health): POB 82, 3738 ZM Maartensdijk; tel. (65) 3515773; e-mail info@nvtg.org; internet www .nvtg.org; f. 1907; supports research; provides education; promotes exchange of expertise and knowledge in the field of tropical medicine and int. health for improvement of health care in low- and middle-income countries; 1,000 mems; Chair. Dr

ANKIE VAN DEN BROEK; Sec. Drs M. G. P. LAGRO; Treas. Drs J. H. M. VISSCHEDIJK.

Vereniging van Orthodontisten (Association of Orthodontists): Simon Vestdijkstraat 67, 3842 LK Harderwijk; tel. (65) 3264175; e-mail info@orthodontist.nl; internet www .orthodontist.nl; f. 1962; Chair. Drs G. P. STEENVOORDEN; Vice-Chair. Drs M. KONING; Sec. Dr M. C. RAADSHEER; Treas. Drs P. ZUURBIER.

Vereniging voor Volksgezondheid en Wetenschap (Netherlands Society of Public Health and Science): Lindelaan 4, 2282 EX Rijswijk; tel. (70) 3030045; e-mail secretariaat@verenigingvenw.nl; internet www.verenigingvenw.nl; f. 1985, fmrly Algemene Nederlandse Vereniging voor Sociale Gezondheidszorg; scientific approach to health and health care questions; 800 mems; Pres. Prof. Dr J. SCHUIT; Sec. Ir I. THIEN; Treas. Ir J. JANSEN; publs *European Journal of Public Health* (4 a year), *Tijdschrift voor Gezondheidswetenschappen* (8 a year).

NATURAL SCIENCES
General

Koninklijke Nederlandse Natuurhistorische Vereniging (Royal Dutch Society for Natural History): POB 310, 3700 AH Zeist; Blvd 12, 3707 BM Zeist; tel. (30) 2314797; e-mail bureau@knnv.nl; internet www.knnv .nl; f. 1901; field biology; supports active participation in and with nature through natural history studies; nature conservation; 8,300 mems; Chair. K. D. WATERREUS; Sec. H. W. ZOLF; Treas. H. TEN GROTENHUIS; publ. *Natura* (6 a year).

Natuurmonumenten: POB 9955, 1243 ZS 's-Graveland; Schaep en Burgh, Noordereinde 60, 1243 JJ 's-Graveland; tel. (35) 6559933; internet www.natuurmonumenten .nl; f. 1905; preserves nature, landscape and cultural history; controls 355 nature reserves; 830,000 mems; Pres. Prof. Dr CEES VEERMAN; Vice-Pres. and Sec. Prof. Dr MARTIN WASSEN; Dir-Gen. Ir JAN JAAP DE GRAEFF; Dir for Finance and Operations Drs FEDDE KOSTER; Treas. JAN VAN DEN BELT; publ. *Natuurbehoud* (4 a year).

Stichting Natuur en Milieu (Society for Nature and Environment): POB 1578, 3500 BN Utrecht; Hamburgerstraat 28A, 3512 NS Utrecht; tel. (30) 2331328; e-mail info@ natuurenmilieu.nl; internet www2 .natuurenmilieu.nl; f. 1972, present location 2007; nature conservation and environmental protection; Chair. M. VAN LIER LELS; Dir TJERK WAGENAAR; publ. *Natuur en milieu* (12 a year).

Thijmgenootschap (Society of Christian Scholars in the Netherlands): Groesbeekseweg 125, 6524 CT Nijmegen; e-mail contact@ thijmgenootschap.nl; internet www .thijmgenootschap.nl; f. 1904 as Vereeniging tot het Bevorderen van de Beoefening der Wetenschap onder de Katholieken in Nederland, current name adopted 1947; promotes scientific reflection from a Christian perspective on devts in culture and soc.; 1,500 mems; Pres. Prof. Dr WIM B. H. J. VAN DE DONK; Sec. Prof. Drs J. S. L. A. W. B. ROES; Treas. ROLAND E. C. VAN DER PLUYM; publ. *Annalen van het Thijmgenootschap* (4 a year).

Biological Sciences

Koninklijke Nederlandse Botanische Vereniging (Royal Botanical Society of the Netherlands): c/o Dr Ir. N. Smits, Alterra WUR, POB 47, 6700 AA Wageningen; e-mail nina.smits@wur.nl; internet www.knbv.eu; f. 1845; promotes knowledge of plants through education and research in areas such as plant ecology, plant molecular biology, plant physiology, plant taxonomy, vegetation science; 350 mems; Chair. Prof. Dr Joop H. J. Schaminée; Vice-Chair. Prof. Dr Theo Elzenga; First Sec. Dr Ton Peeters; Second Sec. Dr Nina Smits; Treas. Dr Tijs Ketelaar; publ. *Plant Biology.*

Koninklijke Nederlandse Dierkundige Vereniging (Royal Dutch Zoological Society): c/o Dr P. H. M. Klaren, Radboud Univ. Nijmegen, Dept of Animal Physiology, Heyendaalseweg 135, POB 30, 6525 AJ Nijmegen; tel. (24) 3653245; e-mail kndv .office@gmail.com; internet www.kndv.nl; f. 1872; promotes zoological research; organizes symposia; travel grants for univ. students; 200 mems; Pres. Dr Jan Kammenga; Sec. Dr Peter H. M. Klaren; Treas. Dr Lia Hemerik; publ. *Animal Biology* (4 a year, online, www.brill.nl/ab).

Natura Artis Magistra (Royal Zoological Society): POB 20164, 1000 HD Amsterdam; Plantage Kerklaan 38–40, Amsterdam; tel. (900) 2784796; e-mail info@artis.nl; internet www.artis.nl; f. 1838; promotes humans' connection with nature, relationship between nature and culture and degree of human interaction in this position; 8,000 mems; Dir Dr Haig Balian; publs *Artis* (5 a year), *Contributions to Zoology, Artis Library* (4 a year), *Tijdschrift van Natura Artis Magistra* (4 a year).

Nederlandse Entomologische Vereniging (Netherlands Entomological Society): Sj. Tiemersma, Vlasakker 2, 8091 MP Wezep; tel. (38) 3758275; e-mail secretaris@nev.nl; internet www.nev.nl; f. 1845; promotes entomology; 5 regional brs; 700 mems; library of 21,000 vols, 4,400 journals, 100,000 reprints; Pres. Dr Matty P. Berg; Vice-Pres. Prof. Dr Marcel Dicke; Sec. Sj. Tiemersma; Treas. Dr P. Oosterbroek; publs *Entomologia Experimentalis et Applicata* (12 a year), *Entomologische Berichten* (6 a year), *Tijdschrift voor Entomologie* (4 a year).

Nederlandse Mycologische Vereniging (Dutch Mycological Society): Centraalbureau voor Schimmelcultures, POB 85167, 3508 AD Utrecht; Uppsalalaan 8, 3584 CT Utrecht; tel. (30) 2122600; e-mail nmv@mycologen.nl; internet www.mycologen.nl; f. 1908; 800 mems; Chair. Rob Chrispijn; Sec. Jac N. J. Gelderblom; Treas. Aad J. Termorshuizen; publ. *Coolia* (4 a year).

Nederlandse Ornithologische Unie (Dutch Ornithological Union): Sloet Marke 41, 8016 CJ Zwolle; e-mail nou.ledenadmin@gmail.com; internet nou.natuurinfo.nl; f. 1901; 1,067 mems; library: 120 periodicals; Pres. Prof. Dr J. M. Tinbergen; Sec. Peter Milders; publs *Ardea* (2 a year), *Limosa* (4 a year).

Nederlandse Vereniging voor Parasitologie (Netherlands Society for Parasitology): c/o Dr J. J. Verweij, Laboratorium voor Parasitologie, L4-Q, LUMC, POB 9600, 2300 RC Leiden; e-mail j.j.verweij@lumc.nl; internet www.parasitologie.nl; f. 1961; promotes and exchanges scientific knowledge of infectious diseases caused by parasites; 250 mems; Pres. Prof. Dr Robert Sauerwein; Sec. Dr Jaco Verweij; Treas. Dr Clemens Kocken.

Nederlandse Zoötechnische Vereniging (Netherlands Association for Animal Husbandry): POB 79, 6700 AB Wageningen; tel. (317) 483487; e-mail info@nzvnet.nl; internet www.nzvnet.nl; f. 1930; network for professionals in the field of animals, people and environment; 550 mems; Pres. Ir Gert Hemke; Sec. Ir G. H. Jansen; Sec. Dr Ir Joost van den Borne.

Mathematical Sciences

Koninklijk Wiskundig Genootschap (Royal Dutch Mathematical Society): CWI, POB 94079, 1090 GB Amsterdam; tel. (20) 5924263; e-mail wiskgenoot@wiskgenoot.nl; internet www.wiskgenoot.nl; f. 1778; organizes confs and symposia; 1,300 mems; library of 16,400 vols and journals of mathematics and its applications; Pres. Prof. Dr Geurt Jongbloed; Sec. Joke Blom; Treas. Dr Fetsje Bijma; publs *Nieuw Archief voor Wiskunde* (4 a year), *Pythagoras* (6 a year).

Vereniging voor Statistiek en Operationele Research (Netherlands Society for Statistics and Operations Research): POB 244, 6700 AE Wageningen; tel. (180) 419572; e-mail admin@vvs-or.nl; internet www.vvs-or .nl; f. 1945; promotes study and application of statistics, operations research, relevant devts in mathematics in service of science and soc.; 800 mems; Chair. Prof. Dr J. J. Meulman; Sec. Dr I. G. Klugkist; Treas. Dr A. A. N. Ridder; publs *Statistica Neerlandica* (4 a year), *Stator* (4 a year).

Physical Sciences

Koninklijk Nederlands Geologisch Mijnbouwkundig Genootschap (Royal Geological and Mining Society of the Netherlands): POB 30424, 2500 GK The Hague; Prinsessegracht 23, 2514 AP The Hague; tel. (70) 3919892; e-mail kngmg@me .com; internet www.kngmg.nl; f. 1912; promotes the interests of earth sciences in the Netherlands; awards Van Waterschoot van der Gracht medal (an award for outstanding scientific achievement); organizes the annual Staring day; sections for petroleum geology, paleobiolology, palynology, mineralogy, sedimentology, engineering geology and geochemistry; section for female professional earth scientists (GAIA) and various regional earth science asscns; 800 mems; Pres. Dr Menno de Ruig; Sec. Drs Barthold Schroot; Treas. Arian Steenbruggen; publs *Geo.brief* (8 a year), *Geologie en Mijnbouw* (Netherlands Journal of Geosciences, 4 a year).

Koninklijk Nederlands Meteorologisch Instituut (Royal Netherlands Meteorological Institute): POB 201, 3730 AE De Bilt; Wilhelminalaan 10, 3732 GK De Bilt; tel. (30) 2206911; internet www.knmi.nl; f. 1854, present location 1897; attached to Min. of Infrastructure and the Environment; meteorology, climatology, oceanography, seismology; conducts research on climate change; library of 140,000 vols, spec. collns incl. Polar expeditions; Dir-Gen. Dr Ir Frits J. J. Brouwer; Exec. Dir Drs D. R. van Hattem; publs *Maandover zicht van het weer*, *Seismological Bulletin*, scientific reports and technical reports, daily weather maps, rain observations.

Koninklijke Nederlandse Chemische Vereniging (Royal Netherlands Chemical Society): POB 249, 2260 AE Leidschendam; Synthesium, Castellum C, Loire 150, 2491 AK The Hague; tel. (70) 3378790; e-mail kncv@kncv.nl; internet www.kncv.nl; f. 1903, present location 2006; promotes molecular sciences; 8,500 mems; Pres. Prof. Dr Saskia van der Vies; Vice-Pres. Drs Jan Apotheker; Sec. and Dir for Bureau Dr Gabriëlle Donné; Treas. Dr Lene Hviid; publs *Chemisch 2 Weekblad* (21 a year), *European Journal of Inorganic Chemistry* (12 a year), *European Journal of Organic Chemistry* (12 a year).

Koninklijke Nederlandse Vereniging voor Weer- en Sterrenkunde (Royal Netherlands Association for Meteorology and Astronomy): Prinses Irenelaan 1, 9765 AL Paterswolde; tel. (30) 3094290; internet www .sterrenkunde.nl/knvws; f. 1901; public lectures, meetings, confs, observing sessions; 5,000 mems; Pres. N. J. J. de Kort; publs *Sterrengids* (1 a year), *Zenit* (12 a year).

Nederlandse Natuurkundige Vereniging (Netherlands Physical Society): POB 41882, 1009 DB Amsterdam; Science Park 105, Kamer N227, 1098 XG Amsterdam; tel. (20) 5922211; e-mail bureau@nnv.nl; internet www.nnv.nl; f. 1921; improves study of physics and safeguards interests of physicists; 3,800 mems; Chair. Prof. Dr J. M. van Ruitenbeek; Sec. Dr J. Klootwijk; Treas. Dr P. Brussaard; publ. *Nederlands Tijdschrift voor Natuurkunde* (12 a year).

PHILOSOPHY AND PSYCHOLOGY

Algemene Nederlandse Vereniging voor Wijsbegeerte (General Netherlands Philosophical Society): c/o Erasmus Universiteit, Faculty of Philosophy, POB 1738, 3000 DR Rotterdam; Faculty of Philosophy, Campus Woudestein, H-Bldg, 5th Fl., Burgemeester Oudlaan 50, 3062 PA Rotterdam; e-mail anvw@fwb.eur.nl; internet www.nl/fw; f. 1933; 150 mems; Pres. Dr J. A. van Ruler; Sec. Dr H. A. Krop; publ. *Algemeen Tijdschrift voor Wijsbegeerte.*

Affiliated Societies:

Internationale School voor Wijsbegeerte (International School of Philosophy): Dodeweg 8, 3832 RD Leusden; tel. (33) 4650700; e-mail info@isvw.nl; internet www.isvw.nl; f. 1916; courses and confs in philosophy; 3,000 mems; library of 3,000 vols; Man. Dir René Gude; Dir for Operations Chantal Orth.

KIVI Aftdeling Filosofie en Techniek: 23 Prinsessegracht, POB 30424, 2500 GK The Hague; f. 1847; Chair. R. E. C. H. Tiepel; Sec. J. Groenhoef.

Nederlands Genootschap voor Esthetica (Dutch Association for Aesthetics): Grevingaheerd 181, 9737 SL Groningen; e-mail info@nge.nl; internet www.nge.nl; f. 1997; asscn for theoretical, philosophical, critical reflection on the arts and aesthetic dimensions of contemporary culture; Chair. Sander van Maas; Vice-Chair. Hans Maes; Sec. Rii Dalitz; publ. *Esthetica: Tijdschrift voor Kunst en Filosofie* (online).

Nederlandse Vereniging voor Godsdienstwijsbegeerte: Ring 34, 3227 AS Oudenhoorn; f. 1995.

Nederlandse Vereniging voor Logica en Wijsbegeerte der Exacte Wetenschappen: POB 407, 9700 AK Groningen; tel. (50) 3636334; e-mail rineke@ai.rug.nl; internet www .verenigingvoorlogica.nl; f. 1947; organizes scientific symposia; 150 mems; Chair. Prof. Dr Rineke Verbrugge; Sec. Dr Femke van Raamsdonk.

Nederlandse Vereniging voor Wetenschapsfilosofie (Dutch Society for Philosophy of Science): Faculty of Philosophy, Univ. of Groningen, Oude Boteringestr. 52 Groningen; tel. (50) 3636148; e-mail info@nvwf.nl; internet www.nvwf .nl; f. 1979; org. of confs, workshops and lectures; 80 mems; Pres. Prof. Dr F. A. Muller; Sec. Prof. Dr Sylvia Wenmackers.

Stichting voor Christelijke Filosofie (Association for Reformational Philosophy): POB 2220, 3800 CE Amersfoort; tel. (33) 4328288; e-mail directie@christelijkefilosofie.nl; internet www .christelijkefilosofie.nl; f. 1935; asscn for Christian philosophy, based on thinking of philosophers such as Dutch Dooyeweerd, Schuurman, Van Riessen, Vollenhoven, foreign philosophers such as Chaplin (UK), Clouser (USA), Strauss (S Africa);

535 mems; Pres. Drs A. BERGER; Vice-Pres. Drs D. A. MEINEMA; Sec. Drs W. VOLLBEHR; Dir HILLIE VD STREEK; publs *Philosophia Reformata* (in English, 2 a year), *Sophie* (in Dutch, 6 a year).

Vereniging 'Het Spinozahuis': Paganinidreef 66, 2253 SK Voorschoten; tel. (71) 5612759; e-mail info@spinozahuis.nl; internet www.spinozahuis.nl; f. 1897; promotes life and works of philosopher Benedictus de Spinoza; cultural monument, library, museum; library of 4,000 vols; 1,100 mems; Pres. L. VAN BUNGE; Sec. THEO VAN DER WERF; publ. *Mededelingen vanwege het Spinozahuis* (3 a year).

Vereniging voor Filosofie en Geneeskunde: p/a Elisa Garcia Concertgebouwplein 17, 1071 LM Amsterdam; tel. (6) 12842555; e-mail m.vanzwol@vumc.nl; internet www.filosofieengeneeskunde.nl; f. 1981; Pres. Prof. Dr MAARTJE SCHERMER; Sec. Drs MARJANNE VAN ZWOL.

Vereniging voor Wijsbegeerte te 's-Gravenhage: Nassau Dillenburgstraat 33, 2596 AC 's-Gravenhage; tel. (70) 3242919; e-mail verenigingvoorwijsbegeerte@gmail.com; internet www.verenigingvoorwijsbegeerte .nl; f. 1907; 100 mems; Pres. Ir J. M. ALBERS; Sec. M. KATER.

Vereniging voor Wijsbegeerte van het Recht (Netherlands Association for Legal Philosophy): Obrechtstraat 188, Lorentzzaal, 2517 XA The Hague; e-mail penningmeester@verenigingrechtsfilosofie .nl; internet www.verenigingrechtsfilosofie .nl; f. 1919; promotes practice of legal philosophy and legal theory; 350 mems; Pres. BART VAN KLINK; Sec. LYANA FRANCOT; publ. *Netherlands Journal for Legal Philosophy* (3 a year).

Wijsgerige Vereniging Thomas van Aquino: POB 37, 5260 AA Vught; Aloysiuslaan 2, 5262 AH Vught; tel. (73) 6579017; f. 1933; philosophical confs; 160 mems; Pres. Prof. Dr A. LEIJEN; Sec. Prof. Dr R. A. TE VELDE.

Bataafsch Genootschap der Proefondervindelijke Wijsbegeerte (Experimental Natural Philosophy Society): POB 597, 3000 AN Rotterdam; tel. (10) 4117947; e-mail secretariaat@bataafschgenootschap.nl; internet www.bataafschgenootschap.nl; f. 1769; organizes 6 lectures for mems each year; awards biannual prizes and an int. Steven Hoogendijk Award every 2 years; 400 mems; Pres. Dr F. B. DE WAARD-VAN DER SPEK; Dir Prof. Dr Ir J. K. VRIJLING; Dir Prof. Ir L. VAN DER SLUIS; Dir Prof. Dr HUUG W. TILANUS.

Nederlands Psychoanalytisch Genootschap (Netherlands Psychoanalytical Association): Maliestraat 1A, 3581 SH Utrecht; tel. (30) 2307080; e-mail npg@ npsai-utrecht.nl; internet www.npg-utrecht .nl; f. 1947; organizes scientific meetings, lectures and symposia; 136 mems; library of 60,000 vols; Sec. ELISE COMES.

RELIGION, SOCIOLOGY AND ANTHROPOLOGY

Fryske Akademy: POB 54, 8900 AB Ljouwert; Doelestraat 8, 8911 DX Ljouwert; tel. (58) 2131414; e-mail fa@fryske-akademy.nl; internet www.fryske-akademy.nl; f. 1938; attached to Royal Netherlands Acad. of Arts and Science; devoted to the scientific study of Friesland, the Frisians and their language, history and culture; 350 mems; library of 20,000 vols; Dir Prof. Dr R. SALVERDA; publs *De Vrije Fries* (history, 1 a year), *It Beaken* (scientific, 4 a year), *Ut de Smidte fan de Fryske Akademy* (information, 3 a year).

TECHNOLOGY

Economisch Instituut voor de Bouw (Economic Institute for the Building): POB 58248, 1040 HE Amsterdam; Basisweg, 10 1043 AP Amsterdam; tel. (20) 5831900; e-mail eib@eib.nl; internet www.eib.nl; f. 1956 as Economic Institute for the Bldg Industry; promotes applied research in org. bldg and economic analysis; Chair. CAREL A. ADRIAANSENS; Dir Drs T. H. VAN HOEK; Deputy Dir Drs O. M. VRIES; Sec. DEBBIE VAN AMERONGEN; Sec. G. KRAMER; publs *Algemene kosten in het bouwbedrijf* (1 a year), *Bedrijfseconomische kencijfers* (1 a year), *Bedrijfseconomische kencijfers in de gww-sector* (1 a year), *Verwachtingen bouwproductie en werkgelegenheid* (1 a year).

Koninklijk Instituut van Ingenieurs (KIVI) (Royal Dutch Society of Engineers (KIVI)): POB 30424, 2500 GK The Hague; Prinsessegracht 23, 2514 AP The Hague; tel. (70) 3919900; e-mail info@kivi.nl; internet www.kivi.nl; f. 2004, by merger of Dutch NIRIA Engineers Asscn and Royal Institute of Engineers; asscn for engineers and engineering students; promotes technology; 20,000 mems; Pres. MARTIN C. J. VAN PERNIS; Vice-Pres. JOOST J. WENTINK; Dir Ir M. V. I. M. DOS RAMOS; Sec. JACKY C. GERSIE; publ. *De Ingenieur Technologiemagazine* (26 a year); publs *Kivi-nieuws* (26 a year), *Technisch Weekblad* (52 a year).

Technologiestichting STW (Technology Foundation): POB 3021, 3502 GA Utrecht; Van Vollenhovenlaan 661, 3527 JP Utrecht; tel. (30) 6001211; e-mail info@stw.nl; internet www.stw.nl; f. 1981; improves and stimulates applied sciences and engineering by sponsoring research at (technical) univs in the Netherlands and promotes cooperation between those institutes and industry; also assists in implementing spec. governmental research programmes; Dir Dr EPPO E. W. BRUINS; Deputy Dir Dr CHRIS A. M. MOMBERS; publ. *!nterval*.

Research Institutes

GENERAL

Adhesion Institute: Kluyverweg 1, 2629 HS Delft; tel. (15) 2785353; e-mail info@ hechtingsinstituut.nl; internet www .adhesioninstitute.com; attached to Faculty of Aerospace Engineering, Delft Univ. of Technology; research focuses on latest devts on surface pre-treatment of metals and plastics, durability of adhesive bonds, the application of adhesive(s) and adhesive bond design, as well as (FEM)-calculations on structural adhesive bonding technology; Dir Dr J. A. POULIS.

Amsterdam Business School Research Institute: Plantage Muidergracht, Room M2.42, 1018 WB Amsterdam; tel. (20) 5257384; e-mail abs-ri@uva.nl; internet absri.uva.nl; f. 2002; attached to Univ. of Amsterdam; research concerning accounting, business, finance, management; Research Dir Prof. BRENDAN O'DWYER.

Amsterdam Center for Career Research (ACCR): De Boelelaan 1105, 1081 HV Amsterdam; tel. (20) 5986000; e-mail loopbanen@feweb.vu.nl; internet www.feweb .vu.nl/en/departments-and-institutes/accr; f. 2006; attached to VU Univ. Amsterdam; researches into factors contributing to growth of careers, in terms of devt and job level, within orgs.

Amsterdam Center for Entrepreneurship at VU: De Boelelaan 1085, 1081 Amsterdam; tel. (20) 5989906; e-mail infoacevu@feweb.vu.nl; internet www.feweb

.vu.nl/acevu; research focuses on entrepreneurship as new venture creation, wealth creation as dominant motive to create new ventures, and entrepreneur as instigator of entrepreneurship; Dir Prof. ENNO MASUREL.

Amsterdam Institute for International Development (AIID): Trinity Bldg C, 3rd Fl., Room XT-3.17, Pietersbergweg 17, 1105 BM Amsterdam; tel. (20) 5661596; e-mail info@aiid.org; internet www.aiid.org; f. 2000; attached to Univ. of Amsterdam, Vrije Univ. Amsterdam; links the two univ. experts in int. devt and engages in policy debates; research on causes and consequences of poverty, human devt, governance and poverty, environment and devt, globalization and devt assistance.

Brabant Centre of Entrepreneurship: POB 513, 5600 MB Eindhoven; Multimedia-Paviljoen, Room 0.21, Horsten 1, 5612 AX Eindhoven; tel. (40) 4663320; e-mail info@ bc-e.nl; internet www.bc-e.nl; attached to Tilburg Univ.; Academic Dir Dr GEERT DUYSTERS; Business Dir KEES KOKKE.

Centre for Innovation Research: Faculty of Social and Behavioural Sciences, POB 90153, 5000 LE Eindhoven; Prisma Bldg, Warandelaan 2, 5037 AB Eindhoven; tel. (13) 4663057; e-mail cir@uvt.nl; internet www .tilburguniversity.nl/cir; attached to Tilburg Univ.; fundamental research on innovation; research themes incl. innovation strategy, org. of innovation, organizational learning; Dir Prof. Dr X. Y. F. MARTIN; Dir Prof. Dr M. T. H. MEEUS.

Centrum voor Justitiepastoraat (Interuniversity Centre for Prison Pastoral Studies): POB 90153, 5000 LE Tilburg; Warandelaan 2, 5037 AB Tilburg; tel. (13) 4662609; e-mail info@ centrumvoorjustitiepastoraat.nl; internet www.centrumvoorjustitiepastoraat.nl; f. 2009; attached to Law School and School of Catholic Theology of Tilburg Univ. and Protestant Theological Univ., Amsterdam; research, education and publs on issues relevant for the work of prison chaplains, like restorative justice, reconciliation, humane detention, punishment; Dir Prof. Dr THEO W. A. DE WIT; Sec. Gen. Dr RYAN A. T. VAN EIJK; publs *Twee Heren Dienen: Geestelijk Verzorgers en hun Beroepseer, Van Kwaad Verhalen*.

Competence Centre for Pension Research: POB 90153, 5000 LE Tilburg; Montesquieu Bldg, Warandelaan 2, Room M612, 5037 AB Tilburg; tel. (13) 4662412; e-mail frw.ccp@uvt.nl; internet www .tilburguniversity.nl/ccp; attached to Faculty of Law, Tilburg Univ.; research in the fields of tax and civil law aspects of pensions and other retirement provisions; Chair. Prof. Dr GERRY DIETVORST; Sec. TONIA NELEN.

European Banking Centre: Tilburg Univ., POB 90153, 5000 LE Tilburg; Koopmans Bldg, Room 3 16, Warandelaan 2, 5037 AB Tilburg; tel. (13) 4662468; e-mail ebc@uvt.nl; internet www.tilburguniversity.nl/ebc; attached to Tilburg Univ.; stimulates and disseminates banking research, with three essential areas of expertise: central banking and financial supervision, European banking and regulation, and int. banking and finance; Chair. Prof. Dr THORSTEN BECK.

European Institute of Retailing and Services Studies (EIRASS): POB 513, Vertigo 8.18, 5600 MB Eindhoven; tel. (40) 2472594; e-mail eirass@bwk.tue.nl; internet w3.bwk.tue.nl/nl/onderzoek/urban_planning/ eirass; attached to Eindhoven Univ. of Technology; organizes confs; progress in retailing and consumer services (tourism, recreation, banking, aspects of transportation, etc.); Dir

Prof. HARRY TIMMERMANS; Sec. LINDA VAN DE VEN.

European Research Institute in Service Science (ERISS): Room K 731, POB 90153, 5000 LE Tilburg; Warandelaan 2, 5037 AB Tilburg; tel. (13) 4663020; e-mail eriss@uvt .nl; internet www.tilburguniversity.nl/eriss; attached to Tilburg Univ.; research in innovation, service science with a focus on critical business process areas that span several knowledge-intensive business services within vertical industries; Chair. of Advisory Board Prof. Dr PIET RIBBERS; Scientific Dir Prof. Dr Ir M. P. PAPAZOGLOU; Man. Dir Prof. Dr W. J. A. M. VAN DEN HEUVEL; Sec. ALICE KLOOSTERHUIS.

European Values Study (EVS): Dept of Sociology, Tilburg Univ., POB 90153, 5000 LE Tilburg; School of Social and Behavioural Sciences, Tilburg Univ., Prisma Bldg, Warandelaan 2, 5037 AB Tilburg; tel. (13) 4662554; e-mail evs@uvt.nl; internet www .europeanvaluesstudy.eu; f. 1981; attached to Tilburg Univ.; research on basic human values; provides insights into the ideas, beliefs, preferences, attitudes, values and opinions of citizens all over Europe; how Europeans think about life, family, work, religion, politics and society; Chair. Prof. Dr PAUL DE GRAAF; Sec. Dr LOEK HALMAN.

EXPres: Van der Boechorststraat 9, 1081 Amsterdam; e-mail expres@fbw.vu.nl; internet www.expertisecentrum-expres.nl; f. 1989; attached to Vrije Univ. Amsterdam; research on rehabilitation, ergonomics and sports.

Globalisation Studies Groningen: Globalisation Studies Groningen, Univ. of Groningen, POB 716, 9700 AS Groningen; tel. (50) 3632391; e-mail gsg@rug.nl; internet www .rug.nl/gsg; attached to Univ. of Groningen; fosters public debate on topics varying from globalization, North–South relations and sustainable devt; Dir Prof. JOOST HERMAN.

Groningen Research Institute for the Study of Culture (ICOG): POB 716, 9700 AS Groningen; Oude Kijk in 't Jatstraat 26, 9712 EK Groningen; tel. (50) 3638195; e-mail icog@rug.nl; internet www.rug.nl/research/ icog; attached to Faculty of Arts, Univ. of Groningen; study of cultural processes in Europe, Americas, E Mediterranean, Asian regions; Dir Prof. Dr E. J. (LIESBETH) KORTHALS ALTES.

Het Zijlstra Center: De Boelelaan 1105, 1081 HV Amsterdam; tel. (20) 5989865; e-mail info@hetzijlstracenter.nl; internet www.feweb.vu.nl/nl/afdelingen-en-instituten/het-zijlstra-center; f. 2009; attached to Univ. of Amsterdam; research focuses on management and operations of non-profits and govts that focus on solving social problems; contributes results to improvement of management of govts and civil soc. orgs; Dir Prof. Dr G. D. MINDERMAN; Sec. ANJA VAN EIJK.

iCRiSP—Centre for Conflict, Risk and Safety Perception: Citadel H 444, POB 217, 7500 AE Enschede; Citadel Bldg, H 444, Drienerlolaan 5, 7522 NB Enschede; tel. (53) 4896052; e-mail icrisp@utwente.nl; internet www.utwente.nl/ibr/icrisp; f. 2009; attached to Univ. of Twente; focuses on the implementation of knowledge from social and behavioural sciences regarding issues of conflict, risk, safety in public and private sectors of soc.; Dir Prof. Dr ELLEN GIEBELS; Dir Dr JAN GUTTELING.

Institute for Sport & Leisure: Univ. of Twente, bld. CTW-Z-115, Drienerlolaan 5, 7522 NB Enschede; tel. (53) 4893606; e-mail info@sportandleisure.nl; internet www .sportandleisure.nl; attached to Univ. of Twente; innovation, devt, prototyping, engineering for products within the field of sport and leisure.

Instituut voor Bedrijfs- en Industriële Statistiek (IBIS) (Institute for Business and Industrial Statistics): Plantage Muidergracht 12, 1018 TV Amsterdam; tel. (20) 5255203; e-mail info@ibisuva.nl; internet www.ibisuva.nl; f. 1994; attached to Univ. of Amsterdam; statistical methodology, business economic context of quality and efficiency improvement, operations management; Man. Dir Prof. Dr RONALD J. M. M. DOES.

International Victimology Institute Tilburg (INTERVICT): Room M634, POB 90153, 5000 LE Tilburg; Montesquieu Bldg, 6th Fl., Warandelaan 2, 5037 AB Tilburg; tel. (13) 4663526; e-mail intervict@ tilburguniversity.edu; internet www .tilburguniversity.nl/intervict; attached to Tilburg Univ.; research areas incl. victims of abuse of power, crime and disaster; rights of victims; psychological effects of victimization; help provided to victims; social reactions to victims; Dir Prof. MARC S. GROENHUIJSEN; Deputy Dir Prof. PETER VAN DER VELDEN; Gen. Man. BARBARA M. VAN GORP.

IPIT Instituut voor Maatschappelijke Veiligheidsvraagstukken: Univ. of Twente, POB 217, 7500 AE Enschede; Capitool 15, Room C-201, Enschede; tel. (53) 4893280; e-mail ipit@bbt.utwente.nl; internet www.ipit.nl; attached to Univ. of Twente; law, public safety studies, law, risk analysis, risk management; research incl. functioning of insecurity and society, public safety maintenance system; Dir Prof. Dr M. JUNGER; Sec. J.L.M. (ANNETTE) VAN DER TUUK.

IVA Beleidsonderzoek en Advies: POB 90153, 5000 LE Tilburg; Campus Tilburg Univ., Bldg T, Warandelaan 2, 5037 AB Tilburg; tel. (13) 4668466; e-mail iva@uvt .nl; internet www.iva.nl; f. 1957; attached to Tilburg Univ.; applied scientific research, consultancy, implementation concerning current social devts, particularly in the domains of education, care and welfare, security, art, media and culture, labour and organizational issues; Pres. Prof. Dr MARC VERMEULEN; Man. Dir and Vice-Pres. MYLÈNE ZWAANS; Exec. Sec. ANNELIES VAN LEEUWEN.

IVO—Instituut voor Ontwikkelingsvraagstukken/Instituto de Estudios Para El Desarrollo (Development Research Institute): POB 90153, 5000 LE Tilburg; Tias Bldg, Office T-231, Warandelaan 2, 5037 AB Tilburg; tel. (13) 4662264; e-mail secr.ivo@ uvt.nl; internet www.uvt.nl/ivo; f. 1963; attached to Tilburg Univ.; applied socio-economic research, training and capacity building in support of poverty alleviation in developing countries; Dir GERARD DE GROOT; Man. MARIA JOSÉ RODIL.

Kohnstamm Instituut (Kohnstamm Institute): POB 94208, 1090 GE Amsterdam; Plantage Muidergracht 24, 1018 TV Amsterdam; tel. (20) 5251226; e-mail secr@ kohnstamm.uva.nl; internet www .kohnstamminstituut.uva.nl; f. fmrly as SCO-Kohnstamm Institute, present status 2009; attached to Univ. of Amsterdam; research areas incl. child rearing, child welfare, education; Man. Dir Drs J. E. KRAMER; Scientific Dir Drs G. LEDOUX; Deputy Dir Drs M. VAN ERP.

Kosmopolis Institute: POB 797, 3500 AT Utrecht; Univ. for Humanistics, Kromme Nieuwegracht 29, 3512 HD Utrecht; tel. (30) 2390100; e-mail kosmopolis@uvh.nl; internet www.uvh.nl; f. 2004; attached to Univ. for Humanistics; focuses on interdisciplinary teaching; training, research, networking on cosmopolitan dimensions of humanism in the world; Gen. Dir Dr CAROLINA SURANSKY; Exec. Sec. DOROTHÉ VAN DRIEL.

Netspar, Network for Studies on Pensions, Ageing and Retirement: POB 90153, 5000 MB Tilburg; Tilburg Univ. Campus, Tias Bldg, Warandelaan 2, 5037 AB Tilburg; tel. (13) 4662109; e-mail secretariaat@netspar.nl; internet www .netspar.nl; f. 2005; attached to Tilburg Univ.; research areas incl. ageing, pensions, retirement; Chair. Prof. Dr FRANK VAN DER DUYN SCHOUTEN; Scientific Dir THEO NIJMAN; Man. Dir DOMINIQUE DE VET; publ. Netspar Magazine (2 a year).

Nexus Instituut (Nexus Institute): POB 90153, 5000 LE Tilburg; Tilburg Univ., Room T203-209, Warandelaan 2, 5037 AB Tilburg; tel. (13) 4663450; e-mail info@ nexus-instituut.nl; internet www .nexus-instituut.nl; f. 1994; attached to Tilburg Univ.; centre for intellectual reflection; organizes confs and lectures; Chair. of Supervisory Board Dr WIM VAN DEN GOORBERGH; Pres. and CEO ROB RIEMEN; Vice-Pres. KIRSTEN WALGREEN; publ. Nexus (3 a year).

Nikos—Dutch Institute for Knowledge Intensive Entrepreneurship: Univ. of Twente, POB 217, 7500 AE Enschede; Drienerlolaan 5, 7522 NB Enschede; tel. (53) 4894512; e-mail nikos@mb.utwente.nl; internet www.utwente.nl/mb/nikos; attached to Univ. of Twente; innovative entrepreneurship, int. management, marketing, strategic management; Scientific Dir Prof. Dr AARD J. GROEN; Sec. GLORIA ROSSINI.

Onderzoekscentrum Preventie Overgewicht Zwolle (Research Centre for the Prevention of Overweight Zwolle): VU-Windesheim, Campus 2–6, POB 10090, 8000 GB Zwolle; tel. (88) 4699096; e-mail preventieovergewicht@windesheim.nl; research on designing, implementing, evaluating and disseminating knowledge related to prevention of obesity in 0–19-year-old children; Man. Dir Dr SASKIA VAN HELDEN.

Rathenau Instituut (Rathenau Institute): POB 95366, 2509 CJ The Hague; Anna van Saksenlaan 51, 2593 HW The Hague; tel. (70) 3421542; e-mail info@rathenau.nl; internet www.rathenau.nl; f. 1986 as Netherlands Org. for Technology Assessment, present name 1994; attached to Royal Netherlands Acad. of Arts and Sciences; supports social and political opinion-forming on issues arising from scientific and technological devt; Chair. GERDI VERBEET; Sec. Drs JAN STAMAN.

Research Center voor Examinering en Certificering (RCEC) (Research Center for Examinations and Certification (RCEC)): POB 217, 7500 AE Enschede; tel. (53) 4893555; e-mail rcec@gw.utwente.nl; internet www.rcec.nl; f. 2007; attached to Univ. of Twente; stimulates and facilitates ind. research into examinations and certification; conducts research projects for public and private orgs; gives training in educational measurement; disseminates information by organizing confs on issues in examinations; Dir BERNARD P. VELDKAMP; Dir Dr PIET F. SANDERS.

Research Institute for Flexicurity, Labour Market Dynamics and Social Cohesion (ReflecT): Tilburg Univ., S 424, POB 90153, 5000 LE Tilburg; Montesquieu Bldg (entrance at Prof. Verbernelaan), 6th Fl., Room M 611, 5000 LE Tilburg; tel. (13) 4662181; e-mail reflect@uvt.nl; internet www .tilburguniversity.edu/research/institutes-and-research-groups/reflect; attached to Tilburg Univ.; combines legal, economic, sociological and psychological approaches and adopts a multi-level perspective in studying the interplay between various regulatory and institutional levels in society: the European/int., nat., sector and company/individual level; Dir Prof. A. C. J. M. (TON) WILTHAGEN; Sec. A. I. (ANNET) VAN HUIJKELOM-FRANKENA.

Tilburg Centre of Finance: Loes de Groot, K 916, POB 90153, 5000 LE Tilburg; tel. (13) 4663041; e-mail tcf@uvt.nl; internet www .tilburguniversity.edu/research/institutes-and-research-groups/tcf; attached to Tilburg Univ.; research areas incl. actuarial profession, finance, governance and supervision; Mem. of Board Prof. Dr BAS WERKER; Mem. of Board Prof. Dr FRANK DE JONG; Mem. of Board Prof. Dr FRANS DE ROON.

Tilburg Sustainability Center (TSC): Tilburg Univ., POB 90153, 5000 LE Tilburg; Tilburg Univ., Koopmans Bldg, K405, Warandelaan 2, 5037 AB Tilburg; tel. (13) 4663479; e-mail tsc@uvt.nl; internet www .tilburguniversity.nl/tsc; f. 2009; attached to Tilburg Univ.; collaborative research between economists, legal scientists, sociologists and related disciplines on fundamental and applied problems in relation to sustainability; Scientific Dir Prof. Dr AART DE ZEEUW; Man. Dir Drs Ir HILDE BAERT.

Transport Infrastructure and Logistics (TRAIL) Research School: POB 5017, 2600 GA Delft; Jaffalaan 5, 2628 BX Delft; tel. (15) 2786046; e-mail info@rstrail.nl; internet www.rstrail.nl; f. 1997; collaboration of five Dutch univ.; research in mobility, transport, logistics, traffic, infrastructure and transport systems; Scientific Dir Prof. BERT VAN WEE; Managing Dir and Deputy Scientific Dir VINCENT A. W. J. MARCHAU.

Tranzo—Scientific Centre for Care and Welfare: Tilburg School of Social and Behavioural Sciences, Tilburg Univ., POB 90153, 5000 LE Tilburg; Room T 515, Tias Bldg, Warandelaan 2, 5037 AB Tilburg; tel. (13) 4662969; e-mail tranzo@uvt.nl; internet www.tilburguniversity.edu/tranzo; attached to Tilburg Univ.; fundamental and applied research in care and services; Chair. Prof. Dr HENK GARRETSEN.

AGRICULTURE, FISHERIES AND VETERINARY SCIENCE

Alterra: POB 47, 6700 AA Wageningen; Droevendaalsesteeg 3, Bldg 101, 6708 PB Wageningen; tel. (317) 480700; e-mail info .alterra@wur.nl; internet www.alterra.wur .nl; f. 2000 by merger of DLO Winand Staring Centre for Integrated Land, Soil and Water Research, Institut voor Bos- en Natuuronderzoek and part of DLO-Instituut voor Agrobiologisch Onderzoek; attached to Wageningen Univ. and Research Centre; practical and scientific research in disciplines related to the green world and the sustainable use of our living environment: knowledge of water, nature, biodiversity, climate, landscape, forest, ecology, environment, soil, landscape and spatial planning, geo-information, remote sensing, flora and fauna, urban green, man and soc. etc.; Man. Dir Ir C. T. (KEES) SLINGERLAND; Dir for Operations Ir AUKE H. DE BRUIN; publ. *Alterra Scientific Contributions.*

Centre for Development Innovation: POB 88, 6700 AB Wageningen; Droevendaalsesteeg 1, Bldg 107, 6708 PB Wageningen; tel. (317) 486800; e-mail info.cdi@wur.nl; internet www.wageningenur.nl/cdi; attached to Wageningen Univ. and Research Centre; works on processes of innovation and change in areas of secure and healthy food, adaptive agriculture, sustainable markets and ecosystem governance; Dir Dr J. C. VERDAAS; Deputy Dir WOUTER LEEN HIJWEEGE; Sec. ANNETTE VAN 'T HULL.

Food & Biobased Research: POB 17, 6700 AA Wageningen; Wageningen Campus, Bornse Weilanden 9, Bldg 118, 6708 WG Wageningen; tel. (317) 480084; e-mail info .fbr@wur.nl; internet www.fbr.wur.nl; attached to Wageningen Univ. and Research Centre; research and devt org. for sustainable innovation in areas of healthy food, sustainable fresh food chains and biobased products; Man. Dir Prof. Dr RAOUL J. BINO; Dir for Operations Drs INGE T. J. GRIMM.

IMARES: POB 68, 1970 AB IJmuiden; Haringkade 1, 1976 CP IJmuiden; tel. (317) 480900; e-mail imares@wur.nl; internet www .imares.wur.nl; f. 1912; attached to Wageningen Univ. and Research Centre; concentrates on research into strategic and applied marine ecology in areas covering aquaculture, coastal zone management, ecology, ecosystem based economy, environmental conservation and protection, fisheries, marine governance; Dir DICK POUWELS; Dir MARTIN SCHOLTEN.

International Institute for Land Reclamation and Improvement (Alterra–ILRI): POB 47, 6700 AA Wageningen; Droevendaalsesteeg 3, Wageningen; tel. (317) 495584; e-mail ilri@ilri.nl; f. 1955; collects and disseminates information on land reclamation and improvement and undertakes supplementary research work; postgraduate courses; Dir Ir C. B. DE ZEEUW.

LEI: POB 29703, 2502 LS The Hague; Alexanderveld 5, 2585 DB The Hague; tel. (70) 3358330; e-mail informatie.lei@wur.nl; internet www.lei.wur.nl; f. 1940; attached to Wageningen Univ. and Research Centre; develops economic expertise for govt and industry in the field of food, agriculture and natural environment; offers a solid basis for socially and strategically justifiable policy choices; library of 20,000 vols; Dir-Gen. Prof. Dr Ir RUUD B. M. HUIRNE; Dir for Operations Ir LAAN C. VAN STAALDUINEN; Sec. R. VAN DEN BERG; Sec. S. FONTIJN; publ. *Leidraad* (6 a year).

Livestock Research: POB 65, 8200 AB Lelystad; Edelhertweg 15, 8219 PK Lelystad; tel. (320) 238238; e-mail info .livestockresearch@wur.nl; internet www .livestockresearch.wur.nl; f. 1970, present status 2008, current name adopted 2009; attached to Wageningen Univ. and Research Centre; 9 experimental farms in the Netherlands; develops knowledge, solutions for contemporary issues in the livestock sector; areas incl. animal nutrition, animal behaviour and welfare, genetics and genomics, innovation processes, livestock and environment; 140 mems; library of 20,000 vols; Gen. Dir Ir PAUL W. J. VRIESEKOOP; Man. for Operations JAN DIJK; publs *Rapporten* (6 a year), *Publikaties* (10 a year), *Jaarverslag* (1 a year), *Periodiek* (6 a year).

Nederlands Agronomisch-Historisch Instituut (Dutch Institute of Agricultural History): Oude Kijk in 't Jatstraat 26, 9712 EK Groningen; POB 716, 9700 AS Groningen; tel. (50) 3637672; e-mail nahi@rug.nl; internet www.rug.nl/let/nahi; f. 1949, present status 1998; scientific research in agricultural history; institute at Groningen Univ. and Wageningen Univ. and Research Centre; library of 12,000 vols; Dir Prof. Dr PIM KOOIJ (acting); Man. Dir Dr ERWIN H. KAREL; publ. *Historia Agriculturae* (1 or 2 a year).

Plant Research International: POB 16, 6700 AA Wageningen; Droevendaalsesteeg 1, Radix (Bldg 107), 6708 PB Wageningen; tel. (317) 486001; e-mail info.plant@wur.nl; internet www.pri.wur.nl; f. 1991; attached to Wageningen Univ. and Research Centre; strategic and applied research in agrosystems, bioinformatics, crop ecology, crop pro-

tection, genetics and reproduction, genomics, metabolomics, proteomics; offers unique new perspectives for govts and private cos, for agriculture and horticulture, and for rural and environmental devt; library of 50,000 vols; Dir-Gen. Dr ERNST VAN DEN ENDE; Dir for Management Ir TON VAN SCHEPPINGEN; publs *Descriptive List of Fruit Varieties* (every 5 years), *Descriptive List of Ornamental Crops* (every 2 years), *Descriptive List of Trees* (every 5 years), *Descriptive List of Varieties of Field Crops*, *Descriptive List of Varieties of Vegetable Crops* (1 a year).

Plantenziektenkundige Dienst (Plant Protection Service): Geertjesweg 15, POB 9102, 6700 HC Wageningen; tel. (317) 496911; f. 1899; activities incl. phytosanitary inspection of plants, issue of plant health certificates and design of laws for disease and pest prevention and control, integrated plant protection, diagnostics of diseases and pests; Dir Prof. Dr. L. VAN VLOTEN-DOTING; publ. *Verslagen en Mededelingen Plantenziektenkundige Dienst* (Reports and Communications of the Plant Protection Service).

ARCHITECTURE AND TOWN PLANNING

Netherlands Graduate School of Urban and Regional Research: POB 80115, 3508 TC Utrecht; Willem C. van Unnikgebouw, Room 725A, Heidelberglaan 2, 3584 CS Utrecht; tel. (30) 2532250; e-mail nethur .geo@uu.nl; internet www.nethur.nl; urban, regional, housing research; jt initiative of 6 univs; Scientific Dir Prof. Dr PIETER HOOIMEIJER; Dir for Education Dr BAS SPIERINGS.

Onderzoeksinstituut OTB (OTB Research Institute for the Built Environment): POB 5030, 2600 GA Delft; Jaffalaan 9, Bldg 30, 2628 BX Delft; tel. (15) 2783005; e-mail mailbox@otb.tudelft.nl; internet www.otb2 .tudelft.nl; attached to Delft Univ. of Technology; research in the field of housing, construction, built environment; Academic Dir Prof. Dr PETER J. BOELHOUWER; Dir Prof. WILLEM KORTHALS ALTES; publ. *European Journal of Spatial Development.*

ECONOMICS, LAW AND POLITICS

Amsterdam Center for Entrepreneurship: Roetersstraat 11, Room E 2.28, 1018 WB Amsterdam; tel. (20) 5254110; e-mail ace-feb@uva.nl; internet www .ace-amsterdam.org; f. 2006; attached to Univ. of Amsterdam; research on understanding the determinants of successful entrepreneurship; Scientific Dir CELINE MIRJAM VAN PRAAG; Exec. Dir ERIK BOER.

Amsterdam Center for Finance and Insurance: Finance Group, UvA Business School, Faculty of Economics and Business, Univ. of Amsterdam, Roetersstraat 11, 1018 WB Amsterdam; tel. (20) 5254256; e-mail acfi@uva.nl; internet www.feb.uva.nl/acfi; attached to Univ. of Amsterdam; researches in areas of quantitative finance and insurance and stimulates interaction between practitioners and academic researchers; Dir ANTOON PELSSER.

Amsterdam Center for Law & Economics (ACLE): Univ. van Amsterdam, Roetersstraat 11, 1018 WB Amsterdam; tel. (20) 5254162; e-mail acle@uva.nl; internet www .acle.nl; attached to Univ. of Amsterdam; research areas incl. foundations of law and economics, competition and regulation, corporate governance and law; Dir Prof. Dr ARNOUD BOOT.

Amsterdam Centre for Corporate Finance (ACCF): Chandra Doest, Roetersstraat 11, 1018 WB Amsterdam; tel. (20) 5254162; e-mail office@accf.nl; internet www .accf.nl; promotes research on the interface between financial theory and corporate policy; provides a forum for dialogue between academics and practitioners; Dir Prof. Dr ARNOUD BOOT; Dir Prof. Dr JOSEPH MCCAHERY.

Amsterdam Centre for Environmental Law and Sustainability (ACELS): POB 1030, 1000 BA Amsterdam; Oudemanhuispoort 4–6, 1000 BA Amsterdam; tel. (20) 5253075; e-mail milieurecht-fdr@uva.nl; internet www.jur.uva.nl/cvm; f. 1988, fmrly Centre for Environmental Law, current name adopted 2010; attached to Faculty of Law, Univ. of Amsterdam; research focuses on environmental law as a means of orienting market processes towards sustainable devt, especially problem of climate change; Dir Prof. ROSA UYLENBURG.

Amsterdam Centre for International Law (ACIL): Faculty of Law, Univ. of Amsterdam, POB 1030, 1000 BA Amsterdam; Faculty of Law, Univ. of Amsterdam, Oudemanhuispoort 4, 1012 CN Amsterdam; tel. (20) 5253361; e-mail acil-fdr@uva.nl; internet www.jur.uva.nl/aciluk/home.cfm; attached to Faculty of Law, Univ. of Amsterdam; research on int. constitutional law (incl. human rights law), int. responsibility, int. criminal justice, reception of int. law in domestic legal order; Exec. Dir Dr YVONNE DONDERS; publ. *Legal Issues of Economic Integration.*

Amsterdam Centre for Research in International Finance (CIFRA): Univ. of Amsterdam, Business Studies, Finance Group, Room E4.26, Roetersstraat 11, 1018 WB Amsterdam; tel. (20) 5254256; e-mail j.a .p.gompel@uva.nl; internet www1.fee.uva.nl/ fm/cifra/cifra.htm; f. 1998; research areas incl. int. capital market integration and corporate finance and banking; Dir Prof. Dr ENRICO PEROTTI; Dir Prof. Dr STIJN CLAESSENS; Sec. JOLINDA GOMPEL.

Amsterdam Centre for Service Innovation (AMSI): Amsterdam Business School, Faculty of Economics and Business, Univ. of Amsterdam, Roetersstraat 11, 1018 WB Amsterdam; tel. (20) 5258620; e-mail w .vanderaa@uva.nl; internet www.abs.uva.nl/ amsi/home.cfm; f. 2008; attached to Univ. of Amsterdam; research focuses on management of innovation in service firms and service orgs; Dir Dr WIETZE VAN DER AA; Chair. Prof. Dr M. W. DE JONG.

Amsterdam Institute for Business and Economic Research Foundation (AMBER): Main Bldg, VU Univ., 5th Fl., Room 5A-38, De Boelelaan 1105, 1081 HV Amsterdam; tel. (20) 5986080; e-mail amber@feweb.vu.nl; internet www.feweb.vu .nl/amber; attached to Faculty of Economics and Business Admin., VU Univ. Amsterdam; supports application for nat. and int. grants for research; Man. Dir Dr A. M. GROENENDIJK; Chair. Prof. Dr E. J. BARTELSMAN.

Amsterdams Instituut voor ArbeidsStudies (AIAS) (Amsterdam Institute for Advanced Labour Studies): Univ. of Amsterdam, Plantage Muidergracht 12, 1018 TV Amsterdam; tel. (20) 5254199; e-mail aias@ uva.nl; internet www.uva-aias.net; f. 1998; attached to Univ. of Amsterdam; combines law, economics, sociology, psychology, occupational health studies for labour studies; Dir Dr WIEMER SALVERDA.

Amsterdam School of Economics Research Institute: Universiteit van Amsterdam, Roetersstraat 11, 1018 WB Amsterdam; tel. (20) 5254276; e-mail ase-ri@uva.nl; internet www.ase.uva.nl; f. fmrly as Research in Economics & Econometrics Amsterdam (RESAM); attached to Univ. of Amsterdam; research focuses to improve understanding of the operation of economic systems, behaviour of agents in the economy and the effects of economic policies; Dir Prof. Dr PETER BOSWIJK.

CentER Applied Research: Tilburg Univ., POB 90153, 5000 LE Tilburg; tel. (13) 4662347; internet www.tilburguniversity.nl/ center-ar; f. 1931; attached to Tilburg Univ.; applied economic research; Dir Prof. Dr H. FLEUREN; Dir Drs J. DE RANITZ.

Center for Company Law: Tilburg Univ., Tilburg Law School, Dept of Business Law, POB 90153, 5000 LE Tilburg; Montesquieu Bldg, Warandelaan 2, 5037 AB Tilburg; tel. (13) 4662672; e-mail a.huijben@ tilburguniversity.edu; internet www .tilburguniversity.edu/ccl; attached to Tilburg Univ.; research in the fields of corporate, property, securities, tax, insolvency law; also focuses on doing research in nat., int. and European aspects of the 'firm', its various legal forms, financing, governance, reorganization and accounting; Dir Assoc. Prof. GER J. H. VAN DER SANGEN; Dir Prof. Dr P. H. J. ESSERS; Dir Prof. E. P. M. VERMEULEN.

Center for e-Government Studies (CFES): Univ. of Twente, Cubicus Bldg, POB 217, 7500 AE Enschede; Univ. of Twente, Cubicus Bldg, Drienerlolaan 5, 7522 NB Enschede; tel. (53) 4893299; e-mail an.vandijk@utwente.nl; internet www .utwente.nl/ibr/cfes; f. 2009; attached to Univ. of Twente; research on the electronic govt; advises governmental agencies, policy makers, politicians, stakeholders; Dir Prof. Dr JAN VAN DIJK.

CentER for Economic Research: POB 90153, 5000 LE Tilburg; tel. (13) 4663050; e-mail center@uvt.nl; internet center.uvt.nl; f. 1988, present status 1992; attached to Tilburg Univ.; academic research into economics, econometrics, finance and accounting, information management, marketing, operations research, organization; Dir Prof. Dr A. VAN WITTELOOSTUIJN.

Center for Nonlinear Dynamics in Economics and Finance (CeNDEF): Faculty of Economics and Econometrics, Univ. of Amsterdam, Roetersstraat 11, 1018 WB Amsterdam; tel. (20) 5254217; e-mail kesec-feb@uva.nl; internet www1.fee.uva.nl/ cendef; f. 1998; research areas incl. nonlinear dynamics in economics and finance; Dir Prof. Dr CARS HOMMES.

Center for Research in Experimental Economics and Political Decision-Making (CREED): Faculty of Economics and Econometrics, Univ. of Amsterdam, Bldg E2, 6th Fl., Roetersstraat 11, Amsterdam; tel. (20) 5254126; e-mail creed-fee@uva.nl; internet www1.fee.uva.nl/creed; attached to Univ. of Amsterdam; research programmes incl. economics of political decision making, bounded rationality and institutions, experimental economics; Dir ARTHUR SCHRAM.

Centraal Bureau voor de Statistiek (Central Bureau of Statistics): POB 24500, 2490 HA The Hague; Henri Faasdreef 312, 2492 JP The Hague; tel. (70) 3373800; e-mail persdienst@cbs.nl; internet www.cbs.nl; f. 1899, present status 2004; economic and social statistical research; br. office in Heerlen; library not accessible to public; library of 410,000 vols, 100,000 microfiche; Dir-Gen. G. VAN DER VEEN; Deputy Dir G. BRUINOOGE; publs *Historical Statistics of the Netherlands, Statistical Yearbook of the Netherlands.*

Centre for International Cooperation (CIS): De Boelelaan 1105, 1081 HV Amsterdam; Metropolitan Bldg, 4th Fl., Buitenveldertselaan 3–7, 1082 VA Amsterdam; tel. (20) 5989090; e-mail cis@vu.nl; internet www .cis.vu.nl; attached to VU Univ. Amsterdam; int. devt cooperation with partners in Asia, Africa and Latin America; contributes to capacity bldg efforts in developing countries; Dir KEES KOUWENAAR.

Centre for the Study of Democracy (CSD): Univ. of Twente, POB 217, 7500 AE Enschede; tel. (53) 4893270; internet www .utwente.nl/mb/csd; attached to Univ. of Twente; research on functioning of contemporary democracies; provides insight on innovation of democratic institutions; Dir Prof. Dr J. J. A. THOMASSEN; Exec. Dir Dr A. K. WARNTJEN; Exec. Dir Dr M. ROSEMA; Sec. RIA LUSCHEN.

Centre for Transboundary Legal Development: Tilburg Univ., POB 90153, 5000 LE Tilburg; Tilburg Univ., Montesquieu Bldg, 5th Fl., Warandelaan 2, 5037 AB Tilburg; tel. (13) 4668033; e-mail frw.eip.secretariaat@ uvt.nl; internet www.tilburguniversity.nl/ ctld; f. 2000; attached to Tilburg Univ.; ethics and jurisprudence, history of law, int. and European law, philosophy of law, social law; Dir Prof WILLEM VAN GENUGTEN; Coordinator Asst Prof. ANNA MEIJKNECHT.

Centrum van Procesrecht (Centre for Legal Procedure and Litigation): Tilburg Univ., POB 90153, 5000 LE Tilburg; Tilburg Univ., Montesquieu Bldg, Warandelaan 2, 5037 AB Tilburg; tel. (13) 4662254; e-mail j .w.dejong@uvt.nl; internet www.uvt.nl/cvp; attached to Tilburg Univ.; research in criminal law; Dir Prof. Dr C. J. C. F. FIJNAUT; Dir Prof. M. S. GROENHUIJSEN.

Centrum voor Recht, Bestuur en Samenleving (CRBS) (Centre for Law, Administration and Society): POB 716, 9700 AS Groningen; Harmonie, Bldg 11, Oude Kijk in't Jatstraat 26, 9712 EK Groningen; tel. (50) 3636145; e-mail b.m.e.hallebeek@rug.nl; internet www.rug.nl/crbs/index; f. 1990; attached to Faculty of Law, Univ. of Groningen; 3 legal areas transcending, interdisciplinary and internationally orientated research lines are brought together in 3 research centres; Admin. Dir Dr JOOP HOUTMAN; Academic Dir Prof. Dr O. COUWENBERG.

Economics Network for Competition and Regulation (ENCORE): Faculty of Economics, Univ. of Amsterdam, Roetersstraat 11, 1018 WB Amsterdam; tel. (20) 5257162; e-mail info@encore.nl; internet www.encore.nl; f. 2003; attached to Faculty of Economics, Univ. of Amsterdam; int. research network; researches on available scientific knowledge on competition and regulation to benefit and improve policy making; Dir Prof. Dr MAARTEN PIETER SCHINKEL.

Ecorys: POB 4175, 3006 AD Rotterdam; Watermanweg 44, 3067 GG Rotterdam; tel. (10) 4538800; e-mail netherlands@ecorys .com; internet www.ecorys.com; f. 1929 as Netherlands Economic Institute (NEI), present name and status 2000; economic research and policy advice; consulting and training; programme management and implementation; monitoring and evaluation; areas covered incl. economics and competitiveness, regions, cities and real estate, transport, mobility and infrastructure, social policy and govt; Man. Dir Dr KOEN BERDEN.

Fiscaal Instituut Tilburg (FIT) (Tilburg Institute of Fiscal Law): POB 90153, 5000 LE Tilburg; Warandelaan 2, Montesquieu Bldg, Room M612, 5037 AB Tilburg; tel. (13) 4662412; e-mail fit@uvt.nl; internet www .uvt.nl/fit; f. 1968; attached to Tilburg Univ.; research in the field of Dutch and int. taxation, tax law system.

Groningen Centre for Law and Governance: Attn. Eleonora Goljan, POB 716, 9700 AS Groningen; Harmonie bldg, Oude Kijk in 't Jatstraat 26, 9712 EK Groningen; tel. (50) 3635685; e-mail gcl@rug.nl; internet www .rug.nl/gcl; f. 2008; attached to Faculty of

Law, Univ. of Groningen; contributes to legal research into the relationship between public and private interests; focuses on the interaction between public and private law and the function of law in the regulatory state; Academic Dir Prof. Dr AURELIA COLOMBI CIACCHI; Academic Dir Prof. Dr LEON VERSTAPPEN; Sec. ELEONORA GOLJAN.

Groningen Centre of Energy Law: POB 716, 9700 AS Groningen; tel. (50) 3635736; e-mail m.m.roggenkamp@rug.nl; internet www.rug.nl/rechten/onderzoek/gcel/index; f. 2007; attached to Faculty of Law, Univ. of Groningen; research covers the entire energy chain and incl. all legislation and regulation applying to the production, transmission and supply of energy, promotion of renewable energy sources, need to secure energy supply as well as issues concerning climate change and environmental protection; Dir Prof. MARTHA ROGGENKAMP.

Hugo Sinzheimer Instituut (HSUIK) (Hugo Sinzheimer Institute): Faculty of Law, Univ. of Amsterdam, Oudemanhuispoort 4–6, 1012 CN Amsterdam; tel. (20) 5253400; e-mail hsi-fdr@uva.nl; internet www.jur.uva.nl/hsiuk; f. 1993; attached to Faculty of Law, Univ. of Amsterdam; coordinates, implements and stimulates interdisciplinary research in labour law and social security law; Scientific Dir Dr ROBERT KNEGT.

Institute for Innovation and Governance Studies (IGS): Univ. of Twente, POB 217, 7500 AE Enschede; Univ. of Twente, Bldg Ravelijn, 7522 NH Enschede; tel. (53) 4893423; e-mail info@igs.utwente.nl; internet www.utwente.nl/igs; attached to Univ. of Twente; faculty of behavioural sciences, engineering technology, geo-information science and earth observation; multidisciplinary research, postgraduate research training in the field of governance and management of technological and social innovation; Scientific Dir Prof. Dr KEES AARTS; Exec. Dir SJOERD VAN TONGEREN; Sec. MARCIA CLIFFORD.

Institute for Management Research: POB 9108, 6500 HK Nijmegen; Thomas van Aquinostraat 1-5, 6525 GD Nijmegen; tel. (24) 3615995; e-mail imr@fm.ru.nl; internet www.ru.nl/imr; f. 2000; attached to Radbound Univ. Nijmegen; conducts fundamental and applied research on devt, design and effectiveness of the public and private structures that regulate, govern, manage human interaction; Vice-Dean for Research Prof. Dr ALLARD VAN RIEL.

Institute of Social Studies: see under Colleges.

Instituut voor Informatierecht (Institute for Information Law): Kloveniersburgwal 48, 1012 CX Amsterdam; Korte Spinhuissteeg 3, 1012 CG Amsterdam; tel. (20) 5253406; e-mail ivir@ivir.nl; internet www.ivir.nl; f. 1989; attached to Faculty of Law, Univ. of Amsterdam; information society related to legal areas such as advertising law, commercial speech, digital consumer issues, domain names, freedom of expression, intellectual property law, internet regulation, media law, privacy, patents, telecommunications and broadcasting regulation, etc.

International Institute for Asian Studies: POB 9500, 2300 RA Leiden; Rapenburg 59, 2311 GJ Leiden; tel. (71) 5272227; e-mail iias@iias.nl; internet www.iias.nl; f. 1993 by Royal Netherlands Acad. of Arts and Sciences and 3 Dutch univs; postdoctoral research in humanities and social sciences; promotes interdisciplinary and comparative study of Asia on nat. and int. cooperation; Chair. Prof. H. SCHULTE NORDHOLT; Dir

PHILIPPE PEYCAM; Deputy Dir MANON OSSEWEIJER; Sec. AMPARO DE VOGEL.

Nederlands Instituut voor Internationale Betrekkingen 'Clingendael' (Netherlands Institute of International Relations 'Clingendael'): POB 93080, 2509 AB The Hague; Clingendael 7, 2597 VH The Hague; tel. (70) 3245384; e-mail info@clingendael.nl; internet www.clingendael.nl; f. 1983; research and training on int. relations especially int. diplomacy, Europe, int. security and conflict management and int. energy; debates, courses and publs; library of 26,000 vols, 300 periodicals, 150 current journals; Pres. Dr BERNARD R. BOT; Vice-Pres. Lt. Gen. M. L. M. URLINGS; Gen. Dir Prof. Dr KO COLIJN; publ. *Internationale Spectator* (12 a year).

Nederlands Interdisciplinair Demografisch Instituut (NIDI-KNAW) (Netherlands Interdisciplinary Demographic Institute): POB 11650, 2502 AR The Hague; Lange Houtstraat 19, 2511 CV The Hague; tel. (70) 3565200; e-mail info@nidi.nl; internet www.nidi.nl; f. 1970, present status 2003; attached to Royal Netherlands Acad. of Arts; research, training, information and documentation in the field of population studies; library of 6,000 vols, 2,500 reprints, 15,000 articles; Dir Prof. Dr LEO J. G. VAN WISSEN; Deputy Dir Drs NICO VAN NIMWEGEN; Sec. JACQUELINE VAN DER HELM; publs *Bevolking en Gezin* (3 a year), *Demos* (10 a year, online).

Nederlands Studiecentrum Criminaliteit en Rechtshandhaving (NCSR) (Netherlands Institute for the Study of Crime and Law Enforcement): POB 71304, 1008 BH Amsterdam; Room 0D-07, De Boelelaan 1105, 1081 HV Amsterdam; tel. (20) 5985239; e-mail nscr@nscr.nl; internet www.nscr.nl; f. 1992, reorganized 1999; attached to Netherlands Org. for Scientific Research; fundamental research, dissemination of knowledge in the field of crime and law enforcement; Chair. Prof. Y. BURUMA; Scientific Dir Prof. Dr G. J. N. BRUINSMA; Sec. ARIENA H. VAN POPPEL-VAN DIJK.

Research Group for Methodology of Law and Legal Research: Faculty of Law, Tilburg Univ., Room M412, Montesquieu Bldg, POB 90153, 5000 LE Tilburg; Montesquieu Bldg, Warandelaan 2, Room M412, 5037 AB Tilburg; tel. (13) 4662745; e-mail frw.methodology@uvt.nl; internet www.tilburguniversity.nl/research/law/institutes/; f. 2007; attached to Faculty of Law, Tilburg Univ.; research in methodology of judicial lawmaking and legal research; Dir Dr GIJS VAN DIJCK; Dir ROB VAN GESTEL.

SEO Economisch Onderzoek (SEO Economic Research): Univ. of Amsterdam, Gijsbert van Tienhoven Bldg, Roetersstraat 29, 1018 WB Amsterdam; tel. (20) 5251630; e-mail secretariaat@seo.nl; internet www.seo.nl; f. 1949; attached to Univ. of Amsterdam; ind. applied economic research for govt and industry; Chair. JACQUES SCHRAVEN; Dir Prof. Dr B. E. BAARSMA; Treas. WALTER ETTY.

SOM Research Institute: POB 800, 9700 AV Groningen; Nettelbosje 2, Duisenberg Bldg, 9747 AE Groningen; tel. (50) 3633749; e-mail a.c.koning@rug.nl; internet www.rug.nl/som/index; attached to Faculty of Economics and Business, Univ. of Groningen; coordinating institute of 6 research programmes: human resource management and organizational behaviour; int. economics, business and management; economics, econometrics and finance; innovation and org.; marketing; operations management and operations research; Chair. Prof. ELMER STERKEN; Scientific Dir Prof. Dr TAMMO BIJMOLT.

Tilburg Graduate Law School: Tilburg Univ., POB 90153, 5000 LE Tilburg; Montesquieu Bldg, Warandelaan 2, 5037 AB Tilburg; tel. (13) 4668901; e-mail law.tgls@uvt.nl; internet www.tilburguniversity.nl/law/graduateschool; f. fmrly as Schoordijk Institute; attached to Tilburg Univ.; interdisciplinary study of law, legal methodology; Dir Prof. J. HAN SOMSEN.

Tilburg Institute for Behavioral Economics Research (TIBER): Tilburg Univ., POB 90153, 5000 LE Tilburg; tel. (13) 4668394; e-mail d.a.stapel@uvt.nl; internet www.tilburguniversity.nl/tiber; attached to Tilburg Univ.; interdisciplinary research in psychological processes underlying individual choice and economic decision; Dir Prof. DIEDERIK A. STAPEL; Man. Dir Dr TON HEINEN.

Tilburg Institute for Interdisciplinary Studies of Civil Law and Conflict Resolution Systems (TISCO): Faculty of Law, Tilburg Univ., Montesquieu Bldg, Room M 928, POB 90153, 5000 LE Tilburg; Montesquieu Bldg, Warandelaan 2, Room M 928, 5037 AB Tilburg; tel. (13) 4662281; e-mail law.tisco@uvt.nl; internet www.tilburguniversity.nl/tisco; attached to Faculty of Law, Tilburg Univ.; interdisciplinary, empirical-based research in civil law; develops, integrates and applies insight from negotiation theory, conflict research, dispute system design, (comparative) legal research, network theory, behavioural law, and law and economics; Academic Dir Prof. J. M. (MAURITS) BARENDRECHT; Man. Dir C. M. C. (CORRY) VAN ZEELAND.

Tilburg School of Politics and Public Administration: Tilburg School of Politics and Public Admin., Tilburg Univ., POB 90153, 5000 LE Tilburg; Montesquieu Bldg, Warandelaan 2, 5037 AB Tilburg; tel. (13) 4662128; e-mail frw.tspb.secretariaat@tilburguniversity.edu; internet www.tilburguniversity.nl/tspb; attached to Tilburg School of Politics and Public Admin., Tilburg Univ.; researches into legitimacy, multiplicity, vitality of public sector; Dept Chair. Prof. Dr G. J. M. (GABRIËL) VAN DEN BRINK; Dir Prof. Dr P. H. A. FRISSEN.

TILEC—Tilburg Law and Economics Centre: Tilburg Univ., POB 90153, 5000 LE Tilburg; Prof. Cobbenhagenlaan 221, Montesquieu Bldg, Room M512A, 5037 DE Tilburg; tel. (13) 4668789; e-mail tilec@uvt.nl; internet www.tilburguniversity.nl/tilec; attached to Tilburg Univ.; Dir Prof. Dr ERIC VAN DAMME; Dir Prof. Dr PIERRE LAROUCHE; Man. NICOLA HEEREN.

Tinbergen Institute: Gustav Mahlerplein 117, 1082 MS Amsterdam; tel. (20) 5251600; e-mail tinbergen@tinbergen.nl; internet www.tinbergen.nl; f. 1987; also located in Rotterdam; research areas incl. behavioural and experimental economics; cooperative behaviour, strategic interaction and complex systems; econometrics and operations research: finance; labour, health, education and devt; macroeconomics and int. economics; org. and markets; spatial, transport and environmental economics; Gen. Dir Prof. BAUKE VISSER.

EDUCATION

Centre for European Studies (CES): POB 217, 7500 AE Enschede; tel. (53) 4894106; e-mail n.s.groenendijk@utwente.nl; internet www.utwente.nl/mb/ces; f. 1998; attached to School of Management and Governance, Univ. of Twente; Dir Prof. Dr NICO GROENENDIJK.

Centre for Higher Education Policy Studies (CHEPS): POB 217, 7500 AE Enschede; tel. (53) 4893263; e-mail cheps@

mb.utwente.nl; internet www.utwente.nl/mb/cheps; f. 1986; attached to Univ. of Twente; research on dynamics of the transformation of higher education and research in the knowledge soc.; Dir Prof. Dr J. J. (Hans) Vossensteyn; Sec. Karin van der Tuin.

Centre for International Cooperation: De Boelelaan 1105, 1081 HV Amsterdam; Metropolitan Bldg, 4th Fl., Buitenveldertselaan 3–7, 1082 VA Amsterdam; tel. (20) 5989090; e-mail cis@vu.nl; internet www.cis.vu.nl; attached to Vrije Univ.; education and devt in higher education; ICT in teaching and research; management and org. in higher education; natural resource management; Chair. Prof. Dr H. A. Verhoef; Dir Kees Kouwenaar; Sec. Henny Keppel.

Groningen Institute for Educational Research: Grote Rozenstraat 3, 9712 TG Groningen; tel. (50) 3636631; internet www.rug.nl/gion/index; attached to Faculty of Behavioural and Social Studies, Univ. of Groningen; fundamental and contract research in teaching and education; Scientific Dir Prof. Dr Roel Bosker.

ICT in het Onderwijs (ICTO) (ICT in Education): Kanaalweg 2b, 2628 EB Delft; tel. (15) 2784686; e-mail icto@tudelft.nl; internet www.icto.tudelft.nl; attached to Delft Univ. of Technology.

Instituut voor Internationale Studien (Institute for International Studies): POB 9555, 2333 AK Leiden; tel. 5273411; f. 1970; attached to Leiden Univ.; promotes cooperation in teaching between univ. depts; research on contemporary int. affairs; Dir Dr Ph. P. Everts.

Top Institute for Evidence Based Education Research (TIER): Roetersstraat 11, 1018 WB Amsterdam; tel. (20) 5254311; e-mail s.m.postma@uva.nl; internet www.tierweb.nl; conducts and promotes research in the field of evidence-based education; Scientific Coordinator Prof. Dr Henriëtte Maassen van den Brink.

Twente Centre for Career Research (TCCR): Univ. of Twente, Bldg Cubicus, POB 217, 7500 AE Enschede; Univ. of Twente, Bldg Cubicus, Drienerlolaan 5, 7522 NB Enschede; tel. (53) 4893580; e-mail k.sanders@utwente.nl; internet www.utwente.nl/ibr/tccr; attached to Univ. of Twente; research programmes in the field of professional devt of teachers within education and health care; Dir Prof. Dr Karin Sanders.

FINE AND PERFORMING ARTS

Piet Zwart Institute: POB 1272, 3000 BG Rotterdam; Mauritsstraat 36, 3012 CJ Rotterdam; tel. (10) 7947405; internet pzwart.wdka.nl; attached to Willem de Kooning Acad.; Rotterdam Univ.; offers int. Masters study and research programmes into professional practice of art, design, media and education.

HISTORY, GEOGRAPHY AND ARCHAEOLOGY

Centrum voor Technische Geowetenschappen (Centre for Technical Geoscience): Stevinweg 1, 2628 CN Delft; tel. (15) 2789511; e-mail ctg@tudelft.nl; internet www.ctg.tudelft.nl; attached to Delft Univ. of Technology; integration of applied geosciences.

Groningen Institute of Archaeology: Poststraat 6, 9712 ER Groningen; tel. (50) 3636712; e-mail gia@rug.nl; internet www.rug.nl/let/onderzoek/onderzoekinstituten/gia/index; f. 1995; attached to Faculty of Arts, Univ. of Groningen; fundamental archaeo-

logical research with strong ecological component in Eurasia, Mediterranean and Arctic; stimulates and integrates fundamental research on past human societies and their environments, from the level of Palaeolithic hunter-gatherers to that of historical complex urban societies; library of 20,000 ejournals; Dir Prof. D. C. M. Raemaekers; publs *Paleo-aktueel* (Dutch, 1 a year), *Palaeohistoria* (English, 1 a year), *Tijdschrift voor Mediterrane Archeologie* (Dutch, 1 a year).

Instituut voor Milieuvraagstukken (IVM) (Institute for Environmental Studies): De Boelelaan 1087, 1081 HV Amsterdam; De Boelelaan 1085, 1081 HV Amsterdam; tel. (20) 4449555; e-mail info@ivm.falw.vu.nl; internet www.ivm.vu.nl; f. 1971; attached to Vrije Univ.; multidisciplinary research in chemistry and biology, environmental economics, environmental policy and governance, spatial analysis and decision support; Dir Prof. Dr Frans G. H. Berkhout.

Koninklijk Instituut voor Taal-, Land- en Volkenkunde (Royal Netherlands Institute of Southeast Asian and Caribbean Studies): POB 9515, 2300 RA Leiden; Reuvensplaats 2, 2311 BE Leiden; tel. (71) 5272295; e-mail kitlv@kitlv.nl; internet www.kitlv.nl; f. 1851; attached to Royal Netherlands Acad. of Arts and Sciences; advances the study of the social sciences and humanities of SE Asia and the Caribbean, particularly the fmr Dutch colonies of Indonesia and Suriname, and the fmr Netherlands Antilles and Aruba; library of 750,000 vols; spec. collns incl. Indonesia; Chair. Prof. Dr S. Legêne; Vice-Chair. M. Plomp; Dir Prof. Dr G. J. Oostindie; publs *Bijdragen tot Taal-, Land- en Volkenkunde* (3 a year, in English), *Nieuwe West-Indische Gids* (New West Indian Guide, 2 a year, in English), *Journal of Indonesian Social Sciences and Humanities* (2 a year, in Dutch).

NIOD Instituut voor Oorlogs-, Holocaust- en Genocide Studies (NIOD Institute for War, Holocaust and Genocide Studies): Herengracht 380, 1016 CJ Amsterdam; tel. (20) 5233800; e-mail info@niod.knaw.nl; internet www.niod.knaw.nl; f. 1945, merger of Center for Holocaust and Genocide Studies and Netherlands Institute for War Documentation in 2010; attached to Royal Netherlands Acad. of Arts and Sciences; Dutch, German and Allied collns on the history of the Second World War; conducts research on war, large-scale violence in the 20th century; library of 60,000 vols; Dir Prof. Dr Marjan Schwegman.

Roosevelt Study Center: POB 6001, 4330 LA Middelburg; Abdij 8, 4331 BK Middelburg; tel. (118) 631590; e-mail rsc@zeeland.nl; internet www.roosevelt.nl; f. 1986; research institute, conf. centre and library on modern US history and European–US relations; Pres. George R. J. van Heukelom; Sec. Rein Jan Hoekstra; Treas. Kees Storm; Dir Prof. Dr Cornelis A. van Minnen; Asst Dir Dr Hans Krabbendam; publ. *The Roosevelt Herald* (1 a year).

Spatial Information Laboratory (SPINlab): De Boelelaan 1087, 1081 HV Amsterdam; tel. (20) 5989569; e-mail spinlab@vu.vu.nl; internet www.feweb.vu.nl/gis/spinlab_website; attached to Vrije Univ.; research on spatial, geo-information with emphasis on their added value to environmental protection, health care, emergency and risk management, field work, transport, distribution, logistics, and marketing; Scientific Dir Henk Scholten; Sec. Jessica Endendijk.

Vening Meinesz Research School of Geodynamics: c/o Institute of Earth Sciences, Budapestlaan 4, 3584 CD Utrecht; tel.

(30) 2535031; e-mail vmsg@geo.uu.nl; internet vmsg.geo.uu.nl; promotes and carries out geodynamic research, with spec. attention for the integration of geophysical, geological and Earth-oriented space research; Scientific Dir Prof. Dr Rinus Wortel; Exec. Sec. Drs Jan-Willem de Blok.

LANGUAGE AND LITERATURE

Amsterdam Centre for Language and Communication (ACLC): Spuistraat 210–212, Room 1.11, 1012 VT Amsterdam; tel. (20) 5252543; e-mail aclc-fgw@uva.nl; internet www.hum.uva.nl/aclc; attached to Faculty of Humanities, Univ. of Amsterdam; focuses on study of both functionally and formally oriented linguistic research; Academic Dir Prof. Dr Kees Hengeveld; Man. Dir Dr Marten Hidma; Vice-Dir Dr Rob Schoonen; publ. *Linguistics in Amsterdam series*.

Center for Language and Cognition Groningen (CLCG): POB 716, 9700 AS Groningen; e-mail clcg@rug.nl; internet www.rug.nl/research/clcg; f. 1994; attached to Faculty of Arts, Univ. of Groningen; linguistic research; interaction between other linguistic research groups; Dir Prof. Dr Petra Hendriks.

Centre for Language Studies: POB 9103, 6500 HD Nijmegen; Erasmusplein 1, 6525 HT Nijmegen; tel. (24) 3611807; e-mail cls@let.ru.nl; internet www.ru.nl/cls; attached to Faculty of Arts, Radboud Univ. Nijmegen; research in linguistics, language and speech technology and communication studies; Dir Prof. Paula Fikkert.

Max Planck Institute for Psycholinguistics: POB 310, 6500 AH Nijmegen; Wundtlaan 1, 6525 XD Nijmegen; tel. (24) 3521911; e-mail info@mpi.nl; internet www.mpi.nl; f. 1980; attached to German Max Planck Soc.; basic research on psychological, social and biological foundations of language; library of 30,000 vols, 20,000 bound journals, 30,000 online journals; Dir Prof. Dr Antje Meyer.

MEDICINE

Academic Centre for Dentistry Amsterdam: Gustav Mahler Laan 3004, 1081 LA Amsterdam; tel. (20) 5980380; e-mail info@acta.nl; internet www.acta.nl; br. at Almere; conducts scientific research, provides educational programmes, and delivers patient care in field of dentistry; research focuses on physiology and pathology of tissues in and around oral cavity; Dean Prof. Dr A. J. Feilzer; Dir for Research Prof. Dr V. Everts.

Academisch Medisch Centrum (AMC): POB 22660, 1100 DD Amsterdam; Meibergdreef 9, 1105 AZ Amsterdam; tel. (20) 5669111; internet www.amc.uva.nl; f. 1983; attached to Univ. van Amsterdam; clinical and translational research; works as medical centre; Pres. and Dean Prof. Dr M. M Levi; Vice-Pres. Dr R. J. M. Hopstaken; publ. *AMC Magazine* (10 a year).

Centre for Healthcare Operations Improvement & Research (CHOIR): c/o Univ. of Twente, POB 217, 7500 AE Enschede; tel. (53) 4893447; e-mail e.w.hans@utwente.nl; internet www.utwente.nl/choir; attached to Univ. of Twente; research on healthcare; research areas incl. decision theory, logistics and operations management, information technology and management, operations research, purchase management, quality and safety management.

Centre of Research on Psychology in Somatic Diseases (CoRPS): POB 90153, 5000 LE Tilburg; Warandelaan 2, 5037 AB Tilburg; tel. (13) 4668720; e-mail corps@

tilburguniversity.edu; internet www .tilburguniversity.edu/corps; f. 2008; attached to Tilburg Univ.; research on issues in the interface between medical and behavioural sciences; Academic Dir Prof. Dr JOHAN DENOLLET; Man. Dir J. H. (HANS) DIETEREN.

Centrum voor Ouderenonderzoek (CVO) (Center for Research on Aging): De Boelelaan 1081, 1081 HV Amsterdam; Metropolitan, Room Z-427, Buitenveldertselaan 3, 1081 HV Amsterdam; tel. (20) 5986891; internet www.cvo.vu.nl; f. 1996; attached to Vrije Univ. Amsterdam; research and education in gerontology and geriatrics; Head Dr F. J. M. MEILAND.

EMGO+ Institute for Health and Care Research: van der Boechorststraat 7, 1081 BT Amsterdam; tel. (20) 4448180; e-mail secretariaat.emgo@vumc.nl; internet www .emgo.nl; attached to VU Univ.; research in public and occupational health, primary care, rehabilitation, long-term care; Dir Prof. ECO DE GEUS; Vice-Dir Prof. WILLEM VAN MECHELEN; Vice-Dir Prof. HENRIËTTE VAN DER HORST.

Graduate School of Neurosciences Amsterdam, Rotterdam: De Boelelaan 1085, 1081 HV Amsterdam; tel. (20) 4449641; e-mail els.borghols@cncr.vu.nl; internet www.onwar.nl; research in the field of neurosciences; Chair. of Advisory Board Prof. Dr F. H. LOPES DA SILVA; Dir Prof. Dr A. B. SMIT; Chair. of Teaching Cttee Dr C. N. LEVELT.

GUIDE—Research Institute for Chronic Diseases and Drug Innovation: POB 196, 9700 AD Groningen; Ant. Deusinglaan 1, Bldg 3217 'De Brug', Room 7.31, 9713 AV Groningen; tel. (50) 3633163; e-mail guideoffice@med.umcg.nl; internet www .graduateschoolguide.nl; attached to Univ. of Groningen; integrates clinical, biomedical and pharmaceutical research, which promotes education of researchers with a keen eye on the complete spectrum of biomedical research in a unique research and teaching environment: from bed to bench to drugs; Scientific Dir Prof. Dr HAN MOSHAGE.

Het Nederlands Kanker Instituut— Antoni van Leeuwenhoek Ziekenhuis (Netherlands Cancer Institute—Antoni van Leeuwenhoek Hospital): POB 90203, 1006 BE Amsterdam; Plesmanlaan 121, 1066 CX Amsterdam; tel. (20) 5129111; e-mail nkilib@ nki.nl; internet www.nki.nl; f. 1913; basic and translational cancer research, clinical cancer research, diagnostic, surgical and medical oncology, radiotherapy; library of 15,000 vols; Patron HKH PRINCESS BEATRIX; Chair. and Scientific Dir Prof. Dr R. MEDEMA; Sec. M. DIEPEVEEN; Library Dir JOERI BOTH; publ. *Scientific Report* (1 a year).

Institute for Cardiovascular Research VU: POB 7057, 1007 MB Amsterdam; van der Boechorststraat 7, 1081 BT Amsterdam; tel. (20) 4448111; e-mail icar@vumc.nl; internet www.vumc.com/branch/icar-vu; f. 1992; attached to VU Univ. Amsterdam; research into aspects of cardiovascular diseases, cardiovascular function; Dir Prof. Dr V. W. M. VAN HINSBERGH.

Institute for Genetic and Metabolic Disease: Radboud Univ. Nijmegen Medical Centre, Geert Grooteplein Zuid 10, POB 9101, 6500 HB Nijmegen; Radboud Univ. Nijmegen Medical Centre, Geert Grooteplein 10, 6525 GA Nijmegen; tel. (24) 3619118; internet www.igmd.nl; attached to Radboud Univ. Nijmegen Medical Centre; clinical, applied and fundamental research on genetic and metabolic diseases; Dir Prof. Dr JAN SMEITINK.

Institute of Technical Medicine: Noordhorst, POB 217, 7500 AE Enschede; tel. (53) 4893300; e-mail j.a.dutrieux-schuit@utwente .nl; internet www.utwente.nl/tnw/itm; attached to Univ. of Twente; basic science and technology with clinical practice in medicine.

Instituut Beleid & Management Gezondheidszorg (iBMG) (Institute of Health Policy & Management): POB 1738, 3000 DR Rotterdam; J-Bldg, Campus Woudestein, Burgemeester Oudlaan 50, 3062 PA Rotterdam; tel. (10) 4081169; e-mail research@bmg .eur.nl; internet www.bmg.eur.nl; f. 1982; attached to Erasmus Univ.; research school and educational programmes of Netherlands Institute for Health Sciences (NIHES) and Netherlands School of Public Health (NSPH); researches on competition and regulation in health care, quality and efficiency in health care, management and org. of health care delivery; Vice-Dean Prof. Dr WERNER BROUWER; Man. Dir Drs GEERT GERRITSE; Dir for Research Prof. Dr ERIK SCHUT.

Instituut voor Fundamentele en Klinische Bewegingswetenschappen (Institute for Fundamental and Clinical Human Movement Sciences): van der Boechorststraat 9, 1081 BT Amsterdam; tel. (20) 5982000; e-mail ifkb@fbw.vu.nl; internet www.ifkb.nl; f. 1995; attached to Vrije Univ.; research into nature and significance of human movement; research themes incl. control, mechanics, metabolism; Chair. of Board Prof. Dr P. J. BEEK; Dir Dr Ir L. BLANKEVOORT; Dir Prof. Dr ARNOLD DE HAAN; Dir Prof. Dr Ir D. F. STEGEMAN.

Interuniversitair Cardiologisch Instituut Nederland (Interuniversity Cardiology Institute of the Netherlands): POB 19258, 3501 DG Utrecht; Catharijnesingel 52, 3511 GC Utrecht; tel. (30) 2333600; e-mail info@icin.knaw.nl; internet www.icin .nl; attached to Royal Netherlands Acad. of Arts and Sciences; scientific research in the field of cardiovascular diseases; alliance of 8 univ. cardiology depts; Dir Prof. Dr WIEK H. VAN GILST; Dir Prof. Dr ERNST E. VAN DER WALL; Gen. Man. JAN WEIJERS.

Koninklijk Instituut voor de Tropen (KIT) (Royal Tropical Institute): POB 95001, 1090 HA Amsterdam; Mauritskade 63, 1092 AD Amsterdam; tel. (20) 5688711; e-mail ils@kit.nl; internet www.kit.nl; f. 1910 as Colonial Institute, present bldg 1926, current name adopted 1950; health policy and tropical medicine; int. research and training org. that focuses on improving communication between the W and non-W world; collects and disseminates information on the developing world; library: see under Libraries and Archives; Chair. Prof. Dr RUDY RABBINGE; Vice-Chair. PETER J. GROENENBOOM; Pres. Dr JAN DONNER.

Nederlands Herseninstituut (Netherlands Institute for Neuroscience): Meibergdreef 47, 1105 BA Amsterdam; tel. (20) 5665500; e-mail secretariaat@nin.knaw.nl; internet www.herseninstituut.nl; f. 2005; attached to Royal Netherlands Acad. of Arts and Sciences; carries out fundamental neuroscience research with spec. emphasis on the brain and the visual system; 18 research groups; Scientific Dir Dr PIETER R. ROELFSEMA; Man. Dir Dr RONALD VAN DER NEUT; Vice-Dir Dr CHRIS I. ZEEUW.

Nijmegen Centre for Evidence Based Practice (NCEBP): Radboud Univ. Nijmegen Medical Centre, Post 148, NCEBP, POB 9101, 6500 HB Nijmegen; Radboud Univ. Nijmegen Medical Centre, NCEBP, Geert Grooteplein 21, 6525 EZ Nijmegen; tel. (24) 3614639; e-mail info@ncebp.umcn.nl; internet www.ncebp.eu; attached to Radboud

Univ. Nijmegen; conducts research that is aimed at individual patients and patient population; Scientific Dir Prof. Dr PAUL SMITS; Asst Scientific Dir Dr. GERDI EGBERINK.

Nijmegen Intitute for Infection, Inflammation and Immunity: POB 9101, Route 463, 6500 HB Nijmegen; tel. (24) 3668015; e-mail a.peters@aig.umcn.nl; internet www .n4i.nl; attached to Radboud Univ. Nijmegen Medical Centre; performs clinical translational and basic research on the interaction between microorganisms and the host, the inflammatory response and immune mechanisms as occur in autoimmune disorders and transplantation; Scientific Dir Prof. Dr JOS VAN DER MEER; Sec. GONNY PETERS.

Onderzoekschool Oncologie Amsterdam (Oncology Graduate School): c/o Dr. Esther M. Ruhé-Hoogervorst, De Boelelaan 1117, 1081 HV Amsterdam; tel. (20) 4443113; e-mail e.ruhe@vumc.nl; internet www .ooa-graduateschool.org; attached to Vrije Univ.; research in basic and clinical oncology; Chair. of Board Prof. Dr ANTON BERNS; Chair. Prof. Dr GERRIT A. MEIJER.

TNO Gezond Leven (TNO Healthy Living): POB 2215, 2301 CE Leiden; Wassenaarseweg 56, 2333 AL Leiden; tel. (88) 8669000; e-mail info-zorg@tno.nl; internet www.tno.nl; f. 1932; scientific research in the fields of public health and prevention of illness; postgraduate courses in occupational health; library of 20,000 vols; Chair. Ir JAN H. J. MENGELERS; Chair for Defence Research Board JAN WILLEM KELDER; Chair for Supervisory Board Dr C. A. LINSE; Exec. Sec. MARIAN NIEUWENHOUT; publ. *TNO Magazine* (4 a year).

VU Medisch Centrum (VU University Medical Center): POB 7057, 1007 MB Amsterdam; De Boelelaan 1117, 1081 HV Amsterdam; tel. (20) 4444444; e-mail uhp@ vumc.nl; internet www.vumc.nl/meg; f. 2001 by merger of medical school and VU hospital; attached to Vrije Universiteit Medical Centre; research into magnetoencephalography; Chair. Drs E. B. MULDER; Vice-Chair. Prof. Dr T. J. F. SAVELKOUL; Dean Prof. Dr W. A. B. STALMAN.

W. J. Kolff Institute for Biomedical Engineering and Materials Science: Antonius Deusinglaan 1, FB41, 9713 AV Groningen; tel. (50) 3633140; e-mail h.j .busscher@med.umcg.nl; internet www.rug .nl/umcg/onderzoek/interfacultaireinstituten/bmsa/index; f. 1997; establishes a centre of expertise for the entire stage of biomedical materials science and its application involving basic materials science, medical product devt and clinical evaluation that contributes to the long-lasting well-being of patients in need of biomaterials implants and extracorporal support systems; Scientific Dir Prof. Dr H. J. BUSSCHER.

W. Kahn Institute of Theoretical Psychiatry and Neuroscience: Henk van Tienhovenstraat 67, 6543 JB Nijmegen; tel. (247) 505829; e-mail wimkahn1@hotmail.com; internet kahn-institute.tripod.com; f. 1997; 25 mems; develops theoretical models in the fields of psychiatry, psychology, neuroscience and philosophy, for the diagnosis and treatment of mental health disorders; 10 depts; Chair. Dr WILLEM H. J. MARTENS; Pres. Prof. Dr W. KAHN; Sec. W. A. TUIJTEN; publ. *WKITPN–Publication* (4 a year).

NATURAL SCIENCES
General

CEDLA—Centrum voor Studie en Documentatie van Latijns-Amerika (CEDLA—Centre for Latin American

Research and Documentation): Keizersgracht 395–397, 1016 EK Amsterdam; tel. (20) 5253498; e-mail secretariat@cedla.nl; internet www.cedla.uva.nl; f. 1964, present status 1971; social science research on Latin America; library: see Libraries and Archives; Dir Prof. Dr MICHIEL BAUD; publ. *ERLACS: European Review of Latin American and Caribbean Studies* (Revista Europea de Estudios Latinoamericanos y del Caribe, 2 a year, in English and Spanish).

CentERdata—Instituut voor Dataverzameling en Onderzoek (CentERdata—Institute for Data Collection and Research): POB 90153, 5000 LE Tilburg; Tias Bldg, Warandelaan 2, 5037 AB Tilburg; tel. (13) 4668325; e-mail centerdata@uvt.nl; internet www.centerdata.nl; attached to Tilburg Univ.; data colln, methodological and applied research; Dir Prof. Dr MARCEL DAS.

Groningen Research Institute of Pharmacy (GRIP): Dept of Pharmacy, Antonius Deusinglaan 1, 9713 AV Groningen; tel. (50) 3633275; internet www.rug.nl/farmacie/index; attached to Faculty of Mathematics and Natural Sciences, Univ. of Groningen; organizes research in 11 pharmacy research groups; Scientific Dir Prof. Dr W. J. QUAX.

Kapteyn Astronomical Institute: POB 800, 9700 AV Groningen; Landleven 12, Zernike Bldg, 9747 AD Groningen; tel. (50) 3634073; internet www.rug.nl/sterrenkunde/onderzoek/index; f. 1896 as an astronomical laboratory; Scientific Dir Prof. Dr J. M. VAN DER HULST.

Nederlandse Organisatie voor Toegepast—Natuurwetenschappelijk Onderzoek (TNO) (Netherlands Organization for Applied Scientific Research): POB 6050, 2600 JA Delft; Schoemakerstraat 97, 2628 VK Delft; tel. (88) 8660000; e-mail wegwijzer@tno.nl; internet www.tno.nl; f. 1932; strategic policy and innovation consultancy; bldg, materials and information technology, mechanical and production engineering, product design and development, telecommunications, quality control, health and safety, nutrition, environment and energy; library of 16,000 vols; Chair. JAN MENGELERS; Sec. Drs S. J. VLAAR; publs *TNO Magazine* (in English), *Toegepaste Wetenschap* (in Dutch).

Nederlandse Organisatie voor Wetenschappelijk Onderzoek (NWO) (Netherlands Organization for Scientific Research): POB 93138, 2509 AC The Hague; Laan van Nieuw Oost-Indië 300, 2593 CE The Hague; tel. (70) 3440640; e-mail nwo@nwo.nl; internet www.nwo.nl; f. 1988; stimulates and coordinates pure and applied research in all fields of learning; funds researchers; Chair. Dr JOS ENGELEN; Dir-Gen. and Sec. Dr CEES DE VISSER; publ. *Jaarboek*.

Netherlands Graduate Research School of Science, Technology and Modern Culture (WTMC): Univ. Maastricht, Faculteit der Cultuur-en Maatschappijwetenschappen, WTMC, POB 616, 6200 MD Maastricht; e-mail wtmc@maastrichtuniversity.nl; internet www.wtmc.net; science and technology studies; study of devt of science, technology and modern culture; Scientific Dir Prof. Dr SALLY WYATT.

Netherlands Research School in Process Technology: OSPT Secretariat, Faculty of Engineering Technology, Bldg 'De Meander', POB 217, 7500 AE Enschede; OSPT Office, Univ. of Twente, Bldg 'De Meander', Room ME-116, 7500 AE Enschede; tel. (53) 4894626; e-mail ospt@tudelft.nl; internet ospt.tnw.utwente.nl; research in chemical engineering and process technology; 5 participant univs; Scientific Dir Prof. Dr H. E. A. VAN DEN AKKER.

Oldendorff Research Institute: POB 90153, 5000 LE Tilburg; Prisma Bldg, Warandelaan 2, 5037 AB, Tilburg; tel. (13) 4663140; e-mail e.j.simons@uvt.nl; f. 2001; attached to Tilburg Univ.; int., multi-disciplinary, multi-level research in social sciences; Dir Prof. Dr KLAAS SIJTSMA; Man. A. G. J. J. (TON) HEINEN.

Radionuclide Centre (RNC): De Boelelaan 1085c, 1081 HV Amsterdam; tel. (20) 4449101; internet www.rnc.vu.nl; attached to Vrije Univ. Amsterdam; research on chemical, biological and medical research with radionuclides at Type-2-level; facilitation and cooperation in processing and transport of radioactive waste and first aid with radioactive accidents; laundering of radioactive working clothes.

Stichting voor Wetenschappelijk Onderzoek van de Tropen (WOTRO) (WOTRO Science for Global Development): POB 93120, 2509 AC The Hague; Laan van Nieuw Oost Indië 300, 2593 CE The Hague; tel. (70) 3440763; e-mail wotro@nwo.nl; internet www.nwo.nl; f. 1964; attached to Netherlands Org. for Scientific Research (NWO); research granting org.; focuses on programming, funding and monitoring research on global issues; supports scientific research on devt issues; Chair. Prof. WILLEM J. M. VAN GENUGTEN.

Stratingh Institute for Chemistry: Nijenborgh 4, 9747 AG Groningen; tel. (50) 3634233; e-mail stratingh@rug.nl; internet www.rug.nl/stratingh; f. 1997; attached to Faculty of Mathematics and Natural Sciences, Univ. of Groningen; research in molecular chemistry; Scientific Dir Prof. Dr J. C. HUMMELEN.

Tilburg Centre for Logic and Philosophy of Science (TILPS): POB 90153, 5000 LE Tilburg; Dante Bldg, Warandelaan 2, 5037 AB Tilburg; e-mail tilps@tilburguniversity.nl; internet www.tilburguniversity.nl/tilps; f. 2007; attached to Tilburg Univ.; Dir Prof. STEPHAN HARTMANN.

Van der Waals-Zeeman Institute: POB 94485, 1090 GL Amsterdam; Science Park 904, 1098 XH Amsterdam; tel. (20) 5255663; e-mail secr-wzi-science@uva.nl; internet www.science.uva.nl/research/wzi; attached to Univ. of Amsterdam; research areas incl. atomic physics, hard condensed matter, materials science, quantum optics, soft condensed matter; Dir Prof. Dr M. S. GOLDEN; Man. L. LUSINK.

Biological Sciences

Center for Behaviour and Neurosciences: Nijenborgh 7, 9747 AG Groningen; tel. (50) 3632053; e-mail d.g.m.beersma@rug.nl; internet www.rug.nl/research/cbn; attached to Faculty of Mathematics and Natural Sciences, Univ. of Groningen; integral part of the Research School for Behavioural and Cognitive Neurosciences (BCN) of Univ. of Groningen; Dir Prof. Dr DOMIEN BEERSMA.

Centraalbureau voor Schimmelcultures (CBS—KNAW Fungal Biodiversity Centre): POB 85167, 3508 AD Utrecht; Uppsalalaan 8, 3584 CT Utrecht; tel. (30) 2122600; e-mail info@cbs.knaw.nl; internet www.cbs.knaw.nl; f. 1904, present location 2000; attached to Royal Netherlands Acad. of Arts and Sciences; researches on biosystematics of the fungal kingdom; maintains a world-renowned colln of filamentous fungi, yeasts and bacteria; research focus on the taxonomy and evolution of fungi, functional aspects of fungal biology and ecology, using molecular and genomics approaches; Dir Prof. Dr PEDRO W. CROUS; publs *CBS Biodiversity*

Series (2–3 a year), *IMA Fungus* (2 a year), *Persoonia* (2 a year), *Studies in Mycology* (3 a year).

Centre for Synthetic Biology: Nijenborgh 4, 9747 AG Groningen; tel. (50) 3633385; e-mail syntheticbiology@rug.nl; internet www.rug.nl/fwn/onderzoek/instituten/csb/index; f. 2008; attached to Faculty of Mathematics and Natural Sciences, Univ. of Groningen; design, construction of cellular and biohybrid systems; Scientific Dir Prof. Dr BERT POOLMAN.

Donders Institute for Brain, Cognition and Behaviour: POB 9101, 6500 HE Nijmegen; Montessorilaan 3, 6525 HR Nijmegen; tel. (24) 3615617; e-mail info@donders.ru.nl; internet www.ru.nl/donders; attached to Radboud Univ. Nijmegen; consists of the Centre of Cognition, the Centre for Cognitive Neuroimaging and the Centre for Neuroscience; Man. Dir SASKIA SCHEPERS.

Groningen Biomolecular Science and Biotechnology Institute: Nijenborgh 7, 9747 AG Groningen; tel. (50) 3634203; e-mail t.hummel@rug.nl; internet www.rug.nl/gbb/organisation/index; f. 1993; attached to Faculty of Mathematics and Natural Sciences, Univ. of Groningen; originates from collaboration between dept of biology and chemistry; composed of 13 research groups; Dir Prof. Dr A. J. M. DRIESSEN.

Hortus Botanicus: POB 9500, 2300 RA Leiden; Rapenburg 73, 2311 GJ Leiden; tel. (71) 5275144; e-mail hortus@hortus.leidenuniv.nl; internet www.hortusleiden.nl; f. 1590; attached to Univ. Leiden; Prefect/Dir Dr P. J. A. KESSLER; Scientific Dir Prof. Dr E. F. SMETS.

Hortus Haren Holland: POB 179, 9750 AD Haren; Kerklaan 34, 9751 NN Haren; tel. (50) 5370053; e-mail info@hortusharen.nl; internet www.hortusharen.nl; f. 1642, renewed 1929; CEO Drs J. C. KAPPENBURG.

Hubrecht Institute: POB 85164, 3508 AD Utrecht; Uppsalalaan 8, 3584 CT Utrecht; tel. (30) 2121800; e-mail library@hubrecht.eu; internet www.hubrecht.eu; f. 1916 as Hubrecht Laboratory, present location 2000, current name adopted 2007; attached to Royal Netherlands Acad. of Arts and Sciences; research on developmental and stem cell biology of animals; 21 research groups; Dir Prof. ALEXANDER VAN OUDENAARDEN; Man. Dir Dr MARIËTTE OOSTERWEGEL; Deputy Dir for Research Prof. JEROEN DEN HERTOG.

Instituut voor Plantenziektenkundig Onderzoek (IPO–DLO) (DLO–Research Institute for Plant Protection): POB 9060, 6700 WG Wageningen; tel. (317) 476000; e-mail info@ipo.dlo.nl; f. 1949; prevention, management and control of plant diseases and pests; library of 24,000 vols; Dir Dr Ir N. G. HOGENBOOM.

Nationaal Herbarium Nederland (National Herbarium of the Netherlands): POB 9514, 2300 RA Leiden; Van Steenis Bldg, Einsteinweg 2, 2333 CC Leiden; tel. (71) 5273515; e-mail dewolf@nhn.leidenuniv.nl; internet www.nhn.leidenuniv.nl; f. 1999 by merger of Herbarium Vadense, Rijksherbarium Leiden and Utrecht Univ. Herbarium; attached to Universiteit Leiden; investigation of flora (taxonomy, geography), particularly of the Netherlands and the Tropics; br and research centre in Wageningen; library of 45,000 vols, 100,000 journal vols, 100,000 reprints, 90,000 microfiches, 40,000 plant illustrations; Chair. Prof. Dr S. B. MENKEN; Dir Prof. Dr E. F. SMETS; Sec. Dr J. B. MOLS; publs *Blumea* (in English), *Flora Malesiana* (Phanerog., ferns), *Flora Malesiana Bulletin*, *Gorteria* (Netherlands flora), *IAWA Journal* (4 a year), *Persoonia* (Mycology).

Nederlands Instituut voor Onderzoek in de Katalyse (Netherlands Institute for Catalysis Research): 300 Laan van Nieuw Oost-Indië, POB 93460, 2509 AL Hague; tel. (70) 3440523; e-mail office@niok.nl; internet www.niok.eu; f. 1991; virtual institute consists of major catalysis groups of 8 Dutch univs; Scientific Dir Prof. BERT WECKHUYSEN.

Radboud Institute for Molecular Life Sciences (RIMLS): 259 RIMLS, POB 9101, 6500 HB Nijmegen; Geert Grooteplein 28, 6525 GA Nijmegen; tel. (24) 3610707; e-mail rimls@radboudumc.nl; internet www.rimls .nl; attached to Radboud Univ. Nijmegen Medical Centre; multidisciplinary research within molecular mechanisms of disease and molecular medicine, cell biology, translational research; Dir Prof. Dr RENÉ BINDELS.

Research School of Behavioural and Cognitive Neurosciences: POB 196, 9700 AD Groningen; Ant. Deusinglaan 1, HPC FA30, Bldg 3217, Room 731, 9713 AV Groningen; tel. (50) 3634734; e-mail e.t .kuiper-drenth@umcg.nl; internet www.rug .nl/bcn; f. 1987; attached to Univ. of Groningen; integrates fundamental research and education; addresses neurobiological basis of behavioural and cognitive events; studies the physiological and pathological processes of the nervous system; 5 faculties of the Univ. of Groningen participate with a number of research institutes; focuses on bringing together clinical and pre-clinical researchers from different research institutes; offers Masters and doctorate programmes; Scientific Dir Prof. Dr H. W. G. M. BODDEKE.

Swammerdam Institute for Life Sciences: POB 94216, 1090 GE Amsterdam; Science Park 904, 1098 XH Amsterdam; tel. (20) 5257678; e-mail info-science@uva.nl; internet www.science.uva.nl/sils; attached to Univ. of Amsterdam; research related to cellular processes and interactions; multidisciplinary research in biology, (bio)chemistry, (bio)physics, data analysis technology, information technology, medicine; Dir Prof. Dr WILLEM. J. STIEKEMA.

Mathematical Sciences

Casimir Onderzoekschool (Casimir Research School): Management Office, Casimir Research School, Oortgebouw, kamer 154 Niels Bohrweg 2, 2333 CA Leiden; tel. (15) 275955; e-mail info@casimir .researchschool.nl; internet casimir .researchschool.nl; f. 2004 by Leiden Institute of Physics and Kavli Institute of Nanoscience; graduate school for interdisciplinary physics and strong focus on nanoscience; Dir Prof. Dr JAN VAN RUITENBEEK.

Centre for Theoretical Physics: Nijenborgh 4, 9747 AG Groningen; tel. (50) 3634950; e-mail secrctn@rug.nl; internet www.rug.nl/research/centre-theoretical-physics; consists of 4 research groups: computational physics, theory of condensed matter, high energy physics.

Centrum Wiskunde & Informatica (CWI) (Centre for Mathematics and Computer Science): POB 94079, 1090 GB Amsterdam; Science Park 123, 1098 XG Amsterdam; tel. (20) 5929333; e-mail info@cwi.nl; internet www.cwi.nl; f. 1946; fundamental scientific research in mathematics and computer science; library: see Libraries and Archives; Gen. Dir Prof. Dr JOS C. M. BAETEN; Chair. PETER VAN LAARHOVEN.

Euler Institute for Discrete Mathematics and its Applications: c/o Dept of Mathematics and Computing Science, Eindhoven Univ. of Technology, POB 513, 5600 MB Eindhoven; tel. (40) 2472254; e-mail eidma@tue.nl; internet www.win.tue.nl/wsk/

eidma; f. 1994; attached to Eindhoven Univ. of Technology; coding theory, combinatorial optimization and algorithms, discrete algebra and geometry, graph theory, information theory and cryptology; Chair. Prof. Dr A. M. COHEN; Scientific Dir Prof. Dr Ir HENK C. A. VAN TILBORG.

Eurandom: POB 513, 5600 MB Eindhoven; MF 4.081, Den Dolech 2, 5612 AZ Eindhoven; tel. (40) 2478100; e-mail info@eurandom.tue .nl; internet www.eurandom.nl; attached to Eindhoven Univ. of Technology; probability theory, statistics, stochastic operations research; Chair. Prof. Dr FRANK VAN DER DUYN SCHOUTEN; Scientific Dir Prof. Dr Ir ONNO J. BOXMA; Man. Dir Drs CONNIE M. M. CANTRIJN.

Institute for Mathematics, Astrophysics and Particle Physics: POB 9010, 6500 GL Nijmegen; Huygens Bldg, Room HG03.830, Heyendaalseweg 135, 6525 AJ Nijmegen; tel. (24) 3652099; e-mail secr@hef.ru.nl; internet www.ru.nl/imapp; f. 2005; attached to Faculty of Science, Radbound Univ. Nijmegen; research in mathematics, astrophysics and elementary particle physics; Dir Prof. Dr SIJBRAND DE JONG.

Instituut voor Hoge Energie Fysica (IHEF) (Institute for High Energy Physics): POB 41882, 1009 DB Amsterdram; Science Park 105, 1098 XG Amsterdam; tel. (20) 5925169; e-mail j.berger@nikhef.nl; internet www.nikhef.nl/onderwijs/universitaire-partners/uva-ihef; attached to Univ. of Amsterdam; high energy particle physics, subatomic physics, instrumentation; Dir Prof. Dr S. C. M. BENTVELSEN.

Instituut voor Programmatuurkunde en Algoritmiek (Institute for Programming Research and Algorithmics): Eindhoven Univ. of Technology, Dept of Mathematics and Computing Science, IPA Secretariat, POB 513, 5600 MB Eindhoven; Den Dolech 2, Room HG 7.22, 5600 MB Eindhoven; tel. (40) 2474124; e-mail ipa@tue.nl; internet www.win.tue.nl/ipa; attached to Eindhoven Univ. of Technology; research areas incl. algorithms and complexity, formal methods, software technology and engineering; Scientific Dir Prof. Dr J. C. M. BAETEN.

Instituut voor Theoretische Fysica (Institute for Theoretical Physics): POB 94485, 1090 GL Amsterdam; Science Park 904, Amsterdam; tel. (20) 5255773; e-mail itf@science.uva.nl; internet www.science.uva .nl/research/itf; f. 1949; attached to Univ. of Amsterdam; Dir Prof. Dr KARELJAN SCHOUTENS.

Johann Bernoulli Institute of Mathematics and Computing Science (JBI): POB 407, 9700 AK Groningen; Nijenborgh 9, 9747 AG Groningen; tel. (50) 3633973; e-mail jbiboard@rug.nl; internet www.rug.nl/ informatica/onderzoek/bernoulli; attached to Faculty of Mathematics and Natural Science, Univ. of Groningen; 6 mathematics, 6 computer research programmes.

Kernfysisch Versneller Instituut (KVI) (Nuclear Physics Accelerator Institute): Zernikelaan 25, 9747 AA Groningen; tel. (50) 3633600; e-mail info@kvi.nl; internet www .rug.nl/kvi/index; f. 1971; attached to Univ. of Groningen; int. institute in fundamental and applied atomic and subatomic physics; Dir Prof. Dr KLAUS JUNGMANN.

Korteweg—de Vries Instituut voor Wiskunde (Korteweg-de Vries Institute for Mathematics): POB 94248, 1090 GE Amsterdam; Fl. 4C, Science Park 904, 1098 XH Amsterdam; tel. (20) 5255217; internet www .science.uva.nl/research/math; f. 1997, present location 2009; attached to Univ. of Amsterdam; research in mathematics; Dir Prof. Dr JAN J. O. O. WIEGERINCK; Man. Dr

M. KRANENBURG; Man. L. STOLTE; Sec. EVELIEN WALLET.

Sterrenkundig Instituut Anton Pannekoek (Anton Pannekoek Astronomical Institute): POB 94249, 1090 GE Amsterdam; Science Park 904, 1098 XH Amsterdam; tel. (20) 5257491; e-mail secr-astro-science@uva .nl; internet www.astro.uva.nl; attached to Univ. of Amsterdam; research in high-energy astrophysics; Dir Prof. Dr MICHIEL VAN DER KLIS.

Physical Sciences

Centre for Ecological and Evolutionary Studies (CEES): POB 11103, 9700 CC Groningen; Nijenborgh 7, 9747 AG Groningen; tel. (50) 3638357; e-mail cees-office@rug .nl; internet www.rug.nl/research/cees; attached to Faculty of Mathematics and Natural Sciences, Univ. of Groningen; 9 research groups; coordinates the local research school ecology and evolution; Dir Prof. Dr HAN OLFF.

Green Energy Initiative: Meander Bldg, POB 217, 7500 AE Enschede; Meander Bldg, Drienerlolaan 5, 7500 AE Enschede; tel. (53) 4892489; e-mail m.h.steenbergen@utwente .nl; internet www.utwente.nl/greenenergy; f. 2012; attached to Univ. of Twente; works to strengthen collaboration between the various scientific disciplines in renewable energy research at the Univ. of Twente; promotes successful implementation of innovations; enables a better contact for external parties; Scientific Dir Prof. Dr Ir L. LEFFERTS; Programme Dir Ir J. P. EMMERZAAL; Sec. MARION H. STEENBERGEN.

Institute for Molecules and Materials (IMM): POB 9010, 6500 GL Nijmegen; Huygens Bldg, Heyendaalseweg 135, 6525 AJ Nijmegen; tel. (24) 3653189; e-mail imm@ science.ru.nl; internet www.ru.nl/imm; f. 2005; attached to Faculty of Science, Radbound Univ. Nijmegen; research in functional molecular structures and materials; Dir Prof. Dr ELIAS VLIEG; Man. Dir Dr IWAN HOLLEMAN; Sec. ERNA GOUWENS.

Institute for Wetland and Water Research (IWWR): POB 9010, 6500 GL Nijmegen; Heijendaalseweg 135, 6525 AJ Nijmegen; tel. (24) 3652294; e-mail m .frieling@science.ru.nl; internet www.ru.nl/ iwwr; attached to Faculty of Science, Radbound Univ. of Nijmegen; joint research in microbiology, ecology, plant and environmental sciences; Dir Prof. Dr HANS DE KROON.

Instituut voor Biodiversiteit en Ecosysteem Dynamica (Institute for Biodiversity and Ecosystem Dynamics): POB 94248, 1090 GE Amsterdam; Science Park 904, 1098 XH Amsterdam; tel. (20) 5256635; e-mail ibed-dir-science@uva.nl; internet www .science.uva.nl/ibed; attached to Univ. of Amsterdam; research on biodiversity and evolution, geo-ecology and community dynamics; Dir Prof. Dr PETER TIENDEREN.

Nationaal Instituut voor Subatomaire Fysica (NIKHEF) (National Institute for Subatomic Physics): POB 41882, 1009 DB Amsterdam; Science Park 105, 1098 XG Amsterdam; tel. (20) 5922000; e-mail info@ nikhef.nl; internet www.nikhef.nl; f. fmrly Nat. Institute for Nuclear Physics and High-Energy Physics, current name adopted 1998; 900 MeV pulse stretcher and storage ring (AmPs) and auxiliary instrumentation for basic research in (astro) particle physics; Dir F. LINDE.

Nederlands Instituut voor Ecologie (Netherlands Institute of Ecology): POB 1299, 3600 BG Maarssen; Rijksstraatweg 6, 3631 AC Nieuwersluis; tel. (294) 239300; e-mail m.albers@nioo.knaw.nl; internet www.nioo.knaw.nl; f. 1992 as Netherlands

Institute for Ecological Research, current name adopted 2002; attached to Royal Netherlands Acad. of Arts and Sciences; studies animal ecology, plant ecology, microbial ecology in terrestrial, freshwater and marine environments; incorporates Centre for Estuarine and Coastal Ecology (in Yerseke), Centre for Limnology (in Nieuwersluis) and Centre for Terrestrial Ecology (in Heteren); Dir Prof. Dr L. E. M. VET.

Netherlands Institute of Applied Geoscience TNO—National Geological Survey: POB 80015, 3508 TA Utrecht; Princetonlaan 6, 3584 CB Utrecht; tel. (30) 2564256; e-mail info@nitg.tno.nl; f. 1903; Dir Dr M. J. VAN BRACHT; publs *Geological Maps*, *Netherlands Journal of Geosciences* (4 a year).

NIOZ Koninklijk Nederlands Instituut voor Onderzoek der Zee (NIOZ Royal Netherlands Institute for Sea Research): POB 59, 1790 AB Den Burg, Texel; Landsdiep 4, 1797 SZ 't Horntje, Texel; tel. (222) 369300; e-mail cpr@nioz.nl; internet www .nioz.nl; f. 1876, present bldg 1976; attached to Netherlands Org. for Scientific Research; scientific marine research; ships; Chair. Prof. Dr PIER VELLINGA; Gen. Dir Prof. Dr HENK BRINKHUIS; Deputy Dir Prof. Dr Ir HERMAN RIDDERINKHOF; Sec. Prof. Dr E. A. KOSTER; Treas. GUUS F. C. VAN DER KAMP; publ. *Journal of Sea Research* (4 a year).

SRON Netherlands Institute for Space Research: Sorbonnelaan 2, 3584 CA Utrecht; tel. (88) 7775600; e-mail info@sron .nl; internet www.sron.nl; f. 1983 as Space Research Org. Netherlands, current name adopted 2005; attached to Netherlands Org. for Scientific Research; develops and exploits equipment for space research and for terrestrial research from space; br. in Groningen; Chair. Ir P. A. O. G. KORTING; Vice-Chair. Prof. Dr W. J. VAN DER ZANDE; Scientific Dir and Gen. Dir Prof. Dr RENS WATERS; Man. Dir and Deputy Gen. Dir Dr ROEL GATHIER.

Stichting voor Fundamenteel Onderzoek der Materie (FOM) (Foundation for Fundamental Research on Matter): POB 3021, 3502 GA Utrecht; Van Vollenhovenlaan 659, 3527 JP Utrecht; tel. (30) 6001211; e-mail info@fom.nl; internet www.fom.nl; f. 1946; promotes, coordinates and finances fundamental physics research in the Netherlands through 200 univ. teams in 2 institutes of its own, and 1 used jtly with univs; Chair. Prof. Dr N. J. LOPES CARDOZO; Vice-Chair. Prof. Dr C. W. J. BEENAKKER; Dir Dr Ir WIM VAN SAARLOOS; Sec. PETRA VAN LULING..

Attached Institutes:

FOM—Dutch Institute for Fundamental Energy Research (DIFFER): POB 1207, 3430 BE Nieuwegein; Edisonbaan 14, 3439 MN Nieuwegein; tel. (30) 6096999; e-mail info@differ.nl; internet www.differ.nl; f. 1959; research in plasma physics, plasma containment, heating, plasma surface interaction, EUV mirrors, solar fuels; library of 7,000 vols, 13,000 reports; Dir Dr M. C. M. VAN DE SANDEN.

FOM—Instituut AMOLF (FOM Institute AMOLF): POB 41883, 1009 DB Amsterdam; Science Park 104, 1098 XG Amsterdam; tel. (20) 7547100; e-mail info@amolf .nl; internet www.amolf.nl; f. 1949 as FOM Laboratory for Mass Spectrography, present name 1966; facilities incl. mass-spectrometers, spectrographs, molecular beam apparatus, microwave interferometers, laser equipment, beam plasma experiments, a PDP 11 computer and a nanocentre; library of 2,200 vols; Gen. Dir Prof. Dr VINOD SUBRAMANIAM; Man. BART VAN LEIJEN.

KVI (Nuclear-Physics Accelerator Institute): Zernikelaan 25, 9747 AA Groningen; tel. (50) 3633600; e-mail info@kvi.nl; internet www.kvi.nl; f. 1968; fundamental and applied atomic and subatomic physics; AVF cyclotron, ion sources, traps for short-living isotopes; Chair. Prof. K. DUPPEN; Dir Prof. KLAUS JUNGMANN; Exec. Sec. Dr MARJAN KOOPMANS.

Twente Water Centre: Horst Bldg, W 114, POB 217, 7500 AE Enschede; Horst Bldg, Drienerlolaan 5, 7522 NB Enschede; tel. (53) 4894320; e-mail water@utwente.nl; internet www.utwente.nl/water; attached to Univ. of Twente; water systems and governance; Chair. for Scientific Programme Council Prof. Dr Ir ARJEN Y. HOEKSTRA; Sec. JOKE MEIJER-LENTELINK.

Van't Hoff Institute for Molecular Sciences: POB 94157, 1090 GD Amsterdam; Science Park 904, 1098 XH Amsterdam; tel. (20) 5255265; e-mail r.b.hippert@uva.nl; internet www.science.uva.nl/hims; research themes incl. sustainable chemistry, computational chemistry, macromolecular and biosystems analysis and molecular photonics; Scientific Dir Prof. Dr JOOST N. H. REEK.

Zernike Institute for Advanced Materials: POB 221, 9700 AE Groningen; Nijenborgh 4, 9747 AG Groningen; tel. (50) 3634843; e-mail t.t.m.palstra@rug.nl; internet www.rug.nl/zernike/index; f. 2007 by merger of Materials Science Centre and Materials Science Centre plus; attached to Faculty of Mathematics and Natural Sciences, Univ. of Groningen; symbiotic studies of functional materials involving researchers from different disciplines; Scientific Dir Prof. Dr T. T. M. PALSTRA.

PHILOSOPHY AND PSYCHOLOGY

Amsterdam Centre for Child Studies: c/o Dr Dorien Graas, Van der Boechorststraat 1, 1081 BT Amsterdam; tel. (20) 5988785; e-mail info@ack.vu.nl; internet www.ack.vu .nl; f. 2002; attached to Vrije Univ., Amsterdam; research on insights in disturbed processes of child rearing and devt, and application and implementation of findings for policies and programmes concerning parents and children.

Behavioural Science Institute: POB 9104, 6500 HE Nijmegen; Montessorilaan 3, A.08.29, 6525 HR Nijmegen; tel. (24) 3610082; e-mail secr@bsi.ru.nl; internet www.ru.nl/bsi; attached to Faculty of Social Sciences, Radboud Univ., Nijmegen; research on principles and processes of human behaviour; Dir Prof. Dr A. H. N. CILLESSEN.

Centre for Philosophy of Technology and Engineering Science: POB 217, 7500 AE Enschede; tel. (53) 4893297; e-mail p .bruulsma@utwente.nl; internet www .utwente.nl/gw/ceptes; attached to Univ. of Twente; research in philosophy of engineering science, technology; Dir PHILIP BREY; Sec. PETRA BRUULSEMA.

Heymans Institute for Psychological Research: Grote Kruisstraat 2/1, 9712 TS Groningen; tel. (50) 3638210; e-mail secr-onderzoekpsych@rug.nl; internet www .rug.nl/psy/onderzoek; attached to Dept of Psychology, Univ. of Groningen; psychological research conducted within 7 research programmes, participates in 6 research schools; Dir for Research Prof. Dr ERNESTINE GORDIJN.

Psychology Research Institute: Diamantbeurs, Weesperplein 4, 1018 XA Amsterdam; tel. (20) 5256739; e-mail ozipsychologie-fmg@ uva.nl; internet psyres.uva.nl; attached to Univ. of Amsterdam; research, Bachelors and Masters courses in psychology; Scientific Dir

Prof. Dr A. H. FISCHER; Sec. Dr J. J. W. VAN DER MEER.

Research Institute for Philosophy: POB 9103, 6500 HD Nijmegen; Erasmusplein 1, 6525 HT Nijmegen; tel. (24) 3612474; e-mail secretariaat@unie.ru.nl; internet www.ru.nl/ english/research/research_institutes/vm/ research_institute_0; research programmes: rationality and cognition, hermeneutic philosophy, natural philosophy to science; includes centre for ethics.

RELIGION, SOCIOLOGY AND ANTHROPOLOGY

Amsterdam Institute for Social Science Research: Kloveniersburgwal 48, 1012 CX Amsterdam; Nieuwe Prinsengracht 130, 1018 VZ Amsterdam; tel. (20) 5252262; e-mail aissr@uva.nl; internet www.aissr.uva .nl; f. 2010 by merger of Amsterdam Institute for Metropolitan and Int. Devt, Amsterdam School for Social Science Research, Institute for Migration and Ethnic Studies; attached to Univ. of Amsterdam; research in social sciences incl. anthropology, int. devt studies, geography and planning, political science, sociology, urban studies; Academic Dir Prof. Dr ANITA HARDON; Exec. Dir JOSÉ KOMEN.

Amsterdam School for Cultural Analysis: Spuistraat 210, Room 113, 1012 VT Amsterdam; tel. (20) 5253874; e-mail asca-fgw@uva.nl; internet www.hum.uva.nl/ asca; attached to Univ. of Amsterdam; interdisciplinary, comparative studies across cultural and linguistic areas; Academic Dir CHRISTOPH LINDNER; Man. Dir Dr ELOE KINGMA; Vice-Dir Dr WANDA STRAUVEN.

Babylon, Centre for the Study of Superdiversity: POB 90153, 5000 LE Tilburg; Tilburg Univ., Warandelaan 2, Dante Bldg, 2nd Fl., 5037 AB Tilburg; tel. (13) 4663563; e-mail babylon@uvt.nl; internet www .tilburguniversity.edu/research/institutes-s-and-research-groups/babylon; f. 2002; attached to Tilburg Univ.; research on characteristics and management of cultural, linguistic, religious diversity in multicultural society; Dir Prof. Dr JAN BLOMMAERT; Assoc. Dir Prof. Dr FONS VAN DE VIJVER; Sec. KARIN BERKHOUT.

Centrum voor Patristisch Onderzoek (Centre for Patristic Research): POB 80101, 3508 TC Utrecht; tel. (30) 2532928; e-mail info@patristiek.eu; internet www.patristiek .eu; attached to Tilburg Univ.; research themes incl. early devt of Christian thinking about man, soc., creation, the triune God; Dir Prof. Dr PAUL VAN GEEST.

Globus Competence Centre for Globalization and Sustainable Development: POB 90153, 5000 LE Tilburg; Warandelaan 2, 5037 AB Tilburg; tel. (13) 4668010; e-mail viv.mestdagh@tiasnimbas.edu; internet www.tiasnimbas.edu/globus; f. 1998; attached to TiasNimbas Business School, Tilbug Univ.; globalization, sustainable devt; Chair. Prof. Dr K. ZOETEMAN; Exec. Dir Prof. Dr PAUL VAN SETERS.

Institute for Historical, Literary and Cultural Studies: POB 9103, 6500 HD Nijmegen; Erasmusplein 1, 6525 HT Nijmegen; tel. (24) 3612336; e-mail hlcs@let.ru.nl; internet www.ru.nl/hlcs; f. 1998; attached to Faculty of Arts, Radboud Univ. Nijmegen; research programmes on ancient world, memory, cultural and religious identities; history of politics and human life courses; literary criticism.

Institute for Migration and Ethnic Studies: Oudezijds Achterburgwal 185, 1012 DK Amsterdam; tel. (20) 5252504; e-mail imes@ uva.nl; internet www.imes.uva.nl; attached to Univ. of Amsterdam; debates on migration as a social science issue; fosters dialogue across academic disciplines; promotes intellectual reflexivity; Co-Dir BARAK KALIR; Co-Dir OLGA SEZNEVA; Co-Dir FLORIS VERMEULEN.

Instituut voor Rituele en Liturgische Studies (IRiLiS) (Institute for Ritual and Liturgical Studies): POB 90153, 5000 LE Tilburg; Dante Bldg, Room 229, Warandelaan 2, 5037 AB Tilburg; tel. (13) 4663553; e-mail irilis@uvt.nl; internet www.tilburguniversity.nl/irilis; f. 1992; attached to Tilburg Univ.; research areas incl. rituals, Christian liturgy, sacred places, sacraments, folk religious rites, religious music, abbeys; Dir Prof. Dr P. POST; Sec. Dr PETRA VERSNEL; publs *Jaarboek voor Liturgieonderzoek, Liturgia Condenda, Meander, Netherlands Studies in Ritual and Liturgy.*

Interuniversity Centre for Social Science Theory and Methodology (ICS): ICS, Department of Sociology, Grote Rozenstraat 31, 9712 TG Groningen; tel. (50) 3636469; e-mail s.simon@rug.nl; internet www.ics-graduateschool.nl; f. 1986; jt project of Univ. of Groningen, Utrecht Univ. and Radboud Univ., Nijmegen; located in sociology dept. of all three univs; Scientific Dir Prof. RAFAEL WITTEK.

LUCE—Centrum voor Religieuze Communicatie (LUCE—Centre for Religious Communication): POB 80101, 3508 TC Utrecht; Nieuwegracht 61, Utrecht; tel. (30) 4663800; e-mail luce-crc@uvt.nl; internet www.luce-crc.nl; f. 2007; attached to Tilburg Univ.; Dir HENK VAN HOUT.

Meertens Instituut: POB 94264, 1090 GG Amsterdam; Joan Muyskenweg 25, 1096 CJ Amsterdam; tel. (20) 4628500; e-mail info@meertens.knaw.nl; internet www.meertens.knaw.nl; f. 1926, present status 1952; attached to Royal Netherlands Acad. of Arts and Sciences; research into diversity and documentation of Dutch language and culture; incl. ethnological studies, structural, dialectological and sociolinguistic study of language variation; organizes workshops, symposiums and confs; library of 70,000 vols, 4,000 journals; Dir Prof. Dr H. J. BENNIS.

Nederlandse Onderzoekschool voor Theologie en Religiewetenschap (NOSTER) (Netherlands School for Advanced Studies in Theology and Religion): POB 80.105, 3508 TC Utrecht; Janskerkhof 13, 3512 JK Utrecht; tel. (30) 2533105; e-mail noster@uu.nl; internet www.noster.org; attached to Utrecht Univ.; research in theology, religious studies; Pres. Prof. Dr PETER J. A. NISSEN; Exec. Sec. Dr CHARLOTTE VAN DER LEEST; Dir Prof. Dr A. J. A. C. M. (ANNE-MARIE) KORTE; 200 teachers; 50 students; publ. *Studies in Theology and Religion (STAR).*

Netherlands Institute for Advanced Study in the Humanities and Social Sciences (NIAS): Meijboomlaan 1, 2242 PR Wassenaar; tel. (70) 5122700; e-mail nias@nias.knaw.nl; internet www.nias.knaw.nl; f. 1970, present status 1998; attached to Royal Netherlands Acad. of Arts and Sciences; encourages research in the humanities and social sciences; fellowships awarded annually (25 to foreign scholars, 25 to Dutch scholars); Rector Prof. AAFKE HULK; publs *Jelle Zijlstra Lecture* (1 a year), *KB Lecture* (1 a year), *Ortelius Lecture* (every 2 years), *Uhlenbeck Lecture* (1 a year), *Willem F. Duisenberg Lecture* (1 a year).

Nijmeegs Instituut voor Sociaal en Cultureel Onderzoek (NISCO) (Nijmegen Institute for Social and Cultural Research): POB 9104, 6500 HE Nijmegen; Thomas van Aquinostraat 4, 6525 GD Nijmegen; tel. (24)

3615568; e-mail e.vanwijk@maw.ru.nl; internet www.ru.nl/english/research/research_institutes/vm/nijmegen_institute; f. 2003; attached to Faculty of Social Sciences, Radboud Univ. Nijmegen; comparative questions on cohesion, inequality, rationalization within and between societies; Dir PAUL HOEBINK.

Research Institute for Theology and Religious Studies: POB 9103, 6500 HD Nijmegen; Erasmusplein 1, 6525 HT Nijmegen; tel. (24) 3612474; e-mail secretariaat@unie.ru.nl; internet www.ru.nl/english/research/research_institutes/vm/research_-institute; attached to Radboud Univ., Nijmegen; study of religious identities in multi-religious societies.

SISWO—Instituut voor Maatschappijwetenschappen (SISWO—Institute for the Social Sciences): Plantage Muidergracht 4, 1018 TV Amsterdam; tel. (20) 5270600; e-mail siswo@siswo.uva.nl; internet www.siswo.uva.nl/angloam; f. 1960; initiates and coordinates policy-relevant social science research; Dir Prof. Dr H. G. DE GIER; publs *FACTA, KWALON, Tijdschrift voor Criminologie.*

Telos Brabants Centrum voor Duurzame Ontwikkeling (TELOS—Brabant Centre for Sustainable Development): POB 90153, 5000 LE Tilburg; Warandelaan 2, 5037 AB Tilburg; tel. (13) 4668712; e-mail telos@uvt.nl; internet www.telos.nl; f. 1999; attached to Tilburg Univ.; research into sustainable system innovations, transitions in Brabant; Chair Prof. Dr Ir J. T. MOMMAAS.

Thomas Instituut te Utrecht: Heidelberglaan 2, 3584 CS Utrecht; tel. (73) 6135665; e-mail info@instituut-thomas.nl; internet www.thomasinstituut.nl; f. 1990, present status 2006; attached to Tilburg Univ.; study of work of St Thomas Aquinas; Dir Prof. Dr H. J. M. SCHOOT; Sec. for Studies Dr C. M. PUMPLUN.

TECHNOLOGY

3TU Centre for Ethics and Technology: Delft Univ. of Technology, Faculty of TPM, Philosophy Section, POB 5015, 2600 GA Delft; tel. (15) 2787210; e-mail info@ethicsandtechnology.eu; internet www.ethicsandtechnology.eu; studies ethical issues in devt, use and regulation of technology; Man. Dir Dr SABINE ROESER.

Advanced School for Computing and Imaging: TU Delft, EWI, Mekelweg 4, 2628 CD Delft; tel. (15) 2788032; e-mail asci@ewi.tudelft.nl; internet www.asci.tudelft.nl; research in computer systems; Scientific Dir Prof. Dr Ir A. W. M. SMEULDERS.

BatchKennisCentrum (Batch Knowledge Centre): POB 5015, 2600 GA Delft; Jaffalaan 5, 2628 GX Delft; tel. (15) 2781147; e-mail bkc@batchcentre.tudelft.nl; internet www.batchcentre.tudelft.nl; attached to Delft Univ. of Technology; provides information on batch literature, batch research, batch software, batch tutorials; Project Leader Dr Z. VERWATER-LUKSO.

Beta Research School for Operations Management and Logistics: Paviljoen C 07, POB 513, 5600 MB Eindhoven; tel. (40) 2474733; e-mail beta@tue.nl; internet beta.ieis.tue.nl; f. 1995, present status 1998; attached to Eindhoven Univ. of Technology; operational processes, computer science, labour psychology, mathematics, organizational behaviour; Scientific Dir Prof. Dr Ir G. J. VAN HOUTUM.

CIM Centrum Delft (CIM Centre Delft): Mekelweg 2, 2628 CD Delft; tel. (15) 2786876; e-mail b.r.meijer@tudelft.nl; f. 1985; attached to Delft Univ. of Technology;

training and knowledge centre in the fields of computer integrated manufacturing (CID), automated production systems, robotics in corporate economic and organizational context.

Centre for Plasma Physics and Radiation Technology: Dept of Applied Physics, POB 513, 5600 MB Eindhoven; tel. (40) 2472779; e-mail office.cps@tue.nl; internet www.phys.tue.nl/cps; attached to Eindhoven Univ. of Technology; research in the field of astrophysical plasmas, cold etching and deposition plasmas, hot thermonuclear plasmas, micro-discharges, physics; devt, applications of radiation sources; Scientific Dir Prof. Dr M. C. M. VAN DE SANDEN; Sec. A. M. M. LOONEN.

Centre for Telematics and Information Technology: POB 217, 7500 AE Enschede; Zilverling Bldg, Drienerlolaan 5, 7522 NB Enschede; tel. (53) 4898031; e-mail office@ctit.utwente.nl; internet www.ctit.utwente.nl; attached to Univ. of Twente; research on design of advanced ICT systems and their application in a variety of application domains; Chair. of Supervisory Board Prof. Dr E. H. L. AARTS; Scientific Dir PETER M. G. APERS; Man. Dir IDDO BANTE.

Centrum voor Schone Technologie en Milieubeleid (Twente Centre for Studies in Technology and Sustainable Development): POB 217, 7500 AE Enschede; Ravelijn Bldg, Drienerlolaan 5, 7522 NB Enschede; tel. (53) 4893203; e-mail secr@cstm.utwente.nl; internet www.utwente.nl/mb/cstm; f. 1988; attached to Univ. of Twente; environmental quality, governance, sustainable devt, technological innovation; Scientific Dir Prof. Dr HANS TH. A. BRESSERS; Man. Dir Dr MAARTEN J. ARENTSEN.

CIM Centrum Delft (CIM Centre Delft): Mekelweg 2, 2628 CD Delft; tel. (15) 2786876; e-mail b.r.meijer@tudelft.nl; f. 1985; attached to Delft Univ. of Technology; training and knowledge centre in the fields of computer integrated manufacturing (CID), automated production systems, robotics in corporate economic and organizational context.

Communication Technology Basic Research and its Applications (COBRA): Bldg Potentiaal, Room PT 11.28, POB 513, 5600 MB Eindhoven; Bldg Potentiaal, Room PT 11.28, Den Dolech 2, 5612 AZ Eindhoven; tel. (40) 2473880; e-mail cobra@tue.nl; internet www.cobra.tue.nl; f. 1994; attached to Eindhoven Univ. of Technology; communication technologies basic research and applications; Scientific Dir Prof. Dr H. J. S. DORREN.

Delft Centre for Aviation: Jaffalaan 5, 2628 BX Delft; tel. (12) 2787553; e-mail a.r.c.dehaan@tudelft.nl; internet www.tudelft.nl; attached to Delft Univ. of Technology; researches air traffic systems, aviation processes, airport systems, landslide accessibility, sustainability analysis; Managing Dir Dr ALEXANDER DE HAAN.

Delft Centre for Engineering Design: Mekelweg 2, 2628 CD Delft; tel. (15) 2786794; e-mail j.w.m.tournoij@tudelft.nl; internet www.tudelft.nl; attached to Delft Univ. of Technology; Advanced Masters in Engineering Design; industry research; Dir Prof. Dr T. TOMIYAMA.

Delft Institute for Earth-Oriented Space Research: POB 5058, Delft; Kluyverweg 1, 2600 GB Delft; tel. (15) 2782558; e-mail teunissen@deos.tudelft.nl; attached to Delft Univ. of Technology; incorporates field of spacecraft system integration and design that is essential for the devt of earth observation systems; Scientific Dir Prof. Dr Ir P. J. G. TEUNISSEN.

Delft Institute for Information Technology in Service Engineering: Stevinweg 1, 2628 CN Delft; tel. (15) 2785170; e-mail info@duwind.tudelft.nl; attached to Delft Univ. of Technology; Dir Prof. Dr H. G. SOL.

Delft Institute of Microsystems and Nanoelectronics (Dimes): Feldmannweg 17, 2628 CT Delft; tel. (15) 2786234; e-mail info@dimes.tudelft.nl; internet www.dimes.tudelft.nl; attached to Delft Univ. of Technology; research and education in microsystems and nanoelectronics through PhD programme; Scientific Dir Prof. Dr KEES BEENAKKER.

Delft University Research Centre of Intelligent Sensor Microsystems: POB 5031, 2600 GA Delft; Mekelweg 4, EWI Bldg, 2628 CD Delft; tel. (15) 2785745; e-mail disens@tudelft.nl; internet www.disens.tudelft.nl; attached to Delft Univ. of Technology; research on sensors and actuators in microsystem technology; Dir Prof. Dr P. M. SARRO; Man. Dir Prof. Dr Ir J. H. HUIJSING; Sec. G. HOUWELING.

Delft University Wind Energy Research Institute: Kluyverweg 1, 2629 HS Delft; tel. (15) 2785170; e-mail duwind@tudelft.nl; internet www.duwind.tudelft.nl; f. 1999; attached to Delft Univ. of Technology; research on modern wind turbine technology.

Dutch National Research School Combination Catalysis Controlled by Chemical Design (NRSC-Catalysis): POB 513, 5600 MB Eindhoven; Den Dolech 2, Helix W 3.23, Eindhoven; tel. (40) 2473071; e-mail m.j.m.j.jong@tue.nl; internet www.nrsc-catalysis.nl; f. 1999; attached to Eindhoven Univ. of Technology; Dir Prof. Dr RUTGER A. VAN SANTEN; Man. Dr GABRIELA E. DIMA.

Energieonderzoek Centrum Nederland (ECN) (Energy Research Centre of the Netherlands (ECN)): POB 1, 1755 ZG Petten; Westerduinweg 3, 1755 LE Petten; tel. (22) 4564949; e-mail info@ecn.nl; internet www.ecn.nl; f. 1955 as Reactor Centrum Nederland—RCN; carries out energy research; under contract from the govt, nat. and int. orgs and industry; Man. Dir Ir PAUL A. O. G. KORTING; Dir Dr C. A. M. (KEES) VAN DER KLEIN; Dir PEDRO J. SAYERS.

Graduate School on Engineering Mechanics: c/o Dr Ir J. A. W. van Dommelen, Dept of Mechanical Engineering, Eindhoven Univ. of Technology, POB 513, W-hoog 4.133, 5600 MB Eindhoven; tel. (40) 2474060; e-mail engineering.mechanics@tue.nl; internet www.em.tue.nl; f. 1996; attached to Eindhoven Univ. of Technology; description, analysis, optimization of static and dynamic behaviour of materials, products, processes in a variety of engineering applications; Scientific Dir Prof. MARC G. D. GEERS.

Hechtingsinstituut (The Adhesion Institute): Kluyverweg 1, 2629 HS Delft; tel. (15) 2785353; e-mail info@hechtingsinstituut.nl; internet www.adhesioninstitute.com; f. 1990; attached to Faculty of Aerospace Engineering, Delft Univ. of Technology; research in the field of structural adhesive bonds; Dir Dr J. A. POULIS.

IBR Centre for eHealth Research and Disease Management: Citadel H 411, POB 217, 7500 AE Enschede; Citadel Bldg H 411, Drienerlolaan 5, 7522 NB Enschede; tel. (53) 4892398; e-mail j.vangemert-pijnen@utwente.nl; internet www.utwente.nl/ibr/ehealth; attached to Univ. of Twente; examines technology's contribution to healthy lifestyle.

IBR Research Institute for Social Sciences and Technology: Citadel Bldg H 411, POB 217, 7500 AE Enschede; tel. (53) 4892398; e-mail ibr@utwente.nl; internet www.utwente.nl/ibr; attached to Univ. of Twente; research on human behaviour; research themes incl. health assessment and promotion, learning, organization and communication, product design, safety and security, technical cognition; Scientific Dir Prof. Dr E. R. SEYDEL; Man. Dir Dr O. PETERS; Sec. M. G. STEGEHUIS-DE VEGTE.

Institute for Biomedical Technology and Technical Medicine: Zuidhorst Bldg, POB 217, 7500 AE Enschede; Zuidhorst Bldg, Drienerlolaan 5, 7522 NB Enschede; tel. (53) 4893367; e-mail mira@utwente.nl; internet www.utwente.nl/mira; attached to Univ. of Twente; Scientific Dir Prof. Dr CLEMENS A. VAN BLITTERSWIJK; Man. Dir Dr Ir MARTIJN KUIT; Medical Dir Prof. Dr G. P. (PETER) VOOIJS; Dir for Education Drs HELEEN A. T. MIEDEMA.

Institute for Computing and Information Sciences: POB 9010, 6500 GL Nijmegen; Heyendaalseweg 135, 6525 AJ Nijmegen; tel. (24) 3652643; e-mail info@cs.ru.nl; internet www.ru.nl/icis; attached to Faculty of Science, Radboud Univ. Nijmegen; research on computer systems through model based system devt, digital security and intelligent systems; Research Dir Prof. Dr T. M. HESKES.

Institute for Logic, Language and Computation: POB 94242, 1090 GE Amsterdam; Science Park 904, 1098 XH Amsterdam; tel. (20) 5256051; e-mail illc@uva.nl; internet www.illc.uva.nl; f. 1986 as Institute for Language, Logic and Information, present status 1991; attached to Univ. of Amsterdam; research in fundamental principles of encoding, transmission and comprehension of information; Dir Prof. Dr YDE VENEMA; Man. Drs JENNY BATSON; publ. *ILLC magazine* (1 a year).

Institute for Medical Technology Assessment (iMTA): POB 1738, 3000 DR Rotterdam; Burgemeester Oudlaan 50, 3062 PA Rotterdam; tel. (10) 4088571; e-mail vanoorschot@bmg.eur.nl; internet www.bmg.eur.nl/imta; f. 1988; attached to Erasmus Univ.; medical technology assessment, incl. health economics and health outcomes research; provides teaching and training in economic evaluation and MTA research; Vice-Dir Prof. Dr MAUREEN RUTTEN-VAN MÖLKEN; Sec. KARIN VAN OORSCHOT-LÖWENTHAL.

Institute for Science, Innovation and Society (ISIS): POB 9010, 6500 GL Nijmegen; Huygens Bldg, Room 02.832, Heijendaalseweg 135, 6525 AJ Nijmegen; tel. (24) 3653155; e-mail h.zwart@science.ru.nl; internet www.ru.nl/science/isis; f. 2005; attached to Faculty of Science, Radboud Univ. Nijmegen; analyses, assesses and improves societal embedding of science and technology; Dir Prof. Dr HUB ZWART.

Instituut voor Milieu en Agritechniek (IMAG-DLO) (Institute of Agricultural and Environmental Engineering): POB 43, 6700 AA Wageningen; Mansholtlaan 10–12, 6708 PA Wageningen; tel. (317) 476300; e-mail postkamer@imag.dlo.nl; f. 1974; Dir Dr Ir AAD A. JONGEBREUR.

International Research Centre for Telecommunications and Radar: c/o Delft Univ. of Technology, POB 5031, 2600 GA Delft; Mekelweg 4, EWI Bldg, 2628 CD Delft; tel. (15) 2781034; e-mail d.a.u.meijer@tudelft.nl; f. 1994; attached to Delft Univ. of Technology; Dir Prof. Dr Ir LEO P. LIGTHART; Sec. DOMINIQUE A. U. MEIJER.

International Research Institute for Simulation, Motion and Navigation: POB 5058, 2600 GB Delft; Anthony Fokkerweg 1, 2629 HC Delft; tel. (15) 2782094; e-mail info@simona.tudelft.nl; attached to Delft Univ. of Technology; research institute in the field of simulation and transport; Man. Dir Ir MEINE P. OOSTEN; Management Asst VERA M. VAN BRAGT.

J. F. Schouten School for User–System Interaction Research: POB 513, 5600 MB Eindhoven; Paviljoen, R. 1.40, ingang Het Eeuwsel, Eindhoven; tel. (40) 2475938; e-mail jfs@tue.nl; internet www.industrialdesign.tue.nl/jfschouten; f. 1993; attached to Eindhoven Univ. of Technology; Scientific Dir Prof. Dr DON G. BOUWHUIS.

J. M. Burgerscentrum—Onderzoekschool voor Stromingsleer (JMBC) (J. M. Burgerscentrum—Research School for Fluid Mechanics): c/o TU Delft, Mekelweg 2, 2628 CD Delft; tel. (15) 2783216; e-mail jmburgerscentrum@tudelft.nl; internet www.jmburgerscentrum.nl; 60 research groups; Dir Prof. Dr Ir G. OOMS.

Kavli Institute of Nanoscience: Postbus 5046, 2600 GA Delft; Lorentzweg 1, 2628 CJ Delft; tel. (15) 2783163; e-mail nanoscience@tnw.tudelft.nl; internet www.tnw.tudelft.nl; f. 2004; attached to Delft Univ. of Technology; 6 research units, 1 nanofacility cleanroom; founded on grant by Kavli Foundation; Dir Prof. Dr H. S. J. VAN DER ZANT.

Koiter Institute Delft: Kluyverweg 1, 2629 HS Delft; tel. (15) 2785460; e-mail r.deborst@lr.tudelft.nl; internet www.kid.tudelft.nl; attached to Delft Univ. of Technology; promotes mono-disciplinary activity in engineering mechanics.

Materials Innovation Institute (M2i): POB 5008, 2600 GA Delft; Mekelweg 2, 2628 CD Delft; tel. (15) 2782535; e-mail info@m2i.nl; internet www.m2i.nl; devt of new materials for sustainable economic growth; partnership between industry, govt, academia.

MESA+ Institute for Nanotechnology: POB 217, 7500 AE Enschede; NanoLab Bldg, Hallenweg 15, 7522 NB Enschede; tel. (53) 4892715; e-mail info@mesaplus.utwente.nl; internet www.utwente.nl/mesaplus; attached to Univ. of Twente; research in nanotechnology; Scientific Dir Prof. Dr Ing DAVE BLANK.

Nationaal Lucht- en Ruimtevaartlaboratorium (NLR) (National Aerospace Laboratory): POB 90502, 1006 BM Amsterdam; Anthony Fokkerweg 2, 1059 CM Amsterdam; tel. (20) 5113113; e-mail info@nlr.nl; internet www.nlr.nl/public; f. 1919; fluid dynamics, flight mechanics, flight testing and operations, structures and materials, space research, remote sensing, information technology, electronics and instrumentation; br. in Flevoland; library of 7,000 vols, 4,800 conf. proceedings, 2,596 theses, 112,000 reports, etc.; Chair. Drs ARIE KRAAIJEVELD; Gen. Dir Ir MICHEL PETERS; Gen. Sec. ERNST FOLKERS.

National Dutch Graduate Research School of Polymer Science and Technology (PTN): POB 6284, 5600 HG Eindhoven; tel. (40) 2475262; e-mail info@ptn.nu; internet www.ptn.nu; cooperation foundation stage for polymer research in univ. and industry.

National Dutch Graduate School of Polymer Science and Technology (PTN): POB 6284, 5600 HG Eindhoven; tel. (40) 2475262; e-mail nfo@ptn.nu; internet www.ptn.nu; Chair. Ir DICK MEDEMA.

Onderzoekschool Engineering Mechanics (Graduate School on Engineering Mechanics): c/o Dr Ir J. A. W. van Dommelen, POB 513, WH 4.125, 5600 MB Eindhoven; tel. (40) 2474521; e-mail engineering.mechanics@tue.nl; internet www.em.tue.nl; f. 1996; research and education in engineering mechanics; works with Eindhoven Univ. of Technology, Delft Univ. of technology and Univ. of Twente; Scientific Dir Prof. Dr Ir M. G. D. (MARC) GEERS.

OnderzoekSchool ProcesTechnologie (Research School in Process Technology): Groen van Prinstererlaan 37, 3818 JN Amersfoort; tel. (53) 7009797; e-mail ospt@ispt.eu; internet www.ospt.eu; chemical engineering, process technology; Chair. of the Academic Advisory Board Prof. Dr J. A. M. KUIPERS; Exec. Sec. DANIELLA VRIJLING.

Onderzoekschool voor Integrale Product Vernieuwing (Graduate School of Integrated Product Innovation): Univ. Twente, Faculteit der Werktuigbouwkunde, Centrum voor Integrale, Productie Vernieuwing, POB 217, 7500 AE Enschede; tel. (53) 4892520; research programme for research groups in product innovation; Dir Prof. Dr Ir F. J. A. M. VAN HOUTEN.

Reactor Institute Delft: Mekelweg 15, 2629 JB Delft; tel. (15) 2785052; e-mail secretary-rid@tudelft.nl; attached to Delft Univ. of Technology; fundamental and applied scientific research in various fields, both nationally and internationally; houses Hoger Onderwijs Reactor (HOR); Dir Prof. Dr Ir TIM H. J. J. VAN DER HAGEN; Gen. Man Drs Ir RIK J. LINSSEN; Sec. LINDA HOOGEN-DONK-DEN OTTER.

Research School Integral Design of Structures: POB 5048, 2600 GA Delft; Faculty of Civil Engineering and Geosciences, Delft Univ. of Technology, Stevinweg 1, 2628 CN Delft; tel. (15) 2784578; e-mail info@osbouw.nl; internet www.osbouw.nl; f. 1994; inter-univ. research institute for structural design, structural engineering and building processes; Dir Prof. Dr Ir J. C. WALRAVEN.

School for Information and Knowledge Systems: Utrecht Univ., Dept of Information and Computing Sciences, Corine Jolles, Buys Ballot Laboratory, Princetonplein 5, Office 574, 3584 CC Utrecht; tel. (30) 2534083; e-mail office@siks.nl; internet www.siks.nl; f. 1996; research school for information and communication technology; network institute with 11 collaborating univs; Man. Dir Dr R. J. C. M. STARMANS.

ThermoPlastic Composite Research Centre: Palatijn 15, 7521 PN Enschede; tel. (88) 8773877; e-mail info@tprc.nl; internet www.tprc.nl; f. 2009; attached to Univ. of Twente; research and devt of thermoplastic composites materials and technologies for mems; Gen. Man. HARALD HEERINK.

TICER—Tilburg Innovation Centre for Electronic Resources: POB 90153, 5000 LE Tilburg; tel. (13) 4662620; e-mail m.a .schuurman@uvt.nl; internet www .tilburguniversity.nl/ticer; f. 1995; attached to Tilburg Univ.; digital libraries and IT infrastructure; Man. JOLA PRINSEN; Logistics Man. MERRILEE SCHUURMAN.

Tilburg Centre for Cognition and Communication (TICC): POB 90153, 5000 LE Tilburg; Dante Bldg, Warandelaan 2, 5037 AB Tilburg; tel. (13) 4668118; e-mail ticc@uvt .nl; internet www.tilburguniversity.nl/ticc; attached to Tilburg Univ.; artificial intelligence, cognitive modelling, gaming, human–computer interaction, cognition and communication, creative computing and social signal processing; Dir Prof. Dr FONS MAES.

Tilburg Institute for Law, Technology and Society (TILT): POB 90153, 5000 LE Tilburg; Montesquieu Bldg, Warandelaan 2, 5037 AB Tilburg; tel. (13) 4668199; e-mail v .carter@uvt.nl; internet www .tilburguniversity.nl/tilt; attached to Tilburg Univ.; transnational study of law, society,

technology; research areas incl. devts in ICT, biotechnology, other technologies; Gen. Dir Prof. Dr HAN SOMSEN; Dir for Research and Deputy Dir Prof. Dr RONALD E. LEENES; Dir for Studies Dr ANTON H. VEDDER; Dir for Human Resources Dr SIMONE VAN DER HOF; Sec. VIVIAN CARTER.

Twente Embedded Systems Initiative: POB 217, 7500 AE Enschede; tel. (53) 4894173; e-mail t.krol@cs.utwente.nl; internet www.tesi.utwente.nl; attached to Univ. of Twente; research activities in the field of embedded systems, embedded systems design; Head Prof. Dr Ir THIJS KROL.

Vakgroep Verkeer, Vervoer & Ruimte (Centre for Transport Studies): POB 217, 7500 AE Enschede; Bldg Horst, Drienerlolaan 5, 7522 NB Enschede; tel. (53) 4894322; e-mail d.alink-olthof@utwente.nl; internet www.vvr.ctw.utwente.nl; attached to Univ. of Twente; provides traffic engineering courses in Bachelors programme; civil engineering and track traffic engineering and management within the Masters programme; Head Prof. Dr ERIC VAN BERKUM; Sec. DORETTE ALINK-OLTHOF.

Vermogenselektronica en Elektromagnetisch Conversie Centrum (Power Electronics and Electromagnetic Power Conversion Centre): Mekelweg 4, 2628 CD Delft; tel. (15) 2786259; attached to Delft Univ. of Technology.

Virtual Reality Initiative Twente: c/o Dr Ir H. van der Kooij, POB 217, 7500 AE Enschede; tel. (53) 4894779; internet vrint .ctit.utwente.nl; attached to Univ. of Twente; platform for all research groups involved with the devt and application of virtual reality tools.

Libraries and Archives

Alkmaar

Regionaal Archief Alkmaar (Regional Record Office Alkmaar): POB 9232, 1800 GE Alkmaar; Bergerweg 1, 1815 AC Alkmaar; tel. (72) 8508200; e-mail regionaal@archiefalkmaar.nl; internet www .archiefalkmaar.nl; f. 1990; municipal archives, books about Alkmaar and N Holland; also regional archives for the area; pictures, prints, maps, relating to Alkmaar and surroundings; 50,000 vols; Librarian M. JOUSTRA.

Amersfoort

Bibliotheek van het Oud-Katholiek Seminarie (Library of the Old Catholic Seminary): Koningin Wilhelminalaan 3, 3818 HN Amersfoort; tel. (33) 4617569; e-mail seminariebibliotheek@okkn.nl; internet seminarie.okkn.nl; f. 1725; attached to Dept of Theology, Utrecht Univ.; Old Catholicism, Jansenism, Port-Royal, Church history of the Netherlands and Old-Catholic churches, ecumenism, titles edited before 1900 have been moved to the Library of Utrecht Univ.; 12,000 vols; Librarian LUBERTUS NIEUWENHUIZEN.

Openbare Leeszaal en Bibliotheek (Public Library): Zonnehof 12, 3811 ND Amersfoort; tel. (33) 631914; f. 1913; 190,000 vols; Librarian E. A. MURRIS.

Amsterdam

Bibliotheca Philosophica Hermetica (Library of Hermetic Philosophy in Amsterdam): Bloemgracht 13–19, 1016 KC Amsterdam; tel. (20) 6258079; e-mail bph@ritmanlibrary.nl; internet www .ritmanlibrary.nl; f. 1984; specializes in early printed books and MSS in the field of the

Christian-Hermetic tradition (alchemy, Hermetism, mysticism and Rosicrucianism); modern biographical and bibliographical reference works, text-editions, scholarly works, books on the modern esoteric tradition; 22,000 vols, incl 5,000 vols printed before 1800, 600 MSS, 17,000 modern titles; Man. Dir and Librarian ESTHER OOSTERWIJK-RITMAN; Curator Dr CIS VAN HEERTUM; Curator Drs JOSÉ BOUMAN.

Bibliotheek Centrum Wiskunde & Informatica (Library of the Centre for Mathematics and Computer Science): POB 94079, 1090 GB Amsterdam; Science Park 123, 1098 XG Amsterdam; tel. (20) 5924027; e-mail bibl@cwi.nl; internet www.cwi.nl/library; f. 1946; spec. scientific library on non-elementary mathematics and its applications and computer science; 45,700 vols, 1,000 current periodicals, 10,000 e-books, 158,000 reports; Library Man. AY-LING ONG.

Bibliotheek van het Koninklijk Instituut voor de Tropen (Library of the Royal Tropical Institute): POB 95001, 1090 HA Amsterdam; Mauritskade 63, 1092 AD Amsterdam; tel. (20) 5688462; e-mail library@kit.nl; internet www.kit.nl; f. 1910; 450,000 vols, 12,000 periodicals, 27,000 maps; Head of Information, Library and Documentation Drs J. H. W. VAN HARTEVELT.

Boekmanstichting Bibliotheek (Library of the Boekman Foundation): Herengracht 415, 1017 BP Amsterdam; tel. (20) 6243739; e-mail library@boekman.nl; internet www .boekman.nl; f. 1963; all fields of art and culture and related policy; 65,000 vols, 150 current periodicals; Head of Library HILDE KLEIN; publ. *Boekman*.

Centre for Latin American Research and Documentation: Keizersgracht 395–397, 1016 EK Amsterdam; tel. (20) 5253248; e-mail library@cedla.nl; internet www.cedla .uva.nl/60_library/library_index.html; attached to Univ. of Amsterdam; social sciences, economy and history of Latin America; 1,222 journals, spec. collns incl. 20,000 microfiches, 3,500 microfilms.

Economisch-Historische Bibliotheek Amsterdam (Economic-History Library Amsterdam): Cruquiusweg 31, 1019 AT Amsterdam; tel. (20) 6685866; e-mail info@neha.nl; internet www.neha.nl; f. 1914; attached to Netherlands Economic-Historical Archives Foundation; 120,000 vols, spec. colln of 16th–18th-century books on commerce and book-keeping, and on Dutch business history and companies, 3,000 periodicals; Librarian JACQUES VAN GERWEN; publ. *Tijdschrift voor Sociale en Economische Geschiedenis*.

Historical Documentation Centre for Dutch Protestantism: De Boelelaan 1105, 1081 HV Amsterdam; tel. (20) 5985270; e-mail hdc@vu.nl; internet www.hdc.vu.nl; f. 1971; attached to Vrije Univ. Amsterdam; collects and manages archives of persons and instns in protestant circles; promotes historical research, organizes symposia and workshops and publs; provides information and advice, and collaborates in educational and academic projects; Dir Prof. Dr G. HARINCK; Archivist J. F. SEIJLHOUWER.

KIT Library—Royal Tropical Institute: POB 95001, 1090 HA Amsterdam; Mauritskade 63, 1092 AD Amsterdam; tel. (20) 5688298; e-mail ils@kit.nl; internet www.kit .nl/smartsite.shtml?id=27569; information on int. cooperation, sustainable social and economic devt, poverty alleviation, health, cultural exchange and heritage, capacity building, and on the history of the former Dutch colonies; 260,000 vols, 4,500 journals, 30,000 articles, 25,000 maps, 800 atlases; Dir HANS VAN HARTEVELT.

Openbare Bibliotheek Amsterdam (Amsterdam Public Library): Oosterdoksstraat 110, 1011 DK Amsterdam; Oosterdokskade 143, 1011 DL Amsterdam; tel. (20) 5230701; e-mail dir@oba.nl; internet www.oba.nl; f. 1919; central library, 27 br libraries; 1.7m. vols and pieces of sheet music, spec. collns incl. AdamNet libraries, Hella Haasse, children's books in Spanish and home language, Europe Direct centres, international gay and lesbian information centre and archives, music collns; Dir HANS VAN VELZEN.

Rijksakademie van Beeldende Kunsten Bibliotheek (Library of the State Academy of Fine Arts): Sarphatistraat 470, 1018 GW Amsterdam; tel. (20) 5270303; e-mail infodesk@rijksakademie.nl; internet www.rijksakademie.nl; f. 1870, present status 1999; art historic library; large colln of monographs, catalogues of exhibitions and books on visual arts, photography, video, applied art and architecture; 33,000 vols, 85 magazines, 1,400 video cassettes and DVDs; Head MARIETTA DIRKER.

The Academy Library: POB 2169, 1000 CD Amsterdam; Cruquiusweg 31, 1019 AT Amsterdam; tel. (20) 6685866; e-mail ask@iisg.nl; internet socialhistory.org/en/collections/academy-library-collection-guide; f. 1808; attached to International Institute of Social History; formerly part of Library KNAW; contains library collns of Royal Netherlands Academy of Arts and Sciences collected in 19th century; 200,000 vols; spec. collns incl. collns of Willem Bilderdijk, Jacob van Lennep, Johannes Wertheim Salomonson; 15th, 16th century printings; western, eastern MSS; travel accounts and expedition reports; numismatics; Head CO SEEGERS.

Universiteitsbibliotheek Amsterdam (University of Amsterdam Library): POB 19185, 1000 GD Amsterdam; Singel 425, 1012 WP Amsterdam; tel. (20) 5252301; e-mail secr-uba@uva.nl; internet www.uba.uva.nl; f. 1578; incl. Bibliotheca Rosenthaliana (f. 1880, 100,000 vols, 850 MSS), Réveil-Archives, Vondel, Frederik van Eeden and Albert Verwey collns; Tetterode colln; several historical Church collns; libraries of Royal Dutch Book Trade Asscn, Royal Geographical Soc., Royal Netherlands Soc. of Medicine; 4m. vols, 145,000 maps, 160 medieval and 70,000 modern MSS, 500,000 letters; Dir Drs M. A. M. HEIJNE; Man. for Spec. Collns Drs S. C. G. T. SCHOLTEN.

Universiteitsbibliotheek Vrije Universiteit (University Library Vrije Universiteit Amsterdam): De Boelelaan 1103, 1081 HV Amsterdam; De Boelelaan 1105, 1081 HV Amsterdam; tel. (20) 5985200; e-mail vraag.ub@vu.nl; internet www.ub.vu.nl; f. 1880; 1.5m. book titles in print, 3,01,479 ebooks, 27,045 ejournals, 70,000 documents produced prior to 1901, 36,000 maps; Chief Librarian JOSJE CALFF.

Arnhem

Gelders Archief (Gelders Archives): Markt 1, 6811 CG Arnhem; tel. (26) 3521600; e-mail info@geldersarchief.nl; internet www.geldersarchief.nl; f. 1877; contains archives of the Dukes of Gelders and succeeding provincial admins, and of other regional and local authorities; of private persons, families, enterprises, religious bodies, etc. (since 12th century); archive material for northern Limburg before 1580; Dir-Gen. Dr FRED J. W. VAN KAN.

Stichting Arnhemse Openbare en Gelderse Wetenschappelijke Bibliotheek (Arnhem Public and Learned Library): POB 1168, 6801 ML Arnhem; Koningstraat 26, 6811 DG Arnhem; tel. (26) 3543111; e-mail

secretariaat@bibliotheekarnhem.nl; internet www.biblioarnhem.nl; f. 1856; dist. libraries in Kronenburg, Presikhaaf; 14 regional libraries; 750,000 vols, 130 MSS; Library Dir RIA OUDEGA.

Assen

Drents Archief (Drenthe Archive): POB 595, 9400 AN Assen; Brink 4, 9401 HS Assen; tel. (59) 2313523; e-mail info@drentsarchief.nl; internet www.drentsarchief.nl; f. 1879, present status 2005; public records of the Province of Drenthe; archives of private persons, institutions and enterprises; 7,500 vols; Dir DOUWE HUIZING.

Breda

De Bibliotheek Breda (Breda Public Library): POB 90192, 4800 RN Breda; Molenstraat 6, 4811 GS Breda; tel. (76) 5299500; e-mail aam.weterings@breda.nl; internet www.bibliotheekbreda.nl.

Sifria—van de Joodse Gemeente Breda (Sifria—Library of the Jewish Congregation of Breda): NIG Breda, POB 1934, 4801 BX Breda; tel. (13) 5086008; e-mail info@joodsbreda.nl; internet www.joodsbreda.nl/bibliotheek.html; f. 1997; books on Jewish religion, tradition, history, philosophy; collns on holocaust, anti-Semitism, contemporary history of Israel; nonfiction science books, reference dept; works by Jewish writers; antiques works; 4,000 vols.

Breukelen

Nyenrode Business Universiteit Library: Straatweg 25, POB 130, 3620 AC Breukelen; tel. (346) 291310; e-mail library@nyenrode.nl; internet www.nyenrode.nl/library; attached to Nyenrode Business Univ.; library colln covers relevant areas of management studies; 25,000 vols; 350 printed journals; Library Head ONNO MASTENBROEK.

Bussum

Bibliotheek Narden-Bussum (Nard-Bussum Library): Wilhelminaplantsoen 18, 1404 JB Bussum; tel. (35)-6973000; e-mail info@bibliotheeknaardenbussum.nl; internet www.bibliotheeknaardenbussum.nl.

Brunssum

Parkstad Limburg Bibliotheken: Rumpenerstraat 147, 6443 CC Brunssum; tel. (45) 4007560; e-mail info@parkstadlimburgbibliotheken.nl; internet www.obparkstad.nl; consortium of 23 brs in Bocholtz, Brunssum, Heerlen, Hoensbroek, Hulsberg, Kerkrade, Klimmen, Landgraaf, Merkelbeek, Nuth, Ransdaal, Schimmert, Schinveld, Simpelveld and Voerendaal.

De Bilt

Bibliotheek van het Koninklijk Nederlands Meteorologisch Instituut (Library of the Royal Netherlands Meteorological Institute): POB 201, 3730 AE De Bilt; Wilhelminalaan 10, 3732 GK De Bilt; tel. (30) 2206855; e-mail bibliotheek@knmi.nl; internet www.knmi.nl/bibliotheek; f. 1854; holds the nat. meteorological colln; 180,000 vols on meteorology, physical oceanography and geophysics (esp. seismology, ionosphere and geomagnetism); Librarian W. J. JANSEN.

Delft

Erfgoed Delft en Omstreken (Heritage of Delft and Surroundings): POB 78, 2600 ME Delft; Schoolstraat 7, 2611 HS Delft; tel. (15) 2602358; e-mail erfgoeddelft@delft.nl; internet www.erfgoed-delft.nl; f. 1859; protects cultural heritage of Delft and its surroundings; consists of Archaeology of Delft, Archives of Delft, Museum Lambert van

Meerten, Museum Het Prinsenhof, Kouwenhoven's little shop; 40,000 vols mainly on history of Delft, genealogy and heraldry; spec. collns: Delft early printed books, House of Orange-Nassau, Naundorff, 17th century Dutch art, vols about Indonesia, contemporary art, archeology; Dir PATRICK VAN MIL J. A. METER; Head Librarian M. P. SCHOEMAKER-VAN WEESZENBERG.

TU Delft Library (Library of the Delft University of Technology): POB 98, 2600 MG Delft; Prometheusplein 1, 2628 ZC Delft; tel. (15) 2785678; e-mail library@tudelft.nl; internet www.library.tudelft.nl; f. 1842; technical and scientific library; 635,000 vols, 30,900 e-books, 37,000 books published before 1900, 1,500 journals subscriptions, 13,500 ejournal subscriptions, 27,000 TU Delft Open Access publs, 14,000 online photos and video cassettes, 4,000 data sets; Librarian Ir WILMA VAN WEZENBEEK.

Deventer

Stadsarchief en Athenaeumbibliotheek Deventer (City Archives and Deventer Municipal Library): POB 351, 7400 AJ Deventer; Klooster 12, 7411 NH Deventer; tel. (570) 693887; e-mail info.sab@saxion.nl; internet www.sabinfo.nl; f. 1560; library for town of Deventer and province of Overijssel and Saxion Univ. of Applied Sciences; 250,000 vols, 550 MSS, 380 incunabula, 400 post-incunabula; municipal archives 1241–1950, judicial archives 1423–1811, archives of chapter 1123–1591, church registers 1542–1811, notarial archives 1811–1905; Dir G. E. TULP.

Dordrecht

Regionaal Archief Dordrecht (Regional Archives Dordrecht): Stek 13, 3311 XS Dordrecht; tel. (78) 7705301; e-mail studiezaal@dordrecht.nl; internet www.regionaalarchiefdordrecht.nl; f. 1885, current name adopted 2013; archives of the City of Dordrecht and of nearby towns; books and prints of Dordrecht and its environs; 40,000 vols, 800 periodicals; Archivist Drs TEUN DE BRUIJN; Librarian JAN ALLEBLAS.

Eindhoven

Informatie Expertise Centrum/Bibliotheek Technische Universiteit Eindhoven (Information Expertise Centre/Library of the Eindhoven University of Technology): POB 90159, 5600 RM Eindhoven; MetaForum Bbldg, Den Dolech 2, 5612 AZ Eindhoven; tel. (40) 2472381; e-mail iec.helpdesk@tue.nl; internet w3.tue.nl/en/services/library; f. 1956; 415,000 vols, 550 current print journals, 14,700 ejournals, 3,200 full-text TU/e dissertations, 1,500 microfiches and 66,000 other items; Head Librarian Drs JEANNE C. M. FIGDOR; Sec. CAROLA M. J. L. TAK.

Openbare Bibliotheek Eindhoven (Eindhoven Public Library): POB 488, 5600 AL Eindhoven; Gebouw de Witte Dame, Emmasingel 22, 5611 AZ Eindhoven; tel. (40) 2604260; e-mail info@bibliotheekeindhoven.nl; internet www.bibliotheekeindhoven.nl; f. 1916; 9 brs; 800,000 vols; Man. and Dir Drs THIJS TORREMAN.

Enschede

ITC Library (Faculty of Geo-Information Science and Earth Organization Library): POB 217, 7500 AE Enschede; Hengelosestraat 99, Third Fl., Room 3-036, 7514 AE Enschede; tel. (53) 4874202; e-mail library-utc@utwente.nl; internet www.itc.nl/pub/home/library; attached to Univ. of Twente; specialized scientific library on remote sensing and geographical information sciences; Archivist HOMME MARTINUS; Librarian M. TH. KOELEN.

University of Twente Library and Archive: POB 217, 7500 AE Enschede; Drienerlolaan 5, 7522 NB AE Enschede; tel. (53) 4892777; e-mail infoub@utwente.nl; internet www.utwente.nl/ub; f. 1964; 375,000 vols, 2,700 periodicals, 250 printed journals, 14,000 ejournals; Librarian Drs P. G. G. M. DAALMANS; Sec. J. VROOM-VAN GORCUM.

Gouda

De Bibliotheek Gouda (Gouda Library): Spieringstraat 1, 2801 ZH Gouda; tel. (82) 590101; internet www.bibliotheekgouda.nl; central library and 3 br. libraries; 119,892 materials incl. 300,000 CDs, 10,000 music DVDs; Dir NAN VAN SCHENDEL.

Groningen

Bibliotheek der Rijksuniversiteit te Groningen (Library of the State University): POB 559, 9700 AN Groningen; Broerstraat 4, 9712 CP Groningen; tel. (50) 3635020; e-mail bibliotheek@rug.nl; internet www.rug.nl/bibliotheek; f. 1615; 3m. vols, 1,100 MSS, 210 incunabula; Librarian MARJOLEIN NIEBOER.

Regionaal Historisch Centrum Groninger Archieven (RHC Groninger Archives): POB 30040, 9700 RM Groningen; Cascadeplein 4, 9726 AD Groningen; tel. (50) 5992000; e-mail info@groningerarchieven.nl; internet www.groningerarchieven.nl; f. 2002 by merger of Nat. Archives Groningen and Municipal Archive Groningen; information centre for history of city and province of Groningen; about 12.5 miles of documents, maps, prints, books, newspapers, photos, film and video cassettes from governmental bodies and private individuals; 35,000 vols; Chair. Dr J. A. J. STAM; Dir EDDY DE JONGE; Deputy Dir HARRY ROMIJN.

Haarlem

Bibliotheek van Teylers Museum (Teyler Museum Library): Spaarne 16, 2011 CH Haarlem; tel. (23) 5160960; e-mail info@teylersmuseum.nl; internet www.teylersmuseum.nl; f. 1784; 125,000 vols (natural sciences); Head Librarian Drs M. A. M. VAN HOORN.

De Bibliotheek Haarlem en Omstreken: POB 204, 2000 AE Haarlem; Gasthuisstraat 32, 2011 XP Haarlem; tel. (23) 5115300; e-mail stadsbibliotheek@haarlem.nl; internet www.sbhaarlem.nl; f. 1596, present status 2008; 452,000 vols, 280 MSS, 192 incunabula; Dir L. SLUYSER.

Hbo-opleidingen Hogeschool Inholland Bibliotheek (Inholland University of Applied Sciences Library): Inholland University Haarlem, attn Library, POB 558, 2003 RN Harleem; Bijdorplaan 15, 2015 CE Harleem; tel. (23) 5412700; e-mail bibliotheek@inholland.nl; internet www.inholland.nl/bibliotheek; Head of Library RIA PAULIDES.

Noord-Hollands Archief (North Holland Archives): POB 3006, 2001 DA Haarlem; Jansstraat 40, 2011 RX Haarlem; tel. (23) 5172700; e-mail info@noord-hollandsarchief.nl; internet www.noord-hollandsarchief.nl; f. 2005 by merger of Archives of Kennemerland and State Archives in N Holland; documentary heritage of province of N Holland, Kennemerland region (in particular the municipalities of Aalsmeer, Beverwijk, Bloemendaal, Haarlemmerliede and Spaarnwoude, Haarlemmermeer, Heemskerk, Heemstede, Uitgeest, Uithoorn, Velsen and Zandvoort) and of provincial capital Haarlem; Chair. B. B. SCHNEIDERS; Dir Drs L. ZOODSMA.

Kampen

Gemeentearchief Kampen (Record Office Kampen): Molenstraat 28, 8261 JW Kampen; tel. (38) 3370770; e-mail gemeentearchief@kampen.nl; internet www.gemeentearchiefkampen.nl; archives of the town 1251–1955; Dir Drs M. VINK-BOS; publ. *De Archieven der Gemeente Kampen, I, II, III.*

Leeuwarden

Historisch Centrum Leeuwarden (Leeuwarden History Centre): Groeneweg 1, 8911 EH Leeuwarden; tel. (58) 2338399; e-mail historischcentrum@leeuwarden.nl; internet www.historischcentrumleeuwarden.nl; f. 1838, fmrly Leeuwarden Municipal Archives; archives, publs, MSS about Leeuwarden; topographical colln, mainly historical; 18,000 vols; Man. Drs G. DE VRIES; Librarian W. VAN RIJNSOEVER.

TRESOAR Fries Historisch en Letterkundig Centrum (TRESOAR Frisian Historical and Literary Centre): POB 2637, 8901 AC Leeuwarden; Boterhoek 1, 8911 DH Leeuwarden; tel. (58) 7890789; e-mail info@tresoar.nl; internet www.tresoar.nl; f. 2002 by merger of the Frysk Letterkundich Museum en Dokumintaasjesintrum (FLMD), the Provincial and Buma library (PBF) and the Public Records Office in Friesland (RAF); collns mainly relating to Frisian literature and history; Chair. Drs J. A. DE VRIES; Dir Drs B. LOOPER; publ. *Letterhoeke.*

Leiden

Bibliotheek van de Maatschappij der Nederlandse Letterkunde (Library of the Society of Dutch Literature): POB 9501, 2300 RA Leiden; tel. (71) 5272109; e-mail mnl@library.leidenuniv.nl; internet www.maatschappijdernederlandseletterkunde.nl/bibliotheek.php; f. 1766, managed by Leiden Univ. Library since 1876; awards prizes for literary debuts, cultural and historical works; organizes meetings and lectures; 110,000 vols, 3,300 MSS; Librarian Dr KURT DE BELDER; publs *Nieuwe Letterkundig Magazijn* (2 a year), *Tijdschrift voor Nederlandse Taal-en Letterkunde* (4 a year).

Naturalis Biodiversity Center Library: POB 9517, 2300 RA Leiden; Darwinweg 2, 2333 CR Leiden; tel. (71) 5687668; e-mail library@naturalis.nl; internet science.naturalis.nl/library; research library of the Naturalis Biodiversity Center; collns incl. biodiversity literature (flora and fauna), geology, mineralogy and palaeontogy; focus on the Netherlands, Europe and SE Asia; 100,000 vols, 8,000 journals, 200,000 zoology and geology papers; Head CAROLINE PEPERMANS; publs *Blumea: Biodiversity, evolution and biogeography of plants* (online, www.ingentaconnect.com/content/nhn/blumea), *Contributions to Zoology* (online, www.ctoz.nl), *Gorteria: Tijdschrift voor onderzoek aan de wilde flora, Persoonia: Molecular phylogeny and evolution of fungi* (online, www.persoonia.org), *Scripta Geologica* (online, www.scriptageologica.nl), *Zoologische mededelingen* (online, www.zoologischemededelingen.nl).

Universitaire Bibliotheken Leiden (Leiden University Libraries): POB 9501, 2300 RA Leiden; Witte Singel 27, 2311 BG Leiden; tel. (71) 5272814; e-mail helpdesk@library.leidenuniv.nl; internet library.leiden.edu; f. 1575; 4.3m. vols, 1m. ebooks, 40,500 ejournals, 50,000 MSS, 70,000 maps, 700 databases; Librarian KURT DE BELDER; Deputy Dir BAS VAT.

Maastricht

Regionaal Historisch Centrum Limburg (Regional Historic Centre Limburg): St Pieterstraat 7, 6211 JM Maastricht; tel. (43) 3285500; e-mail info@rhcl.nl; internet www.rhcl.nl; f. 2004 by merger of State Archives in Limburg and Municipal Archives; 60,000 vols; Dir Drs LITA WIGGERS.

Stadsbibliotheek Maastricht, Centre Céramique (Municipal Library): POB 1992, 6201 BZ Maastricht; Ave Céramique 50, 6221 KV Maastricht; tel. (43) 3505600; e-mail mail@sbm.nl; internet www.centreceramique.nl; f. 1662; 774,000 vols, incl. 107 incunabula, 297 post-incunabula, 1,600 periodicals, spec. collns and documentation relating to the Province of Limburg, devotional material and chess literature; Dir Dr ERIC P. G. WETZELS; publ. *Limburgensia.*

Universiteitsbibliotheek Maastricht (Maastricht University Library): POB 616, 6200 MD Maastricht; Inner City Library, Grote Looiersstraat 17, 6211 JH Maastricht; Randwyck Library, Universiteitssingel 50, 6229 ER Maastricht; tel. (43) 3885000; e-mail i.wijk@maastrichtuniversity.nl; internet www.maastrichtuniversity.nl/web/library/home.htm; attached to Maastricht Univ.; includes digital library; 11,703 ejournals, 11,279 digital univ. publs; spec. collns incl. Jesuit colln of 265,000 vols; Univ. Librarian I. WIJK.

Middelburg

Zeeuws Archief (Zeeland Archives): POB 70, 4330 AB Middelburg; Hofplein 16, 4331 CK Middelburg; tel. (118) 678800; e-mail info@zeeuwsarchief.nl; internet www.zeeuwsarchief.nl; f. 2000 by merger of State Archives in the province of Zeeland, Middelburg Municipal Archives and Veere Municipal Archives; contains documents on the history of Zeeland in gen.; Man. Dir Dr J. L. KOOL-BLOKLAND.

Zeeuwse Bibliotheek (Zeeland Library): POB 8004, 4330 EA Middelburg; Kousteensedijk 7, 4331 JE Middelburg; tel. (118) 654000; e-mail info@zeeuwsebibliotheek.nl; internet www.zeeuwsebibliotheek.nl; f. 1985; 880,000 vols, 7,500 MSS, 2,900 periodicals; Pres. Drs G. A. EGAS REPÁRAZ; Dir Drs H. HOFMEIJER.

Nijkerk

Bibliotheek Nijkerk (Nijkerk Library): POB 198, 3860 AD Nijkerk; Frieswijkstraat 99, 3861 BK Nijkerk; tel. (33) 2451756; e-mail info@bibliotheeknijkerk.nl; internet www.bibliotheeknijkerk.nl.

Nijmegen

Universiteitsbibliotheek, Radboud Universiteit Nijmegen (Library of Radboud University Nijmegen): POB 9100, 6500 HA Nijmegen; Erasmuslaan 36, Nijmegen; tel. (24) 3612437; e-mail secretariaat@ubn.ru.nl; internet www.ru.nl/library; f. 1923; 6 library brs; 2m. vols; Librarian Drs N. J. GRYGIERCZYK.

Oss

Bibliothek Oss (Oss Library): POB 815, 5340 AV Oss; Raadhuislaan 10, 5341 GM Oss; tel. (12) 622618; e-mail contact@oboss.nl; internet www.oboss.nl; brs in Berghem, Heesch, Heeswijk-Dinther, Nistelrode, Lith, Ravenstein, Schaijk and Zeeland.

Rotterdam

de Bibliotheek Rotterdam (Rotterdam Library): Hoogstraat 110, 3011 PV Rotterdam; tel. (10) 2816100; e-mail klantenservice@bibliotheek.rotterdam.nl; internet www.bibliotheek.rotterdam.nl; f. 1604; 23 dist. brs; 1,550,000 vols, 200 MSS, Erasmus colln 5,000 vols, 1,500 journals, 450,000 CDs, 15,000 music DVDs and 300,000 records; Dir Ir F. H. MEIJER.

Rotterdamsch Leeskabinet (Rotterdam Reading Cabinet): POB 1738, 3000 DR Rotterdam; Burgemeester Oudlaan 50, 3062 PA Rotterdam; tel. (10) 4081195; e-mail kabinet@ubib.eur.nl; internet www .leeskabinet.nl; f. 1859; attached to Erasmus Univ.; history, art, art history, language and literature, biography, theology, philosophy, social sciences, geography; 260,000 vols; Librarian PIERRE N. G. PESCH; publ. *Kwartaalbericht*.

Stadsarchief Rotterdam (Municipal Archives of Rotterdam): POB 71, 3000 AB Rotterdam; Hofdijk 651, 3032 CG Rotterdam; tel. (10) 2675555; e-mail infogar@rotterdam.nl; internet www.stadsarchief.rotterdam.nl; f. 1857; city archives, church records, notariate archives, Chamber of Commerce records 1797–1922, family archives, business archives, topographical collns, sound archives, historical library; 19.7 linear km of archives; Archivist and Man. Dir Drs JANTJE STEENHUIS.

Universiteitsbibliotheek Erasmus Universiteit Rotterdam (Library of the Erasmus University of Rotterdam): POB 1738, 3000 DR Rotterdam; Burgemeester Oudlaan 50, 3062 PA Rotterdam; tel. (10) 4081223; e-mail documentverwerking@ubib.eur.nl; internet www.eur.nl/ub; f. 1913; economics and management, medicine and health, law, culture and soc.; 1m. vols, 5,400 current journals; Univ. Librarian Dr PAUL E. L. J. SOETAERT; Deputy Librarian Drs G. GORIS; Deputy Librarian Drs J. L. DE VRIES.

's-Hertogenbosch

Brabants Historisch Informatie Centrum (Brabant Historical Information Centre): POB 81, 5201 AB 's-Hertogenbosch; Zuid-Willemsvaart 2, 5211 NW 's-Hertogenbosch; tel. (73) 6818500; e-mail info@bhic.nl; internet www.bhic.nl; f. 1860 as Rijksarchief in de Provincie Noord-Brabant; records since 13th century; record office contains approx. 200,000 vols; 50,000 vols, 8,000 charters; Dir Drs R. BASTIAANSE; Librarian F. VAN DE POL; publ. *Inventarisreeks*.

Openbare Bibliotheek 's-Hertogenbosch: POB 1253, 5200 BH 's-Hertogenbosch; Hinthamerstraat 72, 5211 MR 's-Hertogenbosch; tel. (73) 6802900; e-mail info@bibliotheekdenbosch.nl; internet www .bibliotheekdenbosch.nl; f. 1915; 270,000 vols, 18,000 CDs; Dir J. J. T. E. (HANS) DERKS; Deputy Dir P. C. J. M. (ELLY) HUFF-MEULENBROEKS.

The Hague

Bibliotheek Den Haag (The Hague Public Library): POB 12653, 2500 DP The Hague; Spui 68, 2511 BT The Hague; tel. (70) 3534455; e-mail secr@dobdenhaag.nl; internet www.dobdenhaag.nl; f. 1906; 16 br., 2 mobile libraries; 980,000 vols, 190,000 children's books, music library of 55,000 vols and 60,000 CDs, 21,000 audiovisual items; Dir CHARLES NOORDAM.

Bibliotheek van het Centraal Bureau voor de Statistiek (Library of Statistics Netherlands): POB 24500, 2490 HA The Hague; Henri Faasdreef 312, 2492 JP The Hague; tel. (70) 3375151; e-mail acquisitiev@cbs.nl; internet www.cbs.nl; f. 1899; not accessible to public from 2005; available for scientific research with prior appointment; 380,000 vols; Librarian D. L. M. WEIJERS.

Bibliotheek van het Vredespaleis (Peace Palace Library): Carnegieplein 2, 2517 KJ The Hague; tel. (70) 3024242; e-mail peacelib@ppl.nl; internet www.ppl.nl; f. 1913; int. public and municipal law, diplomatic history, int. relations; Grotius Colln; 700,000 vols; Dir JEROEN VERVLIET.

Koninklijke Bibliotheek (National Library of the Netherlands): POB 90407, 2509 LK The Hague; Prins Willem-Alexanderhof 5, 2595 BE The Hague; tel. (70) 3140310; internet www.kb.nl; f. 1798, present status 1993; responsible for the devt, documentation and management of the nat. cultural heritage; depository for all Dutch publs and the nat. bibliography; research library for the humanities and social sciences; centre of expertise in preservation and restoration; focal point of inter-library cooperation; 2.2m. books, 15,000 current periodicals, newspapers, MSS; spec. collns incl. chess, cookery, children's books; Chair. Drs L. C. BRINKMAN; Dir-Gen. Drs J. S. M. (BAS) SAVENIJE; publ. *Nederlandse Bibliografie*.

Nationaal Archief (National Archives): POB 90520, 2509 LM The Hague; Prins Willem Alexanderhof 20, 2595 BE The Hague; tel. (70) 3315400; e-mail info@nationaalarchief.nl; internet www .nationaalarchief.nl; f. 1802; 93 km of archives; 80,000 vols, 700 journals; Gen State Archivist MARTIN BERENDSE; publ. *Inventories of Archives*.

Tweede Kamer der Staten-Generaal; Dienst Bibliotheek en Dienst Documentatie (Dutch House of Representatives; Library Department and Documentation Department): Plein 2, POB 20018, 2500 EA The Hague; tel. (70) 3183040; internet www .houseofrepresentatives.nl; f. 1815; 100,000 vols; Librarian J. C. KEUKENS; Head of Documentation P. VAN RIJN.

Tilburg

Universiteit van Tilburg Bibliotheek (Tilburg University Library): POB 90153, 5000 LE Tilburg; Warandelaan 2, 5037 AB Tilburg; tel. (13) 4662124; e-mail library@uvt .nl; internet www.tilburguniversity.edu/nl/over-tilburg-university/bibliotheek; f. 1927; economics, applied computer sciences, social sciences, law, history, philosophy, linguistics and theology; 900,000 vols; Dir Ir M. J. VAN DEN BERG.

Utrecht

Bibliotheek Utrecht (Public Library): POB 80, 3500 AB Utrecht; Oude Gracht 167, Utrecht; tel. (30) 2861800; e-mail klantenservice@bibliotheek-utrecht.nl; internet www.bibliotheek-utrecht.nl; f. 1892; 14 br libraries and art library; 795,000 vols, music library; Dir A. G. J. VAN VLIMMEREN.

Het Utrechts Archief (Utrecht Archives): POB 131, 3500 AC Utrecht; Hamburgerstraat 28, 3512 NS Utrecht; tel. (30) 2866611; e-mail inlichtingen@hetutrechtsarchief.nl; internet www .hetutrechtsarchief.nl; f. 1805; records of the City and Province of Utrecht, church history, political pamphlets, regional newspapers, nat. railway history; 70,000 vols, 500,000 maps, drawings, prints and photographs, 18 km of archival documents; Chair. ALEID WOLFSEN; Deputy Chair. VINCENT VAN DER BURG; Dir Drs CHANTAL C.A.E. KEIJSPER; Head Archivist Dr K. VAN VLIET; Librarian Dr J. J. MAMMEN.

Universiteitsbibliotheek Utrecht (Library of Utrecht University): POB 80124, 3508 TC Utrecht; Heidelberglaan 3, 3584 CS Utrecht; tel. (30) 2536601; e-mail info@library.uu.nl; internet www.uu.nl/university/library; f. 1584; 4.5m. vols, 2,500 MSS, 900 incunabula, 110,000 vols printed before 1800, MSS and printed books of the medieval libraries of the Utrecht churches and religious houses, 2 16th century private libraries; special collns in the fields of literature, theology, history, botany, medicine, 18th and 19th century science libraries, and on the province and city of Utrecht; Univ. Librarian Drs H. P. A. SMIT.

Vlaardingen

Vlaardingen City Archives: Plein Emaus 5, 3135 JN Vlaardingen; tel. (10) 2484999; e-mail stadsarchief@vlaardingen.nl; internet www.vlaardingen.nl/stadsarchief; f. 1948; 500 archives and collns related to city; oldest document from 1276.

Wageningen

Bibliotheek Wageningen UR (Wageningen UR Library): POB 9100, 6700 HA Wageningen; Droevendaalsesteeg 2, Wageningen; tel. (31) 7484440; e-mail servicedesk .facilities@wur.nl; internet www .wageningenur.nl/library; f. 1873; colln of scientific literature esp. in fields of agrotechnology, food sciences, plant and animal sciences, soil science, geo-information, landscape and spatial planning, water and climate, ecosystem studies; 1.5m. vols, 15,000 current periodicals; Chief Librarian H. G. M. KREKELS; publ. *Wageningen Agricultural University Papers*.

Zwolle

Historisch Centrum Overijssel (Historic Centre of Overijssel): POB 1510, 8001 BM Zwolle; Eikenstraat 20, 8021 WX Zwolle; tel. (38) 4266300; e-mail infohco@historischcentrumoverijssel.nl; internet www.historischcentrumoverijssel.nl; f. 2000; 60,000 vols; 18 km archive, 15,000 charters; 15,000 maps, prints, posters and drawings; 150,000 photographs; collns incl. provincial archives 1528–1948, judicial archives 1333–1979, notarial archives 1811–1915, old church registers and civil registers 1592–1942, archives of monasteries 1225–1811, industrial archives 1850–1980, Zwolle municipal archives 1265–1970, notarial archives 1811–1925, cadastral archives 1811–1980, family archives since 13th century; Chair. C. G. A. A. BREKELMANS; Dir Drs A. G. DE VRIES.

Museums and Art Galleries

Alkmaar

Stedelijk Museum Alkmaar: Canadaplein 1, 1811 KE Alkmaar; tel. (72) 5489789; e-mail info@museumalkmaar.nl; internet stedelijkmuseumalkmaar.nl; f. c. 1550; municipal museum; antiquarian and art colln from Alkmaar and its environs, paintings by van Heemskerck, van de Velde the Elder, Allart and Caesar B. van Everdingen, Honthorst; objects incl. old silver, glass, pottery, porcelain, tiles and modern art; colln of antique toys and dolls; Dir LIDEWIJ DE KOEKKOEK; Curator CHRISTI KLINKERT.

Amstelveen

Cobra Museum voor Moderne Kunst (Cobra Museum of Modern Art): POB 2028, 1180 EA Amstelveen; Sandbergplein 1, 1181 ZX Amstelveen; tel. (20) 5475050; e-mail info@cobra-museum.nl; internet www .cobra-museum.nl; works by artists of CoBrA group (1948–51) and Dutch artists, incl. artists of Vrij Beelden (1945) and Creatie (1950–55) movements; Artistic Dir Dr K. WEITERING; Exec. Dir E. OTTENHOF.

Museum Jan van der Togt: Dorpsstraat 50, 1182 JE Amstelveen; tel. (20) 6415754; e-mail info@jvdtogt.nl; internet www.jvdtogt .nl; f. 1991; colln of paintings, sculpture and glass; incl. architectural museum designs;

temporary exhibitions; Curator Tomas Hillebrand.

Amsterdam

Allard Pierson Museum: POB 94057, 1090 GB Amsterdam; Oude Turfmarkt 127, 1012 GC Amsterdam; tel. (20) 5252556; e-mail allard.pierson.museum@uva.nl; internet www.allardpiersonmuseum.nl; f. 1934, present location 1994; attached to Univ. of Amsterdam; archaeological museum; scientific research centre for students of archaeology and history of art, and public museum; archaeology of ancient Egypt, Near East, Greece, Etruria, Roman Empire; Dir-Gen. Prof. Dr W. Hupperetz; Scientific Dir Prof. Dr H. A. G. Brijder; publ. *Mededelingenblad van de Vereniging van Vrienden*.

Amsterdam Museum (Amsterdam Museum): POB 3302, 1001 AC Amsterdam; Nieuwezijds Voorburgwal 357, Kalverstraat 92, Amsterdam; tel. (20) 5231822; e-mail info@amsterdammuseum.nl; internet www .amsterdammuseum.nl; f. 1926; exhibits of the city's history over 700 years incl. archaeological finds, artefacts, paintings, prints and models; library of 18,000 vols on history of Amsterdam, Dutch art history and applied industrial arts; spec. colln: Jan and Casper Luyken colln; Chair. Drs Henk J. Brouwer; Vice-Chair. Ben van der Veer; Dir Rutger J. Graaf Schimmelpenninck; Curator Laura van Hasselt.

Anne Frank Museum: POB 730, 1000 AS Amsterdam; Prinsengracht 267, 1000 AS Amsterdam; tel. (20) 5567100; internet www.annefrank.org; f. 1960; Anne's hiding place, secret annexe; original MSS of diaries and samples of other writings Anne produced during her time in hiding; film exhibition; Exec. Dir Hans Westra; Man. Dir Kleis Broekhuizen.

Hermitage Amsterdam: POB 11675, 1001 GR Amsterdam; Amstel 51, 1001 GR Amsterdam; tel. (20) 5307488; e-mail mail@ hermitage.nl; internet www.hermitage.nl; exhibition devoted to Alexander the Great; has archive; Dir Prof. Dr Mikhail Piotrovski.

Hortus Botanicus Amsterdam: Plantage Middenlaan 2A, 1081 DD Amsterdam; tel. (20) 6259021; e-mail info@dehortus.nl; internet en.dehortus.nl; f. 1638, present status 1987; colln of species of plants from different countries; greenhouse; historic herb garden; Dir Lena Euwens; publs *Het Hortusbericht, Hortuskrant* (4 a year).

Joods Historisch Museum (Jewish Historical Museum): POB 16737, 1001 RE Amsterdam; Nieuwe Amstelstraat 1, 1001 RE Amsterdam; tel. (20) 5310310; e-mail info@ jhm.nl; internet www.jhm.nl; f. 1930; colln of 13,000 works of art, ceremonial items and historical objects related to Jewish history and culture; library of 43,000 vols; Dir Joël Cahen.

Museum Van Loon: Keizersgracht 672, 1017 ET Amsterdam; tel. (20) 6245255; e-mail info@museumvanloon.nl; internet www.museumvanloon.nl; f. 1672; colln of paintings, furniture, precious silver and porcelain from different centuries; canal house, coach house and garden; Chair. Philippa van Loon.

Nederlands Scheepvaartmuseum Amsterdam (Netherlands Maritime Museum Amsterdam): POB 15443, 1001 MK Amsterdam; Kattenburgerstraat 7, Amsterdam; tel. (20) 5232222; e-mail info@ scheepvaartmuseum.nl; internet www .scheepvaartmuseum.nl; f. 1916; closed until mid-2011 for reconstruction; models, paintings, charts, globes, technical drawings, nautical instruments, arms and relics, full-

size replica East-Indiaman; library of 60,000 vols, spec. collns: early navigation textbooks, voyages and travel, navigation, Dutch sea atlases; Dir Dr Willem Bijleveld; Business Dir Karin Brandt; Dir for Collns Drs Henk Dessens; publ. *Zee Magazijn* (4 a year).

NEMO: POB 421, 1000 AK Amsterdam; Oosterdok 2, 1011 VX Amsterdam; tel. (20) 5313233; e-mail info@e-nemo.nl; internet www.e-nemo.nl; f. 1997; science centre; organizes exhibitions, theatre performances, films, workshops and demonstrations related to science and technology; Gen. Dir Michiel Buchel; Dir R. V. M van Hattum.

Ons' Lieve Heer op Solder Museum (Our Lord in the Attic Museum): Oudezijds Voorburgwal 40, 1012 GE Amsterdam; tel. (20) 6246604; e-mail info@opsolder.nl; internet www.opsolder.nl; f. 1888; merchant's house of 1661 with a clandestine Catholic church in the attic; exhibits of ecclesiastical art since 16th century; library of 1,500 vols; Chair. Drs M. A. M. Elsenburg; Dir Drs J. Kiers; Exec. Sec. M. Aardewijn; Curator Drs T. Boers.

Persmuseum: Zeeburgerkade 10, 1019 HA Amsterdam; tel. (20) 6928810; e-mail info@ persmuseum.nl; internet www.persmuseum .nl; f. 1902; colln of newspapers and magazines from 1600, posters and other advertisements in press, political cartoons and press graphics, archives, photos of journalists, editors and publishers and library; Dir Angelie Sens; publs *Jaarverslag, Persvrijheidlezing*.

Rembrandthuis Museum (Rembrandt House Museum): Jodenbreestr. 4, 1011 NK Amsterdam; tel. (20) 5200400; e-mail museum@rembrandthuis.nl; internet www .rembrandthuis.nl; f. 1907; Rembrandt's etchings and drawings, and paintings by his teacher and pupils; the artist lived here 1639–58; Dir Marie-José Grotenhuis; Deputy Dir Michiel Kersten; Curator Bob van den Boogert; publ. *Kroniek van het Rembrandthuis* (Rembrandt House Chronicle, 2 a year).

Rijksmuseum (State Museum): POB 74888, 1070 DN Amsterdam; Stadhouderskade 42, 1071 ZD Amsterdam; tel. (20) 6621440; e-mail info@rijksmuseum.nl; internet www .rijksmuseum.nl; f. 1800 as Nationale Kunst-galerij; colln incl. major works by Rembrandt, Vermeer, Jan Steen, Frans Hals and other artists; colln of paintings, sculpture, drawings, history, porcelain, glass, costumes, silver, furniture, Asiatic art, weapons and ship models; library of 80,000 vols; Chair. Prof. J. G. de Hoop Scheffer; Gen. Dir Prof. Drs W. M. J. Pijbes.

Stedelijk Museum: POB 75082, 1070 AB Amsterdam; Van Baerlestraat 31, 1071 AN Amsterdam; tel. (20) 5732911; e-mail info@ stedelijk.nl; internet www.stedelijk.nl; f. 1895; modern paintings and sculpture, esp. American and European trends since 1950; graphics and drawings; applied arts and industrial design; temporary exhibitions on contemporary art; library of 190,000 vols, 200 periodicals; Dir Karin van Gilst (acting).

Tropenmuseum (Museum of the Royal Tropical Institute): POB 95001, 1090 HA Amsterdam; Linnaeusstraat 2, 1092 CK Amsterdam; tel. (20) 5688200; e-mail info@ tropenmuseum.nl; internet www .tropenmuseum.nl; f. 1916, present location 1926; attached to Royal Tropical Institute; 175,000 objects, 155,000 photographs and 10,000 drawings, paintings, documents, etc.; presents a picture of life and work in the tropics and sub-tropics; children's museum; library of 18,000 vols; Dir Lejo Schenk.

Van Gogh Museum: POB 75366, 1070 AJ Amsterdam; Stadhouderskade 55, 1072 AB Amsterdam; tel. (20) 5705200; e-mail info@ vangoghmuseum.nl; internet www

.vangoghmuseum.nl; f. 1973; collns of the Vincent van Gogh Foundation; paintings and drawings by van Gogh and his contemporaries; van Gogh's personal colln incl. English and French prints and graphics, Japanese woodcuts, documents and personal correspondence with his brother, Theo van Gogh; Theo's personal colln; Western paintings, sculptures, drawings and prints from the period 1840 to 1920; archives of the art historian M. E. Tralbaut; spec. colln: 19th century literature (mainly French) read by van Gogh; library of 24,000 vols; Chair. Trude Maas-de Brouwer; Dir Axel Rüger; Treas. Peter Tieleman; publ. *Cahier Vincent* (scientific research, 1 a year).

Verzetsmuseum Amsterdam: Plantage Kerklaan 61, 1018 CX Amsterdam; tel. (20) 6202535; e-mail info@verzetsmuseum.org; internet www.verzetsmuseum.org; f. 1985; colln of objects, photos and documents, film and sound fragments related to the Second World War; temporary exhibitions on historical or contemporary themes; Pres. Hans Blom; Sec. Carla Bastiaansen; Treas. Hans Hoek.

Apeldoorn

CODA Museum: Vosselmanstraat 299, 7311 CL Apeldoorn; tel. (55) 5268400; e-mail mail@coda-apeldoorn.nl; internet www .coda-apeldoorn.nl; f. 2003; colln exhibits contemporary art and regional history, esp. jewellery and paper art; image bank; Dir Dr Carin E. M. Reinders.

Paleis Het Loo Nationaal Museum (Palace Het Loo): Koninklijk Park 1, 7315 JA Apeldoorn; tel. (55) 5772400; e-mail info@ paleishetloo.nl; internet www.paleishetloo .nl; f. 1984; colln of portraits, furniture, documents, etc., relating to the Dutch royal family, the House of Orange-Nassau; library of 20,000 vols; Man. Dir Drs M. van Maarseveen.

Arnhem

Historisch Museum Arnhem (Arnhem Historical Museum): Bovenbeekstraat 21, 6811 CV Arnhem; tel. (26) 3775300; e-mail hma@arnhem.nl; internet www.hmarnhem .nl; f. 1995; pre-1900 applied art, history, archaeology, glass and silver, Delftware, topographic colln of Gelderland; currently closed due to re-location; Head of Public Affairs Peter de Kok; publ. *Museumkrant* (2 a year).

Museum voor Moderne Kunst (Museum for Modern Art): Utrechtseweg 87, 6812 AA Arnhem; tel. (26) 3775300; e-mail mmka@ arnhem.nl; internet www.mmkarnhem.nl; f. 1920; post-1900 sculpture, Dutch realist paintings, design, jewellery, contemporary art; Dir M. Meyer; Head of Public Affairs Peter de Kok.

Nederlands Openluchtmuseum (Netherlands Open Air Museum): POB 649, 6800 AP Arnhem; Schelmseweg 89, 6816 SJ Arnhem; tel. (26) 3576111; e-mail info@ openluchtmuseum.nl; internet www .openluchtmuseum.nl; f. 1912, present status 1991; history of daily life; information retrieval; library of 26,000 vols, 146 periodicals; Chair. Ir Drs Jeroen van der Veer; Dir-Gen. Drs Pieter-Matthijs Gijsbers; Man. Dir Adelheid M. C. J. Ponsioen.

Assen

Drents Museum: POB 134, 9400 AC Assen; Brink 8, 9401 HS Assen; tel. (592) 377773; e-mail info@drentsmuseum.nl; internet www .drentsmuseum.nl; f. 1854, present status 1999; exhibits bog bodies, Pesse dugout canoe, Terracotta army of Xi'an; colln of art nouveau, art deco and figurative art; photo archive; Dir Michel van Maarseveen.

Brill

Historisch Museum Den Briel: Markt 1, 3231 AH Brill; tel. (181) 475475; e-mail info@ historischmuseumdenbriel.nl; internet www .historischmuseumdenbriel.nl; f. 1912, present status 1998; colln of art historical prints by patron Alexander Verhuell; Curator Dr MARIJKE HOLTROP.

Delft

Leger Museum (Army Museum): POB 90004, 3509 AA Delft; Korte Geer 1, 2611 CA Delft; tel. (15) 2150500; e-mail info@ legermuseum.nl; internet www .legermuseum.nl; f. 1913, present location 1984; contains more than 500,000 objects, incl. personal books, handwritten documents, prints and photographs, vehicles; exhibition covering 2,000 years of Netherlands' military history; weapons from prehistory to the present; uniforms, equipment, medals, paintings; library of 225,000 vols and colln of prints; Dir-Gen. CHRIS RONTELTAP; Dir for Collns DIRK STAAT; publ. *Armamentaria* (1 a year).

Museum Het Prinsenhof: POB 78, 2600 ME Delft; St Agathaplein 1, 2611 HR Delft; tel. (15) 2602358; e-mail gemeentemusea@ delft.nl; internet www.prinsenhof-delft.nl; f. 1948; historical colln of City of Delft, paintings of the Delft School, Eighty Years' War, William the Silent; Dir ERIK DE GROOT.

Museum Lambert van Meerten: POB 78, 2600 ME Delft; Oude Delft 199, 2611 HD Delft; tel. (15) 2602358; e-mail erfgoeddelft@ delft.nl; internet www .lambertvanmeerten-delft.nl; f. 1909; museum has been temporarily closed due to structural and internal renovations, it is unknown when the museum will be accessible to the public; Dir PATRICK VAN MILL; Curator Drs RONALD E. BROUWER.

Museum Nusantara: POB 78, 2600 ME Delft; Sint Agathaplein 4, 2611 HR, Delft; tel. (15) 2602358; e-mail erfgoeddelft@delft.nl; internet www.nusantara-delft.nl; f. as Ethnographic Museum of Delft; history and culture of the Indonesian archipelago; colln incl. exhibitions of Dutch involvement in Indonesia since the 17th century, incl. the Dutch East India Co. (1602–1799) and the Colonial Period (1800–1949); Indonesian art, culture, religion, musical instruments, puppets, jewellery, wooden carvings, masks, textiles; maquettes of 19th century, Indonesian houses and ships; Dir ERIK DE GROOT.

Den Helder

Marinemuseum (Dutch Naval Museum): Hoofdgracht 3, 1781 AA Den Helder; tel. (223) 657534; e-mail info@marinemuseum.nl; internet www.marinemuseum.nl; f. 1962; attached to Min. of Defence; history of the Royal Netherlands Navy since 1813, collns of models, navigational instruments, paintings, photographs, etc.; three-cylinder submarine 'Tonijn' (1966), minesweeper 'Abraham Crynssen' (1937), ironclad ram ship 'Schorpioen' (1868), and other craft; Dir Cmdr HARRY DE BLES.

Deventer

Gemeentemusea Deventer (Municipal Museums of Deventer): POB 5000, 7400 GC Deventer; tel. (570) 693783; e-mail info@ deventermusea.nl; internet www .deventermusea.nl; f. 1963; Dir C. F. C. G. BOISSEVAIN..

Associated Museums:

  Historisch Museum Deventer (Historical Museum Deventer): POB 5000, 7400 GC Deventer; Brink 56, 7411 BV Deventer; tel. (570) 693780; e-mail info@ deventermusea.nl; internet www .historischmuseumdeventer.nl; f. 1913; local history, paintings, drawings, applied arts, bicycles; Dir C. F. C. G. BOISSEVAIN.

  Speelgoedmuseum Deventer (Deventer Toy Museum): POB 5000, 7400 GC Deventer; Brink 47, 7411 BV Deventer; tel. (570) 693786; e-mail info@deventermusea.nl; internet www.speelgoedmuseumdeventer .nl; f. 1982; dolls, mechanical toys, toys, trains; Dir C. F. C. G. BOISSEVAIN.

Dordrecht

Dordrechts Museum: POB 1170, 3300 BD Dordrecht; Museumstraat 40, 3311 XP Dordrecht; tel. (78) 7708708; internet www .dordrechtsmuseum.nl; f. 1842; colln of paintings, drawings, prints, photos, sculptures and ceramics; conducts research and restoration work; Man. Dir P. J. SCHOON.

Drechterland

Museum Mohlmann for Representational Art: Westersingel 102–104, 9901 GK Appingedam; tel. (596) 682856; e-mail info@ museummohlmann.nl; internet www .robmohlmann.nl; f. 1995; 3 permanent collns: Canto-colln (124 works), Møhlmann-colln-I (250 present-day realistic and figurative works), Møhlmann-colln-II (40 works of painter), Mankes-colln (graphic works, letters and documents about the life of Jan Mankes); 3 exhibitions per year; Dir ROB MØHLMANN.

Eindhoven

Museum Kempenland: St. Antoniusstraat 7, 5616 RT Eindhoven; tel. (40) 2529093; e-mail secretariaat@museumkempenland.nl; internet www.museumkempenland.nl; f. 1932; closed until mid-2011; colln of material culture of Eindhoven and region, Brabant painting, drawing and graphic arts and photography, Dutch small sculpture from 19th and 20th centuries; organizes lectures, choir performances, publ., courses, tours; library; Man. JAN VAN LAARHOVEN.

Van Abbemuseum: POB 235, 5600 AE Eindhoven; Bilderdijklaan 10, 5611 NH Eindhoven; tel. (40) 2381000; e-mail info@ vanabbemuseum.nl; internet www .vanabbemuseum.nl; f. 1936; large colln of modern and contemporary art incl. works and archives by Lissitzky, Picasso, Kokoschka, Chagall, Beuys, McCarthy, Daniëls and Körmeling; library of 130,000 vols; Dir CHARLES ESCHE; Deputy Dir ULRIKE ERBSLÖH.

Enschede

Rijksmuseum Twenthe, Enschede (Twenthe Estate Museum, Enschede): Lasondersingel 129–131, 7514 BP Enschede; tel. (53) 4358675; internet www .rijksmuseumtwenthe.nl; f. 1930, present status 1994; 8,000 art objects from the 13th century to the present day; library of 15,000 vols; Dir LISETTE PELSERS; Curator for Fine Arts PAUL KNOLLE; Curator for Modern Art TON GEERTS; publ. *MUSE Rijksmuseum Twenthe* (2 a year).

Gouda

Museum Gouda: Achter de Kerk 14, 2801 JX Gouda; tel. (182) 331000; e-mail info@ museumgouda.nl; internet www .museumgouda.nl; f. 1874; 18th-century town dispensary; antique toys, surgeons' Guild Room, decorative art since late 16th century, Gasthuis kitchen and chapel, important colln of art since 15th century; Dir GERARD DE KLEIJN.

Nationaal Farmaceutisch Museum (National Pharmaceutical Museum): Westhaven 29, 2801 PJ Gouda; tel. (182) 687142; e-mail info@farmaceutischmuseum .nl; internet www.farmaceutischmuseum.nl; f. 1938 reopened in 2008; exhibiting the history of Dutch apothecaries and the devt of the pharmaceutical profession; fmrly 'The Blackmoor' Stedelijk Museum containing and managing authentic 18th century tobacco shop, colln of Dutch clay pipes and Gouda pottery now transferred to Het Catharina Gasthuis en De Moriaan; Chair. Prof. Dr A. H. L. M. PIETERS; Deputy Chair. Dr R. H. A. SOREL; Dir Drs P. H. VREE; Treas. Drs C. B. M. HEERKENS.

Groningen

Groninger Museum: POB 90, 9700 ME Groningen; Museumeiland 1, 9711 ME Groningen; tel. (50) 3666555; e-mail info@ groningermuseum.nl; internet www .groningermuseum.nl; f. 1894; prehistory and history; paintings of local school; Dutch and Flemish of 16th and 17th centuries: Fabritius, Jordaens, Rubens, Sweerts, Teniers; drawings: Rembrandt, Averkamp, Van Goyen, Cuyp, Lievens; painting since 19th century; extensive colln of Far-Eastern ceramics; colln of applied art; photography, design and fashion collns; library of 38,000 vols incl. book colln on modern art and artists and colln of modern art since 1979; Man. Dir KEES VAN TWIST; Dir PATTY WAGEMAN.

Noordelijk Scheepvaartmuseum (Northern Maritime Museum): Brugstraat 24, 9711 HZ Groningen; tel. (50) 3122202; e-mail info@noordelijkscheepvaartmuseum.nl; internet www.noordelijkscheepvaartmuseum .nl; f. 1932; colln related to N Dutch shipping and shipbuilding history from Middle Ages to present, archives, library, photographs; Dir J. W. VAN VEEN; Curator and Deputy Dir W. KERKMEIJER.

Haarlem

Frans Hals Museum (Frans Hals Museum): POB 3365, 2001 DJ Haarlem; Groot Heiligland 62, 2011 ES Haarlem; tel. (23) 5115775; e-mail office@franshalsmuseum.nl; internet franshalsmuseum.nl; f. 1913; pictures since 15th century, focusing on the Haarlem school and Frans Hals; applied arts; Dir ANN DEMEESTER; Sec. ANNEKE BAKKER.

Teylers Museum: Spaarne 16, 2011 CH Haarlem; tel. (23) 5160960; e-mail info@ teylersmuseum.nl; internet www .teylersmuseum.nl; f. 1784; paintings, drawings, palaeontology, geology, mineralogy, natural history, physics, numismatics; library of 125,000 vols (natural science); Dir Drs M. SCHARLOO; publs *Archives du Musée Teyler, Verhandelingen van Teylers Godgeleerd Genootschap, Verhandelingen van Teylers Tweede Genootschap.*

Heerlen

Thermenmuseum Heerlen: POB 1, 6400 AA Heerlen; Coriovallumstraat 9, 6411 CA Heerlen; tel. (45) 5605100; e-mail info@ thermenmuseum.nl; internet www .thermenmuseum.nl; f. 1977; colln incl. Roman bath house excavated in 1940–41 and other objects from Roman period; Curator Dr KAREN JENESON.

Helmond

Gemeentemuseum Helmond: Kasteelplein 1, 5701 PP Helmond; tel. (492) 587716; e-mail info@ gemeentemuseumhelmond.nl; internet www .gemeentemuseumhelmond.nl; colln of int. modern and contemporary art incl. works from 1970 to present; exhibits popular visual culture, incl. film and advertising; works of Alma, Burtynsky, Heijenbrock, Isaac Israels, Kollwitz, Meunier, Jan en Chartley Toorope and Van der Leck; Curator ANNEMIEKE HOGERVORST.

Hoorn

Westfries Museum: Achterom 2–4, 1621 KV Hoorn; Roode Steen 1, 1621 CV Hoorn; tel. (229) 280028; e-mail info@wfm.nl; internet www.wfm.nl; f. 1879, baroque bldg dates from 1632; 17th and 18th century painting, prints, oak panelling, glass, pottery, silver, furniture, costumes, interiors, objects of trade, navigation and business, folk art, historical objects from Hoorn and W Friesland, prehistoric finds; Dir AD GEERDINK.

Leerdam

Nationaal Glasmuseum—De Glasblazerij (National Glass Museum—The Glass Factory): POB 78, 4140 AB Leerdam; Lingedijk 28–30, 4142 LD Leerdam; tel. (345) 614960; e-mail info@stichtingglas.nl; internet www.nationaalglasmuseum.nl; f. 1953, present status 2007; art glass, industrial glass and bottles, contemporary Dutch colln and works from other European countries and America; small library; Chair. AUBERT VAN ENGELEN; Dir ARNOUD ODDING; Curator HÉLÈNE BESANÇON.

Leeuwarden

Fries Museum: POB 1239, 8900 CE Leeuwarden; Turfmarkt 11, 8911 KS Leeuwarden; tel. (58) 2555500; e-mail info@friesmuseum.nl; internet www.friesmuseum.nl; f. 1827; painting, local history, archaeology, decorative arts, prints and drawings, Second World War, Mata Hari gallery, modern art; Chair. Prof. Dr L. KOOPMANS; Dir-Gen. Drs SASKIA BAK; Man. Dir Ir ROEL WOERING; publ. *Visitor's Guide* (in English, French and German).

Keramiekmuseum Princessehof (Princessehof National Museum of Ceramics): Grote Kerkstraat 11, POB 1239, 8900 CE Leeuwarden; tel. (58) 2948958; e-mail info@princessehof.nl; internet www.princessehof.nl; f. 1917; Asian and European ceramics and tiles, contemporary ceramics; library of 20,000 vols; Dir-Gen. Drs SASKIA BAK; Man. Dir Ir ROEL WOERING; publ. *Keramika* (3 a year).

Leiden

Museum Boerhaave/Rijksmuseum voor de Geschiedenis en van de Natuurwetenschappen en van de Geneeskunde (Museum Boerhaave/National Museum of the History of Science and Medicine): POB 11280, 2301 EG Leiden; Lange St Agnietenstraat 10, 2312 WC Leiden; tel. (71) 5214224; e-mail informatie@museumboerhaave.nl; internet www.museumboerhaave.nl; f. 1907; historical scientific and medical instruments and documents, anatomical preparations, portraits; library of 25,000 vols, 75 periodicals, MSS; Dir Prof. Dr DIRK VAN DELFT; Exec. Sec. FRANCISCA PARMENTIER.

Museum Volkenkunde (National Museum of Ethnology): POB 212, 2300 AE Leiden; Steenstraat 1, 2312 BS Leiden; tel. (71) 5168800; e-mail pr@volkenkunde.nl; internet www.volkenkunde.nl; f. 1837 as Ethnographic Museum in Leiden; collns from Africa, the Middle East, the Islamic and Indian cultural areas, the Far East, Pacific, SE Asia, the Americas and the circumpolar regions; library of 60,000 vols; Dir Dr STEVEN B. ENGELSMAN; Business Dir MIEP HUIVENAAR; Dir for Public Programmes and Devt JOHN SIJMONSBERGEN; publ. *Mededelingen*.

Naturalis Biodiversity Center (Naturalis Biodiversity Center): POB 9517, 2300 RA Leiden; Darwinweg 2, 2333 CR Leiden; tel. (71) 5687600; e-mail contact@naturalis.nl; internet www.naturalis.nl; f. 1820, by merger of Zoological Museum Amsterdam, Nat.

Museum of Natural History Naturalis and brs of Nat. Herbarium of the Netherlands; colln incl. more than 11m. objects related to fossils, insects, invertebrates, vertebrates; library of 108,000 vols, 8,000 periodical (zoology library 78,000 vols, 5,000 periodicals; geology and paleontology library 30,000 vols, 3,000 periodicals); Gen. Dir Drs EDWIN VAN HUIS; Scientific Dir Prof. Dr ERIK F. SMETS; publs *Blumea, Entomologische tabellen, Nederlandse Faunistische Mededelingen, Persoonia, Scripta Geologica, Zoölogische Bijdragen, Zoölogische Mededelingen, Zoölogische Verhandelingen.*

Rijksmuseum van Oudheden (National Museum of Antiquities): POB 11114, 2301 EC Leiden; Rapenburg 28, 2311 EW Leiden; tel. (71) 5163163; e-mail info@rmo.nl; internet www.rmo.nl; f. 1818; prehistoric, Roman and Medieval periods in the Netherlands; Egyptian, Mesopotamian, Greco-Roman and ancient European collns; library of 30,000 vols, 25 periodicals; Dir Drs WIM WEIJLAND.

Stedelijk Museum de Lakenhal Leiden (Cotton Hall Museum, Leiden): POB 2044, 2301 CA Leiden; Oude Singel 28–32, 2312 RA Leiden; tel. (71) 5165360; e-mail postbus@lakenhal.nl; internet www.lakenhal.nl; f. 1874; pictures of Leiden school; memorial table (triptych) and altar pieces by Lucas van Leyden and C. Engebrechtsz; Rembrandt, Jan Steen, Jan van Goyen, van Mieris, Dou, modern Leiden school: Verster, Kamerlingh Onnes and contemporary Dutch art; furniture, silver, glass, tapestry, etc.; period rooms; history of the town; library of 4,604 vols, 10,500 catalogues; Dir META KNOL.

Limburg

Museum Het Domein Sittard: POB 230, 6130 AE Sittard; Kapittelstraat 6, 6131 ER Sittard; tel. (46) 4513460; e-mail info@hetdomein.nl; internet www.hetdomein.nl; colln of archaeological and historical artefacts, int. avant-garde, with emphasis on photography, video and crossover art; Dir PETER FRANSMAN.

Maastricht

Bonnefantenmuseum (Provincial Museum): POB 1735, 6201 BS Maastricht; Ave Céramique 250, 6221 KX Maastricht; tel. (43) 3290190; e-mail info@bonnefanten.nl; internet www.bonnefanten.nl; f. 1863, refounded 1968; early Italian paintings (1300–1550); Neutelings colln (medieval sculpture and applied arts); Maasland sculpture (incl. works by Jan van Steffeswert); contemporary art (incl. works by René Daniëls, Peter Duig, Gary Hume, Sol LeWitt and Roman Signer); Chair. Drs J. H. H. MANS; Vice-Chair. Prof. Dr K. OTTENHEYM; Artistic Dir ALEXANDER M. U. VAN GREVENSTEIN; Man. Dir HARRIE DRAGSTRA; Treas. L. J. J. RULKENS; Sec. Drs J. VAN DEN BELT.

Natuurhistorisch Museum Maastricht (Maastricht Natural History Museum): De Bosquetplein 6–7, 6211 KJ Maastricht; De Bosquetplein 7, 6211 KJ Maastricht; tel. (43) 3505490; e-mail museum@maastricht.nl; internet www.nhmmaastricht.nl; f. 1912; colln of 550,000 objects; flora, fauna and soils of the Limburg area, late Cretaceous fossils; library of 30,000 vols; Dir-Gen. Drs ERIC P. G. WETZELS; Man. CORRIEN DERKSEN; publ. *Natuurhistorisch Maandblad* (12 a year).

Muiden

Muiderslot: Stichting Rijksmuseum Muiderslot, Herengracht 1, 1398 AA Muiden; tel. (294) 256262; e-mail info@muiderslot.nl; internet www.muiderslot.nl; 13th century castle furnished in early 17th century style: paintings, tapestries, furniture and armoury;

Dir Drs BERT BOER; Chair. H. J. E. BRUINS SLOT.

Naarden

Comenius Museum: Kloosterstraat 33, 1411 RS Naarden; tel. (35) 6943045; e-mail info@comeniusmuseum.nl; internet www.comeniusmuseum.nl; f. 1924; J. A. Comenius mausoleum and museum; library of 2,500 vols; Chair. H. VAN OOSTVEEN; Dir HANS VAN DER LINDE; Sec. H. VERHOEF; Treas. A. OVERDIEP.

Nijmegen

Museum Het Valkhof: POB 1474, 6501 BL Nijmegen; Kelfkensbos 59, 6511 TB Nijmegen; tel. (24) 3608805; e-mail mhv@museumhetvalkhof.nl; internet www.museumhetvalkhof.nl; f. 1999; archaeology, cultural history and fine art, mainly related to Nijmegen and the province of Gelderland; modern art, mainly related to the Netherlands; library of 22,400 vols in art library and 11,000 titles in archaeological library; Dir Drs MARIJKE BROUWER; Chair. R. MIGO.

Opmeer

Scheringa Museum voor Realisme (Scheringa Museum of Realist Art): Spanbroekerweg 162, 1715 GV Spanbroek; tel. (226) 351111; e-mail info@scheringamuseum.nl; internet www.scheringamuseum.nl; f. 1997; colln of paintings and drawings by Carel Willink, paper, sculptures, fashion creations, photographs, objects, and contemporary works of Realism; Dir BELIA VAN DER GIESSEN.

Oss

Museum Jan Cunen: Molenstraat 65, 5341 GC Oss; tel. (412) 629328; e-mail museumjancunen@oss.nl; internet www.museumjancunen.nl; f. 1935; exhibits contemporary art focused on local history, archeology and industrial history; Dir NICOLETTE BARTELINK.

Otterlo

Kröller-Müller Museum: POB 1, 6730 AA Otterlo; Houtkampweg 6, 6731 AW Otterlo; tel. (318) 591241; e-mail info@kmm.nl; internet www.kmm.nl; f. 1938; large colln of paintings by van Gogh, paintings and sculpture since 19th century, old masters, open-air modern sculpture colln (Moore, Serra, Volten), ceramics, drawings, graphic art; library of 40,000 vols; Dir Dr LISETTE PELSERS; Exec. Sec. Drs WANDA VERMEULEN.

Nederlands Tegelmuseum (Dutch Tile Museum): Eikenzoom 12, 6731 BH Otterlo; tel. (318) 591519; e-mail info@nederlandstegelmuseum.nl; internet www.nederlandstegelmuseum.nl; f. 1963; extensive colln of Netherlands tiles since 1500; library of 930 vols; Dir M. H. VAN MEURS.

Roermond

Het Cuypershuis (The House of Cuypers): POB 900, 6040 AX Roermond; Pierre Cuypersstraat 1, 6041 XG Roermond; tel. (475) 359102; e-mail museum@roermond.nl; internet www.cuypershuisroermond.nl; f. 1932; architecture and art of Dr P. J. H. Cuypers (1827–1921) and art and design; Head Dr HANS VAN DE MORTEL.

Rotterdam

Chabotmuseum Rotterdam: Museumpark 11, 3015 CB Rotterdam; tel. (10) 4363713; e-mail mail@chabotmuseum.nl; internet www.chabotmuseum.nl; f. 1993, present status 2000; private Grootveld colln incl. paintings, sculptures, drawings and graphics by Chabot; Schortemeijer colln; enthnographic objects; artists' works, notes, letter, photographs and original sketches.

Historisch Museum Rotterdam (Rotterdam Historical Museum): Korte Hoogstraat 31, 3011 GK Rotterdam Centrum; tel. (10) 2176767; e-mail info@hmr.rotterdam.nl; internet www.hmr.rotterdam.nl; more than 100,000 objects; archaeology, art, domestic life, history, technology; Dir HANS WALGENBACH; publ. *Historisch Nu*.

Kunsthal Rotterdam: POB 23077, 3015 AA Rotterdam; Westzeedijk 341, 3015 AA Rotterdam; tel. (10) 4400301; e-mail communicatie@kunsthal.nl; internet www .kunsthal.nl; works of impressionism, Leonardo da Vinci, Blackfoot Indians, jewels of the orient, pop-art; 2 annual exhibitions: for children and on historico-cultural theme; Dir EMILY ANSENK; Curator JANNET DE GOEDE; Curator CHARLOTTE VAN LINGEN.

Maritiem Museum Rotterdam (Rotterdam Maritime Museum): POB 988, 3000 AZ Rotterdam; Leuvehaven 1, 3011 EA Rotterdam; tel. (10) 4132680; e-mail info@ maritiemmuseum.nl; internet www .maritiemmuseum.nl; f. 1874, new bldg 1986; models of ships since 15th century, globes, atlases, 20,000 books; ironclad warship 'Buffel'; spec. children's exhibition; library of 35,000 vols, 25,000 journals; Chair. Ir P. O. VERMEULEN; Dir-Gen. FRITS LOOMEIJER; Man. Dir MARIEKE VAN BOMMEL; publ. *Maritiem Museum Magazine* (2 a year).

Museum Boijmans Van Beuningen: POB 2277, 3000 CG Rotterdam; Museumpark 18–20, 3015 CX Rotterdam; tel. (10) 4419400; e-mail info@boijmans.nl; internet www .boijmans.nl; f. 1849; approx. 140,000 objects; Dutch School incl. paintings by van Eyck, Bosch, Pieter Brueghel, Hals, Rembrandt, van Ruysdael, Hobbema, Jan Steen; Baroque School, French School, Impressionists; old, modern and contemporary paintings and sculpture; drawings since 15th century from Dutch, Flemish, French, German, Italian and Spanish schools, old and modern prints; glass, Dutch silver, old pewter, laces and ceramics, among which an important colln of Persian, Spanish, Italian and Dutch pottery and tiles; furniture, industrial design; sculpture garden; library of 125,000 vols and catalogues, 200 periodical titles; Chair. H. R. OKKENS; Gen. Man. SJAREL EX.

Nederlands Architectuurinstituut: POB 237, 3000 AE Rotterdam; Museumpark 25, 3015 CB Rotterdam; tel. (10) 4401358; e-mail collection@nai.nl; internet www.nai.nl; f. 1988, by merger of Stichting Architectuurmuseum, Nederlands Documentatiecentrum voor de Bouwkunst, and Stichting Wonen; Sonneveld house museum; maintains archive; library of 42,000 vols, 1,000 periodicals; Chair. WILLEM HEIN SCHENK; Vice-Chair. SANDER MIRCK.

Nederlands Fotomuseum: POB 23383, 3001 KJ Rotterdam; Wilhelminakade 332, 3072 AR Rotterdam; tel. (10) 2030405; e-mail info@nederlandsfotomuseum.nl; internet www.nederlandsfotomuseum.nl; 3m. negatives and colln of slides, prints and documents about life and work of Dutch photographers, amateur photography exhibition; archives of Katharina Eleonore Behrend and Hein Wertheimer; conserves and restores photographic material and provides advice about archival storage material; library of 11,000 vols; Dir RUUD VISSCHEDIJK.

Stedelijk Museum Schiedam: POB 208, 3100 AE Schiedam; Hoogstraat 112–114, 3111 HL Schiedam; tel. (10) 2463666; e-mail info@stedelijkmuseumschiedam.nl; internet www.stedelijkmuseumschiedam.nl; f. 1899; Major Gerrit Visser Bastiaansz's private

colln of modern and contemporary art and historical artefacts; Dir DIANA A. WIND.

Wereldmuseum Rotterdam (World Museum Rotterdam): POB 361, 3000 AJ Rotterdam; Willemskade 25, 3016 DM Rotterdam; tel. (10) 2707172; e-mail info@ wereldmuseum.nl; internet www .wereldmuseum.nl; f. 1885; non-western traditional art collns from Asia and Oceania; Dir STANLEY BREMER.

Witte de With Centre for Contemporary Art: Witte de Withstraat 50, 3012 BR Rotterdam; tel. (10) 4110144; e-mail info@ wdw.nl; internet www.wdw.nl; f. 1990; contemporary art and theory in context of Rotterdam and Netherlands; explores devts in contemporary art worldwide through exhibitions, theoretical and educational programmes, public events and publs; Dir DEFNE AYAS; Curator ZOË GRAY; Assoc. Curator AMIRA GAD.

's-Hertogenbosch

Noordbrabants Museum (North Brabant Museum): POB 1004, 5200 BA 's-Hertogenbosch; Verwersstraat 41, 5211 HT 's-Hertogenbosch; tel. (73) 6877877; e-mail info@ noordbrabantsmuseum.nl; internet www .noordbrabantsmuseum.nl; f. 1981; North Brabant prehistorical, historical and folklore collns, paintings, sculpture, metalwork, prints, coins, etc.; Chair. W. M. VAN DEN GOORBERGH; Dir CHARLES DE MOOIJ; Gen. Man. LEO VAN ROZENDAAL.

The Hague

Escher in Het Paleis (Escher in The Palace): Lange Voorhout 74, 2514 EH The Hague; tel. (70) 4277730; e-mail info@ escherinhetpaleis.nl; internet www .escherinhetpaleis.nl; f. 2002; works of Escher; exhibits works of art with biographical material incl. slide show, photographs, letters, studies of divisions of plane and preliminary sketches.

Fotomuseum Den Haag (The Hague Museum of Photography): POB 72, 2501 CB The Hague; Stadhouderslaan 43, 2517 HV The Hague; tel. (70) 3381144; e-mail info@ fmdh.nl; internet www.fotomuseumdenhaag .nl; f. 2002; attached to Stichting Gemeentemuseum Den Haag; contemporary photography as well as photographs from the colln of the Gemeentemuseum; Dir BENNO TEMPEL; Deputy Dir HANS BUURMAN; Curator WIM VAN SINDEREN.

Gemeentemuseum Den Haag: POB 72, 2501 CB The Hague; Stadhouderslaan 41, 2517 HV The Hague; tel. (70) 3381111; e-mail info@gemeentemuseum.nl; internet www .gemeentemuseum.nl; f. 1862, present status 1999; Modern Art (since 19th century); Decorative Arts (ceramics, glass, silver, furniture) and design since early 20th century; costumes and fashion from 1750 to the present; musical instruments from 15th century to the present; art and music library; Chair. JOOP N. A. VAN CALDENBORGH; Dir BENNO TEMPEL; Deputy Dir HANS BUURMAN.

Mauritshuis, Het Koninklijk Kabinet van Schilderijen Mauritshuis (Mauritshuis, Royal Picture Gallery): POB 536, 2501 CM The Hague; Korte Vijverberg 8, 2513 AB The Hague; tel. (70) 3023456; e-mail communicatie@mauritshuis.nl; internet www.mauritshuis.nl; f. 1822, present status 1995; 15th, 16th and 17th century Dutch and Flemish masters (Rembrandt, Vermeer, Hals, Rubens, Ruisdael, Ter Borch, van Dyck, Holbein, R. v. d. Weyden); Chair. A. BURGMANS; Sec. J. W. WINTER; Dir E. E. S. GORDENKER; Deputy Dir V. J. E. MOUSSAULT.

Museon: POB 30313, 2500 GH The Hague; Stadhouderslaan 37, 2517 HV The Hague;

tel. (70) 3381338; e-mail info@museon.nl; internet www.museon.nl; f. 1904 as Museum for Education, present name and status 1985; astronomy and geology, biology and ecology, history and archaeology, geography and ethnology, science and technology; Dir MARIE-CHRISTINE VAN DER SMAN.

Museum Bredius: Lange Vijverberg 14, 2513 AC The Hague; tel. (70) 3620729; e-mail info@museumbredius.nl; internet www.museumbredius.nl; f. 1895; colln of paintings, drawings, German and Chinese ceramics, Dutch and English silver; Chair. Prof. Dr P. SCHNABEL; Man. R. R. D. SWART; Sec. A. H. VERMEULEN; Treas. F. CH. M. TILMAN; Curator Dr J. HOOGSTEDER.

Museum Meermanno—Huis van het Boek: Prinsessegracht 30, 2514 AP The Hague; tel. (70) 3462700; e-mail info@ meermanno.nl; internet www.meermanno .nl; f. 1848; medieval MSS, incunabula; modern typography, book plates, private press books; Dir MAARTJE DE HAAN; publ. *Leeslint* (2 a year).

Museum Mesdag: Laan van Meerdervoort 7F, 2517 AB The Hague; tel. (70) 3621434; e-mail uildriks@vangoghmuseum.nl; internet www.museummesdag.nl; f. 1903; attached to Van Gogh Museum, Amsterdam; Dutch pictures 1860–1920; French pictures of the Barbizon school; Oriental objects; Dir AXEL RÜGER; publs *Catalogue de l'école française XIX siècle, Museum Mesdag Nederlandse 19e eeuwse Schilderijen*.

Museum Rijswijk: Herenstraat 67, 2282 BR Rijswijk; tel. (70) 3903617; e-mail info@ museumrijswijk.nl; internet www .museumrijswijk.nl; f. 1940; temporary exhibitions; colln of excavated artefacts, mementos of the poet Hendrik Tollens, engravings, medals and treaty documents commemorating 1697 event; Curator ARJAN KWAKERNAAK.

Museum voor Communicatie (Museum of Communication): Zeestraat 82, 2518 AD The Hague; tel. (70) 3307500; e-mail info@ muscom.nl; internet www.muscom.nl; f. 1929, current name adopted 1999; objects and documents, etc., concerning the history and working of the services of posts, telegraphs and telephones in the Netherlands; int. stamp gallery; library of 20,000 vols; Dir TITUS YOCARINI.

Utrecht

Cavaleriemuseum: Barchman Wuytierslaan 198, Amersfoort; tel. (33) 4661996; internet www.cavaleriemuseum.nl; colln of uniforms, small arms, silver, paintings, miniatures, scale, cavalry vehicles, tanks and armoured cars.

Centraal Museum Utrecht: POB 2106, 3500 GC Utrecht; Nicolaaskerkhof 10, 3512 XC Utrecht; tel. (30) 2362362; e-mail info@ centraalmuseum.nl; internet www .centraalmuseum.nl; f. 1838; oldest municipal museum in the Netherlands; colln divided into 5 depts: old masters, modern art, design, fashion and local history; paintings and sculpture incl. old masters works by Saenredam, van Scorel and the Utrecht Caravaggists, incl. Ter Brugghen and van Honthorst; modern art colln from 20th century incl. works by van Doesburg, van der Leck and the Magic Realists Koch, Willink and Moesman; doll's house, 11th century Utrecht ship, applied art and design; Rietveld colln, Dick Bruna colln; Dir EDWIN JACOBS; Deputy Dir MARCO GROB.

Geld Museum (Money Museum): POB 2407, 3500 GK Utrecht; Leidseweg 90, 3531 BG Utrecht; tel. (30) 2910492; e-mail info@ geldmuseum.nl; internet www.geldmuseum .nl; f. 1816 as Rijksmuseum Het Koninklijk

Penningkabinet, merged with Nederlands Muntmuseum 2004; coins from Greek and Roman times to the present, medals, paper money, engraved gems: serves as nat. and int. monetary institute for the main Dutch numismatics; library of 12,000 vols on numismatics and glyptics; Chair. Drs CEES MAAS; Dir HELEEN BUIJS; Curator Drs A. POL; Man. Div. Collns and Research CHRITSEL SCHOLLAARDT; Librarian ANS TER WOERDS; publs *De Beeldenaar* (6 a year), *Jaarboek voor Munt- en Penningkunde.*

Mondriaanhuis: POB 699, 3800 SR Amersfoort; Kortegracht 11, 3811 KG Amersfoort; tel. (33) 4600170; internet www .mondriaanhuis.nl; f. 1992; works of art from early figurative period of Piet Mondrian; exhibition of works by contemporary artists; colln of geometric abstract art and structural concrete art.

Veere

Museum 'De Schotse Huizen' (Museum of Scottish Homes): Kaai 25–27, 4351 AA Veere; tel. (118) 501744; e-mail info@deltacultureel .nl; internet www.schotsehuizen.nl; f. 1950; Chinese and Japanese ceramics; prints, nat. costumes, furniture, statues, exhibitions of paintings; sited in 16th century merchants' houses; Dir JAN VAN DEN BROEKE.

Polderhuis Westkapelle Dijk- en Oorlogsmuseum: Zuidstraat 154–156, 4631 AK Westkapelle; tel. (118) 570700; e-mail info@ polderhuiswestkapelle.nl; internet www .polderhuiswestkapelle.nl/wie-zijn-we; f. 1999; presentation of history of dam village and its inhabitants; history of dike village: Second World War with bombing of dikes in Walcheren in 1944, flooding, closing dike and reconstruction of dike village; liberty bridge; temporary exhibitions in art and cultural and historical heritage; publ. *Polderhuisblad.*

Stadhuismuseum De Vierschaar (Town Hall Museum Vierschaar): Markt 5, 4351 AA Veere; tel. (118) 506064; e-mail info@ deltacultureel.nl; internet www .schotsehuizen.nl/devierschaar; f. 1881; tribunal, council-chamber and exhibition rooms; old standards and flags; pictures; golden cup of Maximilian from Burgundy (1546); memorabilia from the house of Oranje-Nassau; Dir PETER BLOM.

Venlo

Limburgs Museum: POB 1203, 5900 BE Venlo; Keulsepoort 5, 5911 BX Venlo; tel. (77) 3522112; e-mail info@limburgsmuseum.nl; internet www.limburgsmuseum.nl; f. 2000; prehistory, Roman and medieval colln, history of Limburg, art and applied art; coins and medals; Chair. W. AERTS; Vice-Chair. M. DE LOO; Sec. and Treas. S. S. HUIJS; Dir Drs JOS SCHATORJÉ.

Vlissingen

Zeeuws Maritiem Muzeeum Vlissingen (Maritime Museum of Zeeland in Vlissingen): Nieuwendijk 15, 4381 BV Vlissingen; Nieuwendijk 11, 4381 BV Vlissingen; tel. (118) 412498; e-mail info@muzeeum.nl; internet www.muzeeum.nl; f. 2002, originally Stedelijk Museum Vlissingen (f. 1890); maritime colln (pilotage, lighthouses, marine archaeology, fishery); local history (souvenirs of Admiral de Ruyter, paintings, ceramics, wood carvings, engravings, tiles, coins and medals); library of 700 vols; Dir Drs ANNELIES VISSER; Gen. Man. POL VERBEECK.

Universities

DE HAAGSE HOGESCHOOL
(The Hague University of Applied Sciences)

Johanna Westerdijkplein 75, 2521 EN The Hague

Telephone: (70) 4458888
Internet: www.dehaagsehogeschool.nl

Chair.: ROB K. BRONS

Number of teachers: 1,700
Number of students: 20,000

ERASMUS UNIVERSITEIT ROTTERDAM
(Erasmus University)

POB 1738, 3000 DR Rotterdam
Burgemeester Oudlaan 50, 3062 PA Rotterdam

Telephone: (10) 4081111
E-mail: info@smc.eur.nl
Internet: www.eur.nl

Founded 1973 by merger of Nederlandse Economische Hogeschool (f. 1913) and Medische Faculteit Rotterdam (f. 1966)
Academic year: September to July

Chair. of Supervisory Board: Drs A. VAN ROSSUM
Chair. of Exec. Board: P. F. M. VAN DER MEER MOHR
Rector Magnificus: Prof. HENK SCHMIDT
Sec. of Supervisory Board: J. T. A. VAN MAURIK
Librarian: Dr P. E. L. J. SOETAERT

Library: see Libraries and Archives
Number of students: 23,867

DEANS

Erasmus MC (Medical Center): Prof. Dr HUIB POLS
Erasmus School of Economics: Prof. PHILIP HANS FRANSES
Erasmus School of Law: Prof. MAARTEN KROEZE
Faculty of History and Arts: Prof. Dr DICK DOUWES
Faculty of Philosophy: Prof. L. (WIEP) VAN BUNGE
Faculty of Social Sciences: Prof. Dr H. T. VAN DER MOLEN
Rotterdam School of Management: Prof. Dr GEORGE S. YIP

FONTYS HOGESCHOLEN
(Fontys University of Applied Sciences)

POB 347, 5600 AH Eindhoven

Telephone: (877) 877877
E-mail: info@fontys.nl
Internet: www.fontys.nl

Pres.: MARCEL J. G. WINTELS
Sec.: H. J. M. (LENY) SCHEEPERS
Sec.: PIETER G. JANSSEN

Number of teachers: 3,111
Number of students: 38,313

HOGESCHOOL LEIDEN

POB 382, 2300 AJ Leiden
Zernikedreef 11, 2333 CK Leiden

Telephone: (71) 5188800
E-mail: infohl@hsleiden.nl
Internet: www.hsleiden.nl

Br. in Rotterdam

Chair.: PAUL VAN MAANEN
Sec.: LISETTE VAN DE WEIJER

Number of teachers: 700
Number of students: 7,300

HOGESCHOOL ZEELAND
(HZ University of Applied Sciences)

Edisonweg 4, 4382 NW Vlissingen

Telephone: (118) 489155
E-mail: study@hz.nl
Internet: hz.nl
State control

Chair.: Drs H. J. SIMONS
Pres.: Drs PETER C. A. VAN DONGEN
Sec.: M. (RIEN) DE KLERK
Number of students: 4,000

HOGESCHOOL ZUYD
(Zuyd University)

POB 550, 6400 AN Heerlen
Nieuw Eyckholt, Heerlen

Telephone: (45) 4006060
E-mail: info@hszuyd.nl
Internet: www.hszuyd.nl

Campuses in Maastricht, Sittard-Geleen

Chair.: J. J. FRANSEN VAN DE PUTTE
Sec.: BERT NELISSEN

Number of teachers: 1,099
Number of students: 13,955

HOTELSCHOOL THE HAGUE— INTERNATIONAL UNIVERSITY OF HOSPITALITY MANAGEMENT

Brusselselaan 2, 2587 AH The Hague

Telephone: (70) 3512481
E-mail: info@hdh.nl
Internet: www.hotelschool.nl

Founded 1929

Campus in Amsterdam
Private control

Pres.: WIM DOOGE

Number of teachers: 180
Number of students: 1,900

NYENRODE BUSINESS UNIVERSITEIT
(Nyenrode Business University)

POB 130, 3620 AC Breukelen
Straatweg 25, 3621 BG Breukelen

Telephone: (346) 291211
E-mail: info@nyenrode.nl
Internet: www.nyenrode.nl

Founded 1946
Private control
Languages of instruction: Dutch, English
Academic year: September to July

Rector: Prof. Dr MAURITS VAN ROOIJEN
Dean: Prof. Dr LEEN PAAPE
Registrar: R. GUIJT
Librarian: Dr ONNO MASTENBROEK

Library of 25,000 vols, 350 printed journals
Number of teachers: 68
Number of students: 350

OPEN UNIVERSITEIT
(Open University)

POB 2960, 6401 DL Heerlen
Valkenburgerweg 177, 6419 AT Heerlen

Telephone: (45) 5762888
E-mail: info@ou.nl
Internet: www.ou.nl

Founded 1984
State control
Language of instruction: Dutch

Chair.: Drs T. J. F. M. BOVENS
Chair. of Supervisory Board: A. H. BROUWER-KORF
Rector: Prof. Dr Ir F. MULDER
Pro-Rector: Prof. Dr W. M. G. JOCHEMS
Registrar: Y. SMEETS-BERKERS
Librarian: Y. SMEETS-BERKERS

Library of 30,000 vols

Number of teachers: 751
Number of students: 26,182
Publications: *Modulair, OnderwijsInnovatie* (4 a year)

DEANS

Educational Technology Expertise Centre: Prof. Dr W. M. G. JOCHEMS
School of Cultural Studies: Prof. Dr JAAP VAN MARLE
School of Education: Prof. Dr ELS BOSHUIZEN
School of Informatics: Prof. Dr A. (LEX) BIJLSMA
School of Law: Prof. EVERT STAMHUIS
School of Management: Prof. Dr HERMAN VAN DEN BOSCH
School of Natural Science: Prof. Dr PAQUITA PÉREZ SALGADO
School of Psychology: Prof. Dr R. VAN HEZE-WIJK

PROFESSORS

Educational Technology Expertise Centre:
 JOCHEMS, W. M. G.
 KIRSCHNER, P. A.
 KOPER, E. J. R.
 VAN MERRIENBOER, J. J. G.

Rude de Moor Centre:
 COONEN, H. W. A. M.
 STIJNEN, P. J. J.
 VERMEULEN, M. J. M.
 ZWANEVELD, G.

School of Cultural Studies:
 MARLE, J. VAN
 VAN DER DUSSEN, W. J.
 WESSEL, L. H. M.

School of Education:
 BOSHUIZEN, H. P. A.

School of Informatics:
 BAKKER, R. R.
 JEURING, J. T.
 JOOSTEN, S. M. M.
 UDINK TEN CATE, A.
 VAN DE CRAATS, J.

School of Law:
 BOON, P. J.
 RINKES, J. G. J.
 SLOOT, B. P.
 SPOORMANS, H. C. G.

School of Management:
 HEEMSTRA, F. J.
 HERST, A. C. C.
 HOMAN, T.
 JEPMA, C. J.
 KORSTEN, A. F. A.
 KUSTERS, R. J.
 PEER, H. W. G. M.
 SEMEIJN, J. J. S.
 STORM, P. M.
 VAN DEN AARDEMA, H. M. J.
 VAN DEN BOSCH, H. M. J.
 VAN DEN HEIJDEN, B. I. J. M.
 VERSTEGEN, B. H. J.

School of Psychology:
 CLAESSEN, J. F. M.
 VAN DER MOLEN, H. T.
 VAN HEZEWIJK, R. W. J.
 VAN KEMENADE, J. A.
 VON GRUMBKOW, J.

School of Science:
 GLASBERGEN, P.
 MARTENS, P.
 PEREZ SALGADO, F.
 REIJNDERS, L.
 VAN DAM-MIERAS, M. C. E.

RADBOUD UNIVERSITEIT NIJMEGEN
(Radboud University, Nijmegen)

POB 9102, 6500 HC Nijmegen
Comeniuslaan 4, 6525 HP Nijmegen
Telephone: (24) 3616161
E-mail: info@communicatie.ru.nl
Internet: www.ru.nl

Founded 1923 as Katholieke Universiteit Nijmegen, current name adopted 2004
Private control
Languages of instruction: Dutch, English
Academic year: September to July

Trustees: STICHTING KATHOLIEKE UNIV.
Pres. of the Univ. Board: Prof. Dr G. J. M. MEIJER
Vice-Pres. of the Univ. Board: W. L. M. DE KONING-MARTENS
Rector Magnificus: Prof. Dr S. C. J. J. KORTMANN
Sec. Gen.: Drs J. J. A. VAN DE RIET
Librarian: Dr N. J. GRYGIERCZYK

Number of teachers: 2,632
Number of students: 19,103

Publications: *Radboud Magazine* (4 a year), *Vox* (6 a year)

DEANS

Faculty of Arts: Prof. Dr TH. L. M. ENGELEN
Faculty of Law: Prof. Dr P. P. T. BOVEN-D'EERT
Faculty of Medical Sciences: Prof. Dr A. B. M. SMIT
Faculty of Philosophy, Theology and Religious Studies: Prof. Dr J. THIJSSEN
Faculty of Science: Prof. C. C. A. M. GIELEN
Faculty of Social Sciences: Prof. D. H. J. WIGBOLDUS
Nijmegen School of Management: Prof. Dr Ir R. E. C. M. VAN DER HEIJDEN

RIJKSUNIVERSITEIT GRONINGEN
(University Of Groningen)

POB 72, 9700 AB Groningen
Broerstraat 5, 9700 AB Groningen
Telephone: (50) 3639111
E-mail: communicatie@rug.nl
Internet: www.rug.nl

Founded 1614
State control
Languages of instruction: Dutch, English
Academic year: September to September

Chair.: Prof. Dr SIBRAND POPPEMA
Chair. of Supervisory Board: R. J. HOEKSTRA
Rector Magnificus: Prof. Dr ELMER STERKEN
Registrar: BERT VERVELD
Librarian: MARJOLEIN NIEBOER

Number of teachers: 413
Number of students: 27,699

Publication: *Broerstraat 5* (4 a year)

DEANS

Faculty of Arts: Prof. Dr GERRY C. WAKKER
Faculty of Behavioural and Social Sciences: Prof. Dr HENK A. L. KIERS
Faculty of Economics and Business: Prof. Dr J. H. GARRETSEN
Faculty of Law: Prof. Dr JAN BEREND WEZE-MAN
Faculty of Mathematics and Natural Sciences: Prof. Dr JASPER S. KNOESTER
Faculty of Medical Science: Prof. Dr FOLKERT KUIPERS
Faculty of Philosophy: Prof. Dr MARTIN V. B. P. M. VAN HEES
Faculty of Spatial Sciences: Prof. Dr INGE HUTTER
Faculty of Theology: Prof. Dr GEURT HENK VAN KOOTEN

TECHNISCHE UNIVERSITEIT DELFT
(Delft University of Technology)

POB 5, 2600 AA Delft
Mekelweg 5, 2628 CC Delft
Telephone: (15) 2789111
E-mail: info@tudelft.nl
Internet: www.tudelft.nl

Founded 1842, current name adopted 1986
State control
Language of instruction: Dutch
Academic year: September to July

Pres.: Drs D. J. VAN DEN BERG
Vice-Pres. and Rector Magnificus: Prof. Ir K. CH. A. M. LUYBEN
Vice-Pres. for Education: Drs P. M. M. RULLMANN
Sec.-Gen.: Drs J. L. MULDER
Librarian: Ir W. J. S. M. VAN WEEZENBEEK
Library: see Libraries and Archives
Number of teachers: 2,683
Number of students: 16,427

Publications: *Delft Integraal, Delft Outlook, Delta, Jaarverslag, Quarterly Progress Report, Statistisch Jaarboek, Studiegids, Wetenschappelijk Verslag*

DEANS

Faculty of Aerospace Engineering: Prof. Dr Ir JACCO M. HOEKSTRA
Faculty of Applied Sciences: Prof. Dr Ir TIM VAN DER HAGEN (acting)
Faculty of Architecture: Prof. Ir KARIN LAGLAS
Faculty of Civil Engineering and Geosciences: Prof. Dr Ir BERT M. GEERKEN
Faculty of Electrical Engineering, Mathematics and Computer Science: Prof. Dr Ir ROB H. J. FASTENAU
Faculty of Industrial Design Engineering: (vacant)
Faculty of Mechanical, Maritime and Materials Engineering: (vacant)
Faculty of Technology, Policy and Management: Prof. Dr THEO A. J. TOONEN

TECHNISCHE UNIVERSITEIT EINDHOVEN
(Eindhoven University of Technology)

POB 513, 5600 MB Eindhoven
Den Dolech 2, 5612 AZ Eindhoven
Telephone: (40) 2479111
E-mail: cec@tue.nl
Internet: www.tue.nl

Founded 1956
State control
Languages of instruction: Dutch, English
Academic year: September to August

Chair. of Supervisory Board: Ir R. L. VAN IPEREN
Pres. of Exec. Board: Dr Ir A. J. H. M. PEELS
Sec. of Univ.: Dr M. M. N. UMMELEN
Rector Magnificus: Prof. Dr Ir C. J. VAN DUIJN
Chair. of the Univ. Council: J. P. VAN HAM
Librarian: Drs J. C. M. FIGDOR
Library: see under Libraries and Archives
Number of teachers: 2,032
Number of students: 7,700

Publication: *Slash* (3 a year)

DEANS

Dept of Applied Physics: Prof. Dr Ir K. KOPINGA
Dept of Architecture, Building and Planning: Prof. Ir E. S. M. NELISSEN
Dept of Biomedical Engineering: Prof. Dr P. A. J. HILBERS
Dept of Chemical Engineering and Chemistry: Prof. Dr J. C. SCHOUTEN
Dept of Electrical Engineering: Prof. Dr Ir A. C. P. M. BACKX

Dept of Industrial Design: Prof. Dr Ir A. C. BROMBACHER
Dept of Industrial Engineering and Innovation Sciences: Prof. Dr A. G. L. ROMME
Dept of Mathematics and Computer Science: Prof. Dr A. M. COHEN
Dept of Mechanical Engineering: Prof. Dr Ir L. P. H. DE GOEY

UNIVERSITEIT MAASTRICHT
(University of Maastricht)

POB 616, 6200 MD Maastricht
Minderbroedersberg 4–6, 6211 LK Maastricht
Telephone: (43) 3882222
E-mail: communicatie@maastrichtuniversity.nl
Internet: www.maastrichtuniversity.nl
Founded 1976 as State Univ. of Limburg, current name adopted 2008, Univ. of Limburg (www.tul.edu) was est. in 2001, in partnership with Hasselt Universiteit (see chapter on Belgium)
State control
Languages of instruction: Dutch, English
Academic year: September to June
Chair. of Supervisory Board: Drs A. H. A. VEENHOF
Pres. of Exec. Board: Dr Ir J. M. M. RITZEN
Rector: Prof. Dr G. P. M. F. MOLS
Vice-Pres. of Exec. Board: Drs A. POSTEMA
Librarian: Dr I. M. WIJK
Library of 410,000 vols, 2,400 current periodicals
Number of teachers: 3,500
Number of students: 14,500
Publication: *Doc UM ent* (research and devts in problem-based learning, 2 a year)

DEANS

Faculty of Arts and Social Sciences: Prof. Dr. REIN DE WILDE
Faculty of Cultural Studies: Prof. Dr Ir W. E. BIJKER, Prof. Dr P. TUMMEC
Faculty of Health, Medicine and Life Sciences: Prof. Dr MARTIN PAUL
Faculty of Humanities and Sciences: Prof. Dr LOUIS BOON
Faculty of Law: Prof. Dr A. W. HERINGA
Faculty of Psychology and Neurosciences: Prof. Dr BERNADETTE JANSMA
School of Business and Economics: Prof. Dr JOS LEMMINK

UNIVERSITEIT TWENTE
(University of Twente)

POB 217, 7500 AE Enschede
Drienerlolaan 5, 7522 NB Enschede
Telephone: (53) 4899111
E-mail: info@utwente.nl
Internet: www.utwente.nl
Founded 1961
Chair. of Supervisory Board: Drs H. J. VAN ESSEN
Pres.: Dr A. H. FLIERMAN
Rector Magnificus: Prof. Dr H. BRINKSMA
Vice-Pres.: Ir K. J. VAN AST
Sec. of the Univ.: ERIK VAN KEULEN
Librarian: Drs P. G. G. M. DAALMANS
Library: see Libraries and Archives
Number of students: 9,000

DEANS

Faculty of Behavioural Sciences: Prof. Dr KAREN VAN OUDENHOVEN-VAN DER ZEE
Faculty of Electrical Engineering, Mathematics and Computer Science: Prof. Dr Ir TON MOUTHAAN
Faculty of Engineering Technology: Prof. Dr RIKUS EISING
Faculty of Geo-Information Science and Earth Observation: Prof. Dr Ir TOM VELDKAMP (Man. Dir)
Faculty of Science and Technology: Prof. Dr GERARD VAN DER STEENHOVEN
School of Management and Governance: Prof. Dr RAMSES WESSELS

UNIVERSITEIT UTRECHT
(Utrecht University)

POB 80125, 3508 TC Utrecht
Heidelberglaan 8, 3584 CS Utrecht
Telephone: (30) 2539111
E-mail: studievoorlichting@uu.nl
Internet: www.uu.nl
Founded 1636
Languages of instruction: Dutch, English
Academic year: September to July
Pres.: YVONNE C. M. T. VAN ROOY
Chair. of Supervisory Board: M. H. (RIEN) MEIJERINK
Rector Magnificus and Vice-Pres.: Prof. HANS STOOF
Sec.-Gen.: Dr JOOP J. M. KESSELS
Library: see Libraries and Archives
Number of teachers: 3,000
Number of students: 29,927
Publication: *Ublad* (univ. magazine, 52 a year)

DEANS

Faculty of Geosciences: Prof. Dr BERT VAN DER ZWAAN
Faculty of Humanities: Prof. Dr WILJAN VAN DEN AKKER
Faculty of Law, Economics and Governance: Prof. H. R. B. M. (HENK) KUMMELING
Faculty of Science: Prof. Dr JAN VAN REE
Faculty of Social and Behavioural Sciences: Prof. Dr WILLEM KOOPS
Faculty of Veterinary Medicine: Prof. Dr A. PIJPERS
University Medical Centre: Prof. Dr F. MIEDEMA

PROFESSORS

Faculty of Arts (Kromme Nieuwegracht 46, 3512 HJ Utrecht):

BRAIDOTTI, R., Comparative Women's Studies
DE GROOT, R., Music of the Low Countries after 1600
DE JONG, F., Islamic Languages and Cultures
EDEL, D. R., Celtic Languages
GERRITSEN, W. P., Dutch Medieval Literature
HART, P., Utrecht Studies
HECHT, P. A., History of Visual Arts in Renaissance and Modern Times
HERRLITZ, W., German Language
JANSSEN, H. L., Studies of Medieval Castles
JONG, M. B., Medieval History
KLAMT, J. C. J. A., History of Medieval Art
KLOEK, J. J., Social History of Literature
LANDSBERGEN, S. P. J., Language and Speech Automation
LASARTE, F. J., Latin-American Studies
MEYER, B. W., Visual Arts during the Renaissance in Italy and the Netherlands and their Underlying Relationship
MIJNHARDT, W. W., Post-Middle Ages History
MOORTGAT, J., Linguistics, Language Informatics
NOOTEBOOM, S. G., Linguistics, in particular Phonetics
OP DE COUL, P. M., History of Music after 1600
ORBÁN, A. P., Vulgar and Medieval Latin
OTTENHEYM, K. A., History of Architecture
POLLMANN, M. M. W., Social Functions of Language Disciplines
PRAK, M. R., Post-Medieval History (Social Relationships)
REULAND, E. J., Linguistics, specifically Syntax
RIGHART, J. A., Post-Medieval History, in particular Internal Political Relations
SANCISI-WEERDENBURG, H. W. A. M., Ancient History and Culture
SCHENKEVELD VAN DER DUSSEN, M. A., Dutch Renaissance Literature
SCHOENMAKERS, H., Theatre Science
SCHWEGMAN, M. J., Women's History
SICCAMA, J. G., History of Security Issues
STUMPEL, J. F. H. J., Iconology and Art Theory
URICCHIO, W., History of Film and Television
VAN BUUREN, M. B., Modern Literature (French)
VAN DEN HOVEN, P. J., Linguistics
VAN DER VOORT, C. M. M.
VAN EIJCK, D. J. N., Logical Aspects of Computational Linguistics
VAN ZANDEN, J. L., Post-Medieval History (Social Relationships)
VELLEKOOP, C., History of Music before 1600
VERKUIJL, H. J., Dutch Language
VOOGD, P. J. DE, Modern Literature
WESTHOFF, G. J., Didactics of Modern Languages
ZONNEVELD, W., Linguistics, in particular Phonology, English Linguistics

Faculty of Biology (Sorbonnelaan 16, 3584 CA Utrecht; tel. (30) 2532276):

BOERSMA, K. TH., Didactics of Biology
DURSTON, A. J., Organismal Embryology
GOOS, H. J. TH., Comparative Endocrinology
HOEKSTRA, W. P. M., Microbiology
HOGEWEG, P., Theoretical Biology
KOLLÖFFEL, CHR., Botany
LAAT, S. W. DE, Developmental Biology
LAMBERS, J. T., Ecophysiology
SAYER, J. A., International Aspects of Nature Protection
SEINEN, W., Biological Toxicology
VAN DAMME, J. M. M., Ecological Population Genetics
VAN DE GRIND, W. A. P. F. L., Comparative Physiology
VAN DEN BIGGELAAR, J. A. M., Experimental Embryology
VAN DER HORST, D. J., Metabolic Physiology
VAN DER MAAS, P. J. M., Plant Taxonomy
VAN HOOFF, J. A. R. A. M., Comparative Physiology
VAN LEEUWEN, C. J., Biological Toxicology (Ecological Risk Assessment)
VAN LOON, L. C., Phytopathology
VAN NOORDWIJK, A. J., Population Ecology of Animals
VERKLEIJ, A. J., Electromicroscopy
VERRIPS, C. T., Applied Molecular Biology
VISSCHER, H., Palaeobotany
VOORMA, H. O., Molecular Biology
WEISBEEK, P. J., Molecular Genetics
WERGER, M. J. A., Botanical Ecology

Faculty of Chemistry (Sorbonnelaan 16, 3584 CA Utrecht; tel. (30) 2533791):

BRANDSMA, L., Organic Chemistry
DE HAAS, G. H., Biophysics
DE KRUIJF, H. A. M., Toxicology and Society
DE KRUIJFF, B., Molecular Biology of Biomembranes
EGMOND, M. R., Applied Enzymology
FRENKEL, D., Physical Computer Simulation
GEUS, J. W., Inorganic Chemistry
HAVERKAMP, J., Analytical Chemistry
HOLLANDER, J. A., In vivo NMR Spectroscopy
JENNESKENS, L. W., Physical Organic Chemistry

KAMERLING, J. P., Organic Chemistry of Natural Substances
KAPTEIN, R., NMR Spectroscopy
KELLY, J. J., Electrochemistry
KONINGSBERGER, D. C., Inorganic Chemistry
KROON, J., Chemistry
LEKKERKERKER, H. N. W., Physical Chemistry
MEIJERINK, A., Chemistry of Solids
PHILIPSE, A. P., Physical Chemistry
TURKENBURG, W. C., Science and Society
VAN DE VEN, J., Materials Science
VAN DEN BOSCH, H., Biochemistry
VAN DER MAAS, J. H., Spectrochemical Analysis
VAN DUIJNEVELDT, F. B., Theoretical Chemistry
VAN EERDEN, J. P. J. M., Macroscopic Physical Chemistry
VAN EIJNDHOVEN, J. C. M., Technological Research of Aspect
VAN KOTEN, G., Organic Chemistry
VELDINK, G. A., Organic Aspects of Bio-Catalysis
VERHEIJ, H. M., Biochemistry
VLIEGENTHART, J. F. G., Bio-Organic Chemistry
WIRTZ, K. W. A., Biochemistry

Faculty of Earth Sciences (Budapestlaan 4, 3584 CD Utrecht; tel. (30) 2535050):

DAS, H. A., Radioanalysis in Geochemistry
EISMA, D., Marine Sedimentology
JONG, B. M. W. S. DE, Petrology and Experimental Petrology
LEEUW, J. W. DE, Organic Geochemistry
MEULENKAMP, J. E., Stratigraphy and Palaeontology
MONDT, J. C., Exploratory Geophysics
OONK, H. A. J., Thermodynamics
PRIEM, H. N. A., Isotope Geology
SNIEDER, R. K., Seismology
SPIERS, CH. J., Experimental Rock-Deformation
VAN DER WEIJDEN, C. H., Marine Geochemistry and Hydrochemistry
WHITE, S. H., Structural Geology and Tectonics
WONG, TH. E., Sedimentary Geology of Subsoils in the Netherlands
WORTEL, M. J. R., Tectonophysics

Faculty of Geosciences (Heidelberglaan 2, 3584 CS Utrecht; tel. (30) 2532044):

BURROUGH, P. A., Physical Geography of Landscapes
DIELEMAN, F. M. J., Human Geography of Urban Industrialized Countries
GLASBERGEN, P., Environmental Policies
GROENEWEGEN, P. P., Environmental and Social Aspects of Health and Health Care
HAUER, J., Methods and Techniques in Geographical Research
HOEKVELD, G. A., Education and Regional Geography
HOOIMEIJER, P., Regional Aspects of Population Issues
KOSTER, E. A., Landscape Architecture
KREUKELS, A. M. J., Urban and Regional Planning
LAMBOOY, J. G., Geographical Economics
LUNING, H. A., Town and Country Planning in Developing Countries
NIEUWENHUIS, J. D., Soil Mechanics of Natural Systems
ORMELING, F. J., Cartography
OTTENS, H. F. L., Human Geography
SCHILDER, G. G., History of Cartography
TERWINDT, J. H. J., Physiogeographical Processes
VAN DEN AKKER, C., Ground and Surface Water Quality
VAN DEN BERG, M., Urban and Regional Planning
VAN GINKEL, J. A., Human Geography

VAN RIJN, L. C., Mechanics of Fluids (Geographical Modelling)
VAN WEESEP, J., Human Geography
VELLINGA, M. L., Human Geography (Developing Countries)
VONKEMAN, G. H., Environmental Studies
WEVER, E., Human Geography (Economic Geography and International Economics)

Faculty of Law (Janskerhof 3, 3512 BK Utrecht; tel. (30) 2537017):

ANDRIESSEN, F. H. J. J., European Integration
BACKES, CH. W., Environmental Law
BAEHR, P. R., Human Rights
BAHLMAN, J. P., Business Economics
BOELE-WOELKI, K. S. R. D., International and Comparative Private Law
BOON, D., Animals and Law
BOVENKERK, F., Criminology
BOVENS, M. A. P., Philosophy of Law
BRANTS, C. H., Penal Law and Law of Criminal Procedure
BRINKHOFF, J. J., Industrial Property
BRUINSMA, J. F., Sociology of Law
CURTIN, D. M., Law of International Organizations
DALHUISEN, J. H., International Commercial Law
GROSHEIDE, F. W., Private Law
HARTKAMP, A. S., Private Law, particularly Civil Law
HEYMAN, H. W., Notarial Law
HOL, A. M., Theory of Law
HONDIUS, E. H., Civil Law
IDENBURG, PH. A., Management Sciences
IN 'T VELD, R. I., Management of Public Government
JASPERS, A. PH. C. M., Social Law
KABEL, J. J. C., Mass Media Law
KELK, C., Penitentiary Law
KOERS, A. W., International Law
KUMMELING, H. R. B. M., Constitutional and Administrative Law
KWIATKOWSKA, B., International Maritime Law
MEIJKNECHT, P. A. M., Civil Law
MOOIJ, A. W. M., Forensic Psychiatry
MORTELMANS, K. J. M., Social Economic Law
NIEUWENBURG, C. K. F., Political Economy
ROSCAM ABBING, H. D. C., Health Law
SCHILFGAARDE, P., Business Law
SIEGERS, J. J., Economics
SOONS, A. H. A., International Law
SPRUIT, J. E., History of Roman Law
STILLE, A. L. G. A., Notarial Law
SWART, A. H. J., Penitentiary Law
TEN BERGE, J. B. J. M., Administrative Law
VAN BUUREN, P. J. J., Governmental Law
VAN DEN BERGH, R., Economics of Law
VAN HALL, A., Law of Public Water and Water Boards
VAN HOOF, G. J. H., Social Economic Law
VAN HUIZEN, P. H. J. G., Commercial Traffic Law
VAN MENS, K. L. H., Fiscal Law
VAN REENEN, P., Causes of Violations of Human Rights
VERVAELE, J. A. E., Maintenance of Law and Order
VREE, J. K. DE, International and Political Relations

Faculty of Mathematics and Informatics (Budapestlaan 6, 3584 CD Utrecht; tel. (30) 2531515):

DE LANGE, J., Didactics of Teaching Mathematics and Computer Science
DIEKMANN, O., Applied Mathematics
DUISTERMAAT, J. J., Pure and Applied Mathematics
GILL, R. D., Stochastics
HAZEWINKEL, M., Algebraic Chemistry
LOOIJENGA, E. J. N., Pure Mathematics
MARS, J. G. M., Mathematics

MEERTENS, L. T. G., Programming Technology
MEIJER, J. J. CH., Informatics
OORT, F., Mathematics
OVERMARS, M. H., Computer Science
SIERSMA, D., Mathematics
SWIERSTRA, S. D., Informatics
TREFFERS, A., Field-Specific Education
VAN DALEN, D., Logic and Philosophy of Mathematics
VAN DER VORST, H. A., Mathematics
VAN LEEUWEN, J., Informatics
VERHULST, F., Quantitative Analysis of Dynamic Systems
ZAGIER, D. B., Pure Mathematics

Faculty of Medicine (Universiteitsweg 100, 3584 CG Utrecht; tel. (30) 2538888):

AKKERMANS, L. M. A., Gastrointestinal Physiology
BÄR, P. R., Experimental Neurology
BATTERMAN, J. J., Radiotherapy
BAX, N. M. A., Paediatric Surgery
BEEMER, F. A., Clinical Genetics
BERGER, R., Chemistry of Hereditary Metabolic Diseases
BERNARDS, R. A., Molecular Carcinogenesis
BIJLSMA, J. W. J., Rheumatology
BLIJHAM, G. H., Clinical Medicine
BORST, C., Experimental Cardiology
BOS, J. L., Physiological Chemistry
BOSMAN, F., Dental Physics
BOUMA, B. N., Biochemistry of Haemostasis
BREDEE, J. J., Cardio-Pulmonic Surgery
BRUYNZEEL-KOOMEN, C. A. F. M., Dermatology-Allergology
BUITELAAR, I. K., Biopsychosocial Determinants in Human Behaviour
BURBACH, J. P. H., Molecular Biology of Neuropeptides
CAPEL, P. J. A., Experimental Immunology
CLEVERS, J. C., Clinical Immunology
COHEN-KETTENIS, P. T., Gender Development and Child and Youth Psychopathology
DEJONCKERE, P. H., Speech Therapy and Phoniatrics
DE PUTTER, C., Special Dental Surgery
DE WILDT, D. J., Medical Pharmacology
DUIJNSTEE, M. S. H., Innovations in Home Care
DUURSMA, S. A., Clinical Medicine
EIKELBOOM, B. C., Vascular and Transplant Surgery
ERKELENS, D. W., Clinical Medicine
FELDBERG, M. A. M., Radiodiagnostics
GAST, G. C. DE, Haematology
GEUZE, J. J., Cytology
GISPEN, W. H., Molecular Pharmacology and Neuro-Pharmacology
GOOSZEN, H. G., Surgery
GROBBEE, D. E., Clinical Epidemiology
GRYPDONCLE, M. H. F., Nursing Science
HAUER, R. N. W., Clinical Electrophysiology
HEEREN, TH. J., Psychogeriatrics
HEINTZ, A. P. M., Oncological Gynaecology
HELDERS, P. J. M., Physiotherapy
HENGEVELD, M. W., Sexology
HILLEN, B., Functional Anatomy
HORDIJK, G. J., Oto-rhino-laryngology
HUIZING, E. H., Oto-rhino-laryngology
JONGSMA, H. J., Medical Physiology
KAHN, R. S., Clinical and Biological Psychiatry
KATER, L., Clinical Immunopathology
KNAPE, J. TH. A., Anaesthesiology
KOERSELMAN, G. F., Psychotherapy
KON, M., Plastic and Reconstructive Surgery
KOOMANS, H. A., Nephrology
LAMMERS, J. W. J., Pulmonary Diseases
MALI, W. P. TH. M., Radiodiagnostics
MARX, J. J. M., General Internal Medicine
MOSTERD, W. L., Clinical Sports Medicine

OKKEN, A., Paediatrics
PEARSON, P. L., Medical Molecular Genetics
PETERS, A. C. B., Paediatric Neurology
PETERS, P. W. J., Teratology
POLL-THE, B. E., Clinical Congenital Metabolic Diseases
ROBLES DE MEDINA, E. O., Clinical Cardiology
SANGSTER, B., Health Protection
SAVELKOUL, T. J. F., Toxicology
SCHRIJVERS, A. J. P., General Health Care
SCHULPEN, T. W. J., Social Paediatrics
SITSEN, J. M. A., Clinical Pharmacology
SIXMA, J. J., Haematology
SLOOTWEG, P. J., Oral Pathology
SMOORENBURG, G. F., Experimental Audiology
SMOUT, A. J. P. M., Pathophysiology
STAAL, G. E. J., Enzymology
STILMA, J. S., Ophthalmology
STROUS, G. J. A. M., Cellular Biology
SUSSENBACH, J. S., Molecular Biology
TEN HORN, G. H. M. M., Psychiatric Care-Management
TE VELDE, E. R., Desirable Fertility
THIJSSEN, J. J. H., Clinical Chemistry
TREFFERS, W. F., Ophthalmology
TULLEKEN, C. A. F., Neurosurgery
VAN BEL, F., Neonatology
VAN BERGE HENEGOUWEN, G. P., Gastroenterology
VAN BRONSWIJK, J. E. M. H., Biological Agents in Domestic Hygiene
VAN DE WAL, H. J. C. M., Cardiopulmonic Surgery of Infants and Children
VAN DEN TWEEL, J. G., Pathology
VAN DER DONK, J. A. W. M., Cell Biology
VAN DER VLIET, P. C., Physical Chemistry
VAN DER WERKEN, CHR., Acute Surgery
VAN DER WINKEL, J. G. J., Immunotherapy
VAN ENGELAND, H., Psychiatry of Children
VAN GIJN, J., Neurology
VAN HUFFELEN, A. C., Clinical Neurophysiology
VAN LONDEN, J., General Health Care
VAN NIEUWENHUIZEN, O., Paediatric Neurology in relation to Functional Morphology
VAN NORREN, D., Ophthalmological Physics
VAN REE, J. M., Psychopharmacology
VAN VEELEN, C. W. M., Functional Neurosurgery
VAN VLOTEN, W. A., Dermatology
VAN VROONHOVEN, TH. J. M. V., General Surgery
VAN WAES, P. F. G. M., Röntgen Diagnostics
VAN WIMERSMA GREIDANUS, TJ. B., Neuroendocrinology
VELDMAN, J. E., Experimental Otology and Otoimmunology
VERBOUT, A. J., Orthopaedic Aspects of Spinal and Neuromuscular Disorders
VERHEIJ, T. J. M., Family Medicine
VERHOEF, J., Clinical Microbiology
VERSTEEG, D. H. G., Medical Pharmacology
VIERGEVER, M. A., Image-processing in Medicine
VISSER, G. H. A., Obstetrics
VOORN, TH. B., General Practice
WESTENBERG, H. G. M., Neurochemical Aspects of Psychiatry
WINNUBST, J. A. M., Psychology of Health and Illness
WOKKE, J. H. J., Neurology focusing on Neuromuscular Diseases
WOLTERS, W. H. G., Paediatric Psychology
ZEGERS, B. J. M., Paediatric Immunology
ZONNEVELD, F. W., Medical Representation Techniques

Faculty of Pharmacy (Sorbonnelaan 16, 3584 CA Utrecht; tel. (30) 2532525):

BAKKER, A., Pharmaceutical Practice
BEIJNEN, J. H., Bio-Analysis (Research in Clinical Medicine)
BULT, A., Pharmaceutical Analysis
CLERCK, F. F. P., Applied Pulmonary and Cardiovascular Pharmacology
CROMMELIN, D. J. A., Biopharmacy
DE JONG, J. G. A. M., Management Aspects of Pharmaceutical Practice
GLERUM, J. H., Clinical Pharmacy
HENNINK, W. E., Pharmaceutical Technology
JANSSEN, L. H. M., Pharmaceutical Chemistry
LABADIE, R. P., Pharmacognosy
LISKAMP, R. M. J., Molecular Medicinal Chemistry
MAES, R. A. A., Toxicology
NIJKAMP, F. P., Molecular Pharmacology
OLIVIER, B., Applied Pharmacology of the Central Nervous System
PORSIUS, A. J., Pharmacotherapy
RUITER, A., Food Chemistry and Bromatology
THIJSSEN, J. H. H., Clinical Chemistry
TOLLENAERE, J. P. A. E., Computational Medicinal Chemistry
VAN DIJK, H., Immunology of Phytochemicals
VERBATEN, M. N., Human Psychophysiology and Psychopharmacology

Faculty of Philosophy (Heidelberglaan 8, 3584 CS Utrecht; tel. (30) 2531831):

BERGSTRA, J. A., Applied Logic
GEERTSEMA, H. P., Calvinist Philosophy
MANSFELD, J., History of Philosophy in the Ancient World and the Middle Ages
MIDDELBURG, C. A., Applied Logic
RUNIA, D. T., The Tradition of Platonism in Relation to Early Christianity
SCHUHMANN, K. J., History of Modern and Renaissance Philosophy
VAN DALEN, D., Logic and Philosophy
VAN REIJEN, W. L., Political and Social Philosophy
VERBEEK, TH. H. M., 17th-Century Ideology from the Dutch Perspective

Faculty of Physics and Astronomy (Princetonplein 5, 3584 CC Utrecht; tel. (30) 2533284):

ANDRIESSE, C. D., Electricity Supplies
BEIJERINCK, H. C. W., Atomic and Interface Physics
BLEEKER, J. A. M., Space Research
BUIJS, A., Experimental Physics
BUILTJES, P. J. H., Chemistry of the Atmosphere
CROWE, A., Medical and Physiological Physics
DE RUIJTER, W. P. M., Physical Oceanography
DE WIJN, H. W., Solid State Physics
DE WIT, B. Q. P. J., Theoretical Physics
DE WITT HUBERTS, P. K. A., Reactor Physics
DIEKS, D. G. B. J., Foundations and Philosophy of the Natural Sciences
DIJKHUIS, J. I., Semiconductor Laser Optics
DRONKERS, J., Physics of Coastal Systems
ERKELENS, C. J., Human Physics
ERNÉ, F. C., Current Issues in Physics
ERNST, M. H. J., Theoretical Physics
FEINER, L. F., Theory of Condensed Materials
HABRAKEN, F. H. P. M., Physics Education
HEARN, A. G., Astrophysics
HEIDEMAN, H. G. M., Experimental Physics
HOLTSLAG, A. A. M., Meteorology (Forecasting) Techniques
HOOFT, T. W. J. M., Theory of Solids
KAMERMANS, R., Experimental Physics and Experimental Nuclear Physics
KOENDERINK, J. J., Human Physics
KUPERUS, M., Astrophysics
LAMERS, H. J. G. L. M., Astronomy
LELIEVELD, J., Atmospheric Chemistry
LEVINE, Y. K., Biophysics
LIJNSE, P. L., Development of Physics Concepts and Methods in Education

LOURENS, W., Physics Informatics
NIEHAUS, A., Experimental Physics
OERLEMANS, J., Dynamics of the Climate
POLMAN, A., Advancement of Atomic and Interface Physics
RUIJGROK, TH. W., Theoretical Physics and Mechanics
SARIS, F. W., Atomic and Molecular Physics
SCHÜLLER, F. C., Plasma Physics
SCHUURMANS, C. J. E., Meteorology
SINKE, W. C., Physical and Chemical Properties of Thin Layers
SMIT, J., Theoretical High-Energy Physics
'T. JANSSEN, G., Theoretical Physics
TJON, J. A., Theoretical Physics
VAN BEIJEREN, H., Theoretical Physics
VAN DER WEG, W. F., Technical Physics
VAN HIMBERGEN, J. E. J. M., Theoretical Physics
VERBUNT, F. W. M., High-Energy Astrophysics
VERLINDE, E. P., Theoretical Physics
ZIMMERMAN, J. TH. F., Physical Oceanography

Faculty of Social Sciences (Heidelberglaan 1, 3584 CS Utrecht):

ADRIAANSENS, H. P. M., Social Sciences and Social Processes and Structures
BANCK, G. A., Anthropology of Brazil
BECKER, H. A., Sociology
BENSING, J. M., Clinical Psychology and Health Psychology
BIERMAN, D. J., Parapsychology
BRINKGEVE, C. D. A., Primary Forms of Cohabitation, Life-Course and Identity
COENEN, H. M. H., Labour Issues
DEEN, N., Theory and Practice of Pupil Accompaniment
DERCKSEN, W. J., Social Sciences (Socio-Economic Policy)
DUBBELDAM, L. F. B., Education in Developing Countries
ELBERS, E. P. J. M., Communication, Thought and Culture Issues
ENGBERSEN, G. B. M., Welfare State System
ENTZINGER, H. B., Studies of Multi-Ethnic Societies
GRIENSVEN, G. J. P., Social Epidemiology with respect to HIV/AIDS
GROEBEL, F. J., Social Sciences (Psychology of Mass Communication)
HAAN, E. H. F. DE, Applied Experimental Psychology
HAGENDOORN, A. J. M. W., Social Sciences
HART, H. 'T, Statistics and Methodology of Pedagogical Research
HEIJMANS, P. G., Life Psychology
HOKSBERGEN, R. A. C., Adoption
HOX, J. J., Survey Research
IDENBURG, PH. A., Management Sciences
IMELMAN, J. D., Principles of Pedagogics
INGLEBY, J. D., Life Psychology
KANSELAAR, G., Educational Sciences, in particular Educational Psychology
KNULST, W. P., Education in Arts and Cultural Participation
KRUIJT, D. A. N. M., Development Issues
LAGERWEIJ, N. A. J., Pedagogics and Innovation in Teaching
LEEUW, F. L., Empirical Theoretical Analysis of the Social Effects of Government Policy
MANTE MEIJEE, E. A., Management and Renewal Processes in Large Organizations
OOSTINDIE, G. J., Anthropology of Comparative Sociology (Caribbean)
PILOT, A., Didactics
RAUB, W., Theoretical Sociology
RISPENS, J., Education of Problem Children
ROBBEN, A. C. G. M., Anthropology of Comparative Sociology (Latin America)
RUIJTER, A. DE, Social Anthropology

SCHAUFELI, W. B., Organizational Psychology

SCHETTKAT, R., Social and Institutional Economics

SCHNABEL, P., Mental Health Care

SCHOFFELEERS, J. H., Socio-Economic Changes and Forms of Meaning-Making

SEVENHUYSEN, S. L., Comparative Women's Studies

STEVENS, L. M., Orthopedagogics

STROEBE, W., Social and Organizational Psychology

TAZELAAR, F., Sociology

THIJSSEN, J. G. L., Business and Professional Education

TIELMAN, R. A. P., Social and Cultural Aspects of Humanism

TREFFERS, A., Field-Specific Education

VAN DEN BOUT, J., Bereavement Acceptance Process

VAN DER HEIJDEN, P. G. M., Statistics for Social Sciences

VAN DER LAAN, G., Foundations of Social Work

VAN DER ZWAN, A., Development of Views on the Adjustment of the Welfare State

VAN SON, M. J. M., Clinical and Health Care Psychology

VAN WAARDEN, B. F., Intervention, Organization and Policy Issues in Social Sciences

VAN WIJNGAARDEN, P. J., Sociological Aspects of Social Security Issues

VAN WYNGAARDEN, P. J., Social Security Issues

VAN ZANTWIJK, R. A. M., Anthropology and Ethno-History of the Indian Peoples of Latin America

VEENHOVEN, R., Humanism

VERMEER, A., Remedial Education

VRIENS, L. J. A., Peace Studies

VROON, P., Theoretical Psychology

WERTHEIM, A. H., Cognitive Ergonomics

WILTERDINK, N. A., Study of Long-term Processes in Social Sciences

WINTER, M. DE, Innovations in Primary Parent and Child Care

WUBBELS, TH., Teacher Behaviour as a Factor in the Learning Environment

Faculty of Theology (Heidelberglaan 2, 3584 CS Utrecht; tel. (30) 2531853):

ANDREE, T. G. I. M., Ideological Upbringing and Formation in a Multi-Religious Context

BECKING, B. E. H. J., Old Testament

BRÜMMER, V., Philosophy of Religion

DE REUVER, A., Education in Calvinist Theology

DEN BOEFT, J., Religious History of Hellenism

HEEGER, F. R., Ethics

HOUTEPEN, A. W. P., Ecumenics

IMMINK, F. G., Practical Theology

JONGENEEL, J. A. B., Missiology

KLOPPENBORG, M. A. G. T., History of Religions and Comparative Religious Studies

MAAS, T. A., Relationships between Christianity and Modern Culture

MUIS, J., Dogmatics

OTTEN, W., Church History

SCHROTEN, E., Christian Ethics

TIELEMAN, H. J., Sociology of Religions

VAN BELZEN, J. A., Psychology of Religion

VAN DER HORST, P. W., New Testament

VAN LEEUWEN, TH. M., Science of the Old Testament and History of Israelite Religion

VRIES, O. H. DE, History and Dogmas of the Baptism

Faculty of Veterinary Medicine (Yalelaan 1, 3584 CL Utrecht; tel. (30) 2534851):

BARNEVELD, A., General Surgery and Surgery of Large Domestic Animals

BEYNEN, A. C., Experimental Animals

BREUKINK, H. J., Clinical Veterinary Medicine

COLENBRANDER, B., Fertility

CORNELISSEN, A. W. C. A., Parasitology

DE VRIES, H. W., Medicine of Small Domestic Animals

DEN OTTER, W., Cell Biology and Histology

DIK, K. J., Radiology

EVERTS, M. F., Veterinary Physiology

FERON, V. J., Biological Toxicology

FINK-GREMMELS-GEHRMANN, J., Pharmacology of Domestic Animals

GIELKENS, A. J. L., Veterinary Medicine for Poultry Farms

GROMMERS, F. J., Relationship between Man and Animal

GRUYS, E., Pathology of Domestic Animals

HELLEBREKERS, L. J., Anaesthesiology of Laboratory Animals

HORZINEK, M. C., Virology

HUIS IN 'T VELD, J. H. J., Microbiology of Food Products of Animal Origin

JANSSEN, J., Knowledge of Veterinary Law

KROES, R., Biological Toxicology

MELOEN, R. H., Biomedical Identification

MOUWEN, J. M. V. M., Pathology

OSTERHAUS, A. D. M. E., Environmental Virology

PIJPERS, A., Veterinary Medicine for Poultry Farms

ROTTIER, P. J. M., Molecular Virology

RUITENBERG, E. J., Veterinary Immunology

RIJNBERK, A., Medicine of Small Domestic Animals

SCHALKEN, J. A., Veterinary Oncology

SLUYS, F. J., Medicine of Domestic Animals, Reproduction and Surgery

SPRUIJT, B. M., Good Health of Animals

TIELEN, M. J. M., Lodging and Provision of Animals

VAN DER WEYDEN, G. C., Obstetrics

VAN DER ZEIJST, B. A. M., Veterinary Bacteriology

VAN DER ZUTPHEN, L. F. M., Animals and Experimental Application

VAN DIJK, J. E., Pathology of Rare Animals/Spontaneous Laboratory Animal Pathology

VAN EDEN, W., Veterinary Immunology

VAN GOLDE, L. M. G., Veterinary Biochemistry

VAN KNAPEN, F., Hygiene of Food of Animal Origin

VAN MIERT, A. S. J. P. A. M., Veterinary Pharmacology

VAN OIRSCHOT, J. T., Veterinarian Vaccinology

VAN OOST, B. A., Clinical and Molecular Genetics of Domestic Animals

VERHEIJDEN, J. H. M., Medicine of Pigs

VOS, J. G., Toxicological Pathology

WEIJS, W. A., Veterinary Anatomy and Embryology

UNIVERSITEIT VAN AMSTERDAM
(University of Amsterdam)

POB 19268, 1000 GG Amsterdam
Spui 21, 1012 WX Amsterdam

Telephone: (20) 5259111
E-mail: info@uva.nl
Internet: www.uva.nl

Founded 1632 as Athenaeum Illustre, present name and status 1877
State control
Languages of instruction: Dutch, English
Academic year: September to July

Pres.: Dr LOUISE GUNNING-SCHEPERS
Rector Magnificus: Prof. DYMPH VAN DEN BOOM
Vice-Pres.: HANS AMMAN
Sec.-Gen.: MIEKE ZAANEN
Library Dir: Drs MARIA HEIJNE

Library: see under Libraries and Archives
Number of teachers: 2,626

Number of students: 32,165

Faculty of Dentistry: Prof. A. J. FEILZER
Faculty of Economics and Business: Prof. H. G. VAN DISSEL
Faculty of Humanities: Prof. F. P. I. M. VAN VREE
Faculty of Law: Prof. C. E. DU PERRON
Faculty of Medicine: Prof. M. M. LEVI
Faculty of Science: Prof. K. I. J. MAEX
Faculty of Social and Behavioural Sciences: Prof. E. H. F. DE HAAN

TILBURG UNIVERSITY

POB 90153, 5000 LE Tilburg
Warandelaan 2, 5037 AB Tilburg

Telephone: (13) 4669111
E-mail: info@tilburguniversity.edu
Internet: www.tilburguniversity.edu

Founded 1927 as Roomsch Katholieke Handelshoogeschool, present status 2006
State control
Languages of instruction: Dutch, English
Academic year: September to August

Chair.: R. F. M. LUBBERS
Pres. of Exec. Board: K. M. BECKING
Rector: Prof. Dr PHILIP EIJLANDER
Chief Admin. Officer: Drs M. H. VAN IEPEREN
Chief Information Officer: Ir M. VAN DEN BERG
Sec.-Gen.: Drs E. A. C. M. ZWAANS

Library of 800,000 vols, 11,000 periodical vols
Number of teachers: 929
Number of students: 12,952

Publications: *Tilburg Research* (irregular), *UNIVERS* (online), *Until* (irregular)

Law School: Prof. Dr CORINE PRINS
School of Economics and Management: Prof. Dr LEX MEIJDAM
School of Humanities: Prof. Dr ARIE DE RUIJTER
School of Social and Behavioural Sciences: Prof. Dr KLAAS SIJTSMA
School of Theology: Prof. Dr MARCEL SAROT
TiasNimbas Business School: Prof. Dr KEES KOEDIJK

UNIVERSITEIT LEIDEN
(Leiden University)

POB 9500, 2300 RA Leiden
Rapenburg 70, 2311 EZ Leiden

Telephone: (71) 5272727
E-mail: info@leidenuniv.nl
Internet: www.leidenuniv.nl

Founded 1575
State control
Language of instruction: Dutch
Academic year: September to July

Rector Magnificus and Pres.: Prof. Dr C. J. J. M. STOLKER
Vice-Rector: Prof. Dr S. E. BUITENDIJK
Vice-Pres.: Drs H. W. TE BEEST
Librarian: KURT DE BELDER

Library: see under Libraries and Archives
Number of teachers: 1,141
Number of students: 20,712

Faculty of Archaeology: Prof. Dr WILLEM J. H. WILLEMS
Faculty of Humanities: Prof. Dr H. W. VAN DEN DOEL
Faculty of Science: Prof. G. R. DE SNOO
Faculty of Social Science: Prof. Dr J. T. SWAAB-BARNEVELD
Leiden Law School: Prof. R. A. LAWSON
Leiden University Medical Center: Prof. Dr P. C. W. HOGENDOORN (Chair. of Exec. Bd)

UNIVERSITEIT VOOR HUMANISTIEK
(University for Humanistics)

POB 797, 3500 AT Utrecht
Kromme Nieuwegracht 29, 3512 HD Utrecht
Telephone: (30) 2390100
E-mail: info@uvh.nl
Internet: www.uvh.nl

Founded 1989
State control
Academic year: September to June
Chair.: Prof. Dr ARIE DE RUIJTER
Rector: Prof. Dr HANS A. ALMA
Librarian: M. A. M. BOERBOOM
Library of 22,000 vols
Number of teachers: 100
Number of students: 350

PROFESSORS

COENEN, H. L. M., Sciences of Man, Society and Culture
ELDERS, A. D. M., Theories of World Views
HOUTEN, D. J. VAN, Social Policy, Planning and Organization
KUNNEMAN, H. P., Practical Humanist Studies
MANSCHOT, H. A. M., Philosophy and Ethics
MASO, I., Philosophy of Science, Methodology and the Theory of Research
VRIES, T. DE, Regional Health Care

VRIJE UNIVERSITEIT, AMSTERDAM
(Free University, Amsterdam)

De Boelelaan 1105, 1081 HV Amsterdam
Telephone: (20) 5989898
E-mail: international@dienst.vu.nl
Internet: www.vu.nl

Founded 1880
Languages of instruction: Dutch, English
Academic year: September to September
Chair. of Supervisory Board: P. BOUW
Chair. of Exec. Board: R. M. SMIT
Rector: LEX BOUTER
Mem. of Exec. Board: H. J. RUTTEN
Library: see under Libraries and Archives
Number of teachers: 2,000
Number of students: 25,000
Publication: *VU Magazine*

DEANS

Faculty of Arts: Prof. Dr DOUWE G. YNTERNA
Faculty of Dentistry: Prof. A. FEILZER
Faculty of Earth and Life Sciences: Prof. BAUKE OUDEGA
Faculty of Economics and Business Administration: Prof. H. VERBRUGGEN
Faculty of Human Movement Sciences: Prof. P. J. BEEK
Faculty of Law: Prof. Dr E. SLIEDREGT
Faculty of Medicine: Prof. W. STALMAN
Faculty of Philosophy: Prof. R. VAN WOUDENBERG
Faculty of Psychology and Education: Prof. J. PASSCHIER
Faculty of Sciences: Prof. Dr H. IRTH
Faculty of Social Sciences: Prof. ANTON C. HEMERIJCK
Faculty of Theology: Prof. Dr WIM JANSE

WAGENINGEN UNIVERSITEIT
(Wageningen University)

POB 9101, 6700 HB Wageningen
Bldg no. 400, Costerweg 50, 6701 BH Wageningen
Telephone: (317) 480100
E-mail: info@wur.nl
Internet: www.wageningenuniversity.nl

Founded 1876, present status 1918; attached to Wageningen Univ. and Research Centre
State control
Languages of instruction: Dutch, English
Academic year: September to August

Chair.: Dr LOUISE O. FRESCO
Rector Magnificus and Vice-Pres.: Prof. Dr M. J. KROPFF
Mem. of Exec. Board: Dr IJ. J. H. (TIJS) BREUKINK
Chair. of Supervisory Board: M. DE BOER
Chief Librarian: VAN D. ZAANE
Information Officer: S. VINK
Library: see under Libraries and Archives
Number of teachers: 500
Number of students: 6,430
Publication: *Wb*

PROFESSORS

ANTONIDES, G., Economics of Consumers and Households
BAKKER, J., Nematology, Physiology and Molecular Ecology of Nematodes
BEERS, G., Supply Chain Management
BERENDSE, F., Nature Conservation and Plant Ecology
BEULENS, A. J. M., Information Technology
BIGMAN, D., Global Food Security and International Trade
BINDELS, J., Nutrition during Growth and Development
BINO, R. J., Metabolomica of Plants
BISSELING, A. H. J., Molecular Biology, Devt Biology of Plants
BLANS, G. H. T., Philosophy
BONGERS, F., Forest Ecology and Forest Management Group
BOOM, R. M., Food Process Engineering
BOT, G. P. A., Technical Physics
BREGT, A. K., Geo-Information Science, Geographical Information Systems
BRUSSAARD, L., Soil Biology and Biological Soil Quality
CAPELLE, A., Agrification
CLEEF, A. M., Tropical Nature Conservation and Vertebrate Ecology
COHEN STUART, M. A., Physical Chemistry and Colloid Chemistry
CROUS, P. W., Evolutionary Phytopathology
DENNY, P., Aquatic Ecology
DICKE, M., Entomology
DONS, H. J. M., Entrepreneurship in Life Sciences
ELFRING, T., Innovative Entrepreneurship
EMONS, A. M. C., Plant Cell Biology
FEDDES, R. A., Soil Physics, Ecohydrology and Groundwater Management
FLEER, G. J., Physical and Colloid Chemistry
FOLMER, H., General Economics
FOLSTAR, P., Knowledge Management of Innovation Processes in Food Production
FRERKS, G. E., Disaster Management
FREWER, L. J., Food Safety and Consumer Behaviour
GIJZEN, H. J., Environmental Biotechnology
GILLER, K. E., Plant Production Systems
GOEWIE, E. A., Social Aspects of Biological Farming
GOLDBACH, R. W., Virology
GORRIS, L. G. M., Food Safety Microbiology
GOVERDE, H. J. M., Political Science in Agriculture and Environment
GRASMAN, J., Mathematical and Statistical Methods
GROENEN, M. A. M., Animal Breeding and Genetics
HAMER, R. J., Technology of Cereal Proteins
HARTOG, L. A. DEN, Developments in Animal Production
HEIJMAN, W. J. M., Rural Economics, Spatial Aspects of Rural Devt and Transformation
HEYTING, C., Molecular Cell Genetics
HIDDINK, G. J., Nutritional Extension by Intermediary
HOEKSTRA, R. F., Genetics, Populations and Quantitative Genetics
HOLTSLAG, B., Meteorology and Air Quality
HOOG, C. DE, Sociology of the Family
HOWARD-BORJAS, P. L., Gender Studies in Agriculture

HUIRNE, R. B. M., Economics of Animal Health and Food Safety
JACOBSEN, E., Plant Breeding
JONGEN, W. M. F., Product Design and Quality Management
KATAN, M. B., Nutrition and Epidemiology
KEMP, B., Adaptation Physiology
KOK, F. J., Nutrition and Health
KOOIJ, P., Agricultural History
KOORNNEEF, M., Genetics
KORTHALS, H. J. J. A. A., Applied Philosophy
KROEZE, J. H. A., Psychological and Sensorial Aspects of Food and Nutrition
KROMHOUT, D., Public Health Research
KROPFF, M. J., Crop and Weed Ecology
LANKVELD, J. M. G., Dairy Science
LEEMANS, R., Analysis of Environmental Systems
LEENTVAAR, J., Integrated Water Management
LEEUWIS, C., Communication and Innovation Studies
LEIJNSE, A., Groundwater Quality
LENGKEEK, J., Socio-Spatial Analysis of Land Use (Recreation and Tourism)
LEUNISSEN, J. A. M., Bio-informatics
METZ, J. H. M., Technical Design of Farm Systems in Animal Husbandry
MILITZ, H., Wood Science
MOHREN, G. M. J., Forest Ecology and Forest Management Group
MOL, A. P. J., Environmental Policy
MULDER, B. M., Theoretical Cell Physics
MULDER, M., Agricultural Education
MÜLLER, J., Farm Technology
MÜLLER, M., Nutrition, Metabolism and Genomics
NIEHOF, A., Sociology of Consumers and Households
OENEMA, O., Management of Nutrient Fluxes and Soil Fertility
OMTA, S. W. F., Management Studies
OPDAM, P. F. M., Landscape Ecology, Spatial Population Ecology
OSKAM, A. J., Agricultural Economics and Rural Policy
OUDE LANSINK, A. G. J. M., Business Economics
PENNINGS, J. M. E., Future Markets
PERDOK, U. D., Soil Technology
PRINS, H. H. T., Resource Ecology
RAATS, P. A. C., Continuum Mechanics
RABBINGE, R., Sustainable Devt and System Innovation
RICHARDS, P., Technology and Agrarian Devt
RIETJENS, I. M. C. M., Toxicology
RULKENS, W. H., Environmental Technology
SANDERS, J. P. M., Valorisation of Plant Production Chains
SAVELKOUL, H. F. J., Cell Biology and Immunology
SCHAAFSMA, G. J., Nutrition and Food
SCHAEPMAN, M. E., Geo-information Science, Remote Sensing
SCHANZ, H., Forest Policy and Forest Management
SCHEFFER, J. J. C., Medicinal and Aromatic Plant Science
SCHEFFER, M., Aquatic Ecology and Water Quality
SCHIPPERS, J. C., Water Supply Technology (IHE)
SCHOUTEN, M. G. C., Ecology of Nature Conservation
SCHULTZ, E., Land and Water Devt (IHE)
SCHUURMAN, E., Reformational Philosophy
SKIDMORE, A. K., Vegetation and Agricultural Land Use Survey
SLANINA, J., Measuring Methods in Atmospheric Research
SMIT, G., Molecular Flavour Science
SMITS, M. A., Animal Breeding and Genetics
SNOO, G. R. DE, Agri-Environment Schemes
SOSEF, M., Biosystematics
SPIERTZ, J. H. J., Crop Ecology, Nutrient and Metabolic Flows

SPRUIJT, B. M., Ethology and Animal Welfare
STAM, P., Plant Breeding, Selection Methods and Sustainable Resistance
STAMS, A. J. M., Microbiology
STEIN, A., Spatial Statistics
STIEKEMA, W. J., Genome Informatics
STROOSNIJDER, L., Erosion and Soil and Water Conservation
STRUIK, P. C., Crop Physiology
SUDHÖLTER, E. J. R., Organic Chemistry
SYKORA, K. V., Ecological Organisation and Management of Infrastructure
TAMMINGA, S., Animal Nutrition, Ruminants
TERPSTRA, M. J., Consumer Technology and Product Use
TRAMPER, J., Bioprocess Engineering
TROCH, P. A., Hydrology and Quantitative Water Management
VAN ARENDONK, J. A. M, Animal Genetics and Breeding
VAN BOEKEL, M. A. J. S., Product Design and Quality Management
VAN BLADEREN, P. J., Toxico-Kinetics and Biotransformation
VAN BREEMEN, N., Soil Formation and Ecopedology
VAN DEN BERG, J. A., Genomics
VAN DEN BRINK, A., Policy and Management in Land Use Planning
VAN DEN BRUGGEN, A. H. C., Biological Farming Systems
VAN DER HEIDE, D., Human and Animal Physiology
VAN DER KOOIJ, D., Environmental Microbiology, Drinking Water Supply
VAN LENTEREN, J. C., Entomology
VAN DER LINDEN, E., Food Physics
VAN DER MAESEN, L. J. G., Plant Taxonomy and Geography
VAN DER MEULEN, B. M. J., Law and Governance
VAN DER MUISWINKEL, W. B., Cell Biology and Immunology
VAN DER PLAS, L. H. W., Plant Physiology
VAN DER PLOEG, J. D., Rural Sociology
VAN DER PUTTEN, W. H., Functional Biodiversity
VAN DER VALK, A. J. J., Land Use Planning
VAN DER ZEE, S. E. A. T. M., Soil Chemistry and Chemical Soil Quality
VAN DER ZIJPP, A. J., Animal Production Systems
VAN DIJK, G., Theory and Practice of Agricultural Cooperative Organizations
VAN IERLAND, E. C., Environmental Economics and Natural Resources
VAN KOOTEN, O., Horticultural Production Chains
VAN LEEUWEN, J. L., Experimental Zoology
VAN OOYEN, A. J. J., Genetics in Food Technology
VAN RIEMSDIJK, W. H., Soil Chemistry and Chemical Soil Quality
VAN STAVEREN, W. A., Nutrition and Gerontology
VAN STRATEN, G., Systems and Control
VAN TRIJP, J. C. M., Marketing and Consumer Behaviour
VAN VIERSSEN, W., Aquatic Ecology
VAN WAGENBERG, A. F., Facility Management
VAN WOERKUM, C. M. J., Communication Management
VEER, P. VAN T, Human Nutrition and Epidemiology
VELDKAMP, A., Soil and Land Evaluation
VERRETH, J. A. J., Fish Culture and Fisheries
VERSTEGEN, M. W. A., Animal Nutrition, Monogastrics
VERVLOET, J. A. J., Historical Geography of Landscaping in the Netherlands
VET, L. E. M., Evolutionary Ecology
VINCENT, L. F., Irrigation and Water Engineering
VISSER, L. E., Rural Development Sociology
VISSER, R. G. F., Plant Breeding
VLAK, J. M., Virology

VORAGEN, A. G. J., Food Chemistry
VOS, W. M. DE, Microbiology
VRIES, S. C. DE, Biochemistry
WIT, P. J. G. M. DE, Phytopathology, Plant-Pathogen Interactions
ZACHARIASSE, L. C., Strategic Economics in Agribusiness
ZWIETERING, M. H., Food Microbiology

Institutes of University Standing

ABC HOGESCHOOL

POB 8118, 3301 CC Dordrecht
Telephone: (78) 6186662
E-mail: info@abc-opleidingen.nl
Internet: www.abc-opleidingen.nl; attached to ABC Opleidingen

ACADEMIE VERLOSKUNDE MAASTRICHT
(University of Midwifery Education and Studies Maastricht)

POB 1256, 6201 BG Maastricht
Universiteitssingel 60, 6229 ER Maastricht
Telephone: (43) 3885410
E-mail: info@av-m.nl
Internet: www.av-m.nl
Founded 1913
Man. Dir: R. W. A. A. VAN CRIMPEN
Sec.: S. NORDHAUSEN

ACADEMIE VOOR OVERHEIDSJURISTEN
(Academy for Government Lawyers)

Lange Voorhout 62, 2514 EH The Hague
Telephone: (70) 3129850
E-mail: academie@acjur.nl
Internet: www.academievooroverheidsjuristen.nl
Founded 2009
Chair.: R. J. HOEKSTRA
Dean: Drs PETER VAN LOCHEM

ACADEMIE VOOR WETGEVING
(Academy for Legislation)

Lange Voorhout 62, 2514 EH The Hague
Telephone: (70) 3129830
E-mail: academie@acwet.nl
Internet: www.academievoorwetgeving.nl
Founded 2001
Chair.: R. J. HOEKSTRA
Dean: Drs PETER VAN LOCHEM

AMSTERDAM SCHOOL OF REAL ESTATE

POB 140, 1000 AC Amsterdam
Huys Azië, Jollemanhof 5, 1019 GW Amsterdam
Telephone: (20) 6681129
E-mail: info@asre.nl
Internet: www.asre.nl
Founded 1987
Chair.: Ir J. D. DOETS
Dir and Sec of the Board: Drs L. B. UITTENBOGAARD

BUSINESS SCHOOL NETHERLANDS

POB 709, 4116 ZJ Buren
De Raadskamer, Herenstraat 25, 4116 BK Buren
Telephone: (344) 579030
E-mail: international@bsn.eu
Internet: www.bsn.eu

Founded 1988
Dean: FRANCIS BLUM

BUSINESS SCHOOL NOTENBOOM— INSTITUTE FOR BUSINESS, HOTEL AND LEISURE MANAGEMENT

POB 307, 5600 AH Eindhoven
Telephone: (40) 2520620
E-mail: hogeschool@notenboom.nl
Internet: www.notenboom.nl
Brs in Hilversum, Maastricht
Man.: JAN THEO MELLEMA
Number of teachers: 120

CHRISTELIJKE AGRARISCHE HOGESCHOOL DRONTEN

De Drieslag 1, 8251 JZ Dronten
Telephone: (321) 386100
E-mail: info@cah.nl
Internet: www.cah.nl
Br. in Almere
Dir: Ir W. VAN DE WEG
Exec. Sec.: DAALMEIJER VAN VUUREN

CHRISTELIJKE HOGESCHOOL EDE

POB 80, 6710 BB Ede
Oude Kerkweg 100, 6717 JS Ede
Telephone: (318) 696300
E-mail: info@che.nl
Internet: www.che.nl
Founded 1950, present status 1994, current name adopted 1997
State control
Chair. of Supervisory Board: R. C. ROBBERTSEN
Head: Dr C. P. (KEES) BOELE
Number of teachers: 400
Number of students: 4,000

CHRISTELIJKE HOGESCHOOL WINDESHEIM

POB 10090, 8000 GB Zwolle
Campus 2–6, 8017 CA Zwolle
Telephone: (88) 4699777
E-mail: info@windesheim.nl
Internet: www.windesheim.nl
State control
Chair.: Prof. Dr A. W. C. A. CORNELISSEN
Sec.: Drs W. A. HOBBELEN
Number of teachers: 1,700
Number of students: 20,000

DRIESTAR HOGESCHOOL
(University for Teacher Education)

POB 368, 2800 AJ Gouda
Burg. Jamessingel 2, 2803 PD Gouda
Telephone: (182) 540333
E-mail: internationaloffice@driestar-educatief.nl
Internet: www.driestar-hogeschool.nl
Founded 1944, present status 2005; attached to Driestar Educatief
Chair.: Drs L. N. (RENS) ROTTIER
Number of teachers: 275
Number of students: 1,400

EUROPORT BUSINESS SCHOOL

POB 21510, 3001 AM Rotterdam
Complex Weenahof, Schaatsbaan 61–91, Rotterdam
Telephone: (10) 2012320
E-mail: info@epbs.nl
Internet: www.epbs.nl
Chair.: JELLE MARCHAND

FACULTEIT KATHOLIEKE THEOLOGIE TE UTRECHT (School of Catholic Theology, Tilburg University)

POB 80101, 3508 TC Utrecht
Heidelberglaan 2, 3584 TC Utrecht
Telephone: (13) 4663800
E-mail: bureaufkt@uvt.nl
Internet: www.tilburguniversity.edu/nl/over-tilburg-university/schools/theologie

Founded 2007 by merger of Catholic Theological Univ. in Utrecht and Tilburg Faculty of Theology; attached to Tilburg Univ.
Academic year: September to September
Chair. of the Board: H. M. C. M. VAN OORSCHOT
Dean: Prof. Dr. A. J. DENAUX
Vice-Dean for Education: Dr. H. J. M. SCHOOT
Vice-Dean for Research: Prof. Dr P. H. A. I. JONKERS
Registrar: Drs G. A. VAN DER VELDEN-WESTERVELT

Number of teachers: 45
Number of students: 140

PROFESSORS

BEENTJES, P. C., Old Testament
FRISHMAN, J., Rabbinic Literature and Judaism
HELLEMANS, G. A. F., Social Sciences
JONKERS, P. H. A. I., Philosophy and History of Philosophy
MENKEN, M. J. J., New Testament
MÜLLER, D., Church History
POORTHUIS, M. J. H. M., Inter-Religious Dialogue
RIKHOF, H. W. M., Systematic Theology and History of Theology
ROUWHORST, G. A. M., History of Liturgy
SAROT, M., Fundamental Theology
VAN GEEST:, P. C., Church History and History of Theology
VOSMAN, F. J. H., Moral Theology
WISSINK, J. B. M., Practical Theology

FEDERATIE BELASTINGACADEMIE BV

Brenkmanweg 6, 4105 DH Culemborg
Telephone: (345) 547024
E-mail: fba@rb.nl
Internet: www.fbacademie.nl

FONTYS BESTUURSACADEMIE— INSTITUUT VOOR BESTUURLIJKE INNOVATIE

POB 90903, 5000 GD Tilburg
Professor Gimbrerelaan 16, 5037 EK Tilburg
Telephone: (13) 4651351
E-mail: bestuursacademie@fontys.nl
Internet: www.bazn.nl

Founded 2002 as BAZN de bestuursacademie, present name and status 2011
Br. in Amsterdam
Dir: PIETER BON

GEREFORMEERDE HOGESCHOOL

POB 10030, 8000 GA Zwolle
Grasdorpstraat 2, 8012 EN Zwolle
Telephone: (38) 4255542
E-mail: info@gh-gpc.nl
Internet: www.gh.nl

Chair.: A. VAN DER VEER
Vice-Chair.: B. WESSELING
Sec.: D. DE JONGE

Number of teachers: 125
Number of students: 1,450

GERRIT RIETVELD ACADEMIE

Frederik Roeskestraat 96, 1076 ED Amsterdam
Telephone: (20) 5711600
E-mail: secretariaatcvb@grac.nl
Internet: www.gerritrietveldacademie.nl

Founded 1924, present status 1968, current name adopted 1965
Private control
Chair.: TIJMEN VAN GROOTHEEST
Dir for Education: BEN ZEGERS
Dir for Operations: ANNELIES VAN EENNENNAAM
Dir for Sandberg Institute: JURGEN BEY
Sec.: STEVEN JONGEJAN
Dean of Fine Arts and Design: BEN ZEGERS
Library of 8,000 vols
Number of students: 1,000

HANZEHOGESCHOOL GRONINGEN, UNIVERSITY OF APPLIED SCIENCES (Hanze University Groningen, University of Applied Sciences)

POB 30030, 9700 RM Groningen
Zernikeplein 7, 9747 AS Groningen
Telephone: (50) 5955555
E-mail: info@org.hanze.nl
Internet: www.hanze.nl

Founded 1798, present status 1993
Brs in offices in Amsterdam, Assen, Leeuwarden; 21 attached institutes
Chair.: Drs H. J. PIJLMAN

Number of teachers: 24,000
Number of students: 2,700

HBO NEDERLAND

Kortestraat 1, 6811 EN Arnhem
Telephone: (26) 3516379
E-mail: info@hbonederland.com
Internet: www.hbonederland.com

Founded 1987
Private control
Language of instruction: Dutch
Number of students: 3,000

HOGESCHOOL DIRKSEN ARNHEM

POB 3090, 6802 DB Amsterdam
Parkstraat 27, 6828 JC Arnhem
Telephone: (26) 3544644
E-mail: info@dirksen.nl
Internet: www.dirksen.nl

HOGESCHOOL E3 ICT

Oranjeplein 97, 6224 KV Maastricht
Telephone: (43) 3638333
E-mail: info@e3.nl
Internet: www.e3.nl
Private control
Dir: MARCEL SNEL

HOGESCHOOL EDITH STEIN— ONDERWIJSCENTRUM TWENTE

POB 568, 7550 AN Hengelo
M.A. de Ruyterstraat 3, 7556 CW Hengelo
Telephone: (74) 8516100
E-mail: info@edith.nl
Internet: www.edith.nl

Founded 1984, by merger of Pedagogische Academie Hoogveld and KLOS (Kleuter-Leidster Opleidingsschool), current name adopted 1986
Private control
Language of instruction: Dutch
Dir: MANON KETZ
Chair.: HENK MULDERS
Number of teachers: 110

Number of students: 1,100

HOGESCHOOL HAS DEN BOSCH

POB 90108, 5223 DE 's-Hertogenbosch
Onderwijsboulevard 221, 5223 DE 's-Hertogenbosch
Telephone: (73) 6923600
E-mail: has@has.nl
Internet: www.hasdenbosch.nl
Languages of instruction: Dutch, English
Chair.: STEF VALK (acting)
Number of teachers: 300
Number of students: 1,700
Publication: HAS Beats Hogeschoolgeluiden (10 a year)

HOGESCHOOL INHOLLAND

POB 93043, 2509 AA The Hague
Theresiastraat 8, 2593 AN The Hague
Telephone: (70) 3120100
E-mail: info@inholland.nl
Internet: www.inholland.nl
Private control
Chair.: D. TERPSTRA
Pres.: GEERT DALES
Number of teachers: 2,900
Number of students: 37,500

HOGESCHOOL IPABO

POB 90506, 1006 BM Amsterdam
Jan Tooropstraat 136, 1061 AD Amsterdam
Telephone: (20) 6137079
E-mail: receptie@hs-ipabo.edu
Internet: www.hs-ipabo.edu
Private control
Language of instruction: Dutch
Chair.: Dr Ing. JAN W. M. A. HOUBEN
Number of teachers: 120
Number of students: 1,000

HOGESCHOOL ISBW

POB 266, 5300 AG Zaltbommel
E-mail: info@isbw.nl
Internet: www.isbw.nl
Founded 1931
Private control
Language of instruction: Dutch

HOGESCHOOL IVA DRIEBERGEN

POB 33, 3970 AA Driebergen
Hogesteeg 2A, 3972 JT Driebergen
Telephone: (343) 512780
E-mail: info@iva-driebergen.nl
Internet: www.iva-driebergen.nl
Founded 1930
Private control
Publication: LIVA Post

HOGESCHOOL NOVI

POB 2068, 3500 GB Utrecht
Kobaltweg 44, 3542 CE Utrecht
Telephone: (30) 7115615
E-mail: info@novi.nl
Internet: www.novi.nl
Founded 1958, present status 1997
Dir: KEES LOUWMAN

HOGESCHOOL NTI

POB 2222, 2301 CE Leiden
Schipholweg 101, 2301 XC Leiden
Telephone: (71) 7501040
E-mail: vragen@nti.nl
Internet: www.nti.nl
Founded 1997, present status 2000

Head: MARIANNE VAN WESTRIENEN
Number of teachers: 125
Number of students: 70,000

HOGESCHOOL PBNA

POB 68, 3330 AB Zwijndrecht
H.A. Lorentzstraat 1A, 3331 EE Zwijndrecht
Telephone: (78) 6253889
E-mail: examens@pbna.com
Internet: www.pbna.com
Founded 1912, present status 1999
Private control
Languages of instruction: Dutch, English, Polish, Portugese
Number of students: 50,000

HOGESCHOOL THIM VAN DER LAAN

Newtonbaan 6, 3439 NK Nieuwegein
Telephone: (30) 2886670
E-mail: info@thimvanderlaan.nl
Internet: www.thim.nl
Founded 1974, as Thim van der Laan Hogeschool voor Fysiotherapie
Private control
Languages of instruction: Dutch, German
Dir of Education Affairs: R. M. VAN ECK
Number of students: 650

HOGESCHOOL TIO

Oudenoord 2, 3513 ER Utrecht
Telephone: (30) 6668836
E-mail: internationaloffice@tio.nl
Internet: www.tio.nl
Private control
Languages of instruction: Dutch, English
Dir: Ir M. W. DÜTHLER
Number of teachers: 250

HOGESCHOOL UTRECHT (HU)

Oudenoord 330, 3513 EX Utrecht
Telephone: (88) 4818181
E-mail: info@hu.nl
Internet: www.hu.nl
Founded 1995, current name adopted 2005
Private control
Chair.: GERI BONHOF
Number of teachers: 3,500
Number of students: 30,000
Publication: *magazine van Hogeschool Utrecht*

HOGESCHOOL VAN AMSTERDAM

POB 1025, 1000 BA Amsterdam
Spui, 21 1021 WX Amsterdam
Telephone: (20) 5953200
E-mail: voorzittercvb@uva.nl
Internet: www.hva.nl
Chair.: Dr LOUISE GUNNING-SCHEPERS
Exec. Sec.: J. M. KERSBERGEN
Sec.: ARJAN P. TROMMEL
Number of teachers: 3,101
Number of students: 41,770

HOGESCHOOL VAN ARNHEM EN NIJMEGEN

POB 5375, 6802 EJ Arnhem
Ruitenberglaan 31, 6826 CC Arnhem
Telephone: (26) 3691555
E-mail: info@han.nl
Internet: www.han.nl
Founded 1996, by merger of 3 instns
Chair.: Drs RON BORMANS
Number of teachers: 2,900
Number of students: 28,000

HOGESCHOOL VAN HALL LARENSTEIN
(Van Hall Larenstein University of Applied Sciences)

POB 9001, 6880 GB Velp
Larensteinselaan 26A, 6882 CT Velp
Telephone: (58) 3695749
E-mail: info@vanhall-larenstein.nl
Internet: www.vanhall-larenstein.nl
Founded 2003; attached to Wageningen UR
Languages of instruction: English, Dutch
Campuses in Velp, Wageningen
Man. Dir: ELLEN MARKS
Man Dir: RIEN KOMEN
Dir of Education: HANS HARDUS
Dir of Education: GERRIT JEURING
Dir of Education: GEARTSJE OOSTERHOF
Dir of Education: HANS VAN HAEREN
Dir of Education: HANS VAN ROOIJEN
Dir of Education: JAN VAN DER VALK
Dir of Education: JOS WINTERMANS
Dir of Education: WENDY ZUIDEMA
Number of teachers: 450
Number of students: 4,500

HOGESCHOOL WEST-NEDERLAND VOOR VERTALER EN TOLK

Chr. Scholengemeenschap Zandvliet, Bezuidenhoutseweg, 40, 2594 AW The Hague
Internet: www.west-nederland.nl
Founded 1994
Gen. Man.: A. MINKMAN

HOGESCHOOL WITTENBORG

Laan van de Mensenrechten 500, 7331 VZ Apeldoorn
Telephone: (88) 6672688
E-mail: info@wittenborg.nl
Internet: www.wittenborg.nl
Founded 1987
State control
Language of instruction: English
Chair.: PETER BIRDSALL
Gen. Man.: KAREN PENNINGA
Number of teachers: 22
Number of students: 220

INHOLLAND SELECT STUDIES

POB 23145, 3001 KC Rotterdam
Posthumalaan 90, 3072 AG Rotterdam
Telephone: (10) 4399491
E-mail: selectstudies@inholland.nl
Internet: www.inholland.nl/select+studies

INSTITUUT VOOR PSYCHOSYNTHESE

Biltstraat 200, 3572 BS Utrecht
Telephone: (30) 2714634
E-mail: info@psychosynthese.nl
Internet: www.psychosynthese.nl
Founded 1985, present status 1999
Dir-Gen.: DIEDERIK VAN ROSSUM
Dean of Student Affairs: INGRID VAN BEEK-VELDKAMP

INTERCOLLEGE BUSINESS SCHOOL

Zeestraat 62, 2518 AC The Hague
Telephone: (70) 3451110
E-mail: denhaag@intercollege.nl
Internet: www.intercollege.nl
Founded 1979
Private control
Campuses in Amsterdam, Rotterdam, Utrecht

ITV HOGESCHOOL VOOR TOLKEN & VERTALEN
(ITV School of Interpretation and Translation)

POB 14007, 3508 SB Utrecht
Padualaan 97, 3508 SB Utrecht
Telephone: (30) 2730818
E-mail: admin@itv-hogeschool.nl
Internet: www.itv-h.nl
Founded 1983
Private control
College of translation; uses premises, facilities of Utrecht univ.
Dir: SJOKEAN OOSTERBAAN
Number of teachers: 70
Number of students: 750

LANDELIJK EXPERTISECENTRUM SOCIALE INTERVENTIE

c/o Utrecht Univ., FSW/ASW, POB 80140, 3508 TC Utrecht
Van Unnikgebouw, Heidelberglaan 2, 3584 CS Utrecht
Telephone: (30) 2534920
E-mail: nfo@lesi.nl
Internet: www.lesi.nl
Founded 2004; attached to Utrecht Univ.
Dir: Prof. Dr ROELOF HORTULANUS
Publication: *Tijdschrift voor Sociale Interventies*

MARKUS VERBEEK BUSINESS ACADEMY

POB 6546, 4802 HM Breda
Telephone: (76) 5499998
E-mail: info@mvba.nl
Internet: www.mvba.nl
Private control
Masters courses in business, management and finance
Dir: W. HAIR

MARKUS VERBEEK PRAEHEP

Paasheuvelweg 35, 1105 BG Amsterdam Zuidoost
Telephone: (20) 5677800
E-mail: amsterdam@mvp.nl
Internet: www.markusverbeek.nl
Founded 1896
Private control
Brs in Amsterdam, Rotterdam, Rijswijk, Zwolle, Eindhoven, Utrecht; provides Bachelors, Masters and training in finance-related courses

NHL HOGESCHOOL
(NHL University)

POB 1080, 8900 CB Leeuwarden
Rengerslaan 10, 8917 DD Leeuwarden
Telephone: (58) 2511888
E-mail: infocentrum@nhl.nl
Internet: www.nhl.nl
Private control
Language of instruction: Dutch
Academic year: September to September
Number of students: 10,500

NHTV INTERNATIONAAL HOGER ONDERWIJS BREDA
(NHTV Breda University of Applied Sciences)

POB 3917, 4800 DX Breda
Telephone: (76) 5332203
E-mail: communicatie@nhtv.nl
Internet: www.nhtv.nl

Founded 1966 as the Dutch Scientific Institute for Tourism

Private control

Specialist disciplines of games and media, hotel and facility, leisure, tourism, urban devt, logistics and mobility

Rector Magnificus: Prof. Dr JAAP LENGKEEK

Number of students: 7,000

PRO EDUCATION

POB 22799, 1100 DG Amsterdam

Atlas Complex, Gebouw Azië, Hoogoorddreef 5, 1101 BA Amsterdam

Telephone: (20) 5677999

E-mail: info@proeducation.nl

Internet: www.proeducation.nl

Founded 2002 by Univ. of Amsterdam; ind. in 2004

Private control

PROTESTANTSE THEOLOGISCHE UNIVERSITEIT
(Protestant Theological University)

POB 5021, 8260 GA Kampen

Koornmarkt 1, Kampen

Telephone: (38) 3371600

E-mail: bureau@mail.thuk.nl

Internet: www.thuk.nl

Founded 2007 by merger of Theological University Kampen (ThUK), Theological Research Institute (ThWI), Utrecht and Leiden, Evangelical Lutheran Seminary (ELS), Utrecht, Theological Seminary, Doorn; attached to Protestant Church in The Netherlands

Languages of instruction: Dutch, English

Academic year: September to August

Pres.: Dr HENK C. VAN DER SAR

Rector: Prof. Dr F. G. IMMINK

Dean of Students: Drs T. A. STRUIK

Head Librarian: J. W. PUTTENSTEIN

Library of 187,500 vols

Number of teachers: 30

Number of students: 172

Publications: *Documentatieblad voor de Geschiedenis van de Nederlandse zending en overzeese kerken* (2 a year, in Dutch), *Zeitschrift für Dialektische Theologie* (2 a year, in German)

PROFESSORS

DE LANGE, F., Ethics

HOLTROP, P. N., Missiology

HOUTMAN, C., Old Testament

JONKER, E. R., Pastoral Theology

KIRN, H.-M., Church History

KOFFEMAN, L. J., Church Polity

NEVEN, G. W., Dogmatics

ROUKEMA, R., New Testament

SAXION HOGESCHOLEN
(Saxion University of Applied Sciences)

POB 501, 7400 AM Deventer

Handelskade 75, 7417 DH Deventer

Telephone: (70) 603663

E-mail: info@saxion.nl

Internet: www.saxion.nl

Founded 1998 by merger of Hogeschool Enschede and Hogeschool IJselland

State control

Campuses in Deventer, Enschede and Apeldoorn

Chair.: WIM BOOMKAMP

Number of teachers: 1,200

Number of students: 22,000

Publication: *Sax* (11 a year, online, sax.nu)

SCHOEVERS

Papiermolen 10, 3994 DK Houten

Telephone: (30) 2808770

E-mail: info@schoevers.nl

Internet: www.schoevers.nl

Founded 1913

Dir: RIA VAN 'T KLOOSTER

SOD-OPLEIDINGEN

POB 544, 3440 AM Woerden

De Bleek 6, 3447 GV Woerden

Telephone: (348) 485151

E-mail: info@sod-opleidingen.nl

Internet: www.sod-opleidingen.nl

Private control

Languages of instruction: Dutch, English

Pres.: Drs J. C. M. COX

Sec.: R. DE NIEUWE

Dir: CASPER MOLMANS

STENDEN HOGESCHOOL

POB 1298, 8900 CG Leeuwarden

Rengerslaan 8, 8917 DD Leeuwarden

Telephone: (58) 2441441

E-mail: info@stenden.com

Internet: www.stenden.com

Founded 2008 by merger of Christelijke Hogeschool Nederland with Hogeschool Drenthe

Private control

Pres.: PIM BREEBAART

Number of students: 11,000

STICHTING OPLEIDINGEN MUSCULOSKELETALE THERAPIE
(Musculoskeletal Therapy Foundation Training)

POB 585, 3800 AN Amersfoort

Softwareweg 5, 3821 BN Amersfoort

Telephone: (33) 4560737

E-mail: info@somt.nl

Internet: www.somt.nl

Education, research and clinic; offers Masters in manual therapy, basin physiotherapy, sports physiotherapy, physiotherapy in geriatrics and ultrasound

Dir: WILY SMEETS

STOAS HOGESCHOOL

POB 245, 6710 BE Ede

Bovenbuurtweg 27, 6710 BE Ede

Telephone: (318) 675611

E-mail: info@stoashogeschool.nl

Internet: www.stoashogeschool.nl

Founded 1981

Number of teachers: 71

Number of students: 774

THEOLOGISCHE UNIVERSITEIT APELDOORN
(The Theological University of Apeldoorn)

Wilhelminapark 4, 7316 BT Apeldoorn

Telephone: (55) 5775700

E-mail: info@tua.nl

Internet: www.tua.nl

Founded 1894, current name adopted 1992

Pres.: Ir J. J. EBERWIJN

Rector: Prof. Dr G. C. DEN HERTOG

Vice-Rector: Prof. H. G. L. PEELS

Librarian: Prof. Dr N. VAN DER MIJDEN-GROENENDIJK

Library of 45,000 vols

Number of teachers: 11 (6 full-time, 10 part-time)

Number of students: 98 full-time

Publications: *Apeldoornse Studies* (2 a year), *Oikodomē* (4 a year), *TUA Conned* (3 a year)

THEOLOGISCHE UNIVERSITEIT VAN DE GEREFORMEERDE KERKEN
(Theological University of the Reformed Churches)

POB 5026, 8260 GA Kampen

Broederweg 15, 8261 GS Kampen

Telephone: (38) 4471710

E-mail: secretariaat@tukampen.nl

Internet: www.tukampen.nl

Founded 1854

Rector: Prof. Dr M. TE VELDE

Man. Dir: Drs J. DE JONG

Dir for Education: Prof. P. H. R. VAN HOUWELINGEN

Librarian: Drs G. D. HARMANNY

Library of 150,000 vols

Number of teachers: 16

Number of students: 130

PROFESSORS

DE BRUIJNE, A. L. TH., Ethics and Spirituality

DE RUIJTER, C. J., Pastoral Theology

KAMPHUIS, B., Dogmatics

KWAKKEL, G., Old Testament Exegesis

TE VELDE, M., Church History and Polity

VAN DER POL, F., Church History and History of Dogma

VAN HOUWELINGEN, P. H. R., New Testament Exegesis

TIASNIMBAS BUSINESS SCHOOL

POB 90153, 5000 LE Tilburg

Tias Bldg, Warandelaan 2, 5037 AB Tilburg

Telephone: (13) 4668600

E-mail: information@tiasnimbas.edu

Internet: www.tiasnimbas.edu

Founded 1982 as Tilburg Institute for Advanced Studies; attached to Tilburg Univ.

Br in Bonn, Eindhoven, Taipei, Utrecht

Private control

Chair.: Prof. Dr KEES KOEDIJK

Chair. of Supervisory Board: RICK HARWIG

Deputy Chair. of Supervisory Board: PHILIP EIJLANDER

Vice-Dean: Prof. Dr PHILIP JOOS

Vice-Dean: Prof. Dr DIRK BROUNEN

TRANSFERGROEP ROTTERDAM
(Transfer Group Rotterdam)

POB 420, 3000 AK Rotterdam

Hogeschool Rotterdam, locatie Museumpark, Burgemeester s'Jacobplein 1, 3015 CA Rotterdam

Telephone: (10) 7946800

E-mail: transfergroep@hro.nl

Internet: www.transfergroep.nl

Founded 1996; attached to Hogeschool Rotterdam

Private control

Undergraduate and postgraduate courses in business and management, coaching skills, health, education and training, welfare; specialist in organizational consulting and individual counselling programmes

UNIVERSITY COLLEGE UTRECHT

POB 80145, 3508 TC Utrecht

Campusplein 1, 3584 ED Utrecht

Telephone: (30) 2539900

E-mail: ucu.info@uu.nl

Internet: www.uu.nl/university/college

Founded 1997; attached to Utrecht Univ.

State control

Dean: ROB VAN DER VAART

Number of teachers: 165
Number of students: 723

WEBSTER UNIVERSITY LEIDEN

Boommarkt 1, 2311 EA Leiden

Telephone: (71) 5168000
E-mail: info@webster.nl
Internet: www.webster.nl

Founded 1983
Private control

Dir: Prof. Dr JEAN MARISSING

Library of 19,000 ebooks, 23,000 academic journals
Number of students: 400

Institutes of International Education

EUROPEAN INSTITUTE OF PUBLIC ADMINISTRATION

POB 1229, 6201 BE Maastricht

Telephone: (43) 3296222
E-mail: info@eipa.eu
Internet: www.eipa.eu

Founded 1981
Languages of instruction: English, French, German

Centres in Luxembourg, Barcelona; supported by mem. states of the EU and the Commission of the EU; personal and organizational devts and policy support in European policy-making and implementation, EU institutions and political integration, European public management, community policies and internal markets, legal systems of the EU

Chair.: HENNING CHRISTOPHERSEN
Dir-Gen.: Prof. Dr MARGA PRÖHL
Dir for Finance and Org.: WIM VAN HELDEN

Library of 30,000 vols, 350 periodicals; European documentation centre; depositing library of the Council of Europe
Number of teachers: 60
Number of students: 15,000

Publications: *Conference Proceedings*, *Current European Issues*

HOGESCHOOL ROTTERDAM
(Rotterdam University, University of Applied Sciences)

POB 25035, 3001 HA Rotterdam
Kralingse Zoom 91, 3063 ND Rotterdam

Telephone: (10) 7949494
E-mail: tudievoorlichting@hr.nl
Internet: www.hro.nl

Founded 1988, present status 2002
State control
Languages of instruction: English, Dutch
Academic year: September to July

Pres.: Drs J. A. C. F. TUYTEL
Asst Dir: MARJOLEIN BAKKER
Dir for Gen. and Admin. Affairs: HERMAN A. VEENEMA
Dir for Communications and External Relations: Drs J. E. (ANS) HUURMAN-VAN BUREN

Number of teachers: 3,000
Number of students: 28,500

Publication: *Profielen* (College Profiles Magazine)

INTERNATIONAL INSTITUTE OF SOCIAL STUDIES

POB 29776, 2502 LT The Hague
Kortenaerkade 12, 2518 AX The Hague

Telephone: (70) 4260460
E-mail: info@iss.nl

Internet: www.iss.nl

Founded 1952, present status 2009; attached to Erasmus Univ. Rotterdam
Language of instruction: English

Rector: Prof. LEO DE HAAN
Deputy Rector for Teaching: Dr JOS MOOIJ
Deputy Rector for Research: Prof. MOHAMED SALIH
Exec. Sec.: LINDA JOHNSON

Library of 100,000 vols, 400 print journals, 20,000 ejournals
Number of teachers: 60
Number of students: 300

Publication: *Development and Change* (5 a year)

PROFESSORS

ARTS, C. J. M., States, Societies and World Development
BEDI, A. S., Economics of Sustainable Development
BERGEIJK, P. A. G. VAN, Economics of Sustainable Development
DIJK, M. P. VAN, Human Resources and Local Development
DOORNBOS, M. R., States, Societies and World Development
FOWLER, A. F., States, Societies and World Development
GASPER, D., States, Societies and World Development
GRIMM, M., Economics of Sustainable Development
HAAR, G. TER, States, Societies and World Development
HELMSING, A. H. J., Human Resources and Local Development
HOEVEN, R. E. VAN DER, Human Resources and Local Development
HOUT, W., States, Societies and World Development
KAY, C., Rural Development, Environment and Population Studies
KNORRINGA, P., Human Resources and Local Development
MURSHED, S. M., Economics of Sustainable Development
PRONK, J. P., Economics of Sustainable Development
SAITH, A., Rural Development, Environment and Population Studies
SALIH, M. A. R. M., States, Societies and World Development
SPOOR, M. N., Rural Development, Environment and Population Studies
STAVEREN, I. P. VAN, Human Resources and Local Development
VOS, R. P., Economics of Sustainable Development
WHITE, B., Rural Sociology

MAASTRICHT SCHOOL OF MANAGEMENT (MSM)

POB 1203, 6201 BE Maastricht
Endepolsdomein 150, 6229 EP Maastricht

Telephone: (43) 3870808
E-mail: info@msm.nl
Internet: www.msm.nl

Founded 1952
Private control
Language of instruction: English
Academic year: September to September

Chair. of the Board: Prof. P. R. H. M. VAN DER LINDEN
Vice-Chair. of the Board: F. J. M. TUMMERS
Dir and Dean: Prof. Dr W. NAUDE

Library of 10,000 vols
Number of teachers: 140 (40 resident, 100 visiting)
Number of students: 2,500

Publication: *MSM Research Papers: Management & Development* (2 a year)

PROFESSORS

ANKOLEKAR, SURESH, e-Business
ENGEL, PAUL G. H., Public Policy and Innovations
HELING, GEERT W. J., Organizational Behaviour
NAUDÉ, WIM A., Development Economics and Entrepreneurship
SANDER, HARALD, Economics
VAN DIJK, MEINE PIETER, Entrepreneurship in Emerging Countries
VAN MOURIK, AAD, Economics

TRANSNATIONALE UNIVERSITEIT LIMBURG

c/o Maastricht Univ., POB 616, 6200 MD Maastricht

Telephone: (43) 3882222
E-mail: info@maastrichtuniversity.nl
Internet: www.tul.edu

Founded 2001

UNESCO–IHE, INSTITUTE FOR WATER EDUCATION

POB 3015, 2601 DA Delft
Westvest 7, 2611 AX Delft

Telephone: (15) 2151715
E-mail: info@unesco-ihe.org
Internet: www.unesco-ihe.org

Founded 1957 as IHE, present name and status 2003
State control
Language of instruction: English
Academic year: October to September

Postgraduate and PhD programmes; short courses; online courses in environmental science and technology, environmental planning and management, limnology and wetland ecosystems, water quality management, sanitary engineering, urban water engineering and management, water supply engineering, water quality management, water services management, water resources management, water conflict management, hydrology and water resources, hydraulic engineering and river basin devt, hydraulic engineering—coastal engineering and port devt, hydraulic engineering—land and water devt, hydroinformatics—modelling and information systems for water management

Rector: Prof. ANDRÁS SZÖLLÖSI-NAGY
Vice-Rector for Academic Affairs: Prof. STEFAN UHLENBROOK

Library of 25,000 vols
Number of teachers: 100
Number of students: 500

Schools of Art, Architecture and Music

Academie van Bouwkunst (Academy of Architecture): Waterlooplein 211, 1011 PG Amsterdam; tel. (20) 5318218; e-mail info@bwk.ahk.nl; internet www.ahk.nl/bouwkunst; f. 1908, present status 1987; attached to Amsterdam School of the Arts; offers courses in architecture, urban design and landscape architecture; library: 10,000 vols; 150 teachers; 200 students; Dir Drs AART OXENAAR.

Academie van Bouwkunst Maastricht (Maastricht Academy of Architecture): Brusselsestraat 75, 6211 PC Maastricht; tel. (43) 3219645; e-mail abm@hszuyd.nl; internet www.academievanbouwkunst.com; f. 1947, present status 2002; attached to Zuyd Univ.; offers Masters degree in architecture and related fields; 43 teachers; 55 students; Dir NIEK BISSCHEROUX.

Academie voor Architectuur en Stedebouw (School of Architecture and Urban Design): POB 90907, 5000 GJ Tilburg; Bisschop Zwijsenstraat 5, 5038 VA Tilburg; tel. (877) 874922; e-mail aas@fontys.nl; internet www .fontyshogeschoolvoordekunsten.nl/architectuur_stedenbouw.aspx; f. 1936; attached to Fontys Univ. of Arts; architecture and town planning/design; library: 8,000 vols; 50 teachers; 80 students; Dir MARC K. T. M. GLAUDEMANS.

AKV – St Joost Breda: POB 90116, 4800 RA Breda; Beukenlaan 1, 4834 CR Breda; tel. (76) 5250302; e-mail info.akvstjoost@avans .nl; internet www.akvstjoost.nl; f. 1945; attached to Avans Univ.; br. in 's-Hertogenbosch; offers Bachelors and Masters courses in fine art, design; publ. *Leporello*.

Amsterdamse Hogeschool voor de Kunsten (Amsterdam School of the Arts): POB 15079, 1001 MB Amsterdam; Jodenbreestraat 3, Amsterdam; tel. (20) 5277710; e-mail info@ahk.nl; internet www.ahk.nl; f. 1987 by merger of Academy of Fine Art in Education, Amsterdam Academy of Architecture, Conservatorium van Amsterdam, Netherlands Film and Television Academy, Reinwardt Academy, Theatre School; offers Bachelors and Masters degrees in architecture, dance, film and television, fine art and design, music, theatre, museum studies; Chair. OLCHERT BROUWER; 750 teachers; 3,000 students.

ArtEZ Academie voor Art & Design (ArtEZ Academy of Art & Design): POB 1440, 7500 BK Enschede; Campus Univ. of Twente, Hallenweg 5, 7522 NH Enschede; tel. (53) 4824400; e-mail artdesign .enschede@artez.nl; internet www.artez.nl; f. 1949; attached to ArtEZ Institute of the Arts; fine arts, design, fashion, architecture; library: 8,000 vols; Chair. DINGEMAN KUILMAN; Dir S. HUISMANS.

ArtEZ Hogeschool voor de Kunsten (ArtEZ Institute of the Arts): POB 49, 6812 CE Arnhem; Onderlangs 9, 6812 CE Arnhem; tel. (26) 3535600; e-mail communicatie@artez.nl; internet www.artez .nl; f. 2002; architecture, design, dance, drama, fine arts, fashion, music; institutes in Arnhem, Enschede, Zwolle; Chair. DINGEMAN KUILMAN; Sec. LAURIEN TIMMERMANS; 600 teachers (420 f.t.e.); 3,059 students.

Avans Hogeschool (Avans University of Applied Sciences): POB 732, 5201 AS 's-Hertogenbosch; Onderwijsboulevard 215, 5223 DE 's-Hertogenbosch; tel. (73) 6295295; e-mail internationaloffice@avans .nl; internet www.studyatavans.com; f. 2004 by merger of Hogeschool Brabant and Hogeschool 's-Hertogenbosch; offers courses in painting, sculpture, graphic art, ceramics, environmental art, illustration, graphic design; brs in Breda, Tilburg; 19 attached schools, 4 support units, 1 learning and innovation centre; library: 10,000 vols; 2,000 teachers; 23,000 students; Chair. Drs PAUL L. A. RÜPP; Vice-Chair. Drs FRENCH J. M. VAN KALMTHOUT.

Codarts, Hogeschool voor de Kunsten (Codarts University for the Arts): Kruisplein 26, 3012 CC Rotterdam; tel. (10) 2171100; e-mail codarts@codarts.nl; internet www .codarts.nl; consists of the Rotterdams' Conservatorium and the Rotterdamse Dansacademie; library: 15,000 copies of sheet music; 300 teachers; 1,100 students; Pres. CAREL VAN EYKELENBURG; Dir JIKKIE VAN DER GIESSEN; publ. *Codarts Magazine* (4 a year).

Conservatorium Maastricht (Hogeschool Zuyd): Bonnefantenstraat 15, 6211 KL Maastricht; tel. (43) 3466680; e-mail info .conservatorium@hszuyd.nl; internet www .hszuyd.nl; f. 1956; library: 30,000 vols; 110 teachers; 450 students; Dir HARRY CUSTERS (acting)..

Attached Institutes:

> **Conservatorium Gent:** Hoogpoort 64, 9000 Ghent, Belgium; Dir JAN RISPENS.

> **Fontys Conservatorium:** Postbus 90907, 5000 GJ Tilburg; Dir JAN WIRKEN.

Conservatorium van Amsterdam: POB 78022, 1070 LP Amsterdam; Oosterdokskade 151, 1011 DL Amsterdam; tel. (20) 5277550; e-mail cva-info@ahk.nl; internet www.ahk .nl/conservatorium; f. 1884, present bldg 2008; attached to Amsterdam School of the Arts; offers courses in classical music, early music, jazz, opera, latin and popular music; library: 30,000 vols; 200 teachers; 800 students; Dir HANS VAN BEERS; Vice-Dir MICHEL DISPA; Vice-Dir RUUD VAN DIJK; publ. *Gebouwd voor Muziek*.

Design Academy Eindhoven: POB 2125, 5600 CC Eindhoven; Emmasingel 14, 3rd Fl., 5611 AZ Eindhoven; tel. (40) 2393939; e-mail info@designacademy.nl; internet www .designacademy.nl; f. 1950; offers Bachelors and Masters courses in contextual design, information design, social design; 200 teachers; 700 students; Chair. ANNE MIEKE EGGENKAMP.

Hogeschool Dansacademie Lucia Marthas (Dance Academy Lucia Marthas): Rustenburgerstraat 436, 1072 HK Amsterdam; tel. (20) 6761370; e-mail info@ luciamarthas.nl; internet www.luciamarthas .nl; f. 1983; offers accredited HBO (higher vocational education) degrees and MBO degrees (intermediate vocational education); Man. C. VAN DER LOOP-MEESTERMAN; Man. LUCIA MARTHAS; Man. RUUD VAN DER KOOIJ.

Hogeschool der Kunsten (University of the Arts): Juliana van Stolberglaan 1, 2595 CA The Hague; tel. (70) 3151515; e-mail info@koncon.nl; internet www.koncon.nl; f. 1826 by merger of Royal Conservatory and Royal Acad. of Fine Arts 1990, current name adopted 2010; faculties of fine arts and design, music and dance; interfaculty of art and science; school for young talent; library: 50,000 vols; 265 teachers; 1,023 students; Chair. JACK VERDUYN LUNEL; Dir HENK VAN DER MEULEN.

Hogeschool voor de Kunsten Utrecht (Utrecht School of the Arts): POB 1520, 3500 BM Utrecht; Lange Viestraat 2B, Utrecht; tel. (30) 2349440; e-mail info@ssc .hku.nl; internet www.hku.nl; f. 1987 by merger of Utrechts Conservatorium, Academie voor Beeldende Kunsten Utrecht and Academie voor Expressie en door Woord en Gebaar; faculties of art and economics; art, media and technology; music; theatre; visual arts and design; interfaculty of art and economics; library: 36,000 vols; 350 teachers; 3,800 students; Chair. of Supervisory Board Drs P. C. KLAVER; Deputy Chair. of Supervisory Board Drs W. KARDUX; Pres. AD WISMAN; Dir CÉCILE DE VOS; publ. *Mahkuzine* (2 a year).

IHS—Institute for Housing and Urban Development Studies: Burgemeester Oudlaan 50, Bldg T, 14th Fl., 3062 PA Rotterdam; POB 1935, 3000 BX Rotterdam; tel. (10) 4089825; e-mail admission@ihs.nl; internet www.ihs.nl; f. 1948, current name adopted 1991, present status 2003; attached to Erasmus Univ.; library: 15,000 vols; 53 teachers; 120 students; Dir KEES VAN ROOIJEN; Deputy Dir JAN FRANSEN.

Rijksakademie van Beeldende Kunsten (State Academy of Fine Arts): Sarphatistraat 470, 1018 GW Amsterdam; tel. (20) 5270300; e-mail info@rijksakademie.nl; internet www .rijksakademie.nl; f. 1870, present location 1992, present status 1999; 1 and 2 year courses; organizes the Prix de Rome, the Netherlands; library: 33,000 vols, 85 magazines, 1,400 video cassettes and DVDs, large colln of monographs, catalogues of exhibitions and art theory books on visual arts, photography, video, applied art and architecture; Chair. of Board of Supervisors Prof. Dr L. J. GUNNING-SCHEPERS; Dir ELS VAN ODIJK; Librarian MARIETTA DIRKER.

Rotterdamse Academie van Bouwkunst (Rotterdam Academy of Architecture): POB 25035, 3001 HA Rotterdam; Heijplaatstraat 23, 3089 JB Rotterdam; tel. (10) 7944855; e-mail info@ravb.nl; internet www.ravb.nl; f. 1965; attached to Rotterdam Univ.; architecture and urban design; library: 10,000 vols; 225 students; Dir CHRIS VAN LANGEN; Business Dir BERT HOOIJER.

Sandberg Instituut: Fred. Roeskestraat 98, 1076 ED Amsterdam; tel. (20) 5882400; e-mail contact@sandberg.nl; internet www .sandberg.nl; f. 1990; attached to Gerrit Rietveld Acad.; Masters programmes in fine arts, applied arts and design; courses validated by accreditation cttee NVAO; 41 students; Dir JURGEN BEY.

University of the Arts, The Hague: Juliana van Stolberglaan 1, 2595 CA The Hague; tel. (70) 3151515; e-mail secrcvb@ kabk.nl; internet www.koncon.nl; f. 1990 as Academy of Fine Arts, Music and Dance by merger of The Royal Conservatory and Royal Academy of Arts; current name adopted 2010; Bachelors and Masters courses in classical music, early music, jazz, composition, sonology, art of sound, art science, music education, theory of music and dance, master in opera and PhD (Arts); bachelors, masters and preparatory courses in fine arts, design etc.; Dir HENK MEULEN.

Willem de Kooning Academie (Willem de Kooning Academy): POB 1272, 3000 BG Rotterdam; Blaak 10 and Wijnhaven 61, Rotterdam; tel. (10) 7904750; e-mail wdka .communicatie@hro.nl; internet abk.hro.nl; f. 1773, current name adopted 1998; attached to Rotterdam Univ.; library: 6,000 vols; Pres. RICHARD E. OUWERKERK.

NETHERLANDS SPECIAL MUNICIPALITIES

BONAIRE

Learned Society
NATURAL SCIENCES
Biological Sciences

Stichting Nationale Parken Bonaire (STINAPA Bonaire): POB 368, Bonaire; tel. 7178444; e-mail info@stinapa.org; internet www.stinapa.org; 2 protected areas: Bonaire Nat. Marine Park (BNMP) and Washington Slagbaai Nat. Park (WSNP); protects Bonaire's natural and historical heritage; Dir ELSMARIE BEUKENBOOM.

Research Institutes
NATURAL SCIENCES
Biological Sciences

Bonaire National Marine Park: POB 368, Bonaire; tel. 7178444; e-mail marinepark@ stinapa.org; internet www.bmp.org; f. 1979; attached to STINAPA Bonaire; marine and ecological research; spec. in reef surveys; protects and manages natural, cultural and historical resources; Man. RAMON DE LEON.

CIEE Research Station Bonaire: Kaya gobernador n. Debrot 26, Kralendijk, Bonaire; tel. 7174140; internet www .cieebonaire.org; research on marine ecology and conservation; provides scientific data, analysis and support to Bonaire's environmental, educational and governmental bodies; Dir Dr RITA PEACHEY; publ. *Physis*.

University

SAINT JAMES SCHOOL OF MEDICINE

Bonaire Plaza Juliana 4, Kralendijk, Bonaire
Telephone: 7172150

E-mail: info@mail.sjsm.org
Internet: www.sjsm.org
Founded 1999
Private control
Language of instruction: English
Academic year: January to December (3 semesters)

Campus in Anguilla; offers Doctor of Science programme

Pres.: Dr KALLOL GUHA
Dean of Student Affairs: Dr BRUCE DAVIDSON
Registrar: SHIRSHA GUHA
Librarian: OSCAR ANDRADE

Library of 2,600 vols, 30 print periodical titles, 1,474 e-periodicals
Number of teachers: 28
Number of students: 410

DEANS

Basic Sciences: Dr RAVINDER KENUE
Clinical Sciences: JAY K. PANDIT

SABA

Regulatory Body
GOVERNMENT

Department of Education: Power Street One, The Bottom, Saba; tel. 4163365; Commr CHRIS JOHNSON.

Learned Society
NATURAL SCIENCES
Biological Sciences

Saba Conservation Foundation: POB 18, The Bottom, Saba; tel. 4163295; e-mail info@ sabapark.org; internet www.sabapark.org; f. 1987; preserves and enhances marine and terrestrial environment through education, scientific research and monitoring; 10 mems.

College

Saba University School of Medicine: POB 1000, Church St, The Bottom, Saba; tel. 4163456; e-mail admissions@saba.edu; internet www.saba.edu; f. 1986; offers programmes in basic and clinical sciences; library: 8,600 books, 155 periodicals; 79 teachers; 585 students (postgraduate); Chair. of the Board of Trustees Dr PAUL L. DALBEC; Pres. JOSEPH CHU; Exec. Dean Dr HUGH K. DUCKWORTH; Assoc. Dean for Basic Sciences JAMES G. LEWIS; Assoc. Dean for Clinical Sciences MICHAEL ELIASTAM; Dir of Admissions Dr ALAN L. BERNSTEIN; Registrar BERNICE M. OUELLET; Library Dir SAMUEL JOHNSON.

SINT EUSTATIUS

Regulatory Body
GOVERNMENT

Department of Education, Culture and Sports: Govt Bldg, Oranjestad, Sint Eustatius; tel. 3182382; e-mail comm.ctearr@ statiagov.com; internet www .statiagovernment.com/directory.html; Commr C. TEARR.

Learned Societies
HISTORY, GEOGRAPHY AND ARCHAEOLOGY

St Eustatius Centre for Archaeological Research (SECAR): Oranjestad, Sint Eustatius; internet www.secar.org; f. 2000; protects and develops historical resources; educates children, locals and visitors; Dir R. GRANT GILMORE, III.

NATURAL SCIENCES
Biological Sciences

St Eustatius National Parks Foundation (STENAPA): Gallows Bay, Sint Eustatius; tel. 3182884; e-mail info@statiapark.org; internet www.statiapark.org; f. 1988; 3 nat. parks: St Eustatius Nat. Marine Park, Quill/ Boven Nat. Park and Miriam Schmidt Botanical Gdn; protects biodiversity and tropical ecosystems; Pres. IRVING BROWN; Dir KATE

WALKER; Sec. INGRID WALTHER; Treas. RUTH PANDT.

Museum

Oranjestad

Simon Doncker Museum: Simon Doncker House, Oranjestad, Sint Eustatius; tel. 3182693; e-mail secar@hotmail.com; internet www.statiatourism.com/museum; 2 galleries: colonial history and pre-Columbian history; spec. Granny Statia room.

University

UNIVERSITY OF SINT EUSTATIUS SCHOOL OF MEDICINE

POB 73, Goldenrock, Sint Eustatius
Telephone: 3182600
E-mail: info@eustatiusmed.edu
Internet: www.eustatiusmed.edu

Founded 1999

Medical degree programme, incl. training in basic sciences and clinical education
State control
Language of instruction: English
Academic year: September to August

Chair.: Dr CLYDE B. JENSEN
Pres.: LEONARD A. WISNESKI
Provost: Dr EZZELDIN NASSER
CEO: MICHAEL KNOPF
Vice-Pres. for Academic Devt: MARC POULIN
Vice-Pres. for Finance: JOHN BLUETHGEN
Dean of Int. Affairs: THAM NIMAL-RAJ

ARUBA

The Higher Education System

There is one public university in the Dutch Dependency of Aruba, the Universiteit van Aruba (founded in 1988), which comprises four faculties—the Faculty of Arts and Science, the Faculty of Accounting, Finance and Marketing, the Faculty of Law, and the Faculty of Hospitality and Tourism Management Studies. There is also the Instituto Pedagogico Arubano (Aruban Teacher Training College), as well as a number of private institutions, including two medical schools—the Aureus University School of Medicine (formerly the All Saints University of Medicine, founded in 2004) and the Xavier University School of Medicine at Aruba (founded in 2004). However, the majority of Aruban students who pursue higher education choose to do so abroad, generally in the Netherlands, although a significant number attend institutions in North America, South America or mainland Europe. In 2010 there was a total of 2,330 students enrolled in tertiary-level education. The main language of instruction is Dutch, but Papiamento is used in the lower levels of technical and vocational education.

Supervision of higher education is the responsibility of the Education Inspectorate, which assesses, monitors and promotes quality in education. Institutions are responsible for their own internal quality assurance and are encouraged to organize and access their activities from this perspective. There is currently no national qualifications framework in place in Aruba.

Admission to degree programmes at the Universiteit van Aruba requires students to hold the Voorbereidend Wetenschappelijk Onderwijs (VWO—Preparatory Scientific Education), the Hoger Algemeen Voortgezet Onderwijs (HAVO—Higher General Continued Education) or the Middelbaar Beroepsonderwijs (MBO—Middle Applied Education). Undergraduate Bachelors degree programmes last between three and four years, and grant access to postgraduate Masters programmes, which generally last between one and two years.

The Instituto Pedagogico Arubano offers the qualification of Graad van Volledig Bevoegd Leerkracht (Fully Qualified Teacher Qualification), which is comparable to a Bachelors degree in primary education in the Netherlands, or the Akte van Bekwaamheid van de tweede graad tot het geven van voortgezet onderwij (Teaching Certificate in Secondary Teaching, Level Two), which is comparable to a Bachelors degree in secondary education in the Netherlands. Both teacher training qualifications require a period of four years' study.

Regulatory Bodies

GOVERNMENT

Ministry of Economy, Social Affairs and Culture: L. G. Smith Blvd 76, Oranjestad; tel. 5885455; e-mail minszi@setarnet.aw; Minister Drs MICHELLE JANICE HOOYBOER-WINKLAAR.

Ministry of Justice and Education: L. G. Smith Blvd 76, Oranjestad; tel. 5830004; e-mail macs@setarnet.aw; Minister ARTHUR LAWRENCE DOWERS.

Libraries and Archives

Oranjestad

Archivo Nacional Aruba (National Archives of Aruba): Sabana Banco 60, Oranjestad; tel. 5834880; e-mail ana@aruba.gov.aw; f. 1994; preservation and conservation of nat. and cultural heritage of Aruba; manages transferred govt and private records; supervises and inspects governmental archives; makes archival information accessible for public use; supplies information about records to public; conducts historical research and publishes result; promotes historical interest of the public by organizing exhibitions, presentations regarding history and culture; Dir Dr RAYMOND R. HERNANDEZ.

Biblioteca Nacional Aruba (National Library of Aruba): George Madurostr. 13, Oranjestad; tel. 5821580; e-mail info@bibliotecanacional.aw; internet www.bibliotecanacional.aw; f. 1908 as first Public Library of Aruba 1949, mobile library 1968, present bldg 1982, present name and status 1986; nat. library, with functions of public library and nat. information centre; br. in San Nicolas; 2 bookmobiles; 100,000 books; Dir ASTRID J. T. BRITTEN.

Museums and Art Galleries

Oranjestad

Museo Arquelogico Nacional Aruba (National Archaeological Museum of Aruba): J. E. Irausquinplein 2A, Oranjestad; tel. 5828979; e-mail info@namaruba.org; internet www.namaruba.org; attached to Instituto di Cultura Aruba; permanent colln of ceramic artefacts, shell and stone tools, ornaments from the first cultures of Aruba; research, documentation, preservation of heritage and indigenous culture of Aruba.

Museo Historico Arubano (Aruban Historical Museum): Fort Zoutman z/n, Oranjestad; tel. 5885199; e-mail museohistoricoarubano@hotmail.com; internet www.institutodicultura-aruba.com; f. fort built in 1798, est. as museum by Cultureel Centrum van Aruba 1983, admin. by Fundacion Museo Arubano since 1992; attached to Instituto di Cultura Aruba; archaeology, architecture, history.

Museo Numismatico Aruba (Aruba Numismatic Museum): Timbalstr. 11, Tarabana, Oranjestad; tel. 5828831; e-mail numisaruba@hotmail.com; internet www.museumaruba.org; f. 1981; attached to Instituto di Cultura Aruba; holds private colln of Juan Mario Odor; colln of 35,000 items from 400 countries; Pres. for J. M. Odor colln RAQUEL MADURO-ODOR; Dir for J. M. Odor colln DESIREE CROES.

San Nicolas

Aruban Model Trains Museum: Koolbaaibergstr. 12, San Nicolas; tel. 5847321; e-mail auacultura@setarnet.aw; internet www.institutodicultura-aruba.com; f. 2001;

attached to Instituto di Cultura Aruba; colln of miniature trains; Dir J. DE VRIES.

Universities and Colleges

AUREUS UNIVERSITY SCHOOL OF MEDICINE

Wayaca 31c, Oranjestad
Telephone: 5832126
E-mail: info@aureusuniversity.com
Internet: www.aureusuniversity.com

Founded 2004, fmrly All Saints Univ. of Medicine
Private control
Language of instruction: English
Academic year: January to December
Exec. Dean: Dr GURMIT CHILANA
Dean for Academic Affairs: Dr FRANK NAVAR-RETE
Dean for Clinical Affairs: Dr RICHARD SCOTT
Number of teachers: 17
Number of students: 190 medical, 77 pre-medical

Arubaanse Muziekschool (Aruban School of Music): Vondellaan 2, Oranjestad; tel. 5822888; e-mail arumuziekschool@setarnet

.aw; f. 1953; educational and recreational activities; centre for information and archive of musical pieces; Dir FELIX RAIMOND HOEK.

UNIVERSIDAD DI ARUBA (University of Aruba)

Dr Schaepmanstr. z/n, San Nicholas
Telephone: 5845287
E-mail: osa@ua.aw
Internet: www.ua.aw

Founded 1970
Private control
Language of instruction: English
Academic year: September to June
Pres.: Dr CARLIN I. BROWNE
Registrar: HILTONIA PETER
Librarian: LISA WEBB

Library of 6,000 vols
Number of teachers: 20
Number of students: 300

DEANS

College of Business Administration: Dr CAR-LIN I. BROWNE
College of Education: Dr RACHEL JONES
College of Languages: Dr JOSSY MANSUR
College of Liberal Arts: Rev. Fr WILLIAM LAKE

UNIVERSITEIT VAN ARUBA (University of Aruba)

J. Irausquinplein 4, POB 5, Oranjestad
Telephone: 5823901
E-mail: info@ua.aw
Internet: www.ua.aw

Founded 1988
State control
Languages of instruction: Dutch, English
Academic year: September to June

Pres.: FREDERIC GIBBS
Rector: GLENN THODÉ
Librarian: LEONIE BOERKAMP

Library of 20,000 vols
Number of teachers: 40
Number of students: 500

Publication: *Aruba Iuridica* (2 a year)

DEANS

Faculty of Arts and Science: PAULA KIBBE-LAAR
Faculty of Accounting, Finance and Market-ing: JOOST JACOBS
Faculty of Hospitality and Tourism Manage-ment Studies: JOHN WARDLAW
Faculty of Law: CARLOS BOLLEN

CURAÇAO

The Higher Education System

Following the dissolution of the Netherlands Antilles and Curaçao's establishment as an autonomous constituent country within the Netherlands in October 2010, the provision of higher education on the island has been the responsibility of the newly created Ministry of Education, Science, Culture and Sports. There is one public university on Curaçao—the University of Curaçao Mr Dr Moises Frumencio da Costa Gomez (founded in 1970 as the Law College of the Netherlands Antilles; name changed and university status adopted in 1979, current name

adopted 2011). In 2011/12 enrolment at the University totalled 2,211 students. Degree programmes are also available at the Inter-Continental University of the Caribbean (formerly the Curaçao Institute for Social and Economic Studies, which was a constituent division of the University of the Netherlands Antilles prior to becoming an independent institution in 2009; current name adopted 2010) and at two private institutions—the University of the Dutch Caribbean and the Caribbean International University. In 2002/03 some 6,088 students were enrolled in vocational education.

Regulatory Body

GOVERNMENT

Ministry of Education, Science, Culture and Sports: Scharlooweg 102, Willemstad; tel. (9) 4615133; e-mail info.sae@gobiernu .cw; Minister IRENE DICK (acting).

Learned Societies

HISTORY, GEOGRAPHY AND ARCHAEOLOGY

National Archaeological and Anthropo-logical Memory Management (NAAM): Johan van Walbeeckplein 13, Pietermaai, Willemstad; tel. (9) 4621933; e-mail info@ naam.an; internet www.naam.an; f. 1998 fmrly Archaeological–Anthropological Insti-tute of the Netherlands Antilles; current name adopted 2008; promotes nat. and int. cooperation; knowledge acquisition; under-standing of Caribbean heritage issues; incl.

10,000 artefacts of the Afro-Caribbean cul-ture; archeological colln incl maritime arte-facts; heritage management; library of 2,000 vols; Chair. LIONEL JANGA; Dir RICHENEL ANSANO; Sec. ALCA SINT JAGO; Treas. FLOR-ENTINO OVERMAN.

NATURAL SCIENCES

Biological Sciences

CARMABI Foundation: Piscaderabaai z/n, POB 2090, Willemstad; tel. (9) 4624242; e-mail info@carmabi.org; internet www .carmabi.org; f. 1955 as a marine biological research station, merged with STINAPA 1996; terrestrial and marine ecology; Chris-toffel Park, Curaçao Marine Park, Savonet Museum, Research Station Carmabi, Car-mabi Education (environmental education programmes); library of 3,000 vols; Chair. DITO ABBAD; Dir Ir. PAUL STOKKERMANS; Sec. JEFFREY SYBESMA; Treas. PETER BONGERS.

Physical Sciences

Meteorological Department Curaçao: Seru Mahuma, Willemstad; tel. (9) 8393366; e-mail admin-cur@meteo.an; internet www .weather.an; f. 1953, fmrly Meteorological Service of the Netherlands Antilles and Aruba, present location 1976, present name and status 2010; attached to Min. of Traffic, Transport and Urban Planning; provides weather forecasts and warnings for Curaçao and Caribbean islands; offers services to sustain social-economic devt; Dir Dr A. A. E. MARTIS.

Libraries and Archives

Willmestad

Biblioteka Públiko Kòrsou/Openbare Bibliotheek Curaçao/Biblioteca Pública Curazao (Public Library Curaçao): Abra-ham. M. Chumaceiro Blvr 17, Willemstad; tel. (9) 4345200; e-mail publiclibrary@onenet

.an; internet www.curacaopubliclibrary.an; f. 1922 as part of Govt Service of Culture and Education, present location 1988, present status 1997; Antillean and Caribbean colln; adult, children's, mobile and schools' library services, 1 br. library, 2 mobile libraries; 180,000 vols and small colln of audiovisual material; Chair. SHIK-TONG CHAN; Librarian R. M. DE PAULA; Sec. M. ROJER; Treas. D. PIMENTEL.

Mongui Maduro Library: POB 480, Landhuis Rooi Catootje, Willemstad; tel. (9) 7375119; e-mail info@madurolibrary.org; internet www.madurolibrary.org; 3,000 vols.

Nationaal Archief (National Archives): Scharlooweg 75–79, Willemstad; tel. (9) 4614866; e-mail na@nationalarchives.an; internet www.nationalarchives.an; f. 1969; repository for all non-current govt records; collns of originals and microfilm copies of archives from 1713; 15,000 vols, 400,000 photographs and negatives and audiovisual materials; Dir Drs N. C. ROMER-KENEPA; publ. *Lantèrnu*.

Museums
Willmestad

Curaçao Museum: Van Leeuwenhoekstr z/n, Willemstad; tel. (9) 4623873; e-mail curmuseum@gmail.com; f. 1946 as The Curaçao Museum Foundation, present name and status 1948; colln of antique furniture, local and int. art; traditional Curaçaoan kitchen; paintings by early 20th-century Dutch masters and contemporary Curaçao artists; carillon with 47 bells; botanical and sculpture garden and music pavilion; cockpit of first KLM airplane that crossed the Atlantic Ocean in 1934; Pres. C. WEEBER; publ. *De Museumbode* (4 a year).

Jewish Historical Cultural Museum: POB 322, Willemstad; tel. (9) 4611067; e-mail museum@snoa.com; internet www.snoa.com/snoa.html; f. 1970; cultural objects collected over 350 years of Jewish life in Curaçao.

Maritiem Museum Curaçao (Curaçao Maritime Museum): Van der Brandhofstraat One, Willemstad; tel. (9) 4652327; e-mail info@curacaomaritime.com; internet www.curacaomaritime.com; f. 1998; exhibits 500 years of maritime history of Curaçao; authentic nautical charts, ship models and navigation equipment; Dir LEO HELMS.

Money Museum Yotin Kòrtá: Scharlooweg 11, Willemstad; tel. 4612404; e-mail info@moneymuseum.cw; internet www.moneymuseum.cw; f. 1993; attached to Centrale Bank van Curaçao en Sint Maarten; displays Antillean currency from barter deals; use of coins from different countries; incl. commemorative coins.

Tele Musuem: Wilhelminaplein Four, Punda, Willemstad; tel. (9) 4652844; attached to UTS; history of telephone from the 1880s to the late 20th-century inventions, incl. fibre optic cables, computerization and teleconferencing.

Universities

AVALON UNIVERSITY SCHOOL OF MEDICINE (AUSOM)

Scharlooweg 25, Willemstad
Telephone: (9) 7173967
E-mail: admissions@avalonu.org
Internet: www.avalonu.org
Language of instruction: English
Academic year: January to December

Offers programmes in premedicine, doctor of medicine and clinical sciences

Chancellor: Dr SHOKAT FATTEH
Pres.: Dr SAMIR FATTEH
Vice-Pres.: DILU DINANI
Dean of Academic Affairs: Dr SIREESHA BALA ARJA
Dean of Admissions: Dr SALEEM UMAR
Exec. Dir: Dr SATEESH BABU ARJA
Dir for Admissions and Registrar: MICHELLE RICHARDS
Number of students: 450

CARIBBEAN INTERNATIONAL UNIVERSITY

World Trade Center Curaçao, Piscadera Bay
Telephone: (9) 4636192
E-mail: info@ciucuracao.info
Internet: www.ciucuracao.org
Private control
Language of instruction: Dutch

Offers Bachelors and Masters degrees in banking, economy and finance and management; doctoral programmes in social sciences, education sciences and legal sciences; language courses in English and Spanish

INTER-CONTINENTAL UNIVERSITY OF THE CARIBBEAN (ICUC)

Plaza Brion One, Otrobanda
Telephone: (9) 7666300
E-mail: info@icuc.org
Internet: www.icuc.org
Founded 1994, present status 2009, current name adopted 2010
Private control

Schools of financial management, hospitality and tourism management, management and leadership, int. business and school of language studies

ST. MARTINUS UNIVERSITY— FACULTY OF MEDICINE

Brionplein One, POB 2050, Otrobanda
E-mail: info@martinus.edu
Internet: www.martinus.edu

Founded 1842 as St. Martinus College
Private control
Academic year: January to May, July to November (2 semesters)

Offers Bachelors programme in medicine; provides undergraduate and graduate research opportunities

Dean of Academics: Dr THOMAS GEST
Dean of Basic Sciences: Dr KALICHARAN MISRA

Dean of Clinical Sciences: Dr REBECCA K. KARTJE
Vice-Pres. for Academic and Admin. Affairs: J. M. PARBHOO

UNIVERSITY OF CURAÇAO MR DR MOISES FRUMENCIO DA COSTA GOMEZ

Jan Noorduynweg 111, Curaçao
Telephone: (9) 8442222
E-mail: una@una.an
Internet: www.una.an

Founded 1970 as The Law College of the Netherlands Antilles, univ. status 1979 as Univ. of the Netherlands Antilles, current name adopted 2011
State control
Languages of instruction: English, Dutch
Academic year: September to June

Pres.: Ir H. J. BEHR
Rector: Dr F. DE LANOY (acting)
Gen. Dir: H. DE FRANÇA
Chief Admin. Officer: R. RAVENSTEIN
Library and Research Head: Drs M. GROENEWOUD

Library of 100,000 vols
Number of teachers: 235
Number of students: 2,096

DEANS

Faculty of Engineering: R. BULBAAI
Faculty of General Arts: Dr E. ECHTELD
Faculty of Law: Dr P. KLICK
Faculty of Social and Behavioural Sciences: (vacant)
Faculty of Social Sciences and Economics: R. SOPHIA (acting)

UNIVERSITY OF THE DUTCH CARIBBEAN

Landhuis Groot Davelaar, Willemstad
Telephone: (9) 7383300
E-mail: info@udc.an
Internet: www.udc.an
Private control
Language of instruction: Dutch

Offers business economics, commercial economics, higher legal education, higher tourism and recreational education, int. business and management studies

College

Akademia di Músika 'Edgar Palm' (Edgar Palm Music Academy): Koninginnelaan z/n, Emmastad, Curaçao; tel. (9) 7373682; e-mail info@sentrokultural-korsou.org; internet www.sentrokultural-korsou.org; f. 1960; attached to Sentro Kultural Kòrsou (Cultureel Centrum Curaçao); 550 students; Dir ETZEL PROVENCE.

SINT MAARTEN

The Higher Education System

Following the dissolution of the Netherlands Antilles and Sint Maarten's establishment as an autonomous constituent country within the Netherlands in October 2010, the Sint Maarten Department of Education was reorganized as the Ministry of Education, Culture, Youth and Sports Affairs; the Ministry is the national agency responsible for the provision of higher education. The Government maintains a comprehensive bursary programme for university students, at both local and foreign institutions. A significant number of students who choose to pursue higher education do so at institutions based in North America, South America or the European mainland. The University of St Martin, based in Sint Maarten, caters for students both in Sint Maarten and in the French Overseas Collectivity of Saint-Martin, and offers programmes in conjunction with universities in other Caribbean islands, including Associate and Bachelors degree courses in business, liberal arts, applied science, education, and hospitality. In 2006/07 there were 217 students enrolled in the university. Medical education is available at the American University of the Caribbean School of Medicine (founded in 1978), which follows curricula equivalent to those taught in US medical colleges and is accredited by the Accreditation Commission of Colleges of Medicine. Graduates from the institution are able to obtain residency and licensure throughout the USA.

Regulatory Body

GOVERNMENT

Ministry of Education, Culture, Youth and Sports Affairs: Government Administration Building, POB 943, Clem Labega Sq., Philipsburg; tel. 5429344; internet www.sintmaartengov.org; Minister PATRICIA D. LOURENS-PHILIP.

Learned Societies

HISTORY, GEOGRAPHY AND ARCHAEOLOGY

St Maarten National Heritage Foundation and Museum: POB 631, Front St Seven, Philipsburg; tel. 5424917; e-mail heritage@caribserve.net; internet www.museumsintmaarten.org; f. 1993, by merger of St Maarten Nat. Park Foundation and St Maarten Museum Foundation; promotes, protects and studies history, culture and natural environment of St Maarten; incl. reference library.

MEDICINE

Mental Health Foundation: Leopard Rd One, Cay Hill; tel. 5421677; e-mail admin@mhf-sxm.com; internet www.mhf-sxm.com; f. 2006; psychiatric clinical care, prevention of mental health diseases; psychiatric home health care; Dir EILEEN HEALY; Pres. Dr FELIX HOLIDAY; Sec. FENNA ARNELL; Treas. ERIC VAN DER HOEK.

St Maarten AIDS Foundation: c/o Gerard van Osch, Union Rd, 144A, Cole Bay; tel. 5445374; e-mail info@sxmaidsfoundation.org; internet www.sxmaidsfoundation.org; f. 1991; promotes awareness about AIDS and sexually transmittable disease; prevention and reduction of AIDS epidemic.

NATURAL SCIENCES

Biological Sciences

Nature Foundation St Maarten: POB 863, Philipsburg; Wellsberg St 1A, Unit 25–26 Fisherman's Wharf Complex, Cole Bay; tel. 5444267; internet www.naturefoundationsxm.org; f. 1987; promotes conservation of St Maarten's environment; Chair. JAN BEAUJON; Sec. FRANK BOEKHOUT; Treas. MALOU CARTY.

Library

Philipsburg

Philipsburg Jubilee Library: Ch. E. W. Vogestreet 12, Philipsburg; tel. 5422970; e-mail info@stmaartenlibrary.org; internet www.stmaartenlibrary.org; f. 1923; books on biography, health and computers; bookmobile outreach programme; Chair. CHANTAL SCHAMINEE; Dir MONIQUE ALBERTS; Sec. MONIQUE HOFMAN; Treas. CLAYTON HOLIDAY.

Universities

AMERICAN UNIVERSITY OF THE CARIBBEAN SCHOOL OF MEDICINE

Medical Science Campus, One Univ. Dr., Jordan Rd, Cupecoy

Telephone: 5452298

E-mail: registrar@aucmed.edu

Internet: www.aucmed.edu

Founded 1978, present location 1995

Academic year: January to December (3 semesters)

Medical sciences at St Maarten campus and clinical sciences in affiliated hospitals in the USA and UK

Chancellor: Dr PAUL S. TIEN

Chief Academic Officer: BRUCE KAPLAN

Chief Financial Officer: PAUL R. SUID

Dean of Medical Sciences: Dr RONALD J. TESTA

Dir of Admissions: MINDY GREENE

Librarian: CHRIS WILLIAMS

Registrar: DIMPLE AMARNANI

Library of 5,000 vols incl. books, video cassettes, DVDs, CDs and 75 journals

Number of teachers: 500

Publication: *AUC Connections*

UNIVERSITY OF ST MARTIN

One Soualiga Rd, POB 836, Philipsburg

Telephone: 5425171

E-mail: president@usmonline.net

Internet: www.usmonline.net

Founded 1989

Academic year: August to July (3 semesters)

Offers Bachelors degrees in arts in education, hospitality, tourism management

Pres.: ANNELIES VAN DEN ASSEM

Dean for Academic Affairs: GLEN YEUNG (acting)

Dir for Admissions: ANGELIQUE HAZEL

Librarian: MARK PAUL

Registrar: GLENDA BRAZIER

NEW ZEALAND

The Higher Education System

New Zealand became a dominion, under the British Crown, in 1907 and achieved full independence in 1947, when it accepted the 1931 Statute of Westminster. Most of the major institutions of higher education were founded during the second half of the 19th century, notably the University of Otago (founded in 1869), the University of Canterbury (founded in 1873), Lincoln University (founded in 1878; current name and status since 1990) and the University of Auckland (founded in 1883; current status since 1962). Higher education consists of universities, institutes of technology and polytechnics (ITPs), colleges of education (all of which had merged with universities by 2007) and schools of art and music. In 2011/12 there were eight state universities and 18 ITPs. In 2011 there were 175,719 students enrolled at the universities and 157,319 students in the polytechnic system. There were also some 74,825 students enrolled in private training establishments. There is a parallel education system for the indigenous Maori population, who account for 20% of school enrolment. Three Maori institutions (wānanga) in the tertiary sector provide higher learning in ahuatanga Māori (Maori tradition) according to tikanga Māori (Maori custom). In 2011 38,629 students were enrolled in the wānanga. Students from the Dependent Territory of Tokelau and the Associated States of the Cook Islands and Niue may receive higher education either through branches and campuses of the University of the South Pacific or through scholarships to study in New Zealand, Australia, Fiji and other Pacific countries.

Under the Education Act (1989) the Ministry of Education is the supreme body for the provision of education at all levels. The Tertiary Education Commission determines public higher education policy and administers funding, and the New Zealand Qualifications Authority (NZQA) oversees private education providers and government training establishments. The NZQA has established a New Zealand Register of Quality Assured Qualifications ('The Register'), which lists all quality-assured programmes of study and their international equivalency. It accredits and audits tertiary education providers, excluding universities, and other registered learning establishments that offer approved courses and award credits for registered qualifications. The universities are autonomous institutions, each governed by a Council, consisting of elected, appointed or co-opted members, and headed by a Vice-Chancellor. The Senate is an academic board with responsibility for academic affairs. Some 80% of the universities' funds are state-provided. In addition to government funding dispersed by the Tertiary Education Commission, the universities are also financed by tuition fees, which are subsidized by the State. Universities in New Zealand are not self-accrediting and must apply to offer new qualifications or new subjects to the Committee on University Academic Programmes of the New Zealand Vice-Chancellors' Committee, which acts under statutory authority in lieu of NZQA in the university sector. Following the Education Amendment Act (1990), the polytechnics, colleges of education and wānanga became autonomous institutions and award their own degrees.

Admission to higher education is on the basis of the National Certificate of Educational Achievement. The standard university-level degree system consists of Bachelors, Masters and Doctorate degrees, but aspects such as period of study and criteria for award vary among the institutions owing to their autonomy. The Bachelors is often a three-year degree (although some disciplines such as medicine require upwards of five years) and is awarded on the basis of 'credits' accrued. An 'Honours' Bachelors degree is a four-year programme of study. The Masters is the first postgraduate degree, and varies in length from one to three years of full-time (or equivalent part-time) study. The PhD or DPhil is the highest university-level degree, awarded after a minimum of two years of research-based study leading to submission of a thesis. There are also 'higher' doctorates such as the DSc or DLitt awarded after publication of a corpus of work. Institutions of higher education operate a credit-transfer system, which allows students to complete their degree in an institution other than the one in which they started.

Post-secondary technical and vocational education is offered by the universities, institutes of technology, polytechnics, colleges of education, professional institutes, wānanga and private training establishments. The main qualifications are the National Certificate (four levels) and National Diploma. In 2011 it was estimated that there were over 700,000 students (including international students) in the tertiary education system.

During 2009 the Government strengthened the performance of institutes of technology and polytechnics by reshaping the nature of their governing councils and introducing a new investment-based approach to quality assurance.

Regulatory and Representative Bodies

GOVERNMENT

Ministry for Culture and Heritage: POB 5364, Wellington 6145; Level 4, ASB House, 101 The Terrace, Wellington 6011; tel. (4) 499-4229; e-mail info@mch.govt.nz; internet www.mch.govt.nz; Minister Hon. CHRISTOPHER FINLAYSON.

Ministry of Education: POB 1666, Thorndon, Wellington 6140; Level 3, 45–47 Pipitea St, Thorndon, Wellington 6140; tel. (4) 463-8000; e-mail info@minedu.govt.nz; internet www.minedu.govt.nz; Minister Hon. HEKIA PARATA.

Science+Innovation Group: Level 3, 33 Bowen St, POB 5762, Wellington, 6145; tel. (4) 917-0199; e-mail info@msi.govt.nz; internet www.msi.govt.nz; attached to Min. of Business, Innovation and Employment (MBIE); Minister STEVEN JOYCE.

ACCREDITATION

ENIC/NARIC New Zealand: POB 160, Wellington 6140; Level 13, 125 The Terrace, Wellington 6011; tel. (4) 463-3000; e-mail pamela.hulston@nzqa.govt.nz; internet www.nzqa.govt.nz; f. 1990; secondary school examinations and qualifications; quality assurance of tertiary instns; assessment and benchmarking of overseas qualifications; Man. PAMELA HULSTON.

New Zealand Qualifications Authority: POB 160, Wellington 6140; Level 13, 125 The Terrace, Wellington 6011; tel. (4) 463-3000; e-mail helpdesk@nzqa.govt.nz; internet www.nzqa.govt.nz; coordinates the admin. and quality assurance of nat. qualifications in NZ; responsible for quality assurance services to Institutes of Technology and Polytechnics; Board Chair. SUE SUCKLING; Chief Exec. Dr KAREN POUTASI.

NATIONAL BODIES

DEANZ: New Zealand Association for Open, Flexible, and Distance Learning: c/o Kalina Vladinova-Aylor, Open Polytechnic of NZ. Private Bag 31914, Lower Hutt 5011; tel. (3) 388-5148; e-mail admin@deanz.org.nz; internet www.deanz.org.nz; Pres. MARK NICHOLS (acting); Sec. ANDREW HIGGINS; publ. *Journal of Open, Flexible and Distance Learning* (1 a year).

New Zealand Educational Institute/ NZEI Te Riu Roa: 178–182 Willis St, POB 466, Wellington 6140; tel. (4) 382-2736; e-mail nzei@nzei.org.nz; internet www.nzei.org.nz; f. 1883; teachers and support staff working in primary, area and secondary schools and early childhood centres, spec. education and school advisory services; Nat.

.nzarchaeology.org; f. 1954; associated with Historic Places Trust, Dept of Conservation and Min. of Culture and Heritage; annual conf.; 350 mems; Pres. R. WALTER; Sec. LYNDA WALTER; publs *Archaeology in New Zealand* (4 a year), *Journal of Pacific Archaeology* (2 a year).

New Zealand Cartographic Society: ENV, Univ. of Auckland, Private Bag 92019, Auckland; tel. (9) 373-7599; e-mail info@cartography.org.nz; internet www .cartography.org.nz; f. 1971; Pres. GEOFF AITKEN; Sec. ANTONI MOORE.

New Zealand Geographical Society Inc.: c/o School of People, Environment and Planning, Massey Univ., Private Bag 11222, Palmerston North 4410; tel. (6) 356-9099; e-mail admin@nzgs.co.nz; internet www.nzgs .co.nz; f. 1944; brs in Auckland, Christchurch, Dunedin, Hamilton, Palmerston North and Wellington; biennial conf.; mem. of the Int. Geographical Union via its membership of the Royal Society of New Zealand; 400 mems (375 in NZ, 25 overseas); Pres. Prof. JOHN OVERTON; Sec. Dr MARIA BOROVNIK; publ. *New Zealand Geographer* (3 a year).

New Zealand Historical Association: c/o Dept of History and Art History, Univ. of Otago, POB 56, Dunedin 9054; internet www .nzha.org.nz; f. 1979; works with the NZ History Teachers' Assцn; holds regular nat. and regional confs; gives financial or other assistance to the publication of historical research in NZ; expresses opinions on issues of public policy which concern historical study, teaching or research; 300 mems; Pres. KATIE PICKLES; Sec. JOANNA COBLEY.

New Zealand Historic Places Trust/Pouhere Taonga: Antrim House, 63 Boulcott St, POB 2629, Wellington 6140; tel. (4) 472-4341; e-mail information@historic.org.nz; internet www.historic.org.nz; f. 1955; autonomous crown entity with statutory responsibilities; identifies, investigates, registers and preserves historic places, incl. archaeological sites, traditional sites and old European and Maori heritage; 48 historic sites; 20,000 nat. mems; Chair. SHONAGH KENDERDINE; Chief Exec. BRUCE CHAPMAN; publ. *Heritage New Zealand* (4 a year).

LANGUAGE AND LITERATURE

Alliance Française: POB 11141 Manners Central, Wellington 6142; Level 3, Old Dominion Bldg, 78 Victoria St, Wellington 6140; tel. (4) 472-1272; e-mail alliance@ french.co.nz; internet www.french.co.nz; offers courses and examinations in French language, promotes cultural exchange with France; centres in Auckland, Christchurch, Dunedin, Hamilton, Nelson, North Shore, Palmerston North, Timaru and Whangerei; library of 7,000 vols, 1,500 books for children, 150 audio books, 880 CDs, 750 DVDs, 15 magazines; Pres. STEPHEN HAY; Dir NATHALIE BUCKRELL; Librarian FLORENCE LAIGLE.

British Council: POB 91488 AMC, Victoria St, Auckland 1142; 5E Endeans Bldg, 2 Queen St, Auckland; tel. (9) 302-3560; e-mail enquiries@britishcouncil.org.nz; internet www.britishcouncil.org.nz; offers courses and exams in English language and British culture and promotes cultural exchange with the UK; Dir INGRID LEARY.

New Zealand Society of Authors (PEN NZ Inc.): POB 7701 Wellesley St, Auckland 1141; Level 14, Oracle Tower, 56 Wakefield St, Auckland; tel. (9) 379-4801; e-mail office@ nzauthors.org.nz; internet www.authors.org .nz; f. 1934 as the New Zealand PEN Centre, current name adopted 1994; promotes cooperation and support amongst writers; encourages writing and works to protect the interests of writers; awards annual and biannual prizes; has representatives on major literary bodies; 1,522 mems; Pres. KYLE MEWBURN; Chief Exec. JACKIE DENNIS; publ. *The New Zealand Author* (6 a year).

MEDICINE

Dietitians NZ: POB 13468, Johnsonville, Wellington 6440; Level 3 Survey House, 23–29 Broderick Rd, Johnsonville, Wellington; tel. (4) 477-4704; e-mail office@dietitians.org .nz; internet dietitians.org.nz; f. 1943; professional asscn of registered dietitians and assoc. nutrition professionals; promotes good health through appropriate food and nutrition, using evidence-based scientific research; 7 brs and 14 spec. interest groups; 570 mems; Pres. CHRISTINE STEWART; CEO PETRINA TURNER-BENNY; publ. *Nutrition & Dietetics* (published jtly with Dietitians Asscn of Australia).

New Zealand Medical Association: POB 156, Wellington 6140; 26 The Terrace, Wellington; tel. (4) 472-4741; e-mail nzma@nzma .org.nz; internet www.nzma.org.nz; f. 1886; provides advocacy on behalf of doctors and their patients and provides support and services to mems and their practices; 5,000 mems; Chair. Dr PAUL OCKELFORD; Pres. Dr AINE McCOY; Chief Exec. CAMERON McIVER; publ. *New Zealand Medical Journal* (20 a year).

Physiological Society of New Zealand: Private Bag 913, Dunedin; c/o Dept of Physiology, Otago School of Medical Sciences, Univ. of Otago, Dunedin; tel. (3) 479-7330; internet www.physoc.org.nz; f. 1972; aims to enhance the quality of physiological and related research and to establish links with similar research socs throughout the world; 180 mems; Pres. Assoc. Prof. COLIN BROWN; Sec. Dr DARYL SCHWENKE; publ. *Proceedings* (1 a year).

NATURAL SCIENCES

General

New Zealand Association of Scientists: POB 1874, Wellington 6140; e-mail contact@ scientists.org.nz; internet www.scientists.org .nz; f. 1940; promotes and increases public awareness of science; debates scientific issues and influences govt science policy; improves working conditions for scientists and promotes the free exchange of knowledge and int. cooperation; Pres. NICOLA GASTON; Sec. Dr FIONA McDONALD; publ. *New Zealand Science Review* (4 a year).

Biological Sciences

Entomological Society of New Zealand: School of Biological Sciences, Univ. of Auckland, Private Bag 92019, Auckland 1142; tel. (9) 373-7599; e-mail secretary@ento.org.nz; internet ento.org.nz; f. 1951; 250 mems; Pres. Dr STEPHEN PAWSON; Hon. Sec. Dr GREG HOLWELL; publ. *New Zealand Entomologist* (1 a year).

New Zealand Ecological Society (Inc.): POB 5075, Christchurch 8542; tel. (3) 318-1056; e-mail nzecosoc@paradise.net.nz; internet nzes.org.nz; f. 1951; promotes the study of ecology and the application of ecological knowledge; membership open to any person interested in ecology; holds annual conf.; 600 mems; Pres. CHRIS BYCROFT; Vice-Pres. DEB WILSON; Sec. LAURA YOUNG; Treas. CLAYSON HOWELL; publ. *New Zealand Journal of Ecology* (2 a year).

New Zealand Freshwater Sciences Society (Inc.): c/o Janine Wech, NIWA, Private Bag 8602, Christchurch; tel. (3) 348-8987; internet freshwater.science.org.nz; f. 1968 as New Zealand Limnological Soc., present name 2005; promotes interest in all aspects of fresh and brackish water research; awards the NZFSS Medal; 420 mems; Pres. Prof. DAVID HAMILTON; Sec. and Treas. JANINE WECH; publ. *New Zealand Journal of Marine and Freshwater Research*.

New Zealand Marine Sciences Society: Private Bag 2, Nelson 7042; e-mail conference@nzmss.org; internet nzmss.org; f. 1960; 400 mems, 47 instn mems; Pres. Dr MARY LIVINGSTON; Sec. WILLIAM ARLIDGE; publ. *Marine Sciences Review* (1 a year).

New Zealand Microbiological Society (Inc.): c/o Dept of Oral Sciences, Otago School of Medical Sciences, Univ. of Otago, POB 56, Dunedin 9016; tel. (3) 479-9254; e-mail treasurer@nzms.org.nz; internet www .nzms.org.nz; f. 1956; organizes annual meetings and workshops; 422 mems; Pres. Prof. STEVE FLINT; Sec. DANIEL POWER; Treas. Dr NICK HENG; publs *NZBioscience* (1 a year), *New Zealand Microbiology* (3 a year).

New Zealand Society for Parasitology Inc.: c/o Caroline Costall, Private Bag 11008, Palmerston North 4442; tel. (6) 351-8685; e-mail caroline.costall@agresearch.co.nz; internet nzsp.science.org.nz; f. 1972; study of parasites of plants and animals; encourages the dissemination of information and new devt in Parasitology for education and betterment of society; 100 mems; Pres. Dr IAN SCOTT; Sec. Dr CAROLINE COSTALL; Treas. Dr ALLEN HEATH; publ. *Proceedings* (1 a year).

New Zealand Society of Plant Biologists: Private Bag 11 600, Palmerston North; tel. (6) 356-8300; e-mail secretary@plantbiology .science.org.nz; internet plantbiology.science .org.nz; f. 1974 as New Zealand Soc. of Plant Physiologists, current name adopted 2006; 160 mems; Pres. Prof. BRIAN JORDAN; Sec. Dr MARIAN McKENZIE.

Ornithological Society of New Zealand (Inc.)/Birds New Zealand: c/o POB 834, Nelson 7040; tel. (3) 545-0835; e-mail secretary@osnz.org.nz; internet www.osnz .org.nz; f. 1939; assists the conservation and management of birds; 1,000 mems; Pres. DAVID LAWRIE; Sec. PETER GAZE; publ. *Notornis* (4 a year).

Mathematical Sciences

New Zealand Mathematical Society: c/o Dr Emily Harvey, Institute of Natural and Mathematical Sciences, Massey Univ., Private Bag 102 904, North Shore City 0745; internet nzmathsoc.org.nz; f. 1974; 226 mems; Pres. Dr WINSTON SWEATMAN; Sec. Dr EMILY HARVEY; publ. *NZ Journal of Mathematics* (2 a year).

New Zealand Statistical Association: POB 1731, Wellington; internet www.stats .org.nz; f. 1948; holds annual conf.; 400 mems; Pres. Prof. JAMES CURRAN; Sec. BEATRIX JONES; publ. *Australian and New Zealand Journal of Statistics* (published jtly with Statistical Soc. of Australia (Inc.), 4 a year).

Physical Sciences

Geoscience Society of New Zealand: POB 306, Takaka, 7142; e-mail admin@gsnz.org .nz; internet www.gsnz.org.nz; f. 1955 by merger of New Zealand Geophysical Soc.; confs, lecture series, field trips, br. meetings; 8 brs; 900 mems; Pres. Dr ANDREW GORMAN; Sec. CATHERINE REID.

Meteorological Society of New Zealand: POB 6523, Te Aro, Wellington; e-mail info@ metsoc.rsnz.org; internet www.metsoc.org .nz; f. 1979; addresses any contentious issue involving weather or climate; 300 mems; Pres. Dr S. M. DEAN; Sec. Dr K. RICHARDS; publ. *Weather and Climate* (1 a year).

New Zealand Institute of Chemistry: c/o Richard Rendle, POB 39-112, Harewood,

Christchurch; tel. (3) 359-7275; e-mail nzic .office@nzic.org.nz; internet www.nzic.org .nz; f. 1931; 6 brs and 10 specialist groups; 1,000 mems; Pres. MICHAEL PRINSEP; Hon. Gen. Sec. RICHARD RENDLE; Treas. COLIN FREEMAN; publ. *Chemistry in New Zealand* (4 a year).

New Zealand Institute of Physics: c/o Bill Williams, Institute of Fundamental Sciences, Massey Univ., Private Bag 11222, Palmerston North; tel. (6) 356-9099; e-mail secretary@nzip.org.nz; internet www.nzip .org.nz; sponsors high school Physics prizes, 6 brs; 310 mems; Pres. Prof. PETER DERRICK; Sec. Prof. BILL WILLIAMS.

New Zealand Society for Biochemistry and Molecular Biology: c/o Wayne Patrick, Dept of Biochemistry, Univ. of Otago, POB 56, Dunedin 9054; internet nzsbmb.science .org.nz; f. 1972; 400 mems (230 full mems, 170 student mems); Pres. WAYNE PATRICK; Sec. KERRY LOOMES; Treas. RENWICK DOBSON; publ. *NZ BioScience* (4 a year).

Royal Astronomical Society of New Zealand: POB 3181, Wellington 6140; e-mail secretary@rasnz.org.nz; internet www.rasnz.org.nz; f. 1920 as NZ Astronomical Soc., Royal Charter 1946; sections for astrophotography, aurora and sun, comets and meteors, occultation; dark sky group; holds annual conf.; 180 mems; Pres. G. HUDSON; Exec. Sec. RORY O'KEEFFE; publ. *Southern Stars* (4 a year).

PHILOSOPHY AND PSYCHOLOGY

New Zealand Psychological Society: Level 7 The Grand Annex, 84 Boulcott St, POB 25 271, Wellington 6146; tel. (4) 473-4884; e-mail office@psychology.org.nz; internet www.psychology.org.nz; f. 1967; promotes the discipline of psychology as a science, high standards of ethical and professional practice, and provides professional support to mems; 1,000 full mems, 300 student and subscriber mems; Pres. PETER COLEMAN; Exec. Dir Dr PAMELA HYDE; publs *NZ Journal of Psychology* (3 a year, online), *Professional Practice of Psychology in Aotearoa New Zealand*, *Psychology Aotearoa* (2 a year).

RELIGION, SOCIOLOGY AND ANTHROPOLOGY

Polynesian Society: Maori Studies Dept, Univ. of Auckland, Private Bag 92019, Auckland; tel. (9) 373-7599; e-mail jps@auckland .ac.nz; internet www.thepolynesiansociety .org; f. 1892; promotes studies and publs about the Polynesians and other Pacific peoples past and present; library deposited in the Alexander Turnbull Library; 1,000 mems; Pres. RICHARD BENTON; Sec. and Treas. RANGIMARIE RAWIRI; publs *Journal of the Polynesian Society* (4 a year), *Memoirs* (irregular).

TECHNOLOGY

Institute of IT Professionals New Zealand: POB 10044, Wellington 6143; L24, Grand Plimmer Tower, 2 Gilmer Terrace, Wellington 6011; tel. (4) 473-1043; e-mail info@iitp.org.nz; internet www.iitp.org.nz; f. 1960; 6 brs; 1,650 mems; Pres. RAY DELANY; Chief Exec. PAUL MATTHEWS.

Institution of Professional Engineers New Zealand: POB 12 241, Wellington 6144; 158 The Terrace, Wellington 6011; tel. (4) 473-9444; e-mail ipenz@ipenz.org.nz; internet www.ipenz.org.nz; f. 1914; 12,000 mems; 16 brs and 1 br. in UK; Pres. KEVIN THOMPSON; Chief Exec. Dr ANDREW CLELAND; publ. *e.nz* (Engineering Insight, 6 a year).

New Zealand Hydrological Society: POB 12300, Thorndon, Wellington 6144; tel. (6) 357-1605; e-mail admin@hydrologynz.org.nz; internet www.hydrologynz.org.nz; f. 1961; publishes books; organizes annual conf.; 600 mems; Pres. JOSEPH THOMAS; Sec. GIL ZEMANSKY; publ. *Journal of Hydrology (New Zealand)* (2 a year).

New Zealand Society for Earthquake Engineering: POB 2193, Wellington 6140; tel. (4) 565-3650; e-mail exec@nzsee.org.nz; internet www.nzsee.org.nz; f. 1968; promotes the advancement of the science and practice of earthquake engineering, and cooperation among scientists, engineers and other professionals in the field; 700 mems; Pres. Prof. STEFANO PAMPANIN; Exec. Officer WIN CLARK.

Operational Research Society of New Zealand: POB 6544, Wellesley St, Auckland 1141; e-mail president@orsnz.org.nz; internet www.orsnz.org.nz; f. 1965; promotes operational research and management science in both academic and industrial aspects; 150 mems; Pres. GOLBON ZAKERI; Sec. GEOFFREY PRITCHARD.

Research Institutes

AGRICULTURE, FISHERIES AND VETERINARY SCIENCE

AgResearch: Private Bag 3115, Hamilton 3240; 5th Fl., Tower Block, Ruakura Research Centre, Bisley Rd, Hamilton 3240; tel. (7) 834-6600; internet www.agresearch.co .nz; f. 1992 as NZ Pastoral Agriculture Research Institute Ltd; 6 research groups: animal nutrition and health, animal productivity, food and bio-based products, forage improvement, innovative farm systems, land and environment; Chair. SAM ROBINSON; CEO Dr TOM RICHARDSON; Research Dir Prof. WARREN MCNABB; publs *AgResearch Now* (2 a year), *Science Review* (1 a year).

New Zealand Institute for Plant & Food Research Ltd: Private Bag 92169, Auckland Mail Centre, Auckland 1142; 120 Mt Albert Rd, Sandringham, Auckland 1025; tel. (9) 925-7000; e-mail media@plantandfood.co.nz; internet www.plantandfood.co.nz; f. 2008 by merger of HortResearch—Horticulture and Food Research Institute of New Zealand, Ltd (f. 1992) and New Zealand Institute for Crop and Food Research Ltd (f. 1992); conducts research to enhance the value and productivity of horticultural, viticultural, arable, seafood and food and beverage industries; library of 16,000 monograph titles, 5,500 periodical titles; Chair. MICHAEL AHIE; CEO PETER LANDON-LANE.

New Zealand Institute of Food Science and Technology (Inc.): POB 5574, Terrace End, Palmerston North 4441; Shop 9, Rossmont Shopping Centre, 57 Vogel St, Palmerston North 4414; tel. (6) 356-1686; e-mail rosemary@nzifst.org.nz; internet www.nzifst .org.nz; f. 1965; professional body for the food science and technology industry in NZ; divs of dairy, food marketing, food safety, nutrition and sensory evaluation; regular br. meetings, technical sessions and an annual conf.; education and vocational guidance for young people; 9 brs; 1,000 student, standard and professional mems; Pres. DAVID EVERETT; Exec. Man. ROSEMARY HANCOCK; Hon. Treas. MARGOT BUICK; publ. *Food New Zealand* (6 a year).

Scion Research/New Zealand Forest Research Institute Ltd: Private Bag 3020, Rotorua 3046; Te Papa Tipu Innovation Park, 49 Sala St, Rotorua 3010; tel. (7) 343-5899; e-mail enquiries@scionresearch .com; internet www.scionresearch.com; f.

1947 as Forest Experimental Station, renamed Forest Research Institute 1949, current name adopted 2005; govt-owned Crown Research Institute providing research and technology devt for the forestry and wood product industries; focuses on the devt of biomaterials from plants; wood colln and herbarium; offices in Christchurch and Wellington; library of 300,000 vols (incl. monographs and periodicals); CEO Dr WARREN PARKER; Librarian CLAIRE MILLER; publ. *New Zealand Journal of Forestry Science* (1 a year, print and online, www.nzjforestryscience.com).

ECONOMICS, LAW AND POLITICS

New Zealand Institute of Economic Research: POB 3479, Wellington 6140; L13, Grant Thornton House, 215 Lambton Quay, Wellington 6011; tel. (4) 472-1880; e-mail econ@nzier.org.nz; internet www .nzier.org.nz; f. 1958; non-profit inc. society; provides economic consultation, forecasting and research in NZ and overseas; presents annual NZIER Economics Award; Chair. MICHAEL WALLS; Sec. J. MATTHEWSON; publs *New Zealand Industry and Regions* (1 a year), *Quarterly Predictions* (4 a year), *Quarterly Survey of Business Opinion* (4 a year).

EDUCATION

New Zealand Council for Educational Research: POB 3237, Wellington 6140; 10th Fl., W Block, Education House, 178–182 Willis St, Wellington; tel. (4) 384-7939; e-mail library@nzcer.org.nz; internet www .nzcer.org.nz; f. 1934; fosters the study of, and research into, educational matters; prepares and publishes reports for teachers and others in the profession; library of 7,900 vols; Dir and Chief Exec. ROBYN BAKER; publs *Curriculum Matters* (1 a year), *New Zealand Annual Review of Education* (2 a year), *New Zealand Journal of Educational Studies* (2 a year), *Set—Research Information for Teachers* (2 a year).

MEDICINE

Auckland Medical Research Foundation: POB 110139, Auckland Hospital, Auckland 1148; Ground Fl., 89 Grafton Rd, Auckland 1010; tel. (9) 923-1701; e-mail amrf@medicalresearch.co.nz; internet www .medicalresearch.org.nz; f. 1955; financed by public subscription to sponsor and encourage medical research; 2 museum collns of anatomy and pathology; Exec. Dir KIM MCWILLIAMS.

Canterbury Medical Research Foundation: Level 1/230 Antigua St, Christchurch 8011; tel. (3) 353-1240; e-mail health@cmrf .org.nz; internet www.cmrf.org.nz; f. 1960; privately financed; funds health research; Patron ROBERT STEWART; Chair. MIKE STENHOUSE; Exec. Dir GUY JOHNSON.

Hawke's Bay Medical Research Foundation (Inc.): POB 596, Napier; tel. (6) 879-9199; e-mail secretary@hbmrf.org.nz; internet hbmrf.org.nz; f. 1961; works to foster and support medical research and health education in and outside Hawke's Bay; acts as agent for various trusts; Pres. ANDREW WARES; Sec. J. M. BAXTER.

Health Research Council of New Zealand: POB 5541, Wellesley St, Auckland 1141; Level 3, ProCARE Bldg, Grafton Mews, 110 Stanley St, Auckland 1010; tel. (9) 303-5200; e-mail info@hrc.govt.nz; internet www.hrc.govt.nz; f. 1990; initiates, funds and supports health research; advises the govt on issues of health research ethics; monitors the data and safety of large clinical trials; Chair. ROBERT STEWART; Chief. Exec. Dr ROBIN OLDS.

Palmerston North Medical Research Foundation: c/o The Secretary, POB 949, Palmerston North 4440; tel. (6) 357-0640; e-mail sb@naylorlawrence.co.nz; internet www.pnmrf.org.nz; f. 1959; privately financed; gen. medical research; offers the Wilson grant for research; Pres. JOHN CHRISP; Vice-Pres. Prof. H. BLAIR; Vice-Pres. Dr R. ISAACS; Sec. MICHAEL LAWRENCE.

Wellington Medical Research Foundation: c/o The Secretary, POB 51-211, Wellington; tel. (4) 232-5475; e-mail info@wmrf.co.nz; internet www.wmrf.co.nz; f. 1960; privately financed; provides grants for research to both medical and non-medical researchers; Pres. of the Foundation and Chair. of Council Prof. J. NACEY; Sec. and Treas. K. ROSS MACDONALD.

NATURAL SCIENCES
Biological Sciences

Cawthron Institute: Private Bag 2, Nelson 7042; 98 Halifax St E, Nelson 7010; tel. (3) 548-2319; e-mail info@cawthron.org.nz; internet www.cawthron.org.nz; f. 1919; scientific and technological research into the management and devt of NZ's coastal and freshwater systems; community and education programmes; library of 4,500 vols; Chair. IAN KEARNEY; Chief Exec. Dr CHARLES EASON; publ. *Cawthron Lectures* (1 a year).

Institute of Environmental Science and Research Ltd (ESR): POB 50-348, Porirua 5240; Kenepuru Science Centre, 34 Kenepuru Dr., Porirua 5240; tel. (4) 914-0700; e-mail enquiries@esr.cri.nz; internet www.esr.cri.nz; f. 1992; provides scientific research and consulting services related to public health, environmental health and forensic science to public and private sectors and the Asia-Pacific region; research centres in Auckland, Wellington and Christchurch; library of 34,000 vols; CEO Dr KEITH MCLEA.

Landcare Research: POB 69040, Lincoln 7640; Canterbury Agriculture and Science Centre, Gerald St, Lincoln; tel. (3) 321-9999; internet www.landcareresearch.co.nz; f. 1992 as a Crown Research Institute; research, consultancy services and technology devt focused on enhancing natural, productive and urban environments to ensure the future economic prosperity of NZ; other activities incl. environmental sciences, informatics, biosystematics, nationally significant databases and collns, remote-sensing and GIS; specialist library; 9 brs; Chair. PETER SCHUYT; Chief Exec. Dr RICHARD GORDON.

Physical Sciences

Carter Observatory: POB 893, Wellington 6140; tel. (4) 910-3140; e-mail carter@wmt.org.nz; internet www.carterobservatory.org; f. 1941; the nat. observatory; astronomical research and planetarium; cooperation with schools, colleges and univs for education in astronomy; library of 20,000 vols, 434 journals; Dir BRETT MASON.

GNS Science/Institute of Geological and Nuclear Sciences Ltd: POB 30-368, Lower Hutt 5040; 1 Fairway Dr., Avalon, Lower Hutt 5010; tel. (4) 570-1444; e-mail webmaster@gns.cri.nz; internet www.gns.cri.nz; f. 1865 as New Zealand Geological Survey, current name adopted 2006; Crown Research Institute; earth and isotope research and consultancy; maintains collns of rocks, minerals and fossils, incl. Suter colln of NZ Mollusca; responsible for nat. geological mapping, geophysics and hazard studies, and all applied geology incl. petroleum exploration, geothermal energy, groundwater; library of 40,000 vols, 15,000 photos; Chair. TOM CAMPBELL; Chief Exec. MIKE

McWILLIAMS; publs *Globe Magazine* (1 a year), *NZ Volcanological Record* (1 a year).

Mount John University Observatory: POB 56, Lake Tekapo 7945; 422 Godley Peaks Rd, Lake Tekapo; tel. (3) 680-6000; e-mail hod-secretary@phys.canterbury.ac.nz; internet www.phys.canterbury.ac.nz/research/mt_john; f. 1963; operated by Univ. of Canterbury; research esp. into variable stars, stellar spectroscopy and gravitational microlensing; 4 research telescopes with apertures of 1.8 m, 1.0 m and 2 of 0.6 m; Dir Prof. KAREN POLLARD.

National Institute of Water and Atmospheric Research Ltd (NIWA): Private Bag 99940, Newmarket, Auckland 1149; 41 Market Pl., Viaduct Harbour, Auckland Central 1010; tel. (9) 375-2050; e-mail enquiries@niwa.co.nz; internet www.niwa.co.nz; f. 1992; Crown Research Institute; manages and makes use of the natural environment in a sustainable manner; 7 subsidiaries; Chair. CHRIS MACE; Chief Exec. JOHN MORGAN.

New Plymouth Astronomical Society: POB 818, New Plymouth; Marsland Hill, Robe St, New Plymouth; e-mail nickandviv@gmail.com; internet www.marsland.info; f. 1920; organises public nights; Pres. NICK GLADSTONE.

TECHNOLOGY

New Zealand Institute for Industrial Research and Development (Industrial Research Ltd): Gracefield Research Centre, 69 Gracefield Rd, POB 31-310, Lower Hutt 5040; tel. (4) 931-3000; e-mail info@irl.cri.nz; internet www.irl.cri.nz; f. 1992; Crown Research Institute; conducts research and devt into science and technology, and advises on implementing its results commercially; Chair. MICHAEL LUDBROOK; Chief Exec. SHAUN COFFEY; Dir JAN EVANS-FREEMAN.

Libraries and Archives
Auckland

Auckland Libraries: Private Bag 92300, Auckland 1142; tel. (9) 301-0101; internet www.aucklandlibraries.govt.nz; f. 2010 by merger of 7 local authorities in Auckland region; 55 community libraries, 4 mobile libraries, 4 research centres, central library; 3.5m. vols (incl. books, lending magazines, reference serials, UN and FAO depository colln, music sound recordings, DVD and video cassettes), 133 online databases; spec. collns incl. founding donation from Sir George Grey, medieval MSS, incunabula, early printed books, maps, sheet music, photographs, early Maori MSS and printed works; Man. ALLISON DOBBIE.

University of Auckland Library: Private Bag 92019, Auckland Mail Centre, Auckland 1142; tel. (9) 373-7599; e-mail lending.library@auckland.ac.nz; internet www.library.auckland.ac.nz; f. 1890; consists of a General Library, 9 divisional libraries and 12 subject specialist libraries; 2.1m. print vols, 127,000 ejournals, 670,000 ebooks, 15,000 electronic course readings, 330,000 microfilms, 46,000 maps, 34,000 visual recordings, 30,000 audio recordings, 47,500 photographs and drawings, 40,000 slides and multimedia, 2,200 m of archives and MSS; Univ. Librarian JANET COPSEY.

Christchurch

Christchurch City Libraries: POB 73045, Christchurch 8154; tel. (3) 941-7923; e-mail library@ccc.govt.nz; internet christchurchcitylibraries.com; f. 1859; 20 libraries, 2 mobile libraries and 1 digital

library; 1,265,832 vols; Library Man. CAROLYN ROBERTSON; Librarian for Serials and Preservation COLLEEN FINNERTY.

Library, Teaching and Learning George Forbes Memorial Library Lincoln University: POB 85064, Lincoln University, Lincoln, Canterbury 7647; tel. (3) 423-03334; e-mail serials@lincoln.ac.nz; internet library.lincoln.ac.nz; f. 1960; specializes in agriculture, commerce and management, primary production, science and engineering, social sciences incl. landscape architecture, and tourism, environment and natural resource management; 229,657 vols, 114,504 books, 1,357 current print periodicals, 53,336 electronic periodicals; Univ. Librarian Prof. PENNY CARNABY; publ. *Lincoln University Research Archive* (online, researcharchive.lincoln.ac.nz).

University of Canterbury Library: Private Bag 4800, Christchurch 8140; Warehouse, 20 Kirkwood Ave, Ilam, Christchurch 8041; tel. (3) 364-2198; e-mail lending@libr.canterbury.ac.nz; internet library.canterbury.ac.nz; f. 1879; colln. distributed across 4 libraries; 1,831,995 vols, 7,000 rare books, 4,000 linear m of documentary archives, art colln with 4,985 works and 100,000 architectural drawings; spec. collns incl. Macmillan Brown Colln of New Zealand and Pacific Materials; Assoc. Univ. Librarian CORAL BLACK (acting).

Dunedin

Dunedin Public Libraries: POB 5542, Dunedin 9058; 230 Moray Pl., Dunedin 9016; tel. (3) 474-3690; e-mail library@dcc.govt.nz; internet www.dunedinlibraries.govt.nz; f. 1908; network of 5 libraries and 2 bookbuses; 709,992 vols, 30,000 books and 15,000 magazines; heritage collns incl. McNab New Zealand colln (90,509 vols); MSS and Bibles, hymn books and autographed letters; Library Services Man. BERNIE HAWKE.

New Zealand Law Society Library, Otago Branch: Level 4, John Wickliffe House, 265 Princes St, Private Bag 1901, Dunedin; tel. (3) 477-0596; e-mail otago@nzlslibrary.org.nz; internet www.lawsociety.org.nz/law-library; f. 1859; private library for use by mems and assoc. mems of the New Zealand Law Soc., the Judiciary and the Ministry of Justice Court staff and Law Faculty members; 13,500 vols, consisting of statutes, regulations, law reports, unreported judgments, treaties; and a rep. selection of New Zealand secondary sources (textbooks, law journals, dictionaries and encyclopaedias; Asst Librarian NICOLA STEDMAN.

University of Otago Library: POB 56, Dunedin 9054; 65 Albany St, Dunedin; tel. (3) 479-8910; e-mail library@otago.ac.nz; internet www.library.otago.ac.nz; f. 1869; consists of several libraries: Central (arts, commerce, humanities, social sciences), Dental, Education, Hocken (NZ and Pacific research collns), Law, Medical, Science, Southland Campus, Canterbury Medical and Wellington Medical & Health Sciences; spec. collns incl. early European imprints, de Beer Exhibition Gallery and Otakou Press; 1,123,098 vols, 542,518 serials, 6,030 titles, 2,613,176 e-titles; Univ. Librarian HOWARD AMOS.

Hamilton

University of Waikato Library: Private Bag 3105, Hamilton 3240; Hillcrest Rd, Hamilton; tel. (7) 838-4111; e-mail library@waikato.ac.nz; internet www.waikato.ac.nz/library; f. 1964; incorporates Central, Education, Law libraries and NZ colln; 1,059,000 vols, 2,144 print serial titles and 187,870 electronic resources; Univ. Librarian ROSS HALLETT.

Palmerston North

Palmerston North City Library and Community Services: Private Bag 1948, Palmerston North 4440; 4 The Square, Palmerston North; tel. (6) 351-4100; e-mail pncl@pncc.govt.nz; internet citylibrary.pncc.govt.nz; f. 1876; 5 brs; 1 mobile library; community centre; 250,000 vols; Library Gen. Man. ANTHONY LEWIS.

Tauranga

Tauranga City Libraries: Private Bag 12022, Tauranga 3110; Library Arcade, Cnr Wharf and Willow St, Tauranga; tel. (7) 577-7177; e-mail library@tauranga.govt.nz; internet library.tauranga.govt.nz; f. 1906 from Mechanics Institute (f. 1871); NZ and local history collns; 4 brs and 1 mobile library; 325,000 vols; Man. for Libraries JILL BEST.

Wellington

Archives New Zealand: POB 12-050, Wellington; 10 Mulgrave St, Thorndon, Wellington 6011; tel. (4) 499-5595; e-mail general.enquiries@dia.govt.nz; internet www.archives.govt.nz; f. 1926; attached to Dept of Internal Affairs; Nat. War Art Colln; originals from Treaty of Waitangi; Walter Nash Exhibition; public reference services in Wellington and at regional offices in Auckland, Christchurch and Dunedin; gateway at Wellington office; 102,000 linear m of archives, 1,579,000 photographs, 42,603 films and video cassettes, 540,000 maps and plans; 6,000,000 legislative, exec. and judicial records of NZ govt incl. provincial govts; ministerial papers; specialist library collns; Chief Archivist and Gen. Man. MARILYN LITTLE.

National Library of New Zealand/Te Puna Matauranga o Aotearoa: POB 1467, Wellington 6140; tel. (4) 474-3000; e-mail information@natlib.govt.nz; internet www.natlib.govt.nz; f. 1965; receives all New Zealand publs (conventional and electronic) on legal deposit; collns of NZ MSS, sound recordings, music, prints, paintings, drawings and ephemera; oral history and the works of John Milton; 940,863 vols, 10,466 current print periodical titles, 12 main microform collns, 16,812 audio titles in the gen. collns, 778 ebooks, 35 databases, 33,418 ejournals, 593,249 items in the schools collns; Nat. Librarian BILL MACNAUGHT..

Constituent Library:

Alexander Turnbull Library: POB 12–349, Wellington 6144; tel. (4) 474-3120; e-mail alexander.turnbull-library@dia.govt.nz; internet www.natlib.govt.nz/atl; f. 1920; spec. collns incl. New Zealand and the Pacific, Milton, Katherine Mansfield; 30,000 oral history audio cassettes; 10,000 linear m of MSS; 105,000 drawings, paintings, prints and cartoons; 4,964,446 photographic prints, negatives and albums; 60,000 maps; 50,000 sound recordings; 7,000 video cassettes; 1,100 computer files; 195,000 items of ephemera (incl. 19,500 posters); 458,000 newspaper issues; 1,216,000 vols of periodicals; 3,740 music scores; 30,000 online publs; 3,500 websites; 387,500 vols, incl. 32,000 rare books, chiefly in English literature; Chief Librarian CHRIS SZEKELY; publs *Off the Record* (1 a year), *Turnbull Library Record* (1 a year).

Parliamentary Library: Private Bag 18041, Parliament Bldgs, Wellington 6160; tel. (4) 817-9999; e-mail parlinfo@parliament.govt.nz; internet www.parliament.nz; f. 1858; research, reference and information services for mems of parliament and parliamentary staff; services to the public incl. Parliamentary Information Service and Int. Documents Service; 500,000 vols, incl. NZ parliamentary colln, official publs, overseas official and parliamentary publs; Parliamentary Librarian BARBARA MCPHEE (acting); publs *Bills Digests* (irregular, online), *Electorate Profiles* (online), *Monthly Economic Review* (12 a year, online), *Overseas Parliamentary News* (12 a year, online), *Research Papers* (irregular, online).

Te Aka Matua Research Library: POB 467, Wellington 6011; 55 Cable St, Wellington 6011; tel. (4) 381-7000; e-mail library@tepapa.govt.nz; internet www.tepapa.govt.nz/researchattepapa/libraryandinfocentre/; f. 1867; attached to Museum of New Zealand, Te Papa Tongarewa; NZ, Māori, and Pacific history, natural history, art, photography and museum studies; 150,000 vols; Knowledge Man. SHARMAN BUCKLE; publ. *Tuhinga: Records of the Museum of New Zealand Te Papa* (1 a year).

Victoria University of Wellington Library: POB 3438, Wellington; tel. (4) 463-6186; e-mail library@vuw.ac.nz; internet library.victoria.ac.nz; f. 1899; 5 constituent libraries: Architecture and Design Library, Kelburn Library, Commerce Library, Law Library, W. J. Scott Education Library; 1.3m. vols and 70,000 print and electronic periodical titles; Univ. Librarian NOELLE NELSON.

Wellington City Libraries: POB 1992, Wellington 6140; 65 Victoria St, Wellington 6011; tel. (4) 801-4040; e-mail enquiries@wcl.govt.nz; internet www.wcl.govt.nz; f. 1893; 11 br. libraries, 1 central library; 600,000 vols, 450,000 magazines, 85,000 CDs, DVDs, video cassettes and other items; Libraries and Community Spaces Man. JOHN STEARS.

Museums and Art Galleries

Auckland

Auckland Art Gallery Toi o Tāmaki: POB 5449, Wellesley St, Auckland 1141; Cnr of Kitchener and Wellesley St, Auckland 1010; tel. (9) 379-1349; e-mail library@aucklandartgallery.govt.nz; internet www.aucklandartgallery.com; f. 1888; 15,000 works; European paintings since 12th century, sculpture, works by Māori and Pacific Island artists, prints and drawings, Frances Hodgkins colln, Colin McCahon colln, Fuseli drawings, New Zealand painting since 19th century, sculpture and prints; photographs and artists' books, audio and video cassettes; John Weeks archive; library of 33,000 vols; Dir RHANA DEVENPORT; publ. *Gallery Quarterly*.

Auckland War Memorial Museum: Private Bag 92018, Victoria St W, Auckland 1142; The Auckland Domain, Parnell, Auckland; tel. (9) 309-0443; e-mail info@aucklandmuseum.com; internet www.aucklandmuseum.com; f. 1852; natural history, ethnology (esp. NZ Maori and Oceanic), applied arts (esp. Asian, European and NZ ceramics, English furniture, textiles), society and war history, botanical and marine specimens, 1.2m. photographs; conservation laboratory; war memorial for the province; library of 100,000 vols; Dir ROY CLARE; Library Services Man. BRUCE RALSTON; publ. *Records* (1 a year).

Museum of Transport and Technology (MOTAT): POB 44-114, Point Chevalier, Auckland 1246; 805 Great North Rd and Meola Rd, Western Springs, Auckland 1022; tel. (9) 815-5800; e-mail enquiries@motat.org.nz; internet www.motat.org.nz; f. 1964; operates on 2 sites, exhibiting vehicles, aircraft, machinery and equipment of historical and technical interest, incl. an extensive aircraft colln, bus colln, rail colln, vintage agricultural and military vehicles, steam and diesel engines, a working tram line and travelling exhibitions; library: Walsh Memorial Library 12,000 vols, 1,500 serial titles, technical manuals, photographs, maps, plans, archives, Whites Aviation Photographic colln, archives relating to pioneer aviators Jean Batten and Richard Pearse, Les Downey rail photograph colln, Air New Zealand, TEAL, Nat. Airways Corpn and New Zealand Flying School Archives; Dir MICHAEL FRAWLEY.

Christchurch

Canterbury Museum: Rolleston Ave, Christchurch 8013; tel. (3) 366-5000; e-mail info@canterburymuseum.com; internet www.canterburymuseum.com; f. 1870; 2.1m. items from cultural and natural history of the Canterbury region, NZ and global contexts; Antarctic age of discovery and exploration; archaeology, ethnology, geology, zoology, extinct bird studies; Asian and European arts; Canterbury archives; pictorial history; research library; spec. research library on the Antarctic; documentary research centre; Dir ANTHONY E. WRIGHT; publ. *Records of the Canterbury Museum* (1 a year).

Christchurch Art Gallery Te Puna o Waiwhetu: Cnr Worcester Blvd and Montreal St, POB 2626, Christchurch 8140; 58 Gloucester St, Christchurch 8140; tel. (3) 941-7300; e-mail info@christchurchartgallery.org.nz; internet christchurchartgallery.org.nz; f. 1932 as Robert McDougall Art Gallery, current name adopted 2003; nat. and int. touring exhibitions; works by local artists; 6,000 works of art; currently closed for repairs; library of 10,000 vols, 1,200 artist files; Dir JENNY HARPER; publ. *Bulletin* (4 a year).

Dunedin

Dunedin Public Art Gallery: 30 The Octagon, Dunedin; tel. (3) 474-3240; e-mail dpagmail@dcc.govt.nz; internet www.dunedin.art.museum; f. 1884; maintains conservation laboratory; holdings incl.: 14th–19th century European paintings, NZ paintings from 1870, Australian paintings 1900–70, British watercolours, portraits and landscapes; Japanese prints since 18th century, NZ prints since 19th century; old and modern masters, incl. artworks by Machiavelli, Claude Lorrain, Rosa, Pissarro, Reynolds, Gainsborough, Turner, Burne-Jones and Monet; Japanese prints and 20th century Australian art; decorative arts collns; Frances Hodgkins colln; Dir CAM MCCRACKEN.

Otago Museum: POB 6202, Dunedin 9059; 419 Great King St, Dunedin; tel. (3) 474-7474; e-mail mail@otagomuseum.govt.nz; internet www.otagomuseum.govt.nz; f. 1868; colln of over 2m. natural science specimens and human history artefacts; NZ and Pacific anthropology, classical archaeology, European and Asian ceramics, Discovery World Science Centre, Tropical Forest immersive gallery, Southern NZ marine life, geology and fossils, Tangata Whenua—the indigenous Maori people of S New Zealand, Animal Attic—a Victorian taxonomy gallery; Dir IAN GRIFFIN.

Theomin Gallery: 'Olveston', 42 Royal Terrace, Dunedin; tel. (3) 477-3320; e-mail reception@olveston.co.nz; internet www

.olveston.co.nz; built 1904–06; Jacobean-style house designed by British architect Sir Ernest George for David Edward Theomin; bequeathed to the city by his daughter, Dorothy, 1966; opened to the public 1967; antique furniture, ceramics, crystal, bronzes, Persian rugs, silver, early English, European and NZ oils and watercolours; Man. JEREMY SMITH.

Gisborne

Tairawhiti Museum: POB 716, Gisborne 4040; Kelvin Rise, 10 Stout St, Gisborne 4010; tel. (6) 867-3832; e-mail info@tairawhitimuseum.org.nz; internet www.tairawhitimuseum.org.nz; f. 1954; social history, Maori treasures (taonga Maori), fine arts, photography, surfboards, 'Star of Canada' wreck colln, natural history, oral history archive, textiles; local archives, cards and postcards, maps, plans, theatrical programmes, Maori cultural festivals; temporary exhibitions of fine arts and crafts, C. Company Maori (28) Battalion; Te Moana maritime museum; Dir LAURA VODANOVICH.

Gore

Eastern Southland Gallery: POB 305, Gore 9740; Cnr Hokonui Dr. and Norfolk St, Gore; tel. (3) 208-9907; e-mail jgeddes@goredc.govt.nz; internet www.esgallery.co.nz; f. 1984; exhibitions: art works, craft work, historical displays; cultural centre for presentation of films, lectures, music, poetry; 300 works in John Money colln, 60 works in Ralph Hotere colln, 300 works in District colln; Dir JIM GEDDES.

Hokitika

Hokitika Museum: 17 Hamilton St, PMB 704, Hokitika 7842; tel. (3) 755-6898; e-mail enquiries@hokitikamuseum.co.nz; internet www.hokitikamuseum.co.nz; f. 1973; soc. exhibits, working models; audiovisual programme on 19th century W Coast goldmining industry and colonial settlement; Poutini Maori and 19th century immigrant histories; pounamu (NZ greenstone), gold; maintains research centre with local history archives and large photograph colln; Museum Dir JULIA BRADSHAW.

Invercargill

Anderson Park Art Gallery: POB 5095, Invercargill 9843; 91 McIvor Rd, Waikiwi, Invercargill 9876; tel. (3) 215-7432; e-mail andersonparkgallery@xtra.co.nz; internet www.andersonparkgallery.co.nz; f. 1951; 1,000 pieces of NZ art; ceramics, carvings, sculptures and mixed media pieces; currently closed for public viewing; Man. and Curator STEPHEN DAVIES.

Southland Museum and Art Gallery: POB 1012, Invercargill 9840; Queens Park, 108 Gala St, Invercargill 9810; tel. (3) 219-9069; e-mail office@southlandmuseum.co.nz; internet www.southlandmuseum.com; f. 1915; natural history; Maori and colonial history; 'Victoriana'; 4 art galleries; Tuatara breeding colony; sub-Antarctic centre; education programmes; Man. PAUL HORNER; Operations Man. TRACEY WEDGE.

Napier

Hawke's Bay Cultural Trust: POB 248, Napier 4140; tel. (6) 833-9935; e-mail info@mtghawkesbay.com; internet www.mtghawkesbay.com; f. 1989; Man. DOUGLAS LLOYD JENKINS..

Institutions Under the Trust's Control:

Faraday Centre: POB 7021, Napier 4141; 1 Faraday St, Napier; tel. (6) 835-2338; e-mail dprebensen@gmail.com; internet www.faradaycentre.org.nz; f. 1979; science and technology education (stationary, hot-air and steam engines, horse-drawn phaeton and hearse, bath-chairs; audio recording and broadcasting equipment; printing presses; early hospital equipment; high voltage displays, Wimshurst machine, Tesla coil); workshops for school groups; Man. DAVID PREBENSEN.

Hawke's Bay Museum and Art Gallery: POB 248, Napier 4140; 1 Tennyson St, Napier 4110; tel. (6) 835-7781; e-mail info@mtghawkesbay.com; internet www.mtghawkesbay.com; f. 1936; Hawke's Bay Museum and Art Gallery is now closed order to undertake a redevt project; 100,000 objects from Maori and NZ art and material culture, painting, pottery and sculpture, decorative arts, 1931 earthquake and dinosaur exhibitions; regional archives; library; Dir DOUGLAS LLOYD JENKINS.

Nelson

Nelson Provincial Museum: POB 853, Nelson 7040; Town Acre 445, Cnr Trafalgar and Hardy Sts, Nelson; tel. (3) 548-9588; e-mail enquiries@museumnp.org.nz; internet www.nelsonmuseum.co.nz; f. 1841; Maori and European history, Kingdon-Tomlinson Silver colln, Bett colln and Marsden colln; research facility in Isle Park incl. reference library, 1,200,000 photographs (since 1860s), archives (since 1840s); Chief Exec. PETER MILLWARD.

Suter Art Gallery/Te Aratoi o Whakatu: 208 Bridge St, POB 751, Nelson; tel. (3) 548-4699; e-mail info@thesuter.org.nz; internet www.thesuter.org.nz; f. 1899; not-for-profit community org.; local and int. art works; early New Zealand watercolours; programme of exhibitions, events, performances and films; Dir JULIE CATCHPOLE (acting); publ. *The Suter Programme* (4 a year).

Oamaru

Forrester Gallery: Waitaki Dist. Council, Private Bag 50058, Oamaru 9444; 9 Thames St, Oamaru 9400; tel. (3) 433-0853; e-mail info@forrestergallery.com; internet www.forrestergallery.com; f. 1983; housed in a neo-classical bldg constructed in 1884; works of art and architectural drawings related to N Otago and NZ; programme of exhibitions and cultural events; Dir JANE MACKNIGHT; Curator ALICE LAKE-HAMMOND.

Paihia

Waitangi Treaty Grounds: POB 48, Paihia 0247; Tau Henare Dr., Paihia 0200; tel. (9) 402-7437; e-mail info@waitangi.org.nz; internet www.waitangi.org.nz; f. 1840; historic Treaty House; carved Maori meeting house and war canoe; exhibits of NZ historical interest up to 1840; visitor centre complex and audiovisual programme on signing of Treaty of Waitangi between Maori Chiefs and British Crown on 6 February 1840; live Maori theatre and spec. education programmes; CEO GREG MCMANUS.

Timaru

Aigantighe Art Gallery: 49 Wai-iti Rd, Timaru 7910; tel. (3) 688-4424; e-mail gallery@timdc.govt.nz; internet www.timaru.govt.nz/art-gallery; f. 1956; NZ and European paintings, prints, sculpture and ceramics; Dir FIONA CIARAN.

Wanganui

Sarjeant Gallery: POB 998, Wanganui 4540; Queen's Park, Wanganui; tel. (6) 349-0506; e-mail info@sarjeant.org.nz; internet www.sarjeant.org.nz; f. 1919; 5,500 artworks; 16th century European art through to 21st century NZ art; collns incl. works in all media; historic and modern works on paper; NZ and int. sculptures, pottery, ceramics and glass; bronze works; video art and paintings by contemporary artists and old masters; photography exhibitions; Edith Marion Collier Loan Colln incl. 500 pieces; Curator and Public Programmes Man. GREG DONSON.

Whanganui Regional Museum: Watt St, POB 352, Wanganui 4540; tel. (6) 349-1110; e-mail info@wrm.org.nz; internet www.wrm.org.nz; f. 1895; Taonga Maori, natural history, local social history; art colln; archives; Dir Dr ERIC DORFMAN.

Wellington

Museum of New Zealand Te Papa Tongarewa (Te Papa): Cable St, POB 467, Wellington 6011; tel. (4) 381-7000; e-mail mail@tepapa.govt.nz; internet www.tepapa.govt.nz; f. 1992; museum opened 1998; art, history, Maori culture, natural environment; colln of Maori taonga, incl. Te Hau-ki-Turanga (oldest extant Maori building in NZ); Polynesian, Micronesian and Melanesian art and culture; paintings, drawings, graphic art, photography and sculpture by NZ and foreign artists; collns of works by Natalia Gontcharova, Frances Hodgkins, Raymond McIntyre and Colin McCahon; maintains Hector Library (systematic biology, ethnology, early European S Pacific exploration and art reference material); Chief Exec. and Dir MICHAEL HOULIHAN; publ. *Tuhinga: Records of the Museum of New Zealand Te Papa Tongarewa*.

New Zealand Academy of Fine Arts: 1 Queens Wharf, Wellington 6011; tel. (4) 499-8807; e-mail info@nzafa.com; internet www.nzafa.com; f. 1882; art gallery promoting NZ artists and the visual arts in NZ through 8 annual exhibitions; Gen. Man. and Curator NATALIE JONES.

Universities

AUCKLAND UNIVERSITY OF TECHNOLOGY

Private Bag, 92006, Auckland 1142
55 Wellesley St East, Auckland
Telephone: (9) 921-9999
E-mail: info@aut.ac.nz
Internet: www.aut.ac.nz

Founded 1895 as Auckland Technical School, current name adopted 2000
State control
Language of instruction: English
Academic year: January to December

Chancellor: JOHN MAASLAND
Pro-Chancellor: LEX HENRY
Vice-Chancellor: Dr DEREK MCCORMACK
Deputy Vice-Chancellor: Prof. ROB ALLEN
Pro-Vice-Chancellor for Innovation and Enterprise: Prof. JOHN RAINE
Pro-Vice-Chancellor for Int. Relations: Prof NIGEL HEMMINGTON
Pro-Vice-Chancellor for Learning and Teaching and Pro-Vice-Chancellor for Maori Advancement: Assoc. Prof. PARE KEIHA
Pro-Vice-Chancellor for North Shore: Prof. MAX ABBOTT
Pro-Vice-Chancellor for Research: Prof. RICHARD BEDFORD
Pro-Vice-Chancellor: DESNA JURY
Pro-Vice-Chancellor: Dr GEOFF PERRY
Pro-Vice-Chancellor: Prof. PHILIP SALLIS
Pro-Vice-Chancellor: Prof. IAN SHIRLEY
Gen. Counsel: Dr ANDREA VUJNOVICH
Univ. Librarian: Dr LARRAINE SHEPHERD

Library of 241,228 vols, 178,598 electronic resources
Number of teachers: 1,000 f.t.e.
Number of students: 27,299

DEANS

Faculty of Business and Law: Dr GEOFF PERRY

Faculty of Culture and Society: Prof. NIGEL HEMMINGTON

Faculty of Design and Creative Technologies: DESNA JURY

Faculty of Health and Environmental Sciences: Prof. MAX ABBOTT

Law School: Prof. IAN EAGLES

Te Ara Poutama—Faculty of Maori Development: Assoc. Prof. PARE KEIHA

LINCOLN UNIVERSITY

POB 85084, Lincoln Univ., Lincoln 7647
Ellesmere Junction Rd/Springs Rd, Lincoln

Telephone: (3) 325-2811
E-mail: info@lincoln.ac.nz
Internet: www.lincoln.ac.nz

Founded 1878, fmrly Canterbury Agricultural College, renamed Lincoln College 1961, present name and status 1990

State control

Academic year: February to October

Vice-Chancellor: Dr ANDREW WEST

Asst Vice-Chancellor for Academic Programmes and Student Experience: Prof. SHEELAGH MATEAR

Asst Vice-Chancellor for Business Devt: JEREMY BAKER

Asst Vice-Chancellor for Communities: Prof. HIRINI MATUNGA

Asst Vice-Chancellor for Scholarship and Research: Dr STEFANIE RIXECKER

Librarian: PENNY CARNABY

Library of 110,000 vols, 190,000 ebooks, 57,000 serials, 245 databases; art colln

Number of teachers: 220
Number of students: 3,300

Publication: *Infolinc* (12 a year)

DEANS

Faculty of Agriculture and Life Sciences: Prof. BRUCE MCKENZIE

Faculty of Commerce: Assoc. Prof. HUGH BIGSBY

Faculty of Environment, Society and Design: Assoc. Prof. GREG RYAN

PROFESSORS

BOND, S., Property Studies
CONDRON, L., Biochemistry
CULLEN, R., Resource Economics
DI, H., Soil and Environmental Science
EASON, C., Wildlife Management
EDWARDS, G., Dairy Production
FALLOON, R., Plant and Food
HUGHLEY, K., Environmental Management
LIYANARACHICHI, G., Accounting
MCKENZIE, B., Agronomy
MATEAR, S., Marketing
MATUNGA, H., Maori Studies
MOOT, J., Crop and Pasture Physiology
PALMER, D., Biochemical Pathology
PERKINS, H., Human Geography
SAUNDERS, C., Economics
SMALLMAN, C., Business Management

MASSEY UNIVERSITY

Private Bag 11-222, Palmerston North 4442
Tennent Dr., Palmerston North 4474

Telephone: (6) 350-5701
E-mail: contact@massey.ac.nz
Internet: www.massey.ac.nz

Founded 1928 as Massey Agricultural College and merged with the Palmerston North br. of the Victoria Univ. of Wellington 1963; current name adopted 1964, absorbed Wellington Polytechnic 1999

State control

Academic year: February to November

3 Campuses: Albany, Manawatu, Wellington

Chancellor: CHRIS KELLY
Pro-Chancellor: MICHAEL AHIE
Vice-Chancellor: Prof. STEVE MAHAREY
Deputy Vice-Chancellor: Prof. ROBERT ANDERSON
Asst Vice-Chancellor for External Relations: CAS CARTER
Asst Vice-Chancellor for Māori, Pasifika and New Migrants: Dr SELWYN KATENE
Asst Vice-Chancellor for Operations, International and Univ. Registrar: STUART MORRISS
Asst Vice-Chancellor for People and Organisational Devt: ALAN DAVIS
Asst Vice-Chancellor for Research, Academic and Enterprise: Prof. BRIGID HEYWOOD
Asst Vice-Chancellor for Strategy, Finance, IT and Commercial Operations: ROSE ANNE MACLEOD
Librarian: LINDA PALMER

Number of teachers: 1,250
Number of students: 40,000

PRO-VICE-CHANCELLORS

College of Business: Prof. THEODORE ZORN
College of Creative Arts: Assoc. Prof. CLAIRE ROBINSON
College of Health: Prof. PAUL MCDONALD
College of Humanities and Social Sciences: Distinguished Prof. PAUL SPOONLEY
College of Science: Prof. ROBERT ANDERSON

PROFESSORS

ANDERSON, R. D., Sciences
BAILEY, W. C., Food Nutrition and Human Health
BARRY, T., Veterinary, Animal and Biomedical Sciences
BIRKBECK, J., Food Nutrition and Human Health
BLAIR, H. T., Veterinary, Animal and Biomedical Sciences
BODDY, J., Health Sciences
BRIGHT, G., Mechatronics
BRODIE, A. M., Fundamental Sciences
BROWN, I., History
CAHAN, S. F., Accountancy
CARRYER, J. B., Health Sciences
CHAMBERLAIN, K. P., Psychology
CHAPMAN, J. W., Learning and Teaching
CHATTERJEE, S., Applied and International Economics
CHETTY, S., Commerce
CHISTI, Y., Biotechnology
CLELAND, D. J., Technology and Engineering
CODD, J. A., Social and Policy Studies in Education
CORBALLIS, R. P., English and Media Studies
CRESSWELL, M. J., History, Philosophy and Politics
CROPP, G. M., Language Studies
CULLEN, J. L., Learning and Teaching
DAVIES, C., Particle Technology
DE BRUIN, A., Commerce
DEVLIN, M., Management
DURIE, M. H., Maori Studies
ENGELBRECHT, H.-J., Applied and International Economics
EVANS, I., Psychology
FIRTH, E. C., Veterinary, Animal and Biomedical Sciences
FLENLEY, J. R., People, Environment and Planning
FREYBURG, C., Information Systems
GARRICK, D. J., Veterinary, Animal and Biomedical Sciences
GENDALL, P. J., Marketing
GILL, H. S., Food, Nutrition and Animal Health
GUILFORD, W. G., Veterinary, Animal and Biomedical Sciences
HARGREAVES, R. V., Finance, Banking and Property Studies
HARKER, R. K., Education
HAWICK, K., Computer Science

HENDY, M. D., Mathematics
HERMANSSON, G. L., Health and Human Development
HEWETT, E. W., Food, Nutrition and Human Health
HODGSON, J., Natural Resources
HODGSON, R. M., Information Sciences and Technology
HOLMES, C. W., Veterinary, Animal and Biomedical Sciences
HOWE, K. R., History, Philosophy and Politics
HUNT, G. J., Aviation
HUNTER, J. J., Information and Mathematical Sciences
INKSON, J. H., Management and International Business
INKSON, K., Management and International Business
JAMESON, P., Plant Biology
LAGROW, S. J., Health Sciences
LAMBERT, D. M., Molecular Biosciences
LASWAD, F., Accountancy
LEATHERN, J., Neuropsychology
LOCK, A. J., Psychology
LONG, N., Psychology
MACDONALD, B. K., Humanities and Social Sciences
MCKIBBIN, R., Information and Mathematical Sciences
MCLACHLAN, R., Mathematics
MADDOX, I., Industrial Bioscience
MALLON, M., Human Resource Management
MEISTER, A. D., Applied and International Economics
MELLOR, D. J., Food, Nutrition and Human Health
MERRICK, P. L., Psychology
MILNE, K. S., Sciences
MOORE, C. I., Finance, Banking and Property Studies
MORGAN, S., Fine Arts
MORRIS, R. S., Veterinary, Animal and Biomedical Sciences
MOUGHAN, P. J., Food, Nutrition and Human Health
MUNFORD, R. E., Sociology, Social Policy and Social Work
MURPHY, B., Commerce
NASH, R., Social and Policy Studies in Education
OFFICER, D., Chemistry
ONO, K., Language Studies
OPENSHAW, R., Social and Policy Studies in Education
OVERTON, J. D., People, Environment and Planning
PARRY, D. A., Fundamental Sciences
PEARCE, N. E., Public Health Research
PENNY, E. D., Molecular Biosciences
PERERA, H. M. B., Accountancy
RAE, A. N., Applied and International Economics
REEVES, R., Chemistry
ROCHE, M., Health Sciences
ROSE, L. C., Commerce
SCHEWE, K.-D., Information Systems
SCOTT, D. B., Molecular Biosciences
SHOUKSMITH, G., Psychology
SIGNAL, A., Physics
SINGH, H., Food, Nutrition and Human Health
SISSONS, J. D., People, Environment and Planning
SPOONLEY, P., Social and Cultural Studies
SPRINGETT, B. P., Natural Resources
STABLEIN, R., Management
SULLIVAN, P. A., Molecular Biosciences
TENNANT, M., Health Sciences
THOMSON, D. W., History, Philosophy and Politics
TILLMAN, R. W., Natural Resources
TRAWICK, M. J., People, Environment and Planning
TUNMER, W. E., Learning and Teaching
VAN DER WALT, N. T., Management and International Business

VITALIS, T., Management
WATERS, J., Chemistry
WILLIAMSON, N. B., Veterinary, Animal and Biomedical Sciences
WINGER, R. J., Food, Nutrition and Human Health

UNIVERSITY OF AUCKLAND

Private Bag 92019, Auckland 1142
Telephone: (9) 373-7999
E-mail: studentinfo@auckland.ac.nz
Internet: www.auckland.ac.nz

Founded 1883 as Auckland Univ. College, present name and status 1962
Academic year: January to November

Chancellor: Dr I. PARTON
Pro-Chancellor: P. KIELY
Pro-Chancellor for Equal Opportunities: TRUDIE MCNAUGHTON
Pro-Vice-Chancellor for Māori: JIM PETERS
Vice-Chancellor: Prof. STUART MCCUTCHEON
Deputy Vice-Chancellor for Academic Affairs: Prof. JOHN MORROW
Deputy Vice-Chancellor for Research: Prof. JANE HARDING
Deputy Vice-Chancellor for Strategic Engagement: Prof. JENNY DIXON
Dir for Admin. and Registrar: ADRIENNE CLELAND

Library: see under Libraries and Archives
Number of teachers: 2,200
Number of students: 41,000

Publication: *University of Auckland Research Report* (1 a year)

DEANS

Business School: Prof. GREG WHITTRED
Faculty of Arts: Assoc. Prof. ROBERT GREENBERG
Faculty of Education: Prof. GRAEME AITKEN
Faculty of Engineering: Prof. NICHOLAS SMITH
Faculty of Law: Dr ANDREW STOCKLEY
Faculty of Medical and Health Sciences: Prof. JOHN FRASER
Faculty of Science: Prof. GRANT GUILFORD
National Institute of Creative Arts and Industries: Prof. DIANE BRAND

PROFESSORS

ADAMS, P., Applied Behavioural Science
ANAE, M., Pacific Studies
ANDERSON, C. A., Medicine
ASHER, I., Paediatrics
AUSTIN, G. L., Physics
BAKER, E. N., Biological Sciences, Chemistry
BAKER, M., Sociology
BELICH, J. C., History
BELLAMY, A. R., Biological Sciences
BHATTACHARYYA, D., Mechanical Engineering
BISHOP, J. C., Philosophy
BLACK, P. M., Geology
BOOTH, G., Creative and Performing Arts
BOOTH, R., Molecular Medicine and Pathology
BOWMAKER, G., Chemistry
BOWMAN, R. G., Accounting and Finance
BOXALL, P., Management and Employment Relations
BOYS, J. T., Electrical and Electronic Engineering
BRIMBLE, M. A., Chemistry
BRODIE, R. J., Marketing
BROWETT, P., Pathology
BROWNE, P., Geology
BYBLEW, W., Sport and Exercise Science
CALUDE, C. S., Computer Science
CANNELL, M., Physiology
CARMICHAEL, H., Physics
CARTER, I. R., Sociology
CARTWRIGHT, R. W., International Business
CHEN, J. J. J., Chemical and Materials Engineering

CHEN, X. D., Chemical and Materials Engineering
CLARK, G., Chemistry
CLARK, P. J. A., Chinese
CLARK, R. G., Molecular Medicine
COLLINS, I. F., Engineering Science
COOPER, G. J. S., Biological Sciences and Medicine
CORBALLIS, M. C., Psychology
CORRADO, C., Accounting and Finance
COSTER, G. D., General Practice
COVIELLO, N., Marketing
CRAIG, J. L., Geography and Environmental Science
CROSIER, K. E., Molecular Medicine and Pathology
CROSTHWAITE, J., European Languages and Literatures
DANAHER, P. J., Marketing
DAVISON, M. C., Psychology
DENNY, W., Auckland Cancer Society Research Centre
DIXON, J., Planning
DRAGUNOW, M., Pharmacology and Clinical Pharmacology
DUFFY, G. G., Chemical and Materials Engineering
DUNN, M. R., Fine Arts
DUNN, W., Business
DURING, M. J., Molecular Medicine
EAGLES, I. G., Commercial Law
ELLIS, R., Applied Language Studies and Linguistics
EMANUEL, D. M., Accounting and Finance
EVANS, P. J., Law
FAULL, R. L. M., Anatomy
FERGUSON, L., Auckland Cancer Society Research Centre
FERGUSON, W. G., Chemical and Materials Engineering
FLAY, R., Mechanical Engineering
FORER, P. C., Geography and Environmental Science
FRASER, J., Molecular Medicine
GAO, W., Chemicals and Materials Engineering
GARDNER, R. C., Biological Sciences
GAULD, D. B., Mathematics
GEERTSHUIS, S., Continuing Education
GILMOUR, R. S., Liggins Institute
GLUCKMAN, P. D., Liggins Institute
GONZALEZ-CASANOVAS, R., Spanish
GORMAN, D., Medicine
GRANTHAM, R., Commercial Law
GRAY, V. J., Classics and Ancient History
GRUNDY, J., Computer Science
GUSTAFSON, B. S., Political Studies
HAARHOF, E. J., Architecture
HARDING, J. E., Obstetrics and Gynaecology
HARRIS, B. V., Law
HARVEY, J. D., Physics
HATCHER, S., Psychiatry
HATTIE, J. A., Education
HAWORTH, N. A. F., International Business
HAZLEDINE, T. J., Economics
HOLLIS, S., English
HOOL, R. B., Economics
HORROCKS, R., Film, Television and Media Studies
HOSKING, J., Computer Science
HOUSLEY, G., Physiology
HUNT, J. G., Architecture
HUNTER, P. J., Bioengineering Institute
HURSTHOUSE, R., Philosophy
IRWIN, G. J., Anthropology
JACKSON, M. P., English
JACKSON, P. S., Mechanical Engineering
JACKSON, R., Community Health
JACOBS, R., Optometry and Vision Science
JENSEN, C., Anatomy with Radiology
KALLONIATIS, M., Optometry
KELSEY, J., Law
KILPATRICK, J., Nursing
KIRKNESS, A. C., Applied Language Studies and Linguistics
KISTLER, J., Biological Sciences

KLETTE, R., Computer Science
KYDD, R. R., Psychiatry
LARSEN, K., English
LEES, H., Music
LE HERON, R. B., Geography and Environmental Science
LENNON, D. R., Paediatrics
LIPSKI, J., Physiology
LORRIGAN, G., Business
LUCIANO, B., Italian
MCCARTHY, D. C., Psychology
MCCORMICK, R., Goodfellow Unit
MCGHEE, C., Ophthalmology
MCKECHNIE, P., Classics and Ancient History
MCNAUGHTON, S., Education
MACPHERSON, C., Sociology
MANTELL, C. D., Maori and Pacific Health
MARTIN, G. J., Mathematics
MARTIN, I., Surgery
MAXTON, J. K., Law
MELLSOP, G., South Auckland Clinical School
MELVILLE, B., Civil and Resource Engineering
MERRY, A., Anaesthesiology
MITCHELL, E. A., Paediatrics
MITCHELL, M. D., Pharmacology and Clinical Pharmacology
MOLLOY, M. A., Women's Studies
MONTGOMERY, J. C., Biological Sciences
MORIARTY, S., Accounting and Finance
MORROW, J., Political Studies
MUTU, M., Maori Studies
MYERS, M., Management Science and Information Systems
NEICH, R., Anthropology
NEILL, M. A. F., English
NEVILLE, R., Property
NICHOLSON, T., Education
O'CONNOR, C. J., Chemistry
O'SULLIVAN, M., Engineering Science
OWENS, R. G., Psychology
PARRY, B. R., Surgery
PAVLOV, B., Mathematics
PAXTON, J., Pharmacology and Clinical Pharmacology
PENDER, M. J., Civil and Resource Engineering
PERRY, N., Film, Television and Media Studies
PETERS, M., Education
PETRIE, K., Health Psychology
PHILPOTT, A., Engineering Science
POWELL, M. J., Management and Employment Relations
RAMSAY, R. L., French
RANKIN, E. A., Art History
REA, H. H., Medicine
REAY, B. G., History
REID, I. R., Medicine
REILLY, I. L., Mathematics
ROBINSON, V., Education
RUSSELL, D. K., Chemistry
RYAN, D. M., Engineering Science
SALCIC, Z., Electrical and Electronic Engineering
Dame SALMOND, M. A., Anthropology, Maori Studies
SCHWERDTFEGER, P., Chemistry
SCOTT, A. J., Statistics
SCOTT, D., Statistics
SCRIVEN, M., Education
SHARP, R. A., Political Studies
SHAW, J., Pharmacy
SHEPHEARD, C., Fine Arts
SIMPSON, I. J., Medicine
SLEIGH, J., Anaesthesia
SMALL, J., Economics
SMITH, G., Education
SMITH, L., Education
SMITH, W., Geography and Environmental Science
SPALINGER, A., Classics and Ancient History
SPICER, B. H., Accounting and Finance
SRINIVASAN, A., Management Science and Information Systems
STONE, P., Obstetrics and Gynaecology

STURM, T. L., English
SUTTON, D. G., Anthropology
TAGGART, M. B., Law
THOMAS, D. R., Community Health
THOMBORSON, C. D., Computer Science
THORNE, P., Audiology
TIBBLES, J., Music
TINDLE, C., Physics
VALE, B. A., Architecture
VOIT, F., German Languages and Literature
VOWLES, J., Political Studies
WAINWRIGHT, E., Theology
WATTS, P., Law
WELLS, R. M. G., Biological Sciences
WENDT, A., English
WILD, C., Statistics
WILLIAMS, P. W., Geography and Environmental Science
WILLIAMSON, A. G., Electrical and Electronic Engineering
WILSON, M. G., Management and Employment Relations
WILSON, M. J., Classics and Ancient History
WILSON, W., Auckland Cancer Society Research Centre
WILTON, R., Accounting and Finance
WONG, J., Accounting and Finance
ZHANG, Y., Asian Studies

UNIVERSITY OF CANTERBURY

Private Bag 4800, Christchurch 8140
Warehouse, 20 Kirkwood Ave, Ilam, Christchurch 8041
Telephone: (3) 366-7001
E-mail: info@canterbury.ac.nz
Internet: www.canterbury.ac.nz
Founded 1873 as Canterbury College
State control
Academic year: February to November
Vice-Chancellor: Dr ROD CARR
Deputy Vice-Chancellor for Academics: Dr HAMISH COCHRANE
Deputy Vice-Chancellor for Research: Prof. STEVE WEAVER
Asst Vice-Chancellor for Māori Affairs: DARRYN RUSSELL
Pro-Vice-Chancellor for Arts: Prof. JONATHAN LE COCQ
Pro-Vice-Chancellor for Business and Law: Prof. SONIA MAZEY (acting)
Pro-Vice-Chancellor for Education: Prof. GAIL GILLON
Pro-Vice-Chancellor for Engineering: Prof. JAN EVANS-FREEMAN
Pro-Vice-Chancellor for Science: Prof. PAUL FLEMING
Univ. Registrar: JEFF FIELD
Librarian: (vacant)
Library: see under Libraries and Archives
Number of teachers: 547 (f.t.e.)
Number of students: 14,617

DEANS

College of Commerce: Dr ROSS JAMES (acting)
College of Education: Dr JULIE MACKEY
College of Engineering and Forestry: Dr CONAN FEE
College of Science: Prof. CATHERINE MORAN
Faculty of Creative Arts Faculty of Humanities and Social Sciences: Prof. JONATHAN LE COCQ
Postgraduate Research: Prof. LUCY JOHNSTON
School of Law: Assoc. Prof. CHRIS GALLAVIN

PROFESSORS

College of Arts:

BERCOVITCH, J., Political Science
CARSTAIRS-MCCARTHY, A. D., Linguistics
COPELAND, B. J., Philosophy and Religious Studies
FRANCIS, M., Political Science
HEMPENSTALL, P. J. A., History
KUIPER, K., Linguistics

MACDONALD, G. F., Philosophy
MCNAUGHTON, H. D., English
MAJOR, M., Music
MONDRY, H., Russian
ROCHFORT, A. D., Fine Arts
THORNS, D. C., Sociology and Anthropology
WILLIAMS, M., Culture, Literature and Society
ZANKER, G., Classics

College of Business and Economics:

BALL, A., Accountancy
CLARKE, B. J., Accountancy, Finance and Information Systems
CRAGG, P., Accountancy
HALL, C. M., Management
HAMILTON, R. T., Management
MILNE, M., Accountancy
OXLEY, L., Economics

College of Engineering and Forestry:

BLAKIE, R. J., Electrical and Computer Engineering
BODGER, P., Electrical and Computer Engineering
BRIDGES, D. S., Mathematics and Statistics
BUCHANAN, A. H., Civil Engineering
CARR, A. J., Civil and Natural Resources
DAVID, T., Mechanical Engineering
FEE, C. J., Chemical and Process Engineering
GOUGH, P. T., Electrical and Computer Engineering
MILLANE, R. P., Electrical and Computer Engineering
PAWLIKOWSKI, K., Computer Science and Software Engineering
SIRISENA, H. R., Electrical and Computer Engineering
STEEL, M., Mathematics and Statistics
TAKOAKA, T., Computer Science and Software Engineering
TAYLOR, D. P., Electrical and Electronic Engineering
WALKER, J. C., Forestry
WALL, D., Mathematics and Statistics

College of Science:

BAGGALEY, W. J., Physics and Astronomy
BLUNT, J. W., Chemistry
BUTLER, P. H., Physics and Astronomy
COLE, J. W., Geological Sciences
COXON, J. M., Chemistry
DAVIDSON, W., Biological Sciences
FLETCHER, G., Psychology
GERRARD, J., Biological Sciences
HARLAND, P. W., Chemistry
HEARNSHAW, J., Physics and Astronomy
HUGHES, R., Psychology
JACKSON, R. R., Biological Sciences
JAMESON, P. E., Biological Sciences
KELLY, D., Biological Sciences
KEMP, S., Psychology
MCEWAN, M., Chemistry
MUNROE, M. H., Chemistry
PAWSON, E. J., Geography
PHILLIPS, L. F., Chemistry
ROBB, M. P., Communication Disorders
SCHIEL, D. R, Biological Sciences
STEEL, P., Chemistry
STURMAN, A. P., Geography
TAYLOR, R. P., Physics and Astronomy
WEAVER, S. D., Geology
WILLIAMSON, B., Chemistry

School of Law:

FINN, J., Law
JOSEPH, P. A., Law
TODD, S. M. D., Law
WEBB, D., Law

UNIVERSITY OF OTAGO

POB 56, Dunedin 9054
Telephone: (3) 479-1100
E-mail: university@otago.ac.nz
Internet: www.otago.ac.nz

Founded 1869
State control
Language of instruction: English
Academic year: February to November
Chancellor: JOHN WARD
Pro-Chancellor: S. J. MCLAUCHLAN
Vice-Chancellor: Prof. HARLENE HAYNE
Deputy Vice-Chancellor for Academic and Int. Affairs: Prof. VERNON SQUIRE
Deputy Vice-Chancellor for Research and Enterprise: Prof. RICHARD BLAIKIE
Pro-Vice-Chancellor for Commerce: Prof. GEORGE BENWELL
Pro-Vice-Chancellor for Health Sciences: Prof. PETER CRAMPTON
Pro-Vice-Chancellor for Humanities: BRIAN MOLOUGHNEY
Pro-Vice-Chancellor for Int. Affairs: Prof. HELEN NICHOLSON
Pro-Vice-Chancellor for Sciences: Prof. KEITH HUNTER
Dean of Univ. of Otago, Christchurch: PETER JOYCE
Dean of Univ. of Otago, Wellington: CATHERINE COLLINGS
Registrar and Sec. to the Council: Prof. JAN FLOOD
Librarian: HOWARD AMOS
Library: see under Libraries and Archives
Number of teachers: 1,488
Number of students: 21,113

DEANS

College of Education: LISA SMITH
Dunedin School of Medicine: BARRY TAYLOR
Faculty of Law: MARK HENAGHAN
Faculty of Medicine: PETER CRAMPTON
Otago School of Medical Sciences: (vacant)
School of Dentistry: (vacant)
School of Maori, Pacific and Indigenous Studies: MICHAEL REILLY
School of Pharmacy: STEPHEN DUFFULL
School of Physical Education: DOUGLAS BOOTH
School of Physiotherapy: DAVID BAXTER
School of Surveying: Prof. CHRISTINA HULBE

PROFESSORS

ABRAHAM, W. C., Psychology
ACKERLEY, C. J., English
ADLER, R. W., Accounting
AHDAR, R. J., Law
ALBERT, M. H., Computer Science
ALDRED, R. E. L., Pure Mathematics
AN HUEF, A., Pure Mathematics
ANDERSON, J. S., Law
ANDERSON, T. J., Medicine
ARDAGH, M.W, Surgery
BAIRD, M. A., Pathology
BAKER, M. G., Public Health
BALLAGH, R. J., Physics
BALLANTYNE, A. J., History
BARKER, R. J., Statistics
BARUSCH, A. J., Social Work
BAUCUS, M. S., Management
BAXTER, G. D., Physiotherapy
BEGG, E. J., Medicine
BENNETT, J. A., History
BENWELL, G. L., Information Science
BHATIA, M., Pathology
BILKEY, D. K., Psychology
BINNS, J. A., Geography
BLAIKIE, R. J., Physics
BLAKELY, A. A., Public Health
BLAKIE, P. B., Physics
BOOTH, D. G., Physical Education
BRAITHWAITE, A. W., Pathology
BREMER, P. J., Food Science
BROOKER, S. A., Chemistry
BROOKES, B. L., History
BROOKING, T. W. H., History
BROUGHTON, J. R., Dentistry and Preventive and Social Medicine
BURNS, C. W., Zoology
CAMERON, A. V., Medicine

CAMPBELL, H. R., Sociology
CAMPBELL-HUNT, C., Management
CANNON, R. D., Oral Sciences
CHAMBERS, S. T., Pathology
CHARLES, C. J., Medicine
CHETTY, S., Entrepreneurship
CLEMENTS, K. P., Peace and Conflict Studies
COLLINGS, C. D., Psychological Medicine
COLOMBO, M. W., Psychology
CONNOR, J. L., Preventive and Social Medicine
COOK, G. M., Microbiology
CRACK, T. F., Finance
CRAMPTON, P. R., General Practice
CRANE, J., Medicine
CRANEFIELD, S. J. S., Information Science
CRAW, D., Geology
CROWE, M. T., Psychological Medicine and Nursing
CRUMP, J. A., Preventive and Social Medicine
DARLOW, B. A., Paediatrics
DAVIS, L. S., Science Communication
DAWKINS, K. E., Law
DAWSON, J. B., Law
DAWSON, S. M., Marine Science
DAY, A. S., Paediatrics
DAY, C. L., Biochemistry
DE RIDDER, D., Neurosurgery
DELAHUNT, B., Pathology
DENNIS, J. T., Music
DICKINSON, K. J. M., Botany
DOMINIK, W. J., Classics
DOVEY, S. M., General Practice
DOWELL, A. C., General Practice
DOYLE, T. C., Medicine
DRUMMOND, B. K., Oral Sciences
DRUMMOND, J. D., Music
DUFFULL, S. B., Pharmacy
EATON-RYE, J. J., Biochemistry
ECCLES, R. M., Cancer Pathology
EDWARDS, P. R., Public Health
ELDER, D. E., Paediatrics and Child Health
ELLIS, P. M., Psychological Medicine
ESPINER, E. A., Medicine
EVANS, J. J., Obstetrics and Gynaecology
EVERETT, A. M., Management
FARELLA, M., Orthodontics
FERGUSSON, D. M., Psychological Medicine
FIELDING, D. J., Economics
FITZSIMONS, S. J., Geography
FLEMING, J. S., Science Communication
FLYNN, J. R., Politics
FORDYCE, R. E., Geology
FRANZ, E. A., Psychology
FRAUENDIENER, J. T., Applied Mathematics
FREW, R. D., Chemistry
FRIZELLE, F. A., Surgery
GARDNER, R. J. M., Paediatrics
GAULD, R. D. C., Preventive and Social Medicine
GEARE, A. J., Management
GEDDIS, A. C., Law
GEMMELL, N. J., Anatomy
GERRARD, D. F., Medicine
GIBSON, R. S., Human Nutrition
GILLETT, W. R., Obstetrics and Gynaecology
GILLETT, G. R., Bioethics
GLUE, P., Psychological Medicine
GNOTH, J., Marketing
GORDON, K. C., Chemistry
GRATTAN, D. R., Anatomy
GRAY, B. J., Marketing
GREEN, D. P. L., Anatomy
GRIFFIN, J. F. T., Immunology
GROVER, S., Management
GUILFORD, P. J., Biochemistry
HALBERSTADT, J. B., Psychology
HALL, G. G., Law
HAMPTON, M. B., Pathology
HANTON, L. R., Chemistry
HARLAND, A. D., Higher Education
HARRIS, W. W., Politics
HAUG, A. A., Economics
HAYNE, H., Psychology
HENAGHAN, R. M., Law
HENDY, M. D., Mathematics

HERBISON, A. E., Physiology
HERBISON, G. P., Preventive and Social Medicine
HIGGINS, S. J., Botany
HIGHAM, C. F. W., Anthropology and Archaeology
HIGHAM, J. E. S., Tourism
HIGHTON, J., Medicine
HILL, P. C., Preventive and Social Medicine
HODGE, K. P., Physical Education
HOEK, J. A., Marketing
HOLLOWAY, L. J., Pathology
HOOK, S. M., Pharmacy
HOOPER, G. J., Orthopaedic Surgery
HOWDEN-CHAPMAN, P. L., Public Health
HULBE, C. L., Surveying
HUNTER, K. A., Chemistry
HUTTON, J. D., Obstetrics and Gynaecology
HYLAND, B. I., Physiology
JACKSON, R. D. W., Peace and Conflict Studies
JACKSON, S. J., Physical Education
JAMIESON, I. G., Zoology
JOHNSON, H. M., Music
JONES, D. G., Anatomy and Bioethics
JOYCE, P. R., Psychological Medicine
KENNEDY, M. A., Pathology
KETTLE, A. J., Pathology
KIESER, J. A., Dental Research
KNIGHT, J. G., Marketing
KNIGHT, R. G., Psychology
KRAUSE, K. L., Biochemistry
KUCH, P. R., Irish Studies
LAI, K., Education
LAING, R. M., Clothing and Textile Sciences
LAMONT, I. L., Biochemistry
LAWSON, R. W., Marketing
LONT, D. H., Accounting
LOVE, R. M., Oral Rehabilitation
LYONS, K. M., Restorative Dentistry
MACDONELL, S. G., Information Science
MAHONEY, R. R., Law
MANN, J. I., Human Nutrition
MATISOO-SMITH, E. A., Anatomy
MAY, H., Education
MCCALL, J. L., Clinical Science
MCCARTHY, A. H., Scottish and Irish History
MCGEE, R. O., Preventive and Social Medicine
MCILVANNEY, L. A., Scottish Studies
MCLENNAN, I. S., Anatomy
MCMILLAN, J. R., Bioethics
MCNAUGHTON, N., Psychology
MCQUILLAN, A. J., Chemistry
MEHIGAN, T. J., German
MERCER, A. A., Viral Pathogenesis
MERCER, A. R., Zoology
MILLER, J. O., Psychology
MILLER, A., Philosophy
MOLLER, H., Geography
MOLOUGHNEY, B. D., History
MOLTENO, A. C. B., Ophthalmology
MORGAN, R. K., Geography
MORISON, I. M., Pathology
MULDER, R. T., Psychological Medicine
MURDOCH, D. R., Pathology
MUSGRAVE, A. E., Philosophy
NACEY, J. N., Surgery
NEL, E. L., Geography
NEL, P. R., Politics
NICHOLSON, H. D., Anatomy
NORRIS, P. T., Pharmacy
OEY, I., Food Science
OWEN, P. D., Economics
PATMAN, R. G., Politics
PEART, N. S., Law
PORTER, R. J., Psychological Medicine
POULIN, R., Zoology
POULTON, R. G., Preventive and Social Medicine
PRINGLE, K. C., Obstetrics and Gynaecology
PRIOR, D. J., Geology
PURVIS, M. K., Information Science
RADNER, H. A., Film and Media Studies
RAE, M. A., Theology
RAEBURN, I. F., Pure Mathematics

REESE, J. E., Psychology
REEVE, A. E., Biochemistry
REILLY, M. P. J., Maori Studies
RICH, A. M., Oral Diagnostic and Surgical Sciences
RICHARDS, A. M., Medicine
ROAKE, J. A., Surgery
ROBERTSON, S. P., Paediatrics
ROBINS, A. V., Computer Science
ROBINSON, B. A., Cancer Medicine
ROBINSON, B. H., Chemistry
RODGER, C. J., Physics
ROMANS, S. E., Psychological Medicine
RONSON, C. W., Genetics
ROSE, E. L., Management
ROTH, P. A., Law
ROTHWELL, A. G., Obstetrics and Gynaecology
RUFFMAN, K. E., Psychology
SCOTT, S. R., Law
SEDDON, P. J., Zoology
SELLMAN, J. D., Psychological Medicine
SHEPHARD, K. L., Higher Education
SHIPTON, E. A., Anaesthesia
SKEAFF, C. M., Human Nutrition
SKEGG, D. C. G., Preventive and Social Medicine
SKEGG, P. D. G., Law
SMILLIE, J. A., Law
SMITH, J. K., Education
SMITH, L. F., Education
SMITH, P. F., Pharmacology and Toxicology
SONG, J. J., English
SPENCER, H. G., Zoology
SPRONKEN-SMITH, R. A., Higher Education
SQUIRE, V. A., Applied Mathematics
STAMP, L. K., Medicine
STILLMAN, S. E., Economics
SULLIVAN, S. J., Physiotherapy
SUMMERHAYES, G. R., Anthropology
TANNOCK, G. W., Microbiology
TAPSELL, P. J., Maori Studies
TATE, W. P., Biochemistry
TAYLOR, B. J., Paediatrics
THEIS, J., Surgical Sciences
THOMSON, W. M., Oral Sciences
TILYARD, M. W., General Practice
TOOP, L. J., Practice
TOWNSEND, C. R., Zoology
TREBILCO, P. R., Theology
TRIBBLE, E. B., English
TROUGHTON, R. W., Medicine
TUCKER, I. G., Pharmacy
VAN RIJ, A. M., Surgical Sciences
VISSERS, M. C. M., Pathology
WALKER, R. J., Medicine
WALLIS, G. P., Zoology
WALTER, R. K., Archaeology
WARD, V. K., Virology
WATERS, J. M., Zoology
WEATHERALL, M., Medicine
WELLS, J. E., Biostatistics
WHARTON, D. A., Zoology
WHITE, K. G., Psychology
WILKINSON, T. J., Medicine
WILLIAMS, M. J. A., Medicine
WILSON, G. S., Marine Science
WILSON, P. D., Obstetrics and Gynaecology
WING, S. R., Marine Science
WINIKOFF, M., Information Science
WINTERBOURN, C. C., Pathology
ZHANG, J., Finance

UNIVERSITY OF WAIKATO

Private Bag 3105, Hamilton 3240
Te Whare Wānanga o Waikato, gate one, Knighton Rd, Hamilton 3240

Telephone: (7) 856-2889
E-mail: info@waikato.ac.nz
Internet: www.waikato.ac.nz

Founded 1964
State control
Academic year: February to November

Chancellor: Rt Hon JAMES B. BOLGER
Vice-Chancellor: Prof. ROY CRAWFORD

Deputy Vice-Chancellor: Prof. ALISTER JONES
Pro-Vice-Chancellor for Education: Prof. ROBYN LONGHURST
Pro-Vice-Chancellor for Int. Affairs: Assoc. Prof. ED WEYMES
Pro-Vice-Chancellor for Māori: Prof. LINDA SMITH
Pro-Vice-Chancellor for Postgraduate Affairs: Prof. KAY WEAVER
Pro-Vice-Chancellor for Research: Prof. AL GILLESPIE
Univ. Librarian: ROSS HALLETT
Library: see under Libraries and Archives
Number of teachers: 639
Number of students: 12,344

DEANS

Faculty of Arts and Social Sciences: Prof. Dr ROBERT HANNAH (acting)
Faculty of Computing and Mathematical Sciences: Prof. GEOFF HOLMES
Faculty of Education: Prof. Dr ROGER MOLTZEN
Faculty of Science and Engineering: Prof. Dr BRUCE CLARKSON
School of Maori and Pacific Development: Prof. LINDA SMITH
Te Piringa—Faculty of Law: Prof. BRADFORD W. MORSE
Waikato Management School: JOHN TRESSLER (acting)

PROFESSORS

APPERLEY, M. D., Computing and Mathematical Sciences
BARRATT, A. A. T., English
BARTON, B., Law
BEARDON, C., Computer Sciences
BEDFORD, R. D., Geography
BING, D., Political Science and Public Policy
BISHOP, R., Maori Education
BOOTH, D., Sport and Leisure Studies
CARY, C., Biological Sciences
CLARK, D., Management
CLEARY, J. G., Computer Sciences
CORNER, J., Management Systems
CRAIG, I., Mathematics
CUBITT, S., Screen and Media Studies
DANIEL, R. M., Biological Sciences
EGGLETON, I., Accounting
ERICKSEN, N., International Global Change Institute
FARRAR, J. H., Law
FARRELL, R. L., Biological Sciences
FOULDS, L. R., Management Systems
GILLESPIE, A. M., Law
GILSON, C. H. J., Strategic Management and Leadership
GLYNN, E. L., Human Development and Counselling
GRANT, B., Sport and Leisure Studies
GREEN, T. G. A., Biological Sciences
HAMILTON, D., Biological Sciences
HARCOURT, M., Strategic Management and Leadership
HEALY, T. R., Earth Sciences
HOLMES, M. J., Economics
JOHN, N., Statistics
JONES, A. T., Wilf Malcolm Institute of Educational Research
KALNINS, E. G., Mathematics
KAMP, P. J. J., Earth Sciences
KOOPMAN-BOYDEN, P. G., Arts and Social Sciences
LAWRENCE, S., Accounting
LEITCH, S., Public Relations and Marketing
LOWE, A., Accounting
McGEE, C., Wilf Malcolm Institute of Educational Research
McKIE, D., Management Communication
McQUEEN, B., Management Systems
MAY, S., Arts and Language Education
MIDDLETON, S. C., Policy, Cultural and Social Studies in Education
MOLAN, P. C., Biological Sciences

MORGAN, H. W., Biological Sciences
MOTION, J., Management Communication
NELSON, C. S., Earth Sciences
NICHOLSON, B. K., Chemistry
O'DRISCOLL, M., Psychology
POOL, D. I., Population Studies
POOT, J., Population Studies
PRATT, M. J., Management Studies
PRICE, R., Science and Engineering
QUICK, S. P., Biological Sciences
REEDY, T., Maori Sustainable Enterprise
REEVES, S., Computer Science
RICHARDSON, N. A., Management
RITCHIE, J., Psychology
ROA, T. C., Maori and Pacific Development
RYAN, C. A., Tourism Management
SCARPA, R., Economics
SCRIMGEOUR, F. G., Economics
SILVESTER, W. B., Biological Sciences
SMYTH, J., Wilf Malcolm Institute of Educational Research
SNEYD, A. D., Mathematics
SPILLER, P. R., Law
STOKES, E. M., Geography, Tourism and Environmental Planning
TE AWEKOTUKWU, N. A., Maori and Pacific Development
VAREY, R. J., Marketing and International Management
VOS, E. A. J., Finance
WALKER, G. M., English
WILKINS, A. L., Chemistry
WILKINS, R. J., Biological Sciences
WITTEN, I. H., Computer Science
YATES-SMITH, G. R. A., Maori and Pacific Development
ZIRKER, D., Arts and Social Sciences
ZORN, T. E., Management Communication

VICTORIA UNIVERSITY OF WELLINGTON

POB 600, Wellington 6140
Telephone: (4) 472-1000
E-mail: info-desk@vuw.ac.nz
Internet: www.victoria.ac.nz
Founded 1897 as Victoria College, current name adopted 1961
Languages of instruction: English, Maori
Academic year: March to February (3 trimesters)
4 Wellington-based campuses: Kelburn, Pipitea, Te Aro and Karori
Chancellor: IAN D. MCKINNON
Pro-Chancellor for Univ. Council: GRAEME R. MITCHELL
Vice-Chancellor: Prof. GRANT GUILFORD
Deputy Vice-Chancellor for Academics: Prof. PENNY BOUMELHA
Deputy Vice-Chancellor for Research: Prof. NEIL QUIGLEY
Pro-Vice-Chancellor for Commerce: Prof. BOB BUCKLE
Pro-Vice-Chancellor for Law: Prof. TONY SMITH
Pro-Vice-Chancellor for Humanities and Social Sciences: Prof. DEBORAH WILLIS
Pro-Vice-Chancellor for Maori: Prof. PIRI SCIASCIA
Pro-Vice-Chancellor for Engineering, Science; Architecture and Design: Prof. MIKE WILSON
Chief Operating Officer: ANDREW SIMPSON
Sec. to Council: CAROLINE WARD
Library: see under Libraries and Archives
Number of teachers: 1,824
Number of students: 16,787
Publications: *Staff and Student Research* (1 a year), *Victorious* (3 a year)

DEANS

Faculty of Architecture and Design: Prof. ROBIN SKINNER (acting)

Faculty of Education: Assoc. Prof. DAVID CRABBE
Faculty of Engineering: Prof. JOHN HINE
Faculty of Graduate Research: Prof. PETER WHITEFORD
Faculty of Humanities and Social Sciences: Prof. DEBORAH WILLIS
Faculty of Law: TONY SMITH
Faculty of Maori: Prof. PIRI SCIASCIA
Faculty of Science: Prof. MIKE WILSON
Victoria Business School: Prof. BOB BUCKLE

PROFESSORS

Faculty of Architecture and Design (tel. (4) 463-6200; e-mail architecture@vuw.ac.nz; internet www.victoria.ac.nz/architecture):
FRASER, S., Design
MOLONEY, J., Architecture

Faculty of Education (tel. (4) 463-9500; e-mail teaching@vuw.ac.nz; internet www.victoria.ac.nz/education):
HALL, C. G. W.
MEYER, L.
SIGAFOOS, J.

Faculty of Humanities and Social Sciences (tel. (4) 463-5208; e-mail hum-socsci-office@vuw.ac.nz; internet www.victoria.ac.nz/fhss):
BAUER, L., Linguistics and Applied Language Studies
CLARK, M., History, Philosophy, Political Science and Int. Relations
DAVIDSON, J. F., Art History, Classics and Religious Studies
HOLMES, J., Linguistics and Applied Language Studies
LEVINE, S., Political Science and Int. Relations
MORRIS, P., Religious Studies
NATION, P., Linguistics and Applied Languages
PRATT, J., Social and Cultural Studies
STERELNY, K., Philosophy

Faculty of Law (tel. (4) 463-6366; e-mail law-enquiries@vuw.ac.nz; internet www.victoria.ac.nz/law):
ANDERSON, G.
ANGELO, T.
ATKIN, B.
McLACHLAN, C.
McLAUCHLAN, D. W.
PREBBLE, J.
SMITH, T.

Faculty of Science (tel. (4) 463-5101; e-mail science-faculty@vuw.ac.nz; internet www.victoria.ac.nz/science):
BARRETT, P. J., Antarctic Research Centre
DOWNEY, R., Mathematics, Statistics and Operations Research
GARNOCK-JONES, P., Biological Sciences
GOLDBLATT, R. I., Mathematics, Statistics and Operations Research
HINE, J., Engineering and Computer Science
JOHNSTON, J., Chemical and Physical Sciences
KAISER, A., Chemical and Physical Sciences
KHMALADZE, E., Mathematics, Statistics and Operations Research
LEKNER, J., Chemical and Physical Sciences
SCHENK, S., Psychology
SMITH, E., Geography, Environment and Earth Sciences
WARD, C., Psychology
WARD, T., Psychology
WHITTLE, G., Mathematics, Statistics and Operations Research

Victoria Business School (tel. (4) 463-5376; e-mail fca-sao@vuw.ac.nz; internet www.victoria.ac.nz/fca):
BOSTON, J., Govt
BROCKLESBY, J., Management
CORBETT, L., Management

CUMMINGS, S., Management
DAVIES, J., Management
EVANS, L. T., Economics and Finance
HALL, V. B., Economics and Finance
HUFF, S., Information Management
PEARCE, D., Tourism Management
SCOTT, C. D., Govt
VAN ZIJL, T., Commerce

Other Higher Education Institutions

Bay of Plenty Polytechnic: Private Bag 12001, Tauranga 3143; 70 Windermere Dr., Poike, Tauranga 3112; tel. (7) 571-0190; e-mail info@boppoly.ac.nz; internet www.boppoly.ac.nz; f. 1982 as Bay of Plenty Community College, current name adopted 1988; schools of applied science, applied technology, business studies, design and humanities; 2 campuses: Edgecumbe and Windermere; Road Transport, Warehousing and Logistics Training Centre, Bongard Centre; 561 teachers; 6,822 students (3,204 full-time); Chair. IAN TURNER; Chief Exec. Dr ALAN HAMPTON.

Christchurch Polytechnic Institute of Technology: POB 540, Christchurch Mail Centre, Christchurch 8140; 130 Madras St, Christchurch; tel. (3) 940-8000; e-mail info@cpit.ac.nz; internet www.cpit.ac.nz; f. 1965; specializes in information technology, with pathways to Monash Univ. (Australia) Masters programmes; library: 48,000 items; 1,180 teachers (350 full-time, 830 part-time); 17,600 students; Chief Exec. KAY GILES.

Manukau Institute of Technology: Private Bag 94006, Manukau 2241; Cnr of East Tamaki Rd and Newbury St, Otara, Manukau City 2023; tel. (9) 968-8000; e-mail info@manukau.ac.nz; internet www.manukau.ac.nz; f. 1970; faculties of business and information technology, consumer services, creative arts, education and social sciences, engineering and trades, maritime and logistics, nursing and health studies; school of secondary-tertiary studies; library: 55,000 vols; 400 teachers; 32,700 students; Chief Exec. Dr PETER BROTHERS.

Nelson Marlborough Institute of Technology: Private Bag 19, Nelson 7042; 322 Hardy St, Nelson 7010; tel. (3) 546-9175; e-mail info@nmit.ac.nz; internet www.nmit.ac.nz; campus in Marlborough; 3,500 students; Chief Exec. TONY GRAY.

Open Polytechnic of New Zealand: Private Bag 31914, Lower Hutt 5040; 3 Cleary St, Lower Hutt 5011; tel. (4) 913-5300; e-mail customerservices@openpolytechnic.ac.nz;

internet www.openpolytechnic.ac.nz; f. 1946 as Technical Correspondence School; current name adopted 1990; schools of business, commerce and enterprise, education studies, engineering, trades and construction, health and community, science and technology, social sciences; open polytechnic library; 120 teachers; 37,000 students; Chief Exec. Dr CAROLINE SEELIG.

Otago Polytechnic: Private Bag 1910, Dunedin 9054; F Block Forth St, Dunedin 9016; tel. (3) 477-3014; e-mail info@op.ac.nz; internet www.otagopolytechnic.ac.nz; f. 1870; 3 campuses: Dunedin, Central Otago and Auckland; library: 30,000 vols; 700 teachers; 6,700 students; Chief Exec. PHIL KER.

Southern Institute of Technology: Private Bag 90114, 133 Tay St, Invercargill 9840; tel. (3) 211-2699; e-mail info@sit.ac.nz; internet www.sit.ac.nz; f. 1971 as Southland Polytechnic; 4 campuses: Christchurch, Gore, Invercargill, Queenstown; Chief Exec. PENNY SIMMONDS.

Te Wānanga o Aotearoa: POB 22037, Christchurch 8011; 105 Gasson St, Christchurch 8011; tel. (3) 365-9874; e-mail studentsupport@twoa.ac.nz; internet www.twoa.ac.nz; f. 1984; 80 locations in NZ; CEO JIM MATHER.

Te Wananga O Raukawa: POB 119, Ōtaki, Aotearoa 5542; 144 Tasman Rd, Ōtaki, Aotearoa 5512; tel. (6) 364-9011; e-mail tetomonga@twor-otaki.ac.nz; internet www.wananga.com; f. 1981; Chief Exec. MEREANA SELBY.

Te Whare Wananga o Awanuiarangi: Ground Fl., 13 Domain Rd, Whakatāne; e-mail enquiries@wananga.ac.nz; internet www.wananga.ac.nz; f. 1991; 3 locations: Whakatāne, Auckland, Northland; Mark Laws media centre; library; CEO and Vice-Chancellor Prof. HINGANGAROA SMITH; Chair. Prof. Sir SIDNEY MOKO MEAD.

UNITEC Institute of Technology: Private Bag 92025, Victoria St West, Auckland 1142; Carrington Rd, Mt Albert, Auckland; tel. (9) 849-4180; e-mail study@unitec.ac.nz; internet www.unitec.ac.nz; f. 1976 as the Carrington Technical Institute, current name adopted 1994; faculties of architecture and design, arts and social sciences, business, health and environmental sciences; applied technology institute; 3 campuses: Mt Albert, Northern campus and Waitakere; library: 88,834 vols; 1,100 teachers; 23,000 students; Chief Exec. Dr RICK EDE.

Waikato Institute of Technology: Private Bag 3036, Waikato Mail Centre, Hamilton 3240; City Campus, A Block, Gate 3, Tristram St, Hamilton; tel. (7) 838-6399; e-mail info@wintec.ac.nz; internet www.wintec.ac

.nz; f. 1924 as Hamilton Technical College; became Waikato Technical Institute 1968, Waikato Polytechnic 1987; current name adopted 2001; courses at Masters degree, diploma, certificate, professional technician and trades levels; community education; 2 campuses: City campus and Rotokauri; library: 62,800 vols; 365 teachers; 13,100 students (4,500 full-time, 8,600 part-time); Chief Exec. Officer MARK FLOWERS.

Wellington Institute of Technology: Private Bag 39803, Wellington Mail Centre, Lower Hutt 5045; 11 Kensington Ave, Petone, Lower Hutt; tel. (4) 920-2400; e-mail information@weltec.ac.nz; internet www.weltec.ac.nz; f. 2001 by an amalgamation between the Central Institute of Technology and the Hutt Valley Polytechnic; provides diplomas and degrees; faculties incl. addiction, counselling and health Studies, art, design and multimedia, business, construction trades, engineering technology, exercise science, funeral services, hairdressing, beauty therapy and make-up artistry, social services, hospitality, information technology; 5 campuses: Petone, Wellington, Auckland, Christchurch and WelTec School of Hospitality; 11,000 students; Chief Exec. Dr LINDA SISSONS; Electronic Services and Reference Librarian ANNE GRANT.

Schools of Art and Music

Elam School of Fine Arts: Faculty of Fine Arts, Univ. of Auckland, Private Bag 92019, Auckland; Main Fine Arts, Bldg 431, Level 4, 20 Whitaker Pl., Auckland; tel. (9) 373-7599; e-mail info-creative@auckland.ac.nz; internet www.creative.auckland.ac.nz; f. 1889 as Elam School of Art and Design; attached to Univ. of Auckland; fine arts instn; art and design activities in a interdisciplinary studio environment; George Fraser Gallery, Elam Projectspace Gallery; library: 35,000 vols; 35 teachers; 450 students; Head of School DERRICK CHERRIE.

SAE Institute: 12 Heather St, Parnell, Auckland; tel. (9) 373-4712; e-mail auckland@sae.edu; internet auckland.sae.edu; f. 1976; Man. LEYLAND BOTTOMLEY (acting); publ. *SAE Magazine*.

School of Fine Arts: Univ. of Canterbury, Private Bag 4800, Christchurch 8140; tel. (3) 364-2159; internet www.fina.canterbury.ac.nz; f. 1882 as Canterbury College School of Art; attached to Univ. of Canterbury; library: 10,000 vols, incl. index of NZ historic buildings, 100,000 slides, 4,985 works in the art colln and 100,000 architectural drawings; 20 teachers; 785 students; Dir HUBERT KLAASSENS.

NICARAGUA

The Higher Education System

The oldest institution of higher education in Nicaragua is the Universidad Nacional Autónoma de Nicaragua (founded in 1812), which dates from the Spanish colonial period. Nicaragua became part of the Central American Federation in 1821 and declared its independence in 1838. There are currently 10 universities that are full members of the Consejo Nacional de Universidades (National Council of Universities—CNU), of which four are state-run, and a further 59 universities which are authorized by the CNU. In 2003/04 a total of 103,577 students attended universities and other higher education institutes. In 2010 there were 137,254 students enrolled in the universities.

The CNU is the body responsible for all strategic planning. The principal officer of each university is a Rector, who is assisted by a number of Vice-Rectors; individual Faculties are headed by Deans. The Comisión de Evaluación y Acreditación advises the CNU on matters of evaluation and accreditation of the universities.

Admission to higher education is on the basis of the Bachillerato, the leading secondary school qualification, and an entrance examination. The Licenciado, the main undergraduate degree, is a four- or five-year course of study; a professional title may also be awarded, depending on the subject. Following the Licenciado, the first postgraduate degree is the Maestría, which lasts two years and culminates with the submission of a thesis.

Institutions of higher education also offer two- and three-year courses in technical and vocational education. The main qualification studied for is the Técnico Superior. Since its founding in 2002, the Asociación de Colegios Profesionales (Association of Professional Colleges), as well as the four public universities and two private universities (Universidad Centroamericana and Universidad Americana) are all members of the Consejo Centroamericano de Acreditación de la Educación Superior (Central American Accreditation Council for Higher Education), a regional body whose purpose it is to harmonize and improve higher education in Central America.

Regulatory and Representative Bodies

GOVERNMENT

Ministry of Education: Apdo 505, Managua; Centro Cívico, Módulo 'K', Planta Alta, Managua; tel. 2253-8490; e-mail valdiviam@mined.gob.ni; internet www.mined.gob.ni; Minister Dr MIRIAM RÁUDEZ.

NATIONAL BODY

Consejo Nacional de Universidades (National Council of Universities): Los Robles, de donde fue el Chamán una cuadra al Este, media al Norte, Managua; tel. 2278-1053; e-mail administracion@cnu.edu.ni; internet www.cnu.edu.ni; f. 1990; 14 mems; Pres. Dr TELÉMACO TALAVERA SILES; Sec. Ing. ALBERTO SEDILES; publ. *Universidad y Sociedad*.

Learned Societies

BIBLIOGRAPHY, LIBRARY SCIENCE AND MUSEOLOGY

Asociación Nicaragüense de Bibliotecarios y Profesionales Afines (Nicaraguan Association of Librarians and Related Professionals): Apdo postal 3257, calle F. Guzman Bolanos, Altamira del Est, Casa 120, Managua; e-mail anibipa@yahoo.com; f. 1982; Pres. Lic. NUBIA MANZANAREZ.

LANGUAGE AND LITERATURE

Academia Nicaragüense de la Lengua (Nicaraguan Academy of Language): Apdo 2711, Managua; Avda del Campo 42, Las Colinas, Managua; e-mail pavsa@munditel.com.ni; internet www.anilengua.com; f. 1928; corresp. of the Real Academia Española (Madrid); 13 mems; Dir FRANCISCO JOSE ARELLANO OVIEDO; Sec. PEDRO XAVIER SOLÍS CUADRA.

Alianza Francesa (Alliance Française): Apdo 2370, Managua; Planes de Altamira, De la Embajada de México ½ cuadra al Norte, Managua; tel. 2267-2811; e-mail informacion@alianzafrancesa.org.ni; internet www.alianzafrancesa.org.ni; f. 1951; offers courses and examinations in French language and culture and promotes cultural exchange with France; attached teaching centres in León and Granada; Dir MÉLANIE BOUCHARD.

MEDICINE

Asociación Nicaraguense de Cirugía Plástica Reconstructiva y Estética (Nicaraguan Association of Reconstructive Plastic and Cosmetic Surgery): Clinicentro Ciudad Jardín, ITR 1/2 cuadras al Norte, Managua; tel. 8850-9269; internet www.cirujanosplasticosnicaragua.com; Pres. Dra SANDRA M. GUTIÉRREZ GÓMEZ; Sec. Dr EDGARD IBARRA.

Sociedad Nicaragüense de Oftalmología (Nicaraguan Society of Ophthalmology): Altamira D. Este No 99 Cl principal, Managua; f. 1949; Pres Dr DIEGO A. VALLE GONZÁLEZ.

Research Institutes

ECONOMICS, LAW AND POLITICS

Instituto Nicaragüense de Investigaciones Económicas y Sociales (INIES) (Nicaraguan Institute of Economic and Social Research): Apdo 663, Managua; tel. 2266-8502; e-mail inies@turbonett.com.ni; internet www.unan.edu.ni/index.php/i-d/92-centros-investigacion/113-inies; f. 1982; attached to Universidad Nacional Autónoma de Nicaragua; informs and conducts research on developing alternatives for the vulnerable sectors of the nat. population; Dir Dr GUSTAVO RAMÓN SILES GONZÁLEZ; publ. *Cuadernos de Investigación* (irregular).

HISTORY, GEOGRAPHY AND ARCHAEOLOGY

Instituto de Historia de Nicaragua y Centroamérica (Institute of History of Nicaragua and Central America): Apdo C-186, Managua; Rotonda Rubén Darío 150 m al Oeste, Managua; tel. 2278-7317; e-mail ihnca.uca@ihnca.edu.ni; internet www.ihnca.edu.ni; f. 1987, affiliated to Universidad Centroamericana 1990; attached to Universidad Centroamericana; 29 mems; Dir Dra MARGARITA VANNINI; publ. *Revista de Historia*.

Libraries and Archives

Chinandega

Biblioteca 'Eduardo Montealegre' ('Eduardo Montealegre' Library): Parque Las Rosas 2 cuadras al Sur, Chinandega; tel. 2341-2950; Librarian ANA LUISA PANIAGUA GONZÁLEZ.

León

Biblioteca Central de la Universidad Nacional Autónoma de Nicaragua, León (Central Library of the National Autonomous University of Nicaragua, León): Edif. Central UNAN-León, Apdo 68, León; tel. 2311-0588; f. 1816; 39,000 vols, 2,778 theses and 363 units of non-book materials; Dir NORMA FLORES.

Managua

Archivo Nacional de Nicaragua (National Archive of Nicaragua): Del Cine Cabrera 2½ cuadras al Lago, Managua; tel. 2222-6290; e-mail binanic@tmx.com.ni; internet manfut.org/museos/archivonacional.html; f. 1882; 41,000 vols, 10m. documents; Dir ALFREDO GONZÁLEZ VILCHEZ; publ. *Gaceta Oficial*.

Biblioteca Nacional 'Rubén Darío' (National Library 'Rubén Darío'): Apdo Postal 3514, Managua; Palacio Nacional de la Cultura, Antigua Catedral, Managua; tel. 222-2722; e-mail b.n.rd@hotmail.com; internet www.abinia.org/nicaragua; f. 1880; 80,000 vols; Dir JIMMY ALVARADO MORENO.

Centro Nacional de Información y Documentación Agrícola (National Centre for Agricultural Information and Documentation): Km 12 1/2 Carretera Norte, Managua; e-mail cenida@una.edu.ni; internet cenida.una.edu.ni; f. 1984; Dir RUTH VELIA GÓMEZ.

Museums and Art Galleries

Carazo

Museo Ecológico de Trópico Seco (Ecological Museum of Dry Tropics): Costado Sur policía nacional Diriamba, Carazo; tel. 2534-2129; e-mail museoeco@ideay.net.ni; internet www.adeca.org.ni/museo_eco; f. 1996; permanent ecological exhibitions, documentation centre, training materials.

Chinandega

Museo Chorotega-Nicarao 'Enrique Berio Mantica' (Museum Chorotega-Nicarao 'Enrique Berio Mantica'): Reparto Los Angeles, de donde fue Multicable, 11/2 cuadras al Sur, Chinandega; tel. 2341-4291; e-mail egretta01@yahoo.com; f. 2006; pre-Columbian art in ceramics, lithics and gold.

Granada

Mi Museo (My Museum): Calle Atravesada 505, Granada; tel. 2552-7614; e-mail mimuseo@hotmail.com; internet mimuseo .org; f. 2005; archaeological treasures and ceramic artifacts from Pre-Columbian era; Owner PEDER KOLIND; publ. *Mi Museo y Vos*.

León

Museo Entomologico de León (Entomology Museum of León): Apdo 527, León; tel. 2311-6586; e-mail jmmaes@ibw.com.ni; internet www.bio-nica.info; f. 1988; library of 30,000 vols; Dir JEAN-MICHEL MAES.

Museo y Archivo 'Ruben Darío' (Museum and Archive 'Ruben Darío'): De la Iglesia San Francisco, 1 cuadra al Oeste, León; tel. 2311-2388; e-mail museorubendario@yahoo.com; internet rubendario.enriquebolanos.org; f. 1964; Exec. Dir Dr EDGARDO BUITRAGO.

Managua

Museo Nacional de Nicaragua (National Museum of Nicaragua): Apdo 416, Col. Dambach, Managua; tel. 2222-4820; e-mail museo@inc.gob.ni; internet manfut.org/museos/nacional.html; f. 1897; archaeology, ceramics, zoology, botany and geology; library of 500 vols; Dir LEONOR MARTÍNEZ DE ROCHA.

Masaya

Museo Arqueológico 'Tenderí' (Archaeological Museum 'Tenderí'): Biblioteca Municipal 1 cuadra Oeste, Nindirí, Masaya; tel. 2522-4026; f. 1910; archaeological remains from the Chorotega Indian culture; coins and medals from the Spanish colonial era.

Museo Comunitario y Etnográfico 'Insurreccion de Monimbó' (Community and Ethnography Museum 'Insurreccion de Monimbó'): Damas Salesianas 1 1/2 cuadra Este, Masaya; tel. 2522-4368; e-mail museoetnogaficomonimbo@yahoo.com; f. 2009.

Matagalpa

Museo Nacional del Café (National Museum of Coffee): Del Parque Morazán 1 cuadras y 10 varas al sur, Matagalpa; tel. 2772-0587; e-mail sturismo@alcaldiamatagalpa.gob.ni; internet www .alcaldiamatagalpa.gob.ni/museo_del_cafe; f. 2002.

Rivas

Museo de Antropología e Historia de Rivas (Museum of Anthropology and History of Rivas): Farmacia Miranda 1 cuadras Norte, Rivas; tel. 2463-3663; e-mail mnndc@ibw.com.ni; f. 1975; archaeology, natural history and fauna of Rivas.

Universities

BLUEFIELDS INDIAN AND CARIBBEAN UNIVERSITY

Avda Universitaria, Barrio San Pedro, Bluefields

Telephone: 2572-1910
E-mail: bicu@bicu.edu.ni
Internet: www.bicu.edu.ni
Private control
Language of instruction: Spanish
Academic year: March to December

Rector: GUSTAVO CASTRO JO

KEISER UNIVERSITY

Gasolinera Texaco 2 cuadras, San Marcos

Telephone: 2535-1214
E-mail: admissionslac@keiseruniversity.edu
Internet: www.keiseruniversity.edu/san-marcos.php
Founded 2007 as Ave Maria College of the Americas; transferred to Keiser Univ. 2013
Private control
Language of instruction: Spanish
Academic year: March to December

Rector: MATHEW ANDERSON
Dean of Students: EMILIA LILLY BERMUDEZ

UNIVERSIDAD ADVENTISTA DE NICARAGUA
(Adventist University of Nicaragua)

Km 12 carretera vieja a León, 1500 mts, al sur, Managua

Telephone: 2264-4492
E-mail: unadenic_0609@hotmail.com
Founded 2003
Private control
Language of instruction: Spanish
Academic year: March to December

Rector: GABRIEL GÁMEZ HERNÁNDEZ

UNIVERSIDAD AMERICAN COLLEGE
(American College University)

Plaza España, De la Rotonda el Gueguense 2 cuadras al Oeste 1cuadra al Norte, Managua

Telephone: 2268-7555
E-mail: info@americancollege.edu.ni
Internet: www.americancollege.edu.ni
Founded 2005
Private control
Language of instruction: Spanish
Academic year: March to December

Rector: Dr MAURICIO HERDOCIA S.
Librarian: FABIOLA CEPEDA

DEANS

Faculty of Economic Sciences and Administration: Lic. SERGIO GONZALEZ
Faculty of Engineering: Ing. GUILLERMO JACOBY S.
Faculty of Political Sciences and Humanities: RICARDO DE LEON BORGE
Faculty of Tourism: Lic. AUSBERTO NARVÁEZ

UNIVERSIDAD AMERICANA
(American University)

Costado Noroeste, Camino de Oriente, Managua

Telephone: 2278-3800
E-mail: ernesto.medina@uam.edu.ni
Internet: www.uam.edu.ni
Founded 1992
Private control
Language of instruction: Spanish
Academic year: March to December

Rector: Dr ERNESTO MEDINA

Dean for College of Univ. Studies in English
UAM-CUSE: GISELLE POVEDA MONTERREY
Library of 35,000 vols and 200 multimedia discs

DEANS

Faculty of Dentistry: Dr NIDIA ROA GAMBOA
Faculty of Design and Communication: MARÍA FABIOLA ESPINOSA
Faculty of Diplomacy and International Relations: MARÍA JESÚS FUENTES FRAILE
Faculty of Engineering: MARTÍN GUEVARA CANO
Faculty of Law and Social Sciences: Dr ALEJANDRO AGUILAR ALTAMIRANO
Faculty of Management and Economic Sciences: Dr ÁLVARO PORTA
Faculty of Medicine: Dr FEDERICO MUÑOZ FERNÁNDEZ

UNIVERSIDAD CATÓLICA AGROPECUARIA DEL TRÓPICO SECO 'PRESBITERO FRANCISCO LUIS ESPINOZA PINEDA'
(Catholic Agricultural University of the Dry Tropics 'Presbyter Francisco Luis Espinoza Pineda')

Apdo 81, Estelí
Telephone: 2719-7600
E-mail: ucatse@ucatse.edu.ni
Internet: www.ucatse.edu.ni
Founded 2002; univ. status 2002
Private control
Language of instruction: Spanish
Academic year: March to December

Faculties of agricultural sciences, medical sciences and theology

Rector: Mgr JUAN ABELARDO MATA GUEVARA
Assoc. Rector: LEONARDO GUEVARA, Dra SANDRA MARGARITA LÓPEZ BENITEZ

UNIVERSIDAD CATÓLICA 'REDEMPTORIS MATER'
(Catholic University 'Redemptoris Mater')

Km 9 ½ Carretera a Masaya, 500 vrs, Sur Oeste, Managua
Telephone: 2276-0004
Internet: www.unica.edu.ni
Founded 1992
Private control
Language of instruction: Spanish
Academic year: March to December

Rector: MICHELLE RIVAS REYES

DEANS

Faculty of Humanities: HÉCTOR COTTE
Faculty of Medical Sciences: OMAR ARAGÓN

UNIVERSIDAD CENTRAL DE NICARAGUA
(Central University of Nicaragua)

De los semáforos del Zumen 3 Cuadras abajo, 1 cuadra al lago, Managua
Telephone: 2279-1160
E-mail: ccentral@ucn.edu.ni
Internet: www.ucn.edu.ni
Founded 1998
Private control
Language of instruction: Spanish
Academic year: March to December

Also faculty of engineering and psychology; campuses in Estelí, Jinotepe and Managua

Rector: Ing. GILBERTO CUADRA SOLÓRZANO
Gen. Vice-Rector: Dr FRANCISCO LÓPEZ PÉREZ

DEANS

Faculty of Law: Dr MIRNA ELIZABETH DELGADILLO CASTRO

Faculty of Management Sciences and Business: JOSÉ MANUEL SEQUEIRA HERNÁNDEZ
Faculty of Medicine: Dr FRANCISCO ANTONIO SOMARRIBA HERNÁNDEZ
Faculty of Veterinary Medicine: Dr ELIAZAR CAMPOS MÉNDEZ

UNIVERSIDAD CENTROAMERICANA
(Centroamerican University)

Apdo 69, Managua
Rotonda Rubén Darío 150 metros al Oeste, Managua
Telephone: 2278-3923
E-mail: dci@ns.uca.edu.ni
Internet: www.uca.edu.ni

Founded 1961
Private control
Language of instruction: Spanish
Academic year: February to December

Rector: Dra MAYRA LUZ PÉREZ DÍAZ
Vice-Rector for Gen. Affairs: Fr JOSÉ ALBERTO IDIÁQUEZ GUEVARA
Vice-Rector for Academic Affairs: Dra RENATA RODRIGUEZ
Vice-Rector for Admin.: Lic. RÓGER URIARTE GÓMEZ
Sec.-Gen.: VERA AMANDA SOLÍS
Librarian: Lic. GLORIA MARÍA MORALES

Publications: *Cuadernos de Sociología*, *Diakonía*, *Encuentro* (3 a year, print and online, encuentro.uca.edu.ni), *Envío* (12 a year, print and online, www.envio.org.ni), *WANI* (4 a year)

DEANS
Faculty of Economic Sciences and Business: GUILLERMO BORNEMANN MARTÍNEZ
Faculty of Humanities and Communication: IRIS PRADO
Faculty of Law: MANUEL ARKUZ ULLOA
Faculty of Science, Technology and Environment: TARSILIA ELDINEY SILVA

UNIVERSIDAD CENTROAMERICANA DE CIENCIAS EMPRESARIALES
(Central American University of Business Studies)

Costado Norte del INVUR, 29a Avda SO, Managua
Telephone: 2268-0337
E-mail: informacion@ucem.edu.ni
Internet: www.ucem.edu.ni

Founded 1997
Private control
Language of instruction: Spanish
Academic year: March to December

Rector: Ing. RAFAEL JOSÉ CHAMORRO FLETES

UNIVERSIDAD CRISTIANA AUTÓNOMA DE NICARAGUA
(Christian Autonomous University of Nicaragua)

Avda central. Catedral 2 1/2 cuadras al Norte, Managua
Telephone: 2311-0353
E-mail: ucanleon@ucan.edu.ni
Internet: www.ucan.edu.ni

Founded 2001
Private control
Language of instruction: Spanish
Academic year: March to December

Campuses in Chinandega, Chontales, Estelí, Masaya and Matagalpa

Rector: JEANNETTE BONILLA
Vice-Rector for Academic Affairs: Lic. WILBER MIRANDA
Vice-Rector for Postgraduate Research and Social Projection: JAIRO RODRÍGUEZ B

DEANS
Faculty of Economics and Administrative Sciences: Lic. RODOLFO ÁLVAREZ
Faculty of Engineering and Architecture: Arq. MIGUEL SUAZO
Faculty of Law and Social Sciences: Lic. WILBER MIRANDA
Faculty of Medical Sciences: Dr OSCAR REAL

UNIVERSIDAD DE ADMINISTRACIÓN, COMERCIO Y ADUANA 'MARÍA GUERRERO'
(University of Administration, Commerce and Customs 'María Guerrero')

Rotonda Jardines de Veracruz, 2 cuadras Sud, 1 cuadra Oeste, Managua
Telephone: 2289-2372
E-mail: unacad@hotmail.com
Internet: www.unacad.net

Founded 1991
Private control
Language of instruction: Spanish
Academic year: March to December

Rector: Lic. JUAN ALEGRÍA

UNIVERSIDAD AUTÓNOMA DE CHINANDEGA
(Autonomous University of Chinandega)

Club Edén 1/2 cuadra, Oeste, 505, Chinandega, Chinandega
Telephone: 2341-0439
E-mail: uach@alfa.com.ni
Internet: www.uach-chinandega.site90.net

Founded 1997
Private control
Language of instruction: Spanish
Academic year: March to December

Rector: Lic. ALVARO ALBERTO FAJARDO SALGADO

UNIVERSIDAD DE CIENCIAS COMERCIALES
(University of Commercial Sciences)

Frente al polideportivo España, Managua
Telephone: 2277-1931
E-mail: ucc@ucc.edu.ni
Internet: www.ucc.edu.ni

Founded 1964
Private control
Language of instruction: Spanish
Academic year: March to December

Campuses in León, Managua and Matagalpa; also faculty of architecture, engineering and computing and political science business

Rector: Dr GILBERTO BERGMAN PADILLA
Vice-Rector for Academics: MARÍA LOURDES GÓMEZ

DEANS
Faculty of Agricultural Sciences: Dr LUIS BORRELL
Faculty of Business Administration, Tourism and Hospitality: JOSEFINA SÁNCHEZ CARGO
Faculty of Communication and Public Relations: Dr ADRIAN URIARTE
Faculty of Economic Sciences and Business: JUANITA LÓPEZ BRAVO
Faculty of Graduate Studies: Dr MARÍA LOURDES GÓMEZ MEZA
School of Marketing, Design and Advertising: MARCIA GONZÁLEZ BARBERENA (Dir)

UNIVERSIDAD DE LAS AMÉRICAS
(University of the Americas)

Apdo A-279, Managua
km 2.5-Carretera Norte, Antigua Pepsi 1 cuadra hacia el Sur y 1 cuadra Oeste, Managua
Telephone: 2248-3081
E-mail: ulam@ulam.edu.ni
Internet: www.ulam.edu.ni

Founded 1996
Private control
Language of instruction: Spanish
Academic year: March to December

Rector: Lic. JOSÉ EVENOR ESTRADA GARCÍA
Sec. Gen.: Dr ARIEL OTERO CASTAÑEDA
Librarian: Ing. RICARDO SÁNCHEZ

UNIVERSIDAD DE LAS REGIONES AUTÓNOMAS DE LAS COSTA CARIBE NICARAGÜENSE
(University of the Autonomous Regions of the Nicaraguan Caribbean Coast)

Apdo 0891, Managua
Puente El Eden, 1 cuadra al Este, 2 cuadras al Sur, Barrio Ducualí, Managua
Telephone: 2248-2119
E-mail: rectoria@uraccan.edu.ni
Internet: www.uraccan.edu.ni

Founded 1992
Private control
Language of instruction: Spanish
Academic year: March to December

Campuses in Bilwi, Bluefields, Siuna and Nueva Guinea

Rector: ALTA HOOKER BLANDFORD

Publication: *La Revista Ciencia e Interculturalidad de URACCAN*

UNIVERSIDAD DE MANAGUA
(University of Managua)

Hospital Vélez Paiz 1 1/2 arriba, Managua
Telephone: 2265-0240
E-mail: webmaster@udem.edu.ni
Internet: www.udem.edu.ni

Founded 1998
Private control
Language of instruction: Spanish
Academic year: March to December

Rector: Ing. DORIS MEZA CORNAVACA

UNIVERSIDAD DE OCCIDENTE-LEÓN
(University of West-León)

Apdo 615, León
Telephone: 2887-8843
E-mail: udoleon@yahoo.es

Founded 1994
Private control
Language of instruction: Spanish
Academic year: March to December

Campuses in León and Managua

Rector: Lic. ARMANDO GUTIÉRREZ

UNIVERSIDAD DEL NORTE DE NICARAGUA
(University of the North of Nicaragua)

De la Avon 1/2 cuadras al Oeste, Matagalpa
Telephone: 2772-7207
E-mail: j_zeledon@unnnicaragua.org
Internet: www.unnnicaragua.org

Founded 1997
Private control
Language of instruction: Spanish
Academic year: March to December

Faculties of agricultural sciences, economic sciences, humanities, and political sciences

Rector: EVERTH BOANERGES RIVAS BEJARANO
Vice-Rector: JOSE AUGUSTO ZELEDÓN IBARRA

UNIVERSIDAD DEL VALLE
(University of the Valley)

Rotonda el periodista 25 varas al Sur, Managua

Telephone: 2278-8626

E-mail: mercadeo@univalle.edu.ni

Internet: www.univalle.edu.ni

Founded 2011

Private control

Language of instruction: Spanish

Academic year: March to December

Rector: KATHIA SEHTMAN

Sec.-Gen.: Lic. ARNOLDO ARREAGA

Dir for Library: Lic. ESMELDA OROZCO

UNIVERSIDAD EVANGÉLICA NICARAGÜENSE
(Nicaraguan Evangelical University)

Robles Frente a Plaza el Sol, Managua

Telephone: 2270-1600

E-mail: rector@uenicmlk.edu.ni

Internet: www.uenicmlk.edu.ni

Founded 1999

Private control

Language of instruction: Spanish

Academic year: March to December

Campuses in Bonanza, Juigalpa, Masaya, Matagalpa, Nagarote, Rio Blanco and Rafael del Sur

Rector: Dr BENJAMIN CORTES

Vice-Rector: Lic. OMAR ANTONIO CASTRO

Publication: *Revista Electrónica UENIC MLK* (3 a year)

UNIVERSIDAD HISPANOAMERICANA
(Spanish American University)

Apdo 531, Managua

Reparto Bolinia de Canal 2 de TV, 2 cuadras abajo, Managua

Telephone: 2268-4496

E-mail: ltc@uhispam.edu.ni

Internet: www.uhispam.edu.ni

Founded 1999

Private control

Language of instruction: Spanish

Academic year: March to December

Campuses in Camoapa, Granada, Jinotepe, Masaya and Rivas

Rector: Dr LEONARDO TORRES CÉSPEDES

Gen. Vice-Rector: Dr ADAM BERMÚDEZ URCUYO

Vice-Rector for Academics: GABRIEL TORRES ESPINOZA

Sec. Gen.: Lic. CARLOS ADAN BERMÚDEZ

DEANS

Faculty of Business Administration, Tourism and Hospitality: Dr ADAM GAITAN JIMÉNEZ

Faculty of Economic Sciences and Administration: JAIME SUÁREZ GARCÍA

Faculty of Journalism: Lic. FERNANDO CENTENO CHIONG

Faculty of Political and Social Science: Dr IVÁN ESCOBAR FORNOS

UNIVERSIDAD IBEROAMERICANA DE CIENCIA Y TECNOLOGÍA
(Latin American University of Science and Technology)

Rotonda Universitaria 100 m al Sur, Managua

Telephone: 2278-7231

E-mail: unicit@unicit.edu.ni

Internet: www.unicit.edu.ni

Founded 1995

Private control

Language of instruction: Spanish

Academic year: March to December

Pres.: Dr LUIS ENRIQUE LACAYO

Rector: Dra ALINA SÁLOMON SANTOS

Vice-Rector for Admin.: HÉCTOR LACAYO H.

Vice-Rector for Academic Affairs: Ing. FÁTIMA ALEMÁN

Librarian: Lic. REYNA SOZA

DEANS

Faculty of Economic Sciences: ERICK ARIAS

Faculty of Electronics and Computer Science: MARÍA MERCEDES OROZCO

Faculty of Engineering and Architecture: RENÉ TERRAZAS

Faculty of Health Sciences: Dra ALMA LILA PASTORA

Faculty of Law: MANUEL IGNACIO LACAYO

International Relations: ORLANDO LÓPEZ SELVA

UNIVERSIDAD INTERNACIONAL DE LA INTEGRACIÓN DE AMERICA LATINA
(International University of Latin American Integration)

Reparto San Juan, calle el Carmen, Managua

Telephone: 2278-1417

E-mail: info@unival.edu.ni

Internet: www.universidadunival.com

Founded 1995

Private control

Language of instruction: Spanish

Academic year: March to December

Departmental coordination offices in Chinandega, Estelí, Jalapa, Jinotega, Juigalpa, León, Matagalpa and Ocotal

Rector: Dr SERGIO BONILLA DELGADO

UNIVERSIDAD INTERNACIONAL PARA EL DESARROLLO SOSTENIBLE
(International University for Sustainable Development)

Apdo A-275, Managua

Embajada Alemana 2 cuadras al Oeste 1/2 cuadras al Norte, Managua

Telephone: 2266-9948

E-mail: informacion@unides.edu.ni

Internet: www.unides.edu.ni

Founded 2005

Private control

Language of instruction: Spanish

Academic year: March to December

Rector: ROBERTO GARCÍA BOZA

Gen. Vice-Rector: PABLO LANZAS AYÓN

Vice-Rector for Finance and Institutional Devt: JUAN JOSÉ RAMÍREZ VALLADARES

DEANS

Faculty of Business: Dr RADOSLAV BARZEV

Faculty of Medical Sciences: Dr GERARDO GARCÍA BOZA

UNIVERSIDAD JEAN JACQUES ROUSSEAU
(Jean Jacques Rousseau University)

Puente Larreynaga 2 cuadras abajo, 1 1/2 al lago, Managua

Telephone: 2248-3411

E-mail: unijjar@yahoo.com

Internet: www.unijjar.edu.ni/universidad .htm

Founded 2002

Private control

Language of instruction: Spanish

Academic year: March to December

Rector: Lic. ANIBAL LANUZA RODRÍGUEZ

UNIVERSIDAD JUAN PABLO II
(John Paul II University)

Costado Norte del Polideportivo España, 2 cuadras al lago, Managua

Telephone: 2278-7548

E-mail: rectoriajuanpablo@hotmail.com

Founded 2002

Private control

Language of instruction: Spanish

Academic year: March to December

Rector: VÍCTOR MANUEL RIVAS BUSTAMANTE

UNIVERSIDAD LA ANUNCIATA
(Anunciata University)

Iglesia el Calvario 50 m al Este Frente al MAGFOR, Rivas

Telephone: 2563-3320

E-mail: uanunciata@gmail.com

Internet: www.colegiofatima.edu.ni

Founded 2002

Private control

Language of instruction: Spanish

Academic year: March to December

Rector: Sis. ANA MARÍA EXPÓSITO

UNIVERSIDAD MARTÍN LUTERO
(Martin Luther University)

Km 10 carretera vieja a León 200 m al Norte, frente a las oficinas de las Asambleas de Dios, Managua

Telephone: 2265-4938

E-mail: rectoria@uml.edu.ni

Internet: www.uml.edu.ni

Founded 2002

Private control

Language of instruction: Spanish

Academic year: March to December

Rector: Dr JOSÉ MOISÉS ROJAS TALAVERA

UNIVERSIDAD METROPOLITANA
(Metropolitan University)

Contiguo donde fue el cine Cabrera, calle 27 de Mayo, Managua

Telephone: 2268-0749

E-mail: unimet@unimet.edu.ni

Internet: www.unimet.edu.ni

Founded 2002

Private control

Language of instruction: Spanish

Academic year: March to December

Rector: Ing. ELMER ACEVEDO SÁNCHEZ

UNIVERSIDAD NACIONAL AGRARIA
(National Agricultural University)

Km 12½ Carretera Norte, Managua

Telephone: 233-1619

Internet: www.una.edu.ni

Founded 1929, present name and status 1990

State control

Language of instruction: Spainsh

Academic year: March to December

Campuses in Carazoa, Camoapa and Juigalpa

Rector: Ing. FRANCISCO TELÉMACO TALAVERA SILES

Vice-Rector Gen.: Ing. ROBERTO BLANDINO OBANDO

Registrar: Lic. RONALD QUIROZ OCAMPO

Library of 12,000 vols, 500 periodicals

Publication: *La Calera* (2 a year)

DEANS

Faculty of Agronomy: Dr DENNIS SALAZAR CENTENO

Faculty of Animal Sciences: Ing. CARLOS RUIZ FONSECA

Faculty of Natural Resources and the Environment: Lic. ESTHER CARBALLO MADRIGAL

Faculty of Rural Development: Dr ELGIN VIVAS VILLACHICA

UNIVERSIDAD NACIONAL AUTÓNOMA DE NICARAGUA-LEÓN
(National Autonomous University of Nicaragua-León)

Apdo 68, León

Edif. Central, Contiguo a Iglesia La Merced, León

Telephone: 2311-5013

E-mail: admingral@ac.unanleon.edu.ni

Internet: www.unanleon.edu.ni

Founded 1812

State control

Language of instruction: Spanish

Academic year: March to December

Regional centres in Jinotega, San Carlos, Somoto and Somotillo

Rector: OCTAVIO GUEVARA

Vice-Rector for Academic Affairs: Dra AZUCENA NAVAS

Vice-Rector for External Relations: MARITZA VARGAS PAÍZ

Vice-Rector for Research and Graduate Studies: Dra FLOR DE MARIA VALLE ESPINOZA

Sec.-Gen.: SONIA RUIZ

Library: see under Libraries and Archives

DEANS

Faculty of Chemistry: AZUCENA MONTENEGRO REYES

Faculty of Dentistry: Dr HUMBERTO ALTAMIRANO REYES

Faculty of Economics and Business: FRANCISCO VALLADARES RIVAS

Faculty of Education and Humanities: FRANCISCO JAVIER PARAJON

Faculty of Law and Social Sciences: MAURICIO CARRIÓN MATAMOROS

Faculty of Medical Sciences: Dr ARMANDO MATUTE MORENO

Faculty of Science and Technology: JOSE ALBERTO CERDA CAMPOS

UNIVERSIDAD NACIONAL AUTÓNOMA DE NICARAGUA
(National Autonomous University of Nicaragua)

Apdo 6631, Managua

De la Rotonda Universitaria, 2½ km al sur, Villa Fontana, Managua

Telephone: 2278-6764

E-mail: unan@unan.edu.ni

Internet: www.unan.edu.ni

Founded 1812

State control

Language of instruction: Spanish

Academic year: June to March

Rector: ELMER CISNEROS MOREIRA

Vice-Rector for Academic Affairs: Dr ISABEL BENAVIDES GUTIÉRREZ

Vice-Rector for Admin. Affairs: Lic. JAVIER PICHARDO RAMÍREZ

Vice-Rector for Gen. Affairs: RAMONA RODRÍGUEZ PÉREZ

Vice Rector for Research, Graduate and Univ. Extension: LUIS ANTONIO RODRÍGUEZ PÉREZ

Dean for Regional Multidisciplinary Faculty, Carazo: PEDRO ALBERTO ABURTO JARQUÍN

Dean for Regional Multidisciplinary Faculty, Chontales: EMILIO JOSÉ LÓPEZ JARQUÍN

Dean for Regional Multidisciplinary Faculty, Estelí: REYNA ISABEL SEVILLA MIDENCE

Dean for Regional Multidisciplinary Faculty, Matagalpa: VÍCTOR GUTIÉRREZ LAGUNA

Sec.-Gen.: Lic. JAIME LÓPEZ LOWERY

Library Dir: MARITZA DEL SOCORRO VALLECILLO

Library: see Libraries and Archives

Number of teachers: 850

Number of students: 33,000

Publications: *Cuadernos Universitarios* (4 a year), *Gaceta Universitaria* (6 a year), *Revista Cátedra*, *Revista Científica de la FAREM-Estelí* (4 a year, online, www.farem.unan.edu.ni/revistas/index.php/RCientifica/index), *Revista Electrónica de Investigación en Ciencias Económicas* (2 a year, print and online, revistacienciaseconomicas.unan.edu.ni), *Revista Médica* (2 a year), *Revista Tierra*, *Revista Universidad y Ciencia* (2 a year, print and online, revistauniversidadyciencia.unan.edu.ni)

DEANS

Faculty of Economics: ISABEL DEL CARMEN LANUZA OROZCO

Faculty of Education and Language: Lic. ALEJANDRO GENET CRUZ

Faculty of Humanities and Legal Sciences: LUIS ALFREDO LOBATO BLANCO

Faculty of Medical Sciences: Dr FREDDY ALBERTO MEYNARD MEJÍA

Faculty of Science and Engineering: Lic. HUGO A. GUTIÉRREZ OCÓN

UNIVERSIDAD NACIONAL DE INGENIERÍA
(National University of Engineering)

Apdo 5595, Managua

Avda Universitaria Frente Escuela de Danza, Managua

Telephone: 2277-1650

Internet: www.uni.edu.ni

Founded 1983

State control

Academic year: March to December

Rector: Arq. VICTOR ARCIA GÓMEZ

Vice-Rector for Academic Affairs: Arq. ANA ULMOS VADO

Vice-Rector for Admin. Affairs: Ing. NÉSTOR GALLO ZELEDÓN

Vice-Rector for Research and Devt: Dr LEONEL PLAZAOLA PRADO

Sec.-Gen.: Ing. DIEGO ALFONSO MUÑOZ LATINO

Librarian: Lic. MARTHA PEREZ GARCIA

Publications: *Campus* (6 a year), *Nexo* (4 a year), *Teckno* (6 a year)

DEANS

Faculty of Architecture: Arq. LUIS ALBERTO CHÁVEZ QUINTERO

Faculty of Chemical Engineering: Ing. LEONARDO ANTONIO CHAVARRÍA CARRIÓN

Faculty of Construction Technology: Dr OSCAR ISAAC GUTIÉRREZ SOMARRIBA

Faculty of Electrotechnology and Computer Science: Ing. RONALD TORRES

Faculty of Industrial Technology: Ing. DANIEL AUGUSTO CUADRA HORNEY

Faculty of Sciences and Systems: CARLOS SÁNCHEZ

UNIVERSIDAD NICARAGÜENSE DE CIENCIA Y TECNOLOGIA
(Nicaraguan University of Science and Technology)

Apdo 2301, Managua

Semáforos de Rubenia 700 m al Norte, Managua

Telephone: 2240-0789

E-mail: contacto@ucyt.edu.ni

Internet: www.ucyt.edu.ni

Founded 2003

Private control

Language of instruction: Spanish

Academic year: March to December

Rector: Lic. FERNANDO ROBLETO LANG

Dir for Library: Lic. PATRICIA GUTIÉRREZ

Publication: *Revista uCyt*

UNIVERSIDAD PAULO FREIRE
(Paulo Freire University)

Semaforos de linda vista, 6 1/2 al Sur, sobre la pista, reparto miraflores, Managua

Telephone: 2250-3850

E-mail: rector@upf.edu.ni

Internet: www.upf.edu.ni

Founded 1998; univ. status 2001

Private control

Language of instruction: Spanish

Academic year: March to December

Rector: Dr ADRIAN MEZA SOSA

Gen. Vice-Rector: SUSY DURIEZ GONZALEZ

Vice-Rector for Academics: Ing. SANDRA LORENA VILLALOBOS CRUZ

Vice-Rector for Planning and Quality Assurance: Dr CESAR LARGAESPADA PALLAVICINI

Vice-Rector for Territories Care: Lic. JOSÉ LEÓN ROMÁN ALVAREZ

Dir for Library: Lic. GLADIS GÓMEZ FERNANDEZ

DEANS

Faculty of Law and Political Science: Dr CESAR LARGAESPADA PALLAVICCINI

Faculty of Psychology and Social Work: Lic. LILLIANA LARGAESPADA GARCIA

UNIVERSIDAD POLITÉCNICA DE NICARAGUA
(Polytechnic University of Nicaragua)

Apdo 3595, Managua

Costado Sur Col. Rubén Darío, Managua

Telephone: 2289-7740

E-mail: rectoria@upoli.edu.ni

Internet: www.upoli.edu.ni

Founded 1967 as institute, university status 1977

Private control

Language of instruction: Spanish

Academic year: March to December

Campuses in Boaco, Estelí and Rivas

Rector: Ing. EMERSON PÉREZ SANDOVAL

Vice-Rector: Dra LIDIA RUTH ZAMORA

Vice-Rector for Academic Affairs: Dra MIRNA CUEVAS RUIZ

Vice-Rector for Students: Lic. BLANCA ROSA GALARZA

Registrar: TOMÁS HANDELL TÉLLEZ RUIZ

Librarian: Licda AURA CELA CORTEZ SILVA

DEANS

School of Administration, Commerce and Finance: MIGUEL MURILLO

School of Design: D. I. EDUARDO VANEGAS

School of Economics: EYRA REYES

School of Engineering: Licda GLADYS AGUILAR

School of Law: Dr OSCAR CASTILLO GUIDO

School of Nursing: MARGARITA GUEVARA

School of Tourism: AMPARO MENDOZA

UNIVERSIDAD POPULAR DE NICARAGUA
(Peoples University of Nicaragua)

Bolonia Esq. opuesta Hotel Mansion Teodolinda, Managua

Telephone: 2266-1166

E-mail: uponic@ns.tmx.com.ni

Internet: www.uponic.edu.ni

Founded 1992

Private control

Language of instruction: Spanish

Academic year: March to December

Rector: Dra OLGA SOZA BRAVO

Gen. Vice-Rector: Ing. HULASKO MEZA SOZA

Vice-Rector for Strategic Areas: Lic. MARIA SOLEDAD MEZA SOZA

Sec.-Gen.: Lic. OLGA ASUNCIÓN MEZA SOZA

UNIVERSIDAD SANTO TOMAS DE ORIENTE Y MEDIO DIA
(University Saint Thomas of the East and Mid-Day)

Iglesia la Merced 1 cuadra al Norte, 1 cuadra al Oeste, calle el consulado, Granada

Apdo 41, Granada

Telephone: 2552-2545

E-mail: ustom@cablenet.com.ni

Founded 2003

Private control

Language of instruction: Spanish

Academic year: March to December

Rector: Dr ROBERTO FERREY

UNIVERSIDAD TECNOLÓGICA NICARAGÜENSE
(Nicaraguan Technological University)

Rotonda Metro Centro 150, Al Oeste en el 'CIPRES', en el sector de la Avda Universitaria, Managua

Telephone: 2278-6338

E-mail: universidadtecnologicanic@yahoo.es

Internet: utn-nicaragua.es.tl

Founded 1997

Private control

Language of instruction: Spanish

Academic year: March to December

Campuses in Léon and Managua

Rector: Lic. ANTONIA NÁJERA ARAGÓN

UNIVERSIDAD THOMAS MORE
(Thomas More University)

Semáforos del Club Terraza 150 vrs. al Sur, Managua

Telephone: 2277 0114

E-mail: informacion@unithomasmore.edu.ni

Internet: www.unithomasmore.edu.ni/sitio

Founded 2003

Private control

Language of instruction: Spanish

Academic year: March to December

Rector: Ing. IRENE ROJAS ĎFRANCO

Pres.: Dr SILVIO DE FRANCO MONTALVÁN

Colleges

Escuela Internacional de Agricultura y Ganadería (International School of Agriculture and Livestock): Apdo 5, Rivas; tel. 2563-3551; e-mail eiag@turbonet.com.ni; internet www.eiag.edu.ni; academic programmes in agriculture, management, veterinary science and zootechnology; Rector Fr CARLOS IRIAS AMAYA.

Instituto de Estudios Superiores de Medicina Oriental Japón-Nicaragua (Institute for Advanced Studies in Eastern Medicine Japan-Nicaragua): Semáforos de Rubenia 7 C abajo, Managua; tel. 2253-0344; e-mail relacionespúblicas@iesmojn.edu.ni; internet www.iesmojn.edu.ni; f. 2003; Rector Dr HARUO YAMAKI.

Instituto Latinoamericano de Computación (Latin American Institute of Computing): Semáforos del Colonial 1 ½ al lago, Managua; tel. 2249-3716; e-mail ilcomp@ilcomp.edu.ni; internet www.ilcomp.edu.ni; campuses in Matagalpa and Masaya; Rector Ing. HÉCTOR ANTONIO LACAYO HERNÁNDEZ.

The Higher Education System

The Republic of Niger was formerly part of French West Africa and obtained independence from France in 1960. The Ecole Nationale d'Administration et de Magistrature du Niger (founded in 1963 as the Ecole Nationale d'Administration; new status 2005) is the oldest current institution of higher education and the Université Abdou Moumouni (founded in 1971; formerly Université de Niamey) was the first university-level institution. The other leading institution is the Université Islamique du Niger (founded in 1986). In 2011 there were 18,328 students enrolled in tertiary education.

The principal officer of a university is the President or Rector, elected by the faculty to serve three-year, renewable terms of office. A Vice-President is also elected to assist the President. Deans of Faculty and Heads of Department are also elected to their posts and serve for three years and two years, respectively. The Ministry of Higher Education and Scientific Research is responsible for all tertiary education. In 2010, however, the Ministry of Professional Training and Employment was created to oversee the vocational education sector.

The entry requirement for higher education courses is the Baccalauréat; however, students who do not hold the Baccalauréat can gain admission by taking an entrance examination. In 2009 the Government introduced the LMD (Licence/Master/Doctorat) reforms, in order to bring the university degree system closer into line with the European model under the Bologna Process in a bid to harmonize degree structures, credit systems and quality assurance procedures in all higher education programmes and institutions in Niger, as well as in the other seven member states of the West African Economic and Monetary Union, all of which have implemented, or have pledged to implement by 2013, the LMD degree system. In 2012 the Niger Government adopted a decree making the LMD system compulsory for all higher education institutions. Under the new simplified structure, there is a three-year first cycle of study leading to the award of the Licence, followed by a second-cycle, two-year Master degree (merging the previous Maîtrise and Diplôma qualifications) and a third-cycle, three-year Doctorat course. The new structure also introduced a credit-transfer system, enabling students to complete their degree in a department or institution other than the one in which they started, or to leave university and complete their studies at a later date.

Specialist non-university education is offered by institutes attached to the relevant Ministries, including schools and centres for administration, public health, civil aviation and information technology. The Brevet de Technicien Supérieur is awarded to those completing between two and three years of vocational post-secondary education.

Regulatory Bodies

GOVERNMENT

Ministry of Higher Education and Scientific Research: BP 628, Niamey; tel. 20-72-26-20; e-mail mesnt@intnet.ne; Minister ASMANE ABDOU.

Ministry of National Education, Literacy and the Promotion of National Languages: BP 557, Niamey; tel. 20-72-28-33; e-mail scdameb@intnet.ne; Minister ALI MARIAMA ELHADJ IBRAHIM.

Ministry of Professional Training and Employment: Immeuble ex-HCCT, blvd, Mali Béro, BP 628, Niamey; tel. 20-72-59-51; Minister CHAIBOU DAN INNA.

Ministry of Youth, Sports and Culture: BP 452, Niamey; tel. 20-72-32-35; Minister OUSMANE ABDOU.

Learned Society

LANGUAGE AND LITERATURE

Alliance Française: BP 126, Agadez; tel. (20) 44-05-82; offers courses and examinations in French language and culture and promotes cultural exchange with France; attached teaching centre in Maradi; Dir M. ABDOURAHAMANE TOURAWA.

Research Institutes

GENERAL

Institut de Recherche pour le Développement (IRD): Ave de Maradi BP 11416, Niamey; tel. 20-75-38-27; e-mail irdniger@ird.ne; internet www.ird.ne; medical entomology, hydrology, genetics, ecology, soil sciences, botany, agronomy, economics, linguistics, sociology; in cooperation with Org. for Co-ordination and Co-operation in the Fight against Endemic Diseases; see main entry under France; library: documentation centre of 2,500 vols; Dir FRANCIS KAHN.

Institut de Recherches en Sciences Humaines (IRSH) de l'Université Abdou Moumouni: BP 318, Niamey; tel. 20-73-51-41; f. 1975 as successor to Institut Français d'Afrique Noire and Centre Nigérien de Recherches en Sciences Humaines; 6 sections: art and archaeology, history and popular traditions, linguistics and nat. languages, Arabic MSS, geography and environmental devt, sociology of devt, devt economics; library of 30,000 vols; Dir ABDOULAYE MAGA; publs *Etudes Nigériennes* (irregular), *Mu Kara Sani* (2 a year).

AGRICULTURE, FISHERIES AND VETERINARY SCIENCE

Institut de Recherches sur les Fruits et Agrumes (IRFA): BP 886, Niamey; see main entry under France; Dir C. LENORMAND.

Institut National de la Recherche Agronomique du Niger (INRAN): BP 429, Niamey; tel. (20) 72-53-89; e-mail dginran@yahoo.com; internet inran.refer.ne; f. 1975; soil science; stations at Tarna and Kolo; Dir J. NABOS.

HISTORY, GEOGRAPHY AND ARCHAEOLOGY

Centre d'Etudes Linguistiques et Historiques par Tradition Orale: BP 878, Niamey; tel. (20) 73-54-14; internet www.celhto.org; f. 1974; 25 mems; library of 1,250 vols; oral tradition, African languages and cultures; publishes works in African languages, French and English; Coordinator TUBLU KOMI N'KEGBE FOGA; publ. *Les Cahiers du CELHTO*.

TECHNOLOGY

Bureau de Recherches Géologiques et Minières (BRGM): BP 11458, Niamey; tel. 20-72-23-25; see main entry under France; Dir G. BERNERT.

Office National de l'Energie Solaire: BP 621, Niamey; tel. 20-73-45-05; f. 1965; Dir Eng. ALBERT WRIGHT.

Libraries and Archives

Niamey

Archives de la République du Niger: BP 550, Niamey; tel. 20-72-26-82; f. 1913; documents to the end of the 19th century; Dir IDRISSA YANSAMBOU.

Centre d'Information et de Documentation Economique et Sociale (CIDES): Ministère des Finances et du Plan, BP 862, Niamey; tel. 20-72-33-11; f. 1988; attached to Min. of Economy, Finance and Planning; 10,500 vols; Dir MALIKI ABDOULAYE; publ. *CIDES-Flash* (6 a year).

Museum

Niamey

Musée National du Niger: BP 248, Niamey; tel. (20) 73-43-21; f. 1959; representative colln of tribal costumes, crafts, tribal houses; incl. park and zoo, geological and mineral exhibition, ethnographic museum, palaeontology and pre-history museums; also Handicrafts Centre and Cultural Activities Centre; Curator NÉINO CHAÏBOU.

Universities

UNIVERSITÉ ABDOU MOUMOUNI DE NIAMEY

BP 237, 10896 Niamey

Telephone: 20-31-57-13

Founded 1971, univ. status as Univ. de Niamey 1973, present name 1999

State control

Language of instruction: French

Academic year: October to June

Rector: Prof. HABIBOU ABARCHI

Vice-Rector for Academic Affairs: BOUREIMA AMADOU

Vice-Rector for Research and Int. Affairs: BARAGÉ MOUSSA

Sec.-Gen.: Dr SALIFOU MAÎMOUNA

Librarian: SAIDOU HAROUNA

Library of 62,000 vols

Number of teachers: 326

Number of students: 13,078

Publications: *Annales de l'Université Abdou Moumouni* (1 a year), *Etudes Nigériennes*, *Mu Kara Sani* (2 a year)

DEANS

Faculty of Agronomy, Arts and Humanities: ADAM TOUDOU

Faculty of Arts and Humanities: TANDINA OUSMANE

Faculty of Economics and Law: ALOU MAHAMANE TIDJANI

Faculty of Health Sciences: SAIDOU MAMADOU

Faculty of Science: ABDOULAYE ALHASSANE

UNIVERSITÉ ISLAMIQUE DU NIGER
(Islamic University in Niger)

BP 11507, Niamey, Say

Telephone: 20-72-39-03

E-mail: unislam@intnet.ne

Internet: www.universite.say.ne

Founded 1986 by the Org. of the Islamic Conf.

Language of instruction: Arabic

Number of teachers: 20

Number of students: 350

Faculties of Arabic Language and Islamic Studies

Rector: Prof. ABDEL JAOUAD SEKKAT

College

Ecole Nationale d'Administration et de Magistrature: Rue Martin Luther King Jr, BP 542, Niamey; tel. 20-72-31-83; e-mail enam.niger@yahoo.fr; internet enam.refer.ne; f. 1963; trains civil servants and other officials; library: 27,000 vols; 120 teachers; 430 students; Dir BOUCAR ABBA KAKA; publ. *Revue* (2 a year).

The Higher Education System

The oldest institution of higher education in Nigeria is the Federal College of Agriculture, Ibadan (founded in 1921), while the oldest university is the University of Ibadan (founded in 1948; formerly University College, Ibadan), originally founded in conjunction with the University of London (United Kingdom). Expansion of the university system began following Nigeria's independence in 1963, and the universities established during 1960–70 are referred to as the 'first generation' universities, among them the University of Nigeria (founded in 1960), Obafemi Awolowo University (founded in 1961; present name since 1987), Ahmadu Bello University (founded in 1962), the University of Lagos (founded in 1962) and the University of Benin (founded in 1970). Education is partly the responsibility of the state governments, although the Federal Government has played an increasingly important role since 1970, and universities may be federally, state or privately administered. In 2005 there were 724,856 students enrolled in 80 universities and 237,708 in 178 poly/monotechnics. There are three kinds of university: federal universities, the majority of which were formed during the 15 years immediately following independence; state universities, which were established from 1979 in each of Nigeria's 36 states; and private universities, the establishment of which was enabled by legislation approved by the Government in 1993. In 2012 there were 37 federal universities, 38 state universities and 50 private universities. Degrees from the federal universities are generally more highly regarded than those from state or private universities.

The Governing Board or Council is the governing body of the federal universities, and its members are government appointees. The chief executive role is taken by the Vice-Chancellor in universities, the Rector in polytechnics and the Provost in colleges of education. Funding for public universities is channelled through different parastatal agencies for different types of institution, namely the National Universities Commission (NUC—universities), the National Board for Technical Education (NBTE—polytechnics) and the National Commission for Colleges of Education (colleges). The NUC is also responsible for accreditation and quality assurance for all institutions with degree-awarding powers, which takes place on a six-yearly cycle.

Admission to higher education is made on the basis of sufficient passes in the Senior School Certificate (SSC) and the University Matriculation Examination (UME), administered by the Joint Admissions and Matriculation Board. However, students with acceptable GCE A Level qualifications may enter directly into the second year of a four-year undergraduate course, negating the need for the UME, although GCEs have now been replaced by the SSC in all but a few private schools. Most undergraduate Bachelors degrees last four years, but programmes leading to the award of professional titles last five years and degrees in medicine and dentistry take six years to complete. A student awarded a first- or second-class Bachelors degree with Honours may be admitted to the first postgraduate degree, the Masters, study for which lasts for one to two years. Following the Masters, the Doctorate is the highest university-level degree, and consists of a two- or three-year period of research, submission of a thesis and an oral examination (viva).

Polytechnics and colleges offer post-secondary technical and vocational education. The most popular qualifications offered by these institutions are the two-year Ordinary National Diploma, the two-year Higher National Diploma, entry to which requires the Ordinary National Diploma and one year of relevant work experience, and the Full Professional Diploma, which is open only to holders of the Higher National Diploma and lasts for a minimum of 18 months. Programmes are accredited by the NBTE, which sets standards for non-university further and higher education. Additionally, the Ministry of Health offers professional courses in a number of related fields, including community health, environmental health, food hygiene and public health nursing, completion of which leads to professional registration either with the Ministry or with the West Africa Health Examinations Board.

A number of universities were severely afflicted by a six-month strike in 2010–11; the industrial action was provoked by a memorandum of understanding (MOU), signed in 2009, which sought to increase wages and improve working and living conditions on university campuses. Federal and private universities moved to implement the MOU in 2010, but many state universities, particularly in southern Nigeria, declared themselves unable to do so owing to financial constraints. Following protracted negotiations with staff unions, the administration of President Goodluck Jonathan was reported to have agreed to increase central government funding to help the universities to implement the MOU. Academic activities were subsequently resumed at the affected universities from early 2011. However, the universities in question were prohibited from admitting students for the 2011/12 academic year, having failed to complete the previous year's academic schedule.

Regulatory and Representative Bodies

GOVERNMENT

Federal Ministry of Culture and Tourism: Phase II Federal Secretariat, Block A, 1st Floor, Shehu Shagari Way, Abuja; tel. (9) 2348311; e-mail akayode@nigeria.gov.ng; Minister EDEM DUKE.

Federal Ministry of Education: New Federal Secretariat Complex, Shehu Shagari Way, Central Business Dist., PMB 146, Abuja; tel. (9) 5237838; e-mail inquiries@fme.gov.ng; internet www.fme.gov.ng; Minister (vacant).

Federal Ministry of Science and Technology: 5th and 9th Fl., New Federal Secretariat, Shehu Shagari Way, Central Area, PMB 331, Garki, Abuja; tel. (9) 5233397; e-mail info@fmst.gov.ng; internet www.fmst.gov.ng; Minister OMOBOLA JOHNSON (acting).

ACCREDITATION

National Universities Commission: Aja Nwachukwu House, Plot 430, Aguiyi Ironsi St, Maitama District, PMB 237, Garki GPO, Abuja; tel. (9) 4133176; e-mail webmaster@nuc.edu.ng; internet www.nuc.edu.ng; f. 1962; Exec. Sec. Prof. JULIUS OKOJIE.

FUNDING

National Board for Technical Education: PMB 2239, Plot B, Bida Rd, Kaduna; tel. (62) 246554; e-mail enquiries@nbte.gov.ng; internet www.nbte.gov.ng; provides standardized minimum guide curricula for technical and vocational education and training; accredits programmes offered by technical instns at secondary and post secondary levels; strengthens machinery for educational devt in the country; Exec. Sec. Dr MASA'UDU ADAMU KAZAURE.

National Commission for Colleges of Education: Plot 829, Cadastral Zone A01, Ralph Shodeinde St, PMB 0394, Garki, Abuja; tel. (9) 2346531; e-mail info@ncceonline.org; internet www.ncceonline.org; ensures quality assurance in teacher education; lays down minimum standards for all programmes of teacher education and accredits their certificates and other academic awards; acts as agency for channelling all external aids to colleges of education; Exec. Sec. Prof. M. I. JUNAID.

Learned Societies

GENERAL

UNESCO Office Abuja: PMB 424, Garki, Abuja; located at: Plot 777, Bouake St (off Herbert Macauley Way), Wuse Zone 6, Abuja; tel. (9) 4618502; e-mail abuja@unesco.org; Dir HUBERT CHARLES.

AGRICULTURE, FISHERIES AND VETERINARY SCIENCE

Fisheries Society of Nigeria: PMB 2607, Apapa, Lagos; Old College (NIOMR), Wilmot Point Rd, Bar Beach Bus Stop, Ahmadu Bello Way, Victoria Island, Lagos; tel. (802) 3325185; e-mail info@fison.org.ng; internet www.fison.org.ng; f. 1976; 500 mems; Pres. FOLUKE AREOLA; publ. *Nigerian Journal of Fisheries.*

Forestry Association of Nigeria: POB 4185, Ibadan, Oyo State; tel. (64) 626535; internet www.forestrynigeria.org; f. 1970 to further interest in forests and forest resources management and utilization; 1,078 mems (incl. 17 corporate mems, 61 life mems and 1000 ordinary mems); Pres. BELLOI ABBA YAKASA; Sec. P. C. OBIAGA; publs *FAN Newsletter, Nigerian Journal of Forestry, Proceedings of Annual Conference.*

Nigerian Veterinary Medical Association: Veterinary Council Bldg, No 8 Zambezi Crescent, Maitama, Abuja; tel. (808) 8576282; e-mail nvma-ng@org; internet www.nvma.org.ng; f. 1963; 5,000 mems; Pres. Dr GANI ENAHORO; Gen. Sec. Dr MONDAY OJEAMIREN; publs *Nigerian Veterinary Journal* (2 a year), *Tropical Veterinarian* (2 a year), *Zariya Veterinarian* (2 a year).

West African Association of Agricultural Economics: c/o Dept of Agricultural Economics, University of Ibadan, Ibadan, Oyo State; f. 1972; 250 mems from Benin Republic, Burkina Faso, Cameroon, Côte d'Ivoire, Ghana, Liberia, Mali, Nigeria, Senegal, Sierra Leone and Togo; Pres. Prof. Dr ANTHONY E. IKPI; Sec. Dr THOMAS EPONOU; publ. *West African Journal of Agricultural Economics.*

ARCHITECTURE AND TOWN PLANNING

Nigerian Institute of Architects: 2 Kukawa Close, Garki II, Abuja; tel. (9) 4802518; e-mail info@niarchitects.org; internet www.niarchitects.org; f. 1960; 1,370 full mems; 874 graduate mems and 87 fellows; Pres. Arc. ERIC CHUKWUKA; publs *NIA Journals, NIA Yearbook and Diary, Shelter for Nigerians.*

BIBLIOGRAPHY, LIBRARY SCIENCE AND MUSEOLOGY

Nigerian Library Association: c/o National Library of Nigeria, Sanusi Dantata House, Business Central District, PMB 1, Garki GPO 900001, Abuja; tel. (9) 2346773; e-mail info@nla-ng.org; internet www.nla-ng.org; f. 1962; 5,000 mems; Pres. VICTORIA OKOJIE; publs *Nigerian Libraries* (2 a year), occasional papers.

ECONOMICS, LAW AND POLITICS

Nigerian Bar Association: Plot 1261, Adeola Hopewell St, Victoria Island, Lagos; tel. (1) 4618287; e-mail nigerianbar@nba.org.ng; internet www.nigerianbar.com; f. 1962; Pres. Chief BAYO OJO; Gen. Sec. NIMI WALSON-JACK.

Nigerian Economic Society: Dept of Economics, Univ. of Ibadan, Ibadan; tel. (2) 7800395; e-mail adminofficer@nigerianeconomicsociety.org; internet www.nigerianeconomicsociety.org; f. 1957; advances the study and promotes investiga-

tion of economic and social problems, with spec. reference to Nigeria; 3,600 mems; library of 52 vols; Pres. Prof. AKIN IWAYEMI; Sec. Dr DOUGLASON G. OMOTOR; publs *Nigerian Journal of Economic and Social Studies (NJESS)* (3 a year), *Proceedings of Annual Conferences.*

Nigerian Institute of International Affairs: 13 Kofo Abayomi Rd, Victoria Island, POB 1727, Lagos; tel. (1) 9500983; e-mail dgeneral@niianet.org; internet www.niianet.org; f. 1961; 2,344 mems; library of 69,324 vols, 1,707 periodicals, 20,509 pamphlets, 333,085 press clippings; Dir-Gen. Prof. BOLA A. AKINTERINWA (acting); publs *Nigerian Forum* (12 a year), *Nigerian Journal of International Affairs* (4 a year).

Nigerian Institute of Management: Plot 22, Idowu Taylor St, POB 2557, Victoria Island, Lagos; tel. (1) 2615105; e-mail registrar@managementnigeria.org; internet www.managementnigeria.org; f. 1961; academic programmes offered incl. the Professional Diploma in Management and Postgraduate Diploma in Management (with Obafemi Owalowo University, Ile-Ife—see Federal Universities); 20,000 mems; library of 2,300 vols; Dir-Gen. Chief L. E. A. AIMIUWU; publ. *Management in Nigeria* (4 a year).

Nigerian Political Science Association (NPSA): Dept of Political Science, Uthman Danfodiyo Univ., Sokoto; tel. (803) 3376328; e-mail info@npsanigeria.org; internet www.npsanigeria.org; f. 1973; 200 mems; Pres. Dr ABDULLAHI SULE-KANO; Sec. Dr YAHAYA T. BABA.

EDUCATION

Committee of Vice-Chancellors of Nigerian Federal Universities: 4 Parakou St, Wuse II, Abuja; tel. (9) 5237655; e-mail cvc_nigeria@yahoo.com; f. 1962; acts as a coordinating body for Federal Univs; offers advice to govt and univ. governing councils on educational matters; 24 fed. univ. mems; Sec. Gen. Prof. MUSA ABDULLAHI.

HISTORY, GEOGRAPHY AND ARCHAEOLOGY

Historical Society of Nigeria: c/o Dept. of History, University of Lagos, Lagos; internet www.hsnonline.org; f. 1955; Pres. Prof. MONDAY B. ABASIATTAI; Sec. Dr I. R. AMADI; publs *Journal, Tarikh* (2 a year).

Nigerian Geographical Association: c/o Dept of Geography, University of Ibadan, Ibadan; tel. (22) 400550; f. 1955; 500 mems; Pres. Prof. ADETOYE FANIRAN; publ. *Nigerian Geographical Journal.*

LANGUAGE AND LITERATURE

Alliance Française: c/o French Consulate, Maison de France 2, Aromire Rd (on Kingsway Rd, opp. Ikoyi Hotel), Ikoyi, Lagos; tel. (1) 2692365; e-mail aflagos@alliancefrancaise-ng.org; internet www.maisondefrance-ng.com; offers courses and exams in French language and culture and promotes cultural exchange with France; attached teaching centres in Enugu, Ibadan, Ikoyi, Ikoyi-Yaba, Ilorin, Jos, Kaduna, Kano, Lagos, Lagos-Yaba, Maiduguri, Owerri and Port Harcourt.

British Council: Plot 2935, IBB Way, Maitama, PMB 550, Garki, Abuja; tel. (9) 41378707; e-mail infonigeria@ng.britishcouncil.org; internet www.britishcouncil.org/nigeria; offers courses and exams in English language and British culture and promotes cultural exchange with the UK; attached offices in Lagos and Kano;

Dir, Nigeria and Regional Dir, West Africa Dr JOHN RICHARDS.

Goethe-Institut: 10, Ozumba Mbadiwe Ave, opp. 1004 Flats, Victoria Island, Lagos State; tel. (1) 2610717; internet www.goethe.de/af/lag/deindex.htm; offers courses and exams in German language and culture and promotes cultural exchange with Germany; library of 6,000 vols; Dir MICHAEL MÜLLER-VERWEYEN.

MEDICINE

Nigerian Dental Association: c/o Dept of Oral Pathology and Biology, School of Dental Sciences, Univ. of Lagos, PMB 12003, Lagos; e-mail ndass1966@yahoo.co.uk; Pres. Dr KOFO WINFUNKE SAVAGE; Sec.-Gen. Dr O. A. OREBANJO.

Nigerian Medical Association: POB 1108, Adeniyi Jones Ave, Ikeja, Marina, Lagos; tel. (1) 4801569; e-mail info@nigeriannma.org; internet www.nigeriannma.org; f. 1951; 35,000 mems; Chair. (vacant); Pres. Dr WOLE ATOYEBI; Sec.-Gen. Dr WAPADA INUWA BALAMI.

Nigerian Society for Microbiology: c/o Prof. Nduka Okafor, Anambra State University of Technology, PMB 1660 Enugu State; f. 1973; holds annual conferences in the Nigerian universities; 130 mems; Pres. Dr A. O. EIIOFOR; publ. *Nigerian Journal for Microbiology* (2 a year).

Nutrition Society of Nigeria: c/o Dept of Human Nutrition, Faculty of Public Health, College of Medicine, University of Ibadan, Ibadan, Oyo State; e-mail nutrisocng@yahoo.com; f. 1963; 350 mems; Pres. Prof. ISAAC O. AKINYELE; publ. *Nigerian Nutrition Newsletter.*

NATURAL SCIENCES

General

Nigerian Academy of Science: NSPRI House, 32–36 Barikisu Iyede St, PMB 1004, University of Lagos Post Office, Akoko, Yaba, Lagos; tel. (1) 7916130; e-mail info@nas.org.ng; internet www.nas.org.ng; f. 1977; 120 fellows; Pres. Prof. D. U. U. OKALI; Academic Sec. for Physical Sciences Prof. A. O. ESOGBUE; Academic Sec. for Biological Sciences Prof. N. M. GADAZAMA; publs *Discourses* (2 a year), *Nigerian Journal of Agricultural Sciences* (1 a year), *Nigerian Journal of Medical Sciences* (1 a year), *Nigerian Journal of Natural Sciences* (1 a year), *Proceedings of the Nigerian Academy of Science* (4 a year).

Biological Sciences

Ecological Society of Nigeria: c/o Department of Biological Sciences, University of Lagos, Lagos; f. 1973; 373 mems; Pres. Prof. J. K. EGUNJOBI; Sec. C. CHIKE OKAFO; publs *Newsletter, Proceedings.*

Entomological Society of Nigeria: c/o Department of Crop Protection, Ahmadu Bello University, PMB 1044, Samaru, Zaria, Kaduna State; f. 1965; 250 mems; Pres. Prof. S. N. OKIWELU; Sec. O. O. ADU; publs *Nigerian Entomologists' Magazine* (1 a year), *Nigerian Journal of Entomology* (1 a year).

Genetics Society of Nigeria: c/o The Director, National Centre for Genetic Resources and Biotechnology, PMB 5382, Ibadan, Oyo State; f. 1972; 75 mems; Pres. Prof. W. AKINHASSAN; Sec.-Gen. Dr NGOZI E. ABU; publ. *Nigerian Journal of Genetics.*

Physical Sciences

Nigerian Geological Survey Agency: 31, Shettima A Mongunu Crescent (Behind Julius Berger's Head Office), Utako, Abuja; tel. (62) 212003; f. 1919; geological mapping; mineral exploration; geophysical and geochemical surveys and consultation on geological problems; library of 34,000 vols; Dir-Gen. Eng. ALEXANDER NDUBUISI NWEGBU.

TECHNOLOGY

Nigerian Society of Engineers: National Engineering Centre, Off National Mosque-Labour House Road, Central Business Area, Abuja, Abuja; tel. (1) 4766686; e-mail info@nse.org.ng; internet www.nse.org.ng; f. 1958; 30,000 mems; library of 1,500 vols; Pres. Eng. OLUMUYIWA ALADE AJIBOLA; publs *Technical Transactions*, *The Nigerian Engineer* (4 a year), *The Wisdom of Nigerian Engineers*.

Research Institutes

GENERAL

Lake Chad Research Institute (LCRI): Maidugur, PMB 1293, Maiduguri, Borno State; tel. (76) 960300; e-mail executivedirector@lcresmaid.org; internet www.lcresmaid.org; f. 1975; ecology and methods of control of crop pests and diseases of economic importance; improvement of the methods of control of dry farming and livestock husbandry in the severe environmental conditions around the lake; improvement of cultivation of wheat, barley, and other crops by irrigation; the socio-economic and public health effects of the introduction of large-scale irrigation schemes and improved methods of animal husbandry and fishing on the rural populations around the lake; genetic improvement, investigation of problems of all agricultural food crops grown, agricultural extension and research services with relevant fed. and state ministries, primary agricultural producers, industries and other users, technical services to farmers, agro-based industries; library of 16,000 vols; Exec. Dir Prof. BUKAR BABABE.

AGRICULTURE, FISHERIES AND VETERINARY SCIENCE

Cocoa Research Institute of Nigeria: Onigambari, PMB 5244, Ibadan, Oyo State; tel. (22) 410040; f. 1964; research aspects incl. entomology, plant-breeding, plant pathology, soil chemistry and biochemistry; library of 15,000 vols; Dir S. T. OLATOYE; publ. *Progress Report* (4 a year).

Forestry Research Institute of Nigeria (FRIN): PMB 5054, Ibadan, Oyo State; tel. (2) 413327; e-mail dfrin@skannet.com; internet www.frin-ng.org; f. 1954; Federal Colleges of Forestry at Ibadan and Jos, Federal College of Wildlife Management at New Bussa and Federal College of Forestry Mechanization at Afaka in Kaduna State; library of 17,798 vols, 590 periodicals; Exec. Dir Prof. S. O. O. BADEJO; publ. *Journal of Forestry Research and Management* (2 a year).

Institute for Agricultural Research (IAR): Ahmadu Bello University, PMB 1044, Samaru, Zaria, 810261; tel. (69) 551335; e-mail iar20002001@yahoo.com; internet www.iarsamaru.org; f. 1924; improvement of production of sorghum, millet, wheat, groundnuts, cotton and fibres, cowpea, sesame, soyabean and vegetables; maintenance of soil fertility; land resources assessment; crop environment; cropping systems and intercropping; crop-livestock integration; mechanization; soil and water management; socio-economic studies of small farm management, marketing, credit, supply systems and extension; sub-stations at: Kano in Kano State, Kadawa in Kano State and Talata Mafara in Zamfara State; library of 18,000 vols; Dir Prof. SHEHU GARKI ADO;

publs *Samaru Journal of Agricultural Research* (1 a year), *Samaru Miscellaneous Papers* (2 a year), *Samaru Research Bulletins* (4 a year), *Soil Survey Reports*.

Institute of Agricultural Research and Training (IART): Obafemi Awolowo University, Moor Plantation, PMB 5029, Ibadan, Oyo State; tel. (2) 2312523; e-mail drart@infoweb.abs.net; f. 1921, univ. institute 1970; comprises research div. and 2 federal colleges of agriculture and animal health production; serves as nat. centre for research into crops, cereals, grains, soyabean, jute, kenaf, livestock, soils and water management; library of 45,000 vols; Dir Prof. E. A. ADEBOWALE; publ. *Moor Journal of Agricultural Research* (2 a year).

National Agricultural Extension and Research Liaison Services: Ahmadu Bello University, PMB 1067, Zaria; tel. (69) 879449; e-mail director@naerls.gov.ng; internet www.naerls.gov.ng; f. 1963; agricultural performance and evaluation, agricultural economics and resources management, agricultural extension research, extension training and outreach and agricultural communication research; library of 2,000 vols, 1,400 periodicals; Exec. Dir Dr SADIQ ZUBAIAR ABUBAKAR; Exec. Dir Dr O. A. OYEDOKUN; publ. *The Nigerian Journal of Agricultural Extension* (2 a year).

National Animal Production Research Institute (NAPRI): Ahmadu Bello University, Shika, POB 1096, Zaria; tel. (69) 550435; e-mail nsapnet@nsapng.net; f. 1928; research into dairy, beef, sheep, goat, swine, rabbit and poultry production, management and breeding, range and pasture research and improvement, livestock economics and rural sociology of pastoral nomadic peoples; library of 23,624 vols; Dir Prof. A. M. ADAMU; publ. *Journal of Animal Production Research* (1 a year).

National Centre for Agricultural Mechanization: Federal Ministry of Agriculture, PMB 1525, Ilorin, Kwara State; tel. (33) 649168; e-mail info@ncam.gov.ng; internet www.ncam.gov.ng; f. 1977; Exec. Dir Ing. IKE AZOGU.

National Centre for Genetic Resources and Biotechnology (NACGRAB): Moor Plantation, PMB 5382, Ibadan, Oyo State; tel. (2) 2312622; e-mail info@nacgrab.gov.ng; internet www.nacgrab.gov.ng; f. 1986; research, data gathering and dissemination of information on matters relating to plant genetic resources, genetic engineering and biotechnology; library of 1,500 vols; Project Man. LANRE GBADAMOSI.

National Cereals Research Institute (NCRI): PMB 8, Badeggi, Bida, Niger State; tel. (66) 461233; e-mail ncri@skannet.com; f. 1975, fmrly Federal Dept of Agricultural Research; conducts research into the production, processing and industrial capacity utilization of rice, digitaria, oilseeds (soybean and beniseed) and sugarcane; mechanization and improvement of methods of cultivating, harvesting, processing and storage of crops; improving the utilization of by-products; ecology of crop pests and diseases and improved methods of their control; integration of crop cultivation into farming systems in different ecological zones and its socio-economic effects on the rural population; distributes farming implements, machinery and cultivated varieties of rice and soybean; incl. a Plant Quarantine Training Centre; library of 6,078 vols; Head of Station A. S. GANA; publs *Information Papers* (12 a year), *Memoranda* (irregular), *Research Bulletins* (4 a year).

National Horticultural Research Institute (NIHORT): Idi-Ishin, PMB 5432, Iba-

dan, Oyo State; tel. (2) 2412230; e-mail nihortinfo@yahoo.com; internet www.nihort.org; f. 1975; two sub-stations at Mbato, near Okigwe, Imo State and at Bagauda, near Tiga, Kano State; conducts research into fruit and vegetable production and consumption, in particular improvement of the genetic potentials of the cultivated, semi-cultivated and wild crops; improvement of agronomic and husbandry practices; mechanization and improvement of methods of cultivating, harvesting, processing and storage; improvement of the utilization of by-products; ecology of crop pests and diseases and improved methods of their control; integration of crop cultivation into farming systems in different ecological zones of the country; library of 23,000 vols; Dir ADEMOLA ADESEYE IDOWU; publs *Information Papers* (12 a year), technical bulletins, production guides, training manuals (irregular).

National Institute for Freshwater Fisheries Research (NIFFR): PMB 6006, New Bussa, Niger State; tel. (31) 670 444; e-mail contact@niffrnigeria.org; f. 1968; research into the limnological behaviour and characteristics of the man-made lakes and their effects on the fish and other aquatic life; the abundance, distribution and other biological characteristics of species of fish and practical methods of their exploitation; the socio-economic effects of the construction of man-made lakes on rural populations; technical and vocational training in freshwater fishing and related fields; library of 20,000 vols, 40 periodicals; Dir Prof. B. M. B. LADU; publ. *Nigerian Fisheries and Aquatic Sciences Abstract* (1 a year).

National Root Crops Research Institute (NRCRI): Umudike, PMB 7006, Umuahia, Abia State; tel. (82) 440471; e-mail keninwrosu_nrcri@yahoo.com; internet www.nrcri.org.ng; f. 1923; research for the genetic improvement of yams, cocoyams, cassava, sweet potato, Irish potato, ginger and other root-crops; library of 3,113 books, 25,665 periodicals; Dir Dr KEN I. NWOSU; publs *Advisory Bulletins* (12 a year), *Gazette*, *Programmes of Work* (1 a year).

National Veterinary Research Institute (NVRI): PMB 01, Vom, near Jos, Plateau State; tel. (55) 578876; e-mail edvr@nvri.gov.ng; f. 1924; all aspects of animal nutrition; production of vaccine and sera; introduction of exotic stock to improve meat, milk and egg production; standardization and quality control of manufactured animal feeds; training livestock superintendents, laboratory technicians and technologists; library of 14,000 vols, 4,000 reports, etc.; Exec. Dir Dr MOHAMMED SANI AHMED; publs *Index of Veterinary Research* (1 a year), *Research Papers* (irregular).

Nigerian Institute for Oil Palm Research (NIFOR): PMB 1030, Benin City, Edo State; tel. (52) 602485; f. 1939; library of 13,000 vols; Dir Dr U. OMOTI; publ. *Nigerian Journal of Palms and Oil Seeds* (irregular).

Nigerian Stored Products Research Institute (NSPRI): Km 3, Asa Dam Rd, PMB 1489, Ilorin, Kwara State; tel. (31) 222143; e-mail nspriheadquarters@yahoo.com; internet www.nspriilorin.com; f. 1960; 450 mems; library of 3,610 vols; Exec. Dir Dr M. A. ADESIDA; publs *Journal* (4 a year), *Nigerian Post-Harvest Technology Abstract* (1 a year), *Research News* (4 a year).

Rubber Research Institute of Nigeria (RRIN): Iyanomo, PMB 1049, Benin City, Edo State; tel. (68) 226592; e-mail rubberresearchnig@yahoo.com; internet www.rrin.org; f. 1961; researches into the production and products of natural rubber

(Hevea brasilliensis), gum arabic (Acacia spp.) and other latex bearing plants of economic importance; disseminates research information to the target farmers; library of 1,000 vols; Exec. Dir Prof. OSAYANMO IGBINOSA EGUAVOEN; publs *Information Booklets* (4 a year), *RRIN's Advisory Leaflets* (12 a year).

BIBLIOGRAPHY, LIBRARY SCIENCE AND MUSEOLOGY

Institute of Archaeology and Museum Studies: PMB 2031, Jos, Plateau State; tel. (73) 453516; e-mail iamsjos2000@yahoo.co .uk; f. 1963; library of 1,500 vols, 500 journals; Dir MONICA ABADOM; publ. *The Museologist* (1 a year).

ECONOMICS, LAW AND POLITICS

Centre for Management Development: PMB 21578, Ikeja, Lagos; tel. (80) 37120043; e-mail info@cmd.gov.ng; internet www.cmd .gov.ng; f. 1973; promotes and coordinates activities of institutions engaged in the education and training of managerial manpower; advises govt on policy, formulates policies and guidelines, monitors standards of management education, accredits and registers management trainers, assesses training programmes, provides advisory and consultancy service to Nigerian businesses; library of 50,000 vols (incl. books and monographs), 1,000 periodicals, also general publs and serials, teaching materials library, and audiovisual unit; Dir-Gen. and Chief Exec. Dr KABIR KABO USMAN; publs *Journal of Economic Management*, *Nigerian Management Review* (2 a year).

Nigerian Institute of Social and Economic Research: PMB 5, University Post Office, Ibadan; tel. (2) 8102904; e-mail dg@ niser.org.ng; internet www.nisernigeria.org; f. 1950 as WA Institute of Social and Economic Research, present name 1960; govt-financed; applied research on problems of immediate and long-term relevance to Nigerian devt: economic planning and devt, agricultural and industrial devt, business and technology, foreign and int. trade, public finance and social, physical and manpower planning and devt; political devt, population studies; training for staff of planning orgs; consultancy service for fed. and state govts, private orgs and int. bodies; library of 75,000 vols; Dir-Gen. Prof. BANKOLE ONI; publ. *Research for Development* (1 a year).

EDUCATION

Nigerian Educational Research and Development Council: POB 91, Abuja; Km 135, Lokoja-Kaduna Rd, Sheda, Abuja; tel. (803) 4511393; e-mail info@nerdc.gov.ng; internet www.nerdc.gov.ng; f. 1988 by merger of Nigerian Educational Research Council, Comparative Education Study and Adaptation Centre, Nigerian Book Devt Council and Nigerian Language Centre; curriculum devt and general educational research; library of 12,000 vols; Exec. Sec. Prof. GODSWILL OBIOMA; publ. conference and workshop reports.

MEDICINE

National Institute of Pharmaceutical Research and Development (NIPRD): PMB 21, Idu, Abuja; tel. (9) 5239089; f. 1989; research into medical plants, herbs and drug development and formulary; drug information centre; nat. centre for drugs; regulates the standardization of pharmaceutical substances; library of 2,350 vols, 2,389 journals, 6,000 CD-ROMs; Dir Dr UFORD S. INYANG; publ. *Journal of Phytomedicine and Therapeutics (JOPAT)* (1 a year).

Nigerian Institute for Trypanosomiasis Research (NITR): PMB 2077, Kaduna, Kaduna State; tel. (62) 238074; e-mail nitrng@yahoo.com; internet www.nitr-ng .org; f. 1951; research into trypanosomiasis and onchocerciasis generally; the pathology, immunology and methods of treatment of the diseases; the ecology and life-cycle of the vectors and the mode of transmission of the disease; chemical, biological and other methods of vector control, the socio-economic effects of the disease on the rural populations; maintains 6 zonal offices, 2 field stations; library of 10,000 vols; Dir Prof. M. MAMMAN.

Nigerian Institute of Medical Research (NIMR): Edmund Crescent, PMB 2013, Yaba, Lagos; tel. (1) 800090; e-mail director@nimr-ng.org; internet www.nimr-ng .org; f. 1973; library of 13,000 vols; Dir-Gen. Dr ONI IDIGBE.

NATURAL SCIENCES

General

Nigerian Institute for Oceanography and Marine Research (NIOMR): Victoria Island, PMB 12729, Lagos; tel. (1) 2617385; e-mail niomr@linkserve.com.ng; f. 1975; library of 10,000 vols; Dir J. G. TOBOR; publ. *Newsletter* (4 a year).

TECHNOLOGY

Federal Institute of Industrial Research (FIIRO): PMB 21023, Ikeja, Lagos; Blind Centre St, Cappa Bus Stop, off Agege Motor Rd, Oshodi, Ikeja, Lagos; tel. (1) 8947094; e-mail info@fiiro.gov.ng; internet www.fiiro .gov.ng; f. 1956; food technology, industrial fermentation through biotechnology, pulp and paper research, domestic and industrial water treatment, environmental studies, ceramic and engineering materials research, machinery and equipment design and fabrication; consultancy, analytical services, technical services to industry, scientific and industrial information service; library of 14,500 vols; Dir-Gen. and CEO Dr OLUWOLE OLATUNJI; publs *Journal of Industrial Research and Technology* (irregular), *Profile on FIIRO Commercializable Technologies* (irregular), *Research Report* (irregular).

National Centre for Energy Research and Development: University of Nigeria, Nsukka, Enugu State; tel. (42) 771853; e-mail ncerdunn@yahoo.com; f. 1982; attached to Univ. of Nigeria Nsukka; fed. govt-funded centre for research and devt of solar and other renewable and non-renewable energy such as photovoltaic, photothermal, wind energy, radiation measurement, biomass, coal, energy management, etc.; Dir Dr P. E. UGWUOKE.

National Research Institute for Chemical Technology (NARICT): PMB 1052, Zaria, Kaduna State; tel. (69) 334503; e-mail info@narict.gov.ng; f. 1988; research and development work in chemicals, leather and allied fields; short-term training courses in chemical technology, laboratory management, chemistry laboratory practicals, safety; four extension centres, at Kano, Jos, Maiduguri and Sokoto for extension services; serves as national information centre on leather and chemical technology; Dir-Gen. Dr E. M. OKONKWO; publ. *Journal of Leather and Chemical Technology* (1 a year).

Nigerian Building and Road Research Institute (NBRRI): PMB 5065, Wuse General Post Office, Abuja FCT; 3 Gabes str., Wuse Zone 2, Abuja FCT; tel. (9) 5237466-7; e-mail servicomunit@nbrri.gov.ng; internet www.nbrri.gov.ng; f. 1978; conducts applied research and devt into the use of local

materials and methods in road and bldg construction; library of 12,000 vols; Dir-Gen. Dr J. A. ALI; publs *Journal of Construction and Materials Technology* (2 a year), *Technical Digest* (2 a year).

Projects Development Institute (PRODA): Emene Industrial Layout, PMB 01609, Enugu State; tel. (98) 811745; e-mail info@proda-ng.org; internet www.proda-ng .org; f. 1970 as Project Devt Agency, present status 1977; accredited by Federal Min. of Science and Technology; conducts research into various areas of science, ceramics, energy and engineering with the aim of advancing industialization; promotes the establishment of new industrial projects through laboratory and pilot investigations to the construction of large-scale commercial plants, uses local raw materials and labour; library of 4,500 vols; Dir-Gen. Prof. G. N. ONUOHA; publs *PRODA Investment Opportunities, PRODA Technological Innovations*.

Raw Materials Research and Development Council (RMRDC): Plot 17, Aguiyi Ironsi St, Maitama District, PMB 232, Garki, Abuja; tel. (9) 8213090; e-mail ceo@rmrdc.gov .ng; internet www.rmrdc.gov.ng; f. 1987; supports and expedites industrial devt and self-sufficiency through maximum utilization of local materials; draws up policy guidelines and action programmes on raw materials acquisition, exploitation and devt; advises on adaptation of machinery and process for raw materials utilization; library of 3,000 vols; Chief Exec. and Dir-Gen. Prof. PETER AZIKIWE ONWUALU; publs *Journal of Raw Materials* (1 a year), *Research Reports* (8 a year).

Libraries and Archives

Abeokuta

Ogun State Library: PMB 2060, Abeokuta, Ogun State; f. 1976; 21,736 vols; Chief Librarian Alhaji BAYO YISA ODULAJA.

Akure

Ondo State Library Board: PMB 719, Akure; tel. (34) 230561; f. 1976, current name adopted 1985; reading and reference services, mobile and school library services, training of library assistants; 62,546 vols; Dir T. A. AJUMOBI.

Bauchi

Bauchi State Library Board: PMB 0141, Abdulkadri Ahmed Rd, Off Bank Rd, Bauchi; tel. (77) 542959; f. 1976; lending and reference services, special services to rehabilitation centres, training of library staff; 35,000 vols, 3,475 periodicals; Dir MUSA M. DEDE.

Benin

Edo State Library Board: Sapele Rd, PMB 1127, Benin City; tel. (52) 234-255176; f. 1971; 311,680 vols; Central Reference Library with emphasis on the needs of the State Govt; Readers Services Div. (22 brs). Technical Service Div.; School Library Div.; hospital trolley services; Dir JOSEPH O. UDUEBOR; publs *Edo Library Accessions List* (2 a year), *Legal Deposit Bulletin* (2 a year), *Index to The Observer* (2 a year).

Enugu

Enugu State Library Board: PMB 01026, Enugu; tel. (42) 254103; f. 1955; Dir for Library Services ISAAC OGBONNA..

Attached Library:

State Central Library: Market Rd, Enugu; f. 1956; lending and reference library activities; legal deposit and regional centre for bibliographical information and research; Nigeriana colln; 1

mobile library unit; divisional library at Onueke; zonal libraries at Awgu, Agbani and Nsukka; 83,000 vols.

Ibadan

Forestry Research Institute of Nigeria Library: PMB 5054, Ibadan; tel. (2) 2414441; e-mail dfrin@skannet.com; internet www.frin-ng.org; f. 1954; spec. collns: Nigerian silvicultural records and working plans, postgraduate theses colln, and Harold Young Library of rare materials on forest mensuration, biometrics, photogrammetry and technometrics; 17,798 vols, 590 periodicals; Head of Library Dr B. A. AKINTOLA; publs *Current Awareness Service on Agricultural Research and Development Bulletin* (12 a year), *Current Contents* (12 a year), *Library Accession Lists* (4 a year).

Kenneth Dike Library, University of Ibadan: University of Ibadan, Ibadan; tel. (2) 8101100; e-mail librarykdl@mail.ui.edu .ng; internet www.ui.edu.ng/unitslibrary .htm; f. 1948; depository for OAU and UN specialized agencies publs; spec colln of Africana, private papers of eminent Nigerians; 700,000 vols, 1,500 current periodicals; Librarian OLUFUNMILAYO G. TAMUNO; publ. *Library Record*.

National Archives of Nigeria: PMB 4, University of Ibadan Post Office, Ibadan; f. 1951, legally recognized 1957; charged with colln, rehabilitation, reproduction and preservation of all public records incl. private papers under the Min. of Information and Nat. Orientation; 3 major (zonal) offices at Enugu, Ibadan and Kaduna; other brs are located at Abeokuta, Akure, Benin, Calabar, Ilorin, Jos, Lagos Maiduguri, Oweri, Port-Harcourt and Sokoto; 8,500 vols; Dir COMFORT AINA UKWU; publ. *Special Lists*.

Ife

Hezekiah Oluwasanmi Library, Obafemi Awolowo University: Ile-Ife; tel. (36) 230290; e-mail librarian@oauife.edu.ng; internet library.oauife.edu.ng; f. 1962; spec. collns of Africana, audiovisual materials and govt documents; 673,263 vols, 7,400 periodicals; Librarian BUKKY O. ASUBIOJO; publs *Abstracts of Theses* (1 a year), *Research in Progress at the Obafemi Awolowo University* (1 a year).

Ikeja

Industrial Information Centre and Extension Services (FIIRO Indices): PMB 21023, Ikeja, Cappa Bus Stop, Agege Motor Rd, Lagos State; tel. (1) 4522905; f. 1956; scientific, technical and industrial information, documentation and dissemination, current awareness, publication services; spec. collns: UNIDO, NTIS, FOS publs, nat. and int. standards; 14,500 vols; Librarian P. O. DEKWE; publs *Journal of Industrial Research and Technology*, industrial and corporate profiles, reports on selected FIIRO technologies for rural industrialization.

Ilorin

Kwara State Library Board: Sulu Gambari Rd, PMB 1561, Ilorin, Kwara State; f. 1968; 45,000 vols; Dir Deacon BENSON BABATUNDE ODEWALE.

Jos

Plateau State Library Board: c/o Bureau for Information, POB 2053, Jos, Plateau State; f. 1976; 45,293 vols; brs at Akwanga, Keffi, Lafia, Pankshin and Shendam; Librarian TIMOTHY P. A. ANGBA (acting).

Kaduna

Kaduna State Library Board: PMB 2061, No 6 Bida Rd, Kaduna; tel. (802) 3051338; f.

1953, current name adopted 1976; 200,000 vols; Dir ABDULLAHI MUSA; publs *Bibliographies*, *Legal Deposit Collection*, *Public Enlightenment*, *Readers' Guides*.

Kano

Kano State Library Board: PMB 3094, Ahmadu Bello Way, Kano; tel. (64) 645614; e-mail nassarawa2001@yahoo.com; f. 1968; incl. mobile and school library services, cultural programmes, outreach services to govt depts, reference and documentation services, audiovisual services, internet services; 1m. vols; Exec. Dir Alhaji SANUSI ABDULLAH NASSARAWA.

Lagos

Central Medical Library: Federal Ministry of Health, PMB 2003, Yaba, Lagos; f. 1946; 30,000 vols, 600 journals; Librarian M. O. ORIMOLADE.

Lagos City Libraries: PMB 2025, Lagos; f. 1950; 229,150 vols; Librarian B. B. OGUNLANA.

National Library of Nigeria: 4 Wesley St, PMB 12626, Lagos; tel. (1) 2600220; f. 1964; 12 brs; spec. collns of Nigerian and UK govt publications, UN documents, Rhodes House Library Colln (private papers of past colonial civil servants), Ranfurly Library Colln; depository for UN, OAU and Canadian colln; 140,000 vols in main library, 18,000 at brs; Chair. FRANCIS Z. GANA; Nat. Librarian Alhaji MU'AZU H. WALI.

University of Lagos Library: Lagos; tel. (1) 4932552; internet www.unilag.edu; f. 1962; legal depository for Lagos State; depository for all publications of ECA, GATT, ICJ and ILO; collections on UNESCO, WHO and FAO; 375,000 vols, 4,500 periodicals; Librarian Dr S. O. OLANLOKUN (acting); publs *Library Notes*, *Reader's Guide*.

Maiduguri

Borno State Library Board: PMB 14434, Maiduguri, Borno State; tel. (76) 231389; f. 1968, became library board 1984; 11 brs; provides information for the public, trains library staff, organizes school libraries, annual book exhibition; 86,535 vols; Dir JOHN YADU MALGWI.

Nsukka

University of Nigeria, Nsukka Libraries: Nnamdi Azikiwe Library, Nsukka, Enugu State; tel. (42) 771444; e-mail misunn@aol .com; f. 1960; 717,000 vols at Nsukka and Enugu campuses, medical library at Enugu with 42,000 vols, Africana colln of 30,000 vols; Librarian EMENIKE IKEGBUNE (acting); publs *Nsukka Library Notes* (irregular), *UNLAN*.

Owerri

Imo State Library Board: PMB 1118, Owerri, Imo State; tel. (83) 230280; f. 1976; lending, reference, children's library and library for the disabled, bibliographic and information consultancy services, rural library services and school library resource centre; 123,000 vols; Dir for Library Services AGATHA C. NWACHUKWU; publ. *The Light* (1 a year).

Port Harcourt

British Council Information Centre: Plot 127, Olu Obasanjo Way, GRA II, Port Harcourt; tel. (84) 237173; e-mail info .portharcourt@ng.britishcouncil.org; Centre Man. PATIENCE EZINWOKE.

Museums and Art Galleries

Benin

National Museum, Benin: Benin; tel. (52) 252675; e-mail natmusben@yahoo.com; f. 1973; Benin antiquities, bronzes, ivory, terracotta, wood, beads, masks, masquerades, ancestral figures, materials for warfare, etc.; Curator MARTINS OGUNTAYO AKANBIEMU.

Esie

Esie Museum: PMB 301, Kwara State; f. 1945; stone antiquities (800 half life-size human figures); Dir (vacant).

Ife

Natural History Museum, Obafemi Awolowo University: Ile-Ife, Osun State; tel. (36) 230291; e-mail bogunfol@oauife.edu.ng; internet www.oauife.edu.ng/museum; f. 1971 as sub-unit of Dept of Biological Sciences of Univ. of Ife, present status 1982, present bldg 2011; research, outreach activities, teaching, exhibition and identification of animal and plant specimens; botanical, entomological, geological, palaeontological and zoological collns; archaeological artifacts; offers MSc in conservation and MSc and PhD in biosystematics; library of 2,500 vols; Dir Dr ADISA OGUNFOLAKAN.

Jos

National Museum, Jos: PMB 2031, Jos, Plateau State; f. 1982; ethnography, architecture and archaeology of Nigeria; terracotta Nok figurines, modern and traditional Nigerian pottery; zoological and botanical gardens; museum of traditional architecture; transport museum; craft village; open-air theatre; library of 10,000 vols and 2,000 Arabic MSS; Dir M. DANDAURA.

Kaduna

National Museum, Kaduna: PMB 2127, Kaduna; tel. (62) 211180; f. 1975; archaeology and ethnography; houses the 'Craft Village', where traditional hair-plaiting, weaving, pottery, calabash decoration, wood carving, leather work, brass casting and smithery are done; library of 1,500 vols; Dir Dr K. S. CHAFE; publ. *Tambari*.

Kano

Gidan Makama Museum: POB 2023, Kano; tel. (64) 645170; e-mail yusufadamu2000@yahoo.com; internet www .kanoonline.com/gidan_makama; f. 1959; local art work; history of Kano and the Kanawas from 15th–19th centuries; Curator MUSA O. HAMBOLU.

Lagos

National Museum, Lagos: Onikan Rd, Lagos; tel. (1) 2634045; e-mail museumlagos@yahoo.com; f. 1957; ethnography, archaeology and traditional art; library of 9,247 vols; Dir-Gen. MALLAM YUSUF ABDALLAH USMAN; publ. *Nigerian Heritage* (1 a year).

Oron

National Museum, Oron: PMB 1004, Oron, Akwa Ibom State; f. 1958; rebuilt after civil war in 1975; wooden sculptures and ethnographic artefacts and materials; Chief Curator ANIEFIOK UDO AKPAN.

Owo

Owo Museum: Federal Dept of Antiquities, POB 84, Owo, Ondo State; f. 1959; arts and crafts; some ethnographic relics mainly from the Eastern part of the Yoruba region; Curator E. OLA ABEJIDE.

Universities

FEDERAL UNIVERSITIES

ABUBAKAR TAFAWA BALEWA UNIVERSITY

PMB 0248, Bauchi
Telephone: (77) 543500
E-mail: info@atbunet.org
Internet: www.atbu.edu.ng
Founded 1988
federal govt control
Language of instruction: English
Academic year: October to September

Vice-Chancellor: Prof. MUHAMMAD HAMISU MUHAMMAD
Deputy Vice-Chancellor for Academic Affairs: Prof. MOHAMMAD IBRAHIM ONOGU
Deputy Vice-Chancellor for Admin.: Prof. USMAN ALIYU EL-NATATY
Bursar and Registrar: Alhaji ALI A. DEBA
Librarian: Prof. MANSUR USMAN MALUMFASHI
Number of teachers: 260
Number of students: 12,000 (8,000 full-time, 4,000 part-time)

DEANS

School of Agriculture and Agricultural Technology: Prof. ISYAKU MUHAMMAD
School of Engineering Technology: Prof. GERRY EGBO
School of Environment and Environmental Technology: Prof. UMAR ABDULLAHI
School of Management Technology: ABUBAKAR YUSUF DUTSE
School of Science and Science Education: Prof. EDIGA B. AGBO
School of Technology Education: Prof. JOSEPH D. ENEMALI

PROFESSORS

ABAYEH, O. J., Chemistry
ABUBAKAR, M. M., Animal Science
ADEBITAN, S. A., Crop Production
ADEGBOLA, T. A., Animal Science
ALIYU, U. O., Electrical Engineering
BABAJI, G. A., Crop Production
BOGOVO, S., Crop Production
DIKE, E. F. C., Geology
ELINWA, A. U., Civil Engineering
GANI, A. M., Biological Sciences
HAQUE, M. F., Physics
IBRAHIM, S. A., Crop Production
JATAU, J. S., Mechanical and Production Engineering
KELA, S. L., Biological Sciences
MATAWAL, D. S., Civil Engineering
MBAP, S. T., Animal Production
OCHI, J. E., Agricultural Economics and Extension
OGIDI, J. A., Biological Sciences
ONOGU, M. I., Electrical Engineering and Electronics
ORAZULIKE, D. M., Geology
OYAWOYE, E. O., Animal Production
OYAWOYE, E. O., Biological Sciences
SANI, R. M., Agricultural Economics and Extension
SAWA, F. J., Biological Sciences
SESAY, M. S., Mathematical Sciences
SHEHU, L. M., Animal Production
SHEHU, Y., Animal Production
SULEIMAN, M. M., Biological Sciences
UBA, A., Biological Sciences
YUSUF, I. Z., Biological Sciences

AHMADU BELLO UNIVERSITY

Zaria
Telephone: (69) 550581
E-mail: registrar@abu.edu.ng
Founded 1962
federal control
Language of instruction: English
Academic year: November to August

Vice-Chancellor: Prof. ABDULLAHI MUSTAPHA
Deputy Vice-Chancellor for Academic Affairs: Prof. ALI MOSES ADAMU
Deputy Vice-Chancellor for Admin.: Prof. IDRIS ISA FUNTUA
Registrar: Dr ISAH MOHAMMED ABBASS
Librarian: Prof. ZAKARI MOHAMMAD

Number of teachers: 2,064
Number of students: 35,783

Publications: *Inaugural Lectures* (4 a year), *University Gazette, University Public Lectures* (12 a year), *University Research Report*

DEANS

Faculty of Administration: Dr B. SABO
Faculty of Agriculture: Prof. M. C. DIKE
Faculty of Arts: Dr M. L. AMIN
Faculty of Education: Prof J. GWANI
Faculty of Engineering: Prof. O. J. MUDIARE
Faculty of Environmental Design: Prof. M. B. YUNUSA
Faculty of Law: Prof. N. M. JAMO
Faculty of Medicine: Dr S. SHEHU
Faculty of Pharmaceutical Sciences: Dr M. I. SLE
Faculty of Science: Prof. A. J. NOK
Faculty of Social Sciences: Prof. R. A. DUNMOYE
Faculty of Veterinary Medicine: Prof. N. D. G. IBRAHIM
School of Postgraduate Studies: Prof. J. ADEBAYO

PROFESSORS

Faculty of Administration (Kongo Campus, Zaria):

ABDULLAHI, S., Business Administration
ABDULSALAMI, I., Public Administration

Faculty of Agriculture (Agricultural Complex, A. B. U. Main Campus, Zaria):

ATALA, T. K., Rural Sociology
DIKE, M. C., Crop Protection
OGUNLELA, V. B., Agronomy
OLAREWAJU, J. D., Plant Science
OLUFAJO, O. O., Agronomy
OLUKOSI, J. O., Agricultural Economics
VOH, J. P., Rural Sociology

Faculty of Arts (tel. (69) 551540):

ABAH, O. S., English
MAHADI, A., History
MOHAMMED, A., English
NASIDI, Y. A., English

Faculty of Education (e-mail deaneduc@yahoo.com):

ADEYANJU, F. B., Physical and Health Education
CHADO, M. A., Physical and Health Education
KOLO, F. D., Education
LADAN, B. A., Physical and Health Education
OLAOFE, I. A., Education
VENKATESWARLU, K., Physical and Health Education
ZAKARI, M., Library Science

Faculty of Engineering (e-mail deaneng@abu.edu.ng):

ADEFILA, S. S., Chemical Engineering
AKU, S. Y., Mechanical Engineering
FOLAYAN, C. O., Mechanical Engineering
OKUOFU, C. A., Water Resources and Environmental Engineering

OYINOLA, A. K., Metallurgical Engineering

Faculty of Environmental Design (e-mail deanen@abu.edu.ng):

OGUNTONA, T., Industrial Design
SA'AD, H. T., Architecture

Faculty of Law:

CHUKKOL, K., Public Law

Faculty of Medicine:

ADEKEYE, E. A., Dental Surgery
AHMED, M. H., Psychiatry
AIKHIONBARE, H. A., Paediatrics
ALI, M. A., Human Physiology
OGALA, W. N., Paediatrics
ONYEMELUKWE, G. C., Medicine
YAKUBU, A. M., Paediatrics

Faculty of Pharmaceutical Sciences (tel. (69) 951209; e-mail emabdu@abu.edu.ng):

AGUYE, I. A., Pharmacy and Clinical Pharmacy
HUSSEIN, I., Pharmacology and Clinical Pharmacy
ILYAS, M., Pharmacy and Medicinal Chemistry
MUSTAPHA, A., Pharmaceutical and Medicinal Chemistry
ONAOLAPO, J. A., Pharmaceutical Science and Microbiology

Faculty of Science (tel. (69) 551886; e-mail science@abu.edu.ng):

AHMAD, A., Microbiology
AMUPITAN, J. O., Chemistry
ARIYO, J. A., Geography
AWODI, S., Biological Sciences
BELLO, K. O., Textile Science and Technology
IKE, E. C., Geology
IYUN, J. F., Chemistry
KOLAWOLE, E. G., Textile Science and Technology
NKEONYE, P. O., Textile Science and Technology
OSAZUWA, I. B., Physics

Faculty of Social Sciences (tel. (69) 551540):

DUNMOYE, A., Political Science
KWANASHIE, M., Economics
NKOM, S., Sociology

Faculty of Veterinary Medicine (tel. (69) 551358; e-mail deanvet@abu.edu.ng):

ABDULLAHI, U., Veterinary Surgery and Medicine
AGBEDE, R. I. S., Parasitology and Entomology
ESIEVO, K. A. N., Veterinary Pathology and Medicine
GHAJI, A., Veterinary Anatomy
HAMBOLU, J. O., Anatomy
KWAGA, J. P. K., Veterinary Public Health and Preventive Medicine
OGWU, D., Veterinary Surgery and Medicine
OJO, S. A., Veterinary Anatomy
UMOH, J. U., Veterinary Public Health and Preventive Medicine
ZARIA, L. T., Veterinary Pathology and Microbiology

Centres:

ABUBAKAR, S., National Agricultural Research and Liaison Services
ADAMU, A. M., National Animal Production Research Institute
ADEGBEHIN, J. D., National Agricultural Research and Liaison Services
ALIYU, J. S., Institute of Education
BAIKIE, A., Institute of Education
EDUVIE, L. V., National Animal Production Research Institute
GEFU, J. O., National Animal Production Research Institute
OTCHERE, E. O., National Animal Production Research Institute
VOH, A., National Animal Production Research Institute

BAYERO UNIVERSITY

PMB 3011, Kano
Telephone: (64) 666023
E-mail: registrar@buk.edu.ng
Founded 1977
federal control
Language of instruction: English
Academic year: October to July (2 semesters)
Chancellor: HRH OBA SIJUWADE OKUNADE OLUBUSE, II (Ooni of Ife)
Chair. of Ccl: MUHD ADAMU JUMBA
Vice-Chancellor: Prof. ABUBAKAR ADAMU RASHID
Deputy Vice-Chancellor for Academic Affairs: Prof. MUHD YAHUZA BELLO
Deputy Vice-Chancellor for Admin.: Prof. ABDULRASHID GARBA
Registrar: SANI IBRAHIM AMIN
Librarian: Prof. IBRAHIM LUKMAN DISO
Library of 170,000 vols, 2,200 periodicals
Number of teachers: 793
Number of students: 28,941

Publications: *Bayero University Quarterly News*, *University Public Lectures* (1 a year)

DEANS

Faculty of Agriculture: Prof. AUWALU MANSUR BINDAWA
Faculty of Arts and Islamic Studies: Prof. SAIDU A. BABURA
Faculty of Education: Dr IBRAHIM M. YAKASAI
Faculty of Law: Dr A. B. AHMAD
Faculty of Medicine: Dr ABDU LAWAN
Faculty of Science: M. S. SULE
Faculty of Social and Management Sciences: Prof. SULEIMAN ALIYU KANTUDU
Faculty of Technology: Dr A. U. ALHAJI
General Studies Unit: Dr LAWAN S. TAURA (Dir)
Postgraduate School: Prof. SADIQ ISA RADDA

PROFESSORS

ABBA, I. A., History
ABDULKADIR, D., Centre for the Study of Nigerian Languages
ABDULKADIR, M. S., History
ABDULLAHI, M., Sociology
ABUBAKAR, M. A., Arabic
ABUBAKAR, M. M.
ADAMU, U. A., Education
AHMED, K., Geography
AJIBERO, M., Library Science
AYODELE, J. T., Chemistry
AZARE, G. D., Education
BICHI, A. Y., Centre for the Study of Nigerian Languages
BICHI, M. Y., Education
DAMBATTA, B. B., Chemistry
DANGAMBO, A., Nigerian Languages
DISO, S. I., Mechanical Engineering
DUZE, M. C., Sociology
EGBON, M., Mass Communication
ESSIET, E. U., Geography
FAGBEMI, A. O., Education
FALOLA, J. A., Geography
FATOPE, M. O., Physics
GUSAU, S. M., Nigerian Languages
HASHIM, I., Political Science
IBRAHIM, M., Paediatrics
JEGA, A. M., Political Science
JIBRIL, M. M., English Language
JOWITT, D. R., English and European Languages
KATANDE, J., Electrical Engineering
MAIWAQDA, D. A., Education
MUHAMMAD, A. R., History
OCHOGWU, M., Library Science
OLOFIN, E. A., Geography
PEDRO, I. A., Economics
RUJBANI, S. M., Mathematics
SALIHI, A., Mechanical Engineering
SALIM, B. A., Nigerian Languages
SANI, M. A. Z., Nigerian Languages
SHEA, P. J., History

SULEIMAN, M. D., History
TABI'U, M., Islamic Law
UMAR, I. H., Physics
YADUDU, A. H., Law
YAHAYA, D., History
ZAHRADEEN, M. S., Islamic Studies
ZAHRADEEN, U., Management Science

FEDERAL UNIVERSITY OF TECHNOLOGY, AKURE

PMB 704, Akure, Ondo State
Telephone: (34) 243744
E-mail: registrar@futa.edu.ng
Internet: futa-edu.ng
Founded 1981
public control
Language of instruction: English
Academic year: October to September
Chancellor: Emir of Lafia ISA MUSTAPHA AGWAI II
Vice-Chancellor: Prof. ADEBIYI G. DARAMOLA
Deputy Vice-Chancellor for Academic Affairs: Prof. E. A. FASAKIN
Deputy Vice-Chancellor for Devt: Prof. T. L. AKINBOGUN
Registrar: Dr M. O. AJAYI
Librarian: F. Z. OGUNTUASE
Library of 64,822 vols
Number of teachers: 683
Number of students: 15,563

Publications: *Journal of Applied Tropical Agriculture* (4 a year), *Journal of Urban and Environmental Research* (every 2 years), *Nigerian Journal of Pure and Applied Physics* (4 a year)

DEANS

School of Agriculture and Agricultural Technology: Prof. J. A. FUWAPE
School of Engineering and Engineering Technology: Prof. C. O. ADEGOKE
School of Environmental Technology: Prof. D. O. OLANREWAJU
School of Management Technology: Prof. E. E. OKOKO
School of Mines and Earth Sciences: Prof. J. S. OJO
School of Sciences: Prof. K. O. IPINMOROTI
School of Postgraduate Studies: Prof. V. A. ALETOR

FEDERAL UNIVERSITY OF TECHNOLOGY, MINNA

PMB 65, Minna, Niger State
Telephone: (66) 222422
E-mail: info@futminna.edu.ng
Internet: www.futminna.edu.ng
Founded 1983
federal control
Language of instruction: English
Academic year: October to September (2 semesters)
Chancellor: The Olu of Warri, HRH OGIAME ATUWASE II
Pro-Chancellor: Prof. RUFA'I AHMED ALKALI
Vice-Chancellor: Prof. MUHAMMED SALIHU AUDU
Deputy Vice-Chancellor: Dr AKIM O. OSUNDE
Registrar: MALLAM M. D. USMAN
Bursar: M. A. BELLO
Librarian: MUHAMMAD IBN MUHAMMAD
Number of teachers: 698
Number of students: 13,589

Publications: *Journal of Agricultural Technology* (2 a year), *Journal of Science, Technology and Mathematics Education* (2 a year), *Nigeria Journal of Technological Research* (2 a year), *Proceedings of the National Engineering Conference* (1 a year)

DEANS

School of Agriculture and Agricultural Technology: Prof. K. M. BABA
School of Engineering and Engineering Technology: Prof. J. O. ODIGUORE
School of Environmental Technology: Prof. O. O. MORENKEJI
School of Science and Science Education: Prof. MUSA GALADIMA
Postgraduate School: Prof. SAMUEL L. LAMAI

FEDERAL UNIVERSITY OF TECHNOLOGY, OWERRI

PMB 1526, Owerri, Imo State
Telephone: (83) 233228
E-mail: vc@futo.edu.ng
Founded 1980
federal control
Language of instruction: English
Academic year: October to July
Chancellor: HRH Dr SHEKARAU ANGYU MASSA-IBI
Pro-Chancellor: VITA O. ABBA
Vice-Chancellor: Prof. CELESTINE O. E. ONWULIRI (acting)
Deputy Vice-Chancellor for Academic Affairs: Prof. E. T. ESHETT
Deputy Vice-Chancellor for Admin.: Prof. M. I. NWUFO
Registrar: C. O. OMEIRE
Bursar: R.-U. AKUJOBI
Librarian: J. E. NWOGU
Library of 68,345 vols
Number of teachers: 699
Number of students: 21,307

Publications: *Annual Review*, *Centre for Industrial Studies*, *Erosion News* (4 a year)

DEANS

School of Agriculture and Agricultural Technology: Prof. C. C. ASIABAKA
School of Engineering and Engineering Technology: Prof. O. N. OGUOMA
School of Management Technology: Prof. G. E. NWORUH
School of Science: Dr F. C. EZE (acting)
Postgraduate School: Prof. C. D. OKEREKE

PROFESSORS

ACHI, P., Mechanical Engineering
AGBOGU, A., Political Science
AGWU, E., Transport Management Technology
AKPAN, E., Engineering
AKUJOR, C., Astrophysics and Space Physics
ALAEZI, O., Curriculum and Vocational Education
ANANABA, S., Geophysics
ANEKE, L., Chemical Engineering
ANUNUSO, C., Analytical Chemistry
ANYANWU, B., Microbiology
ANYANWU, E., Mechanical Engineering
ARIRIATU, L., Industrial Microbiology
ASIABAKA, C., Agricultural Extension
ASIEGBU, L., Ethical Philosophy
DURU, J., Water Resources Engineering
EHEDURU, G., Information Management Technology
EJIKE, E., Chemistry
EMEHAROLE, P., Public Health Technology
ENYIEGBULAM, M., Polymer Science and Technology
ESHETT, E., Pedology
ESONU, B., Animal Nutrition
EZE, F., Physics
IBE, K., Geology
IHEONYE, A., Polymer and Textile Engineering
ILOEJE, M., Animal Genetics
IWUAGWU, C., Geology
IWUALA, M., Biology
IWUOHA, C., Food Science and Technology

MBAKWE, R., Forestry and Wildlife Management

NDUKA, A., Theoretical Physics and Applied Mathematics

NJOKU, J., Agricultural Economics

NJOKU, O., Biology

NJIRIBEAKO, I., Chemical Engineering

NTAMERE, C., Economics

NWABUEZE, R., Microbiology

NWACHUKWU, B., Civil Engineering

NWACHUKWU, E., Computer Science

NWADIARO, C., Fisheries and Aquaculture

NWAFOR, O., Mechanical Engineering

NWANKITI, A., Crop Science and Technology

NWANKWOR, G., Geology

NWIGWE, H., Biotechnology

NWORUH, G., Statistics

NWUFO, M., Plant Pathology

OBAH, B., Petroleum Engineering

OBIEFUNA, J., Horticulture

OFOH, M., Crop Science Technology

OGBOBE, O., Polymer and Textile Engineering

OGBOGU, S., Electrical/Electronic Engineering

OGBULIE, J., Microbiology

OGUOMA, O., Mechanical Engineering

OGWEUEGBU, M., Industrial Chemistry

OGWUDE, I., Transport Management

OGWUDE, S., English Literature

OKEREKE, C., Environmental Engineering

OKPALA, K., Chemical Engineering

OKORAFOR, O., Metallurgical Engineering

ONONIWU, J., Solid State Physics

ONU, N., Geophysics

ONUOHA, G., Chemistry

ONWUAGBA, B., Physics

ONWULIRI, C., Zoology/Parasitology/Biotechnology

ONWULIRI, V., Biochemistry

ONYEAGORO, E., Mechanical Engineering

ONYEJEKWE, D., Mechanical Engineering

ONYEJEKWE, E., Public Health Technology

ONYEMAOBI, O., Material and Metallurgical Engineering

ONYEZE, G., Industrial Biochemistry

ONYIRIUKA, S., Organic Chemistry

OREBIYI, J., Agricultural Economics

OSONDU, K., Pure Mathematics

OSUALA, F., Biotechnology

OSUAGWU, O., Information Management Technology

OSUJI, G., Soil Science

OWUAMA, O., Environmental Technology

OZOH, P., Environmental Management and Toxicology

UBBAONU, C., Food Processing and Product Development

UDEDIBIE, A., Animal Nutrition

UFODIKE, E., Fisheries and Aquaculture

UKOHA, A., Biochemistry

FEDERAL UNIVERSITY OF TECHNOLOGY, YOLA

PMB 2076, Yola, Adamawa State

Telephone: (75) 624416

E-mail: vcfuty@yahoo.com

Internet: www.futy.edu.ng

Founded 1981, present status 1988

federal control

Language of instruction: English

Academic year: October to September

Chancellor: HH Oba GABRIEL ADEKUNLE AROMOLARAN II

Vice-Chancellor: Prof. ABDULLAHI YUSUFU RIBADU

Registrar: Alh. AHMED USMAN W/CHEKKE

Librarian: Prof. B. S. H. WOMBOH

Library of 29,000 vols

Number of teachers: 345

Number of students: 9,701

Publication: *Technology and Development* (1 a year)

DEANS

School of Agriculture and Agricultural Technology: Prof. A. KADAMS

School of Engineering and Engineering Technology: Prof. P. B. OMAJI

School of Environmental Sciences: Dr F. ILLESANMI

School of Management and Information Technology: Prof. S. O. ANYANWU

School of Pure and Applied Sciences: Dr A. OKOLO

School of Technology and Science Education: Dr L. C. EZUGU

School of Postgraduate Studies: Prof. G. FAKUADE

MICHAEL OKPARA UNIVERSITY OF AGRICULTURE, UMUDIKE

PMB 7267, Umuahia, Umuahia, Abia State

Telephone: (82) 440555

E-mail: info@mouau.edu.ng

Internet: www.mouau.edu.ng

Founded 1992 as Federal Univ. of Agriculture, Umudike; present name and status 2000

Vice-Chancellor: Prof. OGBINNAYA C. ONWUDIKE

Deputy Vice-Chancellor: Prof. HILARY O. EDEOGA

Registrar: JULIA N. UCHE

Librarian: ALOYSIUS ONONOGBO

Library of 8,500 vols

Number of teachers: 158

Number of students: 1,248

DEANS

College of Agricultural Economics, Rural Sociology and Extension: Prof. ALOYSIUS NWOSU

College of Animal Science and Animal Health: Prof. JOHN IBEAWUCHI

College of Biological and Physical Sciences: Dr OBIOHA EZEREONYE

College of Crop and Soil Sciences: Dr CHIDA AMADIOHA

College of Food Processing and Storage Technology: Prof. ENOCH AKOBUNDU

College of Natural Resources and Environmental Management: Prof. EME AKACHUKU

School of Postgraduate Studies: Prof. SYLVESTER IBE

PROFESSORS

AKACHUKU, E. A., Natural Resources and Environmental Management

AKOBUNDU, E. N. T., Food Processing and Storage Technology

ALUKO, P., Natural Resources and Environmental Management

ANASO, H. U., Crop and Soil Sciences

ASIEGBU, J. C., Crop and Soil Sciences

CHIBOKA, V. O., Biological and Physical Sciences

EDEOGA, H. O., Biological and Physical Sciences

EKWUEME, B. N., Biological and Physical Sciences

ELUWA, M. C., Biological and Physical Sciences

IBE, S. N., Animal Science and Animal Health

IBEAWUCHI, J. A., Animal Science and Animal Health

MENKITI, A. I., Biological and Physical Sciences

NJOKU, P. C., Animal Science and Animal Health

NWAGBO, E. C., Agricultural Economics, Rural Sociology and Extension

NWOKE, B. E. B., Biological and Physical Sciences

NWOSU, A. C., Agricultural Economics, Rural Sociology and Extension

OBIZOBA, I. C., Food Processing and Storage Technology

OKERE, L. C., Agricultural Economics, Rural Sociology and Extension

OKOH, P. N., Biological and Physical Sciences

ONWUDIKE, O. C., Animal Science and Animal Health

ONYENWEAKU, C. E., Agricultural Economics, Rural Sociology and Extension

UWAEGBUTE, A. C., Food Processing and Storage Technology

UWAKAH, C. T., Agricultural Economics, Rural Sociology and Extension

NATIONAL OPEN UNIVERSITY OF NIGERIA

14–16 Ahmadu Bello Way, PMB 80067, Victoria Island, Lagos

Telephone: (1) 8188849*Kaduna Campus* Fmr NETC Campus, Kaduna-Zaria Rd, Rigachikun, Kaduna

E-mail: centralinfo@nou.ed.ng

Internet: www.nou.edu.ng

Founded 1983; suspended by govt 1984; reopened 2001

Courses for adults by correspondence and distance teaching at 40 study centres serving each state and local govt area of Nigeria; Schools of Arts and Social Sciences, Business and Human Resource Management, Education and Science and Technology; Centre for Continuing Education; Regional Training and Research Institute for Open and Distance Learning (RETRIDAL)

Vice-Chancellor: Prof. OLUGBEMIRO JEGEDE

Registrar: JOSEPHINE O. AKINYEMI

Number of students: 78,935

NNAMDI AZIKIWE UNIVERSITY

PMB 5025, Awka, Anambra State

Telephone: (80) 60492273

E-mail: info@unizik.edu.ng

Founded 1992

federal govt control

Languages of instruction: English, French, Hausa, Igbo, Yoruba

Academic year: October to June

Chancellor: Emir of Ilorin Alhaji SULU GAMBARI

Pro-Chancellor: SENAS UKPANAH

Vice-Chancellor: Prof. GREG NWAKOBY

Deputy Vice-Chancellor for Academic Affairs: Prof. J. E. AHANEKU

Deputy Vice-Chancellor for Admin.: Prof. BEN C. OKEKE

Registrar: C. C. OKEKE (acting)

Librarian: EMMA ONWUKA (acting)

Provost for College of Health Sciences: Prof. OKEY IKPEZE

Bursar: U. J. AGU (acting)

Library of 65,000 vols

Number of teachers: 842

Number of students: 36,000

Publications: *Journal of Arts and Humanities*, *Journal of Economic Studies*, *Journal of Education Management*, *Journal of Management Studies*, *Journal of Vocational and Adult Education*, *Tropical Journal of Medical Research*, *UNIZIK Law Journal*

DEANS

Faculty of Agriculture: Prof. NONSO NNABUIFE

Faculty of Arts: Prof. DAN AGU

Faculty of Basic Medical Sciences: Prof. ED NWOBODO

Faculty of Education: Prof. SAM OKEKE

Faculty of Engineering and Technology: Prof. D. O. ONUKWULI

Faculty of Environmental Sciences: Prof. C. C. EGOLUM

Faculty of Health Sciences and Technology: Dr C. C. ONYENEKWE (acting)
Faculty of Law: Prof. KEN NWOGU
Faculty of Management Sciences: Prof. C. I. ONWUCHEKWA
Faculty of Medicine: Prof. A. M. E. NWOFOR
Faculty of Natural Sciences: Prof. P. A. C. OKOYE
Faculty of Pharmaceutical Sciences: Prof. C. O. ESIMONE
Faculty of Physical Sciences: Prof. F. C. ODIBO
Faculty of Social Sciences: Prof. E. A. EGBOH
Postgraduate School: Prof. LUKE ANIKE

PROFESSORS

Confucius Institute:
  NENGWEN, J.

Faculty of Arts:
  AGBODIKE, C.
  AGU, D.
  ANAGBOGU, P.
  ANIZOBA, O.
  DUKOR, E.
  EKPUNOBI, D.
  EYISI, J.
  MADU, J.
  MBANUGO, C.
  NDUKA, D.
  NZOMIWU, J.
  OKEKE, D.
  ONYEKAONWU, G.
  UMEASIEGBU, R.
  UMEH, O.

Faculty of Education:
  ABONE, O.
  AKUDOLU, L.
  AKUEZUILO, E.
  ANAGBOGU, M.
  EBENEBE, R.
  EZE, T.
  IKE, A.
  NDINECHI, G.
  NDU, A.
  NNADOZIE, J.
  OGBALU, A.
  OKAFOR, J.
  OKONKWO, O.
  ORAEMESI, J.
  UMEDUM, S.
  UMEASIEGBU, G.
  UNACHUKWU, G.

Faculty of Engineering and Technology:
  IGBOKWE, P.
  IJOMAH, M.
  INYIAMA, H.
  KATCHY, E.
  NNUKA, E.
  NWOBU, R.
  OFODILE, E.
  OGBUAGU, J.
  OKEKE, S.
  ONUKWULI, O.
  UBA NWUBA, E.

Faculty of Law:
  OKAFOR, I.

Faculty of Management Sciences:
  IKEZUE, C.
  MBACHU, A.
  NZE, F.
  OKAFOR, F.
  ONWUCHEKWA, C.
  OSISIOMA, B.
  UMEBALI

Faculty of Medicine:
  ADINMA, J.
  AGBATA, A.
  AHANEKU, J.
  ANYANWU, S.
  EGBUONU, I.
  EKEJINDU, G.
  EMELE, F.

EZECHUKWU, C.
IKPEZE, O.
MBONU, O.
MELUDU, S.
NWOFOR, A.
NWOFOR, A.
NWOSU, S.
OFIAELI, R.
OKAFOR, P.
OKONKWO, J.
ORAKWE, J.
OSUIGWE, A.
UMEH, B.
UWAKWE, R.

Faculty of Natural Sciences:
  AJIWE, V.
  AKPUAKA, M.
  ANASO, H.
  ANENE, G.
  ANIZOBA, M.
  ANYAKOHA, M.
  CHUKWURAH, E.
  EBOATU, A.
  EKEJIUBA, I.
  EKPUNOBI, A.
  ENEANYA, C.
  EZEKWE, N.
  EZEONU, E.
  MBANUGO, J.
  MOORE, C.
  NWAORGU, O.
  ODIBO, F.
  OGUM, G.
  OKAKA, A.
  OKEREKE, G.
  OKOYE, P.
  ONOCHIE, C.
  ONYALI, O.
  ONYEAGU, S.
  ORAJAKA, I.
  OYEKA, C.
  OYEKA, I.
  UMEGO, M.
  UMEH, C.

Faculty of Pharmaceutical Sciences:
  ESIMONE, C. O.

Faculty of Social Sciences:
  DIKE, M.
  EYIUCHE, A.
  NWANUNOBI, C.
  NWUNELI, O.
  OBI, A.
  OKUNNA, C.

OBAFEMI AWOLOWO UNIVERSITY

Ile-Ife
Telephone: (36) 230290
E-mail: registra@oauife.edu.ng
Internet: www.oauife.edu.ng
Founded 1961 as Univ. of Ife, present name 1987
federal control
Language of instruction: English
Academic year: September to July
Chancellor: Alhaji KABIR USMAN
Pro-Chancellor: Alhaji SHETIMA A. M. LIBERTY
Vice-Chancellor: Prof. ROGER MAKANJUOLA
Deputy Vice-Chancellor for Academic Affairs: Prof. A. A. ADEDIRAN
Deputy Vice-Chancellor for Admin.: Prof. L. O. KEHINDE
Registrar: B. O. ILUYOMADE
Univ. Bursar: O. ODEYEMI
Univ. Librarian: M. O. AFOLABI
Library: see under Libraries and Archives
Number of teachers: 1,343
Number of students: 22,742
Publications: *Calendar, Gazette, Handbook, Ife Studies in English Language, Odu: A Journal of West African Studies* (2 a year),

Quarterly Journal of Administration, Second Order (2 a year)

DEANS

Faculty of Administration: O. OJO
Faculty of Agriculture: R. ADEYEMO
Faculty of Arts: O. T. AKINRINADE
Faculty of Basic Medical Sciences: M. A. DUROSINMI
Faculty of Clinical Sciences: J. A. OWA
Faculty of Dentistry: O. D. OTUYEMI (acting)
Faculty of Education: D. K. AKANBI
Faculty of Environmental Design and Management: C. A. AJAYI
Faculty of Law: M. O. ADEDIRAN
Faculty of Pharmacy: A. O. OGUNDAINI
Faculty of Science: M. A. BADEJO
Faculty of Social Sciences: J. A. FABAYO
Faculty of Technology: M. O. FABORODE

PROFESSORS

Faculty of Administration:
  ERERO, E. J., Public Administration
  OJO, O., International Relations
  OMOPARIOLA, O., Management and Accounting
  ORIBABOR, P. E., Management and Accounting
  SESAY, A., International Relations
  SOREMEKUN, O., International Relations

Faculty of Agriculture:
  ADEBAYO, A. A., Soil Science
  ADEPETU, J. A., Soil Science
  ADERIBIGBE, A. O., Animal Science
  ADEYEMO, R., Agricultural Economics
  ADUAYI, E. A., Soil Science
  AINA, P. O., Soil Science
  AJOBO, O., Agricultural Economics
  AKINGBOHUNGBE, A. E., Plant Science
  AKINYEMIJU, O. A., Plant Science
  ALOFE, C. O., Plant Science
  FAKOREDE, M. A., Plant Science
  ILORI, J. O., Animal Science
  JIBOWO, A. A., Agricultural Extension and Rural Sociology
  LADIPO, J. L., Plant Science
  LAOGUN, E. A., Agricultural Extension and Rural Sociology
  MATANMI, B. A., Plant Science
  OBISESAN, I. O., Plant Science
  OKUSAMI, T. A., Soil Science
  OLAYINKA, A., Soil Science
  SONAIYA, E. B., Animal Science

Faculty of Arts:
  ADEDIRAN, A. A., History
  ADEWOLE, L. O., African Languages and Literature
  AJUWON, B., African Languages and Literature
  AKINRINADE, O. T., History
  IBITOKUN, B. M., English
  ILESANMI, T. M., Religious Studies
  KOLAWOLE, M. E. M., English
  MAKINDE, M. A., Philosophy
  MANUS, C. U., Modern European Languages
  NWEZEH, E. C., Foreign Languages
  OLANIYAN, R. A., History
  OLAYIWOLA, D. O., Religious Studies
  OLOMOLA, G. O. I., History
  OLORUNFEMI, A., History
  OMOSINI, O., History
  ONIBERE, S. G. A., Religious Studies
  VIDAL, A. O., Music

Faculties of Basic Medical Sciences, Clinical Sciences and Dentistry:
  ADEJUYIGBE, O., Surgery
  ADELEKAN, D. A., Community Health
  ADEYEMO, A. O., Surgery
  AKINOLA, D. O., Surgery
  AKINSOLA, A., Medicine
  ARIGBABU, O., Surgery
  BALOGUN, M. O., Medicine

Pres. JUDITH NOWOTARKSI; Nat. Sec. PAUL GOULTER.

Tertiary Education Commission: POB 27048, Wellington 6141; Level 10, 44 The Terrace, Wellington 6141; tel. (9) 263-1735; e-mail servicecentre@tec.govt.nz; internet www.tec.govt.nz; f. 2003; leads the govt's relationship with the tertiary sector and makes investments in tertiary education and training on the govt's behalf; Chair. JOHN SPENCER; Chief Exec. TIM FOWLER.

Universities New Zealand/Te Pōkai Tara: POB 11915, Manners St, Wellington 6142; Level 9, 142 Lambton Quay, Wellington; tel. (4) 381-8500; e-mail jackie.bailey@universitiesnz.ac.nz; internet www.universitiesnz.ac.nz; f. 1961; responsible for the quality of univ. programmes; administers a range of scholarships and represents the univs in the public interest, both nationally and internationally; Chair. Prof. HARLENE HAYNE; Exec. Dir CHRIS WHELAN.

Learned Societies

GENERAL

Royal Society of New Zealand: POB 598, Wellington 6140; 11 Turnbull St, Thorndon, Wellington 6011; tel. (4) 472-7421; e-mail academy@royalsociety.org.nz; internet www.royalsociety.org.nz; f. 1867; nat. academy of scholars representing the applied, biological, earth, engineering, information, medical, physical and social sciences; mathematics, technology, and humanities; awards scholarships, grants and medals; 1,167 mems, 373 fellows, 65 constituent socs; Pres. Prof. Sir DAVID SKEGG; publs *Journal of the Royal Society of New Zealand* (4 a year), *Kotuitui: New Zealand Journal of Social Sciences Online* (2 a year), *New Zealand Journal of Agricultural Research* (4 a year), *New Zealand Journal of Botany* (4 a year), *New Zealand Journal of Crop and Horticultural Science* (4 a year), *New Zealand Journal of Geology and Geophysics* (4 a year), *New Zealand Journal of Marine and Freshwater Research* (4 a year), *New Zealand Journal of Zoology* (4 a year).

AGRICULTURE, FISHERIES AND VETERINARY SCIENCE

Agronomy Society of New Zealand: c/o Paul Johnstone, Private Bag 1401, Havelock North 4157; e-mail secretary@agronomysociety.org.nz; internet www.agronomysociety.org.nz; f. 1970; annual conf. and occasional symposia; 150 mems; Pres. Dr BRUCE SEARLE; Sec. PAUL JOHNSTONE; publ. *Agronomy New Zealand* (1 a year).

New Zealand Institute of Agricultural and Horticultural Science Inc.: POB 121-063, Henderson, Auckland; tel. (9) 812-8506; e-mail secretariat@agscience.org.nz; internet www.agscience.org.nz; f. 1954; 800 mems; Pres. Dr DAVID LEWIS; publ. *AgScience* (6 a year).

New Zealand Institute of Forestry (NZIF)/Te Putahi Ngaherehere o Aotearoa Inc.: POB 10-513, Wellington 6143; Level 9, 93 The Terrace, Wellington 6143; tel. (4) 974-8421; e-mail admin@nzif.org.nz; internet www.nzif.org.nz; f. 1927; promotes the best use of NZ's resources and encourages wise use of forest lands; gives Chavasse Travel Award, NZIF student awards and Kirk Horn Award; 824 mems; Pres. ANDREW MCEWEN; Sec. DAVID EVISON; publs *New Zealand Journal of Forestry* (4 a year), *Forestry Handbook* (1 a year).

New Zealand Society of Animal Production (Inc.): c/o Kate Crookston, POB 955, Cambridge; tel. (7) 823-9345; e-mail nzsap.inc@gmail.com; internet nzsap.org.nz; f. 1940; fosters research in all areas of animal production incl. production systems, nutrition, meat science, animal welfare, wool science, animal breeding and genetics; offers awards and grants; 200 mems; Pres. DAVID PACHECO; Exec. Sec. KATE CROOKSTON; publs *Proceedings* (1 a year), occasional publs.

New Zealand Society of Soil Science Inc.: c/o Groundwork Associates, POB 7067, Hamilton 3247; tel. (7) 855-7163; e-mail nzsss@groundworkassociates.co.nz; internet nzsss.science.org.nz; f. 1952; organizes annual conf.; lobbies govt on science funding and scientific issues; gives prizes and bursaries for research; 400 mems; Pres. TRISH FRASER; Sec. TIM CLOUGH.

New Zealand Veterinary Association: POB 11-212, Wellington 6142; Level 2, 44 Victoria St, Wellington 6011; tel. (4) 471-0484; e-mail nzva@vets.org.nz; internet www.nzva.org.nz; f. 1923; 15 regional brs and 14 spec. interest brs; 1,900 mems; CEO JULIE HOOD; Pres. STEVE MERCHANT; publs *New Zealand Veterinary Journal* (6 a year, print and online, www.vetjournal.org.nz), *Vetscript* (11 a year, print and online, vetscript.nzva.org.nz).

Royal Agricultural Society of New Zealand: POB 54, Woodend 7641; tel. (3) 313-1004; e-mail debbie@ras.org.nz; internet www.ras.org.nz; f. 1924; promotes the devt of agricultural, pastoral, horticultural, stock-raising and forestry resources in NZ; organizes competitions; 1,000 individual mems, 170 institutional mems; library of 1,000 vols; Pres. JOHN GRIGG; CEO DEBBIE CAMERON; publ. *On Show* (2 a year).

ARCHITECTURE AND TOWN PLANNING

New Zealand Institute of Architects: POB 2516, Shortland St, Auckland 1140; Level 5, Zurich House, 21 Queen St, Auckland 1010; tel. (9) 623-6080; internet www.nzia.co.nz; f. 1905; offers professional devt programmes to mem. architects; 2,800 mems; Chief Exec. TEENA HALE PENNINGTON; Pres. PIP CHESHIRE.

New Zealand Institute of Surveyors: POB 831, Wellington 6140; Level 5, 114 The Terrace, Wellington; tel. (4) 471-1774; e-mail nzis@surveyors.org.nz; internet www.surveyors.org.nz; f. 1888; monitors and maintain the professional and ethical conduct of surveyors; offers awards; 1,300 mems; Pres. JEFF NEEDHAM; CEO HADYN SMITH; publs *New Zealand Surveyor* (1 a year), *Survey Quarterly*.

BIBLIOGRAPHY, LIBRARY SCIENCE AND MUSEOLOGY

Museums Aotearoa Te Tari o Nga Whare Taonga o Te Motu/The Museums of New Zealand (Inc.): POB 10-928, Wellington 6143; Level 8, 104 The Terrace, Wellington 6011; tel. (4) 499-1313; e-mail mail@museumsaotearoa.org.nz; internet www.museumsaotearoa.org.nz; f. 1947; ind. professional body; represents museums and museum employees in NZ; 327 mems; Chair. THÉRÈSE ANGELO; publs *Museums Aotearoa Quarterly*, *New Zealand Directory of Museums* (1 a year), *Te Ara—Journal of Museums Aotearoa* (2 a year).

New Zealand Book Council: POB 65392, Mairangi Bay, Auckland 0630; Stephenson and Turner House, 156–158 Victoria St, Te Aro, Wellington 6011; tel. (4) 801-5546; e-mail admin@bookcouncil.org.nz; internet www.bookcouncil.org.nz; f. 1972; promotes love for books and reading through a wide

range of programmes; provides free writer visits; 2,500 mems (individuals, schools, libraries, booksellers, publishers); Chair. PETER BIGGS; Chief Exec. CATRIONA FERGUSON; publ. *Booknotes Unbound* (online, www.booknotes-unbound.org.nz).

New Zealand Library Association Inc.: POB 12212, Thorndon, Wellington 6144; Level 4, Stephenson & Turner House, 156–158 Victoria St, Wellington 6011; tel. (4) 801-5542; e-mail officeadmin@lianza.org.nz; internet www.lianza.org.nz; f. 1910; also known as Library and Information Asscn of New Zealand Aotearoa (LIANZA); annual conf.; 1,962 mems (1,638 individual mems, 324 institutional mems); Pres. LAURINDA THOMAS; publs *Library Life* (26 a year), *The NZ Library & Information Management Journal* (2 a year, online).

ECONOMICS, LAW AND POLITICS

New Zealand Institute of International Affairs: c/o Victoria Univ. of Wellington, POB 600, Wellington 6140; Room 507, Level 5, Railway West Wing, Victoria Univ. of Wellington, Pipitea Campus, Bunny St, Wellington; tel. (4) 463-5356; e-mail nziia@vuw.ac.nz; internet www.nziia.org.nz; f. 1934; promotes understanding of nat. and int. questions and problems, particularly related to the Pacific, Asia, and the Commonwealth; 10 brs; Pres. Hon. Sir DOUGLAS KIDD; Dir PETER KENNEDY; Exec. Officer SYNONNE RAJANAYAGAM; publ. *New Zealand International Review* (6 a year).

New Zealand Law Society: POB 5041, Wellington 6145; 26 Waring Taylor St, Wellington 6011; tel. (4) 472-7837; e-mail inquiries@lawsociety.org.nz; internet www.lawsociety.org.nz; f. 1869; responsible for regulating the legal profession (barristers and solicitors); 11,100 mems; Pres. CHRIS MOORE; Exec. Dir and Sec. CHRISTINE GRICE; publ. *LawTalk* (23 a year).

Population Association of New Zealand: POB 225, Wellington; tel. (9) 484-6247; e-mail secretary@population.org.nz; internet www.population.org.nz; f. 1974; promotes population research, understanding and policy devt; annual conf.; 122 mems; Pres. ALISON REID; Sec. SHEFALI PAWAR; publs *New Zealand Population Review* (1 a year), *Technical Papers*.

FINE AND PERFORMING ARTS

Creative New Zealand (Arts Council of New Zealand Toi Aotearoa): Old Public Trust Bldg, Level 2, 131–135 Lambton Quay, POB 3806, Wellington 6011; tel. (4) 473-0880; e-mail info@creativenz.govt.nz; internet www.creativenz.govt.nz; f. 1994; invests in a wide variety of artists and artistic orgs involved with all areas of the arts; brs in Auckland, Christchurch, Wellington and Rotorua; 7 mems; Chair. ALAN SORRELL; Chief Exec. STEPHEN WAINWRIGHT.

New Zealand Maori Arts and Crafts Institute: POB 334, Rotorua 3040; Te Puia, Hemo Rd, Rotorua; tel. (7) 348-9047; e-mail info@tepuia.com; internet www.tepuia.com; f. 1963; works towards the promotion, preservation and perpetuation of Maori arts, crafts and culture; Kiwi Conservation Centre; 70 mems; Chief Exec. ANDREW TE WHAITI.

HISTORY, GEOGRAPHY AND ARCHAEOLOGY

New Zealand Archaeological Association: POB 6337, Dunedin 9059; tel. (3) 474-7474; e-mail publications@nzarchaeology.org; internet www

CAXTON-MARTINS, A. E., Anatomy and Cell Biology
DARE, F. O., Obstetrics and Gynaecology
DUROSINMI, M. A., Haematology and Immunology
ELEGBE, R. A., Physiological Sciences
FAJEWONYOMI, B. A., Community Health
FAKUNLE, J. B., Chemical Pathology
JINADU, M. I., Nursing
MAKANJUOLA, R. O. A., Mental Health
ODESANMI, W. O., Morbid Anatomy and Forensic Medicine
OGUNBODEDE, E. O., Preventive Dentistry
OGUNNIYI, S. O., Obstetrics and Gynaecology
OJO, O. S., Morbid Anatomy and Forensic Medicine
OJOFEITIMI, E. O., Community Health and Nutrition
ONWUDIEGWU, U., Obstetrics and Gynaecology
OTUYEMI, O. D., Child Dental Health
OWA, J. A., Paediatrics and Child Health
OYEDEJI, G. A., Paediatrics and Child Health

Faculty of Education:
ADEYANJU, S. A., Physical and Health Education
AKANBI, D. K., Educational Technology
EHINDERO, O. J., Institute of Education
FASOKUN, T. O., Continuing Education
FAWOLE, J. O., Physical Education
OBIDI, S. S., Education, Foundation and Counselling
OGUNDARI, J. T., Physical and Health Education
OKUNROTIFA, E. B., Physical and Health Education

Faculty of Environmental Design and Management:
AJAYI, C. A., Estate Management
AMOLE, S. A., Architecture
AREMU, P. S. O., Fine Arts
FADARE, S. O., Urban and Regional Planning
IGHALO, J. I., Estate Management
OGUNJUMO, A., Urban and Regional Planning
OLAJUYIN, L. O., Urban and Regional Planning

Faculty of Law:
ADEDIRAN, M. O., Public Law
FABUNMI, J. O., Business Law
OKORODUDU-FUBARA, M. T., International Law

Faculty of Pharmacy:
ADESANYA, S. A., Pharmacognosy
ADESINA, S. K., Drug Research
ADEWUNMI, C. O., Drug Research
ALADESANMI, J. A., Pharmacognosy
ELUJOBA, A. A., Pharmacognosy
LAMIKANRA, A., Pharmaceutics
OGUNBONA, F. A., Pharmaceutical Chemistry
OGUNDAINI, A. O., Pharmaceutical Chemistry
OGUNDARI, O., Pharmaceutical Chemistry
OLUGBADE, T. O., Pharmaceutical Chemistry
ONAWUNMI, G. O., Pharmaceutics
ONYEJI, O. C., Pharmaceutical Chemistry
ORAFIDIYA, O. O., Pharmaceutics
SOFOWORA, E. A., Pharmacognosy

Faculty of Science:
ADEDOKUN, J. A., Physics
ADEGOKE, J. A., Zoology
ADESULU, E. A., Zoology
ADEWUSI, S. R. A., Chemistry
AFOLAYAN, A., Biochemistry
AFUWAPE, M. A., Mathematics
AJAYI, E. O. B., Physics
AJAYI, T. R., Geology
AKANNI, M. S., Chemistry

AKINRELERE, E. A., Mathematics
AKO, B. D., Geology
AKO-NAI, K. A., Microbiology
ALADEKOMO, J. B., Physics
AMIRE, O. A., Chemistry
AMUSA, A., Physics
ARAWOMO, G. A. O., Zoology
ASAOLU, S. O., Zoology
AUBICJO, F. O. I., Chemistry
BALOGUN, E. E., Physics
BALOGUN, R. A., Zoology
FAKUNLE, C. O., Chemistry
IGE, W. J., Chemistry
IMORU, C. O., Mathematics
ISAWUMI, M. A. (Natural History Museum)
ISICHEI, A. O., Botany
KOLAWOLE, D. O., Microbiology
NWACHUKWU, J. I., Geology
OBAFEMI, C. A., Chemistry
ODEYEMI, O., Microbiology
ODU, E. A., Botany
OGUNKOYA, L. O., Chemistry
OJO, J. F., Chemistry
OKON, E. E., Zoology
OLANIYI, H. B., Physics
OLAREWAJU, V. O., Geology
OLOMO, J. B., Physics
OLORODE, O., Botany
OLORUNFEMI, M. O., Geology
OLUTIOLA, P. O., Microbiology
ONAJOBI, F. D., Biochemistry
OSADEBE, F. A. N., Physics
OSHOBI, E. O., Mathematics
RAHAMAN, M. A., Geology
SALAMI, M. B., Geology
SALAU, A. A. M., Physics
SHONUKAN, O. O., Microbiology

Faculty of Social Sciences:
ADESINA, F. A., Geography
ADEWUYI, A. A., Demography and Social Statistics
AFONJA, S., Sociology and Anthropology
EBIGBOLA, J. A., Demography and Social Statistics
EKANADE, O., Geography
FABAYO, J. A., Economics
JEJE, L. K., Geography
ODEBIYI, A. I., Sociology and Anthropology
OGUNBADEJO, F. O., Political Science
OGUNKOYA, O. O., Geography
OLORUNTIMEHIN, O., Sociology and Anthropology
OLOWU, A. A., Psychology
TOGONU-BICKESTETH, T., Psychology

Faculty of Technology:
ADEGBOYEGA, G. A., Electronic and Electrical Engineering
ADEKOYA, L. O., Mechanical Engineering
AFONJA, A. A., Metallurgical and Materials Engineering
AJAYI, G. O., Electronic and Electrical Engineering
AJIBOLA, O. A., Agricultural Engineering
BURAIMAH-IGBO, L. A., Electronic and Electrical Engineering
FABORODE, M. O., Agricultural Engineering
FAPOHUNDA, M. O., Agricultural Engineering
FASHAKIN, J. B., Food Science and Technology
IGE, M. T., Agricultural Engineering
ILLORI, M. O., Technology, Planning and Development Unit
KEHINDE, L. O., Electronic and Electrical Engineering
KUKU, T. A., Electronic and Electrical Engineering
LASISI, F., Agricultural Engineering
LAYOKUN, S. K., Chemical Engineering
MAKANJUOLA, G. A., Agricultural Engineering
MOJOLA, O. O., Mechanical Engineering
OGEDENGBE, M. O., Civil Engineering
OGUNSUA, A. O., Food Science and Technology

SANNI, S. A., Chemical Engineering
SOLOMON, B. O., Chemical Engineering
TAIWO, O., Chemical Engineering

AFFILIATED INSTITUTES
Institute of Agricultural Research and Training (IART), Ibadan: see under Research Institutes.

Institute of Education: Ile-Ife; f. 1962; sponsored by the University, the Oyo State Min. of Education and the Asscn of Principals of Teacher Training Colleges and Secondary Schools in the State; a mobile library equipped with books, audiovisual aids and film aids for demonstration among colleges and secondary schools; Dir O. J. EHINDERO

UNIVERSITY OF ABUJA

PMB 117, Abuja, Federal Capital City

Telephone: (9) 8821380

E-mail: info@uniabuja.edu.ng

Internet: www.uniabuja.edu.ng

Founded 1988

public control

Language of instruction: English

Academic year: October to September

Faculties of management sciences, veterinary medicine

Chancellor: (vacant)

Vice-Chancellor: Prof. JAMES S. ADEBOWALE ADELABU

Registrar: YAKUBU HASSAN HABI

Librarian: Dr FAB. A. J. AKHIDIME

Library of 19,866 vols

Number of teachers: 150

Number of students: 5,400

DEANS
College of Health Science: J. A. M. OTUBU (Provost)
Faculty of Agriculture: E. A. SALAKO
Faculty of Arts: EFFIOK B. UWATT
Faculty of Education: J. Y. MAISAMARI
Faculty of Engineering: FOLORUNSO O. AKINBODE
Faculty of Law: C. U. ILEGBUNE
Faculty of Science: N. R. ISU
Faculty of Social Science: ABDULHAMEED A. UJO
Postgraduate School: FUNKE WASILAT ABDUL-RAHMAN

PROFESSORS
ADELABU, J. A., Physics
AMDII, I. E. S., Political Science
BIRAI, U. M., Political Science
IKEOTUONYE, A. I., Education
OKWUTE, S. I., Chemistry
UJO, A. A., Political Science

UNIVERSITY OF AGRICULTURE, ABEOKUTA

PMB 2240, Abeokuta, Ogun State

Telephone: (39) 08033490946

E-mail: registrar@unaab.edu.ng

Internet: www.unaab.edu.ng

Founded 1988, fmrly a college of Univ. of Lagos

federal control

Language of instruction: English

Academic year: October to July

Chancellor: Prof. JOSEPH CHIKE EDOZIEN

Vice-Chancellor: Prof. OLUWAFEMI OLAIYA BALOGUN ADU

Deputy Vice-Chancellor for Academic Affairs: Prof. C. F. I. ONWUKA

Deputy Vice-Chancellor for Devt: Prof. S. T. O. LAGOKE

Registrar: A. O. ADEBOYE (acting)

Librarian: A. T. AGBOOLA

Number of teachers: 519

Number of students: 9,723

Publications: *Agricultural Sciences, Science, Environment and Technology (ASSET)* (2 a year), *UNAAB News*

DEANS

College of Agricultural Management, Rural Development: Prof. S. O. APANTAKU

College of Animal Science and Livestock Production: Prof. D. ERUVBETINE

College of Engineering: Prof. E. S. A. AJISE-GIRI

College of Environmental Resources Management: Prof. T. A. AROWOLO

College of Food Science and Human Ecology: Prof. F. O. HENSHAW

College of Natural Sciences: Prof. T. O. S. POPOOLA

College of Plant Science and Crop Production: Prof. O. B. KEHINDE

College of Veterinary Medicine: Prof. M. DIPEOLU

Postgraduate School: Prof. S. O. AFOLAMI

Student Affairs: Prof. S. A. OLUWALANA

PROFESSORS

ADAMSON, I., Chemistry

ADDO, A. A., Home Science and Management

ADEBAMBO, O. A., Animal Breeding and Genetics

ADETUNJI, M. T., Soil Science and Agricultural Mechanisation

ADU, I. F., Animal Nutrition

AKINGBALA, J. O., Food Science and Technology

AKINLADE, O., Physics

ARIYO, O. J., Plant Breeding and Seed Technology

AWONORIN, S. O., Food Science and Technology

BAMIRO, F. O., Chemistry

BELLO, N. J., Water Management and Agricultural Meteorology

EROMOSELE, I. C., Chemistry

ERUVBETINE, D., Animal Nutrition

KADIRI, M., Biological Sciences

LADEINDE, T. A. O., Plant Breeding and Seed Technology

MARTINS, O., Water Management and Agricultural Meteorology

OGUNTONA, C. R. B., Home Science and Management

OJANUGA, A. G., Soil Science and Agricultural Mechanisation

OKUNEYE, P. A., Agricultural Economics and Farm Management

OLADOKUN, M. A. O., Horticulture

OLAGOKE, S. T. O., Crop Protection

OLASANTAN, F. O., Horticulture

ONWUKA, C. F., Animal Nutrition

PHILLIP, D., Agricultural Economics and Farm Management

TAYO, T. O., Plant Physiology and Crop Production

UNIVERSITY OF AGRICULTURE, MAKURDI

PMB 2373, Makurdi, Benue State

Telephone: (44) 533204

E-mail: info@uam.edu.ng

Internet: www.uam.edu.ng

Founded 1988, fmrly campus of the Univ. of Jos, now a fully independent univ.

federal control

Language of instruction: English

Academic year: October to September

Chancellor: HRH Igwe (Barr) I. U. NNAJI (Eze Odezurigbo III of Nike, Enugu)

Vice-Chancellor: Prof. D. V. UZA

Registrar: Dr S. A. EDE

Librarian: SUGH LOHO

Number of teachers: 446

Number of students: 7,654

Publication: *Journal of Agriculture, Science and Technology* (2 a year)

DEANS

College of Agricultural Economics and Mgt: Prof. O. J. OKWO

College of Agricultural Engineering and Engineering Technology: Dr I. O. AGBEDE

College of Agricultural Science Education: Prof. A. A. EKOJA

College of Agronomy: Dr M. O. ADEYEMO

College of Animal Science: Prof. O. I. A. OLUREMI

College of Food Science and Technology: Prof. C. C. ARIAHU

College of Forestry and Fisheries: Dr L. O. TIAMIYU

College of Veterinary Medicine: Prof. P. A. ONYEYILI

School of Postgraduate Studies: Prof. E. I. KUCHA

UNIVERSITY OF BENIN

Ugbowo-Lagos Rd, Ugbowo, PMB 1154, Benin City

Telephone: (52) 600443

E-mail: registrar@uniben.edu

Internet: www.uniben.edu

Founded 1970

federal control

Language of instruction: English

Academic year: October to June

Chancellor: HRH Alhaji Dr MUHAMMADU BARKINDO ALIYU MUSDAFA

Pro-Chancellor: Sir GABRIEL TOBY

Vice-Chancellor: Prof. O. G. OSHODIN

Deputy Vice-Chancellor for Academic Affairs: Prof. E. A. ONIBERE

Deputy Vice-Chancellor for Admin.: Prof. J. A. OKHUOYA

Registrar: G. O. OGBOGHODO

Librarian: S. A. OGUNROMBI (acting)

Library of 265,144 vols

Number of teachers: 1,182

Number of students: 31,247

Publications: *Benin Journal of Educational Studies*, *Faculty of Arts Journal* (4 a year), *Faculty of Education Journal* (2 a year), *Journal of the Humanities*, *Physical Health Education and Recreational Journal*, *University of Benin Law Journal* (1 a year)

DEANS

Faculty of Agriculture: Prof. U. J. IKHATUA

Faculty of Arts: Prof. A. O. ASAGBA

Faculty of Education: Prof. MON NWADIANI

Faculty of Engineering: Prof. F. O. EDEKO

Faculty of Law: Prof. A. ATSEGBUA

Faculty of Life Sciences: Prof. C. C. OSUBOR

Faculty of Management Sciences: Prof. B. A. AGBONIFOH

Faculty of Pharmacy: Prof. E. O. OSAZUWA

Faculty of Physical Sciences: Prof. S. M. OGBONNWAN

Faculty of Social Sciences: Prof. C. O. OKOLOCHA

School of Dentistry: Prof. B. D. O. SAHEED

School of Medicine: Prof. D. E. OVIASU

School of Postgraduate Studies: Prof. R. O. ELAIHO

PROFESSORS

ABIODUN, P. O., Child Health

ADEMOROTI, C. M. A., Chemistry

AFE, J. O., Educational Psychology and Curriculum Studies

AGBADUDU, A. B., Business Administration

AGBAKWURU, E. O. P., Pharmaceutical Chemistry

AGHENTA, J. A., Educational Administration and Foundations

AHONKHAI, S. I., Chemistry

AJISAFE, M. O., Physical and Health Education

AKERELE, A., Business Administration

ALAKIJA, W., Community Health

ANAO, A. R., Accounting

ASALOR, J. O., Mechanical Engineering

AUDU, T. O. K., Chemical Engineering

AWANBOR, D., Educational Psychology and Curriculum Studies

AWARITEFE, A. A., Mental Health

AYANRU, D. K. G., Microbiology

AYANRU, J. O., Ophthalmology

BADMUS, G. A., Educational Psychology and Curriculum Studies

BAFOR, B. E., Geology

EBEIGBE, A. B., Physiology

EBEWELE, R. O., Chemical Engineering

ECHENIM, K., Modern Languages

EGHAFONA, N. O., Microbiology

EGUDU, R. N., English and Literature

EHIAMETALOR, E. T., Educational Administration and Foundations

EKUNDAYO, J. A., Microbiology

GRILLO, B. O., Anatomy

HUGBO, P. G., Pharmaceutical Microbiology

IGBAFE, A. I., History

IGENE, J. O., Animal Science

IKEDIUGWU, F. E. O., Microbiology

IKENEBOMEH, M. J., Microbiology

IKHATUA, J. U., Animal Science

ILOHA, M. A., Economics and Statistics

IMEOKPARIA, G. E., Geology

IMOGIE, A. I., Educational Psychology and Curriculum Studies

IREMIREN, G. O., Crop Science

IWU, G. O., Chemistry

KUALE, P. A., Civil Engineering

NDIOKWERE, C. L., Chemistry

NWAGWU, N. A., Educational Administration and Foundations

NWANZE, E. C., Biochemistry

NWOKOYE, D. N., Civil Engineering

OBADAN, M. I., Economics and Statistics

OBASEIKI-EBOR, E. E., Pharmaceutical Microbiology

OBASOHAN, A. O., Medicine

OBIANWU, H. O., Pharmacology and Toxicology

OBIKA, L. F., Physiology

OBUEKWE, C. O., Microbiology

ODEBUNMI, A., Educational Psychology and Curriculum Studies

ODIME, O., Surgery

OFOEGBU, R. O., Surgery

OFUANI, O. A., English and Literature

OGBEIDE, N. O., Chemistry

OGBEIDE, O., Community Health

OGBIMI, A. O., General Studies

OGONOR, J. I., Pharmaceutical Chemistry

OGUDE, S. E., English and Literature

OHWOVORIOLE, E. N., Mechanical Engineering

OJOGWU, L. I., Medicine

OKAFOR, F. C., Geography and Regional Planning

OKEH, P. I., Modern Languages

OKEKE, E. O., Mathematics

OKHAMAFE, A. O., Pharmaceutics and Pharmaceutical Technology

OKHUOYA, J. A., Botany

OKIEIMEN, F. E., Chemistry

OKOH, S. E. N., Economics and Statistics

OKOJIE, C. E., Economics and Statistics

OKOLO, A. A., Child Health

OKOLOKO, G., Botany

OKONFUA, F. E., Obstetrics and Gynaecology

OKOR, R. S., Pharmaceutics and Pharmaceutical Technology

OLA, R. F., Physics

OLOMU, J. M., Animal Science

OMIUNU, F. G. I., Geography and Regional Planning

OMU, F. I. A., History

OMUTA, G. E. D., Geography and Regional Planning

ONOKERHORAYE, A. G., Geography and Regional Planning
OPUTE, F. I., Botany
OROBATOR, S. E., Physics
ORONSAYE, A. U., Obstetrics and Gynaecology
OSAGIE, A. U., Biochemistry
OSAZE, R. E., Business Administration
OSHODIN, O. G., Physical and Health Education
OWIE, I., Physical and Health Education
OYAIDE, W. J., Agricultural Economics and Extension Services
SADA, P. O., Geography and Regional Planning
SALAMI, L. A., Mechanical Engineering
SANNI, B. S., Chemistry
UCHE, C., Sociology and Anthropology
UFOMATA, D., Restorative Dentistry
URAIH, N., Microbiology
WEMAMBU, S. N. C., Medical Microbiology

UNIVERSITY OF CALABAR

PMB 1115, Calabar, Cross River State
Telephone: (87) 232790
E-mail: webadmin@unicaledu.org
Internet: www.unicaledu.org

Founded 1975
federal control
Language of instruction: English
Academic year: October to July

Chancellor: HRH IGWE KINGSLEY CHIME (Eze of Abia)
Vice-Chancellor: Prof. IVARA EJEMOT ESU
Deputy Vice-Chancellor for Academic Affairs: Prof. A. I. ESSIEN
Deputy Vice-Chancellor for Admin.: Prof. JOHN O. OFEM
Registrar: E. E. EFFIOM
Librarian: Dr OLU OLAT LAWAL
Number of teachers: 707
Number of students: 22,678 (full-time)

DEANS

College of Medical Sciences: Prof. SPENCER EFEM
Faculty of Agriculture: Prof. A. I. ESSIEN
Faculty of Arts: Prof. CHRIS NWAMUO
Faculty of Basic Medical Sciences: Prof. I. B. UMOH
Faculty of Clinical Sciences: Dr C. E. ANTIA-OBONG (acting)
Faculty of Education: Prof. S. C. UCHE (acting)
Faculty of Laboratory and Allied Health Sciences: Prof. A. E. UDOH (acting)
Faculty of Law: N. O. ITA (acting)
Faculty of Science: Prof. JOHN O. OFFEM
Faculty of Social Sciences: Prof. JOHN E. NDEBBIO
Graduate School: Prof. EBONG W. MBIPOM

PROFESSORS

College of Medical Sciences:
AKPAN, J. O., Pharmacology
ANDY, J. J., Medicine
ATTAH, E. B., Pathology
BASSEY, O. O., Surgery
BOLARIN, D. M., Chemical Pathology
BRAIDE, V. B., Pharmacology
EFEM, S., Surgery
EJEZIE, G. C., Medical Microbiology and Parasitology
EKA, O. U., Biochemistry
ESSIEN, E. U., Biochemistry
ONUBA, O. O., Surgery
OSIM, E. E., Physiology
OTU, A. A., Surgery
UMOH, I. B., Biochemistry
UTSALO, S. J., Medical Microbiology, Parasitology

Faculty of Agriculture:
AMALU, U. C., Soil Science
ASUQUO, B. O., Animal Science

ESSIEN, A. I., Animal Science
ESU, I., Soil Science

Faculty of Arts:
ABASIATTAI, M. B., History
EKO, E. O., English and Literary Studies
ERIM, E. O, History
ESSIEN, O. E. A., Languages and Linguistics
IKONNE, C. U. E., English and Literary Studies
IWE, N. S. S., Religious Studies and Philosophy
JOHN, E. E., Languages and Linguistics
NOAH, M. E., History
NWAMUO, C. I., Theatre Arts
ORISAWAYI, D., English and Literary Studies
UKA, K., Theatre Arts
UYA, O. E., History

Faculty of Education:
ABODERIN, A. O., Curriculum and Teaching
AMADI, L. E., Curriculum and Teaching
DENGA, D. I., Educational Foundations and Administration
ENUKOHA, O. I.
ESU, A. E.
IKPAYA, B. O.
NWACHUKWU, D. N., Guidance and Counselling
OMOJUWA, J. O.
UCHE, S. C.

Faculty of Science:
AKPAN, E. B., Geology
BRAIDE, E. I., Parasitology
EKPA, O. D., Chemistry
EKPE, U. J., Chemistry
EKWERE, S. J., Geology
EKWUEME, B. N., Geology
IBOK, U. J., Chemistry
LIPCSY, Z.
MBIPOM, E. W., Physics
MENKITI, A. I., Physics
OFFEM, J. O., Chemistry
OKWUEZE, E. E., Physics
PETERS, S. W., Geology
USUA, E. J., Biological Sciences
UWAH, E. J., Physics

Faculty of Social Sciences:
BASSEY, C. O., Political Science
EBONG, M. O., Geography, Regional Planning
ETUK, E. J., Management Studies
NDEBBIO, J. E. U., Economics
OBOT, J. U., Geography, Regional Planning
OTTONG, J. G., Sociology
SULE, R. A. O., Geography, Regional Planning

Institute of Oceanography:
ANTAI, E. E.
HOLZLONER, S.
OBIEKEZIE, A. I.

Institute of Public Policy and Administration:
UYA, O. E.

UNIVERSITY OF IBADAN

Ibadan
Telephone: (2) 7511988
E-mail: vc@mail.ui.edu.ng
Internet: www.ui.edu.ng

Founded 1948 as Univ. College, Ibadan, a constituent College of the Univ. of London, UK, present name and status 1962
federal control
Language of instruction: English
Academic year: September to July

Chancellor: HH ALHAJI ADO BAYERO
Vice-Chancellor: Prof. OLUFEMI A. BAMIRO
Deputy Vice-Chancellor for Academics: Prof. A. A. B. AGBAJE

Deputy Vice-Chancellor for Admin.: Prof. ELIJAH A. BAMGBOYE
Registrar: OMOTAYO O. IKOTUN
Librarian: Dr B. A. OLADELE

Library: see under Libraries and Archives
Number of teachers: 1,214
Number of students: 19,521

Publications: *Digest of Statistics, Ivory Tower, Official Gazette, Order of Proceedings, Pocket Statistics, Research Bulletin of the Centre for Arabic Documentation* (2 a year), *Student Information Handbook, University Calendar*

DEANS

Faculty of Agriculture and Forestry: Prof. F. K. EWETE
Faculty of Arts: Prof. P. A. OGUNDEJI
Faculty of Basic Medical Sciences: Prof. O. D. OLALEYE
Faculty of Clinical Sciences: Prof. O. M. OLUWATOSIN
Faculty of Dentistry: Prof. GHEMISOLA A. OKE
Faculty of Education: Prof. J. B. BABALOLA
Faculty of Law: Prof. OLUYEMISI A. BAMGBOSE
Faculty of Pharmacy: Prof. J. O. MOODY
Faculty of Science: Prof. K. O. ADEBOWALE
Faculty of Social Sciences: Prof. KASSEY GARBA
Faculty of Technology: Prof. A. E. OLULEYE
Faculty of Veterinary Medicine: Prof. V. O. TAIWO
Postgraduate School: Prof. L. POPOOLA
Student Affairs: Prof. A. E. FALAYE

PROFESSORS

Faculty of Agriculture and Forestry:
ADEJUMO, O., Animal Science
ADEOYE, G., Agronomy
AIYELARI, E., Agronomy
AKEN'OVA, M., Agronomy
AKINSOYINU, A., Animal Science
AKORODA, M., Agronomy
ATIRI, G., Crop Protection and Environmental Biology
AYODELE, A., Wildlife and Fisheries
BADA, S., Forest Resources Management
EKPO, E., Crop Protection and Enviromental Biology
EWETE, F., Crop Protection and Enviromental Biology
FALAYE, A., Wildlife and Fisheries
FALUSI, A., Agricultural Economics
FATUROTI, E., Wildlife and Fisheries
FAWOLE, B., Crop Protection and Enviromental Biology
IKOTUN, B., Crop Protection and Enviromental Biology
IKPI, A., Agricultural Economics
IYAYI, E., Animal Science
LADELE, A., Agricultural Extension and Rural Development
LONGE, O., Animal Science
LUCAS, E., Agronomy
OGUNKUNLE, A., Agronomy
OGUNYEMI, S., Crop Protection and Enviromental Biology
OLAWOYE, J., Agricultural Extension and Rural Development
OLOGHOBO, A., Animal Science
OMUETI, J., Agronomy
OSHO, J., Forest Resources Management
POPOOLA, L., Forest Resources Management
TEWE, O., Animal Science
TIJANI-ENIOLA, H., Agronomy
TOGUN, A., Crop Protection and Enviromental Biology

Faculty of Arts:
ABDULRAHMON, M., Arabic and Islamic Studies
ADEBAYO, A., European Studies
ADEKOYA, O., English

ADESANOYE, F., Communication and Language Arts
AKINYEYE, O., History
DASYLVA, A., English
DRURGBA, A., Religious Studies
EGBOKHARE, F., Linguistics and African Languages
ELUGBE, B., Linguistics and African Languages
IRELE, J., Philosophy
LAWAL, O., History
ODEJIDE, I., Communication and Language Arts
OGUNDEJI, P., Linguistics and African Languages
OLADIPO, O., Philosophy
OMAMOR, P., Linguistics and African Languages
OMOSINI, O., History
OSOFISAN, B., Theatre Arts
OWOLABI, D., Linguistics and African Languages
OYELEYE, A., English
OYETADE, S., Linguistics and African Languages

Faculty of Basic Medical Sciences:
ADENIYI, F., Chemical Pathology
AGBEDANA, E., Chemical Pathology
AKANG, E., Pathology
AKEN'OVA, Y., Haematology
BAKARE, R., Medical Microbiology and Parasitology
BOLARINWA, A., Physiology
FAROMBI, E., Biochemistry
MADUAGWU, E., Biochemistry
OGUNBIYI, J., Pathology
OLALEYE, D., Virology
OLORUNSOGO, O., Biochemistry
OSOTIMEHIN, B., Chemical Pathology
OYEBOLA, D., Physiology
SHOKUNBI, W., Haematology
SHOKUNBI, M., Anatomy
SOWUNMI, A., Pharmacy and Therapeutics

Faculty of Clinical Sciences:
ADEBAMOWO, C., Surgery
ADEGBOYE, V., Surgery
ADEKUNLE, A., Obstetrics and Gynaecology
ADEWOLE, I., Obstetrics and Gynaecology
AJAIYEOBA, A., Ophthalmology
AKINYINKA, O., Paediatrics
AMANOR-BOADU, S., Anaesthesia
ARIJE, A., Medicine
AROWOJOLU, A., Obstetrics and Gynaecology
ASUZU, M., Community Medicine
BAIYEROJU, A., Ophthalmology
BAIYEWU, O., Psychiatry
CAMPBELL, O., Radiotherapy
FALADE, A., Paediatrics
GEORGE, A., Medicine
GUREJE, O., Psychiatry
IJADUOLA, G., Otorhinolaryngology
ILESANMI, A., Obstetrics and Gynaecology
KADIRI, S., Medicine
NWAORGU, O., Otorhinolaryngology
OGUNNIYI, A., Medicine
OGUNSEYINDE, A., Radiology
OJENGBEDE, O., Obstetrics and Gynaecology
OLUWATOSIN, O., Surgery
OMIGBODUN, A., Obstetrics and Gynaecology
OMOKHODION, S., Paediatrics
OMOKHODION, F., Community Medicine
OSINUSI, K., Paediatrics
SALAKO, B., Medicine
SANYA, A., Physiotherapy
SHITTU, O., Surgery
SOYANNWO, O., Anaesthesia

Faculty of Dentistry:
AROWOJOLU, M. O., Preventive Dentistry
LAWOYIN, J. O., Oral Pathology
OBIECHINA, A. E., Oral & Maxillofacial Surgery

OKE, G. A., Preventive Dentistry

Faculty of Education:
AJAYI, E., Educational Management
AKINTAYO, M., Adult Education
ALEGBELEYE, G., Library, Archival and Information Studies
ATINMO, M., Library, Archival and Information Studies
AYODELE-BAMISAIYE, O., Teacher Education
BABALOLA, J., Educational Management
MABAWONKU, I., Library, Archival and Information Studies
NWAZUOKE, A., Special Education
OGUNDELE, B., Human Kinetics and Health Education
OGUNSANYA, M., Educational Management
UWAKWE, C., Guidance and Counselling

Faculty of Law:
AGBEDE, I., Private and Business Law
ANIFALAJE, J., Private and Business Law
BAMGBOSE, O., Private and Business Law
OMOROGBE, O., Public and International Law
OWOADE, M., Public and International Law

Faculty of Pharmacy:
AJAIYEOBA, E. O., Pharmacognosy
BABALOLA, C. P., Pharmaceutical Chemistry
ERHUN, W. O., Clinical Pharmacy and Pharmacy Administration
ITIOLA, O. A., Pharmaceutical and Industrial Pharmacy
JAIYEOBA, K. T., Pharmaceutical and Industrial Pharmacy
MOODY, J. O., Pharmacognosy

Faculty of Public Health:
AKINYELE, I. O., Human Nutrition and Dietetics
ATINMO, T., Human Nutrition and Dietetics
AYENI, O., Epidemiology, Medical Statistics and Environmental Health
BAMGBOYE, E. A., Epidemiology, Medical Statistics and Environmental Health
OLADEPO, O., Health Promotion and Education

Faculty of Science:
ADEBOWALE, K., Chemistry
ADELEKE, B., Chemistry
ADESOMOJU, A., Chemistry
BAMIRO, F., Chemistry
EKHAGUERE, S., Mathematics
EKUNDAYO, O., Chemistry
ELUEZE, A., Geology
FARAI, I., Physics
FOLORUNSO, C., Archaeology and Anthropology
HASSAN, A., Zoology
HUSSAIN, L., Physics
ILORI, S., Mathematics
LAWUYI, O., Archaeology and Anthropology
ODAIBO, A., Zoology
ODERINDE, R., Chemistry
ODIAKA, T., Chemistry
ODUNFA, S., Botany and Microbiology
OKUNADE, A., Physics
OLADIRAN, E., Physics
OLAYINKA, A., Geology
ONIANWA, P., Chemistry
OSIBANJO, O., Chemistry
OSOFISAN, A., Computer Science
OSONUBI, O., Botany and Microbiology
OYELARAN, P., Archaeology and Anthropology
SANNI, A., Botany and Microbiology
UGWUMBA, O., Zoology
WOODS, J., Chemistry

Faculty of Social Sciences:
ADENIKINJU, A., Economics
AFOLAYAN, A., Geography
AGBAJE, A., Political Science
AGBOLA, S., Urban and Regional Planning
ARIYO, A., Economics

AWETO, A., Geography
AYENI, M., Geography
BALOGUN, S., Psychology
EGWAIKHIDE, F., Economics
EHIGIE, B., Psychology
GARBA, A., Economics
GARBA, P., Economics
GBADEGESIN, A., Geography
GBOYEGA, E., Political Science
IKPORUKPO, C., Geography
ISIUGO-ABANIHE, U., Sociology
IWAYEMI, A., Economics
OGUNKOLA, E., Economics
OKAFOR, S., Geography
OKE, E., Sociology
OKUNADE, A., Political Science
OLOFIN, S., Economics
OSINOWO, H., Psychology
OYEJIDE, T., Economics
SOYIBO, A., Economics
SUBERU, R., Political Science
SUNMOLA, A., Psychology

Faculty of Technology:
ADEGOKE, G., Food Technology
ADEKOYA, L., Mechanical Engineering
AGBEDE, O., Civil Engineering
ALABI, B., Mechanical Engineering
AWORH, O., Food Technology
BAMIRO, O., Mechanical Engineering
CHARLES-OWABA, O., Industrial and Production Engineering
OLORUNSOLA, A., Agricultural Engineering
OLULEYE, A., Industrial & Production Engineering
ONILUDE, M., Agricultural Engineering
SANGODOYIN, A., Agricultural Engineering

Faculty of Veterinary Medicine:
ABATAN, M., Veterinary Physiology and Pharmacy
ADEYEFA, C., Veterinary Medicine
AGBEDE, S., Veterinary Public Health
AKINBOADE, O., Veterinary Microbiology and Parasitology
AKPAVIE, S., Veterinary Pathology
ANOSA, V., Veterinary Pathology
AROWOLO, R., Veterinary Physiology and Pharmacy
FAGBEMI, B., Veterinary Microbiology and Parasitology
FAYEMI, O., Veterinary Surgery and Reproduction
NOTTIDGE, H., Veterinary Medicine
OBI, T., Veterinary Medicine
OGUNDIPE, G., Veterinary Public Health
OKE, B., Veterinary Anatomy
OLADOSU, L., Veterinary Medicine
OLUFEMI, B., Veterinary Medicine
ONWUKA, S., Veterinary Anatomy
OYEWALE, J., Veterinary Physiology and Pharmacy
TAIWO, V., Veterinary Pathology

UNIVERSITY OF ILORIN

PMB 1515, Ilorin, Kwara State
Telephone: (31) 221691
E-mail: registra@unilorin.edu.ng
Internet: www.unilorin.edu.ng

Founded 1975
federal control
Language of instruction: English
Academic year: September to June

Chancellor: HRH AMBROSE ALLAGOA
Vice-Chancellor: Prof. SHAMSUDEEN ONYILOKWU ONCHE AMALI
Deputy Vice-Chancellor for Academic Affairs: Prof. ISHAQ OLANREWAJU OLOYEDE
Deputy Vice-Chancellor for Admin.: Prof. LUKE DAYO EDUNGBOLA
Registrar: O. O. OYEYEMI
Librarian: Prof. M. I. AJIBERO

Library of 155,000 vols, 2,800 periodicals
Number of teachers: 644
Number of students: 18,488

Publication: *University Calendar*

DEANS

Faculty of Agriculture: Prof. J. O. ATTEH
Faculty of Arts: Prof. R. D. ABUBAKRE
Faculty of Business and Social Sciences: Prof. I. O. TAIWO
Faculty of Education: Prof. E. A. OGUNSAKIN
Faculty of Engineering and Technology: Prof. O. A. ADETIFA
Faculty of Health Sciences: Prof. M. A. ARAOYE
Faculty of Law: Prof. Z. O. AJE
Faculty of Science: Prof. T. O. OPOOLA
Post-Graduate School: Prof. J. A. MORAKINYO

UNIVERSITY OF JOS

PMB 2084, Jos, Plateau State
Telephone: (73) 610514
Internet: www.uiowa.edu/intlinet/unijos

Founded 1975
federal control
Language of instruction: English
Academic year: September to June (2 semesters)

Chancellor: HRH Oba Dr FESTUS IBIDAPO ADEDINSEWO ADESANOYE OSEMAWE OF ONDOLAND
Pro-Chancellor: Prof. MUSA ABDULLAHI
Vice-Chancellor: Prof. MONDAY MANGVWAT
Deputy Vice-Chancellor for Academic Affairs: Prof. A. O. MALU
Deputy Vice-Chancellor for Admin.: Prof. J. O. A. ONYEKA
Registrar: Z. D. GALAM
Librarian: Dr A. OCHAI

Number of teachers: 745
Number of students: 14,378

DEANS AND DIRECTORS

Faculty of Arts: Prof. E. B. AJULO
Faculty of Education: Prof. I. J. IHENACHO
Faculty of Environmental Sciences: Prof. A. A. ADEPETU
Faculty of Law: Dr J. M. NASIR
Faculty of Medical Sciences: Prof. J. O. OGUNRANTI
Faculty of Natural Sciences: Prof. M. S. AUDU
Faculty of Pharmaceutical Sciences: Prof. F. OKWUASABA
Faculty of Social Sciences: Prof. S. G. TYODEN
School of Postgraduate Studies: Prof. G. A. UBOM
Institute of Education: Dr A. Y. MALLUM
Centre for Continuing Education: Dr E. A. ABAMA
Centre for Development Studies: Dr J. S. ILLAH

PROFESSORS

Faculty of Arts:
AIRE, Y. O., Languages and Lingusitics
AJE, A. O., Languages and Linguistics
AJULO, E. B., English
AMALI, S. O. O., Theatre Studies
BASHIR, I. L., History
CYRIL, I. O., Religious Studies
JAMES, I., History
JEMKUR, J. F., History
MANGVWAT, M. Y., History
YAHYA, M. T., Religious Studies

Faculty of Education:
ABANG, T., Special Education
ADEWOLE, M. A., Philosophy of Education
AKINNADE, C. T. O., Science and Technical Education
AKPAN, E. U. U., Science and Technology Education
AWOTUNDE, P. O., Science Education
IHENACHO, I. J., Special Education
LASSA, P. N., Mathematics Education
MALLUM, M. P., Guidance and Counselling
OZOJI, E., Special Education

UDOH, S. U., Social Science Education
Faculty of Environmental Sciences:
ADEPETU, A. A., Geography and Planning
KOLAWOLE, J. O., Building
Faculty of Law:
ADUBA, J. N., Public and Law
Faculty of Medical Sciences:
ADOGA, G. I., Biochemistry
ANAKWE, G. E., Biochemistry
IDOKO, J. A., Medicine
IHEZUE, C. H., Surgery
ISICHEI, H. U., Psychiatry
MALU, A. O., Medicinal Radiology
OKOYE, Z. S. C., Biochemistry
UBOM, G. A., Enzymology and Molecular Biology
Faculty of Natural Sciences:
AGINA, S. E., Botany
AJAYI, J., Zoology
AKUESHI, C. O., Plant Pathology
AUDU, M. S., Mathematics
DUHLINSKA, D. D., Protozoology, Insect Pathology
EGILA, J. N., Chemistry
EKPENYONG, K. I., Chemistry
EKWENCHI, M. M., Chemistry
HUSAINI, S. W. H., Plant Taxonomy and Cytogenetics
IFENKWE, O. P., Botany
LIVERPOOL, L. S. O., Mathematics
NWUFO, B. T., Chemistry
OGBONNA, C. I., Botany
OGEZI, I. E., Geology and Mining
OJOJEKWU, P. C., Zoology
ONUMANYI, P., Mathematics
ONWULIRI, C. O. E., Zoology
ONYEKA, J. O. A., Zoology
POPOV, T. V., Zoology
SHAMBE, T. S., Chemistry
UFODIKE, E. B. C., Zoology
UTAH, E. U., Physics
Faculty of Pharmaceutical Sciences:
IRANLOYE, T. A., Pharmacology and Pharmaceutical Technology
OKWUASABA, F., Pharmacology and Clinical Pharmacy
SOKOMBA, E. N., Pharmacology
Faculty of Social Sciences:
ALLI, W. O., International Relations
ALUBO, S. O., Sociology
ETANNIBI, E. O., Sociology
IBANGA, U. A., Sociology
NWEZE, A., Psychology
TYODEN, G. S., Political Economy
Centre for Development Studies:
OJOWU, O., Economics

UNIVERSITY OF LAGOS

Lagos
Telephone: (1) 4932660
E-mail: vc@unilag.edu
Internet: www.unilag.edu

Founded 1962
federal control
Language of instruction: English
Academic year: October to June

Chancellor: HRH Alhaji Dr ALIYU O. OBAJE (the Attah Igala)
Pro-Chancellor: Chief AFE BABALOLA
Vice-Chancellor: Prof. OYE IBIDAPO-OBE
Deputy Vice-Chancellor for Academic Affairs and Research: Prof. OLUSOGA A. SOFOLA
Deputy Vice-Chancellor for Management: (vacant)
Registrar: C. F. A. OLUMIDE
Librarian: S. O. OLANLOKUN
Library: see under Libraries and Archives
Number of teachers: 969
Number of students: 39,783

Publications: *Imodoye, A Journal of Africa Philosophy* (1 a year), *Journal of Economics and Policy Analysis* (1 a year), *Journal of Engineering Research* (1 a year), *Journal of Private and Property Law* (1 a year), *Journal of Society, Development and Public Health* (1 a year), *LAANGBASA (Jona Ise Akadani Ede Yoruba)* (African Studies, 1 a year), *Lagos Historical Review* (1 a year), *Lagos Journal of Environmental Studies* (1 a year), *Lagos Review of English Studies* (1 a year), *Nigerian Journal of Business and Social Science* (1 a year), *Nigerian Journal of Health and Biomedical Sciences* (2 a year), *Nigerian Journal of Industrial Relations* (1 a year), *Nigerian Journal of Management Studies* (1 a year), *Nigerian Journal of Philosophy* (1 a year), *UNILAG Communication Review* (1 a year), *UNILAG Journal of Business* (1 a year), *UNILAG Journal of Politics* (1 a year), *UNILAG Sociological Review* (1 a year)

DEANS

College of Medicine: Prof. S. O. ELEHSA (Provost)
Faculty of Arts: Prof. C. S. MOMOH
Faculty of Business Administration: Prof. W. ADEWUNMI
Faculty of Education: Prof. DURO ADENAYO AJEYALEMI
Faculty of Engineering: Prof. O. O. AKINDELE
Faculty of Environmental Sciences: Prof. R. O. IYAGBA
Faculty of Law: Prof. CHIOMA AGOMO
Faculty of Pharmacy: Prof. H. A. B. COKER
Faculty of Science: Prof. O. O. AMUND
Faculty of Social Sciences: Prof. L. OLURODE
School of Basic Medical Sciences: Prof. S. A. ADIGUN
School of Clinical Sciences: Prof. A. O. GRANGE
School of Dental Sciences: Prof. J. A. AKINWANDE
School of Postgraduate Studies: Prof. F. O. OLATUNJI

PROFESSORS

ABAELU, A. M., Biochemistry
ABASS, O., Computer Science
ABIDOYE, R. O., Community Health
ABUDU, O. O., Obstetrics and Gynaecology
ADEBAYO, N., Sociology
ADEDIMILA, A. S., Civil Engineering
ADEGBENRO, O., Electrical and Electronics Engineering
ADEGBOLA, O., Geography
ADEGOKE, K. A., Curriculum Studies (Education)
ADEJUGBE, M. O. A., Economics
ADEKOLA, S. A., Electrical and Electronics Engineering
ADELEMO, I. A., Geography
ADENIYI, P. O., Geography
ADEOGUN, A. A., Commercial and Industrial Law
ADE-OJO, S., European Languages
ADEPOJU, J. A., Mathematics
ADEROGBA, K., Mathematics
ADEWALE, A. O., Adult Education
ADEWUNMI, W., Banking and Finance
ADEYEMI, A. A., Public Law
ADEYEMI, J. D., Psychiatry
ADEYEMI, S. D., Surgery
ADEYEMI-DORO, H. O., Surgery
ADIGUN, S. A., Physiology
ADU, D. I., Mathematics
AGOMO, C. K., Commercial and Industrial Law
AJAYI, O., Mathematics
AJEYALEMI, S. D., Curriculum Studies (Education)
AKEJU, T. A., Civil Engineering
AKERE, J. F., English
AKINDELE, O. O., Mechanical Engineering

AKINFELEYE, R. A., Mass Communication
AKINGBADE, J. F., Business Administration
AKINOLA, M. O., European Languages (French)
AKINSETE, I., Haematology and Blood Transfusion
AKINTOLA-ARIKAWE, J. O., Geography
AKINTONWA, A., Pharmacology
AKINWADE, J. A., Oral and Maxillofacial Surgery
AKINWANDE, A. I., Biochemistry
AKO, C. T., Chemical Engineering
AKPATA, T. V. I., Botany and Microbiology
ALABA, I. O., African Languages and Literature (Yoruba)
ALABA, O., Political Science
ALO, B. I., Chemistry
AMUND, O. O., Botany and Microbiology
ARIGBABU, S. O., Surgery
ASIKA, M. N., Business Administration
AWONUSI, V. O., English
AWOSOPE, C. O., Electrical and Electronics Engineering
AYENI, J. O., Computer Science
AYENI, O. O., Surveying
BALOGUN, O. Y., Geography
BALOGUN, S. A., Metallurgical Engineering
BANDELE, E. O., Medicine
BELLO, R. A., Chemical Engineering
COKER, A. O., Medical Microbiology and Parasitology
COKER, H. A. B., Pharmaceutical Chemistry
DA ROCHA-AFODU, J. T., Surgery
DANESI, M. A., Medicine
DENLOYE, A. O., Chemical Engineering
DON-PEDRO, K., Zoology, Marine Biology and Fisheries
DUROSIMI-ETTI, F. A., Radiation Biology, Radiotherapy and Radiodiagnosis
EDEBIRI, U., European Languages (French)
EGBERONGBE, F. O. A., Surveying and Geoinformatics
EJIOGU, A. M., Educational Administration
ELESHA, S. O., Morbid Anatomy
ERUVBETINE, A. E., English
EZE, L. N., Psychology
EZEIGBO, C. U., Surveying and Geoinformatics
EZEIGBO, T. A., English
FAGBAMIYE, E. O., Educational Administration
FAGBENRO-BEYIOKU, A. F., Microbiology and Parasitology
FAJEMIROKUN, F. A., Surveying and Geoinformatics
FAMUYIWA, O. O., Psychiatry
FOGAM, P. K., Commercial and Industrial Law
FOLARIN, B. A., Psychology
FOLAWIYO, A. F. A., Physical and Health Education
GBADAMOSI, T. G. O., History
GIWA-OSAGIE, O. O. F., Obstetrics and Gynaecology
GRANGE, A. O., Clinical Pathology
IBIDAPO-OBE, O., Systems Engineering
IFUDU, N. D., Pharmacy and Pharmaceutical Technology
IGWILO, C. I., Pharmacy and Pharmaceutical Technology
IJAOLA, O. O., Electrical and Electronics Engineering
IKULAYO, P. B., Physical and Health Education
ISIEKWE, M. C., Dental Sciences
IYAGBA, R. O., Building
IYIEGBUNIWE, W. C., Finance
JEBODA, S. O., Preventive Dentistry
JOHNSON, M. A., European Languages (French)
JOHNSON, T. O., Medicine
KAMMA, C. M., Mechanical Engineering
KAZEEM, A. A., Clinical Pathology
KENKU, M. A., Mathematics
KUKOYI, A. A., European Languages (French)
KUSEMIJU, K., Marine Science

KWOFIE, E. N., European Languages (French)
LAWAL, A. A., History
LAWAL, O. O., Education
MAJEKODUNMI, A. A., Surgery
MAKANJU, O. O. A., Psychology
MAKANJUOLA, W. A., Zoology
MALAKA, S. L. O., European Languages (French)
MOMOH, C. S., Philosophy
MOREGBE, J. I., Philosophy
NINALOWO, A., Sociology
NWANKO, D. I., Zoology, Marine Biology and Fisheries
OBEBE, B. J., Curriculum Studies
ODEIGAH, P. G. C., Zoology, Marine Biology and Fisheries
ODIETE, W. O., Zoology, Marine Biology and Fisheries
ODUGBEMI, T., Medical Microbiology and Parasitology
ODUKOYA, O. O., Oral Pathology
ODUTOLA, T. A., Medicine
OGBOJA, O., Chemical Engineering
OGEDENGBE, O. K., Obstetrics and Gynaecology
OGUNDOWOLE, E. K., Philosophy
OGUNLESI, M. M., Chemistry
OGUNSANWO, A. C. A., Political Science
OGUNTOYE, A. O., Educational Administration
OHWOVORIOLE, A. E., Medicine
OJO, S. A., European Languages (French)
OJO, S. O., Geography
OKENIMKPE, M. N., Adult Education
OKEOWO, P. A., Surgery
OKORO, C. C., Electrical and Electronics Engineering
OKOTORE, R. O., Biochemistry
OLATUNJI, F. O., Chemical Engineering
OLOWOKUDEJO, J. O., Botany and Microbiology
OLUKOJU, A. O., History
OLUMIDE, Y. M., Medicine
OLUNLOYO, V. O. S., Mechanical Engineering
OLURODE, O., Sociology
OLUSANYA, O., Architecture
OLUWAFEMI, C. O., Physics
OMOLUABI, P. F., Psychology
OMO-MALAKA, S. L., Zoology, Marine Biology and Fisheries
OMOREGBE, J., Philosophy
OMOTOLA, J. A., Private and Property Law
OSEGBE, D. N., Surgery
OSIBOGUN, A. O., Community Health
OSINBAJO, Y., Public Law
OSIPITAN, T. A. I., Public Law
OSUNTOKUN, J. O., History
OTOBO, D., Industrial Relations and Personnel Management
OWHOTU, V. B., Curriculum Studies
OWOEYE, I. O., Physiotherapy
OYEBANDE, L., Geography
OYEBODE, A., Jurisprudence and International Law
OYEDIRAN, M. A., Child Health and Primary Care
OYEKANMI, F. A. D., Sociology
OYELELE, D. A., Geography
SOFOLA, O. A., Physiology
SOFOLUWE, A. B., Computer Science
SOTE, E. O., Child Dental Health
SOTE, G. A., Psychology
SOWEMIMO, G. O. A., Surgery
SUSU, A. A., Chemical Engineering
TALABI, S. O., Mechanical Engineering
TAYO, F., Clinical Pharmacy
TOMORI, S., Economics
UCHE, L. U., Mass Communication
UCHEGBU, A., Jurisprudence and International Law
UNAH, J. I., Philosophy
UTUAMA, A. A., Private and Property Law
UZOCHUKWU, S., African Languages and Literature (Igbo)
UZODIKE, E. N. U., Private and Property Law
VINCENT, T., English

WILLIAMS, G. O., Zoology, Marine Biology and Fisheries

UNIVERSITY OF MAIDUGURI

PMB 1069, Maiduguri, Borno State
Telephone: (76) 232949
E-mail: root@unimaid.edu.ng
Internet: www.unimaid.edu.ng
Founded 1975
federal control
Language of instruction: English
Academic year: October to June

Chancellor: His Royal Majesty Dr EKPENYONG OKONKO UDOUTUN
Pro-Chancellor and Chair. of Council: Dr BOLANLE OLAWALE BABALAKIN
Vice-Chancellor: Prof. IBRAHIM ABUBAKAR NJODI
Deputy Vice-Chancellor for Academic Services: (vacant)
Deputy Vice-Chancellor for Central Admin.: (vacant)
Registrar: Dr LAWAN BUKAR ALHAJI
Librarian: JAMES ABAYOMI AGAJA (acting)

Number of teachers: 700
Number of students: 30,000

Publications: *Annals of Borno, Inaugural Lecture and Convocation Speeches*

DEANS

College of Medical Sciences: Prof. A. A. TAHIR
Faculty of Agriculture: Prof. J. D. KWARI
Faculty of Arts: Prof. YAKUBU MUKHTAR
Faculty of Education: Prof. IBRAHIM NJODI
Faculty of Engineering: Prof. M. I. BUGAJE
Faculty of Law: Dr YUSUF M. YUSUF (acting)
Faculty of Management Sciences: Prof. AMINU AYUBA (acting)
Faculty of Science: Prof. M. Y. BALLA (acting)
Faculty of Social Sciences: Prof. S. S. IFAH (acting)
Faculty of Veterinary Medicine: Prof. A. G. AMBALI

PROFESSORS

ABAH, J. O., English
ABUBAKAR, A., Languages and Linguistics
ABUBAKAR, S., History
ADENIJI, F. A., Agricultural Engineering
AGUOLU, C. C., Library Science
AL-AMIN, J.D.
AMALI, I. O. O., English
AMBALI, A. G., Veterinary Medicine
ANASO, A. B., Crop Science
AYUBA, A., Management Science
AZEKE, T. O., Education
BABU, S. S., Veterinary Medicine, Microbiology and Parasitology
BADEJO, B. R., Languages and Linguistics
BRANN, C. M. B., Language and Linguistics
BWALA, S. A., Medicine
CAREW, P. F. C., Education
CHHANGANI, R. C., Common Law
CHIBUZO, G. A., Veterinary Anatomy
DAWHA, E. M. K., Library Science
DLAKWA, H., Social Science
EGWU, G. O., Veterinary Anatomy
ENYIKWOLA, O., Human Physiology
GADZAMA, M. N., Science
GOPAL, B. V., Biological Sciences
GUKAS, G. H., Industrial Design
HARRY, T. O., Microbiology
HASSAN, A. W., Surgery
HUSSAINI, I. M., Pharmacy
IDOKO, E. F., Theatre Arts
IGBOKWE, I. O., Veterinary Pathology
IGUN, U. A., Sociology and Anthropology
JACKS, J. W., Medicine
JIBOYEWA, D. A., Education
KAGU, B., Education
KALU, A. U., Veterinary, Public Health and Preventive Medicine
KOROMA, D. S. M., History

MALGWI, D., Physics
MBAHI, A. A., Creative Arts
MOHAMMED, I., Medicine
MSHELIA, B., P. H. E.
MSHELIA, E. D., Physics
NUR, A. M., History
ODO, P. E., Crop Science
OGUNBAMERU, B. O.
OHU, J. O., Agricultural Engineering
OMOTARA, B., Community Medicine
ONI, A., Continuing Education
PATE, U., Mass Communication
PINDIGA, H. U., Medicine
RICHARDS, W. S., Biological Sciences
SHEHU, U., Community Medicine
SODIPO, W., Biochemistry
TIJANI, K., Political Science and Administration
UBOSI, C. O., Animal Science
WAZIRI, I., History
ZARIA, L. T., Veterinary Microbiology and Parasitology

UNIVERSITY OF NIGERIA

Nsukka, Enugu State
Telephone: (42) 771911
Internet: www.unn.edu.org

Founded 1960
federal control
Language of instruction: English
Academic year: September to June

Chancellor: Emir of Zazzau Alhaji Dr SHEHU IDRIS
Pro-Chancellor: Prof. BOLANLE AWE
Vice-Chancellor: Prof. BARTO N. OKOLO
Deputy Vice-Chancellor for Academic Affairs: Prof. I. U. ASUZU
Deputy Vice-Chancellor for Admin.: Prof. EGBEKE AJA
Deputy Vice-Chancellor (Enugu Campus): Prof. R. E. UMEH
Registrar: A. I. OKONTA (acting)
Librarian: Dr CHARLES O. OMEKWU

Library: see Libraries and Archives
Number of teachers: 1,122
Number of students: 29,482

DEANS

College of Medicine: Prof. B. J. C. ONWUBERE
Faculty of Agriculture: Prof. K. P. BAIYERI
Faculty of Arts: Prof. I. U. NWADIKE
Faculty of Biological Sciences: Prof. C. E. A. OKEZIE
Faculty of Business Administration: Prof. IKE E. NWOSU
Faculty of Dentistry: Prof. E. NDIOKWELU
Faculty of Education: Prof. S. A. EZEUDU
Faculty of Engineering: Prof. J. C. AGUWAMBA
Faculty of Environmental Studies: Prof. J. U. OGBUEFI
Faculty of Health Sciences and Technology: Prof. G. C. OKOYE
Faculty of Law: Prof. F. N. MONYE
Faculty of Medical Sciences: Prof. F. U. EZEPUE
Faculty of Pharmaceutical Sciences: Prof. P. O. OSADEBE
Faculty of Physical Sciences: Prof. M. O. OYESANYA
Faculty of Social Sciences: Prof. E. O. EZEANI
Faculty of Veterinary Medicine: Prof. C. N. UCHENDU
School of General Studies: Prof. E. OGBONNA
School of Postgraduate Studies: Prof. A. N. AKWANYA

PROFESSORS

ADEILUYI, J. O., Civil Engineering
AGAJELU, S. I., Geoinformatics and Surveying
AGHAJI, M. A. C., Medical Sciences and Dentistry
AGU, C. C., Economics
AGUWA, C. N., Clinical Pharmacy and Pharmacy Management

AKAH, P. A., Pharmacology and Toxicology
AKAMIGBO, F. O. R., Soil Science
AKUBUE, A. U., Educational Foundations
ALI, A., Institute of Education
AMAZIGO, J., Mathematics
AMUCHEAZI, E. C., Political Science
AMUCHIE, F. A., Health and Physical Education
ANATSUI, E. K., Fine and Applied Arts
ANIAKOR, C. C., Fine and Applied Arts
ANIKA, S. M., Veterinary Physiology and Pharmacology
ANYADIKE, R. N. C., Geography
ANYANWU, S. U., Health and Physical Education
ARUA, E. O., Agricultural Economics
ASIEGBU, J. E., Crop Science
ASUZU, I. U., Veterinary Physiology and Pharmacology
ATTAH, C. A., Surgery
AZUBUIKE, J. C., Paediatrics
CHIDEBELU, S. A. N. D., Agricultural Economics
CHIDUME, C. E., Mathematics
CHIEJINA, S. N., Veterinary Parasitology and Entomology
CHIKWENDU, V. E., Archaeology
CHUKWU, C. C., Veterinary Medicine
EBIGBO, P. O., Psychological Medicine
EDOKA, B. E., Library and Information Science
EGBUNIWE, N., Civil Engineering
EGONU, I. T. K., Foreign Languages and Literature
EGWIM, P. O., Medical Biochemistry
EJIOFOR, L. J. C., Political Science
EKE, E. I., Educational Foundations
EKECHUKWU, O. V., Mechanical Engineering
ENEKWE, O., English
ESEDEBE, P. O., History
EYO, I. E., Psychology
EZEASOR, D. N., Veterinary Anatomy
EZEILO, B. N., Psychology
EZEJI, S. C. O. A., Vocational Teacher Education
EZEKWE, C. I., Mechanical Engineering
EZEOKE, A. C. J., Chemical Pathology
EZEPUE, M. C., Geology
EZE-UZOMAKA, O. J., Civil Engineering
HARBOR-PETERS, V. F., Science Education
IBEMESSI, J. A., Pure and Industrial Chemistry
IGBOELI, G., Animal Science
IGWILO, B. N., Fine and Applied Arts
IHEKORONYE, A. I., Food Science and Technology
IHEZUE, U. H., Psychological Medicine
IJOMA, J. O., History
IKEJIANI-CLARK, M. I. O., Public Administration and Local Government
IKENE, A. I., Home Science and Technology
IKPEZE, A. I., Economics
ILOABACHIE, G. C., Obstetrics and Gynaecology
ILOBA, C., Crop Science
ILOEJE, O. C., Mechanical Engineering
IMAGA, E. U. L., Management
KENE, R. O. C., Veterinary Surgery and Obstetrics
MADUBUNYI, L. C., Veterinary Parasitology and Entomology
MADUEWESI, E. J., Educational Foundations
MBAGWU, J. S. C., Soil Science
MODUM, E. P., Languages
MODUM, U., Accountancy
NGODDY, P. O., Food Science and Technology
NJOKO, O. N., History
NWABUEZE, E. P., Dramatic Arts
NWACHUKWU, P A., Linguistics and Nigerian Languages
NWACHUKWU, T. A., Educational Foundations
NWAFOR, J. C., Geography
NWAGBO, E. C., Agricultural Economics
NWAKOBY, B. A. N., Community Medicine
NWALA, T. U., Philosophy
NWANKITI, O. C., Botany

NWOSU, I. E., Marketing
NZE, C. B., Philosophy
NZEAKO, A. N., Electronic Engineering
OBANU, Z. A., Food Science and Technology
OBI, I. U., Crop Science
OBI, M E., Soil Science
OBI, S. K. C., Microbiology
OBIANYO, N. E. N., Surgery
OBIDOA, O., Biochemistry
OBIKEZE, D. S., Sociology and Anthropology
OBIZOBA, I. C., Home Science and Nutrition
OBOEGBULAM, S. I., Veterinary Pathology and Microbiology
ODIGBOH, E. U., Agricultural Engineering
ODUKWE, A. O., Mechanical Engineering
OGBAZI, J. N., Vocational Teacher Education
OGBUJI, R. O., Crop Science
OHAEGBU, A. U., Languages
OKAFOR, B. C., Otolaryngology
OKAFOR, C. O., Pure and Industrial Chemistry
OKAFOR, E. C., Pure and Industrial Chemistry
OKAFOR, F. C., Zoology
OKAFOR, F. O., Banking and Finance
OKAFOR, F. U., Philosophy
OKEKE, C. E., Physics and Astronomy
OKEKE, E. A. C., Education
OKEKE, F. N., Physics and Astronomy
OKEKE, P. N., Physics and Astronomy
OKOGBUE, C. O., Geology
OKOLI, F. C., Public Administration and Local Government
OKONKWO, P. O., Pharmacology and Therapeutics
OKORAFOR, A. E., Economics
OKORE, A. O., Economics
OKORIE, J. U., Vocational Teacher Education
OKORJI, E. C., Agricultural Economics
OKORO, B. A., Paediatrics
OKORO, O. M., Vocational Teacher Education
OKOYE, J. O. A., Veterinary Pathology and Microbiology
OKPALA, J. I. N., Education
OKPARA, E., Psychology
OKPOKO, A. I., Archaeology
OLAITAN, S. O., Vocational Teacher Education
OLI, J. M., Medicine
OLOIDI, O., Fine and Applied Arts
ONAH, J. O., Marketing
ONONOGBU, I. C., Biochemistry
ONUKOGU, I. B., Statistics
ONUOHA, K. M., Geology
ONWU, N., Religion
ONYEGEGBU, S. O., Mechanical Engineering
ONYEJEKWE, D. C., Mechanical Engineering
ORANU, R. N., Vocational Teacher Education
OSUAGWU, C. C., Electronic Engineering
OSUALA, E. C., Vocational Teacher Education
OSUALA, J. D. C., Adult Education and Extramural Studies
OYEOKU, O. K., Fine and Applied Arts
OZIOKO, J. O. C., Psychology
OZUMBA, B. C., Obstetrics and Gynaecology
PAL, S., Physics and Astronomy
SOLUDO, C. C., Economics
UCHE, J. I., Statistics
UKAEJIOFO, E. O., Medical Laboratory Science
UME, J. A., Estate Management
UMEH, L. C., Urban and Regional Planning
UMEH, T. A., Adult Education and Extramural Studies

ATTACHED INSTITUTES

Centre for Energy Research and Development: Nsukka; internet unn.edu.ng/centres/centre-energy-research-and-development; Dir Prof. E. C. OKORJI (acting).

Centre for Equipment Maintenance and Development: Nsukka; Dir Prof. I. C. OBIZOBA.

Institute of African Studies: Nsukka; e-mail ias.unn@unn.edu.ng; internet unn

.edu.ng/institutes/institute-african-studies;
Dir Prof. O. O. ENEKWE.

Institute for Development Studies: Univ.
of Nigeria, Enugu Campus, Enugu; f. 1963;
library of 4,000 vols; Dir Prof. OSITA OGBU;
Deputy Dir BONIFACE UMOH; Librarian
CHIOMA MBAEKWE; publ. *Nigerian Journal
of Development Studies*.

Institute of Education: Nsukka; internet
unn.edu.ng/institutes/institute-education;
Dir Prof. E. A. C. OKEKE.

Veterinary Teaching Hospital: Nsukka;
internet   unn.edu.ng/department/
veterinary-teaching-hospital; Dir Dr L. J. E.
ORAJAKA (acting)

UNIVERSITY OF PORT HARCOURT

PMB 5323, Port Harcourt, Rivers State
Telephone: (84) 335218
E-mail: registrar@uniport.edu.ng
Internet: www.uniport.edu.ng

Founded 1975
federal control
Language of instruction: English
Academic year: October to July

Chancellor: HRH Alhaji MUSTAPHA UMAR EL-
KANEMI (Shehu of Borno)
Pro-Chancellor: Prof. (Emer.) ALHAJI L. A. K.
JIMOH
Vice-Chancellor: Prof. NIMI DIMPKA BRIGGS
Deputy Vice-Chancellor for Academic
Affairs: Prof. J. D. OKOH
Deputy Vice-Chancellor for Admin.: Prof. M.
O. C. ANIKPO
Registrar: Dr CHRIS ALAFONYEKA TAMUNO
Librarian: Prof. E. O. AYALOGU

Library of 90,000 vols, 220 foreign current
journals, depository rights for UN publications
Number of teachers: 560
Number of students: 26,672

Publications: *Biologia Africana* (2 a year),
*Journal of Education in Developing
Areas—JEDA* (1 a year), *Kiabara* (2 a
year), *Library Waves* (2 a year)

DEANS

Faculty of Basic Medical Sciences: Prof. O. O.
EBONG
Faculty of Clinical Sciences: Prof. K. E. O.
NKANGINIEME
Faculty of Dentistry: Prof. F. OKOISOR
Faculty of Engineering: Prof. C. UMEZURIKE
Faculty of Humanities: Prof. S. I. UDOIDEM
Faculty of Management Sciences: Prof. D. P.
S. ASECHEMIE
Faculty of Pharmacy: Prof. O. K. UDEALA
Faculty of Science: Prof. C. M. OJINNAKA
Faculty of Social Sciences: Prof. W. J. OKOWA
School of Graduate Studies: Prof. W. I. BELL-
GAM

PROFESSORS

College of Health Sciences:
ANAH, C. O., Cardiology
ASOGWA, S. E., Preventative and Social
Medicine
BRAMBAIFA, N., Pharmacology
BRIGGS, N. D., Obstetrics and Gynaecology
DATUBO-BROWN, D. D., Surgery
EBONG, O. O., Pharmacology
EKE, F., Paediatrics
EKE, N., Surgery
ELECHI, E. N., Surgery
ESSIEN, E. N., Haematology
JOHN, T., Obstetrics and Gynaecology
NKANGINIEME, K. E. O., Paediatrics
NWANKWOALA, R. N. P., Pharmacology
ODIA, O. J., Medicine
OKOISOR, F., Dentistry
ORUAMABO, R. S., Paediatrics
UDEALA, O. K., Pharmacy

WAKWE, V. C., Chemical Pathology

Faculty of Education:
AWOTUA-EFEBO, E. B., Educational Tech-
nology
BARIKOR, C. N., Adult Education
DIENYE, N. E., Science Education
DIKE, H. I., Curriculum and Educational
Technology
EHEAZU, B. A., Adult and Non-Formal
Education
ENAOWHO, J. O., Educational Management
and Planning
GBAMANJA, S. P. T., Curriculum and Edu-
cational Technology
JOE, A. I., Psychology, Guidance and
Counselling
OKEKE, B. S., Education Administration
OKOH, J. D., History and Philosophy of
Education
UKWUIJE, R. P. I., Educational Psychology,
Guidance and Counselling

Faculty of Engineering:
AJIENKA, J. A., Petroleum Engineering
EBONG, M. B., Civil Engineering
KUYE, A. O., Chemical Engineering
NWAOGAZIE, I. L., Civil Engineering
ONYEKONWU, M. A., Petroleum Engineer-
ing
UMEZURIKE, C., Mechanical Engineering

Faculty of Humanities:
BESTMAN, M. T., French
CHUKWUMA, H. O., Oral Literature
EJITUWU, N. C., History
EJIZU, C. I., Religious Studies
EKWELIE, S. A., Linguistics
EMENANJO, E. N., Linguistics
IKONNE, C., English
ILEGA, D., Religious Studies
MADUKA, C. T., Comparative Literature
NNOLIM, C. E., Literature
NWODO, C. S., Philosophy
UDOIDEM, S. I., Philosophy

Faculty of Management Sciences:
ASECHEMIE, D. P. S., Accounting
BARIDAM DON, O. M., Management
NWACHUKWU, C. C., Management

Faculty of Science:
ABBEY, B. W., Biochemistry
AKPOKODJE, E. A., Geology
AMAJOR, L. C., Geology
ANOSIKE, E. O., Enzymology and Protein
Chemistry
ANUSIEM, A. C. I., Thermochemistry and
Biophysical Chemistry
ARENE, F. O. I., Animal and Environmental
Biology
ARINZE, A. E., Plant Science and Biotech-
nology
AYALOGU, E. O., Biochemistry
EBENIRO, J. O., Physics
EFIU-VWEVWERE, B. J. O., Biodegradation
and Environmental Toxicology
EKEKE, G. I., Biochemistry
ETU-EFEOTOR, J. O., Sedimentology, Sedi-
mentary Geochemistry
KINAKO, P. D. S., Botany
LALE, N. E. S., Crop Science
NYANANYO, B. L., Plant Science and Bio-
technology
OJINNAKA, C. M., Organic and Natural
Products Chemistry
OKIWELU, S. N., Entomology
OKOLI, B. S., Genetics
OKPOKWASILI, G. S. C., Microbiology
OTI, M. N., Geology

Faculty of Social Sciences:
AGIOBENEBO, T. J., Economics
ANIKPO, M. O. C., Sociology
BELL-GAM, W. I., Geography
EKPENYONG, S., Sociology
ETENG, I. A., Sociology
GBOSI, A. A., Economics

IBODJE, S. W. E., Political and Administra-
tive Studies
OKOKO, K. A. B., Political and Administra-
tive Studies
OJO, O. J. B., Political and Administrative
Studies
OKOWA, W. J., Economics

UNIVERSITY OF UYO

1 Ikpa Rd, PMB 1017, Uyo, Akwa Ibom State
Telephone: (85) 200303
E-mail: vc@uniuyo.edu.ng
Internet: www.uniuyo.edu.ng

Founded 1983 as Univ. of Cross River State,
then renamed Univ. of Akwa Ibom State;
present name 1991
federal control
Language of instruction: English
Academic year: October to July

Chancellor: The Emir of Fika, Haj. Dr
MUHAMMADU ABALI MUHAMMADU IBN
IDRISSA
Vice-Chancellor: Prof. COMFORT MEMFIN
EKPO
Deputy Vice-Chancellor for Academic
Affairs: Prof. ANTHONY AKPAN
Deputy Vice-Chancellor for Admin.: Prof.
CHARLES UKO
Dean for Student Affairs: ENO IBANGA
Registrar: Prof. EDAK UMONDAK
Librarian: Prof. FELICIA ETIM

Library of 84,628 vols, 271 periodicals
Number of teachers: 800
Number of students: 18,082

Publications: *Journal of Humanities, Journal of Research in Education and the
Humanities, Uyo Social Science Journal*

DEANS

Faculty of Agriculture: Prof. ENEFIOK UDO
Faculty of Arts: Prof. DESMOND WILSON
Faculty of Basic Medical Sciences: Prof.
ENOMFON AKPAN
Faculty of Business Administration: Dr ENE-
FIOK ESSIEN
Faculty of Clinical Sciences: Dr TIMOTHY
NOTTIDGE
Faculty of Education: Prof. QUEENDOLEEN
OBINAJU
Faculty of Engineering: Dr LINUS ASUQUO
Faculty of Environmental Studies: Prof. GOD-
FREY UDO
Faculty of Law: Prof. NSONGURUA UDOMBANA
Faculty of Pharmacy: Prof. SABINA OFUEFULE
Faculty of Science: Prof. ALFRED ITAH
Faculty of Social Sciences: Prof. INNOCENT
MODO
Post-Graduate Studies: Prof. JOSEPH OBINAJU
School of Continuing Education: Prof. TREN-
CHARD IBIA

PROFESSORS

ABASIATTAI, M. B., History
ABASIEKONG, E. M., Sociology
ABODERIN, A., Chemistry
ACHALU, O. E., Health Education
AFOLABI, M., Library Science
ANWANA, U. I., Guidance and Counselling
EKA, D., English
EKONG, E. E., Sociology
EKPENYONG, S., Sociology and Anthropology
EKPO, A. H., Economics
EKPO, N. M., Physics
EKPO, O. E., Curriculum Studies
ENOH, C. O. E., Geography
ESHIET, I. T., Chemistry and Education
ESSIEN, E. E., Pharmaceutical Chemistry
ETTE, S. I., Biochemistry
ETUK, U. A., Philosophy
EZE, O. C., Law
IBE-BASSEY, G. S., Educational Technology
IKKIDEH, I. S., English
IWOK, E. R., Accounting

NWA, E. U., Engineering
OKON, E. D., Zoology
UDO, E. J., Soil Science
UDOFOT, M. A., Curriculum Studies
UKPONG, I. I., Economics
UMOH, J. E., Animal Science
UMOH, P. U., Law
USORO, E., Geography

USMANU DANFODIYO UNIVERSITY

Dundaye Village, PMB 234, Sokoto
Telephone: (60) 234042
E-mail: registrar@udusok.edu.ng
Internet: www.udusok.edu.ng
Founded 1975
federal control
Language of instruction: English
Academic year: November to July
Chancellor: (vacant)
Vice-Chancellor: Prof. A.S. MIKAILA
Deputy Vice-Chancellor for Academic Affairs: Dr A. A. ZURU
Registrar: A. S. USMAN
Librarian: AHMED ABDU BALARABE (acting)
Number of teachers: 371
Number of students: 11,617
Publications: *Calendar*, *Convocation Speeches*, *Student Handbook* (1 a year), *University Lecture Series*

DEANS

Faculty of Agriculture: Dr H. M. TUKUR (acting)
Faculty of Arts and Islamic Studies: Dr M. M. DANGANA (acting)
Faculty of Education and Extension Services: Dr F. A. KALGO (acting)
Faculty of Law: Mal. M. I. SAID
Faculty of Management and Administration: Prof. S. A. DIYO
Faculty of Science: Dr U. ABUBAKAR
Faculty of Social Sciences: (vacant)
Faculty of Veterinary Medicine: Dr A. I. DANEJI
College of Health Sciences: Dr W. E. K. OPARA
Postgraduate School: Dr R. A. SHEHU

PROFESSORS

ABDULKAREEM, A., Health Sciences
ABDULRAHMAN, D. A., Sociology
ABDULRAHMAN, F. W., Chemistry
ABUBAKAR, M. K., Biochemistry
ADAMU, M., History
ADEYANJU, J. B., Veterinary Medicine
AGALEA, A. S., Arabic
AUDU, M. S., Mathematics
BADEJO, O. A., Health Sciences
BANDE, T. M., Political Science
BASHAR, M. L. A., Economics
BASHIR, A. M., Accounting
BILBIS, L. S., Biochemistry
BIRNIWA, H. A., Nigerian Languages
DANIEL, S. O., Community Health
DORA, J. S., Geography
ILIYA, M. A., Geography
IPINJOLU, J. K., Forestry and Fisheries
JUNAID, M. I., Education
KALGO, F. A., Education
KAURA, J. M., Islamic Studies
KYIOGWON, U. B., Agricultural Economics and Extension
MAGAJI, M. D., Crop Science
MAJEED, Q., Biological Sciences
MAMMAN, A. B., Geography
MIKAILU, A. S., Business Administration
MUKOSHY, I. A., Nigerian Languages
OBEMBE, A. Y. O., Medicine
OPARA, W. E., Surgery
SALAWU, A. A., Education
SHEHU, B., Surgery
SHEIDU, A. D., Accounting
YAQUB, N. O., Political Science

ZURU, A. A., Chemistry

STATE UNIVERSITIES

ABIA STATE UNIVERSITY

PMB 2000, Uturu, Abia State
Telephone: (88) 220785
Internet: absu.edu.ng
Founded 1981 as Imo State University; present name c. 1993
State control
Language of instruction: English
Academic year: October to August
Chancellor: Ambassador Dr Chief M. T. MBU
Vice-Chancellor: Prof. OGWO E. OGWO
Deputy Vice-Chancellor: Prof. STELLA OGBUAGU
Pro-Chancellor: EMEKA NWANKPA
Registrar: O. E. ONUOHA
Librarian: HERBERT I. IWUJI
Library of 27,000 vols
Number of teachers: 640
Number of students: 7,050

DEANS

College of Agriculture and Veterinary Medicine: Dr V. O. IMOH
College of Biological and Physical Sciences: Dr C. I. OGBONNAYA
College of Business Administration: Dr I. AJA-NWACHUKU
College of Education: Prof. V. C. NWACHUKU
College of Engineering and Environmental Studies: Dr M. A. IJIOMA (acting)
College of Humanities and Social Sciences: Prof. J. O. J. NWACHUKWU-ABADA
College of Legal Studies: M. O. UNEGBU (acting)
College of Medicine and Health Sciences: A. U. MBANASO (Provost)

PROFESSORS

AKPUAKA, F. C., Medicine and Health Sciences
ALEZI, O., Education
EBEOGU, A. N., Humanities and Social Sciences
EKE, F., Medicine and Health Sciences
MADUABUM, M. A., Education
MBATA, G. N., Biological and Physical Sciences
MKPA, M. A., Education
NWACHUKU, V. C., Education
NWACHUKWU-AGBADA, J. O. J., Humanities and Social Sciences
OGBONNAYA, C. I., Biological and Physical Sciences
OGBUAGU, S. C., Humanities and Social Sciences
OGWO, E. O., Marketing
ONOFEGHARA, N., Education
ONOH, J. K., Finance
ONUIGBO, W. I., Medicine and Health Sciences
OPARA-NADI, O. I., Agriculture and Veterinary Medicine
UWAKAH, C. T., Agriculture and Veterinary Medicine

ADAMAWA STATE UNIVERSITY

PMB 25, Mubi, Adamawa State
Telephone: (805) 8421126
E-mail: info@adsu.edu.ng
Internet: www.adsu.edu.ng
Founded 2002
State control
Language of instruction: English
Academic year: October to August (2 semesters)
Vice-Chancellor: Prof. ALKASUM ABBA
Deputy Vice-Chancellor: Dr SAIDU IBRAHIM
Registrar: J. M. GARNVWA
Bursar: KUMTHI EZRA ANJILI

Univ. Librarian: BELLO Y. DAHIRU
Dir for Academic Planning: Dr S. M. MORUPPA
Library of 35,089 vols, 60 journals, 5,000 vols of ebooks, 2,000 ejournals
Number of teachers: 760
Number of students: 6,519
Publications: *Adamawa Business Journal* (2 a year), *Adamawa Journal of Management and Decision Analysis* (2 a year), *ADSU Journal of Social and Development Studies* (2 a year)

DEANS

Faculty of Agriculture: Prof. W. NDAHI
Faculty of Science: Dr MOSES ZIRA ZARUWA
Faculty of Social and Management Sciences: Dr ABDULSALAM JIBRIL
Postgraduate School: Prof. MERCY OGUNSOLA-BANDELE
School of Remedial and Basic Studies: IDRIS ATADASHI (Dir)

AMBROSE ALLI UNIVERSITY

PMB 14, Ekpoma, Edo State
Telephone: (55) 98448
E-mail: swsupportaau@gmail.com
Internet: www.myaau.com
Founded 1981
State control
Language of instruction: English
Academic year: September to August
Chancellor: HRH Alhaji Dr UMARU FARUQ BAHAGO (Emir of Minna)
Vice-Chancellor and Chief Executive: Prof. D. O. AIGBOMIAN
Deputy Vice-Chancellor for Academic Affairs: Dr G. B. EFOGHE
Deputy Vice-Chancellor for Admin.: (vacant)
Provost for College of Medicine: Prof. G. O. AKPEDE
Registrar: G. T. OLAWOLE
Librarian: M. E. OJO-IGBINOBA
Library of 94,000 vols
Number of teachers: 500
Number of students: 18,000
Publications: *AAU* (journal of the Faculty of Education, 1 a year), *Iroro* (journal of the Faculty of Arts and Social Sciences, 1 a year)

DEANS

Faculty of Agriculture: Dr P. O. ONOLEMHEMHEN (acting)
Faculty of Arts: Prof. F. I. EMORDI
Faculty of Clinical Sciences: F. ALUFOHAI
Faculty of Education: Prof. M. O. OMO-OJUGO
Faculty of Engineering and Technology: Prof. C. A. AJUWA
Faculty of Environmental Studies: Dr Ing. S. O. IZOMOH (acting)
Faculty of Law: Prof. A. D. BADAIKI
Faculty of Medicine: Dr C. P. ALOAMAKA
Faculty of Natural Sciences: Prof. F. EGHAREVBA (acting)
Faculty of Social Sciences: Prof. B. E. AIGBOKHAN

PROFESSORS

AGBONLAHOR, D. E., Microbiology
AIGBOKHAN, B. E., Economics
AIGBOMIAN, D. O., Educational Foundations
AKINBODE, A., Geography and Regional Planning
ALOAMAKA, C. P., Physiology
DIME, C. A., Religious and Cultural Management
ECHEKWUBE, A. O., Philosophy
EFOGHE, G. B., Psychology
EGUAVOEN, O. I., Chemistry
EMIOLA, A., Law
EMORDI, F. I., Modern Languages
IJOMAH, B. I. C., Sociology

IMOBIGHE, T. A., Political Science
KURNOW, K., History
LONGE, J. B., Economics
OAIKHINAN, E. P., Engineering, Technology and Development
OKECHA, S. A., Chemistry
OMO-OYUGO, M. O., Curriculum and Instruction
OSEMEIKHIAN, J. E. A., Physics
REMISON, S. U., Crop Science
SEGYNOLA, A. A., Geography and Regional Planning
UNOMAH, A. C., History
YESUFU, A. K., Electrical and Electronic Engineering

BENUE STATE UNIVERSITY

PMB 102119, Makurdi, Benue State
Telephone: (44) 533811
E-mail: root@bensu.edu.ng
Founded 1992
Language of instruction: English
Vice-Chancellor: Prof. AKASE P. SORKA
Deputy Vice-Chancellor for Academic Affairs: Prof. TYOHDZUAH P. AKOSU (Academic)
Deputy Vice-Chancellor for Admin.: Prof. TONY EDOH
Registrar: TIMOTHY I. UTILE
Librarian: JOHNATHAN A. OCHEIBI
Library of 67,000 vols
Number of teachers: 558
Number of students: 13,649 (12,070 full-time, 1,579 part-time)
Publications: *Faculty of Arts Journal, Faculty of Education Journal*

DEANS

Faculty of Allied Sciences: EMMANUEL O. NWOKEDI
Faculty of Arts: Dr JOSEPH T. KERKER
Faculty of Clinical Sciences: MARGARET M. ARAOYE
Faculty of Education: Dr NANCY AGBE
Faculty of Law: AKAA T. IMBWASEH
Faculty of Management Science: SYLVESTER ORSAAH
Faculty of Science: Prof. EMMANUEL AGBA
Faculty of Social Science: Prof. ADAGBA OKPAGA
Postgraduate School: Prof. JOSEPH FIASE

PROFESSORS

ACHUA, J., Accounting
ADEJIR, T., Languages and Linguistics
AGBA, E. H., Physics
ANGYA, C. A., Theatre Arts
ANYANDE, G., Economics
APAM, J., Political Science
CHIAWA, M., Maths and Computer Science
GAFFA, T., Biological Science
GYUSE, T., Geography
KEGHKU, T., Mass Communication
KPELAI, T., Business Management
MOTI, J. S., Religion and Philosophy
NEVKAA, J. N., Educational Foundations
NYITSE, L. M., English
ODEY, M. O., History
SAMBA, J. N., Commercial and Property Law
SHINDI, J. A., Psychology
UTULU, R. E., Curriculum and Teaching
WEGH, F. S., Sociology
YIASE, S. G., Chemistry

EBONYI STATE UNIVERSITY

PMB 053, Abakaliki, Ebonyi State
Telephone: (43) 221093
E-mail: vc@ebsu-edu.net
Internet: www.ebsu-edu.net
Founded 1999
Language of instruction: English
Vice-Chancellor: Eng. Prof. FRANK I IDIKE

Deputy Vice-Chancellor: Prof. EGWU U. EGWU
Registrar: SAM NTE EGWU
Librarian: FRIDAY U. IBIAM
Library of 27,000 vols
Number of teachers: 792
Number of students: 22,029 (11,441 full-time; 10,588 part-time)

DEANS

Faculty of Agriculture and Natural Resources Management: Prof. EKUMA O. EKUMANKAMA
Faculty of Applied and Natural Sciences: Prof. JAMES C. OGBONNA
Faculty of Arts: Dr CLEMENT MGBADA
Faculty of Basic Medical Sciences: Prof. SUNDAY O. ELOM
Faculty of Biological Sciences: Dr IBIAM UDU
Faculty of Clinical Medicine: Prof. ESTHER U. AJULUCHUKWU
Faculty of Education: Prof. BERNARD ALUMODE
Faculty of Health Science and Technology: Asst Prof. C. O. EDEOGU
Faculty of Law: M. AJA NWACHUKWU
Faculty of Management Sciences: Dr FIDELIS OKPATA
Faculty of Physical Sciences: Prof. OBINI EKPE
Faculty of Social Sciences: Dr EUGENE NWEKE
School of Postgraduate Studies: Prof. SUNDAY N. AGWU

PROFESSORS

AKUBILO, C. J. C., Agricultural Economics, Management and Extension
ALAKU, S. O., Animal Production and Fisheries Management
ALI, A., Computer Science Education
AMUCHIE, F. A., Human Kinetics and Health Education
ANEZI-ONWU, O. N., Medicine
ATTAH, C. A., Surgery
AZUBUIKE, M. M., Computer Science Education
DIRIBE, C. O., Medical Biochemistry
EGWU, E. U., Management and Marketing
EGWUATU, V. E., Obstetrics and Gynaecology
EKUMANKAMA, E. O., Food Science
EZEIFEKA, G. O., Applied Microbiology
EZEILO, J. O., Industrial Mathematics and Applied Statistics
IBE, S., Animal Production and Fisheries Management
IBEMISI, J. A., Industrial Chemistry
IHEME, B. A., Law
INYIAMA, H. C., Computer Science
MARIRE, B. N., Animal Production and Fisheries Management
MGBODILE, M. U. K., Chemical Pathology
NDU, U., Applied Biology
NNOKE, F. N., Soil and Environmental Management
OBI, I. U., Crop Production and Landscape Management
OBIAKO, M. N., Surgery
OBIDOA, O., Medical Biochemistry
OBINNA, O. E., Economics
OBIONU, C. N., Community Medicine
OGAH, F., Crop Production and Landscape Management
OGBONNA, J. C., Biochemistry and Biotechnology
OJI, C., Surgery
OKAGBUE, R. N., Applied Microbiology
OKAKA, A. N. C., Biochemistry and Biotechnology
OKAKA, J. C., Food Science
OKANY, M. C., Law
OKOGBUE, C. O., Geology and Exploration Geophysics
OKOLI, E. C., Food Science
OKOLI, F. C., Political Science and Public Administration

OKORJI, E. C., Agricultural Economics, Management and Extension
OLUIKPE, B. O., English
ONUAGULUCHI, G., Pharmacology and Therapeutics
ONYENEKE, C. E., Biochemistry and Biotechnology
OSISIOMA, B. C., Accountancy
UBAH, C. N., History and International Relations
UCHE, C. U., Banking and Finance
UKPABI, S. C., History and International Relations
UKWU, U. I., Economics
UMEH, E. D., Crop Production and Landscape Management
UMEJI, A. C., Geology and Exploration Geophysics
UMEZUIKE, I. A., Law
UMOH, S. M., Management and Marketing

ENUGU STATE UNIVERSITY OF SCIENCE AND TECHNOLOGY

PMB 01660, Enugu
Telephone: (42) 451244
E-mail: esut@compuserve.com
Internet: www.esut.edu.ng
Founded 1980
State control
Campuses at Enugu and Nsukka
Academic year: January to October (two semesters)
Language of instruction: English
Chancellor: Dr Chief ERNEST ADEGUNLE OLADEINDE SHONEKAN
Pro-Chancellor: Igwe Dr C. A. ABANGWU
Vice-Chancellor: Prof. SAMUEL CHUKWU
Deputy Vice-Chancellor: Rev. Prof. Canon CHINEDU NEBO
Registrar: B. N. UZOIGWE
Librarian: Dr N. ENE
Number of teachers: 472
Number of students: 29,827
Publication: *Journal of Science and Technology* (2 a year)

DEANS

Faculty of Agriculture: Prof. B. N. MARIRE
Faculty of Applied Natural Sciences: Prof. A. C. OKONKWO
Faculty of Basic Medical Sciences: Prof. S. E. ASOGWA
Faculty of Education: Prof. O. O. ONOWOR
Faculty of Law: Dr OBI S. OGENE
Faculty of Management Sciences: P. E. EMEKEKWUE
Faculty of Social Sciences: Dr D. N. NWATU
School of Engineering: Prof. G. N. ONOH
School of Environmental Sciences: Prof. A. N. AGU
School of Postgraduate Studies: Prof. R. C. OKAFOR

PROFESSORS

ADIBE, E. C., Geography and Meteorology
AGAJELU, S. I., Surveying and Photography
AGU, N., Geography and Meteorology
AKUBUILO, C. J. C., Agriculture
ALAKU, S. O., Animal Science
ANEKE, L. E., Chemical Engineering
ANOWOR, O. O., Foundations of Education
ASOGWA, S. E., Community Medicine
CHIDOBEM, I. J., Animal Science
CHUKWU, S. C., Cooperatives
ENE, J. C., Applied Natural Sciences
MADUEWESI, J. N. C., Applied Natural Sciences
MARIRE, B. N., Animal Science
MOGBO, J. O., Foundations of Education
NEBO, C. O., Mechanical and Materials Engineering
NWORGY, O. C., Applied Biology
OCHO, L. O., Foundations of Education

OHUCHE, R. O., Industrial Mathematics and
Statistics
OKAFOR, N., Applied Microbiology and Brew-
ing
OKAFOR, R. C., Foundations of Education
OKAKA, J. C., Agriculture
OKONKWO, C. A. C., Applied Biology
OKORIE, B. A., Mechanical and Materials
Engineering
ONOH, G. N., Electrical and Electronic Engin-
eering
ONYEHALU, A. S., Foundations of Education
UGWU, I. C., Urban and Regional Planning
UMEH, E. D., Applied Biology

IMO STATE UNIVERSITY

PMB 2000, Owerri, Imo State
Telephone: (83) 221687
Internet: imsupostumeportal.org

Founded 1981

Vice-Chancellor: Prof. TONY G. ANWUKAH
Registrar: FRANCIS E. NWANKWO
Number of teachers: 230
Number of students: 15,991

DEANS

College of Medical and Health Sciences: B. C.
JIBURUM
Faculty of Agriculture and Veterinary Medi-
cine: A. ONWEAGBA
Faculty of Business Administration: INNO-
CENT OKONKWO
Faculty of Education: D. A. ONYEJEMEZI
Faculty of Engineering and Environmental
Sciences: U. O. NKWOGU
Faculty of Humanities: ROSE ACHOLONU
Faculty of Law: U. S. F. NNABUE
Faculty of Science: E. N. MGBENU
Faculty of Social Sciences: C. B. NWACHUKWU
Postgraduate School: F. N. MADUBUIKE

KANO STATE UNIVERSITY OF TECHNOLOGY, WUDIL

PMB 3244, Kano, Kano State
Telephone: (64) 241149
E-mail: info@kustportal.edu.ng

Founded 2001

Chancellor: ALHAJI ALIKO DANGOTE
Vice-Chancellor: SHAWKI A. A. SEOUD
Registrar: A. U. ABDURAHIM

LADOKE AKINTOLA UNIVERSITY OF TECHNOLOGY

PMB 4000, Ogbomoso, Oyo State
Telephone: (38) 720285
E-mail: contact@lautech.edu.ng
Internet: www.lautech.edu.ng

Founded 1990 as Oyo State Univ. of Technology; present name 1991

Vice-Chancellor: Prof. AKINOLA M. SALAU
Registrar: Y. O. GBADAMOSI
Library of 19,604 vols
Number of teachers: 439
Number of students: 12,245

DEANS

Faculty of Agriculture: J. I. OLAIFA
Faculty of Engineering and Technology: J. O.
OJEDIRAN (acting)
Faculty of Environmental Sciences: R. O. R.
KALILU
Faculty of Medical Sciences: P. O. AKINWISU
(acting)
Faculty of Pure and Applied Sciences: R. O.
AYENI

LAGOS STATE UNIVERSITY

PMB 1087, Apapa, Lagos State
Telephone: (1) 5884048

E-mail: veecee@lasu.org

Founded 1983
State control
Language of instruction: English
Academic year: October to July

Vice-Chancellor: Prof. JOHN OLADAPO OBA-
FUNWA
Registrar: OLUWATOYIN GLADSTONE OSHUN
Librarian: T. A. B. SERIKI
Library of 63,000 vols
Number of teachers: 513
Number of students: 35,544 (16,422 full-
time, 19,122 part-time)

Publications: *ECOFLASH*, *Educational Per-
spectives*, *Enhancing Quality Education in
Nigeria*, *Journal of Humanities* (2 a year),
Journal of Prospects in Science, *LASU
Jurist*, *LASU Law Journal*, *LASU Social
Science Journal*, *Nigerian Journal of
Research & Review in Science*

DEANS

College of Medicine: Prof. WOLE ALAKIJA
Faculty of Arts: Dr KUMLE LAWAL
Faculty of Education: Prof. ADEMOLA ONIFADE
Faculty of Engineering: Prof. P. A. O.
ADEGBUYI
Faculty of Law: Prof. B. A. SUSU
Faculty of Management Science: Prof. O. J.
FAPOHUNDA
Faculty of Sciences: Prof. MARTIN A. ANATE-
KHAI
Faculty of Social Sciences: Prof. TAYO ODU-
MOSU
Postgraduate School: Prof. C. O. OSHUN

PROFESSORS

ABDUL-KUREEM, H., Medical Biochemistry
ADARAMOLA, F., International Law and Jur-
isprudence
AJAJA, O., Mechanical Engineering
AJOSE, S. O., Electronics and Computer
Engineering
AKINRIMISI, E. O., Haematology and Blood
Transfusion
ALAKIJA, W., Community and Primary
Healthcare
ANETEKHAI, M. A., Fisheries Science
ASHIRU, O. A., Anatomy
BAMGBOYE, O. A., Chemistry
DADA, O. A., Chemical Pathology
FAPOHUNDA, O. J., Business Administration
HUNPONU-WUSU, O. O., Community and Pri-
mary Healthcare
IKHARIALE, M. A., Public Law
MATANMI, S. O., Industrial Relations and
Personnel Management
OBAFUNWA, J. O., Pathology
ODERINDE, B. B., Curriculum Studies
ODUBUNMI, E. O., Curriculum Studies
ODUMOSU, A. O., Geography and Planning
ODUMOSU, T., Communications
OKANLAWON, A., Anatomy
OKEBUKOLA, P. A. O., Curriculum Studies
OLUKOYE, A. O., Chemical Pathology
ONABANJO, A. O., Medical Microbiology
ONIFADE, A., Public Law
OSINBAJO, O. O., Public Law
OYERINDE, J. P. O., Medical Biochemistry
SAGOE, A. O., Haematology and Blood Trans-
fusion
TUNDE, S., Communications and Educational
Management
YEROKUN, O. A., Business Law

NIGER DELTA STATE UNIVERSITY

PMB 1, Abraka, Delta State
Telephone: (54) 66027
E-mail: pro@ndu.edu.ng

Founded 1992

Vice-Chancellor: Prof. F. M. A. UKOLI
Registrar: E. E. AVBIOROKOMA
Librarian: LAWRENCE OGBENI

OLABISI ONABANJO UNIVERISTY

PMB 2002, Ago-Iwoye, Ogun State
Telephone: (37) 432384
Internet: www.oou-ng.com

Founded 1982
State control
Academic year: October to July

Chancellor: Dr AYOOLA OBA OTUDEKO
Pro-Chancellor: Prof. BIYI AFONJA
Vice-Chancellor: Prof. AFOLABI SOYODE
Deputy Vice-Chancellors: Prof. E. O. A. AJAYI
Deputy Vice-Chancellors: Prof. ODUTOLA OSI-
LESI
Registrar: APOSTLE SAMUEL O. AJAYI
Librarian: O. K. ODUSANYA

Library of 106,709 vols
Number of teachers: 699
Number of students: 43,382 (28,221 full-
time, 15,161 part-time)

Publications: *Ago-Iwoye Journal of Social
and Behavioural Sciences* (2 a year),
GEGE Journal of the English Department
(1 a year), *International Journal of
Accountancy, Finance and Management
Sciences* (2 a year), *Journals of History
and Diplomatic Studies* (1 a year), *Journal
of Philosophy and Development.* (1 a year),
Journal of Public Law and Practice (1 a
year), *Journal of Social and Management
Sciences* (1 a year), *Nigerian Journal of
Private and Commercial Law* (1 a year),
OSU Journal of Educational Studies (1 a
year), *OYE Journal of Arts* (1 a year),
*Private and Commercial Law Additional
Information* (1 a year), *Studies in Curricu-
lum* (4 a year)

DEANS

College of Agricultural Sciences: Prof. S. F.
ADEDOYIN (Provost)
College of Engineering and Technology: Prof.
R. O. FAGBENLE (Provost)
Faculty of Agricultural Management and
Rural Development: Dr AIHONSU JOHN
(Provost)
Faculty of Agricultural Production and
Renewable Resources: Prof. S. O. OSUNLAJA
Faculty of Arts: Prof. KAMALDEEN BALOGUN
Faculty of Basic Medical Sciences: Prof. JIDE
OLOWOOKERE
Faculty of Clinical Sciences: Prof. FEMI
ADELOWO
Faculty of Education: Prof. OLATUNJI ODE-
DEYI
Faculty of Engineering: Prof. J. AKINYEMI
Faculty of Environmental Technology: Prof.
TOYIN OGUNTONA
Faculty of Law: Prof. JUSTUS SOKEFUN
Faculty of Management Sciences: Dr S. A.
TELLA (acting)
Faculty of Pharmacy: Prof. M. N. FEMI-
OYEWO
Faculty of Science: Prof. AFOLABI ADEBANJO
Faculty of Social Sciences: Dr WALE OLAITAN
Obafemi Awolowo College of Health Sciences:
Prof. M. A. OLANREWAJU (Provost)
Postgraduate School: Prof. O. O. KEHINDE
PHILLIPS (Provost)

PROFESSORS

ADEBANJO, A., Chemical Sciences
ADEDIPE, V. O., Educational Foundations and
Management
ADEDOYIN, S. F., Agricultural Extension and
Rural Sociology
ADEJONWO, K. O., Crop Production
ADESEMOWO, P. O., Educational Foundations
and Management
ADESIMI, A. A., Agribusiness and Farm Man-
agement
ADETORO, O. O., Obstetrics and Gynaecology
AFEJUKU, D. H., Private and Commercial
Law

AJAYI, E. O. A., Educational Foundations and Management
AJIBADE, E. S., Educational Foundations and Management
ALAUSA, O. K., Community Medicine and Primary Care
AWODERU, V. A., Biological Sciences
AYANLAJA, S. A., Soil Science and Farm Mechanisation
BALOGUN, K A., Religious Studies
BENEDICT, J. N., Curriculum Studies and Instructional Technology
DADA, O. A., Haematology and Blood Transfusion
DADA, S. S., Earth Sciences
EJIWUNMI, A. B., Anatomy
ERINOSHO, O. A., Sociology
FEMI, O. M. N., Pharmaceutics and Pharmaceutical Technology
HASSAN, T., Educational Foundations and Management
IYANIWURA, J. O., Mathematical Sciences
JAYESIMI, A. E. A., Medicine
KEHINDE-PHILLIPS, O. O., Earth Sciences
ODEDEYI, TUNJI, Sports Science and Health Education
ODUGBEMI, O. O., Geography and Regional Planning
ODUMUYIWA, E. A., Religious Studies
OGUNBA, OYIN, English
OGUNDERO, V. W., Biological Sciences
OGUNYEMI, E. O., Chemical Pathology and Haematology
OLAGUNJU, O. P., Educational Foundations and Management
OLANREWAJU, D. M., Paediatrics
OLOWOOKERE, J. O., Biochemistry
OLOWU, A. O., Paediatrics
OLUDIMU, O. L., Agricultural Economics
OSILESI, O., Biochemistry
OSONUBI, O., Biological Sciences
OSUNLAJA, S. O., Crop Production
OWORU, O. O., Crop Production
OYEDEJI, O. A., Curriculum Studies and Instructional Technology
OYEGUNLE, O. A., Anaesthesia
OYESIKU, O. O., Geography and Regional Planning
SANWO, J. O., Crop Production
SOSANWO, O. A., Mathematical Sciences
SULE-ODU, A. O., Obstetrics and Gynaecology
TAIWO, A., Educational Foundations and Management

RIVERS STATE UNIVERSITY OF SCIENCE AND TECHNOLOGY

PMB 5080, Port Harcourt, Rivers State
Telephone: (84) 233288
E-mail: info@ust.edu.ng
Founded 1971, univ. status 1980
State control
Language of instruction: English
Academic year: October to July

Chancellor: (vacant)
Pro-Chancellor: Hon. Justice (retd) ADOLPHUS KARIBI-WHYTE
Vice-Chancellor: Prof. B. B. FAKAE
Deputy Vice-Chancellor: Prof. H. I. HART
Registrar: DABA C. ODIMABO
Librarian: Dr B. E. AHIAUZU

Library of 2,000 vols
Number of teachers: 496
Number of students: 20,060

DEANS

Faculty of Agriculture: Prof. J. P. ALAWA
Faculty of Engineering: Prof. ALEX J. AKOR
Faculty of Environmental Sciences: VICTOR A. AKUJURU (acting)
Faculty of Law: F. O. AKAAKAR (acting)
Faculty of Management Sciences: Prof. SETH ACCRA-JAJA (acting)
Faculty of Science: Prof. FRIDAY B. SIGALO

Faculty of Technical and Science Education: Prof. W. AMAEWHULE (acting)
Postgraduate School: Prof. EMMANUEL N. AMADI

PROFESSORS

Faculty of Agriculture:
  ACHINEWHU, S. C., Food Science
  AMAKIRI, M. A., Soil Science
  AMAKIRI, S. F., Animal Science
  GIAMI, S., Food Science
  IGBEN, M. S., Agricultural Economics/ Extension
  ISIRIMAH, N. O., Crop/Soil Science
  MONSI, A., Animal Science
  OGBURIA, M. N., Food Science
  ONUEGBU, B. A., Crop/Soil Science
  OPUWARIBO, E. E., Crop/Soil Science
  ORUWARI, B. M., Animal Science
  WAHUA, T. A. T., Crop/Soil Science
  WEKHE, S. N, Animal Science

Faculty of Engineering:
  ABOWEI, M. F. N.
  CHINWAH, J. G.
  HART, H. I., Mechanical Engineering
  IDERIAH, F. J. K., Mechanical Engineering
  IDONIBOYE-OBU, K. I., Chemical/Petrochemical Engineering
  JOHNARRY, T., Civil Engineering
  ODI-OWEI, S., Mechanical Engineering
  WAMI, E. N.

Faculty of Environmental Sciences:
  FUBARA, D. M. J., Geodesy
  TEME, S. C., Geology

Faculty of Management Sciences:
  ACCRA-JAJA, S., Business Administration
  AHIAUZU, A. I., Business Administration
  FUBARA, B. A., Business Administration
  GBOSI, A. N., Management Science
  JOHNNIE, P. B., Business Administration
  ONOH, J. K., Banking & Finance

Faculty of Science:
  ABBEY, S. D., Medical Laboratory
  AMADI, E. N., Biology
  EKWEOZOR, I. K. E., Biology
  NWANKWO, S. I., Chemistry
  OKWAKPAM, B. A., Biology
  OMUARU, V. O. T., Chemistry

Faculty of Technical and Science Education:
  AHIAKWO, M. J., Science and Technical Education
  AMAEHULE, W. A., Business Education
  KOKO, M. N., Business Education
  WOKOCHA, A. M., Educational Foundations

UNIVERSITY OF ADO-EKITI

PMB 5363, Ado-Ekiti, Ekiti State
Telephone: (30) 250026
E-mail: registrar@unad.edu.ng
Internet: www.unadportal.com
Founded 1982

Vice-Chancellor: Prof. DIPO KOLAWOLE
Deputy Vice-Chancellor for Academics: Prof. O. OLAOFE
Deputy Vice-Chancellor for Devt: Prof. J. A. ADEGUN
Dir for Directorate of Distance Learning: Prof. R. O SEWEJE
Dir for Gen. Studies Unit: Prof. K. AJAYI
Dir for Pre-Degree Programmes: Prof. E. O. OLANIPEKUN
Registrar: OMOJOLA AWOSUSI
Bursar: F. M. FAPOHUNDA
Librarian: G. O. OGUNLEYE

Library of 110,000 vols
Number of teachers: 445
Number of students: 20,352 (14,652 fulltime, 5,700 part-time)
Publication: *Nigerian Journal of Banking and Financial Issues* (2 a year)

DEANS

College of Medicine: Prof. D. D. OYEBOLA
Faculty of Agricultural Sciences: Prof. A. S. FASINA
Faculty of Arts: Dr T. F. JEMIRIYE (acting)
Faculty of Education: Prof. G. A. AKINLEYE
Faculty of Engineering: Dr S. B. ADEYEMO (acting)
Faculty of Law: T. I. AKOMOLEDE
Faculty of Management Sciences: Prof. J. A. OLOYEDE
Faculty of Science: Prof. S. S. ASAOLU
Faculty of Social Sciences: Prof. A. L. ADESINA (acting)
School of Postgraduate Studies: Prof. J. O. ARIBISALA

PROFESSORS

ADEBAYO, W., Social Sciences
ADELOWO, E., Arts
ADERIBIGBE, E., Science
ADERIBIGBE, F., Science
ADERIYE, J., Science
ADETIFA, O., Engineering
ADEYOJU, K., Agricultural Sciences
AFOLABI, F., Social Sciences
AGAGU, A., Political Science
AJAJA, O., Engineering
AKINDUTIRE, I., Education
AKINLEYE, G., Education
AKINTAYO, E., Science
ALONGE, M., Education
BANDELE, S., Education
ESAN, G., Medicine
FAKUNLE, J., Science
FALUYI, M., Science
FAMUREWA, O., Science
IBIJOLA, E., Mathematical Sciences
KAYODE, J., Science
KOLAWOLE, D., Social Sciences
LUCAS, E., Agricultural Sciences
MUKOLU, I., Physics
OGUNLADE, A., Education
OGUNSINA, J., Arts
OJO, S., Engineering
OKE, G., Law
OLOMOLA, G., History and International Studies
OLORUNSOLA, S., Science
OMOSINI, O., Arts
OWOLABI, I., Electrical and Electronic Engineering
OWUAMANAM, D., Education
OWUAMANAM, T., Education
OYINLOYE, A., Science
UKOYEN, J., Arts

PRIVATE UNIVERSITIES

ABTI AMERICAN UNIVERSITY OF NIGERIA

2 Ahmed Onibudo St, POB 73688, Victoria Island, Lagos
Telephone: (1) 3200695
E-mail: abtiuniversity@yahoo.com
Internet: www.abti-american.edu.ng
Founded 2005 in partnership with the American Univ., Washington DC, USA
Number of students: 200

Pres.: Dr DAVID HUWILER
Dean for Students and Registrar: Dr BARRY MORRIS

BABCOCK UNIVERSITY

Ilishan-Remo, Ogun
Telephone: (1) 7613797
E-mail: registrar@babcockuni.edu.ng
Internet: www.babcockuni.edu.ng
Founded 1999, fmrly Adventist Seminary of West Africa
Seventh-Day Adventist Church control
Language of instruction: English

Pres. and Vice-Chancellor: Prof. JAMES KAYODE MAKINDE

Number of teachers: 233
Number of students: 5,600
Library of 58,000 vols, 664 periodicals

DEANS

School of Education and Humanities: Prof. JOSHUA M. A. OYINLOYE
School of Law and Security Studies: ZAC O. OLOMOJOBI
School of Management and Social Sciences: (vacant)
School of Science and Technology: Prof. GRACE OLUWATOYIN TAYO

PROFESSORS

School of Education and Humanities
  Department of History and International Studies:
    ADEWOYE, O., Legal History
    NENGEL, J. G., Intergroup Relations
  Department of Languages and Literary Studies:
    AKPOROBARO, I. A., Literary Studies, African and European Literature
    OSISANWO, I. A., English Language, Phonetics and Grammar
  Department of Mass Communication:
    AKANBI, D. K., Instructional Media and Communication
    ALAO, D., Journalism and International Communication
    KIO, J., Speech Communication and Human Relations

School of Law and Security Studies:
    AGEDE, I. S., Alternative Dispute Resolution, Arbitration, Conflict of Law and Jurisprudence
    OLIYIDE, S., Banking, Commercial Law and Law of International Trade
    OLOMOJOBO, Z. O., Military and Constitutional Law

School of Management and Social Sciences:
    AINA, A., Political Science, Political Strategies
    AJAYI, F., Political Science
    AKINOLA, J., Educational Management
    ASIKA, N., Business Management, Research Methods
    MAKINDE, J., Political Science, Political History
    OGUNDAIRO, M., Economics
    OLALOKU, F., Economics

School of Science and Technology
    Department of Agriculture:
      DARAMOLA, D. S., Soil Science
      TAYO, G. O., Animal Nutrition
    Department of Biosciences and Biotechnology:
      FAPOHUNDA, S. O., Industrial Microbiology
      KOLAWOLE, D. O., Medical Microbiology
    Department of Chemical and Environmental Sciences:
      ESAN, E. B., Botany and Biotechnology
      OGUNWENMO, K. O., Biosystematics and Cytogenetics
      ONAJOBI, F. D., Lipids and Membrane Biochemistry
    Department of Computer and Mathematics:
      ADELODUN, J. F., Mathematics
      OMOTOSHO, O. J., Computer Engineering and Instrumentation
    Department of Nursing Sciences:
      FASHINA, E. M., Clinical Psychology and Nursing
    Department of Public and Allied Health:
      AKINBOYE, D. O., Medical Parasitology

FAJEWONYOMI, B. A., Community Health and Epidemiology

BENSON IDAHOSA UNIVERSITY

PMB 1100, University Way, Off Upper Adesuwa Grammar School Rd, Benin City
Telephone: (52) 253764
E-mail: president@biu.edu.ng
Internet: www.biu.edu.ng
Founded 2002
Private control
Language of instruction: English
Vice-Chancellor: Prof. MACDONALD IDU
Chief Financial Officer: ANDY AKEN'OVA
Librarian: W. MOKOGWU (acting)
Library of 48,000 vols, 450 periodicals
Number of teachers: 211
Number of students: 2,821 (f.t.e.)

DEANS

Faculty of Agriculture and Agricultural Technology: Prof. J. O. OYEDEJI
Faculty of Basic Sciences: Dr C. L. IGELEKE
Faculty of Law: Prof. C. C. OHURUOGU

COVENANT UNIVERSITY

10 km Idiroko Rd, Canaan Land, Ota, Ogun State
Telephone: (1) 7900724
E-mail: contact@covenantuniversity.com
Internet: www.covenantuniversity.com
Founded 2002
Colleges of business and social sciences, human devt, science and technology
Chancellor: Dr DAVID OYEDEPO
Vice-Chancellor: Prof. AIZE OLOHIGBE IMOUO-KHOME OBAYAN

IGBINEDION UNIVERSITY

PMB 0006, Okada, Benin-City
Telephone: (52) 260005
E-mail: pefs@skannet.com
Internet: www.igbinedionuniversity.edu.ng
Founded 1999
Vice-Chancellor: Prof. EGHOSA EMMANUEL OSAGHAE
Deputy Vice-Chancellor: Prof. L. C. CHIEDOZI
Dean for Student Affairs: Prof. GILBERT O. NWOBU
Registrar: Dr SALLY AKWUGO ASAGWARA
Librarian: Dr R. OLORUNSOLA (acting)

DEANS AND PROVOSTS

College of Agriculture: Prof. ADETOKUNBO ADEOLA (Dean)
College of Arts and Social Sciences: Dr ANGELU M. ONWUEJEOGU (Dean)
College of Business and Management Studies: Prof. A. E. OKOYE (Dean)
College of Engineering: Dr T. S. WARA (acting) (Dean)
College of Health Sciences: Prof. TUNDE DARAMOLA (Provost)
College of Law: Prof. M. O. OGUNGBE (Dean)
College of Natural and Applied Sciences: Prof. ALEXANDER E. ODAIBO (Dean)
College of Pharmacy: Prof. SAMSON ESEZOBOR (Dean)
School of Basic Medical Sciences: Prof. A. A. ODUTOGA (Dean)
School of Clinical Medicine: Prof. L. C. CHIEDOZIE (Dean)
School of Postgraduate Studies: Prof. ABAYOMI ONI (Dean)

PROFESSORS

ADELUSI, Pharmacy
ADEOLA, A., Wildlife and Forestry
AGBA, M., Microbiology

AGBONLAHOR, D., Microbiology and Medical Laboratory Sciences
AIBONI, S., Law
AWOGUN, I., Medical Microbiology
BAXTER-GRILLO, D., Anatomy
CHIEDOZIE, L., Surgery
DARAMOLA, T., Community Health
EKEH, J., Electrical and Electronic Engineering
EKUNDARE, R., Economics
ESEZOBOR, S., Pharmacy
NAREBO, D., Law
NWOBU, G., Medical Laboratory Sciences
ODAIBO, A., Zoology
ODUTUGA, A., Biochemistry
OFUOROFO, I., Chemical Pathology
OGUNBIYI, J., Morbid Anatomy
OGUNGBE, M., Law
OKOYE, A., Accountancy
OLUOHA, U., Chemical Pathology
ONI, A., Mechanical Engineering
ONWUJEOGWU, A., Sociology and Anthropology
OSAGHAE, Political Science
OSENI, T., Agronomy
OSIFO, N., Pharmacology
PADONU, M., Community Health
YESUFU, English

PAN-AFRICAN UNIVERSITY

2 Ahmed Onibudo St, POB 73688, Victoria Island, Lagos
Telephone: (1) 3200695
E-mail: info@pau.edu.ng
Founded 2002
Postgraduate degree programmes in business administration and economics
Vice-Chancellor: Prof. ALBERT J. ALOS

Polytechnics and Colleges

Akanu Ibiam Federal Polytechnic, Unwana: PMB 1007, Afikpo, Ebonyi State; tel. (90) 500180; f. 1981; schools of business, engineering technology, environmental studies, industrial technology, science and general studies; library: 36,200 vols, 350,000 ebooks; 290 teachers; 5,200 students; Rector F. O. OTUNTA; Registrar A. D. OKONO.

Auchi Polytechnic: PMB 13, Benin–Okene Rd, Auchi, Edo State; tel. (57) 200159; e-mail registrar@auchipoly.edu.ng; internet www.auchipoly.edu.ng; f. 1963 as technical college, current status 1973; schools of applied sciences and technology, art and design, business studies, engineering technology, environmental studies; library: 38,250 vols; 310 teachers; 9,500 students; Rector Dr PHILIPA O. IDOGHO; Registrar Dr M. AASHIK-PELOKHA.

Benue State Polytechnic, Ugbokolo: PMB 01, Okpokwu, Ugbokolo, Benue State; Km 45, Otukpo-Enugu Rd, Okpokwu, Ugbokolo, Benue State; tel. (44) 661930; e-mail inquiry@benpolyonline.edu.ng; internet www.benpolyonline.edu.ng; f. 1976 as Murtala College of Arts, Science and Technology, current name adopted 1983; schools of administrative and vocational studies, art, design and printing, business and management studies, engineering technology, environmental sciences, general and preliminary studies, technology; 200 teachers; 5,000 students; Rector H. O. A. OLUMA; Registrar MOSES ABAH EGWU.

Federal College of Agriculture, Akure: Ado-Ekiti Rd, Akure, Ondo State; tel. (34) 240891; e-mail info@feca.edu.ng; internet www.feca.edu.ng; f. 1957; library: 10,000 vols; 30 teachers; 1,000 students; Prin. Dr A. O. AYODELE.

Federal College of Agriculture, Ibadan: PMB 5029, Moor Plantation, Ibadan; tel. (2) 3444165; internet www.fcaib.edu.ng; f. 1921; 33 teachers; 319 students; Provost T. A. ADEGBULUGBE.

Federal College of Forestry: c/o Forestry Research Institute of Nigeria, PMB 5054, Ibadan; tel. (22) 411035; f. 1941; library: 5,251 vols; 178 teachers; 830 students; Exec. Dir S. O. BADEJO; Deputy Provost Dr BENSON OSIKABOR.

Federal Polytechnic, Ado-Ekiti: PMB 5351, Ado-Ekiti, Ekiti State; tel. (30) 250523; e-mail fedpolyado@fedpolyado.org; internet www.fedpolyado.org; f. 1977; schools of business studies, engineering, environmental studies, science and computer studies; library: 15,706 vols, 845 periodicals; 290 teachers; 6,161 students; Rector Prof. O. AJAJA; Registrar A. I. AJAYI; publs *Expertus* (2 a year), *Research Journal* (1 a year).

Federal Polytechnic, Bauchi: PMB 0231, Bauchi; Along Dass Rd, Gwallameji Village, Bauchi; tel. (77) 543630; e-mail info@fptb.edu.ng; internet fptb.edu.ng; f. 1979; schools of business studies, engineering technology, environmental technology, general studies, technology; library: 35,900 vols; 257 teachers; 8,667 students; Rector Dr SHUAIBU MUSA; Registrar ALHAJI LABARAN IBRAHIM.

Federal Polytechnic, Bida: PMB 55, Bida, Niger State; tel. (66) 461707; internet www.fedpolybida.edu.ng; f. 1977; schools of applied arts and sciences, business and management studies, engineering technology, environmental studies, preliminary studies; library: 26,105 vols; 380 teachers; 10,000 students; Rector ABDULLAHI SULE; Registrar S. F. IKO; publ. *Polymath Journal.*

Federal Polytechnic, Ede: PMB 231, Ede, Osun State; Polytechnic Rd, Ede, Osun State; tel. (06) 7448642; e-mail admissions@federalpolyede.edu.ng; internet www.federalpolyede.edu.ng; f. 1992; Rector and CEO PATRICK HUSSAIN; Registrar O. A. OGUNLEYE.

Federal Polytechnic, Idah: PMB 1037, Idah, Kogi State; tel. (58) 800128; internet www.federalpolyidah.edu.ng; f. 1977; schools of business studies, engineering, environmental studies, preliminary studies and continuing education, technology; library: 19,490 vols; 140 teachers; 3,200 students; Rector MATTHEW ITOPA AKPATA; Registrar J. A. ELAIGWU.

Federal Polytechnic, Ilaro: PMB 50, Ilaro, Ogun State; tel. (39) 440005; internet www.federalpolyilaro.edu.ng; f. 1979; schools of applied science, engineering, environmental studies, management studies, part-time studies; library: 16,000 vols; 3,000 students; Rector Dr R. A. OLOYO; Registrar R. O. EGBEYEMI.

Federal Polytechnic, Kaura Namoda: PMB 1012, Kaura-Namoda, Zamfara State; tel. (63) 60452; e-mail namodapoly@plet.net; f. 1983; schools of business management, engineering, environmental studies, general studies, science and technology; library: 11,450 vols; 152 teachers; 3,268 students; Rector Eng. NA'INNA MOHAMMAD AUDI; Registrar A. DANBOYI; publs *Kanajoge* (2 a year), *Namoda Telescope* (2 a year).

Federal Polytechnic, Mubi: PMB 35, Mubi, Adamawa State; tel. (75) 882771; e-mail info@federalpolytechnicmubi.edu.ng; internet www.federalpolytechnicmubi.edu.ng; f. 1979; schools of business studies and general studies, engineering, science and technology; library: 23,601 vols; 184 teachers; 3,338 students; Rector ALHAJI M. A. ABBA; Registrar B. BELLO; publs *Applied*

Science and Management (1 a year), *Sabon Dale* (1 a year).

Federal Polytechnic, Nasarawa: PMB 001, Nasarawa, Nasarawa State; tel. (47) 66707; e-mail fpnas@yahoo.com; f. 1983; Rector Dr IDRIS BUGAJE.

Federal Polytechnic, Nekede: PMB 1036, Owerri, Imo State; tel. (83) 231516; internet www.federalpolynekede.net; f. 1978; schools of business and public administration, engineering technology, environmental design, general studies, industrial sciences; library: 24,837 vols; 257 teachers; 30,000 students; Rector Eng. O. I. NWANKWO; Registrar C. D. ONUKOGU.

Federal Polytechnic, Offa: PMB 420, Offa, Kwara State; tel. (31) 800160; internet www.fedpoffa.edu.ng; f. 1979; Rector Dr ABDUL-RAZAQ BELLO.

Federal Polytechnic Oko: PMB 21, Aguata, Anambra State; tel. (48) 911144; e-mail registrar@federalpolyoko.edu.ng; internet www.federalpolyoko.edu.ng; f. 1979; schools of applied science technology, arts, design and printing technology, business, engineering technology, environmental design and technology, financial studies, general studies, information technology; library: 210,000 vols; 9,298 students; Rector GODWIN ONU; Registrar TONY OLIH NWAOKO-LOBIA; Librarian F. O. OBODOEZE; publs *Federal Polytechnic Library* (4 a year), *Journal of Accountancy* (2 a year), *The Polytechnic Accountant* (1 a year).

Federal School of Dental Technology and Therapy, Enugu: PMB 01473, Enugu; tel. (42) 290926; e-mail fedsdtten@fedsdtten.edu.ng; internet www.fedsdtten.edu.ng; f. 1955 as Federal School of Dental Technology and Hygiene, current name adopted 1978; Rector Dr KEHINDE SOFOLUWE; Registrar ANIGBO P. O.

Hassan Usman Katsina Polytechnic: PMB 2052, Katsina; tel. (65) 32816; f. 1983; colleges of administration and management studies, legal and general studies, science and technology; library: 18,000 vols; 501 teachers; 3,506 students; Rector KABIR IBRA-HIM MATAZU; Registrar ABDU HALLIRU ABDUL-LAHI.

Institute of Management and Technology: PMB 01079, Enugu, Enugu State; tel. (42) 250416; e-mail imtregistry@imt.edu.ng; internet www.imt.edu.ng; f. 1973; schools of business studies, communication arts, distance learning and continuing education, engineering, financial studies, general studies, technology; library: 50,000 vols; 360 teachers; 20,000 students; Rector Prof. E. C. ONYENEJE; Registrar BARTH O. EZEA; publs *Journal of Financial Studies* (1 a year), *Journal of Technology Education* (1 a year).

Kaduna Polytechnic: PMB 2021, Kaduna; tel. (62) 211551; e-mail info@kadunapolytechnic.edu.ng; internet kadunapolytechnic.edu.ng; f. 1968; library: 56,000 vols; 1,413 teachers; 20,000 students; Rector Dr MOHAMMED BELLO IBRAHIM; Registrar ZAYYANA I. KUKASHEKA.

Kano State Polytechnic: PMB 3401, B. U. K. Rd, Kano; tel. (64) 666058; internet www.kanostatepoly.net; f. 1976; schools of environmental studies, general studies, management studies, rural technology and entrepreneurship development, technology; library: 30,276 vols; 510 teachers; 12,826 students; Rector Arch. HAMZA SAID; Registrar SULAIMAN ABDULLAHI.

Kwara State Polytechnic: PMB 1375, Ilorin; tel. (31) 221441; internet www.kwarapolytechnic.com; f. 1972; library: 50,155 vols; 650 teachers; 17,000 students;

Rector ALHAJI MAS'UD ELELU; Registrar M. O. SALAMI; publ. *Techforum* (2 a year).

Lagos State Polytechnic: PMB 21606, Ikeja, Lagos State; tel. (1) 523528; e-mail support@laspotech.net; internet www.laspotech.net; f. 1977; schools of agriculture, engineering, environmental technology, management technology, technology; library: 29,558 vols, 1,880 spec. collns; 800 teachers; 30,000 students; Rector Dr ABDULAZEEZ A. LAWAL; Registrar OLUWOLE O. OJIKUTU; publ. *Poly Handbook* (1 a year).

Moshood Abiola Polytechnic, Abeokuta: PMB 2210, Abeokuta,, Ogun State; tel. (80) 33230941; e-mail mapolylib2002@yahoo.com; internet www.mapoly.educ.ng; f. 1979; schools of business and management studies, communication and general studies, engineering, environmental studies, pure and applied science; centre for part-time studies; library: 22,097 vols; 165 teachers; 15,000 students; Rector ALHAJI WAHEED A. KADIRI; Registrar A. B. BADMOS; publs *Liberal Forum* (1 a year), *Polymath* (1 a year), *Social Philosophy* (1 a year).

National Eye Centre: Off Nnamdi Azikiwe Way, PMB 2267, Kaduna; tel. (62) 313956; e-mail neckad@yahoo.com; f. 1979; provides postgraduate ophthalmic training (medical and surgical), TOT IOL microsurgical course, ophthalmic nursing training, clinical services; 9 teachers; 16 students; Chief Medical Dir Dr C. P. OZEMELA.

Petroleum Training Institute: PMB 20, Effurun, Delta State; tel. (53) 250774; e-mail info@pti.edu.ng; internet www.pti.edu.ng; f. 1972; library: 54,013 vols; 189 teachers; 2,520 students; Principal and Chief Exec. N. C. DENNAR; Registrar A. S. EWERE.

Plateau State Polytechnic, Barkin Ladi: PMB 02023, Bukuru, Plateau State; internet www.plapoly.edu.ng; f. 1978, current status 1980; schools of administration and business studies, engineering technology, environmental studies, general studies, management studies, science and technology; centre for continuing education, consultancy and applied research div.; library: 11,393 vols; 130 teachers; 2,260 students; Rector DUADA G. GYEMANG.

Polytechnic, Calabar: PMB 1110, Calabar, Cross River State; tel. (87) 222303; f. 1973; schools of agriculture, applied science, business and management, communication arts, education, engineering, environmental studies; computer centre, continuing education centre, centre for general and preliminary studies, industrial coordination and public relations unit, polytechnic industrial consultancy services unit; library: 25,000 vols; 213 teachers; 5,000 students; Rector Eng. R. E. EKANEM; Registrar G. F. A. ONUGBA.

Polytechnic, Ibadan: PMB 22, U. I. Post Office, Ibadan; tel. (22) 8133356769; e-mail rector@polyibadan.edu.ng; f. 1961, polytechnic status 1971; faculties of business and communication studies, engineering, environmental studies, financial and management studies, science; library: 68,000 vols; 576 teachers; 9,250 students; Rector Prof. O. A. ODUNOLA; Registrar TOSHO AYANWALE.

Rufus Giwa Polytechnic, Owo: Km 46, Owo-Benin Rd, Owo, Ondo State; tel. (803) 4730783; internet www.rugipo.edu.ng; f. 1978, renamed Ondo State Polytechnic 1984, current name adopted 2003; faculties of agricultural technology, business studies, engineering technology, environmental studies, food technology, information technology; centre of research and development; library: 25,000 vols; 180 teachers; 9,800 students; Rector Prof. IGBEKELE AJIBEFUN; Registrar P.T. AKINLABI; publ. *RUGIPO Journal.*

Waziri Umaru Federal Polytechnic, Birnin Kebbi: PMB 1034, Birnin Kebbi, Kebbi State; tel. (68) 320597; e-mail info@wufpbk .com; f. 1976; schools of accounting and finance, business and public administration, environmental design, industrial engineering, natural resources engineering, sciences, surveying and land administration, vocational and technical education; library: 13,761 vols; 350 teachers; 3,678 students; Rector MUHAMMAD KABIR NABADE; Registrar BELLO BAGUDU ABUBAKAR.

Yaba College of Technology: PMB 2011, Yaba, Lagos State 234; tel. (1) 7742155; e-mail registrar@yabatech.edu.ng; internet www.yabatech.edu.ng; f. 1948; schools of art, design and printing, engineering, environmental studies, management, science, technology; library: 70,000 vols; 800 teachers; 14,000 students; Rector O. OWOSO; Registrar F. F. TAIWO; publ. *YCT Academic Journal.*

NORWAY

The Higher Education System

The oldest current institutions of higher education were founded before Norway declared its independence from Swedish rule in 1905. The state Universitetet i Oslo (founded in 1811) is the oldest university; the next oldest university is the state Universitetet for Miljø- og Biovitenskap (Norwegian University of Life Sciences—founded in 1859). The first institution founded in the independent period was the private Teologiske Menighetsfakultet (Norwegian Lutheran School of Theology—founded in 1907). In 2012 there were seven public universities, six specialized institutions at university level (five public and one private), and 24 public and two private university colleges. The latter category offer three-year professional Bachelors programmes in engineering or nursing, for example. In addition there are 25 private higher education institutions which receive public funding. In 2010 some 224,706 students were enrolled in tertiary education.

Higher education is administered according to Act No. 15 on Universities and University Colleges (2005, amended 2009). Norway participates in the Bologna Process to establish a European Higher Education Area, the first phase of which is to adopt a credit-based system of comparable degrees with two main cycles (undergraduate and graduate). The Norwegian Agency for Quality Assurance in Education (NOKUT) is an independent government body established in 2003 to monitor and develop the quality of higher education in Norway through evaluation, accreditation and recognition of quality assurance systems, institutions and study programmes. The primary responsibility for quality assurance rests with the individual higher education institution, but internal quality assurance systems must adhere to nationally set standards and are externally evaluated by NOKUT. Institutions and programmes are not accredited for a defined period; accreditation is valid until revoked. NOKUT makes its decisions independently of the Ministry of Education and Research. Norway is the only country in Europe that still adheres to the policy of free higher education for all students regardless of country of origin. As a result, Norwegian institutions have reported significant increases in the number of applications received from foreign students in recent years. There have been increasingly vocal calls for universities to be afforded greater economic autonomy, with the right to determine how best to divest funding from the Government.

Admission to higher education is on the basis of successful completion of secondary education; however, since 2000 applicants have also been admitted with non-formal qualifications. In 2003 a two-tier Bachelorgrad and Mastergrad degree system was implemented in accordance with the principles of the Bologna Process. Norwegian institutions award degrees on the basis of the European Credit Transfers System, with each year equivalent to 60 'credits'. The standard undergraduate degree is the Bachelorgrad, which lasts three years, and the first postgraduate degree is the Mastergrad, a course lasting one-and-a-half to two years. The final postgraduate and highest university degree is the Doktorgrad, awarded after three to four years of study; the title of the degree awarded may vary depending on the subject area.

Post-secondary vocational and technical education is available at technical colleges (Teckniske Fagskoler), university colleges and state colleges. Programmes at these institutions last for two to three years.

Regulatory and Representative Bodies

GOVERNMENT

Ministry of Culture: POB 8030 Dep., 0030 Oslo; Akersgt. 59, Oslo; tel. 22-24-90-90; e-mail postmottak@kud.dep.no; internet www.regjeringen.no/kud; Minister THORHILD WIDVEY.

Ministry of Education and Research: POB 8119 Dep., 0032 Oslo; Kirkegata 18, Oslo; tel. 22-24-90-90; e-mail postmottak@kd.dep.no; internet www.regjeringen.no/kd; Minister TORBJØRN RØE ISAKSEN.

ACCREDITATION

ENIC/NARIC Norway: NOKUT—Norwegian Agency for Quality Assurance in Education, POB 1708, 1327 Lysaker; tel. 21-02-18-60; e-mail postmottak@nokut.no; internet www.nokut.no; f. 2003; Dir-Gen. TERJE MØRLAND.

Nasjonalt Organ for Kvalitet i Utdanningen (Norwegian Agency for Quality Assurance in Education): POB 1708 Vika, 0121 Oslo; Kronprinsensgt. 9, Oslo; tel. 21-02-18-00; e-mail postmottak@nokut.no; internet www.nokut.no; f. 2003; controls and develops the quality of Norwegian higher education instns through the evaluation, accreditation and recognition of quality assurance systems, instns and education programmes; Chair. Prof. BORGHILD BARTH-H ROALD; Dir-Gen. TERJE MØRLAND.

NATIONAL BODIES

Norges Forskningsråd (The Research Council of Norway): POB 2700, St Hanshaugen, 0131 Oslo; Stensberggt 26, Oslo; tel. 22-03-70-00; e-mail post@forskningsradet.no; internet www.forskningsradet.no; attached to Min. of Education and Research; promotes and supports basic and applied research in all areas of science, technology, medicine and the humanities; awards research grants and fellowships and runs its own research establishments (see under Research Institutes); Chair. INGVILD MYHRE; Dir-Gen. ARVID HALLÉN; publ. *Forskning* (4 a year).

Norsk Forbund for Fjernundervisning og Fleksibel Utdanning (NFF) (Norwegian Association for Distance Education and Flexible Education): Lilleakerveien 23, 0283 Oslo; tel. 22-51-04-80; e-mail nade@nade-nff.no; internet www.nade-nff.no; f. 1968; works for propagation and devt of distance learning methods; promotes research and devt regarding distance education; organizes meetings and confs; 37 mems; Chair. SVEIN QVIST-ERIKSEN; Exec. Dir TORHILD SLÅTTO; publ. *Synkron* (magazine).

Riksantikvaren (Directorate for Cultural Heritage): Dronningensgt. 13, POB 8196 Dep., 0034 Oslo; tel. 22-94-04-00; e-mail postmottak@ra.no; internet www.riksantikvaren.no; f. 1912; attached to Min. of the Environment; directorate responsible for nat. monuments and sites, medieval bldgs; archives; library of 60,000 vols, 700,000 photographs; special collns incl. Norwegian churches, restoration and conservation of paintings and sculptures; Dir-Gen. JØRN HOLME; publs *La stå!* (Let Stand!, 2 a year), *Arringer* (Tree Rings, 1 a year).

Senter for Internasjonalisering av Utdanning (SIU) (Norwegian Centre for International Cooperation in Education): POB 1093, 5809 Bergen; Vaskerelven 39, 5014 Bergen; tel. 55-30-38-00; e-mail siu@siu.no; internet siu.no; f. 2004; promotes int. cooperation in education and research; Chair. Prof. Dr DORIS JORDE; Dir-Gen. ALF RASMUSSEN (acting); publ. *Global Knowledge* (magazine on politics and global implication in research and higher education).

Universitets- og Høgskolerådet (Norwegian Association of Higher Education Institutions): Pilestredet 46, 0167 Oslo; tel. 22-45-39-50; e-mail postmottak@uhr.no; internet www.uhr.no; f. 2000 by merger of the Norwegian Ccl of State Colleges and the Norwegian Ccl of Univs; 46 mem. instns; Chair. JAN I. HAALAND; Gen. Sec. OLA STAVE.

Learned Societies

GENERAL

Det Kongelige Norske Videnskabers Selskab (Royal Norwegian Society of Sciences and Letters): Erling Skakkesgt. 47c, Postuttak, 7491 Trondheim; tel. 73-59-21-57; e-mail post@dknvs.no; internet www.dknvs.no; f. 1760, current name adopted and status 1767; promotes scholarship by arranging lecture meetings, demonstrations and debates on scholarly topics; disseminates scholarly knowledge to the general public; supports scholarly projects financially; 686 mems (541 Norwegian mems, 145 foreign mems, 1 hon. mem., 18 assoc. mems); Pres. Prof. HELGE HOLDEN; Sec.-Gen. KRISTIAN OVERSKAUG; publ. *Skrifter*.

Norske Videnskaps-Akademi (Norwegian Academy of Science and Letters): Drammensveien 78, 0271 Oslo; tel. 22-12-10-90; e-mail dnva@online.no; internet www.dnva .no; f. 1857; sections of mathematics and natural sciences, historical and philosophical sciences; 895 mems; Pres. Prof. KIRSTI STRØM BULL; Sec.-Gen. Prof. ØIVIND ANDERSEN; publs *Årbok, Avhandlinger, Physica Scripta* (12 a year), *Zoologica Scripta* (6 a year).

ARCHITECTURE AND TOWN PLANNING

Norske Arkitekters Landsforbund (NAL) (Norwegian Architects' Association): Josefines gt. 34, 0351 Oslo; tel. 23-33-25-00; e-mail nal@arkitektur.no; internet www .arkitektur.no; f. 1911; works to improve the framework for architecture within various public and private instns; 3,600 mems; Pres. KIM SKAARA; Man. Dir PÅL STEPHENSEN; publs *Arkitektnytt* (20 a year), *Byggekunst* (8 a year), *Norske Arkitektkonkurranser*.

BIBLIOGRAPHY, LIBRARY SCIENCE AND MUSEOLOGY

Norsk Bibliotekforening (Norwegian Library Association): POB 6540, Etterstad, 0606 Oslo; tel. 23-24-34-30; e-mail nbf@ norskbibliotekforening.no; internet www .norskbibliotekforening.no; f. 1913; promotes devt of library, documentation and information activities; 3,200 mems; Pres. INGEBORG RYGH HJORTHEN; Sec.-Gen. HEGE NEWTH NOURI; publ. *Bibliotekforum* (10 a year).

ECONOMICS, LAW AND POLITICS

Norsk Forening for Internasjonal Rett (Norwegian Branch of the International Law Association): c/o Wiersholm Mellbye and Bech, POB 1400 Vika, 0115 Oslo; Ruseløkkveien 26, 0115 Oslo; tel. 21-02-10-00; e-mail veem@wiersholm.no; internet foreninger.uio .no/nfir; f. 1925; discussion of questions of int. law, incl. int. and civil law; supports efforts to develop int. law; 77 mems; Pres. ROLF EINAR FIFE; Sec. SIV MYRVOLD.

Statsøkonomisk Forening (Economic Association of Norway): Ullern Alle 59, 0381 Oslo; tel. 63-90-05-76; f. 1883; 300 mems; Pres. Prof. KJELL STORVIK; Sec. BJÖRN STENSETH.

FINE AND PERFORMING ARTS

Arts Council Norway: POB 8052, Dep, 0031 Oslo; tel. 21-04-58-00; e-mail post@ kulturrad.no; internet www.kulturradet.no; f. 1965, merged with ABM-utvikling—Statens Senter for Arkiv, Bibliotek og Museum 2011; attached to Min. of Culture; encourages artistic life and cultural activities in Norway; distributes the resources of Cultural Fund in grants and subsidies; Chair. YNGVE SLETTHOLM; Dir ANNE AASHEIM; publs *Notatserien* (irregular), *Rapportserien* (irregular).

Norske Billedkunstnere (Norwegian Visual Artists Association): Grubbegt. 14, 0179 Oslo; tel. 23-25-60-30; e-mail nbk@ billedkunst.no; internet www.billedkunst.no/ nbk; f. 1889, reorganized 1979 and 1988; the Norwegian Govt's Advisory Bd on questions relating to graphic arts; mem. of UNESCO's Int. Asscn of Art (IAA); promotes and secures intellectual, social, legislative and economic interest of the professional visual artist; incl. 14 regional orgs, 5 nat. asscns and a society for the younger artists; 2,700 mems; Chair.

HILDE ROGNSKOG; Sec. GJERT GJERTSEN; publ. *Billedkunstneren* (7 a year).

HISTORY, GEOGRAPHY AND ARCHAEOLOGY

Fortidsminneforeningen (Foreningen til norske Fortidsminnesmerkers Bevaring) (Society for the Preservation of Norwegian Ancient Monuments): Dronningensgt. 11, 0152 Oslo; tel. 23-31-70-70; e-mail post@fortidsminneforeningen.no; internet www.fortidsminneforeningen.no; f. 1844; works towards protecting Norwegian cultural heritage sites and creating a common understanding of their value; owns and cares for 40 properties, among those 8 stave churches incl. the World Heritage site at Urnes; 7,500 mems; Dir LEIF KAHRS JAEGER; Sec.-Gen. ELI-SOFIE THORNE (acting); publs *Årbok* (1 a year), *Fortidsvern* (4 a year), *Gode Råd serien* (irregular).

Kirkehistorisk Samfunn (Church History Society): Jernbaneveien 127, 1369 Stabekk; f. 1956; 39 mems; Pres. Prof. JAN SCHUMACHER; Sec. Prof. Dr PEDER A. EIDBERG.

Landslaget for Lokalhistorie (National Association of Local History): Institutt for Historie og Klassiske Fag, NTNU, 7491 Trondheim; tel. 73-59-64-33; e-mail post@ historielag.org; f. 1920; 415 mem. historical socs; Pres. KURT TVERLI; Man. JOSTEIN MOLDE; publs *Heimen* (4 a year), *Lokalhistorisk* (4 a year).

Norsk Arkeologisk Selskap (Norwegian Archaeological Society): Huk Aveny 35, 0287 Oslo; tel. 22-43-87-92; e-mail nas@arkeologi .no; internet www.arkeologi.no; f. 1936; supports archaeological research; 800 mems; Pres. OLE RIKARD HØISÆTHER; Sec.-Gen. EGIL MIKKELSEN; publ. *Viking* (1 a year).

Den Norske Historiske Forening (Norwegian Historical Association): IHR, UiT Norges Arktiske Universitet, POB 6050, Langnes, 9037 Tromso; tel. 77-66-03-06; e-mail post@hifo.no; internet www.hifo.no; f. 1869; works for Norwegian historical research; 11 local brs; 1,000 mems; Pres. KARI AGA MYKLEBOST; Sec. CHRISTEL MISUND DOMAAS; publ. *Historisk Tidsskrift* (4 a year).

Norsk Lokalhistorisk Institutt (Norwegian Institute of Local History): POB 8045 Dep, 0031 Oslo; Observatoriegata 1B, 0254 Oslo; tel. 22-92-51-30; e-mail nli@ lokalhistorie.no; internet www.lokalhistorie .no; f. 1955; guidance for local historians, research in local history incl. publication of sources; library of 20,000 vols; Dir KNUT SPRAUTEN.

Norsk Slektshistorisk Forening (Norwegian Genealogical Society): Øvre Slottsgt. 2B, 0157 Oslo; tel. 47-77-06-77; e-mail kontor@ genealogi.no; internet www.genealogi.no; f. 1926; 1,680 mems; Chair. RUNE NEDRUD; Sec. JAN I. KRISTIANSEN; publs *Genealogen* (2 a year), *Norsk Slektshistorisk Tidsskrift* (2 a year).

LANGUAGE AND LITERATURE

Alliance Française: POB 34, Sentrum, 5803 Bergen; Vågsallmenningen 12, Gamle Norges Bank, 3. etasje, Bergen; e-mail alliance.francaise@uib.no; internet www .france-bergen.no; f. 1898; offers courses and examinations in French language and culture; promotes cultural exchange with France; 100 mems; Pres. BERNADETTE MOUTTE; Sec. ANNE-BERIT HAGEN.

British Council: c/o Kontorfellesskapet, Bogstadveien 6, 0355 Oslo; tel. 19-57-77-55; e-mail norway.enquiries@britishcouncil.org; internet www.britishcouncil.org/norway; offers courses and examinations in English language and British culture and promotes

cultural exchange with the UK; Country Dir SARAH PROSSER.

Den Norske Forfatterforening (Norwegian Authors' Union): POB 327 Sentrum, 0103 Oslo; tel. 23-35-76-20; e-mail post@ forfatterforeningen.no; internet www .forfatterforeningen.no; f. 1893; protects and promotes Norwegian literature; safeguards Norwegian interests of authors; 615 mems; Chair. SIGMUND LØVÅSEN; Gen. Sec. METTE MØLLER.

Det Norske Akademi for Sprog og Litteratur (Norwegian Academy for Language and Literature): Rosenborggaten 3, 0356 Oslo; tel. 22-60-88-59; e-mail akademiet@ riksmalsforbundet.no; internet www .riksmalsforbundet.no; f. 1953; protects and authorizes dictionaries of the traditional 'Riksmaal'; 50 mems; Chair. NILS HEYERDAHL; Treas. TOR GUTTU.

Goethe-Institut: Grønland 16, 0188 Oslo; tel. 22-05-78-80; e-mail info@oslo.goethe.org; internet www.goethe.de/ins/no/osl; offers courses and examinations in German language and culture and promotes cultural exchange with Germany; library of 6,000 vols, 30 periodicals; Dir Dr KRISTIAN ZAPPEL.

Norsk PEN (Norwegian Centre of International PEN): Wergelandsveien 29, 0167 Oslo; tel. 22-60-74-50; e-mail pen@norskpen .no; internet www.norskpen.no; f. 1922; contact for Norwegian writers with the rest of the writing world; defends freedom of expression worldwide, with focus on Afghanistan, Belarus, People's Republic of China, Tunisia, Turkey and the Middle East; 400 mems; Pres. ANDERS HEGER; Sec.-Gen. CARL MORTEN IVERSEN.

MEDICINE

Norske Laegeforening (Norwegian Medical Association): POB 1152 Sentrum, 0107 Oslo; Akersgata 2, 0158 Oslo; tel. 23-10-90-00; e-mail legeforeningen@legeforeningen .no; internet legeforeningen.no; f. 1886; works for professional, social and economic interests of its mems; promotes quality in medical education and medical scientific devt; promotes medical science work with health policy issues; 28,510 mems; Pres. Dr HEGE GJESSING; Sec.-Gen. Dr GEIR RIISE; publ. *Tidsskrift for den norske lægeforening* (24 a year).

Norske Medicinske Selskab (Norwegian Medical Society): POB 1130 Blindern, 0318 Oslo; tel. 22-85-06-73; e-mail oivind.larsen@ medisin.uio.no; internet www.dnms.no; f. 1833 as continuation of a medical reading soc.; organizes open medical lectures, medical and cultural programmes; 250 mems; Chair. Prof. Dr ØIVIND LARSEN; Sec. Dr ASTRID NYLENNA; publ. *Michael Quarterly* (4 a year).

Norske Tannlegeforening (NTF) (Norwegian Dental Association): POB 2073 Vika, 0125 Oslo; Haakon VIIs gt 6, 0161 Oslo; tel. 22-54-74-00; e-mail post@tannlegeforeningen .no; internet www.tannlegeforeningen.no; f. 1884; maintains professional, economic and social interests of dentists; 6,228 mems; Pres. STEINUM CAMILLA HANSEN; Sec.-Gen. RICHARD R. NÆSS (acting); publ. *Den norske tannlegeforenings Tidende* (15 a year).

Norsk Farmasøytisk Selskap (Norwegian Pharmaceutical Society): POB 5070, Majorstuen, 0301 Oslo; Apotekernes Hus, Slemdalsveien 1, 0369 Oslo; tel. 21-62-02-23; e-mail post@nfs.no; internet www.nfs.no; f. 1924; furthers scientific and practical devt of pharmacy; 550 mems; Chair. Dr HEGE HELM; Sec. RØNNAUG LARSEN.

Norsk Kirurgisk Forening (Norwegian Surgical Association): POB 1152 Sentrum,

0107 Oslo; Legenes hus, Akersgt. 2, Oslo; tel. 23-10-90-00; e-mail trazumo@legeforeningen.no; internet legeforeningen.no/nkf; f. 1911; 1,171 mems; Chair. OLAUG INGUNN VILLANGER; Sec. OLE-ANDERS STENSEN; publs *Journal of the Norwegian Medical Association* (24 a year), *Vitenskapelige forhandlinger* (1 a year).

NATURAL SCIENCES

General

Polytekniske Forening (Norwegian Polytechnical Society): Rosenkrantzgt. 7, 0159 Oslo; tel. 22-42-68-70; e-mail polyteknisk@polyteknisk.no; internet www.polyteknisk.no; f. 1852; 7,000 mems; Chair. SVERRE LODGAARD; Sec.-Gen. FREDRIK EVJEN; publ. *Teknisk Ukeblad* (52 a year).

Selskapet til Vitenskapenes Fremme (Society for the Advancement of Science): Noreidstraumen 31, c/o Guldborg, 5251 Søreidgrend; e-mail guldborg.sovik@biomed.uib.no; f. 1927; promotes and encourages intellectual activities generally by regular series of lectures, excursions; 200 mems; Pres. ANDREAS STEIGEN; Gen. Sec. Prof. GULDBORG SØVIK.

Biological Sciences

Norsk Botanisk Forening (Norwegian Botanical Association): Naturhistorisk Museum, POB 1172 Blindern, 0318 Oslo; tel. 92-68-97-95; e-mail post@botaniskforening.no; internet www.botaniskforening.no; f. 1935; promotes interest and knowledge of botanical studies through lectures and field trips; 1,500 mems; Gen. Man. TORBORG GALTELAND; publ. *Blyttia* (4 a year).

Physical Sciences

Norsk Geologisk Forening (Geological Society of Norway): c/o NGU, POB 6315 Sluppen, 7491 Trondheim; tel. 73-90-40-00; e-mail ngf@geologi.no; internet www.geologi.no; f. 1905; organizes interdisciplinary conf. every year; 1,400 mems; Pres. GUNN MANGERUD; Sec.-Gen. GUNN KRISTIN HAUKDAL; publ. *Norsk Geologisk Tidsskrift* (Norwegian Journal of Geology, 4 a year).

Norsk Kjemisk Selskap (Norwegian Chemical Society): POB 1107 Blindern, 0317 Oslo; tel. 22-85-55-56; e-mail medlem@kjemi.no; internet www.kjemi.no; f. 1893; promotes chemistry advancement in science, technology and education; represents Norwegian chemists in int. forums; 8 local brs and 6 professional divs; organizes meetings, excursions, scientific seminars, exhibitions; 2,000 mems; Pres. KENNETH RUUD; Gen. Sec. HARALD WALDERHAUG; publ. *Kjemi*.

TECHNOLOGY

Norges Tekniske Vitenskapsakademi (Norwegian Academy of Technological Sciences): Lerchendal Gård, 7491 Trondheim; NTVA Strindvegen 2, Trondheim; tel. 73-59-54-63; e-mail ntvamail@ntva.ntnu.no; internet www.ntva.no; f. 1955; promotes research, education and devt within the fields of technology and natural sciences; 500 mems; Pres. EIVIND HIIS HAUGE; Sec.-Gen. HEIN JOHNSON.

Teknisk-Naturvitenskapelig Forening (Tekna) (Norwegian Society of Graduate Technical and Scientific Professionals (Tekna)): POB 2312 Solli, 0201 Oslo; Dronning Mauds gate 15, Oslo; tel. 22-94-75-00; e-mail post@tekna.no; internet www.tekna.no; f. 1874; promotes research and devt; represents engineering profession in relation with other orgs and countries; 61,000 mems; Pres. MARIANNE HARG; Gen. Sec. IVAR HORNELAND KRISTENSEN; publs *Magasinet Tekna* (10

a year), *Sivilingeniøren* (10 a year), *Teknisk Ukeblad* (52 a year), *Våre Veger* (10 a year).

Research Institutes

GENERAL

Chr. Michelsens Institute: POB 6033 Bedriftssenteret, 5892 Bergen; Jekteviksbakken 31, Bergen; tel. 47-93-80-00; e-mail cmi@cmi.no; internet www.cmi.no; f. 1930; research on cultures and politics of faith, democracy and governance, devt aid, gender politics, global health and devt, natural resources, poverty dynamics, rights and legal instns, tax and public finance management, politics of violence and security; library of 70,000 vols; Dir Dr OTTAR MÆSTAD.

Nordlandsforskning (Nordland Research Institute): POB 1490, 8049 Bodø; Mørkvedtråkket 30, Inngang A, 3. etg, 8049 Bodø; tel. 75-51-76-00; e-mail nf@nforsk.no; internet nordlandsforskning.no; f. 1979; inter-disciplinary research across a wide range of fields, with particular focus on social sciences and business management; Dir HANNE ØSTERDAL.

Norsk Samfunnsvitenskapelig Datatjeneste (NSD) (Norwegian National Social Science Data Services): Harald Hårfagres gate 29, 5007 Bergen; tel. 55-58-21-17; e-mail nsd@nsd.uib.no; internet www.nsd.uib.no; f. 1971; attached to Universitetet i Bergen; works as resource centre assisting researchers with regard to data gathering, data analysis, issues of methodology, privacy and research ethics; works to improve possibilities and working conditions for empirical research that is primarily dependent on the access to data by reducing financial, technical, legal and administrative barriers between users and data sources; Dir BJØRN HENRICHSEN.

Stein Rokkan Senter for Flerfaglige Samfunnsstudier (Stein Rokkan Centre for Social Studies): Nygårdsgaten 5, 5015 Bergen; tel. 55-58-97-10; e-mail rokkansenteret@uni.no; internet rokkan.uni.no; f. 2002 by merger of Centre for Social Science Research and Norwegian Centre for Research in Organization and Management; attached to Univ. of Bergen; multi-disciplinary research centre for social and cultural studies; Dir Prof. JAN ERIK ASKILDSEN; publ. *Tidsskrift for Velferdsforskning* (Journal of Social Research, 4 a year).

ECONOMICS, LAW AND POLITICS

Norske Nobelinstitutt (Norwegian Nobel Institute): Henrik Ibsens gate 51, 0255 Oslo; tel. 22-12-93-00; e-mail postmaster@nobel.no; internet nobelpeaceprize.org; f. 1903; follows devt of int. relations (esp. work for the pacific settlement of them) in order to advise the Nobel Peace Prize Cttee; research dept; library of 200,000 vols, 200 periodicals; Dir Prof. Dr GEIR LUNDESTAD.

Norsk Utenrikspolitisk Institutt (Norwegian Institute of International Affairs): POB 8159 Dep., 0033 Oslo; C. J. Hambros pl. 2D, Oslo; tel. 22-99-40-00; e-mail info@nupi.no; internet www.nupi.no; f. 1959; int. economics, devt studies, European integration, collective security, Russian studies, UN, peacekeeping; library of 20,000 vols; Dir Prof. Dr ULF SVERDRUP; publs *Forum for Development Studies* (3 a year), *Hvor Hender Det?* (24 a year), *Internasjonal Politikk* (4 a year), *Nordisk Østforum* (4 a year).

Peace Research Institute Oslo (PRIO): POB 9229 Grønland, 0134 Oslo; Hausmanns gate 7, 0186, Oslo; tel. 22-54-77-00; e-mail info@prio.no; internet www.prio.no; f. 1959; multi-disciplinary research on peace- and conflict-related topics; conducts graduate

training; library of 22,000 vols, 340 journals; Chair. BERNT AARDAL; Dir Dr KRISTIAN BERG HARPVIKEN; publs *Journal of Peace Research* (6 a year), *Security Dialogue* (6 a year).

Senter for fredsstudier (Centre for Peace Studies): Faculty of Humanities, Social Sciences and Education, Univ. of Tromsø, 9037 Tromsø; tel. 77-64-43-00; e-mail mail@peace.uit.no; internet www.peace.uit.no; f. 2002; attached to Univ. of Tromsø; examines, promotes and facilitates dialogue pertaining to non-violent conflict resolution and the creation of peace; Dir CHRISTINE SMITH-SIMONSEN.

Statistisk Sentralbyrå (Statistics Norway): POB 8131 Dep., 0033 Oslo; Kongens gt. 6, Oslo; tel. 21-09-00-00; e-mail ssb@ssb.no; internet www.ssb.no; f. 1876; provides statistics on Norwegian soc.; responsible for coordinating all official statistics in Norway; acts as a driving force for int. statistics work; library of 70,000 vols; Dir-Gen. HANS HENRIK SCHEEL; publs *Norges offisielle statistikk* (series, Official Statistics of Norway, irregular), *Økonomiske analyser* (Economic Survey), *Sosiale og Økonomiske studier* (Social and Economic Studies), *Statistiske analyser* (Statistical Survey), *Statistisk årbok* (Statistical Yearbook).

HISTORY, GEOGRAPHY AND ARCHAEOLOGY

Roald Amundsen Centre for Arctic Research: c/o Univ. of Tromsø, Eriksen Bldg, 9037 Tromsø; tel. 77-64-52-40; e-mail arctic.info@uit.no; f. 1989; attached to Univ. of Tromsø; aims to encourage inter-disciplinary cooperation in Arctic research and teaching; Head of Admin. GEIR GOTAAS.

LANGUAGE AND LITERATURE

Center for Advanced Study in Theoretical Linguistics-CASTL: Faculty of Humanities, Social Sciences and Education, Univ. of Tromsø, 9037 Tromsø; tel. 77-64-47-51; e-mail jorun.nordmo@uit.no; internet castl.uit.no; f. 2002; attached to Univ. of Tromsø; aims to foster a greater understanding of the nature of syntactic, morphological and phonological variation, in order to be able to determine along which grammatical parameters any 2 languages vary; Chair. Prof. KIRSTI KOCH CHRISTENSEN; Dir Prof. PETER SVENONIUS.

MEDICINE

Helseøkonomi Bergen (HEB) (Health Economics Bergen): Herman Fossgt. 6, 5007 Bergen; tel. 55-58-92-00; e-mail oddvar.kaarboe@econ.uib.no; internet heb.rokkan.uib.no; attached to Univ. of Bergen; economic analysis of health; assessment of profitability and distributional effects of health care and treatment; Dir Prof. Dr KJELL HAUG.

Nasjonalt Forskningssenter innen Komplementær og Alternativ Medisin (NaFKAM) (National Research Centre in Complementary and Alternative Medicine): Forskningsparken I, Sykehusveien 23, 9037 Tromsø; tel. 77-64-66-50; e-mail nafkam@helsefak.uit.no; internet www.nafkam.no; f. 2000; conducts and coordinates Norwegian research in complementary and alternative medicine; Chair. and Man. VINJAR MAGNE FØNNEBØ; publ. *NAFKAM skriftserie* (irregular).

Nasjonalt Senter for Distriktsmedisin (NSDM) (National Centre of Rural Medicine): Institutt for Samfunnsmedisin, Universitetet i Tromsø, 9037 Tromsø; Universitetssykehuset Nord-Norge, Blokk C0, plan 6 (inngang fra blokk C, plan 4),

9037 Tromsø; tel. 77-64-48-16; e-mail ivar
.aaraas@uit.no; internet www.nsdm.no; f.
2007; attached to Universitetet i Tromsø;
promotes research, professional devt projects, education and networking among physicians and health personnel in rural and
remote areas to bridge the gap between
academia; contributes to quality, recruitment
and stability in rural health services; Gen.
Man. Prof. Dr IVAR J. AARAAS.

**Research Centre for Health Promotion
and Resources HiST/NTNU:** 7491 Trondheim; Dragvoll Univ. Centre, Bldg 11, Level
5, 7491 Trondheim; tel. 90-16-51-53; e-mail
mail@svt.ntnu.no; internet www.rchpr.org;
attached to Norwegian Univ. of Science and
Technology and SørTrøndelag Univ. College;
works to establish knowledge about factors
that contribute towards health and well-
being; Dir Prof. GEIR ARILD ESPNES.

Senter for Samisk Helseforskning
(Centre for Sami Health Research): c/o
Univ. of Tromsø, Breivika, 9037 Tromsø;
tel. 77-64-63-05; e-mail saminor@ism.uit.no;
f. 2001; attached to Univ. of Tromsø; aims to
promote inter-disciplinary and multi-disciplinary research and devt on the health and
living conditions among the Sami population
in Norway; Dir RAGNHILD V. KALSTAD.

NATURAL SCIENCES

Biological Sciences

Espeland Marine Biological Station:
Espelandsveien 232, 5258 Blomsterdalen;
tel. 55-58-39-20; internet www.uib.no/bio/en/
research/infrastructure-at-bio/espeland-mar-
ine-biological-station; attached to Universitetet i Bergen; equipped for large-scale
experimental work on primary and secondary production; Man. AGNES AADNESEN.

Havforskningsinstituttet (Institute of
Marine Research): POB 1870 Nordnes, 5817
Bergen; Nordnesgaten 50, 5005 Bergen; tel.
55-23-85-00; e-mail post@imr.no; internet
www.imr.no; f. 1900; attached to Min. of
Fisheries and Coastal Affairs; provides
advice to Norwegian authorities on aquaculture and the ecosystems of the Barents Sea,
the Norwegian Sea, the N Sea and the
Norwegian coastal zone; library of 80,000
vols; Man. Dir TORE NEPSTAD; publs *Facts
and Figures* (every 2 years), *Fisken og Havet*.

**Norwegian Structural Biology Centre
(NorStruct):** Dept of Chemistry Research
Park 3, Faculty of Sciences, Univ. of Tromsø,
9037 Tromsø; Dept of Chemistry Research
Park 3, Sykhusvegen 23, Univ. of Tromsø,
9019 Tromsø; tel. 77-64-40-00; e-mail
norstruct@chem.uit.no; internet uit.no/
norstruct; nat. research and service centre
working for functional genomics; offers consulting, service, courses and collaboration to
the Norwegian research community in structural biology techniques; attached to Universitetet i Tromsø; Dir Prof. ARNE O.
SMALÅS; Man. Dr RONNY HELLAND.

Physical Sciences

**Centre for Theoretical and Computa-
tional Chemistry:** Univ. of Oslo, Dept of
Chemistry, POB 1033 Blindern, 0315 Oslo;
Univ. of Tromsø, Dept of Chemistry, 9037
Tromsø; tel. 77-62-31-00; e-mail post@ctcc
.no; internet www.ctcc.no; f. 2007; collaborative project between Univ. of Oslo and the
Univ. of Tromsø; works towards the devt and
application of quantum-mechanical modelling in chemistry and materials science;
Head of Admin. STIG EIDE.

Meteorologiske Institutt (Norwegian
Meteorological Institute): POB 43 Blindern,
0313 Oslo; Henrik Mohns plass 1, 0313 Oslo;
tel. 22-96-30-00; e-mail post@met.no;
internet www.met.no; f. 1866; promotes

meteorology to protect life, property and the
environment; provides the meteorological
services required by soc.; library of 30,000
vols; Dir ANTON ELIASSEN; publs *Klimatolo-
gisk månedsoversikt* (12 a year), *Technical
Report* (irregular).

**Nansen Environmental and Remote
Sensing Center:** Thormøhlens gate 47,
5006 Bergen; tel. 55-20-58-00; e-mail
admin@nersc.no; internet www.nersc.no; f.
1986; attached to Univ. of Bergen; aims to
make significant contribution to the understanding, monitoring and forecasting of the
environment and climate on regional and
global scales through coordination and participation in nat. and int. research programmes; Chair. ANTON KJELAAS; Dir Dr
STEIN SANDVEN.

Norges Geologiske Undersøkelse (Geological Survey of Norway): POB 6315 Sluppen, 7491 Trondheim; Leiv Eirikssons vei 39,
7040 Trondheim; tel. 73-90-40-00; e-mail
ngu@ngu.no; internet www.ngu.no; f. 1858;
works to ensure that geoscientific knowledge
is utilised for effective and sustainable management of the nation's natural resources
and environment; library of 120,000 vols and
950 periodicals; Man. Dir MORTEN SMELROR;
publs *Bulletin* (irregular, in English, online
only), *Gråsteinen* (irregular, in Norwegian).

Norsk Polarinstitutt (Norwegian Polar
Institute): Fram Centre, Hjalmar Johansens
gt. 14, 9296 Tromsø; tel. 77-75-05-00; e-mail
post@npolar.no; internet www.npolar.no; f.
1928; research, monitoring and topographic
mapping of Norwegian polar regions; advises
Norwegian authorities on matters concerning polar environmental management; scientific investigations in the fields of geology,
geophysics and biology; topographical mapping, responsible for Norwegian Antarctic
Research expeditions; scientific logistical
support; admin. and maintenance of all-
year scientific stations in Ny-Alesund, Sval-
bard (Sverdrup Station) and Dronning Maud
Land, Antarctica (Troll Station); library of
15,000 vols and 5,000 journals; Dir Dr JAN-
GUNNAR WINTHER; publ. *Polar Research*
(irregular).

RELIGION, SOCIOLOGY AND ANTHROPOLOGY

**Instituttet for Sammenlignende Kultur-
forskning** (Institute for Comparative
Research in Human Culture): POB 2832
Solli, 0204 Oslo; Drammensveien 78, Oslo;
tel. 22-85-81-02; e-mail post@iskf.no; internet
iskf.no; f. 1922; comparative study of languages, religions, folklore, law, ethnology,
archaeology, and sociology, sponsoring
research programmes and publishing; Chair.
Prof. ARNE BUGGE AMUNDSEN; Sec. IDA
SLETTA; publ. *Institute for Comparative
Research in Human Culture. Series B*
(irregular).

**Regionalt kunnskapssenter for barn og
unge (RKBU Nord)** (Regional Centre for
Child and Youth Mental Health and Child
Welfare-North): Det helsevitenskapelige
fakultet, Univ. of Tromsø, 9037 Tromsø;
Gimlevegen 78, 9037 Tromsø; tel. 77-64-58-
50; e-mail post.rbup@fagmed.uit.no; f. 2011
by merger of Centre for Child and Adolescent
Mental Health, North Region (RBUP North)
and Child Devt in Northern Norway (BUS);
provides training about child and adolescent
mental health in the N Norway; Dir Prof.
TOM MIKALSEN.

**Senter for Kvinne og Kjønnsforskning
(Kvinnforsk)** (Centre for Women's and Gen-
der Research): Univ. of Tromsø, 9037
Tromsø; Øvre Lysthus, First Floor, Univ. of
Tromsø, 9037 Tromsø; tel. 77-64-52-40;
e-mail kvinnforsk@skk.uit.no; internet uit

.no/kvinnforsk; f. 1995; attached to Univ. of
Tromsø; works to strengthen competence and
to stimulate gender and women research
within different disciplines at the univ.;
Chair. Prof. JØRGEN LORENTZEN; Man. LISE
NORDBRØND; publ. *Kvinnforsk Skritserie*
(irregular).

**Senter for Kvinne og Kjønnsforskning
(SKOK)** (Centre for Women's and Gender
Research): POB 7805, 5020 Bergen; Ida
Bloms hus, Allégt. 34, 5007 Bergen; tel. 55-
58-24-71; e-mail post@skok.uib.no; internet
www.uib.no/skok; attached to Univ. of Bergen; research fields incl. feminist theory,
gender theory, women's studies, philosophy,
sociology, anthropology, cultural studies,
psychoanalysis, sexuality, devt studies,
migration studies and family history; Dir
Prof. ELLEN MORTENSEN.

TECHNOLOGY

**FALCK NUTEC—Norsk Undervannste-
knologisk Senter A/S** (FALCK NUTEC—
Norwegian Underwater Technology Centre):
Gravdalsveien 255, POB 6, Ytre Laksevåg,
5848 Bergen; tel. 55-94-20-00; e-mail
companymail@falcknutec.no; internet www
.falck.com/nutec_no; f. 1976, current name
adopted 1981; test and research centre for
underwater technology; library of 5,000 vols,
170 periodicals; Man. Dir ELI SÆTERSMOEN.

Institutt for Energiteknikk (Institute for
Energy Technology): POB 40, 2027 Kjeller;
Instituttveien 18, 2007 Kjeller; tel. 63-80-60-
00; e-mail firmapost@ife.no; internet www.ife
.no; f. 1948; int. research institute for energy
and nuclear technology; undertakes research
and devt within the energy and petroleum
sectors, carries out assignments in nuclear
technology, safety and environmental
research; Pres. EVA S. DUGSTAD; Research
Dir for Energy and Environmental Technology ARVE HOLT; Research Dir for Nuclear
Safety and Reliability MARGARET MCGRATH;
Research Dir Nuclear Technology and Physics BRIT S. FARSTAD; Research Dir for Petroleum Technology TORE BJERKELUND GIMSE;
Research Dir for Safety Man-Technology-
Organisation JON KVALEM.

**NIVA—Norsk Institutt for Vannforskn-
ing** (NIVA—Norwegian Institute for Water
Research): Gaustadalléen 21, 0349 Oslo; tel.
22-18-51-00; e-mail niva@niva.no; internet
www.niva.no; f. 1958; research, monitoring,
assessment and studies on freshwater,
coastal and marine environments in addition
to environmental technology; environmental
contaminants, biodiversity and climate
related issues; library of 5,000 vols, 25 periodicals in print, 3,900 online periodicals;
Chair. ANNE ENGER; publ. *Arbok*.

Norges Geotekniske Institutt (NGI) (Norwegian Geotechnical Institute): POB 3930
Ullevaal Stadion, 0806 Oslo; Sognsveien 72,
0855 Oslo; tel. 22-02-30-00; e-mail ngi@ngi
.no; internet www.ngi.no; f. 1953; soil, rock
and snow mechanics, foundation engineering, dams, offshore structures, instrumentation, rock engineering, geoenvironmental
engineering; library of 20,000 vols, 300 periodicals, Terzaghi Library, Peck Library;
Man. Dir LARS ANDRESEN.

NORSAR: POB 53, 2027 Kjeller; Gunnar
Randers vei 15, 2007 Kjeller; tel. 63-80-59-
00; e-mail info@norsar.no; internet www
.norsar.no; f. 1968, present status 1999;
conducts research and devt in the areas of
geophysics and geophysical software; Dir
ANDERS DAHLE; publ. *Technical Summary* (2
a year).

**Norsk Institutt for By- Og Regionforskn-
ing** (Norwegian Institute for Urban and
Regional Research): Gaustadalléen 21, 0349
Oslo; tel. 22-95-88-00; e-mail nibr@nibr.no;

internet www.nibr.no; f. 1967; acts as nat. centre for urban and regional research; conducts and promotes research and devt activities for Norwegian community and business sector; library of 23,000 vols, 200 periodicals; Chair. JAN SANDAL; Dir-Gen. Dr HILDE LORENTZEN; publ. *Regionale Trender* (irregular).

Norsk Institutt for Luftforskning (Norwegian Institute for Air Research): POB 100, 2027 Kjeller; Instituttveien 18, 2027 Kjeller; tel. 63-89-80-00; e-mail nilu@nilu.no; internet www.nilu.no; f. 1969; nat. and int. research and consultation in air pollution, atmospheric dispersion and measurements, meteorological measurements and analysis, instrumentation and chemical analysis; library of 16,000 vols, 150 periodicals; Man. Dir KARI NYGAARD.

Norsk Marinteknisk Forskningsinstitutt AS (Norwegian Marine Technology Research Institute): POB 4125 Valentinlyst, 7450 Trondheim; Otto Nielsens veg 10, 7052 Trondheim; tel. 46-41-50-00; e-mail info@marintek.sintef.no; internet www.marintek.sintef.no; f. 1939 as Ship Model Tank in Trondheim, current name adopted 1984; research, devt and technical consultancy in the maritime sector for industry and the public sector; develops and verifies technological solutions for the shipping, marine equipment, ocean energy and petroleum industries; subsidiaries in Houston, Texas and Rio de Janeiro, Brazil; library of 11,000 vols, 365 periodicals; Pres. ODDVAR EIDE; publ. *Marintek Review* (irregular).

Norsk Regnesentral (Norwegian Computing Centre): POB 114, Blindern, 0314 Oslo; Gaustadalléen 23 A-B, 0373 Oslo; tel. 22-85-25-00; e-mail nr@nr.no; internet www.nr.no; f. 1952; contract research and devt projects in information and communication technology and applied statistical modelling; library of 4,000 vols, 250 periodicals; Man. Dir LARS HOLDEN.

Papirindustriens Forskningsinstitutt (PFI) (Paper and Fibre Research Institute): Høgskoleringen 6B, 7491 Trondheim; tel. 73-60-50-65; e-mail firmapost@pfi.no; internet www.pfi.no; f. 1923; conducts research within wood fibre, pulp, paper, new biobased materials and biofuels; Dir Dr PHILIP ANDRÉ REME; Sec. ELIN BREMSETH.

Senter for Internasjonal Økonomi og Skipsfart (SIØS) (Centre for International Economics and Shipping): Norwegian School of Economics and Business Administration, Helleveien 30, 5035 Bergen; tel. 55-95-92-62; e-mail sasamndm@debetmhs.no; f. 1958; aims to provide a centre for research fellows in sea transport, shipping economics and int. economics from Norway and abroad; promotes cooperation with similar institutions; library of 3,500 vols, 1,600 periodicals, reports, etc.; Dir Prof. GUTTORM SCHJELDERUP; Sec. ANNE LIV SCRASE.

SINTEF: POB 4760, Sluppen, 7465 Trondheim; Strindveien 4, Trondheim; tel. 73-59-30-00; e-mail info@sintef.no; internet www.sintef.no; f. 1950 as Foundation for Scientific and Industrial Research at the Norwegian Institute of Technology, present name 2007; undertakes contracts in science and technology research for industry and others; 8 affiliated research institutes; Pres. UNNI M. STEINSMO.

SINTEF Byggforsk (SINTEF Building and Infrastructure): POB 124 Blindern, 0314 Oslo; Forskningsveien 3B, Oslo; tel. 22-96-55-55; e-mail byggforsk@sintef.no; internet www.sintef.no/byggforsk; f. 1953, reorganized 1985 as an ind. institute, merged with Norges byggforskningsinstitutt (NBI) 2007; encourages research and devt, research-based expert consultancy, certification and knowledge dissemination; library of 25,000 vols, 250 periodicals; Exec. Vice-Pres. HANNE RØNNEBERG.

SINTEF Energi (SINTEF Energy Research): POB 4760, Sluppen, 7465 Trondheim; tel. 73-59-72-00; e-mail energy.research@sintef.no; internet www.sintef.no/sintef-energi-as; f. 1958 as Elektrisitetsforsyningens Forskningsinstitutt, present name 2010; research and devt in the field of energy, esp. electricity generation, transmission, distribution and consumption; Exec. Vice-Pres. MARIE BYSVEEN.

Transportøkonomisk Institutt (Institute of Transport Economics): Gaustadalléen 21, 0349 Oslo; tel. 22-57-38-00; e-mail toi@toi.no; internet www.toi.no; f. 1958 as a govt dept, reorganized as ind. institute 1964; carries out applied research on issues connected with transport; promotes application of research results by advising authorities, transport industry and public; library of 30,000 vols, 200 periodicals; Chair. SIGURD LARSEN; Man. Dir Dr GUNNAR LINDBERG; publ. *Samferdsel* (Communication, 10 a year).

VilVite, Bergen Vitensenter (VilVite, Bergen Science Centre): Thormøhlensgt. 51, 5006 Bergen; tel. 55-59-45-00; e-mail post@vilvite.no; internet www.vilvite.no; f. 2005; attached to Univ. of Bergen; research and learning centre of technology, natural sciences and mathematics; Man. Dir SVEIN ANDERS DAHL.

Libraries and Archives

Arendal

Arendal Bibliotek (Arendal Library): POB 786, 4809 Arendal; Torvet 6, 4836 Arendal; tel. 37-01-39-13; e-mail arendal@arendal.folkebibl.no; internet www.arendal.folkebibl.no; f. 1832, inc. East Agder County Library 1972; 200,000 vols; Head Librarian OLA EIKSUND.

Ås

Universitetet for Miljø- og Biovitenskap, Biblioteket (Norwegian University of Life Sciences, Library): POB 5003, 1432 Ås; Chr. M. Falsens vei 18, Tårnbygningen, Ås; tel. 64-96-50-00; e-mail biblioteket@umb.no; internet www.umb.no/biblioteket; f. 1859; literature concerning all brs of agricultural science and forestry, conservation of natural resources, biology, etc.; 500,000 vols; Head Librarian GEIR ARNE ROSVOLL (acting).

Bergen

Bergen offentlige Bibliotek (Municipal and County Library): Strømgt. 6, 5015 Bergen; tel. 55-56-85-05; e-mail post@bergenbibliotek.no; internet bergenbibliotek.no; f. 1872; Grieg colln of 135 MSS and 5,700 letters; 6 brs and 1 mobile library; 700,000 vols; incl. books, magazines, sheet music, CDs and movies; City Librarian LEIKNY HAGA INDERGAARD.

Universitetsbiblioteket i Bergen (University of Bergen Library): POB 7808, 5020 Bergen; Stein Rokkans hus, Nygårdsgt. 5, 5015 Bergen; tel. 55-58-25-32; e-mail post@ub.uib.no; internet www.uib.no/ub; f. 1825 as Bergens Museums Bibliotek; 1.8m. vols incl. books and periodicals, 3,600 MSS and diplomas, 43,000 maps and atlases and 16,600 journals; Library Dir OLE GUNNAR EVENSEN.

Drammen

Drammensbiblioteket (Drammen Library): POB 3554, 3007 Drammen; Grønland 58B, 3045 Drammen; tel. 32-04-54-00; e-mail bibliotek@drmk.no; internet www.dbib.no; f. 1916 as Drammen Bibliotek, present name adopted 2007 following merger with Buskerud County Library and the library at Buskerud Univ. College; 300,000 vols; Faculty Librarian HUGO HØYMO.

Hamar

Riksarkivet (National Archives of Norway): Sognsveien 221, POB 4013, Ullevål Stadion, 0806 Oslo; tel. 22-02-26-00; e-mail biblioteket@arkivverket.no; internet www.arkivverket.no; f. 1817; takes charge of the archives of the mins and other brs of the central admin.; collns incl. medieval documents, maps and drawings, MSS and transcripts; 70,000 vols; Dir-Gen. IVAR FONNES; Head Librarian ARNE REED; publ. *Arkivmagasinet* (3 a year).

Statsarkivet i Hamar (Regional State Archives in Hamar): Lille Strandgate 3, 2317 Hamar; tel. 62-55-54-40; e-mail sahamar@arkivverket.no; internet www.arkivverket.no/arkivverket/hamar; f. 1917; public record office, archives; 30,000 vols; Chief Archivist VIGDIS STENSBY.

Kristiansand

Kristiansand Folkebibliotek (Kristiansand Public Library): POB 476, 4664 Kristiansand; Rådhusgt. 11, 4611 Kristiansand; tel. 38-12-49-10; e-mail post.folkebibliotek@kristiansand.kommune.no; internet www.kristiansand.folkebibl.no; f. 1909; 3 brs; 300,000 vols; Librarian ANNE KRISTIN UNDLIEN.

Oslo

Deichmanske Bibliotek (Oslo Public Library): Arne Garborgs plass 4, 0179 Oslo; tel. 23-43-29-00; e-mail postmottak.deichman@kul.oslo.kommune.no; internet www.deichmanske-bibliotek.oslo.kommune.no; f. 1785; 1,378,109 vols, incl. 1,118,274 books, 22,231 audio books, 31,438 music recordings, 19,239 video cassettes and DVDs; Chief Librarian LIV SÆTEREN.

Patentstyret (Norwegian Industrial Property Office): POB 8160 Dep., 0033 Oslo; Sandakerveien 64, 0484 Oslo; tel. 22-38-73-00; e-mail mail@patentstyret.no; internet www.patentstyret.no; f. 1911; 25,000 vols of scientific and technical books and periodicals of reference for patent research; Head of Dept OTTO SCHARFF; publs *Designtidende* (Design Gazette), *Norsk Varemerketidende*, *Patenttidende* (Patent Gazette, 52 a year), *Varemerketidende* (Trademark Gazette, 52 a year).

Statistisk Sentralbyrås Bibliotek og Informasjonssenter (Statistics Norway, Library and Information Centre): POB 8131 Dep., 0033 Oslo; Akersveien 26, Oslo; tel. 21-09-46-42; e-mail biblioteket@ssb.no; internet www.ssb.no/biblioteket; f. 1917; open to the public; OECD deposit library; European Statistical Data Support; 80,000 vols: mainly economic, demographic and statistical literature (incl. official and int. statistics); Librarian ELSA GRANVOLL.

Stortingsbiblioteket (Library of the Norwegian Parliament): Stortinget, 0026 Oslo 1; Prinsensgt. 26, Oslo; tel. 23-31-36-90; e-mail bibl@stortinget.no; internet www.stortinget.no/no/stottemeny/kontakt/stortingsbiblioteket; f. 1871; reference library mainly for mems of Parliament and govt officials; open to the public on application; 200,000 vols; literature on political and social science, law, and economics; reports from official and semi-official institutions; Head Librarian GRO SANDGRIND.

Universitetsbiblioteket i Oslo (University of Oslo Library): POB 1085, Blindern, 0317 Oslo; Georg Sverdrup bldg, Third Floor,

Moltke Moes vei 39, 0315 Oslo; tel. 22-85-40-50; e-mail postmottak@ub.uio.no; internet www.ub.uio.no; f. 1811; academic library; depositary library; 3,800,000 vols; spec. collns of papyri and orientalia; Library Dir BENTE R. ANDREASSEN.

Utenriksdepartementets Dokumentasjonssenter (Documentation Centre of the Ministry of Foreign Affairs): POB 8114 Dep., 0032 Oslo; 7 Juni-Plassen 1, Oslo; tel. 22-24-36-00; e-mail post@mfa.no; internet www.ud.dep.no; f. 1900; literature on foreign affairs, int. law and int. relations; not open to the public; Head Librarian RITA AARS-NICOLAYSEN.

Rjukan

Rjukan Bibliotek (Public Library of Rjukan): POB 93, 3661 Rjukan; Torget 1, 3660 Rjukan; tel. 35-08-25-60; e-mail bibliotek@tinn.kommune.no; internet www.tinn.kommune.no; f. 1914; 3 brs; 100,000 vols; colln on history, philosophy and sociology of the working class; colln on local and regional history; Head Librarian TINE K. ANDERSEN.

Stavanger

Stavanger Bibliotek (Stavanger Library): POB 310, 4002 Stavanger; Sølvberggt. 2, Stavanger; tel. 51-50-74-65; e-mail biblioteket@stavanger-kulturhus.no; internet www.stavanger-kulturhus.no/stavanger_bibliotek; f. 1885; municipal library for the town of Stavanger, central library for the county of Rogaland; 500,000 vols; Library and Cultural Dir MARIT EGAAS.

Tønsberg

Tønsberg og Nøtterøy Bibliotek (Tønsberg and Nøtterøy Public Library): Storgaten 16, 3126 Tønsberg; tel. 33-35-49-00; e-mail tbg@tnb.no; internet www.tnb.no; f. 1909; 220,000 vols; Chair. ROLF STORM-SOLBERG.

Trondheim

NTNU Universitetsbiblioteket (Norwegian University of Science and Technology library): Høgskoleringen 1, 7491 Trondheim; Høgskoleringen 1, 7034 Trondheim; tel. 73-59-51-10; e-mail post@ub.ntnu.no; internet www.ntnu.no/ub; f. 1768; receives deposit copies of all Norwegian books; 11 br. libraries; 2,878,000 vols of books and periodicals, 421,500 photographs, 84,500 e-books, 32,500 maps, 19,500 MSS, 12,000 e-journals; Dir LISBETH TANGEN.

Ulefoss

Telemark Fylkesbibliotek/Nome Folkebibliotek (Telemark/Nome County Library): Ringsevja 2, 3830 Ulefoss; tel. 35-94-89-20; e-mail telfy@t-fk.no; internet www.tm.fylkesbibl.no; f. 1942; 150,000 vols, 200 periodicals; Library Dir TOVE FJERDINGSTAD.

Museums and Art Galleries

Bergen

Bergenhus Festningsmuseum (Bergen Fortress Museum): POB 100 (K-14), Haakonsvern, 5886 Bergen; tel. 55-54-63-87; e-mail bhusmus@gmail.com; internet forsvaretsmuseer.no/nor/bergenhus/om-bergenhus; f. 2006; devoted to the resistance movement during the Second World War and shortly after the war; Dir GUNNAR SØNSTEBY.

University Museum of Bergen: POB 7800, 5020 Bergen; H. Hårfagresgt. 1, 5007 Bergen; tel. 55-58-00-00; e-mail post@um.uib.no; internet www.uib.no/bergenmuseum; f. 1825; part of University 1948; comprises two units,

Cultural History Collns (Norwegian culture and folk art) and Natural History Collns (anthropology, archaeology, botany, geology and zoology); Dir HENRIK VON ACHEN; publ. *Årbok for Bergen Museum* (Bergen Museum Yearbook).

Vestlandske Kunstindustrimuseum (West Norway Museum of Decorative Art): Rasmus Meyers allé 9, 5015 Bergen; tel. 55-56-80-00; e-mail post@kunstmuseene.no; internet www.vk.museum.no; f. 1887; 20,000 objects incl. Norwegian and European furniture, glass, porcelain, silver and textiles from the Renaissance to modern times; Gen. Munthe's colln of Chinese art; library of 20,000 vols; Dir ERLEND G. HØYERSTEN; Chief Curator KNUT ORMHAUG.

Bodø

Norsk Luftfartsmuseum (Norwegian Aviation Museum): POB 1124, 8001 Bodø; Olav 5 gate, 8004 Bodø; tel. 75-50-78-50; e-mail flymuseum@luftfart.museum.no; internet luftfart.museum.no; f. 1994; depicts cultural and technical background of Norway's civil and military aviation history; Dir ERLING KJÆRNES; publ. *Flyhistorie*.

Salten Museum: Prinsensgt. 116, 8005 Bodø; tel. 75-50-35-00; e-mail post@nordlandsmuseet.no; internet www.saltenmuseum.no; f. 1888; covers most aspects of life in the county of Nordland; 80,000 items, specialities: fisheries, boats, etc.; 9 br. museums; library of 6,000 vols; Dir HARRY ELLINGSEN.

Drammen

Drammens Museum–Fylkesmuseum for Buskerud: Konnerudgt. 7, 3045 Drammen; tel. 32-20-09-30; e-mail post@drammens.museum.no; internet www.drammens.museum.no; f. 1908, merged with Drammen Art Soc. 1996; 50,000 artefacts of art and cultural history, incl. paintings, furniture, glass, ceramics; library of 16,000 vols; Dir ASMUND THORKILDSEN; publ. *Årbok* (Yearbook).

Fredrikstad

Fredrikstad Museum: Tøihusgaten 41, 1632 Fredrikstad; tel. 69-30-40-30; e-mail postmottak@ostfoldmuseene.no; internet ostfoldmuseene.no/museene/fredrikstad_museum; f. 1903; cultural and military history of the town and district; Curator TOVE M. THØGERSEN.

Hamar

Hedmarksmuseet: Strandvegen 100, 2315 Hamar; tel. 62-54-27-00; e-mail post@domkirkeodden.no; internet www.hedmarksmuseet.no; f. 1906 as Opplandenes Folkemuseum, renamed Hedmarksmuseet og Domkirkeodden 1945, and subsequently as above; comprises 50,000 artefacts; colln of 2m. photographs; open-air museum and medieval colln; ruins of the medieval cathedral, bishop's palace (now housing a modern exhibition), other medieval ruins; excavations in progress; farm bldgs depicting local history and domestic life; library of 14,000 vols; Dir STEINAR BJERKESTRAND; Chief Curator BJØRN SVERRE HOL HAUGEN; publ. *Årbok Fra Kaupang og bygd*.

Attached Museums:

Kirsten Flagstad Museum: POB 1053, Storhamar, 2305 Hamar; Kirkegt. 11, 2317 Hamar; tel. 62-54-27-00; e-mail post@kirsten-flagstad.no; internet www.kirsten-flagstad.no; f. 1985; dedicated to the life and work of opera singer Kirsten Flagstad (1895–1962), born in Hamar; Chair. RAGNHILD NYHUS.

Norsk Utvandrermuseum (Norwegian Emigrant Museum): Åkershagan, 2312 Ottestad; tel. 62-57-48-50; e-mail admin@emigrantmuseum.no; internet www.emigrantmuseum.no; f. 1955; Chair. JON GUNNAR ARNTZEN.

Horten

Forsvarets Marinemuseet (Marine Museum): MMU, POB 215, 3192 Horten; Captain Klinck vei 9, 3183 Horten; tel. 33-03-33-97; e-mail mar-mus@online.no; internet forsvaretsmuseer.no/nor/marinemuseet/om-marinemuseet; f. 1853; preserves, documents and disseminates Naval tangible heritage and Norwegian naval history; Dir JAN INGAR HANSEN.

Lillehammer

Lillehammer Kunstmuseum (Lillehammer Art Museum): Stortorget 2, POB 264, 2602 Lillehammer; tel. 61-05-44-60; e-mail post@lillehammerartmuseum.no; internet www.lillehammerartmuseum.com; f. 1927 as Lillehammer City Colln of Paintings, present name 1994; collns of Norwegian paintings, sculpture and graphic art, historical and contemporary art exhibitions; Chair. GUNNAR K. HAGEN.

Maihaugen (Maihaugen Open Air Museum): Maihaugvegen 1, 2609 Lillehammer; tel. 61-28-89-00; e-mail post@maihaugen.no; internet www.maihaugen.no; f. 1887; open-air museum with 200 bldgs of historical interest from 1200 till 2001; exhibitions of Norwegian history and folk culture; library of 20,000 vols; Dir GAUTE JACOBSEN.

Oslo

Astrup Fearnley Museet for Moderne Kunst (Astrup Fearnley Museum of Modern Art): POB 2074 Vika, 0125 Oslo; Strandpromenaden 2, 0252 Oslo; tel. 22-93-60-60; e-mail info@fearnleys.no; internet afmuseet.no; f. 1993; colln of Norwegian and int. contemporary art; Dir GUNNAR B. KVARAN.

Forsvarsmuseet (Armed Forces Museum): Oslo mil Akershus, 0015 Oslo; tel. 23-09-35-82; e-mail post.fmu@mil.no; internet forsvaretsmuseer.no/nor/forsvarsmuseet; f. 1978; 70,000 artefacts depict technical and historical progress of the Norwegian military from Viking era to cold war years; library of 175,000 vols; Dir Col RUNAR GJERALD; Curator NINI FRITZNER; publs *Fosvarsmuseets Årbok* (1 a year), *Forsvarsmuseets skrifter* (irregular).

Kon-Tiki Museet (Kon-Tiki Museum): Bygdøynesveien 36, 0286 Oslo; tel. 23-08-67-67; e-mail kon-tiki@kon-tiki.no; internet www.kon-tiki.no; archaeology of Easter Island, E Polynesia, the Galapagos Islands and Peru; boats and artefacts from Thor Heyerdahl's expeditions; library of 12,000 vols; Man. Dir MAJA BAUGE.

Kulturhistorisk Museum (Museum of Cultural History): POB 6762 St Olavs plass, 0130 Oslo; Frederiks gate 2, 0164 Oslo (Historical Museum); tel. 22-85-19-00; e-mail postmottak@khm.uio.no; internet www.khm.uio.no; f. 1904; attached to Univ. of Oslo; exhibits colln of nat. antiquities with the Viking treasures, weapons and everyday utensils, the medieval colln with its church art, coin cabinet, treasure chest, ancient Egypt exhibition, the American exhibition, the Arctic and Subarctic and East Asia; library of 70,000 vols; Dir RANE WILLERSLEV; publs *KHM skrifter* (1 a year), *Norske Oldfunn* (Norwegian Archaeological Finds, irregular), *Varia* (irregular).

Munch Museum: POB 2823 Tøyen, 0608 Olso; Tøyengt. 53, 0578 Oslo; tel. 23-49-35-00; e-mail info.munch@munch.museum.no;

internet www.munch.museum.no; f. 1963; 28,000 artefacts incl. 1,150 paintings, 17,800 prints, 7,700 drawings (incl. Edvard Munch's 200 sketchbooks), 21 sculptures and photographs taken by Edvard Munch; library of 22,000 vols, incl. colln of Munch's private letters, notes and diaries, Munch's private book colln; Dir STEIN OLAV HENRICHSEN.

Nasjonalmuseet for Kunst, Arkitektur og Design (National Museum of Art, Architecture and Design): POB 7014, St Olavs plass, 0130 Oslo; Kristian Augusts gt. 23, Oslo; tel. 21-98-20-00; e-mail info@ nasjonalmuseet.no; internet www .nasjonalmuseet.no; f. 2003 by merger of the Norwegian Museum of Architecture, the Museum of Decorative Arts and Design, the Museum of Contemporary Art, the Nat. Gallery; exhibition venues: Nat. Gallery, the Museum of Contemporary Art, Nat. Museum–Architecture, Museum of Decorative Arts and Design; library of 30,000 vols; Dir AUDUN ECKHOFF.

Naturhistorisk museum, Universitetet i Oslo (Natural History Museum, University of Oslo): POB 1172 Blindern, 0318 Oslo; tel. 22-85-16-30; e-mail informasjon@nhm.uio .no; internet www.nhm.uio.no; houses 7.4m. artefacts (c. 65% of the total natural history collns nationwide); Dir Prof. ARNE BJØRLYKKE..

Constituent Museums:

Botanisk hage og Botanisk museum (Botanical Garden and Botanical Museum): POB 1172 Blindern, 0318 Oslo; Sarsgt. 1, 0562 Oslo; tel. 22-85-50-50; e-mail postmottak@nhm.uio.no; internet www.nhm.uio.no/om/bygninger/botanisk-museum; f. 1814 (garden), 1863 (museum); taxonomy and plant ecology; museum not open to the general public; library of 45,000 vols; Dir Prof. ARNE BJØRLYKKE; publ. *Sommerfeltia* (irregular).

Geologisk museum (Geological Museum): POB 1172 Blindern, 0318 Oslo; Sarsgt. 1, 0562 Oslo; tel. 22-85-50-50; e-mail postmottak@nhm.uio.no; internet www.nhm.uio.no/om/bygninger/geologisk-museum; f. 1920; rocks, minerals and fossils; research laboratories in mineralogy, petrology, geochemistry and palaeontology, dinosaurs, meteorites and Ida; library of 75,000 vols; Dir Prof. ARNE BJØRLYKKE.

Zoologisk museum (Zoological Museum): POB 1172 Blindern, 0318 Oslo; Sarsgt. 1, 0562 Oslo; tel. 22-85-50-50; e-mail postmottak@nhm.uio.no; internet www .nhm.uio.no/om/bygninger/zoologisk-mu seum; f. 1910; public exhibitions of Norwegian and world fauna; Norwegian vertebrates and invertebrates, Arctic, Antarctic and exotic, particularly Australian, research collns; library of 28,000 vols, 53,000 pamphlets; Dir Prof. ARNE BJØRLYKKE.

Norges Hjemmefrontmuseum (Norway's Resistance Museum): Oslo mil/Akershus, 0015 Oslo; Bldg 21, Akershus Fortress, 0015 Oslo; tel. 23-09-31-38; e-mail post .nhm@gmail.com; internet forsvaretsmuseer .no/nor/hjemmefrontmuseet; f. 1995; presentation of the German occupation during the Second World War; Dir Prof. IVAR KRAGLUND.

Norsk Folkemuseum (Norwegian Museum of Cultural History): POB 720 Skøyen, 0214 Oslo; Museumsveien 10, Bygdøy, 0287 Oslo; tel. 22-12-37-00; e-mail post@ norskfolkemuseum.no; internet www .norskfolkemuseum.no; f. 1894; consists of indoor and open-air sections comprising 230,000 artefacts; library of 45,000 vols; Dir OLAV AARAAS; Librarian TONE ODDEN.

Norsk Maritimt Museum (Norwegian Maritime Museum): Bygdøynesveien 37, 0286 Oslo; tel. 24-11-41-50; e-mail fellespost@marmuseum.no; internet www .marmuseum.no; f. 1914; museum opened 1974; Norwegian maritime history and coastal culture; colln of ship portraits, maritime paintings, models, instruments, historic ships and traditional small craft, full-size original ship interiors; library of 55,000 vols, archives of photographs and plans, MSS, maps, occasional papers, research reports, 200 periodicals; Dir ESPEN WÆHLE; publs *Norsk Maritimt Museum. Arbok* (Yearbook), *Norsk Maritimt Museum. Rapport* (irregular), *Norsk Maritimt Museum. Skrifter* (irregular).

Norsk Teknisk Museum (Norwegian Museum of Science and Technology): Kjelsåsveien 143, 0491 Oslo; tel. 22-79-60-00; e-mail post@tekniskmuseum.no; internet www.tekniskmuseum.no; f. 1914; nat. museum of technology, industry, science and medicine; library of 40,000 vols; Man. Dir HANS WEINBERGER; publ. *Yearbook*.

Vigeland-museet: POB 1453, Vika, 0166 Oslo; Nobels gate 32, 0268 Oslo; tel. 23-49-37-00; e-mail postmottak.vigeland@vigeland .museum.no; internet www.vigeland .museum.no; f. 1947; life and work of sculptor Gustav Vigeland; colln comprises 1,600 sculptures, 12,000 drawings and 420 woodcarvings; library of 5,000 vols of books, 2,500 magazines; Dir JARLE STRØMODDEN; Curator GURI SKUGGEN; Curator TRINE OTTE BAK NIELSEN.

Sandefjord

Hvalfangstmuseet (Sandefjord Whaling Museum): POB 396, 3201 Sandefjord; Museumsgt. 39, 3210 Sandefjord; tel. 94-79-33-41; e-mail hvalfangstmuseet@ vestfoldmuseene.no; internet www .hvalfangstmuseet.no; f. 1917; shows the devt of whaling from primitive to modern times; geography, ethnology, zoology, maritime history; incl. photograph colln of 150,000 images; Dir SIDSEL HANSEN.

Skien

Telemark Museum: Øvregt. 41, 3715 Skien; tel. 35-54-45-00; e-mail post@ telemark.museum.no; internet telemarkmuseum.no; f. 1909 as Fylkesmuseet for Telemark og Grenland (County Museum of Telemark and Grenland), present name 1998; conservation and research on items of historical interest from the Telemark region; situated in Brekkeparken, with open-air museum (log houses dating from the Middle Ages) and a manor house furnished in 17th-, 18th- and 19th-century styles; collns on folk art, handicrafts, navigation, church art, Ibsen Colln and Ibsen's childhood home, Venstøp Farm; operates and manages 7 museums; library of 6,000 vols; Dir JORUNN SEM FURE; publ. *Magasinet Lundetangen*.

Stavanger

Arkeologisk Museum i Stavanger (Museum of Archaeology, Stavanger): POB 478, 4002 Stavanger; Peder Klows gate 30A, 4010 Stavanger; tel. 51-83-26-00; e-mail post-am@uis.no; internet www.ark.museum .no; f. 1975; own library, scientific archive; Dir TOVE FRANTZEN (acting); publ. *Frá haug ok heiðni* (scientific magazine, 4 a year).

Stavanger Museum: Muségt. 16, 4010 Stavanger; tel. 51-84-27-00; e-mail post@ stavanger.museum.no; internet www .museumstavanger.no; f. 1877; urban and rural culture, zoology, ornithology; incl. maritime museum, canning museum, medical museum, children's museum, printing museum and the mansions of Ledaal and

Breidablikk; library of 65,000 vols; Dir Dept of Cultural History OVE MAGNUS BORE; Dir for Dept of Natural History Dr ATLE FISKÅ.

Tromsø

Tromsø Museum (Universitetetsmuseet) (Tromso University Museum): Lars Thøringsvei 10, 9037 Tromsø; tel. 77-64-50-00; e-mail museumspost@uit.no; internet uit.no/ tmu; f. 1872; attached to Univ. of Tromsø; 6 sections: Archaeology, Botany, Cultural History, Geology, Sami Ethnography, Zoology; library of 180,000 vols; Dir MARIT ANNE HAUAN; publs *Ottar* (5 a year, in Norwegian), *Skrifter* (irregular, in Norwegian), *Tromura* (scientific reports, irregular, in Norwegian), *Way North* (irregular, in English).

Trondheim

Nordenfjeldske Kunstindustrimuseum (National Museum of Decorative Arts): Munkegt. 5, 7013 Trondheim; tel. 73-80-89-50; e-mail post@nkim.museum.no; internet www .nkim.no; f. 1893; depts of furniture, textiles, glass, ceramics, metalwork from the 14th century onwards; special colln of Japanese art and textiles; Dir ÅSHILD ADSEN.

NTNU Vitenskapsmuseet (Museum of Natural History and Archaeology of the Norwegian University of Science and Technology): 7491 Trondheim; Erling Skakkes gt. 47A, Trondheim; tel. 73-59-21-45; e-mail post@vm.ntnu.no; internet www.ntnu.no/ vitenskapsmuseet; f. 1760; graduate and research instn of the univ.; archaeological, botanical and zoological depts; mineralogical and numismatic collns; marine station; incl. Ringve Botanical Gardens and Kongsvoll Alpine Garden; Dir Prof. AXEL CHRISTOPHERSEN; publs *Chironomus Newsletter* (1 a year, in English), *Fauna norvegica* (peer-reviewed journal, 1 a year, in English), *Gunneria* (irregular, in English and Norwegian), *Vitark—Acta Archaelogica Nidrosiensi* (Norwegian and Nordic research and insight into archaeological problems, irregular, in English and Norwegian).

Universities

NORGES TEKNISK-NATURVITENSKAPELIGE UNIVERSITET (NTNU)
(Norwegian University of Science and Technology)

7491 Trondheim

Telephone: 73-59-50-00
E-mail: postmottak@adm.ntnu.no
Internet: www.ntnu.edu

Founded 1996
Academic year: August to June

Chair: SVEIN RICHARD BRANDTZÆG
Rector: GUNNAR BOVIM
Pro-Rector for Education and Quality of Learning: BERIT KJELDSTAD
Pro-Rector for External Relations and Innovation: JOHAN E. HUSTAD
Pro-Rector for Research: KARI MELBY
Dir for Finance and Property: FRANK ARNTSEN
Dir for Organization: IDA MUNKEBY
Library: see under Libraries and Archives
Number of teachers: 3,000
Number of students: 20,000

Publications: *Gemini* (irregular), *Spor* (2 a year)

DEANS

Faculty of Architecture and Fine Art: FREDRIK SHETELIG

Faculty of Engineering Science and Technology: INGVALD STRØMMEN
Faculty of Humanities: ANNE KRISTINE BØRRESEN
Faculty of Information Technology, Mathematics and Electrical Engineering: GEIR ØIEN
Faculty of Medicine: STIG A. SLØRDAHL
Faculty of Natural Sciences and Technology: ANNE BORG
Faculty of Social Sciences and Technology Management: MARIT REITAN

PROFESSORS

Faculty of Architecture and Fine Art (tel. 73-55-02-75; e-mail fak-adm@ab.ntnu.no; internet www.ntnu.no/ab):

ANDRESEN, I.
BJØRBERG, S.
BLAKSTAD, S. H.
BOOKER, C. A.
FRØYEN, Y. K.
FURUNES, A.
GAMDRUP, M.
GRYTLI, E. R.
GUSTAVSEN, A.
HESTNES, A. G.
HÖGER, K.
JAUKKURI, M. H.
JOHNER, J.
KITTANG, D.
LUND, F.
MATUSIAK, B.
MEDALEN, T.
MÖLLER, R.
MONSEN, P. K.
MØYSTAD, O.
MURPHY, J. M.
OLSSON, N.
RAMSTAD, K.
RINTALA, S. J.
SHETELIG, C. F. L.
SIEM, J. H.
SKIBNES, S. E.
STØA, E.

Faculty of Engineering Science and Technology (tel. 73-59-45-01; e-mail postmottak@ivt.ntnu.no; internet www.ntnu.edu/ivt):

AARSNES, J. V.
ABERLE, J.
AKSELSEN, O. M.
ALFREDSEN, K.
ALVES-FILHO, O.
AMDAHL, J.
AMUNDSEN, L.
ANDERSEN, B.
ANDERSSON, H. I.
ARNTSEN, B.
ASBJØRNSLETT, B. E.
ASHEIM, H. A.
AVSETH, P. A.
BAKKEN, L. E.
BAUER, A.
BENZ, T.
BERG, T. E.
BERG-EDLAND, R.
BJØRBERG, S.
BJØRGE, T.
BJØRKUM, P. A.
BOKS, C.
BOLLAND, O.
BØRVIK, T.
BRATTEBØ, H.
BRATTLI, B.
BRATVOLD, R. B.
BREDESEN, A. M.
BRULAND, A.
BUNGER, U.
CLAUSEN, A. H.
DAGESTAD, S.
DAHLHAUG, O. G.
DORAO, C. A.
DREYER, H. C.
ECHTERMEYER, A.
EGELAND, O.

EHLERS, S.
EIKEVIK, T. M.
EIKSUND, G. R.
ELLINGSEN, H.
ERIKSTAD, S. O.
ERTESVÅG, I. S.
FAGERHOLT, K.
FALTINSEN, O. M.
FICHLER, C.
FJÆR, E.
FJELDAAS, S.
GEIKER, M. R.
GEVING, S.
GJERSVIK, T. B.
GODHAVN, J.
GOLAN, M.
GRAN, I. R.
GRANDE, L. O.
GRECO, M.
GRØV, E.
GUDMESTAD, O. T.
GUDMUNDSSON, J. S.
GUNDERSEN, T.
HAAVALDSEN, T.
HAGEN, A.
HANSSEN, S. O.
HÄRKEGÅRD, G.
HAUGE, M.
HAUGEN, S.
HAUGEN, S.
HAVER, S.
HELLEVIK, L. R.
HENDRIKS, M.
HEPSØ, V.
HERTWICH, E.
HILDRE, H. P.
HOFF, I.
HØIER, L.
HØISETH, K. V.
HOKSTAD, K.
HOLDEN, E.
HOLT, R. M.
HOLTHE, K. H.
HOMB, A.
HOPPERSTAD, O. S.
HØYLAND, K. V.
HUSTAD, O. S.
HVOLBY, H.
JACOBSEN, S.
JELLE, B. P.
JELMERT, T. A.
JOHANNESSEN, S.
JOHANSEN, S. E.
JOHANSEN, S. T.
JOHNSEN, R.
KANSTAD, T.
KAYNIA, A. M.
KILLINGTVEIT, Å.
KLAKEGG, O. J.
KLEIV, R. A.
KLEPPE, J.
KNUDSEN, O. Ø
KOCH, W. H.
KRILL, A. G.
KROGSTAD, P.
KVANDE, T.
LADEMO, O.
LANDRØ, M.
LANDRØ, H.
LANGØY, M. A.
LANGSETH, M.
LARSEN, C. M.
LEIKNES, T. O.
LEIRA, B. J.
LI, C. C.
LIA, L.
LIPPARD, S. J.
LØSET, S.
LØVÅS, T.
MALO, K. A.
MATHISEN, H. M.
MATHISEN, K. M.
McENROE, S.
MIDTBØ, T.
MIDTTØMME, G. H.
MOAN, T.

MØRK, A.
MØRK, M. B. E.
MUELLER, D. B.
MÜLLER, B.
MYHR, O. R.
MYRDAL, R.
MYRHAUG, D.
NADIM, F.
NÆSS, E.
NAHAVANDCHI, H.
NEKSÅ, P.
NIELSEN, T. K.
NILSEN, B.
NORDAL, S.
NOVAKOVIC, V.
NYDAL, O. J.
ØIEN, K.
OLSEN, N. R. B.
OLSSON, N.
ØSTERHUS, S. W.
PEDERSEN, E.
PETTERSEN, B.
PETTERSEN, J.
RAUSAND, M.
REMSETH, S. N.
REYES, A. G. R.
RINGROSE, P.
RØDLAND, A.
ROLSTADÅS, A.
RØLVÅG, T.
SÆGROV, S.
SÆTRAN, L. R.
SÆVIK, S.
SAGER, T. Ø.
SAMSET, K. F.
SANGESLAND, S.
SIGBJÖRNSSON, R.
SIVERTSEN, O. I.
SKALLERUD, B. H.
SKJETNE, R.
SMEPLASS, S.
SØRBY, K.
SØRENSEN, A. J.
SØRENSEN, S. I.
STEEN, S.
STENSEN, J. A.
STØLE, H.
STOVAS, A.
STRANDHAGEN, J. O.
STRØMMAN, A. H.
STRØMMEN, E. N.
SVENSVIK, B.
SYVERTSEN, T. G.
THAULOW, C.
THUE, J. V.
TJELFLAAT, P. O.
TORSÆTER, O.
TRYLAND, T.
TUKKER, A.
UGARELLI, R. M.
URSIN, B.
UTNE, I. B.
VALBERG, H. S.
VATN, J.
VINNEM, J. E.
VIOLA, G.
WALLACE, S. W.
WANG, K.
WELO, T.
WHITE, M. F.
WHITSON, C. H.
WIGUM, B. J.
YANG, Z. L.
ZHANG, Z.

Faculty of Humanities (tel. 73-59-65-95; e-mail postmottak@hf.ntnu.no; internet www.ntnu.no/hf):

AASLESTAD, P.
AFARLI, T. A.
AMIDU, A. A.
ANDERSEN, B.
ANDERSEN, H. W.
ANNFELT, T.
BAKKA, E.
BERGMANN, S.

BERKER, T.
BJØRKØY, K.
BORGERSEN, T.
BØRRESEN, A. K.
BRANDTSEGG, Ø.
BREIVIK, M.
BRUMO, J.
BULL, I.
CARUSI, A.
CHABERT, G.
COLLETT, J. P.
DYBDAHL, A.
DYRENDAL, A.
EIDE, K. M.
ELIASSEN, K. O.
EVENSEN, L. S.
FINDAL, W.
FINKE, S. R. S.
FOSS, G.
FRØLAND, H. O.
FURUSETH, S.
GJELSVIK, A.
GLADSØ, S.
GORING, P. M.
GREENALL, A. K.
HAGLAND, J. R.
HANKELN, R.
HAUKIOJA, J.
HELLAN, L.
HELLAND, H. P.
HERNÆS, P. O.
HETLAND, J.
HODNE, L.
HØIBRAATEN, H.
HOWLAND, J.
IMSEN, S.
IVERSEN, G.
JASINSKI, M. E.
JONSSON, L. S.
JØRGENSEN, L. B.
KAISER, W.
KALDAL, S. I.
KEUL, I.
KJELDSTADLI, K.
KLEIBERG, S.
KNOWLES, J.
KOREMAN, J.
KRUGER, S. V.
LAGESEN, V. A.
LIE, M.
MÆHLUM, B. K.
MÁRTENSSON, U.
MATERSTVEDT, L. J.
MEHLUM, H.
MITCHELL, D. M.
MOLANDER, B. A.
MYSKJA, B. K.
NEUMANN, B. O.
NYLANDER, L.
ØSTBY, P.
OVERSAND, K.
PETERI, G. G.
PETERSEN, T. T.
RASMUSSEN, B. K.
RISE, H.
RYGHAUG, M.
SEIP, I.
SELVIK, R. M.
SOGNNES, K.
SØRENSEN, K. H.
SØRENSSEN, B.
STAVNEBREKK, S. J.
STUGU, O. S.
THOMASSEN, Ø.
THORSEN, M.
THORSETH, M.
TOPSØE, E. M.
TORVIK, R.
TRETVIK, A. M.
ULRICHSEN, J. H.
VAN DOMMELEN, W.
VULCHANOVA, M. D.
WAADELAND, C. H.
WAHLGREN, S.
WALLERSTRØM, T.
WYLLER, T. E.

YTTREDAL, T.

Faculty of Information Technology, Mathematics and Electrical Engineering (tel. 73-59-42-02; e-mail postmottak@ime.ntnu.no; internet www.ntnu.no/ime):

AAGESEN, F. A.
AAMO, O. M.
AAMODT, A.
AKSNES, A.
ANDRESEN, S. H.
AUDESTAD, J. A.
AUNET, S.
BAAS, N. A.
BALASINGHAM, I.
BERGH, P. A.
BERNSTEIN, R. W.
BLAKE, R.
BRÆK, R.
BRATBERGSENGEN, K.
BRATSBERG, S. E.
BUAN, A. B.
CARLSEN, T. M.
CELLEDONI, E.
CONRADI, R.
DIGERNES, T.
DIVITINI, M.
DO, V. T.
DONG, H.
DOORMAN, G. L.
DOWNING, K.
ENGEN, S.
FIMLAND, B.
FJELDLY, T. A.
FORNÆSS, J. E.
FOSS, B. A.
FOSSEN, T. I.
FOSSO, O. B.
GAMBÄCK, B.
GLIGOROSKI, D.
GRAVDAHL, J. T.
GREPSTAD, J.
GULLA, J. A.
HADDOW, P.
HALAAS, A.
HALLINGSTAD, O.
HEEGAARD, P. E.
HELVIK, B. E.
HERRMANN, P. M.
HJELME, D. R.
HØIDALEN, H. K.
HOLDEN, H.
HOLTE, N.
HOVD, M.
HVASSHOVD, S.
ILDSTAD, E.
IMSLAND, L. S.
JACCHERI, M. L.
JAKOBSEN, E. R.
JIANG, Y.
JOHANSEN, T. A.
KJELDSBERG, P. G.
KJØLLE, G. H.
KNAPSKOG, S. J.
KOUZAEV, G.
KRISTENSEN, Å.
KRISTIANSEN, L.
KRISTIANSEN, U. R.
KROGSTIE, J.
KURE, Ø.
KVÆRNØ, A.
LANDSTAD, M. B.
LANGSETH, H.
LINDQVIST, B. H.
LINDQVIST, L. P.
LORENTZEN, L.
LUNDHEIM, L. M.
LYUBARSKII, Y.
MIDTGÅRD, O.
MJØLSNES, S. F.
MOLDEKLEV, K.
MOLINAS, M. M. C.
MONTEIRO, E.
MULLER, R. R.
NÆSS, A.
NATVIG, L.

NILSSEN, R.
NORUM, L. E.
NØRVÅG, K.
NYGÅRD, M.
NYSVEEN, A.
OMHOLT, G. J. G.
OMRE, K. H.
ONSHUS, T. E.
OPPERMANN, S.
ØSTERBERG, U. L.
OWREN, B.
PAXAL, V. M.
PERKIS, A.
PETTERSEN, K. Y.
PETTERSEN, O. K.
RANDEBERG, L. L.
RØNNING, F.
RØNNINGEN, L. A.
RØNQUIST, E.
RUE, H.
SÆLID, S.
SÆTROM, P.
SAGATUN, S. V.
SAND, K.
SEIP, K.
SELBERG, S.
SHIRIAEV, A.
SINDRE, G.
SKAAR, J.
SKRAMSTAD, T.
SMALØ, S. O.
SOLBERG, Ø.
SØLVBERG, I.
SØRDALEN, O. J.
STÅLHANE, T.
STENSØNES, B.
STRAUME, E.
SVANÆS, D.
SVARSTAD, K.
SVENDSEN, T.
SVENSSON, P.
THEOHARIS, T.
TJELMELAND, H.
TOUSSAINT, P. J.
TUFTO, J.
TYBELL, T.
UHLEN, K.
UNDELAND, T. M.
USHAKOV, N.
WANG, A. I.
WANGENSTEEN, I.
WEMAN, H.
YDSTIE, B. E.
YTTERDAL, T.

Faculty of Medicine (tel. 73-59-88-59; e-mail dmf-post@medisin.ntnu.no; internet www.ntnu.no/dmf):

AADAHL, P.
AAKHUS, S.
AAMODT, A.
AASLY, J.
ALBREKTSEN, G.
ANGELSEN, A.
ANGELSEN, B. A. J.
ANTHONSEN, M. W.
AUGUSTO, C.
AUSTGULEN, R.
BENTZEN, N.
BERGH, K.
BJERVE, K. S.
BJØRNGAARD, J. H.
BØNAA, K. H.
BORCHGREVINK, P. C.
BOVIM, G.
BRATLID, D.
BRENNA, E.
BRODTKORB, E.
BRUBAKK, A.
BRUM, P. C.
CARLSEN, S. M.
CHEN, D.
DALE, A.
DALE, O.
DAMÅS, J. K.
DRABLØS, F.

EIK-NES, S.
ELSÅS, T. B.
ESPEVIK, T.
FARUP, P. G.
FAYERS, P.
FINSEN, V.
FJØSNE, H. E.
FORSMO, S.
GETZ, L.
GISVOLD, S. E.
GRIBBESTAD, I.
GRILL, V.
GRIMSMO, A.
GRØNBECH, J. E.
GUSTAFSSON, B.
HAGEN, B.
HAGEN, K.
HALAAS, Ø.
HALGUNSET, J.
HALLAN, S.
HAMMERSTRØM, J.
HARALDSETH, O.
HAUGEBERG, G.
HEERSCHAP, A.
HELGERUD, J.
HERNES, T. A. N.
HETLEVIK, I.
HILT, B.
HOFF, J.
HOLEN, A.
HOLM, S.
HOLMEN, J.
HOLMEN, J.
HOLMEN, T. T. L.
HVEEM, K.
INDREDAVIK, B.
INDREDAVIK, M. S.
IVERSEN, O.
JACOBSEN, G. W.
KAASA, S.
KIRKENGEN, A. L.
KLEIN, G.
KLEPP, O.
KLEPSTAD, P.
KLEVELAND, P. M.
KLUNGLAND, H.
KLUNGLAND, H.
KOLMANNSKOG, S.
KRISTOFFERSEN, K.
KROKAN, H. E.
LÆGREID, A.
LARSSON, B. S.
LARSSON, E.
LARSSON, H.
LEIVSETH, G.
LEREIM, I.
LIEN, E.
LINAKER, O. M.
LINDE, M.
LØVIK, M.
LUNDGREN, S.
LYDERSEN, S.
MARHAUG, G.
MATTSSON, E.
MEHTA, M.
MIDELFART, A.
MIDTHJELL, K.
MØRK, C.
MORKEN, G.
MØRKVED, S.
MØRKVED, S.
MOSER, E. I.
MOSER, M.
NILSEN, A. M.
NILSEN, O. G.
NORDGÅRD, S.
NORDRUM, I. S.
NYGAARD, Ø. P.
NYLENNA, M.
OTTERLEI, M.
ROMUNDSTAD, P. R.
RYGG, M.
RYGNESTAD, T.
SÆTHER, O. D.
SÆTROM, P.
SALVESEN, K. A.

SAND, T.
SANDVIK, A. K.
SCHEI, B.
SCHØNBERG, S. M.
SEIM, A.
SELLEVOLD, O.
SKOGVOLL, E.
SKOGVOLL, E.
SKORPEN, F.
SKRANES, J.
SLETVOLD, O.
SLØRDAL, L.
SLUPPHAUG, G.
SMITH, G. L.
SOLBERG, B.
SONNEWALD, U.
SPIGSET, O.
STEINER, T. J.
STEINSBEKK, A.
STEINSHAMN, S. L.
STENMARK, H.
STENSETH, R.
STØYLEN, A.
STRØMSKAG, K. E.
SUND, A. M.
SUNDAN, A.
SYVERSEN, U.
TORP, S. H.
TORP, H.
TRETLI, S.
TREVES, A.
UNSGÅRD, G.
USSERY, D. W.
VASSELJEN, O.
VATTEN, L. J.
VIK, T.
VIK, A.
VOGT, C.
WAAGE, A.
WAHBA, A.
WALDUM, H.
WESTIN, S.
WHITE, L.
WIBE, A.
WISETH, R.
WISLØFF, U.
WITTER, M.
ZIEGLER, C. M.

Faculty of Natural Sciences and Technology
(tel. 73-59-41-97; e-mail postmottak@nt.ntnu
.no; internet www.ntnu.no/nt):

ALMAAS, E.
ALSBERG, B. K.
AMUNDSEN, T.
ANDERSEN, J. O.
ARMBRUSTER, W. S.
ARNBERG, L.
ARUKWE, A.
ÅSTRAND, P. O.
AUNE, R. E.
AURSAND, M.
BECH, C.
BERG, O. K.
BERG, T.
BLEKKAN, E. A.
BONES, A. M.
BORG, A.
BRANDVIK, P. J.
BRATAAS, A.
BRESME, F.
CHEN, D.
CHRISTENSEN, B. E.
DAVIES, C.
DRAGET, K. I.
DYKYY, O.
EINARSRUD, M.
EINUM, S.
ELLINGSEN, T. E.
ESPY, P. J.
FIKSDAHL, A.
FLATEN, T. P.
FORSGREN, E.
FORSMAN, L. K.
FOSSUM, J. O.
FURU, T.

GIBSON, U.
GRAAE, B. J.
GRANDE, T.
GREGERSEN, Ø. W.
GRONG, Ø.
HAARBERG, G. M.
HÄGG, M.
HANSEN, A.
HAUGEN, A.
HIBBINS, R.
HILLESTAD, M.
HJELEN, J.
HOLMEDAL, B.
HOLMESTAD, R.
HØYE, J. S.
JAKOBSEN, H. A.
JENSRUD, O.
JENSSEN, B. M.
JOHANSEN, B.
JOHNSEN, G.
JUSTNES, H.
KACHELRIESS, M.
KARLSEN, M.
KILDEMO, M.
KJELSTRUP, S.
KJØRSVIK, E.
KNUDSEN, K. D.
KOCH, H.
KOLBEINSEN, L.
KUIPER, M. T. R.
KVITTINGEN, L.
LANDE, R.
LINDGREN, M.
LINDMO, T.
LJONES, T.
LUNDER, O.
MARTHINSEN, K.
M'HAMDI, M.
MIKKELSEN, A.
MIKKELSEN, Ø.
MOLJORD, K.
MORK, J.
MYRHEIM, J.
NAQVI, K. R.
NICHOLSON, D. G.
NILSSEN, K. J.
NISANCIOGLU, K.
OLAUSSEN, K.
OLSEN, Y.
ØSTGAARD, K.
OTTESEN, R. T.
ØYE, G.
PARTALI, V.
PELABON, C.
PREISIG, H. A.
RAAEN, S.
REINERTSEN, R. E.
REISO, O.
RØNNING, M.
ROSENQVIST, G.
RØSKAFT, E.
ROVEN, H. J.
RUSTAD, T.
RYTTER, E.
SÆTHER, B.
SAMSETH, J.
SIKORSKI, P. T.
SIMONSEN, I.
SJØBLOM, J.
SKAGERSTAM, B.
SKJÅK-BRÆK, G.
SKOGESTAD, S.
SÖDERSTRÖM, L.
SOLBERG, J. K.
SOLLIE, R.
SOROKINA, I. T.
STOKKE, B. T.
STRAND, B. L.
SUDBØ, A.
SUNDE, S.
SVENDSEN, H. F.
SVENSSON, A. M.
TANGSTAD, M.
TVEIT, H.
VADSTEIN, O.
VALLA, S.

VÅRUM, K. M.
VENVIK, H. J.
VERSTEEG, G. F.
WALMSLEY, J.
WIIK, K.
WRIGHT, J.
YSTENES, M.
ZOTCHEV, S.

Faculty of Social Sciences and Technology Management (tel. 73-59-19-00; e-mail postmottak@svt.ntnu.no; internet www.ntnu.no/svt):

AALBERG, T.
ALMÅS, R.
ASPELUND, A.
AUGESTAD, L. B.
BAILEY, J. L.
BÅRDSEN, G.
BERG, B.
BERG, N. I. G.
BLEKESAUNE, A.
BONESRØNNING, H.
BORGE, L.
BRANDTH, B.
BUHAUG, H.
CARLSEN, F.
CHRISTIANSEN, M.
DAHL-JØRGENSEN, C.
DALE, B. E.
DE, S. I. S.
DE, B. L.
DROTTZ, S. B.
ERRING, B. B.
ESPNES, G. A.
ETTEMA, G. J.
FAGERHOLT, K.
FALCH, T.
FET, A. M.
FLETEN, S.
FROSTAD, P.
GABRIEL, U.
GAIVORONSKI, A. A.
GATES, S. G.
GLEDITSCH, N. P.
GYNNILD, V.
HAGEN, I.
HAMMER, T. H.
HESTAD, K.
HJELMELAND, H. M.
HJEMDAL, O.
HOHR, H.
HOVDEN, J.
HOVDEN, J.
HVATTUM, L. M.
IMSEN, G.
INNSTRAND, S. T.
IRGENS, E. J.
IYENGAR, S.
JACOBSEN, K. H.
JENSEN, A.
JENSSEN, A. T.
JOHANSEN, K.
JONES, M. R. H.
KARLSDOTTIR, R.
KARLSEN, A.
KJELLEN, U. A. G.
KJØRHOLT, A. T.
KLØCKNER, C.
KNIZEK, B. L.
KNUTSEN, T. L.
KRISTIANSEN, K.
KROKAN, A.
KROPOTOV, Y.
KVALSUND, R.
KVANDE, E.
LEIN, H.
LEIULFSRUD, H.
LEVIN, M.
LINDSET, S.
LINDSTRØM, B.
LISTHAUG, O.
LUND, R.
MADSEN, T. K.
MATSEN, E.
MEHMETOGLU, M.

MIDFORD, P.
MOEN, T.
MOEN, Ø.
MOSES, J.
MOXNES, K.
NILSEN, T. I. L.
NILSEN, R. D.
NORDAHL, H. M.
NYGREEN, B.
OLSEN, B.
ØSTERN, A.
PEDERSEN, A.
PETERSEN, T. K. A.
PIJL, S. J.
POSTHOLM, M. B.
RAMET, S. P.
RASMUSSEN, B.
RASMUSSEN, K.
RATTSØ, J.
REITAN, M.
RINGDAL, K.
RINGDAL, G. I.
RISMARK, M.
ROELEVELD, K.
ROGSTAD, J.
RUNDMO, T.
RYE, J. F.
SÆTNAN, A. R.
SÆTRE, A. S.
SAKSVIK, P. Ø.
SCHIEFLOE, P. M.
SIGMUNDSSON, H.
SIMKUS, A. A.
SKONHOFT, A.
SOHLBERG, P.
SOLHAUG, T.
SØRHEIM, R.
STAVIK-KARLSEN, G.
STEINSHOLT, K.
STENØIEN, J. M.
STILES, T. C.
STRØM, B.
SVENDSEN, K. V. H.
THORSVIK, J.
TINGSTAD, V.
TJORA, A.
TOMASGARD, A.
TORVIK, R.
TØSSEBRO, J.
VAN DER MEER, A.
VAN DER WEEL, F.
VAN DER WIJST, D.
VEREIJKEN, E.
VETTENRANTA, S.
VIKAN, A.
VOGEL, P. A.
WELLS, A.
WESTGAARD, R. H.
WICHSTRØM, L.
WRENCH, J.
YTTERHUS, B.

Museum of Natural History and Archaeology (tel. 73-59-21-45; e-mail post@vm.ntnu.no; internet www.ntnu.no/vitenskapsmuseet):

CHRISTOPHERSEN, A., Archaeology
FLATBERG, K. I., Botany
HOGSTAD, O., Zoology
JASINKSI, M. E., Maritime Archaeology
JOHANSEN, A. B., Archaeology
MOEN, A., Botany
MORK, J., Population Genetics
OLSEN, Y., Marine Physiology
SAKSHAUG, E., Marine Botany
SOGNES, K., Archaeology
SOLEM, J. O., Zoology

UNIVERSITETET FOR MILJØ—OG BIOVITENSKAP (UMB)
(Norwegian University of Life Sciences)

POB 5003, 1432 Ås
Universitetstunet 3, 1432 Ås
Telephone: 64-96-50-00
E-mail: postmottak@umb.no

Internet: www.umb.no

Founded 1859 as State College, present name and status 2005
Languages of instruction: English, Norwegian
Academic year: August to August

Depts of animal and aquacultural sciences, chemistry, biotechnology and food science, ecology and natural resource management, economics and resource management, international environment and development studies/noragric, landscape architecture and spatial planning, mathematical sciences and technology, plant and environmental sciences

Rector: Prof. HANS FREDRIK HOEN
Pro-Rector for Education: MARI SUNDLI TVEIT
Pro-Rector for Research: RUTH HAUG
Univ. Dir: SIRI MARGRETHE LÖKSA
Dir for Acad. Affairs: OLE-JØRGEN TORP
Dir for Research: RAGNHILD SOLHEIM
Library Dir: GEIR ARNE ROSVOLL

Library: see under Libraries and Archives
Number of teachers: 640
Number of students: 4,420

UNIVERSITETET I AGDER
(University of Agder)

POB 422 Kristiansand, 4604 Grimstad

Telephone: 38-14-10-00
E-mail: post@uia.no
Internet: www.uia.no

Founded 1994 as Agder Univ. College by merger of 6 regional colleges, present name and status 2007

Rector: Prof. Dr TORUNN LAUVDAL
Vice-Rector for Education: Dr MARIT AAMODT NIELSEN
Vice-Rector for Research, Dissemination and Innovation: Dr DAG G. AASLAND
Univ. Dir: TOR A. AAGEDAL
Chief Librarian: HANNE G. MOVIG

Library of 200,000 vols, 1,500 periodicals
Number of teachers: 600
Number of students: 10,000

DEANS

Faculty of Economics and Social Sciences: Dr SIGBJØRN SODAL
Faculty of Engineering and Science: Prof. Dr FRANK REICHERT
Faculty of Fine Arts: PER KVIST
Faculty of Health and Sports Sciences: Prof. Dr STEPHEN SEILER
Faculty of Humanities and Education: Dr ERNST HAKON JAHR

UNIVERSITETET I BERGEN
(University of Bergen)

POB 7800, 5020 Bergen

Telephone: 55-58-00-00
E-mail: post@uib.no
Internet: www.uib.no

Founded 1946
State control
Academic year: August to June

Rector: Prof. SIGMUND GRØNMO
Pro-Rector: Prof. BERIT ROKNE
Vice-Rector for Education: Prof. KUVVET ATAKAN
Vice-Rector for Int. Relations: Prof. ASTRI ANDRESEN
Univ. Dir: KARI TOVE ELVBAKKEN
Library Dir: RANDI ELISABETH TAXT

Library: see under Libraries and Archives
Number of teachers: 1,999
Number of students: 14,500

Publications: *Ilicifolia* (irregular), *Naturen* (6 a year, popular scientific review), *Sarsia* (6 a year)

DEANS

Faculty of Humanities: Prof. GJERT KRISTOF-FERSEN
Faculty of Law: Prof. ASBJØRN STRANDBAKKEN
Faculty of Mathematics and Natural Sciences: Prof. DAG RUNE OLSEN
Faculty of Medicine and Dentistry: Prof. NINA LANGELAND
Faculty of Psychology: Prof. JARLE EID
Faculty of Social Sciences: Prof. KNUT HELLAND

PROFESSORS

Faculty of Humanities (POB 7805, 5020 Bergen; tel. 55-58-93-80; e-mail post@hf.uib.no; internet www.uib.no/hf):

ÅDLAND, E., General Literature
AKSELBERG, G., Nordic Language
ALVER, B. G., Folklore
ANGVIK, B., Spanish
ARMSTRONG, C. I., British Literature
ÅRSETH, A., Nordic Language
BAGGE, S. H., History
BELL, J. N., Arabic
BERGGREEN, B., Ethnology
BJØRGO, N., Archaeology
BJØRKELO, A., History
BONDEVIK, J., Nordic Language
BØRTNES, J., Russian Literature
BREIVIK, L. E., English Philology
BROWN, E., Philosophy
BUVIK, P., General Literature
CHRISTENSEN, K. K., General Linguistics
DANBOLT, G., History of Art
DE CUZZANI, P. M., Philosophy
DYRVIK, S., History
DYVIK, H. J., General Linguistics
ENDSJØ, D., Religious Studies
FJELL, T. I., Cultural Studies and History of Art
FLØTTUM, K., French Language
FORSBERG, L. L., Archaeology
GILHUS, A. I. S., Religion
GRØNLIE, T., History
GULLVEIG, B. A., Folklore
HAAVERT, I. E., History
HÄGG, T., Classical Philology
HÅLAND, R., African Archaeology
HALMØY, O., French Language
HALVERSEN, S., Philology
HAUG, E., History
HAUGEN, O. E., Nordic Language
HELLE, L. J., Russian Language
HENSHILWOOD, C., Archaeology
HESTVIK, A., General Linguistics
HOLGERNES, B., Philosophy
HOLM, H. V., Philology
HOVLAND, E., History
HUBBARD, W. H., History
JANICKI, K., English Philology
JOHANNESSEN, H., Philosophy
JOHANNESSEN, K. S., Philosophy
JOHNSEN, K. O., Philosophy
KIILERICH, B. K., History of Art
KITTANG, A., General Literature
KOLLER, W., German Language
KRISTOFFERSEN, G., Nordic Language
KROEPELIEN, B., History of Art
LIE, R. K., Philosophy
LINNEBERG, A., General Literature
LUNDE, I., Russian Language and Literature
MCCAFFERTY, K., British Literature
MELVE, L., History
MEYER, J. C., History of Art
MEYER, S., European Culture
MIKAELSSON, L., Religion
MORTENSEN, E., General Literature
MUNDAL, E., Nordic Languages
NAGEL, A.-H., History
NORDENSTAM, T., Philosophy
O'FAHEY, R. S., History
ØSTBY, E., Archaeology
ØVERLAND, O., American Literature
ØYE, I., Archaeology

PIERCE, R., Egyptology
QUESEDA-PACHECO, M. A., Spanish
ROKSTAD, K., Philosophy
RYDVING, L. O. H., Religion
SÄÄTELÄ, S. T. S., Philosophy
SÆTRE, L., General Literature
SANAKER, J. K., French Language
SANDBERG, B., German Literature
SANDØY, H., Nordic Language
SCHRØTER, H. G., History
SELBERG, T., Folklore
SILLARS, S. J., English Philology
SKÅNLAND, M. H., Linguistics
SKARSTEN, R., Humanistic Informatics
SKILLEÅS, O. M., Philosophy
SKIRBEKK, G., Philosophy
SKULSTAD, A. S., English Philology
STEGANE, I., Nordic Language
STRAUSBERG, M., Religion
SVENDSEN, L. F., Philosophy
THOMASSEN, E., Religion
UTAKER, A., Philosophy
VELAND, R. M., French Language
VENNESLAN, K., Philosophy
VIKØR, K. S., History
WINTHER, T., French Language
WÆRNESS, K. E., Sociology

Faculty of Law (POB 7806, 5020 Bergen; tel. 55-58-95-00; e-mail post@jurfa.uib.no; internet www.uib.no/jur):

ÅLL, J.
ÅSEN, H. S.
ASKELAND, B.
BERNT, J. F.
FRANTZEN, T.
GIERTSEN, J.
HOLGERSEN, G.
HUSABØ, E. J.
KONOW, B.-E.
KRÜGER, K.
LUNDE, T.
MÆLAND, H. J.
MONSEN, E.
NORDTVEIT, E.
NYGAARD, N.
RASMUSSEN, Ø.
SÆBO, R.
SØVIG, K. H.
SUNDE, J.
TRUYEN, F.

Faculty of Mathematics and Natural Sciences (POB 7803, 5020 Bergen; tel. 55-58-20-62; e-mail post@mnfa.uib.no; internet www.uib.no/matnat):

AKSNES, D., Chemistry
AKSNES, D. L., Fisheries Biology
ANDERSEN, Ø. M., Chemistry
BÅMSTEDT, U., Fisheries Biology
BERG, C. C., Botany
BERGE, G., Mathematics
BERNTSEN, J., Mathematics
BEZEM, M. A., Computer Science
BIRKELAND, N.-K., Microbiology
BIRKS, H. J. B., Botany
BJØRSTAD, P. E., Computer Science
BRATBAK, G., Microbiology
BRIX, O., Zoology
CSERNAI, L., Physics
DAHLE, H. K., Mathematics
DYSTHE, K., Mathematics
ECKHOFF, K. S., Mathematics
ECKHOFF, R. K., Physics
EIGEN, G., Physics
ENDRESEN, C., Fisheries Biology
ENGEVIK, L. E., Mathematics
ESPEDAL, M., Mathematics
ESPELID, T. O., Computer Science
FERNØ, A., Fisheries Biology
FJOSE, A., Molecular Biology
FOSSEN, F., Geology
FRANCIS, G. W., Organic Chemistry
FRODESEN, A. G., Physics
FURNES, H., Petroleum Geology
FYHN, H. J., Milieu Physiology
GABRIELSEN, R., Petroleum Geology

GADE, H. G., Physical Oceanography
GAMMELSRØD, T., Physical Oceanography
GISKE, J., Fisheries Biology
GRAHL-NIELSEN, O., Chemistry
GRAUE, A., Physics
GRØNÅS, S., Meteorology
GUDMUNDSSON, A., Geology
HAMMER, E. A., Physics
HANSEN, J. P., Physics
HANYGA, A., Applied Geophysics
HAUGAN, P. M., Geophysics
HAVSKOV, J., Applied Geophysics
HELLAND, D. E., Molecular Biology
HELLAND-HANSEN, W., Geology
HELLESETH, T., Computer Science
HEUCH, I., Mathematics
HOBÆK, H., Physics
HOFFMAN, A. C., Physics
HØGSTEDT, G., Zoology
HØILAND, H., Physical Chemistry
HOLME, A., Mathematics
HUSEBYE, E., Applied Geophysics
HUSEBYE, S., Chemistry
JAKOBSEN, P. J., Zoology
JANSEN, E., Geology
JENSEN, H. B., Molecular Biology
JOHANNESEN, O. M., Physical Oceanography
JOHNSEN, T., Mathematics
JØRGENSEN, P. M., Botany
KALAND, P. E., Botany
KLØVE, T., Computer Science
KNUDSEN, L. R., Computer Science
KNUTSEN, G., Microbiology
KOCBACH, L., Physics
KOLLTVEIT, K., Physics
KRISTOFFERSEN, Y., Seismology
KRYVI, H., Zoology
KVALHEIM, O. M., Chemistry
KVAMME, B., Physics
LARSSON, P., Zoology
LAURITZEN, S.-E., Geology
LIEN, T., Microbiology
LILLEHAUG, J., Molecular Biology
LILLESTØL, E., Physics
LØVLIE, R., Geomagnetism
MAALØE, S. B., Geology
MÆLAND, E., Applied Geophysics
MALYSHEV, A., Computer Science
MANGERUD, J., Quaternary Geology
MANNE, R. E., Chemistry
MJELDE, R., Applied Geophysics
MOE, D., Botany
MUNTHE-KAAS, H., Computer Science
MYKLEBOST, K., Physics
NÆVDAL, G., Fisheries Biology
NEMEC, W., Geology
NESJE, A., Geology
NYLUND, A., Fisheries Biology
ØIEN, A. H., Mathematics
OSLAND, P., Physics
PAULSEN, J., Mathematics
PEDERSEN, R.-B., Geology
RAAE, A. J., Molecular Biology
ROBINS, B., Geology
RØDSETH, Ø. J., Mathematics
RØHRICH, D., Physics
RYE, N. M., Geology
SÆTHER, O. A., Zoology
SÆTHRE, L. J., Chemistry
SALVANES, A. G. V.
SCHRADER, H., Geology
SEJRUP, H. P., Geology
SKARTVEIT, A., Physical Oceanography
SKOGEN, A., Botany
SKORPING, A., Zoology
SLETTEN, E., Physical Chemistry
SLETTEN, J., Inorganic Chemistry
SONGSTAD, J., Inorganic Chemistry
SØRÅS, F., Physics
SØREVIK, T., Computer Science
STAMNES, J. J., Physics
STEFANSSON, S., Fisheries Biology
STEIHAUG, T., Informatics
STORETVEDT, K. M., Geomagnetism
STORØY, S., Computer Science

STRAY, A., Mathematics
STRØMME, S. A., Mathematics
STUGU, B., Physics
SUNDVOR, E., Seismology
SVENDSEN, H., Physical Oceanography
SVENDSEN, J.-I., Geology
SYDNES, L. K., Chemistry
TAI, X.-C., Mathematics
TALBOT, M. R., Petroleum Geology
TELLE, J. A., Computer Science
THINGSTAD, T. F., Microbiology
TJØSTHEIM, D. B., Statistics
TØNSBERG, T., Botany
TORSVIK, V. L., Microbiology
TOTLAND, G. K., Zoology
TVERBERG, H., Mathematics
ULLTANG, Ø., Fisheries Biology
VÅGEN, J. S., Physics
WALTHER, B. T., Molecular Biology
WILLASSEN, E., Zoology
YTREHUS, Ø., Computer Science

Faculty of Medicine and Dentistry (POB 7804, 5020 Bergen; tel. 55-58-20-86; e-mail post@mofa.uib.no; internet www.uib.no/mofa):

AKSNES, L., Clinical Medicine
ÅRLI, J. A., Clinical Medicine
ÅRSTAD, H. J., Surgical Sciences
ARVIDSON, K. F., Dentistry
ÅSTROM, A. N., Dentistry
BÆRHEIM, A., General Practice
BAKKE, M., Biomedicine
BAKKEN, V., Oral Microbiology
BERG, E., Prosthesis
BERGE, M. E., Prosthodontics
BERGE, T. I., Dentistry
BERGGREEN, E., Biomedicine
BINDOFF, L., Clinical Medicine
BJERKNES, R., Clinical Medicine
BJERKVIG, R., Biomedicine
BJØRGE, T., Epidemiology
BJØRVATN, B., General Practice
BLYSTAD, A., Nursing Science
BØ, L., Clinical Medicine
BOLSTAD, A. I., Dental Research
BOMAN, H., Clinical Medicine
BRAMHAM, C. R. E., Biomedicine
BRÅTVEIT, M., Physiology
BRUDVIK, P., Dentistry
DALTVEIT, A. K., Epidemiology
DØSKELAND, S. E., Biomedicine
EIDE, R., Dental Materials
ENGESÆTER, L. B., Surgical Sciences
ESPELID, I., Paedodontics
FASMER, O. B., Clinical Medicine
GERDES, H.-H., Biomedicine
GJENGEDAL, E., Praxeology
GJERDET, N. R., Dental Materials
GJESDAL, S., Public Health
GREVE, G., Clinical Medicine
GRONG, K., Surgical Sciences
GULLBERG, D., Biomedicine
HAAVIK, R., Biomedicine
HALSE, A., Oral Radiology
HARTVEIT, J., Biomedicine
HAUG, K., General Practice
HAUKAAS, S. A., Surgical Sciences
HAVER, B., Clinical Medicine
HELLE, K. B., Biomedicine
HELLEM, S., Oral Surgery
HOLSTEN, F., Clinical Medicine
HØVDING, G., Clinical Medicine
HUSBY, P., Surgical Sciences
IVERSEN, O.-E., Clinical Medicine
JOHANNESSEN, A. C., Oral Pathology
JONUNG, J. A. T., Surgical Sciences
JØRGENSEN, H., Clinical Medicine
KETTUNEN, P., Biomedicine
KISERUD, T., Clinical Medicine
KLOCK, K., Dentistry
KROHN, J., Clinical Medicine
KRÜGER, P. G., Biomedicine
KUSCHE-GULLBERG, M., Biomedicine
LARSEN, T., Biomedicine
LEKNES, K., Dentistry

LEKVEN, J., Surgical Sciences
LORENS, J., Biomedicine
LUND, A., Clinical Medicine
LUNDERVOLD, A., Biomedicine
LUND-JOHANSEN, M., Surgical Sciences
LUUKKO, K. A., Biomedicine
MÆLAND, J., Social Medicine
MARTINEZ, A., Biomedicine
MELAND, E., General Practice
MOE-NILSSEN, R., Physiotherapy
MOEN, B. E., Occupational and Environmental Medicine
MØLLER, P., Surgical Sciences
MUSTAFA, K., Dentistry
MYKLEBUST, R., Biomedicine
NATVIG, G., Nursing Science
NJØLSTAD, P. R., Clinical Medicine
NORGÅRD, G., Clinical Medicine
NORHEIM, O. F., Medical Ethics
NYLAND, H. I., Clinical Medicine
OLOFSSON, J., Surgical Sciences
ØYMAR, K., Clinical Medicine
PETERSEN, K. A., Praxeology
PRYME, I. F., Biomedicine
RÅDAL, M. J., Odontophobia and Paedodontics
RASMUSSEN, S., Clinical Medicine
RØDAHL, E., Clinical Medicine
RØRVIK, J., Surgical Sciences
ROSLAND, J. H., Surgical Sciences
SALVESEN, H. B., Clinical Medicine
SARASTE, J., Biomedicine
SØNDENAA, K., Surgical Sciences
STEEN, V. M., Clinical Medicine
STRAND, G., Dentistry
TANG, T., Clinical Medicine
TAXT, T., Biomedicine
TENSTAD, O., Biomedicine
TJØLSEN, A., Biomedicine
VASSTRAND, E., Dentistry
VEDELER, A., Biomedicine
VISTE, A., Surgical Sciences
WESTER, K., Surgical Sciences
WIIG, H., Biomedicine
WIK, G., Clinical Medicine
WISTH, P. J., Orthodontics

Faculty of Psychology (POB 7807, 5020 Bergen; tel. 55-58-27-10; e-mail post@psyfa.uib.no; internet www.uib.no/psyfa):

AARØ, L. E., Social Psychology
ANDERSSEN, N., Social Psychology
ASBJØRNSEN, A E., Biological and Medical Psychology
BØHM, G., Social Psychology
DALLAND, T., Social Psychology
EID, J., Social Psychology
EINARSEN, S., Social Psychology
HAVIK, O. E., Clinical Psychology
HELLAND, T., Biological and Medical Psychology
HUGDAHL, K., Somatic Psychology
JOHNSEN, B. H., Social Psychology
KVALE, G., Clinical Psychology
LABERG, J. C., Clinical Psychology
LÆNG, B., Biological and Medical Psychology
LINSTRØM, T. C., Social Psychology
LUNDERVOLD, A., Biological and Medical Psychology
MANGER, T., Social Psychology
MATTHIESEN, S., Social Psychology
MURISON, R., Physiological Psychology
NIELSEN, G. H., Clinical Psychology
NORDHUS, I. H., Clinical Psychology
PALLESEN, S., Social Psychology
REBER, R., Biological and Medical Psychology
SAM, D. L., Personal Psychology
SANDAL, G. M., Social Psychology
SKOGSTAD, A., Social Psychology
STORMARK, K. M., Child Psychology
SUNDBERG, H., Physiological Psychology
VOLLMER, F., Personal Psychology
WICKLUND, R. A., Social Psychology

Faculty of Social Sciences (POB 7802, 5020 Bergen; tel. 55-58-90-50; e-mail post@svfa.uib.no; internet www.uib.no/svf):

AMUNDSEN, E. S., Economics
ÅRRESTAD, J., Economics
ÅSE, T. H., Geography
BAKKE, M., Media Studies
BJELLAND, A. K., Social Anthropology
BLEIKLIE, I., Administration and Organization Theory
DAVIDSEN, P., Geography
EIDE, M., Media Studies
FIMREITE, A., Administration and Organization Theory
FLÅM, S. D., Economics
FLØYSAND, A., Geography
GOODNOW, K. J., Media Studies
GRAN, T., Administration and Organization Theory
GRIPSRUD, J., Media Studies
GRØNHAUG, R., Social Anthropology
GRØNMO, S., Sociology
GULBRANDSEN, Ø., Social Anthropology
HENRIKSEN, G., Social Anthropology
HOLT-JENSEN, A., Geography
HVIDING, E., Social Anthropology
HÅLAND, G., Social Anthropology
JOHANSEN, A., Media Studies
KAPFERER, B., Social Anthropology
KAPFERER, J., Sociology
KJELDSEN, J. E., Media Studies
KNUDSEN, J. C., Social Anthropology
KORSNES, O., Sociology
KUHNLE, S., Comparative Politics
LÆGREID, P., Administration and Organization Theory
LARSEN, P. L., Media Studies
LILLEHAUG, B. W., Media Studies
LINDSTRØM, U. A., Comparative Politics
LINDKVIST, K. B., Geography
LITHMAN, Y., Sociology
LOMMERUD, K. E., Economics
LUNDBERG, A., Geography
MANGER, L. O., Social Anthropology
MIDTBØ, T., Comparative Politics
MOXNES, E., Geography
NILSEN, A., Sociology
OPDAHL, A. L., Information Science
ØSTBYE, H., Media Studies
RISA, A. E., Economics
RONESS, P. G., Administration and Organization Theory
RUSTEN, G., Geography
SÆTREN, H., Administration and Organization Theory
STRAND, T., Administration and Organization Theory
SVÅSAND, L. G., Comparative Politics
STRAND, T., Administration and Organization Theory
TESSEM, B., Information Science
TJØTTA, S., Economics
TORSVIK, G., Economics
TVEDT, T., Geography
UHDE, A., Economics
ØYEN, E., Sociology

Bergen Museum (tel. 55-58-93-60; e-mail publikum@bm.uib.no; internet www.uib.no/bergenmuseum):

ACHEN, H. VON, Art History
BERG, C. C., Botany
FOSSEN, H., Geology
INDRELID, S., Archaeology
JØRGENSEN, P. O., Botany
MOE, D., Botany
ØVSTEDAL, D. O., Botany
SÆTHER, O. A., Zoology
TØNSBERG, T., Botany
WILLASSEN, E., Zoology

UNIVERSITETET I NORDLAND
(University of Nordland)

POB 1490, 8049 Bodø

Universitetsalleen 11, 8049 Bodø

Telephone: 75-51-72-00

E-mail: postmottak@uin.no

Internet: www.uin.no

Founded 1972 as Bodø Univ. College, present name and status 2011

State control

Languages of instruction: English, Norwegian

Academic year: August to June

Rector: PÅL A. PEDERSEN

Dir: STIG FOSSUM

Head Librarian: GUNNLAUG HANSTEEN

Library of 90,000 vols of books and periodicals

Number of teachers: 318

Number of students: 5,707

DEANS

Bodø Graduate School of Business: BJØRN OLSEN

Faculty of Biosciences and Aquaculture: Dr REID HOLE

Faculty of Professional Studies: ARNE FJALSTAD

Faculty of Social Sciences: HANNE THOMMESEN

UNIVERSITETET I OSLO
(University of Oslo)

POB 1072, Blindern, 0316 Oslo

Telephone: 22-85-50-50

E-mail: informasjon@uio.no

Internet: www.uio.no

Founded 1811

State control

Academic year: August to June (2 semesters)

Rector: Prof. OLE-PETTER OTTERSEN

Pro-Rector: Dr INGA BOSTAD

Univ. Dir: Dr GUNN-ELIN AA. BJØRNEBOE

Vice-Rectors: Prof. RAGNHILD HENNUM

Library Dir: BENTE R. ANDREASSEN

Library: see under Libraries and Archives

Number of teachers: 3,327

Number of students: 27,414

Publications: *Apollon* (4 a year, in Norwegian; 1 a year, in English), *Uniforum* (16 a year)

DEANS

Faculty of Dentistry: Prof. PÅL BARKVOLL

Faculty of Educational Sciences: Prof. BEIT KARSETH

Faculty of Humanities: Prof. TRINE SYVERTSEN

Faculty of Law: Prof. Dr HANS PETTER GRAVER

Faculty of Mathematics and Natural Sciences: Prof. MORTEN DÆHLEN

Faculty of Medicine: Prof. Dr FRODE VARTDAL

Faculty of Social Sciences: Prof. FANNY DUCKERT

Faculty of Theology: Prof. TRYGVE E. WYLLER

PROFESSORS

Faculty of Dentistry (Geitmyrsvn. 69/71, POB 1142 Blindern, 0317 Oslo; tel. 22-85-20-00; e-mail postmottak@odont.uio.no; internet www.odont.uio.no):

BARKVOLL, P., Dental Surgery

BJØRNLAND, T., Oral Surgery and Medicine

BRODIN, P., Physiology

BRYNE, M., Oral Biology

DEMBIK, Z., Dentistry

ELLINGSEN, J. E., Prosthetic Dentistry

ERIKSEN, H. M., Cariology

ESPELAND, L. V., Dentistry

ESPELID, L., Dentistry

GRYTTEN, J. I., Community Dentistry, Health Economics

HALTENSEN, T. S., Oral Biology

HANSEN, B., Periodontology

HOLST, D. J., Social Dentistry

HAANÆS, H. R., Dental Surgery

HAAPASALO, M., Endodontics

JACOBSEN, I., Pedodontics

JOKSTAD, A., Dentistry

KLINGE, R. F., General and Oral Anatomy

KOPPANG, H. S., General and Oral Pathology

KOPPANG, R., Material Sciences

LARHEIM, T. A., Dentistry

LYNGSTADAAS, S. P., Dentistry

ØGAARD, B., Orthodontics

OLSEN, I., Microbiology

OSMUNDSEN, H., Biochemistry

PREUS, H. R., Periodontology

RISNES, S., General and Oral Anatomy

RYKKE, M., Dentistry

RØED, A., Physiology

SCHEIE, A. AA, Microbiology

SCHENCK, K., Immunology

SKOGLUND, L. A., Dental Pharmacology

SOLHEIM, T., Oral Pathology

STENVIK, A., Orthodontics

THRANE, P. S., Oral Pathology

TRONSTAD, L., Endodontics

TVEIT, A. B., Dentistry

VASSEND, O., Behavioural Science

WÅLER, S. M., Dentistry

Faculty of Educational Sciences (Helga Engs hus, Sem Sælands vei 7, POB 1161 Blindern, 0318 Oslo; tel. 22-85-82-76; e-mail postmottak@uv.uio.no; internet www.uv.uio.no):

BEFRING, E., Special Education

BIRKEMO, A., Pedagogy

BRÅTEN, I., Pedagogy

BROCK-UTNE, B., Pedagogy

DALE, E. L., Pedagogy

DALEN, M., Special Education

ENGELSEN, B. U., General Didactics

GJESME, T., Pedagogy

GJONE, G., Teacher Education and School Development

HAGTVET, B. E., Education, Dyslexia

HANDAL, G., Pedagogy

HAUGE, T. E., Pedagogy

HERTZBERG, F., Teacher Education

JENSEN, K., Pedagogy

JORDE, D., Teacher Education

JORDELL, K. Ø., Pedagogy

LAHN, L. C., Pedagogy

LIE, S., Pedagogy

LIEBERG, S., Pedagogy

LUND, T., Special Education

LYCKE, K. H., Pedagogy

LØVLIE, L., Pedagogy

MARTINSEN, H., Psychology

NIELSEN, H. B., Pedagogy

OSTAD, S., Pedagogy

ØSTERUD, S., Pedagogy

ØZERK, K., Pedagogy

RUDBERG, M., Pedagogy

RYE, H., Special Education

SIMENSEN, A. M., Teacher Education

SJØBERG, S., Pedagogy (Natural Science)

SKOGEN, K., Special Education

STAFSENG, O., Pedagogy

TELLEVIK, J. M., Special Education

TJELDVOLL, A., Pedagogy

TVEIT, K., Pedagogy

ULVUND, S. E., Pedagogy

VONEN, A. M., Pedagogy, Linguistics

WIGGEN, G., Pedagogy

Faculty of Humanities (Administrasjonsbygn., 8 et., POB 1079 Blindern, 0316 Oslo; tel. 22-85-62-93; e-mail postmottak@hf.uio.no; internet www.hf.uio.no):

AKSNES, H., Musical Theory

ALLERN, S., Media and Communication Research

AMUNDSEN, A. B., Folklore

ANDERSEN, Ø., Classical Philology (Greek)

ANDERSEN, P. T., Nordic Literature

ASHEIM, O., Philosophy

ASKEDAL, J. O., German Language

ASZTALOS, M. M., Classical Philology (Latin)

AUESTAD, R. A., Japanese Language

AÚKRÚST, K. H., History of Religions

BACHE-WIIG, H., Nordic Literature

BAUNE, Ø., Philosophy

BENSKIN, M., English Language

BERGE, K. L., Nordic Language

BJERKE, Ø. L. S., Fine Art History

BJØRDAL, F., Philosophy

BJØRGUM, J., History

BJØRKVOLD, J. R., Musicology

BJØRNFLATEN, J. J., Slavonic Languages

BJORVAND, H., German Linguistics

BLIKSRUD, L., Nordic Literature

BØ, G., Norwegian Literature

BØ-RYGG, A., General Aesthetics

BRAAVIG, J., History of Religion

BRANDT, J. R., Classical Archaeology

BRENDEMOEN, B., Turkish Language

BRULAND, K., History

BRYNHILDSVOLL, K., Research on Ibsen

COLLETT, F. P., History

DAHL, H. F., Media and Communication Research

DIMAS, P., Philosophy

EDZARD, L. E., Hebrew and Semitic Languages

EGGE, A., History

EIFRING, H., Modern Chinese Languages

ELSNESS, J., English Language

EMILSSON, E. K., Ancient Philosophy

ENGER, H.-O., Scandinavian Languages and Linguistics

ERIKSEN, A., Folklore

ERIKSEN, T. B., History of Ideas

FAARLUND, J. T., Nordic Language and Literature

FARNER, G., Dutch

FEHR, D., Literature

FJELD, R. E. V., Lexicography

FØRLAND, T. E., History

FREIIN VON VILLIEZ, C., Philosophy

FRELLESVIG, B., Japanese Language and Culture

FRICKE, C., Philosophy

FRIEDMAN, R. M., History

FUGLESTAD, F., History

GAMMELGAARD, K., Central and Eastern European Languages

GJELSVIK, O., Philosophy

GLAMBEK, I., Art History

GODØY, R. I., Musical Theory

GULDBRANDSEN, E. E., Music History

GUNDERSEN, K., French Literature

GUSTAVSSON, A., Ethnology

GUTH, S., Arabic and Middle Eastern Studies

HAARBERG, F., Nordic Literature

HAGEMANN, G., History

HANSEN, C. F., German Language

HANSEN, J. E. E., History of Ideas

HARBSMEIER, C. H., East Asian Languages

HAREIDE, J., Nordic Literature

HAREIDE, S., Philosophy

HASSELGÅRD, H., English Language

HAWKINS, S., Music

HEDEAGER, L., Nordic Archaeology

HELLAND, H. P., French

HEYERDAHL, G. B., History of Ideas

HJELDE, S., History of Religions

HOBÆK HAFF, M., French Language

HODNE, B., Folklore

HOEL, K., Fine Art History

IMENES, O., Philosophy

IVERSEN, I., General Literary Science

JERVELL, H. R., Computer Science

JOHANNESSEN, F. E., History

JOHANNESSEN, J. B., Linguistics

JOHANSEN, K. E., Philosophy

JOHANSSON, A., Modern Economic History

JØRGENSEN, J. G., Nordic Literature

KAARE, B. H., Folklore
KELLER, J. C., Nordic Archaeology
KJELDSTADLI, K., Modern History
KJETSAA, G., Russian Literature
KOLSTØ, P., Russian and East European Studies
KRISTOFFERSEN, K. E., Linguistics, Philology
KROGH, T., History of Ideas
KROGSETH, O., History of Christianity
KVÆRNE, P., History of Religions
KVIFTE, T., Folk Music
LANGE, E., History
LANGHOLM, T., Computer Science
LANZA, E., Linguistics
LAÚK, E., Media and Communication
LIE, S., Norwegian Language
LIEPE, L., Art History
LØDRUP, H., Linguistics
LØNNING, J. T., Computer Science
LOTHE, J., British Literature
LYCHE, C., French, Phonetics
MELBERG, B. A. E., Literature
MOEN, I., Linguistics
MØNNESLAND, S., Slavonic Languages
MORGAN, N., Fine Art History
MYHRE, J., History
NAGUIB, S. N., Cultural History, Cultural Analysis
NEDKVITNE, A., History
NYGAARD, J., Theatre Science
OTTOSSON, K., Icelandic
PEDERSEN, A., Philosophy
PETTERSON, E. R., Fine Art History
PHARO, H., History
PRELL, H.-P., German Language
PRICE, P. G., History
QUILLER, B., History of Ideas
RAMBERG, B., Philosophy
RAND, K. A., English Language
RASMUSSEN, T., Media and Communication
REINTON, R., Literary Theory
REM, T., English Literature
RIAN, Ø., History
RINDAL, M., Nordic Onomastics
ROGAN, B., Ethnology
RØNNING, H., Media and Communication Research
RUUD, E., Musicology
SÆBØ, K. J., German Language
SAGMO, I., German Literature
SALBERG, T. K., French
SANDE, S., Classical Archaeology
SAÚGSTAD, F., Philosophy
SCHAANNING, E., History of Ideas
SCHMIDT, T., Nordic Literature
SERCK-HANSSEN, C., Philosophy
SIMONSEN, H. G., Linguistics
SIRGES, T., German Language
SKATTURN, I., Francophone Studies
SKAUG, E., Art Conservation
SKEI, H. H., Literary Theory
SKOGERBØ, E., Media and Communication Research
SKRE, D., Archaeology
SLETSJØE, A., Portuguese Language
SØRENSEN, Ø., Modern History
STEINFELD, T., Nordic Language and Literature
STEINSLAND, G. S., History of Religions
STENE-JOHANSEN, K., Literary Theory
STENGAARD, B., Ibero-Romance Philology
STENSVOLD, A., History of Religions
SYVERTSEN, T., Media and Communication
TEEUWEN, M. J., Japanese
THEIL, R., English Literature
THORSEN, L. E., Ethnology
TORP, A., Nordic Languages
URSTAD, T. S., British Literature
VETLESEN, A. J., Philosophy
VIKØR, L. S., Nordic Linguistics
VOLLSNES, A., Music
WALDAHL, R., Media and Communication Research
WERENSKIOLD, M., Fine Art History
WICHSTRØM, A., Fine Art History

WIKSHÁLAND, S., Musicology
WORREN, D., Nordic Linguistics
YSTAD, V., Nordic Literature
YTREBERG, E., Media and Communication
ZOLLER, C. P., South Asian Studies
ZWARTJES, O., Spanish Language

Faculty of Law (POB 6706 St Olavs plass 5, 0130 Oslo
Karl Johans gt. 47, 0162 Oslo; tel. 22-85-95-00; e-mail info@jus.uio.no; internet www.jus.uio.no):

ANDENÆS, K., Sociology of Law
ANDENÆS, M., European Law
ANDREASSEN, B., Human Rights and Governance
ARNESEN, F., European Law
BAILLIET, C. M., International Law
BING, J., Law
BOE, E., Law
BUGGE, H. CHR., Law
BULL, H. J., Law
BULL, K. S., Law
CORDERO-MOSS, G., International Law
EIDE, E., Economics and Statistics
ENG, S., Law
ERICSSON, K., Criminology
ESKELAND, S., Criminal Law
EVJU, S., Civil Law
FAUCHALD, O. K., International Law
FINSTAD, L., Criminology
FØLLESDAL, A., Human Rights Law
GIERTSEN, H., Criminology
GJEMS-ONSTAD, O., Tax Law
GRAVER, H. P., Sociology of Law
HAGSTRØM, V., Civil Law
HELLUM, A., Women's Law
HJELMENG, E. J., Tort Law
HØIGÅRD, I. C., Criminology
HOV, J., Civil Law
JOHANSEN, P. O., Criminology
JOHNSEN, J. T., Law
KAASEN, K., Law
KJØNSTAD, A., Law
LARSEN, A., Criminology
LILLEHOLT, K., Civil Law
MESTAD, O., European Law
MICHALSEN, D., Law History
PRIEUR, A. I., Criminology
ROBBERSTAD, A., European Law
ROGNSTAD, O.-A., Private Law
RØSÆG, E., Transportation Law
SAND, I. J., Public Law
SANDBERG, K., Children's and Women's Law
SCHARTUM, D. W., Administrative Informatics
SEJERSTED, F., European Law
SIMONSEN, L., Private Law
SMITH, E., Constitutional Law
STENVIK, A., Private Law
STRIDBECK, U., Criminology
SVERDRUP, T., Family Law
TORVUND, O., Private Law
TRONVOLL, K., Law
ULFBECK, V., Law
ULFSTEIN, G., International Law
WILHELMSEN, T. L., Insurance Law
WOXHOLTH, G., Civil Law
ZIMMER, F., Tax Law

Faculty of Mathematics and Natural Sciences (Fysikkbygn., POB 1032 Blindern, 0315 Oslo
Sem Sælands vei 24, 0371 0371; tel. 22-85-52-00; e-mail postmottak@mn.uio.no; internet www.matnat.uio.no):

AAGAARD, P., Geology
AALEN, R., Biology
AARNES, H., Biology
AASEN, A. J., Pharmacy
AASHAMAR, K., Physics
AKSNES, D., Astrophysics
ALBREGTSEN, F., Computer Science
ALVE, E., Geology
ANDERSEN, T. B., Geology
ANDERSSON, K. K., Biochemistry

ANDRESEN, A., Geology
AUSTRHEIM, H., Geology
BAKKE, O., Biology
BEDOS, E. CHR., Mathematics
BENNECHE, T., Chemistry
BERG, T., Cell Biology
BERG, Y., Informatics
BERTELSEN, A., Mechanics
BEUTH, F. E., Mathematics
BJØRLYKKE, K. O., Geology
BØLVIKEN, E., Statistics
BORGAN, Ø., Statistics
BRATTELI, O., Mathematics
BRAVINA, L., Physics
BRODERSEN, H., Mathematics
BUGGE, L., Physics
BURAN, T., Physics
BYE, R., Chemistry
CARLSSON, M., Astrophysics
CHRISTOPHERSEN, N., Informatics
CORFU, F., Geology
DÆHLEN, M., Mathematical Modelling
DAHL, G., Informatics
DAHLBACK, A., Physics
DALE, B., Geology
DØVING, K., Zoophysiology
EEG, J. O., Physics
ELIASSEN, F., Computer Science
ELLINGSRUD, G., Mathematics
ELVERHØI, A., Quaternary Geology
ENGVOLD, O., Astrophysics
ESKILD, W., Biochemistry
FÆGRI, K., Chemistry
FALEIDE, J. I., Geology
FEDER, J. G., Physics
FINSTAD, T., Physics
FJELLVÅG, H., Chemistry
FLEKKØY, E. G., Physics
FLOATER, M. S., Informatics
FURUSETH, S., Chemistry
GABRIELSEN, O. S., Biochemistry
GALPERINE, I., Physics
GELIUS, L.-J., Geophysics
GJESSING, S., Computer Science
GJEVIK, B., Hydrodynamics
GOEBEL, V. H., Informatics
GØRBITZ, C. H., Chemistry
GOTTSCHALK, L., Geophysics
GRAY, J. S., Marine Zoology
GREIBROKK, T., Analytical Chemistry
GRUE, J., Mechanics
GUNDERSEN, G., Chemistry
GUNDERSEN, K., Biology (Physiology)
GUNDERSEN, L.-L., Chemistry
GUTTORMSEN, M., Physics
HAALAND, A., Chemistry
HAGELBERG, E., Zoology
HAGEN, J. O. M., Geography
HANSEN, E. W., Chemistry
HANSEN, F. K., Chemistry
HANSETH, O., Informatics
HANSTEEN, V., Astrophysics
HELGAKER, T., Chemistry
HELLAND, I., Statistics
HELLESLAND, J., Mechanics
HESSEN, D., Zoology
HESTMARK, G., Biology
HJORT, N. L., Statistics
HJORTH-JENSEN, M., Nuclear Physics
HØEG, K., Geology
HOFF, P., Chemistry
HØGÅSEN, H., Theoretical Physics
HØILAND, K., Biology
HOLE, E. O., Physics
HOLM, P., Mathematics
HOLM, S., Signal Processing
HOLTET, J. A., Physics
HUMLUM, O., Geography
INGEBRETSEN, F., Physics
ISAKSEN, I., Meteorology
IVERSEN, T., Geophysics
JAHREN, B., Mathematics
JAKOBSEN, K. S., Biology
JAMTVEIT, B., Geology
JOHANSEN, H. T., Pharmacy
JOHANSEN, T. H., Physics

JØRGENSEN, M., Informatics
KAARTVEDT, S., Marine Biology
KAASBØLL, F. F., Informatics
KAREN, P., Chemistry
KARLSEN, J., Pharmacy
KJELDSETH-MOE, O., Astrophysics
KLAVENESS, D., Biology
KLAVENESS, J., Pharmacy
KOLSTØ, A. B., Microbiology
KOOMEY, J. M., Pharmacology
KRISTENSEN, T. A., Biochemistry
KRISTJANSSON, F. E., Geophysics
KROGDAHL, S., Computer Science
LAANE, C. M., Botany
LAMBERTSSON, A., Genetics
LAMPE, H. M., Biology
LANDE, T. S., Computer Science
LANGTANGEN, H. P., Informatics
LEER, E., Astrophysics
LEINAAS, H. P., Zoology
LEINAAS, J. M., Physics
LIESTØL, K., Mathematical Modelling
LILJE, P. V., Astrophysics
LILLERUD, K. P., Chemistry
LINDQVIST, B. H., Zoology
LINDSTRØM, T., Mathematics
LØVHØIDEN, G., Physics
LØW, E., Mathematics
LUND, W., Chemistry
LUNDANES, E., Chemistry
LUTKEN, C. A., Physics
LYCHE, T. J. W., Mathematical Modelling
LYSNE, O., Communication Systems
MÅLØY, K. J., Physics
MALTERUD, K. E., Pharmacognosy
MARTINSEN, Ø. G., Physics
MAUPIN, V., Geophysics
MOEN, J. I., Physics
MØLLENDAL, H., Chemistry
MØLLER-PEDERSEN, B., Informatics
MØRKEN, K., Numerical Analysis
MYHRE, A. M., Geology
NAGY, J., Geology
NATVIG, B., Mathematical Statistics
NEUMANN, E. R., Geology
NIELSEN, C. J., Chemistry
NILSSON, G. E., Biology (Physiology)
NISSEN-MEYER, J., Biochemistry
NORBY, P. Æ., Chemistry
NORBY, T. E., Chemistry
NORDAL, I., Botany
NORMANN, D., Mathematical Logic
NYSTRØM, B., Organic Chemistry
ØKSENDAL, B., Mathematics
OLSBYE, U., Chemistry
OLSEN, A., Physics
OMTVEDT, F. P., Chemistry
OSNES, E., Physics
OWE, O., Computer Science
PAULSEN, B. S., Pharmacognosy
PAULSEN, R. E., Pharmacy (Microbiology)
PECSELI, H., Physics
PEDERSEN, G. K., Mathematics
PEDERSEN-BJERGAARD, S., Pharmacy
PETTERSEN, E. O., Physics
PIENE, R., Mathematics
PLAGEMANN, T. P., Informatics
PODLADTCHIKOV, Y., Geology
PRYDZ, K., Biochemistry
RANESTAD, K., Mathematics
RASMUSSEN, K. E., Pharmaceutical Analysis
RAVNDAL, F., Theoretical Physics
READ, A. L., Physics
REKSTAD, J. B., Physics
RISE, F., Chemistry
RISEBRO, N. H., Mathematics
ROGNES, J., Mathematics
ROOS, N., Cell Biology
ROOTS, J., Chemistry
RUENESS, J., Marine Biology
RUSTAN, A., Pharmacy
SAATCIOGLU, F., Biology
SÆTRE, G.-P., Biology
SAGSTUEN, E., Physics
SAHAY, S., Informatics

SAMDAL, S., Chemistry
SAND, O., Zoophysiology
SANDE, S. A., Pharmacy
SANDHOLT, P. E., Physics
SANDLIE, I., Biology
SCHUMACHER, T., Botany
SEIP, H. M., Chemistry
SIREVÅG, R., Microbiology
SJØBERG, D., Informatics
SKAALI, T. B., Physics
SKRAMSTAD, J., Chemistry
SLAGSVOLD, T., Zoology
SMISTAD, G., Pharmacy
SØRÅSEN, O., Microelectronics
SPILLING, P., Telematics and Telecommunications
STABELL, B., Geology
STABELL, R., Astrophysics
STAPNES, S., Physics
STEEN, H., Biology
STENERSEN, J. H. V., Biology
STENSETH, N. C., Zoology
STØLEN, S., Chemistry
STORDAL, F., Meteorology
STØRMER, E., Mathematics
SUDBØ, AA., Optoelectronics
SVENSSON, B. G., Physics
SWENSEN, A. R., Mathematics (Statistics)
TAFTØ, J., Physics
THRONDSEN, J., Marine Biology
TILSET, M., Chemistry
TOMTER, P., Mathematics
TØNNESEN, H. H., Clinical Pharmacy
TOVERUD, E., Pharmacy
TRULSEN, J., Astrophysics
TVEITO, A., Informatics
TVETER, T. S., Physics
UGGERUD, E., Chemistry
VESETH, L., Physics
VØLLESTAD, A. L., Biology (Zoology)
WEBER, J. E., Geophysics
WINTHER, R., Mathematical Modelling

Faculty of Medicine (POB 1078, 0316 Oslo; tel. 22-84-53-00; e-mail postmottak@medisin.uio.no; internet www.med.uio.no):
AALEN, O. O., Statistics
AASEN, A., Surgery
AGARTZ, I., Psychiatry
AURSNES, I. A., Pharmacology
BENESTAD, H. B., Physiology
BERG, O. T., Health Administration
BERG, T., Physiology
BJERTNESS, E., Epidemiology
BJUNE, G. A., International Health
BJÅLIE, E. G., Anatomy
BLOMHOFF, H. K., Medical Biochemistry
BLOMHOFF, R., Nutrition Research
BOE, J., Respiratory Medicine
BOGEN, B., Immunology
BOTTEN, G. S., Health Administration
BRANTZAEG, P., Immunology
BREIVIK, H., Anaesthesiology
BRODAL, P., Anatomy
BROSSTAD, F. R., Internal Medicine Research
BRUUSGAARD, D., Social Security Medicine
BUKHOLM, G., Bacteriology
CARLSEN, K.-H., Paediatrics
CHRISTOFFERSEN, T., Pharmacology
CLAUSEN, O. P. F., Pathology
COLLAS, P., Biochemistry
COLLINS, A. R., Nutrition Research
DANBOLT, N. C., Physiology
DREVON, C., Nutrition Research
DUTTAVOY, A. K., Nutrition Research
EVENSEN, S. A., Haematology
FINSET, A., Medical Behavioural Research
FOSSUM, S., Anatomy
FRIGESSI, A., Medical Statistics
FRØLAND, S. S., Clinical Medicine
FUGELLI, P., Social Medicine
FYRAND, O. L., Dermatology
GEIRAN, O., Cardiovascular Surgery
GIESDAL, K., Cardiology
GLOVER, J., Physiology

GORDELADZE, J. O., Medical Biochemistry
GRØHOLT, B., Psychiatry
GRØTTUM, P., Medical Computer Science
HAGEN, T. P., Health Administration
HANSSON, V., Medical Biochemistry
HAUG, F. M., Anatomy
HEGGELUND, P., Neurophysiology
HEIBERG, A. N., Psychiatry
HJORTDAHL, P., Medicine
HØGLEND, P. A., Psychiatry
HOLCK, P., Anatomy
HORN, R., Medical Biochemistry
HØSTMARK, T. A., Preventive Medicine
HUITFELDT, H., Pathology
HUSBY, G., Rheumatology
ILEBEKK, A. B., Experimental Medicine
INGSTAD, B., Social Medicine
IVERSEN, I. G. H., Physiology
IVERSEN, P. O., Nutrition Research
IVERSEN, T., Health Economics
JAHNSEN, T., Biochemistry
JELLUM, E., Clinical Biochemistry
KASE, B. F., Paediatrics
KIERULF, P., Clinical Chemistry
KIRKEVOLD, M., Medicine
KJEKSHUS, J., Cardiology
KLEPP, K. I., Nutrition Research
KOLBENSTVEDT, A. N., Radiology
KOLSET, S. O., Nutrition Research
KVITTINGEN, E. A., Clinical Biochemistry
LAAKE, P., Medical Statistics
LÆRUM, F., Clinical Medicine
LARSEN, Ø., Medical History
LEVY, F. O., Pharmacology
LIE, S. O., Paediatrics
LINDEGAARD, K., Neurosurgery
LOGE, F. H., Medical Behavioural Research
LORENSEN, M., Nursing Science
LØVSTAD, R., Medical Biochemistry
MADSHUS, I. H., Molecular Biology
MENGSHOEL, A. M., Health Science
MEYER, H. E., Social Medicine
MOUM, T., Medical Behavioural Research
MULLER, F., Pharmacology
NAFSTAD, P., Social Medicine
NATVIG, J. B., Immunology
NICOLAYSEN, G., Physiology
NJÅ, A., Neurophysiology
NYBERG-HANSEN, R., Neurology
NÆSS, O., Pathology
ORMSTAD, K., Forensic Medicine
OS, I., Pharmacology
OSNES, J. B., Pharmacology
ØSTVOLD, A. C., Neurochemistry
OTTERSEN, O. P., Anatomy
PEDERSEN, J. I., Nutrition Research
REIBERÅS, O., Orthopaedics
REIKVAM, Å., Pharmacotherapy
REINHOLT, F. P., Pathology
RINVIK, E., Anatomy
ROGDE, S., Forensic Medicine
ROGNUM, T. O., Forensic Medicine
ROLLAG, H., Bacteriology
ROLSTAD, B., Anatomy
SAGVOLDEN, T., Neurophysiology
SANDANGER, B., Medical Behavioural Research
SANDNES, D. L., Pharmacology
SAUGSTAD, O. D., Paediatrics
SEJERSTED, O. M., Experimental Research
SKOMEDAL, T., Pharmacology
SOLBAKK, J. H., Medical Ethics
SOLLID, L. M., Transplantation Immunology
STEEN, P. A., Anaesthesiology
STOKKE, O., Clinical Biochemistry
STORM, J., Physiology
STORM-MATHISEN, J., Anatomy
STRAAND, F., Social Medicine
STRAY-PEDERSEN, B., Obstetrics and Gynaecology
SØRENSEN, T., Psychiatry
TASKÉN, K., Medical Biochemistry
TELLNES, G., Social Security Medicine
TØNJUM, T., Microbiology
UNDLIEN, D. E., Medical Genetics

URSIN, G., Nutrition Research
VAAGE, I. F., Traumatology
VAGLUM, P., Psychiatry
VATN, M. H., Clinical Epidemiology
VØLLESTAD, N. K., Health Science
WAAL, H., Psychiatry
WALAAS, S. I., Biochemistry
WALLØE, L., Physiology
WANDEL, M., Nutrition Research

Faculty of Social Sciences (POB 1084 Blindern, 0317 Oslo; tel. 22-85-62-64; e-mail postmottak@sv.uio.no; internet www.sv.uio.no):

ALBUM, D., Sociology
ANDRESEN, S. E., Political Science
ARCHETTI, E. P., Social Anthropology
ASHEIM, G. B., Economics
BALDERSHEIM, H., Political Science
BERKAAK, O. A., Social Anthropology
BIRKELUND, G. E., Sociology
BIØRN, E., Economics
BJERKHOLT, O., Economics
BJØRKLÚND, R., Psychology
BJØRKLÚND, T., Political Science
BLAKAR, R. M., Social Psychology
BORGE, A. I. H., Psychology
BREKKE, K. A., Economics
BRENNEN, T., Psychology
BROCH, H. B., Social Anthropology
BROCHMANN, G., Sociology
CHECKEL, F. T., Political Science
CHRISTENSEN, T., Political Science
CHRISTIANSEN, V., Economics
DUCKERT, F., Psychology
EGEBERG, M., Political Science
ENGELSTAD, F., Sociology
ERIKSEN, G. T. H., Social Anthropology
FEHR, N. H., Economics
FJELL, A., Psychology
FØRSUND, F., Economics
FRØNES, I., Sociology
FURST, E. L., Social Anthropology
GULLESTAD, S. E., Psychology
HAAVIND, H., Psychology
HAGTVET, B., Political Science
HAGTVET, K. A., Psychology
HANSEN, M. N., Sociology
HANSEN, T., Political Science
HARTMANN, E. F., Psychology
HEIDAR, K., Political Science
HELLEVIK, O., Political Science
HESSELBERG, J., Social Geography
HOEL, M. O., Economics
HOLDEN, S., Economics
HOVI, J., Political Science
HOWELL, S. L., Social Anthropology
HVEEM, H., Political Science
HYLLAND, AA., Economics
KALLAND, A., Social Anthropology
KALLENBERG, R., Sociology
KEILMAN, N. W., Demography
KIRKEBØEN, G., Psychology
KNUTSEN, O., Political Science
KRAVDAL, Ø., Demographics
KROGSTAD, A., Sociology
LANDRØ, N. I., Psychology
LEIRA, A., Sociology
LUND, D., Economics
LUND, S. E., Social Anthropology
MAGNUSSEN, S. J., Psychology
MALNES, R. S., Political Science
MASTEKAASA, A., Sociology
MATLARY, F. H., Political Science
MEHLUM, H., Economics
MELHUS, M., Social Anthropology
MJØSET, L., Sociology
MOENE, K. O., Economics and Statistics
MONSEN, J., Psychology
MYDSKE, P. K., Political Science
NARUD, H. M., Political Science
NIELSEN, T. H., Social Sciences and Humanities
NILSSEN, T., Economics
NORDBY, T., Political History
NYBORG, K., Economics

NYMOEN, R., Economics
OMMUNDSEN, R., Psychology
ØSTERUD, Ø., Conflict and Peace Research
OTNES, P., Sociology
PEDERSEN, W., Social Geography
PONS, F., Psychology
RASCH, B. E., Political Science
REINVANG, I., Psychology
RØDSETH, A., Economics
RØNNESTAD, H., Psychology
ROSE, L. E., Political Science
RØYSAMB, E., Psychology
SCHWEDER, T., Statistics
SKJEIE, H., Political Science
SKOE, E. E. A., Psychology
SKOG, O., Sociology
STEEN, A., Political Science
STOKKE, K., Social Geography
STORESLETTEN, K., Economics
STRAND, J., Economics
SUNDET, J. M., Psychology
SUNDET, K. S., Psychology
SYDSÆTER, K., Mathematics
SØRENSON, T., Sociology
SØRUM, A., Social Anthropology
TALLE, A., Social Anthropology
TEIGEN, K. H., Psychology
TETZCHNER, S. V., Psychology
TJERSLAND, O. A., Psychology
TORGERSEN, S. O., Psychology
TØRNQUIST, O., Political Science
ULLTVEIT-MOE, K. H., Economics
UNDERDAL, A., Political Science
VASSEND, O., Psychology
VISLIE, J., Economics
VOLLRATH, M., Psychology
WALHOVD, K., Psychology
WESSEL, T., Social Geography
WIDERBERG, K., Sociology
WIKAN, U., Social Anthropology
WILLASSEN, Y., Economics
WOLD, A. H., Psychology

Faculty of Theology (POB 1023 Blindern, 0315 Oslo
Domus Theologica, Blindernvn. 9, 0371 Oslo; tel. 22-85-03-00; e-mail info@teologi.uio.no; internet www.tf.uio.no):

CHRISTOFFERSEN, S. A., Systematic Theology
DOKKA, T. S., New Testament and Systematic Theology
ELSTAD, H., Church History and Religious Sociology
FRØYSHOV, S. R., Liturgy and Ancient Christianity
HAFSTAD, K., Systematic Theology
KVANVIG, H. S., Old Testament
LEIRVIK, O. B., Inter-Religious Studies
MOXNES, H., New Testament
NODERVAL, Ø., Ancient Christianity
RASMUSSEN, T., History of the Church
RUYTER, K., Religious Ethics
SALOMONSEN, J., Religious Anthropology
STORDALEN, T., Old Testament
THORKILDSEN, D., Church History
TØNNESEN, A. V., Church History
WYLLER, T. E., Systematic Theology

Biotechnology Centre of Oslo (EMBIO) (POB 1125 Blindern, 0317 Oslo
Forskringsparken, Gaustadalleen 21, 0349 Oslo; tel. 22-84-05-00; e-mail postmottak@biotek.uio.no; internet www.biotek.uio.no):

TASKÉN, K. (Dir)

Natural History Museum and Botanical Gardens (POB 1172 Blindern, 0318 Oslo
Sars' gt. 1, Monradgt., 0562 Oslo; tel. 22-85-16-30; e-mail informasjon@nhm.uio.no; internet www.nhm.uio.no):

ANDERSEN, K. I., Zoology
BACHMANN, L., Zoology
BAKKE, T. A., Zoology
BJORKLUND, K. R., Palaeontology
BORGEN, L., Botany
BROCHMANN, C., Botany

BRUTON, D. L., Palaeontology
ELVEN, R., Botany
GULDEN, G., Botany
HALVORSEN, O., Zoology
LIFJELD, J. T., Zoology
ØKLAND, R. H., Botany
SUNDING, P., Botany
VAN BERGEN, I. J., Mineralogy
WIIG, Ø., Zoology and Mammalogy

Kulturhistorisk Museum (POB 6762 St Olavs plass, 0130 Oslo; tel. 22-85-19-00; e-mail postmottak@khm.uio.no; internet www.khm.uio.no):

CHRISTENSEN, A. E., Scandinavian Archaeology
KNIRK, J. E., Medieval History
MIKKELSEN, E., Nordic Archaeology
ØSTMO, E., Stone Age and Bronze Age
PLATHER, U., Art Conservation Chemistry
RESI, H. G., Iron Age
SVENSSON, T. G., Social Anthropology

UNIVERSITET I STAVANGER
(University of Stavanger)

4036 Stavanger
Arne Rettedal hus, Kjell Arholmsgt. 41, Stavanger

Telephone: 51-83-10-00
E-mail: post@uis.no
Internet: www.uis.no

Founded 1994 as Høgskolen i Stavanger, present name and status 2005
State control
Languages of instruction: English, Norwegian

Rector: MARIT BOYESEN
Pro-Rector: TOR H. HEMMINGSEN
Univ. Dir: JOHN BRANEM MØST
Dir for Strategy and Communication: ANNE SELNES
Librarian: TERJE BLÅSTERNES

Library of 250,000 vols, 3,000 periodicals
Number of teachers: 1,200
Number of students: 9,200

DEANS

Faculty of Arts and Education: TOR HAUKEN
Faculty of Science and Technology: OLE RINGDAL
Faculty of Social Sciences: EINAR MARNBURG

UNIVERSITETET I TROMSØ
(University of Tromsø)

9037 Tromsø
Telephone: 77-64-40-00
E-mail: postmottak@uit.no
Internet: uit.no

Founded 1968, merged with Høgskolen i Tromsø (Tromsø Univ. College) 2009
State control
Languages of instruction: English, Norwegian
Academic year: August to June (2 semesters)

Rector: Prof. JARLE AARBAKKE
Pro-Rector for Education: Prof. BRITT VIGDIS EKELI
Pro-Rector for Research and Devt: CURT RICE
Univ. Dir: LASSE LØNNUM
Librarian: UNN ALSTAD

Number of teachers: 2,500
Number of students: 9,000

Publications: *Journal of Department of Community Medicine*, *Journal of Faculty of Law*, *Nordlit* (literature), *Ottar* (popular science), *Poljarnyj Vestnik* (Russian language and literature), *Ravnetrykk* (univ. library journal), *Speculum Boreale* (history), *Troll* (literature), *Uvett* (education)

DEANS

Faculty of Biosciences, Fisheries and Economics: EDEL ELVEVOLL
Faculty of Fine Arts: KJELL MAGNE MÆLEN
Faculty of Health Sciences: ARNFINN SUNDSFJORD
Faculty of Humanities, Social Sciences and Education: PETTER NAFSTAD
Faculty of Law: HEGE BRÆKHUS
Faculty of Science and Technology: MORTEN HALD

PROFESSORS

Faculty of Biosciences, Fisheries and Economics (tel. 77-64-60-00; e-mail postmottak@bfe.uit.no):

AMUNDSEN, P.-A., Aquatic Biology
BØGWALD, J., Marine Biotechnology
CLARK, D., Economics and Management
EILERTSEN, H. C., Aquatic Biology
ELVEVOLL, E. O., Marine Biotechnology
FALK-PETERSEN, I. B., Aquatic Biology
FEVOLDEN, S.-E., Aquatic Biology
FLÅTEN, O., Economics and Management
GULLIKSEN, B., Aquatic Biology
HERSOUG, B., Economics and Management
HOLM, P., Economics and Management
JENTOFT, S., Economics and Management
JOBLING, M., Aquatic Biology
JOHNSEN, H. K., Aquatic Biology
JØRGENSEN, E., Aquatic Biology
JØRGENSEN, J. B., Marine Biotechnology
JØRGENSEN, T. ø., Marine Biotechnology
KLEMETSEN, A., Aquatic Biology
KRISTIANSEN, S., Aquatic Biology
OLAFSEN, J. A., Marine Biotechnology
OLSEN, K. K., Aquatic Biology
OLSEN, R. L., Marine Biotechnology
OLSEN, S. O., Economics and Management
ROBERTSEN, B., Marine Biotechnology
SCHULZ, C.-E., Economics and Management
TANDE, K., Aquatic Biology
TRONDSEN, T., Social and Marketing Studies
VASSDAL, T., Economics and Management
WASSMANN, P., Aquatic Biology

Faculty of Fine Arts (tel. 77-66-03-04; e-mail postmottak@kunstfak.uit.no):

LUNDBERG, L., Creative Writing
SIEPEN, N., Contemporary Art
SONJASDOTTER, A., Contemporary Art

Faculty of Health Sciences (tel. 77-64-46-01; e-mail postmottak@helsefak.uit.no):

ANDERSEN, T., Community Medicine
ARNESEN, E., Community Medicine
BJØRKLID, E., Medical Biology
BLIX, A. S., Medical Biology
BRANDL, M., Pharmacy
DAHL, S. G., Medical Biology
EL-GEWELY, M. R., Medical Biology
FOLKOW, L., Medical Biology
FØNNEBØ, V., Community Medicine
FØRDE, O. H., Community Medicine
GRAM, I. T., Community Medicine
GREINER-TOLLERSRUD, O. K., Medical Biology
HASVOLD, T., Community Medicine
HOLTEDAHL, K., Community Medicine
HUSEBEKK, A., Medical Biology
HUSEBY, N.-E., Medical Biology
HØYER, G., Community Medicine
JACOBSEN, B. K., Community Medicine
JENSEN, E., Pharmacy
JOHANSEN, S., Medical Biology
JOHANSEN, T., Medical Biology
LARSEN, T., Medical Biology
LOENNECHEN, T., Pharmacy
NIELSEN, K. M., Pharmacy
LUND, E., Community Medicine
MERCER, J., Medical Biology
MELBYE, H., Community Medicine
MJØS, O. D., Medical Biology
MOENS, U., Medical Biology

NIELSEN, K. M., Pharmacy
NJØLSTAD, I., Community Medicine
NORDØY, E., Medical Biology
OLSEN, J. A., Community Medicine
OLSVIK, Ø., Medical Biology
ØRBO, A., Medical Biology
REKVIG, O.-P., Medical Biology
RINNE, A., Medical Biology
SAGER, G., Medical Biology
SMEDSRØD, B., Medical Biology
STOKKAN, K.-A., Medical Biology
SUNDSFJORD, A., Medical Biology
SYLTE, I., Medical Biology
WILLASSEN, N. P., Medical Biology
WINBERG, J.-O., Medical Biology
YTREHUS, K., Medical Biology

Faculty of Humanities, Social Sciences and Education (tel. 77-64-43-00; e-mail postmottak@hsl.uit.no):

AARSÆTHER, N.
ANDERSSON, D. T.
ALHAUG, G.
BARSTAD, G.
BERTELSEN, R.
BLANKHOLM, P.
BOUVRIE, S. DES
BULL, T.
DAMM, C.
DRIVENES, E.-A.
EGEBERG, E. H.
ENGELSTAD, E.
GAASLAND, R.
HOFSTEN, H. W. VON
KARLSEN, O.
KONSTANTINOV, Y.
LIEPE, L.
LINDGREN, A.-R.
LUND, N. W.
LÖNNGREN, L.
MØRCK, E.
MYRSTAD, A.
NESSET, T.
OLSEN, B.
RAMCHAND, G.
RICE, C.
SCHMIDT, M.
STARKE, M.
SVENONIUS, P.
SVONNI, M.
SWAN, T.
TARALDSEN, K. T.
VALESTRAND, H.
WESTVIK, O. M. J.
WÆRP, H. H.

Faculty of Law (tel. 77-64-41-97; e-mail postmottak@jus.uit.no):

CHRISTIANSEN, P.
HAUGLI, T.

Faculty of Science and Technology (tel. 77-64-40-01; e-mail postmottak@nt.uit.no):

ANDERSEN, J., Biology
ANSHUS, O. J., Computer Science
ASLAKSEN, T., Physics
BERGH, S., Geology
BHUVANESWARI, T. V., Biology
CARLSON, R., Chemistry
DAHL, D., Chemistry
ELTOFT, T., Physics
ESSER, R., Physics
FLÅ, T., Mathematics and Statistics
FOLSTAD, I., Biology
GHOSH, A., Chemistry
GODTLIBSEN, F., Mathematics and Statistics
HALD, M., Geology
HANSEN, L. K., Chemistry
HANSSEN, A., Physics
HARTVIGSEN, G., Computer Science
HAVNES, O., Physics
HOUGH, E., Chemistry
IMS, R. A., Biology
JACOBSEN, S., Physics
JOHANSEN, D., Computer Science
JOHNSEN, B., Mathematics and Statistics

JUNTILLA, O., Biology
KRUGLIKOV, B., Mathematics and Statistics
LA HOZ, C., Physics
LYCHAGIN, V., Mathematics and Statistics
MELANDSØ, F., Physics
MIENERT, J., Geology
MJØLHUS, E., Mathematics and Statistics
OLSON, L., Mathematics and Statistics
PRASOLOV, A., Mathematics and Statistics
RAVNA, E. K., Geology
RUUD, K., Chemistry
RYPDAL, K., Physics
RØEGGEN, I., Physics
SMALÅS, A., Chemistry
SVENDSEN, J. S., Chemistry
SVENNING, M., Biology
VORREN, K.-D., Biology
VORREN, T., Geology
YOCCOZ, N., Biology

University Colleges

Ansgar Teologiske Høgskole (Ansgar School of Theology and Mission): Fredrik Fransons vei 4, 4635 Kristiansand; tel. 38-10-65-00; e-mail post@ansgarskolen.no; internet www.ansgarhogskole.no; f. 1913 as Det Norske Misjonsforbunds—Missionsskole; provides BA in intercultural understanding, music, practical theology, psychology with religion and health, theology with Christianity, religions and worldviews; library: 29,000 vols of books, 300 movies, journals, newspapers and trade papers; Prin. HARALD NYGAARD; Dir for Admissions RANDI HAUGLAND; Librarian BIRGIT MYRENE.

Atlantis Medisinske Høgskole (Atlantis Medical College): POB 4290 Nydalen, 0402 Oslo; Sandakerveien 116, 0484 Oslo; tel. 23-00-73-50; e-mail atlantismed@amh.no; internet www.amh.no; f. 1987; BA degrees in nutrition and medicine; Dir TOMM-ESPEN STRØM; Rector MOHSEN ZANGANI.

Barratt Due musikkinstitutt (Barratt Due Institute of Music): POB 5344, Majorstuen, 0304 Oslo; Lyder Sagens gt 2, Oslo; tel. 22-06-86-86; e-mail post@bdm.no; internet www.barrattdue.no; f. 1927; Artistic Dir STEPHAN BARRATT-DUE.

Betanien Diakonale Høgskole (Betanien Diaconal University College): Vestlundveien 19, 5145 Fyllingsdalen; tel. 55-50-73-00; e-mail bdh@betanien.no; internet www .betaniensykepleierhogskole.no; f. 1923; offers bachelor in nursing; library: 1,000 vols incl. books, 60 journals; Rector ANNELINE RØSSLAND; Head Librarian MARGRETHE B. SØVIK.

Bjørknes Høyskole (Bjørknes College): Lovisenberggata 13, 0456 Oslo; tel. 23-23-38-20; e-mail info@bjorkneshoyskole.no; internet www.bjorkneshoyskole.no; offers bachelor degrees in medicine, physiotherapy, chiropractic studies and communications; Man. Dir SVEINUNG LUNDE; Rector Dr LINN SKOGLUND.

Diakonhjemmet Høgskole (Diakonhjemmet University College): POB 184 Vinderen, 0319 Oslo; Diakonveien 14–16, 0370 Oslo; tel. 22-45-19-45; e-mail post@diakonhjemmet .no; internet www.diakonhjemmet.no; offers bachelors in occupational therapy, nursing, social education, social work, social education; 2,200 students; Rector INGUNN MOSER; Man. for Admin. and Finance STÅLE SØBYE; Chief Librarian HILDE TRYGSTAD.

Dronning Mauds Minne Høgskolen (Queen Maud University College): Thoning Owensgt. 18, 7044 Trondheim; tel. 73-80-52-00; e-mail post@dmmh.no; internet www .dmmh.no; f. 1947; offers BA in early childhood education and care; 120 teachers; 1,000 students; Rector ELIN ALVESTRAND; Pro-Rector IVAR SELMER-OLSEN; Pro-Rector for Education LIV AASTAD; Pro-Rector for Research and Devt ELSE BERIT SKAGEN; Head Librarian KJERSTI LANGSLET RYGH.

Fjellhaug Internasjonale Høgskole (Fjellhaug International University College): Sinsenveien 15, 0572 Oslo; tel. 23-23-24-00; e-mail post@fjellhaug.no; internet fih .fjellhaug.no; f. 1898 as Fjellhaug Misjonshøgskole, current name adopted 2011; offers bachelor degrees in religious and ethical education, theology and mission; library: 26,000 vols of books in theology, mission, religion, education and music, 100 periodicals; Rector Prof. HANS AAGE GRAVAAS; Library Dir TOM ERIK HAMRE.

Forsvarets høgskole (FHS) (Norwegian Defence University College): POB 800, Postmottak, 2617 Lillehammer; tel. 23-09-57-49; e-mail post.fhs@mil.no; internet hogskolene .forsvaret.no/forsvarets-hogskole; consists of 5 units: Norwegian National Defence College, Norwegian Defence Command and Staff College, Norwegian Institute for Defence Studies, Norwegian Defence Centre for Skills and Education, Norwegian School of Sports Science, Defence Institute; Chief Head LOUISE K. DEDICHEN; Dean TORUNN L. HAALAND; Library Dir HEGE UNDEM STORE.

Høgskolen i Ålesund (Aalesund University College): POB 1517, 6025 Aalesund; Larsgårdsveien 2, 6009 Aalesund; tel. 70-16-12-00; e-mail postmottak@hials.no; internet www.hials.no; faculties of engineering and natural sciences, health sciences, international marketing, life sciences, maritime technology and operations; 200 teachers; 2,000 students; Rector MARIANNE SYNNES; Pro-Rector WEBJØRN REKDALSBAKKEN; Dir LASSE GALLEFOSS (acting); Head Librarian ASTRID ENGELSEN.

Høgskolen i Bergen (Bergen University College): POB 7030, Nygårdsgaten 112, 5020 Bergen; tel. 55-58-75-00; e-mail post@hib.no; internet www.hib.no; faculties of education, engineering, health and social sciences; library: 120,000 vols, 1,000 journals; 7,000 students; Rector OLE-GUNNAR SØGNEN; Deputy Rector BJØRG KRISTIN SELVIK; Vice-Rector JAN MAGNUS BJORDAL; Dir AUDUN RIVEDAL; Head Librarian TOVE PEMMER SÆTRE.

Høgskolen i Buskerud (Buskerud University College): POB 235, 3603 Kongsberg; tel. 32-86-95-00; e-mail postmottak@hibu.no; internet www.hibu.no; faculties of health sciences, teacher education, technology; school of business and social sciences; library: 65,000 vols, 261 periodicals in print, 11,000 e-journals, 70,000 e-books; 178 full-time teachers; 3,780 full-time students; Rector KRISTIN ØRMEN JOHNSEN; Pro-Rector GUNNAR HORGEN; Pro-Rector KÅRE SANDVIK; Chief of BUC Library KARI FAGERJORD.

Høgskolen i Finnmark (Finnmark University College): Follumsvei 31, 9509 Alta; tel. 78-45-05-00; e-mail postmottak@hifm.no; internet www.hifm.no; f. 1994; courses in business and tourism, education and humanities, health, social studies and sports and science; 1,800 students; Rector SVEINUNG EIKELAND; Pro-Rector CARSTEN ROLLAND; College Dir PÅL MARKUSSON; Dir for Academic Affairs ANNE MARI RØDDE HARPER; Main Librarian KARI HEITMANN.

Høgskolen i Gjøvik (Gjøvik University College): POB 191, 2802 Gjøvik; tel. 61-13-51-00; e-mail postmottak@hig.no; internet www.hig.no; f. 1994 after merger of Gjøvik College of Engineering and College of Nursing in Oppland; faculties of computer science and media technology; health, care and nursing; technology, economy and management; library: 34,500 vols; 3,000 students;

Rector Prof. Dr JØRN WROLDSEN; Pro-Rector for Education, Study and Learning GRO IREN KVANLI DÆHLIN; Pro-Rector for Research MORTEN IRGENS; College Dir INGE ØYSTEIN MOEN; Univ. Librarian KLAUS JØRAN TOLLAN.

Høgskolen i Harstad (Harstad University College): Havnegata 5, 9480 Harstad; tel. 77-05-81-00; e-mail postmottak@hih.no; internet www.hih.no; f. 1983; depts of business administration and social sciences, health and social studies; 1,300 students; Rector BODIL OLSVIK; Pro-Rector SVEIN TVEDT JOHANSEN; Man. Dir KARL ERIK ARNESEN.

Høgskolen i Hedmark (Hedmark University College): POB 400, 2418 Elverum; Terningen Arena, Hamarveien 112, 2418 Elverum; tel. 62-43-00-79; e-mail postmottak@hihm.no; internet www.hihm .no; faculties of business administration, education and natural sciences, forestry and wildlife management, health and sports; campuses at Elverum, Evenstad, Hamar and Rena; 5,000 students; Rector LISE IVERSEN KULBRANDSTAD; Vice-Rector for Education ANNA OTTOSEN; Vice-Rector for Research TORSTEIN STORAAS; Dir PÅL EINAR DIETRICHS; Dir for Admin. Staff HANS OVE HJELSVOLD; Library Dir ANNA LØKEN.

Høgskolen i Lillehammer (HiL) (Lillehammer University College): POB 952, 2604 Lillehammer; Gudbrandsdalsvegen 350, 2624 Lillehammer; tel. 61-28-80-00; e-mail post@hil.no; internet www.hil.no; faculties of business and organizational sciences, education and social work, social sciences; dept of television subjects; Norwegian Film School; library: 50,000 vols, 380 journals, 18,700 e-journals, 50,000 e-books; 4,500 students; Rector BENTE OHNSTAD; Pro-Rector JENS UWE KORTEN; Vice-Rector for Research YVONNE FRITZE; College Dir KARI KJENNDALEN; Head Librarian SIGBJØRN HERNES.

Høgskolen i Narvik (Narvik University College): POB 385, 8505 Narvik; Lodve Langes St 2, 8505 Narvik; tel. 76-96-60-00; e-mail postmottak@hin.no; internet www.hin .no; f. 1994; faculties of health and society, technology; library: 20,000 vols incl. books, reports and journals; 170 teachers; 1,600 students; Vice-Chancellor ARNE ERIK HOLDØ; Admin. Dir BJØRNAR STORENG; Library Dir UNNI TRONDSEN.

Høgskolen i Nesna (Nesna University College): 8700 Nesna; tel. 75-05-78-00; e-mail postmottak@hinesna.no; internet www .hinesna.no; f. 1918 as a Teacher Training College; offers bachelors in sports, information systems, nursing; 1,100 students; Rector SVEN ERIK FORFANG; Pro-Rector MARGRETE NORHEIM; Head Librarian KARI PETTERSEN.

Høgskolen i Nord-Trøndelag (Nord-Trøndelag University College): POB 2501, 7729 Steinkjer; tel. 74-11-20-00; e-mail postmottak@hint.no; internet www.hint.no; faculties of agriculture and information technology, economics, organization and leadership, education of driving instructors, health sciences, teacher education; 4,460 students; Rector STEINAR NEBB; Pro-Rector HANNE SOLHEIM HANSEN; Dir BEATE ASPDA.

Høgskolen i Oslo og Akershus (Oslo and Akershus University College of Applied Sciences): POB 4, St Olavs plass, 0130 Oslo; tel. 67-23-50-00; e-mail postmottak@hioa.no; internet www.hioa.no; f. 2011 by merger of Oslo Univ. College and Akershus Univ. College; faculties of education and international studies, health sciences, social sciences, technology, art and design; 17,000 students; Rector KARI TOVERUD JENSEN; Pro-Rector for Education and Regional Cooperation OLGUNN RANSEDOKKEN; Pro-Rector for Research and Internationalisation FRODE EIKA SANDNES; Dir ANN ELISABETH WEDØ.

Høgskolen i Østfold (Østfold University College): 1757 Halden; tel. 69-21-50-00; e-mail postmottak@hiof.no; internet www .hiof.no; f. 1994; faculties of business, social sciences and foreign languages, computer sciences, education, engineering, health and social studies; library: 125,000 vols; 4,500 students; Rector Dr HANS ANDREAS BLOM; Pro-Rector VIGDIS ABRAHAMSEN GRØNDAHL (acting); Dir CARL-MORTEN GJELDNES; Head Librarian ELSE NORHEIM.

Høgskolen i Sør-Trøndelag (Sør-Trøndelag University College): POB 2320, 7004 Trondheim; tel. 73-55-90-00; e-mail postmottak@hist.no; internet hist.no; faculties of engineering, health education and social work, informatics and e-learning, nursing, teacher and interpreter education, technology; Trondheim Business School; 8,000 students; Rector TROND MICHAEL ANDERSEN; Pro-Rector ARNULF OMDAL.

Høgskolen i Telemark (Telemark University College): POB 203, 3901 Porsgrunn; tel. 35-02-62-00; e-mail postmottak@hit.no; internet www.hit.no; faculties of art, folk culture and teacher education, arts and sciences, health and social work studies, technology; library: 236,000 vols of books, 10,000 e-periodicals and 700 current periodicals; 6,500 students; Rector KRISTIAN BOGEN; Vice-Rector for Education ASHILD KISE; Vice-Rector for Research, Internationalisation and External Relations PÅL AUGESTAD; Dir JOHN W. VIFLOT; Chief Librarian FRODE BAKKEN.

Høgskolen i Vestfold (Vestfold University College): POB 2243, 3103 Tønsberg; tel. 33-03-10-00; e-mail postmottak@hive.no; internet www.hive.no; f. 1994; faculties of business and social sciences, education and humanities, health science, technology and maritime science; library: 58,000 vols; 4,500 students; Rector PETTER AASEN; Pro-Rector JORUN ULVESTAD; Vice-Rector for Education ANNE FÆNGSRUD; Dir OLAV REFSDAL; Univ. Librarian HEIDI KRISTIN OLSEN.

Høgskolen Stord/Haugesund (Stord/Haugesund University College): Klingenbergvegen 8, 5414 Stord; tel. 53-49-13-00; e-mail postmottak@hsh.no; internet www.hsh.no; faculties of health education; teacher and cultural education; technical, economic and maritime education; f. 1994; 3,000 students; Rector LIV REIDUN GRIMSTVEDT; Dir TAGE BÅTSVIK; Head of Library MARIANNE NESBJØRG TVEDT.

Høgskulen for Landbruk og Bygdeutvikling (University College for Agriculture and Rural Development): POB 213, 4353 Klepp; tel. 51-79-94-00; e-mail post@hlb.no; internet www.hlb.no; f. 2005; offers BA in rural development; Rector Dr DAG JØRUND LØNNING.

Høgskulen i Sogn og Fjordane (Sogn og Fjordane University College): POB 133, 6851 Sogndal; tel. 57-67-60-00; e-mail post@hisf .no; internet www.hisf.no; faculties of engineering and sciences, health studies, social sciences, teacher education and sports; 3,000 students; Rector ÅSE LØKELAND; Vice-Rector ERIK KYRKJEBØ; Vice-Rector for Education TERJE BJELLE; Head of Library ASTRID SANDNES.

Høgskulen i Volda (HVO) (Volda University College): POB 500, 6101 Volda; Joplassvegen 11, Berte Kanutte bldg, 6101 Volda; tel. 70-07-50-00; e-mail postmottak@hivolda .no; internet www.hivolda.no; faculties of art and physical education, humanities and education, media and journalism, social sciences and history; library: 100,000 vols, 100,000 ebooks, 350 print journals and 17,000 full text ejournals; 4,000 students; Rector Dr PER

HALSE; Pro-Rector Marie Nedregotten Sørbø; Dir Jacob Kjøde jr.

Høyskolen Campus Kristiania: POB 1155, Sentrum, 0107 Oslo; Kirkegata 24, 0153 Oslo; tel. 22-59-60-00; e-mail info@c-k .no; internet www.c-k.no; f. 1976; schools of creative studies, health, management; 7,000 students; Rector Trond Blindheim; Managing Dir Solfrid Lind.

Høyskolen Diakonova (Diakonova University College): POB 6716, St. Olavs plass, 0130 Oslo; Fredensborgveien 24Q, 0177 Oslo; tel. 22-98-63-00; e-mail post@diakonova.no; internet www.diakonova.no; f. 1916; offers a bachelor degree in nursing; 500 students; Dir Gunhild Hagesæther; publ. *Diakonova*.

Høyskolen for Ledelse og Teologi (Norwegian School of Leadership and Theology): Michelets vei 62, 1368 Stabekk; tel. 67-10-35-40; e-mail post@hoyskolen.org; internet hoyskolen.org; f. 2008; Dean Dr Kai Tore Bakke.

Krigsskolen (Army Academy): POB 42, Linderud, 0517 Oslo; Utfartsveien 2, 0593 Oslo; tel. 23-09-90-00; e-mail ks.kontakt@mil .no; internet hogskolene.forsvaret.no/ krigsskolen; f. 1750; provides BA in professional courses.

Lovisenberg Diakonale Høgskole (Lovisenberg Diaconal University College): Lovisenberggt. 15B, 0456 Oslo; tel. 22-35-82-00; e-mail admin@ldh.no; internet www.ldh.no; f. 1868; offers bachelors degrees within the field of nursing; professional continuation programmes; 800 students; Rector Lars Mathisen; College Dir Hallgeir Lien; Dir for Academic Affairs Else Berit Øren; Head Librarian Turid Brandsdal.

Luftkrigsskolens (Air Force Academy): Trondhiem; tel. 73-99-54-00; internet hogskolene.forsvaret.no/luftkrigsskolen; f. 1949; offers bachelors degree; library: 15,000 vols and 150 periodicals; Chief Oberst Ole-Asbjørn Fauske; Dean of the Air force Academy Karl Erik Haug; Head Librarian Nina Beck Anderssen.

NLA Høgskolen (NLA University College): POB 74 Sandviken, 5812 Bergen; tel. 55-54-07-00; e-mail post@nla.no; internet www.nla .no; f. 1966 merged with NLA Lærerhøgskolen in 2010; 2,000 students; Rector Bjarne Kvam; Vice-Rector Jan Gossner; Vice-Rector Lars Dahle; Pro-Rector for Education Svenning Bjørke; Pro-Rector for Research Erik Waaler; Dir for Int. Affairs Siri Elisabeth Haug; publs *Hilsen* (4 a year), *M-link*, *Staffeldtsnytt*.

Norges Dansehøyskole (Norwegian College of Dance): PBO 2956, Tøyen, 0608 Oslo; Borggata 7, 0650 Oslo; tel. 23-24-18-00; e-mail info@ndh.no; internet www.dnbk .no; f. 1966 as Ballettinstituttet, present name 2011; bachelor study programme for dance with pedagogy; Rector Ann Kristin Norum; Vice-Rector Dr Ole von Wowern-Carstensen Egeberg.

Norges Informasjonsteknologiske Høgskole AS (Norwegian School of Information Technology): Schweigaardsgate 14, 0185 Oslo; tel. 22-05-99-99; e-mail oslo@nith.no; internet nith.no; offers bachelors degree in information technology; library: 5,000 vols; 650 students; Dean Bjørn Jarle Hanssen; Librarian Trude Westby.

Norske Eurytmihøyskole (University College of Eurythmy): Professor Dahls gate 30, 0260 Oslo; tel. 22-44-32-90; e-mail dne@ eurytmi.no; internet www.eurytmi.no; f. 1983; provides BA degrees and diplomas in the education of eurythmy.

Sámi allaskuvla (Sámi University College): Hánnoluohkká 45, 9520 Guovdageaidnu; tel. 78-44-84-00; e-mail postmottak@samiskhs .no; internet www.samiskhs.no; f. 1989; offers bachelor programmes in journalism; Rector Jelena Porsanger; Pro-Rector Inger Marie Gaup Eira; Dir Maaren Palismaa; Library Dir Mette Irene Hætta.

Sjøkrigsskolen (Naval Academy): POB 800, Postmottak, 2617 Lillehammer; Sjøkrigsskoleveien 32, Gravdal, 5164 Laksevåg; tel. 55-50-20-00; e-mail sksk@mil.no; internet hogskolene.forsvaret.no/sjokrigsskolen; f. 1996; promotes navigation safety; works towards increasing the combat capability of the Navy; Chief Thomas T. Wedervang.

Westerdals Høyskole (Westerdals School of Communication (WSoC)): Maridalsveien 17D, 0178 Oslo; tel. 22-99-97-50; e-mail post@ westerdals.no; internet www.westerdals.no; f. 1965 as Westerdals Advertising School, present name 2001 after the merger of Westerdals School of Communication, School of Graphic Design and Sverre Wolff Advertising and Decoration School; offers bachelor degrees in text and copywriter, art direction, film and television, visual merchandising and commercial interior, graphic design, event and experience design; 500 students; Rector Tom Kvisle.

Colleges of University Standing

ARKITEKTUR- OG DESIGNHØGSKOLEN I OSLO
(Oslo School of Architecture and Design)

POB 6768 St Olavs plass, 0130 Oslo
Maridalsveien 29, 0175 Oslo

Telephone: 22-99-70-00
E-mail: postmottak@aho.no
Internet: www.aho.no

Founded 1945
State control
Academic year: September to June

Institutes of architecture, design, form, theory and history, urbanism and landscape

Rector: Karl Otto Ellefsen
Dir for Gen. Admin.: Einar Fagerå
Head of Academic Services: Berit Skjærvold
Head of Library: Sidsel Moum

Library of 40,000 vols
Number of teachers: 120
Number of students: 700

Publication: *Research Magazine* (1 a year)

PROFESSORS

Dahl, K. E., Urbanism and Landscape
Dahle, E., Architectural Design
Dobloug, M., Architectural Design
Dunin-Woyseth, H., Form, Theory and History
Edeholt, H., Design
Fjeld, P. O., Architectural Design
Gerstlauer, R., Architectural Design
Hermansen, C., Architectural Design
Hjeltnes, K., Architectural Design
Hølmebakk, B., Form, Theory and History
Hvattum, M., Form, Theory and History
Jensen, J., Architectural Design
Kleven, B., Architectural Design
Løkse, O., Form and Design
Michl, J., Industrial Design
Morrison, A., Design
Robbins, E., Urbanism and Landscape
Sandaker, B., Building Technology
Sevaldson, B., Design
Skjønsberg, T., Form and Design
Thiis-Evensen, T., Architectural Theory and History
Tostrup, E., Form, Theory and History
Tvilde, D., Urbanism and Landscape

BERGEN ARKITEKTHØGSKOLE
(Bergen School of Architecture)

POB 39, 5841 Bergen
Sandviksboder 59–61A, 5035 Bergen

Telephone: 55-36-38-80
E-mail: adm@bas.org
Internet: www.bas.org

Founded 1986, fully recognized 1990
Private control
Languages of instruction: English, Norwegian

Offers masters in architecture

Rector: Cecilie Andersson
Pro-Rector: Sixten Rahlff
Head of Student Affairs: Siv Gjerde Aardal
Head of Library: Line Frøyland

Library of 3,000 vols, 20 int. magazines
Number of teachers: 50 (incl. part-time)
Number of students: 150

HANDELSHØYSKOLEN BI
(BI Norwegian Business School)

0442 Oslo
Nydalsveien 37, 0484 Oslo

Telephone: 46-41-00-00
E-mail: info@bi.no
Internet: www.bi.no

Founded 1943
Private control
Languages of instruction: English, Norwegian
Academic year: September to June

Depts of accounting, auditing and law, communication, culture and languages, economics, financial economics, innovation and economic organisation, leadership and organisational behaviour, marketing, strategy and logistics

Pres.: Tom Colbjørnsen
Provost: Dag Morten Dalen
Sr Vice-Pres.: Ulf Henning Olsson
Exec. Vice-Pres. for Communication: Yngve Kveine (acting)
Exec. Vice-Pres. for Exec. Education: Lise Hammergren
Exec. Vice-Pres. for Human Resources: Wenche Nlisen
Exec. Vice-Pres. for Individual Education: Jens Petter Øndel
Library Dir: Dagmar Langeggen

Number of teachers: 340
Number of students: 20,049

HØGSKOLEN I MOLDE—VITENSKAPELIG HØGSKOLE I LOGISTIKK
(Molde University College—Specialized University in Logistics)

POB 2110, 6402 Molde
Britvegen 2, 6410 Molde

Telephone: 71-21-40-00
E-mail: post@himolde.no
Internet: www.himolde.no

Founded 1994, present status 2010
State control
Languages of instruction: English, Norwegian

Rector: Prof. Dr Solfrid Vatne
Pro-Rector: Prof. Dr Kjetil Kåre Haugen

Library of 90,000 vols
Number of students: 2,000

DEANS

Faculty of Economics, Informatics and Social Sciences: Ottar Ohren
Faculty of Health and Social Care: Heidi V. Haavardsen

MISJONSHØGSKOLEN (MHS)
(MHS–School of Mission and Theology)

POB 226, 4001 Stavanger
Misjonsmarka 12, 4024 Stavanger
Telephone: 51-51-62-10
E-mail: post@mhs.no
Internet: www.mhs.no
Founded 1843; attached to Norwegian Mission Soc.
Private control
Divs of Biblical studies, church history and systematic theology, science of religion and science of culture, theology of mission and practical theology
Rector: Prof. Dr BÅRD MÆLAND
Pro-Rector for Education: Prof. Dr TOMAS SUNDNES DRØNEN
Pro-Rector for Research: Prof. Dr KNUT HOLTER
Dir: Prof. Dr KRISTIN FJELDE TJELLE
Dean for Studies: Prof. Dr TORREY SELAND
Sr Research Librarian: ARNE B. SAMUELSEN
Library of 90,000 vols of books, 1,000 journals
Number of teachers: 24
Number of students: 350

NORGES HANDELSHØYSKOLE
(Norwegian School of Economics)

Helleveien 30, 5045 Bergen
Telephone: 55-95-90-00
E-mail: nhh.postmottak@nhh.no
Internet: www.nhh.no
Founded 1936
State control
Academic year: September to June
Depts of accounting, auditing and law, business and management science, economics, finance, professional and intercultural communication, strategy and management
Rector: Dr JAN I. HAALAND
Deputy Rector: Dr GUNNAR E. CHRISTENSEN
Vice-Rector: Dr METTE H. BJØRNDAL
Man. Dir: Dr OLE HOPE
Library Dir: SISSEL HAFSTAD
Library of 280,000 vols, 1,600 periodicals
Number of teachers: 210
Number of students: 3,000

PROFESSORS

Faculty of Accounting, Auditing and Law:
BJØRNENAK, T., Management Accounting
EILIFSEN, A., Financial Accounting and Auditing
GJESDAL, F., Management and Financial Accounting
JOHNSEN, A., N., Financial Accounting
MONSEN, N., Governmental Accounting
ÖSTERGREN, K., Cost Accounting and Project Management
STUART, I., Auditing
Faculty of Economics:
BASBERG, B., Economic History
BIVAND, R., Economic and Quantitative Geography
BJORVATN, K., Economic Development and Geography
BREKKE, K., Health Economics
BRUNSTAD, R., Macroeconomics
BRUNT, L., Economic History
CAPPELEN, A., Experimental Economics
GRYTTEN, O., Macroeconomic History
HAGEN, K. P., Public Economics
HANNESSON, R., Fisheries Economics
HÅLAND, J. I., International Economics
KIND, H. J., Industrial Organization and International Economics
KLOVLAND, J. T., Macroeconomics and Economic History
KRISTIANSEN, E. G., Microeconomics

MATHIESEN, L., General Equilibrium Modelling
NILSEN, O. A., Labour Economics and Investment
NORMAN, V. D., International Economics
SALVANES, K. G., Labour Economics and Industrial Organization
SCHROTYEN, F., Public Economics
SØRGARD, L., Industrial Organization
STEEN, F., Econometrics and Industrial Organization
STRANDENES, S. P., International and Shipping Economics
THØGERSEN, O., Macroeconomics and Social Security
TUNGODDEN, B., Social Choice Theory and Development Economics
VATNE, E., Economic Geography
Faculty of Finance and Management Science:
ÅSE, K. K. P., Finance and Insurance Mathematics
BJERKSUND, P., Investment and Risk Management
BJØRNDAL, M. H., C., Operations Research and Management
EKERN, S., Finance
ESKELAND, G. S., Environmental Economics and Public Finance
FOROS, O., Industrial Organization and Management Science
GJERDE, O., Finance and Operations Management
HANSEN, T., Personal Finance and Management Control Systems
JOHNSEN, T., Finance
JÖRNSTEN, K., Finance
JÖRNSTEN, K., Production Planning and Control
LEITE, T., Financial Markets and Intermediation
LENSBERG, T., Decision Theory
LILLESTØL, J., Statistics and Probability
MØEN, J., Microeconometrics and Productivity Analysis
OLSEN, T. E., Financial Contracting
PERSSON, S.-A., Finance and Economics of Insurance
RÖNNQVIST, M., Operations Research and Logistics
SÆTTEM, F., Finance
SANDAL, L. K., Applied Mathematics and Management Science
SCHJELDERUP, G., Microeconomics
STENSLAND, G., Investment and Risk Management
UBØE, J., Mathematics and Statistics
Faculty of Professional and Intercultural Communication:
DAHL, T., English
MARTÍNEZ, J. A., Spanish
SIMONNÆS, I., German
WHITTAKER, S., French
Faculty of Strategy and Management:
BREIVIK, E., Brand Management and Consumer Trends
BROCHS-HAUKEDAL, W., Management and Organizational Behaviour
ESPEDAL, B., Organizational Learning and Adaptation
FOSS, K., Competitive Strategy
FUGLSETH, A.-M., System Development
GOODERHAM, P., International and Knowledge Management
GREVE, A., Organization Theory
HAUGLAND, S., Strategic Management and Organization Theory
HEM, L., Brand Management and Consumer Trends
IMS, K., Business Ethics and Management
LINES, R., Market Research and Strategy
MEYER, C., Strategy, Merger and Acquisitions
NORDHAUG, O., Organization Theory and Management

NYSVEEN, H., Interactive Marketing and Product Development
PEDERSON, P. E., Innovation and Information Management
ROGNES, J. K., Negotiation
SELART, M., Organizational Behaviour and Human Resources Management
SUPPHELLEN, M., Brand Management and Consumer Trends
THORBJØRNSEN, H., Consumer Psychology and Trends
TROYE, S., Market Research and Consumption Patterns

NORGES IDRETTSHØGSKOLE
(Norwegian School of Sport Sciences)

POB 4014 Ullevål Stadion, 0806 Oslo
Sognsveien 220, Oslo
Telephone: 23-26-20-00
E-mail: postmottak@nih.no
Internet: www.nih.no
Founded 1968
State control
Academic year: August to June
Depts of coaching and psychology, cultural and social studies, physical education, physical performance, sport medicine
Rector: Prof. Dr SIGMUND LOLAND
Vice-Rector: INGER-ÅSHILD BY
Dir: BAARD WIST
Head Librarian: HEGE UNDERTHUN
Library of 70,000 vols
Number of teachers: 100
Number of students: 1,300
Publication: *Moving Bodies* (2 a year)

NORGES VETERINÆRHØGSKOLE
(Norwegian School of Veterinary Science)

POB 8146 Dep, 0033 Oslo
Ullevålsvn 72, 0033 Oslo
Telephone: 22-96-45-00
E-mail: post@nvh.no
Internet: www.nvh.no
Founded 1935
Academic year: August to June
Depts of basic sciences and aquatic medicine, food safety and infection biology, production animal clinical sciences, companion animal clinical sciences
Rector: YNGVILD WASTESON
Pro-Rector: HALVOR HEKTOEN
Dir-Gen.: BIRGER KRUSE
Chief Librarian: ANNE CATHRINE MUNTHE
Library of 82,500 vols incl. books and journals
Number of teachers: 114
Number of students: 470

PROFESSORS

ALESTRØM, P., Biochemistry
ANDRESEN, Ø., Reproduction
ANSOK, S. B., Anatomy and Pathology
AULIE, A., Physiology
BERG, K. A., Reproduction
BJERKÅS, I., Anatomy
DOLVIK, N. I., Large Animal Clinical Sciences
ELIASSEN, K., Biochemistry and Physiology
EVENSEN, ø., I., Aquatic Medicine and Nutrition
FARSTAD, W., Reproduction
FRØSLIE, A., Forensic Medicine
GJERDE, B., Parasitology
GODFROID, J., Arctic Veterinary Medicine
GRANUM, P. E., Food Hygiene
GRAVE, K., Pharmacology and Toxicology
GRØNDALEN, J., Small Animal Clinical Sciences
GRØNSTØL, H., Large Animal Clinical Sciences
HARBITZ, I., Biochemistry

HORSBERG, T. E., Pharmacology
KARLBERG, K., Reproduction
KROGDAHL, A., Nutrition
LANDSVERK, T., Pathology
LARSEN, J. J., Microbiology
LINGAAS, F., Animal Genetics
LØKEN, T., Large Animal Clinical Sciences
MOE, L., Small Animal Clinical Sciences
NESBAKKEN, T., Food Hygiene
ØDEGAARD, S., Reproduction
PAULSON, J. E., Food Hygiene
POPPE, T., Anatomy and Pathology
REIMERS, E., Anatomy and Pathology
REITE, O. B., Aquaculture and Fish Diseases
RIMSTAD, E., Virology
RØED, K. H., Animal Genetics
RØNNINGEN, K., Animal Genetics
ROPSTAD, E., Reproduction
SIMENSEN, E., Research Farm
SJAASTAD, Ø., Physiology
SKJERVE, E., Food Hygiene
SMITH, A., Laboratory Animals
SØLI, N., Pharmacology and Toxicology
SØRUM, H., Microbiology
TEIGE, J., Pathology
TRANULIS, M., Biochemistry and Physiology
TRYLAND, M., Arctic Veterinary Medicine
TVERDAL, A., Animal Genetics
ULVUND, M., Sheep and Goat Research
WALDELAND, H., Sheep and Goat Research
WASTESON, Y., Food Hygiene
YNDESTAD, M., Food Hygiene

TEOLOGISKE MENIGHETSFAKULTET
(MF Norwegian School of Theology)

POB 5144 Majorstuen, 0302 Oslo
Gydasvei 4, Majorstuen, 0302 Oslo

Telephone: 22-59-05-00

E-mail: post@mf.no

Internet: www.mf.no

Founded 1907

Private control

Languages of instruction: English, Norwegian

Academic year: August to June

Depts of religion and society, religious education and pedagogical studies, theology

Pres. and Rector: Prof. Dr VIDAR L. HAANES

Dir: BEATE PETTERSEN
Dean for Research: Prof. JAN-OLAV HENRIKSEN
Dean for Studies: ATLE O. SØVIK
Chief Librarian: ELNA OLINE STRANDHEIM

Library of 72,000 vols and 520 periodicals
Number of teachers: 50
Number of students: 950

Publications: *Studia Theologica* (2 a year), *Nordic Journal for Religion and Society* (2 a year)

PROFESSORS

AAVITSLAND, K. B., Church History
AFDAL, G., Philosophy of Religious Education
CZAIKA, O., Church History
ENGEDAL, L. G., Psychology of Religion
FRETHEIM, K., Systematic Theology
HANNES, V. L., Church History
HEGSTAD, H., Systematic Theology
HEIENE, G., Systematic Theology
HENRIKSEN, J.-O., Systematic Theology
HVALVIK, R., The New Testament
LEGANGER-KROGSTAD, H., Philosophy of Religious Education
LIED, L. I., Religious Studies
MOGSTAD, S. D., Philosophy of Religious Education
SANDNES, K. O., The New Testament
THORBJØRNSEN, S. O., Systematic Theology
WEYDE, K. W., The Old Testament

Schools of Art and Music

Griegakademiet (Grieg Academy): Dept of Music, Faculty of Humanities, POB 7805, 5020 Bergen; Lars Hilles gate 3, 5015 Bergen; tel. 55-58-69-50; e-mail post@grieg.uib.no; internet www.uib.no/grieg; f. 1905; education of musicians, music teachers and organists; offers teacher-training and Bachelors and Masters degree courses; 120 students; Head of Dept FRODE THORSEN.

Kunstakademiet i Trondheim, Norges Teknisk-Naturvitenskaplige Universitet (Trondheim Academy of Fine Art, Norwegian University of Science and Technology): NTNU, 7491 Trondheim; Innherredsveien 7, Trondheim; tel. 73-59-79-00; e-mail adm@kit.ntnu.no; internet www.kit.ntnu.no; f. 1946, present status 1996; offers Bachelors and Masters degree courses in fine arts; library: 5,000 vols; 11 teachers; 58 students; Pres. IVAR SMEDSTAD; publ. *Kitsch* (4 a year).

Kunst- og designhøgskolen i Bergen (Bergen Academy of Art and Design): Strømgaten 1, 5005 Bergen; tel. 55-58-73-00; e-mail postmottak@khib.no; internet www.khib.no; library: 15,000 vols, 200 periodicals; 100 part-time and full-time teachers; 340 students; Rector PAULA CRABTREE; Pro-Rector JOHAN SANDBORG; College Dir CECILIE OHM; Dir for Academic Affairs INGJALD SELLAND; Head Librarian SIGRUN ASK.

Kunsthøgskolen i Oslo (KHiO) (Oslo National Academy of the Arts): POB 6853 St Olavs plass, 0130 Oslo; Fossveien 24, 0551 Oslo; tel. 22-99-55-00; e-mail postmottak@khio.no; internet www.khio.no; f. 1996 by merger of Nat. College of Art and Design, Nat. Academy of Fine Arts, Nat. College of Ballet, State Univ. of Theatre, State Opera Academy; 6 depts of design, visual art, academy of fine art, academy of dance, academy of opera, academy of theatre; library: 75,000 vols; 200 students; 550 students; Prin. CECILIE BROCH KNUDSEN; Head of Library and Archive HANNE STORM OFTELAND.

Norges Musikkhøgskole (Norwegian Academy of Music): POB 5190, Majorstua, Slemdalsveien 11, 0302 Oslo; tel. 23-36-70-00; e-mail mh@nmh.no; internet www.nmh.no; f. 1973, merged with Eastern Norway Conservatory of Music 1996; offers Bachelors, Masters and PhD degree courses; library: 16,000 vols of books, 160 journals, 1,000 video cassettes, 60,000 items incl. scores, chamber music sets, orchestral/choral sets and scholarly editions; 130 teachers; 541 students; Academy Dir TOVE TVEDT BLIX; Rector EIRIK BIRKELAND; Pro-Rector INGRID MARIA HANKEN; Vice-Rector KJELL TORE INNERVIK; Vice-Rector SIW GRAABRÆK NIELSEN; Head Librarian TONE M. ELOFSSON.

OMAN

The Higher Education System

Until independence was confirmed in 1951, Oman had a special relationship with the United Kingdom. The first institutions of higher education were founded in the 1980s, notably Sultan Qaboos University (founded 1986). In 2009/10 there were 15,357 students enrolled at the university. The Colleges of Education, which were established in the 1970s to provide training for teachers, were transformed in 2007 into Colleges of Applied Sciences (of which there are six) offering Bachelor degrees. In 2011 there were 89,230 students enrolled in the tertiary education sector.

The Ministry of Education has supreme authority over general education, but the Ministry of Higher Education is responsible for tertiary education, the Ministry of Manpower oversees most vocational and technical training and the Ministry of Health coordinates health sciences, nursing and pharmaceutical education. The Ministries sponsor an estimated 6,000 students per year to attend higher education.

Success in the secondary thanawiya amma (school leaving certificate) examinations is the main basis for admission to higher education. Prior to commencing the undergraduate Bachelors degree, students are required to take a one-year Foundation course; this consists of English language, information technology (IT) and study skills training. The Bachelors degree is usually a four-year course and students must accrue at least 120 'credits' in order to graduate. Medical students must first complete a four-year Bachelor of Health Sciences degree before proceeding to a three-year postgraduate programme in Clinical Medicine. The first postgraduate degree is the Diploma, which is approximately equivalent to half a Masters degree. Following completion of the Masters, the PhD is the highest university degree. In 2009 there were 15 doctoral programmes on offer at Sultan Qaboos University.

Technical and vocational education at the post-secondary level is offered by technical industrial colleges, vocational training centres, professional institutes and seven higher colleges of technology. The technical industrial colleges award National Diplomas after upwards of two years of study and workplace training; admission is on the basis of the thanawiya amma. However, the National Diploma system is gradually to be phased out in favour of a system of vocational and occupational training. The vocational training centres offer one- or two-year programmes of training for skilled and semi-skilled workers, and qualifications are equivalent to the United Kingdom National Vocational Qualification (NVQ). The Ministry of Health administers 16 institutes to train nursing and medical science professionals; these include 12 nursing institutes, as well as the Institute of Health Sciences, the Oman Assistant Pharmacy Institute, the Oman Institute of Public Health and the Oman Medical Records Institute. The Nursing and Midwifery Council of Oman, established by the Ministry of Health in 2001, is charged with regulating the nursing profession and the education of its members. The higher colleges of technology, the principal of which is the Higher College of Technology in Muscat, offer a one-year Certificate, a two-year Diploma and a three-year Higher Diploma, all of which require a foundation year (covering English, Mathematics and IT) following successful completion of the thanawiya amma. The Higher College of Technology in Muscat also offers a four-year Bachelor of Technology degree.

In 2011 there were 27 private tertiary education providers under licence from the Ministry of Higher Education with an estimated enrolment of 35,000 students. These institutions are classified into private universities, private university colleges and private colleges. Most of these were established by foreign providers to meet the demand of school leavers entering higher education as the existing provision for higher education in the public sector is insufficient. The three private university colleges—Caledonian College of Engineering, Majan College and Sur University College—are affiliated to recognized overseas degree providers. Caledonian College of Engineering offers an undergraduate Diploma, a Bachelors (Ordinary) and a Bachelors (Honours) degree in Engineering validated by Glasgow Caledonian University. The awards align to levels within the Scottish Credit and Qualifications Framework. Majan University College offers Bachelors (Honours) degrees in IT, Business and Marketing and Finance, which are validated by the University of Bedfordshire. Sur University College offers Australian Bachelors (Honours) degrees in IT and Commerce, which are validated by Bond University in Queensland. The private colleges in Oman, some of which have ties with overseas institutions, do not offer Bachelors degrees but two-year Diploma and three-year Advanced Diploma programmes, the majority of which are in Business, IT and Engineering.

Established in 2001, the Oman Accreditation Council (OAM) is responsible for the external quality assurance and quality enhancement of higher education institutions and programmes. The OAM created a National Qualifications Framework in 2005 to standardize qualifications offered by tertiary education providers in terms of level, learning outcomes and volume of study.

Regulatory and Representative Bodies

GOVERNMENT

Ministry of Education: POB 3, Muscat 113; tel. 24561134; e-mail moe@moe.gov.om; internet www.moe.gov.om; Minister Dr MADEEHA BINT AHMED BIN NASIR AL-SHIBANIYAH.

Ministry of Heritage and Culture: POB 668, Muscat 113; tel. 24641300; e-mail info@mhc.gov.om; internet www.mhc.gov.om; Minister SAYYID HAITHM BIN TARIQ AL-SAID.

Ministry of Higher Education: POB 82, Ruwi 112; tel. 24340999; e-mail info_dept@mohe.gov.om; internet www.mohe.gov.om; Minister Dr RAWYA BINT SAUD BIN AHMAD AL-BUSAIDIYAH.

ACCREDITATION

Oman Accreditation Council: POB 1255, Al Khuwair 133; tel. 24475170; e-mail enquiries@oac.gov.om; internet www.oac.gov.om; accredits public institutes, and public and private colleges and univs; 11 mems; Chair. Dr HAMED AL-DHAHAB.

Learned Societies

HISTORY, GEOGRAPHY AND ARCHAEOLOGY

Historical Association of Oman: POB 3941, Ruwi 112; tel. 24141674; e-mail artsdean@hotmail.com; internet www.hao.org.om; f. 1971; 200 mems; library of 400 vols; Pres. Dr ISAM BIN ALI BIN AHMED AL-RAWAS; publs Geology of Oman, The Journal of Oman Studies, The Sambuq, Traditional Spinning and Weaving in the Sultanate of Oman, Turtles in the Sultanate of Oman.

LANGUAGE AND LITERATURE

British Council: Rd One, Madinat al Sultan, Qaboos West, POB 73, Muscat 115; tel. 24681000; e-mail bc.muscat@om.britishcouncil.org; internet www.britishcouncil.org/me-oman.htm; teaching centre; offers courses and exams in English language and British culture and promotes cultural exchange with the UK; attached office in Seeb; Dir JIM SCARTH; Dir for Teaching and Examination Services MARY STANSFIELD.

Research Institute

AGRICULTURE, FISHERIES AND VETERINARY SCIENCE

Marine Sciences and Fisheries Centre: c/o Ministry of Agriculture and Fisheries, POB 467, Muscat; tel. 24740062; f. 1986; biological research, conservation, ecology, food technology, oceanography; incl. library and aquarium.

Libraries and Archives

Bowshar

Central Medical Library: Min. of Health-Royal Hospital, POB 1331, Seeb, Bowshar 111; tel. 24595971; f. 1970; 7,000 vols, 122 periodicals; spec. collns: Min. of Health reports, health reports, WHO collns; Head of Medical Library AFFRA SAID AL SHAMSI; Librarian IMAN MAHFOODH AL HARTHY.

Muscat

Archives of the Directorate General of Heritage: Min. of Heritage and Culture, POB 668, Muscat 113; f. 1976; 5,000 MSS, 50,000 archives; Dir-Gen. MOHAMMED SAID AL-WOHAIBI.

Museums and Art Galleries

Muscat

Oman Natural History Museum (ONHM): Ministry of Heritage and Culture, Al Khuwair, Muscat; tel. 24641510; f. 1983; incl. the Nat. Herbarium of Oman and the Nat. Shell and Coral Colln, and the Insect and Osteological Collns.

Qurm

Oman Museum, Qurm: c/o Min. of Heritage and Culture, POB 668, Muscat 113; Al Alam St, behind Ministry of Information, Madinat Sultan Qaboos, Muscat; tel. 24600946; attached to Min. of Heritage and Culture; Oman's 5,000-year history with displays on shipbuilding, Islam and fort architecture.

Ruwi

National Museum at Ruwi: Way 3123, off Al'Noor St, near Al Fallaj Hotel, Ruwi, Muscat; tel. 24701289; f. 1978; attached to Min. of Heritage and Culture; fmrly the Museum of Bait Assayed, Nadir bin Faisal bin Turki; exhibits incl. silver ornaments, copper crafts and samples from Omani ships; holy relics incl. a letter sent by The Prophet to the rulers of Oman A'bd and Jaiifer, sons of Al Julanda, dated 8th century Hijri; belongings of the Al Busaidi dynasty, rulers of Zanzibar.

Universities

DHOFAR UNIVERSITY

POB 2509, Salalah 211
Telephone: 23225061
E-mail: du@du.edu.om
Internet: www.du.edu.om
Founded 2004
Vice-Chancellor: MUHAMMAD FAOUR

DEANS

College of Arts and Applied Sciences: HUSSEIN YAGHI

College of Commerce and Business Administration: NIMR EID
College of Engineering: FARID CHAABAN

GERMAN UNIVERSITY OF TECHNOLOGY IN OMAN

POB 1816, Athaibah 130
Telephone: 24493051
E-mail: info@gutech.edu.om
Internet: www.gutech.edu.om
Founded 2006; attached to RWTH Aachen University, Germany
Private control
Faculties of economics and planning, information technology and mathematics, sciences

SOHAR UNIVERSITY

POB 44, Sohar 311
Telephone: 26720101
E-mail: soharuni@omantel.net.om
Internet: www.soharuni.edu.om
Founded 1998 as Sohar College of Applied Sciences; univ. status 2001
Private control
Affiliated to Queensland University, Australia
Vice-Chancellor: Dr ABOOD HAMAD AL SAWAFI

DEANS

Faculty of Business: Dr MOHIT KUMAR KOLAY
Faculty of Computing and Information Technology: Dr WAIL M. OMAR
Faculty of Engineering: (vacant)
Faculty of Humanities and Social Sciences: (vacant)

SULTAN QABOOS UNIVERSITY

POB 50, 123, Al-Khod, Muscat
Telephone: 24141111
E-mail: webmaster@squ.edu.om
Internet: www.squ.edu.om
Founded 1986
State control
Academic year: September to May
Vice-Chancellor: Dr ALI AL-BEMANI
Dean for Admissions and Registration: Dr HAIDER ALI RAMADAN
Library Dir: Dr MOOSA NASSER AL-MUFARAJI
Library of 120,698 vols
Number of teachers: 964
Number of students: 12,591
Publications: *Journal of Scientific Research: Agricultural Marine Sciences* (2 a year), *Journal of Scientific Research: Medical Sciences* (2 a year), *Journal of Scientific Research: Science and Technology* (2 a year)

DEANS

College of Agriculture and Marine Sciences: Dr SANMUGAM A. PRATHAPAR
College of Arts and Social Sciences: Dr ISSAM ALI AL-RAWAS
College of Commerce and Economics: Dr DARWISH AL-MOHARBY
College of Education: Dr THUWAYBA AHMED AL-BARWANI
College of Engineering: Dr ALI AL-HARETHI
College of Law: Dr MOHAMED SAMI GAMALELDIN
College of Medicine and Health Sciences: Dr BAZDAWI AL-RIYAMI
College of Nursing: Prof. BAZDAWI M. S. AL-RIYAMI (acting)
College of Science: Dr ADEL YOUSSEF

DIRECTORS

Centre for Environmental Studies and Research: Prof. REGINALD VICTOR

Centre for Human Resources and Staff Development: ABDUL BASIT TALIB RAJAB AL-HAMMADI
Centre of Educational Technology: KHALID KHAMIS AL-SAADI
Centre of Information Systems: ALI OBAID AL-MAJEENI
Language Centre: Dr WILLIAM HARSBARGER
Remote Sensing Centre: Dr ANDY KWARTENG
Student Counselling Centre: SAUD MOHAMMAD ALI SULAIMAN
Water Research Centre: Dr SANMUGAM A. PRATHAPAR

UNIVERSITY OF NIZWA

POB 33, Birkat Al Mouz PC 616
Telephone: 25446234
E-mail: rose@unizwa.edu.om
Internet: www.unizwa.edu.om
Founded 2004
Private control
Languages of instruction: Arabic, English
Academic year: September to July
Chancellor: Prof. AHMED KHALFAN AL RAWAHI
Vice-Chancellor for Academic Affairs: Prof. ABDULAZIZ YAHYA AL KINDI
Vice-Chancellor for Graduate Studies and Research: Dr ABDALLAH MOHAMMED OMEZZINE

DEANS

College of Arts and Sciences: Dr ABDULLAH SAIF AL TOBI
College of Economics, Management and Information Systems: Dr AHMED MASOUD AL KINDI
College of Engineering and Architecture: Prof. WALEED A. THANOON
College of Pharmacy and Nursing: Prof. NAFSIAH BINTI SHAMSUDIN

Colleges

Al Buraimi University College: POB 77, Al Buraimi 512; tel. 25641866; e-mail info@buc.edu.om; internet www.buc.edu.om; diploma, advanced diploma and Bachelor degree levels; depts of business administration and accounting, English language and literature, information technology; Dir YAQOOB M. FAKEER.

College of Banking and Financial Studies: POB 3122, Ruwi 112; tel. 24505796; e-mail info@cbfs.edu.om; internet www.cbfs.edu.om; f. 1998 as Institute of Banking and Financial Studies; present name and status 2004; courses in accounting, banking, business, computing, English, insurance; Chair. IQBAL ALI KHAMIS AL LAWATI; Dean Dr ASHRAF NABHAN AL NABHANI.

Higher College of Technology: POB 74, Al Khuwair 133; tel. 24473600; internet www.hct.edu.om; f. 1984 as Oman Technical Industrial College; present name and status 2001; Bachelors degree; depts of applied sciences, business studies, engineering, fashion design, information technology, pharmacy, photography; 600 teachers; 7,300 students; Dean Dr OBAID AL SAEEDI.

Institute of Health Sciences: POB 3720, 112 Ruwi, Muscat; tel. 24560085; f. 1982; attached to Min. of Health; library: 5,000 vols; 36 teachers; 244 students; Dean ALYA MOHAMMED MUSALLEM AL-RAWAHY; publ. *Quarterly Medical News Journal.*

Institute of Public Administration: POB 1994, Ruwi 112; tel. 24600205; e-mail ipa@ipa.gov.om; internet www.ipa.gov.om; f. 1977; training, research and consultancy; library: 12,000 Arabic vols, 3,800 foreign; 70 Arabic periodicals, 5 foreign periodicals; 57

teachers; 1,000 students; Dir-Gen. SULEIMAN BIN HILAL AL-ALAWI; publ. *Al-Edari* (4 a year).

Mazoon University College: POB 101, Muscat 133; tel. 24513301; e-mail mazoonco@omantel.net.om; internet www .mazooncollege.edu.om; f. 1999; affiliated to Missouri University of Science and technology, USA in partnership with Banasthali Vidyapith, Jaipur, India; Masters Degree, Bachelors Degree and Assoc. Dipl. in accounting, business administration, computer science, economics, English, information science and technology, management information systems and psychology; Man. Dir Dr JUMA S. AL GHAILANI; Dir for Student Affairs and Registration JIHAD IBRAHIM JABARIN.

Middle East College of Information Technology: POB 79, al Rusayl 124; tel. 24446698; e-mail info@mecit.edu.om; internet www.mecit.edu.om; f. 2000; affiliated to Coventry Univ., UK; depts of business studies, computing, cultural studies, design technology, electronics and communication, mathematics and applied sciences.

Modern College of Business and Science: POB 100, al Khuwair 133; tel. 24482802; e-mail info@mcbs.edu.om; internet www.mcbs.edu.om; f. 1996; Assoc. of Science in business administration, computer science, information communication technology; BA in arts; BSc in business administration, computer science; Dean BADR EL DIN A. IBRAHIM.

Muscat College: POB 2910, Ruwi 112; tel. 24503821; e-mail info@mctcollege.com; internet www.mctcollege.com; f. 1996; attached to Univ. of Stirling, UK and Scottish Qualifications Authority; Bachelor degrees in accountancy and finance, business studies, computing science; Chair. Dr AHMED BIN ABDULLA AL-GHAZALI.

Oman Dental College: POB 835, Muscat 116; tel. 24696171; e-mail info@ omandentalcollege.org; internet www .omandentalcollege.org; affiliated to AB Shetty Memorial Institute of Dental Sciences, India.

Oman Medical College: POB 620, Azaiba 130; tel. 24504608; e-mail admissions@omc .edu.om; internet www.omc.edu.om; f. 2000; affiliated to West Virginia Univ., USA; degrees in Doctor of Medicine and Bachelor of Pharmacy; Dean for Boshwar Campus Dr DIANA BEATTIE; Dean for Sohar Campus Dr SALEH MOHAMMED AL KHUSAIBY.

Oman Tourism and Hospitality Academy: POB 822, al Khoud 132; tel. 521105; e-mail office@otha.edu.om; internet www .otha.edu.om; f. 2001; affiliated to the Int. Institute of Tourism and Management, Krems and the Int. Management Centre, Univ. of Applied Sciences, Krems, Austria.

Salalah College of Technology: Thumrait Rd, Salalah, Dhofar 211; e-mail webmaster@ sct.edu.om; internet www.sct.edu.om; f. 1979 as a Vocational Training Centre; 1993 became Technical Industrial College; present name 2001; attached to Min. of Manpower; depts of business, engineering, information technology; 197 teachers; 2,132 students; Dean Dr HASSAN KASHOOB.

Sur University College: POB 400, Sur 411; tel. 25542888; internet www.suc.edu.om; affiliated to Bond Univ., Australia; depts of business administration and commerce, information systems and technology; Chair. MUBARAK JUMA BAHWAN; Dean Dr AHMAD ABDEL-AZIZ SHARIEH.

Waljat Colleges of Applied Sciences: POB 197, Muscat 124; tel. 24446660; e-mail info@waljatcolleges.edu.om; internet www .waljatcolleges.edu.om; in partnership with Birla Institute of Technology; Dean Dr A. M. AGRAWAL.

PAKISTAN

The Higher Education System

In 1947 Pakistan declared its independence from the former British Indian Empire. The oldest current institutions of higher education were established during the period of British rule, among them the Government College University (founded in 1897), Liaquat University of Medical and Health Sciences (founded in 1881; present name and status since 2001) and the University of the Punjab (founded in 1882). Consequently, the university system is closely based on the late 19th-century British model (particularly the University of London) of federal institutions, consisting of a centralized administration and affiliated colleges. Universities and degree-awarding institutions are broadly divided into 'general' and 'professional' categories. In 2010/11 there were 135 universities and degree-awarding institutions. In 2011/12 there were an estimated 1,414,000 students enrolled at such institutions. In the same year there were also 3,600 arts and science colleges and 1,700 professional colleges; enrolment totalled 1,291,000 and 1,015,000, respectively. The Allama Iqbal Open University has been established with the technical support of the British Open University. With the assistance of the Asian Development Bank, 11 polytechnic institutes and a national teacher-training college have been established by the Government. Training is provided for teachers at polytechnic, commercial and vocational institutes. In 2009 the Government announced an initiative calling for an increase in the percentage of the 17–23-year-old age group with access to higher education, from the existing level of 5% to 10% by 2015. If the objective were to be achieved, significant government funding and other support would be required.

In late 2002 the Higher Education Commission (HEC) replaced the University Grants Commission as the national controlling body of higher education. The HEC is responsible for, inter alia, dispersal of government funding, formation of higher education policy, evaluation, accreditation and quality assurance. Government proposals, announced in mid-2011, to disband the HEC and transfer its functions to various ministries, so as to ensure that budgetary and other higher education matters go through proper parliamentary channels for approval, received a mixed response, with some arguing that it would be detrimental to the higher education sector, while others contended that the Government should go further and create a new government ministry devoted exclusively to higher education. In the mean time, however, the HEC still has authority over both public and private institutions, although universities are still autonomous institutions. The chairman of the university is the Chancellor, while the chief executive and academic officer is the Vice-Chancellor, aided by Pro-Vice-Chancellors. Bodies of institutional and academic control include the Senate, Syndicate, Academic Council, Boards of Faculty and Study, Selection Board, Advanced Studies and Research Board, Finance and Planning Committee, Affiliation Committee and Disciplinary Committee.

Admission to higher education is based on the secondary school leaving certificate. From the mid-2000s the Bachelors degree programme was reformed from two- or three-year programmes—Bachelors (Pass) and Bachelors (Honours), respectively—to a four-year course of study. Specialist degrees leading to professional titles in architecture and medicine are five-year programmes of study. Bachelors degrees in law, education and library science are postgraduate degrees, admission to which are based upon completion of an undergraduate Bachelors degree. Postgraduate diplomas are one-year courses taken following a relevant first degree. The Masters is a postgraduate degree requiring two years of study following the Bachelors; it consists of coursework and final examinations. The Master of Philosophy (MPhil) lasts two years, and is a research-based degree taken after a Masters in arts, commerce or science. The highest university degree is the PhD, requiring a minimum of three years of study after award of the Masters.

Technical and vocational education at the post-secondary level is available at polytechnics and colleges of technology, which are the responsibility of the National Institute of Science and Technical Education. At a provincial level, Boards of Technical Education are the responsible bodies. Polytechnics specialize in three-year Diploma courses and colleges of technology offer degree courses to holders of the Polytechnic Diplomas (in addition to the Diploma). Several professional bodies are authorized to issue Diplomas and certificates, among them the College of Physicians and Surgeons Pakistan, the Institute of Chartered Accountants of Pakistan, the Institute of Cost and Management Accountants of Pakistan and the Pakistan Nursing Council.

Regulatory and Representative Bodies

GOVERNMENT

Federal Directorate of Education: Rohtas Rd, Muave Ave, Sector G-9/4, Islamabad; tel. (51) 9260230; e-mail info@fde.gov.pk; internet www.fde.gov.pk; f. 1967; attached to Min. of Capital Admin. and Devt; Dir-Gen. Dr SHAHNAAZ ANJUM RIAZ.

Ministry of Education, Trainings & Standards in Higher Education: First Fl., C Block, Pak Secretariat, Islamabad; tel. (51) 9213933; e-mail secretary@moent.gov.pk; internet moptt.gov.pk; Minister (vacant).

Ministry of Science and Technology: Fourth Fl., Evacuee Trust Complex, Aga Khan Rd, F-5/1, Islamabad; tel. (51) 9202790; e-mail minister@most.gov.pk; internet www.most.gov.pk; Minister ZAHID HAMID.

ACCREDITATION

Higher Education Commission: Sector H-9, E Service Rd, Islamabad; tel. (51) 9040000; e-mail info@hec.gov.pk; internet www.hec.gov.pk; f. 2002; evaluates, improves and promotes Pakistan's higher education and research sector; est. accreditation ccls in areas of computing, agricultural education, teachers education and business education; est. quality assurance agency to develop policies and guidelines to ensure improvement in the quality of higher education throughout the country; 17 mems; library of 41,000 vols, 232 periodicals; Chair. Dr JAVAID R. LAGHARI; Exec. Dir Prof. Dr SYED SOHAIL H. NAQVI; publs *Guide to the Equivalence of Qualifications in Pakistan* (irregular), *Handbook of Centres of Excellence and Advanced Studies*, *Handbook of Colleges*, *Handbook of Universities of Pakistan* (every 2 years), *Higher Education News* (4 a year), *Statistics on Higher Education in Pakistan*.

Pakistan Engineering Council: Attaturk Ave (E), G-5/2, POB 1296, Islamabad; tel. (51) 2829348; e-mail chairman@pec.org.pk; internet www.pec.org.pk; f. 1976; statutory functions incl. registration of engineers, consulting engineers, constructors/operators; accreditation of engineering programmes run by univs/instns; ensures and manages continuing professional devt; assists the Fed. govt as think tank; establishes standards for engineering products and services; safeguarding the interest of its mems; Chair. SYED ABDUL QADIR SHAH.

Learned Societies

GENERAL

Quaid-i-Azam Academy: 297 M. A. Jinnah Rd, Karachi 74800, Sindh; tel. (21) 99215238; e-mail qaak@quaidiazamacademy.com; internet www.quaidiazamacademy.com; f. 1976; Min. of Inter Provincial Coordination; research on Quaid-i-Azam Mohammad Ali Jinnah, on the historical background (incl. cultural, religious, literary, linguistic, social, economic and political aspects) of the Pakistan Movement, and various aspects of Pakistan; gives scholarships and professorships; awards Quaid-i-Azam Academic and Literary Prizes for scholarly works; holds seminars and lectures; photostat vols of Archives of Freedom Movement; photostat files of Quaid-i-Azam Papers; 52 photostat vols of Shamsul Hasan collns, Sadar Abdur Rab Nishtar collns, 2,000 microfilms of various pre-partition newspapers and other collns; publishes bibliographies, research studies, biographies, monographs and documents (in English, Urdu and dialects); library of 30,000 vols; Exec. Head MUHAMMAD ARIF AZIM; Dir Dr SHEHLA KAZMI (acting).

UNESCO Office Islamabad: St 8 House 17 Sector F 7/3, Islamabad 2034; tel. (51) 2611170; e-mail islamabad@unesco.org; internet unesco.org.pk; f. 1945; education, basic sciences, culture, communication and information, natural sciences, social and human sciences; Dir Dr KOZUE KAY NAGATA; Deputy Dir Dr ROSHAN CHITRAKAR.

ARCHITECTURE AND TOWN PLANNING

Pakistan Council of Architects and Town Planners: Suite 111, First Fl., R. S. M. Sq., E-1 Shaheed-e-Millat Rd, Karachi 75350, Sindh; tel. (21) 4523129; internet www.pcatp.org.pk; f. 1983 as a statutory body by the Govt of Pakistan; regulates professions of architecture and town planning; 797 mems; Chair. SHAMA USMAN.

BIBLIOGRAPHY, LIBRARY SCIENCE AND MUSEOLOGY

Library Promotion Bureau: 1239/9 Dastgir Soc., Fed. B Area, Karachi 75270, Sindh; tel. (21) 6321959; f. 1965; promotes librarianship in Pakistan; coordinates with all orgs engaged in promotional activities; publs reference books, books on library and information science, textbooks on library science, bibliographies, directories, etc.; Pres. M. ADIL USMANI; Sec.-Gen. Dr NASIM FATIMA; publ. *Pakistan Library and Information Science Journal* (4 a year).

National Book Foundation: 6 Mauve Area, G-8/4, Taleemi Chowk, POB 1169, Islamabad; tel. (51) 2255572; e-mail books@nbf.org.pk; internet www.nbf.org.pk; f. 1972; attached to Min. of Education; promotes writing, research and publ, promotes literacy, organizes book festivals and exhibitions, operates book promotion schemes, publishes Braille books; 128 mems; Man. Dir Prof. Dr INAM-UL-HAQ JAVEID; Sec. AFTAB AHMED SOOMRO; publ. *Kitab* (in English and Urdu).

Pakistan Library Association: c/o Office of Executive Committee, PLA HQ, Quetta Balochistan; tel. (51) 9214041; e-mail info@pla.org.pk; f. 1957; represents librarians in Pakistan; develops and improves libraries; office of Exec. council rotates every 2 years between PLA brs in Balochistan, Sindh, Punjab, Khyber Pakhtunkhwa; 1,329 mems; Pres. Prof. MALAHAT KALEEM SHERWANI; Vice-Pres. NUZHAT YASMEEN; Sec. RIAZ ALI KHASKHELI; publs *Conference Proceedings* (1 a year), *PLA Journal* (4 a year).

Regional Branches:

Balochistan Branch: Quetta, Balochistan; e-mail bb@pla.org.pk; Pres. ABDUR RAHMAN QAISARANI.

Federal Branch: c/o Pakistan Library Association Islamabad; e-mail fb@pla.org.pk; Pres. MUSHAHID HUSSAIN.

Khyber Pakhtunkhwa Branch: Peshawar, Khyber Pakhtunkhwa; e-mail nwfp@pla.org.pk; Pres. MUHAMMAD KHAN MARAWAT.

Punjab Branch: Punjab Univ. Library, Quaid-e-Azam Campus, Lahore 54000, Punjab; tel. (42) 99230863; e-mail info@plapunjab.org; internet plapunjab.org; Pres. CHAUDHRY MUHAMMAD HANIF.

Sindh Branch: Liaquat Memorial Library Bldg, Stadium Rd, Ground Fl., Karachi, Sindh; tel. (333) 2658156; e-mail plasindh@gmail.com; internet pla-sindhbranch.weebly.com; Pres. Prof. SHEREEN GUL SOOMRO.

ECONOMICS, LAW AND POLITICS

Institute of Cost and Management Accountants of Pakistan: St 18/C, Block-6, Gulshan-e-Iqbal, POB 17642, Karachi 75300, Sindh; tel. (21) 99243900; e-mail ed@icmap.com.pk; internet www.icmap.com.pk; f. 1951; regulates cost and management accountancy profession in Pakistan; arranges professional devt programmes; 4,620 mems; library of 32,000 vols; Pres. ZIA UL MUSTAFA AWAN; Vice-Pres. GHULAM MUSTAFA QAZI; Exec. Dir MUSHTAQ AHMED MADRASWALA; publs *Cost Audit Handbook*, *Glossary of Management Accounting*, *History of Management Accounting Profession in Pakistan*, *Students' Handbook* (1 a year).

Pakistan Institute of International Affairs: Aiwan-e-Sadar Rd, POB 1447, Karachi 74200, Sindh; tel. (21) 35682891; e-mail info@piia.org.pk; internet www.piia.org.pk; f. 1947; 650 mems; library: see Libraries and Archives; studies int. affairs and promotes scientific study of int. politics, Pakistan foreign policy, economics, jurisprudence; conducts research and surveys; maintains clipping files of chronology of events; organizes lectures, round-table discussions, and seminars on relevant subjects; Chair. Dr MASUMA HASAN; Hon. Sec. SYED ABDUL MINAM JAFRI; publ. *Pakistan Horizon* (4 a year).

EDUCATION

Punjab Bureau of Education: Punjab Public Service Commission, 2 Agha Khan (Davis Rd), Lahore, Punjab; tel. (42) 9202762; e-mail info@ppsc.gop.pk; internet www.ppsc.gop.pk; f. 1958; clearing house for information on education of all aspects and levels, within Pakistan and abroad; Documentation Section, Statistical Section, Publication Section and Research Section; library of 10,000 vols and periodicals; Dir SAJJAD HUSSAIN NAQVI; publ. *Educational Statistics* (1 a year).

FINE AND PERFORMING ARTS

Arts Council of Pakistan: M. R. Kayani Rd, Karachi 74200, Sindh; tel. (21) 99213090; e-mail art_council_khi@yahoo.com; f. 1956; promotes and develops fine arts and crafts, drama, music; 6,597 mems; Chair. SHOAIB AHMED SIDDIQUI; Pres. Prof. EJAZ AHMED FAROOQI; Deputy Dir MUHAMMAD ASHRAF; publ. *Khabar Nama*.

Lok Virsa/National Institute of Folk and Traditional Heritage: Garden Ave, Shakarparian, POB 1184, Islamabad; tel. (51) 9252106; e-mail info@lokvirsa.org.pk; internet lokvirsa.org.pk; f. 1974; preserves and promotes traditional culture, folk arts and folklore of Pakistan; museum, publishing house, media centre, sound archive; library of 10,000 vols; Exec. Dir KHALID JAVAID; publs *Lok Punjab*, *Mai Ni Main Kinno Akhan*, *Rag Swaroop*.

Pakistan National Council of the Arts: Plot 5, F-5/1, Islamabad; tel. (51) 9205273; e-mail pncaoaisb@gmail.com; internet www.pnca.org.pk; f. 1973; promotes visual and performing arts, nat. heritage; offices in

Karachi, Lahore; library of 3,000 vols; Dir-Gen. TAUQEER AHMED NASIR.

HISTORY, GEOGRAPHY AND ARCHAEOLOGY

Department of Archaeology and Museums: First Floor, Block 4, Sitara Market, G-7 Markaz, Islamabad; tel. (51) 9206236; e-mail doam@cyber.net.pk; f. 1947; explores, excavates and scientifically conserves archaeological, historical and cultural heritage of Pakistan; develops a documentary and published record; exhibits material in the museums for educational research and amusement; Dir-Gen. Dr FAZAL DAD KAKAR; publ. *Pakistan Archaeology* (1 a year).

Pakistan Historical Society: Bait al-Hikmah, Hamdard Univ. campus, Madinat al-Hikmah, Karachi 74600, Sindh; tel. (21) 36616001; e-mail phs@hamdard.edu.pk; f. 1950; historical studies and research, particularly history of Islam and the sub-continent; library of 10,000 vols, 80 MSS; Pres. SADIA RASHID; Gen. Sec. Dr ANSAR ZAHID KHAN; publ. *Journal of the Pakistan Historical Society (Historicus)* (4 a year).

LANGUAGE AND LITERATURE

Alliance Française d'Islamabad: House 9, St 49, F 6/4, Islamabad; tel. (51) 2825218; e-mail contact@afislamabad.org; internet www.afislamabad.org; offers courses and exams in French language and culture and promotes cultural exchange with France; attached teaching centres in Karachi, Lahore and Peshawar; library of 1,500 vols; Dir MATTHIEU DECLERCQ; Asst Dir NAUMAN AHMED.

Anjuman Taraqqi-e-Urdu Pakistan: D-159, Block 7, Gulshan-e-Iqbal, Karachi 75300, Sindh; tel. (21) 34973296; e-mail anjumantarraqieurdu@hotmail.com; f. 1903 in pre-partition India, 1948 in Pakistan; promotes Urdu language and literature; prepares a 6-volume bibliography of Urdu books in collaboration with UNESCO; library of 30,000 vols, research library of 48,000 vols and 6,000 MSS; Pres. AFTAB AHMED KHAN; Hon. Sec. JAMILUDDIN AALI; publs *Qaumi Zaban* (12 a year), *Urdu* (4 a year).

Balochi Academy: Adalat Rd, Quetta, Balochistan; tel. (81) 2829566; e-mail academy@balochiacademy.org; internet www.balochiacademy.org; f. 1958; promotes Balochi language and literature, publishes books on Balochi history, poetry, culture, folk stories, and a Balochi–Urdu dictionary and encyclopaedia; 48 mems; library of 40,000 vols; Chair. MUHAMMAD SIDDIQ BALOCH; Gen. Sec. ABDUL QADIR SHAHWANI ASEER.

British Council: POB 1135, Islamabad; tel. (21) 35839932; e-mail info@britishcouncil.org.pk; internet www.britishcouncil.org/pakistan; offers courses and exams in English language and British culture and promotes cultural exchange with the UK; attached offices in Faisalabad, Karachi, Lahore, Multan, Peshawar and Quetta; Dir DAVID MARTIN.

Goethe-Institut: 2 Brunton Rd, Civil Lines, Karachi; tel. (21) 35661633; e-mail info@karachi.goethe.org; internet www.goethe.de/karachi; f. 1956; offers courses and exams in German language; cultural activities incl. lectures, seminars, workshops and concerts from Germany; library of 3,715 vols, 20 periodicals; Dir Dr MARKUS LITZ; Admin. Man. S. A. FAROOQ.

Institute of Islamic Culture: 2 Club Rd, Lahore, Punjab; tel. (42) 36363127; e-mail iic-lhr@hotmail.com; f. 1950; publishes books on Islamic subjects in English and Urdu; Dir

KAZI JAVED; publ. *Al-Ma'arif* (in Urdu, 4 a year).

Iqbal Academy: POB 1308, 6th Fl., Academy Block, Aiwan-e-Iqbal Complex, off Egerton Rd, Lahore, Punjab; tel. (42) 6314510; e-mail info@iap.gov.pk; internet www.allamaiqbal.com; f. 1951; promotes, disseminates study and understanding of works and teachings of Dr Allama Iqbal; publishes books and pamphlets on Dr Allama Iqbal; library of 30,000 vols; Dir MUHAMMED SUHEYL UMAR; publs *Iqbaliyat* (2 a year, in Urdu; 1 a year, in Arabic, Farsi and Turkish), *Iqbal-nama*, *Iqbal Quarterly*, *Iqbal Review* (2 a year, in English).

National Language Authority: Pitras Bukhari Rd, H-8/4, Islamabad; tel. (51) 9250311; e-mail secretary@nla.gov.pk; internet www.nla.gov.pk; f. 1979; promotes Urdu as the nat., official, judicial and instructional language of Pakistan; organizes seminars and conferences; offers courses; develops Urdu terminology in various disciplines; compiles dictionaries; library of 25,000 vols; Chair. Dr ANWAR AHMED; Sec. SARFARAZ TARIQ; publ. *Akhbar-e-Urdu* (12 a year).

Attached Centre:

Centre of Excellence for Urdu Informatics: tel. (51) 9250317; e-mail nlauit@apollo.net.pk; Urdu IT Wing of the NLA; develops Urdu keyboard layouts for computers and computer codes (Standardized Urdu Code Plate), and localization of Microsoft Urdu Office and Windows XP; mem of UNICODE, Inc.; Project Dir Dr ATTASH DURRANI; Project Man. AGHA ABID HUSSAIN MEMON.

Pakistan Academy of Letters: H 8/1, Islamabad; tel. (51) 9250570; e-mail pakistanacademyoflettersisb@gmail.com; internet www.pal.gov.pk; f. 1976; promotes literary works; determines research priorities in literature; evaluates the performance of literary bodies; sets up Bureau of Translation; introduces Pakistani literature to foreign readers; organizes seminars on literary and academic issues; advises the Govt on int. literary gatherings; nominates recipients for various literary awards and distinctions; provides financial assistance to scholars; library of 20,000 vols; Chair. ABDUL HAMEED; Dir-Gen. (vacant); publs *Adbiyat* (4 a year, in Urdu), *Bibliography of Pakistani Literature*, *Pakistani Literature* (2 a year), *Selection of Pakistani Literature* (12 a year).

Regional Offices:

Balochistan Office: Espeni Rd, Quetta; tel. (81) 2823473; Resident Asst Dir AFZAL MURAAD.

Khyber Pakhtunkhwa Office: Attached Dept Complex, Block 15, Khyber Rd, Peshawar; tel. (91) 9211139; Resident Asst Dir Dr MUHAMMAD AZAM AZAM.

Punjab Office: House 74/A3-1, Abu Bakar Block, New Garden Town, Lahore, Punjab; tel. (42) 35852974; Resident Asst Dir ALTAF AHMAD QURESHI.

Sindh Office: 80A, Block 2, P. E. C. H. S., Khalid Bin Waleed Rd, Karachi; tel. (21) 4531588; Resident Asst Dir AGHA NOOR MUHAMMAD PATHAN.

Pakistan American Cultural Centre: 11 Fatima Jinnah Rd, Karachi, Sindh; tel. (21) 35215305; e-mail info@pacc.edu.pk; internet www.pacc.edu.pk; f. 1959; promotes relation between people of Pakistan and USA; offers language services, cultural activities; Exec. Dir MUHAMMAD SIKANDER IQBAL.

Pakistan Writers Guild: Guild House, 1 Montgomery Rd, Lahore, Punjab; tel. (42) 6367124; e-mail info@pakwritersguild.org; internet www.pakwritersguild.org; f. 1959; 4 regional offices; promotes authorship, dispenses literary prizes, concerned with welfare of writers; Sec. AHMED OMAR SHARIF; publs *Ham Qalam* (12 a year), *Khaber Namay* (12 a year).

Pashto Academy: Univ. of Peshawar, Peshawar, Khyber Pakhtunkhwa; tel. (91) 9216486; e-mail pashtoacademy@yahoo.com; internet pashto.upesh.edu.pk; f. 1955; research into Pashto language and literature, history, art and culture; research cell for study of life and works of Khushal Khan Khattak and his contemporaries; research library; Dir Prof. Dr SALMA SHAHEEN; Librarian SARFARAZ KHAN MARWAT; publ. *Pukhto* (12 a year).

Sindhi Adabi Board: POB 12, Jamshorro 76070, Sindh; tel. (22) 9213421; e-mail sindhiab@yahoo.com; internet www.sindhiadabiboard.org; f. 1951; autonomous literary and cultural instn; fosters the language, literature and culture of the Sindh region; publishes books in English, Sindhi, Urdu, Persian and Arabic; library of 10,000 vols, 450 MSS; Chair. MAKHDOOM JAMEELUZ-ZAMAN; publs *Gul Phul* (12 a year), *Mehran* (4 a year), *Sartyoon* (12 a year).

Urdu Academy: 33C Model Town 'A', Bahawalpur, Punjab; f. 1959; develops Urdu literature and language; publishes books in English and Urdu; Sec. MASUD HASSAN SHIHAB; publ. *Az-Zubair* (4 a year, in Urdu).

Urdu Dictionary Board: ST-18/A, Block 5, Gulshan-e-Iqbal, Off University Rd, Karachi 75300, Sindh; tel. (21) 34988887; internet www.udb.gov.pk; f. 1958 as Urdu Devt Board, present name 1982; publishes books and dictionaries in Urdu; projects incl. a comprehensive, 23-vol. Urdu Dictionary; library of 15,638 vols; Chair. FED. MIN. OF EDUCATION; Pres. Dr FARMAN FATEH PURI; Chief Editor FAHMID RIAZ.

Urdu Science Board: 299 Upper Mall, Lahore 54000, Punjab; tel. (42) 5758674; e-mail u_s_board@hotmail.com; f. 1962; removes deficiencies in Urdu language, particularly in the fields of technology, natural and social sciences; coordinates work of other orgs engaged in related fields; prepares standard dictionaries of scientific and technical terms; library of 10,000 vols; Dir-Gen. KHALID IQBAL YASIR; publ. *Urdu Science Magazine* (4 a year).

MEDICINE

College of Physicians and Surgeons Pakistan: Seventh Central St, Defence Housing Authority Phase II, Karachi 75500, Sindh; tel. (21) 99207100; e-mail administration@cpsp.edu.pk; internet www.cpsp.edu.pk; f. 1962; promotes specialist practice of medicine, surgery and gynaecology and allied disciplines by means of improvement in hospital teaching and methods; arranges postgraduate medical, surgical and other specialist training; provides for medical research and organizes scientific confs for Pakistani and foreign medical experts; awards diplomas of MCPS and FCPS; 9,366 mems (MCPS), 6,900 fellows (FCPS); short course on research methodology, biostatistics, medical writing and computer learning, CME for medical and allied health teachers, CME in RH primary care providers (medical), computer training workshop for medical librarians in Pakistan, diploma in health system management; 12 regional centres; library of 10,000 books, 10,000 journals, 7,000 periodicals, 7,500 dissertations, 375 CD-ROMs, 1,300 audio journals, 1,322 video cassettes, 600 WHO books and monographs, 171 slides, 1,835 x-rays, medical databases and journals; 18,390 mems; Pres. Prof. ZAFARULLAH CHAUDHRY; Vice-Pres. Prof. TARIQ MAHMOOD KHAN; Vice-Pres. Prof. KHALID MASOOD GONDAL; Sec. Capt. Dr QAZI JALALUDDIN AHMED; Registrar Prof. GHULAM ASGHAR CHANNA; Chief Librarian BAIBA AWAN; publ. *Journal of the College of Physicians and Surgeons Pakistan* (12 a year).

Pakistan Academy of Medical Sciences: c/o Prof. Anwar-ul Gilani, Aga Khan Univ. Hospital, Stadium Rd, POB 3500, Karachi 74800; tel. (21) 48594571; f. 1975; promotes medical sciences and arts; awards annual Gold Medal; holds annual PAMS Lecture; 56 fellows; Pres. Prof. KHALID J. AWAN; Sec. Gen. IFTIKHAR A. MALIK; publ. *Pakistan Journal of Ophthalmology* (4 a year).

Pakistan Medical Association: PMA House, Garden Rd, POB 7267, Karachi 74400; tel. (21) 2226443; e-mail jpma_jpma@hotmail.com; f. 1948; Pres. Dr TIPU SULTAN; Sec.-Gen. Dr MIRZA ALI AZHAR; publ. *Journal of Pakistan Medical Association* (12 a year).

NATURAL SCIENCES

General

Pakistan Academy of Sciences: 3 Constitution Ave, G-5/2, Islamabad; tel. (51) 9225159; e-mail pas.editor@gmail.com; internet www.paspk.org; f. 1953; promotes research in pure and applied sciences; establishes and maintains libraries; awards grants, fellowships and gold medals; 117 mems (87 fellows, 22 foreign fellows, 8 gen.); Pres. Prof. Dr ATTA-UR-RAHMAN; Vice-Pres. Prof. Dr KHALID MAHMOOD KHAN; Vice-Pres. Prof. Dr M. QASIM JAN; Sec.-Gen. Prof. Dr G. A. MIANA; publs *Proceedings of Symposia, Monographs* (irregular), *Proceedings of the Pakistan Academy of Sciences* (4 a year), *Yearbook*.

Pakistan Association for the Advancement of Science: First Fl., 67 Shadman Plaza, Shadman Market, Lahore, Punjab; tel. (42) 37578770; internet www.paas.com.pk; f. 1947; promotes science in all its brs, incl. its application to practical problems and research; organizes nat. conferences; publishes journals, 1,500 mems. Pres. Prof. Dr MUHAMMAD ARSHAD; Vice-Pres. Prof. Dr MUHAMMAD AMJAD; Gen. Sec. Prof. Dr MUHAMMAD SALEEM CHAUDHRY; publs *Pakistan Journal of Science* (4 a year), *Pakistan Journal of Scientific Research* (4 a year), *Proceedings of the All Pakistan Science Conference* (every 3 years), *Proceedings of the National Seminars* (every 3 years).

Mathematical Sciences

Centre for Advanced Studies in Mathematics: Opposite Sector U, D. H. A., Lahore Cantt, Lahore 54792, Punjab; tel. (42) 35608013; e-mail casm@lums.edu.pk; internet casm.lums.edu.pk; attached to Lahore Univ. of Management Sciences; promotes interaction between mathematicians and experts of other disciplines; holds workshops, confs; 16 mems, 10 assoc. mems; Dir Dr FAQIR M. BHATTI; Sec. NOREEN IRSHAD.

PHILOSOPHY AND PSYCHOLOGY

Pakistan Philosophical Congress: Dept of Philosophy, Univ. of the Punjab, New Campus, Lahore, Punjab; tel. (42) 99230884; e-mail secretary.ppc@pu.edu.pk; f. 1954; Pres. Dr ABDUL KHALIQ; Gen. Sec. SHAHID MEHMOOD GUL; publ. *Pakistan Philosophical Journal* (1 a year).

RELIGION, SOCIOLOGY AND ANTHROPOLOGY

Hamdard Foundation Pakistan: Al Majeed, Hamdard Centre, Nazimabad 3, Karachi 74600, Sindh; tel. (21) 36616001;

e-mail hfp@hamdardfoundation.org; internet www.hamdardfoundation.org; f. 1964; administers and controls charitable and philanthropic work from the voluntary contribution of Hamdard Laboratories (WAQF) Pakistan; oversees the establishment of academic and educational institutes; 7 mems; library: see under Libraries and Archives; Pres. SADIA RASHID; Vice-Pres. Dr NAVAID UL ZAFAR; Dir of Admin. SYED SHAMIM AKHTER RIZVI; publs *Hamdard-i-Sehat* (12 a year), *Hamdard Islamicus* (4 a year), *Hamdard Medicus* (4 a year), *Hamdard Naunehal* (12 a year), *Historicus* (4 a year).

Heritage Foundation: E-6 Fourth Gizri St, DHA 4, Karachi 75500, Sindh; tel. (21) 5834215; e-mail info@heritagefoundationpak.org; internet www.heritagefoundationpak.org; f. 1980; engages in research, publication and conservation of Pakistan's cultural heritage; outreach programme *KaravanPakistan* (est. 2000) involves youth and communities in safeguarding heritage; attached research institute; Chair. and CEO YASMEEN LARI.

Jamiyat-ul-Falah: Akbar Rd, Saddar, POB 7141, Karachi 74400, Sindh; f. 1950; Tamizuddin Khan Memorial Library (8,000 vols); Koran, Tafseer, Hadees and Seerat colln; Falah Islamic Centre, Falah Social Service Centre, Falah Majlis-e-Adab (literary soc.), Falah Pakistan Studies Centre, Falah Muslim World Studies Centre, Falah Science Studies Centre; Sec.-Gen. SHAMSUDDIN KHALID AHMED; publ. *Voice of Islam* (12 a year, in English).

Karachi Theosophical Society: Jamshed Memorial Hall, M. A. Jinnah Rd, Karachi 74200; tel. (21) 2721275; e-mail daramirza@cyber.net.pk; internet tospakistan.com.pk/khi_tos_society.html; f. 1896; activities incl. study of comparative religion, philosophy and science; investigation of unexplained laws of nature; 150 mems; library of 20,000 vols; Pres. AMANULLAH AMIR; Vice-Pres. JAMIL AHMAD; Hon. Sec. KAIKOBAD J. DINSHAW; publs *The Karachi Theosophist* (6 a year), *Theosophy in Karachi* (6 a year).

Shariah Academy: Sector H-10, Islamabad; tel. (51) 9258060; e-mail director.dawah@iiu.edu.pk; f. 1981, present status 1985; attached to Int. Islamic Univ.; promotes Islamic legal philosophy and orientation in Islamic law; Dir-Gen. Dr SAHIBZADA SAJID-UR-REHMAN.

TECHNOLOGY

Institution of Electrical and Electronics Engineers Pakistan (IEEEP): C-2, Mezzanine Fl., 15th Commercial St, Phase II DHA, Karachi, Sindh; tel. (21) 35392965; e-mail ieeepkhi@yahoo.co.uk; internet www.ieeepkhi.org; f. 1979; head office in Lahore; promotes dissemination of knowledge and improves professional standard; lectures, seminars and publs on electrical and electronic telecommunication engineering; 4,450 (2,300 corporate mems, 2,150 individual mems); library of 2,050 vols, 6,000 periodicals; Chair. TAHIR SALEEM; Vice-Chair. OBAID UR REHMAN; Vice-Pres. S. S. A. JAFRI; publs *Quarterly Electrical Journal*, *The Electrical Engineer* (12 a year).

Institution of Engineers (Pakistan): IEP Bldg, Ground Fl., Gulberg III, Lahore 54660, Punjab; tel. (42) 35754043; e-mail iephqr@gmail.com; internet www.iep.com.pk; f. 1948; promotes and advances science, practice and business of engineering in all its brs; regional offices in Faisalabad, Hyderabad, Islamabad, Karachi, Peshawar and Quetta; sub-centres

in Bahrain, Jeddah and Riyadh; 50,000 mems (corporate and individual); Pres. ZAFARUDDIN A. ZUBERI; Dir RAJA MUHAMMAD RAFIQUE KHAN; publ. *The Pakistan Engineers* (12 a year).

Research Institutes

GENERAL

Area Study Centre: Peshawar, Khyber Pakhtunkhwa; tel. (91) 9216764; e-mail ascpesh@gmail.com; internet asc.upesh.edu.pk; f. 1978; attached to Univ. of Peshawar; research on Central Asia; Dir Prof. Dr SARFARAZ KHAN; library of 18,880 vols; publ. *Central Asia* (2 a year).

Pakistan Study Centre: Main Univ. Rd, Karachi 75270, Sindh; tel. (21) 9261300; e-mail psc@uok.edu.pk; f. 1983; attached to Univ. of Karachi; research in social sciences; Dir Prof. Dr SYED JAFFAR AHMED; publ. *Pakistan Perspectives*.

AGRICULTURE, FISHERIES AND VETERINARY SCIENCE

Central Cotton Research Institute: Pakistan Central Cotton Committee, 47-A Hussain Centre, Darul Aman Housing Soc., Main Shahrah-e-Faisal, Karachi, Sindh; tel. (61) 9201128; e-mail pccc@super.net.pk; f. 1970; divs: agronomy, breeding and genetics, cytogenetics, entomology, pathology, physiology, fibre technology, statistics, transfer of technology; processing of cotton varieties and their release for cultivation in the local environment; library of 1,530 vols; Dir Dr M. ARSHAD; publ. *The Pakistan Cottons*.

Pakistan Agricultural Research Council: Plot 20 Sector G-5/1, Islamabad; tel. (51) 9203966; e-mail chair@comsats.net.pk; internet www.parc.gov.pk; f. 1978; aims to undertake, aid, promote and coordinate agricultural research; sets up research ests; arranges training of high-level scientists in agricultural sciences; generates, acquires and disseminates information relating to agriculture; library of 21,000 vols, 1,166 periodicals; Chair. Dr IFTIKHAR AHMAD; publs *Pakistan Journal of Agricultural Research* (4 a year), *Pakistan Journal of Agricultural Social Sciences* (2 a year), *PARC News* (12 a year), *Progressive Farming* (6 a year).

Pakistan Forest Institute: Univ. of Peshawar Campus, Peshawar 25000, Khyber Pakhtunkhwa; tel. (91) 49580; tel. (91) 71260; f. 1947; library: see Libraries and Archives; Forestry Museum; training courses leading to BSc and MSc in Forestry; Dir-Gen. Dr K. M. SIDDIQUI; publ. *Pakistan Journal of Forestry* (2 a year).

Punjab Veterinary Research Institute: Ghazi Rd, Lahore Cantonment, Punjab; tel. (42) 9220140; f. 1963; promotes and improves devt of the livestock industry and control diseases; production of vaccines, research on animal health problems; disease diagnosis and investigation; development of improved laboratory techniques; part of the Punjab Livestock and Dairy Devt Dept.

Rice Research Institute Dokri: Dokri, Larkana 77080, Sindh; tel. (74) 4080328; f. 1938; research on various aspects of rice incl. varietal improvement, control of insect pests,

diseases and weeds, grain quality; library of 4,426 vols, 1,523 periodicals.

Veterinary Research Institute: Bacha Khan Chowk, Charsadda Rd, POB 367, Peshawar 25000, Khyber Pakhtunkhwa; tel. (91) 9210218; e-mail directorvri@hotmail.com; f. 1949; research on livestock and poultry diseases, production of veterinary biologics and diagnostic agents; 45 mems; library of 1,000 vols; Dir Dr SAADULLAH JAN; publ. *Journal of Animal Health and Production* (4 a year).

ECONOMICS, LAW AND POLITICS

Applied Economics Research Centre: Univ. of Karachi, POB 8403, Karachi 75270, Sindh; tel. (21) 99261541; e-mail aerc@cyber.net.pk; internet www.aerc.edu.pk; f. 1973; policy-orientated quantitative research on problems in applied economics; courses leading to MPhil and PhD in Economics; library of 40,000 vols; 250 periodicals; Dir Prof. Dr NUZHAT AHMAD; publ. *Pakistan Journal of Applied Economics* (2 a year).

Centre for South Asian Studies: Univ. of the Punjab, Quaid-i-Azam Campus, Lahore 54590, Punjab; tel. (42) 99231143; e-mail director.csas@pu.edu.pk; f. 1973, present 1975; interdisciplinary research on S Asia, incl. economics, politics, sociology, foreign affairs, and other social devts of the area; programme incl. data collection and analysis; sponsors seminars; library of 12,000 vols; Dir Dr UMBREEN JAVAID; publ. *South Asian Studies* (2 a year, in English).

Federal Bureau of Statistics: Statistics Div., Govt of Pakistan, 5-SLIC Bldg, F-6/4, Blue Area, Islamabad; tel. (51) 9208489; e-mail statpak@statpak.gov.pk; internet www.statpak.gov.pk; f. 1950; library of 4,600 vols, 41,200 periodicals; Dir-Gen. Dr NOOR MUHAMMAD LARIK; publs *Census of Manufacturing Industries* (1 a year), *Foreign Trade Statistics of Pakistan* (separate series for imports and exports, each 1 a year), *Macro Economic Indicators of Pakistan* (4 a year), *Monthly Statistical Bulletin*, *National Accounts* (1 a year), *Pakistan Statistical Yearbook* (1 a year), *Reviews of Foreign Trade* (12 a year), *Statistical Pocket Book of Pakistan* (1 a year).

Institute of Strategic Studies: Sector F-5/2, Islamabad; tel. (51) 9204423; e-mail strategy@issi.org.pk; internet www.issi.org.pk; f. 1973; provides a broad-based and informed public understanding of vital strategic and allied issues affecting Pakistan and the int. community at large; library of 14,000 vols and 70 journals; Chair. KHALID MAHMOOD; Dir-Gen. RASUL BAKHSH RAIS; Dir of Americas NAJAM RAFIQUE; publ. *Strategic Studies* (4 a year).

National Institute of Public Administration: 78 Shahrah-e-Quaid-e-Azam, Lahore; tel. (42) 9200921; e-mail nipa@nipa-khi.edu.pk; internet www.niplahore.gov.pk; f. 1961; training in public admin. for officers of fed. and provincial govt; research in public admin.; consultancy services to the govt; library of 30,000 vols; Dir-Gen. SIKANDAR SHAMI; publ. *Public Administration Review* (4 a year).

Pakistan Institute of Human Rights: Centre 177, St 68, F-10/3, Islamabad 46000; tel. (51) 2294601; e-mail info@pihr.org.pk; internet www.pihr.org.pk; f. 1998; non-profit, non-aligned research-based academic instn promoting human rights; Chair. and Founder Dr SYED MOHAMMED ANWER; Dir ABDUR REHMAN, FAZAL I RABBI; Dir FAZAL I RABBI; Dir

HINA BASHARAT; Dir MUHAMMAD RAUF CHAUDHRY; Dir NIAZ. A. ABASSI; Dir SYED TANVER HAIDER.

Punjab Economic Research Institute (PERI): 24 Mianmir Rd, Upper Mall Scheme, Lahore, Punjab; f. 1955; attached to Planning and Development Dept, Govt of Punjab; undertakes socioeconomic investigations and coordinates research in economic problems of Pakistan; collects, compiles and interprets statistical data; publishes the results and findings of investigations; Dir AZIZ A. ANWAR; Sec. A. R. ARSHAD.

HISTORY, GEOGRAPHY AND ARCHAEOLOGY

National Centre of Excellence in Geology: Peshawar 25120, Khyber Pakhtunkhwa; tel. (91) 9216427; e-mail masifk@upesh.edu.pk; internet nceg.upesh.edu.pk; f. 1974; attached to Univ. of Peshawar; research in earth sciences; library of 9,192 vols; Dir Prof. Dr MUHAMMAD ASIF KHAN; publ. *Journal of Himalayan Earth Sciences* (2 a year).

National Institute of Historical and Cultural Research: Quaid-e-Azam Univ., New Campus, Shadara Rd, Islamabad; tel. (51) 2896153; e-mail nihcr@yahoo.com; internet www.nihcr.edu.pk; f. 1973 as Nat. Commission on Historical and Cultural Research, present name and status 1983; promotes studies on the history and culture of S Asian Muslims, genesis and growth of Muslim freedom movement; publishes research studies in history and culture, bibliographies, indices etc.; library of 50,000 vols, colln of historical records, old newspapers, journals, photocopies of rare material, microfilms, microfiches; Dir SYED UMAR HAYAT (acting); Librarian HAZOOR BAKHSH CHANNA; publs *Majallah-i-Tarikh wa Thaqafat* (2 a year, in Urdu), *Pakistan Journal of History and Culture* (2 a year, in English).

Research Society of Pakistan: c/o the Vice-Chancellor, Univ. of the Punjab, Lahore, Punjab; tel. (42) 9211631; f. 1963; research on cultural, political, literary, linguistic, economic, historical, topographical and archaeological features of Pakistan; library of 12,000 vols; Pres. Prof. Dr MUJAHID KAMRAN; Vice-Pres. IRSHAD AHMAD HAQQANI; Dir AFZAL HAQ; publ. *Journal of the Research Society of Pakistan* (2 a year).

MEDICINE

Cancer Research Institute: Dept and Institute of Radiotherapy, Jinnah Postgraduate Medical Centre, Rafiqui (H.J.) Shaheed Rd, Karachi 75510, Sindh; tel. (21) 9201300; e-mail edojpmc@jpmc.com.pk; f. 1954.

Pakistan Medical Research Council: Shahrah-e-Jamhuriat, G-5/2, Islamabad; tel. (51) 9216793; e-mail pmrc@comsats.net.pk; internet www.pmrc.org.pk; f. 1962; promotes research in fields of medicine and public health; disseminates and arranges utilization of this research; establishes liaison with nat. and int. orgs; research centres in medical colleges in Lahore, Karachi, Peshawar, Islamabad, Multan and Quetta; library of 4,800 vols; Pres. MIR AIJAZ HUSSAIN JAKHRANI; Exec. Dir Dr HUMA QURESHI; Librarian FAYYAZ AHMAD PIRZADO; publ. *Pakistan Journal of Medical Research* (4 a year).

NATURAL SCIENCES
General

Fazl-i-Omar Research Institute: Rabwah, Chenabnagar, Jhang 35460, Punjab; tel. (4524) 211082; f. 1946; promotes study of science and the devt of industries in Pakistan; library of 10,000 vols; Dir MUBARAK MUSLEH-UD-DIN AHMAD.

Pakistan Council for Science and Technology: Shahrah-e-Jamhuriat, off Constitution Ave, Sector G-5/2, Islamabad; tel. (51) 9205157; e-mail info@pcst.org.pk; internet www.pcst.org.pk; f. 1961; advises the govt on science and technology policy; devises measures for promotion, devt and application of science and technology in Pakistan; library of 1,200 vols; Chair. Dr TARIQ-UR-RAHMAN; Librarian SHAGUFTA SHAHEEN; publs *Science, Science and Technology in the Islamic World* (4 a year), *Science, Technology and Development* (6 a year).

Pakistan Council of Scientific and Industrial Research (PCSIR): Constitution Ave, Sector G-5/2, Islamabad 74200; tel. (51) 9225395; e-mail chairman@pcsir.gov.pk; internet www.pcsir.gov.pk; f. 1953; attached to Min. of Science and Technology; promotes scientific and industrial research and its applications to the devt of the nat. industries and the utilization of the natural resources of the country; laboratories in Islamabad, Karachi, Lahore, Peshawar, Quetta, Skardu; Scientific and Technical Information Centre; library: see under Libraries and Archives; Chair. Dr SHOUKAT PARVEZ; Sec. AHMAD SAGHIR; publ. *Pakistan Journal of Scientific and Industrial Research* (6 a year).

Biological Sciences

Centre for Molecular Genetics: Main Univ. Rd, Karachi 75270, Sindh; tel. (21) 4966045; e-mail cmg@uok.edu.pk; attached to Univ. of Karachi; advanced research in genetic engineering, microbial genetics, molecular genetics; Dir Dr NUZHAT AHMED.

Centre of Biotechnology and Microbiology: Peshawar, Khyber Pakhtunkhwa; tel. (91) 9216485; e-mail biotech@upesh.edu.pk; internet biotech.upesh.edu.pk; f. 2001; attached to Univ. of Peshawar; research areas incl. genetics, physiology, medicinal plants and biotechnology, microbiology; Dir Prof. Dr BASHIR AHMAD.

Centre of Excellence in Marine Biology: Univ. of Karachi, Karachi 75270, Sindh; tel. (21) 9261300; e-mail info@cemb-pk.edu.pk; internet www.cemb-ku.edu.pk; f. 1969, present status 1975; research in marine biology; library of 5,210 vols, 1,670 journals; Chair. Prof. Dr PIRZADA QASIM RAZA SIDDIQUI; Dir Prof. Dr JAVED MUSTAQUIM; publs *CEMB News* (2 a year), *Pakistan Journal of Marine Biology* (2 a year).

Department of Plant Protection: Jinnah Ave, Malir Halt, Karachi, Sindh; tel. (21) 9248612; e-mail info@plantprotection.gov.pk; internet www.plantprotection.gov.pk; f. 1947; attached to Min. of Food, Agriculture and Livestock; survey and control of desert locust population, control of crop pests by air; executes Plant Quarantine Act 1976 and Pakistan Agriculture Pesticide Ordinance 1971 and its rules 1973; advises Fed. and Provincial govts on plant protection matters; library of 22,085 vols, 13 current periodicals; Dir-Gen. Dr TASNEEM AHMAD.

Institute of Industrial Biotechnology: GC Univ., Lahore, Punjab; tel. (42) 99211634; e-mail ikmhaq@yahoo.com; f. 1990 as Biotechnology Research Centre, Dept of Botany, present status 2005; attached to GC Univ.; research in microbiology and biotechnology; library of 10,000 vols; Dir Prof. Dr IKRAM UL HAQ.

Institute of Sustainable Halophyte Utilization: Main Univ. Rd, Karachi 75270, Sindh; tel. (21) 34820253; e-mail majmalk@uok.edu.pk; internet www.halophyte.org; attached to Univ. of Karachi; research areas incl. biochemistry and molecular biology,
ecology, ecophysiology, halophyte utilization; Dir Dr M. AJMAL KHAN.

National Nematological Research Centre: Main Univ. Rd, Karachi 75270, Sindh; tel. (21) 99261387; e-mail nnrc@uok.edu.pk; attached to Univ. of Karachi; research areas incl. molecular taxonomy, biology, pathogenicity, population dynamics, control of plant parasitic nematodes, use of marine nematodes as pollution indicators, entomopathogenic nematodes, nematodes in biological control of insect pests, human nematology; library of 800 vols; Dir Prof. Dr SHAHINA FAYYAZ; publ. *Pakistan Journal of Nematology (PJN)* (2 a year).

Zoological Survey Department: Govt of Pakistan, Kalma Chowk, Bhara Kahu, Islamabad 44000; tel. (51) 2233121; internet www.zsd.gov.pk; f. 1948; research in ecology, biodiversity, marine biology, and wildlife of Pakistan; library of 10,810 vols, 125 periodicals, 1,600 reprints; Dir ABDUL WAHAB; publ. *Records/Zoological Survey of Pakistan* (1 a year).

Research Laboratory:

Marine Biological Research Laboratory: Block 67, Pakistan Secretariat, Shahrah-e-Iraq, Saddar, Karachi 74200; tel. (21) 9203334; e-mail zsd6167@imulti.net.pk; f. 1962.

Mathematical Sciences

Abdus Salam School of Mathematical Sciences (ASSMS): GC Univ., 68-B, New Muslim Town, Lahore 54600; tel. (42) 99231859; e-mail info@sms.edu.pk; internet www.sms.edu.pk; f. 2003; attached to GC Univ.; fundamental research in mathematical and allied sciences; library of 2,000 vols; Dir-Gen. Dr A. D. RAZA CHOUDHARY; publs *Journal of Prime Research in Mathematics (JPRM)* (Mathematics Magazine), *Math Track* (Mathematics Magazine).

Physical Sciences

Astronomical Observatory of the University of the Punjab: c/o Dept of Space Science, Quaid-i-Azam Campus, Univ. of the Punjab, Lahore 54590, Punjab; tel. (42) 99239294; e-mail chairman.spsc@pu.edu.pk; f. 1920, reorganized in 1986 within the Univ. Dept of Space Science; teaching and research in astronomy, remote sensing, GIS, telecommunication and atmospheric science; courses at undergraduate and graduate level; works in cooperation with nat. and int. institutes; Chair. Dr MUHAMMAD ALI.

Centre for Advanced Studies in Physics (CASP): 1 Church Road, GC Univ., Lahore, Punjab; tel. (42) 99211589; e-mail ahriaz@gcu.edu.pk; f. 1954; attached to GC Univ.; research in Atomic and Nuclear Physics; Dir Prof. Dr RIAZ AHMAD.

H. E. J. Research Institute of Chemistry: c/o Int. Centre for Chemical and Biological Sciences, Main Univ. Rd, Karachi 75270, Sindh; tel. (21) 99261701; e-mail hej@cyber.net.pk; internet www.iccs.edu/hej; attached to Univ. of Karachi; research areas incl. biosynthesis, cancer, computational chemistry, genetic engineering, plant biotechnology, textile and food chemistry, tropical disease, spectroscopy; library of 7,000 vols, 177 journals; Dir Prof. Dr ATTA-UR-RAHMAN.

Institute of Chemical Sciences: Peshawar 25120, Khyber Pakhtunkhwa; tel. (91) 9216652; e-mail chemistry@upesh.edu.pk; f. 1955; attached to Univ. of Peshawar; research in analytical chemistry, biochemistry, fuel and applied chemistry, inorganic chemistry, physical chemistry, organic chemistry; Dir Prof. Dr IMDAD ULLAH.

Institute of Environmental Studies: Main Univ. Rd, Karachi 75270, Sindh; tel.

(21) 9261386; e-mail ies@uok.edu.pk; f. 1982; attached to Univ. of Karachi; research on environment and related fields; library of 5,000 vols; Dir Dr MOAZZAM ALI KHAN.

Institute of Marine Science: Main Univ. Rd, Karachi 75270, Sindh; tel. (21) 99261300; e-mail ims@uok.edu.pk; f. 1981; attached to Univ. of Karachi; research in ecological, biological and geological aspect of marine environment; Dir Dr RASHIDA QARI.

National Centre of Excellence in Physical Chemistry: Univ. of Peshawar Peshawar 25120, Khyber Pakhtunkhwa; tel. (91) 9216766; e-mail ncepc@upesh.edu.pk; internet ncepc.upesh.edu.pk; f. 1978; attached to Univ. of Peshawar; research areas incl. advance oxidation technology for water treatment, coal and biomass as alternate fuel, electrochemistry, fine particles science, hetrogeneous catalysis, macromolecular chemistry, polymer chemistry, radiation and photochemistry, solution and gas phases kinetics, surface chemistry, tribology; Dir Prof. Dr HASAN M KHAN; publ. *Physical Chemistry*.

Pakistan Atomic Energy Commission (PAEC): POB 1114, Islamabad; tel. (51) 9204276; e-mail sipr@paec.gov.pk; internet www.paec.gov.pk; f. 1956; responsible for the devt of nuclear technology as part of Pakistan's nuclear power programme; operates nuclear power plants in Karachi and Chashma; promotes peaceful use of atomic energy in agriculture, medicine, industry and hydrology; searches for indigenous mineral deposits suitable for the production of atomic energy; trains project personnel; Chair. Dr ANSAR PARVEZ; Sec. JAVED IQBAL KHWAJA; publ. *The Nucleus* (4 a year).

Pakistan Meteorological Department: Pitras Bukhari Rd, Sector H-8/2, Islamabad 44000; tel. (51) 9250367; e-mail pakmet_islamabad@yahoo.com; internet www.pmd.gov.pk; f. 1947; provides hydrometeorological and geophysical services for protection of life, property and the environment; issues weather and flood forecasts and warnings; investigates behaviour of atmosphere to predict short- and long-term weather conditions; undertakes research and devt activities in weather modifications and wind potential of coastal and N Pakistan; Dir-Gen. ARIF MAHMOOD; publ. *Pakistan Journal of Meteorology* (2 a year).

PHILOSOPHY AND PSYCHOLOGY

Institute of Clinical Psychology: Main Univ. Rd, Karachi 75270, Sindh; tel. (21) 34613584; e-mail icp@uok.edu.pk; f. 1983; attached to Univ. of Karachi; research and professional training in clinical psychology, psychotherapy, psychological assessment, diagnostic testing, speech therapy, occupational therapy, rehabilitation and other related areas; Dir Dr RIYAZ AHMAD; publs *Pakistan Journal of Clinical Psychology (PJCP)* (2 a year), *Pakistan Journal of Psychology (PJP)* (official journal).

RELIGION, SOCIOLOGY AND ANTHROPOLOGY

Centre of Excellence for Women's Studies: Main Univ. Rd, Karachi 75270, Sindh; tel. (21) 99261654; e-mail cews@uok.edu.pk; f. 1989; attached to Univ. of Karachi; library of 4,000 vols; Dir Dr NASREEN ASLAM SHAH; publ. *Pakistan Journal of Gender Studies*.

Dawah Academy: Shah Faisal Complex, Islamabad; tel. (51) 9258060; e-mail director .dawah@iiu.edu.pk; internet dawah.iiu.edu .pk; f. 1985; attached to Int. Islamic Univ.; research in Islamic studies, Dawah; library of 25,000 vols, 166 journals; Dir-Gen. Dr SAHIBZADA SAJID-UR-REHMAN.

Institute of Sindhology: Allama I. I. Kazi Campus, University of Sindh, Jamshoro 76070, Sindh; tel. (22) 2771386; e-mail director@sindhology.usindh.edu.pk; internet www.sindhology.com.pk; f. 1962 as Sindhi Academy, present name 1964; publishes research material in foreign languages; develops working tools (dictionaries, historical surveys, etc.) for scholars; research in history, culture, literature and fine arts; incl. bureau of production, publn and translation, documentation, information and research cell, research library, dept of preservation of documents and rare material, anthropological research centre with Sindh Art Gallery and Museum, dept of performing arts, sound and film with ethnomusical gallery; photographic and microform sections; library: see Libraries; Dir SHOUKAT HUSSAIN SHORO; publs *Sindhi Adab* (1 a year, in Sindhi), *Sindhological Studies* (2 a year, in English).

Islamic Research Institute: POB 1035, Islamabad 44000; Sector H-10, Islamabad; tel. (51) 2281289; e-mail dgiri@iiu.edu.pk; internet iri.iiu.edu.pk; f. 1960, present status 1980; attached to Int. Islamic Univ.; develops and disseminates methodology for research in various fields of Islamic learning; interprets teachings of Islam; studies contemporary problems of Islam; contributes to the revival of Islamic heritage; organizes study groups, seminars, conferences, etc.; serves as a clearing house on various aspects of Islam; library of 55,000 vols and periodicals, 550 microfilms, 140 MSS, 760 photostats, 150 cassettes; Chair. Dr ANWAR HUSSAIN SIDDIQI; Dir-Gen. Dr MUHAMMAD KHALID MASUD; publs *Al-Dirasat al-Islamiyyah* (4 a year), *Fikr-o-Nazar* (4 a year), *Islamic Studies* (4 a year, in English).

Shaykh Zayed Islamic Centre: Peshawar 25120, Khyber Pakhtunkhwa; tel. (91) 9216746; e-mail szic@upesh.edu.pk; internet www.szic.pk; f. 1985; attached to Univ. of Peshawar; research in Arabic language, Islamic studies; library of 15,000 vols; Dir Prof. Dr DOST MUHAMMAD KHAN.

Sheikh Zayed Islamic Centre: Main Univ. Rd, Karachi 75270, Sindh; tel. (21) 99261081; e-mail szic@uok.edu.pk; internet szic.edu.pk; attached to Univ. of Karachi; research in Islamic studies; Dir Dr NOOR AHMED SHAHTAAZ; publ. *As–Saqafat–ul Islamia* (4 a year, in Arabic, English, Urdu).

Sustainable Development Study Centre: Science Blk Bldg, GC Univ., Lahore; tel. (42) 9213357; e-mail dr.aminulhaq@gcu.edu.pk; f. 2003; attached to GC Univ.; research areas incl. sustainable livelihoods, environmental management, community devt; library of 400 vols; Dir Prof. Dr AMIN-UL-HAQ KHAN.

TECHNOLOGY

Hydrocarbon Development Institute of Pakistan: Plot 18, St 6, Sector H-9/1, POB 1308, Islamabad; tel. (51) 9258301; e-mail info@hdip.com.pk; internet www.hdip.com .pk; f. 1975; attached to Min. of Petroleum and Natural Resources; research and services in petroleum geology and geochemistry, resource estimation, enhanced oil recovery, petroleum products testing and evaluation, petroleum processing technology, coal utilization technology, interfuel substitution, energy conservation, environmental control, compressed natural gas, energy database, oil and gas advisory and training services; laboratories in Islamabad, Karachi; library of 1,500 vols, 44 periodicals; Dir-Gen. IRSHAD ALI KHOKHAR; Sec. SHAHID ALI KHAN; publs *Pakistan Energy Yearbook* (1 a year), *Pakistan Journal of Hydrocarbon Research* (every 2 years).

Institute of Industrial Electronics Engineering: ST-22/c, Block-6, Gulshan-e-Iqbal, Karachi 75300, Sindh; tel. (21) 99244218; e-mail info@iiee.edu.pk; internet iiee.edu.pk; f. 1989; research in field of industrial electronics engineering; library of 2,500 vols; Prin. Dr RIAZUDDIN ABRO.

Irrigation Research Institute: Shahrah-e-Quaid-e-Azam, Lahore, Punjab; f. 1925; deals with irrigation and allied engineering problems in Pakistan; 2 field model stations, 2 sub-stations and subsidiary laboratories for soils, foundation engineering, tube well experiments, etc.; library of 20,000 vols; Admin. SAAD HARROON.

Pakistan Council of Research in Water Resources: Khyaben-e-Johar Rd, Sector H 8/1, Islamabad; tel. (51) 9101282; e-mail pcrwr_ibd@yahoo.com; internet www.pcrwr .gov.pk; f. 2007; attached to Min. of Science and Technology; promotes research in fields of water and environment, hydraulics, irrigation, drainage, reclamation, tube wells and flood control; regional centres in Bahawalpur, Lahore, Peshawar, Quetta, Tando Jam; library of 10,000 vols; Chair. Dr MUHAMMAD ASLAM TAHIR; Dir-Gen. CH. MUHAMMAD AKRAM; Dir LUBNA NAHEED BUKHARI; publs *Fresh Arrivals and Periodicals Content Service* (4 a year), *Journal of Drainage and Water Management* (2 a year), *Pakistan Journal of Water Resources* (2 a year).

Pakistan Institute of Cotton Research and Technology: Moulvi Tamizuddin Khan Rd, Karachi 74200, Sindh; tel. (21) 9202558; e-mail pccc@super.net.pk; f. 1956; fundamental and applied research on cotton fibres, yarns and fabrics; provides testing facilities and training to agriculture, trade and industry; library of 30,000 vols, 350 periodicals; Dir I. H. RESHAMWALA; publ. *The Pakistan Cottons* (4 a year).

Pakistan Institute of Management: Management House, Shahrah-e-Iran, Clifton, Karachi 75600, Sindh; tel. (21) 9251711; e-mail registration@pim.com.pk; internet www.pim.com.pk; f. 1954; offers 140 short courses in functional and integrated aspects of management each year; research on management issues; br. in Lahore; library of 6,000 vols, 60 films, 60 periodicals; Dir ZARRAR R. ZUBAIR; publ. *Pakistan Management Review* (4 a year).

Pakistan Standards and Quality Control Authority: St 7/A, Block 3, Scheme 36, Gulistan-e-Juhar, Karachi, Sindh; tel. (21) 34023842; e-mail dgeneral@psqca.com.pk; internet www.psqca.com.pk; f. 1996; attached to Min. of Science and Technology; mem. of ISO, International Electrotechnical Commission (IEC), Organisation Internationale de Métrologie Légale (OIML); fosters and promotes standards and conformity assessment; recommends nat. standards for the measurement of length, weight, volume and energy, prepares and promotes general adoption of standards on nat. and int. basis relating to materials and commodities, simplification in industry and commerce, enforcement of standards, etc.; library of 1,852 vols, 148,955 nat. and int. standards; Dir-Gen. PIR BAKHSH KHAN JAMALI; publs *Pakistan Standards Specification, PSI Yearbook, Test Methods and Code of Practice*.

Libraries and Archives
Bahawalpur

Central Library: Bahawalpur, Punjab; tel. (621) 80658; f. 1948; mobile library; audiovisual and microfiche sections; language laboratory; collections: books, newspapers and periodicals since 1948; some 19th-century newspapers and periodicals; map gallery; children's library; braille library; 105,960 vols (36,070 Urdu, 61,730 English, 8,160 other languages), 175 MSS (120 Arabic, 55 Persian and Urdu); 34 microfilms, 70 films; Chief Librarian MUHAMMAD ASHRAF JALAL.

Sir Sadiq Muhammad Khan Library: Bahawalpur, Punjab; tel. (62) 9255483; e-mail chief.librarian@iub.edu.pk; internet library.iub.edu.pk; f. 1975; attached to Islamia Univ. of Bahawalpur; 225,000 vols, 40,000 e-books; Chief Librarian MUHAMMAD RAFIQ AWAN; publs *Journal of Educational Research, Journal of Social Sciences and Humanities* (2 a year), *Ulum-e-Islamia Research Journal.*

Dera Ismail Khan

Gomal University Central Library: Dera Ismail Khan, Khyber Pakhtunkhwa; tel. (966) 750424; f. 1974; 60,000 vols; Librarian MUHAMMAD SADIQ JAVAID.

Faisalabad

University of Agriculture Library: Faisalabad 38040, Punjab; tel. (41) 9200161; e-mail luaf98@yahoo.com; internet www.uaf .edu.pk/library/lib_overview.html; f. 1961; audiovisual section, Global Information Centre (GIC), Information Resource Centre (IRC), access to HEC Digital Library; depository library for FAO and World Bank publs; 262,000 vols, 23,890 MSS; Prin. Officer of Library Prof. M. ASLAM KHAN.

Hyderabad

Pakistan National Central Library and Culture Centre: Hyderabad, Sindh; f. 1958; 19,000 vols; Dir M. R. SIDDIQI.

Shamsul Ulema Daudpota Sindh Government Library: Hyderabad; f. 1951; attached to Culture and Tourism Dept, Sindh; 59,000 vols; Librarian (vacant).

Islamabad

Allama Iqbal Open University Central Library: Sector H-8, Islamabad; tel. (51) 9250040; e-mail reacmsf@gmail.com; internet www.aiou.edu.pk; f. 1974; 1m. vols; colln of theses, monographs and term papers; archives and govt papers colln; Librarian Dr SHAH FARRUKH (acting); publs *Ilm Ki Roshni* (2 a year, in Urdu), *Journal of Social Sciences and Humanities* (2 a year), *Maarif-e-Islami* (2 a year, in Urdu), *Pakistan Journal of Education* (2 a year).

Dr Raziuddin Siddiqi Memorial Library: Islamabad 45320; tel. (51) 90642071; e-mail librarian@qau.edu.pk; internet www.qau.edu .pk/lib; f. 1966; attached to Quaid-i-Azam Univ.; 240,000 vols, 223 current periodicals, 11,200 online journals; spec. colln of 29,000 vols on Indo–Pakistani history and Oriental literature; 269 MSS; 20,000 abstracts provided by Higher Education Commission of Pakistan; Librarian MUHAMMAD ANWAR EJAZ.

International Islamic University Central Library: POB 1243, H-10 Campus, Islamabad; tel. (51) 9257955; e-mail library@iiu.edu.pk; internet www.iiu.edu.pk; f. 1980; teaching, research facilities; 350,000 vols, 108 periodicals and journals; Chief Librarian SHER NOWROOZ KHAN; Prin. Librarian CH. MUHAMMAD ZULQARNAIN AKHTAR (acting); Librarian for Reader Services QARI MUHAMMAD MAQBOOL SIDDIQUI.

Islamabad Public Library: Block 12-A, G-8 Markaz, Islamabad; tel. (51) 9260795; e-mail nlpiba@isb.paknet.com.pk; f. 1950; 34,000 vols; spec. collns incl. central and provincial govt publs; Deputy Dir HAFIZ KHUBAIB; Sr Librarian MUHAMMAD TARIQ.

National Archives of Pakistan: Admin. Block Area, Block N, Pakistan Secretariat, Islamabad; tel. (51) 9202044; e-mail info@ nap.gov.pk; internet www.nap.gov.pk; f. 1951; acquisition, classification and preservation of public and private records of permanent and historical value; provides reference service and assistance to accredited scholars; promotes ideology of Pakistan by projecting the Muslim efforts in acquiring independence; 35,000 vols, 1,859 MSS, 450 oral archives (300 audio cassettes, 150 video cassettes), 1,614 titles of newspapers and periodicals, gazetteers of 109 dists, 31,000 govt publs, Quaid-i-Azam Papers, All India Muslim League Records; Dir-Gen. HABIB AHMED KHAN; Deputy Dir IRSHAD AHMED; Deputy Dir TAHIRA TANVEER; Deputy Dir ZAHIR GUL; publs *Archival Sources in South Asia, The Pakistan Archives* (2 a year).

National Assembly Library: Islamabad; tel. (51) 9205626; e-mail haji.hattar@yahoo .com; internet www.na.gov.pk/en/library .php; f. 1947; 80,000 vols, 160 current periodicals, UN publs; Librarian Haji HATTAR.

National Library of Pakistan: Constitution Ave, POB 1982, Islamabad 44000; Nat. Library Bldg, Sharah-e-Jamhoriat, G-5, Islamabad; tel. (51) 9214523; e-mail nlpiba@isb .paknet.com.pk; internet www.nlp.gov.pk; f. 1993; depository library for all Pakistani publs, ISBN agency for Pakistani publs; 180,000 vols, 600 MSS, 80,000 microfiches, 500,000 pages on microfilm; Dir-Gen. CH. MUHAMMAD NAZIR; publs *Directory of Periodicals and Newspapers* (irregular), *Pakistan National Bibliography* (1 a year).

Pakistan Scientific and Technological Information Centre (PASTIC): PASTIC Nat.Centre, Quaid-i-Azam Univ. Campus, POB 1217 Islamabad 44000; tel. (51) 9248103; e-mail dg@pastic.gov.pk; internet www.pastic.gov.pk; f. 1956 as PANSDOC under Pakistan Council of Scientific and Industrial Research, reorganized 1974 under Pakistan Science Foundation; sub-centres at Faisalabad, Karachi, Lahore, Peshawar, Quetta, Muzaffarabad; facilities incl. documentation services, scientific and technical information services, scientific and technical publs and compilation of scientific bibliographies, patent services, environmental information service, reprographic services; 8,000 vols, 900 journals, 300 current periodicals, 300,000 patents, 1,340 NTIS reports; Dir-Gen. Dr KHALIL AHMAD IBUPOTO; Dir NAGEEN AINUDDIN; Sr Librarian SYED HABIB AKHTAR JAFRI; publ. *Pakistan Science Abstracts* (agriculture (1 a year), animal sciences (1 a year), biology and biotechnology (1 a year), chemistry (1 a year), earth sciences (1 a year), information (1 a year), communication and space sciences (1 a year), mathematics and statistics (1 a year), medicine (1 a year), pharmaceutics (1 a year), plant sciences (1 a year)).

Jamshoro

Allama I. I. Kazi Central Library: Allama I. I. Kazi Campus, Jamshoro 76080, Sindh; tel. (22) 2771681; e-mail info@library.usindh .edu.pk; internet www.library.usindh.edu .pk; f. 1947 as Sindh Univ. Library; attached to Univ. of Sindh; 356,843 vols, 23 current periodicals, 700 MSS; Librarian MUHAMMAD AZAM ROONJHO; Asst Librarian ASGHAR ALI.

Institute of Sindhology Library: Allama I. I. Kazi Campus, Univ. of Sindh, Jamshoro 76070; tel. (22) 2771386; e-mail director@ sindhology.usindh.edu.pk; internet www .sindhology.com.pk; f. 1962; 109,000 vols (Arabic, Balochi, English, Pashito, Persian, Sindhi, Urdu and other languages), 14,500 periodical bound vols, 32,000 rare books, 500 microfilms; 2,200 audio cassettes, 3,500

slides, 1,700 MSS, 700 bound vols; 3,800 bound vols of newspapers; Librarian GUL MUHAMMED N. MUGHAL; publs *Sindhi Adab* (2 a year, in Sindhi), *Sindhological Studies* (2 a year, in English).

Mehran University of Engineering & Technology Library: Jamshoro, Sindh; tel. (22) 2771169; e-mail librarian@admin .muet.edu.pk; internet www.muet.edu.pk/ academics/library; f. 1977; attached to Mehran Univ. of Engineering & Technology; 125,000 vols, incl. journals; Librarian AZAM ALI HALEPOTA.

Karachi

All Pakistan Educational Conference Library: 1-5-45/100 Altaf Brelvi Rd, Karachi 74600, Sindh; tel. (21) 621195; f. 1886; 35,000 vols on Aligarh and Pakistan Movement; Sec. SAYED MUSTAFA ALI BRELVI.

Bait al-Hikmah Library: Madinat al-Hikmah, Muhammad bin Qasim Ave., off Sharae Madinat al-Hikmah, Karachi 74700, Sindh; tel. (21) 36440056; e-mail baitalhikmah@ hotmail.com; internet www.baitalhikmah .com; f. 1989; attached to Hamdard Foundation; specializes in education, herbal science, history, Indo-Pakistani history, information technology, Islamic studies, literature, medical science, management, social sciences, traditional medicine; 516,436 vols, 29,525 periodicals, 915 current periodicals, 1,767 MSS, 3,000 rare books, 690 microfilms, 455 video cassettes, 2,821 audio cassettes, 39,180 photographs, 16,357 stamps, coins, maps and charts; 3,680,000 newspaper clippings covering 1,300 subjects; Chief Librarian JAVED HUSSAIN; Admin. Man. MUHAMMAD ARSALAN SYED.

Dr Mahmud Husain Library: Karachi 75270, Sindh; tel. (21) 9261300; e-mail librarian@uok.edu.pk; internet www.uok.edu .pk/library; f. 1952; attached to Univ. of Karachi; depository of personal book colln of Muhammad Ali Jinnah; UN colln; 360,000 vols, 110,000 journals, 22,000 vols in seminar libraries, 8,000 theses and reports; Head Librarian Prof. MALAHAT KALEEM SHERWANI; Chief Librarian RASHIDA AMAN.

Islamic Documentation and Information Centre (IDIC): SS College of Liberal Arts and Social Sciences, Univ. Rd, Karachi 75000, Sindh; tel. (21) 4978274; f. 1983; 5,250 vols in English and Urdu, 60 current periodicals; Dir-Gen. Dr MANZOOR AHMAD.

Khalikdina Hall Library Association: M. A. Jinnah Rd, Karachi, Sindh; tel. (21) 7732228; f. 1856; language classes, social and cultural events; 50,218 vols; Pres. TARIQ RAHMANI; Chief Librarian QARI HILAL AHMED RABBANI.

Liaquat Hall Library: Bagh-e-Jinnah, Abdullah Haroon Rd, Karachi, Sindh; f. 1852 as Frere Hall Library; 52,000 vols; Asst Dir SYEDA SHAHANA ALVI.

Liaquat Memorial Library: c/o Tourism and Cultural Dept, Govt of Sindh, Stadium Rd, Karachi, Sindh; tel. (21) 9230116; f. 1950; 150,000 vols; Dir SHAHZOR TABANI.

National Bank of Pakistan, Head Office Library: Central Directorate of State Bank of Pakistan, I. I. Chundrigar Rd, Karachi, Sindh; tel. (21) 2414783; f. 1949; colln of books, technical reports, govt documents, periodicals and magazines relating mainly to the subjects of economics, banking, finance, management and commerce; 60,000 vols (45,000 English, 15,000 Oriental); Librarian SALIHA MOIN; publs *Index of Economic Literature* (12 a year), *List of Acquisitions* (4 a year).

NED University of Engineering and Technology Central Library: University

Rd, Karachi 75270, Sindh; tel. (21) 9243261; e-mail libadmin@neduet.edu.pk; internet www.neduet.edu.pk/library; f. 1977; 160,305 vols, 121 current periodicals; Chief Librarian MEHER YASMEEN KHAN.

Pakistan Institute of International Affairs Library: Aiwan-e-Sadar Rd, POB 1447, Karachi 74200, Sindh; tel. (21) 35682891; e-mail info@piia.org.pk; internet www.piia.org.pk; f. 1947; rare collns of books and periodicals, newspaper clippings since 1948 on int. politics, economics and jurisprudence; 34,900 vols, 100 journals, 44 microfilms, 210 audio cassettes; Information Resource Librarian MUNAWAR SULTANA RAZIUDDIN; Chief Librarian ISHRATULLAH SIDDIQUI; publ. *Pakistan Horizon* (scholarly articles, chronology of events and other documents relating to Pakistan, 4 a year).

Scientific Information Centre: PCSIR Laboratories Campus, Shahrah-e-Dr Salimuzzaman Siddiqui, Karachi 75280, Sindh; tel. (21) 34651739; e-mail info@pjsir.org; f. 1958; attached to Pakistan Ccl of Scientific and Industrial Research; Dir Dr KANIZ FIZZA AZHAR; publs *Pakistan Journal of Scientific and Industrial Research* (6 a year), *PCSIR Research and Development Programme* (1 a year).

State Bank of Pakistan Library: I. I. Chundrigar Rd, Karachi 74000, Sindh; tel. (21) 99212460; e-mail bashir.zia@sbp.org.pk; internet www.sbp.org.pk/library; f. 1949; 85,000 books, 40,000 bound periodicals; Chief Librarian BASHIR AHMAD ZIA.

Lahore

Atomic Energy Minerals Centre Library: POB 658, Lahore, Punjab; tel. (42) 5758661; f. 1961; Dir MUHAMMAD MANSOOR.

Dyal Singh Trust Library: 25 Nisbet Rd, Lahore, Punjab; tel. (42) 7229483; e-mail info@dyalsingh.org.pk; internet www.dyalsingh.org.pk; f. 1908; 146,000 vols; Sr Librarian NUSRAT ALI ATHEER; publ. *Minhaj* (4 a year).

Ewing Memorial Library: Forman Christian College, Ferozepur Rd, Lahore 54600, Punjab; tel. (42) 9231581; e-mail contact@fccollege.edu.pk; f. 1943; attached to Forman Christian College; 100,000 vols; Chief Librarian BUSHRA ALMAS JASWAL.

Gad & Birgit Rausing Library: Opposite Sector U, D. H. A, Lahore, Punjab; tel. (42) 35608169; e-mail library@lums.edu.pk; internet library.lums.edu.pk; attached to Lahore Univ. of Management Sciences; 200,000 vols, 35,000 journals; Library Dir Dr MUHAMMAD RAMZAN.

Government College University Library: GC Univ. Library, Katchery Rd, Lahore 54000, Punjab; tel. (42) 99213348; e-mail chieflibrary@gcu.edu.pk; internet www.gcu.edu.pk/library; f. 1872 as Fazal-i-Hussain Library; 312,800 vols, 236 journals; Chief Librarian ABDUL WAHEED; publ. *GCU Lahore Newspapers Index*.

Government Punjab Public Library: Library Rd, Shahra-e-Quaid-e-Azam (Mall Rd), Lahore, Punjab; tel. (42) 99211649; e-mail info@gppl.org.pk; internet gppl.org.pk; f. 1884; Bait-ul-Quran section with Quranic MSS, rare material on the Quran, audiovisual units; ladies' and children's section; arranges seminars and lectures for the promotion of library activities; 350,000 vols, 5,100 bound vols of periodicals, 1,800 MSS, 75 English and 100 Oriental language periodicals; Chief Librarian AZRA USMAN (acting).

Islamia College Library: Civil Lines, Lahore 54000, Punjab; f. 1958; 50,061 vols, 53 current periodicals; Librarian MUNIR AHMAD NAEEM; publ. *Faran* (1 a year).

National Library of Engineering Sciences: Univ. of Engineering and Technology, Grand Trunk Rd, Lahore 54890, Punjab; tel. (42) 9029243; e-mail lib@uet.edu.pk; internet www.uet.edu.pk; f. 1961; attached to Univ. of Engineering and Technology; 125,000 vols, 60,000 bound copies of scientific and technical periodicals; Librarian MANZOOR A. K. ANJUM.

Punjab University Library: Quaid-e-Azam Campus, Lahore 54590, Punjab; tel. (42) 99231126; e-mail chieflibrarian@pu.edu.pk; internet www.pulibrary.edu.pk; f. 1873 as Punjab Univ. College Library, present name 1882; attached to Univ. of the Punjab; 535,000 vols, incl. 20,000 MSS; Chief Librarian CH. MUHAMMAD HANIF.

Quaid-e-Azam Library: Bagh-e-Jinnah, Shahra-e-Quaid-e-Azam, Lahore, Punjab; tel. (42) 99201007; e-mail qallahore@gmail.com; internet www.qal.org.pk; f. 1984; research and reference facilities; spec. colln: dissertations on Pakistan and Islam; 110,000 vols, 350 current periodicals; Dir-Gen. of Punjab Libraries SAEED AHMAD NAWAZ; Chief Librarian ABID ALI GILL; publs *Informit* (4 a year), *Makhzan* (2 a year).

Multan

Bahauddin Zakariya University Library: Bosan Rd, Multan; e-mail librarysc@bzu.edu.pk; f. 1975; attached to Bahauddin Zakariya Univ.; 109,000 vols, 20 current periodicals, 20 slides; Librarian MAQBOOL AHMAD CHAUDHRY; publs *Journal of Research* (humanities), *Journal of Research* (sciences), *Law Research Journal*.

Muzaffarabad

University of Azad Jammu and Kashmir Central Library: Muzaffarabad, Azad Jammu and Kashmir; tel. (300) 5228090; e-mail chief.librarian@ajku.edu.pk; f. 1980; attached to Univ. of Azad Jammu and Kashmir; 120,000 vols; Chief Librarian SARDAR MUHAMMAD SALEEM.

Peshawar

Archival Museum: Directorate of Archives, Govt of NWFP, Peshawar, Khyber Pakhtunkhwa; tel. (521) 274831; f. 1950; 71,000 vols; Dir TARIQ MANSOOR JALALI.

Central Forest Library: Pakistan Forest Institute, Peshawar, Khyber Pakhtunkhwa; tel. (91) 9216196; e-mail dg_pfi@yahoo.com; f. 1947; 25,000 vols, 20,000 periodicals; Librarian YOUSAF KHAN; publ. *Pakistan Journal of Forestry* (2 a year).

Central Library—University of Peshawar: Peshawar, Khyber Pakhtunkhwa; tel. (91) 9216701; f. 1951; also houses Oriental colln of valuable and rare books, MSS; 2,000,000 vols, 10,400 periodicals, 693 Persian, Arabic and Pashto MSS; Librarian IBRAR MOHAMMAD.

Quetta

University of Balochistan Library: Sariab Rd, Quetta, Balochistan; tel. (81) 9211247; internet www.uob.edu.pk/library.htm; f. 1971; 120,000 vols, 1,000 rare books, 4,000 microfiche cards, periodicals, depository library of World Bank, UNESCO and UNICEF; Librarian ABDUL JALIL KHAN.

Rawalpindi

Archaeological Library: Taxila Museum, Taxila, Rawalpindi, Punjab; f. 1960; 1,450 vols on history and arts, especially the ancient history and archaeology of Pakistan; Custodian GULZAR MOHAMMAD KHAN.

Museums and Art Galleries

Harappa

Archaeological Museum: Dist. Sahiwal, Harappa, Punjab; f. 1926, re-established 1967; antiquities from site of the pre-historic and proto-historic site (3500–1500 BC); Curator MUHAMMAD HASSAN KHOKHAR.

Karachi

National Museum of Pakistan: Burns Garden, Dr Ziauddin Ahmed Rd, Karachi 74200, Sindh; tel. (21) 9212839; f. 1950; Pakistan's cultural heritage from Stone Age to the birth of Pakistan; Superintendent QASIM ALI QASIM; publs *Museum Journal*, *Pakistan Archaeology*.

Quaid-i-Azam Birthplace, Reading Room, Museum and Library: Wazir Mansion, Chagla St, Kharadar, Karachi, Sindh; tel. (21) 2434904; f. 1953; library of 5,000 vols (incl. spec. colln on Indo-Pakistani history); Custodian TAHIR SAEE.

Lahore

Directorate of Archives and Archival Museum: Punjab Civil Secretariat, Lahore, Punjab; tel. (42) 7322381; f. 1924; consists of Historical Record Office, Central Record Office and Museum; library of 150,000 vols; Dir SYED ISHRAT ALI SHAH; publ. *Urdu Nama* (12 a year).

Industrial and Commercial Museum: Poonch House, Multan Rd, Lahore, Punjab; f. 1950; permanent colln of raw material resources, handicrafts, art-ware and manufactured products of Pakistan; industrial library, reading-room, auditorium attached; provides free economic intelligence to trade and industry; Curator MUSHTAQ AHMAD.

Lahore Fort Museum: Lahore 54000, Punjab; Mughal Gallery: Mughal paintings, coins, calligraphy, MSS, carving; Sikh Gallery: arms and armour, paintings of Sikh period; Sikh Painting Gallery: oil paintings from the Princess Bamba colln; Curator ANJUM JAVED; Asst Curator SHA-BANO.

Lahore Museum: Opp. old Univ. Hall, Shahrah-e-Quaid-i-Azam, Lahore, Punjab; tel. (42) 7322835; internet www.lahoremuseum.org; f. 1864; collns of Graeco-Buddhist sculpture, Indo-Pakistani coins and miniature paintings of the Mughal, Rajput, Kangra and Pahari schools; Hindu, Buddhist and Jaina sculpture, local arts, Chinese porcelain, armoury, fabrics, Pakistani postage stamps, modern paintings, Oriental MSS, Islamic calligraphy, archives and photographs on Pakistan Movement; library of 35,000 vols; Dir Dr SAIFUR RAHMAN DAR; publs *Catalogue of Coins*, *Catalogue of Miniatures*, *Guide Book*, *Guide to Gandhara Gallery*, *Guide to Manuscripts*.

Lahore Zoo: 92 Shahrah-e-Quaid-i-Azam, Mall Rd, Lahore, Punjab; tel. (42) 36314684; e-mail info@lahorezoo.com.pk; internet www.lahorezoo.com.pk; f. 1872; houses animals of 136 species incl. 82 species of birds, 8 species of reptiles and 45 species of mammals; Dir SHAFQAT ALI.

Larkana

Archaeological Museum: Mohenjodaro, Larkana, Sindh; tel. (741) 459051; f. 1924; variety of antiquities unearthed from the prehistoric site of Mohenjodaro, dating from 3,000 BC; Curator SAEED JATOI.

Peshawar

Peshawar Museum: Near Old Dean's Hotel, Peshawar, Khyber Pakhtunkhwa; f. 1907; collns incl. sculptures of the Gandhara

School; colln of images of the Buddha, the Bodhisattvas, Buddhist deities, reliefs illustrating the life of the Buddha and Jataka stories, architectural pieces and minor antiquities excavated at Charsadda, Sahri-Bahlol, Shahji-ki-Dheri, Takht-i-Bahi and Jamal Garhi; Muslim gallery of Quranic MSS and MSS in Arabic and Persian languages; ethnological section; Curator NIDAUL-LAH SEHRAI.

Rawalpindi

Archaeological Museum: Taxila, Rawalpindi, Punjab; tel. (51) 9315476; e-mail nasiraladand2003@yahoo.com; f. 1928; Gandhara sculptures in stone and stucco; gold and silver ornaments; household utensils, pottery; antiquities of every description from the sites of Taxila and monastic area from 6th century BC to 5th century AD; library: see under Libraries and Archives; Curator ABDUL NASIR KHAN.

Universities

ABASYN UNIVERSITY

Ring Rd (Charsadda Link), Peshawar
Telephone: (91) 2247264
E-mail: vc@abasyn.edu.pk
Internet: www.abasynuniv.edu.pk
Founded 2007
Private control
Academic year: January to December (3 semesters)
Offers Masters degree in computer sciences, management studies
Chancellor: IMRAN ULLAH
Vice-Chancellor: Prof. Dr FIDA MUHAMMAD KHAN
Registrar: MUHAMMAD IQBAL
Controller of Examinations: MUHAMMAD IFTIKHAR
Publication: *Journal of Social Sciences*

AGA KHAN UNIVERSITY

Stadium Rd, POB 3500, Karachi 74800
Telephone: (21) 34930051
E-mail: aku@aku.edu
Internet: www.aku.edu
Founded 1983
Private control
Language of instruction: English
Academic year: January to August
Chancellor: HE AGA KHAN
Pres.: FIROZ RASUL
Provost and Chief Academic Officer: Dr GREG MORAN
Vice-Pres. for Health and Operational Services: ALLAUDIN MERALI
Vice-Pres. for Human Resources: CAROL JOAN ARIANO
Dir-Gen. for Resource Devt: ZAHIR JANMOHAMED (acting)
Dir-Gen. and Chief Financial Officer: AL-KARIM HAJI
Registrar: LOUIS R. ARIANO
Librarian: NORMAND DEMERS
Library of 137,000 vols 265 print journal titles, 70,500 online books, 27,000 online periodicals
Number of teachers: 650
Number of students: 2,300

DEANS

Faculty of Arts and Sciences, East Africa: Dr RAFIQUE KESHAVJEE
Institute for Educational Development, East Africa: Prof. PAULINE REA-DICKINS
Institute for Educational Development, Karachi: Dr MUHAMMAD MEMON

Institute for the Study of Muslim Civilizations: Dr FAROUK TOPAN (Dir)
Medical College: Dr FARHAT ABBAS
Medical College, East Africa: ROBERT ARMSTRONG
Nursing and Midwifery, East Africa: Dr YASMIN AMARSI
Research and Graduate Studies: Dr EL-NASIR MA LALANI
School of Nursing, Karachi: Dr ROZINA KARMALIANI

PROFESSORS

AMARSI, Y., Nursing
BADRUDDIN, S. H., Community Health Sciences
BAIG, S. M., Medicine
BHUTTA, A. B., Paediatrics
BILLOO, A. G., Paediatrics
CHOHAN, U., Anaesthesia
CONNOR, J. D., Pharmacology
FARAH, I., Education
FILALI-ANSARY, A., Education (London)
FROSSARD, P., Biochemistry
GILANI, A. H., Pharmacology
HAMID, S., Medicine
HARLEEH-JONES, B. A., Education
HASAN, R., Microbiology
HASAN, S. H., Pathology
HUSSAIN, R., Microbiology
IQBAL, M. P., Biochemistry
JABBAR, A., Medicine
JAFRI, S. M. W., Medicine
KAMAL, R., Anaesthesia
KARIM, M. S., Community Health Sciences
KAYANI, N., Pathology
KHAN, F. A., Anaesthesia
KHAN, F. H., Anaesthesia
KHAN, I. A., Paediatrics
KHAN, J. A., Medicine
KHAN, K. M., Anatomy
KHAN, M. A., Medicine
KHAN, M. M., Psychiatry
KHAN, S. M., Surgery
KHURSHID, M., Pathology
KING, L., Nursing (Kenya)
MACLEOD, G., Education
MEMON, M., Education
NIZAMI, S. Q., Paediatrics
PARDHAN, S., Education
PERVEZ, S., Pathology
QURESHI, R. H., Family Medicine
RAJA, A. J., Surgery (Kenya)
REES, J., Radiology (Kenya)
RIZVI, J. H., Obstetrics and Gynaecology
SIDDIQUI, A. A., Biochemistry
TALATI, J., Surgery
VELLANI, C. W., Medicine
ZUBERI, R. W., Family Medicine

ATTACHED RESEARCH INSTITUTES

Institute for Educational Development: IED-PDC, 1-5/B-VII, F.B. Area, POB 13688, Karimabad, Karachi 75950; tel. (21) 6347611; e-mail ied@aku.edu; f. 1993; Dir Prof. MUHAMMAD MEMON; publ. *Research and Policy Studies*.
Institute for the Study of Muslim Civilizations: 210 Euston Rd, London NW1 2DA, United Kingdom; tel. (20) 7380-3800; e-mail ismc@aku.edu; Dir Dr DAVID TAYLOR; Librarian WASEEM FAROOQ

AIR UNIVERSITY

Sector E–9, PAF Complex, Islamabad 44000
Telephone: (51) 9262557
E-mail: admissions@mail.au.edu.pk
Internet: www.au.edu.pk
Founded 2002
State control
Academic year: September to August (3 semesters)
Vice-Chancellor: Dr IJAZ AHMAD MALIK
Registrar: ZAFAR AHMED

Dir for Academic Affairs: Dr Q. ISA DAUDPOTA
Librarian: MAMOONA KOUSAR
Library of 13,000 vols, 22 journals
Number of teachers: 120
Number of students: 2,100

DEANS

Faculty of Administrative Sciences: Dr IKRAMULLAH SHAD
Faculty of Basic and Applied Sciences: Dr ABDULLAH SADIQ
Faculty of Engineering: Dr ZAFAR-ULLAH KORESHI
Faculty of Social Sciences and Humanities: ABIDA HASSAN (acting)

AL-KHAIR UNIVERSITY

Gujrat Rd, Bhimber, Azad Jammu and Kashmir
Telephone: (5828) 201611
Internet: www.alkhair.edu.pk
Founded 1994
Private control
Chancellor: PRES. OF AZAD JAMMU AND KASHMIR
Pro-Chancellor: Dr MUHAMMAD BASHIR GORAYA
Rector and Vice-Chancellor: Prof. Dr A. Q. ANSARI
Pro-Vice-Chancellor: IMTIAZ AQDAS
Registrar: MANZOOR HUSSAIN SHEIKH
Controller of Examinations: CH. MUHAMMAD BASHIR

DEANS

Faculty of Computer Sciences: Dr ISHTIAQ AHMED GONDAL
Faculty of Education: Prof. Dr M. MAHMOOD HUSSAIN AWAN

ALHAMD ISLAMIC UNIVERSITY

Zarghoon Rd, Quetta
Telephone: (81) 2451342
E-mail: president@aiu.edu.pk
Internet: www.aiu.edu.pk
Founded 2005
Private control
Faculties of arts, education, engineering, Islam, law, science, technology
Pres.: Prof. SHAKEEL AHMED ROSHAN
Dean: Prof. MEHRU NISA KHAN
Registrar: URWA JAWED
Controller of Examinations: MOHSIN JAVED

ALLAMA IQBAL OPEN UNIVERSITY

Sector H–8, Islamabad 44000
Telephone: (51) 9057816
E-mail: director_sac@aiou.edu.pk
Internet: www.aiou.edu.pk
Founded 1974 as People's Open Univ., current name adopted 1977
State control
Languages of instruction: English, Urdu
Academic year: April to March
Chancellor: PRES. OF ISLAMIC REPUBLIC OF PAKISTAN
Pro-Chancellor: MIN. OF EDUCATION
Vice-Chancellor: Prof. Dr NAZIR AHMED SANGI
Registrar: HAFEEZ ULLAH
Librarian: Prof. Dr SHAH FARRUKH (acting)
Library: see under Libraries and Archives
Number of teachers: 170
Number of students: 512,000
Publications: *Ilm Ki Roshni* (2 a year), *Jamia Nama* (12 a year, in English and Urdu), *Journal of Social Sciences and Humanities* (2 a year), *Marif-I-Islami* (2 a year), *Pakistan Journal of Education* (2 a year), *Sehen Ujala* (2 a year)

DEANS

Faculty of Arabic and Islamic Studies: Prof. Dr ALI ASGHAR CHISHTI
Faculty of Education: Prof. Dr REHANA MASRUR
Faculty of Sciences: Prof. Dr NOWSHAD KHAN
Faculty of Social Sciences and Humanities: Prof. Dr ABDUL HAFEEZ

BAHAUDDIN ZAKARIYA UNIVERSITY

Univ. Campus, Bosan Rd, Multan 60800

Telephone: (61) 9210097
E-mail: regbzu@brain.net.pk
Internet: www.bzu.edu.pk

Founded 1975 as Univ. of Multan; present name 1979
State control
Languages of instruction: English, Urdu
Academic year: October to September

Chancellor: GOV. OF PUNJAB
Vice-Chancellor: Prof. Dr SYED KHAWAJA ALQAMA
Registrar: Prof. Dr SYED MUHAMMAD ALI
Controller of Examination: MALIK MUNIR HUSSAIN
Librarian: ABDUL MAJEED

Library: see under Libraries and Archives
Number of teachers: 500
Number of students: 20,000

Publications: *Journal of Research (Humanities), Journal of Research (Science), Journal of Research of Business Management, Journal of Research of the Faculty of Islamic Studies and Languages*

DEANS

Faculty of Arts and Social Science: Prof. Dr S. KHAWAJA ALQAMA
Faculty of Commerce, Law and Business Administration: Prof. Dr HAYAT M. AWAN
Faculty of Engineering and Technology: Prof. Dr ABDUL AZIZ MAZHAR
Faculty of Islamic Studies and Languages: Prof. Dr ZAFAR IQBAL
Faculty of Medicine and Dentistry: Prof. Dr SHABBIR AHMAD NASIR
Faculty of Pharmacy: Prof. Dr KHALID HUSSAIN JANBAZ
Faculty of Science and Agriculture: Prof. Dr HUMAYUN PERVEZ
Faculty of Veterinary Sciences: Prof. Dr CH. SIKANDAR HAYAT

BAHRIA UNIVERSITY

Main Campus: Shangrila Rd, Sector E-8, Islamabad 44000

Telephone: (51) 9260271

Karachi Campus: 13 Nat. Stadium Rd, Karachi

Telephone: (21) 9240002
E-mail: info@bahria.edu.pk
Internet: www.bahria.edu.pk

Founded 2000
State control
Language of instruction: English
Academic year: January to June

Pro-Chancellor: MOHAMMAD ASIF SANDILA
Rector: SHAHID IQBAL
Pro-Rector: MUHAMMAD EHSAN SAEED
Registrar: Dr MOHAMMAD JAVED KHAN
Head of Libraries: SHER AFZAL KHAN

Library of 45,000 vols
Number of students: 9,500

Publications: *Bahria Journal of Professional Psychology, Bahria University Journal of Information & Communication Technology, Journal of Bahria University Medical & Dental College (BUMDC)*

DEANS

Islamabad Campus:
Internet: www.bci.edu.pk
Faculty of Engineering: Prof. Dr MUHAMMAD ALTAF MUKATI
Faculty of Sciences: Dr MUHAMMAD RIAZ
Karachi Campus:
E-mail: src@bimcs.edu.pk
Internet: www.bimcs.edu.pk
Computer Science and Engineering: Prof. NAEEM JANJUA
Management Sciences: NAVEED MOHAMMAD KHAN

BALOCHISTAN UNIVERSITY OF ENGINEERING AND TECHNOLOGY

Khuzdar, Balochistan

Telephone: (848) 412524
E-mail: registrar@buetk.edu.pk
Internet: www.buetk.edu.pk

Founded 1987 as Balochistan Engineering College, present name and status 1994
State control
Language of instruction: English
Academic year: March to December

Vice-Chancellor: Dr ZAHOOR AHMAD BALOCH
Registrar: SHER AHMED QAMBRANI
Controller of Examinations: MUHAMMAD ALAM BALOCH
Librarian: MOHAMMAD ANWAR

Number of teachers: 78
Number of students: 904

DEANS

Faculty of Engineering: Dr MUSHTAQ AHMED SHAH

BALOCHISTAN UNIVERSITY OF INFORMATION TECHNOLOGY, ENGINEERING AND MANAGEMENT SCIENCES (BUITEMS)

Airport Rd, Belili, Quetta, Balochistan

Telephone: (81) 2881042
E-mail: vc@buitms.edu.pk
Internet: www.buitms.edu.pk
State control
Language of instruction: English
Academic year: March to February

Vice-Chancellor: Eng. AHMED FAROOQ BAZAI
Pro-Vice-Chancellor: Prof. Dr M. A. K. MALGHANI
Registrar: JAMAL MUSTAFA
Librarian: GULAM MURTAZA SHAHWANI

Library of 30,000 vols
Number of teachers: 330
Number of students: 6,500

Publication: *Journal of Emerging Sciences*

DEANS

Faculty of Arts and Basic Sciences: Dr HAMDULLAH KHAN
Faculty of Engineering: Prof. Dr AHSANULLAH KAKAR
Faculty of Information and Communication Technology: Prof. Dr AFTAB AHMED SHEIKH
Faculty of Life Sciences and Informatics: Prof. Dr DOST M. BALOCH
Faculty of Management Sciences: Dr ABDUL RAZIQ

BAQAI MEDICAL UNIVERSITY

51 Deh Tor, Gadap Rd, Super Highway, POB 2407, Karachi 74600

Telephone: (21) 34410293
E-mail: info@baqai.edu.pk
Internet: www.baqai.edu.pk

Founded 1988 as Baqai Medical College, present name and status 1996
Private control

Institutes of cardiovascular diseases, clinical nutrition, diabetology and endocrinology, health sciences, health management sciences, haematology, pharmaceutical sciences, reproduction and devt, information technology, medical technology, oncology, physical therapy rehabilitation, pathology; Baqai Medical College; Baqai Dental College

Chancellor: Prof. Dr FAREED UDDIN BAQAI
Vice-Chancellor: Prof. Dr SYED AZHAR AHMED
Pro-Vice-Chancellor: Prof. Dr ZAHIDA BAQAI
Registrar: Prof. KHURSHEED ALI KHAN

BEACONHOUSE NATIONAL UNIVERSITY

3-C Zafar Ali Rd, Gulberg V, Lahore

Telephone: (42) 35718260
E-mail: info@bnu.edu.pk
Internet: www.bnu.edu.pk

Founded 2003
Private control

Vice-Chancellor: SARTAJ AZIZ
Librarian: NIGHAT SALEEMI

Number of teachers: 80

DEANS

School of Architecture: Prof. Dr GULZAR HAIDER
School of Computer and Information Technology: Prof. Dr KHAVER ZIA
School of Education: Dr TARIQ RAHMAN
School of Liberal Arts: Dr HAFIZ A. PASHA
School of Media and Mass Communication: Prof. Dr MEHDI HASAN
School of Social Science: Dr HAFIZ A. PASHA
School of Visual Arts and Design: Prof. SALIMA HASHMI

CECOS UNIVERSITY

Hayatabad, Peshawar, Khyber Pakhtunkhwa

Telephone: (91) 5860291
Internet: www.cecos.edu.pk

Founded 1986, present status 2001
Private control

Pres.: MUHAMMAD TANVEER JAVED
Vice-Chancellor: Prof. Dr RIAZ A. KHATTAK

College of Engineering and Information Technology; Institute of Management and Information Sciences; CECOS Data Institute; CECOS-Frontier College of Business Education; CECOS London College

Number of teachers: 150
Number of students: 1,800

CITY UNIVERSITY OF SCIENCE & INFORMATION TECHNOLOGY

Dalazak Rd, Peshawar, Khyber Pakhtunkhwa

Telephone: (91) 2584161
E-mail: info@cusit.edu.pk
Internet: www.cityuniversity.edu.pk

Founded 2001
Private control

Depts of chemistry, computer science, education, electrical engineering, English, Islamic studies, management science, mathematics, Urdu

Pres.: MUHAMMAD SABUR SETHI
Vice-Pres.: Prof. Dr MUHAMMAD ASRAR KHATTAK
Vice-Chancellor: Prof. Dr ANWAR F. CHISHTI
Registrar: ZAFAR AHMED
Controller of Examinations: AMJAD ALI
Librarian: ABDUL HAMEED
Number of students: 21,000

COMSATS INSTITUTE OF INFORMATION TECHNOLOGY (CIIT)

Park Rd, Chak Shahzad, Islamabad

Telephone: (51) 9247000
E-mail: registrar@comsats.edu.pk
Internet: www.comsats.edu.pk

Founded 1998, present status 2000
State control
Language of instruction: English
Academic year: July to June

Rector: Dr SYED MUHAMMAD JUNAID ZAIDI
Pro-Rector: Dr HAROON RASHID
Registrar: Prof. Dr IZHAR HUSSAIN
Controller of Examinations: MUHAMMAD SOHAIL GHANI WARAICH

Library of 45,000 vols, 7,000 CDs, DVDs, audio and video cassettes
Number of teachers: 2,200
Number of students: 21,500

Publication: *South Asian Journal of Global Business Research*

DEANS

Faculty of Architecture and Design: Prof. ZAIN UL-ABEDIN
Faculty of Business Administration: Prof. Dr QAISAR ABBAS
Faculty of Engineering: Prof. Dr SHAHZAD A. MALIK
Faculty of Information Science and Technology: Prof. Dr SAJJAD MOHSIN
Faculty of Sciences: Prof. Dr ARSHAD SALEEM BHATTI

PROFESSORS

Faculty of Architecture and Design:
ABEDIN, Z. UL, Architecture
AHMAD, E., Architecture
BAJWA, K. W., Architecture
KHALID, N., Architecture

Faculty of Business Administration:
ABBAS, Q., Management Sciences
AFZA, T., Management Sciences
AHMAD, K. F., Management Sciences
AMJAD, S. N., Development Studies
HASNU, S. A. F., Management Sciences
KALEEM, A., Management Sciences
NASR, A. H. M., Management Sciences
RIAZ, K., Management Sciences

Faculty of Engineering:
FAROOQ, R., Chemical Engineering
KHAN, A. U., Chemical Engineering
KHAN, L. K., Chemical Engineering
KHAN, N., Chemical Engineering
KHAN, S. A., Chemical Engineering
KHATTAK, S., Chemical Engineering
MALIK, S. A., Chemical Engineering

Faculty of Information Science and Technology:
HABIB, Z., Computer Science
HUSSAIN, S. A., Computer Science
MOHSIN, S., Computer Science

Faculty of Science:
ASGHAR, S., Mathematics
AZAM, A., Mathematics
BHATTI, A. S., Physics
HAFEEZ, F. Y., Biosciences
HAROON, T., Mathematics
HASEEB, M. Q., Physics
JADOON, I. A. K., Earth Sciences
JAMIL, M., Meteorology
KHAN, A., Mathematics
KHAN, A. R., Chemistry
KHAN, M. A., Physics
KHAN, M.-UD-D., Mathematics
NOOR, K. I., Mathematics
NOOR, M. A., Mathematics
OLIMOV, K., Physics
PERVAIZ, A., Environmental Sciences
QAMAR, R., Biosciences
QAMAR, S., Physics
RAJA, I. A., Environmental Sciences
REHMAN, N., Pharmacy
SHAH, M. M., Environmental Sciences
SHAHALIYEV, E., Physics
SHAHBAZ, M. Q., Mathematics
SHAUKAT, S. F., Physics
SULEYNANOV, M., Physics

DADABHOY INSTITUTE OF HIGHER EDUCATION

SNPA-17/B, Block 3, KCHSU Ltd, off Shaheed-e-Millat Rd, Karachi

Telephone: (21) 34389102
E-mail: admission@dadabhoy.edu.pk
Internet: www.dadabhoy.edu.pk

Founded 2000, present status 2003
Private control

Rector: Prof. Dr S. ALTAF HUSSAIN

DEANS

Faculty of Computer and Mathematical Sciences: Dr JAWAID QUAMAR
Faculty of Management, Media and Social Sciences: Dr M. M. H. SIDDIQUI

DAWOOD COLLEGE OF ENGINEERING AND TECHNOLOGY

M. A. Jinnah Rd, Karachi 74800, Sindh

Telephone: (21) 99231195
E-mail: registrar@dcet.edu.pk
Internet: www.dcet.edu.pk

Founded 1962, present status 2007
State control

Faculties of architecture and planning, basic sciences, mathematics and humanities, chemical engineering, computer system engineering, electronic engineering, energy and environment engineering, industrial engineering and management, metallurgy and materials engineering, petroleum and gas engineering, telecommunication engineering

Prin.: Dr MUHAMMAD ALI SHEIKH
Dean of Dawood College of Electronic Engineering: Prof. RASHID BAIG
Registrar: GHULAM SHABBIR BHOGIO
Controller of Examinations: GUL MUHAMMAD BHAYO

Library of 30,269 vols
Number of teachers: 70
Number of students: 1,450

DOW UNIVERSITY OF HEALTH SCIENCES

Baba-E-Urdu Rd, Karachi 74200

Telephone: (21) 99215754
E-mail: vc@duhs.edu.pk
Internet: www.duhs.edu.pk

Founded 2003
State control

Offers Bachelors degree in dental technology, medical technology, nursing, physical medicine; Masters courses incl. biostatistics and epidemiology, diabetes and endocrinology, dental surgery, health profession education, jurisprudence, nursing, physiotheraphy

FATIMA JINNAH WOMEN UNIVERSITY

Old Presidency, The Mall, Rawalpindi 4600, Punjab

Telephone: (51) 9270050
E-mail: registrar@fjwu.edu.pk
Internet: www.fjwu.edu.pk

Founded 1998
State control

Vice-Chancellor: Prof. Dr SAMINA AMIN QADIR
Registrar: Dr MARYAM RAB
Controller of Examinations: Dr MUSSARET ANWAR SHEIKH

Librarian: ZAFAR JAVED NAQVI
Library of 23,000 vols

DEANS

Faculty of Arts and Social Sciences: Prof. Dr SAMINA AMIN QADIR
Faculties of Law, Commerce, Management and Admin. Sciences, Science and Technology: Prof. Dr NAHEED ZIA KHAN

FEDERAL URDU UNIVERSITY OF ARTS, SCIENCE AND TECHNOLOGY

MSC Block, Block 9, University Rd, Gulshan-e-Iqbal, Karachi 75300

Telephone: (21) 99244141
E-mail: info@fuuast.edu.pk
Internet: www.fuuast.edu.pk

Founded 2002
State control

Vice-Chancellor: Prof. Dr MUHAMMAD QAISER
Registrar: Prof. Dr QAMR-UL-HAQ
Controller of Examinations: WAQAR-UL-HAQ
Librarian: MUKHTAR ASHRAF

Number of teachers: 450
Number of students: 12,000

DEANS

Faculty of Arts: FAROOQ PERVAIZ MUGAL (acting)
Faculty of Business Admin., Commerce and Economics: Dr SULAMAN D. MUHAMMAD (acting)
Faculty of Law: Dr JUSTIS
Faculty of Pharmacy: Dr ALI AKBAR SIAL (acting)
Faculty of Science and Technology: Prof. Dr JAMAL HAIDER

FORMAN CHRISTIAN COLLEGE

Ferozepur Rd, Lahore 54600

Telephone: (42) 99231581
E-mail: contact@fccollege.edu.pk
Internet: www.fccollege.edu.pk

Founded 1864 as Lahore Mission College, current name adopted 1894, present status 2004
Private control

depts of biological sciences, chemistry, computer science, economics, education, English, geography, health and physical education, history, mass communication, mathematics, philosophy, physics, political science, psychology, religious studies, sociology, statistics, Urdu

Rector: Dr PETER H. ARMACOST
Exec. Vice-Rector: Dr C. J. DUBASH
Exec. Vice-Rector: Dr JIM TEBBE
Prin.: Dr CHRISTY MUNIR
Registrar: Dr HAMID SAEED
Dean of Students: CHERYL BURKE
Controller of Examinations: Dr MIAN WAJAHAT HUSSAIN
Librarian: BUSHRA ALMAS JASWAL

Library: see under Libraries and Archives
Number of students: 4,660

FOUNDATION UNIVERSITY ISLAMABAD

Defense Ave, Phase-I, DHA, Islamabad

Telephone: (51) 5788446
E-mail: registrar@fui.edu.pk
Internet: www.fui.edu.pk

Founded 2002
Private control

Chancellor: NAEEM KHALID LODHI
Pres.: MUHAMMAD MUSTAFA KHAN
Rector: Prof. Dr BELAL A. KHAN
Registrar: TANWIR-UL-ISLAM
Dir: ZAHID PARVEZ (acting)

Library of 6,000 vols

DEANS

Faculty of Education: Prof. Dr MAQSUD ALAM BUKHARI

FRONTIER WOMEN UNIVERSITY

Asamia Rd, Peshawar, Khyber Pakhtunkhwa

Telephone: (91) 9212422
E-mail: info@fwu.edu.pk
Internet: www.fwu.edu.pk

Founded 2005
State control
Academic year: December to June

Faculties of Arabic, bioinformatics, computer science, economics, English language and literature, Islamiyat, mathematics, microbiology, statistics

Vice-Chancellor: Prof. Dr SYEDA FARHANA JAHANGIR

GANDHARA UNIVERSITY

Canal Rd, University Town, Peshawar, Khyber Pakhtunkhwa

Telephone: (91) 5844429
E-mail: info@gandhara.edu.pk
Internet: www.gandhara.edu.pk

Founded 2002
Private control

Offers Bachelors and Masters degrees in medicine, dentistry

Chair.: ROEEDA KABIR
Vice-Chancellor: Dr R. A. K. TAHIRKHAILI

GC UNIVERSITY

Katchery Rd, Lahore 54000, Punjab

Telephone: (42) 99213340
E-mail: registrar@gcu.edu.pk
Internet: www.gcu.edu.pk

Founded 1864, present status 2002
State control

Vice-Chancellor: Prof. Dr MUHAMMAD KHALEEQ-UR-RAHMAN
Registrar: SYED ANJUM NISAR
Controller of Examinations: ASHRAF SHABBIR BOKHARI
Chief Librarian: ABDUL WAHEED

Library: see under Libraries and Archives
Number of teachers: 430
Number of students: 7,380

DEANS

Faculty of Arts and Social Sciences: Prof. Dr M. KHALID PERVAIZ
Faculty of Languages, Islamic and Oriental Learning: Prof. Dr SOHAIL AHMAD KHAN
Faculty of Science and Technology: Prof. Dr IKRAM UL HAQ

GHULAM ISHAQ KHAN INSTITUTE OF ENGINEERING SCIENCES AND TECHNOLOGY

Topi 23640, Khyber Pakhtunkhwa

Telephone: (938) 271858
E-mail: rector@giki.edu.pk
Internet: www.giki.edu.pk

Founded 1993
Private control
Language of instruction: English
Academic year: August to July (3 semesters)

Bachelors degree courses incl. engineering sciences, management sciences and humanities

Pres.: SHAMS-UL-MULK
Rector: JEHANGIR BASHAR
Pro-Rector for Academics: Prof. Dr F. AHMAD KHALID
Dean of Student Affairs: Dr JUNAID MUGHAL

Controller of Examinations and Registrar: MUHAMMAD FAHEEM AKHTAR
Library of 17,000 vols
Number of teachers: 35

GIFT UNIVERSITY

GIFT Univ. Chowk, Gujranwala 52250

Telephone: (55) 3892989
E-mail: president@gift.edu.pk
Internet: www.gift.edu.pk

Founded 2002
Private control

Faculties of accounting and finance, art, design and architecture, arts and social sciences, business and commerce, computer sciences, management sciences

Pres.: MUHAMMAD ANWAR DAR
Rector: Prof. Dr MOHAMMAD IQBAL TAHIR
Registrar: NAVEED AHMAD MUGHAL
Dean: Dr SURRAYA SHAFI MIR
Librarian: SAJIDA BASHIR

Library of 10,500 vols

GOMAL UNIVERSITY

Dera Ismail Khan, Khyber Pakhtunkhwa

Telephone: (966) 750424
E-mail: vc@gu.edu.pk
Internet: www.gu.edu.pk

Founded 1974
State control
Languages of instruction: English, Urdu
Academic year: September to June

Chancellor: GOV. OF KHYBER PAKHTUNKHWA
Vice-Chancellor: Prof. Dr MANSOOR AKBAR KUNDI
Registrar: MUHAMMAD JAN KHAN
Controller of Examinations: MUSHATQUREHMAN
Dir of Academics: FARIDULLAH KHAN
Librarian: MUHAMMAD SADIQ JAVAID

Library: see under Libraries and Archives
Number of teachers: 340
Number of students: 6,700

Publication: *Gomal University Journal of Research* (2 a year)

DEANS

Faculty of Agriculture: Dr SAID MIR KHAN
Faculty of Arts: Dr UMER ALI KHAN
Faculty of Pharmacy: Dr GUL MAJID KHAN
Faculty of Sciences: Dr MUSA KALEEM BALOCH

PROFESSORS

AHMAD, H. K., Agriculture
BALOCH, J. J., Physics
KHAN, A. G., Agriculture
KHAN, A. S., Pharmacy
KHAN, I. U., Pharmacy
KHAN, K. Z., Economics
KHAN, L. U., Agriculture
KHAN, M. A., Physics
KHAN, M. F., Pharmacy
KHAN, M. K., Chemistry
KHAN, M. Q., Agriculture
KHAN, Z. A., Chemistry
QAZI, N. S., Pharmacy
SAEED, A., Biological Sciences

GOVERNMENT COLLEGE UNIVERSITY, FAISALABAD

Allama Iqbal Rd, Faisalabad

Telephone: (41) 9200886
E-mail: info@gcuf.edu.pk
Internet: www.gcuf.edu.pk

Founded 1897, present status 2002
State control

Vice-Chancellor: Dr ZAKIR HUSSAIN
Registrar: MUHAMMAD AKRAM

Controller of Examinations: JAVED ASLAM BAJWA
Librarian: MUHAMMAD ASHFAQ
Library of 80,400 vols
Number of teachers: 460
Number of students: 13,570

DEANS

Faculty of Arts and Social Science: Dr PARVAIZ AZEEM
Faculty of Islamic and Oriental Learning: Prof. Dr HAFEEZ-UR-REHMAN
Faculty of Management and Admin. Sciences: Dr MUHAMMAD SHAHBAZ ARIF
Faculty of Science and Technology: Prof. Dr NAUREEN AZIZ QURESHI

GREENWICH UNIVERSITY

Greenwich House, DK-10, 38th St, Darakshan, Phase VI Defence Housing Authority, Karachi 75500

Telephone: (21) 35840397
E-mail: gu@greenwichuniversity.edu.pk
Internet: www.greenwichuniversity.edu.pk
Private control

Vice-Chancellor: SEEMA MOGHUL

DEANS

Faculty of Management Sciences and Information Studies: Prof. Dr MUNIR ALI SHAH RIZVI
Faculty of Social Sciences and Humanities: Prof. Dr MUNIR WASTI

HAJVERY UNIVERSITY

43–52 Industrial Area, Gulberg III, Lahore, Pakistan

Telephone: (42) 35717130
E-mail: registrar@hup.edu.pk
Internet: www.hup.edu.pk

Founded 2002
Private control

Chair.: ATIF MUSHTAQ
Dir for Admin.: MUHAMMAD LATIF

Number of teachers: 240
Number of students: 5,000

DEANS

HU Business School: Prof. Dr MUHAMMAD ASLAM
HU School of Commerce and Banking: Prof. Dr MUHAMMAD ASLAM
HU School of Engineering and Computer Sciences: Prof. Dr NAEEM AKHTER KHAN AFRIDI

HAMDARD UNIVERSITY

Sharae Madinat Al-Hikmah, Muhammad bin Qasim Ave, Karachi 74600

Telephone: (21) 36440017
E-mail: huvc@hamdard.edu.pk
Internet: www.hamdard.edu.pk

Founded 1991
Private control

Chancellor: S. M. ZAFAR
Vice-Chancellor: Prof. Dr NASIM A. KHAN
Registrar: Col (retd) RAFIQ AHMED

Library of 500,000 vols, 1,629 MSS
Number of students: 5,000

DEANS

Faculty of Eastern Medicine: Prof. Dr HK. ABDUL HANNAN
Faculty of Engineering Sciences and Technology: Prof. Dr ABDUL REHMAN MEMON
Faculty of Health and Medical Sciences: Prof. Dr ALEY HASAN ZAIDI
Faculty of Humanities and Social Sciences: Dr SYED ABDUL AZIZ
Faculty of Legal Studies: NASIR ASLAM ZAHID

Faculty of Management Sciences: Prof. Dr
MATIN A. KHAN
Faculty of Pharmacy: Prof. Dr JAVEID IQBAL

HAZARA UNIVERSITY

Mansehra, Khyber Pakhtunkhwa
Telephone: (997) 530732
E-mail: registrar@hu.edu.pk
Internet: www.hu.edu.pk
Founded 2002
State control
Language of instruction: English
Academic year: January to December (2
semesters)
Vice-Chancellor: Prof. Dr SYED SAKHAWAT
SHAH
Registrar: Prof. Dr MUQARRAB SHAH

DEANS

Faculty of Arts: Prof. Dr SAEED ANWAR
Faculty of Health Sciences: Prof. Dr MUQAR-
RAB SHAH
Faculty of Law and Admin. Sciences: Prof. Dr
SOHAIL SHAHZAD
Faculty of Science: Prof. Dr BAKHTIAR
MUHAMMAD

HITEC UNIVERSITY

Taxila Cantt
Telephone: (51) 490814650
E-mail: registrar@hitecuni.edu.pk
Internet: www.hitecuni.edu.pk
Founded 2007, present status 2009
Private control
Language of instruction: English
Academic year: September to August
Depts of computer science engineering, elec-
trical engineering, humanities and basic
sciences, Islamic studies, management sci-
ences, mathematics, mechanical engineering
Vice-Chancellor: QAMAR ZAMAN
Registrar: MUHAMMAD HAFEEZ
Controller of Examinations: MAHMOOD
AHMED SIDDIQUI
Dir of Student Affairs: ZAHOOR SULTAN
Number of teachers: 87
Number of students: 1,683

DEANS

Faculty of Engineering and Technology: Dr
EJAZ MUHAMMAD

IMPERIAL COLLEGE OF BUSINESS STUDIES

C Block, Izmir Society, Canal Rd, Lahore
53800
Telephone: (42) 37499301
E-mail: registrar@imperial.edu.pk
Internet: www.imperial.edu.pk
Founded 1991, present status 2002
Private control
Chair.: MUNAWAR AHMAD
Pro-Rector: ASIM N. AHMAD

DEANS

Department of Management and Business
Studies: Dr NISAR AHMAD
Faculty of Computing and Information Sci-
ences: Prof. Dr M. A. PASHA

INDUS INSTITUTE OF HIGHER EDUCATION

ST-2D, Block-17, Karachi, Sindh
Telephone: (21) 4801430
E-mail: indus@indus.edu.pk
Internet: www.indus.edu.pk
Private control
Chair.: KHALID AMIN
Rector: Prof. Dr MUNEER QURESHI

Registrar: AYUB SHEIKH
Dir: WAHID FAROOQUI
Librarian: FARHANA MAQSOOD

DEANS

Faculty of Business Admin.: Prof. Dr HANIF
MUHAMMAD
Faculty of Engineering: Dr SYED FAISAL
AHMED BUKHARI
Faculty of Fashion and Textile Design: Dr
AHMED NIAZ

INDUS VALLEY SCHOOL OF ART AND ARCHITECTURE

ST-33, Block 2, Scheme 5, Clifton, Karachi,
Sindh
E-mail: info@indusvalley.edu.pk
Internet: www.indusvalley.edu.pk
Founded 1989, present status 1994
Private control
Architecture, communication design, fine art,
interior design, liberal arts; postgraduate
degrees offered in apparel design, photog-
raphy, textile design
Exec. Dir: SAMINA RAEES KHAN
Registrar: RASHID RAZA
Librarian: ABID KHAN
Library of 9,500 vols
Number of students: 440

INSTITUTE OF BUSINESS ADMINISTRATION

University Rd, Karachi 75270, Sindh
Telephone: (21) 38104700
E-mail: info@iba.edu.pk
Internet: www.iba.edu.pk
Founded 1955, present status 1994
State control
Faculties of business admin., computer sci-
ence
Patron: GOV. OF SINDH
Dean and Dir: Dr ISHRAT HUSAIN
Registrar: AHMED ZAHEER
Librarian: MUHAMMAD ANWAR
Library of 40,000 vols, 50 journals
Number of teachers: 170
Number of students: 1,600

INSTITUTE OF BUSINESS AND TECHNOLOGY (BIZTEK)

Main Ibrahim Hydri Rd, Korangi Creek,
Karachi, Sindh
Telephone: (21) 35120461
E-mail: info@biztek.edu.pk
Internet: www.biztek.edu.pk
Founded 2001
Private control
Academic year: June to April (3 semesters)
Chancellor: NOMAN ABID LAKHANI
Rector: Dr SYED KASHIF RAFI (acting)
Librarian: SYEDA ZAREEN NAZ

DEANS

Faculty of Computer Sciences and Informa-
tion Technology: Dr MANSOOR UZ ZAFAR
DAWOOD
Faculty of Management Sciences and Social
Sciences: Dr MUHAMMAD ALI SIDDIQUI

INSTITUTE OF BUSINESS MANAGEMENT

Korangi Creek, Karachi 75190, Sindh
Telephone: (21) 35090961
E-mail: iobm@iobm.edu.pk
Internet: www.iobm.edu.pk
Founded 1995
Private control
Chancellor: AFTAB AHMED KHAN

Pres.: SHAHJEHAN S. KARIM
Rector: TALIB SYED KARIM
Exec. Dir of Admissions and Finance: SABINA
MOHSIN
Controller of Examinations: NAZ SOOMRO
Librarian: MUNOVER AZMATULLAH
Library of 25,000 vols

DEANS

College of Business Management: Prof. Dr
JAVED A. ANSARI

INSTITUTE OF MANAGEMENT SCIENCES

23 E-III, Gulberg-III, Lahore 54600, Punjab
Telephone: (42) 35751115
E-mail: info@pakaims.edu.pk
Internet: www.pakaims.edu.pk
Founded 1986 as Canadian School of Man-
agement-Lahore Learning Centre, present
name and status 2002
Private control
Language of instruction: English
Academic year: January to December
Depts of business administration, computer
science
Rector: Dr KHALID RANJHA
Pro-Rector: Prof. Dr ZAFAR ALTAF
Dean: Prof. Dr M. AFZAL BEG
Registrar: HASSAN MUJTABA

INSTITUTE OF MANAGEMENT SCIENCES

1-A, Sector E-5, Phase VII, Hayatabad,
Peshawar, Khyber Pakhtunkhwa
Telephone: (91) 5861024
E-mail: info@imsciences.edu.pk
Internet: www.imsciences.edu.pk
Founded 1995, present status 2005
State control
Centres of computer sciences, information
technology, management sciences; school of
liberal arts
Dir: Dr NASSER ALI KHAN
Jt Dir: Dr MUHAMMAD MOHSIN KHAN
Deputy Dir: FAYAZ AHMAD
Controller of Examinations: SYED MABOOD
GUL KAKA KHEL

INSTITUTE OF SPACE TECHNOLOGY

POB 2750, Islamabad 44000
Telephone: (51) 9075401
E-mail: info@ist.edu.pk
Internet: www.ist.edu.pk
Founded 2002
State control
Faculties of aeronautics and astronautics,
communication systems engineering,
humanities and sciences, materials science
and engineering, research and devt; campus
in Karachi
Vice-Chancellor: IMRAN RAHMAN
Dean: Dr ABDUL AZIZ MAZHAR
Registrar: FAROUQUE KHOKHAR
Library of 6,300 vols, 59 periodicals

INTERNATIONAL ISLAMIC UNIVERSITY

POB 1243, Islamabad
Sector H-10, Islamabad
Telephone: (51) 9258067
E-mail: rector@iiu.edu.pk
Internet: www.iiu.edu.pk
Founded 1980 as Islamic Univ., current
name adopted 1985
State control
Academic year: September to August
Chancellor: PRES. OF PAKISTAN

Pro-Chancellor: (vacant)
Rector: Prof. FATEH MUHAMMAD MALIK
Pres.: Dr MUMTAZ AHMAD
Vice-Pres. for Admin., Finance and Planning: Dr SAHIBZADA SAJID-UR-REHMAN
Dir for Academics: SHAGUFTA HAROON
Chief Librarian: SHER NOWROZ KHAN
Library: see under Libraries and Archives
Number of teachers: 100
Number of students: 17,000

Publications: *Al-Dirasat Al-Islamiya* (4 a year, in English), *Fikr-O-Nazar* (4 a year, in Urdu), *Insights* (4 a year), *Islamic Studies* (4 a year, in English), *Journal of Business and Management Sciences* (2 a year), *Mayar* (in Urdu)

DEANS

Faculty of Arabic Language: Dr MUHAMMAD MAKHLOF
Faculty of Basic and Applied Sciences: Prof. Dr MUHAMMAD IRFAN KHAN
Faculty of Engineering and Technology: Prof. Dr GHULAM YASIN CHOHAN
Faculty of Languages, Literature and Humanities: Dr RASHEED AMJAD
Faculty of Management Sciences: Prof. Dr M. BASHIR KHAN
Faculty of Shariah and Law: Prof. Dr MUHAMMAD ZIA-UL-HAQ
Faculty of Social Sciences: Prof. Dr N. B. JUMANI
Faculty of Usuluddin: Dr ZAFAR ULLAH BAIG

IQRA UNIVERSITY

Defence View, Shaheed-e-Millat Rd, Karachi 75500, Sindh
E-mail: info@iqra.edu.pk
Internet: www.iqra.edu.pk

Founded 1998
Private control

Chancellor: HUNAID H. LAKHANI
Vice-Chancellor: Dr U. A. G. ISANI
Exec. Sec.: ANWER ALI
Registrar: Dr S. AKIF HASAN
Controller of Admin.: M. KAMRAN KHAN
Controller of Examinations: NAJEEB US SAQLAIN
Librarian: MAHWISH KHAN
Number of teachers: 125

DEANS

Faculty of Engineering Sciences and Technology: KAMRAN RAZA (acting)
Faculty of Management Sciences: Dr M. A. K. CHISHTY

ISLAMIA COLLEGE, PESHAWAR

Univ. Campus, Jamrod Rd, Peshawar 25120, Khyber Pakhtunkhwa
Telephone: (91) 5850235
E-mail: registrar@icp.edu.pk
Internet: www.icp.edu.pk

Founded 1913
State control

Vice-Chancellor: AJMAL KHAN
Registrar: Dr GOHAR ZAMAN
Controller of Examinations: JAVED KHAN
Librarian: SAJJAD HUSSAIN
Library of 90,000 vols, 1,261 MSS

DEANS

Faculty of Social and Behavioural Sciences: Prof. Dr NAUSHAD KHAN

ISLAMIA UNIVERSITY OF BAHAWALPUR

Bahawalpur
Telephone: (62) 9250231
E-mail: vc@iub.edu.pk

Internet: www.iub.edu.pk
Founded 1975
State control
Languages of instruction: English, Urdu
Academic year: September to August

Chancellor: GOV. OF PUNJAB
Vice-Chancellor: Prof. Dr MUHAMMAD MUKHTAR
Registrar: MUHAMMAD ALI WALLANA
Chief Librarian: AMIR RASOOL (acting)
Library: see under Libraries and Archives
Number of teachers: 590
Number of students: 18,500

Publications: *Journal of Educational Research* (2 a year), *Journal of Social Sciences and Humanities* (2 a year), *Ulum–e–Islamia* (2 a year, in English, Persian and Urdu)

DEANS

Faculty of Arts: Prof. Dr MAMUNA GHANI
Faculty of Education: Prof. Dr ASGHAR HASHMI
Faculty of Islamic Learning: Prof. Dr SALEEM TARIQ KHAN
Faculty of Management Sciences: Prof. Dr MUHAMMAD MUKHTAR
Faculty of Pharmacy and Alternative Medicine: Prof. Dr MAHMOOD AHMED
Faculty of Science: Prof. Dr ASGHAR HASHMI

ISRA UNIVERSITY

Hala Rd, Hyderabad, Sindh
Telephone: (22) 2030181
E-mail: admissions@isra.edu.pk
Internet: www.isra.edu.pk
Founded 1997
Private control

Chancellor: Prof. Dr ASADULLAH KAZI
Vice-Chancellor: Prof. Dr GHULAMQADIR KAZI
Pro-Vice-Chancellor of Engineering and Management Studies: Dr HAMEEDULLAH KAZI
Pro-Vice-Chancellor of Health Sciences: Dr ABDUL GHANI KAZI
Pro-Vice-Chancellor of Islamabad Campus: Prof. Dr ALTAF ALI G. SHAIKH
Pro-Vice-Chancellor of Karachi Campus: Prof. Dr GHULAM HUSAIN SIDDIQI
Library of 10,000 vols
Number of students: 1,500

DEANS

Faculty of Commerce, Economics and Management Sciences: Prof. Dr MOHAMMAD IQBAL BHATTI
Faculty of Dentistry: Prof. Dr RAFIQUE AHMED MEMON
Faculty of Engineering, Science and Technology: Prof. Dr MOHAMMAD IQBAL BHATTI
Faculty of Medicine and Allied Medical Sciences: Prof. Dr NAZIR ASHRAF LAGHARI

JINNAH UNIVERSITY FOR WOMEN

5C Nazimabad, Karachi 74600, Sindh
Telephone: (21) 36620857
E-mail: info@juw.edu.pk
Internet: www.juw.edu.pk
Founded 1998
Private control
Academic year: January to November (2 semesters)

Chancellor: Prof. NOOR-US-SABAH CHUGHTAI
Vice-Chancellor: Prof. Dr NAEEM FAROOQUI
Registrar: Dr QAZI NAWAB MANZAR
Controller of Examinations: SHAHID ALI KHAN

Library of 30,000 vols
Number of teachers: 150
Number of students: 3,000

DEANS

Faculty of Arts: JAMILA KHANUM
Faculty of Pharmacy: Prof. Dr GHULAM SARWAR
Faculty of Science: Dr NEELOFAR SHAUKAT

KARACHI INSTITUTE OF ECONOMICS AND TECHNOLOGY

Korangi Creek, Karachi 75190, Sindh
Telephone: (21) 35091114
E-mail: info@pafkiet.edu.pk
Internet: www.pafkiet.edu.pk

Founded 2000
Private control

Colleges of computing and information sciences, engineering, English and communication skills, humanities and sciences, management sciences, media and arts

Chancellor: Dr MOHAMMAD IZHAR-UL-HASAN
Pres.: M. KHALID HUSAIN
Vice-Pres. and Dean of Academics: Prof. Dr SYED IRFAN HYDER
Dir of Admin.: UBAID M. ABBASI
Librarian: SYED MUHAMMAD IDREES

KARAKORAM INTERNATIONAL UNIVERSITY

University Rd, Gilgit 15100, Khyber Pakhtunkhwa
Telephone: (5811) 960440
E-mail: vcoffice@kiu.edu.pk
Internet: www.kiu.edu.pk
Founded 2002
State control

Chancellor: PRES. OF ISLAMIC REPUBLIC OF PAKISTAN
Vice-Chancellor: Prof. Dr NAJMA NAJAM
Number of teachers: 190
Number of students: 1,170

DEANS

Sciences: Prof. Dr AQUILA ISLAM
Social Sciences and Humanities: Prof. Dr SHAFIQ JULLUNDHRY

KHADIM ALI SHAH BUKHARI INSTITUTE OF TECHNOLOGY (KASBIT)

Bldg 1, 84-B S. M. C. H. S., off Shahrah-e-Faisal, Karachi 74400, Sindh
Telephone: (21) 4314970
E-mail: info@kasbit.edu.pk
Internet: www.kasbit.edu.pk
Founded 1999
Private control

Chancellor: ARIF ALI SHAH BUKHARI
Vice-Chancellor: SYED ALI ABBAS ABIDI

Publications: *Journal of Economics and Business Research* (1 a year), *KASBIT Business Journal*

DEANS

Faculty of Management Sciences: Prof. Dr MUHAMMAD MAHMUD

KHYBER MEDICAL UNIVERSITY

PDA Bldg, Block IV, Phase 5, Hayatabad, Peshawar, Khyber Pakhtunkhwa
Telephone: (91) 9217703
Internet: www.kmu.edu.pk
Founded 2006
State control
Academic year: September to June (2 semesters)

Institutes of basic medical science, health professional education, physical medicine and rehabilitation, public health and social science; postgraduate college of nursing

Vice-Chancellor: Prof. Dr MOHAMMAD HAFI-ZULLAH
Registrar: FAZAL MAHMOOD KHAN
Dir of Academics, Admissions and Quality Assurance: Prof. Dr SHAD MOHAMMAD
Controller of Examinations: Prof. Dr SHAHNAZ AKHTAR

KING EDWARD MEDICAL UNIVERSITY

Nelagumbad, Anarkali, Lahore 54000, Punjab

Telephone: (42) 9211145
E-mail: kemcol@brain.net.pk
Internet: www.kemu.edu.pk
Founded 1860, fmrly King Edward Medical College, present name and status 2005
State control

Chancellor: GOV. OF PUNJAB
First Vice-Chancellor: Prof. MUMTAZ HASAN
Vice-Chancellor and Pro-Vice-Chancellor: Prof. ASAD ASLAM KHAN

Library of 50,279 vols

DEANS

Faculty of Public Health and Preventive Medicine: Prof. Dr MAAZ AHMAD

KOHAT UNIVERSITY OF SCIENCE & TECHNOLOGY

Bannu Rd, off Jerma, Kohat 26000, Khyber Pakhtunkhwa

Telephone: (922) 554565
Internet: www.kust.edu.pk
Founded 2001
State control
Academic year: November to August (2 semesters)

Vice-Chancellor: Dr NASIR JAMAL KHATTAK
Registrar: Prof. Dr IHSAN ELLAHI
Dir for Works: ALTAF HUSSAIN
Dir for Finance: MUHAMMAD ZAFAR KHAN
Librarian: MURAD ALI

Library of 25,000 vols

DEANS

Faculty of Biological Sciences: Prof. Dr SHAFIQ UR REHMAN
Faculty of Physical Sciences: Prof. FIDA YOUNUS KHATTAK

LAHORE COLLEGE FOR WOMEN UNIVERSITY

Jail Rd, Lahore 54000, Punjab
Telephone: (42) 99201950
E-mail: registrar@lcwu.edu.pk
Internet: www.lcwu.edu.pk
Founded 1922, present name and status 2002
State control

Vice-Chancellor: Prof. Dr SABIHA MANSOOR
Registrar: RIFFAT SAQLAIN
Librarian: HINA AZIZ

Number of teachers: 510 (455 full-time, 58 part-time)
Number of students: 6,450 (5,534 full-time, 916 part-time)

DEANS

Faculty of Engineering, Technology and Management Sciences: Prof. Dr FARHAT SALEEMI
Faculty of Humanities, Islamic and Oriental Learning: NAUSHABA FAROOQ (acting)
Faculty of Natural Sciences: Prof. Dr KAUSER JAMAL CHEEMA
Faculty of Social Sciences: Prof. RIFFAT SAQLAIN

PROFESSORS

ALI, Y., Physics

CHEEMA, K. J., Environmental Sciences
CHEEMA, K. J., Zoology
GOHAR, K., Economics
MAHMOOD, A. S., Mathematics
MATEEN, B., Environmental Sciences
NAVQI, R. F., Fine Arts
NAWAZ, R., Islamic Studies

LAHORE SCHOOL OF ECONOMICS

Intersection Main Blvd, Phase VI DHA, Burki Rd, Lahore 53200, Punjab
Telephone: (42) 36560938
Internet: www.lahoreschoolofeconomics.edu.pk
Founded 1993, present status 1997
Private control

Rector: SHAHID AMJAD CHAUDHRY
Registrar: VIQAR AHMED
Controller of Examinations: ROMANA NOOR
Librarian: QAISAR SULTANA

Publication: Lahore Journal of Economics (2 a year)

DEANS

Faculty of Business Admin.: Prof. SOHAIL ZAFAR
Faculty of Economics: AZAM CHAUDHRY

LAHORE UNIVERSITY OF MANAGEMENT SCIENCES

Opposite Sector U, D. H. A., Lahore Cantt, Lahore 54792, Punjab
Telephone: (42) 5722670
E-mail: admissions@lums.edu.pk
Internet: www.lums.edu.pk
Founded 1985
Private control
Language of instruction: English
Academic year: September to June

Chancellor: PRES. OF ISLAMIC REPUBLIC OF PAKISTAN
Pro-Chancellor: SYED BABAR ALI
Vice-Chancellor: ADIL NAJAM
Pro-Vice-Chancellor: Dr AHMAD J. DURRANI
Rector: ABDUL RAZAK DAWOOD
Chief Librarian: MUHAMMAD RAMZAN

Library: see under Libraries and Archives
Number of teachers: 120
Number of students: 1,750

Publications: Asian Journal of Management Cases (2 a year), LUMS Business Recorder (1 a year), PLUMS (1 a year)

DEANS

School of Humanities, Social Sciences and Law: Dr ANJUM ALTAF
School of Science and Engineering: ASAD A. ABIDI
Suleman Dawood School of Business: ARIF NAZIR BUTT

PROFESSORS

ALI, I., Business History and Business Policy
BABRI, H. A., Computer Science
BEG, I., Mathematics
GHANI, J. A., Strategy and Marketing
HASSAN, S. Z., Management Information Systems and Management of Technology
IQBAL, M. A., Computer Science and Mathematics
KHURSHID, A., Technology and Organizational Management
MAUD, M. A., Computer Science
NASIM, A., Business–Government Relations
SARWAR, S. M., Computer Science
SIPRA, N., Finance
ZAMAN, A., Econometrics
ZAMAN, A., Mathematics

LASBELA UNIVERSITY OF AGRICULTURE, WATER AND MARINE SCIENCES

Uthal, Lasbela 90150, Balochistan
Telephone: (853) 610847
E-mail: info@luawms.edu.pk
Internet: www.luawms.edu.pk
Founded 2005
State control

Chancellor: GOV. OF BALOCHISTAN
Vice-Chancellor: Dr ABDUL HAMEED BAJOI
Registrar: SHER AHMED QAMBRANI
Dir of Student Affairs: TAIMOOR KHAN
Librarian: YAHYA HABIB

DEANS

Faculty of Agriculture: Prof. Dr ABDUL JABBAR MALIK
Faculty of Marine Sciences: Dr JAVED MUSTAQUIM
Faculty of Veterinary and Animal Sciences: Prof. Dr M. SHARIF PHULLAN
Faculty of Water Resources Management: Prof. Dr MUHAMMAD ISHAQ GHAZNAVI

LIAQUAT UNIVERSITY OF MEDICAL & HEALTH SCIENCES

Jamshoro, Sindh
Telephone: (22) 9213305
E-mail: registrar@lumhs.edu.pk
Internet: www.lumhs.edu.pk
Founded 1881, present name and status 2001
State control
Language of instruction: English
Academic year: November to November

Vice-Chancellor: Prof. Dr MASHOOR ALAM SHAH
Registrar: MUHAMMAD SALEH RAJAR
Additional Registrar: Dr MOHAMMAD ALI PIR

Library of 110,621 vols of books, 13,645 vols of periodicals
Number of teachers: 370

Publication: Journal of Liaquat University of Medical and Health Sciences (JLUMHS)

DEANS

Faculty of Basic Medical Sciences: Prof. SHAHEEN SHAH
Faculty of Community Medicine and Public Health Sciences: Prof. RAFIQUE AHMED SOOMRO
Faculty of Dentistry: Prof. RAFQUE AHMED MEMON
Faculty of Medicine and Allied Sciences: Prof. ALLAH BACHAYO MEMON
Faculty of Surgery and Allied Sciences: Prof. GHULAM ALI MEMON

MEHRAN UNIVERSITY OF ENGINEERING & TECHNOLOGY

Jamshoro, 76062 Sindh
Telephone: (22) 2772250
E-mail: vc@admin.muet.edu.pk
Internet: www.muet.edu.pk
Founded 1963 as constituent college of Univ. of Sindh, present status 1977
State control
Language of instruction: English
Academic year: October to August

Chancellor: GOV. OF SINDH
Vice-Chancellor: Prof. Dr MUHAMMAD ASLAM UQAILI
Registrar: Prof. Dr TAUHA HUSSAIN ALI
Librarian: AZAM ALI HALEPOTA

Library: see under Libraries and Archives
Number of teachers: 270
Number of students: 3,700

Publication: Research Journal of Engineering and Technology (4 a year)

DEANS

Faculty of Architecture and Civil Engineering: Prof. Dr GHOS BUX KHASKELI

Faculty of Electrical, Electronics and Computer Engineering: Prof. Dr BHAWANI SHANKAR CHOWDHRY

Faculty of Engineering: Prof. Dr HAFEEZ-U-REHMAN MEMON

Faculty of Science, Technology and Humanities: Prof. ROSHAN ALI SHAH RASHDI

MINHAJ UNIVERSITY, LAHORE

Near Hamdard Chowk, Township, Lahore, Punjab

Telephone: (42) 35145621

E-mail: info@mul.edu.pk

Internet: www.mul.edu.pk

Founded 2005

Private control

Chancellor: GOV. OF PUNJAB

Vice-Chancellor: Prof. Dr ALI MUHAMMAD

Registrar: MUHAMMAD AHMAD

Controller of Examinations: MUHAMMAD YAQUB

Librarian: SHAHID MEHMOOD

Library of 50,000 vols

DEANS

Faculty of Basic Sciences and Mathematics: Prof. Dr ALI MUHAMMAD

Faculty of Commerce and Management Sciences: Prof. Dr MUHAMMAD ASLAM GHOURI

Faculty of Computer Science and Information Technology: Prof. Dr ALI MUHAMMAD

Faculty of Islamic Studies: Prof. Dr OBED ULLAH

Faculty of Languages: Prof. Dr ZAHOOR AHMAD AZHAR

Faculty of Social Sciences: Prof. Dr SYED RAZA UL HAQ

MIRPUR UNIVERSITY OF SCIENCE & TECHNOLOGY

Allama Iqbal Rd, Mirpur 10250, Azad Jammu and Kashmir

Telephone: (5827) 961037

E-mail: info@must.edu.pk

Internet: www.must.edu.pk

Founded 1980 as Ali Ahmed Shah Univ. College of Engineering and Technology, present name and status 2008

State control

Faculties of arts, engineering, sciences; campuses in Mirpur, Bhimber

Chancellor: PRES. OF AZAD JAMMU AND KASHMIR

Vice-Chancellor: Prof. NAIB HUSSAIN CH.

Registrar: MUHAMMAD SHABIR MIRZA

Controller of Examinations: MUHAMMAD KHALID

Chief Librarian: MUHAMMAD WARIS

MOHAMMAD ALI JINNAH UNIVERSITY

Islamabad Expressway, Kahuta Rd, Zone-V, Islamabad

Telephone: (51) 2512800

E-mail: info@jinnah.edu.pk

Internet: www.jinnah.edu.pk

Founded 1998

Private control

Chancellor: MIAN AMER MAHMOOD

Pres.: Prof. Dr ABDUL WAHAB

Exec. Vice-Pres.: Prof. Dr M. MANSOOR AHMED

Registrar: G. A. NAQI SYED

Controller of Examinations: SAQIB NAVEED

Library of 90,000 vols

DEANS

Faculty of Engineering and Applied Sciences: Dr ABDUL QADIR

Faculty of Management and Social Sciences: Dr ANWAR FAZIL CHISHTI

MOHI-UD-DIN ISLAMIC UNIVERSITY, NERIAN SHARIF

Plot 2A, I-9 Markaz, Islamabad

Telephone: (51) 4859658

E-mail: miuuniversity@hotmail.com

Internet: www.miu.edu.pk

Private control

Academic year: September to March (2 semesters)

Faculties of education and social sciences, health and medical sciences, management sciences and information technology

Chancellor: ALLA-UD-DIN SIDDIQUI

Vice-Chancellor: MUHAMMAD KHURSHID

Library of 17,400 vols

NATIONAL COLLEGE OF ARTS

4 Shahrah-e-Quaid-Azam, Lahore, Punjab

Telephone: (42) 99210599

E-mail: info@nca.edu.pk

Internet: www.nca.edu.pk

Founded present name 1958, present status 1985

State control

Bachelor degrees in fine arts, design and architecture; Masters degree in interior design

Prin.: Prof. SAJJAD KAUSAR (acting)

Registrar: NADEEM HASAN KHAN

Librarian: RUBINA IMTIAZ

Publication: *Journal of Contemporary Arts and Culture*

NATIONAL COLLEGE OF BUSINESS ADMINISTRATION & ECONOMICS

40 E/I Gulberg-III, Lahore, Punjab

Telephone: (42) 35752716

E-mail: info@ncbae.edu.pk

Internet: www.ncbae.edu.pk

Founded 1994, present status 2002

Private control

Faculties of applied economics, applied mathematics, applied statistics, business admin., computer science, environmental management, fine arts

Chair.: MIAN SHAMIM HAIDER

Rector: Dr MUNIR AHMAD

NATIONAL DEFENCE UNIVERSITY

E-9, Islamabad

Telephone: (51) 9260651

E-mail: presidentndu@ndu.edu.pk

Internet: ndu.edu.pk

State control

Depts of govt and public policy, int. relations, leadership studies, peace and conflict studies, strategic and nuclear studies

Chancellor: PRES. OF ISLAMIC REPUBLIC OF PAKISTAN

Pres.: AGHA MUHAMMAD UMER FAROOQ

Registrar: Dr M. F. K. LODHI

Controller of Examinations: Dr S. Q. M. ZAIDI

Library of 70,000 vols

Publication: *NDU Journal* (2 a year)

NATIONAL TEXTILE UNIVERSITY

Sheikhupura Rd, Faisalabad 37610, Punjab

Telephone: (41) 9230099

E-mail: info@ntu.edu.pk

Internet: www.ntu.edu.pk

Founded 1959 as Institute of Textile Technology, renamed Nat. College of Textile Engineering 1976, current name and status 2002

State control

Rector: Dr NIAZ AHMAD AKHTAR

Staff Officer: JALIL UD DIN BUTT

Registrar: Prof. MUHAMMAD ASHFAQ (acting)

Librarian: MUSHTAQ AHMAD

Library of 16,000 vols, 33 journals

Number of teachers: 35

Number of students: 600

DEANS

Faculty of Engineering and Technology: Dr TANVEER HUSSAIN

Faculty of Humanities and Social Sciences: Dr MUMTAZ HASSAN MALIK

Faculty of Management Sciences: Dr MUHAMMAD ABRAR

Faculty of Sciences: Prof. TAHIR HUSSAIN

NATIONAL UNIVERSITY OF COMPUTER AND EMERGING SCIENCES

A. K. Brohi Rd, H-11/4, Islamabad

Telephone: (51) 8314100

E-mail: info@nu.edu.pk

Internet: www.nu.edu.pk

Founded 2000

Private control

Academic year: January to December (2 semesters)

Campuses in Karachi, Lahore, Peshawar

Chancellor: WASIM SAJJAD

Rector: Dr AMIR MUHAMMED

Pro-Rector: SYED REFAQAT

Dean: Dr M. AYUB ALVI

Registrar: Dr M. LATIF VIRK

Number of students: 4,000

NATIONAL UNIVERSITY OF MODERN LANGUAGES

Main Campus, Sector H–9, Islamabad 44000

Telephone: (51) 9257646

E-mail: info@numl.edu.pk

Internet: www.numl.edu.pk

Founded 1970, present name and status 2000

State control

Academic year: January to December (2 semesters)

Chancellor: PRES. OF ISLAMIC REPUBLIC OF PAKISTAN

Rector: MASOOD HASAN

Dir-Gen.: AZAM JAMAL

Dir of Academic Affairs: RIASAT HUSSAIN

Dir of Admin.: MUHAMMAD YASIN

Library Dir: MUHAMMAD ABBAS

Dir of Int. Relations: KAMRAN JAHANGIR

Dir of Student Affairs: TAJ MUHAMMAD

Registrar: SAJIDA TAHIR

Library of 115,000 vols

Number of teachers: 320

Number of students: 12,420

Publications: *Daryaft* (1 a year), *Research Magazine* (2 a year), *Takhleeqi Adab* (1 a year)

DEANS

Faculty of Advanced Integrated Studies and Research: Dr SHAZRA MUNNAWER

Faculty of Engineering and Information Technology: Dr MUHAMMAD AKBAR

Faculty of English Language, Literature and Applied Linguistics: Dr RUBINA KAMRAN

Faculty of Management Sciences: Prof. Dr RASHID AHMAD KHAN

Faculty of Near Eastern Language and Culture: Dr SYED ALI ANWAR

Quality Enhancement Cell: Dr SOHAILA JAVED

NATIONAL UNIVERSITY OF SCIENCES AND TECHNOLOGY

H–12, Islamabad
Telephone: (51) 90851001
E-mail: info@nust.edu.pk
Internet: www.nust.edu.pk
State control

Campuses in Rawalpindi, Karachi and Risalpur; colleges of aeronautical engineering (Risalpur), civil engineering (Risalpur), electrical and mechanical engineering (Rawalpindi), marine engineering (Karachi), medical sciences (Rawalpindi), telecommunication engineering (Rawalpindi)

Rector: MUHAMMAD ASGHAR
Pro-Rector for Academics: Dr ASIF RAZA
Registrar: SALIM DAUD
Dir of Admin.: NASIR HUSSAIN
Dir of Research: SALMAN ABSAR
Dir of Student Affairs: MAHMUD BASHIR BAJWA

NED UNIVERSITY OF ENGINEERING AND TECHNOLOGY

Main University Rd, Karachi 75270
Telephone: (21) 99261261
E-mail: vc@neduet.edu.pk
Internet: www.neduet.edu.pk
Founded 1922 as NED Govt Engineering College, univ. status 1977
State control
Language of instruction: English
Academic year: February to December

Chancellor: GOV. OF SINDH
Pro-Chancellor: EDUCATION MIN. OF SINDH
Vice-Chancellor: Eng. ABUL KALAM
Pro-Vice-Chancellor: Prof. Dr MUZZAFFAR MAHMOOD
Pro-Vice-Chancellor: Dr SAHIBZADA FAROOQ AHMAD RAFEEQI
Registrar: Eng. JAVED AZIZ KHAN
Chief Librarian: MEHER YASMEEN KHAN
Library: see under Libraries and Archives
Number of teachers: 460
Number of students: 8,000

Publications: NED University of Engineering and Research (2 a year), Research Journal (4 a year), Versity News (12 a year)

DEANS

Faculty of Biomedical Engineering: Prof. NEELOFUR MASTER (acting)
Faculty of Chemical and Process Engineering: Prof. Dr MUHAMMAD TUFAIL
Faculty of Civil Engineering and Architecture: Prof. Dr. SAROSH HASHMAT LODI
Faculty of Electrical and Computer Engineering: Prof. Dr MUZZAFFAR MAHMOOD
Faculty of Information Sciences and Humanities: Prof. Dr MAHMOOD KHAN PATHAN
Faculty of Mechanical and Manufacturing Engineering: Prof. Dr NAZIMUDDIN QURESHI

PROFESSORS

AHMED, N., Architecture and Planning
ALI, A., Materials Engineering
ALI, M., Urban and Infrastructure Engineering
ALI, S., Polymer and Petrochemical Engineering
ALTAF, T., Electrical Engineering
ANJUM, S., Physics
BAIG, M., Mathematics
FAROOQUI, R., Civil Engineering
HAQUE, S., Computer Science and Information Technology
HASHMI, S., Automotive and Marine Engineering
IQBAL, S., Industrial and Manufacturing Engineering
JAFRI, A., Biomedical Engineering
KHALID, A., Mechanical Engineering
KHAN, A., Civil Engineering
KHAN, R., Earthquake Engineering
KHATOON, H., Computer and Information Systems Engineering
MAHMOOD, K., Materials Engineering
MEMON, I., Chemical Engineering
MURTAZA, A., Petroleum Engineering
NAEEM, A., Architecture and Planning
PASHA, K., Textile Engineering
QADIR, A., Urban and Infrastructure Engineering
QAZI, S., Electrical Engineering
RAFI, M., Earthquake Engineering
SATTAAR, S., Computer Science and Information Technology
SHAIKH, A., Environmental Engineering
SIDDIQUI, M., Mechanical Engineering
SYED, K., Polymer and Petrochemical Engineering
TARIQ, Q., Computer and Info. Systems Engineering
WAHAB, Q., Electronic Engineering
YASMIN, F., Bio-Medical Engineering
ZAIDI, S., Electronic Engineering

NEWPORTS INSTITUTE OF COMMUNICATIONS AND ECONOMICS

159/O, Block-3, Kashmir Rd, PECHS, Karachi, Sindh
Telephone: (21) 34541067
E-mail: info@newports.edu.pk
Internet: www.newports.edu.pk
Founded 1993 as Karachi Campus of Newport Univ. of California, present status 2002
Private control

Chair.: SADIQ JAMAL
Rector: HUMA BUKHARI
Registrar: SALMAN JAMAL

DEANS

Faculty of Business and Admin.: Prof. Dr M. WASIM
Faculty of Computer Science: SAJJAD HUSSAIN MAHESRI

NORTHERN UNIVERSITY

Watter Wallai Ziarat Kaka Sahib Road, Nowshera, Khyber Pakhtunkhwa
Telephone: (923) 613485
E-mail: registrar@northern.edu.pk
Internet: www.northern.edu.pk
Founded 2002
Private control

Pres.: SAWAR KHAN
Rector: Dr ABDUL MAJEED
Registrar: MUHAMMAD ASHRAF
Controller of Examinations: ZAFAR IQBAL

DEANS

Faculty of Administrative Sciences: Prof. SALMA S. ASHRAF
Faculty of Arts and Social Sciences: Prof. Dr R. A. FAROOQ
Faculty of Engineering and Information Technology: Prof. Dr SULEMAN ASHRAF
Faculty of Sciences: Prof. Dr MUHAMMAD ULLAH

NWFP UNIVERSITY OF ENGINEERING AND TECHNOLOGY

POB 814, Univ. Campus, Peshawar 25120, Khyber Pakhtunkhwa
Telephone: (91) 9216796
E-mail: registrar@nwfpuet.edu.pk
Internet: www.nwfpuet.edu.pk
Founded 1980
State control
Language of instruction: English
Academic year: November to September

Chancellor: GOV. OF KHYBER PAKHTUNKHWA
Vice-Chancellor: SYED IMTIAZ HUSSAIN GILANI
Registrar: IMTIAZ AHMAD KHAN
Dean: Prof. AZZAM UL ASSAR
Librarian: ABDUR RASHID

Campuses at Abbottabad, Bannu and Mardan

Library of 14,000 vols
Number of teachers: 350
Number of students: 3,360

Publication: Journal of Engineering and Applied Sciences (2 a year)

PROFESSORS

AKBAR SHAH, S. R., Mechatronics Engineering
GUL JADOON, K., Mining Engineering
HUSSAIN, I., Industrial Engineering
INAYATULLAH KHAN BABAR, M., Computer Science and Information Technology (Non Engineering)
JADOON, K. G., Chemical Engineering
MAHMOOD, Z., Agricultural Engineering
NAEEM KHAN, A., Civil Engineering
TAJIK, S. J., Mechanical Engineering
UR REHMAN, S., Basic Science and Islamiat
YAHYA, K. M., Computer System Engineering
ZAHIR KHAN, M., Electrical and Electronics Engineering

PAKISTAN INSTITUTE OF DEVELOPMENT ECONOMICS

POB 1091, Islamabad 44000
Telephone: (51) 9248051
E-mail: pide@pide.org.pk
Internet: www.pide.org.pk
Founded 1957, present status 2006
State control

Chancellor: Dr NADEEM UL HAQUE
Vice-Chancellor: Dr RASHID AMJAD
Registrar: Dr ABDUL QAYYUM
Controller of Examinations: Dr MUHAMMAD IQBAL

DEANS

Dept of Business Studies: Dr ZAFAR MUEEN NASIR
Dept of Economics: Dr EJAZ GHANI
Faculty of Devt Studies: Dr MUNIR AHMAD

PIMSAT UNIVERSITY

177/2, IEP Bldg, Shahrah-e-Faisal, Karachi, Sindh
Telephone: (21) 2789888
E-mail: info@pimsat-khi.edu.pk
Internet: www.pimsat-khi.edu.pk
Private control

Chair. and Rector: MUNAWAR AHMAD
Exec. Dir and Registrar: ASIM N. AHMAD
Controller of Examinations: SYED MASOOD RAZA
Librarian: SAADIA TAYYABA

DEANS

Dept of Applied Technologies: Dr S. N. IQBAL
Dept of Management of Science: Dr Z. A. KHAN

PIR MEHR ALI SHAH ARID AGRICULTURE RAWALPINDI

Shamsabad, Muree Rd, Rawalpindi
Telephone: (51) 9290466
E-mail: registrar@uaar.edu.pk
Internet: www.uaar.edu.pk
Founded 1979; present name and status 1994
State control

Vice-Chancellor: Prof. Dr KHALID MEHMOOD KHAN
Registrar: MALIK MAQBOOL HUSSAIN AWAN
Controller of Examinations: MUHAMMAD NISAR

Librarian: ZAMMURAD AHMAD IQBAL

DEANS

Faculty of Crop and Food Sciences: Dr ABDUL KHALIQ

Faculty of Forestry Range Management and Wildlife: Prof. Dr SARWAT NAZ MIRZA

Faculty of Sciences: Dr AZRA KHANUM

Faculty of Veterinary and Animal Sciences: Prof. Dr NEMAT ULLAH

PRESTON UNIVERSITY

15 Banglore Town, Shahrah-e-Faisal, Karachi, Sindh

Telephone: (21) 4534663

E-mail: karachi@preston.edu.pk

Internet: www.preston.edu.pk

Founded 1984 as School of Business and Commerce, present status 2004

Private control

Academic year: September to August (3 semesters)

Campuses at Faisalabad, Islamabad, Kohat, Lahore, Peshawar

Chancellor: Dr ABDUL BASIT

Pro-Chancellor: SYED DEEDAR HUSSAIN SHAH

Vice-Chancellor: Dr NAZIR A. MUGHAL

Library of 8,000 vols

Number of teachers: 50

DEANS

Faculty of Business Administration: Dr IBRAHIM SHAH BUKHARI

Faculty of Education: Dr FATIMA RAZI

Faculty of Engineering and Technology: Prof. Dr ABDUL RAZZAQUE MEMON

Faculty of Social Sciences: Dr IBRAHIM SHAH BUKHARI

QUAID-E-AWAM UNIVERSITY OF ENGINEERING, SCIENCE AND TECHNOLOGY

Nawabshah 67480, Sindh

Telephone: (244) 9370387

E-mail: info@quest.edu.pk

Internet: www.quest.edu.pk

Founded 1963 as constituent college of Univ. of Sindh, present name and status 1996

State control

Language of instruction: English

Academic year: January to December

Vice-Chancellor: Prof. Dr ALI BUX SOOMRO

Pro-Vice-Chancellor: Prof. Dr SALEEM RAZA SAMO

Registrar: SOHAIL MUSHTAQUE SOOMRO

Controller of Examinations: NAZIR AHMED DURRANI

Dir for Library: GHULAM FAROOQUE CHANNAR

Library of 52,000 vols and 45,000 ebooks

Number of teachers: 170

Number of students: 2,750

Publication: *Quaid-e-Awam University Research Journal of Engineering, Science and Technology* (2 a year)

DEANS

Faculty of Electrical, Electronics and Computer Engineering: Prof. Dr MUHAMMAD USMAN KEERIO

Faculty of Engineering: Prof. Dr BASHIR AHMED MEMON

Faculty of Technology: Prof. Dr NOOR AHMED MEMON

QUAID-I-AZAM UNIVERSITY

Islamabad 45320

Telephone: (51) 90644050

E-mail: vco@qau.edu.pk

Internet: www.qau.edu.pk

Founded 1967 as Univ. of Islamabad, current name adopted 1976

State control

Language of instruction: English

Chancellor: PRES. OF ISLAMIC REPUBLIC OF PAKISTAN

Vice-Chancellor: Prof. Dr MASOOM YASINZAI

Registrar: Dr SHAFEEQ UR REHMAN

Controller of Examination: MUHAMMAD AQEEL GILLANI

Librarian: MEHBOOB HUSSAIN KHAN

Library: see under Libraries and Archives

Number of teachers: 200

Number of students: 4,000

Publications: *Journal of Science* (2 a year), *Journal of Social Science, Scrutiny* (2 a year)

DEANS

Faculty of Biological Sciences: Dr ABDUL HAMEED

Faculty of Medicine: Dr SYED FAZLE HADI

Faculty of Natural Sciences: Dr QAISER MUSHTAQ

Faculty of Social Sciences: Dr EATZAZ AHMED

ATTACHED INSTITUTES

Area Study Centre for Africa, North & South America: Quaid-i-Azam Univ. Campus, Islamabad 45320; tel. (51) 2896006; e-mail ascqau@yahoo.com; attached to Quaid-i-Azam Univ.; conducts research in fields of American, Latin American, Canadian and African Studies; library of 30,000 vols; Dir Prof. RUKHSANA QAMBER; publ. *Pakistan Journal of American Studies* (2 a year).

National Institute of Pakistan Studies: c/o Quaid-i-Azam Univ., Islamabad 45320; tel. (51) 90644010; e-mail trahman@nips.qau .edu.pk; internet www.qau.edu.pk/nips; f. 1983; attached to Quaid-i-Azam Univ.; Dir Prof. Dr TARIQ RAHMAN.

National Institute of Psychology: c/o Quaid-i-Azam Univ., Shahdra Rd, Islamabad; tel. (51) 90644031; e-mail nip@nip.edu .pk; internet www.nip.edu.pk; f. 1976; attached to Quaid-i-Azam Univ.; research in psychology; library of 9,500 vols; Dir Prof. Dr ANILA KAMAL; publ. *Pakistan Journal of Psychological Research* (2 a year)

QURTUBA UNIVERSITY OF SCIENCE AND INFORMATION TECHNOLOGY

K-1, Phase III, Hayatabad, Peshawar, Khyber Pakhtunkhwa

Telephone: (91) 5812117

E-mail: query@qurtuba.edu.pk

Internet: www.qurtuba.edu.pk

Founded 2001

Private control

Depts of botany, education, English, management sciences and information technology, pharmacy, political science and int. relations, Urdu; campus at Dera Ismail Khan

Pres.: Dr MUHAMMAD ZULFIQAR KHAN NIAZI

Vice-Chancellor: Prof. Dr HAMEEDULLAH KHAN ALIZAI

Registrar: SHER BAHADUR

Publications: *Journal of Managerial Sciences* (2 a year), *The Dialogue* (4 a year)

RIPHAH INTERNATIONAL UNIVERSITY

Sector I-14, Hajj Complex, Peshawar Rd, Islamabad

Telephone: (51) 8446000

E-mail: admissions@riphah.edu.pk

Internet: www.riphah.edu.pk

Founded 2002

Private control

Chancellor: MUHAMMAD ZULFIQAR KHAN

Pro-Chancellor: M. HASSAN KHAN

Vice-Chancellor: Prof. Dr ANIS AHMAD

Library of 80,000 vols, 20,000 journals

DEANS

Faculty of Computing: SAAD NAEEM ZAFAR

Faculty of Engineering and Applied Sciences: Prof. Dr MIRZA MUHAMMAD JAVED

Faculty of Management Sciences: Prof. M. AMANULLAH KHAN

Faculty of Pharmaceutical Sciences: Dr INAMUL HAQ

SARDAR BAHADUR KHAN WOMEN'S UNIVERSITY

Brewery Rd, Quetta, Balochistan

Telephone: (81) 9213304

E-mail: vc_secretariat@sbkwu.edu.pk

Internet: www.sbkwu.edu.pk

Founded 2004

State control

Faculties of management and computer sciences, natural sciences, social sciences

Chancellor: GOV. OF BALOCHISTAN

Vice-Chancellor: SULTANA BALOCH

Registrar: Prof. JAMILA QAZI

Number of students: 3,000

SARHAD UNIVERSITY OF SCIENCE & INFORMATION TECHNOLOGY

Landi Akhun Ahmad, Ring Rd (Hayatabad Link), Peshawar, Khyber Pakhtunkhwa

Telephone: (91) 5230931

E-mail: vc@suit.edu.pk

Internet: suit.edu.pk

Founded 2001, present status 2008

Private control

Language of instruction: English

Academic year: September to August

Vice-Chancellor: Prof. Dr SALIM-UR-REHMAN

Registrar: MUHAMMAD NASIR

Controller of Examinations: SALMAN FAIZ

Dir for Distance Education: MASOOD AHMAD KHAN

Library of 30,000 vols

Number of teachers: 250

Number of students: 5,000

DEANS

Faculty of Arts, Social Sciences and Education: Prof. Dr WAHEED A. MUGHAL

Faculty of Engineering: Prof. GHULAM RUHULLAH

Faculty of Life Sciences: Prof. Dr KAMRAN AHMAD CHISTI

Faculty of Management Sciences: Prof. Dr GHIAS UL HAQ SAHIBZADA

Faculty of Sciences, Computer Science and Information Tecnology: Prof. Dr NAZIR SHAH KHATTAK

SHAH ABDUL LATIF UNIVERSITY

Khairpur, Sindh

Telephone: (243) 9280051

E-mail: info@salu.edu.pk

Internet: www.salu.edu.pk

Founded 1975, present status 1987

State control

Languages of instruction: English, Sindhi, Urdu

Academic year: September to June

Chancellor: GOV. OF SINDH

Vice-Chancellor: Prof. Dr NILOFER SHAIKH

Pro-Vice-Chancellor: Prof. Dr ABDULLAH PHULPOTO

Registrar: Prof. SYED AHMED HUSSAIN SHAH

Librarian: MUHAMMAD SALEH BHATTI

Library of 40,311 vols

Number of teachers: 190

Number of students: 5,000

Publications: *Aashikar* (1 a year, in Sindhi, research), *Almas* (online), *Ancient Sindh* (1 a year, research), *Bhittai* (1 a year, in Sindhi, research), *ELF Annual Research Journal* (in English), *Indus Journal of Mathematical Sciences*, *International Journal of Chemical & Biological Science*, *Scientific Sindh* (1 a year, research), *The Commerce and Economic Review* (1 a year, research), *The Diplomat* (2 a year)

DEANS

Faculty of Arts and Social Sciences: Prof. SYED AHMED HUSSAIN SHAH
Faculty of Commerce and Business Admin.: Prof. SHAH MUHAMMAD LUHRANI
Faculty of Law: Prof. QALANDAR BUX PHULPOTO
Faculty of Natural Sciences: Prof. MIANDAD ZARDARI

SHAHEED BENAZIR BHUTTO UNIVERSITY

Sheringal, Dir (Upper), Khyber Pakhtunkhwa
Telephone: (944) 885529
Internet: www.sbbu.edu.pk
Founded 2009
State control

Vice-Chancellor: Prof. Dr JEHANDAR SHAH
Registrar: BADSHAH HUSSAIN
Controller of Examinations: MUHAMMAD ROZ KHAN

Depts of botany, biotechnology, computer science, English, environmental science, forestry, management studies, pharmacy, sociology, zoology

SHAHEED MOHTARMA BENAZIR BHUTTO MEDICAL UNIVERSITY

Larkana, Sindh
Telephone: (74) 9410724
E-mail: info@smbbmu.edu.pk
Internet: www.smbbmu.edu.pk
Founded 2009
State control

Vice-Chancellor: Prof. AKBAR HAIDER SOOMRO
Registrar: Prof. AMANULLAH JOKHIO
Controller of Examinations: Prof. SAIFULLAH JAMRO

Publication: *Journal of SMBBMU*

DEANS

Faculty of Basic Medical Sciences: Prof. MUHAMMAD ASHRAF MEMON
Faculty of Medicine and Allied Sciences: Prof. ABRAR SHAIKH
Faculty of Surgery and Allied Sciences: Prof. SYED IMTIAZ ALI SHAH

SHAHEED ZULFIKAR ALI BHUTTO INSTITUTE OF SCIENCE AND TECHNOLOGY

90 and 100 Clifton, Karachi 75600, Sindh
E-mail: info@szabist.edu.pk
Internet: www.szabist.edu.pk
Founded 1995
Private control

Pres.: Dr SAQIB RIZAVI
Vice-Pres. for Academics: Dr AMANAT ALI JALBANI
Controller of Examinations: ALIYA SALEEM
Dir of Admin.: SHAFQAT MUHAMMEDALLY
Librarian: MUHAMMAD ARIF

Campuses at Hyderabad, Islamabad, Larkana, Dubai
Number of students: 2,200

Publication: *Journal of Independent Studies and Research*

DEANS

Faculty of Management Sciences: Prof. Dr AMANAT ALI JALBANI
Faculty of Social and Media Sciences: Dr FOUZIA NAEEM KHAN

SINDH AGRICULTURE UNIVERSITY, TANDOJAM

Tandojam Dist., Hyderabad, Sindh
Telephone: (22) 2765870
E-mail: info@sau.edu.pk
Internet: www.sau.edu.pk
Founded 1977
State control
Language of instruction: English
Academic year: October to March

Chancellor: GOV. OF SINDH
Vice-Chancellor: Dr A. Q. MUGHAL
Registrar: HAFIZULLAH MEMON
Controller of Examinations: AHMED KHAN NAGRAJ
Librarian: ABDUL LATIF ANSARI

Library of 75,000 vols, 10,500 foreign journals, 6,500 Pakistani journals
Number of teachers: 220
Number of students: 3,930

Publications: *Pakistan Journal of Agriculture, Agricultural Engineering and Veterinary Sciences* (2 a year, in English), *SARANG Magazine* (1 a year, in English, Sindhi and Urdu), *SAUNI News* (4 a year, in English, Sindhi and Urdu), *Seerat Supplement* (1 a year, in English, Sindhi and Urdu), *Zarat Sindh* (4 a year)

DEANS

Faculty of Agricultural Engineering: Prof. Dr MUHAMMAD SAFFAR
Faculty of Agricultural Social Science: KHALID AHMED MAHAR
Faculty of Animal Husbandry and Veterinary Sciences: Dr AMIR BUX KALHORO
Faculty of Crop Production: Prof. Dr SHAMSUDDIN TUNIO
Faculty of Crop Protection: Dr MAQSOOD ANWAR RUSTAMANI

PROFESSORS

ABRO, G. H., Entomology
ABRO, H. K., Plant Breeding and Genetics
ANSARI, N. N., Poultry Husbandry
ARAIN, M. H., Plant Pathology
BALOCH, A. F., Horticulture
BALOCH, G. M., Animal Nutrition
BHUTTO, H. B., Irrigation and Drainage
BURIRO, U. A., Agronomy
CHANDIO, B. A., Land and Water Management
CHANG, M. A., Plant Breeding and Genetics
CHANNA, A. N., Plant Physiology and Biochemistry
DEHO, N. A., Horticulture
DEVERAJANI, B. T., Land and Water Management
JAKHARO, A. A., Soil Science
KADRI, A. A., English
KALHORO, A. B., Surgery and Obstetrics
KHAN, M. M., Entomology
KUMBAHAR, M. I., Animal Breeding and Genetics
KUMBHAR, M. B., Plant Breeding and Genetics
LARIK, A. S., Plant Breeding and Genetics
LEGHARI, N. H., Farm Power and Machinery
LOHAR, M. K., Entomology
MAHAR, S., Farm Power and Machinery
MEMON, K. S., Soil Science
MEMON, M. A., Animal Physiology and Biochemistry
MEMON, N. A., Land and Water Management
MEMON, R. A., Agricultural Education Extension and Short Courses
MIRBAHAR, K. B., Animal Reproduction

MIRBAHAR, R. B., Plant Physiology and Biochemistry
MIRJAT, M. S., Irrigation and Drainage
MUGHAL, A. Q., Farm Power and Machinery
NENWANI, K. L., Soil Science
NIZAMANI, S. M., Plant Protection
PARDEHI, M., Anatomy and Histology
PATHAN, M. A., Plant Pathology
PHULLAN, M. S., Parasitology
PHULPOTO, P. B., Agricultural Economics
PUNO, H. K., Soil Science
QAYYUN KHAN, S. M., Agronomy
RAHU, G. M., Entomology
RAJPER, M. M., Biotechnology
RIZVI, N.-ul-H., Entomology
SAIF, M. S., Soil Science
SHAH, A. J., Plant Breeding and Genetics
SHAIKH, B. A., Animal Physiology and Biochemistry
SIDDIQUI, L. A., Veterinary Microbiology
SIYAL, N. B., Soil Science
SOOMRO, A. L., Soil Science
SOOMRO, M. S., Energy and Environment
TNIO, K., Agronomy
WAGGAN, M. R., Soil Science

SIR SYED UNIVERSITY OF ENGINEERING & TECHNOLOGY

University Rd, Karachi 75300, Sindh
Telephone: (21) 34988000
E-mail: registrar@sssuet.edu.pk
Internet: www.ssuet.edu.pk
Founded 1993
Private control

Chancellor: Z. A. NIZAMI
Vice-Chancellor: Prof. Dr SAIYID NAZIR AHMAD
Registrar: SHAH MAHMOOD H. SYED
Librarian: MAQSOOD ALAM SIDDIQUI

Library of 56,000 vols
Number of teachers: 210
Number of students: 4,500

DEANS

Faculty of Basic and Applied Sciences: Prof. Dr S. JAWAID HASAN RIZVI
Faculty of Engineering: Prof. Dr S. M. MAKHDUMI

SUKKUR INSTITUTE OF BUSINESS ADMINISTRATION

Air Port Rd, Sukkur, Sindh
Telephone: (71) 5630272
E-mail: info@iba-suk.edu.pk
Internet: www.iba-suk.edu.pk
Founded 1994
State control

Faculties of computer science, engineering, management science

Chancellor: GOV. OF SINDH
Dir: Dr NISAR AHMED SIDDIQUI
Registrar: ZAHID HUSSAIN KHAND
Controller of Examinations: IMRAN KHAN
Librarian: IMDAD HUSSAIN ABRO

Library of 15,000 vols

SUPERIOR GROUP OF COLLEGES

Main Raiwind Rd,
Telephone: (42) 35330361
E-mail: admissions@superior.edu.pk
Internet: www.superior.edu.pk
Founded 2004
Private control

Faculties of business and management sciences, economics and commerce, engineering and technology, information technology and computer sciences, law, medical and health sciences, pharmacy

Chair. and Rector: Prof. Dr CH. ABDUL REHMAN

Pro-Rector for Academics: Prof. Dr ZAFAR IQBAL

Pro-Rector for Research: Prof. Dr SIKANDAR KHAN

Registrar: PIRZADA SAMI ULLAH SABRI

Controller of Examinations: ASIM MASOOD

Librarian: MUHAMMAD RAFIQ KHAN

Library of 18,000 vols

TEXTILE INSTITUTE OF PAKISTAN

EZ/1/P-8, Eastern Zone, Bin Qasim, Karachi, Sindh

Telephone: (21) 38109641

E-mail: info@tip.edu.pk

Internet: www.tip.edu.pk

Founded 1994, present status 2001

Private control

Undergraduate degree courses in business, design, science; programmes incl. textile science, textile design technology, textile management and marketing, textile technology

Chancellor: ARIF HASAN

Pres.: Dr ANBAHAN ARIADURAI

Library of 20,000 vols

UNIVERSITY OF AGRICULTURE

Peshawar, Khyber-Pakhtunkhwa

Telephone: (91) 9216518

E-mail: registraraup@yahoo.com

Internet: www.aup.edu.pk

Founded 1981

State control

Language of instruction: English

Academic year: January to December

Chancellor: GOV. OF KHYBER PAKHTUNKHWA

Vice-Chancellor: Prof. Dr KHAN BAHADAR MARWAT

Registrar: Dr MOHAMMAD ZULFIQAR

Librarian: ATTAULLAH

Library of 113,600 vols

Number of teachers: 200 full-time, 77 part-time

Number of students: 8,000

Publications: *Journal of Development Studies* (irregular), *Pakistan Journal of Weed Science Research* (4 a year), *Sarhad Journal of Agriculture* (4 a year)

DEANS

Faculty of Animal Husbandry and Veterinary Sciences: Prof. Dr M. SUBHAN QURESHI

Faculty of Crop Production Sciences: Prof. Dr ZAHOOR A. SWATI

Faculty of Crop Protection Sciences: Prof. Dr MIAN INAYATULLAH

Faculty of Nutrition Sciences: Prof. Dr ALAM ZEB

Faculty of Rural Social Sciences: ZAHID HUSSAIN

UNIVERSITY OF AGRICULTURE, FAISALABAD

Faisalabad

Telephone: (41) 9200161

E-mail: vc@uaf.edu.pk

Internet: www.uaf.edu.pk

Founded 1909 as Punjab Agricultural College, current name adopted 1973

State control

Language of instruction: English

Academic year: October to September

Chancellor: GOV. OF PUNJAB

Vice-Chancellor: Prof. Dr IQRAR AHMAD KHAN

Registrar: CH. MUHAMMAD HUSSAIN

Controller of Examinations: Prof. Dr TANWIR AHMAD MALIK

Librarian: Prof. Dr ASGHAR ALI

Library: see under Libraries and Archives

Number of teachers: 600

Number of students: 11,750

Publications: *Journal of Agricultural Sciences* (4 a year), *Journal of Veterinary Science, Pakistan Entomologist, Research Studies*

DEANS

Faculty of Agricultural Economics and Rural Sociology: Prof. Dr MUHAMMAD IQBAL ZAFAR

Faculty of Agricultural Engineering and Technology: Prof. Dr RAI NIAZ AHMAD

Faculty of Agriculture: Prof. Dr MUHAMMAD ASHFAQ

Faculty of Animal Husbandry: Prof. Dr MUHAMMAD SARWAR

Faculty of Sciences: Prof. Dr MUHAMMAD ASHRAF

Faculty of Veterinary Science: Prof. Dr LAEEQ AKBAR LODHI

PROFESSORS

Division of Education and Extension (tel. (41) 9200186):

Department of Rural Home Economics:

ALMAS, K.

Faculty of Agricultural Economics and Rural Sociology (tel. (41) 9200196):

Department of Agricultural Economics:

HUSSAIN, Z.

Faculty of Agricultural Engineering and Technology (tel. (41) 9200194; e-mail mssabir_uaf@yahoo.com):

Department of Farm Machinery and Power:

SABIR, M. S.

Department of Food Technology:

ANJUM, F. M.

Department of Irrigation and Drainage:

CHAUDHRY, M. R.

Department of Structural and Environmental Engineering:

ALI, M. A.

SIAL, J. K.

Faculty of Agriculture (tel. (41) 9200193; e-mail deanagri@fsd.paknet.com.pk):

Department of Agricultural Entomology:

RANA, M. A.

Department of Agronomy:

AKHTAR, M.

ALI, A.

ATTA, Z.

HUSSAIN, A.

MALIK, M. A.

Department of Horticulture:

IBRAHIM, M.

KHAN, I. A.

KHAN, M. A.

Department of Plant Breeding and Genetics:

AZHAR, F. M.

ASLAM, M.

KHAN, I. A.

MEHDI, S.

SALEEM, A.

SALEEM, M.

Department of Plant Pathology:

CHOHAN, R. A.

KHAN, S. M.

Department of Soil Science:

ARSHAD, M.

GHAFOOR, A.

GILL, M. A.

HASSAN, A. U.

RANJHA, A. M.

Faculty of Animal Husbandry (tel. (41) 9200195):

Department of Animal Nutrition:

SARWAR, M.

Department of Livestock Management:

GONDAL, K. Z.

YOUNAS, M.

Department of Poultry Husbandry:

HAQ, A.

Faculty of Sciences (tel. (41) 9200197):

Department of Botany:

ASHRAF, M.

Department of Chemistry:

NAWAZ, R.

SHEIKH, M. A.

Department of Mathematics and Statistics:

KHAN, M. I.

Department of Physics:

CHAUDHRY, M. A.

Department of Zoology and Fisheries:

QURESHI, J. I.

Faculty of Veterinary Science (tel. (41) 9200725; e-mail drmsakhter@hotmail.com):

Department of Animal Reproduction:

LODHI, L. A.

SAMAD, H. A.

Department of Physiology and Pharmacology:

AKHTAR, M. S.

NAWAZ, M.

Department of Veterinary Microbiology:

SIDDIQU, M.

Department of Veterinary Pathology:

ANJUM, A. D.

UNIVERSITY OF AZAD JAMMU AND KASHMIR

City Campus, CMH Rd, Muzaffarabad 13100

Telephone: (5822) 960418

E-mail: registrar@ajku.edu.pk

Internet: www.ajku.edu.pk

Founded 1980

State control

Languages of instruction: English, Urdu

Academic year: September to October

Vice-Chancellor: Prof. Dr HABIB-UR-REHMAN

Registrar: Prof. Dr MUHAMMAD QAYYUM KHAN

Controller of Examinations: Prof. Dr MUHAMMAD RUSTAM KHAN

Chief Librarian: SARDAR MUHAMMAD SALEEM

Library: see under Libraries and Archives

Number of teachers: 260

Number of students: 1,800

Publications: *Al-Muhaqqiq* (1 a year), *Kashmir Economics Review* (1 a year), *Kashmir Journal of Geology* (1 a year), *Kashmir Journal of Language Research* (1 a year), *Kashmir Research Journal of Natural Sciences* (1 a year)

DEANS

Muzaffarabad Campus (Main Campus):

Faculty of Arts: Prof. Dr RAJA NASIM AKHTAR

Faculty of Sciences: Prof. Dr MUHAMMAD HALEEM KHAN

Kotli Campus:

Faculty of Admin. Sciences: Prof. Dr MUSHTAQ AHMED MALIK

Mirpur Campus:

Faculty of Engineering and Technology: Prof. CH. NAIB HUSSAIN

Faculty of Home Economics: RAFIA KHANAM

Rawalakot Campus:

Faculty of Agriculture: Dr DILNAWAZ AHMED GARDAZI

UNIVERSITY OF BALOCHISTAN

Sariab Rd, Quetta

Telephone: (81) 9211008

E-mail: netadmin@uob.edu.pk
Internet: www.uob.edu.pk

Founded 1970
State control
Languages of instruction: English, Urdu
Academic year: March to December

Chancellor: MUHAMMAD KHAN ACHAKZAI
Vice-Chancellor: Prof. Dr JAVEID IQBAL
Pro-Vice-Chancellor: Prof. Dr MEHRAB KHAN
  BALOCH
Registrar: TARIQ JOGEZAI
Librarian: ABDUL JALIL KHAN BAZAI

Number of teachers: 300
Number of students: 6,000

Publications: *Balochistan Review*, *Takatoo*

DEANS

Faculty of Basic Sciences: Prof. Dr SYED
  MOSHIN RAZA
Faculty of Earth and Environmental Sci-
  ences: Prof. Dr AKHTAR M. KASI
Faculty of Life Science: Prof. Dr RASOOL
  BAKHSH TAREEN
Faculty of Literature and Languages: Prof.
  Dr HAMEED SHAHWANI
Faculty of Management Science and Infor-
  mation Technology: ABDUL LATIF DURANI
Faculty of Pharmacy: Prof. Dr JAVEID IQBAL
Faculty of Social Sciences: Prof. Dr ABDUL
  MALIK

UNIVERSITY OF CENTRAL PUNJAB

1 Khayaban-e-Jinnah Rd, Johar Town,
  Lahore, Punjab
Telephone: (42) 35880007
E-mail: info@ucp.edu.pk
Internet: www.ucp.edu.pk

Founded 1999, present status 2002
Private control

Chair.: MIAN AMER MAHMOOD
Pro-Rector: Prof. Dr MUHAMMAD ZAFARULLAH

Library of 20,000 vols
Number of students: 8,000

DEANS

Faculty of Arts and Social Sciences: Dr
  KHALID ZAHEER
Faculty of Commerce: MUHAMMAD AZHAR
  IKRAM AHMAD
Faculty of Engineering: Dr TABREZ A. SHAMI
Faculty of Information Technology: Dr ABDUL
  AZIZ
Faculty of Law: Dr HADIA AWAN
Faculty of Pharmacy: Dr MUHAMMAD JAM-
  SHAID

UNIVERSITY OF EAST

Latifabad, Hyderabad, Sindh
Telephone: (22) 3868612
E-mail: info@uoe.edu.pk
Internet: www.uoe.edu.pk

Founded 1999
Private control
Academic year: July to August (3 semesters)

Depts of business administration, civil technology, computer science and information
technology, education, electrical technology,
mechanical technology, Urdu

Chancellor: Dr KHALIDA MANDHRO
Pres.: ZAFAR UL ISLAM
Vice-Chancellor: Prof. ABDUL QADEER
Registrar: Prof. Dr M. A. CHANG
Controller of Examinations: MIR MUHAMMAD

Library of 10,000 vols

UNIVERSITY OF EDUCATION

Township Campus, College Rd, Township,
  Lahore 5400, Punjab
Telephone: (42) 5216530

E-mail: registrar@ue.edu.pk
Internet: www.ue.edu.pk

Founded 2002
State control

3 Campuses in Lahore; further campuses in
Attock, Faisalabad, Jauharabad, Multan,
Okara and Vehari; 33 affiliated colleges

Vice-Chancellor: Prof. Dr FAIZ-UL-HASAN
Registrar: MUHAMMAD SAEED AKHTAR (acting)
Librarian: NAEEM SARWAR

Publication: *Journal of Research and Reflections in Education* (2 a year)

UNIVERSITY OF ENGINEERING AND TECHNOLOGY, LAHORE

Grand Trunk Rd, Lahore 54890, Punjab
Telephone: (42) 99029227
E-mail: registrar@uet.edu.pk
Internet: www.uet.edu.pk

Founded 1921 as Mughalpura Technical
  College
State control
Language of instruction: English
Academic year: January to December

Chancellor: GOV. OF PUNJAB
Pro-Chancellor: MIN. OF EDUCATION
Vice-Chancellor: Lt-Gen. (retd) MUHAMMAD
  AKRAM KHAN
Registrar: Lt-Col (retd) ABDUL RAUF
Controller of Examinations: M. ASIF
Librarian: MANZOOR AHMAD KHAN ANJUM

Library: see under Libraries and Archives
Number of teachers: 900
Number of students: 9,690

Publications: *ECHO* (1 a year), *Varsity News*
  (26 a year)

DEANS

Faculty of Architecture and Planning: Prof.
  Dr EHSAN ULLAH BAJWA
Faculty of Chemical, Mineral And Material
  Science: Prof. Dr A. R. SALEEMI
Faculty of Civil Engineering: Prof. Dr ABDUL
  SATTAR SHAKIR
Faculty of Electrical Engineering: Prof. Dr
  ZUBAIR KHAN
Faculty of Mechanical Engineering: Prof. Dr
  SALIM ABID TABASSUM
Faculty of Natural Sciences, Humanities and
  Islamic Studies: Prof. Dr FAZEELAT TAHIRA

PROFESSORS

Department of Architecture (tel. (42)
99029223; e-mail sakbar@gmail.com):

  AKBAR, S.
  AWAN, M. Y.
  GELANI, I. A. S.
  HUSSAIN, M.
  MALIK, R. A.
  REHMAN, A.

Department of Chemical Engineering (tel.
(42) 99029488; e-mail pd_govsect@yahoo
.com):

  AHMAD, M. M.
  KHAN, J. R.
  MAMOOR, G. M.
  NAVEED, S.
  SALARYA, A. K.
  SALEEMI, A. R.

Department of Chemistry (tel. (42) 99029200;
e-mail saeed_a786@hotmail.com):

  AMJAD, M.
  HAQ, I. U.
  TAHIRA, F.

Department of City and Regional Planning
(tel. (42) 99029203):

  ANJUM, G. A.
  BAJWA, E. U.
  ISLAM, Q. U.
  MALIK, T. H.
  ZAIDI, S.-UL-H.

Department of Civil Engineering (tel. (42)
99029202; e-mail ilyas@uet.edu.pk):

  ASHRAF, M.
  CHAUDHRY, M. Y.
  CHISHTY, F. A.
  ILYAS, M.
  MIAN, Z.
  RIZWAN, S. A.
  SHAKIR, A. S.
  SHEIKH, A. S.
  TAHIR, M. A.

Department of Computer Science and Engineering (tel. (42) 99029260; e-mail mamaud@
uet.edu.pk):

  ASIM, M. R.
  MALIK, A. A.

Department of Electrical Engineering (tel.
(42) 99029229; e-mail mna@uet.edu.pk):

  BUKHARI, S. H.
  CHUGHTAI, M. A.
  KHAN, Z. A.
  QURESHI, S. A.
  SALEEM, M. M.
  SHAH, A. H.
  SHAMI, T. A.
  SHEIKH, N. M.

Department of Humanities and Social Sciences (tel. (42) 99029493; e-mail
chairmanhmss@uet.edu.pk):

  ZAIDI, M. H.

Department of Islamic Studies (tel. (42)
99029246; e-mail misraeel@yahoo.com):

  YAHYA, M. A.

Department of Mathematics (tel. (42)
99029210; e-mail ffffz_khan@hotmail.com):

  AHMAD, M. O.
  CH., N. M.
  SHAH, N. A.

Department of Mechanical Engineering (tel.
(42) 99029467; e-mail chairmanmech@uet
.edu.pk):

  ALI, S.
  CHAUDHRY, I. A.
  HUSSAIN, I.
  KHAN, M. I.
  MIRZA, M. R.
  PIRACHA, J. L.
  QURESHI, A. H.
  SHAH, F. H.
  TABASSUM, S. A.

Department of Metallurgical and Materials
Engineering (tel. (42) 99029207; e-mail
mohammad_ajmal@hotmail.com):

  AJMAL, M.
  HASSAN, F.
  IQBAL, J.
  ZAIDI, S. Q. H.

Department of Mining and Geological Engineering (tel. (42) 99029212; e-mail akram@uet
.edu.pk):

  AKRAM, M.
  CHATTAH, N. H.
  HUSSAIN, S. A.
  KIRMANI, F. A.
  RANA, M. T.

Department of Petroleum and Gas Engineering (tel. (42) 99029471; e-mail
chairmanpetroleum@uet.edu.pk):

  KHAN, A. S.

Department of Physics (tel. (42) 99029204;
e-mail chairmanphy@uet.edu.pk):

  REHMAN, M. K. (Chair)

Institute of Environmental Engineering and
Research (tel. (42) 99029248; e-mail
ajbari57@hotmail.com):

  AHMAD, K.
  ALI, W.
  AZIZ, J. A.
  BARI, A. J.
  HYAT, S.

ZIAI, K. H.

UNIVERSITY OF ENGINEERING AND TECHNOLOGY, TAXILA

Taxila 47050, Punjab
Telephone: (596) 9314216
E-mail: registrar@uettaxila.edu.pk
Internet: web.uettaxila.edu.pk/uet
State control

Vice-Chancellor: Prof. Dr MUHAMMAD ABBAS CHOUDHARY
Registrar: AZIZ UR REHMAN
Controller of Examinations: MAHMOOD AKHTAR
Librarian: MUHAMMAD ANWAAR
Library of 25,000 vols
Publication: *Taxila Engineering Journal*

DEANS

Faculty of Basic Sciences and Humanities: Prof. Dr MUMTAZ AHMAD KAMAL
Faculty of Civil and Environmental Engineering: Prof. Dr MUMTAZ AHMAD
Faculty of Electronics and Electrical Engineering: Prof. Dr AHMAD KHALIL KHAN
Faculty of Industrial Engineering and Management Sciences: Prof. Dr SHAHAB KHUSHNOOD
Faculty of Mechanical and Aeronautical Engineering: Prof. Dr SHAHAB KHUSHNOOD
Faculty of Telecommunications and Information Engineering: Prof. Dr ADEEL AKRAM

PROFESSORS

AHMAD, S., Mechanical Engineering
AHMED, S., Civil Engineering
AMIN, M., Electrical Engineering
CHOWDHRY, M. A., Electrical Engineering
FAROOQ, U., Electrical Engineering
GHUMMAN, A. R., Civil Engineering
IQBAL ALVI, M. S., Mechanical Engineering
JAMAL, H., Electrical Engineering
JAVAID, M. A., Basic Sciences
KAMAL, M. A., Civil Engineering
KHAN, A. K., Electrical Engineering
KHAN, M. A., Mechanical Engineering
KHAN, S. A., Civil Engineering
KHUSHNOOD, S., Mechanical Engineering
NISAR, H., Civil Engineering
SAHIR, M. H., Mechanical Engineering
ZAFRULLAH, Electrical Engineering

UNIVERSITY OF FAISALABAD

4 km Sargodha Rd, Faisalabad 38850, Punjab
Telephone: (41) 8868326
E-mail: info@tuf.edu.pk
Internet: www.tuf.edu.pk
Founded 2002
Private control

Chair.: MIAN MUHAMMAD HANIF
Vice-Chair.: MIAN MUHAMMAD RASHEED
Pro-Rector: Prof. Dr ABDUL KARIM BALOCH
Registrar: IZHAR UL AHSAN
Controller of Examinations: HAMID NAWAZ SHIEKH

DEANS

Faculty of Arts and Social Sciences: Prof. Dr ZAHOOR AHMED AZHAR
Faculty of Engineering and Technology: Prof. Dr A. D. CHAUDARY
Faculty of Health Sciences: Prof. Dr A. G. REHAN
Faculty of Management Studies: Prof. Dr M. ASLAM CHAUDHRY

UNIVERSITY OF GUJRAT

Hafiz Hayat Campus, Jalalpur Jattan Rd, Gujrat, Punjab
Telephone: (53) 3643112

E-mail: info@uog.edu.pk
Internet: uog.edu.pk
Founded 2003
State control

Faculties of basic sciences, computer science and information technology, engineering and technology, Oriental and Islamic Studies, social sciences; schools of art and design, business and management sciences, law

Chancellor: GOV. OF PUNJAB
Vice-Chancellor: Prof. Dr MOHAMMAD NIZAMMUDDIN
Registrar: MUHAMMAD AKRAM BHATTI
Dir of Admin. and Coordination: AZRA ZULFIQAR GHANI
Controller of Examinations: Prof. MAQSOOD AKHTER

UNIVERSITY OF HEALTH SCIENCES

Shaikh Zayed Hospital Medical Complex, Khayaban-e-Jamia, Lahore 54600, Punjab
Telephone: (42) 99231304
E-mail: info@uhs.edu.pk
Internet: www.uhs.edu.pk

Founded 2002
State control

Offers medical, dental, nursing, biomedical engineering, paramedic education

Chancellor: GOV. OF PUNJAB
Vice-Chancellor: Prof. MALIK HUSSAIN MUBBASHAR
Registrar: Prof. MUHAMMAD ZAFAR IQBAL
Librarian: ABID ALI GILL
Number of students: 39,000

UNIVERSITY OF KARACHI

Main Univ. Rd, Karachi 75270, Sindh
Telephone: (21) 99261300
E-mail: info@uok.edu.pk
Internet: www.uok.edu.pk
Founded 1951
State control
Language of instruction: English, Urdu
Academic year: September to August

Chancellor: GOV. OF SINDH
Vice-Chancellor: Prof. Dr PIRZADA QASIM RAZA SIDDIQUI
Pro-Vice-Chancellor: Prof. Dr NASIRUDDIN KHAN
Pro-Vice-Chancellor for Academic Affairs: Prof. Dr SHAHANA UROOJ KAZMI
Registrar: Prof. M. KALEEM RAZA KHAN
Head Librarian: Prof. MALAHAT KALEEM SHERWANI

Library: see under Libraries and Archives
Number of teachers: 800
Number of students: 24,000

Publications: *Jareeda* (Journal of the Bureau of Composition, Compilation and Translation, 1 a year), *Journal of Science* (2 a year), *Pakistan Journal of Botany* (2 a year), *Pakistan Journal of Nematology* (2 a year), *Pakistan Journal of Psychology* (4 a year)

DEANS

Faculty of Arts: Prof. Dr ZAFAR IQBAL
Faculty of Education: Prof. Dr M. ISMAIL BROHI
Faculty of Engineering: Prof. Dr DARAKHSHAN J. HALEEM
Faculty of Islamic Studies: Prof. Dr REHANA FIRDOUS
Faculty of Law: Prof. KHURSHEED A. HASHMI
Faculty of Management and Administration Sciences: Prof. Dr M. ABUZAR WAJIDI
Faculty of Medicine: Prof. Dr S. M. ABBAS HUSSAIN
Faculty of Pharmacy: Prof. Dr GHAZALA H. RIZWANI

Faculty of Science: Prof. Dr DARAKHSHAN J. HALEEM

PROFESSORS

Faculty of Arts:
AHMED, N., Islamic History
ANSARI, A. M. S., Urdu
ARAB, A. K., Arabic
FATIMA, N., Library and Information Science
HAQ, I., Arabic
HUMAYUN, S., Public Administration
HUSAIN, F., Sindhi
HUSAIN, S. M. A., Economics
HUSSAIN, J., General History
MEHDI, S. S., International Relations
MEMON, S., Sindhi
MIRZA, S. Q., Mass Communication
MURTAZA, M. R., Mass Communication
REHMAN, K., Sociology
SAJDIN, M., Commerce
SHAHEED, M. A., Arabic
SHAMSUDDIN, M., Mass Communication
SHERWANI, M. K., Library and Information Science
TAFHIMI, S., Persian
WAJIDI, M. A., Public Administration
WAZARAT, T. A., International Relations

Faculty of Islamic Studies:
RASHID, A., Islamic Studies
SIDDIQUI, M. A. S., Islamic Learning

Faculty of Pharmacy:
AHMED, M., Pharmacognosy
AHMED, M. A., Pharmaceutics
AHMED, S. P., Pharmacology
AHMED, T., Pharmaceutics
ALI, S. A., Pharmaceutics
BAIG, A. E., Pharmaceutics
HUSSAIN, W., Pharmaceutical Chemistry
MANZAR, K. N., Pharmaceutical Chemistry
REHMAN, S. B., Pharmacology
SAIFY, S. Z., Pharmaceutical Chemistry
SHAIKH, D., Pharmaceutics
SULTANA, N., Pharmaceutical Chemistry

Faculty of Science:
AFTAB, N., Biochemistry
AHMED, A., Applied Chemistry
AHMED, E., Statistics
AHMED, F., Physics
AHMED, I., Zoology
AHMED, I. K., Physics
AHMED, N., Genetics
AHMED, S., Botany
AKHTAR, S. K., Physics
AKHTAR, W., Physics
ALI, S. I., Applied Chemistry
ANIS, K., Physics
ANSARI, A. A., Applied Physics
ARAYN, M. S., Chemistry
ARSHAD, R., Physiology
ATHAR, H. S. A., Biochemistry
AZEEM, A., Physiology
AZHAR, A., Biochemistry
AZIZ, K., Botany
AZMATULLAH, M., Geology
BARKATI, S., Zoology
BURNI, S. M. A., Computer Science
FAHIMUDDIN, Chemistry
FARID, A., Philosophy
HALEEM, M. A., Biochemistry
HAMEED, S., Applied Chemistry
HASAN, H., Zoology
HASNAIN, S. N., Biochemistry
HASNI, S., Biochemistry
HUSAIN, V., Geology
HUSSAIN, M. R., Physics
IQBAL, M., Zoology
IQBAL, Z., Botany
JABEEN, D., Biochemistry
JAHANGIR, S., Biochemistry
JAVED, W., Zoology
KAZMI, M. A., Zoology
KAZMI, Q. B., Zoology
KAZMI, S. A., Chemistry

KAZMI, S. U., Microbiology
KHAN, A. F., Microbiology
KHAN, F., Applied Chemistry
KHAN, K. R., Physiology
KHAN, M. A., Botany
KHAN, M. ALTAF, Microbiology
KHAN, M. I., Botany
KHAN, N., Mathematics
KHANUM, A., Biochemistry
KHATOON, H., Microbiology
KHATOON, K., Botany
MAHMOOD, Z., Statistics
MALIK, A., Research Institute of Chemistry
MALIK, S. A., Chemistry
MAQSOOD, Z. T., Chemistry
MEHDI, F., Botany
MOHSIN, S. I., Geology
MUHAMMAD, I., Biochemistry
NAEEM, R. K., Mathematics
NAQVI, I. I., Chemistry
NAQVI, S. M. M. R., Physics
NAQVI, S. R. R., Chemistry
NAZAMI, S. S., Chemistry
NOOR, F., Chemistry
NUSRAT, J., Microbiology
QADEER, A., Applied Physics
QADRI, M. U., Geology
QAISER, M., Botany
QAMAR, J., Mathematics
QASIM, R., Biochemistry
QIDWAI, A. A., Physics
QIDWAI, I. M., Biochemistry
QURESHI, M. A., Physiology
QURESHI, N. M., Physiology
RAFI, F., Physiology
RAOOF, M. A., Physics
RASOOL, S. A., Microbiology
RAZZAQI, T. F., Biotechnology
REHMAN, A. U., Research Institute of Chemistry
RIZVI, N., Zoology
SAIFULLAH, S. M., Botany
SHAIKH, S. A., Geology
SHAHEEN, B., Research Institute of Chemistry
SHAMEEL, M. M., Botany
SHAMS, N., Applied Chemistry
SHAUKAT, S. S., Botany
SIDDIQI, J. S., Statistics
SIDDIQI, N. S., Biochemistry
SIDDIQI, P. A., Zoology
SIDDIQI, P. Q. R., Physiology
SIDDIQI, R., Microbiology
SIDDIQI, S. A., Chemistry
SIDDIQI, Z., Chemistry
SIDDIQUI, A. J., Statistics
SIDDIQUI, K. A., Physics
ULLAH, N., Geology
USMAN, M., Botany
USMANI, A. A., Chemistry
VAHIDY, A. A., Genetics
VAHIDY, R., Microbiology
YASMEN, N., Zoology
ZAIDGHAM, N. A., Geology
ZAIDI, S. A. H., Applied Chemistry
ZAIDI, S. S. H., Applied Physics
ZEENAT, I., Psychology

UNIVERSITY OF LAHORE

1 km Raiwind Rd, Lahore, Punjab
Telephone: (42) 35963421
E-mail: info@uol.edu.pk
Internet: uol.edu.pk
Private control

Faculties of civil engineering, computer science and information technology, electrical engineering, electronics, health sciences, law, mechanical engineering, nursing, pharmacy; institute of molecular biology and biotechnology; Lahore business school; school of creative arts

Rector: Dr SALEEM SHUJA

UNIVERSITY OF MALAKAND

Chakdara, Malakand, Khyber Pakhtunkhwa
Telephone: (936) 763441
E-mail: vicechancellor@uom.edu.pk
Internet: www.uom.edu.pk
Founded 2001
State control

Depts of biotechnology, botany, chemistry, computer science and information technology, economics, education, English, Islamic studies, law, management studies, mathematics, pharmacy, physics, political science, sociology and social work, software engineering, statistics, tourism and hotel management, zoology

Vice-Chancellor: Prof. Dr M. RASUL JAN
Registrar: Dr MIR AZAM KHAN (acting)
Dean of Studies: Prof. Dr RAHMAT ALI KHAN

Library of 9,655 vols
Number of students: 2,030

UNIVERSITY OF MANAGEMENT AND TECHNOLOGY

C-II, Johar Town, Lahore, Punjab
Telephone: (42) 35212801
E-mail: info@umt.edu.pk
Internet: umt.edu.pk
Founded 1990 as Institute of Leadership and Management, present status 2002, present name 2004
Private control

Rector: Dr HASAN SOHAIB MURAD
Pro-Rector: Dr A. R. KAUSAR
Registrar: SALMAN SAEED QURESHI
Controller of Examinations: ASIF SAEED HAIDER
Librarian: SOHAIL ASLAM

Library of 50,000
Number of teachers: 200
Number of students: 4,500

DEANS

School of Business and Economics: FAHEEM UL ISLAM
School of Science and Technology: Dr ABDUL AZIZ BHATTI
School of Social Sciences and Humanities: Prof. Dr ABDUL HAMEED

UNIVERSITY OF PESHAWAR

Peshawar, Khyber Pakhtunkhwa
Telephone: (91) 9216701
E-mail: vice_chancellor@upesh.edu.pk
Internet: www.upesh.edu.pk
Founded 1950
State control
Language of instruction: Arabic, English, Pashto, Persian, Urdu
Academic year: September to June

Chancellor: GOV. OF KHYBER PAKHTUNKHWA
Vice-Chancellor: Prof. Dr RASUL JAN
Registrar: Dr S. FAZL-I-HADI
Provost: Dr ALAM KHAN
Controller of Examination: Dr RASHID KHAN
Dir of Admin.: ISHTIAQULLAH KHAN
Treas.: IFTEKHAR HUSSAIN KHAN
Librarian: IBRAR MOHAMMAD

Library: see under Libraries and Archives
Number of teachers: 600
Number of students: 14,060

Publications: *Geological Bulletin* (1 a year), *Journal of Humanities and Social Sciences* (1 a year), *Journal of Law and Society* (1 a year), *Peshawar University Review* (1 a year)

DEANS

Faculty of Arts and Humanities: Prof. Dr M. FAROOQ SWATI
Faculty of Islamic and Oriental Studies: Prof. Dr QIBLA AYAZ

Faculty of Life and Environmental Sciences: Prof. Dr AMIR NAWAZ KHAN
Faculty of Management and Information Sciences: Prof. Dr ABDUL QAIYUM
Faculty of Numerical and Physical Sciences: Prof. Dr MUHAMMAD RIAZ KHAN
Faculty of Social Sciences: Prof. Dr NAEEM-UR-REHMAN

PROFESSORS

ABBASI, J. A., Geology
ADEEL, M. A., Institute of Education and Research
ALI, A., Law
ALI, T., Archaeology
AYAZ, Q., Islamic Studies
BANGASH, G. T., History
GILANI, S. Z., Education (Psychology)
HANIF, M., Islamic Studies
HUSSAIN, F., Biotechnology
IQBAL, M., Statistics
JAN, A.-H., Zoology
JAN, M. Q., Geology
KHAN, A., Geography
KHAN, M., Chemistry
KHAN, M. A., Chemistry
KHAN, M. J., Geology
KHAN, Z. A., Mathematics
KHATTAK, N. S., Electronics
MAJID, M., Geology
MIAN, I., Geology
NAWAZ, A., Geography
NASIR, G., Persian
NOOR, I., Mathematics
QAZI, S., Islamic Studies
RAFIQ, M., Geology
RAHMAN, C., English
RAHMAN, F., Physics
RAHMAN, M., English
RASHID, H., Chemistry
REHANA, N., Chemistry
REHMAN, S. S., Environmental Sciences
RIAZ, M., Physics
RIAZ, M. N., Psychology
SHAH, R., Pashto
SULAIMAN, M., Zoology

UNIVERSITY OF SARGODHA

Sargodha, Punjab
Telephone: (451) 9230811
E-mail: info@uos.edu.pk
Internet: www.uos.edu.pk
Founded 2002
State control

Vice-Chancellor: Prof. Dr MOHAMMAD AKRAM CHAUDHARY
Acting Registrar and Dir of Academics: Prof. Dr SHAUKAT ALI
Dir of Student Affairs: IJAZ ASGHAR BHATTI
Controller of Examinations: MUHAMMAD IQBAL QURESHI

Number of teachers: 700
Number of students: 16,000

DEANS

Faculty of Agriculture: Prof. Dr MUHAMMAD AFZAL
Faculty of Arts, Social Sciences and Law: Prof. Dr RASHID AHMED KHAN
Faculty of Islamic and Oriental Learning: Prof. Dr MAQBOOL HUSSAIN SIAL
Faculty of Management and Admin. Sciences: Prof. Dr MAQBOOL HUSSAIN SIAL
Faculty of Medical and Health Sciences: Prof. Dr MUHAMMAD ZAHOOR UL HASSAN DOGAR

PROFESSORS

AHMED, I., Arts and Social Sciences
ALI, M., Chemistry
ARIF, S., English
BUKHARI, A., Islamic and Oriental Learning
HAQ, F., Chemistry
IQBAL, M., Science and Technology
SULTANA, N., Mathematics

TAHIR, M., Chemistry

UNIVERSITY OF SCIENCE AND TECHNOLOGY, BANNU

Bannu, Khyber Pakhtunkhwa
Telephone: (928) 633825
E-mail: vc@ustb.edu.pk
Internet: www.ustb.edu.pk
State control

Depts of botany, biotechnology, chemistry, English, physics, Islamic studies and research

Vice-Chancellor: Prof. Dr ASMATULLAH KHAN

UNIVERSITY OF SINDH

Allama I. I. Kazi Campus, Dadu Dist., Jamshoro 76080, Sindh
Telephone: (22) 9213150
E-mail: vc@usindh.edu.pk
Internet: www.usindh.edu.pk

Founded 1947 in Karachi
State control
Languages of instruction: English, Sindhi, Urdu

Chancellor: GOV. OF SINDH
Vice-Chancellor: Prof. Dr NAZIR A. MUGHAL
Pro-Vice-Chancellor: Prof. Dr PARVEEN SHAH
Registrar: AKHTAR AHMED MEMON
Controller of Examinations: MUHAMMAD ALI PATHAN
Librarian: MUHAMMAD AZAM ROONJHO
Library: see under Libraries and Archives
Number of teachers: 650
Number of students: 19,000

Publications: *Ariel* (1 a year, in English), *Grassroot* (2 a year, English), *Kinjhar* (1 a year, in Sindhi), *Sindhi Arab* (1 a year, in Sindhi), *Sindhological Studies* (1 a year, in English), *Sindh University Journal of Education* (1 a year, in English), *Sindh University Research Journal (Science)*, *Sindh University Research Journal (Social Sciences)* (1 a year, in English), *Tahqiq* (1 a year, in Urdu), *University of Sindh Arts Research Journal* (1 a year, in English)

DEANS

Faculty of Arts: Prof. Dr KHUWAJA NOOR AFROZE
Faculty of Commerce and Business Admin.: Prof. Dr NOOR MUHAMMAD JAMALI (acting)
Faculty of Education: Prof. Dr MUNSHI PARVEEN (acting)
Faculty of Islamic Studies: Prof. Dr SANAULLAH BHUTTO
Faculty of Law: JHAMAT
Faculty of Natural Sciences: Prof. Dr RAJPUT MUHAMMAD TAHIR
Faculty of Pharmacy: Prof. Dr DAYO ABDULLAH
Faculty of Social Sciences: Prof. Dr IQBAL AHMED PANHWAR

PROFESSORS

Department of Botany:
ABRO, H.
AHMED, B.
HASSANI, S. S.
MEMON, A. H.
RAJPUT, M. T.
SAHITO, M. A.
SHAIKH, W.
TIRMIZI, S. A.
YASMIN, S.

Department of Comparative Religion and Islamic Culture:
BHUTTO, S.

Department of Fine Arts:
BHATTI, M. A.

Department of Muslim History:
ANSARI, A. S.
BHUTTO, M.
BUGHIO, M. M.

Department of Sindhi:
BUGHIO, M. Q.
HUSSAIN, K. K.
IMDAD, S.
KHUWAJA, N. A.

UNIVERSITY OF SOUTH ASIA

47 Tufail Rd, Lahore Cantonment, Punjab
Telephone: (42) 36672942
E-mail: info@usa.edu.pk
Internet: www.usa.edu.pk

Founded 2004
Private control

Faculties of art and fashion design, computer sciences, engineering and technology, health sciences, humanities and social sciences, law, management sciences; depts of intermediate studies, teaching

Chancellor: GOV. OF PUNJAB

UNIVERSITY OF THE PUNJAB

Quaid-e-Azam Campus, POB 54590, Lahore, Punjab
Telephone: (42) 99231102
E-mail: registrar@pu.edu.pk
Internet: pu.edu.pk

Founded 1882
State control
Languages of instruction: English, Urdu

Chancellor: GOV. OF PUNJAB
Vice-Chancellor: Prof. Dr MUJAHID KAMRAN
Pro-Vice-Chancellor: (vacant)
Registrar: Prof. Dr MUHAMMAD AKHTAR
Controller of Examinations: Prof. Dr LIAQAT ALI
Chief Librarian: CH. MUHAMMAD HANIF
Library: see under Libraries and Archives
Number of teachers: 740
Number of students: 30,608

DEANS

Faculty of Arts and Humanities: Prof. Dr S. QALB-I-ABID
Faculty of Behavioural and Social Sciences: Prof. Dr MUHAMMAD HAFEEZ
Faculty of Commerce: Prof. Dr MUHAMMAD EHSAN MALIK
Faculty of Economics and Management Sciences: Prof. Dr MUHAMMAD EHSAN MALIK
Faculty of Education: Prof. Dr HAFIZ MUHAMMAD IQBAL
Faculty of Engineering and Technology: Prof. Dr JAVAID AHMAD
Faculty of Islamic Studies: Prof. Dr HAFIZ MAHMOOD AKHTAR
Faculty of Law: Prof. Dr MUHAMMAD EHSAN MALIK
Faculty of Life Sciences: Prof. Dr MUHAMMAD EHSAN MALIK
Faculty of Medicine and Dentistry: (vacant)
Faculty of Oriental Learning: Prof. Dr HAFIZ MAHMOOD AKHTAR
Faculty of Pharmacy: Prof. Dr S. QALB-I-ABID
Faculty of Science: Prof. Dr HARIS RASHID

PROFESSORS

Faculty of Arts and Humanities (Quaid-e-Azam Campus, Lahore, Punjab; tel. (42) 9231167; e-mail dean.ahs@pu.edu.pk):
ABID, M., Pakistan Studies Centre
ABID, Q., History
AHMAD, A., Philosophy
AHMAD, N., Philosophy
AHSAN, A. S., Research Society of Pakistan
BUTT, A. R., Economics
CHAUDHRY, M. A., Economics
GILL, S. A., History

HAFEEZ, M., Philosophy
HASNAT, S. F., Political Science
JABEEN, N., Administrative Sciences
JADOON, M. Z. I., Administrative Sciences
JAVED, M. A., Sports Sciences and Physical Education
JULLANDHRY, M. S., Mass Communication
MALIK, M. E., Business Administration
MALIK, M. H., Social Sciences
MIRZA, M. S., Women Studies
SHEIKH, M. D., Mass Communication
SIRAJUDDIN, S. S., English Language and Literature
ZAKAR, M. Z., Sociology

Faculty of Commerce (Quaid-e-Azam Campus, Lahore, Punjab; tel. (42) 9231154; e-mail dean.commerce@pu.edu.pk):
ALI, L.
BUTT, Z. A.
CHAUDHARY, N. A.
SAEED, K. A.

Faculty of Education (Quaid-e-Azam Campus, Lahore, Punjab; tel. (42) 9231264; e-mail dean.education@pu.edu.pk):
HAMEED, A.
IQBAL, M. Z.
KHALID, M. I.
KHAN, Z. A.
MIRZA, M. S.
ZAIDI, S. N. R.

Faculty of Engineering and Technology (Quaid-e-Azam Campus, Lahore, Punjab; tel. (42) 9230343; e-mail dean.engg@pu.edu.pk):
AHMAD, J.
AKHTAR, N. A.
BUTT, M. A.
BUTT, M. T. Q.
DILAWARI, A. H.
NAWAZ, S.
RIZVI, S. Z. H.

Faculty of Islamic Studies (Allama Iqbal Campus, Lahore, Punjab; tel. (42) 9210837; e-mail dean.is@pu.edu.pk):
AKHTAR, H. M., Islamic Studies
CHAUDHARY, M. A., Arabic
FATIMA, S., Islamic Studies
HASAN, M., Urdu
HASHMI, R., Urdu
KHAN, S. A., Urdu
MOEEN, M., Arabic
SHAH, M. A., Iqbal Studies
SHAUKAT, J., Islamic Studies

Faculty of Law (Quaid-e-Azam Campus, Lahore, Punjab; tel. (42) 9231276; e-mail dean.ems@pu.edu.pk):
MALIK, D. M.
NAEEM, M.

Faculty of Pharmacy (Allama Iqbal Campus, Lahore, Punjab; tel. (42) 9211617; e-mail dean.pharmacy@pu.edu.pk):
RIAZ, M.

Faculty of Science (Quaid-e-Azam Campus, Lahore, Punjab; tel. (42) 9231162; e-mail dean.science@pu.edu.pk):
ABBASI, G. Q., Mathematics
ABDULLAH, T., Solid-State Physics
AHMAD, Z., Geology
AKHTAR, M. W., Biochemistry and Biotechnology
AKHTER, A. S., Statistics
ALEEM, F., High-Energy Physics
ANWAR, C. J., Chemistry
ASGHAR, R., Business and Information Technology
AZHAR, S., Business and Information Technology
BHATTI, S. A., Mathematics
BUTT, A. R., Business and Information Technology
DIN, S., Business and Information Technology

DIN, S., Mathematics
FAROOQ, U., Geology
GHAZANFAR, M., Geology
GULZAR, F., Geography
HAFEEZ, M., Business and Information Technology
HASNAIN, S., Botany
IDREES, M., Business and Information Technology
IKRAM, N., Solid-State Physics
IQBAL, J., Chemistry
JAMAL, K., Business and Information Technology
KAMRAN, M., Physics
KHAN, Z. A., Business and Information Technology
LATIF, S., Business and Information Technology
MANSOOR, G. D., Business and Information Technology
NAZAR, F. M., Solid-State Physics
RAO, A. A., Business and Information Technology
RASHID, K. H., High-Energy Physics
RAZA, A., Business and Information Technology
RIAZUDDIN, S., Advanced Molecular Biology
SHAKOORI, A. R., Microbiology and Molecular Genetics
SIDDIQI, S. A., Solid-State Physics
SOHAIL, M., Business and Information Technology
SOHAIL, S., Business and Information Technology
ZAIDI, N. R., Business and Information Technology

UNIVERSITY OF VETERINARY AND ANIMAL SCIENCES

Syed Abdul Qadir Jillani Rd, Lahore 54600, Punjab

Telephone: (42) 99211374
E-mail: webmaster@uvas.edu.pk
Internet: www.uvas.edu.pk
Founded 1882; present name and status 2002
State control

Chancellor: GOV. OF PUNJAB
Vice-Chancellor: Prof. Dr TALAT NASEER PASHA
Registrar: Dr MUHAMMAD AFZAL
Controller of Examinations: SAJJAD HYDER
Librarian: MIAN MUHAMMAD ILYAS

DEANS

Faculty of Animal Production and Technology: Prof. Dr MUHAMMAD ABDULLAH
Faculty of Biosciences: Prof. Dr IJAZ AHMAD
Faculty of Fisheries and Wildlife: Prof. Dr MUHAMMAD AKRAM
Faculty of Life Sciences Business Management: Prof. Dr HABIB-UR-REHMAN
Faculty of Veterinary Science: Prof. Dr NASIM AHMAD

UNIVERSITY OF WAH

The Mall, Quiad Ave, Wah Cantonment, Punjab

Telephone: (51) 905522255
E-mail: info@uow.edu.pk
Internet: uow.edu.pk
Founded 2005, present status 2009
Private control

Chancellor: GOV. OF PUNJAB
Vice-Chancellor: Prof. Dr M. MAQBOOL AHMAD

Controller of Examinations: Dr SIKANDAR AZAM
Library of 51,000 vols

DEANS

Faculty of Basic Sciences: Prof. Dr M. MAQBOOL AHMAD

VIRTUAL UNIVERSITY OF PAKISTAN

M. A. Jinnah Campus, Defence Rd, Off Raiwind Rd, Lahore, Punjab
E-mail: registrar@vu.edu.pk
Internet: www.vu.edu.pk

Founded 2002
State control

Depts of computer science, economics, English, Islamic studies, management sciences, mass communication, mathematics, Pakistan studies, physics, psychology, sociology, statistics; uses free-to-air satellite television broadcasts, internet to provide education

Chancellor: PRES. OF ISLAMIC REPUBLIC OF PAKISTAN
Rector: Dr NAVEED A. MALIK

ZIAUDDIN UNIVERSITY

4/B, Shahrah-e-Ghalib, Block 6, Clifton, Karachi 75600, Sindh

Telephone: (21) 35862937
E-mail: info@zu.edu.pk
Internet: www.zu.edu.pk
Founded 2005
Private control

Chancellor: Dr ASIM HUSSAIN
Rector: YUSUF HAROON
Vice-Chancellor: Dr ANWER EJAZ BEG (acting)
Registrar: MUHAMMAD YOUSUF
Librarian: SYED AHMED NAQVI

DEANS

Postgraduate Clinical: Dr EJAZ AHMED VOHRA
Ziauddin College of Nursing: SEEMA REHAN AFGHANI
Ziauddin College of Pharmacy: Dr KHWAJA ZAFAR AHMED
Ziauddin Medical College: Dr KAMRAN HAMEED

Colleges

Bolan Medical College: Quetta, Balochistan; e-mail principal@bmc.edu.pk; internet www.bmc.edu.pk; f. 1972; offers graduate courses in medical and dental sciences; Prin. Prof. Dr SHANAZ NASEER BALOCH; Vice-Prin. Prof. SHAH MUHAMMAD MARRI.

Government College of Technology: Mandi Bahauddin, Rasul, Punjab; tel. (546) 553216; e-mail gctrasul@yahoo.com; internet www.gctrasul.edu.pk; f. 1873, present status 1972; diploma and degree courses in technology and civil engineering; library: 25,076 vols; 90 teachers; 4,062 students; Prin. MAZHAR ABBAS NAQVI.

Government Polytechnic Institute: Paris Rd, Sialkot, Punjab; tel. (52) 9250199; 3-year diploma courses in electrical, mechanical, civil engineering, auto and diesel technologies; library: 12,999 vols.

Islamabad Medical and Dental College: Main Muree Rd, Bhara Kahu, Islamabad; tel. (51) 2807201; e-mail info@imdcollege.com; internet www.imdcollege.com; f. 2007; offers

courses in dental and medical sciences; library: 10,000 vols, 27 periodical titles; 100 teachers; Dean Prof. Dr M. NASEEMULLAH; Man. Dir YASIR NIAZI.

Jinnah Postgraduate Medical Centre: Rafiqui (H. J.) Shaheed Rd, Karachi 75510, Sindh; tel. (21) 9201300; e-mail edojpmc@jpmc.com.pk; internet www.jpmc.com.pk; f. 1958; provides postgraduate training and education (incl. doctorate) in basic medical subjects; also degrees in medical technology, occupational therapy and physiotherapy, diplomas in general and postgraduate nursing, other full-time certificate courses; library: 19,000 books, 21,000 bound periodicals, 500,000 loose periodicals; Exec. Dir Dr TASNEEM AHSAN; Dir SIMI JAMALI; publ. *Annals* (4 a year).

Kinnaird College for Women: 93 Jail Rd, Lahore, Punjab; tel. (42) 9203781; e-mail info@kinnaird.edu.pk; internet www.kinnaird.edu.pk; f. 1913; offers intermediate, undergraduate, Masters programmes; depts of accounting and finance, Arabic, biochemistry, biotechnology, botany, business studies, chemistry, computer sciences, economics, English, environmental sciences, fine arts, food sciences and nutrition, French, geography, int. relations and Pakistan studies, Islamic studies, mathematics, media studies, music, philosophy, physical education, physics, political science, psychology, social work, statistics, Urdu, zoology; library: 28,000 vols; 3,300 students; Prin. Dr RUKHSANA DAVID.

National School of Public Policy: Shahrah-i-Quaid-i-Azam, Upper Mall, Lahore 54000, Punjab; tel. (42) 99202943; e-mail info@nspp.gov.pk; internet www.nspp.gov.pk; f. 1960 as Pakistan Admin. Staff College; present name and status 2002; training in admin. management for sr execs from govt and public enterprises, private sector, Commonwealth and third world countries; also research and publs on the subject; consultancy and advisory service in public admin.; campuses in Islamabad, Karachi, Lahore, Peshawar, Quetta; Rector. MUHAMMED ISMAIL QURESHI; publ. *Pakistan Administration* (2 a year).

Pakistani Swedish Institute of Technology: Landhi, GPOB 186, Karachi, Sindh; f. 1957; training in electrical, mechanical, woodworking, welding and clothing technology; library: 20,000 vols; 35 teachers; 2,000 students; Dir IMAM ALI SOOMRO.

Rawalpindi Government College of Technology: Shahrah-e-Shershah, Rawalpindi, Punjab; f. 1958; 3-year diploma courses in various subjects, degree courses in electrical power technology, electronics and communication technology; library: 22,000 vols; 1,700 students; Prin. MUHAMMAD AFSAR; publ. *Technician* (1 a year).

Swedish–Pakistani Institute of Technology: Rehman Shaheed Rd, Near Service More, Gujrat 50700, Punjab; tel. (53) 3524819; e-mail contact@spitgujrat.com; internet www.spitgujrat.com; f. 1966; 3-year diploma courses in electrical engineering, mechanical engineering, electronics, instrumentation, foundry, pattern making, metallurgy and welding technology, auto and diesel technology, automation and control technology; 1-year post-diploma course in biomedical technology; library: 15,000 vols; 50 teachers; 600 students; Prin. MUHAMMAD IQBAL DUGAL.

PALAU

The Higher Education System

The Republic of Palau's independence in 1994, under a Compact of Free Association with the USA, marked the end of the US-administered Trust Territory of the Pacific Islands that had been established in 1947. The Ministry of Education is the responsible body of higher education. The Palau National Scholarship Board offers assistance to selected students who wish to pursue their post-secondary education abroad but intend to return to Palau. The Palau Community College (formerly the Micronesian Occupational College) is the sole institution of higher education and is accredited by the Western Association of Schools and Colleges (USA). Its current name and status were adopted following implementation of the Palau Higher Education Act of 1993, which established it as an independent college with its own governing board. The College offers associate degrees (approximately equivalent to the first two years of a four-year degree in the USA) and certificates in a number of fields including agricultural science, business, criminal justice, liberal arts and nursing. According to the results of the 2005 census, there were 545 students in tertiary education that year. The Bureau of Curriculum and Programme Development, a division of the Ministry of Education, is responsible for the provision of adult and community education.

Regulatory Bodies

GOVERNMENT

Ministry of Community and Cultural Affairs: POB 100, Koror 96940; tel. 767-1126; e-mail mcca@palaunet.com; internet palaugov.org/executive-branch/ministries/community; Minister BAKLAI TEMENGIL.

Ministry of Education: POB 189, Koror 96940; tel. 767-1464; e-mail moe@palaumoe.net; internet www.palaumoe.net; Minister MASA-AKI EMESIOCHEL.

FUNDING

Palau National Scholarship Board: POB 1608, Koror 96940; tel. 488-3608; e-mail pnsb@palaunet.com; internet www.palaumoe.net/pnsb; provides financial assistance to the citizens of the Republic of Palau for education and training; Chair. STEVEN VICTOR.

Learned Societies

BIBLIOGRAPHY, LIBRARY SCIENCE AND MUSEOLOGY

Palau Association of Libraries (PAL): Koror; e-mail palau.libraries@gmail.com; internet palaulibraries.weebly.com; dedicated to improvement and devt of Palau libraries; Pres. SANDY FERNANDEZ; Vice-Pres. MARGA B. ATEN; Sec. MEGAN K. BEARD; Treas. LORI ISAO.

NATURAL SCIENCES

Biological Sciences

Palau Conservation Society: POB 1811, Bai Ra Maibrel, Koror 96940; tel. 488-3993; e-mail pcs@palaunet.com; internet www.palauconservation.org; f. 1994; works with the community to preserve the nation's unique natural environment and perpetuate its conservation ethic for the economic and social benefit of present and future generations of Palauans and for the enjoyment and education of all; Chair. Dr CALEB OTTO; Exec. Dir ELBUCHEL SADANG; Sec. SANDRA S. PIERANTOZZI; Treas. KEOBEL SAKUMA.

Research Institutes

NATURAL SCIENCES

Biological Sciences

Coral Reef Research Foundation (CRRF): POB 1765, Koror 96940; tel. 488-5255; e-mail crrf@palaunet.com; internet www.coralreefresearchfoundation.org; f. 1991; special emphasis on species diversity work, colln for biomedical screening, environmental monitoring, reef fish spawning biology and devt of new techniques for marine research work; focus on increasing knowledge of coral reefs and other tropical marine environments to allow intelligent conservation and management decisions; Dir and Pres. Dr PATRICK L. COLIN.

Palau International Coral Reef Center: POB 7086, Koror 96940; tel. 488-6950; e-mail picrc@palaunet.com; internet www.picrc.org; f. 1999; aims to protect and conserve marine biodiversity; educates public about ecological, economic and cultural importance of coral reefs; provides facilities for research, professional training, workshops and conferences on marine research and management; centre for marine research, training and educational activities; indoor gallery displays several closed-system aquariums exhibiting marine organisms; outdoor marine park features open-system aquariums that exhibit different plant and animal dwellers of these habitats; Chair. Dr PATRICK TELLEI; CEO SANDRA S. PIERANTOZZI; Sec. and Treas. LOLITA K. GIBBONS-DECHERONG.

Libraries and Archives

Koror

Palau Congress Library: POB 8, Koror 96940; tel. 488-2507; f. 1981; 5,000 vols of committee reports, journals and legislative history on all public laws enacted by the Palau Nat. Congress; Librarian HARRY BESEBES.

Palau National Archives: POB 100, Koror 96940; tel. 488-4720; e-mail archives@palaunet.com; internet www.palaugov.net/palaugov/executive/ministries/mcca/archive.htm; f. 1988; 2,200 16-mm and 110 35-mm cartridges/rolls of microfilms processed during the Trust Territory era; Chief Archivist NAOMI NGIRAKAMERANG.

Palau Public Library: POB 6088, Koror 96940; tel. 488-2973; e-mail library@palaumoe.net; internet www.palaumoe.net/publib/about.html.xhtml; 13,000 vols; spec. collns: Pacific area, legislative records of Palau House of Delegates, nuclear topics; Head Librarian MARY ARIUS.

Singichi Ikesakes Law Library: POB 248, Koror 96940; tel. 488-4979; e-mail palaujudiciary@palaunet.com; internet www.palaugov.net/judiciary/judiciary_llibrary.html; 16,000 vols incl. sources of Palauan and int. law; houses legal vols, treatises and reference books; Law Librarian LORI ISAO.

Museums

Koror

Belau National Museum: POB 666, Koror 96940; Ngerbeched Hamlet, Koror; tel. 488-2265; e-mail bnm@palaunet.com; internet www.belaunationalmuseum.org; f. 1955; preserves, promotes nat. heritage; exhibits natural, cultural, social and historical values; develops arts at all levels; 4,500 cultural objects relating to anthropology, traditional and contemporary art, history and natural history, media colln of 25,000 photographic slides, 6,000 prints, negatives, films, video cassettes and sound recordings, traditional men's meeting hall, botanical garden; library of 5,000 vols, and periodicals, maps, posters, research papers and articles; Dir and Curator OLYMPIA ESEL MOREI.

Etpison Museum: POB 7049, Koror 96940; tel. 488-6730; e-mail info@etpisonmuseum.org; internet www.etpisonmuseum.org; f. 1999; colln incl. tools, artefacts, heirlooms, traditional Pacific and Palauan currency, childbirth ceremony of Palau, archaeological sites, rare shells and antique maps; Curator and Dir MANDY THIJSSEN ETPISON.

College

Palau Community College: POB 9, Koror 96940; tel. 488-2470; e-mail alvina@palau.edu; internet www.palau.edu; f. 1969 as Micronesian Occupational Center; independent, two-year post-secondary vocational/technical instn; school of arts and sciences, business, technical education; library: 30,000 items, incl. books, periodicals, govt documents, video cassettes, maps and CD-ROMs; 34 teachers; 650 students; Pres. Dr PATRICK U. TELLEI.

PALESTINIAN TERRITORIES

The Higher Education System

Palestinian education has been severely disrupted since 1987, when the university sector in the Gaza Strip and the West Bank was closed by Israeli military order. The universities were not re-opened until 1992. Since late 2000 the al-Aqsa intifada (uprising) has led to further strain on relations between the Palestinian Authority (PA) and Israel. All aspects of political, social and economic life in the occupied territories have been affected by the deteriorating security situation, including the higher education sector. In 2010 the Government announced a drive intended to modernize the sector; plans included expanding access to higher education, which was to involve the provision of additional funding to institutions and students alike, the development of five international programmes with foreign universities, and the improvement of quality control across the higher education system. The oldest university is Hebron University, which was founded in 1971. In 2010 there were 11 universities (including Al-Quds Open University), nine university colleges and 20 community colleges in the Palestinian Territories. In 2011 there were a total of 213,973 students enrolled in tertiary education.

In May 1994 the PA assumed responsibility for education in Gaza and parts of the West Bank. Higher education is regulated by the Ministry of Education and Higher Education, while the Ministry of Labour is responsible for vocational training centres. The specific requirements for the completion of undergraduate and postgraduate degrees are set out in Article 20 of Law No. 11 of 1998 for Higher Education. The Accreditation and Quality Assurance Commission (AQAC) was established in 2002 as an autonomous body functioning under the Ministry of Education and Higher Education. Its main duties include the licensing and accreditation of new higher education institutions, the accreditation of undergraduate and postgraduate programmes and the promotion of quality assurance within the higher education sector. Programme accreditation is not yet compulsory at all institutions.

Admission to higher education requires students to pass the Tawijihi (secondary school certificate) examinations. Arts and science undergraduate degree programmes require a score of at least 65% in the Tawijihi for entry, while engineering, medical technology, pharmacy and veterinary degrees require at least 80%, and medicine and dental programmes require at least 90%. Some programmes, e.g. medicine and dentistry, also require the applicant to pass an English proficiency test, as well as an interview for entry.

Undergraduates may study for a Diploma, which lasts between a few months and three years. Some Diplomas represent roughly half of the content of a Bachelors degree in the same subject. Others are more vocational in their nature and are regarded as post-secondary non-tertiary qualifications. The main undergraduate qualification is the Bachelors degree, which is generally awarded after four years of study, and requires the completion of at least 120 credit hours following the Tawijihi. Students are required to select three categories of subjects: those specific to a degree programme (offered by the appropriate departments), those relevant to a degree programme (offered by faculties) and those of a more general nature (offered centrally by the university). Examples of the latter include Islamic studies and the History of Jerusalem. With the exception of dentistry, only two degree titles are awarded on completion of a Bachelor degree—Bachelor of Arts and Bachelor of Science. Degrees in dentistry, engineering, pharmacy and veterinary medicine require five years' study, and degrees in medicine six years'. Degree programmes in these subjects are available only at selected universities.

The first postgraduate qualification is the Higher Diploma, which is awarded after the completion of at least 30 credit hours (one year) of study following the Bachelors degree. Higher Diplomas are offered only by the Birzeit University and are available only in selected subjects (development, gender studies, law, medical laboratory technology, primary health care supervision and training).

Study for a Masters degree is generally one to two years in length following the award of the Bachelors degree, and may include the submission of a thesis. For most Masters programmes, taught courses constitute the majority of the required credit hours. At some universities where a thesis is required, candidates may be awarded a Higher Diploma, should their thesis not meet the required standard, or if the comprehensive examination is failed.

Doctoral studies are typically three years in duration, and require the completion of a minimum of 45 credit hours following the completion of a Masters degree (with a minimum grade of 'very good'). Doctoral degrees are offered only by the Faculty of Graduate Studies at An-Najah National University, and currently the only doctorate available is in the field of chemistry. This doctorate is divided evenly between taught courses and a research project. Candidates must obtain a grade of at least 75% in the taught courses in order to proceed to the research component. A submitted dissertation must be defended by the candidate in front of a panel of specialists from the department.

Regulatory Bodies

GOVERNMENT

Ministry of Culture: POB 147, Ramallah; tel. (2) 2413860; e-mail moc@moc.pna.ps; internet moc.pna.ps; Minister ANWAR JAMAL ABDUL MOHSEN ABU AISHA.

Ministry of Education and Higher Education: POB 576, Al-Masyoun, Ramallah; tel. (2) 2983200; e-mail moehe.p@gmail.com; internet www.moehe.gov.ps; Minister of Education LAMIS AL-ALAMI; Minister of Higher Education Dr ALI AL-JARBAWI.

ACCREDITATION

Accreditation and Quality Assurance Commission: Ministry of Education and Higher Education, POB 1932, Ramallah; tel. (2) 2980140; e-mail aqac@p-ol.com; internet www.aqac.mohe.gov.ps; f. 2002; autonomous body attached to the Min.; board of 12 mems; Dir Prof. MOHAMMED M. A ALSUBU; Sec. GHADEER A'LI ZA'AL AHMAD.

Learned Societies

GENERAL

UNESCO Office Ramallah: POB 2154, Ramallah, West Bank; 35 Ahliyya College St, Ramallah, West Bank; tel. (2) 2959740; e-mail ramallah@unesco.org; internet www.unesco.org/new/en/bfc/office-in-ramallah; Admin. & Finance (HR Focal) MANHAL QARSHOLI.

LANGUAGE AND LITERATURE

Alliance Française: Peace Centre, POB 1166, Bethlehem; e-mail afbeth@p-ol.com; tel. (2) 2750777; offers courses and exams in French language and culture and promotes cultural exchange with France; Pres. PAULINE ANASTAS.

British Council: 31 Nablus Rd, POB 19136, 97200 Jerusalem; tel. (2) 6267111; e-mail information@ps.britishcouncil.org; internet www.britishcouncil.org/ps.htm; offers courses and exams in English language and British culture; promotes cultural exchange with the UK; attached offices in Gaza (building destroyed during civil unrest in March 2006), Hebron, Khan Yunis, Nablus and Ramallah; Dir-Gen. KEN CHURCHILL.

Research Institutes

GENERAL

Applied Research Institute, Jerusalem: Caritas St., Bethlehem; tel. (2) 2741889; e-mail pmaster@arij.org; internet www.arij.org; f. 1990; dedicated to promoting applied research, technology transfers, sustainable devt and the self-reliance of the Palestinian people through greater control over their natural resources; Pres. Eng. DAOUD ISTANBULI; Vice-Pres. SALIM ZUGBI; Treas. Dr NASRI QUMSIYEH; Sec. Dr NABEEL 'EDEILY; publ. *Report* (12 a year).

Health, Development, Information and Policy Institute: POB 1351, Ramallah; tel. (2) 2985372; e-mail hdip@hdip.org; internet www.hdip.org; f. 1989; policy research and planning regarding the Palestinian health care and development system in the West Bank and Gaza Strip.

Muwatin/The Palestinian Institute for the Study of Democracy: POB 1845, Ramallah; tel. (2) 2951108; e-mail muwatin@muwatin.org; internet www.muwatin.org; f. 1992 to promote the study and development of democracy in Palestine; Dir Dr GEORGE GIACAMAN.

Palestinian Academic Society for the Study of International Affairs: POB 19545, Jerusalem; 18 Hatem Al-Ta'i St, Wadi Al-Joz; tel. (2) 6264426; e-mail passia@passia.org; internet www.passia.org; f. 1987; deals with nat., Arab and int. aspects of the Palestinian Question through academic research, dialogue and publs; library of 2,000 vols; Chair. Dr MAHDI ABDUL HADI.

ECONOMICS, LAW AND POLITICS

Institute of Law: POB 14, Birzeit, West Bank; tel. (2) 2982009; e-mail iol.programs@birzeit.edu; internet lawcenter.birzeit.edu; research areas incl. comparative law, law and society, constitutional law and legislative support; Dir Dr GHASSAN FARAMAND.

MEDICINE

Institute of Community and Public Health: POB 14, Birzeit; tel. (2) 2982019; e-mail icph@birzeit.edu; internet icph.birzeit.edu; f. 1982; attached to Birzeit Univ.; research for devt of health-related issues and health system; 5 units: child health, epidemiology, mental health, women's health and health systems management; Dir Dr ABDULLATIF HUSSEINI.

NATURAL SCIENCES

Institute of Environmental and Water Studies: POB 14, Birzeit; tel. (2) 2982120; e-mail wsi@birzeit.edu; internet iews.birzeit.edu; f. 2001 as Water Studies Institute, present name 2007; attached to Birzeit Univ.; research for developing technologies on water resources management, distribution and wastewater treatment; Dir Dr NIDAL MAHMOUD.

RELIGION, SOCIOLOGY AND ANTHROPOLOGY

Institute of Women's Studies: POB 14, Birzeit, West Bank; tel. (2) 2982013; e-mail swadi@birzeit.edu; internet home.birzeit.edu/wsi; f. 1994; research on women's rights, gender relations and social policy in the local and regional context; library of 6,262 vols; Dir Dr ISLAH JAD; publ. *Institute of Women Studies*.

Libraries

Nablus

Nablus Municipality Public Library: Shwetreh St, Nablus, West Bank; tel. (9) 2383356; e-mail nab_lib@nablus.org; internet www.nablus.org; f. 1969; 70,000 vols, mainly in Arabic and English; Librarian ALI TOUQAN.

Ramallah

Public Library: Ramallah, West Bank; f. 1962; 3,500 vols; Librarian ADEL UWAIS.

Museums

Bethlehem

Baituna al-Talhami Museum/Bethlehem Folklore Museum: c/o Arab Women's Society, POB 19, Star St, Bethlehem; tel. (2) 2742431; f. 1948 as centre for Palestinian refugees, museum established 1979; 2 houses of typical Palestinian architecture, furnished with colln of traditional Palestinian household items and colln of photographs, furniture, and works of art illustrating life of Bethlehem residents in 1900–1932; open daily, except Thursdays and Sundays.

Gaza

Al-Math'af/Recreational Cultural House: Sodaniya, Rasheed St, Gaza; tel. (8) 2858444; e-mail info@almathaf.ps; internet www.almathaf.ps; f. 2008; archaeology and antiquities; Dir JAWDAT AL-KHOUDARY.

Universities

AL-AQSA UNIVERSITY

POB 4051 Gaza

Telephone: (8) 282826809
E-mail: it_affairs@alaqsa.edu.ps
Internet: www.alaqsa.edu.ps

Founded 1991
State control
Academic year: July to January

Faculties of administration sciences, arts, education, fine arts, media, physical education, sciences

Pres.: SALAM ALAGHA

Number of teachers: 350
Number of students: 21,000
Library of 113,200 vols

AL-AZHAR UNIVERSITY

POB 1277, Jamal Abdl Naser St, Gaza

Telephone: (8) 2824020
E-mail: alazhar@alazhar-gaza.edu
Internet: www.alazhar-gaza.edu

Founded 1991
State control
Languages of instruction: Arabic, English

Pres.: Prof. Dr ABED AL KHALEQ AL FARAH
Vice-Pres. for Academic Affairs: Prof. Dr SAMI MUSLEH
Vice-Pres. for Admin. and Financial Affairs: Prof. Dr ALI AL NAJAR
Vice-Pres. for Planning and Quality Assurance: Dr NABEEL ABU SHAABAN

Number of teachers: 400
Number of students: 18,200

DEANS

Faculty of Agriculture: Prof. Dr NSER ABU FOUL
Faculty of Applied Sciences: Prof. Dr OMAR ABU TIAM
Faculty of Arts and Human Sciences: Dr MOHAMMED SALAH ABU HAMAIDA

Faculty of Economics and Administrative Sciences: Dr SAMIR ABU MUDALALAH
Faculty of Dentistry: Dr ABDEL NASSER ABU SHAHLA
Faculty of Education: Dr SOHAIB EL-AGHA
Faculty of Engineering and Information Technology: Prof. Dr SAMY ABU NASSER
Faculty of Intermediate Studies: Dr MOHAMMAD AJOUR
Faculty of Law: Dr ABED AL RAHMAN ABU AL NSIR
Faculty of Medicine: Dr SAMIR ISMAIL
Faculty of Pharmacy: Dr SULIMAN AL JBUR
Faculty of Science: Dr OMAR MILAD
Faculty of Shari'a: Dr NAEIM EL MASRY

ATTACHED CENTRES

Centre for Continuing Education: Dir Dr WAEL THABET.

Centre for Drug Analysis and Research: Dir Dr SULAIMAN AL JOBOUR.

Centre for Food Analysis: Dir Dr ABED EL-RAZEQ SALAMA.

Centre for Information Technology: Dir Dr MONTASER EL HALABI.

Institute of Water and Environment: Dir Dr YOUSIF ABU MAYLA

AL-QUDS OPEN UNIVERSITY

POB 51800, Sheikh Jarrah, Musa Feidi St, East Jerusalem

Telephone: (2) 5816239
E-mail: administrative@qou.edu
Internet: www.qou.edu

Founded 1991
State control

Programmes in agriculture, education, management and entrepreneurship, social and family devt and technology and applied science; campus in Riyadh, Saudi Arabia, open to Palestinian nationals or people of Palestinian origin; 22 educational regions and study centres in the West Bank and Gaza Strip, in addition to a br. in Saudi Arabia; also has 5 centres that deal with IT, media production and education

Pres.: Prof. YOUNIS AMIR
Vice-Pres. for Academic Affairs: Prof. SUFIAN KAMAL
Vice-Pres. for Admin.: Dr SAMIR NAJDI

Library of 20,800 vols (16,000 in Arabic, 4,800 in English), 80 periodicals
Number of teachers: 360 academic supervisors apart from part-time instructors
Number of students: 60,700

AL-QUDS UNIVERSITY

POB 51000, Jerusalem

Telephone: (2) 5838652
E-mail: president@alquds.edu
Internet: www.alquds.edu

Founded 1979
Private control
Language of instruction: English
Academic year: October to August

Pres.: Prof. SARI NUSSEIBEH
Vice-Pres.: Prof. HASAN DWEIK
Asst to the Pres. for Academic Affairs: Dr SAED ZEEDANI
Asst to the Pres. for Planning and Devt: Dr BADIE SARTAWI
Dean of Scientific Research: Dr SAMIRA BARGHOUTHI
Librarian: HAKIM BESHAWI

Library of 100,000 vols
Number of teachers: 440
Number of students: 11,700

DEANS

Faculty of Admin. and Economic Sciences: Dr MAHMOOD ALJAFARE

Faculty of Arts: Dr MUNTHER DAJANI
Faculty of Dentistry: Dr MUSA BAJALI
Faculty of Engineering: Dr HUSSEIN JADDU
Faculty of Health Professions: Dr VARSEEN SHAHEEN
Faculty of Islamic Studies: Dr SAID AL-QEEQ
Faculty of Law: Prof. ALI KHASHAN
Faculty of Medicine: Prof. HANI ABDEEN
Faculty of Pharmacy: Dr RAFIK KARAMAN
Faculty of Public Health: Dr SHAHEEN MOHAMMAD
Faculty of Science and Technology: Dr AMIN AHMAD LEGHROUZ

ATTACHED RESEARCH INSTITUTES

Abu-Jihad Centre for Political Prisoners' Affairs: tel. (2) 2792515; e-mail info@aj-museum.alquds.edu; internet www.aj-museum.alquds.edu.

Al-Quds Human Rights Clinic: tel. (2) 2790417; e-mail info@aqhrclinic.alquds.edu; f. 2006; Dir MUNIR NUSEIBAH.

Al-Quds Nutrition and Health Research Institute: tel. (2) 6289798; e-mail enquire@anahri.alquds.edu; internet anahri.alquds.edu; Dir ZIAD ABDEEN.

American Studies Institute: tel. (2) 2989184; e-mail info@americanstudiespalestine.org; internet asi.arts.alquds.edu; Dir Prof. MOHAMMED S. DAJANI DAOUDI.

Centre for Chemical and Biological Analysis: tel. (2) 2796961; f. 1999; Dir Dr MUSTAFA KHAMIS.

Centre for Development in Primary Health Care: tel. (2) 2952767; e-mail cdphc@palnet.com; internet cdphc.alquds.edu.

Centre for Human Rights and Humanitarian Law: e-mail info@aqhrclinic.alquds.edu; f. 2006; Dir Dr MOHAMMAD SHALALDEH.

Centre for Jerusalem Studies: tel. (2) 6287517; e-mail huda@planet.edu; internet www.jerusalem-studies.alquds.edu; Dir HUDA IMAM.

Centre for Radiation Science and Technology: e-mail lahham@crst.alquds.edu; internet www.crst.alquds.edu; Dir Dr A. LAHHAM.

Child Institute: tel. (2) 5859955; e-mail pci@admin.alquds.edu; Dir Dr KHULOUD KHAYYAT DAJANI.

Community Action Centre: internet www.cac-alquds.org.

Ethnomusicology Research and Studies Centre: e-mail adileh@art.alquds.edu; Dir Prof. MUTASEM ADILEH.

INSAN Centre for Gender and Women's Studies: tel. (2) 2791344; e-mail fadwal@arts.alquds.edu; Dir Dr FADWA ALLABADI.

Institute of Archaeology: tel. (2) 2959276; Dir Dr MARWAN ABU KHALAF.

Institute of Area Studies: Dir Dr AZIZ HEIDER.

Institute of Business and Economic Studies: tel. (2) 2799497; e-mail mjafari@admin.alquds.edu; Dir MAHMOUD K. EL-JAFARI.

Institute of Modern Media: tel. (2) 2964213; e-mail info@imm.ps; internet www.imm.ps.

Islamic Research Centre: tel. (2) 6275228; f. 1987; Dir Dr MOSTAFA ABU SWAI.

Issam Sartawi Centre: tel. (2) 5859955; e-mail msdajani@art.alquds.edu; f. 1998; Dir Prof. MUNTHER S. DAJANI.

Jericho Local Urban Observatory Centre: tel. (2) 2799753; e-mail juoc@admin.alquds.edu; internet www.jluo.alquds.edu; Dir Dr FAYEZ FREIJAT.

Language Resource Centre: tel. (2) 6275228; f. 1995; Dir Dr OMAR ABU HOMOS.

Medical Research Centre: Dir Dr MYSA EL-AZZEH.

Said Khoury IT Centre of Excellence: tel. (2) 2790852; internet www.itce.alquds.edu.

Science and Technology Centre: tel. (2) 2799234; f. 1998; Dir Dr HASAN DWEIK.

Science Discovery Centre: e-mail info@sep.alquds.edu; internet www.sep.alquds.edu

AN-NAJAH NATIONAL UNIVERSITY

Omar Ibn Khattab St, POB 7, Nablus, West Bank

Telephone: (9) 2345113
E-mail: info@najah.edu
Internet: www.najah.edu

Founded 1977
State control
Languages of instruction: Arabic, English
Academic year: September to June
Chair., Board of Trustees: SABIH AL-MASRI
Pres.: Prof. RAMI HAMDALLAH
Vice-Pres. for Academic Affairs: Prof. MAHER NATSHEH
Vice-Pres. for Admin. Affairs: Dr SA'ED AL-KONI
Vice-Pres. for Community Affairs: Dr MOHAMAD HANOON
Deputy Pres. for Graduate Affairs: Prof. JAWAD FATAYER
Deputy Pres. for Planning, Devt and Quality Assurance: Dr ALLAM MOUSA
Deputy Pres. for Strategic and Int. Affairs: Dr KHERIEH RASSAS
Dean of Admission and Registration: ABDULLAH ALNASSER
Dean of Student Affairs: MUSA ABU DIYEH
Librarian: HANI JABER
Library of 300,000 vols, 27,000 periodicals
Number of teachers: 1,340 (820 full-time, 520 part-time)
Number of students: 20,000
Publications: *An-Najah 'A base of Science and Technology'* (in Arabic and English), *An-Najah Journal of Research* (separate series for natural sciences and humanities)

DEANS

Faculty of Agriculture: Dr MUNQEZ SHTAYA
Faculty of Arts: Prof. MAHER ABU ZANT
Faculty of Economics and Administrative Sciences: Dr NAFEZ ABU BAKER
Faculty of Educational Sciences: Dr SAMI AL-KAILANI
Faculty of Engineering: Dr ABED RAHIM ABU SAFA
Faculty of Fine Arts: Dr HASAN M. N'ERAT
Faculty of Graduate Studies: Dr MOHAMMAD ABU JAFAR
Faculty of Information Technology: Dr BAKER ABDALHAQ
Faculty of Islamic Law (Shari'a): Dr JAMAL AL-KILANI
Faculty of Law: Dr AKRAM DAOUD
Faculty of Media: Dr ATEF SALAMEH
Faculty of Medicine and Health Sciences: Prof. ANWAR DUDIN
Faculty of Science: Prof. SULAIMAN KHALIL
Faculty of Veterinary Medicine: Dr HATEM ATALLA
Hisham Hijjawi College of Technology: Dr SHAKER BITAR

ATTACHED RESEARCH INSTITUTES

Academic Programme for the Study of Involuntary Migration: e-mail frc@najah.edu; Dir SAMER AQROUQ.

Central Medical Laboratory: e-mail cml@najah.edu; Dir Dr SULAIMAN KHALIL.

Centre for Continuing Education: e-mail cec@najah.edu; Dir Dr MUSADDAQ ALMASRI.

Centre for Urban and Regional Planning: e-mail abhamid@najah.edu; Dir Dr ALI ABDUL HAMEED.

Chemical, Biological and Drugs Analysis Centre: e-mail nidalzatar@najah.edu; Dir Dr NIDAL ZATAR.

Community Service Centre: Dir BILAL SALAMEH.

Computer Research Centre: e-mail cc@najah.edu; Dir NAJEH ABU SAFYYEH.

Construction and Transport Research Centre: e-mail alsahili@yahoo.com; Dir Dr KHALED AL-SAHILI.

Earth Sciences and Seismic Engineering Centre: e-mail seiscen@najah.edu; Dir Dr JALAL ALDABEEK.

Energy Research Centre: Dir Dr EMAD BRAIK.

Korean Palestinian IT Institute of Excellence (KPITIE): e-mail kaitie@najah.edu; Dir Dr KHALID BARHAM.

Measurement and Evaluation Centre: e-mail mec2006@najah.edu; Dir Dr ABDELNASSER ALQADDOUMI.

Opinion Polls and Survey Studies Centre: e-mail polls@najah.edu; Dir Dr HUSSEIN AHMAD.

Poison Control and Drug Information Centre (PCDIC): e-mail poison@najah.edu; Dir Dr ANSAM SAWALHA.

UNESCO Chair on Human Rights and Democracy: e-mail uchrdn@najah.edu; Dir SAMER AQROUQ.

Water and Environmental Studies Institute: e-mail wesi@najah.edu; Dir Dr MARWAN HADDAD

ARAB AMERICAN UNIVERSITY—JENIN

Jenin
E-mail: asaleh@aauj.edu
Internet: www.aauj.edu

Founded 2000
Private control
Faculties of admin. and financial sciences, allied medical sciences, arts and sciences, dentistry, engineering and information technology, law
Pres.: Dr ADLI SALEH
Vice-Pres. for Academic Affairs: Dr NASER HAMAD
Vice-Pres. for Planning and Devt: Dr ZAKI M. SALEH
Library of 60,000 vols

BETHLEHEM UNIVERSITY

POB 9, Bethlehem, West Bank
Rue des Frères, Bethlehem, West Bank

Telephone: (2) 2741241
E-mail: info@bethlehem.edu
Internet: www.bethlehem.edu

Founded 1973
Private control (Roman Catholic)
Languages of instruction: Arabic, English
Academic year: September to June
Chancellor: Archbishop ANTONIO FRANCO
Vice-Chancellor: Br DANIEL CASEY
Pres.: Archbishop FOUD TWAL
CEO: Br PETER BRAY
Vice-Pres. for Academic Affairs: Br ROBERT SMITH
Vice-Pres. for Devt: Br JACK CURRAN
Vice-Pres. for Finance and Planning: SAMI EL-YOUSEF
Dean for Students: MAHMOUD HAMMAD
Registrar: MARY JUHA
Librarian: Dr MELLIE BRODRETH

Library of 90,000 vols
Number of teachers: 184 (132 full-time, 52 part-time)
Number of students: 3,000

DEANS

College of Arts: JAMAL DAIBES
College of Business Administration: Dr FADI KATTAN
College of Education: RIZEK SLEIBI
College of Nursing and Health Sciences: AMAL ABU NIJMEH
College of Sciences: Dr HAIFA KONKAR

ATTACHED RESEARCH INSTITUTES

Hereditary Research Laboratory: tel. (2) 2744233; e-mail mkanaan@bethlehem.edu; internet hrl.bethlehem.edu; f. 1993; Dir Dr MOIEN KANAAN.

Institute for Community Partnership: tel. (2) 2770936; e-mail icp@bethlehem.edu; internet icp.bethlehem.edu; f. 1989; Dir MOUSSA RABADI.

UNESCO Biotechnology Educational and Training Centre: tel. (2) 2765404; e-mail niraki@bethlehem.edu; f. 1995; Dir Dr NAIM IRAKI.

Water and Soil Environmental Research Unit: e-mail wseru@bethlehem.edu; internet wseru.bethlehem.edu; f. 1988; Dir Dr ALFRED ABED RABBO

BIRZEIT UNIVERSITY

POB 14, Birzeit, West Bank
Telephone: (2) 2982000
E-mail: pr@birzeit.edu
Internet: www.birzeit.edu

Founded 1924 as school, 1951 college, present status 1975
Private control
Languages of instruction: Arabic, English
Academic year: September to August (2 semesters), 2 summer sessions

Pres.: Prof. KHALIL HINDI
Vice-Pres. for Academic Affairs: Dr ADNAN AL-YEHYA
Vice-Pres. for Admin. Affairs: Dr ADEL ZAGHA
Vice-Pres. for Community Outreach: Dr SAMIA HULEILEH
Vice-Pres. for Financial Affairs: BISHARA DABBAH
Head Librarian: Dr GHASSAN AL KHATIB
Library of 312,313 vols
Number of teachers: 441 (405 full time, 36 part-time)
Number of students: 10,200

DEANS

Faculty of Arts: Dr MAHDI ARAR
Faculty of Business and Economics: Dr MOHAMMED NASR
Faculty of Education: Dr HASAN ABELKAREEM
Faculty of Engineering: Dr AFIF HASAN
Faculty of Graduate Studies: Dr TALAL SHAHWAN
Faculty of Information Technology: Dr ALI JABER
Faculty of Law and Public Admin.: Dr ASEM KHALIL
Faculty of Nursing and Allied Health Professions: Dr TAMER ESSAWI
Faculty of Science: Dr WAE'L QARAE'EN

HEBRON UNIVERSITY

POB 40, Hebron, West Bank
Telephone: (2) 2220995
E-mail: info@hebron.edu
Internet: www.hebron.edu

Founded 1971
Ind. nat. univ.
Languages of instruction: Arabic, English
Academic year: September to June

Chair., Board of Trustees: Dr NABIL AL-JABARI
Pres.: Dr SAMIR A. ABUZNAID
Vice-Pres. for Academic Affairs: Prof. RADWAN BARAKAT
Vice-Pres. for Admin. Affairs: ZIAD AL JABARI
Vice-Pres. for External Affairs: Dr NIMER ABUZAHRA
Vice-Pres. for Quality Assurance: Dr HASAN IFLAIFEL
Registrar: AMAL AL-NATSHEH
Librarian: SALAH ABU SNANEH
Library of 65,000 vols
Number of teachers: 350
Number of students: 7,800

DEANS

Faculty of Agriculture: Dr SABRI SAGHIR
Faculty of Arts: Dr SALAH ALSHROUF
Faculty of Education: Dr JAMAL ABU MARAQ
Faculty of Finance and Management: Dr MUHAMMED AL-JABARI
Faculty of Graduate Studies: Prof. FAKHRI HASAN
Faculty of Islamic Studies: Prof. HUSSEIN AL-TARTORI
Faculty of Nursing: Dr HUSSEIN JABAREEN
Faculty of Pharmacy: Dr TAWFEQ KAIMARI
Faculty of Science and Technology: Dr NABIL HASASNEH

ISLAMIC UNIVERSITY OF GAZA

POB 108, Gaza
Telephone: (8) 2860700
E-mail: pres@iugaza.edu.ps
Internet: www.iugaza.edu.ps

Founded 1978
Academic year: September to June

Pres.: Dr KAMALAIN SHAATH
Vice-Pres. for Academic Affairs: Prof. MOHAMMED SHABAT
Vice-Pres. for Admin. Affairs: Prof. SALEM HELLES
Vice-Pres. for External Relations: Prof. RIFAT RUSTOM
Dean of Library: Dr WALEED AL-AMOUDY
Dean of Planning and Devt: Dr ABDELMAJEED NASSAR
Dean of Student Affairs: Dr KAMAL GHNAIM
Library of 100,300 vols in central library
Number of students: 20,900

Publication: *Journal* (2 a year)

DEANS

College of Arts: Prof. MAHMOUD EL-AMOUDI
College of Business: Prof. MAJED EL-FARRA
College of Education: Prof. ELYAN AL-HOLY
College of Engineering: Prof. SHAFIQ JENDYA
College of Foundations of Religion: Dr SALEM SALAMEH
College of Information Technology: Prof. NABEEL HEWAIHY
College of Islamic Law: Dr MAHER AL-HOLY
College of Medicine: Dr MOFEED MOKHALLATI
College of Nursing: Dr ASHRAF EL-JEDI
College of Religion Foundation: Dr MOHAMMED BKHAIT
College of Science: Dr NIZAM AL-ASHQAR

PROFESSORS

College of Arts:
  ABO ALI, N. KH.
  AMOUDI, M. A.
  OLWAN, M. SH.
  OLWAN, N. S.
College of Business:
  EDWAN, A. I.
College of Education:
  ASQOUL, M.
  EL-HELOU, M. W.
College of Engineering:
  AWAD, M.

ENSHASSI, A.
KUHAIL, Z. S.
College of Religion Foundation:
  HALABIYA, A. A.
  HAMMAD, N. H.
College of Science:
  ABDEL-LATIF, M.
  ASHOUR, M. M.
  EL-ATRASH, M. S.
  EL-AZIZ, E. E. A.
  EL-NAKHAL, H. A.
  HABIL, E.
  SARSOUR, M. E.
  SHABAT, M. M.
  SHUBAIR, M. E.

PALESTINE POLYTECHNIC UNIVERSITY

Hebron, West Bank
Telephone: (2) 2229812
E-mail: info@ppu.edu
Internet: www.ppu.edu

Founded 1978
State control
Colleges of admin. sciences and informatics, applied professions, applied sciences, engineering and technology

Pres.: DAWOD AL-ZATARY
Number of students: 5,000

Colleges

Bethlehem Bible College: POB 17166, 91190 Jerusalem; tel. (2) 2741190; e-mail info@bethlehembiblecollege.edu; internet www.bethlehembiblecollege.edu; f. 1979; Private control; Christian Bible College; accredited by Ministry of Education and Higher Education and Middle East Association of Theological Education; Pres. Prof. BISHARA AWAD.

Community College of Applied Sciences: POB 1415, Gaza; tel. (8) 2868999; e-mail info@ccast.edu.ps; internet www.ccast.edu.ps; f. 1998; State control; accredited by Ministry of Education and Higher Education; Dean YEHIA ROSHDI SIRAJ.

Ibrahimieh Community College: POB 19014, 91190 Jerusalem; tel. (8) 6286361; e-mail icc@ibrahimieh.edu; internet www.ibrahimieh.edu; f. 1998; State control; accredited by Ministry of Education and Higher Education.

National Institute for Administration: Al-Bireh; f. 2004; Palestinian Economic Council for Development and Construction; public admin. training for Palestinian Ministries, public orgs, private sector; Dir Dr MOHAMMED DAJANI.

National Institute for Technology: Ramallah; f. 2001; Palestinian Economic Council for Development and Construction; higher education courses in software engineering, web and e-commerce solutions devt, system engineering, database devt and network engineering; English language courses; Dir ADEL LAFI.

Palestine Technical College, Deir al-Balah: POB 6037, Deir al-Balah; tel. (8) 2531171; e-mail eng_ptc@ptcdb.edu.ps; internet www.ptcdb.edu.ps; State control; accredited by Ministry of Education and Higher Education.

Tulkarm Community College: West Bank; f. 1931; library: 30,000 vols; 27 teachers; 400 students; teacher training college preparing teachers of agriculture, science, mathematics, computer science, Arabic, Islamic and social studies, English and physical education; Dean Dr M. Z. GHAZALEH.

PANAMA

The Higher Education System

In 1821 Panama became independent from Spain as part of Gran Colombia, declaring its separate independence in 1903. The Universidad de Panamá (founded in 1935) is the oldest and largest university, with an enrolment of 54,121 students in 2010 . In 2010 a total of 139,116 students were enrolled in tertiary education. In 2013 there were 17 universities operating with official accreditation, of which four are public institutions, with regional centres in the provinces. However, the actual number of universities operating is reported to be as high as 40, although there are only 11 universities (public and autonomous) represented on the Consejo de Rectores de Panamá (CRP—Council of Rectors) and nine private universities listed as members of the Asociación de Universidades Privadas de Panamá (AUPPA—Association of Private Universities) .

Under the Organic Educational Law 47 of 1946, amended by Law 34 of 1995, higher education is centralized under the authority of the Ministry of Education. In 2006 Law 30 repealed Law 16 of 1963 to bring into existence the Consejo Nacional de Evaluación y Acreditación Universitaria (CONEAUPA— National Council for the Evaluation and Accreditation of University Education), which in 2010 launched the first nation-wide initiative to evaluate and accredit tertiary institutions in Panama, in an attempt to identify those institutions failing to meet standards set by the Ministry of Education. In 2012 some 27 universities had submitted to the process, although only 17 were accredited. However, in 2013 both the CRP and the AUPPA called on the President of the Republic to suspend the second round of evaluations as they deemed the process flawed. As a consequence, three public universities (Universidad de Panamá [UP], Universidad Tecnológica de Panamá [UTP] and Universidad Marítima Internacional de Panamá) and two private universities (Universidad del Arte Ganexa and Universidad Americana de Panamá) announced that they would be withdrawing from CONEAUPA. UP and UTP, however, remain members of the larger regional accreditation system, the Consejo Centroamericano de Acreditación de la Educación Superior (Central American Accreditation Council for Higher Education).

Admission to higher education is made on the basis of a Bachillerato (specialized secondary school certificate) relevant to the intended field of study. Applicants must also pass an entrance examination. Undergraduates study for four or five years for the Licenciado (Bachelors) degree or a professional title (five years for dentistry, six years for medicine). Postgraduate study after the Licenciado is offered at Especialización (Specialization), Maestría (Masters) and Doctorado (Doctorate) levels of one year, one and a half years, and a minimum of two years respectively.

Technical and vocational education is offered by institutions of higher education; the leading programme of study is the Técnico, which requires two to three years of study. Adult education is administered by the Instituto Nacional de Formación Profesional y Capacitación para el Desarrollo Humano (Institute for Training and Utilization of Human Resources).

Regulatory and Representative Bodies

GOVERNMENT

Ministry of Education: Apdo 0816-04049, Panamá 3; Villa Cárdenas, Ancón, Panamá 3; tel. 511-4400; e-mail lucy.molinar@meduca .gob.pa; internet www.meduca.gob.pa; Minister LUCY MOLINAR.

NATIONAL BODY

Consejo de Rectores de Panamá (Panama Rectors' Council): Albrook, Ancón, Edif. 868, 2°, Panamá; tel. 315-0959; e-mail rectores@ cwpanama.net; internet www.consejo.ac.pa; f. 1995; Pres. Dr BRUNO GARISTO PETROVICH; Sec. Dra XIOMARA DE ARROCHA.

Learned Societies

LANGUAGE AND LITERATURE

Academia Panameña de la Lengua (Panamanian Academy of Language): Apdo 0816-06740, Zona 1, Panamá; Calle Manuel María Icaza, Esq. con Calle 50, Panamá; tel. 223-0717; e-mail aplengua@cwpanama.net; internet www.aplengua.com.pa; corresp. of the Real Academia Española (Madrid); 4 mems, 14 elected mems; Dir BERNA PÉREZ AYALA DE BURRELL; Sec. MARGARITA J. VÁSQUEZ Q.

Alliance Française: Apdo Postal 4305, Zona 5, Panamá; Calle 44 con Avda Justo Arosemena, Edif. Casa Blanca, Bella Vista, Panamá; tel. 223-7376; e-mail alliance@ afpanama.org; internet www.afpanama.org; offers courses and exams in French language and culture and promotes cultural exchange with France; attached teaching centre in David; Dir FABRICE PLACET.

Research Institutes

AGRICULTURE, FISHERIES AND VETERINARY SCIENCE

Instituto de Investigación Agropecuaria de Panamá (Agricultural Research Institute of Panama): Edif. 161 y 162, Ciudad del Saber, Clayton Calle Carlos R. Lara, Panamá 6-4391; tel. 500-0519; e-mail idiap.panama@ idiap.gob.pa; internet www.idiap.gob.pa; f. 1975; helps increase the yields and productivity of agricultural producers; advises govt on formulation and application of scientific policies and agricultural technology; promotes technical training; Gen. Dir Dr PAULO DUCASA C; Sec. JAVIER RODRÍGUEZ.

EDUCATION

Instituto para la Formación y Aprovechamiento de los Recursos Humanos (Institute for the Training and Development of Human Resources): Apdo 6337, Zona 5, Panamá; Vía España, Avda Ramón Arias y Calle 1ra El Carmen, Panamá; tel. 500-4757; internet www.ifarhu.gob.pa; f. 1965; 9 regional agencies, 9 student centres and an Information and Documentation Centre; Dir-Gen. Licda SONIA DE LUZCANDO; Sec.-Gen. EUSEBIA MORÁN; publs Cidinforma (12 a year), Mujer al Cambio (1 a year), Orientifarhu (4 a year).

MEDICINE

Instituto Conmemorativo Gorgas de Estudios de la Salud (Gorgas Commemorative Institute of Health Studies): Avda Justo Arosemena entre Calle 35 y 36, Apdo 0816-02593, Panamá; tel. 527-4800; e-mail informatica@gorgas.gob.pa; internet www .gorgas.gob.pa; f. 1921; library of 6,000 vols, 590 titles of scientific journals; Dir Dr NESTOR SOSA.

NATURAL SCIENCES

Biological Sciences

Instituto Smithsonian de Investigaciones Tropicales (Smithsonian Tropical Research Institute): Apdo Postal 0843-03092, Balboa, Panamá; Roosevelt Avda, Building 401, Tupper, Ancón, Balboa, Panamá; tel. 212-8000; e-mail stribci@si.edu; internet www.stri.org; f. 1923; researches and promotes tropical biology, education and conservation; marine and terrestrial research facilities; library of 66,000 vols, 850 periodicals; Dir Dr WILLIAM WCISLO.

Libraries and Archives

Panamá

Archivo Nacional de Panamá (National Archives of Panama): Apdo 6618, Zona 5, Panamá; Avda Perú entre Calle 31 y 32, Frente a la Plaza de La Loteria, Panamá 6618; tel. 501-6150; e-mail arnapa@ cwpanama.net; internet www .archivonacional.gob.pa; f. 1912; documents from Hispanic era, Republican era and Colombian Union period; 3,400 vols; Dir BETSY DE LEÓN.

Biblioteca del Instituto Nacional de Estadística y Censo (Library of National Institute of Statistics and Census): Apdo 0816–01521, Panamá; Edif. Contraloría General, Avda Balboa, Planta Baja, lado izquierdo, Panamá; tel. 510-4777; e-mail cie_dec@contraloria.gob.pa; internet www.contraloria.gob.pa/inec; f. 1949; compiles and publishes statistical information about Panama and its provinces incl. details of the Nat. Census; 40,000 vols; Dir DANIS P. CEDEÑO H.; Librarian ELSI P. DE MEJÍA; publs *Censo Nacional Agropecuario* (every 10 years), *Censos Nacionales de Población y Vivienda* (every 10 years), *Censos Nacionales Económicos* (every 10 years), *Estadística Panameña* (1 a year), *Informe del Contralor* (1 a year).

Biblioteca Interamericana Simón Bolívar (Interamerican Library Simon Bolivar): Estafeta Universitaria, Panamá; tel. 223-8786; e-mail biblis1@ancon.up.ac.pa; f. 1935 as Biblioteca de la Universidad de Panamá, current name adopted 1978; maintains interchange with 200 instns; 286,000 vols incl. 9,000 vols in medical library; Dir OCTAVIO CASTILLO; publ. *Boletín Bibliográfico* (2 a year).

Biblioteca Nacional de Panamá (National Library of Panama): Apdo 7906, Zona 9, Panamá; Parque Recreativo y Cultural Omar, Vía Porras, San Francisco, Panamá; tel. 224-9466; e-mail referencia@binal.ac.pa; internet www.binal.ac.pa; f. 1892 as Biblioteca Colón, reorganized as Biblioteca Nacional 1942; br. of the Ministry of Education's Public Libraries system; 200,000 vols (incl. bound reviews and periodicals); Admin. Dir MARÍA MAJELA BRENES; publ. *LOTERIA*.

Centro de Información y Documentación Institucional (Institute for Training and Development of Human Resources): Apdo 6337, Zona 5, Panamá; tel. 262-2109; e-mail cidi@ifarhu.gob.pa; internet www.ifarhu.gob.pa; f. 1980; attached to Instituto para la Formación y Aprovechamiento de Recursos Humanos; 5,000 vols; Dir Lic. INES PERALTA DE VARGAS; publs *Orientifarhu*, *Cidinforma*, *Alertas*, *Mujer al Cambio* (1 a year).

Museums and Art Galleries

Coclé

Museo De Parque Arqueológico El Caño (Museum of El Caño Archaeological Park): El Caño, Natá de los Caballeros, Coclé; tel. 228-6231; f. 1979; stone carvings and ornaments of the pre-Columbian era; Dir MERCEDES MENESES.

Colon

Museo de Aduana de Portobelo (Museum of Customs of Portobelo): Frente al Parque de Portobelo, Colón; tel. 448-2024; f. 1998; weapons, objects and historic elements from the 16th, 17th and 18th centuries; Dir ALBERTO HERRERA.

Herrera

Museo de Herrera Fabio Rodriguez (Herrera Museum Fabio Rodriguez): Calle Manuel María Correa y Avda Julio Arjona, Chitré, Herrera; tel. 996-0077; f. 1984; archaeology, pre-Columbian pottery, costumes; dances, dresses and traditions of the countryside; Dir ERILCA MELGAR.

Los Santos

Museo de la Nacionalidad de la Heroica Villa de Los Santos (National Museum of the Heroic Los Santos Villa): Calle José Vallarino, Villa de Los Santos, Los Santos; tel. 966-8192; f. 1974; archaeological objects from Tonosí Valley, pre-Hispanic culture, weapons used in War for Independence; Dir MANUEL MORENO.

Panamá

Centro Natural Punta Culebra (Punta Culebra Nature Centre): Punta Culebra, a unos 3.5 km de la entrada a la Calzada de Amador, Panamá; tel. 212-8793; e-mail puntaculebra@si.edu; internet www.stri.si.edu/english/visit_us/culebra/index.php; f. 1996; attached to Smithsonian Tropical Research Institute; open air museum; exhibits marine biodiversity, conservation and interpretation of marine coastal environments; Admin. Asst DAYRA NAVARRO.

Dirección Nacional del Patrimonio Histórico (National Directorate of Historical Heritage): Apdo 0816-07812, Zona 5, Panamá; tel. 501-4710; e-mail direcciongeneral@inac.gob.pa; internet www.inac.gob.pa/direcciones/patrimonio-historico/; f. 1974; library of 8,000 vols; Nat. Dir SANDRA CERRUD.

Museo de Arte Contemporáneo (Museum of Contemporary Art): Apdo 4211, 0816-00417, Zona 5, Panamá; Avda de los Mártires, Calle San Blas, Ancón, Panamá; tel. 262-8012; e-mail info@macpanama.org; internet www.macpanama.org; f. 1962; library of 3,000 vols; Exec. Dir SILVIA ESTARÁS MANZANO.

Museo Afro-Antilleano (Afro-Antillian Museum): Calle 24 Este y Justo Arosemena, Calidonia, Panamá; tel. 501-4131; e-mail info@samaap.org; internet www.samaap.org; f. 1910; exhibits history and living conditions of West Indian immigrants through photographs and domestic items.

Museo de Arte Religioso Colonial (Museum of Colonial Religious Art): Apdo 662, Zona 1, Panamá; Avda A y Calle 3, San Felipe, Panamá; tel. 228-2897; internet www.inac.gob.pa/museos/105-museo-de-arte-religioso; f. 1974; sited in restored 17th-century Dominican chapel; varied colln of objects of religious art of the Colonial period; cultural programmes and lectures; Dir Prof. NORIS NÚÑEZ DE ALVAREZ.

Museo de Ciencias Naturales (Museum of Natural Sciences): Apdo 662, Zona 1, Panamá; Avda Cuba, Calle 29 y 30, Calidonia, Panamá; tel. 225-0645; e-mail museociencianaturales@yahoo.com; internet www.inac.gob.pa/museos/100-museo-de-ciencias-naturales; f. 1975; natural history, geology and palaeontology; fauna of Panama and other countries; library of 300 vols; Dir Profa NURIA ESQUIVEL DE BARILLAS.

Museo de Historia de Panamá (History Museum of Panama): Apdo 662, Zona 1, Panamá; Avda 6a Central, Plaza Catedral, Palacio Municipal, Planta Baja, San Felipe, Panamá; tel. 501-4128; internet www.inac.gob.pa/museos/99-museo-de-historia; f. 1977; Dir Licda NILKA FUENTES; publ. guide books.

Museo del Canal Interoceánico de Panamá (Museum of the Inter Oceanic Canal of Panama): Calle 5a y 6a Avda Este, San Felipe, Plaza de la Independencia, Apdo 0816-06779, Casco Viejo, Panamá; tel. 211-1649; e-mail info@museodelcanal.com; internet www.museodelcanal.com; f. 1997; exhibits history of canal construction and technology.

Universities

COLUMBUS UNIVERSITY

Edif. Vigamar I, Avda Justo Arosemena y Calle 39 y Edif. Vigamar II, Avda Cuba y Calle 34, Panamá

Telephone: 263-3888
E-mail: columbus@columbus.edu
Internet: www.columbus.edu

Founded 1992
Private control
Language of instruction: Spanish
Academic year: March to December

Campuses in Azuero, Chiriquí and Veraguas

Rector: Dr CARLOS ARELLANO LENNOX
Vice-Rector for Academic Affairs: Mag. CARLOS A. BONILLA G.
Vice-Rector for Admin. and Gen. Dean: Dra MARISSA E. DE MEDINA
Vice-Rector for Research and Graduate Studies: Dra MARÍA EUGENIA CASTAÑEDA V.
Vice-Rector for Outreach and Student Affairs: Dr LUIS DE LEÓN ARIAS

DEANS

Faculty of Administrative Sciences, Economics and Trade: Mag. ANAYANSI O. DE GARCÍA
Faculty of Education Sciences and Language: ELVIA E. CASTILLO C.
Faculty of Law and Political Sciences: Dr LUIS DE LEÓN ARIAS
Faculty of Marine Science and Technology: Capt. PEDRO J. COIDURAS
Faculty of Medicine and Health Sciences: Dr RAFAEL ANDRADE ALEGRE
Faculty of Natural Sciences and Architecture: Dr MARÍA DE LA CRUZ LOMBARDO S.
Faculty of Social Science and Information: Mag. RAÚL ANTONIO LÓPEZ A.

FLORIDA STATE UNIVERSITY

POB 0819-05390, Panamá
Bldg 227, City of Knowledge, Clayton, Panamá

Telephone: 317-0367
E-mail: clangoni@mailer.fsu.edu
Internet: panama.fsu.edu

Founded 1851
Private control
Academic year: March to December

Rector: CARLOS LANGONI
Vice-Rector: ALEXANDRA ANYFANTI

UNIVERSIDAD ABIERTA Y A DISTANCIA DE PANAMÁ (Open and Distance Learning University of Panama)

Apdo 0823-03130, Panamá 7
Calle 39 Este, Edif. 5–57 entre Avda Cuba y Avda Perú, Panamá

Telephone: 227-7242
E-mail: generalunadp@cwpanama.net
Internet: www.unadp.ac.pa

Founded 1994
Private control
Language of instruction: Spanish
Academic year: March to December

Centres in Penonomé and Santiago

Founder: DELIA SÁNCHEZ PONCE
Rector: ROSA ELIDA SÁNCHEZ PONCE
Vice-Rector for Academic Affairs: ÁNGELA MARTÍNEZ
Vice-Rector for Planning, Research and Graduate Studies: ZOBEIDA E. DE BETHANCOURT
Sec.-Gen.: Ing. OSVALDO AGUILAR

UNIVERSIDAD AMERICANA
(American University)

Avda Las Américas-Plaza Panamá Oeste, frente al Mc Donalds de la Chorrera, Panamá

Telephone: 282-1900
E-mail: info@uam.ac.pa
Internet: www.uam.ac.pa

Founded 2002
Private control
Language of instruction: Spanish
Academic year: March to December

Campuses in El Carmen and Los Pueblos

Rector: VERONICA DE BARRIOS
Vice-Rector for Academic Affairs: Dr GUS-TAVO QUINTERO-BARRETO

DEANS

Faculty of Education: NEREIDA SOO NÚÑEZ
Faculty of Law and Political Science: MAR-ITZA MAXWELL
Faculty of Medical and Health Sciences: Dr JOSÉ PAREDES

UNIVERSIDAD AUTÓNOMA DE CHIRIQUÍ
(Autonomous University of Chiriquí)

El Cabrero, David, Chiriquí

Telephone: 730-5300
E-mail: rectoria@unachi.ac.pa
Internet: www.unachi.ac.pa

Founded 1994; present name and status 1995
State control
Language of instruction: Spanish
Academic year: March to December

Campuses in Barú, Boquete, Oriente and Volcán; also faculty of humanities

Rector: ETELVINA DE BONAGAS
Vice-Rector for Academic Affairs: JOSÉ COR-ONEL
Vice-Rector for Admin. Affairs: ROSA MORENO
Vice-Rector for Research and Postgraduate Affairs: Dra ROGER SANCHEZ
Sec.-Gen.: MARIO LUIS PITTÍ

Number of teachers: 1,056

Publications: *Bitacora* (4 a year), *Econometrín*, *El Observator*, *Revista*, *Senda Universitaria* (12 a year), *Supra*

DEANS

Faculty of Business Administration and Accountancy: Dr RAFAEL BOLÍVAR AGUILAR
Faculty of Economics: ÁNGEL GÓMEZ
Faculty of Education: ALEXIS VILLALAZ
Faculty of Law and Political Science: ABEL BULTRÓN
Faculty of Medicine: Dr FÉLIX G. RODRÍGUEZ
Faculty of Natural Sciences: PEDRO CABALLERO
Faculty of Nursing: LIANA DEL CID
Faculty of Public Administration: ROSA NELY MÉNDEZ
Faculty of Social Communication: HERIBERTO CABALLERO

UNIVERSIDAD CATÓLICA SANTA MARÍA LA ANTIGUA
(Catholic University St Mary the Ancient)

Via Ricardo J. Alfaro, Apdo 0819-08550, Panamá

Telephone: 230-8206
E-mail: rectoria@usma.ac.pa
Internet: www.usmapanama.com

Founded 1965, reorganized 1973
Private control
Languages of instruction: Spanish, English
Academic year: January to December (3 semesters)

Chancellor: Mgr JOSÉ DOMINGO ULLOA MENDIETA
Rector: Mgr CARLOS ALBERTO VOLOJ PEREIRA
Vice-Rector for Academic Affairs: Mgr PAULINA FRANCESCHI
Vice-Rector for Admin. Affairs: Prof. LUIS PABÓN ORDOÑES
Vice-Rector for Research and Postgraduate Affairs: Mgr MARÍA EUGENIA PÉREZ DE ALEMÁN
Sec.-Gen.: Mgr INGRID MIROSLAVA CHANG VALDÉS
Librarian: Licda IRENE DE CARVAJAL

Library of 65,000 vols
Number of teachers: 400
Number of students: 4,500

Publications: *Iustitia et Pulchritudo* (1 a year), *Revista La Antigua* (2 a year)

DEANS

Faculty of Architecture and Design: Arq. ALCIDES PONCE
Faculty of Business: Prof. EDUARDO PAZMIÑO
Faculty of Engineering and Technology: Prof. KARIMA RACHEL
Faculty of Humanities and Religious Studies: Prof. FRANCISCO JAVIER BLANCO
Faculty of Law and Political Science: Prof. VICTOR DELGADO
Faculty of Social Sciences: Mag. FLORENCIA ORTEGA

UNIVERSIDAD DE PANAMÁ
(Panama University)

Estafeta Universitaria, Apdo 3366, Panamá 4, Panamá
Urb. El Cangrejo, Vía Simón Bolívar (Transístmica) con la intercepción de la Vía Manuel Espinoza Batista y José De Fábrega, Panamá

Telephone: 523-5000
E-mail: upweb@up.ac.pa
Internet: www.up.ac.pa

Founded 1935
State control
Language of instruction: Spanish
Academic year: March to December

Campus also in Harmodio Arias Madrid; regional centres in Azuero, Bocas del Toro, Coclé, Colón, Darién, Los Santos, Panamá Oeste, San Miguelito and Veraguas

Rector: Dr GUSTAVO GARCÍA DE PAREDES
Vice-Rector for Academic Affairs: Dr JUSTO MEDRANO
Vice-Rector for Admin. Affairs: Dr JOSÉ CHEN BARRIA
Vice-Rector for Extension: Dr MARÍA DEL CARMEN TERRIENTES DE BENAVIDES
Vice-Rector for Research and Graduate Studies: Dr JUAN ANTONIO GÓMEZ H.
Vice-Rector for Student Affairs: ELDIS BARNES
Sec.-Gen.: Dr MIGUEL ANGEL CANDANEDO
Librarian: Prof. DAYSI DE JEAN FRANÇOISE

Number of teachers: 8,772
Number of students: 51,627

Publications: *Campus*, *ECO*, *EDU*, *Hacia La Luz*, *Memoria*, *Revistas Jurídicas Panameñas*, *Revista Universidad*, *Scientia*

DEANS

Faculty of Agricultural Sciences: Dr JUAN MIGUEL MIGUEL OSORIO
Faculty of Architecture: Prof. RICARDO ORTEGA
Faculty of Business Administration and Accountancy: ROLDÁN ADAMES
Faculty of Computer Science, Electronics and Communication: Dra DIANA CHEN
Faculty of Economics: Mag. ROLANDO GORDÓN CANTO
Faculty of Education: Dra MIGDALIA BUSTAMANTE DE AVILÉS

Faculty of Fine Arts: Mag. LUIS TROETSCH
Faculty of Humanities: Dr CARMEN G. CÓRDOBA
Faculty of Law and Political Sciences: Dr ROLANDO MURGAS TORRAZZA
Faculty of Medicine: Dr ENRIQUE MENDOZA
Faculty of Natural and Exact Sciences and Technology: Prof. CARLOS RAMOS DELGADO
Faculty of Nursing: Mag. ALCIRA TEJADA ANRIA
Faculty of Odontology: Dr LUIS BATRES MÉNDEZ
Faculty of Pharmacy: Dra LEIDA BARRIOS
Faculty of Psychology: Dr MARIA ELENA S. DE CANO
Faculty of Public Administration: NICOLÁS JEROME
Faculty of Social Communication: Mag. RAFAEL AYALA BOLÍVAR
Faculty of Veterinary Medicine: Dr CARLOS G. MORÁN R.

UNIVERSIDAD DEL ISTMO
(University of Istmo)

Avda Justo Arosemena, Calle 40 y 41, Panamá

Telephone: 227-8822
E-mail: informacion@udi.edu
Internet: www.udi.edu

Founded 1963
Private control

Campuses in Chitré, Changuinola, Colón, David, La Chorrera, Las Tablas, Los Pueblos, Penonomé and Santiago

Rector: JOSÉ LEONARDO VALENCIA MOLANO
Dean for Academic Devt: Dr JUAN LUIS CORREA

DEANS

Faculty of Business: Lic. PEDRO DÍAZ ALFARO
Faculty of Communication Sciences: Licda ANNETTE CLEMENT
Faculty of Engineering and Information Technology: Ing. LEONIDAS ANZOLA
Faculty of Law and Political Science: Dr OYDÉN ORTEGA DURÁN
Faculty of Maritime Business: Dr OYDÉN ORTEGA DURÁN
Faculty of Marketing and Advertising: Mag. ALEJANDRO FERNÁNDEZ
Faculty of Tourism and Technical Courses: Mag. FIDEL REYES ESQUER

UNIVERSIDAD ESPECIALIZADA DE LAS AMERICAS
(Specialized University of the Americas)

Albrook Edif. 806-808-809-830-850, Apdo 0843-01041, Panamá

Telephone: 501-1000
E-mail: rectoria@udelas.ac.pa
Internet: www.udelas.ac.pa

Founded 1997
State control
Language of instruction: Spanish
Academic year: March to December

Campuses in Azuero, Chiriquí, Coclé, Colón and Veraguas

Rector: Dra BERTA TORRIJOS DE AROSEMENA
Vice-Rector: Dr JUAN BOSCO BERNAL
Gen. Sec.: ERIC GARCÍA
Librarian: YISELA ARROCHA
Dean for Postgraduate Studies: OCAR SITTÓN
Dean for Research: Dr ALEXIS RODRIGUEZ

Library of 10,000 vols
Number of teachers: 873
Number of students: 7,000

DEANS

Faculty of Integrated Health and Rehabilitation: Dr PEDRO ARCIA

Faculty of Social and Special Education: Dr WALTER SERRANO

UNIVERSIDAD INTERAMERICANA DE PANAMÁ
(Inter-American University of Panama)

Avda Manuel Espinosa Batista, Panamá

Telephone: 208-4444
E-mail: crai@uip.edu.pa
Internet: www.uip.edu.pa
Founded 1992
Private control
Language of instruction: Spanish
Academic year: January to December
Campuses in Chorrera and Plaza Conquistador
Pres.: WILLIAM J. SALOM
Rector: STANLEY MUSCHETT
Vice-Rector for Academics: FRANCISCO MONDINO
Sec.-Gen.: MIRIAM PÉREZ DE ESPINO

UNIVERSIDAD LATINA DE PANAMÁ
(Latin University of Panama)

Apdo 87-0887, Via Ricardo J. Alfaro, Calle Aragón, Catilla, Panamá 7

Telephone: 230-8600
E-mail: web@ulatina.ac.pa
Internet: www.ulat.ac.pa
Founded 1989, present status 1991
Private control
Language of instruction: Spanish
Academic year: March to December
Campuses in Chitré, David, Penonomé and Santiago
Rector: Dr MODALDO TUÑON
Registrar: CLAUDIA MARÍN
Library Dir: AURA AROSEMENA

Publications: *Info Latina* (print and online, www.ulat.ac.pa/revista), *Latina News*

DEANS

Faculty of Business: GUSTAVO QUINTERO-BARRETTO
Faculty of Communication Sciences: NEDELKA GALVEZ
Faculty of Education Sciences: GLADYS DE JAÉN
Faculty of Engineering: Ing. BETZY PINTO
Faculty of Health Sciences Dr William C. Gorgas: Dr JORGE MEDRANO
Faculty of Law and Political Sciences: Lic. OCTAVIO DEL MORAL

UNIVERSIDAD LATINOAMERICANA DE CIENCIA Y TECNOLOGÍA
(Latin American University of Science and Technology)

Vía España Calle 74E, Carrasquilla, Panamá

Telephone: 323-6600
E-mail: narosemena@ulacit.ac.pa
Internet: www.ulacit.ac.pa
Founded 1991
Private control
Language of instruction: Spanish
Academic year: March to December
Also faculties of business studies, engineering, law and political science
Rector: Dr STANLEY MUSCHETT
Vice-Rector for Academic Affairs: GLORIELA ORO
Sec.-Gen.: MIRIAM PÉREZ DE ESPINO
Dean for Graduate Studies: CESAR CONSTANTINO

Library of 40,000 vols, 80,000 periodical titles

DEANS

Faculty of Health Sciences: Dr FERNANDO GRACIA

UNIVERSIDAD LATINOAMERICANA DE COMERCIO EXTERIOR
(Latin American University of Foreign Trade)

Calle F al lado del Teatro la Cúpula, El Cangrejo, Panamá

Telephone: 223-7941
E-mail: info@ulacex.com
Internet: www.ulacex.com
Private control
Language of instruction: Spanish
Academic year: March to December
Rector: Ing. BRUNO GARISTO PETROVICH

UNIVERSIDAD MARÍTIMA INTERNACIONAL DE PANAMÁ
(International Maritime University of Panama)

Apdo 0843-03561, Panamá
Campus Universitario, La Boca, Panamá

Telephone: 314-3700
E-mail: info@umip.ac.pa
Internet: www.umip.ac.pa
Founded 2005
State control
Language of instruction: Spanish
Academic year: March to December
Rector: Ing. VÍCTOR LUNA BARAHONA
Vice-Rector for Academic Affairs: CARLOS AYÚ PRADO
Vice-Rector for Admin.: Lic. GIUSEPE BONISSI
Vice-Rector for Research, Graduate Studies and Extension: MARÍA DELGADO
Sec.-Gen.: Lic. ANGEL ATENCIO

Library of 1,500 vols, 771 geographical maps and nautical charts

DEANS

Faculty of Civil and Maritime Engineering: Capt. JUSTO REYES ALLARD
Faculty of Marine Sciences: Dr HUMBERTO GARCÉS
Faculty of Maritime Transport: Capt. ERNESTO CORDOVEZ
Faculty of Nautical Sciences: Ing. FAUSTINO GONZÁLEZ

UNIVERSIDAD PANAMERICANA
(Pan American University)

Edif. No 23, Vía Argentina Calle No 49 Oeste, El Cangrejo, Panamá

Telephone: 203-9991
E-mail: direccion-administrativa@upam.ac.pa
Internet: www.upampanama.com
Founded 2001
Private control
Language of instruction: Spanish
Academic year: March to December
Rector: ROLANDO MUÑOZ
Vice-Rector for Admin.: ELIZABETH DE BARAHONA
Dean: ANDRÉS BARRIOS LÓPEZ
Librarian: LEYDI SANTANA
Sec.-Gen.: DAMARIS CANDANEDO

UNIVERSIDAD TECNOLOGICA DE PANAMÁ
(Technological University of Panama)

Apdo 0819-07289, El Dorado, Panama
Campus 'Víctor Levi Sasso', Panama

Telephone: 560-3246
E-mail: rectoria@utp.ac.pa
Internet: www.utp.ac.pa
Founded 1981

State control
Languages of instruction: English, Spanish
Academic year: March to December
7 Regional centres in Azuero, Bocas del Toro, Chiriquí, Coclé, Colón Veraguas and Panamá Oeste
Rector: PhD OSCAR M. RAMÍREZ R.
Vice-Rector for Academic Affairs: PhD OMAR AIZPURUA
Vice-Rector for Admin. Affairs: Ing. ESMERALDA HERNÁNDEZ
Vice-Rector for Research and Graduate Studies: PhD GILBERTO A. CHANG C.
Dir of External Affairs: PhD VICTOR SÁNCHEZ
Sec.-Gen.: Ing. LUIS A. BARAHONA G.
Librarian: Licda EDILDA F. DE MORALES

Number of teachers: 1,547
Number of students: 19,580

Publications: *Memorias* (1 a year), *Reflejos* (6 a year, print and online, www.fisc.utp.ac.pa/reflejos), *Revista de I+D Tecnológico* (2 a year, print and online, www.utp.ac.pa/publicaciones-digitales-de-la-revista-de-id-tecnologico), *Revista El Tecnológico* (2 a year, print and online, www.utp.ac.pa/revista-el-tecnologico), *Revista Mente & Materia* (2 a year, print and online, cei.utp.ac.pa/revista-mente-materia), *Revista 'Prisma Tecnológico'* (2 a year, print and online, www.utp.ac.pa/revista-prisma-tecnologico), *Revista Tecnología Hoy*

DEANS

Faculty of Civil Engineering: Ing. ÁNGELA LAGUNA
Faculty of Computer Science Engineering: PhD NICOLÁS SAMANIEGO
Faculty of Electrical Engineering: PhD JULIO QUIEL
Faculty of Industrial Engineering: Ing. SONIA SEVILLA
Faculty of Mechanical Engineering: Ing. MIRTHA MOORE
Faculty of Science and Technology: Mag. ÁNGELA ALEMÁN

Schools of Arts and Music

Centro Educativo en Artes Diversificadas (Diversified Arts Education Centre): Calle Hospital, Edif. 6548 y 6550, Los Ríos, Corozal, Ancón, Panamá; tel. 317-6943; e-mail ebadinac@hotmail.com; f. 1997 as Escuela de Bachillerato en Artes Diversificadas; current name adopted 2013; Dir ALBERTO OLMOS (acting).

Escuela de Folklore de San Miguelito (School of Folklore of San Miguelito): Entrada de Paraíso, Esq. Calle de Circunvalación con calle J, Antigua Caja de Ahorros de San Miguelito, Panamá; tel. 501-4156; e-mail efosanmiguelito@hotmail.com; f. 2001; Dir JETZABE SANDOVAL.

Escuela Nacional de Danzas (National School of Dance): Apdo 662, Zona 1, Ancón, Panamá; Edif. 5553, Diablo, Corregimiento Ancón, Panamá; tel. 232-0572; e-mail escueladedanzas.isba.inac@gmail.com; f. 1948; Dir ANA ACELA SMITH.

Escuela Nacional de Teatro (National School of Theatre): Apdo 662, Zona 1, Panamá; Antiguo Museo del Hombre Panameño, Plaza 5 de Mayo, Panamá; tel. 501-4121; e-mail escueladeteatro-inac@hotmail.com; f. 1974; 10 teachers; 40 students; Dir EIRA LEDEZMA.

Instituto Nacional de Música (National Institute of Music): Edif. 800, Albrook, Corregimiento Ancón, Panamá; tel. 501-4113; e-mail inam-inac@hotmail.com; f. 1904; Dir ROBERTO FLÓREZ (acting).

PAPUA NEW GUINEA

The Higher Education System

In 1906 the Territory of Papua came under Australian control, and in 1914 the former German possession of New Guinea became a Trust Territory, also under Australian control. A joint administration for the two territories was established by Australia in July 1949, and the name Papua New Guinea was adopted in 1971. Independence was achieved in 1975. Major institutions of higher education were first established in the 1960s, including the Papua New Guinea Institute of Public Administration—founded in 1963—and the University of Papua New Guinea, the University of Vudal—renamed the Papua New Guinea University of Natural Resources and Environment in 2005—and the Papua New Guinea University of Technology (all founded in 1965). The Office of Higher Education, which was established by the Higher Education Act of 1983, is the administrative and executive agency for higher education in Papua New Guinea. In 2012 there were 32 authorised higher and technical education institutions. The enrolment figures for the University of Papua New Guinea in that year were 5,043 students and for the University of Technology 2,856 students. However, according to the Minister for Higher Education, Research, Science and Technology, the country's universities had exceeded their designed infrastruc-ture capacity and a new National Higher Education Plan III (2013–23) was being designed to review, among other issues, the 1983 Higher Education Act, the student financial support scheme, and the quality standards of institutions.

Admission to higher education is on the basis of the Grade 12 Higher School Certificate. However, students with the Grade 10 Secondary School Certificate may enter a degree course after completing a foundation year. In addition to the standard undergraduate Bachelors degree, which is a four-year pro-gramme of study, universities offer two- to four-year diploma and certificate-level courses. Degree courses in medicine and law are five years in duration. Following the Bachelors, the Masters is the first postgraduate degree and lasts between one and three years. Finally, the PhD is the highest university-level degree and requires students to undertake a period of relevant training prior to starting the course. The PhD itself requires a minimum of three years' study and research for the preparation and submission of a thesis.

Most technical and vocational education starts at the secondary Grade 10-level, and consists of one- to two-year certificate and three-year diploma programmes at technical colleges and specialized professional institutes.

Regulatory Body

GOVERNMENT

Department of Education: FinCorp Haus, POB 446, Waigani, NCD; tel. 3013555; internet www.education.gov.pg; Minister Hon. JAMES MARAPE (acting).

Department of Higher Education, Research, Science and Technology: Mutual Rumana Bldg, Boroko, NCD; tel. 3277528; Minister Hon. DELILAH GORE.

Department of Tourism, Arts and Cul-ture: Port Moresby, NCD; Minister BOKA KONDRA.

ACCREDITATION

Office of Higher Education: Level Two, Mutual Rumana Waigani Dr., POB 5117, Boroko, 111 NCD; tel. 3012051; internet www.ohe.gov.pg; Dir-Gen. Dr WILLIAM TAGIS.

Learned Societies

BIBLIOGRAPHY, LIBRARY SCIENCE AND MUSEOLOGY

Papua New Guinea Library Association: c/o National Library Service, POB 734, Waigani, NCD; f. 1973; 200 mems; Pres. MARGARET J. OBI; Sec. JENNY WAL; publs *Directory of Libraries in Papua New Guinea*, *PNGLA Nius* (2 a year), *Toktok bilong haus buk* (Journal, 4 a year).

ECONOMICS, LAW AND POLITICS

Papua New Guinea Institute of Banking and Business Management: ToRobert Centre, Vanama Crescent, POB 1721, Lawes Rd, Port Moresby NCD; tel. 3212088; e-mail customerservice@ibbm.com.pg; internet www.ibbm.com.pg; f. 1965; training in admin., finance, banking, commerce, super-visory and management skills; Exec. Dir SWETA SUD.

LANGUAGE AND LITERATURE

Alliance Française: UPNG Campus, Kuri Dom Bldg, Port Moresby; tel. 3267120; e-mail info@afportmoresby.org; internet www .afportmoresby.org; offers courses and exams in French language and culture and pro-motes cultural exchange with France; library of 1,500 vols.

NATURAL SCIENCES

General

Papua New Guinea Scientific Society: c/o National Museum and Art Gallery, POB 5560, Boroko; tel. 3252422; e-mail pngmuseum@global.net.pg; f. 1949; promotes sciences, exchanges scientific information, preserves scientific collns and establishes museums; 203 mems; Pres. H. SAKULAS; publ. *Proceedings*.

Research Institutes

GENERAL

National Research Institute: POB 5854, Boroko, NCD; tel. 3260300; e-mail nri@nri .org.pg; internet www.nri.org.pg; f. 1961 as New Guinea Research Unit, present name 1989; research in social, political, economic, educational and cultural issues in Papua New Guinea; research focus on wealth cre-ation, universal basic education, governance and public sector and environment and people; library of 10,000 vols; Dir Dr THOMAS WEBSTER; publ. *TaimLain: A Journal of Contemporary Melanesian Studies*.

AGRICULTURE, FISHERIES AND VETERINARY SCIENCE

Lowlands Agricultural Experiment Sta-tion: Kerevat, POB 204, Kokopo, East New Britain Province; tel. 9839145; f. 1928; food crops, spices, soil and land management, entomology and plant pathology.

ECONOMICS, LAW AND POLITICS

Institute of National Affairs: POB 1530, Port Moresby NCD; tel. 3211045; internet www.inapng.com; f. 1979; conducts research in economy, taxation, land, trade, coastal shipping, industrialization, law and order, agriculture, mining, small business, govt expenditure, fisheries, forestry, human cap-ital formation and labour; publishes smaller research papers and speech series papers; Pres. DAVID PEATE; Exec. Dir and Treas. and Sec. PAUL BARKER.

MEDICINE

Papua New Guinea Institute of Medical Research: POB 60, Goroka, 411 EHP; tel. 5322800; e-mail info@pngimr.org.pg; internet www.pngimr.org.pg; f. 1968; brs: Goroka, Madang, Maprik and Wewak; research in matters relating to research into human health and disease within Papua New Guinea incl. medical, human biological, nutritional and sociological research; library of 5,000 vols; Dir Prof. PETER SIBA.

Libraries and Archives

Boroko

National Archives and Public Records Service: POB 1089, Boroko; tel. 3256200; f. 1957; br. of Nat. Library Service, Division of the Dept of Education; repository for the public archives and records of Papua New Guinea; Reference Service and Microfilm Unit, Records Management Service and Records Centre Service for govt offices and statutory bodies; br. repository in Lae: 10,000 linear m and 1,000 maps and plans, and photographic archives; Chief Archivist JACOB HELEVAWA; publs *Guides to Groups of Records in the National Archives* (irregular), *Patrol Reports* (microfiche, irregular).

Lae

Matheson Library, Papua New Guinea University of Technology: PMB, Lae, 411; tel. 4734351; e-mail ikisikel@lib.unitech.ac.pg; f. 1965; 600 serial titles, 4,000 audiovisual items; spec. colln: Papua New Guinea; microfilm unit produces microfiche edns of all major PNG serial publs; 99,250 vols (Taraka campus); Univ. Librarian ISMAEL ISIKEL KAVANAMUR (acting).

Waigani

National Library Service: POB 734, Waigani; tel. 3256200; f. 1975; nat. reference library; legal deposit library; ISBN agency for Papua New Guinea; advisory services, lending and educational services; important holdings of New Guinea, particularly govt publs; Papua New Guinea colln; films and video cassettes of Papua New Guinea; mobile school library service; 50,000 vols, 4,000 films and video recordings; Dir-Gen. DANIEL PARAIDE; publs *Directory of Libraries in Papua New Guinea* (irregular), *OLA Nius* (6 a year), *Papua New Guinea Directory of Information Sources in Science and Technology* (irregular), *Papua New Guinea National Bibliography* (1 a year), *Selective Times Index to PNG* (1 a year).

University of Papua New Guinea 'Michael Somare Library': c/o Univ. of Papua New Guinea, POB 320, University Post Office, Waigani; tel. 3260900; f. 1965; 500,000 vols, 2,000 current journals, 25,000 vols in law section; Librarian IVARATURE KIVIA; publs *New Guinea Archives: A Listing* (microfiche), *New Guinea Photographic Index* (microfiche).

Subordinate library:

    Medical Library: POB 5623, Boroko; f. 1976; 65,000 vols; Librarian L. WANGATAU; publ. *Papua New Guinea Medical Journal*.

Museum and Art Gallery

Boroko

Papua New Guinea National Museum and Art Gallery: POB 5560, Boroko; tel. 3252422; e-mail pngmuseum@global.net.pg; f. 1954; field research in archaeology, cultural anthropology, natural history; educational tours, public programmes, broadcasts, etc.; aims to implement the National Cultural Property (Preservation) Act to protect Papua New Guinea's cultural heritage, and establish museums; library of 4,500 vols; Dir SIMON PAUL PORAITUK.

Universities

DIVINE WORD UNIVERSITY

POB 483, Madang
Telephone: 4222907
E-mail: info@dwu.ac.pg
Internet: www.dwu.ac.pg
Founded 1979 as Divine Word Institute, present status 1996
Private control
Language of instruction: English
Academic year: February to October (2 semesters)

Campuses in Modilon, Port Moresby, St Benedict and Mt Hagen; academic programmes incl. faculty of theology

Pres.: JAN CZUBA
Vice-Pres.: Dr CECILIA NEMBOU
Vice-Pres. for Academic Affairs: Prof. PAMELA NORMAN
Vice-Pres. for Admin.: BENJAMIN NAING
Vice-Pres. for Corporate Services, Devt and Self-Reliance: NEIL HERMES

Vice-Pres. for Research and Postgraduate Studies: Dr MARETTA KULA SEMOS
Vice-Pres. for Student Affairs: ANDREW SIMPSON
Dean of Students: ANDREW POHON
Dean of Studies: PAMELA NORMAN
Registrar: CECILIA N'DROWER
Dir of Library: DAVID LLOYD
Library of 43,320 vols, 1,350 ebooks and 1,659 ejournals

Publication: *DWU Research Journal* (2 a year)

DEANS

Faculty of Arts: Dr LINDA SUE CROWL
Faculty of Business and Management: Dr ROMULO LINDIO
Faculty of Education: Dr CATHERINE NONGKAS
Faculty of Flexible Learning: Dr LYNUS YAMUNA
Faculty of Health Sciences: Dr PASCAL MICHON

PACIFIC ADVENTIST UNIVERSITY

PMB, Boroko, 111 NCD
Telephone: 3280200
E-mail: administration@pau.ac.gp
Internet: www.pau.ac.pg
Founded 1984 as Pacific Adventist College, present status 1997
Private control
Language of instruction: English
Academic year: February to August

Campuses in Koiari Park and Boroko; affiliated campuses: Fiji and Sonoma

Chancellor: Dr BARRY OLIVER
Vice-Chancellor: Dr BEN THOMAS
Deputy Vice-Chancellor: TRACIE MAFILE'O
Dir of Research and Postgraduate Studies: Dr LALEN SIMEON
Dir of Student Services: THOMAS DAVAI (acting)
Registrar: PELE ALU
Number of teachers: 50
Number of students: 380

Publication: *Davaria*

DEANS

School of Arts and Humanities: Dr JENNIFER LITAU
School of Business: Dr KHIN MAUNG KYI
School of Education: Dr KURESA TAGA'I
School of Health Science: NINA PANGIAU
School of Science and Technology: ELISAPESI MANSON (acting)
School of Theology: Dr DAVID THIELE

PAPUA NEW GUINEA UNIVERSITY OF NATURAL RESOURCES AND ENVIRONMENT

UNRE PMB Service, Rabaul, E New Britain Province
Telephone: 9839144
Internet: www.unre.ac.pg
Founded 1965 as Vudal Agricultural College, present status 1997, present name 2005
State control
Language of instruction: English
Academic year: February to November

Campuses in Vudal, Popondetta, Sepik Central and Kavieng, depts of management studies, agriculture, fisheries, forestry

Chancellor and Chair.: (vacant)
Pro-Chancellor: MARGARET ELIAS
Pro-Vice-Chancellor for Academic Affairs and Planning: (vacant)
Pro-Vice-Chancellor for Admin. and Devt: (vacant)
Vice-Chancellor: Prof. Dr PHILIP SIAGURU
Registrar: HENRY GIOVEN

Bursar: JACKSON RODGERS
Librarian: BRUCE NINGAKUN
Library of 25,000
Number of teachers: 20
Number of students: 380

DEANS

School of Natural Resources: Dr ALAN QUARTERMAN

PAPUA NEW GUINEA UNIVERSITY OF TECHNOLOGY

PMB, Lae
Telephone: 4734206
E-mail: lfugre@admin.unitech.ac.pg
Internet: www.unitech.ac.pg
Founded 1965 as Papua New Guinea Institute of Higher Technical Education, present name and status 1973
State control
Language of instruction: English
Academic year: February to November (2 semesters)

Depts of agriculture, applied physics, applied science, architecture and bldg, business studies, communications and devt studies, civil engineering, electrical and communication engineering, forestry, mathematics and computer science, mechanical engineering, mining engineering and surveying and lands

Chancellor: A. TOLOLO
Pro-Chancellor: R. KEKEDO
Vice-Chancellor and Pro-Vice Chancellor for Admin.: Dr MISTY BALOILOI
Pro-Vice Chancellor for Academic Affairs: Dr MUHAMMED A. SATTER
Registrar: ALLAN J. Q. SAKO
Univ. Librarian: ISMAEL ISIKEL KAVANAMUR (acting)
Library: see under Libraries and Archives
Number of teachers: 100
Number of students: 2,600

Publications: *UniTech Reporter* (12 a year), *Research Report*, *Vice-Chancellor's Report*

UNIVERSITY OF GOROKA

POB 1078, Goroka, EHP
Telephone: 5311727
Internet: www.uog.ac.pg
Founded 1997 by merger of two faculties of Univ. of Papua New Guinea (UPNG) and Goroka Teacher's College (GTC)
State control
Language of instruction: English
Academic year: January to December

Chancellor: PETER BAKI
Vice-Chancellor: Dr GAIRO ONAGI (acting)
Pro-Vice-Chancellor for Academic Affairs and Devt: Dr MICHAEL MEL (acting)
Pro-Vice-Chancellor for Admin.: Dr JAMES YOKO (acting)
Dir of Student Admin.: E. MAKARAI
Dir of Student Services: MONICA PUSAL
Librarian and Head of Dept: LEAH KALAMOROH
Library of 100,000 vols of monographs, 110 periodicals, 400 serials and 1,000 visual items
Number of teachers: 80
Number of students: 1,800

Publication: *Papua New Guinea Journal of Teacher Education* (1 a year)

DEANS

Faculty of Education: Dr KAPA DARIUS KELEP-MALPO
Faculty of Humanities: DAVID AWAY HOSEA
Faculty of Science: Dr POORANALINGHAM JEYARATHAN
School of Graduate Studies: Dr SAM NAJIKE

UNIVERSITY OF PAPUA NEW GUINEA

Box 320, University Post Office, Waigani
Telephone: 3260900
E-mail: pr&m@upng.ac.pg
Internet: www.upng.ac.pg
Founded 1965
State control
Language of instruction: English
Academic year: February to September (2 semesters)
Campuses: Waigani (HQ) and Taurama
Chancellor: Sir ALKAN TOLOLO

Pro-Chancellor: Dr ROSEMARY KEKEDO
Vice-Chancellor: Prof. ROSS HYNES
Deputy Vice-Chancellor: N. R. KUMAN
Registrar: VINCENT MALAIBE
Library: see under Libraries and Archives
Number of teachers: 700
Number of students: 4,416
Publications: *Melanesian Law Journal* (2 a year), *PNG Law*, *Research in Melanesia* (2 a year), *Science in New Guinea* (4 a year), *South Pacific Journal of Psychology* (1 a year), *Yagl-Ambu*

DEANS

Centre for Research and Postgraduate Studies: Dr Prof. SIMON SAULEI
School of Business Admin.: Prof. Dr ALBERT MELLAM
School of Humanities and Social Science: Prof. Dr KENNETH SUMBUK
School of Law: S. KAIPU (acting)
School of Medicine and Health Sciences: Prof. Dr ISI KEVAU
School of Natural and Physical Sciences: Prof. Dr L. HILL (acting)

PARAGUAY

The Higher Education System

Paraguay, ruled by Spain from the 16th century, achieved independence in 1811. The oldest institution of higher education is the Universidad Nacional de Asunción founded in 1889. The next oldest university, the Universidad Católica Nuestra Señora de la Asunción, was not opened until the 1960s. Following the end of military rule in 1989, several universities were established in the 1990s. Until 2013 the governing law of higher education was Law 136/93 (1993), which led to the creation of the Consejo de Universidades (Council of Universities). However, on 2 August 2013 the Ley de Educación Superior (Law 4995/13) was promulgated, providing for the establishment of a new body, the Consejo Nacional de Educación Superior (National Council of Higher Education). This organization, whose aim was to improve the quality of higher education in Paraguay and to restrain the proliferation of new tertiary institutions, many of which were believed to be providing education of variable standards, held its inaugural meeting on 2 November 2013. In 2010, according to UNESCO, there were 236,000 students enrolled in tertiary-level education, of whom 67% were at private institutions. In 2012 a total of 53 university-level institutions (eight public, 45 private) were officially registered in Paraguay.

Applicants must have the Bachillerato in order to gain admission to higher education, and universities may set individual entry requirements. The Título de Licenciatura is the main undergraduate degree, and is awarded after four years of study. Under Law 136/93 the Título de Licenciatura is both an academic and a professional title. Undergraduate degrees in professional fields of study, such as economics, engineering, law and medicine, last between four and six years. In some professional areas an intermediate level qualification, the Título Intermedio, may be awarded after between one and three years of undergraduate study, although this does not confer any professional rights. There is no uniform system of postgraduate degrees, which were not available in Paraguay before 1991. However, the Universidad Nacional de Asunción has established a system that is being considered by the Consejo de Universidades, consisting of: Diplomado (Diploma), a postgraduate short course in a professional field of study; Especialización (Specialization), undertaken as part of the undergraduate degree; Maestría (Masters), which lasts two years; and Título de Doctorado (Doctorate) or Doctor en Ciencias (Doctor of Sciences), which were available at nine universities (four public and five private) in 2005.

Post-secondary technical and vocational education is available mainly at Instituciones Técnicas Superiores (higher technical institutions). A total of four such institutions were officially registered in 2012. The Título de Técnico Superior is awarded after completion of two years.

The Agencia Nacional de Evaluación y Acreditación de la Educación Superior (ANEAES—National Agency for Evaluation and Accreditation of Higher Education) was founded in 2003 following the enactment of Law 2072/03. ANEAES is the national body for quality assurance and accreditation of higher education at undergraduate and postgraduate levels. Paraguay also participates in the Mecanismo Experimental de Acreditación de Carreras del Mercosur.

Regulatory and Representative Bodies

GOVERNMENT

Consejo Nacional de Educación y Cultura (CONEC) (National Council for Education and Culture): Sgto. Martinez 240 entre Dr Telmo Aquino, Asunción; tel. (21) 660-763; e-mail secretaria@conec.gov.py; internet www.conec.gov.py; formulates and implements nat. policy on education and culture; proposes ways to develop and improve the educational system; 12 mems; Pres. MARTA LAFUENTE; Admin. Dir Lic. MIRTA ELIZABETH ARMOA.

Dirección General de Educación Superior (Directorate General of Higher Education): Avda Mariscal López 735 casi Tacuary, Asunción; tel. (21) 443-040; e-mail info@educacionsuperior.mec.gov.py; internet educacionsuperior.mec.gov.py; attached to Min. of Education and Culture; outlines policies and strategies to ensure quality training of professionals; Dir-Gen. CARLOS GARAY.

Ministry of Education and Culture: Edif. La Consolidada, Chile 719, Casi Eduardo V. Haedo, Asunción; tel. (21) 450-014; e-mail comunicacion@mec.gov.py; internet www.mec.gov.py; Minister MARTA LAFUENTE.

ACCREDITATION

Agencia Nacional de Evaluación y Acreditación de la Educación Superior (ANEAES) (National Agency for Evaluation and Accreditation of Higher Education): Jejuí No 530 entre 14 de Mayo y 15 de Agosto, Asunción; tel. (21) 445-362; e-mail info@aneaes.gov.py; internet www.aneaes.gov.py; f. 2003; Pres. Dra CARMEN QUINTANA-HORÁK.

Learned Societies

GENERAL

Academia de la Lengua y Cultura Guaraní (Academy of the Guaraní Language and Culture): Calle España y Mompox, Asunción; f. 1975; Pres. Dr RUFINO AREVALO PARIS; Sec. ANTONIO E. GONZÁLEZ; publ. *Revista*.

LANGUAGE AND LITERATURE

Academia Paraguaya de la Lengua Española (Paraguayan Academy of the Spanish Language): Avda 25 de Mayo 972, Asunción; tel. (21) 205-330; e-mail aparle1927@hotmail.com; internet www.aparle.org; f. 1927; corresp. of the Real Academia Española (Madrid); 23 mems; Pres. RENÉE FERRER; Gen. Sec. ESTELA APPLEYARD DE ACUÑA; publ. *Anales*.

Alliance Française: Mariscal Estigarribia 1039, Calle Estados Unidos, Asunción; tel. (21) 210-503; f. 1956; offers courses and exams in French language and culture and promotes cultural exchange with France; Dir FERNAND DEFOURNIER.

MEDICINE

Sociedad Paraguaya de Pediatría (Paraguayan Paediatrics Society): Mcal Estigarribia 1764 c/ Rca Francesa, Asunción; tel. (21) 447-493; e-mail sppsecre@spp.org.py; internet www.spp.org.py; f. 1938; Pres. Dr SALIM EGUIAZU FLORENTÍN; Gen. Sec. Dra MÓNICA RODRÍGUEZ; publ. *Pediatría* (3 a year).

RELIGION, SOCIOLOGY AND ANTHROPOLOGY

Asociación Indigenista del Paraguay (Indigenous Association of Paraguay): Mompox y Manuel Gondra, Asunción; tel. (21) 448-592; e-mail aindigenistadelpy@tigo.com.py; internet www.aip.org.py; f. 1942; anthropology, devt of indigenous communities; 170 mems; library of 1,640 vols; Pres. Dr RICARDO AZORERO MORENO; Sec. MARIA JOSÉ MORENO.

Research Institutes

ECONOMICS, LAW AND POLITICS

Centro Interdisciplinario de Derecho Social y Economía Política (CIDSEP) (Interdisciplinary Centre of Social Law and Political Economy): Alberdi 855 casi Piribebuy, Asunción; tel. (21) 445-429; e-mail cidsep@conexion.com.py; internet www.cidsep.org; f. 1986; attached to Universidad Católica 'Nuestra Señora de la Asunción'; Dir Dr CARLOS ALBERTO GONZÁLEZ.

Centro Paraguayo de Estudios de Desarrollo Económico y Social (Paraguayan Centre for the Study of Economic and Social Development): Mariscal Estigarribia entre Estados Unidos y Brasil, 1050 Asunción; tel. (21) 211-779; Pres. CELIA GRUTOS.

HISTORY, GEOGRAPHY AND ARCHAEOLOGY

Instituto Geográfico Militar (Military Geographical Institute): Avda Artigas 920 casi Saltos del Guaira, Asunción; tel. (21) 222-443; e-mail disergemil@highway.com.py; Dir ÓSCAR ANTONIO NÚÑEZ; Sec. E. LÓPEZ MOREIRA.

MEDICINE

Instituto Nacional de Parasitología (National Institute of Parasitology): Instituto de Microbiología, Facultad de Medicina, Casilla Correo 1102, Asunción; f. 1963; Dir Dr ARQUIMEDES CANESE; publ. *Revista Paraguaya de Microbiología* (1 a year).

RELIGION, SOCIOLOGY AND ANTHROPOLOGY

Centro de Estudios Antropológicos de la Universidad Católica (Anthropological Studies Centre of the Catholic University): Casilla de Correo 1718, Asunción; e-mail ceaduc@uca.edu.py; internet www.ceaduc .uca.edu.py; f. 1950, affiliated to Universidad Católica 'Nuestra Señora de la Asuncion' 1971; Dir Prof. Dr JOSÉ ZANARDINI; Sec. MYRIAN AURORA GAONA MARTÍNEZ; publs *Estudios Paraguayos, Suplemento Antropológico, Universidad Católica* (2 a year).

Centro Paraguayo de Estudios Sociológicos (Paraguayan Centre of Sociological Studies): Eligio Ayala 973, Casilla de Correo 2157, Asunción; tel. (21) 443-734; e-mail cpes@cpes.org.py; f. 1964; research and devt in social sciences: migration, bilingualism, population structure, rural devt, role of women in the workforce, education; library of 5,000 vols, 4,000 documents; Dir MARÍA MAGDALENA RIVAROLA; publ. *Revista Paraguaya de Sociología* (3 a year).

TECHNOLOGY

Centro Paraguayo de Ingenieros (Paraguayan Centre of Engineers): Avda España 959 casi Washington, Asunción; tel. (21) 202-424; e-mail cpi@cpi.org.py; internet www.cpi .org.py; f. 1939; Pres. Ing. MARIA TERESA PINO; Sec. Ing. CÉSAR MANUEL LÓPEZ BOSIO; publ. *Ingeniería 2000* (1 a year).

Instituto Nacional de Tecnología, Normalización y Metrología (INTN) (National Institute of Technology, Standardization and Metrology): Avda Artigas 3973, y Gral Roa, Asunción; tel. (21) 290-160; e-mail intn@intn.gov.py; internet www.intn .gov.py; f. 1963; carries out research and technological studies, and sets technical norms; Dir Ing. OSCAR SALAZAR YARYES; publ. *Normas Técnicas Paraguayas*.

Libraries and Archives

Asunción

Archivo del Ministerio de Relaciones Exteriores (Archive of the Ministry of Foreign Affairs): Calle Juan E. Oleary 222 esq. Pdte Franco, Asunción; tel. (21) 493-928; e-mail smareski@mre.gov.py; internet www .mre.gov.py; contains 200 linear m of documents incl. Colecciones de los Documentos Diplomáticos from 1870 and the Archivo General de las Indias from 1545.

Archivo Nacional de Asunción (National Archive of Asunción): Mcal. Estigarribia esq. Iturbe, Asunción; tel. (21) 447-311; e-mail archivonacionaldeasunción@gmail.com; internet archivonacionaldeasuncion.org; f. 1534; attached to Dirección General de Archivos, Bibliotecas y Museos of the Secretaría de Cultura; c. 7,000 vols of documents

and 2.5m. records dating from 1534; Dir NORMA IBÁÑEZ DE YEGROS.

Biblioteca Americana (American Library): Mariscal Estigarribia e Iturbe, Asunción; attached to the Museo Nacional de Bellas Artes (*q.v.*).

Biblioteca de la Sociedad Científica del Paraguay (Library of the Scientific Society of Paraguay): Andrés Barbero 230 esq. Artigas, Asunción; tel. (21) 205-438; f. 1921; 29,300 vols.

Biblioteca Nacional del Paraguay (National Library of Paraguay): De la Residenta casi Perú, Asunción; tel. (21) 204-670; e-mail info@bibliotecanacional.org; internet www.bibliotecanacional.org; f. 1887; 44,000 vols; Dir Lic. ZAYDA CABALLERO.

Biblioteca Pública del Ministerio de Defensa Nacional (Public Library of the Ministry of Defence): Avda Mariscal López y Vicepresidente Sánchez, Planta baja, Asunción; tel. (21) 223-965; e-mail mendozah@cu .com.py; internet www.mdn.gov.py; 2,000 vols, 7,000 photographs; Dir Col HUGO RAMÓN MENDOZA MARTÍNEZ.

Museums and Art Galleries

Asunción

Casa de la Independencia (Independence House Museum): 14 de Mayo esq. Presidente Franco, Asunción; tel. (21) 493-918; e-mail casa.independencia.py@hotmail.com; internet www.casadelaindependencia.org.py; f. 1965; historical museum of the colonial period; Pres. Dr GERARDO FOGEL.

Museo de la Fundación Carlos Alberto Pusineri Scala (Museum of the Carlos Alberto Pusineri Scala Foundation): Lugano 1153 entre Hernandarias y Don Bosco, Asunción; tel. (21) 420-370; e-mail museocarlospusineri@gmail.com; internet www.museopusineri.org; f. 1950; collns of Guaraní archaeology, trophies of Paraguayan wars, colonial objects; small library of Paraguayan history, numismatics and anthropology.

Jardín Botánico y Museo de Historia Natural (Botanical Gardens and Natural History Museum): Artigas y Avda Primer Presidente, Asunción; tel. (21) 290-269; f. 1914; herbarium, zoological garden and museum, bacteriological laboratory, agricultural experimental station; Dir Ing. GILDO INSFRÁN GUERROS; publ. *Revista*.

Museo Etnográfico 'Andrés Barbero' (Ethnographic Museum 'Andrés Barbero'): Avda España 217, Asunción; tel. (21) 441-696; e-mail museobarbero@museobarbero .org.py; internet www.museobarbero.org.py; f. 1929; archaeology, ethnography, ethnology, history, archives, MSS, photographs, world music; library of 30,000 vols; Dir Prof. ADELINA PUSINERI; Vice-Dir Lic. RAQUEL ZALAZAR.

Museo Histórico Militar (Museum of Military History): Avda Mariscal López 140 y Vicepresidente Sánchez, Planta baja del edificio del Ministerio de Defensa Nacional, Asunción; tel. (21) 223-965; e-mail mendozah@cu.com.py; internet www.mdn .gov.py; f. 1942; recent war collns; Dir Col HUGO RAMÓN MENDOZA MARTÍNEZ.

Museo Nacional de Bellas Artes de Asunción (National Museum of Fine Arts of Asunción): Mariscal Estigarribia esq. Iturbe, Asunción; tel. (21) 447-716; f. 1887; paintings and sculptures of Juan Silvano Godoy; Dir JOSÉ LATERZA PARODI.

Yaguarón

Museo Dr Gaspar Rodríguez de Francia (Dr Gaspar Rodríguez Museum of France): Km 49 dela Ruta I Mcal. Estigarribia, Yaguarón; f. 1968; relics of Paraguay's first dictator, 'El Supremo'; Dir ESTELA PEREIRA.

Universities

UNIVERSIDAD ADVENTISTA DEL PARAGUAY
(Adventist University of Paraguay)

Pai Perez 950 c/ Pettirossi, Asunción

Telephone: (21) 210-569
E-mail: informes@unapy.edu.py
Internet: www.unapy.edu.py

Founded 2009
Private control

Faculties of economics and health sciences

UNIVERSIDAD AMERICANA
(American University)

Avda Brasilia 1100, Asunción

Telephone: (21) 288-8000
E-mail: universidad@uamericana.edu.py
Internet: www.uamericana.edu.py

Founded 1994
Private control

Faculties of agribusiness, communication arts and technological sciences, economics and administrative sciences, health sciences and law, political and social sciences

Pres.: Lic. GUSTAVO PARINO
Rector: Dr BENJAMÍN FERNÁNDEZ BOGADO
Vice-Rector for Acad. Affairs: Ing. EDMUNDO DURÁN
Vice-Rector for Admin. and Finance: Ing. RODOLFO CORTHORN
Vice-Rector for Int. Relations: Lic. SERGIO SOMERVILLE

Library of 9,000 vols, 100 periodicals
Number of teachers: 200
Number of students: 4,000

UNIVERSIDAD AUTÓNOMA DE ASUNCIÓN
(Autonomous University of Asunción)

Jejuí 667, entre O'Leary y 15 de Agosto, 1255 Asunción

Telephone: (21) 495-873
E-mail: info@uaa.edu.py
Internet: www.uaa.edu.py

Founded 1978 as Escuela Superior de Administración de Empresas; current name and status 1991
Private control
Languages of instruction: English, Portuguese, Spanish
Academic year: March to February

Rector: Dra KITTY GAONA
Vice-Rector: JUAN DE DIOS GARBETT
Sec.-Gen.: Lic. MARÍA LUISA PUERTAS
Library Dir: REINA AGUILAR

Library of 16,895 vols, 549 periodicals
Number of teachers: 350
Number of students: 6,000

Publications: *La Ley-Revista Jurídica Paraguaya, Revista Internacional de Investigación en Ciencias Sociales, Revista Koreana*

DEANS

Faculty of Economics and Business Administration: Dr SALVIO GÓMEZ ZORRILLA
Faculty of Health Sciences: Dr FRANCISCA ROMERO DE FLORES
Faculty of Humanities and Communication Sciences: MARIEN PEGGY MARTÍNEZ

Faculty of Law, Politics and Social Science:
Dr ANTONIO SOLJANCIC
Faculty of Science and Technology: Lic. HUGO
CORREA EDWARDS

UNIVERSIDAD AUTÓNOMA DE ENCARNACIÓN
(Autonomous University of Encarnación)

Padre José Kreusser, Independencia Nacional, Encarnación

Telephone: (71) 200-257
E-mail: rectorado@unae.edu.py
Internet: www.unae.edu.py

Founded 2008
Private control

Rector: NADIA CZERANIUK
Vice-Rector for Admin. Affairs: Lic. HELMUT SCHAEFER
Sec.-Gen.: Lic. FRANCISCO CANTONI

DEANS

Faculty of Business Studies: SUSANA ROMERO
Faculty of Legal Sciences: Abog. PEDRO CZERANIUK
Faculty of Science, Art and Technology: Prof. RITA THIBEHAAD (Coordinator)

UNIVERSIDAD AUTÓNOMA DEL PARAGUAY
(Autonomous University of Paraguay)

Gen. Díaz 1053, Colón 658, Asunción

Telephone: (21) 447-579
E-mail: info@uap.edu.py
Internet: www.uap.edu.py

Founded 1991

Rector: Dr ÁNGEL LIRD OLMEDO
Vice-Rector: Dr REINALDO BARRETO MEDINA
Sec.-Gen.: Dr CARLOS LAHAYE

DEANS

Faculty of Behavioural Sciences: Lic. FRANCA LA CARRUBA
Faculty of Business: Lic. FRANCO BELLI
Faculty of Optics and Contacts: Lic. GLADYS NESSI
Institute of Dental Prosthetics: Dr ORLANDO PUSINERI
Pierre Fauchard Faculty of Dentistry: Dra MIRTHA PERDOMO
School of Audiology: Lic. PATRICIA GIUNTA
School of Nutrition: Dra BLANCA GOMPERTT GIANGRECO
School of Physiotherapy and Podiatry: Dra CELESTE LATAZA

UNIVERSIDAD CATÓLICA 'NUESTRA SEÑORA DE LA ASUNCIÓN'
(Catholic University of 'Our Lady of the Assumption')

Cantaluppi y G. Molinas, Asunción

Telephone: (21) 334-650
E-mail: info@uca.edu.py
Internet: www.uc.edu.py

Founded 1960
Private control
Language of instruction: Spanish
Academic year: March to December

Campuses in Alto Paraná, Asunción, Caaguazú, Carapegúa, Concepción, Guairá, Itapúa

Grand Chancellor: Mgr IGNACIO GORGOZA (Bishop of Encarnación)
Rector: Prof. Dr MICHEL MARCEL GIBAUD WESTERMANS
Vice-Rector for Acad. Affairs: Profa Dra CARMEN QUINTANA DE HORAK
Vice-Rector for Admin. Affairs: Prof. Lic. CARLOS LEÓN AYALA VERA
Sec.-Gen.: Prof. CÉSAR RUFFINELLI

Librarian: Licda MARGARITA KALLSEN
Number of teachers: 1,900
Number of students: 18,000
Publications: *Cuadernos de Discusión, Estudios Antropológicos, La Quincena, Lila, Revista Jurídica, Universitas, Ventana Abierta*

DEANS

Faculty of Accounting and Administration (Alto Paraná): Prof. Lic. ARMÍN NICOLÁS VILLAGRA
Faculty of Accounting, Administration and Economics (Asunción): Prof. Lic. HÉCTOR ENRIQUE ALMIRÓN FIGUEREDO
Faculty of Accounting, Administration and Economics (Concepción): Lic. MARCELINO FRETES ROA
Faculty of Accounting and Administration (Guairá): Prof. Lic. RAMÓN MIERES
Faculty of Agriculture (Caaguazú): Ing. Agr. PAULINO INVERNIZZI
Faculty of Agricultural Sciences (Itapúa): Prof. Ing. MÓNICA LUCÍA RAMÍREZ PAREDES
Faculty of Chemistry (Guairá): Prof. Dr CÉSAR MONGES
Faculty of Education (Concepción): Profa Licda MARÍA CRISTINA MEDINA DE SAMUDIO
Faculty of Health Sciences (Alto Paraná): Prof. EDUARDO ESPINOLA
Faculty of Health Sciences (Asunción): Prof. Dr JOSÉ CORVALÁN
Faculty of Law (Alto Paraná): Prof. WALTER SHULZ
Faculty of Law (Caaguazú): Abog. SILVIO MARTÍNEZ JIMÉNEZ
Faculty of Law (Concepción): Prof. Dr FÉLIX CORONEL CRISTALDO
Faculty of Law (Guairá): Dr JANICE AYALA DE GIRALA
Faculty of Law (Itapúa): Profa Abog. GLADYS MARGARITA BARRIOS CÁCERES
Faculty of Law and Diplomatic Science (Asunción): Prof. Abog. JOSÉ MARÍA CABRAL ALCARAZ
Faculty of Medicine (Guairá): Prof. CARLOS BERNAL
Faculty of Philosophy and Human Sciences (Asunción): Prof. Lic. ILDE SILVERO ÁLVAREZ
Faculty of Philosophy and Human Sciences: Prof. Lic. VICTORIA MARTINEZ
Faculty of Science and Technology (Alto Paraná): Prof. Ing. CÉSAR LÓPEZ BADO
Faculty of Science and Technology (Asunción): Prof. Dr LUCA CARLO CERNUZZI
Faculty of Science and Technology (Itapúa): Prof. Arq. CÉSAR OSCAR PERRUPATO
Higher Institute of Theology (Asunción): Pbro JOAQUÍN MEDINA (Dir)

UNIVERSIDAD CENTRAL DEL PARAGUAY
(Central University of Paraguay)

J. Eulogio Estigarribia esq. Monseñor Bogarin, Asunción

Telephone: (21) 605-700
E-mail: info@central.edu.py
Internet: www.central.edu.py

Founded 2006
State control
Academic year: March to February

Faculties of business studies, communication, arts and technology, engineering, health sciences, humanities, social sciences

UNIVERSIDAD CENTRO MÉDICO BAUTISTA
(University Baptist Medical Centre)

Rca. Argentina 635 entre Manuel, Castillo y Pacheco, Asuncion

Telephone: (21) 603-655

E-mail: info@ucmb.edu.py
Internet: www.ucmb.edu.py
Founded 1999
Private control
Faculties of business, health sciences and human sciences
Pres.: NELSON PERALTA
Rector: Prof. Abog. MANUEL CÉSPEDES LAGUARDIA
Sec.-Gen.: Lic. MIRTHA FIGUEREDO DE BARRETT

UNIVERSIDAD COLUMBIA DEL PARAGUAY
(Columbia University of Paraguay)

25 de Mayo 658 y Antequera, Asunción

Telephone: (21) 490-811
Internet: www.columbia.edu.py

Founded 1991
Private control

Rector: Dr ROBERTO ELÍAS CANESE
Vice-Rector: Lic. JAVIER BATTILANA URBIETA

UNIVERSIDAD COMUNERA
(Comunera University)

San José 630 y Artigas, Asunción

Telephone: (21) 223-892
E-mail: educom@ucom.edu.py
Internet: www.ucom.edu.py

Founded 1992
Private control

Rector: Dr ALEX BEATRIZ PRIETO DE MARTINEZ
Library of 8,002 vols

DEANS

Faculty of Agricultural Administration: Ing. GERARDO LÓPEZ
Faculty of Public Administration: Dr ARNALDO MARTINEZ PRIETO
Faculty of Public Relations and Marketing: MARTÍN LLANO DOMECQ
Faculty of Social Economy: Lic. JUAN CARLOS SPIESS
Faculty of Tourism Development and Environment: Arq. SHIRLEY AMARILLA DE SÁNCHEZ (Coordinator)

UNIVERSIDAD DE DESARROLLO SUSTENTABLE
(University of Sustainable Development)

Mcal. López No 2929 esq. Gómez de Castro, Asunción

Telephone: (21) 600-973
E-mail: informes@uds.edu.py
Internet: www.uds.edu.py

Founded 1997
Private control

UNIVERSIDAD DE LA INTEGRACIÓN DE LAS AMÉRICAS
(Integration University of the Americas)

Avda. Venezuela 1353 c/ Tte. Insaurralde, Asunción

Telephone: (21) 288-9000
Internet: www.unida.edu.py
Private control

Brs in Concepción, Ciudad del Este, Luque and Villarrica

Rector: LEILA RACHID LICHI
Library of 10,000 vols

UNIVERSIDAD DEL CONO SUR DE LAS AMÉRICAS
(University of the Southern Cone of the Americas)

Avda España 443 Calle Brasil, Asunción

Telephone: (21) 221-103
E-mail: ucsa@ucsa.edu.py
Internet: www.ucsa.edu.py

Founded 1996
Private control

Offers degrees in business, engineering and humanities

Rector: Ing. LUIS ALBERTO LIMA MORRA
Academic Dir: Lic. ANDRÉS ANTONIO VILLALBA COLMÁN
Vice-Rector for Research and Devt: Prof. JOSÉ BLÁS RAMÓN VILLALBA GIMÉNEZ
Sec.-Gen.: Prof. Lic. CAROLINA SCHOLZ LOPPA-CHER

UNIVERSIDAD DEL NORTE
(University of the North)

Avda España 676, casi Boquerón Asunción

Telephone: (21) 229-450
E-mail: info@uninorte.edu.py
Internet: www.uninorte.edu.py

Founded 1991
Private control
Academic year: March to December

Rector: JUAN MANUEL MARCOS

Library of 20,000 vols
Number of students: 20,000

Publication: *Revista de Ciencias Empresariales*

DEANS

Faculty of Business Administration: CÉSAR CRUZ ROA
Faculty of Chemistry: ANA KALENIUSKA
Faculty of Education and Humanities: SERGIO MARCOS GUSTAFSON
Faculty of Engineering: LUIS FERNANDO MEYER CANILLAS
Faculty of Health Sciences: CARLOS MICHELETTO
Faculty of Law and Politics: CARMEN GUBETICH DE CATTONI
Faculty of Medicine: JUAN CARLOS CHAPARRO
Faculty of Technology: CARLOS CABALLERO
Postgraduate Faculty: JUAN MANUEL MARCOS

UNIVERSIDAD DEL PACÍFICO PRIVADA
(Private Pacific University)

Avda San Martin 961 c/Avda España, Asunción

Telephone: (21) 615-490
E-mail: promocion@upacifico.edu.py
Internet: www.upacifico.edu.py

Founded 1991
Private control

Rector: Dr MARIA ELENA PISCOYA CABREJOS
Vice-Rector: Prof. RUBÉN DARÍO ROMERO ASTETE
Vice-Rector for Admin. Affairs: Lic. JULIO PISCOYA CABREJOS
Sec.-Gen.: Lic. LOURDES SEGADO
Head of Library: MERCEDES SALINAS

DEANS

Faculty of Agricultural Sciences: Ing. DORA DIGNA GONZÁLEZ AYALA (Dir)
Faculty of Business: Prof. CYNTIA C. CABELLO AGUIRRE (Dir)
Faculty of Communication: Prof. ENRIQUE MARINI (Dir)
Faculty of Dentistry: Dra FANNY AYALA RATTI
Faculty of Law and Social Sciences: Prof. CARLOS NEFFA

Faculty of Medical Sciences: Prof. Dr CÉSAR MANUEL SISA

UNIVERSIDAD EVANGÉLICA DEL PARAGUAY
(Evangelical University of Paraguay)

Pacheco No 4546 c/ Legión Civil Extranjera, Asunción

Telephone: (21) 609-141
E-mail: academico@universidadevangelica.edu.py
Internet: www.universidadevangelica.edu.py

Founded 1994
Private control
Academic year: February to December

Faculties of accounting, administration and economics, health sciences, humanities and educational sciences, modern languages, music, nursing, psychology and human development, theology

Rector: DIONISIO ÓRTIZ MUTTI
Vice-Rector: MELITA WALL
Sec.-Gen.: ESTEBAN MISSENA DEL CASTILLO

Number of teachers: 193
Number of students: 1,374

UNIVERSIDAD NACIONAL DE ASUNCIÓN
(National University of Asunción)

Avda España, No 1098, Asunción 910

Telephone: (21) 227-682
E-mail: sgeneral@rec.una.py
Internet: www.una.py

Founded 1889
State control
Language of instruction: Spanish
Academic year: March to December

Rector: Prof. Ing. Agr. PEDRO GERARDO GONZÁLEZ
Vice-Rector: Prof. Arq. AMADO FRANCO NAVONI
Gen. Sec.: Prof. Ing. Agr. JULIO RENÁN PANIAGUA ALCARAZ
Librarian: Lic. JULIA ROMÁN RODRÍGUEZ

Library of 184,810 vols, 54,260 periodicals, 3,010 audiovisual materials
Number of teachers: 8,234
Number of students: 49,715

Publications: *Researches and UNA studies* (2 a year), *UNA Revista* (2 a year, online)

DEANS

Faculty of Agricultural Engineering: Prof. Ing. Agr. LORENZO MEZA LÓPEZ
Faculty of Architecture, Design and Art: Prof. Arq. RICARDO MANUEL MEYER CANILLAS
Faculty of Chemistry: Prof. Dr ANDRÉS AMARILLA
Faculty of Dentistry: Prof. Dr RUBÉN DI TORE AQUINO
Faculty of Economics: Prof. Dr ANTONIO RAMÓN RODRÍGUEZ ROJAS
Faculty of Engineering: Prof. Ing. ISACIO EUSEBIO VALLEJOS AQUINO
Faculty of Exact and Natural Sciences: Prof. CONSTANTINO NICOLÁS GUEFOS KAPSALIS
Faculty of Law and Social Sciences: Prof. Dr ANTONIO FRETES
Faculty of Medicine: Prof. Dr ANÍBAL HERIBERTO PERIS MANCHINI
Faculty of Philosophy: Prof. Lic. MARÍA ANGÉLICA GONZÁLEZ DE LEZCANO
Faculty of Veterinary Sciences: Prof. Dr FROILÁN ENRIQUE PERALTA TORRES
Institute 'Dr. Andrés Barbero': Prof. Lic. ROSALÍA RODRÍGUEZ DE LÓPEZ (Dir)
Institute of Social Work: Prof. Lic. NORMA BENÍTEZ
Polytechnic Faculty: Prof. ABEL CONCEPCIÓN BERNAL CASTILLO

UNIVERSIDAD NACIONAL DE CAAGUAZU
(National University of Caaguazu)

Juan Manuel Frutos, Coronel Oviedo
Internet: www.unca.edu.py

Founded 2007
State control
Language of instruction: Spanish
Academic year: March to November

Rector: Prof. Dr PABLO MARTÍNEZ ACOSTA
Vice-Rector: Prof. Lic. HUGO ALFREDO RECALDE

Number of students: 2,937

DEANS

Faculty of Dentistry: Prof. Dr ULISES ARMANDO VILLASANTI TORALES
Faculty of Economics: Prof. Lic. JULIO CÉSAR MENDOZA AQUINO
Faculty of Health Sciences: Prof. Lic. GUIOMAR VIVEROS DE CABELLO
Faculty of Medical Sciences: Prof. Dr CARLOS ALBERTO CANO FLEITAS
Faculty of Production: Prof. M. V. JAIME TORALES KENNEDY
Faculty of Social and Political Sciences: Prof. OSCAR ESCOBAR TOLEDO
Faculty of Technology: Prof. Ing. ROBERTO CHÁVEZ AYALA

UNIVERSIDAD NACIONAL DE CONCEPCIÓN
(National University of Concepción)

Km 2 Ruta V Gral. Bernardino Caballero, Concepción

Telephone: (21) 240-069
Internet: www.unc.edu.py

Founded 2002
State control

Faculties of agricultural sciences, dentistry, economic and administrative sciences, exact sciences, humanities and educational science, medicine

Rector: Dr CLARITO ROJAS MARIN
Vice-Rector: Dr LUIS GILBERTO ROMERO

UNIVERSIDAD NACIONAL DE ITAPÚA
(National University of Itapúa)

Abog. Lorenzo Zacarías López 255 y Ruta 1, Barrio Ca'aguy Rory. Encarnación, Itapúa

Telephone: (71) 206-990
E-mail: dcom@uni.edu.py
Internet: www.uni.edu.py

Founded 1995
State control

Rector: Prof. Ing. HILDEGARDO GONZÁLEZ IRALA
Vice-Rector: Profa Dra YILDA AGÜERO DE TALAVERA
Library Dir: Lic. INGRID PAREDES BENÍTEZ

Library of 10,017 vols

Publication: *Revista*

DEANS

Faculty of Agriculture and Forestry: Ing. Agr. RUBÉN GENCIANO FERREIRA
Faculty of Economics and Administrative Sciences: Dr RENÉ DAMIÁN ARRÚA TORREANI
Faculty of Engineering: Ing. OSCAR DIONISIO TROCHEZ VALDEZ
Faculty of Humanities, Social Sciences and Guarani Culture: Dr ANTONIO KIERNYEZNY
Faculty of Law: Abog. GUSTAVO MIRANDA VILLAMAYOR
Faculty of Medicine: Prof. Dr ELIGIO FRETES ESPÍNOLA
Faculty of Science and Technology: Dr HERMENEGILDO COHENE VELÁZQUEZ

UNIVERSIDAD NACIONAL DE PILAR
(National University of Pilar)

Calle Mello esq. Iturbe, Pilar, Neembucu

Telephone: (786) 232-148
E-mail: rectorado@unp.edu.py
Internet: www.unp.edu.py

Founded 1994
State control

Rector: Dr VÍCTOR RÍOS OJEDA
Vice-Rector: Dr ADOLFO VILLASBOA

DEANS

Faculty of Accounting, Management and Economics: Prof. Dr DIOSNEL AGUILERA ROJAS
Faculty of Agricultural Sciences and Rural Development: Prof. Ing. GUSTAVO ADOLFO RETAMOZO
Faculty of Applied Sciences: Prof. Ing. ROGELIO ENCINA ROMÁN
Faculty of Humanities and Education: Prof. CECILIA AGUILERA ESTIGARRIBIA
Faculty of Law and Political Science: Prof. Dr VICTOR H. ENCINA SILVA
Faculty of Science, Technology and Arts: Lic. ELIDA DUARTE

UNIVERSIDAD NACIONAL DE VILLARRICA DEL ESPÍRITU SANTO
(Villarrica National University of the Holy Spirit)

Alejo García No 1498 esq. Mómpox, Villarrica

Telephone: (541) 44-407
Internet: www.unves.edu.py

Founded 2007
State control

Rector: Prof. Ing. JOSÉ FÉLIX GONZÁLEZ FERNÁNDEZ
Vice-Rector: Prof. Abog. SIMÓN BENITEZ ORTIZ
Sec.-Gen.: Prof. Lic. SINDULFO GARCIA BENITEZ

Number of teachers: 1,000
Number of students: 7,000

DEANS

Faculty of Agricultural Sciences: Prof. Lic. SINDULFO GARCÍA BENÍTEZ
Faculty of Architecture and Engineering: Arq. ERNESTO MEZA LAGRAVE
Faculty of Arts and Culture: DIEGO SÁNCHEZ HAASE
Faculty of Basic Sciences: Prof. MIGUELA BEATRÍZ DENIS DOLDÁN
Faculty of Economic Sciences: Prof. Lic. GLORIA MERCEDES SANTOS DE TORRES
Faculty of Food, Hospitality and Tourism: Prof. OSCAR HERIBERTO LAVIOSA
Faculty of Health Sciences: Prof. Dr ANTOLIANO WUYK CABRERA
Faculty of Philosophy and Humanities: Prof. Lic. ALBA MARÍA GONZÁLEZ LÓPEZ
Faculty of Physics, Chemistry and Mathematics: NOELIA CRISTINA SANTOS DE GONZÁLEZ
Faculty of Social and Political Sciences: Prof. Abog. GUSTAVO ALBERTO BATTAGLIA CÁCERES
Faculty of Science (Caazapá): Prof. Lic. JUANA EVANGELISTA GIMÉNEZ DE BOGGINO
Faculty of Science (Carapeguá): Prof. Lic. CIRILO ALBERTO DÁVALOS PORTILLO
Faculty of Science (Paraguarí): Prof. Lic. JOSÉ MANUEL GONZÁLEZ FORTEZA
Faculty of Science (Pedro Juan Caballero): Prof. Abog. OSCAR ORFILIO SERRÁN TOLEDO
Faculty of Science (Yuty): Prof. Abog. PATERNIO EMILIANO VERA GONZÁLEZ
Graduate School: Prof. Dr CARLOS ALBERTO ARESTIVO BELLASSAI
Polytechnic Faculty: Prof. Ing. ERNESTO SEBASTIÁN MONTALBETTI RUIZ DÍAZ
School of Digital Platform: Prof. DAXI SILVANA DUARTE DE GARCÍA

UNIVERSIDAD NACIONAL DEL ESTE
(Eastern National University)

Barrio San Juan, Ciudad del Este, Alto Paraná

Telephone: (61) 575-478
E-mail: rectorado@une.edu.py
Internet: www.une.edu.py

Founded 1993
State control
Language of instruction: Spanish

Rector: Dr VÍCTOR ALFREDO BRÍTEZ CHAMORRO
Vice-Rector: Ing. GERÓNIMO LAVIOSA GONZÁLEZ
Sec.-Gen.: Lic. JULIO CÉSAR MEAURIO LEIVA

Publication: *Revista UNE*

DEANS

Faculty of Agricultural Engineering: Prof. Ing. Agr. RAFAEL VÁZQUEZ TORRES
Faculty of Economics: Dr GUSTAVO ADOLFO PANIAGUA FORMIGLI
Faculty of Health Sciences: Dr HUGO FERNANDO CASARTELLI OREGGIONI
Faculty of Law and Social Sciences: NELSON RAMÓN RIVEROS VERA
Faculty of Philosophy: Lic. BLANCA TOTTIL DE MORENO
Polytechnic School: Lic. LIDIA GRACIELA BENÍTEZ DE PÉREZ

UNIVERSIDAD POLITÉCNICA Y ARTÍSTICA DEL PARAGUAY
(Polytechnic and Artistic University of Paraguay)

14 de Mayo 1628 calle Roma, Asunción

Telephone: (21) 448-831
E-mail: info@upap.edu.py
Internet: www.upap.edu.py

Founded 1996
Private control

Faculties of arts and technology, economics and business, health sciences, law, social sciences and humanities, sports

Rector: Prof. MANUEL VIEDMA ROMERO

Library of 20,000 vols

UNIVERSIDAD PRIVADA DEL ESTE
(Private University of the East)

Avda Los Lapachos entre Francisco Chávez Delvalle, Ciudad del Este

Telephone: (61) 552-304
E-mail: recepcion@upe.edu.py
Internet: www.upe.edu.py

Founded 1992
Private control

Rector: Abog. JUAN BAUTISTA GONZÁLEZ FLORES
Sec.-Gen.: Lic. NICOLÁS FLORES GONZÁLEZ

DEANS

Faculty of Architecture: Arq. FRANCISCO RUFFINELLI
Faculty of Computer Science: Ing. GERMANO SOAREZ DOCUMET
Faculty of Dentistry: Dra DIONISIA DÁVALOS DE VARGAS
Faculty of Educational Sciences: Lic. FELISA RODRÍGUEZ DE MEDINA
Faculty of Law: Dr LUCIO VICENTE GAMARRA MEDINA
Faculty of Management and Accounting: Lic. VICENTE FERNÁNDEZ PANIAGUA
School of Environmental Science: Ing. Agr. LUCIANO DUARTE

UNIVERSIDAD SAN CARLOS
(San Carlos University)

Gral. Garay 798 c/ España, Barrio Villa Morra, Asunción

Telephone: (21) 615-500
E-mail: info@sancarlos.edu.py
Internet: www.sancarlos.edu.py

Founded 2007
Private control

Pres.: Lic. JUAN MANUEL BRUNETTI MARCOS
Rector: Prof. Ing. Agr. RONALDO ENO DIETZE
Vice-Rector: Lic. ARTURO VILLATE

UNIVERSIDAD TÉCNICA DE COMERCIALIZACIÓN Y DESARROLLO
(Technical University of Marketing and Development)

Avda Santa Teresa esquina Avda. Mcal. López, Asunción

Telephone: (21) 614-456
E-mail: info@utcd.edu.py
Internet: www.utcd.edu.py

Founded 1993, current name adopted 1996
Private control

Pres.: Dr DANIEL FRETES VENTRE
Rector: Ing. Agr. RUBÉN FRETES VENTRE
Sec.-Gen.: Lic. NILDA MYRIAM LLEDÓ

DEANS

Faculty of Business Sciences: Prof. Dr ROBERTO FORMIGLI
Faculty of Education Sciences: Dra INÉS LÓPEZ DE SUGASTTI
Faculty of Health Sciences: MARIANO ARIAS
Faculty of Social Sciences: Lic. IDALINA SEGOVIA
Notarial Law School: Abog. MÓNICA PORZIA
Polytechnic Faculty: Abog. RUBÉN FRETES COCIAN

UNIVERSIDAD TECNOLÓGICA INTERCONTINENTAL
(Intercontinental Technological University)

Atyrá 1750 Calle Capitán Rivas, Fernando de la Mora, Zona Sur, Asunción

Telephone: (21) 590-353
Internet: www.utic.edu.py

Founded 1996
Private control

Faculties of business, computer technology and sciences, health sciences, human sciences, law and social sciences

Rector: Prof. Dr HUGO FERREIRA GONZÁLEZ
Vice-Rector for Scientific Research: Dr RICARDO BENÍTEZ

Higher Education Institutes

Instituto de Altos Estudios Estratégicos (Institute of Strategic Studies): Avda Mariscal Francisco Solano López esquina 22 de Septiembre Edificio del Ministerio de Defensa Nacional, Bloque B, 4 Piso, Asunción; tel. (21) 223-392; e-mail iaeepy@hotmail.com; internet www.iaee.gov.py; f. 1968 as Colegio Nacional de Guerra, current name adopted 1999; prepares leaders with capacity for research and analysis of nat. issues; Dir-Gen. ROGELIO CANO MENDOZA.

Instituto Nacional de Salud (National Institute of Health): Avda Santísima Trinidad y Pasaje Francia, Asunción; tel. (21) 296-210; internet www.ins.gov.py; f. 1958; promotes and develops the education and training of human resources; Dir-Gen. Dr ANGILBERTO PAREDES; Librarian Lic. MARÍA ANTONIA MENDOZA; publ. *Revista Salud Pública del Paraguay* (1 a year).

Instituto Superior de Educación 'Dr Raúl Peña' (Higher Institute of Education 'Dr Raúl Peña'): Km 4 ½ de la Avda Eusebio Ayala, Barrio Hipódromo, Asunción; tel. (21) 503-012; e-mail ise-mec@sce.cnc.una.py; internet www.ise.edu.py; f. 1968; Dir-Gen. MARÍA VICTORIA ZAVALA SAUCEDO; publ. *Kuaapy Ayvu* (2 a year).

PERU

The Higher Education System

The oldest universities in Peru date from the 16th century when the country was under Spanish rule, notably the Universidad Nacional Mayor de San Marcos de Lima (founded in 1551) and the Universidad Nacional de San Cristóbal de Huamanga (founded in 1677). The Universidad Nacional de la Libertad (founded in 1824) was the first university established after independence; its founder was Simón Bolívar. The Universidad Nacional de San Agustín de Arequipa (founded in 1828) followed shortly thereafter. The Constitution of 1993 abolished the right to free university education. Public universities, however, are generally free, while private universities often charge high tuition fees, resulting in intense competition for entrance to public institutions. In 2012 there were 33 public and 68 private universities. In 2010, according to UNESCO, total enrolment in tertiary level institutions stood at some 1,207,000 students. Enrolment in universities in 2012 totalled 435,637, at other tertiary institutes was 376,782, and at vocational establishments totalled 230,421.

The Ministry of Education is responsible for certain higher education institutions, but universities are largely autonomous and not supervised directly by any public agency. However, the Asamblea Nacional de Rectores (ANR—National Assembly of Rectors) is responsible for the coordination of universities at a national level and for ensuring that national standards are met. The Consejo Nacional para la Autorización y Funcionamiento de Universidades (CONAFU—National Council for the Authorization and Functioning of Universities) oversees the licensing of new universities. University institutions are entitled to award degrees under the Ley Universitaria (Law 23733) of 1983.

Technical and vocational education is provided under the supervision of the Dirección General de Educación Superior y Técnico Profesional (General Directorate of Higher and Technical and Professional Education). The number and diversity of private institutes has increased significantly since the 1980s.

Students must hold the Certificado de Educación Secundaria Común Completa (Certificate of Completion of Common Secondary Education) in order to sit the university entrance examination. The first undergraduate degree is the Bachiller (Bachelors degree), awarded after a 10-semester or five-year period of study. Upon completion of additional study and a thesis, the Licenciado or professional title is then awarded. Some of the larger public universities offer postgraduate degrees, which are primarily the Maestría (Masters degree) and the Doctorado (Doctorate—the highest academic qualification in the education system); both degrees require completion of at least two years of study. In addition, graduates with at least two years' work experience in an area related to their Bachiller may study for the Diploma de Especialista or Título de Segunda Especialidad Profesional (Specialist Diploma or Second Specialist Professional Title).

Post-secondary technical and vocational education, leading to professional qualifications, is provided by Institutos Superiores Pedagógicos (Teacher Training Institutes), Institutos Superiores Tecnológicos (ISTs—Higher Technological Institutes) and Escuelas Superiores (Higher Schools), which specialize in the arts, music and drama. The Especialista Profesional and Título de Bachiller Profesional are the main qualifications offered by the ISTs.

The Sistema Nacional de Evaluación, Acreditación y Certificación de la Calidad Educativa (SINACE—National System of Evaluation, Accreditation and Certification of Educational Quality) was established in 2005. The Consejo de Evaluación, Acreditación y Certificación de la Calidad de la Educación Superior Universitaria (CONEAU—Council for Evaluation, Accreditation and Certification for Quality Assurance in Higher University Education) and the Consejo de Evaluación, Acreditación y Certificación de la Calidad de la Educación Superior no Universitaria (CONEACES—Council for Evaluation, Accreditation and Certification for Quality Assurance in Higher non-University Education) were both established as functioning bodies within SINACE to oversee institutions at their respective levels. In December 2012 a loan of US $25m. was approved by the World Bank, in order to reform the system of evaluation and accreditation in Peru's higher education institutes. The PROCALIDAD programme, as it was known, was to be implemented with the cooperation of SINACE, with the aim of improving quality throughout the sector.

Regulatory and Representative Bodies

GOVERNMENT

Ministry of Education: Biblioteca Nacional del Perú, Avda de la Poesía 160, San Borja, Lima 41; tel. (1) 6155800; e-mail webmaster@minedu.gob.pe; internet www.minedu.gob.pe; Minister EMMA PATRICIA SALAS O'BRIEN.

Ministry of Culture: Avda Javier Prado Este 2465, San Boria, Lima 41; tel. (1) 6189393; e-mail comunicaciones@mcultura.gob.pe; internet www.mcultura.gob.pe; Minister Dr DIANA ALVAREZ-CALDERÓN GALLO.

NATIONAL BODY

Asamblea Nacional de Rectores (Rectors' National Assembly): Calle Aldabas 337, Urb. Las Gardenias, Surco, Lima 33; tel. (1) 2754608; e-mail webmaster@anr.edu.pe; internet www.anr.edu.pe; f. 1983; 34 mems; library of 30,000 vols; Pres. Dr ORLANDO VELÁSQUEZ BENITES; Exec. Sec. Ing. VÍCTOR RAÚL AGUILAR CALLO; publs *Universidad, Escuelas y/o Carreras Profesionales*.

Learned Societies

GENERAL

Academia Peruana de la Lengua (Peruvian Academy of Language): Palacio de Osambela, Conde de Superunda 298, Lima 1; internet www.academiaperuanadelalengua.org.pe; f. 1887; corresp. of the Real Academia Española (Madrid); 30 mems; Dir Dr LUIS JAIME CISNEROS; Sec. Dr MARTHA HILDEBRANDT.

UNESCO Office Lima: Apdo 41–0192 Lima; Avda Javier Prado Este 2465, San Borja, Lima 41; tel. (1) 4769871; e-mail lima@unesco.org; internet www.unesco.org/lima; f. 1995; Rep. JORGE SEQUEIRA.

ARCHITECTURE AND TOWN PLANNING

Colegio de Arquitectos del Perú (College of Architects of Peru): Avda San Felipe 999, Jesús María, Lima 11; tel. (1) 2654098; e-mail cap@cap.org.pe; internet www.cap.org.pe; f. 1962; 3,717 mems; library of 3,500 vols; Dean SHIRLEY EMPERATRIZ CHILET CAMA; publ. *Arquivisión* (12 a year).

BIBLIOGRAPHY, LIBRARY SCIENCE AND MUSEOLOGY

Colegio de Bibliotecólogos del Perú (College of Librarianship of Peru): Avda 2 de Mayo 1545, Of. 218, Lima 27; e-mail informes@bibliotecologos.pe; internet www.bibliotecologos.pe; f. 1990; 320 mems incl. 3 hon. mems and 9 emeritus mems; Dean Dr CÉSAR AUGUSTO CASTRO ALIAGA.

FINE AND PERFORMING ARTS

Asociación de Artistas Aficionados (Association of Amateur Artists): Jr. Ica 323, Centro Histórico, Lima; tel. (1) 4280432; e-mail aaaasociacion@yahoo.com; internet www.aaalima.blogspot.com; f. 1938; 254 mems; presentation of plays, classical ballet and varied music programmes.

Instituto de Arte Peruano 'José Sabogal' (José Sabogal Institute of Peruvian Art): Avda Alfonso Ugarte 650, Apdo 3048, Lima 1; tel. (1) 4235892; e-mail mncp@inictel.gob.pe; internet museodelacultura.perucultural.org.pe; f. 1946; publ. *Revista del Museo Nacional* (1 a year).

Instituto Peruano de Cultura Hispánica (Peruvian Institute of Hispanic Culture): Calle de la Riva 426, Lima; f. 1947; 280 mems; Pres. HUGO ALBERTO SAN ROMÁN NÚÑEZ.

HISTORY, GEOGRAPHY AND ARCHAEOLOGY

Centro de Estudios Histórico-Militares del Perú (Centre of Historical—Military Studies of Peru): Paseo Colón 150, Lima 1; tel. (1) 230415; e-mail info@cehmp.org; internet www.cehmp.org; f. 1944; 1,098 mems; library of 13,800 vols; Pres. Brig. Gen. EPHERRMANN HAMANN CARRILLO; Sec. Dr MIGUEL A. SEMINARIO OJEDA; publ. *Revista*.

Instituto Geográfico Nacional (National Geographical Institute): Avda A. Aramburú 1190–1198, Surquillo, Lima 34; tel. (1) 4753030; e-mail comercializacion@ign.gob .pe; internet www.ign.gob.pe; f. 1921; 300 mems; library of 3,200 vols; Head Brig. Gen. PEDRO ARTURO OCHOA CHOCANO; publ. topographical, physical and political maps of Peru.

Sociedad Geográfica de Lima (Geographical Society of Lima): Jr. Puno 450, Apdo 100-1176, Lima 100; tel. (1) 4273723; e-mail antunez@socgeolima.org; internet www .socgeolima.org.pe; f. 1888; 750 mems, incl. corresp. and hon.; library of 13,400 vols, also archives, maps and museum; Pres. Ing. ZANIEL NOVOA GOICOCHEA; Vice-Pres. Dra NICOLE BERNEX WEISS; publs *Anuario Geográfico del Perú*, *Diccionario Geográfico del Perú*, *Forjando los Genios del Mañana* (1 a year).

LANGUAGE AND LITERATURE

Alliance Française de Lima: Avda Arequipa 4595, Casilla 18, 1667, Lima; tel. (1) 6108000; e-mail informes@alianzafrancesa .org.pe; internet www.alianzafrancesa.org .pe; offers courses and exams in French language and culture and promotes cultural exchange with France; attached teaching centres in Arequipa, Chiclayo, Cusco, Huancayo, Iquitos, Piura and Trujillo; library of 26,000 vols of books, 52 journal titles, 4,000 DVDs and 2,000 CDs; Dir-Gen. PAUL-ELIE LÉVY.

Goethe-Institut: Jr. Nazca 722, Jesús María, Lima 100; tel. (1) 4333180; e-mail info@lima.goethe.org; internet www.goethe .de/ins/pe/lim/esindex.htm; f. 1966; offers courses and exams in German language and promotes cultural exchange with Germany; library of 7,500 vols, 24 periodicals; Dir Dra CAROLA DÜRR; Dir for Admin. FRANK MEYER.

MEDICINE

Academia de Estomatología del Perú (Peruvian Academy of Stomatology): Calle Los Próceres 261, 2°, Urb. Sta Constanza, Lima 33; tel. (1) 4351623; e-mail academiadeestomatologia@terra.com.pe; internet www .academiadeestomatologiadelperu.com; f. 1929; 165 mems; library of 600 vols; Pres. Dra ESTHER FLORES MUBARAK; Sec. PATRICIA FRY OROPEZA; publ. *Estomatología Integrada* (2 a year).

Academia Nacional de Medicina (National Academy of Medicine): Avda 28 de Julio No 776, 6°, Miraflores, Lima; tel. (1) 6523819; e-mail academia.nac@speedy.com .pe; internet www.acadnacmedicina.org.pe; f. 1884; 40 academicians; 80 academic assocs; honorary mems, emeritus mems and corresp. mems; Pres. Dr ROGER GUERRA-GARCÍA CUEVA; Permanent Sec. Dr JAIME ESPINOZA A. N. SOLIS; publ. *Annals* (2 a year).

Academia Peruana de Cirugía (Peruvian Academy of Surgery): Malecón Armendáriz 791, Miraflores, Lima; tel. (1) 7196104; e-mail consultas@academiaperuanadeciugia .org; internet www .academiaperuanadecirugia.org; f. 1940; 100 titular mems and unlimited number of associates; Pres. Dr EDUARDO PAYET MEZA; Sec. Gen. Dr EDUARDO ANCHANTE CASTILLO; publ. *Revista*.

Asociación Médica Peruana (Peruvian Medical Association): Jr. Camaná 381, Of. 207, Lima 1; tel. (1) 4274590; e-mail amp@ amp.pe; internet www.amp.pe; f. 1920; 1,499 mems; Pres. Dr HERBERTH CUBA GARCÍA; Gen. Sec. Dr JULIO CÉSAR SÁNCHEZ TONOHUYE; publ. *Revista Médica Peruana*.

Federación Médica Peruana (Peruvian Medical Federation): Jr. Almirante Guisse 2165, Lince, Lima; tel. (1) 4705036; e-mail federacion_medica_peruana@yahoo.es; internet www.federacionmedicaperuana.org; f. 1942; 1,230 mems; Pres. Dr CÉSAR PALOMINO COLINA; Gen. Sec. Dr GODOFREDO TALAVERA CHÁVEZ.

Sociedad Peruana de Neumología (Peruvian Society of Pneumology): Avda Guardia Civil 236, San Isidro, Lima 27; tel. (1) 2262867; e-mail spneumologia@terra.com .pe; internet www.spneumologia.org.pe; f. 1935; 280 mems; Pres. Dr OSCAR GAYOSO CERVANTES; Gen. Sec. Dr CARLOS SAAVEDRA LEVEAU; publ. *Revista SPN*.

NATURAL SCIENCES

Biological Sciences

Sociedad Entomológica del Perú (Entomological Society of Peru): Apdo 14-0413, Lima; Universidad Nacional Agraria La Molina, Avda La Universidad s/n, Museo de Entomología, Lima 14; tel. (1) 6147800; e-mail sepperu@sepperu.net; internet www .sepperu.net; f. 1956; 700 mems; library of 9,500 vols; Pres. BENJAMÍN REY TORDOYA; Sec. NORMA NOLAZCO ALVARADO; publ. *Revista Peruana de Entomología* (1 a year).

Mathematical Sciences

Instituto Nacional de Estadística (National Institute of Statistics): Avda General Garzón N° 654-658, Jesús María, Lima 11; tel. (1) 6520000; e-mail infoinei@inei.gob .pe; internet www.inei.gob.pe; f. 1975; involved in population, housing, socio-economic and agricultural censuses and surveys; plans statistical policy of country; library of 9,000 vols; Chief ALEJANDRO VILCHEZ DE LOS RÍOS; publs *Compendio Económico* (1 a year), *Cuentas Nacionales—PBI Nacional* (1 a year), *Indice de Precios al Consumidor* (12 a year), *Informe Económico Mensual* (12 a year).

Physical Sciences

Asociación Peruana de Astronomía (Peruvian Association of Astronomy): Morro Solar s/n, Chorrillos, Lima 9; e-mail wcentauri@apa.com.pe; internet www.apa .com.pe; f. 1946; 550 mems; library of 1,500 vols, 1,000 periodicals; Pres. Ing. VÍCTOR ESTREMADOYRO; Sec. Dr JOSÉ DOMINGO GÓMEZ SÁNCHEZ.

Sociedad Geológica del Perú (Peruvian Geological Society): Apdo 2559, Avda 28 de Julio 745, Miraflores 18, Lima; tel. (1) 6281150; internet sgp.escueladigital.pe; f. 1924; 800 mems; library of 40,000 vols; Pres. JOSÉ ARCE ALLEVA; Sec. ALEJANDRO CHALCO LUNA.

Sociedad Peruana de Espeleología y Carstología (Peruvian Speleological and Karstological Society): Casilla 18-1209, Lima 18; La Mariscala 115, Lima 27; e-mail peru.spec@gmail.com; f. 1965; Pres. Ing.

CARLOS MORALES-BERMÚDEZ LÁMPARO; publ. *Cavernas Peruanas*.

Sociedad Química del Perú (Chemical Society of Peru): Avda Nicolás de Aranibar 696, Sta Beatriz, Lima; tel. (1) 4723925; f. 1933; 1,200 mems; library of 5,600 vols; Pres. Dr JUAN JOSÉ LEÓN CAM; Gen. Sec. Dr JORGE REINALDO ANGULO CORNEJO; publ. *Revista* (4 a year).

RELIGION, SOCIOLOGY AND ANTHROPOLOGY

Centro Amazónico de Antropología y Aplicación Práctica (CAAAP) (Amazon Centre of Anthropology and Practical Application): Apdo 14-0166, Lima 14; Avda González Prada 626, Magdalena del Mar, Lima; tel. (1) 4600763; e-mail caaapdirec@caaap .org.pe; internet www.caaap.org.pe; f. 1974; defends cultural identity and way of life of marginalized Amazonian people and protects natural resources in the Amazonian region; library of 15,000 vols, 2,000 titles of brochures, 2,000 articles in Spanish, maps and photographs; Dir ADDA VICTORIA CHUECAS CABRERA; publs *Amazonía Peruana* (2 a year), *El Trueno* (4 a year), *Nuestra Tierra—Nuestra Vida* (4 a year).

Instituto de Estudios Etnológicos (Institute of Ethnological Studies): Avda Alfonso Ugarte 650, Apdo 3048, Lima 1; tel. (1) 4235892; e-mail mncp@inictel.gob.pe; internet museodelacultura.perucultural.org .pe; f. 1946; publ. *Revista del Museo Nacional* (1 a year).

TECHNOLOGY

Asociación Electrotécnica Peruana (Peruvian Electrotechnical Association): Avda República de Chile 284, Of. 201, Jesús María, Lima; tel. (1) 3304635; e-mail informes@ aep-peru.org; internet www.aep-peru.org; f. 1943; Pres. Ing. MANUEL ZELADA RODRÍGUEZ; Sec. Ing. MARÍA JULIA SÁNCHEZ MUNARRIZ; publ. *Revista Electrotécnica* (irregular).

Sociedad de Ingenieros del Perú (Society of Peruvian Engineers): Avda Nicolás Piérola 788, Casilla 20085, Lima, Cercado; tel. (1) 4247517; e-mail soc_ing_peru@terra.com.pe; internet www.apelimaperu.com; f. 1898; library of 15,000 vols; Pres. Ing. RAUL GUERRA PÉREZ; Exec. Sec. Arq. CÉSAR SILVA HURTADO; publ. *Ingenería* (3 a year).

Research Institutes

GENERAL

Institut de Recherche pour le Développement (IRD) (Research Institute for Development—IRD): Casilla 18–1209, Lima 18; Calle Diecisiete No 455–Corpac, San Isidro, Lima 27; tel. (1) 7199855; e-mail perou@ird.fr; internet www.peru.ird.fr; f. 1967; research in agronomy, archaeology, botany, ecology, economy, geography, geology; natural history museum; see main entry under France; Rep. JEAN LOUP GUYOT.

AGRICULTURE, FISHERIES AND VETERINARY SCIENCE

Estación Experimental Vista Florida (Experimental Station Vista Florida): Km 8 Carretera a Ferreñafe, Chiclayo, Lambayeque; tel. (74) 238753; e-mail vflorida@inia.gob .pe; internet www.inia.gob.pe/vista-florida/ introduccion; f. 1970; crops research (plant protection, rice, corn, beans, sorghum); library of 5,000 vols; Dir Ing. SEGUNDO FERNÁNDEZ ROMERO.

MEDICINE

Instituto de Cultura Alimentaria Bircher-Benner (Food Culture Institute Bircher-Benner): Jr. Diez Canseco 487, Miraflores, Lima; tel. (1) 4444250; f. 1979; research into diet, especially of meat-substitutes and high-nutrition and low-cost food mixtures; warns about inadequate diet; promotes agriculture by biological methods; film and sound archives; Pres. CÉSAR MORALES GARCÍA; Sec. MARCELA CÁRDENAS.

Instituto de Investigaciones Alérgicas 'Dr Luis E. Betetta' ('Dr Luis E. Betetta' Allergy Research Institute): Avda La Marina 2501, San Miguel, Lima; tel. (1) 5781083; e-mail www.alergia.betetta@speedy.com.pe; f. 1965.

Instituto Nacional de Salud (National Institute of Health): Cápac Yupanqui No 1400, Jesús Maria, Lima 11; tel. (1) 7481111; e-mail postmaster@ins.gob.pe; internet www.ins.gob.pe; f. 1936; communicable diseases, occupational diseases, nutritional disorders, food and drug quality control, research, production of vaccines and reagents, traditional medicine; library of 5,000 vols, 30,000 journals, 1,000 theses; Head CABEZAS SÁNCHEZ CÉSAR AUGUSTO; publ. *Revista Peruana de Medicina Experimental y Salud Pública* (4 a year).

NATURAL SCIENCES
General

Instituto del Mar del Perú (IMARPE) (Peruvian Marine Institute): Esq. Gral. Valle y Gamarra, Apdo 22, Callao; tel. (51) 2088650; e-mail webmaster@imarpe.gob.pe; internet www.imarpe.gob.pe; f. 1964; oceanography, marine biology, fisheries, aquaculture, aquatic ecotoxicology, hydroacoustics, biodiversity; library of 75,000 vols; Pres. Rear-Admiral GERMÁN ABRAHAM VASQUEZ SOLÍS TALAVERA; Exec. Scientific Dir ANDRÉS ROBERTO CHIPOLLINI MONTENEGRO; publs *Informe* (6 a year), *Informe Progresivo* (12 a year).

Biological Sciences

Instituto de Biología Andina (Institute of Andean Biology): Facultad de Medicina de San Fernando, Universidad Nacional Mayor de San Marcos, Avda Grau 755, Lima 1; tel. (1) 6197000; e-mail ofinfmed@unmsm.edu.pe; f. 1930; attached to Facultad De Medicina, San Marcos Univ.; laboratories in Lima, Morococha and Puno; mobile laboratory research on physiology of inhabitants of the Andes and their resistance to high altitudes; library of 1,091 vols, 400 periodicals; Dir Dr ELYDIA CORNELIA MUJICA ÁLBAN; publ. *Archivos del Instituto de Biología Andina* (4 a year).

Physical Sciences

Dirección General de Meteorología del Perú (National Meteorological Service of Peru): Jr. Cahuide 785, Jesús María, Lima 11; tel. (1) 6141414; e-mail webmaster@senamhi.gob.pe; internet www.senamhi.gob.pe; f. 1928; 79 primary stations.

Instituto Geofísico del Perú (Geophysical Institute of Peru): Calle Badajoz 169, Mayorazgo IV Etapa, Lima; tel. (1) 3172300; e-mail web@geo.igp.gob.pe; internet www.igp.gob.pe; f. 1919 as Huancayo Magnetic Observatory of the Carnegie Instn of Washington, transferred to Peruvian govt 1947; education sector; observatories in Huancayo, Jicamarca, Ancón, Arequipa and Lima; int. programmes in geomagnetism, seismology, atmospheric sciences, solar activity and natural hazards; Pres. Dr RONALD WOODMAN POLLIT.

TECHNOLOGY

Instituto Geológico, Minero y Metalúrgico (Institute of Geology, Mining and Metallurgy): Apdo 889, Avda Canadá 1470, San Borja, Lima; tel. (1) 6189800; e-mail info@ingemmet.gob.pe; internet www.ingemmet.gob.pe; f. 1978; carries out and coordinates geological mapping at regional scale and evaluates mineral resources; environmental assessment and ecological zonification; provides mining and metallurgical information; library of 37,000 vols; Pres. Ing. SUSANA GLADIS VILCA ACHATA; Sec. Gen. ELIZABETH RAMOS DE LA CRUZ; publs *Boletín Serie A: Carta Geológica Nacional* (irregular), *Boletín Serie B: Geología Económica* (irregular), *Boletín Serie C: Geodinámica e Ingeniería Geológica* (irregular), *Boletín Serie D: Estudios Regionales* (irregular).

Instituto Peruano de Energía Nuclear (Peruvian Nuclear Energy Institute): Avda Canadá 1470, San Borja, Lima 41; tel. (1) 2260030; e-mail sege@ipen.gob.pe; internet www.ipen.gob.pe; f. 1975; researches peaceful uses of nuclear energy in medicine, biology, agriculture and industry, prospecting, mining and processing of uranium ores; management of nuclear reactor and operation of a radioisotope production plant; nucleo-electricity planning; training and research; library of 75,000 vols, periodicals, monographs; Pres. SUSANA MARGARITA PETRICK CASAGRANDE; Exec. Dir Dr CARLOS ALFREDO ESPINOZA ALEGRÍA; publ. *Informe Científico Tecnológico* (1 a year).

Affiliated Institute:

Centro Superior de Estudios Nucleares: Avda Canadá 1470, San Borja, Lima 41; tel. (1) 2260030; e-mail csen@ipen.gob.pe; f. 1972; information and training centre on nuclear energy and its applications; Dir EDUARDO MEDINA GIRONZINI.

Libraries and Archives
Arequipa

Biblioteca de la Universidad Nacional de San Agustín (Library of the National University of San Agustin): Calle Santa Catalina 117, Arequipa; tel. (54) 239261; e-mail bibsoc@unsa.edu.pe; internet www.bvirtual-unsa.edu.pe; f. 1900; 430,000 vols, 1,204 pamphlets and 535 periodicals; 12 specialized libraries; Dir-Gen. Dr VICTOR HUGO LINARES HUACO; publ. *Revista de Investigación de la Universidad.*

Biblioteca Pública Municipal de Arequipa (Municipal Public Library of Arequipa): Portal de la Municipalidad 110, Arequipa; f. 1879; also houses *Casa de la Cultura*; 57,500 vols; Librarian WALTER ALVAREZ THOMAS.

Callao

Biblioteca de la Escuela Naval del Perú (Naval School Library of Peru): Calle Medina s/n La Punta, Callao; tel. (14) 6130400; internet 200.60.17.99/cgi-bin/koha/opac-main.pl; f. 1914; Librarian ABEL ULLOA FERNÁNDEZ-PRADA; specialized library of 6,500 vols.

Biblioteca Pública Municipal Piloto (Municipal Piloto Public Library): Esq. Ruiz y Colón, Apdo 270, Callao; tel. (14) 290558; f. 1936, reorganized 1957; 48,312 vols; 42 mems; Dir ROSA SÁNCHEZ DE WU.

Lima

Archivo General de la Nación (National Archives of the Nation): Jr. Camaná 125 con Psje Piura, Lima; tel. (1) 4267221; e-mail pmaguina@agn.gob.pe; internet www.agn.gob.pe; f. 1861; 2 sections, Administrative and Historical; Dir Dr PABLO ALFONSO MAGUIÑA MINAYA; publs *Legislación Archivística Peruana*, *Revista del AGN*.

Biblioteca Central de la Universidad Nacional de Ingeniería (Central Library of the National University of Engineering): Apdo 3864, Lima 25; Avda Tupac Amaru 210, El Rimac, Lima 25; tel. (1) 4811070; e-mail oceb@uni.edu.pe; internet www.bibliotecacentral.uni.edu.pe; 29,000 vols; Librarian Ing. MARY APOLAYA ARNAO.

Biblioteca Central 'Pedro Zulen' (Central Library 'Pedro Zulen'): Avda Germán Amézaga s/n, Lima 1; tel. (1) 6197000; e-mail sisbiblio@unmsm.edu.pe; internet sisbib.unmsm.edu.pe; f. 1551; attached to Universidad Nacional Mayor de San Marcos; Peruvian Section has rare material on history, law and literature; Head of Library System Lic. BELIZARIO ARICOCHEA ZAMBRANO; 450,000 vols.

Biblioteca del Ministerio de Relaciones Exteriores (Library of the Ministry of Foreign Affairs): Palacio Torre-Tagle, Jr. Ucayali 363, Lima; tel. (1) 3112952; f. 1921; 30,000 vols; Dir MANUEL G. GALDO; publ. *Maris Aestus.*

Biblioteca Nacional del Perú (National Library of Peru): Avda Abancay 4ta Cdra s/n, Lima 01; tel. (1) 5136900; e-mail contactobnp@bnp.gob.pe; internet www.bnp.gob.pe; f. 1821; possesses copies of the first printed works in Peru and the Americas; 737,000 vols, 32,500 MSS, 12,500 maps, 11,000 photographs; Dir RAMÓN ELÍAS MUJICA PINILLA; publs *Bibliografías de Intelectuales Peruanos* (irregular), *Bibliografía Peruana* (1 a year), *Gaceta Bibliotecaria del Perú* (irregular), *Fénix* (1 a year), *Revista Libros y Artes* (4 a year).

Biblioteca y Archivo Histórico Municipal de Lima (Municipal Library and Historical Archive of Lima): Jr. Conde de Superunda 141, 2° Piso, Palacio Municipal, Lima; tel. (1) 3151540; e-mail biblioteca@munlima.gob.pe; internet www.munlima.gob.pe/biblioteca/archivo_municipal; f. 1963; documents, certificates from the 19th century, municipal reports, Peruvian literature; Librarian SANDRO COVARRUBIAS LLERENA.

Sistema de Bibliotecas de la Pontificia Universidad Católica del Perú (Library System of the Pontifical Catholic University of Peru): Apdo 1761, Lima; tel. (1) 6262000; e-mail khanza@pucp.edu.pe; internet biblioteca.pucp.edu.pe; f. 1917; 800,000 vols, 26,049 audiovisual items, 2,260 electronic items and 369,000 monographs; Dir KATHIA HANZA.

Museums and Art Galleries
Arequipa

Museo Arqueológico (Archaeological Museum): Avda Independencia s/n, Ciudad Universitaria, Arequipa; tel. (54) 229719; f. 1933; ceramics, mummies; Dir Dr E. LINARES MÁLAGA.

Ayacucho

Museo de Sitio Wari (Wari Site Museum): Complejo Arqueológico de Wari, km 23 Carretera Ayacucho – Quinua, Huamanga, Ayacucho; tel. (66) 312056; e-mail ayacucho@mcultura.gob.pe; exhibits devt of Wari culture; collns include ceramics, bones, stone objects obtained during research excavations.

Museo Histórico Regional 'Hipólito Unanue' (Regional Historical Museum 'Hipólito Unanue'): Calle 28 de Julio Noi 106, Ayacucho; tel. (66) 312056; e-mail ayacucho@mcultura.gob.pe; f. 1946; archaeology, anthropology, history and popular crafts; library of 4,724 vols incl. bound periodicals; Dir FREDY LAGOS ARRIARÁN; publ. *Anuario.*

Callao

Museo del Ejército del Perú (Army Museum of Peru): Fortaleza del Real Felipe, Plaza de la Independencia s/n, Callao; tel. (14) 4290532; e-mail fortalezadelrealfelipe@hotmail.com; f. 1984; colln of weapons incl. carbines, grenade launchers, handguns, machine guns, mortars, rifles and tanks used by the army; Dir LUIS LOAYZA MORALES.

Museo Naval del Perú (Naval Museum of Peru): Avda Jorge Chávez 123, Plaza Grau, Callao; tel. (14) 6136868; e-mail informes@museonaval.com.pe; internet www .museonaval.com.pe; f. 1958; library of 7,948 vols; Dir Contralmirante FERNANDO CASARETTO ALVARADO; publ. *Fuentes para la Historia Naval.*

Cusco

Museo Arqueológico (Archaeological Museum): Cuesta del Almirante 103 Esq. Calle Ataúd, Cusco; tel. (84) 237380; remains from the Inca period incl. stone objects, funerary metalwork, ceramics, textiles, vessels, evidence of trepanning, embalming, gold, silver, copper and turquoise idols, ceremonial objects, jugs; 17th-century portraits of Incas and Indian chiefs; Dir Dr LUIS A. PARDO.

Museo Histórico Regional del Cusco (Regional Historical Museum of Cusco): Calle Heladeros s/n, Cusco; tel. (84) 223245; e-mail museos@drc-cusco.gob.pe; f. 1946; Peruvian colonial art, Cusco schools of painting affiliated to Inst. Nacional de Cultura; Dir ANTONIA VEGA CENTENO B.; publ. *Revista del Museo Histórico Regional.*

Huancavelica

Museo Arqueológico 'Daniel Hernández Morillo' (Archaeological Museum 'Daniel Hernández Morillo'): Plazoleta de San Juan de Dios, Huancavelica; tel. (67) 453420; e-mail huancavelica@mcultura.gob.pe; tertiary fossils, quaternary remains of various marine species; works of Peruvian painters incl. Daniel Hernandez, Fernando de Szislo and Hilmer Cajahuaringa.

Huancayo

Museo Arqueológico 'Federico Gálvez Durand' de la Gran Unidad Escolar 'Santa Isabel' (Archaeological Museum 'Federico Gálvez Durand'of the Great School Unit 'Santa Isabel'): Jr. Santa Isabel 567, San Carlos, Huancayo, Junín; tel. (64) 231061; f. 1952; 1,654 archaeological specimens from Nazca and other Peruvian cultures; examples of weaving, gold and bronze ornaments, fossils; Head ROBERTH ARROYO HUAMÁN.

Huánuco

Museo Regional 'Leoncio Prado' (Regional Museum 'Leoncio Prado'): Calle 2 de Mayo 680, Huánuco; tel. (62) 519698; e-mail museo@unheval.edu.pe; internet www .unheval.edu.pe/museo; f. 1945; attached to Nat. Univ. of Hermilio Validizán; natural history; Dir JOSÉ WUENCISLAO CONDEZO MARTEL.

Huaráz

Museo Arqueologico de Ancash (Archaeological Museum of Ancash): Avda Luzuriaga 762, Plaza de Armes, Huaráz, Ancash; tel. (44) 721551; e-mail ancash@mcultura.gob.pe; internet www.mcultura.gob.pe; f. 1935; pre-Hispanic history of the Ancash region; exhibits incl. ceramics, metalwork, textiles, human remains; collns from the Chavín, Recuay, Moche, Wari, Chimu and Inca cultures; largest Lithic Park in S America, incl. stone carvings and megalithic statues from the Recuay culture; Dir Arq. ROSA MARÍA VALVERDE; publ. *Cuadernillo de Difusión.*

Ica

Museo Científico Javier Cabrera (Scientific Museum Javier Cabrera): Plaza de Armas, Calle Bolívar 174, Ica; tel. (56) 227676; e-mail informes@museocientificojaviercabrera.com; internet www.museocientificojaviercabrera.com; f. 1966; colln of ancient engraved stones and pottery; library of 100,000 vols; Dir ERNESTO CABRERA CLAUX.

Lambayeque

Museo Nacional Sicán (National Museum Sicán): Avda Batán Grande cuadra 7 s/n Carretera Pítipo–Ferreñafe, Lambayeque; tel. (74) 286469; e-mail museosican@hotmail .com; internet sican.perucultural.org.pe; f. 2001; artefacts related to Sicán soc.; Dir Dr CARLOS G. ELERA ARÉVALO.

Museo Regional Arqueológico 'Bruning' de Lambayeque (Bruning Regional Archaeological Museum of Lambayeque): Avda Huamachuco s/n, Lambayeque; tel. (74) 232110; f. 1924; 8,000 exhibits, of which 1,366 gold, 110 silver; textile, ceramic, wooden and stone pieces; 2 unique blue and black granite mortars incised with mythological figures in 'Chavin' style; Dir CARLOS WESTER LA TORRE.

Lima

Casa de la Gastronomía Peruana (Peruvian Gastronomy House): Jr. Conde de Superunda 170, Cercado de Lima, Lima; tel. (1) 4267264; e-mail aleon@mcultura.gob.pe; f. 2011; culinary culture of Peru in pre-Hispanic, colonial, republican and contemporary eras.

Museo Amazónico (Amazon Museum): Malecón Tarapacá No 382, Iquitos, Maynas, Loreto; tel. (65) 234031; e-mail loreto@mcultura.gob.pe; f. 1996; sculptures of native communities of the Amazon, photographic gallery, portraits.

Museo de Arte de Lima (Museum of Art): Paseo Colón 125, Parque de la Exposición, Lima 1; tel. (1) 2040000; e-mail informes@mali.pe; internet www.mali.pe; f. 1961; exhibits of Peruvian art from its origins to the present day; Pre-Columbian Dept: ceramics, carvings, Paracas woven material dating from 400BC; Colonial Dept: furniture, sculpture, paintings, religious art, silver; Modern Dept: furniture and paintings since 19th century; film archive; studio art courses; restoration and conservation laboratory; library of 4,000 vols; Dir NATALIA MAJLUF BRAHIM.

Museo de Arte Italiano (Museum of Italian Art): Paseo de la República 250, Lima 1; tel. (1) 4239932; e-mail museodearteitaliano@mcultura.gob.pe; f. 1923; 1920s Italian art donated by the Italian colony in Peru; organizes courses and conferences; library of 500 vols; Dir Dra MARGARITA GHINNOCHO LAINEZ LOZADA.

Museo de Historia Natural de la Universidad Nacional Mayor de San Marcos (Natural History Museum of the National University of San Marcos): Apdo 14-0434, Lima 14; Avda Arenales 1256, Jesús María, Lima; tel. (1) 4710117; e-mail museohn@unmsm.edu.pe; internet museohn.unmsm .edu.pe; f. 1918; incl. Herbario San Marcos (USM), with 300,000 specimens largely of Peruvian flora and units of zoology, botany, ecology and geosciences; zoological collns; library of 8,000 vols; Dir Prof. Dr BETTY MILLÁN SALAZAR; publs *Serie 'A' Zoología, Serie 'B' Botánica, Serie 'C' Geología.*

Museo de la Nación (Museum of the Nation): Avda Javier Prado Este 2465, San Borja, Lima; tel. (1) 4769878; e-mail museodelanacion@mcultura.gob.pe; internet www.museodelanacion.pe; overview of Peruvian civilizations: archaeological, ethnographic and contemporary art; Dir Arq. MARGARITA GINOCCHIO LAINEZ LOZADA.

Museo del Virreinato (Museum of the Viceroys): Quinta de Presa Jr. Chira 344, Rímac, Lima 25; tel. (1) 4813867; e-mail etl@mail.cosapidata.com.pe; f. 1935; sited in an 18th-century mansion; exhibits from the Spanish Viceroys period; Dir JOSÉ FLORES ARAOS; publ. *Revista.*

Museo de Mineralogía y Paleontología (Museum of Mineralogy and Paleontology): Campus Universitario, Avda Túpac Amaru km 4.5, 210 Rimac, Lima 25; tel. (1) 4811070; e-mail museomineralogico@uni.edu.pe; internet www.uni.edu.pe; f. 2011; attached to Faculty of Geological, Mining and Metallurgical Engineering (FIGMM), Nat. Univ. of Engineering; colln of fossils and 6,000 mineral specimens; Dir Ing. GUIDO DEL CASTILLO ECHEGARAY.

Museo Larco (Larco Museum): Avda Bolívar 1515, Pueblo Libre, Lima 21; tel. (1) 4611312; e-mail webmaster@museolarco.org; internet www.museolarco.org; f. 1926; Peruvian pre-Columbian history; colln of gold, silver, erotica; 45,000 classified archaeological objects; library of 10,000 vols; Pres. LARCO ISABEL ALVAREZ CALDERÓN; Exec. Dir ANDRÉS ALVAREZ CALDERÓN..

Branch Museum:

Museo de Arte Precolombino (Museum of Pre-Columbian Art): Plaza de Las Nazarenas 231, Cusco; tel. (84) 233210; e-mail amap@infonegocio.net.pe; internet map.museolarco.org; f. 2003; arts of ancient Peruvian cultures; 450 objects from 1250BC to AD 1532; Dir ANDRÉS ALVAREZ CALDERÓN; Exec. Dir EDGAR CASAVERDE.

Museo Nacional de Arqueología, Antropología e Historia del Perú (National Museum of Archaeology, Anthropology and History of Peru): Plaza Bolívar s/n, Pueblo Libre, Lima 21; tel. (1) 4635070; e-mail mnaahp@mcultura.gob.pe; f. 1945; library of 30,000 vols; colln contains pre-Inca and Inca remains, and artefacts from colonial and republican periods; Dir Dra CARMEN ARELLANO HOFFMANN; publs *Arqueológicas, Historia y Cultura, Cuadernos de Investigaciones.*

Museo Nacional de la Cultura Peruana (National Museum of Peruvian Culture): Avda Alfonso Ugarte 650, Apdo 3048, Lima 1; tel. (1) 4235892; e-mail mncp@mcultura .gob.pe; internet www.mcultura.gob.pe; f. 1946; responsible for Instituto de Estudios Etnológicos and the Instituto de Arte Peruano 'José Sabogal'; popular art and ethnography; ethno-historical archive; photographic archive; Dir MANUEL RUIZ RETAMOZO; publ. *Revista del Museo Nacional* (1 a year).

Museo Postal y Filatélico del Perú (Postal and Philatelic Museum): Jr. Conde de Superunda Nº 170, Lima 1; tel. (1) 4280400; f. 1931; library of 100 vols; Dir DORA IBERICO CASTRO.

San Martín

Museo Departamental de San Martín (Departmental Museum of San Martin): Jr. Benavides Nº 380 Barrio Calvario, Moyobamba, San Martín; tel. (42) 562281; e-mail sanmartin@mcultura.gob.pe; archaeological remains of the Chachapoyas culture, artefacts from colonial and republican era.

Trujillo

Museo de Arqueología, Antropología e Historia de la Universidad Nacional de Trujillo (Museum of Archaeology, Anthropology and History of the University of Trujillo): Jr. Junín 682, Trujillo, La Libertad; tel. (44) 474850; e-mail museoarqueologiaunt@gmail.com; f. 1939; displays devt of the historical process of the N coast; collns incl. prehistoric ceramics, textiles, metals, organic material and stone; Dir Arq. ENRIQUE VERGARA MONTERO; publ. *Chimor*.

Museo de Sitio de Chan Chan (Site Museum of Chan Chan): Jr. Torre Tagle 178, Urb. San Andres, Trujillo; tel. (44) 227705; e-mail hgayoso@chanchan.gob.pe; internet www.chanchan.gob.pe; Chimu civilization, colln includes stone artefacts, idols, wood, ceramics, textiles, metalwork and construction materials; Dir Dr HENRY FERNAN GAYOSO PAREDES.

Universities

ASOCIACIÓN UNIVERSIDAD PRIVADA SAN JUAN BAUTISTA
(Private University Association St John the Baptist)

Avda José Antonio Lavalle s/n Hacienda Villa, Distrito Chorrillos, Lima

Telephone: (1) 2142500
E-mail: rafael.urrelo@upsjb.edu.pe
Internet: www.upsjb.edu.pe
Founded 1997
Private control
Language of instruction: Spanish
Academic year: March to December

Rector: Dr RAFAEL URRELO GUERRA
Vice-Rector for Academics: ABILIO PASCACIO ANAYA PAJUELO
Sec. Gen.: Dr REYNALDO CHÁVEZ RÍOS

DEANS

Faculty of Engineering: Dr ALBERTO GARCÍA CÁCERES
Faculty of Health Sciences: Dr ALBERTO GARCÍA CÁCERES
Faculty of Law: Dr JOSÉ DE LA VIRGEN MARÍA URQUIZO OLAECHEA
School of Communication and Management Sciences: Dr ALBERTO GARCÍA CÁCERES

FACULTAD DE TEOLOGÍA PONTIFICIA Y CIVIL DE LIMA
(Pontifical Faculty of Theology and Civil of Lima)

Apdo postal 1801, Lima
Jr. Carlos Bondy No 700-Pueblo Libre, Lima
Telephone: (1) 4610013
E-mail: rectorado@ftpcl.edu.pe
Internet: www.ftpcl.edu.pe
Founded 1548, independent univ. status 1994
Private control
Language of instruction: Spanish
Academic year: March to December

Incl. Limense Institute of Theological Sciences

Chancellor: CARDENAL JUAN LUIS CIPRIANI THORNE

Rector: Dr CARLOS ROSELL DE ALMEIDA
Vice-Rector for Academics: Dr LEONARDO ALCAYHUAMÁN ACCOSTUPA
Vice-Rector for Admin.: Dr JOSÉ CALDERÓN MOQUILLAZA
Sec. Gen.: GABRIEL ROMERO
Librarian: Dr DICK TONSMANN VÁSQUEZ
Library of 18,500 vols
Publications: *Revista Teológica Limense* (3 a year), *Revista Verba Hominis* (1 a year)

PONTIFICIA UNIVERSIDAD CATÓLICA DEL PERÚ
(Pontifical Catholic University of Peru)

Avda Universitaria 1801, San Miguel, Lima 32

Telephone: (1) 6262000
E-mail: secgen@pucp.edu.pe
Internet: www.pucp.edu.pe
Founded 1917
Private control
Language of instruction: Spanish
Academic year: March to December (2 semesters)

Rector: Dr MARCIAL RUBIO CORREA
Vice-Rector for Academic Affairs: Dr EFRAÍN GONZALES DE OLARTE
Vice-Rector for Admin.: CARLOS FOSCA PASTOR
Vice-Rector for Research: Dra PEPI PATRÓN COSTA
Sec. Gen.: Dr RENÉ ORTIZ CABALLERO
Librarian: Dra CARMEN VILLANUEVA
Library: see under Libraries and Archives
Number of teachers: 2,500
Number of students: 19,000

Publications: *Agenda Internacional* (2 a year), *Análisis Económico de Coyuntura* (12 a year), *Anthropológica* (1 a year), *Areté* (2 a year), *Debates en Sociología* (2 a year), *Derecho* (1 a year), *Economía* (1 a year), *Educación* (2 a year), *Electro Electrónica* (2 a year), *Espacio y Desarrollo* (1 a year), *Histórica* (2 a year), *Lexis* (2 a year), *Pensamiento Constitucional* (1 a year), *Pro Matemática* (2 a year), *Revista de Psicología* (2 a year), *Revista de Química* (2 a year), *Synergies Pérou* (1 a year), *Tren de Sombras* (4 a year)

DEANS

Arts (General Studies Programme): Prof. PABLO QUINTANILLA PÉREZ-WICHT
Faculty of Administration and Accounting: OSCAR DÍAZ BECERRA
Faculty of Architecture and Planning: FREDERICK COOPER LLOSA
Faculty of Arts: ALBERTO AGAPITO ABURTO
Faculty of Arts and Human Sciences: SUSANA REISZ CANDREVA
Faculty of Communication Arts and Sciences: Prof. JUAN GARGUREVICH REGAL
Faculty of Education: CARMEN COLOMA MANRIQUE
Faculty of Humanities: Prof. SUSANA REISZ CANDREVA
Faculty of Law: Prof. CÉSAR LANDA ARROYO
Faculty of Management: Prof. MÓNICA BONIFAZ CHIRINOS
Faculty of Science and Engineering: DANIEL TORREALVA DÁVILA
Faculty of Social Sciences: ALAN FAIRLIE REINOSO
Graduate School: Prof. PATRICIA MARTÍNEZ URIBE
Science (General Studies Programme): Prof. CARLOS PIZARRO ORTIZ

UNIVERSIDAD ANDINA 'NÉSTOR CÁCARES VELÁSQUEZ'
(Andean University 'Néstor Cácares Velásquez')

Edif. 'El Campin', Of. 208 Psje la Cultura, Juliaca, Puno
Telephone: (51) 322213
Internet: www.uancv.edu.pe
Founded 1981
Private control
Academic year: March to December
Study centres in Arequipa, Azángaro, Ilave, Juliaca and Puno

Rector: Dr HUAMÁN MEZA VICTOR JULIO
Vice-Rector for Academics: Dra BUTRON ZEVALLOS UDELIA
Vice-Rector for Admin.: Dr CARI ORTÍZ LEOPOLDO
Sec.-Gen.: RONAL MADERA TERAN

DEANS

Faculty of Accounting and Financial Sciences: Dr OBDULIO COLLANTES MENIS
Faculty of Administrative Sciences: HUGO BARRANTES SANCHEZ
Faculty of Education Science: Dr PASCUAL HUACASI SUCASACA
Faculty of Engineering and Pure Sciences: ZEGARRA BUTRON ALFREDO
Faculty of Health Sciences: CHAMBI CATACORA MARÍA AMPARO
Faculty of Legal and Political Sciences: VICTOR NIÑO DE GUZMÁN PINO
Faculty of Systems Engineering: LAZO ROJAS ADONIS HUBERT

UNIVERSIDAD ANTONIO RUÍZ DE MONTOYA
(Antonio Ruíz de Montoya University)

Paso de los Andes 970, Pueblo Libre, Lima
Telephone: (1) 7195990
E-mail: informes@uarm.edu.pe
Internet: www.uarm.edu.pe
Founded 2003
Private control
Language of instruction: Spanish
Academic year: March to December

Rector: Dr JUAN CARLOS MORANTE BUCHHAMMER
Vice-Rector for Academics: Dr JUAN MANUEL BURGA DÍAZ
Sec.-Gen.: Abog. ENRIQUE DURÁN PADRÓS
Dir for Humanities Programme: Dr RAFAEL VEGA-CENTENO SARA-LAFOSSE
Dir for Research and Advocacy: Dr ERNESTO CAVASSA CANESSA
Dir for Library: RITA MINAYA ESPINOZA
Library of 50,000 vols, 350 magazines, 2,500 brochures and handouts, 69 maps and audiovisual material

DEANS

Faculty of Engineering and Management: Ing. FERNANDO VILLARÁN DE LA PUENTE
Faculty of Philosophy and Humanities: Dr RAFAEL FERNÁNDEZ HART
Faculty of Social Sciences: Dr ALDO VÁSQUEZ RÍOS

UNIVERSIDAD CATÓLICA DE SANTA MARÍA
(Catholic University of Santa Maria)

Urb. San José s/n Umacollo, Arequipa
Telephone: (54) 382038
E-mail: cempos@ucsm.edu.pe
Internet: www.ucsm.edu.pe
Founded 1961
Private control
Language of instruction: Spanish
Academic year: March to December

Rector: Dr ABEL TAPIA FERNÁNDEZ

Vice-Rector for Academics: Dr MANUEL VÁSQUEZ HUERTA

Vice-Rector for Admin.: Dr GASPAR DEL CARPIO RODRIGUEZ

Publications: *Revista Medica Galénica, Revista Científica de Ciencias Biológicas, Revista de Derecho Procesal Penal, Revista Inteligencia Mecanica*

DEANS

Faculty of Accounting and Finance: Dr JORGE VALDEZ CORNEJO

Faculty of Architecture, Civil Engineering and the Environment: Arq. CARLOS RODRÍGUEZ QUIROZ

Faculty of Biological Science and Chemical Engineering: Dr CAYETANO RIVERA RIVERA

Faculty of Dentistry: Dr HERBERT MARIO GALLEGOS VARGAS

Faculty of Economics and Administrative Sciences: Dr JOSÉ MANUEL PATRICIO QUINTANILLA PAULET

Faculty of Engineering Physics and Formal Science: CESAR CASTILLO CÁCERES

Faculty of Humanities and Social Technology: (vacant)

Faculty of Human Medicine: Dr JUAN CAMPOS NIZAMA

Faculty of Law and Political Sciences: Dr LUIS VARGAS FERNANDEZ

Faculty of Medicine: RUTH ROMERO SANTOS DE RODRÍGUEZ

Faculty of Obstetrics and Child Care: RICARDINA FLORES FLORES

Institute of Informatics: Ing. JOSÉ SULLA TORRES (Dir)

UNIVERSIDAD CATÓLICA DE TRUJILLO BENEDICTO XVI
(Catholic University of Trujillo Benedicto XVI)

Panamericana Norte No 555-Moche, Trujillo, La Libertad

Telephone: (44) 607430

E-mail: informes@uct.edu.pe

Internet: www.uct.edu.pe

Founded 2000

Private control

Language of instruction: Spanish

Academic year: March to December

Faculties of engineering, health sciences, humanities, law and political science, management and economics, theology

Chancellor and Founder: Dr HÉCTOR MIGUEL CABREJOS VIDARTE

Rector: Dr ALCIBÍADES HELÍ MIRANDA CHÁVEZ

Vice-Chancellor and Vice-Rector for Academics: Mgr RICARDO EXEQUIEL ANGULO BAZAURI

Rector for Admin. and Finance: Ing. MARCO DÁVILA CABREJOS

Sec. Gen.: JORGE ISAAC MANRIQUE CATALÁN

UNIVERSIDAD CATÓLICA LOS ÁNGELES DE CHIMBOTE
(Catholic University Los Ángeles of Chimbote)

Avda Bolognesi No 835, Chimbote, Ancash

Telephone: (43) 343444

E-mail: webmaster@uladech.edu.pe

Internet: www.uladech.edu.pe

Founded 1985

Private control

Language of instruction: Spanish

Academic year: March to December

Rector: Dr JULIO B. DOMÍNGUEZ GRANDA

Vice-Rector: Dr VICENTE VALDEZ MORANTE

Sec. Gen.: CARMEN ROSA BARRETO RODRÍGUEZ

Librarian: MARÍA MARILUZ RISCO FLORES

DEANS

Faculty of Accountancy, Finance and Administration: ROBERTO REYNA MÁRQUEZ

Faculty of Education and Humanities: Dr JUAN ROGER RODRIGUEZ RUIZ

Faculty of Engineering: Ing. EULOGIO FRANCISCO HUAMBACHANO SÁNCHEZ

Faculty of Health Sciences: Dr C. D. JOSÉ LUIS ROJAS BARRIOS

Faculty of Law and Political Sciences: DIÓGENES JIMÉNEZ DOMÍNGUEZ

UNIVERSIDAD CATÓLICA SAN PABLO
(Catholic University of St Paul)

Campus Campiña Paisajista s/n Quinta Vivanco, Barrio de San Lázaro, Arequipa

Telephone: (54) 605630

E-mail: institucional@ucsp.edu.pe

Internet: www.ucsp.edu.pe

Founded 1996

Private control

Language of instruction: Spanish

Academic year: April to December

Rector: Dr GERMÁN CHÁVEZ CONTRERAS

Pro-Rector: Dr ALONSO QUINTANILLA PÉREZ-WICHT

Vice-Rector and Dir of the Graduate School: Dr JOSÉ MARÍA CORRALES-NIEVES LAZARTE

Sec. Gen.: Abog. JUAN IGNACIO ANGULO CUBA

Dir for Research: Mag. ALEJANDRO ESTENÓS LOAYZA

Publication: *Revista de Investigación* (1 a year)

DEANS

Faculty of Business and Economic Sciences: Mag. JORGE ANGULO PAULET

Faculty of Engineering and Computer Science: Dr ERNESTO CUADROS VARGAS

Faculty of Human Sciences: Mag. JORGE PACHECO TEJADA

Faculty of Law: Dr RAFAEL SANTA MARÍA D'ANGELO

UNIVERSIDAD CATÓLICA SANTO TORIBIO DE MOGROVEJO
(Catholic University of St Toribio of Mogrovejo)

Avda Panamericana Norte No 855, Chiclayo

Telephone: (74) 606200

E-mail: informacion@usat.edu.pe

Internet: www.usat.edu.pe

Founded 1996

Private control

Language of instruction: Spanish

Founder: Mgr IGNACIO MARÍA DE ORBEGOZO Y GOICOECHEA

Chancellor: Bishop JESÚS MOLINÉ LABARTA

Vice-Chancellor: CARLOS MUNDACA GUERRA

Rector: Dr HUGO CALIENES BEDOYA

Vice-Rector for Academics: Dra SOFÍA LAVADO HUARCAYA

Vice-Rector for Admin.: CARLOS CAMPANA MARROQUÍN

Vice Rector for Professors: Dra MIRTHA FLOR CERVERA VALLEJOS

Vice-Rector for Student Affairs: JAVIER ESPINOZA ESCOBAR

Sec. Gen.: JORGE PÉREZ URIARTE

Dir for the Graduate School: Dr JORGE ANTONIO HEREDIA PÉREZ

Publication: *Flumen* (2 a year, print and online, intranet.usat.edu.pe/usat/flumen)

DEANS

Faculty of Business: JULIA MATURANA CORONEL

Faculty of Engineering: ROBERTO RUIDIAS SEMINARIO

Faculty of Humanities: WILLAM ANTONIO RUIZ CORONADO

Faculty of Law: ERIKA VALDIVIESO LÓPEZ

Faculty of Medicine: Dra PATRICIA CAMPOS OLAZÁBAL

UNIVERSIDAD CATÓLICA SEDES SAPIENTIAE
(Seat of Wisdom Catholic University)

Esq. Constelaciones y Sol de Oro s/n Urb., Sol de Oro, Los Olivos, Lima

Telephone: (1) 5330008

E-mail: laliaga@ucss.edu.pe

Internet: www.ucss.edu.pe

Founded 1998

Private control

Language of instruction: Spanish

Centres of biological research, business advice, language; institute of transport; territorial development observatory

Chancellor: Mgr LINO PANIZZA RICHERO

Rector: Dr JOAQUÍN MARTÍNEZ VALLS

Vice-Chancellor: Dr ROGER RAFAEL RODRÍGUEZ ITURRI

Vice-Rector for Academics: LUIS HUMBERTO ALIAGA RODRÍGUEZ

Vice-Rector for Admin.: Dr GIAN BATTISTA FAUSTO BOLIS

Sec. Gen.: Dr GIANCARLO MASCELLARO LUPERDI

DEANS

Faculty of Agricultural Engineering: JUAN IGNACIO PASTÉN MONARDEZ

Faculty of Economics and Business: Dr PAOLO BIDINOST

Faculty of Education and Humanities: Dra GIULIANA CONTINI

Faculty of Engineering: JOSÉ HIGINIO PÉREZ FERNÁNDEZ

Faculty of Health Sciences: Dr LUIS SOLARI DE LA FUENTE

UNIVERSIDAD CÉSAR VALLEJO
(César Vallejo University)

Avda Larco cuadra 1770, Trujillo

Telephone: (44) 485000

E-mail: trujillo@ucv.edu.pe

Internet: www.ucv.edu.pe

Founded 1991

Private control

Language of instruction: Spanish

Academic year: March to December

Campuses in Callao, Chiclayo, Chimbote, Huaraz, San Juan de Lurigancho, Lima East, Lima Norte, Moyobamba, Piura, Tarapoto

Rector: Dr BRIJALDO SIGIFREDO ORBEGOSO VENEGAS

Vice-Rector for Academics: Dra ANA TERESA FERNÁNDEZ GILL

Sec. Gen.: Prof. VÍCTOR RAFAEL SANTISTEBAN CHÁVEZ

DEANS

Faculty of Architecture: ADELI ZAVALETA PITA

Faculty of Business Studies: Dra ROSA MORENO RODRIGUEZ

Faculty of Communication Sciences: Dr DENNIS VARGAS MARÍN

Faculty of Education and Languages: Dra HELVIDIA CASTILLO

Faculty of Engineering: RICARDO DELGADO ARANA

Faculty of Humanities: JUAN QUIJANO PACHECO

Faculty of Law: Dr ROBERTO PALACIOS BRAND

Faculty of Medical Sciences: Dra EVELYN GOICOCHEA

UNIVERSIDAD CIENTÍFICA DEL PERÚ
(Science University of Peru)

Avda Abelardo Quiñones km 2.5 San Juan Bautista, Iquitos, Loreto

Telephone: (65) 261088
E-mail: mail.ucp@edu.pe
Internet: www.ucp.edu.pe

Founded 1990
Private control
Language of instruction: Spanish
Academic year: April to December

Also faculty of education and humanities; cultural centre

Rector: Dr JUAN REMIGIO SALDAÑA ROJAS
Vice-Rector for Academics: Dr HUGO SIGFREDO CRUZ ULLOA
Vice-Rector for Research and Innovation: Dr JOSÉ RONY VALERA SUÁREZ

DEANS

Faculty of Architecture and Urbanism: Arq. JAIME RUIZ DE LOAYZA
Faculty of Business: Dr JESÚS AQUILES GAMARRA RAMÍREZ
Faculty of Health Sciences: Mag. JESÚS JACINTO MAGALLANES CASTILLA
Faculty of Law and Political Science: Mag. ROGER ALBERTO CABRERA PAREDES
Faculty of Science and Engineering: Ing. ULISES OCTAVIO IRIGOIN CABRERA

UNIVERSIDAD CIENTÍFICA DEL SUR
(Scientific University of the South)

Antigua Panamericana Sur, km 19, Villa, Lima

Telephone: (1) 6106400
E-mail: informes@cientifica.edu.pe
Internet: www.cientifica.edu.pe

Founded 1998
Private control
Language of instruction: Spanish
Academic year: March to December

Pres.: JOSÉ CARLOS DEXTRE CHACÓN
Founder Rector: Dr FERNANDO CABIESES MOLINA
Rector: Dr JOSÉ AMIEL PÉREZ
Vice-Rector for Academics: Dra JOSEFINA TAKAHASHI SATO

Publications: Científica, Cultura Sur, Desde el Sur, Habla Científico, Solar, Sur Económico

DEANS

Faculty of Environmental Sciences: Dra JOSEFINA TAKAHASHI SATO
Faculty of Health Sciences: Dr RAFAEL ELGEGREN REÁTEGUI
Faculty of Humanities: LUIS GUILLERMO SICHERI MONTEVERDE
Faculty of Veterinary Sciences and Biology: MANUEL EFRAÍN ROSEMBERG BARRÓN

UNIVERSIDAD CONTINENTAL
(Continental University)

Huancayo Campus: Avda San Carlos 1980, Huáncayo

Telephone: (64) 481430

Arequipa Campus: Calle Las Beatas 203-Yanahuara, Arequipa
E-mail: comunicaciones@continental.edu.pe
Internet: www.universidad.continental.edu.pe

Founded 1998
Private control
Language of instruction: Spanish
Academic year: March to December

Rector: ESAÚ CARO MEZA
Pres.: FERNANDO BARRIOS IPENZA
Exec. Vice-Pres.: JOSÉ BARRIOS IPENZA

Dir of Research Institute: WILFREDO BULEGE GUTIÉRREZ

Library of 15,000 vols

Publications: Revista Científica Yachayninchic (2 a year), Revista Científica Apuntes de Ciencia & Sociedad (2 a year)

DEANS

Faculty of Business: WILLIAM RODRÍGUEZ GIRÁLDEZ
Faculty of Engineering: RICARDO SALCEDO ZÁRATE
Faculty of Health Sciences: RIGOBERTO ZÚÑIGA MERA
Faculty of Law: ARMANDO PRIETO HORMAZA

UNIVERSIDAD DE CHICLAYO
(University of Chiclayo)

Ciudad Universitaria km 3.5 Carretera a Pimentel, Chiclayo, Lambayeque

Telephone: (1) 265889
E-mail: rectorado@udch.edu.pe
Internet: www.udch.edu.pe

Founded 1985
Private control
Language of instruction: Spanish
Academic year: March to December

Rector: Dr ROGER PINGO JARA
Vice-Rector for Academics: Dr ALCIDES RODAS SÁNCHEZ
Vice-Rector for Research: Dr SOLEDAD TORRES ELERA
Sec. Gen.: HEBER VARGAS ASCURRA

DEANS

Faculty of Communication Sciences: JULIO LÁZARO VILLACORTA
Faculty of Education: Dr MAXIMILIANO LARREA PORTILLA
Faculty of Law: Dr VÍCTOR ROJAS HERRERA
Faculty of Management Sciences, Computing and Systems: LUIS FERNANDO CAMPOS CONTRERAS

UNIVERSIDAD DE HUÁNUCO
(Huanuco University)

Jr. Hermilio Valdizán 871, 2°, Huánuco

Telephone: (62) 519773
E-mail: info@udh.edu.pe
Internet: www.udh.edu.pe

Founded 1984

Rector: Dr JOSÉ ANTONIO BERAÚN BARRANTES
Vice-Rector for Academics: JULIA PALACIOS ZEVALLOS
Sec. Gen.: BERNABÉ MATO CORI
Librarian: MARY DIAZ PAIVA

Number of teachers: 60
Number of students: 1,700

DEANS

Faculty of Forestry Engineering: NILO LÓPEZ TELLO
Faculty of Law and Politics: EMERICO ISRAEL OLIVERA
Faculty of Obstetrics: MANUEL ISRAEL OLIVERA

UNIVERSIDAD DE LIMA
(University of Lima)

Apdo 852, Lima 100, Lima
Avda Javier Prado Este cuadra 46, Urb. Monterrico, Lima 33, Lima

Telephone: (1) 4376767
E-mail: usim@ulima.edu.pe
Internet: www.ulima.edu.pe

Founded 1962
Private control
Language of instruction: Spanish
Academic year: April to December

Rector: Dra ILSE WISOTZKI LOLI

Vice-Rector: Mag. CÉSAR VIALARDI SACÍN
Admin. and Gen. Services: Ing. JOSÉ ANTONIO LIZÁRRAGA
Librarian: NELLY CASAS PASTOR

Number of teachers: 900
Number of students: 14,000

Publications: Ciencia Económica (2 a year), Contratexto (1 a year), Ingeniería Industrial, Ius et Praxis (2 a year), Lienzo (1 a year), Persona (1 a year)

DEANS

Accounting: JAIME FLORES CÓRDOVA (Dir)
Architecture: ENRIQUE BONILLA DI TOLLA (Dir)
Faculty of Administration: CARLOS JOSÉ MARÍA BRESANI TAMAYO
Faculty of Communication Sciences: ÓSCAR QUEZADA MACCHIAVELLO
Faculty of Economics: JAVIER FRANCISCO ZÚÑIGA QUEVEDO
Faculty of Industrial Engineering: JAIME LEÓN FERREYRA
Faculty of Law: OSWALDO HUNDSKOPF EXEBIO
Faculty of Psychology: OSCAR QUEZADA MACCHIAVELLO
General Studies: JOSÉ VALDIZÁN AYALA (Dir)
International Business: NORKA PATRICIA STUART ALVARADO (Dir)
Systems Engineering: JAIME LEÓN FERREYRA (Dir)

UNIVERSIDAD DE PIURA
(University of Piura)

Piura Campus: Avda Ramón Mugica 131, Urbanización San Eduardo, POB 353, Piura

Telephone: (73) 284500
E-mail: info@udep.pe

Miraflores Campus: Calle Bellavista 199, Miraflores, Lima

Telephone: (1) 2139600
E-mail: campuslima@udep.pe
Internet: www.udep.edu.pe

Founded 1969
Private control
Language of instruction: Spanish
Academic year: March to December

Chancellor: JAVIER ECHEVARRÍA RODRÍGUEZ
Vice-Chancellor: EMILIO ARIZMENDI ECHECOPAR
Rector: Dr SERGIO BALAREZO SALDAÑA
Vice-Pres.: ANTONIO MABRES TORELLÓ
Vice-Pres. for Professors: MARIELA GARCÍA ROJAS
Vice-Pres. for Research and Academics: MARÍA PÍA CHIRINOS MONTALBETTI
Vice-Pres. for Lima Campus: Dr JOSE STOCK CAPELLA
Gen. Sec.: WILLIAM ZAPATA JIMÉNEZ
Librarian: Dr MARÍA JOSÉ ANDRADE DE HAKANSSON

Library of 197,725 vols
Number of teachers: 240
Number of students: 8,200

Publications: Coleccion Jurídica, Colección Persona y Comunicación, Cuaderno de Humanidades, Mercurio Peruano, Revista Amigos, Revista de Derechos Humanos, Revista Ita Ius Esto (online)

DEANS

Faculty of Communications: MELA SALAZAR VELARDE
Faculty of Economics and Business Administration: ALVARO TRESIERRA
Faculty of Education: MARÍA DEL CARMEN BARRETO PÉREZ
Faculty of Engineering: Dra SUSANA VEGAS CHIYÓN
Faculty of Humanities: JULISSA GUTIÉRREZ RIVAS

Faculty of Law: Dr Luis Castillo Córdova
School of Management PAD: José Garrido-Lecca Arimana

UNIVERSIDAD DE SAN MARTÍN DE PORRES
(University of San Martin of Porres)

Lima Campus: Ciuadad Universitaria, Avda Las Calandrias s/n, Santa Anita, Lima

Telephone: (1) 3620064

Chiclayo Campus: Calle Nazareth 621 con Esq. Avda Balta, Chiclayo, Lambayeque

Telephone: (074) 222206
E-mail: rectorado@usmp.edu.pe
Internet: www.usmp.edu.pe

Founded 1962
Private control
Language of instruction: Spanish
Academic year: March to December

Institutes for art, quality education, human rights and devt, wine

Rector: Dr Jose Antonio Chang Escobedo
Vice-Rector: Dr Raúl Eduardo Bao García
Sec. Gen.: Dr Rodolfo Gavilano Oliver

Library of 160,000 vols
Number of teachers: 4,100
Number of students: 34,000

Publications: *Correspondencias & Análisis* (1 a year, print and online, www.correspondenciasyanalisis.com/es), *Gobernabilidad*, *Horizonte Medico*, *Martín*, *Revista Cultura* (1 a year, print and online, www.fcctp.usmp.edu.pe/cultura/index.php), *Revista KIRU* (2 a year), *Revista Peruana de Obstetricia y Enfermería*, *Revista SAPERE* (1 a year), *Turismo y Patrimonio* (1 a year), *Vox Juris*

DEANS

Faculty of Accounting, Economy and Finance: Dr Domingo Sáenz Yaya
Faculty of Administration and Human Resources: Dr Daniel Hernán Valera Loza
Faculty of Communication, Tourism and Psychology: Dr Johan Leuridan Huys
Faculty of Dentistry: Dr Carlos Enrique Cava Vergiu
Faculty of Engineering and Architecture: Ing. Manuel Alejandro Cáceres Lampen
Faculty of Human Medicine: Dr Frank Lizaraso Caparó
Faculty of Law: Dr Rubén Darío Sanabria Ortiz
Faculty of Obstetrics and Nursing: Mag. Hilda Baca Neglia

UNIVERSIDAD DEL PACÍFICO
(University of the Pacific)

Avda Salaverry 2020, Jesús María, Apdo 4683, Lima 11

Telephone: (1) 2190100
E-mail: ori@up.edu.pe
Internet: www.up.edu.pe

Founded 1962
Private control
Language of instruction: Spanish
Academic year: March to December

Rector: Prof. Felipe Portocarrero Suárez
Vice-Rector: Prof. María Matilde Schwalb Helguero
Gen. Sec.: Prof. Luis Alfredo Agusti Pacheco-Benavides
Librarian: Rosa Dorival

Library of 50,000 vols, 1,500 periodicals, 500 multimedia titles, theses and entrepreneurial projects
Number of teachers: 900
Number of students: 3,400 (2,800 full-time undergraduate, 600 part-time graduate)

Publications: *Apuntes*, *Punto de Equilibrio*

DEANS

Faculty of Economics and Finance: Prof. Gustavo Yamada Fukusaki
Faculty of Engineering: Prof. Oscar de Azambuja
Faculty of Law: Prof. Fernando Cantuarias
Graduate School: Prof. Elsa Del Castillo
School of Business: Prof. Eduardo Mindreau

UNIVERSIDAD ESAN
(University ESAN)

Alonso de Molina 1652, Monterrico, Surco, Lima

Telephone: (1) 7127200
E-mail: jtalavera@esan.edu.pe
Internet: www.ue.edu.pe

Founded 2003
Private control
Language of instruction: Spanish
Academic year: March to December

Also institutes of economic development, governance and corporate governance, international business, regulation and finance

Rector: Jorge Talavera
Vice-Rector for Academics: Nancy Matos
Head of Library and Information Centre: Cecilia Alegre Castro

Library of 60,000 vols of books

Publication: *Journal of Economics, Finance and Administrative Science* (2 a year, in Spanish and English, print and online, jefas.esan.edu.pe/index.php/jefas/index)

DEANS

Faculty of Economics and Administrative Sciences: Jorge Alberto Cortez Cumpa
Faculty of Engineering: Javier Fernando del Carpio Gallegos
Graduate School of Business Administration: Jaime Félix Serida Nishimura

UNIVERSIDAD FEMENINA DEL SAGRADO CORAZÓN
(Women's University of the Sacred Heart)

Avda Los Frutales 954, Urb. Santa Magdalena Sofia, La Molina, Apdo 0005, Lima 41

Telephone: (1) 4364641
E-mail: webmaster@unife.edu.pe
Internet: www.unife.edu.pe

Founded 1962
Private control
Language of instruction: Spanish
Academic year: April to December (2 semesters)

Rector: Dra R. M. Elga García Aste
Vice-Rector for Academic Affairs: Dra Victoria García García
Vice-Rector for Admin.: Dr Fernando Élgegren Reátegui
Sec.-Gen.: Lucrecia Villanueva Paz
Librarian: Licda María La Serna de Más

Library of 67,300 vols

Publications: *Avances en Psicología*, *Comunifé*, *Consensus*, *Cuaderno de Psicología*, *Puente*, *Revista de Educación*, *Revista de Psicología*, *Revista Sistémica*

DEANS

Faculty of Architecture: Arq. Daniel Maya Garavito
Faculty of Educational Sciences: Dr Mónica Escalante Rivera
Faculty of Engineering, Nutrition and Management: Mgr Juan Manuel Fernández Chavesta
Faculty of Law and Political Sciences: Abog. Sylvia Torres Morales
Faculty of Management Sciences: Dra Eulalia Calvo Bustamante

Faculty of Psychology and Humanities: Dra Elena Carmen Morales Miranda
Faculty of Translation, Interpreting and Communications: Licda Rossana Sorlano Vergara
Postgraduate School: Dr Agustín Campos Arenas

UNIVERSIDAD INCA GARCILASO DE LA VEGA
(Inca Garcilaso de la Vega University)

Avda San Felipe 890, Jesús María, Lima

Telephone: (1) 4711784
E-mail: vrac@uigv.edu.pe
Internet: www.uigv.edu.pe

Founded 1964
Private control
Language of instruction: Spanish
Academic year: March to December (2 semesters)

Rector: Dr Luis Cervantes Linan
Vice-Rector: Dr Jorge Manuel Lazo Manrique
Sec. Gen.: Dr Óscar Romero Aquino
Librarian: Nancy Harman de Alvarado

Number of teachers: 240
Number of students: 7,000

Publication: *Garcilaso*

DEANS

Faculty of Accountancy and Corporate Finance: Dr Julio Vargas Arbieto
Faculty of Communication Sciences, Tourism and Hospitality: Dr Ramiro Gómez Salas
Faculty of Education: Dr Carlos Oyola Martinez
Faculty of Foreign Trade and International Relations: Dr Julio Villar Castillo
Faculty of Industrial Engineering and Engineering Management: Dr Victor Rojas Hernández
Faculty of Law and Political Science: Dr Antonio Jesús Rivera Oré
Faculty of Management and Economics: Dr Raúl Gonzales Herrera
Faculty of Nursing: Dra Sonia Vela Gonzales
Faculty of Pharmacy and Biochemistry: Dr Jorge Lazo Manrique
Faculty of Psychology and Social Work: Dra Graciela Villegas García
Faculty of Stomatology: Dr Juan Wilder Ponte Lucio
Faculty of Systems Engineering, Computing and Telecommunications: Dr Eduardo Ugaz Burga

UNIVERSIDAD JOSÉ CARLOS MARIÁTEGUI
(José Carlos Mariátegui University)

Calle Ayacucho 393 Moquegua, Lima

Telephone: (1) 461110
E-mail: correo@ujcm.edu.pe
Internet: www.ujcm.edu.pe

Founded 2002
Private control
Language of instruction: Spanish
Academic year: March to December

Rector: Dra Elvira Ofelia Rodríguez Antinori
Vice-Rector for Academics: Dr Miguel Fuentes Chávez
Vice-Rector for Admin.: Dr Denesy Pelagia Palacios Jimenez
Sec. Gen.: Oscar Paredes Vargas

DEANS

Faculty of Engineering: Elar Ordoñez Carpio
Faculty of Health Sciences: Dra Hilda Guevara Gómez

Faculty of Political Sciences, Business and Education: Dr DELFÍN BERMEJO PERALTA

UNIVERSIDAD LAS AMÉRICAS
(University of the Americas)

Avda Garcilaso de la Vega No 1880, Lima

Telephone: (1) 4171415

E-mail: imagen.institucional@ulasamericas.edu.pe

Internet: www.ulasamericas.edu.pe

Founded 2003

Private control

Language of instruction: Spanish

Academic year: March to December

Rector: Dr LUIS EFRAÍN HURTADO VALENCIA

Vice-Rector for Academics: Dr ENRIQUE LOO AYNE

Sec. Gen.: JOSÉ LUIS ZEGARRA ESCALANTE

DEANS

Faculty of Business: Dra LILY CHAN SÁNCHEZ

Faculty of Communication: ELEODORO ORLANDO MENÉNDEZ GALLEGOS

Faculty of Engineering: Dr LUIS MIGUEL ROMERO ECHEVARRÍA

Faculty of Law: Dr JORGE RODRÍGUEZ VÉLEZ

UNIVERSIDAD MARCELINO CHAMPAGNAT
(University Marcelino Champagnat)

Avda Mariscal Castilla 1270, Santiago de Surco, Lima

Telephone: (1) 4490449

E-mail: informes@umch.edu.pe

Internet: www.umch.edu.pe

Founded 1990

Private control

Language of instruction: Spanish

Academic year: March to December

Faculties of accounting, administration, education, psychology

Rector: PABLO GONZÁLEZ FRANCO

Vice-Rector: Dr NICANOR MARCIAL COLONIA VALENZUELA

Vice-Rector for Admin.: ANA SOLIMANO NAVARRO

Sec. Gen.: JOSÉ TICÓ MÁRQUEZ

Library of 23,000 vols

UNIVERSIDAD NACIONAL AGRARIA DE LA SELVA
(National Agricultural University of the Selva)

Avda Universitaria s/n km 1.5, Tingo María, Huánuco

Telephone: (62) 562190

E-mail: webmaster@unas.edu.pe

Internet: www.unas.edu.pe

Founded 1964

State control

Language of instruction: Spanish

Academic year: April to December

Rector: Dr SEGUNDO CLEMENTE RODRÍGUEZ DELGADO

Vice-Rector for Academics: Dr MÁXIMO ALFREDO DIONISIO GARMA

Vice-Rector for Admin.: Ing. CÉSAR AUGUSTO MAZABEL TORRES

Sec.-Gen.: TITO F. GONZÁLEZ MANRIQUE DE LARA

Central Library Dir: KARINA DEL AGUILA VELA

Number of teachers: 200

Number of students: 1,500

Publication: *Tropicultura*

DEANS

Faculty of Agronomy: DAVID GUARDA SOTELO

Faculty of Animal Husbandry: Dr JORGE RÍOS ALVARADO

Faculty of Computers and Systems Engineering: Dr CÉSAR LINDO PIZARRO

Faculty of Economics and Administration: Lic. LUIS ABANTO MORALES Y CHOCANO

Faculty of Food Industries: Ing. DOLORES WASHINGTON PAREDES PEREDA

Faculty of Renewable Natural Resources: Ing. CÉSAR SAMUEL LOPÉZ LOPÉZ

UNIVERSIDAD NACIONAL AGRARIA LA MOLINA
(National Agricultural University of La Molina)

Avda La Molina s/n, La Molina, Lima 12

Telephone: (1) 6147800

E-mail: rrpp@lamolina.edu.pe

Internet: www.lamolina.edu.pe

Founded 1902, fmrly Escuela Nacional de Agricultura

State control

Language of instruction: Spanish

Academic year: April to December (2 semesters)

Rector: Dr JESÚS ABEL MEJÍA MARCACUZCO

Vice-Rector for Academics: Dr JORGE ALIAGA GUTIÉRREZ

Vice-Rector for Admin.: Ing. EFRAÍN DONALD MALPARTIDA INOUYE

Dir for Postgraduate School: Dr MARIANO GONZALO ECHEVARRÍA ROJAS

Sec. Gen.: Dr ÁNGEL FAUSTO BECERRA PAJUELO

Dir-Gen. for Library Services: LIZ ARANIBAR CAMPANA

Number of teachers: 500

Number of students: 4,100

Publications: *Anales Científicos* (3 a year), *Revista Agronegocios* (2 a year, print and online, www.lamolina.edu.pe/revista-agronegocios), *Revista Ecología Aplicada* (2 a year, print and online, www.lamolina.edu.pe/ecolapl), *Revista Natura@economía* (2 a year, print and online, ojournal.lamolina.edu.pe/index.php/natura)

DEANS

Faculty of Agriculture: ANDRÉS VIRGILIO CASAS DÍAZ

Faculty of Agricultural Engineering: Dr MIGUEL ÁNGEL SÁNCHEZ DELGADO

Faculty of Animal Science: CARLOS ALFREDO GÓMEZ BRAVO

Faculty of Economics and Planning: Dr LUIS ALBERTO JIMÉNEZ DÍAZ

Faculty of Fisheries: Dr PATRICIA LILIANA GIL KODAKA

Faculty of Food Industries: Dr FANNY EMMA LUDEÑA URQUIZO

Faculty of Forestry: Ing. GILBERTO DOMÍNGUEZ TORREJÓN

Faculty of Sciences: Dr ANDRÉS VIRGILIO CASAS DÍAZ

UNIVERSIDAD NACIONAL AMAZÓNICA MADRE DE DÍOS
(Amazon National University of Madre de Dios)

Avda Jorge Chávez s/n Tambopata, Tambopata 082, Madre de Dios

Telephone: (082) 573186

E-mail: webmaster@unamad.edu.pe

Internet: www.unamad.edu.pe

Founded 2000

Private control

Language of instruction: Spanish

Academic year: March to December

Rector: Dr MILTHON HONORIO MUÑOZ BERROCAL

Vice-Rector for Academics: Dra ELA LEILA ESTRADA ORÉ

Vice-Rector for Admin.: Dr MANUEL ISRAEL HERNÁNDEZ GARCÍA

Sec. Gen.: GERMÁN CORREA NUÑEZ

DEANS

Faculty of Eco-Tourism: YOLANDE PAREDES VALVERDE

Faculty of Education: Dr JUAN HUYALLANI MOSCOSO

Faculty of Engineering: JOEL PEÑA VALDEIGLESIAS

UNIVERSIDAD NACIONAL DANIEL ALCIDES CARRIÓN
(Daniel Alcides Carrión National University)

Edif. Estatal No 3, San Juan Pampa, Cerro de Pasco, Pasco

Telephone: (63) 421365

E-mail: informatica@undac.edu.pe

Internet: www.undac.edu.pe

Founded 1965

Faculties of agricultural sciences, dentistry, economics, accountancy and administration, education sciences, communication and law, engineering, health sciences, medicine, mining

Rector: Dr RICARDO ARTURO GUARDIÁN CHÁVEZ

Vice-Rector for Academics: Dr FLAVIANO ARMANDO ZENTENO RUIZ

Vice-Rector for Research: LEONIDAS FÉLIX VILLAORDUÑA CALDAS

Sec. Gen.: Dr RAMÓN SOLÍS HOSPINAL

UNIVERSIDAD NACIONAL DE CAJAMARCA
(National University of Cajamarca)

Avda Atahualpa 1050, Cajamarca

Telephone: (76) 363263

E-mail: webmaster@unc.edu.pe

Internet: www.unc.edu.pe

Founded 1962

State control

Language of instruction: Spanish

Academic year: March to December (2 semesters)

Campuses in Bambamarca, Cajabamba, Celendin, Chiclayo, Chota Contumaza, Cutervo, Guadalupe, Huamachuco, San Marcos and Jaén

Rector: Ing. CARLOS SEGUNDO TIRADO SOTO

Vice-Rector for Academics: Dr ÓSCAR SILVA RODRÍGUEZ

Vice-Rector for Admin.: Ing. JOSÉ FRANCISCO HUAMÁN VIDAURRE

Sec. Gen.: AMANDA RODRÍGUEZ SÁNCHEZ

Librarian: JOSE LUIS VARGAS BAZAN

DEANS

Faculty of Agricultural Sciences: Dr VICTOR VÁSQUEZ ARCE

Faculty of Animal Husbandry: Dr ANGEL FRANCISCO DAVILA ROJAS

Faculty of Economics, Administration and Accountancy: Prof. EDWARD FREDY TORRES IZQUIERDO

Faculty of Education: Dr LETICIA NOEMÍ ZAVALETA GONZALES

Faculty of Engineering: Ing. JOSÉ LUIS MARCHENA ARAUJO

Faculty of Health Sciences: Dr MARÍA EUGENIA URTEAGA BECERRA

Faculty of Human Medicine: Dr SEGUNDO BUENO ORDOÑEZ

Faculty of Law and Political Science: JOSÉ LEONIDAS CASTILLO ROMÁN

Faculty of Social Sciences: Dr JOSÉ ALINDOR PÉREZ MUNDACA

Faculty of Veterinary Medicine: Dr JORGE BERNARDO GAMARRA ORTIZ

UNIVERSIDAD NACIONAL DE EDUCACIÓN 'ENRIQUE GUZMÁN Y VALLE'
(National University of Education 'Enrique Guzmán y Valle')

Avda Enrique Guzmán y Valle s/n, La Cantuta, Chosica, Lima 15

Telephone: (1) 3133700
E-mail: webmaster@une.edu.pe
Internet: www.une.edu.pe

Founded 1967
State control
Language of instruction: Spanish

Also faculty of management sciences and tourism

Pres.: Dra FREDDY ALBERTO APONTE GUERRERO
Vice-Pres. for Academic Affairs: Dra DENESY PELAGIA PALACIOS JIMÉNEZ
Vice-Pres. for Research: Dr EDWIN GUILLERMO AURIS MELGAR
Gen. Sec.: LUIS MAGNO BARRIOS TINOCO
Librarian: MARGARITA LÓPEZ M.

Library of 16,500 vols
Number of teachers: 190
Number of students: 10,000

Publication: *Cantuta*

DEANS

Faculty of Agriculture and Nutrition: Dra MARÍA HILDA SÁNCHEZ CHARCAPE
Faculty of Education: DONATILA TOBALINO LÓPEZ
Faculty of Humanities: HUMBERTO VARGAS SALGADO
Faculty of Pedagogy and Physical Culture: Dr JOSÉ FRANCISCO MORÁN DE LOS SANTOS
Faculty of Sciences: RAMÓN CAJAVILCA
Faculty of Technology: JOSÉ RAUL CORTEZ BERROCAL
Postgraduate School: Dr JORGE JHONCON KOOYIP (Dir)

UNIVERSIDAD NACIONAL DE HUANCAVÉLICA
(National University of Huancavélica)

Ciudad Universitaria Paturpampa, Huancavélica

Telephone: (67) 454014
E-mail: rectorado@unh.edu.pe
Internet: www.unh.edu.pe

Founded 1990

Rector: Dra ZEIDA PATRICIA HOCES LA ROSA
Vice-Rector for Academic Affairs: Dr AGUSTÍN PERALES ANGOMA
Vice-Rector for Admin.: ADOLFO R. CORTAVARRIA
Sec.-Gen.: Lic. VÍCTOR GUILLERMO SÁNCHEZ ARAUJO
Number of students: 4,300

DEANS

Faculty of Agricultural Sciences: Dr DAVID RUIZ VILCHEZ
Faculty of Business Administration: EDGARDO FÉLIX PALOMINO TORRES
Faculty of Civil Mining: Ing. FREDDY PAREDES RODRÍGUEZ
Faculty of Education: Dr HONORATO VILLAZANA RASUHUAMAN
Faculty of Electronic Systems: Ing. LUCIO QUIPE CARRIÓN
Faculty of Engineering: Dr NICASIO VALENCIA MAMANI
Faculty of Nursing: Dra TARCILA H. CRÚZ SANCHEZ

UNIVERSIDAD NACIONAL DE INGENIERÍA
(National University of Engineering)

Avda Túpac Amaru 210, Rimac, Lima 25

Telephone: (1) 4811070
E-mail: webmaster@uni.edu.pe
Internet: www.uni.edu.pe

Founded 1896 as Escuela Nacional de Ingenieros del Perú, present name 1955
State control
Language of instruction: Spanish
Academic year: April to December

Rector: Dr AURELIO MARCELLO PADILLA RÍOS
Primary Vice-Rector: GEOLOGO JOSÉ SIGFREDO MARTÍNEZ TALLEDO
Secondary Vice-Rector: Ing. WALTER ZALDIVAR ÁLVAREZ
Sec.-Gen.: Dr NELSON CACHO ARAUJO
Librarian: MARY APOLAYA ARNAO
Library: see under Libraries and Archives
Number of teachers: 1,000
Number of students: 12,000

Publications: *Revista Técnica 'Tecnia', Revista Artes y Ciencias 'Amaru'*

DEANS

Faculty of Architecture, Town Planning and Fine Arts: Arq. LUIS ARMANDO N. CABELLO ORTEGA
Faculty of Chemical and Textile Engineering: JULIA VICTORIA SALINAS GARCÍA
Faculty of Civil Engineering: Ing. JOSE WILFREDO GUTIÉRREZ LAZARES
Faculty of Economics and Social Sciences: Dr ULISES HUMALA TASSO
Faculty of Electrical and Electronic Engineering: Ing. LUIS FERNANDO JIMÉNEZ ORMEÑO
Faculty of Environmental Engineering: Ing. FRANCISCA BEATRIZ CASTAÑEDA SALDAÑA
Faculty of Geology, Mining and Metallurgical Engineering: Ing. EDWILDE YOPLAC CASTROMONTE
Faculty of Industrial and Systems Engineering: Ing. ERNESTO FLORES CISNEROS
Faculty of Mechanical Engineering: Dr GILBERTO BECERRA AREVALO
Faculty of Petroleum Engineering, Natural Gas and Petrochemicals: Dr GERMÁN GRAJEDA REYES
Faculty of Science: Dr WALTER FRANCISCO ESTRADA LOPEZ

UNIVERSIDAD NACIONAL DE LA AMAZONÍA PERUANA
(National University of the Peruvian Amazon)

Apdo 496, Iquitos, Loreto
Sargento Lores 385, Iquitos, Loreto

Telephone: (65) 232186
E-mail: infounap@unapiquitos.edu.pe
Internet: www.unapiquitos.edu.pe

Founded 1962
State control
Language of instruction: Spanish
Academic year: April to February (2 terms)

Rector: Dr ANTONIO PASQUEL RUIZ
Vice-Rector for Academic Affairs: Dr CARLOS HERNÁN ZUMAETA VÁSQUEZ
Vice-Rector for Admin.: Dr HEITER VALDERRAMA FREYRE
Sec. Gen.: Ing. MARÍA ISABEL MAURY LAURA
Librarian: MARGARITA FASANANDO VÁSQUEZ

Number of teachers: 400
Number of students: 3,200

Publication: *Conocimiento*

DEANS

Faculty of Agronomy Science: Dr PEDRO ANTONIO GRATELLY SILVA
Faculty of Biological Science: Dr ALVARO BENJAMÍN TRESIERRA AYALA

Faculty of Chemical Engineering: Ing. GUSTAVO ADOLFO MALCA SALAS
Faculty of Dentistry: ALEJANDRO CHÁVEZ PAREDES
Faculty of Economic Sciences and Business: Lic. ALICIA OFELIA PINEDO SANTILLÁN
Faculty of Educational Sciences and Humanities: Dr RICARDO DÍAZ RAMÍREZ
Faculty of Food Sciences: Ing. RÓGER RUIZ PAREDES
Faculty of Forestry: Ing. RODIL TELLO ESPINOZA
Faculty of Human Medicine: Dr JORGE ANTONIO REYES DÁVILA
Faculty of Husbandry: Ing. ESTHER RUIZ REÁTEGUI
Faculty of Law and Political Science: Abog. RAFAEL AUGUSTO VALDEZ MARÍN
Faculty of Nursing: Dra RUTH VÍLCHEZ RAMÍREZ
Faculty of Pharmacy and Biochemistry: LUIS ALBERTO VILCHEZ ALCALÁ
Faculty of Systems and Computer Engineering: CARLOS GARCÍA CORTEGANO

UNIVERSIDAD NACIONAL DE PIURA
(National University of Piura)

Apdo 295, Castilla, Piura
Campus Universitario, Urb. Miraflores s/n, Castilla, Piura

Telephone: (73) 285251
E-mail: webmaster@unp.edu.pe
Internet: www.unp.edu.pe

Founded 1961
State control
Language of instruction: Spanish
Academic year: March to December

Rector: Dr JOSÉ RAÚL RODRÍGUEZ LICHTENHELDT
Vice-Rector for Academics: Dr EDDY WILLIAM GIVES MUJICA
Vice-Rector for Admin.: Dr OSCAR ARMANDO VÁSQUEZ RAMOS
Sec. Gen.: Lic. ALFREDO SULLÓN LEÓN
Librarian: Dr ELAR NILTON TORRES QUIROZ

Publication: *Universalia* (2 a year)

DEANS

Faculty of Accounting and Finance: RONALD SAVITSKY MENDOZA
Faculty of Administrative Sciences: Lic. YOHANI MARIA ABAD SULLÓN
Faculty of Agronomy: JAVIER JAVIER ALVA
Faculty of Animal Husbandry: Dr VICENTE PAREDES MURO
Faculty of Architecture: Arq. MIGUEL ADRIANZÁN HUANCAS
Faculty of Civil Engineering: Ing. CARMEN CHILÓN MUÑOZ
Faculty of Economics: Dr JAIME ROMERO ZAPATA
Faculty of Fisheries Engineering: CÉSAR AUGUSTO RAMOS CHUNGA
Faculty of Human Medicine: Dr ARTURO SEMINARIO CRUZ
Faculty of Industrial Engineering: Lic. RIGO FÉLIX REQUENA FLORES
Faculty of Law and Political Sciences: Dr FLORENTINO ALBERTO CALLE ENRIQUEZ
Faculty of Mining Engineering: Dr GUILLERMO RAMIREZ GARCÍA
Faculty of Sciences: SANTOS MONTAÑO ROALCABA
Faculty of Social Sciences and Education: Dr AMANCIO MARTINEZ GOMEZ
Postgraduate School: Dr CESAR REYES PEÑA (Dir)

UNIVERSIDAD NACIONAL DE SAN AGUSTÍN DE AREQUIPA
(National University of St Augustin of Arequipa)

Calle Santa Catalina 117, Arequipa

Telephone: (54) 237808

E-mail: postulantes@unsa.edu.pe

Internet: www.unsa.edu.pe

Founded 1828

State control

Language of instruction: Spanish

Academic year: April to December

Rector: Dr VALDEMAR MEDINA HOYOS

Vice-Rector for Academics: Dr VÍCTOR HUGO LINARES HUACO

Vice-Rector for Admin.: Dra ELISA CASTAÑEDA HUAMÁN

Gen. Sec.: FRANCISCO GARCÍA CALISAYA

Library: see Libraries

Number of teachers: 1,500

Number of students: 23,000

DEANS

Faculty of Accountancy and Financial Sciences: Dr GILBERTO LEÓN HIDALGO ALADZEME

Faculty of Administration: Dr JUAN ARMIN BECERRA GUZMÁN

Faculty of Architecture and Town Planning: Arq. HUGO WELLINGTON MUELLE VALDEZ

Faculty of Biological and Agricultural Sciences: JUAN MARIO GERMÁN VILLEGAS PAREDES

Faculty of Civil Engineering: Dr JOSÉ ENRIQUE FLORES CASTRO LINARES

Faculty of Economics: Dr EDGAR JUAN BOLÍVAR DÍAZ

Faculty of Education Sciences: Dr WALTER FERNÁNDEZ GAMBARINI

Faculty of Geology and Geophysics: Dr LUIS ALBERTO ARANIBAR ROSAS

Faculty of History and Social Sciences: Dra JUANA EVA ALEJANDRINA DÍAZ GAMERO DE SALAS

Faculty of Law: Dr JORGE JUAN DE MATA GUZMÁN RODRÍGUEZ

Faculty of Medicine: Dr EDGAR RIVERA DÍAZ

Faculty of Natural and Formal Sciences: Dr EPIFANIO WILFREDO LICONA GUTIÉRREZ

Faculty of Nursing: Dra CRISTINA LINARES RASMUSSEN

Faculty of Philosophy and Humanities: Dr EDMUNDO FREDY CÁCERES CUADROS

Faculty of Process Engineering: Dr ELÍAS DAVID ESQUICHA LARICO

Faculty of Production and Services Engineering: Dr LUIS ALBERTO ALFARO CASAS

Faculty of Psychology, Industrial Relations and Communication Sciences: Dra ELIANA ELBA ARANÍBAR MELGAR

Postgraduate School: Dr JUAN LAZO ANGULO

UNIVERSIDAD NACIONAL DE SAN ANTONIO ABAD DEL CUSCO
(National University of San Antonio Abad of Cusco)

Apdo 921, Cusco

Avda de la Cultura 733, Cusco

Telephone: (84) 604100

E-mail: webmaster@unsaac.edu.pe

Internet: www.unsaac.edu.pe

Founded 1962, reorganized 1969

Rector: Dr GERMÁN ZECENARRO MADUEÑO

Vice-Rector for Academics: Dr TEÓFILO POMPEYO COSSIO CUENTAS

Vice-Rector for Research: Dra GLADYS CONCHA FLORES

Sec. Gen.: ELEAZAR CRUCINTA UGARTE

Number of teachers: 450

Number of students: 16,000

Publication: *Revista Universitaria* (1 a year)

DEANS

Faculty of Accounting and Finance: ZENON LATORRE VALDEIGLESIAS

Faculty of Agriculture and Animal Science: Ing. ROGER ALEX ROMERO DE LA CUBA

Faculty of Architecture and Fine Arts: Arq. WILBERT SANDY SALAZAR MUÑIZ

Faculty of Biological Sciences: LUCIANO JULIAN CRUZ MIRANDA

Faculty of Chemical Engineering and Metallurgy: Dr ABEL FRANKLIN CANAL CESPEDES

Faculty of Chemistry, Physics and Mathematics: VÍCTOR AYMA GIRALDO

Faculty of Civil Engineering: Dr JOSÉ FELIPE MARIN LOAYZA

Faculty of Economics: Dr CARLOS ARTURO DAVILA ROJAS

Faculty of Education: Dr AUGUSTA CARMEN SALAS DEL CASTILLO

Faculty of Electrical, Electronic, Mechanical and Mines Engineering: MIGUEL VERA MIRANDA

Faculty of Geological Engineering and Geography: Ing. FREDY VICTOR BUSTAMANTE PRADO

Faculty of Human Medicine: Dr OSTWALT ULPIO AVENDAÑO TAPIA

Faculty of Law and Political Science: Dr JORGE EFRAÍN POLO Y LA BORDA GONZÁLES

Faculty of Management and Tourism: Dr RAUL ABARCA ASTETE

Faculty of Nursing: Dr NOEMI ÁLVAREZ PAREDES

Faculty of Social Communication and Languages: Dr ANTERO VIDAL CHÁVEZ RIVERA

Faculty of Social Sciences: Dr OSCAR PAREDES PANDO

UNIVERSIDAD NACIONAL DE SAN CRISTÓBAL DE HUAMANGA
(National University of San Cristóbal of Huamanga)

Portal Independencia No 57, Ayacucho

Telephone: (66) 312230

E-mail: postmaster@unsch.edu.pe

Internet: www.unsch.edu.pe

Founded 1677, reopened 1959

State control

Language of instruction: Spanish

Academic year: March to July, August to December

Rector: Dr HUMBERTO HERNÁNDEZ ARRIBASPLATA

Vice-Rector for Academic Affairs: Dra RUTH E. ALARCÓN MUNDACA

Vice-Rector for Admin.: Dr PELAYO HILARIO VALENZUELA

Gen. Sec.: Ing. J. ALEJANDRO BERNEDO NAVARRO

Librarian: MARÍA ISABEL MATTA DURAN

Publications: *Guamangengis*, *Signos y Obras*

DEANS

Faculty of Agricultural Sciences: Dr JUAN RAMIRO PALOMINO MALPARTIDA

Faculty of Biological Sciences: Dr SEGUNDO TOMÁS CASTRO CARRANZA

Faculty of Chemical and Metallurgical Engineering: Ing. CIPRIANO MENDOZA ROJAS

Faculty of Economics, Administration and Accounting: Dr JULIO GÓMEZ MÉNDEZ

Faculty of Education: Dr RANULFO CAVERO CARRASCO

Faculty of Law and Political Sciences: Abog. OSCAR OBDULIO GALVÁN OVIEDO

Faculty of Mining, Geological and Civil Engineering: Dr JAIME ALBERTO HUAMÁN MONTES

Faculty of Nursing: Prof. CELIA BERENICE MAURTUA GALVÁN

Faculty of Obstetrics: Dra LUISA ALCARRAZ CURI

Faculty of Social Sciences: MANUEL ULDARICO MAYORGA SÁNCHEZ

UNIVERSIDAD NACIONAL 'SAN LUIS GONZAGA' DE ICA
(National University 'San Luis Gonzaga' of Ica)

Prolongación Ayabaca C-9, Urb. San José, Ica

Telephone: (56) 228406

E-mail: webmaster@unica.edu.pe

Internet: www.unica.edu.pe

Founded 1961

Rector: Dr ALEJANDRO GABRIEL ENCINAS FERNÁNDEZ

Vice-Rector for Academics: Dr GUSTAVO REYES MEJÍA

Vice-Rector for Admin.: Dr MAXIMO SEVILLANO DÍAZ

Sec. Gen.: Dr LUIS ALBERTO MASSA PALACIOS

Number of teachers: 500

Number of students: 6,300

Publications: *Educación Dental*, *Letras y Educación*

DEANS

Faculty of Accountancy: Mag. CÉSAR AURELIO MARTÍNEZ GARCÍA

Faculty of Agronomy: Dr MEDARDO ANTONIO NAVARRO EURIBE

Faculty of Architecture: Dr ROSARIO BENDEZÚ HERENCIA

Faculty of Economics: Dr MARCO ANTONIO FARFÁN GUERRA

Faculty of Education and Humanities: Dr BERNAOLA RAMOS MANUEL RENÉ

Faculty of Engineering, Environment and Health: Dr LUIS ALBERTO MASSA PALACIOS

Faculty of Chemical Engineering and Petrochemicals: Dra ROSA LUZ GALINDO PASACHE

Faculty of Civil Engineering: Ing. JOSÉ CLAUDIO GUEVARA BENDEZÚ

Faculty of Communication, Tourism and Archaeology: Mag. HERNAN MARCELO CABREJAS FARFÁN

Faculty of Dentistry: Mag. CARMEN ROSA CHANG VDA DE GARABITO

Faculty of Fisheries and Food Engineering: Ing. EDILBERTO ENRIQUE SILVA SANTISTEBAN ACEVEDO

Faculty of Human Medicine: Dr TOLMOS REGAL LUIS ANTONIO

Faculty of Law and Political Science: Mag. WENCESLAO MIGUEL QUISPE SEGOVIA

Faculty of Management: Dr ACASIETE APARCANA MANUEL ANTONIO

Faculty of Mechanical and Electrical Engineering: Dr MARTÍN RAYMUNDO ALARCÓN QUISPE

Faculty of Mining and Metallurgical Engineering: Mag. BENDEZÚ BENAVIDES ROGER NEMESIO

Faculty of Nursing: Dra ISABEL NATIVIDAD URURE VELAZCO

Faculty of Obstetrics: Dra CARMEN LAOS ANCHANTE

Faculty of Pharmacy and Biochemistry: Mag. UNFREDO PABEL APUMAYTA VEGA

Faculty of Psychology: Dra LUISA VARGAS REYES

Faculty of Science: Mag. VARGAS MAYA NÉSTOR MANUEL

Faculty of Systems Engineering: Mag. EDGAR LEONARDO PEÑA CASAS

Faculty of Veterinary Medicine: Dra MARIA EMILIA DÁVALOS ALMEYDA

Postgraduate School: C. P. C. C. WILLIAM EBERTH RÍOS ZEGARRA (Dir)

UNIVERSIDAD NACIONAL DE SAN MARTÍN
(National University of San Martín)

Jr. Maynas 177, Tarapoto, San Martín

Telephone: (42) 524253
E-mail: informes@unsm.edu.pe
Internet: www.unsm.edu.pe

Founded 1979

Rector: Dr JULIO ARMANDO RÍOS RAMÍREZ
Vice-Rector for Academics: Dra EVANGELINA AMPUERO FERNÁNDEZ
Vice-Rector for Admin.: Dra NELLY REÁTEGUI LOZANO
Librarian: JORGE YUNGBLUTH ZEGARRA

DEANS

Faculty of Agricultural Sciences: CESAR ENRIQUE CHAPPA SANTA MARIA
Faculty of Agroindustrial Engineering: Ing. WILSON ERNESTO SANTANDER RUIZ
Faculty of Civil Engineering and Architecture: Dr SERVANDO SOPLOPUCO QUIROGA
Faculty of Ecology: ASTRIHT RUIZ RÍOS
Faculty of Economics: RÉNIGER SOUSA FERNÁNDEZ
Faculty of Education and Humanities: ALCIVIADES VIVAS CAMPUSANO
Faculty of Law and Political Science: VICTOR ANDRES PRETTEL PAREDES
Faculty of Health Sciences: Dra MARINA HUAMANTUMBA PALOMINO
Faculty of Human Medicine: Dr ALICIA BARTRA REATEGUI
Faculty of Systems Engineering: CARLOS RODRÍGUEZ GRÁNDEZ

UNIVERSIDAD NACIONAL DE TRUJILLO
(National University of Trujillo)

Diego de Almagro No 344, Trujillo, La Libertad

Telephone: (44) 205513
E-mail: rectorado@unitru.edu.pe
Internet: www.unitru.edu.pe

Founded 1824
State control
Language of instruction: Spanish
Academic year: April to December

Rector: Dr ORLANDO VELÁSQUEZ BENITES
Vice-Rector for Academics: Dra VILMA JULIA MÉNDEZ GIL
Vice-Rector for Admin.: Dra FLOR MARLENE LUNA VICTORIA MORI
Sec. Gen.: Dr PEDRO LUIS LAVALLE DIOS
Librarian: Dr CÉSAR GAMARRA SÁNCHEZ

Library of 28,000 vols
Number of teachers: 980
Number of students: 15,000

Publications: Amauta—Archivos de Oftalmología del Norte del Perú, Lenguaje y Ciencia, Memoria Rectoral, Revista de Derecho, Revista del Museo de Arqueología y Antropología

DEANS

Faculty of Agricultural Sciences: Dr VÍCTOR JAVIER VÁSQUEZ VILLALOBOS
Faculty of Biological Sciences: Dr HERMES MARIO ESCALANTE AÑORGA
Faculty of Chemical Engineering: Dr MANUEL ISAÍAS VERA HERRERA
Faculty of Economic Sciences: Dr EBERTH VALVERDE VALVERDE
Faculty of Education and Communication Sciences: Dr ALBERTO SANTIAGO MOYA OBESO
Faculty of Engineering: Ing. RANULFO DONATO CÁRDENAS ALAYO
Faculty of Law and Political Sciences: Dr CARLOS ALBERTO VÁSQUEZ BOYER
Faculty of Medical Sciences: Dr EDUARDO ROJAS HIDALGO

Faculty of Nursing: Dra SOLEDAD MARLENE PESANTES SHIMAJUKO
Faculty of Pharmacy and Biochemistry: Dr RAMÓN PIMINCHUMO CARRANZA
Faculty of Physical and Mathematical Sciences: Dr HUMBERTO ANÍBAL VERDE OLIVARES
Faculty of Social Sciences: Dr JOSÉ FERNANDO ELÍAS MINAYA

UNIVERSIDAD NACIONAL DE TUMBES
(National University of Tumbes)

Avda Universitaria s/n, C U, Pampa Grande, Tumbes

Telephone: (72) 522810
E-mail: oginf@untumbes.edu.pe
Internet: www.untumbes.edu.pe

Founded 1984

Rector: Dr JOSÉ DE LA ROSA CRUZ MARTÍNEZ
Vice-Rector for Academics: Dra MIRIAM NOEMÍ OTINIANO HURTADO
Vice-Rector for Admin.: Dr DANTE ENRÍQUEZ RODRÍGUEZ RUIZ

DEANS

Faculty of Agricultural Sciences: CARLOS DEZA NAVARRETE
Faculty of Economics: GILMER RUBEN MURGA FERNÁNDEZ
Faculty of Fisheries Engineering: Dr AUBERTO HIDALGO MOGOLLON
Faculty of Health Sciences: JOSÉ LUIS SALY ROSAS SOLANO
Faculty of Social Sciences: ELBER LINO MORAN CORONADO

UNIVERSIDAD NACIONAL DE UCAYALI
(National University of Ucayali)

Carretera Federico Basadre s/n km 6, Pucallpa

Telephone: (61) 579962
E-mail: rector_unu@unu.edu.pe
Internet: www.unu.edu.pe

Founded 1979
State control
Language of instruction: Spanish

Rector: Dr ROLY BALDOCEDA ASTETE
Vice-Rector for Academics: Dra OTILIA HERNÁNDEZ PANDURO
Vice-Rector for Admin.: Dr JAIME ALBERTO PASTOR SEGURA
Sec. Gen.: Dr JAIME ALBERTO PASTOR SEGURA
Librarian: RAUL JAVIER GUTIÉRREZ PINEDA

DEANS

Faculty of Administration, Economics and Accountancy: Lic. Admin. MIGUEL ÓSCAR LÓPEZ Y OJEDA
Faculty of Agricultural Sciences: GUSTAVO HORACIO CELI ARÉVALO
Faculty of Civil and Systems Engineering: ROMEL PINEDO RÍOS
Faculty of Education and Health Sciences: HÉCTOR QUISPE CERNA
Faculty of Forest and Environment Sciences: Dr ÓSCAR ANTONIO BARRETO VÁSQUEZ
Faculty of Health Sciences: JAIME ALBERTO PASTOR SEGURA
Faculty of Human Medicine: ANTONIO ALBERTO PEÑA TORRES
Faculty of Law and Political Sciences: Abog. JORGE ANIANO RUIZ ROJAS

UNIVERSIDAD NACIONAL DEL ALTIPLANO
(National University of the Altiplano)

Avda Sesquicentenario No 1150, Puno, Puno

Telephone: (51) 599430
E-mail: webmaster@unap.edu.pe

Internet: www.unap.edu.pe

Founded 1856
Academic year: March to December

Rector: Dr LUCIO ÁVILA ROJAS
Admin. Vice-Rector for Academics: Dr GERMÁN YÁBAR PILCO
Vice-Rector for Admin.: Dr EDGARDO PINEDA QUISPE
Librarian: Prof. SERAFÍN CALSIN MAMANI

Publications: Revistas Problemáticas, Revista Universitaria, Revista Visión Agraria

DEANS

Faculty of Accounting and Administration: ANTONIO ESPILLICO CHIQUE
Faculty of Agricultural Engineering: LORENZO GABRIEL CIEZA CORONEL
Faculty of Agricultural Sciences: JULIO MAYTA QUISPE
Faculty of Biological Sciences: Dra MARIA TRINIDAD ROMERO TORRES
Faculty of Chemical Engineering: WALTHER B. APARICIO ARAGÓN
Faculty of Civil Engineering and Architecture: ELISEO ZAPANA QUISPE
Faculty of Economic Engineering: CRISTOBAL YAPUCHURA SAICO
Faculty of Educational Sciences: SAMUEL MONRROY GALLEGOS
Faculty of Health Sciences: JOSÉ OSCAR ALBERTO BEGAZO MIRANDA
Faculty of Human Medicine: JULIAN A. SALAS PORTOCARRERO
Faculty of Law and Political Science: JOVIN HIPÓLITO VALDEZ PEÑARANDA
Faculty of Mechanical, Electrical, Electronics and Systems Engineering: GREGORIO MEZA MAROCHO
Faculty of Metallurgy and Geological Engineering: ÁLVARO E. GALLEGOS PASCO PEDRO
Faculty of Mining Engineering: MARIO SERAFÍN CUENTAS ALVARADO
Faculty of Nursing: CHRISTIAN WILLIAM JARA ZEVALLOS
Faculty of Social Sciences: PORFIRIO ENRIQUEZ SALAS
Faculty of Social Work: MARI YOLANDA AVILA CAZORLA
Faculty of Statistics and Information: VLADIMIRO IBAÑEZ QUISPE
Faculty of Veterinary Medicine: Prof. MARTÍN URVIOLA SÁNCHEZ
Postgraduate School: Dr EDMUNDO MORENO TERRAZAS (Dir)

UNIVERSIDAD NACIONAL DEL CALLAO
(National University of Callao)

Avda Juan Pablo II 306, Bellavista, Callao

Telephone: (51) 4299740
E-mail: rector@unac.edu.pe
Internet: www.unac.edu.pe

Founded 1966
State control
Language of instruction: Spanish
Academic year: April to December (2 terms)

Rector: Dr MANUEL ALBERTO MORI PAREDES
Vice-Rector for Research: Dr JOSÉ RAMÓN CÁCERES PAREDES
Vice-Rector for Admin.: Dr CÉSAR AUGUSTO RODRÍGUEZ ABURTO
Sec. Gen.: Ing. CHRISTIAN JESÚS SUÁREZ RODRÍGUEZ
Librarian: LUIS CARRASCO VEREGAS

Publications: Catálogo de Informes de Investigación (1 a year), Ciencia y Tecnología (1 a year)

DEANS

Faculty of Accountancy: Dr VÍCTOR MEREA LLANOS

Faculty of Administration: JUAN MORENO SAN MARTÍN

Faculty of Chemical Engineering: PABLO BELIZARIO DÍAZ BRAVO

Faculty of Economic Sciences: Dr JUAN NUNURA CHULLY

Faculty of Electrical and Electronic Engineering: Dr JUAN GRADOS GAMARRA

Faculty of Environmental and Natural Resources Engineering: EDUARDO TRUJILLO FLORES

Faculty of Fisheries and Food Engineering: Dr DAVID VIVANCO PEZANTES

Faculty of Health Sciences: Dra ANGÉLICA DÍAZ TINOCO

Faculty of Industrial and Systems Engineering: Dr CÉSAR LORENZO TORRE SIME

Faculty of Mathematics and Natural Sciences: VENANCIO GÓMEZ JIMÉNEZ

Faculty of Mechanical and Energy Engineering: FELIX GUERRERO ROLDÁN

Postgraduate School: LIDA SANÉZ FALCÓN

UNIVERSIDAD NACIONAL DEL CENTRO DEL PERÚ
(National University of Central Peru)

Ciudad Universitaria, Avda Mariscal Castilla No 3909, El Tambo, Huáncayo

Telephone: (64) 481062
E-mail: rrpp@uncp.edu.pe
Internet: www.uncp.edu.pe

Founded 1959
State control
Language of instruction: Spanish
Academic year: April to December (2 terms)

Rector: Dr JESÚS EDUARDO POMACHAGUA PAÚCAR

Vice-Rector for Academic Affairs: Dr JORGE CASTRO BEDRIÑANA

Vice-Rector for Admin.: Dr CARLOS PRIETO CAMPOS

Sec. Gen.: MAURO RODRÍGUEZ CERRÓN

Librarian: Dr OCTAVIO CARHUAMACA RODRÍGUEZ

Publications: *Ciencias Agrarias*, *Proceso* (irregular)

DEANS

Faculty of Accountancy: Dr CISINIO PARIONA CONTRERAS

Faculty of Agricultural Sciences: Mgr DAVID ALFONSO AMAYA CUBAS (Satipo)

Faculty of Agronomy: Mgr EFRAÍN BERNABÉ LINDO GUTARRA

Faculty of Anthropology: Lic. VÍCTOR MARÍN PRIETO GUZMÁN

Faculty of Applied Sciences: LUIS ANTONIO PACHECO ACERO (Tarma)

Faculty of Architecture: Dr LUIS ARMANDO CHÁVEZ BELLIDO

Faculty of Business Administration: Lic. AMÉLIDA FLORES GAMBOA

Faculty of Chemical Engineering: Ing. ROMÁN CALDERÓN CÁRDENAS

Faculty of Civil Engineering: RUBÉN CORTÉZ GALINDO

Faculty of Communication Sciences: Dr JOSÉ VILCAPOMA CHAMBERGO

Faculty of Economics: JUAN TARSICIO LINO QUISPE

Faculty of Education: Lic. LUIS HUAYTALLA TORRES

Faculty of Electrical Engineering and Electronics: BARTOLOMÉ SAENZ LOAYZA

Faculty of Engineering and Humanities: Dr FELIZA CHIPANA BELTRAN (Junin)

Faculty of Food Engineering: Ing. EMILIO FREDY YABAR VILLANUEVA

Faculty of Forest Sciences and Environment: Dra ROSA HAYDEE ZÁRATE QNIÑONES

Faculty of Human Medicine: Dr JULIO ENRIQUE HUAMAN BERRÍOS

Faculty of Husbandry: EVELIO SAAVEDRA PEÑA

Faculty of Mechanical Engineering: Ing. VALERIANO MÁXIMO HUAMÁN ADRIANO

Faculty of Metallurgical and Materials Engineering: Ing. TORIBIO VARGAS AGUIRRE

Faculty of Mining Engineering: Ing. ELI TEOBALDO CARO MEZA

Faculty of Nursing: Dra ANA LUCILA GIRÓN VARGAS

Faculty of Social Work: Dra LAYLI MARAVÍ BALDEÓN

Faculty of Sociology: LUIS VICENTE MANRIQUE ALVAREZ

Faculty of Stockbreeding: Ing. HUMBERTO RODRÍGUEZ LANDEO

Faculty of Systems Engineering: Dr HÉCTOR HUAMÁN SAMANIEGO

Postgraduate School: Dr PABLO MOSOMBITE PINEDO

UNIVERSIDAD NACIONAL DEL SANTA
(National University of Santa)

Avda Pacífico 508, Urb. Buenos Aires Apdo 10, Nuevo, Chimbote, Ancash

Telephone: (43) 310445
E-mail: rectorado@uns.edu.pe
Internet: www.uns.edu.pe

Founded 1984, present status 1998

Rector: Dra AMÉRICA ODAR ROSARIO

Vice-Rector for Academic Affairs: Dra SUSANA GUTIÉRREZ SALDAÑA

Vice-Rector for Admin.: Dra ELSA AGUIRRE VARGAS

Sec. Gen.: Dr HERMES ARNALDO LOZANO LUJÁN

DEANS

Faculty of Education and Humanities: Licda ROSENDO DANIEL RAMOS

Faculty of Engineering: Dr SIXTO DÍAZ TELLO

Faculty of Science: Licda LUZ FALLA JUÁREZ

UNIVERSIDAD NACIONAL FEDERICO VILLARREAL
(National University of Federico Villarreal)

Jr. Carlos Gonzáles 285, Maranga, San Miguel, Lima

Telephone: (1) 7480888
E-mail: ceuci@unfv.edu.pe
Internet: www.unfv.edu.pe

Founded 1963
State control
Language of instruction: Spanish
Academic year: April to December

Rector: Dr JOSÉ MARÍA VIAÑA PÉREZ

Vice-Rector for Academic Affairs: Dr NANCY OLIVERO PACHECO

Vice-Rector for Research: Dr FELICIANO TIMOTEO ONCEVAY ESPINOZA

Gen. Sec.: Dr ECKERMAN PANDURO ANGULO

Number of teachers: 2,354
Number of students: 22,449

Publications: *Gaceta el Villarrealino, Hipótesis, Villarreal al Futuro, Villarreal en el Tercer Milenio, Síntesis Académica, Wiñay Yachay, Yachaywasi*

DEANS

Faculty of Administration: Dr GUDELIA DOMITILA VIGO SÁNCHEZ

Faculty of Architecture and Urbanism: Dr LUIS ALBERTO LEÓN ESPINOZA

Faculty of Civil Engineering: Dr ROQUE ALBERTO SÁNCHEZ CRISTOBÁL

Faculty of Economic Sciences: Dr ÓSCAR PONGO ÁGUILA

Faculty of Education: Dr MANUEL JESÚS ASMAT ASMAD

Faculty of Electronic Engineering and Computing: Dr JUSTO PASTOR SOLÍS FONSECA

Faculty of Financial and Accounting Sciences: Dra PEDRO JUAN ANTON DE LOS SANTOS

Faculty of Geographical Engineering, Environment and Ecotourism: Dr ELÍAS ALFONSO VALVERDE TORRES

Faculty of Humanities: LORGIO ADALBERTO GUIBOVICH DEL CARPIO

Faculty of Industrial and Systems Engineering: Dr CRISTINA ASUNCIÓN ALZAMORA RIVERO

Faculty of Law and Political Science: Dr VÍCTOR TAQUÍA VILA

Faculty of Medical Technology: Dr REGINA MEDINA ESPINOZA

Faculty of Medicine: Dr LUIS ALBERTO HUARACHI QUINTANILLA

Faculty of Natural Sciences and Mathematics: Mag. CARLOS MARCO SANTA CRUZ CARPIO

Faculty of Oceanography, Fisheries and Food Sciences: Dr LUIS ALBERTO DÁVILA SOLAR

Faculty of Odontology: Mag. ALEJANDRO SALAZAR FUERTES

Faculty of Psychology: Lic. FLORITA PINTO HERRERA

Faculty of Social Sciences: Dr ISAAC ROBERTO ÁNGELES LAZO

UNIVERSIDAD NACIONAL HERMILIO VALDIZÁN
(National University Hermilio Valdizán)

Avda Universitaria 601–607, Cayhuayna, Huánuco

Telephone: (62) 591060
E-mail: webmaster@unheval.edu.pe
Internet: www.unheval.edu.pe

Founded 1964
State control
Language of instruction: Spanish
Academic year: April to July;August to December (2 semesters)

Rector: Dr GUILLERMO AUGUSTO BOCANGEL WEYDERT

Vice-Rector for Academics: Dr LORENZO PASQUEL LOARTE

Vice-Rector for Admin.: Dr HERNÁN LÓPEZ ROJAS

Sec. Gen.: JANETH L. TELLO CORNEJO

Librarian: Lic. AURORA AMPUDIA DÁVILA

Library of 26,000 vols
Number of teachers: 600
Number of students: 9,600

DEANS

Faculty of Accountancy and Financial Sciences: Dr EDWIN T. ORTEGA GALARZA

Faculty of Administrative Sciences and Tourism: Dr ROGER WILFREDO CÉSPEDES REVELO

Faculty of Agricultural Sciences: Dr RUBÉN LIMAYLLA JURADO

Faculty of Business Management: ARTURO RIVERA Y CALDAS

Faculty of Civil Engineering and Architecture: RICARDO SÁNCHEZ MURRUGARRA

Faculty of Economic Sciences: TEODOLFO ENCIZO GUTIÉRREZ

Faculty of Educational Sciences: Dr ARTURO LUCAS CABELLO

Faculty of Health Sciences: EDILBERTO ENRIQUE SUERO ROJAS

Faculty of Industrial and Systems Engineering: Ing. GUADALUPE RAMÍREZ REYES

Faculty of Law and Political Science: Dr CIRO TORRES SALCEDO

Faculty of Medical Sciences: Dr LILIA CAMPOS

Faculty of Nursing: Dra NANCY GUILLERMINA VERAMENDI VILLAVICENCIO

Faculty of Obstetrics: DIGNA AMALIA MANRIQUE DE LARA SUÁREZ

Faculty of Social Sciences: ENMA REEVES HUAPAYA

Faculty of Veterinary Medicine and Zootechnics: RICHARD TASAYCO ALCÁNTARA

Postgraduate School: Dr LORENZO PASQUEL LOARTE (Dir)

UNIVERSIDAD NACIONAL JORGE BASADRE GROHMANN
(National University Jorge Basadre Grohmann)

Calle Alto Lima 1594, Tacna

Telephone: (52) 583000

E-mail: sredo@unjbg.edu.pe

Internet: www.unjbg.edu.pe

Founded 1971 as Universidad Nacional de Tacna

State control

Language of instruction: Spanish

Academic year: April to December

Chancellor: Dr CARLOS VALENTE ROSSI

Rector: Dr MIGUEL ÁNGEL LARREA CÉSPEDES

Vice-Rector for Academics: Dr LORENZO WALTER IBARCENA FERNÁNDEZ

Vice-Rector for Admin.: RAMÓN VERA ROALCABA

Sec. Gen.: Mgr RAUL PAREDES MEDINA

Librarian: Ing. ALBERTO PACHECO PACHECO

Library of 29,000 vols

Publications: *Ciencia y Tecnología* (1 a year), *Memoria de Gestión* (1 a year), *Revista Materno Infantil* (1 a year)

DEANS

Faculty of Agricultural Sciences: Dr QUITERIO VALENCIA MECOLA

Faculty of Civil Engineering, Architecture and Geotechnics: Ing. LUIS ALBERTO ALFARO RAVELLO

Faculty of Education, Communication and Humanities: GREGORIO PEDRO TEJADA MONROY

Faculty of Engineering: Dr DANTE ULISES MORALES CABRERA

Faculty of Health Sciences: Dra VICTORIA NORA VELA DE CÓRDOVA

Faculty of Legal and Business Studies: Mgr BETTY ESTHER COHAILA CALDERÓN

Faculty of Science: Lic. CÉSAR EFRAÍN RIVASPLATA CABANILLAS

UNIVERSIDAD NACIONAL JOSÉ FAUSTINO SÁNCHEZ CARRIÓN
(National University José Faustino Sánchez Carrión)

Ciudad Universitaria, Avda Mercedes Indacochea s/n, Huacho, Lima

Telephone: (1) 2322918

E-mail: rectorado@unjfsc.edu.pe

Internet: www.unjfsc.edu.pe

Founded 1968

Rector: Dr LUIS ALBERTO BALDEOS ARDÍAN

Vice-Rector for Academics: Dr MANUEL ANTONIO LEÓN JULCA

Vice-Rector for Research: Dr JULIO MACEDO FIGUEROA

Sec. Gen.: Abog. JAIME ANDRÉS RODRÍGUEZ CARRANZA

Librarian: LINO ROLANDO RODRÍGUEZ ALEGRE

Library of 5,000 vols

DEANS

Faculty of Agricultural Engineering, Food and Environment: JESÚS EGO AMARO PALOMINO

Faculty of Business: Dr FELIPE CALDAS BERMÚDEZ

Faculty of Chemical Engineering and Metallurgy: Dr JOSÉ ANTONIO LEGUA CARDENAS

Faculty of Economic Science, Accountancy and Finance: Dr JORGE HORACIO ROMERO HERBOZO

Faculty of Education: CLIMACO MARCELINO VERGARA GUADALUPE

Faculty of Fisheries Engineering: FIDEL ALBERTO REYES ULFE

Faculty of Human Medicine: Dr ELSA CARMEN OSCUVILCA TAPIA

Faculty of Industrial Engineering and Information Systems: ALEJANDRO HIJAR TENA

Faculty of Law and Political Science: Dr SILVIO MIGUEL RIRVERA JIMÉNEZ

Faculty of Science: Dr WILLIAM ANDRÉS GUZMÁN SÁNCHEZ

Faculty of Social Sciences: JUAN MARIO SARMIENTO RAMOS

UNIVERSIDAD NACIONAL MAYOR DE SAN MARCOS
(National University of San Marcos)

Edif. Jorge Basadre, Ciudad Universitaria, Lima 1

Telephone: (1) 6197000

E-mail: cooperacion.unmsm@gmail.com

Internet: www.unmsm.edu.pe

Founded 1551

State control

Language of instruction: Spanish

Academic year: March to December

Rector: Dr PEDRO ATILIO COTILLO ZEGARRA

Vice-Rector for Academics: Dra ANTONIA CASTRO RODRÍGUEZ

Vice-Rector for Research: Dr BERNARDINO RAMÍREZ BAUTISTA

Sec. Gen.: Dr JOSÉ NIÑO MONTERO

Library of 470,448 vols

Publications: *Compendios*, *Revista de San Marcos*

DEANS

Faculty of Administrative Sciences: Dra ELIZABETH CANALES AYBAR

Faculty of Biological Sciences: OLGA BRACAMONTE GUEVARA

Faculty of Chemistry and Chemical Engineering: Dr CESARIO CONDORHUAMÁN CCORIMANYA

Faculty of Dentistry: Dr MARGOT GUTIÉRREZ ILAVE

Faculty of Economics: Dr JORGE OSORIO VACCARO

Faculty of Education: Dra ELSA BARRIENTOS JIMÉNEZ

Faculty of Electronic and Electrical Engineering: Dra TERESA NÚÑEZ ZÚÑIGA

Faculty of Engineering and Information Systems: PERCY EDWIN DE LA CRUZ VÉLEZ DE VILLA

Faculty of Geology, Mining, Metallurgy and Geographical Engineering: Dr CARLOS CABRERA CARRANZA

Faculty of Human Medicine: Dr HERMAN VILDÓZOLA GONZALES

Faculty of Industrial Engineering: Dr ORESTES CACHAY BOZA

Faculty of Law and Political Science: Dr JOSÉ HORNA TORRES

Faculty of Letters and Human Sciences: Dr RAIMUNDO PRADO REDONDEZ

Faculty of Mathematical Sciences: Dra DORIS GÓMEZ TICERÁN

Faculty of Pharmacy and Biochemistry: Dr JULIO LÓPEZ CASTILLO

Faculty of Physical Sciences: Dr ÁNGEL BUSTAMANTE DOMÍNGUEZ

Faculty of Psychology: Dr CARLOS ALBERTO ARENAS IPARRAGUIRRE

Faculty of Social Sciences: Dr JORGE AQUILES RUEDA HUERTA

Faculty of Veterinary Medicine: Dr FELIPE SAN MARTÍN HOWARD

UNIVERSIDAD NACIONAL MICAELA BASTIDAS DE APURIMAC
(National University Micaela Bastidas of Apurimac)

Avda Arenas 121, Abancay, Apurímac

Telephone: (83) 322577

E-mail: unambapurimac@yahoo.es

Internet: www.unamba.edu.pe

Founded 2000

State control

Language of instruction: Spanish

Academic year: April to December

Rector: Dr ALEJANDRO NARVÁEZ LICERAS

Vice-Rector for Academics: Dr LUCY MARISOL GUANUCHI ORELLANA

Vice-Rector for Admin.: Dr FREDDY VEGA LOAYZA

Sec. Gen.: Abog. ADALBERTO CRUZ GARCÍA

Number of teachers: 134

Number of students: 3,200

DEANS

Faculty of Business Administration: Lic. PERCY FRITZ PUGA PEÑA

Faculty of Education: Dr WILBER JIMÉNEZ MENDOZA

Faculty of Engineering: Dr LEONCIO TEIÓFILO CARNERO CARNERO

Faculty of Veterinary Medicine and Animal Science: LILIAN ROCÍO BÁRCENAS RODRÍGUEZ

UNIVERSIDAD NACIONAL PEDRO RUIZ GALLO
(National University Pedro Ruiz Gallo)

Avda Juan XXIII 339, Lambayeque

Telephone: (74) 283146

E-mail: webmaster@unprg.edu.pe

Internet: www.unprg.edu.pe

Founded 1970

State control

Language of instruction: Spanish

Rector: Dr MARIANO AGUSTÍN RAMOS GARCÍA

Vice-Rector for Academics: Dr LUIS JAIME COLLANTES SANTISTEBAN

Vice-Rector for Admin.: Dr LEOPOLDO POMPEYO VÁSQUEZ NÚÑEZ

Sec. Gen.: Ing. MIGUEL ÁNGEL JIMÉNEZ GAMARRA

Librarian: Dr GUILLERMO BACA AGUINAGA

Publication: *Universidad* (1 a year)

DEANS

Faculty of Agricultural Engineering: Dr JULIO OSWALDO VIVAR PÁRRAGA

Faculty of Agronomy: RICARDO CHAVARRY FLORES

Faculty of Animal Husbandry Engineering: FRANCIS VILLENA RODRÍGUEZ

Faculty of Biological Sciences: MARTHA ARMINDA VERGARA ESPINOZA

Faculty of Chemical Engineering and Food Industries: Dr ADOLFO DIAZ EYZAGUIRRE

Faculty of Civil Engineering, Systems and Architecture: Dr CARLOS ADOLFO LOAYZA RIVAS

Faculty of Economic Sciences, Administration and Accountancy: Dr MARIANO LARREA CHUCAS

Faculty of History, Social Sciences and Education: Dr JOSE WILSON GOMEZ CUMPA

Faculty of Human Medicine: Dra BLANCA SANTOS FALLA ALDANA

Faculty of Law and Political Sciences: Dr MIGUEL ARCANGEL ARANA CORTEZ

Faculty of Mechanical and Electrical Engineering: Dr ANIBAL SALAZAR MENDOZA

Faculty of Nursing: Dra TANIA ROBERTA MURO CARRASCO

Faculty of Physical Sciences and Mathematics: LEANDRO AGAPITO AZNARÁN CASTILLO

Faculty of Veterinary Medicine: VICTOR RAVILLET SUAREZ

UNIVERSIDAD NACIONAL SANTIAGO ANTÚNEZ DE MAYOLO
(National University of Santiago Antunez de Mayolo)

Avda Centenario No 200, Independencia, Huaraz, Ancash

Telephone: (43) 421452
E-mail: webmaster@unasam.edu.pe
Internet: www.unasam.edu.pe

Founded 1977
Private control
Language of instruction: Spanish
Academic year: March to December

Faculties of agricultural sciences, civil engineering, economics and accounting, education and communication, environmental sciences, food industries engineering, law and political science, management and tourism, medical sciences, mining engineering, geology and metallurgy, science and social sciences

Rector: Dr DANTE ÉLMER SÁNCHEZ RODRÍGUEZ
Sec. Gen.: Abog. ANTONIO GARCÍA HUESA

UNIVERSIDAD NACIONAL TORIBIO RODRÍGUEZ DE MENDOZA DE AMAZONAS
(National University Toribio Rodriguez de Mendoza of Amazon)

El Franco-Barrio de Higos Urco, Chachapoyas

Telephone: (041)-477955
E-mail: informes@untrm.edu.pe
Internet: www.untrm.edu.pe

Founded 2000
Private control
Language of instruction: Spanish
Academic year: March to December

Language centre

Rector: Dr VICENTE MARINO CASTAÑEDA CHÁVEZ
Vice-Rector for Academics: Dr ROBERTO JOSÉ NERVI CHACÓN
Vice-Rector for Admin.: Dr EVER SALOMÉ LÁZARO BAZÁN
Sec. Gen.: POLICARPIO CHAUCA VALQUI

DEANS

Faculty of Engineering and Agricultural Sciences: Dr MIGUEL ANGEL BARRENA GURBILLÓN
Faculty of Nursing: Dr BERNADETTE GLADYS LEÓN MONTOYA
Faculty of Social Sciences and Humanities: JOSÉ LEONCIO BARBARÁN MOZO
Faculty of Tourism and Economic Sciences, Management and Accounting: Dra MARITHZA REVILLA BUELOT

UNIVERSIDAD PERUANA CAYETANO HEREDIA
(Peruvian University Cayetano Heredia)

Avda Honorio Delgado 430, Urb. Ingeniería, Lima

Telephone: (1) 3190000
E-mail: web@oficinas-upch.pe
Internet: www.upch.edu.pe

Founded 1961
Private control
Language of instruction: Spanish
Academic year: April to March

Institutes of tropical medicine, gerontology

Rector: Dra FABIOLA LEÓN-VELARDE SERVETTO
Vice-Rector for Academic Affairs: Dr ALEJANDRO BUSALLEU RIVERA
Vice-Rector for Research: Dr CIRO MAGUIÑA VARGAS
Sec. Gen.: JUAN JIMÉNEZ BENDEZU

Library of 25,000 vols, 9,000 thesis
Number of teachers: 500

Number of students: 4,300
Publications: Acta Herediana, HONTANAR, Revista Acta Andina, Revista de Enfermería Herediana, Revista de Neuro-Psiquiatría, Revista Estomatológica Herediana, Revista Médica Herediana, Revista Psicológica Herediana

DEANS

Faculty of Education: Dr MAÑUEL BELLO DOMINGUEZ
Faculty of Medicine: Dra MARÍA PAOLA LUCÍA LLOSA ISENRICH
Faculty of Nursing: Dra YESENIA MUSAYÓN OBLITAS
Faculty of Psychology: Dr HUGO SALAZAR JÁUREGUI
Faculty of Public Health and Administration: Dra PATRICIA J. GARCÍA
Faculty of Sciences and Philosophy: Dr PATRICIA HERRERA VELIT
Faculty of Stomatology: Dr FERNANDO SALAZAR SILVA
Faculty of Veterinary and Husbandry Sciences: Dr ARMANDO HUNG
School of Postgraduate Studies: Dr JOSÉ R ESPINOZA BABILÓN (Dir)

UNIVERSIDAD PERUANA DE CIENCIAS APLICADAS
(Peruvian University of Applied Sciences)

Prolongación Primavera 2390, Monterrico, Lima

Telephone: (1) 3133333
E-mail: webmaster@upc.edu.pe
Internet: www.upc.edu.pe

Founded 1994
Private control
Language of instruction: Spanish
Academic year: March to December

Campuses in Monterrico, Segura, San Isidro and Villa

Rector: Dr GONZALO GALDOS JIMÉNEZ
Vice-Rector for Academics: Dr JOSÉ PEREYRA LÓPEZ
Vice-Rector for Planning and Devt: Dr GUSTAVO GUERRERO VÁSQUEZ
Vice-Rector for Univ. Services: MILAGROS MORGAN ROZAS
Sec. Gen.: ANA CECILIA MAC LEAN MARTINS
Dir for Library: JORGE BOSSIO MONTES DE OCA

DEANS

Faculty of Architecture: Arq. MIGUEL CRUCHAGA BELAUNDE
Faculty of Business: JACK ZILBERMAN FLEISCHMAN
Faculty of Communications: ÚRSULA FREUNDT-THURNE FREUNDT
Faculty of Economics: CARLOS ADRIANZEN CABRERA
Faculty of Engineering: JORGE CABRERA BERRÍOS
Faculty of Health Sciences: Dra GRACIELA RISCO DE DOMÍNGUEZ
Faculty of Hotel Management and Tourism: URS SCHAERER
Faculty of Human Sciences: LILIANA GALVÁN ORÉ
Faculty of Law: Dr JOSÉ LUIS SARDÓN

UNIVERSIDAD PERUANA DE CIENCIAS E INFORMÁTICA
(Peruvian University of Science and Informatics)

Jesús María Campus: Jr. Talara No 752-Jesús María, Lima
Telephone: (1) 3307087

Miraflores Campus: Calle María Parado de Bellido 129, Miraflores, Lima
Telephone: (1) 4456292

E-mail: contactenos@upci.edu.pe
Internet: www.upci.edu.pe

Founded 2002
Private control
Language of instruction: Spanish
Academic year: March to December

Also faculty of law and political sciences

Rector: Dr HÉCTOR PRISCILIANO VILCA PALACIOS
Vice-Rector for Academics: Dr FÉLIX H. VALVERDE ORCHÉS
Sec. Gen.: Dr MARIO PELÁEZ PÉREZ

Library of 4,000 vols, 1,200 serial titles and 300 electronic journals

DEANS

Faculty of Management Sciences and Accountancy: Dr FELIX H. VALVERDE ORCHÉS
Faculty of Science and Engineering: AIDA ALICIA CÓRDOVA QUINTEROS

UNIVERSIDAD PERUANA LOS ANDES
(Los Andes Peruvian University)

Avda Giraldes No 230, Huancayo, Junín

Telephone: (064) 224479
E-mail: rectoradoupla@yahoo.es
Internet: www.upla.edu.pe

Founded 1983
Private control
Language of instruction: Spanish
Academic year: March to December

Faculties of engineering, health sciences, human sciences, law and political sciences, management sciences and accountancy, medicine; graduate school

Rector: Dr JOSÉ MANUEL CASTILLO CUSTODIO
Vice-Rector for Academics: Dr JESÚS ARMANDO CAVERO CARRASCO
Vice-Rector for Admin.: Dr CASIO AURELIO TORRES LÓPEZ
Sec. Gen.: JULIO VILLARREAL SIFUENTES

Publications: Revista Científicas de la Facultad de Medicina Humana (2 a year), Revista Científicas Los Andes, Revista Innovación 2013, Quod Dictum Est-Revista de Derecho

UNIVERSIDAD PERUANA UNIÓN
(Peruvian Union University)

Altura km 19.5 Carretera Central, Ñaña, Lima

Telephone: (1) 6186300
E-mail: webmaster@upeu.edu.pe
Internet: www.upeu.edu.pe

Founded 1983
Private control
Language of instruction: Spanish
Academic year: March to December

Campuses in Juliaca and Tarapoto

Rector: Dra MAXIMINA CONTRERAS CASTRO
Vice-Rector: VICTOR CHOROCO CARDENAS
Sec. Gen.: Dr SALOMÓN VÁSQUEZ VILLANUEVA

Publications: Estrategias para el Cumplimiento de la Misión, Revista Berit Olam, Revista Científica de Ciencias de la Salud, Revista de Investigación En Ciencia y Tecnología de Alimentos, Revista de Investigación Universitaria

DEANS

Faculty of Business Studies: EDWIN CISNEROS GONZALES
Faculty of Engineering and Architecture: Dr JULIO PAREDES GUZMAN
Faculty of Health Sciences: LILI FERNANDEZ MOLOCHO
Faculty of Humanities and Education: QUELEON MAMANI QUISPE

Faculty of Theology: EDGARD HORNA SANTILLÁN

UNIVERSIDAD PRIVADA ANTENOR ORREGO
(Private University Antenor Orrego)

Apdo postal 1075, Trujillo, La Libertad
Trujillo Campus: Avda América Sur 3145 Monserrate, Trujillo, La Libertad

Telephone: (44) 604444

Piura Campus: Avda Los Tallanes Zona Los Ejidos s/n Piura, Piura

Telephone: (73) 607614
E-mail: imagen_institucional@upao.edu.pe
Internet: www.upao.edu.pe
Founded 1988
Private control
Language of instruction: Spanish
Academic year: March to December

Rector: Dr VÍCTOR RAÚL LOZANO IBÁÑEZ
Vice-Rector for Academics: Dr LUIS ANTONIO CERNA BAZÁN
Vice-Rector for Research: Dr JULIO LUIS CHANG LAM
Sec. Gen.: Dra BERTHA MALABRIGO REYES

DEANS

Faculty of Agricultural Sciences: Dr CÉSAR LOMBARDI PÉREZ
Faculty of Architecture, Urbanism and Arts: Arq. NELLY AMEMIYA HOSHI
Faculty of Communication Sciences: DANTE PADILLA ZÚÑIGA
Faculty of Economic Sciences: Dra YOLANDA PERALTA CHÁVEZ
Faculty of Education and Humanities: Dr JAIME MANUEL ALBA VIDAL
Faculty of Engineering: Dr ELMER HUGO GONZÁLEZ HERRERA
Faculty of Health Sciences: Dr ALFONSO VILLANUEVA VASQUEZ
Faculty of Human Sciences: Dr RAMEL ULLOA DEZA
Faculty of Law and Political Sciences: Dr CARLOS ANGULO ESPINO

UNIVERSIDAD PRIVADA ANTONIO GUILLERMO URRELO
(Private University Antonio Guillermo Urrelo)

Jr. José Sabogal No 913, Cajamarca
Telephone: (076) 365819
E-mail: informes@upagu.edu.pe
Internet: www.upagu.edu.pe
Founded 1998
Private control
Language of instruction: Spanish
Academic year: March to December

Rector: Dr WILMAN MANUEL RUIZ VIGO
Vice-Rector for Research and Graduate Affairs: Dr HOMERO BAZÁN ZURITA
Vice-Rector for Academics: Dr LUIS VÁSQUEZ RODRÍGUEZ
Sec. Gen.: ÉDGAR GUTIÉRREZ PORTAL
Head of Library Services: CÉSAR SILVA

DEANS

Faculty of Engineering: Dr LUIS VÁSQUEZ RODRÍGUEZ
Faculty of Law and Political Science: JORGE LUIS SALAZAR SOPLAPUCO
Faculty of Management Sciences: CARMEN DÍAZ CAMACHO
Faculty of Pharmacy and Biochemistry: IVÁN TORRES MARQUINA
Faculty of Psychology: Dr LUIS VÁSQUEZ RODRÍGUEZ

UNIVERSIDAD PRIVADA DE TACNA
(Private University of Tacna)

Avda Bolognesi No 1177, Tacna
Telephone: (52) 427212
E-mail: rectorado@upt.edu.pe

Internet: www.upt.edu.pe
Founded 1985
Private control
Language of instruction: Spanish
Academic year: March to December

Rector: Dr HUGO CIRILO CALIZAYA CALIZAYA
Vice-Rector for Academics: Dr JAVIER RÍOS LAVAGNA
Vice-Rector for Admin.: Dr PEDRO RIVEROS VALDERRAMA
Sec. Gen.: Dr NORIBAL JORGE ZEGARRA ALVARADO

DEANS

Faculty of Architecture: Dra NELLY GONZALES MUÑIZ
Faculty of Business: ARCADIO ATENCIO VARGAS
Faculty of Education, Communication Sciences and Humanities: PATRICIA ROSA MARÍA NUÉ CABALLERO
Faculty of Engineering: Dr OSCAR ANGULO SALAS
Faculty of Health Sciences: Dr PEDRO CÁRDENAS RUEDA
Faculty of Law and Political Science: Dr RAFAEL SUPO HALLASI

UNIVERSIDAD PRIVADA DEL NORTE
(Private University of the North)

Avda El Ejército No 920, Urb. El Molino, Trujillo, La Libertad
Telephone: (44) 606222
E-mail: informes_lima@upnorte.edu.pe
Internet: www.upnorte.edu.pe
Founded 1993
Private control
Language of instruction: Spanish
Academic year: March to December

Campuses in Cajamarca, Lima and Trujillo

Rector: ANDRÉS VELARDE TALLERI
Vice-Rector for Academics: GUILLERMO SÁNCHEZ HERNÁNDEZ
Vice-Rector for Quality Education: ARIADNA HERNÁNDEZ DE TEJEDA
Sec. Gen.: CARMEN ALICIA NACARINO PÉREZ

DEANS

Faculty of Architecture and Design: JOSÉ IGNACIO PACHECO DÍAZ
Faculty of Business Studies: JORGE ARBULÚ BERNAL
Faculty of Communications: PATRICIA SÁNCHEZ URREGO
Faculty of Engineering: OSWALDO SIFUENTES BITOCCHI
Faculty of Law and Political Science: ALBERTO VILLANUEVA

UNIVERSIDAD PRIVADA NORBERT WIENER
(Norbert Wiener Private University)

Jr. Larrabure y Unanue 110 Urb. Santa Beatriz, Lima
Telephone: (1) 7065100
E-mail: info@uwiener.edu.pe
Internet: www.uwiener.edu.pe
Founded 1996
Private control
Language of instruction: Spanish
Academic year: March to December

Rector: Dr LUIS ALBERTO BULLÓN SALAZAR
Vice-Rector: Dr VÍCTOR LUIS IZAGUIRRE PASQUEL
Sec. Gen.: Dra DORINA RIVERA GALLEGOS

DEANS

Faculty of Business Studies: MARTÍN EDUARDO PALACIOS CABEL
Faculty of Engineering: EMIGDIO ALFARO
Faculty of Health Sciences: Dr JOSÉ LEONARDO PISCOYA ARBAÑIL

Faculty of Law and Political Science: IVÁN NOGUERA RAMOS
Faculty of Pharmacy and Biochemistry: Dr ENRIQUE LEÓN SORIA

UNIVERSIDAD PRIVADA SAN PEDRO
(San Pedro Private University)

Los Pinos Manzana B s/n, Chimbote, Ancash
Telephone: (43) 323505
E-mail: jhuaman@usanpedro.edu.pe
Internet: www.usanpedro.edu.pe
Private control
Language of instruction: Spanish
Academic year: March to December

Also postgraduate school

Rector: Dr JOSÉ MARÍA HUAMÁN RUIZ
Vice-Rector for Academics: Dr GILMER DÍAZ TELLO
Vice-Rector for Admin.: Dra MANUELA PORTALES PAIRAZAMÁN
Sec. Gen.: Dr ÁNGEL PAREDES QUIPUSCOA
Librarian: PEDRO RAFAEL ARROYO

Publications: *Avances en Salud, Conocimiento para el Desarrollo, Revista Científica San Pedro*

DEANS

Faculty of Education and Humanities: Dr JULIO LANDERAS RODRÍGUEZ
Faculty of Engineering: ALEJANDRO CARRERA SORIA
Faculty of Health Sciences: Dra ANA MARÍA NAZARIO GARCÍA
Faculty of Human Medicine: Dr ELMER QUEZADA REYES
Faculty of Law and Political Science: ÁNGEL QUEZADA TOMÁS
Faculty of Management Sciences and Accountancy: Dr OSCAR CRUZ CRUZ

UNIVERSIDAD PRIVADA TELESUP
(Private University Telesup)

Avda 28 de Julio No 1056, Lima
Telephone: (1) 5148400
E-mail: dead@utelesup.com
Internet: www.utelesup.com
Founded 2004
Private control
Language of instruction: Spanish
Academic year: March to December

Faculties of engineering and architecture, health and nutrition, law and social sciences, management sciences and accountancy, tourism, hotel and gastronomy

Rector: Dr ELÍAS CASTILLA ROSA PÉREZ
Vice-Rector for Academics: Dr LUIS ALBERTO COLÁN VILLEGAS
Sec. Gen.: LOURDES MORALES FERNÁNDEZ

UNIVERSIDAD RICARDO PALMA
(Ricardo Palma University)

Apdo postal 1801, Lima
Avda Benavides 5440, Urb. Las Gardenias, Santiago de Surco, Lima 33
Telephone: (1) 7080000
E-mail: webmaster@urp.edu.pe
Internet: www.urp.edu.pe
Founded 1969
Private control
Language of instruction: Spanish
Academic year: April to December

Rector: Dr IVÁN RODRÍGUEZ CHÁVEZ
Vice-Rector for Academics: Dr LEONARDO ALCAYHUAMÁN ACCOSTUPA
Vice-Rector for Admin.: Dr JOSÉ CALDERÓN MOQUILLAZA
Sec. Gen.: Lic. SAMUEL GERARDO CHOQUE MARTÍNEZ
Librarian: Mag. ROSARIO VALDIVIA PAZ SOLDÁN

Publications: *Revista Arquitextos, Revista Biotempus, Revista de la Facultad de Lenguas Modernas, Revista de la Facultad de Medicina Humana* (1 a year), *Revista de la Facultad de Psicología, Revista Economia, Revista Perfiles de Ingeniería, Revista Virtual de la Facultad de Derecho y Ciencia* (1 a year), *Tradición, Yuyaskusun Revista* (1 a year)

DEANS

Faculty of Architecture and Town Planning: Arq. OSWALDO VELÁSQUEZ HIDALGO

Faculty of Biological Sciences: Dra HUGO GONZALES FIGUEROA

Faculty of Business Studies and Economic Sciences: Dr C. P. C. JOSÉ GUILLERMO CALDERÓN MOQUILLAZA

Faculty of Engineering: Mag. LEONARDO ALCAYHUAMAN ACCOSTUPA

Faculty of Humanities and Modern Languages: Dr PEDRO DÍAZ ORTIZ

Faculty of Human Medicine: Dr MANUEL HUAMÁN GUERRERO

Faculty of Law and Political Science: Dra MAGDIEL GONZALES OJEDA

Faculty of Psychology: Dra NELLY RAQUEL UGARRIZA CHÁVEZ

UNIVERSIDAD SAN IGNACIO DE LOYOLA
(University St Ignatius of Loyola)

Avda La Fontana 550, La Molina, Lima

Telephone: (1) 3171000

E-mail: eroekaert@usil.edu.pe

Internet: www.usil.edu.pe

Founded 1995

Private control

Language of instruction: Spanish

Academic year: March to December

Rector: Dr EDWARD ROEKAERT EMBRECHTS

Vice-Rector for Academics: RODOLFO J. CREMER

Vice-Rector for Student Services: Dr HENRY BARCLAY REY DE CASTRO

Vice-Rector for Int. Affairs: RAMIRO SALAS BRAVO

Sec. Gen.: CARLOS A. SOTOMAYOR BERNOS

Publication: *Revistas de Investigación Universidad San Ignacio de Loyola* (1 a year, print and online, investigacion.usil.pe/ojs)

DEANS

Faculty of Business Studies: JOSÉ AUGUSTO GONZÁLEZ ELÍAS

Faculty of Education: Dra CARMEN BLÁZQUEZ QUINTANA

Faculty of Engineering and Architecture: Arq. ANTONIO ALEJANDRO TACCHINO DEL PINO

Faculty of Entrepreneurship: Dra DANIEL HUGH DIEZ CANSECO TERRY

Faculty of Hotel Management, Tourism and Gastronomy: Dr GUILLERMO GRAGLIA ROLAND

UNIVERSIDAD SEÑOR DE SIPÁN
(University of Sipan)

Carretera a Pimentel km. 5, Chiclayo, Lambayeque

Telephone: (74) 481610

E-mail: hllempen@uss.edu.pe

Internet: www.uss.edu.pe

Founded 1999

Private control

Language of instruction: Spanish

Academic year: March to December

Rector: Dr LLEMPÉN CORONEL HUMBERTO

Vice-Rector: Dr ALCIBIADES SIMÉ MÁRQUES

Vice-Rector for Student Affairs: Dra SUSANA TOSO DE VERA

Sec. Gen.: EDGAR ROLAND TUESTA TORRES

Publications: *Docencia y Memoria, Revista Hatun Runa, Revista Paian, Revista Ssias, Revista Tzhoecoen*

DEANS

Faculty of Business Studies: ALFREDO DÍAZ JAVE

Faculty of Engineering, Architecture and Urbanism: Arq. JORGE EDUARDO LUJÁN LÓPEZ

Faculty of Health Sciences: LEOPOLDO ACUÑA PERALTA

Faculty of Humanities: Dr NICOLAS VALLE PALOMINO

Faculty of Law: Dra DANIEL GUILLERMO CABRERA LEONARDINI

UNIVERSIDAD TECNOLÓGICA DE LOS ANDES
(Technological University of the Andes)

Avda Perú No 700, Abancay, Apurímac

Telephone: (83) 321559

E-mail: jvillafuerterecharte@utea.edu.pe

Internet: www.utea.edu.pe

Founded 1984

Private control

Language of instruction: Spanish

Academic year: March to December

Brs in Andahuaylas, Aymaraes, Cusco and Curahuasi

Rector: Dr JUAN VITALIANO RODRÍGUEZ PANTIGOSO

Vice-Rector for Academics: Dr JORGE EDUARDO VILLAFUERTE RECHARTE

Vice-Rector for Admin.: Dr JORGE LESCANO SANDOVAL

Sec. Gen.: JULIA FARFÁN TANAKA

DEANS

Faculty of Agricultural Sciences: BRAULIO PÉREZ CAMPANA

Faculty of Accountancy and Financial Sciences: GUILLERMO BUSTILLO PALOMINO

Faculty of Education Sciences and Humanities: Dr HUMBERTO COLLADO ROMÁN

Faculty of Law and Political Science: Abog. BONIFACIO ROBLES AGUIRRE

Faculty of Nursing: AYDEÉ ESPINOZA PALOMINO

Faculty of Stomatology: Abog. URIEL CARRIÓN HERRERA

UNIVERSIDAD TECNOLÓGICA DEL PERÚ
(Technological University of Peru)

Esq. Avda 28 de Julio y Avda Petit Thouars, Lima

Telephone: (1) 3159600

E-mail: admision@utp.edu.pe

Internet: www.utp.edu.pe

Founded 1997

Private control

Language of instruction: Spanish

Academic year: March to December

Rector: Dr ENRIQUE BEDOYA SÁNCHEZ

Academic Vice-Rector for Engineering: BEATRIZ ZAKIMI MIYASATO

Academic Vice-Rector for Humanities and Management: MÓNICA JACOBS MARTÍNEZ

Sec. Gen. and Vice-Rector for Int. Relations and Govt: JORGE GONZÁLEZ BOLAÑOS

DEANS

Faculty of Accountancy and Finance: CÉSAR URBANO VENTOCILLA

Faculty of Business Studies and Management: ALBERTO BULLÓN SÁNCHEZ

Faculty of Communication Sciences: ALEJANDRO GUERRERO TORRES

Faculty of Industrial and Mechanical Engineering: HUMBERTO CARRANZA

Faculty of Law, Political Science and International Relations: MIGUEL ÁNGEL RODRÍGUEZ MACKAY

Faculty of Systems and Electronics Engineering: FELIPE ONCHI

School of Postgraduate Studies: CÉSAR FERRADAS

Colleges

Conservatorio Nacional de Música (National Conservatory of Music): Jr. Carabaya 421-429, Lima; tel. (1) 4269677; e-mail informes@cnm.edu.pe; internet www.cnm.edu.pe; f. 1908 as Academia Nacional de Música 'Alcedo', autonomous since 1966; performance, musicology, education, composition; choir and orchestra; library: 14,000 books and musical scores, and record library; Dir-Gen. FERNANDO DE LUCCHI FERNALD; Acad. Dir JUAN CHÁVEZ ALVARADO; publ. *Conservatorio* (1 a year).

Escuela Nacional Superior Autónoma de Bellas Artes del Perú (Autonomous National School of Fine Arts): Jr. Ancash 681, Lima; tel. (1) 4272200; e-mail ensabap@ensabap.edu.pe; internet www.ensabap.edu.pe; f. 1918; library: 5,000 vols; Dir-Gen. DAVID SIXTO DURAND ATO; Academic Dir SISSI OLENKA HAMANN TURKOWSKY; publ. *Anuario Académico*.

Escuela Superior Autónoma de Bellas Artes 'Diego Quispe Tito' de Cusco (Autonomous School of Fine Arts of Cusco 'Diego Quispe Tito'): Calle Márquez 271, Cusco; tel. (84) 231491; e-mail info@bellasartescusco.edu.pe; internet www.bellasartescusco.edu.pe; Dir-Gen. LUCIO VITA GUTIERREZ MENDOZA; Academic Dir AMÓS DAVID PILCO LOAIZA.

Schools of Art and Music

Conservatorio de Lima 'Josafat Roel Pineda' (Conservatory of Lima 'Josafat Roel Pineda'): Avda Alejandro Bertello 1092, Lima 1; tel. (1) 5640350; e-mail josafat@conservatoriodelima.edu.pe; internet www.conservatoriodelima.edu.pe; f. 1986; Dir-Gen Dr RUBÉN VALENZUELA ALEJO; Academic Dir YHASMÍN VALENZUELA TORRES.

Conservatorio Regional de Música del Norte Público 'Carlos Valderrama' (Regional Public Conservatory of Music North 'Carlos Valderrama'): Jr. Independencia 572 (2°), Trujillo, La Libertad; tel. (44) 246941; e-mail informes@conservatoriotrujillo.edu.pe; internet conservatoriotrujillo.edu.pe; f. 1946 as Escuela Regional de Música del Norte; current name adopted 2003; Dir-Gen CARLOS PAREDES ABAD.

Conservatorio Regional de Música 'Luis Duncker Lavalle' (Regional Conservatory of Music 'Luis Duncker Lavalle'): Lambramani Calle 4 s/n, J. L. Bustamante y Rivero, Arequipa; tel. (54) 430241; e-mail crmduncklerlavalle@hotmail.com; internet www.luisdunckerlavalle.com; f. 2010; Dir-Gen. Lic. JAIME CHARRES VARGAS.

Escuela Nacional Superior de Folklore 'José María Arguedas' (National School of Folklore 'José María Arguedas'): Jr. Ica 143, Cercado de Lima, Lima; tel. (1) 3210032; e-mail webmaster@escuelafolklore.edu.pe; internet www.escuelafolklore.edu.pe; Dir-Gen. AMADO BENJAMÍN LOAYZA SANDOVAL; Academic Dir ENRIQUE BLANCO TERCERO.

Escuela Superior de Formación Artística 'Gudelia Alarco de Vargas'

(Artistic Training School 'Gudelia Alarco de Vargas'): Prolongacion Trujillo No 1160, Avda San Carlos Cuadra 16 Con San Judas Tadeo, El Tambo, Huáncayo; internet www .esfagav.edu.pe; f. 1994; Dir ELIZABETH VARGAS CARBAJAL.

Escuela Superior de Formación Artística Pública 'Condorcunca' (Public School of Art Education 'Condorcunca'): Jr.

28 de julio N° 120, Ayacucho; tel. (66) 314493; e-mail esmacondorcunca@hotmail.com; internet www.esfa-c.edu.pe; f. 1946; 25 teachers; Dir-Gen. Lic. PEDRO RAMÓN CASTILLA HUAYHUA.

Escuela Superior de Formación Artística Pública 'José Maria Valle Riestra' (Training School of Public Art 'José Maria Valle Riestra'): Calle Libertad 324,

Piura; tel. (73) 307114; e-mail contacto@ esfapjmvr.com; internet www.esfapjmvr .com; f. 1951; Admin. Dir GLADYS LACHIRA LEÓN.

Escuela Superior Pública de Arte Carlos Baca Flor (School of Arts Carlos Baca Flor): Calle Sucre 111, Cercado, Arequipa; tel. (54) 281291; f. 1951.

PHILIPPINES

The Higher Education System

From the 16th century until 1898 the Philippines were under Spanish control. They were ceded to the USA under the terms of the Treaty of Paris (1898) and remained under US control until independence was achieved in 1946. The Philippines' colonial inheritance is reflected in its higher education system. The two oldest institutions, the University of San Carlos (founded in 1595; current status since 1948) and the University of Santo Tomás (founded in 1611), are both private Catholic universities, while universities founded during or after the period of US control are modelled on US institutions. In 2011/12 there were 1,183,145 students enrolled in the public universities and colleges; in total there were 2,247 higher education institutions (643 public, 1,604 private).

More than 80% of higher education institutions in the Philippines are privately run. The Commission on Higher Education (CHED), established by the Higher Education Act of 1994 as part of a broad reform programme of the education system, is the supreme national body for public and private universities. It is responsible, inter alia, for quality assurance, accreditation (which is mandatory), and policy formulation and planning. Higher education institutions (both public and private) that are deemed by the CHED to have reached the highest standard of teaching and research in specific subject areas are designated as Centres of Excellence and receive additional funding from the Government. Additional accreditation and quality assurance may be sought from one of four agencies, namely: Philippine Accrediting Association of Schools, Colleges and Universities; Philippine Association of Colleges and Universities, Commission on Accreditation; Association of Christian Schools and Colleges—Accrediting Agency, Inc.; and Accrediting Agency of Chartered Colleges and Universities in the Philippines. All four bodies are members of the Federation of Accreditating Agencies of the Philippines.

Admission to higher education is on the basis of satisfactory performance in the High School Diploma and the university entrance examination. For most Filipino degrees, students are expected to accrue a specified number of credits each semester throughout the duration of the degree in order to graduate. Associate degrees are offered by community colleges and universities and are two-year programmes of study in the arts and sciences. The first full undergraduate degree is the Bachelors, usually a four-year course, but certain subjects may require longer periods of study, such as law and medicine (both eight years). The postgraduate degrees are the Masters and PhD. The Masters lasts for two years and consists of full-time study and the submission of a thesis. For a PhD, students are required to undertake at least three years of study and research, and to complete a dissertation.

The Technical Education and Skills Development Authority (TESDA) is the controlling body of post-secondary technical and vocational education, which is offered by public and private technical/vocational institutes and specialist institutions. The duration of programmes varies from one to three years; in some instances programmes are geared towards a Certificate system of four levels. All technical and vocational education providers must be accredited by the TESDA.

Regulatory and Representative Bodies

GOVERNMENT

Department of Education: DepED Complex, Meralco Ave, Pasig City, 1600 Metro Manila; tel. (2) 636-1663; e-mail action@deped.gov.ph; internet www.deped.gov.ph; Sec. of Education ARMIN A. LUISTRO.

Department of Science and Technology: DOST Bldg, Gen. Santos Ave, Bicutan, Taguig City, 1631 Metro Manila; tel. (2) 837-2071; e-mail mgmontejo@dost.gov.ph; internet www.dost.gov.ph; Sec. MARIO G. MONTEJO.

ACCREDITATION

Accrediting Agency of Chartered Colleges and Universities in the Philippines, Inc. (AACCUP): 812 Future Point Plaza 1, 112 Panay Ave, South Triangle, Quezon City; tel. (2) 415-9016; e-mail aaccup@axti.com; internet www.aaccupqa.org.ph; f. 1987; accredits curricular programmes in the Philippines, particularly for state univs and colleges; 107 mems (104 state univs and colleges, 3 local colleges); Pres. and Chair. of Board of Trustees Dr RUPERTO S. SANGALANG; Exec. Dir Dr MANUEL T. CORPUS.

Federation of Accrediting Agencies of the Philippines (FAAP): Unit 302 Puno Building, 47 Kalayaan Ave, Diliman, Quezon City; tel. (2) 927-9645; f. 1976; NGO founded to improve the quality of education by means of voluntary accreditation for private higher education instns; Pres. Dr FELICIANA A. REYES.

Philippine Accrediting Association of Schools, Colleges and Universities (PAASCU): Unit 107, The Tower at Emerald Sq., J. P. Rizal cnr P. Tuazon Sts, 1109 Quezon City; tel. (2) 911-2845; e-mail info@paascu.org.ph; internet www.paascu.org.ph; f. 1957; private org. accrediting academic programmes that meet commonly accepted standards of quality education; has accredited programmes in 229 instns; Chair. of Board of Dirs Dr RAMON C. REYES; Exec. Dir CONCEPCION V. PIJANO.

Philippine Association of Colleges and Universities, Commission on Accreditation (PACUCOA): Suite 7M Eagle Star Condominium, Dela Rosa St, Loyola Heights, Katipunan Ave, Quezon City; tel. (2) 426-0089; e-mail pacucoa@yahoo.com; f. 1967; accredits private colleges and univs; 125 mem. schools with 799 programmes; Chair. Dr ROSITA L. NAVARRO; Exec. Dir Dr ADLAI C. CASTIGADOR.

FUNDING

Fund Assistance to Private Education (FAPE): 5th Fl., Salamin Bldg, Salcedo St, Legaspi Village, Makati City; tel. (2) 845-0169; internet www.fape.org.ph; f. 1968; perpetual trust fund set up by the Philippines govt with help from the US govt; funds are provided by interest earned on the initial capital augmented by donations and grants; Exec. Dir CAROLINA PORIO.

NATIONAL BODIES

Association of Catholic Universities of the Philippines, Inc.: c/o Office of Public Affairs, Univ. of Santo Tomás (Room 104, Main Bldg), España St, Manila 1008; tel. (2) 731-3544; f. 1973; Pres. Fr HERMINIO V. DAGOHOY; Sec. Gen. Prof. GIOVANNA V. FONTANILLA.

Catholic Educational Association of the Philippines (CEAP): 7 Road 16, Bagong Pag-asa, 1105 Quezon City; tel. (2) 426-2679; e-mail ceap@edsamail.com.ph; internet www.eccceonline.org/ceap; f. 1941; Pres. Fr RODERICK SALAZAR, Jr.

Commission on Higher Education: Higher Education Development Center (HEDC) Bldg, C. P. Garcia St, U. P. Diliman, Quezon City; tel. (2) 351-7413; e-mail info@ched.gov.ph; internet www.ched.gov.ph; f. 1994; governing body covering public and private higher education instns as well as degree-granting programmes in all tertiary educational insts in the Philippines; Chair. Dr PATRICIA B. LICUANAN; Exec. Dir Dr WILLIAM C. MEDRANO.

Coordinating Council for Private Educational Association (COCOPEA): 89-C 9th Ave, Cubao, Quezon City; tel. (2) 913-2932; promotes excellence in private higher education instns; Pres. JUANITO M. ACANTO.

Philippine Association of Colleges and Universities (PACU): Unit 601 Richmonde Plaza, Ortigas Centre, San Miguel Ave, Pasig City; tel. (2) 638-5635; e-mail pacuinc@yahoo.com; internet www.pacu.org.ph; f. 1932; Pres. Dr PATRICIA LAGUNDA; Sec. Dr CAROLINE MARIAN ENRIQUEZ.

Philippine Association of Private Schools, Colleges and Universities (PAPSCU): 10th Fl., Bldg 7, Emilio Aguinaldo College, 113 Gonzales cnr San Marcelino Sts, UN Ave, Ermita, Manila; tel. (2) 522-0097; e-mail papscu2005@yahoo.com.ph;

internet www.papscu.org.ph; f. 1956; Pres. Dr JOSE PAULO E. CAMPOS.

Philippine Association of State Universities and Colleges: 2nd Fl., ITC Bldg, EARIST Compound, Valencia St, Sta Mesa, Manila; tel. (2) 716-0944; f. 1967; ind. but attached to Dept of Education; aims to foster excellence in higher education, to promote communication among its mem. institutions, to encourage studies on higher education, to secure adequate government support for education, to encourage inter-institutional assistance through fellowships, grants, teacher exchange, accreditation; 75 mem. institutions; library with spec. collns on education; Pres. ELDIGARIO D. GONZALES; Exec. Dir Dr FREDERICK S. PADA; publ. *Baliham* (4 a year).

Learned Societies
GENERAL

Academia Filipina (Philippine Academy): 47 Juan Luna St, San Lorenzo Village, 1200 Makati, Metro Manila; tel. (2) 817-1128; f. 1924; corresp. of the Real Academia Española (Madrid); 15 mems; Dir ALEJANDRO ROCES; Sec. SALVADOR B. MALIG.

AGRICULTURE, FISHERIES AND VETERINARY SCIENCE

Crop Science Society of the Philippines: c/o Phil Rice, Los Baños, Pili Drive, College, Laguna; tel. (49) 536-3635; e-mail asian@laguna.net; internet www.cssp.org.ph; f. 1970; 3,000 mems; Pres. NORVIE L. MANIGBAS; Vice-Pres. RENATO A. REANO; publ. *Philippine Journal of Crop Science* (3 a year).

Philippine Society of Agricultural Engineers: ATI Bldg Elliptical Rd, Diliman, Quezon City; tel. (2) 920-4071; e-mail contact@psae.net; internet psae.net; f. 1950; 5,800 mems; Pres. Dr TERESITO G. AGUINALDO.

Philippine Veterinary Medical Association: Unit 233, Union Square Condominium, 15th Ave, Cubao, Quezon City; tel. (2) 911-3159; e-mail secretariat@pvma.com.ph; internet www.pvma.com.ph; f. 1907; 5,274 mems; Pres. Dr TOMAS C. LAZARO, II.

ARCHITECTURE AND TOWN PLANNING

United Architects of the Philippines (UAP): 53 Scout Rallos St, Diliman, Quezon City 1103; tel. (2) 412-6374; e-mail uap@united-architects.org; internet www.united-architects.org; f. 1974 following merger of Philippine Institute of Architects, League of Philippine Architects and Association of Philippine Government Architects; Pres. EDRIC MARCO C. FLORENTINO; Sec.-Gen. GIL C. EVASCO.

BIBLIOGRAPHY, LIBRARY SCIENCE AND MUSEOLOGY

Association of Special Libraries of the Philippines (ASLP): Room 301, National Library Bldg, Kalaw St, Ermita, Manila; tel. (2) 524-4611; e-mail ladladj@dlsu.edu.ph; internet www.aczafra.com; f. 1954; 556 mems; Pres. JOCELYN L. LADAD; Sec. ARLENE Y. GONZALES; publs *ASLP Bulletin* (4 a year), *ASLP Newsletter* (4 a year), *Directory of Special Libraries*.

HISTORY, GEOGRAPHY AND ARCHAEOLOGY

Philippine Historical Association: c/o Office of External Affairs, St Mary's College, 37 M. Ignacia Ave, 1103 Quezon City; tel. 413-4076 ext. 222; e-mail glo.santos@yahoo .com; f. 1955; 500 mems; Pres. Prof. AMBETH OCAMPO; Exec. Dir Dr GLORIA M. SANTOS; publs *PHA Balita* (2 a year), *Philippine Historical Bulletin* (1 a year).

LANGUAGE AND LITERATURE

Alliance Française: POB 2899, 128 Manila; located at: 209 Nicanor Garcia St, Bel Air II, 1209 Makati City; tel. (2) 895-7585; e-mail info@alliance.ph; internet www.alliance.ph; offers courses and examinations in French language and culture and promotes cultural exchange with France; Dir PHILIPPE NORMAND.

British Council: 10th Fl., Taipan Pl., F. Ortigas Jr Ave, Ortigas Centre, Pasig City, Manila, 1605; tel. (2) 914-1011; e-mail britishcouncil@britishcouncil.org.ph; internet www.britishcouncil.org/philippines; teaching centre; offers courses and examinations in English language and British culture; promotes cultural exchange with the UK; library; Dir GILL WESTAWAY.

Goethe-Institut: POB 1744, Makati Central Post Office, 1257 Makati City; 4-5/F Adamson Centre, 121 Leviste St, Salcedo Village, 1227 Makati City; tel. (2) 817-0978; e-mail info@manila.goethe.org; internet www .goethe.de/manila; f. 1961; offers courses and examinations in German language and culture and promotes cultural exchange with Germany; library of 3,000 vols; Dir RICHARD KÜNZEL.

Instituto Cervantes: 855 T. M. Kalaw St, Ermita, 1000 Manila; tel. (2) 526-1482; e-mail cenmni@cervantes.es; internet manila.cervantes.es; f. 1991; offers courses and examinations in Spanish language and culture and promotes cultural exchange with Spain and Spanish-speaking countries; library of 23,000 vols, 1,500 CDs and audio cassettes, 2,000 video cassettes and 500 DVDs; Dir EDUARDO CALVO; Sec. KATERINA VENERACIÓN.

Komisyon sa Wikang Filipino: Watson Bldg, 1610 J. P. Laurel St, San Miguel, Manila; tel. (2) 734-5546; e-mail komfil .gov@gmail.com; internet www.komfil.gov .ph; f. 1991, fmrly Institute of Philippine Languages; develops, promotes and standardizes Filipino and other Philippine languages; library of 5,000 vols; Chair. Dr PONCIANO B. P. PINEDA.

MEDICINE

Manila Medical Society: 800 Taft Ave, Manila; tel. (2) 524-9944; e-mail mmsi@yahoo .com; internet www.geocities.com/mmsi1902; f. 1902; 1,249 mems; Pres. Dr ASCENSION F. BAUTISTA; Sec. Dr FELICISIMA B. BACON.

Philippine Medical Association: PMA Bldg, North Ave, Quezon City; tel. (2) 929-6366; e-mail medical@pma.com.ph; internet www.pma.com.ph; f. 1903; 107 component societies, 60 affiliated speciality societies; Pres. Dr MODESTO O. LLAMAS; Sec.-Gen. Dr REY MELCHOR SANTOS; publ. *Journal*.

Philippine Paediatric Society, Inc.: POB 3527, Manila; e-mail ppsinc@pps.org.ph; f. 1947; 620 mems; Pres. Dr JOEL S. ELISES; Sec. Dr VICTOR S. DOCTOR; publ. *Philippine Journal of Paediatrics* (6 a year).

Philippine Pharmacists Association: 815 R. Papa St. Sampaloc, 1008 Manila; tel. (2) 734-4820; f. and incorporated 1920; 8,000 mems; Pres. Dr LOURDES TALAG ECHAUZ; Exec. Sec. Dr NORMA V. LERMA.

NATURAL SCIENCES
General

National Academy of Science and Technology: 3rd Level, Science Heritage Bldg, DOST Complex, Gen. Santos Ave, Bicutan, Taguig City, 1631 Metro Manila; tel. (2) 837-2071; e-mail secretariat@nast.ph; internet www.nast.ph; f. 1976; advises the Pres. and Cabinet of the nat. govt on policies concerning science and technology; Pres. Dr WILLIAM G. PADOLINA; Sec. Dr EVELYN MAE TECSON-MENDOZA.

TECHNOLOGY

Philippine Institute of Mining, Metallurgical and Geological Engineers: POB 1595, Manila; f. 1940; 117 mems; Pres. JONES R. CASTRO; Sec.-Treas. LEOPOLDO F. ABAD.

Philippine Institute of Civil Engineers: No 4, Albany St, Aurora Cubao, 1109 Quezon; tel. (2) 709-3936; e-mail picenatl@pice .org.ph; internet www.pice.org.ph; f. 1918 as Philippine Soc. of Civil Engineers, merged with Philippine Asscn of Civil Engineers, current name adopted 1972; Hon. Pres. FIDEL V. RAMOS; Sec. MARIANO R. ALQUIZA; publ. *Philippine Journal of Civil Engineering* (4 a year).

Philippine Society of Mechanical Engineers: 19 Scout Bayoran St, S Triangle, Quezon City; tel. (2) 371-1819; e-mail info@psme.org; internet www.psme.org; f. 1952; Pres. Eng EDIMAR V. SALCEDO.

Research Institutes
GENERAL

Advanced Science and Technology Institute: ASTI Bldg., C. P. Garcia Ave., Technology Park Complex, U.P. Campus, Diliman, 1101 Quezon City; tel. (2) 426-9755; e-mail info@asti.dost.gov.ph; internet www.asti.dost.gov.ph; conducts research and devt in information and communications technology and microelectronics; Dir DENIS F. VILLORENTE.

Institute of Philippine Culture, Ateneo de Manila University: Frank Lynch Hall, Social Devt Complex, Loyola Heights, 1108 Quezon City; tel. 426-6067; e-mail ipc@admu .edu.ph; internet www.ipc-ateneo.org; f. 1960 as a univ. research org.; undertakes studies directed towards solving devt problems, particularly in the areas of upland devt, local governance, agrarian reform, community health, resources management, irrigation, forestry, women and sustainable agriculture; assists devt agencies; trains agency personnel and local communities in the use of research methodologies; library of 7,000 vols, 3,000 reprints and 104 multimedia vols; Dir Dr WILFREDO F. ARCE; publs *Culture and Development Series*, *IPC Discussion Papers*, *IPC Final Reports*, *IPC Monograph Series*, *IPC Papers*, *IPC Social Explorations Series*.

National Research Council of the Philippines: General Santos Ave, Bicutan, Taguig City; tel. (2) 837-6141; e-mail nrcpinfo@dost.gov.ph; internet mis.dost.gov .ph/nrcp; f. 1933; supports basic research in a wide variety of fields; 12 scientific divisions; 2,250 mems; library of 1,300 vols; Pres. Prof. FORTUNATO T. DELA PEÑA; Exec. Dir Dr PACIENTE A. CORDERO, Jr; publs *Newsletter* (4 a year), *NRCP Research Journal* (4 a year), *Technical Bulletin* (irregular).

AGRICULTURE, FISHERIES AND VETERINARY SCIENCE

Bureau of Plant Industry: 692 San Andres St, Malate, Manila; tel. (2) 525-7857; e-mail cu.bpi@da.gov.ph; internet bpi.da.gov.ph; f. 1930; conserves and develops Philippine plant genetic resources and ensures the protection and devt of the plant industry;

library of 10,000 vols; Dir Dr CLARITO M. BARRON.

Forest Products Research and Development Institute (FPRDI): Narra St, Forestry Campus, UP College, Los Baños, 4031 Laguna; tel. (49) 536-2360; e-mail fprdi@dost .gov.ph; internet www.fprdi.dost.gov.ph; f. 1957; conducts basic and applied research on forestry, forest products and other related areas; undertakes the transfer of completed research; provides technical services and industrial manpower training; library of 17,000 vols, 8,170 books, 3,708 reports, 4,650 vols of periodicals; Dir Dr ROMULO T. AGGANGAN; Sec. Dr MARIO G. MONTEJO; publs *Forest Products Technoflow*, *FPRDI Journal* (1 a year), *Lexicon of Philippine Trees*.

Philippine Rice Research Institute: Central Experiment Station Maligaya, Science City of Muñoz, Nueva Ecija; tel. (44) 456-0277; e-mail prri@philrice.gov.ph; internet www.philrice.gov.ph; f. 1960; aims to sustain the country's self-sufficiency in rice; undertakes and funds a national research and development programme for rice and rice-based farming systems; trains scientists, farmer leaders and agribusiness managers; Exec. Dir Dr LEOCADIO S. SEBASTIAN.

EDUCATION

Science Education Institute: c/o Department of Science and Technology, 3rd PTRI Bldg, Bicutan, Taguig, 1604 Metro Manila; tel. (2) 837-1359; e-mail webmaster@sei.dost .gov.ph; internet www.sei.dost.gov.ph; Dir Dr ESTER B. OGENA.

Southeast Asian Ministers of Education Organization Regional Center for Educational Innovation and Technology (SEAMEO INNOTECH): Commonwealth Ave, Diliman, 1101 Quezon City; tel. (2) 924-7681; e-mail info@seameo-innotech.org; internet www.seameo-innotech.org; f. 1970; identifies basic educational problems common to the SE Asian region and assists the SE Asian Mins of Education Org. mem. countries in the solution of these problems; conducts training, devt, research, evaluation, information and communications technology and other spec. programmes; library of 18,000 vols; Dir Dr ERLINDA C. PEFIANCO; publs *INNOTECH Journal* (2 a year), *INNOTECH Newsletter* (2 a year).

MEDICINE

Food and Nutrition Research Institute: c/o Department of Science and Technology, Gen. Santos Ave, Bicutan, 1604 Taguig, Metro Manila; tel. (2) 837-2934; e-mail mvc@fnri.dost.gov.ph; internet www.fnri .dost.gov.ph; f. 1987; Dir Dr MARIO V. CAPANZANA.

NATURAL SCIENCES
Physical Sciences

Philippine Institute of Volcanology and Seismology: PHIVOLCS Bldg, C. P. Garcia Ave, U.P. Campus, Diliman, Quezon City; tel. (2) 426-1468; e-mail phivolcs@x5.phivolcs .dost.gov.ph; internet www.phivolcs.dost.gov .ph; f. 1952; library of 3,000 vols; Dir RENATO U. SOLIDUM, Jr.

TECHNOLOGY

Industrial Technology Development Institute: DOST Compound, Gen. Santos Ave, Bicutan, 1631 Taguig, Metro Manila; tel. (2) 837-2071; e-mail nea@dost.gov.ph; internet www.mis.dost.gov.ph/itdi; f. 1951; carries out research and development in the areas of food processing, materials science, chemicals and minerals, electronics and process control, fuels and energy, microbiology

and genetics, and the environment; Dir Dr NUNA E. ALMANZOR.

Metals Industry Research and Development Centre: MIRDC Compound, Gen. Santos Ave, Bicutan, 1604 Taguig, Metro Manila; tel. (2) 837-0431; e-mail adcruz@dost .gov.ph; internet www.mirdc.dost.gov.ph; f. 1972; research and devt, quality control, and testing of metal products; Exec. Dir ARTHUR LUCAS D. CRUZ; publ. *Metals Industry Trends and Events* (newsletter, 3 a year).

Mines and Geosciences Bureau: North Ave, Diliman, 1100 Quezon City, Metro Manila; tel. (2) 920-9120; e-mail central@ mgb.gov.ph; internet www.mgb.gov.ph; f. 1898; administers the utilization and management of the country's mineral wealth; conducts geological, mining, metallurgical, chemical and other research; undertakes geological and mineral exploration surveys; library of 4,200 vols; Dir JEREMIAS DOLINO; publs *Mineral Gazette* (2 a year), *Mineral Industry Indicators* (2 a year), *National Directory of Producing Mines and Quarries in the Philippines* (1 a year), *Philippine Mineral Industry Review* (4 a year), *Philippine Mineral Statistics* (1 a year).

Philippine Nuclear Research Institute: Commonwealth Ave, Diliman, 1101 Quezon City; tel. (2) 920-8787; e-mail nrlsd@pnri.dost .gov.ph; internet www.pnri.dost.gov.ph; f. 1958; peaceful applications of nuclear energy; library of 19,069 vols; Dir Dr ALUMANDA M. DELA ROSA (acting); publ. *Philippines Nuclear Journal* (1 a year).

Philippine Textile Research Institute: Gen. Santos Ave, Bicutan, Taguig City, Metro Manila; tel. (2) 837-1325; e-mail ptri@dost.gov.ph; internet www.ptri.dost.gov .ph; f. 1967; conducts applied research and devt for textile industry; undertakes transfer of completed researches to end-users or via linkage units of other govt agencies; provides technical services and training programmes; Dir Dr CELIA B. ELUMBA.

Libraries and Archives
Bacalod City
Bacalod City Library: Bacalod City, Negros Occidental; e-mail mcorpuz@ bacolodcity.gov.ph; 50,000 vols.

Cagayan de Oro City
Cagayan de Oro City Public Library: Apolinar Velez St, Cagayan de Oro City; tel. (8822) 72-5560; Librarian MYRNA F. ACEDERA.

Xavier University Library: Ateneo de Cagayan, Corrales Ave, Cagayan de Oro City 9000; tel. (8822) 72-3116 ext. 2302; e-mail librarytech@xu.edu.ph; internet library.xu.edu.ph; f. 1933; 121,500 vols, 376 periodicals; Dir, Univ. Libraries ANNABELLE P. ACEDERA; publ. *Kinaadman*.

Cebu City
Cebu City Public Library: Osmeña Blvd., Cebu City; tel. (32) 253-1526; Librarian CIRILA A. DELOS REYES.

University of San Carlos Library: P. del Rosario St, 6000 Cebu City; tel. (32) 253-1000 ext. 133; e-mail information@usc.edu.ph; internet www.usc.edu.ph; f. 1947; 269,705 vols incl. 21,320 vols of Filipiniana, 3,360 titles of periodicals (44,992 vols total); 3,502 audiovisual items; spec. colln for local studies held in Cebuano Studies Centre at above address; Dir of Libraries Dr MARILOU P. TADLIP.

Davao City
Davao City Library: 3rd Fl., SP Building, San Pedro St, Davao City; tel. (82) 227-3137; e-mail citylib@davaocity.gov.ph; Librarian NORA FE ALAJAR.

Dumaguete
Silliman University Library: 6200 Dumaguete City, Negros Oriental; tel. (35) 422-7208; e-mail sulib@su.edu.ph; internet su .edu.ph; f. 1906; outreach activities; organizes seminars, workshops, lectures; information literacy programme; 200,000 items; Univ. Librarian LORNA YSO; publs *Convergence* (arts and sciences, irregular), *Silliman Journal* (humanities, social sciences and sciences, 2 a year), *The Educator* (every 3 years).

Makati City
Asian Institute of Management, Knowledge Resource Centre—Library: 123 Paseo de Roxas, Makati City 1229; tel. (2) 892-4011; e-mail vong@aim.edu; internet www.aim.edu; f. 1968; 25,000 vols; Chief Librarian VIRGINIA ONG.

Filipinas Heritage Library: 6F Ayala Museum, Makati Ave cnr, Dela Rosa St, 1224 Makati City; tel. (2) 759-8288; e-mail asklibrarian@filipinaslibrary.org.ph; internet www.filipinaslibrary.org.ph; f. 1996; research library specializing in Philippine art and culture; photography; museology; migration; 13,000 vols; Himig colln of vintage Philippine music; Elpidio Quirino presidential papers; spec. collns: Roderick Hall colln on Second World War in the Philippines; Memorare colln on the Liberation of Manila; Armengol colln; Man. SUZANNE YUPANGCO; Librarian MARIA CECILIA AYSON.

Manila
Adamson University Library: 900 San Marcelino St, Ermita, 1000 Manila; tel. (2) 524-2011 ext. 131; e-mail hdecastro@ adamson.edu.ph; internet www.adamson .edu.ph; f. 1933; Dir of Libraries HELEN C. DE CASTRO.

Ateneo de Manila University Rizal Library: Katipunan Ave, Loyola Heights, 1108 Quezon City; tel. (2) 426-6001; e-mail ltdavid@ateneo.edu; internet rizal.lib.admu .edu.ph; f. 1967; 240,000 vols, 36,000 bound periodicals, 325,000 microforms; preservation of spec. collns, incl. Filipiniana colln, Rizaliana, American Historical colln, Pardo de Tavera colln and the Ateneo Library of Women's Writings; Dir Prof. LOURDES T. DAVID; publs *Asian Perspectives in the Humanities and the Arts, Journal of Philippine Studies*.

Far Eastern University Library: POB 609, Quezon Blvd, 1008 Manila; 3rd Fl., NRH Bldg, Nicanor Reyes Sr St, Sampaloc, 1008 Manila; tel. (2) 735-5649; e-mail evelyn_sf@hotmail.com; f. 1928; 82,243 vols; Librarian Dr EVELYN S. FABITO.

Manila City Library: 2nd Fl., Sining Kayumanggi Bldg, Mehan Garden, Malate, Manila; tel. (2) 523-8688; Chief Librarian FILEMON L. GECOLEA.

National Library of the Philippines: POB 2926, T. M. Kalaw St, 1000 Ermita, Manila; tel. (2) 310-5032; e-mail antonio .santos@nlp.gov.ph; internet web.nlp.gov.ph; f. 1887; 1,691,030 vols, 6,250 periodicals, 813,095 MSS, 51,680 vols of theses and dissertations, 10,332 audio cassettes, 6,004 microfilms, 2,190 sheet maps, 388 CD-ROMs; also 762,459 vols in public libraries and 8,579 vols in bookmobiles; Dir ANTONIO M. SANTOS; publ. *Philippine National Bibliography* (1 a year).

Philippine Women's University Library: 1743 Taft Ave, 1004 Manila; tel. 526-8421; e-mail library@pwu.edu.ph; internet www .pwu.edu.ph; f. 1919; 4 br. libraries: social sciences, pure sciences, applied sciences, music, arts, literature, history, Filipiniana, women's colln, Asian colln, archive colln; 80,056 vols; Chief Librarian DIONISIA M. ANGELES; publs *PWU Research Journal, The Philippine Educational Forum*.

Science and Technology Information Institute, Department of Science and Technology: DOST Complex, Gen. Santos Ave, Upper Bicutan, Taguig City, Metro Manila; tel. (2) 837-2191; e-mail monliboro@ yahoo.com; internet www.stii.dost.gov.ph; f. 1988; acquisition of science and technology information materials, technical information processing, library and reference services, science information services, databanking, training in science and technology information and computer applications; training on ScINET Integrated Library Management System (SILMS); provides communication and publication services, prepares audiovisual materials on science and technology, press releases, documentary films/video, coordinates and facilitates radio and television interviews of scientists and science managers; 10,534 vols, 2,549 periodicals, 1,903 theses and dissertations, 1,661 non-prints, 32,708 analytics and 251 investigative projects, 411 technical reports; Dir RAYMUND E. LIBORO; publs *Philippine Journal of Science* (2 a year), *Philippine Men of Science* (1 a year), *Philippine Science and Technology Abstracts* (2 a year), *S&T Post* (4 a year), *Specialized Bibliographies*.

Technological University of the Philippines Library: Ayala Blvd, Ermita, 1000 Manila; tel. (2) 302-7750 ext. 601; internet www.tup.edu.ph; 34,170 items; Dir Dr WILHELMINA G. BORJAL.

University of the East Library: 2219 Claro M. Recto Ave, 2806 Manila; internet online.ue.edu.ph/manila/library; 183,000 vols; Dir of Libraries NORMA I. JHOCSON.

University of Manila Central Library: 546 Dr M. V. de los Santos St, Sampaloc, Manila; e-mail library@dlsu.edu.ph; internet www.dlsu.edu.ph/library; f. 1913; 28,600 vols; other libraries; 23,000 vols; Assistant Chief Librarian JUAN MARTIN GUASCH.

University of the Philippines Manila, University Library: 650 Pedro Gil St, Ermita, 1000 Manila; tel. (2) 526-4253; e-mail tdugenia@mail.upm.edu.ph; internet lib.upm.edu.ph; main library and 9 br. libraries; Librarian THERESA P. DUGENIA.

Miguel de Benavides Library: España St, 1015 Manila; tel. (2) 731-3034; e-mail library@mnl.ust.edu.ph; internet library.ust .edu.ph; attached to Univ. of Santo Tomas; 391,120 vols; collns of Filipiniana and rare and ancient books; spec. libraries of Ecclesiastical faculties, medicine, music, engineering, fine arts and commerce; Prefect of Libraries Fr ANGEL A APARICIO; Chief Librarian ESTRELLA S. MAJUELO.

Quezon City

Loyola School of Theology Library: POB 240, U.P. Quezon City; tel. (2) 426-5966; e-mail lwakefield@admu.edu.ph; internet www.lst.edu/library.asp; f. 1965; 69,000 vols, 18,000 vols of periodicals; Librarian CRISANTA C. ROSALES; publ. *Landas (The Way)* (2 a year).

University of the Philippines Diliman University Library: Gonzalez Hall, Diliman, 1101 Quezon City; tel. (2) 926-1877; e-mail salvacion.arlante@up.edu.ph; internet www.mainlib.upd.edu.ph; f. 1922; 1,055,048 vols, 32,671 periodical titles; 26 brs; Dir SALVACION M. ARLANTE; publ. *Index to Philippine Periodicals* (4 a year).

Museums and Art Galleries

Cebu City

CAP Art Centre and President Osmeña Memorabilia: 60 Osmeña Blvd, Cebu City; tel. (32) 217-519; f. 1986; work by artists from all parts of the Philippines; memorabilia concerning the late President Osmeña; Curator MARY F. ABAD.

Casa Gorordo Museum: 35 Lopez Jaena St, Cebu City; tel. (32) 255-5645; fmr home of the first Filipino Bishop of Cebu, now restored as a typical 19th-century residence; furniture, paintings, religious relics, pottery and ceramics; Exec. Dir CHARLES MUERTEGUI.

Southwestern University Museum: Urgello Rd, 6000 Cebu City; tel. (32) 253-6500; internet www.cebu-online.com/swum; prehistoric, archaeological, ethnographic, ecclesiastical and art objects; Dir TONETTE S. PAÑARES.

University of San Carlos Museum: P. del Rosario St, 6000 Cebu City; tel. (32) 253-1000 loc 191; e-mail museum@usc.edu.ph; internet www.usc.edu.ph; f. 1967; Spanish colonial, ethnographic, archaeological and natural science objects; Curator MARLENE SOCORRO SAMSON.

Davao City

Davao Museum: Zonta Bldg, Insular Village Phase I, Lanang, Davao City; f. 1977; tribal art, local costumes, jewellery, textiles, handicrafts, musical instruments; Curator Dr HEIDI K. GLORIA.

Makati City

Ayala Museum: Makati Ave, Greenbelt Park, Ayala Center, 1224 Makati City; tel. (2) 757-7117; e-mail museum_inquiry@ayalamuseum.org; internet www .ayalamuseum.org; f. 1967; archaeological, ethnographic and fine arts collections; paintings by Philippine artists Juan Luna, Fernando Amorsolo and Fernando Zobel; 60 dioramas illustrating Philippine history; models of ships and watercraft; Dir Dr FLORINA H. CAPISTRANO-BAKER.

Makati Museum: J. P. Rizal St, Población, Makati City; tel. (2) 896-0277; native arts and crafts, paintings by contemporary Filipino artists; Curator LINGLING CERVANTES.

Manila

Lopez Memorial Museum: Benpres Bldg, Ground Floor, Exchange Rd, cnr Meralco Ave, Ortigas Centre, Pasig City, Manila; tel. (2) 631-2417; e-mail pezseum@gmail.com; internet www.lopez-museum.org.ph; f. 1960; paintings by the Filipino painters Juan Luna, Felix Resurreccion Hidalgo and others; letters and MSS of Jose Rizal; library of 16,000 vols, including rare Filipiniana; Dir MERCEDES LOPEZ VARGAS.

Malacañang Palace Presidential Museum: J. P. Laurel St, San Miguel, Manila; tel. 521-2301; internet www.op.gov .ph/museum; f. 1993; memorabilia of all former Philippine presidents; Dir MA. EDNA S. GAFFUD.

Metropolitan Museum of Manila: Bangko Sentral ng Pilipinas Complex, Roxas Blvd, Manila 1004; tel. (2) 708-7829; e-mail info@metmuseum.ph; internet metmuseum.ph; f. 1976; fine arts museum: painting, sculpture, graphic arts, decorative arts, prehistoric gold, pottery, contemporary art; Museum Pres. FLORENTINA COLAYCO; Museum Dir SANDRA PALOMAR-QUAN.

Museo ng Arkidiyosesis ng Maynila (MANA): POB 132, 1099 Manila;; tel. (2) 527-7631; e-mail rcam@pldtdsl.net; internet www.rcam.org; f. 1987, fmrly Archdiocesan Museum of Manila; history of the Catholic Church in the Philippines; Dir Fr ALBERT C. A. FLORES.

National Museum of the Philippines: P. Burgos Ave, Padre Burgos St, 1000 Manila; tel. (2) 527-1215; e-mail directornatmuse@ yahoo.com; internet www.nationalmuseum .gov.ph; f. 1901; divs of anthropology, archaeology, botany, geology, zoology, museum education, restoration and engineering, arts, cultural properties, planetarium; 19 br. museums and sites; museology training, workshops, outreach activities, lectures; library of 5,442 vols; Dir JEREMY R. BARNS; Dir CECILIO G. SALCEDO; Dir MAHARLIKA A. CUEVAS; Chief Admin. Officer DIONISIO O. PANGILINAN; publ. *National Museum Papers* (scientific journal, 1 a year).

Attached Sites:

Angono Petroglyphs Site Museum: National Museum, Binangonan Branch, Binangonan, Rizal, (Region IV) Luzon; tel. (2) 527-4192; e-mail nm_asbmd@ yahoo.com; the most ancient Filipino work of art, dating from c. 1000BC; 127 drawings of human and animal figures; declared a nat. cultural treasure.

Balanghai Shrine: National Museum, Butuan Branch, Libertad, Butuan City, Mindanao (Region XIII); e-mail nm_asbmd@yahoo.com; remains of the earliest known watercraft in the country, dating from AD 320.

Bolinao Branch Museum: National Museum, Bolinao Branch, Bolinao, Pangasinan, (Region I) Luzon; e-mail nm_asbmd@yahoo.com; archaeological and general museum; Head GINA DE VERA.

Butuan Branch Museum: National Museum Butuan Branch, Doongan, Butuan City, Mindanao (Region XIII); tel. 527-4192; e-mail nm_asbmd@yahoo.com; archaeological artefacts from Agusan del Norte and ethnographic materials from several local ethnic communities; Head MARGARITA CEMBRANO.

Cagsawa Branch: Albay, Luzon; geological materials from the Mayon volcano, archaeological and ethnographic collns; Head ALICE ALAURIN.

Cotabato City Branch: Cotabato City, Mindanao; ethnographic colln of local tribal materials; Head DANIEL LACERNA.

Fort Pilar Branch Museum: National Museum, Fort Pilar Branch, Fort Pilar, Zamboanga City, Mindanao (Region IX); tel. (2) 527-4192; e-mail nm_asbmd@yahoo .com; f. 1985; material culture of 3 ethnic groups, traditional boats; dioramas depicting 400 species of marine life; Head EUFEMIA CATOLIN.

Fort San Pedro Branch: Cebu City, Cebu; ceramics, archaeological artefacts depicting the history of a sunken 16th-century Spanish galleon; Head VICENTE SECUYA.

Jolo Branch Museum: National Museum, Jolo Branch, Jolo, Sulu, Mindanao; tel. (2) 527-4192; e-mail nm_asbmd@ yahoo.com; material culture of Sulu; Head BELEN UDDIN.

Kabayan Branch: National Museum, Kabayan Branch, Kabayan, Benguet, (Region I) Luzon; tel. (2) 527-4192; e-mail nm_asbmd@yahoo.com; material culture of the Ibalois and the Kankana-ey; Head JULIET IGLOSO.

Kiangan Branch: National Museum, Kiangan Bran, Kiangan, Ifugao, Luzon; tel. (2) 527-4192; e-mail nm_asbmd@yahoo.com; anthropological materials, Ifugao house.

Lubuagan Branch: Lubuagan, Kalinga, Luzon; ethnographic colln on culture of the Kalinga.

Magsingal Branch: National Museum, Magsingal Branch, Vigan City, Ilocos Sur, (Region I) Luzon; tel. (2) 527-4129; e-mail nm_asbmd@yahoo.com; ethnographic colln on the Ilocano people and liturgical arts; Head REMEDIOS PALACPAC.

Peñablanca Branch: Peñablanca, Cagayan, Luzon; finds from the cave sites of Peñablanca.

Puerto Galera Branch: Puerto Galera, Oriental Mindoro, Luzon; archaeological history of Puerto Galera; Head MAMERTO CONTRERAS.

Tabon Cave Complex: National Museum, Quezon Branch, Tawa-tawa, Quezon, Palawan (Region IV); tel. (2) 527-4192; natural heritage of the region; ethnographic materials from 3 local ethnic groups; archaeological artefacts from the Tabon Caves; Head VIVIAN BROWN.

Tuguegarao Branch: Tuguegarao City, Cagayan, Luzon; prehistory of the Cagayan Valley; ethnographic exhibits; Head AIREEN MELAD.

Vigan Branch: National Museum, Vigan Branch, Vigan City, Ilocos Sur, Luzon (Region I); tel. (75) 554-2065; e-mail nm_asbmd@yahoo.com; culture of the Ilocano people through archaeological and ethnographic materials; Head REMEDIOS PALACPAC.

San Agustín Museum: POB 3366, General Luna St, Intramuros, 1002 Manila; tel. (2) 527-4060; f. 1972; located in 400-year-old San Agustín monastery; Hispano-Philippine religious art (paintings, sculptures, etc.); library of 3,000 vols; Dir Dr PEDRO G. GALENDE.

University of Santo Tomas Museum (UST Museum): 3rd Fl., Main Bldg, Univ. of Santo Tomás, España Blvd, Sampaloc 1015 Manila; tel. (2) 781-1815; e-mail museum@mnl.ust.edu.ph; internet www.ustmuseum.ust.edu.ph; f. 1871; sections on natural history, Philippine ethnography, Philippine religious images, coins, medals and memorabilia, visual arts, and archeology; Dir Fr ISIDRO C. ABAÑO; publ. *UST Museum Newsletter* (2 a year).

Marikina City

Philippine Science Centrum: E-Com Bldg, Riverbanks Centre, 84 Andres Bonifacio Ave, Barangka, Marikina City, 1803 Metro Manila; tel. (2) 942-5136; e-mail pfst@science-centrum.ph; internet www.science-centrum.ph; f. 1990; attached to Philippine Foundation for Science and Technology; promotes science education; interactive museum with sections on lights, bodyworks, mathematics, electricity and magnetism, water, vision and perception, bioethics and biotechnology, earth science, space; Exec. Dir MAY PAGSINOHIN; Head of Operations EDICEL HERRERA; publs *DISCOVER!* (4 a year), *PSC Manual of Exhibits* (4 a year).

Pasay City

Cultural Centre of the Philippines Museum/Museo ng Kalinangang Pilipino: CCP Complex, Roxas Blvd, Pasay City, Metro Manila; tel. (2) 832-5094; e-mail museo@culturalcenter.gov.ph; internet www.culturalcenter.gov.ph; f. 1988; traditional Filipino art and traditional Asian musical instruments; exhibitions of modern art; tableaux and artefacts of Philippine traditional and folk cultural practices; lectures by artists and curators; Officer-in-Charge VICTORIA T. HERRERA.

Quezon City

Ateneo Art Gallery: Level 2 Rizal Library Spec. Collns Bldg, Ateneo de Manila Univ., Katipunan Ave, Loyola Heights, 1108 Quezon City; tel. (2) 426-6001; e-mail rtalamayan@ateneo.edu; internet www.ateneoartgallery.org; f. 1960; works by Filipino artists since 1945; Dir and Chief Curator RAMON E. S. LERMA.

Jorge B. Vargas Museum and Filipiniana Research Centre: Roxas Ave, Univ. of the Philippines, Diliman, 1101 Quezon City; tel. (2) 928-1927; e-mail vargasmuseum@gmail.com; internet vargasmuseum.upd.edu.ph; f. 1987; Philippine oil paintings, watercolours, pastels, drawings and sculpture from the 1880s to the 1960s, incl. work by the artists Lorenzo Guerrero, Simon Flores, Juan Luna, Felix Resurrecion Hidalgo, Fabian de la Rosa, Fernando Amorsolo, Jorge Pineda, Vicente Rivera y Mir, Victorio Edades, Juan Aralleno and Diosdado Lorenzo, and by the sculptors Guillermo Tolentino and Graciano Nepomuceno; archives, newspaper cuttings, photographs; colln also incl. Vargas archives and philatelic and numismatic memorabilia; library of 3,193 vols, 1,542 vols of periodicals; Curator Dr PATRICK FLORES.

Universities

ADAMSON UNIVERSITY

900 San Marcelino St, Ermita, 1000 Manila
Telephone: (2) 524-2011
E-mail: glbanaga@adamson.edu.ph
Internet: www.adamson.edu.ph

Founded 1932
Private (Roman Catholic)
Languages of instruction: English, Filipino
Academic year: June to March

Pres.: Fr GREGORIO L. BAÑAGA
Vice-Pres. for Finance: Fr MAXIMINO RENDON
Vice-Pres. for Academic Affairs: Fr FRANCISCO NICOLAS MAGNAYE, JR
Vice-Pres. for Student Affairs: Fr ANDREW BAYAL
Registrar: Sr NILDA IBAÑEZ
Librarian: HELEN DE CASTRO
Library: See Libraries and Archives
Number of teachers: 460
Number of students: 28,390

Publications: *Adamson Chronicle* (12 a year), *Adamson News* (12 a year), *Touchstone* (4 a year)

DEANS

College of Architecture: Arch PETER VILLANUEVA
College of Business Administration: Dr VIRGINIA CALABRIA
College of Education: Dr SERVILLANO MARQUEZ
College of Engineering: JESUS MANALASTAS
College of Law: ANTONIO ABAD
College of Liberal Arts: Dr SERVILLANO MARQUEZ
College of Nursing: Prof. NARESSIA BALLENA
College of Pharmacy: RYAN PEKSON
College of Sciences: Dr GLADIOLA SANTOS
Graduate School: JOSE GENARO YAP-AYSON

AKLAN STATE UNIVERSITY

Banga, Aklan 5601, Western Visayas
Telephone: (36) 267-6567
E-mail: webmaster@asu.edu.ph
Internet: www.asu.edu.ph

Founded 1918 as Capiz Farm School, present name and status 2001
State control
Academic year: June to March

Pres.: Dr BENNY A. PALMA
Vice-Pres. for Academic Affairs: Dr ERSYL T. BIRAY
Vice-Pres. for Admin.: Eng. MERLINE I. MARCELINO
Vice-Pres. for Research, Extension, Training and ICT: ROBERTO L. SALADAR
Univ. Sec.: MICHELLE M. TAN
Dir for Library and Information Technology: EDELINA L. MATEO
Dir for Student Affairs: EDILBERTO L. SOLIDUM

DEANS

College of Agriculture, Forestry and Environmental Sciences: Dr MARILYN E. ROMAQUIN (acting)
College of Fisheries and Marine Sciences: Prof. EDUARDO B. PASTRANA (acting)
College of Hospitality and Rural Resource Management: Prof. MARIVEL S. VILLORENTE (acting)
College of Industrial Technology: Eng. LESLIE S. CABANEZ (acting)
College of Teacher Education: Dr EDNA I. GONZALES
School of Arts and Sciences: Dr MARY EDEN M. TERUEL (acting)
School of Management Sciences: Dr CECILE O. LEGASPI
School of Veterinary Medicine: Dr CECILIA T. REYES (acting)

ANGELES UNIVERSITY FOUNDATION

Angeles City
Telephone: (632) 246-8383
Internet: www.auf.edu.ph

Founded 1962
Private control
Languages of instruction: English, Filipino
Academic year: June to March

Chancellor: Dr EMMANUEL Y. ANGELES
Pres.: JOSEPH EMMANUEL L. ANGELES
Vice-Pres. for Academic Affairs: Dr ARCHIMEDES T. DAVID
Vice-Pres. for Admin.: Prof. SYLVIA M. SORIANO
Vice-Pres. for Finance: Dr LORETO A. CANLAS
Registrar: Prof. MELLANY M. PUNU
Librarian: AMOR MARTIN
Library of 100,000 vols
Number of teachers: 400
Number of students: 8,000

Publications: *Alumnews, AUF Journal, AUF News, Datalink, MPA Perspective, Nurscene, The Pioneer*

DEANS

College of Allied Medical Professions: CONSUELO P. MACALALAD
College of Arts and Sciences: Dr NUNILON G. AYUYAO
College of Business Administration: LEONIDA F. CAYANAN
College of Computer Science: CAESAR R. MAÑALAC
College of Criminology: LUCIA M. HIPOLITO
College of Education: LUCENA P. SAMSON
College of Engineering and Technology: Eng. JOSÉ L. MACAPAGAL, JR
College of Medicine: Dr REYNALDO V. LOPEZ
College of Nursing: ZENAIDA S. FERNANDEZ
Graduate School: Dr CONCESA MILAN BADUEL

Law: JOSE C. VITUG

AQUINAS UNIVERSITY OF LEGAZPI

Rawis, 4500 Legazpi City
Telephone: (52) 482-0540
E-mail: secgen@aq.edu.ph
Internet: www.aq.edu.ph
Founded 1948, present status 1968
Private (Roman Catholic) control
Languages of instruction: Bikol, English, Filipino
Academic year: June to May
Pres.: Very Rev. Dr RAMONCLARO G. MENDEZ
Vice-Pres.: Fr ROBERTO G. REYES
Sec.-Gen.: VIRGILIO S. PERDIGON, Jr
Registrar: LETICIA R. ROQUE
Librarian: JANE L. BEBENG
Library of 54,992 vols
Number of teachers: 237
Number of students: 4,137
Publications: *Aquinas University Research Journal*, *Balintataw* (Mind; student ccl newsletter), *Gimata* (New Moon; Awakening; admin. newsletter), *Tagba* (Harvest; research journal), *Phoenix* (college student organ), *The Prism* (high school student organ)

DEANS

College of Arts, Sciences and Education: Dr SUSAN G. BOBADILLA
College of Business Administration: Dr JEAN C. DELA TORRE
College of Law: Atty EMERSON B. AQUENDE
College of Nursing and Health Sciences: VICENTE B. PERALTA
Graduate School: Dr ROSALINDA B. BARQUEZ
Polytechnic Institute (Engineering, Architecture, Computer Science): MARIA TERESA P. BONDAD

ARELLANO UNIVERSITY

Legarda St, Sampaloc, 2600 Manila
Telephone: 734-7371
E-mail: inp@arellano.edu.ph
Internet: www.arellano.edu.ph
Founded 1938
Language of instruction: English
Private control
Chair. and Pres.: FRANCISCO PAULINO V. CAYCO
Vice-Pres. for Academic Affairs: MARIA TERESA N. RIVERA
Vice-Pres. for Admin.: FLORENTINO S. CAYCO III
Vice-Pres. for Finance: ALMA C. CURATO
Vice-Pres. for Int. Programmes: MARIO F. SALES
Vice-Pres. for Marketing: VALENTE V. CAYCO
Vice-Pres. for Human Resources Div.: FREDERICK G. DEDACE
Registrar: ROLAND A. NIEDO
Librarian: PATRICIA T. CRUZ
Number of teachers: 340
Number of students: 10,330
Publications: *Arellano Standard*, *Philippine Education Quarterly*

DEANS

Arellano Law College: Atty MARIANO M. MAGSALIN
College of Arts and Sciences: CORAZON OSORIO
College of Commerce: FRANCISCO P. CAYCO
College of Education: Dr EDUARDO O. DE LA CRUZ, JR
Florentino Cayco Memorial School of Graduate Studies: MARIA TERESA F. CALDERON
Graduate School: Dr AMPARO S. LARDIZABAL
Graduate School of Nursing: Dr REMEDIOS L. FERNANDEZ

School of Business and Technology: ALEX LAVINIA
School of Law: VIRGILIO B. GESMUNDO

ATENEO DE DAVAO UNIVERSITY

E. Jacinto St, 8016 Davao City
Telephone: (82) 221-2411
E-mail: admissions@addu.edu.ph
Internet: www.addu.edu.ph
Founded 1948
Private control
Language of instruction: English
Academic year: June to March
Pres.: Fr JOEL E. TABORA
Registrar: EDGAR PASCUA II
Dir of Libraries: LEONISA P. SALES
Library of 104,857 vols
Number of teachers: 512 (372 full-time, 140 part-time)
Number of students: 7,925
Publications: *Journal of Business and Governance* (4 a year), *Tambara* (1 a year)

DEANS

College of Engineering and Architecture: Dr RANDELL ESPINA
College of Law: MANUEL P. QUIBOD
College of Nursing: Dr PATRIA MANALAYSAY
School of Arts and Sciences: Fr Dr DANIEL McNAMARA
School of Business and Governance: ARLENE COSAPE

ATENEO DE MANILA UNIVERSITY

POB 154, Manila
Telephone: 426-6001
Internet: www.ateneo.edu
Founded 1859, present status 1959
Languages of instruction: English, Filipino
Private control
Academic year: June to March (2 semesters and a summer term)
Pres.: Rev. JOSE RAMON T. VILLARIN
Vice-Pres. for Admin. and Planning: Dr EDNA P. FRANCO
Vice-Pres. for Finance and Treas.: JOSE SANTOS
Vice-Pres. for Loyola Schools: Dr JOHN PAUL C. VERGARA
Vice-Pres. for Professional Schools: Dr ALFREDO R. A. BENGZON
Dir of Library: LOURDES T. DAVID
Library of 219,562 vols, 309,659 vols of non-print resources, 37 databases, 45,000 ebooks, 25,000 ejournals, 22,801 vols of microforms, 3,872 vols of audiovisual materials
Number of teachers: 1,026 (609 f.t.e.)
Number of students: 8,000
Publications: *Asian Perspectives on the Arts and Humanities*, *Budhi*, *Kritika Kultura*, *Landas—Journal of Loyola School of Theology*, *Loyola Schools Review*, *Philippine Studies*

DEANS

Ateneo Graduate School of Business: ALBERT BUENVIAJE
Ateneo Law School: Atty CESAR VILLANUEVA
Ateneo School of Medicine and Public Health: Dr ALFREDO R. A. BENGZON
John Gokongwei School of Management: RODOLFO P. ANG
School of Government: Dr ANTONIO G. LA VINA
School of Humanities: Dr MARIA LUZ C. VILCHES
School of Science and Engineering: Dr FABIAN C. DAYRIT
School of Social Sciences: Fr JOSE M. CRUZ

BATANGAS STATE UNIVERSITY

Rizal Ave, 4200 Batangas City
Telephone: (43) 778-2170
E-mail: bsu@batstate-u.edu.ph
Internet: www.batstate-u.edu.ph
Founded 1903 as Manual Training School; present name and status 2001
State control
Academic year: June to March
Pres.: Dr ERNESTO M. DE CHAVEZ
Sr Exec. Vice-Pres.: Dr ROLANDO L. LONTOC, Sr
Exec. Vice-Pres.: Dr PORFIRIO C. LIGAYA
Vice-Pres.: Dr MARITESS D. MANLOÑGAT (Academic Affairs), LUZVIMINDA ROSALES (Admin. and Finance), Dr FELIX M. PANOPIO (Extension Campus Operation), Dr JESSIE A. MONTALBO (ICT, Infrastructure Devt and External Affairs), Dr ROLANDO M. LONTOK, Jr (Research, Public Relations, Planning and Devt, and Univ. Sec.)
Dir (Library Services): Prof. ARACELI H. LUNA
Central campuses in Batangas City (Don Pablo Borbon Campuses 1 and 2) and extension campuses in Balayan, Calaca, Lipa City (Don Claro M. Recto Campus), Lobo, Malvar (Jose P. Laurel Polytechnic College Campus), Nasugbu (ARASOF Campus), Padre Garcia, Rosario, San Juan and Taysan

DEANS

College of Accountancy (Don Pablo Borbon Campus 1 and Lipa City): Prof. MARIA CARMEN L. VIDAL
College of Arts and Science: Prof. RACHEL EVANGELIO
College of Engineering (Lipa City): Eng. ERMA QUINAY
College of Engineering, Architecture and Fine Arts (Don Pablo Borbon Campus 2): Prof. ROGELIO A. ANTENOR
College of Industrial Technology (Don Pablo Borbon Campuses 1 and 2): Dr ROLANDO M. LONTOK, Jr
College of Industrial Technology (Balayan, Calaca, and Lipa City Campuses): Prof. MAXIMO PANGANIBAN
College of Liberal Arts: Dr GLORIA G. MENDOZA
College of Physical Education and Human Kinetics: Prof. EDUARDO EVANGELIO
Graduate School: Dr ROLANDO L. LONTOC
School of Business and Economics: Prof. MARITESS D. MANLOÑGAT
School of Developmental Communication: Prof. CYNTHIA Q. MANALO
School of Energy, Earth and Transportation Engineering: Dr JESSIE A. MONTALBO
School of Food and International Hospitality Management: Prof. TERESA KALALO
School of Governance, Peace and Development Studies: Prof. RACHEL EVANGELIO
School of Informatics and Computing Sciences: Dr JESSIE A. MONTALBO

ATTACHED RESEARCH CENTRE

Batangas Centre for Research and Special Studies: Dir Prof. JOCELYN R. CASTILLO

BENGUET STATE UNIVERSITY

La 2601 Trinidad, Benguet
Telephone: (74) 422-2401
E-mail: cip@bsu.edu.ph
Internet: www.bsu.edu.ph
Founded 1916, univ. status 1985
Language of instruction: English
Academic year: June to May
Pres.: Dr CIPRIANO C. CONSOLACION
Vice-Pres.: Dr FRANCO T. BAWANG
Designated Vice-Pres.: Dr MARCOS A. BULIYAT (Academic Affairs), Dr ROGELIO D. COLTING (Research and Extension), Dr TESSIE M. MERESTELA (Planning and Devt)

Dir of Admissions: VIRGINIA R. DUGAT
Dir of Student Affairs: Prof. WILFREDO B. MINA
Registrar: (vacant)
Librarian: Dr NORA J. CLARAVALL
Library of 34,000 vols
Number of teachers: 290
Number of students: 6,598 on degree courses
Publications: *BSU Extension*, *BSU Research Journal*, *Highland Express*, college publications

DEANS

College of Agriculture: Dr DANILO P. PADUA
College of Arts and Sciences: Dr EDNA A. CHUA
College of Engineering and Applied Technology: GENARO W. MACASIEB, Jr
College of Forestry: MELECIO A. BALANGEN
College of Home Economics and Technology: Dr JANE K. AVILA
College of Nursing: Dr FLORENCE C. CAWAON
College of Teacher Education: Dr PERCYVER-ANDA A. LUBRICA
College of Veterinary Medicine: Dr RUTH C. DIEGO
Graduate School: Dr DOMINADOR S. GARIN

BICOL UNIVERSITY

Rizal St, 4500 Legazpi City
Telephone: (052) 480-0167
E-mail: bicol_university1969@yahoo.com
Internet: www.bicol-u.edu.ph
Founded 1970
State control
Languages of instruction: English, Filipino
Academic year: June to May (2 semesters and a summer term)
Campuses in Gubat, Polangui and Tabaco
Pres.: Dr FAY LEA PATRIA M. LAURAYA
Vice-Pres. for Admin.: Dr AMELIA A. DOROSAN
Vice-Pres. for Academic Affairs: Dr HELEN M. LLENARESAS
Vice-Pres. for Resource Generation and Assets Management: Prof. JERRY S. BIGORNIA
Registrar: ERLINDA O. LORINO
Librarian: Prof. NERIA E. GOMEZ
Library of 35,400 vols
Number of teachers: 570
Number of students: 12,600
Publications: *Graduate Forum* (2 a year), *Outreach* (4 a year), *R & D E-Journal* (1 a year, online, journal.bicol-u.edu.ph/index.php/ejournal), *Research Monitor* (2 a year), *The Bicol Universitarian* (4 a year), *The Cassette*, *The Gearcast*, *The Mentor*, *The Net*

DEANS

College of Agriculture and Forestry: Dr MARISSA N. ESTRELLA
College of Arts and Letters: Dr MARIA JULIETA B. BORRES
College of Business Economics and Management: Dr RAMESIS M. LORINO
College of Education: Dr EPIFANIA B. NUÑEZ
College of Engineering: Ing. EDMUNDO O. ESTOR
College of Industrial Technology: Dr ERLINDA C. RELUCIO
College of Medicine: Dr RUBEN CARAGAY
College of Nursing: Dr EMERLINDA E. ALCALA
College of Science: Dr LUCY P. ESTIOKO
College of Social Science and Philosophy: Dr NOEMI L. IBO
Graduate School: Dr NORA L. LICUP
Institute of Physical Education, Sports and Recreation: Prof. MARY LOU C. BORJA

BULACAN STATE UNIVERSITY

Malolos, 3000 Bulacan
Telephone: (44) 791-0153
E-mail: bsu-ice@bulsu.edu.ph
Internet: www.bulsu.edu.ph
Founded 1904 as Bulacan Trade School, present name and status 1993
Regional campuses in Bustos, Hagonoy, Meneses and Sarmiento
State control
Academic year: June to March
Pres.: Dr MARIANO C. DE JESUS
Vice-Pres. for Academic Affairs: Dr DANILO S. HILARIO
Vice-Pres. for Admin. and Finance: EVANGELINA G. CUSTODIO
Vice-Pres. for Planning, Research and Extension: Dr ANTONIO L. DEL ROSARIO
Dean for Student Affairs: NICANOR DE LA RAMA
Registrar: LEILANI M. LIZARDO
Librarian: VIRGINIA C. MIRANDA
Number of teachers: 973 (391 full-time, 582 part-time)
Number of students: 30,873

DEANS

College of Architecture and Fine Arts: SATURNINA PARUNGAO
College of Arts and Letters: VICTOR RAMOS
College of Business Administration: HELEN BAESA
College of Criminal Justice Education: AMANDO VICENTE
College of Education: Dr LUZVIMINDA TANTOCO
College of Engineering: Dr NICANOR DE LA RAMA
College of Home Economics: CECILIA PASCUAL
College of Industrial Technology: Dr ALEXANDER DELA PAZ
College of Information and Communications Technology: FAUSTO HILARIO
College of Law: PASCUAL LACAS
College of Nursing: LOIDA CRESPO
College of Physical Education, Recreation and Sports: RAQUEL MENDOZA
College of Science: NORA TAN
College of Social Sciences and Philosophy: REYNALDO NAGUIT
Graduate School: Dr VICTORIA P. VALENZUELA

CAGAYAN STATE UNIVERSITY

Carig, 3500 Tuguegarao City
Telephone: (78) 844-0107
E-mail: abcortes@scan.com.ph
Founded 1978 by merger of Northern Luzon State College of Agriculture and Cagayan Valley College of Arts and Trades
Academic year: June to March
Colleges of agriculture, arts and sciences, engineering, fisheries, industrial technology, medicine, teacher training, graduate school
Pres.: Dr ARMANDO B. CORTES
Vice-Pres. for Academic Affairs: Dr ELEUTERIO C. DE LEON
Dir for Research: ROMILLO N. TRINIDAD
Number of teachers: 500
Number of students: 10,300
Publications: *CSU Research Journal* (2 a year), *Faculty Journal* (1 a year), *Research Journal of the Graduate School*

CAVITE STATE UNIVERSITY

Bancod, Indang, 4122 Cavite
Telephone: (46) 4150-010
E-mail: cvsu_rc@cavite.net
Founded 1906; fmrly Don Severino Agricultural College; present name and status 1998

Colleges of arts, trades, fisheries; courses in agriculture, business administration, development studies, economics, education, engineering, environmental studies, food technology, hotel and restaurant management, mass communication, mathematics and computer science, natural sciences and technology
Pres.: Dr RUPERTO S. SANGALANG

CEBU NORMAL UNIVERSITY

Osmeña Blvd, Cebu City, 6000 Cebu
Telephone: (32) 253-7915
E-mail: cnu2@cnu.edu.ph
Internet: www.cnu.edu.ph
Founded 1902, as Cebu Normal Secondary School; present name and status 1998
State control
Languages of instruction: English, Filipino
Academic year: June to March
Pres.: Dr MARCELO T. LOPEZ
Vice-Pres. for Academic Affairs: Dr BIBIANA T. ISOK
Vice-Pres. for Admin.: Dr GLEN M. PESOLE
Registrar: FLORDELYNN E. ESCARDA
Dean for Student Affairs: GWENDELINA A. VILLARANTE
Univ. Librarian: Dr MARILYN L. LASPIÑAS
Number of students: 6,910

DEANS

College of Arts and Sciences: Dr FLORIZA N. LAPLAP
College of Nursing: Dr DAISY R. PALOMPON (acting)
College of Teacher Education: Dr FILOMENA T. DAYAGBIL

CENTRAL LUZON STATE UNIVERSITY

Muñoz, 3120 Nueva Ecija
Telephone: (6344) 456-0107
Internet: www.clsu.edu.ph
Founded 1907, attained univ. status 1964
State control
Languages of instruction: English, Filipino
Academic year: June to March
Pres.: Dr RODOLFO C. UNDAN
Vice-Pres.: Dr RUBEN C. SEVILLEJA (Academic Affairs), Prof. REYNALDO S. GUTIERREZ (Admin.), Prof. ONOFRE F. RINGOR (Business Affairs), Dr HONORATO L. ANGELES (Research, Extension and Training)
Dean of Students: Dr ZENAIDA M. SERNA
Dir of Admissions: Dr MELISSA E. AGULTO
Librarian: Prof. CELIA D. DE LA CRUZ
Number of teachers: 373
Number of students: 6,489
Publications: *CLSU Collegian* (2 a year), *CLSU Newsletter* (12 a year), *CLSU Research Digest* (2 a year), *CLSU Scientific Journal* (2 a year)

DEANS

College of Agriculture: Dr FEDERICO O. PEREZ
College of Arts and Sciences: Dr MARILOU G. ABON
College of Business Administration and Accountancy: Dr DANILO S. CASTRO
College of Education: Dr DANILO G. TAN
College of Engineering: Dr IRENEO C. AGULTO
College of Fisheries: Dr ARSENIA G. CAGAUAN
College of Home Science and Industry: Dr HILARIA T. CUARESMA
College of Veterinary Science and Medicine: Dr JESUS S. DE LA ROSA
Institute of Graduate Studies: Dr CYNTHIA C. DIVINA

CENTRAL MINDANAO UNIVERSITY

University Town, Musuan, 8710 Bukidnon
Telephone: (88) 356-1910
E-mail: cmu.musuan@eudora.com
Internet: www.cmu.edu.ph
Founded 1952 as the Mindanao Agricultural
College; Univ. 1965
State control
Languages of instruction: English, Filipino
Academic year: June to March (2 semesters
and a summer school)
Pres.: Dr MARDONIO M. LAO
Vice-Pres.: Dr EMMANUEL A. LARIOSA (Aca-
demic Affairs), Dr PORFERIO M. BALANAY
(Admin.), Dr HERMINIO M. PAUA (Research
and Extension)
Registrar: Prof. NELLIE C. LASTIMOSA
Librarian: Prof. ESTHER E. DINAMPO
Library of 23,000 vols
Number of teachers: 311
Number of students: 5,371
Publications: *CMU Journal of Food, Agricul-
ture and Nutrition* (4 a year), *Barangay
Balita* (4 a year), *Newsletter* (4 a year)

DEANS

College of Agriculture: Dr CELSO C. TAUTHO
College of Arts and Sciences: Dr CECILIA B.
AMOROSO
College of Education: Dr MARINA I. LIZARDO
College of Engineering: Prof. REYNALDO G.
JUAN
College of Forestry: Dr JAMES O. LACANDULA
College of Home Economics: Dr NERISSA A.
MACARAYAN
College of Veterinary Medicine: Dr JOSE
ALEXANDER C. ABELLA
Graduate School: Dr EVELYN L. BARRIDO

CENTRAL PHILIPPINE UNIVERSITY

POB 231, 5000 Iloilo City

Telephone: (33) 329-1971
E-mail: admin@cpu.edu.ph
Internet: www.cpu.edu.ph
Founded 1905
Language of instruction: English
Private control
Academic year: June to March (2 terms)
Pres.: Dr TEODORO C. ROBLES
Treas.: ROSALENE J. MADERO
Vice-Pres. for Academic Affairs: ELMA S.
HERRADURA
Registrar: RUTH G. FERNANDEZ
Dir for Libraries: MELDA L. ESTEMBER
Number of teachers: 280
Number of students: 9,300
Publications: *Centralite, Link, Southeast
Asia Journal*

DEANS

College of Agriculture Resources and Envir-
onmental Sciences: Dr REYNALDO N.
DUSARAN
College of Arts and Sciences: LYNN J. PAREJA
College of Business and Accountancy: Dr
TERESITA E. CRUCERO
College of Computer Studies: Dr CIRILO C.
CALIBJO
College of Education: NELSON A. POMADO
College of Engineering: WALDEN S. RIO
College of Hospitality Management: PERLA A.
SUYO
College of Law: ZACARIAS BEDONA
College of Medicine: Dr GLENN A. M. CATE-
DRAL
College of Nursing: LILY LYNN V. SOMO
College of Theology: BERNABE C. PAGARA
School of Graduate Studies: FELY P. DAVID

CENTRO ESCOLAR UNIVERSITY

9 Mendiola St, San Miguel, Manila
Telephone: (2) 735-5991
E-mail: ceu1@galileo.fapenet.org
Internet: www.ceu.edu.ph
Founded 1907
Languages of instruction: English, Filipino
Private control
Academic year: June to March
Pres.: Dr ROSITA L. NAVARRO
Vice-Pres.: Dr ROSITA L. NAVARRO (Academic
Affairs, concurrent with Univ. Presidency),
LUCILA C. TIONGCO (Alumni Affairs), CAR-
MELITA E. LA O' (Business Affairs), Dr
MARIA L. AYUYAO (Exec.), JOSEPHINE E.
MAPE (Finance)
Registrar: LUCIA D. GONZALES
Librarian: Dr TERESITA G. HERNANDEZ
Number of teachers: 800
Number of students: 22,691
Publications: *Academe, Ciencia y Virtud* (4 a
year), *Graduate and Faculty Studies* (1 a
year), *Rose and the Leaf* (1 a year), *The
Clarion* (4 a year)

DEANS

College of Dentistry: Dr RENATO M. SISON
College of Medical Technology: Dr PRISCILLA
A. PANLASIGUI
College of Nursing: MERLINA V. LOCQUIAO
College of Optometry: Dr JESSICA L. FLOR
College of Science: Dr ZENAIDA M. AUSTRIA
Graduate School: Dr ROSITA L. NAVARRO
School of Accountancy, Business, Secretarial
and Public Administration: Dr CONRADO E.
IÑIGO, Jr
School of Arts and Humanities: Dr CECILIA G.
VALMONTE
School of Education, Music and Social Work:
Dr PAZ I. LUCIDO
School of Pharmacy: Dr OLIVIA M. LIMUACO
School of Tourism, Family Economics and
Nutrition: Dr CARMINA P. CATAPANG

DE LA SALLE UNIVERSITY

2401 Taft Ave, Malate, 1004 Manila
Telephone: (2) 523-4148
E-mail: quebengcoc@dlsu.edu.ph
Internet: www.dlsu.edu.ph
Founded 1911
Private control
Languages of instruction: English, Filipino
Academic year: May to April
Pres.: Bro. ARMIN A. LUISTRO
Chancellor: Dr CARMELITA I. QUEBENGCO
Vice-Chancellor for Academics: Dr JULIUS B.
MARIDABLE
Vice-Chancellor for Admin.: Dr CARMELITA I.
QUEBENGCO
Vice-Chancellor for Research: Dr WYONA C.
PATALINGHUG
Asst Vice-Chancellor for Academic Services:
AGNES G. YUHICO
Asst Vice-Chancellor for Campus Services:
ENRICO J. CORDERO
Asst Vice-Chancellor for Campus Devt: AUR-
ELLANO O. DE LA CRUZ, Jr
Registrar: EDWIN P. SANTIAGO
Dir of Library: ANA MARIA B. FRESNIDO
Library of 258,591
Number of teachers: 950
Number of students: 14,400 (12,000 under-
graduate, 2,400 postgraduate)
Publications: *Asia–Pacific Education
Researcher* (2 a year), *Asia-Pacific Social
Science Review* (2 a year), *DLSU Business
and Economics Review* (2 a year), *Ideya* (2
a year), *Journal of Research in Science,
Computing and Engineering* (3 a year),
Malay (2 a year), *URCO Digest* (3 a year)

DEANS

College of Business and Economics: Dr
MYRNA S. AUSTRIA
College of Computer Studies: Dr CASLON L.
CHUA
College of Education: Dr ROSE MARIE SALA-
ZAR-CLEMEÑA
College of Engineering: Dr PAG-ASA D. GAS-
PILLO
College of Liberal Arts: Dr ANTONIO P.
CONTRERAS
College of Science: Dr GERARDO C. JANAIRO

PROFESSORS

ABELLA, L. C., Chemical Engineering
AUSTRIA, M. S., Economics
AZCARRAGA, A. P., Software Technology
BERNARDO, A. B. I., Counselling and Educa-
tional Psychology
CABRERA, E. C., Biology
CARANDANG, J. S. R. V., Biology
CLAVERIA, F. G., Biology
CONTRERAS, A. P., Political Science
CORPUZ, C. C., History
CRUZ, I. R., Literature
CULABA, A. B., Mechanical Engineering
DADIOS, E. P., Manufacturing Engineering
Management
DEL MUNDO, JR, C. A., Communication
DIESTO, S. D., Mathematics
EDRALIN, D. M., Business Management
ESTAÑERO, R. A., Civil Engineering
EVASCO-PERNIA, M., Literature
GALLARDO, S. M., Chemical Engineering
GARCIA, JR, L. R., Marketing Management
GASPILLO, P. D., Chemical Engineering
GERVACIO, S. V., Mathematics
GRIPALDO, R. M., Philosophy
HILA, A. C., History
INTAL, JR, P. S., Economics
JANAIRO, G. C., Chemistry
LAMBERTE, E. E., Behavioural Sciences
LICUANAN, W. R. Y., Biology
MAGLAYA, A. B., Mechanical Engineering
ORETA, A. W. C., Civil Engineering
PALISOC, S. T., Physics
PASCASIO, A. A., Mathematics
PATALINGHUG, W. C., Chemistry
PRUDENTE, M. S., Science Education
RAGASA, C. Y., Chemistry
ROBLES, JR, A. C., International Studies
ROCES, S. A., Chemical Engineering
SALAZAR-CLEMEÑA, R. M., Counselling and
Educational Psychology
SANTOS, P. V. M., Literature
SISON, R. C., Software Technology
TULLAO, JR, T. S., Economics
UNITE, A. A., Economics

DON MARIANO MARCOS MEMORIAL STATE UNIVERSITY

Bacnotan, 2515 La Union
Telephone: (72) 888-5677
Internet: www.dmmmsu.edu.ph
Founded 1960 as La Union Agricultural
School; present name and status 1980
State control
Academic year: June to March
Pres.: Dr ERNESTO R. GAPASIN
Vice-Pres. (Academic Affairs): Dr AMELIA O.
BACUNGAN
Vice-Pres. (Admin.): (vacant)
Vice-Pres. (Planning and Devt): Dr ELVI C.
BUGAOAN
Vice-Pres. (Research and Public Relations):
Dr FLORENTINA S. DUMLAO

HEADS OF OPERATING UNITS

Apiculture Training and Development Cen-
ter: Dr APOLONIO S. SITO (Dir)
Graduate College: Dr NORMA B. NATINO
(Dean)
Mid La Union Campus: Dr RODOLFO R. APIGO
(Chancellor)

North La Union Campus: Dr ORLANDO O. ALMOITE (Chancellor)
Open University System: Dr CONCEPCION L. BEDERIO (Dir)
Sericulture Research Development Institute: Dr RICARDO C. BRIONES (Dir)
South La Union Campus: Dr INOCENCIO I. MANGAOANG, Jr

EASTERN VISAYAS STATE UNIVERSITY

Salazar St, Quarry Dist., 6500 Tacloban
Telephone: (53) 321-1084
E-mail: helpdesk@evsu.edu.ph
Internet: www.evsu.edu.ph
Founded 1965 as Leyte Institute of Technology; Univ. status 2004
State control
Languages of instruction: English, Filipino
Pres.: DOMINADOR O. AGUIRRE
Vice-Pres. for Academic Affairs: SEGUNDA A. LACABA
Vice-Pres. for Admin.: MA. SOCORRO C. GICAIN
Vice-Pres. for Research and Extension Services: MANUEL L. PACAÑA
Registrar: GREGORIA C. DELA CRUZ
Librarian: ERLINDA G. AYLES

DEANS

College of Architecture and Allied Discipline: DEANNA B. FUENTES
College of Arts and Sciences: EVANGELINE Z. HIDALGO
College of Business and Entrepreneurship: FELIXBERTO E. AVESTRUZ (acting)
College of Education: ROSARIO E. GARCIA
College of Engineering: DANILO B. PULMA
College of Technology: MA. CRISTINA I. CAINTIC
Graduate School: EVANGELINE H. CAYANONG

FAR EASTERN UNIVERSITY

POB 609, Manila
Nicanor Reyes St, Sampaloc, Manila
Telephone: (2) 735-5621
E-mail: registrar@feu.edu.ph
Internet: www.feu.edu.ph
Founded 1928 as Institute of Accountancy, incorporated in 1934 as Far Eastern Univ.
Private control
Language of instruction: English
Academic year: June to March
Pres.: Dr MICHAEL M. ALBA
Sr Vice-Pres. for Academic Affairs: Dr MARIA TERESA TRINIDAD P. TINIO
Vice-Pres. for Corporate Affairs: Atty GIANNA R. MONTINOLA
Vice-Pres. for Academic Services: Dr MIGUEL M. CARPIO
Vice-Pres. for Academic Devt: Dr AUXENCIA A. LIMJAP
Vice-Pres. for Facilities and Technical Services: Eng. RUDY M. GASPILLO
Registrar: GRACE C. SIPIN (acting)
Chief Librarian: TERESITA C. MORAN
Library: see under Libraries and Archives
Number of teachers: 1,300
Number of students: 25,100
Publications: Ambon (1 a year), Arts and Science Review (2 a year), Cultural Forum (irregular), Far Eastern University Journal (2 a year), Papers Etcetera (2 a year), Transition (1 a year)

DEANS

Institute of Accounts, Business and Finance: Dr CELITO C. MACACHOR
Institute of Architecture and Fine Arts: Dr LORELEI D. C. DE VIANA
Institute of Arts and Sciences: Dr MYRNA P. QUINTO
Institute of Education: Dr ELSA F. GERARDO

Institute of Graduate Studies: JOVITO B. CASTILLO (Co-ordinator)
Institute of Law: Atty MELENCIO STA. MARIA
Institute of Nursing: Dr BELINDA BUENAFE
Institute of Tourism and Hotel Management: Dr MELINDA D. TORRES

FOUNDATION UNIVERSITY

6200 Dumaguete City
Telephone: (35) 422-9167
E-mail: op@foundationu.com
Internet: www.foundationu.com
Founded 1949
Language of instruction: English
Private control
Academic year: June to March (2 semesters)
Pres.: Dr MIRA D. SINCO (acting)
Vice-Pres. for Academic Affairs: Dr EVA C. MELON
Vice-Pres. for Finance and Admin.: VICTOR VICENTE G. SINCO
Vice-Pres. for Student Life and External Affairs: DINNO WILLIE D. DEPOSITARIO
Registrar: GLENE MAY D. LUSARES
Librarian: LILIBETH D. BUSLON
Library of 55,023 vols
Number of teachers: 169
Number of students: 4,000
Publications: Foundation Time (12 a year), FU Recorder (12 a year), Graduate Journal (2 a year), Greyhound (Magazine), Law Forum (2 a year), Pillar (1 a year), University Recorder (2 a year)

DEANS

College of Agriculture: LILIAN P. SUMAGAYSAY
College of Arts and Sciences: Dr MIRA D. SINCO
College of Business and Economics: Dr EVA C. MELON
College of Education: Dr THELMA E. FLORENDO
College of Law and Jurisprudence: ELEUTERIO E. CHIU (RETD)
College of Nursing: NENITA P. TAYKO
Graduate School: Dr APARICIO H. MEQUI
Habalo School of Hospitality Management: CHARLOTTE V.
School of Computer Studies: DAE P.
School of Industrial Engineering: Eng. MARLON A. TANILON

DE LA SALLE ARANETA UNIVERSITY

Araneta University Post Office, Malabon, Metro, 1404 Manila
Telephone: 366-9053
E-mail: gauf@gauf.curricula.net
Internet: www.dlsau.edu.ph
Founded 1946; reorganized as a foundation 1965; current name adopted 2002
Private control
Languages of instruction: English, Filipino
Academic year: June to March

Colleges of arts, science and technology, business, education, graduate studies, veterinary medicine and agricultural science
Pres.: Bro. NARCISCO S. ERGUIZA, JR
Exec. Vice-Pres.: Dr ROSENDA A. DE GRACIA
Vice-Chancellor. for Academics and Research: Dr ROSEMARIE L. MONTAÑANO
Vice-Chancellor. for Admin.: CHRISTOPHER N. POLANCO
Vice-Chancellor. for Students and Missions: MARIE ALLISON E . PARPAN
Registrar: Prof. TERESITA R. GUTIERREZ
Librarian: Prof. FELISA W. DADOR
Number of teachers: 160
Number of students: 3,000
Publications: Araneta Research Journal (4 a year), Compendium of Veterinary Research (1 a year), Harvest (1 a year), The Philippine Veterinarian (4 a year), Tinig (12 a year)

ISABELA STATE UNIVERSITY

San Fabian, Echague, 1318 Isabela
Telephone: 22013
Internet: isu.edu.ph
Founded 1978
State control
Language of instruction: English
Academic year: June to April
Pres.: Dr ALETH M. MAMAUAG
Vice-Pres. for Academic Affairs: Dr EDMUND C. GUMPAL
Vice-Pres. for Admin. and Finance: Dr RELLI PABLEO
Vice-Pres. for Research, Devt and Training: Dr WILLIAM MEDRANO
Registrar: THELMA T. LANUZA
Librarian: ROMULA P. ROMERO
Library of 11,818 vols
Number of teachers: 477
Number of students: 4,340
Publications: CVIARS Monitor, Forum, Geyser, Hexachord, Mediator, Research Journal

DEANS

College of Agriculture: Dr FLORANTE BALICO
College of Arts and Sciences: Dr WILLIAM EUSTAQUIO
College of Business Accountancy and Public Administration: Dr ROBINSON M. PEREZ
College of Engineering: Dr JOEL ALCARAZ
College of Forestry: Dr TOMAS C. REYES
College of Teacher Education: Dr ELIZA P. DELA CRUZ
Graduate Studies: Dr CATALINA M. RODRIGO
School of Development Communication: Dr THERESA M. AGGABAO
School of Veterinary Medicine: Dr JULPHA M. AGUSTIN

LEYTE NORMAL UNIVERSITY

Paterno St, Tacloban City, 6500 Leyte
Telephone: (53) 321-2176
Internet: lnu.evis.net.ph
Founded 1921 as Leyte Normal School; present name and status 1995
State control
Academic year: June to March
Colleges of arts and sciences, commerce, education, engineering and management, development and entrepreneurship
Pres.: Dr CRESCENCIA V. CHAN-GONZAGA
Publication: LNU Research Journal (1 a year)

MANILA CENTRAL UNIVERSITY

Edsa, 1400 Caloocan
Telephone: 364-1071
Internet: www.mcu.edu.ph
Founded 1904
Private control
Language of instruction: English
Academic year: June to March
Pres.: Dr ARISTOTLE T. MALABANAN
Vice-Pres. for Academic Affairs: Dr LYDIA L. TAGANGUIN
Vice-Pres. for Admin. Affairs: Dr RENATO C. TANCHOCO, Jr
Dir for Finance: MILA PEREZ
Registrar: AINI SALVADORA
Librarian: OPHELIA ENRIQUEZ
Number of teachers: 240
Number of students: 5,500
Publications: Gold and Purple, Research Journal, The Pharos, The Pulse

DEANS

College of Arts and Sciences: Dr Eva Javier
College of Business Administration: Dr Dennis Sandoval
College of Dentistry: Dr Jerome Alcazaren
College of Medical Technology: Petrona Benitez
College of Medicine: Dr Divina Beato
College of Nursing: Dr Lina Salarda
College of Optometry: Dr Francisco Baetiong, Jr
College of Pharmacy: Maricon Boie
College of Physical Therapy: Eduardo Peregrino
Graduate School: Dr Jose Mallari
School of Midwifery: Dr Lina Salarda

MANUEL L. QUEZON UNIVERSITY

1015 R. Hidalgo, Quiapo, 1001 Manila
Telephone: (2) 734-0121
E-mail: mlq@mlqu.edu.ph
Internet: www.mlqu.edu.ph

Founded 1947

Pres.: Atty Eduardo D. de Los Angeles
Vice-Pres. for Academic Affairs: Atty Antonio A. Agustin
Vice-Pres. for Admin.: Arq. Ma. Victoria O. Chan
Vice-Pres. for Planning and Devt: Candido S. Dizon
Registrar: Gregorio A. del Valle
Chief Librarian: Prof. Flordeliza M. Torres
Number of teachers: 290
Number of students: 8,350

Publications: *Junior Quezonian, MLQU Graduate Journal, MLQU Law Quarterly*

DEANS

School of Accountancy and Business Arts: Virginia C. Corpuz (acting)
School of Architecture: Arq. Rudy O. Ferrer
School of Criminal Justice: Angelito Q. Tan
School of Education, Arts & Sciences: Dr Erlinda G. Dejarme
School of Engineering: Eng. Rogelio M. Avenido
School of Graduate Studies: Dr Nilda G. Woolsey
School of Information Technology: Dr Carlo B. Monterey
School of Law: Atty Antonio A. Agustin

MARIANO MARCOS STATE UNIVERSITY

No 16 Quiling Sur, Batac 2906, Ilocos Norte
Telephone: (77) 792-3191
E-mail: op@mmsu.edu.ph
Internet: www.mmsu.edu.ph

Founded 1978
State control
Language of instruction: English
Academic year: June to March

Pres.: Dr Miriam E. Pascua
Vice-Pres. for Academic Affairs: Dr Wilma C. Natividad
Vice-Pres. for Admin. and Business: Atty Ramon A. Leaño
Vice-Pres. for Research, Extension and Linkages: Dr Prima Fe R. Franco
Registrar: Dr Felina J. Isaac
Librarian: Prof. Lucena R. Felipe
Library of 55,511 vols
Number of teachers: 500
Number of students: 12,000

Publication: *S & T Journal* (2 a year, print and online, research.mmsu.edu.ph/journal)

DEANS

College of Agriculture, Food and Sustainable Devt: Dr Artemio B. Alcoy

College of Aquatic Science and Applied Technology: Prof. Facundo B. Asia
College of Arts and Sciences: Dr Marivic M. Alimbuyuguen
College of Business, Economics and Accountancy: Prof. Lorna Olivia F. Salmasan
College of Engineering: Eng. Edmund Edison A. Esteban
College of Health Sciences: Dr Manolita S. Crisostomo
College of Industrial Technology: Prof. Cesario Y. Pacis
College of Law: Ramon A. Leaño (acting)
College of Teacher Education: Dr Eliza T. Samson
Graduate School: Dr Joselito L. Lolinco

ATTACHED CENTRES

Climate Resilient Agriculture: tel. (77) 670-1898; e-mail natzalibuyog@yahoo.com; Head Dr Nathaniel R. Alibuyog

Gender and Development: gender related research.

Ilocos Agriculture and Resources Research and Development Consortium (ILARRDEC): tel. (77) 792-3420; f. 1979 as Ilocos Agricultural Research Center (ILIARC); current name adopted 1988; farmers information and technology services (FITS), 18 agencies; affiliated renewable energy, business resources and devt, regional centre for Filipino language and regional centre for poverty studies; Dir Prof. Leonardo T. Pascua.

Higher Education Regional Research Centers (HERRC): tel. (77) 670-1898; e-mail mmsu_herrc@gmail.com; CHED (Commission on Higher Education) Teaching Excellence and Centre for Iloko and Amianan Studies; Dir Dr Nathaniel R. Alibuyog.

Intellectual Property Office: tel. (77) 792-3507; regional centre for bio-energy research and Tuklas Lunas Devt Centre for Luzon; Dir Dr Dionisio S. Bucao

MINDANAO STATE UNIVERSITY

MSU Campus, 9700 Marawi City
Telephone: (63) 352-1002
E-mail: op@msumain.edu.ph
Internet: www.msumain.edu.ph

Founded 1961
Language of instruction: English
Academic year: June to May

Pres.: Dr Camar A. Umpa
Exec. Vice-Pres. and Chancellor: Dr Datumanong A. Sarangani
Vice-Pres. for Academic Affairs: Prof. Yusoph Latip
Vice-Pres. for Admin. and Finance: Dr Datumanong Sarangani (acting)
Vice-Pres. for Planning and Devt: Prof. Saidale Mohamad
Registrar: Jessie Silang
Librarian: Lawansan Mangorac

Number of teachers: 1,220
Number of students: 12,000

Publications: *Alumni Monitor, CSSH Graduate Research Journal, Darangen, Mindanao Arts and Culture Professional Papers Publication, Mindanao Journal, Mindanao Varsitarian* (12 a year), *Ongangen, OVCRE Bulletin, Pagsibol, Piglas, Unirescent*

DEANS

College of Agriculture: Dr Camar Mikunug
College of Business Administration: Dr Merlyn Tan
College of Education: Dr Pendililang Gunting
College of Engineering: Prof. Rodrigo Baid (acting)

College of Fisheries: Dr Julieta Lagmay
College of Forestry and Environmental Sciences: Dr Gerardo Gavine
College of Health Sciences: Dr Mindamora Mutin
College of Hotel and Restaurant Management: Dr Cecille Mambuay
College of Law: Basari D. Mapupuno
College of Medicine: Dr Angelo Manalo
College of Natural Sciences and Mathematics: Prof. Rambe Ramel
College of Public Affairs: Dr Nasroden Guro
College of Social Sciences and Humanities: Prof. Bonifacio R. Tacata
College of Sports and Physical Recreation: Prof. Hasan Maranda
Graduate School: Dr Cosain Derico
Institute of Science Education: Dr Emerita Moti
King Faisal Centre for Islamic and Arabic Studies: Prof. Talib Benito
Regional Science Training Centre: Dr Dolores Pattuinan
School of Information Technology: Dr Pepe L. Madrid

ATTACHED INSTITUTE OF TECHNOLOGY

Iligan Institute of Technology of the Mindanao State University

Andres Bonifacio Ave, Tibanga, 9200 Iligan City

Telephone: (63) 221-4056
E-mail: mpsalazar50@gmail.com
Internet: www.msuiit.edu.ph

Founded 1968
State control
Languages of instruction: English, Filipino
Academic year: June to April

Chancellor: Prof. Marcelo P. Salazar
Vice-Chancellor for Academic Affairs: Dr Arnulfo P. Supe
Vice-Chancellor for Admin. and Finance: Dr Polaus M. Bari
Vice-Chancellor for Research and Extension: Dr Olga M. Nuñeza
Registrar: Dr Lydie D. Paderanga
Librarian: Meles F. Castillano

Library of 58,975 vols
Number of teachers: 490
Number of students: 7,778

Publications: *Gazette* (4 a year), *Mindanao Forum* (1 a year)

DEANS

College of Arts and Social Sciences: Prof. Nora A. Clar
College of Business Admin.: Dr Julita W. Bokingo
College of Education: Prof. Esmar N. Sedurifa
College of Engineering: Dr Feliciano B. Alagao
College of Science and Mathematics: Dr Jinky B. Bornales
Integrated Development School: Dr Manuel B. Barquilla
School of Engineering Technology: Prof. Santiago R. Evasco
School of Graduate Studies: Dr Jerson N. Orejudos

NATIONAL UNIVERSITY

551 Mariano F. Jhocson St, Sampaloc, 1008 Manila

Telephone: (2) 743-7951
Internet: www.national-u.edu.ph

Founded 1900
Language of instruction: English
Private control
Academic year: June to March

Pres.: TEODORO JHOCSON-OCAMPO
Registrar: LETICIA J. PAGUIA
Head of Graduate Studies: ZENAIDA N. MAGIBA
Librarian: CONSUELO J. MIGUEL

DEANS

College of Architecture: FERNANDO ABAD
College of Civil, Chemical and Sanitary Engineering: ROMULO D. COLOMA
College of Commerce: LETICIA J. PAGUIA (acting)
College of Dentistry: Dr GREGORIO D. GABRIEL
College of Education: DOMINGO L. DIAZ
College of Electrical, Industrial and Mechanical Engineering: ROMULO D. COLOMA
College of Liberal Arts: ZENAIDA N. MAGIBA
College of Pharmacy: CELIA V. LANSANG

NAVAL STATE UNIVERSITY

Naval, 6543 Biliran
Telephone: (53) 500-9045
E-mail: nsu_oicpres@yahoo.com
Internet: www.nsu.edu.ph
Founded 1972 as Naval Institute of Technology; univ. status 2009
State control

Pres.: Dr MINERVA EBAJAN SAÑOSA
Vice-Pres. for Admin.: NENITA S. SEREÑO
Vice-Pres. for Academic and External Affairs: Dr SUSAN S. BENTOR
Vice-Pres. for Planning, Research, Extension and Production Services: Dr JOHN ANTHONY D. ROMAGOS
Registrar: Dr NISA T. LUMBAB
Librarian: CONCEPCION M. GAYRAMA
Library of 10,000 vols
Number of teachers: 386
Number of students: 6,421

DEANS

College of Arts and Sciences: Dr ROLAND A. NIEZ
College of Education: Dr VICTOR C. CAÑEZO, JR
College of Engineering: Dr ROSSINI B. ROMERO
College of Industrial, Information, and Communication Technology: Dr NORMA M. DUALLO
College of Maritime Education: Capt. FEDERICO P. JAMIN
College of Tourism: Dr ERLINDA F. RALAR
Graduate School: Dr SUSAN S. BENTOR

NUEVA ECIJA UNIVERSITY OF SCIENCE AND TECHNOLOGY

Gen. Tinio St, 3100 Cabanatuan City, Central Luzon
Telephone: (44) 463-1201
E-mail: president@nuest.edu.ph
Internet: www.nuest.edu.ph
Founded 1929 as Nueva Ecija Trade School; present name and status 1998
State control
Academic year: June to March

Campuses at Fort Magsaysay, Gabaldon, San Isidro and Sumacab; Colleges of arts and science, business and management technology, computer studies, education, engineering and industrial technology; Graduate School

Pres.: Dr GEMILIANO C. CALLING

PALAWAN STATE UNIVERSITY

Tiniguiban Heights, 5300 Puerto Princesa City
Telephone: (48) 433-2379
Internet: www.psu.itgo.com

Founded 1972 as Palawan Teacher's College; present name and status 1994
State control
Academic year: June to March
Pres.: Dr TERESITA L. SALVA
Exec. Vice-Pres.: Dr CARLOS A. ALCANTARA
Vice-Pres. for Academic Affairs: Dr ELIZABETH J. MAGAY
Vice-Pres. for Admin.: MARILYN GONZALES PABLICO
Vice-Pres. for Finance: DESTIDCHADO S. VILLASARIO
Registrar: VENERANDA L. LAGROSA
Univ. Librarian: LOURDES C. SALVADOR

PAMANTASAN NG LUNGSOD NG MAYNILA
(University of the City of Manila)

Intramuros, 1002 Manila
Telephone: (2) 527-7941
E-mail: info@plm.edu.ph
Internet: www.plm.edu.ph
Founded 1965
State control
Languages of instruction: English, Filipino
Academic year: June to March (2 semesters); summer term for graduate schools; trimestral for graduate programmes in management and engineering

Pres. (CEO): Atty ARTEMIO TUQUERO
Exec. Vice-Pres. (Chief Operating Officer): Dr VIRGINIA SANTOS
Vice-Pres. for Academic Affairs: Dr OLIVER STA. ANA
Vice-Pres. for Admin.: ELSA MARTINEZ
Vice-Pres. for Finance and Planning: ANGELITA SOLIS
Univ. and Board Sec.: Atty CARLOS CARLOS
OSDS Dean: Atty ALEXANDER ERESE
Registrar: BERNADETTE SACOP
Univ. Treas.: ANGELES RAMOS
Chief Librarian: FE HAICO
Library of 70,000 vols, 3,400 periodicals
Number of teachers: 822 incl. 301 full-time, 521 part-time
Number of students: 10,048

Publications: CAE Digest, Pantas, PLM Research Bulletin, PLM Review, PLM Star Post

DEANS

College of Accountancy and Economics: Prof. ELOISA MACALINAO
College of Architecture and Urban Planning: GIL C. EVASCO
College of Engineering and Technology: Eng. JUAN TALLARA, JR
College of Human Development: JIMMY ROMERO
College of Law: Atty ERNESTO P. MACEDA, JR
College of Liberal Arts: Dr ERLINDA CAYAO
College of Management and Entrepreneurship: Prof. NEIL GAMUS
College of Mass Communication: Prof. LUDMILA R. LABAGNOY
College of Medicine: Dr ANCHELA BIAG
College of Nursing: Dr GILMORE SOLIDUM
College of Physical Education, Recreation and Sports: Dr SUSAN C. MERCADO
College of Physical Therapy: Prof. PRIME ROSE TEODULICE M. LANETE
College of Science: Prof. ROBERTO DELA CRUZ
College of Tourism, Hotel and Travel Industry Management: Dr OLIVER A. PANDILE
Emeritus College: Prof. ESPERANZA BAUTISTA
Graduate School of Arts, Sciences, Education and Nursing: Dr FLORDELIZA FERRER
Graduate School of Engineering: Eng. FELIX F. ASPIRAS
Graduate School of Law: ANGELINA SANDOVAL-GUTIERREZ
Graduate School of Management: Dr ROSALINDA EVANGELISTA

PANGASINAN STATE UNIVERSITY

Alvear St, Lingayen, Pangasinan
Telephone: (75) 542-4261
E-mail: webadmin@psu.edu.ph
Internet: www.psu.edu.ph
Founded 1979
State control
Languages of instruction: English, Filipino
Academic year: June to May

9 Campuses in Alaminos, Asingan, Bayambang, Binmaley, Infanta, Lingayen, San Carlos, Santa Maria and Urdaneta

Pres.: Dr VICTORIANO C. ESTIRA
Vice-Pres. for Academic Affairs: Dr MANOLITO C. MANUEL
Vice-Pres. for Research and Auxillary Services: Dr HONORIO L. CASCOLAN
Vice-Pres. for Admin. and Planning: ALEX N. MORES
Vice-Pres. for Business and Resource Generation: Dr ARTEMIO M. REBUGIO
Dean of Graduate School: Dr ZENAIDA U. SUYAT
Librarian (Lingayen): ARACELI P. UNTALAN
Library of 50,000 vols
Number of teachers: 310
Number of students: 5,830

Publications: Banyuhay (2 a year), PSU Chronicle, PSU Graduate School Journal, Research and Extension Bulletin (4 a year), The Aqua Sounds, The Farm Breeze, The Golden Harvest, The Green Hills, The Ocean View, The Reflections, The Technologist, The Technotrends

PARTIDO STATE UNIVERSITY

San Juan Bautista, Goa, 4422 Camarines Sur
Telephone: (54) 453-0235
E-mail: psu-goa@asia.com
Internet: ecommunity.ncc.gov/psu
Founded 1941 as Partido High School; present name and status 2001
State control
Academic year: June to March

Campuses in Caramoan, Lagonoy, Sagñay, Salogon, San Jose and Tinambac; depts of business education, engineering, graduate studies, teacher education and technology

Pres.: Dr MODESTO D. DETERA
Vice-Pres. for Academic Affairs: Dr MINDA P. FORMALEJO
Vice-Pres. for Admin.: LEONCIO P. OBIAS

PHILIPPINE NORMAL UNIVERSITY

Taft Ave, Cnr Ayala Blvd, 1000 Manila
Telephone: (2) 527-0374
Internet: www.pnumanila.com.ph
Founded 1901; present name and status 1991
State control
Academic year: June to March
Pres.: Dr NILO L. ROSAS

PHILIPPINE WOMEN'S UNIVERSITY

1743 Taft Ave, 1004 Manila
Telephone: (2) 4651-777
E-mail: registrar@pwu.edu.ph
Internet: www.pwu.edu.ph
Founded 1919
Private control
Language of instruction: English
Academic year: June to March
Chair. of the Board of Trustees: Hon. HELENA Z. BENITEZ
Pres.: Dr JOSE FRANSISCO BENITEZ
Chancellor, Cavite Campus: Dr AMELIA REYES
Chancellor, Manila Campus, and Vice-Pres. for Academic Affairs: Dr DOLORES LASAN

Chancellor, Quezon City Campus: Dr SYLVIA MONTES
Vice-Pres. for Admin. and Finance: JULITA DADO
Vice-Pres. for Planning, Devt and External Affairs: ENCARNACION RARALIO
Registrar: Dr LIWAYWAY O. DAPITO
Librarian: DIONISIA ANGELES
Library: see under Libraries and Archives
Number of teachers: 479
Number of teachers: 480
Number of students: 10,700
Publications: *Journal on the Environment and Habitat, Journal on Women's Health, Philippine Educational Forum* (2 a year), *PWU Research Journal* (2 a year), *The Maroon and White* (1 a year), *The Philwomenian* (12 a year)

DEANS

Conrado Benitez Institute of Business Education: Dr LORENZO LORENZO
Helena Z. Benitez School of International Relations and Diplomacy: ROSARIO MANALO
Philippine School of Social Work: Dr NENITA M. CURA
School of Arts and Sciences: Dr MELISSA ALCAZAREN
School of Education: Dr ADELAIDA ALMEIDA
School of Fine Arts and Design: JOSEPHINE TURALBA
School of Food Science and Technology: LIGAYA BRAGANZA
School of Habitat and Environment: LEONORA GONZALES
School of Hospitality Management: Dr LIGAYA BRAGANZA
School of Medical Technology: Dr NINI LIM
School of Music: KRISTINA BENITEZ (Officer-in-Charge)
School of Nursing: EDNA DOMINGUEZ
School of Nutrition: Dr LEONORA PANLASIGUI
School of Pharmacy: Dr JULIET UY
School of Tourism: Dr EVELYN B. PANTIG

POLYTECHNIC UNIVERSITY OF THE PHILIPPINES

Anonas St, Sta Mesa, 1016 Manila
Telephone: (2) 716-7832
E-mail: registrar@pup.edu.ph
Internet: www.pup.edu.ph
Founded 1904
State control
Languages of instruction: English, Filipino
Academic year: June to March
Pres.: EMANUEL C. DE GUZMAN
Exec. Vice-Pres.: MANUEL M. MUHI
Vice-Pres. for Academic Affairs: Dr SAMUEL M. SALVADOR
Vice-Pres. for Admin.: ALBERTO C. GUILLO
Vice-Pres. for Student Services: JUAN C. BIRION
Vice-Pres. for Finance: MARISSA J. LEGASPI
Vice-Pres. for Research, Extension, Planning and Devt: MANUEL M. MUHI
Vice-Pres. for Branches and Campuses: JOSEPH MERCADO
Registrar: FLORDELIZA E. ALVENDIA
Library Officer: DIVINA T. PASUMBAL
Library of 205,400 vols
Number of teachers: 1,400
Number of students: 43,000
Publications: *BISIG, Campus Circular, CLMC Update, Graduate Forum, Journal of Economics and Politics* (4 a year), *Journal of Open and Distance Education, PUP Monograph* (1 a year), *PUP Open University Newsletter* (12 a year), *PUP Studies, The Catalyst* (12 a year), *Trends* (4 a year)

DEANS

College of Accountancy and Finance: SYLVIA A. SARMIENTO

College of Architecture and Fine Arts: Arq. TED VILLAMOR G. INOCENCIO
College of Arts and Letters: Dr JOSEFINA U. PARENTELA
College of Business Administration: LEOPOLDO FRANCISCO T. BRAGAS
College of Communication: EDNA T. BERNABE
College of Computer and Information Sciences: Prof. GISELA MAY A. ALBANO
College of Education: Prof. MILAGRINA A. GOMEZ
College of Engineering: GUILLERMO O. BERNABE
College of Human Kinetics: REMUS M. LAGLAGARON
College of Languages and Mass Communication: Prof. WILHELMINA N. CAYANAN
College of Law: Atty GEMY LITO L. FESTIN
College of Office Administration and Business Teacher Education: Prof. AVELINA C. BUCAO
College of Physical Education and Sports: Prof. MARIPRES P. PASCUA
College of Political Science and Public Administration: SANJAY P. CLAUDIO
College of Science: THERESITA V. ATIENZA
College of Social Sciences and Development: NENITA F. BUAN
College of Tourism, Hospitality and Restaurant Management: SHEILA M. SISON-GANCHERO
Graduate School: EMANUEL C. DE GUZMAN
Institute of Technology: Eng. DANTE V. GEDARIA

RAMON MAGSAYSAY TECHNOLOGICAL UNIVERSITY

Iba, Zambales 2201, Central Luzon
Telephone: (47) 811-1683
E-mail: rmtupresident@rmtu.edu.ph
Founded 1910; present name and status 2001
State control
Courses in biology, education, engineering, hotel and restaurant management, mathematics and computer science, psychology, public administration, technology
Academic year: June to March
Pres.: Dr FELICIANO S. ROSETE

RIZAL TECHNOLOGICAL UNIVERSITY

Boni Ave, 1550 Mandaluyong City
Telephone: (2) 533-6041
E-mail: riztech@mnl.cyberspace.com.ph
Founded 1969
State control
Academic year: June to March
Courses in architecture, business administration, education, engineering, English, industrial and organizational psychology, mathematics, natural sciences, political science, statistics, technology
Pres.: Dr JOSÉ Q. MACABALLUG

SAINT LOUIS UNIVERSITY

POB 71, 2600 Baguio City
Telephone: (74) 442-2793
E-mail: picrodir@slu.edu.ph
Internet: www.slu.edu.ph
Founded 1911
Private control (Roman Catholic)
Languages of instruction: English, Filipino
Academic year: June to March (2 semesters)
Pres.: Fr PAUL VAN PARIJS
Vice-Pres. for Academic Affairs: Engr JOSE MARIA PANGILINAN
Vice-Pres. for Admin.: ARNULFO SORIANO
Vice-Pres. for Finance: EVANGELINE O. TRINIDAD
Registrar: VIOLETA GARCIA

Dean, Student Affairs: GIL ESPIRITU
Dir of Libraries (College-Level): VIRGILIO C. FUERTE
Library of 107,214 vols
Number of teachers: 669
Number of students: 23,584
Publications: *Buhay SLU* (12 a year), *Cordillera Researches and Studies* (1 a year), *SLU Chronicle* (4 a year), *SLU Research Journal* (2 a year)

DEANS

College of Accountancy and Commerce: NOEL B. DE LEON
College of Education: ROQUE Q. BERNARDEZ
College of Engineering and Architecture: JOSELITO BUHANGIN
College of Human Sciences: TERESITA AZARCON
College of Information and Computing Sciences: RANDY FLORES
College of Law: CEAZAR ORACION
College of Medicine: ROBERTO LEGASPI
College of Natural Science: GAUDELIA A. REYES
College of Nursing: MARY GRACE LACANARIA

SILLIMAN UNIVERSITY

6200 Dumaguete City, Negros Oriental
Telephone: (35) 422-6002
E-mail: oip@su.edu.ph
Internet: www.su.edu.ph
Founded 1901
Private control
Language of instruction: English
Academic year: June to May
Pres.: Dr BEN S. MALAYANG, III
Vice-Pres. for Academic Affairs: Dr BETSY JOY B. TAN
Vice-Pres. for Devt: Prof. JANE ANNETTE L. BELARMINO
Vice-Pres. for Finance and Admin.: Prof. CLEONICO Y. FONTELO
Registrar: ANNABELLE E. PAA
Librarian: LORNA TUMULAK-YSO
Library: see under Libraries and Archives
Number of teachers: 430
Number of students: 9,000
Publications: *Convergence* (1 a year), *Educator* (every 5 years), *Graduate Currents, Infoline* (12 a year), *Ingenium* (2 a year), *Insights* (2 a year), *Nurse* (2 a year), *Sands and Corals* (literary magazine, 1 a year), *Scoop* (1 a year), *Silliman Journal* (humanities, social sciences and sciences, 2 a year), *Sillimanian Magazine* (1 a year), *Stones and Pebbles* (1 a year), *SUCN Abstracts* (irregular)

DEANS

College of Agriculture: Dr JOSE EDWIN C. CUBELO
College of Arts and Sciences: Dr MARGARET HELEN U. ALVAREZ
College of Business Administration: Prof. JANE ANNETTE L. BELARMINO
College of Computer Studies: Dr DAVE E. MARCIAL
College of Education: Dr EARL JUDE PAUL L. CLEOPE
College of Engineering and Design: Dr TESSIE A. CABIJE
College of Law: MIKHAIL LEE MAXINO
College of Mass Communication: Dr MARIA CECILIA M. GENOVE
College of Nursing: Prof. FLORENDA F. CABATIT
College of Performing and Visual Arts: Dr ELIZABETH SUSAN V. SUAREZ
Divinity School: Dr LOPE B. ROBIN
Graduate Programme: Dr BETSY JOY B. TAN
Institute of Clinical Laboratory Sciences: Prof. TEODORA A. CUBELO (Dir)

Institute of Rehabilitative Sciences: Dr Lyn L. Olegario (Dir)
Medical School: Dr Jonathan C. Amante
School of Basic Education: Dr Earl Jude Paul L. Cleope
School of Public Affairs and Governance: Dr Reynaldo Y. Rivera

SOUTHWESTERN UNIVERSITY

Villa Aznar, Urgello St, 6000 Cebu

Telephone: (32) 415-5555
E-mail: president@swu.edu.ph
Internet: www.swu.edu.ph

Founded 1946
Private control
Languages of instruction: English, Filipino
Academic year: June to March

Pres.: Dr Elsa A. Suralta
Vice-Pres. for Academic Affairs: Dr Carmen M. Eturma
Vice-Pres. for Admin.: Jonah P. Lafuente
Registrar: Francisco B. Bacalla
Librarian: Virginia P. Mollaneda

Number of teachers: 540
Number of students: 10,800

Publications: SWU Graduate School Journal (1 a year), SWU Research Digest (2 a year)

DEANS

College of Arts and Sciences: Arceli P. Villacarlos
College of Commerce: Flordelis R. Rivera
College of Computer Studies: Ira T. Pongasi
College of Criminal Justice Education: Belinda R. Comahig
College of Dentistry: Rodivick O. Docor
College of Engineering: Concordia L. Naldoza
College of Medical Technology: Marvi D. Niog
College of Medicine: Dr Marilyn T. Zarraga
College of Nursing: Dr Belinda R. Rosales
College of Optometry: Ruth M. Ortiz
College of Pharmacy: Marilou S. Basa
College of Veterinary Medicine: Dr Jocelyn A. Tingson
Graduate School: Dr Alicia P. Cabatingan
Maritime College: Capt. Reynaldo M. Abella
School of Business: Cecille O. Rasada

TARLAC STATE UNIVERSITY

Romulo Blvd, Tarlac City, 2300 Tarlac

Telephone: (45) 982-0110
E-mail: tsu@mozcom.com.ph

Founded 1906 as Tarlac Trade School; present name and status 1989
State control
Academic year: June to March

Courses in architecture, business administration, education, engineering, fine arts, journalism, mathematics and computer science, natural sciences, nutrition, social sciences, technology, theatre

Pres.: Dr Dolores G. Matias

TECHNOLOGICAL UNIVERSITY OF THE PHILIPPINES

POB 3171, Ayala Blvd, Ermita, Metro Manila

Telephone: (2) 523-2293
Internet: www.tup.edu.ph

Founded 1901
State control
Languages of instruction: English, Filipino
Academic year: June to March

Pres.: Dr Fedeserio C. Camarao
Vice-Pres. for Academic Affairs: Prof. Josefino P. Gascon

Vice-Pres. for Admin. and Finance: Prof. Radames M. Doctor
Vice-Pres. for Planning and Devt: Prof. Perla S. Roxas
Vice-Pres. for Research and Extension: Dr Emiliana V. R. Tadeo
Dir, TUP Cavite: Prof. Enrico R. Hilario
Dir, TUP Taguig: Dr Federico Ramos
Dir, TUP Visayas: Dr Leoncio Jamera
Registrar: Dr Milagros I. Cachola
Library Dir: Dr Wilhelmina G. Borjal

Library: see Libraries and Archives
Number of teachers: 573
Number of students: 18,915

Publications: Philippine Journal of Industrial Education and Technology (2 a year), TUP.com (4 a year), TUP Graduate Journal (1 a year)

DEANS

College of Architecture and Fine Arts: Dr Dionisio A. Espression, Jr
College of Engineering: Prof. Florencio G. Balanay, Jr
College of Industrial Education: Dr Olympio V. Caparas
College of Industrial Technology: Prof. Buenaventura V. Sabater
College of Liberal Arts: Dr Marcelo B. Apar
College of Sciences: Dr Adora S. Pili

PROFESSORS

Agbayani, J., Economics
Alto, R., Education
Apar, M., Filipino
Arrieta II, C., Tool and Die Technology
Baluyut, F., Education
Belen, V., English
Belgica, A., Career Education
Buaquiña, V., Mathematics
Cachola, M., Foods
Calo, R., Physical Education
Camaro, G., Research, Life Sciences, Ecology
Caparas, O., Industrial Arts
De Leon, L., Education
Delos Reyes, V., Education
Dimayuga, Z., Education
Domantay, D., Education
Gabriel, P., English
Galang, E., Family and Community Education
Garino, N., Electrical Technology, Technology Management
Gatmaytan, R., Chemistry
Gollayan, R., Chemistry
Graza, N., Mechanical Engineering
Hilario, E., Education
Huang, A., Mathematics
Ignacio, M., Mathematics
Imlan, J., Public Administration
Janier, J., Mathematics
Joaquin, A., Drafting Technology
Labuguen, F., Foods
Lejano, B., Civil Engineering
Macam, Jr, V., Civil Engineering
Manalastas, J., Civil Engineering
Manalastas, S., Chemistry Education
Mangao, F., Mathematics
Matic, V., Chemistry
Mendoza, M., Social Studies
Obnamia, C., English, Journalism, Education
Pacio, A., Mathematics Education
Pangan, M., Mathematics
Pangilinan, M., Social Studies
Pereda, P., Education
Perez, J., Sociology
Pili, A., Chemistry
Rivera, A., Education
Rolluqui, G., Electronic Engineering Technology, Computer Technology
Saltivan, L., Physics
Tabanera, M. D., Physics
Tracena, M., English
Valderrama, L., Public Administration
Velas, F., Cultural Affairs

Verayo, E., Education
Villamejor, S., English
Zaratan, L., Education Research

UNIVERSITY OF BAGUIO

General Luna Rd, 2600 Baguio City

Telephone: (74) 442-3071
E-mail: ub@ubaguio.edu
Internet: www.ubaguio.edu

Founded 1948 as a Technical School
Private control; granted deregulated status by the Philippine Comm. on Higher Education
Languages of instruction: English, Filipino
Academic year: June to March

Pres.: Herminio C. Bautista
Vice-Pres. for Academic Affairs: Dr Perfecto M. Lopez
Vice-Pres. for Admin.: Dr Rebecca C. Cajilog
Registrar: Eng. Melba E. Baliwan
Librarian: Birgit S. Santiago

Library of 75,223 vols
Number of teachers: 415
Number of students: 18,085

Publications: The Leaven (4 a year), University of Baguio Journal (2 a year)

DEANS

College of Commerce: Mary Haydee Agnes E. Dabucol
College of Dentistry: Dr Veronica S. Garcia
College of Education: Dr Agnes T. Bautista
College of Engineering: Eng. Renato D. Tandoc
College of Hotel and Restaurant Management: Jane P. Liu
College of Information and Communications Technology: Eng. Lakan-asa R. Bautista
College of Law: Daniel T. Fariñas
College of Liberal Arts: Dr Teresita De Guzman
College of Medical Technology: Constantino Wi
College of Nursing: Catalina B. Alinduza
College of Physical Therapy and Optometry: Esmerelda M. Gatchallan
Graduate School: Dr Agnes T. Bautista
Law Enforcement Academy: Dr Miller F. Peckley

UNIVERSITY OF EASTERN PHILIPPINES

6400 University Town, Northern Samar

Telephone: (55) 251-8611
E-mail: admin@uep.edu.ph
Internet: www.uep.edu.ph

Founded 1918
State control
Languages of instruction: English, Filipino
Academic year: June to March

Pres.: Dr Mar P. De Asis
Vice-Pres. for Academic Affairs: Dr Felisa L. Sanico
Vice-Pres. for Admin. and Finance: Dr Baltazar Martires
Vice-Pres. for External Affairs: Dr Mindanilla B. Broto
Vice-Pres. for Research and Extension: Dr Rolando A. Delorino
Registrar: Dr Rogelio Banagbanag
Librarian: Fe G. Baoy

Library of 22,823 vols
Number of teachers: 496
Number of students: 9,492

Publications: The Pacific Journal of Science and Technology, The Pillar, UEP Graduate Journal

DEANS

College of Agriculture: Pio Tuan

College of Arts and Communication: Dr ESTRELLITA PINCA
College of Business Administration: Dr AURORA CALADES
College of Education: Dr RONATO BALLADO
College of Engineering: ROMEO D. ATENCIO
College of Law: Atty MARLON FRITZ BROTO
College of Nursing: Prof. MA. LINDA S. AGUS
College of Science: Dr ABRAHAM HERIALES
College of Veterinary Medicine: Dr GERRY CAMER
Graduate School: Dr VIRGINIA BALANON

UNIVERSITY OF MANILA

546 Dr M. V. de los Santos St, Sampaloc, 1008 Manila
Telephone: 741-3637
E-mail: admin@um.edu.ph
Internet: www.um.edu.ph
Founded 1913
Private, non-sectarian instn
Language of instruction: English
Academic year: June to May (three terms)
Pres.: Dr VIRGILIO DE LOS SANTOS
Exec. Vice-Pres.: Atty ERNESTO LL. DE LOS SANTOS
Vice-Pres. for Academic Affairs: Dr EMILY D. DE LEON
Registrar: Dr VIRGILIO DE LOS SANTOS
Chief Librarian: CORAZON G. PAYTE
Number of teachers: 250
Number of students: 7,500
Publications: *The Gold Leaf, The UM Law Gazette, The University of Manila Graduate School Journal*

DEANS

College of Business Administration and Accountancy: NELSON S. ABELEDA
College of Criminology: FORTUNATO S. RIVERA
College of Education: EMILY D. DE LEON
College of Engineering: ARSENIO A. RONQUILLO
College of Foreign Service: BENJAMIN D. QUINERI
College of Law: MICHAEL P. MORALDE
College of Liberal Arts: ROSALIA V. MOLINA
Graduate Studies: EMILY D. DE LEON

UNIVERSITY OF MINDANAO

Bolton St, Davao City, Mindanao
Telephone: (82) 227-5456
E-mail: um@mozcom.com
Internet: www.umindanao.edu.ph
Founded 1946
Private control
Language of instruction: English
Academic year: June to March
Pres.: GUILLERMO P. TORRES, JR
Exec. Vice-Pres. for Academic Affairs: Dr PEDRO B. SAN JOSE
Exec. Vice-Pres. for Operations: GLORIA E. DETOYA
Sr Vice-Pres. for Academic Planning and Services: Dr EUGENIO S. GUHAO, JR
Sr Vice-Pres. for Treasury: SANDRA G. ANGELES
Vice-Pres. for ICT: EDGARDO O. CASTILLO
Vice-Pres. for Institutional Affairs: MARIA JULIETA R. TORRES
Vice-Pres. for Physical Plant: FELICISIMO RAMOS
Vice-Pres. for Student Personnel Services/Registrar: Dr CARMENCITA E. VIDAMO
Number of teachers: 620
Number of students: 19,720
Publications: *Communique, Journal of Arts and Sciences, The Frontier, Journal of the Graduate School, UM Research and Publication Journal*

DEANS

Arts and Sciences: GERLIETA S. RUIZ
College of Architecture: ILUMINADO C. QUINTO
College of Business Administration: VICENTE SALVADOR E. MONTAÑO
College of Criminology: Dr CARMELITA B. CHAVEZ
College of Education: Dr MARILOU T. LOZARITA (Asst Dean)
College of Engineering: LEO LARGO
College of Law: MELCHOR QUITAIN
College of Nursing: OFELIA B. LARIEGO
Graduate School: EUGENIO S. GUHAO
Technical School: GERARDO SALAS

UNIVERSITY OF NEGROS OCCIDENTAL-RECOLETOS

Lizares Ave, POB 214, 6100 Bacolod City
Telephone: 433-2449
E-mail: unorpro@yahoo.com
Internet: www.uno-r.edu.ph
Founded 1941
Private control
Language of instruction: English
Academic year: June to March
Pres.: Fr DIONISIO CACHERO
Comptroller: Fr EDUARDO CELIZ
Registrar: Dr CARMENDA LEONORAS
Librarian: ARABELLA M. ANANORIA
Number of teachers: 330
Number of students: 7,879
Publications: *The Tolentine Star* (2 a semester), *UNO-R Journal of the Graduate School (Raison d'Etre)* (4 a year)

DEANS

College of Arts and Sciences: NIEVES HIBALER-PEPITO
College of Business and Accountancy: Dr JOHN CLIFFORD SALUGSUGAN
College of Criminal Justice Education: JASMIN PARRENO
College of Education: Dr OFELIA POSECION
College of Engineering: Eng. CHRISTOPHER G. TACLOBOS
Elementary Dept: SUNYA PHI SUMALDE
Graduate School: JOEL A. ALVE
High School Dept: SOL ABELLAR
School of Agriculture: Dr EVANGELINE O. ABOYO
School of Law: Atty JOHN PAOLO VILLASOR

UNIVERSITY OF NORTHERN PHILIPPINES

Vigan, Ilocos Sur
Telephone: (77) 722-2810
E-mail: op@unp.edu.ph
Internet: www.unp.edu.ph
Founded 1965
State control
Languages of instruction: English, Filipino
Pres.: Dr GILBERT R. ARCE
Vice-Pres. for Academic Affairs: LUMEN H. ALMACHAR
Vice-Pres. for External Affairs: JIMMY R. SORIA
Dir of Research: Prof. PETRONILA E. FLORENDO
Registrar: SEGUNDINA S. AGAM
Head of Library Services: VICENTA R. PILORIN
Library of 28,369 vols
Number of teachers: 390
Number of students: 7,020
Publications: *New Vision* (4 a year), *Tandem* (6 a year), *UNP Research Journal* (1 a year)

DEANS

College of Architecture: FATIMA NICETAS R. ALONZO

College of Arts and Sciences: MARIE ROSE Q. RABANG
College of Business Administration and Accountancy: CRISTINA R. BUNDOC
College of Criminology: TRINIDAD P. ROJO
College of Engineering: REY M. BASILIO
College of Fine Arts: ASHLEY S. MARTINEZ
College of Health Sciences: LARGUITA P. REOTUTAR
College of Information Technology: MILAGROS R. REMULAR
College of Law: GILBERT R. ARCE (Officer-in-Charge)
College of Social Work: AGUSTIN B. GUINID
College of Nursing: BRIGIDA F. DE LEON
College of Teacher Education: AGUSTINA R. TACTAY
College of Technology: JOSELITO A. TOTAAN
Graduate School: GORGONIA N. PINOL

UNIVERSITY OF NUEVA CACERES

Jaime Henandez Ave, 4400 Naga
Telephone: (54) 472-6100
Internet: www.unc.edu.ph
Founded 1948
Private control
Languages of instruction: English, Filipino
Academic year: June to March (two semesters)
Also college of education
Pres.: Dr DOLORES H. SISON
Exec. Vice-Pres.: PERFECTO O. PALMA
Vice-Pres. for Admin.: JAIME HERNÁNDEZ, Jr
Registrar: NELIA E. SAN JOSE
Librarian: Dr PERPETUA S. PORCALLA
Number of teachers: 330
Number of students: 8,060
Publications: *Nueva Caceres Bulletin* (6 a year), *Nueva Caceres Review, Red and Gray* (1 a year), *Sed Vitae* (1 a year), *The Trailblazer* (12 a year)

DEANS

College of Arts and Sciences: Dr JOSEPHINE B. ALBA
College of Business and Accountancy: Dr NORA ELIZABETH F. MANIQUIZ
College of Engineering: MAXIMINO O. PANELO, Jr
College of Law and Commerce: PERFECTO O. PALMA
School of Graduate Studies and Research: MILAGROS Z. REYES

PROFESSORS

ALMOITE, G. E. O., Public Administration
ANONAS, L. S., Methods of Research
BARIAS, A. M.
CADAG, D., Engineering Management, Highway Engineering, Water Resources Engineering, Hydrology
CONDA, A., Development of the Novel
ENOJADO, V. F., Human Relations, Principles of Guidance
EVORA, M., Electrical Engineering, Refrigeration Engineering
FORTUNO, R. Z., Production, Planning Control
GROYON, S., Psychology
PALMA, M. B., Civil Procedure, Special Proceedings
PORCALLA, P., Library Science
REYES, M., Educational Planning, Personnel Administration, Inferential Statistics
SEPTIMO, C., Power Plant Design, Steam Power Engineering, Industrial Plant Design

UNIVERSITY OF PANGASINAN

Arellano St, Dagupan City
Telephone: (75) 522-5635
E-mail: info@upang.phinma.edu.ph
Internet: www.up.phinma.edu.ph

Founded 1925; Univ. status 1968
Private control
Languages of instruction: English, Filipino
Academic year: June to March

Pres.: MELITON B. SALAZAR, JR
Chief Academics Officer: FRANCIS L. LARIOS
Chief Finance Officer: DAISY C. MONTINOLA
Chief Operations Officer: MARK C. MACA-
VENTA
Dean of Faculty and Academic Affairs: LIB-
ERTY SORIANO
Registrar: ALBERT F. AQUINO
Librarian: IDA F. ROSARIO

Library of 20,500 vols
Number of teachers: 220
Number of students: 10,340

Publication: *The Researcher* (2 a year)

DEANS

College of Arts and Sciences: SHEILA P.
CAYABYAB
College of Criminal Justice Education:
JOSEPH O. MEJIA
College of Education: Dr JOSEPH O. MEJIA
College of Engineering and Architecture:
JOHN T. ZAMORA
College of Health Sciences: M. TERESA R.
FAJARDO
College of Information Technology Educa-
tion: Dr ARISTOTLE B. LIWANAG
College of Law: ALBINO L. GONZALES
College of Management and Accountancy:
CHRISTINE O. RESULTAY
College of Social Sciences: JOSEPH O. MEJIA
Graduate School: Dr ALELI N. CORNISTA

UNIVERSITY OF RIZAL SYSTEM

URS Tanay Main Campus, J. P. Rizal St,
Sampaloc, Tanay, 1980 Rizal

Telephone: (2) 401-4900URS Morong Campus, Sumulong St, Morong, 1960 Rizal

Telephone: (2) 653-1735
E-mail: urstanay_main@yahoo.com
Internet: www.urs.edu.ph

Founded 1959 as Rizal Agricultural School;
present name and status 2001
State control
Academic year: June to May (2 semesters)

Number of teachers: 15,407
Number of students: 582

Pres.: Dr OLIVIA F. DE LEON
Vice-Pres. for Academic Affairs: Dr ARACELI
M. BOBADILLA
Vice-Pres. for Admin. and Finance: Dr DEME-
TRIA A. SAN JUAN
Vice-Pres. for Research, Devt, Extension and
Production: Dr HERMY D. ESTRABO
Chancellor for Cluster 1 (Tanay, Cardona,
Rodriguez): Dr ALLEN U. BAUTISTA
Chancellor for Cluster 2 (Morong, Cainta,
Taytay): Dr RENEECILIA B. PAZ DE LEON
Chancellor for Cluster 3 (Angono, Antipolo,
Binangonan, Pililla): Dr GLORIA P. SARABIA

CAMPUS DIRECTORS

URS Main Campus (Tanay): Dr FLORIE B.
GAPIDO
URS Angono: Dr ROWENA A. LAROZA
URS Antipolo: Prof. ALLEN U. BAUTISTA
URS Binangonan: Dr DEMETRIA A. SAN JUAN
URS Cainta: Dr MANUEL S. ORDONEZ
URS Morong: Dr HERMY D. ESTRABO
URS Pililla: Dr GLORIA P. SARABIA
URS Rodriguez: Dr TERESITA BUENVIAJE

UNIVERSITY OF SAN AGUSTÍN

General Luna St, 5000 Iloilo City
Telephone: (33) 337-4841
E-mail: info@usa.edu.ph
Internet: www.usa.edu.ph

Founded 1904, Univ. status 1953

Private control
Languages of instruction: English, Filipino
Academic year: June to March

Pres.: Fr RAUL M. MARCHAN
Vice-Pres. for Academic Affairs: Fr GENEROUS
P. GONESTO
Vice-Pres. for Admin.: Fr EDGARDO L. LAZO
Vice-Pres. for Student Affairs: Fr PEDERITO
A. APARECE
Registrar: GEMMA B. HALILI
Librarian: EPIFANIA A. PACLIBAR

Number of teachers: 524
Number of students: 10,250

Publications: *Augustinian Interdisciplinary
Journal* (2 a year), *Augustinian Legacy* (1 a
year), *Augustinian Research Journal* (1 a
year), *Communitas* (2 a year), *The Augustinian* (6 a year), *The Augustinian Mirror*
(2 a year)

DEANS

College of Arts and Sciences: Dr ISIDORO
CRUZ
College of Business Admin. and Account-
ancy: Dr LUCIO ENCIO
College of Commerce: NEOMISIA GONZALES
College of Education: Dr ALEX FACINABAO
College of Engineering and Architecture: Ing.
REYNALDO ASUNCION
College of Law: JUANA JUDITA P. NAFARRETE
College of Nursing: SOFIA COSETTE MONTE-
BLANCO
College of Pharmacy and Medical Technol-
ogy: VICTORIA SUSTENTO
Conservatory of Music: Fr JONAS MEJARES
Graduate School: Dr RUBY CATALAN

UNIVERSITY OF SAN CARLOS

6000 Cebu City
P. del Rosario St, Cebu City, 6000
Telephone: (32) 253-1000
E-mail: president@usc.edu.ph
Internet: www.usc.edu.ph

Founded 1595, present status 1948
Private control
Language of instruction: English
Academic year: June to March (2 terms)

Pres.: Fr DIONISIO M. MIRANDA
Vice-Pres. for Academic Affairs: Fr ANTHONY
SALAS
Vice-Pres. for Admin.: Fr ELENO BUCIA
Vice-Pres. for Finance: Fr GENEROSO RICARDO
Jr REBAYLA
Registrar: ROMEO E. YAP
Dir of Library System: MAXIE DOREEN L.
CABARRON

Library of 309,446 vols, 42,024 periodicals
Number of teachers: 1,051 (810 full-time,
241 part-time)
Number of students: 18,824

Publications: *Journal of Business Studies* (2
a year), *Philippine Quarterly of Culture
and Society* (4 a year), *Philippine Scientist*
(1 a year), *USC Graduate Journal* (2 a
year)

DEANS

College of Architecture and Fine Arts:
JOSEPH MICHAEL P. ESPINA
College of Arts and Sciences: Dr RAMON S.
DEL FIERRO
College of Education: Dr ANTONIO E. BATO-
MALAQUE
College of Engineering: ANDRESA S. ALLERA
School of Business and Economics: Dr CHALL-
ONER MATERO
School of Health Care Professions: ANTONIA
F. PASCUAL
School of Law and Governance: Atty ALEX L.
MONTECLAR

UNIVERSITY OF SAN JOSE-RECOLETOS

Cnr Magallanes and P. Lopez Sts, 6000 Cebu
City

Telephone: (32) 253-7900
E-mail: usjr@usjr.edu.ph
Internet: www.usjr.edu.ph

Founded 1947, univ. status 1984
Private (Roman Catholic) control
Language of instruction: English
Academic year: June to March

Pres.: Rev. Fr CONSTANTINO B. REAL
Vice-Pres. for Admin.: Rev. Fr CORNELIO E.
MORAL
Vice-Pres. for Academics: Rev. Fr SIXTO M.
BITANGJOL
Vice-Pres. for Business and Finance: Rev. Fr
LEONARDO P. PAULIGUE
Vice-Pres. for Student Welfare: Rev. Fr
ANTHONY A. MORILLO
Dir of Basak Campus: Rev. Fr RAUL M.
BUHAY
Registrar: DEMETRIO QUIRANTE
Librarian: EVELYN A. LIM

Library of 190,000 vols
Number of teachers: 500
Number of students: 13,000

Publications: *Faculty Research Journal* (1 a
year), *Forward* (1 a year), *Josenian* (1 a
year), *Precedent* (2 a year), *USJ-R Journal
of Research* (Graduate School publication,
2 a year), *USJ-R Updates* (newsletter, 4 a
year)

DEANS

College of Arts and Sciences: Dr CORAZON A.
TAN
College of Commerce: Dr SUSAN CHUNG
College of Education: Dr ALMA ANG
College of Engineering: Dr EVANGELINE EVAN-
GELISTA
College of Law: ALICIA E. BATHAN
College of Nursing: RAOUL
Graduate School: (vacant)
Grade School Department: PURA S. WAGAS
High School Department: SONIA F. PAGLINA-
WAN
Religious Education Centre: Fr CORNELIO E.
MORAL

UNIVERSITY OF SANTO TOMAS

España St, Manila
Telephone: 731-3101
E-mail: opa@mnl.ust.edu.ph
Internet: www.ust.edu.ph

Founded 1611
Private control
Academic year: June to March

Chancellor: Rev. Fr BRUNO CADORÉ
Vice-Chancellor: Rev. Fr GERARD FRANCISCO
P. TIMONER
Rector: Rev. Fr HERMINIO V. DAGOHOY
Vice-Rector: Prof. CLARITA D. L. CARILLO
Vice-Rector: Rev. Fr RICHARD G. ANG
Vice-Rector for Finance and Treasurer: Rev.
Fr MANUEL F. ROUX
Vice-Rector for Religious Affairs: Rev. Fr
FILEMON I. DELA CRUZ, JR
Sec. Gen.: Rev. Fr WINSTON F. CABADING
Registrar: CESAR M. VELASCO, JR
Prefect of Libraries: Fr ANGEL APARICO
Chief Librarian: ESTRELLA S. MAJUELO

Library: see under Libraries and Archives
Number of teachers: 1,440
Number of students: 32,060

Publications: *Academia, Acta Manilana,
Commerce Journal, Education Journal,
Journal of Graduate Research, Journal of
Medicine, Law Review, Nursing Journal,
Philippiniana Sacra, Science Journal,
Thomasian, Unitas, Varsitarian*

DEANS

College of Architecture: Assoc. Prof. John Joseph T. Fernandez

College of Commerce and Business Administration: Asst Prof. Mary Hildence M. Baluyot (acting)

College of Education: Prof. Clotilde N. Arcangel

College of Fine Arts and Design: Assoc. Prof. Cynthia B. Loza

College of Nursing: Assoc. Prof. Susan N. Maravilla

College of Rehabilitation Sciences: Assoc. Prof. Cheryl R. Peralta

College of Science: Prof. John Donnie A. Ramos

College of Tourism and Hospitality Management: Asst Prof. Ma. Cecilia A. Tio Cuison

Conservatory of Music: Prof. Raul M. Sunico

Faculty of Arts and Letters: Prof. Michael Anthony C. Vasco

Faculty of Canon Law: Fr Jose Ma. B. Tinoko

Faculty of Civil Law: Atty Nilo T. Divina

Faculty of Engineering: Prof. Philipina A. Marcelo

Faculty of Medicine and Surgery: Prof. Jesus V. Valencia

Faculty of Pharmacy: Assoc. Prof. Ma. Elena J. Manansala

Faculty of Philosophy: Fr Richard G. Ang

Faculty of Sacred Theology: Fr Rodel E. Aligan

Graduate School: Prof. Marilu R. Madrunio

UST-AMV College of Accountancy: Assoc. Prof. Patricia M. Empleo (acting)

UNIVERSITY OF SOUTHEASTERN PHILIPPINES

F. Iñigo St, Bo. Obrero, 8000 Davao City

Telephone: (82) 225-4696

E-mail: pio@usep.edu.ph

Internet: www.usep.edu.ph

Founded 1978

State control

Language of instruction: English

Academic year: June to March

Pres.: Dr Perfecto A. Alibin

Univ./Board Sec.: Marnie Grace I. Sonico

Chancellor (Tagum-Mabini Campus): Prof. Ceferino T. Bastian

Vice-Pres. for Academic Affairs: Dr Marcelo M. Angelia

Vice-Pres. for Admin.: Dr Rodulfo C. Sumugat

Vice-Pres. for Research, Devt and Extension: Dr Sophremiano B Antipolo

Registrar: Vic Jean A. Soller

Librarian: Prof. Restituta D. Macarayo

Library of 20,933 vols

Number of teachers: 592

Number of students: 13,000

Publications: *Headlight* (2 a year), *USeP Official Publication, Southeastern Philippines Journal of Research and Development* (ejournals.ph/index.php?journal=cjkdshafjsdbcvnmxbAJSDNJKSNCSDKA)

DEANS

College of Arts and Sciences: Dr Eveyth Deligero

College of Education: Dr Bonifacio Gabales

College of Engineering: Dr Lyndon Roble

College of Governance Business and Economics: Dr Sherlito Sable

College of Technology: Dr Annweda C. Mina

Institute of Computing: Val A. Quimno (acting)

School of Applied Economics: Dr Agustina Tan-Cruz

UNIVERSITY OF SOUTHERN MINDANAO

Kabacan 9407, N Cotabato

Telephone: (64) 248-2138

Internet: www.usm.edu.ph

Founded 1954 as Institute of Technology, present name 1980

State control

Languages of instruction: English, Filipino

Academic year: June to December (2 semesters)

Colleges of agriculture, engineering, home and ecological sciences, education, arts and sciences, trade and industry; institutes of veterinary science, Middle Eastern and Asian studies, development economics management, animal science and aquaculture, nursing

Pres.: Dr Jesus Antonio Gamido Derije

Vice-Pres.: Abraham G. Castillo

Vice-Pres.: Dr Palasig U. Ampang

Registrar: Dr Priscilla P. Costes

Vice-Pres.: Antonio N. Tacardon

Vice-Pres.: Dr Naomi G. Tangonan

Librarian: Anita Sornito

Number of teachers: 434

Number of students: 9,152

Publications: *CA Research Journal, USMARC Monitor, USM Research and Development Journal* (2 a year)

UNIVERSITY OF SOUTHERN PHILIPPINES FOUNDATION

Salinas Dr., Lahug, Cebu

Telephone: (32) 414-8773

E-mail: uspfimo@uspf.edu.ph

Internet: www.uspf.edu.ph

Founded 1927; Univ. status 1949

Private control

Pres.: Dr Alicia P. Cabatingan

Vice-Pres. for Academic Affairs: Dr Alicia P. Cabatingan

Vice-Pres. for Comptrollership: Geronimo D. Staana

Vice-Pres. for External Affairs: Lourdes D. Jereza

Vice-Pres. for Treasury: Eng. Rolando L. Villa

Registrar: Susan C. Ferguson

Dir for Libraries: Remedios M. Estella

Number of teachers: 200

Number of students: 7,400

DEANS

College of Accountancy: Michael Angelo Abarcar (Officer-in-Charge)

College of Arts and Sciences: Charles Roy P. Baguio

College of Computer Studies: Dr Paz C. Jumalon

College of Education: Dr Lucila S. Bonilla (acting)

College of Engineering and Architecture: Mario Arnaiz (Officer-in-Charge)

College of Law: Atty Alicia E. Bathan

College of Nursing: Merlyn Ouano

College of Pharmacy: Dr Althea R. Arenajo

Graduate School: Dr Alicia P. Cabatingan

School of Business and Management: Dr Venus M. Empuerto

UNIVERSITY OF THE EAST

Main Campus, 2219 Claro M. Recto Ave, Manila 1008

Telephone: (2) 735-5471

E-mail: admission@ue.edu.ph

Internet: www.ue.edu.ph *Caloocan Campus*, 105 Samson Rd, Caloocan City, Metro Manila 1400

Telephone: (2) 367-4572

E-mail: admissions_cal@ue.edu.ph

Internet: www.ue.edu.ph/caloocan

Academic year: June to April

Founded 1946 as the Philippine College of Commerce and Business Admin., present name 1951

Private control

Chair. of the Board and Chief Exec. Officer: Lucio C. Tan

Pres. and Chief Academic Officer: Dr Ester A. Garcia

Exec. Vice-Pres. and Chief Admin. Officer: Carmelita G. Mateo

Chancellor of UE Caloocan: Dr Zosimo M. Battad

Chancellor of UE Manila: Dr Linda P. Santiago

Dir for Student Affairs of Caloocan: Clemente A. Diwas

Dir for Student Affairs of Manila: Mercy L. Candelaria

Registrar: Erwin B. Bermillo

Dir of Libraries: Loreto Garcia

Library: see under Libraries and Archives

Number of teachers: 725

Number of students: 19,000

Publications: *Graduate School Research Journal, Law Update, Research Bulletin, UE Panorama Yearbook, UE Today*

DEANS

Caloocan Campus:

College of Arts and Sciences: Julian E. Abuso

College of Business Administration: Dr Rogelio V. Paglomutan

College of Engineering: Dr Victor R. Macam Jr

College of Fine Arts: Celino B. Santiago

Elementary and Secondary Laboratory Schools: Benilda L. Santos (Principal)

Physical Education Department: Fernando Z. Olona (acting)

Manila Campus:

College of Arts and Sciences: Justina M. Evangelista

College of Business Administration: Dr Veronica N. Elizalde (acting)

College of Computer Studies and Systems: Rodany A. Merida

College of Dentistry: Dr Rhodora H. Luciano

College of Education: Dr Evelina M. Vicencio

College of Engineering: Dr Dominador S. Pagbilao

College of Fine Arts: Gerardo M. Tan

College of Law: Justice Amado D. Valdez

Elementary and Secondary Laboratory Schools: Nieva J. Discipulo (Principal)

Graduate School: Dr Avelina A. De La Rea

Physical Education Department: Rodrigo M. Roque (acting) (Asst Dir)

AFFILIATED MEDICAL CENTRE

University of the East Ramon Magsaysay Memorial Medical Centre

64–68 Aurora Blvd, Barangay Doña Imelda, 1113 Quezon City

Telephone: (2) 715-0861

E-mail: registrar@uerm.edu.ph

Internet: www.uerm.edu.ph

Founded 1957

Affiliated to Univ. of the East

Chief Librarian: Juliana M. Noces-Gasmen

Library of 31,150 vols, 342 periodicals

DEANS

Graduate School: Dr Teresa S. Ludovice-Yap

College of Medicine: Dr Alfaretta Luisa T. Reyes

College of Nursing: Dr CARMELITA C. DIVINA-GRACIA

College of Physical Therapy: Dr RAQUEL S. CABAZOR

UNIVERSITY OF THE PHILIPPINES SYSTEM

UP Diliman, Quezon City

Telephone: (2) 926-1572

E-mail: op@up.edu.ph

Internet: www.up.edu.ph

Founded 1908

State control

Languages of instruction: English, Filipino

Academic year: June to May (2 terms, 1 summer session)

Pres.: Dr ALFREDO PASCUAL

Vice-Pres. for Academic Affairs: Prof. GISELA CONCEPCION

Vice-Pres. for Admin.: Prof. ARLENE A. SAMANIEGO

Vice-Pres. for Devt: Prof. ARMIN B. SARTHOU Jr

Vice-Pres. for Legal Affairs: Prof. MARAGTAS AMANTE

Vice-Pres. for Planning and Finance: Prof. EDGARDO G. ATANACIO

Vice-Pres. for Public Affairs: Prof. ISABELITA O. REYES

Sec.: Prof. LILIAN DE LAS LLAGAS

Library: see under Libraries and Archives

Number of teachers: 3,952

Number of students: 50,668

Publications: *The Carillon* (online), *UP Forum* (28 a year), *UP Newsletter* (12 a year), *UP Statistics* (1 a year)..

CONSTITUENT CAMPUSES

UP at Baguio

Baguio

Telephone: (74) 442-3888

E-mail: opa@upb.edu.ph

Internet: www.upb.edu.ph

State control

Language of instruction: English

Academic year: June to March

Chancellor: Prof. RAYMUNDO ROVILLOS

Vice-Chancellor for Academic Affairs: Prof. WILFREDO ALANGUI

Vice-Chancellor for Admin.: Prof. JESSICA CARIÑO

Registrar: Prof. JOCELYN RAFANAN

Librarian: BRENDA MARIE DOGUP

Library of 81,964 vols

Number of teachers: 140

Number of students: 2,528

DEANS

College of Arts and Communication: Prof. PURIFICACION DELIMA

College of Science: Prof. WILFREDO ALANGUI

College of Social Sciences: Prof. RAYMUNDO ROVILLOS

Institute of Management: Prof. CORAZON ABANSI

University of the Philippines, Cebu

Gorordo Ave, Lahug, Cebu City

Telephone: (2) 231-3086

E-mail: dean.upcebu@gmail.com

Internet: www.upcebu.edu.ph

Language of instruction: English

Academic year: June to May

Officer-in-Charge: Prof. TERESITA RODRIGUEZ

College Sec. and Registrar: PATRICIA ANNE NAZARENO

College Librarian: MYLAH PEDRANO

Library of 28,009

Number of teachers: 123

Number of students: 1,289

UP at Diliman

E-mail: updio@upd.edu.ph

Internet: www.upd.edu.ph

Chancellor: SERGIO S. CAO

Vice-Chancellor for Academic Affairs: Prof. LORNA I. PAREDES

Vice-Chancellor for Admin.: Prof. MARY DELIA G. TOMACRUZ

Vice-Chancellor for Community Affairs: Prof. CYNTHIA GRACE C. GREGORIO

Vice-Chancellor for Research and Devt: Prof. LUIS G. SISON

Vice-Chancellor for Student Affairs: Prof. ELIZABETH L. ENRIQUEZ

Registrar: Prof. PAMELA C. CONSTANTINO

Librarian: SALVACION M. ARLANTE

DEANS

Archaeological Studies Program: Prof. VICTOR J. PAZ

Asian Centre: Prof. MARIO I. MICLAT

Asian Institute of Tourism: Prof. CORAZON P. RODRIGUEZ

College of Architecture: Prof. DANILO A. SILVESTRE

College of Arts and Letters: Prof. FLORA ELENA R. MIRANO

College of Business Administration: Prof. ERLINDA S. ECHANIS

College of Education: Prof. VIVIEN M. TALISAYON

College of Engineering: Prof. ROWENA CRISTINA L. GUEVARA

College of Fine Arts: Prof. LEONARDO C. ROSETE

College of Home Economics: Prof. ADELAIDA V. MAYO

College of Human Kinetics: Prof. LEILANI L. GONZALO

College of Law: Prof. MARVIC MARIO VICTOR F. LEONEN

College of Mass Communication: Prof. ROLAND B. TOLENTINO

College of Music: Prof. RAMÓN MA. G. ACOYMO

College of Science: Prof. CAESAR A. SALOMA

College of Social Science and Philosophy: ZOSIMO E. LEE

College of Social Work and Community Development: Prof. AMERYLLIS TORRES

Institute of Islamic Studies: Prof. MASHUR BIN-GHALIB JUNDAM

National College of Public Administration and Governance: Prof. ALEX B. BRILLANTES Jr

School of Economics: EMMANUEL S. DE DIOS

School of Labour and Industrial Relations: Prof. JORGE V. SIBAL

School of Library and Information Science: Prof. VYVA AGUIRRE

School of Statistics: Prof. ERNIEL BARRIOS

School of Urban and Regional Planning: Prof. CANDIDO A. CABRIDO Jr

UP Extension Programme in Pampanga: Prof. JULIETA C. MALLARI

UP at Los Baños

E-mail: learnmore@uplb.edu.ph

Internet: www.uplb.edu.ph

Chancellor: Prof. LUIS REY I. VELASCO

Vice-Chancellor for Admin.: Prof. ROBERTO F. RAÑOLA, Jr

Vice-Chancellor for Community Affairs: Prof. VIRGINIA R. CARDENAS

Vice-Chancellor for Instruction: Prof. RITA P. LAUDE

Vice-Chancellor for Planning and Devt: Prof. RUBEN D. TANQUECO

Vice-Chancellor for Research and Extension: Prof. ENRICO P. SUPANGCO

Registrar: Prof. MYRNA G. CARANDANG

Librarian: CONCEPCION D. L. SAUL

DEANS

College of Agriculture: Prof. DOMINGO E. ANGELES

College of Arts and Sciences: Prof. ASUNCION K. RAYMUNDO

College of Development Communication: Prof. CLEOFE S. TORRES

College of Economics and Management: Prof. LIBORIO S. CABANILLA

College of Engineering and Agro-Industrial Technology: Prof. VICTOR B. CRUZ

College of Forestry and Natural Resources: Prof. REX VICTOR O. CRUZ

College of Human Ecology: Prof. SUE LIZA C. SAGUIGUIT

College of Public Affairs: Prof. AGNES C. ROLA

College of Veterinary Medicine: Prof. CONRADO A. VALDEZ

Graduate School: Prof. OSCAR B. ZAMORA

School of Environmental Science and Management: Prof. MARIA VICTORIA O. ESPALDON

UP at Manila

Internet: www.upm.edu.ph

Chancellor: Prof. Dr RAMON L. ARCADIO

Vice-Chancellor for Academic Affairs: Prof. JOSEFINA G. TAYAG

Vice-Chancellor for Admin.: Prof. ORLINO O. TALENS

Vice-Chancellor for Planning and Devt: Prof. ZORAYDA E. LEOPANDO

Vice-Chancellor for Research: Prof. LULU C. BRAVO

Registrar: SUSAN B. VILLEGAS

Librarian: THERESA P. DUGENIA

Library: see Libraries and Archives

DEANS

College of Allied Medical Professions: Prof. CONCEPCION C. CABATAN

College of Arts and Sciences: Prof. REYNALDO H. IMPERIAL

College of Dentistry: Prof. VICENTE O. MEDINA

College of Medicine: Prof. ALBERTO B. ROXAS

College of Nursing: Prof. JOSEFINA A. TUAZON

College of Pharmacy: Prof. JOCELYN S. BAUTISTA-PALACPAC

College of Public Health: Prof. NINA G. GLORIANI

Graduate School: LILIA A. REYES

National Institutes of Health: Prof. LULU C. BRAVO

National Teacher-Training Centre for the Health Professions: Prof. ERLYN A. SANA

School of Health Sciences: Prof. JUSIE LYDIA J. SIEGA-SUR

UP on Mindanao

E-mail: oc@upmin.edu.ph

Internet: www.upmin.edu.ph

Chancellor: Prof. GILDA C. RIVERO

Vice-Chancellor for Academic Affairs: Prof. EMMA RUTH V. BAYOGAN

Vice-Chancellor for Admin.: Prof. MIGUEL D. SOLEDAD

Registrar: Prof. KAREN JOYCE G. CAYAMANDA

Librarian: BRICCIO M. MERCED

DEANS

College of Humanities and Social Sciences: Prof. MA. ARACELI DANS-LEE

College of Science and Mathematics: Prof. REYNALDO G. ABAD

School of Management: Prof. SYLVIA B. CONCEPCION

UP in the Visayas

E-mail: upvoc09@gmail.com

Internet: www.upv.edu.ph

Chancellor: Prof. MINDA J. FORMACION

Vice-Chancellor for Academic Affairs: Prof. LEONOR M. SANTOS

Vice-Chancellor for Admin.: Prof. LOUISE ANNETTE B. ESCOTO

Vice-Chancellor for Planning and Devt: Prof. ALICE JOAN G. FERRER

Vice-Chancellor for Research and Extension: Prof. JANE S. GEDUSPAN

Registrar: Prof. MARILYN Z. ALCARDE

Librarian: ANA T. MONES

DEANS

College of Arts and Sciences: Prof. ROMMEL A. ESPINOSA

College of Fisheries and Ocean Sciences: Prof. CARLOS C. BAYLON

College of Management: Prof. JOY C. LIZADA

School of Technology: Prof. LUZETTE T. TERUEL

UPV Cebu College: Prof. ENRIQUE M. AVILA

UPV Tacloban College: Prof. MARGARITA DELA CRUZ

UP Open University

E-mail: admissions@upou.edu.ph

Internet: www2.upou.edu.ph

Chancellor: Prof. GRACE JAVIER ALFONSO

Vice-Chancellor for Academic Affairs: Prof. MARIA FE V. MENDOZA

Vice-Chancellor for Finance and Admin.: Prof. MELINDA F. LUMANTA

Registrar: Prof. RICARDO T. BAGARINAO

Librarian: AUDREY ANDAY

DEANS

Faculty of Education: Prof. MA. THERESA DE VILLA

Faculty of Information and Communication Studies: Prof. MELINDA D. P. BANDALARIA

Faculty of Management and Development Studies: Prof. INOCENCIO E. BUOT, JR

UNIVERSITY OF THE VISAYAS

Colon St, 6000 Cebu

Telephone: (32) 255-2434

E-mail: info@uv.edu.ph

Internet: www.uv.edu.ph

Founded 1919

Private control

Languages of instruction: English, Filipino

Academic year: June to May

Pres.: EDUARDO R. GULLAS

Exec. Vice-Pres.: JOSE R. GULLAS

Comptroller and Sr Vice-Pres.: GLICERIA GULLAS-LUCERO

Vice-Pres. for Admin.: ELADIO C. DIOKO

Vice-Pres. for Academics: JACQUELINE GULLAS-WECKMAN

Vice-Pres. for External Affairs: JOSEPH M. BADUEL

Vice-Pres. for Finance: JOSELITO F. GULLAS

Dir of Centre for Research, Planning and Development: BRIAN VASQUEZ

Registrar: LAKAMBINI RELUYA

Librarian: AILEEN B. CATACUTAN

Number of teachers: 600

Number of students: 18,200

Publications: *Spectrum*, *Strategies*, *The Visayanian*

DEANS

College of Arts and Sciences: Dr ESTRELLA CABILUNA NAVARRO

College of Business Administration: ROSEMARIE CRUZ-ESPAÑOL

College of Computer Studies: ELIZALDE J. DURAN

College of Criminal Justice: DONALD B. NARRA

College of Dentistry: Dr JELBERT F. SENO

College of Education: Dr NERISSA S. LOPEZ

College of Engineering and Architecture: Dr GAMALIEL B. VICENTE, JR

College of Nursing: Dr RESTY L. PICARDO

College of Pharmacy: Dr EMMA A. YAUN

Graduate School: Dr ELADIO C. DIOKO

Gullas College of Medicine: LEONARD RAYMUND CIMAFRANCA

Gullas Law School: Atty TEODORO A. ALMASE

Maritime College: Capt. SIEGFREDO G. LANTICSE

VISAYAS STATE UNIVERSITY

Visca, Baybay, 6521 Leyte

Telephone: (53) 335-2601

Internet: www.vsu.edu.ph

Founded 1924 as Baybay Agricultural School, present name and status 2001

State control

Languages of instruction: English, Filipino

Academic year: June to March

Colleges of agriculture, arts and science, education, engineering and agri-industries, forestry and veterinary medicine, management and economics, nursing; Graduate School; Open Univ. system

Pres.: Dr JOSE L. BACUSMO

Number of teachers: 400

WEST VISAYAS STATE UNIVERSITY

Luna St, La Paz, Iloilo City, 5000 Iloilo

Telephone: (33) 320-0870

Internet: www.wvsu.edu.ph

Founded 1924 as Iloilo Normal School; present name and status 1986

State control

Academic year: June to March

Colleges of arts and sciences, education, mass communications, medicine and nursing; Institute of information and communications technology

Pres.: Dr LOURDES C. ARAÑADOR

WESTERN MINDANAO STATE UNIVERSITY

Normal Rd, Baliwasan, 7000 Zamboanga

Telephone: (62) 991-1040

E-mail: wmsu@wmsu.edu.ph

Internet: www.wmsu.edu.ph

Founded 1918

State control

Languages of instruction: English, Filipino

Academic year: June to March (2 semesters)

Pres.: Dr MILABEL ENRIQUEZ-HO

Vice-Pres. for Academic Affairs: Dr CARLA A. OCHOTORENA

Vice-Pres. for Planning, Admin. and Finance: Dr EDERLINDA M. FERNANDEZ

Vice-Pres. for Research Extension and Devt: (vacant): Dr ROBERTO B. TORRES

Registrar: Prof. AURORA O. MANZON

Dean for Admissions: Dr CARLA A. OCHOTORENA

Dean for External Studies Unit: Dr RICARDO A. SOMBLINGO

Dean for Research Devt and Evaluation: Dr CHONA Q. SARMIENTO

Dean for Student Affairs: Dr MILA YOSORES

Librarian: SALUD C. LAQUIO

Library of 50,000 vols

Number of teachers: 552

Number of students: 15,368

DEANS

College of Agriculture: Dr ERIBERTO D. SALANG

College of Architecture: Arq. DOMINGO A. ABARRO, III

College of Asian and Islamic Studies: Prof. EDDIE M. LADJA

College of Communications and Humanities: Dr SOCORRO YVONNE H. RAMOS

College of Criminal Justice Education: Prof. EFFRENDY M. ESTIPONA

College of Education: Dr EDGARDO H. ROSALES

College of Engineering and Technology: Eng. DANTE JESUS P. VILLAREAL

College of Forestry and Environmental Studies: Prof. DINO A. SABELLINA

College of Home Economics: Prof. LUCIA M. SANTOS

College of Law: Atty EDUARDO F. SANSON

College of Nursing: Prof. LEILA B. BENITO

College of Physical Education, Recreation and Sports: Prof. JESUS O. TUBOG, JR

College of Public Administration and Developmental Studies: Dr FREDE MORENO

College of Science and Mathematics: Dr MARILOU C. ELAGO

College of Social Sciences: Dr RUFINA A. CRUZ

College of Social Work and Community Development: VICTORIA G. ALOJADO

Department of Extension Services and Community Development: Prof. LUCIO C. SOMBLINGO

XAVIER UNIVERSITY—ATENEO DE CAGAYAN

Corrales Ave, 9000 Cagayan de Oro City

Telephone: (8822) 72-3116

E-mail: pres@xu.edu.ph

Internet: www.xu.edu.ph

Founded 1933

Private control

Language of instruction: English

Academic year: June to March (2 terms)

Pres.: Rev. Fr ROBERTO C. YAP

Registrar: VERNA A. LAGO

Dir for Library: ESTRELLA CALDAMO CABUDOY

Library of 148,307 vols

Number of teachers: 608

Number of students: 10,921

Publications: *Kinaadman (Wisdom)* (1 a year), *XU Graduate School Journal* (2 a year)

DEANS

College of Agriculture: ROEL R. RAVANERA

College of Arts and Sciences: Dr DULCE R. DAWANG

College of Computer Studies: GERARDO S. DOROJA

College of Engineering: Ing. ELISEO B. LINOG, JR

College of Law: RAUL R. VILLANUEVA

College of Nursing: Dr RAMONA HEIDI C. PALAD

Graduate School: Dr ISAIAS S. SEALZA

School of Business and Management: Dr VIRGINIA LOURDES C. YACAPIN

School of Education: Dr LOURDES G. TOLOD

School of Medicine: Dr RUTH S. BELTRAN

Colleges
GENERAL

San Beda College: 638 Mendiola St, San Miguel, Manila; tel. (2) 735-6011; e-mail sbc@dns.sbc.edu.ph; internet www.sanbeda.edu.ph; f. 1901; campus in Rizal; colleges of arts and sciences, law, medicine, nursing; graduate school of business, law and liturgy; library: 120,464 vols; 280 teachers; 6,010 students; Rector and Pres. Rev. Fr ALOYSIUS MA. A. MARANAN; Head of College Library ROSALINDA P. ROBLES.

St Paul College of Manila: 680 Pedro Gil St, Malate, Manila, POB 3062; tel. (2) 524-

5687; e-mail spcm@spcm.edu.ph; internet www.spcm.edu.ph; f. 1912; Private control; first degree courses in computer science, hotel and restaurant management, psychology, education, commerce, secretarial administration, nursing, communication arts, music; library: 47,898 vols; 148 teachers; 2,800 students; Pres. Sis. NATIVIDAD DE JESUS FERAREN.

St Scholastica's College: 2560 Leon Guinto St, Malate, Metro 1004 Manila, POB 3153; tel. (2) 524-7686; e-mail maryjohn@ssc.edu.ph; internet www.ssc.edu.ph; f. 1906; Private control (sectarian); schools of accountancy, arts and sciences, commerce, music, music education; 516 teachers; 6,601 students; Pres. Sis. MARY JOHN MANANZAN.

State Polytechnic College of Palawan: Aborlan, 5302 Palawan; tel. 433-4480; f. 1910; courses in agriculture, forestry, fisheries, environmental management, engineering and technology, education, arts, science, rural development; library: 22,500 vols; Pres. Dr CONCEPTO B. MAGAY; publs *SPCP-IMS Research Journal* (2 a year), *SPCP Research Journal* (irregular).

ECONOMICS

Asian Institute of Management: Eugenio Lopez Foundation Bldg, Joseph R. McMicking Campus, 123 Paseo de Roxas, 1260 Makati City; tel. (632) 892-4011; e-mail admissions@aim.edu.ph; internet www.aim.edu.ph; f. 1968 by Ateneo de Manila Univ., De La Salle University, the Harvard Business School and the Ford Foundation; academic units and degree programmes: Washington SyCip Graduate School of Business (MBA, Masters in Management), Centre for Development Management (Masters in Development Management), Asian Centre for Entrepreneurship (Masters in Entrepreneurship), Executive Education and Life Long Learning Centre (Executive MBA, Certificate Programmes); library: more than 25,000 books and periodicals, more than 30,000 learning material items; 61 teachers;

Pres. ROBERTO F. DE OCAMPO; Dean VICTORIA S. LICUANAN.

MEDICINE

Ago Medical Educational Center-Bicol Christian College of Medicine: Rizal St, Old Albay, 4501 Legazpi; tel. (52) 820-5877; e-mail admission@amec-bccm.com; internet amec-bccm.com; f. 1980; library: 30,050 vols; Pres. ANGELITA F. AGO; Dean for College of Medicine Dr SONIA G. ROSARIO.

Cebu Doctors' University College of Medicine: CDU Administrative Offices Bldg, Gov. M. Roa St, 6000 Cebu City; tel. (32) 253-4919; e-mail cdu-cm@cebudoctorsuniversity.edu; internet www.cebudoctorsuniversity.edu/medicine; f. 1977; library: 11,800 vols; 160 staff; 360 students; Pres. POTENCIANO V. LARRAZABAL; Sec. POTENCIANO S. D. LARRAZABAL, III; Treas. PHILIP ANTHONY S. D. LARRAZABAL; Dean ENRICO B. GRUET; publ. *Proceedings* (2 a year).

TECHNOLOGY

Lyceum of the Philippines: Real and Muralla Sts, Intramuros, POB 1264, Manila; tel. (2) 527-5548; internet www.lyceumphil.edu.ph; f. 1952; Private control; faculties of law, graduate studies, mechanical engineering, communication, journalism, arts and sciences, foreign service, economics, business administration, office management, technical vocational, hotel and restaurant management, secretarial science, computer engineering, electronics and communication engineering, political science, legal studies, Filipino, literature, history, humanities, mathematics, psychology, biology, tourism, accountancy, legal secretarial administration, computer science, secondary education, banking and finance, management, marketing, computer data management and processing, tax and customs administration, cruise line management, nursing and med-

ical transcription; library: 45,000 vols; 300 teachers; 10,000 students; Pres. ROBERTO P. LAUREL.

Mapùa Institute of Technology: Muralla St, Intramuros, 1002 Manila; tel. (2) 247-5000; e-mail registrar@mapua.edu.ph; internet www.mapua.edu.ph; f. 1925; campus in Makati; schools of architecture and planning; industrial design and the built environment; chemical engineering and chemistry; civil engineering and environmental and sanitary engineering; electrical engineering, electronics and communications engineering; computer engineering; graduate studies; industrial engineering and engineering management; information technology; languages, humanities and social sciences; mechanical and manufacturing engineering; multimedia and visual arts; E. T. Yuchengco School of Business and Management; San Lorenzo School of Health Sciences; 13,000 students; Pres. and CEO REYNALDO B. VEA; Registrar LOBELLA G. DAMIAN.

Namei Polytechnic Institute: 123 A Mabini St, Mandaluyong, Metro Manila; tel. (2) 531-7328; internet www.namei.ph; f. 1947; BSc in naval architecture and marine engineering, marine transportation, and marine engineering; Pres. MA. CELEDONIA PATAG; Registrar PERLA G. CRUZ.

Naval Institute of Technology: Naval, 6543 Biliran; f. 1972; library: 10,000 vols; 83 teachers; 2,500 students; Pres. Dr JUANITO S. SISON.

Palompon Institute of Technology: Palompon, Leyte; tel. (53) 555-9841; e-mail pit@glinesnx.com.ph; internet foo.ncc.gov.ph/ecommunity/pit; f. 1972; courses in marine transportation and engineering; engineering technology; technical and vocational education; customs administration; radio communication; domestic science; industrial technology, shipping management, teacher education, information technology, industrial engineering, Doctor and Masters programmes; library: 10,434 vols; 114 teachers; 2,776 students; Pres. Dr JUANITO S. SISON.

POLAND

The Higher Education System

Higher education in Poland dates from the 14th century, with the establishment of Uniwersytet Jagielloński (Jagiellonian University—founded in 1364), the country's oldest university. Several institutions of higher education were founded in the 18th and 19th centuries, including Uniwersytet Wrocławski (the University of Wrocław—founded in 1702), Uniwersytet Muzyczny Fryderyka Chopina (Fryderyk Chopin University of Music—founded in 1810) and Uniwersytet Warszawki (the University of Warsaw—founded in 1816). Many institutions of higher education were founded during the period of Communist rule (1948–89) and still more have been created since the fall of Communism; by 2011/12 there were 450 higher education establishments in Poland with a total of more than two million students.

The Ministry of Science and Higher Education is the state authority responsible for higher education. Higher education is provided by universities (uniwersytet), technical universities (politechnika) and non-university level institutions (wyzsze szkoly zawodowe). Public universities are funded from the state budget, with allocations determined by the Minister of National Education, while private universities are mainly funded by the student tuition fees. Poland has one of the highest rates globally of private sector higher education, with around one-third of all students enrolled in private institutions. However, in recent years the private sector has appeared to be in decline; at the beginning of the 2011/12 academic year, the number of students enrolled in private institutions had fallen by 80,000 compared with 2007, and 17 private institutions were in various stages of liquidation. As a result, there has been a series of mergers, as well as concerted efforts to attract greater numbers of foreign students. Poland participates in the Bologna Process to establish a European Higher Education Area, the first phase of which was to adopt a credit-based system of comparable degrees with two main cycles (undergraduate and graduate). The 2003 Act on Academic Degrees and Academic Titles and 2005 Act on Higher Education were finally fully implemented at the beginning of the 2011/12 academic year.

The main criterion for admission to higher education is the Świadectwo dojrzałości (secondary school 'maturity' certificate) and some institutions may set entrance examinations. Poland has implemented a two-tier Bachelors and Masters degree system, in accordance with the principles of the Bologna Process, but some old-style degree programmes are still offered, mostly by institutions of professional education. The primary examples of these types of degree are the Licencjat (Bachelors) and Inzynier, which are awarded after three- to four-year courses of higher professional education. The undergraduate Bachelors degree is a three- or four-year course of study equivalent to the initial stages of the old-style Magister (Masters). The new Masters is now a separate postgraduate degree lasting one to two years; however, students in mainly professional fields of study continue to work towards integrated Masters programmes. Admission to the highest level of university degree, the Doktor (Doctorate), requires the Masters. The Doctorate is awarded following the submission and defence of a thesis and success in doctoral examinations.

Technical and vocational education at the post-secondary level is offered by post-secondary schools (szkoly policealne or, in the case of nursing and midwifery institutes, szkoly pomaturalne) and schools of higher professional education (wyzsze szkoly zawodowe); the latter were established following the Act on Schools of Higher Vocational Education (1997) and offer Licencjat and Inzynier qualifications. Admission to post-secondary schools requires students to hold the Swiadectwo ukończenia liceum ogólnokształcącego (certificate of completion of lyceum); some courses may also require the Świadectwo dojrzałości.

The Act on Schools of Higher Vocational Education of 1997 established the Accreditation Commission for Higher Vocational Education, and the State Accreditation Committee (created on the basis of the amended Higher Education Act of 1990) has been in operation since 2002.

Regulatory and Representative Bodies

GOVERNMENT

Ministry of Culture and National Heritage: ul. Krakowskie Przedmieście 15/17, 00-071 Warsaw; tel. (22) 4210240; e-mail minister@mkidn.gov.pl; internet www.mkidn.gov.pl; Minister BOGDAN ZDROJEWSKI.

Ministry of National Education: al. J. Ch. Szucha 25, 00-918 Warsaw; tel. (22) 3474100; e-mail informacja@men.gov.pl; internet www.men.gov.pl; Minister JOANNA KLUZIK-ROSTKOWSKA.

Ministry of Science and Higher Education: 20 Hoża St, 1/3 Wspólna St, 00-529 Warsaw; tel. (22) 5292718; e-mail sekretariat.minister@nauka.gov.pl; internet www.nauka.gov.pl; Minister Prof. Dr LENA KOLARSKA-BOBIŃSKA.

ACCREDITATION

Biuro Uznawalności Wykształcenia i Wymiany Międzynarodowej (Bureau for Academic Recognition and International Exchange): ul. Ogrodowa 28/30, 00-896 Warsaw; tel. (22) 8288161; e-mail biuro@buwiwm.edu.pl; internet www.buwiwm.edu.pl; reports to the minister responsible for higher education; acts as contact point for the EU directives of gen. system of recognition of professional qualifications.

Centralna Komisja do Spraw Stopni i Tytułów (Central Commission for Degrees and Titles): pl. Defilad 1 (PKiN), 00-091 Warsaw; tel. (22) 8268238; e-mail kancelaria@ck.gov.pl; internet www.ck.gov.pl; defines fields and disciplines within sciences and the arts in which academic and professional titles and degrees are awarded; grants relevant instns the right to award such titles and degrees; ratifies awards of Dr hab. degrees; Pres. Prof. Dr Hab. TADEUSZ KACZOREK; Sec. Prof. HUBERT IZDEBSKI.

ENIC/NARIC Poland: Dept of Strategy, Min. of Science and Higher Education, ul. Wspólna 1/3, 00-529 Warsaw; tel. (22) 5292266; e-mail enic-naric@nauka.gov.pl; internet www.enic-naric.net/index.aspx?c=poland; responsible for the recognition of foreign credentials for both academic and professional purposes; gives opinions and information on documents of higher education obtained abroad; provides information on the recognition procedures of foreign education in Poland; assists those who wish to seek recognition of Polish educational credentials abroad; promotes implementation of Diploma Supplement in Poland; Head HANNA RECZULSKA.

Polska Komisja Akredytacyjna (Polish Accreditation Committee): Żurawia 32/34 str., 00-515 Warsaw; tel. (22) 6220718; e-mail biuro@pka.edu.pl; internet www.pka.edu.pl; f. 2001; supports Polish public and non-public higher education instns in the devt of educational standards matching the best models adopted in Europe and the world; conducts obligatory assessments of the quality of higher education and gives opinions on applications submitted by higher education instns to provide degree programmes; Pres. Dr Hab. MAREK ROCKI; Sec. Dr Hab. JÓZEF ROGOWSKI.

Uniwersytecka Komisja Akredytacyjna (University Accreditation Commission): Adam Mickiewicz Univ., Wieniawskiego 1, 61-712 Poznań; Hostel 'JOWITA', Zwierzyniecka 7C, room 215, Poznań; tel. (61) 8292502; e-mail pkaz@amu.edu.pl; internet www.uka.amu.edu.pl; f. 1998; matches the quality of univ. education in Poland with that in the EU; promotes high-quality courses of study and the univs offering them; harmonizes the standards of educational quality at univs; aims to create accreditation system of courses of studies at univs; 20 mems; Chair.

Prof. Dr Hab. MAREK WĄSOWICZ; Sec. Prof. Dr Hab. ZBIGNIEW PALKA.

FUNDING

Komitet Badań Naukowych (State Committee for Scientific Research): 53 Wspólna Str. 1/3, 00-529 Warsaw; tel. (22) 5292718; e-mail dg@kbn.gov.pl; internet kbn.icm.edu .pl; f. 1991; draws up guidelines on scientific policy and presents them to govt; submits plans for budgetary expenditure in the area of science and technology; distributes funds among instns and research teams and controls spending; signs int. agreements on cooperation in the field of science and technology; 19 mems; Chair. MICHAŁ KLEIBER; Gen. Dir KRYSTYN WEREMOWICZ.

NATIONAL BODIES

Konferencja Rektorów Akademickich Szkół Polskich (Conference of Rectors of Academic Schools in Poland): Uniwersytet Warszawski, ul. Krakowskie Przedmieście 26/28, 00-927 Warsaw; tel. (22) 5520352; e-mail biuro@krasp.org.pl; internet www .krasp.org.pl; f. 1997; voluntary asscn of rectors representing those instns of higher education awarding doctorates (or equivalent) in at least one scientific discipline; inspires and coordinates cooperation of mem. instns; represents common interests of the schools and undertakes activities leading to creation of integrated system of nat. education; acts for the benefit of higher education, science and culture devt; 107 mems, 9 assoc. mems; Pres. Prof. Dr Hab. WIESŁAW BANYŚ; Sec.-Gen. Prof. Dr Hab. ANDRZEJ KRASNIEWSKI.

Rada Główna Nauki i Szkolnictwa Wyższego (Central Council for Science and Higher Education): ul. Wspólna 1/3, 00-529 Warsaw; tel. (22) 5292216; e-mail radaglowna@mnisw.gov.pl; internet www .rgnisw.nauka.gov.pl; formulates and expresses opinions on how higher education, science, culture and education should be developed; helps govt to set state policy in the field of higher education, science policy and innovation policy; Pres. Prof. Dr Hab. JÓZEF LUBACZ.

Learned Societies

GENERAL

Bydgoskie Towarzystwo Naukowe (Bydgoszcz Scientific Society): ul. Jezuicka 4, 85-102 Bydgoszcz; tel. (52) 3222268; e-mail btn@um.bydgoszcz.pl; internet www.btn.utp .edu.pl; f. 1959; promotes, develops and cultivates scientific studies in Bydgoszcz; initiates and facilitates scientific research work in Bydgoszcz and Kujawsko-Pomorskie region; organizes readings, lectures, confs, sessions and exhibitions; 400 mems; library of 17,500 vols; Pres. Prof. Dr Hab. MAREK BIELIŃSKI; Sec.-Gen. Dr ARKADIUSZ KUZIEMSKI; publs *Bydgostiana Kolokwium Wiedzy o Ziemi* (irregular), *Ekologia i Technika* (6 a year), *Prace Wydziału Nauk Humanistycznych* (1 a year), *Prace Wydziału Nauk Przyrodniczych* (1 a year), *Prace Wydziału Nauk Technicznych* (1 a year), *Przegląd Bydgoski* (1 a year).

Gdańskie Towarzystwo Naukowe (Gdańsk Scientific Society): ul. Bielanska 5 pokoj 41, 80-851 Gdańsk; tel. (58) 3012124; e-mail biuro@gtn.gda.pl; internet www.gtn .gda.pl; f. 1922 as Gdańsk Soc. of Friends of Science and Art; sections of social sciences and humanities, biological and medical sciences, mathematical, physical and chemical sciences, technical sciences, earth sciences;

organizes research work from different fields of knowledge and disseminates results; 572 mems; Pres. Prof. Dr Hab. MAREK WESOLOWSKI; Sec.-Gen. Prof. Dr Hab. JERZY BŁAŻEJOWSKI; publ. *Acta Biologica et Medica*.

Kieleckie Towarzystwo Naukowe (Kielce Scientific Society): ul. Zamkowa 5, 25-009 Kielce; tel. (41) 3445453; e-mail ktn@pu .kielce.pl; internet www.ujk.edu.pl/ktn; f. 1958; regional scientific research in history, philology, medicine, geology, geography and nature conservation, psychology, sociology and education, physics, mathematics, engineering; conducts research, disseminates research results and knowledge about the region; 464 mems; library of 4,620 vols; Pres. Prof. Dr Hab. TOMASZ LECH STAŃCZYK; Sec. Dr JANUSZ DETKA; publs *Rocznika Świętokrzyskiego* (Yearbook), *Studiów Kieleckich* (irregular).

Łomżyńskie Towarzystwo Naukowe im. Wagów (The Brothers Waga Łomża Scientific Society): ul. Długa 13, 18-400 Łomża; tel. (86) 2163256; e-mail zegalska@poczta.onet .pl; internet www.ltn.lomza.pl; f. 1975; promotes and nurtures devt of science, culture, education, esp. among young people; inspires and supports scientific research in the region; agriculture, economics, environmental protection, ethnology, geography, history, linguistics, natural history, veterinary science, settlement of NE Poland, sociology; 215 mems; library of 18,000 vols; Pres. Prof. Dr Hab. HALINA KARAŚ; Sec. Mgr Inż ELŻBIETA ŻEGALSKA; publs *Archiwalia badauia regianalne* (1 a year), *Pogranicze w Jezyku i Kulturze* (1 a year), *Polszczyzna Mazowsza i Podlasia* (1 a year), *Studia Gwolroznewdze* (1 a year), *Studia Łomżyńskie* (1 a year).

Lubelskie Towarzystwo Naukowe (Lublin Scientific Society): Plac Litewski 2, 20-080 Lublin; tel. (81) 5321300; e-mail biuro@ltn.lublin.pl; internet www.ltn.lublin .pl; f. 1957; 5 sections: humanities, biology, mathematics–physics–chemistry, technical science, mining and geography; initiates and promotes research in all science depts with particular emphasis on region; develops academic life in Lublin region; 722 mems; Pres. Prof. Dr Hab. ARTUR KOROBOWICZ; Sec.-Gen. Prof. Dr Hab. MARIAN WIELOSZ.

Polska Akademia Nauk (PAN) (Polish Academy of Sciences): Pałac Kultury i Nauki, Plac Defilad 1, Skrytka Pocztowa 24, 00-901 Warsaw; tel. (22) 6204970; e-mail akademia@ pan.pl; internet www.pan.pl; f. 1952; divs: biological and agricultural sciences, engineering sciences, humanities and social sciences, mathematics, physics, chemistry and earth sciences, medical sciences; attached research institutes: see under Research Institutes; colln: science and technology, future studies, praxiology, library and information science, bibliography; comprises 79 research institutes; 7 territorial brs in Gdańsk, Katowice, Kraków, Lublin, Łódź, Poznań and Wrocław; 515 mems (incl. 171 ordinary, 145 corresponding, 199 foreign); library of 413,697 vols; Pres. Prof. MICHAL KLEIBER; Vice-Pres Prof. ANDRZEJ GORSKI; Vice-Pres Prof. MAREK CYPRIAN CHMIELEWSKI; Vice-Pres Prof. MIROSLAWA MARODY; Vice-Pres Prof. RYSZARD GORECKI; publs *ACADEMIA* (4 a year, in English and Polish), *Acta Arithmetica* (4 a year), *Acta Biochimica Polonica* (4 a year), *Acta Geologica Polonica* (4 a year), *Acta Neurobiologicale Experimentalis* (4 a year), *Acta Physica Polonica* (4 a year), *Acta Physiologiae Plantarum* (4 a year), *Acta Poloniae Historica* (2 a year), *Acta Protozoologica* (4 a year), *Archeologia* (1 a year), *Archives of Metallurgy and Materials* (4 a year), *Archivum Immunologiae et Therapiae Experimentalis* (6 a year), *Bulletin of the Polish Academy of Sciences*: Series: *Tech-*

nical Sciences (4 a year), *Chemia Analityczna* (4 a year), *Chemical and Process Engineering* (4 a year), *Ethnologia Polonia* (1 a year), *Etudes et Travaux* (1 a year), *Folia Neuropathologica* (4 a year), *Fundamenta Mathematicae* (4 a year), *Journal of Animal and Feed Sciences* (4 a year), *Nauka* (Science, 4 a year), *Nauka dla Polski* (Science for Poland), *Oceanologia* (4 a year), *Onomastica* (1 a year), *Pamiętnik Literacki* (4 a year), *Polish Journal of Food and Nutrition Sciences* (4 a year), *Polish Journal of Pharmacology* (6 a year), *Polish Journal of Veterinary Sciences* (4 a year), *Studia Logica* (4 a year), *Studia Mathematica* (4 a year).

Poznańskie Towarzystwo Przyjaciół Nauk (Poznań Society of Friends of Arts and Sciences): ul. Seweryna Mielżyńskiego 27/29, 61-725 Poznań; tel. (61) 8527441; e-mail sekretariat@ptpn.poznan.pl; internet www.ptpn.poznan.pl; f. 1857; divs of agricultural and forestry science, history and social sciences, mathematics and natural sciences, medicine, philology and philosophy, science of art, technical sciences; 1,070 mems; library of 330,000 vols, 5,024 periodical titles, 1,432 MSS, 15,157 old books incl. incunabula, 1,839 maps and atlases, 711 microfilms; Pres. Prof. Dr Hab. HANNA KOČKA-KRENZ; Sec.-Gen. Prof. Dr Hab. LESZEK MROZEWICZ; publs *Archiwum Historii i Filozofii Medycyny* (Archives of the History and Philosophy of Medicine), *Badania Fizjograficzne nad Polską Zachodnią* (Series A (Geography) Series B (Botany) Series C (Zoology)), *Biological Letters* (in English, online), *Interdisciplinary Studies in Musicology*, *Lingua Posnaniensis*, *Neuroskop*, *Our Europe*. *Ethnography Ethnology Anthropology of Culture*, *Res Facta Nova*, *Roczniki Dziejów Społecznych i Gospodarczych*, *Roczniki Historyczne*, *Slavia Antiqua*, *Slavia Occidentalis*, *Studia Europaea Gnesnensia Gnieźnieńskie Studia Europejskie*, *Studia z Automatyki i Informatyki* (1 a year, 4 vols), *Sprawozdania Poznańskiego Towarzystwa Przyjaciół Nauk*, *Symbolae Philologorum Posnaniensium Graecae et Latinae* (2 a year).

Towarzystwo Naukowe Płockie (Płock Scientific Society): plac Narutowicza 8, 09-402 Płock; tel. (24) 3669950; e-mail aktnp@ interia.pl; internet www.tnp.org.pl; f. 1820; fosters and promotes scientific education; conducts and supports research and scientific colln of materials, in particular the Plock and land associated with the region of Mazovia; has brs in Sierpc and Łęczyca; 369 mems; library of 391,508 vols, 5,688 magazine titles; Pres. Prof. Dr Hab. Inż. ZBIGNIEW PAWEŁ KRUSZEWSKI; Sec.-Gen. Dr WIESŁAW KOŃSKI; publs *Notatki Płockie* (4 a year), *Sprawozdanie z działalności* (Yearbook).

Towarzystwo Naukowe Warszawskie (Warsaw Scientific Society): ul. Nowy Świat 72, 00-330 Warsaw; tel. (22) 6572718; e-mail sekretariat@tnw.waw.pl; internet www.tnw .waw.pl; f. 1907; promotes and develops scientific research in all brs of knowledge; organizes scientific meetings, lectures, readings and competitions for academic papers and awards; 462 mems; Pres. Prof. Dr Hab. JANUSZ LIPKOWSKI; Sec.-Gen. Prof. Dr Hab. LESZEK ZASZTOWT; publ. *Rocznik TNW* (1 a year).

Towarzystwo Naukowe w Toruniu (Scientific Society of Toruń): ul. Wysoka 16, 87-100 Toruń; tel. (56) 6223941; e-mail tnt .biuro@wp.pl; internet www.tnt.torun.pl; f. 1875; promotes practice of science and its results, in particular scientific research and the lands of Pomerania historically associated with it; concerned with historical, legal and social studies, philology, philosophy and natural sciences; 490 mems; library of 117,200 vols; Pres. Prof. Dr Hab. JAN KOPCE-

WICZ; Sec.-Gen. Prof. Dr Hab. ROMAN CZAJA; publs *Fontes* (irregular), *Prace Archaeologiczne* (irregular), *Prace Popularnonaukowe* (irregular), *Prace Wydziału Filologiczno-Filozoficznego* (irregular), *Roczniki, Sprawozdania* (1 a year), *Studia Iuridica* (irregular), *Studia Societatis Scientiarum Toruniensis* (various series: geography and geology, botany, zoology, astronomy, physiology, medicine, all irregular), *Zapiski Historyczne* (4 a year, concerned chiefly with Pomeranian problems).

Towarzystwo Przyjaciół Nauk w Przemyślu (Society of Science and Letters of Przemyśl): ul. Kościuszki 7, 37-700 Przemyśl; tel. (16) 6785601; e-mail tpntpn@wp.pl; internet www.tpn.pbp.webd.pl; f. 1909; supports and conducts research work in all scientific disciplines and popularizes science, knowledge and culture in the region; works for devt of scientific research and education; 266 mems; library of 60,000 vols; Pres. Dr TOMASZ PUDŁOCKI; Sec. Dr IZABELA WODZIŃSKA; publs *Acta Medica Premisliensia, Biblioteka Przemyska, Polska południowo-wschodnia w epoce nowożytnej Zródła dziejowe, Rocznik Przemyski*.

Towarzystwo Wiedzy Powszechnej (Universal Education Society): Pałac Kultury i Nauki, Plac Defilad 1, Sixth Fl., Room 602, 00-901 Warsaw; tel. (22) 8265630; e-mail twp@twp.pl; internet www.twp.pl; f. 1950; general adult education; runs private schools providing vocational, secondary and post-secondary education; founded 5 schools of higher education, of which 2 award Masters qualifications; organizes discussions, lectures, seminars, confs, popular science and training sessions; disseminates knowledge for the protection of environmental and public health and knowledge and training; 5,000 mems; library of 2,000 vols; Pres. BALAWEJDER EDWARD; Dir-Gen. ZENON GAWORCZUK; publ. *Edukacja Dorosłych* (12 a year).

Towarzystwo Wolnej Wszechnicy Polskiej (Society of the Polish Free University): ul. Górnośląska 20, 00-484 Warsaw; tel. (22) 6217355; e-mail mlipowski@mercury.ci.uw.cdu.pl; f. 1882; permanent education, research and application services, specialized interests clubs; brs in 14 cities; operates research, awareness, teaching and publishing in the field of social policy and education; 1,000 mems; library of 10,000 vols; Pres. Dr Inż. MIKOŁAJ Ł. LIPOWSKI; publs *Człowiek w Społeczeństwie* (irregular), *Kalendarz Samorządowy* (1 a year), *Zeszyty Naukowe* (irregular).

Wrocławskie Towarzystwo Naukowe (Wrocław Scientific Society): ul. Parkowa 13, 51-616 Wrocław; tel. (71) 3484061; e-mail wtn@wtn.wroc.pl; internet www.wtn.wroc.pl; f. 1946; promotes devt of science in all areas; initiates and stimulates creative research; develops and promotes scientific methods and work together in the promotion of scientific thought; organizes scientific meetings, lectures and readings, confs, symposia; 482 mems; Pres. Prof. Dr Hab. ANDRZEJ MULAK; Sec.-Gen. Prof. Dr Hab. JAN ZARZYCKI; publs *Annales Silesiae, Litteraria, Prace Wrocławskiego Towarzystwa Naukowego, Rozprawy Komisji Historii Sztuki, Rozprawy Komisji Językowej, Sląskie Prace Bibliologiczne i Bibliotekoznawcze, Seminaria Naukowe WTN*.

AGRICULTURE, FISHERIES AND VETERINARY SCIENCE

Polskie Towarzystwo Gleboznawcze (Polish Society of Soil Science): ul. Wiśniowa 61, 02-520 Warsaw; tel. (22) 8494816; e-mail ptg@ptg.sggw.pl; internet www.ptg.sggw.pl; f. 1937; has 14 regional divs; mem. of the Int.

Union of Soil Sciences (IUSS); works in the fields of classification of forest soils, forest habitat breeding grounds, principles of forest habitat mapping and soil science research for the proposed open-pit mine near Konin; 450 mems; Pres. Prof. Dr Hab. ZBIGNIEW ZAGÓRSKI; Sec. Prof. Dr Hab. JÓZEF CHOJNICKI; publ. *Roczniki Gleboznawcze* (Soil Science Annual, 4 a year, in Polish and English).

Polskie Towarzystwo Leśne (Polish Forest Society): ul. Bitwy Warszawskiej 1920 r. nr 3, 02-362 Warsaw; tel. (22) 8221470; e-mail sylwan@ibel.waw.pl; internet www.ptl.pl; f. 1882, present name 1925; promotes devt of scientific research in forestry; works towards effective implementation of scientific solutions to forest management problems; promotes knowledge of forest and forestry; organizes lectures, readings, discussion meetings, confs and publications related to problems of forest management; 20 regional brs; 4,314 mems; library of 3,611 vols; Pres. Prof. Dr ANDRZEJ GRZYWACZ; Sec. Dr JAN ŁUKASZEWICZ; publ. *Sylwan* (12 a year).

Polskie Towarzystwo Nauk Weterynaryjnych/Societas Polona Scientiarum Veterinariarum (Polish Society of Veterinary Sciences): ul. Nowoursynowska 159c, 02-776 Warsaw; tel. (22) 5931606; e-mail ptnw@sggw.pl; internet www.ptnw.pl; f. 1952; works for devt and dissemination of veterinary science knowledge; inspires scientific research work; promotes implementation of programmes of education and specialization in the veterinary profession; 14 sections and 13 brs; organizes lectures and seminars; holds congress every 4 years; 1,360 mems; library of 2,500 vols; Pres. Prof. Dr Hab. ANDRZEJ KONCICKI; Admin. Sec. Dr DARIUSZ BARSKI; Scientific Sec. Dr Hab. IWONA MARKOWSKA-DANIEL; publ. *Medycyna Weterynaryjna* (12 a year, online, www.medycynawet.edu.pl).

Polskie Towarzystwo Zootechniczne (Polish Society of Animal Production): ul. Kaliska 9, 02-316 Warsaw; tel. (22) 8221723; e-mail ptzph@neostrada.pl; internet ptz.icm.edu.pl; f. 1922; initiates and undertakes studies on animal production science; organizes scientific meetings, sessions, discussion; organizes teams of experts to develop opinions and judgements of breeding and animal production on request of the competent authorities and instns or of its own initiative; 1,200 mems; library of 2,630 vols; Pres. Prof. Dr Hab. ZYGMUNT LITWIŃCZUK; Sec. Prof. Dr Hab. STANISŁAW KONDRACKI; publs *Przeglądu Hodowlanego* (12 a year), *Roczników Naukowych PTZ* (1 a year).

ARCHITECTURE AND TOWN PLANNING

Stowarzyszenie Architektów Polskich (Association of Polish Architects): ul. Foksal 2, 00-950 Warsaw; tel. (22) 8278712; e-mail sarp@sarp.org.pl; internet www.sarp.org.pl; f. 1934, present name 1952; draws attention to quality architecture and environment, natural and built, in public interest; creates conditions for devt of architectural creation and its protection; organizes devt workshop and protects profession of architect; holds competition, workshops, seminars, confs; 5,100 mems; Pres. JERZY GROCHULSKI; Sec.-Gen. ANNA BORYSKA; publs *ARCH* (6 a year), *Komunikat SARP* (12 a year).

Towarzystwo Urbanistów Polskich (Society of Polish Town Planners): ul. Lwowska 5/100, 00-660 Warsaw; tel. (22) 8759756; e-mail zg@tup.org.pl; internet www.tup.org.pl; f. 1923; conducts and supports activity serving spatial management of Poland; realizes principles of sustainable devt and ensures spatial order; advertises new research and design methods; organizes

confs, seminars, workshops and training and urban competitions; initiates and supports research programmes; 1,300 mems; Pres. Prof. Dr Hab. TADEUSZ MARKOWSKI; Sec.-Gen. Dr Ing. TOMASZ MAJDA; publs *Biblioteka Urbanisty, Przeglad Urbanistyczny* (4 a year).

BIBLIOGRAPHY, LIBRARY SCIENCE AND MUSEOLOGY

Stowarzyszenie Archiwistów Polskich (Polish Archivists Association): ul. Bonifraterska 6 lok. 21, 00-213 Warsaw; tel. (22) 8318363; e-mail sap@sap.waw.pl; internet www.sap.waw.pl; f. 1965; has 27 brs; supports devt of archival science; disseminates information about archives and the legislation concerning records management; 1,265 mems; Pres. KAZIMIERZ JAROSZEK; Sec.-Gen. MARLENA KOTER; publ. *Archiwista Polski* (4 a year).

Stowarzyszenie Bibliotekarzy Polskich (Polish Librarians' Association): National Library, al. Niepodleglosci 213, 02-086 Warsaw; tel. (22) 8258374; e-mail biuro@sbp.pl; internet www.sbp.pl; f. 1917 as Polish Librarians Union, present name 1953; works for devt of librarianship, improvement of professional identity and social image, integration of the librarians' community; 7,500 mems; Pres. ELŻBIETA STEFAŃCZYK; Sec. MARZENA PRZYBYSZ; publs *Bibliotekarz* (Librarian, 12 a year), *Biuletyn Informacyjny Zarządy Głównego SBP* (PLA General Board Bulletin), *Poradnik Bibliotekarza* (Librarian's Guide, 12 a year), *Przegląd Biblioteczny* (Library Review, 4 a year), *Zagadnienia Informacji Naukowej* (Information Science Issues, 4 a year).

ECONOMICS, LAW AND POLITICS

Polskie Towarzystwo Demograficzne (Polish Demographic Society): Al. Niepodległości 164, room 3, 02-554 Warsaw; tel. (22) 3379272; e-mail ewaf@sgh.waw.pl; f. 1982; disseminates information about regularities that govern the processes of demographic and social, economic and cultural conditions of these processes; 250 mems; Pres. ZBIGNIEW STRZELECKI; Sec. LUCYNA NOWAK; publ. *Polish Population Review* (2 a year).

Polskie Towarzystwo Ekonomiczne (Polish Economic Society): Nowy Swiat 49, 00-042 Warsaw; tel. (22) 5515401; e-mail admin@pte.pl; internet www.pte.pl; f. 1945; 24 regional brs; promotes devt of economic thought and culture; disseminates economic ideas; organizes scientific confs, research projects, training programmes, competitions and education at post-secondary schools and colleges; 6,220 mems (incl. 6,000 ordinary mems and 220 supporting mems); Pres. Prof. Dr Hab. ELŻBIETA MACZYNSKA; Dir STANISŁAW GLIŃSKI; publ. *Ekonomista* (6 a year).

Polskie Towarzystwo Towaroznawcze (Polish Society for Commodity Science): ul. Sienkiewicza 4, 30-033 Cracow; tel. (12) 6330821; e-mail adamczyw@ae.krakow.pl; f. 1963; 500 mems; Pres. Prof. WACŁAW ADAMCZYK; Sec. Dr STANISŁAW POPEK; publ. *Towaroznawstwo—Problemy Jakości* (1 a year).

EDUCATION

Polskie Towarzystwo Pedagogiczne (Polish Pedagogical Association): ul. Smulikowskiego 6/8, 00-389 Warsaw; tel. (22) 3189100; e-mail biuro@ptp-pl.org; internet www.ptp-pl.org; f. 1981; 19 brs; contributes to devt and popularization of science; develops standards for educational research and practice with a focus on ethical issues; organizes congresses, confs and meetings of research; participates in nat. and int. research projects and services; 240 mems;

Pres. Prof. Dr Hab. JOANNA MADALINSKA-MICHALAK; Sec. Gen. Prof. Dr Hab. MARIAN WALCZAK; publs *Forum Oświatowe* (Educational Forum, 4 a year), *Problemy Wczesnej Edukacji* (Problems of Early Education, 2 a year), *Przegląd Historyczno-Oświatowy* (Historical-Educational Review, 2 a year), *Studia Pedagogiczne* (Pedagogic Studies, 1 a year).

FINE AND PERFORMING ARTS

Polskie Stowarzyszenie Filmu Naukowego (Polish Scientific Film Association): pl. Żelaznej Bramy 2, 00-136 Warsaw; tel. (22) 6290832; internet galaxy.uci.agh.edu.pl/~kpfn; f. 1958; Pres. Mgr GRZEGORZ KOWALEWSKI; Sec.-Gen. Dr STANISŁAW ŚLEDŹ; publ. *Film Naukowy* (2 a year).

Stowarzyszenie Historyków Sztuki (Art Historians Association): Rynek Starego Miasta 27, 00-272 Warsaw; tel. (22) 6359699; e-mail shs@shs.pl; internet www .shs.pl; f. 1934; unites art historians and those involved professionally or socially in the study of art and monuments; represents interests of mems; promotes scientific research in the field of the arts; organizes meetings, confs and scientific projects; 1,406 mems; library of 34,000 vols, 280 journals; Pres. Prof. Dr Hab. WOJCIECH WŁODARCZYK; Sec.-Gen. Dr ANNA SYLWIA CZYŻ; publs *Materiały do Dziejów Rezydencji w Polsce*, *Materiały Seminariów Metodologicznych*, *Materiały Sesji SHS*, *Materiały Sesji Oddziałowych*.

Towarzystwo im. Fryderyka Chopina (Fryderyk Chopin Society): 43 Tamka Str., 00-355 Warsaw; tel. (22) 8266549; tel. (22) 8279589; e-mail info@chopin.pl; internet www.tifc.chopin.pl; f. 1934 as Fryderyk Chopin Institute, present name 1950; permanent Secretariat of the Int. Chopin Record Competitions 'Grand Prix du Disque-Frédéric Chopin'; central Chopin museum, library, phototheque and phonotheque for study of Chopin's life and preparation of complete edition of his works; organization of concerts; 400 soc. mems; library of 20,000 vols; Pres. Prof. KAZIMIERZ GIERŻOD; Gen. Dir ANTONI GRUDZIŃSKI; publs *Annales Chopin* (Chopin Annual), *Chopin Studies*.

Warszawskie Towarzystwo Muzyczne (Music Society in Warsaw): ul. Morskie Oko 2, 02-511 Warsaw; tel. (22) 8496856; e-mail wtm@wtm.org.pl; internet www.wtm.org.pl; f. 1871; organizes concerts, exhibitions, programmes for children and youth, educational activities in schools; runs library, museum and archive; 300 mems; library of 47,500 vols; Pres. ANNA MALEWICZ-MADEY; Sec. EMILIAN MADEY.

HISTORY, GEOGRAPHY AND ARCHAEOLOGY

Polskie Towarzystwo Geograficzne (Polish Geographical Society): ul. Krakowskie Przedmieście 30, 00-927 Warsaw; tel. (22) 8261794; e-mail ptg@uw.edu.pl; internet www.ptg.pan.pl; f. 1918; organizes congresses, geographic olympiad, competition and confs; promotes devt of geographical science and teaching of geography; undertakes studies on local and regional scale; promotes principles of proper management of the geographical environment; 1,500 mems; library of 17,000 vols; Pres. Prof. Dr JERZY BAŃSKI; Sec. Dr TOMASZ WITES; Treas. Dr KONRAD CZAPIEWSKI; publs *Czasopismo Geograficzne* (Geographical Journal, 4 a year), *Polski Przegląd Kartograficzny* (Polish Cartographical Review, 4 a year), *Prace Komisji Geografii Komunikacji* (1 a year), *Studia Obszarów Wiejskich* (Rural Studies, 1 a year), *Teledetekcja Środowiska* (1 a year).

Polskie Towarzystwo Historyczne (Polish Historical Society): Rynek Starego Miasta 29/31, 00-272 Warsaw; tel. (22) 8316341; e-mail pth@ihpan.edu.pl; internet www.pth .net.pl; f. 1886; 48 regional brs and 3 research centres; promotes and organizes research on regional history; promotes devt of history and historical consciousness of soc.; preserves historical heritage; disseminates knowledge about history; organizes meetings, confs, scientific meetings and Polish historians' reunions every 5 years; 4,137 mems; Pres. Prof. Dr Hab. KRZYSTOF MIKULSKI; Sec.-Gen. Prof. Dr Hab. JACEK WIJACZKA; publs *Komunikaty Mazursko-Warmińskie* (4 a year), *Przegląd Historyczny* (4 a year), *Sobótka-Śląski Kwartalnik Historyczny* (4 a year), *Studia i Materiały do dziejów Wielkopolski i Pomorza* (series).

Polskie Towarzystwo Numizmatyczne (Polish Numismatic Society): ul. Jezuicka 6/8, skr. poczt. 2, 00-281 Warsaw; tel. (22) 8313928; e-mail ptn@ptn.pl; internet www .ptn.pl; f. 1991; promotes numismatic research; organizes sessions, scientific meetings, lectures and public meetings, exhibitions and demonstrations; 2,000 mems; library of 4,200 vols, 184 titles of periodicals; Pres. ZBIGNIEW NESTOROWICZ; Sec. Gen. ADAM ZAJĄC.

Stowarzyszenie Miłośników Dawnej Broni i Barwy (Historic Arms and Uniforms Association): al. 3 Maja 1, 30-062 Cracow; tel. (12) 2955577; e-mail kontakt@broniibarwa.org.pl; internet www.broniibarwa .org.pl; f. 1957; studies devt and dissemination of knowledge in military in the areas of protective and offensive weapons, clothing, military signs, architecture, military, air force and navy, genealogy, weapons and species; 9 local brs; 300 mems; Pres. Prof. Dr Hab. ALEKSANDER GUTERCH; Sec. MICHAL DZIEWULSKI; publ. *Studia do dziejów dawnego uzbrojenia i ubioru wojskowego*.

Towarzystwo Miłośników Historii i Zabytków Krakowa (Society of Friends of the History and Monuments of Cracow): ul. Sw. Jana 12, 31-018 Cracow; tel. (12) 4212783; e-mail tmhzk@tmhzk.krakow.pl; internet www.tmhzk.krakow.pl; f. 1897; promotes research on the history, art and culture of Cracow and its environment; organizes meetings and lectures; collects and preserves historical material; 650 mems; Pres. Prof. Dr Hab. JERZY WYROZUMSKI; Sec. Dr KAMILA FOLLPRECHT; publs *Biblioteka Krakowska*, *Fontes Cracovienses*, *Krakowa w dziejach narodu*, *Rocznik Krakowski*.

LANGUAGE AND LITERATURE

Alliance Française: BUW, ul. Dobra 56/66, 00-312 Warsaw; tel. (22) 5527165; e-mail alliance.francaise@neostrada.pl; offers courses and exams in French language and culture and promotes cultural exchange with France; attached offices in Białystok, Cieszyn, Gdańsk, Gorzow, Katowice, Łódź, Lublin, Opole, Poznań, Rybnik, Rzeszów, Szczecin, Toruń, Wałbrzych and Wrocław; Dir PATRICK RENARD.

British Council: Al. Jerozolimskie 59, 00-697 Warsaw; tel. (22) 6955900; e-mail info@britishcouncil.pl; internet www .britishcouncil.pl; f. 1938; teaching centre and library; offers courses and exams in English language and British culture; promotes cultural exchange with the UK; attached teaching centre in Cracow; Dir ANDY WILLIAMS.

Goethe-Institut: ul. Chmielna 13A, Zugang ul. Chmielna 11, 00-021 Warsaw; tel. (22) 5059000; e-mail info@warschau.goethe.org; internet www.goethe.de/warschau; f. 1990;

offers courses and exams in German language and culture and promotes cultural exchange with Germany; attached centre in Cracow; library of 16,000 vols, 7,500 online journals; Dir Dr GEORG M. BLOCHMANN.

Instituto Cervantes: ul. Nowogrodzka 22, 00-511 Warsaw; tel. (22) 5013900; e-mail cenvar@cervantes.es; internet varsovia .cervantes.es; offers courses and exams in Spanish language and culture and promotes cultural exchange with Spain and Spanish-speaking Latin and Central America; library of 21,000 vols; Dir SOLER ONÍS.

Polskie Towarzystwo Filologiczne/Societas Philologa Polonorum (Polish Philological Society): ul. Szewska 49, PL, 50-139 Wrocław; tel. (71) 3418901; e-mail sekretariat@ptf.edu.pl; internet www.ptf.edu .pl; f. 1893; promotes classical studies; preserves science of ancient culture, esp. Greek and Roman; organizes confs, congresses, lectures and meetings; 500 mems; library of 2,500 vols; Pres. Prof. Dr Hab. GOŚCIWIT MALINOWSKI; Sec. Dr KATARZYNA OCHMAN; publ. *EOS Commentarii Societatis Philologae Polonorum* (2 a year, in Polish and English, online, www.eos.uni.wroc.pl).

Polskie Towarzystwo Fonetyczne (Polish Phonetic Association): Collegium Novum, Instytut Językoznawstwa UAM, ul. Aleja Niepodległości 4, 61-874 Poznań; tel. (61) 8292706; e-mail ptfon@ptfon.pl; internet ptfon.pl; f. 1980; promotes and popularizes science of linguistic phonetics, phonetics in medicine and technology and conducts educational activities; organizes scientific meetings, readings, lectures, courses and seminars; 112 mems; Chair. Prof. GRAŻYNA DEMENKO; Sec. Mgr MARIUSZ OWSIANNY; publ. *Technologia Mowy i Języka/Speech and Language Technology (SLT)*.

Polskie Towarzystwo Językoznawcze (Polish Linguistic Society): al. Adama Mickiewicza 31, 31-120 Cracow; tel. (60) 1759153; e-mail ptj@civ.pl; internet www.ptj.civ.pl; f. 1925; organizes meetings for mems and annual scientific confs; contributes to devt of linguistic knowledge, with focus on scientific findings and practical innovations; 585 mems; Pres. Prof. RENATA PRZYBYLSKA; Sec. Dr PATRYCJA PAŁKA; publ. *Biuletyn* (1 a year).

Polskie Towarzystwo Neofilologiczne (Modern Language Association of Poland): UAM, Collegium Novum, al. Niepodległości 4, pok. 014, 61-874 Poznań; tel. (50) 5230164; e-mail poltowneo@gmail.com; internet www .poltowneo.org; f. 1929; promotes and develops theoretical and practical knowledge of modern languages and cultures, esp. in the field of language teaching; collaborates with the Min. of Nat. Education; organizes conf.; 302 mems; Pres. Prof. Dr Hab. HALINA WIDŁA; Sec.-Gen. Prof. Dr Hab. MIROSŁAW PAWLAK; publ. *Neofilolog* (2 a year).

Towarzystwo Literackie im. Adama Mickiewicza (Mickiewicz Literary Society): ul. Nowy Świat 72, pok. 14A, 00-330 Warsaw; tel. (22) 6572879; e-mail towarzystwo-literackie@wp.pl; internet www .towarzystwo-literackie.org; f. 1886; studies history of Polish literature with particular reference to works of Adam Mickiewicz and of contemporary literature and culture; arranges public lectures, meetings, sessions, academic and cultural events; 28 regional brs; 1,600 mems; Pres. Prof. Dr Hab. GRAŻYNA BORKOWSKA; Sec. Dr IRENA SZYPOWSKA; publ. *Wiek XIX* (yearbook).

Związek Literatów Polskich (Union of Polish Writers): Krakowskie Przedmieście 87/89, 00-079 Warsaw; tel. (22) 8265785; e-mail owzlp@o2.pl; internet www.literaci .eu; f. 1920; safeguards the dignity, rights and obligations of the clerical state; represents the writing community on nat. and int. level; grants financial, legal and social assistance to writers and their families; supports communities through brs and literary clubs; 1,300 mems; library of 40,000 vols and cuttings; Pres. MAREK WAWRZKIEWICZ; Sec.-Gen. ZBIGNIEW MILEWSKI.

MEDICINE

Polskie Lekarskie Towarzystwo Radiologiczne (Polish Medical Society of Radiology): ul. Chałubińskiego 5, 00-928 Warsaw; e-mail marek.sasiadek@am.wroc.pl; internet www.polradiologia.org; f. 1925; fosters devt and promotion of Polish radiology and other visualization techniques in the field, inspiring mems to creative scientific work and constant improvement of their professional skills and use of new knowledge into practice; organizes scientific confs, symposia, meetings, lectures and congress every 3 years; 1,700 mems; Pres. Prof. MAREK SĄSIADEK; Sec. Dr ANNA CHODOROWSKA; Treas. Dr BARBARA HEINRICH; publ. *Polish Journal of Radiology* (4 a year).

Polskie Towarzystwo Anatomiczne (Polish Anatomical Society): Uniwersytet Medyczny w Poznaniu, Katedra i Zakład Anatomii Prawidłowej, ul. Święcickiego 6, 60-781 Poznań; tel. (61) 6546565; e-mail pta@pta.info.pl; internet www.pta.info.pl; f. 1923; promotes scientific work in the field of morphology and related disciplines; organizes scientific meetings and conventions; conducts competitions, courses and lectures; 304 mems; Pres. Prof. Dr Hab. BOGDAN CISZEK; Sec. Dr PAWEŁ SZARO; publs *Folia Morphologica* (4 a year, print and online, www.fm.viamedica.pl), *Postępy Biologii Komórki* (Advances in Cell Biology, online, www.pbkom.pl/pbkom/index_pl.htm).

Polskie Towarzystwo Anestezjologii i Intensywnej Terapii (Polish Society of Anaesthesiology and Intensive Therapy): ul. Bytnara 13 a m 65, 02-645 Warsaw; tel. (81) 7244332; e mail ptaiit05@amp.edu.pl; internet www.anestezjologia.org.pl; f. 1959; conducts and supports research activities in the field of anaesthesiology and intensive care, pain management; cooperates to improve professional skills of mems and medical staff; disseminates knowledge in the field of anaesthesiology, intensive care, resuscitation and pain management; initiates and supports nat. and int. scientific exchange; organizes congresses, symposia, confs, scientific meetings, lectures, exhibitions; 13 regional brs and 6 sections; Pres. Prof. Dr Hab. MARIA WUJTEWICZ; Sec. Dr Hab. RADOSŁAW OWCZUK; publ. *Anestezjologia Intensywna Terapia* (6 a year).

Polskie Towarzystwo Badań Radiacyjnych im. Marii Skłodowskiej-Curie (Polish Radiation Research Society): Nat. Institute of Public Health, Nat. Institute of Hygiene, ul. Chocimska 24, 00-791 Warsaw; tel. (22) 8497774; e-mail ptbr@pzh.gov.pl; internet ptbr.org.pl; f. 1967; unites scientists involved and interested in radiation research and applications; promotes and popularizes devt of radiation research; facilitates exchange of ideas and research results among mems and between scientific circles and gen. public; awards Maria Skłodowska-Curie medal; organizes scientific meetings every 3 years; 229 mems; Pres. Prof. MAREK JANIAK; Sec. Dr KRZYSZTOF PACHOCKI.

Polskie Towarzystwo Chirurgów Dziecięcych (Polish Association of Paediatric Surgeons): Dept of Surgery and Urology for Children and Adolescents, Medical Univ. of Gdańsk, ul. Nowe Ogrody 1–6, 80-804 Gdańsk; tel. (58) 7640321; e-mail pedsurg@gumed.edu.pl; internet www.ptchd.pl; f.

1965; 300 mems; Pres. PIOTR CZAUDERNA; Sec. MARCIN ŁOSIN; publs *Standardy Medyczne-Problemy Chirurgii Dziecięcej* (4 a year), *Surgery in Childhood International* (4 a year).

Polskie Towarzystwo Chorób Płuc (Polish Phthisiopneumonological Society): ul. Płocka 26, 01-138 Warsaw; tel. (69) 2399149; e-mail biuroptchp@ptchp.org; internet www.ptchp.org; f. 1934 as Polskie Towarzystwo Badań Naukowych nad Gruźlicą, present name 2006; supports and encourages research into tuberculosis and chest diseases; 17 regional brs; 1,100 mems; Pres. DOROTA GÓRECKA; Sec. EWA JASSEM; publ. *Pneumonologia i Alergologia Polska* (12 a year).

Polskie Towarzystwo Diagnostyki Laboratoryjnej (Polish Laboratory Diagnostics Society): c/o Dr Piotr Paluch, Zakład Diagnostyki Szpital Uniwersytecki, Kopernika 15A, 31-501 Cracow; tel. (12) 4248375; e-mail ppaluch@su.krakow.pl; internet www.ptdl.pl; f. 1964; disseminates scientific and training activities for professional devt and to support research activities of its mems; organizes congresses and scientific confs, courses and lectures, workshops and presentations, laboratory equipment, competitions; 18 regional brs; 5,000 mems; Pres. Dr Hab. BOGDAN SOLNICA; Sec. Dr PIOTR PALUCH; publ. *Diagnostyka Laboratoryjna* (4 a year).

Polskie Towarzystwo Epidemiologów i Lekarzy Chorób Zakaźnych (Polish Society of Epidemiology and Infectious Diseases): ul. Koszarowa 5, 51-149 Wrocław; tel. (52) 3255605; e-mail kikchzak@cm.umk.pl; internet www.pteilchz.org.pl; f. 1958; promotes devt of programmes for the prevention and treatment of infectious diseases; disseminates medical knowledge, with emphasis on infectious diseases and epidemiology; promotes ethical and professional conduct; gives awards and scholarships; organizes meetings, confs, training; 1,100 mems; Pres. Prof. Dr Hab. MALGORZATA PAWLOWSKA; Sec. Dr EWA SMUKALSKA; publ. *Przegląd Epidemiologiczny* (4 a year).

Polskie Towarzystwo Farmaceutycznego (Polish Pharmaceutical Society): ul. Długa 16, 00-238 Warsaw; tel. (22) 8311542; e-mail zarzad@ptfarm.pl; internet www.ptfarm.pl; f. 1947; promotes progress of science among pharmacists; encourages and assists pharmacists to implement scientific work; rep. of science and the pharmaceutical profession at nat. and int. level; organizes meetings, conventions and confs, exhibitions and research trips, lectures and training courses; 7,000 mems; Chair. Prof. Dr Hab. JANUSZ PLUTA; publs *Acta Poloniae Pharmaceutica* (6 a year), *Bromatologia i Chemia Toksykologiczna* (4 a year), *Farmacja Polska* (12 a year).

Polskie Towarzystwo Farmakologiczne (Polish Pharmacological Society): Siedziba stała Zarządu Głównego, ul. Krakowskie Przedmieście 26/28, 00-927 Warsaw; tel. (22) 8262116; e-mail ptf.webpage@yahoo.pl; internet www.ptf.info.pl; f. 1965; contributes to devt of research and scientific studies in the field of experimental and clinical pharmacology and toxicology; organizes scientific meetings, congresses, symposia, confs; 8 regional brs; 341 mems; Pres. Prof. Dr WLADYSLAW LASON; Sec. Prof. Dr BOGUSLAWA BUDZISZEWSKA; publ. *Pharmacological Reports* (abstracts of the Int. Congresses of the Polish Pharmacological Soc.).

Polskie Towarzystwo Fizjologiczne (Polish Physiological Society): 16 Grzegórzecka St, 31-531 Cracow; tel. (12) 4211006; e-mail zgptf@cm-uj.krakow.pl; internet ptf.krakow.pl; f. 1936; promotes scientific activity in

all fields of physiology incl. most gastrointestinal, endocrine, cardiovascular, neural, respiratory and kidney physiology; awards Napoleon Cybulski Honorary Medal; organizes scientific meetings, public readings, lectures, congresses, symposia and confs; 300 mems; Pres. Prof. Dr Hab. WIESLAW W. PAWLIK; Sec.-Gen. AGATA PTAK-BELOWSKA; publ. *Journal of Physiology and Pharmacology* (online, jpp.krakow.pl).

Polskie Towarzystwo Fizyki Medycznej (Polish Society of Medical Physics): Centrum Onkologii-Instytut im. Marii Skłodowskiej-Curie, Zakład Fizyki Medycznej, ul. Roentgena 5, 02-781 Warsaw; Polskie Towarzystwo Fizyki Medycznej im. Cezarego Pawłowskiego, ul. Sw. Andrzeja Boboli 8, 02-525 Warsaw; tel. (22) 5462775; e-mail karo@pum.edu.pl; internet ptfm.ire.pw.edu.pl; f. 1965; promotes devt and popularization of applications in medical physics, biomedical engineering, radiation protection; organizes symposia, scientific meetings, lectures, training and competitions; makes rules, regulations and guidelines on use of technical measures and conditions of use of medicines, esp. in the area of infrastructure quality and safety of medical technologies related to medical physics, through participation in the implemented systems, accreditation, inspection and information; 150 mems; Pres. Dr Hab. PAWEŁ KUKOŁOWICZ; Sec. Dr GRAŻYNA KOSICKA; publ. *Polish Journal of Medical Physics and Engineering*.

Polskie Towarzystwo Gerontologiczne (Polish Society of Gerontology): Wisniowa St 41/66D, 02-520 Warsaw; ul. Kleczewska 61/63, 01-826 Warsaw; tel. (22) 5649117; e-mail gerontologia@gerontologia.org.pl; internet www.gerontologia.org.pl; f. 1973; develops science in the field of gerontology; promotes popularization of social, clinical and theoretical gerontology; initiates, organizes and supports scientific research in the field of gerontology in different specialized disciplines; facilitates contacts and organizes cooperation of individuals and orgs working on different sections of theoretical and applied gerontology; organizes scientific meetings, lectures, readings, scientific confs, seminars and courses; 12 regional brs; 320 mems; Pres. Prof. Dr Hab. PIOTR BŁĘDOWSKI; Sec. Dr PAWEŁ KUBICKI; publ. *Gerontologia Polska* (4 a year).

Polskie Towarzystwo Ginekologiczne (Polish Gynaecological Society): Katedra i Oddział Kliniczny Ginekologii i Położnictwa, Śląskiego Uniwersytetu Medycznego w Katowicach, ul. Edukacji 102, 43-100 Tychy; tel. (32) 3255301; e-mail zgptg@ginekologia.tychy.pl; internet www.poltowgin.pl; f. 1902; Pres. Prof. Dr Hab. RYSZARD PORĘBA; Sec. Prof. Dr Hab. JERZY SIKORA; publ. *Ginekologia Polska* (12 a year, online, ginekolpol.com).

Polskie Towarzystwo Higieniczne (Polish Hygiene Society): ul. Karowa 31, 00-324 Warsaw; tel. (22) 8266320; e-mail biuro@pth.pl; internet www.pth.pl; f. 1898; creates professional opinion on devt of social hygiene, environmental health, health education, preventive medicine and public health; organizes scientific meetings, symposia, confs, congresses, lectures and specialized training courses; Pres. Prof. Dr Hab. JERZY T. MARCINKOWSKI; Treas. Dr ANETA KLIMBERG; publs *Druk Bibliofilski 'Hygeia'*, *Problemy Higieny*, *Problemy Higieny i Epidemiologii* (4 a year, online, www.phie.pl/index.php), *Problemy Higieny Pracy*.

Polskie Towarzystwo Higieny Psychicznej (Polish Mental Health Society): ul. Targowa 59/16, 03-729 Warsaw; tel. (22) 8186599; e-mail pthp@poczta.onet.pl;

internet www.pthp.org.pl; f. 1948; develops and disseminates appropriate hierarchy of values, principles and standards of moral health and life through publications, training and mass media to create social awareness; initiates and organizes scientific research works in the field of mental health; 6 regional brs; organizes scientific meetings every 3 years; 1,250 mems; library of 2,500 vols; Pres. Prof. Dr Hab. ANDRZEJ BAŁANDYNOWICZ; publ. *Zdrowie Psychiczne* (4 a year).

Polskie Towarzystwo Immunologii Doświadczalnej i Klinicznej (Polish Society for Experimental and Clinical Immunology): ul. Czysta 18, 31-121 Cracow; tel. (12) 6339431; e-mail mmmarcin@cyf-kr.edu.pl; internet immuno.net.pl; f. 1969; promotes devt and implementation of research in the field of experimental and clinical immunology; organizes congresses, scientific meetings, symposia, scientific confs and competitions, public readings and lectures; 9 regional brs; 500 mems; Pres. Prof. JANUSZ MARCINKIEWICZ; Sec. Mgr MARTA CISZEK-LENDA; publs *Central European Journal of Immunology* (4 a year, in English), *Integryna—Biuletyn PTI* (4 a year, in Polish).

Polskie Towarzystwo Kardiologiczne (Polish Cardiac Society): ul. Stawki 3A lok. 1–2, 00-193 Warsaw; tel. (22) 8871856; e-mail zarzad.glowny@ptkardio.pl; internet www.ptkardio.pl; f. 1954; disseminates knowledge about the progress of cardiology and cardiac surgery among physicians and other health care workers; initiates and supports research in the field of heart and blood diseases; organizes congresses, confs and scientific meetings and teaching; 6,198 mems; Pres. Prof. Dr Hab. JANINA STĘPIŃSKA; Sec. Prof. Dr Hab. ADAM WITKOWSKI; publs *Folia Cardiologica* (12 a year), *Kardiologia Polska* (12 a year).

Polskie Towarzystwo Lekarskie (Polish Medical Association): al. Ujazdowskie 22, 00-478 Warsaw; tel. (22) 6288699; e-mail ptl@interia.pl; internet www.ptl.org.pl; f. 1951; develops knowledge and awareness of scientific and professional qualifications of doctors and mems; promotes and develops principles of medical ethics and care for their adherence; 25,000 mems; Pres. Prof. Dr Hab. JERZY WOY-WOJCIECHOWSKI; Sec.-Gen. Prof. Dr Hab. EDWARD TOWPIK; Sec. Dr FELIKSA ŁAPKIEWICZ; publs *Polski Merkuriusz Lekarski* (52 a year), *Przegląd Lekarski* (12 a year), *Wiadomości Lekarskie* (26 a year).

Polskie Towarzystwo Medycyny Pracy (Polish Society of Occupational Medicine): ul. Teresy 8, 90-950 Łódź; tel. (42) 6314775; e-mail jolantaw@imp.lodz.pl; f. 1969; facilitates cooperation among people working for devt and dissemination of science in occupational medicine; participates in the organization of occupational health services; br. in Warsaw; Pres. Prof. Dr Hab. RYSZARD ANDRJEZAK; Sec. Dr JOLANTA WALUSIAK; publs *International Journal of Occupational Medicine and Environmental Health* (4 a year, in English), *Medycyna Pracy* (6 a year).

Polskie Towarzystwo Medycyny Sądowej i Kryminologii (Polish Society of Forensic Medicine and Criminology): ul. Sędziowska 18A, 91-304 Łódź; tel. (42) 6544536; e-mail ptmsik@ptmsik.pl; internet www.ptmsik.pl; f. 1938; works for devt and research in the field of forensic medicine, toxicology, genetics, other forensic sciences; 200 mems; Pres. Prof. JAROSŁAW BERENT; Sec. AGNIESZKA PAULA JURCZYK; publ. *Archiwum Medycyny Sądowej i Kryminologii* (4 a year, online, www.amsik.pl).

Polskie Towarzystwo Medycyny Społecznej i Zdrowia Publicznego (Polish Association of Social Medicine and Public Health): ul. Chodźki 1, 20-093 Lublin; tel. (81) 7405753; e-mail mchbt@eskulap.am.lublin.pl; f. 1916; 1,800 mems; Pres. Prof. Dr Hab. n. med. LESZEK WDOWIAK; publ. *Problemy Medycyny Społecznej* (Problems in Social Medicine, 2 or 3 a year).

Polskie Towarzystwo Medycyny Sportowej (Polish Society of Sports Medicine): 1 pl. Hallera St, 90-647 Lódź; tel. (42) 6393399; e-mail ptms@ptms.org.pl; internet www.ptms.org.pl; f. 1937; 7 regional divs; encourages research, disseminates information on scientific basis for understanding physiological and pathological processes taking place in the human body under the influence of exercise or lack of it; cooperates to improve professional skills; organizes congresses and education; Pres. Prof. Dr ANNA JEGIER; Sec. Dr WITOLD JULIUSZ FURGAŁ; publs *Chirurgia Kolana Artroskopia Traumatologia Sportowa* (4 a year, online, www.sportmed.com.pl/wydawnictwo.php), *Medicina Sportiva* (online, www.medycynasportowa.edu.pl), *Medycyna Sportowa* (Polish Journal of Sports Medicine, 4 a year, online, www.medycynasportowa.edu.pl).

Polskie Towarzystwo Nauk Żywieniowych (Polish Society of Nutritional Sciences): ul. Nowoursynowska 159C, 02-776 Warsaw; tel. (22) 5937110; e-mail ptnz@sggw.pl; internet ptnz.sggw.pl; f. 1980; organizes and promotes activities to develop nutritional science; disseminates and promotes scientific achievements in the field of nutrition; organizes meetings, symposia and scientific confs, lectures, readings and exhibitions; 5 regional brs; 300 mems; Pres. Prof. Dr Hab. ANNA BRZOZOWSKA; Sec. Prof. Dr Hab. JULIUSZ PRZYSLAWSKI; publ. *Polish Journal of Food and Nutrition Sciences* (4 a year).

Polskie Towarzystwo Neurochirurgów (Polish Society of Neurosurgeons): Katedra i Kliniczny Oddział Neurochirurgii, ŚlAM, Wojewódzki Szpital Specjalistyczny Nr 5 im. Sw. Barbary, Pl. Medyków 1, 41-200 Sosnowiec; tel. (32) 3682024; e-mail sekr_nch@wss5.pl; internet www.neurochirurgia-polska.org; f. 1964; advances knowledge in the sciences related to the nervous system, particularly surgery of the nervous system; encourages research and scientific work in this area; promotes principles of medical deontology; organizes nat. and int. scientific meetings, public readings and lectures; 279 mems; Pres. Prof. Dr Hab. HENRYK MAJCHRZAK; Sec. Dr PIOTR ŁADZIŃSKI; publ. *Neurologia i Neurochirurgia Polska* (6 a year).

Polskie Towarzystwo Neurologiczne (Polish Neurological Society): Klinika Neurologii Szpital Kliniczny im. Heliodora Swiecickiego ul. Przybyszewskiego 49, 60-355 Poznan; tel. (61) 8691535; e-mail sekretarz@ptneuro.pl; internet www.ptneuro.pl; f. 1934; promotes devt of science in the field of neuroscience and related brs of science; organizes congresses and scientific meetings; 16 regional brs; 2,800 mems; Pres. Prof. W. KOZUBSKI; Sec. Dr JAN MEJNARTOWICZ; publ. *Neurologia i Neurochirurgia Polska* (6 a year).

Polskie Towarzystwo Onkologiczne (Polish Society of Oncology): ul. Dębinki 7, 80-211 Gdańsk; tel. (12) 4228760; e-mail ptoportal@gmail.com; internet www.pto.med.pl; f. 1921; stimulates research and propagates scientific achievements in the field of oncology; improves professional skills of the staff of oncological centres and spreads health education and prophylactic principles; organizes conventions, symposia, confs and scientific meetings; 1,000 mems; Pres. Prof. Dr Hab. JACEK JASSEM; Sec. Dr Hab. MARZENA WEŁNICKA-JAŚKIEWICZ; publ. *Nowotwory* (Journal Of Oncology, 6 a year, online, www.nowotwory.edu.pl).

Polskie Towarzystwo Ortopedyczne i Traumatologiczne (Polish Orthopaedic and Traumatological Society): c/o Prof. Dr Hab. Paweł Stanisław Małdyk, Instytut Reumatologii im. Prof. Dr Hab.Eleonory Reicher, ul. Spartańska 1, 02-637 Warsaw; tel. (22) 8444241; e-mail kontakt@ptoitr.pl; internet www.ptoitr.pl; f. 1928; 16 local brs; assists mems in their professional work and research; facilitates asscn of doctors interested in orthopaedics, traumatology; cooperates with the authorities in solving health problems; organizes scientific meetings, symposia, discussions and scientific training; Pres. Prof. Dr Hab. DAMIAN KUSZ; Sec. MARIUSZ NOWAK; publs *Chirurgia Narządów Ruchu i Ortopedia Polska* (6 a year), *Kwartalnik Ortopedyczny* (4 a year).

Polskie Towarzystwo Patologów (Polish Society of Pathologists): Zakład Patomorfologii Centralnego Szpitala Klinicznego MSWiA, ul. Wołoska 137, 02-507 Warsaw; tel. (22) 5081230; internet www.pol-pat.pl; f. 1958; raises level of academic and professional qualifications of mems; initiates and promotes research in the field of pathology; promotes scientific work; disseminates updated knowledge; cooperates in the social organization of healthcare; organizes meetings, conventions, confs and symposia; training and courses; 13 brs; 581 mems; Pres. Prof. Dr Hab. ANNA NASIEROWSKA-GUTTMEJER; Sec. Dr KRZYSZTOF BARDADIN; publ. *Polish Journal of Pathology* (4 a year, in English).

Polskie Towarzystwo Pediatryczne (Polish Paediatric Society): Klinika Transplantacji Szpiku, Onkologii i Hematologii Dziecięcej AM we Wrocławiu, ul. Bujwida 44, 50-345 Wrocław; tel. (71) 7703216; e-mail pedhemat@am.wroc.pl; internet www.ptp.edu.pl; f. 1908; 25 regional brs; disseminates medical knowledge with particular emphasis on children and adolescents; creates health protection programmes for children and young people; encourages raising the level of academic and professional qualifications of paediatricians; promotes principles of professional conduct and ethics; 4,500 mems; Pres. Prof. Dr Hab. ALICJA CHYBICKA; Treas. Prof. Dr Hab. WOJCIECH SŁUŻEWSKI; publs *Pediatria Polska* (12 a year), *Przegląd Pediatryczny* (4 a year).

Polskie Towarzystwo Pielęgniarskie (Polish Nurses Association): Reymonta 8/12, 01-842 Warsaw; tel. (22) 3981872; e-mail zgptpiel@gmail.com; internet www.ptp.na1.pl; f. 1924, revived 1954; popularizes scientific achievements in the field of nursing and related sciences; supports professional and scientific devt of nurses and midwives; conducts research and implements their results to the practice of nursing and midwifery; 3,000 mems; library of 3,000 vols; Pres. Dr MARIA CISEK (acting); Sec. Mgr GRAZYNA WYSIADECKA; publ. *Problemy Pielęgniarstwa* (Nursing Topics).

Polskie Towarzystwo Psychiatryczne (Polish Psychiatric Association): ul. Sobieskiego 9, 02-957 Warsaw; tel. (22) 8424087; e-mail ptp@psychiatria.org.pl; internet www.psychiatria.org.pl; f. 1920; 15 brs; promotes cooperation among psychiatrists; works for mental health legislation to establish rules and organization of mental health care; 1,400 mems; Pres. Dr Hab. JANUSZ HEITZMAN; Sec. WOJCIECH KOSMOWSKI; publs *Archives of Psychiatry and Psychotherapy* (4 a year, online, www.archivespp.pl), *Psychiatria i Psychoterapia* (online (psychiatriapsychoterapia.pl)), *Psychiatria Polska* (6 a year, online, www.psychiatriapolska.pl), *Psychoterapia* (4 a year, online, www.psychoterapiaptp.pl).

Polskie Towarzystwo Stomatologiczne (Polish Dental Association): ul. Montelupich 4, Małopolska, 31-155 Cracow; tel. (12) 4245442; e-mail biurozgpts@gmail.com; internet www.pts.net.pl; f. 1951; promotes devt of medical knowledge in the field of dental disciplines; organizes scientific meetings and training, courses, symposia, confs, scientific seminars and congress every 5 years; 24 brs and 7 sections; 8,000 mems; Pres. Dr Hab. BARTLOMIEJ W. LOSTER; Sec.-Gen. Dr Hab. JOLANTA PYTKO-POLOŃCZYK; publs *Dental and Medical Problems* (4 a year), *Dental Forum* (2 a year), *Implantoprotetyka* (4 a year), *Journal of Stomatology / Czasopismo Stomatologiczne* (12 a year), *Protetyka Stomatologiczna* (6 a year).

Polskie Towarzystwo Toksykologiczne (Polish Society of Toxicology): Nofer Institute of Occupational Medicine, 8 Teresy St, 91-348 Lodz; tel. (42) 63146266; e-mail impx@imp.lodz.pl; internet www.pttox.lodz.pl; f. 1978; organizes and supports activities aiming at devt of toxicological research; disseminates recent scientific achievements in toxicological research; 11 regional sections; organizes nat. and int. scientific congresses, confs, symposia, training and methodological seminars and courses; 300 mems; Pres. Prof. WOJCIECH WĄSOWICZ; Sec. Dr JOLANTA GROMADZIŃSKA; publ. *Acta Poloniae Toxicologica* (2 a year).

Polskie Towarzystwo Urologiczne (Polish Urological Association): ul. Łowicka 19, 02-574 Warsaw; tel. (22) 8456919; e-mail sekretariat@ptu.net.pl; internet www.pturol.org.pl; f. 1949; represents the interests of its mems and doctors working in the field of urology; cooperates with reps of other disciplines of science and technology for devt of urology; encourages ethical behaviour among mems; participates in preparation of agenda and organization of teaching pre- and postgraduate and professional training in the field of urology; 9 regional brs; 800 mems; Pres. Prof. MAREK SOSNOWSKI; Dir IWONA SRIBNIAK; publs *Central European Journal of Urology, Przegląd Urologiczny* (6 a year), *Urologia Polska* (4 a year).

Polskie Towarzystwo Walki z Kalectwem (Polish Society for Rehabilitation of the Disabled): ul. Oleandrów 4/10, 00-629 Warsaw; tel. (22) 8259839; e-mail twk@twk.org.pl; internet www.twk.org.pl; f. 1960; provides social assistance and equal opportunities to people with disabilities and their families; promotes scientific and organizational prevention, treatment, rehabilitation, orthopaedic, psychology and pedagogy and prevention of social pathologies; popularizing progressive ideas in prophylaxis and changing social attitudes towards the disabled; 34 br. offices; Pres. ANNA BEDNARZ-ŚLIWOWSKA; Sec. ELŻBIETA SZADURA-URBAŃSKA; publs *Life of the Polish Society for Rehabilitation of the Disabled Information Bulletin, Ty i Swiat* (12 a year).

Stowarzyszenie Neuropatologów Polskich (Polish Association of Neuropathologists): 5 Pawińskiego str., 02-106 Warsaw; tel. (61) 6686560; e-mail jszymas@ampat.amu.edu.pl; internet snp.amu.edu.pl; f. 1964; fosters devt of science in the field of neuropathology and related disciplines; issues scientific, organizational and expert opinions in matters concerning neuropathology; organizes scientific congresses, meetings and competitions; 101 mems; Pres. Prof. Dr Hab. JANUSZ SZYMAŚ; Sec. AGNIESZKA KALISZEK; publ. *Folia Neuropathologica* (4 a year).

Towarzystwo Chirurgów Polskich (Society of Polish Surgeons): ul. Banacha 1A, 02-097 Warsaw; tel. (22) 5991129; e-mail biuro@tchp.pl; internet www.tchp.pl; f. 1889; encourages and implements scientific work of surgeons; promotes and facilitates contacts with surgical centres on nat. and int. level; participates in the appointment of consultants for surgery and staffing coordinators surgical wards; provides opinions on curriculum of pre- and postgraduate in the field of surgery and specialization programs; organizes scientific meetings every 2 years; conducts training; 3,150 mems; Pres. Prof. Dr Hab. MAREK KRAWCZYK; Sec.-Gen. Prof. MAREK MARUSZYŃSKI; publ. *Polski Przegląd Chirurgiczny* (12 a year).

Towarzystwo Internistów Polskich (Polish Society of Internal Medicine): ul. Skawińska 8, 31-066 Cracow; tel. (12) 4305415; e-mail tip@mp.pl; internet tip.org.pl; f. 1906; advances knowledge of internal medicine, represents Polish internal medical physicians; organizes Congress every 4 years, annual Nat. Educational Conf. on Internal Medicine and Polish–Slovak Conf. on Internal Medicine; 21 local brs; 3,000 mems; Pres. Prof. Dr Hab. TOMASZ GUZIK; Sec. Dr PIOTR GAJEWSKI; publ. *Polskie Archiwum Medycyny Wewnętrznej* (Polish Archives of Internal Medicine, 12 a year, in English).

NATURAL SCIENCES

Biological Sciences

Polskie Towarzystwo Biochemiczne (Polish Biochemical Society): ul. L. Pasteura 3, 02-093 Warsaw; tel. (22) 5892499; e-mail biuro@ptbioch.edu.pl; internet www.ptbioch.edu.pl; f. 1958; holds nat. and int. scientific confs, symposia, meetings, discussions, lectures and workshops; promotes and supports molecular and cellular life sciences, incl. biochemistry, pathobiochemistry, clinical biochemistry, molecular biology, molecular medicine, biotechnology; 12 regional brs; 1,200 mems; Pres. Prof. Dr Hab. ANDRZEJ DZUGAJ; Sec. Prof. Dr Hab. PAWEŁ POMORSKI; publs *Acta Biochimica Polonica* (4 a year, online, www.actabp.pl), *Postępy Biochemii* (Advances in Biochemistry, 4 a year, online, www.postepybiochemii.pl).

Polskie Towarzystwo Biofizyczne (Polish Biophysical Society): pl. M. Curie-Skłodowskiej 1 p. 201, 20-031 Lublin; tel. (81) 5376252; e-mail zg.ptbf@gmail.com; internet ptbf.pl; f. 1971; promotes devt and popularization of the biophysical sciences; encourages research and grants scholarships; holds scientific meetings and discussions, readings, lectures, exhibitions, competitions and polls, scientific and educational meetings; 250 mems; Pres. Prof. Dr Hab. WIESŁAW I. GRUSZECKI; Sec. Dr WOJCIECH GRUDZIŃSKI; publ. *Current Topics in Biophysics* (2 a year, in English, supplement in Polish).

Polskie Towarzystwo Biometryczne (Polish Biometric Society): Poznań Univ. of Life Sciences, ul. Wojska Polskiego 28, 60-637 Poznań; tel. (61) 8487140; e-mail polbiom@up.poznan.pl; internet www.polbiom.up.poznan.pl; f. 1961; promotes devt of biometry, applied mathematical statistics in medicine, agriculture, biology, genetics, ecology; organizes int. colloquium; 230 mems; Pres. Prof. Dr Hab. STANISŁAW MEJZA; Sec Dr KATARZYNA AMBROZY; publs *Biometrical Letters* (2 a year, online, www.au.poznan.pl/biometrical.letters), *Colloquium Biometricum* (1 a year, online, collbiom.up.lublin.pl).

Polskie Towarzystwo Botaniczne (Polish Botanical Society): c/o Dr Wojciech J. Szypuła, Warszawski Uniwersytet Medyczny, Zakład Biologii a Botaniki Farmaceutycznej, ul. Banacha 1, 02-097 Warsaw; tel. (22) 5720932; e-mail secretary@pbsociety.org.pl; internet pbsociety.org.pl; f. 1922; 15 regional brs; contributes to devt of botanical science and dissemination of botanical knowledge; works to improve the level of scientific mems and their business relationship with the needs of the nat. economy and culture; organizes scientific meetings, conventions, confs, scientific expeditions; initiates and supports research; 1,320 mems; library of 47,139 vols (incl. 22,342 vols of periodicals, 18,023 prints and brochures), 815 journal titles; Pres. Prof. Dr Hab. ADAM ROSTAŃSKI; Sec. Gen. Dr WOJCIECH J. SZYPUŁA; publs *Acta Agrobotanica* (4 a year, in English), *Acta Mycologica* (2 a year, in English), *Acta Societatis Botanicorum Poloniae* (4 a year, in English), *Biuletyn Ogrodów Botanicznych Muzeów i Zbiorów, Monographiae Botanicae, Wiadomości Botaniczne.*

Polskie Towarzystwo Entomologiczne (Polish Entomological Society): ul. Dabrowskiego 159, 60-594 Poznań; tel. (61) 8487916; e-mail carabus@au.poznan.pl; internet pte.up.poznan.pl; f. 1923 as Polish Entomological Union, present name 1965; research work on theoretical and applied entomology; 500 mems; library of 11,000 vols; Pres. Dr Hab. MAREK BUNALSKI; Gen. Sec. Dr PAWEŁ SIENKIEWICZ; publs *Fauna Polski* (Fauna of Poland), *Klucze do Oznaczania Owadów Polski* (Keys for Identification of Polish Insects, irregular), *Polskie Pismo Entomologiczne* (Polish Entomological Papers, 4 a year), *Wiadomości Entomologiczne* (Entomological News, 4 a year).

Polskie Towarzystwo Fitopatologiczne (Polish Phytopathological Society): ul. Wojska Polskiego 71C, 60-625 Poznań; tel. (61) 8487711; internet www.up.poznan.pl/ptfit; f. 1971; holds scientific meetings, field days, confs and symposia of sections incl. nomenclature and teaching, biological control of plant diseases, plant virology, seed pathology, mycology and mycotoxins, biochemistry and genetics of plant pathogens, woody plant diseases, bacteriology, new pathogens and diseases; 8 divs; 300 mems; Pres. Prof. Dr Hab. MAŁGORZATA MAŃKA; Sec. Dr Ing. DOROTA SZOPIŃSKA; publ. *Phytopathologia* (4 a year, in English).

Polskie Towarzystwo Genetyczne (Polish Genetics Society): c/o Dr Anna Skorupska, Zakład Genetyki i Mikrobiologii UMCS, ul. Akademicka 19, 20-033 Lublin; tel. (81) 5375972; e-mail anna.skorupska@poczta.umcs.lublin.pl; internet www.ptgen.pl; f. 1966; 10 regional brs; promotes devt of genetics; works for improvement of scientific mems; promotes modern genetic knowledge; holds scientific meetings and confs; 762 mems; Pres. Prof. Dr Hab. ANNA SKORUPSKA; Sec. Prof. Dr Hab. WANDA MAŁEK; publs *Biuletyn, Genetica Polonica* (4 a year).

Polskie Towarzystwo Hydrobiologiczne (Polish Hydrobiological Society): ul. Banacha 2, 02-097 Warsaw; tel. (22) 5546443; e-mail sekretarz@pth.home.pl; internet www.pth.home.pl; f. 1959; 12 nat. brs; promotes devt and dissemination of achievements of hydrobiology and related sciences; promotes and supports research into the biology and ecology of aquatic organisms, analysis of functioning and protection of aquatic ecosystems and wetlands; mem. of Int. Soc. of Limnology; organizes scientific expeditions; 400 mems; Vice-Pres. Dr IWONA JASSER; Sec. Dr JAN IGOR RYBAK; publs *Biuletynu DNO, Fauna Słodkowodna Polski, Wiadomości Hydrobiologiczne* (online).

Polskie Towarzystwo Mikrobiologów (Polish Society of Microbiologists): ul. Płocka 26, Warsaw; tel. (22) 5854480; e-mail kizmikrob@cm.umk.pl; internet www.microbiology.pl; f. 1927 as Polish Soc. of Microbiologists and Epidemiologists, current name and status 1951; promotes basic and applied research in microbiology; 14 regional brs; holds nat. congress every 4 years; 900 mems; Pres. Prof. Dr Hab. EUGENIA GOSPO-DAREK; Sec. Dr AGNIESZKA MIKUCKA; publs *Journal of Polish Microbiology* (4 a year, in English, online, www.pjm.microbiology.pl), *Medycyna Doświadczalna i Mikrobiologia* (Experimental Medicine and Microbiology, 4 a year, in Polish), *Postępy Mikrobiologii* (Advances in Microbiology, 4 a year, in Polish, online, www.pm.microbiology.pl).

Polskie Towarzystwo Parazytologiczne (Polish Parasitological Society): ul. Twarda 51/55, 00-818 Warsaw; tel. (22) 6206226; internet www.ptparasit.org.pl; f. 1948; develops various fields of parasitology; works with state and social instns to promote issues related to parasitology in the community; sections of gen., medical and veterinary parasitology; organizes scientific meetings and confs; maintains specialized museums and libraries; 235 mems; Pres. Prof. Dr Hab. PIOTR KURNATOWSKI; Sec. Prof. Dr Hab. ANNA ROCKA; publs *Annals of Parasitology* (4 a year, online, annals-parasitology.eu), *Katalog Fauny Pasozytniczej Polski* (irregular).

Polskie Towarzystwo Zoologiczne (Polish Zoological Society): ul. H. Sienkiewicza 21, 50-335 Wrocław; tel. (71) 3754049; e-mail ptzol@biol.uni.wroc.pl; f. 1935; develops and popularizes zoological sciences; 13 regional brs; 1,372 mems; library of 55,000 vols; Pres. Dr Hab. Prof. JACEK JÓZEF NOWAKOWSKI; Sec. ANDRZEJ JABŁOŃSKI; publs *Notatki Ornitologiczne*, *Przegląd Zoologiczny*, *The Ring* (4 a year), *Zoologica Poloniae*.

Mathematical Sciences

Polskie Towarzystwo Matematyczne (Polish Mathematical Society): ul. Sniadeckich 8, 00-956 Warsaw; tel. (22) 5228146; e-mail zgptm@ptm.org.pl; internet www.ptm .org.pl; f. 1919; promotes mathematical research and applied mathematics; promotes mathematical culture, incl. support for mathematics education and popularization of mathematics; organizes meetings, discussions, lectures, confs, seminars and training courses; 1,300 mems; Pres. Prof. STEFAN JACKOWSKI; Sec. KRYSTYNA JAWORSKA; publs *Annales Societatis Mathematicae Polonae: Series I Commentationes Mathematicae*, *Popularny Miesięcznik Matematyczno-Fizyczno-Astronomiczny DELTA* (Mathematical-Physical-Astronomical Popularizing Monthly Journal, 12 a year), *Series II Wiadomości Matematyczne* (Mathematical News), *Series III Matematyka Applicanda* (Applied Mathematics), *Series IV Fundamenta Informaticae*, *Series V Didactica Mathematicae* (Didactics of Mathematics), *Series VI Antiquitates Mathematicae* (History of Mathematics).

Polskie Towarzystwo Statystyczne (Polish Statistical Association): al. Niepodległości 208, 00-925 Warsaw; tel. (22) 6083274; internet www.stat.gov.pl/pts; f. 1912; works for devt and promotion of statistics, informatics, economics and econometrics; 17 regional brs; 750 mems; Pres. Prof. Dr Hab. CZESŁAW DOMAŃSKI; Sec. Prof. Dr Hab. ZOFIA RUSNAK; publs *Biuletyn Informacyjny* (Bulletin of Information, 4 a year), *Statistics in Transition* (2 a year, in print and online), *Wiadomości Statystyczne* (Statistical News, 12 a year, in print and online).

Physical Sciences

Polskie Towarzystwo Astronomiczne (Polish Astronomical Society): ul. Bartycka 18, 00-716 Warsaw; tel. (22) 8410041 ext. 146; e-mail zarzad@pta.edu.pl; internet www .pta.edu.pl; f. 1923; promotes advancement of science of astronomy and its teaching; holds

conventions, symposia, scientific meetings; awards medals and prizes; evaluates state and needs of nat. astronomy; 251 mems; Pres. Dr AGNIESZKA KRYSZCZYŃSKA; Sec. Dr WALDEMAR OGLOZA; publs *Delta*, *Urania-Postepy Astronomii* (Progress in Astronomy, 6 a year, online, urania.pta.edu.pl).

Polskie Towarzystwo Chemiczne (Polish Chemical Society): ul. Freta 16, 00-227 Warsaw; tel. (22) 8311304; e-mail ptchem@ ptchem.pl; internet www.ptchem.pl; f. 1919; promotes devt of chemical sciences and its knowledge; organizes confs, meetings, seminars, public lectures and training; maintains Marii Skłodowskiej-Curie museum; 2,350 mems; library of 2,400 vols; Pres. Prof. Dr Hab. BOGUSŁAW BUSZEWSKI; Sec. Prof. Dr Hab. MONIKA MICHEL; publs *Chemical Analysis* (6 a year), *Orbital* (Society News, 6 a year), *Polish Journal of Chemistry*, *Wiadomości Chemiczne* (Chemical News).

Polskie Towarzystwo Fizyczne (Polish Physical Society): ul. Hoża 69, 00-681 Warsaw; tel. (22) 5532154; e-mail ptf@fuw.edu.pl; internet www.polskie-towarzystwo-fizyczne .pl; f. 1920; 19 regional brs; promotes devt of physics and dissemination of information to popularize physics in soc.; 1,991 mems; library of 1,300 vols; Pres. Prof. Dr Hab. WIESŁAW A. KAMINSKI; Gen. Sec. Prof. BOHDAN GRZADKOWSKI; publs *Acta Physica Polonica A* (12 a year, in English, French, German and Russian, online, info.ifpan.edu.pl/acta), *Acta Physica Polonica B* (12 a year, in English, French, German and Russian, online, th-www.if.uj.edu.pl/acta), *Delta* (12 a year, in Polish, online, www.deltami.edu.pl), *Fizyka i przyroda* (Physics and Nature, online, www.fip.elbi.pl)), *Foton/Neutrino* (online, www2.if.uj.edu.pl/Foton), *Moja Fizyka* (My Physics), *Postępy Fizyki* (Advances in Physics, 6 a year, online, postepy.polskie-towarzystwo-fizyczne.pl), *Reports on Mathematical Physics* (6 a year, in English).

Polskie Towarzystwo Geofizyczne (Polish Geophysical Society): ul. Podleśna 61, 01-673 Warsaw; tel. (22) 5694562; e-mail ptgeof@imgw.pl; internet www.imgw.pl/ internet/zz/zz_xpages/ptg; f. 1947; works for devt and popularization of geophysical sciences and their applications; 10 brs; 377 mems; library of 5,000 vols; Pres. Dr ALFRED DUBICKI; Sec.-Gen. Dr JERZY SZKUTNICKI; publ. *Przegląd Geofizyczny* (Geophysical Review, 4 a year).

Polskie Towarzystwo Geologiczne (Polish Geological Society): ul. Oleandry 2A, 30-063 Cracow; tel. (12) 6332041; e-mail ptg@uj .edu.pl; internet www.ptgeol.pl; f. 1921; 14 brs; works for devt and popularization of geological sciences and environmental protection; organizes meetings and confs; 866 mems; library of 9,397 vols, 25,883 journals; Pres. Prof. Dr Hab. MARIAN ADAM GASINSK; Sec. Prof. Dr Hab. JOZEF CHOWANIEC; publ. *Annales Societatis Geologorum Poloniae/ Rocznik Polskiego Towarzystwa Geologicznego/Annals of the Polish Geological Society* (3 a year).

Polskie Towarzystwo Miłośników Astronomii (Polish Amateur Astronomical Society): ul. św. Tomasza 30/8, 31-027 Cracow; tel. (12) 4223892; e-mail zgptma@gmail.com; internet www.ptma.pl; f. 1919; works in the field of amateur observations, instrument-making, popularization of astronomy; establishes and maintains astronomical observatories and planetariums, specialized libraries; organizes lectures and scientific confs; 16 local brs; 3,000 mems; Pres. Dr HENRYK BRANCEWICZ; Sec. Mgr ANDRZEJ BOROŃ; publ. *Urania-Postępy Astronomii* (12 a year).

Polskie Towarzystwo Mineralogiczne (Mineralogical Society of Poland): al. Mickiewicza 30, 30-059 Cracow; tel. (12) 6172513; e-mail ptmin@ptmin.pl; internet www.ptmin .pl; f. 1969; propagates and supports devt of mineralogical sciences; 4 regional brs; organizes confs and meetings and recognizes doctoral theses with awards; 210 mems; Pres. Prof. Dr Hab. LESZEK MARYNOWSKI; Sec. Dr TADEUSZ SZYDŁAK; publs *Elements* (6 a year, online, www.elementsmagazine.org), *Mineralogia* (4 a year, in English, online, www.mineralogia.pl), *Mineralogia Polonica-Special Papers* (in English).

Polskie Towarzystwo Nautologiczne (Polish Nautological Society): ul. 3 Maja 12a m 7, 81-357 Gdynia; tel. (58) 6204975; e-mail ptngdynia@poczta.wp.pl; f. 1958; history of human involvement with the sea; 150 mems; library of 2,800 vols; Pres. Prof. Dr DANIEL DUDA; Sec. Dr ELŻBIETA SKUPIŃSKA-DYBEK; publ. *Nautologia* (4 a year).

PHILOSOPHY AND PSYCHOLOGY

Polskie Towarzystwo Filozoficzne (Polish Philosophical Society): Pałac Staszica, ul. Nowy Swiat 72, pok.160, 00-330 Warsaw; tel. (22) 6572759; e-mail olimpiad@ifispan.waw .pl; internet www.ptfilozofia.pl; f. 1904; study of all traditional philosophical disciplines; promotes practice and teaching of philosophy; holds meetings, discussions and scientific lectures; 22 regional brs; 826 mems; library of 7,200 vols; Pres. Prof. Dr Hab. WŁADYSŁAW STRÓŻEWSKI; Sec. Mgr MAGDALENA GAWIN; publ. *Ruch Filozoficzny* (Philosophical Movement, 4 a year, online, www.filozofia.umk.pl).

Polskie Towarzystwo Psychologiczne (Polish Psychological Association): ul. Stawki 5/7, 00-183 Warsaw; tel. (22) 8311368; e-mail ptp@psych.uw.edu.pl; internet www.ptp.org .pl; f. 1948; works for devt and popularization of psychology as science and profession; encourages and conducts research; organizes scientific meetings, confs, seminars, competitions; 24 regional brs; 2,000 mems; Pres. Dr MAŁGORZATA TOEPLITZ-WINIEWSKA; Sec.-Gen. Dr WIESŁAWA MACHALICA; publs *Nowiny Psychologiczne* (Psychological News, 4 a year), *Przegląd Psychologiczny* (Psychological Review, 4 a year).

Polskie Towarzystwo Semiotyczne (Polish Semiotic Society): c/o Institute of Philosophy, Warsaw Univ., ul. Krakowskie Przedmieście 3, 00-927 Warsaw; tel. (22) 8265734; e-mail pts2@pts.edu.pl; internet www.pts.edu.pl; f. 1968; studies and propagates all aspects of semiotics: signs, sign systems, information, communication, indirect cognition; applied semiotics; philosophy of language, linguistics, logic; 150 mems; library of 1,700 vols; Pres. Dr Hab. JOANNA ODROWĄŻ-SYPNIEWSKA; Sec. Dr TADEUSZ CIECIERSKI; publ. *Studia Semiotyczne* (irregular).

RELIGION, SOCIOLOGY AND ANTHROPOLOGY

Polskie Towarzystwo Antropologiczne (Polish Anthropological Society): ul. Umultowska 89, 61-614 Poznań; tel. (61) 8295713; e-mail pta@amu.edu.pl; internet www .ptantropologiczne.pl; f. 1925; 10 local brs; disseminates knowledge in the field of anthropology; holds symposia and confs; conducts and supports research; organizes education and training for mems; 317 mems; library of 10,000 vols; Pres. Prof. Dr Hab. MARIA KACZMAREK; Sec. Dr ANITA SZWED; publ. *Anthropological Review* (1 a year, in English, print and online).

Polskie Towarzystwo Kryminalistyczne (Polish Forensic Association): ul. Zgoda 11 lok. 300, 00-018 Warsaw; tel. (22) 6924385;

e-mail biuro@kryminalistyka.pl; internet www.kryminalistyka.pl; f. 1973; performs forensic examinations and gives expert opinions; organizes training courses in forensic science; undertakes research projects; popularizes forensic science and related disciplines; provides assistance to aggrieved persons and victims of crimes; organizes scientific symposia, confs, lectures, presentations and training; 6 regional sections; 350 mems; Pres. BRONISŁAW MŁODZIEJOWSKI; Sec. RYSZARD ZIELIŃSKI; publ. *Problemy Współczesnej Kryminalistyke* (Issues of Contemporary Forensic Science).

Polskie Towarzystwo Ludoznawcze (Polish Ethnological Society): ul. Szczytnicka 11, 50-382 Wrocław; tel. (71) 3211610; e-mail ptl@ptl.info.pl; internet www.ptl.info.pl; f. 1895; supports and popularizes devt of anthropology; 17 regional divs; conducts scientific research; organizes sessions, scientific confs, lectures, training and excursions; maintains archive; 735 mems; library of 50,000 vols; Pres. Prof. Dr Hab. MICHAŁ BUCHOWSKI; Sec.-Gen. Dr JERZY ADAMCZEWSKI; publs *Archiwum Etnograficzne*, *Atlas Polskich Strojów Ludowych*, *Biblioteka Literatury Ludowej*, *Biblioteka Popularna*, *Biblioteka Zesłańca*, *Dziedzictwo Kulturowe*, *Dzieła Wszystkie O. Kolberga*, *Komentarze do Polskiego Atlasu Etnograficznego*, *Literatura Ludowa* (6 a year), *Łódzkie Studia Etnograficzne* (1 a year), *Lud* (1 a year), *Prace Etnologiczne*, *Prace i Materiały Etnograficzne*.

Polskie Towarzystwo Orientalistyczne (Polish Oriental Society): ul. Krakowskie Przedmieście 26/28, Wydział Orientalistyczny UW, 00-927 Warsaw; tel. (22) 5520353; e-mail pto.orient@uw.edu.pl; internet www.pto.orient.uw.edu.pl; f. 1922; conducts and supports research into Asia and Africa; disseminates knowledge about the East; organizes scientific meetings and conventions; 160 mems; Pres. Prof. Dr Hab. MAREK DZIEKAN; Sec.-Gen. MARIA KOZLOWSKA; publ. *Przegląd Orientalistyczny* (4 a year).

Polskie Towarzystwo Religioznawcze (Polish Society for the Study of Religions): Pałac Staszica, ul. Nowy Świat 72 pok. 010, 00-330 Warsaw; tel. (22) 6252642; e-mail redakcja@ptr.edu.pl; internet www.ptr.edu.pl; f. 1958; diseminates information on history, theory, methodology, sociology, psychology of religions; 165 mems; Pres. Prof. Dr Hab. ZBIGNIEW STACHOWSKI; Scientific Sec. Prof. Dr Hab. JERZY KOJKOŁ; publ. *Przegląd Religioznawczy* (4 a year).

Polskie Towarzystwo Socjologiczne (Polish Sociological Association): ul. Nowy Świat 72, 00-330 Warsaw; tel. (22) 8267737; e-mail pts@ifispan.waw.pl; internet www.pts.org.pl; f. 1956; supports devt of sociology; propagates sociological knowledge within soc.; fosters professional ethics among sociologists and represents the interests of its mems in the scope of their academic activity; 5 regional depts; 1,300 mems; Pres. Prof. Dr Hab. GRAŻYNA SKĄPSKA; Gen. Sec. Prof. ZBIGNIEW RYKOWSKI; publs *Informacja Bieżąca* (Current Bibliographical Information, 2 a year), *Polish Sociological Review* (4 a year, in English).

Polskie Towarzystwo Teologiczne (Polish Theological Society): ul. Kanonicza 3, 31-002 Cracow; tel. (12) 3945676; e-mail zarzad@ptt.net.pl; internet www.ptt.net.pl; f. 1924; devt of the ecclesiastical sciences, esp. theology; holds scientific meetings, lectures and readings; 7 local brs; Pres. Rev. Prof. Dr Hab. KAZIMIERZ PANUŚ; Sec. Rev. KAZIMIERZ MOSKALA; publ. *Ruch Biblijny i Liturgiczny* (4 a year).

Towarzystwo Naukowe Organizacji i Kierownictwa (Scientific Society for Organization and Management): ul. Górska 6/10 lok. 71 00-740 Warsaw; tel. (22) 6254485; e-mail bzg@tnoik.org; internet www.tnoik.org; f. 1925, present name 1948; propagates and disseminates information about professional management; 16 brs; organizes and participates in confs, seminars, symposia, lectures and scientific research works; 4,300 mems (incl. 4,000 individual mems and 300 supporting mems); library of 15,000 vols; Pres. Prof. Dr Hab. ZBIGNIEW DWORZECKI; Vice-Pres. Dr ERYK GŁODZIŃSKI; Vice-Pres. Prof. Dr Hab. LESZEK KIEŁTYKA; publ. *Przegląd Organizacji* (12 a year, online, www.przegladorganizacji.pl).

TECHNOLOGY

Akademia Inżynierska w Polsce (Academy of Engineering in Poland): ul. Czackiego 3/5, 00-043 Warsaw; tel. (22) 8142609; e-mail aip@akademiainzynierska.pl; internet www.akademiainzynierska.pl; f. 1992; promotes devt of new technologies and entrepreneurial innovation and technology transfer to industry; encourages innovation of technical culture to adapt to strategy of sustainable devt; fosters and participates in the implementation of the priority programmes of research, devt and application; 254 mems (incl. 239 individual mems, 12 foreign mems and 3 assoc. mem. instns); Pres. Prof. Dr Hab. LESZEK RAFALSKI; Sec.-Gen. Dr Hab. ANDRZEJ PACHUTA.

Federacja Stowarzyszeń Naukowo-Technicznych–Naczelna Organizacja Techniczna (FSNT-NOT) (Polish Federation of Engineering Associations): ul. Czackiego 3/5, 00-043 Warsaw; tel. (22) 3361260; e-mail sekretariatsg@not.org.pl; internet www.not.org.pl; f. 1835 as Polish Polytechnical Soc.; provides cooperation, integration and mutual support to mem. asscns in their tasks to develop interests; develops ethics of the use of resources and the environment in accordance with the principles of sustainable devt; maintains museum of technology; 37 br. asscns; 230,000 individual mems; Pres. EWA MAŃKIEWICZ-CUDNY; Sec.-Gen. JERZY GUMIŃSKI; publ. *Przegląd Techniczny* (Technical Review, 52 a year).

Polskie Towarzystwo Akustyczne (Polish Acoustical Society): Umultowska 85, 61-614 Poznań; c/o Politechnika Wrocławska, Wybrzeże Wyspiańskiego 27, 50-370 Wrocław; tel. (71) 3203068; internet www.ippt.gov.pl/akustyka/; works for devt of acoustics and its related depts and disciplines; promotes acoustics with particular emphasis on areas important for science, culture, soc., nat. economy and environmental protection; 7 brs; organizes meetings, nat. and int. confs and scientific courses; awards Marka Kwieka medal; Pres. Prof. GRAŻYNA GRELOWSKA; Sec. Prof. Dr Hab. ANDRZEJ DOBRUCKI; publ. *Archives of Acoustics*.

Polskie Towarzystwo Astronautyczne (Polish Astronautical Society): ul. Bartycka 18A, 00-716 Warsaw; tel. (22) 8403766; e-mail poczta@ptastronaut.org.pl; internet www.ptastronaut.org.pl; f. 1954; develops, promotes and popularizes theoretical and practical knowledge of space science and space; works in the field of scientific, educational, and popular astronautics, planetology, bioastronautics, space physics, CETI, and space law; conducts research and organizes scientific confs and meetings, symposia, seminars, meetings, discussions, readings and lectures; 40 mems; Pres. Dr MACIEJ MROCZKOWSKI; Vice-Pres. ANDRZEJ KOTARSKI; Vice-Pres. KRYSTIAN GÓRSKI; Vice-Pres. Prof. Dr Hab.

RUDOLF KLEMENS; publ. *Postępy Astronautyki* (Progress in Astronautics, irregular).

Polskie Towarzystwo Elektrotechniki Teoretycznej i Stosowanej (Polish Society for Theoretical and Applied Electrical Engineering): Politechnika Warszawska, Wydz. Elektryczny, Gmach Electrotechniki p. 310, ul. Koszykowa 75, 00-662 Warsaw; tel. (22) 2347563; e-mail ptetis@ien.pw.edu.pl; internet ptetis.ee.pw.edu.pl; f. 1961; promotes and encourages devt of theoretical and applied electrical engineering; organizes confs, symposia, seminars, readings; 14 regional brs; 750 mems; Pres. Prof. Dr Hab. KRZYSZTOF KLUSZCZYŃSKI; Sec. Dr MARCIN WESOŁOWSKI.

Polskie Towarzystwo Ergonomiczne (Polish Ergonomics Society): ul. Narbutta 85, 02-524 Warsaw; tel. (22) 8499798; e-mail sekretariat@ergonomia-polska.com; internet www.ergonomia-polska.com; f. 1977; 14 local brs; develops and disseminates science of ergonomics; popularizes principles and achievements of ergonomics for optimal adaptation of tools, machines, devices, technology, organization and work environment and material objects; promotes teaching of science of ergonomics in primary and higher education instns; organizes scientific meetings, confs, symposia, readings, lectures, seminars; Pres. Dr Hab. EWA GÓRSKA; Sec.-Gen. TOMASZ TOKARSKI; publs *Biuletyn Publikacji Członków Polskiego Towarzystwa Ergonomicznego*, *Ergonomia* (2 a year).

Polskie Towarzystwo Mechaniki Teoretycznej i Stosowanej (Polish Society of Theoretical and Applied Mechanics): Gmach Inżynierii Lądowej, Politechniki Warszawskiej, al. Armii Ludowej 16, p. 650, 00-637 Warsaw; tel. (22) 8257180; e-mail biuro@ptmts.org.pl; internet www.ptmts.org.pl; f. 1958; promotes and encourages devt and dissemination of theoretical and applied mechanics; initiates discussion and expressions of opinion on topics related to the curriculum, research programmes and the use of scientific achievements in practice; 17 local brs; 1,000 mems; Pres. Prof. Dr Hab. ARKADIUSZ MĘŻYK; Sec.-Gen. Prof. Dr Hab. KATARZYNA KOWAL-MICHALSKA; publs *Biuletyn PTMTS*, *Journal of Theoretical and Applied Mechanics* (4 a year, online, www.ptmts.org.pl/jtam.html).

Research Institutes
GENERAL

Instytut Kultur Śródziemnomorskich i Orientalnych PAN (Institute of Mediterranean and Oriental Cultures, Polish Academy of Sciences): Nowy Świat 72, 00-330 Warsaw; tel. (22) 826-63-56; e-mail csnec@zkppan.waw.pl; internet www.iksio.pan.pl; f. 1978; attached to Polish Acad. of Sciences; library of 17,000 vols; Dir Prof. JERZY ZDANOWSKI; Librarian DOROTA DOBRZYNSKA; publs *Acta Asiatica Varsoviensia* (1 a year, in English and German), *Hemispheres* (4 a year, in English and French).

Instytut Kultury (Institute of Culture): e-mail info@instytutkultury.pl; internet instytutkultury.pl; f. 1974; library of 35,000 vols; Dir JAN STANISŁAW WOJCLECHOWSKI; publ. *Prace Instytutu Kultury*.

Instytut Podstaw Inżynierii Środowiska PAN (Institute of Environmental Engineering of the Polish Academy of Sciences): ul. M. Skłodowskiej-Curie 34, 41-819 Zabrze; tel. (32) 2716481; e-mail kanc@ipis.zabrze.pl; internet www.ipis.zabrze.pl; f. 1961 as Dept of the Polish Academy of Sciences for Scientific Investigations of Upper Silesian Industrial Region, present name and status 1975; research in the areas of air and water pollution control, land reclamation, energy conservation, influence of pollutants on plants; library of 14,000 vols; Exec. Dir Dr Eng. FRANCISZEK PISTELOK (acting); publs *Archives of Environmental Protection* (4 a year, with summaries in English and Russian), *Prace i Studia* (Works and Studies, irregular).

Instytut Slawistyki PAN (Institute of Slavic Studies of Polish Academy of Sciences): ul. Bartoszewicza 1B/17, 00-337 Warsaw; tel. (22) 8267688; e-mail sekretariat@ispan.waw.pl; internet www.ispan.waw.pl; f. 1954; attached to Polish Acad. of Sciences; confers doctoral degrees in linguistics and humanities; 4 dpts: history, linguistics, literary and cultural studies, study of nationalities; library of 112,872 vols (incl. 91,596 books and 21,276 journals), 1,065 vols of spec. colln (incl. microfilms and copies of old prints); Dir Dr ANNA ENGELKING; publs *Acta Baltico-Slavica*, *Adeptus*, *Cognitive Studies/Etudes Cognitives*, *Colloquia Humanistica*, *Slavia Meridionalis*, *Sprawy Narodowościowe*, *Studia Litteraria et Historica*, *Studia z Filologii Polskiej i Słowiańskiej*.

Instytut Sportu (Institute of Sport): ul. Trylogii 2/16, 01-982 Warsaw; tel. (22) 8340812; e-mail insp@insp.waw.pl; internet www.insp.pl; f. 1978; carries out research for sports; conducts diagnostic tests and services for sports asscns and other bodies; develops expertise for orgs and sports asscns; carries out doping tests in accordance with relevant regulations; designs and constructs test equipment for sports; certification of products for sports and recreation; library of 6,130 vols; Dir Dr ANDRZEJ POKRYWKA; publ. *Biology of Sport* (4 a year, print and online, www.biolsport.com).

AGRICULTURE, FISHERIES AND VETERINARY SCIENCE

Instytut Agrofizyki im. Bohdana Dobrzańskiego PAN (Bohdan Dobrazański Institute of Agrophysics Polish Academy of Sciences): ul. Doświaczalna 4, 20-290 Lublin; tel. (81) 7445061; e-mail sekretariat@ipan.lublin.pl; internet www.ipan.lublin.pl; f. 1968, present name 1990; carries out fundamental and applied research on topics related to environmental management and protection, sustainable agriculture, post-harvest and food processing; conducts PhD studies in agricultural sciences; library of 3,000 vols; Dir Prof. Dr Hab. JÓZEF HORABIK; publs *Acta Agrophysica* (2 a year, online, www.acta-agrophysica.org), *International Agrophysics* (4 a year, online, www.international-agrophysics.org), *Polish Journal of Soil Science* (2 a year, online, www.pjss.org).

Instytut Badawczy Leśnictwa (Forestry Research Institute): 3 Braci Leśnej St, Sękocin Stary, 05-090 Raszyn; tel. (22) 7150300; e-mail ibl@ibles.waw.pl; internet www.ibles.pl; f. 1930 as Experimental Station of the State Forests Org., present name and status 1945; carries out scientific research for forests, forestry and for afforested areas and wooded lands; brs at Cracow and Białowieża; scientific depts of forest ecology, silviculture and genetics, forest protection, forest management, chemical analysis, forest fire protection, natural forests, mountain forestry; library of 69,000 vols; Dir Prof. Dr TOMASZ ZAWIŁA-NIEDŹWIECKI; publs *Folia Forestalia Polonica* (Series A—Forestry, in English, irregular), *Leśne Prace Badawcze* (Forest Research Papers, 4 a year, online, www.lesne-prace-badawcze.pl), *Notatnik Naukowy, Nowości Piśmiennictwa Leśnego* (12 a year).

Instytut Biotechnologii Przemysłu Rolno—Spożywczego (Institute of Agricultural and Food Biotechnology): ul. Rakowiecka 36, 02-532 Warsaw; tel. (22) 8490224; e-mail ibprs@ibprs.pl; f. 1949; biotechnology: improvement of microbial strains, fermentation processes (beer, wine, spirits, organic acids), malt, yeasts, enzymatic preparations, microbial preparations; technology of fruit and vegetable products, food analysis, food concentration, storage and processing of grain, bread and pastry baking; culture collection of industrial micro-organisms; library of 22,000 vols; Dir Prof. ROMAN GRZYBOWSKI; publ. *Prace Instytutów i Laboratoriów Badawczych Przemysłu Spożywczego* (in Polish with summaries in English, 1 a year).

Instytut Budownictwa, Mechanizacji i Elektryfikacji Rolnictwa (Institute for Building, Mechanization and Electrification in Agriculture): ul. Rakowiecka 32, 02-532 Warsaw; tel. (22) 5421100; e-mail selian@ibmer.waw.pl; f. 1950; research into the mechanization of farming, economics and management, land reclamation, farm building and energy sources; library of 47,783 vols; Dir Prof. Dr Hab. ANDRZEJ MYCZKO; publs *Inżynieria Rolnicza* (irregular), *Prace Naukowo Badawcze IBMER* (1 a year), *Problemy Inżynierii Rolniczej* (4 a year), *Przegląd Dokumentacyjny—Technika Rolnicza* (6 a year).

Instytut Ekonomiki Rolnictwa i Gospodarki Żywnościowej—Państwowy Instytut Badawczy (Institute of Agricultural and Food Economics): ul. Świętokrzyska 20, 00-002 Warsaw; tel. (22) 5054444; e-mail ierigz@ierigz.waw.pl; internet www.ierigz.waw.pl; f. 1950 as Agricultural Economics Institute, present name and status 1983; carries out scientific and research work into issues of economic production and social situation of rural areas, agriculture and broadly conceived food economy; library of 41,000 vols; Dir Prof. Dr ANDRZEJ KOWALSKI; publs *Analizy Rynkowe* (Market Analyses, 2 a year for main commodities), *Rynek Rolny* (Agricultural Market, 12 a year), *Zagadnienia Ekonomiki Rolnej* (Problems of Agricultural Economics, 6 a year).

Instytut Fizjologii i Żywienia Zwierząt im. Jana Kielanowskiego PAN (Kielanowski Institute of Animal Physiology and Nutrition): ul. Instytucka 3, 05-110 Jabłonna; tel. (22) 7653300; e-mail office@ifzz.pan.pl; internet www.ifzz.pl; f. 1955 as research unit of the Polish Academy of Sciences, present name 1990; attached to Polish Acad. of Sciences; conducts research into 3 main fields: nutrition and its effects on the devt, health and wellbeing of animals and on environment, quality of animal products as a function of nutritional and endogenous factors, molecular and endocrine regulation of physiological processes; library of 5,000 vols; Dir Dr TOMASZ MISZTAL; publ. *The Journal of Animal and Feed Sciences* (4 a year).

Instytut Fizjologii Roślin im. Franciszka Górskiego PAN (Franciszek Górski Institute of Plant Physiology of the Polish Academy of Sciences): ul. Niezapominajek 21, 30-239 Cracow; tel. (12) 4251833; e-mail ifr@ifr-pan.krakow.pl; internet www.ifr-pan.krakow.pl; f. 1956 as Dept of Plant Physiology of the Polish Academy of Sciences, present name and status 2003; maintains laboratories; conducts research into plant growth and devt, photosynthesis, biology of stress, metabolism of fungi; myxomycetes; Dir Prof. Dr Hab. JOLANTA BIESAGA-KOŚCIELNIAK; publ. *Acta Physiologiae Plantarum* (4 a year).

Instytut Genetyki i Hodowli Zwierząt PAN (Institute of Genetics and Animal Breeding of the Polish Academy of Sciences): Jastrzębiec, ul. Postępu 1, 05-552 Magdalenka; tel. (22) 7561711; e-mail director@ighz.pl; internet www.ighz.edu.pl; f. 1955 as Dept of Experimental Animal Breeding, present name and status 1969; conducts theoretical research into molecular genetics, cytogenetics, experimental embryology and biotechnology, genetic background to the physiology of stress and animal etiology; library of 13,904 vols (incl. 7,097 books and 6,478 vols of bound periodicals); Dir Prof. Dr JAROSŁAW HORBAŃCZUK; publs *Animal Science Papers and Reports* (4 a year, in English), *Prace i Materiały Zootechniczne* (irregular, in Polish).

Instytut Genetyki Roślin PAN (Institute of Plant Genetics of the Polish Academy of Sciences): ul. Strzeszyńska 34, 60-479 Poznań; tel. (61) 6550200; e-mail office@igr.poznan.pl; internet www.igr.poznan.pl; f. 1961 as Dept of Plant Genetics, present name and status 1979; carries out basic genetic research into cultivated plants, genomics, biometrics, molecular biology, plant stresses; library of 35,300 vols (incl. 14,840 vols of books and 20,460 vols of periodicals); Dir Prof. BOGDAN WOLKO; publ. *Journal of Applied Genetics* (4 a year).

Instytut Meteorologii i Gospodarki Wodnej—Państwowy Instytut Badawczy (Institute of Meteorology and Water Management—National Research Institute): ul. Podleśna 61, 01-673 Warsaw; tel. (22) 5694100; e-mail imgw@imgw.pl; internet www.imgw.pl; f. 1973 by merger of State Hydrological and Meteorological Institute and Institute of Water Management; work on research and devt into the fields of meteorology, hydrology, oceanology, water management and engineering, water resources quality, wastewater management and sewage utilization; collections of data from 61 meteorological stations, 149 meteorological posts, 893 hydrological posts, 1,027 pluviometric posts and 100 groundwater posts; library of 95,000 vols (incl. 31,000 books and 53,000 periodicals); Dir-Gen. Prof. Dr Eng. MIECZYSŁAW S. OSTOJSKI; publs *Gazeta Obserwatora IMGW* (Journal of IMGW Observer, 6 a year), *Meteorology Hydrology and Water Management-Research and Operational Application* (in English), *Wiadomości Instytutu Meteorologii i Gospodarki Wodnej* (Reports, 4 a year).

Instytut Nawozów Sztucznych (Fertilizers Research Institute): al. Tysiąclecia Państwa Polskiego 13A, 24-110 Puławy; tel. (81) 4731400; e-mail sekretariat@ins.pulawy.pl; internet www.ins.pulawy.pl; f. 1935 as Research Laboratory at United Works of Nitrogen Compounds in Mościce and Chorzów, present name and status 1958; research and devt work into synthesis gases and hydrogen, carbon dioxide, nitrogen oxides, nitric acid and its salts, mineral fertilizers, catalysts and sorbents, derivatives of methanol and urea, super-critical carbon dioxide extraction; environmental protection; unit operations; devises new processes and products; library of 36,990 vols; Gen. Dir Dr CEZARY MOŻEŃSKI; publ. *Przemysł Nawozowy* (4 a year).

Instytut Ogrodnictwa (Research Institute of Horticulture): ul. Konstytucji 3 Maja 1/3, 96-100 Skierniewice; tel. (46) 8332021; e-mail io@inhort.pl; internet www.inhort.pl; f. 2011 by merger of Research Institute of Pomology and Floriculture (f. 1951) and Institute of Vegetable Crops (f. 1964); 4 divs: beekeeping, floriculture, pomology, vegetable crops; 6 field stations; 3 accredited laboratories; organizes confs and seminars; confers doctoral degrees and postdoctoral agricultural sciences in the field of horticulture; library of 37,578 vols; Dir Prof. Dr Hab. FRANCISZEK ADAMICKI; publs *Journal of Fruit and Ornamental Plant Research* (2 a year), *Nowości Warzywnicze* (2 a year), *Pszczelnicze Zeszyty Naukowe* (Journal of Apiculture Science, 2 a year), *Zeszyty Naukowe Instytutu Sadownictwa i Kwiaciarstwa* (1 a year).

Instytut Przemysłu Cukrowniczego (Institute of the Sugar Industry): ul. Inzynierskiej 4, 05-084 Leszno k Blonia, Warsaw; tel. (22) 7259088; e-mail dyrektor@inspcukr .pl; internet www.inspcukr.bip.waw.pl; f. 1898; research into all brs of sugar production, protection and use; raw product, sugar beet, technological, analytical, mechanical, environmental protection depts; gives training and awards; library of 1,500 vols; Dir Dr ANDRZEJ BARYGA; publs *Burak cukrowy-gazeta dla plantatorów* (irregular), *Informacja dekadowa z przebiegu Kampanii* (9 a year), *Informacja o wynikach produkcyjnych i danych techniczo-technologicznych przemysłu cukrowniczego* (1 a year).

Instytut Rozwoju Wsi i Rolnictwa PAN (Institute of Rural and Agricultural Development PAS): Nowy Swiat 72, 00-330 Warsaw; tel. (22) 8266371; e-mail irwir@irwirpan.waw .pl; internet www.irwirpan.waw.pl; f. 1971; research into the process of developing agriculture and rural soc. and multi-functional devt of rural areas; works to define conditions for long-term devt strategies of rural areas and transformation of agriculture; library of 7,000 vols, 1,400 vols of journals; Dir Dr MIROSŁAW DRYGAS; publ. *Wieś i Rolnictwo* (Village and Agriculture, 4 a year in Polish, 1 a year supplement of selected papers in English).

Instytut Rybactwa Śródlądowego im. Stanisława Sakowicza (Inland Fisheries Institute): ul. Oczapowskiego 10, 10-719 Olsztyn; tel. (89) 5240171; e-mail irs@infish .com.pl; internet www.infish.com.pl; f. 1951, present name 1987; conducts research and prepares studies on inland fisheries and disseminates research results; confers doctoral degrees and postdoctoral agricultural sciences in the field of fisheries; library of 16,000 vols, 770 journal titles, 2,000 items of MSS; Dir Prof. Dr Hab. BOGUSŁAW ZDANOWSKI; publs *Archives of Polish Fisheries* (2 a year, print and online, www.infish .com.pl/wydawnictwo/archives/arch_fish_pol.html), *Komunikaty Rybackie* (6 a year, print and online).

Instytut Środowiska Rolniczego i Leśnego PAN (Institute for Agricultural and Forest Environment of Polish Academy of Sciences): ul. Bukowska 19, 60-809 Poznań; tel. (61) 8475603; e-mail isrl@man.poznan.pl; internet www.isrl.poznan.pl; f. 1975 as Research Center of Agricultural and Forest Biology, present name and status 2009; research in the areas of climate and water resources, climate change impacts, extreme weather events, geochemical cycles, biodiversity, landscape structure, biogeochemical barriers, sustainable devt; library of 26,935 vols (incl. 7,500 books, 18,156 periodical vols and 1,279 cartographic elaboration); Dir Dr Hab. PIOTR KOWALCZAK.

Instytut Technologiczno-Przyrodniczy (Institute of Technology and Life Sciences): Falenty, al. Hrabska 3, 05-090 Raszyn; tel. (22) 7200531; e-mail itep@itep.edu.pl; internet www.itep.edu.pl; f. 2010; carries out advocacy, devt, education, research, training and innovation in agriculture; flood and drought management, grassland farming, land devt, sustainable devt of rural areas, rural sanitation, water management in agriculture; library of 20,000 vols, 15,000

vols of journals, and 8,600 vols in spec. collns; Dir Prof Dr Hab. Inż. EDMUND KACA; publs *Journal of Water and Land Development* (1 a year, in English), *Problemy Inżynierii Rolniczej* (Problems of Agricultural Engineering, 4 a year), *Woda-Srodowisko-Obszary Wiejskie* (Water-Environment-Rural Areas, 4 a year).

Instytut Technologii Drewna (Wood Technology Institute): Winiarska Str. 1, 60-654 Poznań; tel. (61) 8492400; e-mail office@ itd.poznan.pl; internet www.itd.poznan.pl; f. 1952; research for solving problems of the wood processing industry and for developing new technical processes and application and creation of new composites based on wood; library of 27,000 vols, 18,000 vols of standards, 6,200 vols of accounts of research; Gen. Dir Dr WŁADYSŁAW STRYKOWSKI; publ. *Drewno (Wood)* (2 a year).

Instytut Uprawy, Nawożenia i Gleboznawstwa w Puławach—Państwowy Instytut Badawczy (Institute of Soil Science and Plant Cultivation—State Research Institute): ul. Czartoryskich 8, 24-100 Puławy; tel. (81) 8863421; e-mail sekretariat@iung.pulawy.pl; internet www .iung.pulawy.pl; f. 1917 as State Research Institute of Rural Husbandry, present name 1950, present status 2005; research into the field of pedology; utilization and protection of agricultural land; soil chemistry, plant physiology, biochemistry, microbiology, soil and crop management, production technology of cereals, forage crops, tobacco and hops; Exec. Dir Prof. Dr Hab. WIESŁAW ALEKSANDER OLESZEK; publs *Pamiętnik Puławski* (2 or 3 a year), *Polish Journal of Agronomy* (2–4 a year), *Studia i Raporty IUNG-PIB* (in Polish), *Zalecenia Agrotechniczne* (every 5 years).

Instytut Warzywnictwa im. Emila Chroboczkaw Skierniewicach (Research Institute of Vegetable Crops): ul. Konstytucji 3 Maja 1/3, 96-100 Skierniewice; tel. (46) 8332211; e-mail iwarz@iwarz.pl; internet www.iwarz.pl; f. 1964; research into genetic, plant breeding and biotechnology; vegetable production both in the field and under cover and mushroom growing; plant protection against pests, diseases and weeds; storage technology; vegetable quality and nutritional value evaluation; develops practical guidelines for the rational and economic devt of vegetable production; library of 10,890 vols (incl. books, brochures and spec. collns); Dir Prof. Dr Hab. FRANCISZEK ADAMICKI; publs *Nowości Warzywnicze* (Vegetable Crops News, 2 a year), *Vegetable Crops Research Bulletin (VCRB)* (1 a year, in English with Polish summaries).

Instytut Zootechniki Państwowy Instytut Badawczy (National Research Institute of Animal Production): 1 Krakowska St, 32-083 Balice; tel. (12) 3572500; e-mail izooinfo@ izoo.krakow.pl; internet www.izoo.krakow .pl; f. 1950; carries out research and devt work on issues of breeding of all species of farm animals and animal production issues; library of 125,000 vols; Dir Prof. Dr Hab. JĘDRZEJ KRUPIŃSKI; publs *Annals of Animal Science* (4 a year), *Reports on Animal Performance Testing* (1 a year), *Wiadomosci Zootechniczne* (4 a year).

Morski Instytut Rybacki—Państwowy Instytut Badawczy (National Marine Fisheries Research Institute): ul. Kołłątaja 1, 81-332 Gdynia; tel. (58) 7356232; e-mail sekrdn@mir.gdynia.pl; internet www.mir .gdynia.pl; f. 1921 as Sea Fisheries Laboratory, present name and status 2011; establishes effective paths for providing scientific advice to fishery admin. and relevant int. orgs; performs and promotes physical, chem-

ical, biological and interdisciplinary research intof the marine environment and in the fields of processing technology, marine foodstuff safety, fishery economics and fishery technology; creates public awareness about functioning and rational utilization of marine ecosystems; library of 24,000 vols; Dir Dr Hab. TOMASZ LINKOWSKI; publ. *Bulletin of the Sea Fisheries Institute*.

Państwowy Instytut Weterynaryjny—Państwowy Instytut Badawczy (National Veterinary Research Institute): 57 Partyzantów ave, 24-100 Pulawy; tel. (81) 8893000; e-mail sekretariat@piwet.pulawy.pl; internet www.piwet.pulawy.pl; f. 1945; confers degrees of doctor of science (ScD) and PhD (PhD) in veterinary sciences; runs postgraduate training and professional specialization; carries out applied research in veterinary medicine; acts as the nat. reference laboratory; 16 scientific depts incl. those at Bydgoszcz and Zduńska Wola; library of 21,000 vols, 116 journal titles; Dir-Gen. Dr KRZYSZTOF NIEMCZUK; publ. *Bulletin of the Veterinary Institute in Pulawy* (4 a year, in English).

ARCHITECTURE AND TOWN PLANNING

Instytut Gospodarki Przestrzennej i Mieszkalictwa (Institute of Spatial Management and Housing): ul. Targowa 45, 03-728 Warsaw; tel. (22) 6191350; e-mail igpim@ igpim.pl; internet www.igpim.pl; f. 1986, present name 2002; offers research work, ongoing process monitoring, changes forecasting, urban planning and design study methodology, system and detailed solution concepts, legal solution proposal creation, standardization and normalization of spatial management and housing issues and environment protection; library of 70,000 vols, incl. spec. collns; Head SŁAWOMIR ANUSZ; publs *Człowiek i Srodowisko* (4 a year, online), *Geospatial information–key asset of spatial planning* (2 a year).

Instytut Rozwoju Miast (Institute Of Urban Development): ul. Cieszyńska 2, 30-015 Cracow; tel. (12) 6342953; e-mail sekretariat@irm.krakow.pl; internet irm .krakow.pl; f. 2002 by merger of Instytutu Gospodarki Przestrzennej i Komunalnej (f. 1977) and Instytutu Gospodarki Mieszkaniowej (f. 1950); carries out research and devt in urban planning, spatial planning, architecture, geography, law, economy, biology, civil engineering, hydro-engineering, sanitary engineering, land reclamation, transportation, computer science, organization and management; Dir Mgr JERZY ADAMSKI; publ. *Urban Development Issues-Research Quarterly*.

Instytut Techniki Budowlanej (Building Research Institute): ul. Filtrowa 1, 00-611 Warsaw; tel. (22) 8250471; e-mail instytut@ itb.pl; internet www.itb.pl; f. 1945; conducts research and devt work into issues of sustainability in the construction sector, safety, durability and reliability of structures, rationalization of energy utilization inside bldgs; approves and certifies new non-standardized bldg products; 10 laboratories; library of 104,000 vols; Dir Dr JAN BOBROWICZ; publ. *Prace Instytutu Techniki Budowlanej* (4 a year).

ECONOMICS, LAW AND POLITICS

Instytut Badań Rynku, Konsumpcji i Koniunktur (Institute for Market, Consumption and Business Cycles Research): al. Jerozolimskie 87, 02-001 Warsaw; tel. (22) 6285585; e-mail sekretariat@ibrkk.pl; internet ibrkk.pl; f. 2007 by merger of Foreign Trade Research Institute (f. 1969) and Institute of Home Market and Consumption;

conducts scientific and research work to analyze and forecast foreign economic relations; carries out surveys on effect of the globalization factors of enterprise management, determinants, devt and transformations of franchise systems, devt of processes of concentration in trade, strategies for devt of foreign commercial enterprises, forecasting of effects of locality of large trade facilities on the environment, forecasting of business situation in retailing; library of 40,000 vols; Dir Dr Hab. RYSZARD MICHALSKI; publs *Handel Wewnętrzny* (6 a year), *Konsumpcja i Rozwój* (2 a year), *Unia Europejska.pl* (6 a year).

Instytut Ekspertyz Sądowych im. Prof. dra Jana Sehna (Institute of Forensic Research): ul. Westerplatte 9, 31-033 Cracow; tel. (12) 4228755; e-mail ies@ies.krakow.pl; internet ies.krakow.pl; f. 1929, present name 1966; conducts research into the field of forensic science, toxicology, traffic accidents, DNA analysis and psychology; depts of criminalistics, traffic accident investigation, forensic toxicology, forensic psychology, forensic haemogenetics; organizes confs, postgraduate studies; library of 10,149 vols; Dir Dr MARIA KAŁA; publs *Paragraf na Drodze* (12 a year, in Polish), *Problems of Forensic Sciences* (4 a year, in English and Polish).

Instytut Nauk Ekonomicznych PAN (Institute of Economics of the Polish Academy of Sciences): Pałac Staszica, ul. Nowy Świat 72, pok. 266, 00-330 Warsaw; tel. (22) 6572707; e-mail inepan@inepan.waw.pl; internet www.inepan.waw.pl; f. 1980; researches contemporary economic theory, economic policy, analysis, forecasts and strategic studies concerning the Polish economy; analyses global economy and European integration and their influence on the devt of the Polish economy; organizes postgraduate and doctoral studies; library of 15,000 vols; Dir Prof. LESZEK JASIŃSKI; publs *Gospodarka Polski-Prognozy i Opinie* (Polish Economy-Forecasts and Opinions, 2 a year, in Polish and summary in English), *Opera Minora* (irregular), *Raport o Innowacyjności Gospodarki* (Report on Innovation in the Polish Economy, 1 a year), *Studia Ekonomiczne* (4 a year), *Working Papers* (irregular).

Instytut Nauk Prawnych PAN (Institute of Law Studies of the Polish Academy of Sciences): Pałac Staszica, ul. Nowy Świat 72, 00-330 Warsaw; tel. (22) 8267853; e-mail inp@inp.pan.pl; internet www.inp.pan.pl; f. 1956; conducts basic theoretical and practical research into the area of legal studies and criminology; grants PhD and habilitation academic titles; organizes postgraduate studies; library of 50,000 vols, 300 journals; Dir Prof. Dr Hab. WŁADYSŁAW CZAPLIŃSKI; publs *Archiwum Kryminologii* (irregular, in Polish with abstracts of articles in English and Russian), *Droit Polonais Contemporain/Polish Contemporary Law* (4 a year, in French and English), *Orzecznictwo Sądów Polskich* (12 a year), *Polish Yearbook of International Law* (in English, online, www.inp.pan.pl/pyil), *Studia Prawnicze* (4 a year).

Instytut Organizacji i Zarządzania w Przemyśle 'ORGMASZ' (Institute of Organization and Management in Industry): ul. Żelazna 87, 00-879 Warsaw; tel. (22) 6546061; e-mail instytut@orgmasz.eu; internet www.orgmasz.pl; f. 1953; conducts research and devt work for govt and companies related to restructuring, privatization, marketing, analysis and exploitation of opportunities of Polish accession to the EU, incl. fund-raising, implementation of quality systems in companies and laboratories, training of scientific personnel; confers doctoral degrees in economics in management

science; organizes confs and seminars; library of 11,200 vols, spec. collns; Dir Dr WITOLD WITOWSKI; publ. *Ekonomika i Organizacja Przedsiębiorstwa* (Business Economics and Organization, 12 a year).

Instytut Pracy i Spraw Socjalnych (Institute of Labour and Social Studies): ul. Bellottiego 3B, 01-022 Warsaw; tel. (22) 5367511; e-mail instprac@ipiss.com.pl; internet www.ipiss.com.pl; f. 1963; conducts statutory research, research grants, int. projects, seminars, confs; research into labour, wages, income distribution, living standards, social security and social insurance, labour law, human resources management, collective labour relations, family problems and family policy; Gen. Dir Prof. KAZIMIERZ W. FRIESKE; publs *Biuletynu*, *Materiały z Zagranicy* (irregular), *Opracowania PCZ* (irregular), *Polityka Społeczna* (Social Policy, 12 a year, print and online, www.ipiss.com.pl/polityka-spoleczna), *Raport IPiSS* (irregular), *Zarządzanie Zasobami Ludzkimi* (Human Resources Management, 6 a year, print and online, www.ipiss.com.pl/wydawnictwo/zarzadzanie-zasobami-ludzkimi).

Instytut Przedsiębiorstwa (Institute of Enterprise): ul. Madalińskiego 6/8, pok.106, 02-513 Warsaw; tel. (22) 5648671; internet www.sgh.waw.pl/instytuty/ip; f. 2006; research into enterprise devt and competitiveness of enterprises and regions; organizes lectures for gen. audience, doctoral seminars and confs; Dir Prof. Dr Hab. IRENA LICHNIAK; publs *Studia i Analizy* (3 or 4 a year), *Szara Seria* (3 or 4 a year).

Instytut Studiow Politycznych PAN (Institute of Political Studies of Polish Academy of Sciences): ul. Polna 18/20, 00-625 Warsaw; tel. (22) 8255221; e-mail politic@isppan.waw.pl; internet www.isppan.waw.pl; f. 1990; develops theoretical work and empirical studies of post-communist socs; carries out studies of Poland's int. security in globalization and changing world order; offers doctoral programme in political science jtly with Collegium Civitas; library of 19,000 vols, 161 periodicals; Dir Prof. EUGENIUSZ C. KRÓL; publs *Civitas-Studia z Filozofii Polityki* (1 a year, online, www.isppan.waw.pl/ksiegarnia/civ.htm), *Europa Srodkowo-Wschodnia* (Central-Eastern Europe Yearbook, online, www.isppan.waw.pl/ksiegarnia/eur.htm), *Kultura i Społeczeństwo* (Culture and Society, 4 a year, online, www.isppan .waw.pl/ksiegarnia/kis.htm), *Rocznik Polsko-Niemiecki* (Polish-German Yearbook, online, www.isppan.waw.pl/ksiegarnia/rpn.htm), *Studia Polityczne* (Political Studies, 2 a year, online, www.isppan.waw.pl/ksiegarnia/sp.htm).

Instytut Turystyki (Institute of Tourism): ul. Merliniego 9A, 02-511 Warsaw; tel. (22) 8446347; e-mail it@intur.com.pl; internet www.intur.com.pl; f. 1972; interdisciplinary research and devt of social, economic and spatial aspects of tourism; conducts professional training, cultural activities, market research, seminars and dissemination of information; library of 12,609 vols, 3,304 periodicals, spec. collns of 3,280 vols; Pres WACŁAW CZEPIŃSKI; publ. *Problemy Turystyki* (4 a year).

Instytut Wymiaru Sprawiedliwości (Institute of Justice): ul. Krakowskie Przedmieście 25, 00-071 Warsaw; tel. (22) 8260363; e-mail iws@iws.org.pl; internet www.iws.org .pl; f. 1990; conducts permanent empirical studies of the practice of courts and prosecution offices and monitors the trends of crime, crime policy and functioning of the country's justice system; financed and supervised by the Min. of Justice, but operates independently; sections of civil law, criminal law and

criminology, statistical analysis and methodology; library of 5,500 vols; Dir Prof. Dr Hab. ANDRZEJ SIEMASZKO; publs *Atlas Przestępczości* (Crime Atlas), *Prawo w Dzialaniu* (Law in Action).

Instytut Zachodni im. Zygmunta Wojciechowskiego (Institute for Western Affairs): ul. Mostowa 27, 61-854 Poznań; tel. (61) 8527691; e-mail izpozpl@iz.poznan.pl; internet www.iz.poznan.pl; f. 1944; research into int. relations in Europe, esp. Polish-German relations up to the acquisition of Polish western territories, and since 1945 and of Western European economic, political, historical, juridical, social and cultural matters; library of 110,000 vols (incl. books, periodicals and spec. inventories); Man. Dir Dr MICHAŁ NOWOSIELSKI; publs *Biuletyn*, *Przegląd Zachodni* (4 a year).

Państwowy Instytut Naukowy–Instytut Śląski w Opolu (Government Research Institute–Silesian Institute in Opole): ul. Piastowska 17, 45-081 Opole; tel. (77) 4536032; e-mail instytutslaski@wp.pl; internet www.instytutslaski.com; f. 1957; conducts research into the field of history of science, sociology, geography, science, philology, economics, legal science; library of 56,921 vols, 23,362 vols of journals, spec. collns of 754 maps and 118 MSS maps, 7,242 MSS, 3,942 iconography items; Dir Dr Ing. KATARZYNA WIDERA; publs *Region and Regionalism* (in English, jrregular), *Śląsk Opolski* (4 a year), *Studia Śląskie* (1 a year), *Zeszyty Odrzańskie* (1 a year).

Polski Instytut Spraw Międzynarodowych (Polish Institute of International Affairs): POB 1010, ul. Warecka 1A, 00-950 Warsaw; tel. (22) 5568000; e-mail pism@pism.pl; internet www.pism.pl; f. 1996; conducts interdisciplinary and comparative research into int. relations and foreign policy, Poland's membership of the EU and NATO, int. and energy security, Poland's bilateral relations with neighbouring countries; courses for civil servants, confs; UN depository library; library of 160,000 vols; Dir Dr MARCIN ZABOROWSKI; Deputy Dir Dr BEATA WOJNA; Head of Library ANDRZEJ KAMINSKI; publs *Bulletin*, *Polish Quarterly of International Affairs* (4 a year, in English), *Polski Przegląd Dyplomatyczny* (Polish Diplomatic Review, 4 a year, in Polish), *Rocznik Polskiej Polityki Zagranicznej* (Yearbook of Polish Foreign Policy, 1 a year, in Polish), *Sprawy Międzynarodowe* (International Affairs, 4 a year, in Polish).

EDUCATION

Centrum Badań Polityki Naukowej i Szkolnictwa Wyższego (Centre for Science Policy and Higher Education): ul. Nowy Świat 69, 00-046 Warsaw; tel. (22) 8260746; e-mail dziekanat@wsnsir.uw.edu.pl; f. 1973; attached to Faculty of Applied Social Sciences and Resocialisation, Univ. of Warsaw; plans and forecasts devt of higher education; modernization of instruction and organization of higher education; Dir Prof. IRENEUSZ BIAŁECKI; publ. *Nauka i Szkolnictwo Wyższe* (Science and Higher Education, 2 a year).

Instytut Badań Edukacyjnych (Educational Research Institute): ul. Górczewska 8, 01-180 Warsaw; tel. (22) 2417100; e-mail ibe@ibe.edu.pl; internet www.ibe.edu.pl; f. 1952; conducts interdisciplinary research and devt work on functioning and effectiveness of the education system; prepares analyses, expert opinions, reports and forecasts for the Min. of Nat. Education; library of 57,670 vols; Dir Prof. MICHAŁ FEDEROWICZ; publs *Edukacja* (4 a year, online, www.edukacja.ibe.edu.pl), *Edukacja Biologiczna i Srodowiskowa* (4 a year, online, www.ebis.ibe.edu.pl).

Instytut Kształcenia Zawodowego (Institute of Vocational Education): ul. Jana Pawła II 14, 47-220 Kędzierzyn-Koźle; tel. (77) 4834053; f. 1972; library of 18,000 vols; Dir STANISŁAW KACZOR; publs *Biblioteka Kształcenia Zawodowego*, *Pedagogika Pracy* (1 a year), *Szkoła-Zawód-Praca* (1 a year).

FINE AND PERFORMING ARTS

Instytut Sztuki Polskiej Akademii Nauk (Institute of Art of the Polish Academy of Sciences): ul. Długa 28, 00-950 Warsaw; tel. (22) 5048200; e-mail ispan@ispan.pl; internet www.ispan.pl; f. 1949; conducts interdisciplinary research and documentation of Polish art and artistic culture in the field of fine arts and architecture, music, theatre, film and audiovisual art; awards doctoral and postdoctoral titles in history and art studies; library of 140,000 vols, photographic archive of 450,000 negatives, phonographic library of 80,000 items, 16,000 audio cassettes; Dir Prof. Dr Hab. ELŻBIETA WITKOWSKA-ZAREMBA; publs *Almanach Sceny Polskiej* (Almanac of the Polish Stage, 1 a year), *Biuletyn Historii Sztuki* (Bulletin of Art History, 4 a year), *Dagerotyp* (Daguerrotype, 1 a year), *Konteksty. Polska Sztuka Ludowa* (Context-Polish Folk Art, 4 a year), *Kwartalnik Filmowy* (Film Quarterly, 4 a year), *Muzyka* (Music, 4 a year), *Pamiętnik Teatralny* (Theatre Diary, 4 a year), *Rzeczy Teatralne* (Theatre Miscellaneous, 1 a year).

HISTORY, GEOGRAPHY AND ARCHAEOLOGY

Instytut Archeologii i Etnologii PAN (Institute of Archaeology and Ethnology of the Polish Academy of Sciences): Aleje Solidarności 105, 00-140 Warsaw; tel. (22) 6202881; e-mail director@iaepan.edu.pl; internet www.iaepan.edu.pl; f. 1953 as Institute for History of Material Culture PAN, present name 1992; conducts research in the fields of primeval and medieval archeology of the Polish land, Mediterranean archeology, cultural anthropology, ethnology, history of material culture in the Middle Ages and modern history; library of 185,000 vols; Dir Prof. Dr ANDRZEJ BUKO; publs *Archaeologia Polona* (1 a year, in English, online, www.iaepan.edu.pl/archaeologia-polona), *Archaeologia Urbium*, *Archaeological Reports*, *Archaeological Review*, *Archaeology*, *Archaeology of Poland*, *Bibliotheca Antiqua*, *Culture of Early Medieval Europe*, *Ethnologia Polona* (scientific yearbook), *Inventaria Archaeologica*, *Library of Polish Ethnography*, *Polish Archaeological Abstracts*, *Polish Archaeological Researches*, *Polish Ethnographic Atlas*, *Polish Ethnography*, *Quarterly Journal of the History of Material Culture*, *Studia Ethnica*, *Studies and Materials of the History of Material Culture*.

Instytut Geodezji i Kartografii (Institute of Geodesy and Cartography): ul. Modzelewskiego 27, 02-679 Warsaw; tel. (22) 3291900; e-mail igik@igik.edu.pl; internet www.igik.edu.pl; f. 1945; conducts research and devt work for the application of geodetic and cartographic practices for state and local govt, environmental protection, agriculture, forestry, land use planning and management; library of 40,000 vols (incl. 16,000 books; Dir Dr MAREK BARANOWSKI; publs *Geoinformation Issues*, *Informacja Bibliograficzna Geodezji i Kartografii* (12 a year), *Prace IGIK* (2–3 a year), *Proceedings of Institute of Geodesy and Cartography* (1–3 a year), *Rocznik Astronomiczny* (1 a year), *Technicznej i Ekonomicznej Geodezji i Kartografii* (4 a year).

Instytut Geografii i Przestrzennego Zagospodarowania im. S. Leszczyckiego PAN (Stanisław Leszczycki Institute of Geography and Spatial Organization of the Polish Academy of Sciences): ul. Twarda 51/55, 00-818 Warsaw; tel. (22) 6978841; e-mail igipzpan@twarda.pan.pl; internet www.igipz.pan.pl; f. 1953 as Institute of Geography PAS; conducts research in the fields of geomorphology, hydrology, climatology, geoecology, economic geography, urban and population studies, geography of agriculture and rural areas, global development, political geography, regional planning, environmental management, eco-development, European studies, cartography, geographic information systems; library of 293,977 vols (incl. 140,580 vols of books, 53,501 vols of periodicals, 98,672 items of spec. collns of maps, atlases and antique prints); Dir Prof. MAREK DEGÓRSKI; publs *Atlas Warszawy* (Atlas of Warsaw, irregular), *Bibliografia Geografii Polskiej* (Bibliography of Polish Geography, 1 a year, online, www.cbgios.pan.pl/bazy/bgp), *Dokumentacja Geograficzna* (Geographical Documentation, irregular), *Europa XXI* (irregular), *Geographia Polonica* (2 a year), *Geopolitical Studies* (irregular), *Prace Geograficzne* (Geographical Studies, irregular), *Przegląd Geograficzny* (Polish Geographical Review, 4 a year).

Instytut Historii im. Tadeusza Manteuffla Polskiej Akademii Nauk (Tadeusz Manteuffel Institute of History of the Polish Academy of Sciences): Rynek Starego Miasta 29/31, 00-272 Warsaw; tel. (22) 8310261; e-mail ihpan@ihpan.edu.pl; internet www.ihpan.edu.pl; f. 1953; studies political and social history from the Middle Ages to the modern era; specific fields of research: Poland and Central-Eastern Europe, origins and history of modern Poland, history of Polish culture, social changes in post-Second World War Poland, history of mass migrations in 19th and 20th centuries, history of totalitarian systems and the Second World War; library of 40,000 vols, 21,000 vols of serials and periodicals, 633 titles of foreign academic journals and doctoral theses; Dir Prof. Dr Hab. WOJCIECH KRIEGSEISEN; publs *Acta Poloniae Historica* (2 a year, in English), *Czasopismo Prawno-Historyczne* (2 a year), *Dzieje Najnowsze* (4 a year), *Kwartalnik Historyczny* (4 a year), *Odrodzenie i Reformacja w Polsce* (1 a year), *Roczniki Dziejów Społecznych i Gospodarczych* (1 a year), *Roczniki Historyczne* (1 a year), *Studia z Dziejów Rosji i Europy Środkowo-Wschodniej* (1 a year), *Studia Źródłoznawcze. Commentationes* (1 a year).

Zakład Archeologii Śródziemnomorskiej PAN (Research Centre for Mediterranean Archaeology of the Polish Academy of Sciences): Pałac Staszica, Room 33, ul. Nowy Świat 72, 00-330 Warsaw; tel. (22) 8266560; e-mail zaspan@zaspan.waw.pl; internet zaspan.waw.pl; f. 1956; conducts research, excavation, documentation and surveys in the archaeology of Egypt, Nubia and Hellenistic and Roman Near East; library of 13,600 vols, 6,900 vols of periodicals; Dir Prof. Dr Hab. KAROL JAN MYŚLIWIEC; Vice-Dir Prof. Dr Hab. ZSOLT KISS; publs *Alexandrie* (irregular), *Deir el-Bahari* (irregular), *Etudes et Travaux*, *Nea Paphos* (irregular), *Nubia* (irregular), *Saqqara* (irregular), *Tell Atrib* (irregular), *Travaux du Centre d'Archéologie Méditerranéenne*.

LANGUAGE AND LITERATURE

Instytut Badań Literackich PAN (Institute of Literary Research of the Polish Academy of Sciences): ul. Nowy Świat 72, 00-330 Warsaw; tel. (22) 8269945; e-mail ibadlit@ibl.waw.pl; internet ibl.waw.pl; f. 1948, present status 1952; 20 scientific depts and sections in Poznań, Toruń and Wrocław; research in the theory of literature, history of Polish literature, sociology of literature; library of 450,000 vols, spec. collns: 85,000 vols; Dir Prof. Dr Hab. MIKOŁAJ SOKOŁOWSKI; publs *Pamiętnik Literacki* (Literary Journal, 4 a year), *Teksty Drugie* (Texts, 6 a year).

Instytut Języka Polskiego PAN (Institute of the Polish Language at Polish Academy of Sciences): al. Mickiewicza 31, 31-120 Cracow; tel. (12) 6325692; e-mail ijp@ijp-pan.krakow.pl; internet www.ijp-pan.krakow.pl; f. 1973; conducts studies in grammatical construction and history of the Polish language, dialectology, onomastics, sociolinguistics, theory and methodology of linguistics, lexicography, corpus linguistics, relations of the Polish language with other Slavic languages and Latin; library of 27,000 vols; Dir Prof. Dr Hab. PIOTR ŻMIGRODZKI; publs *Antroponimia Polski od XVI do końca XVIII w*, *Nazwy miejscowe Polski*, *Nazwy wodne Polski* (electronic version), *Onomastica* (1 a year, online, onomastica.ijp-pan.krakow.pl), *Polonica* (1 a year, online, polonica.ijp-pan.krakow.pl), *Prace* (series), *Prace Instytutu Języka Polskiego PAN* (series), *Słownik Gwar Polskich* (1 a year), *Słownik Gwar Ostródzkiego*, *Słownik Języka Polskiego XVII i I Polowy XVIII Wieku*, *Słownik Laciny Sredniowiecznej w Polsce*, *Słownik Polskich Leksemów Potocznych*, *Słownik Polszczyzny Jana Kochanowskiego*, *Socjolingwistyka* (1 a year), *Studies in Polish Linguistics* (1 a year), *Wielki Słownik Języka Polskiego* (Great Dictionary of the Polish language, online, www.wsjp.pl).

MEDICINE

Centrum Onkologii—Instytut im. Marii Skłodowskiej-Curie w Warszawie (Marie Skłodowska-Curie Memorial Cancer Centre and Institute of Oncology): ul. W. K. Roentgena 5, 02-781 Warsaw; tel. (22) 5462000; internet www.coi.pl; f. 1932; brs at Cracow and Gliwice; conducts fundamental cancer research, clinical research, diagnosis and treatment, epidemiology; coordinates Nat. Cancer Programme; library of 23,458 vols; Dir Prof. Dr Hab. KRZYSZTOF WARZOCHA; publ. *NOWOTWORY Journal of Oncology* (4 a year, online, www.nowotwory.edu.pl).

Instytut Biocybernetyki i Inżynierii Biomedycznej im. Macieja Nałęcza PAN (Nałęcz Institute of Biocybernetics and Biomedical Engineering PAS): ul. Trojdena 4, 02-109 Warsaw; tel. (22) 6599143; e-mail ibib@ibib.waw.pl; internet www.ibib.waw.pl; f. 1975; collaborates with WHO; mem. of UNESCO Global Network for Molecular and Cell Biology; field of activities: biomeasurements, artificial internal organs, mathematical and physical modelling of physiological systems and processes, computerized image analysis, computer-aided medical diagnosis; Int. Centre of Biocybernetics to facilitate and encourage research and devt and to organize int. scientific meetings and seminars and disseminate information; library of 23,800 vols; Dir Prof. Dr JAN M. WÓJCICKI; publs *Biocybernetics and Biomedical Engineering* (4 a year), *Lecture Notes of the ICB Seminars*, *Prace IBIB PAN* (IBIB PAN Reports, irregular).

Instytut Farmaceutyczny (Pharmaceutical Research Institute): ul. Rydygiera 8, 01-793 Warsaw; tel. (22) 4563900; e-mail kontakt@ifarm.eu; internet www.ifarm.waw.pl; f. 1952; conducts research and devt on comprehensive technology devt and commercialization of medicinal products incl. API synthesis, drug dosage form, analytical services, registration; organizes multidisciplinary conf. on drug research every 2 years;

library of 12,200 vols, 350 periodical titles; Man. Dir Prof. Dr LUKASZ KACZMAREK.

Instytut Farmakologii PAN (Institute of Pharmacology of the Polish Academy of Sciences): ul. Smętna 12, 31-343 Cracow; tel. (12) 6374022; e-mail ifpan@if-pan.krakow.pl; internet www.if-pan.krakow.pl; f. 1954 as Dept of Pharmacology of the Polish Academy of Sciences, present status 1974; conducts research in the fields of behavioural neuroscience and drug devt, brain biochemistry, experimental neuroendocrinology, medicinal chemistry, molecular neuropharmacology, neurobiology, neurochemistry, neuro- and psychopharmacology, pharmacokinetics and drug metabolism, pharmacology, pharmacology of pain, physiology, phytochemistry; library of 9,403 vols, 15,738 vols of journals, 592 journal titles, 118 current journals; Dir Prof. Dr Hab. KRZYSZTOF WEDZONY; publ. *Pharmacological Reports* (6 a year, online, www.if-pan.krakow.pl/pjp).

Instytut Genetyki Człowieka PAN w Poznaniu (Institute of Human Genetics of the Polish Academy of Sciences): ul. Strzeszyńska 32, 60-479 Poznań; tel. (61) 6579100; e-mail igcz@man.poznan.pl; internet www.igcz.poznan.pl; f. 1974; depts of reproductive biology and stem cells, nucleic acids, molecular and clinical genetics, molecular pathology, environmental mutagenesis; organizes confs and seminars; Dir Prof. Dr Hab. JERZY NOWAK.

Instytut Hematologii i Transfuzjologii (Institute of Haematology and Blood Transfusion): ul. Indiry Gandhi 14, 02-776 Warsaw; tel. (22) 3496100; e-mail sekihit@ihit.waw.pl; internet www.ihit.waw.pl; f. 1951, present name 1992; provides medical services; conducts scientific and clinical research and devt for the advancement of science in the field of haematology, transfusion and related disciplines; confers doctoral degrees in medical science; Dir Prof. Dr Hab. KRZYSZTOF WARZOCHA; publs *Acta Haematologica Polonica* (4 a year), *Sprawozdania Roczne z Działalności Instytutu* (1 a year).

Instytut Immunologii i Terapii Doświadczalnej im. Ludwika Hirszfelda PAN (Ludwik Hirszfeld Institute of Immunology and Experimental Therapy of the Polish Academy of Sciences): ul. Rudolfa Weigla 12, 53-114 Wrocław; tel. (71) 3371172; e-mail bednorz@iitd.pan.wroc.pl; internet www.iitd.pan.wroc.pl; f. 1952; research work in basic and clinical immunology, microbiology, immunochemistry, immunogenetics, experimental and bacteriophage therapy; library of 24,000 vols; Dir Prof. Dr DANUTA DUŚ; publs *Archivum Immunologiae et Therapiae Experimentalis* (6 a year, in English), *Postępy Higieny i Medycyny Doświadczalnej* (6 a year, in Polish).

Instytut Kardiologii im. Prymasa Tysiąclecia Stefana Kardynała Wyszyńskiego (Cardinal Stefan Wyszyński Institute of Cardiology): ul. Alpejska 42, 04-628 Warsaw; tel. (22) 3434600; e-mail dyrektor@ikard.pl; internet www.ikard.pl; f. 1979; carries out research related to health monitoring and evaluation of the epidemiology of cardiovascular disease at nat. and regional level; contributes to postgraduate training and education in cardiology; library of 5,887 vols, 4,203 journals; Dir Prof. Dr Hab. WITOLD RUŻYŁŁO; publ. *Biblioteka Kardiologiczna* (Cardiological Library, irregular).

Instytut Matki i Dziecka (Mother and Child Research Institute): ul. Kasprzaka 17A, 01-211 Warsaw; tel. (22) 3277000; internet www.imid.med.pl; f. 1948; research into the physiology and medicine of reproduction; provides consultative, educational and training services; Dir Dr TOMASZ MACIE-

JEWSKI; publ. *Development Period Medicine* (4 a year).

Instytut Medycyny Doświadczalnej i Klinicznej im. M. J. Mossakowskiego PAN (Mossakowski Medical Research Centre of the Polish Academy of Sciences): ul. Pawińskiego 5, 02-106 Warsaw; tel. (22) 6685250; e-mail sekretariat@cmdik.pan.pl; internet www.imdik.pan.pl; f. 1967; conducts research on neurogenetics, neurochemistry, neuropathology, experimental pharmacology, and renal physiology; coordinates Mazovian Peptide Cluster to promote economic devt and cooperation of Polish science with the business sector in Mazovia, to increase the number of commercialized products and innovative technologies and to foster improvement of scientific research capacity and innovations; 4 laboratories; library of 10,000 vols, 164 periodicals; Dir Prof. Dr Hab. ANDRZEJ W. LIPKOWSKI; publ. *Folia Neuropathologica* (4 a year, jtly with Asscn of Polish Neuropathologists).

Instytut Medycyny Morskiej i Tropikalnej (Institute of Maritime and Tropical Medicine): ul. Powstania Styczniowego 9B, 81-519 Gdynia; tel. (58) 6223354; e-mail mimmit@gumed.edu.pl; internet www.mimmit.gumed.edu.pl; f. 1939; attached to Medical Univ. of Gdańsk; research in maritime occupational health, tropical medicine and epidemiology, toxicology, microbiology, travel medicine; clinic; postgraduate courses; WHO Inter-Regional Collaborating Centre on Maritime Occupational Health; Dir Prof. Dr Hab. BOGDAN JAREMIN; publ. *International Maritime Health* (4 a year).

Instytut Medycyny Pracy im. prof. J. Nofera (Nofer Institute of Occupational Medicine): ul. Sw. Teresy od Dzieciątka Jezus 8, 91-348 Łódź; tel. (42) 6314502; e-mail impx@imp.lodz.pl; internet www.imp.lodz.pl; f. 1954; research in occupational medicine and hygiene, physiology, psychology, toxicology, neurotoxicology, carcinogenesis, pathology and epidemiology; management of occupational health service; radiation protection and the diagnosis and treatment of occupational diseases and acute poisoning; scientific information; Dir Prof. Dr KONRAD RYDZYŃSKI; publs *Informacja Expresowa–Ostre Zatrucia* (Express Information–Acute Poisoning, 4 a year), *International Journal of Occupational Medicine and Environmental Health* (in English, 4 a year), *Medycyna Pracy* (Occupational Medicine, 6 a year).

Instytut Medycyny Pracy i Zdrowia Srodowiskowego (Institute of Occupational Medicine and Environmental Health): ul. Kościelna 13, 41-200 Sosnowiec; tel. (32) 2660885; internet www.imp.sosnowiec.pl; f. 1950 as Silesian Institute of Occupational Medicine, current name and status 1992; conducts research and implementation studies, training, diagnostic and treatment activities in the field of occupational medicine and environmental health; Dir Dr PIOTR BREWCZYŃSKI; publ. *Medycyna Srodowiskowa–Environmental Medicine* (4 a year, online, www.medycynasrodowiskowa.pl).

Instytut Medycyny Wsi im. Witolda Chodźki (W. Chodźko Institute of Rural Health): ul. Jaczewskiego 2, 20-090 Lublin; tel. (81) 7184400; e-mail imw@galen.imw.lublin.pl; internet www.imw.lublin.pl; f. 1951 as Institute of Occupational Medicine in Lublin, present status 1984; conducts scientific studies, research and devt activities and projects for implementation; evaluates state of health of the rural population and provides diagnosis, treatment and rehabilitation; organizes training courses for primary healthcare physicians; confers doctoral

degrees in medical sciences; library of 20,000 vols of monographs; Man. Dr ANDRZEJ HOROCH; publs *Annals of Agricultural and Environmental Medicine* (2 a year, online, aaem.pl), *Journal of Pre-Clinical and Clinical Research (JP-CCR)* (online, jpccr.eu), *Medycyna Ogólna i Nauki o Zdrowiu* (4 a year, in Polish with abstracts and articles in English, Russian and Ukrainian, online, monz.pl).

Instytut Psychiatrii i Neurologii (Institute of Psychiatry and Neurology): ul. Sobieskiego 9, 02-957 Warsaw; tel. (22) 4582800; e-mail ipin@ipin.edu.pl; internet www.ipin.edu.pl; f. 1951; conducts research in the field of neurology, drug and psychiatry; develops new methods of treatment and rehabilitation of mental and neurological disorders; library of 28,645 vols, 555 journals; Dir Prof. Dr Hab. DANUTA RYGLEWICZ; publs *Alkoholizm i Narkomania* (Alcohol and Drug Abuse, 4 a year, online, ain.ipin.edu.pl), *Farmakoterapia w Psychiatrii i Neurologii* (4 a year, online, fpn.ipin.edu.pl), *Postępy Psychiatrii i Neurologii* (Advances of Psychiatry and Neurology, 4 a year, online, ppn.ipin.edu.pl).

Instytut Żywności i Żywienia im. Prof. Dr. med. Aleksandra Szczygła (National Food and Nutrition Institute): ul. Powsińska 61/63, 02-903 Warsaw; tel. (22) 5509771; internet www.izz.waw.pl; f. 1963; multidisciplinary scientific research in the field of human nutrition, food health quality and safety, prevention of food-related diseases; library of 14,000 vols, 68 journal subscriptions; Dir Prof. Dr MIROSŁAW JAROSZ; publs *Żywienie Człowieka i Metabolizm* (4 a year), *Żywność, Żywienie a Zdrowie* (4 a year).

Narodowy Instytut Leków (National Medicines Institute): ul. Chełmska 30/34, 00-725 Warsaw; tel. (22) 8410652; e-mail sekretariat@il.waw.pl; internet www.nil.gov.pl; f. 1951, present status 2002; carries out research and devt on quality control of medicinal products and medical devices, methods of identification, elimination and prevention of biological threats; develops methods in the area of pharmacoeconomics and for improvement of drug compliance; library of 7,000 vols; Dir Prof. Dr Hab. ZBIGNIEW E. FIJAŁEK; publs *Biuletyn Informacyjny Instytutu Leków* (irregular), *Biuletyn Leków* (4 a year).

Narodowym Instytut Zdrowia Publicznego—Państwowy Zakład Higieny (National Institute of Public Health—National Institute of Hygiene): ul. Chocimska 24, 00-791 Warsaw; tel. (22) 5421200; e-mail pzh@pzh.gov.pl; internet www.pzh.gov.pl; f. 1918; conducts scientific and research work for biological, chemical and physical risk factors in nutrition, water, air in rooms and contagious diseases and infections; library of 38,094 vols; Dir-Gen. Prof. Dr MIROSŁAW J. WYSOCKI; publs *Medycyna Doświadczalna i Mikrobiologia* (4 a year), *Przegląd Epidemiologiczny* (4 a year, online, www.pzh.gov.pl/oldpage/przeglad_epimed/index.html), *Roczniki Państwowego Zakładu Higieny* (4 a year).

Zakład Amin Biogennych PAN (Department of Biogenic Amines of Polish Academy of Sciences): ul. Tylna 3, skr. poczt. 225, 90-364 Łódz; tel. (42) 6817007; f. 1958; conducts research into metabolic and allergic diseases; role of biogenic amines, polyamines and respective enzymes in fast growing tissue; the visual system; mast cells devt, differentiation and functions; library of 7,000 vols; Dir Prof. Dr JANINA WYCZÓŁKOWSKA.

NATURAL SCIENCES
General

Instytut Historii Nauki im. Ludwika i Aleksandra Birkenmajerów PAN (L. and A. Birkenmajer Institute for the History of Science of the Polish Academy of Sciences): ul. Nowy Świat 72, pok. 9, 00-330 Warsaw; tel. (22) 8268754; e-mail ihn@ihpan.waw.pl; internet www.ihpan.waw.pl; f. 1954, present name 1994; conducts research into the history of Polish and European science and letters with focus on sources from the European Middle Ages, conditions of devt and reception of modern science, comparative investigation into the history of education, environmental factors, European relations, Polish scientific elite, contribution of Polish scientists to the devt of modern science and technology, reception of scientific theories in the context of social changes and nat. movements in central and E Europe; library of 16,000 vols, 80 journals; Dir Prof. Dr LESZEK ZASZTOWT; publs *ANALECTA. Studia i Materiały z Dziejów Nauki* (2 a year), *Archiwum Dziejów Oświaty* (1 a year), *Kwartalnik Historii Nauki i Techniki* (Quarterly Journal of the History of Science and Technology, 4 a year, online, www.wiw.pl/wielcy/kwartalnik), *Medycyna Nowożytna* (2 a year), *Organon* (1 a year, in French, English and Russian), *Rozprawy z Dziejów Nauki i Techniki* (1 a year).

Instytut Oceanologii PAN (Institute of Oceanology of the Polish Academy of Sciences): ul. Powstańców Warszawy 55, POB 148, 81-712 Sopot; tel. (58) 5517281; e-mail office@iopan.gda.pl; internet www.iopan.gda.pl; f. 1953 as Marine Station of the Academy, present name and status 1983; scientific and technological research into marine physics, hydrodynamics, marine chemistry, marine ecology, genetics of marine organisms; library of 6,450 vols, 7,270 journals; Dir Prof. JANUSZ PEMPKOWIAK; publ. *Oceanologia* (4 a year, in English, online, www.iopan.gda.pl/oceanologia/index.html).

Biological Sciences

Centrum Badań Ekologicznych PAN (Centre for Ecological Research of the Polish Academy of Sciences): ul. M. Konopnickiej 1, 05-092 Łomianki; tel. (22) 7513046; e-mail cbe@cbe-pan.pl; internet www.cbe-pan.pl; f. 2002; conducts research work on population and community studies, landscape ecology, ecological bioenergetics, biogeochemistry, agroecology, polar research, hydrobiology, plant ecology, soil ecology, vertebrate ecology, modelling of ecological processes; incl. hydrobiological station in Mikołajki and research station in Lublin; library of 75,000 vols; Dir Prof. JANUSZ UCHMAŃSKI; publ. *Polish Journal of Ecology* (original papers in English, 4 a year, online, www.pol.j.ecol.cbe-pan.pl).

Instytut Biochemii i Biofizyki PAN (Institute of Biochemistry and Biophysics of the Polish Academy of Sciences): ul. Pawińskiego 5A, 02-106 Warsaw; tel. (22) 6597072; e-mail secretariate@ibb.waw.pl; internet www.ibb.waw.pl; f. 1957; research work in the fields of molecular genetics, biotechnology, biochemistry, biophysics, bioinformatics; library of 6,500 vols of books, 67,190 vols of periodicals; Dir Prof. PIOTR ZIELENKIEWICZ.

Instytut Biologii Doświadczalnej im M. Nenckiego PAN (Nencki Institute of Experimental Biology of the Polish Academy of Sciences): ul. Pasteura 3, 02-093 Warsaw; tel. (22) 5892207; e-mail dyrekcja@nencki.gov.pl; internet www.nencki.gov.pl; f. 1918; depts of biochemistry, cell biology, molecular and cellular neurobiology, neurobiology, neu-rophysiology; library of 25,130 vols of books, 48,817 vols of journals, 441 doctoral and postdoctoral theses, 126 titles of periodicals; Dir ADAM SZEWCZYK; Deputy Dir for Scientific Research URSZULA SŁAWIŃSKA; publ. *Acta Neurobiologiae Experimentalis* (4 a year, print and online, www.ane.pl).

Instytut Biologii Ssaków PAN (Mammal Research Institute of the Polish Academy of Sciences): ul. Gen. Waszkiewicza 1C, 17-230 Białowieża; tel. (85) 6827750; e-mail mripas@zbs.bialowieza.pl; internet www.zbs.bialowieza.pl; f. 1952; scientific research in biomorphology, ecology, ecophysiology, genetics, taxonomy and fauna of mammals; colln of 190,000 specimens; library of 34,000 vols; Dir Dr Hab. KRZYSZTOF SCHMIDT; publ. *Acta Theriologica* (4 a year, print and online, www.ibs.bialowieza.pl/artykul/587.html).

Instytut Botaniki im. Władysława Szafera PAN (W. Szafer Institute of Botany of the Polish Academy of Sciences): ul. Lubicz 46, 31-512 Cracow; tel. (12) 4241700; e-mail sekretariat@botany.pl; internet www.botany.pl; f. 1954; depts of ecology, phycology, mycology, palaeobotany, systematics, bryology, lichenology; laboratory of molecular analyses; library of 163,510 vols, incl. 121,635 vols of books, 34,835 vols of journals, 7,040 maps, microforms and slides; Dir Prof. Dr Hab. KONRAD WOŁOWSKI; publs *Acta Palaeobotanica* (International Journal of Palaeobotany and Palynology, 2 a year, print and online, www.botany.pl/en/ibwyd/acta_paleo/act-p.htm), *Fragmenta Floristica et Geobotanica Polonica* (Material on the Flora and Vegetation of Poland, 2 a year, in Polish, print and online), *Polish Botanical Journal* (2 a year, print and online, www.botany.pl/en/ibwyd/pol-b-j/pol-b-j.htm), *Polish Botanical Studies* (irregular, in English, print and online).

Instytut Chemii Bioorganicznej PAN (Institute of Bioorganic Chemistry of the Polish Academy of Sciences): ul. Z. Noskowskiego 12/14, 61-704 Poznań; tel. (61) 8528503; e-mail ibch@ibch.poznan.pl; internet www.ibch.poznan.pl; f. 1980; bioorganic chemistry, crystallochemistry of nucleic acids, proteins and their components; molecular biology, genetics and genetic engineering of plants, applied phytochemistry, biochemistry, bioinformatics; library of 3,300 vols; Dir Prof. Dr Hab. MAREK FIGLEROWICZ; Deputy Dir for Scientific Affairs Prof. Dr Hab. JERZY BORYSKI.

Instytut Dendrologii PAN (Institute of Dendrology of the Polish Academy of Sciences): ul. Parkowa 5, 62-035 Kórnik; tel. (61) 8170033; e-mail idkornik@man.poznan.pl; internet www.idpan.poznan.pl; f. 1933, present status 1952, present name 1975; dendrology, acclimatization, systematics and geography of woody plants, tree genetics, tree physiology, seed physiology, tree resistance to pathogens, frost and pollution; library of 47,029 vols, incl. 25,750 vols of books, 9,645 vols of periodicals; spec. colln of 1,634 items; Dir Prof. JACEK OLEKSYN; publ. *Dendrobiology* (2 a year, print and online).

Instytut Ochrony Przyrody PAN (Institute of Nature Conservation of the Polish Academy of Sciences): al. A. Mickiewicza 33, 31-120 Cracow; tel. (12) 3703500; e-mail sekretariat@iop.krakow.pl; internet www.iop.krakow.pl; f. 1920; research on problems relating to nature conservation, biological conservation, landscape ecology, interaction between human activity and the biosphere; field stations in Wrocław and Zakopane; library of 21,000 vols, 18,300 periodicals, 19,500 maps and photographs; Dir Dr Hab. HENRYK OKARMA; publs *Chrońmy Przyrodę Ojczystą* (Let Us Protect the Nature of Our Homeland, 6 a year), *Nature Conservation* (1 a year, in English), *Studia Naturae* (irregular).

Instytut Paleobiologii im. Romana Kozłowskiego PAN (Institute of Paleobiology of the Polish Academy of Sciences): ul. Twarda 51/55, 00-818 Warsaw; tel. (22) 6978850; e-mail paleo@twarda.pan.pl; internet www.paleo.pan.pl; f. 1952; conducts biologically oriented research on fossil biota and comparative studies of their recent counterparts; research covers vertebrates, invertebrates and microfossils of various origins; library of 30,000 vols of books, 25,000 vols of periodicals; Dir Prof. Dr Hab. JERZY DZIK; publs *Acta Palaeontologica Polonica* (4 a year, print and online, www.app.pan.pl), *Ewolucja* (Evolution, irregular, print and online), *Rocznik Muzeum Ewolucji* (Yearbook).

Instytut Parazytologii im Witolda Stefańskiego PAN (Witold Stefański Institute of Parasitology of the Polish Academy of Sciences): ul. Twarda 51/55, 00-818 Warsaw; tel. (22) 6206226; e-mail iparpas@twarda.pan.pl; internet www.ipar.pan.pl; f. 1952, present name 1983; scientific research work in parasitology, incl. animal parasitism, its origin, prevalence, manifestations and effects in natural and experimental parasite-host systems; depts of biodiversity, deer farming, epizootiology, molecular biology and pathology; library of 25,000 vols, 533 periodicals; Dir Prof. Dr Hab WŁADYSŁAW CABAJ; Vice-Dir for Scientific Affairs Prof. Dr Hab ALEKSANDER W. DEMIASZKIEWICZ; publ. *Acta Parasitologica* (4 a year, print and online, www.actaparasitologica.pan.pl).

Instytut Systematyki i Ewolucji Zwierząt PAN (Institute of Systematics and Evolution of Animals of the Polish Academy of Sciences): ul. Sławkowska 17, 31-016 Cracow; tel. (12) 4221901; e-mail office@isez.pan.krakow.pl; internet www.isez.pan.krakow.pl; f. 1865; research on animal systematics, paleontology, faunistics, and cytology with focus on zoology of vertebrates, zoology of invertebrates and experimental zoology; library of 107,000 vols, incl. 53,000 books, 52,000 journals, 2,000 maps, tables; spec. colln of 539 old prints; Dir Prof. ZBIGNIEW BOCHEŃSKI; publs *Acta Zoologica Cracoviensia* (4 a year, in English, print and online, www.isez.pan.krakow.pl/journals/azc.htm), *Folia Biologica* (4 a year, print and online, www.isez.pan.krakow.pl/journals/folia.htm).

Instytut Włókien Naturalnych i Roślin Zielarskich (Institute of Natural Fibres and Medicinal Plants): ul. Wojska Polskiego 71B, 60-630 Poznań; tel. (61) 8455800; e-mail sekretariat@iwnirz.pl; internet iwnirz.pl; f. 2009 by merger of Institute of Natural Fibres (f. 1930) and Research Institute of Medicinal Plants (f. 1947); research depts of biotechnology, botany, breeding and agricultural technology, innovative textile technologies, pharmacology and experimental biology, research and processing of seed, quality testing for medicinal products and dietary supplements, innovative biomaterials and nanotechnology; 2 accredited laboratories; Dir Prof. Dr Hab. GRZEGORZ SPYCHALSKI; publs *Herba Polonica* (4 a year, online, www.herbapolonica.pl), *Journal of Natural Fibers* (4 a year).

Mathematical Sciences

Instytut Matematyczny PAN (Institute of Mathematics of the Polish Academy of Sciences): ul. Sniadeckich 8, POB 21, 00-956 Warsaw; tel. (22) 5228100; e-mail instytut.matematyczny@impan.pl; internet www.impan.pl; f. 1948, present name and status 1952; scientific research work in mathematics and applications; local brs in Cracow,

Gdańsk, Katowice, Łódź, Poznań, Toruń and Wrocław; library of 134,000 vols; Dir Prof. Dr Hab. FELIKS PRZYTYCKI; publs *Acta Arithmetica* (24 a year, print and online, journals.impan.gov.pl/aa), *Annales Polonici Mathematici* (9 a year, print and online, journals.impan.gov.pl/ap), *Applicationes Mathematicae* (4 a year, print and online, journals.impan.gov.pl/am), *Bulletin* (3 a year, print and online, journals.impan .gov.pl/ba), *Colloquium Mathematicum* (8 a year, print and online, journals.impan.gov.pl/ cm), *Fundamenta Mathematicae* (12 a year, print and online, journals.impan.gov.pl/fm), *Studia Mathematica* (18 a year, print and online, journals.impan.gov.pl/sm).

Attached Centre:

Międzynarodowe Centrum Matematyczne im. Stefana Banacha (Stefan Banach International Mathematical Centre): ul. Sniadeckich 8, POB 21, 00-956 Warsaw; tel. (22) 5228232; e-mail banach.center.office@impan.pl; internet www.impan.pl/bc; f. 1972 by an agreement of Academies of East European countries; br. of the Institute of Mathematics; promotion of int. cooperation in mathematics through organizing research and training semesters, workshops, confs and symposia in different fields of mathematics; Dir Prof. STANISŁAW JANECZKO.

Physical Sciences

Centrum Astronomiczne im. Mikołaja Kopernika PAN (Nicolaus Copernicus Astronomical Centre of the Polish Academy of Sciences): ul. Bartycka 18, 00-716 Warsaw; tel. (22) 8410041; e-mail camk@camk.edu.pl; internet www.camk.edu.pl; f. 1956, present name 1978; astronomy and astrophysics; library of 20,000 vols; Dir Prof. Dr Hab. MAREK SARNA.

Centrum Badań Kosmicznych PAN (Space Research Centre of the Polish Academy of Sciences): ul. Bartycka 18A, 00-716 Warsaw; tel. (22) 4966200; e-mail cbk@cbk .waw.pl; internet www.cbk.waw.pl; f. 1977; space physics, planetary geodesy, remote sensing; library of 15,000 vols; Dir Prof. Dr Hab. MAREK BANASZKIEWICZ; publ. *Artificial Satellites—Journal of Planetary Geodesy* (4 a year, print and online, artsat.cbk.waw.pl).

Centrum Badań Molekularnych i Makromolekularnych PAN (Centre of Molecular and Macromolecular Studies of the Polish Academy of Sciences): ul. Sienkiewicza 112, 90-363 Łódź; tel. (42) 6847113; e-mail cbmm@ cbmm.lodz.pl; internet www.cbmm.lodz.pl; f. 1972; hetero-organic chemistry, organic chemistry of sulphur, bio-organic chemistry, polymer physics, polymer chemistry, heteroorganic polymers, instrumental and elemental analysis; library: over 16,950 vols, 18 current periodicals; Dir Prof. Dr Hab. STANISLAW SLOMKOWSKI; Deputy Dir for Research Prof. Dr Hab. MAREK POTRZEBOWSKI.

Centrum Fizyki Teoretycznej PAN (Centre for Theoretical Physics of the Polish Academy of Sciences): al. Lotników 32/46, 02-668 Warsaw; tel. (22) 8470920; e-mail cft@cft .edu.pl; internet www.cft.edu.pl; f. 1980; classical and quantum field theory, gravitational theory, gen. relativity, statistical physics, quantum and atom optics, particle astrophysics; Dir Prof. LECH MANKIEWICZ.

Centrum Materiałów Polimerowych i Węglowych PAN (Centre of Polymer and Carbon Materials of the Polish Academy of Sciences): ul. Marii Curie-Skłodowskiej 34, 41-819 Zabrze; tel. (32) 2716077; e-mail sekretariat_naukowy@cmpw-pan.edu.pl; internet www.cmpw-pan.edu.pl; f. 1968 as the Institute of Coal Chemistry and Polymers, current name adopted 2007; research

to develop new polymers, carbon-polymer materials, carbon materials and to examine their properties for use in biotechnology, microtechnology, optoelectronics, protection of the environment and healthcare; library of 10,685 vols, 4,291 periodicals; Exec. Dir Prof. Dr Hab. ANDRZEJ DWORAK; Scientific Sec. Dr AGNIESZKA KOWALCZUK.

Instytut Chemii Fizycznej PAN (Institute of Physical Chemistry of the Polish Academy of Sciences): Kasprzaka 44/52, 01-224 Warsaw; tel. (22) 3432000; e-mail ichf@ichf.edu .pl; internet ichf.edu.pl; f. 1955; research work in physico-chemical fundamentals incl. chemical engineering and chemical technology: physical chemistry of metal-hydrogen systems incl. surface science and heterogeneous catalysis, analytical physical chemistry and instrumentation, experimental thermodynamics of organic mixtures, spectroscopy, calorimetry, theory of chemical kinetics, electrochemistry and corrosion, fuel cells, molten salts, process kinetics, statistical mechanics and thermodynamics of irreversible phenomena; library of 99,147 vols; Dir Prof. Dr Hab. ROBERT HOŁYST.

Instytut Chemii Organicznej PAN (Institute of Organic Chemistry of the Polish Academy of Sciences): ul. Kasprzaka 44/52, 01-224 Warsaw; tel. (22) 3432000; e-mail icho-s@icho.edu.pl; internet www.icho.edu .pl; f. 1954; research in synthetic organic chemistry and natural products chemistry; library of 28,648 vols; Gen. Dir Prof. SŁAWOMIR JAROSZ; Research Dir Prof. WITOLD DANIKIEWICZ.

Instytut Fizyki Jądrowej im. Henryka Niewodniczańskiego PAN (Henryk Niewodniczański Institute of Nuclear Physics of the Polish Academy of Sciences): ul. Radzikowskiego 152, 31-342 Cracow; tel. (12) 6628000; e-mail dyrektor@ifj.edu.pl; internet www.ifj.edu.pl; f. 1955; particle physics and astrophysics, nuclear physics and strong interactions physics, condensed matter physics, interdisciplinary research, physics methods in radiation and environmental biology, environmental physics, medical physics, dosimetry, nuclear geophysics, econophysics, radiochemistry and engineering of nano-materials; library of 19,000 vols, 8,000 periodicals; Gen. Dir Prof. Dr Hab. MAREK JEŻABEK; publ. *Raporty IFJ PAN* (Reports, 1 a year, print and online).

Instytut Fizyki Molekularnej PAN (Institute of Molecular Physics of the Polish Academy of Sciences): ul. Mariana Smoluchowskiego 17, 60-179 Poznań; tel. (61) 8695100; e-mail office@ifmpan.poznan .pl; internet www.ifmpan.poznan.pl; f. 1975; scientific divs of physics of dielectrics and molecular spectroscopy, physics of magnetics and cooperative phenomena, soft matter physics and functional materials; library of 23,500 vols; Dir Prof. Dr Hab. ANDRZEJ JEZIERSKI; Vice-Dir for Scientific Affairs Prof. Dr Hab. ROMAN SWIETLIK.

Instytut Fizyki PAN (Institute of Physics of the Polish Academy of Sciences): Al. Lotników 32/46, 02-668 Warsaw; tel. (22) 8437001; e-mail dir@ifpan.edu.pl; internet www.ifpan.edu.pl; f. 1953; research in condensed matter physics: semiconductors, magnetics, superconductors, atomic and molecular physics, quantum optics, spectroscopy, X-ray crystallography, crystal growth; library of 28,000 vols; Dir Prof. Dr Hab. LESZEK SIRKO; publs *Acta Physica Polonica A* (12 a year, print and online, info.ifpan.edu.pl/ ACTA/acta.home.html), *Proceedings of Conferences in Physics* (irregular).

Instytut Fizyki Plazmy i Laserowej Mikrosyntezy (Institute of Plasma Physics and Laser Microfusion): ul. Hery 23, 01-497

Warsaw; tel. (22) 6381460; e-mail office@ ipplm.pl; internet www.ifpilm.pl; f. 1976; attached to Min. of Science and Higher Education; basic plasma physics studies and its implementation in the area of magnetic confinement fusion, inertial confinement fusion and pulsed high power technology; library of 1,000 vols; Dir Dr Hab. ANDRZEJ GALKOWSKI.

Instytut Geofizyki PAN (Institute of Geophysics of the Polish Academy of Sciences): ul. Księcia Janusza 64, 01-452 Warsaw; tel. (22) 6915950; e-mail office@igf.edu.pl; internet www.igf.edu.pl; f. 1952; seismology and physics of earth's interior, geomagnetism, palaeomagnetism, physics of the atmosphere, hydrology and polar research; incl. seismological observatories, physics of the atmosphere observatories, magnetic observatories; library of 32,700 vols, 115 current periodicals, 306 maps and atlases, 4,200 ejournals; Dir Prof. Dr Hab. PAWEŁ ROWIŃSKI; publ. *Acta Geophysica Polonica* (4 a year, print and online, agp.igf.edu.pl).

Instytut Katalizy i Fizykochemii Powierzchni im. Jerzego Habera PAN (Jerzy Haber Institute of Catalysis and Surface Chemistry of the Polish Academy of Sciences): ul. Niezapominajek 8, 30-239 Cracow; tel. (12) 6395101; e-mail ncikifp@cyf-kr .edu.pl; internet www.ik-pan.krakow.pl; f. 1968; kinetics and mechanism of heterogeneous, homogeneous and enzymatic catalytic reactions, solid state chemistry, properties and dynamics of colloids, inter-facial phenomena, electrochemistry of interfaces; library of 11,091 vols; Dir Prof. Dr Hab. MAŁGORZATA WITKO; Deputy Dir for Research Prof. Dr Hab. ROMAN KOZŁOWSKI.

Instytut Mechaniki Górotworu PAN (Strata Mechanics Research Institute of the Polish Academy of Sciences): ul. Reymonta 27, 30-059 Cracow; tel. (12) 6376200; e-mail biuro12@img-pan.krakow.pl; internet www .img-pan.krakow.pl; f. 1954; mechanics of granular media, rock deformation, gas and rock-mass outbursts, low-speed flow of fluids, dynamics of air flow, flow through porous media, micromeritics; library of 23,000 vols; Dir Prof. Dr Hab. WACŁAW DZIURZYŃSKI; publs *Archives of Mining Sciences* (4 a year, print and online, mining.archives.pl), *Prace Instytutu Mechaniki Górotworu* (Transactions of the Strata Mechanics Research Institute, 4 a year, print and online, www.img-pan.krakow.pl/index.php/en/publishing/transactions-of-img-pan.html).

Instytut Nauk Geologicznych PAN (Institute of Geological Sciences of the Polish Academy of Sciences): ul. Twarda 51/55, 00-818 Warsaw; tel. (22) 6978700; e-mail ingpan@twarda.pan.pl; internet www.ing .pan.pl; f. 1956; conducts basic geological research on the origin and formation of rocks and minerals, evolution of selected orogens and reconstruction of ancient environments; areas of research incl. isotope geochemistry (esp. geochronology), mineralogy, petrology, quaternary geology, sedimentology, stratigraphy and hydrogeology; tectonics; library of 57,709 vols of books, 194,615 periodicals, 7,978 maps; Exec. Dir Prof. Dr Hab. MAREK LEWANDOWSKI; publs *Annales Societatis Geologorum Poloniae* (3 a year, print and online, www.asgp.pl), *Geologia Sudetica* (1 a year, print and online, gs.ing.pan.pl), *Studia Geologica Polonica* (irregular, print and online, sgp.ing.pan.pl), *Studia Quaternaria* (1 a year, print and online, www.studia.quaternaria.pan.pl).

Instytut Niskich Temperatur i Badań Strukturalnych PAN im. Włodzimierza Trzebiatowskiego we Wrocławiu (W. Trzebiatowski Institute of Low Temperature and Structure Research of the Polish Academy of Sciences in Wrocław): POB 1410, 50-950 Wrocław 2; ul. Okólna 2, 50-422 Wrocław; tel. (71) 3435021; e-mail intibs@int.pan.wroc.pl; internet www.int.pan.wroc.pl; f. 1966; physics and chemistry of solids: electronic and crystallographic structure, low temperature phenomena, magnetism, superconductivity; library of 22,000 vols; Dir Prof. Dr Hab. ANDRZEJ JEŻOWSKI; Scientific Sec. ANDRZEJ KOCZARSKI.

Instytut Wyokich Ciśnień PAN/UNI-PRESS (Institute of High Pressure Physics of the Polish Academy of Sciences): ul. Sokołowska 29/37, 01-142 Warsaw; tel. (22) 6325010; e-mail dyrekcja@unipress.waw.pl; internet www.unipress.waw.pl; f. 1972; effects of high pressure on metals and semiconductors, high pressure metal formation and crystal growth, cold isostatic pressing, hot isostatic pressing and sintering; manufacture of high pressure laboratory equipment; Dir Prof. IZABELLA GRZEGORY.

Państwowy Instytut Geologiczny—Państwowy Instytut Badawczy (Polish Geological Institute—National Research Institute): ul. Rakowiecka 4, 00-975 Warsaw; tel. (22) 4592000; e-mail sekretariat@pgi.gov.pl; internet www.pgi.gov.pl; f. 1919; geological, hydrogeological and geo-environmental mapping; geological and hydrogeological national survey; central chemical laboratory; 8 brs; geological museum; library of 160,000 vols, 32,000 bound periodicals, 520,000 maps and atlases, 326,000 geological documents; Dir Prof. Dr Hab. JERZY NAWROCKI; Scientific Sec. Dr Hab. GRZEGORZ PIEŃKOWSKI; publs *Bibliografia Geologiczna Polski* (Geological Bibliography of Poland, 1 a year), *Biuletyn Państwowego Instytutu Geologicznego* (irregular, print and online), *Geological Quarterly* (4 a year, print and online, gq.pgi.gov.pl), *Przegląd Geologiczny* (Polish Geological Review, 12 a year, print and online), *Volumina Jurassica* (1 a year, print and online, voluminajurassica.org).

PHILOSOPHY AND PSYCHOLOGY

Instytut Filozofii i Socjologii PAN (Institute of Philosophy and Sociology of the Polish Academy of Sciences): ul. Nowy Świat 72, 00-330 Warsaw; tel. (22) 8267181; e-mail secretar@ifispan.waw.pl; internet www.ifispan.waw.pl; f. 1956; carries out advanced research in philosophy and sociology, cognitive and communication fields; library of 182,267 vols, 41,937 journals; spec. colln of 15,228 items; Dir Prof. Dr Hab. ANDRZEJ RYCHARD; publs *Archiwum Historii Filozofii i Myśli Społecznej* (Archive of the History of Philosophy and Social Thought, 1 a year, print and online, www.ahf.ifispan.pl), *Ask: Research and Methods* (irregular, in English, print and online, askresearchandmethods.org), *Prakseologia* (irregular, print and online), *Studia Antyczne i Mediewistyczne* (1 a year, print and online, ifispan.waw.pl/saim), *Studia Logica* (4 a year, in English, print and online, www.ifispan.waw.pl/studialogica), *Studia Socjologiczne* (4 a year, print and online, www.studiasocjologiczne.pl).

Instytut Psychologii PAN (Institute of Psychology of the Polish Academy of Sciences): Jaracza 1, 00-378 Warsaw; tel. (22) 5831380; e-mail sekretariat@psych.pan.pl; internet www.psych.pan.pl; f. 1980, present name and status 1989; social psychology, personality, general psychology, psycholinguistics, cognitive and decision processes, political psychology, ecological psychology, cross-cultural psychology; grants doctoral degrees and habilitations; library of 7,800 vols; Dir Dr Hab. URSZULA JAKUBOWSKA; Scientific Dir Dr Hab. PIOTR SZAROTA; publ.

Studia Psychologiczne (4 a year, print and online, studiapsychologiczne.pl).

RELIGION, SOCIOLOGY AND ANTHROPOLOGY

Polska Akademia Nauk Zakład Antropologii (Polish Academy of Sciences Institute of Anthropology): ul. Kuźnicza 35, 50-951 Wrocław 56; tel. (71) 3438675; e-mail sekretariat@antro.pan.wroc.pl; internet www.antro.pan.wroc.pl; f. 1952; biological aspects of social stratification, human growth and devt, indicators of individual biological conditions, biological basis of human behaviour and reproduction; library of 18,438 vols; Dir Dr Hab. SŁAWOMIR KOZIEŁ.

Żydowski Instytut Historyczny im. Emanuela Ringelbluma (Emanuel Ringelblum Jewish Historical Institute): ul. Tłomackie 3/5, 00-090 Warsaw; tel. (22) 8279221; e-mail secretary@jhi.pl; internet www.jhi.pl; f. 1947; research in Jewish history, educational activities, public lectures, film shows, seminars, workshops and exhibitions; incl. a museum of Jewish art and martyrology, archives and library; library of 80,000 vols, 600 MSS; Dir Prof. Dr Hab. PAWEŁ SPIEWAK; publ. *Kwartalnik Historii Żydów* (Jewish History Quarterly, 4 a year, print and online).

TECHNOLOGY

Centralny Instytut Ochrony Pracy–Państwowy Instytut Badawczy (CIOP-PIB) (Central Institute for Labour Protection—National Research Institute): ul. Czerniakowska 16, 00-701 Warsaw; tel. (22) 6234601; e-mail dakor@ciop.pl; internet www.ciop.pl; f. 1950; research and devt on occupational health and safety; determination of exposure limits; standardization; testing and certification of machinery and manufacturing devices and personal and collective protective equipment; implementation and certification of occupational health and safety management systems; certification of the competence of personnel and educational bodies active in occupational health and safety; education and training; consultations; promotion; information and publishing; library of 30,000 vols, 4,000 reference vols, 300 journals; Dir Prof. Dr Hab. DANUTA KORADECKA; publs *Bezpieczeństwo Pracy—Nauka i Praktyka* (Occupational Safety—Science and Practice, 12 a year), *International Journal of Occupational Safety and Health (JOSE)* (4 a year, in English), *Podstawy i Metody Oceny Srodowiska Pracy* (Principles and Methods of Assessing the Working Environment, 4 a year).

Główny Instytut Górnictwa (Central Mining Institute): pl. Gwarków 1, 40-166 Katowice; tel. (32) 2581631; e-mail gig@gig.eu; internet gig.eu; f. 1945; research work in rock mechanics, mining systems, blasting techniques, gas, dust, water and rock burst hazards, clean coal technologies utilization and recovery of waste water, material engineering, noise and vibration control, environmental protection; library of 390,000 vols; Gen. Dir Prof. Dr JÓZEF DUBIŃSKI; publs *Prace Naukowe* (Transactions, irregular, about 20 papers a year), *Prace Naukowe—Górnictwo i Srodowisko* (4 a year, print and online, www.kwartalnik.gig.eu).

Instytut Automatyki Systemów Energetycznych (Institute of Power Systems Automation): ul. Wystawowa 1, 51-618 Wrocław; tel. (71) 3484221; e-mail sekretariat@iase.wroc.pl; internet www.iase.wroc.pl; f. 1949; automatic control systems, computer systems and networks, database systems, data communication for electric power system operation, expert systems, exploitation and

management; library of 21,000 vols, 5,400 vols of reports; Chair EDWARD ZIAJA; publs *Biuletyn IASE* (2 a year in 12 a year *Energetyka* journal), *Informator Patentowy Energetyki* (4 a year), *Prace IASE* (1 a year).

Instytut Badań Systemowych PAN (Systems Research Institute of the Polish Academy of Sciences): ul. Newelska 6, 01-447 Warsaw; tel. (22) 3810275; e-mail ibs@ibspan.waw.pl; internet www.ibspan.waw.pl; f. 1977; depts of modelling and optimization of dynamical systems, optimization methods and algorithms, intelligent systems, stochastic methods, decision support in the presence of risk, computer modelling; library of 45,000 vols; Dir Prof. Dr Hab. ZBIGNIEW NAHORSKI; Deputy Dir for Research Prof. Dr Hab. SŁAWOMIR ZADROŻNY; publs *Badania Systemowe* (Systems Studies, irregular, in Polish), *Control and Cybernetics* (4 a year), *Working Papers IBS PAN*.

Instytut Badawczy Dróg i Mostów (Road and Bridge Research Institute): ul. Instytutowa 1, 03-302 Warsaw; tel. (22) 6980606; e-mail ibdim@ibdim.edu.pl; internet ibdim.edu.pl; f. 1955 as Institute of Road Building, present name 1974; research and devt projects in construction and maintenance of road and bridge structures and facilities, spec. roads and road bridges, railway subgrades, railway bridges and underground structures; Gen. Dir Prof. Dr LESZEK RAFALSKI; publs *Informacje, Instrukcje* (irregular), *Prace Instytutu Badawczego Dróg i Mostów* (4 a year), *Roads and Bridges—Drogi i Mosty* (4 a year, in English and Polish), *Studia i Materiały* (irregular).

Instytut Biopolimerów i Włókien Chemicznych (Institute of Biopolymers and Chemical Fibres): ul. Marii Skłodowskiej-Curie 19/27, 90-570 Łódź; tel. (42) 6380300; e-mail ibwch@ibwch.lodz.pl; internet www.ibwch.lodz.pl; f. 1952; chemistry, technology, application of chemical fibres, environmental protection, natural polymers, their modification, applied biotechnology, medical and agricultural applications of polymers and fibres; library of 13,184 vols, 1,025 periodicals; Man. Dir Dr DANUTA CIECHAŃSKA; publ. *Fibres and Textiles in Eastern Europe* (6 a year, in English with Polish abstracts, print and online, www.fibtex.lodz.pl).

Instytut Budownictwa Wodnego PAN (Institute of Hydroengineering of the Polish Academy of Sciences): ul. Kościerska 7, 80-328 Gdańsk; tel. (58) 5222900; e-mail sekr@ibwpan.gda.pl; internet www.ibwpan.gda.pl; f. 1953; river, estuary and reservoir hydraulics, maritime hydraulics, soil mechanics and foundation engineering, environmental engineering; library of 25,000 vols; Dir Prof. Dr Hab. ANDRZEJ SAWICKI; publs *Archives of Hydroengineering and Environmental Mechanics (AHEM)* (4 a year), *Proceedings* (irregular).

Instytut Ceramiki i Materiałów Budowlanych (Institute of Ceramics and Building Materials): ul. Postępu 9, 02-676 Warsaw; tel. (22) 8437421; e-mail info@icimb.pl; internet www.icimb.pl; f. 2007 by merging Institute of Glass and Ceramics (f. 1951), Institute of Refractory Materials in Gliwice (f. 1953) and Institute of Mineral Building Materials in Opole (f. 1954); mineral processing, ceramic material and glass production technology, refractory and building materials, mineral binders and concrete products; three divs: glass and bldg materials div. in Cracow, refractory materials div. in Gliwice, bldg materials engineering div. in Opole; library of 60,000 vols; Dir Dr STANISŁAW TRACZYK; Scientific Sec. and Deputy Dir for Research Prof. Dr Hab. KRZYSZTOF SZAMAŁEK; publs *Cement Wapno Beton* (6 a year), *Prace*

ICiMB (The Scientific Works of the Institute, irregular), *Przegląd Dokumentacyjny Materiałów Ogniotrwałych i Ceramiki Specjalnej* (Review of Refractory and Special Ceramics Publications, 12 a year), *Szkło i Ceramika* (Glass and Ceramics, 6 a year).

Instytut Chemii i Techniki Jądrowej (Institute of Nuclear Chemistry and Technology): ul. Dorodna 16, 03-195 Warsaw; tel. (22) 5041205; e-mail sekdyrn@ichtj.waw.pl; internet www.ichtj.waw.pl; f. 1955; library of 36,000 vols, 775 periodicals; Dir-Gen. Prof. Dr Hab. ANDRZEJ GRZEGORZ CHMIELEWSKI; publs *INCT Reports* (irregular), *Nukleonika* (4 a year), *Postępy Techniki Jadrowej* (4 a year, in Polish).

Instytut Chemii Przemysłowej im. Prof. Ignacego Mościckiego (Industrial Chemistry Research Institute): ul. Rydygiera 8, 01-793 Warsaw; tel. (22) 5682000; e-mail ichp@ichp.pl; internet www.ichp.pl; f. 1922; research into carbo- and petrochemistry, organic synthesis, polymer and plastics technology, industrial catalysis, household chemistry products and disinfectants, environmental impact technology, process safety, chemical process engineering, instrumental analysis, medical diagnostic tests, biotechnology; Bureau for Ozone Layer Protection; Nat. Centre for Ecological Management in the Chemical Industry; library of 49,891 vols, 55,846 periodicals, 1,050 microfilms; spec. collns of 215,646 items; Man. Dir Dr REGINA JEZIÓRSKA; publ. *Polimery* (12 a year, print and online).

Instytut Elektrotechniki (Electrotechnical Institute): ul. Pożaryskiego 28, 04-703 Warsaw; tel. (22) 8122000; e-mail iel@iel.waw.pl; internet www.iel.waw.pl; f. 1946; research and manufacture of electric machines, apparatus and appliances; library of 50,000 vols, 16,000 periodicals; spec. collns of 20,000 items; Gen. Dir Dr Hab. WIESŁAW WILCZYŃSKI; publ. *Prace Instytutu Elektrotechniki* (Proceedings of the Electrotechnical Institute).

Instytut Energetyki (Institute of Power Engineering): ul. Mory 8, 01-330 Warsaw; tel. (22) 3451200; e-mail instytut.energetyki@ien.com.pl; internet www.ien.com.pl; f. 1953; divs of thermal, electric, mechanical; unit of Energy Research Integration Centre; 5 brs; library of 53,000 vols; Dir Prof. Dr JACEK WAŃKOWICZ; publs *Biuletyn Instytutu Energetyki* (6 a year), *Prace Instytutu Energetyki* (irregular).

Instytut Informatyki Teoretycznej i Stosowanej PAN (Institute of Theoretical and Applied Informatics of the Polish Academy of Sciences): ul. Bałtycka 5, 44-100 Gliwice; tel. (32) 2317319; e-mail office@iitis.gliwice.pl; internet www.iitis.gliwice.pl; f. 1969; research areas: performance evaluation of computer networks, computer vision, quantum informatics, multimedia systems; library of 6,000 vols; Dir Prof. Dr Hab. TADEUSZ CZACHÓRSKI; Deputy Dir for Research Prof. Dr Hab. JERZY KLAMKA; publ. *TAAI—Theoretical and Applied Informatics* (4 a year, print and online, taai.iitis.gliwice.pl).

Instytut Inżynierii Chemicznej PAN (Institute of Chemical Engineering of the Polish Academy of Sciences): ul. Bałtycka 5, 44-100 Gliwice; tel. (32) 2346915; e-mail secret@iich.gliwice.pl; internet www.iich.gliwice.pl; f. 1958; research on adsorption and membrane separation, catalysis and chemical kinetics, diffusional processes and conversion of solar energy, intensification of heat and mass transfer, multiphase reactors and biotechnological processes, nanoporous materials, simultaneous heat and mass transfer in condensation and evaporation;

library of 6,677 vols; Dir Prof. Dr Hab. KRZYSZTOF WARMUZIŃSKI; Deputy Dir for Scientific Affairs Prof. Dr Hab. GRAŻYNA BARTELMUS; publs *Chemical and Process Engineering-Inżynieria Chemiczna i Procesowa* (4 a year), *Prace Naukowe Instytutu Inżynierii Chemicznej PAN*.

Instytut Łączności Państwowy Instytut Badawczy (National Institute of Telecommunications): ul. Szachowa 1, 04-894 Warsaw; tel. (22) 5128100; e-mail info@itl.waw.pl; internet www.itl.waw.pl; f. 1951; telecommunications, data transmission, satellite telecommunications, optical transmission, information technology, radiocommunications, EMC; library of 56,405 vols; Dir WOJCIECH HALKA; Deputy Dir for Research Prof. Dr Hab. WOJCIECH BURAKOWSKI; publs *Journal of Telecommunications and Information Technology* (4 a year, print and online), *Telekomunikacja i Techniki Informacyjne* (4 a year, print and online).

Instytut Lotnictwa (Institute of Aviation): al. Krakowska 110/114, 02-256 Warsaw; tel. (22) 8460011; e-mail ilot@ilot.edu.pl; internet www.ilot.edu.pl; f. 1926; library of 80,000 vols, 18,000 journals, 5,500 microfilms; Dir Dr WITOLD WIŚNIOWSKI; Scientific Dir Dr CEZARY GALIŃSKI; publs *Biblioteka Historyczna* (1 a year), *Biblioteka Naukowa* (Scientific Library, 2 a year), *Prace Instytutu Lotnictwa* (Transactions of the Institute of Aviation, 6 a year), *Przegląd Dokumentacyjny* (12 a year), *Tematy Prac Wykonawczych w Instytucie Lotnictwa* (1 a year).

Instytut Maszyn Matematycznych (Institute of Mathematical Machines): ul. Ludwika Krzywickiego 34, 02-078 Warsaw; tel. (22) 6217817; e-mail sekretariat@imm.org.pl; internet www.imm.org.pl; f. 1957; computer science and technology, training and education; develops systems of work-time registration and access control, identification systems (biometric and proximity readers), modelling and simulation; library of 28,000 vols; Dir Dr MAREK HOŁYŃSKI; publs *Elektronika* (1 a year, online), *Prace Naukowo-Badawcze IMM* (Proceedings of IMM, irregular, print and online), *Techniki Komputerowe—Biuletyn Informacyjny* (Computer Technologies—IMM Bulletin, irregular, print and online).

Instytut Maszyn Przepływowych im. Roberta Szewalskiego PAN (Szewalaski Institute of Fluid-Flow Machinery of the Polish Academy of Sciences): ul. Fiszera 14, 80-231 Gdańsk; tel. (58) 3411271; e-mail imp@imp.gda.pl; internet www.imp.gda.pl; f. 1956; fundamental research, design methods, construction and devt of machines and equipment for energy conversion in flow, measuring techniques and instrumentation in connection with fluid-flow machines, solid-state mechanics, machinery diagnostics, plasma physics; library of 23,000 vols; Dir Prof. Dr Hab. JAROSŁAW MIKIELEWICZ; Deputy Dir for Scientific Issues Prof. Dr Hab. JAN KICIŃSKI; publs *Archives of Thermodynamics* (4 a year), *Archiwum Energetyki* (Archives of Energetics, 2 a year), *Transactions of the Institute of Fluid-Flow Machinery* (2 a year), *Zeszyty Naukowe* (Bulletin of the Institute of Fluid-Flow Machinery, irregular).

Instytut Mechanizacji Budownictwa i Górnictwa Skalnego (Institute for Mechanized Construction and Rock Mining): ul. Racjonalizacji 6/8, 02-673 Warsaw; tel. (22) 8430201; e-mail imb@imbigs.pl; internet www.imbigs.org.pl; f. 1951; mechanized construction, industry of construction material machinery; rock mining machinery; waste management and recycling; normalization, using systems and techniques of machines and equipment; quality systems and product

certification; protection of man and environment in construction; training of building machinery operators; library of 6,997 vols, 49 periodicals; Dir Prof. Dr Hab. STEFAN GORALCZYK; publs *Działalność Instytutu Mechanizacji Budownictwa* (1 a year), *Przegląd Mechaniczny*, *Wiadomości IMB* (4 a year).

Instytut Metali Nieżelaznych Gliwice (Institute of Non-Ferrous Metals in Gliwice): ul. Sowińskiego 5, 44-100 Gliwice; tel. (32) 2380200; e-mail imn@imn.gliwice.pl; internet www.imn.gliwice.pl; f. 1952; research depts of analytical chemistry, environmental protection, hydrometallurgy, material science and powder metallurgy, metallurgy, minerals treatment and waste utilization, processing of metals and alloys; library of 35,000 vols, 270 current periodicals, 15,000 reports; Man. Dir Prof. Dr ZBIGNIEW ŚMIESZEK; Sec. ALICJA FOLEK; publ. *Biuletyn Instytutu Metali Nieżelaznych* (12 a year).

Instytut Metalurgii i Inżynierii Materiałowej im. Aleksandra Krupkowskiego PAN (Institute of Metallurgy and Materials Science of the Polish Academy of Sciences): ul. W. Reymonta 25, 30-059 Cracow; tel. (12) 2952800; e-mail office@imim.pl; internet www.imim.pl; f. 1952; depts of anisotropic structures, chemical physics of materials, functional and structural materials, metallurgical processes, multilayer materials, plastic deformation of metals, surface engineering and biomaterials; library of 16,328 vols, 9,317 journals; Dir Prof. Dr Hab. PAWEŁ ZIĘBA; Research Dir Prof. Dr Hab. WŁADYSŁAW GĄSIOR; publ. *Archives of Metallurgy and Materials* (4 a year, print and online, www.i-mim.pl/archives).

Instytut Metalurgii Żelaza im. Stanisława Staszica w Gilwicach (Stanisław Staszic Institute of Ferrous Metallurgy): ul. K. Miarki 12–14, 44-100 Gliwice; tel. (32) 2345205; e-mail imz@imz.pl; internet www.imz.pl; f. 1945; provides scientific research, consulting and training services for steel producers, steel users and public instns involved in the steel business; library of 34,800 vols, 21,850 periodicals; Dir Dr ADAM SCHWEDLER; Deputy Dir for Scientific Affairs Prof. Dr Hab. JÓZEF PADUCH; publ. *Prace Instytutu Metalurgii Żelaza* (Transactions of the Institute of Ferrous Metallurgy, 4 a year, print and online, www.imz.pl/periodical.html).

Instytut Morski w Gdańsku (Maritime Institute in Gdańsk): ul. Długi Targ 41/42, 80-830 Gdańsk; tel. (58) 3011641; e-mail im@im.gda.pl; internet www.im.gda.pl; f. 1950; economic and technical research in shipping, harbour and coastal engineering, corrosion, maritime law; library of 80,000 vols; Dir Dr KAZIMIERZ SZEFLER; Scientific Sec Mgr MAŁGORZATA SŁOMIANKO-WASILEWSKA; publs *Informacja Ekspresowa*, *Materiały Instytutu Morskiego*, *Prace Instytutu Morskiego*, *Przegląd Informacji*, *Zeszyty Problemowe Gospodarki Morskiej*.

Instytut Nafty i Gazu (Oil and Gas Institute): ul. Lubicz 25A, 31-503 Cracow; tel. (12) 4210033; e-mail office@inig.pl; internet www.inig.pl; f. 1945, present name 2004; divs of hydrocarbon deposits devt, gas engineering, petroleum processing, prospecting of hydrocarbon deposits; library of 102,300 vols, 10,000 periodicals; Man. Dir Prof. Dr Hab. MARIA CIECHANOWSKA; publs *INiG Bulletin* (4 a year), *Nafta-Gaz* (Oil and Gas, 12 a year), *Prace Naukowe INiG* (INiG Works), *Przegląd Bibliograficzno-Faktograficzny 'Nafta-Gaz'* (4 a year), *Rynek Polskiej Nafty i Gazu* (Market of Polish Oil and Gas, 1 a year).

Instytut Nawozów Sztucznych (Fertilizer Research Institute): al. Tysiąclecia Państwa

Polskiego 13A, 24-110 Puławy; tel. (81) 4731400; e-mail sekretariat@ins.pulawy.pl; internet www.ins.pulawy.pl; f. 1935, present name 1958; depts of fertilizers, catalysts, nitrogen technologies, organic technologies, research support, supercritical extraction; attached div. of inorganic chemistry in Gliwice; Dir Prof. Dr CEZARY MOŻEŃSKI.

Instytut Obróbki Plastycznej (Metal Forming Institute): ul. Jana Pawła 14, 61-139 Poznań; tel. (61) 6570555; e-mail inop@inop.poznan.pl; internet www.inop.poznan.pl; f. 1948; research and devt works on non-metallurgical metal forming; library of 11,000 vols, 150 current journals; spec. colln of 8,000 items; Dir Dr HANNA WISNIEWSKA-WEINERT; Deputy Dir for Research Dr JACEK BOROWSKI; publs *Informacja Ekspresowa Obróbki Plastycznej* (12 a year, print and online), *Obróbka Plastyczna Metali* (4 a year, print and online).

Instytut Odlewnictwa (Foundry Research Institute): ul. Zakopiańska 73, 30-418 Cracow; tel. (12) 2618324; e-mail iod@iod.krakow.pl; internet www.iod.krakow.pl; f. 1946; research into foundry materials, technological processes, alloys and additives; library of 10,000 vols, 45 periodicals; Gen. Dir Prof. Dr JERZY JÓZEF SOBCZAK; Deputy Dir for Research and Technology Dr JÓZEF TURZYŃSKI; publs *Odlewnictwo Współczesne—Polska Świat* (Modern Foundry—Poland and the World, 6 a year), *Prace Instytut Odlewnictwa* (Transactions of the Foundry Research Institute, 4 a year, print and online, www.prace.iod.krakow.pl).

Instytut Podstaw Informatyki PAN (Institute of Computer Science of the Polish Academy of Sciences): ul. Jana Kazimierza 5, 01-248 Warsaw; tel. (22) 3800500; e-mail ipi@ipipan.waw.pl; internet www.ipipan.waw.pl; f. 1976; depts of theoretical foundations of computer science and artificial intelligence; library of 16,400 vols, 250 periodicals; Dir Prof. Dr Hab. JACEK KORONACKI; Deputy Dir for Scientific Affairs Dr Hab. BEATA KONIKOWSKA; publs *Journal of Language Modelling* (2 a year, print and online, nlp.ipipan.waw.pl/ojs/index.php/JLM/), *Prace IPI PAN* (ICS PAS Reports, irregular).

Instytut Podstawowych Problemów Techniki PAN (Institute of Fundamental Technological Research of the Polish Academy of Sciences): ul. Pawińskiego 5B, 02-106 Warsaw; tel. (22) 8261281; e-mail director@ippt.gov.pl; internet www.ippt.gov.pl; f. 1953; depts of computational science, intelligent technologies, mechanics and physics of fluids, mechanics of materials, strength of materials, theory of continuous media, ultrasound; library of 82,400 vols, 200 periodicals; Dir Prof. Dr Hab. ANDRZEJ NOWICKI; Deputy Dir for Research Prof. Dr Hab. TOMASZ A. KOWALEWSKI; publs *Archives of Acoustics* (4 a year, in English, print and online, acoustics.ippt.gov.pl), *Archives of Mechanics* (6 a year, print and online, am.ippt.gov.pl), *CAMES–Computer Assisted Mechanics and Engineering Sciences* (4 a year, print and online, cames.ippt.gov.pl), *Prace IPPT* (IFTR Reports on Fundamental Technological Research, print and online, prace.ippt .gov.pl), *Rozprawy Inżynierskie* (Engineering Transactions, 4 a year, print and online, et.ippt.gov.pl).

Instytut Przemysłu Organicznego (Institute of Industrial Organic Chemistry): ul. Annopol 6, 03-236 Warsaw; tel. (22) 8111231; e-mail ipo@ipo.waw.pl; internet www.ipo .waw.pl; f. 1947; research on plant pesticides and biocides, auxiliary chemical products, organic intermediate products, blasting materials, chemical safety, toxicology and ecotoxicology; library of 30,000 vols; spec.

colln of 24,000 items; Gen. Dir Mgr URSZULA WYRZYKOWSKA; Scientific Sec. Dr Hab. LESZEK KONOPSKI; publs *Central European Journal of Energetic Materials* (4 a year, print and online, www.wydawnictwa.ipo.waw.pl/CEJEM.html), *Materiały Wysokoenergetyczne* (High-Energetic Materials, 1 a year, print and online, www.wydawnictwa.ipo .waw.pl/materiały-wysokoenergetycz-ne.html), *Pestycydy* (Pesticides, 4 a year, print and online, www.wydawnictwa.ipo .waw.pl/pestycydy.html).

Instytut Spawalnictwa (Institute of Welding): ul. Bł. Czesława 16–18, 44-100 Gliwice; tel. (32) 2310011; e-mail is@is.gliwice.pl; internet www.is.gliwice.pl; f. 1945; fundamental and developmental research, acceptance tests, certification, consulting, training, safety of welders, standardization, manufacture; library of 12,000 vols, 36 periodicals; Dir Prof. Dr Hab. JAN PILARCZYK; publ. *Biuletyn Instytutu Spawalnictwa* (6 a year, print and online, www.bis.is.gliwice.pl).

Instytut Technologii Elektronowej (Institute of Electron Technology): al. Lotni-ków 32/46, 02-668 Warsaw; tel. (22) 5487700; e-mail cambroz@ite.waw.pl; internet www .ite.waw.pl; f. 1966; research and devt in physics and technology of low dimensional semiconductor structures for photonics, silicon semiconductor nanostructures and microsystems, sensors; designing of integrated schemes and systems; hybrid microelectronics; characterization of nanostructures; library of 11,000 vols, 9,000 periodicals; spec. colln of 1,800 items; Dir Mgr ZBIGNIEW POZNAŃSKI; Vice-Dir for Research and Devt Prof. Dr Hab. JERZY KĄTCKI; publ. *Biblioteka Elektroniki* (irregular).

Instytut Technologii Materiałów Elektronicznych (Institute of Electronic Materials Technology): ul. Wólczyńska 133, 01-919 Warsaw; tel. (22) 8349003; e-mail itme@itme .edu.pl; internet www.itme.edu.pl; f. 1979; research and devt in electronics, microsystems, optoelectronics, micromechanics, metrology; library of 10,100 vols, 230 periodicals, 44 theses and dissertations; Gen. Man. Dr ZYGMUNT ŁUCZYŃSKI; Scientific Man. Prof. Dr ANDRZEJ JELEŃSKI; publs *Materiały Elektroniczne* (4 a year, print and online), *MST News–Poland* (4 a year), *Prace ITME*.

Instytut Transportu Samochodowego (Motor Transport Institute): ul. Jagiellońska 80, 03-301 Warsaw; tel. (22) 4385400; e-mail info@its.waw.pl; internet www.its.waw.pl; f. 1952; focuses on operation of motor transport in the market economy, road traffic organization, environmental protection; library of 22,000 vols, 50 periodicals; Dir-Gen. Dr ANDRZEJ WOJCIECHOWSKI; publs *Bezpieczeństwo Ruchu Drogowego* (4 a year), *Transport Samochodowy* (Motor Transport, 4 a year, print and online, www.its.waw.pl/transportsamochodowy).

Instytut Włókiennictwa (Textile Research Institute): ul. Brzezińska 5/15, 92-103 Łódź; tel. (42) 6163100; e-mail info@iw.lodz.pl; internet www.iw.lodz.pl; f. 1945; textile raw materials, technology of yarn manufacturing, non-woven fabrics, textile chemical processing, colour determination and formulation; library of 17,559 vols; spec. colln of 12,879 items; Dir Prof. Dr JADWIGA SÓJKA-LEDAKO-WICZ; publ. *Prace Instytutu Włókiennictwa* (1 a year).

Narodowe Centrum Badań Jądrowych Swierk (National Centre for Nuclear Research Swierk): ul. Andrzeja Sołtana 7, 05-400 Otwock-Swierk; tel. (22) 7180001; e-mail ncbj@ncbj.gov.pl; internet www.ncbj .gov.pl; f. 2011 by merger of Institute of Atomic Energy and Institute for Nuclear

Studies (both f. in 1983); electronics and detectors, accelerator physics, plasma physics and technology, nuclear physics, dosimetry in radiation protection, reactor technology, radiation medical physics; library of 44,420 vols, 2,183 periodicals; Dir-Gen. Prof. Dr Hab. GRZEGORZ WROCHNA; Deputy Dir for Scientific Matters Prof. Dr Hab. EWA RONDIO.

Przemysłowy Instytut Maszyn Rolniczych (Industrial Institute of Agricultural Engineering): ul. Starołęcka 31, 60-963 Poznań; tel. (61) 8712200; e-mail office@pimr .poznan.pl; internet www.pimr.poznan.pl; f. 1946; design and testing of agricultural machines and equipment; library of 11,000 vols; Man. Dir Dr TADEUSZ PAWŁOWSKI; Deputy Dir for Research Dr Hab. JAN SZCZEPANIAK; publs *Ciągniki i Maszyny Rolnicze* (every 2 years), *Journal of Research and Applications in Agricultural Engineering* (4 a year, print and online), *Technika Rolnicza Ogrodnicza Lesna* (Agricultural, Horticultural and Forest Engineering, 6 a year, print and online).

Przemysłowy Instytut Motoryzacji (Automotive Industry Institute): ul. Jagiellońska 55, 03-301 Warsaw; tel. (22) 7777000; e-mail instytut@pimot.org.pl; internet www .pimot.org.pl; f. 1972; attached to Min. of Economy; scientific research and devt work in the field of automotive industry; basic research in natural sciences, engineering and biotechnology; braking systems laboratory in Łódź; library of 12,000 vols, 110 titles of periodicals; Dir Dr ANDRZEJ MUSZYŃSKI; publ. *Archiwum Motoryzacji* (Archives of Automotive Engineering, 4 a year, print and online, archiwummotoryzacji.pl).

Libraries and Archives

Białystok

Biblioteka Politechniki Białostockiej (Library of Białystok University of Technology): ul. Zwierzyniecka 16, 15-333 Białystok; tel. (85) 7469330; e-mail biblioteka@pb.edu .pl; internet biblioteka.pb.edu.pl; f. 1951; 254,768 vols, 523 periodicals; spec. collns: 77,925 items; Man. Dir Mgr JOANNA PUTKO; publs *Acta Mechanica et Automatica* (4 a year), *Advances in Computer Science Research* (irregular), *Architecturae et Artibus* (4 a year), *Budownictwo i Inżynieria Środowiska* (4 a year), *Ekonomia i Zarządzanie* (4 a year).

Bydgoszcz

Wojewódzka i Miejska Biblioteka Publiczna im. Dr Witolda Bełzy w Bydgoszczy (Bydgoszcz Dr W. Bełza Voivodship and Public Municipal Library): ul. Długa 39, 85-034 Bydgoszcz; tel. (52) 3287390; e-mail sekretariat@wimbp .bydgoszcz.pl; internet www.wimbp .bydgoszcz.pl; f. 1903; 1,133,919 vols, incl. old books, maps and atlases, MSS, CDs; Dir Mgr EWA STELMACHOWSKA; publ. *Bibliotekarz Kujawsko-Pomorski* (2 a year).

Cracow

Archiwum Nauki PAN i PAU w Krakowie (Archive of Science of the Polish Academy of Sciences and the Polish Academy of Arts and Sciences in Cracow): ul. Jana 26, 31-018 Cracow; tel. (12) 4232328; e-mail archiwum@archiwum-nauki.krakow.pl; internet www.archiwum-nauki.krakow.pl; f. 2002; collects archival material of Polish Acad. of Sciences and Polish Acad. of Arts and Sciences; private papers, photographs, photo albums of acads and scientists; Dir Dr RITA MAJKOWSKA.

Biblioteka Główna Uniwersytet Pedagogicznej im. KEN w Krakowie (Main Library of Pedagogical University of Cracow): ul. Podchorążych 2, 30-084 Cracow; tel. (12) 6626375; e-mail info@tessa.up.krakow.pl; internet libproxy.up.krakow.pl; f. 1946; 654,504 vols, 48,526 periodicals, 1,857 sound recordings; also audiovisual materials, CD-ROMs and microforms; Dir Dr STANISŁAW SKÓRKA.

Biblioteka Jagiellońska (Jagiellonian Library): al. Mickiewicza 22, 30-059 Cracow; tel. (12) 6330903; e-mail ujbj@uj.edu.pl; internet www.bj.uj.edu.pl; f. 1364; colln: nat. library for books before 1800, central library of general scientific, Polish affairs, humanities, Polish writing of the 15th–18th centuries; 44 univ. institute libraries; 5,279,566 vols, 2,483,206 books, 958,333 periodicals, 53,798 online journals, 106,752 old prints (3,666 incunabula), 33,208 MSS, 44,332 music prints, 59,301 drawings and items of graphic art, 57,301 maps and atlases, flysheets and microforms; 1,838,027 units; Dir Prof. Dr ZDZISŁAW PIETRZYK; publ. *Bibliotheca Iagellonica, Fontes et Studia* (irregular).

Biblioteka Naukowa PAU i PAN w Krakowie (Scientific Library of Polish Academy of Arts and Sciences and Polish Academy of Sciences in Cracow): ul. Sławkowska 17, 31-016 Cracow; tel. (12) 4310021; e-mail biblioteka@pau.krakow.pl; internet biblioteka.pau.krakow.pl; f. 1856; periodicals relating to the social and biological sciences; 718,431 vols, 345,637 vols of periodicals, 168,429 MSS, old prints, cartography, graphic arts; Dir Dr KAROLINA GRODZISKA; publ. *Rocznik Biblioteki Naukowej PAU i PAN w Krakowie* (Yearbook).

Wojewódzka Biblioteka Publiczna w Krakowie (Cracow Voivode Public Library): ul. Rajska 1, 31-124 Cracow; tel. (12) 3752200; e-mail biblioteka@wbp.krakow.pl; internet www.rajska.info; f. 1945; 771 regional brs; 550,000 vols; Dir Mgr JERZY WOŹNIAKIEWICZ; publ. *Notes Biblioteczny* (2 a year).

Częstochowa

Biblioteka Główna Politechniki Częstochowskiej (Main Library of Częstochowa University of Technology): al. Armii Krajowej 36, 42-200 Częstochowa; tel. (34) 3614473; e-mail biblioteka@adm.pcz.czest.pl; internet www.bg.pcz.pl; f. 1950; 507,191 vols, incl. 162,562 books, 77,614 journals; 267,015 spec. collns (standards, patents, microforms, edocuments, dissertations); Dir Dr DAGMARA BUBEL.

Gdańsk

Biblioteka Główna Politechniki Gdańskiej (Main Library of Gdańsk University of Technology): ul. G. Narutowicza 11/12, 80-952 Gdańsk; tel. (58) 3472758; e-mail library@pg.gda.pl; internet www.bg.pg.gda .pl; 1,200,000 vols incl. books, printed series of course lectures and academic handbooks, scientific and technical journals, standards, patents, technical business literature and database; Dir HAKUĆ BOŻENA; publs *Bibliografia Publikacji Pracowników Naukowych Politechniki Gdańskiej* (Bibliography of Publications of Scientific Workers of the Technical University of Gdańsk, irregular), *Newsletter Biblioteki Głównej PG* (4 a year, print and online), *Raport Politechniki Gdańskiej* (Report of the Technical University of Gdansk, 1 a year), *Wykaz Nabytków* (List of Acquisitions, 12 a year).

Biblioteka Uniwersytetu Gdańskiego (Library of the University of Gdańsk): ul. Wita Stwosza 53, 80-308 Gdańsk; tel. (58) 5233210; e-mail bib@bg.ug.edu.pl; internet www.bg.ug.edu.pl; f. 1970; 938,725 vols, 301,424 periodicals; spec. collns: 160,807 units; Dir GRAŻYNA JAŚKOWIAK.

Polska Akademia Nauk Biblioteka Gdańska (Polish Academy of Sciences Gdańsk Library): ul. Wałowa 15, 80-858 Gdańsk; tel. (58) 3015523; e-mail bgpan@bgpan.gda.pl; internet www.bgpan.gda.pl; f. 1596; research and public library; colln: humanities, social sciences, maritime, Pomeranian and Gdańsk affairs; 579,657 vols, incl. 60,446 old books, 664 incunabula, 96,631 periodicals, 9,779 MSS, 10,765 maps, 8,119 graphics; Dir Dr ZOFIA TYLEWSKA-OSTROWSKA; publ. *Libri Gedanenses* (1 a year).

Gliwice

Biblioteka Główna Politechniki Śląskiej w Gliwicach (Central Library of Silesian University of Technology): ul. Kaszubska 23, 44-100 Gliwice; tel. (32) 2371551; e-mail bg .sekr@polsl.pl; internet www.bg.polsl.pl; f. 1945; collns incl. technical and technology sciences, mathematics, physics, chemistry, materials technology, metallurgy, chemistry, building, architecture, mineral and mining, geology, traffic, sanitary, environmental, civil, power, electrical and electronics, informatics, telecommunications and mechanical engineering, bioengineering; 796,482 vols in main library and 201,198 vols in departmental libraries, 92,223 journals and periodicals, 198,704 spec. collns; Dir Dr KRZYSZTOF ZIOLO; publ. *Biuletyn Głównej Politechniki Śląskiej* (Bulletin of the Silesian University of Technology, 12 a year, print and online, biuletyn.polsl.pl).

Katowice

Biblioteka Główna Śląskiego Uniwersytetu Medycznego w Katowicach (Main Library of the Medical University of Silesia): ul. Warszawska 14, 40-006 Katowice; tel. (32) 2083537; internet www.sum.edu.pl; f. 1948; 183,848 vols; Head of Library Mgr EWA NOWAK; Librarian JUSTYNA SEIFFERT.

Biblioteka Śląska (Silesian Library): Pl. Rady Europy 1, 40-021 Katowice; tel. (32) 2083740; e-mail info@bs.katowice.pl; internet www.bs.katowice.pl; f. 1922; colln: arts, social science, economics, literature relating to Silesia; 1,760,161 books (incl. 28,716 old vols), 269,079 vols of periodicals, 27,950 MSS, 22,868 maps and atlases, 11,348 drawings and prints, 47,168 postcards, 29,211 photographs, 320,555 documents of social life; Dir Prof. JAN MALICKI; publs *Bibliografia Bieżąca Województwa Śląskiego* (4 a year, print and online), *Książnica Śląska* (irregular).

Kielce

Biblioteka Główna Politechniki Świętokrzyskiej (Central Library of Świętokrzyska Technical University): al. Tysiąclecia Państwa Polskiego 7, 25-314 Kielce; tel. (41) 3424483; e-mail library@tu .kielce.pl; internet lib.tu.kielce.pl; f. 1966; 115,425 books, 34,468 vols of periodicals, 50,881 standards; Dir DANUTA KAPINOS.

Łódź

Biblioteka Uniwersytetu Łódzkiego (Library of Łódź University): ul. Jana Matejki 32/38, 90-237 Łódź; tel. (42) 6356002; e-mail sekretariat@lib.uni.lodz.pl; internet www.lib.uni.lodz.pl; f. 1945; 1,387,564 vols, 527,325 vols of periodicals, 4,062 MSS, 25,417 maps and atlases, 44,103 vols of music, 23,888 music records, 54,548 iconographic items, 28,705 old prints, 99,111 public relations documents, 3,800 microfilms, 32,729 microfiches, 6,386 CDs; Dir Mgr TOMASZ PIESTRZYŃSKI.

Wojewódzka i Miejska Biblioteka Publiczna im. Marszałka Józefa Piłsudskiego w Łodzi (Jozef Pilsudski Regional and Municipal Public Library in Lodz): ul. Gdańska 100/102, 90-508 Łódź; tel. (42) 6630300; e-mail sekretariat@hiacynt2 .wimbp.lodz.pl; internet www.wimbp.lodz.pl; f. 1917; spec. subjects: social sciences and humanities; 755,000 vols, 545,000 periodicals, 129,000 vols in special collns; Dir-Gen. Mgr BARBARA CZAJKA; publs *Biuletyn Informacji Bibliotecznych i Kulturalnych (BIBiK)* (irregular), *Sprawozdanie z działalności WiMBP* (1 a year).

Lublin

Biblioteka Główna Uniwersytetu Marii Curie Skłodowskiej (Main Library of Maria Curie-Skłodowska University): ul. Idziego Radziszewskiego 11, 20-031 Lublin; tel. (81) 537-58-35; e-mail bgumcs@umcs .lublin.pl; internet bg.umcs.lublin.pl; f. 1944; 20 faculty libraries; 2,445,947 vols, incl. 343,399 periodicals, 19,252 old prints, 826 MSS, 41,533 maps and atlases, 24,131 icons, 10,564 posters, 178,012 patents, 19,853 music scores, 10,596 social life documents, 7,395 microforms, 3,384 dissertations; Dir Dr BOGUSŁAW KASPEREK.

Wojewódzka Publiczna im. Hieronima Łopacińskiego w Lublinie (Hieronim Łopacinski Voivodship Public Library): ul. Narutowicza 4, 20-950 Lublin; tel. (81) 5287400; e-mail info@hieronim.wbp.lublin .pl; internet www.wbp.lublin.pl; f. 1907; regional, humanistic, scientific and educational colln; 480,240 vols, 11,898 old vols, 43,620 periodicals, 2,897 MSS, 4,245 maps and atlases, 97,944 ephemera, 40,501 drawings and illustrations, 3,861 microfilms; Dir Mgr ZOFIA CIURUŚ; publs *Bibliotekarz Lubelski* (1 a year), *Dostrzegacz Biblioteczny* (4 a year).

Poznań

Biblioteka Kórnicka PAN (Kórnik Library of the Polish Academy of Sciences): Zamkowa 5, 62-035 Kórnik; tel. (61) 8170081; e-mail bkpan@bkpan.poznan.pl; internet www .bkpan.poznan.pl; f. 1828, present status 1953; collns on history, history of Polish literature, history of art, history of culture; attached literary museum; 350,000 vols, 15,000 MSS, 30,000 old prints, periodicals, newspapers; Dir Prof. Dr Hab. TOMASZ JASIŃSKI; publ. *Pamiętnik Biblioteki Kórnickiej*.

Biblioteka Raczyńskich (Raczyńsky Library): pl. Wolności 19, 61-739 Poznań; tel. (61) 8529442; e-mail sekret@bracz.edu.pl; internet www.bracz.edu.pl; f. 1829; scientific and educational colln; 1,592,654 vols, 17,854 old books, 44,851 periodicals, 10,038 MSS, 11,596 maps and atlases, 37,083 ex-libris, 21,374 photos, 1,514 drawings and illustrations, 164 microfilms, 84,517 audiovisual items; Dir WOJCIECH SPALENIAK.

Biblioteka Uniwersytecka w Poznaniu Uniwersytet im. Adama Mickiewicza (Library of Adam Mickiewicz University): ul. Ratajczaka 38/40, 61-816 Poznań; tel. (61) 8293817; e-mail library@amu.edu.pl; internet lib.amu.edu.pl; f. 1919; supports academic programmes of the Univ. and its curriculum in natural sciences, humanities, mathematics, chemistry, physics, social science, law and languages; supports research activity of the academic community; acquisition, organization and dissemination of information; provides training in computer literacy and web-based searches; 2,731,000 vols in central library, incl. 100,240 ancient vols, 5,600 MSS, 30,000 maps and atlases, 2,059,000 vols in deptl libraries; Dir Dr Hab. ARTUR JAZDON; publ. *Biblioteka* (1 a year).

Rzeszów

Biblioteka Główna Politechniki Rzesz-owskiej im. Ignacego Łukasiewicza (Central Library of Ignacy Łukasiewicz Rzeszow University of Technology): al. Powstańców Warszawy 12, 35-959 Rzeszów; tel. (17) 8651264; e-mail bgprz@prz.edu.pl; internet biblio.prz.edu.pl; f. 1951; colln covers following subjects: architecture, aviation, chemistry, computer science, construction, electrical engineering, electronics, environmental engineering, environmental protection, logistics, management, mathematics, mechanics, mechatronics, physics; 161,000 vols, 37,000 periodicals; spec. colln of 155,000 items; Dir Dr MONIKA ZUB.

Szczecin

Biblioteka Główna Uniwersytetu Szczecińskiego (Main Library of the University of Szczecin): ul. Mickiewicza 16, 70-384 Szczecin; tel. (91) 4442361; e-mail info@bg.szczecin.pl; internet bg.szczecin.pl; f. 1985; 1.3m. vols; Dir Prof. Dr Hab. RADOSŁAW GAZIŃSKI; publs *Bibliografia Publikacji Pracowników Uniwersytetu Szczecińskiego*, *Wykaz Ważniejszych Nabytków* (irregular).

Książnica Pomorska im. Stanisława Staszica w Szczecinie (Pomeranian Library in Szczecin): ul. Podgórna 15/16, 70-205 Szczecin; tel. (91) 4819110; e-mail ksiaznica@ksiaznica.szczecin.pl; internet www.ksiaznica.szczecin.pl; f. 1905; 848,087 vols, 157,930 vols of periodicals, 3,243 MSS, 30,410 early books, 250,010 govt documents, 38,287 standards, 9,036 maps and atlases, 19,032 records, 4,755 audio cassettes, 2,407 CDs, 3,986 microforms; Dir LUCJAN BĄBO-LEWSKI; publs *Bibliografia Pomorza Zachodniego. Piśmiennictwo polskie i Piśmiennictwo Zagraniczne* (Bibliography of Western Pomerania. Polish Literature and Foreign Literature), *Bibliotekarz Zachodniopomorski* (The West Pomeranian Librarian, 4 a year).

Toruń

Wojewódzka Biblioteka Publiczna–Książnica Kopernikańska w Toruniu (Copernicus Library of Toruń): ul. Słowackiego 8, 87-100 Toruń; tel. (56) 6226642; e-mail ksiaznica@ksiaznica.torun.pl; f. 1923; int. exchange of information, bibliographical enquiries, archival research, research on cultural and political history of Pomerania; 769,419 vols of books, incl. 26,300 old books, 92,926 vols of periodicals, 700 MSS, 3,807 cartographic units; Dir Mgr TERESA E. SZYMOROWSKA; publs *Folia Toruniensia* (irregular), *Regional Bibliography of Kujawy-Pomerania* (on CD-ROM, 1 a year).

Warsaw

Archiwum Akt Nowych (Central Archive of Modern Records in Warsaw): ul. Hankiewicza 1, 02-103 Warsaw; tel. (22) 5893118; e-mail sekretariat@aan.gov.pl; internet www.aan.gov.pl; f. 1919; 25,000 m of records in 2,400 archival collns of records of central and state instns; social, political records from the period of Polish independence; Dir Dr TADEUSZ KRAWCZAK.

Archiwum Główne Akt Dawnych w Warszawie (Central Archives of Historical Records in Warsaw): ul. Długa 7, 00-263 Warsaw; tel. (22) 8315491; e-mail sekretariat@agad.gov.pl; internet www.agad.archiwa.gov.pl; f. 1808; archives from 13th century to 1918; 22,946 vols, 412,704 records; Dir Dr HUBERT WAJS.

Archiwum Polskiej Akademii Nauk (Archives of the Polish Academy of Sciences): ul. Nowy Świat 72, 00-330 Warsaw; tel. (22) 8268130; e-mail apan2@apan.waw.pl; internet www.petea.home.pl/apan; f. 1953; spec. collns of medals, photographs, private

papers, microfilms; brs in Cracow, Poznań, Katowice; 26,000 vols; Dir Dr HANNA KRAJEWSKA; publ. *Biuletyn Archiwum PAN* (1 a year).

Biblioteka Narodowa (National Library of Poland): al. Niepodległości 213, 02-086 Warsaw; tel. (22) 6082999; e-mail kontakt@bn.org.pl; internet www.bn.org.pl; f. 1928; state central library; colln of writings in Polish and relating to Poland; basic foreign publications in social sciences and humanities; library science literature; houses the Bibliographic Institute and the Book and Reader's Institute; 8.7m. vols, incl. 2,565,098 books, 895,804 periodicals, 2,257,565 items of ephemera, 218,973 vols on librarianship and information science, 27,198 MSS, 161,548 old prints, 120,239 printed music, 485,770 fine prints and drawings, 121,234 maps and atlases, 126,092 recorded sound and audiovisual documents, 20,068 edocuments, 268,005 microfilms; Dir-Gen. Dr TOMASZ MAKOWSKI; publs *Biuletyn Informacyjny Biblioteki Narodowej* (Information Bulletin, 4 a year, print and online), *Polish Libraries Today* (in English, irregular, print and online), *Rocznik Biblioteki Narodowej* (National Library Yearbook, scientific library science periodical, with English summaries, print and online).

Biblioteka Publiczna m. st. Warszawy–Biblioteka Główna Województwa Mazowieckiego (Warsaw Public Library—Central Library of Masovia Province): ul. Koszykowa 26/28, POB 365, 00-950 Warsaw; tel. (22) 5374158; e-mail biblioteka@koszykowa.pl; internet www.biblpubl.waw.pl; f. 1907; 1,249,083 vols, 13,000 old prints, 4,000 MSS, 18,400 maps and atlases, 39,600 standards, 3,933 drawings, 5,900 records; Dir Dr MICHAŁ STRĄK; publ. *Bibliotekarz* (The Librarian, 12 a year).

Biblioteka Sejmowa (Sejm Library): ul. Wiejska 4/6/8, 00-902 Warsaw; tel. (22) 6941073; e-mail parlib@sejm.gov.pl; internet libr.sejm.gov.pl/bibl; f. 1919; economics, law, modern history, political and social sciences; 526,000 vols, 303,000 books, 110,800 vols of periodicals, 106,000 parliamentary, official and int. publs, 1,240 m. archival documents, 70,500 sound and video recordings of Sejm meetings; Dir-Gen. Dr WOJCIECH KULISIE-WICZ.

Biblioteka Szkoły Głównej Handlowej (Library of Warsaw School of Economics): ul. Rakowiecka 22B, 02-521 Warsaw; tel. (22) 5648690; e-mail infnauk@sgh.waw.pl; internet www.sgh.waw.pl; f. 1906; colln: economics, sociology, social policy, geography, economic history, politics, statistics and demography, accounting, finance, cooperative movement, law, labour problems, foreign trade, marketing, industry, agriculture, transport, business and management; 1,003,112 vols, incl. 786,334 vols of books, 216,778 vols of journals, 30,000 ejournals; Head Librarian Dr MARIA REKOWSKA; publs *Bibliografia Opublikowanego Dorobku Pracowników Naukowo-Dydaktycznych SGH*, *Przegląd Bibliograficzny Czasopiśmiennictwa Ekonomicznego* (4 a year).

Biblioteka Uniwersytecka w Warszawie (University of Warsaw Library): ul. Dobra 56/66, 00-312 Warsaw; tel. (22) 5525178; e-mail oin.buw@uw.edu.pl; internet www.buw.uw.edu.pl; f. 1816; 2,619,269 vols, 1,924,204 books, 695,065 jounals; 393,761 units of spec. collns, incl. 162,528 items of ephemera, 50,000 vols of old prints (master and architectural drawings, single leaf prints and bound vols of prints from 16th–20th centuries), 5,000 MSS, 1,500 doctoral theses, 20,000 vols of printed music, 10,000 globes, maps and atlases, 143 items of incunabula;

Gen. Dir Prof. Dr JOLANTA TALBIERSKA; publ. *Prace Biblioteki Uniwersyteckiej w Warszawie* (irregular).

Centralna Biblioteka Rolnicza im. Michała Oczapowskiego (Central Agricultural Library of Michał Oczapowski): POB 360, 00-950 Warsaw; ul. Krakowskie Przedmieście 66, 00-950 Warsaw; tel. (22) 8266041; e-mail listy@cbr.net.pl; internet www.cbr.edu.pl; f. 1955; br. at Puławy; mem. of Agris-FAO, IAALD; centre for information and documentation in agriculture and for exchange with scientific instns abroad; 380,000 vols, incl. 207,000 books, 131,000 journals; 42,000 spec. collns, incl. 798 vols of old prints; Dir Dr RYSZARD MIAZEK; publs *Bieżąca Informacja o Rolnictwie na Swiecie* (Current Information on Agriculture in the World, 52 a year, online), *Rolniczy Magazyn Elektroniczny* (6 a year, online, rme.cbr.net.pl).

Centralna Biblioteka Statystyczna (Central Statistical Library): al. Niepodległości 208, 00-925 Warsaw; tel. (22) 6083347; e-mail b.lazowska@stat.gov.pl; internet statlibr.stat.gov.pl; f. 1918; colln: scientific and specialized (economic and social subjects, with emphasis on statistics); 489,168 vols incl. 1,500 titles of periodicals, 5,000 atlases, maps and plans; spec. collns: 20,000 vols; Dir Mag. BOZENA LAZOWSKA; publs *Bibliografie Pismiennictwa Demograficznego*, *Bibliografia Polskiego Pismiennictwa Statystycznego* (irregular), *Bibliografia Wydawnictw Głownego Urzedu Statystycznego* (irregular), *Biuletyn Nabytków*, *Roczniki Zagraniczne w Zbiorach Centralnej Biblioteki Statystycznej*.

Centralna Biblioteka Wojskowa im. Marszałka Józefa Piłsudskiego (Marshal Joseph Pilsudski Central Military Library): ul. Ostrobramska 109, 04-041 Warsaw; tel. (22) 6817952; e-mail informacja@cbw.pl; internet www.cbw.pl; f. 1919; 313,736 books, 149,648 periodicals, 1,666 microfilms, 641 CDs; 160,000 units of spec. collns, incl. MSS, incunabula, old prints, maps, drawings and icons; Dir Dr JAN TARCZYŃSKI; publs *Informator Naukowy Centralnej Biblioteki Wojskowej* (irregular), *Polska Bibliografia Wojskowa* (Polish Military Bibliography, 4 a year).

Główna Biblioteka Lekarska im. Stanisława Konopki (Central Medical Library): ul. Chocimska 22, 00-791 Warsaw; tel. (22) 8497851; e-mail sekretariat@gbl.waw.pl; internet www.gbl.waw.pl; f. 1945; colln of medical items, drawings and illustrations; 422,279 vols, 4,000 old vols, 1,156 MSS and 154,442 periodicals, 44,246 microforms; Dir Dr WOJCIECH GIERMAZIAK; publs *Biuletyn Głównej Biblioteki Lekarskiej* (2 a year), *Polska Bibliografia Lekarska* (yearbook).

Główna Biblioteka Pracy i Zabezpieczenia Społecznego (Central Library of Labour and Social Security): ul. Limanowskiego 23, 02-943 Warsaw; tel. (22) 6420473; e-mail gbpizs@gbpizs.gov.pl; internet www.gbpizs.gov.pl; f. 1918; attached to Min. of Labour and Social Policy; colln: labour, wages, social affairs and related matters; 57,000 vols, incl. 17,266 books, 16,000 periodicals; Dir (vacant); Deputy Dir KRYSTYNA CETERA; publs *Bibliography of Economic and Social Problems of Labour* (1 a year), *Documentation Review* (12 a year), *Praca i Polityka Społeczna* (Labour and Social Policy), *Special Bibliographies* (irregular).

Naczelna Dyrekcja Archiwów Państwowych (Head Office of State Archives): ul. Rakowiecka 2D, 02-517 Warsaw; tel. (22) 5654600; e-mail ndap@archiwa.gov.pl; internet www.archiwa.gov.pl; f. 1951; preserves the records of local authorities and state instns, the judiciary organs, admin. and local govt bodies (incl. records of towns), educational, religious and social instns and orgs, industrial enterprises and economic instns, the archives of families and land estates, the papers of individuals, regional collns; 21,433 vols; Gen. Dir Dr Hab. WŁADYSŁAW STĘPNIAK; publs *Archeion* (2 a year, print and online), *Miscellanea Historico-Archivistica* (1 a year, print and online), *Nowe Miscellanea Historyczne* (1 a year, print and online).

Ośrodek Informacji Naukowej Polskiej Akademii Nauk (Centre for Information Science of the Polish Academy of Sciences): Pałac Staszica, ul. Nowy Swiat 72, 00-330 Warsaw; f. 1953; 23,000 vols, 900 int. periodicals on social science and other scientific disciplines; Dir Dr ANDRZEJ GROMEK; publs *Przegląd Informacji o Naukoznawstwie* (Review of Information on Science of Science, 4 a year), *Przegląd Literatury Metodologicznej* (Review of Methodological Literature, 2 a year), *Zagadnienia Informacji Naukowej* (Problems of Information Science, 2 a year).

Ośrodek Przetwarzania Informacji (Information Processing Institute): al. Niepodległości 188B, 00-608 Warsaw; tel. (22) 5701400; e-mail opi@opi.org.pl; internet www.opi.org.pl; f. 1990; attached to Min. of Science and Higher Education; int. cooperation, technology transfer, information services on research and devt; database management; Dir Dr OLAF GAJL; publ. *Informator Nauki Polskiej* (Polish Research Directory, every 2 years).

Wrocław

Biblioteka Ossolineum (Ossolineum): ul. Szewska 37, 50-139 Wrocław; tel. (71) 3444471; e-mail znio@znio.pl; internet www2.oss.wroc.pl; f. 1817; colln incl. MSS, old prints, graphics, drawings, bookplates, postcards, numismatic material, decorative items, badges, social documents, microforms, digitalized objects; 1,870,000 vols, 812,433 books, 194,461 journals, 20,901 MSS, 67,526 old prints, 28,822 maps and atlases, 308,715 misc. documents, 52,846 microforms; Dir Dr ADOLF JUZWENKO; publs *Czasopismo Zakładu Narodowego im. Ossolińskich* (1 a year), *Rocznik Wrocławski* (1 a year).

Biblioteka Uniwersytecka we Wrocławiu (Wrocław University Library): ul. Karola Szajnochy 7/9, 50-076 Wrocław; tel. (71) 3463120; e-mail sekretariat1@bu.uni.wroc .pl; internet www.bu.uni.wroc.pl; f. 1945; Silesiaca and Lusatica; bibliography, int. relations between Poland and other Slavonic countries and Germany; 3,943,593 vols, 1,255,868 books, 370,448 journals, 189,361 restricted colln; 476,974 units of spec. collns, incl. 42,402 microfilms, 128,147 vols of restricted colln; 1,650,952 vols in deptl libraries; Dir Mgr GRAŻYNA PIOTROWICZ; publs *Bibliografia Piśmiennictwa o Uniwersytecie Wrocławskim* (irregular), *Bibliografia Publikacji Pracowników Uniwersytetu Wrocławskiego* (1 a year), *Bibliothecalia Wratislaviensia* (irregular).

Dolnośląska Biblioteka Publiczna im. Tadeusza Mikulskiego we Wrocławiu (T. Mikulski Dolnoslaska Public Library): Rynek 58, 50-116 Wrocław; tel. (71) 3352200; e-mail wbp@wbp.wroc.pl; internet www.wbp.wroc.pl; f. 1945; general library; spec. collns on American, German and Korean studies; 253,000 vols; 128,000 units of spec. collns; Dir ANDRZEJ TYWS; publ. *Książka i Czytelnik* (2 a year).

Museums and Art Galleries

Bydgoszcz

Muzeum Okręgowe im. Leona Wyczółkowskiego w Bydgoszczy (Leon Wyczółkowski District Museum in Bydgoszcz): ul. Gdańska 4, 85-006 Bydgoszcz; tel. (52) 5859966; e-mail muzeum@muzeum .bydgoszcz.pl; internet www.muzeum .bydgoszcz.pl; f. 1880; Polish art since 19th century; paintings and graphic art of Leon Wyczółkowski and gallery of contemporary Polish paintings; Archaeological and Local History brs and Coin Room; library of 47,000 vols; Dir Dr MICHAL F. WOŹNIAK.

Bytom

Muzeum Górnośląskie w Bytomiu (Upper Silesian Museum in Bytom): pl. Jana III Sobieskiego 2, 41-902 Bytom; tel. (32) 281-82-94; e-mail sekretariat@muzeum.bytom.pl; internet www.muzeum.bytom.pl; f. 1927 in Katowice, transferred in 1945; history, archaeology, ethnography, natural history, Polish and foreign art; br. museum (ul. W. Korfantego 34, Bytom); library of 53,000 vols; Dir Dr DOMINIK ABŁAMOWICZ; publ. *Rocznik Muzeum Górnośląskiego w Bytomiu* (Yearbook).

Cracow

Muzeum Archeologiczne w Krakowie (Archaeological Museum in Cracow): ul. Senacka 3, 31-002 Cracow; tel. (12) 4227560; e-mail mak@ma.krakow.pl; internet www.ma.krakow.pl; f. 1850; archaeological remains from palaeolithic age, clay figurines, painted dishes, coins, Peruvian and Egyptian collns; library of 11,753 vols, 16,726 periodicals; Dir Dr JACEK GÓRSKIS; publs *Materiały Archeologiczne* (1 a year), *Materiały Archeologiczne Nowej Huty* (1 a year).

Muzeum Etnograficzne im. Seweryna Udzieli w Krakowie (Seweryn Udziela Ethnographic Museum in Cracow): ul. Krakowska 46, 31-066 Cracow; tel. (12) 430-60-23; e-mail sekretariat@etnomuzeum.eu; internet etnomuzeum.eu; f. 1910; folk art and folk culture of Poland; collns of art works from Europe, Asia, Africa, S. America; archives; library of 30,000 vols; Dir Dr ANTONI BARTOSZ; publ. *Rocznik Muzeum Etnograficznego w Krakowie* (1 a year).

Muzeum Historyczne Miasta Krakowa (Historical Museum of the City of Cracow): Krzysztofory, Rynek Główny 35, 31-011 Cracow; tel. (12) 4223264; e-mail dyrekcja@ mhk.pl; internet www.mhk.pl; f. 1899; traditions, history and culture of Cracow, model houses, arms and clocks, history of theatre in Cracow, history and culture of Jews in Cracow, history of Cracow Fowler Brotherhood, upheaval and martyrdom of Polish people from 1936–1956; spec. colln of 1,171 items; library of 23,810 vols; Dir MICHAŁ NIEZABITOWSKI; publ. *Krzysztofory* (1 a year).

Muzeum Narodowe w Krakowie (National Museum in Krakow): 3 Maja Ave 1, 30-062 Cracow; tel. (12) 2955637; e-mail dyrekcja@muz-nar.krakow.pl; internet www .muzeum.krakow.pl; f. 1879; colln of 780,000 artefacts; history, fine art, costume and textiles, arms and armour, numismatics, house-museums of Matejko, Wyspiański, Mehoffer and Szymanowski, Japanese art and technology; library of 125,000 vols; Dir ZOFIA GOŁUBIEW; publs *Notae Numismaticae Zapiski Numizmatyczne* (Numismatic Notes, 1 a year), *Rozprawy i Sprawozdania Muzeum Narodowego w Krakowie* (Yearbook).

Muzeum Uniwersytetu Jagiellońskiego: ul. Jagiellońska 15, 31-010 Cracow; tel. (12) 4220549; e-mail info@maius.in.uj.edu.pl; internet www.maius.uj.edu.pl; museum housed in Collegium Maius, the oldest structure of the Jagiellonian Univ.; collns of scientific instruments, paintings, photographs, sculptures, woodcuts; Dir Prof. Dr Hab. KRZYSZTOF STOPKA; publ. *Opuscula Musealia* (1 a year).

Zamek Królewski na Wawelu (Wawel Royal Castle): Wawel 5, 31-001 Cracow; tel. (12) 4225155; e-mail zamek@wawel.edu.pl; internet www.wawel.krakow.pl; f. 1930; collns of art in the Royal Castle: Italian Renaissance furniture, King Sigismund August's 16th-century colln of Flemish tapestries, Italian and Dutch painting, Polish carpets; Royal treasury: crown jewels, historical relics, banners, gold objects; armoury: Polish and West European weapons; objects of Oriental art: Persian and Turkish weaponry and tents; oriental rugs, Chinese and Japanese pottery; colln relating to the history of Wawel Hill, Polish stove tiles from 15th to 18th centuries; 18th-century Meissen porcelain; library of 16,000 vols, 390 periodicals; Dir Prof. Dr JAN K. OSTROWSKI; publs *Acta Archaeologica Waweliana* (4 a year), *Biblioteka Wawelska*, *Studia Waweliana* (1 a year).

Frombork

Muzeum Mikołaja Kopernika (Nicolaus Copernicus Museum): ul. Katedralna 8, 14-530 Frombork; tel. (55) 2440071; e-mail frombork@softel.elblag.pl; internet www .frombork.art.pl; f. 1948; biographical exhibits; history of astronomy; astronomical observatory; example of Foucault's pendulum; planetarium; modern art gallery; history of medicine; herb garden; library of 20,500 vols; Dir Mgr HENRYK SZKOP; publ. *Komentarze Fromborskie* (1 a year).

Gdańsk

Centralne Muzeum Morskie w Gdańsku (Polish Maritime Museum in Gdańsk): ul. Olowianka 9–13, 80-751 Gdańsk; tel. (58) 3018611; e-mail sekretariat@cmm.pl; internet www.cmm.pl; f. 1960; depts of ports devt, history of shipbuilding, history of maritime shipping and trade, marine fine arts, history of yachting, underwater archaeology, educational services; special vessel for underwater archaeological investigations; laboratory for conservation of artefacts recovered from sea; Lighthouse Museum in Rozewie; also br. in Hel (history of Polish fishery; open-air exhibition of types of fishing boats); br. in Tczew (history of Polish inland navigation); 4 historic ships (incl. sailing ship 'Dar Pomorza', fmr Polish school-ship); archives: plans, drawings, photos, documents; library of 50,000 vols of books and journals; Dir JERZY LITWIN.

Muzeum Archeologiczne w Gdańsku (Archaeological Museum in Gdańsk): ul. Mariacka 25/26, 80-958 Gdańsk; tel. (58) 3222100; e-mail mag@archeologia.pl; internet www.archeologia.pl; f. 1953; collects, preserves and exhibits archaeological remains of the Pomerania region from the Stone Age to modern times; library of 23,000 vols; Dir HENRYK PANER; publs *Gdańsk Archaeological Museum African Reports*, *Pomorania Antiqua*.

Muzeum Historyczne Miasta Gdańska (Gdańsk History Museum): ul. Długa 46/47, 80-831 Gdańsk; tel. (58) 7679100; e-mail kancelaria@mhmg.pl; internet www.mhmg .pl; f. 1970; Dir ADAM KOPERKIEWICZ.

Muzeum II Wojny Światowej (Museum of the Second World War): ul. Długa 81–83, 80-831 Gdańsk; tel. (58) 3237520; e-mail sekretariat@muzeum1939.pl; internet www .muzeum1939.pl; f. 2009; 18,000 items for exhibition; open air exhibition chronicling the Battle of Westerplatte using plans, drawings, photographs and documents; Dir Prof. Dr Hab. PAWEŁ MACHCEWICZ.

Muzeum Narodowe w Gdańsku (National Museum in Gdańsk): ul. Toruńska 1, 80-822 Gdańsk; tel. (58) 3016804; e-mail info@ muzeum.narodowe.gda.pl; internet www .muzeum.narodowe.gda.pl; f. 1870; art since 12th century, craftwork since 15th century, photography, ethnography (collns held at various locations); library of 21,000 vols, 440 journals; Dir WOJCIECH BONISŁAWSKI.

Katowice

Muzeum Śląskie (Silesian Museum): al. W. Korfantego 3, 40-005 Katowice; tel. (32) 7799300; e-mail dyrekcja@muzeumslaskie .pl; internet www.muzeumslaskie.pl; f. 1929; permanent exhibitions: Polish painting since 1800, war industry in Silesea in the 19th and 20th centuries; hand typesetting and printing machines from mid 20th century, a linotype and a graphics press; collns of archaeology, ethnography, photography, history, art; Dir LESZEK JODLIŃSKI (acting); Deputy Dir JANUSZ GAWRON.

Kielce

Muzeum Narodowe w Kielcach (National Museum in Kielce): pl. Zamkowy 1, 25-010 Kielce; tel. (41) 3444015; e-mail poczta@mnki .pl; internet mnki.pl; f. 1908; brs: Museum of Stefan Żeromski's early years, Henryk Sienkiewicz Museum in Oblęgorek; library of 40,000 vols; Dir Dr ROBERT KOTOWSKI; publ. *Rocznik Muzeum Narodowego w Kielcach* (1 a year).

Kołobrzeg

Muzeum Oręża Polskiego w Kołobrzegu (Museum of Polish Arms in Kołobrzeg): ul. Armii Krajowej 13, 78-100 Kołobrzeg; tel. (94) 3525253; e-mail muzeum@muzeum .kolobrzeg.pl; internet www.muzeum .kolobrzeg.pl; f. 1963; permanent exhibition of ancient, medieval and modern Polish arms and armament; library with a spec. colln of old prints, photographs, postcards, audiovisual materials, iconographic documents, microforms, periodicals; Dir PAWEŁ PAWŁOWSKI; publ. *Gazeta Muzealna* (Bulletin, 4 a year).

Łódź

Centralne Muzeum Włókiennictwa w Łodzi (Central Museum of Textiles in Łódz): ul. Piotrkowska 282, 93-034 Łódź; tel. (42) 6832684; e-mail sekretariat@ muzeumwlokiennictwa.pl; internet www .muzeumwlokiennictwa.pl; f. 1960; collns of ancient and modern clothes, folk textiles, documents of history of textile industry, industrial textiles, Polish and foreign artistic textiles, textile tools and machines; Łódź Wooden Architecture Open-Air Museum; library of 15,000 vols, 2,000 journals; Dir MARCIN OKO (acting).

Muzeum Archeologiczne i Etnograficzne w Łódźi: pl. Wolności 14, 91-415 Łódź; tel. (42) 6328440; e-mail maie@maie .art.pl; internet www.maie.lodz.pl; f. 1956; archaeology, ethnography, numismatics; radio-chemical laboratory; 227,438 artefacts; library of 47,000 vols; Dir Prof. Dr Hab. RYSZARD GRYGIEL; publ. *Prace i Materiały Muzeum Archeologicznego i Etnograficznego w Łódźi* (archaeology, ethnography, numismatics and conservation series).

Muzeum Sztuki w Łodzi (Museum of Art in Łodz): ul. Więckowskiego 36, 90-734 Łódź; tel. (42) 6339790; e-mail muzeum@msl.org .pl; internet msl.org.pl; f. 1931; Gothic art;

foreign painting of the 15th to 19th centuries; Polish painting since 17th century; int. modern and contemporary art; Księży Młyn house with late 19th-century interior décor; library of 40,000 vols; Dir JAROSŁAW SUCHAN.

Lublin

Muzeum Lubelskie w Lublinie (Lublin Province Museum): ul. Zamkowa 9, 21-117 Lublin; tel. (81) 5325001; e-mail dyrektor@ zamek-lublin.pl; internet www.zamek-lublin .pl; f. 1906; regional archaeological, historical and ethnographic colln, Polish and foreign paintings and decorative art; armoury; numismatics; conservation dept; 14th century Holy Trinity Chapel, with 15th century paintings; 13th century dungeon; 157,000 artefacts; 5 regional br. museums; library of 20,000 vols; Dir ZYGMUNT NASALSKI; publ. *Studia i Materiały Lubelskie*.

Muzeum Wsi Lubelskiej (Open Air Village Museum in Lublin): al. Warszawska 96, 20-824 Lublin; tel. (81) 5333051; e-mail skansen@skansen.lublin.pl; internet skansen .com.pl; f. 1970; open air exhibits depicting Polish rural life; Jewish exhibition; organizes symposia and social meetings; Dir MIECZYSŁAW KSENIAK.

Państwowe Muzeum na Majdanku (State Museum at Majdanek): ul. Droga Męczenników Majdanka 67, 20-325 Lublin; tel. (81) 7102821; e-mail sekretariat@majdanek.eu; internet www.majdanek.eu; f. 1944; fmr Nazi concentration camp; historical colln incl. authentic objects from the concentration camp in Majdanek; contemporary art collns incl. works of art presenting the issue of martyrdom and anti-totalitarianism, produced between 1945 and 2008; library of 15,000 vols; Dir Dr TOMASZ KRANZ; publ. *Zeszyty Majdanka* (irregular).

Olsztynek

Muzeum Budownictwa Ludowego— Park Etnograficzny w Olsztynku (Folk Architecture Museum and Ethnographic Park in Olsztynek): ul. Leśna 23, 11-015 Olsztynek; tel. (89) 519-21-64; e-mail dyrektor@muzeumolsztynek.com.pl; internet www.muzeumolsztynek.com.pl; f. 1909 in Kaliningrad, present location 1937; protection of folk culture; over 10,000 exhibits; library of 10,768 vols; Dir EWA WROCHNA.

Oświęcim

Miejsce Pamięci i Muzeum Auschwitz-Birkenau (Memorial and Museum Auschwitz-Birkenau): ul. Więźniów Oświęcimia 20, 32-603 Oświęcim; tel. (33) 8448003; e-mail muzeum@auschwitz.org.pl; internet www .auschwitz.org.pl; f. 1947; fmr Nazi concentration camp at Auschwitz-Birkenau, illustrating system of mass extermination; colln incl. concentration camp documents and objects; library of 30,000 vols, 2,500 periodicals and archives; Dir Dr PIOTR M. A. CYWIŃSKI; publs *Pro Memoria* (irregular, in Polish and English), *Zeszyty Oświęcimskie* (irregular, in Polish and German).

Poznań

Muzeum Archeologiczne w Poznaniu (Poznań Archaeological Museum): ul. Wodna 27-Pałac Górków, 61-781 Poznań; tel. (61) 8528251; e-mail muzarp@man.poznan.pl; internet www.muzarp.poznan.pl; f. 1857, present location 1967; archaeology of Greater Poland and the Nile basin; library of 54,087 vols; Dir Prof. Dr Hab. MARZENA SZMYT; publs *Biblioteka Fontes Archaeologici Posnanienses* (irregular), *Fontes Archaeologici Posnanienses* (1 a year), *Studies in African Archaeology* (irregular).

Muzeum Narodowe w Poznaniu (National Museum in Poznań): Aleje Marcin-

kowskiego 9, 61-745 Poznań; tel. (61) 8568000; e-mail mnp@mnp.art.pl; internet www.mnp.art.pl; f. 1857, present name 1950; medieval art, European paintings 14th–19th centuries, Polish paintings since 15th century, prints and drawings, sculpture, numismatics, modern art; br. museums specializing in ethnography, Poznań history, military history, musical instruments, applied arts; gallery of painting and sculpture; library of 67,000 vols; Dir Prof. Dr Hab. WOJCIECH SUCHOCKI; publ. *Studia Muzealne* (1 a year).

Sanok

Muzeum Budownictwa Ludowego w Sanoku (Museum of Folk Architecture in Sanok): ul. Traugutta 3, 38-500 Sanok; tel. (13) 4635381; e-mail sekretariat@mblsanok .eu; internet skansen.mblsanok.pl; f. 1958; traditional architecture, interiors, folk arts and crafts, icons; library of 18,900 vols on the Orthodox church and ethnography; Man. Mgr JERZY GINALSKI; publs *Acta Scansenologica* (every 2 years), *Materiały Muzeum Budownictwa Ludowego w Sanoku* (every 2 years).

Szczecin

Muzeum Narodowe w Szczecinie (National Museum in Szczecin): ul. Staromłyńska 27, 70-561 Szczecin; tel. (91) 4315200; e-mail biuro@muzeum.szczecin.pl; internet www.muzeum.szczecin.pl; f. 1945; Pomeranian art and archaeology, Polish art since 19th century, African and Asian art, maritime and ethnological collns; library of 85,000 vols; Dir LECH KARWOWSKI; publ. *Materiały Zachodniopomorskie* (1 a year).

Sztutowo

Muzeum Stutthof w Sztutowie (State Museum in Sztutowo): ul. Muzealna 6, 82-110 Sztutowo; tel. (55) 2478353; e-mail sekretariat@stutthof.org; internet stutthof .org; f. 1962; fmr Nazi concentration camp of Stutthof; 69,000 archival units; Dir PIOTR TARNOWSKI; publ. *Zeszyty Muzeum Stutthof* (1 a year).

Toruń

Muzeum Etnograficzne im. Marii Znamierowskiej-Prüfferowej w Toruniu (Ethnographical Museum in Toruń): Wały gen. Sikorskiego 19, 87-100 Toruń; tel. (56) 6228091; e-mail kontakt@etnomuzeum.pl; internet www.etnomuzeum.pl; f. 1959, present name 1999; folk culture of N Poland; library of 18,142 vols; Dir Dr HUBERT CZACHOWSKI; publ. *Rocznik Muzeum Etnograficznego w Toruniu* (1 a year).

Muzeum Okręgowe w Toruniu (District Museum in Toruń): Rynek Staromiejski 1, 87-100 Toruń; tel. (56) 6605612; e-mail muzeum@muzeum.torun.pl; internet www .muzeum.torun.pl; f. 1861; 14th- to 20th-century art (painting, graphics, sculpture, handicrafts), Far-Eastern art, history, archaeology, militaria, numismatics, Copernicus museum; library of 30,000 vols, incl. 39 antique books by Euclides, Nicolaus Copernicus, Hartmann Schedel, etc.; Man. Dir Dr MAREK RUBNIKOWICZ; publ. *Rocznik Muzeum Okręgowego w Toruniu* (Toruń Museum Yearbook).

Warsaw

Muzeum Historyczne m. st. Warszawy (Historical Museum of Warsaw): Rynek Starego Miasta 28–42, 00-272 Warsaw; tel. (22) 6351625; e-mail mhw@mhw.pl; internet www.mhw.pl; f. 1936 as Museum of Old Warsaw, present name 1948; exhibits relating to the history of Warsaw since 10th century; depts of archaeology, art, historical colln, photography, inventory, medals and coins; library: vols, 4,500 vols of periodicals; Dir EWA NEKANDA-TREPKASS; publ. *Almanach Muzealny* (every 2 years).

Muzeum i Instytut Zoologii PAN (Museum and Institute of Zoology of the Polish Academy of Sciences): ul. Wilcza 64, 00-679 Warsaw; tel. (22) 6293221; e-mail sekretariat@miiz.waw.pl; internet www.miiz .waw.pl; f. 1819; research in various fields of zoology; molecular and 3-dimensional morphometrics laboratory; research station at Łomna near Warsaw; zoological collns of 8,178,000 specimens; archives and documents; library of 44,876 vols of books, 74,065 vols of reprints, 116,760 vols of journals, 6,123 titles, 776 serial publications, 4,953 cartographic colln, 134 phonographic colln; Dir Prof. Dr Hab. DARIUSZ IWAN; publs *Acta Chiropterologica* (2 a year, print and online), *Acta Ornithologica* (2 a year, print and online), *Annales Zoologici* (4 a year, print and online), *Fragmenta Faunistica* (2 a year, print and online).

Muzeum Literatury im. Adama Mickiewicza (Adam Mickiewicz Museum of Literature): Rynek Starego Miasta 20, 00-272 Warsaw; tel. (22) 8317692; e-mail sekretariat@muzeumliteratury.pl; internet muzeumliteratury.pl; f. 1951; museum of literary history of Poland esp. 19th and 20th centuries; library of 110,000 vols; Dir Dr JAROSŁAW KLEJNOCKI; publ. *Blok-Notes Muzeum Literatury im. Adama Mickiewicza.*

Muzeum Narodowe w Warsawie (National Museum in Warsaw): al. Jerozolimskie 3, 00-495 Warsaw; tel. (22) 6211031; e-mail muzeum@mnw.art.pl; internet www .mnw.art.pl; f. 1862; paintings and sculpture; prints and drawings; numismatics; decorative arts and crafts; photography; Egyptian, Greek, Roman and Byzantine (Nubian) art; medieval and modern Polish art since 12th century; 14th- to 19th-century foreign painting; also administers the Poster Museum at Wilanów, Królikarnia Palace in Warsaw and outside Warsaw, Nieborów Palace; Otwock Palace; library of 130,000 vols; Dir AGNIESZKA MORAWIŃSKA; publ. *Bulletin du Musée National de Varsovie* (4 a year).

Muzeum Niepodległości (Museum of Independence): al. Solidarności 62, 00-240 Warsaw; tel. (22) 8269091; e-mail sekretariat@ muzeumniepodleglosci.art.pl; internet muzeum-niepodleglosci.pl; f. 1990; history of Polish independence and social movements; library of 29,230 vols, 3,960 periodicals; Dir Dr TADEUSZ SKOCZEK; publ. *Niepodległość i Pamięć* (1 a year).

Muzeum Sportu i Turystyki (Museum of Sports and Tourism): ul. Wybrzeże Gdyńskie 4, 01-531 Warsaw; tel. (22) 5603780; e-mail muzsport@muzeumsportu.waw.pl; internet www.muzeumsportu.waw.pl; f. 1952; collects and exhibits sport trophies incl. medals, tokens, badges and cups; coins, flags, pennants and emblems, dresses, sports equipment, travel accessories, sports and tourism posters, artwork and stamps; library of 16,500 vols; spec. colln of 50,000 photographs, incl. 4,000 photographs taken before 1939; Dir TOMASZ JAGODZIŃSKI; publ. *Wiadomości Muzealne* (4 a year, print and online).

Muzeum Techniki (Warsaw Museum of Technology): Pałac Kultury i Nauki, pl. Defilad 1, 00-901 Warsaw; tel. (22) 6566759; e-mail informacja@muzeumtechniki .warszawa.pl; internet muzeumtechniki .warszawa.pl; f. 1875; popularization of science and technology and their history, preservation of monuments of technology; planetarium; cinema; local brs: Museum of Ancient Metallurgy in Nowa Słupia, Museum of the old Polish Basin in Sielpia, waterpowered forges in Stara Kuźnica and

Gdańsk, 19th-century blast furnace in Chlewiska, Museum of Industry in Old Rolling Mill, Warsaw; library of 14,000 vols, 150 titles of journals; Dir JERZY JASIUK.

Muzeum Wojska Polskiego (Polish Military Museum): al. Jerozolimskie 3, 00-495 Warsaw; tel. (22) 6295271; e-mail muzeumwp@muzeumwp.pl; internet www .muzeumwp.pl; f. 1920; colln of 79,000 weapons, uniforms, banners, decorations, etc; permanent exhibition showing Polish military history since 10th century; militaria from Asia, Africa, Australia; colln of modern paintings, sculptures and graphics; iconographic colln; conservation workshops for metal, textile, wooden, leather and paper exhibits; library of 40,000 vols; Dir Prof. ZBIGNIEW WAWER; publ. *Muzealnictwo Wojskowe* (Military Museology, irregular).

Państwowe Muzeum Archeologiczne w Warszawie (State Archaeological Museum): ul. Długa 52, 00-241 Warsaw; tel. (22) 5044800; e-mail pma@pma.pl; internet www .pma.pl; f. 1923; prehistoric and proto-historic exhibits; organizes regional and field exhibitions and carries out archaeological excavations throughout Poland; archaeological stores at Rybno; library of 48,000 vols, 335 titles of periodicals; Dir Dr WOJCIECH BRZEZIŃSKI; publ. *Wiadomości Archeologiczne* (1 a year, in Polish with summaries in English).

Państwowe Muzeum Etnograficzne w Warszawie (State Ethnographic Museum in Warsaw): ul. Kredytowa 1, 00-056 Warsaw; tel. (22) 8277641; e-mail sekretariat@ ethnomuseum.pl; internet ethnomuseum .website.pl; f. 1888; Polish and non-European ethnographical colln; library of 26,000 vols, 30 titles of periodicals; Dir Dr ADAM CZYŻEWSKI; publs *Etnografia Nowa* (The New Ethnography, 4 a year, print and online), *Zeszyty Państwowego Muzeum Etnograficznego w Warszawie* (Reports, 1 a year).

Polska Akademia Nauk Muzeum Ziemi w Warszawie (Polish Academy of Sciences Museum of the Earth in Warsaw): Aleja Na Skarpie 20/26, 27, 00-488 Warsaw; tel. (22) 6297497; e-mail sekretariat@mz.pan.pl; internet www.mz.pan.pl; f. 1932; collns incl. Polish minerals, rocks, meteorites, fossil flora and fauna, Baltic amber; library of 21,000 vols of books, 24,000 vols of journals, 1,044 titles of periodicals, 6,500 units of old prints and maps; Dir Dr RYSZARD SZCZĘSNY; publ. *Prace Muzeum Ziemi.*

Polska Akademia Nauk Ogród Botaniczny—Centrum Zachowania Różnorodności Biologicznej w Powsinie (Polish Academy of Sciences Botanical Garden—Centre for Biological Diversity Conservation in Powsin): ul. Prawdziwka 2, 02-973 Warsaw 76; tel. (22) 6483856; e-mail ob .sekr@obpan.pl; internet ogrod-powsin.pl; f. 1974; conservation and evaluation of genetic resources of plants; library of 8,000 vols; Dir Prof. Dr Hab. JERZY PUCHALSKI; publs *Biuletyn* (1 a year), *Prace Ogrodu Botanicznego Polskiej Akademii Nauk* (Reports of the Botanical Garden, irregular, in Polish with summaries in English).

Zamek Królewski w Warszawie (Royal Castle in Warsaw): pl. Zamkowy 4, 00-277 Warsaw; tel. (22) 6572170; e-mail informacja@zamek-krolewski.pl; internet www.zamek-krolewski.pl; f. 1980; applied arts, carpets and rugs, drawings, furniture, numismatics, paintings, sculpture; library of 25,000 vols; Dir Prof. Dr Hab. ANDRZEJ ROTTERMUND; publ. *Kronika Zamkowa* (2 a year).

Wieliczka

Muzeum Żup Krakowskich Wieliczka (Cracow Saltworks Museum in Wieliczka): ul. Zamkowa 8, 32-020 Wieliczka; tel. (12) 4221947; e-mail podziemne@muzeum .wieliczka.pl; internet www.muzeum .wieliczka.pl; f. 1951; history, archaeology, geology, history of art and ethnography, archives, metal conservation laboratory; library of 20,000 vols, 4,500 vols of archival documents, spec. collns: photographs, mining maps; Dir Prof. Dr ANTONI JODŁOWSKI; publ. *Studia i Materiały do Dziejów Żup Solnych w Polsce* (Studies and Materials on the History of Saltworks, 1 a year).

Wrocław

Muzeum Architektury we Wrocławiu (Museum of Architecture in Wrocław): ul. Bernardyńska 5, 50-156 Wrocław; tel. (71) 3433675; e-mail muzeum@ma.wroc.pl; internet www.ma.wroc.pl; f. 1965; Polish and other architecture; modern art; library of 7,000 vols; Dir Dr JERZY ILKOSZ.

Muzeum Miejskie Wrocławia (City Museum of Wrocław): ul. Sukiennice 14/15, 50-107 Wrocław; tel. (71) 3471690; e-mail sekretariat@mmw.pl; internet www.muzeum .miejskie.wroclaw.pl; f. 1970, present status 2000; Dir Dr MACIEJ ŁAGIEWSKI..

Attached Museums:

Muzeum Archeologiczne (Museum of Archaeology): Arsenał Miejski, ul. Cieszyńskiego 9, 50-136 Wrocław; tel. (71) 3471696; f. 1815; Man. Dr MACIEJ TRZCIŃSKI.

Muzeum Historyczne we Wrocławiu (Historical Museum): Pałac Królewski, ul. Kazimierza Wielkiego 35, 50-077 Wrocław; tel. (71) 3916940; f. 1948; Man. HALINA OKÓLSKA.

Muzeum Militariów (Wrocław Military Museum): Arsenał Mikołajsk, ul. Cieszyńskiego 9, 50-136 Wrocław; tel. (71) 3471696; f. 1971, present status 2000; Man. Dr MARIUSZ CIEŚLA.

Muzeum Sztuki Cmentarnej (Museum of Cemetery Art): Stary Cmentarz Żydowski, ul. Ślężna 37/39, 50-301 Wrocław; tel. (71) 7915904; e-mail cmentarz@ mmw.pl; f. 1991; Man. JAN KLUŹNIAK.

Muzeum Sztuki Medalierskiej (Museum of Medallic Art): Pałac Królewski, ul. Kazimierza Wielkiego 35, 50-077 Wrocław; tel. (71) 3916940; e-mail b .kozarskaorzeszek@mmw.pl; f. 1965; Man. BARBARA KOZARSKA-ORZESZEK.

Muzeum Sztuki Mieszczańskiej (Museum of Bourgeois Art): Stary Ratusz, Rynek, 50-107 Wrocław; tel. (71) 3471691; e-mail janek@mmw.pl; f. 2000; Man. JAN TRZYNADLOWSKI.

Muzeum Narodowe we Wrocławiu (National Museum in Wrocław): Pl. Powstańców Warszawy 5, 50-153 Wrocław; tel. (71) 3435643; e-mail muzeumnarodowe@wr.onet .pl; internet www.mnwr.art.pl; f. 1948; colln of medieval art, Polish painting since 17th century, European painting since 16th century, decorative arts, prints, photographs, ethnography and history relating to Silesia, panoramic painting 'Battle of Racławice'; numismatics; library of 92,889 vols; Dir MARIUSZ HERMANSDORFER; publ. *Roczniki Sztuki Śląskiej* (1 a year).

Zakopane

Muzeum Tatrzańskie im. Dra Tytusa Chałubińskiego w Zakopanem (Tatra Museum in Zakopane): ul. Krupówki 10, 34-500 Zakopane; tel. (18) 2015205; e-mail biuro@muzeumtatrzanskie.pl; internet www .muzeumtatrzanskie.pl; f. 1888; main museum: geology, regional flora, fauna, history and ethnography; glass paintings, pottery, sculpture, wooden, metal and leatherware, costumes, musical instruments, etc.; museum of the Zakopane style—inspirations (local culture sources of the style); museum of the Zakopane style (architecture, furniture, textiles, ceramics and jewellery and pastels by St Ignacy Witkiewicz); Wł. Hasior Art Gallery; Kornel Makuszyński Museum; art gallery in Koziniec (temporary exhibitions) and 4 brs across Podhale and Spisz regions; library of 27,000 vols of books, 2,000 periodicals; spec. collns: maps, musical records and scores, photographic archive (positives, negatives and transparencies), print colln (printed iconographic materials), technical documentation; Dir ANNA WENDE-SURMIAKS; publ. *Rocznik Podhalański* (irregular).

Universities

GDAŃSKI UNIWERSYTET MEDYCZNY
(Medical University of Gdańsk)

ul. M. Skłodowskiej-Curie 3A, 80-210 Gdańsk
Telephone: (58) 3491000
E-mail: rektor@gumed.edu.pl
Internet: www.gumed.edu.pl

Founded 1945

Chancellor: MAREK LANGOWSKI
Rector: Prof. Dr JANUSZ MORYŚ
Vice-Rector for Clinical Affairs: Prof. Dr ANDRZEJ BASINSKI
Vice-Rector for Education: Prof. Dr LESZEK BIENIASZEWSKI
Vice-Rector for Science: Prof. Dr TOMASZ BACZEK
Vice-Rector for Student Affairs: Prof. Dr MARCIN GRUCHALA
Dir for Library: ANNA GRYGOROWICZ

Library of 608,032 vols incl. 368,445 books, 103,769 periodicals, 106,269 spec. collns and 29,549 fictional books
Number of teachers: 1,700
Number of students: 6,800

Publication: *Annales Academiae Medicae Gedanensis*

DEANS

Faculty of Health Sciences: Prof. Dr PIOTR LASS
Faculty of Medicine: Prof. Dr MARIA DUDZIAK
Faculty of Pharmacy: Prof. Dr WIESŁAW SAWICKI
Intercollegiate Faculty of Biotechnology UG-MUG: Prof. Dr IGOR KONIECZNY

KATOLICKI UNIWERSYTET LUBELSKI JANA PAWŁA II
(John Paul II Catholic University of Lublin)

ul. Racławickie 14, 20-950 Lublin
Telephone: (81) 4454101
E-mail: kul@kul.pl
Internet: www.kul.pl

Founded 1918
Private control
Academic year: October to June

Chancellor: Rev. Prof. Dr Hab. STANISŁAW BUDZIK
Rector: Rev. Prof. ANTONI DEBINSKI
Vice-Rector for Admin. and Finances: Prof. Dr Hab. PAWEŁ SMOLELEŃ
Vice-Rector for Promotion and Int. Cooperation: Prof. Dr Hab. URSZULA PAPROCKA-PIOTROWSKA
Vice-Rector for Research and Devt: Rev. Prof. ANDRZEJ DERDZIUK

Vice-Rector for Students: Prof. Dr Hab. KRZYSZTOF NARECKI
Dir for Library: Dr BARBARA ZEZULA
Library of 2,172,395 vols (incl. dept libraries) of which 1,678,185 books, 51,253 old books, 4,94,210 vols of periodicals, 6,902 MSS, 10,639 maps and atlases, 10,162 music scores, 2,225 audio cassettes and records, 15,518 graphic items
Number of teachers: 1,185
Number of students: 19,000

Publications: *Acta Mediaevalia, Człowiek i Przyroda* (2 a year), *Ethos* (4 a year), *KERYGS* (2 a year), *Law–Administration–Church* (4 a year), *Przegląd Uniwersytecki* (6 a year), *Roczniki Filozoficzne* (1 a year), *Roczniki Humanistyczne* (1 a year), *Roczniki Nauk Prawnych* (1 a year), *Roczniki Nauk Społecznych* (1 a year), *Roczniki Psychologiczne* (1 a year), *Roczniki Teologiczne* (1 a year), *Studia Norwidiana* (1 a year), *Studia Polonijne* (1 a year), *Summarium, Zeszyty Naukowe KUL* (4 a year), *Vox Patrum* (2 a year)

DEANS

College of Interdisciplinary Individual Studies in Humanities and Social Sciences: Prof. Dr Hab. AGNIESZKA DZIUBA (Dir)
Faculty of Biotechnology and Environment Sciences: Prof. Dr Hab. RYSZARD SZYSZKA
Faculty of Humanities: Prof. Dr Hab. HUBERT ŁASZKIEWICZ
Faculty of Law, Canon Law and Administration: Prof. Dr Hab. PIOTR STANISZ
Faculty of Mathematics, IT and Landscape Architecture: Prof. Dr Hab. RYSZARD SMARZEWSKI
Faculty of Philosophy: Rev. Prof. MARCIN TKACZYK
Faculty of Social Sciences: Prof. Dr Hab. STANISŁAW FEL
Faculty of Theology: Prof. Dr Hab. MIROSŁAW KALINOWSKI
Institute of Lexicography: Dr EDWARD GIGILEWICZ (Dir)
Off-Campus Faculty of Law and Economic Sciences in Stalowa Wola: Prof. Dr Hab. TOMASZ RAKOCZY
Off-Campus Faculty of Legal and Economic Sciences in Tomaszów Lubelski: Prof. Dr PAWEŁ MARZEC
Off-Campus Faculty of Social Sciences in Stalowa Wola: Prof. Dr Hab. ANDRZEJ KUCZUMOW

PROFESSORS

Faculty of Humanities (tel. (81) 4454145; e-mail wydz_nh@kul.lublin.pl):

ANDRUSIW, S., Ukrainian Literature
CHODKOWSKI, R., Classical Linguistics, Greek Literature
DEPTUA, C., History of Medieval Culture
ECKMANN, A., Classical Linguistics, Ancient Christian Literature
KACZMAREK, W., Drama and Theatre
KNAPIŃSKI, R., Art History
KONEFAŁ, J., 19th–20th Century History of Social and Political Movements
KUCZYŃSKA, J., Medieval Polish Art
LAMENSKI, L., Modern Art History
MAKARSKI, W., Linguistics
MAZURCZAK, M., General Medieval Art History
OŁDAKOWSK, M., Contemporary Literature
PODBIELSKI, H., Classical Greek Philology
WOŹNIAK, A., Russian Literature

Faculty of Law, Canon Law and Administration (tel. (81) 4453731; e-mail wppkia@kul.pl):

CIOCH, H., Civil Law
DĘBIŃSKI, A., Roman Law
HRYSZCZUK, W., Medical Law and Forensic Medicine

KOŚĆ, A., Philosophy of Law
KRUKOWSKI, J., Canon Law
ŁĄCZKOWSKI, W., Financial Law, Administrative Law
MISZTAL, H., Canon Law, Law and Religion
SZAJKOWSKI, A., Commercial Law
TYSZCZYK, B., History of State and Law
WITCZAK, W., Forensic Medicine
ZUBERT, B., Canon Law

Faculty of Mathematics, IT and Landscape Architecture (tel. (81) 4454552):

CICHOCKA, E., Agriculture
FISCHER-MALANOWSKA, Z., Ecology
GOSZCZYŃSKI, W., Horticulture
HOŁUBIEC, J., Numerical Analysis and Programming
JANICKI, A., Information Technology
MATUS, P., Mathematics
RZYMOWSKI, W., Mathematics Application
SKOWRONSKI, T., Toxicology
STĘPNIEWSKA, Z., Agricultural Engineering
SZESZKO, M., Mathematics and Computer Science
SZYSZKA, R., Molecular Biology
URBANOWICZ, P., Computer Science
WOJCIECHOWSKA, W., Ecology, Hydrobiology
ZIĘBA, S., Humanistic Ecology

Faculty of Philosophy (tel. (81) 4454032; e-mail filozofia@kul.lublin.pl):

BRONK, A., Philosophy of Science
GAŁKOWSKI, J., Ethics, Political Philosophy
KICZUK, S., Logic
MARYNIARCZYK, A., Metaphysics
SZOSTEK, A., Ethics
WIELGUS, S., History of Philosophy, Medieval Philosophy
ZIELIŃSKI, E., History of Ancient and Medieval Philosophy
ŻYCIŃSKI, J., Philosophy of Nature, Philosophy of Science

Faculty of Social Sciences (tel. (81) 4453548; e-mail wns@kul.lublin.pl):

BIELA, A., Experimental Psychology, Industrial Psychology, Environmental Psychology
BRAUN-GAŁKOWSKA, M., Educational Psychology, Family Psychology
DYCZEWSKI, L., Sociology of Culture, Sociology of Family
GILOWSKA, Z., Economics, Local Finance
MARIAŃSKI, J., Sociology of Religion, Sociology of Morals
SĘKOWSKI, A., Rehabilitative Psychology
WÓJCIK, S., Sociology, Local Policy
ZALESKI, Z., Experimental Psychology

Faculty of Theology (tel. (81) 4453842; e-mail teolog@kul.lublin.pl):

DRĄCZKOWSKI, F., Patristics
GŁOWA, W., Pastoral Theology, Liturgy
KAMIŃSKI, R., Pastoral Theology, Organization of Pastoral Care
PACIOREK, A., Biblical Studies
RUBINKIEWICZ, R., Biblical Studies
RUSECKI, M., Fundamental Theology
TRONINA, A., Biblical Studies
WITCZYK, H., Biblical Studies
WILK, S., History of Monasteries
ZASĘPA, T., Contemporary Forms of Communication of the Faith
ZIMOŃ, H., Religious Studies

Off-Campus Faculty of Legal and Economic Sciences (ul. Lwowska 80, 22-600 Tomaszow Lubelski; tel. (84) 6642680):

ANTONOWICZ, L., International Public Law
CZEREWKO, G., Theory of Economics
KOSSAK, W., Civil Law
KRUKOWSKI, J., Theory of Law
MISZTAL, H., Canon Law
SRUTWA, J., Church History of Law
WOJCIECHOWSKI, W., Econometrics and Statistics

POMORSKI UNIWERSYTET MEDYCZNY W SZCZECINIE (Pomeranian Medical University)

ul. Rybacka 1, 70-204 Szczecin

Telephone: (91) 4800801
E-mail: rektor@pum.edu.pl
Internet: www.pum.edu.pl

Founded 1948, present name 1992
Academic year: September to October

Chancellor: JERZY ŁUCZAK
Vice-Chancellor: ANDRZEJ GAJEWSKI
Rector: Prof. Dr PRZEMYSŁAW NOWACKI
Vice-Rector for Clinical Affairs: Dr MAREK BRZOSKO
Vice-Rector for Didactic Affairs: Prof. Dr BARBARA WISZNIEWSKA
Vice-Rector for Scientific Affairs: Prof. Dr ANDRZEJ CIECHANOWICZ

Dir for Library: DAGMARA BUDEK

Library of 270,000 vols
Number of teachers: 620
Number of students: 4,100

DEANS

Faculty of Health Sciences: Dr ANDRZEJ STARCZEWSKI
Faculty of Medicine: Prof. Dr BOGUSŁAW MACHALIŃSKI
Faculty of Medicine and Dentistry: Dr MARIUSZ LIPSKI

SZKOŁA GŁÓWNA GOSPODARSTWA WIEJSKIEGO W WARSZAWIE (Warsaw University of Life Sciences– SGGW)

ul. Nowoursynowska 166, 02-787 Warsaw

Telephone: (22) 5931000
E-mail: rektor@sggw.pl
Internet: www.sggw.pl

Founded 1816
Languages of instruction: English, Polish
Academic year: October to June

Chancellor: Dr WŁADYSŁAW W. SKARŻYŃSKI
Rector: Prof. Dr Hab. ALOJZY SZYMAŃSKI
Pro-Rector for Devt: Prof. Dr Hab. WIESŁAW BIELAWSKI
Pro-Rector for Didactics: Prof. Dr Hab. BOGDAN KLEPACKI
Pro-Rector for Int. Cooperation: Prof. Dr Hab. MAREK STEFAN SZYNDEL
Pro-Rector for Research: Prof. Dr Hab. JAN NIEMIEC

Dir for Library: Dr JAN SANDECKI

Library of 430,000 vols
Number of teachers: 1,300
Number of students: 27,110

Publication: *Annals* (in 8 series)

DEANS

Faculty of Agriculture and Biology: GRAŻYNA GARBACZEWSKA
Faculty of Animal Sciences: Dr Hab. WANDA OLECH-PIASECKA
Faculty of Applied Informatics and Mathematics: Dr Hab. ARKADIUSZ ORŁOWSKI
Faculty of Civil and Environmental Engineering: Prof. Dr Hab. JERZY JEZNACH
Faculty of Economic Sciences: Dr Hab. JAROSŁAW GOŁĘBIEWSKI
Faculty of Food Sciences: Prof. Dr Hab. DOROTA WITROWA-RAJCHERT
Faculty of Forestry: Dr Hab. MICHAŁ ZASADA
Faculty of Horticulture, Biotechnology and Landscape Architecture: Prof. Dr Hab. KATARZYNA NIEMIROWICZ-SZCZYTT
Faculty of Human Nutrition and Consumer Sciences: Prof. Dr Hab. KRYSTYNA GUTKOWSKA
Faculty of Production Engineering: Prof. Dr Hab. TOMASZ NUREK
Faculty of Social Sciences: Prof. Dr Hab. FRANCISZEK KAMPKA

Faculty of Veterinary Medicine: Prof. Dr Hab. MARIAN BINEK
Faculty of Wood Technology: Prof. Dr KRZYSZTOF KRAJEWSKI

PROFESSORS

Faculty of Agriculture and Biology (ul. Nowoursynowska 159, 02-776 Warsaw; tel. (22) 5932510; e-mail dwrb@sggw.pl; internet agrobiol.sggw.waw.pl):

BIELAWSKI, W., Biochemistry
BLASZCZYK, M., Biochemistry
BOGATEK-LESZCZYNSKA, R., Plant Physiology
CHOJNICKI, J., Soil Science
CZEPINSKA-KAMINSKA, D., Soil Science
GARBACZEWSKA, G., Botany
GOLINOWSKI, W., Botany
GWOREK, B., Soil Science
KOZANECKA, T., Soil Science
KUSINSKA, A., Soil Science
LABETOWICZ, J., Agrochemistry
LENART, S., Soil and Land Management
LOBOCKA, M., Biochemistry
MADRY, W., Mathematical Statistics And Experimentation
PIETKIEWICZ, S., Plant Physiology
PODLASKI, S., Plant Physiology
PRACZ, J., Soil Science
RADECKI, A., Soil and Land Management
ROZBICKI, J., Crop Production
RUSSEL, S., Biochemistry
RUTKOWSKA, B., Agrochemistry
STYPINSKI, P., Agronomy
WYSZYNSKI, Z., Crop Production
ZAGDANSKA, B., Biochemistry
ZAGORSKI, Z., Soil Science

Faculty of Animal Science (ul. Ciszewskiego 8, 02-786 Warsaw; tel. (22) 5936500; e-mail dwnz@sggw.pl; internet animal.sggw.pl):

BRZOZOWSKI, M., Fur Animal Breeding
BRZOZOWSKI, P., Cattle Breeding
CHARON, K., Animal Genetics
CHRZANOWSKI, S., Horse Breeding
DYMNICKA, M., Animal Nutrition
GRODZKI, H., Cattle Breeding
KALETA, T., Animal Genetics
KAMIONEK, M., Zoology
KOSLA, T., Animal Hygiene
KULISIEWICZ, J., Swine Breeding
MICHALSKA, E., Animal Genetics
NALECZ-TARWACKA, T., Cattle Breeding
NIEMIEC, J., Poultry Breeding
NIZNIKOWSKI, R., Sheep and Goats Breeding
OLECH-PIASECKA, W., Animal Genetics
OSTASZEWSKA, T., Ichthyobiology and Fisheries
PEZOWICZ, E., Zoology
RADZIK-RANT, A., Sheep and Goat Breeding
REKIEL, A., Animal Breeding
SAWOSZ-CHWALIBOG, E., Animal Nutrition, Biotechnology
SCIESINSKI, K., Animal Breeding
SKOMIAL, J., Animal Nutrition
SOKOL, J., Economics, Animal Nutrition
ZARSKI, T., Animal Hygiene

Faculty of Applied Informatics and Mathematics (ul. Nowoursynowska 159, 02-776 Warsaw; tel. (22) 5937210; e-mail wzim@sggw.pl; internet www.wzim.sggw.pl):

BINDERMAN, Z., Mathematics
BORKOWSKI, B., Econometrics
CHMIELEWSKI, L., Informatics
CIARKOWSKI, A., Computer Applications
JANOWICZ, M., Physics
JEZIERSKI, J., Mathematics
LAUDANSKI, Z., Biometrics
ORŁOWSKI, A., Physics
RUSEK, M., Physics
SMOLIK, S., Econometrics
STRASBURGER, A., Mathematics
SZCZESNY, W., Informatics
TWARDOWSKA, K., Mathematics

WIERZBICKI, E., Technical Applications
WITKOWSKA, D., Econometrics, Financial Engineering
ZAWISTOWSKI, Z., Computer Applications
ZIELINSKI, W., Statistics and Biometrics
ZUBEREK, W., Informatics

Faculty of Civil and Environmental Engineering (ul. Nowoursynowska 159, 02-776 Warsaw; tel. (22) 5935000; e-mail dwiks@sggw.pl; internet wbis.sggw.pl):

BANASIK, K., Hydrology, Erosion and Sedimentation
BUCZKOWSKI, W., Civil Engineering
GARBULEWSKI, K., Environmental Geotechnics
HEWELKE, P., Environmental Improvement
IGNAR, S., Hydrology, Water Management
JEZNACH, J., Environmental Improvement, Drainage and Irrigation
KERNYTSKYY, I., Descriptive Geometry
KUBRAK, J., Hydraulics
LECHOWICZ, Z., Environmental Geotechnics
MOSIEJ, J., Environmental Improvement
NAGORKO, W., Civil Engineering
OKRUSZKO, T., Hydrology
PIEKUT, K., Natural Bases of Environmental Engineering
PIERZGALSKI, E., Environmental Improvement, Drainage and Irrigation
POLONSKI, M., Engineering Management
POPEK, Z., Water Engineering
SZYMANSKI, A., Geotechnical Engineering
WAGROWSKA, M., Civil Engineering
WYSOCKI, J., Geodesy
ZELAZO, J., Water Engineering
ZOLTOWSKI, W., Civil Engineering

Faculty of Economic Sciences (ul. Nowoursynowska 166, 02-776 Warsaw; tel. (22) 5934010; e-mail dwne@sggw.pl; internet www.wne.sggw.pl):

BAGIENSKI, S., Organization and Management
JEDRZEJCZYK, I., Law and Finance
JUSZCZYK, S., Banking
KLEPACKI, B., Economics of Production and Logistics
KRZYZANOWSKA, K., Communication
KRZYZANOWSKI, J., International Economic Relations
MAJEWSKI, E., Organization and Management
MANTEUFFEL, H., International Economic Relations
PODSTAWKA, M., Law and Finance
PUDELKIEWICZ, E., Marketing
RUNOWSKI, H., Organization and Management
SAWICKA, J., Agrarian Policy and Law
SIKORSKA-WOLAK, I., Rural Development
STANKO, S., Agricultural Economics
SZWACKA-MOKRZYCKA, J., Marketing
WASILEWSKI, M., Accountancy, Banking
WOJCICKI, W., Economic Policies
WOLOSZYN, J., Organization
ZIETARA, W., Organization and Management

Faculty of Food Sciences (ul. Nowoursynowska 159, 02-776 Warsaw; tel. (22) 5937510; e-mail dwnoz@sggw.pl; internet wnoz.sggw.pl):

BIALECKA-FLORJANCZYK, E., Organic Chemistry
BLAZEJAK, S., Biotechnology, Microbiology
CEGLINSKA, A., Crop Technology
GNIEWOSZ, M., Biotechnology, Microbiology
KAZIMIERCZUK, Z., Food Chemistry
KOWALCZYK, R., Food Engineering
KOWALSKI, B., Food Chemistry
KRYGIER, K., Fats and Oils Technology
LENART, A., Food Engineering
MITEK, M., Fruit and Vegetables Technology
MROCZEK, J., Meat Technology
OBIEDZINSKI, M., Food Quality

ORESZKO, A., Organic Chemistry
PALACHA, Z., Food Engineering
PISULA, A., Meat Technology
RACZYNSKA, E., Organic Chemistry
SLOWINSKI, M., Meat Technology
WITROWA-RAJCHERT, D., Food Engineering

Faculty of Forestry (ul. Nowoursynowska 159, 02-776 Warsaw; tel. (22) 5938010; e-mail wl@sggw.pl; internet w1.cem.sggw.pl):

ALEKSANDROWICZ-TRZCINSKA, M., Mycology and Forest Pathology
ANDRZEJCZYK, T., Silviculture
BEDKOWSKI, K., GIS in Forestry
BORECKI, T., Forest Management
BOROWSKI, J., Forest Entomology
BRZEZIECKI, B., Silviculture, Forest Management
DUDEK, A., Dendrometry
GOSZCZYNSKI, J., Forest Zoology
GRZYWACZ, A., Mycology and Forest Pathology
KLAPEC, B., Forestry Economics
MAZUR, S., Entomology and Forest Protection
MISCICKI, S., Forest Management
MOSKALIK, T., Forest Resources Utilization
MOZGAWA, J., GIS in Forestry
OLENDEREK, H., GIS in Forestry
PASCHALIS-JAKUBOWICZ, P., Forest Resources Utilization
PLOTKOWSKI, L., Forestry Economics
PORTER, B., Forest Resources Utilization
SKLODOWSKI, J., Entomology and Forest Protection
STEPIEN, E., Forest Management
TARASIUK, S., Silviculture, Forest Management
TRACZ, H., Forest Entomology and Ecology
WASILEWSKI, M., Forest Zoology
WERKA, J., Forest Zoology
ZAJACZKOWSKI, S., Botany, Tree Physiology
ZAKRZEWSKI, J., Botany
ZYBURA, H., Silviculture, Forest Management

Faculty of Horticulture, Biotechnology and Landscape Architecture (ul. Nowoursynowska 159, 02-776 Warsaw; tel. (22) 5932005; e-mail dwoa@sggw.pl; internet woiak.sggw.pl):

BURZA, W., Plant Genetics, Breeding and Biotechnology
DABROWSKI, Z., Applied Entomology
GAJC-WOLSKA, J., Vegetable and Medicinal Plants
GAJEWSKI, M., Vegetable and Medicinal Plants
GAWRONSKA, H., Natural Sciences in Horticulture
GAWRONSKI, W., Natural Sciences in Horticulture
IGNATOWICZ, S., Applied Entomology
JABLONSKA, L., Horticultural Economics
JADCZUK-TOBJASZ, E., Pomology
KARPINSKI, S., Plant Genetics, Breeding and Biotechnology
KIELKIEWICZ, M., Applied Entomology
KOBRYN, J., Vegetable and Medicinal Plants
KOSMALA, M., Landscape Art
KOZLOWSKI, M., Applied Entomology
KROLIKOWSKI, J., Landscape Art
LUKASZEWSKA, A., Ornamental Plants
MALESZY, S., Plant Genetics, Breeding and Biotechnology
NIEMIROWICZ-SZCZYTT, K., Plant Genetics, Breeding and Biotechnology
OSINSKA, E., Vegetable and Medicinal Plants
PADUCH-CICHAL, E., Plant Pathology
PLANDER, W., Plant Genetics, Breeding and Biotechnology
PRZYBECKI, Z., Plant Genetics, Breeding and Biotechnology
PRZYBYLA, A., Pomology

RAKOCZY-TROJANOWSKA, M., Plant Genetics, Breeding and Biotechnology
RYLKE, J., Landscape Art
SZULCZEWSKA, B., Landscape Architecture
SZYNDEL, M., Plant Pathology
SZYSZKO, J., Evaluation and Assessment of Natural Resources
TOMALA, K., Pomology
TOMCZYK, A., Applied Entomology
WAKULINSKI, W., Plant Pathology
WEGLARZ, Z., Vegetable and Medicinal Plants
WYSOCKI, C., Environmental Protection
ZARSKA, B., Environmental Protection

Faculty of Human Nutrition and Consumer Sciences (ul. Nowoursynowska 159C, 02-776 Warsaw; tel. (22) 5937010; e-mail dwnzck@sggw.pl; internet wnzck.sggw.pl):

BRZOZOWSKA, A., Human Nutrition
FILIP, R., Gastroenterology, Dietetics
GROMADZKA-OSTROWSKA, J., Nutritional Physiology, Dietetics, Reproductive Regulation
GRONOWSKA-SENGER, A., Human Nutrition
GUTKOWSKA, K., Consumer Behaviour, Marketing Research
KAWECKA, W., Human Immunology, Medical Mycology
KOLOZYN-KRAJEWSKA, D., Food Technology, Food Hygiene and Microbiology
KOWRYGO, B., Food Policy and Management
LASKOWSKI, W., Consumption Research
OZIMEK, I., Consumer Protection, Consumer Behaviour
PRZYBYLSKI, W., Catering Technology, Meat Science
REMBIALKOWSKA, M., Organic Agriculture, Food Quality
ROSOLOWSKA-HUSZCZ, D., Dietetics, Nutritional Physiology
SWIDERSKI, F., Functional Food and Commodities
WASZKIEWICZ-ROBAK, B., Functional Food and Commodities
WIERZBICKA, A., Food Engineering, Food Quality

Faculty of Production Engineering (ul. Nowoursynowska 164, 02-787 Warsaw; tel. (22) 5934500; e-mail dwip@sggw.pl; internet wip.sggw.pl):

BULINSKI, J., Agricultural and Forest Machinery
CHOCHOWSKI, A., Energy Management
FABIRKIEWICZ, A., Production Engineering
GACH, S., Farm Machinery
JAROS, M., Agricultural Engineering
KALETA, A., Technical Sciences
KLIMKIEWICZ, M., Technical Infrastructure
KRAWIEC, F., Production Organization and Management
KUPCZYK, F., Production Organization and Management
LISOWSKI, A., Agricultural and Forest Machinery
MAJEWSKI, Z., Production Engineering
SKROBACKI, A., Production Engineering
SZTYBER, J., Forestry Mechanization
TRAJER, J., Technical Sciences
WASCINSKI, T., Production Organization and Management
WASZKIEWICZ, C., Farm Machinery
WOJDALSKI, J., Technical Infrastructure

Faculty of Social Sciences (ul. Nowoursynowska 166, 02-787 Warsaw; tel. (22) 5934710; e-mail dwnh@sggw.pl; internet wnh.sggw.pl):

BLESZYNSKA, K., Pedagogy
BOBRYK, J., Psychology
CZAPLIGO-SIKORSKA, J., Sociology
GRYKO, C., Sociology
JEDRZEJKO, M., Pedagogy
KAMPKA, F., Sociology, Political Science

KORAB, K., Rural Sociology, Social Communication
LASTAWSKI, K., Political Science
PODEDWORNA, H., Sociology
PRZYCHODZEN, Z., Pedagogy, Sociology
SNIHUR, S., Philosophy
STEPKA, S., Political Science, History
WALKIEWICZ, W., Political Science
WOJTOWICZ, A., Sociology
ZANIEWSKA, T., Pedagogy, Sociology of Culture

Faculty of Veterinary Medicine (ul. Nowoursynowska 159, 02-776 Warsaw; tel. (22) 5936010; e-mail dwmw@sggw.pl; internet wmw.sggw.pl):

BINEK, M., Bacteriology, Molecular Biology
BORYCZKO, Z., Animal Gynaecology, Animal Reproduction
DEBSKI, B., Biochemistry
FRYMUS, T., Veterinary Epidemiology
GRALAK, M., Animal Physiology
KANIA, B., Animal Physiology
KATKIEWICZ, M., Animal Gynaecology, Animal Reproduction
KLECZKOWSKI, M., Clinical Diagnosis, Internal Medicine
KLUCINSKI, W., Clinical Diagnosis, Internal Medicine
KOBRYN, H., Anatomy
LECHOWSKI, R., Internal Medicine
LEONTOWICZ, H., Animal Dietetics
MALINOWSKI, E., Livestock Disease, Internal Medicine
MOTYL, T., Animal Physiology
NIEMIALTOWSKI, M., Preclinical Science, Animal Immunology
ORZECHOWSKI, A., Animal Physiology
OSTASZEWSKI, P., Animal Dietetics
SYSA, P., Histology and Embryology
SZCZAWINSKI, J., Hygiene of Food of Animal Origin
WEDRYCHOWICZ, H., Parasitology
WIECHETEK, M., Pharmacology, Toxicology
ZABIELSKI, R., Animal Physiology

Faculty of Wood Technology (ul. Nowoursynowska 159, 02-776 Warsaw; tel. (22) 5938500; e-mail dwtd@sggw.pl; internet wtd.sggw.pl):

BAJKOWSKI, B., Mechanical Processing of Wood
BEER, P., Furniture Quality and Technology
DOLOWY, K., Physics
DZBENSKI, W., Wood Science
GORSKI, J., Mechanical Processing of Wood
KRAJEWSKI, A., Wood Protection
KRAJEWSKI, J., Wood Protection
KRUTUL, D., Wood Science
NICEWICZ, D., Composite Wood Products
OSIPIUK, J., Mechanization and Automatization
SWACZYNA, I., Construction and Technology of Final Wood Products
ZIELONKA, P., Economics

UNIWERSYTET ARTYSTYCZNY W POZNANIU
(University of Arts in Poznań)

POB 191, ul. Marcinkowskiego 29, 60-967 Poznań 9

Telephone: (61) 8522771
E-mail: office@uap.edu.pl
Internet: uap.edu.pl

Founded 1919, present name and status 2010
State control

Rector: Prof. MARCIN BERDYSZAK
Vice-Rector for Art Affairs: Prof. JACEK JAGIELSKI
Vice-Rector for Int. Programmes and Research Affairs: Prof. ANDRZEJ SYSKA
Vice-Rector for Quality of Education: Prof. Dr Hab. KONSTANCJA PLESKACZYŃSKA

Vice-Rector for Student Affairs: Prof. JACEK ADAMCZAK

Dir for Library: Dr BOGUMIŁA TWARDOSZ

Number of teachers: 220

DEANS

Faculty of Architecture and Design: Prof. BOGUMIŁA JUNG

Faculty of Artistic Education: Dr Hab. JOANNA IMIELSKA

Faculty of Graphics: Prof. KRZYSZTOF KOCHNOWICZ

Faculty of Multimedia Communication: Prof. ANDRZEJ FLORKOWSKI

Faculty of Painting: Prof. ANDRZEJ ZDANOWICZ

Faculty of Sculpture and Performing Art: Prof. Dr Hab. KAROLINA KOMASA

UNIWERSYTET EKONOMICZNY WE WROCŁAWIU
(Wrocław University of Economics)

ul. Komandorska 118/120, 53-345 Wroclaw

Telephone: (71) 3680100

E-mail: kontakt@ue.wroc.pl

Internet: www.ue.wroc.pl

Founded 1947

State control

Academic year: October to June

Chancellor: EDWARD BRATEK

Rector: Prof. Dr Hab. ANDRZEJ GOSPODAROWICZ

Vice-Rector for Devt and Promotion: Prof. Dr Hab. RYSZARD BROL

Vice-Rector for Didactics: Prof. Dr Hab. EDMUND CIBIS

Vice-Rector for Int. Relations: Prof. Dr Hab. BOGUSLAW FIEDOR

Vice-Rector for Science: Prof. Dr Hab. MARIA WANDA KOPERTYNSKA

Dir for Library: BARBARA ZMIGRODZKA

Library of 400,000 vols

Number of teachers: 790

Number of students: 17,000

DEANS

Faculty of Economic Sciences: Prof. Dr Hab. MAREK LYSZCZAK

Faculty of Economics, Management and Tourism: Prof. Dr Hab. MAREK WALESIAK

Faculty of Engineering and Economics: Prof. Dr Hab. ZBIGNIEW GARNCAREK

Faculty of Management, Information Systems and Finance: Prof. Dr Hab. JANUSZ LYKO

UNIWERSYTET EKONOMICZNY W KATOWICACH
(University of Economics in Katowice)

ul. 1 Maja 50, 40-287 Katowice

Telephone: (32) 2577100

E-mail: kancelaria@ue.katowice.pl

Internet: www.ue.katowice.pl

Founded 1937 as College of Social and Economic Sciences, present name and status 2010

Rector: Prof. Dr LESZEK ŻABIŃSKI

Vice-Rector for Education and Int. Cooperation: Prof. Dr WOJCIECH DYDUCH

Vice-Rector for Organizational Affairs, Finance and Devt: Prof. Dr ROBERT TOMANEK

Vice-Rector for Science, Research and Academic Staff Devt: Prof. Dr JANINA HARASIM

Dir for Library: BARBARA ZAJĄCZKOWSKA

Number of teachers: 480

Number of students: 14,000

DEANS

Faculty of Economics: Prof. Dr BARBARA KOS

Faculty of Finance and Insurance: Prof. Dr ANDRZEJ PIOSIK

Faculty of Informatics and Communication: Prof. Dr JERZY GOLUCHOWSKI

Faculty of Management: Prof. Dr KRYSTYNA JĘDRALSKA

UNIWERSYTET EKONOMICZNY W KRAKOWIE
(Cracow University of Economics)

ul. Rakowicka 27, 31-510 Cracow

Telephone: (12) 2935700

E-mail: rektor@uek.krakow.pl

Internet: uek.krakow.pl

Founded 1925, present name and status 2007

State control

Rector: Prof. Dr Hab. ANDRZEJ CHOCHÓŁ

Vice-Rector for Education and Student Affairs: Prof. Dr Hab. KRZYSZTOF SURÓWKA

Vice-Rector for Organization and Devt: Prof. Dr Hab. ANDRZEJ SOKOŁOWSKI

Vice-Rector for Scientific Research: Prof. Dr Hab. ALEKSY POCZTOWSKI

Dir for Library: ELŻBIETA GOLEC-NYCZ

Library of 330,000 vols, 48,000 periodicals

Number of students: 23,000

DEANS

Faculty of Commodity Science: Prof. Dr Hab. STANISLAW HORNIK

Faculty of Economics and International Relations: Prof. Dr Hab. KAZIMIERZ ZIELIŃSKI

Faculty of Finance: Prof. Dr Hab. BOGUMIŁA SZOPA

Faculty of Management: Prof. Dr Hab. PAWEŁ LULA

UNIWERSYTET EKONOMICZNY W POZNANIU
(Poznan University of Economics)

ul. Niepodległości 10, 61-875 Poznań

Telephone: (61) 8569150

E-mail: rektor@ue.poznan.pl

Internet: www.ue.poznan.pl

Founded 1926

Academic year: September to September

Rector: Prof. Dr Hab. MARIAN GORYNIA

Vice-Rector for Education and Students: Prof. Dr Hab. JACEK MIZERKA

Vice-Rector for Research and Int. Relations: Prof. Dr Hab. MACIEJ ŻUKOWSKI

Vice-Rector for Strategy and Devt: Prof. Dr Hab. CEZARY KOCHALSKI

Number of teachers: 500

DEANS

Faculty of Commodity Science: Prof. Dr Hab. RYSZARD ZIELIŃSKI

Faculty of Economics: Prof. Dr Hab. WALDEMAR CZTERNASTY

Faculty of Informatics and Electronic Economy: Prof. Dr Hab. EMIL PANEK

Faculty of International Business and Economics: Prof. Dr Hab. TOMASZ RYNARZEWSKI

Faculty of Management: Prof. Dr Hab. KAZIMIERZ KRZAKIEWICZ

UNIWERSYTET GDAŃSKI
(University of Gdańsk)

ul. Bażyńskiego 1A, 80-952 Gdańsk

Telephone: (58) 5232043

E-mail: rekug@ug.edu.pl

Internet: www.ug.edu.pl

Founded 1970

State control

Academic year: October to June

Rector: Prof. Dr Hab. BERNARD LAMMEK

Pro-Rector for Devt and Financial Affairs: Prof. Dr Hab. MIROSŁAW SZREDER

Pro-Rector for Educational Affairs: Prof. Dr Hab. ANNA MACHNIKOWSKA

Pro-Rector for Scientific Affairs: Prof. Dr Hab. GRZEGORZ WĘGRZYN

Pro-Rector for Student Affairs: Prof. Dr Hab. JÓZEF ARNO WŁODARSKI

Dir for Library: GRAŻYNA JAŚKOWIAK

Library: see under Libraries and Archives

Number of teachers: 1,700

Number of students: 33,000

Publications: *Prace Habilitacyjne, Skrypty, Zeszyty Naukowe*

DEANS

Faculty of Biology: Prof. Dr Hab. DARIUSZ L. SZLACHETKO

Faculty of Chemistry: Prof. Dr Hab. PIOTR STEPNOWSKI

Faculty of Economics: KRZYSZTOF DOBROWOLSKI

Faculty of History: Prof. Dr hab. WIESŁAW DŁUGOKĘCKI

Faculty of Languages: Prof. Dr Hab. ANDRZEJ CEYNOWA

Faculty of Law and Administration: Prof. Dr Hab. JAKUB STELINA

Faculty of Management: Prof. Dr Hab. JERZY BIELIŃSKI

Faculty of Mathematics, Physics and Informatics: Prof. Dr Hab. PIOTR BOJARSKI

Faculty of Oceanography and Geography: Prof. Dr Hab. WALDEMAR SUROSZ

Faculty of Social Sciences: Prof. Dr Hab. BEATA PASTWA-WOJCIECHOWSKA

Intercollegiate Faculty of Biotechnology of University of Gdańsk and Medical University of Gdańsk: Prof. Dr Hab. IGOR KONIECZNY

UNIWERSYTET IM. ADAMA MICKIEWICZA W POZNANIU
(Adam Mickiewicz University in Poznań)

ul. H. Wieniawskiego 1, 61-712 Poznań

Telephone: (61) 8294000

E-mail: rectorof@amu.edu.pl

Internet: www.amu.edu.pl

Founded 1919

State control

Academic year: October to June (2 semesters)

Rector: Prof. Dr Hab. BRONISŁAW MARCINIAK

Vice-Rector for Cooperation with Business Entities and IT Implementation: Prof. Dr Hab. MAREK NAWROCKI

Vice-Rector for Education: Prof. Dr Hab. KRZYSZTOF KRASOWSKI

Vice-Rector for Human Resources and Institutional Devt: Prof. Dr Hab. ANDRZEJ LESICKI

Vice-Rector for Science and Int. Cooperation: Prof. Dr Hab. JACEK WITKOŚ

Vice-Rector for Student Affairs: Prof. Dr Hab. ZBIGNIEW PILARCZYK

Dir for Library: Dr ARTUR JAZDON

Library: see under Libraries and Archives

Number of teachers: 2,800

Number of students: 50,000

DEANS

Faculty of Biology: Prof. Dr Hab. BOGDAN JACKOWIAK

Faculty of Chemistry: Prof. Dr Hab. HENRYK KORONIAK

Faculty of Educational Studies: Prof. Dr Hab. ZBYSZKO MELOSIK

Faculty of English: Prof. Dr Hab. KATARZYNA DZIUBALSKA-KOŁACZYK

Faculty of Geographical and Geological Sciences: Prof. Dr Hab. LESZEK KASPRZAK

Faculty of Historical Studies: Prof. Dr Hab. KAZIMIERZ ILSKI

Faculty of Law and Administration: Prof. Dr Hab. ROMAN BUDZINOWSKI

Faculty of Mathematics and Computer Science: Prof. Dr Hab. JERZY KACZOROWSKI

Faculty of Modern Languages and Literatures: Prof. Dr Hab. TERESA TOMASZKIEWICZ

Faculty of Pedagogy and Fine Arts in Kalisz: Prof. Dr Hab. MIROSŁAW J. SMIAŁEK

Faculty of Physics: Prof. Dr Hab. ANTONI WÓJCIK

Faculty of Polish and Classical Studies: Prof. Dr Hab. BOGUMIŁA KANIEWSKA

Faculty of Political Sciences and Journalism: Prof. Dr Hab. TADEUSZ WALLAS

Faculty of Social Sciences: Prof. Dr Hab. ZBIGNIEW DROZDOWICZ

Faculty of Theology: Prof. Dr Hab. JAN SZPET

PROFESSORS

Faculty of Biology (ul. Umultowska 89, 61-614 Poznań; tel. (61) 8295556; internet www.biologia.amu.edu.pl):

AUGUSTYNIAK, H., Biochemistry
BALCERKIEWICZ, S., Plant Ecology
BEDNORZ, J., Animal Ecology
BIELAWSKI, J., Animal Cytology
BŁASZAK, Cz., Animal Ecology
BOBOWICZ, M., Plant Genetics
BUJAKIEWICZ, A., Mycology
BURCHARDT, L., Hydrobiology
CIEŚLIK, J., Anthropology
GOŹDZICKA-JÓZEFIAK, A., Biochemistry
GWÓŹDŹ, E., Plant Ecophysiology
HRYNIEWIECKA, L., Biochemistry
JACKOWIAK, B., Botany
KRASKA, M., Hydrobiology
KRZAK, M., Plant Genetics
LATOWSKI, K., Plant Taxonomy
LISIEWSKA, M., Mycology
NIEDBAŁA, W., Animal Ecology
PIONTEK, J., Anthropology
PRUS-GŁOWACKI, W., Plant Genetics
RATAJCZAK, L., Plant Physiology
RATAJCZAK, W., Plant Physiology
STĘPCZAK, K., Zoology
STRZAŁKO, J., Anthropology
SZWEYKOWSKA-KULIŃSKA, Z., Biochemistry
WOJTASZEK, P., Biochemistry
WOŹNY, A., Plant Cytology
ŻUKOWSKI, W., Plant Taxonomy

Faculty of Chemistry (ul. Umultowska 89B, 60-614 Poznań; tel. (61) 8291335; internet chemia.amu.edu.pl):

BRZEZIŃSKI, B., Bio-organic Physical Chemistry
BUREWICZ, A., Teaching of Chemistry
DEGA-SZAFRAN, Z., Physical Organic Chemistry
FIEDOROW, R., Catalysis
GAWROŃSKI, J., Organic Chemistry, Stereochemistry
JARCZEWSKI, A., Physical Organic Chemistry
JASKÓLSKI, M., Crystallography and Biological Chemistry
KATRUSIAK, A., Crystallography
KONARSKI, J., Theoretical Chemistry
KOPUT, J., Physical Chemistry
KORONIAK, H., Synthesis and Structure of Organic Compounds
KOWALAK, S., Catalysis
LIS, S., Rare Earth
ŁOMOZIK, L., Coordination Chemistry, Bioinorganic Chemistry
MARCINIAK, B., Photochemistry
MARCINIEC, B., Organometallic Chemistry, Molecular Catalysis
NAWROCKI, J., Water Treatment Technology
PARYZEK, Z., Organic and Natural Products Chemistry
RADECKA-PARYZEK, W., Coordination and Macrocyclic Chemistry, Bioinorganic Chemistry
ROZWADOWSKA, M., Asymmetric Synthesis, Alkaloid Chemistry
RYCHLEWSKA, U., Crystallography
SARBAK, Z., Adsorption and Catalysis, Environmental Protection

SCHROEDER, G., Organic Chemistry
SIEPAK, J., Water and Soil Analysis
SZAFRAN, M., Physical Organic Chemistry
WACHOWSKA, H., Chemistry of Coal
WASIAK, W., Instrumental Analysis
WOJCIECHOWSKA, M., Heterogeneous Catalysis
WOLSKA, E., Solid-state Chemistry and Magnetochemistry
WYRZYKIEWICZ, E., Mass Spectrometry of Organic Compounds
WYSOCKA, W., Natural Products Chemistry
ZIOŁEK, M., Heterogeneous Catalysis

Faculty of Educational Studies (ul. Szamarzewskiego 89, 60-568 Poznań; tel. (61) 8292331; e-mail dziekwse@amu.edu.pl; internet www.wse.amu.edu.pl):

DUDZIKOWA, M., School Education
FRĄCKOWIAK, T., Social Education
GNITECKI, J., Methodology of Education
MELOSIK, Z., Comparative Education
POTULICKA, E., Comparative Education
PRZYSZCZYPKOWSKI, K., Adult Education
SKRZYPCZAK, J., Adult Education
STRYKOWSKI, W., Educational Technology
ZANDECKI, A., Youth Educational Problems
ŻOŁĄDŹ-STRZELCZYK, D., Pedagogy, History of Education

Faculty of Geographical and Geological Sciences (ul. Fredry 10, 61-701 Poznań; tel. (61) 8296011; e-mail dziego@amu.edu.pl):

CHOIŃSKI, J. A., Hydrology
CIERNIEWSKI, J., Remote Sensing
FEDOROWSKI, J., Palaeozoology
GLAZEK, J., Dynamic and Regional Geology
GŁĘBOCKI, B., Economic Geography
GÓRSKI, J., Hydrogeology
KANIECKI, A., Hydrology
KOSTRZEWSKI, A., Dynamic Geomorphology, Geoecology
KOZACKI, L., Integrated Physical Geography
LORENC, S., Geology, Petrography
MUSZYŃSKI, A., Mineralogy, Petrography
NOWACZYK, B., Geomorphology
PARYSEK, J., Socioeconomic Geography
ROGACKI, H., Spatial Management
SKOCZYLAS, J., Petroarchaeology, Archometry
TOBOLSKI, K., Palaeobotany
WOŚ, A., Climatology, Meteorology

Faculty of Historical Studies (ul. Sw. Marcin 78, 61-809 Poznań; tel. (61) 8294701; e-mail dhist@amu.edu.pl; internet wydzial.historyczny.amu.edu.pl):

BŁASZCZYK, G., East European History
BUCHOWSKI, M., European Ethnology, Theory of Anthropology
FOGEL, J., Bronze and Early Iron Age Prehistory
HAUSER, P., Contemporary History
JASIEWICZ, Z., Ethnology of Poland and Central Asia
JASIŃSKI, T., Medieval History
KOŚKO, A., Prehistory of Poland
KOTŁOWSKI, T., Contemporary History
KOWAL, S., Economic History
LABUDA, A., History of Art
ŁAZUGA, W., Modern History
MOLIK, W., Modern Polish History
MROZEWICZ, L., Ancient History
OLEJNIK, K., Military History
OLSZEWSKI, W., Modern and Contemporary History
PIOTROWSKI, P., History of Contemporary Art
POSERN-ZIELIŃSKI, A., Ethnology of the Americas, Anthropology of Ethnicity
SCHRAMM, T., Modern History
SERWAŃSKI, M., Modern History
SIERPOWSKI, S., Contemporary History
SKIBIŃSKI, S., History of Medieval Art
STRZELCZYK, J., Medieval History
WYRWA, A., History

ZAWADZKI, S., Ancient History

Faculty of Law and Administration (ul. Niepodległości 53, 61-714 Poznań; tel. (61) 8293142; e-mail uamprawo@amu.edu.pl; internet prawo.amu.edu.pl):

CHOBOT, A., Labour Law
GOMUŁOWICZ, A., Financial Law
GULCZ, M., Economics
KĘPIŃSKI, M., European Law
KIJOWSKI, A., Labour Law
KOŁECKI, H., Criminal Law
ŁĄCZKOWSKI, W., Financial Law
MAŁECKI, J., Financial Law
NIEDBAŁA, Z., Labour Law
OWOC, M., Criminal Law
PATRYAS, W., Theory of State and Law
SMYCZYŃSKI, T., Civil Law
SOŁTYSIŃSKI, S., Civil Law
STACHOWIAK, S., Criminal Procedure
SZWARC, A. J., Criminal Law
TYRANOWSKI, J., International Law
WRONKOWSKA-JAŚKIEWICZ, S., Theory of State and Law
ZEDLER, F., Civil Procedure

Faculty of Mathematics and Computer Science (ul. Umultowska 87, 61-614 Poznań; tel. (61) 8295313; e-mail wmiuam@amu.edu.pl; internet web.wmi.amu.edu.pl):

BATÓG, T., Mathematical Logic, Mathematical Linguistics
BUSZKOWSKI, W., Logic, Linguistics, Computation Theory
DOMAŃSKI, P., Functional Analysis
DREWNOWSKI, L., Functional Analysis
HUDZIK, H., Functional Analysis
KACZOROWSKI, J., Number Theory
KĄKOL, J., Functional Analysis, Topology
KAROŃSKI, M., Discrete Mathematics and Probability
KRZYŚKO, M., Mathematical Statistics
KUBIACZYK, I., Mathematics
ŁUCZAK, T., Discrete Mathematics and Probability
MARZANTOWICZ, W., Mathematics
MASTYŁO, M., Functional Analysis
MURAWSKI, R., Mathematical Logic, Philosophy of Mathematics
PYCH-TABERSKA, P., Approximation Theory
RUCIŃSKI, A., Discrete Mathematics and Probability
SZUFLA, ST., Differential Equations
WASZAK, A., Functional Analysis

Faculty of Modern Languages and Literature (ul. Niepodległości 4, 61-874 Poznań; tel. (61) 8293500; e-mail dziekneo@amu.edu.pl; internet neo.amu.edu.pl):

ANDRUSZKO, Cz., Russian Literature
BAŃCZEROWSKI, J., General Linguistics
DARSKI, J., German Linguistics
DZIUBALSKA-KOŁACZYK, K., English Linguistics
FISIAK, J., English Linguistics
GUSSMANN, E., English Linguistics
KALISZAN, J., Russian Linguistics
KAROLAK, Cz., German Literature
KASZYŃSKI, S., Austrian Literature and Culture
KOPCEWICZ, A., American Literature
KOPYTKO, R., English Linguistics
KRYSZTOFIAK-KASZYŃSKA, M., Danish Literature
ŁABĘDZKA, I., Romance Literature
LIPOŃSKI, W., Anglo-Saxon Studies
ŁOBACZ, P., General Linguistics
MAJEWICZ, A., Oriental Linguistics
MALINOWSKI, W., Romance Literature
MARKUNAS, A., Methodology of Russian Language Teaching
ORŁOWSKI, H., German Literature
PAPIÓR, J., German Literature and Culture
PFEIFFER, W., Applied Linguistics
PIOTROWSKI, B., History of Scandinavia
POGONOWSKI, J., Mathematical Linguistics
PUPPEL, S., English Linguistics

SCHATTE, CH., German Linguistics
SIEK-PISKOZUB, T., English Linguistics
SIKORSKA, L., English Literature
SOBKOWIAK, W., English Linguistics
STEFFEN-BATOGOWA, M., General Linguistics
SYPNICKI, J., Romance Linguistics
TOMASZKIEWICZ, T., Romance Linguistics
WĄSIK, Z., General Linguistics
WILCZYŃSKA, W., Applied Linguistics
WÓJTOWICZ, M., Russian Linguistics
ZGÓŁKA, T., General Linguistics

Faculty of Pedagogy and Fine Arts in Kalisz (ul. Nowy Świat 28-30, 62-800 Kalisz; tel. (62) 7670730; e-mail wpa@amu.edu.pl; internet www.wpa.amu.edu.pl):

JANKOWSKI, D., Education
NAWROT, A., Fine Arts
NIEKRASZ, A., Methodology of Art
WERNER, B., Music Arts

Faculty of Physics (ul. Umultowska 85, 61-614 Poznań; tel. (61) 8295202; e-mail fizyka@amu.edu.pl; internet www.fizyka.amu.edu.pl):

BARNAS, J., Solid-state Physics
BŁASZAK, M., Mathematical Physics
BŁASZCZAK, Z., Molecular Optics
DOBEK, A., Biophysics
HOJAN, E., Electroacoustics
JACYNA-ONYSZKIEWICZ, Z., Quantum Physics
JURGA, K., Radiospectroscopy
JURGA, S., Radiospectroscopy and Molecular Physics
KAMIENIARZ, G., Computer Physics
KOZIEROWSKI, M., Nonlinear Optics
KURZYŃSKI, M., Statistical Physics
ŁABOWSKI, M., Molecular Acoustics
MAKAREWICZ, R., Environmental Acoustics
MICNAS, R., Solid-state Physics
MRÓZ, B., Ferroelectrics
NAWROCIK, W., Physics
OZIMEK, E., Psychoacoustics
PARZYŃSKI, R., Quantum Electronics
PATKOWSKI, A., Molecular Biophysics
PUSZKARSKI, H., Solid-state Physics
ROBASZKIEWICZ, S., Solid-state Physics
SCHWARZENBERG-CZERNY, A., Astronomy
SLIWIŃSKA-BARTKOWIAK, M., Physics
STANKOWSKA, J., Molecular Physics
TANAŚ, R., Nonlinear Optics
WĄSICKI, J., Physics
WNUK, E., Astronomy

Faculty of Polish and Classical Studies (ul. A. Fredry 10, 61-701 Poznań; tel. (61) 8293642; e-mail dziewfpk@amu.edu.pl; internet wfpik.amu.edu.pl):

ABRAMOWSKA, J., Polish Literature, Historical Poetics
ADAMCZYK, M., Old Polish Literature
BĄBA, S., Idioms and Culture of Polish Language
BAKUŁA, B., 20th-century Literature
BALCERZAN, E., Polish Literature, Theory of Literature and 20th-century Literature
BARTOL, K., Classical Philology
BOREJSZO, M., Polish Linguistics
CHRZĄSTOWSKA, B., New Teaching Methods, History of Polish Literature
CZAPLIŃSKI, P., Theory of Literature, Literary Criticism
DANIELEWICZ, J., Hellenistic Philology
DWORACKI, S., Hellenistic Philology
HENDRYKOWSKA, M., Film History and Theory
KRĄŻYŃSKA, Z., Polish Linguistics
LEGEŻYŃSKA, A., Theory of Literature
LEWANDOWSKI, I., Latin Philology
LEWANDOWSKI, T., Polish Literature
NOWAK, H., Polish Dialectology
POKRZYWNIAK, J. T., Old Polish Literature
PRZYBYLSKI, R. K., Theory of Literature, History of Literature
RATAJCZAK, D., Polish Drama

RZEPKA, W., Polish Linguistics
SMUSZKIEWICZ, A., Teaching of Polish Language and Literature
TROJANOWICZ, Z., 19th-century Polish Literature
WALCZAK, B., Polish Linguistics
WIEGANDT, E., History of Contemporary Literature
WYDRA, W., Editorial and Bibliography
WYSŁOUCH, S., Polish Literature, Theory of Literature and 20th-century Literature
ZGÓŁKA, T., General Linguistics
ZGÓŁKOWA, H., Polish Linguistics

Faculty of Social Sciences (ul. Szamarzewskiego 89, 60-568 Poznań; tel. (61) 8292100; e-mail socuam@amu.edu.pl; internet www.wns.amu.edu.pl):

ANDRZEJEWSKI, B., History of German Philosophy
BRZEZIŃSKA, A., Development
BRZEZIŃSKI, J., Methodology of Psychology
BUKSIŃSKI, T., Social Philosophy, Philosophy of History
CHYŁA, W., Culture
DROZDOWICZ, Z., Philosophy of Religion
GOLKA, M., Sociology of Culture, Social Anthropology
JAMROZIAKOWA, A., Aesthetics
KOSMAN, M., History
KOSMANOWA, B., History of Science
KOSZEL, B., History and Political Science
MALENDOWSKI, W., Political Science
NOWAK, L., Philosophy of Science, Political Philosophy
NOWAKOWA, I., Philosophy of Science
ORCZYK, J., Economics and History
PAŁUBICKA, A., Theory of Culture
PUŚLECKI, Z., International Economic Relations
SAKSON, A., Sociology of Ethnic Minorities, Sociology of Youth
SĘK, H., Health and Clinical Psychology
SOBCZAK, J., Law
STACHOWSKI, R., History of Psychological Thought
TITTENBRUN, J., Theory and Practice of Privatization
WOŹNIAK, Z., Sociology of Medicine
ZAMIARA, T., Philosophy of Science
ZIÓŁKOWSKI, M., Sociological Theory

Faculty of Theology (ul. Wieżowa 2–4, 61-111 Poznań; tel. (61) 8293990; e-mail thfac@man.poznan.pl):

BRANIAK, J., Sociology
CZESZ, B., Theology, Patristic Theology
LEWEK, A., Theology, Religious Communication
NIPARKO, R., Christian Pedagogy
PONIŻY, B., Theology, Old Testament Exegisis
PYTEL, J., Theology, New Testament Exegisis
STEFAŃSKI, J., Theology
SZPET, J., Theology, Religious Education
TARNOWSKI, K., Philosophy
WĘCŁAWSKI, T., Theology, Fundamental Theology
WEJMAN, H., Theology of Spirituality

UNIWERSYTET JAGIELLOŃSKI W KRAKOWIE
(Jagiellonian University in Crakow)

ul. Gołębia 24, 31-007 Kraków
Telephone: (12) 4221033
E-mail: rektor@uj.edu.pl
Internet: www.uj.edu.pl
Founded 1364
State control
Academic year: October to September (2 semesters)

Chancellor: Mgr EWA PĘDRACKA-KWASKOWSKA (acting)
Rector: Prof. Dr Hab. WOJCIECH NOWAK

Vice-Rector for Educational Affairs: Prof. Dr Hab. ANDRZEJ MANIA
Vice-Rector for Human Resources and Financial Management: Prof. Dr Hab. JACEK POPIEL
Vice-Rector for Medical College: Prof. Dr Hab. PIOTR LAIDLER
Vice-Rector for Research and Structural Funds: Prof. Dr Hab. STANISŁAW KISTRYN
Vice-Rector for Univ. Development: Prof. Dr Hab. MARIA-JOLANTA FLIS
Dir for Library: Prof. Dr ZDZISŁAW PIETRZYK
Library: see under Libraries and Archives
Number of teachers: 3,800
Number of students: 51,610

Publications: *Acta Physica Polonica B* (12 a year), *Ad Americam* (1 a year), *Alma Mater* (12 a year), *Biuletyn Biblioteki Jagiellońskiej* (1 a year), *Cracow Indological Studies* (irregular), *Estetyka i Krytyka* (4 a year), *Eurasian Prehistory* (2 a year), *Forum Europejskie* (4 a year), *Foton* (4 a year), *Kronika* (1 a year), *Kwartalnik Religioznawczy NOMOS* (4 a year), *Management in Culture* (2 a year), *Materiały Edukacyjne Bibliotekoznawstwa i Informacji Naukowej* (1 a year), *MODUS Prace z Historii Sztuki* (1 a year), *Nowy Filomata* (4 a year), *Peregrinus Cracoviensis* (irregular), *Politea* (1 a year), *Prace Archeologiczne* (irregular), *Prace Archeologiczne—Studies in Ancient Art and Civilization* (irregular), *Prace Geograficzne* (irregular), *Prace Historyczne* (1 a year), *Principia* (2 a year), *Przekładaniec* (literary translation, 2 a year), *Recherches Archéologiques* (irregular), *Reports on Mathematical Logic* (1 a year), *Reports on Philosophy* (1 a year), *Romanica Cracoviensia* (1 a year), *Schedae Informaticae, Studia z zakresu Prawa Pracy i Polityki Społecznej* (1 a year), *Universitatis Jagellonicae Acta Mathematica* (1 a year), *Zeszyty Naukowe Uniwersytetu Jagiellońskiego* (1 a year in 26 series), *Zeszyty Prasoznawcze* (4 a year), *Zmieniające się przedsiębiorstwo w zmieniającej się politycznie Europie* (1 a year)

DEANS

Faculty of Biology and Earth Sciences: Dr Hab. MAŁGORZATA KRUCZEK
Faculty of Biochemistry, Biophysics and Biotechnology: Prof. Dr Hab. WOJCIECH FRONCISZ
Faculty of Chemistry: Prof. Dr Hab. GRAŻYNA STOCHEL
Faculty of Health Sciences: Prof. Dr Hab. TOMASZ BRZOSTEK
Faculty of History: Prof. Dr Hab. JAN ŚWIĘCH
Faculty of International and Political Studies: Prof. Dr Hab. BOGDAN SZLACHTA
Faculty of Law and Administration: Prof. Dr Hab. KRYSTYNA CHOJNICKA
Faculty of Management and Social Communication: Prof. Dr Hab. JACEK OSTASZEWSKI
Faculty of Mathematics and Computer Science: Prof. Dr Hab. ARMEN EDIGARIAN
Faculty of Medicine: Prof. Dr Hab. TOMASZ GRODZICKI
Faculty of Pharmacy: Prof. Dr Hab. JAN KRZEK
Faculty of Philology: Prof. Dr Hab. ELŻBIETA GÓRSKA
Faculty of Philosophy: Prof. Dr Hab. JAROSŁAW GÓRNIAK
Faculty of Physics, Astronomy and Applied Computer Science: Prof. Dr Hab. ANDRZEJ WARCZAK
Faculty of Polish Studies: Prof. Dr Hab. RENATA PRZYBYLSKA

PROFESSORS

Faculty of Biology and Earth Sciences (ul. Gronostajowa 7, 30-387 Kraków; tel. (12)

6646755; e-mail binoz@adm.uj.edu.pl; internet www.binoz.uj.edu.pl):

BILIŃSKA, B., Animal Physiology
BILIŃSKI, SZ., Cell Biology
BOBEK, B., Wildlife Research
CHEŁMICKI, W., Geography
DĄBROWSKI, Z., Animal Physiology
DOMANSKI, B., Geography
DZWONKO, Z., Plant Ecology
FALNIOWSKI, A., Malacology
GÓRECKI, A., Ecology
GREGORASZCZUK, E., Animal Physiology
GUZIK, CZ., Population and Agricultural Geography
JACKOWSKI, A., Geography of Religion
KACZANOWSKI, K., Anthropology
KOZŁOWSKI, J., Hydrobiology
KRZEMIEŃ, K., Geomorphology
KUTA, E., Cytology and Embryology of Plants
LASKOWSKI, R., Ecology
LITYŃSKA, A., Glycobiology
ŁOMNICKI, A., Population Ecology
MARCHLEWSKA-KOJ, A., Mammalian Reproduction
MORYCOWA, E., Palaeozoology
MYDEL, R., Geographical Studies on Japan
OBRĘBSKA-STARKEL, B., Climatology
OLECH, M., Plant Taxonomy
OSZCZYPKO, N., Geology
PETRYSZAK, B., Systematic Zoology and Zoological Geography
PŁYTYCZ, B., Evolutionary Immunology
PRZYWARA, L., Plant Cytology and Embryology
RADOMSKI, A., Geology
RAFIŃSKI, J., Evolutionary Biology
SAWICKA-KAPUSTA, K., Ecology, Environmental Protection
SKIBA, S., Soil Geography and Pedology
SLĄCZKA, A., Tectonics and Stratigraphy
SZOŁTYS, M., Zoology
SZYMURA, J. M., Zoology
TRZCIŃSKA-TACIK, H., Botany
TURNAU, K., Plant Taxonomy and Phytogeography
UCHMAN, A., Geology, Sedimentology, Ichnology
WEINER, J., Ecological Bioenergetics and Evolutionary Ecosystems
WIDACKI, W., Geography
WOJTUSIAK, J., Zoology
WOYCIECHOWSKI, M., Ecology and Evolution
ŻABIŃSKI, W., Geology
ZAJĄC, A., Plant Taxonomy and Phytogeography
ZAJĄC, M., Phytogeography
ZEMANEK, A., Botany
ZEMANEK, B., Phytogeography
ZUCHIEWICZ, W., Geology

Faculty of Biochemistry, Biophysics and Biotechnology (ul. Gronostajowa 7, 30-387 Kraków; tel. (12) 6646002; e-mail sekretariat.wbbib@uj.edu.pl; internet www.wbbib.uj.edu.pl):

DUBIN, A., Biochemistry
FRONCISZ, W., Biophysics
GABRYŚ, H., Plant Physiology
KLEIN, A., Biochemistry
KOJ, A., Biochemistry
KOROHODA, WŁ., Cell Biology
ŁUKIEWICZ, S., Biophysics
PASENKIEWICZ-GIERULA, M., Molecular Biophysics
POTEMPA, J., Biochemistry, Biotechnology
PRYJMA, J., Microbiology and Immunology
SARNA, T., Biophysics
STRZAŁKA, K., Biochemistry
WASYLEWSKI, Z., Physical Biochemistry
WIĘCKOWSKI, S., Plant Physiology
ŻAK, Z., Animal Biochemistry

Faculty of Chemistry (ul. Ingardena 3, 30-060 Kraków; tel. (12) 6332277; e-mail sekretar@chemia.uj.edu.pl; internet www.chemia.uj.edu.pl):

BARAŃSKI, A., Chemical Kinetics
BOGDANOWICZ-SZWED, K., Chemistry of Heterocyclic Compounds
DATKA, J., Inorganic Chemistry and Infrared Spectroscopy
DZIEMBAJ, R., Catalysis, Solid-State Chemistry and Technology
HODOROWICZ, S. A., Crystallography and Solid-State Chemistry
JUSZKIEWICZ, A., Physical and Environmental Chemistry
KOŚCIELNIAK, P., Analytical and Forensic Chemistry
NAJBAR, J., Physical Chemistry, Photophysics and Photochemistry
NAJBAR, M., Inorganic and Environmental Catalysis
NALEWAJSKI, R. F., Theoretical Chemistry, Quantum Chemistry
NOWAKOWSKA, M., Physical Chemistry, Photochemistry of Polymers
OLEKSYN, B., Crystallography and Crystal Chemistry
PALUCH, M., Physical Chemistry, Surface Chemistry
PARCZEWSKI, A., Chemometrics and Analytical Chemistry
PAWLIKOWSKI, M., Theoretical Chemistry, Molecular Spectroscopy
PETELENZ, P., Theoretical Chemistry
PRONIEWICZ, L.M., Chemical Physics, Molecular Spectroscopy
SILBERRING, J., Biochemistry and Neurochemistry
STASICKA, Z., Inorganic and Coordination Chemistry
STOCHEL, G., Inorganic and Bioinorganic Chemistry
WÓJCIK, M., Physical Chemistry, Molecular Spectroscopy

Faculty of Health Sciences (ul. Michałowskiego 12, 31-126 Kraków; tel. (12) 4214141; e-mail wnz@cm-uj.krakow.pl; internet www.woz.cm-uj.krakow.pl):

CZABAŁA, J., Psychology
GOLINOWSKA, S., Health Economics
HAŁUSZKA, J., Environmental Health
PILC, A., Pharmacology
SPODARYK, K., Physiotherapy
SZAFRAN, Z., Biochemistry
WŁODARCZYK, W., Health Policy

Faculty of History (ul. Gołębia 24, 31-007 Kraków; tel. (12) 6336377; e-mail historia@adm.uj.edu.pl; internet jazon.hist.uj.edu.pl):

BACZKOWSKI, K., General Medieval History
BAŁUS, K., History of Late Modern Art
BRZOZA, CZ., Modern Polish History
CENTAROWICZ, A., General Modern History
CHOCHOROWSKI, J., Archaeology
CHWALBA, A., Documentation of Polish Independence Movements
CIAŁOWICZ, K, Archaeology
DĄBROWA, E., Ancient History
DYBIEC, J., History of Science and Culture
DZIELSKA, M., Byzantine History
FABIAŃSKI, M., History of Modern Art
GĄSOWSKI, T., Polish Modern History
GEDL, M., Archaeology
GINTER, B., Archaeology
GRYGLEWICZ, T., History of Contemporary Art
JARZĘBSKA, A., 20th-century Polish History
KACZANOWSKI, P., Archaeology
KOZŁOWSKI, J., Archaeology
MAŁKIEWICZA, A., History of Modern Art
MICHALEWICZ, A., Economic and Social History
OSTROWSKI, JAN, History of Art
OSTROWSKI, JANUSZ, Classical Archaeology
PAJA-STACH, J., Contemporary Polish Music
PAPUCI-WŁADYKA, E., Archaeology

PARCZEWSKI, M., Polish and Modern Archaeology
PIROŻYŃSKI, J., General Modern History
QUIRINI-POPŁAWSKA, D., Medieval History
ROBOTYCKI, CZ., Polish Ethnography, Anthropology of Culture
ROJEK, W., General Modern History
ŚLIWA, J., Mediterranean Archaeology
ŚNIEŻYŃSKA-STOLOT, E., History of Ideas
SZCZUR, S., Medieval History

Faculty of International and Political Studies (ul. Gołębia 24, 31-007 Kraków; tel. (12) 6631565; e-mail wsmip@adm.uj.edu.pl; internet www.wsmip.uj.edu.pl):

BABIŃSKI, G., Sociology of Interethnic Relationships
CZIOMER, E., International Relations
FLORKOWSKA-FRANCIĆ, H., History of International Migration Movements
KAPISZEWSKI, A., Middle East Studies
KOZUB-CIEMBRONIEWICZ, M., Modern Political Movements and Political Thought
MACH, Z., Anthropology
MAJCHROWSKI, J. M., Recent Political History of Poland, History of Political and Legal Doctrines, Religious Policy
MANIA, A., World History of the 20th Century
MIODUNKA, W., Applied Linguistics in Polish Language Teaching
PURCHLA, J., Economic History and History of Art
RAŹNY, A., East Slavonic Philology
STAWOWY-KAWKA, I., History of Balkan Countries
SUCHANEK, L., Russian and Soviet Literature
WALASZEK, A., History of International Migration Movements
ZIĘBA, A., Constitutional Law
ZYBLIKIEWICZ, L., International Relations

Faculty of Law and Administration (ul. Gołębia 24, 31-007 Kraków; tel. (12) 4223742; e-mail prawo@adm.uj.edu.pl; internet www.law.uj.edu.pl):

BARAN, KA., General Legal History
BARAN, KRZ., Labour Law
BIERNAT, S., European Law
BŁACHUT, J., Criminology
BRZEZIŃSKI, B., Financial Law
CHOJNICKA, K., History of Political and Legal Thought
ĆWIĄKALSKI, K., Criminal Law
CZAJOWKI, J., Modern Political Systems
DROZD, E., Civil Law, Private International Law
GABERLE, A., Criminology
GAWLIK, B., Civil Law
GIZBERT-STUDNICKI, T., Theory and Philosophy of Law
GRZYBOWSKI, M., Modern Political Systems
HOFMAŃSKI, P., Criminal Procedure
HOŁDA, Z., Sentencing and Penal Procedure
JASKÓLSKI, M., History of Political and Legal Thought
KISIEL, W., Territorial Self-Government
KRAJEWSKLI, K., Criminology
KUBAS, A., Civil Law
LANKOSZ, K., International Public Law
LICHOROWICZ, A., Agricultural Law
MĄCZYŃSKI, A., Civil and International Private Law
MALEC, J., History of Administration
PAŁECKI, K., Theory and Sociology of Law
PLESZKA, K., Theory and Philosophy of Law
PREUSSNER-ZAMORSKA, J., Civil Law
PYZIOŁ, W., Private Business Law
SARKOWICZ, R., Theory and Philosophy of Law
SARNECKI, P., Constitutional Law
SONDEL, J., Roman Law
STEC, M., Private Business Law
STELMACH, J., Theory and Philosophy of Law

ŚWIĄTKOWSKI, A., Labour Law
SZEWCZYK, M., Criminal Law
SZUMAŃSKI, A., International Business Law
TRAPLE, E., Civil Law
URUSZCZAK, W., History of Ecclesiastical Law
WAGNER, B., Labour Law
WALASZEK-PYZIOŁ, A., Public Business Law
WASILEWSKI, A., Environmental Protection Law
WŁUDYKA, T., Economic Policy
WOJCIKIEWICZ, J., Forensic and Police Science
WOŚ, T., Administration Law, Administration Procedures Law
ZAWADA, K., Civil Law and International Private Law
ZIMMERMAN, J., Administrative Procedures
ZOLL, A., Criminal Law

Faculty of Management and Social Communication (ul. Prof. Stanisława Łojasiewicza 4, 30-348 Kraków; tel. (12) 6645507; e-mail orzech@adm.uj.edu.pl; internet www.wzks.uj.edu.pl):

BAŃKA, A., Organizational Psychology
BARTA, J., Copyright Law, Press Law and Information Law
BEDNARCZYK, M., Tourism Management
BOBROWSKI, J., Linguistics, Communication
GOBAN-KLAS, T., Theory of Mass Communication, Public Relations
GODZIC, W., Media and Film Studies
HELMAN, A., Film Studies
LASKOWSKI, R., Linguistics, Slavic Language and Social Communication
LIBERSKA, B., International Economics
LUBASZEWSKI, W., Electrical Transformation of Information
LUBELSKI, T., Film Studies
MAREK, T., Psychology of Work, Organization and Management
MARKIEWICZ, R., Copyright Law, Information Law and Industrial Property Law
MATCZEWSKI, A., Industrial Management
NĘCKI, Z., Social Psychology
OKOŃ-HORODYŃSKA, E., Economics, Management
ORZECHOWSKI, E., Arts Management, History of Theatre
PISAREK, W., Media Research, Social Linguistics
PLEŚNIAROWICZ, K., Arts Management, Performance Theory
PRZEWŁOCKI, R., Medical Science, Neuroscience, Pharmacology
SOWA, K., Management of Higher Education, Sociology
STACHÓWNA, G., Film Studies
STĘPNIEWSKI, J., Accounting, Auditing, Operational Management
SURDYKOWSKA, S., International Accounting and Corporate Finance, Management, Accounting, Comparative Economic Systems
SZUMPICH, S., Management, Accounting, Comparative Economic Systems
SZWAJA, J., Civil and Commercial Law, Industrial Property Law
WIDACKI, J., Criminal Law, Management of Public Security
WILK, E., Media and Film Studies
WITKOWSKI, L., Philosophy, Theory of Arts and Education
WOJCIECHOWSKI, J., Communication and Librarianship

Faculty of Mathematics and Computer Science (ul. Prof. Stanisława Łojasiewicza 6, 30-348 Kraków; tel. (12) 6646629; e-mail matinf@uj.edu.pl; internet www.matinf.uj.edu.pl):

DENKOWSKI, Z., Optimization and Control Theory
DRUŻKOWSKI, L. M., Analytic and Algebraic Geology

FLASIŃSKI, M., Artificial Intelligence Systems
GANCARZEWICZ, J., Differential Geometry
IDZIAK, P. M, Foundations of Computer Science
JARNICKI, M., Complex Analysis
MROZEK, M., Numerical Methods
OMBACH, J., Dynamical Systems
OPOZDA, B., Differential Geometry
PAWŁUCKI, W., Singularity Theory
PELCZAR, A., Analysis, Differential Equations
PLEŚNIAK, W., Complex Analysis, Theory of Approximations
RUSEK, K., Algebraic Geometry
SĘDZIWY, S., Numerical Methods
SICIAK, J., Complex Analysis
SRZEDNICKI, R., Differential Equations
STOCHEL, J., Functional Analysis, Theory of Operators
SZAFIRSKI, B., Differential Equations, Theory of Turbulence
SZAFRANIEC, F. H., Functional Analysis, Theory of Operators
TWOREWSKI, P., Analytical and Algebraic Geometry
WINIARSKI, T., Analytical and Algebraic Geometry

Faculty of Medicine (ul. Św. Anny 12, 31-008 Kraków; tel. (12) 4225414; e-mail dziekwl@cm-uj.krakow.pl; internet www.wl.cm-uj.krakow.pl):

ADAMEK-GUZIK, T., Internal Medicine
ALEKSANDROWICZ, J., Psychotherapy, Psychiatry
ANDRES, J., Anaesthesiology
BASTA, A., Gynaecology and Oncology
BOGDAŁ, J., Gastroenterology, Internal Medicine
BOGDASZEWSKA-CZABANOWSKA, J., Dermatology
BOMBA, J., Psychiatry
BRZOZOWSKI, T., Physiology
CICHOCKI, T., Histology
DEMBIŃSKA-KIEĆ, A., Clinical Biochemistry
DEMBIŃSKI, A., Physiology
DOBROWOLSKI, Z., Urology
DUBIEL, J. S., Cardiology
GIEROWSKI, J., Psychiatry
GRODZIŃSKA, L., Pharmacology
HECZKO, P., Microbiology
KACIŃSKI, M., Neurology
KARCZ, D., Surgery
KAWECKA-JASZCZ, K., Cardiology
KLIMEK, R., Gynaecology, Obstetrics
KONIECZNY, L., Biochemistry
KORBUT, R., Pharmacology
KULIG, J., Surgery
LAUTERBACH, R., Paediatrics
LITWIN, J., Histology
MAJEWSKI, S., Dental Prosthetics
MALEC, E., Paediatric Cardiac Surgery
MARCINKIEWICZ, J., Immunology
MIODOŃSKI, A., Laryngology
MIRECKA, J., Histology
MUSIAŁ, J., Internal Medicine
NASKALSKI, J., Clinical Biochemistry
NIŻANKOWSKA-MOGILNICKA, E., Pulmonology
OBTUŁOWICZ, K., Internal Medicine
PACH, J., Toxicology
PAWLĘGA, J., Oncology
PAWLICKI, R., Histology
PAWLIK, W., Physiology
PIETRZYK, J., Paediatrics
PIWOWARSKA, W., Cardiology
POPIELA, T., Gastroenterological Surgery
RATAJCZAK, M., Transplantology
RERON, E., Laryngology
ROKITA, E., Medical Physics
RYN, Z., Psychiatry
SIERADZKI, J., Metabolic Diseases
SKŁADZIEŃ, J., Otolaryngology
SKOTNICKI, A., Haematology
SŁADEK, K., Internal Medicine

STACHURA, J., Pathomorphology
STARZYCKA, M., Ophthalmology
SUŁOWICZ, W., Nephrology
SZCZEKLIK, A., Internal Medicine
THOR, P., Physiopathology
TOBIASZ-ADAMCZYK, B., Epidemiology and Preventive Medicine
TRACZ, W., Cardiology
WYSOCKI, A., Surgery
ZARZYCKI, D., Orthopaedics
ZEMBALA, M., Microbiology, Immunology
ZIĘBA, A., Psychiatry

Faculty of Pharmacy (ul. Medyczna 9, 30-688 Kraków; tel. (12) 6205414; e-mail dziekanat@farmacja.cm-uj.krakow.pl; internet www.farmacja.cm-uj.krakow.pl):

BOJARSKI, J., Organic Chemistry
BRANDYS, J., Toxicology
BUDAK, A., Pharmaceutical Microbiology
CZARNECKI, R., Pharmacodynamics
JAŚKIEWICZ, J., Biochemical Analysis
KIEĆ-KONOWICZ, K., Chemical Technology of Drugs
PAWŁOWSKI, M., Pharmaceutical Chemistry
RZESZUTKO, W., Inorganic Chemistry
STAREK, A., Biochemical Toxicology
SZYMURA-OLEKSIAK, J., Pharmacokinetics
ZACHWIEJA, Z., Food Chemistry, Nutrition
ZIEJA, A., Pharmaceutical Chemistry

Faculty of Philology (ul. Gołębia 24, 31-007 Kraków; tel. (12) 6631158; e-mail filolog@adm.uj.edu.pl; internet www.filg.uj.edu.pl):

BALBUS, S., Theory of Literature
BOCHENEK-FRANCZAKOWA, R., French Literature
BOROWSKI, A., Polish Philology
BORYŚ, W., Comparative and Historical Slavic Etymology, Serbo-Croatian Linguistics
BRZEZINA, M., Linguistics
BUJNICKI, T., History of Polish Literature
DUNAJ, B., Linguistics
FIUT, A., Polish Philology
GIBIŃSKA-MARZEC, M., English Literature
HOMBEK, D., Polish Philology
JARZĘBSKI, J., History of Polish Literature
JAWORSKI, S., History of Polish Literature
KAPUŚCIK, J., Russian Literature and History
KŁAŃSKA, M., German Philology
KORNHAUSER, J., Slavonic Philology
KORPANTY, J., Classical Philology
KORUS, K., Classical Philology
KORYTOWSKA, M., Comparative Literature
KOWALIKOWA, J., Methodology of Teaching Polish Literature
KULAWIK, A., Theory of Literature
KUREK, H., Polish Philology
LABOCHA, J., Polish Philology
LIPIŃSKI, K., German Philology, History of German Literature, Translation
MAŃCZAK-WOHLFELD, E., English Linguistics
MARKOWSKI, M., History of Polish Literature
MELANOWICZ, M., Japanese Literature
MICHALAK-PIKULSKA, B., Arabic Literature
MICHALIK, J., Theatre Studies
MIODOŃSKA-BROOKES, E., Polish Philology
MUSKAT-TABAKOWSKA, E., Cognitive Linguistics and Theory of Translation
NAUMOW, A., Slavonic Philology
NYCZ, R., Polish Philology
PISOWICZ, A., Iranian and Armenian Linguistics
PRZEBINDA, G., Russian Literature and History, Ukrainian Culture and History
SKARŻYŃSKI, M., Polish Philosophy
ŚLIWIŃSKI, W., Polish Philology
SMOCZYŃSKI, W., General and Indo-European Linguistics
STABRYŁA, S., Classical Philology
STACHOWSKI, M., Turkic and Altaic Linguistics
STALA, M., History of Polish Literature

STYKA, J., Classical Philology
ŚUGIERA, M., Theatre Studies
ŚWIĄTKOWSKA, M., Romance Philology
SZCZUKIN, W., Russian Literature, Culture and History, Theory of Literature
SZTURC, W., Comparative Literature
WALECKI, W., History of Polish Literature
WIDŁAK, S., Romance Philology
WŁODARSKI, M., History of Polish Literature
WRÓBEL, H., Polish and Czech Philology
WYKA, M., History of Polish Literature
ZABORSKI, A., Chamito-Semitic Linguistics
ZAJADA, A., Polish Philology
ZARĘBIANKA, Z., History of Polish Language
ZIEJKA, F., History of Polish Philology

Faculty of Philosophy (ul. Gołębia 24, 31-007 Kraków; tel. (12) 4221136; e-mail filozof@adm.uj.edu.pl; internet www.phils.uj.edu.pl):

ALEKSANDER, T., Adult Education
DRABINA, J., History of Christianity
FLIS, A., Sociology of Culture
FLIS, M., Sociology of Culture, Anthropology
FRYSZTACKI, K., Sociology
GALEWICZ, W., Philosophy
GORLACH, K., Sociology
GROTT, B., Religious Studies
GRYZMAŁA-MOSZCZYŃSKA, H., Psychology of Religion
KOCIK, L., Sociology
KUBIAK, H., Sociology of Politics
LEGUTKO, R., Political Philosophy
LIPIEC, J., Philosophy
MIKLASZEWSKA, J., Philosophy
NÉCKA, E., Psychology
OCHMANN, J., Religious Studies
PACZKOWSKA-ŁAGOWSKA, E., Philosophy
PALKA, S., Methodological Elements of Education
PALUCH, A., Sociology
PERZANOWSKI, J., Philosophy and Logic
PIĄTEK, Z., Philosophy of Natural Sciences
PILECKA, W., Psychology
RODZIŃSKI, S., Pedagogy
SKOCZYŃSKI, J., Philosophy
SLANY, K., Sociology
STRÓŻEWSKI, W., Philosophy, Ontology
SUCHOŃ, W., Philosophy
SZTOMPKA, P., Sociological Theory
SZYMAŃSKA-ALEKSANDROWICZ, B., Philosophy
SZYMAŃSKI, M., Pedagogy, Sociology
URBAN, B., Pedagogy
WILKOSZEWSKA, K., Philosophy of Aesthetics
WOLEŃSKI, J., Philosophy, Epistemology
WROŃSKI, A., Logic and Philosophy

Faculty of Physics, Astronomy and Applied Computer Science (ul. Reymonta 4, 30-059 Kraków; tel. (12) 6635890; e-mail wydzial.fais@uj.edu.pl; internet www.fais.uj.edu.pl):

ARODŹ, H., Field Theory
BAŁANDA, A., Nuclear Physics
BARA, J., Nuclear Physics
BIAŁAS, A., Theory of Elementary Particles, Astrophysics
BLICHARSKI, J. S., Radiospectroscopy, Biophysics
BODEK, K., Nuclear Physics
DOHNALIK, T., Atomic and Optical Physics
FIAŁKOWSKI, K., Theoretical Physics
FULIŃSKI, A., Statistical Physics
GAWLIK, W., Atomic and Optical Physics, Photonics
JURKIEWICZ, J., Theoretical Physics
KAMYS, B., Nuclear Physics
KOTAŃSKI, A., Computer Science, High-Energy Physics
KRÓLAS, K., Nuclear Physics
KULESSA, R., Nuclear Physics
KUTSCHERA, M., Astrophysics
ŁĄTKA, K., Experimental Physics
LONGA, L., Statistical Physics

MACHALSKI, J., Radioastronomy and Extragalactic Astronomy
MAJKA, Z., Hot Matter
MALEC, E., Relativity, Astrophysics
MASŁOWSKI, J., Radioastronomy and Cosmic Physics
MICEK, S., Experimental Computer Physics
MOŚCICKI, J., Soft Matter Physics
MUSIOŁ, K., Atomic Physics
NOWAK, M., Theoretical Physics
OLEŚ, A. M., Theoretical Physics
OSTROWSKI, M., Astronomy
PĘDZIWIATR, A., Experimental Physics
RICHTER-WĄS, E., Applied Numerical Methods, High-Energy Physics
ROKITA, E., Medical Physics, Environmental Physics
ROŚCISZEWSKI, K., Condensed Matter Theory
SPAŁEK, J., Condensed Matter Theory
STANEK, J., Solid State Physics
STARUSZKIEWICZ, A., General Relativity, Electrodynamics, Astrophysics
SZWED, J., Applied Numerical Methods, High-Energy Physics
SZYMOŃSKI, M., Experimental Physics
SZYTUŁA, A., Solid State Physics, Magnetism
TOMALA, K., Radiospectroscopy
URBAN, S., Solid State Physics
WALUŚ, W., Nuclear Physics
WARCZAK, A., Experimental Physics
WITAŁA, H., Nuclear Physics
WOSIEK, J., Theoretical Computer Physics
WRÓBEL, S., Solid State Physics
ZAKRZEWSKI, J., Atomic and Optical Physics, Photonics
ZALEWSKI, K., Particle Theory

UNIWERSYTET KARDYNAŁA STEFANA WYSZYŃSKIEGO W WARSZAWIE
(Cardinal Stefan Wyszyński University in Warsaw)

ul. Dewajtis 5, 01-815 Warsaw

Telephone: (22) 5618800
E-mail: info@uksw.edu.pl
Internet: www.uksw.edu.pl

Founded 1954 as Akademia Teologii Katolickiej, present name and status 1999
State control
Academic year: October to June

Chancellor: Mgr MARIUSZ WIELEC
Rector: Prof. Dr Hab. STANISŁAW DZIEKONSKI
Vice-Rector for Finance and Infrastructure: Prof. Dr Hab. JERZY CYTOWSKI
Vice-Rector for Science and Devt: Prof. Dr Hab. CEZARY MIK
Vice-Rector for Student Affairs and Education: Prof. Dr Hab. MACIEJ BALA
Dir for Library: Mgr PIOTR LATAWIEC

Library of 200,000 vols
Number of teachers: 800
Number of students: 16,000

Publications: *Colloquia Litteraria* (every 2 years), *Collectanea Theologica* (4 a year), *Ius Matrimoniale* (1 a year), *Kroniki UKSW* (4 a year), *Magom* (2 a year), *Prawo Kanoniczne* (4 a year), *Saeculum Christianum* (2 a year), *Studia nad Rodziną* (2 a year), *Studia Philosophiae Christianae* (2 a year), *Studia Psychologica* (1 a year), *Studia Theologica Varsaviensia* (2 a year), *Wiadomości UKSW* (12 a year), *Zeszyty Prawnicze* (1 a year)

DEANS

Faculty of Biology and Environmental Sciences: Prof. Dr Hab. KINGA SUWIŃSKA
Faculty of Canon Law: Prof. Dr Hab. HENRYK STAWNIAK
Faculty of Christian Philosophy: Prof. Dr Hab. ANNA LATAWIEC

Faculty of Family Sciences: Prof. Dr Hab. MIECZYSŁAW OZOROWSKI
Faculty of History and Social Sciences: Prof. Dr Hab. KAZIMIERZ ŁATAK
Faculty of Humanities: Prof. Dr Hab. TOMASZ CHACHULSKI
Faculty of Law and Administration: Prof. Dr Hab. MAREK MICHALSKI
Faculty of Mathematics and Natural Sciences: Prof. Dr Hab. MARIAN TURZAŃSKI
Faculty of Pedagogics: Prof. Dr Hab. JADWIGA KUCZYŃSKA-KWAPISZ
Faculty of Theology: Prof. Dr Hab. PIOTR TOMASIK

PROFESSORS

Faculty of Canon Law (ul. Dewajtis 5, 01-815 Warsaw; tel. (22) 5618812; e-mail prawokan@uksw.edu.pl; internet www.wpk.uksw.edu.pl):

BŁESZYŃSKI, J., Civil Law
BRZOZOWSKI, A., Civil Law
DĘBIŃSKI, A., Roman Law
DYBOWSKI, T., Civil Law
GÓRALSKI, W., Ecclesiastical Matrimonial and Family Law
GRĘŹLIKOWSKI, J., History of Law
JEMIELITY, W., History of Ecclesiastical Polish Law
KAŁOWSKI, J., Law of Consecration Life Institutes and Apostolic Life Associations
KIWIOR, W., Procedural Law
KRUKOWSKI, J., Religion and Concordat Law
PASTUSZKO, M., Law of Sacraments
SOBAŃSKI, R., Theory of Ecclesiastical Law
STAWNIAK, H., Law of Teaching Services
SYRYJCZYK, J., Ecclesiastical Criminal Law
SZTYCHMILER, R., Ecclesiastical Procedural Law
WROCEŃSKI, J., Ecclesiastical Law of Persons

Faculty of Christian Philosophy (ul. Wóycickiego 1/3, 01-938 Warsaw; tel. (22) 5696805; e-mail wfch@uksw.edu.pl; internet www.wfch.uksw.edu.pl):

ANDRZEJUK, A., Philosophy
ARANOWSKA, E., Methodology of Psychological Sciences
BIELECKI, J., Psychology of Religion
BOŁOZ, J., Bioethics
BOMBIK, M., Logic
DOŁĘGA, J., Philosophy of Nature
GAŁUSZKO, K., Preservation of Nature
GASIUL, H., Psychology of Personality
GERAS, G., Judicial and Penitentiary Psychology
HAŁACZEK, B., Anthropology, History and Philosophy of Science
JAKUBIK, A., Clinical Psychology
KLIMSKI, T., History of Philosophy
LATAWIEC, A., Philosophy of Nature
LEMAŃSKA, A., Philosophy of Nature
MACEWICZ, J., Genetics
MATCZAK, A., Developmental Psychology
MORAWIEC, E., Philosophy, Metaphysics
NIEZNAŃSKI, E., Logic, Methodology of Sciences
NOWICKA, G., Biochemistry
PODREZ, E., Ethics
PORĘBSKI, S., History of Polish Philosophy
RYŚ, M., Psychology of Marriage and Family
SAREŁO, Z., Ethics
SINIARSKA-WOLAŃSKA, A., Ecology
SOCHOŃ, J., History of Philosophy, Philosophy of Religion
STOJANOWSKA, E., Social Psychology
STRZAŁECKI, A., General Psychology, Psychodiagnosis
TERELAK, J., Psychology of Labour and Stress
TYLKA, J., Clinical Psychology

ZABŁOCKI, K., Pedagogy, Psychology of Revalidation and Rehabilitation

Faculty of History and Social Sciences (ul. Wóycickiego 1/3, 01-938 Warsaw; tel. (22) 5696828; e-mail wnhis@uksw.edu.pl; internet www.wnhis.uksw.edu.pl):

BALICKI, J., Political Science
BANIA, Z., History of Medieval and Modern Architecture
CYWIŃSKI, B., Contemporary History
DĄBEK, S., Musicology
DĄBROWSKA, T., Archaeology
DADAK-KOZICKA, K., Musicology
DELUGA, W., History of Art
DROZD, J., International Relations
DYLUS, A., Philosophy and Ethics
GRONKIEWICZ-WALTZ, H., Administrative and Banking Law
GROSFELD, J., Political Economy
JANOCHA, M., History of Art
JUROS, H., Moral Theology, Ethics
KOBIELUS, S., History of Art
KOBYLIŃSKI, Z., Archaeology
KOŁOSOWSKI, T., History of Early Christian Literature
KORAL, J., Political Science
KOZŁOWSKI, S., Archaeology
KRASNODĘBSKI, Z., Philosophy and Sociology
MAJKOWSKI, W., Sociology of the Family
MANDZIUK, J., History of the Church
MAZURKIWEICZ, P., Political Science
MIŚKIEWICZ, M., Archaeology
MOISAN-JABLONSKI, CH., History of Art
NAUMOWICZ, J., History of Early Christian Literature
NAWROT, E., History
OCHOCKI, A., Demography
ODZIEMKOWSKI, J., History
POKORA, H., History of Art
POTOCKI, A., Sociology
REKŁAJTIS, E., Arabic Philology
SKOROWSKI, H., Political Science
SZYMONIK, K., Arts of Music
TRZECIAK, M., Sociology
UERTZ, R., Political Science
WILSKA, M., Archaeology
WÓJTOWICZ, A., Sociology
WYSOCKI, W., History
ZBUDNIEWEK, J., History of the Church
ZIEMER, K., Political Science
ŻYRO, T., Political Science

Faculty of Humanities (ul. Dewajtis 5, 01-815 Warsaw; tel. (22) 5618800; e-mail polonistyka@uksw.edu.pl; internet www .wnh.uksw.edu.pl):

BIEŃKOWSKA, E., History of 19th- and 20th-century Literature, Comparative Literature, Literary Criticism
BOBROWSKA, B., History of Literature of the Second Half of the 19th Century
DOPART, B., Romantic Literature
DUMA, J., History of Language
DYBCIAK, K., History of 20th-century Literature, Literary Criticism
JANUS, E., History of Language
KOSTKIEWICZOWA, T., History of 18th-century Literature, Theory of Literature
KUCZYŃSKA-KWAPISZ, J., Education for Handicapped People
ŁUKASZUK-PIEKARA, M, 20th-century Literature
PAWŁOWSKI, K., Classical Philology, Theory of Literature
PISKUREWICZ, J., History of Child-rearing
PRUSSAK, M., Science of Theatre, History of Literature of the Second Half of the 19th Century, Science Publications
SMOLIŃSKA-THEISS, B., Education
SURZYSZKIEWICZ, J., Education
THEISS, W., Social Education
WARZECHA, J., Biblical Studies
WOLNICZ-PAWŁOWSKA, E., History of Language
ZIELIŃSKA, A., Linguistics

Faculty of Law and Administration (ul. Wóycickiego 1/3, 01-938 Warsaw; tel. (22) 5699704; e-mail prawo@uksw.edu.pl; internet www.wpia.uksw.edu.pl):

BORUTA, M., Labour Law
CIEŚLAK, Z., Administrative Law
GRANAT, M., Constitutional Law
JĘDRZEJEWSKA, M., Civil Proceedings
JURCEWICZ, A., Agrarian Law
KACZYŃSKI, L., Labour Law
KALLAS, M., History of the Political System and Law in Poland
LIPOWICZ, I., European Administrative Law
MAJEWSKI, J., Criminal Law
MIK, C., International and European Law
MORAWSKI, L., Theory and Philosophy of Law
NOWAK-FAR, A., Financial Law
OMYŁA, M., Logic and Methodology of Legal Sciences
PRUSAK, F., Criminal Procedure
STOJANOWSKA, W., Family Law
STRZYCZKOWSKI, K., Private Economic Law
SZAJKOWSKI, A., Private Economic Law
SZPOR, G., Informatics Law
ZABŁOCKI, J., Roman Law
ZIELIŃSKI, A., Civil Proceedings

Faculty of Mathematics and Natural Sciences (ul. Wóycickiego 1/3, 01-938 Warsaw; tel. (22) 5699670; e-mail matematyka@uksw .edu.pl; internet www.wmp.uksw.edu.pl):

ALSTER, K., Mathematics
CHEŁMIŃSKI, K., Mathematics
CHOJNACKI, W., Mathematics
CYTOWSKI, J. W., Computer Science
GAJDA, M., Physics
GODLEWSKI, M., Physics
GÓRECKI, J., Chemistry
HERBICH, J., Chemistry
HOŁYST, R., Chemistry
JABŁOŃSKI, A., Chemistry
KARPIŃSKI, Z., Chemistry
KIJOWSKI, J., Physics
KORYBUT-DASZKIEWICZ, B., Chemistry
KOTLARSKI, H., Mathematics
KOWALSKI, M. A., Mathematics
KRYNICKI, M., Mathematics
KULPA, W., Mathematics
KUŚ, M., Physics
KUTNER, W., Chemistry
ŁUNARSKA-BOROWIECKA, E., Chemistry
MACEK, W., Physics
MAINARDI, S., Economy
MAZUR, T., Mathematics
MOSTOWSKI, J., Physics
NANIEWICZ, Z., Mathematics
NOWICKA-TARASZEWSKA, J., Chemistry
RUSINEK, J., Mathematics
RZĄŻEWSKI, K., Physics
SKOŚKIEWICZ, T., Physics
SKWARCZYŃSKI, M., Mathematics
SOCHA, L., Computer Science
TURSKI, L. A., Physics
TURZAŃSKI, M., Mathematics
WALUK, J., Chemistry
ZAGRODNY, D., Mathematics
ZAREMBA, L., Mathematics

Faculty of Theology (ul. Dewajtis 5, 01-815 Warsaw; tel. (22) 5618856; e-mail wtdz@ uksw.edu.pl; internet www.teologia.uksw .edu.pl):

BALTER, L., Dogmatic Theology
BARTNICKI, R., Biblical Studies
BEŁCH, K., Pastoral Theology
BOKWA, I., Dogmatic Theology
CHROSTOWSKI, W., Biblical Studies
CZAJKOWSKI, M., Biblical Studies
DECYK, J., Liturgy
DURAK, A., Liturgy
DZIUBA, A., Moral Theology
GACKA, B., Dogmatic Theology
GÓRALCZYK, P., Moral Theology
GRACZYK, M., Moral Theology
JABŁOŃSKI, S., Mariology

KARWACKI, R., Fundamental Theology
KULISZ, J., Fundamental Theology
LEWANDOWSKI, J., Dogmatic Theology
LEWEK, A., Theology of Mass Media
MATWIEJUK, K., Liturgics
MĘDALA, S., Biblical Studies
MIERZWIŃSKI, B., Pastoral Theology
MISIASZEK, K., Catechesis
MROCZKOWSKI, I., Moral Theology
MURAWSKI, R., Catechesis
NOWAK, J., Liturgy
OGÓREK, P., Theology of Spirituality
OZOROWSKI, E., Dogmatic Theology
PAZERA, W., Homiletics
PIETRZYK, Z., History of the Church
PIKUS, T., Fundamental Theology
PRZYBYŁOWSKI, J., Pastoral Theology
RUMIANEK, R., Biblical Studies
SAKOWICZ, E., Religion
SALIJ, J., Dogmatic Theology
SEWERYNIAK, H., Fundamental Theology
TYLKI-SZYMAŃSKA, A., Family Studies
URBAŃSKI, S., Theology of Spirituality
WARCHOŁ, E., History of the Church
WARZESZAK, J., Dogmatic Theology
ZABIELSKI, J., Moral Theology
ZAŁĘSKI, J., Biblical Studies

UNIWERSYTET KAZIMIERZA WIELKIEGO W BYDGOSZCZY (Kazimierz Wielki University in Bydgoszcz)

ul. Chodkiewicza 30, 85-064 Bydgoszcz

Telephone: (52) 3419200
E-mail: rektor@ukw.edu.pl
Internet: www.ukw.edu.pl

Founded 1969
State control

Rector: Prof. JANUSZ OSTOJA-ZAGÓRSKI
Vice-Rector for Education: Dr Hab. ROMAN LEPPERT
Vice-Rector for Research and Int. Relations: Prof. SLAWOMIR KACZMAREK
Vice-Rector for Univ. Organization and Development: Dr Hab. PIOTR MALINOWSKI
Dir for Library: Dr ALDONA CHLEWICKA

Library of 750,000 vols
Number of teachers: 700
Number of students: 15,000

DEANS

Faculty of Administration and Social Sciences: Prof. Dr Hab. ANNA KOZICZAK
Faculty of Humanities: Prof. Dr Hab. JACEK WOZNY
Faculty of Mathematics, Physics and Technical Sciences: Prof. Dr Hab. ANDRZEJ PROSZYNSKI
Faculty of Natural Sciences: Prof. Dr Hab. GRZEGORZ KLOSOWSKI
Faculty of Pedagogy and Psychology: Prof. Dr Hab. EWA ZWOLINSKA

UNIWERSYTET ŁÓDZKI (University of Łódź)

ul. Narutowicza 65, 90-131 Łódź

Telephone: (42) 6354237
E-mail: rektoratul@uni.lodz.pl
Internet: www.uni.lodz.pl

Founded 1945
State control
Language of instruction: Polish
Academic year: October to September

Rector: Prof. Dr WLODZIMIERZ NYKIEL
Pro-Rector for Curricula and Teaching: Prof. Dr JAROSŁAW PŁUCIENNIK
Pro-Rector for Economic Affairs: Prof. Dr BOGDAN GREGOR
Pro-Rector for Int. Affairs: Prof. Dr ZOFIA WYSOKINSKA
Pro-Rector for Research: Prof. Dr ANTONI RÓŻALSKI

Pro-Rector for Student Affairs: Prof. Dr ZBIGNIEW GÓRAL
Dir for Library: MARIA WROCŁAWSKA
Library: see under Libraries and Archives
Number of teachers: 2,400
Number of students: 45,000

Publications: *Acta Universitatis Lodziensis* (Research Bulletin), *Kronika Uniwersitetu Łódzkiego*

DEANS

Faculty of Biology and Environmental Protection: Dr Hab. ELZBIETA ZADZINSKA
Faculty of Chemistry: Prof. Dr Hab. GRZEGORZ MLOSTOŃ
Faculty of Economics and Sociology: Prof. Dr Hab. PAWEŁ STAROSTA
Faculty of Educational Sciences: Prof. Dr Hab. DANUTA URBANIAK-ZAJĄC
Faculty of Geographical Sciences: Prof. Dr Hab. TADEUSZ MARSZAL
Faculty of International and Political Studies: Prof. Dr Hab. TOMASZ DOMANSKI
Faculty of Law and Administration: Prof. Dr Hab. AGNIESZKA LISZEWSKA
Faculty of Management: Prof. Dr Hab. EWA WALINSKA
Faculty of Mathematics and Computer Science: Prof. Dr Hab. RYSZARD PAWLAK
Faculty of Philology: Prof. Dr Hab. PIOTR STALMASZCZYK
Faculty of Philosophy and History: Prof. Dr Hab. ZBIGNIEW ANUSIK
Faculty of Physics and Applied Informatics: Prof. Dr Hab. ANNA URBANIAK-KUCHARCZYK

PROFESSORS

Faculty of Biology and Environmental Protection (ul. Pilarskiego 14/16, 90-231 Łódź; tel. (42) 6354505; e-mail dziekan@biol.uni.lodz.pl; internet www.biol.uni.lodz.pl):

BAŃBURA, J., Biology, Ecology
BARTOSZ, G., Biophysics
BŁASIAK, J., Molecular Genetics
BRYSZEWSKA, M., Biophysics
DŁUGOŃSKI, J., Microbiology
DUDA, W., Biochemistry
GABARA, B., Cytology and Cytochemistry
GALICKA, W., Ecology and Zoology of Vertebrates
GAŹDZICKI, A., Geology
GRZYBKOWSKA, M., Zoology, Ecology
GWOŹDZIŃSKI, K., Molecular Biology
HEREŹNIAK, J., Biology
JAKUBOWSKA-GABARA, J., Geobotany
JANAS, K., Plant Physiology
JAWORSKI, A., Microbiology
JAŻDŻEWSKI, K., Zoology
JÓŹWIAK, Z., Biochemistry
KACA, W., Microbiology
KILIAŃSKA, Z., Biochemistry
KONOPACKI, J., Neurophysiology
KRAJEWSKA, W., Biochemistry
KUKULSKA-GOŚCICKA, T., Immunology
KWIATKOWSKA, M., Plant Cytology and Cytochemistry
ŁAWRYNOWICZ, M., Botany, Mycology
LIGOWSKI, R., Biology, Oceanography
LIPIŃSKA, A., Biochemistry
LISZEWSKI, S., Economic Geography
MARKOWSKI, J., Biology, Theriology
MASZEWSKI, J., Cell Biology
OLACZEK, R., Plant Systems and Geography
PENCZAK, T., Zoology, Fish Ecology
PIECHOCKI, A., Zoology
ROMANIUK, A., Animal Physiology and Neurophysiology
RÓŻALSKA, B., Infectious Biology
RÓŻALSKI, A., Microbiology
RUDNICKA, W., Immunology
SIDORCZYK, Z., Microbiology
SZWEDA-LEWANDOWSKA, Z., Molecular Biophysics
URBANEK, H., Biochemistry

WACHOWICZ, B., Biochemistry
ZALEWSKI, M., Biology

Faculty of Economics and Sociology (ul. Polskiej Organizacji Wojskowej 3/5, 90-255 Łódź; tel. (42) 6355112; e-mail dziekes@uni.lodz.pl):

BOKSZAŃSKI, Z., Cultural Sociology
BORKOWSKA, S., Business Administrstion
BUCHNER-JEZIORSKA, A., Sociology
DĘBSKI, W., Commerce and International Finance
DOKTÓR, K., Industrial Sociology
DOMAŃSKI, C., Statistics
DURAJ, J., Economics and Organization of Industry
GAJDA, J., Economics
JÓZEFIAK, C., Economics
KOCIK, L., Sociology
KRYŃSKA, E., Economics, Economic Policy
KUCHARSKA-STASIAK, E., Economics of Urban Development
KULPIŃSKA, J., Industrial Sociology
KWIATKOWSKI, E., Economic Theory
LEWANDOWSKA, L., Economics, Industrial Economics
MARSZAŁEK, A., Economics
MILO, W., Econometrics, Statistics
MORTIMER-SZYMCZAK, H., Planning and Economic Policy
PIĄTKOWSKI, W., History of Economic Theory
PIOTROWSKA-MARCZAK, K., Finance
RUDOLF, S., Political Economy of Capitalism
SKODLARSKI, J., International Economic Relations
SUCHECKA, J., Economics
SUŁKOWSKI, B., Cultural Sociology
TOMASZEWICZ, Ł., Econometrics
TRZASKALIK, T., Economics
WARZYWODA-KRUSZYŃSKA, W., Sociology
WELFE, A., Econometrics
WELFE, W., Econometrics and Statistics
WOJCIECHOWSKI, E., Economics of Urban Development

Faculty of Educational Sciences (ul. Pomorska 48/46, 91-408 Łódź; tel. (42) 6390776):

BŁASZCZYK, J., Physical Education
BŁASZCZYK, T., Science of Art
BUCZYŃSKI, A., Physical Education
DOWLASZ, B., Music Education
FLORKOWSKI, A., Psychology
JAŁMUŻNA, T., Pedagogy
KACZOROWSKI, B., Science of Art
KĘDZIORA, J., Biochemistry
KOCUR, J., Psychiatry
MARYNOWICZ-HETKA, E., Social Pedagogy
ORKISZ, S., Physical Education and Health
PAŃCZYK, J., Pedagogy
ŚLIWERSKI, B., Pedagogy
WIERZBIŃSKI, A., Music Education
WÓDKA, B., Science of Art

Faculty of Geographical Sciences (ul. Narutowicza 88, 90-139 Łódź; tel. (42) 6655910; e-mail dziekan@geo.uni.lodz.pl; internet www.geo.uni.lodz.pl):

BACHVAROV, M., Urban Geography and Tourism
HEFFNER, K., Political Geography and Regional Studies
JELONEK, A., Social and Economic Geography
KŁYSIK, C., Climatology and Meteorology
KOTER, M., Environmental Biophysics
KOWALCZYK, A., Urban Geography and Tourism
KOŻUCHOWSKI, K., Physical Geography
LASKOWSKI, S., Pedology
LISZEWSKI, S., Economic Geography
MARSZAŁ, T., Social and Economic Geography
MATCZAK, A., Urban Geography
WERWICKI, A., Economic Geography

Faculty of International and Political Studies (ul. Składowa 43, 90-127 Łódź; tel. (42) 6354265; e-mail interul@uni.lodz.pl; internet wsmip.uni.lodz.pl):

DE LAZARI, A., Eastern Studies
DOMAŃSKI, T., Euromarketing
DUBICKI, T., History
DZIEKAN, M., History of Arabic Literature
KMIECIŃSKI, J., Archaeology
KUCZYŃSKI, K. A., German Literature
MICHOWICZ, W., History of International Relations
OLEKSY, E., American Literature
PRZEBINDA, G., Russian Philology

Faculty of Law and Administration (ul. Kopcińskiego 8/12, 90-232 Łódź; tel. (42) 6354626; e-mail dziekanat@wpia.uni.lodz.pl; internet wpia.uni.lodz.pl):

BIŃCZYCKA-MAJEWSKA, T., Labour Law
BORKOWSKI, J., Administrative Law
BRONIEWICZ, W., Civil Procedure
CHRÓŚCIELEWSKI, W., Administrative Procedure
DĘBOWSKA-ROMANOWSKA, T., Financial Law
GRZEGORCZYK, T., Penal Procedure
HOŁYST, B., Criminology
JANKOWSKI, J., Civil Law
KATNER, W., Civil Law
KMIECIAK, Z., Administrative Procedure
LELENTAL, S., Penal Law
LEWANDOWSKI, H., Labour Law
LEWASZKIEWICZ-PETRYKOWSKA, B., Civil Law
MARCINIAK, A., Civil Procedure
MATUSZEWSKI, J., History of State and Law
MATUSZEWSKI, J., Medieval History, History of Law
NYKIEL, W., Financial Law
PYZIAK-SZAFNICKA, M., Civil Law
RYMASZEWSKI, Z., History of State and the Law
SEWERYŃSKI, M., Labour Law
SZYMCZAK, T., Constitutional Law
TYLMAN, J., Penal Procedure
WŁODARCZYK, W., Social Insurance and Social Policy Law
ZIRK-SADOWSKI, M., Theory of State and Law

Faculty of Management (ul. Matejki 22/26, 90-237 Łódź; tel. (42) 6355044; e-mail wzdziek@uni.lodz.pl):

DIETL, J., Commercial Economics
GREGOR, W., Organization and Management, Marketing
GREGORCZYK, B., Organization and Management, Banking
JANOWSKA, Z., Human Resources, Management Accountancy
JARUGA, A., Cost Accounting, Management Accountancy
KOBYLIŃSKI, W., Quality Management
ŁAŃCUCKI, J., Management
MARKOWSKI, T., Economics of Urban Development
MIKOŁAJCZYK, Z., Theory of Organization and Management
PIASECKI, B., Economics and Organization of Industry
SIKORSKI, C., Organization and Management
SZYMCZAK, J., Management
ZIELIŃSKI, J. S., Computer Science

Faculty of Mathematics and Computer Science (ul. Banacha 22, 90-238 Łódź; tel. (42) 6355949; e-mail facmath@math.uni.lodz.pl; internet www.math.uni.lodz.pl):

BALCERZAK, M., Real Analysis
CHĄDZYŃSKI, J., Complex Variables
GOLDSTEIN, S., Functional Analysis
JAJTE, R., Probability Theory
JAKUBOWSKI, Z., Analytical Functions
MIKOŁAJCZYK, L., Analytical Functions
NOWAKOWSKI, A., Optimization Theory
PASZKIEWICZ, A., Functional Analysis

PAWLAK, R., Functional Analysis
WALCZAK, P., Geometry
WALCZAK, S., Analytical Functions
WALISZEWSKI, W., Geometry
WILCZYŃSKI, W., Real Analysis
WŁODARCZYK, K., Functional Analysis, Complex Analysis

Faculty of Philology (ul. Kósciuszki 65, 90-514 Łódź; tel. (42) 6655260; e-mail filolog@uni.lodz.pl; internet filolog.uni.lodz.pl):

BIEŃKOWSKA, D., Polish Language
BOLECKI, W., Romance Literature and Contemporary Literature
CYBULSKI, M., Polish and Slavonic Languages
CZYŻEWSKI, S., Theory of Literature
DEJNA, K., Polish and Slavonic Languages
DUNIN-HORKAWICZ, J., Research on Books
GALA, A., Polish Language
GAZDA, G., Theory of Literature
HELMAN, A., Film
JABŁKOWSKA, J., German Philology
JANICKA-ŚWIDERSKA, I., English Philology
JANISZEWSKA-ZEIDLER, A., Theory of Literature, Theatre and Film
KAMIŃSKA, M., Polish and Slavonic Languages
KORYTKOWSKA, M., Slavonic Studies
KULIGOWSKA-KORZENIEWSKA, A., History of Theatre
LEWANDOWSKA-TOMASZCZYK, B., English Language
MAŁEK, E., Russian Literature
MUCHA, B., Russian Literature
NOWIKOW, W., Spanish Philology
NURCZYŃSKA-FIDELSKA, E., Theory of Literature
OKOŃ, J., Old Polish Literature
POKLEWSKA, K., Polish Literature
PUSZ, W., History of Polish Literature
RATAJCZAK, D., Theory of Literature
SADZIŃSKI, R., German Philology
STARNAWSKI, J., Old Polish Literature
SYPNICKI, J., French Language
TADEUSIEWICZ, H., Research on Books
TARANTOWICZ, A., German Philology
UMIŃSKA-TYTOŃ, E., Polish Language
WIŚNIEWSKI, B., Classical Philology
WOLSKA, B., History of 18th- and 19th-century Polish Literature
WRÓBLEWSKI, W., Classical Philology and Philosophy

Faculty of Philosophy and History (ul. A. Kamińskiego, 90-219 Łódź; tel. (42) 6354331):

BRZEZIŃSKI, A., Archaeology
CERAN, W., Prehistory and Medieval History
GAJDA-KRYNICKA, J., Philosophy
GŁOSEK, M., Prehistory
GROMCZYŃSKI, W., History of 19th- and 20th-century Philosophy
HASSAN ALI JAMSHEER, Near East Studies
HUNGER, R., History of Art
KAJZER, L., Medieval History, Archaeology
KRAWCZYK-WASILEWSKA, V., Cultural Anthropology, Ethnography
LIPIŃSKA, J., History of Art
MĄCZYŃSKA, M., Archaeology
MALINOWSKI, G., Logic
MATERSKI, W., Recent World History
NOWACZYK, A., Logic
PANASIUK, R., History of 19th-century Philosophy
PIÓRCZYŃSKI, J., Philosophy
PUŚ, P., 19th- and 20th-century Economic History of Poland
SAMUŚ, W., Recent Polish History
STYCZYŃSKI, M., History of Russian Philosophy
SZCZYGIELSKI, W., Modern Polish History
SZTABIŃSKI, G., Aesthetics
SZYNKIEWICZ, S., Ethnology
TUCHAŃSKA, B., Philosophy of Science

WIERUSZEWSKA-ADAMCZYK, M., Ethnography
WIŚNIEWSKI, E., Russian History
ZAJĄCZKOWSKI, S. M., Medieval Polish History

UNIWERSYTET MARII CURIE-SKŁODOWSKIEJ W LUBLINIE
(Maria Curie-Skłodowska University in Lublin)

Pl. Marii Curie-Skłodowskiej 5, 20-031 Lublin

Telephone: (81) 5375100
E-mail: rektor@umcs.lublin.pl
Internet: www.umcs.lublin.pl
Founded 1944
State control
Academic year: October to June

Chancellor: Mgr GRAŻYNA ELŻBIETA FIOK
Rector: Prof. Dr Hab. STANISŁAW MICHAŁOWSKI
Pro-Rector for Education: Prof. Dr Hab. BARBARA HLIBOWICKA-WĘGLARZ
Pro-Rector for Gen. Affairs: Prof. Dr Hab. RYSZARD MOJAK
Pro-Rector for Research and Int. Cooperation: Prof. Dr Hab. RYSZARD DĘBICKI
Pro-Rector for Student Affairs: Prof. URSZULA BOBRYK
Dir for Library: Dr BOGUSŁAW KASPEREK
Library of 1,521,641 vols incl. 861,335 books, 343,399 periodicals and 316,907 spec. collns
Number of teachers: 1,720
Number of students: 34,800

Publication: *Annales Universitatis Mariae Curie-Skłodowska*

DEANS

Faculty of Biology and Biotechnology: Prof. Dr Hab. KAZIMIERZ TRĘBACZ
Faculty of Chemistry: Prof. Dr Hab. WŁADYSŁAW JANUSZ
Faculty of Earth Sciences and Land Management: Prof. Dr Hab. RADOSŁAW DOBROWOLSKI
Faculty of Economics: Prof. Dr Hab. ZBIGNIEW PASTUSZAK
Faculty of Fine Arts: Prof. ARTUR POPEK
Faculty of Humanities: Prof. Dr Hab. ROBERT LITWIŃSKI
Faculty of Law and Administration: Prof. Dr Hab. ANNA PRZYBOROWSKA-KLIMCZAK
Faculty of Mathematics, Physics and Computer Science: Prof. Dr Hab. STEFAN KORCZAK
Faculty of Pedagogy and Psychology: Prof. Dr Hab. RYSZARD BERA
Faculty of Philosophy and Sociology: Prof. Dr Hab. TERESA PĘKALA
Faculty of Political Science: Prof. Dr Hab. GRZEGORZ JANUSZ

PROFESSORS

Faculty of Biology and Biotechnology (pl. Marii Curie-Skłodowskiej 5, 20-031 Lublin; tel. (81) 5375216; e-mail biolbiot@umcs.lublin.pl; internet www.biolbiot.umcs.lublin.pl):

BEDNARA, J., Anatomy and Plant Cytology
BYSTREK, J., Plant Systematics
DĘBICKI, A., Soil Science
DERNAŁOWICZ-MALARCZYK, E., Biochemistry
DROŻAŃSKI, W., Microbiology
FIEDERUK, J., Microbiology
GRANKOWSKI, N., Molecular Biology
HARASIMIUK, M., Geomorphology
JAKUBOWICZ, T., Biochemistry and Immunology
KAŁKOWSKA, K., Animal Physiology
KANDEFER-SZERSZEŃ, M., Microbiology
KRUPA, Z., Plant Physiology
KUREK, E., Environmental Microbiology

LEONOWICZ, A., Biochemistry
MICHALCZYK, Z., Hydrography
PĘKALA, K., Physical Geography and Geomorphology
ROGALSKI, J., Molecular Biology
RUSSA, R., Microbiology
SIRKO, M., Cartography
SKORUPSKA, A., Microbiology
ŚNIEZKO, R., Botany
ŚWIĘS, F., Botany
SZCZODRAK, J., Microbiology
TRĘBACZ, K., Biology and Biophysics
WOJCIECHOWSKI, K., Geography
WOJTANOWICZ, J., Physical Geography and Geomorphology
ZAWADZKI, T., Plant Physiology

Faculty of Chemistry (pl. Marii Curie-Skłodowskiej 2, 20-031 Lublin; tel. (81) 5375716; e-mail chemia@umcs.lublin.pl; internet chemia.umcs.lublin.pl):

BOROWIECKI, T., Chemical Technology
BORÓWKO, M., Physical Chemistry
CHIBOWSKI, E., Physical Chemistry
CHIBOWSKI, S., Physical Chemistry
DĄBROWSKI, A., Theoretical Chemistry
DAWIDOWICZ, A., Physical Chemistry
FERENC, W., Inorganic Chemistry
GAWDZIK, B., Physical Chemistry
GOWOREK, J., Physical Chemistry
HUBICKA, H., Inorganic Chemistry
HUBICKI, Z., Inorganic Chemistry
JAŃCZUK, B., Physical Chemistry
KOZIOŁ, A., Chemistry, X-ray Crystallography
LEBODA, R., Physical Chemistry of Surfaces and Chromatography
MACHOCKI, A., Heterogeneous Catalysis, C1 Chemistry
MATYNIA, T., Organic Chemistry
NARKIEWIEZ-MICHAŁCK, J., Theoretical Chemistry
NAZIMEK, D., Physical Chemistry
PATRYKIEJEW, A., Physical Chemistry
PIETRUSIEWICZ, K., Organic Chemistry
PIKUS, S., X-ray Crystallography-powder Diffraction
PODKOŚCIELNY, W., Organic Chemistry
RAYSS, J., Physical Chemistry
RÓŻYŁŁO, J., Physical Chemistry
RUDZINSKI, W., Theoretical Chemistry
SOKOŁOWSKI, S., Theoretical Chemistry
STASZCZUK, P., Physical Chemistry
WÓJCIK, W., Physical Chemistry
WOLIŃSKI, K., Quantum Chemistry, Methods and Applications

Faculty of Economics (pl. Marii Curie-Skłodowskiej 5, 20-031 Lublin; tel. (81) 5375462; e-mail ekonomia@umcs.lublin.pl; internet ekonomia.umcs.lublin.pl):

GRABOWIECKI, J., Political Economy
KARPUŚ, P., Economics
KOZŁOWSKI, S., Economics
MAMEARZ, M., Economics, Financial Markets
MUCHA-LESZKO, B., Political Economy, Economic Planning
POMORSKA, A., Finance
RONCK, H., Economics
RUDNICKI, M., Economics of Agriculture
SIKORSKI, C., Economics
SKOWRONEK, Cz., Industrial Economics
SKRZYPEK, E., Economics
SOBCZYK, G., Economics
SZYMAŃSKI, Z., Economics, History of Economic Thought
SZYNAL, J., Economics, Banking
WĘCŁAWSKI, J., Economics, Banking
WICH, U., Urban Planning
ZALEWA, J., Agricultural Economics
ZUKOWSKI, M., Economics

Faculty of Fine Arts (ul. Kraśnicka 2B, 20-718 Lublin; tel. (81) 5376900; internet art.umcs.lublin.pl):

BERNATOWICZ, M., Conducting

BOBRYK, U., Conducting
DĄBROWSKA, B., Conducting
GÓRSKI, K., Conducting
GRYKA, J., Graphics
HERMAN, M., Painting
JAWORSKA, A., Conducting
JAWORSKI, L., Conducting
KIERSKI, J., Sculpture
KOŁODZIEJ, R., Graphics
LECH, P., Graphics
MAZUREK, G., Graphics
MIELESZKO, S., Teaching of Sculpture
NALEPKA, J., Music Education
NAWROT-TRZCIŃSKA, I., Photographics
NIEDŹWIEDŹ, Z., Graphics
ORDYK-CZYŻŻEWSKA, E., Conducting
POPEK, A., Graphics
PRZYCHODZIŃSKA-KACICZAK, M., Music Education
RZECHOWSKA-KLAUZA, G., Conducting
SMOCZYŃSKI, M., Painting
SNOCH, M., Graphics
STYKA, A., Painting
ŚWIECA, C., Music Education
WOJCIECHOWSKI, J., Painting
WRÓBLEWSKI, W., Painting
ZAWADZKI, T., Painting
ŻUKOWSKI, S., Painting

Faculty of Humanities (pl. Marii Curie-Skłodowskiej 4, 20-031 Lublin; tel. (81) 5375465; e-mail humanik@umcs.lublin.pl):

BARTMIŃSKI, J., History of Polish Literature
BLAIM, A., English Literature
BONIECKA, B., History of Polish Literature
GMITEREK, M., Modern History
GRABIAS, S., Applied and Sociolinguistics
KARDELA, H., English Philology
KĘSIK, M., French Linguistics
KOKOWSKI, A., Archaeology
KOLEK, L., English Literature
KOLODZIEJ, E., Archiving
KORDELA, H., English Philology
KOSYL, CZ., Polish Philology
KRAJKA, W., Theory of Literature, History of English Literature
KRUK, S., History of Polish Theatre
LEWANDOWSKI, J., Modern History
LEWICKI, R., Linguistics
MAZUR, J., Polish Linguistics
MIKULEC, B., Modern History
MISIEWICZ, J., Theory of Literature
MYRDZIK, B., History of Polish Literature
NIEZNANOWSKI, S., Old Polish Literature
ORŁOWSKI, J., History of Russian Literature
PLISIECKI, J., Film
POMORSKI, J., Methodology and History of Historiography
RADZIK, T., Contemporary History
SAWECKA, H., Theory of Romance Literature
ŚLADKOWSKI, W., Modern History
ŚWIĘCH, W., Modern Polish Literature
STĘPNIK, K., Polish Literature
SZCZYGIEŁ, R., Medieval History
SZYMAŃSKI, J., Auxiliary Sciences of History
TOKARSKI, R., Polish Language
TRELIŃSKA, B., Polish Linguistics
WIŚNIEWSKA, H., Polish Linguistics
WOŹNIAKIEWICZ-DZIADOSZ, M., Theory of Literature

Faculty of Law and Administration (pl. Marii Curie-Skłodowskiej 5, 20-031 Lublin; tel. (81) 5375126; internet pia.umcs.lublin.pl):

BOJARSKI, T., Penal Law
CHORĄŻY, A., Administrative Law
GDULEWICZ, E., Constitutional Law
KIDYBA, A., Economic Law
KMIECIK, R., Penal Law
KOROBOWICZ, A., History of State and Law
KURYŁOWICZ, M., Roman Law
LESZCZYŃSKI, L., Theory of State and Law
OLESZKO, A., Civil Law

POŹNIAK-NIEDZIELSKA, M., Economic Law
SAWCZUK, M., Civil Procedure
SKRĘTOWICZ, E., Penal Law
SKUBISZ, R., European Community Law
SZRENIAWSKI, J., Administrative Law and Administrative Science
TOKARCZYK, R., History of Political Thought
WĄSEK, A., Penal Law and Criminology
WITKOWSKI, W., History of State and Law
WÓJTOWICZ, W., Financial Law
WRÓBEL, A., European Community Law
ZDYB, M., Administrative Law

Faculty of Mathematics, Physics and Computer Science (pl. Marii Curie-Skłodowskiej 1, 20-031 Lublin; tel. (81) 5375212; e-mail mfi@umcs.lublin.pl; internet mfi.umcs.lublin.pl):

ADAMCZYK, B., Physics
BARAN, A., Computer Science
BUDZYŃSKI, M., Experimental Physics
GLADYSZEWSKI, L., Theoretical Physics
GOEBEL, K., Differential Equations
GOWOREK, T., Nuclear Physics
GÓŹDŹ, A., Theoretical Physics
GRUSZECKI, W., Biophysics
HAŁAS, ST., Experimental Physics
JAŁOCHOWSKI, M., Experimental Physics
KAMIŃSKI, W., Nuclear Physics
KOMOROWSKI, T., Differential Equations
KORCZAK, Z., Solid Body Physics
KOZICKI, J., Computer Science
KRAWCZYK, W., Biophysics
KRZYŻ, J., Analytic Functions
KUCZUMOW, T., Differential Equations
KUREK, J., Differential Geometry
MĄCZKA, D., Experimental Physics
MICHALAK, L., Experimental Physics
MIKOŁAJCZAK, P., Solid Body Physics
MURAWSKI, K., Computer Science
NOWAK, M., Analytic Functions
POMORSKA, B., Theoretical Physics
POMORSKI, K., Theoretical Physics
PRUS, S., Functional Analysis
RYCHLIK, Z., Probability Theory
RZYMOWSKI, W., Differential Equations
SIELANKO, J., Nuclear Physics
SIELEWIESIUK, J., Physics and Biophysics
SYZNAL, D., Probability Theory
SZEZERBA, J., Computer Science
TARANKO, E., Theoretical Physics
TARANKO, R., Theoretical Physics
WANIURSKI, J., Analytical Functions
WÓJCIK, L., Experimental Physics
WYSOKIŃSKI, K., Theoretical Physics
ZĄBEK, S., Numerical Methods
ZAŁUŻNY, M., Theoretical Physics
ZIĘBA, W., Probability Theory
ZŁOTKIEWICZ, E., Analytic Functions
ŻUK, J., Experimental Physics

Faculty of Pedagogy and Psychology (ul. Narutowicza 12, 20-004 Lublin; tel. (81) 5370427):

BARTKOWICZ, Z., Pedagogy
CACKOWSKA, M., Didactics
CHODKOWSKA, M., Sociology
GAJDA, M., Pedagogy
GAŚ, Z., Psychopathology
GUZ, S., Pedagogy
HERZYK, A., Neuropsychology
KACZMAREK, B., Psychology
KĘPSKI, CZ., Pedagogy
KIRENKO, J., Pedagogy
KRASOWICZ-KUPIS., G., Psychology
KUCHA, R., History of Learning and Education
KWIATKOWSKA, G., Philosophy
OCHMAŃSKI, M., High School Pedagogy
PALAK, Z., Pedagogy
POPEK, S., Psychology
SARAN, J., Pedagogy
STACHYRA, J., Pedagogy
WĘGLIŃSKI, A., Pedagogy

Faculty of Philosophy and Sociology (pl. Marii Curie-Skłodowskiej 4, 20-031 Lublin;

tel. (81) 5375479; internet wfis.umcs.lublin.pl):

CZARNECKI, Z., History of Philosophy
FILIPIAK, M., Sociology
JEDYNAK, S., Ethics
KOSIŃSKI, S., Sociology
LIBISZEWSKA-ZÓŁTKOWSKA, M., Sociology
MIZIŃSKA, J., Epistemology
OGRYZKO-WIEWIÓROWSKA, M., Sociology
PAŚNICZEK, J., Logic
STYK, J., Sociology
SYMOTIUK, S., Philosophy of Culture
TOKARSKI, S., Sociology of Medicine

Faculty of Political Science (pl. Litewski 3, 20-080 Lublin; tel. (81) 5376023; e-mail politologia@politologia.pl; internet www.politologia.pl):

CHAŁUPCZAK, H., International Relations
CZARNOCKI, A., International Relations
HOŁDA, Z., Human Rights
HUDZIK, J., Political Philosophy
JACHYMEK, J., Political Thought
JANUSZ, G., International Relations
JELENKOWSKI, M., Political Doctrines
KUCHARSKI, W., National Minorities
MAJ, CZ., International Relations
MAJ, F., Contemporary History
MICH, W., Contemporary History
MICHAŁOWSKI, S., Local Government
MIECZKOWSKI, A., Contemporary History
OLSZEWSKI, E., Political Movements
PIETRAŚ, M., International Relations
PIETRAŚ, Z. J., International Relations
STĘPICŃ, S., Contemporary History
SZELIGA, Z., Constitutional Law
WÓJCIK, A., Contemporary History
ŻMIGRODZKI, M., Political Systems

UNIWERSYTET MEDYCZNY IM. KAROLA MARCINKOWSKIEGO W POZNANIU
(Poznań University of Medical Sciences)

ul. Fredry 10, 61-701 Poznań

Telephone: (61) 8546228
E-mail: info@ump.edu.pl
Internet: www.ump.edu.pl

Founded 1919, present name and status 1950

Rector: Prof. Dr JACEK WYSOCKI
Vice-Rector for Clinical Affairs and Postgraduate Studies: Prof. Dr GRZEGORZ OSZKINIS
Vice-Rector for Institutional Organization, Promotion and Advancement: Prof. Dr ANDRZEJ TYKARSKI
Vice-Rector for Science and Int. Relations: Prof. Dr JAROSLAW WALKOWIAK
Vice-Rector for Student Affairs: Prof. Dr EDMUND GRZEŚKOWIAK
Dir for Library: ANIELA PIOTROWICZ
Library of 353,422 vols
Number of teachers: 1,000
Number of students: 8,000

DEANS

Faculty of Health Sciences: Prof. Dr WŁODZIMIERZ SAMBORSKI
Faculty of Medicine I: Prof. Dr RYSZARD MARCINIAK
Faculty of Medicine II: Prof. Dr ZBIGNIEW KRASIŃSKI
Faculty of Pharmacy: Prof. Dr LUCJUSZ ZAPRUTKO

UNIWERSYTET MEDYCZNY IM. PIASTÓW ŚLĄSKICH WE WROCŁAWIU
(Wroclaw Medical University)

ul. Wybrzeże L. Pasteura 1, 50-367 Wrocław

Telephone: (71) 7841001
E-mail: rektor@umed.wroc.pl
Internet: www.umed.wroc.pl

Founded 1950

State control

Chancellor: Mgr ARTUR PARAFIŃSKI

Rector: Prof. Dr Hab. MAREK ZIĘTEK

Vice-Rector for Clinical Affairs: Prof. Dr ROMUALD ZDROJOWY

Vice-Rector for Educational Affairs: Prof. Dr MICHAŁ JELEŃ

Vice-Rector for Scientific Affairs: Prof. Dr Hab. ZYGMUNT GRZEBIENIAK

Vice-Rector for Univ. Development: Prof. Dr Hab. JACEK SZEPIETOWSKI

Dir for Library: RENATA SŁAWIŃSKA

Library of 255,000 vols

Number of teachers: 1,100

Publications: *Advances in Clinical and Experimental Medicine* (24 a year), *Dental and Medical Problems* (4 a year), *Polymers in Medicine* (4 a year)

DEANS

Faculty of Dentistry: Prof. Dr Hab. BEATA KAWALA

Faculty of Health Sciences: Prof. Dr Hab. JERZY HEIMRATH

Faculty of Medicine: Prof. Dr Hab. MAŁGORZATA SOBIESZCZANSKA

Faculty of Pharmacy and Laboratory Medicine: Prof. Dr Hab. HALINA GRAJETA

Faculty of Postgraduate Medical Training: Prof. Dr Hab. JOANNA RYMASZEWSKA

UNIWERSYTET MEDYCZNY W BIAŁYMSTOKU
(Medical University of Białystok)

ul. Jana Kilińskiego 1, 15-089 Białystok

Telephone: (85) 7485404

E-mail: rektor@umb.edu.pl

Internet: www.umb.edu.pl

Founded 1950

Rector: Prof. Dr Hab. JACEK NIKLIŃSKI

Vice-Rector for Clinical Affairs: Prof. Dr Hab. ZENON MARIAK

Vice-Rector for Scientific Affairs: Prof. Dr Hab. ADAM KRĘTOWSKI

Vice-Rector for Student Affairs: Prof. Dr Hab. ADRIAN CHABOWSKI

Library of 130,000 vols, 50,000 periodicals

Number of teachers: 800

Number of students: 4,700

Publications: *Advances in Medical Sciences* (2 a year, online, www.advms.pl), *Progress in Health Sciences* (online, progress.umb.edu.pl)

DEANS

Faculty of Health Sciences: Prof. Dr Hab. SŁAWOMIR JERZY TERLIKOWSKI

Faculty of Medicine: Prof. Dr Hab. IRINA KOWALSKA

Faculty of Pharmacy: Prof. Dr Hab. ELŻBIETA SKRZYDLEWSKA

UNIWERSYTET MEDYCZNY W ŁODZI
(Medical University of Łódź)

ul. Kościuszki 4, 90-419 Łódź

Telephone: (42) 2725803

E-mail: rektor@umed.lodz.pl

Internet: www.umed.pl

Founded 2002 by the merger of Łódź Medical Acad. and Łódź Military Medical Acad.

State control

Rector: Prof. Dr PAWEŁ GÓRSKI

Vice-Rector for Organization and Student Affairs: Prof. Dr RADZISŁAW KORDEK

Vice-Rector for Science: Prof. Dr LUCYNA WOŹNIAK

Vice-Rector for Teaching: Prof. Dr ANNA JEGIER

Vice-Rector for Univ. Development: Prof. Dr DARIUSZ NOWAK

Dir for Library: Dr RYSZARD ŻMUDA

Number of teachers: 1,600

Number of students: 9,530

DEANS

Faculty of Health Sciences: Prof. Dr ANDRZEJ BEDNAREK

Faculty of Medicine: Prof. Dr ADAM ANTCZAK

Faculty of Military Medicine: Prof. Dr JUREK OLSZEWSKI

Faculty of Pharmacy: Prof. Dr ELŻBIETA MIKICIUK-OLASIK

UNIWERSYTET MEDYCZNY W LUBLINIE
(Medical University in Lublin)

ul. Aleje Racławickie 1, 20-059 Lublin

Telephone: (81) 7423759

E-mail: biuro.rektora@umlub.pl

Internet: www.umlub.pl

Founded 1950

State control

Rector: Prof. Dr Hab. ANDRZEJ DROP

Vice-Rector for Clinical Affairs: Prof. Dr Hab. MIROSŁAW JABŁOŃSKI

Vice-Rector for Educational Affairs: Prof. Dr Hab. BARBARA JODŁOWSKA-JĘDRYCH

Vice-Rector for Int. Relations and Postgraduate Education: Dr Hab. HANNA TRĘBACZ

Vice-Rector for Scientific Affairs: Prof. Dr Hab. DARIUSZ MATOSIUK

Dir for Library: RENATA BIRSKA

Library of 130,535 vols, 48,905 spec. collns

Number of teachers: 1,200

Number of students: 5,000

DEANS

Faculty of Medicine I: Prof. Dr Hab. RYSZARD MACIEJEWSKI

Faculty of Medicine II: Prof. Dr Hab. WOJCIECH ZAŁUSKA

Faculty of Nursing and Health Sciences: Prof. Dr Hab. IRENA WROŃSKA

Faculty of Pharmacy: Prof. Dr Hab. RYSZARD KOCJAN

UNIWERSYTET MIKOŁAJA KOPERNIKA
(Nicolaus Copernicus University)

ul. Gagarina 11, 87-100 Toruń

Telephone: (56) 6114010

E-mail: kontakt@umk.pl

Internet: www.umk.pl

Founded 1945

State control

Language of instruction: Polish

Academic year: October to September (2 semesters)

Chancellor: Dr PAWEŁ MODRZYŃSKI

Rector: Prof. Dr Hab. ANDRZEJ TRETYN

Vice-Rector for Collegium Medicum: Prof. JAN STYCZYŃSKI

Vice-Rector for Economy and Devt: Prof. DANUTA DZIAWGO

Vice-Rector for Education: Prof. BEATA PRZYBOROWSKA

Vice-Rector for Research and ICT Infrastructure: Prof. WŁODZISŁAW DUCH

Vice-Rector for Student Affairs and Staff Management: Prof. ANDRZEJ SOKALA

Dir for Library: Dr MIROSŁAW SUPRUNIUK

Library of 1,191,821 vols, 574,465 vols of periodicals, 467,691 spec. collns, 72,367 MSS, 54,945 books, 87,562 sheet music

Number of teachers: 2,230

Number of students: 31,000

Publications: *Bulletin of Geography, Socioeconomic Series, Chaotic and Regular Dynamics, Comparative Law Review, Eastern European Countryside, Logic and Logical Philosophy, Medical and Biological Sciences, Open Systems and Information Dynamics, Prussia Sacra*

(published jointly with Max-Planck-Institut, Göttingen), *Reports on Mathematical Physics, Topological Methods in Nonlinear Analysis, Theoria et Historia Scientiarum, Toruński Rocznik Praw Człowieka i Pokoju*

DEANS

Faculty of Biology and Environment Protection: Prof. Dr Hab. WIESLAW KOZAK

Faculty of Chemistry: Prof. Dr Hab. EDWARD SZŁYK

Faculty of Earth Sciences: Prof. Dr Hab. WOJCIECH WYSOTA

Faculty of Economic Sciences and Management: Prof. Dr Hab. JÓZEF STAWICKI

Faculty of Education Sciences: Prof. Dr Hab. PIOTR PETRYKOWSKI

Faculty of Fine Arts: Prof. Dr Hab. ELŻBIETA BASIUL

Faculty of Health Sciences: Prof. Dr Hab. KORNELIA KĘDZIORA-KORNATOWSKA

Faculty of History: Prof. Dr Hab. JACEK GZELLA

Faculty of Humanities: Prof. Dr Hab. ANDRZEJ SZAHAJ

Faculty of Languages: Prof. Dr Hab. ADAM BEDNAREK

Faculty of Law and Administration: Prof. Dr Hab. TOMASZ JUSTYNSKI

Faculty of Mathematics and Computer Science: Prof. Dr Hab. SLAWOMIR RYBICKI

Faculty of Medicine: Prof. Dr Hab. JACEK KUBICA

Faculty of Pharmacy: Prof. Dr Hab. STEFAN KRUSZEWSKI

Faculty of Physics, Astronomy and Informatics: Prof. Dr Hab. STANISŁAW CHWIROT

Faculty of Political Sciences and International Studies: Prof. Dr Hab. ROMAN BÄCKER

Faculty of Theology: Prof. Dr Hab. DARIUSZ KOTECKI

PROFESSORS

Faculty of Biology and Environment Protection (Lwowska 1, 87-100 Toruń; tel. (56) 6112520; internet www.biol.umk.pl):

BEDNAREK, R., Soil Science

BEDNARSKA, E., Plant Cytology

BUSZKO, J., Entomology, Zoogeography

CAPUTA, M., Animal Physiology

CEYNOWA-GIEŁDON, M., Plant Taxonomy, Geobotany

CHWIROT, B., Plant and Animal Cytology

DAHM, H., Microbiology

DONDERSKI, W., Microbiology, Biotechnology

FALKOWSKI, J., Economic Geography, Spatial Management

GIZIŃSKI, A., Hydrobiology

GNIOT-SZULŻYCKA, J., Biochemistry

GÓRSKA-BRYLASS, A., Plant Cytology

KOPCEWICZ, J., Plant Physiology

KRIESEL, G., Anthropology

MAIK, W., Social Geography

NIEWAROWSKI, W., Physical Geography, Palaeogeography

REJEWSKI, M., Plant Ecology

SADURSKI, A., Hydrobiology and Environmental Protection

SZUPRYCZYŃSKI, J., Geomorphology

TRETYN, A., Plant Physiology

Faculty of Chemistry (ul. Gagarina 7, 87-100 Toruń; tel. (56) 6114302; e-mail wydzial@chem.umk.pl; internet www.chem.umk.pl):

BUSZEWSKI, B., Analytical Chemistry

CHOSTENKO, A., Nuclear Chemistry

GRODZICKI, A., Inorganic Chemistry

KITA, P., Inorganic Chemistry

ROZWADOWSKI, M., Physical Chemistry

RYCHLICKI, G., Physical Chemistry

SADLEJ, A., Theoretical Chemistry

TRYPUĆ, M., Chemical Technology

ZAIDLEWICZ, M., Organic Chemistry

Faculty of Economic Sciences and Management (ul. Gagarina 13A, 87-100 Toruń; tel. (56) 6114608; e-mail dziekan@econ.uni.torun.pl; internet www.econ.umk.pl):

BOGDANIENKO, J., Investment Economics
DREWIŃSKI, M., Management
GŁUCHOWSKI, J., Finance Management
JAWOROWSKI, P., Agricultural Economics
KACZMARCZYK, S., Marketing
MELLER, J., Human Resources Management
SMOLEŃSKI, S., Marketing
SOJAK, S., Accounting
STANKIEWICZ, M., Strategic Management and Planning
SUDOŁ, S., Industrial Management
SZULCE, H., Marketing
WIŚNIEWSKI, Z., Employment Policy
ZIELIŃSKI, Z., Econometrics

Faculty of Fine Arts (ul. Sienkiewicza 30/32, 87-100 Toruń; tel. (56) 6113810; internet www.art.umk.pl):

BEBARSKA, J., Sculpture
CANDER, K., Painting
CHMIELEWSKI, B., Drawing
CHMIELEWSKI, W., Drawing
FLIK, J., Painting
GUTTFELD, A., Painting
KILJAŃSKI, L., Graphics
KRUSZELNICKI, Z., History of Art
LIMONT, W., Art Education
MALINOWSKI, J., History of Art
PAWŁOWSKI, M., Graphics
PRĘGOWSKI, J., Painting
PRZYBYLIŃSKI, B., Graphics
ROUBA, B., Restoration of Painting
SKIBIŃSKI, S., Medieval Art and Architecture
SŁOBOSZ, J., Graphics
STRZELCZYK, A., Conservation of Painting and Leather
SZAŃKOWSKI, M., Sculpture
TAJCHMAN, J., Restoration of Architectural Monuments
WOLSKI, L., Painting
ZIOMEK, M., Painting

Faculty of History (Władysława Bojarskiego 1, 87-100 Toruń; tel. (56) 6113712; internet www.his.umk.pl):

CHUDZIAK, J., Archaeology of Buildings
DYGDAŁA, J., 16th- to 18th-century Polish History
KALEMBKA, S., Polish and General History
KOZŁOWSKI, R., Modern Polish History
KUTZNER, M., Polish and General Medieval History of Art
MALISZEWSKI, K., 16th to 18th century Polish and General History
MAŁŁEK, K., 16th to 18th century Polish and General History
MIELCZAREK, M., Classical Archaeology and Numismatics
NOWAKOWSKI, A., Medieval Archaeology and Military History
OLCZAK, J., Medieval Archaeology and History of Glass
POMIAN, K., Polish and General Modern History of Art and Culture
RADZIMIŃSKI, A., Medieval Church History
REZMER, W., Polish Army between the Two World Wars
STASZEWSKI, J., 16th to 18th century Polish and General History
SUDZIŃSKI, R., Modern Polish History
SYMONIDES, J., EU and International Law
TANDECKI, J., Polish-German Relations
TONDEL, J., History of the Book
WAŻBIŃSKI, Z., History of Art
WENTA, J., Medieval History
WOJCIECHOWSKI, M., 19th- and 20th-century Polish and General History
WOŹNICZKA-PARUZEL, B., Bibliotherapy
ZAREMSKA, H., Cultural History

Faculty of Humanities (ul. Fosa Staromiejska 1A, 87-100 Toruń; tel. (56) 6113610; e-mail whminus@umk.pl; internet www.hum.umk.pl):

ADAMSKI, W., Social Structures and Transformations
BAŃKA, A., Psychology
BOROWICZ, R., Sociology of Education
BYBLUK, M., Teaching of Languages
HUBNER, P., History of Science, Sociology of Institutions
KALETA, A., Rural Sociology
KOWALIK, S., Special Education
KWIECIŃSKI, Z., Sociology of Education
ŁUKASZEWICZ, R., School Education
MELOSIK, Z., General Education
MUCHA, J., Social Anthropology and History of Sociology
NALASKOWSKI, A., General Education
PAWLAK, J., History of Philosophy and Social Thought
PERZANOWSKI, J., Logic and Philosophy
PÓŁTURZYCKI, J., General Education
SCHULZ, R., General Education
SIEMIENIECKI, B., Technology in Education
SZAHAJ, A., Political Philosophy, Philosophy of Culture
SZULAKIEWICZ, M., Political Culture
TEMPCZYK, M., Philosophy of Natural Science
TYBURSKI, W., Ethics
WINCŁAWSKI, W., History of Sociology
ZANDECKI, A., General Education
ZELAZNY, M., Aesthetics, History of Philosophy

Faculty of Languages (ul. Fosa Staromiejska 3, 87-100 Toruń; tel. (56) 6113510; e-mail dziekanat_wf@umk.pl; internet www.fil.umk.pl):

BEZWIŃSKI, A., Russian Literature
BRZOZA, H., Russian Literature
FRIEDEL, T., Slavonic and Polish Linguistics
GROCHOWSKI, M., General Linguistics, Semiotics
HARTMANN, H., German Literature
KALLAS, K., Contemporary Polish Syntax
KRYSZAK, J., Contemporary Polish Poetry
SAUERLAND, K., German Literature
SAWICKA, I., Slavonic Linguistics
SKUCZYŃSKI, J., History of Polish Literature and Theatre
SPEINA, J., 20th-century Polish Prose
SZARMACH, M., Greek Literature, Second Sophistry
SZUPRYCZYŃSKA, M., Contemporary Polish Syntax
WĄSIK, Z., English Linguistics
WISZNIOWSKA-MAJCHRZYK, M., English Drama
WRÓBLEWSKI, W., Classical Philology

Faculty of Law and Administration (ul. Władysława Bojarskiego 3, 87-100 Toruń; tel. (56) 6114005; e-mail wpia@law.umk.pl; internet www.law.umk.pl):

BORODO, A., Financial Law
BRZEZIŃSKI, B., Public Finance Law
BULSIEWICZ, A., Criminal Law
FILAR, M., Penal Law
JASUDOWICZ, T., Human Rights
JUSTYŃSKI, J., Political and Legal Doctrines
KALLAS, M., History of the Polish State
KOLASIŃSKI, K., Labour Law
KULICKI, M., Crime Detection
LANG, A., Theory of Law and State
ŁASZEWSKI, R., History of Law
LUBIŃSKI, K., Civil Law
MAREK, A., Criminal Law
MIK, C., European Law, Human Rights
MORAWSKI, L., Theory of Law and State
NESTEROWICZ, M., Civil Law
OCHENDOWSKI, E., Administrative Law

Faculty of Mathematics and Computer Science (ul. Chopina 12/18, 87-100 Toruń; tel. (56) 6113410; e-mail wmii@mat.umk.pl; internet www.mat.umk.pl):

GÓRNIEWICZ, L., Nonlinear Analysis
JAKUBOWSKI, A., Theory of Probability
KAMIŃSKI, B., Ergodic Theory
KWIATKOWSKI, J., Ergodic Theory
LEMAŃCZYK, M., Ergodic Theory
NAGAJEW, A., Theory of Probability, Statistics
SIMSON, D., Algebra
SKOWROŃSKI, A., Algebra
TYC, A., Algebra

Faculty of Physics, Astronomy and Informatics (ul. Grudziądzka 5, 87-100 Toruń; tel. (56) 6113249; internet www.fizyka.umk.pl):

BĄCZYNSKI, A., Molecular Spectroscopy, Optoelectronics
BALTER, A., Molecular Spectroscopy, Photophysics, Molecular Biophysics
BIELSKI, A., Atomic and Molecular Physics, History of Physics
CHWIROT, S., Atomic and Optical Physics
DEMBIŃSKI, S., Quantum Optics, Chaos Theory
DUCH, W., Computational Intelligence, Cognitive Science and Theoretical Physics
JANKOWSKI, K., Atomic and Molecular Physics, Computational Methods in Physics
JASKÓLSKI, W., Atomic and Molecular Physics, Physics of Low-dimensional Structures
KARWOWSKI, J., Atomic and Molecular Physics
KOSSAKOWSKI, A., Theoretical Physics, Statistical Physics
KREŁOWSKI, J., Astrophysics
KUS, A., Radio Astronomy
MĘCZYŃSKA, H., Solid-State Physics
RACZYŃSKI, A., Atomic and Molecular Physics
ROZPŁOCH, F., Condensed Matter Physics, Physics of Carbon
SZUDY, J., Atomic and Molecular Physics, Optical Collisions
WOJTOWICZ, A., Solid-State Physics, Optoelectronics
WOLSZCZAN, A., Radio Astronomy, Pulsars
WOSZCZYK, A., Astrophysics, Physics of Comets
WYBOURNE, B., Atomic and Molecular Physics
ZAREMBA, J., Atomic and Molecular Physics

Faculty of Theology (ul. Gagarina 37, 87-100 Toruń; tel. (56) 6114990; e-mail teologia@umk.pl; internet www.teologia.umk.pl):

BAGROWICZ, J., Catechetic and Religious Education
GRABOWSKI, M., Christian Philosophy
RYCHLICKI, C., Dogmatic and Ecumenical Theology

UNIWERSYTET MUZYCZNY FRYDERYKA CHOPINA
(Fryderyk Chopin University of Music)

ul. Okólnik 2, 00-368 Warsaw

Telephone: (22) 8277241
E-mail: info@chopin.edu.pl
Internet: www.chopin.edu.pl

Founded 1810
State control

Chancellor: MAGDALENA GIEDROJĆ-JURAHA
Rector: Prof. RYSZARD ZIMAK
Pro-Rector for Artistic Affairs: Prof. KLAUDIUSZ BARAN
Pro-Rector for Foreign and Student Affairs: Prof. Dr Hab. EWA IŻYKOWSKA-KŁOSIEWICZ
Pro-Rector for Teaching Affairs: Prof. ANDRZEJ BANASIEWICZ
Dir for Library: ZOFIA OLSZEWSKA-BAJERA

Library of 100,000 vols
Number of students: 900

DEANS

Faculty of Choir Conducting, Music Education, Church Music, Rhythmics and Dance: Prof. SŁAWEK ADAM WRÓBLEWSKI
Faculty of Composition, Conducting and Theory of Music: Prof. SZYMON KAWALLA
Faculty of Instrumental and Educational Studies in Białystok: Prof. BOŻENNA SAWICKA
Faculty of Instrumental Studies: Prof. TOMASZ STRAHL
Faculty of Piano, Harpsichord and Organ: Prof. ANNA JASTRZĘBSKA-QUINN
Faculty of Sound Engineering: Prof. MAŁGORZATA LEWANDOWSKA
Faculty of Vocal and Acting Studies: Prof. RYSZARD CIESLA

UNIWERSYTET OPOLSKI
(Opole University)

pl. Kopernika 11A, 45-040 Opole
Telephone: (77) 5416070
E-mail: sekretariat@uni.opole.pl
Internet: www.uni.opole.pl

Founded 1994 by the merger of Opole Teacher Training College and the Theological-Pastoral Institute of Opole
State control

Chancellor: EWA RURYNKIEWICZ
Rector: Prof. Dr Hab. STANISŁAW SŁAWOMIR NICIEJA
Vice-Rector for Education and Students: Prof. Dr Hab. MAREK MASNYK
Vice-Rector for Promotion and Management: Prof. Dr Hab. WIESŁAWA PIĄTKOWSKA-STEPANIAK
Vice-Rector for Science and Finance: Prof. Dr Hab. JANUSZ SŁODCZYK
Dir for Library: DANUTA SZEWCZYK-KŁOS

DEANS

Faculty of Chemistry: Prof. Dr Hab. PIOTR P. WIECZOREK
Faculty of Economics: Prof. Dr Hab. STANISŁAWA SOKOŁOWSKA
Faculty of History and Pedagogy: Prof. Dr Hab. JANUSZ HENRYK DOROBISZ
Faculty of Law and Administration: Prof. Dr Hab. PIOTR STEC
Faculty of Mathematics, Physics and Computer Science: Prof. Dr Hab. JACEK NIKIEL
Faculty of Natural and Technical Sciences: Prof. Dr Hab. STANISŁAW KOZIARSKI
Faculty of Philology: Prof. Dr Hab. ANDRZEJ CIUK
Faculty of Theology: Prof. Dr Hab. TADEUSZ DOLA

UNIWERSYTET PEDAGOGICZNY IM. KOMISJI EDUKACJI NARODOWEJ W KRAKOWIE
(Pedagogical University of Cracow)

ul. Podchorążych 2, 30-084 Cracow
Telephone: (12) 6626014
E-mail: info@up.krakow.pl
Internet: www.up.krakow.pl

Founded 1946 as Akademia Pedagogiczna im. Komisji Edukacji Narodowej w Krakowie, present name and status 1999
State control

Rector: Prof. Dr MICHAŁ ŚLIWA
Vice-Rector for Educational Affairs: Dr JERZY WALIGÓRA
Vice-Rector for Research and Int. Relations: Dr KAZIMIERZ KAROLCZAK
Vice-Rector for Student Affairs: Dr JAN SUCHANICZ
Dir for Library: Dr STANISŁAW SKÓRKA
Number of teachers: 800

Number of students: 20,000

DEANS

Faculty of Art: Dr ALICJA PANASIEWICZ
Faculty of Geography and Biology: Prof. Dr ZBIGNIEW DŁUGOSZ
Faculty of Humanities: Prof. Dr ZDZISŁAW NOGA
Faculty of Mathematics, Physics and Technical Science: Dr WŁADYSŁAW BŁASIAK
Faculty of Pedagogy: Dr ZOFIA SZAROTA
Faculty of Philology: Dr BOGUSŁAW SKOWRONEK

UNIWERSYTET PRZYRODNICZY W LUBLINIE
(University of Life Sciences in Lublin)

ul. Akademicka 13, 20-950 Lublin
Telephone: (81) 4456677
E-mail: biuro.rektora@up.lublin.pl
Internet: www.ar.lublin.pl

Founded 1955, present name and status 2008
Rector: Prof. Dr Hab. MARIAN WESOŁOWSKI
Vice-Rector for Personnel and Investment Funds: Prof. ANDRZEJ BOROWY
Vice-Rector for Scientific Research and Int. Cooperation: Prof. STANISŁAW BARAN
Vice-Rector for Student Affairs and Education: Prof. KRZYSZTOF GOŁACKI
Dir for Library: Dr MARIAN BUTKIEWICZ
Library of 380,000 vols
Number of teachers: 800
Number of students: 11,000
Publications: *Annales UMCS*, *Excerpta Veterinaria Lublin* (in English), *Sectio DD Medicina Veterinaria*, *Sectio E Agricultura*, *Sectio EE Zootechnica*, *Sectio EEE Horticulture*

DEANS

Faculty of Agricultural Sciences in Zamosc: Prof. Dr Hab. DANUTA BORKOWSKA
Faculty of Agrobioengineering: Prof. Dr KRZYSZTOF KOWALCZYK
Faculty of Biology and Animal Breeding: Prof. Dr Hab. EUGENIUSZ R. GRELA
Faculty of Food Science and Biotechnology: Prof. Dr BARBARA BARANIAK
Faculty of Horticulture and Landscape Architecture: Prof. Dr ANDRZEJ BOROWY
Faculty of Production Engineering: Prof. Dr Hab. ANDRZEJ MARCZUK
Faculty of Veterinary Medicine: Prof. Dr STANISŁAW WINIARCZYK

UNIWERSYTET PRZYRODNICZY W POZNANIU
(Poznań University of Life Sciences)

ul. Wojska Polskiego 28, 60-637 Poznań
Telephone: (61) 8487001
E-mail: rektorat@up.poznan.pl
Internet: puls.edu.pl

Founded 1951, present name 2014
Chancellor: MAREK KLIMECKI
Rector: Prof. Dr Hab. GRZEGORZ SKRZYPCZAK
Rector for Science and Int. Relations: Prof. Dr Hab. JAN PIKUL
Rector for Studies: Prof. Dr Hab. MONIKA KOZŁOWSKA
Vice-Rector for Staff and Univ. Devt: Prof. Dr CZESŁAW SZAFRANSKI
Dir for Library: Mgr MARIUSZ POLARCZYK
Library of 740,000 vols
Number of teachers: 820
Number of students: 11,320
Publications: *Acta Scientiarum Polonorum*, *Botanika-Steciana*, *Folia Forestalia Polonica*, *Journal of Agrobusiness and Rural Devt* (in English and Polish), *Nauka Przyroda Technologie*

DEANS

Faculty of Agronomy and Bioengineering: Prof. Dr Hab. WIESŁAW KOZIARA
Faculty of Animal Breeding and Biology: Dr Hab. MAŁGORZATA SZUMACHER-STRABEL
Faculty of Economics and Social Sciences: Prof. Dr Hab. WALENTY POCZTA
Faculty of Food Science and Nutrition: Prof. Dr Hab. JAN MICHNIEWICZ
Faculty of Forestry: Prof. Dr Hab. ROMAN GORNOWICZ
Faculty of Horticulture and Landscape Architecture: Dr Hab. BARBARA POLITYCKA
Faculty of Land Reclamation and Environmental Engineering: Prof. Dr Hab. JOLANTA KOMISAREK
Faculty of Wood Technology: Prof. Dr Hab. BARTLOMIEJ MAZELA

UNIWERSYTET PRZYRODNICZY WE WROCŁAWIU
(Wrocław University of Environmental and Life Sciences)

ul. C. K. Norwida 25/27, 50-375 Wrocław
Telephone: (71) 3205020
E-mail: rektor@up.wroc.pl
Internet: www.up.wroc.pl

Founded 1951, present name and status 2006
Academic year: October to June

Rector: Prof. Dr ROMAN KOLACZ
Vice-Rector for Devt: Prof. Dr ANDRZEJ DRABINSKI
Vice-Rector for Int. Relations and Regional Cooperation: Prof. Dr ALINA WIELICZKO
Vice-Rector for Research: Prof. Dr TADEUSZ TRZISZKA
Vice-Rector for Student Affairs and Education: Prof. Dr DANUTA PARYLAK
Dir for Library: GRAŻYNA TALAR
Library of 212,000 vols
Number of teachers: 230
Number of students: 10,800

DEANS

Faculty of Biology and Animal Science: Prof. Dr Hab. ANDRZEJ ZACHWIEJA
Faculty of Environmental Engineering and Geodesy: Prof. Dr Hab. BERNARD KONTNY
Faculty of Food Science: Prof. Dr Hab. JÓZEFA CHRZANOWSKA
Faculty of Life Sciences and Technology: Prof. Dr Hab. ADAM SZEWCZUK
Faculty of Veterinary Medicine: Prof. Dr Hab. KRZYSZTOF KUBIAK

UNIWERSYTET ROLNICZY IM. HUGONA KOŁŁĄTAJA W KRAKOWIE
(University of Agriculture in Cracow)

ul. Mickiewicza 21, 31-120 Cracow
Telephone: (12) 6624280
E-mail: rector@ur.krakow.pl
Internet: www.ur.krakow.pl

Founded 1890, present status 1972, present name 2008

Chancellor: KRZYSZTOF ZIÓŁKOWSKI
Rector: Prof. Dr Hab. WŁODZIMIERZ SADY
Vice-Rector for Education and Student Affairs: Dr Hab. SYLWESTER TABOR
Vice-Rector for Research and Int. Relations: Prof. Dr Hab. STANISLAW MALEK
Vice-Rector for Univ. Organization and Cooperation with the National Economy: Prof. Dr Hab. FLORIAN GAMBUS
Dir for Library: Dr BOŻENA PIETRZYK
Number of students: 13,000

DEANS

Faculty of Agriculture and Economics: Prof. Dr ANDRZEJ LEPIARCZYK
Faculty of Animal Sciences: Prof. Dr CZESLAW KLOCEK

Faculty of Environmental Engineering and Land Surveying: Prof. Dr JAN PAWELEK
Faculty of Food Technology: Prof. Dr TERESA FORTUNA
Faculty of Forestry: Prof. Dr STANISŁAW ORZEŁ
Faculty of Horticulture: Prof. Dr MAREK GRABOWSKI
Faculty of Production and Power Engineering: Prof. Dr SLAWOMIR KURPASKA

UNIWERSYTET RZESZOWSKI
(University of Rzeszów)

ul. Rejtana 16c, 35-959 Rzeszów
Telephone: (17) 8721000
E-mail: info@ur.edu.pl
Internet: www.univ.rzeszow.pl

Founded 2001 by merger of the Pedagogical Univ. of Rzeszów, the Marie Curie Skłodowska Univ., Lublin (Rzeszów br.) and the Economics Faculty of the Agricultural Acad. of Cracow
State control

Chancellor: Mgr Inz. JAROSŁAW SZLĘZAK (acting)
Rector: Prof. ALEKSANDER BOBKO
Vice-Rector for Devt: Prof. CZESŁAW PUCHALSKI
Vice-Rector for Science: Prof. SYLWESTER CZOPEK
Vice-Rector for Student Affairs and Education: Prof. WOJCIECH WALAT
Dir for Library: Dr BOŻENA JASKOWSKA
Library of 755,000 vols, 103,000 periodicals and 23,000 spec. collns
Number of students: 25,000

DEANS

Branch Campus of the Faculty of Biotechnology: MARK KOZIOROWSKI (Dir)
Faculty of Art: Prof. Dr Hab. JOZEF JERZY KIERSKI
Faculty of Biology and Agriculture: Prof. Dr Hab. ZBIGNIEW CZERNIAKOWSKI
Faculty of Economics: Prof. Dr Hab. GRZEGORZ ŚLUSARZ
Faculty of Law and Administration: Prof. Dr Hab. STANISŁAW SAGAN
Faculty of Mathematics and Natural Sciences: Prof. Dr Hab. OŁEH ŁOPUSZANSKI
Faculty of Medicine: Prof. Dr Hab. ARTUR MAZUR
Faculty of Pedagogy and Fine Arts: Prof. Dr Hab. RYSZARD PĘCZKOWSKI
Faculty of Philology: Prof. Dr Hab. ZENON OŻÓG
Faculty of Physical Education: Prof. Dr Hab. WOJCIECH CZARNY
Faculty of Sociology and History: Prof. Dr Hab. ZDZISŁAW BUDZYŃSKI
Institute of Philosophy: Prof. Dr Hab. ANDRZEJ L. ZACHARIASZ (Dir)

UNIWERSYTET ŚLĄSKI W KATOWICACH
(University of Silesia in Katowice)

ul. Bankowa 12, 40-007 Katowice
Telephone: (32) 3591956
E-mail: info@us.edu.pl
Internet: www.us.edu.pl

Founded 1968
State control
Languages of instruction: English, Polish
Academic year: October to June

Chancellor: Dr AGNIESZKA SKOŁUCKA
Rector: Prof. Dr WIESŁAW BANYŚ
Vice-Rector for Education and Student Affairs: Prof. RYSZARD KOZIOŁEK
Vice-Rector for Finance and Devt: Prof. STANISŁAW KUCHARSKI

Vice-Rector for Internationalization, Institutional Affairs and Public Relations: Prof. MIROSŁAW NAKONIECZNY
Vice-Rector for Research and Collaboration with Industry: Prof. ANDRZEJ KOWALCZYK
Dir for Library: Prof. Dr Hab. DARIUSZ PAWELEC
Library of 1,453,658 vols, 69,611 periodicals
Number of teachers: 2,100
Number of students: 30,100

Publications: *Acta Chromotographica, Annales Mathematicae Silesianae, Chowanna, Folia Philosophica, Gazeta Uniwersytecka, Geographia: Studia et Dissertationes, Górnośląskie Studia Socjologiczne, Neophilologica, Postscriptum Polonistyczne, Problemy Prawa Prywatnego Międzynarodowego, Romanica Silesiana, Średniowiecze Polskie i Powszechne, Studia Politicae Universitatis Silesiensis, Wieki Stare i Nowe, Z Dziejów Prawa*

DEANS

Faculty of Biology and Environmental Protection: Prof. Dr Hab. IWONA SZAREJKO
Faculty of Computer and Materials Sciences: Prof. Dr Hab. DANUTA STRÓŻ
Faculty of Earth Sciences: Prof. Dr Hab. ADAM IDZIAK
Faculty of Ethnology and Educational Science: Prof. Dr Hab. ZENON GAJDZICA
Faculty of Fine Arts and Music: Prof. MAŁGORZATA ŁUSZCZAK
Faculty of Law and Administration: Prof. Dr Hab CZESŁAW MARTYSZ
Faculty of Mathematics, Physics and Chemistry: Prof. Dr Hab. ALICJA RATUSZNA
Faculty of Pedagogy and Psychology: Prof. Dr Hab. STANISŁAW JUSZCZYK
Faculty of Philology: Prof. Dr Hab. RAFAL MOLENCKI
Faculty of Radio and Television: Prof. JERZY ŁUKASZEWICZ
Faculty of Social Sciences: Prof. Dr Hab. WIESŁAW KACZANOWICZ
Faculty of Theology: Prof. Dr Hab. ANTONI BARTOSZEK
School of Management: Prof. Dr Hab. BARBARA KOŻUSZNIK (Dir)
School of Polish Language and Culture: Prof. Dr Hab. JOLANTA TAMBOR (Dir)

PROFESSORS

Faculty of Biology and Environmental Protection (ul Jagiellońska 28, 40-032 Katowice; tel. (32) 2009461; e-mail biologia@us.edu.pl; internet www.wbios.us.edu.pl):

BIELAŃSKA-GRAJNER, I., Hydrobiology
CIEPAŁ, R., Ecology
GAJ, M., Genetics
GORCZYCA, J., Zoology
HASTEROK, R., Plant Anatomy and Cytology
HERCZEK, A., Zoology
KARCZ, W., Histology and Animal Embryology
KLAG, J., Cell Biology
KURCZYŃSKA, E., Biophysics and Plant Morphogenesis
KWIATKOWSKA, D., Biochemistry
ŁABUŻEK, S., Plant Anatomy and Cytology
MAŁUSZYŃSKA, J., Genetics
MAŁUSZYŃSKI, M., Animal Physiology and Ecotoxicology
MIGULA, P., Ecology
PALOWSKI, B., Plant Physiology
PIETRUSZKA, M., Microbiology
PIOTROWSKA-SEGET, Z., Microbiology
RADZIEJEWSKA-LEBRECHT, J., Systematic Botany
ROSTAŃSKI, A., Ecology
SKUBAŁA, P., Hydrobiology
STRZELEC, M., Histology and Animal Embryology
ŚWIĄTEK, P., Genetics

SZAREJKO, I., Zoology
WĘGIEREK, P., Geobotany and Nature Protection
WIKA, S., Plant Physiology

Faculty of Computer and Materials Sciences (ul. Żytnia 12, 41-205 Sosnowiec; tel. (32) 2691845; e-mail dwt@us.edu.pl; internet www.wiinom.us.edu.pl):

BOGDANOWICZ, W., Materials Science
BORYCZKA, M., Computer Science
BORYCZKA, U., Computer Science
CYBO, J., Materials Science
CZECH, Z., Computer Science
CZEKAJ, D., Materials Science
DEC, J., Materials Science
DENISZCZYK, J., Materials Science
GROBE, L., Materials Science
ILCZUK, J., Materials Science
KANSY, J., Materials Science
KOTARSKI, W., Computer Science
KUPKA, M., Materials Science
LELĄTKO, J., Materials Science
PORWIK, P., Computer Science
SKONIECZNY, W., Materials Science
SKULSKI, R., Materials Science
STRÓŻ, D., Materials Science
SUROWIEC, M., Materials Science
WAKULICZ-DEJA, A., Computer Science
WOKULSKA, K., Materials Science
WRÓBEL, Z., Computer Science

Faculty of Earth Sciences (ul. Będzińska 60, 41-200 Sosnowiec; tel. (32) 3689400; e-mail wnoz@us.edu.pl; internet www.wnoz.us.edu.pl):

ANDREJCZUK, W., Regional Geography and Tourism
CZAJA, S., Physical Geography
CZYLOK, A., Physical Geography
FABIAŃSKA, M., Geochemistry
GALUSKIN, E., Geochemistry
GŁUCHOWSKI, E., Stratigraphy and Palaeontology
IDZIAK, A., Applied Geology
JANECZEK, J., Geochemistry
JANIA, J., Geomorphology
JANKOWSKI, A., Physical Geography
KARWOWSKI, Ł., Geochemistry
KLIMEK, K., Quaternary Palaeogeography and Palaeoecology
KOWALCZYK, A., Hydrogeology and Engineering Geology
KRUSZEWSKA, K., Geochemistry
MALIK, I., Reconstruction of the Geographical Environment
NIEDŹWIEDŹ, T., Climatology
PULINA, M., Physical Geography
RACKI, G., Stratigraphy and Palaeontology
RAHMONOV, O., Physical Geography
RUNGE, J., Social Geography
RZĘTAŁA, M., Hydrology and Water Management
SZAJNOWSKA-WYSOCKA, A., Settlement Geography
SZCZYPEK, T., Physical Geography
TEPER, L., Applied Geology
TKOCZ, M., Spatial Economy
ZUBEREK, W., Applied Geology

Faculty of Ethnology and Educational Science (ul. Bielska 62, 43-400 Cieszyn; tel. (33) 8546135; e-mail dziekanat.weinoe@us.edu.pl; internet www.weinoe.us.edu.pl):

BUKOWSKA-FLOREŃSKA, I., Ethnology and Cultural Anthropology
GAJDZICA, Z., Pedagogy
KAJFOSZ, J., Ethnology and Cultural Anthropology
KIEDOS, J., Pedagogy
KŁODNICKI, Z., Ethnology and Cultural Anthropology
LEWOWICKI, T., Pedagogy
MRÓZEK, R., Pedagogy
MURZYN, A., Pedagogy
OGRODZKA-MAZUR, E., Pedagogy
OLBRYCHT, K., Cultural Education

REMIN, M., Pedagogy
RUSEK, H., Ethnology and Cultural Anthropology
SMYRNOVA-TRYBULSKA, Y., Pedagogy
SZCZUREK-BORUTA, A., Pedagogy
SZUŚCIK, U., Pedagogy
ZILINEK, M., Pedagogy

Faculty of Fine Arts and Music (ul. Bielska 62, 43-400 Cieszyn; tel. (33) 8546164; e-mail wart@wart.us.edu.pl; internet www.wart.us.edu.pl):

ADAMUS, J., Painting
CIENCIAŁA, W., Music
DANEL-BOBRZYK, H., Music
DELEKTA, E., Graphic Arts
FOBERT, J., Sculpture
GONIEWICZ-URBAŚ, H., Music Education
HOŁARD, J., Graphic Design
JACYKÓW, W., Interdisciplinary Artistic Creation
KNOPEK, J., Graphic Arts
KOŁODZIEJCZYK, L., Music
KORZISTKA, M., Art Theory
KOWALCZYK-KLUS, A., Interdisciplinary Artistic Creation
KULA, K., Painting
KURAJ, E., Music
LASOŃ, A., Painting
ŁUSZCZAK, M., Interdisciplinary Artistic Creation
MACIUSZKIEWICZ, R., Painting
MICHALAK, R., Music
OSTROWSKI, A., Graphic Design
PICHURA, J., Music
PIECH-KALARUS, J., Graphic Arts
PIELESZ, R., Graphic Design
RUS, T., Painting
ŚMIETANA, S., Music
SUTRYK, W., Sculpture
SZAREK, A., Music
TUREK, K., Music
UCHYŁA-ZROSKI, J., Music
WARCHOŁ-SOBIESIAK, M., Music

Faculty of Law and Administration (ul. Bankowa 11B, 40-007 Katowice; tel. (32) 3592060; e-mail wpia@us.edu.pl; internet www.wpia.us.edu.pl):

BIŃCZYCKA-MAJEWSKA, T., Law
BISZTYGA, A., Law
CIĄGWA, J., Law
DOLNICKI, B., Law
DUKIET-NAGÓRSKA, T., Law
FUCHS, B., Law
GLUMIŃSKA-PAWLIC, J., Law
GÓRECKI, J., Law
GRABOWSKA, G., Law
GRABOWSKI, J., Law
KALUS, S., Law
KOWALSKI, W., Law
ŁABNO, A., Law
ŁASZCZYCA, G., Administration
LIPIŃSKI, A., Law
LITYŃSKI, A., Law
MAŁAJNY, R., Law
MARSZAŁ, K., Law
MARTYSZ, C., Law and Administration
MIKOŁAJCZYK, B., Law
MIKOŁAJCZYK, M., Law
MIKOSZ, R., Law
OGIEGŁO, L., Law
PAZDAN, M., Law
PIKULSKA-RADOMSKA, A., Law
POPIOŁEK, W., Law
ROTT-PIETRZYK, E., Law
STRZĘPKA, J., Law
TOBOR, Z., Law
WIDŁA, T., Law
WILK, L., Law
WITOSZ, A., Law
ZACHARKO, L., Law and Administration
ZDEBEL, M., Law
ZGRYZEK, K., Law

Faculty of Mathematics, Physics and Chemistry (ul. Bankowa 14, 40-007 Katowice; tel. (32) 3591550; e-mail dziekanat@mfc.us.edu.pl; internet w3.mfc.us.edu.pl):

BARON, K., Mathematics
BEDNAREKI, L., Astrophysics and Cosmology
BIESIADA, M., Astrophysics and Cosmology
BŁASZCZYK, A., Set Theory
BORGIEŁ, W., Theoretical Physics
BRÓDKA, A., Biophysics and Molecular Physics
BURIAN, A., Biophysics and Molecular Physics
CHEŁKOWSKA, G., Solid-State Physics
CHOLEWA, J., Mathematics
CZYŻ, H., Field Theory and Particle Physics
DAJKA, J., Theoretical Physics
DASZYKOWSKI, M., Chemometrics
DŁOTKO, T., Mathematics
DRZAZGA, Z., Medical Physics
DUDA, H., Physics of Crystals
DZIK, W., Mathematical Logic
FLAKUS, H., Chemistry
FUGIEL, B., Biophysics and Molecular Physics
GBURSKI, Z., Computational Physics and Electronics
GER, R., Mathematics
GLUZA, J., Field Theory and Particle Physics
GROŃ, T., Physics of Crystals
JASTRZĘBSKA, M., Solid-State Physics
JAWORSKA, M., Chemistry
KANIA, A., Ferroelectrics
KISIEL, J., Nuclear Physics
KOCOT, A., Biophysics and Molecular Physics
KOŁODZIEJ, K., Field Theory and Particle Physics
KOMINEK, Z., Mathematics
KOSTUR, M., Theoretical Physics
KOWALSKA, T., Chemistry
KROK-KOWALSKI, J., Physics of Crystals
KROMPIEC, S., Chemistry
KUCHARSKI, S., Chemistry
KUŚ, P., Organic Synthesis
KUSZ, J., Physics of Crystals
LIGĘZA, J., Mathematics
ŁUCZKA, J., Theoretical Physics
MACHURA, B., Crystallography
MARCZAK, W., Chemistry
MAŚKA, M., Theoretical Physics
MATLENGIEWICZ, M., Chemistry
MIERZEJEWSKI, M., Theoretical Physics
MUSIAŁ, M., Chemistry
NOWAK, A., Mathematics
PALUCH, M., Biophysics and Molecular Physics
PISARSKI, W., Chemistry
PLEWIK, S., Mathematics
POLAŃSKI, J., Chemistry
RATUSZNA, A., Solid-State Physics
ROLEDER, K., Experimental Physics
RUDNICKI, R., Mathematics
RZOSKA, S., Biophysics and Molecular Physics
SABLIK, M., Mathematics
SCHAB-BALCERZAK, E., Chemistry
SITKO, R., Chemistry
SKRZYPEK, D., Solid-State Physics
SŁADEK, A., Mathematics
SŁADKOWSKI, J., Astrophysics and Cosmology
ŚLEBARSKI, A., Solid-State Physics
SOCHA, L., Physics
SUŁKOWSKI, W., Chemistry
SZADE, J., Solid-State Physics
SZOPA, M., Theoretical Physics
SZOT, K., Experimental Physics
TALIK, E., Solid-State Physics
UJMA, Z., Experimental Physics
WALCZAK, B., Chemistry
WESTWAŃSKI, B., Theoretical Physics

WRZALIK, R., Biophysics and Molecular Physics
ZAIONC, M., Mathematics
ZIOŁO, J., Biophysics and Molecular Physics
ZIPPER, E., Theoretical Physics
ZRAŁEK, M., Field Theory and Particle Physics

Faculty of Pedagogy and Psychology (ul. Grażyńskiego 53, 40-126 Katowice; tel. (32) 3599811; e-mail pips@us.edu.pl; internet www.wpips.us.edu.pl):

GÓRNIK-DUROSE, M., Psychology
JUSZCZYK, S., Pedagogy
KARANDASHEV, Y., Psychology
KNAPIK, M., Pedagogy
KOŻUSZNIK, B., Psychology
KRASOŃ, K., Pedagogy
KURINCOVA, V., Pedagogy
MANDAL, E., Psychology
NOWAK, A., Pedagogy
SACHER, W., Pedagogy
SEIDLER, P., Pedagogy
SENKO, T., Pedagogy
STANIK, J., Psychology
STANKOWSKI, A., Pedagogy
SYREK, E., Pedagogy
TOKARZ, M., Psychology

Faculty of Philology (pl. Sejmu Śląskiego 1, 40-032 Katowice; tel. (32) 2009263; e-mail filologia@us.edu.pl; internet www.fil.us.edu.pl):

ALEKSANDROWICZ, T., Classical Philology
BANYŚ, W., French Philology
BEDNARSKI, M., Classical Philology
BIAŁAS, Z., English Philology
BORKOWSKA, E., English Philology
CICHOŃSKA, M., Slavonic Philology
CUDAK, R., Polish Philology
CZAPIK-LITYŃSKA, B., Slavonic Philology
CZERWIŃSKI, P., Russian Philology
DUTKA, E., Polish Philology
DZIADEK, A., Polish Philology
FEHR, H., German Philology
FONTAŃSKI, H., Russian Philology
GABRYŚ-BARKER, D., English Philology
GONDEK, E., Scientific Information and Library Science
GÓRSKA, E., English Philology
GUTKOWSKA, B., Polish Philology
GWÓŹDŹ, A., Film and Media Studies
HESKA-KWAŚNIEWICZ, K., Polish Philology
ILUK, J., German Philology
JAKÓBCZYK, J., Polish Philology
JANOWSKA, A., Polish Philology
JARCZYK, M., Polish Philology
JARZĄBEK, K., Slavonic Philology
JASKÓŁA, E., Polish Philology
JĘDRZEJKO, E., Polish Philology
KALAGA, W., English Philology
KISIEL, M., Polish Philology
KITA, M., Polish Philology
KLESZCZ, K., Polish Philology
KŁOSIŃSKA, K., Polish Philology
KOSOWSKA, E., Cultural Studies
KRASUSKI, K., Comparative Literature
KRYZIA, W., Slavonic Philology
KUNCE, A., Cultural Studies
ŁYDA, A., English Philology
MALICKI, J., Polish Philology
MALINOWSKA, E., Polish Philology
MARCINIAK, P., Classical Philology
MAZUREK, H., Russian Philology
MICZKA, T., Polish Philology
MIELCZAREK, Z., German Philology
NAWARECKI, A., Polish Philology
NIESPOREK-SZAMBURSKA, B., Polish Philology
OGIERMAN, L., Scientific Information and Library Science
OLEJNICZAK, J., Polish Philology
OPACKA-WALASEK, D., Polish Philology
OSTASZEWSKA, D., Polish Philology
PAWELEC, D., Polish Philology
PIECHOTA, M., Polish Philology

PIKALA-TOKARZ, B., Slavonic Philology
PYTASZ, M., Polish Philology
ROTT, D., Polish Philology
RÓŻYCKI, E., Scientific Information and Library Science
RYBA, J., Polish Philology
SIERADZKA, D., Scientific Information and Library Science
SKUDRZYK, A., Polish Philology
SŁAWEK, E., Polish Philology
SŁAWEK, T., Comparative Literature
SOBCZYK, J., Polish Philology
SOCHA, I., Scientific Information and Library Science
STAWNICKA, J., Slavonic Philology
SYNOWIEC, H., Polish Philology
SZEWCZYK, G., German Philology
TAMBOR, J., Polish Philology
TERMIŃSKA-KORZON, K., English Philology
UNIŁOWSKI, K., Polish Philology
WĄCHOCKA, E., Cultural Studies
WANDZIOCH, M., French Philology
WARCHALA, J., Polish Philology
WĘŻOWICZ-ZIÓŁKOWSKA, D., Cultural Studies
WIDŁA, H., Romance Philology
WILKOŃ, A., Polish Philology
WILKOŃ, T., Scientific Information and Library Science
WITOSZ, B., Polish Philology
WOŹNICZKA, Z., Cultural Studies
WYSOCKA, M., English Philology
ZABIEROWSKI, S., Cultural Studies
ZELER, B., Cultural Studies
ŻYDEK-BEDNARCZUK, U., Cultural Studies

Faculty of Radio and Television (ul. Bytkowska 1B, 40-955 Katowice; tel. (32) 2597011; e-mail writv@us.edu.pl; internet www.writv.us.edu.pl):

BAJON, F., Film and Television Directing
DOKTOROWICZ, K., Media Management and Production
FIDYK, A., Film and Television Directing
HUDON, W., Cinematography
ŁUKASZEWICZ, J., Cinematography
ŚLĘZAK, P., Media Management and Production
STUHR, J., Film and Television Directing
UHMA, M., Film and Television Production
ŻAKOWICZ, A., Cinematography
ZANUSSI, K., Film and Television Directing

Faculty of Social Sciences (ul. Bankowa 11, 40-007 Katowice; tel. (32) 3591112; e-mail dziekan@wns.us.edu.pl; internet www.wns.us.edu.pl):

BARAŃSKI, M., Political Science
BARCIAK, A., History
BARTOSZEK, A., Sociology
BUDZYŃSKA, E., Sociology
CZAKON, T., Philosophy
DEMBIŃSKI, B., Philosophy
FERTACZ, S., History
GIERULA, M., Political Science
GLIMOS-NADGÓRSKA, A., History
IWANEK, J., Political Science
JACHIMOWSKI, M., Political Science
KACZANOWICZ, W., History
KACZMAREK, R., History
KAUTE, W., Political Science
KIEPAS, A., Philosophy
KOLCZYŃSKI, M., Political Science
KUBOK, D., Philosophy
ŁACIAK, P., Philosophy
ŁOMIŃSKI, B., Political Science
MICHALCZYK, S., Political Science
MIKUŁOWSKI-POMORSKI, J., Political Science
MITRĘGA, M., Political Science
NAWROCKI, T., Sociology
NORAS, A., Philosophy
ONISZCZUK, Z., Political Science
PANIC, I., History
PAWELEC, T., History
SPERKA, J., History
STOLARCZYK, M., Political Science
SWADŹBA, U., Sociology

SZCZEPAŃSKI, M., Sociology
SZOTEK, B., Philosophy
ŚLĘCZEK-CZAKON, D., Philosophy
ŚWIĄTKIEWICZ, W., Sociology
WIECZOREK, K., Philosophy
WÓDZ, J., Sociology
WÓDZ, K., Sociology
WRÓBEL, S., Political Science

Faculty of Theology (ul. Jordana 18, 40-043 Katowice; tel. (32) 3569056; e-mail sekretariat@wtl.us.edu.pl; internet www.wtl.us.edu.pl):

BUDNIAK, J., Theology
CELARY, I., Theology
DROŻDŻ, A., Theology
GÓRECKI, J., Theology
GÓRSKI, J., Theology
KOZYRA, J., Theology
KRĘTOSZ, J., Theology
KRZYSTECZKO, H., Theology
MALINA, A., Theology
MYSZOR, J., Theology
MYSZOR, W., Theology
PASTWA, A., Theology
REGINEK, A., Theology
SŁOMKA, J., Theology
SZYMIK, J., Theology
ŻĄDŁO, A., Theology

UNIWERSYTET SZCZECIŃSKI
(Szczecin University)

ul. Papieża Jana Pawła II 22A, 70-453 Szczecin

Telephone: (91) 4441185
E-mail: rektorat@univ.szczecin.pl
Internet: www.univ.szczecin.pl
Founded 1985
State control
Language of instruction: Polish
Academic year: October to September
Chancellor: Mgr EUGENIUSZ KISIEL
Rector: Prof. Dr EDWARD WŁODARCZYK
Vice-Rector for Education Assoc.: Dr JACEK STYSZYŃSKI
Vice-Rector for Finance and Devt: Prof. Dr WALDEMAR GOS
Vice-Rector for Science and Int. Cooperation: Prof. Dr MAREK GÓRSKI
Vice-Rector for Student Affairs: Dr JACEK BUKO
Dir for Library: Prof. Dr Hab. RADOSŁAW GAZIŃSKI
Library: see under Libraries and Archives
Number of teachers: 1,200
Number of students: 30,000
Publication: *Przegląd Uniwersytecki* (The Univ. Review, 6 a year)

DEANS

Faculty of Biology: Prof. Dr Hab. ANDRZEJ ZAWAL
Faculty of Economics and Management: Prof. Dr Hab. WALDEMAR TARCZYŃSKI
Faculty of Geosciences: Prof. Dr Hab. RYSZARD K. BORÓWKA
Faculty of Humanities: Prof. Dr Hab. BARBARA KROMOLICKA
Faculty of Law and Administration: Prof. Dr Hab. ZBIGNIEW KUNIEWICZ
Faculty of Management and Economics of Services: Prof. Dr Hab. PIOTR NIEDZIELSKI
Faculty of Mathematics and Physics: Prof. Dr Hab. PIOTR KRASOŃ
Faculty of Philology: Prof. Dr Hab. EWA KOMOROWSKA
Faculty of Physical Education and Health Promotion: Prof. Dr Hab. JERZY EIDER
Faculty of Theology: Prof. Dr Hab. HENRYK WEJMAN
Off-Campus Faculty of Administration in Jarocin: Prof. Dr Hab. MIECZYSŁAW STANISZEWSKI

Off-Campus Faculty of Economics and Social Sciences in Gorzów Wielkopolski: Prof. Dr JERZY DUDZIŃSKI
Off-Campus Faculty of Economics in Wałcz: Prof. Dr Hab. WALDEMAR WOLSKI

PROFESSORS

ALEKSIEJENKO, M., Arts
BĄKOWSKI, W., Economics
BIAŁECKI, T., Arts
BRONK, H., Economics
CHMIELEWSKI, Z., Arts
CHWESIUK, K., Economics
CZAPLEWSKI, R., Economics
CZERNIATIN, W., Mathematics
DEPTUŁA, W., Natural Sciences
DOROZIK, L., Economics
DUDZIŃSKI, J., Economics
DZIEDZICZAK, I., Economics
FARYŚ, J., Arts
GIZA, A., Arts
GŁODEK, Z., Economics
GŁOWACKI, A., Arts
GÓRBIEL, A., Law
GRANOWSKI, J., Physics
GRZYWACZ, W., Economics
HADACZEK, B., Arts
HŁYŃCZAK, A. J., Natural Sciences
HOZER, J., Economics
JANASZ, W., Economics
JASKOT, K., Arts
JASZCZANIN, J., Natural Sciences
KARWOWSKI, J., Economics
KĘPCZYŃSKI, J., Natural Sciences
KIZIUKIEWICZ, T., Economics
KOPYCIŃSKA, D., Economics
KOROBOW, W., Mathematics
KOŹMIAN, D., Arts
KUCHARSKA, E., Arts
LUKS, K., Economics
MEJBAUM, W., Arts
MOŁCZANOWA, O., Arts
NOWAKOWSKI, A., Economics
PERENC, J., Economics
PRUSAK, F., Law
RADOMSKA-TOMCZUK, M., Fine Arts
ROGALSKA, S., Natural Sciences
ROGALSKI, M., Natural Sciences
RZEPA, T., Social Sciences
SIERGIEJEW, N., Physics
SŁAWIK, K., Law
ŚLIAŻAS, J., Natural Sciences
STANIELEWICZ, J., Arts
SULIKOWSKI, A., Arts
SUŁKOWSKI, Cz., Economics
SYGIT, M., Medical Sciences
SZAŁEK, B., Economics, Arts
SZLAUER, L., Natural Sciences
URBAŃCZYK, E., Economics
WAŚNIEWSKI, T., Economics
WIERZBICKI, T., Economics
WOŹNIAK, R., Arts
ZALEWSKI, P., Economics
ZAWADZKI, J., Economics

UNIWERSYTET WARMIŃSKO-MAZURSKI W OLSZTYNIE
(University of Warmia and Mazury in Olsztyn)

ul. M. Oczapowskiego 2, 10-719 Olsztyn

Telephone: (89) 5233330
E-mail: rektor@uwm.edu.pl
Internet: www.uwm.edu.pl
Founded 1999 by merger of Olsztyn University of Agriculture and Technology, Higher School of Pedagogy, Warmian Theological Institute
State control
Rector: Prof. Dr Hab. RYSZARD GÓRECKI
Vice-Rector for Devt and Financial Policy: Prof. Dr Hab. MIROSŁAW GORNOWICZ
Vice-Rector for Devt of Education: Prof. Dr Hab. JERZY ANDRZEJ PRZYBOROWSKI

Vice-Rector for Human Resources: Prof. Dr Hab. GRZEGORZ BIAŁUŃSKI

Vice-Rector for Research: Prof. Dr Hab. JERZY JAROSZEWSKI

Vice-Rector for Student Affairs: Prof. Dr Hab. JANUSZ PIECHOCKI

Dir for Library: MAŁGORZATA SZYMAŃSKA-JASIŃSKA

Library of 976,693 vols incl. 741,334 books, 172,772 periodicals and 62,587 spec. collns

Number of teachers: 2,000

Number of students: 31,500

Publications: *Acta Neophilologica* (1 or 2 a year), *Acta Polono-Ruthenica* (1 or 2 a year), *Economic Sciences* (1 or 2 a year), *Echa Przeszłości* (1 or 2 a year), *Forum Oświatowe* (1 or 2 a year), *Forum Teologiczne* (1 or 2 a year), *Humanistyka i Przyrodoznawstwo* (1 or 2 a year), *Natural Sciences* (1 or 2 a year), *Prace Językoznawcze* (1 or 2 a year), *Technical Sciences* (1 or 2 a year)

DEANS

Faculty of Animal Bioengineering: Prof. Dr WIESŁAW SOBOTKA

Faculty of Biology and Biotechnology: Prof. Dr Hab. TADEUSZ KAMIŃSKI

Faculty of Economics: Prof. Dr Hab. JANUSZ HELLER

Faculty of Environmental Management and Agriculture: Prof. Dr Hab. KRZYSZTOF MLYNARCZYK

Faculty of Environmental Sciences and Fisheries: Prof. Dr Hab. MIROSŁAW KRZEMIENIEWSKI

Faculty of Fine Arts: Prof. BENEDYKT BŁOŃSKI

Faculty of Food Sciences: Prof. Dr Hab. BOGUSŁAW STANIEWSKI

Faculty of Geodesy and Land Management: Prof. Dr Hab. RADOSŁAW WIŚNIEWSKI

Faculty of Humanities: Prof. Dr Hab. ANDRZEJ SZMYT

Faculty of Law and Administration: Prof. Dr Hab. BRONISŁAW SITEK

Faculty of Mathematics and Computer Science: Prof. Dr Hab. SZCZEPAN BRYM

Faculty of Medical Sciences: Prof. Dr Hab. WOJCIECH MAKSYMOWICZ

Faculty of Social Sciences: Prof. Dr Hab. MAŁGORZATA SUŚWIŁŁO

Faculty of Technical Sciences: Prof. Dr Hab. ADAM LIPIŃSKI

Faculty of Theology: Prof. Dr Hab. PIOTR DUKSA

Faculty of Veterinary Medicine: Prof. Dr Hab. ANDRZEJ KONCICKI

UNIWERSYTET WARSZAWSKI
(University of Warsaw)

Krakowskie Przedmieście 26–28, 00-927 Warsaw

Telephone: (22) 5520000

E-mail: rektor@adm.uw.edu.pl

Internet: www.uw.edu.pl

Founded 1816

State control

Academic year: October to June

Chancellor: JERZY PIESZCZURYKOW

Rector: Prof. MARCIN PAŁYS

Vice-Rector for Devt and Financial Policy: Prof. ANNA GIZA-POLESZCZUK

Vice-Rector for Human Resources and Lifelong Learning: Prof. TADEUSZ TOMASZEWSKI

Vice-Rector for Research and Liaison: Prof. ALOJZY Z. NOWAK

Vice-Rector for Student Affairs and Quality of Teaching and Learning: Prof. MARTA KICIŃSKA-HABIOR

Dir for Library: EWA KOBIERSKA-MACIUSZKO

Library: see under Libraries and Archives

Number of teachers: 3,300

Number of students: 61,300

Publications: *Acta Philologica* (irregular), *Africana Bulletin* (irregular), *American Studies* (irregular), *Barok* (2 a year), *Filozofia Nauki* (irregular), *Ikonotheka* (irregular), *Japonica* (irregular), *Journal of Juristic Papyrology* (irregular), *Kwartalnik Pedagogiczny* (4 a year), *Novensia* (irregular), *Orientalia Varsoviensia* (irregular), *Phytoocenosis* (irregular), *Polityka Wschodnia* (irregular), *Przegląd Glottodydaktyczny* (irregular), *Przegląd Historyczny* (4 a year), *Przegląd Humanistyczny* (4 a year), *Stosunki Międzynarodowe* (irregular), *Studia Europejskie* (4 a year), *Studia Palmyreńskie* (irregular), *Studia Politologiczne* (irregular)

DEANS

Faculty of Applied Linguistics: Prof. KRZYSZTOF HEJWOWSKI

Faculty of Applied Social Sciences and Resocialisation: Prof. WOJCIECH PAWLIK

Faculty of 'Artes Liberales': Prof. JERZY AXER

Faculty of Biology: Prof. AGNIESZKA MOSTOWSKA

Faculty of Chemistry: Prof. PAWEŁ KULESZA

Faculty of Economic Sciences: Prof. JAN JAKUB MICHAŁEK

Faculty of Education: Prof. ANNA WIŁKOMIRSKA

Faculty of Geography and Regional Studies: Prof. ANDRZEJ LISOWSKI

Faculty of Geology: Prof. EWA KROGULEC

Faculty of History: Prof. ELŻBIETA BARBARA ZYBERT

Faculty of Journalism and Political Science: Prof. JANUSZ ADAMOWSKI

Faculty of Law and Administration: Prof. KRZYSZTOF RĄCZKA

Faculty of Management: Prof. JAN TURYNA

Faculty of Mathematics, Informatics and Mechanics: Prof. ANDRZEJ TARLECKI

Faculty of Modern Languages: Prof. REMIGIUSZ FORYCKI

Faculty of Oriental Studies: Prof. JOLANTA SIERAKOWSKA-DYNDO

Faculty of Philosophy and Sociology: Prof. KRZYSZTOF MARIAN KOSEŁA

Faculty of Physics: Prof. TERESA RZĄCA-URBAN

Faculty of Polish Studies: Prof. ZBIGNIEW GREŃ

Faculty of Psychology: Prof. EWA CZERNIAWSKA

PROFESSORS

Faculty of Applied Linguistics (Szturmowa 4, 02-678 Warsaw; tel. (22) 5534223):

GRUCZA, F., Linguistics

KIELAR, B., Linguistics

KOZAK, S., Ukrainian Philology

KRZESZOWSKI, T., Linguistics

LUKSZYN, J., Russian Philology

NAMOWICZ, T., German Philology

ŠEMCZUK, A., Russian Philology

ŚLIWOWSKI, R., Russian Philology

SZYSZKO, T., Russian Philology

WAWRZYŃCZYK, J., Linguistics

ZMARZER, W., Linguistics

Faculty of Applied Social Sciences and Resocialization (Żurawia 4, 00-503 Warsaw; tel. (22) 6254086):

BAŁANDYNOWICZ, A., Resocialization, Prevention

BOKSZAŃSKI, Z., Sociology

JAWŁOWSKA, A., Sociology

KACZYŃSKA, E., History of Social Economics

KICIŃSKI, K., Sociology of Morals

KRÓL, M., History of Ideas

KULPIŃSKA, J., Sociology

KURCZEWSKI, J., Sociology, Sociology of Law

KWAŚNIEWSKI, J., Labour Law, Deviation Sociology

MISIAK, W., Sociology

PILCH, T., Education

PRZECŁAWSKI, K., Sociology

RZEPLIŃSKI, A., Law, Criminology

ŚWIDA-ZIEMBA, H., Sociology

SZYMANOWSKI, T., Penal Law

TYMOWSKI, A., Social Politics

WOJCIK, P., Political Science, Social Politics

ZABOROWSKI, Z., Psychology

ZIEMBA, Z., Philosophy

Faculty of Biology (Miecznikowa 1, 02-096 Warsaw; tel. (22) 5541104; e-mail dziekanat@biol.uw.edu.pl):

BARTNIK, E., Molecular Biology, Genetics

BRYŁA, J., Biochemistry—Metabolism

CHARZYŃSKA, M., Embryology

CHRÓST, R., Microbiology

CYMBOROWSKI, B., Animal Physiology

DOBROWOLSKI, K., Zoology, Ecology

DOBRZAŃSKA-KACZANOWSKA, J., Zoology

FALIŃSKI, J., Botany, Ecology

GLIWICZ, M., Zoology, Hydrobiology

HREBENDA, J., Microbiology

JERZMANOWSKI, A., Biochemistry

KACPERSKA-LEWAK, A., Plant Physiology, Biochemistry

KACZANOWSKI, A., Zoology

KŁOSOWSKI, S., Ecology of Water Plants

KOZAKIEWICZ, M., Ecology

KURAŚ, M., Experimental Biology

MARKIEWICZ, Z., Microbiology

MORACZEWSKI, J., Zoology

MYCIELSKI, R., Microbiology

PIECZYŃSKA, E., Zoology, Hydrobiology

PIEKAROWICZ, A., Microbiology

POSKUTA, J., Plant Physiology

PREJS, A., Zoology, Hydrobiology

RYCHTER, A., Plant Physiology

SIŃSKI, E., Zoology

STAROŃ, K., Molecular Biology

STĘPIEŃ, P., Molecular Biology, Genetics

SYMONIDES, E., Botany, Ecology

TARKOWSKI, A., Embryology

TOMASZEWICZ, H., Botany

WĘGLEŃSKI, P., Molecular Biology, Genetics

WIŁKOMIRSKY, B., Botany

WŁODARCZYK, M., Microbiology

WOJCIECHOWSKI, Z., Biochemistry

ZIELENKIEWICZ, P., Experimental Biology

Faculty of Chemistry (Pasteura 1, 02-093 Warsaw; tel. (22) 8220975; e-mail dziekan@chem.uw.edu.pl):

BILEWICZ, R., Analytical Chemistry

BORUCKA-BUKOWSKA, J., Physical Chemistry and Molecular Spectroscopy

CHAŁASIŃSKI, G., Theoretical Chemistry

CZERWIŃSKI, A., Physical Chemistry

FIGASZEWSKI, Z., Physical Chemistry

GADOMSKI, W., Physical Chemistry, Optics

GALUS, Z., Mineral Chemistry

GŁĄB, B., Analytical Chemistry

GOLIMOWSKI, J., Analytical Chemistry

IZDEBSKI, J., Organic Chemistry

JAWORSKI, J., Chemistry and Food Technology

JEZIORSKI, B., Analytical Chemistry

JURCZAK, J., Organic Chemistry

KALINOWSKI, M., Physical Chemistry

KASPRZYCKA-GUTTMAN, T., Chemical Technology

KOCZOROWSKI, Z., Electrochemistry

KOLIŃSKI, A., Theoretical Chemistry

KRYGOWSKI, T., Physical Chemistry

KULESZA, P., Electrochemistry

LEŚ, A., Theoretical Chemistry

NIEDZIELSKI, J., Organic Chemistry

OSZCZAPOWICZ, J., Organic Chemistry

PIELA, L., Theoretical Chemistry

SADLEJ, J., Physical Chemistry

SAMOCHOCKA, K., Radiochemistry

STOJEK, Z., Electrochemistry

SZYDŁOWSKI, J., Radiochemistry

TEMERIUSZ, A., Organic Chemistry

TROJANOWICZ, M., Analytical Chemistry

WRONA, P., Analytical Chemistry

ŻYLICZ, M., Biochemistry

Faculty of Economic Science (Długa 44/50, 00-241 Warsaw; tel. (22) 5549144; e-mail wne@wne.uw.edu.pl; internet www.wne.uw.edu.pl):

BAKA, W., Banking and Finance
DANILUK, M., Public Finance
DOBROCZYŃSKI, M., International Economics
GMYTRASIEWICZ, M., Economics, Business
GÓRECKI, B., Econometrics
JEZIERSKI, A., Economic History
KASPRZAK, T., Business, Informatics
KLEER, J., Economics
KOTOWICZ-JAWOR, J., Economics
KOZIŃSKI, W., Banking and Finance
LUBBE, A., International Economics
ŁUKASZEWICZ, A., Economic Policy
MACIEJEWSKI, W., Econometrics
MORECKA, Z., Political Economy
OKÓLSKI, M., Statistics, Demography
OPOLSKI, K., Banking and Finance
RUTKOWSKI, J., Political Economy
SADOWSKI, Z., Theory of Economic Development
SIWIŃSKI, W., International Economics
SZEWORSKI, A., Political Economy
SZTYBER, W., Political Economy, Public Finance
TIMOFIEJUK, I., Statistics
WIECZORKIEWICZ, A., Banking and Finance
WILKIN, J., Political Economy, Agricultural Economics

Faculty of Education (Mokotowska 16/20, 00-561 Warsaw; tel. (22) 5530818; e-mail pedagog@pedagog.uw.edu.pl):

BARTNICKA, K., Education History
FRĄCZEK, A., Psychology
KRUSZEWSKI, K., Education
KUPISIEWICZ, C., Didactics, Comparative Education
KWIATKOWSKA, H., Education
LEWOWICKI, T., Adult Education
MIESZALSKI, S., Didactics
POŁTURZYCKI, J., Education
PRZECŁAWSKA, A., Social Education
THEISS, W., Education
WILGOCKA-OKOŃ, B., Education
WOJNAR, I., Education
WOYNAROWSKA, B., Social Medicine
ZACZYŃSKI, W., Didactics

Faculty of Geography and Regional Studies (Krakowskie Przedmieście 30, 00-927 Warsaw; tel. (22) 5520631; e-mail globus@uw.edu.pl):

CIOŁKOSZ, A., Cartography, GIS
DEMBICZ, A., Economic Geography, Socio-economic Geography of Latin America
GRYGORENKO, W., Cartography
GUDOWSKI, J., Economic Geography
GUTRY-KORYCKA, M., Hydrogeology, Hydrology
KOSTROWICKA, A., Economic Geography, Geography of Tourism
KOWALCZYK, A., Economic Geography
MAKOWSKI, J., Regional Geography
MIKULSKI, Z., Hydrogeography, Hydrology
MYCIELSKA-DOWGIAŁŁO, E., Geomorphology
PLIT, F., Regional Geography of Africa
RICHLING, A., Physical Geography, Landscape Ecology
SOCZYŃSKA, U., Hydrology
STOPA-BORYCZKA, M., Climatology

Faculty of Geology (Żwirki i Wigury 93, 02-089 Warsaw; tel. (22) 8225884; e-mail dziekanat.geol@uw.edu.pl):

BAŁUK, W. A., Palaeontology
DRĄGOWSKI, A., Environmental Protection
GRABOWSKA-OLSZEWSKA, B., Engineering Geology
KACZYŃSKI, R., Engineering Geology
KOWALSKI, W., Geochemistry, Mineralogy
KRAJEWSKI, S., Hydrogeology
KUTEK, J., Tectonics, Stratigraphy

LINDNER, L., Quaternary Geology
MACIOSZCZYK, A., Hydrogeology
MACIOSZCZYK, T., Hydrogeology
MAŁECKA, D., Hydrogeology
MARCINOWSKI, R., Stratigraphy
MARKS, L., Quaternary Geology
MATYSIAK, S., Mechanics of Solids
MYŚLIŃSKA, E., Engineering Geology
ORŁOWSKI, S., Stratigraphy
PINIŃSKA, J., Engineering Geology, Geomechanics
RADWAŃSKI, A., Geology
RONIEWICZ, P., Sedimentology
SPECZIK, S., Geology of Ore Deposits
SZULCZEWSKI, M., Stratigraphy, Sedimentology
WIERZBOWSKI, A., Stratigraphy
WYRWICKI, R., Geology of Ore Deposits

Faculty of History (Krakowskie Przedmieście 26/28, 00-927 Warsaw; tel. (22) 5520545; e-mail wh.dziekanat.sog@uw.edu.pl):

AUGUSTYNIAK, U., History of Culture
BANASZKIEWICZ, J., Modern History
BIEŃKOWSKA, B., History of Culture, Library Science
BRAVO, B., Ancient History
BUCHWALD-PELC, P., Library Science
BUKO, A., Archaeology
BUKOWSKI, Z., Archaeology
CHMIELEWSKI, W., Archaeology
CHRÓŚCICKI, J., History of Art
CZEKANOWSKA-KUKLIŃSKA, A., Musicology
DASZEWSKI, W., Archaeology
FIAŁKOWSKI, K., Library Science
GARLICKI, A., History
GAWLIKOWSKI, M., Archaeology
GODLEWSKI, W., Archaeology
GOŁĄB, M., Musicology
HELMAN-BEDNARCZYK, Z., Musicology
JAŚKIEWICZ, D., History of the USSR
JUSZCZAK, W., History of Art
KARPOWICZ, M., History of Art
KIZWALTER, T., 19th-century History
KOLENDO, J., Archaeology
KOŁODZIEJSKA, J., Library Science
KOZŁOWSKI, S., Archaeology
KULA, M., General History
LASOTA-MOSKALEWSKA, A., Biology, Archaeozoology
LENGAUER, W., History
ŁUKASIEWICZ, J., History
MACISZEWSKI, J., History
MĄCZAK, A., Modern History
MICHAŁEK, K., Modern History, History of the USA
MIKOCKI, T., History of Art
MIŁOBĘDZKI, J. A., History of Art
MODZELEWSKI, K., Medieval History
MURASZKIEWICZ, M., Library Science
MYŚLIWIEC, K., Archaeology
NIWIŃSKI, A. S., History, Egyptology
NOWAKOWSKI, W., Archaeology
OKULICZ-KOZARYN, J., Archaeology
PAPUZIŃSKA-BEKSIAK, J., Literature
PERZ, M., Musicology
POKROPEK, M., Ethnography
PONIATOWSKA, I., History of Music
POPPE, A., Medieval History
POPRZĘCKA, M., History of Art
POTKOWSKI, E., History
RAKOWSKI, A., Musical Acoustics
RUDNICKI, S., 19th- and 20th-century Polish History
RUSINOWA, J., Modern History
SAMSONOWICZ, H., Medieval History
SKUBISZEWSKI, P., Medieval History of Art
SOCHACKI, Z., Archaeology
SOKOLEWICZ, Z., Ethnography
SUCHODOLSKI, S., Archaeology
ŚWIDERKÓWNA, A., Papyrology
SZAFLIK, J., History
TANTY, M., History of Slavonic Countries
TOMASZEWSKI, J., Political Science
TYMOWSKI, M., Modern History
TYSZKIEWICZ, J., Medieval History

WASILEWSKI, T., Medieval History
WAWRYKOWA, M., Modern History
WIERCIŃSKI, A., Archaeology
WIPSZYCKA-BRAVO, E., Ancient History
WOJCIECHOWSKI, M., Modern History
WYROBISZ, A., Medieval History
ZADROŻYŃSKA-BARĄCZ, A., Ethnography
ŻARNOWSKA, A., Modern Polish History
ŻERAŃSKA-KOMINEK, S., Musicology

Faculty of Journalism and Political Science (Krakowskie Przedmieście 3, 00-047 Warsaw; tel. (22) 5520218; e-mail wdinp@uw.edu.pl):

AULEYTNER, J., Economy
BASZKIEWICZ, J., Political Science
BRALCZYK, J., Journalism
DANECKI, J., Political Economy
DOBRZYCKI, W., Law and International Relations
FILIPIAK, T., Political Science
FILIPOWICZ, S., History of Social-Political Thought
GOŁĘBIOWSKI, B., Political Science
GOŁEMBSKI, F., Political Science
GOLKA, B., Journalism
HALIŻAK, M., Political Science
KASPRZYK, L., International Relations
KUKUŁKA, J., Political Science
KUŹNIAR, R., International Relations
ŁUKASZUK, L., International Law
MICHALSKI, B., Journalism
MROZEK, A. B., Political Science
PARZYMIES, S., International Relations
PIEKARA, A., Social Politics
PRZYBYSZ, K., Political Science
RAJKIEWICZ, A., Political Science
SATKIEWICZ, A. H., Theory of Style, Polish Language
SKRZYPEK, A., History
SOBCZAK, J., Law
SYMONIDES, J., International Relations
WŁADYKA, W., Political History
WOJTASZCZYK, K., Political Science
ZIELIŃSKI, E., Modern Political Systems

Faculty of Law and Administration (Krakowskie Przedmieście 26/28, 00-927 Warsaw; tel. (22) 5524304; e-mail dziekan@wpia.uw.edu.pl):

BARDACH, J., History of Law
BŁESZYŃSKI, J., Civil Law
DYBOWSKI, T., Civil Law
ERECIŃSKI, T., Civil Law
FLOREK, L., Labour Law
GARDOCKI, L., Penal Law
GARLICKI, L., Constitutional Law
IZDEBSKI, H., History of Law
JĘDRASIK-JANKOWSKA, I., Labour Law
JĘDRZEJEWSKA, M., Civil Law
KRUSZYŃSKI, P., Penal Law
OKOLSKI, J., Civil Law
PIETRZAK, M., History of Law
PIETRZYKOWSKI, K., Civil Law
PIONTEK, E., International Law
RAJSKI, J., Civil Law
REJMAN, G., Penal Law
SAFJAN, M., Civil Law
SALWA, Z., Labour Law
SKOWROŃSKA-BOCIAN, E., Civil Law
SÓJKA-ZIELIŃSKA, K., History of Law
SZYSZKOWSKA, M., Philosophy of Law
TOMASZEWSKI, T., Penal Law
TRZCIŃSKI, J., Constitutional Law
TURSKA, A., Sociology of Law
WĄSOWICZ, M., History of Law
WIERZBOWSKI, M., Administrative Law
WINCZOREK, P., Theory of State and Law
ZABŁOCKA, M., Roman Law
ZIELIŃSKI, A., Civil Law

Faculty of Management (Szturmowa 3, 02-678 Warsaw; tel. (22) 5534002; e-mail wz@mail.wz.uw.edu.pl):

BOLESTA-KUKUŁKA, K., Sociology of Management

BUCZKOWSKI, L., Techniques of Management
GŁOWACKI, R., Marketing
JAROSZYŃSKI, A., Administrative Law
KISIELNICKI, J., Industrial Economy and Informatics
KRZYŻEWSKI, R., Social Economics
KWIATKOWSKI, S., Theory of Management
MAJCHRZYCKA-GUZOWSKA, A., Financial Law
MUSZALSKI, W., Employment
OBŁÓJ, K., Organization and Management
RYĆ, K., Economic Theory
ŚLIWA, J., Planning
SOBCZAK, K., Administrative Law
SOPOĆKO, A., Theory of Organization
SZPRINGER, W., Administrative Law
ZAWIŚLAK, A., Theory of Management

Faculty of Mathematics, Informatics and Mechanics (Banacha 2, 02-097 Warsaw; tel. (22) 5544214; e-mail mim@mimuw.edu.pl):

BESSAGA, C., Mathematical Analysis
BIAŁYNICKI-BIRULA, A., Mathematics
BOJDECKI, T., Theory of Elasticity
BROWKIN, J., Mathematics
DRYJA, M., Informatics
ENGELKING, R., Mathematics
GRABOWSKI, J., Mathematics
JACKOWSKI, S., Mechanics
KREMPA, J., Mathematics
KWAPIEŃ, S., Mathematics
LIGOCKA, E., Mathematics
MOSZYŃSKA, M., Mathematics
PALCZEWSKI, A., Mathematics
PERADZYŃSKI, Z., Mathematics
POL, R., Mathematics
PUCZYŁOWSKI, E., Mathematics
RYTTER, W., Informatics
SEMADENI, Z., Mathematics
SIEKLUCKI, K., Mathematics
SKOWRON, A., Mathematics
SZAŁAS, A., Informatics
TARLECKI, A., Informatics
TIURYN, J., Mathematics
TORUŃCZYK, H., Mathematics
TURSKI, W., Informatics
WOJTASZCZYK, P., Mathematics
WOŹNIAKOWSKI, H., Informatics
ZBIERSKI, P., Mathematics
ŻOŁĄDEK, H., Mathematics

Faculty of Modern Languages (Krakowskie Przedmieście 32, 00-927 Warsaw; tel. (22) 8267528; e-mail neofilologia@uw.edu.pl):

ASZYK-BANGS, U., Linguistics
BOGACKI, B. K., Italian Philology
BOGUSŁAWSKI, A., Russian Philology
BOJAR, B., Formal Linguistics
BYRSKI, M. K., Oriental Philology
BYSTYDZIEŃSKA, G., English Studies
CZOCHRALSKI, J., German Philology
DANECKI, J., Oriental Philology
KAŁUŻYŃSKI, S., Oriental Philology
KOMOROWSKA-JANOWSKA, H., Linguistics
KOTAŃSKI, W., Oriental Philology
KÜNSTLER, M., Sinology
ŁYCZKOWSKA, K., Oriental Philology
MAJDA, T., Oriental Philology
MAŁCUŻYŃSKI, P., Literature
MANTEL-NIEĆKO, J., Ethiopian Philology
MELANOWICZ, M., Oriental Philology
PIŁASZEWICZ, S., African Philology
POPKO, M., Oriental Philology
RUBACH, J., English Philology
RUSIECKI, J., English Linguistics
SALWA, P., Italian Literature
SAUERLAND, K. K., German Philology
SEMENIUK-POLAKOWSKA, M., Linguistics
SKARŻYŃSKA-BOCHEŃSKA, K., Oriental Philology
SKŁADANEK, B., Iranian Philology
SKŁADANEK, M., Oriental Philology
SŁUPSKI, Z., Oriental Philology
TUBIELEWICZ, J., Oriental Philology
UGNIEWSKA-DOBRZAŃSKA, J., Italian Philology

WEŁNA, J. A., English Philology
WESELIŃSKI, A., English Literature
WIKTOROWICZ, J., German Philology
WIŚNIEWSKI, J., English Literature
ŻABOKLICKI, K., French Philology

Faculty of Philosophy and Sociology (Nowy Swiat 69, 00-046 Warsaw; tel. (22) 5520152):

AUGUSTYNEK, Z., Philosophy
CIUPAK, E., Sociology
DEMBIŃSKA-SIURY, D., Philosophy
JADACKI, J., Philosophy
JANKOWSKI, H., Sociology
JASIŃSKA-KANIA, A., Sociology
KOŹMIŃSKI, A., Sociology
KUCZYŃSKA, A., Philosophy
KUCZYŃSKI, J., Philosophy
MARKIEWICZ, B., Philosophy
MARODY, M., Sociology
MORAWSKI, W., Sociology
NOWICKA-RUSEK, E., Sociology
OMYŁA, M., Logic Philosophy
PELC, J., Logic
ROSIŃSKA-ZIELIŃSKA, Z., Philosophy
SIEMEK, M. J., Philosophy
SIEMIEŃSKA-ŻOCHOWSKA, R., Sociology
SMOLICZ, J. J., Sociology
STANISZKIS, J., Sociology
WIATR, J., Sociology

Faculty of Physics (Hoża 69, 00-681 Warsaw; tel. (22) 5532123; e-mail dziekfiz@fuw.edu.pl):

BADEŁEK, B., Experimental Physics
BAJ, M., Solid Body Physics
BARANOWSKI, J., Experimental Physics
BAŻAŃSKI, S., Theoretical Physics
BIAŁYNICKI-BIRULA, I., Optics and Mechanics
BLINOWSKI, J., Solid Body Physics
CHAŁASIŃSKA-MACUKOW, K., Optics
CIBOROWSKI, J. A., Experimental Physics
CIEŚLAK-BLINOWSKA, K., Medical Physics
DEMIAŃSKI, M., Theoretical Physics
DOBACZEWSKI, J., Theoretical Physics
DZIEMBOWSKI, W., Astronomy
ERNST, K., Atomic Physics
GAJ, J., Solid Body Physics
GRAD, M., Geophysics
GRYNBERG, M., Solid Body Physics
HAMAN, K., Geophysics
KALINOWSKI, J., Molecule Elementary Physics
KAMIŃSKA, M., Solid Body Physics
KIJOWSKI, J., Theoretical Physics
KOPCZYŃSKI, W., High-Energy Physics
KOWALCZYK, P., Experimental Physics
KRÓLIKOWSKI, J., High-Energy Physics
KRÓLIKOWSKI, W., Atomic Physics
KRUSZEWSKI, A., Astronomy
KUBIAK, M., Astrophysics
KURCEWICZ, W., Nuclear Physics
LELIWA-KOPYSTYŃSKI, J., Geophysics
LESYNG, B., Biophysics
MAURIN, K., Mathematical Methods in Physics
MIELNIK, B., Theoretical Physics
NAMYSŁOWSKI, J., Theoretical Physics
NAPIÓRKOWSKI, M., Statistics Physics
NAZAREWICZ, W., Solid Body Physics
PIASECKI, J., Theoretical Physics
POKORSKI, S., Theoretical Physics
RADZEWICZ, C., Experimental Physics
ROHOZIŃSKI, ST., Atomic Physics
RYKACZEWSKI, K., Experimental Physics
SHUGAR, D., Biophysics
SKRZYPCZAK, E., High-Energy Physics
SOSNOWSKA, I., Experimental Physics
STĘPIEŃ, K., Astronomy
STĘPNIEWSKI, R., Solid Body Physics
SYM, A., Physics
SZOPLIK, T., Optics
SZYMACHA, A., Atomic Physics
TRAUTMAN, A., Electrodynamics and Theory of Relativity
TWARDOWSKI, A., Solid Body Physics
UDALSKI, A., Astrophysics

WILHELMI, Z., Atomic Physics
WÓDKIEWICZ, K., Optics
WORONOWICZ, S., Mathematical Methods in Physics
WRÓBLEWSKI, A., Experimental Physics
ZAKRZEWSKI, J., High-Energy Physics
ZYLICZ, J., Experimental Physics

Faculty of Polish Studies (Krakowskie Przedmieście 26/28, 00-927 Warsaw; tel. (22) 5520428; e-mail dziekan.polon@uw.edu.pl):

BARTNICKA, B., Polish Philology, Linguistics
CZAPLEJEWICZ, E., Polish Literature
DOMAŃSKI, J., Classical Philology
DREWNOWSKI, T., History of Polish Literature
DUBISZ, S., Polish Philology
FRYBES, S., Polish Literature
GRZEGORCZYKOWA, R., Polish Philology
HANDKE, R., Theory of Literature
KARWACKA, H., Polish Literature
KOWALCZYK, A., History of Literature
KUPISZEWSKI, W. M., Polish Philology, Linguistics
LAM, A., Polish Philology, Literature
MACIEJEWSKI, J., History of Polish Literature
MAKOWSKI, S., History of Literature
MARKOWSKI, A., Polish Philology, Linguistics
MENCWEL, A., Science of Culture
MITOSEK, Z., Theory of Literature
NOWICKA-JEŻOWA, A., Literature, History of Polish Literature
OSIŃSKI, Z., Science of Culture
OWCZAREK, B., Theory of Literature
PELC, J., History of Literature
PUZYNINA, J., Polish Philology, Linguistics
SIATKOWSKA, E., Slavonic Philology, Linguistics
SIATKOWSKI, J., Slavonic Philology, Linguistics
SMOCZYŃSKI, W., Linguistics
SMUŁKOWA, E., Slavonic Philology, Linguistics
STAROWIEYSKI, M., Classical Philology
SUDOLSKI, Z., Polish Philology, Literature
SULIMA, R., Science of Culture
ŚWIDZIŃSKI, M., Polish Literature, Linguistics
TABORSKI, R., Polish Literature
WOJTCZAK-SZYSZKOWSKI, J., Classical Philology

Faculty of Psychology (Stawki 5/7, 00-183 Warsaw; tel. (22) 5549722; e-mail info@psychology.pl):

GAŁKOWSKI, T., Educational Psychology
GRZELAK, J., Social Psychology
GRZESIUK, L., Psychopathology and Psychotherapy
JARYMOWICZ, M., Personality Psychology
KOFTA, M., Personality Psychology
KOŚCIELSKA, M., Clinical Psychology
KOZIELECKI, J., Cognitive Psychology
MATCZAK, A., Individual Differences
MATYSIAK, J., Biological Psychology
MIKA, S., Social Psychology
STRELAU, J., Individual Differences
WIECZORKOWSKA-NEJTARDT, G., Social Psychology
ZALEWSKA, M., Clinical Psychology

UNIWERSYTET W BIAŁYMSTOKU (University of Bialystok)

ul. Marii Sklodowskiej-Curie 14, 15-097 Białystok

Telephone: (85) 7457000
E-mail: rektorat@uwb.edu.pl
Internet: www.uwb.edu.pl

Founded 1997
State control
Academic year: October to June (2 semesters)

Rector: Prof. Dr Hab. LEONARD ETEL

Vice-Rector for Economic Affairs: Prof. Dr Hab. ROBERT WŁADYSŁAW CIBOROWSKI

Vice-Rector for Research and Int. Relations: Prof. Dr Hab. BEATA GODLEWSKA-ŻYŁKIEWICZ

Vice-Rector for Students and Teaching Affairs: Dr Hab. JERZY HALICKI

Vice-Rector for Univ. Organization and Development: Prof. Dr Hab. DARIUSZ KIJOWSKI

Dir for Library: HALINA BRZEZIŃSKA-STEC

Library of 573,428 vols
Number of teachers: 910
Number of students: 18,310

DEANS

Faculty of Biology and Chemistry: Prof. Dr Hab. IWONA CIERESZKO

Faculty of Economics and Informatics in Vilnius: Prof. Dr Hab. JAROSŁAW WOŁKONOWSKI

Faculty of Economics and Management: Prof. Dr Hab. HENRYK WNOROWSKI

Faculty of History and Sociology: Prof. Dr Hab. WOJCIECH SLESZYŃSKI

Faculty of Law: Prof. Dr Hab. EMIL PŁYWACZEWSKI

Faculty of Mathematics and Informatics: Prof. Dr Hab. ANATOL ODZIJEWICZ

Faculty of Pedagogy and Psychology: Prof. Dr Hab. MIROSŁAW SOBECKI

Faculty of Philology: Prof. Dr Hab. BOGUSŁAW NOWOWIEJSKI

Faculty of Physics: Prof. Dr Hab. EUGENIUSZ ŻUKOWSKI

UNIWERSYTET WROCŁAWSKI
(University of Wrocław)

pl. Uniwersytecki 1, 50-137 Wrocław

Telephone: (71) 3436847
E-mail: rektorat@uni.wroc.pl
Internet: www.uni.wroc.pl

Founded 1702, rebuilt 1945
State control
Language of instruction: Polish
Academic year: October to June (2 semesters)

Rector: Prof. Dr Hab. MAREK BOJARSKI

Vice-Rector for Devt: Prof. Dr Hab. ROBERT OLKIEWICZ

Vice-Rector for Education: Prof. Dr Hab. KAROL KICZKA

Vice-Rector for Research and Int. Relations: Prof. Dr Hab. ADAM JEZIERSKI

Vice-Rector for Student Affairs: Prof. Dr Hab. GRZEGORZ HRYCIUK

Dir for Library: Mgr Inz. GRAŻYNA PIOTROWICZ

Library: see under Libraries and Archives
Number of teachers: 1,720
Number of students: 41,700

Publication: *Acta Universitatis Wratislaviensis*

DEANS

Faculty of Biological Sciences: Dr Hab. DARIUSZ SKARŻYŃSKI

Faculty of Biotechnology: Dr Hab. MARCIN ŁUKASZEWICZ

Faculty of Chemistry: Prof. Dr Hab. ANNA TRZECIAK

Faculty of Earth Science and Environmental Management: Prof. Dr Hab. ZDZISŁAW JARY

Faculty of Historical and Pedagogical Sciences: Dr Hab. ELŻBIETA KOŚCIK

Faculty of Law, Administration and Economics: Prof. Dr Hab. WŁODZIMIERZ GROMSKI

Faculty of Mathematics and Computer Science: Prof. Dr Hab. PIOTR BILER

Faculty of Philology: Prof. Dr Hab. MARCIN CIEŃSKI

Faculty of Physics and Astronomy: Prof. Dr Hab. ANTONI CISZEWSKI

Faculty of Social Sciences: Dr Hab. JERZY JUCHNOWSKI

PROFESSORS

Faculty of Chemistry (ul. F. Joliot-Curie 14, 50-383 Wrocław; tel. (71) 3757290; e-mail dziekanat@chem.uni.wroc.pl; internet www .chem.uni.wroc.pl):

HAWRANEK, J., Electronic Data Processing
JAKUBAS, R., Physical Chemistry
JEZIERSKI, A., Inorganic Chemistry
KISZA, A., Physical Chemistry
KOLL, A., Physical Chemistry
KONOPIŃSKA, D., Organic Chemistry
KOZŁOWSKI, H., Bioinorganic and Biomedicinal Chemistry
LATAJKA, Z., Theoretical Chemistry and Chemical Physics
LATOS-GRAŻYŃSKI, L., General Chemistry
LIS, T., Crystallography
MROZIŃSKI, J., Methodology of Chemistry
PRUCHNIK, F., Environmental Chemistry and Protection
RATAJCZAK, H., Theoretical Chemistry and Chemical Physics
SIEMION, I., Organic Chemistry
SKRZYPIEC-LEGENDZIEWICZ, J., Analytical Chemistry
SOBCZYK, L., Physical Chemistry
SOBOTA, P., Inorganic Chemistry for Natural Scientists
ZIÓŁKOWSKI, J., Inorganic Chemistry

Faculty of Historical and Pedagogical Sciences (ul. Szewska 48, 50-139 Wrocław; tel. (71) 3752223; e-mail dziekanat@wnhip.uni .wroc.pl):

ADAMCZYK, M., Comparative Pedagogy
BANAŚ, P., Science of Art
CIESIELSKI, M., History of Eastern Europe
CZAPLIŃSKI, M., History of Silesia
DERWICH, M., Centre for Studies of Religious Orders and Church Congregations
KULAK, T., General and Polish History since 19th Century
KUSIAK, F., Economic History, Demography and Statistics
MATWIJOWSKI, K., 16th to 18th-century General and Polish History
OCHMAN-STANISZEWSKA, S., 16th to 18th-century General and Polish History
PIETRZAK, J., 16th to 18th-century General and Polish History
POTYRAŁA, B., General Pedagogy
ROK, B., 16th to 18th-century General and Polish History
WACHOWSKI, K., Medieval Archaeology
WRZESIŃSKI, W., Contemporary History
ŻABSKI, E., Philosophical and Methodological Foundations of Psychology
ŻERELIK, R., Centre for Studies of Religious Orders and Church Congregations

Faculty of Law, Administration and Economics (ul. Uniwersytecka 22–26, 50-145 Wrocław; tel. (71) 3437164; internet www.prawo .uni.wroc.pl):

ADAMIAK, B., Administrative Proceedings and Judicial Control of Administrative Activity
BANASZEK, B., Constitutional Law
BEDNARSKI, T., Statistics and Operation Researches
BŁAS, A., Administrative Law
BOĆ, J., Administrative Law
BOGUNIA, L., Criminal Law Practice
BOJARSKI, M., Law of Petty Offences and Penal Fiscal Law
DZIAŁOCHA, K., Constitutional Law
FOJCIK-MASTALSKA, E., Financial Law
FRĄCKOWIAK, J., Economic and Commercial Law
GNIEWEK, E., Civil Law and International Private Law

JENDROŚKA, J., Administrative Proceedings and Judicial Control of Administrative Activity
JONCA, K., Political and Legal Doctrines
KACZMAREK, T., Substantive Penal Law
KAŹMIERCZYK, S., Theory and Philosophy of Law
KEGEL, Z., Crime Detection
KIERES, L., Administrative Economic Law
KOLASA, J., International Economic Relations
KONIECZNY, A., History of Administration
MACIEJEWSKI, M., Political and Legal Doctrine
MĄDRZAK, H., Civil Procedure
MASTALSKI, R., Financial Law
OLSZEWSKI, L., International Economic Relations
ORZECHOWSKI, K., History of Polish State and Law
POŁOMSKI, F., History of Polish State and Law
ŚWIDA, Z., Penal Proceedings
SZURGACZ, H., Labour Law
TRZCIŃSKI, J., Crime Detection

Faculty of Mathematics and Computer Science (ul. F. Joliot-Curie 15, 50-383 Wrocław; tel. 3757890; e-mail dziekan@math.uni.wroc .pl; internet www.math.uni.wroc.pl):

BILER, P., Differential Equations
BOŻEJKO, M., Mathematical Analysis
DAMEK, E., Geometry
DUDA, R., History and Methodology of Mathematics
HULANICKI, A., Functional Analysis
KISIELEWICZ, A., Algebra and Theory of Numbers
KOPOCIŃSKI, B., Applied Mathematics
NARKIEWICZ, W., Algebra and Theory of Numbers
NEWELSKI, Algebra and Theory of Numbers
PACHOLSKI, L., Programming Languages
PYTLIK, T., Functional Analysis
ROLSKI, T., Stochastic Processes
SYSŁO, M., Programming Methods
SZCZOTKA, W., Applications of Mathematics
SZWARC, R., Mathematical Analysis
URBANIK, K., Theory of Probability

Faculty of Philology (pl. Biskupa Nankiera 15, 50-140 Wrocław; tel. (71) 3433029; e-mail dziekanat.fil@uni.wroc.pl):

DĄBROWSKA, A., Applied Linguistics
DEGLER, J., Theory of Culture and Performing Arts
DYNAK, W., Methodology of Teaching Polish Language and Literature
JANIKOWSKI, K., Scandinavian Studies, German Language
JASTRZĘBSKI, J., Theory of Culture
KAMIŃSKA-SZMAJ, I., Contemporary Polish
KLIMOWICZ, T., Russian Literature and Culture
KOLBUSZEWSKI, J., History of Polish Literature before 1918
KUNICKI, W., German Literature before 1848
ŁAWIŃSKA-TYSZKOWSKA, J., New Latin Philology
ŁUGOWSKA, J., Theory of Culture and Performing Arts
MIGOŃ, A., Theory and History of Books
MIGOŃ, K., Theory and History of Books
MIODEK, J., History of Polish
PISAREK, L., Russian Studies
PRĘDOTA, S., Dutch Lexicology and Lexicography
PYSZNY, J., Polish Literature since 1918
SAWICKI, P., Italian Studies
SOKOLSKI, J., History of Early Polish Literature
SZASTYŃSKA-SIEMION, A., Greek Philology
TOMICZEK, E., Applied Linguistics
WIECZOREK, D., Ukrainian Studies
ŻABSKI, T., History of Polish Literature before 1918

ZAWADA, A., Polish Literature since 1918

Faculty of Physics and Astronomy (pl. Maksa Borna 9, 50-204 Wrocław; tel. (71) 3759404; e-mail dziekan@ift.uni.wroc.pl; internet www.wfa.uni.wroc.pl):

CISZEWSKI, A., Microstructure Surface Experimental Physics

CUGIER, H., Astrophysics and Classical Astronomy

CZAPLA, Z., Experimental Physics (Dielectrics Physics)

HABA, Z., Theoretical Physics (Field Theory)

KIEJNA, A., Absorption Experimental Physics

KOŁACZKIEWICZ, J., Experimental Physics (Spectroscopy of Field Emission)

ŁOPUSZAŃSKI, J., Theoretical Physics (Mathematical Methods in Physics)

LUKIERSKI, J., Theoretical Physics (High-Energy Physics and Theory of Fundamental Particles)

MRÓZ, S., Experimental Physics (Electron Spectroscopy)

PĘKALSKI, A., Theoretical Physics (Non-linear Dynamics and Complex Systems)

POPOWICZ, Z., Theoretical Physics (Field Theory)

REDLICH, K., Theoretical Physics (High-Energy Physics and Theory of Fundamental Particles)

Faculty of Social Sciences (ul. Koszarowa 3, 51-149 Wrocław; tel. (71) 3755192; e-mail dziekanat@wns.uni.wroc.pl; internet www.wns.uni.wroc.pl):

ALBIN, B., International Studies (Eastern Europe Research)

ANTOSZEWSKI, A., Political Sciences (Political Systems)

BAL, K., Philosophy (German Philosophy)

BOKAJŁO, W., Contemporary Political Ideas

DĄBROWSKI, S., Political Sciences (Contemporary History and Social Movements)

GAJDA-KRYNICKA, J., Philosophy (History of Philosophy)

GELLES, R., International Studies

HULANICKA, B., Sociology of Political Relations

JABŁONSKI, A., Theory of Politics

KOSIAN, J., History of Philosophy in Silesia

ŁOS-NOWAK, T., International Relations

ŁUKASZEWICZ, R., Studies in Alternatives of Human Education

PISAREK, H., Epistemology and Ontology

SIEMIANOWSKI, A., Philosophy of Science and Culture

STANDTMUELLER, E., European Union Studies

SURMACZYŃSKI, M., Sociology (Sociology of Political Relations)

WOLAŃSKI, M., East European Studies

UNIWERSYTET ZIELONOGÓRSKI
(University of Zielona Góra)

ul. Licealna 9, 65-417 Zielona Góra

Telephone: (68) 3270735

E-mail: rektorat@uz.zgora.pl

Internet: www.uz.zgora.pl

Founded 2001 by merger of Zielona Góra's Pedagogical Univ. and Technical Univ.

State control

Chancellor: FRANCISZEK ORLIK

Rector: Prof. TADEUSZ KUCZYŃSKI

Deputy Rector for Devt: Prof. ANDRZEJ PIECZYŃSKI

Deputy Rector for Education Quality: Prof. MAGDALENA GRACZYK

Deputy Rector for Scientific Research and Int. Cooperation: Prof. JANUSZ GIL

Deputy Rector for Student Affairs: Prof. WOJCIECH STRZYŻEWSKI

Dir for Library: EWA ADASZYŃSKA

Library of 511,145 vols

Number of teachers: 940

Number of students: 15,530

Publications: *Discussiones Mathematicae* (4 series, each 2 a year), *Dyskursy Młodych Andragogów* (1 a year), *International Journal of Applied Mathematics and Computer Science* (4 a year), *International Journal of Applied Mechanics and Engineering* (4 a year), *Management* (2 a year), *Studia Zachodnie* (1 a year), *Zeszyty Naukowe* (irregular)

DEANS

Faculty of Arts: Prof. PIOTR SZUREK

Faculty of Biological Sciences: Prof. LESZEK JERZAK

Faculty of Civil and Environmental Engineering: Prof. JAKUB MARCINOWSKI

Faculty of Economics and Management: Prof. JANINA STANKIEWICZ

Faculty of Education, Sociology and Health Sciences: Prof. EWA NARKIEWICZ-NIEDBALEC

Faculty of Electrical Engineering, Computer Science and Telecommunications: Prof. ANDRZEJ OBUCHOWICZ

Faculty of Humanities: Prof. SŁAWOMIR KUFEL

Faculty of Mathematics, Computer Science and Econometrics: Prof. LONGIN RYBIŃSKI

Faculty of Mechanical Engineering: Prof. SŁAWOMIR KŁOS

Faculty of Physics and Astronomy: Prof. GIORGI MELIKIDZE

WARSZAWSKI UNIWERSYTET MEDYCZNY
(Medical University of Warsaw)

ul. Żwirki i Wigury 61, 02-091 Warsaw

Telephone: (22) 5720913

E-mail: rekrutacja@wum.edu.pl

Internet: www.wum.edu.pl

Founded 1789

Chancellor: MAŁGORZATA KOZŁOWSKA

Rector: Prof. Dr Hab. MAREK KRAWCZYK

Vice-Rector for Clinical Affairs, Devt and Regional Cooperation: Dr SŁAWOMIR NAZAREWSKI

Vice-Rector for Educational Affairs: Prof. Dr MAREK KULUS

Vice-Rector for Human Resources: Prof. Dr RENATA GÓRSKA

Vice-Rector for Science and Int. Relations: Prof. Dr SŁAWOMIR MAJEWSKI

Dir for Library: IRMINA UTRATA

Library of 400,000 vols

Number of teachers: 1,600

Number of students: 8,700

Publication: *Medycyna-dydaktyka-wychowanie* (Medicine-Didactics-Education, 4 a year)

DEANS

Centre of Postgraduate Training: Prof. Dr BOLESŁAW SAMOLIŃSKI

Faculty of Health Sciences: Prof. Dr PIOTR MAŁKOWSKI

Faculty of Medicine and Dentistry: Prof. Dr ELŻBIETA MIERZWIŃSKA-NASTALSKA

Faculty of Pharmacy: Dr PIOTR WROCZYŃSKI

First Faculty of Medicine: Prof. Dr MIROSŁAW WIELGOŚ

Second Faculty of Medicine: Dr MAREK KUCH

Technical Universities

POLITECHNIKA BIAŁOSTOCKA
(Białystok University of Technology)

ul. Wiejska 45A, 15-351 Białystok

Telephone: (85) 7469000

E-mail: rektor@pb.edu.pl

Internet: pb.edu.pl

Founded 1949

State control

Languages of instruction: English, Polish, Russian

Academic year: October to June

Rector: Prof. Dr Hab. LECH DZIENIS

Vice-Rector for Cooperation and Devt: Dr Hab. ROMAN KACZYŃSKI

Vice-Rector for Science: Prof. Dr Hab. JAN DOROSZ

Vice-Rector for Student Affairs and Teaching: Dr Hab. GRAŻYNA ŁASKA

Dir for Library: JOANNA PUTKO

Library: see under Libraries and Archives780

Number of students: 16,500

Publications: *Architektura* (irregular), *Budowa i Eksploatacja Maszyn* (irregular), *Budownictwo* (irregular), *Ekonomia i Zarządzanie* (irregular), *Elektryka* (irregular), *Informatyka* (irregular), *Inżynieria Srodowiska* (irregular), *Matematyka, Fizyka, Chemia* (irregular), *Mechanika* (irregular), *Zeszyty Naukowe* (irregular)

DEANS

Faculty of Architecture: Dr ZDZISŁAW PELCZARSKI

Faculty of Civil and Environmental Engineering: Prof. Dr JÓZEFA WIATER

Faculty of Computer Science: Prof. Dr LEON BOBROWSKI

Faculty of Electrical Engineering: Prof. Dr Hab. MARIAN ROCH DUBOWSKI

Faculty of Forestry in Hajnówka: Prof. Dr Hab. SŁAWOMIR BAKIER

Faculty of Management: Prof. zw. Dr Hab. Inż. JOANICJUSZ NAZARKO

Faculty of Mechanical Engineering: Prof. Dr ANDRZEJ SEWERYN

PROFESSORS

Faculty of Architecture (ul. Oskara Sosnowskiego 11/15, 15-893 Białystok; tel. (85) 7469914; e-mail wa.sekretariat@pb.edu.pl; internet wa.pb.edu.pl):

BARTNICKA, M., Architecture and Urban Planning

BORKOWSKA-LARYSZ, B., Interior Design

DEBIS, J., Visual Arts

DOLISTOWSKA, M., Architecture and Urban Planning

DURMANOW, V., Architecture and Urban Planning

DWORAKOWSKI, A., Architecture and Graphics

JAKUBOWSKI, K., Visual Arts

JEZIERSKA, J., Visual Arts

KUKAWSKI, T., Architecture and Graphics

MOROZOV, V., Architecture and Urban Planning

PELCZARSKI, Z., Architecture and Urban Planning

PERSZKO, J., Visual Arts

RYCHTER, Z., Housing Architecture

SZEWCZYK, J., Architecture and Urban Planning

TURECKI, A., Architecture and Urban Planning

USCINOWICZ, J., Architecture and Urban Planning

Faculty of Civil and Environmental Engineering (ul. Wiejska 45E, 15-351 Białystok; tel. (85) 7469560; e-mail wbiis@pb.edu.pl; internet wb.pb.edu.pl):

BANASZUK, H., Geology and Geomorphology, Soil Science and Soil Protection

BANASZUK, P., Environmental Management

BOŁTRYK, M., Technology of Material and Construction

CHYŻY, T., Structural Mechanics

DYTCZAK, M., Municipal Economy

DZIENIS, L., Wastewater Treatment Systems

GARDZIEJCZYK, W., Road and Traffic Engineering

GRABOWSKI, R. J, Engineering and Industrial Geodesy

HURYNOVICH, A., Water Treatment Systems

ICKIEWICZ, I., Building Physics

JERZY, G., Sculpture

KIRYLUK, A., Environmental Protection and Management

KOBRYN, A., Engineering Geodesy

KOZNIEWSKI, E., Geometry and Engineering Graphics

LEBIEDOWSKI, M., Water Supply Systems and Sewage Disposal Systems

LEWANDOWSKI, W., Inorganic Chemistry

ŁAPKO, A., Concrete Structures

LASKA, G., Geobotanic

LOBODA, T., Biochemistry

MIEDZIAŁOWSKI, C., Structural Engineering

MIŁASZEWSKI, R., Environmental Economics

PIEŃKOWSKI, C., Heating and Ventilation

POGORZELSKI, A. J., Building Physics

ROSOCHACKI, ST. J., Biotechnology

SKORBIŁOWICZ, E., Water Engineering and Protection

SKORBIŁOWICZ, M., Water Engineering and Protection

SORKO, S. A., Technical Mechanics

SULEWSKA, J. M., Geotechnics

SZLENDAK, J., Steel Constructions

SZYPCIO, Z., Soil Mechanics

VALERIY, E., Building Physics

WIATER, J., Environmental Protection and Management

ZABIELSKA-ADAMSKA, K., Geotechnics

ZUKOWSKI, M., Heating and Ventilation

Faculty of Computer Science (ul. Wiejska 45A, 15-351 Białystok; tel. (85) 7469050; e-mail sekretariat@wi.pb.edu.pl; internet wi.pb.edu.pl):

BAGINSKI, C., Mathematics

BARTOSIEWICZ, Z., Mathematics

BOBROWSKI, L., Computer Science

DAŃKO, W., Computer Science

DRUZDZEL, M., Computer Science

GRZESZCZUK, P., Mathematics

KRETOWSKI, M., Computer Science

MACIAK, T., Electronics

MARCHENKO, V., Mathematics

MOZYRSKA, D., Computer Science

RAKOWSKI, W., Electronics

SALAUYOU, V., Computer Science

STEPANIUK, J., Computer Science

YARMOLIK, V., Computer Science

Faculty of Electrical Engineering (ul. Wiejska 45D, 15-351 Białystok; tel. (85) 7469360; e-mail dubowski@pb.edu.pl; internet we.pb.edu.pl):

BADURSKI, J., Internal Medicine, Laboratory Diagnostics

BOLKOWSKI, ST., Electrotechnics and Metrology

BUSŁOWICZ, M., Control Theory, Automatics

CITKO, T., Electrical Engineering, Automatics

CYWIŃSKI, K., Electrotechnology

CZAWKA, G., Electronic Systems

DOROSZ, J., Chemical Technology

DYBCZYŃSKI, W., Lighting

GOŁĄBIOWSKI, J., Electrotechnology

GRISZYN, J., Radiation and Navigation Technology

JORDAN, A., Electrical Engineering, Electrical Metrology

KORNILUK, W., Safety in Electroenergetics

NIEBRZYDOWSKI, J., Electrical Engineering

RAFAŁOWSKI, M., Applied Optics

SIKORSKI, A., Power Electronics

SOWA, A., Electrotechnology

ŚWIERCZ, M., Biocybernetics, Biomedical Engineering

TWARDY, L., Electroenergetics

ZAJĄC, A., Optoelectronics

Faculty of Management (ul.Ojca Tarasiuka 2, 16-001 Kleosin; tel. (85) 7469802; e-mail wz_pb@pb.edu.pl; internet wz.pb.edu.pl):

BARSZCZAK, T., Agricultural Technology

CELMAROWSKI, Cz., Machine Construction

GARBACZEWSKA, G., Biology

IGNATIUK, S., Agricultural Engineering

JĘDRUSZCZAK, M., Agricultural Technology and Agribusiness

JUREWICZ, S., Economics, Mechanics

KLEMENTOWICZ, T., History of Political and Economic Doctrines

KORZUCH, A., Finance and Accountancy

KORZUCH, B., Management

KOWALCZEWSKI, W., Organization and Management, Economics

KUBICKA, H., Agricultural Technology

KURLISZYN-MOSKAL, A., Environment and Tourism Management

ŁAGOWSKA, B., Horticulture

ŁOBODA, T., Biology

MĄDRY, W., Mathematics

MICHAŁOWSKI, K., Environment and Tourism Management

MIŁASZEWSKI, P., Economics, Environmental Engineering and Environmental Protection

NARUSZEWICZ, S., Law, International Economics

NAZARKO, J., Electrical Power Engineering

NICZYPORUK, A., Agricultural Technology

POPŁAWSKI, W. T., Sociology

SADOWSKI, M., Environmental Protection

SASINOWSKI, H., Economics

SOKÓŁ, J., Animal Science

ŚLUSARCZYK, J., Humanities

TOMCZONEK, Z., Humanities, History

WASIAK, A., Chemistry, Materials Engineering, Mechanical Engineering

Faculty of Mechanical Engineering (ul. Wiejska 45C, 15-351 Białystok; tel. (85) 7469200; e-mail wmechaniczny@pb.edu.pl; internet wm.pb.edu.pl):

CZECH, M., Mechanics, Materials Rheology

DĄBROWSKI, J. R., Chemical Engineering, Machine Construction

GAWRYSIAK, M., Mechanical Engineering, Mechatronics

HEJFT, R., Mechanics, Machine Construction

JAWOREK, K., Automatic Control and Robotics

KARPOWICZ, Ś., Automation Engineering

KOWALEWSKI, Z., Applied Mechanical Engineering

KURZYDŁOWSKI, K., Materials Technology

ŁACH, J., Mechanics, Machine Construction

LINDSTEDT, P., Automatic Control and Robotics

MATYSIAK, ST., Computer Techniques

MIATLUK, M., Machine Construction

OSIPIUK, W., Mechanics, Machine Construction

PIWNIK, J., Mechanics, Plastics

PUCIŁOWSKI, K., Mechanics

RAWSKI, F., Automobile Engineering

SEWERYN, A., Mechanics, Resistance of Materials

SIEMIENIAKO, F., Automatic Control and Robotics

SKIEPKO, T., Thermodynamics and Fluid Mechanics

SULYM, H., Applied Mechanical Engineering

POLITECHNIKA CZĘSTOCHOWSKA (Częstochowa University of Technology)

ul. Dąbrowskiego 69, 42-201 Częstochowa

Telephone: (34) 3250498

E-mail: rektor@adm.pcz.czest.pl

Internet: www.pcz.pl

Founded 1949

State control

Academic year: October to June

Chancellor: KATARZYNA PIKULA

Rector: Prof. MARIA NOWICKA-SKOWRON

Vice-Rector for Devt: Prof. JACEK PRZYBYLSKI

Vice-Rector for Education: Prof. ANDRZEJ RUSEK

Vice-Rector for Science and Research: Prof. ZYGMUNT NITKIEWICZ

Dir for Library: Dr DAGMARA BUBEL

Library: see under Libraries and Archives

Number of teachers: 770

Number of students: 14,000

Publication: *Turbulence* (1 a year)

DEANS

Faculty of Civil Engineering: Prof. LUCJAN KURZAK

Faculty of Electrical Engineering: Prof. LECH BOROWIK

Faculty of Environmental Engineering and Biotechnology: Prof. MACIEJ MROWIEC

Faculty of Management: Prof. ARNOLD PABIAN

Faculty of Materials Processing Technology and Applied Physics: Prof. ZBIGNIEW STRADOMSKI

Faculty of Mechanical Engineering and Computer Science: Prof. NORBERT SCZYGIOL

PROFESSORS

Faculty of Civil Engineering (ul. Akademicka 3, 42-200 Częstochowa; tel. (34) 3250930; e-mail wb.dz@adm.pcz.czest.pl; internet bud.pcz.czest.pl):

BOBKO, T., Technology, Organization of Building

CZECH, L., Geometrical Construction, Civil Engineering

DREWNOWSKI, S., Materials Engineering, Structural Engineering

KLEIBER, M., Structural Engineering

KONIECZNY, S., Structural Mechanics

KOSIŃSKI, S., Structural Mechanics

KOZŁOWSKI, R., Civil Engineering

KWIATEK, J., Civil Engineering, Geotechnology

PRZYBYŁO, W., Structural Mechanics, Civil Engineering

PUSZKARIOWA, E., Building Materials

RAJCZYK, J., Civil Engineering

SŁUŻALEC, A., Mathematics, Mechanics

SYGUŁA, S., Bridge Construction, Civil Engineering

Faculty of Electrical Engineering (ul. Armii Krajowej 17, 42-200 Częstochowa; tel. (34) 3250822; e-mail dziekanat@el.pcz.czest.pl; internet www.el.pcz.pl):

BIERNACKI, Z., Electrotechnics, Measurements, Design of Measuring Equipment

BRZOZOWSKI, W., Electrical Engineering, Power Stations

DOBRZAŃSKA, I., Electrical Engineering, Electrical Power Management

ISKIERKA, S., Electrotechnics

JANICZEK, R., Electrotechnology

KRAWCZYK, A., Electrotechnics

KRUCZININ, A. M., Electrotechnology

MINKINA, W., Electronics

POPOV, B., Informatics

ROJEK, R., Electronics, Automatics

ROLICZ, P., Electrotechnics

ROMAN, A., Electronics, Magnetic Materials

RUSEK, A., Electric Motors

SAWICKI, A., Electrotechnology
SOIŃSKI, M., Magnetic Materials, Material Engineering
SOKALSKI, K., Physics
SOWA, P., Electroenergetics
WYSOCKI, J., Electronics, Computer Engineering
ZĄBKOWSKA-WACŁAWEK, M., Electrotechnology

Faculty of Environmental Engineering and Biotechnology (ul. J.H. Dąbrowskiego 73, 42-201 Częstochowa; tel. (34) 3250462; e-mail wiios.dz@adm.pcz.pl; internet www.is.pcz .czest.pl):

BIEŃ, J., Geology, Hydrogeology
BIS, Z., Mechanics, Thermodynamics
BOHDZIEWICZ, J., Environmental Engineering
DEWLATOW, W., Mechanics, Structural Engineering
GIRCZYS, J., Sanitary Engineering
GODZIK, S., Environmental Engineering
GUMNITSKY, J., Biochemistry, Biotechnology
HŁAWICZKA, S., Environmental Engineering
JAGIEŁA, K., Electrotechnology
JANIKOWSKI, R., Environmental Engineering
JANOSZ-RAJCZYK, M., Environmental Engineering
KISIEL, A., Sanitary Engineering
KOSIŃSKI, W., Environmental Engineering
KUCHARSKI, R., Environmental Engineering
MALINA, G., Sanitary Engineering
NOWAK, W., Sanitary Engineering
PISAREK, J., Mechanics, Machine Building Technology
SANITSKY, M., Environmental Engineering

Faculty of Management (ul. Armii Krajowej 19B, 42-200 Częstochowa; tel. (34) 3613876; e-mail dziekan@zim.pcz.czest.pl; internet www.zim.pcz.czest.pl):

ANTOSZKIEWICZ, J., Organization and Management
BARTZ, B., Economics, Logistics
BORKOWSKI, S., Organization and Management, Metallurgy
BOROWIECKI, R., Organization and Management
BUKOWSKI, L., Machine-Building Technology, Management
BUKUVKA, O., Production Engineering
CHRZAN, P., Econometrics, Statistics
DURAJ, J., Organization and Management
DURLIK, I., Marketing
FIEDOROWICZ, K., Economics
GOŁUCHOWSKI, J., Informatics
GORCZYCKA, E., Economics, Organization and Management
GRZESZCZYK, T., Economics, Law
GUBARIENI, N., Informatics
GURGUL, E., Agrotechnology
JASTRZĘBOWSKI-HOFFMAN, Z., History, Politics
KATKOW, A., Informatics
KIEŁTYKA, L., Automatics in Management
KLIBER, J., Materials Engineering, Metallurgy
KLISIŃSKI, J., Economics, Marketing
KONODYBA-SZYMAŃSKI, B., Metallurgy
LEWANDOWSKI, J., Organization and Management, Machine Building Technology
MALISZEWSKI, J., Economics, Organization and Management
MILIAN, L., Sociology, Organization and Management
MOSZKIEWICZ, M., Economics
NOWAK, C., Agricultural Technology
NOWICKA-SKOWRON, M., Economics, Organization and Management
NOWICKI, A., Organization and Management, Informatics
PABIAN, A., Organization of Building

PARTYKA, M., Mathematics, Informatics
RUBACHOW, A., Organization and Management Economics
SITEK, E., Economics
SOBOLAK, L., Organization and Management
SUCHECKA, J., Economics
SZOPA, J., Theoretical and Applied Mechanics, Applied Mathematics, Computers
SZTUKA, J., Marketing
SZUWALSKI, K., Organization and Management
VARKOLY, L., Materials Engineering, Computer Engineering
WOŹNIAK-SOBCZAK, B., Economics, Organization and Management
ZACHOROWSKA, A., Economics
ZAWISŁAWSKA, D., Economics
ŻÓŁTOWSKI, B., Process Engineering and Organization

Faculty of Materials Processing Technology and Applied Physics (ul. Armii Krajowej 19, 42-200 Częstochowa; tel. (34) 3250713; e-mail dziekanat@wip.pcz.pl; internet www.wip.pcz .pl):

BALA, H., Corrosion of Metals
BOCHENEK, A., Metallurgy, Materials Science
BRASZCZYŃSKI, J., Metallurgy, Foundry Technology
BUDZIK, R., Metallurgy of Ferrous Metals
DYJA, H., Plastic Working of Metals
DZILIŃSKI, K., Physics
GOLIS, B., Plastic Working of Metals
HRABAŃSKI, R., Physics
JEZIORSKI, L., Metallurgy, Metals Science
JOWSA, J., Metallurgy
KNAP, F., Plastic Working of Metals
KONOPKA, Z., Metallurgy, Foundry Technology
ŁĘDZKI, A., Metallurgy, Steelmaking
LESIK, L., Metallurgy
LIS, A., Materials Engineering, Metallurgy
MIELCZAREK, E., Thermodynamics in Power Engineering, Heat Engineering
MOREL, S., Heat Engineering
NITKIEWICZ, Z., Metallurgy, Materials Engineering
PIETRZYK, M., Metallurgy
PILARCZYK, J., Metallurgy, Materials Science
PIŁKOWSKI, Z., Foundry, Steelmaking
SIWKA, J., Metallurgy, Steelmaking
SŁUPEK, S., Metallurgy, Heat Engineering
STACHURA, S., Metals Science
WASZKIELEWICZ, W., Organization and Management, Metallurgy
WIERZBICKA, B., Metallurgy, Casting of Non-ferrous Metals
WOLKENBERG, A., Metals Science
WYSŁOCKI, B., Physics of Magnetic Materials
WYSŁOCKI, J., Physics, Physics of Magnetic Materials
ZAPART, M., Physics
ZAPART, W., Physics of Magnetic Materials
ZBROSZCZYK, J., Physics

Faculty of Mechanical Engineering and Computer Science (ul. Dąbrowskiego 73, 42-201 Częstochowa; tel. (34) 3250561; e-mail stacjonarne@wimii.pcz.pl; internet wimii.pcz .czest.pl):

CUPIAŁ, K., Machines and Internal Combustion Engines
DOMAŃSKI, Z., Physics, Biophysics
DROBNIAK, S., Fluid Mechanics, Fluid Flow Machines
GAJEWSKI, W., Thermodynamics
GIERZYŃSKA-DOLNA, M., Mechanical Engineering, Plastics Processing Machines and Technology
JARŻA, A., Fluid Mechanics
KENSIK, R., Welding
KLAJNY, R., Fluid Mechanics
KOMPANEC, L., Informatics

KOSZKUL, J., Plastics Materials
KRIVOI, S., Mathematics
KUBARSKI, J., Mathematics
KUKLA, S., Mathematics, Mechanics
KUKURYK, B., Plastic Working of Metals
MAJCHRZAK, E., Mathematics
MAZANEK, E., Machine Design
MELECHOW, R., Machine-Building Technology
MENDERA, K., Machines and Internal Combustion Engines
MIRKOWSKI, J., Mechanics and Internal Combustion Engines
MOCHNACKI, B., Mathematics
NIESZPOREK, T., Machine-Building Technology
PARKITNY, R., Applied Mechanics and Foundry Technology
PIECH, H., Computer Engineering
POSIADALA, B., Applied Mechanics
RUTKOWSKA, D., Informatics
RUTKOWSKI, L., Informatics, Cybernetics
SCZYGIOL, N., Applied Mechanics
SEWASTJANOW, P., Mathematics
SUBERLAK, O., Plastics Materials
SZOPA, R., Mathematics
TOMSKI, L., Machine Design, Applied Mechanics
TUBIELEWICZ, K., Machine-Building Technology
WIERZBICKI, E., Applied Mathematics, Mechanics
WŁODARSKI, J., Plastics Processing Machines and Technology
WOLAŃSKI, R., Thermodynamics, Thermal Processes in Welding
WOŹNIAK, C., Mathematics, Mechanics
WYRZYKOWSKI, R., Informatics

POLITECHNIKA GDAŃSKA
(Gdańsk University of Technology)

ul. G. Narutowicza 11/12, 80-233 Gdańsk
Telephone: (58) 3471269
E-mail: rektor@pg.gda.pl
Internet: www.pg.gda.pl
Founded 1945
Academic year: October to July

Chancellor: Mgr Inz. MAREK TŁOK
Rector: Prof. Dr Hab. HENRYK KRAWCZYK
Vice-Rector for Cooperation and Innovation: Prof. Dr Hab. JACEK MĄKINIA
Vice-Rector for Devt and Quality: Prof. Dr Hab. KAZIMIERZ JAKUBIUK
Vice-Rector for Education: Prof. Dr Hab. MAREK DZIDA
Vice-Rector for Science: Prof. Dr Hab. JÓZEF E. SIENKIEWICZ
Dir for Library: HAKUĆ BOŻENA

Library: see under Libraries and Archives
Number of teachers: 1,200
Number of students: 27,000

Publications: *Advances in Materials Sciences* (Journal, 4 a year), *Inżynieria Morska i Geotechnika* (Journal, 4 a year), *Pismo PG* (Journal, 12 a year), *Polish Maritime Research* (Journal, 4 a year), *Wykazy Nowych Nabytków Biblioteki* (Library Acquisitions Lists, 4 year), *Zeszyty Naukowe Politechniki Gdańskiej* (Scientific Papers of the Technical Univ. of Gdańsk, irregular)

DEANS

Faculty of Applied Physics and Mathematics: Prof. Dr Hab. WOJCIECH SADOWSKI
Faculty of Architecture: Prof. Dr Hab. ANTONI TARASZKIEWICZ
Faculty of Chemistry: Prof. Dr SLAWOMIR MILEWSKI
Faculty of Civil and Environmental Engineering: Dr Hab. IRENEUSZ KREJA
Faculty of Electrical and Control Engineering: Dr Hab. LEON SWĘDROWSKI

Faculty of Electronics, Telecommunications and Informatics: Prof. Dr Hab. KRZYSZTOF GOCZYŁA

Faculty of Management and Economics: Dr Hab. JULITA WASILCZUK

Faculty of Mechanical Engineering: Prof. Dr Hab. JAN STASIEK

Faculty of Ocean Engineering and Ship Technology: Dr Hab. Inz. JANUSZ KOZAK

PROFESSORS

Faculty of Applied Physics and Mathematics (ul. Gabriela Narutowicz 11/12, 80-233 Gdańsk; tel. (58) 3471310; e-mail dziekanat@mif.pg.gda.pl; internet www.mif.pg.gda.pl):

GŁAZUNOW, J., Mathematical Analysis, Applied Mathematics
GODLEWSKI, J., Physics
KALINOWSKI, J., Physics
KAMONT, Z., Differential Equations
LEBLE, S., Theoretical and Mathematical Physics
MURAWSKI, L., Physics, Solid-State Physics
ROMANOWSKI, A., Algebra
SADOWSKI, W., Solid-State Physics
SIENKIEWICZ, J., Physics, Applied Informatics
SZMYTKOWSKI, Cz., Atomic and Molecular Physics

Faculty of Architecture (ul. Gabriela Narutowicza 11/12, 80-233 Gdańsk; tel. (58) 3472315; e-mail dziekan-arch@pg.gda.pl; internet arch.pg.gda.pl):

GÓRA, J., Painting
KITA, A., Painting
STAWICKA-WAŁKOVSKA, M., Healthy Housing (Urban and Building) and Environmental Assessment of Buildings (Sustainable Buildings)

Faculty of Chemistry (ul. Gabriela Narutowicz 11/12, 80-233 Gdańsk; tel. (58) 3472107; internet www.chem.pg.gda.pl):

BALAS, A., General Chemistry
BIERNAT, J., General Chemistry
BIZIUK, M., Environmental Analytical Chemistry, Elemental Analysis, Spectrophotometric Analysis
BOROWSKI, E., Biochemistry
DAROWICKI, K., Electrochemistry, Corrosion and Corrosion Protection
HĘDRZYCKA, K., Biochemistry
HUPKA, J., Chemical Engineering
KAMIŃSKI, M., Chemical Technology
KAWALEC-PIETRENKO, B., Chemical Engineering
KOŁODZIEJCZYK, A., Organic Chemistry
KONOPA, J., Organic Chemistry
KUR, J., Molecular Biology
LEWANDOWSKI, W., Heat Technology, Chemical Engineering
MAZERSKI, J., Molecular Modelling, Chemometrics, Biophysics
MILEWSKI, S., Biochemistry
NAMIEŚNIK, J., Analytical Chemistry
PACYNA, J., Environmental Chemistry, Environmental Engineering, Environmental Analysis and Monitoring
POŁOŃSKI, T., Organic Chemistry, Stereochemistry, Molecular Modelling, Chiroptical Spectroscopy
RACHOŃ, J., Organic Chemistry
SYNOVIEĆKI, J., Technical Science
WOJNOWSKI, W., Inorganic Chemistry

Faculty of Civil and Environmental Engineering (ul. Gabriela Narutowicz 11/12, 80-952 Gdańsk; tel. (58) 3472205; internet www.wilis.pg.gda.pl):

BOGDANIUK, B., Traffic Engineering
GODYCKI ĆWINKO, T., Theory of Reinforced and Prestressed Concrete Structures
JUDYCKI, J., Road Construction
KOWALCZYK, Z., Technology and Management in Civil Engineering

KOWALIK, P., Geodesy
KRYSTEK, R., Traffic Engineering
OBARSKA-PEMPKOWIAK, H., Environmental Engineering
OLAŃCZUK-NEYMAN, K., Environmental Engineering
SIKORA, Z., Civil Engineering, Soil Mechanics and Geomechanical Computation
SZYMCZAK, Cz., Structural Mechanics
SZYMKIEWICZ, R., Hydrology
ZADROGA, B., Soil Mechanics and Foundation Engineering
ZIÓŁKO, J., Steel Structures

Faculty of Electrical and Control Engineering (ul. Gabriela Narutowicz 11/12, 80-233 Gdańsk; tel. (58) 3471386; e-mail dziekanat@ely.pg.gda.pl; internet eia.pg.gda.pl):

BRDYŚ, M., Control Systems
JAKUBIUK, K., Principles of Electrotechnics, Electrical Apparatus
KOWALSKI, Z., Industrial Automation
KRAWĆZUK, M., Mechanics
KRZEMIŃSKI, Z., Electrical Drives and Power Electronics
MARECKI, J., Electrical Power Engineering
PAZDRO, P., Electrical Apparatus and Traction
SZCZERBA, Z., Electrical Power Engineering
WOLNY, A., High-Voltage Current Switching
ZAJCZYK, R., Power Engineering
ZIMNY, P., Theoretical Electromagnetic Field

Faculty of Electronics, Telecommunications and Informatics (ul. Gabriela Narutowicz 11/12, 80-233 Gdańsk; tel. (58) 3471245; e-mail deans@eti.pg.gda.pl; internet www.eti.pg.gda.pl):

CZYŻEWSKI, A., Sound Engineering
GÓRSKI, J. K., Software Engineering, Informatics
KOWALCZUK, Z., Automatic Control and Robotics
KRAWCZYK, H., Computer Science, Parallel Architectures and Fault-Tolerance
KUBALE, M., Discrete Optimization
MALINA, W., Computer Science and Pattern Recognition
MAZUR, J., Microwave Techniques
MROZOWSKI, M., Electromagnetic Field Theory, Microwaves
NIEDŹWIECKI, MACIEJ, Automatic Control
NOWAKOWSKI, A., Electronics Technology
POLOWCZYK, M., Telecommunications Technology
RUTKOWSKI, D., Principles of Telecommunications
SOBCZAK, W., Cybernetics
SPIRALSKI, L., Electronic Equipment
STEPNOWSKI, A., Marine Acoustics, Telecommunications
WOŹNIAK, J., Telecommunications, Computer Communication Systems
ZIELONKO, R., Electronic Equipment Technology
ZIENTALSKI, M., Electronic Equipment Technology

Faculty of Management and Economics (ul. Gabriela Narutowicz 11/12, 80-233 Gdańsk; tel. (58) 3471899; e-mail dziekan@zie.pg.gda.pl; internet www.zie.pg.gda.pl):

ADAMKIEWICZ, A., Research and Development of Social, Economic and Technological Systems
DASZKOWSKA, M., Principles of Marketing, Services Marketing, the Service Economy

Faculty of Mechanical Engineering (ul. Gabriela Narutowicz 11/12, 80-952 Gdańsk; tel. (58) 3472366; e-mail dziekanat@mech.pg.gda.pl; internet www.mech.pg.gda.pl):

BALCERSKI, A., Marine Diesel Engines and Ship Power Plants

EJSMONT, J., Machine Building and Maintenance
NEYMAN, A., Tribology
PRZYBYLSKI, W., Manufacturing Engineering
PUZYREWSKI, R., Fluid Mechanics
STĄSIEK, J., Thermodynamics and Heat Transfer
WALCZAK, W., Welding
WITTBRODT, E., Mechanics and Machine Dynamics, Applied Mechanics
ZIELIŃSKI, A., Materials Engineering

Faculty of Ocean Engineering and Ship Technology (ul. Gabriela Narutowicz 11/12, 80-233 Gdańsk; tel. (58) 3471567; e-mail dziekoce@pg.gda.pl; internet www.oce.pg.gda.pl):

BRANDOWSKI, A., Engineering Safety and Reliability, Ship Technology
DOMACHOWSKI, Z., Automatic Control of Power Engineering Plants
GIRTLER, J., Ship Power Plants and Diesel Engines
KOLENDA, J., Mechanics of Ship Structures
ROSOCHOWICZ, K., Ship Technology
SZANTYR, J., Mechanics, Ship Hydrodynamics

POLITECHNIKA KOSZALIŃSKA
(Koszalin University of Technology)

ul. Śniadeckich 2, 75-453 Koszalin

Telephone: (94) 3478620
E-mail: jmr@tu.koszalin.pl
Internet: www.tu.koszalin.pl

Founded 1968

Chancellor: Dr ARTUR WEZGRAJ
Rector: Prof. Dr Hab. TADEUSZ BOHDAL
Vice-Rector for Education: Prof. Dr Hab. DANUTA ZAWADZKA
Vice-Rector for Research and Devt: Dr WITOLD GULBINSKI
Vice-Rector for Student Affairs: Prof. Dr Hab. KAZIMIERZ SZYMAŃSKI
Dir for Library: RENATA KISIEL

Library of 177,000 vols incl. 109,800 books and 13,700 periodicals
Number of students: 18,500

DEANS

Faculty of Civil Engineering, Environmental and Geodetic Sciences: Prof. Dr Hab. WIESŁAWA GŁODKOWSKA
Faculty of Economics Science: Prof. Dr Hab. GRZEGORZ SPYCHALSKI
Faculty of Electronics and Computer Science: Prof. Dr Hab. MIROSLAW MALINSKI
Faculty of Mechanical Engineering: Prof. Dr Hab. CZESLAW LUKIANOWICZ

POLITECHNIKA KRĄKOWSKA IM. TADEUSZA KOŚCIUSZKI
(Tadeusz Kościuszko Cracow University of Technology)

ul. Warszawska 24, 31-155 Cracow

Telephone: (12) 6282000
E-mail: kancelaria@pk.edu.pl
Internet: www.pk.edu.pl

Founded 1945, present name and status 1954
State control
Language of instruction: Polish
Academic year: October to September (2 semesters)

Rector: Prof. Dr KAZIMIERZ FURTAK
Vice-Rector for Education and Int. Affairs: Prof. Dr DARIUSZ BOGDAL
Vice-Rector for Gen. Affairs: Dr ANDRZEJ BIALKIEWICZ
Vice-Rector for Research: Prof. Dr JAN KAZIOR
Vice-Rector for Student Affairs: Prof. Dr LESZEK MIKULSKI
Dir for Library: Mgr MAREK M. GÓRSKI

Library of 205,653 vols, 79,278 periodicals, 394,884 standards, patents, etc.

Number of teachers: 1,130

Number of students: 17,800

Publications: *Czasopismo Techniczne* (Technical Bulletin, irregular; series on Architecture, Civil Engineering, Chemistry, Mechanics, Electrotechnics, Environmental Science), *Zeszyty Naukowe i Monografie Politechniki Krakowskiej* (Scientific Papers, irregular; series on Architecture, Civil Engineering, Environmental Engineering, Mechanics, Electrical and Computer Engineering, Chemical Engineering and Technology, Basic Technical Sciences, Human, Economic and Social Sciences)

DEANS

Faculty of Architecture: Prof. Dr Hab. JACEK GYURKOVICH

Faculty of Chemical Engineering and Technology: Prof. Dr Hab. ZYGMUNT KOWALSKI

Faculty of Civil Engineering: Prof. Dr Hab. TADEUSZ TATARA

Faculty of Electrical and Computer Engineering: Prof. Dr Hab. ADAM JAGIEŁŁO

Faculty of Environmental Engineering: Prof. Dr Hab. ELŻBIETA NACHLIK

Faculty of Mechanical Engineering: Prof. Dr Hab. LESZEK WOJNAR

Faculty of Physics, Mathematics and Computer Science: Prof. Dr Hab. MAREK STANUSZEK

PROFESSORS

Faculty of Architecture (ul. Podchorążych 1, 30-084 Cracow; tel. (12) 6282020; e-mail a-0@pk.edu.pl; internet www.pk.edu.pl/arch):

BARTKOWICZ, B., Urban Design and Spatial Planning

BIEDA, K., Urban Design Theory and Practice

BÖHM, A., Architecture, Landscape Architecture

BULIŃSKI, W., Architectural Design

DOUSA, S., Sculpture

GOŁOGÓRSKA-KUCIA, E., Painting and Drawing

KADŁUCZKA, A., History of Architecture and Monument Preservation

KOZŁOWSKI, D., Architectural Design and Theory

KUŚNIERZ, K., History of Urban Design

LENARTOWICZ, J. K., Design of Industrial Architecture

MITKOWSKA, A., History of Architecture and Urban Design

SERUGA, W., Urban and Architectural Design

SIEWNIAK, M., Landscape Architecture

WYŻYKOWSKI, A., Urban and Architectural Design

Faculty of Chemical Engineering and Technology (ul. Warszawska 24, 31-155 Cracow; tel. (12) 6282035; e-mail wiitch@chemia.pk.edu.pl; internet www.chemia.pk.edu.pl):

BARAŃSKI, A., Organic Chemistry and Physical Organic Chemistry

KOWALSKI, Z., Inorganic Chemical Technology

PIELICHOWSKI, J., Chemistry and Technology of Polymers, Organic Synthesis

STOKŁOSA, A., Physical Chemistry, Solid State Physical Chemistry

TABIS, B., Chemical Engineering

ŻUREK, Z., Solid State Chemistry, Materials Science

Faculty of Civil Engineering (ul. Warszawska 24, 31-155 Cracow; tel. (12) 6282023; e-mail l-0@pk.edu.pl; internet www.wil.pk.edu.pl):

ADAMSKI, A., Transport Control Computer Systems, Management and Control Decision-making, Optimization Problems

CHRZANOWSKI, M., Fracture Mechanics and Rheology

CICHOŃ, C., Theory of Structure, Numerical Analysis

CZYCZUŁA, W., Rail and Air Transport Infrastructure, Transportation Systems

DYDUCH, K., Reinforced and Prestressed Concrete Structures, Industrial Buildings, Modernization

FLAGA, A., Structural Mechanics, Building Aerodynamics, Wind Engineering

FLAGA, K., Bridges, Tunnels, Concrete Structures, Technology of Concrete, Nondestructive Testing

FURTAK, K., Bridges, Tunnels, Concrete Structures

KAWECKI, J., Structural Mechanics

ORKISZ, J., Theory of Structure, Structural Mechanics

RUDNICKI, A., Traffic and Highway Engineering, Transportation Systems

ŚLIWIŃSKI, J., Concrete Technology, Building Materials

STACHOWICZ, A., Structural Mechanics, General and Industrial Building, Concrete Structures

SZEFER, G., Solid and Structural Mechanics

TRACZ, M., Traffic and Highway Engineering

WASZCZYSZYN, Z., Structural Mechanics, Strength of Materials, Artificial Intelligence, Neurocomputing and Microcomputing

Faculty of Electrical and Computer Engineering (ul. Warszawska 24, 31-155 Cracow; tel. (12) 628-20-43; internet www.wieik.pk.edu.pl):

JAGIEŁŁO, A., Electrical Machines

LAYER, E., Electrical Metrology

MALECKI, P., Experimental Particle Physics, Online Computing, Detector Control Systems

MOŚCIŃSKI, J., Computer Systems, Large-scale Computing, Network Security, Wireless Networking

SAPIECHA, K., Computer Architecture and Programming

SIWCZYŃSKI, M., Electrotechnics, Circuit Theory and Signals

SOBCZYK, T., Electrical Machines

SZARANIEC, E., Mathematical Geophysics

Faculty of Environmental Engineering (ul. Warszawska 24, 31-155 Cracow; tel. (12) 6282801; e-mail s-0@wis.pk.edu.pl; internet www.wis.pk.edu.pl):

BRYŚ, H., Surveying in Engineering

DĄBROWSKI, W., Water Supply, Waste Water Disposal, Sanitary Engineering

KANDEFER, S., Thermal Engineering, Combustion Processes, Use of Thermal Waste, Air Protection Systems

KOCWA-KALUCH, R., Environmental Biology, Microbiology of Water, Waste Water and Air

MACZEK, K., Refrigeration, Air Conditioning, Environmental Engineering

NACHLIK, E., Hydraulics and Water Management

PIASEK, Z., Geodesy and Cartography for Environmental Engineering, Numerical Geodesy

SŁOTA, H., Water Management

WYSOKIŃSKI, L., Geotechnics, Environmental and Geological Engineering, Civil Engineering

Faculty of Mechanical Engineering (Jana Pawła II 37, 31-864 Cracow; tel. (12) 6283603; e-mail m-0@admin.pk.edu.pl; internet www.mech.pk.edu.pl):

CYKLIS, J., Production Engineering

DYLĄG, M., Chemical Engineering, Chemical Industry Equipment, Environmental Engineering

GAWLIK, J., Machining, Design of Cutting Tools

GOLEC, K., Internal Combustion Engines, Engine Cold-starting, Feeding Systems, Turbocharging

KAMIEŃSKI, J., Industrial Equipment

KAZIOR, J., Machine Technology, Powder Metallurgy, Stainless Steels

KNAPCZYK, J., Motor Vehicles and Tractors, Robotics, Theory of Machines and Mechanisms

KOZŁOWSKI, R., Physical Metallurgy and Heat Treatment, Power Engineering, Materials Science

MATRAS, Z., Fluid Mechanics, Rheology, Chemical Engineering, Power Engineering

MAZURKIEWICZ, S., Experimental Mechanics, Biomechanics

MICHAŁOWSKI, S., Machine Dynamics, Robotics

MUC, A., Plate and Shell Structures, Mechanics of Composite Materials

NIZIOŁ, J., Theoretical and Applied Mechanics, Machine Dynamics

OPRZĘDKIEWICZ, J., Reliability of Mechanical Devices

RUP, K., Fluid Mechanics, Heat and Mass Transfer

RYŚ, J., Machine Design, Gears, Pressure Vessels

SENDYKA, B., Internal Combustion Engines

SKRZYPEK, J., Theory of Plasticity, Rheology, Damage

TALER, J., Power Machines and Engineering, Heat Transfer, Thermodynamics

WANTUCH, E., Production Engineering

WOJNAR, L., Tribology

WOŁKOW, J., Hydraulic and Pneumatic Control and Drives

ZALEWSKI, W., Power Equipment and Systems, Refrigerating and Air-conditioning Systems

ZIELINSKI, A., Computer Methods of Structural Mechanics, Computer-aided Machine Design

Faculty of Physics, Mathematics and Computer Science (ul. Podchorążych 1, 30-084 Cracow; tel. (12) 6380728; e-mail fmi@pk.edu.pl; internet www.fmi.pk.edu.pl):

ARTEMOWICZ, O., Algebra

CISOWSKI, J., Solid State Physics

GRAFIJCZUK, W., Mechanics

KOZARZEWSKI, B., Theoretical Physics, Quantum Computation

ŁAWRENIUK, S., Differential Equations

ŁOPUSZAŃSKI, O., Spectral Theory of Operators

OSTOJA-GAJEWSKI, A., Applied Mechanics

PLICZKO, A., Mathematics

POLITECHNIKA ŁÓDZKA
(Lodz University of Technology)

ul. Żeromskiego 116 90-924 Łódź

Telephone: (42) 6312151

E-mail: rector@adm.p.lodz.pl

Internet: www.p.lodz.pl

Founded 1945

State control

Languages of instruction: English, French, Polish

Academic year: October to June (2 semesters)

Rector: Prof. Dr STANISŁAW BIELECKI

Vice-Rector for Education: Prof. Dr SLAWOMIR WIAK

Vice-Rector for Innovations: Prof. Dr PIOTR KULA

Vice-Rector for Science: Prof. Dr PIOTR PANETH

Vice-Rector for Univ. Development: Prof. Dr PIOTR SZCZEPANIAK

Dir for Library: BŁAŻEJ FERET

Library of 251,000 vols

Number of teachers: 1,500
Number of students: 20,100

Publications: *Budownictwo* (in Polish), *Bulletin* (in Polish), *Chemia* (in Polish and English), *Chemia Spożywcza i Biotechnologia* (in Polish and English), *Cieplne Maszyny Przepływowe* (in Polish and English), *Elektryka* (in Polish and English), *Inżynieria Chemiczna i Procesowa* (in Polish and English), *Journal of Applied Computer Science* (in English), *Mechanics and Mechanical Engineering* (in English), *Organizacja i Zarządzanie* (in Polish), *Physics* (in English), *Rozprawy Naukowe* (in Polish and English), *Włókiennictwo* (in Polish), *Zeszyty Naukowe Politechniki Łódzkiej* (in Polish and English)

DEANS

Faculty of Biotechnology and Food Sciences: Prof. Dr MARIA KOZIOŁKIEWICZ
Faculty of Chemistry: Prof. Dr SŁAWOMIR JANKOWSKI
Faculty of Civil Engineering, Architecture and Environmental Engineering: Prof. Dr DARIUSZ GAWIN
Faculty of Electrical, Electronic, Computer and Control Engineering: Prof. Dr SŁAWOMIR HAUSMAN
Faculty of Material Technologies and Textiles Design: Prof. Dr JÓZEF MASAJTIS
Faculty of Mechanical Engineering: Prof. Dr BOGDAN KRUSZYŃSKI
Faculty of Organization and Management: Prof. Dr RYSZARD GRĄDZKI
Faculty of Process and Environmental Engineering: Prof. Dr IRENEUSZ ZBICIŃSKI
Faculty of Technical Physics, Information Technology and Applied Mathematics: Prof. Dr GRZEGORZ BĄK

PROFESSORS

Faculty of Biotechnology and Food Science (ul. Wólczańska 171/173, 90-924 Łódź; tel. (42) 6313400; e-mail deanbiof@adm.p.lodz.pl; internet snack.p.lodz.pl):

AMBROZIAK, W., Fermentation Technology
ANTCZAK, T., Technical Biochemistry
BIELECKI, S., Technical Biochemistry
BUJACZ, G., Protein Crystallography, Structural Biochemistry
CEDZYŃSKA, K., Organic Chemistry, Environmental Protection
GRABKA, J., Food Engineering, Sugar Technology
ICIEK, J., Chemical Food Technology, Food Engineering
KOZIOŁKIEWICZ, M., Biotechnology, Chemistry, Technical Biotechnology
KRÓL, B., Food Technology
KULA, J., Chemical Technology
LIBUDZISZ, Z., Technical Microbiology
NEBESNY, E., Food Technology
OKRUSZEK, A., Biotechnology, Organic Chemistry
SZOPA, J., Technical Microbiology
TURKIEWICZ, M., Biochemistry, Enzymology
TWARDOWSKI, T., Technical Biochemistry
WYSOCKI, S., Physical And Theoretical Chemistry
ŻAKOWSKA, Z., Technical Microbiology

Faculty of Chemistry (ul. Zeromskiego 116, 90-924 Łódź; tel. (42) 6313100; e-mail deanchem@adm.p.lodz.pl; internet chemia.p.lodz.pl):

ABRAMCZYK, H., Molecular Spectroscopy, Laser Spectroscopy, Physical and Theoretical Chemistry
BEM, H., Physical and Nuclear Chemistry
CZAJKOWSKI, W., Dyes Chemistry and Technology, Organic Chemistry and Technology
GĘBICKI, J. M., Organic Physical Chemistry, Photochemistry, Spectroscopy, Radiation Chemistry, Biocrystallography
GŁÓWKA, M., Biocrystallography
HAWLICKA, E., Physical and Theoretical Chemistry, Computation Chemistry
JANECKI, T., Organic Chemistry
JÓŹWIAK, W., Chemical Catalysis, Environmental Protection
KAMIŃSKI, Z., Organic Chemistry
KAROLAK-WOJCIECHOWSKA, J., Physical and Theoretical Chemistry, Crystallography
MARCINEK, A., Physical Chemistry, Radiation Chemistry
PANETH, P., Physical and Theoretical Chemistry, Biochemistry
ROSIAK, J. M., Biomaterials Engineering, Polymer Chemistry, Radiation Technology
RYNKOWSKI, J., General Chemistry, Chemical Catalysis, Environmental Protection
RZYMSKI, W., Polymer Chemistry and Technology
SOKOŁOWSKA, J., Dyes Chemistry and Technology
ULAŃSKI, J., Physics and Physical Chemistry of Polymers
ZABORSKI, M., Rubber Chemistry and Technology

Faculty of Civil Engineering, Architecture and Environmental Engineering (ul. Politechniki 6, 90-924 Łódź; tel. (42) 6313502; e-mail deanarch@p.lodz.pl; internet bais.p.lodz.pl):

CZKWIANIANC, A., Concrete Structures
JOCZ, J., Sculpture
JUZWA, J., Industrial Architecture, Planning of Industrial Areas
KAMIŃSKA, M., Concrete Structures
KLEMM, P., Building Physics, Building Materials, Acoustics of the Architectural and Urban Environment
PAWŁOWSKI, P., History of Town Planning, Planning for Urban Revitalization
PRZEWŁOCKI, S., Engineering Geodesy, Building Metrology, Cartography, Descriptive Geometry
ROGOWSKI, B., Fracture Mechanics, Contact and Inclusion Mechanics, Mechanics of Piezo-electro-magneto-elastic Materials, 'Smart' Materials and 'Intelligent' Structures, Coupled Fields
SABINIAK, H., Heating, Air Conditioning and Ventilation Engineering, Powerdriving and Exploitation of Machinery

Faculty of Electrical, Electronic, Computer and Control Engineering (ul. Stefanowskiego 18/22, 90-924 Łódź; tel. (42) 6312502; e-mail deanelec@sir.p.lodz.pl; internet wee.p.lodz.pl):

ANDERS, G., Reliability Analysis, Power Cable Thermal Rating, Asset Management, Project Management
BARTOSZEWICZ, A., Control Engineering and Robotics, Control Theory
JEZIERSKI, E., Control of Robots
KACPRZAK, T., Telecommunications, Electronic Devices and Systems, Neural Networks
KOŁACIŃSKI, Z., Electrical Apparatus, Plasma Technologies
KOSZMIDER, A., Instrument Transformers, Applied Electrical Engineering
KUŚMIEREK, Z., Electrical Metrology
KUŹMIŃSKI, K., Control Theory, Automation
LISIK, Z., Semiconductor Devices, Microelectronic Technology, High-Temperature Electronics, Optical and Electrical Integrated Systems
MATERKA, A., Telecommunications, Signals Processing, Medical Electronics
MIELCZARSKI, W., Power Engineering
MOSIŃ, F., Stochastic Processes, High-Voltage Engineering
NAPIERALSKI, A., Microelectronics, Electronic Circuits, Power Electronics, Computer Engineering, Thermography
NOWACKI, Z., Electrical Drive Control, Power Electronics
NOWICZ, R., Electrical Engineering, Transformers
OSTALCZYK, P., Control Engineering and Robotics, Electric Drive Automation
PAWELSKI, W., Electronic Devices and Circuits, Power Electronics
PAWLIK, M., Thermal Power Plant Energy Economics
SANKOWSKI, D., Computerized Data Measurement, Identification and Control of Electrothermal Systems
STRZELCZYK, A., Electrical Engineering, Power Engineering
TADEUSIEWICZ, M., Circuit Theory, Theoretical Electrotechnology
WIAK, S., Computer-aided Design, Electrodynamics
ZAKRZEWSKI, K., Electric Machines and Transformers, Applied Electrodynamics

Faculty of Material Technologies and Textile Design (ul. Zeromskiego 116, 90-924 Łódź; tel. (42) 6313300; e-mail w-4@adm.p.lodz.pl):

CYGAN, W., Tapestry
DEMS, K., Structural Mechanics
FRYDRYCH, I., Mechanical Technology of Textiles, Clothing
GNIOTEK, K., Automation of Textile Processes, Measurement Science and Systems
JANTAS, R., Chemical Technology
KOWALSKI, K., Knitting Technology
KOPIAS, K., Knitting Technology
KRUCIŃSKA, I., Mechanical Technology of Textiles, Metrology
LIPP-SYMONOWICZ, B., Chemical Technology of Textiles
MASAJTIS, J., Mechanical Technology of Textiles
NAWROT, A., Tapestry
RYBICKI, F. E., Chemical Technology of Textiles
SNYCERSKI, M., Mechanical Technology of Textiles
WYSOKIŃSKA, Z., Economics
ZAJACZKOWSKI, J., Mechanics, Textiles

Faculty of Mechanical Engineering (ul. Stefanowskiego 1/15, 90-924 Łódź; tel. (42) 6312200; internet www.mechaniczny.p.lodz.pl):

AWREJCEWICZ, J., Dynamics, Control, Biomechanics
BURCAN, J., Precision Engineering, Medical Engineering
CZOLCZYNSKI, K., Mechanics, Machine Engineering
FODEMSKI, T., Thermodynamics, Heat Transfer
GAWROŃSKI, Z., Materials Engineering
GAZICKI-LIPMAN, M., Materials Engineering
GOŁĄBCZAK, A., Production Engineering
KAPITANIAK, T., Mechanics, Machine Dynamics
KOLAKOWSKI, Z., Applied Mechanics
KRÓLAK, M., Applied Mechanics
KRUSZYŃSKI, B., Machining, Manufacturing and Machine Tools Surface Technology
KRYSIŃSKI, J., Fluid-flow Machinery
KULA, P., Machine Design, Materials Engineering
MITURA, S., Materials Engineering
NIEZGODZINSKI, T., Mechanics, Applied Mechanics
ORYŃSKI, F., Machine Tools, Machine Dynamics
PAWELSKI, Z., Machine Design
PIETROWSKI, S., Materials Engineering, Foundry
TOMCZYK, I., Machine Design, Control
WALKOWIAK, B., Medical Engineering
WIŚNIEWSKI, M., Machine Design, Tribology

Faculty of Organization and Management (ul. Piotrkowska 266, 90-924 Łódź; tel. (42) 6847993; e-mail w-9@adm.p.lodz.pl; internet oizet.p.lodz.pl):

BALENDRA, R., Management
BARANOWSKI, K., Humanities
LACHIEWICZ, S., Management
LECEWICZ-BARTOSZEWSKA, J., Ergonomics
LEWANDOWSKI, J., Management
MARTIN, C., Management
PENC, J., Strategy Management
POMYKALSKI, A., Economics

Faculty of Process and Environmental Engineering (ul. Wólczańska 213, 90-924 Łódź; tel. (42) 6313700; e-mail sekretariat@wipos.p.lodz.pl; internet wipos.p.lodz.pl):

HEIM, A., Mechanical Engineering, Chemical Engineering
KAMIŃSKI, W., Environmental Engineering, Chemical Engineering
LEDAKOWICZ, S., Chemical Engineering and Bioprocess Engineering, Environmental Engineering, Chemical Technology
MUCHA, M., Chemical Engineering, Chemical Technology
PIDDUBNIAK, D., Mechanics
TYCZKOWSKI, J., Materials Science, Chemical Engineering, Chemistry
WODZIŃSKI, P., Chemical Engineering, Mechanical Engineering
ZARZYCKI, R., Environmental Engineering
ZBICIŃSKI, I., Chemical Engineering, Environmental Engineering

Faculty of Technical Physics, Information Technology and Applied Mathematics (ul. Wólczańska 215, 90-924 Łódź; tel. (42) 6313601; e-mail dz-w7-7@adm.p.lodz.pl; internet www.ftims.p.lodz.pl):

BĄK, G., Solid-State Physics, Dielectrics
BALCERZAK, M., Real Analysis
GAJEK, L., Statistics, Financial and Actuarial Mathematics
JACYMIRSKI, M., Signal Processing Methods and Fast Algorithms, Technical and Medical Diagnosis
JEMEC, W., Cytography, Asymptotic Methods, Integral Equations
KUCHARCZYK, W., Solid-State Physics
MIŚKIEWICZ, L., Artistic Composition of Images and Virtual Spaces, Computer Graphics, Visualization
NAKWASKI, W., Semiconductor Laser Physics, Computer Physics
PRZANOWSKI, M., Theory of Relativity, Mathematical Physics
PRZERADZKI, B., Differential Equations, Dynamical Systems
STACHIW, P., Numerical Methods, Methods of Optimization, System Theory
SZCZEPANIAK, P. S., Computational Intelligence, Pattern Recognition, Knowledge Extraction, Technical and Medical Applications

POLITECHNIKA LUBELSKA
(Lublin University of Technology)

ul. Nadbystrzycka 38D, 20-618 Lublin

Telephone: (81) 5384100
E-mail: politechnika@pollub.pl
Internet: www.pollub.pl

Founded 1953
State control
Language of instruction: Polish
Academic year: October to June (2 semesters)
Rector: Prof. Dr PIOTR KACEJKO
Deputy Rector for Scientific Affairs: Prof. Dr MARZENNA DUDZINSKA
Deputy Rector for Student Affairs: Dr ANDRZEJ WAC-WLODARCZYK
Deputy Rector for Univ. Development: Dr BOGUSLAW SZMYGIN
Dir for Library: DOROTA TKACZYK

Library of 150,000 vols
Number of teachers: 550
Number of students: 11,000

DEANS

Faculty of Building and Architecture: Prof. Dr Hab. EWA BLAZIK-BOROWA
Faculty of Electrical Engineering and Computer Science: Prof. Dr Hab. HENRYKA DANUTA STRYCZEWSKA
Faculty of Environmental Engineering: Prof. Dr Hab. JANUSZ OZONEK
Faculty of Fundamentals of Technology: Prof. Dr Hab. KLAUDIUSZ LENIK
Faculty of Management: Prof. Dr EWA BOJAR
Faculty of Mechanical Engineering: Prof. Dr Hab. ZBIGNIEW PATER

PROFESSORS

Faculty of Building and Architecture (ul. Nadbystrzycka 40, 20-618 Lublin; tel. (81) 5384373; e-mail wb.dziekan@pollub.pl; internet wbia.pollub.pl):

BUREK, R., Heating, Ventilation and Automation
CIEŚLAK, W., Mathematics and Engineering Geometry
CIĘŻAK, T., Institute of Civil Engineering and Architecture
FLAGA, A., Structural Mechanics
HALICKA, A., Civil Engineering Structures
KRZOWSKI, Z., Geotechnics
KUKIEŁKA, J., Highway Engineering
OLSZTA, W., Water Supply and Waste Water Removal
POMORSKA, K., Chemical Engineering
SADOWSKI, T., Solid Mechanics

Faculty of Electrical Engineering and Computer Science (ul. Nadbystrzycka 38A, 20-618 Lublin; tel. (81) 5384287; e-mail we.dziekanat@pollub.pl):

BOBROWSKI, A., Mathematics
GRZEGÓRSKI, S., Informatics
JANOWSKI, T., Institute of Electrical Engineering and Electrotechnologies
KOLANO, J., Electrical Drive Systems
KOSMULSKI, M., Electrochemistry
LOZBIN, V., Automatics and Metrology
MAJKA, K., Power Plants and Energy Management
PIETRZYK, W., Computer and Electrical Engineering
RUTKA, Z., Power Networks and Protection
WOJCIK, W., Electronics
ZIELENSKI, W., Mechanics, Polymer Processing
ŻUKOWSKI, P., Electrical Devices and High-Technology Engineering

Faculty of Environmental Engineering (ul. Nadbystrzycka 40B, 20-618 Lublin; tel. (81) 5384402; internet www.wis.pol.lublin.pl):

KWIETNIEWSKI, M., Water Supply and Sewage Disposal
OLSZTA, W., Water Management
OZONEK, J., Indoor Environment Engineering
PAWLOWSKI, L., Institute of Environmental Production Engineering
PAWLOWSKI, L., Water, Waste Water and Waste Technology
SOBCZUK, H., Thermal Techniques
SOLDATOV, V., Sustainable Development
STEPNIEWSKI, W., Land Protection

Faculty of Management (ul. Nadbystrzycka 38, 20-618 Lublin; tel. (81) 5384192; e-mail wz.sekretariat@pollub.pl; internet wz.pollub.pl):

BANEK, T., Quantitative Methods
BAUM, T., Ergonomics
BOJAR, E., Economics
LENIK, K., Principles of Technology
LIPSKI, J., Enterprise Organization
OLCHOWIK, J., Institute of Physics

PAWLAK, M., Organization and Management
SITKO, W., Management
SKOWRON, S., Marketing
WANIURSKI, J., Applied Mathematics

Faculty of Mechanical Engineering (ul. Nadbystrzycka 36, 20-618 Lublin; tel. (81) 5384233; e-mail wm.dziekan@pollub.pl; internet www.wm.pollub.pl):

JONAK, J., Machine Design
KOCZAN, L., Mathematics, Analytical Functions
KUCZMASZEWSKI, J., Production Engineering
NIEWCZAS, A., Internal Combustion Engines and Transportation
OPIELAK, M., Food Processing Engineering
SIKORA, R., Mechanics, Polymer Processing
SWIC, A., Institute of Technical Systems of Information
SZABELSKI, K., Applied Mechanics
TARKOWSKI, P., Tribology, Motor Vehicles and Internal Combustion Engines
WEROŃSKI, A., Physical Metallurgy, Heat Treatment
WEROŃSKI, W., Metal Forming

POLITECHNIKA OPOLSKA
(Opole University of Technology)

ul. Prószkowska 76, 45-758 Opole

Telephone: (77) 4498000
E-mail: rektor@po.opole.pl
Internet: www.po.opole.pl

Founded 1966
State control

Chancellor: BARBARA HETMANSKA
Rector: Prof. Dr Hab. MAREK TUKIENDORF
Vice-Rector for Cooperation and Devt: Prof. Dr Hab. KRZYSZTOF MALIK
Vice-Rector for Education: Prof. Dr Hab. KRYSTYNA MACEK-KAMINSKA
Vice-Rector for Science: Prof. Dr Hab. JANUSZ POSPOLITA
Dir for Library: Dr ELŻBIETA CZERWIŃSKA
Number of students: 12,000

DEANS

Faculty of Civil Engineering: Prof. Dr STEFANIA GRZESZCZYK
Faculty of Economy and Management: Prof. Dr Hab. JOACHIM FOLTYS
Faculty of Electrical Engineering, Automatic Control and Informatics: Prof. Dr MARIAN ŁUKANISZYN
Faculty of Mechanical Engineering: Prof. Dr Hab. TADEUSZ ŁAGODA
Faculty of Physical Education and Physiotherapy: Prof. Dr Hab. ZBIGNIEW BORYSIUK
Faculty of Production Engineering and Logistics: Prof. Dr Hab. WALDEMAR SKOMUDEK

POLITECHNIKA POZNAŃSKA
(Poznań University of Technology)

Pl. Marii Skłodowskiej-Curie 5, 60-965 Poznań

Telephone: (61) 8333881
E-mail: sekretariat.rektora@put.poznan.pl
Internet: www.put.poznan.pl

Founded 1919
State control
Academic year: October to September
Chancellor: Dr Inz. JANUSZ NAPIERAŁA
Rector: Prof. Dr Hab. TOMASZ LODYGOWSKI
Vice-Rector for Continuing Education: Prof. Dr Hab. STEFAN TRZCIELINSKI
Vice-Rector for Economic Cooperation: Prof. Dr Hab. JAN ZUREK
Vice-Rector for Education: Prof. Dr Hab. JACEK GOC
Vice-Rector for Science: Prof. Dr Hab. JOANNA JOZEFOWSKA

Dir for Library: MAŁGORZATA FURGAŁ

Library of 850,000 vols

Number of teachers: 1,200

Number of students: 21,000

Publications: *Fasciculi Mathematici* (in English), *Foundations of Computing and Decision Sciences* (4 a year, in English), *Zeszyty Naukowe Politechniki Poznańskiej* (Faculty Bulletins, in English and Polish)

DEANS

Faculty of Architecture: Prof. Dr Hab. JERZY SUCHANEK

Faculty of Chemical Technology: Prof. Dr Hab. KRZYSZTOF ALEJSKI

Faculty of Civil and Environmental Engineering: Prof. Dr Hab. JANUSZ WOJTKOWIAK

Faculty of Computing: Prof. Dr Hab. JERZY NAWROCKI

Faculty of Electrical Engineering: Prof. Dr KONRAD SKOWRONEK

Faculty of Electronics and Telecommunications: Prof. Dr Hab. KRZYSZTOF WESOLOWSKI

Faculty of Engineering Management: Prof. Dr LESZEK PACHOLSKI

Faculty of Machines and Transportation: Prof. Dr Hab. FRANCISZEK TOMASZEWSKI

Faculty of Mechanical Engineering and Management: Prof. Dr Hab. ROMAN STANIEK

Faculty of Technical Physics: Prof. Dr Hab. RYSZARD CZAJKA

POLITECHNIKA RZESZOWSKA IM. IGNACEGO ŁUKASIEWICZA
(Rzeszów University of Technology)

al. Powstańców Warszawy 12, 35-959 Rzeszów

Telephone: (17) 8651100

E-mail: rekrut@prz.edu.pl

Internet: www.prz.edu.pl

Founded 1951 as High School of Engineering, present name and status 1974

State control

Academic year: October to September

Chancellor: JANUSZ BURY

Rector: Prof. Dr MAREK ORKISZ

Vice-Rector for Devt: Prof. Dr KAZIMIERZ BUCZEK

Vice-Rector for Education: Dr ADAM MARCINIEC

Vice-Rector for Research: Prof. Dr LEONARD ZIEMIAŃSKI

Dir for Library: Dr MONIKA ZUB

Library: see under Libraries and Archives

Number of teachers: 750

Number of students: 17,500

Publications: *Folia Scientiarum Universitatis Technicae Resoviensis, Zeszyty Naukowe*

DEANS

Faculty of Chemistry: Prof. Dr HENRYK GALINA

Faculty of Civil and Environmental Engineering: Prof. Dr PIOTR KOSZELNIK

Faculty of Electrical and Computer Engineering: Dr GRZEGORZ MASŁOWSKI

Faculty of Management: Prof. Dr GRZEGORZ OSTASZ

Faculty of Mathematics and Applied Physics: Dr IWONA WŁOCH

Faculty of Mechanical Engineering and Aeronautics: Dr JAROSŁAW SĘP

POLITECHNIKA ŚLĄSKA
(Silesian University of Technology)

ul. Akademicka 2A, 44-100 Gliwice

Telephone: (32) 2371255

E-mail: r-br@polsl.pl

Internet: www.polsl.pl

Founded 1945

State control

Academic year: October to June

Chancellor: AMELIA BARTNICKA

Rector: Prof. Dr Hab. ANDRZEJ KARBOWNIK

Vice-Rector for Int. Cooperation: Prof. Dr Hab. RYSZARD BIAŁECKI

Vice-Rector for Organization and Devt: Prof. Dr Hab. LESZEK BLACHA

Vice-Rector for Research and Industrial Cooperation: Prof. Dr Hab. LESZEK A. DOBRZAŃSKI

Vice-Rector for Student Affairs and Education: Prof. Dr Hab. STANISŁAW KOCHOWSKI

Dir for Library: Dr KRZYSZTOF ZIOŁO

Library: see under Libraries and Archives

Number of teachers: 1,710

Number of students: 30,100

Publication: *Zeszyty Naukowe Politechniki Śląskiej* (Research Review—various titles)

DEANS

Faculty of Applied Mathematics: Dr RADOSŁAW GRZYMKOWSKI

Faculty of Architecture: Prof. Dr Hab. ZBIGNIEW J. KAMIŃSKI

Faculty of Automatic Control, Electronics and Computer Science: Prof. Dr Hab. ADAM CZORNIK

Faculty of Biomedical Engineering: Prof. Dr Hab. MAREK GZIK

Faculty of Chemistry: Prof. Dr ANDRZEJ JARZĘBSKI

Faculty of Civil Engineering: Prof. Dr Hab. JAN ŚLUSAREK

Faculty of Electrical Engineering: Prof. Dr PAWEL SOWA

Faculty of Materials Engineering and Metallurgy: Prof. Dr Hab. JERZY ŁABAJ

Faculty of Mechanical Engineering: Prof. Dr Hab. ARKADIUSZ MĘŻYK

Faculty of Mining and Geology: Prof. Dr Hab. MARIAN DOLIPSKI

Faculty of Organization and Management: Prof. Dr Hab. MARIAN TUREK

Faculty of Power and Environmental Engineering: Prof. Dr Hab. JANUSZ KOTOWICZ

Faculty of Transport: Dr BOGUSŁAW ŁAZARZ

POLITECHNIKA ŚWIĘTOKRZYSKA
(Kielce University of Technology)

ul. Tysiąclecia Państwa Polskiego 7, 25-314 Kielce

Telephone: (41) 3424444

E-mail: rektor@tu.kielce.pl

Internet: www.tu.kielce.pl

Founded 1965 as Kielce-Radom Evening Higher Engineering School, present name and status 1974

State control

Academic year: October to June

Chancellor: Dr ANDRZEJ SĘK

Rector: Prof. Dr Hab. STANISŁAW ADAMCZAK

Vice-Rector for Innovative Economy and Cooperation with the Industry: Prof. Dr Hab. KRZYSZTOF GRYSA

Vice-Rector for Personnel Devt and Research: Prof. Dr Hab. CZESŁAW KUNDERA

Vice-Rector for Student Affairs and Teaching: Prof. Dr Hab. ZDZISŁAWA OWSIAK

Dir for Library: DANUTA KAPINOS

Library: see under Libraries and Archives

Number of teachers: 450

Number of students: 10,000

DEANS

Faculty of Civil Engineering and Architecture: Prof. Dr Hab. MAREK IWAŃSKI

Faculty of Electrical Engineering, Automatics and Computer Science: Prof. Dr Hab. ANTONI RÓŻOWICZ

Faculty of Environmental Engineering, Geomatics and Power Engineering: Prof. Dr Hab. LIDIA DĄBEK

Faculty of Management and Computer Modelling: Prof. Dr Hab. ARTUR BARTOSIK

Faculty of Mechatronics and Machine Design: Prof. Dr Hab. ZBIGNIEW KORUBA

PROFESSORS

Faculty of Civil Engineering and Architecture (al. Tysiąclecia Państwa Polskiego 7A, 25-314 Kielce; tel. (41) 3424541; e-mail wbia@tu.kielce.pl):

BEZAK-MAZUR, E., Environmental Protection

BOROWICZ, T., Structural Mechanics, Computer Methods in Structural Mechanics

DĄBEK, L., Environmental Chemistry

DĄBKOWSKI, Sz., Water Engineering, Hydraulics

DACHOWSKI, R, Technology and Organization in Civil Engineering

FARYNIAK, L., Civil Engineering

GILEWSKI, W., Structural Mechanics

GOŁASKI, L., Strength of Materials

IWAŃSKI, M., Road Construction Technologies

KOWAL, Z., Metal Constructions and Theory of Structures

KOZŁOWSKI, T., Soil Mechanics, Foundation Engineering

KULICZKOWSKI, A., Environmental Engineering, Trenchless Technologies

ŁOMOTOWSKI, J., Water and Sewage Treatment

MIRSKI, J., Theory of Designing Coatings of Structures

NITA, P., Airfield Construction

ORZECHOWSKI, T., Heat Transfer, Heating and Ventilation

OWSIAK, Z., Concrete Technology

PIASTA, J., Concrete Technology and Prefabrication

PIASTA, W. G., Concrete Technology and Prefabrication

PIOTROWSKI, J. Z., Physics of Buildings, Heating and Ventilation

PURGAL, P., Heating and Ventilation

PROSKURIAKOW, V., Architecture

RUDZIŃSKI, L., Building Repair and Maintenance

RUSIN, Z., Building Materials

RYMASZEWSKI, B., History and Theory of Historical Monuments' Conservation

SERUGA, W., Architecture and Urban Planning

SIKORSKI, M., Land Amelioration

STROJ, A., Heating, Ventilation and Air Conditioning

SZCZEPAŃSKI, W., Art Science

TRĄMPCZYŃSKI, W., Strength of Materials, Mechanics

WAWRZEŃCZYK, J., Building Materials, Concrete Technology

WEHLE-STRZELECKA, S., Architecture and Urban Planning

ŻYGADŁO, M., Waste Management, Waste Disposal and Treatment

Faculty of Electrical Engineering, Automatics and Computer Science (al. Tysiąclecia Państwa Polskiego 7D, 25-314 Kielce; tel. (41) 3424129; e-mail weaii@tu.kielce.pl):

AUGUSTYN, J., Metrology

DENIZIAK, S., Computer Science

GAD, S., Power Electronics, Electrical Engineering

GORZAŁCZANY, M., Electronics and Intelligent Systems, Computer Engineering, Digital Systems

JASTRIEBOW, A., Computer Science

KACZMAREK, Z., Theoretical Electrical Engineering and Metrology

KAPŁON, A., Power Electronics and Electrical Drives, Electrical Engineering

KUŚMIERZ, J., Metrology

ŁASTOWIECKI, J., Power Electronics and Electric Drives

MARCINIAK, M., Telecommunications

NADOLSKI, R., Electrical Machines, Electrical Engineering

NOWICKI, T., Technical Science

RÓŻOWICZ, A., Lighting Technology

SAPIECHA, K., Computer Science

STACHULEC, K., Modern Solid Physics

STEFAŃSKI, T., Management and Control Systems, Identifications and Control Systems

STĘPIEŃ, J., Power Engineering

SUCHAŃSKA, M., Telecommunications and Photonics

SZCZEŚNIAK, Z., Automatization of Technical Process, Components and Devices of Electronics and Control Systems

TUNIA, H., Power Electronics

WCIŚLIK, M., Automatic Control Devices and Systems, Automatic Control, Electrical Engineering

WŁODARCZYK, M., Theoretical Electrical Engineering

WORWA, K., Informatics, Technical Science

Faculty of Management and Computer Modelling (al. Tysiąclecia Państwa Polskiego 7C, 25-314 Kielce; tel. (41) 3424440; e-mail wzimk@tu.kielce.pl):

BEDNARCZYK, J., Economics and Management

BOJCZUK, D., Production Engineering Optimization Methods

CICHOŃ, C., Applied Computer Science

GIERULSKI, W., Production Engineering, Process Modelling

GRYSA, K., Mathematics

JASTRZĘBSKA-SMOLAGA, H., Economic Strategies

KOTOWSKA-JELONEK, M., Economics and Management

MATCZYŃSKI, M., Production Engineering, Process Modelling

MEDUCKI, S., Economic Strategies

OKNIŃSKI, A., Physics

OKSANYCH, A., Economics and Management

PIELORZ, A., Mathematics

PŁOSKI, A., Mathematics

STADNYTSKYY, Y., Economics and Management

Faculty of Mechatronics and Machine Design (al. Tysiąclecia Państwa Polskiego 7B, 25-314 Kielce; tel. (41) 3424420; e-mail wmibm@tu.kielce.pl):

ADAMCZAK, S., Machine Design and Maintenance; Engineering Metrology, Quality Systems, Automated Measurement Systems

AMBROZIK, A., Machine Design and Maintenance, Motor and Tractor Vehicles, Combustion Piston Engines

ANTOSZEWSKI, B., Machine Design and Maintenance, Tribology, Sealing Technologies

CHAŁUPCZAK, J., Metallurgy, Metal Forming, Mechanical Engineering

DINDORF, R., Machine Design and Maintenance, Automation of Fluid Systems, Hydraulic and Pneumatic Automation Systems, Mechatronics, Hydraulic Drive and Control Systems

DZIADOŃ, A., Materials Engineering, Metal Science, Heat Treatment

FARANA, R., Industrial Process and Equipment Control

GAJEWSKI, M., Metallurgy, Foundry Engineering

JANECKI, D., Automation and Robotics, Computer Science, Surface Metrology, Control Theory, Modelling and Simulation

KORUBA, Z., Mechanical Engineering, Mechanical System Dynamics, Numerical Methods, Aerial Vehicle Control

KUNDERA, Cz., Machine Design and Maintenance, Machine Dynamics and Control, Mechanical Engineering, Tribology

LISCAK, S., Transport Technology

MIKO, E., Machine Design and Maintenance, Industrial Process Control

MUCHA, Z., Machine Design and Maintenance, Laser Process Control

MYCZUDA, Z., Automation and Robotics, Computational Methods and Control Systems

NEIMITZ, A., Mechanical Engineering, Mechanics of Solids

OZIMINA, D., Machine Design and Maintenance, Tribology

PŁONECKI, L., Machine Design and Maintenance, Hydraulic and Pneumatic Automation Systems, Machine Control, Laser System Control

RADOWICZ, A., Mechanical Engineering, Mechanics of Solids, Engineering Mechanics

RADZISZEWSKI, B., Theoretical Mechanics, Theory of Stability

RADZISZEWSKI, L., Mechanical Engineering, Vibroacoustics

ROKACH, I., Machine Design and Maintenance, Fracture Mechanics

SPADŁO, S., Machine Design and Maintenance, Industrial Process Control

STAMIROWSKI, J., Automation and Robotics, Computer Science, Information Technology for Business, Computer-aided Engineering

STAŃCZYK, T. L., Machine Design and Maintenance, Machine Dynamics

WESOŁOWSKI, Z., Mechanical Engineering, Dynamics of Continuous Media, Laser Processing of Metals

ZOWCZAK, W., Machine Design and Maintenance, Optimization of Mechanical Systems

POLITECHNIKA WARSZAWSKA
(Warsaw University of Technology)

pl. Politechniki 1, 00-661 Warsaw
Telephone: (22) 2347220
E-mail: jmr@rekt.pw.edu.pl
Internet: www.pw.edu.pl
Founded 1826
State control
Languages of instruction: English, Polish
Academic year: October to September
Rector: Prof. Dr JAN SZMIDT
Vice-Rector for Academic Affairs: Prof. Dr KRZYSZTOF LEWENSTEIN
Vice-Rector for Branch in Plock: Prof. Dr JANUSZ ZIELIŃSKI
Vice-Rector for Devt: Prof. Dr STANISŁAW WINCENCIAK
Vice-Rector for Gen. Affairs: Prof. Dr ZBIGNIEW KLEDYŃSKI
Vice-Rector for Research: Prof. Dr RAJMUND BACEWICZ
Vice-Rector for Student Affairs: Prof. Dr WŁADYSŁAW WIECZOREK
Dir for Library: Mgr JOLANTA STĘPNIAK
Library of 1,151,685 vols, incl. 862,847 books and 288,838 periodicals
Number of teachers: 2,500
Number of students: 33,200
Publication: *Prace naukowe—Politechnika Warszawska* (Scientific Works—Warsaw University of Technology)

DEANS

Business School: Prof. JEAN-PAUL LARCON (Dir)
College of Economics and Social Sciences, Płock Campus: Dr RENATA WALCZAK
Faculty of Administration and Social Sciences: Prof. Dr ZBIGNIEW KRÓL
Faculty of Architecture: Prof. Dr Hab. STEFAN WRONA

Faculty of Automotive and Construction Machinery Engineering: Prof. Dr STANISŁAW RADKOWSKI

Faculty of Chemical and Process Engineering: Prof. Dr EUGENIUSZ MOLGA

Faculty of Chemistry: Prof. Dr ZBIGNIEW BRZÓZKA

Faculty of Civil Engineering: Prof. Dr HENRYK ZOBEL

Faculty of Civil Engineering, Mechanics and Petrochemistry, Płock Campus: Prof. Dr JANUSZ ZIELIŃSKI

Faculty of Electrical Engineering: Prof. Dr LECH GRZESIAK

Faculty of Electronics and Information Technology: Prof. Dr KRZYSZTOF ZAREMBA

Faculty of Environmental Engineering: Prof. Dr KRZYSZTOF WOJDYGA

Faculty of Geodesy and Cartography: Prof. Dr ALINA MACIEJEWSKA

Faculty of Management: Prof. Dr TADEUSZ KRUPA

Faculty of Materials Science and Engineering: Prof. Dr JAROSŁAW MIZERA

Faculty of Mathematics and Information Science: Prof. Dr IRMINA HERBURT

Faculty of Mechatronics: Prof. Dr NATALIA GOLNIK

Faculty of Physics: Prof. Dr MIROSŁAW KARPIERZ

Faculty of Power and Aeronautical Engineering: Prof. Dr JERZY BANASZEK

Faculty of Production Engineering: Prof. Dr ANDRZEJ KOLASA

Faculty of Transport: Prof. Dr WOJCIECH WAWRZYŃSKI

PROFESSORS

College of Economics and Social Sciences, Płock Campus (ul. Łukasiewicza 17, 09-400 Płock; tel. (24) 3672126; e-mail knes@pw.plock.pl; internet www.knes.pw.plock.pl):

BIAŁOŃ-SOCZYŃSKA, L., Economics of Industry, Economics of Science, Marketing

GÓRALSKI, W., Domestic Relations Law, Canon Law

KRAJEWSKA, A., Economics, Fiscal Policy and Taxation Theory

KRAJEWSKI, S., Innovative and Structural Policies, Enterprise Operation and Privatization

MARCINIAK, S., Economics of Innovation, Macroeconomics

OBRĘBSKI, T., Labour Economics, Industrial Relations

PACHO, W., Financing Strategies of Public Limited Companies

SPYCHALSKI, G., History of Economics, Modern Economics

STAWICKI, J., Econometrics and Statistics

WĄSOWICZ, M., Economic Theory, Environmental Economics

WITKOWSKA, J., International Economics, European Integration

ZIELIŃSKI, R., Economic Theory, Defence Economics

Faculty of Administration and Social Sciences (pl. Politechniki 1, 00-661 Warsaw; tel. (22) 2346525; e-mail ans@ans.pw.edu.pl; internet www.ans.pw.edu.pl):

BIAŁOŃ-SOCZYŃSKA, L., Economics of Industry, Economics of Science, Marketing

MARCINIAK, S., Economics of Innovation, Macroeconomics

NIEWIADOMSKI, Z., Public Administration, Self-government, Physical Planning

OBRĘBSKI, T., Economics, Labour Economics, Industrial Relations

ZAWADZKA, Z., Economics, Finance, Banking

Faculty of Architecture (ul. Koszykowa 55, 00-659 Warsaw; tel. (22) 6282887; e-mail dziekan@arch.pw.edu.pl; internet www.arch.pw.edu.pl):

BENEDEK, W., Housing Design and Public Utilities

BRYKOWSKA, M., History of Towns and Architecture

CHMIELEWSKI, J. M., Urban Design and Town Planning

GAWLIKOWSKI, A. Z., Urban Design and Town Planning

GZELL, S., Urban Design and Town Planning

HRYNIAK, Z., Urban Design and Town Planning

KŁOSIEWICZ, L., Contemporary Architecture

KUBICA, B., Fine Arts—Sculpture

KUCZA-KUCZYŃSKI, K., Housing Design and Public Utilities

PAWŁOWSKI, Z., Building Structures

ROGUSKA, J., History of Towns and Architecture

SZPARKOWSKI, Z., Industrial Buildings

SZULBORSKI, K., Building Structures

TOMASZEWSKI, A., Conservation of Monuments, History of Architecture

WERNER, W., Economics of Investment Processes and Management

WIŚNIEWSKA, M., Housing Design and Public Utilities

WRONA, S., Computer-Aided Architectural Design

Faculty of Automotive and Construction Machinery Engineering (ul. Narbutta 84, 02-524 Warsaw; tel. (22) 8490534; e-mail dziekan@simr.pw.edu.pl; internet www.simr.pw.edu.pl):

BIAŁAS, S., Geometrical Accuracy in Machinery Design, Tolerance Technology

BOGACZ, R., Dynamics of Means of Transport

DĄBROWSKI, Z., Machine Design, Vibroacoustics

GOŁOŚ, K., Fatigue in Materials

KURNIK, W., Dynamics of Mechanical Systems, Mechatronics

MADEJ, J., Mechanics of Rail Vehicles

OSIŃSKI, J., Dynamics of Mechanical Systems

RADKOWSKI, S., Safety in Technical Systems, Technical Diagnostics

STARCZEWSKI, Z., Dynamics of Mechanical Systems, Dynamics of Rotors and Journal Bearing System

SZLAGOWSKI, J., Plastics Design of Structures, Automation of Construction Machinery

SZUMANOWSKI, A., Electromechanical Propulsion Systems, Energy Storage, Hybrid and Electric Vehicles

TYLIKOWSKI, A., Dynamics of Mechanical Systems, Mechatronics

WICHER, J., Mechanics, Dynamics of Mechanical Systems

WRÓBEL, J., Theory of Machine Design

Faculty of Chemical and Process Engineering (ul. Waryńskiego 1, 00-645 Warsaw; tel. (22) 2346453; e-mail dziekanat@ichip.pw.edu.pl; internet www.ichip.pw.edu.pl):

BAŁDYGA, J., Chemical Reactor Engineering

BIŃ, A. K., Process Kinetics, Environmental Protection Processes

CHMIELEWSKI, A. G., Environmental Engineering, Separation Processes

GAWROŃSKI, R., Membrane Processes

GRADOŃ, L., Chemical Engineering, Aerosol Mechanics

POHORECKI, R., Chemical Reactor Engineering, Bioprocess Engineering

SIENIUTYCZ, S., Process Thermodynamics, Non-equilibrium Thermodynamics

SZEWCZYK, K. W., Biochemical Technology, Bioprocess Engineering

SZWAST, Z., Process Optimization

WOLNY, A., Chemical Engineering

Faculty of Chemistry (ul. Noakowskiego 3, 00-664 Warsaw; tel. (22) 2345734; e-mail dziekanat@ch.pw.edu.pl; internet www.ch.pw.edu.pl):

BRZÓZKA, Z., Analytical Chemistry

DOMAŃSKA-ŻELAZNA, U., Physical Chemistry

FLORJAŃCZYK, Z., Organic Chemistry, Polymer Science

GRYFF-KELLER, A., Organic Chemistry

GRZYWA, E., General Chemistry

JAROSZ, M., Analytical Chemistry

JOŃCZYK, A., Organic Chemistry and Technology

KASIURA, K., Inorganic and Analytical Chemistry

KIJEŃSKI, J., Organic Chemistry, Catalysis

KSIĄŻCZAK, A., Theory and Technology of Explosives

ŁOBIŃSKI, R., Analytical Chemistry

MĄKOSZA, M., Organic Chemistry and Technology

PLENKIEWICZ, J., Biotransformation in Organic Chemistry

PROŃ, A., Polymer Science, Solid State Technology

ROKICKI, G., Organic Chemistry, Polymer Science

SERWATOWSKI, J., Physical Organic Chemistry

WIECZOREK, W., Solid State Technology

Faculty of Civil Engineering (ul. Armii Ludowej 16, 00-637 Warsaw; tel. (22) 8255937; e-mail dziekanat@il.pw.edu.pl; internet www.il.pw.edu.pl):

ABRAMOWICZ, M., Reinforced Concrete Structures

CHRABACZYŃSKI, G., Building Production and Prefabrication

CZARNECKI, L., Technology of Building Materials

GOMULIŃSKI, A., Structural Mechanics

JAWORSKI, K., Technology of Building Materials

KARCZEWSKI, J., Metal Constructions, Spatial Structures

KNAUFF, M., Building Construction

NAGÓRSKI, R., Structural Mechanics

OBRĘBSKI, J., Structural Mechanics

RADOMSKI, W., Bridge Engineering

RUNKIEWICZ, L., Building Construction

SUCHORZEWSKI, W., Construction of Roads, Streets and Bridges

SZCZEŚNIAK, W., Structural Mechanics

WITKOWSKI, M., Structural Mechanics, Computers in Civil Engineering

WOJEWÓDZKI, W., Theory of Elasticity and Plasticity

ŻÓŁTOWSKI, W., Metal Constructions

Faculty of Civil Engineering, Mechanics and Petrochemistry, Płock Campus (Łukasiewicza 17, 09-400 Płock; tel. (24) 262-62-54; e-mail zielinski@pw.plock.pl; internet www.pw.plock.pl):

BOCHEŃSKI, C., Agricultural Engineering

BUKOWSKI, A., Technology of Plastics

CHOCHOWSKI, A., Solar Power Engineering

DWILIŃSKI, L., Construction and Reliability of Agricultural Machinery

FRĄCZEK, K., Carbon Derivatives Technology, Polymer Chemistry

KAJDAS, Cz., Technology and Processing of Petroleum and its Products, Tribopolymerization

KAMIŃSKI, E., Mechanical Appliances and Machinery

KOSIŃSKI, W., Cartography and Surveying

PONIEWSKI, M., Heat Engines and Thermal Equipment

POWIERŻA, L., Systems Engineering

PYSIAK, J., Physical Solid-State Chemistry

RÓŻYCKI, C., Trace Analysis, Chemometrics

ŚCISŁEWSKI, Z., Durability

URBANIEC, K., Food Industry Machinery

WŁODARCZYK, W., Building Constructions

WOLSKI, L., Physics of Buildings, Sanitary Systems

ZIELIŃSKI, J., Technology of Petroleum and Plastics

ŻUK, D., Agricultural Engineering

Faculty of Electrical Engineering (pl. Politechniki 1, 00-661 Warsaw; tel. (22) 6292531; e-mail dziekanat@ee.pw.edu.pl; internet www.ee.pw.edu.pl):

BĄK, J., Lighting Technology

BARLIK, R., Industrial Electronics and Electrical Drives, Power Electronics

BOLKOWSKI, S., Circuit Theory and Electromagnetic Fields

CELIŃSKI, Z., Nuclear Technology

CICHOCKI, A., Circuit Theory

CIOK, Z., High-voltage Technology

DMOWSKI, A., Industrial Electronics

FLISOWSKI, Z., High-voltage Technology

HERING, M., Electro-heating Technology

KACZOREK, T., Linear Control Systems

KAŹMIERKOWSKI, M., Industrial Electronics and Intelligent Control

KOCZARA, N., Electrical Drives and Generation of Power

KRZEMIŃSKI, S., Circuit Theory

KUJSZCZYK, S., Power Systems and Electrical Networks

MACHOWSKI, J., Power Systems and Electrical Networks

MAKSYMIUK, J., Electrical Apparatus

MIKOŁAJUK, K., Circuit Theory and Electromagnetic Fields

OSOWSKI, S., Artificial Intelligence—Neural Networks

RAWA, H., Circuit Theory and Electromagnetic Fields

SIKORA, J., Circuit Theory and Electromagnetic Fields

SUPRONOWICZ, H., Industrial Electronics

TRZASKA, Z., Circuit Theory and Electromagnetic Fields

TUMAŃSKI, S., Electrical Measurements

WINCENCIAK, S., Circuit Theory and Electromagnetic Fields

Faculty of Electronics and Information Technology (ul. Nowowiejska 15/19, 00-665 Warsaw; tel. (22) 2347497; e-mail dziekanat@elka.pw.edu.pl; internet www.elka.pw.edu.pl):

DĄBROWSKI, M., Computer Networks and Switching

DOBROWOLSKI, J., Computer-aided Design of Microwave Circuits, Monolithic Microwave Integrated Circuits

EBERT, J., High-power Radiotechnology

GALWAS, B., Microwave Electronics and Photonics

GWAREK, P., Microwave Technology

HOLEJKO, K., Telecommunications and Optoelectronics

JACHOWICZ, R., Measurement Systems and Sensors

JAKUBOWSKI, A., Microelectronics, Metal-oxide-semiconductor Devices

KUDREWICZ, J., Theory of Electronic Systems

KUŹMICZ, W., Microelectronics

ŁUBA, T., Computer Engineering, Digital Systems Design

LUBACZ, J., Information and Communication Technologies

MAJKUSIAK, B., Microelectronics

MALINOWSKI, K., Information Engineering and Control Systems

MODELSKI, J., Microwaves, Satellite and Cable Television

MORAWSKI, R. Z., Measurement and Instrumentation

MORAWSKI, T., Microwave Technology

MULAWKA, J., Computer Science, Artificial Intelligence

MURASZKIEWICZ, M., Information and Knowledge Systems, Databases, Networking

PAWŁOWSKI, Z., Medical and Nuclear Electronics

PIÓRO, M., Information and Communication Technologies

ROSŁONIEC, S., Microwave Technology

RYBIŃSKI, H., Information Systems, Databases

SZCZEPAŃSKI, P., Optoelectronics, Laser Physics

TRACZYK, W., Knowledge-based Systems

WIERZBICKI, A., Optimization and Decision Theory

WOJCIECHOWSKI, J., Electronics, Telecommunication Networks, Signals and Systems

WOŹNICKI, J., Electronics, Optoelectronics

ZABRODZKI, J., Computer Science, Computer Graphics

Faculty of Environmental Engineering (ul. Nowowiejska 20, 00-653 Warsaw; tel. (22) 6214560; e-mail dziekanat@is.pw.edu.pl; internet www.is.pw.edu.pl):

BIEDUGNIS, S., Water Supply and Sewerage Systems, Sanitary and Environmental Engineering

JĘDRZEJEWSKA-ŚCIBAK, T., Indoor Air Quality, Ventilation and Air Conditioning

KINDLER, J., Water Resources Management and Environmental Systems

MAŃKOWSKI, S., Heat Engineering

MITOSEK, M., Hydraulics, Fluid Mechanics

MIZIELIŃSKI, B., Ventilation and Air Conditioning

NAWALANY, M., Environmental Engineering, Groundwater Protection

OSIADACZ, A., Gas Engineering

PISARCZYK, S., Building Engineering, Geotechnology

ROMAN, M., Water Supply and Sewerage Systems, Sanitary and Environmental Engineering

Faculty of Geodesy and Cartography (pl. Politechniki 1, 00-661 Warsaw; tel. (22) 6213680; e-mail dziekanat@gik.pw.edu.pl; internet www.gik.pw.edu.pl):

ADAMCZEWSKI, Z., Theory of Adjustment, Geodetic Computation

BARLIK, M., Geodesy, Gravimetry

BIAŁOUSZ, S., Soil Mapping and Remote Sensing, Geographical Information Systems

CZARNECKI, K., Geodesy

CZICHON, H., Technology of Printing

MACIEJEWSKA, A., Soil Conservation and Land Protection

MAKOWSKI, A., Cartography

MARTUSEWICZ, J., Surveying for Tunnelling

MERWIŃSKI, R., Printing Technology

PRÓSZYŃSKI, W., Engineering Surveying, Theory of Adjustment

ROGOWSKI, J., Geodetic Astronomy, Satellite Geodesy

SKŁODOWSKI, P., Soil Science, Soil Conservation

SKÓRCZYŃSKI, A., Surveying, Theory of Adjustment

ŚLEDZIŃSKI, J., Satellite Geodesy

WILKOWSKI, W., Rural Land Management

Faculty of Materials Science and Engineering (ul. Wołoska 141, 02-507 Warsaw; tel. (22) 8499929; e-mail dziekanat@inmat.pw.edu.pl; internet www.inmat.pw.edu.pl):

GRABSKI, M. W., Physics of Plastic Deformation

KURZYDŁOWSKI, K. J., Materials Characterization and Modelling

LEONOWICZ, M., Magnetic Materials

OLSZYNA, A., Ceramic Materials

MICHALSKI, A., Surface Engineering

SZUMMER, A., Functional Construction of Materials

WIERZCHOŃ, T., Surface Engineering

Faculty of Mathematics and Information Science (ul. Koszykowa 75, 00-662 Warsaw; tel. (22) 6219312; e-mail sekretariat@mini.pw.edu.pl; internet www.mini.pw.edu.pl):

JANECZKO, S., Singularity Theory and Symplectic Geometry

KLEIBER, M., Computer Methods in Mechanics

LONC, Z., Discrete Mathematics

MACUKOW, B., Artificial Intelligence

MĄCZYŃSKI, M., Algebra, Mathematical Foundations of Quantum Theory

MARCINIAK, K., Computer Graphics and Geometry

MUSZYŃSKI, J., Differential Equations

PLUCIŃSKA, A., Probability and Stochastic Processes

ROMANOWSKA, A., Algebra

SPIEŻ, S., Topology

Faculty of Mechatronics (ul. Św. Andrzeja Boboli 8, 02-525 Warsaw; tel. (22) 8499936; e-mail dziekanat@mchtr.pw.edu.pl; internet www.mchtr.pw.edu.pl):

CIEŚLICKI, K., Fluid Mechanics

DUNAJSKI, Z., Biomedical Engineering

GAMBIN, W., Mechanics

JANISZOWSKI, K., Automatic Control and Robotics, System Identification

JÓŹWICKI, R., Design of Optical Instruments

KOŚCIELNY, J. M., Automatic Control, Fault Detection

KUJAWIŃSKA, M., Applied Optics, Machine Vision

KUREK, J., Automatic Control and Robotics, Control Theory

MRUGALSKI, Z., Design of Precision Devices

OLEKSIUK, T., Design of Precision Devices

PAŁKO, T., Biomedical Engineering

PATORSKI, K., Applied Optics, Design of Optical Instruments

PAWLICKI, W. G., Biomedical Engineering

RATAJCZYK, E., Measuring Apparatus

Faculty of Physics (ul. Koszykowa 75, 00-662 Warsaw; tel. (22) 2347660; e-mail dziekan@if.pw.edu.pl; internet www.fizyka.pw.edu.pl):

ADAMCZYK, A., Liquid Crystals

BACEWICZ, R., Solid-State Physics

BOGUSZ, W., Solid-State Physics

ĆWIOK, S., Nuclear Physics

HOŁYST, J., Physics of Complex Systems

KOSIŃSKI, R., Physics of Magnetism

KROK, F., Solid-State Physics

SŁOWIŃSKI, B., Nuclear Physics

STRZAŁKOWSKI, I., Solid-State Physics

SUKIENNICKI, A., Physics of Magnetism

WOLIŃSKI, T., Optoelectronics

ŻEBROWSKI, J., Physics of Complex Systems

Faculty of Power and Aeronautical Engineering (ul. Nowowiejska 24, 00-665 Warsaw; tel. (22) 2347354; e-mail dziekan@meil.pw.edu.pl; internet www.meil.pw.edu.pl):

ARCZEWSKI, K., Analytical Mechanics, Multibody Systems

BANASZEK, J., Thermodynamics, Mathematical Methods of Heat Transfer

DIETRICH, M. (acting), Mechanical Engineering, Biomedical Engineering

DOMANSKI, R., Heat Transfer, Thermodynamics, Environmental Engineering

FURMAŃSKI, P., Heat Transfer, Thermodynamics, Thermal Properties of Materials

GORAJ, Z., Aerodynamics, Flight Dynamics, Aircraft Design

JEDRAL, W., Power Engineering, Pumping Machinery and Installations

KĘDZIOR, K., Modelling of Human Movement, Systems Dynamics, Robotics and Biomechanics

LEWANDOWSKI, J., Environmental Engineering, Power Engineering, Control of Power Plants

LEWITOWICZ, J., Aircraft Maintenance, Aerospace Engineering

MARYNIAK, J., Flight Mechanics

MILLER, A., Power Engineering, Gas and Steam Turbines

PORTACHA, J., Power Engineering, Power Plants

RYCHTER, T., Internal Combustion Engines, Combustion

SADO, J., Thermodynamics, Refrigeration, Plasma Physics

STUPNICKI, J., Fundamentals of Machine Construction

STYCZEK, A., Mathematical Methods of Fluid Mechanics

SZOPA, T., Safety Engineering

SZUMOWSKI, A., Fluid Mechanics, Gas Dynamics, Aerodynamic Noise Control

WOLAŃSKI, P., Combustion, Aero Engines

ŻOCHOWSKI, M., Strength of Materials

Faculty of Production Engineering (ul. Narbutta 85, 02-524 Warsaw; tel. (22) 8499795; e-mail dean@wip.pw.edu.pl; internet www.wip.pw.edu.pl):

BOSSAK, M., Computational Mechanics, Computer-aided Design

GRUDZEWSKI, W., Organization and Management

HEJDUK, J., Organization and Management

JEMIELNIAK, K., Production Engineering

KACZOROWSKI, M., Materials Science and Engineering

KISIELNICKI, J., Organization and Management

KLASZTORNY, M., Applied Mechanics

KOCAŃDA, A., Metal-forming

KOZAK, J., Production Engineering

LEWANDOWSKI, J., Economics

MASŁOWSKI, A., Automation and Robotics

MASŁYK-MUSIAŁ, E., Organization and Management

MONKIEWICZ, J., Organization and Management

NOWICKI, B., Production Engineering

PERZYK, M., Casting Technology

SANTAREK, K., Organization and Management

SZAFARCZYK, M., Machine Tools Control and Drive

SZENAJCH, W., Mechanical Engineering, Automatic Control of Industrial Processes

TKACZYK, S., Organization and Management

WILCZYŃSKI, A., Mechanical Engineering

WŁOSIŃSKI, W., Materials Technology

Faculty of Transport (ul. Koszykowa 75, 00-662 Warsaw; tel. (22) 2347364; e-mail dziekanat@it.pw.edu.pl; internet www.it.pw.edu.pl):

BORGOŃ, J., Air Traffic Control

CHUDZIKIEWICZ, A., Dynamics and Diagnostics of Means of Transport

DĄBROWA-BAJON, M., Rail Traffic Control

DYDUCH, J., Control Systems

KISILOWSKI, J., Dynamics and Diagnostics of Mechanical Systems

LESZCZYŃSKI, J., Organization and Technology of Transport

MANEROWSKI, J., Flight Mechanics

NIEDZIELA, T., Image Processing

SMALKO, Z., Maintenance and Operation of Vehicles

POLITECHNIKA WROCŁAWSKA (Wrocław University of Technology)

ul. Wybrzeże Wyspiańskiego 27, 50-370 Wrocław

Telephone: (71) 3202600
E-mail: jmr@pwr.wroc.pl
Internet: www.pwr.wroc.pl

Founded 1945

State control
Languages of instruction: English, Polish
Academic year: October to June

Rector: Prof. Dr TADEUSZ WIĘCKOWSKI
Vice-Rector for Devt: Prof. Dr CEZARY MADRYAS
Vice-Rector for Education: Prof. Dr ANDRZEJ KASPRZAK
Vice-Rector for Gen. Affairs: Prof. Dr JERZY WALENDZIEWSKI
Vice-Rector for Research: Prof. Dr EUGENIUSZ RUSIŃSKI
Vice-Rector for Student Affairs: Dr ZBIGNIEW SROKA
Dir for Library: MIROSŁAW ZIÓŁEK

Library of 900,000 vols
Number of teachers: 2,000
Number of students: 35,300

Publications: *Acta–Bioengineering and Biomechanics* (2 a year), *Architectus Systems* (2 a year), *Badania Operacyjne i Decyzje* (4 a year), *Environmental Protection Engineering* (4 a year), *Fizykochem: Problemy Mineralurgii* (1 a year), *Geometria Wykreślna i Grafika Inżynierska* (1 a year), *Materials Science* (4 a year), *Optica Applicata* (4 a year), *Pryzmat* (12 a year), *Semestr* (12 a year), *Studia Geotechnica et Mechanica* (4 a year), *Systems–Journal of Transdisciplinary Systems Science* (2 a year), *Systems Science* (4 a year)

DEANS

Department of Fundamental Studies: Dr JANUSZ GÓRNIAK (Dir)
Faculty of Architecture: Prof. Dr Hab. ELŻBIETA TROCKA-LESZCZYŃSKA
Faculty of Chemistry: Prof. Dr Hab. ANDRZEJ TROCHIMCZUK
Faculty of Civil Engineering: Prof. Dr Hab. JERZY HOŁA
Faculty of Computer Science and Management: Prof. Dr Hab. ZDZISŁAW SZALBIERZ
Faculty of Electrical Engineering: Prof. Dr Hab. WALDEMAR REBIZANT
Faculty of Electronics: Prof. Dr Hab. JAN ZARZYCKI
Faculty of Environmental Engineering: Prof. Dr Hab. JAN DANIELEWICZ
Faculty of Fundamental Problems of Technology: Dr Hab. MARIAN HOTLOŚ
Faculty of Geoengineering, Mining and Geology: Prof. Dr Hab. WOJCIECH CIĘŻKOWSKI
Faculty of Mechanical and Power Engineering: Prof. Dr Hab. ZBIGNIEW GNUTEK
Faculty of Mechanical Engineering: Prof. Dr Hab. EDWARD CHLEBUS
Faculty of Microsystem Electronics and Photonics: Prof. Dr Hab. ANDRZEJ DZIEDZIC

UNIWERSYTET TECHNOLOGICZNO–HUMANISTYCZNY IM. KAZIMIERZA PUŁASKIEGO W RADOMIU
(Kazimierz Pulaski University of Technology and Humanities in Radom)

ul. Malczewskiego 29, 26-600 Radom
Telephone: (48) 3617010
E-mail: rektor@uthrad.pl
Internet: www.uniwersytetradom.pl
Founded 1950, current name and status 2012
State control
Languages of instruction: English, Polish

Chancellor: MARIUSZ POCZĄTEK
Rector: Prof. Dr Hab. ZBIGNIEW ŁUKASIK
Vice-Rector for Human Resource Devt and Int. Cooperation: Prof. Dr Hab. SŁAWOMIR BUKOWSKI
Vice-Rector for Research: Prof. Dr Hab. ZBIGNIEW KOSMA
Vice-Rector for Teaching and Student Affairs: Prof. Dr Hab. MIROSŁAW LUFT
Dir for Library: STANISŁAW GAŁĘZIA

Library of 170,000 vols, 500 periodicals and 150,000 spec. collns
Number of teachers: 402
Number of students: 8,500

DEANS

Faculty of Art: Prof. Dr Hab. ALEKSANDER OLSZEWSKI
Faculty of Economics: Prof. Dr Hab. JAN BEDNARCZYK
Faculty of Health Sciences and Physical Culture: Prof. Dr Hab. ZBIGNIEW KOTWICA
Faculty of Informatics and Mathematics: Prof. Dr Hab. JANUSZ WALASEK
Faculty of Materials Science, Technology and Design: Prof. Dr Hab. MARIAN WŁODZIMIERZ SUŁEK
Faculty of Mechanical Engineering: Prof. Dr Hab. WOJCIECH BLAJER
Faculty of Philological and Pedagogical Studies: Prof. Dr Hab. DARIUSZ TRZEŚNIOWSKI
Faculty of Transport and Electrical Engineering: Prof. Dr Hab. ELŻBIETA SZYCHTA

UNIWERSYTET TECHNOLOGICZNO-PRZYRODNICZY IM. J. J. ŚNIADECKICH W BYDGOSZCZY
(University of Technology and Life Sciences in Bydgoszcz)

ul. Kordeckiego 20, 85-225 Bydgoszcz
Telephone: (52) 3730280
E-mail: rektor@utp.edu.pl
Internet: www.utp.edu.pl
Founded 1951, present name 2006
Rector: Prof. Dr Hab. ANTONI BUKALUK
Vice-Rector for Cooperation with Economy: Prof. MAREK BIELIŃSKI
Vice-Rector for Organization and Devt: Prof. WOJCIECH KAPELAŃSKI
Vice-Rector for Science: Prof. DARIUSZ BOROŃSKI
Vice-Rector for Teaching and Student Affairs: Prof. JANUSZ PRUSIŃSKI

Library of 293,706 vols, 51,243 periodicals
Number of teachers: 680
Number of students: 10,000

Publications: *Image Processing and Communications* (in English, 4 a year), *Zeszyty Naukowe* (in Polish, with Russian and English summaries, irregular)

DEANS

Faculty of Agriculture and Biotechnology: Prof. EWA SPYCHAJ-FABISIAK
Faculty of Animal Breeding and Biology: Prof. ZENON BERNACKI
Faculty of Chemical Technology and Engineering: Prof. KAZIMIERZ PISZCZEK
Faculty of Civil and Environmental Engineering: Prof. ADAM PODHORECKI
Faculty of Management: Prof. LUDOSŁAW DRELICHOWSKI
Faculty of Mechanical Engineering: Prof. BOGDAN ŻÓŁTOWSKI
Faculty of Telecommunications and Electrical Engineering: Prof. ANTONI ZABŁUDOWSKI
Institute of Mathematics and Physics: Prof. GERARD CZAJKOWSKI (Head)

ZACHODNIOPOMORSKI UNIWERSYTET TECHNOLOGICZNY W SZCZECINIE
(West Pomeranian University of Technology, Szczecin)

ul. Piastów 17, 70-310 Szczecin
Telephone: (91) 4346751
E-mail: rektor@zut.edu.pl
Internet: www.zut.edu.pl
Founded 2009 by merger of Akademia Rolnicza w Szczecinie and Politechnika Szczecińska

Language of instruction: Polish
Academic year: October to September

Chancellor: JAROSŁAW POTACZEK
Rector: Prof. Dr Hab. WŁODZIMIERZ KIERNOŻYCKI
Pro-Rector for Educational Affairs: Prof. Dr Hab. WITOLD BIEDUNKIEWICZ
Pro-Rector for Organization and Academic Devt: Prof. Dr Hab. JAN B. DAWIDOWSKI
Pro-Rector for Scientific Research: Prof. Dr Hab. RYSZARD KALEŃCZUK
Pro-Rector for Student Affairs: Prof. Dr Hab. JACEK WRÓBEL
Dir for Library: ANNA M. GRZELAK-ROZENBERG

Library of 574,399 vols of books and serials, 151,726 spec. collns
Number of teachers: 1,120
Number of students: 13,300

Publications: *Acta Ichthyologica et Piscatoria* (2 a year), *Acta Scientiarum Polonorum. Ser. Piscaria* (4 a year), *Acta Scientiarum Polonorum. Ser. Zootechnica* (4 a year), *Advances in Agricultural Sciences* (irregular), *Electronic Journal of Polish Agricultural Universities. Ser. Fisheries* (4 a year), *Folia Pomeranae Universitatis Technologiae Stetinensis* (4 a year), *Forum Uczelniane* (4 a year), *Polish Journal of Chemical Technology* (4 a year)

DEANS

Faculty of Biotechnology and Animal Husbandry: Prof. Dr Hab. JAN UDAŁA
Faculty of Chemical Engineering: Prof. Dr Hab. JACEK A. SOROKA
Faculty of Civil Engineering and Architecture: Dr Hab. MARIA KASZYŃSKA
Faculty of Computer Science and Information Technology: Prof. Dr Hab. ANTONI WILIŃSKI
Faculty of Economics: Prof. Dr Hab. BARTOSZ MICKIEWICZ
Faculty of Electrical Engineering: Prof. Dr Hab. STEFAN DOMEK
Faculty of Environment Management and Agriculture: Prof. Dr Hab. ALEKSANDER BRZÓSTOWICZ
Faculty of Food Sciences and Fisheries: Prof. Dr Hab. AGNIESZKA TÓRZ
Faculty of Maritime Technology and Transport: Dr Hab. MACIEJ TACZAŁA
Faculty of Mechanical Engineering and Mechatronics: Prof. Dr Hab. STEFAN BERCZYŃSKI

Academies

AKADEMIA GÓRNICZO-HUTNICZA IM. STANISŁAWA STASZICA W KRAKOWIE
(AGH University of Science and Technology)

ul. Mickiewicza 30, 30-059 Cracow
Telephone: (12) 6172002
E-mail: rektorat@agh.edu.pl
Internet: www.agh.edu.pl
Founded 1919
State control
Languages of instruction: English, Polish
Academic year: October to June

Chancellor: HENRYK ZIOŁO
Rector: Prof. TADEUSZ SŁOMKA
Vice-Rector for Cooperation: Prof. TOMASZ SZMUC
Vice-Rector for Education: Prof. ANDRZEJ TYTKO
Vice-Rector for Gen. Affairs: Dr MIROSŁAW KARBOWNICZEK
Vice-Rector for Science: Prof. ZBIGNIEW KĄKOL

Vice-Rector for Student Affairs: Dr ANNA SIWIK

Dir for Library: EWA DOBRZYŃSKA-LANKOSZ

Library of 1,291,260 vols, incl. 427,954 books, 144,382 periodicals, 718,924 spec. collns
Number of teachers: 2,000
Number of students: 39,150

Publications: *Automatyka* (Automatics, 2 a year), *Computer Science* (1 a year), *Elektrotechnika i Elektronika* (Electrical Engineering, 2 a year), *Geodezja* (Mining Surveying, 2 a year), *Geologia* (Geology, 4 a year), *Górnictwo* (Mining, 4 a year), *Inżynieria Środowiska* (Environmental Engineering, 2 a year), *Kliertnictwo Nafta Gaz* (Drilling Oil and Gas, 1 a year), *Mechanika* (Mechanics, 4 a year), *Metallurgy and Foundry Engineering* (2 a year), *Opuscula Mathematica* (1 a year), *Telekomunikacja Cyfrowa* (1 a year)

DEANS

Faculty of Applied Mathematics: Dr VSEVOLOD VLADIMIROV

Faculty of Computer Science, Electronics and Telecommunications: Prof. TADEUSZ PISARKIEWICZ

Faculty of Drilling, Oil and Gas: Prof. ANDRZEJ GONET

Faculty of Electrical Engineering, Automatics, Computer Science and Biomedical Engineering: Dr ANTONI CIEŚLA

Faculty of Energy and Fuels: Dr WOJCIECH SUWAŁA

Faculty of Foundry Engineering: Prof. JÓZEF SZCZEPAN SUCHY

Faculty of Geology, Geophysics and Environmental Protection: Prof. ADAM PIESTRZYŃSKI

Faculty of Humanities: Prof. JANUSZ MUCHA

Faculty of Management: Dr PIOTR ŁEBKOWSKI

Faculty of Materials Science and Ceramics: Prof. JERZY LIS

Faculty of Mechanical Engineering and Robotics: Prof. ANTONI KALUKIEWICZ

Faculty of Metals Engineering and Industrial Computer Science: Dr TADEUSZ TELEJKO

Faculty of Mining and Geoengineering: Prof. PIOTR CZAJA

Faculty of Mining, Surveying and Environmental Engineering: Prof. STANISŁAW GRUSZCZYŃSKI

Faculty of Non-Ferrous Metals: Prof. MARIA RICHERT

Faculty of Physics and Applied Computer Science: Prof. JANUSZ WOLNY

AKADEMIA IM. JANA DŁUGOSZA W CZĘSTOCHOWIE
(Jan Długosz University in Częstochowa)

ul. Waszyngtona 4/8, 42-200 Częstochowa

Telephone: (34) 3784100
E-mail: rektor@ajd.czest.pl
Internet: www.ajd.czest.pl

Founded 1971
State control

Chancellor: MARIOLA PTASZEK
Rector: Prof. Dr Hab. ZYGMUNT BĄK
Pro-Rector for Devt: Prof. Dr Hab. JAROSŁAW KWECLICH
Pro-Rector for Education: Prof. Dr Hab. ELIGIUSZ MAŁOLEPSZY
Pro-Rector for Science: Prof. Dr Hab. JÓZEF DRABOWICZ
Dir for Library: Mgr ALICJA RACZYŃSKA (acting)

Library of 270,000 vols
Number of teachers: 700
Number of students: 8,200

DEANS

Faculty of Art Education: Dr Hab. ROBERT GAWROŃSKI

Faculty of Mathematics and Natural Sciences: Dr Hab. JANUSZ KAPUŚNIAK

Faculty of Pedagogy: Dr Hab. GRAŻYNA RYGAŁ

Faculty of Philology and History: Dr Hab. AGNIESZKA CZAJKOWSKA

Faculty of Social Sciences: Dr Hab. ROMUALD DERBIS

AKADEMIA TECHNICZNO-HUMANISTYCZNA W BIELSKU-BIALEJ
(University of Bielsko-Biala)

ul. Willowa 2, 43-309 Bielsko-Biala

Telephone: (33) 8279349
E-mail: biurorektora@ath.bielsko.pl
Internet: info.ath.bielsko.pl

Founded 2001
Academic year: October to June

Rector: Prof. Dr RYSZARD BARCIK
Vice-Rector for Science and Finance: Prof. Dr KAZIMIERZ NIKODEM
Vice-Rector for Student Affairs and Education: Prof. Dr HENRYK KLAMA
Dir for Library: LILIANA LINEK

Number of teachers: 200
Number of students: 8,000

DEANS

Faculty of Health Sciences: Prof. Dr Hab. MONIKA MIKULSKA

Faculty of Humanities and Social Sciences: Prof. Dr Hab. MAREK BERNACKI

Faculty of Management and Computer Science: Prof. Dr Hab. ANDRZEJ MACZYNSKI

Faculty of Materials and Environmental Sciences: Prof. Dr Hab. JAROSŁAW JANICKI

Faculty of Mechanical Engineering and Computer Science: Prof. Dr Hab. JACEK STADNICKI

Higher Institutes
ECONOMICS, SOCIAL SCIENCES

Szkoła Główna Handlowa w Warszawie (Warsaw School of Economics): al. Niepodległości 162, 02-554 Warsaw; tel. (22) 3379000; e-mail informacja@sgh.waw.pl; internet www.sgh.waw.pl; f. 1906; colleges of business administration, economic analysis, management and finance, social and economic science, world economy; library: see under Libraries and Archives; 900 teachers; 16,451 students (6,544 full-time, 6,131 extra-mural, 2,626 postgraduate, 1,150 PhD); Rector Prof. TOMASZ SZAPIRO; Vice-Rector for Management Prof. MAREK BRYX; Vice-Rector for Research and Int. Relations Prof. MAREK GRUSZCZYŃSKI; Vice-Rector for Teaching and Student Affairs Prof. PIOTR OSTASZEWSKI; Head Librarian Dr MARIA REKOWSKA; publs *National Economy* (12 a year), *Poland: International Economic Report* (1 a year, in English and Polish).

Szkoła Wyższa Psychologii Społecznej (University of Social Sciences and Humanities): ul. Chodakowska 19/31, 03-815 Warsaw; tel. (22) 5179600; e-mail swps@swps.edu.pl; internet www.swps.edu.pl; f. 1996; faculties at Katowice, Poznań, Sopot, Warsaw, Wrocław; library: 88,000 vols; 243 teachers; 8,314 students; Pres. Prof. Dr Hab. ANDRZEJ ELIASZ; Vice-Rector for Academic Affairs and Int. Cooperation Prof. Dr Hab. TERESA GARDOCKA; Vice-Rector for Research Prof. Dr Hab. ROMAN CIEŚLAK; publs *Charaktery* (jt publ., 12 a year), *Czasopismo Psychologiczne* (jt publ., 2 a year), *Kultura Popularna* (2 a year), *Psychologia Jakości Życia* (2 a year), *Studia Psychologiczne* (jt publ., 2 a year).

MEDICINE

Centrum Medyczne Kształcenia Podyplomowego (Medical Centre for Postgraduate Education): ul. Marymoncka 99/103, 01-813 Warsaw; tel. (22) 5693700; e-mail dyrektor@cmkp.edu.pl; internet www.cmkp.edu.pl; f. 1970; faculties of basic sciences, clinical medicine, stomatology, pharmacy, family medicine; school of public health and social medicine; library: 46,000 vols; Dir Prof. Dr Hab. JOANNA JĘDRZEJCZAK; Deputy Dir for Clinical Affairs Prof. Dr Hab. MAREK TAŁAŁAJ; Deputy Dir for Education and Research Prof. Dr Hab. JAROSŁAW CZUBAK; Deputy Dir for Organization and Economic Affairs Mgr Inz. ZBIGNIEW PIOTROWSKI.

Collegium Medicum im. Ludwika Rydygiera w Bydgoszczy (Ludwik Rydygier Collegium Medicum in Bydgoszcz): ul. Jagiellońska 13–15, 85-067 Bydgoszcz; tel. (52) 5853306; e-mail sekretariat@cm.umk.pl; internet www.amb.bydgoszcz.pl; f. 1984; faculties of health sciences, medicine, pharmacy; library: 64,000 vols, 16,000 periodicals; 545 teachers; 3,714 students; Vice-Rector Prof. Dr Hab. JAN STYCZYŃSKI; Vice-Chancellor Mgr MAGDALENA BROŃCZYK.

Collegium Medicum Uniwersytetu Jagiellońskiego (Jagiellonian University, Medical College): ul. Sw. Anny 12, 31-008 Cracow; tel. (12) 4220411; e-mail prorektor@cm-uj.krakow.pl; internet www.cm-uj.krakow.pl; f. 1364; library: 426,000 vols of books, magazines, and spec. collns; 100 teachers; 4,600 students; Vice-Rector Prof. Dr PIOTR LAIDLER; Deputy Chancellor EWA KLEPACZ-ZIELIŃSKA (acting); publs *Annales Collegii Medici Universitatis Jagiellonicae Cracoviensis* (1 a year), *The Methodical Review* (1 a year).

TECHNOLOGY AND ENGINEERING

Akademia Morska w Gdyni (Gdynia Maritime University): ul. Morska 81–87, 81-225 Gdynia; tel. (58) 6217041; e-mail rector@am.gdynia.pl; internet www.am.gdynia.pl; f. 1920; faculties of entrepreneurship and quality science, marine electrical engineering, marine engineering, navigation; library: 89,186 vols, 9,950 vols of old periodicals, 243 titles of journals, 262 units of spec. collns; 370 teachers; 8,500 students; Rector Prof. Dr PIOTR JĘDRZEJOWICZ; Deputy Rector for Education Dr MIROSŁAW CZECHOWSKI; Deputy Rector for Maritime Affairs Dr HENRYK SNIEGOCKI; Deputy Rector for Scientific Research and Devt Prof. Dr JANUSZ MINDYKOWSKI; Library Dir Mgr JOLANTA MACIEJEWSKA; publs *Joint Proceedings*, *Scientific Journal*, *Zeszyty Naukowe* (4 a year, print and online).

Akademia Morska w Szczecinie (Maritime University of Szczecin): ul. Wały Chrobrego 1–2, 70-500 Szczecin; tel. (91) 4809400; e-mail rektor@am.szczecin.pl; internet www.am.szczecin.pl; f. 1947; faculties of economics and transport engineering, marine engineering, navigation; library: 124,000 vols, 7,950 periodicals, 24,400 units of spec. collns; 4,000 students; Chancellor ANDRZEJ DURAJCZYK; Rector Prof. Dr STANISŁAW GUCMA; Vice-Rector for Maritime Affairs Dr ANDRZEJ BĄK; Vice-Rector for Science Prof. Dr ARTUR BEJGER; Vice-Rector for Teaching Dr PIOTR TREICHEL; Library Dir ELŻBIETA EDELMAN; publs *Akademickie Aktualności Morskie* (4 a year, print and online), *Zeszyty Naukowe* (4 a year, print and online).

THEOLOGY

Chrześcijańska Akademia Teologiczna (Christian Theological Academy): ul. Miodowa 21c, 00-246 Warsaw; tel. (22) 8319597; e-mail chat@chat.edu.pl; internet www.chat .edu.pl; f. 1954; faculties of education, theology; library: 55,000 vols; 76 teachers; 955 students; Rector Prof. Dr Hab. Bogusław Milerski; Vice-Rector Prof. Dr Hab. Jerzy Pańkowski; Library Dir Mgr Adam Martynowicz; publ. *Rocznik Teologiczny* (1 a year).

VOCATIONAL SCHOOLS

Karkonoska Państwowa Szkoła Wyższa w Jeleniej Górze (Karkonosze College in Jelenia Góra): ul. Lwówecka 18, 58-503 Jelenia Góra 5; tel. (75) 6453300; e-mail rektorat@kpswjg.pl; internet www.kpswjg.pl; f. 1988 as Kolegium Karkonoskie, present name 2010; faculties of humanities and social sciences, natural sciences and technology; library: 61,200 vols, 91 titles of journals; Chancellor Mgr Grażyna Malczuk; Rector Prof. Dr Hab. Henryk Gradkowski; Vice-Rector Prof. Dr Hab. Tomasz Winnicki; Dir for Library and Scientific Information Centre Mgr Kazimierz Stąpór.

Państwowa Wyższa Szkoła Informatyki i Przedsiębiorczości w Łomży (State College of Computer Science and Business Administration in Lomza): ul. Akademicka 14, 18-400 Łomża; tel. (86) 2155953; e-mail rektor@pwsip.edu.pl; internet www.pwsip .edu.pl; f. 2004; depts of business administration, computer science and automation, food technology and human nutrition, medicine, physical education; Chancellor Mgr Henryk Trojanowski; Rector Prof. Dr Hab. Robert Charmas; Vice-Rector for Research and Int. Relations Prof. Dr Hab. Antoni Jakubczak; Vice-Rector for Teaching and Student Affairs Dr Krystyna Leszczewska.

Państwowa Wyższa Szkoła Techniczno-Ekonomiczna im. ks. Bronisława Markiewicza w Jarosławiu (Bronisław Markiewicz State School of Higher Vocational Education in Jarosław): ul. Czarnieckiego 16, 37-500 Jarosław; tel. (16) 6244620; e-mail pwste@pwste.edu.pl; internet www.pwste .edu.pl; f. 1998; institutes of economics and management, humanities, engineering and technology, health sciences, international relations; library: 40,000 vols; 5,000 students; Chancellor Mgr Robert Wiśniewski; Rector Prof. Dr Hab. Wacław Wierzbieniec; Vice-Rector for Educational Affairs Prof. Dr Hab. Czesław Lewicki; Vice-Rector for Student Affairs and Org. Dr Krzysztof Rejman; publs *Geomatyka i Inżynieria* (4 a year), *Językoznawstwo* (1 a year), *Literatura i Kultura* (1 a year).

Państwowa Wyższa Szkoła Zawodowa im. Jana Grodka w Sanoku (Jan Grodek State Higher Vocational School in Sanok): ul. Mickiewicza 21, 38-500 Sanok; tel. (13) 4655952; e-mail rektorat@pwsz-sanok.edu .pl; internet www.pwsz-sanok.edu.pl; f. 2001; institutes of agriculture, humanities and fine arts, medicine, technology; library: 15,000 vols, 46 titles of journals; Chancellor Lesław Siedlecki; Rector Dr Elżbieta Cipora; Vice-Rector for Devt and Research Dr Rozwoju Nauki; Vice-Rector for Teaching Dr Magdalena Konieczny; publ. *Zeszyty Naukowe PWSZ* (1 a year).

Państwowa Wyższa Szkoła Zawodowa im. Papieża Jana Pawła II w Białej Podlaskiej (Pope John Paul II State School of Higher Education in Biała Podlaska): ul. Sidorska 95/97, 21-500 Biała Podlaska; tel. (83) 3449900; e-mail psw@pswbp.pl; internet www.pswbp.pl; f. 2000; institutes of agriculture, computer science, construction engineering, economics, finance and accounting, management, national security, neophilology, nursing, pedagogy, public health, rescue medicine, sociology, tourism and recreation; library: 22,000 vols; 3,500 students; Chancellor Mgr Leszek Petruczenko; Rector Prof. Dr Hab. Mieczysław Adamowicz; Vice-Rector for Devt Prof. Dr Hab. Józef Bergier; Vice-Rector for Student Affairs Dr Wiesław Romanowicz; Dir for Library Mgr Marzena Dziołak; publs *Bialski Przegląd Akademicki* (4 a year, print and online), *Rozprawy Społeczne* (Social Dissertations), *Studia Ekonomiczne i Regionalne* (Economic and Regional Studies, 1 a year).

Państwowa Wyższa Szkoła Zawodowa im. Prezydenta Stanisława Wojciechowskiego w Kaliszu (President Stanisław Wojciechowski Higher Vocational State School in Kalisz): ul. Nowy Swiat 4, 62-800 Kalisz; tel. (62) 7679500; e-mail rektorat@ pwsz.kalisz.pl; internet www.pwsz.kalisz.pl; f. 1999; institutes of management, nursing and midwifery polytechnic, physiotherapy and emergency medical care; library: 105,000 vols, 325 magazines and professional journals, 1,950 ebooks, magazines and other documents, 75 databases; 366 teachers; 4,036 students; Chancellor Mgr Kazimierz Matusiak; Rector Prof. Dr Jan Chajda; Vice-Rector for Education and Student Affairs Prof. Dr Hab. Stefan Kowal; Vice-Rector for Int. Cooperation Prof. Dr Hab. Magdalena Pisarska-Krawczyk; Dir for Library Dr Małgorzata Całka; publ. *Biuletyn Uczelniany* (4 a year).

Państwowa Wyższa Szkoła Zawodowa im. Rotmistrza Wiltoda Pileckiego w Oświęcimiu (State School of Higher Education in Oświęcim): ul. Kolbego 8, 32-600 Oświęcim; tel. (33) 8430691; e-mail sekretariat@pwsz-oswiecim.edu.pl; internet www.pwsz-oswiecim.edu.pl; f. 2005; institutes of management, nursing, pedagogy, philology, physical education, political sciences; library: 27,000 vols, 8,000 periodicals; Chancellor Mgr Inz. Adam Bilski; Rector Prof. Dr Hab. Witold Stankowski; Vice-Rector Dr Maciej Mączyński; publ. *Pełnym Głosem*.

Państwowa Wyższa Szkoła Zawodowa im. Stanisława Pigonia w Krośnie (State Higher Vocational School in Krosno): ul. Rynek 1, 38-400 Krosno; tel. (13) 4375500; e-mail pwsz@pwsz.krosno.pl; internet www .pwsz.krosno.pl; f. 1999; institutes of economic and social policy, humanities, physical culture, polytechnic; library: 59,000 vols, 100 titles of periodicals; Chancellor Mgr Franciszek Tereszkiewicz; Rector Prof. Dr Hab. Grzegorz Przebinda; Vice-Rector for Devt Dr Inz. Stanisław Rymar; Vice-Rector for Education Prof. Dr Hab. Zbigniew Barabasz; Head of Library Mgr Judyta Zajdel; publ. *Prace* (6 a year).

Państwowa Wyższa Szkoła Zawodowa im. Stanisława Staszica w Pile (Stanisław Staszic State School of Higher Vocational Education in Piła): ul. Podchorążych 10, 64-920 Piła; tel. (67) 3522600; e-mail info@pwsz .pila.pl; internet www.pwsz.pila.pl; f. 2000; institutes of economics, health sciences, humanities, polytechnic; Chancellor Mgr Sylwester Sieradzki; Rector Prof. Dr Hab. Adam Marcinkowski; Pro-Rector for Didactics and Student Affairs Prof. Dr Hab. Donat Mierzejewski; Pro-Rector for Org. and Development Prof. Dr Bolesław Ochodek; Dir for Library Mgr Irena Łosoś.

Państwowa Wyższa Szkoła Zawodowa im. Szymona Szymonowica w Zamościu (Szymon Szymonowic State Higher Vocational School in Zamość): ul. Akademicka 8, 22-400 Zamość; tel. (84) 6383444; e-mail rektorat@pwszzamosc.pl; internet www .pwszzamosc.pl; f. 2005; Humanistic Institute, Nature and Technical Institute, Mathematical and Innovative Technologies Institute; library: 8,000 vols; Chancellor Mgr Jerzy Korniluk; Rector Prof. Dr Hab. Waldemar Martyn; Vice-Rector Dr Kazimierz Chrzanowski.

Państwowa Wyższa Szkoła Zawodowa im. Witelona w Legnicy (Witelon University of Applied Sciences in Legnica): ul. Sejmowa 5a, 59-220 Legnica; tel. (76) 7232150; e-mail pwsz@pwsz.legnica.edu.pl; internet www.pwsz.legnica.edu.pl; f. 1998; faculties of administration, humanities, management and computer science, medicine, pedagogy, tourism and recreation, political science; library: 65,000 vols, 119 titles of periodicals; 7,000 students; Chancellor Mgr Robert Burba; Rector Prof. Dr Hab. Ryszard K. Pisarski; Vice-Rector for Education and Student Affairs Dr Helena Babiuch; Vice-Rector for Science and Int. Cooperation Prof. Dr Hab. Jerzy Pietkiewicz; Dir for Library Danuta Bombik.

Państwowa Wyższa Szkoła Zawodowa w Chełmie (State School of Higher Education in Chełm): ul. Pocztowa 54, 22-100 Chełm; tel. (82) 5658895; e-mail rektorat@pwsz .chelm.pl; internet pwsz.chelm.pl; f. 2001; institutes of agricultural sciences, human sciences, mathematics and computer science, modern languages, technical sciences; library: 28,000 vols; 3,000 students; Chancellor Marian Różański; Rector Prof. Dr Hab. Józef Zając; Vice-Rector for Academic Affairs Dr Beata Fałda; Vice-Rector for Development and Int. Relations Dr Arkadiusz Tofil; Dir for Library Mgr Barbara Polakowska.

Państwowa Wyższa Szkoła Zawodowa w Ciechanowie (State Higher School of Vocational Education in Ciechanów): ul. Narutowicza 9, 06-400 Ciechanów; tel. (23) 6722050; e-mail rektorat@pwszciechanow.edu.pl; internet www.pwszciechanow.edu.pl; f. 2001; faculties of computer science, cultural studies, economics, engineering, health protection, humanities and technology; library: 31,110 vols, 87 titles of periodicals; 2,200 students; Chancellor Mgr Inz. Piotr Wójcik; Rector Dr Leszek Zygner; Pro-Rector Dr Leszek Zygner.

Państwowa Wyższa Szkoła Zawodowa w Elblągu (State School of Higher Professional Education in Elbląg): ul. Wojska Polskiego 1, 82-300 Elbląg; tel. (55) 6290505; e-mail pwsz@pwsz.elblag.pl; internet www.pwsz .elblag.pl; f. 1998; faculties of applied informatics, economics, pedagogy and languages, technology; library: 62,000 vols; 206 teachers; Chancellor Bohdan Niemirycz; Rector Prof. Dr Hab. Zbigniew Walczyk; Vice-Rector for Devt Dr Irena Sorokosz; Vice-Rector for Educational Affairs Prof. Dr Cezary Orlikowski.

Państwowa Wyższa Szkoła Zawodowa we Włocławku (State Higher Vocational School in Włocławek): ul. 3 Maja 17, 87-800 Włocławek; tel. (54) 2316080; e-mail kancelaria@pwsz.wloclawek.pl; internet www.pwsz.wloclawek.pl; f. 2002; institutes of humanities, foreign languages, physical education and sport, social sciences and computer science; library: 36,000 vols, 123 titles of periodicals; Chancellor Mgr Teresa Bieniek; Rector Prof. Dr Hab. Tadeusz Dubicki; Vice-Rector for Teaching and Student Affairs Dr Małgorzata Legiędź-Gałuszka; publs *Ekonomia i Zarządzanie*, *Rozprawy Humanistyczne*, *Zbliżenia Cywilizacyjne*.

Państwowa Wyższa Szkoła Zawodowa w Głogowie (State Higher Vocational School in Głogów): ul. Piotra Skargi 5, 67-200 Głogów; tel. (76) 8353582; e-mail kontakt@

pwsz.glogow.pl; internet pwsz.glogow.pl; f. 2004; depts of economics, foreign languages, humanities, physical education, science and technology; library: 24,000 vols, 75 journals; Chancellor Mgr JAN MIŚKO; Rector Prof. Dr Hab. STANISŁAW CZAJA; Pro-Rector Dr Inz. KATARZYNA PANTOL; publs *Człowiek a Religia* (1 a year), *Człowiek a Tożsamość* (1 a year).

Państwowa Wyższa Szkoła Zawodowa w Gnieźnie (State Higher Vocational School in Gniezno): ul. Ks. Kard. Stefana Wyszyńskiego 38, 62-200 Gniezno; tel. (61) 4242942; e-mail sekretariat@pwsz-gniezno.edu.pl; internet www.pwsz-gniezno.edu.pl; f. 2004; Bachelors degree course in nursing; library: 7,100 vols; Chancellor Mgr MIECZYSŁAW BARANOWSKI; Rector Prof. Dr Hab. JÓZEF GARBARCZYK; Deputy Rector for Studies Prof. Dr Hab. ANDRZEJ URBANIAK.

Państwowa Wyższa Szkoła Zawodowa w Gorzowie Wielkopolskim (State Higher Vocational School in Gorzow Wielkopolski): ul. Teatralna 25, 66-400 Gorzów Wielkopolski; tel. (95) 7216022; e-mail rektor@pwsz.pl; internet www.pwsz.pl; faculties of administration and national security, economics, humanities, technology; library: 70,000 vols; Rector Prof. Dr Hab. ELŻBIETA SKORUPSKA-RACZYŃSKA; Vice-Rector for Org. and Development Dr ARKADIUSZ WOŁOSZYN; Vice-Rector for Student Affairs Dr PRZEMYSŁAW SŁOWINSKI; Dir for Library Mgr SŁAWOMIR JACH.

Państwowa Wyższa Szkoła Zawodowa w Koninie (State School of Higher Professional Education in Konin): ul. Przyjaźni 1, 62-510 Konin; tel. (63) 2497200; e-mail rektorat@konin.edu.pl; internet www.pwsz.konin.edu.pl; f. 1998; faculties of environmental engineering in Turek, physical education and health preservation, social and technical studies; library: 72,000 vols, 130 titles of periodicals; spec. collns: 1,700 CDs, DVDs, audio and video cassettes; 3,000 students; Pres. Prof. Dr Hab. MIROSŁAW PAWLAK; Vice-Pres. Dr JERZY JASIŃSKI; Vice-Pres. Dr JOANNA CHOJNACKA-GÄRTNER; Dir of Administration Mgr ALEKSANDRA ORLIKOWSKA; publ. *Szkiełkiem i Okiem* (1 a year).

Państwowa Wyższa Szkoła Zawodowa w Nowym Sączu (State Higher Vocational School in Nowy Sącz): ul. Staszica 1, 33-300 Nowy Sącz; tel. (18) 4434545; e-mail sog@pwsz-ns.edu.pl; internet www.pwsz-ns.edu.pl; f. 1998; depts of economics, engineering, foreign languages, nursing, pedagogy, physical education; library: 60,000 vols of books, CDs, DVDs, audio and video cassettes, maps, 100 titles of periodicals; 311 teachers; 4,530 students; Rector Prof. Dr Hab. ZBIGNIEW ŚLIPEK; Vice-Rector for Science and Devt Dr MAREK REICHEL; Vice-Rector for Student Affairs and Education Dr JANUSZ PATER; Dir for Library Mgr AGATA WITRYLAK-LESZYŃSKA.

Państwowa Wyższa Szkoła Zawodowa w Nysie (School of Higher Vocational Education in Nysa): ul. Armii Krajowej 7, 48-300 Nysa; tel. (77) 4484703; e-mail rektor@pwsz.nysa.pl; internet www.pwsz.nysa.pl; f. 2001; faculties of architecture and urban planning, internal security, dietetics, English philology, German philology, business English, finance and accounting, computer science, jazz and popular music, cosmetology, nursing, emergency medical rescue, management and production engineering, architectonical objects renovation; library: 33,404 vols, 176 titles of periodicals; spec. collns: 1,143 items; 4,500 students; Chancellor Mgr ZBIGNIEW SZLEMPO; Rector Prof. Dr Hab. ZOFIA WILIMOWSKA; Vice-Rector for Education Dr MARIUSZ KOŁOSOWSKI; Vice-Rector for Gen. Affairs Prof. Dr TOMASZ MALCZYK; Dir for Library

Mgr BOGUMIŁA WOJCIECHOWSKA-MAREK; publ. *Germanistische Studien* (in German).

Państwowa Wyższa Szkoła Zawodowa w Płocku (Higher Vocational State School in Płock): pl. Dąbrowskiego 2, 09-402 Płock; tel. (24) 3665420; e-mail pwsz@pwszplock.pl; internet pwszplock.pl; f. 1999; depts of economics, health sciences, mathematics and information technology, modern languages, pedagogy; library: 32,697 vols, 61 titles of periodicals; Chancellor Mgr RADOSŁAW BANDERA; Rector Prof. Dr Hab. JACEK GRZYWACZ; Vice-Rector for Research and Devt Dr EWA WIŚNIEWSKA; publs *Nauki Ekonomiczne* (2 a year), *Neofilologia, Pedagogika*.

Państwowa Wyższa Szkoła Zawodowa w Raciborzu (State Higher Vocational School in Raciborz): ul. Słowackiego 55, 47-400 Racibórz; tel. (32) 4155020; e-mail rektorat@pwsz.raciborz.edu.pl; internet www.pwsz.raciborz.edu.pl; f. 2001; bachelors in architecture and urban planning, automation and robotics, European studies, mathematics, pedagogy, philology, physical education, sociology; Chancellor Mgr CEZARY RACZEK; Rector Prof. Dr Hab. MICHAŁ SZEPELAWY; Vice-Rector for Devt and Organization Dr Inz. JULIUSZ KIEŚ; Vice-Rector for Educational Affairs Dr BEATA FEDYN; Vice-Rector for Student Affairs Dr TERESA JEMCZURA; publ. *Eunomia* (12 a year).

Państwowa Wyższa Szkoła Zawodowa w Sulechowie (State Higher Vocational School in Sulechow): ul. Armii Krajowej 51, 66-100 Sulechów; tel. (68) 3528303; e-mail rektorat@pwsz.sulechow.pl; internet www.pwsz.sulechow.pl; f. 1998; institutes of law and administration, management and agricultural engineering, tourism and recreation; depts of foreign languages and physical education; library: 28,000 vols, 92 titles of periodicals; Chancellor Inz. STANISŁAW FONTOWICZ; Rector Prof. Dr Hab. WIESŁAW MICZULSKI; Vice-Rector for Devt Dr Inz. IZABELA WOJEWODA; Vice-Rector for Student Affairs Dr Inz. JULIAN JAKUBOWSKI; publs *Biuletyn Informacyjny* (4 a year), *Kształtowanie Terenów Zieleni* (1 a year), *Studia Lubuskie* (1 a year), *Technologia Żywności i Żywienie Człowieka* (1 a year).

Państwowa Wyższa Szkoła Zawodowa w Tarnowie (State Higher Vocational School in Tarnow): ul. Mickiewicza 8, 33-100 Tarnów; tel. (14) 6316500; e-mail pwsz@pwsztar.edu.pl; internet www.pwsztar.edu.pl; f. 1998; Bachelors in chemistry, computer sciences, economics, English, German and Polish philology, environmental protection, mathematics, nursing, physical education, physical therapy, telecommunications; library: 47,000 vols; spec. collns: 2,000 units; 4,500 students; Chancellor Mgr ROMAN ŻOK; Rector Prof. Dr Hab. STANISŁAW KOMORNICKI; Vice-Rector for Devt and Cooperation Dr Hab. WACŁAW RAPAK; Vice-Rector for Student Affairs and Didactics Dr JÓZEF WĘGLARZ.

Państwowa Wyższa Szkoła Zawodowa w Wałczu (State Higher Vocational School in Wałcz): ul. Bydgoska 50, 78-600 Wałcz; tel. (67) 2500187; e-mail rektorat@pwsz.eu; internet www.pwsz.eu; f. 2004; Bachelors in English and German philology, finance and accounting, information science and econometrics, management and production engineering, pedagogy, physical education; library: 37,679 vols, 50 titles of periodicals; 58 teachers; Chancellor Mgr JACEK KASIŃSKI; Rector Prof. Dr Hab. JOLANTA WITEK; Dean Dr Inz. MAREK OLESIAK.

Podhalańska Państwowa Wyższa Szkoła Zawodowa w Nowym Targu (Podhale State Higher Vocational School in Nowy Targ): ul. Kokoszków 71, 34-400 Nowy Targ; tel. (18) 2610700; e-mail ppwsz@

ppwsz.edu.pl; internet www.ppwsz.edu.pl; f. 2001; institutes of architecture and urban planning, environmental engineering, environmental protection, humanities, nursing, physiotherapy, tourism and recreation; library: 14,000 vols, 61 titles of periodicals; Chancellor Mgr ANDRZEJ SASUŁA; Rector Prof. Dr Hab. IWON GRYS; Vice-Rector for Devt Dr MARCIN WROŃSKI; Vice-Rector for Research Dr MACIEJ HODOROWICZ; Vice-Rector for Student Affairs Dr EWA ZIARKO.

Schools of Art and Music

Akademia Muzyczna im. Feliksa Nowowiejskiego w Bydgoszczy (Feliks Nowowiejski Academy of Music in Bydgoszcz): ul. Słowackiego 7, 85-008 Bydgoszcz; tel. (52) 3210582; e-mail sekr@amuz.bydgoszcz.pl; internet www.amuz.bydgoszcz.pl; f. 1974, present name and status 1979; faculties of choir conducting and music education, composition, theory of music and sound engineering, instrumental music, vocal music and drama; library: 63,000 vols, 1,644 old magazines, 1,480 doctoral theses; 100 teachers; 402 students; Rector Prof. JERZY KASZUBA; Deputy Rector for Artistic Affairs Prof. Dr Hab. HANNA MICHALAK; Deputy Rector for Org., Science and Int. Cooperation Prof. MARIA MURAWSKA; Dir for Finance and Admin. MAREK CZERSKI; Library Dir Mgr ELŻBIETA ABRAMEK.

Akademia Muzyczna im. Grażyny i Kiejstuta Bacewiczów w Łodzi (Grażyna and Kiejstut Bacewicz Academy of Music in Łódź): ul. Gdańska 32, 90-716 Łódź; tel. (42) 6621600; e-mail rektorat@amuz.lodz.pl; internet www.amuz.lodz.pl; f. 1945; faculties of composition, theory of music, eurhythmics and art education, instrumental studies, piano, organ, harpsichord and early instruments, piano, organ, harpsichord and early instruments; library: 10,000 vols, 6,000 records and CDs, 300 periodicals, 35,000 scores; 225 teachers; 574 students; Rector Prof. CEZARY SANECKI; Vice-Rector for Didactic Affairs Prof. ELŻBIETA ALEKSANDROWICZ; Vice-Rector for Research and Devt Prof. Dr Hab. AGATA JARECKA; Vice-Rector for Student and Artistic Affairs Prof. BEATA ZAWADZKA-KŁOS.

Akademia Muzyczna im. Ignacego Jana Paderewskiego w Poznaniu (Ignacy Jan Paderewski Academy of Music in Poznań): ul. Święty Marcin 87, 61-808 Poznań; tel. (61) 8568900; e-mail amuz@amuz.edu.pl; internet www.amuz.edu.pl; f. 1920; faculties of choral conducting, music education and church music, composition, conducting, theory of music and eurhythmics, instruments, string instruments, harp, guitar and violin-making, vocal studies; library: 20,000 vols of books and journals, 51,000 music scores; 300 teachers; 800 students; Chancellor MARCIN ELBANOWSKI; Rector Prof. HALINA LORKOWSKA; Vice-Rector for Artistic Affairs and Research Prof. JANUSZ STALMIERSKI; Vice-Rector for Student Affairs Dr Hab. KRZYSZTOF PRZYBYŁOWICZ; Library Dir Dr EWA RZANNA-SZCZEPANIAK.

Akademia Muzyczna im. Karola Lipińskiego we Wrocławiu (Karol Lipinski Academy of Music in Wrocław): pl. Jana Pawła II 2, 50-043 Wrocław; tel. (71) 3100500; e-mail info@amuz.wroc.pl; internet www.amuz.wroc.pl; f. 1948, present name 1981; faculties of composition, conducting, theory of music and music therapy, instruments, voice, music education; library: 120,608 vols, incl. 93,753 music scores, 13,959 books, 2,046 periodicals, 2,439 theses and dissertations, 8,409 vols of archival records; 185 teachers; 685 students; Chancellor Mgr Inz. DANUTA KOPROWSKA; Rector Prof. Dr Hab. KRYSTIAN KIEŁB; Deputy Rector for Scientific Affairs and Foreign Relations Dr Hab. MAGDALENA BLUM-RAK; Deputy Rector for Student Affairs and Didactic Activity Prof. HELENA TOMASZEK-PLEWA; Library Dir Mgr MAGDALENA WIĄCEK.

Akademia Muzyczna im. Karola Szymanowskiego w Katowicach (Karol Szymanowski Academy of Music in Katowice): ul. Zacisze 3, 40-025 Katowice; tel. (32) 7792100; e-mail biurorektora@am.katowice.pl; internet www.am.katowice.pl; f. 1929; faculties of composition, music theory and education, instrumental music, vocal music and theatrical art, jazz and popular music; library: 140,000 vols; spec. colln: music in Silesia; 170 teachers; 745 students; Chancellor Mgr KATARZYNA PLEŚNIAK; Rector Prof. TOMASZ MICZKA; Vice-Rector for Didactics, Science and Personnel Policy Prof. GRZEGORZ BIEGAS; Vice-Rector for Student Affairs, Int. Relations and Development Dr MARCIN TRZĘSIOK; publ. *Klucz* (irregular).

Akademia Muzyczna im. Stanisława Moniuszki w Gdańsku (Stanisław Moniuszko Academy of Music in Gdańsk): ul. Łąkowa 1/2, 80-743 Gdańsk; tel. (58) 3009200; e-mail rektorat@amuz.gda.pl; internet www.amuz.gda.pl; f. 1947; faculties of composition and theory, instruments, choral conducting, musical education, eurhythmics, jazz and church music, vocals and acting; library: 92,000 vols, 15,000 audio recordings; 165 teachers; 433 students; Chancellor PIOTR ŻERKO; Rector Prof. MACIEJ SOBCZAK; Vice-Rector for Artistic Affairs and Int. Relations Prof. RYSZARD MINKIEWICZ; Vice-Rector for Org. and Teaching Prof. MAREK ROCŁAWSKI; Vice-Rector for Student Affairs Prof. ANDRZEJ ARTYKIEWICZ; Library Dir Mgr ANNA MICHALSKA; publs *Bibliografia* (irregular), *Kultura Muzyczna Północnych Ziem Polski* (irregular), *Muzyka Fortepianowa*, *Muzyka Pomorza* (irregular), *Organy iMuzyka Organowa* (every 3 years), *Prace Specjalne* (irregular), *Rocznik Informacyjny* (1 a year), *Skrypty i Podręczniki* (irregular), *Zeszyty Naukowe* (irregular).

Akademia Muzyczna w Krakowie (Academy of Music in Cracow): ul. św. Tomasza 43, 31-027 Cracow; tel. (12) 4220455; e-mail rektor@amuz.krakow.pl; internet www.amuz.krakow.pl; f. 1888; faculties of composition, interpretation and musical education, instruments, voice and drama; library: 47,000 vols; 365 teachers; 644 students; Chancellor Inz. KRZYSZTOF RYMARCZYK; Rector Prof. ZDZISŁAW ŁAPIŃSKI; Vice-Rector for Research and Int. Cooperation Prof. RAFAŁ JACEK DELEKTA; Vice-Rector for Student Affairs Prof. ADAM KORZENIOWSKI; Vice-Rector for Teaching and Human Resources Devt Dr Hab. DARIUSZ BĄKOWSKI-KOIS; Library Dir Mgr CZESŁAWA ZAWROTNIAK; publ. *Teoria Muzyki: Studia, Interpretacje, Dokumentacje*.

Akademia Sztuk Pięknych im. Eugeniusza Gepperta we Wrocławiu (Eugeniusz Geppert Academy of Art and Design in Wrocław): ul. Plac Polski 3/4, 50-156 Wrocław; tel. (71) 3438031; e-mail info@asp.wroc.pl; internet www.asp.wroc.pl; f. 1945; faculties of ceramics and glass, graphic arts and media art, interior design and designing, painting and sculpture; library: 14,000 vols, 1,000 magazines, 3,700 catalogues of Polish and foreign exhibitions; Rector Prof. JACEK SZEWCZYK; Vice-Rector for Artistic Research PIOTR KIELAN; Vice-Rector for Didactics Prof. WACŁAW KOWALSKI.

Akademia Sztuk Pięknych im. Jana Matejki w Krakowie (Jan Matejko Academy of Fine Arts in Cracow): pl. Jana Matejki 13, 31-157 Cracow; tel. (12) 4222450; e-mail rektor@asp.krakow.pl; internet www.asp.krakow.pl; f. 1818; faculties of conservation and restoration of works of art, graphic arts, industrial design, interior design, intermedia, painting, sculpture; library: 150,000 vols, 21,000 graphic items, 13,000 posters; 244 teachers; 845 students; Chancellor ADAM OLESZKO; Rector Prof. STANISŁAW TABISZ; Vice-Rector for Research and Int. Relations Prof. PIOTR BOŻYK; Vice-Rector for Student Affairs JAN TUTAJ; Library Dir JADWIGA WIELGUT-WALCZAK; publs *Studia i Materiały Konserwatorskie* (1 a year), *Wiadomości—ASP* (3 a year, print and online, www.wiadomosciasp.pl).

Akademia Sztuk Pięknych im. Władysława Strzemińskiego w Łodzi (Strzemiński Academy of Art Łódź): ul. Wojska Polskiego 121, 91-726 Łódź; tel. (42) 2547598; e-mail kancelaria@asp.lodz.pl; internet www.asp.lodz.pl; f. 1945; faculties of graphics and painting, industrial design and interior design, textile and fashion, visual arts; library: 30,000 vols; 240 teachers; 1,500 students; Chancellor Mgr ALEKSANDRA SOWIŃSKA-BANASZKIEWICZ; Rector Prof. JOLANTA RUDZKA-HABISIAK; Pro-Rector for Science Prof. Dr Hab. MARIUSZ WŁODARCZYK; Pro-Rector for Teaching Prof. MARIUSZ ŁUKAWSKI; Librarian Mgr HANNA BORT-NOWAK.

Akademia Sztuk Pięknych w Gdańsku (Academy of Fine Arts in Gdańsk): Targ Węglowy 6, 80-836 Gdańsk; tel. (58) 3012801; e-mail rektorat@asp.gda.pl; internet www.asp.gda.pl; f. 1945; faculties of architecture and design, graphic arts, painting, sculpture, interdisciplinary institute of the arts; library: 10,450 vols; 130 teachers; 875 students; Chancellor Mgr ROBERT BERNISZ; Rector Prof. LUDMIŁA OSTROGÓRSKA; Vice-Rector for Devt and Cooperation Prof. KRZYSZTOF GLISZCZYŃSKI; Vice-Rector for Education and Student Affairs Dr Hab. JAROSŁAW SZYMAŃSKI; Head of Library MAŁGORZATA DĄBROWSKA.

Akademia Sztuk Pięknych w Warszawie (Academy of Fine Arts in Warsaw): Krakows-kie Przedmieście 5, 00-068 Warsaw; tel. (22) 3200200; e-mail rektorat@asp.waw.pl; internet www.asp.waw.pl; f. 1904; faculties of conservation and restoration of works of art, graphic arts, industrial design, interior design, painting, sculpture; library: 25,750 vols of books, 5,630 vols of periodicals; 296 teachers; 1,020 students; Rector Prof. ADAM MYJAK; Deputy Rector Prof. Dr JERZY BOGUSŁAWSKI; Deputy Rector for Education Prof. Dr Hab. WOJCIECH ZUBALA; Deputy Rector for the Arts Prof. PAWEŁ NOWAK; Library Dir Mgr IRENA KURNICKA-KĘPA; publs *Rocznik* (1 a year, in English and Russian), *Zeszyty Naukowe ASP* (Scientific Copy Books ASP).

Akademia Teatralna im. Al. Zelwerowicza w Warszawie (Aleksander Zelwerowicz National Academy of Dramatic Art in Warsaw): ul. Miodowa 22/24, 00-246 Warsaw; tel. (22) 8310216; e-mail rektorat@at.edu.pl; internet www.at.edu.pl; f. 1932; depts of acting, directing, theatre studies, puppetry; library: 39,000 vols; 110 teachers; 360 students; Chancellor BEATA SZCZUCIŃSKA; Rector Prof. ANDRZEJ STRZELECKI; Vice-Rector Prof. Dr BARBARA OSTERLOFF-GIERAK; Vice-Rector Dr TOMASZ GROCHOCZYŃSKI; Vice-Rector for Puppetry Faculty in Białystok Prof. Dr Hab. WIESŁAW CZOŁPIŃSKI.

Państwowa Wyższa Szkoła Filmowa Telewizyjna i Teatralna im. Leona Schillera w Łodzi (Polish National Film, Television and Theatre School): ul. Targowa 61/63, 90-323 Łódź; tel. (42) 6345800; e-mail rektorat@filmschool.lodz.pl; internet www.filmschool.lodz.pl; f. 1948; depts of acting, cinematography and television production, film and television directing, film production and management; library: 50,000 vols, 450 int. magazines, 5,000 video cassettes, 2,000 music CDs, 900 DVDs, 2,300 feature films, 400 documentary films, 4,000 student films; 118 teachers (96 full-time, 22 part-time); 825 students (incl. 600 extra-mural); Chancellor IGOR DUNIEWSKI; Rector Prof. MARIUSZ GRZEGORZEK; Curator of Library JAROSŁAW CZEMBROWSKI.

Państwowa Wyższa Szkoła Teatralna im. Ludwika Solskiego w Krakowie (Ludwik Solski State Drama School in Cracow): ul. Strasewskiego 21–22, 31-109 Cracow; tel. (12) 4221855; e-mail sekretariat@pwst.krakow.pl; internet www.pwst.krakow.pl; f. 1946; faculties of acting, direction, dramatic dance in Bytom, puppet theatre in Wrocław; library: 30,000 vols, 100 titles of periodicals; spec. collns: audio and video cassettes, CDs, DVDs, dissertations, MSS of plays, posters, photographs, newspaper clippings of theatre performances; Chancellor Mgr FRANCISZEK GAŁUSZKA; Rector Prof. EWA KUTRYŚ; Vice-Rector Prof. DOROTA SEGDA; Vice-Rector of Wrocław Br. Prof. Dr Hab. ELŻBIETA CZAPLIŃSKA-MROZEK; Dir for Library Mgr EWELINA PORAJ-CHLEBOWSKA.

PORTUGAL

The Higher Education System

Portugal was ruled by a monarchy from the 11th century until it was overthrown in 1910 and a republic was declared. The two oldest current universities, Universidade de Lisboa (founded 1288) and Universidade de Coimbra (founded 1290), date from the late 13th century and were the only such institutions until 1911, when Universidade do Porto was founded. Portugal was governed by a dictatorship during 1932–74, the later years of which saw the establishment of several prominent universities, but most institutions of higher education were founded after the restoration of civilian government in 1975. Higher education is divided into two strands, universities and other institutions (polytechnic institutes, higher schools, professional institutes and schools of art and music). In 2010 there were 383,627 students enrolled in tertiary-level education. In 2012 there were 15 public universities, 37 private universities, 22 public and 51 private non-university higher education institutions, five military and police higher education institutes and one concordatory university (Universidade Católica Portuguesa).

Universities became autonomous institutions under the University Autonomy Law (1988), which granted them the power to devise curricula, award degrees and define the equivalency of foreign awards. The Ministry of Education oversees state universities, polytechnics and specialized tertiary education institutions, while the Ministry of the Economy and Employment is responsible for vocational education. Portugal participates in the Bologna Process to establish a European Higher Education Area; in 2005 the European Credit Transfer System was introduced and by 2010 all institutions had become fully compliant. The Decree Law 369/2007 brought into existence the Agência de Avaliação e Acreditação do Ensino Superior (A3ES—Agency for Assessment and Accreditation of Higher Education), which began operating in 2009 and until 2011 carried out accreditation of all study cycles already in operation. In 2012 the first five-year cycles of accreditation were introduced.

Portuguese students are admitted to higher education on the basis of the Diploma de Ensino Secundário (secondary school diploma) and an entrance examination known as the Concurso nacional (for public institutions) or the Concurso local (for private institutions). Applicants over the age of 23 who do not hold the Diploma de Ensino Secundário may take a special entrance examination, the Exame Extraordinário de Avaliação de Capacidade para Acesso ao Ensino Superior. Following the passage of the Comprehensive Law on Higher Education in 2005, a two-tier degree system, comprising the Licenciado (Bachelors) and Mestre (Masters), was introduced in both universities and polytechnic institutes in accordance with the principles of the Bologna Process. The Licenciado is usually a three- or four-year programme of study, although courses in some subjects may last longer, such as medicine and dentistry (six years). Under the new system, some degrees are integrated courses of study culminating with award of the Mestre, which is otherwise a separate postgraduate degree lasting for one or two years. The Doutor (Doctorate) is the highest academic degree, and is offered only by universities. Students may spend up to five or six years in study and research. Beyond doctoral studies, students who have shown great ability as researchers and who have special teaching expertise in a certain area can take the examinations for the award of the Agregação.

The Decree Law 26/89 (1989) legislated the creation of Escolas Profissionais (professional schools) primarily aimed at upper secondary-level students. Courses are between one and three years in duration, and combine academic education and vocational training.

Regulatory and Representative Bodies

GOVERNMENT

Ministry of Education and Science: Av. 5 de Outubro 107, 1069-018 Lisbon; tel. (21) 781-18-00; e-mail gabinete.ministro@mec.gov.pt; internet www.portugal.gov.pt/pt/os-ministerios/ministerio-da-educacao-e-ciencia.aspx; Minister NUNO CRATO.

ACCREDITATION

ENIC/NARIC Portugal: NARIC Centre, Direcção-Geral do Ensino Superior, Av. Duque de Avila 137, 1069-016 Lisbon; tel. (21) 312-60-00; e-mail info.naric@dges.mctes.pt; internet www.dges.mctes.pt/dges/pt/reconhecimento/naricenic; f. 1986; establishes and carries out nat. policy on higher education; Dir-Gen. Prof. ANTONIO MORÃO DIAS; Sub-Dir-Gen. Dr CRISTINA JACINTO.

NATIONAL BODIES

Associação Portuguesa do Ensino Superior Privado (Portuguese Association of Private Higher Education Institutions): Av. da República 47, 1° dto, 1050-188 Lisbon; tel. (21) 799-48-60; e-mail contactos@apesp.pt; internet www.apesp.pt; works towards the full integration of non-state higher education in the Portuguese educational system; Pres. Prof. JOÃO DUARTE REDONDO; Vice-Pres. Prof. Dr MIGUEL FARIA.

Conselho Coordenador do Ensino Particular e Cooperativo (Coordinating Council for Private and Cooperative Education): Av. 5 de Outubro 89, 2°, 1050-050 Lisbon; tel. (21) 797-29-10; e-mail ccepc@mail.telepac.pt; f. 1980; works for the integration of private and co-operative education into the nat. educational and training system; Pres. Dr ANTÓNIO DE ALMEIDA COSTA; Dir MARIA DE CONCEIÇÃO REIS.

Conselho Coordenador dos Institutos Superiores Politécnicos (Coordinating Council for Polytechnic Institutes): Av. 5 de Outubro 89, 3°, 1050-050 Lisbon; tel. (21) 792-83-60; e-mail ccisp@ccisp.pt; internet www.ccisp.pt; f. 1979; Pres. Dr JOÃO SOBRINHO TEIXEIRA; Sec. CRISTINA ROCHA.

Conselho de Reitores das Universidades Portuguesas (Council of Rectors of the Portuguese Universities): Edifício O, Campus do Lumiar, Estrada do Paço do Lumiar, 1649-038 Lisbon; tel. (21) 360-29-50; e-mail crup@crup.pt; internet www.crup.pt; f. 1979; coordination and global representation of its mems; formulates nat. policies in education, science and culture; prepares legislation and participates in debates; contributes to the devt of education, research and culture; networking; creation, integration, modification or termination of educational public univs; 16 (incl. public mem. univs and 1 Portuguese Catholic Univ.); Pres. Prof. Dr ANTÓNIO RENDAS; Sec.-Gen. Dr JOÃO MELO BORGES.

Conselho Nacional de Educação (National Council for Education): Rua Florbela Espanca, 1700-195 Lisbon; tel. (21) 793-52-45; e-mail cnedu@cnedu.pt; internet www.cnedu.pt; f. 1982; advisory body on all aspects of the Portuguese educational system; Pres. Prof. JOSÉ DAVID JUSTINO; Sec. Gen. MANUEL MIGUÉNS; publs *Estudos e Relatórios*, *Pareceres e Recomendações*.

Direcção-Geral de Inovação e de Desenvolvimento Curricular (DGIDC) (Department for Innovation and Curricular Development): Av. 24 de Julho 140, 1399-025 Lisbon; tel. (21) 393-45-00; e-mail dgidc@dgidc.min-edu.pt; internet www.dgidc.min-edu.pt; educational research, innovation in teaching practice, curriculum devt and evaluation, spec. education, and distance learning; library of 23,000 vols, 1,500 periodicals; Pres. Dra CRISTINA PAULO; Dir-Gen. Dr LUÍS CAPUCHA; publs *Inovação* (3 a year), *Noesis* (4 a year).

Learned Societies

GENERAL

Academia das Ciências de Lisboa (Lisbon Academy of Sciences): Rua da Academia das Ciências 19, 1249-122 Lisbon; tel. (21) 321-97-30; e-mail geral@acad-ciencias.pt; internet www.acad-ciencias.pt; f. 1779; attached to Min. of Science, Technology and Higher Education; establishes ongoing, valuable contacts with other academies to promote cultural exchange, research fellowships and joint programmes to renew their ancestral tradition; weekly lectures on science and humanities topics; 189 nat. mems; library: see Libraries and Archives; Pres. Prof. ADRIANO MOREIRA; Sec.-Gen. Prof. Dr MARIA SALOMÉ PAIS; Librarian LEONOR PINTO; publs *Memórias da Classe de Ciências, Memórias da Classe de Letras*.

Sociedade Científica da Universidade Católica Portuguesa (Scientific Society of the Portuguese Catholic University): Edifício Biblioteca João Paulo II, 5º andar, Universidade Católica Portuguesa, Palma de Cima, 1649-023 Lisbon; tel. (21) 721-41-36; e-mail scientif@lisboa.ucp.pt; internet www.scucp.ucp.pt; f. 1980; attached to Universidade Católica Portuguesa; advances intellectual, artistic, moral and spiritual forms of a Christian-inspired culture as a means to the fulfilment of man, promotes research in a perspective of inter-disciplinarity aiming at a synthesis of knowledge; 15 sections: arts, biology, philosophy, law, history, economics, environmental sciences, literature and linguistics, education, theology, exact and natural sciences, applied sciences and engineering, health sciences and technology, social sciences and politics, communication and information sciences; library of 500 vols; 400 mems; Chair. Prof. MÁRIO JÚLIO BRITO DE ALMEIDA COSTA; Vice-Pres. Prof. Dr ANTÓNIO PEDRO BARBAS HOMEM; Sec. Prof. Dr MARÍLIA PEREIRA LÚCIO DOS SANTOS LOPES HANENBERG; publs *Colecção Cadernos, Lumen Veritatis*.

BIBLIOGRAPHY, LIBRARY SCIENCE AND MUSEOLOGY

Associação Portuguesa de Bibliotecários, Arquivistas e Documentalistas (Portuguese Association of Librarians, Archivists and Documentalists): Rua Morais Soares, 43C, 1° dto, 1900-341 Lisbon; tel. (21) 816-19-80; e-mail bad@bad.pt; internet www.bad.pt; f. 1973; promotes better policy and practice of information management, improved scientific, technical and cultural devt of its mems; organizes training and refresher courses; 1,000 mems; Pres. MARIA PAULA SANTOS; Vice-Pres. MARIA JOSÉ MOURA; Sec. MARIA DULCE CORREIA; Treas. BRUNO DUARTE EIRAS; publ. *Cadernos BAD* (2 a year).

ECONOMICS, LAW AND POLITICS

Ordem dos Economistas (Economists' Association): Rua da Estrela 8, 1200-669 Lisbon; tel. (21) 392-94-70; e-mail geral@ordemeconomistas.pt; internet www.ordemeconomistas.pt; f. 1976; brs in Azores, Madeira and Norte; 12,500 mems; Dir FRANCISCO MURTEIRA NABO; publs *Anuário do Economista* (1 a year), *Cadernos de Economia* (4 a year), *Carta Informativa* (4 a year).

EDUCATION

Associação das Universidades de Língua Portuguesa (Association of Universities of Portuguese Language): Av. Santos Dumont, 67, 2°, 1050-203 Lisbon; tel. (21) 781-63-60; e-mail aulp@aulp.org; internet www.aulp.org; promotes cooperation between univs and educational and research institutions by facilitating exchange of researchers and students, encouraging reflection on the role of higher education and devt of joint scientific and technological research and the widespread exchange of information; Pres. Prof. Dr CLÉLIO CAMPOLINA DINIZ; Vice-Pres. JOÃO TETA; Vice-Pres. ANTÓNIO LEÃO CORREIA E SILVA; Vice-Pres. JOÃO PINTO GUERREIRO; Vice-Pres. RUI MARTINS.

Camões—Instituto da Cooperação e da Língua, I. P. (Camões—Institute of Cooperation and Language, I. P.): Rua Rodrigues Sampaio 113, 1150-279 Lisbon; Av. da Liberdade 270, 1250-149 Lisbon; tel. (21) 310-91-00; e-mail icgeral@instituto-camoes.pt; internet www.instituto-camoes.pt; f. 1929 as Junta de Educação Nacional, present name 2012; attached to the Min. of Foreign Affairs; promotes teaching of Portuguese language and culture abroad; awards grants to foreign students in Portugal; publishes works on Portuguese language and culture; 250 mems; library of 10,000 vols; Pres. ANA PAULA LABORINHO; Vice-Pres. MÁRIO JOSÉ FILIPE DA SILVA; Vice-Pres. MARIA DINAH BANDEIRA SANTOS SILVA AZEVEDO NEVES; publ. *Camões* (irregular).

Instituto Açoriano de Cultura (Azorean Institute of Culture): Apdo 67, 9700-220 Angra do Heroísmo; Alto das Covas, 9700-220 Angra do Heroísmo; tel. (295) 21-44-42; e-mail iac@iac-azores.org; internet www.iac-azores.org; f. 1955; Pres. PAULO ALEXANDRE MARTINS RAIMUNDO; Sec. Dr FILIPA ALEXANDRA DE MOURA MAGALHÃES TAVARES; publs *Atlântida* (1 a year), *Insula* (1 a year).

FINE AND PERFORMING ARTS

Academia Nacional de Belas Artes (National Academy of Fine Arts): Largo da Academia Nacional de Belas Artes, 1200-005 Lisbon; tel. (21) 346-70-91; e-mail geral@academiabelasartes.pt; internet www.academiabelasartes.pt; f. 1932; library of 25,000 vols, incl. some 16th-century work; 20 mems; Pres. Prof. Arq. AUGUSTO PEREIRA BRANDÃO; Sec. Arq. ANTÓNIO MARQUES MIGUEL; publs *Inventário Artístico de Portugal, Revista-Boletim de Belas Artes*.

Instituto Gregoriano de Lisboa (Gregorian Institute of Lisbon): Av. 5 de Outubro 258, 1600-038 Lisbon; tel. (21) 793-37-37; e-mail secretaria@inst-gregoriano.rcts.pt; internet www.inst-gregoriano.rcts.pt; f. 1953 as Centro de Estudos Gregorianos (Gregorian Studies Centre), present name and status 1976; public school of music; courses on Gregorian chant, organ, piano, harpsichord, violin, cello and recorder; 49 mems; library of 1,361 vols, 1,641 scores, 665 CDs, c. 150 DVDs; Dir Dr MARIA LUÍSA OLIVEIRA; Deputy Dir Dr RICARDO MONTEIRO; publ. *Modus* (musicology, irregular).

Sociedade Nacional de Belas Artes (National Society of Fine Arts): Palacio das Belas Artes, Rua Barata Salgueiro 36, 1250-044 Lisbon; tel. (21) 313-85-10; e-mail geral@snba.pt; internet www.snba.pt; f. 1901; exhibitions of painting, sculpture, drawing, etc.; organizes courses in design, painting, drawing, visual education, sociology, aesthetics and history of art; 1,350 assocs; 832 mems; library of 5,200 vols; Pres. EMÍLIA NADAL; Vice-Pres. JOSÉ JOÃO BRITO; Sec. Dr CRISTINA AZEVEDO TAVARES; Treas. AMÉRICO SILVA; publ. *Boletim Informativo* (2 a year).

HISTORY, GEOGRAPHY AND ARCHAEOLOGY

Academia Portuguesa da História (Portuguese Academy of History): Palácio dos Lilases, Alameda das Linhas de Torres 198-200, 1769-024 Lisbon; tel. (21) 754-90-60; e-mail acad.port.historia@sapo.pt; internet www.academiaportuguesadahistoria.gov.pt; f. 1720; research on historical topics; providing historical information; 40 mems, 190 corresp. mems; library of 180,000 vols; Pres. Prof. Dra MANUELA MENDONÇA; Sec.-Gen. Prof. Dr MIGUEL CORRÊA MONTEIRO; publs *Anais, Boletim, Documentos Medievais Portugueses, Fontes Narrativas da História*

Portuguesa, Itinerários Régios, Subsídios para a História Portuguesa.

Associação dos Arqueólogos Portugueses (Association of Portuguese Archaeologists): Largo do Carmo 4, 1° dto, 1200-092 Lisbon; tel. (21) 346-04-73; e-mail aap@mail.pt; internet www.museusportugal.org/aap; f. 1863 as Asscn of Portuguese Civil Architects; 640 mems; library of 10,500 vols; Pres. Dr JOSÉ MORAIS ARNAUD; Vice-Pres. Dr JOÃO JOSÉ FERNANDES GOMES; Sec. Dr PAULO DE ALMEIDA FERNANDES; Treas. Dr JOSÉ BAPTISTA DOMINGOS; publ. *Arqueologia e História* (irregular).

Instituto de Gestão do Património Arquitectónico e Arqueológico (Institute for Management of Architectural and Archaeological Heritage): Palácio Nacional da Ajuda, 1349-021 Lisbon; tel. (21) 361-42-00; e-mail igespar@igespar.pt; internet www.igespar.pt; f. 2007 by merger of Portuguese Architectural Heritage Institute and Portuguese Archaeological Institute; attached to Min. of Culture; manages, safeguards, conserves and enhances those assets that, due to their historical, artistic, landscape, scientific, social and technical value, integrate Portugal's listed architectural and archaeological heritage; Dir GONÇALO COUCEIRO; Deputy Dir JOÃO PEDRO CUNHA RIBEIRO; Deputy Dir LUÍS FILIPE CAPAZ COELHO; publs *Estudos Património* (2 a year), *Portuguesa de Arqueologia*.

Instituto Geográfico Português (Portuguese Geographical Institute): Rua Artilharia Um 107, 1099-052 Lisbon; tel. (21) 381-96-00; e-mail igeo@igeo.pt; internet www.igeo.pt; f. 2002, by merger of Instituto Português de Cartografia e Cadastro and Centro Nacional de Informação Geográfica; attached to Min. of the Environment, Territorial Planning and Regional Devt; nat. cartographic authority, provides official geographical information, fosters training and research; main brs in Ponta Delgada, Beja, Faro, Castelo Branco, Santarém, Funchal and Mirandela; Gen. Dir. Lt-Gen. CARLOS MOURATO NUNES; Librarian MARIA DIAS.

Instituto Histórico da Ilha Terceira (IHIT) (Terceira Island Historical Institute): Convento de São Francisco, Ladeira de São Francisco, Angra do Heroísmo, Terceira, 9700 The Azores; tel. (29) 521-31-47; e-mail ihit@ihit.pt; internet www.ihit.pt; f. 1942, present location 1991; historical, cultural, anthropological, scientific and patrimonial studies and research; consultancy and educational activities; academic partnerships; residential instn for the UNESCO Azores Centre; 70 mems; library of 1,000 vols; Pres. Dr FRANCISCO DOS REIS MADURO-DIAS; Sec. Dr MIGUEL CORTE-REAL DA SILVEIRA MONJARDINO; Treas. Dr ANTÓNIO BENTO FRAGA BARCELOS; publ. *Boletim do Instituto Histórico da Ilha Terceira* (1 a year).

Real Instituto Arqueológico de Portugal (Royal Archaeological Institute of Portugal): Praça Rainha D. Filipa 4, 6° dto, 1600 Lisbon; tel. (21) 759-11-09; e-mail dphadb@sapo.pt; f. 1868; Pres. and Sec.-Gen. Dr JOSÉ ANTÓNIO FALCÃO; publs *Actas, Trabalhos*.

Real Sociedade Arqueológica Lusitana (Royal Lusitanian Archaeological Society): Hospital do Espírito Santo, Praça Conde do Bracial 3, 7540 Santiago do Cacém; tel. (269) 82-63-80; f. 1849; archaeological, historical and ethnological studies; has own museum, archives and library; 150 mems, 97 corresp. mems, 50 fellows; Dir Dr JOSÉ ANTÓNIO FALCÃO; Gen. Sec. Dr LÍLIA RIBEIRO DA SILVA TAVARES; publs *Memórias, Repertorium Fontium Studium Artis Historiae Portugaliae Instaurandum, Trabalhos*.

Sociedade de Geografia de Lisboa (Lisbon Geographical Society): Rua das Portas de

Santo Antão 100, 1150-269 Lisbon; tel. (21) 342-54-01; e-mail geral@socgeografialisboa .mail.pt; internet www.socgeografialisboa.pt; f. 1875; studies geography, history and ethnology of the Portuguese; organizes confs; library of 205,240 vols, 2,020 periodicals, 6,000 MSS, 155 theses/dissertations, 3 sheets printed music, 10,050 maps; 1,500 mems; Pres. Prof. LUÍS AIRES-BARROS; Sec.-Gen. Prof. Dr. JOÃO PEREIRA NETO; Sec.-Gen Prof. ANTÓNIO DIOGO PINTO; Treas. Prof. Dr. CARLOS LOPES BENTO; publs *Boletim* (scientific and literary journal, 1 a year), *Memórias* (irregular), *Relatório* (1 a year).

Sociedade Martins Sarmento (Martins Sarmento Society): Universidade do Minho, Rua Paio Galvão, 4814-509 Guimarães; tel. (253) 41-59-69; e-mail sms@msarmento.org; internet www.csarmento.uminho.pt; f. 1881; archaeology and culture; 600 mems; library of 100,000 vols; Pres. ANTÓNIO AMARO DAS NEVES; publs *Boletim* (4 a year), *Revista de Guimarães* (1 a year).

LANGUAGE AND LITERATURE

Alliance Française: Rua Pinheiro Chagas 60, Apdo 2049, 3000-333 Coimbra; tel. (239) 70-12-52; e-mail afcoimbra@gmail.com; internet www.alliancefr.pt; offers courses and exams in French language and culture and promotes cultural exchange with France; attached offices in the Algarve, Beja, Caldas da Rainha, Entroncamento, Evora, Guimarães, Leiria, Lisbon, Monção, Portalegre, Setúbal, Vila Real and Viseu; Dir of Operations ALAIN DIDIER.

Associação Portuguesa de Escritores (Portuguese Writers' Association): Rua de S. Domingos à Lapa 17, 1200-832 Lisbon; tel. (21) 397-18-99; e-mail a.p.escritores@mail .telepac.pt; f. 1973; protects the interests of Portuguese writers, promotes Portuguese literature abroad, supports cultural activities, conferences, debates, confers several literary prizes, etc.; over 600 mems; library of 7,500 vols; Pres. Dr JOSÉ MANUEL MENDES.

British Council: Rua Luís Fernandes 1–3, 1249-062 Lisbon; tel. (21) 321-45-00; e-mail lisbon.enquiries@pt.britishcouncil.org; internet www.britishcouncil.org/portugal; f. 1938; offers courses and exams in English language and British culture; promotes cultural exchange with the UK; attached teaching centres in Almada, Alverca, Cascais, Coimbra, Foz do Douro, Miraflores, Parede and Porto; Dir ROSEMARY HILHORST; publ. *In English*.

Goethe-Institut: Campo dos Mártires da Pátria 37, 1169-016 Lisbon; tel. (21) 882-45-10; e-mail info@lissabon.goethe.org; internet www.goethe.de/portugal; offers courses and exams in German language and culture and promotes cultural exchange with Germany; attached centre in Porto; library of 14,000 vols, 50 periodicals; Dir Dr JOACHIM BERNAUER.

Instituto Cervantes de Lisboa: Rua Santa Marta 43F, 1169-119 Lisbon; tel. (21) 310-50-20; e-mail cenlis@cervantes.es; internet lisboa.cervantes.es; f. 1991 as Spanish Cultural Centre, present name and status 1993; offers courses and exams in Spanish language and culture and promotes cultural exchange with Spain and Spanish-speaking Latin and Central America; library of 30,000 vols; Dir JOSÉ MARÍA MARTÍN VALENZUELA; Sec. PAULA DE SOUSA PRUDÊNCIO; Head Librarian CECILIA GÁNDARAS PÉREZ.

Sociedade Portuguesa de Autores (Portuguese Society of Authors): Av. Duque de Loulé 31, 1069-153 Lisbon; tel. (21) 359-44-00; e-mail geral@spautores.pt; internet www .spautores.pt; f. 1925 as Sociedade de Escritores e Compositores Teatrais Portugueses;

copyright protection and authors' rights; cultural activities; 21,647 mems; library of 30,000 vols; Pres.and CEO JOSÉ JORGE LETRIA; publ. *Autores* (4 a year).

MEDICINE

Ordem dos Farmacêuticos (Portuguese Pharmaceutical Society): Rua da Sociedade Farmacêutica 18, 1169-075 Lisbon; tel. (21) 319-13-80; e-mail direccao.nacional@ ordemfarmaceuticos.pt; internet www .ordemfarmaceuticos.pt; f. 1835; famous colln of Portuguese pharmacopoeias; unique MS *Historia Pharmaceutica das Plantas Exóticas* by Frei João de Jesus Maria, with permit to print from the Holy Office; 9,950 mems; library of 14,000 vols; Pres. Prof. Dr CARLOS MAURÍCIO BARBOSA; Sec. CARLOS ALBERTO LARANJEIRA HENRIQUES; Sec. MARGARIDA MENDES MARQUES GOMES CARNEIRO; publ. *Revista do Ordem dos Farmacêuticos* (6 a year).

Ordem dos Médicos (Portuguese Medical Association): Av. Almirante Gago Coutinho 151, 1749-084 Lisbon; tel. (21) 842-71-00; e-mail omcne@omcne.pt; internet www .ordemdosmedicos.pt; f. 1938; regulation of medical practice; independence of practitioners; 39,419 mems; Pres. Prof. JOSÉ MANUEL SILVA; publs *Acta Médica Portuguesa* (6 a year), *Revista* (12 a year).

Sociedade Anatómica Portuguesa (Portuguese Anatomical Society): Lab. de Anatomia Normal, Faculdade de Medicina de Coimbra, 3049 Coimbra; f. 1930; 184 mems; Pres. Prof. Dr ANTÓNIO CARLOS MIGUÉIS.

NATURAL SCIENCES
General

Serviço de Informação e Documentação (Information and Documentation Service): Av. D. Carlos I 126, 1249-074 Lisbon; tel. (21) 392-43-00; e-mail biblioteca@fe.up.pt; internet alfa.fct.mctes.pt; f. 1936; attached to Fundação para a Ciência e a Tecnologia; nat. centre of scientific and technical information; library of 3,000 Portuguese, 5,000 foreign books, 350 periodicals; Dir GABRIELA LOPES DA SILVA.

Biological Sciences

Sociedade Broteriana (Botanical Society): Instituto Botânico, Universidade de Coimbra, 3049 Coimbra; tel. (239) 82-28-97; e-mail socbrot@ci.uc.pt; f. 1880; 300 mems; library of 122,000 vols; Chair. Prof. JOSÉ F. M. MESQUITA; publs *Anuário*, *Boletim* (1 a year), *Memórias* (irregular).

Sociedade Portuguesa de Ciências Naturais (Portuguese Natural Science Society): Faculdade de Ciências, Campo Grande, 1749-016 Lisbon; tel. (21) 750-00-00; e-mail spcn@ fc.ul.pt; f. 1907; 938 mems; library of 30,000 vols; Pres. HUMBERTO ROSA; publs *Boletim*, *Natura*, *Naturalia*.

Sociedade Portuguesa de Ecologia (Portuguese Society of Ecology): Faculdade de Ciências da Univ. de Lisboa, Edif. C4, 1°, Sala 4.1.10, Campo Grande 1749-016 Lisbon; tel. (21) 750-04-39; e-mail speco@fc.ul.pt; internet speco.fc.ul.pt; f. 1995; scientific soc. for environmentalists; Pres. HELENA FREITAS; Sec. PAULA SOBRAL; publs *Cadernos de Ecologia* (1 a year), *Revista de Biologia* (1 a year), *Revista Ecologi@* (3 a year).

Mathematical Sciences

Instituto Nacional de Estatística (National Statistical Institute): Av. António José de Almeida, 1000-043 Lisbon; tel. (21) 842-61-00; e-mail ine@ine.pt; internet www .ine.pt; f. 1935; production and dissemination of official statistical information; 750 mems;

library of 12,000 vols, 2,500 periodicals; Pres. ALDA MARIA DAS NEVES CARNEIRO DE CAETANO CARVALHO; Vice-Pres. MARIA HELENA DE SOUSA CORDEIRO; Vice-Pres. PEDRO JORGE NUNES DA SILVA DIAS; publs *Statistical Review*, *Statistical Yearbook* (in English and Portuguese).

Physical Sciences

Sociedade Geológica de Portugal (Portugal Geological Society): Rua da Escola Politécnica, 58, 1269-102 Lisbon; tel. (96) 458-20-09; e-mail webmaster@socgeol.org; internet socgeol.org; f. 1940; asscn of individuals and legal entities that promotes devt of knowledge concerning the geological sciences and cooperates with other stakeholders; 500 mems; library of 1,200 vols; Pres. ROGÉRIO BORDALO DA ROCHA; Vice-Pres. FILOMENA DINIZ; Sec. JOSÉ CARLOS KULLBERG; Sec. JOSÉ MANUEL ROMÃO; Treas. RUI TABORDA; publ. *Boletim da Sociedade Geológica de Portugal*.

Sociedade Portuguesa de Química (Portuguese Chemical Society): Av. da República 45–3, 1050-187 Lisbon; tel. (21) 793-46-37; e-mail sede@spq.pt; internet www.spq.pt; f. 1911; holds Chemistry Olympics; brs in Aveiro, Braga, Oporto, Vila Real, Coimbra, Faro, Covilhã and Braga Meetings; confs and symposiums; 2,000 mems; Pres. MÁRIO NUNO DE MATOS SEQUEIRA BERBERAN E SANTOS; Vice-Pres. MARIA JOSÉ DIOGO DA SILVA CALHORDA; Gen. Sec. JOAQUIM LUÍS BERNARDES MARTINS DE FARIA; Treas. MARIA MANUEL MARTINHO SEQUEIRA BARATA MARQUES; publ. *Química* (4 a year).

RELIGION, SOCIOLOGY AND ANTHROPOLOGY

Academia Internacional da Cultura Portuguesa (International Academy of Portuguese Culture): Rua das Portas de Santo Antão 100, 1150-269 Lisbon; tel. (21) 342-10-81; e-mail aicportuguesa@clix.pt; f. 1965; attached to Min. of Culture; seeks to promote research into the culture of Portuguese communities living outside the nat. territory; 50 mems; Pres. Dr CARLOS MONJARDINO; Vice-Pres. Prof. Dr JUSTINO MENDES DE ALMEIDA; Vice-Pres. Prof. OSCAR BARATA; publ. *Boletim*.

Sociedade Portuguesa de Antropologia e Etnologia (Portuguese Anthropological and Ethnological Society): Faculdade de Ciências do Porto, Praça Gomes Teixeira, 4099-002 Porto; tel. (22) 208-71-49; e-mail vojsoj@sapo.pt; internet spae.no.sapo.pt; stimulates and develops the main anthropological research in its different areas and creates an interdisciplinary perspective; f. 1918; 100 mems; library of 10,000 vols; Pres. Prof. VÍTOR OLIVEIRA JORGE; Sec. PAULO CASTRO SEIXAS; publ. *Trabalhos de Antropologia e Etnologia* (2 a year).

TECHNOLOGY

Ordem dos Engenheiros (Portuguese Association of Engineers): Av. António Augusto de Aguiar 3D, 1069-030 Lisbon; tel. (21) 313-26-00; e-mail secretariageral@ ordemdosengenheiros.pt; internet www .ordemengenheiros.pt; f. 1936; holds seminars, conf. etc. on topics useful to engineers; 28,000 mems; library of 23,000 vols, 500 periodical titles; Pres. Eng. CARLOS ALBERTO MATIAS RAMOS; Vice-Pres. JOSÉ MANUEL PEREIRA VIEIRA; Vice-Pres. VICTOR MANUEL GONÇALVES DE BRITO; publ. *Ingenium* (review, 12 a year).

Research Institutes

GENERAL

Centro de Estudos do Território, Cultura e Desenvolvimento (Territory, Culture and Development Research Centre): Universidade Lusófona de Humanidades e Tecnologias, Av. do Campo Grande 376, 1749-024 Lisbon; tel. (21) 751-55-00; e-mail zoran.roca@ulusofona.pt; internet tercud .ulusofona.pt; f. 2008, fmrly Applied Social Sciences Research Unit; attached to Faculty of Architecture, Urban Planning, Geography and Arts, Univ. Lusófona de Humanidades e Tecnologias; planning, management and evaluation of territorial devt in urban and rural settings; valorization of natural and cultural heritage and other components of territorial identities as devt recourses; Dir Dr ZORAN ROCA; publs *Arquitectura e Educação* (online), *Cadernos de Sociomuseologia* (online), *Malha Urbana* (online).

Centro de Estudos Transdisciplinares para o Desenvolvimento (CETRAD) (Transdisciplinary Studies Centre for Development): Av. Almeida Lucena 1, 5000-660 Vila Real; tel. (25) 930-22-00; e-mail cetrad@ utad.pt; internet www.cetrad.info; f. 2002; attached to Univ. of Trás-os-Montes and Alto Douro; research incl. globalization and state policies; innovation, markets and orgs; society, territory and resources; Dir CHRISTOPHER GERRY; Deputy Dir FRANCISCO DINIZ; Deputy Dir ALBERTO BAPTISTA.

CERAP—Centre d'Étude et de Recherche Appliquée en Psychopédagogie Perceptive (Centre for Applied Research and Study in Perceptual Psychoeducation): Praça 9 de Abril 349, 4249-004 Porto; e-mail info@ cerap.org; internet www.cerap.org; f. 2004; attached to Univ. Fernando Pessoa; studies the particular relationship individuals have to the 'sensible' experience of the body and the place of the 'sensible' body in educational, formative and existential learning processes; Dir Prof. Dr DANIS BOIS; publ. *Réciprocités* (2 a year).

Fundação para a Ciência e a Tecnologia (Science and Technology Foundation): Av. D. Carlos I 126, 1249-074 Lisbon; tel. (21) 392-43-00; e-mail presidencia@fct.mctes.pt; internet www.fct.mctes.pt; f. 1997, fmrly Nat. Board of Scientific and Technological Research; attached to Min. of Science, Technology and Higher Education; evaluates, finances and promotes institutions, programmes and projects in the fields of science and technology; also concerned with the education and qualifications in human resources; library of 15,500 vols; Pres. Prof. JOÃO JOSÉ DOS SANTOS SENTIEIRO.

Instituto de Altos Estudos (Institute for Advanced Studies): c/o Academia das Ciências de Lisboa, Rua Academia das Ciências 19, 1249-122 Lisbon; tel. (21) 321-97-30; e-mail geral@acad-ciencias.pt; internet www.acad-ciencias.pt; f. 1931; attached to Lisbon Acad. of Sciences; Pres. Prof. ADRIANO MOREIRA.

Instituto de Investigação Científica Tropical (Tropical Science Research Institute): Rua da Junqueira 86–1, 1300-344 Lisbon; tel. (21) 361-63-40; e-mail iict@iict .pt; internet www2.iict.pt; f. 1883; develops scientific research in tropical areas of humanities and natural sciences; enhances scientific and technical capacity of countries with which it cooperates; promotes preservation of heritage; Pres. Prof. Dr JORGE BRAGA DE MACEDO; Vice-Pres. Dr ANTÓNIO JOSÉ LOPES DE MELO; Sec. JOÃO NOGUEIRA; publs *Boletim da Filmoteca Ultramarina Portuguesa*, *Comunicações do IICT* (series: Agrarian Sciences; Biological Sciences;

Ethnological and Ethnomuseological Sciences; Geographical Sciences; Earth Sciences), *Estudos de Antropologia Cultural e Social*, *Estudos de Ciências Políticas e Sociais*, *Estudos de História e Cartografia Antiga—Memórias*, *Estudos e Ensaios e Documentos*, *Index Seminum*, *Leba* (quaternary, prehistory, archaeology), *Memórias*, *Revista Internacional de Estudos Africanos*, *Separatas do Centro de Estudos de História e Cartografia Antiga*, *Studia*.

Research Centres:

Centro de Ambiente e Ciências da Terra do Instituto de Investigação Científica Tropical (Environment and Earth Sciences Centre): Aleja D. Afonso Henriques 41, 4° dto, 1000-123 Lisbon; tel. (21) 847-64-05; e-mail cgeol@iict.pt; internet www.iict.pt.

Centro de Antropobiologia do Instituto de Investigação Científica Tropical (Anthropobiology Centre): Av. Óscar Monteiro Torres 34, 1° esq, 1000-219 Lisbon; tel. (21) 796-66-70; e-mail cantp@ iict.pt; internet www.iict.pt; f. 1954; Dir (vacant).

Centro de Antropologia Cultural e Social do Instituto de Investigação Científica Tropical (Cultural and Social Anthropology Centre): Av. Ilha da Madeira, Edifício Museu, 1400-203 Lisbon; tel. (21) 301-52-64; e-mail cacst@iict.pt; internet www.iict.pt; f. 1962; Dir Dra CLARA SARAIVA.

Centro de Botânica do Instituto de Investigação Científica Tropical (Botany Centre): Travessa Conde da Ribeira 9, 1300-142 Lisbon; tel. (21) 361-63-40; e-mail cbotn@iict.pt; internet www.iict.pt; f. 1948; Dir Dra MARIA ADÉLIA DINIZ.

Centro de Cartografia do Instituto de Investigação Científica Tropical (Cartography Centre): Travessa Conde da Ribeira 7–9, 1300-007 Lisbon; tel. (21) 361-63-40; e-mail ccart@iict.pt; internet www.iict.pt; f. 1946; Dir Prof. Eng. ARMANDO SEPÚLVEDA.

Centro de Cristalografia e Mineralogia do Instituto de Investigação Científica Tropical (Crystallography and Mineralogy Centre): Alameda D. Afonso Henriques 41, 4° esq, 1000-123 Lisbon; tel. (21) 847-65-96; e-mail ccris@iict.pt; internet www.iict.pt; f. 1957; Dir Prof. Dra MARIA ONDINA FIGUEIREDO.

Centro de Desenvolvimento Global do Instituto de Investigação Científica Tropical (Global Development Centre): Rua João de Barros 27, 1300-319 Lisbon; tel. (21) 364-27-32; e-mail des@iict.pt; internet www.iict.pt.

Centro de Detecção Remota para o Desenvolvimento do Instituto de Investigação Científica Tropical (Remote Sensing for Development Centre): Travessa Conde da Ribeira 9, 1300-142 Lisbon; tel. (21) 361-63-40; e-mail ccart@ iict.pt; internet www.iict.pt.

Centro de Ecofisiologia, Bioquímica e Biotecnologia Vegetal do Instituto de Investigação Científica Tropical (Ecophysiology, Biochemistry and Vegetal Biotechnology Centre): Av. da República, Quinta do Marquês, 2784-505 Oeiras; tel. (21) 454-46-82; e-mail eco-bio@iict.pt; internet www.iict.pt; Dir. ANTÓNIO EDUARDO BAPTISTA LEITÃO.

Centro de Estudos Africanos e Asiáticos do Instituto de Investigação Científica Tropical (African and Asian Studies Centre): Rua da Junqueira 30, 1°, 1349-007 Lisbon; tel. (21) 362-26-21; e-mail

cestaa@iict.pt; internet www.iict.pt; f. 1983; Dir Prof. Dra JILL REANEY DIAS.

Centro de Estudos de Fitossanidade do Armazenamento do Instituto de Investigação Científica Tropical (Research Centre on Plant Health during Storage): Travessa Conde da Ribeira 9, 1300-142 Lisbon; tel. (21) 361-63-40; e-mail cefa@iict.pt; internet www.iict.pt; f. 1955; Dir Prof. Dr ANTÓNIO MARQUES MEXIA.

Centro de Estudos de História e Cartografia Antiga do Instituto de Investigação Científica Tropical (History and Early Cartography Research Centre): Rua da Junqueira 30, r/c, 1349-007 Lisbon; tel. (21) 360-05-82; e-mail cesth@iict.pt; internet www.iict.pt; f. 1961; history of Portuguese expansion overseas, African history; library of 9,200 vols, 430 periodicals; Dir Dra MARIA EMÍLIA MADEIRA SANTOS; publs *Boletim da Filmoteca Ultramarina Portuguesa* (irregular), *Studia* (2 a year).

Centro de Estudos de Pedologia do Instituto de Investigação Científica Tropical (Pedology Studies Centre): Tapada da Ajuda, 1349-018 Lisbon; tel. (21) 365-31-00; e-mail cestp@iict.pt; internet www.iict.pt; f. 1960; Dir Prof. Eng. RUI PINTO RICARDO.

Centro de Estudos de Produção e Tecnologia Agrícolas do Instituto de Investigação Científica Tropical (Agricultural Technology and Production Studies Centre): Tapada da Ajuda, Edifício das Agro-Indústria e Agronomia Tropical, 1349-018 Lisbon; tel. (21) 361-72-40; e-mail cestt@iict.pt; internet www.iict.pt; f. 1960; Dir (vacant).

Centro de Etnologia Ultramarina do Instituto de Investigação Científica Tropical (Overseas Ethnology Centre): Av. Ilha da Madeira, 1400-203 Lisbon; tel. (21) 301-21-18; e-mail cetno@iict.pt; internet www.iict.pt; f. 1962; Dir Dra MARGARIDA LIMA DE FARIA.

Centro de Fotogrametria do Instituto de Investigação Científica Tropical (Photogrammetry Centre): Rua João de Barros 27, 1300-319 Lisbon; tel. (21) 364-27-32; e-mail cfotg@iict.pt; internet www .iict.pt; f. 1983; Dir Prof. Dr ARMANDO SEPÚLVEDA.

Centro de Geodesia do Instituto de Investigação Científica Tropical (Geodesy Centre): Rua da Junqueira 534, 1300-341 Lisbon; tel. (21) 363-18-62; e-mail cgeod@iict.pt; internet www.iict.pt; f. 1983; Dir Eng. JOSÉ FRIAS DE BARROS.

Centro de Geografia do Instituto de Investigação Científica Tropical (Geography Centre): Rua Ricardo Espírito Santo 7, c/v esq, 1200-790 Lisbon; tel. (21) 395-67-72; e-mail cgeog@iict.pt; internet www.iict.pt; f. 1983; Dir Prof. Dr ILÍDIO DO AMARAL.

Centro de Geologia do Instituto de Investigação Científica Tropical (Geology Centre): Alameda D. Afonso Henriques 41, 4° dto, 1000-123 Lisbon; tel. (21) 847-64-05; e-mail cgeol@iict.pt; internet www .iict.pt; f. 1958; Dir Prof. Dr RICARDO AUGUSTO QUADRADO.

Centro de Investigação das Ferrugens do Cafeeiro do Instituto de Investigação Científica Tropical (Coffee Rusts Research Centre): Quinta do Marquês, 2784-505 Oeiras; tel. (21) 454-46-80; e-mail cferc@iict.pt; internet www.iict.pt; f. 1955; Dir MARIA DO CÉU M. L. SILVA.

Centro de Pré-História e Arqueologia do Instituto de Investigação Científica Tropical (Prehistory and Archaeology

Centre): Travessa Conde da Ribeira 7, 1300-142 Lisbon; tel. (21) 361-63-40; e-mail cphst@iict.pt; internet www.iict.pt; f. 1954; Dir Prof. Dr A. TEODORO DE MATOS.

Centro de Sociedades e Culturas Tropicais do Instituto de Investigação Científica Tropical (Societies and Tropical Cultures Centre): Rua da Junqueira 30, 1°, 1349-007 Lisbon; tel. (21) 360-05-81; e-mail cestaa@iict.pt; internet www.iict.pt.

Centro de Sócio-Economia do Instituto de Investigação Científica Tropical (Socio-Economics Centre): Travessa Conde da Ponte 9, 1°, 1300-141 Lisbon; tel. (21) 363-57-48; e-mail csoec@iict.pt; internet www.iict.pt; f. 1956; Dir Prof. Dr JORGE BRAGA DE MACEDO.

Centro de Veterinária e Zootecnia do Instituto de Investigação Científica Tropical (Veterinary and Zootechnics Centre): Rua João de Barros 27, 1300-319 Lisbon; tel. (21) 364-27-29; e-mail dcn@iict.pt; internet www.iict.pt; f. 1983; Dir Dr LUÍS ALFARO CARDOSO.

Centro de Zoologia do Instituto de Investigação Científica Tropical (Zoology Centre): Rua da Junqueira 14, 1300-343 Lisbon; tel. (21) 363-70-55; e-mail czool@iict.pt; internet www.iict.pt; f. 1948; Dir Dr LUÍS F. MENDES.

Grupo de Florestas e Produtos Florestais do Instituto de Investigação Científica Tropical (Forestry and Forest Products Group-IICT): Tapada da Ajuda, 1349-017 Lisbon; tel. (21) 365-33-74; e-mail jose.rodrigues@iict.pt; internet www2.iict.pt/index.php?idc=98; f. 1948; Dir JOSÉ RODRIGUES.

Instituto de Orientação Profissional da Faculdade de Psicologia da Universidade de Lisboa (Career Guidance and Counselling Institute): Alameda da Universidade, 1649-013 Lisbon; tel. (21) 346-33-57; e-mail geral@iop.ul.pt; internet www.iop.ul.pt; f. 1925, present status 2012; career guidance and counseling intervention, research on career issues; devt of career tools and techniques; nat. and int. scientific exchange; training for practitioners; psychological evaluation and selection procedures; Dir Prof. Dr MARIA EDUARDA DUARTE.

AGRICULTURE, FISHERIES AND VETERINARY SCIENCE

Centro de Ciência Animal e Veterinária (CECAV) (Centre for Animal and Veterinary Sciences (CECAV)): Univ. of Tras-os-Montes and Alto Douro, Apdo 1013, 5001-801 Vila Real; tel. (25) 935-04-08; e-mail arnaldos@utad.pt; internet www.cecav.utad.pt; f. 2002; attached to Univ. of Trás-os-Montes and Alto Douro; fundamental and applied research in veterinary and animal science; disseminates knowledge in animal health and production with emphasis on increasing efficiency and sustainability of livestock production and safety of products of animal origin without compromising on the surrounding environment and economic conditions; main research areas incl. animal production, animal physiology and pathology and quality and food safety of animal products; Dir ARNALDO DIAS DA SILVA; Vice-Dir CRISTINA GUEDES; Vice-Dir JOSÉ MANUEL ALMEIDA.

Centro de Investigação e de Tecnologias Agro-Ambientais e Biológicas (Centre for the Research and Technology of Agro-Environmental and Biological Sciences): Univ. of Trás-os-Montes and Alto Douro, Quinta de Prados, Apdo 1013, 5001-801 Vila Real; tel. (23) 935-04-75; e-mail citab@utad.pt; internet www.citab.utad.pt; f. 2007 by merger of 3 instns; attached to Univ. of Trás-os-

Montes and Alto Douro; ecointegrity, integrative biology and quality and biosystems engineering; research focuses on devt and upgrading of agriculture and forestry production chains; Dir EDUARDO AUGUSTO DOS SANTOS ROSA; Vice-Dir PEDRO JOSÉ DE MELO TEIXEIRA PINTO; Vice-Dir RUI MANUEL VÍTOR CORTES.

Estação Agronómica Nacional (National Agronomical Research Station): Av. República, Quinta do Marquês, Nova Oeiras, 2784-505 Oeiras; tel. (21) 440-35-00; e-mail dir.ean@iniap.min-agricultura.pt; f. 1937; comprises depts of agronomy, entomology, experimental statistics, genetics and plant breeding, pedology, phytopathology, plant physiology, microbiology, systematic botany and plant sociology; library of 172,000 vols; Dir Dr MARIA CRISTINA LOPES; Librarian ROSÁRIO SÁ; publs *Agronomia Lusitana*, *Index Seminum*.

Instituto Nacional de Recursos Biológicos IP (National Institute of Biological Resources IP): Rua Barata Salgueiro 37–4°, 1250-042 Lisbon; tel. (21) 313-17-41; e-mail presidencia@inrb.pt; internet www.inrb.pt; f. 2006; attached to Min. of Agriculture, Rural Devt and Fisheries; supports research of public policies for the valuation of biological resources in the defence of nat. interests and in the continuation and deepening of EU common policies; Pres. Dr MARIA ROSA TOBIAS SÁ.

Unidade de Silvicultura e Produtos Florestais (Forestry Research Unit of INRB): Quinta do Marquês, 2780-159 Oeiras; tel. (21) 446-37-00; e-mail uispf.inia@inrb.pt; f. 1979; forestry research unit of the Instituto Nacional de Recursos Biológicos; 4 research depts; library of 3,500 vols; Dir Dr EDMUNDO SOUSA; publ. *Silva Lusitana*.

ECONOMICS, LAW AND POLITICS

Centro de Estudos Sociais da Faculdade de Economia da Universidade de Coimbra (Centre for Social Studies): Colégio de São Jerónimo, Apdo 3087, 3001-401 Coimbra; tel. (23) 985-55-70; e-mail ces@ces.uc.pt; internet www.ces.uc.pt; f. 1978, present status 2002; attached to School of Economics, Univ. of Coimbra; research and advanced training in social sciences and humanities; library of 13,000 vols, 800 periodicals; Dir Prof. Dr BOAVENTURA SOUSA SANTOS; Pres. PEDRO HESPANHA; Vice-Pres. SILVIA PORTUGAL; Sec.-Gen. LASSALETE PAIVA; publ. *Revista Crítica de Ciências Sociais* (4 a year).

Centro de Investigação do Instituto de Estudos Políticos (Research Centre of the Institute for Political Studies): Univ. Católica Portuguesa, Palma de Cima, 1649-023 Lisbon; tel. (21) 721-41-29; e-mail ciep@iep.lisboa.ucp.pt; internet www.iep.lisboa.ucp.pt; f. 2001; attached to Institute for Political Studies, Univ. Católica Portuguesa; supports scientific research in various brs of science policy, incl. int. relations, comparative politics, public policy, history of political thought and political theory; Scientific Dir Prof. Dr JOÃO CARLOS ESPADA; Scientific Coordinator Dr LÍVIA FRANCO.

EDUCATION

ILG—Instituto Leopoldo Guimarães (Leopoldo Guimarães Institute): Rua Fernando Miguel Cabanas, 2950-616 Palmela; e-mail geral@institutolg.com; internet www.institutolg.com; f. 2008; attached to Univ. Fernando Pessoa; promotes lifelong learning in Portugal, cooperating with such instns for higher education, with public and enterprise dedicated to scientific research; provides teacher training and Masters programmes; Dir Prof. LEOPOLDO GUIMARÃES.

Kie—Associação Conhecimento, Inovação e Educaçã (Kie—Association of Knowledge, Innovation and Education): Edif. Panoramic (Parque das Nações), Av. do Atlântico 1.19.02 A, Escritório 6.05, 1990-096 Lisbon; tel. (21) 894-33-05; e-mail terezaventura@ufp.edu.pt; internet www.kie.pt; f. 2009; attached to Univ. Fernando Pessoa; promotes research and training in continuing education and lifelong learning; provides Masters programmes; Pres. MARIA TEREZA ROMANO VENTURA; Chair. MARIA DE FÁTIMA PAIVA S. COELHO; Treas. HÉLIO JOÃO DA SILVA COELHO.

HISTORY, GEOGRAPHY AND ARCHAEOLOGY

Centro de Estudos do Baixo Alentejo (Centre for Lower Alentejo Studies): c/o Real Sociedade Arqueológica Lusitana, Hospital do Espírito Santo, Praça Conde do Bracial 3, 7540 Santiago do Cacém; tel. (269) 82-63-80; f. 1944; Dir The Pres. of the Royal Lusitanian Archaeological Soc. (*q.v.*); Sec.-Gen. The Gen.-Sec. of the Royal Lusitanian Archaeological Soc. (*q.v.*).

Centro de Estudos Geográficos da Universidade de Lisboa (Centre of Geographical Studies of the University of Lisbon): IGOT - Edif., Faculdade de Letras, Alameda da Universidade, 1600-214 Lisbon; tel. (21) 794-02-18; e-mail ceg@campus.ul.pt; internet www.ceg.ul.pt; f. 1943; funded by the Fundação para a Ciência e a Tecnologia (*q.v.*), the European Commission and other nat. and int. orgs; research into human and regional geography, geoecology, physical and environmental geography and fluvial, coastal dynamics; supports teaching activities; library of 35,000 vols; Pres. CARLOS ALBERTO MEDEIROS; Scientific Dir Prof. Dr DIOGO JOSÉ BROCHADO DE ABREU; Sec. LUÍS MANUEL COSTA MORENO; publ. *Finisterra* (2 a year).

Centro de Estudos Históricos e Etnológicos (Centre for Historical and Ethnological Studies): Serra do Balas, Areias, 2240 Ferreira do Zêzere; tel. (249) 39-14-08; e-mail ferreira.jmr@gmail.com; f. 1983; Pres. Dr JORGE M. RODRIGUES FERREIRA; Sec. Dr ANABELA BENTO; publ. *Série Arqueológica*.

Centro de Geologia da Universidade do Porto (Geology Centre of the University of Porto): Dept de Geologia da FCUP, Rua do Campo Alegre 687, 4169-007 Porto; tel. (22) 040-24-72; e-mail fmnoronh@fc.up.pt; internet www.cguporto.org; f. 1978; attached to Univ. of Porto; devt of research in earth sciences; Coordinator Prof. FERNANDO NORONHA.

Centro de Investigação em Ciência e Engenharia Geológica (Centre for Research in Science and Engineering Geology): Dept de Ciências da Terra, Faculdade de Ciências e Tecnologia, Quinta da Torre 2829-516 Caparica; tel. (21) 294-85-73; e-mail dct.secretariado@fct.unl.pt; internet www.cicege.fct.unl.pt; f. by merger of Centre for Geological Studies (CEG) and the Research Centre for Applied Geoscience (CIGA); attached to Univ. Nova de Lisboa; research in areas of sedimentary geology, stratigraphy, palaeontology, geological mapping, ornamental rocks, applied geology and engineering geology; publ. *Ciências da Terra*.

Centro de Investigação Marinha e Ambiental (Centre for Marine and Environmental Research): Univ. do Algarve, Faculdade de Ciências e Tecnologia, Edif. 7, Campus de Gambelas, 8005-139 Faro; tel. (28) 980-09-00; e-mail cima@ualg.pt; internet cima.ualg.pt; research areas incl. large-scale geological processes and their local record, marine morphosedimentary processes and impact of environmental changes; Gen. Coordinator TOMASZ BOSKI.

Centro de Petrologia e Geoquímica (Centre for Petrology and Geochemistry): Av. Rovisco Pais 1049-001 Lisbon; tel. (21) 840-08-06; e-mail jose.marques@ist.utl.pt; internet cepgist.ist.utl.pt; research, teaching and consulting in hydrogeology, groundwater quality, isotope hydrology, monument stone decay and conservation, environmental geochemistry, applied mineralogy and petrology; Scientific Coordinator JOSÉ MANUEL MARQUES.

Centro de Vulcanologia e Avaliação de Riscos Geológicos (Centre for Volcanology and Geological Risk Assessment): c/o Univ. dos Açores, Edif. do Complexo Científico, 3° Piso, Ala Sul, 9501-801 Ponta Delgada; tel. (29) 665-01-47; e-mail patricia.ij.raposo@ azores.gov.pt; internet www.cvarg.azores.gov .pt; f. 1997; attached to Univ. of Azores; supports research of devt of earth sciences and prediction of disasters, natural calamities; focuses on technical and scientific cooperation nationally and internationally in the field of volcanology and associated phenomena, incl. volcanic eruptions, earthquakes, explosions of steam, toxic gas release, mass movements and tsunamis; mem. of the World Org. of Volcano Observatories (WONO); Dir MARIA GABRIELA PEREIRA DA SILVA.

Evolução Litosférica e Meio Ambiente Superficial: Departamento de Geociências, Universidade de Aveiro, Campus de Santiago, 3810-193 Aveiro; tel. (23) 437-03-57; e-mail sec@geo.ua.pt; internet www.ua.pt/ geo; f. 1998; attached to Geosciences Dept, Univ. of Aveiro; interdisciplinary studies in fundamental and applied aspects of geology and biology; Dir JORGE MEDINA.

'Infante D. Luis' Geophysical Institute: Rua da Escola Politécnica 58, 1250-102 Lisbon; tel. (21) 392-18-63; e-mail presidente.igidl@fc.ul.pt; internet www.igidl .ul.pt; f. 1853; attached to Univ. of Lisbon; geophysics, seismology, meteorology, climatology, solar radiation; maintains Portugal's oldest meteorological series; library of 4,000 vols, 1,075 journals; Pres. JORGE MIGUEL DE MIRANDA; Sec. ANABELA MARTINS.

Instituto Geofísico (Geophysical Institute): Av. Dr Dias da Silva, 3000-134 Coimbra; tel. (23) 979-34-20; e-mail iguc@ci.uc.pt; internet www1.ci.uc.pt/iguc; f. 1864; attached to Univ. of Coimbra; meteorological, magnetic and seismological observatory; library of 16,000 vols; Dir Prof. Dr ANTÓNIO FERREIRA SOARES; publs *Magnéticas e Sismológicas* (1 a year), *Observações Meteorológicas*.

LANGUAGE AND LITERATURE

Centro de Estudos em Letras (Centre for Studies in Letters): Universidade de Trás-os-Montes e Alto Douro Vila Real; tel. (25) 935-07-48; e-mail cel@utad.pt; internet utad.pt/ vpt/area2/investigar/cel/paginas/cel.aspx; f. 2003; research in languages and linguistics, literature and cultural studies; Dir Prof. Dr CARLOS DA COSTA ASSUNÇÃO; Sec. Prof. Dr GONÇALO FENANDES; publ. *Revista de Letras* (www.utad.pt/vPT/Area2/investigar/CEL/ Research/RevistadeLetras/Paginas/revistadeletras.aspx).

Instituto de Estudos Clássicos (Classical Studies Institute): Faculdade de Letras, Universidade de Coimbra, 3004-530 Coimbra; tel. (23) 985-99-81; e-mail classic@ci.uc .pt; internet www.uc.pt/fluc/eclassicos/iec; f. 1944; attached to Faculty of Arts, Univ. of Coimbra; teaching, research, promotion of classics in Portugal; library of 15,000 vols, 500 periodicals; Dir Dr JOSÉ LUIS LOPES

BRANDÃO; Sec. Dr LUÍSA DE NAZARÉ FERREIRA; Sec. Dr SUSANA MARQUES PEREIRA.

Instituto de Lexicologia e Lexicografia da Língua Portuguesa (Institute of Lexicology and Lexicography of the Portuguese Language): c/o Academia das Ciências de Lisboa, Rua da Academia das Ciências 19, 1249-122 Lisbon; tel. (21) 321-97-30; e-mail geral@acad-ciencias.pt; internet www .acad-ciencias.pt; f. 1987; attached to Lisbon Acad. of Sciences; Pres. Prof. Dr ARTUR ANSELMO; Sec. Dr SÉRGIO LOURENÇO.

Instituto Português da Sociedade Científica de Goerres (Portuguese Institute of the Goerres Research Society): Universidade Católica Portuguesa, Reitoria, Palma de Cima, 1649-023 Lisbon; tel. (21) 721-40-00; e-mail mrato@reitoria.ucp.pt; internet www .ucp.pt; f. 1962; research on history, legal history, language and Portuguese literature; also known as Institute Vieira; Office Sec. Dr MARIA EUGÉNIA RATO; library of 9,000 vols; publ. *Portugiesische Forschungen*.

MEDICINE

Association for Innovation and Biomedical Research on Light and Image: Azinhaga Sta. Comba, Celas, 3000-548 Coimbra; tel. (23) 948-01-00; e-mail aibili@aibili .pt; internet www.aibili.pt; f. 1989, present location 1994; develops new products for health imaging, pharmaceutical and biotechnology cos; CEO CECÍLIA MARTINHO; Pres. JOSÉ CUNHA-VAZ.

'Câmara Pestana' Bacteriological Institute: Rua do Instituto Bacteriológico, 1169-110 Lisbon; tel. (21) 882-32-90; e-mail reitoria@reitoria.ul.pt; internet www.ul.pt; f. 1892, present status 1911; attached to Univ. of Lisbon; areas of research incl. several domains of public health, namely diphtheria, streptococci, clinical microbiology and analysis of biology products; nat. lab for antituberculosis vaccine; responsible for Portugal's anti-rabies programme; Dir Prof. JOSÉ MELO CRISTINO.

Centro de Estudos de Vectores e Doenças Infecciosas Doutor Francisco Cambournac (Dr Francisco Cambournac Centre for the Study of Vectors and Infectious Diseases): c/o Instituto Nacional de Saúde Dr Ricardo Jorge, Av. da Liberdade 5, 2965-575 Águas de Moura; tel. (26) 593-82-90; e-mail cevdi@insa.min-saude.pt; internet www.insa.pt; f. 1938 as the Malaria Institute, present name since 1987; attached to Nat. Institute of Health Dr Ricardo Jorge; research and diagnostic activities on vectors and vector-borne diseases incl. hantavirus, arbovirus, phlebovirus, arenavirus, borrelia, francisella, rickettsia, ehrlichia, anaplasma, coxiella and bartonella; vector studies incl. the determination of species present in Portugal and surveillance to prevent or minimize risk of introduction of new species; library of 3,400 vols; Dir Dr MARIA SOFIA NUNCIO.

Centro de Investigação em Desporto, Saúde e Desenvolvimento Humano (Research Centre in Sports, Health and Human Development Science): CIFOP— Sports Dept, Rua Doutor Manuel Cardona, 5000-558 Vila Real; tel. (25) 933-01-05; e-mail cidesd.geral@utad.pt; internet cidesd .org; f. 2007 by merger of 6 research units from the Polytechnic Institute of Bragança; attached to Univ. of Trás-os-Montes and Alto Douro; cross-institutional technical and scientifically multi-disciplinary unity of applied and fundamental research; 3 main domains of sports performance, health, professional and pedagogical intervention; Dir Dr ANTÓNIO JOSÉ SILVA.

Centro de Neurociências e Biologia Celular (Centre for Neuroscience and Cell Biology): Dept of Zoology, Univ. of Coimbra, 3004-51 Coimbra; tel. (23) 985-57-60; e-mail info@cnc.uc.pt; internet www.cnbc.pt; attached to Univ. of Coimbra; translates basic knowledge into clinical applications to improve diagnostics and develop novel therapeutical approaches; Pres CATARINA RESENDE DE OLIVEIRA; Vice-Pres. EUCLIDES PIRES; Vice-Pres. CARLOS FARO; Vice-Pres. LEONOR ALMEIDA.

Instituto de Biologia Molecular e Celular (Institute of Molecular and Cell Biology): Rua do Campo Alegre 823, 4150-180 Porto; tel. (22) 607-49-00; e-mail info@ibmc.up.pt; internet www.ibmc.up.pt; f. 2000; attached to Univ. of Porto; research focuses on genetic diseases, infectious diseases and immunology, neuroscience, stress and structural biology; Dir Prof. CLAUDIO SUNKEL; Vice-Dir Prof. MARIA JOÃO SARAIVA; Vice-Dir Dr MÓNICA SOUSA.

Instituto de Ciências Biomédicas de Abel Salazar (Abel Salazar Biomedical Sciences Institute): Largo Prof. Abel Salazar, 2, 4099-003 Porto; tel. (22) 206-22-00; e-mail conped@icbas.up.pt; internet www.icbas.up .pt; f. 1975; attached to Univ. of Porto; fundamental and applied research in health and life sciences; Dir ANTÓNIO SOUSA PEREIRA.

Instituto de Medicina Molecular (Institute of Molecular Medicine): Faculdade de Medicina da Univ. de Lisboa, Av. Prof. Egas Moniz, 1649-028 Lisbon; tel. (21) 799-94-11; e-mail imm@fm.ul.pt; internet www.imm.ul .pt; f. 2001; attached to Min. of Science, Technology and Higher Education; research into cell and devt biology, immunology and infectious diseases, neurosciences and oncology; Pres. J. LOBO ANTUNES; Sec. PATRÍCIA DA CUNHA.

Instituto de Patalogia e Imunologia da Universidade do Porto (Institute of Molecular Pathology and Immunology of the University of Porto): Rua Dr Roberto Frias s/n, 4200-465 Porto; tel. (22) 557-07-00; e-mail ipatimup@ipatimup.pt; internet www .ipatimup.pt; f. 1989; attached to Univ. of Porto; associated laboratory of Min. of Science, Technology and Higher Education; research focuses on causes and evolution of human oncologic diseases; Dir MANUEL SOBRINHO SIMÕES.

Instituto Gulbenkian de Ciência (Gulbenkian Science Institute): Apdo 14, 2781-901 Oeiras; Rua da Quinta Grande, 6, 2780-156 Oeiras; tel. (21) 440-79-00; e-mail info@ igc.gulbenkian.pt; internet www.igc .gulbenkian.pt; attached to Fundação Calouste Gulbenkian; biomedical research and education in areas of genetic basis of devt and evolution of complex systems; privileged organism-centred approaches in experimental models that incl. plants, yeast, flies and mice, and on the genetics of complex human diseases; library of 16,868 vols; Chair. for Scientific Advisory Board SYDNEY BRENNER; Dir ANTONIO COUTINHO; Deputy Dir JOSÉ MÁRIO LEITE.

Instituto Nacional de Medicina Legal (National Institute of Legal Medicine): Largo da Sé Nova, 3000-213 Coimbra; tel. (23) 985-42-20; e-mail correio@inml.mj.pt; internet www.inml.mj.pt; f. 1919; attached to Faculty of Medicine, Univ. of Coimbra; nat. instn of reference in forensic science; library of 5,000 vols, 45 periodicals; Dir Prof. Dr DUARTE NUNO PESSOA VIEIRA.

Instituto Nacional de Saúde Dr Ricardo Jorge (National Institute of Health Dr Ricardo Jorge): Av. Padre Cruz, 1649-016 Lisbon; tel. (21) 751-92-00; e-mail info@insa

.min-saude.pt; internet www.insa.pt; f. 1899 as Central Institute of Hygiene, present status 1971; attached to Min. of Health; research and technological devt; epidemiological and health services research; external quality assurance for laboratories; diffusion of scientific culture; fostering capacities, knowledge and skills and by providing specialized services, incl. prevention of genetic diseases; nat. reference laboratory and nat. health observatory; Pres. JOSÉ PEREIRA MIGUEL.

Observatório de Medicina Integrativa—Centro de Estudos Avançados em Ciências da Saúde (Centre for Integrative Medicine—Centre for Advanced Studies in Health Sciences): Rua Joaquim Bonifácio, 21–2 Andar, 1150-195 Lisbon; tel. (21) 315-11-43; e-mail cidalia.paradelo@omi.pt; internet www.omi.pt; attached to Univ. Fernando Pessoa; promotes creation and devt of an integrative medicine combining conventional and unconventional medicines through practical work and research of multidisciplinary teams; provides advanced modules, Masters courses in alternative forms of medicine; Pres. Prof. ANGELO LUCAS.

NATURAL SCIENCES

General

Centro de Matemática (CM) (Centre for Mathematics): e-mail egs@utad.pt; internet www.utad.pt/pt/investigacao/c_matematica/index.html; attached to Univ. of Trás-os-Montes and Alto Douro; Dir Prof. Dr EMILIA JOAQUINA GIRALDES SOARES.

Centro de Química—Vila Real (CQVR) (Chemistry Centre—Vila Real): Univ. of Trás-os-Montes and Alto Douro, Chemistry Dept, Edif. de Geociências, 2 stage, 5001-801 Vila Real; tel. (25) 935-02-27; e-mail ptavares@utad.pt; internet home.utad.pt/~cqvr; f. 2001; attached to Univ. of Trás-os-Montes and Alto Douro; develops fundamental and applied chemistry research in areas of organic chemistry, natural products and food chemistry, materials chemistry, environmental chemistry; Dir PEDRO MANUEL DE MELO BANDEIRA TAVARES; Vice-Dir JOSÉ ALCIDES SILVESTRE PERES; Vice-Dir MARIA CRISTINA FIALHO OLIVEIRA.

Centro de Recursos Naturais e Ambiente (Centre for Natural Resources and the Environment): Instituto Superior Técnico, Av. Rovisco Pais 1049-001 Lisbon; tel. (21) 841-74-25; e-mail juliar@ist.utl.pt; internet cerena.ist.utl.pt; f. 2006; attached to Instituto Superior Técnico; multi-disciplinary research and advanced activities in natural resources and environment for modelling and management of natural resources, the benefit of raw materials and solid residues, geoengineering, geotechnics, biomonitoring, environmental modelling and environmental remediation; Pres. AMÍLCAR SOARES.

Institution of Marine Research: 'Centro Interdisciplinar de Coimbra', c/o Dept of Zoology, Univ. of Coimbra, 3000 Coimbra; tel. (23) 983-63-86; e-mail imar@ci.uc.pt; internet www.imar.pt; f. 1991; contributes to the scientific basis of policy support; establishes and promotes key areas of scientific research on a multiyear scale; empowers the Portuguese marine sciences community, making it competitive on a European and int. level; Pres. R. SERRÃO SANTOS; Vice-Pres. Prof. J. C. MARQUES; Vice-Pres. Prof. MANUEL GRAÇA; Vice-Pres. Prof. O. FERREIRA.

Instituto Botânico 'Dr Júlio Henriques' (Botanical Institute): Arcos do Jardim, 3049 Coimbra; tel. (239) 82-28-97; f. 1775; attached to Univ. of Coimbra; botanical garden, study in botany; library of 114,000 vols;

Dir Prof. Dr J. FIRMINO MOREIRA MESQUITA; publs *Boletim*, *Index Seminum*, *Memórias* and *Anuário* of Sociedade Broteriana.

Instituto da Conservação da Natureza e da Biodiversidade (Institute for Nature Conservation and Biodiversity): Rua de Santa Marta 55, 1169-230 Lisbon; tel. (21) 350-79-00; e-mail icnb@icnb.pt; internet www.icnb.pt; f. 1993 as Instituto da Conservação da Natureza (ICN); attached to Min. of Environment and Territorial Planning; sustainable management of wild animal and plant species; designation of land and marine protected areas; integrates the objectives of nature conservation and sustainable use of natural resources into planning policies and sectoral policies; implements nat. strategy for nature conservation and biodiversity and develops nat. programme for nature conservation; warrants compliance with both EU and int. law in matters related to nature conservation and biodiversity; Pres. TITO ROSA; Vice-Pres. FÁTIMA FERNANDES; Vice-Pres. CARLOS FIGUEIREDO.

Instituto de Investigação Científica 'Bento da Rocha Cabral' (Institute of Scientific Research): Calçada Bento Rocha Cabral 14, 1257-047 Lisbon; tel. (21) 388-29-93; e-mail geral@ircabral.org; internet www.ircabral.org; f. 1922; biochemical research, histology and embryology, bacteriology, physiology, history and philosophy of science; Dir MANUEL DIAMANTINO PIRES BICHO; publs *Relatórios*, *Travaux de Laboratoire*.

Sociedade Afonso Chaves (Afonso Chaves Society): Edifício do Museu Carlos Machado, Rua de Santo André, Apdo 258, Ponta Delgada Codex, 9500-903 The Azores; tel. (296) 28-38-14; f. 1932; ethnography, natural history, geophysics and geology of the Azores; Pres. ANTÓNIO MANUEL DE FRIAS MARTINS; Sec. Dr CARLOS MEDEIROS; publ. *Açoreana* (1 a year).

Biological Sciences

Centro de Genómica e Biotecnologia (CGB) (Centre for Genomics and Biotechnology): e-mail reitoria@utad.pt; attached to Univ. of Tras-os-Montes and Alto Douro; Dir Prof. Dr HENRIQUE GUEDES PINTO.

Instituto de Investigação das Pescas e do Mar (INRB) (Institute of Fisheries and Maritime Research): Av. de Brasília, 1449-006 Lisbon; tel. (21) 302-70-00; e-mail ipimar@ipimar.pt; internet inrb.pt/ipimar; f. 1978; attached to Min. of Agriculture, Rural Devt and Fisheries; marine biology, fisheries, aquaculture, marine environment, aquatic products technology; library of 11,000 monographs, 2,000 periodicals; Dir LEONOR NUNES; publs *IPIMAR Divulgação*, *Notícias IPIMAR*, *Publicações Avulsas*, *Relatórios Científicos e Técnicos*.

Jardim Botânico (Botanical Gardens): Jardim Botânico da Universidade de Lisboa, Rua da Escola Politécnica 58, 1250-102 Lisbon; tel. (21) 392-18-00; e-mail jbactividades@museus.ul.pt; internet www.jb.ul.pt; f. 1878; attached to Univ. of Lisbon; taxonomy and systematics, biomonitoring, biodiversity and conservation; library of 18,000 vols; Dir Prof. Dr MARIA AMÉLIA LOUÇÃO; publs *Delectus Sporarum et Seminum* (1 a year), *Portugaliae Acta Biologica* (irregular), *Revista de Biologia* (irregular).

Physical Sciences

Instituto de Plasmas e Fusão Nuclear (Institute for Plasma and Nuclear Fusion): Av. Rovisco Pais, 1049-001 Lisbon; tel. (21) 841-76-96; e-mail ipfn@ipfn.ist.utl.pt; internet www.ipfn.ist.utl.pt; f. 2008, by merger of Centro de Fusão Nuclear (CFN) and

Centro de Física de Plasmas (CFP); attached to Instituto Superior Técnico; carries out research projects and supports formation actions and scientific divulgation in its thematic areas; Pres. CARLOS VARANDAS.

Instituto de Meteorologia (Institute of Meteorology): Rua C do Aeroporto, 1749-077 Lisbon; tel. (21) 844-70-00; e-mail informacoes@meteo.pt; internet www.meteo.pt; f. 1946; provides information to the population, socio-economic activities and public entities adjusted to their needs pursuing nat. politics in meteorology, climate and geophysics; library of 34,000 vols; Pres. ADÉRITO VICENTE SERRÃO; publs *Açores* (1 a year), *Anuário Climatológico de Portugal*, *Anuário Sismológico de Portugal* (1 a year), *Boletim Climatológico Mensal dos Açores* (12 a year), *Boletim Meteorológico para a Agricultura* (36 a year), *Boletim Sismológico Preliminar do Continente e Madeira* (12 a year), *Projecto 12 do PIDDAC* (12 a year), *Resumos Meteorológicos para a Aeronáutica* (12 a year), *Revista do Instituto Nacional de Meteorologia e Geofísica* (4 a year).

Observatório Astronómico da Universidade de Coimbra (Coimbra Univ. Astronomical Observatory): Santa Clara, 3040-004 Coimbra; tel. (239) 80-23-70; e-mail obsastuc@mat.uc.pt; internet www.mat.uc.pt/~obsv; f. 1772, present location 1951; library of 3,500 vols; education and research in astronomy and geophysics; Dir Asst Prof. JOÃO FERNANDES; publs *Anais do Observatorio Astronomico da Universidade de Coimbra* (12 a year), *Efemérides Astronómicas* (1 a year), *Publicações* (60' and 70').

Observatório Astronómico de Lisboa (Lisbon Astronomical Observatory): Tapada da Ajuda, 1349-018 Lisbon; tel. (21) 361-67-30; e-mail info@oal.ul.pt; internet www.oal.ul.pt; f. 1861; part of the Faculty of Sciences, Univ. of Lisbon, since 1995; the country's official timekeeper; carries out scientific research through its attached site; provides astronomical information to the public and civil soc.; promotes teaching of astronomy in schools; library of 13,500 vols; Dir Prof. RUI JORGE AGOSTINHO; Deputy Dir Prof. PAUL CRAWFORD; publs *Dados Astronómicos* (1 a year), *O Observatório* (12 a year).

Attached Site:

Centro de Astronomia e Astrofísica da Universidade de Lisboa (Astronomy and Astrophysics Centre of the University of Lisbon): Tapada da Ajuda, Edifício Leste, 2°, 1349-018 Lisbon; tel. (21) 361-67-39; e-mail caaul@oal.ul.pt; internet caaul.oal.ul.pt; f. 2000; research into extragalactic and galactic astrophysics, the Sun, planetary and space sciences, cosmology and gravitational physics; Dir Dr JOSE AFONSO.

RELIGION, SOCIOLOGY AND ANTHROPOLOGY

Centro de Investigação em Antropologia e Saude (Research Centre for Anthropology and Health): Departamento de Ciências da Vida, Univ. de Coimbra, Apdo 3046, 3001-401 Coimbra; tel. (239) 85-41-00; e-mail cia@ci.uc.pt; internet www.uc.pt/cia; f. 1994; study of human health, disease and well-being in past and living populations from a biocultural perspective; operates through 3 sections: populations and cultures of the past; gene, population and disease; human biology, health and society; library of 44,790 vols, 330 periodicals; Coordinator Prof. Dra CRISTINA PADEZ; publ. *Antropologia Portuguesa*.

Comissão Nacional de Arte Sacra e do Património Cultural da Igreja (National Committee for Sacred Art and the Cultural Heritage of the Church): Santuário de

Fátima, Apdo 31, 2496 Fátima; tel. (249) 53-33-47; f. 1989; Pres. ANTÓNIO FRANCISCO MARQUES; Gen. Sec. Dr JOSÉ ANTÓNIO FALCÃO.

Instituto de Ciências Sociais (Institute of Social Sciences): Av. Prof. Aníbal de Bettencourt 9, 1600-189 Lisbon; tel. (21) 780-47-00; e-mail instituto.ciencias.sociais@ics.ul.pt; internet www.ics.ul.pt; f. 1962, present status 2002, present building 2003; attached to Univ. of Lisbon; studies contemporary socs with spec. emphasis on Portugal and socs and cultures with which Portugal has an historical relationship, either in Europe or in other regions of the world; library of 40,000 vols, 313 periodicals; Dir Prof. JORGE VALA.

Instituto Português de Artes e Tradições Populares (Portuguese Institute of Folk Arts and Traditions): Travessa do Passadiço 1, 7540 Santiago do Cacém; tel. (269) 82-63-80; f. 1979; Dir Prof. Dr PERE FERRÉ; Gen. Sec. Dr JOSÉ ANTÓNIO FALCÃO; publs *Biblioteca de Artes e Tradições Populares*, *Novos Inquéritos*.

TECHNOLOGY

Centro Aquicola do Rio Ave (Inland Fisheries Station): 4481 Vila do Conde; tel. (252) 63-12-41; f. 1886; fresh water fisheries and aquaculture; 15 staff; library of 1,000 vols; Dir EUARDO LENCASTRE.

Instituto Hidrográfico (Hydrographic Institute): Rua das Trinas 49, 1249-093 Lisbon; tel. (21) 094-30-00; e-mail mail@hidrografico.pt; internet www.hidrografico.pt; f. 1960; hydrographic surveys, physical oceanography, magnetic compass adjustments, laboratory; library of 12,000 vols; Dir-Gen. Vice-Admiral AGOSTINHO RAMOS DA SILVA; publs *Anais*, *Hidrográfico* (1 a year), *Hidromar*.

Laboratório Nacional de Energia e Geologia (LNEG) (National Laboratory for Energy and Geology): Estrada do Paço do Lumiar 22, 1649-038 Lisbon; tel. (21) 092-46-00; e-mail info@lneg.pt; internet www.lneg.pt; f. 1977; attached to Min. of the Economy, Innovation and Devt; research and devt in technological innovation for application in the fields of energy, new systems, processes and products, environmental management and sustainability, geological resources and hazards, public health and safety, defence and space, laboratory support and testing; library of 38,000 vols; Pres. MARIA TERESA COSTA PEREIRA DA SILVA PONCE DE LEÃO..

Attached Centres:

Campus de Coimbra (Coimbra Branch): Rua Coronel Júlio Veiga Simão-Loreto, 3020 Coimbra; tel. (239) 82-37-97; e-mail info@lneg.pt; internet www.lneg.pt.

Centro de Dados Geológico-Mineiro Alfragide (Geological and Mining Data Centre, Alfragide): Estrada da Portela, Zambujal-Alfragide, Apdo 7586, 2611-901 Amadora; tel. (21) 092-46-00; e-mail atendimento@ineti.pt; internet www.ineti.pt/campus/campus_frameset.aspx.

Centro de Estudos Geológicos e Mineiros de Bcja (Geological and Mining Studies Centre, Beja): Rua Frei Amador Arrais 39, r/c, Apdo 104, 7801-902 Beja; tel. (28) 431-13-10; e-mail inetibeja@ineti.pt; internet e-geo.ineti.pt/centros/centro_beja.htm; f. 1944.

Laboratório de S. Mamede de Infesta: Rua da Amieira, Apdo 1089, 4466-901 S. Mamede de Infesta; tel. (22) 040-00-00; e-mail atendimento@ineti.pt; internet www.ineti.pt; f. 1953; Dir MÁRIO RUI MACHADO LEITE.

Museu Geológico de Portugal (Geological Museum of Portugal): see under Museums and Art Galleries.

Laboratório Nacional de Engenharia Civil (National Civil Engineering Laboratory): Av. Brasil 101, 1700-066 Lisbon; tel. (21) 844-30-00; e-mail lnec@lnec.pt; internet www.lnec.pt; f. 1946; attached to Min. of Public Works, Transport and Communications; pursues public policies, which are under the responsibility of the various mins; provides expert support to public authorities in various public admin. sectors, particularly with regard to quality and safety of works, protection and re-qualification of natural and built patrimony, as well as technological upgrading and innovation in bldg construction sector; library of 142,000 vols; Pres. CARLOS ALBERTO DE BRITO PINA; publs *Especificações* (standards, regulations), *Memórias* (technical papers).

Libraries and Archives

Agualva-Cacém

Biblioteca Municipal de Agualva-Cacém (Agualva-Cacém Municipal Library): Praceta das Descobertas 20A, 2735-095 Caçem; tel. (21) 432-80-39; f. 1997; 11,452 vols, 21 periodicals.

Amadora

Bibliotecas Municipais da Amadora (Amadora Municipal Libraries): Rua Capitão Plácido de Abreu, Venteira, 2700 Amadora; tel. (21) 494-80-40; e-mail biblioteca.amadora@clix.pt; internet www.cm-amadora.pt/bibliotecas; f. 1960.

Angra do Heroísmo

Biblioteca Pública e Arquivo Regional de Angra do Heroísmo (Public Library and Archives of Angra do Heroísmo): Palácio Bettencourt, Rua da Rosa 49, 9700-171 Angra do Heroísmo, The Azores; tel. (295) 40-10-00; e-mail bpar.angra.info@azores.gov.pt; internet www.bparah.azores.gov.pt/html/bparah-biblioteca+documental+e+publica.html; f. 1956; 250,000 vols, 3.5m. MSS; Dir Dr MARCOLINO CANDEIAS COELHO LOPES; publ. *Arquivo Distrital de Angra do Heroísmo*.

Braga

Arquivo Distrital de Braga (Braga District Archives): Universidade do Minho, Largo do Paço, 4704-553 Braga; tel. (253) 60-11-77; e-mail sec@adb.uminho.pt; internet www.adb.uminho.pt; f. 1917, present status 1976; attached to Universidade do Minho; 4,500 linear m of documents since 9th century; Dir Dr ANTÓNIO ARMANDO FERREIRA DA SILVA E SOUSA.

Biblioteca Pública de Braga (Braga Public Library): Largo do Paço, 4704-553 Braga; tel. (253) 60-11-35; e-mail bpb@bpb.uminho.pt; internet www.bpb.uminho.pt; f. 1841; attached to Universidade do Minho; 500,000 vols, 27,000 periodicals, 53 incunabula; Dir Dr ELÍSIO SILVA MAIA ARAÚJO.

Bragança

Arquivo Distrital de Bragança (Bragança District Archives): Rua Miguel Torga, 5300-037 Bragança; tel. (273) 30-02-70; e-mail mail@adbgc.dgarq.gov.pt; internet adbgc.dgarq.gov.pt; f. 1916; 2,072 linear m of documents; Dir Dr ALDA BERENGUEL.

Cascais

Biblioteca 'Condes de Castro Guimarães': Av. Rei Humberto II de Itália, Parque Marechal Carmona, 2750-327 Cascais; tel. (21) 481-53-26; f. 1930; 25,000 vols; history,

art, philosophy, literature, archaeology, local history; Librarian ANTÓNIO MANUEL GONÇALVES DE CARVALHO; publ. *Arquivo de Cascais—Boletim Cultural do Município* (1 a year).

Coimbra

Arquivo da Universidade de Coimbra (Archives of Coimbra University): Univ. de Coimbra, Rua de S. Pedro 2, 3000-370 Coimbra; tel. (23) 985-98-55; e-mail auc-geral@auc.uc.pt; internet www.uc.pt/auc; f. 1901; Dir Prof. Dr JOSÉ PEDRO MATOS PAIVA; Deputy Dir JÚLIO DE SOUSA RAMOS.

Biblioteca Geral Universidade de Coimbra (General Library University of Coimbra): Largo da Porta Férrea, 3000-447 Coimbra; tel. (23) 985-98-15; e-mail secretaria@bg.uc.pt; internet www.uc.pt/bguc; f. 1291; 800,000 vols, 27,300 periodicals; 7 faculty br. libraries; Dir Prof. Dr CARLOS MANUEL BAPTISTA FIOLHAIS; Deputy Dir ANTÓNIO EUGÉNIO MAIA DO AMARAL; publs *Acta Univ. Conimbrigensis*, *Boletim da Biblioteca Geral da Universidade de Coimbra* (1 a year), *Divulgação Bibliográfica*, *Revista da Universidade de Coimbra* (1 a year), *Sumários das Publicações Periódicas Portuguesas* (10 a year).

Attached Library:

Biblioteca Joanina: Largo da Porta Férrea, 3000-447 Coimbra; tel. (23) 985-98-41; e-mail joanina@bg.uc.pt; internet bibliotecajoanina.uc.pt; f. 1728; 55,953 vols; Dir Prof. Dr JOSÉ AUGUSTO BERNARDES.

Biblioteca Municipal de Coimbra (Coimbra Public Library): Rua Pedro Monteiro, 3000-329 Coimbra; tel. (23) 970-26-30; e-mail biblioteca@cm-coimbra.pt; internet www.cm-coimbra.pt/biblioteca; f. 1922; network of 10 small annexe libraries and a mobile library; 626,314 vols, 3,084 video cassettes and DVDs, 8,798 audio cassettes and CDs, 30,000 journals, 973 books in braille, 1,471 audiobooks; Chief Librarian MARIA-JOSÉ MIRANDA; publ. *Arquivo Coimbrão: boletim da Biblioteca Municipal de Coimbra* (irregular).

Évora

Biblioteca Pública de Évora (Évora Public Library): Largo Conde de Vila Flor, 7000-804 Évora; tel. (26) 676-93-30; e-mail bpevora@bpe.pt; f. 1805; 800,000 vols; Dir ZÉLIA PARREIRA.

Funchal

Arquivo Regional da Madeira (Madeira Regional Archives): Caminho dos Álamos 35, Santo António, 9020-064 Funchal; tel. (29) 170-84-00; e-mail arm@arquivo-madeira.org; internet www.arquivo-madeira.org; f. 1931, present name 1980, present bldg 2005; 8,500 vols on specialized history, 300,000 MSS; memories of admin. of the islands of Madeira and Porto Santo from dawn of their settlement to rise of process of autonomy in 20th century; Dir MARIA FÁTIMA ARAÚJO DE BARROS FERREIRA; publ. *Arquivo Histórico da Madeira*.

Biblioteca Municipal do Funchal (Municipal Library): Palácio de São Pedro, Rua da Mouraria 31, 9000-047 Funchal; tel. (291) 22-28-49; e-mail bmfunchal@gmail.com; f. 1838; 150,000 vols; Librarian RICARDO ARAUJO.

Biblioteca Pública Regional da Madeira (Madeira Regional Public Library): Caminho dos Álamos 35, Santo António, 9020-064 Funchal; tel. (291) 70-84-10; e-mail bpr.drac.srt@gov-madeira.pt; internet www.bprmadeira.org; f. 1979 as Library of Contemporary Documentation, current name adopted 2003, present status 2007; legal deposit library; 200,000 vols; Dir MARIA DA PAZ DE AZEREDO PAIS.

Guimarães

Biblioteca Municipal Raul Brandão (Municipal Library): Largo Cónego José Maria Gomes, 4800-419 Guimarães; tel. (253) 51-57-10; e-mail biblioteca@cm-guimaraes.pt; internet www.bmrb.pt; f. 1992; 70,000 monographs, 6,600 audiovisual documents, about 1,000 electronic documents, 510 periodicals and a local fund with approx. 21,500 vols and postcards, posters, maps, etc.; incl. local studies library.

Horta

Biblioteca Pública e Arquivo Regional João José da Graça—Horta (Public Library and Regional Archive of Horta): Rua Walter Bensaúde 14, 9900-142 Horta, Faial, The Azores; tel. (292) 20-25-50; e-mail bpar.horta.info@azores.gov.pt; internet www .azores.gov.pt/portal/pt/entidades/pgra-drcultura-bpah; f. 1886, present location 2008; 80,000 vols; Librarian LUÍS SÃO BENTO.

Leiria

Arquivo Distrital de Leiria (Leiria District Archive): Rua Marcos Portugal 4, 2400-179 Leiria; tel. (244) 82-00-50; e-mail mail@adlra.dglab.gov.pt; internet adlra.dglab.gov .pt; f. 1916, present bldg 1997; promotes cultural and educational dissemination; 30,000 books, 496 microfilms; Dir PAULA CÂNDIDO.

Lisbon

Arquivo Histórico Militar (Military Historical Archives): Largo dos Caminhos de Ferro 2, 1100-105 Lisbon; tel. (21) 884-25-63; f. 1921; Dir Tenente-Coronel ANICETO AFONSO; publs *Boletim, Noticias* (2 a year).

Arquivo Histórico Parlamentar (Parliamentary Historical Archives): Assembleia da República, Palácio de S. Bento, 1249-068 Lisbon; tel. (21) 391-94-75; e-mail ahp .correio@ar.parlamento.pt; internet www .parlamento.pt; parliamentary activity, history, law, economics, statistics and texts from int. orgs; 180,000 vols; Dir MANUELA MAGALHÃES.

Arquivo Municipal de Lisboa (Municipal Archives of Lisbon): Rua B, Bairro da Liberdade, lote 3A 6,0°, 1070-017 Lisbon; internet arquivomunicipal.cm-lisboa.pt; f. 12th century; publ. *Cadernos.*

Constituent Centres:

Arquivo do Arco do Cego: Rua Nunes Claro 8A, 1000-209 Lisbon; tel. (21) 841-11-70; e-mail arqmun.acego@cm-lisboa.pt; f. 1919; documents since 1834.

Arquivo Fotográfico: Rua da Palma 246, 1100-394 Lisbon; tel. (21) 884-40-60; e-mail arqmun.fotografico@cm-lisboa.pt; f. 1942; images since end of 19th century.

Arquivo Histórico: Rua B, Bairro da Liberdade, lote 3 a 6, piso 1, 1070-017 Lisbon; tel. (21) 380-71-00; e-mail dba .dga@cm-lisboa.pt; f. 1931; documents since 12th century.

Arquivo Intermédio: Rua B, Bairro da Liberdade, lote 3 a 6, piso 0, 1070-017 Lisbon; tel. (21) 380-71-00; e-mail arqmun .intermedio@cm-lisboa.pt; f. 1985; city admin. documents.

Biblioteca Central de Marinha (Naval Library): Praça do Império, 1400-206 Lisbon; tel. (21) 365-85-20; e-mail biblioteca .marinha@marinha.pt; internet www .marinha.pt/pt/amarinha/actividade/areacultural/biblioteca; f. 1835; valuable edns; 126,616 vols; Dir Alm. RUI VILAS BOAS TAVARES.

Biblioteca da Academia das Ciências de Lisboa (Library of the Academy of Sciences): Rua da Academia das Ciências 19, 1249-122 Lisbon; tel. (21) 321-97-30; e-mail biblioteca@acad-ciencias.pt; internet www.acad-ciencias .pt; f. 1779; Portuguese language and culture; 1,000,000 vols, 3,000 MSS, 100 incunabula; Dir Prof. Dr JUSTINO MENDES DE ALMEIDA; Librarian LEONOR PINTO.

Biblioteca da Assembleia da República (Library of the Assembly of the Republic): Palácio de S. Bento, 1249-068 Lisbon; tel. (21) 391-41-41; e-mail bib@ar.parlamento.pt; internet sisgerar.parlamento.pt/sitebib/site/homepage.htm; f. 1836, present name 1974; 200,000 vols; spec. collns: nat. legislation and old books from the libraries of religious orders; offers its services to mems of parliament, admin., parliamentary bodies and officials, and staff of parliamentary groups; also open to gen. public; Dir JOSÉ LUÍS M. TOMÉ.

Biblioteca de Ajuda (Ajuda Library): Palácio Nacional da Ajuda, 1349-021 Lisbon; tel. (21) 363-85-92; e-mail bib_ajuda@bnportugal .pt; f. 1756, present location 1880; 100,000 vols, 30,000 MSS, 5,000 music MSS, 213 incunabula; Dir Dr CRISTINA PINTO BASTO.

Biblioteca de Arte da Fundação Calouste Gulbenkian (Art Library of Calouste Gulbenkian Foundation): Av. de Berna 45A, 1067-001 Lisbon; tel. (21) 782-35-98; e-mail artlib@gulbenkian.pt; internet www.biblarte.gulbenkian.pt; f. 1968; reference library for research in the fields of fine arts and architecture; 353,200 vols specializing in art, monographs, periodicals, architectural drawings, photographs; Dir ANA PAULA GORDO.

Biblioteca do Exército (Army Library): Largo do Outeirinho da Amendoeira, 1100-386 Lisbon; tel. (21) 884-24-56; e-mail bibex .director@mail.exercito.pt; internet www .exercito.pt; f. 1884; 100,000 vols; Dir Col FRANCISCO DIAS COSTA.

Biblioteca e Arquivo Histórico do Ministério das Obras Públicas, Transportes e Comunicações (Library and Historical Archive of the Ministry of Public Works, Transport and Communications): Rua Vale de Pereiro 4, 1250-271 Lisbon; tel. (21) 319-42-00; e-mail biblioteca@sg.moptc.pt; internet www.bahop.moptc.pt; f. 1852; collects, treats and conserves cases completed and printed books and MSS belonging to the min.; 13,000 vols, documents since 16th century, 200,000 textual documents on industry, agriculture, forestry, trade, public works, etc., 1,100 periodicals; Dir Dra PAULA CRISTINA UCHA.

Biblioteca Francisco Pereira de Moura (Higher Institute of Economics and Management Library): Instituto Superior de Economia e Gestão, Rua do Quelhas 6, 1200-781 Lisbon; tel. (21) 392-28-88; e-mail biblio@iseg .utl.pt; internet www.iseg.utl.pt/biblioteca; f. 1911 as Higher Institute of Commerce; attached to Universidade Técnica de Lisboa; European documentation centre of Universidade Técnica de Lisboa and depository library of World Bank; Scientific Dir Prof. Dr JOSÉ PEREIRINHA.

Biblioteca Municipal Central (Central Municipal Library): Palácio Galveias, Largo do Campo Pequeno, 1049-046 Lisbon; tel. (21) 780-30-20; e-mail bib.galveias@cm-lisboa.pt; internet blx.cm-lisboa.pt; f. 1931; 332,673 vols; Dir Dra MANUELA RÊGO.

Biblioteca Nacional de Portugal (National Library of Portugal): Campo Grande 83, 1749-081 Lisbon; tel. (21) 798-20-00; e-mail bn@bnportugal.pt; internet www.bnportugal.pt; f. 1796; 3,000,000 vols, 50,000 newspapers and periodicals, 36,000 MSS; collects, processes and preserves nation's bibliographic heritage and makes it available to intellectual and scientific community; uses latest technologies to conduct online bibliographic research from anywhere in the world; Dir Dr JORGE COUTO; publ. *Leituras* (2 a year).

DGARQ—Direcção-Geral de Arquivos (Directorate General for the Portuguese Archives): Alameda da Universidade, Campo Grande, 1649-010 Lisbon; tel. (21) 781-15-00; e-mail secretariado@dgarq.gov.pt; internet www.dgarq.gov.pt; f. 2007; attached to Min. of Culture; colln dates from 9th century; Nat. Archives network, processing and preservation of conventional and digital records; Dir SILVESTRE LACERDA; publ. *DGARQ Boletim* (news and information, 4 a year).

Serviço de Biblioteca e Documentação Diplomática (Library and Diplomatic Documentation Service): Ministério dos Negócios Estrangeiros, Palácio das Necessidades Largo do Rilvas, 1399-030 Lisbon; tel. (21) 394-63-05; internet www.mne.gov.pt/mne/pt/ministerio/id/biblioteca; f. 1994, present status 2007; attached to Min. of Foreign Affairs; 80,000 vols; Dir MARIA HELENA LOPES DE NEVES PINTO.

Mafra

Biblioteca do Palácio Nacional de Mafra (Mafra National Palace Library): Terreiro de D. João V, 2640-492 Mafra; tel. (261) 81-75-50; e-mail pnmafra@ippar.pt; f. 18th century; 40,000 vols; notable colln of rare books, esp. incunabula and books from the 17th–18th centuries; Dir MARIA MARGARIDA MONTENEGRO.

Ponta Delgada

Biblioteca Pública e Arquivo Regional de Ponta Delgada (Ponta Delgada Public Library and Regional Archive): Largo do Colégio, 9500-054 Ponta Delgada, São Miguel, The Azores; tel. (29) 628-20-85; e-mail bpar.pdelgada.info@azores.gov.pt; internet www.bparpd.azores.gov.pt/index .html; f. 1841; 120,000 vols in spec. collns, 40,000 monographs, 5,000 serials, 3,000 m of archive material; Dir CARLOS GUILHERME RILEY.

Porto

Arquivo Distrital do Porto (District Archives): Rua das Taipas 90, 4050-598 Porto; tel. (22) 339-51-70; e-mail info@adporto.org; internet www.adporto.pt; f. 1931, present location 1995; attached to Min. of Culture; 200,000 vols; Dir MARIA JOÃO PIRES DE LIMA; publ. *Boletim do Arquivo Distrital do Porto.*

Arquivo Histórico Municipal do Porto (Municipal Historical Archives): Rua da Alfândega 10, 4050-029 Porto; tel. (22) 206-04-00; e-mail dmah@cm-porto.pt; internet www.cm-porto.pt; f. 1980; 5,000 vols; colln incl. numerous series handwritten scrolls, illuminated MSS, drawings, photographs, etc.; Head of Section MARIA HELENA DE PAIVA GIL BRAGA.

Biblioteca Pública Municipal do Porto (Municipal Library): Rua D. João IV (ao Jardim de São Lázaro), 4049-017 Porto; tel. (22) 519-34-80; e-mail bpmp@cm-porto.pt; internet www.cm-porto.pt; f. 1833, present location 1842; 1,390,000 vols, 9,411 MSS, 246 incunabula; Dir CARLA FONSECA; publ. *Biblioteca Portucalensis* (1 a year).

Santarém

Biblioteca Municipal de Santarém (Municipal Library of Santarém): Rua Braamcamp Freire, 2000-094 Santarém; tel. (24) 333-02-40; e-mail biblioteca@cm-santarem.pt; internet www.cm-santarem .pt/cultura/biblioteca/paginas/default.aspx; f.

1880; 100,000 vols; Librarian Dr LUISA COTRIM.

Setúbal

Arquivo Distrital de Setúbal (District Archives of Setúbal): Rua Prof. Borges de Macedo, Manteigadas Sul, 2910-001 Setúbal; tel. (26) 570-99-00; e-mail mail@adstb.dgarq .gov.pt; internet adstb.dgarq.gov.pt; f. 1965, present bldg 2001; 4,800 m of documents; documents since 16th century; Dir GLÓRIA SANTOS.

Sintra

Arquivo Municipal de Sintra/Arquivo Histórico (Sintra Municipal Archives/Historical Archives): Palácio Valenças, Rua Visconde de Monserrate 1, 2710-591 Sintra; tel. (21) 923-69-09; e-mail municipe@ cm-sintra.pt; internet www.cm-sintra.pt; f. 1939; 60,000 documents since 14th century.

Biblioteca Municipal de Sintra (Sintra Municipal Library): Rua Gomes de Amorim 12/14, 2710-569 Sintra; tel. (21) 923-61-70; e-mail municipe@cm-sintra.pt; internet www .cm-sintra.pt; f. 1939; 60,000 vols.

Torres Novas

Biblioteca Municipal Gustavo Pinto Lopes (Gustavo Lopes Pinto Municipal Library): Jardim das Rosas, 2350-444 Torres Novas; tel. (249) 81-03-10; e-mail biblioteca@ cm-torresnovas.pt; internet biblioteca .cm-torresnovas.pt; f. 1937; 70,000 vols; Librarian and Dir Dr LUÍS FILIPE CORREIA DIAS.

Vila Nova de Gaia

Biblioteca Municipal de Vila Nova de Gaia (Municipal Library): Rua de Angola, 4430-014 Vila Nova de Gaia; tel. (22) 374-56-70; e-mail bmgaia@gaianima.pt; internet www.bmgaia.gaianima.pt; f. 1933; 101,000 vols, 2,246 periodicals; Coordinator CRISTINA MARGARIDE.

Vila Real

Arquivo Distrital de Vila Real (Vila Real District Archives): Av. Almeida Lucena 5, 5000-660 Vila Real; tel. (25) 933-08-20; e-mail correio@advrl.org.pt; internet www .advrl.org.pt; f. 1965, present status 2007; 31,590 vols, 3,000 m of documents, 180 m of Portuguese legislation since 1715; Dir PAULO MESQUITA GUIMARÃES; publs *Arquivos de Trás-os-Montes e Alto Douro—Instrumentos de Descrição, Estudos Transmontanos e Durienses, Memórias de Vila Real, Memórias do Tempo.*

Viseu

Arquivo Distrital de Viseu (Viseu District Archives): Largo de Santa Cristina, 3504-515 Viseu; tel. (23) 243-03-80; e-mail mail@advis .dgarq.gov.pt; internet www.ad-viseu.com; f. 1932, present bldg 2003; 450,000 documents; collns of scrolls, books, music and books of liturgy; Dir MARIA DAS DORES ALMEIDA HENRIQUES.

Museums and Art Galleries

Alenquer

Museu Municipal 'Hipólito Cabaço' (Municipal Museum 'Hipólito Cabaço'): Rua Maria Milne e Carmo 2, 2580-319 Alenquer; tel. (26) 373-33-04; e-mail museu@ cm-alenquer.pt; f. 1975; archaeological, historical and ethnographical collections; 4,000 exhibits; Dir JOÃO JOSÉ FERNANDES GOMES.

Alpiarça

Casa dos Patudos—Museu de Alpiarça (Alpiarça Museum): Rua José Relvas, 2090-102 Alpiarça; tel. (24) 355-83-21; e-mail museudospatudos@cm-alpiarca.pt; internet www.cm-alpiarca.pt; f. 1960; residence of José Relvas; art collns of José Relvas; furniture, porcelains, paintings, tapestries; library of 4,000 vols incl. historical archive; Dir Dr NUNO PRATES.

Amadora

Centro Ciência Viva de Amadora (Interactive Science Centre of Amadora): Rua Gonçalves Ramos 54B, 2700-036 Amadora; tel. (21) 491-13-13; e-mail info@amadora .cienciaviva.pt; internet amadora.cienciaviva .pt; f. 2003; interactive displays on scientific and technological topics, incl. town planning and electricity; Exec. Dir MARTA VELOSO.

Angra do Heroísmo

Museu de Angra do Heroísmo (Angra do Heroísmo Museum): Ladeira de São Francisco, 9701-875 Angra do Heroísmo, Ilha Terceira, The Azores; tel. (29) 524-08-00; e-mail museu.angra.info@azores.gov.pt; internet museu-angra.azores.gov.pt; f. 1949; historical museum; permanent exhibition on the history of the Azores Islands; paintings, ceramics, furniture, sculpture, ethnography, arms, guns, carriages; Dir MARIA HELENA DE MENESES ORMONDE.

Braga

'D. Diogo de Sousa' Museu Regional de Arqueologia ('D. Diogo de Sousa' Regional Archaeological Museum): Rua dos Bombeiros Voluntários, 4700-025 Braga; tel. (25) 327-37-06; e-mail mdds@imc-ip.pt; internet mdds .imc-ip.pt; f. 1918 as D. Diogo de Sousa Museum of Archaeology and Arts; colln ranges from the Palaeolithic to the Middle Ages; visits to local archaeological sites; library of 8,000 vols; Dir Dra MARIA ISABEL CUNHA E SILVA.

Bragança

Museu do Abade de Baçal (Abbot of Baçal Museum): Rua Conselheiro Abílio Beça 27, 5300-011 Bragança; tel. (27) 333-15-95; e-mail mabadebacal@imc-ip.pt; internet www.ipmuseus.pt; f. 1915 as Regional Museum of Art Works, Parts and Archaeological Numismatics of Bragança, present name 1935; archaeology, epigraphy, sacred art, paintings, gold items, numismatics, furniture, ethnography; Dir ANA MARIA AFONSO.

Cascais

Museu 'Condes de Castro Guimarães': Av. Rei Humberto II de Itália, Parque Marechal Carmona, 2750 Cascais; tel. (21) 481-53-04; e-mail mccg@cm-cascais.pt; internet www.cm-cascais.pt; f. 1931; *Crónica* about the kings of the first dynasty of Duarte Galvão, 16th-century illuminated *Codex* on parchment, 17th-century Indo-Portuguese counting frames, paintings, oriental porcelain; furniture, silverware; library of 2,826 vols; Curator MARIA JOSÉ REGO DE SOUSA.

Castelo Branco

Museu de Francisco Tavares Proença Júnior: Largo Dr José Dias Lopes, 6000-462 Castelo Branco; tel. (27) 234-42-77; e-mail mftpj@ipmuseus.pt; internet www.ipmuseus .pt; f. 1910, present bldg 1971; archaeological colln of objects found in megalithic tombs at Beira Baixa; Bronze-Age weapons and objects from a complete workshop found at Castelo Novo; illustrations of rupestral art in the Tagus sanctuary; Roman epigraphy; art gallery (16th-century Portuguese School and Brussels tapestries); Bishop's Gallery (18th-

and 19th-century paintings); ethnographic collns; ceramic collns; regional embroidery workshop; textiles, incl. oriental and Indo-Portuguese embroidered bedcovers; Dir AIDA RECHENA.

Coimbra

Museu da Ciência da Universidade de Coimbra (Museum of Science, University of Coimbra): Laboratorio Chimico, Largo Marquês de Pombal, 3000-272 Coimbra; tel. (23) 985-43-50; e-mail geral@museudaciencia .org; internet www.museudaciencia.pt; f. 2006; attached to Univ. of Coimbra; 240,000 objects in categories of natural history, ethnography, scientific instruments and models.

Museu Nacional de Ciência e Técnica 'Dr Mário Silva' (National Museum of Science and Technology 'Dr Mário Silva'): Palacete Sacadura Botte, Rua dos Coutinhos 23, 3000 Coimbra; tel. (23) 985-19-40; e-mail mnct@mnct.mces.pt; internet www .museudaciencia.pt; f. 1971; attached to Min. of Science, Technology and Higher Education; information science, medicine, physics, graphic arts, photography, cinema, radio, industrial technology; Dir Prof. Dr PAULO GAMA MOTA.

Museu Nacional de 'Machado de Castro' ('Machado de Castro' National Museum): Largo Dr José Rodriguez, 3000-236 Coimbra; tel. (239) 853070; e-mail mnmachadodecastro@imc-ip.pt; internet mnmachadodecastro.imc-ip.pt; f. 1919; est. in the old Bishop's Palace built over Roman galleries, renewed in the 16th century and recently adapted; antiquities, sculpture, paintings, silver-work, priests' vestments, tapestries, ceramics, glass, furniture; Dir ANA ALCOFORADO.

Coruche

Coruche Museu Municipal (Municipal Museum Coruche): Rua Júlio Maria de Sousa, 2100-192 Coruche; tel. (24) 361-08-20; e-mail museu.municipal@cm-coruche.pt; internet www.museu-coruche.org; f. 2001; 230,398 pieces, mostly archaeological and ethnographic; library of 4,102 vols; Dir ANA SANTOS.

Évora

Museu de Évora: Largo do Conde de Vila Flor, 7000-804 Évora; tel. (26) 670-26-04; e-mail mevora@ipmuseus.pt; internet museudevora.imc-ip.pt; f. 1915; paintings: large collns of 16th-century Flemish and Portuguese works; 17th-century works; local prehistoric tools and Roman art and archaeology; sculpture from middle ages to the 19th century; 18th-century Portuguese furniture and silver; library of 4,000 vols; Dir ANTÓNIO CAMÕES GOUVEIA.

Faro

Museu Marítimo 'Almirante Ramalho Ortigão' (Maritime Museum): Rua da Comunidade Lusíada Capitania do Porto do Faro, 8000-253 Faro; tel. (28) 989-49-90; e-mail biblioteca.dms@clix.pt; f. 1931; regional methods of fishing, instruments, models of ships and equipment, paintings of marine fauna, sailors' handicrafts; Curator Capt. LUÍS FERNANDO TAVARES DOS BEIS ÁGOAS.

Museu Municipal de Faro (Faro Municipal Museum): Largo Afonso III, N.º 14, 8000-167 Faro; tel. (28) 987-08-27; e-mail dmar.dc@ cm-faro.pt; internet www.cm-faro.pt; f. 1894; history, archaeology, ethnography, art from 16th to 19th centuries, photography, toys; Dir Dr MARCO LOPES; publ. *Anais do Municipio do Faro* (1 a year).

Figueira da Foz

Museu Municipal 'Santos Rocha' (Municipal Museum 'Santos Rocha'): Rua Calouste Gulbenkian, 3080-084 Figueira da Foz; tel. (23) 340-28-40; e-mail museu@cm-figfoz.pt; f. 1894; art, archaeology, ethnology, coins and medals, Indo-Portuguese furniture, weapons; library of 14,300 vols; Manager ANA PAULA CARDOSO; Manager MANUELA SILVA; Manager SÓNIA PINTO.

Funchal

Museu da Quinta das Cruzes: Calçada do Pico 1, 9000-206 Funchal, Madeira; tel. (29) 174-06-70; e-mail mqc.drac.srt@gov-madeira .pt; internet www.museuquintadascruzes .com; f. 1946, present status 2013; decorative arts and small clusters of archaeological and ethnographic objects; Dir TERESA PAIS; publs *Porcelana da China—Colecção do Museu Quinta das Cruzes, Um Olhar do Porto.*

Museu de Arte Contemporânea (Museum of Contemporary Art): Fortaleza de São Tiago, Rua do Portão de São Tiago, 9060-250 Funchal, Madeira; tel. (29) 121-33-40; e-mail mac.funchal.drac@madeira-edu.pt; f. 1966, present location 1992; Portuguese art since the 1960s; Dir JOSÉ MANUEL DE FREITAS SAINZ-TRUEVA.

Museu de Arte Sacra (Museum of Sacred Art): Rua do Bispo 21, 9000-073 Funchal, Madeira; tel. (29) 122-89-00; e-mail masf@ netmadeira.com; internet www .museuartesacrafunchal.org; f. 1955; diocesan museum; art of the 15th–18th centuries, Flemish art of the 15th and 16th centuries, sculpture, jewellery; Scientific Dir LUIZA CLODE.

Museu de História Natural do Funchal (Museum of Natural History of Funchal): Rua da Mouraria 31, 9004-546 Funchal, Madeira; tel. (29) 122-97-61; e-mail mmf@ cm-funchal.pt; internet www.cm-funchal.pt/ ciencia; f. 1933; natural history museum and marine aquarium; large colln of marine animals, esp. deep-sea fish and crustaceans; library on marine biology; garden of medicinal and aromatic plants; Dir RICARDO ARAÚJO; publ. *Bocagiana* (irregular).

Guimarães

Museu da Sociedade Martins Sarmento (Museum of the Martins Sarmento Society): Rua Paio Galvão, 4814-509 Guimarães; tel. (25) 341-59-69; e-mail sms@msarmento.org; internet www.csarmento.uminho.pt; f. 1885; archaeology; numerous exhibits relating to Portuguese Celtic, Roman and Visigothic periods; ethnography, numismatics, contemporary art; Dir Dr J. SANTOS SIMÕES.

Museu de Alberto Sampaio (Alberto Sampaio Museum): Rua Alfredo Guimarães, 4800-407 Guimarães; tel. (25) 342-39-10; e-mail masampaio@imc-ip.pt; internet masampaio.imc-ip.pt; f. 1928; religious painting and sculpture, goldsmiths' and silversmiths' art, priestly garments, ceramics; research on industrial archaeology and anthropology; Dir Dr MANUEL SAMPAYO GRAÇA.

Paço dos Duques de Bragança (Palace of the Dukes of Braganza): Rua Conde D. Henrique, 4810-245 Guimarães; tel. (25) 341-22-73; e-mail pduques@imc-ip.pt; internet pduques.imc-ip.pt; f. 1910; attached to Portuguese Institute of Architectural Heritage; 15th-century palace and nat. monument; 17th- and 18th-century art, tapestries, ceramics, faience, furniture; Dir Dra ANTÓNIO PONTE.

Lamego

Museu de Lamego: Largo de Camões, 5100-147 Lamego; tel. (25) 460-02-30; e-mail mlamego@imc-ip.pt; internet www.ipmuseus .pt; f. 1917 as Museum of Works of Art, Archaeology and Numismatics; colln of 16th-century Brussels tapestries, Portuguese painting of 16th–18th centuries, sculpture, religious ornaments; Dir Dr AGOSTINHO PAIVA RIBEIRO.

Leiria

Museu da Imagem em Movimento (Museum of the Moving Image): Largo de São Pedro, Cerca do Castelo, 2400-235 Leiria; tel. (24) 483-96-75; e-mail mimo@cm-leiria .pt; internet mimo.cm-leiria.pt; f. 1996; commemorates the centenary of the creation of cinema; photographic archive, documentation centre.

Lisbon

Casa-Museu Dr Anastácio Gonçalves: Av. 5 de Outubro 6–8, 1050-055 Lisbon; tel. (21) 354-08-23; e-mail cmag@ipmuseus.pt; internet www.cmag-ipmuseus.pt; f. 1980; 2,000 works of Portuguese paintings and foreign furniture; Dir JOSÉ RIBEIRO.

Centro de Arte Moderna—Fundação Calouste Gulbenkian (Centre for Modern Art—Calouste Gulbenkian Foundation): Rua Dr Nicolau de Bettencourt, 1050-078 Lisbon; tel. (21) 782-34-74; e-mail camjap@ gulbenkian.pt; internet cam.gulbenkian.pt; f. 1983; Portuguese and foreign modern art; documentation and research depts, workshops, outdoor amphitheatre; Dir ISABEL CARLOS.

Jardim e Museu Agrícola Tropical do Instituto de Investigação Científica Tropical (Garden and Museum of Tropical Agriculture): Calçada do Galvão, Belém, 1400-171 Lisbon; tel. (21) 363-70-23; internet www.iict.pt/revista/rev06/vrev0603 .htm; e-mail jmat@iict.pt; f. 1906; Dir MARIA CÂNDIDA LIBERATO.

Museu Arqueológico do Carmo (Archaeological Museum): Largo do Carmo, 1200-092 Lisbon; tel. (21) 347-86-29; e-mail carlavf@ mac.pt; internet www.museusportugal.org/ aap; f. 1863; administered by Associação dos Arqueólogos Portugueses; prehistoric, Roman, Visigothic and medieval collns; sarcophagi, religious sculpture, coins, etc.

Museu Calouste Gulbenkian: Av. de Berna 45A, 1067-001 Lisbon; tel. (21) 782-30-00; e-mail info@gulbenkian.pt; internet www.museu.gulbenkian.pt; f. 1969; Gulbenkian art colln containing works since 2800BC; antique classical and oriental art, Egyptian, Assyrian, Greek, Roman, Islamic and Far Eastern art; European painting, sculpture, illuminated MSS, tapestries and fabrics, furniture, silverware, jewellery, glass, medals, coins; Dir Dr JOÃO CASTEL-BRANCO PEREIRA.

Museu da Cidade (City Museum): Palácio Pimenta, Campo Grande 245, 1700-091 Lisbon; tel. (21) 751-32-00; e-mail museudacidade@cm-lisboa.pt; internet www .museudacidade.pt; f. 1942, present location 1979; history of devt of Lisbon shown by archaeological, historical, artistic and ethnological documents and exhibits; an 'ensemble' of the 18th-century period and a large model of Lisbon before the earthquake of 1755; Dir ANA CRISTINA LEITE.

Museu da Música (Music Museum): Estação do Metropolitano Alto dos Moinhos, Rua João de Freitas Branco, 1500-359 Lisbon; tel. (21) 771-09-90; e-mail mmusica@imc-ip.pt; internet www.museudamusica.imc-ip.pt; f. 1994; attached to Instituto dos Museus e da Conservação; more than 1,000 instruments of both classical and popular traditions, European wind, key and percussion instruments of the 16th–19th centuries, Portuguese clavichords, harpsichords and 19th-century string instruments, also African, Asian and Portuguese folk instruments; iconography; sound archive of 6,000 items; printed documents and MSS; Dir MARIA HELENA TRINDADE.

Museu de Arte Popular (Museum of Folk Art): Av. de Brasília, 1400-038 Lisbon; tel. (21) 301-12-82; e-mail museuartepopular@ gmail.com; f. 1948; folk art, ethnology; 13,000 objects; Dir ANDREIA GALVAO.

Museu de Artes Decorativas (Museum of Decorative Arts): Fundação Ricardo do Espírito Santo Silva, Largo das Portas do Sol 2, 1100-411 Lisbon; tel. (21) 888-19-91; e-mail museu@fress.pt; internet www.fress .pt; f. 1953; incl. Ricardo do Espírito Santo Silva's private colln of Portuguese furniture, silver, china, paintings, rugs, tapestries, etc.; workshops in which craftsmen are trained in all aspects of traditional interior arts; Dir MARIA DA CONCEIÇÃO AMARAL.

Museu Nacional de História Natural e da Ciência, Universidade de Lisboa (National Museum of Natural History and Science, University of Lisbon): Rua da Escola Politécnica 58, 1250-102 Lisbon; tel. (21) 392-18-00; e-mail geral@museus.ul.pt; internet www.mnhnc.ul.pt; f. 1768; 10,000 scientific instruments; conducts research and supports postgraduate studies in close collaboration with the Inter-Univ. Centre for the History of Science and Technology (CIUHCT) in the areas of history of science, history of the history of collns and scientific instruments; library of 100,000 vols; Dir Prof. JOSÉ PEDRO SOUSA DIAS.

Museu de São Roque (Museum of São Roque): Largo Trindade Coelho (ao Bairro Alto), 1200-470 Lisbon; tel. (21) 323-50-65; e-mail info@museu-saoroque.com; internet www.museu-saoroque.com; f. 1905; collns of religious paintings, Church vessels in precious metals, embroidered vestments by Italian artists of the 18th century; works from the chapel of St John the Baptist in the adjacent museum of the 16th-century Church of St Roque; educational services and temporary exhibitions; Dir TERESA FREITAS MORNA.

Museu do Chiado (Chiado Museum): Rua Serpa Pinto 4, 1200-444 Lisbon; tel. (21) 343-21-48; e-mail mnac-museudochiado@imc-ip .pt; internet www.museudochiado-ipmuseus .pt; f. 1911; painting and sculpture since 1850; library of 6,000 vols; Dir PEDRO LAPA.

Museu Etnológico da Sociedade de Geografia de Lisboa (Ethnological Museum of Geographical Society of Lisbon): Rua das Portas de St Antão 100, 1150-269 Lisbon; tel. (21) 342-54-01; e-mail geral@ socgeografialisboa.mail.pt; internet socgeografia-lisboa.planetaclix.pt; f. 1875; native arts, arms, clothing, musical instruments from Africa, India, China, Indonesia and Timor, statues of navigators and historians, relics of voyages of discovery, scientific instruments; Curator Dra MANUELA CANTINHO.

Museu Geológico de Portugal (Geological Museum of Portugal): Rua Academia das Ciências 19, 2, 1200-003 Lisbon; tel. (21) 346-39-15; e-mail museugeol@lneg.pt; internet www.lneg.pt; f. 1848; palaeontology, stratigraphy, archaeology and mineralogy; fossils from the Cambrian to the Tertiary period.

Museu Militar (Military Museum): Largo do Museu de Artilharia, 1100-468 Lisbon; tel. (21) 884-25-69; e-mail museumilitar@ portugalmail.pt; internet www.exercito.pt/ sites/musmillisboa/paginas/default.aspx; f. 1851, present name 1926; exhibits of Portuguese military history, light arms, ancient artillery and other equipment, paintings since 18th century; Dir Col Luis Sodre de Albuquerque.

Museu Mineralógico e Geológico (Museum of Mineralogy and Geology): Rua da Escola Politécnica 58, 1250-102 Lisbon; tel. (21) 392-18-24; e-mail smineralogia@fc.ul.pt; internet www.mnhn.ul.pt/geologia/geologia.htm; f. 1837; attached to Museu Nacional de História Natural; geology, petrology, mineralogy, palaeontology and museology; Dir Prof. Fernando José Arraiano de Sousa Barriga; Curator Dr César Lopes; Curator Dra Liliana Póvoas; publs *Gaia* (journal of geosciences), *Memórias de Geociencias* (irregular).

Museu Nacional de Arqueologia do Dr Leite de Vasconcelos (National Museum of Archaeology): Praça do Império, 1400-206 Lisbon; tel. (21) 362-00-00; e-mail mnarq.info@imc-ip.pt; internet www.mnarqueologia-ipmuseus.pt; f. 1893; attached to Secretaria Estado da Cultura; library of 25,000 vols; Dir Dr Luís Raposo; Archaeologist Adolfo Silveira Martins; publ. *O Arqueólogo Português*.

Museu Nacional de Arte Antiga (National Museum of Ancient Art): Rua das Janelas Verdes, 1249-017 Lisbon; tel. (21) 391-28-00; e-mail geral@mnaa.dgpc.pt; internet www.museudearteantiga.pt; f. 1884; Portuguese and foreign plastic and ornamental art from 12th century to 19th century; library of 36,000 vols; Dir Prof. Dr António Filipe Pimentel; Deputy Dir Dr José Alberto Seabra Carvalho.

Museu Nacional de Etnologia (National Ethnological Museum): Av. Ilha da Madeira, 1400-203 Lisbon; tel. (21) 304-11-60; e-mail mnetnologia@ipmuseus.pt; internet www.mnetnologia-ipmuseus.pt; f. 1965; present bldg 1976; Portuguese rural artefacts; collns representing the people and cultures of Lusophone Africa, Mali, Côte d'Ivoire, Ghana, Nigeria, Cameroon, Indonesia, Timor, Macau, and the Amazonian Indians; library: 20,000 books and periodicals; Dir Prof. Dr Joaquim Pais de Brito.

Museu Nacional de História Natural (National Museum of Natural History): Universidade de Lisboa, Rua da Escola Politécnica 58, 1250-102 Lisbon; tel. (21) 392-18-90; e-mail geral@museus.ul.pt; internet www.mnhn.ul.pt; f. 1859; library of 27,000 vols; Dir for Botany Prof. Maria Amelia Martins-Loucão; Dir for Mineralogy and Geology Prof. Fernando Barriga; Dir for Zoology and Anthropology Dra Maria Graça Ramalhinho; publs *Arquivos do Museu Bocage*, *Gaia* (Journal of Geosciences), *Portugaliae Acta Biologica*, *Revista de Biologia* (Lisboa) (1 a year).

Museu Nacional do Azulejo (National Tile Museum): Rua da Madre de Deus 4, 1900-312 Lisbon; tel. (21) 810-03-40; e-mail mnazulejo@imc-ip.pt; internet mnazulejo.imc-ip.pt; f. 1965; colln of 7,271 tiles, 368 ceramics, 698 prints and engravings, 47 tools; library of 6,000 monographs.

Museu Nacional do Teatro (National Theatre Museum): Estrada do Lumiar 10, 1600-495 Lisbon; tel. (21) 756-74-10; e-mail mnteatro@ipmuseus.pt; internet museudoteatro.imc-ip.pt; f. 1982; 250,000 pieces of costumes, props, sets, posters, programmes, records, sheet music, 120,000 photographs; library of 35,000 vols; Dir José Alvarez; Librarian Sofia Patrão.

Museu Nacional do Traje (National Museum of Costume): Largo Júlio de Castilho-Lumiar, 1600-483 Lisbon; tel. (21) 756-76-20; e-mail mntraje@imc-ip.pt; internet museudotraje.imc-ip.pt; f. 1977; colln of garments and accessories of Portuguese people since 1882; Dir Dr Clara Pinto.

Museu Nacional dos Coches (National Coach Museum): Praça Afonso de Albuquerque, Belém, 1300-044 Lisbon; tel. (21) 361-08-50; e-mail mncoches@imc-ip.pt; internet www.museudoscoches.pt; f. 1905 by Queen Amélia in the Riding School of the Royal Palace; comprehensive colln of carriages and coaches since 1619, many by famous craftsmen, incl. those of the Portuguese ex-Royal Family; sedan chairs, harness and equipment, royal liveries, etc., silver trumpets; section of portraits, paintings and engravings; Dir Dra Silvana Bessone.

Museu Numismático Português (Portuguese Numismatic Museum): Imprensa Nacional-Casa da Moeda, Av. António José de Almeida, 1000-042 Lisbon; tel. (21) 781-07-00; e-mail maria.joao.gaiato@incm.pt; f. 1933; important collns of Portuguese and Colonial, Iberian, Roman and Visigothic coins; Portuguese and foreign medals; temporarily closed to the public; library of 20,000 vols; consists of Documentation and Information Centre, and Historical Archives of the Nat. Press and the Lisbon Mint; Dir Maria João Gaiato; publ. *Diário da República*.

Museu Rafael Bordalo Pinheiro (Rafael Bordalo Pinheiro Museum): Campo Grande 382, 1700-097 Lisbon; tel. (21) 817-06-67; e-mail museu.bordalopinheiro@cm-lisboa.pt; internet www.museubordalopinheiro.pt; f. 1916 as a biographical museum; originals and reproductions of famous caricatures, ceramics, satirical documents; library of 1,600 vols; Museum Coordinator Pedro Bebiano Braga; publs *António Maria*, *Lanterna Mágica*, *Pontos nos ii*.

Odivelas

Núcleo Museológico do Posto de Comando do Movimento das Forças Armadas (Command Post of the Armed Forces Movement): Quartel do Regimento de Engenharia 1 Av. do Regimento de Engenharia 1, 1675-103 Pontinha; tel. (21) 932-08-00; e-mail cultura@cm-odivelas.pt; internet www.cm-odivelas.pt; f. 2001; commemorates the revolution of 25 April 1974, covering the main events during 24–26 April 1974.

Pêro Pinheiro

Museu do Ar (Air Museum): Granja do Marquês, 2715-021 Pêro Pinheiro; tel. (21) 967-89-84; e-mail museudoar@emfa.pt; internet www.emfa.pt/www/po/musar/index.php; f. 1969; Air Force museum, 10,000 pieces.

Porto

Museu de Arte Contemporânea de Serralves (Serralves Museum of Contemporary Art): Rua D. João de Castro 210, 4150-417 Porto; tel. (22) 615-65-00; e-mail serralves@serralves.pt; internet www.serralves.com; f. 1999; Portuguese and int. art since the late 1960s; library: reference art library; Dir João Fernandes; Asst Dir Ulrich Loock.

Museu de Etnologia do Porto (Ethnological Museum of Porto): Largo de São João Novo 11, 4000 Porto; f. 1945 as Museum of Ethnography and History of Douro Litora; ethnology, archaeology and history; temporarily closed to the public; Dir (vacant).

Museu do Carro Eléctrico (Tram Museum): Alameda Basílio Teles 51, 4150-127 Porto; tel. (22) 615-81-85; e-mail dsgalmeida@stcp.pt; internet www.museudocarroelectrico.pt; f. 1992; colln of trams used in Portugal for public transport; Dir Cristina Pimentel.

Museu Nacional da Imprensa (National Printing Press Museum): Estrada Nacional 108, 206, 4300-316 Porto; tel. (22) 530-49-66; e-mail mni@museudaimprensa.pt; internet www.museudaimprensa.pt; f. 1997; colln incl. materials of foundry, printing, binding and engraving; Dir Luis Humberto Marcos; Asst Dir Isabel Gonçalves; Sec. Joana Mota.

Museu Nacional de Soares dos Reis (National Museum): Palacio dos Carrancas, Rua D. Manuel II, 4050-342 Porto; tel. (22) 339-37-70; e-mail mnsr.div@imc-ip.pt; internet mnsr.imc-ip.pt; f. 1833; paintings, sculpture, jewellery, furniture, pottery, glass, metalwork; Dir Dra Teresa Viana..

Attached Museums:

Casa Museu Fernando de Castro: Rua de Costa Cabral 716, 4200-211 Porto; tel. (22) 339-37-70; f. 1952; colln of Fernando de Castro; ceramics, sculpture, painting.

Sacavém

Museu de Cerâmica de Sacavém (Museum of Ceramics Sacavém): Urbanização Real Forte, 2685 Sacavém; tel. (21) 940-98-00; e-mail museu_ceramica@cm-loures.pt; internet www.cm-loures.pt/aa_patrimonioredemuseussacavema.asp; f. 2000; colln of ceramics, fine arts and others.

Setúbal

Museu de Setúbal (Setúbal Museum): Rua do Balneário Dr Paulo Borba, 2900-261 Setúbal; tel. (26) 553-78-90; e-mail museu.setubal@mun-setubal.pt; internet www.ipmuseus.pt; f. 1961; 16th-century art, sacred sculpture, decorative arts, archaeology, numismatics; Dir Fernando António Baptista Pereira.

Museu do Trabalho Michel Giacometti (Museum of Labour Michel Giacometti): Largo Defensores da República, 2910-470 Setúbal; tel. (26) 553-78-80; e-mail museu.trabalho@mun-setubal.pt; internet www.mun-setubal.pt/museutrabalho; f. 1995; ethnographic colln of Michel Giacometti; Dir Dr Lucinda Fernandes.

Sintra

Museu Arqueológico de São Miguel de Odrinhas (São Miguel de Odrinhas Archaeological Museum): Av. Prof. Dr D. Fernando d'Almeida, Odrinhas, 2710 Sintra; tel. (21) 961-35-74; e-mail museudeodrinhas@sapo.pt; internet www.museudeodrinhas.com; f. 1955; epigraphs from Etruscan times to the modern age, important colln of Roman inscriptions and carved stones; archaeological artefacts from the Middle Palaeolithic to the 18th century; publ. *Actividades Ludico-didacticas*.

Sintra Museu de Arte Moderna (Sintra Museum of Modern Art): Av. Heliodoro Salgado, 1270 Sintra; tel. (21) 924-81-70; e-mail info@sintramodernart.com; internet www.berardomodern.com; f. 1987; art representing 14 movements; Curator Pedro Aguilar; Sec. Joana de Ávila.

Torres Novas

Museu Municipal Carlos Reis (Carlos Reis Municipal Museum): Rua do Salvador 10, 2350-415 Torres Novas; tel. (24) 981-25-35; e-mail museu.municipal@cm-torresnovas.pt; internet museu.cm-torresnovas.pt; f. 1937; archaeological, historical, fine arts, ethnographical, religious art, numismatics; library of 300 vols; Dir Maria Elvira Marques Teixeira.

Vila Nova de Gaia

Casa Museu Teixeira Lopes (Teixeira Lopes House and Museum): Rua Teixeira Lopes 32, 4400-320 Vila Nova de Gaia; tel. (22) 375-12-24; e-mail cmteixeiralopes@gaianima.pt; internet www.cm-gaia.pt; f.

1933; comprises the home of the sculptor António Teixeira Lopes (1866–1942) and the adjacent Galerias Diogo de Macedo; sculpture and paintings since 19th century, furniture, ceramics, tapestries, decorative arts; Dir DOLPHIN SOUSA.

Vila Viçosa

Museu-Biblioteca da Casa de Bragança (Museum and Library of the House of Bragança): Paço Ducal, Terreiro do Paço, 7160-251 Vila Viçosa; tel. (26) 898-06-59; e-mail palacio.vilavicosa@sapo.pt; internet www.fcbraganca.pt; f. 1933; tapestry, furniture, tiles, European and Chinese ceramics, portraits of the Royal Family, arms, photographs, coaches and carriages; rare 16th-century printed books, Italian 16th-century majolica, 17th-and 18th-century musical archives; library of 40,000 vols; Curator Dra MARIA DE JESUS MONGE.

Viseu

Museu Grão Vasco: Adro da Sé, 3500-195 Viseu; tel. (23) 242-20-49; e-mail mgv@imc-ip .pt; internet www.ipmuseus.pt; f. 1916; furniture, tapestry, plate, ceramics and glassware, prints and Portuguese paintings; Dir Dra ANA PAULA ABRANTES.

Universities

UNIVERSIDADE ABERTA

Palácio Ceia Rua da Escola Politécnica, 141–147, 1269-001 Lisbon

Telephone: (21) 391-63-00
E-mail: contas@univ-ab.pt
Internet: www.uab.pt

Founded 1988
State control
Language of instruction: Portuguese
Academic year: October to July

Number of teachers: 200
Number of students: 9,000

Rector: Dr CARLOS REIS
Vice-Rector: Dr CARLA MARIA BISPO PADREL DE OLIVEIRA
Vice-Rector: ALDA MARIA SIMÕES PEREIRA
Vice-Rector: Dr DOMINGOS JOSÉ ALVES CAEIRO
Pro-Rector: JOÃO CARLOS RELVÃO CAETANO

PROFESSORS

Department of Education and Distance Learning:

AMANTE, L.
BASTOS, G.
FRUTUOSO HENRIQUES, S.
GOULÃO, M. DE F.
GRAVE, L.
IVONE GASPAR, M.
LEBRES AIRES, M. L.
MALHEIRO DA SILVA, S.
MANUEL MARTINS MENDES, A.
MANUELA MALHEIRO FERREIRA, M.
MARGARIDA LOUREIRO CARDOSO, T.
MARIA SIMÕES PEREIRA, A.
MIRANDA, B.
MOREIRA, D.
MOREIRA MARTINS, A.
MORGADO, L.
OLIVEIRA, I.
PAULA MARTINS PEREIRA AFONSO, A.
PINTO MARTINS, A.
TINOCA, L.

Department of Humanities:

ALEXANDRE MAGALHÃES NUNES DA SILVA, P.
ANTÓNIO ALVES DOS REIS, C.
AURÉLIA RODRIGUES DE ALMEIDA, C.
BÄR, G.
BÁRBARA DE SOUSA MONTES RODRIGUES MARQUES DIAS, H.

BATORÉO, H.
CARLOS FERNANDES AVELAR, M.
CARLOS PIMENTA GONÇALVES, L.
CASTILHO PAIS, C.
CHENOLL MORA, A.
DE JESUS CRESPO CANDEIAS VELEZ RELVAS, M.
DO CÉU MARTINS MONTEIRO MARQUES, M.
DO ROSÁRIO DA CUNHA DUARTE, M.
DO ROSÁRIO SAMPAIO SOARES DE SOUSA LEITÃO LUPI BELLO, M.
FILIPA PALMA DOS REIS, M.
FONSECA CLAMOTE CARRETO, C.
GÖTTLICH, K.
ISABEL PEREIRA TEIXEIRA VASCONCELOS, A.
JOAQUIM DE AZEVEDO TEIXEIRA, R.
JOSÉ FILIPE DA SILVA, M.
MALHEIRO, H.
MANUEL LOPES FIRMINO, J.
MARIA DA CONCEIÇÃO FERREIRA DA SILVA, E.
MARIA DE BARROS DIAS, I.
MARIA DE JESUS FERREIRA NOBRE, A.
MARIA DOS SANTOS FALÉ, I.
MARIA FERIN CUNHA DE ALBUQUERQUE VELOSO, M.
MARIA LOUREIRO DE ROBOREDO SEARA, I.
MARIA PONTES CAPITÃO PEDROSA, I.
MARIA SANTOS GRAÇA DE VASCONCELOS RODRIGUES, C.
MARIA SEQUEIRA, R.
MIGUEL GUERREIRO NOBRE, R.
NASCIMENTO PIEDADE, A.
PAULA DA SILVA MACHADO, A.
PAULA S. MENDES COELHO, M.
RITA DE SÁ SOVERAL PADEIRA, A.
SALOMÃO, R.
SCOTT CHILDS, J.
TERESA DE NORONHA CARDOSO ROCHA, M.
VILA MAIOR, D.

Department of Science and Technology:

AMADOR, F.
ARAÚJO, A.
ARAÚJO, J.
AZEITEIRO, U.
BACELAR NICOLAU, P.
BIDARRA DE ALMEIDA, J.
BORGES SEIXAS, S.
CAETANO, F.
CARAPETO, C.
CARDOSO, V.
CARVALHO, G.
CAVIQUE, L.
COELHO, J.
DO ROSÁRIO O. D. RAMOS, M.
FERNANDES MARCOS, A.
GONZAGA ALBUQUERQUE, L.
JOÃO OLIVEIRA, M.
JORGE EDMUNDO, M.
LUCINDA MATOS FERNANDES, M.
LUÍSA CORREIA, A.
MARTINHO MARTINS, C.
MIGUEL MARQUES DE SOUSA, N.
MORAIS, J.
OLIVEIRA, A.
OLIVEIRA, T.
PADREL DE OLIVEIRA, C.
PAULA FERNANDES, A.
PAULA MARTINHO, A.
PESTANA DA COSTA, F.
PINTO DE MOURA, A.
QUARESMA, P.
REMÉDIOS, J.
ROCIO, V.
SÃO MAMEDE, J.
SASPORTES, R.
SHIRLEY, P.
SILVA PEREIRA, P.
SOFIA FERREIRA DA SILVA CAEIRO, S.

Department of Social Sciences and Management:

ALBUQUERQUE, R.
ALEXANDRA GAGO DA CÂMARA, M.
ALEXANDRA GONÇALVES, C.
ALEXANDRE RODRIGUES DIAS DE SOUSA, I.
ALVES, F.

ALVES CAEIRO, D.
ANTÓNIO FERREIRA PORFÍRIO, J.
BÄCKSTRÖM, B.
CAETANO, J.
CARMO, H.
CARRILHO NEGAS, M.
CARRILHO RIBEIRO MENDES, T.
CRISTINA HENRIQUES LOPES DOS REIS, F.
DAS CANDEIAS SALES, J.
DO CARMO TEIXEIRA PINTO, M.
DO ROSÁRIO ALVES DE ALMEIDA, M.
DO ROSÁRIO BASTOS, M.
DO ROSÁRIO DE ABREU DE MATOS BERNARDO, M.
EDUARDO MARTINS, A.
FERREIRA DA SILVA, L.
FILIPE MOUTA LOPES, M.
FILOMENA ANDRADE, M.
FLOR, P.
FONTES, J.
GRONITA, J.
ISABEL DA CONCEIÇÃO JOÃO, M.
JOÃO BRANCO, M.
JOAQUIM, T.
JOAQUIM MARQUES DE ALMEIDA, J.
LUIS CUNHA CARDOSO, J.
MAGANO, O.
MANUEL COSTA, P.
MANUEL TRINDADE, J.
MARIA MILLÁN COSTA, A.
MARIE LUC PHILIPPE JACQUINET, M.
MIGUEL CUSTÓDIO FERRÃO NETO SIMÃO, J.
MIRANDA, J.
NUNES, C.
NUNES, P.
OLIVEIRA RAMOS, P.
PAIVA, A.
PAULA AVELAR, A.
PAULA BEJA HORTA, A.
PAULA CORDEIRO, A.
PAULO GOMES DA SILVA, V.
PEDRO RAMOS DOS SANTOS PINHO, C.
RAFAEL SANTOS BRANCO, C.
RAMOS, N.
RIBEIRO, J.
SOUSA, L.
SOUSA NUNES, T.
TEIXEIRA ISAÍAS, P.
VIDAL, N.
VIEIRA, C.

UNIVERSIDADE ATLÂNTICA
(Atlantic University)

Fábrica da Pólvora de Barcarena, 2730-036 Barcarena

Telephone: (21) 439-82-00
E-mail: geral@uatlantica.pt
Internet: www.uatlantica.pt

Founded 1996
State control
Language of instruction: Portuguese
Academic year: October to December

Pres.: Prof. Dr NELSON LOURENÇO
Sec.-Gen.: Dr NATÁLIA DO ESPÍRITO SANTO

PROFESSORS

Department of Planning, Environment and Society:

ALEXANDRE COELHO, J.
ALMEIDA PINTO, G.
AUGUSTO, R.
BARROSO, P.
CANHOTO DA SILVA, J.
CARNEIRO MARTINS, P.
CATARINA AFONSO, A.
CÉLIA GOMES, A.
DE FÁTIMA GEADA, M.
DO ROSÁRIO JORGE, M.
FÉLIX, S.
FONSECA FERREIRA, A.
LOURENÇO, N.
MEIRELLES, I.
MONTEIRO DA CRUZ, P.
PACHECO, D.

PAULO ZBYSZEWSKI, J.
PINTO DA SILVA, P.
PIRIQUITO COSTA, J.
RODRIGUES, L.
RUSSELL, D.
RUSSO MACHADO, C.
SIMÃO, J.
TABORDA, F.
TEIXEIRA D'AZEVEDO, R.
TIRONE, L.
VALENTIM, A.
VILHENA, J.

Department of Science and Information Technology and Communication:

AGUIAR, A.
ALEXANDRE COELHO, J.
AUGUSTO, R.
BARROSO, P.
CABECINHA, F.
CAÇADOR, D.
CALDAS, A.
CANHOTO, J.
CARNEIRO MARTINS, P.
CÉLIA GOMES, A.
CHAVES, M.
CRUZ, P.
DUTSCHKE, G.
FALCATO, A.
GEADA, F.
MEIRELLES, I.
MIGUEL OLIVEIRA, L.
PINTO, G.
PIRIQUITO COSTA, J.
TABORDA, F.
VALENTIM, A.
VALENTIM, J.

School of Health:

AFONSO, A.
ALMEIDA, C.
ALMEIDA, L.
ALMEIDA, L.
ANTÓNIO PESSOA, J.
ANTUNES, V.
BALTAR, C.
BÁRCIA, S.
BARREIROS, P.
BARROS, R.
BORREGO, M.
BRANDÃO, R.
BREDA, J.
CAIADO GOMES, J.
CALISTO, C.
CARDOSO, J.
CARMO, S.
CARVALHAL, A.
CARVALHO, M.
CARVALHO RODRIGUES, L.
CASASNOVAS, A.
CATARINA AFONSO, A.
CLÁUDIA DE SOUSA, A.
COSTA, M.
COUCEIRO, J.
DA LAPA, M.
DUARTE, D.
DURÃO, C.
FAUSTINO, R.
FELICIANO, E.
FÉLIX, S.
FERNANDES, R.
FERNANDES, S.
FIGUEIREDO, P.
FRAGATA, I.
GERMANO, A.
GODINHO, J.
ISABEL FERREIRA, A.
ISABEL RITO, A.
JACOBSOHN, L.
JOÃO FERNANDES, M.
JOÃO SANTOS, M.
JORGE, R.
KOPKE, R.
LEÃO, J.
LOPES, J.
LOPES, N.
LUCAS, L.

LÚCIA SILVA, A.
LÚCIO, I.
MADEIRA, P.
MAGALHÃES, Z.
MAMEDE, R.
MANUEL VIDAL, M.
MARECO, R.
MARQUES, R.
MARTINS, E.
MAURÍCIO, J.
MENDONÇA LIMA, F.
MENEZES, A.
MERCÊS, A.
MESQUITA, A.
MORAIS, T.
MOURA, J.
NASCIMENTO, G.
NETO, T.
OLIVEIRA, C.
OLIVEIRA, I.
PAIXÃO, P.
PASSÃO, V.
PAULA VITAL, A.
PAZ, S.
PERDIGÃO, E.
PEREIRA COUTINHO, A.
PINHO, M.
PINTO, E.
PIRES, A.
POSTOLACHE, G.
RAINHO, A.
RAMALHO, M.
RAMOS, C.
RAMOS, J.
RATO, J.
RATO, J.
RIBEIRO, H.
SANDE LEMOS, P.
SERRA, S.
SERRANO, M.
SILVA NUNES, J.
TECELÃO, S.
TOMÁS, A.
VALENTE, H.
VALENTIM, A.
VANESSA ANTUNES, A.
VASSALO, P.
VITOR, L.
VITOR, L.

UNIVERSIDADE AUTÓNOMA DE LISBOA
(Autonomous University of Lisbon)

Rua de Santa Marta 56, 1169-023 Lisbon

Telephone: (21) 317-76-46
E-mail: secgeral@universidade-autonoma.pt
Internet: www.universidade-autonoma.pt

Founded 1985
State control
Language of instruction: Portuguese

Rector: Prof. Dr JUSTINO MENDES DE ALMEIDA
Registrar: Prof. Dr JORGE TRACANA DE CARVALHO
Librarian: Prof. Dr MIGUEL FARIA

Library of 20,000 vols
Number of teachers: 500
Number of students: 8,700

DIRECTORS

Department of Architecture: Prof. FLAVIO BARBINI
Department of Communication Science: Prof. Dr ANTÓNIO BERNARDO
Department of Documentation Sciences: Prof. Dr JOSÉ MANUEL SUBTIL
Department of Modern Languages and Literature: Prof. Dr ISABEL MARIA FERNANDES DA SILVA
Department of Psychology and Sociology: Prof. Dr JOÃO HIPÓLITO
Department of Science and Technology: Prof. Dr ALBERTO CARNEIRO
Department of Tourism: GABRIELA MOURA

UNIVERSIDADE CATÓLICA PORTUGUESA
(Catholic University of Portugal)

Palma de Cima, 1649-023 Lisbon

Telephone: (21) 721-40-00
E-mail: info@reitoria.ucp.pt
Internet: www.ucp.pt

Founded 1967
Private control
Language of instruction: Portuguese
Academic year: September to July

Chancellor: Patriarch JOSÉ POLICARPO
Rector: Prof. Dr MANUEL BRAGA DA CRUZ
Vice-Rector: Prof. MARIA LUÍSA HOMEM LEAL DE FARIA GERALDES BARBA
Vice-Rector: Prof. PETER DAMIEN STILWEL
Librarian: Prof. JOSÉ CÂNDIDO DE OLIVEIRA MARTINS

Number of teachers: 1,000
Number of students: 11,300

Publications: *Didaskalia* (2 a year), *Direito e Justiça* (3 a year), *Economia* (3 a year), *Gestão e Desenvolvimento*, *Humanística e Teológica*, *Lusitania Sacra*, *Máthesis*, *Povos e Culturas*, *Revista Portuguesa de Filosofia* (4 a year), *Revista Portuguesa de Humanidades*, *Theologica* (4 a year)

UNIVERSIDADE DA BEIRA INTERIOR
(University of Beira Interior)

Convento de Sto. António, 6201-001 Covilhã

Telephone: (27) 531-97-00
E-mail: geral@ubi.pt
Internet: www.ubi.pt

Founded 1986
State control
Language of instruction: Portuguese

Rector: JOÃO ANTÓNIO DE SAMPAIO RODRIGUES QUEIROZ
Admin. Officer: Dr JOÃO CARLOS CORREIA LEITÃO
Librarian: Dra JOANA LOPES DIAS

Library of 74,000 vols
Number of teachers: 460
Number of students: 6,000

Publication: *Boletim Informativo 'Urbi@Orbi'*

UNIVERSIDADE DA MADEIRA
(University of Madeira)

Colégio dos Jesuitas, Rua dos Ferreiros, 9000-082 Funchal, Madeira

Telephone: (29) 120-94-00
E-mail: pinus@uma.pt
Internet: www.uma.pt

Founded 1988
State control
Academic year: September to August

Rector: Prof. Dr JOSÉ MANUEL NUNES CASTANHEIRA DA COSTA
Vice-Rector: Prof. Dr GONÇALO NUNO RAMOS FERREIRA DE GOUVEIA
Vice-Rector: Profa Dra SANDRA MARIA FREITAS MENDONÇA
Vice-Rector: Prof. Dr MIGUEL XAVIER JESUS JOSEFAT FERNANDES
Pro-Rector: Prof. Dr MORGADO DIAS
Pro-Rector: Prof. Dr BERNARDO GUIDO DE VASCONCELOS
Pro-Rector: Prof. Dr JOAQUIM JOSÉ SANCHES PINHEIRO
Administrator: Dra CARLA CRÓ ABREU
Librarian: Dra MARIA YOLANDA PEREIRA DA SILVA

Library of 129,000 vols
Number of teachers: 252
Number of students: 3,544

UNIVERSIDADE DE AVEIRO
(University of Aveiro)

Campus Universitário de Santiago, 3810-193 Aveiro

Telephone: (23) 437-02-00
E-mail: sre@ua.pt
Internet: www.ua.pt

Founded 1973
State control
Academic year: September to July

Rector: Prof. MANUEL ANTÓNIO ASSUNÇÃO
Vice-Rector: Prof. Dr JOAQUIM DA COSTA LEITE
Vice-Rector: Prof. Dr EDUARDO ANSELMO FERREIRA DA SILVA
Vice-Rector: Prof. Dr CARLOS DE PASCOAL NETO
Vice-Rector: Prof. JOSÉ FERNANDO FERREIRA MENDES
Vice-Rector: Prof. Dr. JOSÉ ALBERTO DOS SANTOS RAFAEL
Pro-Rector: Prof. Dr ARTUR DA ROSA PIRES
Pro-Rector: Prof. Dr JOSÉ CLAUDINO CARDOSO
Pro-Rector: Prof. Dr LILIANA XAVIER DE SOUSA
Pro-Rector: Prof. Dr OSVALDO ROCHA PACHECO
Pro-Rector: Prof. Dr GILLIAN OWEN MOREIRA
Chief Admin. Officer: Dr JOSÉ DA CRUZ COSTA
Librarian: Dra MARIA EMÍLIA M. FERREIRA ARAÚJO

Number of teachers: 952
Number of students: 13,000

Publication: *Lineas* (4 a year)

UNIVERSIDADE DE COIMBRA
(University of Coimbra)

Palácio dos Grilos Rua da Ilha, 3004-531 Coimbra

Telephone: (23) 985-99-00
E-mail: ucadmin@adm.uc.pt
Internet: www.uc.pt

Founded 1290 (in Lisbon)
State control
Language of instruction: Portuguese
Academic year: September to July

Rector: Prof. Dr FERNANDO JORGE RAMA SEABRA SANTOS
Vice-Rector: Prof. Dr HENRIQUE DO CARMO SANTOS MADEIRA
Vice-Rector: Prof. Dr ANTONIO MANUEL DE OLIVEIRA GOMES MARTINS
Vice-Rector: Prof. Dra CRISTINA MARIA SILVA ROBALO CORDEIRO
Pro-Rector: Prof. Dr JOSÉ ANTÓNIO OLIVEIRA BANDEIRINHA
Pro-Rector: Prof. Dr MARGARIDA ISABEL MANO TAVARES SIMÕES LOPES MARQUES DE ALMEIDA
Pro-Rector: Prof. Dr JOSÉ ANTÓNIO RAIMUNDO MENDES DA SILVA
Pro-Rector: Prof. Dr FERNANDO ALBERTO DEOMÉTRIO RODRIGUES ALVES GUERRA
Administrator: CÉLIA CRAVO
Registrar: Dr CARLOS JOSÉ LUZIO VAZ
Gen. Library Dir: Prof. Dr CARLOS MANUEL BAPTISTA FIOLHAIS
Dir of Univ. Archives: Prof. Dr MARIA JOSÉ AZEVEDO SANTOS

Library: see under Libraries and Archives
Number of teachers: 1,472 (incl. 494 profs)
Number of students: 21,165

Publications: *Acta Universitatis Conimbrigensis*, *Anuário da Universidade*, *Biblos*, *Boletim da Biblioteca da Universidade de Coimbra*, *Boletim da Faculdade de Direito*, *Boletim das Ciências Económicas*, *Boletim do Arquivo da Universidade*, *Boletim do Centro de Estudos Geográficos*, *Boletim do Laboratório de Fonética Experimental*, *Brasilia*, *Conimbriga*, *Humanitas*, *Revista Ciência Biológica*, *Revista da Universidade*, *Revista de História Literária de Portugal*, *Revista Portuguesa de Filologia*, *Revista Portuguesa de História*, *Revista Portuguesa de Pedagogia*

DEANS

Faculty of Arts: Prof. Dr CARLOS MANUEL BERNARDO ASCENSO ANDRÉ
Faculty of Economics: Prof. Dr JOSÉ JOAQUIM DINIS REIS
Faculty of Law: Prof. Dr ANTÓNIO DOS SANTOS JUSTO
Faculty of Medicine: Prof. Dr MANUEL AMARO DE MATOS SANTOS ROSA
Faculty of Pharmacy: Prof. Dr AMÍLCAR CELTA FALCÃO RAMOS FERREIRA
Faculty of Psychology and Education: Prof. Dr LUÍSA MARIA ALMEIDA MORGADO
Faculty of Science and Technology: Prof. Dr JOÃO GABRIEL MONTEIRO DE CARVALHO E SILVA
Faculty of Sports Science and Physical Education: Profa Dra JOSÉ PEDRO LEITÃO FERREIRA

UNIVERSIDADE DE ÉVORA
(University of Évora)

Largo dos Colegiais 2, 7004-516 Évora

Telephone: (26) 674-08-00
E-mail: uevora@uevora.pt
Internet: www.uevora.pt

Founded 1559, present status 1973
State control
Language of instruction: Portuguese
Academic year: September to September

Rector: Prof. CARLOS ALBERTO DOS SANTOS BRAUMANN
Vice-Rector: Prof. HERMÍNIA MARIA VASCONCELOS ALVES VILAR
Vice-Rector: Prof. JOSÉ MANUEL MARTINS CAETANO
Vice-Rector: Prof. MANUEL D'OREY CANCELA D'ABREU
Pro-Rector: Prof. JACINTO ANTÓNIO SETÚBAL VIDIGAL DA SILVA
Pro-Rector: Prof. MARTA DA CONCEIÇÃO SOARES SILVA DA CRUZ SILVÉRIO
Pro-Rector: Prof. JOSÉ MANUEL MADEIRA BELBUTE
Library Dir: Prof. SARA MARQUES PEREIRA
Library of 146,000 vols
Number of teachers: 577
Number of students: 7,625

Publication: *UELINE* (online (www.ueline.uevora.pt))

PROFESSORS

BRAUMANN, C. A. S., Stochastic Processes
CARVALHO, M. J. G. P. R., Agricultural Sciences
CLARA, M. I. E. DA, Plant Pathology
CORTE-REAL, J. A. M., Physics
FERREIRA, A. A. C. G., Soil Conservation
LOPES, R. M. E. J., Natural Resource Economics
LOURENÇO, M. E. V., Plant Physiology
MACHADO, J. A. S. G., History of Art
MARQUES, C. A. F., Agricultural Economics
MORAIS, J. M. C., Toxicology
OLIVEIRA, M. R. G., Phytotechnics
PINHEIRO, A. C. A., Agricultural Economics
RAMOS, F. M., Social and Cultural Anthropology
ROSA, R. M. V. N., Energetics, Climatology and Materials
SANTOS, M. A. O. P., Physics
SERRALHEIRO, R. P., Soil and Water Engineering
ZORRINHO, J. C. D., Information Systems Analysis

UNIVERSIDADE DE LISBOA
(University of Lisbon)

Alameda da Universidade, Cidade Universitária, 1649-004 Lisbon

Telephone: (21) 796-76-24
E-mail: reitoria@reitoria.ul.pt
Internet: www.ul.pt

Founded 1288, restored 1911
State control
Academic year: September to July

Rector: Prof. ANTÓNIO SAMPAIO DA NÓVOA
Vice-Rector: Prof. MARIA AMÉLIA BOTELHO DE PAULO MARTINS CAMPOS
Vice-Rector: Prof. ANTÓNIO EMÍLIO PEIXOTO VASCONCELOS TAVARES
Vice-Rector: Prof. CARLOS BAPTISTA LOBO
Administrator: Dra LUÍS PEDRO GOMES COSTA PAULITOS
Librarian: Dra MARIA LEAL VIEIRA

Number of teachers: 1,797
Number of students: 22,245

Publications: *Agenda* (12 a year), *Boletim*

UNIVERSIDADE DE TRÁS-OS-MONTES E ALTO DOURO
(University of Trás-os-Montes and Alto Douro)

Apdo 1013, 5000-801 Vila Real

Telephone: (25) 935-00-00
E-mail: reitoria@utad.pt
Internet: www.utad.pt

Founded 1973, present status 1986
State control
Language of instruction: Portuguese
Academic year: September to July

Rector: Dr CARLOS ALBERTO SEQUEIRA
Vice-Rector: Prof. Dr MARIA SOLINA DE JESUS CURADO QUINTAS DINIS POETA
Vice-Rector: Prof. Dr JORGE MANUEL TEIXEIRA DE AZEVEDO
Vice-Rector: Prof. Dr CARLOS DA COSTA ASSUNÇÃO
Pro-Rector: Prof. Dr ANTÓNIO AUGUSTO FONTAÍNHAS FERNANDES
Pro-Rector: Prof. Dr FERNANDO MANUEL COELHO FRANCO MARTINS
Pro-Rector: Prof. Dr ANTÓNIO JOSÉ ROCHA MARTINS DA SILVA
Pro-Rector: Prof. Dr JOÃO MANUEL PEREIRA BARROSO
Pro-Rector: Prof. Dr ISABEL ALEXANDRA FERREIRA DA SILVA VAZ NICOLAU
Pro-Rector: Prof. Dr ALEXANDRA SOFIA MIGUÉNS FIDALGO ESTEVES
Registrar: Dra ELSA JUSTINO
Administrator: RUI JORGE CORDEIRO DOS SANTOS
Librarian: Dra MARGARIDA CARVALHO

Number of teachers: 502
Number of students: 8,393

Publications: *A UTAD em Números*, *Annals of UTAD*, *Boletim Informativo da UTAD*, *Yearbook of UTAD*

UNIVERSIDADE DO ALGARVE
(University of Algarve)

Campus da Penha, 8005-139 Faro

Telephone: (289) 80-01-00
E-mail: info@ualg.pt
Internet: www.ualg.pt

Founded 1979
State control
Languages of instruction: English, Portuguese
Academic year: September to July

Rector: Prof. Dr ANTÓNIO BRANCO
Administrator: Dr JOÃO MANUEL PAULO RODRIGUES
Dir for Library: Prof. Dr ADRIANA NOGUEIRA

Number of teachers: 820

Number of students: 10,000

Publications: *Jornal Algarve Académico* (1 a year), *Revista Encontros Científicos*, *UALGzine*

DEANS

Engineering Institute: Prof. ILÍDIO MESTRE
Faculty of Economics: Prof. Dr EFIGÉNIO REBELO
Faculty of Human and Social Sciences: Prof. Dr MIRIAN TAVARES
Faculty of Science and Technology: Prof. Dr RUI CABRAL E SILVA
Faro School of Health: Prof. MARIA PALMA MATEUS
School of Education and Communication: Prof. ANTÓNIO GUERREIRO
School of Management, Hospitality and Tourism: Prof. Dr FRANCISCO SERRA

UNIVERSIDADE DO MINHO

Largo do Paço, 4704-553 Braga
Telephone: (25) 360-11-09
E-mail: gcii@reitoria.uminho.pt
Internet: www.uminho.pt
Founded 1973
State control
Language of instruction: Portuguese
Academic year: October to July

Rector: Prof. Dr ANTÓNIO M. DA CUNHA
Vice-Rector: Prof. RUI VIEIRA CASTRO
Vice-Rector: Prof. MARGARIDA PROENÇA
Vice-Rector: Prof. JOSÉ F. MENDES
Vice-Rector: Prof. GRACIETE DIAS
Pro-Rector: Prof. VASCO TEIXEIRA
Pro-Rector: Prof. PAULA CRISTINA MARTINS
Pro-Rector: Prof. FELISBELA LOPES
Pro-Rector: Prof. CLAÚDIA VIANA
Chief Admin. Officer: Eng. JOSÉ F. AGUILAR MONTEIRO
Librarian: Dr ELOY RODRIGUES

Number of teachers: 1,200
Number of students: 16,000

Publications: *Cadernos do Noroeste, Ciência Jurídica, Fórum, Revista Portuguesa de Educação, UM Boletim, UM Jornal*

UNIVERSIDADE DO PORTO
(University of Porto)

Praça Gomes Teixeira, 4099-002 Porto
Telephone: (22) 040-80-00
E-mail: up@up.pt
Internet: www.up.pt
Founded 1911
State control
Academic year: September to July
Language of instruction: Portuguese

Rector: Prof. Dr JOSÉ CARLOS MARQUES DOS SANTOS
Vice-Rector: ANTÓNIO CARDOSO
Vice-Rector: ANTÓNIO MARQUES
Vice-Rector: JORGE GONÇALVES
Vice-Rector: MARIA DE LURDES CORREIA FERNANDES
Pro-Rector: EMÍDIO GOMES
Pro-Rector: JOSÉ SARSFIELD CABRAL
Pro-Rector: LÍGIA MARIA RIBEIRO
Pro-Rector: MANUEL JANEIRA
Pro-Rector: PATRÍCIA TEIXEIRA LOPES
Administrator: JOSÉ ANGELINO BRANCO

Number of teachers: 1,895
Number of students: 29,896 (12,205 undergraduate, 17,691 postgraduate)

Publications: *Arquivos de Medicina* (medicine), *Arquivos Portugueses de Cirurgia* (surgery), *Cadernos de Consulta Psicologica* (consultant psychology), *Cadernos de Literatura Comparada* (comparative literature), *Douro, Estudos CEJD* (sport), *Mediaevalia* (medieval studies), *Revista Africana Studia* (African studies), *Revista*

de Filosofia (philosophy), *Revista de Geografia* (geography), *Revista de História* (history), *Revista de Línguas e Literaturas* (languages and literature), *Revista Educação Sociedade e Cultura* (education, society and culture), *Revista Estudos, Revista Património* (nat. heritage), *Revista População e Sociedade* (population and society), *Revista Portugália, Revista Portuguesa de Ciências do Desporto* (sports sciences), *Sociologia* (sociology), *Terceira Margem* (Brazilian studies)

UNIVERSIDADE DOS AÇORES
(University of the Azores)

Rua da Mãe de Deus s/n, Apdo 1422, 9501-801 Ponta Delgada, The Azores
Telephone: (29) 665-00-00
E-mail: uacgeral@uac.pt
Internet: www.uac.pt
Founded 1976, present status 1980
State control
Language of instruction: Portuguese
Academic year: September to June
3 Campuses: Campus de Ponta Delgada, Campus da Horta, Campus de Angra do Heroísmo

Rector: Prof. Dr AVELINO DE FREITAS DE MENESES
Vice-Rector: Prof. Dr JORGE MANUEL ROSA DE MEDEIROS
Vice-Rector: Prof. Dr. JOSÉ LUÍS VASCONCELOS BRANDÃO DA LUZ
Pro-Rector for Activities Coordination of Angra do Heroísmo Campus: Prof. Dr ALFREDO EMILIO SILVEIRA DE BORBA
Pro-Rector for Activities Coordination of Horta Campus: Dr RICARDO DA PIEDADE ABREU SERRÃO SANTOS
Pro-Rector for Area of Evaluation and Quality: Prof. Dr JORGE MANUEL ÁVILA DE LIMA
Pro-Rector for Coordination of Lifelong Learning: Prof. Dr MARIA TERESA PIRES DE MEDEIROS
Pro-Rector for Mobility and Cooperation: Prof. Dr LUÍS MANUEL VIEIRA DE ANDRADE
Administrator: Dra ANA PAULA CARVALHO HOMEM DE GOUVEIA
Librarian: Dra MARIA JOÃO MOTA MELO

Library of 200,000 vols
Number of teachers: 470
Number of students: 6,068

Publication: *Archipélago* (series on human sciences, natural sciences)

UNIVERSIDADE FERNANDO PESSOA
(University Fernando Pessoa)

Praça 9 de Abril 349, 4249-004 Porto
Telephone: (22) 507-13-00
E-mail: gri@ufp.edu.pt
Internet: www.ufp.pt
Founded present status 1996
Private control
Languages of instruction: Portuguese, English
Academic year: September to June

Rector: Prof. Dr SALVATO TRIGO

Library of 71,502 vols
Number of teachers: 230
Number of students: 3,868

Publications: *A Obra Nasce* (Architecture), *Antropológicas, Cadernos de Comunicação e Linguagem* (Communication and Language), *Cadernos de Estudos Latino-americanos, Cadernos de Estudos Mediáticos, Cibertextualidades* (Informatic Text and Cyber literature), *Consciências, Nuestra America* (Latin American Studies), *Revista da FCHS* (Journal of the Faculty of Human and Social Sciences), *Revista da FCS* (Journal of the Faculty of Health

Sciences), *Revista da FCT* (Journal of the Faculty of Science and Technology)

DEANS

Health Sciences: Prof. Dr LUIS MARTINS
Human and Social Sciences: Prof. INÊS GOMES
Science and Technology: Prof. ALVARO MONTEIRO

UNIVERSIDADE LUSÍADA
(Lusíada University)

Rua da Junqueira 188–198, 1349-001 Lisbon
Telephone: (21) 361-15-00
E-mail: info@lis.ulusiada.pt
Internet: www.ulusiada.pt
Founded 1986 by Cooperativa de Ensino Univ. Lusíada
Private control
Academic year: October to June
Campuses in Lisbon, Oporto and Vila Nova de Famalição

Rector: Prof. Dr DIAMANTINO DURÃO
Vice-Rector: Prof. Dr JOSÉ J. GONÇALVES DE PROENÇA
Librarian: Dr MADALENA FERNANDES

Library of 15,000 vols
Number of teachers: 986
Number of students: 17,041

Publications: *Boletim Informativo, CDE Bulletin, Pólis* (legal-political studies), *Revista Lusíada de Ciência e Cultura*

UNIVERSIDADE LUSÓFONA DE HUMANIDADES E TECNOLOGIAS
(Lusophone University of Humanities and Technology)

Campo Grande 376, 1749-021 Lisbon
Telephone: (21) 751-55-00
E-mail: informacoes@ulusofona.pt
Internet: www.ulusofona.pt
State control
Language of instruction: Portuguese

Rector: Prof. Dr MÁRIO C. MOUTINHO
Vice-Rector: Prof. Dr ÁUREA DO CARMO ADÃO
Pro-Rector: Prof. Dr AUGUSTO PEREIRA BRANDÃO

Library of 1,300 vols, 60,000 monographs

UNIVERSIDADE NOVA DE LISBOA
(New University of Lisbon)

Campus de Campolide, 1099-085 Lisbon
Telephone: (21) 371-56-00
E-mail: unl@unl.pt
Internet: www.unl.pt
Founded 1973
State control
Academic year: October to July

Rector: Prof. Dr ANTÓNIO MANUEL BENSABAT RENDAS
Vice-Rector: JOSÉ PEREIRA
Vice-Rector: MARIA ARMÉNIA CARRONDO
Vice-Rector: MIGUEL DE OLIVEIRA CORREIAL
Vice-Rector: JOÃO PAULO CRESPO
Pro-Rector: LUÍS ESPINHA DA SILVEIRA
Pro-Rector: HENRIQUE TEIXEIRA
Pro-Rector: VÁLTER LÚCIO
Pro-Rector: PAULO JOSÉ JUBILADO SOARES DE PINHO
Administrator: Dra FERNANDA ANTÃO

Number of teachers: 1,449
Number of students: 18,233

Publications: *Faculdade de Ciências Médicas: Annual Report, Faculdade de Ciências Médicas: Nova Medicina* (4 a year), *Faculdade de Ciências Sociais e Humanas: Bulletin, Portuguese and Japanese Studies* (1 a year), *Faculdade de Ciências Sociais e Humanas: Cadernos de Cultura* (irregular), *Faculdade de Ciências Sociais e Humanas: Cadernos de Filosofia* (2 a year), *Faculdade de Ciências Sociais e Humanas: Ethnologia* (irregular), *Faculdade de Ciências Sociais e Humanas: Faces de Eva: estudos sobre a mulher* (2 a year), *Faculdade de Ciências Sociais e Humanas: Fórum Sociológico* (2 a year), *Faculdade de Ciências Sociais e Humanas: Geolnova* (2 a year), *Faculdade de Ciências Sociais e Humanas: Revista da FCSH* (1 a year), *Faculdade de Ciências Sociais e Humanas: Revista de Estudos Anglo-Portugueses* (1 a year), *Faculdade de Ciências Sociais e Humanas: Working Paper* (irregular), *Faculdade de Direito Cultura: Revista de História e Teoria das Ideias* (1 a year), *Frontal* (irregular), *Instituto de Tecnologia Química e Biológica: Revista Portuguesa de Saúde Pública* (2 a year, 1 annual themed journal), *Thémis* (2 a year)

UNIVERSIDADE PORTUCALENSE INFANTE D. HENRIQUE

Rua Dr António Bernardino de Almeida 541, 4200-072 Porto

Telephone: (22) 557-20-00
E-mail: upt@upt.pt
Internet: www.upt.pt

Founded 1986
Private control
Language of instruction: Portuguese
Academic year: September to July

Rector: Prof. Dr GUILHERME OLIVEIRA
Vice-Rector: Prof. Dr PAULA MORAIS
Gen. Sec.: Prof. Dr JOSÉ MANUEL TEDIM
Chief Admin. Officer: Dr MATILDA MACHADO
Librarian: Profa Dra MANUELA BARRETO NUNES

Library of 46,150 vols
Number of teachers: 150
Number of students: 2,100

Publications: *Africana*, *Revista de Ciências da Educação*, *Revista de Ciências Históricas*, *Revista do Departamento de Inovação, Ciência e Tecnologia*, *Revista Jurídica*

UNIVERSIDADE TÉCNICA DE LISBOA
(Technical University of Lisbon)

Alameda de Santo António dos Capuchos 1, 1169-047 Lisbon

Telephone: (21) 881-19-01
E-mail: gre@reitoria.utl.pt
Internet: www.utl.pt

Founded 1930
State control
Language of instruction: Portuguese
Academic year: September to July

Rector: Prof. FERNANDO MANUEL RAMÔA CARDOSO RIBEIRO
Vice-Rector: Prof. LUÍS MANUEL DOS ANJOS FERREIRA
Vice-Rector: Prof. Dr VÍTOR FERNANDO DA CONCEIÇÃO GONÇALVES
Vice-Rector: Prof. HELENA MARGARIDA NUNES PEREIRA
Pro-Rector: Prof. Dr NUNO PAULO DE SOUSA ARROBAS CRATO
Pro-Rector: Prof. Dr MANUEL ALMEIDA RIBEIRO
Pro-Rector: Prof. Dr PAULO JORGE PIRES FERREIRA
Pro-Rector: Prof. Dr JOSÉ MANUEL FRAGOSO ALVES DINIZ
Administrator: Prof. EDUARDO LOPES RODRIGUES
Librarian: D. UMBELINA NASCIMENTO

Library of 500,000 vols, 2,8000 periodicals
Number of teachers: 1,822
Number of students: 22,503

Publications: *DAXIYANGGUO, Portuguese Review of Asiatic Studies*, *Episteme Review*, *European Review of Economics and Finance*, *ISCSP—Estudes Politicos e Sociais*, *ISEG—Estudes de Economia*, *Portuguese Economic Journal*, *Portuguese Review of International and Community Relations*, *Portuguese Review of Veterinary Sciences*

Colleges

Escola Náutica Infante D. Henrique (Infante D. Henrique Nautical School): Av. Eng. Bonneville Franco, 2770-058 Paço d'Arcos; tel. (21) 446-00-10; e-mail enautica@enautica.pt; internet www.enautica.pt; f. 1972; provides training in merchant navy; Pres. ABEL AMORIM.

Escola Superior de Actividades Imobiliárias (School of Real Estate): Praça Eduardo Mondlane, 7C Edifício Coopemi, 1950-104 Lisbon; tel. (21) 836-70-10; e-mail esai@esai.pt; internet www.esai.pt; f. 1990; Dir Prof. Dr LEANDRO PEREIRA.

Escola Superior de Enfermagem da Cruz Vermelha Portuguesa de Oliveira de Azeméis (School of Nursing of the Portuguese Red Cross Oliveira de Azemeis): Rua da Cruz Vermelha, Cidacos, Apdo 1002, 3720-126 Oliveira de Azeméis; tel. (25) 666-14-30; e-mail secretaria@esenfcvpoa.eu; internet www.esenfcvpoa.eu; f. 2002; polytechnic instn of nursing and health sciences education; Pres. HENRIQUE PEREIRA; Vice-Pres. FERNANDA PRÍNCIPE.

Escola Superior de Enfermagem de Coimbra (Nursing School of Coimbra): *Campus A:* Av. Bissaya Barreto, Apdo 55, 3001-901 Coimbra; *Campus B:* Rua 5 de Outubro, Apdo 55, 3001-901 Coimbra; tel. (23) 980-28-50; internet www.esenfc.pt; f. 2004 by merger of Nursing School of Higher Education Dr Angelo da Fonseca (f. 1881) with Nursing School of Higher Education Bissaya Barreto (f. 1971); Pres. MARIA DA CONCEIÇÃO SARAIVA DA SILVA COSTA BENTO; Vice-Pres. FERNANDO MANUEL DIAS HENRIQUES; Vice-Pres. JOSÉ REIS DOS SANTOS ROXO; publ. *Revista Referência.*

Escola Superior de Enfermagem de Lisboa (Lisbon Nursing School): Pólo Maria Fernanda Resende, Parque da Saúde, na Av. do Brasil 53-B, 1700-063 Lisbon; tel. (21) 792-41-00; internet www.esel.pt; f. 2004 by merger of School of Nursing Artur Ravara, School of Nursing Calouste Gulbenkian, Lisbon, School of Nursing and Francisco Garcia College of Nursing Maria Fernanda Resende; library: 22,300 vols, 170 periodicals, 2,500 digital journals; Pres. Prof. Dr MARIA FILOMENA MENDES GASPAR; Vice-Pres. Prof. OLGA MARIA ORDAZ FERREIRA; Vice-Pres. Prof. JOÃO CARLOS BARREIROS DOS SANTOS; publ. *Pensar Enfermagem.*

Escola Superior de Hotelaria e Turismo do Estoril (School of Hospitality and Tourism, Estoril): Av. Condes de Barcelona, 2769-510 Estoril; tel. (21) 004-07-00; e-mail info@eshte.pt; internet www.eshte.pt; offers graduate and postgraduate courses in tourism, travel and hospitality; 110 teachers; Pres. Prof. Dr FERNANDO MOREIRA.

Escola Superior de Saúde Egas Moniz (Egas Moniz School of Health Sciences): Egas Moniz, Cooperativa de Ensino Superior, Crl Campus Universitário, Quinta da Granja, Monte de Caparica, 2829-511 Caparica; tel. (21) 294-68-07; e-mail essem@egasmoniz.edu.pt; internet www.egasmoniz.com.pt; f. 1999; offers Masters courses in health sciences; Dir Prof. Dr JOSÉ A. DE SALIS AMARAL.

Escola Superior de Tecnologia da Saúde de Coimbra (School of Health Technology of Coimbra): Rua 5 de Outubro, S Martinho do Bispo, Apdo 7006, 3046-854 Coimbra; tel. (23) 980-24-30; e-mail geral@estescoimbra.pt; internet www.estescoimbra.pt; f. 1993; clinical analyses, audiology, cardiology, dietetics and nutrition, pharmacy, physiotherapy, radiology and environmental health; library: 4,357 monographs, 6,150 periodicals; 1,000 students; Pres. JORGE CONDE.

Escola Superior de Tecnologia da Saúde do Porto (School of Health Technology Porto): R. Valente Perfeito 322, 4400-330 Vila Nova de Gaia; tel. (22) 206-10-00; e-mail geral@estsp.ipp.pt; internet www.estsp.ipp.pt; f. 1980, present status 2004; offers Masters courses in health technology; Pres. AGOSTINHO CRUZ.

Escola Superior Enfermagem S. José de Cluny (St Joseph of Cluny School of Nursing): Rampa de Quinta de Sant' Ana 22, 9050-282 Funchal, Madeira; tel. (29) 174-34-44; e-mail geral@esesjcluny.pt; internet www.esesjcluny.pt; f. 1940; offers graduate and postgraduate courses in nursing; Pres. IRMÃ SOARES; publ. *O Cluny* (4 a year).

Escola Superior Gallaecia: Largo das Oliveiras, 4920-275 Vila Nova de Cerveira; tel. (25) 179-40-54; e-mail esg@esg.pt; internet www.esg.pt; f. 1992; attached to Fundação Convento da Orada; studies and research in design, ecology and landscape, arts and multimedia; offers Masters degree in architecture and urbanism; Pres. Prof. Dr MARIANA CORREIA.

Escola Universitária Vasco da Gama (Vasco da Gama University School): Mosteiro S. Jorge de Milréu, Estrada da Conraria, Castelo Viegas, 3040-714 Coimbra; tel. (23) 944-44-44; e-mail geral@euvg.net; internet www.euvg.net; f. 2000; attached to Associação Cognitária S. Jorge de Milréu; architecture and veterinary medicine; Pres. Prof. Dr MACHADO FARIA.

Instituto Nacional de Administração (National Institute for Public Administration): Palácio dos Marqueses de Pombal, 2784-540 Oeiras; tel. (21) 446-53-00; e-mail ina@ina.pt; internet www.ina.pt; f. 1979; training and research in public admin., law, European affairs, management, computer science, human resources management; European Documentation Centre; 373 teachers; 11,473 students; library: 19,000 vols, 250 periodicals; Pres. Prof. ANTÓNIO CORREIA DE CAMPOS; publ. *Legislação: Cadernos de Ciência de Legislação* (3 a year).

Instituto Piaget: Quinta de Arreinela de Cima, 2800-305 Almada; tel. (21) 294-62-50; e-mail info@almada.ipiaget.org; internet www.ipiaget.org; f. 1979; offers courses in clinical analysis and public health, social sciences, communications science and intercultural development, chemical sciences and the environment, complementary studies, education, artistic and industrial design, design and management of teaching materials, economics and business, economics and management of health sciences, infant education, nursing, food engineering, civil engineering, contract engineering and maintenance management, electrical engineering, physiotherapy, music, human, social and school nutrition, basic education, psychology, environmental health, sociology..

National Campuses:

Campus Académico de Almada: Quinta de Arreinela de Cima, 2800-305 Almada; tel. (21) 294-62-50; e-mail info@almada.ipiaget.org; internet www.ipiaget.org.

Campus Universitário de Viseu: Estrada do Alto do Gaio, Galifonge, Lordosa, 3515-776 Viseu; tel. (23) 2-91-01-00; e-mail info@viseu.ipiaget.org; internet www.ipiaget.org.

Complexo de Ensino Superior de Macedo de Cavaleiros: Rua Dr António Oliveira Cruz, 5340-257 Macedo de Cavaleiros; tel. (27) 842-00-40; e-mail info@ macedo.ipiaget.org; internet www.ipiaget .org.

Escola Superior de Saúde—Jean Piaget Silves: Enxerim, 8300-025 Silves; tel. (28) 244-01-70; e-mail info@silves.ipiaget .org; internet www.ipiaget.org.

ESS Jean Piaget: Escola Superior de Saúde, Alameda Jean Piaget, Gulpilhares, 4405-678 Vila Nova de Gaia; tel. (22) 753-66-20; e-mail info@gaia.ipiaget.org; internet www.ipiaget.org.

ISEIT Mirandela: Av. 25 de Abril, 5370-202 Mirandela; tel. (27) 820-01-50; e-mail info@mirandela.ipiaget.org; internet www .ipiaget.org.

Santo André: Bairro das Flores, Apdo 38, 7500-999 Vila Nova de Santo André; tel. (26) 970-87-10; e-mail info@standre.ipiaget .org; internet www.ipiaget.org.

Vila Nova de Gaia: Escola Superior de Educação, Rua António Sérgio, Apdo 551, 4410-269 Canelas, Vila Nova de Gaia; tel. (22) 753-76-00; e-mail info@gaia.ipiaget .org; internet www.ipiaget.org.

International Campuses:

Universidade Jean Piaget de Angola: see separate entry in Angola chapter.

Universidade Jean Piaget de Cabo Verde: see separate entry in Cape Verde chapter.

Instituto Politécnico da Guarda: Av. Dr Francisco Sá Carneiro 50, 6300-559 Guarda; tel. (27) 122-01-10; e-mail ipg@ipg.pt; internet twintwo.ipg.pt; f. 1980; courses in education, public relations, computer science, civil engineering, mechanical engineering and business management; 258 teachers; 3,700 students; Pres. Prof. Dr CONSTANTINO MENDES REI; Vice-Pres. Prof. Dr FERNANDO AUGUSTO SÁ NEVES SANTOS; Vice-Pres. Prof. Dr GONÇALO POETA FERNANDES; publs *Educação e Tecnologia* (2 a year), *Revista Egitania Sciencia* (2 a year).

Instituto Politécnico de Beja: Rua Pedro Soares, Campus do Instituto Politécnico de Beja, Apdo 6155, 7800-295 Beja; tel. (28) 431-44-00; e-mail geral@ipbeja.pt; internet www .ipbeja.pt; f. 1987; 231 teachers; 3,500 students; library: 35,000 vols; Dir Dr JOSÉ LUÍS RAMALHO.

Instituto Politécnico de Bragança: Campus de Santa Apolónia, Apdo 1101, 5301-856 Bragança; tel. (27) 333-06-90; e-mail ipb@ipb .pt; internet www.ipb.pt; f. 1983; agriculture, education, technology, management, communication and health; campus in Mirandela; 310 teachers; 7,000 students; Dir Prof. DIONÍSIO A. GONÇALVES.

Instituto Politécnico de Castelo Branco, Escola Superior Agrária: Quinta da Senhora de Mércules, Apdo 119, 6001-909 Castelo Branco; tel. (27) 233-99-00; e-mail esa@ ipcb.pt; internet www.esa.ipcb.pt; f. 1983; higher courses in agriculture (vegetable production, animal production, forestry production, natural resources management, edible oil production); 70 teachers; 1,400 students; library: 22,000 vols; Dir CELESTINO ANTÓNIO MORAIS DE ALMEIDA; publs *AGROforum*, *Bibliografia Temática*, *Boletim Bibliográfico*, *Folha Bibliográfica Mensal*.

Instituto Politécnico de Lisboa: Estrada de Benfica 529, 1549-020 Lisbon; tel. (21) 710-12-00; e-mail academica@sc.ipl.pt; internet www.ipl.pt; f. 1985; 13,000 students;

Pres. Dr ALBERTO A. ANTAS DE BARROS JÚNIOR; Administrator Dr ANTÓNIO JOSÉ CARVALHO MARQUES..

Constituent Institutes:

Escola Superior de Communicação Social: Campus de Benfica do IPL, 1549-014 Lisbon; tel. (21) 711-90-00; e-mail servicos_academicos@escs.ipl.pt; internet www.escs.ipl.pt; f. 1987; academic year September to July; library of 3,919 vols, 8,799 periodicals; 62 teachers; 866 students; Pres. Dr JOÃO PEDRO ABREU.

Escola Superior de Dança: Rua da Academia das Ciências 5, 1200-003 Lisbon; tel. (21) 324-47-70; e-mail geral@esd.ipl.pt; internet www.esd.ipl.pt; f. 1983; academic year September to July; 17 teachers; 83 students; library of 1,270 vols; Pres. Prof. FERNANDO CRESPO; publ. *Dança*.

Escola Superior de Educação: Campus de Benfica do IPL, 1549-003 Lisbon; tel. (21) 711-55-00; e-mail eselx@eselx.ipl.pt; internet www.eselx.ipt.pt; f. 1985; academic year September to July; library of 28,000 vols, 8,500 periodicals; 96 teachers; 1,065 students; Pres. Dra AMÁLIA GARRIDO BÁRRIOS.

Escola Superior de Música: Campus de Benfica do IPL, 1500-651 Lisbon; tel. (21) 322-49-40; e-mail esml@esm.ipl.pt; internet www.esml.ipl.pt; f. 1983; academic year October to June; library of 1,500 vols and 5,000 music scores; 43 teachers; 140 students; Dir Prof. JOSÉ JOÃO GOMES DOS SANTOS.

Escola Superior de Teatro e Cinema: Av. Marquês de Pombal 22B, 2700-571 Amadora; tel. (21) 498-94-00; e-mail estc@ estc.ipl.pt; internet www.estc.ipl.pt; f. 1983; academic year September to July; library of 10,000 vols, 2,000 periodicals; 43 teachers; 208 students; Pres. Prof. FILIPE OLIVEIRA.

Escola Superior de Tecnologia da Saúde de Lisboa (ESTeSL): Av. D João II, Lote 4.69.01, 1990-096 Lisbon; tel. (21) 898-04-00; e-mail estesl@estesl.ipl.pt; internet www.estesl.ipl.pt; f. 1981; Pres. Prof. MANUEL CORREIA; publ. *Saúde & Tecnologia*.

Instituto Superior de Contabilidade e Administração de Lisboa (ISCAL): Av. Miguel Bombarda 20, 1069-035 Lisbon; tel. (21) 798-45-00; internet www.iscal.ipl.pt; f. 1754 as Aula de Comércio, present name 1976; academic year September to July; library of 6,566 vols, 211 periodicals; 202 teachers; 3,334 students; Dir of Services Dr GRACIETTE PINTO CORREIA.

Instituto Superior de Engenharia de Lisboa (ISEL): Rua Conselheiro Emídio Navarro 1, 1959-007 Lisbon; tel. (21) 831-70-00; e-mail isel@isel.ipl.pt; internet www .isel.ipl.pt; f. 1852 as Instituto Industrial de Lisboa, present name 1974; academic year September to July; library of 9,388 vols, 312 periodicals; 551 teachers; 5,495 students; Pres. Dr JOSÉ CARLOS LOURENÇO QUADRADO.

Instituto Politécnico de Portalegre: Praça do Município Apdo 84, 7301-901 Portalegre; tel. (245) 30-15-00; e-mail geral@ipportalegre.pt; internet www .ipportalegre.pt; f. 1985; 250 teachers; 3,000 students; Pres. JOAQUIM MOURATO..

Constituent Schools:

Escola Superior Agrária de Elvas (ESAE): Edifício do Trem Alto, Av. 14 de Janeiro, Apdo 254, 7350-903 Elvas; tel. (26) 862-85-28; e-mail esae@esaelvas.pt; internet www.esaelvas.pt; 5 teachers; 25

students; Dir Eng. GONÇALO J. P. ANTUNES BARRADAS.

Escola Superior de Educação (ESE): Praça da República. Apdo 125, 7300-957 Portalegre; tel. (245) 33-94-00; e-mail esep@mail.esep.ipportalegre.pt; internet www.esep.pt; f. 1985; 72 teachers; 671 students; Pres. Dr CARLOS BRANDÃO; Librarian Dr DOMINGOS BUCHO; publ. *Aprender*.

Escola Superior de Saúde de Portalegre: Av. de Santo António, Apdo 89, 7301-901 Portalegre; tel. (24) 530-04-30; e-mail geral@essp.pt; internet www.essp.pt; Pres. Prof. FRANCISCO ALBERTO MOURATO VIDINHA.

Escola Superior de Tecnologia e Gestão (ESTG): Lugar do Abadessa, Apdo 148, 7301-901 Portalegre; tel. (24) 530-02-00; e-mail estg@estgp.pt; internet baco.estgp.pt; 45 teachers; 695 students; Pres. ARTUR JORGE ROMÃO; Librarian CATARINA ELIAS BARRADAS.

Instituto Politécnico de Santarém: Complexo Andaluz, Apdo 279, 2001-904 Santarém; tel. (24) 330-95-20; e-mail relacoes .publicas@ipsantarem.pt; internet www .ipsantarem.pt; f. 1979; colleges of agriculture, education, management, sport, health; Social Services; library: 38,900 vols; 270 teachers; 3,936 students; Pres. Prof. J. A. GUERRA JUSTINO; Vice-Pres. MARIA TERESA PEREIRA SERRANO; Vice-Pres. HÉLDER ORLANDO CARDOSO PEREIRA.

Instituto Politécnico de Setúbal: Largo Defensores da República 1, 2910-470 Setúbal; tel. (26) 554-88-20; e-mail ips@spr.ips.pt; internet www.ips.pt; f. 1981; 5 colleges: Escola Superior de Tecnologia de Setúbal, Escola Superior de Educação, Escola Superior de Ciências Empresariais, Escola Superior de Tecnologia do Barreiro, Escola Superior de Saúde; courses in education, management and technology; Pres. Prof. Dr ARMANDO PIRES.

Instituto Politécnico de Viana do Castelo (Viana do Castelo Polytechnic Institute): Praça General Barbosa, 4900-347 Viana do Castelo; tel. (25) 880-96-10; e-mail dmoreira@ ipvc.pt; internet www.ipvc.pt; f. 1980; 5 schools offering undergraduate and postgraduate degree courses; teacher-training college, agricultural college, schools of technology and management, nursing, business studies; Pres. Prof. RUI TEIXEIRA.

Instituto Politécnico de Viseu (Polytechnic Institute of Viseu): Av. José Maria Vale de Andrade, 3504-510 Viseu; tel. (23) 248-07-00; e-mail ipv@pres.ipv.pt; internet www.ipv .pt; f. 1979; Schools of education, technology, agrarian, technology and management, health, welfare services; higher training in teacher training, media studies, cultural studies, social service, sports, multimedia, engineering, management, marketing, tourism, agrarian sciences, nursing; 400 teachers; 7,000 students; Dir Eng. FERNANDO LOPES RODRIGUES SEBASTIÃO; publs *Forum Media* (2 a year), *Millenium* (4 a year).

Instituto Superior Bissaia Barreto: Campus do Conhecimento e da Cidadania, Apdo 7049, 3046-901 Coimbra; tel. (23) 980-04-50; e-mail isbb@isbb.pt; internet www .isbb.pt; f. 1927; law and public admin.; Dir Prof. Dr MARIA LUÍSA FERREIRA CABRAL DOS SANTOS VEIGA; Pres. Prof. Dr RUI NOGUEIRA LOBO ALARCÃO E SILVA.

Instituto Superior de Ciências da Saúde-Norte (Institute of Health Sciences-North): Coop. de Ensino Superior, Politécnico e Universitário, CRL R. Central de Gandra 1317, 4585-116 Gandra Prd; tel. (22) 415-71-00; e-mail info@cespu.pt; internet www

.cespu.pt; f. 1984, present name 1993, present location 1995; attached to Cooperative Education, Polytechnic and University (CESPU); higher education in health related courses; 380 profs; Dir Prof. Dr JORGE PROENÇA.

Instituto Superior de Ciências do Trabalho e da Empresa (Higher Institute of Labour and Enterprise): Av. das Forças Armadas, 1649-026 Lisbon; tel. (21) 790-30-00; e-mail geral@iscte.pt; internet iscte.pt; f. 1972; offers Bachelors, Masters and Doctoral courses in management, social and technological sciences; library: 56,000 vols, 17,000 periodicals; 400 teachers; 6,000 students; Dir LUÍS ANTERO RETO; publ. *Portuguese Journal of Social Science.*

Instituto Superior de Línguas e Administração (ISLA): Quinta do Bom Nome, Estrada da Correia 53, 1500-210 Lisbon; tel. (21) 030-99-08; e-mail jose.inacio@lx.isla.pt; internet www.isla.pt; f. 1962; business man-agement, marketing, human resources, computer science for management, applied mathematics, translation, tourism, secretarial studies; library: 20,000 vols; 260 teachers; 3,000 students; Dir Prof. Dr TAWFIQ RKIBI; publ. *Revista Portuguesa de Management.*

Instituto Superior Politécnico Portucalense: Rua do Paço 3, 4560 Penafiel; tel. (25) 571-10-54; f. 1990; courses in local govt admin., accounting, management, computer studies; library: 5,000 vols; 73 teachers; 620 students; Dir Dr JOAQUIM M. SILVA CUNHA.

Schools of Art

Escola Superior Artística do Porto (Art School of Porto): Largo de S. Domingos 80, 4050-545 Porto; tel. (22) 339-21-30; e-mail geral@esap.pt; internet www.esap.pt; f. 1982; 130 teachers; 780 students; Pres. ALEXANDRA TREVISAN DA SIVEIRA PACHECO.

Escola Superior de Belas-Artes (Higher School of Fine Arts): Av. Rodrigues de Freitas 265, 4049-021 Porto; tel. (22) 519-24-00; e-mail directivo@fba.up.pt; internet www.fba.up.pt; f. 1836, present name and status 1994; attached to Univ. of Porto; design, painting, sculpture, art sciences, drawing, geometry; library: 13,300 vols, 11,000 slides, 160 audiovisual titles, 50 electronic documents, antique book colln; Pres. Prof. JOSÉ VAZ; Vice-Pres. HEITOR ALVELOS.

Escola Universitária das Artes de Coimbra (Coimbra University School of Arts): Campus Universitário da ARCA, Lordemão, 3020-244 Coimbra; tel. (23) 949-74-00; e-mail info@arca.pt; internet www.arca.pt; f. 1989, present location 1996; offers Bachelors and Masters degrees in architecture, art and design; Sec. PAULA FONSECA.

QATAR

The Higher Education System

Qatar was part of the Ottoman Turkish Empire until 1916 when it came under British protection. British control was extended in 1934 and in 1971 independence was achieved. The traditional education system was based on Koranic and Shari'a (Islamic law) studies, but in 1973 the largely secular College of Education was founded and it became the University of Qatar in 1977. The University remains the sole national provider of higher education and consists of seven Colleges; degrees are approved by a number of different international accreditation agencies, for example, the College of Arts and Sciences Bachelors and Masters Environmental Sciences Programmes are accredited by the Committee of Heads of Environmental Sciences and the Institute of Environmental Sciences in the UK, while the Biomedical Sciences Programme is accredited by the National Accrediting Agency for Clinical Laboratory Sciences in the USA. A number of courses are taught exclusively to male or female students, for example, the Bachelor of Science in Civil Engineering is open only to male students and the Bachelor of Science in Computer Engineering only to female students. In 2011/12 a total of 8,786 students were enrolled at the University. In the same year a total of 15,352 students were enrolled in tertiary level education. Education City Qatar, the Qatar Foundations' flagship project which opened in 2003, hosts branch campuses of six US universities and numerous other educational and research institutions. A Science and Technology Park, designed to establish Qatar as a regional hub for research and development, was officially opened at Education City in 2009.

Admission to undergraduate courses at the University of Qatar is based upon results achieved in Al-Thanawaya Al-Amah (general secondary certificate) examinations. Students are admitted to the University before their applications are considered by the individual Colleges, some of which require students to sit an entrance examination. Degrees are awarded on a 'credit' basis, and students are required to accumulate a specified number of credits before graduating, depending on the degree applied for. There are mandatory Foundation courses for students in engineering, science, economics and administration, consisting of English, mathematics and IT training. The foremost undergraduate degree is the Bachelors, which generally takes three years to complete, although degrees in some subjects take longer (e.g. the Bachelor of Science in pharmacy, which lasts five years). The main postgraduate courses are the Postgraduate Diplomas and Certificates, Masters and Doctorates. Postgraduate Certificate and Diploma courses are between two and five semesters in duration and are available in education, library science and architectural planning. Masters degree courses last one year and students are required to maintain a specified grade point average. Doctoral degrees (mainly PhD) are not yet widespread.

The main post-secondary qualification for technical and vocational education is the Diploma in Technology, available from Colleges of Technology.

Regulatory Bodies

GOVERNMENT

Ministry of Culture, Arts and Heritage: POB 23700, C-Ring Rd, Doha; tel. 44022211; e-mail communications@moc.gov.qa; internet www.moc.gov.qa; Minister Dr HAMAD BIN ABDULAZIZ BIN ALI AL-KUWARI.

Ministry of Education and Higher Education: POB 80, al-Waqf Tower, al-Dafna, Doha; tel. 44941111; e-mail e.alhorr@moe.edu.qa; internet www.moe.edu.qa; Minister MUHAMMAD ABD AL-WAHID ALI AL-HAMMADI.

Supreme Education Council: POB 35111, al-Dafna, Doha; tel. 44044444; e-mail info@sec.gov.qa; internet www.sec.gov.qa; Minister MUHAMMAD ABD AL-WAHID ALI AL-HAMMADI.

NATIONAL BODY

Qatar Museums Authority: POB 2777, Doha; tel. 4525555; e-mail info@qma.com.qa; internet www.qma.com.qa; coordinating body for nat. museums; incl. Qatar National Museum, Museum of Islamic Art; spec. collns of Orientalist art, Islamic coins, natural history, antique weapons; Chief Exec. Officer ABDULLAH AL-NAJJAR; Exec. Dir Dr ROGER MANDLE.

Learned Societies

GENERAL

UNESCO Office Doha: 66 Lusail St, West Bay, POB 3945, Doha; tel. 4113293; e-mail doha@unesco.org; internet www.unesco.org/doha; designated Cluster Office for Bahrain, Kuwait, Oman, Qatar, Saudi Arabia and United Arab Emirates; Dir HAMED AL-HAMMAMI.

EDUCATION

Qatar Foundation: POB 5825, Doha; tel. 4540000; e-mail info@qf.org.qa; internet www.qf.org.qa; education, scientific research and community devt; responsible for Education City project; f. 1995; Pres. Dr MUHAMMAD FATHY SAOUD.

LANGUAGE AND LITERATURE

British Council: 93 Al-Sadd St, POB 2992, Doha; tel. 4251888; e-mail general.enquiries@qa.britishcouncil.org; internet www.britishcouncil.org/me-qatar.htm; offers courses and examinations in English language and British culture and promotes cultural exchange with the UK.

Research Institutes

ECONOMICS, LAW AND POLITICS

Center for International and Regional Studies: POB 23689, Doha; tel. 4578400; internet cirs.georgetown.edu; attached to School of Foreign Service in Qatar; research into regional and int. issues; Dir MEHRAN KAMRAVA.

RAND-Qatar Policy Institute: POB 23644, Doha; tel. 4927400; e-mail rand-qatarpolicyinstitute@rand.org; internet www.rand.org/qatar; Private control; attached to RAND Corporation and Qatar Foundation; analysis into public policy; Dir RICHARD E. DARILEK.

HISTORY, GEOGRAPHY AND ARCHAEOLOGY

Gulf Cooperation Council Folklore Centre: POB 7996, Doha; tel. 4861999; f. 1982; mem. states: Bahrain, Kuwait, Oman, Qatar, Saudi Arabia, UAE; collect, study, disseminate and protect indigenous local folklore mainly in the fields of literature, customs and traditions, music and dance, arts and crafts; library of 4,853 vols, 110 journals, also video cassettes, cassette recordings and photographic material; Dir-Gen. ABDULRAHMAN AL-MANNAI; publ. Al Ma'thurat Al Sha'biyyah (4 a year).

MEDICINE

Doha International Institute for Family Studies and Development: POB 34080, Doha; tel. (44) 548200; e-mail diifsd@qf.org.qa; internet www.fsd.org.qa; f. 2004; attached to Qatar Foundation; research and scholarship on the legal, sociological and scientific basis of the family as the natural and fundamental group unit of society.

Libraries and Archives

Doha

College of the North Atlantic-Qatar Campus Library System: POB 24449, Doha; tel. 4952051; e-mail reference@cna-qatar.edu.qa; internet cna-qatar.libguides.com/library; incl. Al-Rayyan Library spec. colln of pre-nursing, health sciences, English language learning, engineering, business, information technology and security; Man. CATHLEEN DE GROOT.

Qatar National Library: POB 5825, Doha; tel. 44546039; e-mail qnlps@qf.org.qa;

internet www.qnl.qa; f. 2012; 125,000 vols; 5 brs; reopens in 2015 in new bldg; Project Dir Dr CLAUDIA LUX.

Qatar University Library: POB 2713, Doha; tel. 4852406; e-mail library@qu.edu.qa; internet www.qu.edu.qa/library; f. 1973.

Research and Documents Division: POB 923, Amir's Office, Doha; tel. 4425497; f. 2003; Dir Dr SULTAN JASIM AL-JABER.

Museums and Art Galleries

Doha

Museum of Islamic Art: POB 2777, Doha; tel. 4224444; e-mail infomia@qma.com.qa; internet www.mia.org.qa; attached to Qatar Museums Authority; Early Islamic Art, Iran and Central Asia (12th–19th century), Egypt and Syria (12th–15th century), Turkey (16th–18th century), India (16th–18th century).

Qatar National Museum: QMA Tower, POB 2777, Doha; tel. 44525555; e-mail qnm2000@hotmail.com; internet www.qma.org.qa/en/collections/national-museum-of-qatar; f. 1975; attached to Qatar Museums Authority; collns: ethnography, archaeo-history, geology, botany, zoology, jewellery, numismatics, perfumery; Dir IBRAHIM JABER AL-JABER.

Universities

CARNEGIE MELLON QATAR

POB 24866 Doha

Telephone: 4548400

E-mail: ug-admission@qatar.cmu.edu

Internet: www.qatar.cmu.edu

Founded 2004; attached to Carnegie Mellon Univ., Pittsburgh, USA and the Qatar Foundation

Private control

Business and computer science

Dean: Dr CHUCK THORPE

Librarian: NIKKI KRYSAK

NORTHWESTERN UNIVERSITY IN QATAR

POB 34102, Doha

Telephone: 4545100

E-mail: nu-qadmissions@northwestern.edu

Internet: www.qatar.northwestern.edu

Founded 2004; attached to Northwestern Univ., Illinois, USA and the Qatar Foundation

Private control

Schools of communication and journalism

Dean: JOHN D. MARGOLIS

STENDEN UNIVERSITY QATAR

POB 36037, Doha

Telephone: 4888116

E-mail: info@chn.edu.qa

Internet: www.stenden.com/en/stenden/locations/qatar; attached to Stenden Univ., Netherlands

International hospitality management, tourism management, international business and management studies

TEXAS A&M UNIVERSITY AT QATAR

POB 23874, Doha

Telephone: 4230010

E-mail: info@qatar.tamu.edu

Internet: www.qatar.tamu.edu

Founded 2003; attached to Texas A&M Univ., Texas, USA

Private control

Chemical engineering, electrical and computer engineering, mechanical engineering, petroleum engineering

Dean and CEO: Dr MARK H. WEICHOLD

Librarian: CAROLE THOMPSON

Library of 3,900,000 vols, 90 periodicals

Number of students: 300

UNIVERSITY OF QATAR

POB 2713, Doha

Telephone: 4852222

E-mail: info@qu.edu.qa

Internet: www.qu.edu.qa

Founded 1973 as College of Education, Univ. status 1977

State control

Language of instruction: Arabic

Academic year: September to June

Chair.: HH Sheikh TAMIN BIN HAMAD AL THANI (Heir Apparent)

Pres.: Prof. Dr SHEIKHA ABDULLAH AL-MISNAD

Vice-Pres. and Chief Academic Officer: Dr SHEIKHA JABOR AL-THANI

Vice-Pres. and Chief Financial Officer: Dr HUMAID ABDULLAH AL-MIDFAA

Vice-Pres. for Institutional Planning and Devt: Prof. SAIF SAID AL-SOWAIDI

Vice-Pres. for Research: Dr HASSAN AL-DERHAM

Vice-Pres. for Student Affairs: Dr OMAR MOHAMED AL-ANSARI

Library Dir: TAG ELSIR IBRAHIM S. KARDAMAN

Library of 360,000 vols (Arabic and English), 1,040 periodicals

Number of teachers: 710

Number of students: 7,250

Publication: *Fruits of Knowledge* (1 a year)

DEANS

College of Arts and Science: Dr SIHAM AL-QARADAWI

College of Business and Economics: Prof. Dr MUHAMMAD K. NAJDAWI (acting)

College of Education: Prof. Dr HESSA AL-SADIQ

College of Engineering: Dr MAZEN HASNAH

College of Law: Dr HASSEN ABDULRAHIM AL-SAYED

College of Pharmacy: Prof. Dr PETER JEWESSON

College of Shari'a Law and Islamic Studies: Dr AISHA YOUSIF AL-MANNAI

ATTACHED INSTITUTES

Computer Centre: Dir Dr JIHAD MUHAMMAD AL-JAAM.

Documentation and Humanities Research Centre: colln, classification and preparation of documents pertaining to the field of humanities as a basic source of research, and the issuing of documented research papers; specialized research on the heritage of the Gulf area in all its aspects: social, cultural, linguistic and literary; Dir Dr SAIF AL-MEREIKHI.

Educational Research Centre: educational research and studies that contribute to the devt of education in the State of Qatar, oriented among other things toward improvement of the educational process, curricula and textbooks; Dir Dr NASRA REDA BAGHER.

Educational Technology Centre: Dir Dr JIHAD MOHAMMED AL-JAAM.

Gulf Studies Centre: Dir Dr HASSAN AL-ANSARI.

Scientific and Applied Research Centre: e-mail sarc@qu.edu.qa; to develop experience in scientific, industrial and agricultural fields with spec. reference to industries, natural resources, agriculture and animal resources of Qatar; and to contribute to the transfer of technology and adapt it for application in Qatar; Dir Dr MOHSIN ABDULLAH AL-ANSI.

Sirra and Sunna Research Centre: research related to the *Sirra* of the Prophet Muhammad, i.e. his preaching, moral and spiritual values, and his life, and the *Sunna* of the Prophet Muhammad, i.e. his sayings and acts, which are the second source of guidance for the practice of Islam after the holy Koran; Dir Prof. YOUSUF AL-QARADAWI

VIRGINIA COMMONWEALTH UNIVERSITY IN QATAR

Doha

Telephone: 4927200

E-mail: vcuqadmissions@qatar.vcu.edu

Internet: www.qatar.vcu.edu

Founded 2003; attached to Virginia Commonwealth Univ., USA, and the Qatar Foundation

Private control

Bachelor of Fine Arts degree in fashion design, graphic design, interior design

Dean: ALLYSON VANSTONE

Library of 16,000 vols

Colleges

Centre for GIS: POB 22088 Doha; tel. 4955112; e-mail masoun@gisqatar.org.qa; internet www.gisqatar.org.qa; attached to Urban Planning and Devt Authority; Regional Training Centre for Geospatial Information Systems.

College of the North Atlantic-Qatar: 68 Al-Tarafa, Duhail N, POB 24449, Doha; tel. 4952222; e-mail info@cna-qatar.edu.qa; internet www.cna-qatar.com; f. 2002; attached to College of the North Atlantic, Canada; technical college offering 4 programmes in business studies, engineering technology, health sciences, information technology; security academy, centre for banking and financial studies; 400 teachers; 2,300 students; Pres. Dr HAROLD JORCH.

Language Teaching Institute: POB 3224, Doha; tel. 4657690; f. 1972; part-time courses in Arabic, Persian, English, French, for mature students already in employment; library: 6,000 vols; 29 teachers; 504 students; Dir MUHAMMAD HASSAN AL-SIDDIQI.

Qatar Aeronautical College: POB 4050, Doha; tel. 4408888; e-mail qacadmn@qatar.net.qa; internet www.qac.edu.qa; Dir-Gen. ALI IBRAHIM AL-MALKI; Dir for Academic Affairs Dr SAID ABDULLAH AL-SULEIMAN.

School of Foreign Service in Qatar: POB 23689 Doha; tel. 4578100; e-mail sfsqadmissions@georgetown.edu; internet qatar.sfs.georgetown.edu; Private control; attached to Georgetown Univ., USA; Dean of Academic Affairs VICTORIA PEDRICK; Dir of Library FRIEDE WIEBE; Dir of Public Affairs CHARLES NAILEN.

Weill Cornell Medical College in Qatar: Doha; tel. 4928402; e-mail jadmissions@qatar-med.cornell.edu; internet qatar-weill.cornell.edu; Private control; attached to Cornell Univ., Ithaca, NY, USA; Dir JAVAID I. DHEIKH.

ROMANIA

The Higher Education System

Formerly part of the Ottoman Turkish Empire, Romania became an independent kingdom in 1881. In 1947 King Michael was forced to abdicate and the Romanian People's Republic was proclaimed. Romania became a one-party state under the communist Romanian Workers' Party. Communist rule ended in 1989, when the regime of President Ceauşescu was overthrown in a revolution; multi-party democracy was established in 1991. The oldest current institutions of higher education are mostly specialist establishments dating from the first half of the 19th century, among them the Universitatea 'Politehnica' din Bucureşti (founded in 1818), the Academia de Muzică 'Georghe Dima' (founded in 1819), the Universitatea de Ştiinţe Agronomice şi Medicină Veterinara Bucureşti (founded in 1852) and the Universitatea de Medicină şi Farmacia 'Carol Davila' (founded in 1857; current name since 1990). There was an expansion of higher education during the period of reform (1859–66) initiated by Alexander Ioan Cuza, the first elected Domnitor of the United Principalities of Wallachia and Moldova (which later became independent Romania). Current institutions established during that period include the Unversitatea 'Alexandru Ioan Cuza' Iaşi (founded in 1860), the Universitatea de Arte 'George Enescu' (founded in 1860; current name since 1960), the Universitatea Naţională de Muzică din Bucureşti (founded in 1864) and the Universitatea din Bucureşti (founded in 1864). In 2007/08 there were 106 institutions of higher education. The number of students enrolled at tertiary level in 2010/11 totalled 999,523.

The Ministry of National Education is responsible for higher education, which is governed by the Constitution (1991), the Education Act (1995) and the National Education Law (2011). Education at public institutions is free. Romania participates in the Bologna Process to establish a European Higher Education Area, the first phase of which is to adopt a credit-based system of comparable degrees with three main cycles (undergraduate, postgraduate and doctoral).

Admission to higher education is on the basis of the Bacalaureat (secondary school diploma) and success in the university entrance examination. Since 2005/06 long-term higher education consists of undergraduate and postgraduate degrees, principally the undergraduate Diploma de Licenta (Bachelors) and postgraduate Diploma de Master (Masters) degrees, in accordance with the principles of the Bologna Process. The Diploma de Licenta is a programme of study lasting four to six years, depending on the field of study. Following the Diploma de Licenta, graduates may study for one or two years for the award of, principally, the Diploma de Master or Diploma de Studii postuniversitare (Professional Postgraduate Diploma). Finally, the highest university-level degree is the Doktorat (Doctorate), a programme of study lasting three to seven years.

Post-secondary technical and vocational education (Şcoala Postliceală) consists of one- to three-year training courses at three levels of specialization. Courses are assessed by a practical examination, a written paper and preparation and presentation of a project. The National Authority for Qualifications, established by the 2011 National Education Law, is responsible for developing a National Qualifications Framework in accordance with European standards. The National Centre for Technical and Vocational Education and Training oversees development and strategies in this area. Both instances are subordinated to the Ministry of National Education.

Since 2006 the Agenţia Română de Asigurare a Calităţii în Învăţămantul Superior (ARACIS—Romanian Agency for Quality Assurance in Higher Education) has been in charge of university accreditation. ARACIS is a full member of the European Association for Quality Assurance in Higher Education. Accreditation is a two-stage process. The first step is trust licensing, which gives institutions the right to organize admission examinations. The second step is accreditation, which gives institutions the right to administer degree examinations and issue diplomas (degrees) recognized by the Ministry of National Education.

In 2011 the European University Association announced that it would be working closely with the Romanian Government to support the implementation of a major higher education reform bill that was adopted in February of that year. Under the new law all universities, both public and private, will be grouped into three major categories of institutions—research intensive, teaching and research oriented, and mainly teaching institutions. In a first stage of the reform, that was expected to take three years to complete, universities would be asked to evaluate their competencies in line with one of the three categories.

Regulatory and Representative Bodies

GOVERNMENT

Ministry of Culture: Unirii Blvd 22, Sector 3, 030833 Bucharest; tel. (21) 2232847; e-mail cabinet.ministru@cultura.ro; internet www.cultura.ro; Minister GIGEL-SORINEL ŞTIRBU.

Ministry of National Education: Str. Gen. Berthelot 28–30, Sector 1, 010168 Bucharest; tel. (21) 4056200; e-mail public@min.edu.ro; internet www.edu.ro; Minister REMUS PRICOPIE.

ACCREDITATION

Agenţia Română de Asigurare a Calităţii în Învăţământul Superior (Romanian Agency for Quality Assurance in Higher Education): Spiru Haret St 12, 010176 Bucharest; tel. (21) 2067600; e-mail secretariat@aracis.ro; internet www.aracis.ro; f. 2005; draws up procedures and sets accreditation standards for the assessment of different types of programmes and higher education providers and submits them to the Min. of National Education for approval; carries out assessments and submits accreditation reports to the Min.; draws up and reviews the nat. reference standards and the performance indicators to assess and assure the quality of higher education; devises and promotes policies and strategies to improve the quality of education in Romania; 17 mems; Pres. Prof. Dr IOAN CURTU; Vice-Pres. Prof. Dr ADRIAN MIROIU; Sec.-Gen. Prof. Dr MIHAI ARISTOTEL UNGUREANU; publ. *Quality Assurance Review*.

ENIC/NARIC Romania: c/o Nat. Centre for Recognition and Equivalence of Diplomas Granted Abroad, Str. Gen. Berthelot 28–30, Sector 1, 010168 Bucharest; tel. (21) 3132677; internet www.cnred.edu.ro; f. 1995; Dir GIANINA CHIRAZI.

NATIONAL BODY

Romanian Council of Rectors: Splaiul Independenţei nr. 313, 060042 Bucharest; tel. (21) 3181000; e-mail cnr@rectorat.pub.ro; internet consiliulrectorilor.ro; formulates proposals on higher education devt strategy; advises govt and nat. bodies on issues related to higher education; Pres. Prof. Ing. Dr ECATERINA ANDRONESCU.

Learned Societies

GENERAL

Academia Română (Romanian Academy): Calea Victoriei 125, Sector 1, 010071 Bucharest; tel. (21) 2128640; internet www.acad.ro; f. 1866 as Romanian Literary Soc., present name and status 1879; sections of philology and literature, history and archaeological sciences, mathematical sciences, physical sciences, chemical sciences, biological sciences, geonomical sciences, engineering sciences, agriculture and forestry sciences, medical sciences, economic, law and sociological sciences, philosophical, theological, psychological and pedagogical sciences, arts, architecture and audiovisual, information science and technology; 3 regional brs; attached research institutes: see Research Intitutes; 181 acting mems, 135 hon. mems; library: see under Libraries and Archives; Pres. IONEL HAIDUC; Sec.-Gen. PĂUN ION OTIMAN; publs *Annuaire Roumain d'Anthropologie*, *Anuar de lingvistică şi istorie literară* (Yearbook of Linguistics and Literary History), *Buletinul Societăţii Numismatice Române* (1 a year), *Cahiers de linguistique théorique et appliquée*, *Calitatea vieţii* (Quality of Life), *Cellulose Chemistry and Technology*, *Cercetări de lingvistică* (Linguistic Researches), *Fonetică şi dialectologie* (Phonetics and Dialectology), *Functional and Architectural Electronics*, *Historia Urbana*, *Limba română* (The Romanian Language), *Mathematica*, *Nyelv- és Irodalomtudományi Köziemények*, *Ocrotirea naturii şi a mediului înconjurător* (The Protection of Nature and of the Environment), *Revista de etnografie şi folclor* (Journal of Ethnography and Folklore), *Revista de psihologie* (Journal of Psychology), *Revista română de demografie* (Romanian Journal of Demography), *Revue d'analyse numérique et de théorie de l'approximation*, *Revue des études sud-est européennes*, *Revue Roumaine de biochimie*, *Revue Roumaine de biologie: Série de biologie animale*, *Revue Roumaine de biologie: Série de biologie végétale*, *Revue Roumaine de chimie*, *Revue Roumaine de géologie*, *géophysique et géographie* (3 series), *Revue Roumaine de Linguistique*, *Revue Roumaine de mathématiques pures et appliquées*, *Revue Roumaine de philosophie*, *Revue Roumaine de psychologie*, *Revue Roumaine des sciences économiques*, *Revue Roumaine des sciences juridiques*, *Revue Roumaine des sciences techniques: Série de mécanique appliquée*, *Revue Roumaine des sciences techniques: Série électrotechnique et énergétique*, *Romanian Astronomical Journal*, *Romanian Chemical Quarterly Review*, *Romanian Journal of Biophysics*, *Romanian Journal of Sociology*, *Romanian Neurosurgery*, *Romanian Reports of Physics*, *Studii şi cercetări de antropologie* (Studies and Research in Anthropology), *Studii şi cercetări de biochimie* (Studies and Research in Biochemistry), *Studii şi cercetări de biologie: Seria biologie animală* (Studies and Research in Biology: Series of Animal Biology), *Studii şi cercetări de biologie: Seria biologie vegetală* (Studies and Research in Biology: Series of Plant Biology), *Studii şi cercetări de geologie, geofizică şi geografie* (Studies and Research in Geology, Geophysics and Geography, 3 series), *Studii şi cercetări de mecanică aplicată* (Studies and Research in Applied Mechanics), *Studii şi cercetări lingvistice* (Studies and Research in Linguistics), *Studii şi cercetări matematice* (Studies and Research in Mathematics), *Synthesis–Bulletin du Comité National de Littérature comparée*, *Travaux de l'Institut de Spéléologie 'Emile Racovitza'*.

Asociaţia Culturală 'Pro Basarabia şi Bucovina' (Bessarabia and Bucovina Cultural Association): Str. Blanari 23, Sector 3, 030060 Bucharest; tel. (21) 3122763; e-mail office@probasarabiasibucovina.ro; internet www.probasarabiasibucovina.ro; f. 1990; promotes and fosters the integration of spiritual values, cultural, educational and scientific Romanians in Bessarabia, N Bukovina and Herta Tinutu; 27 nat. brs and 3 in Basarabia; 60,000 mems; Pres. MARIAN CLENCIU; publs *Dor de Basarabia*, *Maluri de Prut'*, *Prutul*.

Centrul European de Cultură, Bucureşti (European Cultural Centre, Bucharest): Sfinţii Voievozi St 49–51, Fourth Fl., Apt. 16, Sector 1, 010968 Bucharest; tel. (21) 6503280; e-mail cti@clicknet.ro; f. 1990; organizes int. postgraduate seminars on European issues; promotes Romania as cultural tourist destination, through research, publs and study tours; promotes colleges and univs in W Europe, the USA, Canada and Australia, offering int. programmes related to undergraduate and postgraduate studies in Romania; 1,300 mems; library of 3,000 vols, 40 periodicals; Pres. DAN BERINDEI; Exec. Dir MARIA BURS-POPESCU.

Institutul Cultural Român (Romanian Cultural Institute): Aleea Alexandru 38, Sector 1, 011824 Bucharest; tel. (31) 7100606; e-mail icr@icr.ro; internet www.icr.ro; f. 2003; promotes Romanian culture abroad; publishes works by Romanian and foreign authors, dictionaries, history texts and other literature; institutes in Berlin, Brussels, Budapest (with a br. in Szeged), Istanbul, Kishinev, Lisbon, London, Madrid, New York, Paris, Prague, Rome, Stockholm, Tel Aviv, Venice, Vienna and Warsaw; 130 mems; Pres. Prof. Dr ANDREI MARGA; Sec.-Gen. NICOLAE BRÎNZEA; publs *Curierul Românesc* (12 a year), *Destin Românesc* (4 a year), *Dilema* (48 a year), *Euresis* (2 a year), *Glasul Bucovinei* (4 a year), *Lettres internationales* (4 a year), *Plural* (2 a year), *România Culturală* (online), *Transylvanian Review* (4 a year).

Societatea Cultural-Ştiinţifică 'Getica' (Getica Cultural Scientific Society): CP 37–149, 70060 Bucharest 37; Str. Plantelor 8–10, 023974 Bucharest; tel. (21) 3214512; e-mail contact.gandirea@yahoo.com; internet getica.8m.com; f. 1990; 87 mems; library of 7,000 vols; Pres. GABRIEL GHEORGHE; Scientific Sec. Prof. ALEXANDRU BADEA; publ. *Getica* (irregular).

AGRICULTURE, FISHERIES AND VETERINARY SCIENCE

Academia de Ştiinţe Agricole şi Silvice 'Gheorghe Ionescu-Şişeşti' (Academy of Agricultural and Forestry Sciences 'Gheorghe Ionescu-Şişeşti'): Bdul Mărăşti 61, Sector 1, 011464 Bucharest; tel. (21) 3184451; e-mail secretariat@asas.ro; internet www.asas.ro; f. 1969; sections of soil science, land reclamation and environmental protection in agriculture, field crops, horticulture, animal husbandry, veterinary medicine, forestry science, agrarian economics and rural devt, food industry, agricultural mechanization; 51 agricultural research and devt stations; 17 institutes; 6 regional brs; 214 mems; library: see under Libraries and Archives; Pres. Prof. Dr GHEORGHE SIN; publs *Buletinul informativ al Academiei de Ştiinţe Agricole şi Silvice* (1 a year), *Bulletin de l'Académie des Sciences Agricoles et Forestières* (1 a year), *Bulletin of the Academy of Agricultural and Forestry Sciences* (1 a year), *Yearbook* (1 a year).

Asociaţia Economiştilor Agrarieni din România (Agrarian Economists Association of Romania): Bdul Mărăşti 61, 011464 Bucharest; tel. (21) 6172180; f. 1990; 42 mems; library of 4,000 vols; Pres. Prof. N. N. CONSTANTINESCU; Gen. Sec. RADU COTIANU.

Societatea Inginerilor Agronomi (Agronomists Society): Bdul Mărăşti 59, 011464 Bucharest; tel. (21) 6182230; f. 1990; 3,500 mems; Pres. Prof. Dr MIHAI VĂJIALĂ; Gen. Sec. Dr RUXANDRA CIOFU.

Societatea Naţională Română pentru Ştiinţa Solului (Romanian National Soil Science Society): Bdul Marasti 61, 071331 Bucharest; tel. (21) 2249442; e-mail snrss@ icpa.ro; internet www.snrss.ro; f. 1961; stimulates scientific research in all soil science areas; organizes scientific reunions, congresses, nat. and int. confs, symposium; 6 comms: soil physics and soil technology, soil chemistry and mineralogy, soil biology, soil fertility and plant nutrition, soil genesis, classification and cartography, soils and environment; 10 regional brs; 330 mems; library of 3,592 vols; Pres. Prof. Dr SEVASTIAN UDRESCU; Sec.-Gen. Dr CONSTANTIN CRACIUN; publs *Bulletin Informativ* (1 a year), *Ştiinţa Solului* (Soil Science, 2 a year).

Societatea Română de Zootehnie (Romanian Society of Animal Production): Bdul Mărăşti 59, 011464 Bucharest; tel. (21) 6182230; f. 1990; 4,500 mems; Pres. Prof. STEFAN POPESCU-VIFOR; Sr Sec. Dr AGATHA POPESCU.

ARCHITECTURE AND TOWN PLANNING

Uniunea Arhitecţilor din România (Union of Architects of Romania): Str. Dem Dobrescu 5, Sector 1, 010025 Bucharest; tel. (21) 3156073; e-mail uar_contact@yahoo.com; internet www.uniuneaarhitectilor.ro; f. 1891; 2,010 mems; library of 13,000 vols; Pres. Dr VIORICA CUREA; publs *Architectura* (4 a year, online, arhitectura-1906.ro), *Buletin Informativ* (12 a year).

ECONOMICS, LAW AND POLITICS

Asociaţia de Drept Internaţional şi Relaţii Internaţionale (Association of International Law and International Relations): Şoseaua Kiseleff 47, 011314 Bucharest; tel. (21) 2224422; f. 1965; 500 mems; library of 8,000 vols; Pres. CORNELIU MANESCU; Sec.-Gen. MIRCEA MALITA.

Asociaţia Română de Drept Umanitar (Romanian Association of Humanitarian Law): Piaţa Haralambie Botescu 11–13, 050892 Bucharest; tel. (21) 3119919; e-mail ardu.association@gmail.com; f. 1990; 200 mems; library of 5,000 vols; Pres. Dr IONEL CLOSCA; Gen. Sec. GHEORGHE BADESCU; publ. *Revista română de drept umanitar*.

FINE AND PERFORMING ARTS

Asociaţia Artiştilor Fotografi din Romania (Association of Photographer Artists of Romania): Str. Dr Turnescu 6, sector 5, 050467 Oradea; tel. (722) 568926; e-mail office@aafro.ro; internet www.aafro.ro; f. 1956; 1,615 mems; library of 12,000 photographic magazines; Pres. EUGEN NEGREA; Vice-Pres. BALASI CSABA; publs *Foto Magazin* (online), *Fotografia şi Video* (6 a year).

Asociaţia Artiştilor Plastici—Bucureşti (Artists Association of Bucharest): Str. Nicolae Balcescu 18, 021051 Bucharest; tel. (21) 6133860; f. 1973; 1,800 mems; Pres. Dr Eng. IOAN CEZAR CORACI; Gen. Sec. DAN SEGARCEANU.

Uniunea Artiştilor Plastici din România (Romanian Union of Fine Arts): Str. Baiculesti 29, Sector 1, 010433 Bucharest; tel. (21) 2127954; e-mail office@uap.ro; internet www.uap.ro; f. 1972; 33 regional brs; 4,170 mems; library of 12,000 vols; Pres. Dr PETRU LUCACI; publs *Arta* (art review, 4 a year), *Info* (12 a year).

Uniunea Cineaştilor din România (Romanian Film Makers Union): Mendeleev St 28–30, Sector 1, 010365 Bucharest; tel. (21) 3168084; e-mail czucin@ucin.ro; internet www.ucin.ro; f. 1963 as Romanian Filmmakers Asscn, current name adopted 1990; 14 asscns; supports its mems socially and professionally; participates in drafting of laws that concerns mems; 850 mems; Pres. Prof. LAURENTIU DAMIAN DUMITRU (acting); publ. *FILM*.

Uniunea Compozitorilor şi Muzicologilor din România—Asociatia Pentru Drepturi De Autor (Romanian Musical Performing and Mechanical Rights Society): Ostasilor St 12, Sector 1, 010071 Bucharest; tel. (21) 3167976; e-mail ada@ucmr-ada.ro; internet www.ucmr-ada.ro; f. 1920, present name 1949; facilitates licensing of musical repertoire by the users; helps collection and distribution of royalties to the right holders; 432 mems; library of 50,000 vols incl. spec. colln of Romanian music (printed scores and MSS); Gen. Man. ANA ACHIM; Sec. ALEXANDRA BILGA; publs *Actualitatea Muzicală* (24 a year), *Muzica* (4 a year).

Uniunea Teatrală din România (Romanian Association of Theatre Artists): Str. George Enescu 2–4, Sector 1, 010306 Bucharest; tel. (21) 3113214; internet www.uniter.ro; f. 1990; 1,900 mems; Pres. ION CARAMITRU; publs *Anuarul teatrului românesc* (Romanian Theatre Yearbook), *Semnal teatral* (Theatre Signal, 4 a year).

HISTORY, GEOGRAPHY AND ARCHAEOLOGY

Comitetul Naţional al Istoricilor (National Committee for Historical Sciences): Calea Victoriei 125, 010071 Bucharest; tel. (21) 2128629; f. 1955; Pres. DAN BERINDEI; Sec.-Gen. CONSTANTIN BUŞE; publ. *Nouvelles d'études d'histoire* (irregular).

Federaţia Filatelică Română (Romanian Philatelic Federation): Str. Boteanu 6, POB 1–29, 010027 Bucharest; tel. (21) 3138921; e-mail federatia_filatelica@yahoo.com; internet www.federatia-filatelica.ro; f. 1891 as Societatea Romana de Timbrologie; provides philatelic expertise and evaluation, bibliographic consulting for specialized articles, philatelic advertising; 25,000 mems; library of 3,000 vols; Pres. LEONARD PASCANU; Sec.-Gen. SERGIU GABUREAC; publ. *Filatelia* (12 a year).

Societatea de Ştiinţe Geografice din România (Society of Geographical Sciences of Romania): Bdul Bălcescu 1, 010041 Bucharest; tel. (21) 6149350; f. 1875; 5,000 mems; library of 4,000 vols; Exec. Pres. POSEA GRIGORE; publs *Bulletin*, *Terra*.

Societatea de Ştiinţe Istorice din România (Society of Historical Sciences of Romania): Blvd Regina Elisabeta 4–12, Sector 3, 030018 Bucharest; tel. (21) 3131329; e-mail ssi_r@yahoo.com; internet www.societateistorie.ro; f. 1949; 29 regional brs; stimulates scientific research and methodology in historical sciences; helps in planning and developing curricula and textbooks; organizes sessions, lectures, confs, study tours; trains specialist teachers in all counties in researching local, nat. and universal history; 5,000 mems; Pres. Prof. Dr BOGDAN MURGESCU; Sec.-Gen Prof. Dr BOGDAN TEODORESCU; publ. *Studii şi articole de istorie* (1 a year).

Societatea Numismatică Română (Romanian Numismatic Society): Str. Popa Tatu 20, 010805 Bucharest; tel. (21) 6422602; internet www.snr-1903.ro; f. 1903; 24 brs; 3,000 mems; library of 4,010 vols; Pres. Dr CONSTANTIN PREDA; Sec.-Gen. AURICĂ SMARANDA; publ. *Buletinul* (1 a year, online, www.snr-1903.ro/bsnr/bsnr.html).

LANGUAGE AND LITERATURE

Alliance Française: Str. Emile Zola 6, 011847 Bucharest; tel. (21) 2310515; offers courses and examinations in French language and culture and promotes cultural exchange with France; attached offices in Braşov, Constanţa, Craiova, Medgidia, Piteşti and Ploieşti.

British Council: Calea Dorobantilor 14, 010572 Bucharest; tel. (21) 3079600; e-mail contact@britishcouncil.ro; internet www.britishcouncil.org/romania.htm; f. 1938; teaching centre; offers courses and examinations in English language and British culture and promotes cultural exchange with the UK; attached offices in Braşov, Cluj, Constanta, Iaşi, Sibiu and Timişoara; library of 16,000 vols; Dir LILIANA BIGLOU; Teaching Centre Man. DIANA BERLINSCHI.

Goethe-Institut: Str. Tudor Arghezi 8–10, 020945 Bucharest; tel. (21) 3119762; e-mail info@bukarest.goethe.org; internet www.goethe.de/bukarest; offers courses and examinations in German language and culture and promotes cultural exchange with Germany; also responsible for Goethe-Institut work in Moldova; library in Chisinau; library of 12,000 vols; Dir BEATE KÖHLER.

Instituto Cervantes din Bucuresti: Blvd Regina Elisabeta 38, 050017 Bucharest; tel. (21) 2102737; e-mail cenbuc@cervantes.es; internet bucarest.cervantes.es; f. 1995; offers courses and examinations in Spanish language and culture and promotes cultural exchange with Spain and Spanish-speaking Latin and Central America; library of 20,000 vols; Dir JUAN CARLOS VIDAL GARCÍA.

Institut Français: Bdul Dacia 77, 020051 Bucharest; tel. (374) 125200; internet www.institutfrancais-roumanie.com; f. 1936; offices in Cluj, Iaşi, Timişoara; library of 35,000 vols; Dir DENIS SORIOT; Sec.-Gen. STÉPHANE BERGEOT.

PEN Centrul Român: Calea Victoriei 115, Sector 1, Bucharest; tel. (21) 3165829; e-mail abalutactin@yahoo.com; internet www.penromania.ro; f. 1924; 81 mems; Pres. MAGDA CARNECI; Sec. SIMONA-GRAZIA DIMA.

Societatea Română de Lingvistică (Romanian Society of Linguistics): Calea 13 Septembrie 13, 050711 Bucharest; tel. (21) 6412757; f. 1941; Pres. Prof. EMANUEL VASILIU; Sec. LAURENTIU THEBAN.

Societatea Română de Lingvistică Romanică (Romanian Society of Romance Linguistics): Str. Edgar Quinet 7, 010017 Bucharest; f. 1962; 250 mems; library of 2,000 vols; Pres. Dr MARIUS SALA; Gen. Sec. SANDA REINHEIMER RIPEANU; publ. *Bulletin* (irregular).

Uniunea Scriitorilor din România (Romanian Writers' Union): Calea Victoriei 133, Sector 1, 010071 Bucharest; tel. (21) 3165829; internet www.uniuneascriitorilor.ro; f. 1949; brs in Bucharest, Iasi, Cluj, Timisoara, Targu-Mures, Brasov, Craiova, Constanta, Bacau, Pitesti, Arad, Sibiu, Galati, Braila, Chisinau; 2,400 mems; Pres. NICOLAE MANOLESCU; Sr Vice-Pres. VARUJAN VOSGANIAN; publs *Apostrof*, *Convorbiri literare* (1 a year), *Helikon*, *Luceafărul de dimineaţă*, *Orizont*, *Ramiuri*, *România Literară*, *Vatra*.

MEDICINE

Academia de Ştiinţe Medicale din Romania (Academy of Medical Sciences): Blvd I. C. Brătianu 1, Sector 3, 061621 Bucharest; tel. (21) 3115380; e-mail adsm@adsm.ro; internet www.adsm.ro; f. 1935; sections of fundamental biomedical sciences, internal medicine, surgery clinic; attached research institutes: see Research Institutes; 6 regional brs; 189 mems, 11 corresp. mems; Pres. Prof. Dr IRINEL POPESCU; Sec.-Gen. Prof. Dr MIRCEA IFRIM; publ. *Buletinul ASM*.

Asociaţia Medicală Română (Romanian Medical Association): Str. Ionel Perlea 10, Sector 1, 010209 Bucharest; tel. (21) 3141062; e-mail asmedro@yahoo.com; internet www.amrorg.ro; f. 1873; promotes improvement in medical practice, medical research and medical education in order to improve the healthcare system; organizes courses and training programmes; 38 affiliated socs; Pres. Prof. Dr C. IONESCU-TIRGOVISTE; publs *Buletin A.M.R.* (4 a year), *Despre MÆDICA—a Journal of Clinical Medicine* (4 a year), *Practica Medicala* (4 a year), *Revista Medicala Romana* (4 a year), *Revista Romana de Boli Infectioase* (4 a year), *Revista Romana de Neurologie* (4 a year), *Revista Romana de Pediatrie* (4 a year), *Revista Romana de Reumatologie* (4 a year), *Revista Romana de Stomatologie* (4 a year).

Societatea de Medici şi Naturalişti Iaşi (Society of Physicians and Naturalists in Iaşi): Bdul Independenţei 16, POB 25, 700098 Iaşi; tel. (232) 216772; e-mail contact@revmedchir.ro; f. 1830; medicine, pharmacy, dentistry; 1,640 mems; Chair. Prof. ION HAULICA; publ. *Revista Medico-Chirurgicală* (multilingual, English abstracts, 4 a year, online, www.revmedchir.ro).

Societatea Română de Stomatologie (Romanian Society of Stomatology): Str. Ionel Perlea 10, 70754 Bucharest; tel. (21) 3142080; e-mail gabidespa@gmail.com; f. 1923; Pres. Prof. Dr EMILIAN HUTU; Sec. Assoc. Prof. ELENA GABRIELA DESPA; publ. *Stomatologia* (4 a year).

NATURAL SCIENCES

General

Asociaţia Oamenilor de Ştiinţă din România (Academy of Romanian Scientists): Splaiul Independenţei 54, Sector 5, 050094 Bucharest; tel. (21) 3147491; e-mail aosromania@yahoo.com; internet www.aos.ro; f. 1956 as Asscn of Romanian Scientists, present name 1996; territorial brs in Cluj-Napoca, Constanta, Iasi, Piatra Neamt, Targoviste, Timisoara; sections of agricultural, forestry and veterinary medicine, biological sciences, chemical sciences, economics, legal and sociological, historical and archaeological sciences, mathematical sciences, medical sciences, military sciences, natural sciences, philosophy, psychology, theology and journalism, science and information technology, technical sciences; Pres. Prof. Dr VASILE CANDEA; Scientific Sec. Prof. Dr DORU-SABIN DELION; publs *Annals of the Academy of Romanian Scientists*, *Anuarul Academiei Oamenilor de Stiinta din Romania*, *Buletin Informativ al Academiei Oamenilor de Stiinta din Romania*, *Conference Proceedings of the Academy of Romanian Scientists*, *International Journal of Communication Research* (4 a year, print and online), *International Journal of Medical Dentistry*, *Romanian Journal of Cardiovascular Surgery / Revista Romana de Chirurgie Cardiovasculara*.

Biological Sciences

Societatea de Ştiinţe Biologice din România (Society of Biological Sciences of Romania): Intrarea Portocalelor 1–3, 060101 Bucharest; f. 1949; 9,000 mems; library of 6,100 vols; Chair. Prof. Dr ION ANGHEL; Sec.-Gen. Dr CONSTANTIN VOICA; publ. *Natura* (4 a year).

Mathematical Sciences

Societatea de Ştiinţe Matematice din România (Romanian Mathematical Society): Str. Academiei 14, Sector 1, 010014 Bucharest; tel. (21) 3144653; e-mail office@rms.unibuc.ro; internet www.rms.unibuc.ro; f. 1910, present name 1990; 53 regional brs; promotes research and mathematical education; 5,000 mems; Pres. RADU GOLOGAN; Sr Vice-Pres. DORU STEFANESCU; publs *Bulletin*

Mathématique de la Societe des Sciences Mathematiques de Roumanie (4 a year), *Gazeta Matematică Seria A, Revista de cultura matematica* (4 a year), *Gazeta Matematică Seria B, Revista de cultura matematica pentru tineret* (12 a year).

Physical Sciences

Societatea Geologică a României (Geological Society of Romania): Str. Caransebeş 1, Sector 1, 70111 Bucharest; tel. (745) 784546; e-mail office@geosociety.ro; internet www.geosociety.ro; f. 1930; promotes scientific research in earth sciences; studies ways and means for rational use and conservation of geological monuments and environment; organizes meetings, reports, symposia, confs, study tours; 500 mems; Pres. Dr ANTONETA SEGHEDI; Sec. VALENTIN PARASCHIV; publ. *Buletinul* (1 a year).

RELIGION, SOCIOLOGY AND ANTHROPOLOGY

Asociaţia Slaviştilor din România (Slav Studies Association of Romania): Str. Pitar Moş 7–13, Sector 1, 010451 Bucharest; tel. (21) 3181579; e-mail romanoslavica@gmail .com; internet www.romanoslavica.ro/ asociatie.htm; f. 1956; promotes comparative Romanian-Slav studies at univ. level, in the fields of culture and civilization, of linguistics, literature, history, anthropology, ethnology, theory and practice of translation; promotes research in the Bulgarian, Croatian, Czech, Polish, Russian, Serbian, Slovakian, Slovenian, Ukrainian languages and literatures; 5 local brs; 150 mems; library of 46 vols; Pres. Prof. Dr CONSTANTIN GEAMBAŞU; Sec. Dr ANDREEA DUNAEVA; publ. *Romanoslavica* (1 a year, online, www.romanoslavica.ro).

Institutul Biblic şi de Misiune Ortodoxe Române (Biblical and Missionary Institute of the Romanian Orthodox Church): Intrarea Miron Cristea 6, Sector 4, 040162 Bucharest; tel. (21) 3352104; e-mail editura@patriarhia .ro; internet www.editurapatriarhiei.ro; f. 1925; publishes the synodal Romanian versions of the Holy Scripture, liturgical books, patristic texts, handbooks and treatises for Romanian theological schools, contemporary Orthodox literature; 14 mems; Dir VASILE BANESCU; Sec.-Gen. ION-DRAGOS VLADESCU; publs *Biserica Ortodoxa Romana* (4 a year), *Ortodoxia* (2 a year).

Societatea de Etnologie din România (Ethnology Society of Romania): Str. Zalomit 12, 010151 Bucharest; tel. (21) 3110323; e-mail rica_org@yahoo.com; f. 1990; 200 mems; Pres. Dr GEORGE ANCA; Sec. ION MOANŢA; publs *Etnologie românească* (4 a year), *Liber* (4 a year), *School of Indology* (4 a year), *Trivium* (4 a year).

TECHNOLOGY

Asociaţia Generală a Inginerilor din România (General Association of Engineers of Romania): Calea Victoriei 118, Sector 1, 70179 Bucharest; tel. (21) 3168994; e-mail office@agir.ro; internet www.agir.ro; f. 1918, present name 1990; advocates and helps in devt of engineering profession; supports free enterprise through consulting engineers, courses and training; contributes to engineering education; 16,300 mems; library of 22,000 vols; Pres. Ing. Dr MIHAI MIHĂIŢĂ; publs *Anuarul AGIR* (1 a year), *Buletinul Tehnic AGIR* (4 a year), *Univers Ingineresc* (24 a year).

Research Institutes

GENERAL

Anastasie Fătu Botanical Garden of Alexandru Ioan Cuza University of Iaşi: Str. Dumbrava Roşie 7–9, 700487 Iaşi; tel. (232) 201373; e-mail gbot.is@uaic.ro; internet www.botanica.uaic.ro; f. 1856; organizes research projects and grants; Dir Prof. Dr CĂTĂLIN TĂNASE; Scientific Sec. Dr CAMELIA IFRIM; publ. *Journal of Plant Development* (1 a year).

Astronomic Observatory: Aleea M. Sadoveanu 5, 700490 Iaşi; internet www.uaic.ro/ uaic/bin/view/resources/observatory; f. 1913; attached to Universitatea 'Alexandru Ioan Cuza' Iaşi; conducts research, didactic and observational activity.

AGRICULTURE, FISHERIES AND VETERINARY SCIENCE

Aquaproiect, SA: Str. Splaiul Independentei 294, Sector 6, 060031 Bucharest; tel. (21) 3160035; e-mail office@aquaproiect.ro; internet www.aquaproiect.ro; f. 1953, present name 1991; design and consulting in environmental engineering and water management; conducts geological, hydrogeological, topographical, geotechnical survey; library of 10,000 vols; Gen. Man. Ing. LILIANA DRAGAN; Technical Dir Ing. GHEORGHE BRĂTIANU.

Centrul de Cercetare—Dezvoltare pentru Combaterea Eroziunii Solului Perieni (Research and Development Centre for Soil Erosion Control Perieni): Bacau Rd, POB 1, 731240 Barlad; tel. (235) 550155; e-mail office@cesperieni.ro; internet www .cesperieni.ro; f. 1954; attached to Acad. of Agricultural and Forestry Sciences, Bucharest; study on soil erosion by means of standard runoff check plots, determination of optimal doses of fertilizers, establishing species and mixtures of perennial herbs necessary to rehabilitate deteriorated pastures; experimental studies on forest shelter belts; research on soil erosion control by agrotechnical methods (conservation agriculture), studies on types of crop rotation on sloping land, establishing crops range (sorts) on sloping land, chemical weed control, water balance on agricultural land deteriorated by gullies and/or landslides; Dir Dr DUMITRU NISTOR; Scientific Sec. Dr NELU POPA.

Centrul de Cercetare—Dezvoltare pentru Cultura Plantelor pe Nisipuri (Central Research Station for Plant Cultivation on Sand): Jud. Dăbuleni, 207220 Dolj; tel. (251) 334402; e-mail ccdcpndabuleni@yahoo .com; internet www.ccdcpndabuleni.ro; f. 1959; attached to Acad. of Agricultural and Forestry Sciences; conducts scientific research and technological devt in crops on sandy soils in Romania through participation in devt strategy; ensures implementation and application of new scientific and technical knowledge in agricultural production; library of 14,315 vols; Dir-Gen. Dr Ing. AURELIA DIACONU; publ. *Anales* (1 a year).

Centrul Naţional de Cartografie (National Centre of Cartography): Bdul Expozitiei 1A, Sector 1, 012101 Bucharest; tel. (21) 2241621; e-mail cnc@ancpi.ro; internet www.cngcft.ro; f. 1958, present name 2012; designs, executes and maintains nat. geodetic networks of permanent GPS stations; establishes and maintains official maps of Romania in analog and digital format and digital terrain model; participates in implementation methodologies and technical specifications with the proposal of technological standards, models and geodetic-cartographic data structures; library of 6,000 vols; Dir ILEANA SPIROU; publs *Analele*

CNGCFT (1 a year), *Buletinul de Fotogrammetrie şi Teledetecţie, Revistei de Geodezie.*

Institutul de Cercetare—Dezvoltare pentru Apicultură (Research and Development Institute for Beekeeping): Bdul Ficusului 42, Sector 1, 013975 Bucharest; tel. (21) 2325060; e-mail secretariat@icdapicultura .ro; internet www.icdapicultura.ro; f. 1974; attached to Acad. of Agricultural and Forestry Sciences; researches on genetics and improvement of bees, beekeeping technologies, resources bees and pollination, chemistry and technology of bee products, apitherapy and bee pathology; library of 11,300 vols, 4,400 periodicals; Dir-Gen. Dr CRISTINA MATEESCU; Scientific Dir Dr Ing. ADRIAN SICEANU; publ. *România apicolă* (12 a year).

Institutul de Cercetare—Dezvoltare pentru Cultura şi Industrializarea Sfeclei de Zahăr şi Substanţelor Dulci (Research and Development Institute for the Cultivation and Processing of Sugar Beet and Sweet Substances): Judeţul Călarasi, 915200 Fundulea; tel. (242) 642423; f. 1981; attached to Acad. of Agricultural and Forestry Sciences; Dir Dr Ing. AURELIAN POPA; publs *Scientific Works—Beet and Sugar* (1 a year), *Health of Plants* (1–3 a year), *Cereal and Technical Plants* (1–3 a year), *Agricultural Papers* (1–4 a year).

Institutul de Cercetare—Dezvoltare pentru Ecologie Acvatica, Pescuit si Acvacultura (Research and Development Institute for Aquatic Ecology, Fishing and Aquaculture): Str. Portului 54, 800211 Galaţi; tel. (236) 416914; e-mail icdeapa@ icdeapa.ro; internet www.icdeapa.ro; f. 1981; attached to Acad. of Agricultural and Forestry Sciences; fundamental and applied research, studies for environmental licences, evaluation in aquaculture and fishing, consulting, technical assistance; Dir Prof. Ing. Dr NECULAI PATRICHE; Scientific Sec. Dr MARILENA TALPES.

Institutul de Cercetare—Dezvoltare pentru Pajisti Brasov (Research—Development Institute for Grasslands Brasov): Str. Cucului 5, 500128 Braşov; tel. (268) 472781; e-mail office@pajisti-grassland.ro; internet www.pajisti-grassland.ro; f. 1969; attached to Acad. of Agricultural and Forestry Sciences; coordinates research programme of grassland cultivation at nat. level; provides scientific and technical information to specialists and farmers involved in utilization of grassland multifunctionality; library of 7,000 vols; Gen. Man. Dr TEODOR MARUSCA; Scientific Man. Dr VASILE MOCANU; publ. *Lucrări ştiinţifice* (Scientific Papers, 1 a year).

Institutul de Cercetare—Dezvoltare pentru Pomicultura Piteşti-Mărăcineni (Research Institute for Fruit Growing Pitesti—Maracineni): CP 73, 110006 Pitesti; Str. Mărului 402, 117450 Arges; tel. (248) 278066; e-mail office@icdp-pitesti.ro; internet www.icdp.ro; f. 1967; attached to Acad. of Agricultural and Forestry Sciences; 7 experimental fruit research stations; research areas incl. breeding studies, biotechnology, pest control and virology; library of 25,000 vols; Dir-Gen. MIHAIL COMAN; Scientific Dir DORIN SUMEDREA; publs *Fruit Growing Research* (1 a year), *Lucrările Ştiinţifice ale Institutul de Cercetare Dezvoltare pentru Pomicultura* (1 a year).

Institutul de Cercetare—Dezvoltare pentru Protecţia Plantelor (Research and Development Institute for Plant Protection): Bdul Ion Ionescu de la Brad 8, Sector 1, 013813 Bucharest; tel. (21) 2693231; e-mail secretariat_stiintific@icdpp.ro; internet www .icdpp.ro; f. 1967; attached to Acad. of Agricultural and Forestry Science; draws up new technologies to increase food chain safety incl. means and methods of biological protection against pathogen attack to accomplish sustainable devt objectives in agriculture and to complete and carry out ecological agriculture systems; application of nat. and int. strategies for research activity in plant protection; devt and improvement of rapid diagnosis techniques for pathogens; eco-toxicology studies and research works necessary to register plant protection products in accordance with EU acquis; library of 9,000 vols; Dir-Gen. Prof. Dr CONSTANTIN HORIA ILIESCU; Scientific Sec. Dr ANA-MARIA ANDREI; publs *Analele ICDPP* (1 a year), *Romanian Journal for Plant Protection* (4 a year).

Institutul de Cercetare şi Dezvoltare pentru Bovine (Institute for Bovine Research and Development): Sect. Agricol Ilfov, 077015 Baloteşti; tel. (21) 2661202; e-mail icpcb@k.ro; f. 1970; attached to Acad. of Agricultural and Forestry Sciences; library of 11,000 vols; Dir Dr Ing. IOAN CUREU; publs *Presentation* (every 5 years), *Taurine—Scientific Works* (1 a year).

Institutul de Cercetare şi Dezvoltare pentru Valorificarea Produselor Horticole (Institute of Research and Development for Marketing Horticultural Products): Intrarea Binelui 1A, POB 1–93, 042146 Bucharest; tel. (21) 3129037; f. 1967; attached to Acad. of Agricultural and Forestry Sciences; library of 3,575 vols; Dir Dr Ing. ANDREI GHERGHI; publs *Lucrări ştiinţifice* (1 a year), *Horticultura* (12 a year).

Institutul de Cercetare şi Inginerie Tehnologică pentru Irigaţii şi Drenaje (Research and Technological Engineering Institute for Irrigation and Drainage): Judeţul Giurgiu, 087010 Băneasa; tel. (246) 285023; e-mail scdid@easynet.ro; f. 1977; attached to Acad. of Agricultural and Forestry Sciences; library of 5,700 vols, 763 periodicals; Dir Dr Ing. GHEORGHE CRUTU; publ. *Scientific Papers on Irrigation and Drainage* (1 a year).

Institutul de Cercetare şi Producţie pentru Creşterea Ovinelor şi Caprinelor (Research and Production Institute for Sheep and Goat Breeding): Str. I. C. Brătianu 248, Judeţul Constanţa Palas, 900316 Constanţa; tel. (241) 639506; e-mail icdcoc@relsys.ro; f. 1897; attached to Acad. of Agricultural and Forestry Sciences; Dir Dr Ing. RADU RĂDUCU.

Institutul de Cercetare şi Producţie pentru Creşterea Păsărilor şi Animalelor Mici (Research and Production Institute for Poultry and Small Animal Breeding): Sect. Agricol Ilfov, 077015 Baloteşti; f. 1970; attached to Acad. of Agricultural and Forestry Sciences; Dir Ing. GRIGORE MUSCALU.

Institutul de Cercetări Dezvoltare pentru Legumicultură şi Floricultură (Research and Development Institute for Vegetable and Flower Growing): Judeţul Ilfov, 077185 Vidra; tel. (21) 3612094; e-mail inclf@mediasat.ro; internet www .icdlfvidra.ro; f. 1967; research into plant breeding and seed production, soil science, plant protection and flower-growing; library of 500 vols; Dir-Gen. Dr MARCEL COSTACHE; publ. *Annals*.

Institutul de Cercetări pentru Cereale şi Plante Tehnice (Research Institute for Cereals and Industrial Crops): Judeţul Fundulea, 915200 Călăraşi; tel. (242) 3110722; f. 1957; attached to Acad. of Agricultural and Forestry Sciences; library of 12,000 vols; Dir GHEORGHE SIN; publs *Analele* (1 a year), *Probleme de agrofitotehnie teoretică şi aplicată*, *Probleme de genetică teoretică şi aplicată*, *Probleme de protecţia plantelor* (4 a year), *Romanian Agricultural Research* (every 2 years).

Institutul de Cercetări pentru Viticultură şi Vinificaţie Valea Calugareasca (Research Institute for Viticulture and Wine-Making): Str. Valea Mantei 2, Judeţul Valea Călugărească, 107620 Prahova; tel. (244) 401900; e-mail icvv@xnet.ro; internet www .icdvv.ro; f. 1967, present name 2002; attached to Acad. of Agricultural and Forestry Sciences; 7 research stations; 3 research laboratories; library of 14,000 vols; Dir-Gen. Dr Ing. ADRIAN SERDINESCU; publ. *Anale* (research papers).

Institutul de Cercetări şi Amenajări Silvice (Forest Research and Management Institute): Sos. Stefanesti 128, 077190 Voluntari; tel. (21) 3503238; e-mail icas@icas.ro; internet www.icas.ro; f. 1933; attached to Acad. of Agricultural and Forestry Sciences; library of 32,000 vols; Man. GHEORGHE DUMITRIU; Man. HEINRICH FLORENTINA; Sec. VIOLETA TIRON; publs *Analele Ilas*, *Bucovina Forestiera*.

Institutul de Chimie Alimentară Research and Development: Splaiul Independentei 202, Sector 6, Bucharest; tel. (21) 3160144; e-mail ica@ccai-ro.com; internet www.ica-rd.ro; f. 1951 as Institute of Food Chemistry; attached to Acad. of Agricultural and Forestry Sciences; library of 25,000 vols; Dir Prof. Dr GHEORGHE MENCINICOPSCHI; publ. *Ştiinţe şi Tehnologii Alimentare* (Food Sciences and Technology, 4 a year).

Institut Pasteur: Calea Giuleşti 333, Sector 6, 77826 Bucharest; tel. (21) 2206915; internet www.pasteur.ro; f. 1895, present name and status 2000; fundamental and applied scientific research in field of pathology, hygiene and animal welfare, veterinary public health, food safety and environmental protection; library of 30,000 vols; Pres. Dr ADRIAN ALEXANDRU; publ. *Studies and Research in Veterinary Medicine* (1 a year).

Institutul Naţional de Cercetare—Dezvoltare Marină 'Grigore Antipa' (National Institute for Marine Research and Development 'Grigore Antipa'): Blvd Mamaia 300, POB 3, 900581 Constanţa 3; tel. (41) 543288; e-mail office@alpha.rmri.ro; internet www.rmri.ro; f. 1970 as Romanian Marine Research Institute, present name 1999; attached to Min. of Nat. Education; carries out basic, applied and technological research on knowledge, protection and management of the coastal zone and marine environment, oceanography, marine and coastal engineering and management of marine living resources in the Black Sea and Planetary Ocean; library of 38,000 vols and periodicals; Dir Dr Ing. SIMION NICOLAEV; Scientific Dir Dr TANIA ZAHARIA; publ. *Cercetări Marine* (1 a year).

Institutul Naţional de Cercetare—Dezvoltare pentru Biologie si Nutriţie Animala (National Research Development Institute for Animal Biology and Nutrition): Calea Bucuresti 1, 077015 Baloteşti; tel. (21) 3512081; e-mail secretariat@ibna.ro; internet www.ibna.ro; f. 1970 as Research Institute for Animal Nutrition, present name 2006; attached to Acad. of Agricultural and Forestry Sciences; provides scientific research, technological devt and innovation in animal nutrition and physiology, forage production technologies, animal biology; library of 5,000 vols; Gen. Man. Prof. Dr HORIA GROSU; Dir of Science Dr CATALIN DRAGOMIR; Sec. of Science Dr Eng. ELENA GHITA; publs *Analele IBNA* (1 a year), *Archiva Zootechnica* (4 a year, in English).

Institutul Naţional de Cercetare-Dezvoltare pentru Cartof si Sfeclă de Zahar Brasov (National Institute of Research and Development for Potato and Sugar Beet Brasov): Str. Fundăturii 2, 500470 Braşov; tel. (268) 476795; e-mail icpc@potato.ro; internet www.potato.ro; f. 1967 as Experimental Agricultural Station, present name 2005; attached to Acad. of Agricultural and Forestry Sciences, Bucharest; basic and applied research on potato, sugar beet and medicinal plants; research network in Târgu-Secuiesc and Miercurea Ciuc; library of 10,000 vols; Gen. Dir Dr SORIN CLAUDIAN CHIRU; Deputy Scientific Dir Dr Ing. VICTOR DONESCU; publs *Anale* (scientific papers, 1 a year), *Cartoful în România* (The Potato in Romania, 4 a year), *Tehnologie* (1 a year).

Institutul Naţional de Cercetare—Dezvoltare pentru Pedologie, Agrochimie şi Protecţia Mediului—ICPA Bucureşti (National Research and Development Institute for Soil Science, Agrochemistry and Environment Protection—ICPA Bucharest): Bdul Mărăşti 61, 71331 Bucharest; tel. (21) 3184463; e-mail office@icpa.ro; internet www .icpa.ro; f. 1970; attached to Acad. of Agricultural and Forestry Sciences; basic, strategic and applied research, survey and long-term monitoring in soil and agrochemistry fields; characterization and quantification of natural resources and environment; inventorying and monitoring natural resources and environment; plant nutrition and soil/plant fertilization; sustainable management of natural resources and environment, soil pollution, global change, rural devt; waste management; standards and methodologies on natural resources and environment; soil/land/environment data computing, agricultural/environment information services; library of 9,000 vols; Gen. Dir Dr MIHAIL DUMITRU; Scientific Dir Dr CATALIN SIMOTA; publ. *Anale* (1 a year).

Staţiunea Centrală de Cercetări pentru Cultura şi Industrializarea Tutunului (Central Research Station for Tobacco Growing and Industrialization): Str. Gârlei 1, 013721 Bucharest; tel. (21) 2304575; f. 1929; Dir MARIANA TIGAU; publ. *Buletinul tutunului* (1 a year).

Staţiunea de Cercetăre—Dezvoltare Agricola Brăila (Brăila Agricultural Research and Development Station): Şoseaua Vizirului km 9, Judeţul Brăila, 810008 Brăila; tel. (239) 684695; f. 1954; 12 mems; Dir Dr Ing. MARCEL BULARDA; Scientific Sec. Dr Ing. VISINESCU IOAN; publ. *Scientific Works* (1 a year).

ARCHITECTURE AND TOWN PLANNING

Centrul pentru Noi Arhitecturei Electronice (Centre for New Electronic Architecture): Bdul Armata Poporului 1–3, Bucharest; tel. (21) 6317800; attached to Romanian Acad.; Dir STEFAN GHEORGHE.

Institutul Naţional de Cercetare—Dezvoltare în Construcţii, Urbanism şi Dezvoltare Teritorială Durabilă URBAN-INCERC (National Institute for Research and Development in Constructions, Urbanism and Sustainable Spatial Development URBAN-INCERC): Şoseaua Pantelimon 266, Sector 2, 021652 Bucharest; tel. (21) 2550270; e-mail urban-incerc@incd.ro; internet www.incd.ro; f. 1957; fundamental and applied research in urban and territorial planning, architecture, constructions and the economy of bldgs; library of 350,000 vols, 200 current periodicals; Dir-Gen. Dr VASILE MEITA; publs *Constructii / Constructions* (2 a year), *Probleme de Economia Constructiilor* (12 a year), *Urbanism. Architectura. Constructii / Urbanism. Architecture. Constructions* (4 a year, online, uac.incerc.ro/EN/index.htm).

Prodomus SA—Institut de Studii şi Proiectare pentru Construcţii Civile

(Institute of Research and Design for Civil Engineering Works): Str. Nicolae Filipescu 53–55, 020961 Bucharest; tel. (21) 2117840; e-mail nicolae@prodomus.com.ro; f. 1949; housing, social bldgs; Dir Eng. CORNELIU VELICU; publs 'bdi' (bulletin of documentation and information), Prodomus—SA.

Proed SA—Institut de Studii şi Proiectare pentru Lucrări Tehnico-Edilitare (Studies and Design Institute for Public Works): Str. Tudor Arghezi 21, 020943 Bucharest; tel. (21) 2115510; f. 1949; water, sewerage and other public facilities, traffic organization and public transport; Man. Dir-Gen. CONSTANTIN HOTULETE; publ. 'bdi' (bulletin of documentation and information, 4 a year).

ECONOMICS, LAW AND POLITICS

Centrul de Cercetări Financiare şi Monetare 'Victor Slăvescu' ('Victor Slăvescu' Centre of Financial and Monetary Research): Calea 13 Septembrie 13, Sector 5, 050711 Bucharest; tel. (21) 3182419; e-mail icfm01@icfm.ro; internet www.icfm.ro; f. 1967 as Centrul de Finanţe, Preţuri şi Probleme Valutare 'Victor Slăvescu', present name and status 2001; attached to Romanian Acad.; research on financial and monetary phenomenology in its theoretical and practical aspects; library of 700 vols; Dir MARIN CONSTANTIN; publs Anuarul Starea financiară a României, Financial Studies (4 a year, online, fs.icfm.ro).

Centrul de Economia Industriei şi Serviciilor al Academiei Române (Centre for the Industrial and Service Economy of the Romanian Academy): Calea 13 Septembrie 13, 050711 Bucharest; tel. (21) 3182418; e-mail office@iei.ro; internet www.iei.ro; f. 1977; attached to Romanian Acad.; fundamental and applied research devt within nat. and int. programs focused on natural resources economics, energy policies, strategies and policies in manufacturing, environmental economics, microeconomics and industrial management, regional devt, services and information society's economics, sustainable devt; Dir Dr MIHAI-SABIN MUSCALU; publs Probleme Economice (Economic Problems, 47 a year), Revista de Economie Industriala (1 a year).

Centrul Român de Economie Comparată şi Consens: Calea 13 September 13, Sector 5, 76117 Bucharest; tel. (21) 4116075; internet www.ince.ro/ecc.htm; f. 1999; attached to Romanian Acad.; Dir Prof. TUDOREL POSTOLACHE.

Institutul de Cercetări Juridice 'Acad. Andrei Rădulescu' ('Acad. Andrei Rădulescu' Legal Research Institute of Romanian Academy): Calea 13 Septembrie 13, Sector 5, 050711 Bucharest; tel. (21) 3188130; e-mail icj_juridic@yahoo.com; internet www.icj.ro; f. 1954, present name 2006; attached to Romanian Acad.; fundamental and applied scientific research within the field of nat. law, comparative law, European law, int. law; library of 15,000 vols, 200 periodicals; Man. Prof. Dr MIRCEA DUTU; Librarian MARIA DUMITRU; publ. Studii de Drept Românesc (4 a year).

Institutul de Economie Mondială (Institute for World Economy): Calea 13 Septembrie 13, Sector 5, 050711 Bucharest; tel. (21) 3182455; e-mail office@iem.ro; internet www.iem.ro; f. 1967 as Institute for Int. Market Research, present name 1976; attached to Romanian Acad.; basic research on economic assessment and monitoring, comparative economic analyses, economic outlook and foresight; World Bank depository library; library of 5,000 vols, 320 periodicals; Dir Dr SIMONA MOAGAR POLADIAN; publs Buletin de

Preţuri şi Cotaţii pe Piaţa Internaţională (144 a year), Conjunctura Economiei Mondiale (1 a year), Euroinfo (2 a year), Eurolex (4 a year), Evoluţia Preţurilor Internaţionale (2 a year), Piaţa Internaţională (96 a year).

Institutul de Economie Naţională (Institute of National Economy): Calea 13 Septembrie 13, Sector 5, 050711 Bucharest; tel. (21) 3182467; e-mail office@ien.ro; internet www.ien.ro; f. 1953 as Institute for Economic Research of the Romanian Acad., present status 1990; attached to Romanian Acad.; Dir GHEORGHE ZAMAN; Scientific Dir VALENTINA VASILE; publ. Revista Româna de Economie (Romanian Economic Review, 2 a year, in English).

Institutul de Prognoză Economică (Institute for Economic Forecasting): Calea 13 Septembrie 13, Sector 5, 050711 Bucharest; tel. (21) 3188148; e-mail ipe@ipe.ro; internet www.ipe.ro; f. 1970 as Centre of Planning Studies and Research (attached to State Planning Cttee), present name and status 1990; conducts fundamental research on economic modeling and forecasting, econometrics, macroeconomics, non-linear modeling, real business cycles, endogenous cycles and deterministic chaos, consumption theory, informal economy modeling; Dir Prof. Dr LUCIAN-LIVIU ALBU; Scientific Sec. Dr MIHAELA-NONA CHILIAN; publ. Romanian Journal for Economic Forecasting (4 a year).

Institutul 'Gheorghe Zane' de Cercetări Economice şi Sociale (Gheorghe Zane Institute for Economic and Social Research): Str. Theodor Codrescu 2, 700481 Iaşi; tel. (332) 408922; internet www.ices.ro; f. 1992; attached to Romanian Acad.; library of 40,000 vols; Dir Prof. TEODOR DIMA; publs Anuarul de Cercetări Economice, Anuarul Idei şi Valori Perene, Anuarului Institutului De Cercetari Economice 'Gheorghe Zane'-Iasi (Yearbook of Gh. Zane Institute of Economic Research-Iasi, 1 a year, online, ices.ro/anuarul_eco/anuarul_eco.htm), Symposion-Revista de Stiinte Socio-Umane (Symposion-Journal of Human Sciences, online, www.symposion.ices.ro).

Institutul Naţional de Cercetări Economice 'Costin C. Kiritescu' (National Institute of Economic Research 'Costin C. Kiritescu'): Calea 13 Septembrie 13, 050711 Bucharest; tel. (21) 3188106; e-mail office@ince.ro; internet www.ince.ro; f. 1990; attached to Romanian Acad.; Dir-Gen. Prof. Dr LUMINITA CHIVU; publs Analele INCE (4 a year), Probleme economice (47 a year), Româna de Economie (2 a year), Romanian Economic Research Observer (6 a year), Romanian Economic Review (2 a year), Studii şi cercetări economice (12 a year).

EDUCATION

Institutul de Cercetari pentru Inteligenţă Artificială 'Mihai Drăgănescu' Academia Romana (Research Institute for Artificial Intelligence 'Mihai Drăgănescu' Romanian Academy): Calea 13 Septembrie 13, 050711 Bucharest; tel. (21) 3188103; e-mail office@racai.ro; internet www.racai.ro; f. 1994 as Centrul de Cercetări Avansate în Invăţarea Automată, Prelucrarea Limbajului Natural şi Modelarea Conceptuală, present name 2002; attached to Romanian Acad.; researches in areas of natural language processing, machine learning, knowledge acquisition, computer-aided instruction, structural-phenomenological modelling; Dir Prof. Dr IOAN DAN TUFIS; Scientific Dir Dr ANGELA IONITA; Hon. Dir GHEORGHE TECUCI.

FINE AND PERFORMING ARTS

Institutul de Arheologie şi Istoria Artei al Academiei Române (Institute of Archaeology and History of Art of the Romanian Academy): Str. M. Kogălniceanu 12–14, 400084 Cluj-Napoca; tel. (264) 591125; e-mail iaiacluj@yahoo.com; internet www.institutarheologie-istoriaarteicj.ro; f. 1990; attached to Romanian Acad.; library of 20,392 vols (incl. 12,616 books and 7,776 periodicals); Dir Dr MARIUS PORUMB; Scientific Sec. Dr IOAN STANCIU; publs Ars Transsilvaniae (1 a year), Ephemeris Napocensis (1 a year).

Institutul de Istoria Artei 'G. Oprescu' (G. Oprescu Institute of the Art History): Calea Victoriei 196, Sector 1, 010098 Bucharest; tel. (21) 3144070; e-mail istartro@yahoo.com; internet www.istoria-artei.ro; f. 1949; attached to Romanian Acad.; Romanian medieval art, Byzantine art, modern art and architecture, theatre, music, cinema; library of 72,000 vols; Dir Dr ADRIAN-SILVAN IONESCU; Deputy Dir Prof. ALIN CIUPALĂ; publs Revue Roumaine d'Histoire de l'Art: Série Beaux-Arts (1 a year), Studii şi Cercetări de Istoria Artei: Artă Plastică (1 a year), Studii şi Cercetări de Istoria Artei: Teatru, Muzică, Cinematografie (1 a year).

HISTORY, GEOGRAPHY AND ARCHAEOLOGY

Centrul de Istorie şi Civilizaţie Europeană (Centre for History and European Civilization): Aleea M. Sadoveanu 3, 700490 Iaşi; tel. (232) 212441; internet www.cice-iasi.ro; f. 1992; attached to Romanian Acad.; researches in nat. and universal history, genealogy and archaeology medieval Romanians role and place in history, historiography; library of 4,050 vols; Dir STELLA CHEPTEA; Scientific Sec. STEPHEN S. GOROVEI; publ. Europa XXI (every 2 years).

Centrul pentru Studiul Istoriei Evreilor din România (Centre for the Study of the History of Jews in Romania): 57B, Calea Calarasilor, sector 3, 030612 Bucharest; tel. (21) 3151045; e-mail csier_fcer@yahoo.com; internet www.csier.jewishfed.ro; f. 1978; attached to the Fed. of Jewish Communities in Romania; Dir Prof. Dr LIVIU ROTMAN.

Institutul de Arheologie, Iaşi (Institute of Archaeology in Iasi): Str. Lascăr Catargi 18, 700107 Iaşi; tel. (332) 106173; e-mail arheoligieiasi@yahoo.com; internet www.arheo.ro; f. 1990; attached to Romanian Acad.; research in archaeology and ancient history; Dir Prof. Dr VICTOR SPINEI; Scientific Sec. Dr DAN APARASCHIVEI; publs Arheologia Moldovei (1 a year), Bibliotheca Archaeologica Iassiensis (irregular), Bibliotheca Archaeologica Moldaviae (irregular), Honoraria (irregular), Studia Et Acta Historiae Iudaeorum Romaniae.

Institutul de Arheologie 'Vasile Pârvan' (Vasile Pârvan Institute of Archaeology): Str. Henri Coandă 11, Sector 1, 010667 Bucharest; tel. (21) 2128862; e-mail iab_vparvan@yahoo.com; internet www.instarhparvan.ro; f. 1956; attached to Romanian Acad.; library of 200,000 vols; Dir Prof. Dr ALEXANDRU VULPE; publs Dacia—Revue d'Archéologie et d'Histoire Ancienne (1 a year, online, www.daciajournal.ro), Materiale şi Cercetări Arheologice (1 a year, online, www.mcajournal.ro), Studii şi Cercetări de Istorie Veche si Arheologie (4 a year, online, www.scivajournal.ro), Studii şi Cercetări de Numismatică (every 2 years, online, www.scnjournal.ro), Thraco-Dacica (online, www.tdjournal.ro).

Institutul de Geografie (Institute of Geography—Romanian Academy): Dimitrie Racoviţă 12, 023993 Bucharest; tel. (21) 3135990; e-mail igar@geoinst.ro; internet www.geoinst.ro; f. 1944; attached to Romanian Acad.; focuses on br. studies, implying physical geography and human geography, integrated studies, involving geographical studies on the environment at nat. level or by geographical units, studies of natural and technological hazards, applied geographical research under contract with various institutions or correlated with global research programmes (IGBP, IHDP) etc.; library of 50,000 vols, 200 periodicals, 1,900 atlases and maps; Dir Prof. DAN BĂLTEANU; Deputy Dir Dr MONICA DUMITRAŞCU; publs *Revue Roumaine De Géographie*/*Romanian Journal of Geography* (1 a year), *Revista Geografică*/*Geographical Journal* (1 a year), *Studii şi Cercetări Geografice*.

Institutul de Istorie 'A. D. Xenopol' Iaşi (A. D. Xenopol Institute of History): Str. Lascăr Catargi 15, 700107 Iaşi; tel. (332) 106172; e-mail institut@xenopol.iasi.astral.ro; internet www.academiaromana-is.ro/adxenopol; f. 1941; attached to Romanian Acad.; Romanian and world history; library of 58,000 vols, 900 titles; Dir Prof. Dr GHEORGHE CLIVETI; Hon. Dir ALEXANDRU ZUB; publs *Anuarul Institutului de Istorie A. D. Xenopol* (1 a year), *Studia et Acta Historiae Iudaeorum Romaniae* (1 a year), *Xenopoliana. Buletinul Fundaţiei Academice A. D. Xenopol* (4 a year).

Institutul de Istorie 'Nicolae Iorga' (Nicolae Iorga Institute of History): Bdul Aviatorilor, Sector 1, 011851 Bucharest; tel. (21) 2125337; e-mail admin@iini.ro; internet www.iini.ro; f. 1937; attached to Romanian Acad.; historical research (middle ages to 20th century); library of 130,000 vols; Dir Dr OVIDIU CRISTEA; Scientific Sec. Dr GHEORGHE LAZĂR; publs *Historical Yearbook* (1 a year), *Revista Istorică* (6 a year), *Revue Roumaine d'histoire* (4 a year), *Studii şi Materiale de Istorie Contemporana* (1 a year), *Studii şi Materiale de Istorie Medie* (1 a year), *Studii şi Materiale de Istorie Modernă* (1 a year).

University '1 December 1918' Alba Iulia Systemic Archaeology Institute 'Iuliu Paul' ('1 December 1918' University of Alba Iulia 'Iulia Paul' Systematic Archaeological Institute): Str. Mihai Viteazul 12, 510010 Alba Iulia; tel. (258) 817071; e-mail arhsis@uab.ro; internet www.bcum.uab.ro; f. 2001; archaeology; preservation and restoration of archaeological sites; Dir Dr MIHAI GLIGOR.

LANGUAGE AND LITERATURE

Institutul de Filologie Română 'Al. Philippide' (Al. Philippide Institute of Romanian Philology): Str. Theodor Codrescu 2, 700481 Iaşi; tel. (332) 106508; e-mail secretariat_philippide@yahoo.com; internet www.academiaromana-is.ro/philippide; f. 1927; attached to Romanian Acad.; depts of lexicology and lexicography, dialectology, toponymy, literature, ethnology; library of 60,000 vols; Dir Prof. Dr EUGEN MUNTEANU; publs *Anuar de Lingvistică şi Istorie Literară*, *Buletinul* (4 a year), *Philologica Jassyensia* (2 a year).

Institutul de Istorie şi Teorie Literară 'G. Călinescu' (G. Călinescu Institute of Literary History and Theory): Calea 13 Septembrie 13, 050117 Bucharest; tel. (21) 3188106; e-mail instcalinescu@yahoo.com; internet www.institutulcalinescu.ro; f. 1949; attached to Romanian Acad.; library of 15,000 vols; Dir Prof. Dr EUGEN SIMION; publs *Revista de Istorie şi Teorie Literară* (4 a year), *Synthesis* (1 a year).

Institutul de Lingvistica 'Iorgu Iordan–Al. Rosetti' (Iorgu Iordan–Al. Rosetti Institute of Linguistics): Calea 13 Septembrie 13, Sector 5, 050711 Bucharest; tel. (21) 3182452; e-mail inst@lingv.ro; internet www.lingv.ro; f. 1949; attached to Romanian Acad.; Dir MARIUS SALA; publs *Fonetică şi Dialectologie* (1 a year), *Limba Română* (6 a year), *Revue Roumaine de Linguistique* (4 a year), *Studii şi Cercetări Lingvistice* (2 a year).

MEDICINE

Centre for Drug Research: 1 Mai Ave 66, 200638 Craiova; tel. (251) 523929; attached to Universitatea de Medicină şi Farmacie din Craiova.

Centrul de Sănătate Publică (Public Health Centre): Gh. Marinescu St 40, 540136 Târgu Mureş; tel. (265) 218360; f. 1956 as Scientific Research Base, present name and status 2001; attached to Acad. of Medical Sciences; library of 12,000 vols; Dir Prof. Dr FRANCISC JESZENSZKY.

Centrul Metodologic de Parodontologie (Paradontology Methodological Centre): 11 Iunie St 10, 040172 Bucharest; tel. (21) 6412079; f. 1968; library of 326 vols; Dir Dr THEODORA GUTU.

Centrul Pentru Studii de Morfologie Microscopică şi Imunologie (Research Centre for Microscopic Morphology and Immunology): Str. Petru Rareş 2, 200349 Craiova; tel. (351) 461458; e-mail cmi@umfcv.ro; internet www.umfcv.ro/centrul-studii-de-morfologie-microscopica-i-munologie; attached to Universitatea de Medicină şi Farmacie din Craiova.

Centrul Regional de Sanatate Publica Iaşi (Regional Center of Public Health Iaşi): Str. Victor Babeş 14, 700465 Iaşi; tel. (232) 410399; e-mail crsp.iasi@insp.gov.ro; internet www.pub-health-iasi.ro; f. 1930; attached to Nat. Institute of Public Health, Min. of Health; library of 17,000 vols; Dir Prof. Dr LUMINIŢA SMARANDA IANCU; publ. *Journal of Preventive Medicine* (4 a year).

Institutul Cantacuzino (Cantacuzino Institute): Splaiul Independenţei 103, Sector 5, 050096 Bucharest; tel. (21) 3069100; e-mail office@cantacuzino.ro; internet www.cantacuzino.ro; f. 1921; attached to Acad. of Medical Sciences; microbiology, immunology and epidemiology of communicable diseases, biotechnology; library of 119,714 vols; Gen. Dir Dr RADU IORDACHEL; Sec.-Gen. FELICIA MARDALE; publ. *Romanian Archives of Microbiology and Immunology* (4 a year).

Institutul de Endocrinologie 'C.I. Parhon' (C. I. Parhon Institute of Endocrinology): Bdul Aviatorilor 34–36, Sector 1, 011863 Bucharest; tel. (21) 3172041; e-mail contact@parhon.ro; internet www.instparhon.ro; f. 1946; attached to Acad. of Medical Sciences; organizes guides and promotes studies and research in theoretical and experimental endocrinology; library of 65,800 vols; Man Dr PAUN DIANA LORETA; Medical Dir Dr GHEMIGIAN ADINA MARIANA; publ. *Romanian Journal of Endocrinology* (4 a year).

Institutul de Fiziologie Normală şi Patologică 'D. Danielopolu' (D. Danielopolu Institute of Normal and Pathological Physiology): Bdul Ion Mihalache 11A, 011171 Bucharest; tel. (21) 3128938; e-mail ifnp@cmb.ro; f. 1949; attached to Acad. of Medical Sciences; library of 49,000 vols; Dir Prof. Dr GR. BENETATO; publ. *Romanian Journal of Physiology* (4 a year).

Institutul de Fonoaudiologie şi Chirurgie Funcţională ORL 'Prof. Dr. D. Hociotă' (Prof. Dr. D. Hociotă Institute of Phono-Audiology and ENT Surgery): Str. Mihai Cioranu 21, Sector 5, 050751 Bucharest; tel. (21) 4102170; e-mail secretariat@ifacforl.ro; internet ifacforl.ro; f. 1972 as Centrul Medical de Fonoaudiologie şi Chirurgie Funcţională O.R.L.; attached to Acad. of Medical Sciences; library of 2,000 vols; Man. MARINESCU ANDREEA; Medical Dir MOCANU BOGDAN.

Institutul de Medicină Internă 'Nicolae Gh. Lupu' (Nicolae Gh. Lupu Institute of Internal Medicine): Şoseaua Ştefan cel Mare 19–21, 020125 Bucharest; tel. (21) 6111370; e-mail cbaicus@clicknet.ro; f. 1949; attached to Acad. of Medical Sciences; library of 72,000 vols; Dir Prof. C. TANASESCU; publ. *Romanian Journal of Internal Medicine* (4 a year).

Institutul de Neurologie şi Psihiatrie (Institute of Neurology and Psychiatry): Şoseaua Berceni 10–12, 041915 Bucharest; tel. (21) 6837831; f. 1950; attached to Acad. of Medical Sciences; library of 7,957 vols; Dir Prof. V. VOICULESCU; publ. *Neurologie et Psychiatrie* (series of *Revue Roumaine de Médecine*, 4 a year).

Institutul de Patologie şi Genetică Medicală 'V. Babeş' (V. Babeş Institute of Pathology and Medical Genetics): Splaiul Independenţei 99–101, 050096 Bucharest; tel. (21) 4115152; f. 1887; attached to Acad. of Medical Sciences; genetics, immunology, pathology and ultra-structure; library of 20,000 vols; Dir Prof. Dr L. M. POPESCU; publ. *Romanian Journal of Morphology and Embryology* (4 a year).

Institutul de Sănătate Publică 'Prof. Dr Iuliu Moldovan' (Prof. Dr Iuliu Moldovan Institute of Public Health): Str. Louis Pasteur 6, 400349 Cluj-Napoca; tel. (264) 594252; e-mail inst@ispcj.ro; f. 1930; monitors public health in 11 Transylvanian counties; provides technical assistance, continuing education, field applied scientific research, public health services; library of 30,150 vols; Dir Prof. Dr IOAN STELIAN BOCŞAN.

Institutul de Sănătate Publică 'Prof. Dr Leonida Georgescu', Timişoara (Prof. Dr Leonida Georgescu Institute of Public Health, Timişoara): Blvd Dr Victor Babeş 16–18, 300226 Timişoara; tel. (256) 492101; internet www.ispt.ro; f. 1946; attached to Acad. of Medical Sciences; library of 14,966 vols; Dir Prof. Dr ROXANA MOLDOVAN; publs *Annals of the Institute of Public Health, Timişoara* (1 a year), *Documentary Booklet* (1 a year).

Institutul de Virusologie Stefan S. Nicolau (Stefan S. Nicolau Institute of Virology): Mihai Bravu Ave 285, Sector 3, POB 201, 030304 Bucharest; tel. (21) 3242590; e-mail office@virology.ro; internet www.virology.ro; f. 1949; attached to Romanian Acad.; researches on HIV/AIDS, hepatitis, HPV, sexually transmitted diseases, arboviruses, influenza, antiviral, anticancer and cell therapy, epigenetics, bioinformatics, funding and scientific life; library of 60,000 vols, 200 periodicals; Dir Dr MIHAI STOIAN; Scientific Sec. Dr C. N. ZAHARIA; publs *Proceedings of the Romanian Academy, series B, Science and Life* (2 a year), *Studii si Cercetari de Virusologie* (2 a year).

Institutul Naţional de Medicină Legală 'Mina Minovici' (Mina Minovici National Institute for Legal Medicine): Şoseaua Vitan-Bârzeşti 9, Sector 4, 042122 Bucharest; tel. (21) 3321156; e-mail contact@legmed.ro; internet www.legmed.ro; f. 1892; forensic genetics, forensic toxicology, forensic pathology, clinical forensic medicine, forensic psychiatry, forensic anthropology; library of 20,000 vols; Dir Prof. Dr DAN DERMENGIU; publ. *Romanian Journal of Legal Medicine* (4 a year, online, www.rjlm.ro).

Institutul National de Sănătate Publică, Bucureşti (National Institute of Public Health, Bucharest): Str. Dr Leonte Anastasievici 1–3, Sector 5, 050463 Bucharest; tel. (21) 3183620; e-mail directie.generala@insp .gov.ro; internet www.insp.gov.ro; f. 1927; attached to Min. of Health; library of 36,000 vols, separate medical history library of 41,000 vols; Dir-Gen. Dr ADRIANA PISTOL; publ. *Sănătate și Prevenție* (4 a year).

Institutul Oncologic 'Prof. Dr Al. Trestioreanu' Bucuresti (Prof. Dr Al. Trestioreanu Institute of Oncology Bucharest): Șoseaua Fundeni 252, Sector 2, 022338 Bucharest; tel. (21) 2271000; e-mail secretariat@iob.ro; internet www.iob.ro; f. 1949; attached to Acad. of Medical Sciences; research, teaching, methodology, training of specialized personnel; library of 41,144 vols; Man. Prof. Dr RODICA ANGHEL; Medical Dir Dr ILEANA CONDREA; publ. *Oncologia* (4 a year).

Institutul pentru Controlul de Stat al Medicamentului și Cercetări Farmaceutice 'Petre Ionescu-Stoian' (Petre Ionescu-Stoian State Institute for Drug Control and Pharmaceutical Research): Aviator Sănătescu St 48, 011478 Bucharest; tel. (21) 2241079; e-mail dd@ns.icsmcf.ro; f. 1929; Dir Prof. Dr DUMITRU DOBRESCU; publ. *Farmacovigilența* (Drug Monitoring, 4 a year).

Research Centre of Gastroenterology and Hepatology: 1 Mai Ave 66, 200638 Craiova; tel. (251) 310287; e-mail ccgh@ umfcv.ro; attached to Universitatea de Medicină și Farmacie din Craiova; Dir TUDOREL CIUREA.

NATURAL SCIENCES
Biological Sciences

Institutul de Biochimie (Institute of Biochemistry): Splaiul Independenței 296, 060031 Bucharest 17; tel. (21) 2239069; internet www.biochim.ro; f. 1952, present name and status 1990; attached to Romanian Acad.; research into protein science, particularly the biosynthesis and function of proteins and glycoproteins; Dir Dr STEFANA M. PETRESCU; Sec. MIRELA PANZARU; publ. *Romanian Journal of Biochemistry* (2 a year, online, journal.biochim.ro).

Institutul de Biologie Bucuresti (Institute of Biology Bucharest): Splaiul Independenței 296, POB 56–53, 060031 Bucharest; tel. (21) 2219202; e-mail biologie@ibiol.ro; internet www.ibiol.ro; f. 1957 as Biological Research Centre, present name and status 1990; attached to Romanian Acad.; depts of ecology, microbiology, plant and animal cytobiology, taxonomy and nature conservation; library of 200,000 vols; Dir Prof. OCTAVIAN POPESCU; Scientific Sec. Dr MEDANA ZAMFIR; publ. *Romanian Journal of Biology* (2 a year).

Institutul de Biologie și Patologie Celulară 'Nicolae Simionescu' (Institute of Cellular Biology and Pathology 'Nicolae Simionescu'): Bogdan Petriceicu Hașdeu St 8, 050568 Bucharest; tel. (21) 3194518; internet www.icbp.ro; f. 1979; attached to Romanian Acad.; 9 laboratories; Dir Dr MAYA SIMIONESCU; Scientific Sec. DOINA POPOV.

Institutul de Cercetări Biologice Cluj-Napoca (Institute of Biological Research Cluj-Napoca): Str. Republicii 48, 400015 Cluj-Napoca; tel. (264) 598084; e-mail office@icbcluj.ro; internet www.icbcluj.ro; f. 1958; attached to Institutul Național de Cercetare-Dezvoltare pentru Științe Biologice; depts of experimental biology and biochemistry, taxonomy and ecology; library of 13,019 vols, 25,120 periodicals; Dir Dr SORINA FARCAS; Sec. VALERIA CALIN; publ. *Contribuții Botanice* (1 a year).

Institutul de Cercetări Biologice Iași (Institute Of Biological Research Iasi): Str.

Lascăr Catargi 47, 700107 Iași; tel. (232) 218121; internet www.icbiasi.ro; f. 1964 as Institute of General and Applied Biology, present name 1996; attached to Institutul Național de Cercetare-Dezvoltare pentru Științe Biologice; library of 35,000 vols; Dir Dr OTILIA IVAN.

Institutul de Cercetări Eco-Muzeale Tulcea (Institute of Eco-Museal Research Tulcea): Str. 14 Noiembrie 1, 820009 Tulcea; tel. (240) 513231; e-mail icemtl@icemtl.ro; internet www.icemtl.ro; f. 1950, present status 1993; attached to Tulcea County Council; archaeology, natural history, history, ethnography, art; library of 50,000 vols; Dir FLORIN GEORGE TOPOLEANU; publ. *Peuce* (1 a year).

Institutul Național de Cercetare-Dezvoltare pentru Științe Biologice (National Institute of Research and Development for Biological Sciences): Splaiul Independenței 296, Sector 6, CP 17–16, 060031 Bucharest; tel. (21) 2207780; e-mail office@ dbio.ro; internet www.dbio.eu; f. 1996; research in life sciences; devt of organisms in specific environmental conditions, biodiversity and preservation of the nat. genofund; Gen. Man. Dr MANUELA ELISABETA SIDOROFF; Scientific Dir Dr ALINA BUTU.

Mathematical Sciences

Institutul de Matematică 'Octav Mayer' (Octav Mayer Institute of Mathematics): Bdul Carol I 8, 700501 Iași; tel. (232) 211150; internet www.math.uaic.ro/~imom; f. 1948; attached to Romanian Acad.; library of 20,000 vols; Dir CATALIN GEORGE LEFTER; publ. *Studii și Cercetări Științifice*.

Institutul de Matematică 'Simion Stoilow' al Academiei Romane (Simion Stoilow Institute of Mathematics of the Romanian Academy): POB 1–764, 014700 Bucharest; Calea Grivitei St 21, 010702 Bucharest; tel. (21) 3196506; internet www .imar.ro; f. 1949, present name 1990; library of 35,000 vols, 121,000 journals; Dir Prof. Dr LUCIAN BEZNEA; Scientific Sec. DANA SAVU; publs *Mathematical Reports* (4 a year), *Revue Roumaine de Mathématiques Pures et Appliquées* (6 a year).

Institutul de Statistică Matematică și Matematică Aplicată 'Gheorghe Mihoc-Caius Iacob' al Academiei Romana ('Gheorghe Mihoc-Caius Iacob' Institute of Mathematical Statistics and Applied Mathematics of Romanian Academy): Calea 13 Septembrie 13, Sector 5, POB 1–24, 050711 Bucharest; tel. (21) 3182439; internet www .csm.ro; f. 2001 by merger of Institute of Applied Mathematics (f. 1991) and Center of Mathematical Statistics (f. 1964); researches on probability and stochastic processes, statistical inference, operational researches, dynamical systems and control theory, fluid mechanics, partial differential equations with applications in environmental and life sciences; Dir MARIUS IOSIFESCU; Man. FLORICA GRIGORE; publs *Mathematical Reports* (1 a year), *Revue Roumaine de Mathématiques Pures et Appliquées* (Romanian Journal of Pure and Applied Mathematics, 1 a year).

Physical Sciences

Institutul Astronomic al Academiei Române (Astronomical Institute of Romanian Academy): Str. Cuțitul de Argint 5, 040557 Bucharest; tel. (21) 3356892; internet www.astro.ro; f. 1990 by merger of observatories of Bucharest, Cluj-Napoca and Timisoara; attached to Romanian Acad.; library of 10,000 vols; Dir Dr VASILE MIOC; publs *Anuarul Astronomic* (Astronomical Yearbook, 1 a year), *Romanian Astronomical Journal* (2 a year).

Institutul de Cercetări Chimice (Institute of Chemical Research): Splaiul Independenței 202, 060021 Bucharest; tel. (21) 3153299; f. 1950; natural and bioactive products, technological engineering, chemical products and technologies; Gen. Man. SEVER ȘERBAN.

Institutul de Chimie Fizică 'Ilie Murgulescu' al Academiei Române ('Ilie Murgulescu' Institute of Physical Chemistry of Romanian Academy): POB 12–194, 060021 Bucharest; Splaiul Independenței 202, 060021 Bucharest; tel. (21) 3188595; e-mail office@icf.ro; internet www.icf.ro; f. 1963, current name adopted 1991; Dir Dr VLAD TUDOR POPA; Deputy Dir Dr OANA CARP; publs *Revue Roumaine de Chimie* (12 a year), *Roumanian Chemical Quarterly Review*.

Institutul de Chimie Macromoleculară 'Petru Poni' al Academiei Romane ('Petru Poni' Institute of Macromolecular Chemistry of Romanian Academy): St Aleea Grigore Ghica Voda 41A, 700487 Iași; tel. (232) 217454; e-mail admin@icmpp.ro; internet www.icmpp.ro; f. 1949; fundamental and applied research in field of organic and inorganic chemistry, polymer chemistry and physics; library of 100,000 vols; Dir Prof. Dr BOGDAN CRISTOFOR SIMIONESCU; Scientific Sec. Dr VALERIA HARABAGIU.

Institutul de Chimie Organică 'Costin D. Nenițescu' al Academiei Române (Costin D. Nenițescu Institute of Organic Chemistry of Romania Academy): Splaiul Independenței 202B, Sector 6, 71141 Bucharest; tel. (21) 3167900; internet www.cco.ro; f. 1949; basic research in organic chemistry, fine organic synthesis and structural analysis of organic compounds; Dir Dr Ing. PETRU IVAN FILIP; Scientific Sec. Dr Ing. CALIN DELEANU.

Institutul de Chimie Timișoara al Academiei Romane (Institute of Chemistry Timisoara of Romanian Academy): Bdul Mihai Viteazul 24, 300223 Timișoara; tel. (256) 491818; internet acad-icht.tm.edu.ro; f. 1967; library of 10,000 vols; Dir Dr OTILIA COSTISOR; Hon. Dir ZENO SIMON; Scientific Sec Dr RAMONA TUDOSE; publ. *Annals of the West University of Timișoara, Chemistry Series* (2 or 3 a year).

Institutul de Geodinamică Sabba S. Ștefănescu al Academiei Romane (Institute of Geodynamics Sabba S. Ștefănescu of Romanian Academy): Jean-Louis Calderon St 19–21, Sector 2, 020032 Bucharest; tel. (21) 3172126; e-mail inst_geodin@geodin.ro; internet www.geodin.ro; f. 1990; geophysical research; study of space-time variations; monitoring of space-time variations of gravitational, geomagnetic, geoelectric fields, modelling of the thermo-mechanical evolution of the lithosphere, non-linear analysis of geodynamic systems, studies of endogeneous processes in the geodynamic evolution of the Romanian territory, study of heliosphere/ geomagnetic field; organizes PhD programmes; library of 12,600 periodicals and 2,300 books; Dir Dr CRISAN DEMETRESCU; Deputy Dir Dr Ing. DUMITRU STANICA; publ. *Revue Roumaine de Geophysique* (1 a year).

Institutul de Speologie 'Emil Racoviță' al Academiei Romane ('Emil Racoviță' Institute of Speleology of Romanian Academy): Calea 13 Septembrie 13, Sector 5, 050711 Bucharest; tel. (21) 3110829; e-mail iser_b@yahoo.com; internet www.iser.ro; f. 1920; depts of biospeleology and karst edaphobiology, geospeleology and paleontology, karstonomy, karst inventory and protection, Cluj-Napoca dept; library of 5,900 vols, 850 periodicals; Dir Dr IOAN POVARA; Librarian IOANA CIUMASU; publs *Theoretical and Applied Karstology* (1 a year), *Travaux de* *l'Institut de Spéologie 'Emile Racovitza'* (1 a year, online, speotravaux.iser.ro).

Institutul Geologic al României (Geological Institute of Romania): Caransebeş 1, Sector 1, 012271 Bucharest; tel. (21) 3181329; e-mail office@igr.ro; internet www .igr.ro; f. 1906; conservation and recovery of drilling cores; colln of minerals, rocks, flowers; monitoring of mining areas; technological devt; studying and forecasting; deciphering geological composition and evolution of the country; defining areas of useful minerals; preparation and editing of geological, hydrogeological, geophysical and geochemical maps; fundamental and basic research in areas of mineralogy, palaeontology, stratigraphy, geochemistry, regional geology, hydrogeology, geotechnics, magnetometry, gravimetry, geoelectricity, seismics; studies on impact of human activities on groundwater pollution; studies on devt of earth sciences according to int. economic situation; expertise in mine flowers, precious stones; research and analysis of geomagnetic field distribution; gravitational, geothermal, electromagnetic fields in Romania; geoinformational system (GIS); geoid; analysis of satellite images; library of 270,000 vols; Dir-Gen. Dr STEFAN MARINCEA; Scientific Dir MARCEL MARUNTIU; publs Romanian journals of mineralogy, petrology, mineral deposits and environmental geochemistry, stratigraphy, palaeontology, tectonics and regional geology, geophysics (1 a year), *Memorii* (irregular).

Institutul National de Cercetare-Dezvoltare 'Delta Dunarii' (Danube Delta National Institute for Research and Development): Str. Babadag 165, 820112 Tulcea; tel. (240) 531520; e-mail office@indd.tim.ro; internet www.ddni.ro; f. 1970 as Research and Design Institute for the Danube Delta, present status 1999; attached to Min. of Environment; promotes conservation of biodiversity and the sustainable devt of wetlands in Romania and the Danube Delta area; library of 40,000 vols; Dir Dr Eng. ROMAN PÎRVULESCU; Scientific Dir Dr LILIANA TÖRÖK; publs *Scientific Annals of the Danube Delta Institute* (1 a year), *Review of Ecological Restoration in the Danube Delta Biosphere Reserve*.

Institutul Naţional de Cercetare Dezvoltare pentru Chimie si Petrochimie (National Institute of Research and Development for Chemistry and Petrochemistry): Splaiul Independentei 202, Sector 6, 060021 Bucharest; tel. (21) 3153299; e-mail office@ icechim.ro; internet www.icechim.ro; f. 2004; scientific research and technological devt; depts of biotechnology, chemical and petrochemical technology; Gen. Man. Eng. SANDA VELEA; Scientific Man. FLORIN OANCEA.

Institutul Naţional de Cercetare-Dezvoltare pentru Fizică Tehnică—IFT Iaşi (National Institute of Research and Development for Technical Physics): Mangeron Blvd 47, 700050 Iaşi; tel. (232) 430680; e-mail info@phys-iasi.ro; internet www .phys-iasi.ro; f. 1955; research in field of magnetism and magnetic materials; design and fabrication of new sensors for biomedical applications, sensors and actuators based on magnetoelastic phenomena, magnetic field sensors and spin-valve devices; devt of medicine and biotechnology, design and fabrication of non-destructive control sensors; library of 5,548 vols; Gen. Man Dr NICOLETA LUPU; Dir of Research Prof. HORIA CHIRIAC.

Institutul Naţional de Meteorologie şi Hidrologie (National Institute of Meteorology and Hydrology): Şoseaua Bucureşti-Ploieşti 97, 013686 Bucharest; tel. (21) 3183240; e-mail relatii@meteo.inmh.ro;

internet www.meteoromania.ro; f. 1884 as Meteorological Service of Romania, present name and status 1970; researches on climatology; physics of atmosphere; agrometeorology; meteorological methodology; numeric modelling; long-range forecasting; remote sensing and GIS laboratory; Dir-Gen. Dr ION SANDU; publs *Bibliografia hidrologică* (1 a year), *Bibliografia meteorologică* (1 a year), *Hydrology Journal* (2 a year), *Meteorology Journal* (2 a year), *Studii şi Cercetări* (in 2 parts: Meteorology, Hydrology; 1 vol. a year).

Institutul Naţional de Metrologie (National Institute of Metrology): Şoseaua Vitan-Bîrzeşti St 11, Sector 4, 042122 Bucharest; tel. (21) 3345520; e-mail office@ inm.ro; internet www.inm.ro; f. 1951; attached to Romanian Bureau of Legal Metrology; devt, maintenance, utilization of nat. measurement standards; providing traceability to the SI; dissemination of units of measurement at nat. level; 5 laboratories; library of 15,000 vols; Dir Dr Eng. MIRELLA BUZOIANU; publ. *Metrologie* (4 a year).

Institutul Naţional pentru Fizică şi Inginerie Nucleară 'Horia Hulubei' (Horia Hulubei National Institute of Physics and Nuclear Engineering): Str. Reactorului 30, 077125 Bucharest; tel. (21) 4042300; internet www.ifin.ro; f. 1949; research and devt in physical and natural sciences; library of 385,000 vols; Dir-Gen. Prof. Dr NICOLAE VICTOR ZAMFIR; Scientific Dir Dr LIVIUS MARIAN TRACHE; publs *Conference Proceedings*, *IFA-Preprints*, *Romanian Journal of Physics* (12 a year), *Romanian Reports in Physics* (12 a year).

PHILOSOPHY AND PSYCHOLOGY

Institutul de Filosofie si Psihologie 'Constantin Rădulescu-Motru' (Institute of Philosophy and Psychology 'Constantin Rădulescu-Motru'): Casa Academiei, Calea 13 Septembrie 13, Sector 5, 050711 Bucharest; tel. (56) 3188106; e-mail secretariat@ ipsihologie.ro; internet www.ipsihologie.ro; f. 2001 by merger of Institute of Philosophy (f. 1953) and Institute of Psychology (f. 1956); attached to Romanian Acad.; research in philosophy, with focus on ethics, aesthetics, logic and ontology, epistemology; research in psychology, with focus on social and cross-cultural psychology, work and organizational psychology, cognitive ergonomics, personality and devt; library of 2,600 vols, 1,657 magazines; Dir ALEXANDRU SURDU; Scientific Sec. Dr BOGDAN DANCIU; publs *Revista de Filosofie* (4 a year), *Revista de Psihologie* (4 a year), *Revue Romaine de Philosophie* (2 a year), *Romanian Journal of Psychology* (2 a year).

RELIGION, SOCIOLOGY AND ANTHROPOLOGY

Association Internationale d'Etudes du Sud-Est Europeen (International Association for South-East European Studies): Nicolae Racota St 12–14, 011393 Bucharest; tel. (21) 2242965; e-mail aiesee@rdslink.ro; internet www.aiesee.org; f. 1963; attached to ICPHS, UNESCO; promotes study of the civilizations spread over the Balkans and SE Europe; social sciences; library of 40,000 vols; Pres. ANDRÉ GUILLOU (France); Sec.-Gen. RAZVAN THEODORESCU (Romania); publ. *Revue de l'AIESEE* (1 a year).

Institutul de Antropologie 'Francisc I. Rainer' al Academiei Romane ('Francisc I. Rainer' Institute of Anthropology of Romanian Academy): Bdul Eroilor Sanitari 8, Sector 5, 050474 Bucharest; tel. (21) 3175072; e-mail franciscrainer@yahoo.com; internet www.antropologia.ro; f. 1937; research on paleoanthropology, socio-cul-

tural and theoretical anthropology, biomedical anthropology; library of 7,000 vols, 25 periodicals; Dir Dr CRISTIANA GLAVCE; Hon. Dir Prof. Dr CONSTANTIN BALACEANU-STOLNICI; publs *Annuaire Roumain d'Anthropologie* (1 a year, online, annuaire.antropologia.ro), *Studii si Cercetari de Antropologie* (4 a year, online, studii.an tropologia.ro).

Institutul de Cercetări Socio-Umane 'C. S. Nicolaescu-Plopsor' ('C. S. Nicolaescu-Plopsor' Institute for Studies in Social Sciences and Humanities): Calea Unirii 68, 200345 Craiova; tel. (251) 523330; e-mail office@icsu.ro; internet icsu.ro; f. 1965, current name adopted 1994; attached to Romanian Acad.; depts of archaeology, history, ethnography, philosophy, philology; library of 71,000 vols, 90,000 periodicals; Dir Prof. Dr AVRAM CEZAR GABRIEL; Scientific Sec. SIMONA LAZAR; publs *Anuarul Institutului de Cercetari Socio-Umane* (1 a year), *Arhivele Olteniei* (1 a year).

Institutul de Cercetări Socio-Umane din Sibiu (Institute of Socio-Human Research—Sibiu): Bdul Victoriei 40, 550024 Sibiu; tel. (269) 212604; e-mail secretariat@icsusib.ro; internet www.icsusib.ro; f. 1956; attached to Romanian Acad.; history and culture of Transylvanian Saxons; their relationship to history and culture of Romanians in the immediate environment and in Transylvania; Transylvanian Saxon dialect; urban history; ethnology; library of 7,850 vols, 10,200 periodicals; Man. Dr PAUL NIEDERMAIER; publs *Anuarul (Yearbook)* (1 a year), *Forschungen zur Volks- und Landeskunde* (2 a year), *Historia Urbana* (2 a year), *Studii şi Comunicări de Etnologie* (1 a year).

Institutul de Cercetări Socio-Umane 'Gheorghe Şincai' al Academiei Române ('Gheorghe Şincai' Institute for Social Sciences and Humanities of Romanian Academy): Str. Al. Papiu Ilarian 10/A, 540074 Târgu Mureş; tel. (265) 260238; e-mail icsu_ms@clicknet.ro; internet www .icsumures.acad-cluj.ro; f. 1957; research on agrarian economic history and private life, intellectual formation history, Transylvanian elite XVIII-XX centuries, history of minorities in the communist regime, church history and religious life, Romania in the context of int. relations, marginal history, Romanian exile history and the history of Romanian literature, imagology and comparative literature; library of 338,290 vols; Dir Prof. Dr CORNEL SIGMIREAN; Scientific Sec. Dr NICOLETA SALCUDEANU; publ. *Anuarul Institutului de Cercetari Socio-Umane 'Gheorghe Şincai'* (1 a year).

Institutul de Etnografie şi Folclor 'Constantin Brăiloiu' ('Constantin Brăiloiu' Institute of Ethnography and Folklore): Str. Dobrescu I Demetru nr. 9, Sector 1, 010025 Bucharest; tel. (21) 3183900; e-mail ief .brailoiu@gmail.com; internet www.acad.ro/ ief; f. 1949; Nat. Folk Archives of sound, image and MSS; fundamental and advanced scientific research and related activities in the fields of folk literature, ethnomusicology, ethnocoreology, ethnography; library of 50,000 vols; Dir Dr CORNELIA-SABINA ISPAS; Scientific Sec. Dr ION GHINOIU; publs *Anuarul Institutului de Etnografie si Folclor*, *Journal of Ethnography and Folklore* (2 a year).

Institutul de Sociologie 'Dimitrie Gusti' ('Dimitrie Gusti' Institute of Sociology): Calea 13 Septembrie 13, 050711 Bucharest; tel. (21) 4118532; e-mail insoc@insoc.ro; f. 1965; attached to Romanian Acad.; Man. Dir Prof. Dr ILIE BĂDESCU; publs *Revue Roumaine des Sciences Sociales—série de Socio-*

logie (4 a year, English edn 2 a year), *Sociologie Românească* (6 a year).

Institutul de Ştiinţe Politice şi Relaţii Internaţionale (Institute of Political Sciences and International Relations): Iuliu Maniu 1–3, Corp A, etaj 7, Sector 6, 061071 Bucharest; tel. (21) 3169661; e-mail ispri@ ispri.ro; internet www.ispri.ro; f. 1990 as Institute of Social Theory and Political Science; attached to Romanian Acad.; depts of systems theory and political instns, political philosophy, int. relations; library: 1m. vols; Dir Prof. Dr DAN DUNGACIU; Scientific Sec. Dr CRISTIAN-ION POPA; publs *Revista de Ştiinţe Politice şi Relaţii Internaţionale* (4 a year), *Revista Romana de Teorie Socială* (4 a year), *Revue Roumaine de Teorie Sociale* (3 a year), *Romanian Journal of Political Science and International Relations* (2 a year).

Institutul de Ştiinţe Socio-Umane (Institute of Social and Human Sciences): Str. T. Codrescu 2, 700481 Iaşi; tel. (232) 115987; f. 1969; attached to Romanian Acad.; library of 35,000 vols; Dir TUDOREL DIMA; publs *Anuar de Ştiinţe Socio-Umane*, *Revista Romana de Sociologie* (2 a year), *Romanian Journal of Sociology*.

Institutul de Studii Banatice 'Titu Maiorescu' (Titu Maiorescu Institute for Research): Str. Mihai Viteazul 24, 300223 Timişoara; tel. (256) 491823; e-mail icsutm@ acad-tim.tm.edu.ro; f. 1970; attached to Romanian Acad.; library of 8,000 vols; Dir Prof. Dr CRISU DASCĂLU; publs *Caietul Cercului de Studii* (2 a year), *Dialectologie* (1 a year), *Limbăliterară* (1 a year), *Poetică* (1 a year), *Revista de Studii Banatice* (2 a year), *Studii de Istorie a Banatului* (1 a year), *Toponimie* (1 a year).

TECHNOLOGY

Institutul de Informatică Teoretică (Institute of Computer Science): Str. T. Codrescu 2, 700481 Iaşi; tel. (332) 106505; internet www.iit.tuiasi.ro; f. 1984, present status 1990; attached to Romanian Acad. Iasi Br.; Dir Prof. H. N. TEODORESCU; Scientific Sec. Dr VASILE APOPEI.

Institutul de Mecanica Solidelor al Academiei Române (Institute of Solid Mechanics of Romanian Academy): Constantin Mille St 15, Sector 1, 10141 Bucharest; tel. (21) 3126736; e-mail imsar@imsar.bu.edu.ro; internet www.imsar.ro; f. 1949 as Institute of Applied Mechanics 'Traian Vuia', present name 1990; control of dynamic systems, mechanics of deformable media, ultrasonics, tribology, mechatronics and robotics; control strategies based on artificial intelligence methods; wave propagation techniques for characterization of mechanical properties; dynamics of elastic structures; direct and inverse methods for biomechanic systems; ultrasonic methods for improvement of non-destructive testing; mechanical and tribological properties investigation for classical and unconventional materials; bio-tribology; methods, strategies for robotics and mechatronics; Dir Dr TUDOR SIRETEANU; Scientific Sec. Dr DAN DUMITRIU; publ. *Revue Roumaine des Sciences Techniques Série de Mécanique appliquée* (Romanian Journal of Technical Sciences-Applied Mechanics, 3 a year).

Institutul National de Cercetare Dezvoltare pentru Metale Neferoase Şi Rare (National Institute of Research And Development for Non-Ferrous and Rare Metals): Bdul Biruintei 102, Pantaleon; tel. (21) 3522046; e-mail imnr@imnr.ro; internet www.imnr.ro; f. 1966, present name 2004; research in nanostructured materials, ecotechnologies and environment protection; Dir

Dr TEODOR VELEA; Scientific Dir Dr Ing. ROXANA MIOARA PITICESCU.

Institutul Naţional de Cercetare-Dezvoltare pentru Protecţia Mediului (National Institute for Research and Development in Environmental Protection): Splaiul Independenţei St 294, 060031 Bucharest; tel. (21) 3052600; e-mail incdpm@incdpm.ro; internet www.incdpm .ro; f. 1952; attached to Min. of Environment; management, control of water, land and air quality; integrated monitoring of environmental factors; control of water pollution; water technologies; technologies and equipment for cleaning sewage; sludge-processing; aquatic ecosystems; biodiversity; fluid mechanics; dispersion of pollutants; noise pollution and vibrations; solid waste management; environmental impact of construction; library of 20,000 vols and journals; Dir-Gen. Prof. Dr Ing. GYÖRGY DEAK; Scientific Dir Dr Ing. LIVIU IANUS; publs *An Environment for the Future* (1 a year), *The Environment* (4 a year).

Institutul Naţional de Informare şi Documentare (National Institute for Information and Documentation): Str. I. D. Mendeleev 21–25, 010362 Bucharest; tel. (21) 3158765; e-mail inid@iniduw.inid.ro; f. 1949; promotes the use of modern equipment for automatic data processing in the area of documentary information; library: see under Libraries and Archives; Dir-Gen. TIBERIUS IGNAT; publs *Asigurerea şi Promovarea Calităţii* (4 a year), *Informarea şi Documentarea Modernă* (4 a year), *Management şi Marketing Coentemporan* (4 a year).

Libraries and Archives

Alba Iulia

Biblioteca Judeţeană 'Lucian Blaga' Alba (Alba 'Lucian Blaga' District Library): Str. Camil Velican 22, 510113 Alba Iulia; tel. (258) 811443; e-mail bjalba@gmail.com; internet www.bjalba.ro; f. 1943; 4 brs; 250,493 vols; Dir MIOARA POP.

Biblioteca Naţională a României, Filiala Batthyaneum (National Library of Romania, Batthyaneum Branch): Str. Gabriel Bethlen 1, 510009 Alba Iulia; tel. (258) 811939; internet www.bibnat.ro/ filiala-batthyaneum-s75-ro.htm; f. 1798, present status 1962; attached to Biblioteca Naţională; mineralogical and numismatic colln; scientific instruments, clocks; religious art; 18th-century astronomical observatory; 115,992 vols of bibliographic items, 4,327 periodicals; spec. collns of 1,778 MSS since 9th century, 571 incunabula, documents, rare books, ex-libris; Dir-Gen. of Nat. Library Dr ELENA TÎRZIMAN.

Alexandria

Biblioteca Judeţeană 'Marin Preda' Teleorman (Teleorman 'Marin Preda' District Library): Str. Bucuresti Bl. T3, 140101 Alexandria; tel. (247) 310706; e-mail bjmarinpreda@yahoo.com; f. 1949; 148,718 vols; Man. VIOREL FOTA.

Arad

Biblioteca Judeţeană 'A. D. Xenopol' Arad (Arad 'A. D. Xenopol' District Library): Str. Gheorghe Popa de Teiuş 2–4, 310022 Arad; tel. (257) 256510; internet www .bibliotecaarad.ro; f. 1913; 5 brs; 500,000 vols; Dir FLORIN DIDILESCU.

Bacău

Biblioteca Judeţeană 'Costache Sturdza' Bacău (Bacău 'Costache Sturdza' District Library): Str. Aleea Parcului 9,

600043 Bacău; tel. (234) 513126; e-mail contact@bjbc.ro; internet www.bjbc.ro:8080/ bjbc; f. 1893; 430,000 vols and periodicals; Dir GABRIELA MURARU; publs *Bibliografia Judeţului Bacău*, *Cartea*, *Ex-Libris*.

Baia Mare

Biblioteca Judeţeană 'Petre Dulfu' Maramureş (Maramureş 'Petre Dulfu' District Library): Bdul Independentei 4B, 430123 Baia Mare; tel. (262) 275583; e-mail biblioteca@bibliotecamm.ro; internet www .bibliotecamm.ro; f. 1951; 433,828 vols; Dir-Gen. TEODOR ARDELEAN.

Bistriţa

Biblioteca Judeţeană Bistriţa-Năsăud (Bistriţa-Năsăud District Library): Str. Garii 2, 420041 Bistriţa; tel. (363) 401356; e-mail bjbndirector@yahoo.com; internet www.bjbn .ro; f. 1950; 209,530 vols; Man. MARCEL SESERMAN; publs *Labirint*, *Specialty Journal* (1 a year).

Blaj

Biblioteca Documentară 'Timotei Cipariu' ('Timotei Cipariu' Documentary Library): Str. Petru Pavel Aron 2–4, 515400 Blaj; tel. (258) 710110; f. 1754; attached to Cluj-Napoca br. library of Romanian Academy; spec. colln of rare and ancient books on history of the Romanian people; 30,000 vols in humanities and sciences.

Botoşani

Biblioteca Judeţeană 'Mihai Eminescu' Botoşani (Botoşani County Library): Calea Naţională 64, 710028 Botoşani; tel. (231) 513334; e-mail biblioteca@bibliotecabotosani .ro; internet www.bibliotecabotosani.ro; f. 1882; 500,000 vols (incl. books, periodicals, records, slides, maps, standards, audiovisual material); Dir Prof. CORNELIA VIZITEU; publs *Catalogul Fondului Documentar*, *Catalogul Fondului Documentar 'Mihai Eminescu'*, *Studii eminescologice / Études sur Eminescu / Eminescu Studies / Eminescu Studien* (1 a year).

Brăila

Biblioteca Judeţeană 'Panait Istrati' Brăila (Brăila 'Panait Istrati' County Library): Calea Călăraşilor 52, 810010 Brăila; tel. (239) 611292; e-mail bjpi@ bjbraila.ro; internet www.bjbraila.ro; f. 1881; 4 brs; coordinates activities of 3 city libraries and 39 village libraries; 388,968 vols; Dir DRAGOS ADRIAN NEAGU; publ. *Ex-libris* (1 a year).

Braşov

Biblioteca Judeţeană 'George Bariţiu' Braşov ('George Bariţiu' County Library Braşov): Bdul Eroilor 33–35, 500036 Braşov; tel. (268) 419338; e-mail biblgb@rdsbv.ro; internet www.bjbv.ro; f. 1835; reading and loan services; organizes cultural and social activities, courses, lectures, confs and workshops; 5 brs; 800,000 vols; Man. Dr DANIEL NAZARE.

Biblioteca Universităţii 'Transilvania' din Braşov (Transylvania University of Braşov Central Library): Str. Iuliu Maniu 41A, 500091 Braşov; tel. (268) 476050; e-mail biblioteca@unitbv.ro; internet but.unitbv.ro; f. 1948; 712,169 vols (incl. 553,763 vols of books, 113,897 vols of periodicals, 44,509 vols of spec. collns); Dir Prof. Ing. Dr ELENA HELEREA.

Bucharest

Arhivele Naţionale ale României (National Archives): Bdul Regina Elisabeta 49, Sector 5, 050013 Bucharest; tel. (21) 3126710; e-mail secretariat.an@mai.gov.ro;

internet www.arhivelenationale.ro; f. 1831; 1,221,500 medieval documents, 22,000 seals, 12,820 MSS, 816,929 ft modern documents, 735,680 vols of plans and maps; Dir Dr IOAN DRAGAN; Deputy Dir Dr ALINA PAVELESCU; publs *Buletine informative*, *Revista Arhivelor* (1 a year).

Attached Library:

Biblioteca Documentară a Arhivelor Naţionale (Documentary Library of the National Archives): Bdul Regina Elisabeta 49, 050013 Bucharest; tel. (21) 3037080; e-mail publicatii.an@mira.gov.ro; internet www.arhivelenationale.ro; f. 1862; 70,000 vols, 50,000 periodicals; Library Coordinator CAMELIA COJOCARU; Librarian VALENTINA DINU; publ. *Revista Arhivelor* (Archives Review).

Biblioteca Academiei Române (Library of the Romanian Academy): Calea Victoriei St, Sector 1, 010071 Bucharest; tel. (21) 2128284; e-mail biblacad@biblacad.ro; internet www.biblacad.ro; f. 1867; collects and preserves the nat. fund of MSS and prints related to history and civilization; UN depository library; 14m. vols, 3.6m. monographs, 5.3m. serials; spec. collns incl. 600,000 historical documents, engravings, numismatic colln, maps, music MSS; Dir-Gen. FLORIN FILIP; publs *Cărţi intrate în reţeaua bibliotecilor Academiei Române* (1 a year), *Periodice intrate în reţeaua bibliotecilor Academiei Române* (1 a year), *Publicaţii Periodice Româneşti*.

Biblioteca Centrală a Academiei de Ştiinţe Agricole şi Silvice 'Gheorghe Ionescu-Şişeşti' (Central Library of the Gheorghe Ionescu-Şişeşti Academy of Agricultural and Forestry Sciences): Bdul Mărăşti 61, 011464 Bucharest; tel. (21) 3184457; f. 1928; 136,000 vols; Chief Librarian ELENA TUDOR; publs *Bibliografia agricolă curentă română* (4 a year), *Cărţi străine intrate in bibliotecile din România—seria Agricultură* (12 a year), *Noutăţi documentare FAO* (12 a year).

Biblioteca Centrală Academiei de Studii Economice (Central Library of the Academy of Economic Studies): Piaţa Romană 6, Sector 1, 010374 Bucharest; tel. (21) 3191900; e-mail rectorat@ase.ro; internet www.biblioteca.ase.ro; f. 1913; 740,000 vols; Dir ALINA CROITORU; publ. *The Bibliographical Bulletin* (2 a year).

Biblioteca Centrală a Universităţii 'Politehnica' din Bucureşti (Central Library of Politehnica University of Bucharest): Splaiul Independentei 313, 060042 Bucharest; tel. (21) 4023982; internet www.library.pub.ro; f. 1868; 1,340,762 vols, incl. books, journals, spec. collns, standards, audiovisual material; Dir Ing. Dr CRISTINA ALBU; publ. *Scientific Bulletin* (4 series: mechanical engineering, electrical engineering, chemistry and materials science, applied mathematics and physics).

Biblioteca Centrală Universitară 'Carol I' (Central University Library 'Carol I'): Str. Boteanu 1, Sector 1, 010027 Bucharest; tel. (21) 3120108; e-mail office@bcub.ro; internet www.bcub.ro; f. 1895, present status 1948; 15 brs; 1,855,424 vols, 10,989 e-books; Dir-Gen. Dr MIREILLE CARMEN RĂDOI; Deputy Dir ŞTEFANIA MAZILU; publs *Ghidul lucrărilor de referinţe în colecţiile Bibliotecii Centrale Universitare 'Carol I' din Bucureşti* (Guide to Reference Works in the Collns of the Library of Bucharest Univ., 2 a year), *Informaţie şi Formaţie* (12 a year), *UniBib* (online).

Biblioteca de Documentare Medicală 'Dr Dimitrie Nanu' (Dr Dimitrie Nanu Medical Documentation Library): Str. Pitar Moş 7–15, 010451 Bucharest; tel. (21)

2110430; f. 1951; attached to Centrul de Calcul, Statistică Sanitară şi Documentare Medicală; 310,556 vols; Dir FELICIA-IOANA DOBRESCU.

Biblioteca Documentară de Istorie a Medicinei (Documentary Library of the History of Medicine): Str. Dr Leonte 1–3, 050463 Bucharest; tel. (21) 6384010; f. 1953; 50,200 vols, 1,100 periodicals, 3,500 MSS and documents, 5,200 museum pieces; Dir Prof. MARIOARA GEORGESCU.

Biblioteca Institutului Naţional de Informare şi Documentare (Library of the National Institute for Information and Documentation): Str. I. D. Mendeleev 21–25, 010362 Bucharest; tel. (21) 3134010; e-mail inid_bucuresti@home.ro; f. 1949; 743,000 vols incl. 135,000 periodicals; Chief Librarian DACIA CRISTIANA STATIE.

Biblioteca Metropolitană Bucureşti (Bucharest Metropolitan Library): Str. Tache Ionescu 4, Sector 1, 010354 Bucharest; tel. (21) 3168304; e-mail secretariat_dirg@bibliotecametropolitana.ro; internet www.bibliotecametropolitana.ro; f. 1831; 6 brs; 1,337,078 vols (periodicals, newspapers, musical scores); Dir-Gen. Dr FLORIN ROTARU; publs *Bibliografia oraşului Bucureşti* (1 a year), *Biblioteca Bucureştilor* (12 a year), *Buletinul Bibliotecilor din Franţa* (12 a year).

Biblioteca Naţională a României (National Library of Romania): Bdul Unirii 22, Sector 3, 030833 Bucharest; tel. (21) 3142434; e-mail biblioteca@bibnat.ro; internet www.bibnat.ro; f. 1838, current name and status 1990; acts as copyright deposit library and nat. bibliographic agency; incorporates research centre for librarianship and book pathology and restoration; 9m. vols; spec. collns of MSS, old and rare books, cartography, musical scores, photographs, maps, prints, old illustrated postcards and drawings; Dir-Gen. Dr ELENA TÎRZIMAN; publs *ABSI—Abstracte în Bibliologie şi Ştiinţa Informării* (4 a year), *Aniversări Culturale* (2 a year), *Bibliografia Naţională Română* (6 series), *Biblioteconomie—Culegere de Traduceri Prelucrate* (4 a year), *Catalogul Colectiv al Cărţilor Străine Intrate în Bibliotecile din România* (4 a year), *Repertoriul Periodicelor Străine Intrate în Bibliotecile din România* (1 a year), *Revista Biblioteca* (12 a year), *Revista Bibliotecii Naţionale a României* (2 a year), *Revista Română de Conservare şi Restaurare* (1 a year), *Revista Română de Istorie a Cărţii* (1 a year).

Biblioteca Pedagogică Naţională 'I. C. Petrescu' ('I. C. Petrescu' National Education Library): Str. Ioan Zalomit 12, 010151 Bucharest; tel. (40) 3110323; internet www.bpn.ro; f. 1880; methodological centre for the nat. network of school libraries; 480,000 educational vols and periodicals; Dir-Gen. Dr GEORGE ANCA; Librarian MANUELA POPA; publs *Bibliografia pedagogică* (1 a year), *Education en Roumanie* (Education in Romania, 1 a year), *Informare tematică* (1 a year), *LIBER. Revistă pentru bibliotecile pedagogice şi şcolare* (4 a year), *Modernizarea învăţămîntului* (1 a year), *Studii de biblioteconomie şi informare documentară* (irregular).

Biblioteca Universităţii de Ştiinţe Agronomice şi Medicină Veterinară Bucureşti (Library of the University of Agronomic Sciences and Veterinary Medicine Bucharest): Bdul Mărăşti 59, Sector 1, 011464 Bucharest; tel. 748025519; e-mail office@biblioteca-usamvb.ro; internet www.biblioteca-usamvb.ro; f. 1868; 480,000 vols; Dir CARMEN CONSTANTIN; publs *Agronomy*,

Biotechnology, *Horticulture*, *Land Reclamation*, *Veterinary Medicine*, *Zootechnics*.

Biblioteca Universităţii Nationala de Arte Bucureşti (Library of the Bucharest National University of Fine Arts): Str. Gen. Budişteanu 19, Sector 1, 010773 Bucharest; tel. (21) 3125429; f. 1864; 60,000 vols, 261,262 slides and photographs; spec. colln of 19th- and 20th-century European fine-art periodicals; Dir GABRIELA BĂJENARU.

Biblioteca Universităţii Naţionale de Muzică din Bucureşti (Library of the National University of Music Bucharest): Str. Ştirbei Vodă 33, Sector 1, 010102 Bucharest; tel. (31) 1029568; e-mail biblioteca@unmb.ro; internet www.unmb.ro/departamente/biblioteca-mediateca; f. 1864; 139,871 vols; Head MARIA CIOPONEA; publs *Acord*, *Musicology Today*.

Centrul de Informare şi Documentare Economică (Centre of Economic Information and Documentation): Casa Academiei Române, Calea 13 Septembrie 13, Sector 5, 050711 Bucharest; tel. (21) 3182438; e-mail cide@zappmobile.ro; internet www.ince.ro/cide.html; f. 1990; attached to Institutului Naţional de Cercetări Economice al Academiei Române; Dir Prof. Dr VALERIU IOAN-FRANC; publs *Analele INCE* (4 a year), *Caiete Critice* (12 a year), *Marketing Management* (6 a year), *Probleme Economice* (48 a year), *Revista de Economie Industriala* (2 a year), *Revista Română de Economie* (2 a year), *Romanian Economic Research Observer* (2 a year), *Romanian Journal of Economic Forecasting* (4 a year), *Studii şi Cercetări Economice* (12 a year).

S. C. Biblioteca Chimiei SA (S. C. Romanian Chemistry Library SA): Calea Plevnei 139B, 060011 Bucharest; tel. (21) 3142447; e-mail biblioteca_de_chimie@syscom18.com; internet www.bch.ro; f. 1956; provides access to nat. and foreign scientific and technical literature; 46,000 vols; Gen. Man. Ing. ION ANDRONACHE; publs *Materiale Plastice* (Plastic Materials Magazine, 4 a year, online, www.revmaterialeplastice.ro), *Revista de Chimie* (Chemistry Magazine, 12 a year, online, www.revistadechimie.ro).

Serviciul de Documentare al Ministerului Învăţământului: Str. Spiru Haret 12, 010716 Bucharest; tel. (21) 6142680; f. 1971; information and documentation on teaching and educational management abroad; Romanian legislation on education; Head EUGENIU TOMA; publs *Buletinul Ministerului Învăţământului* (4 a year), *Educaţie-Învăţământ* (2 a year).

Serviciul de Informare, Documentare şi Informatizare al Academiei de Ştiinţe Agricole şi Silvice 'Gheorghe Ionescu-Şişeşti' (Information, Documentation and Electronic Information Service of the Gheorghe Ionescu-Şişteşti Academy of Agricultural and Forestry Sciences): Bdul Mărăşti 61, 011464 Bucharest; tel. (21) 6182554; f. 1928; attached to Acad. of Agricultural and Forestry Sciences; 147,000 vols and CD-ROMs; Head Dr C. KEVORCHIAN; publ. *Curierul ASAS* (4 a year).

Buzău

Biblioteca Judeţeană 'V. Voiculescu' Buzău (Buzău 'V. Voiculescu' District Library): Bdul Unirii 140, 120360 Buzău; tel. (238) 721509; internet bjvvbuzau.ro; f. 1873, present name 1991; 293,833 vols; Dir SORIN BURLACU.

Călăraşi

Biblioteca Judeţeană 'Al. Odobescu' Călăraşi (Călăraşi 'Al. Odobescu' District Library): Str. Bucureşti 102, 910064 Călăraşi; tel. (242) 316757; e-mail bjc@rdsct

.ro; f. 1883, present name 1992; 265,254 vols; Dir GHIȚA DUMITRU.

Cluj-Napoca

Biblioteca Centrală Universitară 'Lucian Blaga' Cluj-Napoca ('Lucian Blaga' Central University Library Cluj-Napoca): Clinicilor St 2, 400006 Cluj-Napoca; tel. (264) 597092; e-mail informatii@bccluj .ro; internet www.bccluj.ro; f. 1872; 3,665,271 vols; Gen. Dir Prof. Dr DORU RADOSAV; Deputy Dir PORACZKY ROZALIA; publs *BIBLIOREV* (online, www.bccluj.ro/bibliorev), *Buletin Informativ*, *PHILOBIBLON* (online, www.philobiblon.ro).

Biblioteca Centrală 'Valeriu Bologa' ('Valeriu Bologa' Library): Victor Babes St 8, 400012 Cluj-Napoca; tel. (264) 597256; e-mail bibliotecaumf@umfcluj.ro; f. 1949; central library of 'Iuliu Hațieganu' Univ. of Medicine and Pharmacy Cluj-Napoca; 300,000 vols; Dir IOANA ROBU; publ. *Clujul Medical* (4 a year).

Biblioteca Filialei Cluj-Napoca a Academiei Române (Library of the Cluj-Napoca Branch of the Romanian Academy): Str. M. Kogălniceanu 12–14, 400084 Cluj-Napoca; tel. (264) 595027; e-mail biblacadcj@yahoo .com; internet www.acad-cluj.ro/biblioteca_academiei_romane.php; f. 1950; 781,243 vols and periodicals on the humanities and science, 179 incunabula, 2m. documents; spec. collns incl. Romanian, Latin, Hungarian, Slavonic MSS; Man. Prof. Dr IOAN CHINDRIS; publ. *Biblioteca si Cercetarea*.

Biblioteca Județeană 'Octavian Goga' Cluj ('Octavian Goga' Cluj County Library): Calea Dorobanților 104, 400691 Cluj-Napoca; tel. (264) 430323; e-mail bjc@bjc.ro; internet www.bjc.ro; f. 1921; 3 br. libraries; 752,812 vols (incl. 686,178 books and periodicals, 1,579 MSS, 20,287 audiovisual items, 7,291 electronic collns, 37,477 other documents); Dir Prof. Dr SORINA STANCA; Deputy Dir FLOAREA ELENA MOȘOIU; publs *Anul editorial clujean*, *Buletin UE-INFO* (1 a year), *Calendarul evenimentelor și manifestărilor culturale* (1 a year).

Biblioteca Universității Tehnice din Cluj-Napoca (Library of Cluj-Napoca Technical University): Str. C. Daicoviciu nr. 15, 400775 Cluj-Napoca; tel. (264) 401999; internet www.utcluj.ro/biblioteca; f. 1884, reorganized in 1948; 879,000 vols, 65,000 patents; Dir Ing. CĂLIN CÎMPEAN; publ. *Acta Technica Napocensis* (in English, 2 a year).

Constanța

Biblioteca Județeană 'Ioan N. Roman' Constanța ('Ioan N. Roman' Constanța County Library): Str. Mircea cel Batrân 104A, 900592 Constanța; tel. (241) 614482; e-mail biblioteca@biblioteca.ct.ro; internet www.biblioteca.ct.ro; f. 1931, present name 2003; 674,448 vols of encyclopaedic profile, 512,035 books, 80,775 periodicals, 1,428 audiovisual materials, 2,036 spec. collns; Dir CORNELIA PARIZA; publs *Bibliografia Dobrogei* (1 a year), *Biblion* (2 a year).

Craiova

Biblioteca Județeană 'Alexandru și Aristia Aman' Dolj (Public Library 'Alexandru and Aristia Aman' County Dolj): Str. M. Kogălniceanu 9, 200390 Craiova; tel. (251) 523177; e-mail bib@aman.ro; internet www.aman.ro; f. 1908; 4 brs; 466,000 vols; Dir LUCIAN DINDIRICĂ.

Biblioteca Universitatii din Craiova (University of Craiova Library): Str. A. I. Cuza 13, 200585 Craiova; tel. (251) 418844; e-mail bib@central.ucv.ro; internet biblio .central.ucv.ro; f. 1966 by merger of Agronomic Institute Library (f. 1948) and Peda-

gogical Institute Library (f. 1959); 1,071,290 vols; Dir GEORGETA PADUREANU.

Deva

Biblioteca Județeană 'Ovid Densusianu' Hunedoara-Deva (Hunedoara-Deva 'Ovid Densusianu' District Library): Str. 1 Decembrie 26, 330025 Deva; tel. (254) 216457; e-mail bibliotecadeva@upcmail.ro; internet www.bibliotecadeva.ro; f. 1951; 330,000 vols, periodicals and audiovisual items; Dir IOAN SEBASTIAN BARA; publ. *Vox Libri* (4 a year).

Drobeta-Turnu Severin

Biblioteca Județeană 'I. G. Bibicescu' Mehedinți (Mehedinți 'I. G. Bibicescu' District Library): Str. Traian 115, 220134 Drobeta-Turnu Severin; tel. (252) 315682; f. 1921; 450,000 vols; Dir RALUCA ȘTEFANIA GRAF.

Focșani

Biblioteca Județeană 'Duiliu Zamfirescu' Vrancea (Vrancea 'Duiliu Zamfirescu' District Library): Str. Mihail Kogălniceanu 12, 620036 Focșani; tel. (237) 214562; e-mail biblioteca@bjvrancea.ro; internet www .bjvrancea.ro; f. 1906, present name 1951; 211,552 vols (incl. 209,353 books and periodicals); Dir Dr TEODORA FÎNTÎNARU.

Galați

Biblioteca Județeană 'V. A. Urechia' Galați (Galați 'V. A. Urechia' County Library): Str. Mihai Bravu 16, 800208 Galați; tel. (236) 411037; e-mail bvau@bvau.ro; internet www.bvau.ro; f. 1890; 4 brs; 709,434 vols; Dir Prof. ZANFIR ILIE; publs *Asociația* (4 a year), *Buletinul Fundației Urechia* (2 a year), *Revista trimestrială de Cultură: Axis Libri* (4 a year).

Biblioteca Universității 'Dunarea de Jos' din Galați (University of Galați 'Dunarea de Jos' Library): Str. Domnească 47, 800008 Galați; tel. (236) 414112; e-mail biblioteca@ugal.ro; internet www.lib.ugal.ro; f. 1951, present name and status 1974; 480,000 vols mainly on science, technology and engineering, food industry, history, theology, languages and literature, economics; Dir MIOARA VONCILĂ.

Giurgiu

Biblioteca Județeană 'I. A. Bassarabescu' Giurgiu (County Library 'I. A. Bassarabescu' Giurgiu): Soseaua Bucuresti 53, 080033 Giurgiu; tel. (246) 212346; e-mail bibliotecagr@yahoo.com; internet www .bjgiurgiu.ro; f. 1951, present status 1984, present name 1991; 199,178 vols; Dir Prof. ION GAGHII; publ. *Libris*.

Iași

Biblioteca Centrală a Universității de Medicină și Farmacie 'Gr. T. Popa' Iași (Central Library of the 'Gr. T. Popa' University of Medicine and Pharmacy in Iași): Str. Vasile Alecsandri No 7, 700054 Iași; tel. (232) 213701; e-mail library@umfiasi.ro; internet biblio.umfiasi.ro; f. 1882; central library with 80 brs; 273,955 vols; Dir Prof. VIORICA SCUTARIU.

Biblioteca Centrală Universitară 'Mihai Eminescu' Iași ('Mihai Eminescu' Central University Library Iași): Str. Păcurari 4, 700511 Iași; tel. (232) 264245; e-mail bcuis@bcu-iasi.ro; internet www.bcu-iasi.ro; f. 1835; 2,473 vols of bibliographic units; spec. collns of 10,000 documents, MSS, old foreign and Romanian books, atlases, albums, maps, prints, archival pieces and musical scores; Gen. Man. Prof. Dr GHEORGHE TEODORESCU.

Biblioteca Județeană 'Gheorghe Asachi' Iași (Iași 'Gheorghe Asachi' District Library): Bd. Stefan cel Mare si Sfant, nr.

10, 700063 Iași; tel. (332) 110044; e-mail contact@bjiasi.ro; internet www.bjiasi.ro; f. 1920, current name adopted 1983; 606,469 vols, incl. 550,951 books and periodicals, 10 MSS, 12,490 audiovisual documents, 168 electronic collns, 42,850 other documents); Dir DAN NICOLAE DOBOȘ; Deputy Dir VALERIU STANCU; publ. *Bibliographical Annual of the Iași District*.

Biblioteca Universității Tehnice 'Gheorghe Asachi' Iași (Library of the Iași Gheorghe Asachi Technical University): Bdul Carol I 11, 700506 Iași; tel. (232) 212773; e-mail library@library.tuiasi.ro; internet www.tuiasi.ro/biblioteca; f. 1937; 1m. vols; Dir Prof. MIHAELA STIRBU.

Miercurea-Ciuc

Biblioteca Județeană Kájoni János: Piața Libertății 16, CP 32, 530104 Miercurea-Ciuc; tel. (266) 371790; e-mail info@bibliohr.topnet.ro; internet bibliohr.topnet .ro; f. 1950; 195,554 vols (incl. 191,040 vols of books and periodicals, 1,833 audiovisual materials, 371 electronic documents, 2,310 other documents); Man. KATALIN-MARIA KOPACZ.

Năsăud

Biblioteca Documentară Năsăud (Năsăud Documentary Library): Str. Grănicerilor 41, 425200 Năsăud; tel. (263) 362002; f. 1931; attached to Cluj-Napoca br. library of Romanian Acad.; 53,323 vols; Dir MARIA ȘUTEU.

Oradea

Biblioteca Județeană 'Gheorghe Șincai' Bihor Oradea ('Gheorghe Șincai' Bihor Oradea District Library): Str. Armatei Române 1/A, 410100 Oradea; tel. (359) 800368; e-mail bibliobihor@yahoo.com; internet www.bibliobihor.ro; f. 1911; 700,000 vols; Dir Man. Prof. LIGIA-ANTONIA MIRIȘAN.

Piatra-Neamț

Biblioteca Județeană 'G. T. Kirileanu' Neamț (Neamț 'G. T. Kirileanu' District Library): Bdul Republicii 15, 610005 Piatra-Neamț; tel. (233) 210379; e-mail bib_gtk_neamt@yahoo.com; internet www .bibgtkneamt.ro; f. 1956, present status 1974, present name 1992; 286,424 vols; Dir CONSTANTIN BOSTAN.

Pitești

Biblioteca Județeană Argeș 'Dinicu Golescu' (Argeș District Library 'Dinicu Golescu'): Str. Victoriei 18, 110017 Pitești; tel. (248) 223030; e-mail info@bjarges.ro; internet www.bjarges.ro; f. 1880; 500,000 vols; Dir Dr MIHAIL OCTAVIAN SACHELARIE.

Ploiești

Biblioteca Centrala a Universitatii Petrol-Gaze din Ploiesti (Central Library of Petroleum-Gas University of Ploiești): Bdul București 39, CP 22, 100680 Ploiesti; tel. (244) 573171; e-mail biblioteca@upg-ploiesti .ro; internet www.upg-ploiesti.ro/campus/biblioteca; f. 1948; 288,071 vols; Man. GILDA STANCIU; Librarian NICOLAE MADALINA.

Biblioteca 'Nicolae Iorga' Prahova ('Nicolae Iorga' Library): Str. Sublocotenent Erou Călin Cătălin 1, 100066 Ploiești; tel. (244) 521900; e-mail bjprahova@yahoo.com; internet bni.asesoft.ro; f. 1921; 3 brs and 1 subsidiary library; 550,000 vols; Dir MIHAELA RADU.

Râmnicu Vâlcea

Biblioteca Județeană 'Antim Ivireanul' Râmnicu Vâlcea (Vâlcea 'Antim Ivireanul' District Library): Str. Carol I 26, 240591

Râmnicu Vâlcea; tel. (250) 739221; e-mail biblioteca_antim@bjai.ro; internet www.bjai.ro; f. 1950, present status 1974, present name 1991; 400,000 vols; Dir Prof. AUGUSTINA SANDA CONSTANTINESCU; publ. *Biblioteca Vâlceană—Revista de Cultură a Bibliotecii Judeţene 'Antim Ivireanul'*.

Reşiţa

Biblioteca Judeţeană 'Paul Iorgovici' Reşiţa (Reşiţa 'Paul Iorgovici' District Library): Str. Paul Iorgovici 50, 320026 Reşiţa; tel. (55) 212535; e-mail bjpi_resita@yahoo.com; f. 1952; 11 brs; 287,000 vols; Dir NICOLAE SÂRBU; publ. *Revista Noastră*.

Satu Mare

Biblioteca Judeţeană Satu Mare (Satu Mare District Library): Str. Decebal 2, 440006 Satu Mare; tel. (261) 711199; e-mail bibliotecasatumare@yahoo.com; internet www.bibliotecasatumare.ro; f. 1951; 420,000 vols; Dir ANGELA CÂMPIAN.

Sf. Gheorghe

Biblioteca Judeţeană 'Bod Péter' Megyei Könyvtár (Covasna County Public Library): Gábor Áron 14, 520008 Sfantu Gheorghe; tel. (267) 351609; e-mail biblio@kmkt.ro; internet www.kmkt.ro; f. 1880; 221,737 vols; Dir Dr SZABOLCS SZONDA.

Sibiu

Biblioteca Judeţeană 'Astra' Sibiu (Sibiu 'Astra' District Library): Str. G. Baritiu 5–7, 550178 Sibiu; tel. (269) 210551; e-mail bjastrasibiu@yahoo.com; internet www.bjastrasibiu.ro; f. 1861; 4 brs; 544,715 vols, 13,000 multimedia documents, 60,000 periodicals, 66,162 documents of spec. colln, 4,500 legal documents; Dir Dr SILVIU BORŞ; publs *ASTRA, DeLiriKoN* (4 a year), *Mlădite* (4 a year).

Biblioteca Muzeului Brukenthal (Library of Brukenthal Museum): Piaţa Mare 4, 550163 Sibiu; tel. (269) 217691; e-mail info@brukenthalmuseum.ro; internet www.brukenthalmuseum.ro/biblioteca; f. 1817; 280,000 vols, 778 vols of MSS, 382 vols of incunabula, 30,000 rare books, 1,500 rare Romanian books; Gen. Dir Prof. Dr SABIN ADRIAN LUCA; Head of Library Dr CONSTANTIN ITTU.

Slatina

Biblioteca Judeţeană 'Ion Minulescu' Olt (Olt 'Ion Minulescu' District Library): Bdul A. I. Cuza 3B, 230025 Slatina; tel. (349) 407517; e-mail bibljolt@yahoo.com; internet www.bibliotecaslatina.ro; f. 1931, present name 1992; 6 brs; 231,667 vols and periodicals; Dir Dr PAUL MATIU.

Slobozia

Biblioteca Judeţeană 'Ştefan Bănulescu' Ialomiţa (Ialomiţa 'Ştefan Bănulescu' District Library): Bdul Matei Basarab 26, 920031 Slobozia; tel. (243) 230055; e-mail biblioteca_ialomita@bji.ro; internet www.bji.ro; f. 1933; 132,242 vols; Dir MIHAELA RACOVIŢEANU; publ. *Salonul Anual de Carte* (1 a year).

Suceava

Biblioteca Bucovinei 'I. G. Sbierea' (I. G. Sbierea' Library of Bucovina): Str. Mitropoliei 4, 720035 Suceava; tel. (230) 530798; internet www.bbsv.ro; f. 1923, present name 1993; 350,245 vols; Dir GHEORGHE-GABRIEL CĂRĂBUŞ.

Târgovişte

Biblioteca Judeţeană 'Ion Heliade Rădulescu' Dâmboviţa (Dâmboviţa 'Ion Heliade Rădulescu' District Library): Str.

Stelea 2, 130018 Târgovişte; tel. (245) 612316; e-mail office@bjdb.ro; internet www.bjdb.ro; f. 1944, present status 1974, present name 1992; 285,760 vols (incl. books and periodicals), 2,500 MSS, 316 microforms, 9,187 audio cassettes, 27,251 video cassettes, 134 audiovisual documents, 5,554 other documents; Dir Dr AGNES ERICH; publ. *Curier*.

Târgu Jiu

Biblioteca Judeţeană 'Christian Tell' Gorj (Gorj 'Christian Tell' District Library): Calea Eroilor St 23, 210135 Târgu Jiu; tel. (253) 214904; e-mail bibliotell@yahoo.com; f. 1934; 301,582 vols; Dir Dr OLIMPIA BRATU.

Târgu Mureş

Biblioteca Judeţeană Mureş (Mureş County Library): Str. G. Enescu 2, 540052 Târgu Mureş; tel. (265) 262631; e-mail secretariat@bjmures.ro; internet www.bjmures.ro; f. 1913; 900,000 vols; Dir Dr MONICA AVRAM; publs *Biblitheca Marisiana, Libraria*.

Biblioteca 'Teleki-Bolyai' ('Teleki-Bolyai' Library): Str. Bolyai 17, 540067 Târgu Mureş; tel. (265) 261857; e-mail telekiteka.ms@gmail.com; internet telekiteka.ro; f. 1962 by merger of Teleki library (f. 1802) and Bolyai library (f. 1557); books in the natural and social sciences before 19th century; maps, incunabula and MSS; 200,000 vols; Dir DIMITRIE POPTĂMAŞ.

Timişoara

Biblioteca Centrală Universitară 'Eugen Todoran' (Central University Library 'Eugen Todoran'): Bdul Vasile Pârvan 4A, 300223 Timişoara; tel. (256) 494004; e-mail contact@bcut.ro; internet www.bcut.ro; f. 1944 as Biblioteca Universităţii Timişoara, present name 2000; 1,023,616 vols; Dir-Gen. Dr VASILE DOCEA; Deputy Dir-Gen. Ing. DELIA PÂRŞAN.

Biblioteca Judeţeană Timiş (Timiş District Library): Piaţa Libertăţii 3, 300077 Timişoara; tel. (256) 430746; e-mail secretariat@bjt.ro; internet www.bjt.ro; f. 1904; 9 brs; 750,000 vols; Man TUDOR CRETU.

Tulcea

Biblioteca Judeţeană 'Panait Cerna' Tulcea (Tulcea County Library 'Panait Cerna'): Str. Isaccei 20, 820241 Tulcea; tel. (240) 513833; e-mail bjt@tulcealibrary.ro; internet www.tulcealibrary.ro; f. 1879; 303,795 vols, 7,472 audiovisual materials, 17,045 periodicals; Man. OVIDIU GHIONU.

Vaslui

Biblioteca Judeţeană 'Nicolae Milescu Spătarul' Vaslui (Vaslui 'Nicolae Milescu Spătarul' County Library): Str. Hagi Chiriac 2, 730129 Vaslui; tel. (35) 313767; e-mail office@bjvaslui.ro; internet www.bjvaslui.ro; f. 1951; organizes exhibitions and cultural events; 250,000 vols; Man. Prof. GELU VOICU BICHINEŢ.

Zalău

Biblioteca Judeţeană 'Ioniţă Scipione Bădescu' Sălaj (Sălaj 'Ioniţă Scipione Bădescu' District Library): Iuliu Maniu 13, 450016 Zalău; tel. (260) 632007; e-mail ibliosala@yhaoo.com; internet www.bjs.ro; f. 1950, present name 1957, present status 1968; 205,931 vols (incl. 195,539 vols of books and periodicals, 2,998 audiovisual documents, 5,951 electronic collns, 1,321 other documents; Man. Prof. FLORICA POP; publ. *Revista I.D.E.I.*

Museums and Art Galleries

Aiud

Muzeul de Istorie Aiud (Aiud Museum of History): Piaţa Consiliul Europei 24, Judeţul Alba, 515200 Aiud; tel. (258) 865459; internet muzeu-aiud.cimec.ro; f. 1796; 30,000 museum objects; archaeology of the primitive commune, the Dacian-Roman period and the pre-feudal period; library of 1,800 vols; Dir and Curator PAUL VASILE SCROBOTĂ.

Muzeul de Ştiinţele Naturii Aiud (Aiud Natural Sciences Museum): Str. Bethlen Gabor 1, 515200 Aiud; tel. (258) 862569; e-mail muzeustiinte@aiud.ro; internet muzeu-aiud.cimec.ro; f. 1796; collns of geology, mineralogy, palaeontology, botany, zoology; library of 500 vols; Dir PAUL VASILE SCROBOTĂ; Curator JULIA DIANA STEFANESCU.

Alba Iulia

Muzeul Naţional al Unirii (National Museum of Unification): Str. Mihai Viteazul 12–14, 510010 Alba Iulia; tel. (258) 813300; e-mail muzeulalba_relatiipublice@yahoo.com; internet mnuai.ro; f. 1888; exhibits relating to prehistoric and Roman archaeology, medieval era, ecclesiastical history, ethnography and Romanian Union; library of 70,000 vols; Dir Dr GABRIEL TIBERIU RUSTOIU; publs *Apulum—Acta Musei Apulensis* (1 a year), *Bibliotheca Musei Apulensis* (1 a year).

Alexandria

Muzeul Judeţean Teleorman (Teleorman County Museum): 1848th St 1, 140033 Alexandria; tel. (247) 314761; e-mail muzjudteleorman@yahoo.com; internet www.muzeulteleorman.ro; f. 1952 as Alexandria Museum of History; collns of archaeology, art, ethnography, history, numismatics, palaeontology; library of 5,000 vols; Man. Dr PAVEL MIREA.

Arad

Complexul Muzeal Arad (Arad Museum Complex): Piaţa George Enescu 1, 310131 Arad; tel. (257) 281847; e-mail office@museumarad.ro; internet www.museumarad.ro; f. 1893; colln of 125,000 art pieces; permanent exhibitions of archaeology, history, ethnology, natural sciences, fine and applied art; wine museum; Man. Dr PETER HÜGEL; publs *Armonii Naturale* (natural history, every 2 years), *Studii şi Comunicări* (studies and communications of art and architecture, every 2 years), *Zarandul* (ethnology, every 2 years), *Ziridava* (archaeology and history, every 2 years).

Bacău

Complexul Muzeul de Ştiinţele Naturii 'Ion Borcea' Bacău ('Ion Borcea' Natural Sciences Museum Complex of Bacău): Str. Aleea Parcului 9, 600033 Bacău; tel. (234) 512006; e-mail muzstnatbc@yahoo.com; internet www.complexulmuzealionborceabacau.ro; f. 1969; collns on botany, geology, mineralogy, palaeontology, zoology; incl. Natural Sciences Museum of Bacău, vivarium of Bacău, Astronomic Observatory and Ion Borcea Memorial House, Racova, Bacău co; education, research; library of 23,000 vols; Man. Dr GURĂU GABRIELA; publ. *Studii şi Comunicări* (1 a year).

Complexul Muzeul 'Iulian Antonescu' Bacău (Bacău 'Iulian Antonescu' Museum Complex): Str. 9 Mai 7, 600037 Bacău; tel. (234) 512444; e-mail muzeuistorie_bacau@yahoo.com; internet www.cmiabc.ro; f. 1957; collns on history, art, archaeology, ethnography, literature; library of 9,000 vols; Man. MARIANA POPA; publ. *Carpica* (1 a year).

Baia Mare

Muzeul de Mineralogie Baia Mare (Baia Mare Mineralogical Museum): Bdul Traian 8, 430212 Baia Mare; tel. (262) 227517; e-mail muzmin@muzeuminbm.ro; internet www .muzeuminbm.ro; f. 1989; exhibition of rocks; minerals; mineralogical and crystallographic research; library of 900 vols; Man. IOAN BOB.

Muzeul Judeţean de Istorie si Archeologie (County Museum of History and Archeology): Str. Monetăriei 1–3, 430406 Baia Mare; tel. (262) 211924; e-mail mamuresmuzeu@gmail.com; f. 1899; colln on archaeology, ethnography, history, planetary, Romanian art; library of 20,000 vols; Dir Prof. VIOREL RUSU; publ. *Marmaţia* (1 a year).

Bistriţa

Complexul Muzeul Judeţean Bistriţa—Năsăud (Nasaud Bistriţa County Museum Complex): Str. Gen. Grigore Bălan 19, 420016 Bistriţa; tel. (263) 211063; e-mail complexmuzealbn@yahoo.com; internet www .complexulmuzealbn.ro; f. 1950; present status 2002; 14 attached museums; Man. GAVRILAS VASILICHI GEORGE ALEXANDRU; Dir MIHALCA TEODOR; publs *Revista Bistriţei* (history), *Studii şi Cercetări Etnoculturale*, *Studii şi Cercetări Ştiinţele Naturii*.

Botoşani

Muzeul Judeţean Botoşani (Botoşani District Museum): Str. Unirii 15, 710221 Botoşani; tel. (231) 513446; e-mail contabilitate@ muzeubt.ro; internet www.muzeubt.ro; f. 1955; colln on history, archaeology, ethnography, fine arts; incl. 'Nicolae Iorga' and 'George Enescu' memorial houses; library of 6,000 vols; Man. Prof. LUCICA PÂRVAN.

Brad

Muzeul de Istorie şi Etnografie Brad (Brad History and Ethnography Museum): Closca St, 335200 Brad; tel. (254) 616194; f. 1987; traditional arts and crafts, spec. colln of wooden objects; Curator MIHAI DAVID.

Brăila

Muzeul Brăilei (Brăila Museum): Piaţa Traian 3, 810153 Brăila; tel. (339) 401002; e-mail sediu@muzeulbrailei.ro; internet www.muzeulbrailei.ro; f. 1881; exhibition sections of archaeology, history, fine arts, ethnography, natural sciences, memorials; library of 26,000 vols and periodicals; Man. Dr IONEL CÂNDEA; publs *Analele Brăilei* (every 2 years), *ISTROS* (every 2 years).

Bran

Muzeul Bran (Bran Museum): Str. Traian Mosoiu 495–498, 507025 Bran; tel. (268) 238333; e-mail contact@muzeul-bran.ro; internet www.muzeul-bran.ro; f. 1956; 6,000 art objects; Bran castle, history, ethnography, feudal art; Dir NARCIS DORIN ION.

Braşov

Muzeul de Artă Brasov (Art Museum Brasov): Bdul Eroilor 21, 500030 Braşov; tel. (268) 477286; e-mail contact@ muzeulartabv.ro; internet www .muzeulartabv.ro; f. 1949; permanent exhibitions of decorative arts, contemporary Romanian fine arts; Dir BARTHA ÁRPÁD.

Muzeul de Etnografie Brasov (Ethnographical Museum Brasov): Bdul Eroilor 21A, 500030 Braşov; tel. (268) 475562; e-mail muzeu@etnobrasov.ro; internet www .etnobrasov.ro; f. 1990; colln of ethnographic objects of Bran, Rupea, Ţara Oltului, Valea Hârtibaciului, Ţara Bârsei; 21,256 art objects; library of 3,674 vols; Dir Dr LIGIA FULGA.

Muzeul Judeţean de Istorie Braşov (County Museum of History—Brasov): Str. Nicolae Bălcescu 67, 500019 Braşov; tel. (268) 472350; internet istoriebv.ro; f. 1908; incl. council house, bastions, tower; temporary exhibitions; library of 23,000 vols; Dir Dr RADU ŞTEFĂNESCU; publ. *Cumidava*.

Muzeul 'Prima Scoala Romaneasca'—Braşov (Museum 'First Romanian School'—Braşov): Piaţa Unirii 2–3, 500123 Braşov; tel. (268) 511411; e-mail contact@ primascoalaromaneasca.ro; internet www .primascoalaromaneasca.ro; f. 1933; historical museum in bldg of first Romanian school (15th century); incl. 'The youngsters of Brasov' museum, 'Ex-libris' museum, 'Tudor Ciortea' museum, 'St Nicholas' Church; library of 4,000 vols, 30,000 historic documenls; Dir Prof. Dr VASILE OLTEANU.

Bucharest

Muzeul Căilor Ferate Române (Romanian Railway Museum): Calea Griviţei 193A, 010711 Bucharest; tel. (21) 2230660; f. 1939; attached to Min. of Transport; materials, parts, documentary illustrating the evolution of rail transport.

Muzeul de Istorie al Evreilor din România 'Sef Rabin Dr Moses Rosen' (Museum of Jewish History from Romania 'Chief Rabin dr Moses Rosen'): Str. Mămulari 8, 030771 Bucharest; tel. (21) 3110870; e-mail jewishmuseum.bucharest@gmail.com; f. 1978; Pres. Dr Ing. JOSE BLUM; Dir Dr CARMEN DUMITRIU.

Muzeul Militar Naţional 'Regele Ferdinand I' (National Military Museum): Str. Mircea Vulcănescu 125–127, 77116 Bucharest; tel. (21) 3195904; e-mail director@ muzeulmilitar.ro; internet www.mapn.ro/ muzeulmilitar; f. 1923; library of 36,856 vols; Dir Col MARCEL PREDA; publ. *Buletinul Muzeului Militar National*.

Muzeul Municipiului Bucureşti (Bucharest Municipality Museum): Bdul I. C. Bratianu 2, Sector 3, 030174 Bucharest; tel. (21) 3156858; e-mail secretariat@ muzeulbucurestiului.ro; internet www .muzeulbucurestiului.ro; f. 1921; 10 affiliated museums; library of 53,700 vols; Dir Dr IONEL IONITA; publ. *Bucuresti: Materiale de Istorie si Muzeografie*.

Muzeul Naţional al Literaturii Române (National Museum of Romanian Literature): Bdul Dacia 12, Sector 1, 010402 Bucharest; tel. (21) 2129654; e-mail relatiipublice@mnlr .ro; internet www.mlr.ro; f. 1957; 300,000 objects in colln; library of 80,000 vols (books and periodicals), 46,000 MSS and photographs, historical documents, old and rare books, art objects, periodicals, photographs, audiovisual colln; publs *DICE* (2 a year), *Euromuseum* (4 a year), *Manuscriptum* (4 a year).

Muzeul National al Poliţiei Române: c/o Poliţia Română, Str. Mihai Voda 6, Sector 5, Bucharest; tel. (21) 3166655; internet www .politiaromana.ro/muzeul_politiei.htm; f. 2000.

Muzeul Naţional al Satului 'Dimitrie Gusti' (National Village Museum 'Dimitrie Gusti'): Şoseaua Kiseleff 28–30, Sector 1, 011347 Bucharest; tel. (21) 3179068; e-mail contact@muzeul-satului.ro; internet www .muzeul-satului.ro; f. 1936; open-air nat. museum of village life since 17th century; library of 30,000 vols, 130,000 photographs; Dir-Gen. Dr PAULINA POPOIU.

Muzeul Naţional al Ţăranului Român (National Museum of the Romanian Peasant): Şoseaua Kiseleff 3, Sector 1, 011341 Bucharest; tel. (21) 3179660; e-mail info@ muzeultaranuluiroman.ro; internet www .muzeultaranuluiroman.ro; f. 1906; colln of 100,000 items on peasant art and traditions; research in field of ethnology and anthropology; Dir-Gen. Dr VIRGIL STEFAN NITULESCU; publ. *MARTOR* (1 a year, in English and French).

Muzeul Naţional Cotroceni (Cotroceni National Museum): Bdul Geniului 1, Sector 6, 060116 Bucharest; tel. (21) 3173100; e-mail secretariat@muzeulcotroceni.ro; internet www.muzeulcotroceni.ro; f. 1991; colln on Romanian art, medieval architecture, decorative art, history; museum pedagogy; organizes confs, exhibits and workshops; 20,000 art objects; Dir ADINA RENŢEA.

Muzeul Naţional de Artă al României (National Museum of Art of Romania): Calea Victoriei 49–53, 70101 Bucharest; tel. (21) 3133030; e-mail national.art@art.museum .ro; internet www.mnar.arts.ro; f. 1950; European art since 14th century, Romanian religious and secular works of art from 14th–18th centuries, Romanian modern art since 19th century; administers Arts Collections Museum (temporarily closed), Theodor Pallady Museum, K. H. Zambaccian Museum; library of 4,000 vols; Dir-Gen. ROXANA THEODORESCU.

Muzeul Naţional de Istorie a României (National History Museum of Romania): Calea Victoriei 12, 030026 Bucharest; tel. (21) 3158207; e-mail direct@mnir.ro; internet www.mnir.ro; f. 1972; sections on history, archaeology, numismatics and treasure; library of 45,000 vols; Dir Dr CRIŞAN MUŞETEANU; Gen. Man. Dr ERNEST OBERLANDER-TARNOVEANU; publs *Cercetări arheologice*, *Cercetări numismatice*, *Muzeul Naţional*.

Muzeul Naţional de Istorie Naturală 'Grigore Antipa' ('Grigore Antipa' National Natural History Museum): Şoseaua Kiseleff 1, Sector 1, 011341 Bucharest; tel. (21) 3128826; internet www.antipa.ro; f. 1834; colln on zoology, hydrobiology, anatomy, oceanography, ecology, zoogeography, ethnography, anthropology; library of 32,000 vols, 22,465 periodicals; Dir-Gen. Dr DUMITRU MURARIU; publ. *Travaux* (1 a year).

Muzeul Naţional Filatelic (National Philatelic Museum): Calea Victoriei 12, Sector 3, Bucharest; tel. (12) 3127491; e-mail info@ muzeulfilatelic.ro; internet www .muzeulfilatelic.ro; f. 1990; history of stamps and post; exhibits.

Muzeul Naţional 'George Enescu' (National Museum 'George Enescu'): Calea Victoriei 141, Sector 1, 010071 Bucharest; tel. (21) 3181450; e-mail office@georgeenescu .ro; internet www.georgeenescu.ro; f. 1956; preserves and promotes the cultural heritage of the institution; highlights George Enescu's work and cultural inheritance; incl. 'George Enescu' Memorial House, 'Dumitru şi Alice Rosetti-Tescanu George Enescu' dept; Dir ILINCA DUMITRESCU.

Muzeul Tehnic 'Prof. Ing. Dimitrie Leonida' (Prof. Eng. Dimitrie Leonida Museum of Technology): Str. Candiano Popescu 2, Sector 5, 040583 Bucharest; tel. (21) 3367777; e-mail muzel_tehnic_leonida@ yahoo.com; f. 1909; library of 25,000 vols; Dir Dipl. Eng. NICOLAE DIACONESCU; publ. *Anuar*.

Buzău

Muzeul Judeţean Buzău (Buzău County Museum): Bdul Nicolae Bălcescu 50, 120360 Buzău; tel. (238) 710561; e-mail home@ muzeubuzau.ro; internet www.muzeubuzau .ro; f. 1951; colln on history, archaeology, folk art, contemporary and decorative arts; library of 20,875 vols; Man. Dr SEBASTIAN

MATEI; publs *Analele Buzăului* (1 a year), *Mousaios* (1 a year).

Călăraşi

Muzeul Dunării de Jos din Călăraşi (Museum of the Lower Danube in Calarasi): Str. Progresului 4, 910079 Călăraşi; tel. (242) 313161; e-mail coslogeni@yahoo.com; internet www.mdjcalarasi.ro; f. 1951; colln on archaeology, numismatics, medieval history, modern arts, natural history, ethnography of the area; Dir Dr MARIAN NEAGU; Sec. ALAN VIRTEJANU.

Câmpulung

Muzeul Zonal Câmpulung (Câmpulung Zonal Museum): Str. Negru Vodă 119, 115100 Câmpulung; tel. (248) 11737; f. 1880; colln on history, arts, natural science, ethnography, folk art; Dir ŞTEFAN TRÂMBACIU; publs *Istoria Câmpulungului şi a zonei Muscel*, *Studii şi comunicări*.

Câmpulung Moldovenesc

Muzeul Artei Lemnului (Wooden Art Museum): Calea Transilvaniei 10, 725100 Câmpulung Moldovenesc; tel. (230) 311378; f. 1936; colln on ethnography, history, arts, folk art; Dir MARCEL ZAHANICIUC.

Caracal

Muzeul Romanaţiului Caracal (Caracal Museum of the Romanaţiului): Iancu Jianu St 26, 235200 Caracal; tel. (249) 511344; e-mail muzeulromanatiuluicaracal@yahoo .com; f. 1951; colln on history, ethnography, art, lapidarium; Dir PAUL LICĂ.

Caransebeş

Muzeul Judeţean de Etnografie şi al Regimentului de Graniţă-Caransebeş (County Museum of Ethnography and Border Regiment Caransebes): Piaţa Gen. Ion Dragalină 2, 325400 Caransebeş; tel. (255) 512193; e-mail office@muzeul-caransebes.ro; internet www.muzeul-caransebes.ro; f. 1963; colln on history of the border regiment; Banat's history ethnography, folk art, archaeology; incl. Tibiscum, the Roman archaeological site; Man. Prof. Dr ADRIAN ARDET; publs *Studii şi Comunicări de Etnografie şi Istorie*, *Tibiscum/Acta Musei Caransebesiensis-Serie Nouă*.

Cluj-Napoca

Colecţia de Istorie a Farmaciei/Muzeul Farmaciei (Pharmacy Museum): Piaţa Unirii nr. 28, Cluj-Napoca; tel. (264) 597567; e-mail contact@muzeulfarmaciei.ro; internet www.muzeulfarmaciei.ro; f. 1954; attached to Nat. History Museum of Transylvania; museum hosted in the Hintz House, the oldest pharmacy of Cluj-Napoca; colln illustrates pharmaceutical activity of Transylvania from 16th century to 20th century; old pharmaceutical vessels, rare books and documents, registers detailing medicines and their prices; Prof. Iuliu Orient (1869–1940) colln; underground laboratory.

Grădina Botanică Alexandru Borza (The Alexandru Borza Botanical Garden): Republicii St 42, 400015 Cluj-Napoca; tel. (264) 592152; e-mail gradina.botanica@ubbcluj.ro; internet www.ubbcluj.ro/en/structura/sport/botanica.html; f. 1920; attached to Babes-Bolyai Univ.; 10,000 specific plant categories; ornamental, phytogeographic, systematic, economic and medicinal sections; library of 25,000 vols; Dir Dr VASILE CRISTEA; publs *Contribuţii botanice* (1 a year), *Flora Romaniae Exsiccata*, *Delectus seminum* (1 a year), *The Seeds Catalogue and the Botanical Contributions review*.

Muzeul Etnografic al Transilvaniei (Transylvanian Museum of Ethnography):

Memorandum St 21, 400114 Cluj-Napoca; tel. (264) 592344; e-mail contact@muzeul-etnografic.ro; internet www .muzeul-etnografic.ro; f. 1922; incl. open-air nat. ethnographic park 'Romulus Vuia'; Man. TUDOR SALAGEAN; publ. *Anuarul Muzeului Etnografic al Transilvaniei* (Annual of the Transylvanian Museum of Ethnography).

Muzeul Naţional de Artă Cluj-Napoca: Piaţa Unirii 30, 400098 Cluj-Napoca; tel. (264) 596952; e-mail macn@cluj.astral.ro; internet www.macluj.ro; f. 1951; Romanian and foreign art from 16th to 21st century; library of 9,000 vols; Dir Dr CALIN STEGEREAN.

Muzeul Naţional de Istorie a Transilvaniei (National History Museum of Transylvania): Str. Constantin Daicoviciu 2, 400020 Cluj-Napoca; tel. (264) 595677; e-mail secretariat@mnit.ro; internet www.mnit.ro; f. 1859; library of 40,000 vols; Gen. Man. Dr CARMEN CIONGRADI; publ. *Acta Musei Napocensis* (1 a year).

Muzeul Zoologic al Universităţii 'Babeş Bolyai' Cluj-Napoca (Zoological Museum of the Cluj-Napoca 'Babeş Bolyai' University): Str. Clinicilor 5–7, 400006 Cluj-Napoca; tel. (264) 595739; e-mail dceuca@hasdeu.ubbcluj .ro; internet www.ubbcluj.ro/en/structura/muzee/muzeul_zoologic.html; f. 1859; 300,000 art items; integrated in the Faculty of Biology and Geology; incl. exhibits, scientific collns; Curator Dr DANIELA MUREŞAN; Curator DELIA CEUCA; publ. *Studia* (1 a year).

Constanţa

Complexul Muzeal de Ştiinţe ale Naturii (Natural History Museum Complex): Bdul Mamaia 255, 900522 Constanţa; tel. (241) 547055; e-mail office@delfinariu.ro; internet www.delfinariu.ro; f. 1958; aquarium, dolphinarium, planetarium, astronomical observatory, micro-reservation; Dir-Gen. Dr ADRIAN BILBA; Scientific Dir Dr NICOLAE C. PAPADOPOL; publ. *Pontus Euxinus*.

Muzeul de Artă (Art Museum): Bdul Tomis 82–84, 900657 Constanţa; tel. (241) 617012; f. 1961; Romanian paintings and other works of art; Dir DOINA PAULEANU.

Muzeul de Artă Populară (Folk Art Museum): Bdul Tomis 32, 900742 Constanţa; tel. (241) 616133; e-mail muzeuetno@yahoo .com; Dir Dr MARIA MAGIRU.

Muzeul de Istorie Naţională şi Arheologie Constanţa (Constanţa Museum for National History and Archaeology): Piaţa Ovidiu 12, 900745 Constanţa; tel. (241) 618763; e-mail contact@minac.ro; internet www.minac.ro; f. 1879; educational, archaeological activities, affiliated archaeological museums of Histria, Tropaeum Traiani, Harsova and Cernavoda; library of 41,000 vols; Dir Dr GABRIEL CUSTUREA; publs *Analele Dobrogei* (modern and contemporary history, 1 a year), *Pontica* (archaeology, ancient and medieval history, numismatic, 1 a year).

Muzeul Marinei Române (Romanian Naval Museum): Str. Traian 53, 900725 Constanţa; tel. (241) 619035; e-mail naval .museum@yahoo.com; internet www.navy.ro; f. 1969; history of Romanian navy and merchant fleet; 37,800 art objects; Dir Cmdr Dr OLIMPIU MANUEL GLODARENCO.

Corabia

Muzeul de Arheologie şi Etnografie Corabia (Corabia Archaeological and Ethnographical Museum): Str. Cuza Vodă 65, 235300 Corabia; tel. (249) 561364; f. 1951; collns incl. archaeological artefacts, pottery, coins, statues, gravestones, architectural pieces, pieces epigraphic and Byzantine treasures; Dir MIRELA COJOC.

Craiova

Muzeul Olteniei Craiova (Museum of Oltenia Craiova): Str. Popa Sapca 8, 200410 Craiova; tel. (251) 417756; e-mail office@muzeulolteniei.ro; internet www .muzeulolteniei.ro; f. 1915; attached to Dolj Co Ccl; divs of archeology, ethnography, natural sciences; library of 12,000 vols; Gen. Man. Prof. Dr MIHAI VIOREL FIFOR; publ. *Oltenia—Studii şi cercetări*.

Curtea de Argeş

Muzeul de Istorie şi Etnografie (History and Ethnography Museum): Str. Negru Vodă 2, 115300 Curtea de Argeş; tel. (248) 11446; Dir N. MOISESCU.

Deva

Muzeul Civilizaţiei Dacice şi Romane Deva (Deva Museum of Dacian and Roman Civilization): Bdul 1 Decembrie 39, 330005 Deva, Judetul Hunedoara; tel. (254) 216750; e-mail muzeucdr.deva@gmail.com; internet www.mcdr.ro; f. 1882; colln on archaeology, history, natural sciences, numismatics, art, ethnography; incorporates museum of Roman archaeology at Sarmizegetusa and the ethnographical museums at Orăştie and Brad; library of 30,980 vols; Man. TOLAS LILIANA; Dir ARDEU ADRIANA; publ. *Sargetia. Acta Musei Devensis*.

Drobeta-Turnu Severin

Muzeul Regiunii 'Porţile de Fier' ('Iron Gates' Regional Museum): Str. Independenţei 2, 220171 Drobeta-Turnu Severin; tel. (52) 312177; f. 1882; colln on natural history, ethnography, archaeology and Roman ruins; aquarium; Dir Dr ION STINGA; Deputy Dir Dr GABRIEL CRACIUNESCU; publ. *Drobeta* (1 a year).

Focşani

Muzeul Vrancei (Vrancea Museum): Bdul Gării 5, 620233 Focşani; tel. (237) 222890; internet www.muzeulvrancei.ro; f. 1951; incorporates museums of ethnography (open-air); colln on natural history, history and archaeology, ethnography, natural sciences; Dir Dr HORIA DUMITRESCU.

Galaţi

Complexul Muzeal de Ştiinţele Naturii (Natural Science Museum Complex): Str. Regiment 11, Siret 6A, 800340 Galaţi; tel. (236) 411898; e-mail contact@cmsngl.ro; internet www.cmsngl.ro; f. 1956; flora and fauna of the region; incl. botanical and zoological gardens, aquarium, astronomical observatory, planetarium; Dir Eng. CAMELIA GROSU.

Muzeul de Arta Vizuala (Visual Art Museum): Str. Tecuci 7, bl. V3, 800120 Galati; tel. (236) 413452; e-mail contact@mavgl.ro; internet www.mavgl.ro; f. 1967; organizes exhibitions, public events, workshops, art camps; Man. DAN BASARAB NANU.

Muzeul de Istorie Galati (Galati Museum of History): Str. Maior Iancu Fotea 2, 800017 Galaţi; tel. (236) 414228; e-mail muzeuistoriegalati@yahoo.com; internet www.migl.ro; f. 1939; colln on Alexandru Ioan Cuza; presentation on Galaţ city; colln of antique coins and medals, archaeological and ethnographic items, decorative art, philatelic, medals, numanistic; library of 10,000 vols; Dir Prof. CRISTIAN DRAGOS CALDARARU; publ. *Danubius* (1 a year, online, www.revistadanubius.ro).

Gherla

Muzeul de Istorie Gherla (Museum of History—Gherla): Str. Mihai Viteazul 6, 405300 Gherla; tel. (264) 241947; e-mail mihaimester@personal.ro; f. 1881; Daco-

Roman archaeology, ethnography, local history; library of 4,221 vols; Dir RODICA PINTEA.

Giurgiu

Muzeul Județean 'Teohari Antonescu' Giurgiu (Giurgiu District Museum): Str. Constantin Dobrogeanu Gherea 3, 080024 Giurgiu; tel. (246) 216801; e-mail muzeuljudeteangiurgiu@gmail.com; internet www.muzeulgiurgiu.ro; f. 1934; colln on history, ethnography, medieval archaeology, prehistoric archaeology, memorial history; Exec. Dir Prof. ADRIAN NICULAE; publs *Bibliotheca Musei Giurgiuvensis*, *Buletinul Muzeului Judetean 'Teohari Antonescu'-Giurgiu*, *Heritage*.

Golești

Muzeul Viticulturii și Pomiculturii Golești (Golești Viticulture and Tree Growing Museum): Ștefănești Commune, 117715 Golești; tel. (248) 266364; e-mail cmngolesti@yahoo.com; internet www.muzeulgolesti.ro; f. 1939; history of fruit- and vine-growing; library of 13,000 vols; Gen. Man. Dr FILOFTEIA PALLY; Man. IUSTIN DEJANU.

Gura Humorului

Muzeul Obiceiurilor Populare din Bucovina (Museum of Bucovinean Folk Traditions): Piața Republicii 2, 725300 Gura Humorului; tel. (230) 231108; e-mail muzeulhumor@gmail.com; f. 1958; ethnographic colln; colln of numismatics; colln of songs, historic and natural sciences; library of 2,415 vols; Dir ELVIRA ROMANIUC.

Iași

Complexul Muzeal Național 'Moldova' Iași ('Moldova' Iași National Museum Complex): Piața Ștefan cel Mare și Sfânt 1, 700028 Iași; tel. (232) 218383; e-mail contact@muzeul-moldova.ro; internet www.muzeul-moldova.ro; f. 1992; closed for renovation during 2011; incl. Iasi Museum of Art, History Museum of Moldavia, Ethnographic Museum of Moldavia, Museum of Science and Technology 'Stefan Procopiu'; Dir-Gen. Dr LACRAMIOARA STRATULAT; publs *Anuarul Muzeului Etnografic al Moldovei* (1 a year), *Buletinul Centrului de Restaurare-Conservare* (2 a year), *Buletinul Ioan Neculce* (1 a year), *Cercetări istorice* (1 a year).

Muzeul de Istorie Naturală Iași (Iași Natural History Museum): Blvd Independentei 16, 6600 Iași; tel. (232) 201339; e-mail grigore@uaic.ro; internet www.bio.uaic.ro/muzeu/muzeu.html; f. 1834; attached to Alexandru Ioan Cuza Univ.; colln on geology, palaeontology, zoology; Dir Prof. Dr ION COJOCARU.

Muzeul Literaturii Române Iași (Iasi Romanian Literature Museum): Str. Vasile Pogor 4, 700110 Iași; tel. (232) 410340; e-mail mlrpogor@yahoo.com; internet www.muzeulliteraturiiiasi.ro; f. 1990; organizes exhibits, confs; modern and contemporary Romanian literature; incl. 12 museums; Dir DANIEL CORBU; publ. *Dacia literară*.

Mangalia

Muzeul de Arheologie 'Callatis' Mangalia (Callatis Archaeological Museum of Mangalia): Șoseaua Constanței 23, 905500 Mangalia; tel. (341) 146763; e-mail muzeul_callatis@yahoo.com; internet www.muzeulcallatis.ro; f. 1925; colln on prehistory, Greek and Roman periods, ancient Greek colony of Callatis; library of 2,900 vols; Dir Dr SORIN MARCEL COLESNIUC; publ. *Studia Callatiana*.

Mediaș

Muzeul Municipal Mediaș (Mediaș Municipal Museum): Str. M. Viteazu 46, 551034

Mediaș; tel. (269) 841299; f. 1950; colln on history, natural history, ethnography, incl. classical and contemporary arts; Dir Dr PETER WEBER.

Miercurea Ciuc

Muzeul Secuiesc al Ciucului/Csíki Székely Múzeum (Szekler Museum of Ciuc): Piața Cetății nr. 2, 530132 Miercurea Ciuc; tel. (266) 372024; e-mail info@csikimuzeum.ro; internet www.csikimuzeum.ro; f. 1930; colln on history, ethnography, archaeology, 20th-century art history, old books, natural sciences, fine arts; since August 2011 museum has been closed due to restoration; library of 9,000 vols; Dir ZSOLT GYARMATI.

Mogoșoaia

Centrul Național de Cultura Mogoșoaia (Mogoșoaia National Cultural Centre): Brâncoveanu Palace, Ilfov, Str. Valea Parcului 1, Com., 077135 Mogoșoaia; tel. (21) 4904022; e-mail pbpb@xnet.ro; f. 1702; colln of medieval Romanian art; Dir DOINA MANDRU.

Năsăud

Muzeul Năsăudean (Năsăud Museum): Str. Grănicerilor 19, 425200 Năsăud; tel. (263) 362967; colln on history, ethnography; Dir IOAN RADU NISTOR.

Negresti Oas

Muzeul Țării Oașului: Str. Victoriei 140, Negresti Oas, Satu Mare; tel. (261) 854839; internet www.oasmuseum.ro; colln of ethnography and folk art.

Oradea

Muzeul Țării Crișurilor (Criș County Museum): Bdul Dacia 1–3, 410464 Oradea; tel. (259) 412724; e-mail contact@mtariicrisurilor.ro; internet www.mtariicrisurilor.ro; f. 1971; colln on history, art, ethnography, archaeology, natural science; library of 30,000 vols; Dir-Gen. Man. Prof. Dr AUREL CHIRIAC; publs *Biharea* (1 a year), *Crisia* (1 a year), *Nymphaea* (1 a year).

Orăștie

Sectia de Etnografie și Artă Populară Orăștie (Department of Ethnography and Folk Art Orăștie): Piata Aurel Vlaicu 1, 335700 Orăștie; tel. (254) 247300; f. 1952; Curator COSMA AURELIAN.

Petroșani

Muzeul Mineritului (Mining Museum): Str. N. Bălcescu 12, 332026 Petroșani; tel. (254) 541744; f. 1961; history of mining in the Jiu Valley; Dir DUMITRU PELIGRAD.

Piatra-Neamț

Complexul Muzeal Județean Neamț (Neamț District Museums Complex): Str. Mihai Eminescu 10, 610029 Piatra-Neamț; tel. (233) 217496; e-mail muzeupn@yahoo.com; internet www.muzeu-neamt.ro; f. 1978; archaeology, history, arts, memoirs, ethnography, natural sciences colln; affiliated museums: Muzeul de Arta Neamt, Muzeul de Etnografie, Muzeul de Istorie si Arheologie, Muzeul de Stiinte Naturii, Muzeul de Artă Eneolitică Cucuteni, Muzeul Memorial 'Calistrat Hogaș', Expoziția 'Curtea Domnească', Galeriile de Artă 'Lascăr Vorel', Muzeul de Istorie și Etnografie, Muzeul Cetatea Neamț, Muzeul Memorial 'Ion Creangă' Humulești, Casa Memorială 'Veronica Micle', Muzeul de Istorie Bicaz, Muzeul de Istorie Roman, Muzeul de Artă Roman, Muzeul de Stiințele Naturii, Roman; Dir GHEORGHE DUMITROAIA.

Pitești

Muzeul Județean Argeș (Argeș County Museum): Str. Armand Călinescu 44,

110047 Pitești; tel. (248) 212561; e-mail muzeuarges@yahoo.com; internet www.muzeul-judetean-arges.ro; f. 1928; colln on history, art, natural history, archaeology, numismatics, fine arts, planetarium, museum of sports, editorial house (Editura Ordessos); organizes nat. and int. exhibits; library of 22,000 vols; Dir-Gen. Dr SPIRIDON CRISTOCEA; publs *Argessis—Studii și comunicări* (Studies and Reports), *Argessis—Studii și comunicări* (history series and natural science series, 1 a year), *Naturalia* (ecology, 1 a year).

Ploiești

Muzeul Județean de Artă Prahova (Art Museum of Ploiesti City): Bdul Independenței 1, 100028 Ploiești; tel. (244) 522264; e-mail office@artmuseum.ro; internet www.artmuseum.ro; f. 1931; present name 1955; colln of Romanian art from classic and modern periods; Man. FLORIN SICOIE.

Muzeul Județean de Istorie și Arheologie Prahova (Prahova District Museum of History and Archaeology): Str. Toma Caragiu 10, 100042 Ploiești; tel. (244) 514437; e-mail office@histmuseumph.ro; internet www.histmuseumph.ro; f. 1953; 13 permanent exhibitions on history and life and work of famous Romanian scientific and cultural personalities; library of 60,247 vols; Dir-Gen. LIA MARIA VOICU; Dir VALERIA ANGHEL; publs *Studii și comunicări* (1 a year), *Yearbook Museum of History and Archaeology Prahova*.

Muzeul Județean de Stiintele Naturii Prahova (Prahova County Natural Sciences Museum): Str. Erou Calin Catalin 1, 100066 Ploiești; tel. (244) 597896; e-mail office@muzbioph.ro; internet www.muzbioph.ro; f. 1956; incl. laboratory, aquarium; biological and mineralogical colln; Dir-Gen. Prof. Dr EMILIA IANCU; Dir VICTOR PETRESCU; publ. *Comunicări și referate*.

Muzeul Național al Petrolului (National Oil Museum): Str. Dr Bagdazar 8, 100575 Ploiești; tel. (244) 597585; e-mail muzeu.petrol@petrom.ro; f. 1961; history of the Romanian oil industry; library of 3,000 vols; Dir GABRIELA TĂNĂSESCU.

Rădăuți

Muzeul Etnografic Rădăuți (Rădăuți Ethnographic Museum): Piața Unirii 63, 725400 Rădăuți; tel. (230) 462565; internet www.muzeulradauti.ro; f. 1920, present name 1934; collns of old books and MSS, paintings and icons, ceramics, wood, metal, bone and skin, objects and musical instruments, painted eggs, popular jewellery, textiles and folk costumes; Man. TRAIAN POSTOLACHE.

Râmnicu Vâlcea

Muzeul Județean Vâlcea (Valcea County Museum): Calea Traian 143, Râmnicu Vâlcea; tel. (250) 738121; e-mail muzeuljudeteanvalcea@gmail.com; internet www.muzee-valcea.ro; f. 1955, present name 1968; cultural institution specialized in research, conservation, restoration and cultural heritage; publ. *Buridava* (1 a year).

Attached Museums:

Casa Memoriala Anton Pann: Str. Stirbei Voda 4, Râmnicu Vâlcea; tel. (250) 738026.

Colectia de arta plastica Alexandru Balintescu: comuna Costesti, la aprox. 5 km de orasul Horezu, drumul spre m-rea Bistria, Județul Valcea; tel. (250) 738121; colln of fine arts.

Complexul Muzeal Maldaresti: comuna Maldaresti, la aprox. 3 km de orasul Horezu; tel. (250) 861510.

Muzeul de arheologie si arta religioasa Gh. Petre-Govora: Baile Govora, Judeţul Valcea; tel. (250) 738121; e-mail maramuresmuzeu@gmail.com; archeological colln, incl. material, coins, works of art and rare books.

Muzeul de Arta Casa Simian: Strada Carol I 25, Râmnicu Vâlcea; tel. (250) 738121; painting and sculpture from 18th, 19th and 20th centuries.

Muzeul de Istorie a Judetului Valcea: Calea lui Traian 143, Râmnicu Vâlcea; tel. (250) 738121; e-mail muzeuljudeteanvalcea@gmail.com; collns of Palaeolithic, Neolithic and Bronze ages.

Muzeul Satului Valcean: Comuna Bujoreni, Judeţul Valcea; tel. (250) 746869; images of traditional rural settlements.

Reghin

Muzeul Etnografic Reghin (Reghin Ethnographic Museum): Str. Vanatorilor 51, jud. Mures, 545300 Reghin; tel. (265) 512571; e-mail muzeureghin@yahoo.com; internet muzeureghin.xhost.ro; f. 1960; collns of folk art, textiles, wood icons, costumes; library of 2,336 vols, 3,186 slides, 128 ethnological films; Dir MARIA BORZAN; Librarian ADRIAN BUGNAR.

Reşiţa

Muzeul Banatului Montan Resita (Museum of Mountainous Banat Resita): Bdul Republicii 10, 320151 Reşiţa; tel. (355) 401219; e-mail office@muzeulbanatuluimontan.ro; internet www.muzeulbanatuluimontan.ro; f. 1959; 76,000 art objects in the fields of art, ethnography, mineralogy, industrial history, archaeology, numismatics; library of 27,000 vols; Dir and Man. Dr DUMITRU ŢEICU; publ. *Arheologia Medievală*.

Roman

Muzeul de Istorie Roman (Museum of Roman History): Str. Cuza Voda 19, 611009 Roman; tel. (233) 727726; f. 1957; Dir Dr VASILE URSACHI.

Satu Mare

Muzeul Judeţean Satu Mare (Satu Mare District Museum): Bdul Vasile Lucaciu 21, 440031 Satu Mare; tel. (261) 737526; e-mail muzeusm@gmail.com; internet www.muzeusm.ro; f. 1891; depts of archeology, history, ethnography, fine art; library of 60,000 vols; Man. VIOREL CIUBOTA; publs *Satu Mare*, *Studii şi Comunicări*.

Sf. Gheorghe

Székely Nemzeti Múzeum/Muzeul Naţional Secuiesc (Székely National Museum): 10 Kos Karoly St, 520055 Sfântu Gheorghe; tel. (267) 312442; e-mail office .sznm@gmail.com; internet www.sznm.ro; f. 1875; depts of history, ethnography, archaeology, natural history, icons, classical and modern Hungarian art; attached museums: Museum of the History of Guilds, Gyárfás Jenő Art Gallery, Haszmann Pál Museum, Museum of Erdővidék, Csángó Ethnographical Museum; library of 110,000 vols; Dir VARGHA MIHÁLY; Sec. TAMÁS TÜNDE; publs *Acta Margitensia* (1 a year), *Acta Siculica* (1 a year).

Sibiu

Complexul Naţional Muzeal 'ASTRA' (ASTRA National Museum Complex): Piaţa Mică 11, 550182 Sibiu; tel. (269) 202400; e-mail office@muzeulastra.ro; internet www .muzeulastra.ro; f. 1905, present status 1990, present name 2001; incl. Muzeul de Etnografie Universală 'Franz Binder', Muzeul Civilizaţiei Populare Traditionale ASTRA,

Muzeul Civilizaţiei Transilvane Astra, Muzeul de Etnografie şi Artă Populară Săsească 'Emil Sigerus', Proiectul unui Muzeu al Culturii şi Civilizaţiei Rromilor; library of 16,428 vols; Man. VALERIU ION OLARU; publ. *Cibinium* (Romanian museology and the history of traditional folk civilization, every 2 years).

Muzeul Naţional Brukenthal (Brukenthal National Museum): Piaţa Mare 4–5, 550163 Sibiu; tel. (269) 217691; e-mail info@brukenthalmuseum.ro; internet www .brukenthalmuseum.ro; f. 1817; colln on history, ethnography, 15th- to 18th-century; galleries of European painting, Romanian art, contemporary art; library: see under Libraries and Archives; Gen. Dir Prof. Dr SABIN ADRIAN LUCA; publs *Brukenthal Acta Musei* (4 a year), *Cibinium*, *Studii şi Communicări*.

Affiliated Museums:

Muzeul de Istorie a Farmaciei (Museum of Pharmacy of Sibiu): Piaţa Mică 26, Sibiu; tel. (269) 218191; internet www.brukenthalmuseum.ro/farmacie/ index.html; f. 1972; 6,600 artefacts about evolution of medication and pharmaceutical techniques.

Muzeul de Istorie 'Casa Altemberger' (Altemberger House: Museum of History): Str. Mitropoliei 2, Sibiu; tel. (269) 218143; e-mail info@brukenthalmuseum.ro; internet www.brukenthalmuseum.ro/ istorie; permanent exhibition on local history; roman lapidarium, medieval lapidarium, medieval lapidarium, firearms hall, glasswork in Transylvania, guilds of sibiu, coins and medals; Head Dr RALUCA TEODORESCU.

Muzeul de Istorie Naturală din Sibiu (Sibiu Museum of Natural History): Str. Cetăţii 1, 550160 Sibiu; tel. (369) 101782; f. 1849; sectors of palaeontology and mineralogy; ecosystems; library of 65,000 vols; Head Dr RODICA CIOBANU; publ. *Studii şi Comunicări de Ştiinţe Naturale*.

Muzeul de Vânătoare 'August Von Spiess' ('August Von Spiess' Museum of Hunting): Str. Şcoala de Inot 4, Sibiu; tel. (369) 101784; f. 1966; 1,600 artefacts incl. arms and hunting instruments, trophies, memorial room.

Sighetu Marmaţiei

Muzeul Maramureşului, Sighetul Marmaţiei (Sighetul Marmaţiei Maramureş Museum): Piata Libertatii 15, 435500 Sighetul Marmaţiei; tel. (262) 311521; e-mail muzeulmaramuresului@yahoo.com; internet www.muzeulmaramuresului.ro; f. 1873; depts of history, ethnography, natural sciences, open-air museum; memorial houses: Elie Wiesel's memorial house, Dr Ioan Mihaly de Apşa's memorial house, traditional houses preserved in situ; Dir Prof. GHEORGHE TODINCA; publ. *Acta Musei Maramorosiensis* (1 a year).

Sighişoara

Muzeul de Istorie Sighişoara (Sighişoara History Museum): Muzeului Sq. 1, 545400 Sighişoara; tel. (265) 771108; e-mail info@ muzeusighisoara.com; internet www .muzeusighisoara.com; f. 1899; weapon colln; Man. Dr NICOLAE TESCULA.

Slatina

Muzeul Judeţean Olt (Olt District Museum): Str. Ana Ipătescu 1, 230079 Slatina; tel. (249) 415279; e-mail muzeu_olt@yahoo.com; internet www.mjolt .ro; f. 1951; archaeology collns; Dir LAURENTIU GUTICA-FLORESCU.

Slobozia

Muzeul Judeţean Ialomiţa (Ialomiţa District Museum): Bdul Matei Basarab 30, 920055 Ialomita; tel. (243) 230054; e-mail office@mjialomita.ro; internet www .mjialomita.ro; colln on history, ethnography, archaeology, and plastic art; painting, graphics, sculpture; Dir FLORIN VLAD.

Suceava

Muzeul Naţional al Bucovinei (Bucovina National Museum): Str. Ştefan cel Mare 33, 720003 Suceava; tel. (230) 716439; f. 1900; colln on folk art, history, natural history, astronomical observatory, planetarium, Romanian fine arts; library of 91,000 vols; Dir PAVEL BLAJ; publ. *Suceava—Anuarul Muzeului judeţean* (history and natural sciences sections).

Târgovişte

Complexul National Muzeal 'Curtea Domneasca' Târgovişte (National Museum Complex 'The Royal Court' of Târgovişte): Str. Justitiei 7, 130014 Târgovişte; tel. (245) 612877; e-mail contact@ muzee-dambovitene.ro; internet www .muzee-dambovitene.ro; f. 1944; colln on archaeology, ethnography, fine arts, history of books and printing in Romania; Dir GH. BULEI; publ. *Vallachica*.

Târgu Jiu

Muzeul Judeţean Gorj (Gorj District Museum): c/o Muzeul de Istorie şi Arheologie, Str. Geneva 8, 210136 Târgu Jiu; tel. (253) 212044; e-mail muzeulgorjului@gmail .com; internet www.muzeulgorjului.ro; incl. Peştera Polovragi, Muzeul Tudor Arghezi-Targu Carbunesti, Casa Muzeu Maria Lataretu, Casa Cartianu, Casa Memorială Ecaterina Teodoroiu, Casa Memoriala 'Tudor Vladimirescu', Casa Muzeu 'Constantin Brâncuşi' Hobiţa, Muzeul de Arte, Muzeul Arhitecturi Populare din Gorj, Muzeul de Istorie si Arheologie 'Alexandru Ştefulescu'; Dir Dr DUMITRU HORTOPAN.

Târgu Mureş

Muzeul Judeţean Mureş (Mureş County Museum): Str. Marasti 8A, 540328 Târgu Mureş; tel. (365) 430021; e-mail muzeumures@gmail.com; internet www .muzeumures.ro; depts of archeology, fine arts, ethnography and popular arts, history, natural sciences; Gurghiu Castle; library of 25,000 vols; Man. ZOLTÁN SOOS; publ. *Marisia* (1 a year).

Timişoara

Muzeul Banatului Timişoara (Timiş Museum of the Banat): Piaţa Huniade 1, in cladirea monument istoric, Castelul Huniazilor, 300002 Timişoara; tel. (256) 491339; e-mail muzeul.banatului@muzeulbanatului .ro; internet www.muzeulbanatului.ro; f. 1872; sections of archaeology, history, natural sciences; restoration–conservation area laboratory; library of 23,300 vols of books, 11,000 periodicals; Dir DAN LEOPOLD CIOBOTARU; publ. *Analele Banatului* (1 a year).

Vaslui

Muzeul Judeţean 'Ştefan cel Mare' Vaslui (Vaslui District 'Stephen the Great' Museum): Str. Piaţa Independenţei 1, 730141 Vaslui; tel. (235) 311626; e-mail museumvs@yahoo.com; internet www .muzeuvaslui.ro; f. 1975; colln on ancient history and archaeology, ethnography, folk art, modern Romanian art; library of 5,000 vols; Dir Dr LAURENTIU CHIRIAC; publ. *Acta Moldaviae Meridionalis* (5–10 a year).

Zalău

Muzeul Judeţean de Istorie şi Artă Sălaj
(Sălaj District Museum of History and Art):
Str. Unirii 9, 450042 Zalău; tel. (260) 612223;
e-mail muzeulzalau@gmail.com; internet
www.muzeuzalau.ro; f. 1951; library of
15,500 vols; Gen. Man. Dr CORINA BEJINARIU;
publ. *Acta Musei Porolissensis* (1 a year).

Universities

UNIVERSITATEA '1 DECEMBRIE 1918' DIN ALBA IULIA
(1 December 1918 University, Alba Iulia)

Gabriel Bethlen Str. 5, 510009 Alba Iulia
Telephone: (258) 806130
E-mail: cond@uab.ro
Internet: www.uab.ro
Founded 1991
State control
Languages of instruction: English, French, Romanian
Academic year: October to July
Rector: Prof. Dr DANIEL BREAZ
Vice-Rector for Education and Institutional Strategy and Quality: Prof. Dr LUCIA CABULEA
Vice-Rector for Scientific Research and Int. Relations: Prof. Ing. Dr MOISE IOAN ACHIM
Dir for Library: CORINA TATAR
Library of 111,859 vols, 17,000 periodicals
Number of teachers: 159
Number of students: 4,500
Publications: *Acta Universitatis Apulensis* (4 a year, online, www.uab.ro/auajournal), *Annales Universitatis series Apulensis Oeconomica* (2 a year, online, www.oeconomica.uab.ro), *Annales Universitatis Apulensis Series Historica* (1 a year), *Altarul Reîntregirii* (3 a year, online, fto.ro/altarul-reintregirii), *Buletinul Cercurilor Ştiinţifice Studenţeşti* (1 a year), *PANGEEA*, *Pro Cont* (every 2 years), *RevCad Journal of Geodesy and Cadastre* (1 a year, print and online, www.uab.ro/reviste_recunoscute/revcad), *Revista Annales Universitatis Apulensis*

DEANS

Faculty of History and Philology: Prof. Dr ILEANA GHEMES
Faculty of Law and Social Sciences: Prof. Dr IOAN GANFALEAN
Faculty of Orthodox Theology: Prof. Dr EMIL JURCAN
Faculty of Sciences: Prof. Dr MARIA POPA

UNIVERSITATEA 'ALEXANDRU IOAN CUZA' IAŞI

Blvd Carol I nr. 11, 700506 Iaşi
Telephone: (232) 201000
E-mail: contact@uaic.ro
Internet: www.uaic.ro
Founded 1860
State control
Academic year: October to July
Rector: Prof. Dr VASILE IŞAN
Vice-Rector for Information and Evaluation: Prof. Dr CĂTĂLIN TĂNASE
Vice-Rector for Institutional Devt: Prof. Dr Rev. GHEORGHE POPA
Vice-Rector for Int. Relations: Prof. Dr HENRI LUCHIAN
Vice-Rector for MA and PhD Studies: Prof. Dr OVIDIU-GABRIEL IANCU
Vice-Rector for Research and Innovation: Prof. Dr DUMITRU LUCA
Vice-Rector for Student and Graduate Affairs: Prof. Dr CARMEN CREŢU

Vice-Rector for Undergraduate Studies: Prof. Dr GHEORGHE IACOB
Gen. Man.: BOGDAN-EDUARD PLEŞCAN
Dir for Central Univ. Library: Prof. Dr ALEXANDRU CĂLINESCU
Library: see under Libraries and Archives
Number of teachers: 790
Number of students: 31,250
Publication: *Analele Universităţii*

DEANS

Faculty of Biology: Prof. Dr MIRCEA NICUŞOR NICOARA
Faculty of Chemistry: Prof. Dr IONEL MANGALAGIU
Faculty of Computer Science: Dr ADRIAN IFTENE
Faculty of Economics and Business Administration: Prof. Dr DINU AIRINEI
Faculty of Geography and Geology: Prof. Dr CORNELIU IATU
Faculty of History: Prof. Dr PETRONEL ZAHARIUC
Faculty of Law: Prof. Dr TUDOREL TOADER
Faculty of Letters: Prof. Dr CODRIN LIVIU CUTITARU
Faculty of Mathematics: Prof. Dr CĂTĂLIN GEORGE LEFTER
Faculty of Orthodox Theology: Prof. Dr Rev. ION VICOVAN
Faculty of Philosophy: Prof. Dr NICU GAVRILUŢĂ
Faculty of Physical Education and Sports: Prof. Dr MARIN CHIRAZI
Faculty of Physics: Dr SEBASTIAN DUMITRU POPESCU
Faculty of Psychology and Education Sciences: Prof. Dr ION DAFINOIU
Faculty of Roman Catholic Theology: Prof. Dr Rev. EMIL DUMEA

PROFESSORS

Faculty of Biology (Blvd Carol I 20A, 700505 Iaşi; tel. (232) 201072; e-mail admbio@uaic.ro; internet www.bio.uaic.ro):

AILIESEI, O., Microbiology, Immunology
ARTENIE, V., Biochemistry
CHIFU, T., Environmental Protection and Nature Preservation, Environmental Biodiversity, Phylogenesis
COJOCARU, D., Enzymology, Biochemistry
ION, I., Vertebrate Zoology
MIRON, I., Aquaculture, Limnology
MISĂILĂ, C., Animal Physiology
MITITIUC, M., Phytopathology, Biogeography
MOGLAN, I., Invertebrate Zoology
MURARIU, A., Vegetal Physiology, Basis of Environment Protection
MUSTAŢĂ, GH., Evolutionary Biology
NEACŞU, I., Biophysics, Molecular Biology
ŞTEFAN, N., Vegetal Taxonomy, Phytosociology, Phytocenology
TĂNASE, C., Micology, Botany
TOMA, C., Plant Anatomy, Vegetal Cytology, Phylogenesis
TOMA, O., Structural Organization of Proteins and Nucleic Acids
ZAMFIRACHE, M. M., Vegetal Physiology

Faculty of Chemistry (Blvd Carol I nr. 11, 700506 Iaşi; tel. (232) 201363; e-mail infochem@chem.uaic.ro; internet www.chem.uaic.ro):

BÎCU, E., Organic Chemistry
BOURCEANU, G., Physical Chemistry
DROCHIOIU, G., Biochemistry
IORDAN, R., Inorganic Chemistry
MANGALAGIU, I., Organic Chemistry
NEMŢOI, G., Physical Chemistry
PALAMARU, M., Inorganic Chemistry
PUI, A., Inorganic Chemistry

Faculty of Computer Science (Gen. Berthelot St 16, 700483 Iaşi; tel. (232) 201090; e-mail

secretariat@info.uaic.ro; internet www.infoiasi.ro):

CRISTEA, D., Artificial Intelligence, Rule Based Programming
CROITORU, C., Graph Algorithms
FELEA, V., Databases, DBMS Practice
GRIGORAS, GH., Programming, Computer Construction
JUCAN, T., Formal Languages, Petri Nets
LUCANU, D., Formal Methods in Software Engineering, Semantic Web
LUCHIAN, H., Meta-heuristics
MASALAGIU, C., Logic in Computer Science
ŢIPLEA, F. L., Algebraic Foundations of Computer Science, Coding Theory and Cryptography, Computability, Decidability and Complexity, Security Protocols, Programme Analysis

Faculty of Economics and Business Administration (Carol I Blvd 22, 700505 Iaşi; tel. (232) 201070; e-mail feaa@uaic.ro; internet www.feaa.uaic.ro):

AIRINEI, D., Data Warehouses, Business Information Technologies, End-User Computing
ANDONE, I., Accounting Information Systems and Expert Systems in Accounting
ASANDULUI, L., Demography
BEDRULE-GRIGORUŢĂ, V., Public Services Management
BRĂILEAN, T., Economic Politics
BUCĂTARU, D., Business Finances
BUDUGAN, D., Managerial Accounting
CIOBANU, I., Management
COCRIŞ, V., Money and Credit, Risk Management in Banking
DUMITREAN, E., Financial Accounting
DUMITRIU, F., Information Systems Design
FĂTU, T., Business Information Technologies
FILIP, G., Public Finances
FILIP, M., Business Information Technologies, End-User Computing
FOTACHE, D., Groupware, Enterprise Resource Planning, Business Information Technologies
FOTACHE, M., Databases, Information and Knowledge Management
GEORGESCU, I., Fundamentals of Accounting, Managerial Accounting
GEORGESCU, M., Office Information Systems, Business Information Technologies
GRAMA, A., End-User Computing, Business Information Technologies
HOROMNEA, E., Fundamentals of Accounting
IGNAT, I., Macroeconomics
IŞAN, V., Economics
JABA, E., Statistics
JABA, O., Management
LUTAC, G., Political Economics
MAXIM, E., Management and Marketing
MEŞNIŢĂ, G., Project Management, Information Systems Analysis
MIHĂESCU, S., Finances, Finance and Banking Control
MIRONIUC, M., Financial and Accounting Management of the Company
MUNTEANU, A., Information Systems Audit
MUNTEANU, C., Marketing
NECHITA, V., Political Economy
NICA, P., Management
NIŢĂ, V., Merchandising, Hotel Management
ONOFREI, M., Financial Management, Decision in Public Administration
OPREA, D., Information Systems Design, Project Management
PASCARIU, G., European Economics
PEKAR, V., Agricultural Economics
PETRESCU, S., Economic Analysis, Evaluation Concepts and Theories in Business
PINTILESCU, C., Multivariate Statistics, Data Analysis

POHOAȚĂ, I., Economic Doctrines
PRALEA, S., International Economics
PRISACARIU, M., Capital Markets, Modern Management of the Portofolio
PRODAN, A., Human Resource Management
PRUTIANU, S., Business Communication and Negotiations
SASU, C., Marketing
SCORȚESCU, GH., Public Accounting
STOICA, O., European Financial and Monetary Integration, European Financial Markets
STEFURA, G., Public Budgetary Process
TABĂRĂ, N., Fundamentals of Accounting, Compared Accounting Systems
ȚARCĂ, M., Economic Statistics
TOFAN, A., Management
ȚUGUI, A., End-User Computing, Expert Systems
VOINEA, G., International Foreign Exchange and Financial Relations, Local Finances
ZAIT, A., Direct Marketing, Public Relations
ZAIȚ, D., Intercultural Management

Faculty of Geography and Geology (Blvd Carol I nr. 20A, 700505 Iași; tel. (232) 201074; e-mail geoiasi@uaic.ro; internet www.geo.uaic.ro):

APOSTOL, L., Human Geography
BRÂNZILĂ, M., Geology and Palaeontology
GROZA, O., Human Geography
IANCU, O. G., Geochemistry
IAȚU, C., Human Geography
IONIȚĂ, I., Geomorphology
LĂCĂTUȘU, R., Physical Geography
MUNTELE, I., Human Geography
ROMANESCU, GH., Physical Geography
RUSU, C., Physical Geography of Romania
RUSU, E., Human Geography

Faculty of History (Blvd Carol I nr. 11, 700506 Iași; tel. (232) 201056; e-mail istorie@uaic.ro; internet history.uaic.ro):

BĂDĂRĂU, G., Modern History
BÎRLIBA, L., Ancient History
BOUNEGRU, O., Ancient History
CIUPERCĂ, I., Contemporary World History
CLIVETTI, G., Modern History
CRISTIAN, V., Modern World History
GOROVEI, S., Medieval History
IACOB, G., Contemporary History
LÁSZLÓ, A., Ancient History
PLATON, F., Medieval History
PUNGĂ, G., Medieval History
SOLCANU, I., Medieval History
SPINEI, V., Ancient History
SZEKELY, M., Medieval History
URSULESCU, N., Ancient History
ZAHARIUC, P., Medieval History
ZUGRAVU, N., Ancient History

Faculty of Law (Blvd Carol I 11, 700506 Iași; tel. (232) 201058; e-mail drept@uaic.ro; internet laws.uaic.ro):

CIUCĂ, V., Roman Law
DURAC, G., Civil Procedure
MACOVEI, I., International Trade Law
THEODORU, G., Criminal Procedure
TOADER, T., Criminal Law, Special Part

Faculty of Letters (Blvd Carol I 11, 700506 Iași; tel. (232) 201052; e-mail letters@uaic.ro; internet media.lit.uaic.ro):

ALBU, R., English Language
AVĂDANEI, ST., American Literature
BLUMENFELD, O., English Language and Literature
CĂLINESCU, A., French Literature
CĂRĂUȘU, M. L., Romanian Language
CERNĂUȚI GORODEȚCHI, M., Comparative Literature
CIUBOTARU, M., Romanian Language
COTORCEA, L., Russian Literature
CUȚITARU, L. C., English and American Literature

DIACONU, D., Spanish Literature
DIMITRIU, R., English Language
DOROBĂȚ, D., English Literature
GAFTON, A., Romanian Language
GOGĂLNICEANU, C. L., English Language
HOIȘIE, A., German Literature
JEANRENAUD, M., French Literature
LĂCĂTUȘU, T., English Language
MUNTEANU, E., Romanian Language
MUREȘANU, M., French Literature
PETRESCU, M., French Language
PIRVU, S., English Literature
POPESCU, I., French Literature
PORUCIUC, A., English Language
PRICOP, C., Romanian Literature
SECRIERU, M. L., Romanian Language

Faculty of Mathematics (blvd Carol I 11, 700506 Iași; tel. (232) 201060; e-mail admmath@uaic.ro; internet www.math.uaic.ro):

ANASTASIEI, M., Geometry
ANICULĂESEI, GH., Applied Mathematics
ANIȚA, S., Applied Mathematics
ARNĂUTU, V., Applied Mathematics
BARBU, V., Applied Mathematics
BRÂNZEI, D., Geometry
CÂRJĂ, O., Mathematical Analysis
CHIRIȚĂ, S., Applied Mathematics
FLORESCU, L., Mathematical Analysis
HĂVÂRNEANU, T. D., Applied Mathematics
IEȘAN, D., Applied Mathematics
ILIOI, C., Applied Mathematics
LEFTER, C. G., Applied Mathematics
MIRON, R., Applied Mathematics
OPROIU, V., Geometry
POP, I., Geometry
POPA, C. G., Applied Mathematics
POPA, E., Mathematical Analysis
PRECUPANU, A., Mathematical Analysis
PRECUPANU, T., Mathematical Analysis
RĂSCANU, A., Applied Mathematics
TOFAN, I., Algebra
TURINICI, M., Applied Mathematics
VRABIE, I., Applied Mathematics
ZĂLINESCU, C., Mathematical Analysis

Faculty of Orthodox Theology (Str. Cloșca 9, 700066 Iași; tel. (232) 201102; e-mail teologie.ortodoxa@uaic.ro; internet www.teologie.uaic.ro):

ACHIMESCU, N., History and Philosophy of Religions
PETRARU, GH., Missiology and Ecumenism
POPA, GH., Christian Morals and Orthodox Morals
SANDU, I., Branch Orthodox Theology, Cultural Inheritance
SAVA, V., Liturgical Theology and Practice
SEMEN, P., Study and Biblical Exegesis of the Old Testament
TEȘU, I. C., Orthodox Spirituality

Faculty of Philosophy (Blvd Carol I 11, 700506 Iași; tel. (232) 201054; internet www.fssp.uaic.ro):

ADĂMUȚ, A., History of Philosophy
AFLOROAEI, ST., Ontology, Hermeneutics, Metaphysics
BACIU, M., Sociology
BALAHUR, D., Sociology
BEJAN, P., Hermeneutics
CARPINSCHI, A., Political Science
COZMA, C., Ethics
DIMA, T., Logic and Epistemology
DUMITRESCU, P., History of Philosophy
GAVRILUȚA, N., Sociology
GHIDEANU, T., History of Philosophy
IOAN, P., Logic
IONESCU, I., Sociology
MARIN, C., History of Philosophy
MIFTODE, V., Sociology, Social Anthropology
NISTOR, M., Aesthetics, History and Philosophy of Religions
POEDE, G., Political Sciences

RÂMBU, N., Philosophy of Culture and Hermeneutics
SĂLĂVĂSTRU, C., Logic and Semiology
STĂNCIULESCU, T. D., Semiotics and Philosophy of Creation
TEODORESCU, G., Sociology

Faculty of Physical Education and Sports (Str. Toma Cozma nr., 700554 Iași; tel. (232) 201026; e-mail admefs@uaic.ro; internet www.sport.uaic.ro):

BĂLTEANU, V., Massage
DROSESCU, P., Anatomy

Faculty of Physics (tel. (232) 201050; e-mail admphys@uaic.ro; internet www.phys.uaic.ro):

BIBOROSCH, L., Plasma Physics
CĂLȚUN, O. F., Electricity and Magnetism
CREANGĂ, D. E., Biophysics
DARIESCU, C., Quantum Mechanics
DARIESCU, M. A., Quantum Mechanics
DOROHOI, O. D., Optics and Spectroscopy
DUMITRAȘCU, N. V., Plasma Physics
GEORGESCU, V., Solid State Physics
IACOMI, F. D., Solid State Physics
IGNAT, E. M., Theoretical Physics
LOZNEANU, E., Plasma Physics
LUCA, D., Solid State Physics
LUCHIAN, T., Biophysics
MARDARE, D., Biophysics
MELNIG, V., Biophysics
MERCHEȘ, I., Theoretical Physics
MITOȘERIU, L., Electricity and Magnetism
POPA, G., Plasma Physics
RUSU, G., Solid State Physics
RUSU, M., Solid State Physics
SANDULOVICIU, M., Plasma Physics
SINGUREL, G., Spectroscopy and Quantum Optics
STANCU, A., Electricity and Magnetism
STRAT, M., Optics and Spectroscopy
TOMA, M., Plasma Physics

Faculty of Psychology and Education Sciences (Toma Cozma St 3, 700554 Iași; tel. (232) 201028; e-mail secretariat@psih.uaic.ro; internet www.psih.uaic.ro):

ANTONESEI, L., Pedagogy
CONSTANTIN, A., Psychology
CONSTANTIN, T., Psychology
COZMA, T., General Education
CREȚU, C., Psycho-pedagogy of Excellence and Creativity
CUCOȘ, C., Pedagogy
DAFINOIU, I., Medical Psychology
GHEORGHIU, M. D., Psychology
HAVARNEANU, E., Psychology
IACOB, L., Psychology
NECULAU, A., Social Psychology
ȘOITU, L., Pedagogy
TURLIUC, N., Medical Psychology and Special Psycho-pedagogy

Faculty of Roman Catholic Theology (Blvd Carol I nr. 1, 700506 Iași; tel. (232) 201114; e-mail ftrc@uaic.ro; internet www.ftrc.uaic.ro):

DUMEA, E., Church History

UNIVERSITATEA 'ANDREI ȘAGUNA' DIN CONSTANȚA
(Andrei Saguna University of Constanța)

Alexandru Lapusneanu St 13, 900196 Constanța

Telephone: (241) 662520
E-mail: contact@andreisaguna.ro
Internet: www.andreisaguna.ro

Founded 1992
Private control

Rector: Prof. Dr ADRIAN CRISTIAN PAPARI
Pro-Rector: Dr ANDRA SECELEANU
Pro-Rector: Dr GABRIELA MUNTEANU

DEANS

Faculty of Economics: Dr NELUTA MITEA

Faculty of Law and Administrative Sciences: Dr GABRIEL NAGHI

Faculty of Mass Communication and Political Science: Dr IOAN DAMASCHIN

Faculty of Psychosociology: Dr LIVICA FRATIMAN

UNIVERSITATEA 'ATHENAEUM' DIN BUCUREŞTI
(Athenaeum University of Bucharest)

Str. Giuseppe Garibaldi 2A, Sector 2, Bucharest

Telephone: (21) 2305738
E-mail: secretariat@univath.ro
Internet: www.univath.ro

Founded 1990
Private control
Languages of instruction: English, Romanian
Academic year: October to June

Rector: Prof. Dr EMILIA VASILE

Library of 41,925 vols
Number of teachers: 47
Number of students: 1,500

Publication: *Internal Auditing & Risk Management*

DEANS

Faculty of Economic Sciences: Prof. Dr MARIANA BALAN

Faculty of Public Administration: Prof. Dr ARON LIVIU DEAC

UNIVERSITATEA 'AUREL VLAICU' DIN ARAD
('Aurel Vlaicu' University of Arad)

Blvd Revoluţiei nr. 77, POB 2/158, 310130 Arad

Telephone: (257) 283010
E-mail: rectorat@uav.ro
Internet: www.uav.ro

Founded 1972, present status 1990
State control
Academic year: October to July

Rector: Prof. Dr RAMONA LILE

Vice-Rector for Education and Quality: Dr PASTOREL GASPAR

Vice-Rector for Int. Relations: Prof. Dr ALINA ZAMFIR

Vice-Rector for Research: Prof. Dr FLORENTINA MUNTEANU

Number of teachers: 477
Number of students: 15,394

Publications: *Agora Psycho-Pragmatica* (4 a year), *Educatia Plus* (Journal Plus Education, 2 a year), *Journal of Economics and Business Research* (2 a year), *Journal of Humanistic and Social Studies* (2 a year, online, www.jhss.ro), *Proceedings of International Symposium Research and Education in Innovation Era (ISREIE)*, *Revista AGORA* (4 a year), *Scientific and Technical Bulletin*, *Scientific Bulletin of ESCORENA*, *Societal and Political Psychology International Review*, *Theory and Applications of Mathematics & Computer Science* (2 a year, online, www.uav.ro/applications/se/journal/index.php/tamcs)

DEANS

Faculty of Design: Dr LACRIMIOARA-SIMONA IONESCU

Faculty of Economic Sciences: Dr FLORIN ISAC

Faculty of Educational Sciences, Psychology and Social Sciences: Dr ALINA ROMAN

Faculty of Engineering: Prof. DAN OVIDIU GLAVAN

Faculty of Exact Sciences: Dr SORIN NĂDĂBAN

Faculty of Food Engineering, Tourism and Environmental Protection: Ing. Dr VIRGIL CIUTINA

Faculty of Humanities and Social Sciences: Prof. Dr FLOREA LUCACI

Faculty of Physical Education and Sport: Prof. DORIN IOAN GALEA

Faculty of Theology: Prof. Dr IOAN TULCAN

UNIVERSITATEA 'BABEŞ-BOLYAI' CLUJ-NAPOCA

M. Kogălniceanu nr. 1, 400084 Cluj-Napoca
Telephone: (264) 405300
E-mail: rector@ubbcluj.ro
Internet: www.ubbcluj.ro

Founded 1919 as Romanian Univ. of Cluj
State control
Languages of instruction: German, Hungarian, Romanian
Academic year: October to July (2 semesters)

Rector: Prof. Dr IOAN AUREL POP

Vice-Rector for Admin. and Patrimony: Prof. Dr IOAN BOLOVAN

Vice-Rector for Business Relationship: Prof. Dr MIHAELA LUTAS

Vice-Rector for Cooperation with German Cultural Environment: Prof. Dr RUDOLF GRAF

Vice-Rector for Financing and European Programmes: Dr DAN LAZAR

Vice-Rector for Human Resources and Legislation: Dr RADU CATANA

Vice-Rector for Int. Relations: Dr CALIN RUS

Vice-Rector for Quality Assurance and Computerization: Prof. Dr LADISLAU NAGY

Vice-Rector for Research: Prof. Dr SORIN FILIPESCU

Vice-Rector for Training and Competitiveness: Dr CIPRIAN-MARCEL POP

Librarian: Prof. Dr DORU RADUSOV

Library: see under Libraries and Archives
Number of teachers: 1,700
Number of students: 53,000

Publications: *Botanical Contributions*, *Brain and Cognition and Behaviour*, *Colloquia: Journal of Central European History*, *Judaic Library Collection*, *Papers of Transition*, *Studi Italo-Romeni*, *Studia Universitatis Babeş-Bolyai*

DEANS

Faculty of Biology and Geology: Dr IOAN COROIU

Faculty of Business: Prof. IOAN ALIN NISTOR

Faculty of Chemistry and Chemical Engineering: Dr GABRIELA NICOLETA NEMES

Faculty of Economics and Business Management: Prof. Dr MATIS DUMITRU

Faculty of Environmental Science and Engineering: Prof. Ing. Dr ALEXANDRU OZUNU

Faculty of European Studies: Prof. Dr LADISLAU GYÉMÁNT

Faculty of Geography: Prof. Dr PETREA DANUT

Faculty of Greek Catholic Theology: Dr VIRGIL BERCEA

Faculty of History and Philosophy: Dr OVIDIU GHITTA

Faculty of Law: Dr FLORIN STRETEANU

Faculty of Letters: Prof. Dr CORIN BRAGA

Faculty of Mathematics and Computer Science: Prof. Dr ADRIAN PETRUSEL

Faculty of Orthodox Theology: Dr VASILE STANCIU

Faculty of Physical Education and Sports: Prof. Dr BOGDAN VASILE

Faculty of Physics: Prof. Dr AUREL POP

Faculty of Political, Administrative and Communication Sciences: Dr CALIN EMILIAN HINTEA

Faculty of Protestant Theology: Prof. VASILE STANCIU

Faculty of Psychology and Education Sciences: Prof. Dr CALIN FELEZEU

Faculty of Roman Catholic Theology: Prof. Dr JOZSEF MARTON

Faculty of Sociology and Social Work: IRINA CULIC

Faculty of Theatre and Television: Prof. Dr LIVIU MALITA

PROFESSORS

Faculty of Biology and Geology:

BALINTONI, I. C., Geotectonics
BEDELEAN, I., Mineralogy
BUCUR, I., Palaeontology
COMAN, N., Genetics
CRISTEA, V., Botany
DRĂGAN BULARDA, M., Microbiology
MUREŞAN, I., Mineralogy
PÉTERFI, L. S., Botany
PETRESCU, I., Palaeobotany
POPESCU, O., Cell Biology
TARBA, C., Biophysics
TOMESCU, N., Zoology
TRIFU, M., Plant Physiology
TUDORANCEA, C., Ecology
VLAD, Ş. N., Petrology

Faculty of Business:

GIURGIU, A., Finance
VORZSÁK, M., Micro and Macroeconomics

Faculty of Chemistry and Chemical Engineering:

AGACHI, P. Ş., Chemical Engineering
BÂLDEA, I., Physical Chemistry
CORDOŞ, E., Analytical Chemistry
DIUDEA, M., Organic Chemistry
GROSU, I., Organic Chemistry
HOROVITZ, O., Physical Chemistry
MAGER, S., Organic Chemistry
POPESCU, C., Physical Chemistry
SILAGHI-DUMITRESCU, I., Inorganic Chemistry
SILBERG, I. A., Organic Chemistry
SILVESTRU, C., Inorganic Chemistry
VLASSA, M., Organic Chemistry

Faculty of Economics and Business Management:

AVORNICULUI, C., Data Processing in Economics
AVRAM-NIŢCHI, R., Data Processing in Economics
BĂTRÎNCEA, I., Economic Analysis
BEJU, V., Finance
CĂINAP, I., Economic Analysis
CISTELECAN, L., Finance
DIŢU, G., Political Economy
DRĂGOESCU, A., Political Economy
DRĂGOESCU, E., Finance
DUMBRAVĂ, P., Accountancy
FLOREA, I., Statistics
FRĂŢILĂ, R., Manufacture and Marketing of Products
GHIŞOIU, N., Data Processing in Economics
GORON, S., Data Processing in Economics
ILIEŞ, L., Transport Management
IONESCU, T., Political Economy
LAZĂR, D., Marketing
LAZĂR, I., Agricultural Management
MIHUŢ, I., Management
NAGHI, M., Management
NISTOR, I., Finance
NISTOR, L. I., Macroeconomic Forecasting
NIŢCHI, I. Ş., Data Processing in Economics
OPREAN, D., Data Processing in Economics
OPREAN, I., Accountancy
OPREAN, V., Data Processing in Economics
PAINA, N., Marketing
PÂNTEA, P., Accountancy
PLĂIAŞ, I., Marketing
POP, S. I., Management
POPESCU, D., Political Economy
POSTELNICU, G., Political Economy
PURDEA, D., Management
RACOVIŢAN, D., Data Processing in Economics

Roșca, T., Finance
Stăneanu, G., Finance
Temeș, I., Accountancy
Tulai, C., Finance
Vincze, M., Agricultural Economics
Vorzsák, Á., Marketing

Faculty of European Studies:

Bîrsan, M., Management of European Institutions
Gyemant, L., European Studies
Marga, A., Philosophy
Păun, N., Management of European Institutions

Faculty of Geography:

Ciangă, N., Human Geography
Cocean, P., Regional Geography
Gârbacea, V., Regional Geography
Mac, I., Physical Geography
Pop, G., Human Geography
Raboca, N., Economic Geography
Sorocovschi, V. E., Hydrology
Surd, V., Rural Geography

Faculty of Greek Catholic Theology:

Goția, A., Catechetical Theology
Gudea, N., History of the Greek Catholic Church

Faculty of History and Philosophy:

Bărbulescu, M., Ancient History and Archaeology
Bocșan, N., Modern History
Cipăianu, G. A., Contemporary History
Codoban, A. T., Philosophy
Csucsuja, Ș., Contemporary History
Edroiu, N., Medieval History of Romania
Glodariu, I., Ancient History
Iluț, P., Sociology
Magyari, A., Modern History
Muscă, V., History of Philosophy
Pavel, T., Modern History
Piso, I., Ancient History and Archaeology
Pop, I. A., Medieval History
Pușcaș, V., Contemporary History
Rotariu, T., Sociology
Teodor, P., Medieval History of Romania
Țoca, M., History of Art
Vese, V., Contemporary History

Faculty of Law:

Costin, M. N., Commercial Law
Pop, L., Civil Law
Ursa, V., Criminal Law
Zăpîrțan, L., Political Science

Faculty of Letters:

Baciu, I., French Language
Borcilă, M., General Linguistics
Căpușan, M., French Literature
Cseke, É., Hungarian Literature and Society
Dragoș, E., History of the Romanian Language
Fanache, V., History of Romanian Literature
Gruiță, G., Contemporary Romanian Language
Kozma, D., Hungarian Literature
Muthu, M., Theory of Literature and Aesthetics
Oltean, Ș., History of the English Language
Papahagi, M. D., Italian Literature
Péntek, J., General Linguistics
Petrescu, I., History of Romanian Literature
Pop, I., History of Romanian Literature
Pop, R., French Literature
Șeulean, I., Folklore and Cultural Anthropology
Stanciu, V., English Literature
Vartic, I., Comparative Literature and Theory of Drama
Zdrenghea, M., Contemporary English Literature

Faculty of Mathematics and Computer Science:

Andrica, D., Geometry
Blaga, P., Numerical Analysis
Boian, F. M., Informatics
Both, N., Algebra
Breckner, W. W., Functional Analysis and Optimization
Călugăreanu, G., Algebra
Cobzaș, Ș., Functional Analysis
Coman, G., Numerical Analysis
Duca, D., Mathematical Analysis
Dumitrescu, D., Informatics
Frențiu, M., Informatics
Kolumbán, I., Mathematical Analysis
Micula, G., Differential Equations
Mihoc, I., Probability Theory
Mocanu, P., Mathematical Analysis
Moldovan, G., Informatics
Muntean, E., Informatics
Mureșan, A., Applied Mathematics
Németh, A., Mathematical Analysis
Pârv, B., Informatics
Petrila, T., Fluid Mechanics
Pop, M. I., Fluid Mechanics
Pop, V., Astronomy
Purdea, I., Algebra
Rus, A. I., Differential Equations
Sălăgean, G. Ș., Mathematical Analysis
Szilágyi, P., Differential Equations
Tâmbulea, L., Informatics
Trif, D., Differential Equations
Ureche, V., Astronomy
Vasiu, A., Geometry

Faculty of Orthodox Theology:

Ică, I., Fundamental Theology
Moraru, A., History of the Orthodox Church

Faculty of Physical Education and Sports:

Bengeanu, C., Volleyball
Brătucu, L. S., Anatomy and Physiology
Marolicaru, M., Methodology of Scientific Research
Neta, G., Football

Faculty of Physics:

Ardelean, I., Materials Science
Barbur, I., Solid State Physics
Burzo, E., Solid State Physics
Coldea, M., Solid State Physics
Cosma, C., Physics of Radiation
Cozar, O., Atomic and Molecular Physics
Crișan, M., Theoretical Physics
Crișan, V., Solid State Physics
Cristea, G., Solid State Physics
Iliescu, T., Optics and Spectroscopy
Ilonca, G., Solid State Physics
Pop, I., Solid State Physics
Șimon, S., Solid State Physics
Tataru, E., Electronics
Znamirovschi, V., Atomic and Nuclear Physics

Faculty of Political, Administrative and Communication Sciences:

Boari, V., Political Ideology
Stegăroiu, D. C., Management of Human Resources

Faculty of Psychology and Education Sciences:

Goia, V., Methodology
Ionescu, M., Education
Lăscuș, V., Education
Miclea, M., Psychology
Pitariu, H., Psychology
Preda, V., Psychology for Teaching

Faculty of Roman Catholic Theology:

Marton, J., Ecclesiastical History

UNIVERSITATEA BIOTERRA DIN BUCURESTI
(Bioterra University of Bucharest)

Str. Garlei 81, Sector 1, Bucharest

Telephone: (21) 4906128
E-mail: rector@bioterra.ro
Internet: www.bioterra.ro

Founded 1994
Private control
Language of instruction: Romanian

Rector: Prof. Dr Cornel Trandafir
Vice-Rector for Educational Activities: Prof. Dr Catalin Galan
Vice-Rector for Int. Relations: Prof. Dr Livia Nicole Atudosiei
Vice-Rector for Scientific and Research Activities: Prof. Dr Daniela Mariana Stanescu
Scientific Sec.: Dr Razvan Cotianu

Library of 20,547 vols, 3,196 titles

Publication: *Bulletin of Scientific Information*

DEANS

Faculty of Agri-tourism Management: Dr Pirvulescu Mihaela
Faculty of Control and Expertise of Food Products: Dr Daniela Fanuta Mihaila
Faculty of Engineering of Food Products: Prof. Dr Doina Geanina Florescu
Faculty of Law: Prof. Dr Tudor Tanasescu

UNIVERSITATEA 'BOGDAN-VODĂ' DIN CLUJ-NAPOCA
(Bogdan-Vodă University of Cluj-Napoca)

Grigore Alexandrescu St, 26A, Cluj-Napoca

Telephone: (264) 598787
E-mail: ubv@ubv.ro
Internet: www.ubv.ro

Founded 1992
Private control

Rector: Prof. Dr Jaradat Mohammad
Vice-Rector: Prof. Dr Motocu Marius

Library of 12,000 vols, 3,150 unique titles, 61 journals and periodicals

Publication: *Acta Universitatis Bogdan Voda Series Oeconomica* (online, www.ubv.ro/ojs/index.php/oec)

DEANS

Faculty of Economical Sciences: Dr Sirbu Janetta
Faculty of Law: Dr Ban Tiberiu
Faculty of Physical Education and Sports: Dr Sabau Gheorghe

UNIVERSITATEA 'CONSTANTIN BRANCOVEANU' DIN PITEȘTI
(Constantin Brancoveanu University of Pitești)

Calea Bascovului 2A, Pitești

Telephone: (248) 212627
E-mail: pitesti@univcb.ro
Internet: www.univcb.ro

Founded 1991
Private control

Rector: Prof. Dr Ovidiu Puiu
Vice-Rector for Didactic Activity: Prof. Dr Marius Gust
Vice-Rector for Scientific Activity: Dr Sebastian Ene

Library of 55,000 vols

Publication: *Strategii manageriale* (Management Strategies, online, www.strategiimanageriale.ro)

DEANS

Faculty of Administrative and Communication Sciences, Brăila: Dr Liliana Gherman

Faculty of Finance and Accounting, Piteşti: Dr SILVIA DUGAN

Faculty of Juridical, Administrative and Communication Sciences, Piteşti: Prof. Dr RADU GABRIEL PARVU

Faculty of Management Marketing in Economic Affairs, Brăila: Dr CAMELIA VECHIU

Faculty of Management Marketing in Economic Affairs, Piteşti: Dr MIHAELA ASANDEI

Faculty of Management Marketing in Economic Affairs, Râmnicu Vâlcea: Prof. Dr IULIANA CIOCHINA

UNIVERSITATEA 'CONSTANTIN BRANCUSI' DIN TÂRGU JIU

Calea Eroilor nr. 30, Târgu Jiu

Telephone: (253) 214307

E-mail: univ@utgjiu.ro

Internet: www.utgjiu.ro

State control

Language of instruction: English

Academic year: October to June

Faculties of economics and business administration, physical education, humanities and physical therapy, nursing, arts and education sciences

Rector: Prof. Dr BOJINCA MOISE

Pro-Rector: Prof. Ing. Dr MIHAI CRUCERU

Pro-Rector: Dr LIVIU MARIUS CIRTINA

Library of 18,000 vols

Number of teachers: 150

Number of students: 6,000

Publications: *Analele UCB*, *Revista de matematică*, *Revista de mecanică*

DEANS

Dept of Teacher Training: Dr CORNELIA TOMESCU-DUMITRESCU (Dir)

Faculty of Engineering: Prof. Ing. Dr POPESCU LUMINITA

Faculty of International Relations, Law and Administrative Sciences: Dr CORNELIA TOMESCU-DUMITRESCU

UNIVERSITATEA CRESTINA 'DIMITRIE CANTEMIR' ('Dimitrie Cantemir' Christian University)

Splaiul Unirii 176, Sector 4, Bucharest

Telephone: (21) 3307900

E-mail: office@ucdc.ro

Internet: www.ucdc.ro

Founded 1992

Private control

Pres.: Prof. Dr MOMCILO LUBURICI

Rector: Prof. Dr ADRIANA CORINA DUMITRESCU

Pro-Rector: Prof. Dr CRISTIANA CRISTUREANU

Pro-Rector: Dr GABRIELA POHOATA

Pro-Rector: Prof. Dr ION VELCEA

Pro-Rector: Prof. IRINEL POPESCU

Number of students: 20,000

DEANS

Faculty of Foreign Languages and Literatures: Dr CARMEN DUTU

Faculty of Finance, Banking and Accountancy: Dr MARINELLA TURDEAN

Faculty of History: Prof. CONSTANTIN HLIHOR

Faculty of International Business and Economics: Prof. Dr CONSTANCE CHITIBA

Faculty of Juridical and Administrative Sciences: Prof. Dr PETRICA TRUSCA

Faculty of Political Science: Prof. Dr CECILIA TOHĂNEANU

Faculty of Tourism and Commercial Management: Prof. Dr MANOELA POPESCU

UNIVERSITATEA DANUBIUS DIN GALAŢI (Danubius University of Galaţi)

Blvd Galaţi 3, 800654 Galaţi

Telephone: (372) 361207

E-mail: rectorat@univ-danubius.ro

Internet: www.univ-danubius.ro

Founded 1992

Private control

Rector: Dr ANDY PUSCA

Pro-Rector for Educational Activity: Prof. Dr ROMEO IONESCU

Pro-Rector for Research: Dr MARIANA TRANDAFIR

Dir-Gen.: Dr CARMEN SIRBU

Dir for Library: Dr IULIAN GEORGEL SAVENCO

Library of 36,000 vols, 2,000 periodicals

DEANS

Faculty of Administrative Sciences: Dr GABRIELA LUPSAN

Faculty of Communication Sciences: Dr MIRELA ARSITH

Faculty of Economic Sciences: Dr RODICA PRIPOAIE

Faculty of Law: Prof. Dr VASILICA NEGRUŢ

UNIVERSITATEA DE ARTĂ DIN TÂRGU MUREŞ (University of Dramatic Art of Târgu Mureş)

Str. Köteles Sámuel nr. 6, 540057 Târgu Mureş

Telephone: (265) 266281

E-mail: uat@uat.ro

Internet: www.uat.ro

Founded 1954 as Institutul de Teatru 'Szentgyörgyi István'

Rector: Prof. SORIN CRISAN

Pro-Rector: Prof. ANDRAS BALASI

Library of 40,000 vols

Number of teachers: 80

Number of students: 130

Publication: *Symbolon* (2 a year)

DEANS

Faculty of Arts in Hungarian Language: Dr ANNA KOS

Faculty of Arts in Romanian Language: Dr OANA LEAHU

UNIVERSITATEA DE ARTĂ ŞI DESIGN DIN CLUJ-NAPOCA (University of Art and Design Cluj–Napoca)

Pta. Unirii nr. 31, 400098 Cluj-Napoca

Telephone: (264) 598190

E-mail: secretarsef@uad.ro

Internet: www.uad.ro

Founded 1925, present name 2001

State control

Pres.: Prof. Dr IOAN SBÂRCIU

Rector: Prof. Dr RADU SOLOVASTRU

Vice-Rector for Artistic and Scientific Research: Prof. Dr RADU MORARU

Vice-Rector for Statutory Problems and Institutional Collaboration: Dr MARA RATIU

Gen Sec.: ANAMARIA BOCEAN

Librarian: ILYES MARIA

DEANS

Faculty of Decorative Arts and Design: Dr CHRISTIAN CHESUT

Faculty of Fine Arts: Dr DANIELA CHIOREAN

UNIVERSITATEA DE ARTĂ TEATRALĂ ŞI CINEMATOGRAFICĂ 'I. L. CARAGIALE' (I. L. Caragiale National University of Drama and Film)

Str. Matei Voievod 75–77, Sector 2, 021452 Bucharest

Telephone: (21) 2528001

E-mail: rector1@unatc.ro

Internet: www.unatc.ro

Founded 1950, present name 2001

State control

Rector: Prof. Dr ADRIAN IOAN TITIENI

Pro-Rector: Dr DORU NITESCU

Pro-Rector: Prof. Dr TANIA FILIP

Library of 95,000 vols (incl. English theatre library of 5,000 vols)

Number of teachers: 190

Number of students: 680

Publications: *CONCEPT*, *Film Menu*

DEANS

Faculty of Theatre: Dr NICOLAE MANDEA

Faculty of Film: Dr SORIN BOTOSENEANU

UNIVERSITATEA DE ARTE 'GEORGE ENESCU' IASI (University of Arts 'George Enescu' Iaşi)

Str. Cuza Voda 29, 700040 Iaşi

Telephone: (232) 212549

E-mail: rectorat@arteiasi.ro

Internet: www.arteiasi.ro

Founded 1860 as Music and Declamation School in Iaşi, current name adopted 1977

public control

Language of instruction: Romanian

Academic year: October to May

Chancellor: Assoc. Prof. Dr MAGDA SFICLEA

Rector: Prof. Dr ATENA ELENA SIMIONESCU

Vice-Rector for Didatic Activities and Quality Assurance: Assoc. Prof. Dr DORU ALBU

Vice-Rector for Int. Relations and Univ. Image: Assoc. Prof. Dr FLORIN GRIGORAS

Vice-Rector for Scientific Activities: Assoc. Prof. Dr AURELIAN BALAITA

Sec.: Eng. TANIA SCAFARU

Head of Library: IOAN BADULET

Library of 190,000 vols, 36,500 audiovisual items

Number of teachers: 134

Number of students: 1,276

Publication: *Byzantion*

DEANS

Faculty of Fine and Decorative Arts and Design: Prof. Dr MARIA URMĂ

Faculty of Performing, Composition and Musical Theoretical Studies: Prof. Dr LAURA OTILIA VASILIU

Faculty of Theatre: Assoc. Prof. Dr RALUCA BUJOREANU-HUTANU

UNIVERSITATEA DE NORD DIN BAIA MARE (North University of Baia Mare)

Str. Dr Victor Babes 62/A, 430083 Baia Mare

Telephone: (262) 218922

Internet: www.ubm.ro

Founded 1961 as Institute of Higher Education, present status 1991, present name 1996

State control

Academic year: October to June

Rector: Prof. Ing. Dr DAN CALIN PETER

Pro-Rector: Prof. Dr VASILE VIMAN

Pro-Rector: Prof. Dr GEORGETA CORNITA

Scientific Sec.: Prof. Ing. Dr VASILE HOTEA

Library of 2,000,000 vols

Number of teachers: 198

Number of students: 5,520

Publications: *Physics Journal, Proceedings of the Mathematical Creativity Seminar, Scientific Bulletin of Chemistry and Biology, Scientific Bulletin of Economics, Scientific Bulletin of Electrotechnology, Electronics, Automation, Scientific Bulletin of Foreign Languages, Scientific Bulletin of Mathematics and Informatics, Scientific Bulletin of Pedagogy, Psychology and Methodology, Scientific Bulletin of Philology, Scientific Bulletin of Philosophy and Theology, Scientific Bulletin of Tribology and Machine Construction Technology, The Maramureş Orthodoxy*

DEANS

Faculty of Engineering: Prof. Dr NICOLAE UNGUREANU

Faculty of Letters: Prof. Dr GHEORGHE GLODEANU

Faculty of Sciences: Dr NICOLAE POP

Mineral Resources and Environment Faculty: Prof. Ing. Dr VASILE OROS

PROFESSORS

Faculty of Engineering (Str. Dr Victor Babes 62/A, 430083 Baia Mare; tel. (362) 401265):

COTETIU, A.
COTETIU, R.
FILIP, D.
LOBONTIU, M.
NASUI, V.
OPREA, C.
PETER, D. C.
PEREAN, L.
TIPLEA, V.
TISAN, V.
TOADER, C.
UNGUREANU, N.

Faculty of Letters (Str. Victoriei 76, 430122 Baia Mare; tel. (262) 276305):

CORNITA, C.
CORNITA, G.
DUNCA, P.
GLODEANU, G.
ISTRATE, A.
MUNTEANU, C.

Faculty of Mineral Resources and Environment (Str. Dr Victor Babes 62/A, 430083 Baia Mare; tel. (362) 401266):

BANCILA-AFRIM, N.
BUD, I.
DAMIAN, F.
OROS, V.

Faculty of Sciences (Str. Victoriei 76, 430122 Baia Mare; tel. (262) 276059; e-mail decanat_stiinte@ubm.ro; internet www.stiinte.ubm.ro):

ARDELEAN, G.
BERINDE, V.
HUTIRA, T.
MICU, C.
MIHALY-COZMUTH, A.
MODORAN, D.
MORAR, G.
POP, N.
VIMAN, V.

UNIVERSITATEA DE VEST DIN TIMIŞOARA
(West University of Timişoara)

Blvd V. Parvan 4, 300223 Timişoara
Telephone: (256) 592111
E-mail: secretariat@uvt.ro
Internet: www.uvt.ro
Founded 1944, present status 1968
State control
Academic year: October to June
Rector: Dr MARILEN PIRTEA
Pro-Rector for Academic Strategy: Dr MADALIN BUNOIU

Pro-Rector for Financial and Economic Strategy: Prof. Dr PETRU STEFEA
Pro-Rector for Int. Relations and Institutional Communication: Dr DAN D. LAZEA
Pro-Rector for Research: Dr VIOREL NEGRU

Number of teachers: 720
Number of students: 18,600

Publications: *Analele Universităţii de Vest din Timişoara, Seria Drept, Analele Universităţii de Vest din Timişoara, Seria Fizica, Analele Universităţii de Vest din Timişoara, Seria Geografie, Analele Universităţii de Vest din Timişoara, Seria Matematica–Informatica, Analele Universităţii de Vest din Timişoara-Seria Sociologie, Psihologie, Pedagogie şi Asistenta Sociala, Analele Universităţii de Vest din Timişoara, Seria Stiinte Filologice, Analele Universităţii de Vest din Timişoara, Seria Teologie, Annals of West University of Timişoara* (Series of Chemistry), *B. A. S. British and American Studies, BHAUT* (Bibliotheca Historica et Archaeologica Universitatis Timisiensis), *Caiet de Semiotica, Copiii de azi sunt parintii de mâine, Dialogues Francophones, Geographica Timisiensis, Gender Studies, Journal of Social Informatics—Revista de informatică socială, Paradigme, Probleme de Filologie Slavă, Revart* (Specialized Review of Theory and Critique of Art), *Review of Historical Geography and Toponomastics, Revista de Ştiinţe ale Educatie, Romanian Journal of Applied Psychology, Romanian Journal of English Studies, Studii de Istorie a Banatului, Studii de Literatură Romana şi Comparată, Studii de Slavistică, Temeswarer Beiträge zur Germanistik, Timişoara Physical Education and Rehabilitation Journal, Translationes*

DEANS

Faculty of Arts and Design: Dr VICA TILA ADORIAN

Faculty of Chemistry, Biology and Geography: Ing. Dr CONSTANTIN BOLCU

Faculty of Economics and Business Administration: Dr OVIDIU MEGAN

Faculty of Law and Administrative Sciences: Dr LUCIAN BERCEA

Faculty of Letters, History and Theology: Dr DANA PERCEC

Faculty of Mathematics and Informatics: Dr MIRCEA FLORIN DRAGAN

Faculty of Music: Prof. Dr VIOLETA ZONTE

Faculty of Physical Education and Sports: Dr ADRIAN NAGEL

Faculty of Physics: Prof. Dr VULCANOV DUMITRU

Faculty of Political Sciences, Philosophy and Communication Sciences: Dr GHEORGHE CLITAN

Faculty of Sociology and Psychology: Dr ALIN GAVRELIUC

PROFESSORS

Faculty of Arts and Design (Str. Oituz 4, 300086, Timişoara; tel. (256) 592900; e-mail arte@arte.uvt.ro; internet www.arte.uvt.ro):

FÂNTÂNARIU, S., Graphic Arts
FLONDOR, C., Painting
JECZA, P., Sculpture
NUŢIU, R., Painting
SULEA, I., Painting
ZIMAN, M., Textile Arts

Faculty of Chemistry, Biology and Geography (Str. Pestalozzi 16A, 300115 Timişoara; tel. (256) 592622; e-mail cbg@cbg.uvt.ro; internet www.cbg.uvt.ro):

CHIRIAC, A., Physical Chemistry
DOCA, N., Chemical Engineering
MRACEC, M., Physical Chemistry
NUŢIU, R., Organic Chemistry
TRUŢI, S., Geography

Faculty of Economics and Business Administration (Blvd Pestalozzi 16, 300115 Timişoara; tel. (256) 592505; e-mail secretariat@feaa.uvt.ro; internet www.feaa.uvt.ro):

BĂBĂIŢĂ, I., Political Economy
BĂBĂIŢĂ, V., Accounting
BĂILEŞTEANU, GH., Business Economics
BURTICĂ, M., Macroeconomic Forecasting
CĂTINIANU, FL., Prices and Tariffs
CERNA, S., Currency and Credits
CRĂCIUNESCU, V., Management
CRISTEA, H., Business Finance
DĂNĂIAŢĂ, I., Management
EPURAN, M., Accounting
FALNIŢĂ, E., Science of Commodities
GOIAN, M., Management
IONESCU, GH., Marketing
IVAN, ŞT., Informatics
LĂDAR, L., Marketing
LUPULESCU, M., Computer Programming
MARTIN, I., Microeconomic Analysis
MIHAI, I., Financial Analysis
NEGRUT, C., Agrarian Economics and Policy
OPRIŞ, L., Agrarian Policies in the World
POPOVICI, AL., Programming of Production
PUTZ, E., Transport in Tourism
ROTARIU, I., Management of Foreign Trade
SILAŞI, GR., Regional and World Economy
ŞOŞDEANU, A., Accounting
TALPOŞ, I., Public Finance
TRANDAFIR, N., Political Economy
VÂRLAN, GH., Economic Forecasting

Faculty of Law and Administrative Sciences (Blvd. Eroilor 9A, 300575 Timişoara; tel. (256) 592400; e-mail drept@drept.uvt.ro; internet www.drept.uvt.ro):

DRESSLER, M., Forensic Medicine
MIHAI, GH., Philosophy of Law
MOTICA, R. I., Law
POPA, V., Roman Law, Labour Law

Faculty of Letters, History and Theology (Blvd Vasile Parvan 4, 300223 Timişoara; tel. (256) 592164; e-mail litere@litere.uvt.ro; internet www.litere.uvt.ro):

BENEA, D., Ancient History
BIRIŞ, I., History of Culture and Civilization
BUCA, M., Russian Language
CHEIE, I., Romanian Literature
CIOCÂRLIE, L., French Literature
EVSEEV, I., Russian Language
FRĂŢILĂ, V., Dialectology
GRECU, C., Philosophy of Logic
GYURCSIK, M., French Literature
HARANGUŞ, C., Ontology
MIOC, S., Romanian Literature
MUNTEANU, I., Modern Romanian History
OANCEA, I., Romance Philology
PÂRLOG, H., English Linguistics
SÂRBU, R., Russian Language
ŢÂRA, V., History of the Romanian Language

Faculty of Mathematics and Informatics (Blvd Vasile Parvan 4, 300223 Timişoara; tel. (256) 592316; e-mail secretariat@info.uvt.ro; internet www.math.uvt.ro.):

ALBU, A., Differential Geometry
BALINT, Ş., Mathematical Equations
BOROŞ, E., Algebra
CONSTANTIN, GH., Probability Theory
CRAIOVEANU, M., Spectral Geometry
GAŞPAR, D., Functional Analysis, Spectral Theory
IVAN, GH., Algebra
MĂRUŞTER, Ş., Non-Linear Optimization and Computer Science
MEGAN, M., Mathematical Analysis
OBĂDEANU, V., Theoretical Mechanics and Differential Geometry, Operational Research
OPRIŞ, D., Operational Research
PAPUC, D. I., Differential Geometry
PREDA, P., Mathematical Analysis

Puta, M., Differential Equations in Geometry

Radu, V., Stochastic Analysis and Probability Theory

Reghiş, M., Differential Equations

Schwab, E., Homological Algebra

Strătilă, Ş., Mathematical Analysis and Operator Algebras

Suciu, N., Complex Analysis

Faculty of Music (Blvd Vasile Piaţa Libertatii 1, 300077 Timişoara; tel. (256) 592654; e-mail muzica@muzica.uvt.ro; internet www.muzica.uvt.ro):

Stancovici, F., Piano

Vulpe, D., Choral Conducting

Faculty of Physical Education and Sports (Blvd Vasile Pârvan 4, 300223 Timişoara; tel. (256) 592207; e-mail secr_sport@sport.uvt.ro; internet www.sport.uvt.ro):

Gönczi-Raicu, M., Gymnastics

Ionescu, I., Football

Faculty of Physics (Blvd Vasile Pârvan 4, 300223 Timişoara; tel. (256) 592108; e-mail secretary@physics.uvt.ro; internet www.physics.uvt.ro):

Avram, N., Atomic and Molecular Physics and Spectroscopy

Birău, O., Thermodynamics and Molecular Physics

Hrianca, I., Electricity and Magnetism

Muscutariu, I., Electricity and Magnetism, Solid State and Semiconductor Physics

Nicoară, I., Laser Crystals

Schlett, Z., Plasma Physics, Semiconductor Materials and Devices

Faculty of Political Sciences, Philosophy and Communication Sciences (Blvd Vasile Pârvan 4, 300223 Timişoara; tel. (256) 592132; e-mail secr_polsci@polsci.uvt.ro; internet www.polsci.uvt.ro):

Coltescu, G., Political Sciences

Faculty of Sociology and Psychology (Blvd Vasile Pârvan 4, 300223 Timişoara; tel. (256) 592320; internet www.socio.uvt.ro):

Dabu, R., Sociology

Poenaru, R., Pedagogy, Deontology

Vintilescu, D., Educational Theory

UNIVERSITATEA DE VEST 'VASILE GOLDIŞ' DIN ARAD
('Vasile Goldiş' Western University of Arad)

Blvd Revolutiei 94-96, Arad

Telephone: (257) 280260

E-mail: rectorat@uvvg.ro

Internet: www.uvvg.ro

Founded 1990

Private control

Languages of instruction: English, French, Romanian

Academic year: October to June

Univ. Pres.: Prof. Dr Aurel Ardelean

Rector: Prof. Dr Adina Coralia Cotoraci

Vice-Rector for Bachelors, Masters, Quality Assurance and Student Issues: Prof. Dr Cristian Haiduc

Vice-Rector for Int. Scientific Relations: Prof. Dr Anca Hermenean

Vice-Rector for Research Programs, Devt and Innovation: Assoc. Prof. Dr Violeta Turcus

Library: 1m. vols

Number of teachers: 540

Number of students: 12,800

Publications: *Agora Universitaria, Alma Mater Porollissensis, Ecologia Mileniului III, Fiziologia/Physiology, Jurnal Medical Arădean, Natura-Biologie seria III, Probleme curente în Biologia Celulară şi Moleculară* (Current Problems in Cellular

and Molecular Biology), *Revista de Stomatologie, Revista Studii de istorie, Societate si Politica* (Society and Politics, print and online, www.uvvg.ro/socpol), *Studia Iudaica Aradensis, Studia Universitatis Seria Stiinte Ingineresti si Agro-Turism* (Engineering Sciences and Agrotourism Series, 2 a year, print and online, www.facultateadeinginerie.ro/studia), *Studia Universitatis Stiinte Economice* (1 a year, print and online, www.uvvg.ro/studiaeconomia), *Studia Universitatis 'Vasile Goldis' din Arad, seria Stiinţe exacte, Studia Universitatis 'Vasile Goldis' din Arad, Seria Stiintele Vietii* (www.studiauniversitatis.ro/v15/index.php), *Studii de Istorie, Studii de Ştiinta si Cultura* (4 a year, print and online, www.revista-studii-uvvg.ro), *Studii Juridice, Studii şi Comunicări*

DEANS

Faculty of Economics: Prof. Dr Soim Horatiu

Faculty of Education, Psychology, Physical Education and Sport: Prof. Dr Teodor Patrauta

Faculty of General Medicine, Pharmacy and Dental Medicine: Prof. Dr Liana Moş

Faculty of Humanities, Political and Administrative Sciences: Assoc. Prof. Dr Marius Grec

Faculty of Law: Assoc. Prof. Dr Cristian Alunaru

Faculty of Natural Sciences, Engineering and Informatics: Prof. Dr Endre Mathe

UNIVERSITATEA 'DIMITRIE CANTEMIR' DIN TÂRGU MUREŞ
(Dimitrie Cantemir University of Târgu Mureş)

Bodoni Sandor St 3–5, Târgu Mureş

Telephone: (365) 401127

E-mail: universitate@cantemir.ro

Internet: www.cantemir.ro

Founded 1991

Private control

Faculties of economic sciences, geography, law, psychology and educational sciences

Rector: Ing. Dr Alexandru-Bogdan Murgu

Library of 34,000 vols

Number of teachers: 130

UNIVERSITATEA DIN BUCUREŞTI

Blvd Mihail Kogălniceanu 36–46, Sector 5, 050107 Bucharest

Telephone: (21) 3077300

E-mail: office@unibuc.ro

Internet: www.unibuc.ro

Founded 1864

State control

Academic year: October to July

Rector: Prof. Dr Mircea Dumitru

Vice-Rector for Academic Affairs: Prof. Dr Romiţă Iucu

Vice-Rector for Human Resources, Heritage Management and Student Affairs: Prof. Dr Maria Voinea

Vice-Rector for Int. Relations: Prof. Dr Liviu Papadima

Vice-Rector for Quality Management and Business Relations: Prof. Dr Magdalena Iordache-Platis

Vice-Rector for Research and Financial Resources: Prof. Dr Emil Barna

Librarian: Prof. Dr Mircea Regneală

Library: see under Libraries and Archives

Number of teachers: 3,000

Number of students: 30,000

Publications: *Analele Universităţii din Bucureşti* (Chemistry, Law, Geology, Geography, History, Romanian Language and Literature, Physics, 1 a year), *Euroatlantic*

Studies (2 a year, in English), *Geography Communications* (1 a year, in English and French), *Revue Roumaine d'Egyptologie, Science and Technology of Environmental Protection*

DEANS

Faculty of Baptist Theology: Prof. Dr Otniel Ioan Bunaciu

Faculty of Business and Administration: Dr Razvan-Mihail Papuc

Faculty of Biology: Prof. Dr Carmen Postolache

Faculty of Catholic Theology and Social Work: Prof. Dr Wilhelm Danca

Faculty of Chemistry: Dr Constantin Mihailciuc

Faculty of Foreign Languages and Literatures: Prof. Dr Liviu Franga

Faculty of Geography: Dr Laura Comanescu

Faculty of Geology and Geophysics: Prof. Ing. Dr Victor Mocanu

Faculty of History: Prof. Dr Adrian Mihai Cioroianu

Faculty of Journalism and Mass Communication: Dr Viorica Aura Paus

Faculty of Law: Dr Flavius-Antoniu Baias

Faculty of Letters: Prof. Dr Oana Murarus

Faculty of Mathematics and Computer Science: Dr Victor Tigoiu

Faculty of Orthodox Theology: Prof. Dr Stefan Buchiu

Faculty of Philosophy: Prof. Dr Romulus Brancoveanu

Faculty of Physics: Prof. Dr Stefan Antohe

Faculty of Political Science: Prof. Dr Laurentiu Vlad

Faculty of Psychology and Educational Sciences: Prof. Dr Lucian Ciolan

Faculty of Sociology and Social Work: Prof. Dr Marian Preda

PROFESSORS

Faculty of Baptist Theology (Str. Berzei 29, Bucharest; tel. (21) 2248849; e-mail bbts@fx.ro; internet www.unibuc.ro/en/fac_ftb_en):

Bunaciu, I., New Testament

Talpoş, V., Old Testament

Faculty of Biology (Splaiul Independenţei 91–95, Sector 5, 76201 Bucharest; tel. (21) 4115207; e-mail web@bio.bio.unibuc.ro; internet www.bio.unibuc.ro):

Botnariuc, N., Ecology

Costache, M., Biochemistry

Cristurean, I., Botany

Dinischioty, A., Biochemistry

Flonta, M. L., Animal Physiology and Biophysics

Gavrilă, L., Plant Genetics

Georgescu, D., Anatomy

Iga, D. P., Anatomy

Iordăchescu, D., Biochemistry

Lazăr, V., Microbiology

Mailat, I. E., Anatomy

Manolache, V., Animal Biology

Marin, A., Botany

Meşter, L. E., Animal Biology

Mihăescu, G., Microbiology

Mişcalencu, D., Anatomy

Năstăsescu, M., Animal Biology

Sârbu, A., Botany

Sesan, T., Botany

Stoian, V., Genetics

Teodorescu, I., Ecology

Tesio, C., Animal Biology

Toma, N., Botany

Vădineanu, A., Ecology

Vassu, T., Genetics

Voica, C., Plant Physiology

Zărnescu, O., Histology

Faculty of Catholic Theology and Social Work (Str. General Berthelot 19, Sector 1, Bucharest; tel. (21) 3148610; internet www.unibuc.ro/ro/fac_ftrcas_ro):

FERENȚ, E., Theology
MĂRTINCĂ, I., Theology
PETERCĂ, V., Theology
ROBU, I., Theology

Faculty of Chemistry (Bdul Regina Elisabeta 4–12, Sector 1, Bucharest; tel. (21) 3159249; e-mail chimie_secretariat@yahoo.com; internet www.chimie.unibuc.ro):

ANDRUH, M., Inorganic Chemistry
ANGELESCU, E., Chemical Technology and Catalysis
BACIU, I., Organic Chemistry
BĂIULESCU, G.-E., Analytical Chemistry
BALA, C., Analytical Chemistry
BREZEANU, M., Inorganic Chemistry
CENUȘE, A., Physical Chemistry
CERCASOV, C., Organic Chemistry
CIOACĂ, C., Physics
CIOBANU, A., Organic Chemistry
CIOCĂZANU, I., Physical Chemistry
CIUCU, A., Analytical Chemistry
CONSTANTINESCU, E., Physical Chemistry
CONTINEANU, M., Physical Chemistry
CRISTUREAN, E., Inorganic Chemistry
DĂNEȚ, A. F., Analytical Chemistry
DAVID, V., Analytical Chemistry
DUMITRESCU, V., Analytical Chemistry
FIFIRIG, M., Physics
GĂINAR, I., Physical Chemistry
HILLEBRAND, M., Physical Chemistry
IVAN, L., Organic Chemistry
KRIZA, A., Inorganic Chemistry
LECA, M., Physical Chemistry
MAGEARU, V., Analytical Chemistry
MANDRAVEL, L. C., Physical Chemistry
MARIAN, P., Physics
MARINESCU, D., Inorganic Chemistry
MEDVEDOVICI, A., Analytical Chemistry
MELTZER, V., Physical Chemistry
MIHALCEA, I., Physical Chemistry
MUTIHAC, L., Analytical Chemistry
NEGOIU, D., Inorganic Chemistry
NEGOIU, M., Inorganic Chemistry
NICOLAE, A., Organic Chemistry
OANCEA, D., Physical Chemistry
OLTEANU, M. V., Physical Chemistry
ONCESCU, T., Physical Chemistry
PÂRVULESCU, V., Chemical Technology and Catalysis
PATROESCU, C., Analytical Chemistry
PAULINA, M., Physics
POPA, N., Inorganic Chemistry
ROȘU, T., Inorganic Chemistry
SAHINI, V., Physical Chemistry
SĂNDULESCU, I., Chemical Technology and Catalysis
SEGAL, E., Physical Chemistry
SZABÓ, A., Chemical Technology and Catalysis
TĂNASE, I., Analytical Chemistry
UDREA, I., Organic Chemistry
VÂLCU, R., Physical Chemistry
VLĂDESCU, L., Analytical Chemistry
VOLANSCHI, E., Physical Chemistry

Faculty of Foreign Languages and Literatures (Str. Edgar Quinet 5–7, Sector 1, 70106 Bucharest; tel. (21) 3121313; e-mail office@limbi-straine.ro; internet www.limbi-straine.ro):

ANGHELESCU, N., Oriental Languages
BACIU, I., English
BĂDESCU, I., French
BĂLUȚĂ-SKULTETY, M., Classical Languages
BARBORICĂ, C., Slovak Language
CĂLIN, G., Slavic Languages
CIZEK, E. A., Classical Languages
CORNILESCU, A., English
CREȚIA, G., Classical Languages
CUNIȚĂ, A., French
DERER, D., Italian
DOBREA, A., Russian
DOBRIȘAN, N., Oriental Languages
DUMITRIU, G., English
GĂMULESCU, D., Serbo-Croat Language
GUȚU, G., German

HOGEA-VELISCU, I., Oriental Languages
IONESCU, A.-I., Slavic Languages
IRIMIA, M. L., English
MICLĂU, P., French
MIHĂILĂ, GH., Slavic Languages
MIHĂILĂ, R., American Literature
MITU, M., Slavic Languages
MOLNAR, S., Hungarian
MURVAI, O., Hungarian
NICOLAESCU, M., English
NICOLESCU, A., English
PANĂ, I., English
PÂNZARU, I., French
PETRICĂ, I., Slavic Languages
REBUȘAPCĂ, I., Slavic Languages
RÎPEANU, S., Romance Languages
ROȘIANU, N., Russian
SANDU, D., German
SĂULESCU, M., English
SLUȘANSCHI, D. M., Classical Languages
ȘOPTEREANU, V., Russian
ȘTĂNESCU, C., German
SURDULESCU, R., English
SZOBOLCS, A., Hungarian
TOMA, D., French
TOMA, R., French
TUPAN, M., English
TUȚESCU, M., French
VIANU, L., English
VISAN, F., Oriental Languages
VIȘAN, V., French
WALD, L., Classical Languages

Faculty of Geography (Bdul Nicolae Bălcescu 1, Sector 1, Bucharest; tel. (21) 3153074; e-mail secretariat@geo.unibuc.ro; internet www.geo.unibuc.ro):

BĂLTEANU, D., Geomorphology
CÂNDEA, M., Human and Economic Geography
CIULACHE, S., Meteorology and Hydrology
ERDELI, G., Human and Economic Geography
GEANANĂ, M., Geomorphology and Pedology
GRECU, F., Geomorphology and Pedology
GRIGORE, M., Geomorphology and Pedology
IANOȘ, I., Human and Economic Geography
IELENICZ, M., Geomorphology and Pedology
MARIN, I., Regional Geography
POPESCU, N., Geomorphology and Pedology
VESPREMEANU, E., Meteorology and Hydrology

Faculty of Geology and Geophysics (Str. Traian Vuia 6, Sector 6, Bucharest; tel. (21) 2113120; e-mail secr@gg.unibuc.ro; internet www.gg.unibuc.ro):

ANASTASIU, N., Mineralogy
CONSTANTINESCU, E., Mineralogy
DANCHIV, A., Geological Engineering
DINU, C., Geology and Palaeontology
DRĂGĂSTAN, O., Geology and Palaeontology
GEORGESCU, P., Geophysics
GRIGORESCU, D., Geology and Palaeontology
IVAN, M., Geophysics
MĂRUNȚEANU, C., Geological Engineering
MATEI, L., Mineralogy
POPESCU, R., Mineralogy
SCRĂDEANU, D., Geological Engineering
ZAMFIRESCU, F., Geological Engineering

Faculty of History (Bdul Regina Elisabeta 4–12, Sector 5, Bucharest; tel. (21) 3145389; e-mail historybucharest@hotmail.com; internet www.unibuc.ro/ro/fac_fistr_ro):

BABEȘ, M., Prehistory and Archaeology
BARNEA, A., Ancient History, Archaeology and Epigraphy
BOIA, I., Historiography and Modern History
BREZEANU, S., Byzantine History
BULEI, I., Modern Romanian History
BUȘE, C., Contemporary History, Euro-Atlantic Studies
CIUCĂ, M., Medieval Romanian History

GIURESCU, D. C., Contemporary Romanian History
ISAR, N., Modern Romanian History
LUKACZ, A., Medieval History
MAIOR, L., Modern Romanian History
MAXIM, M., Ottoman History
MURGESCU, B., Modern and Economic History
NISTOR, V., Ancient Roman History
PANAITE, V., Ottoman History
PETOLESCU, C. C., Ancient Roman History and Epigraphy
PETRE, Z., Ancient Greek History
PIPPIDI, A., Medieval History
RETEGAN, M., Contemporary Romanian History
SCURTU, I., Contemporary Romanian History
ȘTEFĂNESCU, ȘT., Medieval Romanian History
TEOTEOI, T., Medieval Romanian and Byzantine History
VULPE, A., Prehistory and Archaeology
ZBUCHEA, GH., South-east European History

Faculty of Journalism and Mass Communication (Bdul Iuliu Maniu 1–3, A Bldg, 6th Fl., Sector 5 Bucharest; tel. (21) 3181555; e-mail mcoman53@yahoo.com; internet www.fjsc.unibuc.ro):

COMAN, M., Journalism
FRUMUȘANI, D., Journalism
ZOLTAN, R., Communications

Faculty of Law (Bdul Mihail Kogălniceanu 36–46, Sector 5, 70709 Bucharest; tel. (21) 3157187; internet www.drept.unibuc.ro):

ATHANASIU, A., Private Law
BÂRSAN, C., Private Law
BESTELIU, R., Public Law
BIZIM, A., Sports
BUCUR, I., Economic Sciences
CĂRPENARU, ST., Private Law
CIOBANU, V., Private Law
CIOCLEI, V., Criminal Law
CORNESCU, V., Economic Sciences
CREȚOIU, GH., Economic Sciences
FILIPAȘ, A., Criminal Law
IORGOVAN, A., Constitutional Law
MARINESCU, D., Private Law
MITRACHE, C., Criminal Law
MOLCUȚ, E., Public Law
MURARU, I., Public Law
NĂSTASE, A., Public Law
NEAGU, I., Public Law
POPA, N., Public Law
ȘAGUNA, D., Public Law
SITARU, D., Private Law
STANCIU, S., Economic Sciences
STANCU, E., Criminal Law
VOLONCIU, N. D., Criminal Law

Faculty of Letters (Str. Edgar Quinet 5–7, Sector 1, Bucharest; tel. (21) 3143508; internet www.lit.unibuc.ro):

ANGELESCU, S., Folklore
ANGHELESCU, M., Romanian Literature
BĂLTĂCEANU, I., Hebrew Studies
BANCIU, D., Communication and Public Relations
BERCIU, A., College of Administration
BIDU VRÂNCEANU, A., Romanian Language
BRÎNCUȘI, GR., Romanian Language
CAZIMIR, ȘT., Romanian Literature
CHIVU, GH., Romanian Language
CONSTANTINESCU, N., Folklore
CORNEA, L. P., Romanian Literature
DINDELEGAN, G., Romanian Language
DINU, M. C., Communication and Public Relations
DOCA, GH., Romanian Language
DOMINTE, C., Romanian Language
FILIPAȘ, E., Romanian Literature
FORASCU, N., Romanian Language
GANĂ, G., Romanian Literature
GRIGORESCU, D., Comparative Literature

GUŢU ROMALO, V., Romanian Language
HANŢĂ, A., Romanian Literature
HRISTEA, TH., Romanian Language
MANOLESCU, N. A., Romanian Literature
MANZAS, Z., Romanian Language
MARTIN, M. A., Theory of Literature
MAZILU, D. H., Romanian Literature
MELIAN, A., Romanian Literature
MICU, D., Romanian Literature
MIHĂILESCU, F., Romanian Literature
MORARU, M., Romanian Language
MUNTEANU, R., Comparative Literature
NEGRICI, E., Romanian Literature
NICULESCU, F., Romanian Language
REGNEALA, M., Communication and Public Relations
RUXANDOIU, L., Romanian Language
SARAMANDU, N., Romanian Language
ŞERBAN, I. V., European Studies
SIMION, E., Romanian Literature
SLAMA CAZACU, T., Romanian Language
SPIRIDON, M., Communication and Public Relations
STOICA, I., Library and Information Science
TĂNĂSESCU, A., Theory of Literature
VRÂNCEANU, A., Romanian Language
ZAMFIR, M., Romanian Literature

Faculty of Mathematics and Computer Science (Str. Academiei 14, Sector 1, Bucharest; tel. (21) 3142863; e-mail secretariat@fmi.unibuc.ro; internet www.fmi.unibuc.ro):

ALBU, T., Algebra
ATANASIU, A., Theoretical Computer Science
BĂDESCU, L., Geometry
BOBOC, N., Mathematical Analysis
BUCUR, GH., Mathematical Analysis
CAMENSCHI, G., Mechanics and Equations
CĂZĂNESCU, V., Theoretical Computer Science
CHIŢESCU, I., Mathematical Analysis
CRISTEA, M., Mathematical Analysis
CUCULESCU, I., Probability Theory, Statistics and Operational Research
DĂSCĂLESCU, S., Algebra
DINCĂ, G. I., Mechanics and Equations
DUMITRESCU, M., Probability Theory, Statistics and Operational Research
GEORGESCU, G., Theoretical Computer Science
GEORGESCU, H., Computer Science
IANUŞ, S., Geometry
IFTIMIE, V., Mechanics and Equations
ION, I., Algebra
IONESCU, P., Algebraic Geometry
MIHĂILĂ, I., Mechanics and Equations
MILITARU, G., Algebra
MIRICĂ, S., Mechanics and Equations
MITRANA, V., Theoretical Computer Science
NĂSTĂSESCU, C., Algebra
NICOLESCU, L., Geometry
NIŢĂ, C., Algebra
POPA, N., Mathematical Analysis
POPESCU, D., Algebra
POPESCU, I., Information Technology
POPESCU, L., Informatics
PREDA, V., Probability Theory, Statistics and Operational Research
PROPOAIE, G., Geometry
RUDEANU, S. A., Computer Science
SABAC, M., Mathematical Analysis
ŞANDRU, N., Mechanics and Equations
ŞTEFĂNESCU, A., Probability Theory, Statistics and Operational Research
ŞTEFĂNESCU, GH., Computer Science
STRĂTILĂ ŞERBAN, V., Mathematical Analysis
ŢIGOIU, S., Mechanics and Equations
TOMESCU, I., Computer Science
TUDOR, C., Probability Theory, Statistics and Operational Research
VĂDUVA, I., Statistics and Stochastic Models

Faculty of Orthodox Theology (Str. Sfânta Ecaterina 2, Sector 4, 040155 Bucharest; tel.

(21) 3356117; internet www.unibuc.ro/ro/fac_fto_ro):

CORNIŢESCU, C., Biblical Theology, Cultural Heritage and Church Painting
CORNIŢESCU, E., Biblical Theology, Cultural Heritage and Church Painting
DAVID, P., Systematic Theology
DURA, N., Practical Theology
IONIŢĂ, V., Church History
MOLDOVEANU, N., Practical Theology
NECULA, N., Practical Theology
RĂDUCĂ, P., Systematic Theology
RUS, R., Systematic Theology

Faculty of Philosophy (Splaiul Independenţei 204, Sector 5, 70609 Bucharest; tel. (21) 4102974; e-mail matei@fil.unibuc.ro; internet filosofie.unibuc.ro):

BĂNŞOIU, I., History of Philosophy and Philosophy of Culture
DUMITRU, M., Logic and Theoretical Philosophy
FLONTA, M., Logic and Theoretical Philosophy
IANOŞI, I., History of Philosophy and Philosophy of Culture
ILIESCU, A., Political and Moral Philosophy
MORAR, V., History of Philosophy and Philosophy of Culture
MUREŞAN, V., Political and Moral Philosophy
PÂRVU, I., Logic and Theoretical Philosophy
STOIANOVICI, D., Logic and Theoretical Philosophy
SURDU, A., History of Philosophy and Philosophy of Culture
TONOIU, V., Logic and Theoretical Philosophy
ŢURLEA, M., Logic and Theoretical Philosophy
VIERU, S., Political and Moral Philosophy
VLĂDUŢESCU, GH., History of Philosophy and Philosophy of Culture

Faculty of Physics (Str. Atomistilor 405, 077125 Platforma Magurele, Bucharest; tel. (21) 4574419; e-mail secretariat@fizic.unibuc.ro; internet www.fizica.unibuc.ro):

ALEXANDRU, H., Solid State Physics
ANGELESCU, T., Nuclear Physics and Particle Physics
ANTOHE, ŞT., Electricity, Solid State Physics
ARMEANU, I., Mathematical Physics
BEŞLIU, C., Nuclear Physics
BORŞAN, D., Atmospheric Physics
BRÂNCUŞ, D., Solid State Physics
CIOBANU, GH., Statistical Physics and Thermodynamics
CONSTANTINESCU, A., Nuclear Physics, Computational Physics
CONSTANTINESCU, L. M., Physics of Polymers
COSTESCU, A., Theoretical Physics
COTFAS, N., Mathematical Physics
DOLOCAN, V., Solid State Physics, Electrophysics
DRAGOMAN, D., Solid State Physics
DULIU, O., Nuclear Physics
FLORESCU, V., Quantum Mechanics
GEORGESCU, L., Polymer Physics
GHEORGHE, V., Biophysics
GHIORDĂNESCU, N., Nuclear Physics
GRECU, V., Atomic Physics
IONESCU, A., Atomic Physics
IOVA, I., Optics, Spectroscopy
JIPA, A., Relativistic Nuclear Physics
LAZANU, I., Nuclear Physics
LICEA, I., Solid State Physics
MARIAN, T., Quantum Mechanics
MIHUL, A., Nuclear Physics
MUNTEANU, I., Solid State Physics
MUTIHAC, R., Electricity
NENCIU, GH., Quantum Mechanics
PĂTRAŞCU, ŞT., Earth Physics

PLĂVIŢU, C., Molecular Physics, Polymers
POPA-NIŢĂ, V., Polymer Physics
POPESCU, A., Biophysics
POPESCU, F., Atomic Physics
POPESCU, I., Optics, Spectroscopy, Plasma, Lasers
RĂDUŢA, A., Theoretical Physics
REVEICA, I. M., Nuclear Physics
RUXANDRA, V., Electricity
SIMA, O., Nuclear Physics
ŞTEFĂNESCU, D., Mathematical Physics
TOADER, E., Optics, Plasma Physics
TUDOR, T., Optics, Lasers, Holography
TURBATU, S., Mathematical Physics
TURCU, G., Biophysics
VLĂDUCĂ, G., Nuclear Physics

Faculty of Political Science (Str. Sfântul Ştefan 24, Sector 2, Bucharest; tel. (21) 3139007; e-mail fspub@fspub.ro; internet www.fspub.ro):

ANDREESCU, Ş., International Relations
BARBU, D., Political Sciences
FIDULU, P., International Relations
MELEŞCANU, T., International Relations
MOTOC, I., International Relations
PREDA, C., Political Sciences
STOICA, G., Political Sciences
VLAD, L., International Relations

Faculty of Psychology and Education (Bdul Iuliu Maniu 1–3, A Bldg, 5th Fl., Sector 6, Bucharest; tel. (314) 253452; internet www.fpse.ro):

CREŢU, T., Psychology
CRISTEA, S., Teacher Training
ENĂCHESCU, S., Special Education
FĂTU, S., Teacher Training
LERGHIT, I., Education
MITROFAN, I., Psychology
MITROFAN, N., Psychology
NEACŞU, I., Education
NICOLESCU, V., Education
PĂUN, E., Education
POPESCU, E., Education
POTOLEA, D., Education
RĂSCANU, R., Psychology
ROCO, M., Psychology
SCHIOPU, U., Psychology
STANCIU, I., Education
TOMŞA, G., Education
VERZA, E., Special Education
ZLATE, M., Psychology

Faculty of Sociology and Social Work (Str. Schitu Magureanu 9, Sector 5, Bucharest; tel. (21) 315-83-91; e-mail secretar@sas.unibuc.ro; internet www.sas.swork.unibuc.ro):

ABRAHAM, P., Social Work
ANGHEL, P., Social Work
BĂDESCU, I., Sociology
CHELCEA, S., Sociology
DRĂGAN, I., Sociology
GEANĂ, GH., Sociology
GHEŢĂU, V., Sociology
LARIONESCU, M., Sociology
MĂRGINEAN, I., Sociology
MIHĂILESCU, I., Sociology
SANDU, D., Sociology
VOINEA, M., Sociology
ZAMFIR, C., Sociology
ZAMFIR, E., Social Work

UNIVERSITATEA DIN CRAIOVA

Str. A. I. Cuza nr. 13, 200585 Craiova
Telephone: (251) 414398
E-mail: relint@central.ucv.ro
Internet: www.central.ucv.ro
Founded 1947
State control
Academic year: October to July

Rector: Prof. Dr DAN CLAUDIU DANISOR
Vice-Rector for Academic and Placement Affairs: Prof. Dr CEZAR SPINU

Vice-Rector for Economic Management and Student Affairs: Prof. Dr NICU MARCU
Vice-Rector for Int. Relations: Prof. Dr CRISTIANA NICOLA TEODORESCU
Vice-Rector for Scientific Research: Prof. Ing. Dr DAN POPESCU
Chief Sec.: Dr MIRCEA ZAVALEANU
Librarian: MIHAI COSOVEANU

Library: see under Libraries and Archives
Number of teachers: 1,080
Number of students: 32,000

Publications: *Revista Arhivele Olteniei, Revista de Ştiinţe Juridice, Revista Forum Geografic—Studii şi Cercetari de Geografie şi Protectia Mediului, Studii si Cercetari de Onomastica, University Bulletin* (1 a year, in 16 series according to subject), *Viitorul*

DEANS

Faculty of Agriculture and Horticulture: Prof. Dr MARIN SOARE
Faculty of Automation, Computers and Electronics: Prof. Ing. Dr EUGEN BOBASU
Faculty of Economics and Business Administration: Prof. Dr MARIAN SIMINICA
Faculty of Electrical Engineering: Prof. Dr Eng. MARIAN CIONTU
Faculty of Exact Sciences: Prof. Dr DUMITRU BUŞNEAG
Faculty of Law and Administrative Services: Prof. Dr SEVASTIAN CERCEL
Faculty of Letters: Prof. Dr NICU PANEA
Faculty of Mechanical Engineering: Prof. Dr Eng. NICOLAE DUMITRU
Faculty of Physical Education and Sports: Prof. Dr MARIAN DRAGOMIR
Faculty of Social Sciences: Dr MIHAI RADU COSTESCU
Faculty of Technological System Engineering and Management: Prof. Ing. Dr ION CIUPITU
Faculty of Theology, History and Education Sciences: Prof. Dr IRINEU ION POPA

PROFESSORS

Faculty of Agriculture and Horticulture:
GĂNGIOVEANU, I., Agrotechnology
IONESCU, I., Meadow Cultivation
MARIN, N., Agrochemistry
MATEI, I., Agrotechnics
MOCANU, R., Agrochemistry
NICOLESCU, M., Phytotechnics
PANĂ, D., Management
POP, L., Agrotechnics
ŞOROP, G., Pedology
VASILE, D., Pedology
VOICA, N., Genetics

Faculty of Automation, Computers and Electronics:
BĂDICĂ, C., Computers and Information Technology
BÎZDOACĂ, N., Mechatronics and Robotics
BOBASU, E., Automatics
BREZOVAN, M., Computers and Information Technology
BURDESCU, D., Computers and Information Technology
COJOCARU, D., Mechatronics and Robotics
DIACONU, I., Mechatronics and Robotics
IANCU, E., Automatics
IONETE, C., Automatics
IVANESCU, M., Mechatronics and Robotics
LUNGU, M., Computers and Information Technology
MARIAN, G., Computers and Information Technology
MARIN, C., Automatics
MOCANU, M., Computers and Information Technology
NICULESCU, E., Simulation
NITULESCU, M., Mechatronics and Robotics
PETRE, E., Automatics
POPESCU, D., Automatics
POPESCU, D., Mechatronics and Robotics
PURCARU, D., Electronic Structures for Measuring and Monitoring
RASVAN, V., Automatics
SELISTEANU, D., Automatics
STANESCU, L., Computers and Information Technology
STOIAN, Mechatronics and Robotics
VÎNATORU, M., Automatics

Faculty of Economics and Business Administration (tel. (251) 411317; e-mail stec@central.ucv.ro; internet stec.central.ucv.ro):
AVRAM, M., Accounting
AVRAM, V., Currency and Credits
BĂNDOI, A., Price and Competitiveness
BERCEANU, D., Corporate Finance
BURLEA-SCHIOPOIU, A., Management
BUSE, L., Economic and Financial Analysis
CONSTANTINESCU, D., Management
CRĂCIUN, L., Marketing
DOMNISORU, S., Accounting
DRĂCEA, M., Public Finance
GEORGESCU, V., Statistics
GIURGITEANU, N., Informatics
GRUESCU, R., Economics
IACOB, C., Accounting
IONASCU, C., Statistics
LITOIU, V., Informatics
LOLESCU, E., Economics
MIHAI, M., Accounting
NETOIU, L., Currency and Credits
NISTORESCU, T., Marketing
OPRITESCU, M., Currency and Credits
PETCU, C., Economics
PIRVU, C., Accounting
PIRVU, G., Economics
POPA, S., Informatics
SICHIGEA, N., Corporate Finance
SIMINICĂ, M., Economic and Financial Analysis
SITNIKOV, C., Management
SOAVĂ, G., Informatics
SPULBĂR, C., Banking Management
ZAHARIA, C., Management

Faculty of Electrical Engineering (Bdul Decebal 107, Craiova; tel. (251) 436447; e-mail decanat@elth.ucv.ro; internet elth.ucv.ro):
BROJBOIU, M., Electrical Engineering
CIONTU, M., Energetic Engineering
DIGĂ, S., Energetic Engineering
GOSEA, I., Energetic Engineering
LUNGU, R., Aerospace Engineering
MĂNESCU, L., Energetic Engineering
MIRCEA, I., Energetic Engineering
NICOLAE, P., Electrical Engineering
PASĂRE, S., Electrical Engineering
POPA, I., Electrical Engineering
TOPAN, D., Electrical Engineering
TUSALIU, P., Electrical Engineering

Faculty of Law and Administrative Services (e-mail secretariat@drept.ucv.ro; internet drept.ucv.ro):
CERCEL, S., Civil Law
DĂNIŞOR, D., Political Institutions, Constitutional Law
GĂINĂ, V., Commercial Law
NICULEANU, C., General Criminal Law
OLTEANU, G., Intellectual Property Law
SÂMBRIAN, T., Roman Law
SANDU, A., Political Economy
SCURTU, S., International Commercial Law
TURCULEANU, I., Civil Law Succession

Faculty of Letters (tel. (251) 414468; e-mail litere@central.ucv.ro; internet www.ucv.ro):
AFANA, E., Stylistics, Poetics, Semiotics, Theory of Communication
BUCIU, M., Romanian Literature
BURDESCU, F., English Literature
COSTĂCHESCU, A., French Linguistics, Pragmatics
MURAR, I., English Linguistics
PANEA, N., Anthropology, Romanian Literature
RĂDULESCU, A., French Linguistics, Theory of Translation
SCURTU, G., French Linguistics, General Linguistics
SÎRBULESCU, E., English Literature
TEODORESCU, C., French Linguistics, Theory of Communication
TROCAN, L., French Literature

Faculty of Mechanical Engineering:
ASTEFANEI, I., Fluid Mechanics
BĂGNARU, D., Mechanics
BICĂ, M., Thermotechnics and Thermic Machines
CĂTĂNEANU, A., Machineries
CERNĂIANU, A., Advanced Production Systems
CHERGHINA, G., Technical Drawing and Infographics
CIOLACU, F., Chip Tooling Theory
CREŢU, S., Machineries
DUMITRU, C., Engineering and Design of Products
DUMITRU, N., Machine Elements
GEORGESCU, I., Steel Armed Concrete Buildings
ILINCIOIU, D., Materials Resistance
MARIN, M., Materials Resistance
NANU, G., Mechanics
OŢĂT, V., Automotive Dynamics
RINDERU, P., Mechanical Vibrations
ROŞCA, V., Materials Resistance
STANIMIR, A., Technology of Machine Construction
TĂRÂŢĂ, D., Material Science
TARNIŢĂ, D., Statistics
VINTILĂ, D., Mechanics
ZAMFIRACHE, M., Mechanicals Works

Faculty of Physical Education and Sports (Str. Brestei 156, Craiova; tel. (251) 422743; e-mail efs_kineto@sport.ucv.ro; internet cis01.central.ucv.ro/educatie_fizica-kineto/):
AVRAMESCU, T., Sport Medicine
CĂTĂNEANU, S., Physical Education and Sports
DĂNOIU, M., Sport Medicine
DRAGOMIR, M., Physical Education and Sports
DRAGOMIR, M., Physical Education and Sports
ORTĂNESCU, C., Physical Education and Sports
ORTĂNESCU, D., Physical Education and Sports
RUSU, L., Sport Medicine

Faculty of Social Sciences (tel. (251) 418515; e-mail ifgcraiova@yahoo.com; internet www.ucv.ro):
AVRAM, C., History
CIOBOTEA, D., History
DEACONESCU, I., Philology
GHERGHE, P., History
LUNGU, M., History
OSIAC, V., History
OTOVESCU, D., Sociology
PITURCĂ, A., History-Philosophy
TOMESCU, V., Geography

Faculty of Technological System Engineering and Management:
BENGA, G., Fundamentals of Cutting Technologies, Machining Technologies
CIUPITU, I., Cold Plastic Deformation
GÎNGU, O., Material Science and Engineering
MANGRA, M., Material Science and Engineering

Faculty of Theology, History and Education Sciences:
CHIRILĂ, P., Pastoral Medicine and Bioethics
ISVORANU, A., Old Testament Study
PĂTULESCU, C., Universal Church History
POPA, I., Orthodox Dogmatics
RESCEANU, Ş., Religions History

UNIVERSITATEA DIN ORADEA
(University of Oradea)

University St 1, CP 114, Oradea

Telephone: (259) 408105

E-mail: rectorat@uoradea.ro

Internet: www.uoradea.ro

Founded 1990

State control

Languages of instruction: English, Romanian

Academic year: October to July

Pres.: Prof. SORIN CURILA

Rector: Prof. Dr CONSTANTIN BUNGĂU

Vice-Rector for Academic Management: Prof. Dr MARCEL ROSCA

Vice-Rector for Financial Resources Management: Prof. Dr GHEORGHE TARA

Vice-Rector for Materials and Heritage Resource Management: Dr MARCELA PRADA

Vice-Rector for Research Management and Int. Relations: Prof. Dr SORIN SIPOS

Vice-Rector for Student and Social Service Management: Dr SIMONA TRIP

Gen. Dir: Prof. Dr MIRCEA GORDAN

Library of 280,000 vols

Number of teachers: 1,140

Number of students: 22,420

Publications: *Analele Universităţii din Oradea, Fascicula Agricultură-Horticultură, Analele Universităţii din Oradea, Fascicula Biologie* (bioresearch.ro/bioresearch/revistaen.htm), *Analele Universităţii din Oradea, Fascicula Chimie, Analele Universităţii din Oradea, Fascicula Construcţii si Instalatii Hidroedilitare* (www.arhiconoradea.ro/JAES/Journal_-Archives.htm), *Analele Universităţii din Oradea, Fascicula Drept, Analele Universităţii din Oradea, Fascicula Ecotoxicologie, Zootehnice si Tehnologii de Industrie Alimentara* (protmed.uoradea.ro/facultate/anale/ecotox_zooteh_ind_alim/ecotox_zooteh_ind_alim.htm), *Analele Universităţii din Oradea, Fascicula Educaţie Fizică şi Sport, Analele Universităţii din Oradea, Fascicula Istorie-Arheologie, Analele Universităţii din Oradea, Fascicola Kinetoterapie, Analele Universităţii din Oradea, Fascicula Limba şi Literatura Română, Analele Universităţii din Oradea, Fascicula Limbi şi Literaturi Străine: Engleza, Franceza, Germana, Analele Universităţii din Oradea, Fascicula Matematica* (stiinte.uoradea.ro/en/auofm.htm), *Analele Universităţii din Oradea, Fascicula Protecia Mediului* (protmed.uoradea.ro/facultate/anale/protectia_mediului/protectia_mediului.htm), *Analele Universităţii din Oradea, Fascicula Psihologie* (socioumane.ro/blog/fasciculapsihologie/), *Analele Universităţii din Oradea, Fascicula Silvicultură, Analele Universităţii din Oradea, Fascicula Sociologie-Fiolosie-Asistenta Sociala, Analele Universităţii din Oradea, Fizica, Analele Universităţii din Oradea, Seria Geografie* (istgeorelint.uoradea.ro/Reviste/Anale/anale.htm), *Analele Universităţii din Oradea, Seria Relatii International si Studii Europene, Analele Universităţii din Oradea, Stiinte Economice* (steconomice.uoradea.ro/anale), *Annals of the Oradea University, Fascicle of Management and Technological Engineering* (imtuoradea.ro/auo.fmte), *Annals of the University of Oradea, Fascicle of Textiles-Leatherwork* (textile.webhost.uoradea.ro/Conferinta.html), *Biharean Biologist* (biologie-oradea.xhost.ro/BihBiol/index.html), *Cetatea Bihariei, Eurolimes* (iser.rdsor.ro/eurolimes.htm), *Geojournal of Tourism and Geosites, Herpetologica Romanica* (herpetofauna.uv.ro/herprom.html), *Journal of Computer Science and Control Systems* (electroinf.uoradea.ro/reviste/default.htm), *Journal of Electrical and Electronics Engineering* (electroinf.uoradea.ro/reviste/default.htm), *Journal of Identity and Migration Studies, Journal of Sustainable Energy* (www.energy-cie.ro), *North-Western Journal of Zoology* (herp-or.uv.ro/nwjz), *Orizonturi Teologice, Revista Medicala Oradeana, Revista Română de Geografie Politică* (rrgp.uoradea.ro), *Revista Romana de Kinetoterapie*

DEANS

Faculty of Architecture and Construction: Prof. Dr AURORA-CARMEN MANCIA

Faculty of Arts: Prof. Dr TEODOR MATEOC

Faculty of Economics: Prof. Dr ADRIANA GIURGIU

Faculty of Electrical Engineering and Informatics: Prof. Dr Eng. TEODOR LEUCA

Faculty of Energy Engineering and Industrial Management: Prof. Dr MARCEL ROSCA

Faculty of Environmental Protection: Prof. Dr IOAN CHEREJI

Faculty of Geography, Tourism and Sport: Prof. ALEXANDER ILIES

Faculty of History, International Relations, Information and Communication Sciences: Prof. Dr IOAN HORGA

Faculty of Humanities: Prof. Dr ADRIAN HATOS

Faculty of Law: Prof. Dr VALENTIN MIRIŞAN

Faculty of Management and Technological Engineering: Prof. Dr PELE ALEXANDRU VIOREL

Faculty of Medicine and Pharmacy: Prof. Dr FLORIAN BODOG

Faculty of Orthodox Theology: Prof. Dr NICU DUMITRAŞCU

Faculty of Science: Prof. Dr SANDA MONICA FILIP

Faculty of Technological and Management Engineering: Prof. Dr PELE ALEXANDRU VIOREL

UNIVERSITATEA DIN PETROŞANI
(University of Petroşani)

Str. Universitatii 20, 332006 Petroşani

Telephone: (254) 542580

E-mail: rector@upet.ro

Internet: www.upet.ro

Founded 1864, present name 1995

State control

Academic year: October to July

Rector: Prof. Dr ARON POANTA

Vice-Rector for Academic, Admin. and Financial Management: Dr MARCU MARIUS

Vice-Rector for Education and Int. Relations: Dr CODRUTA DURA

Vice-Rector for Research and Project Management: Prof. Dr VICTOR ARAD

Library of 304,089 vols (incl. 225,805 books, 19,435 periodicals, 56,803 state standards, 1,443 theses and 603 non-publications)

Number of teachers: 200

Number of students: 4,500

Publications: *Annals of Economics* (1 a year), *Annals of Electrical Engineering* (1 a year), *Annals of Mechanical Engineering* (1 a year), *Annals of Mining Engineering* (1 a year), *Annals of Physics* (1 a year), *Annals of Social Sciences* (1 a year), *Informative Gazette* (12 a year), *Library's Informative Gazette* (4 a year), *Mining Magazine* (12 a year), *Revista Minelor* (Mining Revue, 4 a year), *Transylvanian Journal of Mathematics and Mechanics* (print and online, tjmm.edyropress.ro)

DEANS

Faculty of Mechanical and Electrical Engineering: Dr NICOLAE PĂTRĂSCOIU

Faculty of Mining: Dr Eng. IOEL VERES

Faculty of Sciences: Prof. Dr MIRCEA BARON

UNIVERSITATEA DIN PITEŞTI
(University of Piteşti)

Piteşti Str. Targu din Vale 1, 110040 Arges

Telephone: (348) 453102

E-mail: info@upit.ro

Internet: www.upit.ro

Founded 1962, present name and status 1991

State control

Rector: Prof. Dr IONEL DIDEA

Vice-Rector for Int. Relations and European Integration: MIHAI BRASLASU

Vice-Rector for Quality Education and Investment: SEBASTIAN PARLAC

Vice-Rector for Scientific Research: MARIOARA ABRUDEANU

Vice-Rector for Social Affairs and Students: CONSTANTIN DRAGHICI

Dir for Library: ILEANA BALAN

Library of 261,525 vols

Number of teachers: 700

Number of students: 12,000

DEANS

Faculty of Economic Sciences: Dr DANIELA PIRVU

Faculty of Educational Sciences: Prof. Dr LILIANA EZECHIL

Faculty of Electronics, Communications and Computers: Prof. Ing. Dr NICU BIZON

Faculty of Law and Administrative Sciences: Prof. Dr EUGEN CHELARU

Faculty of Letters: Prof. Dr STEFAN GAITANARU

Faculty of Mathematics and Computer Science: Prof. Dr CORNELIU UDREA

Faculty of Mechanics and Technology: Prof. Dr VIOREL NICOLAE

Faculty of Orthodox Theology: Prof. Dr RADU TASCOVICI

Faculty of Physical Education and Sports: Prof. MIHAILESCU LILIANA

Faculty of Sciences: Dr BENEDICT OPRESCU

Faculty of Socio-Humanistic Sciences: Dr CONSTANTIN AUGUSTUS BARBULESCU

UNIVERSITATEA 'DUNAREA DE JOS' DIN GALAŢI

Str. Domnească 47, 800008 Galaţi

Telephone: (336) 130109

E-mail: rectorat@ugal.ro

Internet: www.ugal.ro

Founded 1948, present status 1974, present name 1991

State control

Languages of instruction: English, French, Romanian

Academic year: October to July

Rector: Prof. Ing. Dr IULIAN GABRIEL BIRSAN

Pro-Rector for Academic and Institutional Devt: Prof. Ing. Dr ADRIAN LUNGU

Pro-Rector for Int. Relations and Student Affairs: Prof. Dr ANCA GATA

Pro-Rector for Quality Management: Dr DANA TUTUNARU

Pro-Rector for Scientific Research: Prof. Ing. Dr ANCA NICOLAU

Pro-Rector for Teaching Activities: Prof. Ing. Dr TOADER MUNTEANU

Chief Operating Officer: Ing. ROMEU HORGHIDAN

Dir for Library: MIOARA VONCILA

Library: See under Libraries and Archives

Number of teachers: 670

Number of students: 13,200

DEANS

Faculty of Arts: TEODOR NITA

Faculty of Automation, Computers, Electrical Engineering and Electronics: Ing. Dr EMILIA PECHEANU

Faculty of Economics and Business Administration: Dr EDIT LUKACS

Faculty of Engineering in Brăila: Ing. Dr SILVIU CRISTIAN SIMIONESCU

Faculty of Food Science and Engineering: Prof. Ing. Dr PETRU ALEXE

Faculty of History, Philosophy and Theology: Dr IVAN IVLAMPIE

Faculty of Law, Social and Political Sciences: Dr FLORIN TUDOR

Faculty of Letters: Prof. Dr MICHAELA PRAISLER

Faculty of Mechanical Engineering: Prof. Ing. Dr CATALIN FETECAU

Faculty of Medicine and Pharmacy: Prof. Dr AUREL NECHITA

Faculty of Metallurgy, Materials Science and Environment: Prof. Dr Eng. MARIAN BORDEI

Faculty of Naval Architecture: Prof. Ing. Dr LEONARD DOMNISORU

Faculty of Physical Education and Sport: Dr PLOSTEANU CONSTANTIN

Faculty of Sciences and Environment: Dr JENICA CRINGANU

PROFESSORS

Faculty of Arts:

BULANCEA, G., History of Music, Aesthetics, Folklore
DUMITRIU, M., History of Theatre
NITA, T., Vocal Interpretation

Faculty of Automation, Computers, Electrical Engineering and Electronics:

AIORDĂCHIOAIE, D.
CARAMAN, S.
FILIPESCU, A.
FRANGU, L.

Faculty of Economics and Business Administration:

BUHOCIU, F., Finances
PUSCASU, V., Economy
NISTOR, C., Business Communication
SARPE, D., Economy

Faculty of Engineering in Brăila:

CIUREA, A., Technical Equipment
GOANTA, A., Computer-aided Graphics
OPROESCU, GH., Technical Equipment
PICU, M., Fundamental Sciences

Faculty of Food Science and Engineering:

ALEXE, P., Biochemistry
BAHRIM, G., Bioengineering
BOTEZ, E., Bioengineering
CRISTEA, V., Fishery
OPREA, L., Biochemistry
VIZIREANU, C., Biochemistry

Faculty of History, Philosophy and Theology:

IVAN, I., History of Contemporary Philosophy
LICA, V., History
SISCANU, I., History
TOFAN, S., Philosophy

Faculty of Law, Social and Political Sciences:

RADUCAN, O., Law of Internal Combustion Engines
VICTOR, I., Public Administration

Faculty of Letters:

CROITORU, E., Law of Internal Combustion Engines
GATA, A., Public Administration
IOANA, N., Law of Internal Combustion Engines
MILEA, D., Law of Internal Combustion Engines
PRAISLER, M., Law of Internal Combustion Engines

Faculty of Mechanical Engineering:

ANDREI, G., Machine-parts Design and Graphics
BIRSAN, I., Machine-parts Design
CHIRICA, I., Structures Strength
FETECAU, C., Machine Manufacturing and Robotics

MEREUTA, E., Applied Mechanics

Faculty of Medicine and Pharmacy:

FIRESCU, D., General Surgery, Low-invasive Surgery
MUSAT, C., Physiology and Sports Medicine
NICHITA, A., Paediatrics, Physiology

Faculty of Metallurgy, Materials Science and Environment:

BENEA, L., Environmental and Materials Engineering
CANANAU, N., Plastic Deformation and Heat Treatment
MUSAT, V., Plastic Deformation and Heat Treatment
RADU, T., Environmental and Materials Engineering
VLAD, M., Environmental and Materials Engineering

Faculty of Naval Architecture:

DOMNISORU, L., Naval Structures
LUNGU, A., Naval Structures
OBREJA, C., Naval Hydrodynamics

Faculty of Physical Education and Sport:

LIUSNEA, S., Body Building
NICOLAE, P., Athletics
PACURARU, A., Sport Games and Physical Education

Faculty of Sciences and Environment:

CARAC, G., Chemistry
GEORGESCU, L., Chemistry
GEORGHIES, C., Physics
MORARU, L., Physics
PRAISLER, M., Physics

UNIVERSITATEA ECOLOGICA DIN BUCURESTI
(Ecological University of Bucharest)

Blvd Vasile Milea 1G, Sector 6, 061341 Bucharest

Telephone: (21) 3167932
E-mail: rectorat@ueb.ro
Internet: www.ueb.ro

Founded 1990
Private control

Rector: Prof. Dr ALEXANDRU TICLEA
Pro-Rector: Prof. Dr DORIN JULA
Pro-Rector: Dr NICOLAE GALDEAN
Sec.-Gen.: Ing. VASILE MUSTATEA

Library of 9,820 vols

DEANS

Faculty of Ecology and Environmental Protection: Dr GIULIANO TEVI
Faculty of Economic Sciences: Prof. Dr ANTONIADE-CIPRIAN ALEXANDRU
Faculty of Engineering and Environmental Management: Prof. Dr CRISTIN BIGAN
Faculty of Law and Administrative Sciences: Prof. Dr PETER BUNECI
Faculty of Mass Communication: Dr CONSTANTIN HARIUC
Faculty of Physical Education and Sport: Prof. Dr SANDA TOMA-URICHIANU
Faculty of Psychology: Dr RUXANDRA GHERGHINESCU

UNIVERSITATEA 'EFTIMIE MURGU' DIN REȘIȚA

Piața Traian Vuia 1–4, 320085 Reșița

Telephone: (255) 210227
E-mail: rector@uem.ro
Internet: www.uem.ro

Founded 1971, present name 1992
State control

Rector: Prof. Ing. Dr DOINA FRUNZAVERDE
Pro-Rector for Education: Prof. Ing. Dr JOHN RUJA
Pro-Rector for Research: Prof. Ing. Dr GILBERT-RAINER GILLICH
Chief Operating Officer: Ing. TEODOR GAVRIȘ

Chief Librarian: MIHAELA ARDAI
Library of 71,573 vols, 4,593 journals
Number of students: 3,800

Publications: *Analele Universitatii 'Eftimie Murgu' Resita, Facultatea de Stiinte Economice, Analele Universitatii 'Eftimie Murgu' Resita, Fascicola de Inginerie, Caiete de Drept International* (online, www.caietedrept.eu), *Robotica & Management* (2 a year)

DEANS

Faculty of Administrative Sciences: Dr CLAUDIA ANDRIȚOI
Faculty of Economic Science: Dr VENERA MANCIU
Faculty of Electrical Engineering and Computer Science: Prof. Ing. Dr EUGEN RĂDUCA
Faculty of Engineering and Management: Prof. Ing. Dr CODRUȚA OANA HAMATH
Faculty of Mechanical and Materials Engineering: Prof. Ing. Dr FLORENTINA CZIPLE
Faculty of Theology, Social Sciences and Education: Dr MIHAIL DOBRESCU

UNIVERSITATEA EMANUEL DIN ORADEA
(Emanuel University of Oradea)

Str. Nufarului 87, 410597 Oradea

Telephone: (259) 426692
E-mail: president@emanuel.ro
Internet: www.emanuel.ro

Founded 1989
Private control
Language of instruction: Romanian
Academic year: October to July

Pres.: Prof. Dr CORNELIU C. SIMUȚ
Admin. Dir: Ing. DOREL TIUTIN
Registrar: MARCELA ȚUNDREA
Chief Librarian: ILIE SORIȚĂU

Library of 61,000 vols
Number of teachers: 50
Number of students: 500

Publication: *Perichoresis* (2 a year)

DEANS

'Brian Griffiths' School of Management: Dr SEBASTIAN VĂDUVA
School of Theology: Dr MARIUS DAVID CRUCERU

UNIVERSITATEA EUROPEANĂ 'DRAGAN' DIN LUGOJ
(Dragan European University of Lugoj)

Str. Ion Huniade 2, 305500 Lugoj

Telephone: (256) 359198
E-mail: ued@deu.ro
Internet: www.deu.ro

Founded 1991
Private control
Academic year: October to September

Rector: Prof. Dr PERSIDA CECHIN-CRISTA
Dir: FLORIN MIHAI

Library of 65,992 vols

Publications: *Analele Universității Europene Drăgan din Lugoj. Seria Economică* (1 a year), *Didactica Modernă* (1 a year), *Studium Legis* (1 a year)

DEANS

Faculty of Economics: Prof. Dr SORIN BLAJ
Faculty of Law: Dr DUMITRU CORNEAN

UNIVERSITATEA 'GEORGE BACOVIA' DIN BACĂU
(George Bacovia University of Bacău)

Str. Pictor Aman 96, 600164 Bacău

Telephone: (234) 562600
E-mail: rectorat@ugb.ro
Internet: www.ugb.ro

Founded 1992
Private control

Rector: Prof. Dr TATIANA PUIU
Chief Sec.: Dr MIHAELA MASTACAN
Librarian: PETRU DIMITRIU

Publications: *Acta Universitatis George Bacovia. Juridica* (2 a year, in English and Romanian, online, juridica.ugb.ro), *Economy Transdisciplinarity Cognition* (2 a year, in English, print and online, etc.ugb.ro)

DEANS

Faculty of Economics and Business Administration: Prof. Dr CONSTANTIN COJOCARU
Faculty of Law and Administration: Dr ION CIOCHINA-BARBU

UNIVERSITATEA 'LUCIAN BLAGA' DIN SIBIU
(Lucian Blaga University of Sibiu)

Victoriei Blvd 10, 550024 Sibiu

Telephone: (269) 216062
E-mail: ccom@ulbsibiu.ro
Internet: www.ulbsibiu.ro

Founded 1990, present name 1995
State control
Academic year: October to June

Rector: Prof. Ing. Dr IOAN BONDREA
Vice-Rector for Academic Affairs: Prof. IOAN MARIAN TIPLIC
Vice-Rector for Organizational and Financial Strategy: Prof. Dr LIVIA ILIE
Vice-Rector for Research and Doctoral Studies: Prof. Ing. Dr CLAUDIU V. KIFOR
Vice-Rector for Student Affairs: Prof. Dr MIOARA BONCUȚ
Library Man.: Dr Eng. RODICA VOLOVICI

Library of 600,000 vols (bibliographic units), 14,000 periodicals
Number of teachers: 490
Number of students: 20,000

DEANS

Faculty of Agricultural Sciences, Food Industry and Environmental Protection: Prof. Ing. Dr OVIDIU TITA
Faculty of Economics: Prof. Dr LIVIU MIHĂESCU
Faculty of Engineering: Prof. Ing. Dr LIVIU ROSCA
Faculty of Law: Prof. Dr CĂLINA JUGASTRU
Faculty of Letters and Arts: Dr ALEXANDRA MITREA
Faculty of Medicine: Prof. Dr SILVIU MORAR
Faculty of Sciences: Dr ANGELA BANADUC
Faculty of Social and Human Sciences: Prof. Dr DUMITRU BATÂR
Faculty of Theology: Prof. Dr AUREL PAVEL

UNIVERSITATEA 'MIHAIL KOGALNICEANU' DIN IAȘI
(Mihail Kogalniceanu University of Iași)

Str. Balusescu 2, 700309 Iași

Telephone: (232) 212416
E-mail: rectorat@umk.ro
Internet: www.umk.ro

Founded 1990
Private control
Language of instruction: Romanian
Academic year: October to July

Rector: Assoc. Prof. Dr CRISTIAN SANDACHE

Library of 12,300 vols
Number of teachers: 50
Number of students: 1,000

Publication: *B+ Category*

DEANS

Faculty of Law: Prof. Dr CIUBOTARU BOGDAN-MICHAEL

UNIVERSITATEA NAȚIONALĂ DE ARTE BUCUREȘTI
(National University of Arts Bucharest)

Str. Gen. Budișteanu 19, 010773 Bucharest 1

Telephone: (21) 3125429
E-mail: rectorat@unarte.org
Internet: www.unarte.ro

Founded 1864 as Scoala Națională de Arte Frumoase
Academic year: October to June
State control

Rector: Dr RUXANDRA DEMETRESCU
Chancellor: Dr CATALIN BALESCU

Library: see under Libraries and Archives
Number of teachers: 274
Number of students: 1,000

DEANS

Faculty of Applied Arts and Design: ALEXANDRU GHILDUS
Faculty of Art History and Theory: CORINA POPA
Faculty of Fine Arts: MIHAIL MANESCU

UNIVERSITATEA NAȚIONALĂ DE EDUCAȚIE FIZICĂȘI SPORT DIN BUCUREȘTI
(National University of Physical Education and Sport of Bucharest)

Constantin Noica St 140, Sector 6, 060057 Bucharest

Telephone: (21) 3164107
E-mail: dcre@unefs.ro
Internet: www.unefs.ro

Founded 1923 as Institutul National de Educatie Fizica, present name and status 2009
State control
Language of instruction: Romanian
Academic year: October to July

Rector: Prof. Dr VIOREL COJOCARU
Vice-Rector: Prof. Dr VASILICA GRIGORE
Head of Library: CRISTESCU NADIA

Library of 102,322 vols, 3,563 titles, 39,892 units of monographs, audiovisual material and serials
Number of teachers: 99
Number of students: 1,400

Publication: *Discobolul*

DEANS

Faculty of Kinetotherapy: Prof. Dr MARIANA CORDUN
Faculty of Physical Education and Sports: Prof. Dr ALINA DANIELA MOANTA

UNIVERSITATEA NAȚIONALĂ DE MUZICĂ DIN BUCUREȘTI
(National University of Music in Bucharest)

Știrbei Vodă Str. 33, Sector 1, 010102 Bucharest

Telephone: (21) 3146341
E-mail: rectorat@unmb.ro
Internet: www.unmb.ro

Founded 1864, present name and status 2000
State control
Language of instruction: English, French, German, Romanian
Academic year: October to June

Rector: Prof. Dr DAN DEDIU-SANDU
Chair.: Prof. Dr DOREL PASCU-RĂDULESCU
Pro-Rector: Prof. Dr DANA BORȘAN
Pro-Rector: Prof. Dr TEODOR ȚUȚUIANU
Head of Library: MARIA CIOPONEA

Library of 251,049 vols
Number of teachers: 210
Number of students: 1,250 (full-time)

Publication: *Musicology Today*

DEANS

Faculty of Composition, Musicology and Music Pedagogy: Prof. Dr SMARANDA MURGAN
Faculty of Performing Arts: Dr BIANCA LUIGIA MANOLEANU

PROFESSORS

BARBU BUCUR, S., Byzantine Music
BORSAN, D., Piano
BUCIU, M., Music Theory
DANCEANU, L., Musicology
ENACHESCU, E., Singing
IONOAIA, F., Wind Instruments
PASCU-RADULESCU, D., Conducting
RATIU, O., Violin
ROTARU, D., Composition
VOICU-ARNAUTOIU, R., Chamber Music

UNIVERSITATEA 'NICOLAE TITULESCU' DIN BUCUREȘTI
(Nicolae Titulescu University of Bucharest)

Calea Văcărești 185, Sector 4, 040051 Bucharest

Telephone: (21) 3309032
E-mail: office@univnt.ro
Internet: www.univnt.ro

Founded 1990
Private control

Rector: Prof. Dr GABRIEL BOROI
Pro-Rector: Prof. Dr MIRCEA DAMASCHIN
Registrar: GINA MARIN
Chief Librarian: SANDA GHEORGHIU

Publications: *IPSO FACTO, LESIJ Lex ET Scientia International Journal* (1 a year, online, lexetscientia.univnt.ro), *Romanian Journal of Intellectual Property Law* (4 a year), *Romanian Review of Social Sciences* (2 a year, online, rrss.univnt.ro)

DEANS

Faculty of Economic Sciences: Prof. Dr SERGHEI MARGULESCU
Faculty of Law: Dr BOGDAN MICU
Faculty of Social and Administrative Sciences: Prof. Dr MIHAI HOTCA

UNIVERSITATEA OVIDIUS CONSTANȚA
(Ovidius University of Constanta)

Blvd Mamaia 124, Aleea Universitatii 1, 900527 Constanța

Telephone: (241) 606467
E-mail: rectorat2@univ-ovidius.ro
Internet: www.univ-ovidius.ro

Founded 1990
State control

Rector: Prof. Dr DĂNUT TIBERIUS EPURE
Pro-Rector for Communication and Student Affairs: Prof. Dr ION BORDEIANU
Pro-Rector for Education and Training: Prof. Ing. Dr GABRIELA STANCIU
Pro-Rector for Int. Relations and Foreign Students: Prof. Dr TEODOSIE PETRSECU
Pro-Rector for Research, Devt and Innovation: Prof. Dr VICTOR PLOAE
Pro-Rector for Strategy, Institutional Devt and Quality Management: Dr FLORIN ANGHEL

Number of teachers: 860
Number of students: 16,700

DEANS

Faculty of Arts: Dr DANIELA HANTIU
Faculty of Construction Management: Prof. Ing. Dr MIHAI FLOREA
Faculty of Dental Medicine: Dr AURELIANA CARAIANE
Faculty of Economic Sciences: Prof. Dr ELENA CERASELA SPATARIU

Faculty of History and Political Science: Dr EMANUEL PLOPEANU

Faculty of Law and Administrative Sciences: Dr GEORGE SERBAN

Faculty of Letters: Dr MIHAELA MIRON-FULEA

Faculty of Mathematics and Informatics: Prof. BOSKOFF WLADIMIR-GEORGES

Faculty of Mechanical Engineering, Industrial and Maritime: Prof. Ing. Dr IONEL NICOLAE

Faculty of Medicine: Prof. Dr PETRU BORDEI

Faculty of Natural and Agricultural Sciences: Dr LILIANA PANAITESCU

Faculty of Pharmacy: Prof. Dr SÎRBU RODICA

Faculty of Physical Education and Sports: Prof. Dr GEORGE STANCULESCU

Faculty of Physics, Chemistry, Electronics and Oil Technology: Dr VIORICA POPESCU

Faculty of Psychology and Educational Sciences: Dr VIRGIL FRUNZA

Faculty of Theology: Prof. Dr BOGDAN MOISE

UNIVERSITATEA 'PETRE ANDREI' DIN IAŞI
(Petre Andrei University of Iaşi)

Str. Ghica Vodă 13, 700469 Iaşi

Telephone: (232) 210474

E-mail: office@upa.ro

Internet: www.upa.ro

Founded 1990

Private control

Language of instruction: Romanian

Academic year: October to July

Rector: Prof. Dr DORU TOMPEA

Pres.: Dr SORIN BOCANCEA

Chief Librarian: ALEXANDRINA HULBAN

Library of 29,000 vols, 3,200 periodicals

Number of students: 4,500

Publication: *Journal of Legal Studies* (2 a year, print and online, jls.upa.ro)

DEANS

Faculty of Economics: Dr ALEXANDRU TRIFU

Faculty of Law: Prof. Dr CRISTIAN ANTONIE BOCANCEA

Faculty of Political and Administrative Sciences: Prof. Dr MIHAI BACIU

Faculty of Psychology and Educational Sciences: Prof. Dr MARIANA CALUSCHI

Faculty of Social Work and Sociology: Dr ANCA TOMPEA

UNIVERSITATEA 'PETROL-GAZE' DIN PLOIEŞTI
(Petroleum—Gas University of Ploieşti)

Blvd Bucureşti 39, POB 52, 100680 Ploieşti

Telephone: (244) 573171

E-mail: rectorat@upg-ploiesti.ro

Internet: www.upg-ploiesti.ro

Founded 1948 as Institutul de Petrol şi Gaze, present name 1993

State control

Academic year: October to July

Rector: Prof. Ing. Dr MIHAI PASCU COLOJA

Vice-Rector for Admin. Activities, Social and Human Resources: Dr CORNEL CONSTANTIN LAZAR

Vice-Rector for Degree Programs and Quality Management: Prof. Ing. Dr NICHOLAE PARASCHIV

Vice-Rector for Int. Relations: Dr CRISTIAN MARINOIU

Vice-Rector for Scientific Research: Prof. Ing. Dr ION BOLOCAN

Library of 360,000 vols, 2,879 periodicals

Number of teachers: 730

Number of students: 11,500

Publication: *Bulletin of Petroleum Gas University of Ploiesti* (series on Philology, Mathematics-Informatics, Physics, Eco-

nomics, Educational Sciences, Law and Social Sciences)

DEANS

Faculty of Economical Sciences: Dr MARIANA EFTIMIE

Faculty of Mechanical and Electrical Engineering: Prof. Ing. Dr MIHAI MINESCU

Faculty of Petroleum and Gas Engineering: Prof. Ing. Dr IULIAN NISTOR

Faculty of Petroleum Technology and Petrochemistry: Prof. Ing. Dr PAUL ROSCA

Faculty of Sciences: Dr ANCA MIHAELA DOBRINESCU

PROFESSORS

ALEXANDRU, P.
ANGHEL, A.
ANTONESCU, L.
ANTONESCU, N. N.
AVRAM, L.
BADOIU, D.
BALU, I.
BOLOCAN, I.
BUCUR, C.
CARTOAJE, V.
COLOJA, M. P.
CUTU, I.
DUDA, G.
DUMITRASCU, L.
EPARU, I.
FRUZESCU, D.
GEORGESCU, D.
GEORGESCU, O.
GHEORGHITOIU, M.
GRIGORE, N.
IARCA, I.
IONESCU, M.
IORDACHE, G.
LAMBRESCU, I.
MALUREANU, I.
MARIN, C.
MINESCU, F.
MINESCU, M.
NISTOR, I.
OPREA, F.
OPREA, M.
PANAIT, G.
PARASCHIV, N.
PATARLAGEANU, M.
PETCU, A.
POPA, C.
POPESCU, C.
ROSCA, P.
SIRO, B.
SOARE, A.
STEFAN, G.
STOICESCU, C. C.
STRATULA, C.
TALLE, V.
TOMESCU, D.
TUDOR, I.
ULMANU, V.
VASILESCU, S.
VOICU, I.
ZAHARIA, M.
ZECHERU, G.

UNIVERSITATEA 'PETRU MAIOR' DIN TÂRGU MUREŞ
(Petru Maior University of Târgu Mureş)

Nicolae Iorga Str. 1, 540088 Târgu Mureş

Telephone: (265) 262275

E-mail: rectorat08@upm.ro

Internet: www.upm.ro

Founded 1960

State control

Academic year: October to July

Rector: Prof. Dr CALIN ENACHESCU

Vice-Rector for Scientific Activities: Prof. Dr LIVIU MOLDOVAN

Vice-Rector for Teaching: Prof. Dr TATIANA DANESCU

Library of 150,000 vols

Number of teachers: 160

Number of students: 4,000

Publications: *Buletinul Ştiinţific* (1 a year), *Studia Universitatis—Filologia* (1 a year), *Studia Universitatis—Istoria* (1 a year)

DEANS

Faculty of Economics and Admininstrative Sciences: Prof. Ing. Dr LIVIU MARIAN

Faculty of Engineering: Dr NICOLAE CHIRILA

Faculty of Sciences and Letters: Prof. Dr IULIAN BOLDEA

UNIVERSITATEA ROMÂNĂ DE ŞTIINŢE ŞI ARTE 'GHEORGHE CRISTEA'
(Gheorghe Cristea Romanian University of Sciences and Arts)

Blvd Energeticienilor 9E, block M1, sector 3, Bucharest

E-mail: ugc_rei@ugc.ro

Internet: www.ugc.ro

Founded 1990

Private control

Rector: Prof. Ing. Dr LIDIA CRISTEA

Library of 50,000 vols

DEANS

Faculty of Arts and Sciences: Dr ANDREEA TANASESCU

Faculty of Economics, Law and Administrative Sciences: Dr MARGARETA FLESNER

UNIVERSITATEA ROMĂNO-AMERICANA DIN BUCUREŞTI
(Romanian-American University of Bucharest)

Expozitiei Blvd 1B, Sector 1, 012101 Bucharest

Telephone: (21) 2029500

Internet: www.rau.ro

Founded 1991

Private control

Rector: Prof. Dr OVIDIU FOLCUT

Vice-Pres. for Relations and Social Services: Prof. Dr MIHAI ARISTOTEL UNGUREANU

Vice-Pres. for Scientific Research: Prof. Dr MARIA MOISE

Vice-Pres. for Strategic Management, Quality and Instructional Devt: Prof. Dr DOINITA CIOCIRLAN

Library of 60,000 vols

Publication: *Performance* (12 a year)

DEANS

Faculty of Computer Science for Business Management: Dr CORNELIA BOTEZATU

Faculty of Domestic and International Economy of Tourism: Dr DANIELA FIROIU

Faculty of European Economic Studies: Prof. Dr FLORIN BONCIU

Faculty of Internal and International Commercial and Financial-Banking Relations: Dr GHEORGHE VALERIU POTECEA

Faculty of Law: Prof. Dr GHEORGHE BOTEA

Faculty of Management-Marketing: Dr ALEXANDRU IONESCU

UNIVERSITATEA ROMÂNO-GERMANĂ DIN SIBIU
(Romanian-German University of Sibiu)

Calea Dumbravii 28–31, 550324 Sibiu

Telephone: (269) 233568

E-mail: rectorat@roger-univ.ro

Internet: www.roger-univ.ro

Founded 1998

Private control

Rector: Prof. Dr GEORGE BICHICEAN

Pro-Rector: Dr GEORGE BALAN
Librarian: ROXANA ALEXA

Library of 18,000 vols, 11,500 Romanian, 5,000 German, 1,280 English, 220 other languages

DEANS

Faculty of Economics: Prof. ALINA ANNA CIUHUREANU
Faculty of Law and Administrative Science: Prof. ELIBSABETA BOTIAN

UNIVERSITATEA 'SPIRU HARET' DIN BUCURESTI
(Spiru Haret University of Bucharest)

13 Ion Ghica str., Sector 3, 030045 Bucharest
Telephone: (21) 3149363
E-mail: international@spiruharet.ro
Internet: www.spiruharet.ro
Founded 1991
Private control
Languages of instruction: English, Romanian
Academic year: October to July
Rector: Dr AURELIAN A. BONDREA
Vice-Rector: Prof. Dr GHEORGHE BICA
Vice-Rector: Prof. Dr CARMEN COSTEA
Vice-Rector: Prof. Dr DOINEL DINUICA
Vice-Rector: Prof. Dr MANUELA EPURE
Vice-Rector: Prof. Dr ION GAF DEAC
Vice-Rector: Dr LAURA OANA GORAN
Vice-Rector: Dr IONEL EDUARD IONESCU

Library of 230,553 vols
Number of teachers: 615
Number of students: 12,928

Publications: Annals of Spiru Haret University—7 series: economics, filology, geography, journalism, mathematics-informatics, music, veterinary medicine, *Journal of Economic, Development, Environment and People*

DEANS

Faculty of Accounting and Finance, Câmpulung-Muscel: Dr ODI MIHAELA ZARNESCU
Faculty of Accounting and Finance, Râmnicu-Vâlcea: Dr ELENA DIACONU
Faculty of Architecture, Bucharest: Prof. Dr EMIL CREANGA
Faculty of Arts, Bucharest: Dr GEORGETA PINGHIRIAC
Faculty of Economic Sciences, Blaj: Prof. Dr EMIL M. POPA
Faculty of Financial-Accounting Management, Bucharest: Prof. Dr CICILIA IONESCU
Faculty of Financial and Accounting Management, Constanţa: Dr DRAGOS MIHAI IPATE
Faculty of Financial and Accounting Management, Craiova: Dr ION VIOREL MATEI
Faculty of Finance and Banking, Bucharest: Prof. Dr GHEORGHE PISTOL
Faculty of Geography, Bucharest: Dr GHEORGHE HERISANU
Faculty of International Relations, History and Philosophy, Bucharest: Dr CRISTINA PAIUSAN-NUICA
Faculty of Journalism and Communication Sciences, Bucharest: Dr SOFIA BRATU
Faculty of Law and Public Administration, Bucharest: Dr ILIE MARIN
Faculty of Law and Public Administration, Constanta: Dr MIHNEA CLADIU DRUMEA
Faculty of Law and Public Administration, Craiova: Dr BUJOR FLORESCU
Faculty of Law and Public Administration, Ramnicu Valcea: Dr CEZAR TITA
Faculty of Legal and Administrative Sciences, Braşov: Prof. Dr ALEXANDRU IONAS
Faculty of Letters, Bucharest: Dr VALERIU MARINESCU
Faculty of Management, Braşov: Dr GICA CRUCERU

Faculty of Marketing and International Business, Bucharest: Prof. Dr LUMINITA PISTOL
Faculty of Mathematics and Informatics, Bucharest: Dr MANUELA GHICA
Faculty of Physical Education and Sport, Bucharest: Dr GEORGETA NICULESCU
Faculty of Psychology and Pedagogy, Braşov: Prof. Dr PETRU LISIEVICI
Faculty of Sociology-Psychology, Bucharest: Dr BEATRICE MANU
Faculty of Veterinary Medicine, Bucharest: Dr CARMEN BERGHES

UNIVERSITATEA 'ŞTEFAN CEL MARE' DIN SUCEAVA
(Ştefan Cel Mare University)

Str. Universităţii 13, 720229 Suceava
Telephone: (230) 216147
E-mail: rectorat@usv.ro
Internet: www.usv.ro
Founded 1963 as Pedagogical Institute, present name and status 1990
State control
Language of instruction: Romanian
Academic year: October to July
Rector: Prof. Ing. Dr VALENTIN POPA
Vice-Rector for Didactical Activity and Quality Assurance: Prof. Dr MIRCEA A. DIACONU
Vice-Rector for Material Resources and Students Issues: Prof. Dr GABRIELA PRELIPCEAN
Vice-Rector for Scientific Activity: Prof. Ing. Dr MIHAI DIMIAN
Vice-Rector for Univ. Image, Int. Relations and European Devt: Prof. Dr STEFAN PURICI
Registrar: Ing. MARIA MUSCĂ
Dir for Library: Prof. Dr RODICA NAGY
Library of 300,000 vols, 30,280 periodicals
Number of teachers: 360
Number of students: 11,000

Publications: *Acta Tribologica* (1 a year, online, www.acta.tribologica.usv.ro), *Annals* (philosophy and socio-human disciplines, geography, philology (literature), philology (linguistics), mechanics, electrical engineering, forestry, economic sciences and public admin., education; annals of univ. college, 1 a year), *Atelier de Traduction* (2 a year), *ISTECFILO* (2 a year), *La Lettre 'R'* (2 a year)

DEANS

Faculty of Economic Sciences and Public Administration: Prof. Dr CARMEN NASTASE
Faculty of Educational Sciences: Dr OTILIA CLIPA
Faculty of Electrical Engineering and Computer Science: Prof. Dr STEFAN-GHEORGHE PENTIUC
Faculty of Food Engineering: Prof. Ing. Dr SONIA AMARIEI
Faculty of Forestry: Ing. Dr SERGIU ANDREI HORODNIC
Faculty of History and Geography: Prof. Dr VASILE EFROS
Faculty of Letters and Communication Sciences: Dr LUMINITA-ELENA TURCU
Faculty of Mechanical Engineering, Mechatronics and Management: Prof. Ing. Dr ROMEO IONESCU
Faculty of Physical Education and Sports: Dr PETRU GHERVAN

PROFESSORS

Faculty of Economic Sciences and Public Administration (Universităţii St 13, 720229 Suceava; tel. (230) 522978; e-mail secretariat@seap.usv.ro; internet www.seap .usv.r):

BOSTAN, I., Elements of Discourse Analysis
BURCIU, A., Contemporary English Language

CIUCA, S. A., Translation
HAPENCIUC, C.-V., Forestry
HLACIUC, E., Contemporary French
LUPU, V., French Literature
NASTASE, C. E., Translation
PRELIPCEAN, G., Contemporary German
SCRIPCARU, C., Financial Control
TILIUTE, D. E., Key Concepts of Translation

Faculty of Educational Sciences (tel. (230) 520465):

MUSCA, I., Contemporary Romanian Language, History of Literary Language
NAGY, R., Contemporary Romanian Language, History of Literary Language
OPREA, I., Contemporary Romanian Language, History of Literary Language

Faculty of Electrical Engineering and Computer Science (Universităţii St 13, 720229 Suceava; tel. (230) 524801; e-mail secretariat@eed.usv.ro; internet www.eed .usv.ro):

DIMIAN, M., Optoelectronics, Microwaves, Physics
GAITAN, V. GH., Computer Networks; Operating Systems; Computing Systems
GRAUR, A., Electronics; Electronic Devices
PENTIUC, GH., Computer Programming and Programming Languages; Programming of Distributed Systems
PENTIUC, R. D., Industrial Consumers' Power Alimentation
POPA, V., Applied Electronics; System Input/Output; Identification Systems
POTORAC, A., Computer Networks; Digital Integrated Circuits
TURCU, C. E., Artificial Intelligence, Software Engineering
TURCU, C. O., Systems Theory; Intelligent Systems

Faculty of Food Engineering (Universităţii St 13, 720225 Suceava; tel. (230) 216147; e-mail gutts@usv.ro; internet www.fia.usv.ro):

AMARIEI, S., Food Engineering
GUTT, G. H., Materials Engineering
SOLOMON, N., Equipment for Food Industry, Refrigeration Machinery, Operations and Devices in Food Industry

Faculty of Forestry (Universităţii St 13, 720229 Suceava; tel. (230) 521664; e-mail silvic@usv.ro; internet www.silvic.usv.ro):

CENUSA, R. L., Translation

Faculty of History and Geography (Universităţii St 13, 720229 Suceava; tel. (230) 216147; e-mail sofiap@usv.ro; internet www.fig.usv .ro):

EFROS, V., Quantitative Analysis in Geography
GULICIUC, V., Introduction in Political Sciences
MAXIM, T. S., Economic Geography, Geography of Tourism, Geography of Industry, Transport and Trade
PURICI, S., History of Contemporary Philosophy
RADOANE, M., Applied Geomorphology

Faculty of Letters and Communication Sciences (Universităţii St 13, 720229 Suceava; tel. (230) 216147; e-mail secretariat@litere .usv.ro; internet www.litere.usv.ro):

ARDELEANU, S.-M., Romanian Postwar Poetry: Ideology and Lyricism
CONSTANTINESCU, A. M., Ideology and Exile
DIACONU, M. A., Introduction in Int. Relations, History of Romanians in the XXth century, History of Euroregions
MACIUCA, A., History of French Literature
NAGY, R. M., Romanian literature: Modernism after Modernism, Poetry
STEICIUC, E.-B., Contemporary Romanian Language, History of Literary Language

Faculty of Mechanical Engineering, Mechatronics and Management (Universității St 13, 720225 Suceava; tel. (230) 523743; e-mail secretariat@fim.usv.ro; internet www.fim.usv.ro):

AMARANDEI, D., Manufacturing Technologies

BANCESCU, N., Materials Technology, Thermic Treatments

CIOBANU, M., Metalworking, Quality Assurance

FRUNZA, G., Equipment Maintenance and Repair, Machines Manufacturing Technology

GLOVNEA, M. L., Mechanical Contact, Elasticity and Strength of Materials

IACOB, D., Statistics, Quality Statistic Control

IONESCU, R. D., Robots and Flexible Systems, Industrial Automations

MIHAI, I., Thermodynamics and Thermic Machines

MUSCA, I., Numerical Analysis, Mechanisms and Machines Design, Tribology

RATA, V., Machines Manufacturing Technology, Equipment Maintenance and Repair

SEVERIN, L., Cold Plastic Deformation, Management

Faculty of Physical Education and Sports (Universității 9 C. P., 720225 Suceava; tel. (230) 216147; e-mail petrug@usv.ro; internet fefs.usv.ro):

COVASA, M., Nutrition

UNIVERSITATEA 'TIBISCUS' DIN TIMIŞOARA
(Tibiscus University of Timişoara)

Str. Lascăr Catargiu 4–6, 300559 Timişoara

Telephone: (256) 220689

E-mail: rectorat@tibiscus.ro

Internet: www.tibiscus.ro

Founded 1991, present name 1998

Private control

Rector: Dr CORINA MUSUROI

Pro-Rector: Prof. Dr ADRIAN RACHIERU

Pro-Rector: Prof. Dr CIPRIAN VALCAN

Chief Librarian: ADINA DOMBI-POPOVICI

Library of 135,000 vols

DEANS

Faculty of Computer Science and Applied Informatics: Dr TIBERIU MARIUS KARNYANSZKY

Faculty of Design: Dr DIANA IOVANOVICI

Faculty of Economics: Prof. ALIN MUNTEANU

Faculty of Journalism, Communication and Modern Languages: Dr DORINA CHIS

Faculty of Law and Public Administration: Dr DUMITRU VLĂDUȚ

Faculty of Music: Dr TIBERIU MARIUS KARNYANSZKY

Faculty of Physical Education and Sports: Dr LUCIAN CORIOLAN CODILEAN

Faculty of Psychology: Dr ZVETLANA MÂNDRUȚA ANGHEL

UNIVERSITATEA 'TITU MAIORESCU'
(Titu Maiorescu University)

Calea Văcărești 187, Sector 4, 004051 Bucharest

Telephone: (213) 161646

E-mail: rectorat@utm.ro

Internet: www.utm.ro

Founded 1990

Private control

Language of instruction: Romanian

Academic year: October to June

Rector: Prof. Dr SMARANDA ANGHENI

Pro-Rector: Prof. Dr DUMITRU GHEORGHIU

Registrar: TEOFIL PANC

Library of 1,500,000 vols (central library; there are also separate faculty libraries)

Number of teachers: 400

Number of students: 7,000

DEANS

Faculty of Dental Medicine, Bucharest: Prof. Dr DOINA LUCIA GHERGIC

Faculty of Economic Sciences, Bucharest: Dr FLORIN VADUVA

Faculty of Economic Sciences, Târgu Jiu: Dr ION NEAMTU

Faculty of Informatics, Bucharest: Dr IUSTIN PRIESCU

Faculty of Law, Bucharest: Dr GABRIEL LIVIU ISPAS

Faculty of Law, Târgu Jiu: Dr ANICA MERISESCU

Faculty of Medicine, Bucharest: Dr MCRISTIAN STAN

Faculty of Psychology, Bucharest: Prof. Dr VIOREL IULIAN TANASE

Faculty of Social and Political Science, Bucharest: Prof. Dr SORIN MIREL IVAN

UNIVERSITATEA 'TRANSILVANIA' DIN BRAŞOV
(Transilvania University of Brasov)

Blvd Eroilor 29, 500036 Braşov

Telephone: (268) 412088

E-mail: rector@unitbv.ro

Internet: www.unitbv.ro

Founded 1971 by merger of Polytechnical and Pedagogical Institutes of Braşov, present name 1991

State control

Language of instruction: English, French, German, Romanian

Academic year: October to July

Rector: Prof. Ing. Dr IOAN VASILE ABRUDAN

Vice-Rector for Didactic Activities: Prof. Dr MIHAELA GHEORGHE

Vice-Rector for Internationalization and Quality Evaluation: Prof. Ing. Dr SIMONA LACHE

Vice-Rector for Public Relations: Prof. Dr LILIANA ROGOZEA

Vice-Rector for Scientific Research and IT: Prof. Ing. Dr DORU TALABA

Vice-Rector for Students and Liaison with Economic, Social and Cultural Environment: Prof. Ing. Dr DANIEL MUNTEANU

Deputy Dir for Library: GABRIELA MAILAT

Library: see under Libraries and Archives

Number of teachers: 785

Number of students: 21,122

Publication: *Buletinul Universității 'Transilvania' din Braşov*

DEANS

Faculty of Civil Engineering: Prof. Ing. Dr IOAN TUNS

Faculty of Economic Sciences and Business Administration: Prof. Dr GABRIEL BRATUCU

Faculty of Electrical Engineering and Computer Science: Ing. Dr CARMEN GERIGAN

Faculty of Food and Tourism: Prof. Ing. Dr CAROL CSATLOS

Faculty of Law: Prof. Dr CRISTINEL MURZEA

Faculty of Letters: ADRIAN LACATUS

Faculty of Materials Science and Engineering: Prof. Dr TEODOR PISU-MACHEDON

Faculty of Mathematics and Computer Science: Prof. Dr MARIN MARIN

Faculty of Mechanical Engineering: Prof. Ing. Dr ION CALIN ROSCA

Faculty of Medicine: Dr MARIUS MOGA

Faculty of Music: Prof. Dr STELA DRAGULIN

Faculty of Physical Education and Mountain Sports: Prof. Dr MIRCEA NEAMTU

Faculty of Product Design and Environment: Prof. Ing. Dr OLIMPIU MUNTEANU

Faculty of Psychology and Education Sciences: Dr TOADER PALASAN

Faculty of Silviculture and Forest Engineering: Ing. Dr LUCIAN CURTU

Faculty of Sociology and Communication: Prof. Dr SILVIU COPOSESCU

Faculty of Technological Engineering and Industrial Management: Prof. Ing. Dr VLADIMIR MARASCU-KLEIN

Faculty of Wood Engineering: Prof. Ing. Dr MIHAI ISPAS

PROFESSORS

Faculty of Economic Sciences and Business Administration (Str. Colina Universitatii 1, A Bldg, Third fl., 500068 Braşov; tel. (268) 419304; e-mail f-seaa@unitbv.ro; internet www2.unitbv.ro):

BĂCANU, V. B., Finance, Accounting and Economic Theory

BRÂNZAN, I., Management and Computing

BRĂTUCU, G., Marketing and Tourism

DUGULEANĂ, L., Management and Computing

FORIŞ, T., Management and Computing

LEFTER, C., Marketing and Tourism

LIXĂNDROIU, D. I., Management and Computing

OPREI, I., Management and Computing

POPA, M., Management and Computing

POPESCU, M., Management and Computing

SAON, S., Finance, Accounting and Economic Theory

Faculty of Electrical Engineering and Computer Science (Str. Politehnicii 1, 500024 Braşov; tel. (268) 474718; e-mail f-iesc@unitbv.ro):

ANDONIE, R., Electronics

BIDIAN, D. Ş., Electrical Engineering

BORZA, P. N., Electronics

CERNAT, M., Electrical Engineering

DAN, ŞT., Automation

FRATU, A., Automation

GEORGESCU, M., Electrical Engineering

GOGIOIU, A., Electrical Engineering

HELEREA, E., Electrical Engineering

MĂRGINEANU, I., Automation

MARINESCU, C., Electrical Engineering

MATLAC, I. V., Electrical Engineering

NICOLAIDE, A. C., Electrical Engineering

OLTEAN, I. D., Electronics

PEŞTEANU, O., Electrical Engineering

SCUTARU, GH., Electrical Engineering

SISAK, F., Automation

STOIA, D. D., Electrical Engineering

SZABO, W., Electronics

SZEKELY, I., Electronics

ȚAȚA, M. S., Electrical Engineering

TOACŞE, GH., Electronics

TOPA, I., Automation

Faculty of Law (Blvd Eroilor 25, 500030 Braşov; tel. (268) 471044; e-mail f-dr@unitbv.ro):

BUJDOIU, N., Sociology, Philosophy and Law

CHIRIȚĂ, R., Sociology, Philosophy and Law

POENARU, E., Sociology, Philosophy and Law

Faculty of Materials Science and Engineering (Str. Colina Universității 1, 500068 Braşov; tel. (268) 471626; e-mail f-sim@unitbv.ro):

ANDREESCU, F. G., Welding Equipment

BEJAN, V., Technology of Fabrication and Maintenance of Equipment

BOT, D., Heating Equipment, Foundry Technology

CÂNDEA, V. N., Welding Technology

CHICHERNEA, F., Technological Equipment and Materials Science

CIOBANU, I., Fundamentals of Foundry

CONSTANTINESCU, A., Foundry Equipment

CRIŞAN, A., Technological Equipment and Materials Science

DUȚĂ-CAPRĂ, A., Chemistry

EFTIMIE, L., Welding Technology

ENE, V., Special Proceedings for Foundry
FĂTU, S., Study of Metals
FLOREA, R. G., Welding Technology
GEAMĂN, V., Technological Equipment and Materials Science
GIACOMELLI, I., Equipment and Technologies for Thermal Treatments
IOVANĂȘ, R., Technology of Welding by Pressing
LUCA, V., Study of Metals
MACHEDON, T., Welding Equipment, Non-Destructive Testing, Hydraulic and Pneumatic Engines
MARKOS, Z., Welding Technology
MILOȘAN, I.
MUNTEANU, A., Thermal Treatments and Heat Processing
NOVAC, GH., Welding Equipment
PAȚACHIA, S., Chemistry
POPA, A., Technology of Plastic Deformation
POPESCU, R. M., Welding Technology
SAMOILĂ, C., Furnaces and Equipment for Heating
SCOROBEȚIU, L., Fundamentals of Welding Processes
ȘERBAN, C., Study of Metals
ȚICĂ, E.-R., Chemistry
ȚIEREAN, M., Welding Technology
TRIF, N., Mechanization, Automation and Robots for Welding Processing
TUDORAN, P., Study of Metals
VARGA, B., Technological Equipment
VEȚELEANU, A.

Faculty of Mathematics and Computer Science (Str. Iuliu Maniu 50, 500091 Brașov; tel. (268) 414016; e-mail f-mate-info@unitbv.ro):

ATANASIU, GH., Geometry
CIUREA, E., Computing
COCAN, M., Computing
LUPU, M., Differential Equations
MARIN, M., Differential Equations
MARINESCU, C., Differential Equations
MUNTEANU, GH., Differential Equations
ORMAN, G., Mathematical Analysis and Probability
OVESEA, H., Mathematical Analysis and Probability
PASCU, N., Mathematical Analysis and Probability
PESCAR, V., Geometry
PITIȘ, GH., Differential Equations
RADOMIR, I., Mathematical Analysis and Probability
SCHEIBER, E., Computing
TIȚA, N., Mathematical Analysis and Probability

Faculty of Mechanical Engineering (Str. Politehnicii 1, 500024 Brașov; tel. (268) 474761; e-mail f-im@unitbv.ro):

ABĂITĂNCEI, D., Automotive Technology
BĂCANU, GH., Physics
BALCU, I., Strength of Materials and Vibration
BENCHE, V., Heat Engineering and Fluid Mechanics
BIȚ, C. S., Strength of Materials and Vibration
BOBESCU, GH., Automotive Technology
BOLFA, T. E., Strength of Materials and Vibration
BRĂTUCU, GH., Agricultural and Food-processing Machinery
CÂMPIAN, V., Automotive Technology
CÂNDEA, I., Mechanics
CHIRIACESCU, T. S., Strength of Materials and Vibration
CHIRU, A., Automotive Technology
CIOFOAIA, V., Strength of Materials and Vibration
CIOLAN, GH., Automotive Technology
COFARU, C., Automotive Technology
CONSTANTIN, F., Mechanics
CRISTEA, L., Precision Engineering and Mechatronics

CURTU, T. I., Strength of Materials and Vibration
DELIU, GH., Mechanics
DUMITRIU, A., Precision Engineering and Mechatronics
FETCU, D., Heat Engineering and Fluid Mechanics
GOIA, A. I., Strength of Materials and Vibration
IONESCU, E. GH., Precision Engineering and Mechatronics
IONESCU, E., Agricultural and Food-processing Machinery
MUNTEANU, GH. M., Strength of Materials and Vibration
MUREȘAN, M., Heat Engineering and Fluid Mechanics
NAGY, T., Automotive Technology
NĂSTĂSOIU, S., Automotive Technology
OLTEANU, C., Precision Engineering and Mechatronics
POPA, V. A., Strength of Materials and Vibration
POPARAD, H., Precision Engineering and Mechatronics
POPESCU, S., Agricultural and Food-processing Machinery
POSTELNICU, A., Heat Engineering and Fluid Mechanics
PREDA, I., Automotive Technology
RADU, GH. A., Automotive Technology
RADU, N. GH., Strength of Materials and Vibration
ROȘCA, I. C., Strength of Materials and Vibration
ROȘCA, I. C., Precision Mechanics and Mechatronics
RUS, F., Agricultural and Food-processing Machinery
SĂLĂJAN, C., Automotive Technology
SECARA, E. M., Mechanics
SEITZ, N., Automotive Technology
ȘERBĂNOIU, N., Heat Engineering and Fluid Mechanics
SOARE, I., Automotive Technology
ȘOVA, M., Heat Engineering and Fluid Mechanics
ȘOVA, V., Heat Engineering and Fluid Mechanics
SZÁVA, I., Strength of Materials and Vibration
ȚANE, N., Agricultural and Food-processing Machinery
TOFAN, M., Mechanics
ȚUREA, N., Automotive Technology
ULEA, M., Strength of Materials and Vibration
UNGUREANU, V. B., Heat Engineering and Fluid Mechanics
VEȘTEMEAN, N., Heat Engineering and Fluid Mechanics
VLASE, S., Mechanics

Faculty of Medicine (Str. 6 N. Bălcescu 56t, 500019 Brașov; tel. (268) 412185; e-mail f-med@unitbv.ro):

COMAN, G., Preclinical Medicine
LEAȘU, T., Specialized Medicine
RĂDOI, M., Internal Medicine
RADU, I., Preclinical Medicine

Faculty of Music (Str. Andrei Saguna 2, Brașov; tel. (268) 478884; e-mail f-muzica@unitbv.ro):

BICA, N., Teaching Music
DRĂGULIN, S. D., Instrumental Interpretation
IACOBESCU, L., Instrumental Interpretation

Faculty of Silviculture and Forest Engineering (Șirul Beethoven 1, 500123 Brașov; tel. (268) 475705; e-mail f-silvic@unitbv.ro):

ALEXANDRU, V. M., Forest Exploitation
BELDEANU, E., Forest Exploitation
BOȘ, N.
CHIȚEA, GH., Biostatistics
CIORTUZ, I., Silviculture

CIUBOTARU, A., Forest Exploitation
CLINCIU, I., Flood Control
COSTEA, C.
DANCIU, M. A., Silviculture
FLORESCU, I. I., Silviculture
IONAȘCU, GH., Forest Exploitation
KISS, A., Topography
LEAHU, I., Dendrometry
MARCU, M., Silviculture
MARCU, O., Silviculture
NEGRUȚIU, A., Silviculture
NEGRUȚIU, F., Silviculture
OLTEANU, N., Forest Exploitation
OPREA, I., Forest Exploitation
PARASCAN, D., Silviculture
POPESCU, I., Forest Exploitation
RUSU, A.
SIMON, D., Silviculture
ȘOFLETEA, N., Silviculture
SPÂRCHEZ, GH., Silviculture
TAMAȘ, Ș., Operations Research
TÂRZIU, D., Silviculture
UNGUREANU, Ș., Forest Exploitation

Faculty of Technological Engineering and Industrial Management (Str. Colina Universității 1, 500068 Brașov; tel. (268) 414690; e-mail f-itmi@unitbv.ro):

ALEXANDRU, P., Mechanisms
BOBANCU, Ș., Mechanisms
BONCOI, GH., Automatic Machine Tools
BRANA, M. A., Descriptive Geometry and Technical Drawing
BUZATU, C., Automation of Technological Processes
CALEFARIU, G.
CHIȘU, E., Machine Components
CIOBOTĂ, M., Precision Mechanics
CRUCIAT, P., Technical Measurements
DAJ, I., Machine Components
DEACONESCU, T.
DELIU, M.
DIACONESCU, D. V., Mechanisms
DIȚU, V., Car Construction Technology
DUDIȚĂ, F., Mechanisms
DUMITRU, S., Physics
GAGIONEA, E. L., Descriptive Geometry and Technical Drawing
INȚA, I., Physics
IVAN, M., Machine Tools and Dimensional Control
IVAN, N. V., Machine Engineering Technology
JULA, A., Machine Elements
LUPULESCU, N.-B., Car Construction Technology
MĂNIUȚ, P.
MĂRĂSCU KLEIN, V., Unconventional Materials, Computer-Aided Production Systems Design
MARTINESCU, I., Technology of Cold-pressing
MOGAN, GH. L., Machine Elements
MOLDOVEAN, GH., Machine Elements
NEDELCU, A.
OBACIU, GH., Electric Drive and Machine Tools
PĂUNESCU, T., Car Construction Technology
POPESCU, I., Technical Measurement and Tolerance
ROȘCA, D. M., Metal-cutting Theory
SĂVESCU, D., Machine Elements
SECARĂ, GH., Metal Cutting, Tool Design
SOFONEA, L., Physics
STAREȚU, I., Machine Components
STROE, I., Machine Components
TALABĂ, D., Machine Components
TĂNĂSESCU, I., Machine Elements and Mechanisms
TUREAC, I., Machines for Processing by Deformation
URSUȚIU, D., Physics
VĂSII-ROȘCULEȚ, S., Design of Devices
VELICU, D., Descriptive Geometry and Technical Drawing

VIŞA, I., Mechanisms

Faculty of Wood Engineering (Str. Colina Universităţii 1, 500036 Braşov; tel. (268) 415315; e-mail f-ilemn@unitbv.ro):

BĂDESCU, L. A.-M., Wood-processing Machinery
BARBU, M. C., Wood Technology
BUDĂU, G., Wood-processing Machinery
CISMARU, I., Wood Technology
DOGARU, V., Wood-processing Machinery
ISTRATE, V., Wood Technology
LĂZĂRESCU, C., Wood-processing Machinery
MIHAI, D., Wood Technology
MITIŞOR, A., Wood Technology
NĂSTASE, V., Wood Technology
PETROVICI, V., Wood Technology
ŢĂRAN, N., Wood-processing Machinery
TUDOR, E., Wood-processing Machinery
ZLATE, GH., Wood Technology

UNIVERSITATEA 'VALAHIA' DIN TÂRGOVIŞTE
(Valahia University of Târgovişte)

Blvd Regele Carol I 2, 130024 Târgovişte

Telephone: (245) 206101
E-mail: rectorat@valahia.ro
Internet: www.valahia.ro

Founded 1989

Rector: Dr CALIN D. OROS
Vice-Rector for Education and Quality Assurance: Dr LAURA MONICA GORGHIU
Vice-Rector for Institutional Devt and Int. Relations: Dr LEONARDO BADEA
Vice-Rector for Social and Students Affairs: Ing. Dr IOAN CORNELIU SALISTEANU
Vice-Rector for Univ. Research and Creation: Prof. Dr GABRIELA TEODORESCU
Dir for Library: Dr AGNES ERICH

Number of teachers: 400
Number of students: 11,000

DEANS

Faculty of Economics: Prof. Dr ION STEGAROIU
Faculty of Environmental Engineering and Biotechnology: Prof. Ing. Dr STEFANIA IORDACHE
Faculty of Electrical Engineering: Ing. Dr HENRI-GEORGE COANDA
Faculty of Humanities: Prof. Dr CONSTANTIN PEHOIU
Faculty of Law and Social-Political Sciences: Dr LIVIA MOCANU
Faculty of Materials Engineering, Mechatronics and Robotics: Ing. Dr VASILE BRATU
Faculty of Sciences and Arts: Dr LAURA MONICA GORGHIU
Faculty of Theology and Educational Sciences: Prof. Dr MARIAN VILCIU

UNIVERSITATEA 'VASILE ALECSANDRI' DIN BACĂU
('Vasile Alecsandri' University Of Bacău)

Calea Maraşeşti 157, 600115 Bacău

Telephone: (234) 542411
E-mail: rector@ub.ro
Internet: www.ub.ro

Founded 1961 as Pedagogical Institute, present status 1990, present name 2009
State control
Languages of instruction: English, French, Romanian
Academic year: October to July

Rector: Prof. Ing. Dr VALENTIN NEDEFF
Vice-Rector for Economic and Quality Strategies: Dr CORNELIA-MARCELA DANU
Vice-Rector for Educational Programmes and Student activities: Prof. Dr ADRIANA-GERTRUDA ROMEDEA
Vice-Rector for Ethics and Univ. Image: Prof. Dr CĂTĂLINA ABABEI

Vice-Rector for Research Programmes and Int. Relations: Dr ELENA NECHITA
Registrar and Chief Sec.: ADRIAN APĂVĂLOAIE
Chief Libarian: CECILIA ANGHEL

Library of 176,830 vols, 58,459 periodicals
Number of teachers: 240
Number of students: 5,792 (4,691 undergraduate, 1,028 postgraduate, 31 doctoral, 42 postgraduate specialization)

Publications: Actes du Colloque Franco-Roumain de Chimie Appliquee (COFrRoCA), Cultural Perspectives—Journal for Literary and British Cultural Studies in Romania (1 a year), Gymnasium (2 a year), Interstudia (2 a year), Journal of Engineering Studies and Research (4 a year), Journal of Innovation in Psychology, Education and Didactics, Junimea studenţească băcăuană, Kinetostud, Reste a voir, Ro-Brit, Scientific Study & Research—Chemistry and Chemical Engineering, Biotechnology, Food Industry (4 a year), Scientific Studies and Research—Economic Sciences series, Scientific Studies and Research—Mathematics (12 a year), Scientific Studies and Research—Series Mathematics and Informatics (2 a year), Studenţimea băcăuană, Studii şi Cercetări—Seria Biologie (2 a year), Voxstud

DEANS

Faculty of Economic Sciences: Prof. Dr OVIDIU-LEONARD TURCU
Faculty of Engineering: Prof. Dr Ing. CAROL SCHNAKOVSZKY
Faculty of Letters: Dr SIMINA MASTACAN
Faculty of Movement, Sport and Health Sciences: Dr DĂNUŢ-NICU MÂRZA DĂNILĂ
Faculty of Sciences: Prof. Dr MIHAI TĂLMACIU

Technological Universities

UNIVERSITATEA DE ARHITECTURA ŞI URBANISM 'ION MINCU'
('Ion Mincu' University of Architecture and Urbanism)

Academiei St 18–20, 010014 Bucharest

Telephone: (21) 3077112
E-mail: rectorat.uauim@gmail.com
Internet: www.uauim.ro

Founded 1892 by the Romanian Soc. of Architects as a private school of architecture, present name and status 2000
State control
Academic year: October to July

Rector: Prof. Dr ZENO BOGDANESCU
Vice-Rector for Int. Cooperation: Dr BEATRICE-GABRIELA JOGER
Vice-Rector for Research, Devt and Scientific Innovation: Prof. Dr ANA-MARIA DABIJA
Dir for Library: GABRIELA TABACU

Library of 200,000 vols, 70 periodicals
Number of teachers: 270 (incl. 150 part-time)
Number of students: 3,300

Publications: Analele Arhitecturii, Arhitext Design

DEANS

Faculty of Architecture: Dr MARIAN MOICEANU
Faculty of Interior Architecture: Dr MARIUS MARCU-LAPADAT
Faculty of Urbanism: Dr TIBERIU FLORESCU

UNIVERSITATEA DE MEDICINĂ ŞI FARMACIE 'CAROL DAVILA' DIN BUCURESTI
(University of Medicine and Pharmacy 'Carol Davila' from Bucharest)

Dionisie Lupu St 37, 020021 Bucharest

Telephone: (21) 3180727
E-mail: rectorat@umf.ro

Internet: www.umfcaroldavila.ro

Founded 1857 as Institutul de Medicina si Farmacie, current name adopted 1990
State control
Languages of instruction: English, Romanian

Rector: Acad. IOANEL SINESCU
Vice-Rector for Higher Education and Masters Degree: Prof. Dr ECATERINA IONESCU
Vice-Rector for Int. Relations: Prof. Dr ION FULGA
Vice-Rector for Postgraduate Education: Prof. Dr RUXANDRA IONESCU
Vice-Rector for Scientific Research: Prof. Dr DRAGOS VINEREANU
Vice-Rector for Student Affairs: Prof. Dr CATALIN CIRSTOIU

Library of 580,639 vols
Number of teachers: 1,840
Number of students: 9,300

Publication: Journal of Medicine and Life (4 a year, in English, online, www.medandlife.ro)

DEANS

Faculty of Dentistry: Prof. Dr ALEXANDRU BUCUR
Faculty of Medicine: Prof. Dr DOINA ANCA PLESCA
Faculty of Midwifery and Nurses: Prof. Dr PETRU ARMEAN
Faculty of Pharmacy: Prof. Dr DUMITRU LUPULIASA

UNIVERSITATEA DE MEDICINĂ ŞI FARMACIE DIN CRAIOVA
(University of Medicine and Pharmacy—Craiova)

Str. Petru Rareş 2, 200349 Craiova

Telephone: (351) 443561
E-mail: rectorat@umfcv.ro
Internet: www.umfcv.ro

Founded 1998
Academic year: October to July

Rector: Prof. Dr ION ROGOVEANU
Vice-Rector for Academic Affairs, Postgraduate Education and Quality Assurance: Prof. Dr AUGUSTINE CUPSA
Vice-Rector for Institutional Management, Students and Residents: Prof. Dr MIHAI-RAUL POPESCU
Vice-Rector for Scientific Research and Int. Relations: Dr ANDREI ADRIAN TICA
Head of Library Services: Prof. ALINA CROITORU

Library of 70,000 vols, 59 periodicals
Number of teachers: 450
Number of students: 4,500

Publications: Craiova Medicala (4 a year), Journal of Pharmacology (4 a year), Romanian Journal of Morphology and Embriology

DEANS

Faculty of Dentistry: Prof. Dr VERONICA MERCUT
Faculty of Medicine: Dr CRISTIAN GHEONEA
Faculty of Nursing and Midwives: IULIANA NICOLESCU
Faculty of Pharmacy: Prof. Dr JOHNY NEAMTU

PROFESSORS

Faculty of Dentistry:

BANIŢĂ, I.
CALOTĂ, F.
MANOLESCU, I.
MERCUŢ, V.
PETCU, P.
STOICESCU, I.
SURPĂTEANU, M.

Faculty of Medicine:

ANUŞCA, D.
BADEA, M.

BĂDULESCU, F.
BISTRICEANU, M.
BRĂILA, M.
BUTEICĂ, E.
CÂRSTEA, D.
CERNEA, N.
CIUREA, P.
CIUREA, T.
CRĂIŢOIU, S.
CUPŞA, A.
DINCĂ, M.
ENĂCHESCU, V.
GĂMAN, G.
GEORGESCU, E.
GEORGESCU, I.
IANCĂU, M.
IONESCU, D.
IONIŢA, E.
MARINESCU, D.
MIXICH, F.
MOGOANTĂ, L.
MOGOŞ, D.
MOŢA, E.
MOŢA, M.
NOVAC, L.
PLEŞEA, I.
POPESCU, R.
PREJBEANU, I.
ROGOVEANU, I.
ROŞU, A.
ROŞU, L.
SABETAY, C.
SĂFTOIU, A.
SBÂRCEA, V.
SIMIONESCU, C.
STANCIU, P.
STOICA, Z.
TĂRÂŢĂ, M.
TOMA, I.
UDRIŞTOIU, T.
VASILE, I.
VRABETE, M.
ZAHARIA, C.
ZĂVOI, R.

Faculty of Midwifery and Nursing:
MERCUŢ, D.
NICOLESCU, I.
TRAŞCĂ, E.

Faculty of Pharmacy:
AVRAMESCU, C.
BĂNICERU, M.
GOFIŢA, E.
GORUNESCU, F.
NEAMŢU, J.
PISOSCHI, C.
RADU, S.
TIŢA, I.

UNIVERSITATEA DE MEDICINĂ ŞI FARMACIE 'GR. T. POPA' IASI
(University of Medicine and Pharmacy 'Gr. T. Popa')

Str.Universitatii 16, 700115 Iaşi

Telephone: (232) 267801
E-mail: rectorat@mail.umfiasi.ro
Internet: www.umfiasi.ro

Founded 1879
State control
Languages of instruction: English, French, Romanian
Academic year: October to July

Rector: Prof. Dr VASILE ASTARASTOAE
Vice-Rector for Bachelors and Masters Degree: Prof. Dr IOAN COSTEA
Vice-Rector for Basic Education: Prof. Dr ILEANA CORNELIA COJOCARU
Vice-Rector for Institutional Strategy, Academic Evaluation and Relationships with Student Organizations: Prof. Dr DRAGOS PIEPTU
Vice-Rector for Int. Relations: Prof. Dr MARIN BURLEA

Vice-Rector for Postgraduate and Continuing Training: Prof. Dr MARIA STAMATIN
Vice-Rector for Scientific Research: Prof. Dr ADRIAN COVIC
Chief Sec.: GEANINA CARMEN UNGUREANU
Dir for Library: Prof. VIORICA SCUTARIU
Library of 255,977 vols
Number of teachers: 900
Number of students: 8,290

DEANS

Faculty of Dentistry: Prof. Dr NORINA FORNA
Faculty of Medical Bioengineering: Dr DAN ZAHARIA
Faculty of Medicine: Prof. Dr DOINA AZOICAI
Faculty of Pharmacy: Prof. Dr MONICA HANCIANU

PROFESSORS

Faculty of Medical Bioengineering (Str. Kogalniceanu 9–13, Iaşi; tel. (232) 213573; e-mail pflocea@bioing.umfiasi.ro; internet www.umfiasi.ro):

APOSTOL, I., Clinical Physiology
BALTAG, O., Exact, Metrological and Informatics Sciences
CHIRIAC, H., Biomedical Engineering
DIACONU, I., Exact, Metrological and Informatics Sciences
GROSU, I., General and Applied Physics
PETRESCU, GH., General Management and Marketing
POEATA, I., Biomaterials and Techniques of Prosthetic Systems
UGLEA, C., Applied Chemistry and Physical Chemistry
UNGUREANU, M., Synthetic and Bioactive Substances

Faculty of Medicine (Str. Universitatii 16, 700115 Iaşi; tel. (232) 301615; e-mail gcuciureanu@medgen.umfiasi.ro; internet www.umfiasi.ro):

ALDEA, A. S., Thoracic Surgery
ANTOHE, D. S., Anatomy
ARSENESCU, C., Internal Medicine
ASTARASTOAIE, V., Forensic Medicine
BĂDESCU, A., Histology
BĂDESCU, M., Physiopathology
BALAN, G., Internal Medicine
BILD, E., Oncology and Radiotherapy
BOISTEANU, P., Psychiatry
BRĂNIŞTEANU, D., Physiology
BRUMARU, O., Paediatrics
BUIUC, D., Microbiology
CARASIEVICI, E., Immunology
CHIRIAC, R. M., Rheumatology and Balneophysiotherapy
CHIRIŢA, V., Psychiatry
CHISĂLIŢA, D., Ophthalmology
CIORNIA, T., Forensic Medicine
COLEV, V., Physiopathology
COMAN, G., Microbiology
COSOVANU, A., Internal Medicine
COSTĂCHESCU, GH., Obstetrics and Gynaecology
COSTINESCU, V., Otorhinolaryngology
COTRUTZ, C., Cell Biology
COTUŢIU, C., Histology
COVIC, M., Genetics
COVIC, M., Internal Medicine
DANIIL, C., Radiology
DATCU, G., Internal Medicine
DATCU, M. D., Internal Medicine
DIACONU, C., Surgery
DIMITRIU, A. G., Paediatrics
DRAGOMIR, C., Infant Care
DRAGOMIR, C., Surgery
DRAGOMIR, D., Obstetrics and Gynaecology
FRÎNCU, D. L., Anatomy
FRÎNCU, D. L., Physical Education
GAVĂT, V., Hygiene
GEORGESCU, G., Internal Medicine
GEORGESCU, N. M., Orthopaedics and Traumatology
GHEORGHIŢĂ, N., Biochemistry

GOŢIA, D. G., Paediatric Surgery
GOŢIA, S., Paediatrics
IANOVICI, N., Neurosurgery
IONESCU, C., History of Medicine
IVAN, A., Epidemiology
LUCA, M., Parasitology and Mycoses
LUCA, V., Infectious Diseases
LUCA, V., Physiopathology
MĂTĂSARU, S., Paediatrics
MIHAIESCU, T., Pneumopthisiology
MIHAILOVICI, M. S., Pathological Anatomy
MIHALACHE, C., Occupational Medicine
MIHALACHE, ST., Surgery
MOGOŞ, V., Endocrinology
MORARU, D., Paediatrics
MORARU, E., Paediatrics
MUNGIU, C. O., Pharmacology
PANDELE, G. I., Internal Medicine
PETRESCU, GH., Physiology
PETRESCU, Z., Dermatology
PETROVANU, R., Family Practice Medicine
PLAHTEANU, M., Forensic Medicine
PLEŞA, C., Surgery
POPESCU, D. C., Neurobiology
PRELIPCEAN, C., Internal Medicine
PRICOP, F., Obstetrics and Gynaecology
PRICOP, M., Obstetrics and Gynaecology
RADULESCU, D., Pathological Anatomy
RUSU, V., Biophysics
SINIŢCHI, G., Family Practice Medicine
SLĂTINEANU, S., Physiology
STAN, M., Internal Medicine
STANCIU, C., Internal Medicine
ŞTEFANACHE, F., Neurology
STOIAN, M., Surgery
STRATONE, A., Exploration Physiology
TÎRCOVEANU, E., Surgery
TOPOLICEANU, F., Exploration Physiology
UNGUREANU, G., Internal Medicine
ZAMFIR, M., Anatomy
ZBRANCA, E., Endocrinology

Faculty of Pharmacy (Str. Universitati 16, 700115 Iaşi; tel. (232) 301623; e-mail eonica@farmacie.umfiasi.ro; internet www.umfiasi.ro):

CARAMAN, C., Inorganic Chemistry
CUCIUREANU, R., Environmental Chemistry
DĂNILĂ, GH., Pharmaceutical Chemistry
DORNEANU, M., Organic Chemistry
DORNEANU, V., Analytical Chemistry
GAFIŢEANU, E., Pharmaceutical Technology
HRISCU, A., Pharmacodynamics
LAZAR, M., Drug Control
PĂDURARU, I., Pharmaceutical Biochemistry
PAVELESCU, M. D. G., Pharmacology
POPOVICI, I., Pharmaceutical Technology
PROCA, M., Toxicology
SCUTARIU, M. D., Anatomy and Physiology
STAN, M., Analytical Chemistry
STĂNESCU, U. H., Pharmacognosy
ŞTEFĂNESCU, E., Organic Chemistry

UNIVERSITATEA DE MEDICINA SI FARMACIE IULIU HATIEGANU CLUJ-NAPOCA
(Iuliu Haţieganu University of Medicine and Pharmacy Cluj-Napoca)

Str. Emil Isac 13, 400023 Cluj-Napoca

Telephone: (264) 406841
E-mail: rectoratumf@umfcluj.ro
Internet: www.umfcluj.ro

Founded 1872
State control
Languages of instruction: English, French, Romanian
Academic year: October to July (2 semesters)

Rector: Dr ALEXANDRU IRIMIE
Vice-Rector for Academic Evaluation and Quality Assurance: Prof. Dr DAN DUMITRASCU
Vice-Rector for Academic Management and Devt: Dr VALENTIN CERNEA

Vice-Rector for Residency and Post-Univ. Studies: Prof. Dr GRIGORE BACIUT
Vice-Rector for Scientific Research and Evaluation: Prof. Dr FELICIA LOGHIN
Vice-Rector for Teaching: Prof. Dr IOAN COMAN
Dir for Library: IOANA ROBU
Library of 300,000 vols
Number of teachers: 750
Number of students: 9,000
Publications: *Acta Dermatologica Transilvanica, Acta Neurologica Transilvanicae, Anuarul Universității, Applied Medical Informatics, Biology and Therapy of Cancer Cell, Chirurgia, Clujul Medical, Cosmetic Dentistry—Beauty and Science, Diabetes Management, Diabet, Nutritie, Risc Cardiometabolic, Journal of Clinical Anatomy and Embriology, Journal of Clinical Oncology, Journal of Gastrointestinal and Livers Diseases, Journal of Radiotherapy & Medical Oncology, Jurnalul de Diabet, Jurnalul Roman de Anestezie și Terapie Intensiva, Jurnalul Roman de Pediatrie, Medical Ultrasonography, Minimally Invasive Surgery, Obstetrica si Ginecologia, Palestrica Mileniului III—Civilizatie si sport, Pediatria.ro, Quo Vadis, Radiology and Medical Oncology, Revista de Recuperare, Medicina Fizica si Balneologie, Revista Romana de Chirurgie Rino-sinusala, Romanian Journal of Angiology and Vascular Surgery, Romanian Journal of Gastroenterology, Romanian Journal of Hand and Reconstructive Microsurgery, Romanian Journal of Pathology, The Heart, Transilvania Stomatologica*

DEANS

Faculty of Dental Medicine: Prof. Dr ALIN SERBĂNESCU
Faculty of Medicine: Prof. Dr ANCA DANA BUZOIANU
Faculty of Pharmacy: Dr GIANINA CRISAN

PROFESSORS

Faculty of Medicine:

ACALOVSCHI, I., Anaesthesiology and Intensive Care
ANDERCOU, A., Surgery
BADEA, R., Medical Imaging
BÂRSAN, M., Cardiology
BENGA, G., Cellular and Molecular Biology
BENGA, I., Paediatric Neurology
BOCȘAN, I., Epidemiology
BOLOSIU, H. D., Internal Medicine
CĂLUGĂRU, M., Ophthalmology
CĂPÂLNEANU, R., Cardiology
CÂRSTINA, D., Infectious Diseases
COCÂRLĂ, A., Occupational Health
COSTIN, N., Gynaecology
DEJICA, D., Clinical Immunology
DRAGHICI, A., Internal Medicine
DUNCEA, C., Internal Medicine
FUNARIU, GH., Surgery
GHERMAN, M., Nephrology
GHILEZAN, N., Oncology
GRIGORESCU-SIDO, F., Anatomy
GRIGORESCU-SIDO, P., Paediatrics
HANCU, N., Nutrition and Metabolic Diseases
IONUT, C., Hygiene
JEBELEANU, GH., Biochemistry
KORY, S., Neurology
LAZĂR, L., Oncology
LUCAN, M., Urology
MACREA, R., Paediatric Psychiatry
MAIER, N., Dermatology
MIU, N., Paediatrics
MUREȘAN, A., Physiology
NANULESCU, M., Paediatrics
OLINIC, N., Internal Medicine
OLINICI, C., Morphopathology
PARAIAN, N., Paediatric Surgery

PASCU, O., Gastroenterology
PLESCA-MANEA, L., Physiopathology
POPESCU, A., Neonatology
SANDOR, V., Pharmacology
SASCA, C., Microbiology
SURCEL, I. V., Gynaecology
ȚIGAN, S., Medical Informatics
TOADER RADU, M., Histology
TOMESCU, E., Otorhinolaryngology
TURDEANU, N., Surgery
VLAD, L., Surgery
ZAMORA, C., Pneumophthisiology
ZDRENGHEA, D., Cardiology

Faculty of Pharmacy:

BOJIȚĂ, M., Drug Control
COMAN, M., Drug Industry
LEUCUȚA, S., Pharmaceutical Technology
MOLDOVAN, M., Dermatopharmacy and Cosmeticology
ONIGA, I., Pharmacognosy
ONIGA, O., Pharmaceutical Chemistry
OPREAN, L., Inorganic Chemistry
POLICINENCU, C., Pharmaceutical Legislation, Marketing and Management
PRODAN, A., Informatics
SĂNDULESCU, R., Analytical Chemistry
TĂMAȘ, M., Pharmaceutical Botany
TĂRMURE, C., Biochemistry

Faculty of Stomatology:

BĂCUIȚ, G., Oral and Maxillofacial Surgery
BORZEA, D., Stomatological Propaedeutics
COCÂRLĂ, E., Orthodontics, Paedodontics
FILDAN, F., Oral Radiology
NEGUCIOIU, M., Dental Propaedeutics
POPA, S., Dental Propaedeutics
ROTARU, A., Oral and Maxillofacial Surgery

UNIVERSITATEA DE MEDICINĂ ȘI FARMACIE TIRGU MUREȘ

Gh. Marinescu, 38, 540139 Târgu Mureș
Telephone: (265) 215551
E-mail: rectorat@umftgm.ro
Internet: www.umftgm.ro
Founded 1948, present name and status 1991
State control
Languages of instruction: English, Hungarian, Romanian
Academic year: October to September
Rector: Prof. Dr LEONARD AZAMFIREI
Pro-Rector: Prof. Dr ANGELA BORDA
Pro-Rector: Prof. Dr DAN DOBREANU
Pro-Rector: Prof. Dr DANIELA DOBRU
Pro-Rector: Prof. Dr SZILÁGYI TIBOR
Chief Sec.: ELENA NISTOR
Head of Library: Dr NUȚIU FLORICA-ELISABETA
Library of 190,000 vols
Number of teachers: 420
Number of students: 3,530
Publication: *Revista de Medicină și Farmacie/Orvosi és Gyógyszerészeti Szemle* (4 a year)

DEANS

Faculty of Dentistry: Prof. Dr MARIANA PĂCURAR
Faculty of General Medicine: Dr TUDOR SORIN POP
Faculty of Pharmacy: Prof. Dr DANIELA-LUCIA MUNTEAN

PROFESSORS

Faculty of Dentistry:

KOVÁCS, D.
PĂCURAR, M., Paedodontics and Orthodontics
POPȘOR, S.
SZEKELY, M., Teeth and Dental Arches Morphology

Faculty of General Medicine:

ABRAM, Z., Hygiene
AZAMFIREI, L., Intensive Care

BANCU, S., Surgery
BOJA, R., Urology
BORDA, A., Histology
BRASSAI, Z., Internal Medicine
BRATU, D., Internal Medicine
BURIAN, M., Radiology
CARASCA, E., Internal Medicine
COPOTOIU, C., Surgery
DEAC, R., Cardiac Surgery
DRAȘOVEANU, C., Otorhinolaryngology
EGYED, Z., Pathomorphology
GEORGESCU, C., Internal Medcine
GEORGESCU, L., Physiotherapy
HOBAI, S., Biochemistry
INCZE, A., Internal Medicine
JUNG, I., Pathology
KIKELI, P. I., Family Medicine
KUN, I. Z., Endocrinology
MATHE, I., Biochemistry
MONEA, M., Pharmacology
MUNTEANU, I., Paediatrics
NAGY, Ö., Orthopaedics
NICOLAESCU, I., Biophysics
NIRESTEAN, A., Psychiatry
OLTEANU, G., Internal Medicine
SABĂU, M., Epidemiology
TOGĂNEL, R., Paediatrics

Faculty of Pharmacy:

DOGARU, M. T.
DUDUCZ, G., Medicinal Biotechnology
GYÉRESI, A., Pharmaceutical Chemistry
IMRE, S., Drugs Analysis
KINCSES-AJTAI, M., Toxicology
MUNTEAN, D. L., Drugs Analysis
OROIAN, S.

UNIVERSITATEA DE MEDICINĂ ȘI FARMACIE 'VICTOR BABEȘ' DIN TIMIȘOARA
(University of Medicine and Pharmacy 'Victor Babeș' Timisoara)

Piăta Eftimie Murgu 2, 300041 Timișoara
Telephone: (256) 293389
E-mail: rectorat@umft.ro
Internet: www.umft.ro
Founded 1945 as Institutul de Medicină
State control
Languages of instruction: English, French, Romanian
Academic year: October to July
Rector: Prof. Dr MARIUS RAICA
Pro-Rector for Academic Devt: Prof. Dr OCTAVIAN CRETU
Pro-Rector for Admin.-Social Affairs: Prof. Dr DAN V. POENARU
Pro-Rector for Didactic Activities: Prof. Dr SIMONA DRAGAN
Pro-Rector for Postgraduate Studies: Prof. Dr EUGEN BOIA
Head of Library: SANDOR ADRIANA
Library of 182,000 vols, 31,000 journals
Number of teachers: 770
Number of students: 5,500
Publications: *Cercetări Medico-Chirurgicale* (4 a year), *Fiziologia-Physiology* (4 a year), *Timișoara Medicală* (4 a year)

DEANS

Faculty of Dental Medicine: Prof. Dr MIHAI ROMINU
Faculty of Medicine: Prof. Dr ANASTASIU DORU
Faculty of Pharmacy: Dr CRISTINA DEHELEAN

UNIVERSITATEA DE ȘTIINȚE AGRICOLE ȘI MEDICINĂ VETERINARĂ A BANATULUI DIN TIMIȘOARA
(Banat's University of Agricultural Sciences and Veterinary Medicine, Timișoara)

Calea Aradului 119, 300645 Timișoara
Telephone: (256) 494023

E-mail: usabtm@mail.dnttm.ro
Internet: www.usab-tm.ro

Founded 1945, present name 1995
State control
Languages of instruction: English, Romanian
Academic year: September to September

Rector: Prof. Dr PAUL PÎRŞAN
Vice-Rector for Didactic Activities: Prof. GHEORGHE DĂRĂBUŞ
Vice-Rector for Economic and Social Problems: Prof. OLIMPIA IORDĂNESCU
Vice-Rector for Scientific Research: Prof. Dr TEODOR TRAŞCĂ
Gen. Admin. Dir: Dr TRAIAN BERAR
Librarian: Prof. CONSTANTIN MATEESCU

Library of 368,307 vols, 45 periodicals
Number of teachers: 330
Number of students: 7,040

Publications: *Didactica, Journal of Agroalimentary Processes and Technologies, Journal of Horticulture, Forestry and Biotechnology, Journal of Linguistic Studies, Research Journal of Agricultural Science, Scientific Papers: Animal Sciences and Biotechnologies, Scientific Papers: Farm Management, Scientific Papers of Young Researchers, Scientific Papers: Veterinary Medicine*

DEANS

Faculty of Agricultural Management: Prof. Dr VASILE GOŞA
Faculty of Agriculture: Prof. Dr COSMIN ALIN POPESCU
Faculty of Animal Science and Biotechnology: Prof. Dr NICOLAE PĂCALĂ
Faculty of Food Processing and Technology: Prof. Ing. Dr ADRIAN RIVIŞ
Faculty of Horticulture and Forestry: Prof. Dr ALIN DOBREI
Faculty of Veterinary Medicine: Prof. Dr VIOREL HERMAN

PROFESSORS

Faculty of Agricultural Management (Calea Aradului 119, 300645 Timisoara; tel. (256) 277005; e-mail fma.usabtm@mail.com):

CORNELIA, P., Growth of Products through Processing
IOAN, C., Rural Services
IOAN, P., Production Systems Modulation and Simulation
LIVIU, S., Production Management
NICOLETA, M., Agricultural Policies
PĂUN ION, O., Durable Development Management
VASILE, G., Financial Management

Faculty of Agriculture (Calea Aradului 119, 300645 Timişoara; tel. (256) 277007; e-mail secretariat_agro@usab-tm.ro):

ADRIAN, B., Phytopathology
DORIN, A., Land Evaluation
DORU, P., Entomology
FLORIAN, B., Biodiversity
GICU GABRIEL, A., Botanics
HORTENSIA, R., Policies and Environmental Depopulation Techniques
IACOB, B., General Ecology and Environmental Protection
IOANA, G., Entomology
RADU, P., Comparative Anatomy and Etology
SILVICA, O., Land Improvement
VALERIA, C., Topography

Faculty of Animal Science and Biotechnology (Calea Aradului 119, 300645 Timişoara; tel. (256) 277110; e-mail info@animalsci-tm.ro):

ADRIAN, G., Aquaculture
BENONI, L., Animal Hygiene
CORNELIA, V., Processing and Animal Products Control
DAN, D., Biotechnologies in Animal Nutrition

EUGENIE, G., Management
GHORGHE, N., Animal Husbandry and Nutrition
IOAN, P., Sheep Breeding Technologies
LAVINIA, A., Animal Nutrition
MARIAN, B., Breeding of Fur-Bearing Animals, Bees and Small Animals
NECULAI, D., Fodder Production and Preservation
NICOLAE, P., Animal Reproduction
STELIAN, A., Bovine Breeding Technologies

Faculty of Food Processing and Technology (Calea Aradului 119, 300645 Timişoara; tel. (256) 277004; e-mail secretariattpa@yahoo .com):

ADRIAN, C., Organic Chemistry
ADRIAN, R., Food Contaminants
CONSTANTIN, M., Applied Physics
DOREL, P., Physical and Coloidal Chemistry
ERSILIA, A., Vegetable Origins Food Technologies
IONEL-VASILE, J., Food Industry General Technologies
IOSIF-IOAN, G., Agro-alimentary Products Analysis
MIHAI, D., Food Quality Control
TEODOR-IOAN, T., Food Industry Machines

Faculty of Horticulture and Forestry (Calea Aradului 119, 300645 Timişoara; tel. (256) 277006; e-mail hortimro@yahoo.com):

ALIN, D., Viticulture
ARSENIE, H., Special Vegetable Crops
AUREL, L., Agrotechnology
DAGMAR, V., Dendrology
DORICA, B., Industrial Biotechnologies
EMILIAM, M., Plant Improvement
GHORGHE, C., Soil Work Management
IRINA, P., Genetics
MARIA, B., Floriculture
MIHAELA, C., Genetics
OLIMPIA, I., Fruit Growing
RADU, A., Vegetable Physiology
SIMION, A., Soil Work Maintenance and Preparation Techniques
SORIN, C., Experimental Techniques
VIOREL, B., General Vegetable Crops

Faculty of Veterinary Medicine (Calea Aradului 119, 300645 Timişoara; tel. (256) 277008; e-mail office@fmvt.ro):

ALEXANDRA, T., Toxicology
CARMEN, G., Anatomy
CORNEL, I., Surgery Diseases
EMIL, T., Immunology
EUGENIU, C., Nutrition and Fodder Control
GHEORGHE, D., Parasitology
GHORGHE, B., Medical Genetics
HOREA, S., Physiology
HORIA, C., Reproduction, Obstetrics, Gynaecology
IOAN, A., Entomology
IOAN, O., Forensics
ION, O., Animal Biology and Ecology
MARIAN, C., Pathological Anatomy
MIHAI, D., Animal Protection
NICOLAE, C., Infectious Diseases
ROMEO, C., Pharmacology
TEODOR, M., Medical Pathology
VASILE, A., Reproduction, Obstetrics, Gynaecology
VIOREL, H., Infectious Diseases

UNIVERSITATEA DE ŞTIINŢE AGRICOLE ŞI MEDICINĂ VETERINARĂ CLUJ-NAPOCA
(University of Agricultural Sciences and Veterinary Medicine, Cluj-Napoca)

Calea Mănăştur 3–5, 400372 Cluj-Napoca
Telephone: (264) 596384
E-mail: contact@usamvcluj.ro
Internet: www.usamvcluj.ro

Founded 1869 as Institutul Agronomic, present name and status 1995

State control
Academic year: October to September

Rector: Prof. Dr DORU PAMFIL
Vice-Rector for Academic Affairs: Prof. Dr IOAN ROTAR
Vice-Rector for Institutional Devt: Prof. Dr AUGUSTIN VLAIC
Vice-Rector for Int. Relations: Dr ANDREI MIHALCA
Vice-Rector for Quality Assurance and Human Resource: Dr IOANA POP
Vice-Rector for Research: Prof. Dr CARMEN SOCACIU
Vice-Rector for Social and Student Problems: Dr ADRIAN OROS

Library of 170,000 vols, 10,000 documents
Number of teachers: 270
Number of students: 6,200

Publications: *Agriculture* (magazine), *Bulletin of USAMV Cluj Napoca, Agriculture series (B+), Bulletin of USAMV Cluj Napoca, Animal Science and Biotechnology series (B+), Bulletin of USAMV Cluj Napoca, Horticulture series (B+), Bulletin of USAMV Cluj Napoca, Veterinary Medicine series (B+), Clujul Medical Veterinar, Hops and Medical Plants* (magazine), *Index Seminum, Notulae Botanicae Horti Agrobotanici Cluj Napoca (ISI), Scientia parasitological*

DEANS

Faculty of Agriculture: Prof. Dr ROXANA VIDICAN
Faculty of Animal Science and Biotechnologies: Prof. Dr VIOARA MIRESAN
Faculty of Horticulture: Prof. Dr RADU SESTRAS
Faculty of Veterinary Medicine: Prof. Dr CORNEL CĂTOI

UNIVERSITATEA DE ŞTIINŢE AGRICOLE ŞI MEDICINĂ VETERINARĂ 'ION IONESCU DE LA BRAD' DIN IAŞI
('Ion Ionescu de la Brad' University of Agricultural Sciences and Veterinary Medicine of Iaşi)

Mihail Sadoveanu Alley 3, 700490 Iaşi
Telephone: (232) 213069
E-mail: rectorat@uaiasi.ro
Internet: www.uaiasi.ro

Founded 1912, present name 1996

Rector: Prof. Dr VASILE VÎNTU
Vice-Rector for Didactic Activity: Prof. Dr IOAN TENU
Vice-Rector for Institutional Devt: Prof. Dr PAUL CORNELIU BOISTEANU
Vice-Rector for Int. Relations and Student Affairs: Prof. Dr GHEORGHE SAVUŢA
Vice-Rector for Research Activity, Innovation and Technological Devt: Prof. Dr CONSTANTIN LEONTE
Head of Library: Prof. Dr GILDA ELEONORA DRĂGĂNESCU

Library of 112,597 vols, incl. 105,942 books and 6,655 periodicals
Number of teachers: 159
Number of students: 4,200

Publications: *Cercetari Agronomice in Moldova* (4 a year), *Lucrări Ştiinţifice Editura* (1 a year)

DEANS

Faculty of Agriculture: Prof. Dr TEODOR ROBU
Faculty of Animal Husbandry: Prof. Dr BENONE PĂSĂRIN
Faculty of Horticulture: Prof. Dr LUCIA DRAGHIA
Faculty of Veterinary Medicine: Prof. Dr LIVIU MIRON

UNIVERSITATEA DE ŞTIINŢE AGRONOMICE ŞI MEDICINĂ VETERINARĂ DIN BUCUREŞTI
(University of Agronomic Science and Veterinary Medicine in Bucharest)

Blvd Marasti 59, 011464 Bucharest
Telephone: (21) 3182266
E-mail: post@info.usamv.ro
Internet: www.usamv.ro

Founded 1852 as Institutul Agronomic 'N. Bălcescu', present name 1992
State control
Academic year: October to September (2 semesters)

Rector: Prof. Dr SORIN CÎMPEANU
Vice-Rector: Prof. Dr FLORIN STANICA
Vice-Rector: Dr GINA FINTINERU
Vice-Rector: Prof. Dr NICULAE DOBRESCU
Vice-Rector: Dr VASILICA STAN

Library: see under Libraries and Archives
Number of teachers: 500
Number of students: 4,573 (4,298 undergraduate, 275 postgraduate)
Publication: Lucrări Ştiinţifice (1 a year)

DEANS

Faculty of Agriculture: Prof. Dr COSTICĂ CIONTU
Faculty of Animal Science: Prof. Dr GHEORGHE EMIL MĂRGINEAN
Faculty of Biotechnologies: Prof. Dr PETRUTA CORNEA
Faculty of Horticulture: Prof. Dr DOREL HOZA
Faculty of Land Reclamation and Environmental Engineering: Dr RAZVAN TEODORESCU
Faculty of Management, Economic Engineering in Agriculture and Rural Devt: Prof. Dr TOMA ADRIAN DINU
Faculty of Veterinary Medicine: Prof. Dr GABRIEL PREDOI

UNIVERSITATEA MARITIMĂ DIN CONSTANŢA
(Constanta Maritime University)

Str. Mircea cel Batran 104, 900663 Constanţa
Telephone: (241) 664740
E-mail: info@imc.ro
Internet: www.cmu-edu.eu

Founded 1990, present name and status 2000
State control
Languages of instruction: English, Romanian
Academic year: October to June

Rector: Dr VIOLETA CIUCUR
Vice-Rector for Institutional Devt and Int. Relations: Prof. Dr CORNEL PANAIT
Vice-Rector for Research and Scientific Innovation: Dr EMIL OANTA
Librarian: RALUCA TARACHIU

Library of 71,000 vols, 20 periodicals
Number of teachers: 100
Number of students: 6,400

Publications: Constanta Maritime University Annals (1 a year, online, www.cmu-edu.eu/anale/anale_engleza/anale.html), Ecozoom, Journal of Maritime Technology and Environment (2 a year, online, www.cmu-edu.eu/jmte), Journal of Maritime Transport, Naval Transport

DEANS

Faculty of Naval Electromechanics: Prof. Ing. Dr GEORGE BORDEA
Faculty of Navigation and Naval Transport: Dr COSTEL STANCA

UNIVERSITATEA 'POLITEHNICA' DIN BUCUREŞTI
(University Politehnica of Bucharest)

Splaiul Independenţei 313, Sector 6, 060042 Bucharest
Telephone: (21) 4029100
E-mail: relatii.publice@upb.ro
Internet: www.pub.ro

Founded 1818, present name 1992
State control
Academic year: October to July (2 semesters)

Rector: MIHNEA COSTOIU
Pro-Rector: Prof. Ing. Dr CLAUDIA POPESCU
Pro-Rector: Prof. Ing. Dr GEORGE DARIE
Pro-Rector: Prof. Ing. Dr GIGEL PARASCHIV
Chancellor: Prof. Ing. Dr IULIAN RIPOSAN
Pro-Rector: Prof. Ing. Dr TUDOR PRISECARU
Chief Admin. Officer: MIHAI COROCAESCU
Dir for Library: Ing. Dr CRISTINA ALBU

Library: see under Libraries and Archives
Number of teachers: 1,600
Number of students: 22,000

Publication: The Scientific Bulletin (in 4 series)

DEANS

Faculty of Aerospace Engineering: Prof. Dr VIRGIL STANCIU
Faculty of Applied Chemistry and Materials Science: Prof. Ing. Dr HORIA IOVU
Faculty of Applied Sciences: Prof. Dr VASILE IFTODE
Faculty of Automatic Control and Computer Science: Prof. Ing. Dr ADINA MAGDA FLOREA
Faculty of Biotechnical Systems Engineering: Prof. Ing. Dr GHEORGHE VOICU
Faculty of Electrical Engineering: Prof. Ing. Dr VALENTIN NAVRAPESCU
Faculty of Electronics, Telecommunications and Information Technology: Prof. Ing. Dr CRISTIAN NEGRESCU
Faculty of Engineering in Foreign Languages: Prof. Ing. Dr ADRIAN VOLCEANOV
Faculty of Engineering and Management of Technological Systems: Prof. Ing. Dr CRISTIAN VASILE DOICIN
Faculty of Entrepreneurship, Business Engineering and Management: Prof. Dr CRISTIAN NICULESCU
Faculty of Material Science and Engineering: Ing. Dr NICOLAE GHIBAN
Faculty of Mechanical Engineering and Mechatronics: Prof. Ing. Dr ALEXANDRU DOBROVICESCU
Faculty of Medical Engineering: Prof. Dr ALEXANDRU MOREGA (Head)
Faculty of Power Engineering: Prof. Ing. Dr CONSTANTIN BULAC
Faculty of Transports: Prof. Ing. Dr IULIAN BADESCU

PROFESSORS

Faculty of Aerospace Engineering (George Polizu St 1–7, Sector 1, 011061 Bucharest; tel. (21) 4023812; internet aero.pub.ro):

BERBENTE, C., Aircraft Engineering
GĂLETUŞE, S., Aircraft Engineering
STANCIU, V., Aircraft Engineering

Faculty of Applied Chemistry and Materials Science (Polizu St 1–7, Bucharest; tel. (21) 4023927; internet www.chim.pub.ro):

ANDRONESCU, E., Silicate and Oxide Compounds Chemistry
BANCIU, M., Organic Chemistry
BOZGA, GH., Chemical Reactors
CONSTANTINESCU, I., Inorganic Chemical Technology
DIMONIE, M., Polymer Science
FILIPESCU, L., Inorganic Chemical Technology
GEANĂ, D., Physical Chemistry
GEORGESCU, M., Silicate and Oxide Compounds Chemistry

GURAN, C., Inorganic Chemistry
JINESCU, GH., Chemical Engineering
JITARU, I., Inorganic Chemistry
MEGHEA, A., Physical Chemistry
MUNTEAN, M., Silicate and Oxide Compounds Chemistry
RADU, C., Management in the Chemical Industry
RADU, D., Silicate and Oxide Compounds Chemistry
ROŞCA, S., Organic Chemistry
TARABAŞAN, C., Dyes
VASILESCU, D. S., Polymer Science
VIŞAN, T., Physical Chemistry and Electrochemical Technology
WOINAROSCHY, E. A., Chemical Engineering

Faculty of Automatic Control and Computer Science (Splaiul Independenţei 313, Sector 6, 060042 Bucharest; tel. (21) 4029494; e-mail decanat@acs.pub.ro; internet acs.pub.ro):

ATHANASIU, I., Computer Science
BORANGIU, T., Robotics
CRISTEA, V., Computer Science
CUPCEA, N., Computer Science
DUMITRACHE, I., Control Engineering
GIUMALE, C., Computer Science
ILIESCU, S., Control Engineering
IONESCU, T., Control Engineering
IORGA, V., Computer Science
MOISA, T., Computer Science
NIŢU, C., Control Engineering
PETRESCU, A., Computer Science
POPEEA, C., Control Engineering
POPESCU, D., Control Engineering
STANESCU, A., Control Engineering
TĂPUŞ, N., Computer Science

Faculty of Biotechnical Systems Engineering (Splaiul Independenţei 313, Sector 6, 060042 Bucharest; tel. (21) 4029649; internet isb.pub.ro):

DAVID, L., Agricultural Machines
MURAD, E., Agricultural Machines
PAUNESCU, I., Agricultural Machines

Faculty of Electrical Engineering (Splaiul Independenţei 313, Sector 6, 060042 Bucharest; tel. (21) 4029149; e-mail inginerie.electrica@upb.ro; internet www.electro.pub.ro):

CRĂCIUNESCU, A., Drive Systems
CRISTEA, P., Basic Electrical Engineering
FLUERAŞU, C., Basic Electrical Engineering
GALAN, N., Electrical Machines
GAVRILĂ, H., Basic Electrical Engineering
GOLOVANOV, C., Theory and Design of Electrical Apparatus
HĂNŢILĂ, I. F., Basic Electrical Engineering
IOAN, C. D., Basic Electrical Engineering
IONESCU, F., Theory and Design of Electrical Apparatus
MĂGUREANU, R., Micromachines and Drive Systems
MOREGA, AL., Electrical Materials
NOŢINGHER, P., Electrical Materials
POPESCU, M. O., Theory and Design of Electrical Apparatus
SPINEI, F., Basic Electrical Engineering
TĂNĂSESCU, F., Electrical Engineering
TOMESCU, F., Basic Electrical Engineering
TRUŞCĂ, V., Theory and Design of Electrical Apparatus

Faculty of Electronics, Telecommunications and Information Technology (Iuliu Maniu Blvd 1–3, Sector 6, 061071 Bucharest; tel. (21) 4024618; e-mail decanat@electronica.pub.ro; internet www.electronica.pub.ro):

BĂNICĂ, I., Telecommunications
BODEA, M., Electronic Devices and Circuits
BORCOCI, E., Telecommunications
BREZEANU, GH., Electronic Devices and Circuits
BURILEANU, L., Telecommunications
BUZULOIU, V., Information Theory

CONSTANTIN, I., Telecommunications
DASCĂLU, D., Electronic Devices and Circuits
DRAGULANESCU, N., Reliability
DRAGULIMISCU, M., Reliability
IANCU, O., Reliability
LĂZĂRESCU, V., Information Theory
MANOLESCU, A., Electronic Devices and Circuits
MANOLESCU, A. M., Electronic Devices and Circuits
PROFIRESCU, M., Electronic Devices and Circuits
RUSU, A., Electronic Devices and Circuits
STRUNGARU, R., Medical Engineering
SVASTA, P., Reliability

Faculty of Engineering and Management of Technological Systems (Splaiul Independenţei 313, Sector 6, 060042 Bucharest; tel. (21) 4029302; internet www.imst.pub.ro):

ANTONESCU, P., Mechanism Theory
AURITE, T., Machine Tools
CONSTANTINESCU, I., Strength of Materials
DORIN, A., Machine Tools
GHEORGHE, M., Machine-Building Technology
ILIESCU, N., Strength of Materials
ISPAS, C., Machine Tools
MINCIU, C., Machine Tools
NEAGU, C., Machine-Building Technology
POPESCU, I., Machine-Building Technology
RADEŞ, M., Strength of Materials
ZGURĂ, GH., Technology of Materials

Faculty of Material Science and Engineering (Splaiul Independenţei 313, Sector 6, 060042 Bucharest; tel. (21) 4029624; e-mail decanat@sim.pub.ro; internet www.sim.pub.ro):

BOJIN, D., Metallurgy of Non-Ferrous Metals
BRATU, C., Forge and Foundry Technology
BUNEA, D., Forge and Foundry Technology
COJOCARU, M., Metallurgy of Non-Ferrous Metals
MOLDOVAN, P., Metallurgy of Non-Ferrous Metals
PANAIT, N., Metallurgy of Non-Ferrous Metals
RIPOŞAN, I., Forge and Foundry Technology
TALOI, D., Metallurgy of Non-Ferrous Metals
ZAMFIR, S., Metallurgy of Non-Ferrous Metals

Faculty of Mechanical Engineering and Mechatronics (Splaiul Independenţei 313, Sector 6, 060042 Bucharest; tel. (21) 4029310; internet www.mecanica.pub.ro):

ALEXANDRESCU, N., Fine Mechanics
BRĂTIANU, C., Thermomechanical Equipment
JINESCU, V., Thermomechanical Equipment
MARINESCU, M., Thermodynamics
MICU, C., Fine Mechanics
MIHAIESCU, L., Thermomechanical Equipment
PANA, C., Internal Combustion Engines
PASCOVICI, M., Machine Elements
PASCU, A., Fine Mechanics
PETRESCU, S., Thermodynamics
TUDOR, A., Machine Elements

Faculty of Power Engineering (Splaiul Independenţei 313, Sector 6, 060042 Bucharest; tel. (21) 4029322; e-mail facultatea.energetica@gmail.com; internet www.energ.pub.ro):

ATHANASOVICI, V., Electric Power Plants
BADEA, A., Electric Power Plants
COATU, S., High Voltage Technology
CRISTESCU, D., High Voltage Technology
EREMIA, M., High Voltage Technology
GOLOVANOV, N., High Voltage Technology
HURDUBETIU, S., High Voltage Technology
IONESCU, D. C., Reliability

ISBĂŞOIU, E., Hydraulics
NISTREANU, V., Hydraulics
PANAITESCU, V., Hydraulics
POSTOLACHE, P., High Voltage Technology
ROBESCU, D. N., Hydraulics
SETEANU, I., Hydraulics
VASILIU, N., Hydraulics

Faculty of Transports (Splaiul Independenţei 313, Sector 6, 060042 Bucharest; tel. (21) 4029568; e-mail transport@upb.ro; internet transport.pub.ro):

ALEXANDRESCU, C., Remote Controls and Electronics
FRĂŢILĂ, GH., Automotive Engineering
NEGRUŞ, E., Automotive Engineering
RAICU, Ş., Transport Engineering
SEBEŞAN, I., Railway Vehicles
STOICESCU, A., Automotive Engineering
TANASUICA, I., Transport Engineering

UNIVERSITATEA 'POLITEHNICA' DIN TIMIŞOARA

Piaţa Victoriei 2, 300006 Timişoara
Telephone: (256) 403000
E-mail: rector@rectorat.upt.ro
Internet: www.upt.ro
Founded 1920 as Polytechnic School in Timisoara, present name 1995
State control
Language of instruction: English, French, German, Romanian
Academic year: October to July
Rector: Prof. Ing. Dr VIOREL-AUREL SERBAN
Vice-Rector: Prof. Ing. Dr CORNELIU-MIRCEA DAVIDESCU
Vice-Rector: Ing. Dr DANIEL DAN
Vice-Rector: Prof. Ing. Dr MARIUS-EMIL OTESTEANU
Vice-Rector: Prof. Ing. Dr MIRCEA POPA
Admin. Dir: Dr Eng. FLORENTIU STAICU
Dir for Library: ERICA OTESTEANU
Library of 500,000 vols
Number of teachers: 890
Number of students: 15,000
Publication: *Research Report* (1 a year)

DEANS

Faculty of Architecture: Prof. Dr SMARANDA BICA
Faculty of Automation and Computers: Prof. Ing. Dr HORIA CIOCARLIE
Faculty of Chemistry and Environmental Engineering: Prof. Ing. Dr NICOLAE VASZILCSIN
Faculty of Civil Engineering: Prof. Ing. Dr GHEORGHE LUCACI
Faculty of Communication Sciences: Dr MIRELA-CRISTINA POP
Faculty of Electrical and Power Engineering: Prof. Ing. Dr PETRU ANDEA
Faculty of Electronics and Telecommunications Engineering: Prof. Ing. Dr IVAN BOGDANOV
Faculty of Engineering, Hunedoara: Ing. Dr PANOIU CAIUS
Faculty of Management in Production and Transportation: Prof. Ing. Dr MONICA IZVERCIANU
Faculty of Mechanical Engineering: Prof. Ing. Dr INOCENTIU MANIU

PROFESSORS

Faculty of Automation and Computers (Blvd Vasile Pârvan 2, 300223 Timişoara; tel. (256) 403211; e-mail secretariat@ac.upt.ro; internet www.ac.upt.ro):

BREABAN, F., Biomedical Engineering
CIOCARLIE, H., Numerical Processing of Signals
CRETU, V., Advanced Data Structures and Programming Techniques
CRIŞAN, M., Artificial Intelligence
DRAGOMIR, T.-L., Systems Theory

ELES, P., Programming Techniques
HOLBAN, S., Basis of Artificial Intelligence
JIAN, I., Database Design and Use
JURCĂ, I., Operating Systems Design
PREITL, S., Automatic Adjustment Engineering
PROSTEAN, O., System Identification
ROBU, N., Neuronal Networks
STRATULAT, M., Creation of Interfaces, Circuits
STRUGARU, C., Peripheral Devices and Data Transmission
VLĂDUTIU, M., Computer Reliability

Faculty of Chemistry and Environmental Engineering (Blvd Vasile Parvan 6, 300223 Timişoara; tel. (256) 403063; e-mail secretar.sef@chim.upt.ro; internet www.chim.upt.ro):

BURTICA, G., Mineral Salts Technology
CSUNDERLIK, C., Organic Chemistry
DAESCU, C., Pharmaceutical Products
IOVI, A., Technology of Mineral Fertilizers
LAZĂU, I., Physical Chemistry
LUPEA, A. X., Pharmaceutical Products
NUŢIU, M., Organic Chemistry
OPRESCU, D., General Chemistry
PERJU, D., Process Modelling
PETCA, G., Technology of General Chemistry, Water and Waste Water Technology
PUGNA, I., Chemical Industry

Faculty of Civil Engineering (Traian Lalescu 2, 300223 Timişoara; tel. (256) 404000; internet www.ct.upt.ro):

BĂNCILĂ, R., Steel Structures
BOB, C., Chemistry and Construction Materials
BOTICI, A., Statics, Stability and Dynamics of Constructions
CADAR, I., Reinforced Concrete Structures
CARABA, I., Steel Structures
CIOBANU, G., English
CLIPII, T., Reinforced Concrete Structures
COSTESCU, I., Road Design and Construction
CUTEANU, E., Strength of Materials
DIMOIU, I., Earthquake Engineering
DUBINA, D., Construction
FURDUI, C., Civil Construction
GĂDIANU, L., Steel Structures
GAVRA, C. S., History of Architecture
GHEORGHIU, T., Urbanism, Architecture Design
GIONCU, V. M., Structures
GRUIA, A., Soil Mechanics and Foundation Engineering
HAIDA, V., Soil Mechanics and Foundation Engineering
IANCA, S., Civil Engineering, Architecture and Urbanism
IVAN, M., Statics, Stability and Dynamics
JIVA, C., Concrete Bridges
MARIN, M., Soil Mechanics and Foundation Engineering
MERCEA, G., Steel Structures
NEAMŢU, M., Topography
PATCAS, I., Steel Structures
PODRUMAR, D. G., Heating Installations
REGEP, Z., Steel Structures
RETEZAN, A., Installations
SÂRBU, I., Numerical Methods in Installations Optimization
SCHEIN, T., Soil Mechanics and Foundation Engineering
STOIAN, V., Civil Construction
TOMA, A., Technologies and Mechanization in Civil Engineering
TUDOR, D., Civil Construction

Faculty of Electrical and Power Engineering (Bdul V. Pârvan 2, 300223 Timişoara; tel. (256) 403381; e-mail decanat@et.upt.ro; internet www.et.upt.ro):

ANDEA, P., Electrical Apparatus Technology
ATANASIU, G., Special Electrical Machines
BABESCU, M., Electrical Machines

BANZAR, T., Mathematics
BARTZER, S., Technology of Electrical Products
BIRIESCU, M., Electromechanical Systems Testing
BOJA, N., Mathematics
BOLDEA, I., Electrical Machines
BUTTA, A., Power Delivery
CONSTANTIN, I., Mathematics
CRĂCIUN, P., Physics
CRISTEA, M., Physics
DABA, D., Theoretical Electrotechnics
DELESEGA, I., Electrical Apparatus and Equipment Testing
DOBRE, S., Electrotechnics
DUȘA, V., Optimization Techniques in Industrial Energetics
GHEJU, P., Industrial Power Systems and Networks
HEINRICH, I., Stations and Transformation Posts
HELER, A., Electrotechnics and Electric Machines
IVASCU, C., Automation and Power Systems Protection
KILYENI, S., Numerical Methods in Engineering
LIPOVAN, O., Mathematics
LUSTREA, B., Basis of Energetics and Energy Conversion
MARCU, C., Physics
MIHALCA, I., Physics
MOGA, B., Microprocessors in Electroenergetics
MOLDOVAN, L., Electric Equipment
NEAGU, M., Mathematics
NEGRU, V., High-Voltage Engineering
NEMEȘ, M., Electrical Power Systems
NICA, E., Electrical Machines
POPOVICI, D., Electrical Drives
RADU, D., Non-linear Electrotechnics
SORA, I., Electroheat, Electrotechnology, Electrical Lighting
TOADER, D., Electromechanical Engineering
VASILIEVICI, A., Electrical Equipment
VELICESCU, C., Power Systems and Network Viability
VETRES, I., Basis of Electrotechnics

Faculty of Electronics and Telecommunications Engineering (Bdul Vasile Pârvan 2, 300223 Timișoara; tel. (256) 403291; e-mail secretariat@etc.upt.ro; internet www.etc.upt.ro):

BOGDANOV, I., Robotics
CARSTEA, H., Electronic Equipment Testing and Control
CHIVU, M., Electric and Electronic Measurements
CIUGUDEAN, M., Integrated Circuits and Electronics
CRISAN, S., Electronic Measurements
IGNEA, A., Electric and Electronic Measurements
IONEL, S., Statistics Processing of Signals
ISAR, A., Signals, Circuits, Systems
MUREȘAN, T., Integrated Circuits and Electronics
NAFORNIȚĂ, I., Signals Processing
NAFORNIȚA, M., Data Transfer, Modern Communications Networks
OTESTEANU, M., Television
POLICEC, A., Communication Systems and Techniques
POPESCU, V., Power Electronics
TĂNASE, M., Electronics
TIPONUT, V., Electronic Devices
TOMA, C., Television
TOMA, L., Data Acquisition Systems

Faculty of Engineering, Hunedoara (Str. Revoluției 5, 331128 Hunedoara; tel. (254) 207502; e-mail decan@fih.upt.ro; internet www.fih.upt.ro):

ILCA, I., Technology of Plastic Deformation
SAIMAC, A., Electrotechnics

Faculty of Hydrotechnical Engineering (George Enescu St 1A. 300022 Timișoara; tel. (256) 404081; e-mail decan@hidro.upt.ro; internet www.hidro.upt.ro):

CIOMOCOS, F., Strength of Materials
CRETU, G., Hydrology, Water Resources Supply
DANILESCU, A., Statics, Stability and Dynamics of Construction
DAVID, A., Hydraulics, Transport, Groundwater Pollution Modelling
DOANDES, V., Topography, Road Topography
ION, M., Hydrotechnical Construction
IONESCU, N., Machines for Construction, Irrigation and Drainage
MAN, E. T., Irrigation and Drainage
MARTON, A., Ecology, Ecotoxicology
MIREL, I., Water Supply and Town Drainage
NICOARĂ, T., Hydraulics
POPA, G., Hydrotechnical Construction
PRELUSCHEK, E., Hydrotechnical Construction
ROGOBETE, G., Improvement of Soils and Polluted Areas
WEHRY, A., Irrigation and Drainage

Faculty of Management in Production and Transportation (Str. Remus 14, 300191 Timișoara; tel. (256) 404284; e-mail secretariat@mpt.upt.ro; internet www.mpt.upt.ro):

DĂNILĂ, C., Harvesting Machines
DUMITRESCU, C., Ergonomics, Quality Engineering
GLĂVAN, S., Agrobiological Basis of Agricultural Mechanics
IZVERCIAN, M., Management
NICA, C., Zootechnical Machines
POCINOG, G., Modelling, Simulation and Study of Production
POPA, H., Management and Industrial Engineering
SABAU, C., Finances, Accounting, Ergonomic Analysis, Management
ȘTEFAN, C., Agricultural Engineering
TAROATA, A., Marketing, Industrial Engineering

Faculty of Mechanical Engineering (Blvd Mihai Viteazu 1, 300222 Timișoara; tel. (256) 403521; internet www.mec.upt.ro):

ANCUSA, V., Fluid Mechanics, Transport Phenomena
BABEU, T., Theory of Elasticity and Strength of Materials
BACRIA, V., Mechanics
BAGIU, L., Electromechanical Engineering
BALAȘOIU, V., Hydropneumatic Equipment
BALEKICS, M., Machine Elements
BĂRGLĂZAN, M., Hydraulic Turbines
BRESTIN, A., Technology of Materials
BRÎNDEU, L., Mechanics and Vibration
BUDĂU, V., Materials, Quality Control
CARTE, I., Hydraulic Machines
CARTIS, I., Heat Treatment
CHIRIAC, A., Robotics and Automation in the Textile Industry
CRISTUINEA, C., Theory of Elasticity
CRUDU, M., Mechanisms
CUCURUZ, L., Materials, Casting
DAVID, I., Tolerances
DOBRE, I., Theory of Elasticity and Strength of Materials
DOLGA, V., Mechanical Engineering
DRĂGHICI, G., Manufacturing Engineering
DRĂGULESCU, D., Mechanical Engineering
DUMITRU, I., Technical Mechanics, Strength of Materials
DUNGAN, M., Calculus and Construction of Weight-bearing Structures of Railway Rolling Stock
FAUR, N., Elasticity and Strength of Materials
FLESER, T., Quality Control

GHEORGHIU, M., Mechanics of Fluids and Hydraulic Machines
GLIGOR, O., Components for Precision Mechanics Devices
GLIGOR, T., Mechanics
GLITA, G., Non-Conventional Welding Technologies
HEGEDUS, A., Mechanics
HERMAN, R., Technology Systems and Adjustments
HOANCĂ, V., Thermal Engines
ICLĂNZAN, T., Plastics Manufacturing
IONEL, I., Combustion and Environmental Impact of Stationary Combustion Facilities
IONESCU, N., Mechanisms
IORGA, D., Internal Combustion Engines
JADANEANȚ, M., Thermotechnics
KOVACS, A., Mathematics
LĂNCRĂNGEAN, Z., Technology of Materials
MĂDĂRAS, L., Machine Elements
MANIU, I., Dynamics, Construction and Design of Robotic Systems
MARCUSANU, A., Tolerances
MARINA, M., Mechanisms
MARINCA, V., Mechanics
MESAROȘ, A., Mechatronics, Mechanics
MILOȘ, L., Welding
MITELEA, I., Materials Science
NAGI, M., Thermic Devices, Heat and Mass Transfer
NEGREA, V. D., Internal Combustion Engines
NEGUT, N., Elasticity and Strength of Materials
NICA, C. M., Basic Experimental Research
NICHICI, A., Technology of Materials
NICOARĂ, I., Optical Devices
OPREA, M., Anti-Corrosive Protection Technologies, Materials Technology
PERJU, D., Mechanisms
POMMERSHEIM, A., Programming Languages
POPOVICI, I., Technology of Materials
POPOVICI, V., Welding Equipment
RADULESCU, C., Robotics, Industrial Robots
SAFTA, V., Welding Control and Welded Constructions
SANTĂU, I., Pumping Services
SAVII, G., Computer-Aided Design
SERBAN, V., Materials and Primary Technologies
SMICALĂ, I., Mechanics
SPOREA, I., Materials Technology
SURU, P., Management and Marketing, Computer-Aided Design
TOADER, M., Mechanics
TUCU, D., Technologies and Machines for the Food Industry
URDEA, G., Machine Tools
VACARESCU, I., Biomedical Apparatus

UNIVERSITATEA TEHNICĂ DE CONSTRUCȚII BUCUREȘTI (Technical University of Civil Engineering Bucharest)

Lacul Tei Blvd 122–124, Sector 2, 020396 Bucharest

Telephone: (21) 2421208
E-mail: secretariat@utcb.ro
Internet: www.utcb.ro

Founded 1864, present name and status 1994
State control

Rector: Prof. Ing. Dr IOHAN NEUNER
Vice-Rector: Prof. Ing. Dr RADU SARGHIUTA
Vice-Rector: Prof. Ing. Dr RADU VACAREANU
Vice-Rector: Ing. Dr TEODORA CRETU-LABIS
Dir for Library: DOINA RĂDUCAN

Library of 506,555 vols
Number of teachers: 590
Number of students: 8,600

Publications: *Buletinul Stiintific* (Scientific Bulletin, 4 a year, print and online,

buletinstiintific.utcb.ro/ro/index.html),
Mathematical Modelling in Civil Engineering (4 a year), *Romanian Journal of Mathematics and Computer Science* (online, www.rjm-cs.ro)

DEANS

Faculty of Building Services: Prof. Ing. Dr SORIN BURCHIU
Faculty of Civil, Industrial and Agricultural Buildings: Prof. Ing. Dr DANIELA PREDA
Faculty of Engineering in Foreign Languages: Dr Eng. ALEXANDRU ALDEA
Faculty of Geodesy: Prof. Ing. Dr DUMITRU ONOSE
Faculty of Hydrotechnics: Prof. Ing. Dr IOAN BICA
Faculty of Railway Roads and Bridges: Prof. Ing. Dr MIHAI DICU
Faculty of Technological Equipment: Prof. Ing. Dr ION DAVID

UNIVERSITATEA TEHNICĂ DIN CLUJ-NAPOCA
(Technical University of Cluj-Napoca)

Str. Constantin Daicoviciu 28, 4000114 Cluj-Napoca

Telephone: (264) 401200
E-mail: int.rel.office@staff.utcluj.ro
Internet: www.utcluj.ro

Founded 1947, present name 1992
State control
Languages of instruction: English, German, Romanian
Academic year: October to July
Rector: Prof. Ing. Dr AUREL VLAICU
Vice-Rector for Didactic and Student Activities: Prof. Ing. Dr DANIELA MANEA
Vice-Rector for Int. Relations, Cooperation and Continuous Education: Prof. Ing. Dr CATALIN POPA
Vice-Rector for Resource Management and Financial Policies: Prof. Ing. Dr VASILE TOPA
Vice-Rector for Scientific Research, Computational Infrastructure and Communications: Prof. Ing. Dr SERGIU NEDEVSCHI
Vice-Rector for Technical, Admin. and Patrimony: Ing. Dr HORTENSIU LIVIU CUCU
Vice-Rector for Univ. Management, Masters and Doctoral Studies: Prof. Ing. Dr STELIAN BRAD
Dir for Library: Ing. CALIN CÂMPEAN
Library: see under Libraries and Archives
Number of teachers: 660
Number of students: 15,000

Publications: *ACAM-Automation, Computer Science and Applied Mathematics*, *Acta Technica Napocensis*, *Logi A*, *Scientific Bulletin of the Cluj-Napoca Technical University* (1 a year)

DEANS

Faculty of Architecture and Urban Planning: Dr ROMULUS ZAMFIR
Faculty of Automation and Computer Science: Prof. Ing. Dr LIVIU MICLEA
Faculty of Civil Engineering and Building Services: Dr Ing. MIRCEA BUZDUGAN
Faculty of Electrical Engineering: Prof. Ing. Dr RADU CIUPA
Faculty of Electronics, Telecommunications and Information Technology: Prof. Ing. Dr DAN PITICA
Faculty of Installation: Ing. Dr MIRCEA ION BUZDUGAN
Faculty of Machine Building: Prof. Ing. Dr DANIELA POPESCU
Faculty of Materials Science and Engineering: Prof. Dr Ing. IOAN VIDA-SIMITI
Faculty of Mechanical Engineering: Prof. Ing. Dr NICOLAE BURNETE

PROFESSORS

Faculty of Architecture and Urban Planning (Str. Observatorului 34–36, 3400 Cluj-Napoca; tel. (264) 590255; e-mail moldovanms@hotmail.com):

MATEI, A., Architectural Composition
MOLDOVAN, M., History of World Architecture, Aesthetics, History of Arts
MURADIN, C., Styles of Furniture
SZABO, B., Theory of Structures and Renovation of Constructions

Faculty of Automation and Computer Science (Str. G. Baritiu 26–28, 400027 Cluj-Napoca; tel. (264) 401218; internet www.ac.utcluj.ro):

CÂMPEANU, V., Mathematical Analysis
COLOSI, T., Theory of Systems, Automation
COROVEI, I., Algebra, Special Mathematics
CRIVEI, I., Algebra, Mathematical Analysis
DĂDÂRLAT, T., Digital Circuits
FEŞTILĂ, C., Control Structures and Algorithms
GANSCA, I., Mathematical Analysis
GAVREA, I., Calculus
GORGAN, D., Fundamentals of Computer Graphics
IGNAT, I., Operating Systems
IVAN, D. M., Numerical Analysis, Mathematical Analysis
LAZEA, GH., Theory of Robot Control
LEŢIA, I. A., Real Time Control
LUNG, N., Special Mathematics
NEDEVSCHI, S., Design with Microchips
OPRIŞ, GH., Special Mathematics, Differential Equations
PUSZTAI, K., Computer Networks
RASA, I., Numerical Mathematics
SALOMIE, I., Design Techniques
TOADER, GH., Mathematical Analysis
VORNICESCU, N., Differential Equations, Mathematical Analysis

Faculty of Civil Engineering and Building Services (Str. G. Baritiu 25, 400027 Cluj-Napoca; tel. (264) 594967; internet constructii.utcluj.ro):

ALEXA, P., Theoretical Mechanics, Structural Dynamics, Structural Stability
ANDREICA, H., Timber Structures
BADEA, G., Water Supplies and Sewerage
BÂRSAN, G., Theoretical Mechanics, Structural Dynamics, Structural Stability
BIA, C., Strength of Materials, Theory of Elasticity
BORŞ, I., Theoretical Mechanics, Numerical Methods
BRUMARU, M., Buildings
BUCUR, I., Reinforced Concrete Structures
CĂTĂRIG, A., Structural Analysis
CHIOREAN, T., Economics of the Construction Industry, Management and Organization
CHISĂLIŢĂ, A., Theoretical Mechanics, Numerical Methods, Cable and Hinged Structures, Non-Linear Analysis
COMŞA, E., Buildings
CORDOŞ, GH., Sociology
DOMŞA, J., Construction Technology
DUMITRAŞ, M., Buildings
HOSSU, T., Management in Civil Engineering
ILIESCU, M., Road Engineering
IOANI, A., Strength of Materials, Theory of Elasticity
IONESCU, A., Reinforced Concrete Structures
JURCĂU, N., Psychology
KOPENETZ, L., Computer-Aided Engineering and Design, Structural Analysis, Lightweight Structures
MĂGUREANU, C., Reinforced and Prestressed Concrete
MARŢIAN, I., Strength of Materials, Theory of Elasticity
MOGA, A., Construction Technology
MOGA, I., Thermotechnology

MOGA, P., Metal Bridges
NISTOR, I., History of Culture and Civilization
OLARIU, I., Structural Analysis
ONEŢ, T., Reinforced and Prestressed Concrete
OPRIŢOIU, A., Heat Engineering
PĂCURAR, V., Steel Structures
PANŢEL, E., Strength of Materials, Theory of Elasticity, Numerical Methods
PETRINA, M., Structural Analysis, Computer Programming
POP, F., Electric Installation
POP, I., Seismic Engineering
POPA, A., Soil Mechanics and Foundations
VERDEŞ, D., Agricultural Buildings, Physics of Construction
VIOREL, G., Concrete Bridges

Faculty of Electrical Engineering (Str. G. Baritiu 26–28, 400027 Cluj-Napoca; tel. (264) 401228; e-mail decan.fie@staff.utcluj.ro):

BĂLAN, H., Electrical Equipment
BIRO, K., Electrical Machines
CATANĂ, D., Marketing
CATANĂ, GH., Marketing
CHINDRIŞ, M., Technological Design of Management Systems
CIUPA, R., Principles of Electronics
DARIE, S., Electrical Power Stations, Electrical Apparatus
DRAGOMIR, N., Electrical Measuring
IANCU, V., Electrical Machines
IMECS, M., Theory of Automatic Control Systems
IUGA, A., Electrotechnical Engineering
MAIER, V., Electrothermics
MAN, E., Elements of Electrotechnics
MARSCHALKO, R., Electronics
MICU, D., Electrical Engineering
MUNTEANU, R., Data Acquisition, Sensors and Control
RĂDULESCU, M., Electrical Drives
SIMION, E., Non-linear Circuits, Basic Electrical Engineering
TÂRNOVAN, I. G., Electronic Measurements
TODORAN, GH., Electrical Measurements
TRIFA, V., Applied Informatics and Microprocessor Systems
VIOREL, A., Electrical Machines

Faculty of Electronics, Telecommunications and Information Technology (Str. G. Baritiu 26–28, 400027 Cluj-Napoca; tel. (264) 591689; internet www.etti.utcluj.ro):

BORDA, M., Information Theory
DOBROTĂ, V., Telecommunications
FEŞTILĂ, L., Analogical Integrated Circuits
LUNGU, Ş., Electronics
MIRON, C., Electronics
PITICĂ, D., Applied Electronics
RUSU, C., Signal Processing
TODEREAN, G., Communications Engineering
VAIDA, M., Informatics
VLAICU, A., Multimedia Systems
VOICULESCU, E., Optoelectronics
ZĂHAN, S., Telecommunications

Faculty of Machine Building (B-dul Muncii 103–105, 400641 Cluj-Napoca; tel. (264) 401782; internet cm.utcluj.ro):

ABRUDAN, I., Production Systems
ACHIMAŞ, GH., Metal Forming
ANTAL, A., Machine Components
ARGHIR, M., Computer Programming
BANABIC, D., Manufacturing Technologies
BERCE, P., Manufacturing Technologies
BLEBEA, I., Industrial Robots
BOJAN, I., Management Information Systems
CÂNDEA, D., Industrial Management
CĂZILĂ, A., Machine Components
CREŢU, M., Machine Tools and Industrial Robots
DEACU, L., Hydraulics
GALIŞ, M., Design of Machine Tools

GYENGE, Cs., Manufacturing Technologies
IANCĂU, H., Plastics
ISPAS, V., Mechanics, Robotics
ITU, T., Technical Measurements
MORAR, L., Numerical Control
NEGREAN, L., Mechanics
OLTEANU, R., Manufacturing Technology
PLITEA, N., Mechanics
POP, D., Machine Components
POP, I., Hydraulics
POPA, M., Unconventional Technologies
POPESCU, S., Mechanics
PRUNEA, P., Economics
ROȘ, O., Manufacturing Technologies
SUCALĂ, F., Machine Components
URSU-FISCHER, N., Computer Programming

Faculty of Materials Science and Engineering (Muncii Ave 103–105, 400641 Cluj-Napoca; tel. (264) 415054):

ARGHIR, G., Crystallography
BICSAK, E., Science of Materials, Welded Constructions Technology
BIRIȘ, I., Heat Processes in Metallurgical Furnaces
CÂNDEA, V., Materials Science
CANTA, T., Plastic Deformation Theory
COMAN, S., Mechanical Engineering, Mechanical Technology
COSMA, I., Physics
CULEA, E., Physics
DEMCO, D., Physics
DOMȘA, S., Materials Technology
IANCU, D., Heat and Thermochemical Treatment Technologies
LUCACI, P., Physics
LUPȘA, I., Physics
MILEA, I., Physics
MILITARU, V., Physics
NAGY, E., Steel Casting
NAȘCU, H., Chemistry
ORBAN, R., Materials Technology
PICĂ, M., Chemistry
POP, O., Physics
RUSU, T., Quality Management, Environmental Protection
SOPORAN, V., Technology for Casting Alloys
SPÂRCHEZ, Z., Composite Materials, Metallurgical Physics
VERMEȘAN, G., Heat and Thermochemical Treatment Technologies
VIDA, S., Materials Manufacturing Technology

Faculty of Mechanical Engineering (Blvd Muncii 103–105, 400641 Cluj-Napoca; tel. (264) 401787):

APAHIDEAN, B., Thermodynamics
BĂȚAGĂ, N., Heat Machines
BEJAN, M., Strength of Materials
BRÂNZAȘ, P., Management and Marketing
BURNETE, N., Automobiles and Tractors
CORDOȘ, N., Vehicle Dynamics
CREȚU, A., Strength of Materials
HĂRDĂU, M., Strength of Materials
MĂDĂRĂȘAN, T., Thermodynamics and Thermal Machines
MĂTIEȘ, V., Mechanics
ROȘ, V., Forming Machines

UNIVERSITATEA TEHNICĂ 'GHEORGHE ASACHI' DIN IAȘI
('Gheorghe Asachi' Technical University of Iași)

Str. Prof. Dr Doc. Dimitrie Mangeron 67, 700050 Iași

Telephone: (232) 278683
E-mail: rectorat@staff.tuiasi.ro
Internet: www.tuiasi.ro

Founded 1937, present name and status 1993
State control
Languages of instruction: English, Romanian
Academic year: October to July

Rector: Prof. Ing. Dr ION GIURMA

Vice-Rector for Academic Affairs: Prof. Ing. Dr NECULAI EUGEN SEGHEDIN
Vice-Rector for Informatics: Prof. Ing. Dr DANIEL CONDURACHE
Vice-Rector for Int. Relations and Univ. Image: Assoc. Prof. Ing. Dr IRINA LUNGU
Vice-Rector for Scientific Research: Prof. Ing. Dr CARMEN TEODOSIU
Vice-Rector for Student Problems: Prof. Ing. Dr STEFAN GRIGORAS
Vice-Rector for Univ. Strategy: Prof. Ing. Dr IOAN CIOARA
Dir for Library: Prof. MIHAELA STIRBU
Library: see under Libraries and Archives
Number of teachers: 735
Number of students: 14,851

Publications: *Bulletin of the Technical University of Iasi* (4 a year), *Environmental Engineering and Management Journal* (12 a year, in English), *Iasi Polytechnic Magazine*

DEANS

Faculty of Architecture 'G. M. Cantacuzino': Ing. Dr TANIA MARIANA HAPURNE
Faculty of Automatic Control and Computer Engineering: Prof. Ing. Dr CORNELIU LAZAR
Faculty of Chemical Engineering and Environmental Protection: Prof. Ing. Dr DAN CAȘCAVAL
Faculty of Civil Engineering and Building Services: Prof. Ing. Dr MIHAI BUDESCU
Faculty of Electrical Engineering, Energetics and Applied Informatics: Prof. Ing. Dr DUMITRU-MARCEL ISTRATE
Faculty of Electronics, Telecommunications and Information Technology: Prof. Ing. Dr ION BOGDAN
Faculty of Hydrotechnical Engineering, Geodesy and Environmental Engineering: Prof. Ing. Dr FLORIAN STATESCU
Faculty of Materials Science and Engineering: Dr IULIAN IONITA
Faculty of Mechanical Engineering: Prof. Ing. Dr CEZAR OPRISAN
Faculty of Mechanical Engineering and Industrial Management: Prof. Ing. Dr GHEORGHE NAGIT
Faculty of Textiles and Leather Engineering and Industrial Management: Ing. Dr LILIANA BUHU

PROFESSORS

Department of Teacher Education and Training (Str. Prof. Dr Docent Dimitrie Mangeron 73, 700050 Iași; internet www.tuiasi.ro):

CARCEA, M., Educational Sciences

Faculty of Architecture 'G. M. Cantacuzino' (Str. Prof Dr Docent Dimitrie Mangeron 3, 700050 Iași; tel. (232) 278680; e-mail arhitect@ce.tuiasi.ro; internet www.arhitectura.tuiasi.ro):

BOAZU, R., Urbanism

Faculty of Automatic Control and Computer Engineering (Str. Prof. Dr Docent Dimitrie Mangeron 27, 700050 Iași; tel. (232) 231343; e-mail decanat@ac.tuiasi.ro; internet www.ace.tuiasi.ro):

CRAUS, M., Computer Science
LAZAR, C., Automatic Control and Applied Informatics
MANTA, V., Computer Science
ONEA, A., Automatic Control and Applied Informatics
PANESCU, D., Automatic Control and Applied Informatics
PASTRAVANU, O., Automatic Control and Applied Informatics
UNGUREANU, F., Computer Science

Faculty of Chemical Engineering and Environmental Protection (Str. Prof. Dr Docent Dimitrie Mangeron 73, 700050 Iași; tel. (232) 278683; e-mail decanat@ch.tuiasi.ro; internet www.ch.tuiasi.ro):

CARJA, G., Chemical Engineering
CASCAVAL, D., Organic Substances Engineering and Biochemical Engineering
DAVID, G., Natural and Synthetic Polymers
GAVRILESCU, M., Environmental Engineering and Management
GAVRILESCU, D., Natural and Synthetic Polymers
LUCA, C., Organic Substances Engineering and Biochemical Engineering
POPA, I., Chemical Engineering
POPA, M., Natural and Synthetic Polymers
SIMIONESCU, B., Natural and Synthetic Polymers
SUTIMAN, D., Chemical Engineering
TEODOSIU, C., Environmental Engineering and Management

Faculty of Civil Engineering and Building Services (Blvd Prof. Dr Docent Dimitrie Mangeron 1, 700050 Iași; tel. (232) 278683; e-mail flomar@ce.tuiasi.ro; internet www.ce.tuiasi.ro):

ATANASIU, G., Structural Mechanics
BARBUTA, M., Concrete Structures, Building Materials, Technology and Management
BOBOC, V., Transportation Infrastructure and Foundation
BOTU, N., Transportation Infrastructure and Foundation
BUDESCU, M., Structural Mechanics
COMISU, C., Transportation Infrastructure and Foundation
DIACONU-SOTROPA, D., Structural Mechanics
GALATANU, C., Building Services
HINCU, G., Engineering Graphics
IGNAT, J., Building Services
ISOPESCU, D., Civil and Industrial Engineering
LAZARESCU, D., Building Services
LUNGU, I., Transportation Infrastructure and Foundation
MUSAT, V., Transportation Infrastructure and Foundation
PAULET-CRAINICEANU, F., Structural Mechanics
PAVEL, V., Building Services
PROFIRE, M., Building Services
RUJANU, M., Concrete Structures, Building Materials, Technology and Management
SECU, A., Civil and Industrial Engineering
SERBANOIU, I., Concrete Structures, Building Materials, Technology and Management
STANCIU, A., Transportation Infrastructure and Foundation
STANILA, A., Engineering Graphics
STEFANESCU, D., Civil and Industrial Engineering
TARANU, N., Civil and Industrial Engineering
VELICU, C., Civil and Industrial Engineering

Faculty of Electrical Engineering, Energetics and Applied Informatics (Blvd Prof. Dr Doc. Dimitrie Mangeron 21–23, 700050 Iași; tel. (232) 278680; e-mail decanat@ee.tuiasi.ro; internet www.ee.tuiasi.ro):

ADAM, M., Power Engineering
ASAFTEI, C., Power Engineering
ASANDEI, D., Power Engineering
BAHRIN, V., Electrotechnics
BALUTA, G., Industrial Utilizations, Electric Drives and Industrial Automation
BARABOI, A., Power Engineering
BRENIUC, L., Electrical Measurements and Materials
COJAN, M., Electrotechnics
DAVID, V., Electrical Measurements and Materials
FOSALAU, C., Electrical Measurements and Materials
FURNICA, E., Power Engineering
GAVRILAS, M., Power Engineering

GUSA, M., Power Engineering

ISTRATE, M., Power Engineering

OLARU, R., Industrial Utilizations, Electric Drives and Industrial Automation

PETRESCU, C., Electrotechnics

SALCEANU, A., Electrical Measurements and Materials

SARMASANU, C., Electrical Measurements and Materials

SCHREINER, C., Electrical Measurements and Materials

VARVARA, V., Electrotechnics

VREMERA, E., Electrical Measurements and Materials

Faculty of Electronics, Telecommunications and Information Technology (Blvd Carol I 11, 700506 Iaşi; tel. (232) 270041; e-mail dbarbuta@etti.tuiasi.ro; internet www.etti .tuiasi.ro):

ALEXANDRU, N., Telecommunications

BEJAN, C., Mathematics and Informatics

BOGDAN, I., Telecommunications

CASIAN-BOTEZ, I., Telecommunications

CHIPER, D., Applied Electronics and Intelligent Systems

DIMITRIU, L., Applied Electronics and Intelligent Systems

DUMA, P., Telecommunications

DUMITRIU, N., Mathematics and Informatics

GORAS, L., Fundamentals of Electronics

NEGOESCU, N., Mathematics and Informatics

SARBU, A., Telecommunications

TEODORESCU, H., Applied Electronics and Intelligent Systems

TUDORACHE, R., Mathematics and Informatics

Faculty of Hydrotechnical Engineering, Geodesy and Environmental Engineering (Blvd Prof. Dr Doc. Dimitrie Mangeron 65, 700050 Iaşi; tel. (232) 270804; e-mail decanat@hidro .tuaisi.ro; internet www12.tuaisi.ro/facultati/ hidro):

BARTHA, I., Hydroamelioration and Environmental Protection

GAVRILAS, G., Hydrotechnical Constructions and Sanitary Engineering

LUCA, M., Hydroamelioration and Environmental Protection

STATESCU, F., Hydroamelioration and Environmental Protection

Faculty of Materials Science and Engineering (Blvd Prof. Dr Doc. Dimitrie Mangeron 61A, 700050 Iaşi; tel. (232) 230009; e-mail decanatsim@tuiasi.ro; internet www12.tuaisi .ro/facultati/sim/):

BARBU, G., Materials Science

BUJOREANU, G., Materials Engineering and Industrial Safety

BULANCEA, V., Technologies and Equipment for Materials Processing

CARCEA, I., Materials Science

STANCIU, S., Materials Science

SUSAN, M., Technologies and Equipment for Materials Processing

ZAHARIA, L., Technologies and Equipment for Materials Processing

Faculty of Mechanical Engineering and Industrial Management (Blvd Prof. Dr Doc. Dimitrie Mangeron 59A, 700050 Iaşi; tel. (232) 242109; e-mail secretariat@tcm.tuiasi .ro; internet www.mectuiasi.ro):

AMARIEI, N., Mechanical Engineering, Mechatronics and Robotics

ATANASIU, V., Mechanical Engineering, Mechatronics and Robotics

BERCEA, M., Mechanical Engineering, Mechatronics and Robotics

BIRSANESCU, P., Mechanical Engineering, Mechatronics and Robotics

COMANDAR, C., Mechanical Engineering, Mechatronics and Robotics

COZMA, D., Mechanical Engineering, Automotive Engineering

DOROFTEI, I., Mechanical Engineering, Mechatronics and Robotics

GOLGOTIU, E., Mechanical Engineering, Automotive Engineering

HORBANIUC, B., Mechanical Engineering, Automotive Engineering

LEOHCHI, D., Mechanical Engineering, Mechatronics and Robotics

MOCANU, F., Mechanical Engineering, Mechatronics and Robotics

MUNTEANU, C., Mechanical Engineering, Mechatronics and Robotics

OPRISAN, C., Mechanical Engineering, Mechatronics and Robotics

RAKOSI, E., Mechanical Engineering, Automotive Engineering

Faculty of Textiles and Leather Engineering and Industrial Management (Blvd Prof. Dr Doc. Dimitrie Mangeron 29, 700050 Iaşi; tel. (232) 230491; e-mail practica@tex.tuiasi.ro; internet www12.tuiasi.ro/facultati/tex):

AVASILCAI, S., Engineering and Management

BERTEA, A., Chemical Engineering in Textile and Leather Industries

BLASCU, V., Chemical Engineering in Textile and Leather Industries

BOIER, R., Engineering and Management

BORDEIANU, D., Textile Engineering and Clothing Design

CIOARA, I., Textile Engineering and Clothing Design

CIOARA, L., Textile Engineering and Clothing Design

COMANDAR, C., Knitting and Ready-Made Clothing Engineering

CURTEZA, A., Knitting and Ready-Made Clothing Engineering

FILIPESCU, E., Knitting and Ready-Made Clothing Engineering

HUTU, C., Engineering and Management

LOGHIN, C., Knitting and Ready-Made Clothing Engineering

LUCA, G., Engineering and Management

LUPU, L., Engineering and Management

MUSTATA, A., Textile Engineering and Clothing Design

NICOLAIOV, P., Knitting and Ready-Made Clothing Engineering

PINTILIE, E., Knitting and Ready-Made Clothing Engineering

Other Institutes of Higher Education

Academia de Muzică 'Gheorghe Dima' Cluj-Napoca ('Gheorghe Dima' Music Academy): Str. Ion I. C. Bratianu 25, 400079 Cluj-Napoca; tel. (264) 591241; e-mail conscluj@ gmail.com; internet www.amgd.ro; f. 1919, present name 1990; faculties of musical performance and theory; library: 188,000 vols; 250 teachers; 1,182 students; Rector Dr VASILE JUCAN; Pro-Rector for Artistic Creation and Int. Relations Prof. Dr ADRIANA BERA; Pro-Rector for Didactic Activities Dr VERONICA NEGREANU; Pro-Rector for Scientific Research Prof. Dr NELIDA NEDELCUŢ; Gen. Admin. Dir Ing. CORNEL MIHALCA; publs *Intermezzo* (magazine), *Lucrări de Muzicologie* (Musicology Articles, 1 a year).

Academia de Studii Economice din Bus-curesti (Bucharest University of Economic Studies): Piaţa Romană 6, Sector 1, 010374 Bucharest; tel. (21) 3191900; e-mail rectorat@ase.ro; internet www.ase.ro; f. 1913, present name and status 1967; faculties of accounting and management information systems; administration and public management; agrifood and environment economics; business administration in foreign languages; commerce; cybernetics, statistics and informatics; economics; finance, insurance, banking and stock exchange; international business and economics; management; marketing; library: see under Libraries and Archives; 765 teachers; 49,000 students; Rector Prof. Dr PAVEL NASTASE; Vice-Rector for Admin., Patrimonial, Social Issues and Relationships with Students Prof. Dr CONSTANTIN MITRUT; Vice-Rector for Continuing Education and Training Prof. Dr GABRIELA TIGU; Vice-Rector for Inter-institutional Relations and Socio-Economic Environment Prof. Dr NICOLAE ISTUDOR; Vice-Rector for Int. Relations Dr DOREL MIHAI PARASCHIV; Vice-Rector for Resource Planning and Allocation Dr ROBERT AURELIAN SOVA; Vice-Rector for Scientific Research, Devt and Innovation Prof. Dr ION STANCU; publs *Economic Journal* (in Romanian and English, 4 a year), *Informatica Economică* (4 a year).

Academiei Naţionale de Informaţii 'Mihai Viteazul': Şoseaua Odăi 20–22, Sector 1, Bucharest; tel. (21) 4106560; e-mail ani@sri.ro; internet www.animv.ro; f. 1992, present name 2009; training intelligence officers; offers Bachelors, Masters and doctoral courses; Rector Prof. Dr GHEORGHE TEODORU STEFAN; Dir GEORGE CRISTIAN MAIOR; publ. *Romanian Journal of Intelligence Studies.*

Bulgaria–Romania Interuniversity Europe Center/BRIE—Giurgiu: Str. Mircea cel Batran 36, 080036 Giurgiu; tel. (246) 219161; e-mail brie@ase.ro; internet www .brie.ase.ro; f. 2001; operates through collaboration between Rusenski Universitet 'Angel Kanchev' (see Bulgaria chapter) and the Academia de Studii Economice; Dir Prof. Dr CONSTANTIN APOSTOL.

Institutul Teologic Baptist din Bucureşti (Baptist Theological Institute, Bucharest): Str. Berzei 29, Sector 1, 010251 Bucharest; tel. (21) 3159108; e-mail office@ itb.ro; internet www.itb.ro; f. 1921; library: 23,000 vols of books and magazines in Romanian, English, German, French; Rector Dr DANIEL M. MARIS; Pro-Rector Dr BEN-ONI ARDELEAN; Dean of Student Affairs Dr SORIN BADRAGAN; Admin. Dir TRANDAFIR POPOVICI.

Institutul Teologic Protestant Cluj (Protestant Theological Institute of Cluj): Piaţa Avram Iancu 13, 400124 Cluj-Napoca; tel. (264) 591368; e-mail proteo@proteo.cj.edu.ro; internet www.proteo.cj.edu.ro; f. 1568, present name 1997; offers Bachelors, Masters and doctoral courses; Rector Dr REZI ELEK; publs *Keresztény Magvető*, *Református Szemle* (6 a year, print and online, www.proteo.hu/refszemle), *Studia Doctorum Theologiae Protestantis.*

Institutul Teologic Romano-Catolic 'Sf. Iosif' Iasi: Str. Th. Văscăuţeanu 6, 700462 Iaşi; tel. (232) 410419; e-mail decan@itrc.ro; internet www.itrc.ro; f. 1886; depts of Biblical Christian philosophy and science, systematic theology and practice; 25 teachers; Rector Prof. Dr BENONE LUCACI; Vice-Rector Prof. EDUARD SOARE; Dean Prof. Dr ŞTEFAN LUPU; publs *Dialog Teologic*, *Drumuri Deschise*, *Educatorul Creştin*, *Lasati Copiii Sa Vina La Mine.*

RUSSIA

The Higher Education System

In March 1917 the last Tsar of the Romanov dynasty, which had ruled Russia as an autocracy since 1613, was forced to abdicate and a liberal Provisional Government took power. The Bolsheviks overthrew the Provisional Government in November of the same year and the Russian Soviet Federative Socialist Republic (RSFSR) was proclaimed. In 1922 the RSFSR joined the Union of Soviet Socialist Republics (USSR), which disintegrated in 1991, when the Russian Federation, as the RSFSR was formally renamed, was founded. The oldest current institutions of higher education date from the 18th century, notably St Petersburg State University (founded 1724) and Moscow State University 'M. V. Lomonsov' (founded 1755). Several specialist institutions were founded during the reign of Catherine the Great (1762–96). Major institutions founded during the 19th century include Moscow Agricultural Academy 'K. A. Timiryazev' (founded 1865), Tomsk Polytechnic University (founded 1896) and Nizhnii Novgorod State Technical University (founded 1898 in Warsaw, Poland). Universal education was a fundamental Bolshevik principle, and during the period of Soviet rule (1917–91) more than 340 institutions of higher education were founded. Under Soviet rule all educational institutions were state-owned but a wide range of independent schools and colleges were created in the early 1990s. In 2008/09 there were 474 independent higher education institutions. In 2011/12 there were 6,490,000 students enrolled in 1,080 institutions of higher education.

Higher education institutions are categorized as Academies, Universities, Institutes and Conservatories. Universities are sub-divided by subject area: Agriculture, Humanities and Sciences, Medical, Pedagogical and Technical. The Ministry of Education and Science has overall responsibility for higher education, particularly the licensing and accreditation of institutions. Russia participates in the Bologna Process to establish a European Higher Education Area, the first phase of which is to adopt a credit-based system of comparable degrees with two main cycles (undergraduate and graduate). In 2007 Russia enacted a law that replaced the traditional five-year model of education with a two-tiered approach: a four-year Bachelors degree followed by a two-year Masters. This system was to have been fully implemented by 2010.

Admission was formerly made on the joint basis of the Certificate of Secondary Education (Attestat o srednem obrazovanii) and performance in a competitive entrance examination. In 2007 the Unified State Examination (USE), a standardized common university admission examination replacing the state final school attestation and entrance examinations, was introduced by law. Since 2009 the USE has been adopted nationwide and is compulsory for all applicants. However, in 2009 24 universities received the right to administer their own entrance exams and in 2010 a further 11 Russian universities were allowed to do this as well. The undergraduate degree is the Bakalavr (Bachelors), a four-year programme of study divided into two years of general studies and two years of specialized studies. Graduates holding the Bachelors are eligible to study for the Magistr (Masters), the first postgraduate degree, which is either a one-year taught course or a two-year period of research. Doctoral-level studies have a two-tiered structure, comprising the Aspirantura and Doktorantura. Aspirantura is a period of study following the Masters lasting a minimum of three years and culminating with the defence of a thesis and the award of the title Kandidat Nauk (Candidate of Sciences). Following Aspirantura, Doktorantura lasts for an unspecified period of time that, upon completion, results in the title Doktor Nauk (Doctor of Sciences).

Technical and vocational education is largely offered by specialist institutions and technical colleges at the upper secondary level. The primary qualifications are the Diplom ob okanchanii proftekhuchilishcha (Diploma of Completed Vocational-Technical Education) and the Diplom ob okanchanii srednego spetsial'nogo uchebnogo zavedeniya (Diploma of Completed Specialized Secondary Education—available at both basic and advanced levels). Basic level courses last between two and three years, while advanced level courses generally last an additional year.

The Federal Service for Supervision in Education and Science carries out quality control, licensing, certification and state accreditation of educational institutions. In November 2010 the Government approved a new federal programme for 2011–15 intended to improve the quality of higher education, primarily focusing on Russia's universities. Expected to cost some 137,000m. rubles (US \$4,100m.), the programme was to include improving the quality of teaching staff, the introduction of new technologies and upgrading the infrastructure at the country's leading federal universities.

In late 2012 President Putin announced a reorganization of the university sector, leading to the closure of one in five universities (there were currently more than 600) or their merging with stronger universities. A draft law On Education was submitted outlining the procedures to be put in place so that the restructuring could take place in 2013–14.

Regulatory and Representative Bodies

Association of Russian Higher Education Institutions: 105064 Moscow, 4 Gorokhovsky per.; tel. (499) 261-31-52; e-mail svp@miigaik.ru; Pres. VIKTOR SAVINYKH.

Federal Agency for Education: 115998 Moscow, Lyusinovskaya ul. 51; tel. (495) 237-97-63; e-mail bicab@ed.gov.ru; internet www .ed.gov.ru; manages state property, implements education and training policies, funds higher-education instns; Head NIKOLAI IVANOVICH BULAEV.

Russian Academy of Education: 119121 Moscow, Pogodinskaya ul. 8; tel. (495) 245-16-41; f. 1943; br. depts of philosophy of education and theoretical pedagogy, psychology and physiology in education, general secondary education, culture and education, basic vocational training, higher education; regional depts: Northwest (St Petersburg), Siberia (Krasnoyarsk), Southern (Rostov-on-Don), Central (Moscow), Povolzhskoe (Kazan), Urals (Ekaterinburg); 4 experimental schools, 30 research institutes; see Research Institutes; library: see Libraries and Archives; Pres. Prof. Dr N. D. NIKANDROV; Chief Learned Sec. Prof. Dr I. V. ROBERT; publs *Defektologiya* (Defectology, 6 a year), *Izvestiya RAO* (News, 4 a year), *Pedagogika* (Pedagogics, 12 a year), *Voprosy Psikhologii* (Problems of Psychology, 12 a year).

Russian Rectors' Union: 119991 Moscow, V-234, Vorobievy Gory, Lomonosov Moscow State Univ., Glavnoe Zdanie, Rooms 1001–1003; tel. (495) 939-20-32; e-mail office@rsr-online.ru; internet rsr-online.ru/english; f. 1992; c. 1,000 mems; Pres. VIKTOR A. SADOVNICHY; Sec.-Gen. OLGA V. KASHIRINA.

Learned Societies

GENERAL

Russian Academy of Natural Sciences: 117105 Moscow, Varshavskoye shosse 8; tel. (495) 954-26-11; e-mail info@raen.info; internet www.raen.info; f. 1990; organizes and coordinates pure and applied research; sections: Mathematics; Physics; Chemistry; Earth Sciences; Mining and Metallurgy; Issues in Education; Informatics; Biomedicine; Biology and Ecology; Russian Encyclopedia; Economics and Sociology; Issues in Macroeconomics; Geopolitics and Security; Noosphere Knowledge and Technology; Humanities and Creative Work; Interbranch Ecological and Economic Systems Research; Environmental Sciences; depts: St Petersburg Branch for Education and Science Development; Oil and Gas; Forest Sciences; Eurasia Concept and Culture; Ecology, Hydrogeology, Engineering Geology and Geocryology; Applied Mathematics and Mathematical Physics; Class and National Traditions; 2,500 mems (incl. 100 hon., 250 foreign); Pres. Prof. Dr OLEG LEONIDOVICH KUZNETSOV; Chief Scientific Sec. LIDA V. IVANITSKAYA.

Russian Academy of Sciences: 119991 Moscow, Leninsky pr. 14; tel. (495) 954-29-05; e-mail uvs@pran.ru; internet www.pran .ru; f. 1724; depts of mathematics, physics, power engineering, mechanics and control processes, information science and computer technology, chemistry and materials, biology, earth sciences, social sciences, history and philology; Siberian div. incl. centres in Krasnoyarsk, Irkutsk, Kemerovo, Omsk, Tomsk and Tumen; Far Eastern div.; Urals div. incl. centres in Perm and Komi; additional centres in Makhachkala, Petrozavodsk, Kazan, Nalchik, Ufa and Apatity; attached research institutes: see under

Research Institutes; 1,429 mems (501 academicians, 720 corresp. mems, 208 foreign mems); library: see under Libraries and Archives; Pres. YU. S. OSIPOV; Chief Learned Sec. V. V. KOSTYUK; publs *Izvestiya Rossiiskoi Akademii Nauk* (Bulletin of the Russian Academy of Sciences, in 16 series: Biology, Geography, Literature and Language, Mathematics, Metals, Economics and Society, Mechanics of Liquids and Gases, Solid State Mechanics, Technical Cybernetics, Energy and Transport (6 a year); Geology, Inorganic Materials, Physics of Atmosphere and Ocean, Earth Physics, Physics, Chemistry (12 a year)), *Doklady Rossiiskoi Akademii Nauk* (Proceedings of the Academy, 36 a year), *Izvestiya Sibirskogo Otdeleniya Rossiiskoi Akademii Nauk* (Bulletin of the Siberian Branch of the Russian Academy of Sciences, in 5 series: Biological and Medical Sciences, History, Philology and Philosophy, Economics and Applied Sociology (4 a year); Technical Sciences, Chemical Sciences (6 a year)), *Nauka v Rossii* (Science in Russia, in Russian and English, 6 a year), *Vestnik Rossiiskoi Akademii Nauk* (Journal of the Russian Academy of Sciences, 12 a year), *Vestnik Dalnevostochnogo Otdeleniya RAN* (Journal of the Far Eastern Division of the Russian Academy of Sciences).

UNESCO Office Moscow: 119331 Moscow, ul. Mytnaya 1; tel. (495) 230-10-65; e-mail moscow@unesco.org; internet www.unesco .ru; designated Cluster Office for Armenia, Azerbaijan, Belarus, Moldova and Russia; Dir BADARCH DENDEV.

Union of Scientific and Engineering of Public Associations: 119034 Moscow, Kursovoi per. 17; tel. (495) 695-16-08; e-mail usea@nm.ru; internet www.rusea.h11.ru; 110 mems; Pres. Acad. YURY GULYAEV; Sec. Gen. VLADIMIR SITSEV.

AGRICULTURE, FISHERIES AND VETERINARY SCIENCE

Russian Academy of Agricultural Sciences: 107814 Moscow, Bolshoi Kharitonevsky per. 21; tel. (495) 207-39-42; f. 1992; depts of plant breeding and genetics, arable farming and the use of agricultural chemicals, feed and fodder crops production, plant protection, livestock production, veterinary science, mechanization, electrification and automation in farming, forestry, the Economics and Management of agricultural production, land reform and the organization of land use, land reclamation and water resources, the storage and processing of agricultural products; regional depts in St Petersburg (Non Black Soil Zone), Novosibirsk (Siberia), Khabarovsk (Far East); attached research institutes: see under Research Institutes; 351 mems (incl. 150 mems, 128 corresp. mems, 73 foreign corresp. mems); library: see under Libraries and Archives; Pres. A. A. NIKONOV; Chief Learned Sec. V. P. SHISHKOV; publs *Doklady* (Proceedings), *Mekhanizatsiya i Elektrifikatsiya Selskogo Khozyaistva* (Mechanization and Electrification of Agriculture), *Selektsiya i Semenovodstvo* (Selection and Seed Science), *Selskokhozyaistvennaya Biologiya* (Agricultural Biology), *Sibirskii Vestnik Selskokhozyaistvennoi nauki* (Siberian Agricultural Science Journal), *Vestnik Selskokhozyaistvennoi Nauki* (Agricultural Science Journal).

Society of the Timber and Forestry Industry: 103062 Moscow, ul. Chernyshevskogo 29; tel. (495) 923-95-70; Chair. YU. A. YAGODNIKOV.

Soil Science Society: 109017 Moscow, Pyzhevski per. 7; tel. (495) 231-43-59; attached to Russian Acad. of Sciences; Pres. G. V. DOBROVOLSKY.

ARCHITECTURE AND TOWN PLANNING

Union of Russian Architects: 123001 Moscow, Granatni per. 22; tel. (495) 291-55-78; e-mail sarrus@rambler.ru; f. 1981; 12,000 mems; Pres. YU. P. GNEDOVSKIY; publ. *Vesti SAR* (4 a year).

ECONOMICS, LAW AND POLITICS

Association of International Law: 119841 Moscow, ul. Frunze 10; attached to Russian Acad. of Sciences; Chair. Prof. G. I. TUNKIN.

Association of Orientalists: 103753 Moscow, ul. Rozhdestvenka 12; tel. (495) 928-57-64; attached to Russian Acad. of Sciences; Chair. M. S. KAPITSA.

Association of Political Sciences: 118941 Moscow, ul. Znamenka 10; attached to Russian Acad. of Sciences; Pres. Dr G. K. SHAKHNAZAROV.

Economics Society: 117259 Moscow, B. Cheremushkinskaya ul. 34; tel. (495) 120-13-21; Chair. V. S. PAVLOV.

Municipal Economy and Services Society: 103001 Moscow, Trekhprudny per. 11/13; tel. (495) 299-83-00; Chair. A. F. PORYADIN.

Russian Association of Sinologists: 117218 Moscow, Nakhimovsky pr. 32; tel. (495) 124-08-35; e-mail ifes@cemi.rssi.ru; f. 1992; 700 mems; attached to Russian Acad. of Sciences; Pres. V. S. MYASNIKOV.

EDUCATION

All-Russia 'Znanie' Society: 101990 Moscow, Novaya pl. 3/4; tel. (495) 621-90-58; e-mail znanie@znanie.org; internet znanie .org; f. 1947; co-founder of 30 non-govt instns of higher education and 40 instns or centres of additional education; publishes science-popular brochures and books, educational and methodical literature books for children and parents (incl. those on problems of prevention of drug addiction and AIDS), magazines; 120,000 mems; Pres. Prof. OLEG N. SMOLIN; publ. *New Knowledge* (online, 4 a year).

FINE AND PERFORMING ARTS

Russian Academy of Arts: 119034 Moscow, Ul. Prechistenka 21; tel. (495) 201-39-71; f. 1757; depts of architecture and monumental art, decorative arts, graphic art, painting, sculpture; attached research institutes: see under Research Institutes; 218 mems (100 ordinary, 118 corresp.); library: see under Libraries and Archives; Pres. Z. K. TSERETELY; Chief Learned Sec. M. M. KURILKO-RYUMIN; publ. *Informatsionny Byulleten* (Information Bulletin, 4 a year).

Russian Union of Composers: 125009 Moscow, per. Bryusova 8/10; tel. (495) 629-52-18; e-mail ubioncomposers@mail.ru; internet www.soyuzkompozitorov.ru; f. 1960; organizes music competitions and festivals; 1,600 mems; Chair. VLADISLAV KAZENIN; publs *Musical Life*, *Muzikalnaya Akademia*.

Theatre Union of the Russian Federation: 107031 Moscow, Strastnoy bul., dom 10; tel. (495) 650-28-46; e-mail stdrf@stdrf .ru; internet www.stdrf.ru; 30,124 mems; library of 300,000 vols; Chair. ALYEKSANDR ALYEKSANDROVICH KALYAGIN; publ. *Problems of Contemporary Theatre*.

Union of Arts of the Russian Federation: 103062 Moscow, ul. Pokrovka 37.

Union of Russian Filmmakers: 123056 Moscow, Vasilevskaya 13; tel. (495) 251-53-70; e-mail unikino3@aha.ru; internet www .unikino.ru; Chair. NIKITA MIKHALKOV.

HISTORY, GEOGRAPHY AND ARCHAEOLOGY

Russian Geographical Society: 190000 St Petersburg, tsentr, per. Grivtsova 10; tel. (812) 315-85-35; e-mail rgo@spb.org.ru; internet spb.org.ru/rgo; f. 1845; attached to Russian Acad. of Sciences; 20,000 mems; library of 470,000 vols, archive of 600,000 units; Pres. Prof. SERGEI B. LAVROV; publ. *Izvestiya RGS* (6 a year).

LANGUAGE AND LITERATURE

Alliance Française: 191186 St Petersburg, ul. Zhukovskogo 16; tel. (812) 920-36-53; e-mail info@af.spb.ru; internet www.af.spb.ru; offers courses and exams in French language and culture and promotes cultural exchange with France; attached offices in Ekaterinburg, Irkutsk, Kazan, Nizhnii Novgorod, Novosibirsk, Rostov-on-Don, Samara and Yakutsk; Dir of School GALINA DRAGAN.

British Council: 109189 Moscow, ul. Nikoloyamskaya 1; tel. (495) 287-18-00; e-mail moscow@britishcouncil.ru; internet www.britishcouncil.ru; teaching centre; offers courses and exams in English language and British culture and promotes cultural exchange with the UK; attached centres in Ekaterinburg, Irkutsk, Krasnoyarsk, Nizhnii Novgorod, Novosibirsk, Rostov-on-Don, Samara, Sochi, Tomsk, Yaroslavl and Yuzhno-Sakhalinsk; Dir ADRIAN GREER; Training Centre Man. CLARE JEFFS.

Instituto Cervantes: 121069 Moscow, Novinski bul. 20 bl. 1–2; tel. (495) 937-19-52; e-mail cenmos@cervantes.es; internet moscu.cervantes.es; offers courses and exams in Spanish language and culture and promotes cultural exchange with Spain and Spanish-speaking Latin and Central America; library of 12,000 vols; Dir JUAN CARLOS VIDAL GARCÍA.

International Community of Writers' Unions: 121825 Moscow, Povarskaya ul. 52; tel. (495) 291-63-07; f. 1992; 7,000 mems; Chair. G. M. MARKOV; First Sec. TIMUR PULATOV; publs *Inostrannaya Literatura* (12 a year), *Literaturnaya Gazeta* (52 a year), *Novyi Mir* (12 a year).

Press Society: 103051 Moscow, Petrovka 26; tel. (495) 921-82-98; Chair. B. A. KUZMIN.

Russian Association for Comparative Literature: 121069 Moscow, ul. Vorovskogo 25A; tel. (495) 290-17-09; attached to Russian Acad. of Sciences; Chair. Acad. YU. B. VIPPER.

Russian Linguistics Society: 103009 Moscow, ul. Semashko 1/12; attached to Russian Acad. of Sciences; Chair. Acad. T. V. GAMKRELIDZE.

Russian PEN Centre: 107031 Moscow, ul. Neglinnaya 18/1, str. 2; tel. (495) 625-27-18; e-mail penrussian@mail.ru; internet www.penrussia.org; f. 1989; protection of freedom of expression, int. exchange; writers in prison cttee; 371 mems; Pres. ANDREI BITOV; Dir MIKHAIL DEMCHENKOV; Deputy Dir EKATERINA TURCHANINOVA.

Union of Writers of the Russian Federation: 119087 Moscow, Komsomolsky pr. 13; tel. (495) 246-43-50.

MEDICINE

Federation of Anaesthesiologists and Reanimatologists: 119991 Moscow, 2, Petrovsky per. Petrovsky National Research Center of Surgery; tel. (495) 708-35-67; e-mail admin@far.org.ru; internet far.org.ru; f. 1991 (fmrly All-Union Society, f. 1959); 1,200 mems; Pres. Prof. VIKTOR MIZIKOV.

International Society for Pathophysiology: 125315 Moscow, ul. Baltiiskaya 8; tel. (095) 151-17-56; e-mail 4909.g23@g23.relcom.ru; internet home.ptt.ru/pathophysiology; f. 1991; 1,200 mems; Pres. Prof. OSMO HÄNNINEN; Sec.-Gen. L. SZOLLAR; publ. *Pathophysiology* (4 a year).

National Immunological Society: 115478 Moscow, Kashirskoe shosse 24/2; tel. (499) 611-83-33; f. 1983; 500 mems; Chair. R. V. PETROV; Gen. Sec. S. YU. SIDOROVICH; publ. *Immunologiya* (6 a year).

National Medical and Technical Scientific Society: 129301 Moscow, ul. Kasatkina 3; tel. (495) 283-97-84; f. 1968; 55,000 mems and 512 orgs; library: Central State Scientific Medical Library of 3m. vols; Pres. B. I. LEONOV; Chief Learned Sec. B. E. BELOUSOV; publ. *Biomedical Engineering* (6 a year).

National Ophthalmological Society: 103064 Moscow, ul. Sadovo-Chernogryazskaya 14/19; Chair. E. S. AVETISOV; Chief Learned Sec. T. I. FOROFONOFA; publ. *Vestnik Oftalmologii* (6 a year).

National Pharmaceutical Society: 117418 Moscow, ul. Krasikova 34; Chair. M. T. ALYUSHIN; Chief Learned Sec. R. S. SKULKOVA.

National Scientific Medical Society of Anatomists, Histologists and Embryologists: 117869 Moscow, ul. Ostrovityanova 1; Chair. V. V. KUPRIYANOV; Chief Learned Sec. V. V. KOROLEV.

National Scientific Medical Society of Endocrinologists: 117036 Moscow, ul. Dm. Ulyanova 11; Chair. V. G. BARANOV; Chief Learned Sec. N. T. STARKOVA.

National Scientific Medical Society of Haematologists and Transfusiologists: 125167 Moscow, Novozykovskii pr. 4-a; Chair. V. N. SHABALIN; Chief Learned Sec. M. P. KHOKHLOVA.

National Scientific Medical Society of Hygienists: 103064 Moscow, Mechnikova per. 5; Chair. G. N. SERDYUKOVSKAYA; Chief Learned Sec. A. G. SUKHAREV.

National Scientific Medical Society of Infectionists: 125284 Moscow, 1 Botkinskii pr. 3; Chair. V. N. NIKIFOROV; Chief Learned Sec. N. M. BELYAEVA.

National Scientific Medical Society of Nephrologists: 119021 Moscow, ul. Rossolimo 11-A; tel. (495) 248-53-33; f. 1969; holding of conferences, congresses, symposia; 1,200 mems; Chair. N. A. MUKHIN; Chief Learned Sec. S. O. ANDROSOVA.

National Scientific Medical Society of Obstetricians and Gynaecologists: 113163 Moscow, ul. Shabolovka 57; Chair. G. M. SAVELEVA; Chief Learned Sec. T. V. CHERVAKOVA.

National Scientific Medical Society of Oto-Rhino-Laryngologists: 119435 Moscow, Bol. Pirogovskaya 6; Chair. N. A. PREOBRAZHENSKII; Chief Learned Sec. N. P. KONSTANTINOVA.

National Scientific Medical Society of Paediatricians: 117963 Moscow, Lomonosovskii pr. 2/62; Chair M. YU. STUDENIKIN; Chief Learned Sec. G. V. YATSYK.

National Scientific Medical Society of Phthisiologists: 107564 Moscow, platforma Yauza, ul. 6 km Severnoi Zhcleznoi Dorogi; Chair. A. G. KHOMENKO; Chief Learned Sec. V. V. EROKHIN.

National Scientific Medical Society of Physical Therapists and Health-Resort Physicians: 121099 Moscow, Kalinina pr. 50; Chair. A. N. OBROSOV; Chief Learned Sec. V. D. GRIGOREVA.

National Scientific Medical Society of Physicians-Analysts: 123242 Moscow, ul. Sadovaya-Kudrinskaya 3; Chair. B. F. KOROVKIN; Chief Learned Sec. R. L. MARTSISHEVSKAYA.

National Scientific Medical Society of Physicians in Curative Physical Culture and Sports Medicine: 117963 Moscow, Lomonosovskii pr. 2/62; Chair. S. V. KRUZSHEV; Chief Learned Sec. A. V. SOKOVA.

National Scientific Medical Society of Roentgenologists and Radiologists: 117837 Moscow, ul. Profsoyuznaya 86; Chair. A. S. PAVLOV; Chief Learned Sec. V. Z. AGRANAT.

National Scientific Medical Society of Surgeons: 119874 Moscow, Abrikosovskii per. 2; Chair. B. V. PETROVSKII; Chief Learned Sec. M. I. PERELMAN.

Russian Scientific Medical Society of Physicians: 115088 Moscow, ul. Ugreshskaja 2, Bldg 22, Second Fl., First Entrance, Office 202; e-mail mailbox@rnmot.ru; internet www.rnmot.ru; f. 1909, current name adopted 1993; Pres. ANATOLIJ IVANOVICH MARTYNOV; Scientific Sec. ANDREJ A. SPASSKIJ; publs *Arhiv Internal Medicine* (in Russian, online, medarhive.ru), *Farmateka* (in Russian, online, www.pharmateca.ru).

National Scientific Medical Society of Traumatic Surgeons and Orthopaedists: 125299 Moscow, ul. Priorova 10; tel. (495) 450-24-72; f. 1921; Chair. S. P. MIRONOV; Chief Learned Sec. V. V. TROTSENKO; publ. *N. N. Priorov Journal of Traumatology and Orthopaedics* (4 a year).

National Scientific Medical Society of Urological Surgeons: 105483 Moscow, ul. 3-ya Parkovaya 51; tel. (495) 367-62-62; e-mail urology@cdromclub.ru; f. 1925; 5,506 mems; Chair. N. A. LOPATKIN; Chief Learned Sec. L. M. GORILOVSKI; publ. *Urology and Nephrology* (6 a year).

National Scientific Medical Society of Venereologists and Dermatologists: 107076 Moscow, Korolenko str. 3, bldg 6; tel. (495) 964-26-20; e-mail info@cnikvi.ru; f. 1921; Chair. A. A. KUBANOVA; Chief Learned Sec. I. N. LESNAYA.

Russian Academy of Medical Sciences: 109801 Moscow, ul. Solyanka 14; tel. (095) 298-21-37; e-mail orlov@ramn.ru; f. 1944; depts of preventive medicine, clinical medicine, medical and biological sciences; Siberian dept, North-West dept; 60 specialist research ccls; attached research institutes: see under Research Institutes; 496 mems (191 ordinary, 232 corresp., 73 foreign); library: see under Libraries and Archives; Pres. V. I. POKROVSKY; Gen. Sec. V. A. TUTELIAN; publs *Vesti Meditsyny* (Medical News), *Vestnik Rossiiskoi Akademii Meditsinskikh Nauk* (Journal of the Russian Academy of Medical Sciences), *Arkhiv Patologii* (Pathology Archive), *Byulleten Eksperimentalnoi Biologii i Meditsiny* (Bulletin of Experimental Biology and Medicine), *Voprosy Virusologii* (Problems in Virology), *Voprosy Meditsinskoi Khimii* (Problems in Medical Chemistry), *Immunologiya* (Immunology), *Meditsinskaya Radiologiya* (Medical Radiology and Radiation Safety), *Morfologia* (Morphology), *Patologicheskaya Fiziologiya i Eksperimentalnaya Terapiya* (Pathological Physiology and Experimental Therapy), *Eksperimentalnaya i Klinicheskaya Pharmakologiya* (Experimental and Clinical Pharmacology), *Byulleten Sibirskogo Otdeleniya Rossiiskoi AMN* (Bulletin of the Siberian Division of the Russian Academy of Medical Sciences).

Russian Gastroenterological Association: 119881 Moscow, ul. Pogodinskaya 1/1; tel. (495) 248-35-91; e-mail gastro@orc.ru; f. 1995; 2,500 mems; Pres. Prof. Dr V. T. IVASHKIN; Sec. Dr ALEXANDER S. TRUKHMANOV; publs *Journal of Gastroenterology, Hepatology and Coloproctology* (6 a year).

Russian Medical Association: 125315 Moscow, ul. Baltiskaya 10/3; tel. (495) 151-27-67; e-mail rmass@online.ru; internet www .rmass.ru; f. 1993; 262,000 mems; Chair. Prof. A. G. SARKISIAN; Learned Sec. Dr LEV MALYSHEV; publ. *Vrachebnaya Gazeta* (12 a month).

Russian Neurosurgical Association: 603600 Nizhnii Novgorod, Verkhne-Volskaya nab. 18; tel. (8312) 46-36-48; Pres. A. P. FRAERMAN; Sec. S. N. KOLESOV.

Russian Oncological Society (St Petersburg Branch): 197758 St Petersburg, pos. Pesochnyi-2, ul. Leningradskaya 68; tel. (812) 596-86-54; f. 1954; 460 mems; Chair. Prof. Dr VLADIMIR F. SEMIGLAZOV; Sec.-Gen. Dr EVGENIA V. TSYRLINA; publ. *Voprosi Oncologii* (6 a year).

Russian Pharmacology Society: 125315 Moscow, ul. Baltiyskaya 8; tel. (499) 151-18-81; f. 1958, fmrly All-Union Scientific Medical Soc. of Pharmacologists; 295 mems; library of 10,000 vols; Chair. Prof. Acad. SERGEY SEREDENIN; Sec.-Gen. Prof. ELENA VALDMAN; publ. *Russian Journal of Experimental and Clinical Pharmacology* (in Russian).

Russian Rheumatological Association: 115522 Moscow, Kashirskoye shosse 34A; tel. (495) 114-44-90; e-mail sokrat@irramn .ru; internet www.rheumatolog.ru; f. 1928; 1,860 mems; library of 102,000 vols; Chair. E. NASONOV; Gen. Sec. I. ALEXEEVA; publ. *Clinical-practical Rheumatology* (6 a year).

Russian Society of Cardiology: 121019 Moscow, Gogolevsky Blvd; tel. (495) 500-95-90; e-mail info@scardio.ru; internet www .scardio.ru; f. 1963; cardiology, diagnosis, treatment and prevention of cardiovascular disease; training courses; 3,000 mems; Pres. Prof. EVGENY SHLYAKHTO; Sec.-Gen. Prof. ALEXANDER NEDOSHIVIN; publs *Cardiovascular Therapy and Prevention* (6 a year), *Russian Journal of Cardiology* (6 a year).

Russian Society of Medical Genetics: 115478 Moscow, Moskvorechie ul. 1; tel. (499) 612-86-07; e-mail mgnc@med-gen.ru; internet www.med-gen.ru; f. 1993; human genetics, medical genetics, cytogenetics, clinical genetics, genetic counselling, experimental genetics, ecogenetics, human molecular genetics; 500 mems; Chair. Prof. E. K. GINTER; Chief Learned Sec. V. L. IZHEVSKAYA; publ. *Medical Genetics* (12 a year).

Russian Society of Toxicologists: 117105 Moscow, 19A, Varshavskoye shosse; tel. (495) 633-95-90; e-mail khalidiya@yandex.ru; internet www.rpohv.ru; f. 1996; represents Russian toxicologists in int. orgs; contributes information on advanced studies and achievements among toxicologists in Russia; 200 mems; Chair. Dr B. A. KURLYANDSKIY; Exec. Sec. Dr KHALIDYA KHAMIDULINA; publ. *Toxicological Review*.

Scientific Medical Society of Anatomists-Pathologists: 109801 Moscow, ul. Bolshaya Serpuhovskaya 27; Chair. D. S. SARKISOV.

NATURAL SCIENCES
General

Moscow House of Scientists: 119821 Moscow, Kropotkinskaya ul. 16; tel. (495) 201-45-55; attached to Russian Acad. of Sciences; Dir A. I. DERGACHEV.

St Petersburg M. Gorky House of Scientists: 191065 St Petersburg, Dvortsovaya nab. 26; tel. (812) 315-88-14; attached to Russian Acad. of Sciences; Dir L. M. ANISIMOVA.

Biological Sciences

Biochemical Society: c/o Prof. M. B. Agalarova, Ovchinnikov Institute of Bio-organic Chemistry, 117871 Moscow, Miklukho-Maklaya 16/10; tel. (495) 724-81-44; e-mail biosoc@mail.ibch.ru; f. 1959; attached to Russian Acad. of Sciences; 6,500 mems; Pres. Acad. A. G. GABIBOV; Sec.-Gen. MARIA B. AGALAROVA.

Biotechnology Society: 109044 Moscow, Bol. Kommunisticheskaya ul. 27; tel. (495) 272-67-49; Chair. V. E. MATVEYEV.

Hydrobiological Society: 103050 Moscow, Tverskaya ul. 27; tel. (495) 299-65-04; attached to Russian Acad. of Sciences; Pres. L. M. SUSHCHENYA.

Interregional Russian Microbiological Society: 117312 Moscow, pr. 60-letiya Oktyabrya 7, korp. 2; tel. (499) 135-01-80; e-mail microbsociety@inmi.host.ru; internet www.inmi.ru/microbsociety/news.htm; f. 2004; attached to Russian Acad. of Sciences; 580 mems; Pres. V. F. GALCHENKO; Exec. Sec. NATALY GALCHENKO.

Moscow Society of Naturalists: 125009 Moscow, ul. Bolshaya Nikitskaya 6; tel. (495) 629-48-36; internet www.moipros.ru; f. 1805; sections for biophysics, botany, genetics, geography, geology, gerontology, hydrobiology, palaeontology, zoology; 1,500 mems; library of 500,000 vols; Chair Prof. Dr VICTOR A. SADOVNICHY; publ. *Byulleten Moskovskogo Obshchestva Ispytatelei prirody* (6 a year).

Palaeontological Society: 199106 St Petersburg, Sredny Prospect 74; tel. (812) 328-91-56; e-mail po_ran@vsegei.ru; f. 1916; attached to Russian Acad. of Sciences; 700 mems; Pres. B. S. SOKOLOV.

Russian Botanical Society: 197376 St Petersburg, ul. Prof. Popova 2; tel. (812) 346-47-53; attached to Russian Acad. of Sciences; Pres. R. V. KAMELIN.

Russian Entomological Society: 199034 St Petersburg, Universitetskaya nab. 1; tel. (812) 328-12-12; e-mail reo@zisp.spb.su; f. 1859; attached to Russian Acad. of Sciences; 2,000 mems; library of 80,000 vols; Pres. G. S. MEDVEDEV; publs *Chtenia Pamyati N.A. Kholodkovskogo* (1 a year), *Entomologicheskoe Obozrenie* (4 a year), *Trudy Russkogo Entomologicheskogo Obschestva* (irregular).

Russian Society of Geneticists and Breeders: 117312 Moscow, ul. Fersmana 11, korp. 2; tel. (495) 124-59-52; attached to Russian Acad. of Sciences; Pres. Acad. V. A. STRUNNIKOV.

Society of Helminthologists: 117259 Moscow, Bol. Cheremushkinskaya 28; attached to Russian Acad. of Sciences; Pres. A. S. BESSONOV.

Society of Ornithologists: c/o Russian Academy of Sciences, 117901 Moscow, Leninsky pr. 14; attached to Russian Acad. of Sciences; Pres. V. D. ILICHEV.

Society of Protozoologists: 194064 St Petersburg, Tikhoretsky pr. 4; tel. (812) 247-18-36; e-mail tamara@tb10336.spb.edu; f. 1968 as All-Union Society of Protozoologists; present name 1991; attached to Russian Acad. of Sciences; 200 mems; Pres. (vacant); Sec.-Gen. Prof. Dr TAMARA V. BEYER; publs *Protistology* (4 a year), *Tsitologiya* (Cytology, in Russian with English summaries, 12 a year).

Physical Sciences

Astronomical and Geodesical Society: 103001 Moscow, Sadovo-Kudrinskaya ul. 24; attached to Russian Acad. of Sciences; Pres. YU. D. BULANZHE.

Ferrous Metallurgy Society: 129812 Moscow, pr. Mira 101; tel. (495) 287-83-80; Chair. N. I. DROZDOV.

Gubkin, Acad. I. M., Petroleum and Gas Society: 117876 Moscow, 12-ya Parkovaya ul. 5; tel. (495) 463-93-72; Chair. S. T. TOPLOV.

Mendeleev, D. I., Chemical Society: 101907 Moscow, Krivokolennyi per. 12; tel. (495) 928-43-51; f. 1868; 45 regional orgs; 1,800 mems; Sec.-Gen. NATATYA KOSSINOVA; publs *Chemistry in Russia* (12 a year bulletin), *Russian Chemical Journal* (6 a year).

Russian Geological Society: 113191 Moscow, 2-aya Roshinskaya ul. 10; tel. (495) 954-96-34; f. 1988; 1,025 mems; Pres. V. P. ORLOV.

Russian Mineralogical Society: 199026 St Petersburg, 21st line 2; tel. (812) 328-86-40; e-mail rmo@minsoc.ru; internet www.minsoc .ru; f. 1817; attached to Russian Acad. of Sciences; mineralogy and adjacent sciences; 1,200 mems; library of 85,000 vols; Pres. Prof. DMITRY RUNDQVIST; Vice-Pres. Prof. YURI MARIN; publ. *Zapiski RMO* (Proceedings of the Russian Mineralogical Society).

Society of Non-Ferrous Metallurgy: 103001 Moscow, Sadovaya-Kudrinskaya ul. 18; tel. (495) 291-29-87; Chair. V. S. LOBANOV.

PHILOSOPHY AND PSYCHOLOGY

Russian Philosophical Society: 119991 Moscow, ul. Volhonka 14, Room 102; tel. (495) 609-90-76; e-mail rphs@iph.ras.ru; internet www.dialog21.ru; f. 1971; attached to Russian Acad. of Sciences; 6,131 mems; Pres. V. S. STEPIN; Vice-Pres. A. N. CHUMAKOV; publ. *Bulletin of the Russian Philosophical Society*.

Society of Psychologists: 129366 Moscow, Yaroslavskaya ul. 13; tel. (495) 282-45-03; attached to Russian Acad. of Sciences; Chair. E. V. SHOROKHOVA.

RELIGION, SOCIOLOGY AND ANTHROPOLOGY

Russian Society of Sociologists: 117259 Moscow, ul. Krzhizhanovskogo 24/35 str. 5; tel. (495) 719-09-71; e-mail mansurov@isras .rssi.ru; internet www.isras.rssi.ru; f. 1989; attached to Russian Acad. of Sciences; 1,350 mems; Chair. VALERY A. MANSUROV.

TECHNOLOGY

Aircraft Building Society: 125040 Moscow, Leningradskii pr. 24a; tel. (495) 214-22-88; Chair. A. M. BATKOV.

Civil Engineering Society: 103062 Moscow, Podsosensky per. 25; tel. (495) 297-07-29; Chair. I. I. ISHENKO.

Computers and Informatics Society: 127486 Moscow, Deguninskaya ul. 1, korp. 4; tel. (495) 487-31-61; Chair. I. N. BUKREYEV.

Mapping and Prospecting Engineering Society: 117801 Moscow, ul. Krzhizhanovskogo 14, korp. 2; tel. (495) 124-35-60; Chair. A. A. DRAZHNYUK.

Mechanical Engineering Society: 109004 Moscow, ul. Zemlyanoi Val 64, korp. 1; tel. (495) 297-93-00; Chair. B. N. SOKOLOV.

Mining Engineers' Society: 103006 Moscow, Karetnyi ryad 10/18; tel. (495) 299-88-15; Chair. A. P. FISUN.

Russian Popov Society/A. S. Popov Society: 103907 Moscow, ul. Mokhovaya, 11; tel. (495) 203-49-93; internet www.comsoc.org/ about/sistersocieties/popov; attached to Institute of Radio Engineering and Electronics, Russian Academy of Sciences; Chair. YURY GULYAEV.

Shipbuilding Engineering Society: 191011 St Petersburg, Nevskii pr. 44; tel. (812) 315-50-27; Dir I. V. GORYNIN.

Society of the Food Industry: 103031 Moscow, Kuznetskii Most 19, pod. 2; tel. (495) 924-49-30; Chair. A. N. BOGATYREV.

Society of the Instrument Manufacturing Industry and Metrologists: 103009 Moscow, Tverskaya ul. 12, str. 2; tel. (495) 209-47-98; Chair. G. I. KAVALEROV.

Society of Light Industry: 117846 Moscow, ul. Vavilova 69; tel. (495) 134-90-01; Chair. R. A. CHAYANOV.

Vavilov, S. I., Society of Instrument Manufacturers: 121019 Moscow, Mokhovaya ul. 17, str. 2; tel. (495) 203-34-65.

Water Transport Society: 103012 Moscow, Staropansky per. 3; tel. (495) 921-18-12; Chair. (vacant).

Research Institutes

AGRICULTURE, FISHERIES AND VETERINARY SCIENCE

Adygea Agricultural Research Institute: 352764 Krasnodar krai, Maikop, Podgornoe; attached to Russian Acad. of Agricultural Sciences.

Afanasev, V. A., Research Institute of Fur-Bearing Animals and Rabbits: 140143 Moscow oblast, Ramensky raion, p/o Rodniki; tel. (495) 501-53-55; e-mail niipzk@mail.ru; f. 1932; attached to Russian Acad. of Agricultural Sciences; Dir N. A. BALAKIREV.

Agrarian Institute: 103064 Moscow, Bol. Kharitonevskaya per. 21, korp. 2, POB 34; tel. (495) 207-70-75; e-mail agrin@glas.apc.org; f. 1990; attached to Russian Acad. of Agricultural Sciences; Dir Dr A. V. PETRIKOV.

Agricultural Research Institute for the Central Areas of the Non-Black Soil (Nechernozem) Zone: 143104 Moscow oblast, Odintsovsky raion, Nemchinovka, ul. Agrokhimikov 6; tel. (495) 591-83-91; attached to Russian Acad. of Agricultural Sciences.

Agricultural Research Institute for South-East Region (ARISER): 410010 Saratov, ul. Tulaykova 7; tel. (845) 264-76-88; e-mail saratov@mail.ru; internet www.ariser.narod.ru; f. 1910; attached to Russian Acad. of Agricultural Sciences; library of 350,000 vols, 500 titles; Dir A. I. PRYANISHNIKOV; Scientific Sec. I. N. CHYERNYEVA; publ. *Agrarniy Vyestnik Grarniy Vyestnik Yoogo-Vostoka* (Agricultural Gazette of South-East).

Agrophysical Research Institute: 195220 St Petersburg, Grazhdanskii pr.14; tel. (495) 534-13-24; e-mail office@agrophys.ru; f. 1932; attached to Russian Acad. of Agricultural Sciences; Dir I. B. USKOV.

All-Russia Horticulture Institute for Breeding, Agrotechnology and Nursery: 115598 Moscow, Birulevo-Zagorie, ul. Zagorievskogo; tel. (495) 329-51-66; e-mail vstisp@vstisp.org; internet www.vstisp.org; attached to Russian Acad. of Agricultural Sciences; Dir IVAN KULIKOV; publ. *Fruit Trees and Small Fruits of Russia* (2 a year).

All-Russia Institute of Plant Protection: 196608 St Petersburg, Pushkin, shosse Podbelskogo 3; tel. (812) 470-43-84; e-mail vizrspb@mail333.com; internet www.vizrspb.chat.ru; f. 1929; attached to Russian Acad. of Agricultural Sciences; Dir V. A. PAVLYUSHIN; publ. *Plant Protection News* (3 a year).

All-Russia Legumes and Pulse Crops Research Institute: 302502 Orel, p/o Streletskoe; tel. (0862) 403-224; e-mail office@vniizbk.orel.ru; internet vniizbk.ru; attached to Russian Acad. of Agricultural Sciences; Dir Prof. V. I. ZOTIKOV.

All-Russian Maize Research Institute: 860022 Nalchik, ul. Mechnikova 130A; tel. (86622) 5-03-16; attached to Russian Acad. of Agricultural Sciences.

All-Russian Research Institute of Horticultural Breeding: 302530 Orel, Zhilina; tel. (486) 242-11-39; e-mail info@vniispk.ru; internet www.vniispk.ru; attached to Russian Acad. of Agricultural Sciences; Dir SYERGYEY DMITRIYEVICH KNYAZYEV; publ. *Sovryemyennoye Sadovodstvo* (Contemporary Horticulture, 4 a year, in Russian and English, vniispk.ru/news/zhurnal/article.php).

All-Russia Potato Research Institute: 140052 Moscow oblast, Lyuberetsky raion, pos. Korenevo, ul. Lorkha; tel. (495) 557-10-11; f. 1930; attached to Russian Acad. of Agricultural Sciences; library of 500,000 vols; Dir Prof. A. V. KORSHUNOV.

All-Russia Poultry Research and Technology Institute: Moscow oblast, Sergiev pos.; attached to Russian Acad. of Agricultural Sciences.

All-Russia Research and Technological Institute for Chemical Land Reclamation: 189520 St Petersburg, Pushkin, ul. Lermontova 9; tel. (812) 465-58-75; attached to Russian Acad. of Agricultural Sciences.

All-Russia Research and Development Institute of Agricultural Biotechnology: 127550 Moscow, ul. Timiryazevskaya 42; tel. (495) 977-09-47; attached to Russian Acad. of Agricultural Sciences; Dir P. N. KHARCHENKO.

All-Russia Research and Technological Institute for Chemicalization in Agriculture: 143013 Moscow oblast, Odinstsovsky raion, Nemchinovka, ul. Agrokhimikov 6; tel. (495) 591-91-73; attached to Russian Acad. of Agricultural Sciences.

All-Russia Research and Technological Institute for Mechanization in Livestock Raising: 142004 Moscow oblast, Podolsky raion, p/o Znamya Oktyabrya; 31; tel. (495) 119-74-97; f. 1969; attached to Russian Acad. of Agricultural Sciences; Dir N. M. MOROZOV; publ. *Scientific Research Problems of Mechanization and Automation of Livestock Farming.*

All-Russia Research Institute for Agricultural Biotechnology: 127550 Moscow, Timiryazevskaya ul. 42; tel. (495) 976-65-44; e-mail iab@iab.ac.ru; internet www.agrobiotech.ru; f. 1974; attached to Russian Acad. of Agricultural Sciences; Dir P. N. KHARCHENKO.

All-Russia Research Institute for Agricultural Economics and Standards and Norms: 344006 Rostov on Don, pr. Sokolova 52; tel. (8632) 65-31-81; f. 1980; attached to Russian Acad. of Agricultural Sciences; Dir Dr VLADIMIR V. KUZNETSOV.

All-Russia Research Institute for Beef Cattle Breeding and Production: Orenburg, Yanvarskaya ul. 29; attached to Russian Acad. of Agricultural Sciences.

All-Russia Research Institute for Biological Control: 350039 Krasnodar, a/ya 39; tel. (8612) 50-81-91; attached to Russian Acad. of Agricultural Sciences.

All-Russia Research Institute for Cybernetics in the Agro-industrial Complex: 117218 Moscow, ul. Krzhizhanovskogo 14/1; tel. (495) 124-76-02; attached to Russian Acad. of Agricultural Sciences.

All-Russia Research Institute for Economics, Labour and Management in Agriculture: 111621 Moscow, Orenburgs-kaya ul. 15; tel. (495) 550-06-71; attached to Russian Acad. of Agricultural Sciences.

All-Russia Research Institute for Electrification in Agriculture: 109456 Moscow, 1-i Veshnyakovskii pr. 2; tel. (499) 171-19-20; e-mail viesh@dol.ru; internet www.viesh.ru; f. 1930; attached to Russian Acad. of Agricultural Sciences; rural energy and electrification, solar energy biomass and wind energy; library of 135,000 vols; Dir Acad. D. S. STREBKOV; publ. *Scientific Proceedings* (2 a year).

All-Russia Research Institute for Farm Animal Genetics and Breeding: 196600 St Petersburg-Pushkin, Moskovskoye shosse 55a; tel. (812) 470-76-63; e-mail spbvniigen@mail.ru; attached to Russian Acad. of Agricultural Sciences; Dir Acad. P.N. PROCHORENKO.

All-Russia Research Institute for Floriculture and Subtropical Crops: 354002 Sochi, Jan Fabriziusa str. 2/28; tel. (8622) 96-40-21; e-mail subplod@mail.ru; f. 1894; attached to Russian Acad. of Agricultural Sciences; library of 77,000 vols.

All-Russia Research Institute for Horse Breeding: 391105 Ryazan oblast, Rybnoyek raion; tel. (912) 24-02-65; e-mail vniik08@mail.ru; internet www.ruhorses.ru; f. 1930; attached to Russian Acad. of Agricultural Sciences; library of 47,000 vols; Dir Prof. Dr V. V. KALASHNIKOV; publs *Scientific Works* (1 a year), *Stud Book* (every 4 years, with 1 year supplement).

All-Russia Research Institute for Irrigated Arable Farming: 400002 Volgograd, Timiryazevskaya ul. 9; tel. (8442) 43-49-79; e-mail vniioz@avtlg.ru; f. 1967; attached to Russian Acad. of Agricultural Sciences; library of 138,000 vols; Dir Dr V. V. MELIKHOV.

All-Russia Research Institute for Irrigated Horticulture and Vegetable Crops Production: 416300 Astrakhan oblast, Kamyziak, ul. Lubicha 13; attached to Russian Acad. of Agricultural Sciences.

All-Russia Research Institute for Mechanization in Agriculture: 109389 Moscow, 1-i Institutskii pr. 5; tel. (495) 171-19-33; attached to Russian Acad. of Agricultural Sciences; Dir Acad. V. A. KUIBYSHEV.

All-Russia Research Institute for Sheep and Goat Breeding: 355014 Stavropol, Zootekhnichesky per. 15; tel. (8652) 34-76-88; f. 1932; attached to Russian Acad. of Agricultural Sciences; Dir Prof. VASILY MOROZ.

All-Russia Research Institute for the Agricultural Use of Reclaimed and Improved Land: 170530 Tver oblast, Emmaus; tel. (0822) 37-15-46; e-mail vniimz@mail.ru; internet www.vniimz.newmail; f. 1977; attached to Russian Acad. of Agricultural Sciences; library of 20,000 vols; Dir Dr N. KOVALEV.

All-Russia Research Institute for the Biosynthesis of Protein Substances: 109004 Moscow, Bol. Kommunisticheskaya 27; tel. (495) 912-70-09; e-mail belok@rutenia.ru; attached to Russian Acad. of Agricultural Sciences; Dir Dr ALEXANDER P. ZAKHARYCHEV.

All-Russia Research Institute for Vegetable Breeding and Seed Production: 143080 Moscow oblast, Odintsovsky raion, Lesnoi gorodok; tel. (495) 599-24-42; e-mail vniissok@cea.ru; f. 1920; attached to Russian Acad. of Agricultural Sciences; Dir Prof. VICTOR F. PIVOVAROV.

All-Russia Research Institute for Veterinary Sanitation, Hygiene and Ecology: 123022 Moscow, Zvenigorodskoe shosse 5; tel. (495) 256-35-81; attached to Russian Acad. of Agricultural Sciences.

All-Russia Research Institute of Agricultural Microbiology: 189620 St Petersburg, Pushkin 8, shosse Podbelskogo 3; tel. (812) 470-51-00; f. 1930; attached to Russian Acad. of Agricultural Sciences; Dir Prof. I. A. TIKHONOVICH.

All-Russia Research Institute of Animal Husbandry: 142023 Moscow oblast, Podolskii raion, pos. Dubrovitsy; tel. (495) 546-63-35; attached to Russian Acad. of Agricultural Sciences; Dir Acad. A. P. KALASHNIKOV.

All-Russia Research Institute of Arable Farming and Soil Erosion Control: 305021 Kursk, ul. Karla Marksa 70B; tel. (0712) 53-42-56; e-mail vnizem@kursknet.ru; f. 1970; attached to Russian Acad. of Agricultural Sciences; library of 20,000 vols, 40 periodicals; Dir G. N. CHERKASOV.

All-Russia Research Institute of Economics in Agriculture: 123007 Moscow, Khoroshevskoe shosse 35, korp 3; tel. (495) 195-60-16; attached to Russian Acad. of Agricultural Sciences; Dir I. G. USHCHACHEV.

All-Russia Research Institute of Information, Technological and Economic Research on the Agro-Industrial Complex: c/o Russian Academy of Agricultural Sciences, 107814 Moscow, Bolshoi Kharitonevsky per. 21; attached to Russian Acad. of Agricultural Sciences; Dir Acad. V. I. NAZARENKO.

All-Russia Research Institute of Marine Fisheries and Oceanography: 107140 Moscow, Verkhnyaya Krasnoselskaya 17; tel. (495) 264-93-87; Dir A. S. BOGDANOV.

All-Russia Research Institute of Medicinal and Aromatic Plants: 113628 Moscow, ul. Grina 7; tel. (495) 382-83-18; attached to Russian Acad. of Agricultural Sciences.

All-Russia Research Institute of Organic Fertilizers and Peat: 601390, Vladimir obl., Sudogodskiy region, Vyatkino; tel. (22) 42-60-14; e-mail vnion@vtsnet.ru; f. 1981; attached to Russian Acad. of Agricultural Sciences; Dir Dr LUKIN SERGEY MICHAILOVICH.

All-Russia Research Institute of Phytopathology: 143050 Moscow oblast, Vyazemy; tel. (495) 592-92-87; e-mail vniif@vniif .ru; attached to Russian Acad. of Agricultural Sciences.

All-Russia Research Institute of Pond Fishery: 141821 Moscow oblast, Dmitrovsky raion, p/o Rubnoe; tel. (495) 587-21-98; attached to Russian Acad. of Agricultural Sciences.

All-Russia Research Institute of Tobacco, Makhorka and Tobacco Products: 350072 Krasnodar, Moskovskaya ul. 42; tel. (861) 252-08-82; e-mail vniitti1@mail .kuban.ru; attached to Russian Acad. of Agricultural Sciences; Dir V. A. SALOMATIN.

All-Russia Rice Research Institute: 350921, Krasnodar, Belozerny; tel. (8612) 29-41-98; e-mail arrri_kub@mail.ru; f. 1931; attached to Russian Min. of Agriculture; Dir Prof. EVGENY MIKHAILOVICH KHARITONOV.

All-Russia Vegetable Production Research Institute: 141018 Moscow oblast, Mytishchi, Novomytishchinsky pr. 82; tel. (495) 582-00-15; attached to Russian Acad. of Agricultural Sciences.

All-Russia Veterinary Research Institute for Poultry Diseases: St Petersburg, Moskovsky pr. 99; attached to Russian Acad. of Agricultural Sciences.

All-Russian Plant Quarantine Centre: 140150 Bykovo, Ramenskoe region, Moscow oblast, Pogranichnaya 32; tel. (499) 271-38-24; e-mail vniikr@mail.ru; internet www .vniikr.ru; f. 1979; plant quarantine research

and diagnostics; library of 10,000 vols; Dir Dr ULLUBY MAGOMEDOV; Deputy Dir Dr NATALYA SHEROKOLAVA; Deputy Dir Dr MUZAFAR ABASOV; Deputy Dir Dr EVGENY MAZURIN; publ. *Plant Quarantine Issues.*

All-Russian Rapeseed Research Institute: 398037 Lipetsk, Boevoy proezd 26; tel. (4742) 34-63-61; e-mail rapeseed@yandex.ru; internet rapslipetsk.ru; f. 1986; attached to Russian Acad. of Agricultural Sciences; Head VLADIMIR VLADIMIROVICH KARPACHEV.

All-Russian Scientific Research Institute of Agroforest Reclamation: 400062 Volgograd, Universitetsky pr. 97; tel. (8442) 46-25-67; e-mail vnialmi@avtlg.ru; internet www.vnialmi.ru; f. 1931; attached to Russian Acad. of Agricultural Sciences; research on reclamation of agricultural lands by methods of forest and phytomelioration; combats desertification processes; ecological investigations; library of 93,700 vols; Dir KONSTANTIN N. KULIK; publ. *Scientific Papers* (2 a year).

All-Russian Williams Fodder Research Institute: 141055 Moscow oblast, Lobnya Nauchniy gorodok; tel. (495) 577-73-37; e-mail vniicormov@nm.ru; internet www .vniikormov.ru; f. 1922; attached to Russian Acad. of Agricultural Sciences; scientific research in fields of agriculture, biology, genetics, breeding and seed multiplication of forage crops; grasslands management, fodder production, fodder preservation and utilization; library of 15,000 vols of books, scientific journals, methodological recommendations, brochures, patents, dissertations; Dir Prof. Dr VLADIMIR KOSOLAPOV; publ. *Adaptive Fodder Production (AFP)* (4 a year, online, www.adaptagro.ru).

Altai Experimental Farm: 659739 Altai krai, Gorno-Altaisky autonomous oblast, Shebalinsky raion, selo Cherga; attached to Russian Acad. of Sciences; Dir YU. S. ZEMIROV.

Bashkir Research and Technological Institute for Animal Husbandry and Feed Production: Bashkortostan, 450025 Ufa, Pushkinskaya ul. 86; tel. (3472) 22-17-23; attached to Russian Acad. of Agricultural Sciences.

Bashkir Research Institute for Arable Farming and Field Crops Breeding: 450059 Ufa, ul. Zorge 19; tel. (3472) 24-07-08; attached to Russian Acad. of Agricultural Sciences.

Caspian Research Institute for Arid Arable Farming: 431213 Astrakhan, Solenoe zaimishche; tel. (851) 24-38-36; f. 1991; attached to Russian Acad. of Agricultural Sciences; library of 30,000 vols.

Chelyabinsk Agricultural Research Institute: 456404 Chelyabinsk oblast, Chebarkulsky raion, Timiryazevsky; tel. (3516) 87-14-88; attached to Russian Acad. of Agricultural Sciences; Dir A. V. VRAZHNOV.

Dagestan Agricultural Research Institute: 367014 Makhachkala, pr. K. Marksa, Nauchnyi park; tel. (8722) 3-66-60; attached to Russian Acad. of Agricultural Sciences.

Don Zonal Research and Development Institute of Agriculture: 346714 Rostov oblast, Aksai raion, Rassvet; tel. (863) 503-71-75; e-mail dzniisx@aksay.donpac.ru; attached to Russian Acad. of Agricultural Sciences; Dir V. P. ERMOLENKO.

Flax Research Institute: 172002 Tverskii raion, Torzhok, ul. Lunacharskogo 35; tel. (482) 515-16-45; e-mail vniil@mail.ru; internet www.vniil.narod.ru; f. 1930; library of 50,000 vols; Dir VLADIMIR PAVLOVICH PONAZHYEV; publ. *Trudy VNIL* (1 a year).

Forest Research Institute of the Karelian Research Centre: 185910 Petroza-

vodsk, Pushkinskaya ul. 11; tel. (8142) 76-81-60; e-mail forest@krc.karelia.ru; internet forestry.krc.karelia.ru; f. 1957; attached to Russian Acad. of Sciences; Dir Dr VITALY KRUTOV.

Gorbatov's All-Russia Meat Research Institute: 109316 Moscow, ul. Talilikhina 26; tel. (495) 676-95-11; e-mail info@vniimp .ru; internet www.vniimp.ru; f. 1930; attached to Russian Acad. of Agricultural Sciences; Dir Dr ANDREI LISITSYN; Scientific Sec. NATALIA GORBUNOVA; publ. *All About Meat—The Theory and Practice of Meat Processing* (6 a year).

Institute of Forest Research: 143030 Moscow oblast, Odintsovsky raion, p/o Uspenskoe; tel. (495) 419-52-57; f. 1958; attached to Russian Acad. of Sciences; library of 51,400 vols; Dir Prof. S. E. VOMPERSKY; publ. *Lesovedenie* (Russian Forest Science, 6 a year).

Institute of Forestry: 620134 Ekaterinburg, Bilimbaevskaya ul. 32A; tel. (3432) 52-08-80; attached to Russian Acad. of Sciences; Dir S. A. MAMAEV.

Institute of Soil Science and Agrochemistry: 630099 Novosibirsk, Sovetskaya St. 18; tel. (3832) 22-50-88; e-mail go2siberia@ gmail.com; internet www.siberia-eco.org; f. 1968; attached to Russian Acad. of Sciences; education and research soil science, plant nutrition, pedology, soil chemistry, soil microbiology, int. field courses, summer schools in Siberia, int. annual soil-ecological excursions in Siberia; Dir Dr KONSTANTIN S. BAYKOV; Scientific Sec. for Int. Cooperation Dr PAVEL A. BARSUKOV.

Ya. R. Kovalenko All-Russia Research Institute of Experimental Veterinary Science: 109428 Moscow, Ryazanskiy pr. 24, korp. 1; tel. (495) 970-03-69; e-mail admin@viev.ru; internet www.viev.ru; f. 1898 in St Petersburg; present name and status 1992; attached to Russian Acad. of Agricultural Sciences; Dir MIHAIL IVANOVICH GOOLYOOKIN.

Kursk Research and Development Institute of the Agro-industrial Complex: 305526 Kursk oblast, Cheremushki; tel. (471) 259-53-40; attached to Russian Acad. of Agricultural Sciences; Dir A. YA AIDIEV.

P. P. Lukianenko Krasnodar Research and Development Institute of Agriculture: 350012 Krasnodar; tel. (861) 222-11-20; e-mail kniish@kniish.ru; internet www .kniish.ru; f. 1914; attached to Russian Acad. of Agricultural Sciences; Dir ALYEKSANDR ALYEKSYEYEVICH ROMANYENKO; Scientific Sec. OL'GA FYEDOROVNA KOLYESNIKOVA.

Michurin, I. V., All-Russia Research Institute for Genetics and Breeding in Horticulture: 393740 Tambov oblast, Michurinsk; tel. (47545) 5-78-87; e-mail cglm@rambler.ru; attached to Russian Acad. of Agricultural Sciences; Dir SAVELYEV NIKOLAI IVANOVICH.

Michurin, I. V., All-Russia Research Institute for Horticulture: 393740 Tambov oblast, Michurinsk, ul. Michurina 30; tel. (47545) 2-07-61; e-mail vniis@pochta.ru; f. 1931; attached to Russian Acad. of Agricultural Sciences; Dir Prof. Dr YURI TRUNOV.

N. I. Vavilov All Russian Research Institute of the Plant Industry: 190000 St Petersburg Bolshaya Morskaya St 42–44; tel. (812) 315-50-93; e-mail office@vir.nw.ru; internet vir.nw.ru; f. 1894; attached to Russian Acad. of Agricultural Sciences; depts: computerized information systems; plant biochemistry and molecular biology; laboratory for long-term storage of seeds; rye, barley and oats; fruit crops; industrial crops; experimental stations: Astrakhan, Dagestan, Far

East, Krymsk, Kuban, Maikop, Moscow, Pavlovsk, Polar, Volgograd, Yekaterinino, Zeya; herbarium of 250,000 specimens; Dir Prof. Dr NIKOLAI I. DZYUBENKO.

Nizhne-Volzhsky Agricultural Research Institute: 404013 Volgograd oblast, Nizheznensky; attached to Russian Acad. of Agricultural Sciences.

North Caucasian Mountains and Foothills Agricultural Research Institute: 363110 Mikhailovskoe, N Ossetia, Prigorny raion 1; tel. (867) 273-03-40; attached to Russian Acad. of Agricultural Sciences; Dir A. A. ABAEV.

North Caucasian Zonal Research and Development Institute of Horticulture and Viticulture: 350901 Krasnodar, ul. 40-letiya Pobedy 39; tel. (861) 252-70-74; e-mail kubansad@kubannet.ru; internet www.kubansad.ru; attached to Russian Acad. of Agricultural Sciences; Dir YEVGYENIY ALYEKSYEYEVICH YEGOROV; Scientific Sec. NATALIYA MIHAYLOVNA ZAPOROZHYETS.

Orenburg Research and Development Institute of Agriculture: 460051 Orenburg, ul. Gagarina 27/1; tel. (353) 271-05-50; e-mail orniish@mail.ru; attached to Russian Acad. of Agricultural Sciences; Dir G. I. BELKOV.

Pacific Fisheries Research Centre (TINRO): 690950 Vladivostok, ul. Shevchenko 4; tel. (4232) 400921; e-mail tinro@tinro.ru; f. 1925; ichthyology, oceanography, commercial invertebrates, commercial marine algae, parasitology of marine animals, commercial fisheries, mechanization of fish processing, technology of fish and marine production, aquaculture (marine and freshwater), study of marine pollution; brs at Amur (Khabarovsk) and Chukotka; library of 61,500 vols, 11,000 MSS; Dir Dr L. N. BOCHAROV; publ. *Izvestiya TINRO* (1–3 a year).

Potapenko, Ya. I., All-Russia Research Institute for Viticulture and Winemaking: Rostovsky raion, 346421 Novocherkassk, pr. Baklanovsky 166; tel. (86352) 6-70-88; e-mail ruswine@yandex.ru; internet www.rusvine.com; f. 1936; attached to Russian Acad. of Agricultural Sciences; Dir Dr LEONID VASILIEVICH KRAVCHENKO.

Volga Region Research and Development Institute of Economics and Organization of Agroindustrial Complex: 410010 Saratov, ul. Shekhurdina 12; tel. (845) 264-06-47; e-mail niiapksar@yandex.ru; attached to Russian Acad. of Agricultural Sciences; Dir A. A. CHERNIAEV.

Pryanishnikov, D. N., All-Russia Research Institute of Agrochemistry: 127550 Moscow, ul. Pryanishnikova 31A; tel. (495) 976-37-50; e-mail info@vniia-pr.ru; internet www.vniia-pr.ru; f. 1931; attached to Russian Acad. of Agricultural Sciences; coordination of field experiments with Fertilizers Network, Scientific and Methodical Center of Agrochemical Service, Official Registration Agency for Chemicals and Soils; theory of crop nutrition, soil fertility monitoring of agricultural lands, strategy of fertilizers and chemicals application, geographical principles of fertilizer efficiency, new fertilizers; updating of agrochemical service, integration of agrochemical data; Dir V. G. SYCHEV.

Pustovoit, V. S., All-Russia Research Institute of Oil Crops: 350038 Krasnodar, ul. Filatova 17; tel. (861) 255-59-33; e-mail vniimk-center@mail.ru; internet www.vniimk.ru; f. 1912; attached to Russian Acad. of Agricultural Sciences; breeding and seed growing of oil crops: sunflower, soybean, flax, mustard, rapeseed; library of 100,300

vols; Gen. Dir Dr VYACHESLAV M. LUKOMETS; publ. *Oil Crops Scientific Bulletin* (2 a year).

Research Institute for Animal Nutrition: Moscow oblast, Dmitrovsky raion, pos. Ermolovo.

Research Institute of Chemical Means of Plant Protection: 109088 Moscow, Ugreshskaya 31; tel. (495) 679-55-40; Dir B. P. VASILENKOV.

Research Institute of Farm Animal Physiology, Biochemistry and Nutrition: 249010 Kaluzhskaya oblast, Borovsk; tel. (495) 996-34-15; e-mail bifip@kaluga.ru; internet bifip2006.narod.ru; f. 1960; attached to Russian Acad. of Agricultural Sciences; library of 55,000 vols; Dir Dr A. SH. USHAKOV; publ. *Problems of Productive Animal Biology* (4 a year).

Research Institute of Non-infectious Animal Diseases: Moscow oblast, Istrinsky raion.

Research Institute of Technological Studies in Agricultural Cybernetics: c/o Russian Academy of Agricultural Sciences, 107814 Moscow, Bolshoi Kharitonevsky per. 21; attached to Russian Acad. of Agricultural Sciences.

Research Institute of the Economics and Development of the Agro-industrial Complex in the Central Black Soil (Chernozem) Zone: 394042 Voronezh, ul. Sarafimovicha 26A; tel. (4732) 22-99-40; e-mail niieoapk@mail.ru; internet niieoapk.ru; f. 1930; attached to Russian Acad. of Agricultural Sciences; Dir I. HITSKOV.

All-Russia Research and Development Institute of Veterinary Entomology and Arachnology: 625041 Tyumen, Institutskaya ul. 2; tel. (345) 262-57-00; e-mail vniivea@mail.ru; internet www.vniivea.ru; attached to Russian Acad. of Agricultural Sciences; Dir G. S. SIVKOV.

Russian Institute of Agricultural Radiology and Agroecology: 249032 Kaluga oblast, Obninsk, Kievskoe shosse 109 km; tel. (48439) 6-48-02; e-mail riarae@riar.obninsk.org; f. 1971; attached to Russian Acad. of Agricultural Sciences; library of 70,000 vols; Dir RUDOLF M. ALEXAKHIN; Deputy Dir NATALYA I. SANZHAROVA.

Russian Research Institute of Canning and Vegetable-Drying Industry: 142730 Vidnoye, 78, Shkolnaya Str.; tel. (9163) 28-61-03; e-mail kvlad_46@mail.ru; internet www.vnikop.ru; f. 1938; attached to Russian Acad. of Agricultural Sciences; Dir ANDREY PETROV; Vice Dir of Science Dr VLADIMIR KONDRATENKO.

St Petersburg Forestry Research Institute: 194021 St Petersburg, Institutsky pr. 21; tel. (812) 552-80-21; e-mail spbfriin@nm10043.spb.edu; internet www.spbniilh.ru; f. 1929; 130 mems; library of 90,000 vols; Dir ALEXANDER B. EGOROV (acting).

Samoilov, Ya. V., Research Institute of Fertilizers and Insectofungicides: 119333 Moscow, Leninsky pr. 55/1, bldg 1; tel. (495) 232-96-89; e-mail info@niui.ru; internet www.niuif.ru; f. 1919; technology for production of phosphate fertilisers, sulphuric, phosphoric and nitric acid, and feed phosphates; Gen. Dir V. V. DAVYDENKO; publ. *Mir Sery i NPK (The World of Sulphur & NPK)*.

K. I. Skryabin All-Russia Research and Development Institute of Helminthology: 117218 Moscow, Bolshaya Cheremushkinskaya, 28; tel. (495) 124-56-55; attached to Russian Acad. of Agricultural Sciences; Dir Acad. A. V. USPENSKY.

South Ural Research and Development Institute of Fruit, Vegetable and Potato Growing: 454902 Chelyabinsk, Shershni, ul. Gidrostroy 16; tel. (351) 232-65-10; e-mail potatoes@chel.surnet.ru; attached to Russian Acad. of Agricultural Sciences; Dir T. V. LEBEDEVA.

State Scientific Institution Voronezh Scientific Research Institute of Agriculture: 397463 Voronezh, p/o Institute Dokuchaev, oblast, Talovya raion; e-mail niishi1c@mail.ru; internet www.niidokuchaeva.ru; attached to Russian Acad. of Agricultural Sciences.

Stavropol Research and Development Institute of Agriculture: 356200 Shpakovskoe, Stavropol krai, ul. Nikonovam Dom 1; tel. (865) 295-55-89; e-mail sniish@mail.ru; attached to Russian Acad. of Agricultural Sciences; Dir A. N. ABALDOV.

Tula Research and Development Institute of Agriculture: 301493 Tula oblast, Molochnye dvory, Sadovaya, 7; tel. (487) 525-23-44; f. 1956; attached to Russian Acad. of Agricultural Sciences; Dir Prof. V. I. SEVEROV.

N. M. Tulaykov Samara Research and Development Institute of Agriculture: 446284 Samara, oblast, Bezenchuk, ul. Karl Marksa 41; tel. (846) 762-11-40; e-mail samniish@samtel.ru; attached to Russian Acad. of Agricultural Sciences; Dir S. N. SHEVCHENKO.

Ulyanovsk Research and Development Institute of Agriculture: 433315 Timiryazevskoe, Ulyanovsk oblast, ul. Institutskaya; tel. (842) 241-81-55; e-mail ulniish@mv.ru; attached to Russian Acad. of Agricultural Sciences; Dir N. S. NEMTSEV.

V. N. Sukachev Forest Institute: 660036 Krasnoyarsk, Akademgorodok 50, bldg 28; tel. (3912) 43-36-86; e-mail institute_forest@ksc.krasn.ru; f. 1944; attached to Russian Acad. of Sciences; library of 143,731 vols; Dir ALEXANDER A. ONUCHIN.

V. V. Dokuchaev Soil Science Institute: 109017 Moscow, Pyzhevsky per. 7; tel. (495) 951-50-37; e-mail info@esoil.ru; internet www.esoil.ru; f. 1927; attached to Russian Acad. of Agricultural Sciences; research in field of soil science; Dir ANDREY IVANOV; Vice-Dir IGOR SAVIN.

ARCHITECTURE AND TOWN PLANNING

Central Research and Design Institute of Dwellings: 127434 Moscow, Dmitrovskoe shosse 9, korp. 8; tel. (495) 976-28-19; f. 1962; Dir STANISLAV V. NIKOLAEV.

Central Research and Design Institute of Town Planning: 117944 Moscow, pr. Vernadskogo 29; tel. (495) 138-28-06; f. 1963; library of 25,000 vols; Dir YU. N. MAXIMOV.

Kucherenko, V. A., State Central Research and Experimental Design Institute for Complex Problems of Civil Engineering and Building Structures: 109428 Moscow, 2-ya Institutskaya 6; tel. (495) 171-26-50; f. 1927; Dir VASIL GORPINCHENKO; publs *Earthquake Engineering* (6 a year), *Investigation into Building Structures* (1 a year), *Investigations into Structural Earthquake Resistance* (every 2 years), *Large-Panel and Masonry Structures* (every 3 years), *New Forms and Strength of Metal Structures* (every 3 years), *Numerical Methods of Analysis and Optimization of Building Structures* (every 2 years), *Phosphate Materials* (1 a year), *Strength and Reliability of Structures* (every 2 years), *Structural Dynamics* (every 2 years), *Timber Structures* (every 2 years).

Panfilov, K. D., Academy of Municipal Economics: 123371 Moscow, Volokolamskoe shosse 116; tel. (495) 490-31-66; f. 1931; depts of scientific-technical co-ordination, municipal electrical supply, urban electric transport, anti-corrosion protection of underground metal structures, urban roads maintenance, municipal sanitation, urban landscaping, housing and municipal buildings, information, automation of technological processes, ecology; 5 research institutes (Moscow, St Petersburg, Rostov on Don, Tomsk, Ekaterinburg); 2 experimental factories (Moscow, St Petersburg); library of 740,000 vols; Dir V. F. PIVOVAROV; Scientific Sec. A. N. PROKHOROV.

Research Institute of Foundations and Underground Structures: 109428 Moscow, 2-ya Institutskaya 6; tel. (495) 171-22-40; f. 1931; Dir Prof. V. A. ILYICHEV; publ. *Soil Mechanics and Foundation Engineering* (6 a year).

Scientific and Research Institute for Architecture and Town Planning Theory: 121019 Moscow, pr. Vozdvizhenka 5; tel. (495) 290-36-80.

BIBLIOGRAPHY, LIBRARY SCIENCE AND MUSEOLOGY

All-Russia Research Institute of Restoration: 109172 Moscow, Krestyanskaya ul. 10; tel. (495) 276-99-90.

Book Research Institute: 103473 Moscow, 2-i Volkonsky per. 10; tel. (495) 281-72-58; Dir A. I. SOLOVEV.

ECONOMICS, LAW AND POLITICS

All-Russia Research and Design Institute of the Statistical Information System: 127486 Moscow, Deguninskaya ul. 1/3; tel. (495) 488-14-04.

All-Russia Research Institute of Economic Problems in Development of Science and Technology: 111024 Moscow, Aviamotornaya ul. 26/5; tel. (495) 273-52-31; f. 1986; library of 15,000 vols.

Bank Credit and Finance Research Institute: 103016 Moscow, ul. Alekseya Tolstogo 30/1; tel. (495) 925-61-18.

Central Economics and Mathematics Institute: 117418 Moscow, Nakhimovsky pr. 47; tel. (495) 129-16-44; e-mail director@cemi.rssi.ru; internet www.cemi.rssi.ru; f. 1963; attached to Russian Acad. of Sciences; Dir V. L. MAKAROV; publs *Economics and Mathematical Methods* (4 a year), *Economics of Contemporary Russia* (4 a year).

Central Economics Research Institute: 119898 Moscow, Smolensky bul. 3/5; tel. (495) 246-84-63.

Central Laboratory of Socio-Economic Measurements: c/o Russian Academy of Sciences, 117418 Moscow, ul. Krasikova 32; attached to Russian Acad. of Sciences; Dir A. YU. SHEVYAKOV.

Centre for the Study of Nationality Problems: 117036 Moscow, ul. Dm. Ulyanova 19; tel. (495) 123-90-61; attached to Russian Acad. of Sciences; Head M. N. GUBOGLO.

Federal Service of State Statistics: 107450 Moscow, ul. Myasnitskaya 39; tel. (495) 207-49-02; e-mail stat@gks.ru; internet www.gks.ru; f. 1918 as Central Statistical Board; present name 1991; provides demographic and economic statistical information and analysis to state authorities, the scientific community and commercial and international organizations; Dir VLADIMIR SOKOLIN.

Financial Research Institute: 103006 Moscow, Nastasinsky per. 3 korp. 2; tel. (495) 299-74-14; f. 1937.

Institute for African Studies: 123001 Moscow, ul. Spiridonovka 30/1; tel. (495) 290-27-52; e-mail dir@inafr.ru; f. 1959;

attached to Russian Acad. of Sciences; Dir A. M. VASILIEV; publs *Asia and Africa Today* (jtly with Institute of Oriental Studies, 12 a year), *Vostok-Orience* (jointly with Institute of Oriental Studies, 6 a year).

Institute for Comparative Political Studies: 101831 Moscow, Kolpachnyi per. 9a; tel. (495) 916-37-03; f. 1966; attached to Russian Acad. of Sciences; library of 50,000 vols; Dir T. T. TIMOFEEV; publs *Forum* (1 a year), *Polis* (6 a year).

Institute for Economic Studies: 184209 Murmansk oblast, Apatity, ul. Fersmana 24A; tel. (81555) 7-64-72; e-mail iep .kolasc.net.ru; internet www.ksc.ru; f. 1986; attached to Kola Science Centre (Russian Acad. of Sciences); Dir Prof. FIODOR D. LARICHKIN; publ. *Sever i Rynok* (The North and the Market, 3 a year, in Russian).

Institute for Economics and Mathematics at St Petersburg: 191187 St Petersburg, ul. Tchaikovski 1; tel. (812) 273-7953; e-mail emi@emi.nw.ru; internet emi.nw.ru; f. 1990; attached to Russian Acad. of Sciences; Dir Prof. LEONID A. RUKHOVETS.

Institute for International Economic and Political Studies: 117418 Moscow, Novocheremushkinskaya 46; tel. (495) 128-91-57; e-mail imepi@transecon.ru; internet www.transecon.ru; f. 1960; attached to Russian Acad. of Sciences; Dir Prof. Dr RUSLAN GRINBERG; publ. *The World of Transformations* (4 a year).

Institute for Legislation and Comparative Law: 103728 Moscow, Vozdvizhenka 4/22; tel. (495) 291-02-07; e-mail office@izak.ru; f. 1925, fmrly All-Union Research Institute of Soviet Legislation; library of 180,000 vols; Dir LEV A. OKUNKOV; publs *Commentary on New Russian Legislation* (1 a year), *Legislation of Foreign Countries* (6 or 7 a year), *Materials of Foreign Legislation and International Private Law* (1 a year), *Problems of Perfecting Legislation* (3 a year).

Institute for Socio-Economic Studies of Population: 117218 Moscow, Nakhimovsky pr. 32; tel. (495) 129-04-00; e-mail isesp_ras@mtu-net.ru; internet www.cemi.rssi.ru/isesp; f. 1988; attached to Russian Acad. of Sciences; Dir NATALIA RIMASHEVSKAYA; publ. *Population* (4 a year).

Institute of Economic and Social Problems of the North: 167610 Syktyvkar, Kommunisticheskaya ul. 26; tel. (8212) 42-42-67; e-mail iespn@ksc.komi.ru; attached to Russian Acad. of Sciences; Dir V. N. LAZHENTSEV.

Institute of Economic Research: 680042 Khabarovsk, Tikhookeanskaya ul. 153; tel. (421) 272-48-88; e-mail minakir@ecrin.ru; internet www.ecrin.ru; f. 1976; attached to Russian Acad. of Sciences; Dir Acad. P. A. MINAKIR; publ. *Spatial Economics* (4 a year).

Institute of Economics: 620219 Ekaterinburg, Moskovskaya ul. 29; tel. (3432) 51-45-36; e-mail green@uran.ru; f. 1971; attached to Russian Acad. of Sciences; Dir A. I. TATARKIN.

Institute of Economics: 119991 Moscow, Leninskii Ave 14; tel. (495) 938-03-09; attached to Russian Acad. of Sciences; Dir Acad. RUSLAN S. GRINBERG.

Institute of Europe: 103873 Moscow, Mokhovaya 8–3; tel. (495) 203-73-43; e-mail europe@ieras.ru; f. 1988; attached to Russian Acad. of Sciences; library of 3,000 vols; Dir VITALY V. ZHURKIN.

Institute of Far Eastern Studies: 117218 Moscow, Nakhimovsky pr. 32; tel. (495) 124-01-17; e-mail ifes@cemi.rssi.ru; f. 1966; attached to Russian Acad. of Sciences; Dir M. L. TITARENKO; publ. *Far Eastern Affairs* (6 a year).

Institute of Foreign Economic Research: c/o Russian Academy of Sciences, 117418 Moscow, ul. Krasikova 32; attached to Russian Acad. of Sciences; Dir S. A. SITARYAN.

Institute of National Economic Forecasting: 117418 Moscow, Nakhimovsky pr. 47; tel. (495) 129-34-33; e-mail office@ecfor .ru; internet www.ecfor.ru; f. 1986; attached to Russian Acad. of Sciences; undertakes macroeconomic analysis; short-, medium-, and long-term forecasting of the Russian economy; Dir Prof. VICTOR V. IVANTER; publs *Problemy Prognozirovaniya* (in Russian, 6 a year), *Studies on Russian Economic Development* (in English, 6 a year).

Institute of Philosophy and Law: 620144 Ekaterinburg, ul. 8 Marta 68; tel. (3432) 22-23-46; attached to Russian Acad. of Sciences; Dir S. S. ALEKSEEV.

Institute of Problems of Assimilation of the North: 625003 Tyumen, a/ya 2774; tel. (3452) 7-82-76; attached to Russian Acad. of Sciences; Dir V. P. MELNIKOV.

Institute of Problems of the Marketplace: 117418 Moscow, Nakhimovsky pr. 47; tel. (495) 129-10-00; attached to Russian Acad. of Sciences; Dir N. YA. PETRAKOV.

Institute of Social Sciences: 670042 Ulan-Ude, ul. Marii Sakhyanovoi 6; tel. (3012) 3-66-25; attached to Russian Acad. of Sciences; Dir V. T. NAIDAKOV.

Institute of Socio-Economic Problems of the Development of the Agroindustrial Complex: 401600 Saratov, pr. Lenina 94; tel. (8452) 24-25-38; attached to Russian Acad. of Sciences; Dir V. B. OSTROVSKY.

Institute of Socio-Political Research: 119991 Moscow, Leninsky pr. 32A; tel. (495) 938-53-70; e-mail ispr@ras.ru; internet www .ispr.ru; f. 1991; attached to Russian Acad. of Sciences; Dir Prof. Dr GENNADY OSIPOV; publs *Eurasia* (1 a year), *Science, Culture, Society* (4 a year), *Social and Demographic Policies.*

Institute of State and Law: 119841 Moscow, ul. Znamenka 10; tel. (495) 291-33-81; e-mail igpran@igpran.ru; attached to Russian Acad. of Sciences; Dir B. N. TOPORNIN.

Institute of the Economics of the Comprehensive Assimilation of the Natural Resources of the North: 677891 Yakutsk, ul. Petrovskogo 2; tel. (4112) 3-52-46; attached to Russian Acad. of Sciences; Dir N. V. IGOSHIN.

Institute of USA and Canada Studies: 121814 Moscow, Khlebnyi per. 2/3; tel. (495) 291-20-52; e-mail iskran@glasnet.ru; attached to Russian Acad. of Sciences; Dir SERGEI ROGOV; publs *Ideology* (12 a year), *Policy, US: Economy.*

Institute of World Economics and International Relations: 117957 Moscow, Profsoyuznaya 23; tel. (495) 120-43-32; e-mail imemoran@imemo.ru; internet www.imemo .ru; attached to Russian Acad. of Sciences; 545 mems; Dir Prof. SIMONIA A. NODARI (acting); publs *World Economics and International Relations* (12 a year, in Russian), *Russian Economic Barometer* (4 a year, in English).

International Research Institute for Management Sciences: 117312 Moscow, Pr. 60-letiya Oktyabrya 9; tel. (495) 137-28-57.

Latin America Institute: 115035 Moscow, Bol. Ordynka 21; tel. (495) 951-53-23; e-mail ilac-zan@mtu-net.ru; internet www.mtu-net .ru/ilaran; f. 1961; attached to Russian Acad. of Sciences; Dir Dr V. M. DAVYDOV; publ. *Iberoamerica* (in Spanish, 4 a year).

Peace Research Center of IMEMO: 117859 Moscow, ul. Profsoyuznaya 23; tel.

(495) 128-93-89; e-mail imemoran@online.ru; attached to Russian Acad. of Sciences; Dir A. K. KISLOV; publ. *Ways to Security* (in Russian, 2 or 3 a year).

Pricing Research Institute: 107078 Moscow, Kirovsky pr-d 4/3; tel. (495) 925-50-56.

Research Institute for the Strengthening of the Legal System and Law and Order: 123805 Moscow, GSP 2-ya Zvenigorodskaya ul. 15; tel. (495) 256-54-63.

Research Institute of Planning and Normatives: 125319 Moscow, Kochnovsky pr. 3; tel. (495) 152-45-91; attached to Russian Acad. of Sciences; Dir B. V. GUBIN (acting).

Sochi Research Centre: 354000 Sochi, Teatralnaya 8a; tel. (862) 92-37-71; e-mail snic@sochi.ru; f. 1988; attached to Russian Acad. of Sciences; research into management of the development of recreational areas and tourism; Dir M. M. AMIRKHANOV.

Survey Technique and Applied Research (STAR) Centre of the Institute of Sociology: 117259 Moscow, ul. Krzhizhanovskogo 24/35, str. 5; tel. (495) 719-09-71; e-mail valman@socio.msk.su; f. 1983; attached to Russian Acad. of Sciences; opinion survey design, data collection; Dir Prof. V. MANSUROV.

EDUCATION

Central Sports Research Institute: 107005 Moscow, Elizavetinsky per. 10; tel. (499) 261-50-76.

Centre for Pre-School Education: 113035 Moscow, ul. Osipenko 21; tel. (495) 231-49-28; attached to Russian Acad. of Education; Dir A. S. SPIVAKOVSKAYA.

Centre for Social Pedagogics: 119905 Moscow, Pogodinskaya ul. 8; tel. (495) 246-44-58; attached to Russian Acad. of Education; Dir V. G. BOCHAROVA.

Institute for Advanced Training: 109180 Moscow, ul. Bol. Polyanka 58; tel. (495) 237-31-51; attached to Russian Acad. of Education; Dir Y. A. ROODIE.

Institute for Educational Innovation: 117449 Moscow, ul. Vinokurova 3-в; tel. (495) 126-26-30; attached to Russian Acad. of Education; Dir V. I. SLOBODCHIKOV.

Institute for School Development in Siberia, the Far East and the North: 634050 Tomsk, ul. Gertsena 68; tel. (3822) 21-28-21; attached to Russian Acad. of Education; Dir G. V. ZALEVSKY.

Institute for the Occupational Training of Youth: 119903 Moscow, Pogodinskaya ul. 8; tel. (495) 245-05-13; attached to Russian Acad. of Education; Dir V. A. POLYAKOV.

Institute of Developmental Physiology: 119869 Moscow, ul. Pogodinskaya 8, korp. 2; tel. (495) 245-04-33; attached to Russian Acad. of Education; Dir Dr M. M. BEZRUKIKH.

Institute of Higher Education: 111024 Moscow, Tretya Kabelynaya ul. 1; tel. (495) 273-48-19; e-mail sav@niivo.hetnet.ru; attached to Russian Acad. of Education; Dir ALEXANDER SAVELIEV.

Institute of National Problems of Education: 105077 Moscow, Pervomayskaya 101; tel. (495) 461-92-45; f. 1991; (fmrly Research Institute of National Schools, f. 1949); Dir Prof. M. N. KOUZMIN; publ. *Uchenye Zapiski* (1 a year).

Institute of Secondary Education: 119906 Moscow, ul. Pogodinskaya 8; tel. (495) 245-37-33; attached to Russian Acad. of Education; Dir V. S. LEDNEV.

Institute of Secondary Specialized Education: Tatarstan, 420039 Kazan, ul. Isayeva 12; tel. (8432) 42-63-24; f. 1976;

attached to Russian Acad. of Education; Dir G. V. MUKHAMETZYANOVA; publ. *Professional Education* (4 a year).

Institute of Teaching and Learning Resources: 119903 Moscow, ul. Pogodinskaya 8; tel. (495) 246-35-90; attached to Russian Acad. of Education; Dir T. S. NAZAROVA.

Institute of Theoretical Pedagogics and International Research in Education: 129278 Moscow, ul. Pavla Korchagina 7; tel. (495) 283-09-55; attached to Russian Acad. of Education; Dir B. S. GERSHUNSKY.

Institute of Vocational Education: 119186 St Petersburg, nab. Moiki 48; tel. (812) 311-60-88; attached to Russian Acad. of Education; Dir A. P. BELYAEVA.

Psychological Institute: 125009 Moscow, Mokhovaya ul. 9, Bldg 4; tel. (495) 695-88-76; e-mail pirao@list.ru; internet www.pirao.ru; f. 1912; attached to Russian Acad. of Education; library of 60,000 vols; Dir Prof. VITALY V. RUBTSOV; Vice-Dir for Science Prof. SERGEY MALYKH; publs *New Trends in Psychology* (4 a year, in Russian), *Theoretical and Experimental Psychology* (4 a year, in Russian).

Research Centre for Aesthetic Education: 119034 Moscow, Kropotkinskaya nab. 15; tel. (495) 202-25-97; attached to Russian Acad. of Education; Dir B. P. YUSOV.

Research Centre for the Teaching of Russian: 119903 Moscow, Pogodinskaya ul. 8; tel. (495) 246-05-59; attached to Russian Acad. of Education; Dir E. A. BYSTROVA.

Research Institute of Remedial Education: 119869 Moscow, ul. Pogodinskaya 8, korp. 1; tel. (495) 245-04-52; attached to Russian Acad. of Education; Dir N. N. MALOFEEV.

Siberian Institute of Educational Technologies: 630098 Novosibirsk, Primorskaya ul. 22; tel. (3832) 45-18-32; f. 1985; attached to Russian Acad. of Education; Dir I. M. BOBKO; publ. *Information Technologies in Education* (2 a year).

Family and Education Institute: 119121 Moscow, ul. Pogodinskaya 8; tel. (499) 255-26-06; e-mail niisv@mail.ru; internet www.niisv.ru; f. 1998; attached to Russian Acad. of Education; Dir Acad. SERGEI VLADIMIROVICH DARMODECHIN.

FINE AND PERFORMING ARTS

Research Institute of Film Art: 125009 Moscow, Degtyarny per. 8; tel. (095) 299-56-79; e-mail cineaste@mail.ru; f. 1974; research in the field of history and theory of film and monitoring of the situation in Russian and world cinema; 65 mems; library of 60,000 vols; still photos archive; Dir LIUDMILA BUDYAK; Deputy Dirs DMITRY KARAVAEV, MARK ZAK; publs *Kinograph* (almanac), *Kinovedcheskie Zapisky* (Film Notebooks, 4 a year).

Research Institute of the Theory and History of Fine Arts: 119034 Moscow, ul. Prechistenka 21; tel. (495) 201-42-91; attached to Russian Acad. of Arts; Dir V. V. VANSLOV.

Scientific-Research Museum of the Russian Academy of Fine Arts: St Petersburg, Universitetskaya nab. 17; tel. (812) 328-27-19; e-mail sekretar@nimrah.ru; internet www.nimrah.ru; f. 1758; attached to Russian Acad. of Arts; casts, masterpieces of antique sculpture and models of antique architecture monuments made in 18th century of cork in workshop of Chichi, Roman patternmaker and sculptor; history of Russian artistic school; works of Losenko, Borovikovsky, Bryullov, P.P. Chistyakov, Kustodiyev, Brodsky, A.P. Ostroumova-Lebedeva, sculp-

tors Shubin, Kozlovsky, Shchedrin, Prokofyev, Antokolsky; Saint Petersburg architecture of the 18th–19th centuries in patterns, paintings and drawings; Dir LUDMILA KONDRATENKO.

State Institute for Art Studies: 125009 Moscow, Kozitsky per. 5; tel. (495) 694-03-71; e-mail institut@sias.ru; internet www.sias.ru; f. 1944; research in fine art, theatre, music, architecture, folklore, mass media; studies in sociology, economics and the politics of culture; library of 70,000 vols; Dir Dr NATALIA SIPOVSKAYA; publs *Cultural Transactions* (every 2 years), *Occidental Art of the 20th Century* (every 2 years), *Theory of Culture* (1 a year), *World of Arts* (1 a year).

HISTORY, GEOGRAPHY AND ARCHAEOLOGY

Institute of Archaeology: 117036 Moscow, ul. Dm. Ulyanova 19; tel. (495) 126-47-98; e-mail ia.ras@mail.ru; internet archaeolog.ru; f. 1919; attached to Russian Acad. of Sciences; Dir N. A. MAKAROV; publ. *Russiyskaya Archeologia* (4 a year).

Institute of Geography: 109017 Moscow, Staromonetnii per. 29; tel. (495) 959-00-32; e-mail igras@igras.geonet.ru; internet www.igras.ru; f. 1918; attached to Russian Acad. of Sciences; research into interaction between nature and society at global, regional, and national scales; evolutionary analysis of environment and its components for forecast of global and regional changes; monitors and evaluates efficiency of natural resource utilization; elaboration of ecological and geographical bases of sustainable devt at global, regional, and nat. levels; library of 10,000 vols; Dir Acad. V. M. KOTLYAKOV; publs *Ekologicheskoe Planirovanie i Upravlenie* (6 a year), *Geomorphology* (4 a year), *Izvestiya Akademii Nauk – Seriya Geograficheskaya* (6 a year), *Lyod i Sneg* (2 a year), *Problemy regionalnoi Ekologii* (6 a year).

Institute of History and Archaeology: 620219 Ekaterinburg, ul. R. Lyuksemburg 56; tel. (3432) 22-14-02; e-mail istor@uran.ru; internet www.uran.ru/structure/institutions/history/index.htm; f. 1988; attached to Russian Acad. of Sciences; Dir Prof. V. V. ALEKSEEV; publ. *Ural Historical Journal* (1 a year).

Institute of History, Archaeology and Ethnography of the Peoples of the Far East: 690001 Vladivostok, ul. Pushkinskaya 89; tel. (4232) 22-05-07; e-mail ihae@eastnet.febras.ru; internet ihaefe.org; f. 1971; attached to Russian Acad. of Sciences, Far Eastern Branch; Dir Dr VICTOR LARIN; publ. *Russia and the Pacific* (in Russian, 4 a year).

Institute of History, Language and Literature: 450054 Ufa, pr. Oktyabrya 71; tel. (3472) 35-60-50; e-mail rihll@anrb.ru; internet rihll.ru; f. 1932; attached to Russian Acad. of Sciences; Dir Prof. Dr FIRDAUS G. KHISAMITDINOVA.

Institute of History, Philology and Philosophy: 630090 Novosibirsk, pr. Akad. Lavrenteva 17; tel. (3832) 35-05-37; attached to Russian Acad. of Sciences; Dir Acad. A. P. DEREVYANKO.

Institute of Language, Literature and Arts: 367025 Makhachkala 25, ul. Magomeda Gadjieva 45; tel. (872) 267-06-21; f. 1924; attached to Russian Acad. of Sciences; library of 160,000 vols; Dir M. I. MAGOMEDOV.

Institute of Language, Literature and History: 167610 Syktyvkar, Kommunisticheskaya ul. 26; tel. (8212) 24-55-64; e-mail smetanin@mail.komisc.ru; internet www.komisc.ru/illh; f. 1970; attached to Russian Acad. of Sciences; Dir ALEXANDR F. SMETANIN.

Institute of Linguistics, Literature and History: 185610 Petrozavodsk, Pushkinskaya ul. 11; tel. (8142) 77-44-96; attached to Russian Acad. of Sciences; Dir Yu. A. Savvateev.

Institute of Military History: 117330 Moscow, Universitetskii pr. 14; tel. (495) 147-45-65; attached to Russian Acad. of Sciences; Dir A. N. Bazhenov.

Institute of Oriental Manuscripts: 191186 St Petersburg, Dvortsovaya 18; tel. (812) 315-87-28; e-mail iom@orientalstudies.ru; internet www.orientalstudies.ru; f. 1818; attached to Russian Acad. of Sciences; specialized collns of MSS and early printed books of countries of East; archive of Orientalists; Dir Irina F. Popova; publ. *Pismennye Pamyatniki Vostoka* (2 a year).

Institute of Research in the Humanities: 677007 Sakha Republic, Yakutsk, Petrovskaya ul. 1; tel. (4112) 35-49-96; f. 1935; attached to Acad. of Sciences of the Sakha Republic; history, language and culture of the peoples of the Sakha Republic; Dir Vasily N. Ivanov; publ. *Yakutsky Arkhiv* (12 a year).

Institute of Russian History: 117036 Moscow, ul. Dm. Ulyanova 19; tel. (495) 126-94-49 br. at St Petersburg: 197110 St Petersburg, Petrozavodskaya 7; tel. (812) 235-41-98; attached to Russian Acad. of Sciences; Dir A. N. Sakharov.

Institute of Slavonic Studies: 117334 Moscow, Leninsky pr. 32A; tel. (495) 938-17-80; e-mail ritlen@mail.ru; f. 1947; attached to Russian Acad. of Sciences; Dir V. K. Volkov; publ. *Slavyanovedeniye* (4 a year).

Institute of the History of Material Culture: 191065 St Petersburg, Dvortsovaya nab. 18; tel. (812) 312-14-84; attached to Russian Acad. of Sciences.

Institute of World History: 117036 Moscow, ul. Dm. Ulyanova 19; tel. (495) 126-94-21; attached to Russian Acad. of Sciences; Dir A. O. Chubaryan.

Krasovsky, F. N., Central Research Institute for Geodesy, Aerial Photography, and Cartography: 125410 Moscow, Onezhskaya 26; tel. (495) 456-95-31.

Oceanography Research Institute: 190121 St Petersburg, nab. Moiki 120; Dir I. S. Gramberg.

Pacific Institute of Geography: 690041 Vladivostok, ul. Radio 7; tel. (4232) 32-06-72; f. 1971; attached to Russian Acad. of Sciences; library of 28,000 vols; Dir Prof. P. Ya. Baklanov; publ. *Zov Taigi*.

State Oceanography Institute: 119838 Moscow, Kropotkinskii per. 6; tel. (495) 246-72-88 199026 St Petersburg, V.O., 23-ya liniya 2-a; tel. (812) 218-81-23; Dir F. S. Terziev.

Udmurt Institute of History, Language and Literature: 426004 Izhevsk, ul. Lomonosova 4; tel. (3412) 75-53-21; f. 1931; attached to Russian Acad. of Sciences; library of 60,000 vols; Dir Kuzma I. Kulikov.

V. B. Sochava Institute of Geography: 664033 Irkutsk, Ulanbatorskaya 1; tel. (3952) 42-61-00; e-mail postman@irigs.irk.ru; internet www.irigs.irk.ru; f. 1957; attached to Russian Acad. of Sciences; the state and devt of Siberia's regions; landscape science; devt of the geographical framework for territorial org. of production, and population formation; systemic mapping; creation of the theoretical foundation for forecasting, monitoring and controlling the geosystem; library of 52 vols; Dir Dr Victor M. Plyusnin.

LANGUAGE AND LITERATURE

Gorky, A. M., Institute of World Literature: 121069 Moscow, ul. Vorovskogo 25A; tel. (495) 290-50-30; attached to Russian Acad. of Sciences; Dir F. F. Kuznetsov.

Ibragimov, G., Institute of Language, Literature and Art: 420503 Kazan, ul. Lobachevskogo 2/31; tel. (8432) 38-70-59; attached to Acad. of Sciences of the Republic of Tatarstan; Dir M. Z. Zakiev.

Institute for Linguistic Studies: 199053 St Petersburg, Tuchkov per. 9; tel. (812) 328-16-11; e-mail iliran@mail.ru; internet iling.spb.ru; f. 1921; attached to Russian Acad. of Sciences; research on all aspects of language; library of 140,000 vols; Dir Prof. Dr Nikolay N. Kazansky; publs *Acta Linguistica Petropolitana* (3 a year), *Indoevropeyskoe Yazykoznaniye i Klassicheskaya Filologiya* (1 a year).

Institute of Linguistics: 125009 Moscow, ul. Bol. Kislovsky per. 1, st. 1; tel. (495) 690-35-85; e-mail iling@iling-ran.ru; internet www.iling-ran.ru; f. 1950; attached to Russian Acad. of Sciences; Dir V. A. Vinogradov; Vice-Dir M. Alekseyev; publs *Ural-Altaic Studies* (2 a year), *Voprosy Filologii* (3 a year), *Voprosy Psikholingvistiki* (2 a year).

Institute of Russian Literature (Pushkin House): 199034 St Petersburg, nab. Makarova 4; tel. (812) 328-19-01; e-mail irli@mail.ru; f. 1905; attached to Russian Acad. of Sciences; Dir N. N. Skatov; publ. *Russian Literature* (4 a year).

Russian Institute for Cultural Research: 119072 Moscow, Bersenevskaya nab. 20; tel. (495) 959-09-08; e-mail riku@dol.ru; internet www.ricur.ru; f. 1932; attached to Min. of Culture and the Mass Media; research in theory and history of culture, humanities, applied cultural research; organizes conferences, publs, workshops and festivals; br. in Omsk; library: library of 67,000 books and periodicals; Dir Prof. Kirill E. Razlogov; Deputy Dir Prof. Eleonora A. Shoulepova; Deputy Dir Assoc. Prof. Alexei G. Vasiliev; Deputy Dir Prof. Yuri M. Reznik; publ. *Journal of Cultural Research* (online).

Vinogradov Institute of the Russian Language: 121019 Moscow, Volkhonka 18/2; tel. (495) 202-65-40; f. 1944; attached to Russian Acad. of Sciences; library of 110,000 vols; Dir Dr A. M. Moldovan; publs *Rusistics Today* (4 a year), *Russian Speech* (6 a year).

MEDICINE

All-Russia Antibiotics Research Institute: 113105 Moscow, Nagatinskaya ul. 3a; tel. (499) 611-42-38; f. 1947; library of 65,000 vols; br. in Penza; Dir Prof. S. M. Navashin; publ. *Antibiotics and Chemotherapy.*

All-Russia Research Institute of Pharmaceutical Plants: 113628 Moscow, ul. Grina 7; tel. (495) 382-83-18; Dir P. T. Kondratenko.

All-Russia Research Institute of the Technology of Blood Substitutes and Hormonal Preparations: 109044 Moscow, per. Lavrov 6; tel. (495) 276-43-60.

Allergen State Unitary Enterprise: 355019 Stavropol, Biologicheskaya ul. 20; tel. (8652) 24-40-84; f. 1918; vaccines and sera, allergens, nutrient media, pharmaceuticals; library of 39,500 vols and periodicals; Dir-Gen. V. V. Ermelov.

Bakulev Scientific and Research Centre for Cardiovascular Surgery: 117049 Moscow, Leninskii pr. 8; tel. (495) 236-13-61; e-mail leon@online.ru; internet www.bakoulev.sovintel.ru; f. 1956; attached to Russian Acad. of Medical Sciences; Head Acad. L. A. Boceria; publs *Journal of Thoracic and Cardiovascular Surgery* (in Russian, 6 a year), *Annals of Surgery* (in Russian, 6 a year), *Annals of Arrhythmology* (in Russian, 6 a year).

Blokhin, N. N., Cancer Research Center: 115478 Moscow, Kashirskoe shosse 24; tel. (495) 324-11-14; e-mail info@eso.ru; internet www.cancercenter.ru; f. 1951; attached to Russian Acad. of Medical Sciences; Dir Mikhail V. Davydov; publs *Herald of Moscow Cancer Society* (12 a year), *Journal* (4 a year), *Journal of Biotherapy* (24 a year), *Pediatric Oncology* (24 a year).

Attached Institutes:

Research Institute of Carcinogenesis: 115478 Moscow, Kashirskoe shosse 24; tel. (495) 324-14-70; attached to Russian Acad. of Medical Sciences; Dir David G. Zaridze.

Research Institute of Experimental Therapy and Tumour Diagnosis: 115478 Moscow, Kashirskoe shosse 24; tel. (495) 450-24-72; attached to Russian Acad. of Medical Sciences; Dir Anatoly Y. Baryshnikov.

Research Institute of Pediatric Oncology: 115478 Moscow, Kashirskoe shosse 24; tel. (495) 324-43-09; attached to Russian Acad. of Medical Sciences; Dir Lev A. Durnov.

Russian Institute of Clinical Oncology: 115478 Moscow, Kashirskoe shosse 24; tel. (495) 324-44-16; attached to Russian Acad. of Medical Sciences; Dir Mikhail I. Davydov.

Blood Transfusion Research Institute: 125167 Moscow, Novozykovsky pr-d 4A; tel. (495) 212-45-51.

Burdenko Neurosurgical Institute: 125047 Moscow, ul. Fadeeva 5; tel. (0495) 251-65-26; attached to Russian Acad. of Medical Sciences; Dir A. N. Konovalov.

Central Institute of Traumatology and Orthopaedics: 125299 Moscow, ul. Priorova 10; tel. (495) 450-24-72; f. 1921; 12 clinics; library of 40,000 vols; Dir Prof. S. P. Mironov; publ. *N. N. Priorov Journal of Traumatology and Orthopaedics* (4 a year).

Central Research Institute for the Evaluation of Working Capacity and Vocational Assistance to Disabled Persons: 127486 Moscow, ul. Susanina 3; tel. (495) 906-18-31; f. 1930; library of 50,000 vols; Dir D. I. Lavrova.

Central Research Institute of Dermatology and Venereal Diseases: 107076 Moscow, ul. Korolenko 3; tel. (495) 964-26-20; e-mail info@cnikvi.ru; internet www.cnikvi.ru; f. 1921; attached to Federal Agency for High Technology Medical Care; Dir Prof. Alexei Kubanov; publ. *Vestnik Dermatologii i Venerologii* (Journal of Dermatology and Venereology, 6 a year).

Central Research Institute of Epidemiology: 111123 Moscow, Novogireevskaya 3-a; tel. (495) 176-02-19; Dir A. Sumarokov.

Central Research Institute of Gastroenterology: 111123 Moscow, shosse Enthuziastov 86; tel. (495) 304-19-42; e-mail gastroenter@rambler.ru; internet www.cniig.ru; f. 1973; Dir Prof. Leonid Lazebnik; publ. *Experimental and Clinical Gastroenterology* (12 a year).

Central Tuberculosis Research Institute: 107564 Moscow, Yauzskaya alleya 2; tel. (499) 785-90-19; e-mail cniit@cniitramn.ru; internet www.cniitramn.ru; f. 1921; attached to Russian Acad. of Medical Sciences; Dir Prof. V. V. Erokhin.

Centre for the Chemistry of Drugs—All-Russia Chemical and Pharmaceutical Research Institute: 119815 Moscow, ul. Zubovskaya 7; tel. (495) 246-97-68; f. 1920;

library of 150,000 vols; Dir R. G. GLUSHKOV; publ. *Collection of Proceedings* (1 a year).

Chumakov, M. P., Institute of Poliomyelitis and Virus Encephalitis: 142782 Moscow oblast, Kievskoe shosse, 27 km; tel. (495) 439-90-07; attached to Russian Acad. of Medical Sciences; Dir S. G. DROZDOV.

Chuvash Eye Diseases Research Institute: 428028 Cheboksary, Traktorostroitelei 10; tel. (8350) 26-05-75; f. 1987; Dir Dr NIKOLAI PASHTAEV.

Dagestan Medical Research Centre: 367020 Makhachkala, ul. Gorikogo 53; tel. (87200) 7-49-97; attached to Russian Acad. of Medical Sciences; Dir S.-M. A. OMAROV.

Eastern Siberian Research Centre: 664003 Irkutsk, ul. Timiryazeva 16; tel. (3952) 27-54-48; e-mail sikol@sbamsr.irk.ru; internet www.vsnc.ru; attached to Russian Acad. of Medical Sciences; Chair. of Presidium Acad. S. I. KOLESNIKOV..

Attached Institutes:

Institute of Epidemiology and Microbiology: 664000 Irkutsk, ul. Karla Marksa 3; tel. (3952) 33-34-23; attached to Russian Acad. of Medical Sciences; Dir Prof. V. I. ZLOBIN.

Institute of Industrial Medicine and Human Ecology: 665827 Irkutskaya oblast, Angarsk 27, a/ya 1170; tel. (218) 55-90-70; e-mail rvc@iimhe.irk.ru; attached to Russian Acad. of Medical Sciences; Dir V. S. RUKAVISHNIKOV.

Institute of Paediatrics and Human Reproduction: 664003 Irkutsk, ul. Timiryazeva 16; tel. (3952) 34-73-67; e-mail sikol@sbamsr.irk.ru; attached to Russian Acad. of Medical Sciences; Dir Acad. S. I. KOLESNIKOV.

Institute of Surgery: 664047 Irkutsk, Yubileiny mikroraion 100; tel. (3952) 38-53-31; attached to Russian Acad. of Medical Sciences; Dir Prof. E. G. GRIGOREV.

Institute of Traumatology and Orthopaedics: 664003 Irkutsk, ul. Bortsov Revolyutsii 1; tel. (3952) 27-54-30; attached to Russian Acad. of Medical Sciences; Dir Prof. A. P. BARABASH.

Ekaterinburg Institute of Restorative Surgery, Traumatology and Orthopaedics: Ekaterinburg, Bankovsky per. 7.

Ekaterinburg Region Institute of Dermatology and Venereal Diseases: Ekaterinburg, ul. K. Libknekhta 9.

Ekaterinburg Viral Infections Research Institute: 620030 Ekaterinburg, Letnyaya ul. 23; tel. (3432) 61-99-60; e-mail virus@etel .ru; f. 1920; Dir Prof. NINA P. GLINSKIKH; publ. *Viral Infections: Urgent Problems* (1 a year).

Endocrinology Research Centre: 117036 Moscow, ul. Dm. Ulyanova 11; tel. (495) 500-00-90; e-mail science@endocrincentr.ru; internet www.endocrincentr.ru; f. 1925; attached to Russian Acad. of Medical Sciences; Dir I. I. DEDOV; publ. *Diabetes Mellitus* (in Russian, 4 a year).

Attached Institutes:

Institute of Clinical Endocrinology: Moscow; tel. (495) 129-01-24; e-mail endocrin@endocrincentr.ru; f. 1988; Dir J. A. MELNICHENKO.

Institute of Diabetes: c/o Endocrinology Research Centre, ul. Dmitry Ulyanov 11, Moscow, 117036; tel. (495) 1244500; internet www.endocrincentr.ru/about/ diabed; f. 1988; Dir M. I. BALABOLKIN.

Institute of Experimental Endocrinology: 112255 Moscow, ul. Moskvorechie 1; tel. (495) 324-93-25; f. 1965; Dir V. N. BABICHEV.

Ersman Hygiene Research Institute: 141000 Mytishchi, ul. Semashko 2; tel. (495) 583-82-14.

Far Eastern Scientific Center of Physiology and Pathology of Respiration: 675000 Blagoveshchensk, ul. Kalinina 22; tel. (4162) 77-28-00; e-mail dncfpd@ramn.ru; internet www.cfpd.amursu.ru; f. 1981; attached to Russian Acad. of Medical Sciences; Dir Prof. Dr VICTOR P. KOLOSOV; Vice-Dir Prof. Dr YULIY M. PERELMAN; publ. *Bulletin Physiology and Pathology of Respiration.*

Federal Bureau for Medical and Social Expertise: 127486 Moscow, ul. Ivana Susanina 3; tel. (495) 487-57-11; e-mail fbmse@ inbox.ru; f. 2000 as Federal Scientific and Practical Centre for Medico-Social Expertise and Rehabilitation of Invalids (formed by merger of Central Research Institute of Prosthetics and Prosthesis Design and Central Research Institute for the Evaluation of Working Capacity and Vocational Assistance to Disabled Persons); present name 2005; library of 45,000 vols; Dir Prof. Dr S. N. PUZIN; publ. *Journal of Medical and Social Expertise and Rehabiliation* (4 a year).

Federal Research Institute for Health Education and Health Promotion: 103101 Moscow, ul. A. Mitskevicha 3; tel. (495) 202-18-13; f. 1927; library of 10,000 vols; Dir Dr V. A. POLESKY.

Federal Research Institute of Paediatric Gastroenterology: 603950 Nizhnii Novgorod, ul. Semashko 22; tel. (8312) 36-66-35; e-mail niidegastro@mail.ru; f. 1929; Dir Prof. Dr ANATOLY I. VOLKOV.

Gamalei, N. F., Institute of Epidemiology and Microbiology: 123098 Moscow, ul. Gamalei 18; tel. (495) 193-30-01; e-mail info@riem.ru; attached to Russian Acad. of Medical Sciences; Dir S. V. PROZOROVSKII.

Haematological Research Centre: 125167 Moscow, Novozykovsky pr-d 4A; tel. (495) 212-21-23; attached to Russian Acad. of Medical Sciences; Dir A. I. VOROBIEV.

Herzen, P. A., Moscow Cancer Research Institute: 125284 Moscow, 2-i Botkinsky pr-d 3; tel. (495) 945-19-35; f. 1903; library of 19,336 vols; Dir Prof. V. I. CHISSOV.

Institute of Biomedical Chemistry: 119121 Moscow, ul. Pogodinskaya 10; tel. (495) 246-69-80; internet www.ibmc.msk.ru; f. 1944; attached to Russian Acad. of Medical Sciences; library of 136,000 vols; Dir Prof. ALEXANDER IVANOVICH ARCHAKOV; publ. *Voprosy Meditsinskoy Khimii* (6 a year).

Institute of Biomedical Problems: 123007 Moscow, Khoroshevskoe shosse 76A; tel. (495) 195-23-63; f. 1963; environmental effects on the human body, with emphasis on the effect of space flights; library of 80,000 vols; Dir ANATOLY I. GRIGORIEV; publ. *Aerospatial and Environmental Medicine* (6 a year).

Institute of Biomedical Research and Therapy: 113149 Moscow, Simferopolsky bul. 8; tel. (495) 113-23-51; Dir A. V. KARAULOV.

Institute of Clinical and Experimental Lymphology: 630117 Novosibirsk, ul. Timakova 2; tel. (383) 333-64-09; f. 1991; attached to Russian Acad. of Medical Sciences; library of 1,000 vols; Dir V. I. KONENKOV.

Institute of Clinical and Preventive Cardiology: 625026 Tyumen, ul. Melnikaite 111, POB 4312; tel. (3452) 22-76-08; f. 1985; attached to Russian Acad. of Medical Sciences; Dir V. A. KUZNETSOV.

Institute of Clinical Immunology: 630091 Novosibirsk, ul. Yadrintsovskaya 14;

attached to Russian Acad. of Medical Sciences; Dir V. A. KOZLOV.

Institute of Epidemiology and Microbiology: 690028 Vladivostok, ul. Selskaya 1; tel. (4232) 29-43-03; attached to Russian Acad. of Medical Sciences; Dir N. N. BESEDNOVA.

Institute of Experimental Medicine: 197376 St Petersburg, ul. Akad. Pavlova 12; tel. (812) 234-54-01; e-mail iem@iemrams.ru; internet www.iemrams.spb.ru; f. 1890; attached to Russian Acad. of Medical Sciences; library of 500,000 vols; Dir GENRIKH A. SOFRONOV; Librarian ARINA DZENISKEVICH.

Institute of General Pathology and Pathophysiology: 125315 Moscow, ul. Baltiiskaya 8; tel. (499) 151-17-56; attached to Russian Acad. of Medical Sciences; Dir A. A. KUBATIEV; Scientific Sec. LARISA N. SKURATOVSKAYA.

Institute of Human Morphology: 117418 Moscow, ul. Tsyuryupy 3; tel. (495) 120-80-65; attached to Russian Acad. of Medical Sciences; Dir N. K. PERMYAKOV.

Institute of Immunology: 142380 Moscow oblast, Chekhovsky raion, Lyubuchany; tel. (495) 546-15-55; f. 1980; library of 2,800 vols; Dir V. P. ZAVYALOV.

Institute of Immunology: 115478 Moscow, Kashirskoe shosse 24, korp. 2; tel. (499) 611-83-01; Dir R. M. KHAITOV.

Institute of Influenza: 197022 St Petersburg, ul. Prof. Popova 15/17; tel. (812) 234-58-75; e-mail office@influenza.spb.ru; attached to Russian Acad. of Medical Sciences; Dir O. I. KISELEV.

Institute of Internal Medicine: 630089 Novosibirsk, ul. Bogatkova 175/1; tel. (3832) 64-25-16; e-mail office@iimed.ru; f. 1981; attached to Russian Acad. of Medical Sciences; Dir Prof. M. I. VOEVODA; publ. *Interpress* (4 a year).

Institute of Medical and Biological Cybernetics: 630117 Novosibirsk, ul. Akad. Timakova 2; tel. (3832) 32-12-56; f. 1992; attached to Russian Acad. of Medical Sciences; Dir M. B. SHTARK; publ. *Biofeedback* (every 3 years).

Institute of Medical Climatology and Rehabilitation: 690025 Vladivostok, Sadgorod 25; tel. (4232) 33-05-22; f. 1984; attached to Russian Acad. of Medical Sciences; library of 20,000 vols; Dir Prof. Dr E. M. IVANOV.

Institute of Medical Problems of the North: 660022 Krasnoyarsk, ul. Partizana Zheleznyaka 3G; f. 1976; attached to Russian Acad. of Medical Sciences; Dir VALERY T. MANCHUK.

Institute of Nutrition: 109240 Moscow, Ustinskii pr-d 2/14; tel. (495) 917-44-85; attached to Russian Acad. of Medical Sciences; Dir M. N. VOLGAREV.

Institute of Occupational Health: 105275 Moscow, pr. Budennogo 31; tel. (495) 365-02-09; e-mail niimt@niimt.ru; internet www .niimt.ru; f. 1923; attached to Russian Acad. of Medical Sciences; devt of theoretical basis establishing laws and mechanisms of factors responsible for industrial, general and working process on workers health; aims to find out efficient prevention, diagnosis and treatment of work-related and occupational diseases; research into socio-medical problems and health dynamics of workers due to demographic shifts, changing working conditions, environmental and migration processes; devt and improvement of preventive technologies; Dir Prof. I. V. BUKHTIYAROV; publs *Meditsina Truda i Promyshlennaia Ekologiia* (12 a year), *Occupational Health and Industrial Ecology.*

Institute of Paediatrics: 117296 Moscow, Lomonsovskii pr. 2/62; tel. (495) 134-03-61; attached to Russian Acad. of Medical Sciences; Dir M. YA. STUDENIKIN.

Institute of Paediatrics and Child Surgery of the Ministry of Public Health of the Russian Federation: 127412 Moscow, Taldomskaya ul. 2; tel. (495) 484-02-92; Dir Prof. YURI E. VELTISCHEV; publ. *Vestnik* (Annals of Perinatology and Paediatrics).

Institute of Pharmacology: 125315 Moscow, ul. Baltiiskaya 8; tel. (495) 151-18-41; e-mail niipharm@mail.ru; attached to Russian Acad. of Medical Sciences; Dir S. B. SEREDENIN.

Institute of Physiology: 630117 Novosibirsk, ul. Akad. Timakova 4; attached to Russian Acad. of Medical Sciences; Dir V. A. TRUFAKIN.

Institute of Regional Pathology and Pathomorphology: 630117 Novosibirsk, ul. Timakova 2; tel. (3833) 34-84-38; e-mail pathol@soramn.ru; internet www .pathomorphology.soramn.ru; f. 1992; attached to Russian Acad. of Medical Sciences; diagnostic and training centre; diagnostics of viral hepatitis, tumours, lung, heart, kidney, gastrointestinal chronic diseases; Dir L. M. NEPOMNYASHCHIKH; Deputy Dir for Science and Research ELENA L. LUSHNIKOVA.

Institute of the Brain: 107120 Moscow, per. Obukha 5; tel. (495) 917-80-07; attached to Russian Acad. of Medical Sciences; Dir N. N. BOGOLEPOV.

Institute of the Molecular Pathology and Biochemistry of Ecology: 630117 Novosibirsk, ul. Akad. Timakova 2; attached to Russian Acad. of Medical Sciences; Dir V. V. LYAKHOVICH.

Institute of Toxicology: 192019 St Petersburg Bekhtereva St 1; tel. (812) 365-06-80; e-mail info@toxicology.ru; internet www .toxicology.ru; f. 1935; attached to Federal Medico-Biological Agency of Russia Federal State Scientific Institution; Dir SERGEY P. NECHIPORENKO; Deputy Dir for Research Affairs EVGENY YU. BONITENKO.

Institute of Viral Preparations: 109088 Moscow, 1 Dubrovskaya ul. 15; tel. (495) 274-81-45; attached to Russian Acad. of Medical Sciences; Dir O. G. ANDZHAPARIDZE.

Irkutsk Antiplague Research Institute of Siberia and the Far East: 664047 Irkutsk, ul. Trilissera 78; tel. (3952) 22-01-35; e-mail adm@chumin.irkutsk.ru; internet www.irkutsk.ru/chumin; f. 1934; library of 55,000 vols; Dir Prof. E. P. GOLUBINSKY.

Irkutsk Institute of Orthopaedics and Traumatology: 664003 Irkutsk, ul. Bortzov Revoliutsii 1; tel. (3952) 27-54-30; f. 1946; diseases of the skeleton and bone tissue regeneration; library of 32,000 vols; Dir Prof. A. P. BARABASH.

Irkutsk Research Institute of Epidemiology and Microbiology: 664000 Irkutsk, ul. Karla Marksa 3; tel. (3952) 24-42-30; Dir V. I. ZLOBIN.

Ivanovskii, D. I., Institute of Virology: 123098 Moscow, Gamalei 16; tel. (499) 190-28-74; e-mail lvovdk@virology.ru; attached to Ministry of Health and Soc. Devt of the Russian Federation; Dir DMITRY K. LVOV.

Kazan Institute of Epidemiology, Microbiology and Hygiene: 420015 Kazan, Bol. Krasnaya ul. 67; tel. (8432) 32-25-80; Dir F. Z. KAMALOV.

Kazan State Institute of Orthopaedics and Traumatology: 420015 Kazan, ul. Gorkogo 3; tel. (8432) 38-59-05; f. 1945; library: 13,500 units; publ. *Transactions* (1 a year).

Khabarovsk Research Institute of Epidemiology and Microbiology of Rospotrebnadzor: Khabarovsk, Shevchenko 2, 680610; tel. (4212) 32-54-13; e-mail bovlad@email.kht.ru; internet www.hniiem .rospotrebnadzor.ru; f. 1925; microbiological and epidemiological studies; Head of Institute OLGA E. TROTSENKO; publ. *The Far Eastern Journal of Infectious Pathology* (2 a year).

Laboratory of Experimental Biological Models: 143412 Moscow oblast, p/o Otradnoe, pos. Svetlye Gory; tel. (495) 561-53-70; attached to Russian Acad. of Medical Sciences; Dir T. I. ZAITSEV.

Laboratory of Polar Medicine: 663310 Norilsk 10, ul. Talnakhskaya 7A, p/ya 625; attached to Russian Acad. of Medical Sciences; Dir L. A. NADTOCHII.

Martsinovsky, I. E., Institute of Medical Parasitology and Tropical Medicine: 119435 Moscow, Mal. Pirogovskaya ul. 20; tel. (495) 246-80-49; f. 1920; research into parasitic and tropical diseases, entomology and vectors; undergraduate and postgraduate training; library of 70,000 vols; Dir Prof. EUGENIJ MOROZOV; publ. *Medical Parasitology and Parasitic Diseases* (4 a year).

Mechnikov I. I., Institute of Vaccines and Sera: 103064 Moscow, Mal. Kazenny per. 5A; tel. (495) 917-49-00; e-mail instmech@iitp.ru; f. 1919; attached to Russian Acad. of Medical Sciences; Dir B.F. SEMENOV.

Medical Research Centre for Preventive Medicine and the Protection of the Health of Industrial Workers: 620014 Ekaterinburg, ul. Popova 30; tel. (3432) 71-87-54; e-mail mrc@etel.ru; f. 1929; Dir SERGEY V. KUZMIN; publs *Balneology and Physiotherapy* (1 a year), *Urgent Issues of Preventive Medicine in the Urals* (1 a year).

Moscow G. N. Gabrichevskii Institute of Epidemiology and Microbiology: 125212 Moscow, ul. Admirala Makharova 10; tel. (495) 452-18-16; f. 1895; library of 8,922 vols; Dir Prof. BORIS A. SHENDEROV; publ. *Medical Aspects of Microecology* (1 a year).

Moscow Helmholtz Research Institute of Eye Diseases: 103064 Moscow, ul. Sadovaya-Chernogryazskaya 14/19; tel. (495) 207-23-19; e-mail kanc@igb.ru; f. 1900; library of 69,445 vols; Dir ALEXANDER M. YUZHAKOV.

Moscow Municipal Research First Aid Institute: 129010 Moscow, Sukharevskaya pl. 3; tel. (495) 925-38-97; f. 1923; library of 30,000 vols; Dir Prof. B. D. KOMAROV.

Moscow Research Institute of Psychiatry: 107076 Moscow, Poteshnaya ul. 3; tel. (495) 963-76-26; e-mail krasnov@mtu-net .ru; internet www.mniip.org; f. 1920; social and biological psychiatry; treats mental illness, alcohol and drug addiction; Dir VALERY KRASNOV; publ. *Social and Clinical Psychiatry* (in Russian, 4 a year).

Mother and Child Care Institute: 680022 Khabarovsk, ul.Voronezgskaya, 49, bldg 1; tel. (4212) 98-02-15; f. 1986 collaboration with Far-Eastern State Medical Univ. and other medical instns of Russia and foreign countries (USA, Japan, China, Germany and others); attached to Russian Acad. of Medical Sciences; scientific activities incl. ecological-medical, molecular mechanisms, investigations into aspects of children's and adolescents' healthcare in the Far-Eastern region of Russia, estimation of viral and bacterial infections' influence on the reproductive function and foetus formation; the formation and support of tissue homeostasis at the early stages of ontogenesis; investigations of the immune-dependent peculiarities for pathological states among children and adolescents in the Far-Eastern region of Russia; Dir V. K. KOZLOV.

Nizhnii Novgorod Institute for Skin and Venereal Diseases: Nizhnii Novgorod, ul. Kovalikhinskaya 49; f. 1930; library of 10,000 vols; Dir Prof. T. A. GLAVINSKAYA.

Nizhnii Novgorod Institute of Industrial Hygiene and Occupational Diseases: Nizhnii Novgorod, ul. Semashko 20.

Nizhnii Novgorod Research Institute of Traumatology and Orthopaedics: 603155 Nizhnii Novgorod, V. Volzhskaya nab. 18; tel. (8312) 36-01-60; e-mail gito@pop.sci-nnov.ru; internet www.nniito.ru; f. 1945; 222 mems; library of 38,035 vols; Dir Prof. V. AZOLOV.

Novosibirsk Institute of Tuberculosis: Novosibirsk, ul. Chaplygina 75.

Omsk Research Institute of Naturally Occurring Infections: 644080 Omsk 80, pr. Mira 7; tel. (3812) 65-06-33; Dir A. A. MATUSHENKO.

Ott, D. O., Research Institute of Obstetrics and Gynaecology: 199034 St Petersburg, Mendeleevskaya liniya 3; tel. (812) 328-14-02; f. 1797; attached to Russian Acad. of Medical Sciences; Dir Prof. EDWARD K. AILAMAZYAN.

Pharmacy Research Institute: 117418 Moscow, ul. Krasikova 34; tel. (495) 128-57-88; Dir A. I. TENTSOVA.

PK Anokhin Research Institute of Normal Physiology: Russian Academy of Medical Sciences 125009, Moscow, Mokhovaya St, 11 Blvd 4; tel. (495) 601-22-45; e-mail s-sudakov@nphys.ru; internet nphys.ru; f. 1974; attached to Russian Acad. of Medical Sciences; research in human and animal physiology; Dir Prof. Dr SERGEY SUDAKOV.

Plague Prevention Research Institute for the Caucasus and Transcaucasia: 355106 Stavropol, Sovetskaya ul. 13; tel. (8652) 3-13-12; Dir V. I. EFREMENKO.

Research Centre for Medical Genetics: 115478 Moscow, Moskvorechie 1; tel. (499) 612-86-07; e-mail ekginter@mail.ru; internet www.med-gen.ru; f. 1969; attached to Russian Acad. of Medical Sciences; medical genetics, molecular genetics, cytogenetics, genetics of populations, clinical genetics, genetic counselling, hereditary metabolic diseases, prenatal diagnostics; library of 37,500 vols; Dir Prof. EVGENY K. GINTER; Deputy Dir Dr VERA IZHEVSKAYA; publ. *Medical Genetics* (12 a year).

Attached Institutes:

> **Institute of Clinical Genetics:** Moscow; tel. (499) 611-85-94; attached to Russian Acad. of Medical Sciences; Dir Prof. EVGENY K. GINTER.

> **Institute of Human Genetics:** Moscow, tel. (499) 611-85-87; attached to Russian Acad. of Medical Sciences; Dir S. S. SHISHKIN.

Research Centre for Molecular Diagnostics and Therapy: 117638 Moscow, Simferopolsky bul. 8; tel. (495) 113-23-51; e-mail e .severin@mtu-net.ru; f. 1985; Dir E. S. SEVERIN; publs *Molecular Medicine* (4 a year), *Problems of Biological, Medical and Pharmaceutical Chemistry* (4 a year).

Research Centre for Obstetrics, Gynaecology and Perinatology: 117815 Moscow, GSP-7, ul. Akademika Oparina; tel. (495) 438-51-71; internet www.pregnancy.ru; Dir Prof. VLADIMIR I. KULAKOV; Scientific Sec. Dr TATYANA V. LEOPATINA.

Research Centre of Medical Radiology: 249020 Kaluga oblast, Obninsk, ul. Koroleva 4; tel. (495) 956-14-39; f. 1958; attached to Russian Acad. of Medical Sciences; library of 121,000 vols; Dir A. F. TSYB; publ. *Radiation and Risk* (2 a year).

Research Centre of Mental Health: 115552 Moscow, Kashirskoe shosse 34; tel. (499) 616-61-83; attached to Russian Acad. of Medical Sciences; Dir A. S. TIGANOV.

Research Centre of Neurology: 125367 Moscow, Volokolamskoe shosse 80; tel. (495) 490-20-02; e-mail center@neurology.ru; internet www.neurology.ru; f. 1945; attached to Russian Acad. of Medical Sciences; Dir Z. A. SUSLINA.

Research Centre of Obstetrics, Gynaecology and Perinatology: 117815 Moscow, ul. Akad. Oparina 4; tel. (495) 438-18-00; attached to Russian Acad. of Medical Sciences; Dir VLADIMIR KULAKOV.

Research Centre of Surgery: 119991 Moscow, Abrikosovski per. 2; tel. (499) 246-95-63; e-mail nrcs@med.ru; internet med.ru; attached to Russian Acad. of Medical Sciences; Dir SERGEY L. DZEMESHKEVICH.

Research Institute BIF Rheumatology: 115552 Moscow, Kashirskoe shosse 34-a; tel. (495) 114-44-90; e-mail sokrat@irramn.ru; f. 1958; attached to Russian Acad. of Medical Sciences; br. at Volgograd; Dir E. NASONOV; publ. *Rheumatology Science & Practice* (6 a year).

Research Institute for Complex Problems of Hygiene and Occupational Diseases: 654041 Novokuznetsk, ul. Kutuzova 23; tel. (3843) 79-69-79; e-mail vasiliy .zaharenkov@mail.ru; internet www.ni-kpg .ru; f. 1976; attached to Russian Acad. of Medical Sciences; Dir Dr V. V. ZAKHARENKOV.

Research Institute of Children's Infections: 197022 St Petersburg, ul. Prof. Popova 9; tel. (812) 234-18-62; f. 1927; library of 25,000 vols; Dir V. V. IVANOVA; publ. *Infectious Diseases of Childhood* (1 or 2 a year).

Research Institute of Epidemiology and Microbiology: 603600 Nizhnii Novgorod, Gruzinskaya ul. 44; tel. (8312) 33-40-07; f. 1929; library of 10,000 vols; Dir I. N. BLOKHINA; publ. *Annual Collection of Research Articles*.

Research Institute of Forensic Medicine: 123242 Moscow, ul. Sadovaya-Kudrinskaya 3, Korp. 2; tel. (495) 254-32-49; Dir Prof. V. I. PROZOROVSKY.

Research Institute of Haematology and Intensive Therapy: 125167 Moscow, Novozykovsky pr-d 4A; tel. (495) 212-45-51; f. 1926; library of 50,000 vols; publ. *Sovremennye Problemy Gematologii i Perelivaniya Krovi* (12 a year).

Research Institute of Hygiene and Human Ecology: Samara, Chapaevskaya 87; tel. (846) 332-26-53; e-mail niigigen@ yandex.ru; internet www.samsmu.ru/ university/institutes/eco; f. 1929; sanitary-chemical and microbiological studies of environment objects, biomedical research into iodine content in food; Dir Dr OLGA V. SAZONOVA; publs *Issues of Child Nutrition* (online, elibrary.ru/item.asp?id=19527275), *Public Health and the Environment* (online, elibrary.ru/item.asp?id=18893758), *Quality Management of Health Care* (online, elibrary.ru/item.asp?id=20680149), *World of Science, Culture, Education* (online, elibrary.ru/item.asp?id=18910146).

Research Institute of Laser Medicine: 121165 Moscow, Studencheskaya ul. 40; tel. (495) 249-39-05.

Research Institute of Medical Primatology: 354376 Sochi-Adler, Veseloye 1; tel. (8622) 43-20-28; e-mail primatologia@ramn .ru; internet www.primatologia.ru; f. 1927; attached to Russian Acad. of Medical Sciences; principal research programmes: primatology, maintaining and breeding primates, primate models of human diseases, endocrinology, immunology and cell biology,

pathomorphology, comparative pathology, infectious pathology, infectious virology; library of 7,400 vols; Dir Dr SERGEI VLADIMIROVICH ORLOV; Deputy Dir Dr OLEG IVANOVICH VYSHEMIRSKI.

Research Institute of Occupational Safety under the Auspices of the Independent Russian Trade Unions: 191187 St Petersburg, ul. Gagarinskaya 3; tel. (812) 279-08-13; f. 1927; noise control, respiratory protection, air conditioning, ventilation, air pollution analysis, hygiene and VDUs, certification of personal protective equipment and workplaces; library of 47,000 vols; Dir E. A. KOLODIN.

Research Institute of Phthisiopulmonology of the First Moscow Sechenov Medical University: 127994 Moscow, ul. Dostoevskogo 4; tel. (495) 281-84-22; e-mail tbcripp@mail.ru; f. 1918; research in area of identification, diagnostics, treatment of pulmonary and extrapulmonary tuberculosis and sarcoidosis in children, adolescents and adults; epidemiological surveys and assistance in organization of anti-tuberculosis aid; library of 54,517 vols; Dir Dr SERGEY V. SMERDIN; publ. *Tuberculosis and Ecology* (6 a year).

Research Institute of Radiation Hygiene: 197101 St Petersburg, ul. Mira 8; tel. (812) 233-53-63; e-mail irii@ek6663.spb .edu; f. 1956.

Research Institute of the Technology and Safety of Medicines: 142450 Moscow oblast, Noginsky raion, pos. Staraya Kupavna, ul. Kirova 23; tel. (495) 524-09-36; attached to Russian Acad. of Sciences; Dir YU. V. BUROV.

Research Institute of Traditional Methods of Treatment: 103051 Moscow, Petrovsky bul. 8; tel. (495) 200-27-91.

Research Institute of Transplants and Artificial Organs: 123436 Moscow, Shchukinskaya ul. 1; tel. (495) 190-29-71.

Research Institute of Vaccines and Sera: 614089 Perm, GSP, NIIVS.

Research Institute of Vaccines and Sera: 634004 Tomsk, ul. Lenina 32; tel. (3822) 22-45-12; Dir N. B. CHERNY.

Rostov Institute of Radiology and Oncology: Rostov-on-Don, Voroshilovsky pr. 119; affiliated to the Chelyabinsk Radiation Hygiene Institute.

Rostov Region Paediatric Research Institute: Rostov-on-Don, Dolomanovsky per. 142.

Rostov Research Institute for Plague Control: 344007 Rostov-on-Don, ul. M. Gorkogo 117; tel. (8632) 66-57-03; f. 1934; library of 52,300 vols; Dir Prof. YU. M. LOMOV.

Russian Anti-plague Research Institute 'Microbe': 410005 Saratov, ul. Universitetskaya 46; tel. (8452) 26-21-31; e-mail microbe@san.ru; internet www.microbe.ru; f. 1918; library of 100,000 vols; Dir Dr Prof. V. V. KUTYREV; publ. *Problems of Particularly Dangerous Infections* (4 a year).

Russian Cardiology Research and Production Complex of the Ministry of Health of the Russian Federation: 121552 Moscow, 3rd Cherepkovskaya ul. 15A; tel. (495) 415-00-25; internet www .cardioweb.ru; f. 1945 as Institute of Therapy, present name 1975; attached to Russian Acad. of Medical Sciences; cardiology, cardiosurgery, research in various areas dealing with heart diseases, devt of new effective drugs; library of 250,000 vols; Dir E. I. CHAZOV; publ. *Newsletter of Cardiology* (2 a year).

Attached Institutes:

Institute of Experimental Cardiology: 121552 Moscow, 3 Cherepkovskaya ul. 15A; tel. (495) 415-00-35; attached to Russian Acad. of Medical Sciences; Dir V. N. SMIRNOV.

Myasnikov, A. L., Institute of Cardiology: 121552 Moscow, 3°, Cherepkovskaya ul. 15a; tel. (495) 415-52-05; e-mail c34h@cardio.ru; f. 1945 as Institute of Experimental and Clinical Therapy, present name 1966; attached to Russian Acad. of Medical Sciences; Dir Prof. Dr IRINA YE. CHAZOVA.

Russian Institute of Medical Parasitology: Rostov-on-Don, Moskovskaya 67.

Russian Polenov, A. L., Neurosurgical Institute: 191104 St Petersburg, ul. Mayakovskogo 12; tel. (812) 272-98-79; f. 1926; library of 36,000 vols; Dir V. P. BERSNEV; publ. *Neurosurgery* (1 a year).

Russian Research Centre for Radiology and Surgical Technologies: 197758 St Petersburg, Pesochny, ul. Leningradskaya 70; tel. (812) 596-84-62; e-mail crirr@ peterlink.ru; internet www.crirr.ru; f. 1918; attached to Min. of Health Care of the Russian Federation; Dir Prof. ANATOLY M. GRANOV; publ. *Volume of Conference Reports* (1 a year).

Russian Research Centre of Rehabilitation and Physiotherapy: 121099 Moscow, Novy Arbat 32; tel. (495) 252-18-83; f. 1920; library of 73,500 vols; Dir Dr V. M. BOGOLYUBOV; publs *Problems of Health Resorts, Physiotherapy and Exercise Therapy* (6 a year).

Russian Research Institute of Haematology and Transfusiology: 191024 St Petersburg, 2-a Sovetskaya ul. 16; tel. (812) 274-56-50; e-mail bloodscience@mail.ru; internet www.bloodscience.ru; f. 1932; Dir Dr E. A. SELIVANOV.

Russian Research Institute of Traumatology and Orthopaedics 'Vreden, R. R.': 195427 St Petersburg, ul. Akademika Baykova, dom 8; tel. (812) 670-89-05; e-mail info@rniito.org; internet www.rniito.org; f. 1906; orthopaedic clinical research centre; postgraduate training; library of 57,000 vols; Dir Prof. RASHID TIKHILOV; publ. *Travmatologia i Ortopedia Rossii* (Traumatology and Orthopaedics of Russia, 4 a year).

Russian Scientific Centre of Roentgenoradiology: 117837 Moscow, ul. Profsoyuznaya 86; tel. (495) 333-94-39; e-mail mailbox@rncrr.rssi.ru; internet www.space .ru/rncrr; f. 1924; laser diagnosis and treatment of malignant tumours; library of 51,700 vols; Dir Prof. V.P. KHARCHENKO.

St Petersburg Artificial Limb Research Institute: St Petersburg, pr. K. Marxa 9/12.

St Petersburg Institute of Ear, Throat, Nose and Speech: St Petersburg, Bronnitskaya 9; tel. (812) 316-28-52; e-mail lor-obchestvo@bk.ru; internet www.lornii.ru; f. 1930; attached to Min. of Health; library of 45,000 vols; Dir Prof. Dr JURIJ YANOV.

St Petersburg Institute of Eye Diseases: St Petersburg, Mokhovaya 38.

St Petersburg Institute of Phthisiopulmonology: 193036 St Petersburg, Ligovsky pr. 2–4; tel. (812) 279-25-54; f. 1923; library of 26,000 vols; Dir Prof. ALEXANDR V. VASILEV.

St Petersburg Institute of Tuberculosis: 193130 St Petersburg, Ligovsky pr. 2/4.

St Petersburg Institute of Vaccines and Sera: 198320 Krasnoe Selo, ul. Svobody 52; tel. (812) 741-19-78; e-mail reception@ spbniivs.ru; internet www.spbniivs.ru; Dir R. N. RODIONOVA.

St Petersburg Pasteur Institute of Epidemiology and Microbiology: 197101 St Petersburg, ul. Mira 14; tel. (812) 233-20-92; e-mail intdeppi@ok7368.spb.edu; internet www.pasteur-nii.spb.ru; f. 1923; library of 60,000 vols; Dir Prof. ANATOLY ZHEBRUN.

St Petersburg Petrov, N. N., Research Institute of Oncology: 188646 St Petersburg, Pesochny 2, St Petersburgskaya ul. 68; tel. (812) 237-89-94.

St Petersburg Research Institute of Industrial Hygiene and Occupational Diseases: 193036 St Petersburg, 2-a Sovetskaya ul. 4; tel. (812) 279-40-11; f. 1924.

Saratov Institute of Restorative Surgery, Traumatology and Orthopaedics: Saratov, ul. Chernyshevskogo 148.

Scientific Centre of Clinical and Experimental Medicine: ul. Akad. Timakova 2, 630117 Novosibirsk; tel. (3832) 33-64-56; e-mail sck@cyber.ma.nsc.ru; f. 1970; attached to Russian Acad. of Medical Sciences; Dir Dr V. A. SHKURUPY; publ. *Siberian Consilium* (medical pharmaceuticals, 6 a year).

Scientific Research Institute for General Reanimatology: 103031 Moscow, ul. Petrovka 25; tel. (495) 200-27-08; e-mail miiorramn@mediann.ru; f. 1936; attached to Russian Acad. of Medical Sciences; Dir Prof. V. V. MOROZ; br. at Novokuznetsk.

Scientific Research Institute for the Investigation of New Antibiotics: 119867 Moscow, Bol. Pirogovskaya 11; tel. (495) 246-99-80; attached to Russian Acad. of Medical Sciences; Dir YU. V. DUDNIK.

Scientific Research Institute of Biochemistry: 630117 Novosibirsk, Academician Timakov St. 2; tel. (383) 332-27-35; e-mail ibch@soramn.ru; internet www.ibch .soramn.ru; f. 1988; attached to Russian Acad. of Medical Sciences; Dir L. E. PANIN.

Semashko, N. A., Research Institute of Social Hygiene, Health Service Economics and Management: 103064 Moscow, ul. Vorontsovo Pole 12; tel. (495) 917-48-86; f. 1944; attached to Russian Acad. of Medical Sciences; Dir O. P. SHCHEPIN; publ. *Journal of Social Hygiene and the History of Medicine.*

Serbsky National Research Centre for Social and Forensic Psychiatry: 119034 Moscow, Kropotkinsky per. 23; tel. (495) 201-52-62; internet www.psi.med.ru/sspcen.htm; f. 1921; forensic psychiatry, social and clinical issues of psychiatry; library of 74,000 vols; Dir T. B. DMITRIEVA; publ. *Russian Psychiatric Journal* (contents and summaries in English, 6 a year).

Sochi Health Research Institute: Sochi, Kurortny pr. 110.

State Institute of Natural Curative Factors: 357500 Pyatigorsk, pr. Kirova 30; tel. (87933) 50-050; f. 1920; neurology, rheumatology, pain assessment and management, behavioural therapy; library of 120,000 vols; Dir Prof. KRIVOBOROV.

State Research Institute for the Standardization and Control of Drugs: 117246 Moscow, Nauchni pr-d 14A; tel. (495) 128-26-32; Dir Prof. YU. F. KRYLOV.

State Research Institute of Eye Diseases: 119021 Moscow, ul. Rossolimo 11 A-B; tel. (499) 248-01-28; e-mail info@ eyeacademy.ru; internet www.niigb.ru; f. 1973; attached to Russian Acad. of Medical Sciences; basic and applied research work; devt of new diagnostics techniques, preventive measures, therapeutic, surgical, laser and other methods of eye disease treatment; experimental ophthalmology; approbation and clinical trials of new medications; med-

ical equipment trials; training and education activities; library of 18,000 vols; Dir Prof. S. E. AVETISOV; Scientific Sec. I. I. KUZNETCOVA; publs *Glaucoma* (4 a year), *Polye Zreniya. Journal for Ophthalmologists* (6 a year), *Vestnik Oftalmologii* (Annals of Ophthalmology, 6 a year).

State Scientific Research Institute of Medical Polymers: 117246 Moscow, Nauchni pr-d 10; tel. (495) 120-21-62; internet www.medpol.ru; f. 1966; library of 15,000 vols; Dir Prof. G. A. MATJUSHIN.

State Scientific Research Institute on Medical Problems of the Far North: 629730 Tyumen oblast, Yamalo-Nenets Autonomous Okrug, Nadym, km 107; tel. (34995) 3-03-20; e-mail nii-mpks@mail.ru; internet mpks.ptline.ru; f. 1994; attached to Russian Acad. of Medical Sciences; health service and scientific researches in cardiology, pulmonology, paediatrics, gastroenterology, immunology, genetics, ecology and some other biological and medical brs taking into account the unfavourable conditions of the Far North and influence of extreme northern factors upon people's health; library of 2,000 vols on medical and biological sciences; Dir Prof. A. A. BUGANOV; publ. *Questions of Polar Medicine* (2 a year).

Sysin, A. N., Institute of Human Ecology and Environmental Hygiene: 119833 Moscow, ul. Pogodinskaya 10; tel. (495) 246-58-24; f. 1931; attached to Russian Acad. of Medical Sciences; Dir G. I. SIDORENKO.

Tarasevich, L. A., State Research Institute for the Standardization and Control of Medical Biological Preparations: 121002 Moscow, Sivtsev-Vrazhek 41; tel. (495) 241-39-22; e-mail gisk@glasnet.ru; f. 1919; library of 20,000 vols; Dir Prof. N. V. MEDUNTSIN.

Technological Research Institute for Antibiotics and Medical Enzymes: 198020 St Petersburg, Ogorodnikov pr. 41; tel. (812) 251-19-44; f. 1956; antifungal antibiotics, enzymes for medical use, nucleoside preparation of cardiovascular action; library of 55,000 vols; Dir Dr B. V. MOSKVICHEV.

Tomsk Institute of Physiotherapy and Spa Treatment: Tomsk, ul. Rosa Luxembourg 1.

Tomsk Research Centre: 634012 Tomsk, Kievskaya ul. 111/2; e-mail nii@oncology .tomsk.ru; attached to Russian Acad. of Medical Sciences; Chair. of the Presidium R. S. KARPOV..

Attached Institutes:

Cancer Research Institute: 634050 Tomsk, Kooperativnyi st 5; tel. (3822) 51-10-39; e-mail nii@oncology.tomsk.ru; internet www.oncology.tomsk.ru; f. 1979; attached to Siberian Br. Russian Acad. of Medical Sciences; studies on cancer prevalence and carcinogenesis in the territory of Siberia and the Russian Far E; detects endogenous and exogenous factors in tumour devt; investigates biochemical and molecular-genetic factors reflecting the mechanisms of carcinogenesis and tumour progression for assessing cancer risk and disease prognosis; develops new efficient programmes of the combined modality treatment for cancer patients using high-technology approaches; improves reconstructive plastic and organ-preserving surgeries and approaches for medical-social rehabilitation; Dir EVGENY L. CHOYNZONOV; publ. *Siberian Journal of Oncology* (6 a year).

Institute of Cardiology: 634012 Tomsk, Kievskaya ul. 111/2; tel. (3822) 44-33-97; attached to Russian Acad. of Medical Sciences; Dir R. S. KARPOV.

Institute of Medical Genetics: 634050 Tomsk, pos. Sputnik, nab. Ushaika 10; tel. (3822) 22-22-28; attached to Russian Acad. of Medical Sciences; Dir V. P. PUZYREV.

Institute of Pharmacology: 634028 Tomsk, pr. Lenina 3; attached to Russian Acad. of Medical Sciences; Dir E. D. GOLDBERG.

Laboratory of Experimental Biomedical Models: 634009 Tomsk, Kooperativny per. 7B; tel. (3822) 22-36-26; attached to Russian Acad. of Medical Sciences; Dir S. A. KUSMARTSEV.

Mental Health Research Institute: 634014 Tomsk, Sosnovy Bor, Aleutskaya St, 4; tel. (3822) 72-43-79; e-mail redo@ mail.tomsknet.ru; internet tomsknstitute .mental-health.ru; f. 1981; attached to Siberian Br., Russian Acad. of Medical Sciences; library of 8,120 vols; Dir Acad. VALENTIN SEMKE; Deputy Dir Prof. NIKOLAY BOKHAN; publ. *Siberian Journal of Psychiatry and Addiction Psychiatry* (6 a year).

Turner Scientific Research Institute of Child Orthopaedics and Traumatology: 189620 St Petersburg, ul. Parkovaya 64–68; tel. (812) 465-28-57; e-mail info@rosturner .ru; f. 1932; library of 33,600 vols; Dir Prof. V. L. ANDRIANOV; publ. scientific papers (2–3 a year).

Ufa Eye Research Institute: 450077 Ufa, 90 Pushkin str.; tel. (347) 272-37-75; e-mail eye@anrb.ru; internet www.ufaeyeinstitute .ru; f. 1926; attached to Acad. of Sciences of Republic of Bashkortostan; Dir Prof. M. M. BIKBOV; publ. *Collected Articles* (1 a year).

Ufa Research Institute of Occupational Health and Human Ecology: 450106 Ufa, ul. Kuvykina 94; tel. (3472) 28-53-19; f. 1955; complex development of scientific fundamentals of labour hygiene and physiology, industrial toxicology, occupational pathology, environmental hygiene and aspects of hygiene in juvenile vocational training and the workplace in the oil, petrochemical, gas and microbiological industries; library of 63,000 vols; Dir A. B. BAKIROV; publ. *Production and Environmental Hygiene: Workers' Health Care in Oil and Gas Extracting and Petrochemical Industries* (1 a year).

Ufa Skin and Venereal Diseases Institute: Ufa, ul. Frunze 43.

Urals Research Institute of Maternity and Childhood Care: 620028 Ekaterinburg, ul. Repina 1; tel. (3432) 51-42-02; f. 1877; library of 30,000 vols; Dir Dr G. A. CHERDANTSEVA.

Urals Research Institute of Phthisiopulmonology: 620039 Ekaterinburg, ul. 22 Partsezda 50; tel. (3432) 32-72-20; e-mail urniif@mail.ur.ru; internet www.urniif.okb1 .mplik.ru; f. 1931; library of 5,000 vols; Dir V. A. SOKOLOV.

Urology Research Institute: 105425 Moscow, 3-ya Parkovaya ul. 51; tel. (495) 367-62-62; e-mail urology@cdromclub.ru; f. 1979; Dir Acad. NIKOLAI A. LOPATKIN.

Vishnevsky, A. V., Institute of Surgery: 113811 Moscow, Bol. Serpukhovskaya 27; tel. (495) 236-72-90; attached to Russian Acad. of Medical Sciences; Dir V. D. FEDOROV.

Volgograd Plague Prevention Research Institute: 400131 Volgograd, Golubinskaya ul. 7; tel. (8442) 37-37-74; e-mail vari2@ sprint-v.com.ru; f. 1970; library of 13,320 vols; Dir V. V. ALEKSEEV.

Voronezh Region Radiological and Oncological Institute: Voronezh, ul. Kalyaeva 2.

NATURAL SCIENCES
General

Arctic and Antarctic Research Institute: 199397 St Petersburg, ul. Beringa 38; tel. (812) 352-15-20; e-mail aaricoop@aari.nw.ru; internet www.aari.nw.ru; Dir IVAN YEEGEN-EVICH FROLOV.

Institute of Economic and International Problems of the Assimilation of the Ocean: 690600 Vladivostok, ul. Sukhanova 5-a; tel. (4232) 5-77-31; attached to Russian Acad. of Sciences; Dir R. SH.-A. ALIEV.

Institute of Global Climate and Ecology: 107258 Moscow, Glebovskaya 20B; tel. (495) 169-24-11; e-mail semenov@igce.ru; internet www.igce.ru; f. 1989; attached to Russian Acad. of Sciences; Dir YU. A. IZRAEL.

Institute of Limnology: 196105 St Petersburg, ul. Sevastyanova 9; tel. (812) 387-02-60; e-mail lake@limno.org.ru; internet www.limno.org.ru; f. 1944; attached to Russian Acad. of Sciences; Dir VLADISLAV ALEXANDROVITCH RUMYANTSEV.

Institute of Natural Sciences: 670042 Ulan-Ude, ul. M. Sakhyanovoi 6; tel. (3012) 3-01-62; attached to Russian Acad. of Sciences; Dir K. A. NIKIFOROV.

Institute of the History of Science and Technology 'S. I. Vavilov': 109012 Moscow, Staropanskii per. 1/5; tel. (495) 925-22-80; e-mail postmaster@ihst.ru; internet www.ihst.ru; f. 1953; attached to Russian Acad. of Sciences; research into history of natural sciences and technology (history of maths, physics, mechanics, biology, chemistry, social studies, Earth sciences, ecology and history of space); library of 70,000 vols; Dir Dr YURY M. BATURIN; publ. *Voprosy Istorii Estestvoznaniya i Tekhniki* (4 a year).

Branch:

> **Institute for the History of Science and Technology—St Petersburg Branch:** 199034 St Petersburg, Universitetskaya nab. 5; tel. (812) 328-47-12; e-mail ihst@ihst.nw.ru; internet www.ihst.nw.ru; Dir Prof. EDUARD I. KOLCHINSKY; publs *Sociology of Science and Technology, Studies in the History of Biology*.

Limnological Institute: 664033 Irkutsk, Ulan-Batorskaya ul. 3; tel. (3952) 42-65-04; e-mail info@lin.irk.ru; internet www.lin.irk.ru; attached to Siberian Br., Russian Acad. of Sciences; Dir M. A. GRACHEV.

Mountain Taiga Station: 692533 Primorskii krai, Ussuriisky raion, pos. Gornotaezhnoe; tel. (42341) 9-11-10; attached to Russian Acad. of Sciences; Dir P. S. ZORIKOV.

North-East Interdisciplinary Scientific Research Institute FEB RAS: 685000 Magadan, Portovaya 16; tel. (4132) 63-00-51; e-mail secretary@neisri.ru; internet www.neisri.ru; f. 1960; attached to Russian Acad. of Sciences; geology, geophysics, metallogeny, history, archaeology, economics; library of 450,000 vols; Dir Prof. Dr NIKOLAI ANATOLYEVICH GORYACHEV; Scientific Sec. PLYASHKEVICH ANNA ALEKSEEVNA; publ. *Vestnik NESC* (4 a year).

Pushchino Scientific Centre: 142290 Moscow oblast, Pushchino, pr. Nauki 3; tel. (495) 923-80-03; e-mail nazarova@psn.ru; internet www.psn.ru; f. 1963; attached to Russian Acad. of Sciences; Dir VLADIMIR A. SHUVALOV.

V. I. Il'ichev Pacific Oceanological Institute: 690041 Vladivostok, Baltiiskaya ul. 43; tel. (423) 231-14-00; e-mail pacific@vlad.ru; internet www.poi.dvo.ru; f. 1973; attached to Russian Acad. of Sciences; comprehensive hydrophysical, hydrochemical and hydrobiological studies of water masses in seas and oceans; energy-mass exchange and the interaction of ocean and atmosphere; marine

ecosystems state; studies of geology, geophysics and geochemistry of the Pacific Ocean and its mineral resources; devt of new methods and creation of technical means to study the ocean and atmosphere; devt and application of remote control methods; creation and analysis of oceanography databases; Dir Prof. Acad. V. A. AKULICHEV.

Biological Sciences

All-Russia Research Institute for Nature Conservation: 113628 Moscow, Znamenskoe-Sadki, VNII Priroda; tel. (495) 423-03-22; f. 1981; research, general methodology, environmental protection strategy and coordination at home and internationally; 5 depts: animal protection, plant protection, ecosystem protection and recovery (incl. aquatic ecosystems), utilization of natural resources and nature reserves; library (books, journals, theses); Dir Prof. V. A. KRASILOV.

All-Russia Research Institute of Applied Microbiology: 142279 Moscow oblast, Serpukhovsky raion, Obolensk; tel. (0967) 2-77-61; Dir N. N. URAKOV.

Bakh, A. N., Institute of Biochemistry: Leninsky pr. 33, 119071 Moscow; tel. (495) 952-34-41; e-mail inbi@inbi.ras.ru; internet www.inbi.ras.ru; attached to Russian Acad. of Sciences; 255 mems; Dir Prof. V. O. POPOV; Vice-Dir Prof. B. B. DZANTIEV; publs *Applied Biochemistry and Microbiology* (6 a year), *Uspekhi Biologicheskoi Khimii* (Progress of Biological Chemistry, in Russian, 1 a year).

Bioengineering Research Centre: 117984 Moscow, ul. Vavilova 34/5; tel. (495) 135-73-19; attached to Russian Acad. of Sciences; Dir K. G. SKRYABIN.

Biotechnical Research Institute: 119034 Moscow, ul. Prechistenka 38; tel. (495) 246-16-56; Dir A. M. KARPOV.

Biotechnologia JSC: 117246 Moscow, Nauchny pr-d 8; tel. (495) 332-34-20; f. 1993 as private company (fmrly state enterprise, f. 1986); biotechnology, pharmaceuticals; Gen. Dir RAIF G. VASILOV.

Borissiak Palaeontological Institute of Russia (PIN RAS): 117647 Moscow, Profsoyuznaya 123; tel. (495) 339-05-77; e-mail admin@paleo.ru; internet www.paleo.ru; f. 1930; attached museum: see under Museums and Art Galleries; attached to Russian Acad. of Sciences; library of 20,000 vols; Dirs Acad. A. YU. ROZANOV, Prof. S. V. ROZHNOV, Prof. A. V. LOPATIN; publs *Paleontological Journal* (6 a year, in English and Russian), *Transactions* (3 or 4 a year).

Engelhardt Institute of Molecular Biology: 117984 Moscow, ul. Vavilova 32; tel. (495) 135-23-11; attached to Russian Acad. of Sciences; Dir Acad. A. D. MIRZABEKOV.

Institute of Biological Problems of the North: 685000 Magadan, pr. Portovaya 18; tel. (84132) 63-44-63; e-mail office@ibpn.ru; internet www.ibpn.ru; f. 1972; attached to Russian Acad. of Sciences; study of functioning, organization principles and adaptive strategies of the northern Russian population, communities and ecosystems; study of biological diversity in the NE region of Asia; Dir Dr O. A. RADCHENKO.

Institute of Biology: 630091 Novosibirsk, ul. Frunze 11; tel. (3832) 20-96-14; attached to Russian Acad. of Sciences; Dir V. I. EVSIKOV.

Institute of Biology: 185610 Petrozavodsk, Pushkinskaya ul. 11; tel. (8142) 7-36-15; attached to Russian Acad. of Sciences; Dir S. N. DROZDOV.

Institute of Biology: 167610 Syktyvkar, Kommunisticheskaya ul. 28; tel. (8212) 42-

52-02; f. 1962; attached to Russian Acad. of Sciences; Dir Dr A. I. TASKAEV.

Institute of Biology: 450054 Ufa, 25, pr. Oktyabrya 69; tel. (3472) 34-34-01; attached to Russian Acad. of Sciences; Dir V. M. KORSUNOV.

Institute of Biology and Soil Science: 690022 Vladivostok, pr. Stoletiya Vladivostoka 159; tel. (4232) 31-04-10; e-mail ibss@easnet.febras.ru; internet www.ibss.febras.ru; f. 1962; attached to Russian Acad. of Sciences; library of 80,000 vols; Dir Prof. YU. N. ZHURAVLEV; publ. *Proceedings* (1 a year, in Russian).

Institute of Biophysics: 660036 Krasnoyarsk, Akademgorodok; tel. (3912) 43-15-79; e-mail ibp@ibp.ru; internet www.ibp.ru; f. 1981; attached to Russian Acad. of Sciences; Dir Dr A. G. DEGERMENDZHY; Scientific Sec. Dr EGOR ZADEREEV.

Institute of Biophysics: 123182 Moscow, Zhivopisnaya ul. 46; tel. (495) 190-56-51; e-mail ibphgen@rcibph.dol.ru; f. 1946; radiobiology, radiation protection, health physics, medical radiology, non-ionizing radiation; Dir L. A. ILYIN.

Institute of Cell Biophysics: 142290 Moscow oblast, Pushchino, Institutskaya ul. 3; tel. (495) 625-59-84; f. 1991; attached to Russian Acad. of Sciences; Dir Prof. EVGENII FESENKO.

Institute of Chemical Bioland Fundamental Medicine SB RAS: 630090 Novosibirsk, pr. Akad. Lavrenteva 8; tel. (383) 363-51-50; e-mail vvv@niboch.nsc.ru; internet www.niboch.nsc.ru; f. 1984; attached to Russian Acad. of Sciences; Dir Prof. V. V. VLASOV; Academic Sec. Dr MARSEL KABILOV.

Institute of Cytology: 194064 St Petersburg, Tikhoretsky pr. 4; tel. (812) 247-18-29; e-mail cellbio@mail.cytspb.rssi.ru; attached to the Soc. of Protozoologists, affiliated with the Russian Acad. of Sciences; Dir Prof. Dr VLADIMIR N. PARFENOV.

Institute of Cytology and Genetics: 630090 Novosibirsk, pr. Akad. Lavrenteva 10; tel. (3832) 363-49-80; e-mail icg-adm@bionet.nsc.ru; internet www.bionet.nsc.ru; f. 1957; attached to Russian Acad. of Sciences; Dir Acad. N. A. KOLCHANOV; Scientific Sec. G. V. ORLOVA.

Institute of Food Substances: c/o Russian Academy of Sciences, 117901 Moscow, Leninsky pr. 14; attached to Russian Acad. of Sciences; Dir M. N. MANAKOV.

Institute of General and Experimental Biology, Siberian Branch, Russian Academy of Sciences: 670047 Ulan-Ude, ul. M. Sakhyanovoi 6; tel. (3012) 43-42-11; e-mail ioeb@biol.bscnet.ru; internet www.igaeb.bol.ru; attached to Russian Acad. of Sciences; Dir Prof. L. L. UBUGUNOV.

Institute of Higher Nervous Activity and Neurophysiology of RAS: 117485 Moscow, ul. Butlerova 5a; tel. (495) 334-70-00; e-mail admin@ihna.ru; internet www.ihna.ru; attached to Russian Acad. of Sciences; Dir Prof. PAVEL BALABAN; Sec. Dr NATALIA PASIKOVA.

A. V. Zhirmunsky Institute of Marine Biology: 690041 Vladivostok, ul. Palchevskogo 17; tel. (423) 231-09-05; e-mail inmarbio@mail.primorye.ru; internet www.imb.dvo.ru; f. 1966, current name adopted 1970; attached to Russian Acad. of Sciences; graduate programmes; medico-biological studies; studies of adaptation, ontogenesis and evolution of marine organisms; studies of flora, fauna, ecology and productivity of biota in the seas of the Russian Far East; conservation of biological resources; Dir A. V. ADRIANOV; Scientific Sec. V. E. ZHUKOV; publ. *Biologiya Morya* (Russian Journal of

Marine Biology, 6 a year, in Russian and English, print and online, www.bm.dvo.ru/e_index.htm).

Institute of Marine Biology: 690041 Vladivostok, ul. Palchevskogo 17; tel. (423) 231-09-05; e-mail inmarbio@mail.primorye.ru; internet www.imb.dvo.ru; f. 1970; attached to Russian Acad. of Sciences; library of 40,000 vols; Dir ANDREY V. ADRIANOV; publs *Biologiya Morya* (6 a year), *Russian Journal of Marine Biology* (7 a year, online).

Winogradsky Institute of Microbiology: 117811, Moscow, 7/2, pr. 60-letiya Oktyabrya; tel. (499) 135-21-39; e-mail inmi@inmi.host.ru; internet www.inmi.ru; f. 1930, reorganized and current name adopted in 1934; attached to Russian Acad. of Sciences; incl. 2 depts and 10 laboratories; research in general microbiology and virology–taxonomy, ecology, genetics, and biotechnology of microorganisms and viruses; Dir VALERY F. GALCHENKO; Sec. NINA N. SUDARENKOVA; publ. *Mikrobiologiya* (Microbiology, in Russian and English, print and online).

Institute of Gene Biology (IGB): 119334 Moscow, ul. Vavilova 34/5; tel. (499) 135-60-89; internet www.genebiology.ru; e-mail info@genebiology.ru; f. 1990; attached to Russian Acad. of Sciences; Dir PAVEL GEORGIEVICH GEORGIEV.

Institute of Molecular Genetics: 123182 Moscow, pl. Kurchatova 2; tel. (499) 196-00-00; e-mail img@img.ras.ru; internet www.img.ras.ru; f. 1978; attached to Russian Acad. of Sciences; Dir Prof. SERGEY V. KOSTROV.

A. N. Severtsov Institute of Ecology and Evolution: 119071 Moscow, Leninskii pr. 33; tel. (495) 952-20-88; e-mail admin@sevin.ru; internet www.sevin.ru; f. 1934; attached to Russian Acad. of Sciences; Bird Ringing Centre of Russia, Study Centre for Electron Microscopy, Vivarium, 8 biological stations in Russia, Tropical Centre in Vietnam; research on ecology, biological diversity, ethology, evolutionary morphology and nature conservation; Dir DMITRY S. PAVLOV; Scientific Sec. NATALYA YU. FEOKTISTOVA.

Institute of Physicochemical and Biological Problems in Soil Science: 142290 Moscow oblast, Pushchino; tel. (4967) 73-18-96; e-mail soil@issp.serpukhov.su; internet www.issp.psn.ru; f. 1999; attached to Russian Acad. of Sciences; Dir Prof. V. N. KUDEYAROV.

Institute of Physiologically Active Substances: 142432 Chernogolovka, Moscow oblast, Noginskii raion; tel. (496) 524-95-08; e-mail ipac@ipac.ac.ru; internet www.ipac.ac.ru; f. 1978; attached to Russian Acad. of Sciences; Dir SERGEY O. BACHURIN; Scientific Sec. NIKOLAY S. ZEFIROV.

Pavlov Institute of Physiology: 199034, St Petersburg, Makarova Embankment, 6; tel. (812) 328-07-01; e-mail tch@infran.ru; internet www.infran.ru; f. 1925; attached to Russian Acad. of Sciences; incl. museum; Dir Prof. D. P. DVORETSKY.

Institute of Physiology: 167982 Syktyvkar, Pervomayskaya str. 50; tel. (8212) 24-10-01; e-mail ovoys@physiol.komisc.ru; internet www.physiol.komisc.ru; f. 1988; attached to Russian Acad. of Sciences; Urals br. of the Russian Acad. of Sciences; Dir Prof. Dr Y. S. OVODOV.

Institute of Plant and Animal Ecology, Ural Division of Russian Academy of Sciences: 620144 Ekaterinburg, 8 Marta St 202; tel. (343) 260-82-55; e-mail common@ipae.uran.ru; internet www.ipae.uran.ru; f. 1944; attached to Russian Acad. of Sciences; investigations on regularities of org., functioning, dynamics and stability of living

systems on population, community and ecosystem levels incl. palaeoreconstructions of late quaternary ecosystems of the Urals mountains and adjacent territories (N Eurasia); elaboration of theoretical foundations of rational nature management, ecological regulation, bio-indication, ecotoxicology and radioecology; library of 150,000 vols; Dir Acad. VLADIMIR N. BOLSHAKOV; Deputy Dir VLADIMIR D. BOGDANOV; Deputy Dir EUGENE L. VOROBEICHIK; publ. *Russian Journal of Ecology* (6 a year).

Institute of Problems of the Industrial Ecology in the North (INEP KSC): 184209 Murmansk region, Apatity Fersman St, 14; tel. (81555) 6-10-93; e-mail vandysh@inep.ksc.ru; internet inep.ksc.ru; f. 1989; attached to Kola Science Centre, Russian Acad. of Sciences; library of 400,000 vols; Dir Prof. Dr VLADIMIR A. MASLOBOEV.

Institute of Protein Research: 142290 Moscow oblast, Pushchino ul. 4; tel. (495) 514-02-18; e-mail protres@vega.protres.ru; internet www.protres.ru; f. 1967; attached to Russian Acad. of Sciences; Dir Prof. ALEXANDER S. SPIRIN.

Institute of the Biochemistry and Physiology of Plants and Micro-organisms: 14229 Moscow oblast, Pushchino, pr. Nauki, d. 5; tel. (495) 956-33-70; e-mail rta@ibpm.pushchino.ru; internet www.ibpm.ru; f. 1965; attached to Russian Acad. of Sciences; Dir ALEXANDER M. BORONIN.

Institute of the Biochemistry and Physiology of Plants and Micro-organisms: 410049 Saratov, pr. Entuziastov 13; tel. (8452) 97-04-44; e-mail institute@ibppm.sgu.ru; internet www.ibppm.saratov.ru; f. 1980; attached to Russian Acad. of Sciences; library of 30,000 vols; Dir V. V. IGNATOV.

Institute of the Biology of Inland Waters: 152742 Yaroslavskaya oblast, Nekouzsky raion, p/o Borok; tel. (8547) 24-042; e-mail ibiw@mail.ru; internet www.ibiw.yaroslavl.ru; f. 1956; attached to Russian Acad. of Sciences; Dir Dr SERGEI I. GENKAL; publ. *Biology of Inland Waters* (3 a year).

Institute of the Ecology and Genetics of Micro-organisms: 614081 Perm, ul. Goleva 13; tel. (3422) 44-67-12; internet www.ecology.psu.ru; f. 1988; attached to Russian Acad. of Sciences; library of 3,000 vols; Dir V. A. CHERESHNEV; publ. *Proceedings of Scientific Research* (1 a year).

Institute of the Ecology of the Volga Basin: 445003 Togliatti, ul. Komzina, 10; tel. (8482) 48-99-77; e-mail ievbras2005@mail.ru; internet www.ievbras.ru; attached to Russian Acad. of Sciences; library of 26,120 vols, 36568 periodicals; Dir G. S. ROZENBERG.

Institute of Theoretical and Experimental Biophysics: 142290 Moscow oblast, Serpukhovsky raion, Pushchino; tel. (495) 632-78-69; e-mail office@iteb.ru; attached to Russian Acad. of Sciences; Dir Prof. G. R. IVANITSKY; Asst Dir A. NAUMOV.

Institute of Water and Ecological Problems: 680063 Khabarovsk, ul. Kim Yu Chena 65; tel. (4212) 22-75-73; e-mail iwep@iwep.secna.ru; f. 1968; attached to Russian Acad. of Sciences; Dir Dr B. A. VORONOV; publ. *Biogeochemical and Hydroecological Peculiarities of the Amur River Watershed Ecosystems* (1 a year).

Institute for Water and Environmental Problems: 656038 Barnaul, Molodyozhnaya ul. 1; tel. (3852) 66-64-60; e-mail iwep@iwep.asu.ru; internet www.iwep.asu.ru; f. 1987; research into hydrology, physical geography, cartography, biogeochemistry, geomorphology, limnology, air and water quality, mathematical modelling of contaminant transport in the environment; attached to Russian

Acad. of Sciences; library of 37,000 vols; Dir Prof. YURI I. VINOKUROV; publ. *Polzunovsky Vestnik* (in Russian, 6 a year).

Koltzov Institute of Developmental Biology: 119334 Moscow, ul. Vavilova 26; tel. (499) 135-33-22; e-mail idbras@bk.ru; internet idbras.comcor.ru; f. 1967, current name adopted 1976; attached to Russian Acad. of Sciences; Dir Dr NICKOLAI D. OZERNYUK; Scientific Sec. YELYENA B. ABRAMOVA.

Komarov, V. L., Botanical Institute: 197376 St Petersburg, ul. Prof. Popova 2; tel. (812) 234-12-37; e-mail binadmin@ok3277.spb.edu; internet www.binran.spb.ru; f. 1713; attached to Russian Acad. of Sciences; 460 mems; Dir V. T. YARMISHKO; publs *Botanichesky Zhurnal* (12 a year), *Rastitelnost Rossii* (2 or 3 a year).

Murmansk Marine Biological Institute: 183010 Murmansk, Vladimirskaya ul. 17; tel. (8152) 25-39-63; e-mail mmbi@mmbi.info; internet www.mmbi.info; f. 1935; attached to Russian Acad. of Sciences; oldest instn of the Kola Scientific Centre of the Russian Acad. of Sciences; conducts complex investigations of Nordic seas from Iceland to the Laptev Sea; studies southern seas: the Barents Sea and the Sea of Azov are the focus of ecosystem investigations; addresses problems of climate, marine peri-glacial, quaternary and current ecology, aquaculture, bioresources and environmental safety; monitors the ecosystem of the northern sea route, atomic fleet bases, and other water areas exposed to anthropogenic impacts; develops marine biotechnologies and prediction models for oceanologic processes, and environmental and engineering strategies to be applied to Arctic and southern sea; library of 70,000 vols; Dir Acad. GENNADY MATISHOV.

Pacific Institute of Bio-organic Chemistry: 690022 Vladivostok, pr. 100-letiya Vladivostoka 159; tel. (4232) 31-14-30; e-mail piboc@stl.ru; f. 1964; attached to Russian Acad. of Sciences; Dir Prof. A. STONIK.

Pavlov Institute of Physiology: 199034 St Petersburg, nab. Makarova 6; tel. (812) 328-07-01; e-mail krylov@infran.ru; internet www.infran.ru; f. 1925; attached to Russian Acad. of Sciences; Dir Prof. D. P. DVORETSKY.

Genetika/Research Institute for Genetics and Selection of Industrial Micro-organisms: 117545 Moscow, 1-i Dorozhnyi pr. 1; tel. (495) 315-37-47; e-mail genetika@genetika.ru; internet www.genetika.ru; f. 1968; Dir MIKHAIL BEBUROV; Scientific Dir VLADIMIR DEBABOV.

Research Institute of Food Biotechnology: 111033 Moscow, ul. Samokatnaya Dom 4B; tel. (495) 362-44-95; e-mail vniipbt@com2com.ru; internet www.vniipbt.ru; Dir VIKTOR A. POLYAKOV.

Sechenov Institute of Evolutionary Physiology and Biochemistry: 194223 St Petersburg, pr. Toreza 44; tel. (812) 552-79-01; e-mail office@iephb.ru; internet www.iephb.ru; f. 1950, current name adopted 1956; attached to Russian Acad. of Sciences; Dir NIKOLAI P. VESSELKIN; publ. *Zhurnal Evolyutsionnoi Biokhimii i Fiziologii* (Journal of Evolutionary Biochemistry and Physiology, in English and Russian).

Severtsov, A. N., Institute of Ecology and Evolution: 119071 Moscow, Leninskii pr. 33; tel. (495) 952-20-88; e-mail admin@sevin.ru; attached to Russian Acad. of Sciences; Dir Acad. DMITRI S. PAVLOV; publs *Russian Journal of Aquatic Ecology* (2 a year), *Lutreola* (2 a year).

M. M. Shemyakin and Yu. A. Ovchinnikov Institute of Bioorganic Chemistry: 117997 Moscow, ul. Miklukho-Maklaya 16/

10; tel. (495) 335-01-00; e-mail office@ibch.ru; internet www.ibch.ru; f. 1959; attached to Russian Acad. of Sciences; library of 250,000 vols; br. at Pushchino; Dir VADIM TIKHONOVICH IVANOV; Scientific Sec. VLADIMIR ALEXANDROVICH OLEINIKOV; publ. *Bioorganicheskaya khimiya* (Russian Journal of Bioorganic Chemistry, 12 a year, in Russian and English).

Siberian Institute of Plant Physiology and Biochemistry: 664033 Irkutsk 33, POB 317; tel. (3952) 42-67-21; e-mail matmod@sifibr.irk.ru; internet sifibr.irk.ru; f. 1961; attached to Russian Acad. of Sciences; researches on plant physiology and biochemistry, microbiology and soil science, entomology, botany, geobotany and forestry; Dir Dr VICTOR VOINIKOV; publ. *Journal of Stress Physiology & Biochemistry*.

State Research Centre of Virology and Biotechnology (Vector): 630559 Novosibirsk oblast, Koltsovo; tel. (3832) 36-60-10; e-mail vector@vector.nsk.su; internet www.vector.nsc.ru; f. 1974; library of 90,000 vols; Dir Acad. LEV S. SANDAKHCHIEV.

State Research Institute of Highly Pure Biopreparations (IHPB): 197110 St Petersburg, Pudozhskaya St 7; tel. (812) 235-12-25; e-mail onir@hpb-spb.com; internet www.hpb-spb.com; f. 1974; basic research and applied activities using the latest advances in molecular biology, microbiology, virology, and biotechnology; Dir Prof. VALERIY DOBRITSA.

Timiryazev, K. A., Institute of Plant Physiology: 127276 Moscow, Botanicheskaya 35; tel. (495) 977-80-22; e-mail ifr@ippras.ru; internet www.ippras.ru; f. 1890; attached to Russian Acad. of Sciences; library of 83,000 vols; Dir Prof. VL. V. KUZNETSOV; publ. *Russian Journal of Plant Physiology* (6 a year).

Vavilov Institute of General Genetics: 119991 Moscow, ul. Gubkina 3; tel. (495) 135-62-13; e-mail iogen@vigg.ru; internet www.vigg.ru; f. 1966; attached to Russian Acad. of Sciences; library of 5,000 vols; Dir Prof. YU. P. ALTUKHOV; publs *Russian Journal of Genetics* (12 a year), *Advances in Current Biology* (6 a year).

Zoological Institute: 199034 St. Petersburg, Universitetskaya nab. 1; tel. (812) 328-03-11; e-mail admin@zin.ru; internet www.zin.ru; f. 1832; attached to Russian Acad. of Sciences; Dir O. N. PUGACHEV; Vice-Dir ALEXEY TIKHONOV.

Mathematical Sciences

Euler International Institute of Mathematics: 191023, St Petersburg, Naberezhnaya Fontanki, 27; 197022, St Petersburg, Pesochnaya Naberezhnaya 10; tel. (812) 234-05-74; e-mail admin@euler.pdmi.ras.ru; internet www.pdmi.ras.ru/eimi; f. 1988; attached to Russian Acad. of Sciences; Dir LUDWIG D. FADDEEV.

Institute of Mathematics with Computer Center: 450008 Ufa, ul. Chernyshevsky 112; tel. (347) 272-59-36; e-mail shaig@anrb.ru; internet matem.anrb.ru; f. 1971; attached to Russian Acad. of Sciences; Dir VALENTIN VASILIEVICH NAPALKOV; Scientific Sec. YURY ZAKIROVICH SHAIGARDANOV; publ. *Ufa Mathematical Journal* (4 a year, in English and Russian).

Sobolev Institute of Mathematics: 630090 Novosibirsk, 4 Akad. Koptyuga Ave; tel. (3833) 33-28-92; e-mail im@math.nsc.ru; internet www.math.nsc.ru; f. 1957; attached to Russian Acad. of Sciences; library of 120,000 vols; Dir Prof. SERGEY S. GONCHAROV; Scientific Sec. Dr A. F. VORONIN; publs *Diskretny Analiz i Issledovanie Operatsii* (6 a year), *Matematicheskie Trudy* (2 a year),

Siberian Electronic Mathematical Reports, *Sibirsky Matematichesky Zhurnal* (6 a year), *Sibirsky Zhurnal Industrialnoy Matematiki* (4 a year).

Steklov Mathematical Institute: 119991 Moscow, ul. Gubkina 8; tel. (495) 984-81-41; e-mail steklov@mi.ras.ru; internet www.mi.ras.ru; f. 1921 as Institute of Physics and Mathematics, current name adopted 1926, current status 1932; attached to Russian Acad. of Sciences; library of 30,000 vols, 60,000 journals; Dir VALERII VASIL'EVICH KOZLOV; Academic Sec. ALEXANDER NIKOLAEVICH PECHEN; publ. *Proceedings of the Steklov Institute of Mathematics*.

St Petersburg Department of V. A. Steklov Mathematical Institute: 191023 St Petersburg, nab. Fontanki 27; tel. (812) 312-40-58; e-mail admin@pdmi.ras.ru; internet www.pdmi.ras.ru; f. 1940, ind. instn; attached to Russian Acad. of Sciences; Dir Acad. S. V. KISLYAKOV; Exec. Academic Sec. Dr MAXIM VSEMIRNOV; publs *Journal of Mathematical Sciences* (11 a year), *St Petersburg Math Journal* (24 a year).

Physical Sciences

A. E. Favorsky Irkutsk Institute of Chemistry SD RAS: 664033 Irkutsk, 1 Favorsky Stu; tel. (3952) 51-14-31; e-mail irk_inst_chem@irioch.irk.ru; internet www.inchemistry.irk.ru; f. 1957; attached to Russian Acad. of Sciences; research and devt in organic chemistry; elemento-organic chemistry; chemistry of polymers; wood chemistry; library of 10,000 vols, 55,000 periodicals; Dir Prof. BORIS A. TROFIMOV.

A. N. Frumkin Institute of Physical Chemistry and Electrochemistry: 117071 Moscow, Leninskii pr. 31; tel. (495) 955-46-30; f. 1945; attached to Russian Acad. of Sciences; Dir Prof. A. YU. TSIVADZE.

A. N. Zavaritzky Institute of Geology and Geochemistry: 620075 Ekaterinburg, Pochtovy per. 7; tel. (343) 371-19-97; e-mail director@igg.uran.ru; internet www.igg.uran.ru; f. 1939; attached to Russian Acad. of Sciences; scientific research and applications in geology, geochemistry and geo-ecology; library of 90,000 vols; Dir SERGEY L. VOTYUAKOV; Deputy Dir ELENA V. ANIKINA; publ. *Lithosphere* (6 a year).

All-Russia Geological Oil Research Institute (VNIGNI): 105819 Moscow, shosse Entuziastov 36; tel. (495) 273-26-51; f. 1953; library of 80,000 vols; Dir D-r K. A. KLESCHEV; publs *Geology of Oil and Gas* (1 a year), *Proceedings* (6 a year).

All-Russia Research Institute for the Geology and Mineral Resources of the World's Oceans: 190121 St Petersburg, Angliisky 1; tel. (812) 113-83-79; e-mail okeangeo@vniio.ru; f. 1948; library of 60,500 vols; Dir Prof. I. S. GRAMBERG.

All-Russia Research Institute of Chemical Technology: 115409 Moscow, Kashirskoe shosse 33; tel. (495) 324-61-55.

All-Russian Research Institute of Geological, Geophysical and Geochemical Systems (VNIIgeosystem): 117105 Moscow, Varshavskoe shosse 8; tel. (495) 954-53-50; e-mail geosys@geosys.ru; internet www.geosys.ru; f. 1961; fundamental and applied scientific research; experimental design and technological research in earth sciences and geological exploration; library of 38,000 vols; Dir LEONID E. CHESALOV; Sec. OLGA LYUBIMOVA; publ. *Geoinformatika* (6 a year).

All-Russia Research Institute of Hydrolysis: 198099 St Petersburg, ul. Kalinina 13; tel. (812) 186-29-22; Dir O. I. SHAPOVALOV.

All-Russia Research Institute of Natural Gases and Gas Technology: 142717 Moscow oblast, Leninsky raion, pos. Razvilka; tel. (495) 355-92-06; e-mail vniigaz@vniigaz.gazprom.ru; internet www.vniigaz.ru; f. 1948; library of 100,000 vols.

All-Russia Research Institute of Optical and Physical Measurements: 103031 Moscow, ul. Rozhdestvenka 27; tel. (495) 208-41-83; attached to Russian Acad. of Sciences; Gen. Dir I. G. BARANNIK.

All-Russia Research Institute of Physical-Technical and Radiotechnical Measurements—VNIIFTRI: 147570 Moscow oblast, Solnechnogorsky raion, p/o Mendeleevo; tel. (495) 744-81-12; e-mail director@vniiftri.ru; internet www.vniiftri.ru; f. 1955; attached to Rosstandart and Russian Acad. of Sciences; Dir Prof. S. I. DONCHENKO.

All-Russia Scientific Research Institute of Mineral Resources: 109017 Moscow, Staromonetni per. 31; tel. (495) 231-50-43; f. 1918; prospecting for and estimating ore deposits, research in processing; library of 345,000 vols; Dir Prof. A. N. EREMEEV.

Amur Complex Research Institute: 675000 Amur oblast, Blagoveshchensk, per. Relochnyi 1; tel. (4162) 42-72-32; f. 1980; attached to Russian Acad. of Sciences; geology, minerals; library of 26,000 vols; Dir V. G. MOISEENKO.

Andreev Acoustics Institute: 117036 Moscow, ul. Shvernika 4; tel. (495) 126-74-01; e-mail dubrov@akin.ru; internet www.akin.ru; f. 1953; attached to Russian Acad. of Sciences; Dir N. A. DUBROVSKY.

Arbuzov, A. E., Institute of Organic and Physical Chemistry: 420088 Kazan, ul. Akad. Arbuzova 8; tel. (8432) 73-93-65; e-mail arbuzov@iopc.kcn.ru; internet www.iopc.kcn.ru; f. 1965; attached to Russian Acad. of Sciences; Dir O. G. SINYASHIN.

Baikov, A. A., Institute of Metallurgy: 117911 Moscow, Leninskii pr. 49; tel. (495) 135-86-11; attached to Russian Acad. of Sciences; Dir Acad. N. P. LYAKISHEV.

Bardin, I. P., Central Research Institute of Ferrous Metallurgy: 107005 Moscow, 2-ya Baumanskaya 9/23; tel. (495) 265-72-04; e-mail ferrum.sc@online.ru; f. 1944; library of 65,000 vols; Dir-Gen. VLADIMIR I. MATORIN.

Bochvar, A. A., All-Russia Research Institute of Inorganic Materials: 123060 Moscow, ul. Rugova 5a; tel. (495) 190-82-97; e-mail post@bochvar.ru; internet www.bochvar.ru; f. 1945; Dir-Gen. ALEKSANDR VIKTOROVICH VATULIN; publ. *Materialovedeniye i Novye Materialy* (Materials Science and New Materials, 1 a year).

Boreskov Institute of Catalysis: 630090 Novosibirsk, pr. Akad. Lavrenteva 5; tel. (383) 330-82-69; e-mail bic@catalysis.ru; internet www.catalysis.ru; attached to Russian Acad. of Sciences; Dir V. N. PARMON.

Central Aerological Observatory: 141700 Moscow, 3 Pervomayskaya St, Dolgoprudny; tel. (495) 408-61-48; e-mail caohead@cao-rhms.ru; internet www.cao-rhms.ru; f. 1941; atmospheric physics and chemistry up to 100 km, study and monitoring of ozone layer, cloud physics, applied meteorology, weather modification; use of aircraft, rockets, satellites and radar for atmospheric studies.; library of 61,000 vols; Dir A. A. IVANOV; publ. *CAO Proceedings*.

Central Seismological Observatory: Obninsk; attached to Russian Acad. of Sciences.

Chita Institute of Natural Resources: 672014 Chita, ul. Nedorezova 16, POB 147; tel. (302) 221-25-82; e-mail root@cinr.chita.ru; internet www.chita.ru/public_htm/cinr/

cinr.htm; f. 1981; attached to Russian Acad. of Sciences; library of 6,000 vols; Dir A. B. PTITSYN; publ. *Report on Environmental Conditions in Zabailkalye* (1 a year).

Diamond and Precious Metal Geology Institute of the Siberian Branch of the Russian Academy of Sciences (DPMGI SB RAS): 677890 Yakutsk, pr. Lenina 39; tel. (4112) 33-58-64; e-mail geo@yakutia.ru; internet www.diamond.ysn.ru; f. 1957; attached to Russian Acad. of Sciences; tectonics and geodynamics of Siberian platform and Verkhoyansk-Kolyma folded region; kimberlite magmatism, formation and disposition laws for deposits of diamond, gold, silver, MPG and other; investigation of diamonds; paleontology and stratigraphy of Phanerozoic era; Dir Dr ALEXANDER P. SMELOV.

Far Eastern Institute of Geology: 690022 Vladivostok, pr. Stoletiya Vladivostoka 159; tel. (4232) 31-87-50; e-mail fegi@online.marine.su; f. 1959; attached to Russian Acad. of Sciences; Dir A. I. KHANCHUK.

G. A. Krestov Institute of Solution Chemistry: 153045 Ivanovo, Akademicheskaya ul. 1; tel. (4932) 33-62-59; e-mail adm@isc-ras.ru; internet www.isc-ras.ru; f. 1981; attached to Russian Acad. of Sciences; research in solutions and liquid phase materials; library of 70,000 vols; Dir Prof. ANATOLY ZAKHAROV; Scientific Sec. Dr YURY PUKHOVSKIY; publs *Chemical Thermodynamics and Thermochemistry* (2 a year), *Problems of Solution Chemistry* (4 a year), *Proceedings* (1 a year), *Textile Chemistry* (2 a year).

G. G. Devyatykh Institute of the Chemistry of High-Purity Substances: 603950 Nizhnii Novgorod, ul. Tropinina 49; tel. (831) 462-56-70; e-mail victor@ihps.nnov.ru; internet www.ihps.nnov.ru; f. 1988; attached to Russian Acad. of Sciences; fundamental and applied research of high-purity substances; production of zinc selenide, quartz and chalcogenide optical fibres; Dir Prof. MIKHAIL CHURBANOV; publs *Journal of Optoelectronics and Advanced Materials*, *Optical Letters*.

General Physics Institute: 119991 Moscow, ul. Vavilova 38; tel. (495) 135-82-96; e-mail director@gpi.ru; internet www.gpi.ru; f. 1983; attached to Russian Acad. of Sciences; brs in Tarusa and Troitsk; Dir Prof. IVAN A. SHCHERBAKOV.

Geological Institute: 670047 Ulan-Ude, ul. Sakhyanova 6A; tel. (3012) 43-30-24; e-mail gin@gin.bscnet.ru; internet geo.stbur.ru; f. 1973; attached to Siberian br., Russian Acad. of Sciences; study of structure, history of devt and matter composition of earth crust in the Buryatia and Chita regions by geological, geophysical and geochemical methods; Dir GENNADI TATKOV.

Geological Institute of Kola Science Centre: 184209 Murmansk oblast, Apatity, ul. Fersmana 14; tel. (81555) 79656; e-mail geoksc@geoksc.apatity.ru; internet geoksc.apatity.ru; f. 1951; attached to Russian Acad. of Sciences; Dir YURY L. VOYTEKHOVSKY.

Graphite Research Institute: 111524 Moscow, Elektrodnaya 2; tel. (495) 176-13-06; Dir V. I. KOSTIKOV.

Grebenshchikov, I. V., Institute of Silicate Chemistry: 199155 St Petersburg, ul. Odoevskogo 24, korp. 2; tel. (812) 350-65-16; e-mail ichsran@isc.nw.ru; attached to Russian Acad. of Sciences; Dir Acad. V. J. SHEVCHENKO.

High-Mountain Geophysical Institute: 360030 Nalchik, pr. Lenina 2; tel. (866) 247-00-31; e-mail vgikbr@rambler.ru; f. 1963; meteorology, climatology, glaciology, geophysics, ecology; library of 17,230 vols, 26,288 periodicals; Dir Dr VALERY O. TAPASKHANOV.

Institute for Geothermal Research: 367030 Makhachkala, Shamil pr. 39-A; tel. (8722) 62-93-57; e-mail geoterm@mail.ru; internet www.ipgdncran.ru; f. 1980; attached to Russian Acad. of Sciences; fundamental scientific research on heat physics, hydrodynamics and heat exchange in geothermal systems, mathematical and information models in geothermy, renewable energy; Dir Prof. A. B. ALKHASOV; publ. *Proceedings of the Scientific Training 'Actual problems of renewable energy resources development'* (2 a year).

Institute for High-Energy Physics: 142281 Moscow oblast, Protvino; tel. (4967) 74-04-56; e-mail yury.ryabov@ihep.ru; internet www.ihep.ru; f. 1963; high energy physics; proton accelerators; library of 300,000 vols; Dir NIKOLAI TYURIN.

Institute for Metals Superplasticity Problems of RAS: 450001 Ufa, 39 St Khalturina; tel. (347) 223-64-07; e-mail imsp@anrb.ru; f. 1985; attached to Russian Acad. of Sciences; library of 8,700 vols; Dir R. R. MYLYUKOV.

Institute of Applied Astronomy: 197110 St Petersburg, ul. Zhdanovskaya 8; tel. (812) 275-11-18; e-mail ipa@ipa.nw.ru; internet www.ipa.nw.ru; f. 1988; attached to Russian Acad. of Sciences; Dir Prof. A. V. IPATOV; publs *Trudy IPA RAN* (2 a year, in Russian), *Communications* (10 a year, in Russian and English).

Institute of Applied Physics: 603600 Nizhny Novgorod, ul. Ulyanova 46; tel. (831) 436-58-10; attached to Russian Acad. of Sciences; Dir Acad. A. G. LITVAK.

Institute of Astronomy: 109017 Moscow, Pyatnitskaya ul. 48; tel. (495) 951-54-61; e-mail admin@inasan.rssi.ru; internet www.inasan.rssi.ru; f. 1936; attached to Russian Acad. of Sciences; Dir Prof. BORIS M. SHUSTOV.

Institute of Atmospheric Optics: 634055 Tomsk, Akademicheskii pr. 1; tel. (382) 249-27-38; e-mail mgg@iao.ru; internet www.iao.ru; f. 1969; research and development in physics, laser engineering, aerosol technology and ozone; attached to Siberian br. of the Russian Acad. of Sciences; Dir Prof. GENNADY GRIGOREVICH MATVIENKO.

Institute of Atmospheric Physics: 119017 Moscow, Pyzhevskii per. 3; tel. (495) 951-55-65; e-mail mail_adm@omega.ifaran.ru; f. 1956; attached to Russian Acad. of Sciences; library of 4,000 vols, 40 periodicals; Dir Acad. G. S. GOLITSYN; publ. *Izvestiya—Atmospheric and Oceanic Physics* (6 a year).

Institute of Chemical Kinetics and Combustion: 630090 Novosibirsk, Institutskaya 3; tel. (3832) 34-41-50; f. 1957; attached to Russian Acad. of Sciences; library of 88,000 vols; Dir Prof. YU. D. TSVETKOV.

Institute of Chemistry: 690022 Vladivostok, pr. Stoletiya Vladivostoka 159; tel. (4232) 31-25-90; e-mail chemi@online.ru; f. 1971; attached to Russian Acad. of Sciences; library of 5,000 vols; Dir Prof. Dr V. YU. GLUSHCHENKO.

Institute of Coal and Coal Chemistry: 650610 Kemerovo GSP, ul. Rukavishnikova 21; tel. (3842) 28-14-33; e-mail pvp@kemsc.ru; internet www.kemsc.ru; f. 1983; attached to Russian Acad. of Sciences; library of 40,000 vols; Dir G. I. GRITSKO; publ. *Coalbed Methane* (4 a year).

Institute of Earthquake Prediction Theory and Mathematical Geophysics: 117997 Moscow, Profsoyuznaya str. 84/32; tel. (495) 333-45-13; e-mail mitpan@mitp.ru; internet www.mitp.ru; f. 1990; attached to Russian Acad. of Sciences; predicts earthquakes and geological disasters in complex systems; risk analysis and optimization of disasters preparedness; identification of earthquake-prone areas; theory of seismic waves; inverse problems of geophysics computational geodynamics; inverse retrospective problems of thermal evolution of the Earth's interior; magnetohydrodynamics problems; modelling of dynamics of lithosphere blocks and seismicity; socio-economic predictions; library of 10,400 vols; Dir Dr A. A. SOLOVIEV; Deputy Dir Dr IGOR KUZNETSOV; Scientific Sec. Dr ALEXANDER GORSHKOV; publ. *Computational Seismology* (1 a year).

Institute of Electrophysics: 620219 Ekaterinburg, Amundsena ul. 106; tel. (3432) 67-87-96; e-mail admin@iep.uran.ru; attached to Russian Acad. of Sciences; Dir V. G. SHPAK; Scientific Sec. E. E. KOKORINA.

Institute of Energy Problems of Chemical Physics: 117829 Moscow, Leninskii pr. 38, korp. 2; tel. (495) 137-34-79; attached to Russian Acad. of Sciences; Dir V. L. TALROZE.

Institute of Experimental Meteorology: Obninsk; Dir M. A. PETROSYANTS.

Institute of Experimental Mineralogy: 142432 Moscow oblast, Noginskii raion, Chernogolovka, Institutskaya ul. 4; tel. (496) 524-44-25; e-mail shap@iem.ac.ru; internet www.iem.ac.ru; f. 1969; attached to Russian Acad. of Sciences; 206 mems; Dir YURI B. SHAPOVALOV; publ. *Experiments in Geosciences* (1 a year).

Institute of Geochemistry: 664033 Irkutsk, ul. Favorskogo 1a; tel. (3952) 46-05-00; attached to Russian Acad. of Sciences; Dir M. I. KUZMIN.

Institute of Geology: 367025 Makhachkala, ul. Gadzhieva 45; attached to Russian Acad. of Sciences; Dir V. V. SUETNOV.

Institute of Geology: 109017 Moscow, Pyzhevski per. 7; tel. (495) 230-80-29; f. 1930; attached to Russian Acad. of Sciences; Dir Y. G. LEONOV.

Institute of Geology: 167982 Syktyvkar, Pervomaiskaya ul. 54; tel. (8212) 24-00-37; f. 1958; attached to Russian Acad. of Sciences; Dir A. M. ASKHABOV; publs *Vestnik* (12 a year), *Proceedings* (4 a year).

Institute of Geology: 450000 Ufa 25, ul. K. Marksa 16/2; tel. (3472) 22-82-56; attached to Russian Acad. of Sciences; Dir V. N. PUCHKOV.

Institute of Geology of Karelian Research Centre: 185910 Petrozavodsk, Pushkinskaya ul. 11; tel. (8142) 78-06-02; e-mail geology@krc.karelia.ru; internet geoserv.krc.karelia.ru; f. 1946; attached to Russian Acad. of Sciences; Dir V. V. SHCHIPTSOV (acting).

Institute of Geomechanics: c/o Russian Academy of Sciences, 117333 Moscow, ul. Vavilova 44 (korp. 2, komn. 86); attached to Russian Acad. of Sciences.

Institute of Geophysics: 620016 Ekaterinburg, ul. Amundsena 100; tel. (343) 267-88-68; attached to Russian Acad. of Sciences; Dir P. S. MARTYSHKO.

Institute of High-Pressure Physics: 142092 Moscow oblast, Troitsk; tel. (495) 334-00-10; e-mail hpp@hppi.troitsk.ru; internet www.hppi.troitsk.ru; f. 1958; attached to Russian Acad. of Sciences; Dir Prof. S. M. STISHOV.

Institute of High-Temperature Electrochemistry: 620219 Ekaterinburg, S. Kovalevskaya 22; tel. (343) 374-50-89; e-mail dir@ihte.uran.ru; internet www.ihte.uran.ru; f. 1958; attached to Russian Acad. of Sciences; Dir Prof. YURI ZAIKOV.

Institute of High-Temperature Physics: 127412 Moscow, Izhorskaya 13/19; tel. (495) 485-83-45; attached to Russian Acad. of Sciences; Dir V. M. BATENIN.

Institute of Hydrodynamics: 630090 Novosibirsk, pr. Akad. Lavrenteva 15; tel. (383) 333-16-12; e-mail igil@hydro.nsc.ru; internet www.hydro.nsc.ru; f. 1957; attached to Russian Acad. of Sciences; library of 87,000 vols; Dir Prof. ANATOLY VASILYEV; publs *Combustion Explosions and Shock Waves* (6 a year), *Continuum Dynamics* (1 or 2 a year), *Journal of Applied Mechanics and Technical Physics* (6 a year).

Institute of Macro-Molecular Compounds: 199004 St Petersburg, Bolshoi pr. 31; tel. (812) 213-10-70; attached to Russian Acad. of Sciences; Dir E. F. PANARIN.

Institute of Marine Geology and Geophysics: 693002 Yuzhno-Sakhalinsk, ul. Nauki 5; tel. (4242) 2-21-28; attached to Russian Acad. of Sciences; Dir K. F. SERGEEV.

Institute of Metal Physics: 620041 Ekaterinburg, GSP-170, ul. Sofia Kovalevskaya 18; tel. (343) 374-02-30; e-mail physics@imp .uran.ru; internet www.imp.uran.ru; f. 1932; attached to Russian Acad. of Sciences; library of 18,000 vols, 92,000 periodicals; Dir Prof. Dr V. V. USTINOV; publs *Fizika Metallov i Metallovedenie* (Physics of Metals and Metallography, 12 a year), *Defectoscopiya* (Journal of Non-Destructive Testing, 12 a year).

Institute of Metallo-organic Chemistry: 603600 Nizhnii Novgorod, ul. Tropinina 49; tel. (8312) 66-27-09; f. 1989; attached to Russian Acad. of Sciences; library of 50,000 vols; Dir G. A. ABAKUMOV.

Institute of Metallurgy: Ural Br., 620016 Ekaterinburg, 101, Amundsen St; tel. (343) 2679-124; e-mail admin@imet.mplik.ru; internet www.imet-uran.ru; f. 1955; attached to Russian Acad. of Sciences; devt of physicochemical principles of high temperature processes in ferrous and nonferrous metallurgy; library of 35,000 vols; Dir Dr E. N. SELIVANOV; Scientific Sec. V. I. PONOMAREV; publ. *Rasplavy* (6 a year).

Institute of Metrology named after D. I. Mendeleyev (VNIIM): 190005 St Petersburg, Moskovskii pr. 19; tel. (812) 251-76-01; e-mail info@vniim.ru; internet www.vniim .ru; f. 1842; attached to Fed. Agency of Technical Regulation and Metrology (Rosstandart); centre of scientific and practical metrology; measurements in metrology; centre of nat. measurement standards in Russia; library of 40,000 vols; Dir Dr N. I. KHANOV.

Institute of Mineralogy: 456301 Chelyabinsk oblast, Miass; tel. (35135) 5-35-62; attached to Russian Acad. of Sciences; Dir V. N. ANFILOGOV.

Institute of New Chemical Problems: 142432 Moscow oblast, Noginsky raion, Chernogolovka; tel. (495) 524-50-24; attached to Russian Acad. of Sciences; Dir V. N. TROITSKII.

Institute of Nuclear Physics: 630090 Novosibirsk, pr. Akad. Lavrenteva 11; tel. (3832) 35-97-77 br. in Protvin; attached to Russian Acad. of Sciences; Dir Acad. A. N. SKRINSKY.

Institute of Nuclear Research: 117312 Moscow, pr. 60-letiya Oktyabrya 7a; tel. (499) 135-77-60; attached to Russian Acad. of Sciences; Dir Dr V. A. MATVEEV.

Institute of Organic Chemistry: 630090 Novosibirsk, Akademgorodok, pr. Akad. Lavrenteva 9; tel. (3832) 35-16-52; attached to Russian Acad. of Sciences; Dir Acad. G. A. TOLSTIKOV.

Institute of Organic Chemistry: 450054 Ufa, pr. Oktyabrya 71; tel. (347) 235-55-60; e-mail valeev@anrb.ru; internet w3.chem .anrb.ru; f. 1967; attached to Russian Acad. of Sciences; organic chemistry, physical organic chemistry, high energy chemistry and polymer chemistry; Dir Acad. MARAT S. YUNUSOV.

Institute of Organic Synthesis: 620219 Ekaterinburg, ul. S. Kovalevskoi 20; tel. (3432) 74-11-89; e-mail chupakhin@ios.uran .ru; f. 1993; attached to Russian Acad. of Sciences; Dir Prof. OLEG N. CHUPAKHIN.

Institute of Petroleum Chemistry: 634021 Tomsk, Akademicheskii pr. 4; tel. (3822) 49-16-23; e-mail canc@ipc.tsc.ru; internet www.ipc.tsc.ru; f. 1970; attached to Siberian Br., Russian Acad. of Sciences; chemistry of Russian oils, physicochemical fundamentals of enhanced oil recovery, transformations of oils and their natural components; Dir Prof. Dr LYUBOV K. ALTUNINA; publs *Journal Russian Chemical Reviews, Kinetics and Catalysis*.

Institute of Physics: 367003 Makhachkala 3, ul. 26 Bakinskikh Komissarov 94; tel. (8722) 2-51-60; attached to Russian Acad. of Sciences; Dir I. K. KAMILOV.

Institute of Precambrian Geology and Geochronology: 199034 St Petersburg, 2 nab. Makarova; tel. (812) 328-47-01; e-mail a .b.vrevsky@ipgg.ru; internet www.ipgg.ru; f. 1967; attached to Russian Acad. of Sciences; Dir Dr A. B. VREVSKY; Sec. for Science S. G. SKUBLOV.

Institute of Problems of Chemical Physics: Chernogolovka; tel. (495) 993-57-07; e-mail sma@icp.ac.ru; internet www.icp.ac .ru; attached to Russian Acad. of Sciences; fundamental research in chemistry, chemical physics, biology, applied research; Dir SERGEY ALDOSHIN.

Institute of Semiconductor Physics: 630090 Novosibirsk, pr. Akad. Lavrenteva 13; tel. (383) 333-39-50; f. 1962; attached to Russian Acad. of Sciences; Dir Prof. A. L. ASEEV.

Institute of Solar-Terrestrial Physics: 664033 Irkutsk, ul. Lermontova 126A; tel. (3952) 42-82-65; e-mail uzel@iszf.irk.ru; internet www.iszf.irk.ru; f. 1960; attached to Siberian Br., Russian Acad. of Sciences; current problems in astronomy, astrophysics, and research into outer space, incl. solar physics, physics of interplanetary medium, near-Earth environment, ionosphere, and atmosphere; research into solar-terrestrial relationship, devt of methods and facilities for investigations in the field of astrophysics and geophysics; library of 115,000 books, brochures, periodicals, MSS; Dir Acad. ALEXANDER P. POTEKHINS.

Institute of Solid State Chemistry: 620219 Ekaterinburg, ul. Pervomaiskaya 91; tel. (3432) 74-52-19; e-mail server@ihim .uran.ru; internet www.uran.ru/structure/ institutions/chimtt/issc.htm; f. 1932; attached to Russian Acad. of Sciences; Dir V. G. BAMBUROV.

Institute of Solid State Physics: 142432 Moscow oblast, Chernogolovka; tel. (495) 962-80-54; e-mail adm@issp.ac.ru; internet www.issp.ac.ru; f. 1963; attached to Russian Acad. of Sciences; Dir Prof. V. V. KVEDER.

Institute of Space Physics Research and the Diffusion of Radio Waves: 684034 Kamchatka obl., Elizovsky raion, Paratunka, Mirnaya ul. 7; tel. (41531) 9-31-93; attached to Russian Acad. of Sciences; Dir I. N. AMIANTOV.

Institute of Space Research: 117997 Moscow, Profsoyuznaya 84/32; tel. (495) 333-20-88; internet www.iki.rssi.ru; f. 1965; attached to Russian Acad. of Sciences; Dir Prof. Dr L. M. ZELENYI.

Institute of Spectroscopy: 142092 Moscow oblast, Troitsk; tel. (495) 334-05-79; attached to Russian Acad. of Sciences; Dir E. A. VINOGRADOV.

Institute of Strength Physics and Materials Science: 634021 Tomsk, Akademicheskii pr. 2/1; tel. (3822) 25-94-81; internet www .ispms.tsc.ru; f. 1984; attached to Russian Acad. of Sciences; Dir Acad. V. E. PANIN; publ. *Physical Mesomechanics* (6 a year).

Institute of Structural Macrokinetics and Materials Science: 142342 Moscow oblast, Chernogolovka, Institutsky 8; tel. (495) 962-80-01; e-mail director@ism.ac.ru; internet www.ism.ac.ru; f. 1988; attached to Russian Acad. of Sciences; studies on macroscopic kinetics of chemical reactions; Dir Prof. YURI GORDOPOLOV.

Institute of Tectonics and Geophysics: 680022 Khabarovsk, ul. Kim Yu Chena 65; tel. (4212) 22-71-89; attached to Russian Acad. of Sciences; Dir N. P. ROMANOVSKY; publ. *Tikhookeanskaya Geologiya* (in Russian and English, 6 a year).

Institute of Terrestrial Magnetism, the Ionosphere and Radio Wave Propagation: 142092 Moscow oblast, Troitsk; tel. (495) 334-01-20; f. 1940; attached to Russian Acad. of Sciences; library of 100,000 vols; br. in St Petersburg; Dir Prof. VICTOR N. ORAEVSKY.

Institute of the Chemistry and Technology of Rare Elements and Mineral Raw Materials: 184200 Apatity, ul. Fersmana 26a; tel. (81555) 7-95-49; e-mail office@chemy .kolasc.net.ru; internet www.kolasc.net.ru/ chemy; f. 1957; attached to Russian Acad. of Sciences; Dir V. T. KALINNIKOV.

Institute of the Earth's Crust: 664033 Irkutsk, ul. Lermontova 128; tel. (3952) 42-70-00; e-mail drf@crust.irk.ru; internet www .crust.irk.ru; f. 1949; attached to Russian Acad. of Sciences; 3 sections: geology, geophysics and recent geodynamics, hydrogeology and engineering geology; research areas incl. recent endo and exogeodynamics, geological medium and seismic process, resources and dynamics of underground waters and geoecology, internal structure, paleogeodynamics, endogenous processes and fluid dynamics of the continental lithosphere; library of 400,000 vols; Dir Dr DMITRY P. GLADKOCHUB; publs *American Journal of Sciences, Geodynamics & Tectonophysics, Tectonics*.

Institute of the Geology of Ore Deposits, Petrography, Mineralogy and Geochemistry: 119017 Moscow, Staromonetnyi per. 35; tel. (495) 951-45-79; e-mail director@igem .ru; internet www.igem.ru; f. 1955; attached to Russian Acad. of Sciences; Dir NIKOLAY BORTNIKOV.

Institute of the Mineralogy, Geochemistry and Crystal Chemistry of Rare Elements: 121357 Moscow, ul. Veresaeva 15; tel. (495) 443-84-28; f. 1956; attached to Russian Acad. of Sciences and Min. of Natural Resources; Dir A. A. KREMENETSKY; publ. *Applied Geochemistry* (1 a year).

Institute of Theoretical and Experimental Physics: 117218 Moscow, Bol. Cheremushkinskaya ul. 25; tel. (495) 123-02-88; e-mail director@itep.ru; internet www.itep .ru; f. 1945; Dir M. V. DANILOV.

Institute of Thermal Physics: 620016 Ekaterinburg, Amundsena 106; tel. (3432) 67-88-01; e-mail itp@itp.uran.ru; f. 1988; attached to Russian Acad. of Sciences; Dir V. G. BAIDAKOV.

Institute of Thermophysics: 630090 Novosibirsk, pr. Akad. Lavrenteva 1; tel. (3833)

30-70-50; e-mail web@itp.nsc.ru; internet www.itp.nsc.ru; f. 1957; attached to Russian Acad. of Sciences; undertakes research in the fields of heat and mass transfer, physical hydrodynamics and gas dynamics, thermal physics of ionized gases and physics of low-temperature plasma; library of 100,000 vols; Dir Dr S. V. ALEKSEENKO; publs *Thermophysics and Aeromechanics* (4 a year), *Journal of Engineering Thermophysics* (4 a year).

Institute of Volcanology and Seismology: 683006 Petropavlovsk-Kamchatsky, bul. Piipa 9; tel. (4152) 25-95-13; e-mail volcan@kcs.iks.ru; internet www.kcs.iks.ru; 130 mems; attached to Russian Acad. of Sciences; Dir EVGENY I. GORDEEV.

Institute of Water Problems: 107078 Moscow, Novaya Basmannaya ul. 10, POB 231; tel. (495) 265-97-57; e-mail iwapr@iwapr .msk.su; f. 1968; attached to Russian Acad. of Sciences; library of 35,000 vols; Dir M. G. KHUBLARYAN; publ. *Water Resources* (6 a year).

Institute of Water Problems of the North: Petrozavodsk, pr. Uritskogo 50; tel. (8142) 5-34-71; attached to Russian Acad. of Sciences; Head N. N. FILATOV (acting).

Joint Institute for Nuclear Research: 141980 Moscow oblast, Dubna; tel. (9621) 65-059; e-mail post@jinr.ru; internet www .jinr.ru; f. 1956; conducts studies on the structure of matter, high- and low-energy physics, condensed matter, heavy ion and neutron physics; education programme; library of 434,000 vols; Dir V. A. MATVEEV; publs *Journal of Elementary Particles and the Atomic Nucleus* (6 a year), *Particles and Nuclei—Letters* (7 a year).

Kapitza, P. L., Institute of Physical Problems: 117973 Moscow, GSP-1, ul. A. N. Kosygina 2; tel. (495) 137-32-48; e-mail andreev@kapitza.ras.ru; attached to Russian Acad. of Sciences; Dir Acad. A. F. ANDREEV.

Karpinsky, A. P., All-Russia Geological Research Institute: 199106 St Petersburg, Vasilevsky ostrov, Sredny pr. 74; tel. (812) 321-57-06; e-mail vsegei@vsegei.ru; internet www.vsegei.ru; f. 1882; Dir O. V. PETROV; publ. *Regional Geology and Metallogeny* (2 a year).

Karpov Institute of Physical Chemistry: ul. Vorontsovo Pole 10, 105064 Moscow; tel. (495) 917-32-57; e-mail center@cc.nifhi.ac.ru; internet www.nifhi.ac.ru; f. 1918; 900 mems; library of 38,000 vols; Exec. Dir Prof. ALEXANDER PAVLOVICH SIMONOV.

Khlopin, V. G., Radium Institute: 194021 St Petersburg, 2-i Murinskiy pr. 28; tel. (812) 247-56-41; e-mail moshkov@atom.nw.ru; f. 1922; radiochemistry, nuclear physics; library of 170,000 vols; Dir Dr ALEXANDER A. RIMSKY-KORSAKOV; publ. *Radiochemistry* (in Russian, 6 a year).

Kirensky Institute of Physics: 660036 Krasnoyarsk; tel. (3912) 43-26-35; e-mail dir@iph.krasn.ru; internet www.kirensky.ru; f. 1956; attached to Russian Acad. of Sciences; 300 mems; main fields of activity: physics, magnetic phenomena and magnetic materials; condensed matter physics and materials for electronics; design and engineering of new active elements; components and devices for radio-electronics, acousto-electronics, opto-electronics and quantum electronics; training of higher level material science specialists; Dir Acad. Prof. VASILY F. SHABANOV; Scientific Sec. Dr KIRILL A. SHAIKHUTDINOV.

Konstantinov, B. P., St Petersburg Institute of Nuclear Physics: 188350 Leningrad oblast, Gatchina, Orlova Roscha; tel. (812) 297-91-25; attached to Russian Acad. of Sciences; Dir ANSELM.

Krylov, A. P., All-Russia Oil and Gas Research Institute: 125422 Moscow, Dmitrovsky pr. 10; tel. (495) 976-83-01.

Kurchatov, I. V., Institute of Atomic Energy: 123182 Moscow, ul. Kurchatova 46; tel. (495) 196-61-07; Dir Acad. EVGENII P. VELIKHOV.

Kurnakov Institute of General and Inorganic Chemistry: 119991 Moscow, Leninsky pr. 31; tel. (495) 952-07-87; e-mail 02@igic.ras.ru; internet www.igic.ras.ru; f. 1934; attached to Russian Acad. of Sciences; research areas: analytical chemistry, chemical engineering, coordination chemistry, new inorganic materials; Dir Acad. NIKOLAI T. KUZNETSOV; publs *Coordination Chemistry*, *Inorganic Materials*, *Russian Journal of Inorganic Chemistry*.

L. D. Landau Institute of Theoretical Physics: 117940 Moscow V-234, ul. A. N. Kosygina 2; tel. (495) 137-32-44; e-mail office@itp.ac.ru; f. 1965; attached to Russian Acad. of Sciences; theoretical physics, mathematical physics, condensed matter physics and computational physics; Dir VLADIMIR LEBEDEV.

Lebedev, P. N., Physics Institute: 117924 Moscow, Leninskii pr. 53; tel. (495) 135-14-29; attached to Russian Acad. of Sciences; br. in Kuibyshev; Dir Acad. L. V. KELDYSH.

Lithosphere Institute: 109180 Moscow, Staromonetnyi per. 22; tel. (495) 233-55-88; attached to Russian Acad. of Sciences; Dir N. A. BOGDANOV.

Main Astronomical Observatory: 196140 St Petersburg, Pulkovo; tel. (812) 297-98-41; attached to Russian Acad. of Sciences; br. in Nikolaev oblast; Dir V. K. ABALAKIN.

Melnikov Permafrost Institute: 677010 Yakutsk, ul. Merzlotnaya 36; tel. (4112) 33-44-76; e-mail mpi@ysn.ru; internet mpi.ysn .ru; f. 1961; attached to Russian Acad. of Sciences, Siberian Br.; permafrost research; library of 42,000 vols; Dir MIKHAIL ZHELEZNYAK.

Moscow Radiotechnical Institute: 117519 Moscow, Varshavskoe shosse 132; tel. (495) 315-31-11; e-mail mrti@mrtiran .ru; internet www.mrtiran.ru; f. 1946; attached to Russian Acad. of Sciences; devt of particle accelerators for industrial and medical applications; high-power SHF and x-ray technologies and installations; plasma technologies and installations; computer control and data-processing systems for applications such as accelerators, medicine, ecology and safety; Dir Dr BORIS ALEKSANDROVICH.

Nesmeyanov, A. N., Institute of Elementary Organic Compounds: 119991 Moscow V-334, GSP 1, Vavilova str. 28, INEOS; tel. (495) 135-61-66; e-mail larina@ineos.ac.ru; f. 1954; attached to Russian Acad. of Sciences; Dir Prof. YU. N. BUBNOV.

Nikolaev Institute of Inorganic Chemistry: 630090 Novosibirsk, pr. Akad. Lavrenteva 3; tel. (383) 330-94-90; e-mail niic@niic .nsc.ru; internet www.niic.nsc.ru; f. 1957; attached to Russian Acad. of Sciences; Dir Prof. Dr VLADIMIR P. FEDIN; Scientific Sec. OLGA GERASKO; publ. *Journal of Structural Chemistry* (6 a year).

Noginsk Research Centre: c/o Institute of Solid State Physics, 142342 Moscow oblast, Chernogolovka; attached to Russian Acad. of Sciences; Chair. Acad. YU. A. OSIPYAN.

Oil and Gas Research Institute: 119333 Moscow, Gubkin St, 3; tel. (499) 135-73-71; e-mail a.dmitrievsky@ipng.ru; internet www .ipng.ru; f. 1987; attached to Russian Acad. of Sciences; Dir Prof. Dr A. N. DMITRIEVSKIY.

P. P. Shirshov Institute of Oceanology of the Russian Academy of Sciences: 117997 Moscow, Nakhimovsky pr. 36; tel. (495) 124-59-96; e-mail admin@ocean.ru; internet www.ocean.ru; f. 1946; attached to Russian Acad. of Sciences; brs in Arkhangelsk, Astrakhan, Gelendzhik, Kaliningrad, St Petersburg; library of 275,000 vols; Dir Prof. ROBERT NIGMATULIN; Scientific Sec. Dr MARIYA MARINA; publ. *Oceanology* (6 a year).

Polar Geospace Physics Observatory 'Tiksi': 678400 Bulunsky raion, Tiksi, Leninskaya ul. 25; tel. (41167) 2-17-89; e-mail common@pgo.ysn.ru; attached to Russian Acad. of Sciences; Dir V. N. MEDVEDEV.

Polar Institute of Geophysics: 183023 Murmansk, ul. Khalturina 15; tel. (8152) 6-58-29; e-mail general@pgi.ru; attached to Russian Acad. of Sciences; br. in Apatity; Dir V. G. PIVOVAROV.

Radiophysical Research Institute: 603950 Nizhny Novgorod, Bol'shaya Pecherskaya ul. 25/12a; tel. (831) 436-72-94; e-mail rf@nirfi.sci-nnov.ru; internet www.nirfi.ru; f. 1956; library of 250,000 vols; Dir Dr SERGEY SNEGIREV; Acad. Sec. Dr VLADIMIR FRIDMAN; publ. *Izvestiya Vysshikh Uchebnykh Zavedenii-Radiofizika* (12 a year).

Research Centre for the Study of Properties of Surfaces and Vacuums: c/o Russian Academy of Sciences, 117901 Moscow, Leninsky pr. 14; attached to Russian Acad. of Sciences; Dir L. E. LAPIDUS.

Research Institute of Experimental Physics: 607190 Nizhegorodskaya oblast, Sarov, pr. Mira 37; tel. (83130) 4-44-68; e-mail osv@dc.vniief.ru; f. 1946; Dir Dr RADY I. ILKAEV; publs *Questions of Atomic Science and Technics* (4 a year), *Atom* (4 a year).

Research Institute of Geophysical Research on Exploration Wells: Bashkortostan, 452620 Oktyabrsky, ul. Gorkogo 1; tel. (34767) 5-30-24; e-mail vniigis@poikc .bashnet.ru; internet www.vniigis.bashnet .ru; f. 1956; geophysical well logging; library of 177,000 vols; Dir A. P. POLIAKOV.

Research Institute of Geophysical Shock Waves: Moscow oblast, Ramenskoe, Pryamolineinaya ul. 26.

Research Institute of Gold and Rare Metals: Magadan, ul. Gagarina 2.

Research Institute of the Geochemistry of the Biosphere: 353918 Novorossiisk, Leninsky pr. 54; tel. (8617) 23-03-03; e-mail niigb@mail.kubtelecom.ru; f. 1992; attached to Rostov on Don State University; Dir V. A. ALEKSEENKO; publs *Ecology: Experience, Problems* (irregular), *Geochemistry of the Biosphere* (1 a year).

Russian Research Institute for Integrated Water Management and Protection: 620062 Ekaterinburg, ul. Mira 23; tel. (343) 374-26-79; e-mail wrm@wrm.ru; internet www.wrm.ru; f. 1969; library of 30,000 vols; Dir Prof. Dr N. B. PROKHOROVA; Deputy Dir Y. A. PODZINA; publs *Water of Russia* (12 a year), *Water Sector of Russia* (6 a year).

Schmidt Institute of Physics of the Earth: 123995 Moscow, Bol. Gruzinskaya ul. 10; tel. (495) 766-26-56; e-mail ifz@ifz.ru; internet www.ifz.ru; f. 1928; attached to Russian Acad. of Sciences; fundamental and applied research in internal structure and physical processes in the Earth's interior; global and regional geodynamics, stresses in the Earth's crust and mantle; seismicity, seismic risk assessment and earthquake prediction; magnetic, electromagnetic, gravity and other measurements and analysis of the Earth's physical fields; mathematical geophysics and geoinformatics; Dir SERGEY TIKHOTSKIY.

Semenov, N. N., Institute of Chemical Physics: 117977 Moscow, ul. A. N. Kosygina 4; tel. (495) 939-72-00; e-mail icp@chph.ras .ru; internet www.chph.ras.ru; f. 1931; attached to Russian Acad. of Sciences; Dir A. A. BERLIN; publ. *Khimicheskaya fizika* (12 a year).

Shubnikov, A. V., Institute of Crystallography: 117333 Moscow, Leninskii pr. 59; tel. (495) 135-63-11; attached to Russian Acad. of Sciences; br. in Kaluga; Dir V. I. SIMONOV (acting).

Siberian Research Institute of Geology, Geophysics and Mineral Raw Materials: 630104 Novosibirsk, Krasny pr. 67; tel. (3832) 22-45-03.

Special Astrophysical Observatory: 369167 Karachai-Cherkessian Republic, pos. Nizhnii Arkhyz; tel. (901) 498-29-31; e-mail adm@sao.ru; internet www.sao.ru; f. 1966; attached to Russian Acad. of Sciences; library of 205,247 vols; Dir YU. YU. BALEGA.

State Hydrological Institute: 199053 St Petersburg, V.O., 2-ya liniya 23; tel. (812) 213-89-16; Dir I. A. SHIKLOMANOV.

State Research Institute of Non-ferrous Metals: 129515 Moscow, ul. Akad. Koroleva 13; tel. (495) 215-61-73; e-mail gin@gintsvet .msk.ru; f. 1918; library of 500,000 vols; Dir ANDREI TARASOV; publ. *Gintsvetmet Proceedings* (1 a year).

Titanium Research Institute: 117393 Moscow, ul. Obrucheva 52; tel. (495) 332-95-55.

Troitsk Research Centre: 142092 Moscow oblast, Troitsk, Yubileinaya 3; tel. (495) 334-06-35; e-mail laptev@inr.troitsk.ru; attached to Russian Acad. of Sciences; Chair. Acad. VICTOR A. MATVEEV.

United Institute of Geology, Geophysics and Mineralogy: 630090 Novosibirsk, pr. Akad. Koptyuga 3; tel. (3832) 33-26-00; e-mail dobr@uiggm.nsc.ru; attached to Russian Acad. of Sciences; Dir-Gen. Acad. N. L. DOBRETSOV.

Vernadsky, V. I., Institute of Geochemistry and Analytical Chemistry: 119991 Moscow, ul. A. N. Kosygina 19; tel. (495) 137-14-84; e-mail geokhi.ras@relcom.ru; internet www.geokhi.ru; f. 1947; attached to Russian Acad. of Sciences; library of 33,000 vols, 230 periodicals; Dir Prof. ERIC M. GALIMOV; publs *Geochemical International* (12 a year), *Journal of Analytical Chemistry* (12 a year).

Voeikov, A. I., Main Geophysical Observatory: 194018 St Petersburg, ul. Karbysheva 7; tel. (812) 297-43-90; f. 1849; climatology, atmospheric physics, air pollution; library of 380,000 vols; Dir Dr V. M. KATTSOV; publ. *Trudy GGO*.

Yu. G. Shafer Institute of Cosmophysical Research and Aeronomy: 677980 Yakutsk, pr. Lenina 31; tel. (4112) 39-04-00; e-mail ikfia@ysn.ru; internet ikfia.ysn.ru; f. 1962; attached to Russian Acad. of Sciences; scientific research in field cosmic ray physics and solar-terrestrial physics incl. upper atmosphere physics; library of 40,000 vols; Dir Dr EVGENY G. BEREZHKO.

Zelinsky, N. D., Institute of Organic Chemistry: 119991 Moscow, Leninsky pr. 47; tel. (499) 137-29-44; e-mail secretary@ioc .ac.ru; internet www.ioc.ac.ru; f. 1934; attached to Russian Acad. of Sciences; fundamental research in organic chemistry; library of 213,300 vols; Dir Prof. MIKHAIL P. EGOROV; publs *Mendeleev Communication* (6 a year), *Russian Chemical Bulletin* (12 a year), *Russian Chemical Reviews* (12 a year).

PHILOSOPHY AND PSYCHOLOGY

Institute of Philosophy: 119991 Moscow, Volkhonka ul. 14; tel. (495) 697-92-17; e-mail iph@iph.ras.ru; internet www.iph.ras.ru; f. 1929; attached to Russian Acad. of Sciences; 300 mems; library of 89,500 vols; Dir A. A. GUSEINOV; Acad. Sec. B. O. NIKOLAICHEV; publs *Epistemology and Philosophy of Science* (4 a year), *Personality, Culture, Society* (4 a year), *Philosophical Journal* (2 a year).

Institute of Psychology: 129366 Moscow, Yaroslavskaya ul. 13; tel. (495) 282-51-49; attached to Russian Acad. of Sciences; Dir A. V. BRUSHLINSKY.

RELIGION, SOCIOLOGY AND ANTHROPOLOGY

Institute of Sociology: 117259 Moscow, ul. Krzhizhanovskogo 24/35, korp. 5; tel. (495) 128-91-09 br. in St Petersburg: 198147 St Petersburg, ul. Serpukhovskaya 38; tel. (812) 292-27-65; attached to Russian Acad. of Sciences; Dir V. A. YADOV.

Miklukho-Maklai, N. N., Institute of Ethnology and Anthropology: 117334 Moscow, Leninsky pr. 32A; tel. (495) 938-17-47; e-mail anthpub@iea.ras.ru; internet www .iea.ras.ru; f. 1933; attached to Russian Acad. of Sciences; library of 60,000 vols; Dir V. A. TISHKOV; publs *Etnograficheskoe Obozrenie* (Ethnographic Review, 6 a year), *Bulletin of Ethnological Monitoring* (6 a year).

Research and Training Centre for Problems of Human Activity: 117279 Moscow, ul. Profsoyuznaya 83B; tel. (495) 333-01-02; attached to Russian Acad. of Sciences; Gen. Dir V. A. SHESTAKOV.

TECHNOLOGY

Accounting Machine Building Research Institute: 115230 Moscow, Varshavskoe shosse 42; tel. (499) 611-51-61.

All-Russia Electrotechnical Institute (VEI): 111250 Moscow, Krasnokazarmennaya ul. 12; tel. (495) 362-55-08; e-mail vkozlov@online.ru.

All-Russia Logachev Scientific Research Institute of Exploration Geophysics (VIRG-Rudgeofizika): 193019 St Petersburg, Fayansovaya ul. 20; tel. (812) 567-68-03; internet www.virg.spb.ru; f. 1945; devt of instruments and technology for predicting, exploring, evaluating and mining ores and diamonds, drilling for oil and gas; solving environmental problems; provision of services in these areas; library of 54,000 vols; Dir G. N. MIKHAILOV; publs *Geophysical Instruments* (2 a year), *Russian Journal of Geophysics* (2 a year).

All-Russia Petroleum Research Exploration Institute (VNIGRI): 191104 St Petersburg, Liteinyi pr. 39; tel. (812) 273-43-83; e-mail ins@vnigri.ru; internet vnigri .spb.ru; f. 1929.

All-Russia Research and Design Institute for Atomic Power Station Equipment: 125171 Moscow, ul. Volkova Kosmonavta 6A; tel. (495) 150-83-55.

All-Russia Research and Design Institute for Problems of the Development of Oil and Gas Resources on the Continental Shelf: 107078 Moscow, Kalanchevskaya ul. 11; tel. (495) 971-51-03; Dir I. B. DUBIN.

All-Russia Research and Design Institute of Electroceramics: 111024 Moscow, shosse Entuziastov 17; tel. (495) 273-13-34.

All-Russia Research and Design Institute of Metallurgical Engineering: 109428 Moscow, Ryazansky pr. 8A; tel. (495) 174-37-00; attached to Russian Acad. of Sciences; Gen. Dir V. M. SINITSKY.

All-Russia Research and Design Institute of the Oil-Refining and Petrochemical Industry: 107005 Moscow, ul. Fridrikha Engelsa 32; tel. (499) 261-96-26; e-mail vnipineft@vnipineft.ru; internet www .vnipineft.ru; f. 1929; Dir V. M. NIKITIN.

All-Russia Research, Design and Technological Institute of Lighting Technology: 129626 Moscow, pr. Mira 106; tel. (495) 287-13-52; f. 1953.

All-Russia Research Institute for Nuclear Power Plant Operation: 109507 Moscow, Ferganskaya 25; tel. (495) 376-15-43; f. 1979; Dir-Gen. Prof. A. A. ABAGYAN.

All-Russia Research Institute for Oil Refining JSC: 111116 Moscow, Aviamotornaya ul. 6; tel. (499) 261-52-02; f. 1933; Dir E. F. KAMINSKY; publ. *Mir Nefteproduktov* (The World of Oil Products, 4 a year).

All-Russia Research Institute for the Canned and Vegetable Dry Products Industry: 142703 Moscow oblast, Vidnoe, Shkolnaya 78; tel. (495) 541-08-72; attached to Russian Acad. of Agricultural Sciences.

All-Russia Research Institute for the Dairy Industry: 113093 Moscow, Lyusinovskaya 35; tel. (495) 236-31-64; attached to Russian Acad. of Agricultural Sciences.

All-Russia Research Institute for the Protection of Metals from Corrosion: 125209 Moscow, Baltiiskaya ul. 14; tel. (495) 151-55-01.

All-Russia Research Institute for the Refrigeration Industry: 125422 Moscow, ul. Kostyakova 12; tel. (495) 216-00-04; attached to Russian Acad. of Agricultural Sciences; Dir V. F. LEBEDEV.

All-Russia Research Institute of Electrical Insulating Materials and Foiled Dielectrics: 111250 Moscow, Krasnokazarmennaya ul. 12; tel. (495) 273-24-78.

All-Russia Research Institute of Electromechanics (VNIIEM): 101000 Moscow, Glavpochtamt Box 496 VNIIEM, Khoromny Tupik 4; tel. (495) 208-84-67; e-mail vniiem@ orc.ru; f. 1941; research and devt in space technology, monitoring and control systems for nuclear reactors, electromechanical systems, devices and materials; library of 200,000 vols; Dir Dr S. A. STOMA; publ. *Trudy VNIIEM* (3 a year, proceedings).

All-Russia Research Institute of Exploration Geophysics: 101000 Moscow, ul. Pokrovka 22; tel. (495) 925-45-13; f. 1944; library of 50,000 vols; Dir A. V. MIKHALTSEV; publs *Prikladnaya Geofizika* (2 a year), *Razvedochnaya Geofizika*.

All-Russia Research Institute of Fibre-Optic Systems of Communication and Data Processing: 107066 Moscow, Khiznyaya Krasnoselskaya ul. 13, korp. 1; tel. (499) 267-20-31.

All-Russia Research Institute of Food Biotechnology: 109033 Moscow, Samokatnaya ul. 4B; tel. (495) 362-44-95; attached to Russian Acad. of Agricultural Sciences.

All-Russia Research Institute of Fuel and Energy Problems (VNIIKTEP): 117259 Moscow, Bol. Cheremushkinskaya 34; tel. (495) 128-90-14; f. 1975; library of 63,000 vols; Dir N. K. PRAVEDNIKOV; publ. *The Fuel and Energy Complex of Russia* (1 a year).

All-Russia Research Institute of Helium Technology: 119270 Moscow, Luzhnetskaya nab. 10A; tel. (495) 242-50-77.

All-Russia Research Institute of Mineral Resources and the Use of the Subsurface: 123007 Moscow, 3-ya Magistralnaya 38; tel. (495) 259-69-88; e-mail info@viems .ru; internet www.viems.ru; f. 1964; attached to Russian Acad. of Sciences and Russian

Min. of Natural Resources; Dir-Gen. M. A. KOMAROV.

All-Russia Research Institute of Organic Synthesis (VNIIOS): 105005 Moscow, ul. Radio 12; tel. (499) 261-96-88; e-mail vniios@aha.ru; internet www.vniios.ru; f. 1949; Dir-Gen. V. K. S. CHERNYKH.

All-Russia Research Institute of Problems of Computer Technology and Information Science: 113114 Moscow, 2-i Kozhevnichesky per. 4/6; tel. (495) 235-58-09; Dir V. ZAKHAROV.

All-Russia Research Institute of Radiotechnology: 107005 Moscow, Bol. Pochtovaya ul. 55–59; tel. (499) 267-66-04.

All-Russia Research Institute of Refractory Metals and Hard Alloys: 115430 Moscow, Varshavskoe shosse 56; tel. (495) 113-55-72.

All-Russia Research Institute of Starch Products: 140052 Moscow oblast, pos. Korenevo, ul. Nekrasova; tel. (495) 557-15-00; attached to Russian Acad. of Agricultural Sciences.

All-Russia Research Institute of Television and Radio Broadcasting JSC: 123298 Moscow, 3-ya Khoroshevskaya ul. 12; tel. (495) 192-90-02; e-mail vniitr@online.ru; internet www.vniitr.com; f. 1934; Gen. Dir ALEXANDER S. MKRTUMOV; publ. *Teleraidoveshchaniye* (4 a year).

All-Russia Research Institute of the Cable Industry: 111112 Moscow, shosse Entuziastov 5; tel. (495) 278-02-16.

All-Russia Research Institute of Trunk Pipeline Construction: 105058 Moscow, Okruzhnoi pr-d 19; tel. (495) 366-68-39.

All-Russia Scientific Research Institute for Exploration Methods and Engineering: 199106 St Petersburg, Veselnaya ul. 6; tel. (812) 322-78-53; e-mail vitr@spb.cityline.ru; f. 1955; drilling equipment and techniques for minerals and water; library of 30,000 vols, patents; Dir IVAN S. AFANASYEV; publ. *Collection of Scientific Works* (4–6 a year).

All-Russian Scientific Research Institute of Aviation Materials (VIAM): 105005 Moscow, ul. Radio 17; tel. (499) 261-86-77; e-mail admin@viam.ru; internet www.viam.ru; f. 1932; Dir-Gen. EVGENY N. KABLOV; publ. *Aircraft Materials and Technology* (1 a year).

All-Russia Scientific Research Institute of Fats: 191119 St Petersburg, ul. Chernyakovskogo 10; tel. (812) 164-15-24; e-mail wniig@peterlink.ru; f. 1933; attached to Russian Acad. of Agricultural Sciences; Dir ALEXANDER N. LISITSYN; publ. *Trudy* (works, irregular).

All-Russia Scientific Research Institute of Natural and Synthetic Diamonds and Tools: 129110 Moscow, ul. Giliarovskogo 65; tel. (495) 281-59-07; f. 1948; library of 25,000 vols; Dir N. A. KOLCHEMANOV; publ. *Works of VNIIALMAZ* (1 a year).

All-Russian Scientific Research Institute of Technical Physics and Automation: 115230 Moscow, Varshavskoe shosse 46; tel. (499) 611-2522; e-mail kancelaria@vniitfa.ru; internet www.vniitfa.ru; f. 1960 as Research Institute of Radiation Technology; Dir NIKOLAY KUZELEV.

Blagonravov, A. A., Institute of Machine Science: 101830 Moscow, ul. Griboedova 4; tel. (495) 924-98-00; attached to Russian Acad. of Sciences; brs in St Petersburg, Samara, Saratov, Nizhnii Novgorod; Dir Acad. K. V. FROLOV.

Budnikov, P. P., All-Russia Research Institute of Construction Materials and Structures: 140080 Moscow, pos. Kraskovo, ul. Karla Marksa 117; tel. (495) 557-30-66; f. 1931; library of 180,000 vols; Dir YU. GUDKOV; publs *Autoclaved Materials* (1 a year), *Ceramic Materials* (1 a year), *Gypsum Binders and Products* (1 a year).

Burenie Scientific and Production Co.: 350624 Krasnodar, ul. Mira 34; tel. (8612) 62-23-34; f. 1970; drilling and maintenance of wells; library of 100,000 vols; Gen. Dir Dr SERGEI A. RYABOKON.

Central Boiler and Turbine Institute: 194021 St Petersburg, Politekhnicheskaya ul. 24; tel. (812) 277-95-64; e-mail ckti@neva.spb.ru; internet www.ckti.ru; f. 1927; Dir-Gen. E. K. CHAVCHANIDZE.

Central Design and Research Institute of the Standard and Experimental Design of Livestock Units for the Production of Milk, Beef and Pork: 121002 Moscow, Maly Mogiltsevsky per. 3; tel. (495) 241-36-82.

Central Diesels Research and Development Institute: 196158 St Petersburg, Moskovskoe shosse 25, korp. 1; tel. (812) 291-65-81; f. 1924; library of 62,000 vols; Dir V. BORDUKOV; publ. *Dvigatelstroynie* (4 a year).

Central Electronics Research Institute: 117415 Moscow, pr. Vernadskogo 39; tel. (495) 432-93-30; f. 1964; Dir B. N. AVDONIN.

Central Institute of Aviation Motors: 111116 Moscow, Aviamotornaya ul. 2; tel. (495) 361-64-81; e-mail ibd@ciam.ru; f. 1930; Dir VLADIMIR BABKIN.

Central Marine Research and Design Institute Ltd (CNIIMF): 193015 St Petersburg, Kavalergardskaya ul. 6; tel. (812) 271-12-83; f. 1929; shipbuilding, marine equipment, navigation, transport technology; library of 312,000 vols; Dir VSEVOLOD I. PERESYPKIN; publ. *Transactions*.

Central Paper Research Institute: 141290 Moscow oblast, Pushkinsky raion, pos. Pravdinsky, ul. Lenina 15/1; tel. (495) 584-36-23; f. 1918; library of 90,000 vols; Dir B. V. OREKHOV; publs *Board* (12 a year), *Paper, Pulp, Research Papers of ZNIIB* (1 a year).

Central Research and Design Institute of Fuel Apparatus and Vehicle and Tractor Engines and Stationary Engines: 192302 St Petersburg, Volkovskii pr-d 102; tel. (812) 166-91-11.

Central Research Institute for Machine Building: 141070 Moscow oblast, Korolev, Pionyerskaya ul. 4; tel. (495) 513-50-00; f. 1946; spacecraft and rocket engineering, aero and gas dynamics, heat and mass exchange, strength of materials, reliability, mission control for spacecraft and space stations; library of 100,000 vols; Dir NIKOLAI A. ANFIMOV; publs *Astronautics and Rocket Engineering* (3 or 4 a year), *Rocketry and Space Technology* (52 a year).

Central Research Institute of Coating Materials and Artificial Leathers: 113184 Moscow, ul. Bakhrushina 11; tel. (495) 953-23-55; e-mail cniipik@mail.ru; Dir Dr C. N. KOZLOV.

Central Research Institute of Engineering Technology: 109088 Moscow, Sharikopodshipnikovskaya ul. 4; tel. (495) 275-83-00.

Central Research Institute of Geological Prospecting for Base and Precious Metals: 117545 Moscow, Varshavskoe shosse 129B; tel. (495) 313-18-18; e-mail tsnigri@tsnigri.ru; internet www.tsnigri.ru; f. 1935; forecasting, prospecting, exploration and assessment of deposits of base and precious metals; library of 200,000 vols; Dir Dr IGOR MIGACHEV; publs *Otechestvennaya Geologia* (6 a year, in Russian with English abstracts), *Rudy i Metally* (6 a year, in Russian with English abstracts).

Central Research Institute of Telecommunications: 111141 Moscow, 1-i pr-d Perova Polya 8; tel. (495) 304-57-97.

Central Research Institute of the Ministry of Defence: 141090 Moscow oblast, Bolshevo, V/Ch 25840; tel. (495) 472-92-12; Dir L. I. VOLKOV.

Central Research Laboratory for the Introduction of Personal Computers: c/o Russian Academy of Sciences, 117901 Moscow, Leninsky pr. 14; attached to Russian Acad. of Sciences; Dir A. N. ILIN.

Central Scientific Research and Design Institute of the Wood Chemical Industry: 603603 Nizhnii Novgorod, Moskovskoe shosse 85, GSP 703; tel. (8312) 41-36-98; f. 1932; library of 146,000 vols; Dir VICTOR YA. BONDAREV; publ. *Scientific Works* (1 a year).

Concrete and Reinforced Concrete Research Design and Technological Institute: 109428 Moscow, Vtoraya Institutskaya ul. 6; tel. (495) 171-26-69; e-mail niizhb@niizhb.ru; internet www.niizhb.ru; f. 1927; devt of standards and norms for concrete construction and design; certification testing; postgraduate courses; 400 mems; library of 200,000 vols; Dir Dr A. I. ZVEZDOV; Deputy Dir Dr V. FALIKMAN; Scientific Dir Dr T. MOUKHAMEDIEV; publs *Beton i Zhelezobeton* (Concrete and Reinforced Concrete, 6 a year), *Proceedings of NIIZLB* (1 a year).

Design and Research Institute of the Synthetic Rubber Industry: 105318 Moscow, ul. Ibragimova 15; tel. (495) 366-43-44; Dir S. I. KARTASHOV.

Design and Technological Institute of Monocrystals: 630058 Novosibirsk, Russkaya ul. 43; tel. (3832) 33-22-39; f. 1978; attached to Russian Acad. of Sciences; Head ANATOLY I. CHEPUROV.

Dollezhal, N. A. Research and Development Institute of Power Engineering: 101000 Moscow, POB 788; tel. (499) 263-73-88; e-mail nikiet@nikiet.ru; internet www.nikiet.ru; f. 1952; nuclear power, thermal physics and hydrodynamics; radiation, nuclear and environmental safety of nuclear reactors; strength, reliability and material science; conversion of nuclear technologies; library of 200,000 vols; Dir B. A. GABARAEV.

Dorodnicyn Computing Centre of the Russian Academy of Sciences (CC RAS): 119333 Moscow, ul. Vavilova 40; tel. (499) 135-24-89; e-mail wcan@ccas.ru; internet www.ccas.ru; f. 1955; attached to Russian Acad. of Sciences; scientific divs: mechanics and mathematical physics, informatics and mathematical cybernetics, mathematical systems and decisions modelling, mathematical and programming software, computational technique; Dir Prof. YU. G. EVTUSHENKO; Scientific Sec. SHURSHALOV LEV.

Efremov, D. V., Institute of Electrophysical Apparatus: 196641 St Petersburg, Sovetsky pr. 1; tel. (812) 464-89-63; e-mail glukhikh@niiefa.spb.su; internet www.niiefa.spb.su; f. 1945; Dir V. A. GLUKHIKH; publ. *Plasma Devices and Operations*.

Electronic Control Machines Research Institute: 117812 Moscow, ul. Vavilova 24; tel. (495) 135-32-21; Dir N. L. PROKHOROV.

Energy Systems Institute: 664033 Irkutsk, Lermontova ul. 130; tel. (3952) 42-47-00; e-mail info@isem.sei.irk.su; internet www.sei.irk.ru; f. 1960; attached to Russian Acad. of Sciences; Dir N. I. VOROPAI.

Ershov, A. P., Institute of Informatics Systems: 630090 Novosibirsk, pr. Akad. Lavrenteva 6; tel. (3832) 35-56-52; f. 1990; attached to Russian Acad. of Sciences; library of 100,000 vols; Dir Prof. ALEXANDER G. MARCHUK; publ. *Systems Informatics* (1 a year).

Experimental Factory for Analytical Instrumentation: 198510 St Petersburg, Lomonosov, ul. Fedyuninskogo 3; tel. (812) 473-06-48; attached to Russian Acad. of Sciences; Dir V. I. STEPANOV.

Experimental Factory for Scientific Instrumentation: 142342 Moscow oblast, Noginsk raion, p/o Chernogolovka; tel. (495) 524-50-05; attached to Russian Acad. of Sciences; Dir L. P. KOKURIN.

Experimental Research Institute of Metal-Cutting Machine Tools: 117419 Moscow, 5-i Donskoi pr-d 21B; tel. (495) 952-39-63; Dir V. S. BELOV.

Far Eastern Research Institute of Mineral Raw Materials: 680005 Khabarovsk, ul. Gerasimova 31; tel. (4212) 34-28-43; Dir YU. I. BAKULIN.

Federal State Unitary Enterprise Central Scientific Research Automobile and Engine Institute of the Russian Federation: 125438 Moscow, Avtomotornaya St 2; tel. (495) 456-30-81; e-mail admin@nami.ru; internet www.nami.ru; f. 1918; nat. automobile manufacturing and testing; library of 106,000 vols, spec. colls 93,600 vols; Gen. Dir Prof. A. IPATOV.

Fedorov, E. K., Institute of Applied Geophysics: 129128 Moscow, Rostokinskaya ul. 9; tel. (495) 181-37-14; Dir S. I. AVDYUSHIN.

Gubkin Russian State University of Oil and Gas: 119991 Moscow, Leninsky pr. 65; tel. (499) 233-92-25; e-mail com@gubkin.ru; internet www.gubkin.ru; f. 1930, present status 2010; educational and research and devt programmes through the full process chain of petroleum engineering, 330 journals; library: 1.5m. vols incl. rare monographs, MSS theses and specialized journals; Rector Prof. VICTOR G. MARTYNOV; publs *Chemistry & Technology of Fuels and Oils, Oil, Gas & Business, Proceedings of Gubkin Russian State University of Oil and Gas.*

High-Technology Ceramics Research Centre: 119361 Moscow, Ozernaya ul. 48; tel. (495) 430-77-70; attached to Russian Acad. of Sciences; Dir V. YA. SHEVCHENKO.

Hydrochemical Institute: 344090 Rostov on Don, pr. Stachki 198; tel. (8632) 22-44-70; e-mail ghi@aaanet.ru; f. 1920; library of 40,000 vols; Dir A. M. NIKANOROV; publ. *Gidrokhimicheskiye Materialy* (3 a year).

Image Processing Systems Institute: 443001 Samara, ul. Molodogvardeiskaya 151; tel. (846) 332-56-20; e-mail ipsi@smr.ru; internet www.ipsi.smr.ru; f. 1988; attached to Russian Acad. of Sciences; diffractive optics, nanophotonics, image processing and pattern recognition; library of 1,000 vols; Dir Prof. V. A. SOIFER; publ. *Computer Optics* (4 a year, in Russian).

Institute for Systems Analysis: 117312 Moscow, pr. 60-letia Oktyabrya 9; tel. (495) 135-42-22; e-mail isa@isa.ru; internet www.isa.ru; f. 1976; attached to Russian Acad. of Sciences; Dir YU. S. POPKOV.

Institute of Analytical Instrumentation: 190103 St Petersburg, Rizhsky pr. 26; tel. (812) 251-86-00; e-mail iap@ianin.spb.su; internet www.iai.rssi.ru; f. 1977; attached to Russian Acad. of Sciences; fundamental and applied research aimed at development of new methods, instruments and technologies in the areas of elemental phase and structural analysis; nanotechnology and surface diagnostics; biotechnology, ecology and medicine; Dir Prof. V. E. KUROCHKIN; publ. *Scientific Instrumentation* (4 a year).

Institute of Applied Mathematics: 690041 Vladivostok, ul. Radio 7; tel. (4232) 31-33-30; f. 1988; attached to Russian Acad. of Sciences; library of 21,000 vols; Dir Prof. N. V. KUZNETSOV.

Institute of Applied Mechanics: c/o Russian Academy of Sciences, 119991 Moscow, Leninsky pr.; tel. (495) 938-18-45; attached to Russian Acad. of Sciences; Dir YU G. YANOVSKY; publ. *Journal on Composite Materials and Design* (4 a year).

Institute of Applied Mechanics: 426067 Izhevsk, T. Baramzinoy 34; tel. (3412) 50-88-10; e-mail foipm@udm.ru; internet www.udman.ru; f. 1989; attached to Russian Acad. of Sciences; physics and mechanics of heterogenous media; problems of mechanics of deformed solid and material tribo-technology; new materials; Dir Acad. ALEXEY LIPANOV; publ. *Chemical Physics and Mezoscopy* (4 a year).

Institute of Automation and Control Processes: 690041 Vladivostok, ul. Radio 5; tel. (4232) 31-04-39; e-mail director@iacp.vl.ru; internet www.dvo.ru/iacp; f. 1971; attached to Russian Acad. of Sciences; Dir V. P. MYASNIKOV.

Institute of Automation and Electrometry: 630090 Novosibirsk, Universitetskii pr. 1; tel. (3832) 35-10-52; e-mail malinovsky@iae.nsk.su; attached to Russian Acad. of Sciences; Dir Prof. S. T. VASKOV.

Institute of Biological Instrumentation: 123373 Moscow, Volokalamskoe shosse 91; tel. (495) 491-73-72; Dir V. N. ZLOBIN.

Institute of Chemistry and Chemical Technology: 660049 Krasnoyarsk, ul. K. Marksa 42; tel. (3912) 27-38-31; e-mail chem@krsk.info; internet krsk.info/icct; f. 1981; attached to Russian Acad. of Sciences; Dir Prof. G. L. PASHKOV; publs *Proceedings of Workshops* (every 3 years), *Siberian Gold* (symposium proceedings, every 2 years).

Institute of Computational Technologies: 630090 Novosibirsk, pr. Akad. Lavrenteva 6; tel. (383) 330-61-50; e-mail shokin@ict.nsc.ru; internet www.ict.nsc.ru; f. 1990; attached to Russian Acad. of Sciences, Siberian br.; designs and implements informational-telecommunication technologies in decision-making problems; applies mathematical modelling and computational algorithm devt to a wide range of problems arising in mechanics of continuous media, physics and ecology; Head YURI SHOKIN; publ. *Journal of Computational Technologies* (6 a year).

Institute of Continuous Media Mechanics: 614013 Perm, ul. Akad. Koroleva 1; tel. (3422) 33-07-21; e-mail mvp@admin.icmm.perm.su; f. 1971; attached to Russian Acad. of Sciences; Dir V. P. MATVEYENKO.

Institute of Control Sciences, Automation and Telemechanics: 117806 Moscow, ul. Profsoyuznaya 65; tel. (495) 334-89-10; e-mail vasmac@ipu.rssi.ru; attached to Russian Acad. of Sciences; Dir Acad. I. V. PRANGISHVILI.

Institute of Electronic Measurement Kvarz: 603009 Nizhnii Novgorod, pr. Gagarina 176; tel. (831) 464-03-41; e-mail nnipi_kvarz@sinn.ru; internet www.kvarz.com; f. 1949; research, devt and manufacture of electronic measurement equipment; 1,200 mems; Gen. Dir VLADIMIR MENSHOV; publ. *Electronic Measurements* (1 a year, in Russian).

Institute of Energy Research: 117333 Moscow, ul. Vavilova 44, korp. 2; tel. (495) 127-48-34; attached to Russian Acad. of Sciences; Dir A. A. MAKAROV.

Institute of Engineering Science: 620219 Ekaterinburg, Komsomolskaya ul. 34, GSP-

207; tel. (343) 374-47-25; e-mail ges@imach.uran.ru; internet www.imach.uran.ru; f. 1986; attached to Russian Acad. of Sciences; research into mechanics of solids and structures, advanced materials and technologies; automated systems of measurements, non-destructive testing and diagnostics of machine life; mechanics and control of transportation and traction machines; creation of basic algorithms, software and hardware for systems of automated control of compound objects; library of 16,700 vols; Dir Prof. E. S. GORKUNOV.

Institute of High Current Electronics: 634055 Tomsk, pr. Akademichesky 2–3; tel. (3822) 49-15-44; e-mail contact@hcei.tsc.ru; internet www.hcei.tsc.ru; f. 1977; attached to Russian Acad. of Sciences; library of 50,000 vols; Dir Acad. SERGEI D. KOROVIN.

Institute of Informatics and Mathematical Modelling of Technological Processes: 184200 Murmansk oblast, Apatity, ul. Fersmana 24A; tel. (81555) 7-40-50; e-mail putilov@imm.kolasc.net.ru; f. 1989; attached to Russian Acad. of Sciences; Dir Dr V. A. PUTILOV; publ. *Computer-Aided Simulation.*

Institute of Informatics Problems of the Russian Academy of Sciences (IPIRAN): 119333 Moscow, ul. Vavilova 44-2; tel. (499) 137-34-94; e-mail sshorgin@ipiran.ru; internet www.ipiran.ru; f. 1983; attached to Russian Acad. of Sciences; fundamental and applied research and devt in integrated information-telecommunication networks and systems and stochastic systems; theoretical problems and applied technologies in accumulation, processing and representation of information; creation of computerized information systems; Dir Acad. IGOR SOKOLOV; Deputy Dir SERGEY SHORGIN; publs *Informatics and Applications* (4 a year), *Systems and Means of Informatics* (4 a year).

Institute of Information Science and Automation: 199178 St Petersburg, 14 liniya 39; tel. (812) 218-03-82; attached to Russian Acad. of Sciences; Dir V. M. PONOMAREV.

Institute of Information Transmission Problems (Kharkevich Institute): 127994 Moscow 19/1, Bol. Karetny per.; tel. (495) 650-42-25; e-mail director@iitp.ru; internet www.iitp.ru; f. 1961; attached to Russian Acad. of Sciences; Dir ALEXANDER KULESHOV; publs *Automation and Remote Control* (12 a year), *Information Processes, Problems of Information Transmission* (4 a year).

Institute of Laser and Information Technology: 140700 Moscow oblast, Shatura, Svyatoozerskaya ul. 1; tel. (496) 452-59-95; e-mail center@laser.ru; internet www.laser.ru; f. 1979; attached to Russian Acad. of Sciences; library of 35,000 vols; Dir Prof. V. YA. PANCHENKO.

Institute of Mathematics and Mechanics: 620219 Ekaterinburg, ul. S. Kovalevskoi 16; tel. (3432) 374-83-32; e-mail bvi@imm.uran.ru; internet www.imm.uran.ru; f. 1956; attached to Ural Branch of the Russian Acad. of Sciences; Dir Prof. V. I. BERDYSHEV.

Institute of Medical Instrument Making: 125422 Moscow, Timiryazevskaya ul. 1; tel. (495) 211-09-65; attached to Russian Acad. of Medical Sciences; Dir V. A. VIKTOROV.

Institute of Mining, Khabarovsk: 680000 Khabarovsk, ul. Turgeneva 51; tel. (4212) 33-79-27; attached to Russian Acad. of Sciences; Dir G. V. SEKISOV.

Institute of Mining, Novosibirsk: 630091 Novosibirsk, Krasny pr. 54; tel. (3832) 17-05-36; e-mail admin@misd.nsc.ru; internet www.misd.nsc.ru; f. 1944; attached to Russian Acad. of Sciences; library of 40,000 vols; Dir OPARIN VICTOR NIKOLAEVICH; Academic Sec.

TARASIK T. MIKHAILOVNA; publ. *Journal of Mining Science* (6 a year).

Institute of Mining of the North: 677018 Yakutsk, ul. Lenina 43; tel. (4112) 44-59-30; f. 1980; attached to Russian Acad. of Sciences; Dir Dr M. D. NOVOPASHIN.

Institute of Mining, Perm: 614007 Perm, Sibirskaya ul. 78A; tel. (3422) 16-75-02; e-mail arc@mi-perm.ru; f. 1988; attached to Russian Acad. of Sciences; library of 3,000 vols; Dir Prof. ARKADI E. KRASNO-SHTEIN; publs *Collection of Scientific and Research Works* (1 a year), *Mining Echo* (4 a year), *Proceedings* (1 a year).

Institute of Monitoring of Climatic and Ecological Systems: 634055 Tomsk, Akademicheskii pr. 10/3; tel. (3822) 492265; e-mail post@imces.ru; internet www.imces.ru; f. 1972, fmrly the Institute of Optical Monitoring; attached to Russian Acad. of Sciences; scientific and technological basis for monitoring and modelling climatic and ecosystem changes under impact of natural and anthropogenic factors; Dir V. A. KRUTIKOV; Scientific Sec. for Foreign Relations Dr ELENA YURIEVNA GENINA.

Institute of Petrochemistry and Catalysis: 450075 Bashkortostan, Ufa, pr. Oktyabrya 141; tel. (3472) 31-27-50; e-mail ink@anrb.ru; internet www.anrb.ru/ink/index.html; f. 1992; Dir USAIN M. DZHEMILEV.

Institute of Petroleum Refining and Petrochemistry: 450065 Bashkortostan, Ufa, Initsiativnaya ul. 12; tel. (3472) 43-31-17; e-mail ipnhp@anrb.ru; f. 1956; Dir E. G. TELIASHEV.

Institute of Physical and Technical Problems of the North: 677891 Yakutsk, Oktyabrskaya ul. 1; tel. (4112) 44-66-65; attached to Russian Acad. of Sciences; f. 1970; Dir Acad. V. P. LARIONOV.

Institute of Physics and Power Engineering: Bondarenko pl. 1, 249033 Kaluga oblast, Obninsk; tel. (08439) 98250; e-mail avzrod@ippe.obninsk.ru; internet www.ippe.ru; f. 1946; nuclear systems for civil and defence purposes; nuclear, laser and reactor physics; thermal physics, hydro-, gas and plasma-dynamics, liquid-metal coolant technologies; radiation material science; 3,800 mems; library of 320,000 vols; Dir-Gen. ANATOLY V. ZRODNIKOV.

Institute of Problems in Cybernetics: 117312 Moscow, ul. Vavilova 37; tel. (495) 124-77-67; attached to Russian Acad. of Sciences; Dir (vacant).

Institute of Problems in the Complex Utilization of Mineral Resources: 111020 Moscow, Kryukovskii tupik 4; tel. (495) 360-89-60; e-mail info@ipkonran.ru; internet www.ipkonran.ru; f. 1977; attached to Russian Acad. of Sciences; Dir V. A. CHANTURIA.

Institute of Problems in the Safe Development of Nuclear Energy: 115191 Moscow, Bol. Tulskaya; tel. (495) 952-24-21; attached to Russian Acad. of Sciences; Dir L. A. BOLSHOV.

Institute of Problems of Marine Technology: 690600 Vladivostok, ul. Sukhanova 5A; tel. (4232) 22-64-16; f. 1988; attached to Russian Acad. of Sciences; Dir M. D. AGEEV.

Institute of Problems of Mechanics: 119526 Moscow, pr. Vernadskogo 101; tel. (495) 434-32-38; f. 1965; attached to Russian Acad. of Sciences; library of 150,000 vols; Dir Prof. F. L. CHERNOUSKO.

Institute of Programmable Systems: 152140 Pereslavl-Zalesskii; tel. (08535) 9-81-21; attached to Russian Acad. of Sciences; Dir A. K. AILAMAZYAN.

Institute of Radio Engineering and Electronics: 103907 Moscow, Mokhovaya ul. 8; pr. K. Marksa 18; tel. (495) 203-52-93; attached to Russian Acad. of Sciences; br. in Saratov; Dir Acad. YU. V. GULYAEV.

Institute of Regional Systems Research: Birobidzhan; attached to Russian Acad. of Sciences; (in process of formation).

Institute of Remote Sensing Methods for Geology (VNIIKAM): 199034 St Petersburg, Birzhevoi pr-d 6; tel. (812) 218-28-01; Dir ALEXEI V. PERTSOV.

Institute of Solid State Chemistry and Mechanochemistry: 630128 Novosibirsk, Kutateladze ul. 18; tel. (383) 332-96-00; e-mail root@solid.nsc.ru; internet www.solid.nsc.ru; f. 1944; attached to Russian Acad. of Sciences; topo-chemical, radiation chemical and mechano-chemical methods of the control of the reactivity of solids; chemistry of supramolecular systems; reactions of intercalation; transport properties of composite materials; processes of electro-deposition and electro-dissolution of solid metallic electrodes in water solutions; devt of methods for nano-sized and high-dispersed materials preparation; mechanical alloying and mechano-chemical interaction in organic systems; synthesis of bismuth compounds of high purity and reactivity; library of 50,000 vols; Dir Prof. N. Z. LYAKHOV; publ. *Chemistry for Sustainable Development* (6 a year).

Institute of Synthetic Polymer Materials: 117393 Moscow, Profsoyuznaya 70; tel. (495) 335-91-00; attached to Russian Acad. of Sciences; Dir (vacant).

Institute of Technical Chemistry: 614013 Perm, ul. ak. Koroleva, 3; tel. (342) 237-82-72; e-mail international@itch.perm.ru; internet www.itch.perm.ru; f. 1985; attached to Ural Br. of Russian Acad. of Sciences; areas of research: synthesis of organic monomers, devt of new polymers and composite materials based thereupon, design of chemical processes based on new catalytic systems; library of 17,000 vols (incl. books and journals); Dir Dr V. N. STRELNIKOV; publs *Colloid Polym Sci*, *Journal of Molecular Structure*, *Microporous and Mesoporous Materials*.

Institute of the Automation of Design: 123056 Moscow, 2-ya Brestskaya; tel. (495) 250-02-62; attached to Russian Acad. of Sciences; Dir O. M. BELOTSERKOVSKY.

Institute of the Economics and Organization of Industrial Production: 630090 Novosibirsk, pr. Akad. Lavrenteva 17; tel. (3832) 35-05-36; attached to Russian Acad. of Sciences; Dir (vacant).

Institute of the Geology and Exploitation of Fossil Fuels: 117312 Moscow, ul. Fersmana 50; tel. (495) 124-91-55; attached to Russian Acad. of Sciences; Dir N. KRYLOV.

Institute of Theoretical and Applied Mechanics: 630090 Novosibirsk, Institutskaya ul. 4/1; tel. (3832) 33-35-34; e-mail fomin@itam.nsc.ru; internet www.itam.nsc.ru; f. 1957; attached to Russian Acad. of Sciences; library of 87,000 vols; Dir Prof. V. M. FOMIN; publs *Combustion, Explosion and Shock Waves* (6 a year), *Journal of Applied Mechanics and Technical Physics* (6 a year), *Physical Mesomechanics* (4 a year), *Thermophysics and Aeromechanics* (4 a year).

Institute of Trade Machinery: 127521 Moscow, Scheremetevskaya ul. 47; tel. (495) 218-51-47; f. 1961; Dir VYACHESLAV LVOVICH UMANSKY.

Ioffe, Physical-Technical Institute: 194021 St Petersburg, Politeckhnicheskaya ul. 26; tel. (812) 297-21-45; e-mail post@mail.ioffe.ru; internet www.ioffe.ru; f. 1918; attached to Russian Acad. of Sciences; br. in Shuvalovo; Dir Acad. ZH. I. ALFEROV.

Joint Russian-Vietnamese Tropical Research and Technological Centre: 119071 Moscow, Leninsky pr. 33; tel. (495) 954-12-19; f. 1987; attached to Russian Acad. of Sciences; long-term health consequences of Agent Orange, ecology, tropical resistance of materials and equipment; Head Acad. D. S. PAVLOV.

Kargin, V. A., Polymer Research Institute: 606006 Nizhegorodskaya oblast, Dzerzhinsk; tel. (8313) 25-50-00; e-mail niip@kis.ru; internet www.advtech.ru/nipolymer/nipolymer1.htm; f. 1949; library of 142,000 vols; Gen. Dir Prof. V. V. GUZEEV.

Kazan Physical-Technical Institute: 420029 Kazan, ul. Sibirskii trakt 10/7; tel. (8432) 76-50-44; e-mail phys-tech@kfti.knc.ru; attached to Russian Acad. of Sciences; Dir K. M. SALIKHOV.

Keldysh, M.V., Institute of Applied Mathematics: 125047 Moscow, Miusskaya pl. 4; tel. (495) 972-37-14; attached to Russian Acad. of Sciences; Dir S. P. KURDYUMOV.

Kostyakov, A. N., All-Russian Research Institute of Hydraulic Engineering and Land Reclamation: 127550 Moscow, Bol. Akademicheskaya 44; tel. (499) 153-72-70; library of 8,000 vols; Dir Prof. Dr B. M. KIZYAEV (acting); publ. *Transactions* (1 or 2 a year).

Krylov Shipbuilding Research Institute: 196158 St Petersburg, Moskovskoe shosse 44; tel. (812) 727-93-48; e-mail krylov@krylov.spb.ru; internet www.krylov.com.ru; f. 1894; Science Prin. and Dir V. M. PASHIN; publ. *Proceedings* (1 a year).

Krzhizhanovsky, G. M., State Energy Research Institute: 117927 Moscow, Leninsky pr. 19; tel. (495) 954-37-32; attached to Russian Acad. of Sciences; Dir E. P. VOLKOV.

Lebedev, S. A., Institute of Precision Mechanics and Computing Technology: 117333 Moscow, Leninsky pr. 51; tel. (495) 137-15-67; attached to Russian Acad. of Sciences; Dir G. G. RYABOV.

Lebedev, S. V., All-Russia Synthetic Rubber Research Institute: 198035 St Petersburg, Gapsalskaya ul. 1; tel. (812) 251-40-28; f. 1928; synthetic elastomeric materials, production processes, applications; Dir Prof. VITALY A. KORMER.

Mining Institute: 184209 Murmansk oblast, Apatity, ul. Fersmana 24; tel. (81555) 7-43-42; e-mail root@goi.kolasc.net.ru; internet www.goikolasc.ru; attached to Russian Acad. of Sciences; Dir Acad. N. N. MELNIKOV.

Mints, Acad. A. L., Institute of Radio Technology JSC: 127083 Moscow, ul. 8 Marta 10/1; tel. (495) 214-04-51; e-mail spz@newmail.ru; Gen. Dir V. I. SHUSTOV.

Moscow Scientific-Industrial Association 'Spektr': 119048 Moscow, ul. Usacheva 35; tel. (495) 245-56-56; f. 1964; attached to Russian Acad. of Sciences; research, devt and manufacture of non-destructive-testing equipment and instruments; Gen. Dir V. V. KLYUEV.

National Institute of Aviation Technology: 127051 Moscow, Petrovka 24; tel. (495) 311-05-41; e-mail info@niat.ru; internet www.niat.ru; f. 1920; Dir. O. S. SIROTKIN; publ. *Aviation Industry* (in Russian and English).

Paper Research Institute: 194018 St Petersburg, pr. Shvernika 49; tel. (812) 247-17-03; Dir A. IVANOV.

Pechora Research and Design Institute for the Oil Industry: 169400 Komi, Ukhta, Oktyabrskaya ul. 11; tel. (82147) 6-16-63; Dir A. N. ILIN.

Physical-Technical Institute: 42600 Izhevsk, ul. Kirova 132; tel. (3142) 43-02-03; e-mail fti@fti.udm.ru; internet fti.udm.ru; attached to Russian Acad. of Sciences; Dir Dr VLADIMIR LADYANOV.

Plastics Research Institute: 111112 Moscow, Perovskii pr. 35; tel. (495) 361-64-21; Dir V. I. ILICH.

Polymer Plastics Research Institute: St Petersburg, Polyustrovskii pr. 32; Dir Z. N. POLYAKOV.

Polzunov, I. I., Scientific and Development Association for Research and Design of Power Equipment JSC: 191167 St Petersburg, Atamanskaya str. 3/6; tel. (812) 578-87-13; e-mail general@ckti.ru; f. 1927; attached to Russian Acad. of Sciences; Dir YU. K. PETRENYA; publ. *Proceedings*.

Railway Research Institute-JSC VNIIZHT: 107996 Moscow, 3-ya Mytishchinskaya str. 10; tel. (495) 687-64-23; e-mail mnts@vniizht.ru; internet www.vniizht.ru; f. 1918; Dir-Gen. Dr BORIS LAPIDUS; Deputy Dir-Gen. ALEXANDER KASSAY; publ. *Vestnik VNIIZhT* (6 a year).

Republic Engineering-Technical Centre for the Restoration and Strengthening of Components of Machines and Mechanisms: 634067 Tomsk, Khim ploshchadka; tel. (3822) 1-45-04 br. at Novosibirsk: 630055 Novosibirsk, ul. Musy Dzhalilya 9; tel. (3832) 32-12-49; attached to Russian Acad. of Sciences; Dir V. F. PINKIN (Tomsk); Dir V. M. NEZAMUTDINOV (Novosibirsk).

Research and Design Institute for the Mechanical Processing of Minerals: 199026 St Petersburg, V. O., 21-ya liniya 8A; tel. (812) 321-97-29; f. 1920; Dir VASILY ARSENTIEV; publ. *Obogashcheniye Rud* (Mineral Processing Journal, 6 a year).

Research and Design Institute of Artificial Fibres: 141009 Moscow oblast, Mytishchi, ul. Kolontsova 5; tel. (495) 284-44-78; Dir V. SMIRNOV.

Research and Design Institute of Autogenous Engineering: 109004 Moscow, Shelaputinsky per. 1; tel. (495) 915-09-60; e-mail vniiautogen@newmail.ru; f. 1944; equipment for thermal cutting and spraying; Dir NIKOLAI I. NIKIFOROV; publ. *Research Work* (irregular).

Research and Design Institute of Chemical Engineering: 125015 Moscow, Bol. Novodmitrovskaya 14; tel. (495) 685-56-74; e-mail info@niichimmash.ru; internet niichimmash.ru; f. 1943; Gen. Dir A. TSYGANKOV.

Research and Design Institute of Management Information Technology: 125083 Moscow, ul. Yunnatov 18; tel. (495) 212-60-60.

Research and Design Institute of Metallurgical Engineering: 109428 Moscow, Ryazanskii pr. 8A; tel. (495) 174-37-00.

Research and Design Institute of Polymer Construction Materials: 117419 Moscow, 2-i Verkhny Mikhailovsky pr. 9; tel. (495) 952-30-68; attached to Polymerstroymateriali JSC; Dir ALEXANDER V. POGORELOV.

Research and Design Institute of the Bearings Industry: 109088 Moscow, 2-ya ul. Mashinostroeniya 27; tel. (495) 275-11-59.

Research and Design Institute of Woodworking Machinery: 107082 Moscow, Rubtsovskaya nab. 3; tel. (495) 261-16-73; f. 1948; library of 50,000 vols; publ. *Catalogue of Woodworking Machines* (1 a year).

Research and Design Technological Institute of Heavy Engineering: Ekaterinburg, pl. 1-i Pyatiletki.

Research and Experimental Design Institute of Machinery for the Food Industry: 123308 Moscow, pr. Marshala Zhukova 1.

Research Centre for Fundamental Problems of Computer Technology and Control Systems: 117218 Moscow, ul. Krasikova 25A; tel. (495) 125-77-09; attached to Russian Acad. of Sciences; Chair. of Presidium K. A. VALIEV..

Attached Institutes:

Institute of Computer Technology Problems: 150007 Yaroslavl, Universitetskaya 21; tel. (0852) 35-52-83; attached to Russian Acad. of Sciences; Dir YU. A. MAMATOV.

Institute of Microelectronics Technology and High-purity Materials: 142432 Moscow oblast, Chernogolovka ul. Acad. Ossipyan 6; tel. (49652) 44-060; e-mail general@iptm.ru; internet www.iptm.ru; attached to Russian Acad. of Sciences; Dir V. A. TULIN.

Microelectronics Institute: 150007 Yaroslavl, Universitetskaya 21; tel. (0852) 11-65-52; attached to Russian Acad. of Sciences; Dir V. A. KURCHIDIS.

Physical Technological Institute: 117218 Moscow, ul. Krasikova 25-A; tel. (495) 125-77-09; attached to Russian Acad. of Sciences; Dir K. A. VALIEV.

Research Institute of Systems of Automated Designing of Radioelectronic Apparatus and Very Large Scale Integrated Circuits: 103681 Moscow, Zelenograd, ul. Sovetskaya 3; tel. (495) 531-56-45; attached to Russian Acad. of Sciences; Dir A. L. STEMPKOVSKY.

Special Design Bureau for Microelectronics and Computer Technology: 15007 Yaroslavl, Universitetskaya 21; tel. (0852) 11-81-73; attached to Russian Acad. of Sciences; Dir A. M. GLUSHKOV.

Research Centre for Space Probes: 117810 Moscow, Profsoyuznaya ul. 84/32; attached to Russian Acad. of Sciences; Head N. A. DOLGIKH (acting).

Research, Design and Technological Institute of Electrothermic Equipment: 109052 Moscow, Nizhegorodskaya 29; tel. (495) 278-75-09.

Research Design-Technological Institute for Coal Machinery: 109193 Moscow, ul. Petra Romanova 7; tel. (495) 279-47-66.

Research Institute for Food Concentrates and Food Technologies and Special Food Technology: Leninsky Dist., village of Izmailovo 22, Moscow, 142718; tel. (495) 3831692; e-mail niippspt@gmail.ru; internet niippspt.narod.ru; f. 1981; attached to Russian Acad. of Agricultural Sciences; develops food concentrates, cereal snacks; food rations for Armed Forces and cosmonauts; tea and coffee products, infant foods; library of 7,000 vols; Dir Dr VICTOR F. DOBROVOLSKY; publ. *Tea and Coffee in Russia* (4 a year).

Research Institute for Instrumentation: 125124 Moscow, ul. Raskovoi 20; tel. (495) 214-55-88.

Research Institute for Systems Research: 109280 Moscow, Avtozavodskaya 23; tel. (495) 277-87-31; attached to Russian Acad. of Sciences; Dir V. B. BETELIN.

Research Institute for the Bakery and Confectionery Industry: 107553 Moscow, Bol. Cherkizovskaya ul. 26A; tel. (495) 161-41-44; attached to Russian Acad. of Agricultural Sciences.

Research Institute for the Beer, Soft Drinks and Wine Industry: 119021 Moscow, ul. Rossolimo 7; tel. (495) 246-67-69; attached to Russian Acad. of Agricultural Sciences.

Research Institute for the Organization, Management and Economics of the Oil and Gas Industry: 117420 Moscow, ul. Nametkina 14; tel. (495) 332-00-22.

Research Institute for the Processing of Casing Head Gas: 350550 Krasnodar, Krasnaya ul. 118; tel. (8612) 55-85-52; Dir N. I. KORSAKOV.

Research Institute of Abrasives and Grinding: 197342 St Petersburg, Beloostrovskaya ul. 17; tel. (812) 245-33-05; f. 1931; library of 62,000 vols; Dir S. MOLCHANOV.

Research Institute of Agricultural Engineering: 127427 Moscow, Dmitrovskoe shosse 107; tel. (495) 485-55-81.

Research Institute of Applied Automated Systems: 103009 Moscow, ul. Nezhdanovoi 2A; tel. (495) 229-78-46; attached to Russian Acad. of Sciences; Dir O. L. SMIRNOV.

Research Institute of Atomic Reactors: Ulyanovsk oblast, 433510 Dimitrovgrad; tel. (84235) 3-20-21; e-mail adm@niiar.ru; internet www.niiar.ru; f. 1956; library of 150,000 vols; Dir Dr A. V. BYCHKOV.

Research Institute of Automobile Electronics and Electrical Equipment: 105187 Moscow, Kirpichnaya 39–41; tel. (495) 365-25-66.

Research Institute of Automobile Industry Technology: 115333 Moscow, pr. Andropova 22/30; tel. (495) 118-20-00; Dir S. V. PODOBLYAEV.

Research Institute of Building Ceramics: 143980 Moscow oblast, Zheleznodorozhnyi-1; tel. (495) 527-73-73.

Research Institute of Chemical Fibres and Composite Materials: 195030 St Petersburg, ul. Khimikov 28; tel. (812) 227-61-48; Dir P. E. MIKHAILOV.

Research Institute of Chemical Reagents and Ultrapure Chemical Substances: 107258 Moscow, Bogorodskii val 3; tel. (495) 963-70-70; Dir E. A. RYABENKO.

Research Institute of Chemicals for Polymer Materials: 392680 Tambov, ul. Montazhnikov 3; tel. (0752) 29-51-52; attached to Syntez joint-stock company; Dir B. N. GORBUNOV.

Research Institute of Construction and Road Machinery: 123424 Moscow, Volokolamskoe shosse 73; tel. (495) 491-10-33.

Research Institute of Construction Physics: 127238 Moscow, Lokomotivny pr. 21; tel. (495) 482-40-76; e-mail niisf@ipc.ru; f. 1956; library of 2,000 vols; Dir G. L. OSIPOV.

Research Institute of Current Sources: 129626 Moscow; tel. (495) 287-97-42; attached to Russian Acad. of Sciences; Dir YU. V. SKOKOV.

Research Institute of Drilling Technology: 117957 Moscow, Leninsky pr. 6; tel. (495) 236-01-70; Dir A. V. MNASHCHAKOV.

Research Institute of Earthmoving Machinery: c/o VNIIZEMMASH, 198005 St Petersburg, Petrovskii pr. 2; tel. (812) 235-57-84; attached to VNIIZEMMASH; Dir V. P. KORNEEV.

Research Institute of Elastic Materials and Products: 119048 Moscow, Mal. Trubetskaya ul. 28; tel. (495) 242-53-42; Dir S. V. REZNICHENKO.

Research Institute of Electrical Engineering: 191186 St Petersburg, Dvortsovaya nab. 18; tel. (812) 387-55-22; e-mail jandan@peterlink.ru; f. 1992; attached to Russian Acad. of Sciences; Dir Acad. Y. B. DANILEVICH; publs *Electrichestvo* (12 a year), *Energetics News of RAS* (6 a year).

Research Institute of Electro-welding Technology: 194100 St Petersburg, Litovskaya ul. 10; tel. (812) 245-40-95; Dir V. V. SMIRNOV.

Research Institute of Electromeasuring Equipment: 195267 St Petersburg, pr. Prosveshcheniya 85; tel. (812) 559-51-41.

Research Institute of Foundry Machinery and the Technology and Automation of Foundry Production: 123557 Moscow, Presnenskii val 14; tel. (495) 252-27-25; Dir E. KRAKOVSKII.

Research Institute of Gas Use in the Economy and Underground Storage of Oil, Oil Products and Liquefied Gases: 123298 Moscow, ul. Berzarina 12; tel. (499) 946-89-11.

Research Institute of Hydrogeology and Engineering Geology (VSEGINGEO): 142452 Moscow oblast, Noginskii raion, p/o Kupavna, pos. Zelenyi; tel. (495) 521-20-00; e-mail gvartany@online.ru; f. 1939; Dir Acad. G.S. VARTANYAN.

Research Institute of Instrumentation Technology: 113191 Moscow, Gamsonovskii per. 9; tel. (495) 232-10-41.

Research Institute of Light Alloys: Moscow, ul. Gorbanova 20; Dir N. I. KORYAGINA.

Research Institute of Light and Textile Machinery: 113105 Moscow, Varshavskoe shosse 33; tel. (499) 611-00-30; e-mail vniiltek@mail.magelan.ru; internet www .vimi.ru/vniiltekmash; f. 1932; library of 30,000 vols; Dir Prof. Dr R. M. MALAFEYEV.

Research Institute of Organizational Technology: 119146 Moscow, Komsomolskii pr. 9A; tel. (495) 246-41-21.

Research Institute of Road Traffic Safety: 109389 Moscow, Mal. Lubyanka 16/4.

Research Institute of Rubber and Latex Products: 107564 Moscow, Krasnobogatyrskaya ul. 42; tel. (495) 161-02-92; Dir V. A. BERESTENEV.

Research Institute of Rubber Technical Products: 141300 Moscow oblast, Sergievsky Posad; tel. (496) 544-57-59; f. 1960; library of 15,000 vols; Dir V. V. SHVARTS.

Research Institute of Special Engineering: 107082 Moscow, Cheshikhinsky pr-d 18/20; tel. (499) 261-50-76.

Research Institute of Synthetic Fibres: 170613 Tver, ul. Pashi Savelevoi 45; tel. (08222) 5-36-10; Dir V. F. LOSKUTOV.

Research Institute of Technical Physics: 454070 Chelyabinsk oblast, Chelyabinsk 70; Dir V. Z. NECHAI.

Research Institute of the Cement Industry OJSC (NIICement): 107014 Moscow, 3-i Luchevoy prosek 12; tel. (495) 268-27-21; e-mail riicement@mtu-net.ru; f. 1947; formerly State Research Institute of the Cement Industry; Dir-Gen. Prof. Dr V.I. SHUBIN.

Research Institute of the Chemistry and Technology of Organoelement Compounds: 105118 Moscow, shosse Entuziastov 38; tel. (495) 673-49-53; e-mail eos2004@inbox.ru; internet www.eos.su; f. 1945; Gen. Dir P. A. STOROZHENKO.

Research Institute of the Clock and Watch Industry: 125315 Moscow, Chasovaya 24/1; tel. (495) 151-15-01.

Research Institute of the Factory Technology of Prefabricated Reinforced Concrete Structures and Items: 111524 Moscow, ul. Plekhanova 7; tel. (495) 176-27-04.

Research Institute of the Gas Industry: 142700 Moscow oblast, Vidnoe.

Research Institute of the Metrology Service: 119361 Moscow, G-361, Ozernaya ul.

46; tel. (495) 437-55-77; e-mail office.vniims@relcom.ru; attached to Russian Acad. of Sciences; Dir V. V. SAZHIN.

Research Institute of the Tyre Industry: 105118 Moscow, ul. Burakova 27; tel. (495) 273-69-01; Dir A. A. VOLNOV.

Research Institute of Tooling: 105023 Moscow, Bol. Semenovskaya 49; tel. (495) 366-94-11.

Research Institute of Transport Construction: 129329 Moscow, Kolskaya 1; tel. (495) 180-20-42; e-mail mail@tsniis.com; internet www.tsniis.com; f. 1935; research on bridges, tunnels, railways and associated structures, and development of standards and codes of practice; Dir-Gen. ANATOLY SYCHEV.

Research Institute of Vehicle and Tractor Materials: 113184 Moscow, Ozerkovskaya nab. 22/24; tel. (495) 230-94-59.

Research-Training Centre 'Robototekhnika': 105037 Moscow, Izmailovskaya pl. 7; tel. (495) 165-17-01; e-mail robot@bmstu.ru; internet www.robot.bmstu.ru; f. 1983; attached to Russian Acad. of Sciences and Bauman Moscow State Technical University; Vice-Head for Robotic Systems Dept Prof. A. S. YUSCHENKO; Vice-Head for the Centre Prof. Dr S. L. ZENKEVICH; publs *Mechatronics*, *Priborostroenie*.

Russian Research, Design and Technological Institute for Crane and Traction Electrical Equipment: 109280 Moscow, ul. Masterkova 4; tel. (495) 275-61-66; f. 1960; library of 160,000 vols; Dir ANATOLY D. MASHIKHIN.

Russian Research Institute of Industrial Design: 129223 Moscow, pr. Mira, VVTs, korp. 312; tel. (495) 216-90-10; f. 1962; Dir LEV A. KUZMICHEV; publs *Tekhnicheskaya Estetika* (2 a year), *Designer's Library* (2 a year).

Russian Research Institute of Information Technology and Automated Design Systems: 129090 Moscow, ul. Shchepkina 22; tel. (495) 288-19-24.

Russian Scientific Centre of Applied Chemistry: 197198 St Petersburg, pr. Dobrolyubova 14; tel. (812) 325-66-45; f. 1919; library of 500,000 vols; Gen. Dir Prof. G. F. TERESHCHENKO; publ. *Annual Proceedings*.

Science Production Association 'Orgstankinprom': 105264 Moscow, 5-ya Parkovaya 37, korp. 2; tel. (495) 164-56-53.

Scientific and Engineering Centre 'SNIIP': 123060 Moscow, ul. Raspletina 5; tel. (499) 198-97-64; e-mail support@sniip.ru; internet www.sniip.ru; attached to Rosatom (State Atomic Energy Corporation); systems and instrumentation connected with nuclear power production, electronics and space research; library of 83,000 research vols; Dir-Gen. Dr ALEXANDER F. PELEVIN; publ. *Proceedings* (1 a year).

Scientific and Research Institute for Standardization and Certification in the Engineering Industry: 123007 Moscow, ul. Shenogina 4; tel. (495) 256-04-49; f. 1957; standardization, certification of products.

Scientific and Research Institute of Motor Transport: 123514 Moscow, ul. Geroev-Panfilovtsev 24; tel. (495) 496-55-23; e-mail niiat@niiat.ru; internet www.niiat.ru; f. 1930; research and devt in field of motor transport operation, incl. transport and traffic management, traffic safety, urban transport, transport and the environment, transport economy; library of 250,000 vols.

Scientific and Technical Complex 'Progress': 119034 Moscow, Kropotkinskaya ul.

13/7; tel. (495) 301-23-25; attached to Russian Acad. of Sciences; Gen. Dir L. N. LUPICHEV.

Scientific Centre of Complex Transportation Problems: 113035 Moscow, Sofiiskaya nab. 34, korp. V; tel. (495) 233-89-13; f. 1955; Dir V. ARSENOV.

Scientific-Experimental Centre for the Automation of Air Traffic Control: 123182 Moscow, Volokolamskoe shosse 26; tel. (495) 190-42-18; attached to Russian Acad. of Sciences; Head T. G. ANODINA.

Scientific Research Institute for Systems Studies: 117218 Moscow, pr. Nakhimovsky 36, korp. 1; tel. (495) 719-76-51; e-mail betelin@sistyd.msk.su; internet www .niisi.ru; f. 1989; attached to Russian Acad. of Sciences; Dir V. B. BETELIN; publs *Issues in Cybernetics* (1 a year), *Issues of SRISA* (2 a year).

Scientific Research Institute of Comprehensive Engineering Problems in Animal Husbandry and Fodder Production (VNIIKOMZH): 101509 Moscow, Lesnaya 43; tel. (495) 250-37-90; f. 1974; library of 40,000 vols; Dir-Gen. I. V. ILIN; publ. *Scientific Research Works of VNIIKOMZH* (1 a year).

Scientific Research Institute of Multiprocessor Computer Systems of the Taganrog State University of Radio Engineering: 347928 Taganrog, ul. Chekhova 2; tel. (86344) 36-07-57; internet www.mvs.tsure.ru; f. 1972; attached to Russian Acad. of Sciences; Dir I. A. KALIAEV; publ. *Multiprocessor Computer Structures* (1 a year).

Scientific-Technical Co-operative 'Problems of Mechanics and Technology': 109180 Moscow, ul. Bol. Polyanka 2/10; tel. (495) 251-52-08; attached to Russian Acad. of Sciences; Chair. Acad. V. V. STRUMINSKY.

Siberian Research Institute of the Oil Industry: 625016 Tyumen, ul. 50-let Oktyabrya 118; tel. (3452) 21-19-16; Dir R. I. KUZOVATKIN.

Skochinsky Institute of Mining: 140004 Moscow, Lyubertsy 4; tel. (495) 554-85-13; e-mail igd@igd.ru; internet www.igd.ru; f. 1927; attached to Russian Acad. of Sciences; technology of opencast and underground coal mining; certification of mine electrical equipment and explosion-proof equipment; library of 40,000 vols; Dir ANATOLY DMITRIEVICH RUBAN; publs *Economics of the Coal Industry* (1 or 2 a year), *Technology of Opencast and Underground Coal Mining* (4 a year).

Special Design Bureau for Applied Geophysics: 630058 Novosibirsk, Russkaya ul. 35; tel. (3832) 32-36-45; e-mail geophys@hydromet.ru; attached to Russian Acad. of Sciences; Head N. P. RASHENTSEV.

Special Design Bureau for Automation of Marine Research: 693023 Yuzhno-Sakhalinsk, ul. Gorkogo 25; tel. (424) 255-49-66; e-mail skb-sami@sakhalin.ru; f. 1972; attached to Russian Acad. of Sciences; Head ANATOLY E. MALASHENKO.

Special Design Bureau for High Capacity Electronics: 634055 Tomsk, Akademicheskii pr. 4; tel. (3822) 1-84-59; attached to Russian Acad. of Sciences; Head A. P. KHUZEEV.

Special Design Bureau for Hydroimpulse Technology: 630090 Novosibirsk, ul. Tereshkovoi 29; tel. (3832) 35-72-91; attached to Russian Acad. of Sciences; Head A. A. DERIBAS.

Special Design Bureau for Scientific Instruments: 630058 Novosibirsk, Russkaya ul. 41; tel. (3832) 35-30-41; attached to

Russian Acad. of Sciences; Head YU. V. CHUGUL.

Special Design-Technological Bureau for Special Electronics and Analytical Instrumentation: 630090 Novosibirsk, ul. Akad. Nikolaeva 8; tel. (3832) 32-24-40; attached to Russian Acad. of Sciences; Head K. K. SVITASHCHEV.

Special Design-Technological Bureau 'Nauka': 66049 Krasnoyarsk, pr. Mira 53; tel. (3912) 27-29-12; attached to Russian Acad. of Sciences; Head V. V. MOSKVICHEV.

State Design and Research Institute for the Design of Research Institutes, Laboratories and Research Centres of the Academy of Sciences: 117971 Moscow, ul. Gubkina 3; tel. (495) 135-73-01; e-mail gp@gpran.msk.ru; f. 1938; attached to Russian Acad. of Sciences; Dir A. S. PANFIL.

State Design and Research Institute of Power Systems and Electricity Networks: 107884 Moscow, 2-ya Baumanskaya 7; tel. (499) 261-98-21.

State Institute of Mined Chemical Raw Materials: 140000 Moscow oblast, Lyubertsy, Oktyabrsky pr. 259; tel. (495) 554-42-46.

State Research and Project Development Institute of Maritime Transport: 125319 Moscow, Bol. Koptevsky pr-d 6; tel. (495) 152-36-51; f. 1939; design of port structures and ship repair yards; economic problems of maritime transport; maritime law; Dir FELIX G. ARAKELOV.

State Research Institute for the Nitrogen Industry and the Products of Organic Synthesis: 109815 Moscow, Zemlyanoi val 50; tel. (495) 227-00-04; Dir N. D. ZAICHKO.

State Research Institute for the Operation and Repair of Civil Aviation Equipment: Moscow, ul. Krzhizhanovskogo 7.

State Research Institute of Civil Aviation: 103340 Moscow oblast, Sheremetevo Airport; tel. (495) 578-48-01.

State Research Institute of the Rare Metals Industry: 109017 Moscow, Bol. Tolmachevsky per. 5; tel. (495) 239-90-66.

'Submicron' Research Institute: 103482 Moscow, Zelenograd, korp. 331A; tel. (495) 536-26-17.

Topchiev, A. V., Institute of Petro-Chemical Synthesis: 117912 Moscow, Leninskii pr. 29; tel. (495) 954-22-92; attached to Russian Acad. of Sciences; Dir Acad. N. A. PLATE.

Vavilov State Optical Institute: 199034 St Petersburg, Birzhevaya Liniya 12; tel. (812) 328-48-92; e-mail leader@soi.spb.ru; internet soi.srv.pu.ru; f. 1918; library of 600,000 vols; Dir Dr G. PETROVSKY; publ. *Journal of Optical Technology* (12 a year).

'VNIPIenergoprom' Association JSC: 105094 Moscow, Semenovskaya nab. 2/1; tel. (495) 360-76-40; internet www.vnipiep .ru; f. 1942; design, research and devt of energy transmission systems, combined heating and power plants, project management, devt of heat and power-supply schemes for municipal areas, principally Moscow.

Vologdin, V. P., Research Institute of High-Frequency Currents: 197376 St Petersburg, ul. L. Tolstogo 7; tel. (812) 594-81-23; internet www.vniitvch.spb.ru; f. 1947; Dir F. V. BEZMENOV.

Zhukovsky, N. E., Central Aero- and Hydro-dynamics Institute: 140160 Moscow oblast, Zhukovsky 3; tel. (495) 556-41-79; Dir G. P. SVISHCHEV.

Libraries and Archives

Arkhangelsk

Dobroliubov Arkhangelsk Regional Research Library: 163061 Arkhangelsk, ul. Loginova 2; tel. (8182) 65-11-28; Dir OLGA STIUPINA.

Barnaul

Altai State University Library: 656099 Barnaul, Sotsialisticheskii pr. 68; 159,000 vols; Dir GALINA TRUSHNIKOVA.

Cheboksary

Chuvash State University Library: 428034 Cheboksary, Universitetskaya 38; tel. (8835) 49-79-88; e-mail library@chuvsu .ru; internet library.chuvsu.ru; 1,703,091 vols; Dir NINA D. NIKITINA.

Ekaterinburg

Scientific Library of Ural State University 'M. Gorky': 620083 Ekaterinburg, 51, Lenina ave; tel. (343) 350-75-65; e-mail library@usu.ru; internet lib.usu.ru; f. 1920; incl. rare book dept; institutional repository; 1,261,687 vols; Dir K. P. KUZNETSOVA.

Elista

Kalmyk State University Library: Elista, ul. R. Luksemburg 4; 350,000 vols; Dir P. A. DOLINA.

Grozny

Chechen State University Library: 364907 Grozny, ul. N. Buachidze 34/96; 460,000 vols; Dir R. M. NAZARETYANI.

Ingushetia

National Library of Ingushetia: 386203 Ingushetia, Sunezhsky district, Orjonikidzyevskoye, ul. Lunacharskogo 106; tel. (8734) 72-21-99; e-mail nbri@rambler.ru; internet www.nbri.ru; Dir RADIMA ABDOOLLAYEVNA GAZDIEVA.

Irkutsk

Irkutsk State University Library: 664695 Irkutsk, bul. Gagarina 24; 3.2m. vols; Dir R. V. PODGAICHENKO.

Ivanovo

Ivanovo State University Library: 153377 Ivanovo, ul. Ermaka 37; 410,000 vols; Dir A. N. KRUPPA.

Library of Ivanovo State Chemistry and Technology University: 153000 Ivanovo, ul. Fridrikha Engelsa 7; tel. (4932) 32-73-54; e-mail book@isuct.ru; internet www.isuct.ru/book; 500,000 vols and 78,585 electronic catalogues; Dir VERA V. DMITRIEVA.

Izhevsk

Udmurt State University Library: 426034 Izhevsk, Universitetskaya ul. 1; tel. (3412) 52-60-89; e-mail admin@lib.udsu.ru; internet lib.udsu.ru; f. 1932; 970,647 vols; Librarian L. P. BESKLINSKAYA.

Kaliningrad

Immanuel Kant Baltic Federal University Library: 236040 Kaliningrad, Universitetskaya ul. 2; tel. (4012) 53-31-29; e-mail eafilippova@kantiana.ru; internet lib .kantiana.ru; f. 1968; 624,212 vols; Dir A. N. CHERNYAKOV; Deputy Dir FILIPPOVA ELENA.

Kazan

Kazan Federal University N. I. Lobachevsky Library: 420008 Kazan, Kremlevskaya 35; tel. (843) 264-47-54; e-mail lsl@lsl .ru; internet www.lsl.ksu.ru; f. 1804; 6.1m. vols; Dir Dr EUGENE N. STROUKOV; publs *Opisaniya Rukopisei, Retrospektivnye Bibliograficheskie Ukazately*.

Kemerovo

Kemerovo State University Library: 650043 Kemerovo, Krasnaya ul. 6; tel. (3842) 23-14-26; f. 1928; 350,000 vols; Librarian N. P. KONOVALOVA.

Krasnodar

Kuban State University Library: 350049 Krasnodar, Stavropolskaya ul. 149; tel. (8612) 69-95-52; e-mail gsol@pop.kubsu.ru; internet www.library.kubsu.ru; f. 1920; 1,253,824 vols; Dir G. V. SOLOVEVA.

Krasnoyarsk

Krasnoyarsk State University Library: 660049 Krasnoyarsk, ul. Maerchaka 6; tel. (3912) 21-03-17; 166,000 vols; Librarian E. G. KRIVONOSOVA.

Makhachkala

Dagestan State University Library: 367008 Makhachkala, Batir ul. 1; tel. (8722) 68-02-74; e-mail alieva_li@mail.ru; internet elib.dgu.ru; 780,000 vols; Dir A. M. SHAKHSHAEVA.

Moscow

All-Russia Patent and Technical Library of Federal Institute of Industrial Property of Federal Service for Intellectual Property, Patents and Trademarks (Rospatent): 123995 Moscow, Berezhkovskaya nab. 24; tel. (499) 240-64-25; e-mail vptb@rupto.ru; internet www1.fips .ru/wps/wcm/connect/content_ru/ru/fonds; f. 1896; the only Russian library that receives Russian and all foreign patents; copies of 117,986,700 patent documents; Head O. V. BAKHVALOVA; publs *Guidebook to Funds of Division 'All-Russia Patent and Technical Library', Thematic Bibliographic Indexes of the Literature*.

All-Russia Scientific and Research Institute of Patent Information (VNIIPI): 113035 Moscow, Raushskaya nab. 4; tel. (495) 959-33-13; f. 1964; Dir V. D. ZINOVIEV; publs *Inventions* (36 a year), *Service Marks. Appellations of Origin of Goods* (12 a year), *Trademarks, Utility Models. Industrial Designs* (12 a year).

Archives of the Russian Academy of Sciences: 117218 Moscow, Novocheremushkinskaya ul. 34; tel. (499) 129-19-10; e-mail academ_archive@mail.ru; f. 1728; 9,000 vols; Dir V.Y. AFIANI; publs *Proceedings, Scientific Heritage*.

Central Scientific Agricultural Library of the Russian Academy of Agricultural Sciences: 107139 Moscow, Orlikov byst, 3-B; tel. (495) 607-54-48; e-mail dir@cnshb.ru; internet www.cnshb.ru; f. 1930; centre for bibliographical information on national and foreign agricultural literature, and for scientific and methodological work of agricultural libraries in Russia; 3m. vols, 3,300 periodicals; Dir BUNIN MIKHAIL STANISLAVOVICH; publs *Bibliographic Information* (52 a year), *Selskoe Khozyaistvo* (12 a year), *Selskokhozyaistvennaya Literatura* (12 a year), *Subject Bibliographic Lists* (15 a year).

Central State Archives: 125212 Moscow, Vyborgskaya 3; tel. (495) 159-73-83; Dir A. PROKOPENKO.

Centre for the Preservation of Historical Documentary Collections: Moscow, Vyborgskaya ul. 3; tel. (495) 159-74-71; Dir V. BONDAREV; formerly Central State Archive of the USSR (TsGA SSSR) Special Archive.

Federal Archival Agency: 103132 Moscow, ul. Ilyinka 12; tel. (495) 606-35-31; e-mail rosarhiv@archives.ru; internet www .rusarchives.ru; f. 1991; Head ANDREY ARTIZOV; publ. *Otechestvenniye Archivy* (6 a year).

Gorky, A. M., Archives: 121069 Moscow, ul. Vorovskogo 25a; tel. (495) 291-19-23; f. 1937; Dir VLADIMIR S. BARAKHOV.

Institute of Scientific and Technical Information: 125219 Moscow, ul. Usievicha 20A; tel. (495) 155-43-96; attached to Russian Acad. of Sciences; Dir P. V. NESTEROV.

Institute of Scientific Information for Social Sciences of the Russian Academy of Sciences (INION RAN): Nakhimovsky prospect, 51/21, Moscow, 117997; tel. (499) 128-88-81; f. 1969; sections on philosophy, history, economics, sociology, political science, culture studies, global problems and int. relations, law, science studies, linguistics, theory of literature; 13,500,500 vols; Dir YU. S. PIVOVAROV; publs *Method: Moscow Yearbook of Social Science Studies* (1 a year), *Russian Studies* (1 a year), *Sociological Yearbook* (1 a year), *Symbolic Politics* (1 a year), *The Human Being: Image and Essence* (1 a year), *Theory and Practice of Scientific Information in Social Sciences* (1 a year).

International Centre for Scientific and Technical Information: 125252 Moscow, ul. Kuusinena 21 B; tel. (495) 198-70-21; e-mail alsor@icsti.su; internet www.icsti.su; f. 1969; Dir Dr ZURAB A. YAKOBASHVILI.

Library for Natural Sciences of the Russian Academy of Sciences: 119992 Moscow GSP-2, ul. Znamenka 11/11; tel. (495) 291-22-89; e-mail root@ben.msk.su; internet www.benran.ru/ben_ne2.htm; f. 1973; 12.5m. items in main and associated libraries; Dir Prof. Dr N. E. KALENOV; publ. *Libraries of Academies of Sciences* (in Russian, 1 a year).

Library of the State A. S. Pushkin Museum of Fine Arts: 119019 Moscow, ul. Volkhonka 12; tel. (495) 697-97-28; e-mail bib@artsmuseum.ru; f. 1898; mem of Russian Library Asscn; holds encyclopaedic collns, European art, Egyptian, Greek and Roman art, numismatic, archaeology; art education, architecture, world history, museology; supports research activities; 280,000 vols of books (17th–21st centuries), 405,000 periodicals of 19th–21st centuries, 100,000 reproductions on paper and canvas, 120,000 negatives and photographs, 70,000 slides; Dir OLGA B. MALINKOVSKAYA; publ. *Bulletin of the New Acquisitions* (2 a year, spec. issue for researchers).

Library of the State Central Museum of the Contemporary History of Russia: 103050 Moscow, Tverskaya ul. 21; tel. (495) 299-52-17; e-mail sovrhistory@mtu-net.ru; internet www.sovr.ru; f. 1917 as Museum of the Russian Revolution; 360,000 vols, 825,000 periodicals; Chief Librarian TATYANA N. EREMEEVA.

Library of the State Literature Museum: Moscow, Rozhdestvenskii bul. 16; tel. (495) 621-38-57; e-mail pressa-goslitmuz@yandex .ru; f. 1926; collection of 180,000 books, 27,644 periodicals; Russian and foreign works from 16th to 20th centuries; letters and autographed works; folklore works; periodical collection; Dir ANNA IVANOVNA NIKULINA.

Library of the State Museum of Oriental Arts: 103064 Moscow, Vorontsovo pole 16A; tel. (495) 916-34-29; e-mail dinagnw@ rambler.ru; f. 1918; 75,000 vols; Dir DIANA VAKHTANGOVA; publ. *Scientific Reports* (1 a year).

Library (Book Fund Department) of the State Theatrical A. A. Bakhrushin Museum: 115054 Moscow, Bakhrushin St. 31/12; tel. (495) 953-48-48; e-mail gctm@gctm .ru; internet www.gctm.ru; f. 1894; colln of 1.5m. objects reflecting history of theatre in

Russia since 17th century; 120,000 vols on theatrical art; Head TITANIA BONILYA; Gen. Dir RODIONOV DMITRY.

Library of the Tolstoy State Museum: 119034 Moscow, ul. Prechistenka 11; tel. (499) 766-93-28; e-mail info@tolstoymuseum .ru; f. 1911; 76,000 vols, 86,000 newspaper cuttings; Dir L. M. LUBIMOVA.

Main Library of the Russian Academy of Medical Sciences: 125315 Moscow, Baltiiskaya ul. 8; tel. (495) 151-19-71; e-mail fb@ fbramn.ru; internet www.fbramn.ru; f. 1935; acts as an enquiry, loan, research and guide centre for 42 libraries in the institutes and laboratories of the Acad. of Medical Sciences; 640,000 vols; Dir N. V. KONDRATIEVA.

The M. I. Rudomino, All-Russia State Library for Foreign Literature: 109189 Moscow, Nikoloyamskaya St 1; tel. (495) 915-36-21; e-mail vgbil@libfl.ru; internet www .libfl.ru; f. 1922; research and public library; cultural centre; exchange arrangements with 500 libraries, publishing houses and univs in 90 countries; 4.4m. vols in 140 foreign languages; Dir E. YU. GENIEVA; publ. *Otkrytyj Dostup: Biblioteki za rubezhom* (Open Access: Libraries around the World).

Russian National Public Library for Science and Technology: 107996 Moscow, K-31, GSP-6, Kuznetskii Most 12; tel. (495) 625-95-89; e-mail gpntb@gpntb.ru; internet www.gpntb.ru; f. 1958; permanent contacts with 7,000 enterprises in Russia and other republics of the former USSR; operates Scientific Council; 7m. books, 1.6m. on microcarriers, about 3,000 units; electronic media; Dir JACOB LEONIDOVICH SHRAIBERG; publ. *Journal of Research, Scientific and Technical Libraries*.

Russian Peoples' Friendship University Library: 117198 Moscow, Miklukho-Maklaia 6; tel. (495) 434-86-32; e-mail lib.rudn@ gmail.com; internet lib.rudn.ru; f. 1960, present status 2008; organizes Russian language programme, books and art exhibitions; 1.8m. vols, 280 periodicals; Dir ELENA LOTOVA; Deputy Dir SVETLANA FOMICHEVA.

Russian State Archive of Modern Political History: 109012 Moscow, ul. Ilinka 12; tel. (495) 606-50-30; e-mail rgani@gov.ru; f. 1991; based on the Archive of the General Dept of the Communist Party of fmr USSR; Dir N. G. TOMILINA.

Russian State Archives of Old Documents: 119992 GSP-2 Moscow, G-435, Bolshaya Pirogovskaya ul. 17; tel. (495) 580-87-23; e-mail rgada@archives.ru; annals, charts of grand dukes and independent princes, legal documents of Early Russia (11th–18th centuries), documents of central and patriarchives of nobility and gentry, archives of church establishments and the largest monasteries of Russia; Dir MIKHAIL R. RYZHENKOV.

Russian State Archive of Social-Political History: 109999 Moscow, Bol. Dmitrovka 15; tel. (495) 629-97-26; e-mail rgaspi@inbox.ru; internet www.rgaspi.ru; f. 1920s; 10,000 vols; incl. colln from Central Archive of Komsomol; Dir Dr OLEG VLADIMIROVICH NAUMOV; publ. *Scientific Information Bulletin* (1 a year).

Russian State Archives of Sound Recording: 107005 Moscow, 2-ya Baumanskaya ul. 3, Lefortovskiy Palace; tel. (495) 261-13-00; e-mail rgafd@mail.ru; internet xn–80afe9bwa.xn–p1ai; f. 1932; sound recordings from 1902 of artistic and documentary nature; 135,000 gramophone records, 30,000 audio cassettes, 1,420 matrix moulds, 900 CD-ROMs, 1,136 tonefilms, 591 wax cylinders; Dir VLADIMIR KOLYADA.

Russian State Military Archive: 125212 Moscow, ul. Admirala Makarova 29; tel. (495) 159-80-91; documents of military authorities of the RSFSR and the USSR, of the military areas, detachments, units and establishments of the Soviet Army and Frontier Guards (1918–40); Osobyi Archive; Dir VLADIMIR NIKOLAEVICH KUZELENKOV.

Russian State Art Library: 107031 Moscow, Bol. Dmitrovka 8/1; tel. (495) 692-06-53; e-mail bisk@liart.ru; internet www.liart.ru; f. 1922; 1.7m. items (books, periodicals, press cuttings, engravings, sketches, postcards, photographs, posters); Dir A. A. KOLGANOVA.

Russian State Library for the Blind: 129090 Moscow, Protopopovsky per. 9; tel. (495) 680-26-14; e-mail admin@rgbs.ru; internet www.rgbs.ru; f. 1920; acts as methodical, coordinating and resources centre for special libraries throughout Russia; 1,320,000 vols; Dir T. N. ELFIMOVA; publs *The Visually-impaired and Society* (12 a year), *Correspondence School for the Parents* (2 a year).

Russian State Literature and Art Archives: 125212 Moscow, Vyborgskaya 3, korp. 2; tel. (499) 159-76-85; e-mail rgali@list.ru; internet rgali.ru; f. 1941; MSS, art works and documents of prominent Russian and Soviet writers, composers, artists, theatrical and cinema workers; documents of state and public organizations concerned with the arts since 18th century; 1,503,825 vols; Dir T. M. GORYAEVA; publ. *Vstrechi s Proshlym* (irregular).

Russian State Military Historical Archives: 105005 Moscow, ul. 2-ya Baumanskaya 3; tel. (495) 261-20-70; e-mail rgviarchives@ mtu-net.ru; internet xn–80adcv1b.xn–p1ai; f. 1797; documents of central and district military admins and establishments of the Russian Army, private collns of prominent gens, military leaders and historians (end 17th century–1918); Dir I. O. GARKUSHA.

Scientific Library of Moscow M. V. Lomonosov State University: 119192 Moscow, Lomonosovsky Prosp., 27; tel. (495) 939-22-41; e-mail inf@nbmgu.ru; internet www.nbmgu.ru; f. 1755; 10,000,000 vols; Dir VYACHESLAV VIKTOROVICH MOSYAGIN.

Scientific Library of the State Tretyakov Gallery: 113035 Moscow, 1-i Kadashevskii per. 14; tel. (495) 953-41-85; f. 1899; stock relating to Russian and Soviet art; 400,000 vols; Dir Z. P. SHERGINA.

Scientific S. I. Taneev Library of the Moscow P. I. Tchaikovsky State Conservatoire: 125009 Moscow, ul. B. Nikitskaya 13/6; tel. (495) 629-60-62; e-mail rassina@lib .mosconsv.ru; internet www.taneevlib.ru; f. 1866; Russian and foreign music and books on music; complete files of many Russian and foreign musical periodicals; 1,250,941 vols; Dir E. B. RASSINA.

State Archives of the Russian Federation: 119992 Moscow, Bol. Pirogovskaya ul. 17; tel. (495) 245-12-87; e-mail garf@ statearchive.ru; internet www.statearchive .ru; f. 1992; 6,643,132 vols; Dir SERGEY V. MIRONENKO; publ. *Archive of Contemporary Russian History* (3 series: catalogues, documents, research).

State Central Polytechnic Library: 101000 Moscow, Politekhnicheskii pr-d 2; tel. (495) 928-64-65; f. 1964; 3.5m. vols, incl. periodicals; Dir N. G. REINBERG.

Central Scientific Medical Library: 117997 Moscow, Nakhimovskaya ul. 49; tel. (499) 120-21-03; e-mail loginov@server.scsml .rssi.ru; internet www.mma.ru/en/library/ ?sphrase_id=469699; f. 1919; attached to I.M. Sechenov First Moscow State Medical University; 3m. vols; Dir Dr B. R. LOGINOV; publs

Medicine and Public Health, *New Medical Books*.

State Public Historical Library of Russia: 101990 Moscow, Starosadskii per. 9; tel. (495) 925-65-14; e-mail maf@shpl.ru; internet www.shpl.ru; f. 1938; 3,229,696 vols, including 74,695 in the Dept of Rare Books, 1,107,604 items in the Serials Dept; spec. colln of 10,119 unofficial publs; Dir Dr MIKHAIL AFANASIEV.

Turgenev Library No. 13: 101000 Moscow, Bobrov per. 6, str. 2; tel. (495) 921-00-52; e-mail biblioteka@turgenev.ru; Dir TATYANA KOROBKINA.

Institution of Russian Academy of Education Ushinsky State Pedagogical Library: 119017 Moscow, Bol. Tolmachevskii per. 3; tel. (495) 951-05-85; e-mail gnpbu@gnpbu.ru; internet www.gnpbu.ru; f. 1925; 2m. vols; Dir TAMARA S. MARKAROVA (acting); publ. *Literatura po Pedagogicheskim Naukam i Narodnomu Obrazovaniyu* (4 a year).

Nalchik

Kabardino-Balkar State University Library: 360004 Nalchik, ul. Chernyshevskogo 173; tel. (8662) 42-52-58; e-mail kodzokov@kbsu.ru; 738,000 vols; Dir E. D. MIGUCHKINA.

Nizhnii Novgorod

Nizhnii Novgorod N. I. Lobachevsky State University Central Library: 603091 Nizhnii Novgorod, pr. Gagarina 23; tel. (8312) 31-11-54; 1,210,470 vols; Dir A. I. SAVENKOV.

Novosibirsk

Novosibirsk State University Library: 630090 Novosibirsk, Akademgorodok; tel. (3832) 65-62-60; 450,000 vols; Dir L. G. TORSHENOVA.

Scientific—Technical Centre for Chemical Information: 630090 Novosibirsk, pr. Akad. Lavrenteva 9; tel. (383) 330-96-62; attached to Russian Acad. of Sciences; Head Prof. I. A. GRIGORR'EV.

State Public Scientific and Technical Library of the Siberian Department of the Russian Academy of Sciences: 630200 Novosibirsk, Voskhod 15; tel. (3832) 66-18-60; e-mail office@spsl.nsc.ru; internet www.spsl.nsc.ru; f. 1918; acts as reference, loan, research and coordinating centre for 65 academic institutes located in Siberia and the Far East; 14m. vols; Dir Prof. B. S. ELEPOV.

Omsk

Omsk State University Library: 644077 Omsk, pr. Mira 55A; tel. (3812) 26-84-22; 182,000 vols; Dir L. A. BALAKINA.

Perm

Perm State University Scientific Library: 614990 Perm, ul. Bukireva 15; tel. (3422) 39-64-80; e-mail library@psu.ru; internet www.library.psu.ru; f. 1916; 1,467,000 vols; Dir NATALIA YAKSHINA.

Petrozavodsk

Scientific Library of Petrozavodsk State University: 185910 Petrozavodsk, pr. Lenina 33; tel. (8142) 71-10-44; e-mail lib@psu.karelia.ru; internet library.petrsu.ru; f. 1940; 1,187,908 vols; Dir MARINA P. OTLIVANCHIK.

Rostov-on-Don

'Yu. A. Zhdanov' Zone Scientific Library at Southern Federal University: 344000 Rostov-on-Don, Zorge, 21Zh; tel. (863) 218-40-00; e-mail zaharova@sfedu.ru; internet www.library.sfedu.ru; f. 1915; attached

Museum of the History of Books; 2,515,102 vols; Dir IRINA VALERIEVNA GURBA; publ. *Donskaya Speech*.

St Petersburg

All-Russian Geological Library: 199106 St Petersburg, Srednii pr. 74; tel. (812) 321-72-12; e-mail vgb@vsegei.ru; f. 1882; scientific and technical literature; 1m. books, monographs, periodicals and special maps; Dir OLGA K. ERMILOVA; publ. *Geologicheskaya Literatura* (Geological Literature, 1 a year).

Department of the Art and Museum Book Collections of the State Russian Museum: 191186 St Petersburg, Inzhenernaya ul. 4; tel. (812) 595-42-08; e-mail library@rusmuseum.ru; internet library.rusmuseum.ru; f. 1898; 185,000 vols; Dir YULIA JURKINA.

Library of the Mariinsky State Academic Theatre of Opera and Ballet: 190000 St Petersburg, ul. Zodchego Rossi 2, Teatralnaya pl. 1; tel. (812) 326-41-64; e-mail cml@mariinsky.ru; consists of repertoire and archive sections; Dir Prof. Dr MARIA N. SHCHERBAKOVA.

Library of the National Pushkin Museum: 191186 St Petersburg, nab. Moiki 12; tel. (812) 571-06-19; e-mail vmp@museumpushkin.ru; internet www.museumpushkin.ru; f. 1953; collections of works by Russian authors incl. Pushkin, V. A. Krylov and S. Mazkov; 80,000 vols; Dir M. V. BOKARIUS.

Library of the Russian Academy of Sciences: 199034 St Petersburg, Birzhevaya liniya 1; tel. (812) 328-35-92; e-mail ban@rasl.nw.ru; internet www.ban.ru; f. 1714; 20,353,000 vols; collection of 19,000 MSS, 250,000 rare books, including 834 incunabula; 123,000 maps, 1.8m. publications of the Russian Academy of Sciences; acts as inter-library loan and reference service, exchange centre and book publisher; conducts research in library science, bibliography, palaeography and conservation; co-ordinates network of 31 specialized libraries in the Academy's research institutes; Dir Dr VALERII P. LEONOV; publs *Bibliography of Publications of the Russian Academy of Sciences* (1 a year), *Book in Russia* (1 a year), *Quarterly Bibliography*.

Library of the State Hermitage Museum: St Petersburg, Dvortsovaya nab. 34; f. 1762; over 500,000 vols; on painting, sculpture and all brs of graphic arts throughout the centuries; Dir MAKAROVA.

Mariinsky Theatre Library: 190000 St Petersburg, Teatralnaya pl., 1; tel. (12) 326-4164; e-mail cml@mariinsky.ru; contains one of the largest collns in the world of Russian music in MSS, single copies, first edns, etc., 1,500 copies of Russian vaudeville scores, 200 MSS of ballet scores, and a large colln of opera scores incl. 1,000 foreign operas; Dir Prof. Dr MARIA N. SHCHERBAKOVA.

Music Library of the D. D. Shostakovich St Petersburg Philharmonia: 191186 St Petersburg, Mikhailovskaya ul. 2; tel. (812) 710-49-28; e-mail library@philharmonia.spb.ru; internet www.philharmonia.spb.ru; f. 1882; 150,000 scores and books on music, 300,000 engravings, lithographs and paintings of musicians, composers, etc; 1m. newspaper cuttings; Head Dr PAVEL V. DMITRIEV.

Music Library of the St Petersburg Conservatoire: St Petersburg, Teatralnaya pl. 3; tel. (812) 571-32-23; e-mail admlib@conservatory.ru; internet biblio.conservatory.ru; f. 1862; 583,000 vols, incl. 187,000 Russian and foreign works on music, 338,000 scores, 7,600 MSS, 490 incunabula; Dir HELLEN NEKRASOVA; publs *Musicus* (4 a year), *Opera Musicologica* (4 a year).

National Library of Russia: 191069 St Petersburg, Sadovaya ul. 18; tel. (812) 310-98-50; e-mail office@nlr.ru; internet www.nlr.ru; f. 1795; 32,064,000 items, including a large collection of incunabula and MSS; Dir VLADIMIR N. ZAITSEV; publ. *PNB-Informazia* (12 a year).

Russian State Historical Archives: 190000 St Petersburg, Angliiskaya nab. 4; tel. (812) 311-09-26; f. 1918; documents of central state bodies of the Russian Empire, state and private banks, railways, industrial, trade and other companies; private collns of prominent political and public figures (18th century to 1917); 350,000 vols; Dir A. R. SOKOLOV; publ. *Herald* (irregular).

Russian State Naval Archives: St Petersburg, Millionnaya ul. 36; tel. (812) 315-90-54; f. 1724; documents of central institutions of the Russian pre-revolutionary and Soviet Navy and prominent naval officers (17th century to 1940); 1,219,454 vols; Dir V. G. MISHANOV.

St Petersburg State University M. Gorky Scientific Library: 199034 St Petersburg, Universitetskaya nab. 7/9; tel. (812) 328-27-41; e-mail marina@lib.pu.ru; internet www.lib.pu.ru; f. 1783; 7m. vols, 100,000 rare books, 1,000 MSS; Dir N. A. SHESHINA; publs *Pravovedenie* (6 a year), *Vestnik St. Petersburg* (24 a year).

St Petersburg Theatrical Library: St Petersburg, ul. Zodchego Rossi 2; f. 1756; 800,000 vols of plays and works on theatrical subjects, department of French works with first editions of Corneille; MSS and letters by Chekhov, Turgenev, Diaghilev, Fokine; dept of stage designs by Bakst, Benoit, etc.; dept of classical and contemporary fiction; Dir ANASTASIYA G. GAI.

Scientific Library attached to the Russian Institute for the History of Arts: 190000 St Petersburg, Isaakievskaya pl. 5; tel. (812) 315-55-87; f. 1912; 300,000 books and periodicals on theatre, music, cinematography, history of literature and art, fiction, philosophy, aesthetics, folklore; Chief Librarian I. V. KYTMANOVA.

Scientific Library of the Russian Academy of Arts: 199034 St Petersburg, Universitetskaya nab. 17; Moscow Branch: 119034 Moscow, ul. Prechistenka 21; f. 1757; 471,445 vols on art, architecture, applied and folk arts, including rare 16th- and 17th-century vols and a notable collection of 18th-century works on architecture; Dir L. S. POLAYKOVA; Dir N. V. KOMAROVA.

Samara

Russian State Scientific and Technical Archives: 443096 Samara, ul. Michurina 58; tel. (846) 336-17-81 also: Moscow, Profsoyuznaya ul. 82; tel. (495) 335-00-95; f. 1964; documentation of research and devt projects in industry, construction, transport and communications; invention applications; Dir IRINA N. DAVYDOVA.

Samara State University Library: 443011 Samara, ul. Potapova 64/163; tel. (8469) 28-35-87; e-mail libdirect@samsu.ru; internet www.ssu.samara.ru; f. 1969; 1.2m. vols; Dir IRINA V. GURIYANOVA.

Saransk

Mordovian N. P. Ogarev State University Library: 430000 Saransk, Bolshevistskaya ul. 68; tel. (8342) 4-49-91; f. 1931; 1,954,861 vols; Dir Doc. A. V. SMOLYANOV.

Saratov

V. A. Artisevich Zonal Scientific Library: 410000 Saratov, Universitetskaya ul. 42; tel. (845) 227-14-80; e-mail library@sgu.ru;

internet library.sgu.ru/nbsgu; f. 1909; 2,861,763 vols; Dir IRINA V. LEBEDEVA.

Syktyvkar

Syktyvkar State University Library: 167001 Syktyvkar, Oktyabrskii pr. 55; tel. (8212) 43-94-51; f. 1972; 560,980 vols; 812 MSS and books published in Russia before the 18th century; 22 personal archives of scientists; Dir NONNA F. AKOPOVA; publs *Rubezh* (4 a year), *Vestnik* (1 a year).

Tomsk

Russian State Historical Archive of the Far East: Tomsk, ul. K. Marksa 26; tel. (3822) 2-29-15; formerly Central State Archive of the RSFSR of the Far East (TsGA RSFSR DV).

Tomsk State University Library: 634010 Tomsk, Leninskii pr. 34a; tel. (3822) 2-44-69; 3,320,000 vols; Dir E. SYNTIN.

Tver

Tver State Medical Academy Library: 170000 Tver, ul. Sovetskaya 4; tel. (822) 33-27-26; f. 1954; 468 vols; Dir O. V. TULTSEVA.

Tyumen

Tyumen State University Library: 625036 Tyumen, ul. Volodarskogo 38; tel. (3452) 45-63-09; e-mail inbox@tmnlib.ru; internet www.tmnlib.ru; f. 1930; 2m. vols; Dir L. P. KRYUKOVA.

Ufa

Bashkir State University Library: 450074 Ufa, ul. Zaki Validi 32; tel. (3472) 73-66-26; e-mail jane@ic.bashedu.ru; internet www.bashlib.ru; f. 1909; 1,405,779 vols; Dir E. G. GELVANOVSKAYA.

National Library of Bashkortostan: 450000 Ufa, ul. Lenina 4; tel. (3472) 22-04-89; e-mail bashnl@mail.ru; internet bashnl.ru; f. 1836; collecting, processing, storage, use of information resources; 3.3m. vols; Dir AZAT IBRAGIMOV.

Vladikavkaz

North-Ossetian State University Library: 362000 Vladikavkaz, ul. Vatutina 46; tel. (8672) 53-49-52; e-mail lib_nosu@mail.ru; f. 1920; 1m. vols; Dir K. L. KOCHISOV.

Vladimir

Central State Archives of the Nation's Documentary Films and Photographs: Vladimir, Letneperevozinskaya ul. 9; tel. (0922) 2-79-95 also: Moscow oblast, Krasnogorsk, Rechnaya ul. 1; tel. (495) 563-08-45; topical films, newsreels and historical material that was not included in finished films, negatives of documentary photographs (1854–); Dir L. P. ZAPRYAGAEVA.

Vladivostok

Far Eastern Federal University Research Library: 690652 Vladivostok, Okeanskii pr. 37/41; tel. (4232) 76-22-53; internet www.dvfu.ru/en/web/fefu/library; f. 1899; 2m. vols, 71 nat. and int. edatabases; Dir A. G. TRETYAKOVA.

Voronezh

Scientific Library of Voronezh State University: 394000 Voronezh, pr. Revolyutsii 24; tel. (473) 255-35-59; e-mail minakov@lib.vsu.ru; internet www.lib.vsu.ru; f. 1918; 3,176,406 vols; Dir ARKADY MINAKOV; Chief Librarian LYUBOV KATZ.

Yakutsk

Scientific Library of North-Eastern Federal University: 677018 Yakutsk, Belinsky St 58; tel. (4112) 36-38-82; e-mail libr.ysu@mail.ru; internet www.ysu.ru/library; f. 1934;

compiles and publishes bibliographic indexes; 1,129,971 vols; Dir MAXIMOVA TATIANA SEMENOVNA; Deputy Dir TARABUKINA SARGYLANA KHRISTOPHOROVNA.

Yalutorovsk

Centre for the Preservation of the Reserve Collection: Tyumen oblast, Yalutorovsk, Ishimskaya ul. 136; tel. (34535) 2-29-87; formed from Central State Archive Reserve Collection of Documents of the State Archive Collection of the USSR (TsGA SF SSSR).

Yaroslavl

P. G. Demidov Yaroslavl State University Library: 150000 Yaroslavl, ul. Sovetskaya 14; tel. (4852) 79-16-34; internet www.uniyar.ac.ru; 774,324 vols; Dir I. V. DENEZHKINA.

Museums and Art Galleries

Arkhangelsk

Arkhangelsk State Museum: 163061 Arkhangelsk, pl. V. I. Lenina 2; tel. (8182) 3-66-79; f. 1737; contains 150,000 items featuring the history of the N coast area of Russia, since ancient times; large collection of archaeology, ethnography, documents and photographs; library of 30,000 vols; Dir YU. P. PROKOPEV.

Arkhangelsk State Museum of Fine Arts: 163061 Arkhangelsk, nab. Lenina 79; tel. (8182) 3-26-73; e-mail m1444@mail.museum.ru; internet www.museum.ru/m1444; contains over 150,000 items of ancient North and Western European art; library of 30,000 vols; Dir M. V. MITKEVICH.

Ashaga-stal

Stalsky Memorial Museum: 368765 Dagestan, Suleiman-Stalskii raion, Ashaga-stal; internet www.museum.ru/m1802; f. 1950; exhibits on the history of Dagestan literature, former home of poet Suleiman Stalskii; library of 20,000 vols; Dir LIDIYA M. STALSKAYA.

Astrakhan

Astrakhan State B. M. Kustodiev Gallery: Astrakhan, ul. Sverdlova 81; tel. (8512) 22-66-65; f. 1918; fine arts; library of 15,000 vols; Dir L. J. ILINA.

Barnaul

State Art Museum of Altai Territory: Barnaul, pr. Lenina 88; tel. (3852) 61-25-10; e-mail muzei@ab.ru; internet muzei.ab.ru; f. 1959; large collection since 16th century, of icons, paintings, sculptures, wood carvings, ceramics, national costumes; library of 13,526 vols; Dir I. K. GALKINA.

Belinsky

Belinsky, V. G., State Museum: Penza oblast, Belinsky, ul. Belinskogo 11; f. 1938; 31,280 exhibits on the life and work of the literary critic V. G. Belinsky; Curator I. A. GERASEKIN.

Borodino

Borodino State War and History Museum: 143240 Moscow oblast, Mozhaisk, selo Borodino; tel. (963) 86-32-23; e-mail 1812@borodino.ru; internet www.borodino.ru; f. 1839; researches into 1812 campaign, the Battle of Borodino and the 1941–45 war; 62,780 exhibits incl. material on the Battle of Borodino; library of 13,580 vols; Dir MIKHAIL

R. CHEREPASHENETS; Curator MARINA N. TSELORUNGO.

Bryansk

Bryansk State Museum of Soviet Fine Arts: Bryansk, ul. Gagarina 19; Dir B. F. FAENKOV.

Cheboksary

Chuvash State Art Museum: 428008 Cheboksary, Kalinina 60; tel. (8352) 63-63-11; e-mail tvg@artmuseum.chtts.ru; internet www.artmuseum.ru; f. 1939; 20,000 exhibits, mainly modern Russian, Soviet and Chuvash artists and traditional Chuvash decorative art; library of 12,500 vols; Dir N. SADYUKOV.

Chelyabinsk

Chelyabinsk Region Picture Gallery: Chelyabinsk, ul. Truda 92A; tel. (3512) 33-09-34; e-mail chelmusart@mail.ru; internet gallery.urc.ac.ru; f. 1940; 11,000 items of painting, sculpture, drawing, decorative and applied arts and crafts, incl. house architectural wooden carving of old Chelyabinsk; collns of icon paintings, old printed and hand-written books, plastics cast of brass and wooden sculpture; Chief Keeper SHABILIN SERGEY MIKHAYLOVICH.

Ekaterinburg

Ekaterinburg Picture Gallery: Ekaterinburg, ul. Vainera 11; f. 1746; Western European, Russian and Soviet artists and objects from the Kishisk foundries; Dir E. V. KHAMTSOV.

State Amalgamated Museum of the Writers of the Urals: 620075 Ekaterinburg, Tolmacheva ul. 41; tel. (343) 371-46-52; f. 1940 (amalgamated 1980); study and popularization of the heritage of the writers of the Urals, collns incl. the personal belongings and archives of Mamin-Sibiryak, Bazhov and other Ural writers, illustrations to edns of their works and various other artworks, 34,723 items in all; incorporates the House of D. N. Mamin-Sibiryak in Ekaterinburg, the House of P. P. Bazhov, the House of F. M. Reshetnikov; library of 37,700 vols; Dir V. P. PLOTNIKOV.

Ural Geological Museum: 620144 Ekaterinburg, ul. Kuibysheva 30; tel. (343) 257-31-09; f. 1937; Dir YURI A. POLENOV.

Gagarin

Yurii Gagarin Memorial Museum: 215010 Gagarin, ul. Gerzena 7; tel. (08135) 4-88-37; f. 1970; exhibits depicting the life and career of Yurii Alekseevich Gagarin (the first man in space) and other early Soviet cosmonauts, and the designers of the spaceships; Dir MARIA STEPANOVA.

Ivanovo

Ivanovsky Regional Art Museum: 153002 Ivanovo, pr. Lenina 33; tel. (4932) 32-65-04; e-mail iohm@yandex.ru; f. 1960; Greek, Roman and Ancient Egyptian art, icons, 18th–20th-century Russian art; library of 7,500 vols; Dir L. W. WOLOWENSKAYA.

Kaluga

Kaluga Regional Art Museum: 248610 Kaluga, ul. Lenina 104; tel. (4842) 56-28-30; e-mail artmuseum@kaluga.net; internet artmuseum.kaluga.ru; f. 1918; ancient Russian iconography, western European sculpture; Dir A. V. KAZAK.

Tsiolkovsky, K. E., State Museum of the History of Cosmonautics: Kaluga, ul. Koroleva 2; tel. (842) 57-43-33; e-mail director@mkosmos.kaluga.ru; internet www.museum.ru/gmik; f. 1967; contains K. E. Tsiolkovsky's scientific works, history of rocket technique and cosmonautics, large collection of objects relating to astronautics and rocket technology, including the first experimental rocket launched in 1933, the *Sputniks* and *Luniks*, models of orbital stations; library of 35,600 vols; Dir EVGENY KOUZIN.

Kazan

A. M. Gorky Literary Memorial Museum: 420015 Kazan, ul. Gorkogo 10; tel. (8432) 38-53-73; e-mail musgorky@mail.ru; exhibits illustrating Gorky's life in the flat where he lived and wrote.

National Museum of the Republic of Tatarstan: Tatarstan, 420111 Kazan, Kremlevskaya ul. 2; tel. (8432) 92-71-62; e-mail tatar_museum@mail.ru; internet www.tatar.museum.ru; f. 1894; history, archaeology, ethnography, natural resources and decorative applied art of Tatarstan, Russia and other countries; library of 12,000 vols; 54 brs; Gen. Man. G. S. MYKHANOV.

State Museum of Fine Arts of the Republic of Tatarstan: 420015 Kazan, ul. K. Marksa 64; tel. (8432) 36-69-21; internet www.kcn.ru/tat_en/culture/art_museum/home.htm; f. 1958; large collections of Russian, Western European and Soviet paintings; 10,000 exhibits; Dir ANATOLIY A. SLASTUNIN.

Tatar Historical Museum (House of V. I. Lenin): Tatarstan, Kazan, ul. Ulyanova 58; 10,000 exhibits including documents, photographs, works of art and other exhibits relating to Lenin's life.

Kirov

Kirov Victor and Apollinaris Vasnetsov Museum: 610000 Kirov, ul. K. Marksa 70; tel. (8332) 62-26-46; f. 1910; Russian and Western European sculpture, paintings, engravings and decorative arts; library of 14,000 vols; Dir ALLA A. NOSKOVA.

Kirovsk

Polar Alpine Botanical Garden Institute: 184230 Murmansk region, Kirovsk; tel. (81555) 63350; e-mail pabgi@aprec.ru; attached to Russian Acad. of Sciences; Dir Prof. VLADIMIR K. ZHIROV.

Klin

Tchaikovsky State Museum-Reserve: 141600 Klin, ul. Tchaikovskogo 48; tel. (49624) 5-81-96; e-mail gdmch@mail.ru; internet www.tchaikovsky-house-museum.ru; f. 1894; composer's last residence and first Russian musical museum; contains 217,886 documents and museum treasures associated with the life and work of Tchaikovsky and other Russian musicians; library of 57,375 vols; Dir GALINA I. BELONOVICH.

Komsomolsk-on-Amur

Museum of Fine Arts: 681000 Komsomolsk-on-Amur, pr. Mira 16; tel. (4217) 54-12-62; e-mail museum.kna@mail.ru; internet www.kmsmuseum.ru; f. 1966; 16,000 exhibits; Dir E. Y. TURCHINSKAYA.

Konchanskoe-Suvorovskoe

Suvorov Museum: 174435 Novogorodskaya oblast, Borovichskii raion, selo Konchanskoe-Suvorovskoe; tel. (81664) 9-85-33; internet www.museum.ru/m669; the museum features the main periods in the life of General A. V. Suvorov; Dir V. P. MALYSHEVA.

Kostroma

Kostroma State Museum–Reserve: Kostroma, pr. Mira 5; tel. (4942) 51-43-90; e-mail hudmuseum@kmtn.ru; f. 1913; 5,700 items; collecting, exhibitions, sales, scientific and historical Russian art research, art restoration; library of 6,410 vols; spec. collns of

Ancient Russian religious books and the work of Y. Chestnyakov; Dir N. V. PAVLICHKOVA.

Krasnoyarsk

Krasnoyarsk Regional Museum: 660049 Krasnoyarsk, ul. Dubrovinskogo 84; tel. (3912) 27-25-58; e-mail museum@kkkm.ru; internet www.kkkm.ru; f. 1958; Russian art (incl. icons), Russian pre-revolutionary applied art, Siberian folk art and Soviet art; painting, sculpture, graphic art, applied arts; library of 7,700 vols; Dir A. F. EFIMOVSKII; publ. *Surikov Readings* (2 a year).

Krasnoyarsk Museum Centre: 660097 Krasnoyarsk, pl. Mira 1; tel. (3912) 12-46-63; e-mail adm2123392@gmail.com; internet mira1.ru; f. 1987; Dir MIKHAIL SHUBSKY.

Kursk

Kursk Deineka Picture Gallery: 305016 Kursk, ul. Sovetskaya 3; tel. (4712) 54-87-21; e-mail gallery@sovtest.ru; internet www.deinekagallery.ru; f. 1935; Russian, Soviet and European painting and sculpture; library of 50,000 vols; Dir IGOR A. PRIPACHKIN.

Lermontovo

Lermontov State Museum 'Tarkhany': 442280 Penza oblast, Belinskii raion, Lermontovo; tel. (84153) 2-07-99; e-mail muslerm@sura.ru; internet www.tarhany.ru; f. 1939; life and work of M. Yu. Lermontov; library of 15,000 vols; Dir TAMARA MIKHAILOVNA MELNIKOVA; publ. *Tarkhansky Vestnik* (Bulletin, 1 a year).

Makhachkala

Dagestan Museum of Fine Arts: Makhachkala, ul. Markova 45; tel. (8722) 67-25-99; e-mail uchaltan@mail.ru; internet dmii.ru; f. 1958; 14,000 exhibits.

Maloyaroslavets

Maloyaroslavets Museum of Military History of 1812: 249096 Maloyaroslavets, Moskovskaya ul. 27; tel. (48431) 2-27-11; e-mail m627museum@rambler.ru; internet musey1812.ru; f. 1939; collection and study of exhibits of the 1812 war; library of 4,000 vols; Dir E. A. SHEBIKOVA; publ. *Nashe Nasledie* (Our Heritage, 6 a year).

Melikhovo

Chekhov, A. P. State Literature and Memorial Museum-Reserve: 142326 Melikhovo, Chekhovsky region, Moscow oblast; tel. (496) 723-64-53; e-mail melikhovo@mail.ru; internet www.chekhov-melikhovo.com; f. 1944; house where the writer lived and worked during 1892–99; library of 28,514 vols; Dir K. V. BOBKOV.

Miass

Natural Science Museum of the Ilmen State Reserve: 456301 Chelyabinsk oblast, Miass 1; tel. (35135) 5-48-90; e-mail founds@imin.urc.ac.ru; f. 1930; the museum shows the mineralogical resources of the Ilmen State Reserve, the grounds of which contain more than 250 minerals; library of 17,000 vols; Dir Dr S. N. NIKANDROV; publs *Trudy Ilmenskogo Zapovednika*, *Uralsky Mineralogichesky Sbornik*.

Moscow

A. N. Scriabin Memorial Museum: 119002 Moscow, Bol. Nikolopeskovsky Lane 11; tel. (499) 241-19-01; e-mail scriabinmuseum@mail.ru; f. 1919, opened in 1922 in flat where the composer lived and died; MSS, letters, Skryabin's personal library and magnetictape archive of Skryabin's compositions performed by the composer and famous artists;

excursions, lectures and concerts; library of 708 vols in Skryabin's personal and in scientific libraries; Dir LAZAREV.

Anuchin Institute and Museum of Anthropology of Moscow State University: 125009 Moscow Mokhovaya str. 11; tel. (495) 629-44-49; e-mail anthropos.msu@mail.ru; internet www.antropos.msu.ru; f. 1879; 5 depts: laboratories of anthropogenesis, human diversity, anthropo-ecology, human auxology, human morphology and the Museum of Anthropology; about 470,000 items; anthropology and archaeology of the Stone Age; collns from outstanding Russian explorers; Mousterian Man from Teshik-Tash and Staroseliye; Mesolithic burials from the Dnieper Region in the Ukraine; library of 30,000 vols; Dir Prof. Dr ALEXANDRA BUZHILOVA; publs *Antropologia*, *Vestnik MGU*.

Central House of Aviation and Cosmonautics: 125167 Moscow, Krasnoarmeiskaya 4; tel. (495) 612-54-61; e-mail cdaik@mail.ru; f. 1924; records the national devt of aeronautics and astronautics; contains original full-size aircraft, spacecraft, recovered space exploration vehicles, instruments, flight clothing, accessories of technical, historical and biographical interest; library of 15,800 vols; Dir P. F. VYALIKOV.

Central Museum of Armed Forces of the Russian Federation: 129110 Moscow, ul. Sovetskoi Armii 2; tel. (495) 681-18-80; e-mail cmvs-secretariat@mail.ru; internet www.cmaf.ru; f. 1919; military exhibits; library of 90,000 vols; Dir ALEXANDER K. NIKONOV.

Chekhov, A. P., House-Museum: 103001 Moscow, Sadovaya-Kudrinskaya 6; tel. (495) 291-61-54; e-mail muzchehov@rambler.ru; f. 1954; flat where the writer lived from 1886–1890; br. of the State Literature Museum.

Dostoevsky, F. M., Museum: 127473 Moscow, ul. Dostoyevskogo 2; tel. (495) 681-10-85; e-mail litmuz@arc.ru; f. 1928; affiliated to the State Literature Museum; exhibits illustrating Dostoevsky's life, organized in the flat where he lived until 16 years old; Dir GALINA B. PONOMAREVA.

Earth Science Museum of the Moscow State M. V. Lomonosov University: 119992 Moscow, GSP-2, MGU; tel. (495) 939-14-15; e-mail info@mes.msu.ru; internet www.museum.msu.ru; f. 1955; incl. material on the origin of the face of the earth, its geospheres, surface and underwater landscapes, earth crust, climates, waters, soils, plants, animals, economic resources; on the conservation, utilization and reconstruction of nature; complex geological and geographical characteristics of Russia and of the earth; science-teaching museum for students of the geological, geographical, biological soil science et al depts of Moscow Univ.; 48,000 samples; library of 5,000 vols in library; Dir Prof. A. V. SMUROV; publ. *Zhizn Zemli* (The Life of the Earth, 1 vol. every 1–2 years).

Fersman Mineralogical Museum: 119071 Moscow, Leninsky pr. 18, korp. 2; tel. (495) 954-39-00; e-mail mineral@fmm.ru; internet www.fmm.ru; f. 1716; attached to Russian Acad. of Sciences; 150,000 mineral samples from throughout the world; library of 16,700 vols; Dir Prof. V. K. GARANIN; publ. *New Data on Minerals* (1 a year).

'Glinka, M. I.', State Central Museum of Musical Culture: 125047 Moscow, ul. Fadeeva 4; tel. (495) 972-32-37; e-mail info@glinka.museum; internet www.museum.ru/glinka; f. 1943; based on the Museum of the Moscow Conservatoire; collects archives, MSS and memorabilia; musical instruments; musical iconography; records and tape recordings; music, books, posters, programmes—in all, 800,000 items; exhibits: musical instruments of the world; Russian musical culture; Dir-Gen. A. D. PANIUSHKIN.

Gogol, N. V., House-Museum and Gogol Study Centre: 121019 Moscow, Nikitsky bul. 7; tel. (495) 291-15-50; e-mail vik@systel.ru; f. 1974; exhibits illustrating life and work of Gogol; library of 200,000 vols, Gogol spec. colln of 600 vols and MSS; Dir VERA P. VIKULOVA.

Gorky, A. M., Memorial Museum: Moscow 121069, Malaya Nikitskaya ul. 6/2; tel. (495) 290-05-35; f. 1965 in the house where the author lived; contains Gorky's private library of 10,000 vols, and his collection of Oriental arts (ivory); Dir L. P. BYKOVTSEVA.

Gorky, A. M., Museum: 121069 Moscow, ul. Povarskaya 25A; tel. (495) 291-51-30; f. 1937; 44,500 items, including literary and photographic documents, works of art, memorabilia; Dir L. P. BYKOVTSEVA.

Leo Tolstoy State Museum: 119021 Moscow, ul. Prechistenka 11/8; tel. (499) 766-93-28; e-mail tolstoy@museum.comsat.ru; internet www.tolstoymuseum.ru; f. 1911; MSS section contains 400,000 items of Tolstoy's writings and nearly 600,000 MSS and archive material on Tolstoy and his circle; library of 76,800 works by or about Tolstoy; nearly 87,000 newspaper cuttings, and over 42,000 exhibits in the form of painting, sculpture, photographs, etc.; 4 brs: Literary Museum, urban estate 'Khamovniki', exhibition hall and Leo Tolstoy museum 'Astapovo'; Dir VITALY REMIZOV.

Moscow Kremlin Museums: 103073 Moscow, Kremlin; tel. (495) 695-89-23; e-mail head@kremlin.museum.ru; internet www.kreml.ru; f. 1806; monuments built from late 15th to 20th centuries; incl. cathedrals-museums: Assumption Cathedral, Archangel Cathedral, Annunciation Cathedral, Church of Deposition of Robe of the Holy Virgin, Palace of Patriarch of 17th century with Church of Twelve Apostles, bell tower of Ivan the Great with the belfry and the State Armoury Chamber-treasury; collns of State Historical and Cultural Museum-Preserve comprise more than 60,000 historical, cultural and artistic monuments; library of 49,000 vols; Dir YELENA GAGARINA..

Attached Sites:

Armoury: 103073 Moscow, Kremlin; f. 1857; Museum since 1806; 3,500 artworks: ancient state regalia, diplomatic gifts to Russian Tsars, vestments of Russian Church hierarchs of 14th to 18th centuries, coronation suits of Russian Emperors and dresses of Empresses, artworks by Russian gold and silversmiths of 12th to 20th centuries, monuments of Byzantine and Western European art of 15th to 19th centuries, ceremonial weapons, and ancient carriages.

Kremlin Cathedrals: 103073 Moscow, Kremlin; The cathedrals around the Cathedral Square (Sobornaya ploshchad) include, among others, the following: Cathedral of the Assumption (f. 1479); icons of the 14th to 17th centuries; throne of Ivan the Terrible; Cathedral of the Annunciation (f. 1489); iconostasis by leading artists of the 14th to 15th centuries. Archangel Cathedral (1508); tombs of Ivan Kalita and other Russian Grand Dukes and Czars. Rizpolozhenskii Cathedral (f. 1485). Cathedral of the Twelve Apostles and Patriarch's Palace; 17th-century items of applied decorative art.

Main Botanical Garden 'N. V. Tsitsin': 127276 Moscow, Botanicheskaya ul. 4; tel. (495) 977-90-44; e-mail info@gbsad.ru; internet www.gbsad.ru; f. 1945; attached to

Russian Acad. of Sciences; br. in Cheboksary; Dir Dr ALEXANDER S. DEMIDOV; publs *Bulletin* (2 a year), *Newsletter* (2 a year).

Marx-Engels Museum: c/o Russian State Archive of Modern History, 103132 Moscow, ul. Ilinka 12; f. 1962; 2,000 exhibits descriptive of the lives of Marx and Engels; Dir V. N. KUZNETSOV.

Moscow Art Theatre Museum: 125009 Moscow, pr. Kamergersky 3A; tel. (495) 692-38-66; e-mail muzmxt@rambler.ru; internet www.mxat.ru/museum; f. 1923; Dir MARFA BUBNOVA..

Attached Museums:

K. Stanislavsky's Memorial House: 125009 Moscow, pr. Leontievsky 6; tel. (495) 629-28-55; f. 1948; deals with Stanislavsky's work and the theatrical career of People's Artist, M. P. Lilina.

V. Nemirovitch-Dantchenko's Memorial Apartment: 125009 Moscow, pr. Glinichevsky 5/7, kv. 52; tel. (495) 650-53-91; f. 1944; illustrating career of Nemirovich-Danchenko.

Moscow State University Museum of Zoology: 125009 Moscow, ul. Bol. Nikitskaya 6; tel. (495) 203-64-93; e-mail zmmu@zmmu.msu.ru; internet zmmu.msu.ru; f. 1791; systematics, speciation, zoogeography, fauna research, phylogenetics; library of 190,000 vols; Dir Dr OLGA L. ROSSOLIMO; publs *Archives* (1 a year), *Zoologicheskie Issledovania (Zoological Research)*.

Museum of Frontier Guards: Moscow, ul. Bol. Bronnaya 23; 110,000 exhibits featuring the history of Soviet frontier guards.

Museum of the History of the City of Moscow: 103012 Moscow, Novaya pl. 12; tel. (495) 924-31-45; f. 1896; Dir G. I. VEDEZNIKOVA.

Museum of the Palaeontological Institute: 117647 Moscow, Profsoyuznaya ul. 123; tel. (495) 339-05-77; e-mail admin@paleo.ru; internet www.paleo.ru; f. 1930; attached to Russian Acad. of Sciences; library of 20,000 vols; Dir A. YU. ROZANOV.

Museum of the State Academic Malyi Theatre: 103009 Moscow, Malyi teatr, Teatralnaya pl. 1/6; tel. (495) 921-85-48; e-mail info@maly.ru; f. 1932, being developed out of 1927 exhibition; illustrates and studies history of the Theatre; Dir YU. M. STRUTINSKAYA.

Nikolai Rubinstein Museum: 125009 Moscow, Bol. Nikitskaya 13; tel. (495) 629-90-98; e-mail museumrub@mail.ru; internet www.mosconsv.ru; f. 1992; colln incl. musical instruments and portraits and sculptures of Russian composers; documents, photographs, phonographs, antique furniture; Dir Dr EVGENIA GUREVICH.

Novodevichii Monastery Museum: 119435 Moscow, Novodevichii pr. 1; tel. (495) 246-22-01; e-mail m337@mail.museum.ru; internet www.shm.ru/filials/novodev/fil_nov.htm; Smolensky Cathedral (1524) and other monuments of Russian architecture form the architectural ensemble of the monastery; Russian fine and decorative art (16th and 17th centuries); Dir IRINA G. BORISENKO.

Obraztsov Puppet Museum of the Central State Academic Puppet Theatre: 123473 Moscow Sadovaya-Samotechnaya ul. 3; tel. (495) 699-55-53; e-mail museum@obraztsov.ru; internet www.puppet.ru/museum; f. 1937; Central Puppet Theatre; 5,600 dolls from 50 countries; puppet theatres of the fmr USSR and many other countries; colln of cartoons, sketches, MSS and other documents; library of 15,000 books; Vice-Dir Dr BORIS GOLDOVSKY.

Permanent Tchaikovsky Exhibition in the Tchaikovsky Concert Hall: 125047

Moscow, pl. Triumfalnaya 4/31; exhibits of the composer's life and works.

Petrographic Museum: 109017 Moscow, Staromonetnyi per. 35; tel. (495) 230-82-92; internet www.museum.ru/m417; f. 1934; Dir V. A. PAVLOV.

Pharmaceutical Museum of the Central Drug Research Institute: 117418 Moscow, ul. Krasikova 34; tel. (495) 120-91-51; unique collection of about 6,000 items on the history of pharmacy in Russia and the fmr USSR; Dir B. M. SALO.

Polytechnic Museum: 101000 Moscow, Novaya Sq. 3/4; tel. (495) 625-06-14; e-mail info@polymus.ru; internet www.polymus.ru; f. 1872; over 200,000 exhibits; features history and latest devts in science and technology; belongs to the Ministry of Culture; library: 35m. vols; Dir-Gen. BORIS SALTYKOV.

Rublev, Andrei, Central Museum of Ancient Russian Culture and Art: 107120 Moscow, Andronevskaya pl. 10; tel. (495) 678-14-67; e-mail rublevmuseum@aha.ru; internet www.rublev-museum.ru; f. 1947; Russian art, icons, applied art, MSS, old printed books; library of 23,000 vols; Dir Dr G. V. POPOV.

Shchukin, B. V., Museum-Room: Moscow, Flat 11, ul. Shchukina 8; contains material he had about him during his lifetime as a great actor at the Vakhtangov Theatre.

Shchusev State Museum of Architecture: 121019 Moscow, Vozdvizhenka 5/25; tel. (495) 691-21-09; e-mail info@muar.ru; internet www.muar.ru; f. 1934; study, collection, care and popularization of historical architecture, outstanding contemporary work, monumental sculpture and painting; collection and care of documents on architecture and town planning; over 70,000 sheets of architectural drawings; over 300,000 negatives and 400,000 photographs of architectural monuments throughout the world; library of 50,000 vols; Dir IRINA KOROBINA; Curator I. V. SEDOVA.

State Academic Bolshoi Theatre Museum: 103009 Moscow, Bolshoi Teatr, Okhotnyi Ryad 8/2; tel. (495) 292-00-25; f. 1920; objects: documentation of the work of the Bolshoi Theatre, collection of materials and documents on its history and work, study of history of the theatre; Dir V. I. ZARUBIN.

State Central Museum of Contemporary Russian History: 125009 Moscow, Tverskaya ul. 21; tel. (495) 299-52-17; e-mail 9055.g23@g23.relcom.ru; internet www.sovr.ru; f. 1917; social and political history of Russia since 1850; library of 360,000 vols and 825,000 periodicals; Dir Dr TAMARA SHUMNAYA; publ. *Trudy* (Proceedings).

State Central Theatrical Museum 'A. A. Bakhrushin': 115054 Moscow, ul. Bakhrushina 31/12; tel. (495) 953-48-48; e-mail gctm@gctm.ru; internet www.gctm.ru; f. 1894; collects, houses, studies and exhibits varied materials on history and theory of theatre; approx. 1.5m. exhibits; archives of original MSS of Ostrovsky, Lensky, Stanislavsky, Meyerhold, etc.; library of 120,000 vols; Dir-Gen. DMITRY V. RODIONOV.

State Darwin Museum: 117292 Moscow, Vavilova 57; tel. (495) 135-33-76; e-mail darwin@museum.ru; internet www.darwin.museum.ru; f. 1907; natural history and evolution; total holdings of 360,065 items; library of 30,000 vols; Dir A. I. KLUKINA.

State Historical Museum: 103012 Moscow, Krasnaya pl. 1/2; tel. (495) 692-37-31; e-mail shkurko@shm.ru; internet www.shm.ru; f. 1872; 4.5m. exhibits covering Russian history from pre-history to the present; colln of birch-bark writings; library of 229,000 vols, 29,000 MSS, 25,000 rare books; Dir-Gen. ALEXANDER

SHKURKO; publs *Ezhegodnik GIM, Numizma-ticheskii sbornik* (irregular), *Trudy GIM*.

State Literature Museum: 103051 Moscow, Petrovka ul. 28; tel. (495) 921-38-57; f. 1934; the museum is a research and educational centre that collects, studies and publishes material on the history of Russian and Soviet literature; br. (museums of Lermontov, Herzen, Dostoevsky, Chekhov, Tolstoy, Pasternak, Prishvin, Aksakov and Bryusov); library of 250,000 vols; Gen. Dir NATALYA V. SHAKHALOVA.

State Museum of Ceramics (Country-seat Kuskovo): 111402 Moscow Yunosti ul. 2; tel. (495) 370-01-50; internet www.kuskovo.ru; large colln of Russian art: paintings, furniture, porcelain, pottery; collection of Western European art, tapestries, furniture, paintings, porcelain, pottery; Dir YELENA S. YERITSYAN.

State Museum of Oriental Art: 107120 Moscow, Nikitsky bul. 12A; tel. (495) 291-96-14; e-mail finearts@artsmuseum.ru; internet www.orientalart.ru; f. 1918; large collection of Middle and Far Eastern art, art of the fmr Soviet Central Asian Republics and Transcaucasia, carpets, fabrics, ceramics, etc.; Dir-Gen. V. A. NABACHIKOV.

State Pushkin Museum: 119034 Moscow, ul. Prechistenka 12/2; tel. (495) 202-43-54; f. 1958; 200,000 exhibits; maintains br. in Pushkin's former home (Arbat 53); library of 51,000 vols; Dir E. BOGATYREV.

State Pushkin Museum of Fine Arts: 121019 Moscow, Volkhonka 12; tel. (495) 697-95-78; e-mail finearts@gmii.museum.ru; internet www.arts-museum.ru; f. 1912; about 558,000 items of ancient Eastern, Graeco-Roman, Byzantine, European and American art; numismatic colln of 200,000 items; library of 200,000 vols; Dir MARINA LOSHAK DEVOVNA; Pres. IRINA ANTONOVA ALEXANDROVNA.

State Tretyakov Gallery: 117049 Moscow, Lavrushinskii per. 10; tel. (495) 230-77-88; e-mail tretyakov@tretyakov.ru; internet www.tretyakov.ru; f. 1856; collection of 130,000 Russian icons and works of Russian and Soviet painters, sculptors and graphic artists since 11th century; also 3,200 items from the former Pyotr Zakharov Fine Arts Museum in Grozny; new building at Krymskiy Val houses an exhibition of Russian art from 20th century; Dir VALENTIN A. RODIONOV.

State V. V. Mayakovsky Museum: 101000 Moscow, pr. Serova 3/6; tel. (095) 921-93-87; f. 1974 in the bldg where Mayakovsky lived 1919–30; MSS, documentary material, notebooks, memorial items; library and reading room with c. 200,000 vols, incl. periodicals; Dir S. E. STRIZHNIKOVA.

S. T. Morozov Folk-Art Museum: 103009 Moscow, Leontyevskii per. 7; tel. (495) 290-52-22; f. 1885; three sections devoted to (a) handicrafts connected with peasant daily life; (b) applied arts both ancient and contemporary; (c) experimental decorative applied art; about 800,000 exhibits; under the jurisdiction of the Russian Council of Local Industries; Dir G. A. YAKOVLEVA.

Timiryazev, K. A., Apartment Museum: 103009 Moscow, Romanovski per. 2, str. 2, kv. 29; tel. (495) 202-80-64; f. 1942; cultural and historical memorial to K. A. Timiryazev; 7,545 exhibits and archives on his life and work; library: personal library of 4,871 vols; Dir A. A. DRUCHEK.

Timiryazev State Museum of Biology: 123242 Moscow, Mal. Gruzinskaya 15; tel. (499) 252-55-42; e-mail gbmt@gbmt.ru; internet www.gbmt.ru; f. 1922; collns on botany, ecology, genetics, palaeontology,

physiology, zoology and history of science; library of 70,000 vols; Dir E. A. CHUSOVA.

Tolstoy House Museum: 119021 Moscow, ul. Lva Tolstogo 21; tel. (495) 246-94-44; e-mail info@tolstoymuseum.ru; internet tolstoymuseum.ru; rooms arranged as they were when the author lived there; 4,200 exhibits; Dir A. V. SALOMATIN.

Vakhtangov Theatre Museum: 119002 Moscow, Arbat St 26; tel. (499) 241-37-65; history of the Vakhtangov Theatre; Dir I. L. SERGEEVA.

Vernadsky State Geological Museum: 103009 Moscow, Mokhovaya ul. 11, korp. 11; tel. (495) 692-09-43; e-mail info@sgm.ru; internet www.sgm.ru; f. 1755; attached to Russian Acad. of Sciences; Dir Acad. YURI MALYSHEV.

Zhukovskii, N. E., Memorial Museum: 107005 Moscow, ul. Radio 17; tel. (495) 267-50-54; 25,000 items feature the work of N. E. Zhukovskii, and Soviet contributions to aviation and astronautics; Dir V. I. MASLOV.

Nalchik

Kabarda-Balkar Art Museum: Nalchik, pr. V. I. Lenina 35; 3,500 exhibits; Dir I. Z. BATASHOV.

Nizhnii Novgorod

Nizhnii Novgorod History and Architecture Museum: 603005 Nizhny Novgorod, Verkhnevolzhskaya 7; tel. (831) 419-64-06; 160,000 exhibits incl. collns of archaeology, featuring the history of the Central Volga area since ancient times.

Nizhnii Novgorod State Museum of Art: 603082 Nizhnii Novgorod, korp. 3 Kremlya; tel. (8312) 39-08-55; e-mail art@museum.nnov.ru; internet www.museum.nnov.ru/art; f. 1896; Dir VALENTINA N. KRIVOVA.

State A. M. Gorky Museum of Literature: 603155 Nizhnii Novgorod, ul. Minina 26; tel. (8312) 36-15-29; e-mail danco6@yandex.ru; internet www.museum.nnov.ru/danco; f. 1928; 102,000 exhibits, illustrating the life and work of the writer; library of 40,000 vols; Dir T. A. RIZHOVA.

Novocherkassk

Novocherkassk Museum of the History of the Don Cossacks: 346430 Rostov oblast, Novocherkassk, Atamanskaya ul. 38; tel. (86352) 4-80-59; e-mail m838@mail.museum.ru; internet www.doncossacks.ru; f. 1899; deals with the traditions and exploits of the Don Cossacks; collections of porcelain and painting; library of 17,000 vols; Dir SVETLANA A. SEDINKO.

Novosibirsk

Central Siberian Botanical Garden: 630090 Novosibirsk, Zolotodolinskaya ul. 101; tel. (383) 330-41-01; e-mail botgard@ngs.ru; internet csbg.narod.ru; f. 1946; attached to Russian Acad. of Sciences; Dir Prof. V. P. SEDELNIKOV.

Omsk

Omsk Museum of Fine Arts named after M. A. Vrubel: 644024 Omsk, ul. Lenina 23; tel. (381) 220-00-45; e-mail vrubel_omsk@mail.ru; internet vrubel.ru; f. 1924; 22,000 exhibits; Dir A. A. GERZON.

Orel

Turgenev, I. S., State Literary Museum: 302000 Orel, ul. Turgeneva 11; tel. (8622) 6-27-37; f. 1918; library of 60,000 vols; Dir V. V. SAFRONOVA..

Branch museums:

Andreev Leonid, House Museum: Orel, Pushkarnaya 41; tel. (4862) 76-48-24; f. 1991; Man. O. V. VOLOGINA.

Bunin Museum: 302000 Orel, Oktyabrsky pr. 1; tel. (8622) 6-07-74; e-mail mail@museum.ru; f. 1991; Man. I. A. KOSTOMAROVA.

Granovsky, T. N., Museum: Orel, ul. 7 Noyabrya 24; tel. (8622) 6-34-65; f. 1985; devoted to public figures born in Orel; Man. E. A. IVUSHKINA.

Leskov, N. S., House Museum: 301028 Orel, ul. Oktyabrskaya 9; tel. (8622) 6-33-04; f. 1974; Man. L. S. KAMYSHALOVA.

Literary Museum: 302000 Orel, ul. Turgeneva 11; tel. (8622) 6-35-28; f. 1957; devoted to writers born in Orel; Man. L. E. URAKOVA.

Orenburg

Orenburg Fine Art Museum: Orenburg, ul. Pravdy 6; 3,500 items; Dir L. B. POPOVA.

Palekh

State Museum of Palekh Art: 155620 Ivanovo oblast, Palekh ul. Bakanova 50; tel. (49334) 2-20-54; e-mail m1571@mail.museum.ru; internet www.museum.ru/m1571; f. 1934; library of 16,000 books, photographs and film docs; Dir ALEVTINA G. STRAKHOVA.

Pavlovsk

The State Museum 'Pavlovsk': 196621 St Peterburg Pavlovsk, ul. Sadovaya 20; tel. (812) 452-21-55; e-mail palace@pavlovskmuseum.ru; internet www.pavlovskmuseum.ru; f. 1918; many examples of Russian garden architecture, antique sculpture and sculpture by 18th-century Italian and French masters; European paintings of the 16th to 19th centuries, Russian portraits of the 18th century, Russian decorative art of the 18th and 19th centuries; furniture, porcelain, bronzes and textiles; library of 17,000 vols; Dir N. S. TRETYAKOV.

Penza

Penza Picture Gallery: 660026 Penza, Sovetskaya ul. 3; tel. (8412) 66-64-00; f. 1892; library of 3,200 vols; 7,700 exhibits; also 3 memorial museums; Dir VALERYI SAZONOV.

Perm

Perm State Art Gallery: 614000 Perm, Komsomolskyi Ave 4; tel. (342) 212-95-24; e-mail pghg7@yandex.ru; internet www.permmuseum.com; f. 1922; colln management (conservation, restoration, art expertise); academic work (research, exhibitions, confs, seminars, publs, scholarly exchange); information technologies; devt and fund raising, PR support; colln stocks 50,000 works of art of the 15th to 21st centuries; Russian and foreign art: paintings, graphic, decorative and applied art objects; the Stroganovs school icons and Perm wood carving cult sculptures; library of 28,900 vols; Dir JULYA TAVRIZYAN.

Petrodvorets

Peterhof State Museum Reserve: 198516 St Petersburg, Petrodvorets, ul. Rasvodnaya 2; tel. (812) 427-74-25; e-mail admin@peterhof.org; internet www.peterhof.org; f. 1918; 18th- to 20th-century architecture, painting and landscape gardening; 18th- and 19th-century sculpture, furniture, porcelain, clocks and jewellery; library of 21,000 books, spec. colln of 2,000 rare books, 7,000 Russian book-plates, 1,300 printed graphics; Dir V. V. ZNAMENOV.

Petrozavodsk

Karelian Museum of Fine Arts: 185035 Republic of Karelia, Petrozavodsk, pr. K.

Marksa 8; tel. (8142) 78-37-13; e-mail info@ artmuseum.karelia.ru; internet artmuseum .karelia.ru; f. 1960; Karelian iconic paintings from 15th to 19th centuries, Karelian folk art, modern Karelian art, Russian art since 18th century, western European art; library of 21,000 vols; CEO NATALIA I. VAVILOVA.

Karelian State Regional Museum: 185035 Republic of Karelia, Petrozavodsk, pl. Lenina 1; tel. (8142) 78-02-40; e-mail kgkm@karelia.ru; internet karelia.ru/ ~kgkm; f. 1871; history, economy, science, culture, and natural history of the area; 3 brs; library of 25,700 vols; Dir ELENA ZARINA; publs *Museum Herald* (1 a year), *Museums of Karelia* (4 a year), *Vestnik* (1 a year).

Kizhi State Open-Air Museum of History, Architecture and Ethnography: 185035 Republic of Karelia, Petrozavodsk, 10A, Kirov Sq.; tel. (8142) 78-32-52; e-mail olga@kizhi.karelia.ru; internet kizhi.karelia .ru; f. 1961; wooden architecture, history, ethnography, early Russian and Karelian painting and folklore; library of 10,227 vols; Dir E. V. AVERYANOVA.

Pushkin

Tsarskoe Selo State Museum: 189690 Leningrad oblast, Tsarskoe Selo, Sadovaya ul. 7; tel. (812) 466-66-69; e-mail tzar@spb .cityline.ru; internet www.tzar.ru; f. 1918; former imperial summer residence, incl. Catherine and Alexander Palaces; park and garden architecture and 100 architectural ornaments from 18th to 20th centuries, esp. in Baroque and Classical styles; library of 18,041 vols including collection of rare books of 2,375 vols; Dir I. P. SAUTOV.

Pushkinskie Gory

State Memorial Museum-Reserve of A. S. Pushkin 'Mikhailovskoye': 181370 Pskovskaya oblast, Pushkinskie Gory, Novorzhevskaya 21; tel. (81146) 2-19-50; e-mail pgmuseum@ellink.ru; internet www .pushkin.ellink.ru; f. 1922; 33,000 exhibits on the life in exile of the poet, Aleksandr Pushkin (1799–1837); the preserve incl. the family lands at Mikhailovskoe, Trigorskoe and Petrovskoe, the ancient towns of Voronich and Savkina Gorka and the grave of Pushkin; library of 21,000 vols; Dir GEORGY VASILEVICH.

Pyatigorsk

State Lermontov Literary Memorial Museum: Pyatigorsk, Lermontovskaya ul. 4; tel. (87933) 5-27-10; f. 1912; exhibits feature the life and work of M. Yu. Lermontov in the Caucasus; library of 14,000 vols; Dir L. MOROZOVA.

Roslavl

Roslavl Historical Museum: 216500 Roslavl, ul. Proletarskaya 63; tel. (481) 344-04-06; e-mail roslavlmuseum@mail.ru; f. 1920; colln tracing the history, economy and culture of Russian people from the earliest times; library of 1,300 vols; Dir M. I. IVANOVA.

Rostov-on-Don

Rostov Museum of Fine Art: 344002 Rostov-on-Don, ul. Pushkinskaya 115; tel. (8632) 69-10-88; e-mail romii@mail.ru; f. 1938; old Russian, Soviet and foreign descriptive art; library of 16,697 vols; Dir KRUZE SVETLANA VALEREVNA; publ. *Khudozhnik*.

Ryazan

Ryazan Kremlin Historical and Architectural Museum Reserve: Ryazan, Kreml 118; tel. (0912) 27-60-65; e-mail root@riamz .ryazan.ru; internet www.ryazankreml.ru; f. 1884; over 220,000 items describing the history, culture and art of the peoples of Russia; Dir LUDMILA MAKSIMOVA; publs *Yakhontovsky's Readings* (every 2 years), *Scientific Works* (every 5 years).

Ryazan Regional Art Museum: Ryazan, Svoboda St 57; tel. (4912) 28-04-24; e-mail dirmuzryaz@mail.ryazan.ru; f. 1913; old Russian (15th to 20th centuries), European (16th to 19th centuries) and Soviet art; library of 17,000 vols; Dir M. A. KOTOVA.

St Petersburg

Acad. F. N. Chernyshev Central Scientific Research Geological and Prospecting Museum (CNIGR museum): 199106 St Petersburg, Vasilevskii ostrov, Srednii pr. 74; tel. (812) 321-53-99; e-mail cnigr_museum@vsegei.ru; internet www .vsegei.com; f. 1882, opened 1930; attached to A. P. Karpinsky Russia Geological Research Institute (VSEGEI); 1m. geological specimens incl. examples of mineral deposits from all over the fmr USSR; monographic and palaeontological collns; popularization of geological knowledge; Dir Dr ALEKSEY SOKOLOV.

Botanical Museum: 197376 St Petersburg, ul. Prof. Popova 2; tel. (812) 234-84-39; e-mail bot_museum@mail.ru; internet www.binran .ru/structure/museum; f. 1823; attached to Komarov, V. L., Botanical Institute of the Russian Academy of Sciences; 60,000 specimens; collns incl. carpology, dendrology, economic botany, palaeobotany; photo archive; Dir L. YU. BUDANTSEV.

Central Museum of Railway Transport of Russia: St Petersburg, Sadovaya ul. 50; e-mail cmrt1813@yandex.ru; internet www .railroad.ru/cmrt; f. 1813; traces the history of railway transport in Russia; incl. unique colln of miniature models of engines and carriages; Dir G. ZAKREVSKAYA.

Central Naval Museum: 199034 St Petersburg, Birzhevaya pl. 4; tel. (812) 303-85-11; e-mail info@navalmuseum.ru; internet navalmuseum.ru; f. 1709; relics and other materials from the Russian and Soviet Navies; depts of history of the Russian Navy, history of the Soviet Navy, history of the Navy in the 1941–45 period, history of the Navy in the post-war period; responsible for Kronstadt Fortress, cruiser Aurora and submarine Narodovolets; library of 16,000 vols; Dir E. N. KORCHAGIN.

Dokuchaev Central Soil Museum: St Petersburg, Birzhevoi pr-d 6; tel. (812) 328-54-02; e-mail soilmuseum@bk.ru; internet www.soil-museum.ru; f. 1904; about 5,000 specimens of soil from nearly every soil zone in the world; library of 14,000 vols (Dokuchaev personal library); Dir Dr B. F. APARIN.

Dostoevsky Memorial Museum: 191002 St Petersburg, Kuznechnyi per. 5/2; tel. (812) 571-40-31; e-mail ashimbaeva@md.spb.ru; internet www.md.spb.ru; f. 1971; the house where the author lived 1878–81; MSS, documentary material, memorial items; library of 23,000 vols; Dir Dr NATALIA ASHIMBAEVA.

Literary Museum of the Institute of Russian Literature: 199034 St Petersburg, Pushkinskii Dom, nab. Makarova 4; tel. (812) 328-05-02; e-mail irliran@mail.ru; internet www.pushkinhouse.spb.ru; f. 1905; based on the material of the Pushkin Anniversary Exhibition of 1899; contains 95,000 exhibits and over 120,000 items of reference material; 7 halls containing permanent exhibitions devoted to G. R. Derzhavin, A. S. Pushkin, M. Y. Lermontov, N. V. Gogol, F. M. Dostoevsky, I. S. Turgenev, L. N. Tolstoy and other Russian writers and poets; Dir L. G. AGAMALIAN.

Lomonosov, M. V., Museum: 199164 St Petersburg, Universitetskaya nab. 3; tel. (812) 328-10-11; internet www.kunstkamera .ru/en/museums_structure/research_departments/mv_lomonosov_museum; f. 1947; attached to Museum of Anthropology and Ethnography (Kunstkamera); 3,000 exhibits; Head Prof. MARGARITA F. KHARTONOVICH.

Military-Historical Museum of Artillery, Engineer and Signal Corps: 197046 St Petersburg, Aleksandrovsky park 7; tel. (812) 238-47-04; e-mail artillery@yandex.ru; internet www.artillery-museum.ru; f. 1703; library of 115,000 vols; Chief Dr VALERII MIKHAILOVICH KRYLOV.

Military Medical Museum: 191180 St Petersburg, Lazaretny per. 2; tel. (812) 315-53-58; e-mail m170@mail.museum.ru; internet www.museum.ru/m170; f. 1942; history of Russian and Soviet military medicine; library: research library of 50,000 vols, also collections of rare books; 60m. archive docs on citizens of 45 countries in Europe, Asia, America and Africa; Dir Prof. Dr A. A. BUDKO; publs *History of Medicine in St Petersburg* (1 a year), *History of Military Medicine in Russia* (1 a year), *Memorial Dates of Military Medicine* (1 a year), *Military Medicine Abroad* (6 a year), *Review of the History of Military Medicine* (1 a year).

Mining Museum of the St Petersburg State Mining Institute (Technical University): 199106 St Petersburg, 21-ya liniya 2; tel. (812) 328-84-29; e-mail rectorat@spmi .ru; internet www.gorny-ins.ru; f. 1773; specimens of minerals, rocks, ores, fossils, meteorites; historical mining techniques illustrated by models of the 19th and early 20th century; colln of edged weapons from the Zlatoust Arms Factory; Dir J. POLYARNAYA.

Museum of Sculpture: St Petersburg, pl. A. Nevskogo 1; largest collection of Russian sculpture, collection and care of documents on architecture and town planning; over 150,000 sheets of architectural drawings; Dir N. H. BELOVA.

Museum of the Gorky Bolshoi Drama Theatre: St Petersburg, ul. Fontanka 65.

Museum of the History of Religion: 191186 St Petersburg, Kazanskaya pl. 2; f. 1932; 186,000 exhibits on Russian Orthodox Church, Roman Catholic and other Christian churches, Judaism, Islam and Buddhism; library of 170,000 vols; Dir S. A. KUCHINSKY; publ. *Theses* (1 a year).

Museum of the St Petersburg Mussorgsky Academic Opera and Ballet Theatre: St Petersburg, pl. Iskusstv 1; tel. (812) 595-43-13; internet www.reserve.sp.ru; f. 1935; colln of materials (sketches, posters, photographs, costumes) depicting the history of the theatre and its work; Dir M. KORTUNOVA.

Museum of Zoology: 199034 St Petersburg, Universitetskaya nab. 1; tel. (812) 328-01-12; e-mail museum@zin.ru; internet www.zin.ru; f. 1832; over 30,000 items describe the origin and evolution of the animal world; attached to Zoological Institute of the Russian Acad. of Sciences (see under Research Institutes); Chief ALEXEI TIKHONOV; publ. *Proceedings of the Zoological Institute*.

National Pushkin Museum: 191186 St Petersburg, nab. Moiki 12; tel. (812) 571-38-01; e-mail vmp@museumpushkin.ru; internet www.museumpushkin.ru; f. 1879; under supervision of Ministry of Culture; exhibits illustrating the life and work of the poet and his epoch; Dir S. M. NEKRASOV..

Annexes:

Lyceum Museum: 196600 Pushkin, Sadovaya 2; tel. (812) 476-64-11; e-mail vmp@ museumpushkin.ru; internet www .museumpushkin.ru; f. 1949; Chief Curator M. N. PETAI.

Main Literary Exposition–Life and Creative Work of Alexander Pushkin: 191186 St Petersburg, nab. Moiki 12; tel. (812) 314-00-07; e-mail vmp@museumpushkin.ru; internet www.museumpushkin.ru; f. 1999; Chief Curator N. L. PETROVA.

Museum of Derzhavin and Russian Literature of the 18th Century: 198005 St Petersburg, nab. Fontanki 118; tel. (812) 713-07-17; e-mail vmp@museumpushkin.ru; internet www.museumpushkin.ru; f. 2003; Chief Curator N. P. MOROZOVA.

Nekrasov Apartment Museum: 191104 St Petersburg, Liteiny pr. 36; tel. (812) 272-01-65; e-mail vmp@museumpushkin.ru; internet www.museumpushkin.ru; f. 1946; Chief Curator E. YU. GLEVENKO.

Pushkin Apartment Museum: 191186 St Petersburg, nab. Moiki 12; tel. (812) 117-35-31; e-mail vmp@museumpushkin.ru; internet www.museumpushkin.ru; f. 1925; Chief Curator G. M. SEDOVA.

Pushkin Country House Museum: 196607 Pushkin, Pushkinskaya ul. 2; tel. (812) 476-69-90; tel. (812) 315-73-79; e-mail vmp@museumpushkin.ru; internet www.museumpushkin.ru; f. 1958; Chief Curator T. I. GALKINA.

Permanent Exhibition of Musical Instruments: St Petersburg, 5 Isaakievskaya pl.; about 3,000 exhibits, including a large collection of instruments made by outstanding Russian and foreign craftsmen: Batov, Leman, Nalimov, Krasnoshchekov, Fedorov, Amati, Villaume, Tilke and Denner.

Peter the Great Museum of Anthropology and Ethnography (Kunstkamera): 199034 St Petersburg, Universitetskaya nab. 3; tel. (812) 328-07-12; e-mail info@kunstkamera.ru; internet www.kunstkamera.ru; f. 1714; attached to Russian Acad. of Sciences; ethnographical, archaeological, and anthropological material on the native peoples of all continents; anatomical colln; scientific instruments; Dir Prof. YURI K. CHISTOV; publs *Etnograficheskiye Tetradi* (1 a year), *Forum for Anthropology and Culture* (2 in Russian, 1 in English and 2 online), *Kuryer* (2 a year), *Mauscripta Orientalia* (4 a year), *Sbornik MAE* (1 a year).

Popov, A. S., Central Museum of Communications: 190000 St Petersburg, Pochtamtskaya ul. 7; tel. (812) 315-48-73; e-mail bakayutova@telecommuseum.spb.ru; internet www.rustelecom-museum.ru; f. 1872; over 8m. items representing the development of all types of communication used in Russia and the former USSR; includes the national postage stamp collection; Dir L. BAKAYUTOVA.

Russian Ethnographic Museum: St Petersburg, Inzhenernaya ul. 4/1; tel. (812) 210-47-68; e-mail rme@infopro.spb.ru; internet www.ethnomuseum.ru; f. 1902; 150,000 photographs; library of 105,000 vols; Dir V. M. GRUSMAN; publ. *Collected Articles* (2 a year).

Russian State Museum of the Arctic and the Antarctic: 191040 St Petersburg, ul. Marata 24A; tel. (812) 713-19-98; e-mail boyarsky@norpolex.com; internet www.polarmuseum.ru; f. 1930; exploration, history and environment of polar regions; library of 6,362 vols; Dir Dr VICTOR I. BOYARSKY; Scientific Deputy Dir Dr M. V. DUKALSKAYA.

St Petersburg State Museum of Theatre and Music: 191023 St Petersburg, Ostrovskogo sq. 6; tel. (812) 315-52-43; e-mail theatremuseum@peterlink.ru; internet www.theatremuseum.ru; f. 1918; over 440,000 exhibits depicting the history of Russian,

Soviet and foreign theatre; 31,000 stage designs, 7,000 prints, 900 sculptures, 240,000 photographs, 24,000 MSS and documents, 62,000 posters and programmes, 4,000 theatre costumes; library of 5,000 vols; Dir NATALIA METELITSA.

State Circus Museum: 191011 St Petersburg, ul. Fontanka 3; tel. (812) 313-44-13; e-mail circusmuseum@aport.ru; internet www.circus.spb.ru; f. 1928; 80,000 exhibits of plans, sketches, paintings; section on the circus in Western Europe since 18th century and on Russian and fmr Soviet state circus; library of 4,000 items, Russian and foreign works; 300 videocassettes of circus material; Dir NATALIA KUZNETSOVA.

State Hermitage Museum: 190000 St Petersburg, Dvortsovaya nab. 34; tel. (812) 110-90-79; e-mail chancery@hermitage.ru; internet www.hermitagemuseum.org; f. 1764 as a court museum; opened to public 1852; richest collection in fmr USSR of the art of pre-historic, ancient Eastern, Graeco-Roman and medieval times; preserves 2.8m. *objets d'art*, including 600,000 drawings and engravings; works by Leonardo da Vinci, Raphael, Titian, Rubens and Rembrandt; collection of coins, weapons and applied art; Dir MIKHAIL PETROVSKY.

State Museum of the History of St Petersburg: 197046 St Petersburg, Petropavlovskaya krepost 3; tel. (812) 498-05-11; internet www.spbmuseum.ru; f. 1957; 1.5m. exhibits; shows history and architectural devt of St Petersburg; 7 brs: Peter and Paul Fortress, 'Oreshek' Fortress, Alexander Blok Museum, Museum of Printing, Sergey. Kirov Museum, Monument to Heroic Defenders of Leningrad, Rumyantsev Mansion; Dir ALEXANDER KOLYAKIN.

State Museum of Political History of Russia: 197046 St Petersburg, ul. Kuybysheva 2–4; tel. (812) 233-70-52; e-mail polithistmuseum@mail.ru; internet www.polithistory.ru; f. 1919; history of Russia in the 19th and 20th centuries with reference to political and social devt; Dir E. G. ARTEMOV.

State Russian Museum: 191186 St Petersburg, Inzhenernaya ul. 4; tel. (812) 595-42-40; e-mail info@rusmuseum.ru; internet www.rusmuseum.ru; f. 1895; Russian icons, folk and applied arts, painting, sculpture, 10th to 21st-century drawings; Dir Dr V. A. GUSEV.

Summer Garden and Museum Palace of Peter the Great: 191186 St Petersburg, Letny Sad; tel. (812) 312-77-15; e-mail m126@mail.museum.ru; f. 1934; 18th-century architecture and sculpture; Dir T. D. KOZLOVA.

Samara

Samara A. M. Gorky Memorial Museum: Samara, ul. S. Razina 126; f. 1946; literary museum devoted to the life and work of Gorky; exhibits in the house and furniture which belonged to him; Chief Curator YELENA KOTELNIKOVA.

Samara Art Museum: 443001 Samara 10, pl. Kuibysheva, Palace of Culture; e-mail office@artmus.ru; f. 1897; fine arts museum with 11,000 exhibits; library of 7,000 vols; Dir ANNETA YU. BASS.

Saransk

Mordovian Republic S. D. Erzi Museum of Fine Arts: 430000 Mordoviya Saransk, Kommunisticheskaya ul. 61; tel. (8342) 17-56-38; e-mail m1451@mail.museum.ru; internet www.museum.ru/m1451; f. 1960; painting, sculpture, prints, decorative arts; library of 10,000 vols; Dir M. N. BARANOVA.

Saratov

Chernyshevsky Memorial Museum: 410002 Saratov, ul. Chernyshevskogo 142; tel. (8452) 26-35-83; f. 1920; study of N. G. Chernyshevsky's life, times and literary inheritance; library of 14,232 vols; Dir GALINA P. MURENONA; publs *Propagandist Velikovo Naslediya* (Publicist of the Great Inheritance, every 5 years), *N. G. Chernyshevsky Articles, Investigations and Materials* (every 3 years).

Saratov A. N. Radishchev State Art Museum: 410031 Saratov, Pervomaiskaya 75; tel. (8452) 26-12-09; e-mail radmuseumart@radmuseumart.ru; internet www.radmuseumart.ru; f. 1885; library of 34,000 vols; brs: Victor Borisov-Musatov and Pavel Kuznetsov memorial museums (Saratov), Kuzma Petrov-Vodkin memorial museum (Khvalynsk, Saratov region), Balakovo art gallery (Balakovo, Saratov region), A. A. Mylnikov Engels Art Gallery (Engels, Saratov region); Dir T. V. GRODSKOVA.

Sergievsky Posad

Sergiev Posad State History and Art Museum: 141300 Moscow oblast, Sergiev Posad, pr. Krasnoi Armii 144; tel. (09654) 4-13-58; e-mail sergiev-mus@yandex.ru; internet www.musobl.divo.ru; f. 1920; items dealing with the devt of Russian art since 14th century; icons, embroidery, jewellery, porcelain, glass, vestments; secular applied arts, folk arts; library of 17,000 vols; Dir FELIKS KH. MAKOYEV; Scientific Sec. Dr S. V. NIKOLAEVA.

Starki

Far Eastern State Marine Reserve: 690601 Vladivostok, o. Popova, pos. Starki, Olkhovaya 11; tel. (4232) 9-66-82; attached to Russian Acad. of Sciences; Head V. V. GORLACH.

Stavropol

Stavropol Museum of Fine Arts: Stavropol, ul. Dzerzhinskogo 115–119; tel. (8652) 26-54-78; e-mail izomuz@iskra.stavropol.ru; internet www.museum.ru/m1608; f. 1962; Dir Z. A. BELAYA.

Syktyvkar

National Gallery of the Komi Republic: 167983 Komi Republic, Syktyvkar, ul. Kirova 44; tel. (8212) 42-60-66; e-mail nrgk@list.ru; internet www.komi.com/ngall; f. 1943; Komi, Russian, Soviet and Western European fine art; Dir OLGA TALYANINA.

Taganrog

Chekhov, A. P., Museum: Taganrog, ul. Oktyabrskaya 9; tel. (86344) 6-27-45; rooms arranged as they were when Chekhov lived there in his childhood.

Tambov

Tambov Picture Gallery: 392000 Tambov, Sovetskaya ul. 97; tel. (0752) 2-36-95; f. 1960; 3,500 exhibits; library of 7,000 vols; Dir T. N. SHESTAKOVA.

Tikhvin

Rimsky-Korsakov House-Museum: 187500 Leningrad oblast, Tikhvin, ul Rimskogo Korsakova 12; tel. (81267) 1-15-09; f. 1944 in house where composer was born; main exhibition devoted to composer's childhood; also material on his later life; spec. collns: original scores, etc.

Tobolsk

Tobolsk Picture Gallery: Tobolsk, Krasnaya pl. 2; 1,800 items.

Tula

Tula Art Museum: 300012 Tula, ul. Engelsa 64; tel. (872) 35-42-72; f. 1919; library: specialist art library of 15,000 vols; Dir M. N. KUSINA.

Tula Museum of Regional Studies: Tula, ul. Sovetskaya 68; tel. (0872) 36-22-08; f. 1919; natural sciences, archaeology, literature, architecture, art, history of Tula region; library of 10,806 vols; Dir N. B. NEMOVA.

Tver

Tver Art Gallery: 170640 Tver, ul. Sovetskaya 3; tel. (822) 33-25-61; e-mail art@tversu.ru; internet www.gallery.tversu.ru; f. 1937; library of 33,000 vols; Dir TATYANA S. KUYUKINA.

Tyumen

Tyumen Picture Gallery: Tyumen, ul. Republiki 29; Dir I. S. TERENTEV.

Uglich

Uglich Historical Museum: Uglich, Kreml 3; tel. (08532) 5-17-57; e-mail uglmus@yaroslavl.ru; f. 1892; exhibits on the history of the Russian people; Dir VALERY DENISOV.

Vladikavkaz

North-Ossetian K. L. Khetagurov Memorial Museum: Vladikavkaz, Butirina 19; tel. (86722) 3-62-22; f. 1979; collection of materials on Caucasian poetry and literature; Dir E. A. KESAYEVA.

Vladivostok

Botanical Garden FEB RAS: 690024 Vladivostok, ul. Makovskogo 142; tel. (4232) 38-80-41; e-mail gardens@yandex.ru; internet botsad.ru; f. 1949; attached to Russian Acad. of Sciences; research in botany, plant ecology, plant cultivation, plant resources, investigation of biological diversity of the Russian Far East; environmental education; maintaining exhibits of living plants; landscaping and design; library of 22,000 vols, attached to FEB RAS Central Academical Library, Vladivostok; Dir Dr PAVEL KRESTOV; Deputy Dir Dr OLGA KHRAPKO; publ. *Bulletin of Botanical Garden FEB RAS* (online, botsad.ru/journal).

Oceanarium of the Pacific Research Fisheries Centre: 690950 Vladivostok, Batareinaya ul. 4; tel. (4232) 40-19-65; e-mail oceanariumtinro@mail.ru; internet www.tinro-center.ru; f. 1991; freshwater aquarium; 2,500 exhibits of flora and fauna of the Pacific Ocean; marine museum, 1,950 exhibits; study of hydrobiology and aquaculture; maintenance of zoological colln; library of 3,242 rare vols; Dir B. K. RAZUVAEV.

Voeikovo

Meteorological Museum of the Central Geophysical Observatory: Leningrad oblast, Vsevolozhskii raion, Voeikovo; Dir A. A. VASILIEV.

Volgograd

Volgograd State Museum and Panorama of the Battle of Stalingrad: 400053 Volgograd, ul. Marshal Chuykov 47; tel. (8442) 34-72-72; e-mail panorama_sb@mail.ru; internet www.stalingrad-battle.ru; f. 1937; exhibits feature the defence of the city during the Civil War (1918–20) and the Battle of Stalingrad (1942–43); library of 14,450 vols; Dir B. G. USIK.

Vologda

Vologda Picture Gallery: Vologda, Kremlevskaya pl.; 6,500 exhibits; Dir S. G. IVENSKII.

Vologda State Museum—Preserve of History, Architecture and Decorative Arts: 160000 Vologda, 15 S. Orlov St; tel. (8172) 72-22-83; e-mail museum.admin@vologda.ru; internet vologdamuseum.ru; f. 1885; history, archaeology, ethnography, nature, literature, handicrafts, folk art, decorative and applied art, old Russian painting, modern art of the Vologda region, architecture; library of 27,000 vols, incl. books on history, art, ethnography and archeology; Dir-Gen. ALEXANDR SUVOROV; Deputy Dir-Gen. NATALIA ZOLOTOVA.

Voronezh

Voronezh Art Museum: Voronezh, pr. Revolyutsii 18; tel. (0732) 55-28-43; f. 1933; 22,065 exhibits; library of 18,800 vols; Dir VLADIMIR Y. USTINOV.

Yakutsk

Yakutsk Museum of Fine Arts: 677000 Yakutsk, ul. Khabarova 27; tel. (4112) 2-77-98; f. 1928; folk art, Western European, Russian and Soviet art of 17th to 20th centuries; Dir N. M. VASILEVA.

Yaroslavl

Yaroslavl Historical and Architectural Museum: 150000 Yaroslavl, pl. Bogoyavlenskaya 25; tel. (0852) 30-56-30; e-mail mp@yarmp.yar.ru; internet www.yarmp.yar.ru; f. 1865; over 370,000 exhibits on the history of the Russian people from ancient times to the present; library of 42,000 vols; Dir YELENA A. ANKUDINOVA; publ. *Kraevedcheskiye Zapiski* (irregular).

Yasnaya Polyana

Leo Tolstoy Museum and Estate: 301214 Tula Region, Shchekino Dist., Yasnaya Polyana; tel. (4872) 38-67-10; e-mail yaspol@tula.net; internet yasnayapolyana.ru; f. 1921; memorial house and estate belonging to L. N. Tolstoy; over 33,000 original objects in the Tolstoy House; literary museum devoted to his life and work; estate with park and forest; library of 22,000 vols in Tolstoy's personal library (in the Tolstoy House); c. 60,000 vols in museum library; Dir VLADIMIR I. TOLSTOY; publ. *Yasnaya Polyana* (Writers' Meetings, 1 a year).

Universities

AGRICULTURAL UNIVERSITIES

ALTAI STATE AGRARIAN UNIVERSITY

656099 Barnaul, Krasnoarmeisky pr. 98

Telephone: (3852) 62-83-96

E-mail: rector@asau.ru

Internet: www.asau.ru

Founded 1943 as Altai Agricultural Institute, present name and status 1991

Depts: accounting, agronomy, animal production, economics, irrigation and land reclamation, management, mechanization, veterinary, zoology

Rector: Prof. SERGEI V. ZOLOTAREV

Library of 360,430 vols

Number of teachers: 500

Number of students: 10,000

BASHKIR STATE AGRARIAN UNIVERSITY

450001 Ufa, 50 let Oktyabrya ul. 34

Telephone: (3472) 28-08-98

E-mail: bgau@ufanet.ru

Internet: www.bsau.ru

Rector: Prof. VLADIMIR D. NEDOREZKOV

Number of teachers: 685

CHELYABINSK STATE AGRO-ENGINEERING UNIVERSITY

454080 Chelyabinsk, Lenina Ave 75

Telephone: (3512) 66-65-30

E-mail: mail@csaa.ru

Internet: www.csaa.ru

Founded 1930

Training of engineers, economists, agronomists, teachers and agroecologists for state and private farms and businesses; bachelors and masters for agro-engineering

Rector: YURY B. CHETYRKIN

Library of 550,000 vols

Number of teachers: 350

Number of students: 5,600

Publications: *Trudy Chimeskh*, *Vestnik Akademii*, *Vestnik Universiteta*

DON STATE AGRARIAN UNIVERSITY

346493 Rostov oblast, Oktyabrsky r-n, pos. Persianovsky

Telephone: (863) 603-61-50

E-mail: dgau-web@mail.ru

Internet: www.dongau.ru

Founded 1840

State control

Language of instruction: Russian

Fields of study: agronomy, animal husbandry, biotechnology, economy, processing of agricultural products, veterinary science

Rector: Prof. ANATOLY I. BARANIKOV

Library of 540,000 vols

Number of teachers: 414

Number of students: 3,152

FAR EAST STATE AGRARIAN UNIVERSITY

675005 Blagoveshchensk, Politekhnicheskaya ul. 86

Telephone: (4162) 42-32-06

E-mail: dalgau@tsl.ru

Internet: www.dalgau.ru

Founded 1950

Institutes of agronomy, mechanization, finance and economics, civil engineering, technology, veterinary science and animal husbandry, electrification and the automation of agriculture, forestry, humanities; research institutes of stockbreeding, selection and technology in plant breeding, construction, systems of machinery, technology of the processing of agricultural production

Rector: BORIS I. KASHPURA

Library of 398,000 vols

Number of teachers: 570

Number of students: 8,000

Publications: *Amur Researcher* (2 a year), *Collection of Scientific Publications* (separate series published by each of 14 institutes, each 1 or 2 a year), *Science to Production* (conference report, 1 a year), *Students' Research to Production* (1 a year)

GORSKY STATE AGRICULTURAL UNIVERSITY

362040 Vladikavkaz, ul. Kirova 37

Telephone: (8672) 3-23-04

E-mail: info@gorskigau.ru

Fields of study: agronomy, animal husbandry, mechanization, economics and management, accounting

Rector: BORIS B. BASAEV

Library of 208,000 vols

Number of teachers: 412

Number of students: 6,500

KRASNOYARSK STATE AGRARIAN UNIVERSITY

660049 Krasnoyarsk, 90 Mira pr.
Telephone: (3912) 27-03-86
E-mail: info@kgau.ru
Internet: www.kgau.ru

Founded 1952
State control
Language of instruction: Russian
Academic year: September to June

Rector: Prof. Dr NIKOLAY V. TSUGLENOK
Vice-Rector for Int. Relations and Chief Administrative Officer: Dr GALINA I. TSU-GLENOK
Chief Admin. Officer: Dr VASILY V. MATYUSHEV
Chief Librarian: RAISA ZORINA

Library of 360,442 vols
Number of teachers: 636
Number of students: 5,695

KUBAN STATE AGRARIAN UNIVERSITY

350044 Krasnodar, ul. Kalinina 13
Telephone: (8612) 56-49-42
E-mail: mail@kubsau.ru
Internet: www.kubagro.ru

Founded 1922

Fields of study: agrochemistry and soil science, agronomy, tropical and sub-tropical agriculture, veterinary, horticulture and viticulture, animal husbandry, mechanization, plant protection, electrification, construction, law, economics and management, accountancy

Rector: Dr IVAN T. TRUBILIN

Library of 635,000 vols
Number of teachers: 1,070
Number of students: 17,496

MICHURINSK STATE AGRARIAN UNIVERSITY

393760 Tambov oblast, Michurinsk Internationalnaya 101
Telephone: (47545) 5-26-35
E-mail: info@mgau.ru
Internet: www.mgau.ru

Founded 1931
Language of instruction: Russian

Fields of study: fruit and vegetable production, viticulture, agronomy, selection and genetics of crops, storing and processing of agricultural produce, agroecology, commodity research, horticulture, economics and management of agricultural enterprises, livestock production, commerce, accounting and auditing, banking and finance, catering technologies, municipal management, landscape design

Rector: ALEXANDR V. NIKITIN

Library of 300,000 vols
Number of teachers: 395
Number of students: 7,000

Publication: *Herald of Michurinsk State Agrarian University*

MOSCOW STATE AGRO-ENGINEERING UNIVERSITY, V. P. GORYACHKIN

127540 Moscow, ul. Timiryazevskaya 58
Telephone: (495) 976-36-40
E-mail: rkt@mail.msau.ru
Internet: www.msau.ru

Founded 1930
State control
Language of instruction: Russian
Academic year: September to June

Pres. and Rector: MIKHAIL N. EROKHIN

Library: 1m. vols
Number of teachers: 400
Number of students: 5,500

Publication: *Vestnik*

DEANS

Agricultural Education: VASILIY P. KOSYREV
Economics: VLADIMIR T. VODYANNIKOV
Energy: VLADIMIR I. ZAGINAILOV
Processes and Machines in Agribusiness: ANATOLIY N. SKOROHODOV
Technical Service in Agro-Industrial Complex: SERGEY P. KAZANCEV

MOSCOW STATE UNIVERSITY OF LAND MANAGEMENT

105064 Moscow, ul. Kazakova 15
Telephone: (495) 261-31-46
E-mail: info@guz.ru
Internet: www.guz.ru

Founded 1779

Faculties of architecture, correspondence, further training, land management, land tenure, law, municipal land tenure, retraining

Rector: Prof. SERGEI N. VOLKOV

Library of 220,000 vols

Publications: *Land Boundary Register* (1 a year), *Rural Architecture* (1 a year)

NOVOSIBIRSK STATE AGRARIAN UNIVERSITY

630039 Novosibirsk, ul. Dobrolyubova 160
Telephone: (3832) 67-38-11
E-mail: public@nsau.edu.ru
Internet: www.nsau.edu.ru

Fields of study: agronomy, plant protection, mechanization, economics and management, accounting

Rector: Prof. ANATOLY F. KONDRATOV

Library of 252,000 vols
Number of teachers: 437
Number of students: 9,400

OMSK STATE AGRARIAN UNIVERSITY

644008 Omsk, Institutskaya pl. 2
Telephone: (3812) 65-17-72
E-mail: adm@omgau.ru
Internet: www.omgau.ru

Founded 1918

Faculties of agricultural engineering, agrochemistry, agronomy, dairy production technology, mathematics and social studies, soil science and environment, water resource engineering, humanities; institute of economics and finance, institute of land use planning and tenure, institute of veterinary medicine institute of part-time and continued education

Rector: NIKOLAI M. KOLYCHEV

Library of 622,000 vols
Number of teachers: 979
Number of students: 10,357

Publications: *Kirovets* (12 a year), *Vestnik OmGAU* (4 a year)

OREL STATE AGRARIAN UNIVERSITY

302019 Orel, ul. Generala Rodina 69
Telephone: (0862) 29-40-50
E-mail: pnv@orel.ru
Internet: www.orelsau.ru

Founded 1975 as Orel Agricultural Institute, present name and status 1999

Rector: Prof. NIKOLAI V. PARAKHIN

ORENBURG STATE AGRARIAN UNIVERSITY

460014 Orenburg, ul. Leninskaya 59
Telephone: (3532) 77-52-30
E-mail: orensau@mail.ru
Internet: www.orensau.ru

Founded 1930

Faculties of agronomy, biotechnology, economics and law, forestry, information technology, mechanization of agriculture, veterinary medicine

Rector: VLADIMIR V. KARAKULEV

Library of 842,127 vols
Number of teachers: 600
Number of students: 8,210

Publication: *Works*

ST PETERSBURG STATE AGRARIAN UNIVERSITY

189620 St Petersburg, Pushkin, Peterburgskoe Shosse 2
Telephone: (812) 470-04-22

Founded 1904

Br. in Polessk; depts of agroecology and soil science, agronomy, animal husbandry, economics, engineering, farm electrification, law, plant protection, vegetable growing

Rector: VICTOR EFIMOV

Library of 650,000 vols
Number of teachers: 360
Number of students: 7,500

Publication: *Collection of Scientific Research Works* (8 a year)

SARATOV STATE AGRARIAN UNIVERSITY, N. I. VAVILOV

410034 Saratov, Teatralnaya pl. 1
Telephone: (8452) 26-32-92
E-mail: rector@ssau.saratov.ru
Internet: www.ssau.saratov.ru

Founded 1997

Fields of study: agricultural electrification and automation, agricultural mechanization, agronomy, amelioration and village arrangement, biotechnology, economics, forestry, mechanization of farm production processing, plant protection, technical service, technology, veterinary

Rector: NIKOLAI I. KUZNETSOV

Library: 1.5m. vols
Number of teachers: 1,200
Number of students: 19,000

STAVROPOL STATE AGRARIAN UNIVERSITY

355017 Stavropol, Zootekhnichesky per. 12
Telephone: (8652) 35-22-82
E-mail: rector@stgau.ru
Internet: www.stgau.ru

Founded 1930
Languages of instruction: English, Russian
Academic year: September to June

Rector: Prof. VLADIMIR IV. TRUKHACHEV
Vice-Rector for Education: Dr IVAN V. ATANOV

Library: 3m. vols
Number of teachers: 1,500
Number of students: 17,500

Publication: *Collection of Scientific Works* (1 a year)

DEANS

Accounting and Finance: Prof. IGOR SKLYAROV
Agricultural Mechanization: Dr MIKHAIL DANILOV
Agronomy: Prof. ALEXANDR ESAULKO
Economics: Prof. OLGA KUSAKINA

Electrical Engineering: Dr IVAN ATANOV
Plant Protection: Prof. ALEXANDR ESAULKO
Technological Management: Prof. MARINA
SELIONOVA
Veterinarian Medicine: Dr VALERY BELYAEV

VORONEZH STATE AGRARIAN UNIVERSITY, K. D. GLINKA

Telephone: (732) 52-86-31
E-mail: an@vsau.ru
Internet: www.vsau.ru
Founded 1913
Fields of study: agribusiness, agricultural economics, agricultural engineering, agrochemistry and soil science, agronomy, animal sciences, food-processing technology, land surveying, veterinary science
Rector: VLADIMIR E. SHEVCHENKO
Library of 870,000 vols
Number of teachers: 530
Number of students: 8,700
Publication: *Zapiski* (Notes)

HUMANITIES AND SCIENCES UNIVERSITIES

ADYGHE STATE UNIVERSITY

352700 Republic of Adygheya, Maykop, ul. Universitetskaya 208
Telephone: (8772) 27-02-73
E-mail: adsu@adygnet.ru
Internet: www.adygnet.ru
State control
Founded 1941, present name and status 1993
Brs in Apsheronsk, Belorechensk, Eisk, Novokubansk, Sochi and Koshekhabl
Rector: Prof. RASHID D. KHUNAGOV
Library of 529,000 vols
Number of teachers: 550
Number of students: 7,500

DEANS

Faculty of Economics: RAMAZAN M. TESHEV
Faculty of Foreign Languages: SUSANNA K. BEDANOKOVA
Faculty of Law: AZAMAT M. SHADZHE
Faculty of Pedagogy: FATIMA P. KHAKNOVA
Faculty of Philology: UCHUZHUK M. PANESH

ALTAI STATE UNIVERSITY

656049 Altai Krai, Barnaul, pr. Lenina 61
Telephone: (3852) 29-12-05
E-mail: rector@asu.ru
Internet: www.asu.ru
Founded 1973
State control
Language of instruction: Russian
Academic year: September to June
Rector: Prof. SERGEI ZEMLYUKOV
Vice-Rector for Academic Affairs: Prof. EVGENIY ANICHKIN
Vice-Rector for Devt of Int. Affairs: ROMAN YAKOVLEV
Vice-Rector for Finance: Prof. VITALY MISHCHENKO
Vice-Rector for Safety and General Questions: OLEG ILYNYH
Vice-Rector for Science and Innovations: ALEXEY TISHKIN
Librarian: GALINA TRUSHNIKOVA
Library: 1m. vols, 1,400 periodicals
Number of teachers: 1,000
Number of students: 18,000
Publications: *Chemistry of Vegetative Raw Materials* (4 a year, online), *Proceedings* (8 a year), *Turchaninovia* (4 a year, online)

DEANS

Faculty of Arts: LARISA NEKHVYADOVICH

Faculty of Biology: GALINA SOKOLOVA
Faculty of Chemistry: NATALYA BAZARNOVA
Faculty of Economics: EVGENIY SHVAKOV
Faculty of Geography: GENNADY BARYSHNIKOV
Faculty of History: EVGENIYA DEMCHIK
Faculty of Law: VITALIY SOROKIN
Faculty of Mass Communication, Philology and Political Science: SERGEY MANSKOV
Faculty of Mathematics: ANNA PETROVA
Faculty of Physics and Technology: VICTOR POLYAKOV
Faculty of Psychology and Pedagogics: LYUDMILA DEMINA
Faculty of Sociology: OLGA KOLESNIKOVA

PROFESSORS

Faculty of Arts:
MOSKALYUK, M., History of Domestic and Foreign Art
ROSSINSKIY, A., Music
STEPANSKAYA, T., History of Domestic and Foreign Art

Faculty of Biology:
FILATOVA, O., Zoology and Physiology
KISELEV, V., Zoology and Physiology
SHMAKOV, A., Botany
SILANTIEVA, M., Botany
VOROBIEVA, E., Ecology, Biochemistry and Biotechnology
ZHURAVLEV, V., Zoology and Physiology

Faculty of Chemistry:
BEZNOSYUK, S., Physical and Colloidal Chemistry
CHEBOTAREV, V., Analytical Chemistry
NOVOZHENOV, V., Inorganic Chemistry
PETROV, B., Analytical Chemistry

Faculty of Geography:
BARISHNIKOV, G., Environmental Management and Geoecology
HABIDOV, A., Physical Geography and Geoinformation Systems
KRASNOYAROVA, B., Economic Geography and Cartography
LUZGIN, B., Environmental Management and Geoecology
MALOLETKO, A., Environmental Management and Geoecology

Faculty of History:
ALEXEENKO, A., Regional Studies
ANASHKIN, A., National History
ARSHINTSEVA, O., General History and International Relations
CHERNISHOV, Y., General History and International Relations
GONCHAROV, Y., National History
GORBUNOV, V., Archaeology, Ethnography and Museum Studies
HRAMKOV, A., National History
KOCHETOVA, L., Foreign Languages
KUNGUROV, A., Archaeology, Ethnography and Museum Studies
LISENKO, Y., Oriental Studies
RAZGON, V., National History
SEROV, V., General History and International Relations
SKUBNEVSKIY, V., National History
SOBOLEVA, N., National History
TISHKIN, A., Archaeology, Ethnography and Museum Studies
TSIB, S., Archaeology, Ethnography and Museum Studies
YAKOVLEVA, N., National History

Faculty of Journalism:
FOTIEVA, I., Theory and Practice of Journalism
LUKASHEVICH, E., Theory and Practice of Mass Communications
MANSUROVA, V., Theory and Practice of Journalism
PURGIN, Y., Theory and Practice of Journalism

SEMILET, T., Theory and Practice of Journalism

Faculty of Law:
CHERNENKO, T., Criminal Law and Criminology
DAVIDOV, S., Criminal Trial and Criminalistics
GAVLO, V., Criminal Trial and Criminalistics
KIM, D., Criminal Trial and Criminalistics
LUGOVIK, V., Criminal Trial and Criminalistics
MAZUNIN, Y., Criminal Trial and Criminalistics
MUZYUKIN, V., Labour, Ecological Law and Civil Process
NEVINSKIY, V., Constitutional and International Law
PETUHOV, E., Criminal Trial and Criminalistics
PHILIPPOVA, T., Civil Law
PLAKSINA, T., Criminal Law and Criminology
PLOHOVA, V., Criminal Law and Criminology
RIBALKO, M., Criminal Trial and Criminalistics
ZEMLYUKOV, S., Criminal Right and Criminalogy

Faculty of Mathematics:
BUSHMANOVA, O., Differential Equations
CHESHKOVA, M., Mathematical Analysis
FOSS, S., Mathematical Analysis
GANOV, V., Algebra and Mathematical Logic
GONCHAROVA, O., Differential Equations
KUZIKOV, S., Differential Equations
OSKORBIN, P., Theoretical Cybernetics and Applied Mathematics
PUHNACHEV, V., Differential Equations
RODIONOV, E., Mathematical Analysis

Faculty of Philology:
CHERNISHOVA, T., Modern Russian and Speech Communication
CHUVAKIN, A., Modern Russian and Speech Communication
DESYATOV, V., Russian and Foreign Literature
GREBNEVA, M., Russian and Foreign Literature
HALINA, N., General and Historical Linguistics
KOZLOVA, S., Russian and Foreign Literature
KULYAPIN, A., Russian and Foreign Literature
LEVASHOVA, O., Russian and Foreign Literature
PARUBCHENKO, L., Modern Russian and Speech Communication
ROGOZINA, I., Modern Russian and Speech Communication
SHELEPOVA, L., General and Historical Linguistics

Faculty of Physics and Technology:
KOMAROV, S., Radiophysics and Theoretical Physics
KVEGLIS, L., General and Experimental Physics
MINAKOV, N., Applied Physics, Electronics and Information Security
PAVLOV, V., Computer Facilities and Electronics
SAGALAKOV, A., General and Experimental Physics
SHIDUK, A., General and Experimental Physics
USTINOV, G., Applied Physics, Electronics and Information Security

Faculty of Political Sciences:
BARKALOV, V., Political Sciences
CHERDANTSEVA, I., Social Philosophy, Ontology and Knowledge Theory

DASHKOVSKIY, P., Religious Studies and State and Confessional Relations
DOLZHIKOV, V., Political History
ELCHANINOV, V., Social Philosophy, Ontology and Knowledge Theory
FEDYUKIN, V., Social Philosophy, Ontology and Knowledge Theory
IVANON, A., Political Science
MELNIKOV, A., Social Philosophy, Ontology and Knowledge Theory
SHASHKOVA, Y., Political Science

Faculty of Psychology and Pedagogics:

FROLOVSKAYA, M., Pedagogics of the Higher School and Information Educational Technologies
KAIGORODOVA, N., General and Applied Psychology
KRASNIRYADZEVA, O., Social Psychology
RALNIKOVA, I., Social Psychology
SENKO, Y., Pedagogics of the Higher School and Information Educational Technologies
STROGANOV, A., Clinical Psychology
VERYAEV, A., Pedagogics of the Higher School and Information Educational Technologies
ZALEVSKIY, G., Clinical Psychology

Faculty of Public Relations:

KOVALEVA, A., Advertising and Public Relations

Faculty of Sociology:

ALGAZIN, G., Mathematical Methods in Social Sciences
KOROSTELEVA, O., General Sociology
MAXIMOVA, S., Psychology of Communications and Psychotechnologies
OBOLYANSKIY, G., Empirical Sociology and Conflictology
POPOV, E., General Sociology
SINTSOVA, L., Social Work
SITIH, O., Empirical Sociology and Conflictology

International Institute of Economy, Management and Information Systems:

BELYAEV, V., Business and Marketing
BOCHAROV, S., Business and Marketing
BORTNIKOVA, T., Economy, Sociology of Work and Human Resource Management
BUTAKOVA, M., Business and Marketing
DUBINA, I., International Economy, Mathematical Methods and Business Informatics
GRISCHENKO, N., Finance and Credit
KOZHEVINA, O., Management
LOBOVA, S., Economy Business and Marketing
MATYASH, I., Accounting, Analysis and Audit
MISCHENKO, V., Regional Economy and Management
OREHOVSKIY, P., Regional Economy and Management
SHVETSOV, Y., Crisis Management, Assessment of Business and Innovations
SOKOLOVA, O., Crisis Management, Assessment of Business and Innovations

AMUR STATE UNIVERSITY

675027 Amur Region, Blagoveshchensk, Ignatevskoye shosse 21
Telephone: (4162) 39-46-86
E-mail: master@amursu.ru
Internet: www.amursu.ru
Founded 1975
State control
Language of instruction: Russian
Academic year: September to July
Pres.: ANDREY D. PLOUTENKO
Pro-Rector: VICTOR V. PROKAZIN
Pro-Rector: ILANA B. KASHIRINA

Chief Admin. Officer: TATYANA V. ASTAFUROVA
Librarian: LUDMILA A. PROKAZINA
Library of 232,000 vols
Number of teachers: 600
Number of students: 8,500
Publication: *Bulletin* (3 a year)

DEANS

Design and Technologies: ALEXANDER M. MEDVEDEV
Economics: OLEG A. TCEPELEV
Engineering and Physics: VERA F. ULYANYCHEVA
International Relations: SVETLANA S. KOSIKHINA
Law: SERGEY V. CHERDAKOV
Mathematics and Computer Science: SVETLANA G. SAMOKHVALOVA
Philology: IRINA I. LEIFA
Power Engineering: NATALIA V. SAVINA
Social Sciences: NELLE K. SCHEPKINA

BASHKIR STATE UNIVERSITY

450074 Bashkortostan, Ufa, Z. Validie 32
Telephone: (3472) 72-63-70
E-mail: interdpt@bsu.bashedu.ru
Internet: www.bsunet.ru
Founded 1909
State control
Language of instruction: Russian
Academic year: September to June
Rector: Prof. AHAT G. MUSTAFIN
Vice-Rector for Academic Affairs: Prof. NIKOLAI D. MOROZKIN
Vice-Rector for Education: Prof. YAUDAT T. SULTANAEV
Vice-Rector for Int. Cooperation: ALEXANDR I. SHABRIN
Vice Rector for Science: Prof. RIFKAT TALIPOV
Univ. Library Dir: EVGENIYA GELVANOVSKAYA
Library: 2m. vols
Number of teachers: 1,325
Number of students: 22,300

DEANS

Faculty of Biology: Prof. RINAT I. IBRAHIMOV
Faculty of Chemistry: Prof. RINAT M. AHMETHANOV
Faculty of Economics: Prof. FANIYA S. ISKHAKOVA
Faculty of Geography: Prof. INBER M. YAPPAROV,
Faculty of History: Prof. MARAT M. KULSHARIPOV
Faculty of Mathematics: Prof. TAGIR G. AMALGILDIN
Faculty of Philology: Prof. ALEXANDER A. FEDOROV
Faculty of Philosophy and Sociology: Prof. DAMIR A NURIEV
Faculty of Physics: Prof. ROBERT A. YAKSHIBAEV
Faculty of Romance and Germanic Philology: Prof. RAKHIM Z. MURYASSOV

BELGOROD STATE UNIVERSITY

308015 Belgorod, ul. Pobedy 30
Telephone: (0722) 30-12-11
E-mail: info@bsu.edu.ru
Internet: www.bsu.edu.ru
Founded 1876 as Belgorod Teaching Institute; 1939–1957 as Belgorod State Teaching Institute; 1957–1994 as Belgorod State Pedagogical Institute; as Belgorod State Pedagogical Univ. 1994–1996; present name and status 1996
State control
Rector: Prof. LEONID YA. DYATCHENKO
First Pro-Rector for Admin., Finance and Security: MIKHAIL V. KOSTROV

First Pro-Rector and Pro-Rector for Science: TATYANA M. DAVYDENKO
Pro-Rector for Academic Affairs: VIKTOR N. TKACHEV
Pro-Rector for Distance and Evening Education: VLADIMIR A. SHAPOVALOV
Chief Accountant: NATALYA P. KOZYREVA
Brs in Alekseevka and Stary Oskol, both f. 1999.
Library of 987,987 vols
Number of teachers: 720
Number of students: 13,000

DEANS

Faculty of Biology and Chemistry: GENNADY M. FOFANOV
Faculty of Computer Science and Telecommunications: EVGENY G. ZHILYAKOV
Faculty of Economics: VLADIMIR I. BOLTENKOV
Faculty of Geology and Geography: ALEXANDER N. PETIN
Faculty of History: ELENA YU. PROKOFIEVA
Faculty of Law: EVGENY E. TONKOV
Faculty of Management and Business: VIKTORIA B. TARABAEVA
Faculty of Medicine: YURI I. AFANASEV
Faculty of Pedagogy: NIKOLAI V. PODDUBNY
Faculty of Philology: SVETLANA P. GRINEVA
Faculty of Physical Culture: VASILY V. SOKOREV
Faculty of Physics and Mathematics: OLEG M. PENKIN
Faculty of Psychology: NADEZHDA I. ISAEVA
Faculty of Romance and Germanic Philology: OLGA N. PROKHOROVA
Faculty of Socio-Theology: SERGEI A. KOLESNIKOV
International Faculty: MIKHAIL A. TRUBITSYN

BELGOROD UNIVERSITY OF CONSUMER CO-OPERATIVES

308023 Belgorod, ul. Sadovaya 116A
Telephone: (0722) 6-08-48
E-mail: rector@bukep.ru
Internet: www.bupk.ru
Faculties of economics, trade management; br. in Stavropol
Rector: VITALY I. TEPLOV
Number of teachers: 330
Number of students: 8,000

BRATSK STATE UNIVERSITY

665709 Bratsk, Makarenko ul. 40
Telephone: (3953) 33-20-08
E-mail: rector@brstu.ru
Internet: www.brstu.ru
Founded 1980 as Bratsk Industrial Institute, present name and status 2004
State control
Language of instruction: Russian
Academic year: September to June
Rector: Prof. Dr SERGEY V. BELOKOBYLSKY
Pro-Rector for Economics and Univ. Devt: Prof. YELENA I. LUKOVNIKOVA
Pro-Rector for Education: Prof. Dr LEONID A. MAMAYEV
Pro-Rector for Innovation: Prof. VALERY A. LYUBLINSKY
Pro-Rector for Secondary Professional Education: VLADIMIR P. KALINNIKOV
Pro-Rector for Science: Prof. Dr PETR M. OGAR
Library of 633,114 vols
Number of teachers: 320
Number of students: 8,700
Publications: *Issues of Social-Economic Development of Siberia* (4 a year), *Systems. Methods. Technologies* (4 a year)

DEANS

Faculty of Building Engineering: Assoc. Prof. ALEXANDER A. ZINOVYEV

Faculty of Correspondence Education: Prof. OLEG V. KULIKOV

Faculty of Economics and Management: Prof. MIKHAIL P. GLEBOV

Faculty of Forestry Engineering: Prof. GARIK D. GASPARYAN

Faculty of Humanities and Pedagogical Sciences: Assoc. Prof. SERGEY A. SOLDATOV

Faculty of Intensive Specialists' Training: Assoc. Prof. VLADIMIR B. KASHUBA

Faculty of Masters Degree Programmes: Assoc. Prof. YELENA A. CHEVSKAYA

Faculty of Mechanics: Assoc. Prof. SERGEY A. ZENKOV

Faculty of Natural Sciences: Assoc. Prof. ALLA D. SINEGIBSKAYA

Faculty of Power Engineering and Automation: Assoc. Prof. SVETLANA M. IGNATYEVA

BRYANSK STATE UNIVERSITY

241036 Bryansk, Bezhitskaya ul. 14

Telephone: (083) 246-65-38

Internet: www.bgunet.com

State control

Founded 1974

Rector: Prof. ANDREI V. ANTYUKHOV

Pro-Rector for Academic Affairs: Prof. VLADIMIR V. SHLYK

Number of teachers: 520

Number of students: 15,700

BURYAT STATE UNIVERSITY

670000 Ulan-Ude, ul. Smolina 24A

Telephone: (3012) 21-15-80

E-mail: univer@bsu.ru

Internet: www.bsu.ru

Founded 1932 as Buryat State Teacher Training Institute, present name and status 1995

State control

Languages of instruction: Buryat, Russian

Academic year: August to June

Rector: Prof. Dr STEPAN V. KALMYKOV

First Pro-Rector: Prof. Dr TSYDYPZHAP Z. DORZHIYEV

Pro-Rector for Academic Affairs: Assoc. Prof. ANDREY K MORDOVSKOY

Pro-Rector for Admin.: Assoc. Prof. ALEXANDER G. SHARGAEV

Pro-Rector for Research: Prof. Dr ALEXANDER S. BULDAEV

Pro-Rector for Social Policy and Extra-Curricular Activities: Assoc. Prof. ANDREY V KOZULIN

Academic Ccl's Sec.: Assoc. Prof. TATIANA V. PALIKOVA

Library of 1,150,000 vols

Number of teachers: 1,000

Number of students: 10,000

DEANS

Faculty of Biology and Geography: ERDENI N. ELAEV

Faculty of Chemistry: GALINA N. BATOROVA

Faculty of Eastern Studies: POLINA P. DASHINIMAYEVA

Faculty of Economics and Management: MARIYA V. BADMAEVA

Faculty of Foreign Languages: NINA A. BOKHACH

Faculty of History: ANNA A. BURKINA

Faculty of Law: JAMILYA K. CHIMITOVA

Faculty of Medicine: VLADIMIR E. KHITRIKHEEV

Faculty of Physics and Technology: VALENTINA M. KHALTANOVA

Faculty of Socio-Psychology: TATIYANA S. BAZAROVA

Faculty of Philology: VERA V. BASHKEEVA

Faculty of Physical Culture, Sport and Tourism: GENNADY P. PETRENKO

Institute of Mathematics and Computer Science: IVAN K. SHARANKHAYEV

National Institute: BATOR B. ZANDARAEV

Pedagogical Institute: NINA Z. DAGBAEVA

CHELYABINSK STATE UNIVERSITY

454021 Chelyabinsk, ul. Bratev Kashirinykh 129

Telephone: (3512) 42-05-31

E-mail: postmaster@csu.ru

Internet: www.csu.ru

Founded 1976

Academic year: September to July

Rector: Prof. V. D. BATUKHTIN

Registrar: A. YU. SHATIN

Librarian: L. M. KISELYOVA

Number of teachers: 1,760 (1,410 full-time, 350 part-time)

Number of students: 14,400 (7,800 full-time, 6,600 correspondence)

Publication: *Vestnik*

DEANS

Faculty of Access to Higher Education: E. A. MARTYNOVA

Faculty of Biology: A. L. BURMISTROVA

Faculty of Chemistry: A. V. BELIK

Faculty of Continuing Education: V. A. BURMISTROV

Faculty of Ecology: S. G. AGEEV

Faculty of Economics: T. A. VERESHCHAGINA

Faculty of Eurasia and the East: G. V. SACHKO

Faculty of History: G. A. GONCHAROV

Faculty of Journalism: B. N. KIRSHIN

Faculty of Law: V. A. LEBEDEV

Faculty of Linguistics and Translation: L. A. NEFYODOVA

Faculty of Management: L. A. KUZNETSOVA

Faculty of Mathematics: O. N. DEMENTIEV

Faculty of Original Professions: T. M. KUYASHEVA

Faculty of Philology: I. YU. KARTASHOVA

Faculty of Physics: V. D. BUCHELNIKOV

Institute of Psychology and Pedagogics: S. A. REPIN

PROFESSORS

ABRAMOVSKY, A. P., History

AKHMEDZIANOV, M. G., Physical Education

ALEEV, Physics and Mathematics

ALEVRAS, N. N., History

AZNACHEEVA, E. N., Linguistics

BALYKIN, V. P., Chemistry

BATUKHTIN, V. D., Mathematical Theory of Optimization and Control

BELANKOV, Physics and Mathematics

BELIK, A. V., Chemistry

BENT, M. I., Philology

BLUDENOV, A. F., Economics

BUCHELNIKOV, V. D., Physics and Mathematics

BURMISTROV, V. A., Physics and Mathematics

BURMISTROVA, A. L., Biology

BYCHKOV, I. V., Physics and Mathematics

CHERNETSOV, P. I., Education

DARANKOV, A. Y., Economics

DEMENTIEV, O. N., Physics and Mathematics

DUDOROV, A. Y., Physics and Mathematics

GALIULINA, G. S., History

GOLIKOV, A. A., Economics

GOLOVANOV, V. I., Technology

GORSHKOV, A. V., Economics

GRUDZINSKY, V. V., History

ILYIN, A. M., Physics and Mathematics

JEYT, Physics and Mathematics

KOLOSOVA, O. S., Medicine

KORNEV, N. I., Economics

LAPPA, A. V., Physics and Mathematics

LEBEDEV, V. A., Law

LEZHNEVA, Pedagogics

MARTYNOVA, Pedagogics

MATUSHKIN, S. I., Didactics

MATVEEV, S. V., Topology

MIKHNUKEVICH, V. A., Philology

NARSKY, I. V., History

NEFYODOVA, L. A., Linguistics

NEVELEV, A. B., Philosophy

PAVLENKO, V. N., Physics and Mathematics

PISCHCLIULIN, Pedagogics

PITINA, S. A., Linguistics

PLOKHIKH, N. A., Geology and Mineralogy

POPOV, V. I., Law

POPOVA, N. B., Philology

PRIVEZENTSEV, A. P., Physics and Mathematics

RATANOV, N. E., Physics and Mathematics

REPIN, S. A., Didactics

ROZKOV, A. V., Physics and Mathematics

SABITOV, P. A., Law

SEDOV, V. V., Political Economy

SHATIN, A. YU., Economics

SHISHMARENKOVA, G. YA., Education

SHKATOVA, L. A., Russian Language

SINYAVSKY, V. A., Geology and Mineralogy

SMIRNOV, S. S., History

SOLOVIEV, A. A., Physics and Mathematics

SUKHANOV, K. N., Philosophy

SUROV, Physics and Mathematics

SVIRIDUK, G. A., Physics and Mathematics

TANANA, V. P., Mathematics

TYUMENTSEV, V. A., Physics and Mathematics

UCHOBOTOV, V. I., Physics

YALOVETS, A. P., Physics

YARTSEV, V. M., Physics and Mathematics

ZAGIDULLINA, M. V., Linguistics

CHECHEN STATE UNIVERSITY

Chechnya, 364907 Groznyi, ul. Sheripova 32

Telephone: (87322) 23-40-89

E-mail: mail@chesu.ru

Internet: www.chesu.ru

Founded 1972

Faculties of chemistry and biology, economics, geography, history, mathematics, philology, physics, romance and Germanic philology

Rector: ADNAN D. KHAMZAYEV

Number of teachers: 620

Number of students: 8,000

CHEREPOVETS STATE UNIVERSITY

162600 Cherepovets, ul. Lunacharskogo 5

Telephone: (8202) 55-65-97

E-mail: chsu@chsu.ru

Internet: www.chsu.ru

Founded 1919

Rector: Prof. VLADIMIR S. GRYZLOV

First Pro-Rector: Prof. EVGENY V. ERSHOV

Library of 437,168 vols

CHITA STATE UNIVERSITY

672039 Chita, Aleksandro-Zavodskaya ul. 30

Telephone: (3022) 41-64-44

E-mail: root@chitgu.ru

Internet: www.chitgu.ru

Founded 1966 as a br. of Irkutsk State Polytechnic Institute

State control

Languages of instruction: Chinese, English, French, Russian

Academic year: September to June (2 semesters)

Rector: Prof. YURI N. REZNIK

Vice-Rector: Prof. SERGEY A. IVANOV

Librarian: NINA V. OKUNEVA

Library of 828,057 vols

Number of teachers: 850

Number of students: 12,400

Publications: *ChSU Journal* (6 a year, scientific), *Science: XX1 Century* (1 a year, scientific), *Social Anthropology of North-East Asia* (SCANEA journal, 4 a year, scientific)

DEANS

Automobile Transportation: SERGEI P. OZOR-NIN
Civil Engineering: A.V. KUYDIN
Computer Science and Economics: TATYANA A. PLYUSNINA
Ecology: VLADIMIR V. ZVYAGINTSEV
Economics: S. V. VASILIEVA
Geology: SERGEI V. SMOLICH
International Law: D. S. LUKONIN
Law: V. V. BESSONOVA
Management: N. P. KALASHNIKOVA
Mining: LUDMILA G. NIKITINA
Power Technology: YURI V. ERMOLAEV
Professional Development: M. G. MELKOYAN
Social Policy and Cultural Studies: E. E. KOVALENOK
Social Systems and Regional Forecasting: A. A. RUSANOVA
Technology: VITALY V. GRUSHEV

PROFESSORS

ABAKUMOV, Y., Mathematics
ABRAMOV, V., Philosophy
ABRAMOVA, N., Oriental Studies
BALANDIN, O., Construction Engineering
BEIDINA, T., Political Studies
BERNUKEVICH, T., Social Philosophy
BORODIN, V., Law
BUKIN, A., Anthropology
CHERKASOV, V., Mining
ERDYNEEVA, K., Psychology
FATIANOV, A., Mining Engineering
FOMINA, M., Philosophy
GARMAEV, Y., Law
GERASIMOV, V., Geotechnology
GLAZYRINA, I., Economy
IMETINOV, N., Civil Engineering
IVANOV, S., Power Engineering
KARASEV, K., Chemistry
KOGAN, E., Mathematics
KONDRATIEV, V., Geocryology
KOSTROMIN, M., Mining Engineering
KUZNETSOV, O., Ethnography
LETUNOV, V., Chemistry
LIZUNKIN, V., Geotechnology
LUBIMOVA, L., Linguistic
MAKAROV, A., Law
MALYSHEV, E., Economy
MYAZIN, V., Mining Engineering
OVESHNIKOV, Y., Geoecology
OVSEYCHUK, V., Geotechnology
POLUTOVA, M., Pedagogy
REZNIK, Y., Geotechnology
ROMANOVA, N., Sociology
SEKISOV, G., Geotechnology
SHVETSOV, M., Pedagogy
SUVOROV, I., Engineering
SVININ, V., Engineering
TEREKHOVA, T., Pedagogy
TRUBACHEV, A., Mining Engineering
VASILIEVA, K., Philosophy
VORONOV, E., Geotechnology
ZASLONOVSKY, V., Hydrology

CHUVASH STATE UNIVERSITY

428015 Chuvash Autonomous Republic, Cheboksary, Moskovsky pr. 15

Telephone: (8352) 24-03-79
E-mail: office@chuvsu.ru
Internet: www.chuvsu.ru

Founded 1967
State control
Languages of instruction: Chuvash, Russian
Academic year: September to July

Rector: Prof. Dr LEV P. KURAKOV
First Vice-Rector: NIKOLAI F. GRIGORIEV

Vice-Rector for Academic Affairs: VSEVOLOD G. AGAKOV
Librarian: NINA D. NIKITINA
Library: see under Libraries and Archives
Number of teachers: 1,300
Number of students: 19,400

Publications: *Chuvash Segodny, Ulyanovets* (52 a year)

DEANS

Faculty of Arts: M. N. YACLASHKYN
Faculty of Chemistry: O. Y. NOSAKIN
Faculty of Chuvash Philology and Culture: V. G. RODIONOV
Faculty of Construction: Y. V. CHERNOV
Faculty of Economics: A. E. YAKOVLEV
Faculty of Electrical and Power Engineering: N. A. KOKOREV
Faculty of Electrical Engineering: N. A. KOKOREV
Faculty of Geography: I. N. SHIROKOV
Faculty of History: A. V. ARSENTEVA
Faculty of Journalism: A. P. DANILOV
Faculty of Law: N. V. IVANZOVA
Faculty of Mathematics: V. G. AGAKOV
Faculty of Medicine: V. E. VOLKOV
Faculty of Philology: G. E. KORNILOV
Faculty of Physics: L. K. MYTRUCHIN
Faculty of Psychology and Administration: E. N. KADISHEV
Faculty of Stomatology and Paediatrics: E. V. BUSHUEVA
Higher Business School: L. P. KURAKOV (Dir)
Higher School For Training Engineers: V. A. CHEDRIN (Dir)

DAGESTAN STATE UNIVERSITY

Dagestan, 367000 Makhachkala, 43A Gadzhiyev St

Telephone: (8722) 68-23-26
E-mail: dgu@dgu.ru
Internet: www.dgu.ru

Founded 1931
State control
Language of instruction: Russian
Academic year: September to July

Rector: Prof. M. KH. RABADANOV
Vice-Rector for Academic Affairs: Prof. M. M. GASANOV
Vice-Rector for Research and Innovation: Prof. N. A. ASHURBEKOV
Librarian: L. I. ALIEVA

Library: 2.5m. vols
Number of teachers: 1,100
Number of students: 20,000

Publication: *Herald of Dagestan State University*

DEANS

Faculty of Biology: Dr R. A. KHALILOV
Faculty of Chemistry: Dr A. SH. RAMAZANOV
Faculty of Culture: Dr N. K. ADZHAMATOVA
Faculty of Ecology and Geography: Dr G. M. ABDURAKHMANOV
Faculty of Economics: Dr D. K. DZHAVATOV
Faculty of Foreign Languages: Dr T. I. ASHURBEKOVA
Faculty of History: Dr B. B. BULATOV
Faculty of Information and Information Technologies: Dr S. A. AKHMEDOV
Faculty of International and Pre-University Training: Dr K. G. KHALIKOV
Faculty of Law: Dr SH. B. MAGOMEDOV
Faculty of Mathematics and Computer Science: Dr A. K. RAMAZANOV
Faculty of Oriental Studies: Dr A. R. MAGOMEDOV
Faculty of Philology: Dr SH. A. MAZANAEV
Faculty of Physical Training and Sport: Dr A. SH. RAMAZANOV
Faculty of Physics: Dr V. S. KURBANISMAILOV
Faculty of Professional Development of Teachers: Dr N. SH. ZAGIROV

Faculty of Psychology and Philosophy: Dr M. Y. YAKHIAEV
Faculty of Social Studies: Dr I. I. MAGOMED-SULTANOV

ELETS STATE UNIVERSITY 'I. A. BUNIN'

399770 Lipetsk Region, Elets, ul. Kommunarov 28

Telephone: (07467) 2-21-93
E-mail: main@elsu.ru
Internet: www.elsu.ru

Founded 1939
State control

Rector: VALERY P. KUZOVLEV
First Pro-Rector for Academic Affairs: ANDREY A. ZAITSEV
Second Pro-Rector for Academic Affairs: OLGA N. SARYCHEVA
Pro-Rector for Admin. and Finance: STANISLAV A. KLEIMENOV

DEANS

Faculty of Design: NADEZHDA P. LOGINOVA
Faculty of Economics: SVETLANA A. VOROTYNTSEVA
Faculty of Engineering and Physics: NATALYA A. FORTUNOVA
Faculty of Foreign Languages: IRINA V. ZAITSEVA
Faculty of Further Pedagogic Training: EKATERINA V. CHERNYKH
Faculty of History: DENIS A. LIAPIN
Faculty of Law: SERGEY S. FOMENKO
Faculty of Pedagogy and Primary Education: IRINA A. YELETSKICH
Faculty of Pedagogy and Psychology: TATIANA D. KRASOVA
Faculty of Philology: OLGA A. MESHCHERIAKOVA
Faculty of Physics and Mathematics: ELENA I. TROFIMOVA
Faculty of Sport: VLADIMIR V. MAKAROV

FAR EASTERN FEDERAL UNIVERSITY

690600 Vladivostok, ul. Sukhanova 8

Telephone: (4232) 45-76-87
E-mail: rectorat@dvfu.ru
Internet: www.dvgu.ru

Founded 1899
State control
Language of instruction: Russian
Academic year: September to June

Rector: IWANIEC SERGEY
Vice-Rector for Economics and Finance: ATAMANYUK VIKTOR
Vice-Rector for Campus Devt: ANNA V. BONDARENKO
Vice-Rector for Int. Relations: KURILES VLADIMIR IVANOVICH
Vice-Rector for Science and Innovation: TSHE ALEXEY
Vice-Rector for Strategic Devt: DUBOVITSKII SERGEY
Librarian: N. N. GAIDARENKO

Library: see under Libraries and Archives
Number of teachers: 1,000
Number of students: 16,000

Publications: *News of the Institute of International Studies* (4 a year), *News of the Institute of Oriental Studies* (1 a year), *The Russian Far East* (4 a year)

DEANS

Chemistry and Chemical Ecology: A. A. KAPUSTINA
Correspondence Programme: L. I. ROMANOVA
Economics: R. V. SABITOVA
Entrepreneurial Law: A. S. SHEVCHENKO
German Philology: L. P. BONDARENKO
History and Philosophy: O. V. SIDORENKO

Information Technology: I. V. SOPPA
International Economic Relations and Management: A. A. KHAMATOVA
International Law: V. V. GAVRILOV
International Relations: T. D. KHUZIYATOV
Investigation and Public Prosecution: A. F. REKHOVSKY
Japanese Studies: A. G. SHNYRKO
Journalism: V. V. BAKSHIN
Jurisprudence: A. G. KORCHAGIN
Law (in Petropavlovsk-Kamchatsky): L. A. ZAKHOZHY
Law (in Yuzhno-Sakhalinsk): M. G. SEREBRENNIKOV
Management and Business: S. B. GOLOVACHEV
Mathematics and Computer Science: V. B. OSIPOV
Physics: P. N. KORNYUSHIN
Physics and Engineering: V. G. LIFSHITS
Political Science and Public Administration: A. M. KUZNETSOV
Psychology and Social Work: A. V. STETSIV
Romance Philology: N. S. MOREVA
Russian Philology: V. I. SHESTOPALOVA
Sinology: O. V. KUCHUK
State Law: V. F. SHEKHOVTSOV
Academy of Ecology, Marine Biology and Biotechnology: V. A. KUDRYASHOV
Higher College of Korean Studies: V. V. VERKHOLYAK (Dir)
Institute of Environment: YU. B. ZONOV (Dir)
Institute of Foreign Languages: L. P. BONDARENKO (Dir)
Institute of International Tourism and Hospitality: N. M. PESTEREVA (Dir)
Institute of Law: V. I. KURILOV (Dir)
Institute of Management and Business: A. A. BELUSOV (Dir)
Institute of Military Programmes: S. A. BOGATYRENKO (Dir)
Institute of Oriental Studies: A. A. KHAMATOVA (Dir)
Institute of Physics and Information Technology: V. I. BELOKON (Dir)
Institute of Pre-University Training: N. A. SMAL (Dir)
Institute of Professional Development and In-Service Training: E. M. CHUKHRAYEV (Dir)
Institute for Training Highly Qualified Specialists: B. L. REZNIK (Dir)
Pacific Institute of Distance Education and Technology: V. I. VOVNA (Dir)
Research Institute of Chemistry: N. P. SHAPKIN (Dir)
Research Institute of Regional Studies: B. K. STAROSTIN (Dir)
Vladivostok Institute for International Studies of the Asia-Pacific Region: M. YU. SHINKOVSKY (Dir)
FESU branch in Artem: P. V. KHARITONSKY (Dir)
FESU branch in Hakodate: S. N. ILYIN (Dir)
FESU branch in Nakhodka: A. I. RAZGONOV (Dir)

PROFESSORS

ABAKUMOV, A. I., Mathematics
ABRAMOVA, L. A., Economics
AFINOGENOV, YU. A., Law
AKIMOVA, L. V., Economics
AKIMOVA, T. I., Chemistry
ALEXANDROVSKAYA, L. V., Economics
ALEXEYEV, G. V., Mathematics
ANIKONOV, D. S., Mathematics
ANISIMOV, A. P., Biology
ANISIMOV, N. A., Mathematics
ASHCHEPKOV, L. T., Mathematics
BAKLANOV, P. YA., Physical Geography
BAKSHIN, V. V., Journalism
BELOKON, V. I., Physics
BELOUSOV, A. A., Economics
BEREZNIKOV, K. P., Geophysics
BESSONOVA, V. I., Chemistry
BINDER, A. I., Economics

BINEVSKY, A. A., Philosophy
BONDARENKO, L. P., English Philology
BRESLAVETS, T. I., Japanese Philology
BRODYANSKY, D. L., History
BROVKO, P. F., Geography
BUKIN, O. A., Physics
CHEBOTKEVICH, L. A., Physics
CHIZHOV, L. N., Management
CHUVAKIN, A. A., Russian Philology
DASHKO, N. A., Geophysics
DERBENTSEVA, A. M., Biology
DROZDOV, A. L., Chemistry
DUBININ, V. N., Mathematics
DYUZHIKOVA, E. A., English
EFIMENKO, V. F., Physics
ELANTSEVA, O. P., History
ELYAKOV, G. B., Chemistry
FISENKO, A. I., Economics
FROLOV, N. N., Mathematics
GALKINA, L. V., Korean Philology
GAVRILOVA, T. L., Mathematics
GERASIMENKO, M. D., Physics
GLUSHCHENKO, I. I., History
GRAMM-OSIPOV, L. M., Chemistry
GRAMM-OSIPOVA, V. N., Chemistry
IGNATYUK, V. A., Physics
ILYUSHIN, I. A., Journalism
ISAYEVA, T. S., Law
ISAYEVA, V. V., Biology
IVANKOV, V. N., Biology
IVLEV, A. M., Biology
KAMINSKY, V. A., Chemistry
KAPUSTINA, A. A., Chemistry
KARTAVTSEV, YU. F., Biology
KHAMATOVA, A. A., International Economic Relations and Management
KHRISTOFOROVA, N. K., Biology
KILMATOV, T. R., Oceanology
KLESHCHEV, A. S., Mathematics
KNYAZEV, S. D., Law
KOCHETKOV, V. P., English Language
KOGAN, B. I., Mathematics
KOMAROVA, T. A., Biology
KONDRIKOV, N. B., Chemistry
KORNYUSHIN, P. N., Physics
KOROBEYEV, A. I., Law
KOROTKY, A. M., Physical Geography
KOSTETSKY, E. YA., Biology
KRIVSHENKO, S. F., Russian Philology
KUDRYASHOV, V. A., Biology
KULEBYAKIN, YE. V., Social Work
KULESHOV, YE. L., Physics
KURILOV, V. I., Law
KUSAKIN, O. G., Biology
KUZNETSOV, A. M., Political Science
KUZNETSOV, N. V., Mathematics
KUZNETSOV, N. V., Economy and Finance of Asian Pacific Countries
LEBEDKO, M. G., English
LIFSHITS, V. G., Physics
MEDVEDEVA, E. S., Economics
MEDVEDEVA, K. A., Russian Philology
MEGRABOVA, E. G., English
MELNIKOVA, T. N., English
MIKHAILOV, V. S., International Law
MIKHEEV, R. I., Law
MIRONETS, YU. A., English
NEDOLUZHKO, A. V., Biology
NELEZIN, A. D., Oceanology
NEMOV, R. S., Psychology
NESTERENKO, A. D., Economics
NOMOKONOV, V. A., Law
NURMINSKY, YE. A., Mathematics
OSIPOV, V. B., Mathematics
OSTANIN, V. A., Economics
OVRAKH, G. P., Political Science
PAK, G. K., Mathematics
PECHERITSA, V. F., International Relations
PESTEREVA, N. M., Geophysics
PRIYATKINA, A. F., Russian Philology
PROSHINA, Z. G., English
PSCHENICHNIKOV, B. F., Biology
RAGULIN, P. G., Economics
REZNICHENKO, I. M., Law
REZNIK, B. L., Physics
ROMANOVA, L. I., Law

SABITOVA, R. G., Economics
SAMIGULIN, R. M., History
SARANIN, A. A., Physics
SAZONOV, V. G., International Economics
SEROV, V. M., Japanese Studies
SHAKHOV, V. N., Economics
SHAPKIN, N. P., Chemistry
SHASHKOV, N. I., Philosophy
SHAVKUNOV, E. V., History
SHCHETINNIKOV, P. S., Economics
SHEKHOVTSOV, V. A., Law
SHEPELEVA, R. P., Mathematics
SHEVCHENKO, A. S., Law
SHEVCHENKO, D. K., Mathematics
SHISHMARYOV, YU. E., Mathematics
SHLYK, V. A., Mathematics
SHNYRKO, A. A., Japanese Studies
SOLONITSYNA, A. A., Sociocultural Service and Tourism
SONIN, V. V., Law
SOVASTEEV, V. V., History
STARODUMOVA, YE. A., Russian Philology
STONIK, V. A., Chemistry
SUKHANOV, V. V., Biology
SVYATETSKAYA, T. K., Law
TEREKHOVA, E. V., Foreign Languages
TITOV, A. I., Physics
TKACHEV, V. A., Journalism
TSITSIASHVILI, G. SH., Mathematics
TURCHIN, D. A., Law
VANEEVA, L. A., Law
VASKOVSKY, V. E., Chemistry
VELIKAYA, N. I., Russian Philology
VERISOTSKAYA, YE. V., Japanese Studies
VOLOSHIN, G. YA., Mathematics
VOVNA, V. I., Physics
VYSOTSKY, V. I., Chemistry
YACHIN, S. E., Philosophy
YAKUNIN, L. P., Oceanology
YAROVENKO, V. V., Law
YELANTSEVA, O. P., Economics
YERMAKOVA, E. V., History
YUDIN, V. V., Physics
YUDINA, L. A., Physics
ZAKHOZHY, L. A., Law
ZAYATS, T. S., Chinese Philology
ZHARIKOV, E. P., International Economics
ZHIRMUNSKY, A. V., Biology
ZHURAVLEV, YU. N., Biology
ZOLOTAR, G. YA., Chemistry
ZONOV, YU. B., Geophysics
ZUS, L. B., Law

GORNO-ALTAISK STATE UNIVERSITY

Altai Republic, 649000 Gorno-Altaisk, Lenkina ul. 1

Telephone: (3882) 22-64-39
E-mail: office@gasu.ru
Internet: www.gasu.ru

Founded 1949, present name and status 1993
State control
Language of instruction: Russian
Academic year: September to June (2 semesters)

Rector: Prof. VALERY G. BABIN
Vice-Rector for Academic Affairs: Prof. TATYANA KURILENKO
Vice-Rector for Educational Work: Prof. BORIS V. PAKHAYEV
Vice-Rector for Science and Innovations: Prof. YURY V. TABAKAYEV
Librarian: NATALYA N. VAKHRENEVA
Library of 380,763 vols, 312 periodicals
Number of teachers: 430
Number of students: 5,443 (incl. 2,015 external)

DEANS

College of Agriculture: YELENA V. PIVOVAROVA
Faculty of Agrotechnology and Veterinary Medicine: Dr LYUDMILA SURTAEVA
Faculty of Biology and Chemistry: VERA N. ALEYNIKOVA
Faculty of Economics: JULIA G. GAZUKINA

Faculty of Foreign Languages: TATYANA V. DERBENEVA
Faculty of Geography: ALEXEI V. BONDARENKO
Faculty of History: TATYANA S. PUSTOGACHEVA
Faculty of Law: VERA S. KRASHENININA
Faculty of Philology: TATYANA N. NIKONOVA
Faculty of Physics and Mathematics: IVAN B. DAVYDKIN
Faculty of Psychology and Pedagogy: OLGA V. OSTAPOVICH
Faculty of Social Management: Dr SYVATOSLAV I. GRIGORIEV

IMMANUEL KANT BALTIC FEDERAL UNIVERSITY

236041 Kaliningrad,14 A. Nevskogo Str.
Telephone: (4012) 59-55-77
E-mail: rector@kantiana.ru
Internet: www.kantiana.ru

Founded 1967
State control
Languages of instruction: English, Russian
Academic year: September to June
Rector: Prof. Dr ANDREY KLEMESHEV
Pro-Rector: Dr V. N. KHUDENKO
Librarian: A. D. SHKITSKAYA

Library: see under Libraries and Archives
Number of teachers: 1,000
Number of students: 15,000

Publications: *Kantovsky Sbornik, Vestnik of IKBFU*

DEANS

Faculty of Bioecology: Prof. Dr VIKTOR DEDKOV
Faculty of Economics: Dr ANATOLY CHUIKIN
Faculty of Geography and Geoecology: Dr FATIMA TSEKOEVA
Faculty of History: Dr VALERY GALTSOV
Faculty of Informatics and Applied Mathematics: Prof. Dr SERGEY ISHANOV
Faculty of Law: Dr OLEG ZAYACHKOVSKY
Faculty of Linguistics and Cross-Cultural Communication: Prof. Dr IRINA IERONOVA
Faculty of Medicine: Prof. Dr SERGEY KORENEV
Faculty of Philology and Journalism: Dr NATALYA LIKHINA
Faculty of Physical Culture and Sports: Prof. Dr VIKTOR PELMENEV
Faculty of Physics and Technology: Prof. Dr ALEKSEY IVANOV
Faculty of Psychology and Social Work: Prof. Dr IRINA SIMAEVA
Faculty of Services: Prof. Dr SERGEY KORYAGIN
Institute of Modern Educational Technologies: Dr NATALYA NIKULINA

INGUSH STATE UNIVERSITY

Republic of Ingushetia, 366700 Magas, Aleksandro-Zavodskaya ul. 30
Telephone: (8734) 55-12-64

Founded 1994
Rector: ARSAMAK MARTAZANOV
First Pro-Rector: AKHMED MATIYEV
Pro-Rector for Int. Relations: ZAHIDAT SULTYGOVA
Number of teachers: 320
Number of students: 2,800

IRKUTSK STATE UNIVERSITY

664003 Irkutsk, 3, K. Marksa ul. 1
Telephone: (3952) 24-34-53
E-mail: rector@isu.ru
Internet: www.isu.ru
Founded 1918
State control

Language of instruction: Russian
Academic year: September to May
Rector: Prof. ALEXANDER I. SMIRNOV
Vice-Rector for Academic Affairs: I. GUTNIK
Vice-Rector for Devt: V. SAUNIN
Vice-Rector for Finance and Gen. Affairs: V. I. GLEBETS
Vice-Rector for Scientific Research: A. V. ARGUCHINTSEV
Librarian: R. V. PODGAICHENKO
Library: 3m. vols
Number of teachers: 900
Number of students: 17,230

Publications: *Collected Short Scientific Papers, Proceedings of the Applied Physics Research Institute, Proceedings of the Biological Research Institute, Proceedings of the Oil and Coal Products Research Institute, Transactions*

DEANS

Baikal School of International Business: V. N. SAUNIN
Faculty of Biology and Soil Sciences: Asst Prof. A. N. MATVEYEV
Faculty of Chemistry: Prof. Dr A. YU. SAFRONOV
Faculty of Geography: Asst Prof. A. V. ARGUCHINTSOVA
Faculty of Geology: Asst Prof. S. P. PRIMINA
Faculty of History: Prof. YU. A. ZULYAR
Faculty of Philology: Prof. A. S. SOBENNIKOV
Faculty of Physics: Prof. YU. V. AGRAPHONOV
Faculty of Psychology: Asst Prof. I. A. KOPONAK
Faculty of Service and Advertisement: Asst Prof. V. K. KARNAUKHOVA
Institute of Law: Assoc. Prof. O. P. LICHICHAN
Institute of Mathematics, Economics and Information Science: Prof. YU. D. KOROLKOV
Institute of Social Sciences: Prof. V. A. RASHETNIKOV
International Institute of Economics and Linguistics: Asst Prof. V. YA. ANDRUKHOVA
Siberian-American Faculty of Management: Asst Prof. A. V. DIOGENOV

IVANOVO STATE UNIVERSITY

153025 Ivanovo, ul. Ermaka 39
Telephone: (932) 32-62-10
E-mail: rector@ivanovo.ac.ru
Internet: www.ivanovo.ac.ru
Founded 1974
State control
Faculties of biology and chemistry, economics, history, law, mathematics, philology, physics, romance and Germanic philology
Number of teachers: 429
Number of students: 7,919 (4,452 full-time, 3,467 correspondence)
Rector: Prof. VLADIMIR N. YEGOROV
Pro-Rector for Academic Affairs: ALEXEY I. SCHEGLOV
Pro-Rector for Admin. and Finance: Dr VLADIMIR S. RADNYUK
Pro-Rector for Distance Learning and Further Education: Dr VLADIMIR I. NAZAROV
Pro-Rector for Int. Affairs: Dr NADEZHDA V. USOLTSEVA
Pro-Rector for Public Relations: Dr OLGA M. KARPOVA
Pro-Rector for Scientific Affairs: Dr DMITRY I. POLYVYANNY

KABARDINO-BALKARIAN STATE UNIVERSITY

360004 Kabardino-Balkar Republic, Nalchik, ul. Chernyshevskogo 173
Telephone: (095) 337-99-55
E-mail: kodzokov@kbsu.ru
Internet: www.kbsu.ru

Founded 1932
State control
Language of instruction: Russian
Academic year: September to June
Rector: BARASBI S. KARAMURZOV
Vice-Rector and Head of Studies: ARTUR KAZHAROV
Vice-Rector for Extramural Studies and Postgraduate Studies: MUSLIM BARAZBIEV
Vice-Rector for Scientific Studies and Int. Affairs: ALEKSEY P. SAVINTSEV
Registrar: I. SHOMAKHOVA
Librarian: ROSA N. UNACHEVA
Library: see under Libraries and Archives
Number of teachers: 950
Number of students: 20,600

DEANS

Faculty of Biology: A. M. PARITOV
Faculty of Chemistry: T. KH. LYGIDOV
Faculty of Computer Science and Systems Control: A. S. KSENOFONTOV
Faculty of Economics: R. V. GURFOVA
Faculty of Law: M. KH. GUKEPSHOKOV
Faculty of Mathematics: M. ABREGOV
Faculty of Mechanical Engineering: V. D. BATYROV
Faculty of Medicine: R. M. ZAKHOKHOV
Faculty of Microelectronics: R. SH. TESHEV
Faculty of Pedagogy and Methods of Primary Education: A. ZH. NASIPOV
Faculty of Physical Education and Sport: A. TKHAZEPLOV
Faculty of Physics: A. A. AKHUBEKOV
Institute of Philology: L. A. KHARAEVA
Institute of Social Sciences and Humanities: KH. B. MAMSIROV

KALMYK STATE UNIVERSITY

358000 Elista, ul. Pushkina 11
Telephone: (84722) 5-34-31
E-mail: uni@kalmsu.ru
Internet: www.kalmsu.ru

Founded 1970
Faculties of general engineering, philology, biology, physics, mathematics, oriental studies and agriculture
Rector: G. M. MANDZHIYEVICH
Vice-Rector for Academic Affairs: Prof. ANATOLY V. RUDENKO
Vice-Rector for Admin. and Finance: Prof. VLADIMIR V. UCHUROV
Vice-Rector for Scientific Affairs: Prof. ALEKSANDR A. SOLOVEV
Vice-Rector for Social-Economic Affairs: Prof. VALERY U. MANDZHIEV
Vice-Rector for Univ.–Industry Liaison: Prof. ARKADY K. NATYROV
Number of students: 5,000

KAZAN FEDERAL UNIVERSITY

420008 Tatarstan, Kazan, 18 Kremlevskaya St
Telephone: (843) 292-76-00
E-mail: public.mail@ksu.ru
Internet: www.kpfu.ru

Founded 1804
State control
Languages of instruction: English, Russian, Tatar
Academic year: September to June
Pres.: Prof. MYAKZYUM KH. SALAKHOV
Rector: Prof. ILSHAT R. GAFUROV
Vice-Rector for Admin. Affairs: Dr ANDREY N. KHASHOV
Vice-Rector for Economic Affairs: LENAR S. SAFIULLIN
Vice-Rector for Economic and Strategic Devt: Dr MARAT R. SAFIULLIN
Vice-Rector for Education: Prof. RIYAZ G. MINZARIPOV

Vice-Rector for Finance: RAISA R. MULLA-
KAEVA
Vice-Rector for Innovations: Prof. NAIL F.
KASHAPOV
Vice-Rector for Int. Relations: Dr LINAR N.
LATYPOV
Vice-Rector for Research: Prof. DANIS K.
NURGALIEV
Vice-Rector for Social Education: ARIF M.
MEZHVEDILOV
Head of Library: Dr EVGENIY N. STRUKOV

Library: 6.2m. vols
Number of teachers: 5,200
Number of students: 47,000

Publications: *Education and Self-Develop-
ment, Environmental Radioecology and
Applied Ecology, Georesources, Philology
and Culture, Proceedings of Higher Education Institutions: Mathematics* (print and
online)

DEANS

A. Butlerov Institute of Chemistry: Prof.
VLADIMIR I. GALKIN
Faculty of Law: Prof. ILDAR A. TARKHANOV
Faculty of Philosophy: Prof. MIKHAIL D.
SCHELKUNOV
Higher School of Information Technologies
and Information Systems: Dr AIRAT F.
KHASIYANOV
Institute of Comparative Studies of Mod-
ernity: Dr IRINA B. KUZNETSOVA
Institute of Computer Mathematics and
Information Technologies: Prof. RUSTAM
KH. LATYPOV
Institute of Ecology and Geography: Prof.
SVETLANA YU. SELIVANOVSKAYA
Institute of Economics and Finance: Prof.
SHAMIL M. VALEEV
Institute of Fundamental Medicine and Biol-
ogy: Prof. ANDREI P. KIASOV
Institute of Geology and Petroleum Technol-
ogy: Prof. DANIS C. NURGALIEV
Institute of Management and Territorial
Development: Prof. NAILYA G. BAGAITDI-
NOVA
Institute of Mass Communication and Social
Sciences: Prof. NAIL M. MUKHARYAMOV
Institute of Oriental Studies, History and
International Relations: Prof. RAMIL R.
KHAYRUTDINOV
Institute of Pedagogy and Psychology: Prof.
AIDAR M. KALIMULLIN
Institute of Philology and Arts: Prof. RADIF R.
ZAMALETDINOV
Institute of Physical Education, Sport and
Restorative Medicine: Dr ISKANDER SH.
GALEEV
Institute of Physics: Prof. ALBERT V. AGANOV
N. Lobachevsky Institute of Mathematics
and Mechanics: Prof. VLADIMIR A. CHUGU-
NOV
School of Public Administration: Dr LILIA A.
NURGATINA

PROFESSORS

AGANOV, A. V., Physics
AKHMADULLIN, A. G., Philology
ALATYREV, V. I., Physiology
ANDRAMONOVA, N. A., Russian Philology
ANDREEV, V. I., Education
ARSLANOV, M. M., Mathematics
BAKHTIN, A. I., Mineralogy
BALALYKINA, E. A., Philology
BARABANSHIKOV, B. I., Genetics
BASHKIROV, SH. SH., Physics
BUDNIKOV, G. K., Chemistry
BUKHARAEV, R. G., Cybernetics
BUROV, B. V., Lithology
BUSYGIN, E. P., History
BUTAKOV, G. P., Geomorphology
CHERKASOV, R. A., Chemistry
ERMOLAEV, I. P., History
FARUKSHIN, M. H., Sociology
GABDULKHAEV, B. G., Mathematics

GALIULLIN, T. N., Philology
GOLUBEV, A. I., Zoology
KAIGORODOV, V. R., Physics
KHAIRUTDINOV, R. G., History
KHAKOV, V. H., Turkic Languages
KHALYMBADYA, V. G., Palaeontology
KHOKHLOVA, L. P., Plant Physiology
KOCHELAEV, B. I., Physics
KONOPLEV, YU. G., Mechanics
KOPOSOV, G. F., Soil Studies
KURDYUKOV, G. I., Law
KUZNETSOV, V. A., Ichthyology
LESHCHINSKAYA, I. B., Microbiology
LIASHKO, A. D., Computing Mathematics
LITVIN, A. L., History
LYUBARSKI, E. L., Botany
MAKLAKOV, A. I., Physics
MALKOV, V. P., Law
NAFIGOV, R. I., History
NEPRIMEROV, N. N., Electronics
NIKOLAEV, G. A., Philology
PEREVEDENTSEV, YU. P., Meteorology
RAKHMATULLIN, E. S., Sociology
RESHETOV, YU. S., Law
RYABOV, A. A., Law
SADYKOV, M. B., Philosophy
SAKHIBULLIN, N. A., Astrophysics
SALNIKOV, YU. I., Chemistry
SEMENOV, V. F., Political Economy
SHARIFYANOV, I. I., History
SHERSTNEV, A. N., Mathematics
SHIROKOV, A. P., Geometry
SIDOROV, V. V., Radiophysics
TAGIROV, I. R., History
TEPLOV, M. A., Physics
TEPTIN, G. M., Meteorology
TORSUEV, N. P., Geomorphology
TROFIMOV, A. M., Geomorphology
TUMASHEVA, D. G., Turkic Languages
USMANOV, M. A., History
YEGALOV, V. I., Differential Equations
YIGUNIN, V. D., History
ZABOTIN, YA. I., Computing Mathematics

KEMEROVO STATE UNIVERSITY

650043 Kemerovo, Krasnaya ul. 6
Telephone: (3842) 23-12-26
E-mail: rector@kemsu.ru
Internet: www.kemsu.ru

Founded 1974
State control
Language of instruction: Russian
Academic year: September to July
Faculties of biology, chemistry, economics,
foreign languages, history, law, mathemat-
ics, philology, physics, social sciences and
sport

Rector: YU. A. ZAKHAROV
Pro-Rector: B. A. SECHKARYOV
Pro-Rector: B. P. NEVZOROV
Pro-Rector: K. E. AFANASIEV
Pro-Rector: T. M. CHUREKOVA
Pro-Rector: T. M. PANINA
Pro-Rector: V. A. VOLCHEK
Librarian: N. P. KONOVALOVA

Number of teachers: 780
Number of students: 8,834

KHAKASSIA STATE UNIVERSITY 'N. F. KATANOV'

Khakassia Republic, 655000 Abakan, Lenina
pr. 90
Telephone: (3902) 24-53-29
E-mail: univer@khsu.ru
Internet: www.khsu.ru

Founded 1994
State control

Accredited by Fed. Service of Supervision in
Education and Science of Nat. Accreditation
Agency of Russia

Rector: Prof. GENNADY STANISLAVOVICH SUR-
VILLO

First Vice-Rector, Vice-Rector for Scientific
Work: ANDREY ANATOLYEVICH POPOV
Vice-Rector for Admin. Work: YURY VASILYE-
VICH RYBALCHENKO
Vice-Rector for Pedagogical Work: SVETLANA
AFANASYEVNA SUBRAKOVA
Vice-Rector for Quality Control and Devt:
VASILY VASILJEVICH ANJUSHIN
Vice-Rector for Teaching and Organizational
Work: SVETLANA MIKHAILOVNA KUBRINA

Library: more than 1m. vols in 9 libraries
and 15 reading-halls; more than 700 periodicals
Number of teachers: 590
Number of students: 17,460 (incl. 7,500
external)

Publications: *Herald of Katanov State University of Khakassia, Yearbook of the Institute of Sajan-Altay Turkology*

DEANS AND DIRECTORS

Agrarian Department: ALEXEY NIKOLAEVICH
KADYCHEGOV
Centre of Socio-Political and Humanitarian
Education: TATYANA SERGEEVNA TCHIVERS-
KAJA
College of Agriculture: GALINA ALEKSAN-
DROVNA MINYUHINA
College of Medicine: OLGA VLADIMIROVNA
SHTYGASHEVA
College of Music: NINA NIKOLAEVNA KUSHNIR
College of Pedagogical Education, Computer
Science and Law: NADEZHDA VIKTOROVNA
NADEEVA
College of Service Technologies: NINA VIKTOR-
OVNA SLICHNAYA
Department of Physical Training: ALEXANDER
VICTOROVICH FOMINYKH
Engineering and Technical Department:
OLEG NICOLAEVICH KHEGAY
Institute of Arts: NINA NIKOLAEVNA KUSHNIR
Institute of Computer Science and Tele-
matics: SERGEY VIKTOROVICH SHWETZ
Institute of Continuing Pedagogical Educa-
tion: LYUDMILA ANATOLJEVNA MINDIBEKOVA
Institute of Economics and Management:
NINA FEDOTOVNA DITZ
Institute of History and Law: VLADIMIR
GEORGEVICH KICHEEV
Institute of Medicine, Psychology and Social
Sciences: OLGA VLADIMIROVNA SHTYGA-
SHEVA
Institute of Natural Sciences and Mathemat-
ics: IRINA VICTOROVNA KARPUKHINA
Institute of Philology: IVAN IVANOVICH KRE-
MICH
Institute of Sajan-Altay Turkology: TAMARA
GERASIMOVNA BORGOYAKOVA
Institute of Service and Design Technologies:
MARINA VICTOROVNA KHORTOVA
Institute of Upgrading Skills and Staff
Retraining: LIDIA NIKOLAEVNA CHAIRKINA
Veterinary Medicine Dept: VICTOR YURYEVICH
TCHUMAKOV

KOSTROMA STATE NEKRASSOV UNIVERSITY

156961 Kostroma, ul. Pervogo Maya 14
Telephone: (4942) 31-82-91
E-mail: rgc@ksu.edu.ru
Internet: www.ksu.edu.ru

Founded 1918
State control
Language of instruction: Russian
Academic year: September to July

Rector: Prof. NIKOLAI M. RASSADIN
First Pro-Rector: ANATOLY G. KIRPICHNIK
Pro-Rector for Academic Affairs: IRINA G.
ASADULINA
Pro-Rector for Computerisation: VLADIMIR N.
ERSHOV
Pro-Rector for Household Affairs: VYACHE-
SLAV V. ROGACHEV

Pro-Rector for Int. Relations: Lidia N. Vaulina

Pro-Rector for Science: Alexander R. Naumov

Pro-Rector for Social Affairs: Alexei E. Podobin

Librarian: Natalia A. Smirnova

Library of 614,200 vols
Number of teachers: 500
Number of students: 7,000

Publications: *Educational Economic, Vestnik KSU*

DEANS

Faculty of Art: Marina A. Alekseeva

Faculty of Foreign Languages: Margarita M. Kaplina

Faculty of History: Andrei M. Belov

Faculty of Music: Andrei I. Sakharov

Faculty of Natural Science: Igor G. Krinitsin

Faculty of Philology: Madina A. Fokina

Faculty of Physical Education: Lilia M. Bochkova

Faculty of Physics and Mathematics: Denis L. Legotin

Faculty of Service and Technologies: Natalia B. Tarasova

Institute of Economics: Vladimir V. Bulatov

Institute of Pedagogics and Psychology: Andrei I. Timonin

KUBAN STATE UNIVERSITY

350040 Krasnodar, ul. Stavropolskaya 149
Telephone: (8612) 69-95-02
E-mail: rector@kubsu.ru
Internet: www.kubsu.ru

Founded 1924
State control
Languages of instruction: Russian, English
Academic year: September to July

Pres.: Vladimir A. Babeshko

Chief Vice-Pres. and Vice-Pres. for Information: Alexander G. Ivanov

Vice-Pres. for Academic Affairs: Natalya V. Krasnova

Vice-Pres. for Additional Education: Elena A. Zhuravleva

Vice-Pres. for Capital Construction and Repairs: Elena N. Savenko

Vice-Pres. for Distance Education: Igor D. Bregeda

Vice-Pres. for Science and Research: Alexander A. Gavrilov

Vice-Pres. for Social Affairs: Viktor V. Momotov

Sec. of the Univ. Academic Ccl: Tatyana M. Belokon

Librarian: G. V. Solovieva

Number of teachers: 1,000 (incl. 144 professors and 506 assoc. professors)
Number of students: 16,770

Publications: *Ekologichesky Vestnik Nauchnykh Tsentrov TchES* (Letters of BSEC Research centres, 4 a year), *Ekonomika* (1 a year), *Filologiya* (Philology, 2 a year), *Golos Minuvshego* (The Voice of the Past, 4 a year), *Obshchestvo i Chelovek* (Society and Mankind, 4 a year), *Priroda* (Nature, 4 a year), *Terra Incognita* (2 a year), *Upravleniye* (Management, 1 a year)

DEANS

Faculty of Applied Mathematics: Yu. V. Koltsov

Faculty of Architecture and Design: S. Yu Kochetkova

Faculty of Biology: V. Ya. Nagalevsky

Faculty of Chemistry: V. D. Buyklisky

Faculty of Economics: I. V. Shevchenko

Faculty of Geography: M. Yu. Belikov

Faculty of Graphic Art: Yu. V. Korobko

Faculty of History, Sociology and International Relations: G. M. Achagu

Faculty of Journalism: V. V. Rounov

Faculty of Law: I. A. Nikolaychuk

Faculty of Management: A. M. Zhdanovsky

Faculty of Mathematics: G. F. Sokol

Faculty of Philology: V. P. Abramov

Faculty of Physics and Technology: N. A. Yakovenko

Faculty of Romano-Germanic Philology: V. I. Tkhorik

KURGAN STATE UNIVERSITY

640669 Kurgan, ul. Gogolya 25
Telephone: (3522) 43-26-52
E-mail: rektor@kgsu.ru
Internet: www.kgsu.ru

Founded 1952

Faculties of mathematics and information technology, natural sciences, history, law, philology, economics, health protection, psychology and sport, pedagogy, technology, transport systems

Rector: Prof. Oleg I. Bukhtoyarov

Library: 1m. vols
Number of teachers: 700
Number of students: 8,000

KURSK STATE UNIVERSITY

305000 Kursk, ul. Radischeva 33
Telephone: (4712) 70-05-38
E-mail: info@kurksu.ru
Internet: www.kurksu.ru

Founded 1934 as Kursk State Pedagogical Institute
State control
Language of instruction: Russian
Academic year: September to June

Rector: Prof. Vyacheslav V. Gvozdev

First Vice-Rector: Nikolai N. Grebenkov

Vice-Rector for Academic Affairs: Dr Vladimir V. Zakharov

Vice-Rector for Int. Relations: Dr Elena I. Mikhailina

Vice-Rector for Science and Research: Dr Vitaliy A. Kudinov

Vice-Rector for Technical Support: Igor O. Shulgin

Chief Accountant: Galina E. Klochkova

Library of 65,000 vols
Number of teachers: 900
Number of students: 12,000 (of which 9,000 internal and 3,000 external students)

DEANS

Faculty of Art and Design: Viktor I. Zhilin

Faculty of Computer Science: Dr Vitaliy A. Kudinov

Faculty of Economy and Management: Dr Viktor A. Kriulin

Faculty of Foreign Languages: Nikolai A. Smakhtin

Faculty of Geography: Irina P. Balabina

Faculty of History: Plaksin

Faculty of Law: Dr Vladimir V. Zakharov

Faculty of Philology: Yuri L. Philippov

Faculty of Physics and Mathematics: Vyacheslav V. Melentyev

Faculty of Psychology and Pedagogics: Marina A. Lukina

Faculty of Sport and Physical Education: Dr Tatyana V. Skoblikova

Faculty of Theology and Religion Studies: Anatoliy A. Korzinkin

LENINGRAD STATE UNIVERSITY 'A. S. PUSHKIN'

196605 St Petersburg, Pushkin, Peterburgskoe shosse 10
Telephone: (812) 466-65-58
E-mail: pushkin@infos.ru
Internet: www.lgu-edu.spb.ru

Founded 1992 as Leningrad Regional Pedagogical Institute; as Leningrad State Regional Univ. 1996–1999; as A. S. Pushkin Leningrad State Regional Univ. 1999–2003; present name and status 2003
State control

Rector: Prof. Vyacheslav N. Skvortsov

First Pro-Rector: Prof. Galina P. Chepurenko

Pro-Rector for Academic Affairs: Prof. Tatyana V. Maltseva

Pro-Rector for Economic and Int. Affairs: Dr Leonid L. Bukin

Pro-Rector for External and Further Professional Education: Prof. Tatyana S. Komissarova

Pro-Rector for Science: Dr Ekaterina S. Neryshkina

Number of teachers: 360
Number of students: 13,400

DEANS

Faculty of Arts: Dr Svetlana I. Nazarova

Faculty of Foreign Languages: Prof. Svyatoslav I. Alatortsev

Faculty of Law: Prof. Galina P. Chepurenko

Faculty of Mathematics, Physics and Information Science: Dr Sergei D. Boronenko

Faculty of Natural Sciences, Geography and Tourism: Dr Anatoly M. Makarsky

Faculty of Philology: Prof. Tatyana V. Maltseva

MAGNITOGORSK STATE UNIVERSITY

455043 Magnitogorsk, Lenina pr. 114
Telephone: (3511) 35-15-32
E-mail: masu@masu.ru
Internet: www.masu.ru

Founded 1932
State control

Rector: Prof. Valentin F. Romanov

First Pro-Rector: Prof. Vladimir P. Semenov

Librarian: Ludmila V. Kotelnikova

Library of 443,335 vols

DEANS

Faculty of Advancement of Qualifications and Training of Specialists: Prof. Ludmila A. Miroshnichenko

Faculty of Art and Design: Prof. Vladimir M. Bely

Faculty of History: Prof. Mikhail G. Abramzon

Faculty of Information Technology: Prof. Elmira R. Ipatova

Faculty of Linguistics and Translation: Prof. Galina I. Vasina

Faculty of Pedagogy and Methods of Primary Education: Prof. Yuri D. Korobkov

Faculty of Philology: Prof. Lyubov D. Ponomareva

Faculty of Physics and Mathematics: Prof. Viktor A. Kuznetsov

Faculty of Pre-School Education: Prof. Boris D. Kulanin

Faculty of Psychology: Prof. Elena D. Petrova

Faculty of Social Work: Prof. Flyura A. Mustaeva

MARI STATE UNIVERSITY

424001 Mari-El Republic, Yoshkar-Ola, pl. Lenina 1
Telephone: (8362) 12-59-20
E-mail: postmaster@marsu.ru
Internet: www.marsu.ru

Founded 1972
State control
Academic year: September to July

Rector: V. I. Makarov

Vice-Rector: V. I. Chemodanov

Chief Admin. Officer: L. N. Strelnikova

Number of teachers: 384
Number of students: 4,055

Publication: *Arkheograficheshy Vestnik* (Archaeological News, 2 a year)

DEANS

Faculty of Agriculture: G. S. YUNUSOV
Faculty of Biology and Chemistry: M. G. GRIGORIEV
Faculty of Culture and Arts: R. L. YASHME-TOVA
Faculty of Economics: K. V. SHAKIROV
Faculty of Electric Power Technology: L. M. RIBAKOV
Faculty of History and Philology: A. N. CHIMAEV
Faculty of Law: A. M. LOMONOSOV
Faculty of Linguistics and Intercultural Communication: Z. G. ZORINA
Faculty of Physics and Mathematics: G. A. SITNIKOV

MOSCOW STATE REGIONAL UNIVERSITY

107005 Moscow, ul. Radio 10A
Telephone: (495) 261-22-28
E-mail: mgou@mgou.ru
Internet: www.mgou.ru

Founded 1923 as Moscow State Pedagogical Technical College
State control
Language of instruction: Russian
Academic year: September to June

Faculties of business and technology, decorative arts, economics, further education for higher education specialists, law, linguistics, mathematics and physics, military education, pedagogy, physical education and philology, politics, translation; summer school of Russian language, summer school of Arts

Rector: Prof. PAVEL KHROMENKOV
First Pro-Rector for Academic Affairs and Int. Cooperation: Dr VLADIMIR KLICHNIKOV
Pro-Rector for Education and Youth Politics: VYACHESLAV KHORIHIN
Pro-Rector for Education and Youth Politics: Dr MIKHAIL V. YUDIN
Pro-Rector for Science: Dr MARINA LEV-CHENKO
Pro-Rector for Scientific and Int. Cooperation: Prof. YURI I. YAMALOV

Number of teachers: 800
Number of students: 13,000

Publication: *Vestnik MSRU*

MOSCOW STATE UNIVERSITY 'M. V. LOMONOSOV'

119991 Moscow, GSP-1, Leninskie Gory
Telephone: (495) 939-10-00
E-mail: info@rector.msu.ru
Internet: www.msu.ru

Founded 1755
Academic year: September to June

Rector: Acad. VIKTOR SADOVNICHY
Vice-Rector for Academic Policy and Degree Programmes Man.: PYOTR VRZHESHCH
Vice-Rector for Educational Standards, Curricula and Syllabi: IGOR KOTLOBOVSKY
Vice-Rector for Innovations, Informatization and Int. Scientific Cooperation: ALEXEI KHOKHLOV
Vice-Rector for Int. Cooperation: NIKOLAY SYOMIN
Vice-Rector for Research Policy and Research Man.: VLADIMIR BELOKUROV
Vice-Rector for Social Services and Facilities Devt: ALEXANDER CHERNYAEV
Vice-Rector: NIKITA ANISSIMOV (acting)
Vice-Rector: YURI BELENKOV
Vice-Rector: ALEXEY REYMERS (acting)
Vice-Rector: VICTOR TROFIMOV

Number of teachers: 10,441
Number of students: 40,756

Publications: *Moscow State University* (52 a year), *Vestnik MGU* (20 series, 2 a year)

DEANS

Faculty of Bioengineering and Bioinformatics: VLADIMIR SKULACHEV
Faculty of Biology: MIKHAIL KIRPICHNIKOV
Faculty of Chemistry: VALERY LUNIN
Faculty of Computational Mathematics and Cybernetics: YEVGENY MOISEEV
Faculty of Economics: VASSILI KOLESOV
Faculty of Educational Studies: NIKOLAI ROZOV
Faculty of Fine and Performing Arts: ALEX-ANDER LOBODANOV
Faculty of Foreign Languages and Area Studies: SVETLANA TER-MINASOVA
Faculty of Fundamental Medicine: VSEVOLOD TKACHUK
Faculty of Geography: NIKOLAI KASIMOV
Faculty of Geology: DMITRY PUSHCHAROVSKY
Faculty of Global Processes: V. I. ILIYIN (acting)
Faculty of History: SERGEY KARPOV
Faculty of Journalism: YASEN ZASURSKY
Faculty of Law: ALEXANDER GOLICHENKOV
Faculty of Material Sciences: YURI TRETYA-KOV
Faculty of Mechanics and Mathematics: VLADIMIR CHUBARIKOV (acting)
Faculty of Philology: MARINA REMNYOVA
Faculty of Philosophy: VLADIMIR MIRONOV
Faculty of Physical Chemistry: SERGEY ALDOSHIN
Faculty of Physics: VLADIMIR TRUKHIN
Faculty of Political Science: A. YU. SHUTOV (acting)
Faculty of Psychology: YURI ZINCHENKO
Faculty of Public Administration: (vacant)
Faculty of Sociology: VLADIMIR DOBRENKOV
Faculty of Soil Science: SERGEY SHOBA
Faculty of World Politics: ANDREI KOKOSHIN
Graduate School of Innovative Business: DMITRY KOSHUG
Graduate School of Management and Innovation: VLADIMIR VASSILIEV
School of Business Administration: OLEG VIKHANSKY
School of Comtemporary Social Sciences: G. V. OSIPOV
Moscow School of Economics: ALEXANDER NEKIPELOV (Dir)
School of Television: VITALY TRETYAKOV
School of Translation and Interpretation: NIKOLAI GARBOVSKY
Institute of Asian and African Studies: MIKHAIL MEYER

MOSCOW UNIVERSITY OF CONSUMER COOPERATIVES

141014 Moscow oblast, Mytischi, ul. V. Voloshinoi 12
Telephone: (495) 582-97-37
E-mail: ruc@rucoop.ru
Internet: www.ruc.su

Founded 1913

Areas of study: accounting and auditing, commerce, commodity science, economics, economic information systems, finance and credit, global economics, jurisprudence, management, marketing

Pres. and Rector: Prof. MARIA V. SEROSHTAN

Number of teachers: 500
Number of students: 12,000

N. P. OGAREV MORDOVIAN STATE UNIVERSITY

430005 Mordovia, Saransk, Bolshevistskaya ul. 68
Telephone: (8342) 24-48-88

E-mail: rector@mrsu.ru
Internet: www.mrsu.ru

Founded 1931
State control
Languages of instruction: Mordovian, Russian
Academic year: September to June

Rector: Prof. SERGEY M. VDOVIN
First Vice-Rector for Academic Studies: Prof. NIKOLAY E. FOMIN
Vice-Rector for Extracurricular Activities: Prof. MARINA MARTYNOVA
Vice-Rector for Financial Admin.: Prof. DENIS OKUNEV
Vice-Rector for Further Training and Professional Devt Programmes: SERGEY G. PILIPENKO
Vice-Rector for IT: KONSTANTIN LESHCHANKIN
Vice-Rector for Logistics Accomplishment: Prof. IGOR BULANKIN
Vice-Rector for Major Construction Work: STEPAN P. GUDOZHNIKOV
Vice-Rector for Science: PETR V. SENIN
Registrar: MIKHAIL M. GUDOV
Librarian: IRINA OTSTAVNOVA

Library of 2,196,381 vols, 731 periodicals
Number of teachers: 1,689
Number of students: 26,000

Publications: *Integration of Education* (4 a year), *Regionologiya* (4 a year), *Vestnik Mordovskogo Universiteta* (4 a year)

DEANS

Faculty of Biology: Prof. VIKTOR REVIN
Faculty of Economics: Prof. TATIANA SALI-MOVA
Faculty of Electronic Engineering: IGOR GULAYEV
Faculty of Foreign Languages: Prof. NATALIA V. BURENINA
Faculty of Geography: ANATOLY A. YAMASH-KIN
Faculty of Industrial and Civil Construction: Prof. VLADIMIR EROFEYEV
Faculty of Law: Prof. YULIA SUSHKOVA
Faculty of Lighting Engineering: Prof. OLGA ZHELEZNIKOVA
Faculty of Mathematics and IT: Prof. IVAN CHUCHAYEV
Faculty of Philology: Prof. M. V. MOSIN
Faculty of Pre-Diploma Programmes and Vocational Education: MIKHAIL LOMSHIN

NIZHNII NOVGOROD STATE UNIVERSITY 'N. I. LOBACHEVSKY'

603950 Nizhnii Novgorod, pr. Gagarina 23
Telephone: (831) 462-30-90
E-mail: unn@unn.ru
Internet: www.unn.ru

Founded 1916
State control
Language of instruction: Russian
Academic year: September to June

Rector: Prof. EVGENY V. CHUPRUNOV
Vice-Rector for Academic Affairs: Assoc. Prof. ALEXANDER V. PETROV
Vice-Rector for Int. Relations and Innovations in Education: Prof. ALEXANDER O. GRUDZINSKY
Vice-Rector for Research: Prof. SERGEI N. GURBATOV
Pres.: Prof. ROMAN G. STRONGIN
Librarian: Dr YURI M. SOROKIN

Number of teachers: 1,350
Number of students: 32,000

Publication: *Vestnik of the Nizhnii Novgorod University*

DEANS

Advanced School of General and Applied Physics: Dr M. D. TOKMAN
Faculty of Biology: Dr A. P. VESELOV

Faculty of Business and Management: Dr A. O. GRUDZINSKY
Faculty of Chemistry: Dr A. V. GUSHCHIN
Faculty of Computer Science and Cybernetics: Dr V. P. GERGEL
Faculty of Economics: Dr YU. V. TRIFONOV
Faculty of Finance: Dr V. N. YASENEV
Faculty of History: Dr A. A. KUZNETSOV
Faculty of International Relations: Dr M. I. RYKHTIK
Faculty of Law: Dr V. I. TSYGANOV
Faculty of Mechanics and Mathematics: Dr A. K. LYUBIMOV
Faculty of Philology: Dr L. I. RUCHINA
Faculty of Physical Training and Sport: Dr V. G. KUZMIN
Faculty of Physics: Dr K. A. MARKOV
Faculty of Radiophysics: Dr A. V. YAKIMOV
Faculty of Social Sciences: Dr V. A. BLONIN

NORTH-EASTERN FEDERAL UNIVERSITY

Republic of Sakha (Yakutia), 677000 Yakutsk, ul. Belinskogo 58
Telephone: (4112) 36-14-53
E-mail: oip-yakutsk@mail.ru
Internet: www.s-vfu.ru

Founded 1956
State control
Languages of instruction: English, Russian, Yakut
Academic year: September to July

Rector: Prof. Dr EVGENIYA I. MIKHAYLOVA
Vice-Rector: Prof. Dr VASILY I. VASILYEV
Librarian: TATIANA S. MAKSIMOVA

Library of 1,300,000 vols
Number of teachers: 1,400
Number of students: 20,000

Publications: *Nauka i obrazovaniye* (4 a year), *Vestnik SVFU*

DEANS

Faculty of Geology and Survey: BORIS I. POPOV
Faculty of History: NATALIA A. STRUCHKOVA
Faculty of Law: PETR V. GOGOLEV
Faculty of Mining: BORIS N. ZAROVNYAEV
Faculty of Philology: GALINA E. ZHONDOROVA
Faculty of Pre-Undergraduate Education: SVETLANA V. FEDOROVA
Faculty of Road Construction: MIKHAIL F. SEMENOV
Institute of Additional Professional Education: OLGA M. CHOROSOVA
Institute of Engineering and Technology: TERENTY A. KORNILOV
Institute of Finances and Economics: ALEXANDR A. KUGAEVSKIY
Institute of Foreign Languages and Regional Studies: OLGA A. MELNICHUK
Institute of Languages and Cultures of the Peoples of the North-East: GAVRIL G. FILIPPOV
Institute of Mathematics and Information Science: VERA I. AFANASYEVA
Institute of Medicine: PALMIRA G. PETROVA
Institute of Natural Sciences: ANATOLY N. NIKOLAEV
Institute of Physics and Technologies: NADEZHDA A. SAVVINOVA
Institute of Post-Graduate Education of Physicians: LEONID A. APROSIMOV
Institute of Psychology: ANASTASIA P. OKONESHNIKOVA
Institute of Sports and Physical Education: DMITRY N. PLATONOV
Teacher Training Institute: ALEXEY I. GOLIKOV
Technological Institute: ALEXEY M. BESSMERTNUY

PROFESSORS

ALEXEEV, A. N., History

ANDREEV, V. S., Engineering
ANISIMOV, V. M., Education
ANTONOV, N. K., Philosophy
BASHARIN, K. G., Medicine
BEGIEV, V. G., Medicine
BLOKHIN, I. P., Biology
BURTSEV, A. A., Philology
BURYANINA, N. S., Geology
BUSHKOV, P. N., Surgery
CHEMEZOV, E. N., Geology
DANILOV, D. A., Pedagogics
DIACHKOVSKY, N. D., Yakut Language and Literature
DOBROVOLSKY, G. N., Engineering
EGOROV, I. E., Mathematics
FEDOROV, M. M., Law
FOMIN, M. M., Pedagogics
FRIDOVSKY, V. Y., Geology
GOGOLEV, A. I., General History
GOGOLEV, M. P., Medicine
ILLARIONOV, V. V., Philology
IVANOV, A. I., Medicine
IVANOVA, A. V., Education
IZAKSON, V. Y., Mathematics
KERSHENGOLTS, B. M., Biology
KHANDY, M. V., Medicine
KHATYLAEV, M. M., History
KOCHNEV, V. P., Education
KOLODEZNIKOV, I. I., Geology and Mineralogy
KORNILOVA, A. G., Education
KOZHEVNIKOV, N. N., Philosophy
KYCHKIN, I. S., Theoretical Physics
KYLACHANOV, A. P., Engineering
LUKOVTSEV, V. S., Philosophy
MAKAROV, V. M., Medicine
MAKHAROV, Y. M., Philosophy
MAKSIMOV, G. N., Philosophy
MIKHAILOV, V. D., Philosophy
MISHLIMOVICH, M. Y., Philology
MORDOSOV, I. I., Biology
NEUSTROEV, N. D., Education
NIKOLAEV, N. S., Engineering
NOVIKOV, A. G., Philosophy
OKONESHNIKOVA, A. P., Psychology
PETROV, E. E., Mathematics
PETROV, N. E., Philology
PETROVA, P. G., Medicine
PETROVA, S. M., Education
POPOV, A. A., Economics
POPOV, B. N., Philosophy
PROKOPIEVA, S. M., Philology
SAMOKHIN, A. V., Mining
SAMSONOV, N. G., Philology
SHAMAEV, N. R., Education
SHEPELEV, V. S., Geology
SIVTSEV, I. S., History
SLASTENA, YU. L., Geology
SMIRNOV, V. P., Engineering
SOLOMONOV, N. G., Biology
STOGNY, V. V., Geology
TAZLOVA, R. S., Psychiatry
TIKHONOV, D. G., Medicine
TOBUROKOV, N. N., Linguistics
TOLSTIKHIN, O. N., Permafrost
TOMSKY, I. E., Economics
TYRLYGIN, M. A., Medicine
VASILIEV, E. P., Medicine
VASILIEV, V. I., Mathematics
VASILIEVA-KRALINA, I. I., Biology
VIKULOV, M. A., Engineering
VINOGRADOV, A. V., Chemistry
YAKIMOV, O. D., Journalism
ZAROVNYAEV, B. N., Geology

NORTHERN INTERNATIONAL UNIVERSITY

685014 Magadan, ul. Portovaya 13
Telephone: (41322) 3-00-21
Internet: www.niu.ru

NORTH OSSETIAN STATE UNIVERSITY

362025 Vladikavkaz, ul. Vatutina 46
Telephone: (8672) 53-09-04
E-mail: webmaster@nosu.ru
Internet: www.nosu.ru

Founded 1969
Language of instruction: Russian
Academic year: September to June

Rector: AKHURBEK M. MAGOMETOV
First Pro-Rector, Pro-Rector for Academic Affairs: ANATOLY V. RAITSEV
Pro-Rector for Int. Affairs: OLEG S. KHATSAYEV
Pro-Rector for Science: VALERY G. SOZNANOV
Librarian: KLARA K. KOKAYEVA

Number of teachers: 830
Number of students: 11,700

DEANS

Faculty of Arts and Design: V. N. TSALAGOV
Faculty of Biology and Soil Studies: R. G. ZANGIONOVA
Faculty of Chemistry and Technology: N. I. KALOYEV
Faculty of Economics: Z. G. TEDEEV
Faculty of Education and Elementary Education: V. K. KOCHISOV
Faculty of Foreign Languages: T. T. KAMBOLOV
Faculty of Geography: B. M. BEROYEV
Faculty of History: A. I. ABAYEV
Faculty of Law: E. G. PLIYEV
Faculty of Management: V. G. TSOGOYEV
Faculty of Mathematics: A. A. AZIYEV
Faculty of Ossetian Philology: R. Z. KOMAYEVA
Faculty of Philology: L. M. BESOLOV
Faculty of Physical Education and Sports: F. G. KHAMIKOYEV
Faculty of Physics: A. P. BLIYEV

NOVGOROD STATE UNIVERSITY

173003 Veliky Novgorod, St Petersburgskaya ul. 41
Telephone: (8162) 62-72-44
E-mail: novsu@novsu.ru
Internet: www.novsu.ru

Founded 1993
Academic year: September to June

Faculties of administration, agricultural engineering, agricultural production technology, architecture, arts and design, arts and technology, biology, chemistry and environmental science, child education and psychology, economics, engineering and technology, finance, foreign languages, higher nursing education, history, law, medicine, pharmacy, philosophy, physics and technology, stomatology

Rector: Prof. Dr VIKTOR VEBER

Number of teachers: 900
Number of students: 14,000

Publications: *Chelo* (History and Literature, 4 a year), *Vestnik Novgorodskogo Gosudarstvennogo Universiteta* (Research, 4 a year)

NOVOSIBIRSK STATE UNIVERSITY

630090 Novosibirsk, ul. Pirogova 2
Telephone: (3832) 39-73-78
E-mail: inter@nsu.ru
Internet: www.nsu.ru

Founded 1959
State control
Language of instruction: Russian
Academic year: September to June

Rector: Prof. NIKOLAY S. DIKANSKY
Vice-Rector for Int. Activities: ELENA M. LISMAN

Vice-Rector for Research: Prof. GENNADY YU. SHVEDENKOV
Vice-Rector for Studies: Prof. NATALIA V. DULEPOVA
Registrar: N. I. BOIKOVA
Librarian: L. A. LYAGUSHINA

Library of 815,051 vols
Number of teachers: 2,200
Number of students: 6,000

Publications: *Algebra and Logics* (6 a year), *Critics and Semiotics* (1 a year), *Philosophy of Science* (4 a year), *Siberian Philological Journal* (2 a year), *Vestnik NGU* (3 a year)

DEANS

Department of Economics (tel. (3832) 39-72-42; e-mail dekeko@lab.nsu.ru; f. 1967):

Prof. GAGIK M. MKRTCHAN

Department of Foreign Languages:

Prof. G. G. KURKINA

Department of Geology and Geophysics (tel. (3832) 39-72-18; e-mail shatsky@uiggm.nsu.ru; internet ggd.nsu.ru; f. 1962):

Prof. VLADISLAV S. SHATSKY

Department of the Humanities (tel. (3832) 30-08-62; e-mail info@gf.nsu.ru; internet www.gf.nsu.ru; f. 1962):

Prof. LEONID G. PANIN

Department of Information Technologies (tel. (3832) 39-77-95; e-mail dekanat@ccfit.nsu.ru; internet www.fit.nsu.ru; f. 2000):

Dr MIKHAIL M. LAVRENTIEV

Department of Mechanics and Mathematics (tel. (3832) 39-75-81; e-mail mmf@msu.ru; internet mmfd.nsu.ru):

Prof. SERGEY S. GONCHAROV

Department of Natural Sciences (tel. (3832) 39-74-30; e-mail decan@fen.nsu.ru; internet www.fen.nsu.ru; f. 1959):

Prof. VLADIMIR A. REZNIKOV

Department of Physics (tel. (3832) 39-78-00; e-mail dean@phys.nsu.ru; internet www.phys.nsu.ru; f. 1961):

Prof. ANDREY V. ARZHANNIKOV

OMSK STATE UNIVERSITY

644077 Omsk, pr. Mira 55A
Telephone: (3812) 67-01-04
E-mail: rector@omsu.ru
Internet: www.omsu.ru

Founded 1974
State control
Language of instruction: Russian
Academic year: September to June

Rector: Prof. GENNADY I. GERING
Pro-Rector: Dr MIKHAIL V. KHOROSHEVSKY
Pro-Rector for Academic Affairs: Dr VALERY V. DUBITSKY
Pro-Rector for Finance and Admin.: Dr VLADIMIR P. AVILOV
Pro-Rector for Scientific Affairs: Dr VLADIMIR I. STRUNIN
Librarian: LYUDMILA A. BALAKINA

Number of teachers: 640
Number of students: 10,000

Publications: *Omsky Universitet* (28 a year), *Vestnik Omskogo Universiteta* (4 a year)

DEANS

Faculty of Arts and Culture: NINA M. GENOVA
Faculty of Chemistry: IRINA V. VLASOVA
Faculty of Economics: LYUDMILA N. IVANOVA
Faculty of Foreign Languages: NATALYA G. GICHEVA
Faculty of History: ALEXEY V. YAKUB
Faculty of International Business: YURI P. DRUS
Faculty of Law: MAXIM S. FOKIN

Faculty of Mathematics: VLADIMIR B. NIKOLAEV
Faculty of Philology: NIKOLAI N. MISYUROV
Faculty of Physics: KLIMENTY N. YUGAI
Faculty of Psychology: LYUDMILA I. DEMENTY
Faculty of Theology and World Culture: DMITRY P. SINELNIKOV

PROFESSORS

ADEEV, G. D., Theoretical Nuclear Physics
AKELKINA, E. A., Literature
AZAROV, V. A., Law
BAOURIN, S. N., Law
BORBAT, V. F., Chemistry and Technology of Non-ferrous and Noble Metals
DUBENSKY, U. P., Pedagogics
ELOVIKOV, L. A., Methodology of Local Labour Management
FAIZULLIN, R. T., Mathematics
FISYUK, A. S., Chemistry
FOMENKO, S. V., History
GERING, G. I., Physics
GOOTS, A. K., Geometry
GRIN, A. G., Mathematics
GRINBERG, M. S., Criminal Law
GRISHKOV, A. N., Mathematics
ISSERS, O. S., Linguistics
KASANNIK, A. I., Ecological Law
KLEIMENOV, M. P., Law
KUKIN, G. P., Algebra
KUZMINA, N. A., Linguistics
LAVROV, E. I., Political Economy
MATYUSCHENKO, V. I., Archaeology
MILLER, A. E., Economy
NOVATOROV, V. E., Pedagogics
OSIPOV, B. I., Linguistics
OSTROVSKY, N. M., Chemistry
OVSIANNIKOVA, I. N., Philosophy
PERTSEV, N. V., Mathematics
POSDNIAKOV, N. K., Politology
PRUDNIKOV, V. V., Physics
RAZUMOV, V. I., Philosophy
REMNEV, A. V., History
ROMANKOV, V. A., Mathematics
ROY, O. M., Sociology
SAGITULLIN, R. S., Chemistry of Heterocyclic Compounds
SEMIKOLENOVA, N. A., Physics
SHIROKOV, I. V., Physics
SKOBELKIN, V. V., Labour Law
SOROKIN, U. A., History
STRUGOV, U. F., Mathematics
TIPUKHIN, V. N., Philosophy
TOLOCHKO, A. P., Pre-Revolutionary Native History
TOMILOV, N. A., Ethnography
VERSHININ, V. I., Analytical Chemistry
YUGAI, K. N., Physics
ZOLOTARYOV, I. D., Physics

OREL STATE UNIVERSITY

302015 Orel, Komsomolskaya ul. 95
Telephone: (0862) 77-73-18
E-mail: rector@univ-orel.ru
Internet: www.univ-orel.ru

Founded 1974
State control

Rector: Prof. FEDOR S. AVDEEV
Pro-Rector for Academic Affairs: Prof. NADEZHDA A. ILYINA
Pro-Rector for External Education and Int. Relations: Prof. NADEZHDA A. ILYINA
Pro-Rector for Science: Prof. GENNADY P. VERKEENKO

Number of teachers: 670
Number of students: 11,200

ORENBURG STATE UNIVERSITY

460018 Orenburg, pr. Pobedy 13
Telephone: (3532) 77-67-70
E-mail: oms@mail.osu.ru
Internet: www.osu.ru

Founded 1971
State control
Language of instruction: Russian
Academic year: September to July

Rector: Dr VLADIMIR KOVALEVSKIY
Pro-Rector for Academic Affairs: ALEXANDER D. PROSKURIN
Pro-Rector for Academic Methodology: TATYANA P. PETUKHOVA
Pro-Rector for Admin. Maintenance and Capital Construction: VLADIMIR P. KOLGANOV
Pro-Rector for Informatization and Security: VICTOR V. BIKOVSKY
Pro-Rector for Int. Students Affairs: BALAZHAN M. KARCHAEVA
Pro-Rector for Scientific Research: Dr SERGEY N. LETUTA
Pro-Rector for Social and Educational Affairs: TATYANA A. NOSOVA

Library: 1m. vols
Number of teachers: 2,300
Number of students: 36,600

PACIFIC NATIONAL UNIVERSITY

680035 Khabarovsk, ul. Tikhookeanskaya 136
Telephone: (4212) 72-07-12
E-mail: info@khstu.ru
Internet: www.khstu.ru

Founded 2005, fmrly Khabarovsk State Univ. (f. 1958)
State control
Language of instruction: Chinese, English, Japanese, Korean, Russian
Academic year: September to June

Depts: engineering and construction, nature management and ecology, architecture and design, automation and informational technology, transport and technology, economics and management, social studies and humanities, law, computer and fundamental sciences, extramural training, extension and parallel training, further professional education

Rector: SERGEI N. IVANCHENKO

Library: 1.2m. vols
Number of teachers: 950
Number of students: 25,000

PACIFIC STATE UNIVERSITY OF ECONOMICS

690950 Vladivostok, Okeansky pr. 19
Telephone: (4232) 26-62-21
E-mail: web@psue.ru
Internet: www.psue.ru
State control
Founded 1964

Rector: Prof. VIKTOR G. BELKIN

PENZA STATE UNIVERSITY

440026 Penza, Krasnaya ul. 40
Telephone: (8412) 66-29-27
E-mail: cnit@stup.ac.ru
Internet: www.stup.ac.ru
State control

Founded 1943, present name and status 1998

Rector: Prof. VLADIMIR VOLCHIKHIN
First Pro-Rector: VICTOR A. MESCHERYAKOV
Pro-Rector for Academic Affairs: VICTOR B. MEKHANOV
Pro-Rector for Admin. and Finance: BORIS V. MALSANOV
Pro-Rector for Governance and Personnel: YURI V. KLOCHKOV
Pro-Rector for Science: MIKHAIL A. SCHERBAKOV

Number of teachers: 725
Number of students: 13,895 ..

UNIVERSITY BRANCH
Serdobsk Branch: Penza Region, 442890 Serdobsk, Lenina ul. 285A; Dir IVAN I. IVANOV

PEOPLES' FRIENDSHIP UNIVERSITY OF RUSSIA

117198 Moscow, Miklukho-Maklaya ul. 6

Telephone: (095) 434-70-27
E-mail: rudn@rudn.ru
Internet: www.rudn.ru

Founded 1960 as Patrice Lumumba Peoples' Friendship Univ.
Language of instruction: Russian
Academic year: September to July

Rector: Prof. VLADIMIR M. FILIPPOV (acting)
Vice-Rector: A. D. GLADUSH
Vice-Rector: A. P. YEFREMOV
Vice-Rector: A. V. DOLZIKOVA
Vice-Rector: EL. V. PROTSENKO
Vice-Rector: E. L. SHESHNYAK
Vice-Rector: G. G. SOKOLOV
Vice-Rector: N. S. KIRABAEV
Vice-Rector: N. V. NAZYUTA
Librarian: E. Y. LOTOVA

Number of teachers: 2,200
Number of students: 28,000

Publications: *Druzhba* (52 a year, university newspaper), *Vestnik Rossiiskogo Universiteta Druzhby Narodov* (4 a year)

DEANS

Faculty of Agriculture: Prof. V. G. PLUSHIKOV
Faculty of Ecology: Prof. N. A. CHERNYKH
Faculty of Economics: Prof. M. A. DAVTJAN
Faculty of Engineering: Prof. N. K. PONOMAREV
Faculty of Foreign Languages and General Educational Disciplines: Prof. V. V. YAKUSHEV
Faculty of Humanities and Social Sciences: Prof. V. A. TSVYK
Faculty of Law: Prof. V. F. PONKA
Faculty of Medicine: Prof. V. A. FROLOV
Faculty of Philology: Prof. A. G. KOVALENKO
Faculty of Physical, Mathematical and Natural Sciences: Prof. V. V. DAVYDOV
Institute of Foreign Languages: Prof. N. L. SOKOLOVA
Institute of Hotel Business and Tourism: Prof. S. V. DIKHTYAR
Institute of International Programmes: N. V. SULKOVA
Institute of World Economy and Business (Int. School of Business): Prof. Y. N. MOSEIKYN

PERM STATE UNIVERSITY

614600 Perm, GSP, ul. Bukireva 15

Telephone: 33-61-83
Internet: www.psu.ru

Founded 1916
State control
Language of instruction: Russian
Academic year: September to June

Faculties of biology, chemistry, economics, geology, geography, history and politology, law, mechanics and mathematics, modern foreign languages and literatures, philology, philosophy and sociology and physics

Rector: Prof. IGOR MAKARIKHIN
Vice-Rector: Prof. KRASILNIKOV DMITRIY
Vice-Rector: Dr OLGA P. ILYINYKH
Vice-Rector: Prof. SERGEY O. MAKAROV
Vice-Rector: VALERII N. KATAEV
Vice-Rector: VALERY I. KHIRJUCHIN
Librarian: R. N. ROGALNIKOVA

Number of teachers: 683
Number of students: 9,167

Publications: *Caves Research Problems* (1 a year), *Computer Systems and Processes Modelling* (1 a year), *Geophysical Methods of Oil and Gas Exploration* (1 a year), *Mechanics of Controlled Movement Problems* (1 a year), *Radiospectroscopy* (1 a year), *Statistical Methods of Verifying and Estimating Hypotheses* (1 a year), *Uchenye Zapiski* (Transactions)

PETROZAVODSK STATE UNIVERSITY

185640 Republic of Karelia, Petrozavodsk, Ave Lenina 33

Telephone: (8142) 78-51-40
E-mail: rectorat@psu.karelia.ru
Internet: petrsu.ru

Founded 1940
State control
Languages of instruction: English, Russian
Academic year: September to June

Rector: Prof. ANATOLY VORONIN
Pres.: Prof. VICTOR VASILYEV
Vice-Rector for Admin. and Economic Work: LJUDMILA BEZLATNAYA
Vice-Rector for Education: Prof. VLADIMIR SYUNEV
Vice-Rector for Innovation and Production Activities: Prof. ILYA SHEGELMAN
Vice-Rector for Organizational Work: Prof. SERGEY KORZHOV
Vice-Rector for Pre-Univ. Training and Career Guidance: Assoc. Prof. ANATOLY LOPUHA
Vice-Rector for Research: Prof. Dr ELMIRA ZILBER
Head of Directorate for Int. Cooperation: LYUDMILA KULIKOVSKAYA
Librarian: MARINA OTLIVANCHIK

Library of 1,179,042 vols
Number of teachers: 905
Number of students: 18,616

Publications: *Trudy* (Works, 1 a year), *Uchenye Zapiski* (1 a year)

DEANS

Faculty of Agriculture: NIKITA ONISCHENKO
Faculty of Baltic and Finnish Philology and Culture: TAMARA STARSHOVA
Faculty of Ecology and Biology: ERNEST IVANTER
Faculty of Economics: VLADIMIR AKULOV
Faculty of Forest Engineering: ALEXANDER PITUKHIN
Faculty of History: SERGEY VERIGIN
Faculty of Improvement of Professional Skills: TATYANA AGARKOVA
Faculty of Industrial and Civil Engineering: YURY MARKADANOV
Faculty of Law: SERGEY CHERNOV
Faculty of Mathematics: ALEKSEI VARFOLOMEEV
Faculty of Medicine: ALEKSANDR BALASHOV
Faculty of Mining and Geology: VLADIMIR AMINOV
Faculty of Philology: ANDREY KUNILSKY
Faculty of Physical Engineering: DMITRI BALASHOV
Faculty of Political and Social Sciences: VALENTINA MAKSIMOVA

POMORSKY STATE UNIVERSITY 'M. V. LOMONSOV'

163002 Arkhangelsk, Lomosova pr. 4

Telephone: (8182) 28-07-80
E-mail: psu@pomorsu.ru
Internet: www.pomorsu.ru

Founded 1991, present name and status 1996
State control

Rector: Prof. VLADIMIR N. BULATOV
First Pro-Rector: YURI V. KUDRYASHOV
Pro-Rectors for Academic Affairs: IRINA R. LUGOVSKAYA, LEONID N. SHESTAKOV
Pro-Rector for Admin. and Finance: ALEXANDER G. LESCHIKOV

Pro-Rector for External Academic Affairs: ANATOLY A. SEMIN
Pro-Rector for Int. Affairs: ALEXANDER S. KRYLOV
Pro-Rector for Science: VLADISLAV I. GOLDIN

Library of 700,000 vols
Number of students: 12,419

ROSTOV STATE UNIVERSITY OF ECONOMICS

344002 Rostov-on-Don, Bolshaya Sadovaya Str. 69

Telephone: (8632) 63-30-80
E-mail: rector@rsue.ru
Internet: www.rsue.ru

Founded 1931
State control
Language of instruction: Russian
Academic year: September to July

Rector: ADAM ALBEKOV
Vice-Rector for Science: Prof. Dr LYUDMILA USENKO

Library of 882,000 vols
Number of teachers: 976
Number of students: 18,000

Publications: *Bulletin* (4 a year), *Scientific Notes* (4 a year)

DEANS

Faculty of Accounting: Prof. Dr ELENA MAKARENKO
Faculty of Commerce and Marketing: Prof. Dr DMITRIY KOSTOGLODOV
Faculty of Finance: Prof. Dr ELENA ALIFANOVA
Faculty of Informatization and Control: Prof. Dr MIKHAIL DENISOV
Faculty of Law: Prof. Dr IRINA RUKAVISHNIKOVA
Faculty of Linguistics and Journalism: Prof. Dr TATYANA YEVSYUKOVA
Faculty of National and International Economy: Prof. Dr VLADIMIR DZHUKHA

RUSSIAN STATE SOCIAL UNIVERSITY

107150 Moscow, ul. Losinoostrovskaya 24 Moscow, Vilgelma Pika ul., korp. 1

Telephone: (495) 187-60-25
E-mail: info@mgsu.info
Internet: www.rgsu.net

Founded 1991 as Russian State Social Institute; accredited with univ. status as Moscow State Social Univ. 1994; present name 2004

Rector: Prof. VASILY I. ZHUKOV
Vice-Rector: GENNADY V. SAENKO

DEANS

Faculty of Foreign Languages: IRINA N. TUPITSYNA
Faculty of Further Education: TAMARA S. SUMSKAYA
Faculty of Humanities: LEONID G. LAPTEV
Faculty of Law: DIMITRY V. ILYAKOV
Faculty of Personnel Training and Qualification Improvement: TATYANA V. SHELYAG
Faculty of Socioeconomics: NIKOLAI N. PILIPENKO
Faculty of Social Information Technologies: VITALY M. ARISTOV
Faculty of Social Insurance and Finance: ALEXANDER A. GRUNIN
Faculty of Social Management: OLGA A. URZHA
Faculty of Social Medicine and Rehabilitation Technologies: VALENTINA V. CHESHIKHINA
Faculty of Sociology: DINA T. KABDULLINOVA
Faculty of Social Work, Pedagogy and Psychology: VLADISLAV A. NIKITIN

Faculty of Work and Employment Security: YURI G. SOROKIN

RUSSIAN STATE TRADE AND ECONOMICS UNIVERSITY

125993 Moscow, ul. Smolnaya 36
Telephone: (499) 458-94-79
E-mail: mail@rsute.ru
Internet: www.rsute.ru

Founded 1930
Language of instruction: Russian
Academic year: September to July

Rector: Prof. Dr SERGEY N. BABURIN

Library of 868,960 vols
Number of students: 65,000

Publications: *Caucasian Research Notes* (scientific journal), *Science Horizons*, *Vestnik of RSUTE*

DEANS

Faculty of Commerce and Marketing: Prof. TATYANA PARAMONOVA
Faculty of Computing Technologies: Prof. DMITRY NECHAEV
Faculty of Finance and Economics: Prof. ALEKSANDR LITVINYUK
Faculty of Hospitality, Restaurant Business and Services: Prof. MIKHAIL MOROZOV
Faculty of Law: Prof. OLEG SAULYAK
Faculty of Management: Prof. LYUDMILA NIKITINA
Faculty of Social Technologies: Prof. ALEKSEY CHERNYSHOV
Faculty of Tax and Taxation: Prof. DMITRY RAZUMOVSKY
Faculty of World Economics and Trade: Prof. ELENA VAVILOVA

RUSSIAN STATE UNIVERSITY FOR THE HUMANITIES

125267 Moscow, Miusskaya pl. 6
Telephone: (495) 250-61-18
E-mail: afn@rggu.msk.su
Internet: www.rsuh.ru

Founded 1991

Rector: Prof. YURI N. AFANASYEV

Library: 1.5m. vols
Number of teachers: 484
Number of students: 4,120

ST PETERSBURG STATE UNIVERSITY

199034 St Petersburg, Universitetskaya nab. 7/9
Telephone: (812) 328-20-00
E-mail: office@inform.pu.ru
Internet: www.spbu.ru

Founded 1724
State control
Academic year: September to June (2 terms)

Rector: Prof. NIKOLAY M. KROPACHEV
Vice-Rector: I. A DEMENTYEV
Vice-Rector for Academic Affairs: Prof. EKATERINA G. BABELIUK
Vice-Rector for Academics: Prof. IGOR A. GORLINSKY
Vice-Rector for Economics: Prof. IVAN I. BOYKO
Vice-Rector for Economy and Social Devt: Prof. GENNADIY S. VASILIEV
Vice-Rector for Legal Issues: MIKHAIL N. KUDILINSKY
Vice-Rector for Research: Prof. NIKOLAY G. SKVORTSOV
Librarian: MAXIM GORKY

Library: see under Libraries and Archives
Number of teachers: 6,000
Number of students: 32,400

Publications: *Jurisprudence*, *Vestnik St. Petersburg University* (Journal, in 7 series)

DEANS

Faculty of Applied Communications: Prof. SERGEY N. BOLSHAKOV
Faculty of Applied Mathematics: Dr LEON A. PETROSIAN
Faculty of Arts: VALERY A. GERGIEV
Faculty of Asian and African Studies: Prof. MIKHAIL B. PIOTROVSKY
Faculty of Biology and Soil Science: Prof. ALEXANDRA D. KHARAZOVA
Faculty of Chemistry: Prof. IRINA A. BALOVA
Faculty of Economics: Dr OTAR L. MARGANIYA
Faculty of Geography and Geo-Ecology: Prof. NIKOLAY V. KALDENIN
Faculty of Geology: Prof. SERGEI V. APLONOV
Faculty of History: Assoc. Prof. ABDULLA H. DAUDOV
Faculty of International Relations: Prof. IRINA N. NOVIKOVA
Faculty of Journalism: Prof. LIUDMILA P. GROMOVA
Faculty of Law: Prof. NATALIA A. SHEVELEVA
Faculty of Liberal Arts and Sciences, Smolny College: Prof. ALEXEY L. KUDRIN
Faculty of Management: (vacant)
Faculty of Mathematics and Mechanics: Prof. GENNADY. A. LEONOV
Faculty of Medicine: Prof. PETR K. YABLONSKY
Faculty of Philology: Prof. LUDMILA A. VERBITSKAYA
Faculty of Philosophy: Prof. SERGEY I. DUDNIK
Faculty of Physics: Prof. MIKHAIL V. KOVALCHUK
Faculty of Political Science: Prof. STANISLAV G. EREMEEV
Faculty of Psychology: Assoc. Prof. ALLA V. SHABOLTAS
Faculty of Sociology: Dr VIKTORIA I. DUDINA
Faculty of Stomatology and Medical Technologies: Prof. YURI A. SCHERBUK

ATTACHED INSTITUTES

Botanical Gardens: Dir V. N. NIKITINA.
Institute of Applied Mathematics: Dir Dr D. A. OVSIANNIKOV.
Institute of Astronomy: Dir Dr V. V. VITYAZEV.
Institute of Biology: Dir Dr D. V. OSIPOV.
Institute of Chemistry: Dir Dr YU. E. ERMOLENKO.
Institute of Complex Social Research: Dir Dr V. E. SEMENOV.
Institute of Geography: Dir Dr A. I. CHISTOBAEV.
Institute of Information Technology: Dir Dr A. N. TEREKHOV.
Institute of Laser Research: Dir Dr YU. S. TVERIANOVICH.
Institute of Mathematics and Mechanics: Dir Dr G. A. LEONOV.
Institute of Physics: Dir Dr YE. I. RYUMTSEV.
Institute of Physiology: Dir Dr I. YE. KANUNIKOV.
Institute of Radiophysics: Dir O. V. SOLOVIEV.
Institute of the Earth's Crust: Dir Dr V. V. KURILENKO

ST PETERSBURG STATE UNIVERSITY OF CINEMA AND TELEVISION

191126 St Petersburg, ul. Pravdy 13
Telephone: (812) 315-74-83
E-mail: info@gukit.ru
Internet: www.gukit.ru

Founded 1918

Study areas incl. art of cinema and television, economics, electrical engineering, film equipment, film and photographic materials

Rector: Prof. ALEXANDER A. BELUSOV

Library of 500,000 vols
Number of students: 4,500

Publication: *Proceedings*

ST PETERSBURG STATE UNIVERSITY OF ECONOMICS AND FINANCE

191023 St Petersburg, ul. Sadovaya 21
Telephone: (812) 310-38-23
E-mail: rector@finec.ru
Internet: www.finec.ru

Founded 1930, present name and status 1997

Faculties of accounting, banking, economic theory, finance, industrial economics, international economic relations, management, marketing, statistics; also comprises a Higher Economics School

Rector: LEONID S. TARASEVICH

Number of teachers: 2,000
Number of students: 12,000

Library: 1m. vols

SAKHALIN STATE UNIVERSITY

693008 Yuzhno-Sakhalinsk, ul. Lenina 290
Telephone: (424) 42-43-57
E-mail: admin@sakhgu.sakhalin.ru
Internet: www.sakhgu.ru
State control

Founded 1949 as teacher training institute, reorganized into Yuzhno-Sakhalinsk State Pedagogical Institute in 1954; present name and status 1998

Rector: Dr BORIS R. MISIKOV

Library of 613,099 vols
Number of teachers: 350
Number of students: 7,483

Publications: *Law Journal*, *Maymanovsky Readings*, *Philological Journal*, *Regional Studies Bulletin*

SAMARA STATE UNIVERSITY

443011 Samara, ul. Akademika Pavlova 1
Telephone: (8462) 34-54-02
E-mail: avn@ssu.samara.ru
Internet: www.ssu.samara.ru

Founded 1969
State control
Language of instruction: Russian, English
Academic year: September to June

Rector: GENNADY P. YAROVOY
First Pro-Rector: PETR S. KABYTOV
Pro-Rector for Education: VITALY P. GARKIN
Pro-Rector for Science: YURI N. GORELOV
Chief Librarian: GALINA A. BARSUKOVA

Library of 900,000 vols
Number of teachers: 820
Number of students: 14,000

Publications: *Bulletin* (8 a year), *Physics of Wave Processes and Radio-Technical Systems* (4 a year), *Samara Zemsky Collection* (4 a year)

DEANS

Faculty of Biology: G. L. RYTOV
Faculty of Chemistry: S. V. KURBATOVA
Faculty of History: U. N. SMIRNOV
Faculty of Languages and Literature: A. A. BEZRUKOVA
Faculty of Law: A. A. NAPREENKO
Faculty of Mathematics and Mechanics: V. M. KLIMKIN
Faculty of Physics: V. V. IVAKHNIK
Faculty of Psychology: K. S. LISETSKY
Faculty of Sociology: V. YA. MACHNEV

PROFESSORS

ASTAFIEV, V. I., Mechanics
BLATOV, V. A., Inorganic Chemistry
BREUSOV, Y. G., Economics
BULANOVA, A. V., General Chemistry and Chromatography
FILATOV, O. P., Equations of Mathematical Physics
GIZATULLIN, M. H., Physics and Mathematics
GOLUBKOV, S. A., Russian and Foreign Literature
GORELOV, Y. N., Differential Equations
KABYTOV, P. S., History of Russia
KHRAMKOV, I. V., History of Russia
KLIMKIN, V. M., Functional Analysis
KOMOV, A. N., Electronics
KONEV, V. A., Philosophy of the Humanities Faculties
KOZENKO, B. D., World History
KOZHEVNIKOV, Y. N., Physics and Mathematics
LEONOV, M. I., Russian History
LOBACHEV, A. L., Chemistry and Chromatography
MATVEEV, N. M., Ecology, Botany and Environmental Protection
MERKULOVA, N. A., Human and Animal Physiology
MOLEVICH, E. F., Sociology and Political Science
PLAKSINA, T. I., Ecology, Botany and Environmental Protection
PODKOVKIN, V. G., Biochemistry
PURYGIN, P. P., Organic Chemistry
RUDNEVA, T. I., Education
RYMAR, N. T., Russian and Foreign Literature
SARAEV, L. A., Mathematics and Computers
SEREZHKIN, V. N., Inorganic Chemistry
SEREZHKINA, L. B., Inorganic Chemistry
SHEIFER, S. A., Criminal Court Proceedings and Investigation
SHESTAKOV, A. A., Philosophy
SIKORA, P. E., State and Administrative Law
SKOBELEV, V. P., Russian and Foreign Literature
SKOBLIKOVA, Y. S., Philology, Russian Language
SOBOLEV, V. A., Differential Equations
SOLODYANNIKOV, Y. V., Functional Analysis and Theory of Functions
VOSKRESENSKY, V. E., Algebra and Geometry
YAROVOY, G. P., Radiophysics and Computers
ZAGUZOV, I. S., Mechanics

SARATOV STATE UNIVERSITY 'N. G. CHERNYSHEVSKY'

410012 Saratov, Astrakhanskaya ul. 83

Telephone: (2) 26-16-96
E-mail: rector@sgu.ru
Internet: www.sgu.ru

Founded 1909
State control
Academic year: September to July

Br. in Astrakhan; colleges and institutes: College of Radioelectronics, P. N. Yablochkov; Geological College; College of Management and Service; Pedagogical Institute in Balashov.

Rector: Dr LEONID YU. KOSSOVICH
Vice-Rector for Academic Affairs: Dr ELENA G. YELINA
Vice-Rector for Int. Cooperation: DIMITRY N. KONAKOV
Vice-Rector for Science: Dr DIMITRY A. USANOV
Registrar: IRINA V. FEDUSENKO
Librarian: IRINA V. LEBEDEVA

Library of 2,903,504 vols
Number of teachers: 982
Number of students: 16,000

Publications: *Applied Nonlinear Dynamics, Contemporary Herpetology, Ecological Magazine in the Volga Region, Electrochemical Energetics, Entomological and Parasitological Research in the Volga Region, Hetero-magnetic Electronics, Numbers Theory Research, Problems of Applied Physics*

DEANS

Biology: Dr GENNADIY V. SHLYAKHTIN
Chemistry: Dr OLGA V. FEDOTOVA
Computer Sciences and Information Technologies: ANTONINA G. FEDOROVA
Geography: Dr VLADIMIR Z. MAKAROV
Geology: ELENA N. VOLKOVA
History: Prof. TATYANA V. CHEREVICHKO
Humanities and Social Sciences: Dr SERGEY YU. SHENIN
Mechanics and Mathematics: Dr ANDREY M. ZAKHAROV
Non-Linear Processes: Dr YURIY I. LEVIN
Philology: Dr VALERY V. PROZOROV
Philosophy: MIKHAIL O. ORLOV
Physics: Dr VALERIY M. ANIKIN
Psychology: Dr LIUDMILA N. AKSENOVSKAYA
Sociology: Dr GENNADIY V. DYLNOV

SOUTH URAL STATE UNIVERSITY

454080 Chelyabinsk, 76 Lenin Ave

Telephone: (351) 267-94-56
E-mail: susuniversity@yandex.ru
Internet: www.susu.ac.ru

Founded 1943, fmrly Chelyabinsk State Technical Univ., present name and status 1997
State control
Academic year: September to June

Rector: Prof. ALEXANDER SHESTAKOV
First Vice-Rector for Academics: Prof. MAJOROV VLADIMIR I.
Vice-Rector for Academics: Prof. CHUMANOV ILYA V.
Vice-Rector for Int. Affairs: Prof. VICTOR M. KATOCHKOV
Vice-Rector for Scientific Affairs: Prof. VAULIN SERGEY D.
Registrar: IGOR V. SIDOROV
Dir for Int. Relations Dept: SERGEY G. BARYSHNIKOV
Dir for Library: IRINA P. BERGER

Library: 3m. vols
Number of teachers: 5,000
Number of students: 55,000

DEANS

Architecture and Civil Engineering Faculty: VLADIMIR V. SPASIBOZHKO
Architecture Faculty: SALAVAT G. SHABIEV
Faculty of Chemistry: VYACHESLAV V. AVDIN
Faculty of Computing Mathematics and Computer Science: LEONID B. SOKOLINSKY
Faculty of History: NATALIA V. PARFENTIEVA
Faculty of Journalism: LUDMILA P. SHESTERKINA
Faculty of Physical Education and Sport: EVGENY V. BYKOV
Faculty of Psychology: NIKOLAY A. BATURIN
Instrument-Making Faculty: LEV S. KAZARINOV
International Faculty: VLADIMIR P. GORSHENIN
Law and Finance Faculty: BORIS I. ROVNY
Law Faculty: ALEXANDER N. CLASSEN
Linguistics Faculty: TAMARA N. KHOMUTOVA
Mechanics and Engineering Faculty: VIKTOR I. GUZEEV
Mechanics and Mathematics Faculty: ALEXANDR D. DROZIN
Motor and Tractor Faculty: YURI V. ROZHDESTVENSKY
Physical and Metallurgical Faculty: GENNADY G. MIKHAYLOV
Physical Faculty: NATALIA D. KUNDIKOVA
Power Engineering Faculty: YURI I. KHOKHLOV

Service and Tourism Faculty: VICTOR A. LIVSHITS
Trade and Economics Faculty: IRINA U. OKOLNISHNIKOVA

SOUTHERN FEDERAL UNIVERSITY

344006 Rostov-on-Don, Bolshaya Sadovaya Str. 105/42

Telephone: (863) 272-67-41
E-mail: korn@sfedu.ru
Internet: sfedu.ru

Founded 2006 by merger of Rostov State Acad. of Architecture and Arts, Rostov State Pedagogical Univ. and Taganrog State Radio Engineering Univ. to the Rostov State Univ.
State control
Languages of instruction: English, Russian
Academic year: September to June

Rector: Prof. Dr MARINA BOROVSKAYA
Vice-Rector for Academic Affairs and Further Education: Prof. NIKOLAY MIKHAILOV
Vice-Rector for Admin. and Legal Affairs: SERGEY DYUZHIKOV
Vice-Rector for Bachelors Programmes and Pre-Univ. Studies: IRINA MOSTOVAYA
Vice-Rector for Cooperation with State Agencies: DMITRIY GURTSKOY
Vice-Rector for Int. Relations: NIKOLAY PELIKHOV
Vice-Rector for Masters Programmes and Postgraduate Studies: MARIA SEROSHTAN
Academic Sec.: Dr VALENTINA CHYBAROVA

Library of 3,998,616 vols, (incl. 2,515,102 vols of the main library, 552,741 vols of Pedagogical Institute, 28,809 vols of Institute of Architecture and Arts and 901,964 vols of Taganrog Technological Institute), 32,619 e-books
Number of teachers: 4,109 (2,876 full-time, 1,233 part-time)
Number of students: 43,183 (23,309 full-time, 19,874 part-time)

DEANS

Faculty of Biological Sciences: VITOLD G. PARSHIN
Faculty of Chemistry: VLADIMIR E. GUTERMAN
Faculty of Economics: Prof. VALERY A. ALESHIN
Faculty of Geology and Geography: Prof. NIKOLAY I. BOYKO
Faculty of High Technologies: ANATOLY E. PANICH
Faculty of History: VIKTOR YU. APRYSHCHENKO
Faculty of Information Security: GENNADY E. VESELOV
Faculty of Law: Assoc. Prof. SVETLANA M. LYAKH
Faculty of Mathematics, Mechanics and Computer Science: Prof. MIKHAIL I. KARYAKIN
Faculty of Philology and Journalism: Assoc. Prof. ELENA V. GRIGORYEVA
Faculty of Philosophy and Culture Studies: Prof. GENNADY V. DRACH
Faculty of Physics: VYACHESLAV S. MALYSHEVSKY
Faculty of Psychology: Prof. PAVEL N. ERMAKOV
Faculty of Regional Studies: ANTON V. SERIKOV
Faculty of Social and Political Science: VIKTOR I. FILONENKO

SFEDU INSTITUTES

Institute of Architecture and Art

344082 Rostov-on-Don, Budennovsky pr. 39

Telephone: (8632) 39-09-62
E-mail: rai@aaanet.ru

Founded 1988

Architecture, environmental design, arts and crafts, history of art, fashion design, management in architecture

Library of 300,000 vols
Number of teachers: 181
Number of students: 1,091

Rector: V. A. KOLESNIK

Publication: *Problems of Architectural Education* (1 a year)

SFU Pedagogical Institute

Rostov oblast, 347928 Taganrog, GSP-17a, Nekrasovsky pr. 44

Telephone: (863) 4431-05-98
E-mail: rspu@rspu.edu.ru
Internet: www.rspu.edu.ru

Founded 1869 as Rostov State Pedagogical Univ.

Academic year: September to June

Dir: Dr Sc. Prof. VLADIMIR I. MAREEV

Number of students: 1,746

Taganrog Institute of Technology

Rostov oblast, 347928 Taganrog, GSP-17a, Nekrasovsky pr. 44

Telephone: (863) 439-30-29
E-mail: rector@tsure.ru
Internet: www.tsure.ru

Founded 1952 as Taganrog Institute of Radio Engineering, renamed Taganrog State Univ. of Radio Engineering 1993, present status 2006

Academic year: September to June

Head: ALEKSANDER IVANOVICH SUKHINOV
First Deputy Head: VICTOR ALEKSANDROVICH OBUKHOVETS
Deputy Head for Int. Relations: VADIM P. POPOV

Library of 980,000 vols
Number of teachers: 804
Number of students: 11,300

ACADEMIC INSTITUTES AND RESEARCH INSTITUTES

Institute of Economics and Foreign Economic Relations: 344002 Rostov-on-Don, Soborny 26; tel. (863) 244-15-02; e-mail iecier@sfedu.ru.

Inter-regional Institute of Social Science: 344006 Rostov-on-Don, Bol. Sadovaya 105; e-mail narezhni@mis.sfedu.ru; internet www.rostov.iriss.ru; Acad. Dir ANATOLY IVANOVICH NAREZHNY.

ATTACHED RESEARCH CENTRES

Research and Educational Centre 'Nanotechnologies': integration of education and research as well as improvement of cooperation with scientific orgs and institutes of S Federal Dist.

Research Centre for Nanoscale structure of Matter: 344090 Rostov-on-Don, Sorge 5; tel. (8632) 97-53-26; e-mail asoldatov@phys.rsu.ru; internet www.nano .sfedu.ru; study of 3D local atomic nanoscale geometry and electronic structure in various types of advanced novel materials; Dir Prof. ALEXANDER V SOLDATOV.

14 attached research institutes

STATE UNIVERSITY FOR THE HUMANITIES

119334 Moscow, Leninsky pr-t, 32A

Telephone: (495) 938-10-09
E-mail: gugn@gugn.info
Internet: www.gugn.ru
State control

Founded 1992 as the Republican Centre for Humanities Education; present name 1998

Institutes of advancement of qualifications and teacher training, economics, culture,

history, law, literary culture and management, philosophy, politology, psychology, sociology, world politics

Rector: Prof. ALEXANDER O. CHUBARYAN
First Pro-Rector: Prof. NATALYA N. NIKITINA
Pro-Rector for Gen. Affairs: GEORGY N. KRASNOV
Pro-Rector for Science: Prof. MIKHAIL V. BIBIKOV
Academic Sec.: DENIS V. FOMIN-NILOV

STATE UNIVERSITY OF MANAGEMENT

109542 Moscow, Ryazansky pr. 99

Telephone: (495) 371-13-22
E-mail: rectorat@guu.ru
Internet: www.guu.ru

Founded 1919

Rector: ANATOLY G. PORSHNEV

Library of 280,000 vols
Number of teachers: 700
Number of students: 10,000

STAVROPOL STATE UNIVERSITY

355009 Stavropol, ul. Pushkina 1

Telephone: (8652) 35-72-65
E-mail: stavsu@stavsu.ru
Internet: www.stavsu.ru
State control

Founded 1930 as Stavropol Agro-Pedagogical Institute; 1932–1994 as Stavropol Pedagogical Institute, 1994–1996 as Stavropol State Pedagogical Univ., present name 1996

Academic year: September to June

Rector: Prof. VLADIMIR ALEXANDROVICH
Vice-Rector for Capital Construction: LUBE-NETS YURIY PETROVICH
Vice-Rector for Curriculum: Prof. BELOZEROV VITALY SEMENOVICH
Vice-Rector for Economic Issues and Additional Educational Programmes: Prof. EROKHIN ALEKSEY MIKHAILOVICH
Vice-Rector for Maintenance: VASILENKO ANATOLIY KUZMICH
Vice-Rector for Research: Prof. LIKHOVID ANDREY ALEXANDROVICH
Vice-Rector for Security: Assoc. Prof. TER-ESCHENKO NIKOLAY VIKTOROVICH
Dean of Extra Mural and Externship Dept: Prof. TARANOVA TATYANA NIKOLAEVNA
Dir for Studies: Assoc. Prof. VOLKOVA VALEN-TINA IVANOVNA
Dir for Univ. Scientific Library: KUZMINA ELENA ANATOLIEVNA
Library: 1.2m. vols, 382 periodicals
Number of teachers: 900
Number of students: 15,000

Publication: *Stavropol State University Vestnik*

DEANS

Advanced Training: Prof. GUROV VALERIY NIKOLAEVICH
Arts: Assoc. Prof. MARKOV ALEKSANDR IVANO-VICH
Economics: Prof. AKININ PETR VIKTOROVICH
Geography: Prof. SCHITOVA NATALYA ALEK-SANDROVNA
History: Prof. KUDRYAVSTEV ALEXANDER ABA-KAROVICH
Law: Assoc. Prof. SCHERBAKOVA LUDMILA MIKHAILOVNA
Medicine Biology and Chemistry: Prof. IVA-NOV ALEXANDER LVOVICH
Philology and Journalism: Assoc. Prof. SER-BRYAKOV ANATOLY ALEKSEEVICH
Physical Education: Prof. MAGIN VLADIMIR ALEKSEEVICH
Physics and Mathematics: Assoc. Prof. AGI-BOVA IRINA MARKOVNA

Psychology: Prof. AKHVERDOVA OLGA ALBER-TOVNA
Romance and Germanic Languages: Prof. LOMTEVA TATYANA NIKOLAEVNA

SURGUT STATE UNIVERSITY

628400 Tyumen oblast, Surgut, ul. Energeti-kov 30

Telephone: (3462) 52-47-00
E-mail: info@inao.surgu.ru
Internet: www.surgu.ru

Founded 1993
Private control

Rector: Prof. GEORGY I. NAZIN
Vice-Rector for Academic Affairs: Prof. YURI V. KUZNETSOV
Vice-Rector for Admin. and Finance: Dr BORIS U. SERAZETDINOV
Vice-Rector for Capital Construction: KON-STANTIN S. MOKHOV
Vice-Rector for Distance Learning: Prof. SERGEI F. KOZHUKOV
Vice-Rector for Economic and Social Affairs: VIKTOR I. LYUTY
Vice-Rector for Information Resources: Dr NIKOLAI G. SHEVCHENKO
Vice-Rector for Science: Dr VIKTOR P. SAMSO-NOV
Vice-Rector for Student Affairs: Dr BORIS U. SERAZETDINOV
Librarian: VALENTINA N. SHEVCHENKO

Library of 282,354 vols

DEANS

Biology: VLADIMIR P. STARIKOV
Economics: LEONID A. AVDEEV
Engineering and Physics: NIKOLAI N. BADU-LIN
History: ALEXANDER I. PRISCHEPA
Information Technology: FEDOR F. IVANOV
Law: VLADIMIR V. CHERUSHEV
Linguistics: SVETLANA G. KULAGINA
Medicine: LUDMILA V. KOVALENKO
Physical Culture: SERGEI M. OBUKHOV
Psychology: IRINA P. GREKHOVA

SYKTYVKAR STATE UNIVERSITY

167001 Syktyvkar, Oktyabrskii pr. 55

Telephone: (8212) 43-68-20
E-mail: ssu@syktsu.ru
Internet: www.syktsu.ru

Founded 1972
State control

Languages of instruction: Russian, Komi
Academic year: September to July

Rector: VASILY N. ZADOROZHNY
Vice-Rector: NIKOLAI A. TIKHONOV
Chief Admin. Officer: OLGA P. ZBOROVSKAYA
Librarian: V. PROKURATOVA

Number of teachers: 330
Number of students: 4,250

Publications: *Rubezh* (4 a year), *Vestnik* (1 a year)

DEANS

Faculty of Arts: LUDMILA V. GURLENOVA
Faculty of Chemistry and Biology: IRINA V. PIYR
Faculty of Finance and Economics: EVGENIA A. BADOKINA
Faculty of History: LUBOV A. MAKSIMOVA
Faculty of Humanities: ELENA G. TONKOVA
Faculty of Information Systems and Technologies: DMITRIY A. BELYAEV
Faculty of Law: DMITRIY I. PINAEVSKIY
Faculty of Mathematics: VYACHESLAV G. ANTONOV
Faculty of Management: LUDMILA I. BUSH-UEVA
Faculty of Philology: MIKHAIL V. MELIKHOV
Faculty of Physics and Engineering: YURIY N. BELYAEV

Faculty of Physical Training and Sports: SERGEI A. SOKOLOV
Faculty of Psychology and Social Work: LUDMILA I. BYKOVSKAYA

PROFESSORS
ARAPOV, N., Jurisprudence
BOLOTOV, S., Management
BRACH, B., Chemistry
IRZHAK, L., Physiology
KNJAZEVA, G., Finance
MIKHAILOVSKY, E., Computer Science
NAGAEV, V., Psychology
NIKETENKOV, V., Mathematics
NOVIKOV, Y., Management
POROSHKIN, A., Mathematical Analysis
SEMENOV, V., History
TIKHOMIROV, A., Mathematics
VITYAZEVA, V., Economics
ZADOROZHNIY, V., Economics
ZOLOTAREV, V., History

TAMBOV STATE UNIVERSITY 'G. R. DERZHAVIN'

392000 Tambov, Internatsionalnaya ul. 33
Telephone: (0752) 72-12-29
E-mail: priem1@tsu.tmb.ru
Internet: tsutmb.ru

Founded 1994, on the basis of Tambov State Pedagogical Institute and Tambov State Institute of Culture
State control
Languages of instruction: English, French, Russian
Academic year: September to June

Rector: Prof. VLADISLAV YURIEV
Vice-Rector for Academic Affairs: Prof. VLADIMIR MAMONTOV
Vice-Rector for Educational Policy and Innovation: Prof. MARINA CHVANOVA
Vice-Rector for Int. Relations: Prof. TATIANA OSADCHAYA
Pro-Rector for Research: Prof. NIKOLAY BOLDYREV

Library: 1.5m. vols
Number of teachers: 900
Number of students: 15,000

Publications: *Issues of Cognitive Linguistics, Social-Economic Phenomena and Processes, Vestnik Tambovskogo Universiteta (Tambov University Reports)* (Series: Natural and Technical Sciences; the Humanities)

TOGLIATTI STATE UNIVERSITY

445667 Togliatti, Belorusskaya ul. 14
Telephone: (8482) 54-63-99
E-mail: office@tltsu.ru
Internet: www.tltsu.ru

Founded 1951 as Togliatti Polytechnic Institute, present name and status 2001 following merger with Togliatti State Pedagogical Univ. (f. 1988)
State control
Language of instruction: Russian
Academic year: September to June

Rector: Prof. Dr MIKHAIL M. KRISHTAL
Pro-Rector for Academic Activity: ALEXANDER A. SOLDATOV
Pro-Rector for Admin. Services: ARARAT K. ABRAMYAN
Pro-Rector for Devt: GREGORY RAYTER
Pro-Rector for Extracurricular and Recreational Activity: TATYANA D. ZILPERT
Pro-Rector for Research: SERGEY V. BOLSHAKOV
Head of Int. Cooperation Dept: ELENA KARGINA

Library of 1,093,941 vols
Number of teachers: 570
Number of students: 12,000

Publications: *Herald of the Humanities, Vector of Science*

DEANS
Institute of Architecture and Construction: Assoc. Prof. Dr NIKOLAY USTENKOV
Institute of Chemistry and Environmental Engineering: Prof. Dr ANDREY VASILYEV
Institute of Electrical and Power Engineering: Assoc. Prof. Dr VLADIMIR SHAPOVALOV
Institute of Finance, Economics and Management: Assoc. Prof. Dr MAXIM ISKOSKOV
Institute of Fine, Decorative and Applied Arts: Assoc. Prof. Dr ALEXANDER KOZLYAKOV
Institute of Humanities and Pedagogy: YURIY LIVSHITS
Institute of Law: Assoc. Prof. Dr DMITRY LIPINSKY
Institute of Mathematics, Physics and Information Technologies: Assoc. Prof. Dr SERGEY TALALOV
Institute of Mechanical Engineering: Assoc. Prof. Dr ALEKSANDR SKRIPECHEV
Institute of Physical Education and Sport: Assoc. Prof. Dr VALENTINA BALASHOVA

TOMSK STATE UNIVERSITY

634050 Tomsk, pr. Lenina 36
Telephone: (3822) 52-95-58
E-mail: rector@tsu.ru
Internet: www.tsu.ru

Founded 1878
State control
Academic year: September to June

Faculties of applied mathematics and cybernetics, biology and soil science, chemistry, computer science, economics, foreign languages, geology and geography, history and international relations, journalism, law, mechanics and mathematics, philology, philosophy, physics, political science, psychology, sociology and radio-physics, technical physics; Institute of Culture; International Faculty of Public and Business Administration

Rector: Prof. GEORGY V. MAYER
Sr Vice-Rector: Dr MIKHAIL D. BABANSKY
Vice-Rector for Academic Affairs: Prof. ALEXANDER S. REVUSHKIN
Vice-Rector for Int. Affairs: Dr SERGEY N. KIRPOTIN
Vice-Rector for Research and Postgraduate Studies: Prof. GRIGORY E. DUNAEVSKY
Registrar: N. BUROVA
Librarian: EVGENY N. SYNTIN

Library: see under Libraries and Archives
Number of teachers: 1,400
Number of students: 14,000 (10,000 full-time, 4,000 part-time)

Publications: *Krylovia: Siberian Botanical Journal* (2 a year), *Physics* (4 a year), *Vestnik* (4 a year)

TVER STATE UNIVERSITY

170100 Tver, ul. Zhelyabova 33
Telephone: (4822) 32-11-95
E-mail: rector@tversu.ru
Internet: university.tversu.ru

Founded 1971
State control
Language of instruction: Russian
Academic year: September to June

Rector: ANDREY VLADLENOVICH BELOTSERKOVSKY
Pro-Rector: LIUDMILA NIKOLAEVNA SKAKOVSKAYA
Librarian: OLGA V. VERSHININA

Library: 1m. vols
Number of teachers: 720
Number of students: 10,000

DEANS
Applied Mathematics and Cybernetics: Prof. ALEXANDER YAZENIN
Economics: Prof. DAVID MAMAGULASHVILI
Foreign Languages and International Communication: Prof. LARISA SAPOZHNIKOVA
History: Prof. TATIANA LEONTIJEVA
Law: Prof. LIDIA TUMANOVA
Management and Sociology: Prof. LARISA MOSHKOVA

TYUMEN STATE UNIVERSITY

625003 Tyumen, ul. Semakova 10
Telephone: (3452) 46-01-41
E-mail: international@utmn.ru
Internet: www.utmn.ru

Founded 1930 as Tyumen Pedagogical Institute, present name 1973

Faculties of chemistry and biology, economics, geography, history, philology, physics and mathematics, romance and Germanic philology

Rector: Prof. Dr CHEBOTAREV GENNADY NIKOLAEVITCH
Pres.: Prof. Dr KUTSEV GENNADY PHILIPOVITCH

Number of teachers: 929
Number of students: 40,000

Publications: *Philological Discourse, Siberian Historical Journal, The Journal of Tyumen State University*

UDMURT STATE UNIVERSITY

426034 Udmurt, Izhevsk, Universitetskaya ul. 1
Telephone: (3412) 68-16-10
E-mail: adm@uni.udm.ru
Internet: www.udsu.ru

Founded 1931
State control
Language of instruction: Russian
Academic year: September to June

Rector: Prof. GALINA MERZLYAKOVA
Chief Vice-Rector: Assoc. Prof. SEMEN BUNTOV
Vice-Rector for Academic Affairs: Assoc. Prof. MIKHAIL KIBARDIN
Vice-Rector for Finance, Economics and Investments: GERMAN SERGEEV
Vice-Rector for Int. Relations: MARIA I. BESNOSOVA
Vice-Rector for Public Relations: Assoc. Prof. VLADIMIR A. BAYMETOV
Vice-Rector for Research and Innovation: Dr IGOR MENSHIKOV
Vice-Rector for Social and Educational Work and Extra Curricular Activities: SERGEY V. VOSTROKUTNOV
Head of Int. Relations Office: Assoc. Prof. MARIA BEZNOSOVA
Dir for Library: LYUDMILA BESKLINSKAYA

Library of 1,000,000 vols, 40 periodicals, 50 newspapers
Number of teachers: 1,000
Number of students: 25,000

Publications: *Management: Theory and Practice* (4 a year), *Nonlinear Dynamics* (4 a year), *Problems of Regional Economics* (4 a year), *Quantum, Computers and Computing* (1 a year), *Regular and Chaotic Dynamics)* (English version, 6 series a year), *Udmurt University* (12 a year), *Univer.ru* (12 a year), *Vestnik UdSU* (2 a year, 6 series)

DEANS
Faculty of Biology and Chemistry: NIKOLAY ZUBTSOVSKY
Faculty of Geography: IVAN RYSSIN
Faculty of History: NADEZHA STARKOVA
Faculty of Journalism: VLADIMIR BAYMETOV

Faculty of Mathematics: NIKOLAY PETROV

Faculty of Medical Biotechnology: ALEXEY BARSUKOV

Faculty of Philosophy and Sociology: Prof. MARINA MAKAROVA

Faculty of Physical Education and Sport: ALEXANDER ALABUZHEV

Faculty of Physics and Energetics: VLADIMIR BOVIN

Faculty of Professional Foreign Language Study: RAISA SHISHKINA

Faculty of Russian Philology: ELENA PODSHI-VALOVA

Faculty of Udmurt Philology: LUBOV FYODOROVA

Institute of Arts and Design: MARINA BOTYA

Institute of Civil Defence: VLADIMIR KOLODKIN

Institute of Economics and Management: ANATOLY ANOSHIN

Institute of Foreign Languages and Literature: OLGA GOLUBKOVA

Institute of Law, Social Management and Security: VLADIMIR IVSHIN

Institute of Oil and Gas: ALEXEY VOLKOV

Institute of Psychology, Pedagogics and Social Technology: Prof. ALEXANDER BARANOV

Institute of Social Communications: LARISA BATALOVA

PROFESSORS

Faculty of Biology and Chemistry (tel. (3412) 75-56-48; e-mail bhf@uni.udm.ru):

BARANOVA, O., Botany and Plant Ecology
KORNEV, V., Inorganic and Analytic Chemistry
MAKAROVA, L., Physical and Organic Chemistry
PRONICHEV, I., Anatomy and Human and Animal's Physiology
TUGANAEV, V., General Ecology

Faculty of Geography (tel. (3412) 916070; e-mail rvsin@uni.udm.ru):

RYSSIN, I. I., Physical Geography and Landscape Ecology
STURMAN, V. I., Natural Use and Geo-Ecological Cartography

Faculty of History (tel. (3412) 91-61-84; e-mail history@udsu.ru):

EFREMOVA, T., Native History of Newer Time
GOLDINA, R., Archeology and the History of Primitive Society
SANNIKOV, N., New History and International Relations
SHISHKINA, N., Ancient World and the Middle Ages
VLADYKIN, V. E., Ethnology and Regional Study

Faculty of Information Technology and Computer Engineering (tel. (3412) 91-61-31; e-mail rodionov@uni.udm.ru):

BELTYUKOV, A., Theoretical and Informatic Basis
ISLAMOV, G., Computation and Parallel Programming
KOLODKIN, V., Mathematical Modelling and Forecasting
NIKOLAY, N., Theory and Methodology of Informatics

Faculty of Mathematics (tel. (3412) 91-60-86; e-mail dekanmf@udsu.ru):

BELTYUKOV, A., Mathematical Provision for Computers and Software
DERR, V., Mathematical Analysis
GRYZLOV, A., Algebra and Topology
ISLAMOV, G., Calculus Mathematics
KARPOV, A., Computer Techniques
KONDRATYEV, B., Astronomy and Topology
TONKOV, E., Differential Equation

Faculty of Physics and Energetics (tel. (3412) 91-61-29; e-mail bovin@uni.udm.ru):

TARPEZNIKOV, V., Surface Physics

Faculty of Philology (tel. (3412) 91-61-54; e-mail ktl@udm.ru):

DONETSKIK, L., Contemporary Russian Language and History
PODSHIVOLAVA, E., Russian Literature of the 20th Century and Folklore
SHEIDAEVA, S., Language Theory and Speech
VOROZHTSOVA, I., Lingual Didactics

Faculty of Professional Foreign Languages (tel. (3412) 68-55-57; e-mail profin@udm.ru):

MERZLYAKOVA, A., Romance Languages

Faculty of Sociology and Philosophy (tel. (3412) 916020):

KRUTKIN, V., Philosophy and Sociology of Culture
LADYZHETZ, N., Sociology

Faculty of Udmurt Philology (tel. (3412) 75-59-20):

KELMAKOV, V. K., General and Finno-Ugric Linguistics
SHUTOV, A. F., Udmurt Language and Pedagogy
TARAKANOV, I. V., Udmurt Language and Pedagogy
VLADIKINA, T. G., Russian Philology

Institute of Economics and Management (tel. (3412) 91-60-62; e-mail ier@inem.uni.udm.ru):

BOTKIN, O. I., Economic Theory
LETCHIKOV, A. V., Mathematical Methods in Economics
MATVEEV, V. V., Business Economics
PEREVOSCHIKOV, YU. S., Business Economics

Institute of Foreign Languages and Literature (tel. (3412) 91-61-79; e-mail ifl@pils.uni.udm.ru):

PUSHINA, N. I., Grammar and History of English
UTEKHINA, A. N., German Philology

Institute of Law, Social Management and Security (tel. (3412) 91-60-02; e-mail lawfak@uni.udm.ru; internet www.ipsub.udsu.ru):

IAKOVLEV, V., Ecological and Agrarian Law and Law of Natural Resources
KAMINSKY, M. K., Criminology and Court Examination
POSKONINA, O. V., Philosophy and Sociology of Law
VOYTOVICH, V. YU., Legal Basis of State and Municipal Services
ZINATULLIN, Z. Z., Criminal Procedure

Institute of Pedagogic Philosophy and Social Technology (tel. (3412) 91-61-19; e-mail baranov@ppf.uni.udm.ru):

BARANOV, A., Developmental Psychology and Differential Psychology
KHOTINETS, U., General Psychology
LEONOV, N., Social Psychology

Institute of Social Communications (tel. (3412) 91-60-35; e-mail pr@udsu.ru):

RODIONOV, B., Sociology of Communications
YEROHIN, A., Publishing and Book Studies

ULYANOVSK STATE UNIVERSITY

432700 Ulyanovsk, ul. L. Tolstogo 42
Telephone: (8422) 41-20-88
E-mail: contact@ulsu.ru
Internet: www.ulsu.ru
State control
Founded 1974
Rector: Prof. YURI V. POLYANSKOV
First Pro-Rector and Pro-Rector for Academic Affairs: TOFIK Z. BIKTIMINOV

Pro-Rector for Admin. and Finance: VALERY V. NEFEDKIN

Pro-Rector for Economic and Legal Affairs: NATALYA N. LOMOVYEVA

Pro-Rector for New Information and Teaching Technologies: DIMITRY YU. SHABALKIN

Pro-Rector for Pre-Univ. Education: SERGEI N. MITIN

Pro-Rector for Research: SERGEI V. BULYARSKY

Pro-Rector for Social Devt, Internal Communication and Marketing: TATYANA E. NIKITINA

Number of teachers: 635
Number of students: 10,695

URAL FEDERAL UNIVERSITY

620002 Ekaterinburg, 19 Mira St
Telephone: (343) 374-54-34
E-mail: rector@urfu.ru
Internet: www.urfu.ru
Founded 1920
public control
Languages of instruction: English, Russian
Academic year: September to July
Rector: Dr VICTOR KOKSHAROV
First Vice-Rector: Dr ANATOLY MATERN
First Vice-Rector: Dr DMITRY BUGROV
Vice-Rector for Academic Affairs: Dr SERGEY KNYAZEV
Vice-Rector for Economics and Strategic Devt: Dr DANIIL SANDLER
Vice-Rector for Gen. Affairs: VASILY KOZLOV
Vice-Rector for Information Policy: RAISA IVANITSKAYA
Vice-Rector for Innovations: Dr SERGEY KORTOV
Vice-Rector for Int. Relations: Dr MAXIM KHOMYAKOV
Vice-Rector for Research: Dr VLADIMIR KRUZHAEV
Vice-Rector for Youth and Social Policy: Dr OLEG GUSHIN
Library of 3,067,719 vols
Number of teachers: 4,674
Number of students: 44,323

DEANS

Faculty of Accelerated Education: Dr DMITRY MATYUNIN

Faculty of Professional Development and Retraining: Dr BORIS SEMENOV

Graduate School of Economics and Management: Prof. Dr DANIIL SANDLER

Higher School of Engineering: Dr OLEG REBRIN

Institute of Chemical Engineering: Prof. Dr VLADIMIR RUSINOV

Institute of Civil Engineering: Dr VLADIMIR ALEKHIN

Institute of Fundamental Education: Dr ILYA OBABKOV

Institute of Humanities and Arts: Dr DMITRY BUGROV

Institute of Mathematics and Computer Sciences: Prof. Dr MAGAZ ASANOV

Institute of Metallurgy and Material Studies: Dr VICTOR MALTSEV

Institute of Mechanical Engineering and Machine Building: Dr OLEG BLINKOV

Institute of Military Technical Education and Security: VICTOR BATMAZOV

Institute of Natural Sciences: Dr VLADIMIR KRUZHAEV

Institute of Open Educational Technologies: VASILY TRETYAKOV

Institute of Physical Culture, Sport and Youth Policy: Dr NINA SEROVA

Institute of Physics and Technology: Prof. Dr VLADIMIR RYCHKOV

Institute of Public Administration and Entrepreneurship: Dr ALEXEY KLUYEV

Institute of Radioelectronics and Information Technologies: Dr SERGEY KNYAZEV

Institute of Social and Political Sciences: Dr MAXIM KHOMYAKOV

Ural Power Engineering Institute: Dr YURY BRODOV

PROFESSORS

Faculty of Art Criticism and Culture:
GOLINETS, S. V., History of Art
MIKHAILOV, S. A., Cultural Studies
PIVOVAROV, D. V., History and Philosophy of Religion
TROSHINA, T. M., Museology

Faculty of Biology:
BIBIN, I. A., Human and Animal Physiology
MUKHIN, V. A., Botany
NOVOZHENOV, Y. I., Zoology
PYANKOV, V. I., Plant Physiology

Faculty of Chemistry:
NEUCHADINA, L. N., Analytical Chemistry
NEYMAN, A. YA., Inorganic Chemistry
PETROV, A. N., Physical Chemistry
SUVOROVA, A. I., Higher Molecular Compounds
VSHIVKOV, A. A., Organic Chemistry

Faculty of Economics:
AKBERDINA, R. A., Economics
GREBENKIN, A. V., History and Theory of Management
IVANTSOV, G. B., Theory of Economics
MAZUROV, V. D., Economic Models and Information
NESTEROVA, D. V., Economic History and World Economics
SEMYAKIN, M. N., Economics and Law

Faculty of History:
CHERNUKHOV, A. V., Archives
CHEVTAEV, A. G., Modern History
MIKHAILENKO, V. I., Theory and History of Foreign Affairs
MINENKO, N. A., Ethnology and Special Historical Sciences
POLYAKOVSKAYA, M. A., Ancient and Medieval History
ROMANCHUK, A. I., Archaeology
SHASHKOV, A. G., Russian History

Faculty of Journalism:
BRODSKY, I. S., Television, Radio and Technical Methods of Journalism
KOVALEVA, M. M., History of the Press
LAZAREVA, E. H., Stylistics and Russian Language
OLESHKO, V. F., Periodical Press

Faculty of Mathematics and Mechanics:
ALBREKHT, E. G., Applied Mathematics
ARESTOV, V. V., Mathematical Analysis and Theory of Functions
ASANOV, M. O., Mathematics for Economics
IVANOV, A. O., Mathematical Physics
PROKOPIEV, V. P., Theoretical Mechanics
RYASHKO, L. V., Computational Mathematics
SHEVRIN, L. N., Algebra of Discrete Mathematics
TRETYAKOV, V. E., Computer Information Science and Management Processes

Faculty of Philology:
BABENKO, L. G., Modern Russian Language
BIKOV, L. P., Criticism of 20th-century Literary Theory
BLAZHES, V. V., Folklore
MATVEEV, A. V., General Linguistics
MIKHAILOVA, O. A., Rhetoric and Stylistics of Russian Language
PAVERMAN, V. M., Foreign Literature
SIDOROVA, O. G., Romance and Germanic Philology

Faculty of Philosophy:
BRYANIK, N. V., Ontology and Theory of Cognition

EREMEEV, A. P., Ethics, Aesthetics, History and Theory of Culture
KEMEROV, V. E., Social Philosophy
LYUBUTIN, K. N., History of Philosophy

Faculty of Physics:
BABUSHKIN, A. N., Low-Temperature Physics
BARANOV, N. V., Condensed Matter
BORISOV, S. F., General and Molecular Physics
GULYAEV, S. A., Astronomy and Geodesy
IVANOV, O. A., Magnetic Phenomena
MOSKVIN, A. S., Theoretical Physics
ZVEREV, L. P., Semiconductor Physics, Radiospectroscopy

Faculty of Psychology:
GLOTOVA, G. A., General Psychology and Psychology of Personality
LUPANDIN, V. I., Psychophysiology

Faculty of Sociology and Politics:
BAGIROV, B. B., Social Politics
BARAZGOVA, E. S., Theory and History of Sociology
MERENKOV, A. V., Sociology
MIRONOV, D. A., History of Politics

URAL STATE UNIVERSITY OF ECONOMICS

620219 Yekaterinburg, ul. 8 Marta 62

Telephone: (343) 221-17-90
E-mail: usue@usue.ru
Internet: www.usue.ru

Founded 1967
State control
Languages of instruction: English, Russian
Academic year: September to June

Rector: Prof. Dr MIKHAIL FEDOROV
Vice-Rector: Prof. Dr NATALYA VLASOVA

Library of 624,800 vols, 9,000 periodicals
Number of teachers: 600
Number of students: 26,500

VLADIMIR STATE UNIVERSITY NAMED AFTER ALEXANDER AND NIKOLAY STOLETOVS

600000 Vladimir, Gorkogo St 87

Telephone: (4922) 47-76-83
E-mail: interc.dpt@gmail.com
Internet: www.vlsu.ru

Founded 1958
State control
Language of instruction: Russian
Academic year: September to June

Rector: Prof. ANZOR MIKHAILOVICH SARALIDZE
First Vice-Rector: Dr VALERIY G. PROKOSHEV
Vice-Rector for Capital Building and Material Resources: Dr LEV V. LOGINOV
Vice-Rector for Economics: Prof. SVETLANA M. BASHARINA
Vice-Rector for Education and Social Policy: ALEXANDER YU. VEDEKHIN
Vice-Rector for Methodological Work: Prof. ALEXEI A. PANFILOV
Vice-Rector for Research: Prof. VLADIMIR N. LANTSOV

Number of teachers: 1,200
Number of students: 22,000

DEANS

Faculty of Architecture and Building: Prof. SERGEY N. AVDEEV
Faculty of Automobile Transport: Prof. YURI V. BAZHENOV
Faculty of Chemistry and Ecology: Prof. JURI T. PANOV
Faculty of Economics: Prof. PAVEL ZAKHAROV
Faculty of Information Technologies: Dr ALEXANDER A. GALKIN
Faculty of Mechanical Engineering: Dr ALEXEI YOLKIN

Faculty of Physics and Applied Mathematics: NIKOLAI D. DAVIDOV
Faculty of Radiophysics, Electronics and Medical Engineering: Prof. ALEXANDER G. SAMOILOV
Institute of Human Sciences: Dr ELENA M. PETROVICHEVA
Institute of Law and Psychology: Dr VYACHESLAV YU. KARTUKHIN
Institute of Small and Medium Business: Dr OLGA P. POLOTSKAYA

VLADIVOSTOK STATE UNIVERSITY OF ECONOMICS AND SERVICE

690600 Vladivostok, 41 Gogolya Str.

Telephone: (423) 245-08-53
E-mail: international@vvsu.ru
Internet: www.vvsu.ru

Founded 1967
State control
Language of instruction: Russian
Academic year: September to May

Areas of study: business administration, culture, fashion and design, information technology and technical systems, politics and law of Asian-Pacific countries, service, social and political studies, tourism and hospitality

Rector: Prof. GENNADY I. LAZAREV

Library of 258,170 vols
Number of teachers: 410
Number of students: 24,000

Publication: Russia—21st Century (4 a year)

VOLGOGRAD STATE UNIVERSITY

400062 Volgograd, Pr. Universitetsky 100

Telephone: (8442) 43-81-24
E-mail: endowment@volsu.ru
Internet: www.volsu.ru

Founded 1980
State control
Languages of instruction: English, French, Russian
Academic year: September to June

Rector: Prof. Dr OLEG V. INSHAKOV
Deputy Rector: Dr VASILY V. TARAKANOV
Vice-Rector for Academic Affairs: Dr SERGEI G. SIDOROV
Vice-Rector for Research and Innovations: Dr ALLA E. KALININA
Librarian: LARISA E. YAKOVLEVA

Library of 900,000 vols
Number of teachers: 610
Number of students: 13,500

Publications: Archaeological Vestnik of the Lower Volga (1 a year), Economic History of Russia (1 a year), Junior Faculty and Students' Papers and Reports (1 a year), Proceedings of the Annual Scientific Conference (1 a year), Proceedings of International Conferences (5 a year), Strezhen (1 a year), The Region's Economic Development: Problems, Searches, Prospects (2 a year), Vestnik VolGU (10 series, 1 a year)

DEANS

Faculty of Continuing Education: Dr ALBINA V. GUKOVA
Faculty of Law: Dr ILYA S. DIKAREV
Faculty of Management and Regional Economy: Dr VIKTOR O. MOSEYKO
Faculty of Mathematics and Informational Technologies: Dr ALEXANDER G. LOSEV
Faculty of Natural Sciences: Dr ALEXANDER B. MULIK
Faculty of Philosophy, History, International Relations and Social Technologies: Prof. Dr OLGA Y. REDKINA
Institute of Philology and Intercultural Communication: Dr NIKOLAI L. SHAMNE
Institute of Physics and Telecommunications: KONSTANTIN M. FIRSOV (Dir)

Institute of World Economy and Finances: Dr ELENA G. RUSSKOVA

VORONEZH STATE UNIVERSITY

394006 Voronezh, Universitetskaya pl. 1

Telephone: (0732) 20-75-22
E-mail: office@main.vsu.ru
Internet: www.vsu.ru

Founded 1918
State control
Academic year: September to July

Rector: Prof. IVAN I. BORISOV
First Vice-Rector: SERGEY A. ZAPRYAGAEV
Vice-Rector: VLADIMIR T. TITOV
Vice-Rector for Admin. and Finance: ANATOLY N. PODOBEDOV
Vice-Rector for Information Services: ALEXANDER P. TOLSTOBROV
Vice-Rector for Major Construction Projects: ANATOLY I. BIRYUKOV
Vice-Rector for Organizational and Legal Matters: VALERY P. TROFIMOV
Vice-Rector for Pre-Univ. Training: VLADIMIR N. GLAZYEV
Vice-Rector for Research: ALEXANDER S. SIDORKIN
Librarian: SVETLANA V. YANTS

Library: 3m. vols
Number of teachers: 1,300
Number of students: 21,000
Publication: *Vestnik Voronezhskogo Universiteta*

DEANS

Faculty of Applied Mathematics and Mechanics: A. I. SHASHKIN
Faculty of Biology and Soil Science: V. G. ARTYUKHOV
Faculty of Chemistry: YU. P. AFINOGENOV
Faculty of Computer Science: E. A. ALGAZINOV
Faculty of Economics: V. P. BOCHAROV
Faculty of Geography and Geo-Ecology: V. I. FEDOTOV
Faculty of Geology: V. M. NENAKHOV
Faculty of History: A. Z. VINNIKOV
Faculty of Journalism: V. V. TULUPOV
Faculty of Law: V. A. PANYUSHKIN
Faculty of Mathematics: V. A. KOSTIN
Faculty of Pharmaceutics: A. I. SLIVKIN
Faculty of Philology: V. M. AKATKIN
Faculty of Philosophy and Psychology: YU A. BUBNOV
Faculty of Physics: A. M. VOROBEV
Faculty of Romance and Germanic Philology: N. A. FENENKO

YAROSLAVL STATE UNIVERSITY

150000 Yaroslavl, ul. Sovetskaya 14

Telephone: (0852) 72-51-38
E-mail: depint@uniyar.ac.ru
Internet: www.uniyar.ac.ru

Founded 1970
Academic year: September to July

Rector: Prof. G. S. MIRONOV
First Vice-Rector: A. I. RUSAKOV
Vice-Rector for Economy: R. P. USATYUK
Vice-Rector for Education: I. M. LOKHANINA
Vice-Rector for Innovation: S. A. KASHCHENKO
Vice-Rector for Science: Y. A. BRUKHANOV
Registrar: V. P. ISAYEVA
Librarian: I. V. DENEZHKINA
Number of teachers: 530
Number of students: 6,500
Publications: *Aktualnye Problemy Fiziki* (Current Problems of Physics, 1 a year), *Ekonomichesky Vestnik* (Bulletin on Economics, 1 a year), *Modelirovaniye i Analiz Informatsionnykh System* (Modelling and Analysis of Information Systems, 1 or 2 a

year), *Ocherki po Torgovomy Pravu* (Sketches on Trade Law, 1 or 2 a year), *Problemy Novoi i Noveishei Istorii* (Issues of Modern and Contemporary History), *Put v Nauku* (Road to Science, 1 a year), *Sovremennye Problemy Matematiki i Informatiki* (Modern Problems of Mathematics and Informatics, 1 a year), *Yuridicheskiye zapiski* (Judicial Notes, 1 a year)

DEANS

Faculty of Biology: A. V. EREMEISHVILI
Faculty of Economics: L. B. PARFIONOVA
Faculty of History: N. P. RYAZANTSEV
Faculty of Information Science and Computing Technology: A. V. ZAFIEVSKY
Faculty of Law: N. N. TARUSINA
Faculty of Mathematics: V. G. DURNEV
Faculty of Physics: V. P. ALEKSEYEV
Faculty of Psychology: A. V. KARPOV
Faculty of Social Sciences: G. M. NAZHMUTDINOV

YUGORSKY STATE UNIVERSITY

628012 Khanty-Mansiysk, ul. Chekhova 16

Telephone: (34671) 35-77-13
E-mail: ugrasu@ugrasu.ru
Internet: www.ugrasu.ru
State control

Founded 2001

Rector: Prof. YURI I. REUTOV
First Pro-Rector: TATIANA D. KARMINSKAYA
Pro-Rector for Academic Affairs: OLGA F. SHAPKINA
Pro-Rector for Research: VLADIMIR Z. KOVALEV (acting)
Librarian: NINA I. SMIRNOVA
Library of 170,000 vols, 248 periodicals
Number of teachers: 521
Number of students: 5,138
Publication: *Vestnik of YuSU* (scientific journal)

DEANS

Applied Mathematics, Computer Science and Control: YURIY V. KOLOKOLOV
Economics and Finance: ALEXEY P. ERMILOV
Engineering: VLADIMIR Z. KOVALEV
Further Education: ARKADY V. KRASILNIKOV
Geology, Oil and Gas: TATIANA I. ROMANOVA
Humanities: VLADIMIR A. MISHCHENKO
Language, History and Culture of the Peoples of Yugra: VICTORIA I. SPODINA
Law: STANISLAV V. ROZENKO
Sports and Tourism: SERGEY V. BARBASHOV

MEDICAL UNIVERSITIES

ALTAI STATE MEDICAL UNIVERSITY

656038 Barnaul, pr. Lenina 40

Telephone: (3852) 36-88-48
E-mail: rector@mail.ru
Internet: www.agmu.ru

Founded 1954
Language of instruction: Russian

Rector: VALERY M. BRYUKHANOV

Library of 542,000 vols
Number of teachers: 536
Number of students: 5,079

DEANS

Faculty of General Medicine: Prof. V. G. LICHEV
Faculty of Paediatrics: Prof. G. E. VYKHODTCEVA
Faculty of Pharmaceuticals: Prof. Y. F. ZVEREV
High Qualified Nurses' Education: Assoc. Prof. I. E. GOSSEN
Medico—Preventive Faculty: Prof. E. L. BOBROVSKY

BASHKIR STATE MEDICAL UNIVERSITY

450092 Bashkortostan, Ufa, ul. Lenina 3

Telephone: (3472) 22-41-73
E-mail: admin@bsmu.anrb.ru
Internet: www.bsmu.anrb.ru

Founded 1932

Rector: VIL M. TIMERBULATOV

Library of 600,000 vols
Number of teachers: 650
Number of students: 4,175

IRKUTSK STATE MEDICAL UNIVERSITY

664003 Irkutsk, ul. Krasnogo Vosstaniya 1

Telephone: (3952) 24-38-25
E-mail: rector_ismu@bk.ru
Internet: www.ismu.baikal.ru

Founded 1919

Rector: Prof. ASKOLD A. MAIBORODA

KAZAN STATE MEDICAL UNIVERSITY

420012 Kazan, 49 Butlerov St

Telephone: (843) 236-05-43
E-mail: info@kazansmu.com
Internet: www.kazansmu.com

Founded 1814
State control
Languages of instruction: English, Russian
Academic year: September to June

Faculties of dentistry, general medicine, graduate nursing, medical biochemistry, medical biophysics, paediatrics, pharmacy, prophylactic medicine, social work

Rector: Prof. ALEXEY SOZINOV
Vice-Rector for Int. Affairs: Prof. AYRAT ZIGANSHIN

Library of 20,000 vols
Number of teachers: 500
Number of students: 4,500

Publication: *Kazan Medical Journal* (6 a year)

KURSK STATE MEDICAL UNIVERSITY

305041 Kursk, ul. Karla Marksa 3

Telephone: (0712) 58-81-32
E-mail: main@kgmu.kursknet.ru
Internet: www.kgmu.kursknet.ru

Founded 1935

Rector: Prof. A. LAZAREVA

Library of 320,214 vols

MOSCOW STATE UNIVERSITY OF MEDICINE AND DENTISTRY NAMED AFTER A. I. EVDOKIMOV

127473 Moscow, ul. Delegatskaya 20/1

Telephone: (495) 650-43-94
E-mail: welcome@msmsu.ru
Internet: www.msmsu.ru

Founded 1922
Academic year: September to June

Faculties of dentistry, general medicine, clinical psychology, penitentiary medicine, specialized secondary education, pre-medical school preparation, postgraduate education (internship/residency, fellowship), economic faculty and foreign medical students faculty

Rector: Prof. OLEG YANUSHEVICH

Library of 549,979 vols
Number of teachers: 1,147
Number of students: 6,000

NORTHERN STATE MEDICAL UNIVERSITY

163001 Arkhangelsk, Troitsky pr. 51

Telephone: (8182) 21-00-00
E-mail: info@nsmu.ru
Internet: www.nsmu.ru

Founded 1932 as Arkhangelsk State Medical Institute, present name and status 2000

Faculties of adaptive physical training, ecology, general practice, medical clinical psychology, medical management, paediatrics, pharmaceutics, prophylactic medicine, social work, stomatology; institutes: management, medical education, information technology

Rector: PAVEL I. SIDOROV

Library of 400,000 vols
Number of students: 5,500

Publications: *Human Ecology* (4 a year), *Medik Severa* (12 a year)

ROSTOV STATE MEDICAL UNIVERSITY

344022 Rostov-on-Don, Nakhichevansky per. 29

Telephone: (863) 250-42-00
E-mail: info@geolayfe.ru
Internet: www.rostgmu.ru

Founded 1930

Rector: Prof. SERGEY V. SHLYK

Library of 340,000 vols

RUSSIAN STATE MEDICAL UNIVERSITY

117869 Moscow, ul. Ostrovityanova 1

Telephone: (495) 434-03-29
E-mail: rgmu@rsmu.ru
Internet: www.rsmu.ru

Founded 1906, present name and status 1991

Faculties of biomedicine, medicine, paediatrics

Rector: Prof. Dr VLADIMIR N. YARYGIN

Library of 900,000 vols
Number of teachers: 1,200
Number of students: 6,300

Publication: *Vestnik* (4 a year)

ST PETERSBURG STATE MEDICAL UNIVERSITY 'ACAD. I. P. PAVLOV'

197022 St Petersburg, ul. L. Tolstogo 6/8

Telephone: (812) 238-71-12
E-mail: admission@spmu.rssi.ru
Internet: www.spmu.runnet.ru

Founded 1897

Areas of study: basic sciences, dentistry, medicine, sports medicine

Rector: Prof. NIKOLAI A. YAITSKY
Vice-Rector for Academic Affairs: Prof. U. D. IGNATOV
Vice-Rector for Int. Affairs: Prof. S. H. AL-SHUKRI
Vice-Rector for Research: Prof. E. E. ZVARTAU
Dean of Faculty of Gen. Medicine: Prof. N. N. PETRISHEV
Dean of Foreign Students Affairs: Prof. M. SH. VAKHITOV

Library: 1m. vols

Publications: *Arterial Hypertension* (4 a year), *Nephrology* (4 a year), *Scientific Items* (4 a year), *St Petersburg Medical News* (6 a year)

SAMARA STATE MEDICAL UNIVERSITY

443099 Samara, ul. Chapaevskaya 89

Telephone: (8462) 32-16-34
E-mail: info@samsmu.ru
Internet: samsmu.ru

Founded 1919

Fields of study: cardiology, dentistry, general medicine, gerontology, healthcare, ionizing radiation, medical management, medical prophylactics, military medicine, nursing, paediatrics, pharmaceutics, psychology, surgery, therapy, traumatology; tissue bank

Rector: Prof. Dr GENNADY P. KOTELNIKOV

Library of 570,183 vols
Number of teachers: 700
Number of students: 6,500

Publications: *Annals of Traumatology and Orthopaedics* (6 a year), *Aspirant Herald of Volga Region* (12 a year), *Older Generation* (12 a year), *Samara Medical Archive* (6 a year), *Transregional Association 'Povolzhye Healthcare' Herald* (12 a year)

SARATOV STATE MEDICAL UNIVERSITY

410012 Saratov, Bol. Kazachya 112

Telephone: (8452) 27-33-70
E-mail: meduniv@sgmu.ru
Internet: www.sgmu.ru

Founded 1909

Rector: Dr PETR V. GLYBOCHKO

Library of 950,000 vols

SIBERIAN STATE MEDICAL UNIVERSITY

534050 Tomsk, Moskovsky Trakt 2

Telephone: (3822) 53-04-23
E-mail: office@ssmu.net.ru
Internet: www.ssmu.ru

Founded 1888

Faculties of biological medicine, medicine, military medicine, nursing, paediatrics, pharmaceutics, postgraduate education, preparatory education; institutes: cardiology, genetics, oncology, pharmacology, psychiatric health; attached hospital

Pres.: Prof. Dr VYACHESLAV V. NOVITSKY

Library of 500,000 vols
Number of teachers: 676
Number of students: 3,445

Publications: *Bulletin of Siberian Healthcare* (4 a year), *Questions of Reconstructive and Plastic Surgery* (4 a year), *Siberian Magazine of Gastroenterology and Haematology* (4 a year)

VLADIVOSTOK STATE MEDICAL UNIVERSITY

690600 Vladivostok, pr. Ostryakova 2

Telephone: (4232) 45-16-24
E-mail: webadmin@vgmu.ru
Internet: www.vgmu.ru

Founded 1958

Faculties of therapeutics, medicine and prophylaxis, paediatrics, qualification improvement

Rector: Prof. YURI V. KAMINSKY

Number of teachers: 400
Number of students: 2,717

VOLGOGRAD STATE MEDICAL UNIVERSITY

400066 Volgograd, pl. Pavshikh Bortsov 1

Telephone: (8442) 38-50-05
E-mail: cved@volgmed.ru
Internet: www.volgmed.ru

Founded 1935

Colleges of advanced and continuing education, clinical psychology, general medicine, dentistry, medical biology, paediatrics, pharmacy, social work

Rector: Prof. VLADIMIR I. PETROV

Number of teachers: 657
Number of students: 5,070

PEDAGOGICAL AND LINGUISTIC UNIVERSITIES

BARNAUL STATE PEDAGOGICAL UNIVERSITY

656031 Altai Region, Barnaul, ul. Molodezhnaya 55

Telephone: (3852) 22-85-52
E-mail: rector@bspu.secna.ru
Internet: www.bspu.secna.ru

Rector: Prof. VLADIMIR N. LOPATKIN

Number of teachers: 563
Number of students: 8,534

BLAGOVESHCHENSK STATE PEDAGOGICAL UNIVERSITY

675000 Blagoveshchensk, Amur oblast, ul. Lenina 104

Telephone: (4162) 52-41-64
E-mail: rektorat@bgpu.ru
Internet: www.bgpu.ru

State control

Languages of instruction: French, Russian
Academic year: September to July

Founded 1930, present status 1996

Rector: Prof. Dr YURI P. SERGIENKO
First Vice-Rector: Dr YURY MALINOVSKY
Dir for Foreign Affairs Office: Dr NIKOLAY KUKHARENKO

Library of 700,000 vols
Number of teachers: 350
Number of students: 4,000

Publications: *Geographical Aspects of Upper Amur Area*, *Regional Studies of Amur Area* (in Russian, Chinese, English and French), *Salut! Ça va?*

DEANS

Confucius Institute: Dr NIKOLAY KUKHARENKO
Dept of Foreign Languages: NATALIA KUTCHERENKO
Dept of History and Philology: DMITRY BOLOTIN
Dept of Industry and Pedagogics: LYUDMILA KALNINSH
Dept of Natural Sciences and Geography: IRINA TROFIMTSOVA
Dept of Pedagogics and Elementary Education: TATIANA PLOTNIKOVA
Dept of Physical Culture and Sports: YURY KRETOV
Dept of Physics and Mathematics: VALENTINA NEMILOSTIVA
Dept of Professional Development and Advanced Training: Dr ELENA KALABINA
Dept of Psychology and Pedagogics: SVETLANA ZUEVA
International Dept: VERA PIRKO

IRKUTSK STATE LINGUISTIC UNIVERSITY

664000 Irkutsk, ul. Lenina 8

Telephone: (3952) 20-03-61
E-mail: islu@islu.irk.ru
Internet: www.islu.ru

Founded 1948

Faculties of eastern languages, English language, foreign languages and social science, German language, Romance languages, training of foreign students and advancement of qualifications; external faculty

Rector: Prof. GRIGORY D. VOSKOBOYNIK

MOSCOW STATE LINGUISTIC UNIVERSITY

119034 Moscow, ul. Ostozhenka 38

Telephone: (495) 246-86-03
E-mail: info@linguanet.ru
Internet: www.linguanet.ru

Founded 1930, present name and status 1990
Academic year: September to June

11 Faculties, 6 MSLU educational institutes and 26 MSLU educational and research centres and laboratories

Rector: Prof. IRINA I. KHALEEVA
Vice-Rector for Int. Affairs: VLADIMIR SHLEG

Library: 1m. vols
Number of teachers: 2,025
Number of students: 13,000

NIZHNY NOVGOROD STATE LINGUISTICS UNIVERSITY 'N. A. DOBROLYUBOV'

603155 Nizhny Novgorod, ul. Minina 31A

Telephone: (8314) 36-15-75
E-mail: admdep@lunn.ru
Internet: www.lunn.ru

Founded 1917
State control
Languages of instruction: English, French, German, Italian, Russian, Spanish
Academic year: September to June

Faculties of business admin., economics, int. relations, law, office management, pedagogy, philology, public relations, translation and interpreting, Russian language and culture

Rector: Prof. BORIS A. ZHIGALEV

Library of 406,770 vols
Number of teachers: 329
Number of students: 3,517

Publication: *Sestnik of the Linguistics University of Nizhny Novgorod*

PYATIGORSK STATE LINGUISTIC UNIVERSITY

357532 Pyatigorsk, pr. Kalinina 9

Telephone: (8793) 40-05-05
E-mail: ums@pglu.ru
Internet: www.pglu.ru

Founded 1939
State control
Languages of instruction: English, Russian
Academic year: September to June

Educational programmes: English, French, German, Spanish, Italian, Polish, Turkish, Arabic and Chinese languages, Russian as a foreign language, oriental studies, govt and public admin, business admin, hospitality and tourism management, int. relations, public relations, int. journalism, law, conflict resolution, psychology, theology (Christian and Islam), customs management and advertising

Rector: Prof. ALEXANDER P. GORBUNOV
Vice-Rector: Prof. YURI Y. GRANKIN
Dir for Int. Office: Dr VICTOR E. MISHIN
Chief Librarian: SVETLANA A. CHERNOMOR-DOVA

Library of 850,000 vols
Number of teachers: 562
Number of students: 5,500

Publications: *PSLU Bulletin, PSLU Herald* (4 a year, research journal)

RUSSIAN STATE VOCATIONAL PEDAGOGICAL UNIVERSITY

620012 Ekaterinburg, ul. Mashinostroitelei 11

Telephone: (343) 338-44-47
E-mail: mail@rsvpu.ru
Internet: www.rsvpu.ru

Founded 1979

Rector: GENNADY M. ROMANTSEV

Library of 333,800 vols
Number of teachers: 441
Number of students: 18,124

Publications: *Bulletin of Teaching Research* (2 a year), *Bulletin of the Association of Russian Educational Institutions on Vocational Pedagogics* (1 a year), *Improvement of Educational Processes in Vocational Schools* (1 a year), *Innovations in Industry and Education* (1 a year), *Integrational Processes in Pedagogical Theory and Practice* (1 a year), *Problems of Public Development in the Fields of Sociology and Economics*

SIBERIAN FEDERAL UNIVERSITY

660041 Karsnoyarsk, Svobodny pr. 79

Telephone: (391) 244-82-13
E-mail: rector@sfu-kras.ru
Internet: www.sfu-kras.ru

Founded 2006, reorganized Karsnoyarsk State Univ., Karsnoyarsk State Technical Univ., Karsnoyarsk State Academy of Architecture and Civil Construction, State Univ. of Non-Ferrous Metals and Gold
State control
Language of instruction: Russian
Academic year: September to July

Rector: EVGENY A. VAGANOV
Vice-Rector: NIKOLAY N. DOVZHENKO
Vice-Rector: PAVEL M. VCHERASHINY
Vice-Rector: SERGEY A. PODLESNYI
Vice-Rector: SERGEY V. VERKHOVETS
Vice-Rector: VALENTIN M. ZURAVLEV
Vice-Rector: VLADIMIR I. KOLMAKOV
Vice-Rector: VLADISLAV YU. PANCHENKO
Librarian: EVEGINYA G. KRIVONOSOVA

Library: 3.7m. vols
Number of teachers: 3,300
Number of students: 43,000

Publications: *New University Life* (48 a year), *Scientific Journal of Siberian Federal University* (4 a year, 5 series)

URALS STATE PEDAGOGICAL UNIVERSITY

620219 Ekaterinburg, GSP 135, pr. Kosmonavtov 26

Telephone: (343) 34-12-59
E-mail: root@uspu.ru
Internet: www.uspu.ru

Founded 1930 as Urals Industrial Pedagogical Institute; as Urals State Pedagogical Institute 1932–1993; present name and status 1994
State control

Rector: Prof. VLADIMIR D. ZHAVORONKOV

Number of teachers: 720
Number of students: 7,600

VOLGOGRAD STATE SOCIO—PEDAGOGICAL UNIVERSITY

400066 Volgograd, pr. V. I. Lenina 27

Telephone: (8442) 60-28-12
E-mail: vspu@vspu.ru
Internet: www.vspu.ru
State control
Language of instruction: Russian
Academic year: September to June

Rector: Dr NIKOLAY K. SERGEEV

Number of teachers: 800
Number of students: 10,500

VORONEZH STATE PEDAGOGICAL UNIVERSITY

394043 Voronezh, ul. Lenina 86

Telephone: (0732) 55-19-49
E-mail: rector@vspu.ac.ru
Internet: www.vspu.ac.ru

Founded 1930
State control

Rector: Prof. VYACHESLAV V. PODKOLZIN

Library of 600,000 vols
Number of teachers: 473

TECHNICAL UNIVERSITIES

ADMIRAL MAKAROV STATE UNIVERSITY FOR MARITIME AND INLAND SHIPPING

198035 St Petersburg, ul. Dvinskaya 5/7

Telephone: (812) 251-12-21
E-mail: rector@spbuwc.ru
Internet: www.spbuwc.ru

Founded 1809
State control
Language of instruction: Russian
Academic year: September to June

Rector: Prof. SERGEY BARYSHNIKOV

Library of 1,200,000 vols
Number of teachers: 1,000
Number of students: 10,000 (5,000 full-time, 5,000 evening and distance)

DEANS

Evening and Correspondence Study: Dr YURI EZHOV
Faculty of Arts and Social Sciences: OLEG CHULKOV
Faculty of Economics and Finance: Dr IGOR RASTORGUEV
Faculty of Information Technologies: Dr EVGENIY BARSCHEVSKIY
Faculty of Law: Prof. OLEG KARATAEV
Faculty of Navigation: Dr KIRILL SLATIN
Hydrotechnical Engineering Faculty: SERGEY GOLOVKOV
Marine Engineering: Dr YURI LOPAREV
Port Facilities and Electrical Engineering: Dr EVGENIY ANDRIANOV
Regional and Distance Learning: Dr LARISA ALPEEVA

ARKHANGELSK STATE TECHNICAL UNIVERSITY

163002 Arkhangelsk, Severnaya Dvina nab. 17

Telephone: (8182) 28-76-14
E-mail: public@agtu.ru
Internet: www.agtu.ru

Founded 1929
Academic year: September to June

Faculties of chemical technology, construction, distance learning, forestry, industrial power engineering, law, mechanical engineering, mechanical wood technology, natural resources, re-training and preparatory studies; institutes of chemical technology, economics, finance and business, information technology, law and entrepreneurship, oil and gas; colleges of business, information technology, law; centres of innovative technologies and information science; brs in Naryan-Mar, Kotlas, Velsk, Novodvinsk and Mirny

Rector: ALEXANDER L. NEVZOROV

Library of 720,000 vols, 380 periodicals
Number of teachers: 515
Number of students: 12,040

Publication: *Lesnoi Zhurnal* (Forestry Journal, 6 a year)

ASTRAKHAN STATE TECHNICAL UNIVERSITY

414025 Astrakhan, ul. Tatishcheva 16
Telephone: (8512) 25-09-23
E-mail: astu@astu.org
Internet: www.astu.org

Founded 1930
State control
Language of instruction: Russian
Academic year: September to June

Rector: Prof. Y. T. PIMENOV (acting)

Library of 700,000 vols
Number of teachers: 450
Number of students: 12,000

Publications: *ASTU Herald* (1 a year), *Proceedings*

DEANS

Faculty of Construction: Prof. Dr RAMAZAM ABDULMUMINOVICH NABIEV
Faculty of Law: Prof. Dr IVAN VLADIMIROVICH MAKSIMOV
Institute of Economics: Assoc. Prof. TAMARA FEDOROVNA LOKTEVA
Institute of Fisheries, Biology and Nature Management: Prof. Dr ALEXANDR NIKOLAEVICH NEVALENNYI
Institute of Humanities: Dr ELVIRA ZELETDINOVA
Institute of Information Technologies and Communications: Dr IRINA YURIEVNA KVYATKOVSKAYA
Institute of Oil and Gas: Assoc. Prof. NATALIA NIKOLAEVNA LETICHEVSKAYA
Institute of Marine Sciences, Energy and Transport: SERGEY VLADIMIROVICH VINOGRADOV
Institute of Mechanics and Engineering: Prof. ANATOLY VIKTOROVICH KARABLIN
Preparatory Faculty for Foreign Citizens: NATALIA VITALIEVNA SHTEINIKOVA

BALTIC STATE TECHNICAL UNIVERSITY 'D. F. USTINOV' (VOENMEKH)

198005 St Petersburg, ul. 1-ya Krasnoarmeiskaya 1/21
Telephone: (812) 316-26-13
Internet: www.insu.ru

Founded 1930

Depts of aerospace, applied mechanics and automation, guidance systems, humanities, international industrial management, natural sciences, rocketry and aircraft

Rector: Prof. YURI V. ZAGASHVILI

Library: 1.1m. vols
Number of teachers: 600
Number of students: 5,300

BELGOROD STATE TECHNOLOGICAL UNIVERSITY 'V. G. SHUKOV'

308012 Belgorod, ul. Kostyukova 46
Telephone: (722) 54-20-87
E-mail: rektor@intbel.ru
Internet: www.bstu.ru

Founded 1970
Academic year: September to June

Institutes of building materials, economics and management, mechanical equipment in the building industry; depts of architecture and building technologies, civil engineering, engineering and ecology, highways, machine building, production automation and information technologies; 4 brs across Russia

Rector: Prof. ANATOLY M. GRIDCHIN

Library of 600,000 vols
Number of teachers: 540
Number of students: 9,152

Publication: *Tekhnolog* (newspaper, 6 a year)

BRYANSK STATE TECHNICAL UNIVERSITY

241035 Bryansk, bul. 50-let. Oktyabrya 7
Telephone: (4832) 56-09-05
E-mail: rector@tu-bryansk.ru
Internet: www.tu-bryansk.ru

Founded 1929

Rector: Prof. ALEXANDER V. LAGEREV

Library of 705,668 vols
Number of teachers: 1,131
Number of students: 8,859

Publication: *Vestnik BGTU*

DAGESTAN STATE TECHNICAL UNIVERSITY

367015 Makhachkala, 70 Imama Shamil pr.
Telephone: (8722) 62-37-61
E-mail: dstu@dstu.ru
Internet: www.dstu.ru

Founded 1972 as Dagestan Polytechnical Institute
Academic year: September to July

Rector: Prof. TAGIR A. ISMAILOV
Vice-Rector for Academics: Prof. KADI A. GASANOV
Vice-Rector for Admin. and Supply: MAGOMED G. MEDGIDOV
Vice-Rector for Economy: Prof. NURMAGOMED S. SURAKATOV
Vice-Rector for Educational and Social Work: Assoc. Prof. MARINA E. KOTENKA
Vice-Rector for Informatization: EMRAN E. ILYASOV
Vice-Rector for Science and Innovations: Prof. ELENA I. PAVLYUCHENKO
Head Librarian: TAMILA A. RAGHIMOVA

Library of 832,400 vols, 116,649 periodicals
Number of teachers: 800
Number of students: 13,000

Publications: *Herald of DSTU* (technical sciences, humanities), *Thematic Collected Scientific Papers*

DEANS

Architecture and Construction: Prof. GADGIMAGOMED N. KHADGISHALAPOV
Computer Technology, Computer Engineering and Energetics: Assoc. Prof. ARSLAN G. MUSTAFAEV
Customs and Legal Expertise: Prof. KHADGIMURAD Z. KHALIMBEKOV
Engineering and Economics: Assoc. Prof. NAIDA M. GASANOVA
Finance and Audit: Prof. AMMAKADI R. RABADANOV
Information Systems: Prof. TADZHIDIN E. SARKAROV
Oil, Gas and Environmental Devt: Prof. RASUL M. ALIEV
Radioelectronics, Telecommunications and Multimedia Technologies: Assoc. Prof. KHADGIMURAT M. GADGIEV
Skill Improvement and Personnel Retraining: Asst Prof. AISHAT R. SHAKHMAEVA
Technology: Assoc. Prof. MAGOMED AKHMEDOV
Transport: Assoc. Prof. EDVARD Z. BATAMANOV

DON STATE TECHNICAL UNIVERSITY

344010 Rostov-on-Don, pl. Gagarina 1
Telephone: (822) 38-15-25
E-mail: root@sintez.rud.su

Founded 1930 as Rostov Institute of Agricultural Engineering, present name 1992

Rector: Prof. Dr ANATOLY A. RYZHKIN

Library of 837,000 vols
Number of teachers: 650
Number of students: 6,000

EASTERN SIBERIAN STATE UNIVERSITY OF TECHNOLOGY

670013 Ulan-Ude, ul. Klyuchevskaya 40в
Telephone: (3012) 37-56-00
E-mail: office@esstu.ru
Internet: www.esstu.ru

Founded 1962

Fields of study: mechanics and technology of light industry, construction, mechanical engineering, electrical engineering, power engineering, preparatory faculty; institutes: sustainable development, economics and law, food industry and biotechnology; postgraduate courses, Russian language courses, Russian language summer school, pre-university training courses

Rector: Prof. VLADIMIR E. SAKTOYEV

Library of 715,246 vols
Number of teachers: 868
Number of students: 10,640

FAR EASTERN NATIONAL TECHNICAL UNIVERSITY

690990 Vladivostok, ul. Pushkinskaya 10
Telephone: (4232) 26-51-18
E-mail: festu@festu.ru
Internet: www.festu.ru

Founded 1899

Institutes of architecture, automatics and advanced technologies, civil engineering, continuing and distance education, economics and management, engineering, humanities, information science, maritime engineering, mechanics, mining engineering, natural sciences, oriental studies, politics and law, radioelectronics and electrical engineering, social ecology; brs in Nakhodka, Arseniev, Petropavlovsk-Kamchatsky, Dalnegorsk, Dalnerechensk, Bolshoi Kamen, Artyom, Lesozavodsk, Yuzhno-Sakhalinsk and Kirovsky

Pres.: ANVIR A. FATKULIN

Library of 2,328,000 vols, 300 periodicals
Number of teachers: 109
Number of students: 25,000

Publications: *Pacific Science Review* (jtly with Kangnam Univ., Republic of Korea, annual), *Proceedings* (1 a year)

FAR EASTERN STATE TECHNICAL FISHERIES UNIVERSITY

690600 Vladivostok, ul. Lugovaya 52в
Telephone: (4232) 44-03-06
E-mail: support@dalrybvtuz.ru
Internet: www.dalrybvtuz.ru

Founded 1930

Rector: Prof. GEORGY N. KIM

Library of 450,000 vols
Number of teachers: 266
Number of students: 6,264

Publications: *Dalrybvtuz* (2 a year), *Scientific Papers* (2 a year)

FAR EASTERN STATE TRANSPORT UNIVERSITY

680021 Khabarovsk, ul. Serysheva 47
Telephone: (4212) 40-72-00
E-mail: root@festu.khv.ru
Internet: www.festu.khv.ru

Founded 1937
State control
Languages of instruction: English, Russian
Academic year: September to July

Rector: Prof. BORIS E. DYNKIN (acting)
Vice-Rector: ANDREY N. GANUS (acting)

Library of 960,000 vols
Number of teachers: 520
Number of students: 25,000

Publication: *Social and Humanity Sciences at the Far East*

DEANS

Institute of Economics: Prof. YULIA A. TYUR-INA

GAGARIN STATE TECHNICAL UNIVERSITY, SARATOV (SSTU)

410054 Saratov, Politekhnicheskaya St 77
Telephone: (8452) 99-87-09
E-mail: international@sstu.ru
Internet: www.sstu.ru
Founded 1930
State control
Language of instruction: Russian
Academic year: September to June

Rector: Prof. IGOR PLEVE

Library: 1.5m. vols
Number of teachers: 2,000
Number of students: 25,000

Publications: *The Journal of Innovation Activity* (4 a year), *The Journal of Innovations and Publicity* (4 a year), *The Journal of Saratov State Technical University* (4 a year), *The Journal of Social Policy Studies* (4 a year)

DEANS

Applied Information Technology: Assoc. Prof. OLGA DOLININA
Architecture and Road Construction: Prof. YURIY IVASHCHENKO
Automotive Engineering: Prof. IGOR DANILOV
Ecology and Service: Prof. ALEXEY IVANOV
Economics and Management: Prof. VLADIMIR TREGUBOV
Electronics and Instrumentation Engineering: Prof. MARINA BROVKOVA
Humanities and Social Sciences: Prof. DMITRIY MIKHEL
Mechanical Engineering: Prof. OLEG DAVYDENKO
Physical and Technical Sciences: Prof. ALEXANDER GOROKHOVSKIY
Power Engineering: Assoc. Prof. PAVEL ANTROPOV

GUBKIN RUSSIAN STATE UNIVERSITY OF OIL AND GAS

119991 Moscow, Leninsky pr. 65
Telephone: (4959) 137-81-08
E-mail: com@gubkin.ru
Internet: www.gubkin.ru
Founded 1930
State control
Academic year: September to June

Faculties of automation and computer science, construction and operation, chemical and environmental engineering, economics and management and law, liberal arts and humanities, mechanical engineering, natural science studies, oil and gas fields devt, petroleum geology and geophysics, pipeline network design, reservoir engineering; brs in Ashgabat, Orenburg, Tashkent

Rector: Prof. VICTOR G. MARTYNOV
Vice-Rector for Academic Affairs: Prof. VLADIMIR N. KOSHELEV
Vice-Rector for Int. Affairs: Prof. ANATOLY B. ZOLOTUKHIN

Library: 1.5m. vols
Number of teachers: 900
Number of students: 8,500

Publications: *Chemistry & Technology of Fuels and Oils*, *Oil, Gas & Business*, *Proceedings of Gubkin Russian State University of Oil and Gas*

IVANOVO STATE ENERGY UNIVERSITY

153548 Ivanovo, ul. Rabfakovskaya 34
Telephone: (0932) 32-72-43
E-mail: office@ispu.ru
Internet: www.ispu.ru

Faculties of electrical engineering, heat and power engineering, industrial heat and power engineering, power engineering

Rector: VLADIMIR N. NUZHDIN

Number of teachers: 1,500
Number of students: 8,000

IVANOVO STATE UNIVERSITY OF CHEMISTRY AND TECHNOLOGY

153460 Ivanovo, pr. F. Engelsa 7
Telephone: (0932) 32-92-41
E-mail: rektor@isuct.ru
Internet: www.isuct.ru

Founded 1918 as Ivanovo-Vosnessensk Polytechnic Institute, Ivanovo Institute of Chemistry and Technology 1930–92, as Ivanovo State Acad. of Chemistry and Technology 1992–98, present name and status 1998

Faculties of inorganic chemistry technology, organic chemistry, silicates and engineering

Rector: OSCAR I. KOIFMAN

KALASHNIKOV IZHEVSK STATE TECHNICAL UNIVERSITY

426069 Izhevsk, Studencheskaya St 7
Telephone: (3412) 59-25-55
E-mail: inter@istu.ru
Internet: www.istu.ru

Founded 1952
State control
Languages of instruction: English, Russian
Academic year: September to July

Faculties of advanced technologies and automobiles, advertising and design, civil engineering, computer science, economics, law and humanities, heat engineering, instrumentation engineering, management and marketing, mathematics and natural sciences, mechanical engineering, quality management, institute of sports; brs in Glazov, Kambarka, Sarapul, Tchaikovsky, Votkinsk

Rector: Prof. BORIS YAKIMOVICH

Library of 800,000 vols
Number of teachers: 800
Number of students: 22,000

KALININGRAD STATE TECHNICAL UNIVERSITY

236000 Kaliningrad, Sovietsky pr. 1
Telephone: (0112) 27-22-55
E-mail: ivanov@klgtu.ru
Internet: www.klgtu.ru

Founded 1930
Academic year: September to June

Faculties of biological resources and water usage, commercial fisheries, economics and humanities, mechanics and technology, naval and power engineering, production automation and control

Rector: Prof. VICTOR E. IVANOV

Library of 530,000 vols
Number of teachers: 560
Number of students: 7,000

Publication: *Izvestiya KGTU* (12 a year)

KAZAN STATE TECHNICAL UNIVERSITY 'A. N. TUPOLEV'

420111 Kazan, ul. K. Marksa 10
Telephone: (8432) 31-02-44
E-mail: icd@kai.ru

Internet: www.kai.ru
Founded 1932, present name and status 1992
Rector: Prof. YURIY GORTYSHOV

Library: 3m. vols
Number of teachers: 1,800
Number of students: 24,000

Publications: *Aviatsionaya Tekchnika: Izvestia VUZov* (Russian Aeronautics, 4 a year, in Russian and English), *Non-Linear Analysis Problems in Engineering Systems* (2 a year, in English), *Problemy Nelineinogo Analiza v Inzhenernykh Sistemakh* (Non-Linear Analysis Problems in Engineering Systems, 2 a year, in Russian and English), *Russian Aeronautics* (4 a year, in English), *Radioelectronnye Ustroistva* (Radioengineering Devices, 2 a year, in Russian), *Vestnik KGTU* (Proceedings of KSTU, 4 a year, in Russian)

KAZAN STATE TECHNOLOGICAL UNIVERSITY

420015 Kazan, ul. K. Marksa 68
Telephone: (8432) 38-56-94
E-mail: office@kstu.ru
Internet: www.kstu.ru

Founded 1919

Faculties of light industry engineering, mechanics, chemical engineering, oil and oil refining, polymers, chemical technology, energy engineering and technological engineering, power machinery construction and process equipment, management and automation, humanities and food technology; br. at Nizhnekamsk

Rector: SERGEI G. DYAKONOV

Library: 1.6m. vols
Number of teachers: 950
Number of students: 25,000

Publications: *Economy of Industrial Production*, *Heat and Mass Transfer in Chemical Engineering*

KAZAN STATE UNIVERSITY OF ARCHITECTURE AND CIVIL ENGINEERING

420043 Kazan, ul. Zelenaya 1
Telephone: (843) 510-46-10
E-mail: rector@kgasu.ru
Internet: www.kgasu.ru

Founded 1930 as Kazan Engineering and Civil Engineering Institute; later Kazan State Acad. of Architecture and Civil Engineering; current name adopted 2005
Academic year: September to June

Rector: RASHIT K. NIZAMOV
Vice-Rector: ILFAC E. VILDANOV
Vice-Rector for Academic Affairs: DAMIR K. SHARAFUTDINOV

Library of 583,000 vols
Number of teachers: 540
Number of students: 6,800

DEANS

Architecture: ALEXANDER D. KULIKOV
Building Science Engineering: VLADIMIR S. AGAFONKIN
Construction Technologies: DMITRIY A. SOLDATOV
Design: SERGEY M. MIKHAILOV
Economics: GUZEL M. HARISOVA
Engineering: MUNIR A. VALIULLIN
Engineering Basics: NAIL K. TUKTAMISHEV
Engineering Systems and Ecology: RAIS S. SAFIN
General Architectural and Art Training: HANIFA G. NADIROVA
Part-time and Extended Studies: VICTOR YA. ORLOV

Transport Engineering: ILVERA N. HABIBUL-
LINA

KOMSOMOLSK-ON-AMUR STATE TECHNICAL UNIVERSITY

681013 Komsomolsk-on-Amur, pr. Lenina 27
Telephone: (4217) 53-23-04
E-mail: office@knastu.ru
Internet: www.knastu.ru

Founded 1955

Rector: Prof. YURI KABALDIN
Number of students: 3,500

KOSTROMA STATE TECHNOLOGICAL UNIVERSITY

156005 Kostroma, ul. Dzerzhinskogo 17
Telephone: (4942) 31-48-14
E-mail: info@kstu.edu.ru
Internet: www.kstu.edu.ru

Founded 1932, as Kostroma Textile Institute,
as Kostroma Technological Institute 1962,
present name and status 1995

Rector: ANDREI P. BOLOTNY
Vice-Rector for International Links: VICTOR
P. KALASHNIK

Library of 608,000 vols
Number of teachers: 430
Number of students: 6,520

KUBAN STATE TECHNICAL UNIVERSITY

350072 Krasnodar, ul. Moskovskaya 2
Telephone: (861) 255-84-01
E-mail: adm@kgtu.kuban.ru
Internet: www.kubstu.ru

Founded 1918

Faculties of chemical engineering, civil
engineering, computer technology and automated systems, economics, food technology,
gas and power engineering, highway engineering, oil, mechanical engineering, technology of grain products; Institute of Mechanical
Engineering in Armavir, br. in Novorossiisk

Rector: Prof. A. A. PETRIK

Library of 720,000 vols
Number of teachers: 800
Number of students: 13,000

Publications: *Izvestiya Vuzov*, *Pishevaya
Teckhnologiya* (Food Technology, 6 a year)

KURSK STATE TECHNICAL UNIVERSITY

305040 Kursk, ul. 50-letiya Oktyabrya 94
Telephone: (0712) 22-57-43
E-mail: rector@kstu.kursk.ru
Internet: www.kstu.kursk.ru

Founded 1964

Faculties of civil and industrial construction
engineering, computer engineering and automation systems, economics, environmental
protection, finance and auditing, law, management, machine-building, textile technology

Rector: Prof. IVAN S. ZAKHAROV

Library of 536,000 vols
Number of teachers: 530
Number of students: 4,400

Publication: *Izvestia* (2 a year)

KUZBASS STATE TECHNICAL UNIVERSITY NAMED AFTER T.F. GORBACHEV

650026 Kemerovo, ul. Vesennyaya, 28
Telephone: (3842) 58-33-83
E-mail: rector@kuzstu.ru
Internet: www.kuzstu.ru

Founded 1950
State control
Language of instruction: Russian
Academic year: September to June

Rector: Dr VLADIMIR A. KOVALEV

Library of 650,000 vols
Number of teachers: 761
Number of students: 8,660

DEANS

Chemical Technology: Prof. Dr TATYANA G.
CHERKASOVA
Economics and Service: Prof. Dr VALERIY N.
BOBRIKOV
Machinery Engineering: Prof. Dr ALEXANDER
N. KOROTKOV
Mining and Electrical Engineering: Prof. Dr
VENIAMIN G. KASHIRSKIH
Mining Engineering: Prof. Dr ALEXEY A.
RENEYV
Surface and Underground Construction:
Prof. Dr ANDREY V. UGLYANITCA

LIPETSK STATE TECHNICAL UNIVERSITY

398055 Lipetsk, ul. Moskovskaya 30
Telephone: (0742) 25-00-61
E-mail: mailbox@stu.lipetsk.su
Internet: www.stu.lipetsk.ru

Founded 1956

Rector: Prof. MIKHAIL P. KUPRYANOV

Number of teachers: 500
Number of students: 5,000

MAGNITOGORSK STATE TECHNICAL UNIVERSITY 'G. I. NOSOV'

455000 Magnitogorsk, pr. Lenina 38
Telephone: (3519) 22-12-87
E-mail: mgtu@magtu.ru
Internet: www.magtu.ru

Founded 1932

Rector: Dr BORIS A. NIKIFOROV

Library of 846,656 vols

Br. in Beloretsk

MOSCOW AVIATION INSTITUTE (STATE TECHNICAL UNIVERSITY)

125993 Moscow, A-80, GSP-3, Volokolamskoe
shosse 4
Telephone: (495) 158-04-65
E-mail: aet@mai.ru
Internet: www.mai.ru

Founded 1930

Schools of aerospace engineering, aircraft
engineering, applied mathematics and physics, applied mechanics, control systems, economics and management, flight vehicle
engines, humanities and preparatory studies, informatics and electric power engineering, robotics and intelligent systems, vehicle
flight radioelectronics

Rector: Prof. Dr ALEXANDR M. MATVEENKO

Library of 909,000 vols
Number of teachers: 2,000
Number of students: 14,000

MOSCOW ENGINEERING PHYSICS INSTITUTE (STATE UNIVERSITY)

115409 Moscow, Kashirskoe shosse 31
Telephone: (495) 324-74-91
E-mail: degnn@mephi.ru
Internet: www.mephi.ru

Founded 1942

Rector: Prof. BORIS N. ONYKY

Library: 1m. vols
Number of teachers: 880
Number of students: 6,000

MOSCOW INSTITUTE OF PHYSICS AND TECHNOLOGY (STATE UNIVERSITY)

141700 Moscow oblast, Dolgoprudny, Insti-
tutsky per. 9
Telephone: (495) 408-57-00
E-mail: rector@mipt.ru
Internet: www.mipt.ru

Founded 1951

Depts of aeromechanics and flight engineering (located in Zhukovsky), aerophysics and
space research, applied mathematics and
economics and problems of physics and
power engineering, general and applied
physics, molecular and biological physics,
physical and quantum electronics, radio
engineering and cybernetics

Rector: Prof. NIKOLAY N. KUDRYAVTSEV

Library of 733,000 vols
Number of teachers: 470 full-time, 1,090
part-time
Number of students: 3,500

MOSCOW STATE ACADEMY OF FINE CHEMICAL TECHNOLOGY 'M. V. LOMONOSOV'

117571 Moscow, pr. Vernadskogo 86
Telephone: (495) 434-71-55
E-mail: mitht@mitht.ru
Internet: www.mitht.ru

Founded 1930

Rector: Prof. ALLA K. FROLKOVA

Library of 220,000 vols

DEANS

Faculty of Biotechnology and Organic Syn-
thesis: Prof. A. F. MIRONOV
Faculty of Chemistry and Technology Poly-
mer Processing: Prof. E. E. POTAPOV
Faculty of Chemistry and Technology of Rare
Elements and Materials for Electronic
Technology: Prof. D. V. DROBOT
Faculty of Engineering: Prof. G. I. LAP-
SHENKOV
Faculty of Management, Ecology and Eco-
nomics: Dr I. H. ROZDIN
Faculty of Natural Sciences: Prof. E. M.
KARTASHOV
Preparatory Faculty: V. B. MARGULIS
Evening Classes: Dr A. P. PETRUSENKO

MOSCOW STATE AUTOMOBILE AND ROAD TECHNICAL UNIVERSITY

125829 Moscow, Leningradsky pr. 64
Telephone: (495) 151-03-71
E-mail: info@madi.ru
Internet: www.madi.ru

Founded 1930

Faculties of building and technological
machines, correspondence learning, economics, energy and ecology, design and mechanical engineering, foreign citizen preparation,
humanities, management, military training,
motor transport, natural sciences, pre-admis-
sion preparation, road, road building; institute for the improvement of professional
skills and retraining of personnel in the
transport and road infrastructure; Moscow
Transport Institute; Centre of Engineering
Pedagogy; Centre of Innovations in Engineering Education

Rector: Prof. VYACHESLAV M. PRIKHODKO

Library: 1m. vols
Number of teachers: 850
Number of students: 10,000

MOSCOW STATE FORESTRY UNIVERSITY

141005 Moscow oblast, Mytischi, 1-ya Institutskaya ul. 1

Telephone: (495) 588-55-78
E-mail: mgul@mgul.ac.ru
Internet: www.mgul.ac.ru

Founded 1919

Faculties of forestry, mechanical and chemical wood technology, electronics and technical systems, economics and foreign relations, humanities, landscape architecture, International School of Business and Management

Rector: Prof. VIKTOR G. SANAEV

Library of 550,000 vols
Number of teachers: 627
Number of students: 10,000

MOSCOW STATE INDUSTRIAL UNIVERSITY

115280 Moscow, ul. Avtozavodskaya 16

Telephone: (495) 276-32-98
E-mail: topstaff@msiu.ru
Internet: www.msiu.ru

Founded 1960
State control

Faculties of applied mathematics and engineering physics, automotive engineering, information technology and law, management

Rector: Prof. VALERY KOSHKIN

Number of teachers: 790
Number of students: 7,000

MOSCOW STATE INSTITUTE OF ELECTRONICS AND MATHEMATICS (TECHNICAL UNIVERSITY)

109028 Moscow, Bolshoi Trekhsvyatitelsky per. 1-3/12

Telephone: (495) 917-90-89
E-mail: lenor@miem.edu.ru
Internet: www.miem.edu.ru

Founded 1962

Rector: Dr DMITRY V. BYKOV

Library of 600,000 vols
Number of students: 5,000

MOSCOW STATE INSTITUTE OF RADIO ENGINEERING, ELECTRONICS AND AUTOMATION (TECHNICAL UNIVERSITY)

119454 Moscow, pr. Vernadskogo 78

Telephone: (495) 433-00-44
E-mail: rector@mirea.ru
Internet: www.mirea.ru

Founded 1947
Academic year: September to June
Languages of instruction: Russian, English

Rector: ALEXANDER S. SIGOV

Library: 1.5m. vols
Number of teachers: 1,200
Number of students: 16,000

Publication: *Proceedings of MIREA* (irregular)

DEANS

Faculty of Cybernetics: Prof. MIKHAIL ROMANOV
Faculty of Economy and Management: Prof. ALEXANDER BOLSHAKOV
Faculty of Electronics: Prof. YURI FETISOV
Faculty of Information Technologies: Prof. ANDREY PETROV
Faculty of Radioengineering: Prof. GENNADY KULIKOV
International Faculty of Informatics: Prof. ALEKSEY LOBUZOV

MOSCOW STATE MINING UNIVERSITY

117049 Moscow, Leninsky pr. 6

Telephone: (495) 236-94-80
E-mail: ud@msmu.ru
Internet: www.msmu.ru

Founded 1918

Faculties of applied physics, coal mining and underground construction, mining automation and control, mining electrification and mechanization, mining of mineral and non-mineral deposits

Rector: Prof. Dr LEV A. PUCHKOV

Library of 800,000 vols
Number of teachers: 540
Number of students: 5,270

Publications: *Gornyatskaya Smena* (52 a year), *Scientific Papers* (2 a year)

MOSCOW STATE TECHNICAL UNIVERSITY 'MAMI'

107023 Moscow, ul. Bol. Semenovskaya 38

Telephone: (495) 369-91-53
E-mail: decinter@mami.ru

Founded 1865

Faculties of automation and control, design and technology, economics and engineering economics, machine-building, mechanical engineering, motor vehicles and tractors, power engineering

Rector: Prof. ANATOLY L. KARUNIN

Library: 1m. vols
Number of teachers: 800
Number of students: 7,500

MOSCOW STATE TECHNICAL UNIVERSITY OF CIVIL AVIATION

125838 Moscow, GSP-47, Kronshtadtsky bul. 20

Telephone: (495) 459-07-07
E-mail: rectorat@mail.mstuca.ru
Internet: www.mstuca.ru

Founded 1971 as Moscow Institute of Civil Aviation Engineers, present name and status 1992

Faculties of applied mathematics, computer systems and networks, maintenance of aircraft and engines, maintenance of aircraft electrical systems and avionics, maintenance of transport radio equipment, management, technological processes and safety in the aviation industry

Rector: Prof. VLADIMIR G. VOROBIEV

Library: 1.1m. vols
Number of teachers: 300
Number of students: 5,300

Publication: *Proceedings* (1 a year)

MOSCOW STATE TECHNICAL UNIVERSITY 'N. E. BAUMAN'

107005 Moscow, 2-ya Baumanskaya ul. 5

Telephone: (495) 261-40-55
E-mail: irina@interd.bmstu.ru

Founded 1830

Faculties of basic sciences, electronics and laser technology, engineering business, humanities, informatics and control systems, management, materials and technology, power engineering, robotics and complex automation, special machinery; br. in Kaluga

Rector: Prof. IGOR B. FEDOROV

Library: 3m. vols
Number of teachers: 2,500
Number of students: 18,000

Publications: *Izvestiya Vuzov* (mechanical engineering), *Vestnik MGTU* (issues each

on instrumental engineering and mechanical engineering)

MOSCOW STATE TECHNOLOGICAL UNIVERSITY, STANKIN

101472 Moscow, Vadkovsky per. 3-a

Telephone: (495) 973-30-66
E-mail: rector@stankin.ru
Internet: www.stankin.ru

Founded 1930

Faculties of economics, information technology, innovation technology management, mechanics and control, metrological informatics, technology

Rector: Prof. YURY M. SOLOMENTSEV

Library of 700,000 vols
Number of teachers: 677
Number of students: 5,873

MOSCOW STATE TEXTILE UNIVERSITY

119991 Moscow, ul. Malaya Kaluzhskaya 1

Telephone: (495) 954-70-73
E-mail: office@msta.ac.ru
Internet: www.msta.ac.ru

Founded 1919

Faculties of mechanical technology, textile machinery, chemical technology, applied arts, economics and management, information, automation and energetics

Rector: SERGEI D. NIKOLAEV

Library of 780,000 vols
Number of teachers: 530
Number of students: 5,000

Publication: *Vestnik MGTU* (2 a year)

MOSCOW STATE UNIVERSITY OF CIVIL ENGINEERING

129337 Moscow, Yaroslavskoe shosse 26

Telephone: (495) 183-44-38
E-mail: kanz@mgsu.ru
Internet: www.mgsu.ru

Founded 1921

Faculties of constructional technology, economics organization and management of construction, heat and power construction, heat and ventilation, hydraulic engineering, industrial and civil construction, mechanization and automation of construction, urban construction and services, water and sewerage

Rector: Prof. VALERY I. TELICHENKO

Library: 1.6m. vols
Number of teachers: 1,300
Number of students: 11,000

Publication: *Proceedings of MSUCE* (4 a year)

MOSCOW STATE UNIVERSITY OF ENGINEERING ECOLOGY

105066 Moscow, ul. Staraya Basmannaya 21/4

Telephone: (495) 267-07-01
E-mail: kanc@mami.ru
Internet: www.msuie.ru

Founded 1920 as Moscow State Acad. of Chemical Engineering; present name and status 1997

Faculties of chemical and biological engineering and economics, chemical apparatus manufacture, chemical machine building, cryogenic technology, technical cybernetics and automation of technological processes

Rector: Prof. MIKHAIL B. GENERALOV

Library of 650,000 vols
Number of teachers: 400
Number of students: 3,000

MOSCOW STATE UNIVERSITY OF ENVIRONMENTAL ENGINEERING

127550 Moscow, ul. Pryanishnikova 19

Telephone: (495) 976-10-46
E-mail: mailbox@msuee.ru
Internet: www.msuee.ru

Founded 1930

Rector: Prof. DMITRY V. KOZLOV
Vice-Rector for Academic Affairs: VLADIMIR F. STORCHEVOY
Vice-Rector for Int. Affairs: ANDREI SOROKIN
Vice-Rector for Research: VALENTIN N. KRASNOSHCHEOKOV

Number of teachers: 400
Number of students: 3,700

Publication: *Environmental Engineering* (in Russian)

MOSCOW STATE UNIVERSITY OF GEODESY AND CARTOGRAPHY

105064 Moscow, Gorokhovsky per. 4

Telephone: (495) 261-31-52
E-mail: rector@miigaik.ru
Internet: www.miigaik.ru

Founded 1779

Academic year: September to June

Faculties of applied cosmonautics, cartography, geodesy, humanities, optical instrument manufacture, space surveying and photogrammetry, territorial economics and land management

Rector: Prof. VIKTOR P. SAVINYKH

Library of 800,000 vols
Number of teachers: 400
Number of students: 5,000

Publication: *Geodeziya i Aerofotosiomka* (6 a year)

MOSCOW STATE UNIVERSITY OF RAILWAY ENGINEERING

103055 Moscow, ul. Obraztsova 15

Telephone: (495) 681-31-77
E-mail: mgups@online.ru
Internet: www.miit.ru

Founded 1896, present name and status 1993

Faculties of mechanical engineering, mechanical engineering technology, railway automation, telemechanics and communication, technical cybernetics, industrial and civil construction, traffic management, electrification of railways, railway construction, bridges and tunnels engineering and economics

Rector: Prof. BORIS A. LEVIN

Library: 2m. vols
Number of teachers: 1,300
Number of students: 12,000

Publications: *Inzhener Transporta*, *MREI* (colln of works)

MOSCOW TECHNICAL UNIVERSITY OF COMMUNICATION AND INFORMATICS

111024 Moscow, ul. Aviamotornaya 8A

Telephone: (495) 957-77-09
E-mail: mtuci@mtuci.ru
Internet: www.mtuci.ru

Founded 1921 as Moscow Institute of Electrical Engineering and Communications; present name and status 1992

Faculties of radio communication and radio and television broadcasting, multi-channel communications, postal services automation, automatic telecommunications and engineering and economics; brs in Rostov-on-Don, Nizhnii Novgorod

Rector: Prof. VAGAN V. SHAKHGILDYAN

Library: 1.3m. vols
Number of teachers: 850
Number of students: 14,000

MURMANSK STATE TECHNICAL UNIVERSITY

183010 Murmansk, Sportivnaya ul. 13

Telephone: (8152) 45-46-09
E-mail: webmaster@mstu.edu.ru
Internet: www.mstu.edu.ru

Founded 1950

Rector: Dr ALEXANDER ERSHOV

Library of 350,000
Number of teachers: 394
Number of students: 4,458

NATIONAL RESEARCH IRKUTSK STATE TECHNICAL UNIVERSITY

664074 Irkutsk, ul. Lermontova 83

Telephone: (3952) 40-52-00
E-mail: oms@istu.edu
Internet: www.istu.edu

Founded 1930

State control

Language of instruction: Russian
Academic year: September to June

Rector: Prof. Dr IVAN GOLOVNYKH
Vice-Rector for Int. Relations: Dr ANDREY TANAEV

Library: 1.5m. vols
Number of teachers: 1,450
Number of students: 31,000

Publications: *Geology, Search and Prospecting for Oil and Mineral Deposits, Higher Educational Institutes' News: Geoscience, ISTU Bulletin, Ore Dressing, Problems of the Development of Eastern Siberia's Mineral Base*

DEANS

Faculty of Chemical Engineering and Metallurgy: Prof. SVETLANA DYACHKOVA
Faculty of Computer Sciences: Prof. ALEXANDER PETROV
Faculty of Power Engineering: Dr VADIM FEDCHISHIN
Institute of Architecture and Civil Engineering: Prof. VIKTOR R. CHUPIN
Institute of Aviation Mechanical Engineering and Transport: Dr RASHID AKHATOV
Institute of Economics, Management and Law: Prof. GENNADIY DYKUSOV
Institute of Fine Arts, Social Sciences and Humanities: Dr OLGA IGNATIEVA
Institute of Mineral Resource Management and Processing: Prof. BORIS L. TALGAMER
International Faculty: Dr VITALIY EFREMOV
Physical and Engineering Institute: Prof. NICKOLAY IVANOV

NATIONAL RESEARCH UNIVERSITY 'MOSCOW POWER ENGINEERING INSTITUTE'

111250 Moscow, ul. Krasnokazarmennaya 14

Telephone: (495) 362-73-07
E-mail: uvs@mpei.ru
Internet: www.mpei.ru

Founded 1930

State control

Languages of instruction: English, Russian
Academic year: September to June

Rector: Prof. NIKOLAY ROGALEV
Vice-Rector for Int. Relations: Prof. VLADIMIR ZAMOLODCHIKOV

Library: 2m. vols
Number of teachers: 1,500
Number of students: 15,000

Publication: *Vestnik MPEI* (6 a year)

NATIONAL RESEARCH UNIVERSITY OF ELECTRONIC TECHNOLOGY

124498 Moscow, Zelenograd, Bld 5, Pas. 4806

Telephone: (499) 720-8933
E-mail: netadm@miee.ru
Internet: www.miet.ru

Founded 1965

State control

Language of instruction: Russian
Academic year: September to June

Rector: Prof. YURI A. CHAPLYGIN
Vice-Rector for Int. Affairs and Information Technology: Prof. SERGEY V. UMNYASHKIN
Dean for Computer Science and Telecommunications: Prof. Dr ALEXANDER GUREEV

Library of 680,000 vols
Number of teachers: 530
Number of students: 6,400

Publication: *Collection of Research Work* (12 a year)

DEANS

Electronics and Computer Technologies: Prof. MIKHAIL G. PUTRYA
Electronic Technologies, Materials and Equipment: Prof. VLADIMIR M. ROSHIN

NIZHNII NOVGOROD STATE TECHNICAL UNIVERSITY

603600 GSP 41, Nizhnii Novgorod, ul. Minina 24

Telephone: (8312) 36-23-25
E-mail: nntu@nntu.nnov.ru
Internet: www.nntu.nnov.ru

Founded 1898 in Warsaw as Warsaw Polytechnic Institute; relocated to Moscow 1916, then Nizhnii Novgorod in 1917; re-established as Nizhnii Novgorod Polytechnic Institute; present name and status 1992

Rector: VLADIMIR P. KIRIENKO

Number of teachers: 1,166
Number of students: 12,310

NIZHNII NOVGOROD STATE UNIVERSITY OF ARCHITECTURE AND CIVIL ENGINEERING

603950 Nizhnii Novgorod, ul. Ilyinskaya 65

Telephone: (8312) 33-82-47
E-mail: srec@nngasu.ru
Internet: www.nngasu.ru

Founded 1930

State control

Academic year: September to June

Fields of study: architecture, design, urban development, environmental engineering, economics, law, industrial management, environmental management and occupational safety; distance learning programmes

Rector: Prof. VALENTIN V. NAIDENKO
Vice-Rector for Int. Relations: Dr ALEXANDER PALEEV

Library of 800,000 vols
Number of teachers: 890
Number of students: 8,000

Publication: *Collected Papers and Proceedings of Scientific Conferences* (2 a year)

NORTH CAUCASIAN INSTITUTE OF MINING AND METALLURGICAL (STATE TECHNOLOGICAL UNIVERSITY)

362021 North-Ossetian Republic, Vladikavkaz, ul. Kosmonavta Nikolaeva 44

Telephone: (8672) 74-93-79
E-mail: skgtu@skgtu.ru
Internet: www.skgtu.ru

Founded 1931 as the North Caucasian Institute of Non-Ferrous Metals

Faculties of construction, electromechanical, electronic engineering, metallurgical, mining, management

Rector: Dr VLADIMIR S. VAGIN

Library of 520,000 vols
Number of teachers: 500
Number of students: 4,000

Publications: *Izvestiya Vuzov, Tsvetnaya Metallurgia* (6 a year)

NORTH CAUCASIAN STATE TECHNICAL UNIVERSITY

362021 Stavropol, pr. Kulakova 2
Telephone: (8652) 95-68-08
E-mail: info@ncstu.ru
Internet: www.ncstu.ru

Founded 1958

Rector: Prof. BORIS M. SINELNIKOV

NORTH-WEST STATE TECHNICAL UNIVERSITY

191186 St Petersburg, ul. Millionnaya 5
Telephone: (812) 312-94-84
E-mail: office@nwpi.ru
Internet: www.nwpi.ru

Founded 1930

Rector: ALEXANDER A. KONDRATYEV

Library of 1,544,698 vols
Number of teachers: 400

NOVOSIBIRSK STATE TECHNICAL UNIVERSITY

630092 Novosibirsk, pr. Karla Marksa 20
Telephone: (3832) 46-50-01
E-mail: is@nstu.ru
Internet: www.nstu.ru

Founded 1953

11 Faculties; 80 depts

Rector: Prof. NIKOLAI V. PUSTOVOI

Number of teachers: 1,105
Number of students: 9,354

NOVOSIBIRSK STATE UNIVERSITY OF ARCHITECTURE AND CIVIL ENGINEERING

630008 Novosibirsk-8, ul. Leningradskaya 113
Telephone: (3832) 66-41-25
E-mail: uungas@sibstrin.ru
Internet: www.sibstrin.ru

Founded 1930

Faculties of architecture and construction, building specialists refresher programmes and further training, construction technology, environmental engineering, first stage of higher education, part-time and correspondence education, preliminary training, training of overseas students; institutes: architecture and civil engineering, economics and management, general and basic education, humanities

Rector: Prof. ARKADY P. YANENKO

Library of 553,000 vols
Number of teachers: 580
Number of students: 6,700

Publication: *Izvestiya Vuzov—Stroitelstvo* (Higher School News—Civil Engineering, 12 a year)

OBNINSK STATE TECHNICAL UNIVERSITY FOR NUCLEAR POWER ENGINEERING (TECHNICAL UNIVERSITY)

249020 Kaluga oblast, Obninsk, Studgorodok 1
Telephone: (08439) 7-01-31

E-mail: priem@iate.obninsk.ru
Internet: www.iate.obninsk.ru

Founded 1953 as a br. of Moscow Engineering and Physics Institute; as Obninsk Institute for Nuclear Power Engineering 1985–2002, present name and status 2002

Faculties of advanced education, cybernetics, distance education, economics, evening education, natural science, physics and power engineering

Rector: Prof. NIKOLAI L. SALNIKOV

Library of 140,000 vols
Number of teachers: 340
Number of students: 2,100

OMSK STATE TECHNICAL UNIVERSITY

644050 Omsk, Mira pr. 11
Telephone: (3812) 65-33-89
E-mail: info@omgtu.ru
Internet: inter.omgtu.ru

Founded 1942

State control

Academic year: September to June

Rector: Prof. VICTOR SHALAY
Vice-Rector for Education: Prof. ALEXANDER MYSHLYAVTSEV
Vice-Rector for Research: Prof. ANATOLY KOSYKH

Library of 1,281,294 vols
Number of teachers: 1,000
Number of students: 17,000 (incl. 500 int. students)

Publications: *Analysis and Synthesis of Mechanical Systems* (1 a year), *International Conference: Dynamics of Machines and Mechanisms* (every 2 years), *Omsk Scientific Bulletin* (12 a year)

DEANS

Economics and Management Faculty: Prof. VERA POTUDANSKAYA
Energy Institute: Prof. VLADIMIR GORYUNOV
Humanitarian Education Faculty: Prof. MIKHAIL MASHKARIN
Information Technologies and Computer Systems Faculty: Prof. ANNA ZYKINA
Mechanical Engineering Institute: Prof. EVGENIY EREMIN
Petrochemical Institute: Prof. VLADIMIR YUSHA
Radio Engineering Faculty: Prof. VALERIY LEVCHENKO
Transport, Oil and Gas Faculty: Prof. VALENTIN BELKOV

OMSK STATE TRANSPORT UNIVERSITY

644046 Omsk, pr. Karla Marksa 35
Telephone: (3812) 31-42-13
E-mail: omgups@omgups.ru
Internet: www.omgups.ru

Founded 1930

Faculties of locomotives, railway rolling stock, electric transport, power supply for railways, automation, telemechanics and communication facilities for railway vehicles, technology of machine-building, heat and power engineering, control and information technology in technical systems, information systems, world economy, management, marketing, finance and credit, quality control

Rector: Prof. ILKHAM I. GALIEV

Library of 700,000 vols
Number of teachers: 310
Number of students: 6,000

PENZA STATE UNIVERSITY OF ARCHITECTURE AND CONSTRUCTION

440028 Penza, ul. Titova 28
Telephone: (8412) 48-74-76
E-mail: relay@gasa.penza.com.ru
Internet: www.gasa.penza.com.ru

Founded 1958

Faculties of architecture, automotive engineering, construction, economics and management, engineering ecology, technology

Rector: ALEXANDER I. EREMKIN

Library of 370,000 vols
Number of teachers: 395
Number of students: 5,735

PERM STATE TECHNICAL UNIVERSITY

614600 Perm, Komsomolsky pr. 29A
Telephone: (3422) 12-87-53
E-mail: rector@pstu.ac.ru
Internet: www.pstu.ac.ru

Founded 1953 as Perm Mining Institute

Faculties of aerospace technology, applied mathematics and mechanics, chemical technology, construction, electrical engineering, humanities, mining, road transport

Rector: VASILY YU. PETROV

Library: 1.4m. vols
Number of teachers: 932
Number of students: 12,500

PETERSBURG STATE TRANSPORT UNIVERSITY

190031 St Petersburg, Moskovsky pr. 9
Telephone: (812) 310-25-21
Internet: www.pgups.ru

Founded 1809

Faculties of bridge and tunnel construction, construction, electrical engineering, electrification, mechanics, traffic management; br. in Velikie Luki

Rector: Prof. VALERY I. KOVALEV

Library: 1.5m. vols
Number of teachers: 700

Publication: *Proceedings* (1 a year)

POLZUNOV ALTAI STATE TECHNICAL UNIVERSITY

656038 Barnaul, Lenina pr. 46
Telephone: (3852) 26-05-42
E-mail: nikonov@mail.altstu.ru
Internet: www.altstu.ru

Founded 1942

State control

Language of instruction: Russian

Academic year: September to August

Faculties of automotive, part-time studies, civil engineering, extramural education, food and chemical engineering, humanities, information technologies, innovation technologies in machine building, military training, natural science, power engineering, concurrent training, social science and tourism; institutes of architecture and design, economics and management, further professional education devt, intensive education, textile and light industry; brs: Biysk Technological Institute, Rubtsovsk Industrial Institute

Rector: Prof. ALEXANDR SITNIKOV (acting)
Dean for Faculty of Foreign Students: Prof. ALEXEY T. EVTUSHENKO

Library of 992,456 vols
Number of teachers: 1,500
Number of students: 21,000

Publication: *Polzunovsky Vestnik*

ROSTOV STATE UNIVERSITY OF CIVIL ENGINEERING

344022 Rostov-on-Don, Sotsialisticheskaya ul. 162

Telephone: (8632) 01-90-02
E-mail: interzentrum@rgsu.ru
Internet: www.rgsu.ru

Founded 1943
State control
Academic year: September to June

Institutes of civil and urban engineering, engineering and ecological systems, economics and management, engineering technologies and materials, highways and transport and architecture and design

Rector: VLADIMIR S. VAGIN

Library of 710,000 vols
Number of students: 8,816

Publication: *Izvestiya* (4 a year)

ROSTOV STATE UNIVERSITY FOR RAILWAY TRANSPORTATION

344038 Rostov-on-Don, pl. Narodnogo Opolcheniya 2

Telephone: (8632) 45-06-13
E-mail: rek@rgups.ru
Internet: www.rgups.ru

Founded 1929

Areas of study: automation and telemechanics, power engineering, electromechanical engineering, railway construction, traffic and transport management, road building machinery, humanities; Institute of Management and Law

Rector: VLADIMIR I. KOLESNIKOV

Library of 980,000 vols
Number of teachers: 550
Number of students: 5,000

RUSSIAN STATE HYDROMETEOROLOGICAL UNIVERSITY

195196 St Petersburg, Malookhtinsky pr. 98

Telephone: (812) 372-50-92
E-mail: rector@rshu.ru
Internet: www.rshu.ru

Founded 1930
Languages of instruction: English, Russian
Academic year: September to July

Rector: Prof. LEV N. KARLIN
Pro-Rector: Prof. ANDREI V. BELOTSERKOVSKY
Vice-Rector for Int. Relations: Dr ANATOLY I. BOGUSH
Vice-Rector for Research: VLADIMIR N. VOROBYEV
Vice-Rector for Undergraduate and Graduate Education: Dr VLADIMIR M. SAKOVICH

Library of 408,000 vols
Number of teachers: 250
Number of students: 5,500

Publication: *Proceedings* (4 a year)

DEANS

Correspondence Education: Prof. VADIM G. ORLOV
Economic and Social-Humanitarian Faculty: Prof. MIKHAIL M. GLAZOV
Faculty of Ecology and Natural Physics: Dr ANNA L. SKOBLIKOVA
Faculty of Information Systems and Geo-Technologies: Prof. Dr EVGENY P. ISTOMIN
Hydrological Faculty: Dr ARKADY DOGANOVSKY
Meteorological Faculty: Prof. LEONID DIVINSKY
Oceanological Faculty: Dr ALEXANDER S. AVERKIYEV

BRANCHES

RSHU Aleksin: 301351 Tula oblast, Aleksin District, Kolosovo; tel. (8753) 7-34-17; Dir VALERY M. BORTYAKOV.

RSHU Rostov-on-Don: 344025 Rostov-on-Don, 31-aya Liniya 4; tel. (8632) 91-41-05; Dir SERGEY S. ANDREEV.

RSHU Tuapse: 352800 Krasnodar oblast, Tuapse, ul. Morskaya 4; tel. (8616) 72-37-63; Dir YARVANT O. YAILY

RUSSIAN STATE OPEN TECHNICAL UNIVERSITY OF RAILWAY TRANSPORT

125993 Moscow, ul. Chasovaya 22/2

Telephone: (495) 151-14-51
E-mail: org@rgotups.ru
Internet: www.rgotups.ru

Founded 1951

Faculties of railway traffic and management, railway construction and civil engineering, economics and general technology; brs in Nizhnii Novgorod, Voronezh, Yaroslavl, Smolensk, Saratov, Bryansk, Tula, Novomoskovsk, Ryazan, Murom, Elets, Vologda, Vladimir, Kirov, Izhevsk, Lisky, Kotlas, Kaliningrad, Orel, Rtitshevo, Labytnangy, Astrakhan, Volgograd, Uhta

Rector: Prof. Dr A. T. DEMCHENKO
Vice-Rector: Prof. Dr V. I. APATZEV

Library of 930,453 vols
Number of teachers: 508
Number of students: 21,573

RUSSIAN STATE TECHNOLOGICAL UNIVERSITY 'K. E. TSIOLKOVSKY' (MATI)

103767 Moscow, ul. Orshanskaya 3

Telephone: (495) 141-18-40
E-mail: intdep@intedu.mati.msk.ru
Internet: www.mati.ru

Founded 1932

Faculties of aerospace engineering and technology, applied mathematics and mechanics, avionics, computer science, economics and business, ecology, materials science and technology, satellite communications and technology

Rector: ANATOLY P. PETROV

Library of 800,000 vols
Number of teachers: 1,103
Number of students: 9,000

RUSSIAN UNIVERSITY OF CHEMICAL TECHNOLOGY 'D. MENDELEEV'

125047 Moscow, Miusskaya pl. 9

Telephone: (495) 978-87-33
E-mail: rector@muctr.edu.ru
Internet: www.muctr.edu.ru

Founded 1920

Faculties of chemical technology of inorganic substances, chemical technology of organic substances, chemical technology engineering, chemical technology of polymers, cybernetics of chemical technological processes, ecological engineering, physical chemistry engineering, general engineering and economics; br. in Novomoskovsk

Rector: Dr PAVEL D. SARKISOV

Library: 1.7m. vols
Number of teachers: 1,003
Number of students: 8,416

Publication: *Trudy* (6 a year)

ST PETERSBURG ELECTROTECHNICAL UNIVERSITY 'LETI' (ETU)

197376 St Petersburg, ul. Prof. Popova 5

Telephone: (812) 234-35-53
E-mail: oso@etu.ru
Internet: eltech.ru

Founded 1886
Academic year: September to June

Faculties of electrical engineering and automatics, electronics, computing and information technologies, humanities, measurement and biotechnical systems, radio engineering and telecommunications

Chancellor: VLADIMIR M. KUTUZOV

Library of 1,063,000 vols
Number of teachers: 1,000
Number of students: 9,000

Publications: *Izvestiya ETU* (10 a year), *Izvestiya Vuzov Rossii—Radioelektronika* (6 a year)

ST PETERSBURG STATE MARINE TECHNICAL UNIVERSITY

190008 St Petersburg, ul. Lotsmanskaya 3

Telephone: (812) 114-41-68
E-mail: inter@smtu.ru
Internet: www.smtu.ru

Founded 1930

Faculties of natural and social sciences and humanities, naval architecture and ocean engineering, marine engineering, marine electronics and control systems, business and management

Rector: Dr KONSTANTIN P. BORISENKO

Library of 862,380 vols
Number of teachers: 600
Number of students: 5,500

ST PETERSBURG STATE MINING INSTITUTE (TECHNICAL UNIVERSITY)

199026 St Petersburg, Vasilevskii ostrov, 21-ya Liniya 2

Telephone: (812) 213-60-78
E-mail: rectorat@spmi.ru
Internet: www.spmi.ru

Founded 1773

Rector: Prof. VLADIMIR S. LITVINENKO

Library of 1,209,266 vols
Number of students: 8,000

ST PETERSBURG STATE POLYTECHNICAL UNIVERSITY

195251 St Petersburg, Politekhnicheskaya ul. 29

Telephone: (812) 297-20-95
E-mail: office@spbstu.ru
Internet: www.spbstu.ru

Founded 1899
State control
Languages of instruction: Russian, English
Academic year: September to July

20 Int. research centres; historical and technical museums

Rector: ANDREY I. RUDSKOY
Pres.: YURIY S. VASILIEV
Vice-Rector for Academic Affairs: KONSTANTIN V. SHVETSOV (acting)
Vice-Rector for Admin. and Economic Activity: VLADIMIR V. GLOUKHOV
Vice-Rector for Admin. Services and Construction: SERGEY V. ROMANOV
Vice-Rector for Capital Construction: VLADIMIR K. SLASTENKO
Vice-Rector for Distance and Part-time Education: ALEXANDER V. IVANOV

Vice-Rector for Int. Relations: DMITRY G. ARSENIEV

Vice-Rector for Perspective Projects: ALEXEY I. BOROVKOV

Vice-Rector for Research: DMITRY Y. RAYCHUK

Vice-Rector for Safety and Security: VALERY G. SILIN

Vice-Rector for Secondary and Vocational Education: MICHAEL V. LOPATIN

Vice-Rector for Teaching and Learning Enhancement: ALEXANDER V. RECHINSKY

Library: 2.5m. vols
Number of teachers: 3,250
Number of students: 30,200

Publications: *Scientific and Engineering News, Transactions*

DIRECTORS

Institute of Applied Linguistics: Prof. MARIA A. AKOPOVA

Institute of Applied Mathematics and Mechanics: Prof. ALEXANDER K. BELYAEV

Institute of Civil Engineering: Prof. NIKOLAY I. VATIN

Institute of Computing and Control: Prof. IGOR G. CHERNORUTSKIY

Institute of Industrial Economics and Management: VALERY A. LEVENTSOV

Institute of International Educational Programs: ANDREI M. ALEXANKOV

Institute of Machine-Building (LMZ): Prof. MICHAIL V. AFANASIEV

Institute of Metallurgy, Mechanical Engineering and Transport: Prof. ANATOLIY A. POPOVICH

Institute of Military Engineering and Safety Research: Prof. MICHAEL V. SILNIKOV

Institute of Physics, Nanotechnology and Telecommunications: Prof. SERGEY B. MAKAROV

Institute of Power Engineering and Transportation: NIKOLAY A. ZABELIN

ST PETERSBURG STATE TECHNOLOGICAL UNIVERSITY OF PLANT POLYMERS

198095 St Petersburg, ul. Ivan Chernykh 4

Telephone: (812) 786-58-09

E-mail: zsv@gturp.spb.ru

Internet: www.gturp.spb.ru

Founded 1931, present name and status 1993

State control

Language of instruction: Russian

Academic year: September to July

Rector: Prof. PAVEL LUKANIN (acting)

Vice Rector for Advanced Training: ALEXANDER IVANOV

Vice-Rector for Economics: IVAN GRIGORIEV

Vice-Rector for Management: Prof. ALEXANDER ASHKALUNIN

Vice-Rector for Science: Prof. VICTOR KUROV

Vice-Rector for Studies: Prof. EVGENIY KHARDIKOV

Library of 740,000 vols
Number of teachers: 250
Number of students: 4,000

Publications: *JPPS, Pulp Paper Board Magazine, TAPPI*

DEANS

Faculty of Automated Process Control Systems: Assoc. Prof. ANNA CHERNIKOVA

Faculty of Chemical Engineering: Prof. ALEKSEY KOMISSARENKOV

Faculty of Economics and Management: Prof. TATIANA TERESHKINA

Faculty of Environmental Engineering: Prof. LEV ISYANOV

Faculty of Industrial Power Engineering: Prof. NIKOLAY GLADYSHEV

Faculty of Mechanical Engineering: Prof. ALEXANDER GAUZE

ST PETERSBURG STATE UNIVERSITY OF ARCHITECTURE AND CIVIL ENGINEERING

190005 St Petersburg, 2nd Krasnoarmeiskaya ul., 4

Telephone: (812) 316-58-72

E-mail: rector@spbgasu.ru

Internet: www.spbgasu.ru

Founded 1832

Advanced training and retraining institute; faculties of architecture, civil engineering, automobile and road building, environment engineering, economics and management, urban construction and public utilities, correspondence faculty

Rector: Prof. YEVGENY I. RYBNOV

Library of 855,000 vols
Number of teachers: 870
Number of students: 8,775

Publications: *Masterok* (4 a year), *Za Stroitel'nye Kadry* (12 a year)

ST PETERSBURG STATE UNIVERSITY OF INFORMATION TECHNOLOGY, MECHANICS AND OPTICS

197101 St Petersburg, ul. Sablinskaya 14

Telephone: (812) 233-00-89

E-mail: rector@mail.ifmo.ru

Internet: www.ifmo.ru

Founded 1900

Rector: Prof. VLADIMIR N. VASILEV

Library of 900,000 vols
Number of teachers: 500
Number of students: 4,000

Publication: *Izvestiya Vuzov (Priborostroenie)* (4 a year)

ST PETERSBURG STATE UNIVERSITY OF REFRIGERATION AND FOOD ENGINEERING

191002 St Petersburg, ul. Lomonosova 9

Telephone: (812) 315-36-17

E-mail: refr@gunipt.spb.ru

Internet: www.gunipt.edu.ru

Founded 1931

Academic year: September to June

Rector: ALEXANDER V. BARANENKO

Vice-Rector for Int. Contacts: OLGA N. RUMYANTSEVA

Library: 1m. vols
Number of teachers: 340
Number of students: 6,300

DEANS

Faculty of Correspondence and Extramural: Prof. DMITRY P. MALYAVKO

Faculty of Cryogenics and Conditioning Systems: Dr IGOR V. BARANOV

Faculty of Economics and Environmental Management: Dr VICTOR L. VASILYONOK

Faculty of Food Manufacturing Facilities: Prof. ELENA V. VERBOLOZ

Faculty of Food Technologies: Dr ALEXANDER L. ISHEVSKY

Faculty of Refrigeration Engineering: Prof. VLADIMIR A. KOROTKOV

ST PETERSBURG STATE UNIVERSITY OF TECHNOLOGY AND DESIGN

191186 St Petersburg, Bol. Morskaya ul. 18

Telephone: (812) 315-12-10

E-mail: international@sutd.ru

Internet: www.sutd.ru

Founded 1828, present name and status 1992

Academic year: September to June

Rector: Prof. ALEXEY V. DEMIDOV

Head of Library: O. TEROVA

Library of 1,245,684 vols

Number of teachers: 900

Number of students: 12,000 (incl. 6,500 full-time)

DEANS

Faculty of Applied Chemistry and Ecology: Prof. N. NOVOSELOV

Faculty of Information Technologies and Machine Science: Prof. V. ENTIN

Faculty of Natural Sciences and Humanities: S. IVANOVA

Faculty of Textiles and Clothing: Prof. E. SURZHENKO

ST PETERSBURG STATE UNIVERSITY OF TELECOMMUNICATIONS 'PROF. M. A. BONCH-BRUYEV'

191065 St Petersburg, nab. Moiki 61

Telephone: (812) 315-01-18

E-mail: rector@sut.ru

Internet: www.sut.ru

Founded 1930

Faculties of biomedical electronics, economics and management, multi-channel telecommunication systems, radio broadcasting and television, radio communication, switching systems and computer technology, telecommunication networks, telecommunication technologies

Rector: Prof. ALEXANDER A. GOGOL

Library of 90,000 vols

SAMARA STATE AEROSPACE UNIVERSITY 'S. P. KOROLEV'

443086 Samara, Moskovskoye shosse 34

Telephone: (846) 334-57-22

E-mail: intdep@ssau.ru

Internet: www.ssau.ru

Founded 1942

State control

Language of instruction: Russian

Academic year: September to June

Rector: EVGENIY SHAKHMATOV

Library of 1,092,955 vols
Number of teachers: 750
Number of students: 11,790

DEANS

Aircraft Design: Prof. VICTROR KIRPICHEV

Aircraft Engines Design: Prof. ALEXANDER ERMAKOV

Aircraft Maintenance: Assoc. Prof. ALEKSEI TIKHONOV

SAMARA STATE TECHNICAL UNIVERSITY

443010 Samara, ul. Molodogvardeiskaja 244

Telephone: (846) 278-43-00

E-mail: postman@samgtu.ru

Internet: www.samgtu.ru

Founded 1914

State control

Language of instruction: Russian

Faculties of automation and information technology, chemical technology, economics and humanities, electrotechnology, engineering technology, machine building, oil technology, physical technology, thermal power

Rector: Prof. DMITRY BYKOV

Number of teachers: 2,500
Number of students: 18,000

Publication: *Vestnik SamGTU*

SAMARA STATE UNIVERSITY OF ARCHITECTURE AND CIVIL ENGINEERING

443001 Samara, Molodogvardeiskaya ul. 194

Telephone: (8462) 42-17-84

E-mail: sgasu@sgasu.smr.ru
Internet: www.sgasu.smr.ru
State control
Languages of instruction: Russian, English
Academic year: September to June

Founded 1930 as Samara State Acad. of Architecture and Civil Engineering, present name and status 2004

Rector: Prof. MIKHAIL I. BALZANNIKOV
Pres.: VSEVOLOD A. SHABANOV
Vice-Rector: NATALYA G. CHUMACHENKO
Library Dir: LYUDMILA I. KORYTINA

Library: 1m. vols, incl. 300,000 specialist books
Number of teachers: 420
Number of students: 8,000

DEANS

Centre for Linguistic Training and Translation/Interpretation: Prof. EUPHYM G. VYSHKIN
Construction Institute: Prof IGOR S. KHOLOPOV
Faculty of Architecture: Assoc. Prof ELINA V. DANILOVA
Faculty of Construction Engineering: Assoc. Prof. KONSTANTIN S. GALITSKOV
Faculty of Design: Assoc. Prof SVETLANA G. MALYSHEVA
Faculty of Engineering Economics: Assoc. Prof VALERY A. PROTSENKO
Faculty of Engineering Systems and Environment Protection Construction: Assoc. Prof. MIKHAIL V. SHUVALOV
Faculty of Industrial and Civil Engineering: Assoc. Prof VALERY M. KAZAKOV
Faculty of Information Systems and Technologies: Prof. SEMYON A. PIYAVSKIY
Faculty of Transport and Town Development: Assoc. Prof. TATYANA E. GORDEYEVA
Institute of Architecture and Design: Prof. YELENA A. AKHMEDOVA
Institute of Ecology and Engineering Life Support Systems: Prof. ALEKSANDR K. STRELKOV
Institute of Economics and Management: Prof. IRINA P. SCHEGOLEVA

SIBERIAN STATE AEROSPACE UNIVERSITY 'M. F. RESHETNEV'

660014 Krasnoyarsk, 31 Krasnoyarsky Rabochy pr.

Telephone: (391) 264-00-14
E-mail: info@sibsau.ru
Internet: www.sibsau.ru

Founded 1959
State control
Languages of instruction: Russian, English
Academic year: September to June

Rector: Prof. IGOR V. KOVALEV
Vice-Rector for Academic Affairs: ANNA A. LUKIANOVA
Vice-Rector for Admin. and Social Affairs: SERGEY N. SKOTNIKOV
Vice-Rector for Devt: VLADIMIR A. KURESHOV
Vice-Rector for General Affairs and Public Relations: BORIS V. VERBENKO
Vice-Rector for Int. Cooperation and Additional Education: ANNA A. VOROSHILOVA
Vice-Rector for Pre-Univ. Training and Educational Work: VADIM V. KOLGA
Vice-Rector for Research and Innovations: YURIY Y. LOGINOV

Library of 858,424 vols, 427 titles
Number of teachers: 810
Number of students: 11,400

Publication: Vestnik Sibsau

DEANS

Faculty of Distance and Additional Learning: LILIYA V. ERYGINA
Faculty of Economics and Finance: YURIY V. ERYGIN

Faculty of Humanities: SVETLANA Y. PISKORSKAYA
Faculty of Physical Education and Sport: IGOR A. TOLSTOPYATOV
Faculty of Professional Devt of Teaching Staff: VALERIY A. LEVKO
Faculty of Retraining and Professional Devt of Specialists: GRIGORIY B. DOBRETSOV
Institute of Civil Aviation: VLADIMIR L. MEDVEDEV
Institute of Information Science and Telecommunication: ALEKSEY M. POPOV
Institute of Machine Science and Innovation: EVGENIY V. SUGAK
Institute of Space Research and High Technologies: VASILIY F. SHABANOV
Institute of Space Technology: NIKOLAY A. TEREKHIN
International Higher School of Innovating Business and Administration: OLGA E. PODVERBNYKH
Military Institute: EVGENIY I. DOBRYAKOV

SIBERIAN STATE TECHNOLOGICAL UNIVERSITY

660049 Krasnoyarsk, pr. Mira 82

Telephone: (391) 227-63-82
E-mail: repyakh@sibstu.kts.ru
Internet: www.sibstu.kts.ru

Founded 1930

Faculties of automation and robot technology, chemical technology, engineering economics, engineering for chemical technology, forestry, humanities and mechanics, woodworking technology, timber technology and equipment; brs in Lesosibirsk and 5 representative offices in major Siberian cities

Rector: Prof. EDUARD S. BUKA

Library of 243,000 vols
Number of teachers: 682
Number of students: 12,912

SIBERIAN STATE UNIVERSITY OF TELECOMMUNICATIONS AND INFORMATICS

630102 Novosibirsk, ul. Kirova 86

Telephone: (3832) 66-10-38
E-mail: rectorat@neic.nsk.ru
Internet: www.sibsutis.ru

Founded 1953

Faculties of automatic electrical communication, engineering economics and informatics, multi-channel electrical communication, radio communication and broadcasting; brs in Khabarovsk, Ekaterinburg, Ulan-Ude

Rector: Prof. VALERY P. BAKALOV

Library of 463,638 vols
Number of teachers: 650
Number of students: 10,000

SIBERIAN TRANSPORT UNIVERSITY

630023 Novosibirsk, ul. D. Kovalchuk 191

Telephone: (3832) 28-74-70
E-mail: inter_sgups@stu.ru
Internet: www.stu.ru

Founded 1932

Faculties of accounting and auditing, bridges and tunnels, civil engineering, construction and track machinery, economics and building management, economics and transport management, management and world economics, railway construction, railway traffic management, water supply and sewerage

Rector: Dr VLADIMIR D. VERESKUN

Library of 773,000 vols
Number of teachers: 600
Number of students: 12,000

Publication: Proceedings (5 or 6 a year)

SOUTH RUSSIA STATE TECHNICAL UNIVERSITY (NOVOCHERKASSK POLYTECHNIC INSTITUTE)

346428 Novocherkassk, ul. Prosveshcheniya 132

Telephone: (8635) 25-55-14
E-mail: ngtu@novoch.ru
Internet: www.npi-tu.ru

Founded 1907
State control
Language of instruction: Russian
Academic year: September to June

Rector: Prof. VLADIMIR G. PEREDERIY
Vice-Rector: Prof. NIKOLAY I. GORBATENKO
Vice-Rector for Admin. Work: URIY I. KLIMENKO
Vice-Rector for Educational Activities: Prof. LIDIA I. SHERBAKOVA
Vice-Rector for Research and Innovation: Prof. ALEXANDER V. PAVLENKO
Vice-Rector for Strategic Devt: Dr VALERY V. SHMATKOV

Library of 3,162,689 vols, 300 periodical titles
Number of teachers: 2,111
Number of students: 24,616

Publications: Izvestiya SK NC Visshey Shkoly (4 a year), Izvestiya Vuzov Severo-Cavkazskogo Regiona: Elektromekhanika (12 a year)

DEANS

Department of Electromechanics: Prof. Dr BORIS N. LOBOV
Department of Energy: Prof. Dr VLADIMIR I. NAGAY
Department of Geology, Mining and Petroleum Engineering: Prof. Dr URIY I. RAZARENOV
Department of Innovation and Production Organization: Prof. Dr EVGENIY B. KOLBYSHEV
Department of Open and Distance Learning: Prof. Dr VLADIMIR S. ISAKOV
Faculty of Automation and Control: Prof. Dr VALERIY L. KANDRASHOV
Faculty of Chemical Technology: Prof. Dr ELENA A. YACENKO
Faculty of Civil Engineering: Prof. Dr GENADIY M. SKIBIN
Faculty of Information Technology: Prof. Dr VALERIY M. GRINSHENKOV
Faculty of Mechanical Engineering: Prof. Dr VITALIY M. BERDNIK
Faculty of Physics and Mathematics: Prof. Dr VIKTOR V. NEFEDOV

STATE EDUCATIONAL INSTITUTION OF HIGHER PROFESSIONAL EDUCATION ULYANOVSK STATE TECHNICAL UNIVERSITY

432027 Ulyanovsk, ul. Severny Venets 32

Telephone: (8422) 43-06-43
E-mail: rector@ulstu.ru
Internet: www.ulstu.ru

Founded 1957 as Ulyanovsk Evening Polytechnic Institute; reorganized into Ulyanovsk Polytechnic Institute 1962, renamed Ulyanovsk State Technical University 1994, present name and status 2002

Rector: Prof. Dr ALEXANDER D. GORBOKONENKO
Vice-Rector: N. YARUSHKINA
Librarian: TAMARA M. SMIRNOVA

Library of 1,411,507 vols
Number of teachers: 637
Number of students: 13,318

Publication: Vestnik Ulyanovsk State Technical University (4 a year)

Faculties of information systems and technology, radio engineering, power engineering, civil engineering, mechanical engineering, aircraft engineering, humanities, economics, mathematics, correspondent (evening) studies, open education centres and distance education; open business school at Dimitrovgrad

TAMBOV STATE TECHNICAL UNIVERSITY

392000 Tambov, Sovetskaya ul. 106
Telephone: (4752) 63-10-19
E-mail: tstu@admin.tstu.ru
Internet: www.tstu.ru

Founded 1958
State control
Language of instruction: Russian
Academic year: September to July

Rector: Prof. Dr STANISLAV I. DVORETSKY (acting)
Vice-Rector: Dr VYACHESLAV F. KALININ
Vice-Rector: Dr ELENA S. MISCHENKO
Librarian: IRINA V. SCHUKINA

Library: 1.5m. vols
Number of teachers: 700
Number of students: 12,000

Publications: *Problems of Contemporary Science and Practice* (4 a year), *TSTU Transactions* (4 a year)

DEANS

Architecture and Civil Engineering: PAVEL MONASTYREV
Correspondence Study and External Studies: VALERIY ODNOLKO
Economics: BORIS GERASIMOV
Information Technologies: YURIY GROMOV
International Education: MAXIM PROMOTOV
Law: SERGEY YESIKIV
Masters Programmes: OLGA A. KORCHAGINA
Motor Transport: OLEG DMITRIEV
Nanotechnologies: ALEXANDER MAYSTRENKO
Power Engineering: TATYANA CHERNYSHEVA
Pre-University Training: VLADIMIR PLOTNIKOV

PROFESSORS

BELYAEV, P.
BRUSENTOV, Y.
BYKOVSKIY, V.
CHERNYSHEVA, T.
CHERNYSHEV, V. N.
DEMIN, O. B.
DMITRIEV, O.
DVORETSKIY, S. I.
DZUBA, S.
FROLOV, S.
GATAPOVA, N. T.
GERASIMOV, B. I.
GROMOV, Y.
KALININ, V. F.
KILIMNIK, A.
KLIMOV, A. M.
KLINKOV, A.
KONOVALOV, V.
KULIKOV, G.
KULIKOV, N.
KUROCHKIN, I. M.
LAZAREV, S.
LEDENEV, V.
LEONTYEVA, A. I.
MAKEEVA, M.
MALYGYN, E.
MARTEMYANOV, Y. F.
MATVEYKIN, V.
MOLOTKOVA, N
MILOVANOV, I. V.
MISCHENKO, S. V.
MOLOTKOV, N.
NIKULIN, V. V.
ODNOLKO, V. G.
PARKHOMENKO, L.
PENKOV, V.
PERSHIN, V.
PODOLSKIY, V. Y.

POPOVA, I.
POPOV, N. S.
PROMTOV, M. A.
PUCHKOV, N. P.
PUDOVKIN, A.
ROMANOV, A. P.
SHAMKIN, V. N.
SLEZIN, A.
TKACHEV, A.
VANIN, V.
VOROBYEV, Y.
VORONKOVA, O.
YESIKOV, S. A.
ZHARIKOV, V.
ZHUKOV, N. P.

TOMSK POLYTECHNIC UNIVERSITY

634050 Tomsk, 30 Lenin Ave
Telephone: (3822) 70-17-77
E-mail: tpu@tpu.ru
Internet: www.tpu.ru

Founded 1896
State control
Languages of instruction: English, Russian
Academic year: September to July

Rector: Prof. PETR CHUBIK

Library: 2.7m. vols
Number of teachers: 2,300
Number of students: 22,800

DEANS

Institute of Cybernetics: Prof. MIKHAIL SONKIN
Institute of High Technology Physics: Prof. ALEXEY YAKOVLEV
Institute of Natural Resources: Prof. ANDREY DMITRIEV
Institute of Non-Destructive Testing: Prof. VASILIY KLIMENOV
Institute of Physics and Technology: Prof. VALERI KRIVOBOKOV
Institute of Power Engineering: Prof. YURI BOROVIKOV

TOMSK STATE UNIVERSITY OF CONTROL SYSTEMS AND RADIOELECTRONICS

634050 Tomsk, pr. Lenina 40
Telephone: (3822) 51-05-30
E-mail: office@tusur.ru
Internet: www.tusur.ru

Founded 1962
State control

Pres.: Prof. Dr ANATOLY V. KOBZEV
Rector: Prof. Dr YURY A. SHURYGIN

Library of 620,000 vols
Number of teachers: 600
Number of students: 13,000

DEANS

Faculty of Advanced Training: Prof. VYACHESLAV I. EFANOV
Faculty of Computer Systems: Assoc. Prof. MIKHAIL V. CHERKASHIN
Faculty of Control Systems: Assoc. Prof. PAVEL V. SENCHENKO
Faculty of Distance Learning: IRINA P. LEVSHENKOVA
Faculty of Economics: Prof. Dr ARKADY G. BUIMOV
Faculty of Electronic Engineering: Assoc. Prof. VIKTOR M. GERASIMOV
Faculty of Extramural and Evening Education: Assoc. Prof. IGOR V. OSIPOV
Faculty of Human Sciences: Prof. Dr TATYANA I. SUSLOVA
Faculty of Innovation Technologies: Assoc. Prof. YURI M. LIRMAK
Faculty of Law: Assoc. Prof. SERGEY L. KRASINSKY
Faculty of Radio Design: Assoc. Prof. DENIS V. OZERKIN

Faculty of Radio Engineering: Assoc. Prof. ANATOLY Y. DEMIDOV
Higher College of Informatics, Electronics and Management: Prof. Dr VYACHESLAV M. DMITRIEV

TULA STATE UNIVERSITY

300600 Tula, pr. Lenina 92
Telephone: (0872) 35-21-55
E-mail: info@tsu.tula.ru
Internet: www.tsu.tula.ru

Founded 1930

Faculties of mechanics and control systems, mechanics and mathematics, applied physics, engineering, cybernetics, mining and construction, medicine, natural sciences, humanities, economics and law, technological, physical culture, sport and tourism, int. students' faculty

Rector: Prof. MIKHAIL V. GRYAZEV

Library: 1m. vols
Number of teachers: 1,386
Number of students: 17,000

Publication: *Izvestiya* (4 a year)

TVER STATE TECHNICAL UNIVERSITY

170026 Tver, nab. A. Nikitina 22
Telephone: (0822) 31-15-09
E-mail: common@tstu.tver.ru
Internet: www.tstu.tver.ru

Founded 1922

Faculties of machine building, automatic control systems, civil and industrial engineering, environmental engineering, humanities, postgraduate, evening and distance education

Rector: Prof. VYACHESLAV A. MIRONOV

Library: 2m. vols

TYUMEN STATE OIL AND GAS UNIVERSITY

625000 Tyumen, ul. Volodarskogo 38
Telephone: (3452) 25-08-61
E-mail: general@tgngu.tyumen.ru
Internet: www.tgngu.tyumen.ru

Founded 1963

Faculties of geology and geoinformatics, oil and gas fields, pipeline engineering, transport, technical cybernetics, oil and gas refining, management, drilling and mechanical engineering

Rector: NIKOLAI N. KARNAUKHOV

Library of 677,000 vols
Number of teachers: 1,230
Number of students: 30,000

UFA STATE AVIATION TECHNICAL UNIVERSITY

450000 Bashkortostan, Ufa, ul. K. Marksa 12
Telephone: (347) 256-96-93
E-mail: root@admin.ugatu.ac.ru
Internet: www.ugatu.ac.ru

Founded 1932

Faculties of aircraft engines, aircraft machine building technology, aircraft technological systems, general sciences, informatics and robotics, economics, management and finance, social sciences

Rector: Prof. MURAT B. GUZAIROV

Library of 700,000 vols

Publication: *Higher School Collections on Research* (irregular)

UFA STATE PETROLEUM TECHNOLOGICAL UNIVERSITY

450062 Bashkortostan, Ufa, ul. Kosmonavtov 1

Telephone: (3472) 42-03-70
E-mail: info@rusoil.net
Internet: www.ugntu.ru

Founded 1941

Faculties of oil and mining, pipeline transport, petrochemical, oil equipment, construction, technology, economics and management, automation of production processes, humanities, military studies; brs in Oktyabrsky, Salavat, Sterlitamak

Rector: Ayrat M. Shammazov

Library of 1,031,930 vols
Number of teachers: 802
Number of students: 14,000

URALS STATE MINING UNIVERSITY

620144 Ekaterinburg, ul. Kuibysheva 30

Telephone: (3432) 22-25-47
E-mail: office@usmga.ru
Internet: www.usmga.ru

Founded 1914 as Ekaterinburg Mining Institute; as Sverdlovsk Mining Institute 1934–1993; as Urals State Acad. of Mining and Geology 1993–2004; present name and status 2004

Faculties of economics, environmental engineering, geology, geophysics, mining engineering, mining technology

Rector: Prof. Nikolai P. Kosarev

Library of 800,000 vols
Number of teachers: 1,500
Number of students: 6,000

URALS STATE TECHNICAL UNIVERSITY

620002 Ekaterinburg, ul. Mira 19

Telephone: (343) 374-54-34
E-mail: inter@inter.ustu.ru
Internet: www.ustu.ru

Founded 1920

Faculties of chemical technology, civil engineering, construction materials, economics and management, electrical engineering, heat and power engineering, mechanical engineering, metallurgy, physical engineering, humanities, physical training and sport, radio engineering

Rector: Prof. Stanislav S. Naboichenko

Library: 2m. vols
Number of teachers: 2,233
Number of students: 35,000

URALS STATE UNIVERSITY OF RAILWAY TRANSPORT

620034 Ekaterinburg, ul. Kolmogorova 66

Telephone: (343) 245-34-67
E-mail: rector@usart.ru
Internet: www.usart.ru

Founded 1956
State control; attached to Min. of Transport of the Russian Federation
Academic year: September to June

Faculties of construction, economics, electrical engineering, electrification, mechanics, traffic management

Rector: Prof. Alexander V. Efimov
Vice-Rector for Int. Affairs: Boris M. Gotlib

Library of 600,000 vols
Number of teachers: 580
Number of students: 10,186 (6,000 full-time, 4,186 correspondence)

Publication: *Research Reviews* (every 2 years)

URALSKIY GOSUDARSTVENNYY LESOTEHNICHESKIY UNIVERSITET (Ural State Forest Engineering University)

260100 Ekaterinburg, ul. Sibirsky Trakt 37

Telephone: (343) 254-65-06
E-mail: general@usfeu.ru
Internet: www.usfeu.ru

Founded 1930
State control
Language of instruction: Russian
Academic year: September to June

Rector: Prof. Andrey V. Mekhrentsev
Pro-Rector for Educational Work: Sergey I. Kolesnikov
Pro-Rector for Innovation Activity and Int. Cooperation: Natalia A. Shpak
Pro-Rector for Scientific Work: Prof. Sergey V. Zalesov
Librarian: Ludmila K. Bukvareva

Library of 878,000 vols, 260 periodical titles
Number of teachers: 473
Number of students: 8,400

DEANS

Faculty of Complementary Education: Prof. Leo G. Shvamm
Faculty of Correspondence: Prof. Anatoly V. Kapralov
Faculty of Ecological Engineering: Prof. Alesja V. Vurasko
Faculty of Economics and Management: Prof. Victor P. Chasovskih
Faculty of Forestry: Prof. Zufar Ya. Nagimov
Faculty of Forestry Engineering: Prof. Edward F. Guerz
Faculty of Humanities: Irina G. Svetlova
Faculty of Mechanical Engineering: Prof. Valery P. Sivakov
Faculty of Professional Education: Olga A. Udachina
Faculty of Wood Technology: Prof. Yury I. Trakalo

VOLGA STATE UNIVERSITY OF TECHNOLOGY

424024 Yoshkar-Ola, 3 Lenin pl.

Telephone: (8362) 41-08-72
E-mail: rector@volgatech.net
Internet: www.volgatech.net

Founded 1932
State control
Language of instruction: Russian
Academic year: September to June

Rector: Evgeny M. Romanov

Library: 1m. vols
Number of teachers: 591
Number of students: 12,406

VOLGA STATE UNIVERSITY OF TELECOMMUNICATIONS AND INFORMATICS

443010 Samara, ul. L. Tolstogo 23

Telephone: (8463) 33-58-56
E-mail: priem@psati.ru
Internet: www.psuti.ru

Founded 1956

Faculties of basic telecommunications education, distance education, information systems and technology, telecommunications and radio engineering; Telecom College of PSATI, Samara Telecommunications Training Centre; brs in Kazanskiy, Orenburg and Stavropol

Rector: Vladimir A. Andreev

Library of 461,000
Number of teachers: 300
Number of students: 4,100

VOLGOGRAD STATE TECHNICAL UNIVERSITY

400005 Volgograd, pr. Lenina 28

Telephone: (8442) 23-00-76
E-mail: rector@vstu.ru
Internet: www.vstu.ru

Founded 1930
Academic year: September to June

Faculties of automated systems and technological informatics, automobile transport, chemical engineering, economics and management, electronics and computer science, engineers' training, food engineering, foreign students' training, mechanical and metallurgical, postgraduate studies, pre-university training, structural materials technology, vehicle and weapon systems; Kirovsky Evening Faculty, Institute for Retraining and Advanced Training

Rector: Prof. Vladimir I. Lysak
Vice-Rector for Int. Cooperation: Prof. Alexander V. Navrotskiy

Library of 1,235,810 vols
Number of teachers: 1,112
Number of students: 18,000

Publication: *Polytekhnik* (26 a year)

DEANS

A. V. Belov
A. E. Godenko
V. F. Kablov
Vasiliy G. Karaban
Yuri Y. Komarov
Oleg D. Kosov
S. M. Ledenev
A. P. Mantoroshin
Yuri P. Mukha
Yuri I. Osadshy
O. P. Otchenashev
A. N. Savkin
N. I. Zuban

VOLGOGRAD STATE UNIVERSITY OF ARCHITECTURE AND CIVIL ENGINEERING

400074 Volgograd, Akademicheskaya ul. 1

Telephone: (8442) 97-48-72
E-mail: info@vgasu.ru
Internet: www.vgasu.ru

Founded 1952, present name and status 2003

5 Br. institutes: Institute of Architecture and Civil Engineering, Institute of Traffic Engineering, Institute of Economics and Law, Institute of Ecology, Institute of Distance Education; attached institute: Volzhsky Institute of Civil Engineering and Technologies

Rector: Sergey Yu. Kalashnikov

Library: 1.1m. vols
Number of teachers: 879
Number of students: 12,026

VOLOGDA STATE TECHNICAL UNIVERSITY

160000 Vologda, ul. Lenina 15

Telephone: (8172) 72-46-45
E-mail: rector_s@mh.vstu.edu.ru
Internet: www.vstu.edu.ru

Founded 1975 as Vologda Polytechnic Institute
State control
Language of instruction: Russian
Academic year: August to June

Faculties of power engineering, industrial management, construction engineering, ecology, humanities, economics, correspondence and distance learning, secondary technical training mechanical engineering technikum branch in Cherepovets

Rector: Prof. Dr Leonid Sokolov

Library of 1,328,342 vols
Number of teachers: 451
Number of students: 9,242

VORONEZH STATE TECHNICAL UNIVERSITY

394026 Voronezh, Moskovsky pr. 14

Telephone: (0732) 21-09-19
E-mail: rector@vorstu.ru
Internet: www.vorstu.ru

Faculties of automation and mechanization of engineering, aviation, automation and electrical engineering, engineering economics, radio engineering, physical engineering

Rector: Prof. VADIM N. FROPOV

Library of 700,000 vols

VYATKA STATE TECHNICAL UNIVERSITY

610601 Kirov, GSP (Centre), Moskovskaya ul. 36

Telephone: (8332) 62-65-71
E-mail: root@kpicnit.vyatka.su

Founded 1963

Faculties of electrical engineering, automation and computer technology, chemical technology, construction engineering, socioeconomics and machine engineering

Rector: Prof. VASILY M. KONDRATOV

Library: 1m. vols

Publication: *Transactions*

YAROSLAVL STATE TECHNICAL UNIVERSITY

150053 Yaroslavl, Moskovsky pr. 88

Telephone: (0852) 44-15-19
E-mail: webmaster@ystu.ru
Internet: www.ystu.ru

Founded 1944; present name and status 1994

Rector: Prof. YURI A. MOSKVICHEV

Number of students: 5,000

Academies

ARCHITECTURE AND CIVIL ENGINEERING

Ivanovo Academy of Civil Engineering and Architecture: 153002 Ivanovo, ul. 8 Marta 20; tel. (0932) 32-85-40; e-mail post@iisi.asinet.ivanovo.su; f. 1981; facilities: construction technology, economics, architecture; library: 250,000 vols; Rector Prof. Dr S. V. FEDOSOV.

Tomsk State Academy of Civil Engineering: 634003 Tomsk, Solyanaya pl. 2; tel. 75-39-30; f. 1952; faculties: architecture, civil and industrial construction engineering, road building, mechanical engineering, technology; library: 638,000 vols; 458 teachers; 5,086 students; Rector G. M. ROGOV.

Tyumen Civil Engineering and Architectural Academy: 625001 Tyumen, ul. Lunacharskogo 2; tel. (3452) 46-10-10; e-mail tumgasa@sbtx.tmn.ru; internet www.tumgasa.ru; f. 1971; faculties: construction, engineering networks and systems, road building, economics and management; 360 teachers; 5,000 students; Rector Dr TCHIKICHEV.

Ural State Academy of Architecture and Arts: 620075 Ekaterinburg, ul. Karla Libknekhta 23; tel. (3432) 51-33-69; e-mail vgafurov@usaaa.ru; internet www.usaaa.ru; f. 1972 (fmrly Sverdlovsk Architectural Institute); depts of architecture, applied decorative art, design, fashion design, monumental decorative art, urban planning; library:

80,000 vols; 1,100 students; Rector A. A. STARIKOV; publ. *Architecton* (4 a year).

Voronezh State University of Architecture and Civil Engineering: 394006 Voronezh, 20-Letiya Oktyabrya ul. 84; tel. (0732) 71-52-68; e-mail rectorat@vgasu.vrn.ru; internet www.vgasu.vrn.ru; f. 1930; academic year September to July; faculties of arts, automation and information systems, architecture, construction, construction technology, engineering economics, engineering systems and buildings, mechanical engineering and highway construction; distance learning courses available; Rector Igor S. SUROVTSEV; library: 500,000 vols; 485 teachers; 7,981 students; publ. *Scientific Bulletin* (colln of scientific articles, 1 a year).

AGRICULTURE AND VETERINARY SCIENCE

Belgorod State Agricultural Academy: 309103 Belgorod oblast, pos. Maiskii, Vavilova ul. 1; tel. (0722) 39-21-79; e-mail bsaa@csn.ru; internet www.bsaa.edu.ru; f. 1978; 490 teachers; 4,500 students; Rector ALEXANDR V. TURIANSKY.

Bryansk State Agricultural Academy: 243365 Bryansk oblast, Vygonichesky r-n, pos. Kokino; tel. (8341) 2-43-21; e-mail bgsha@bitmcnit.bryansk.su; internet www.bgsha.com; f. 1980; library: 385,000 vols, 150 periodicals; Rector Prof. NIKOLAI M. BELUS; publ. *Collection of Scientific Papers* (1 a year).

Buryat State Agricultural Academy: 670024 Ulan-Ude, Pushkina ul. 8; tel. (3012) 34-26-11; e-mail bgsha@eastsib.ru; f. 1932; depts: animal husbandry, agronomy, veterinary medicine, economics, farm mechanization, land tenure regulations, accounting, management; library: 582,000 vols; 325 teachers; 4,800 students; Rector Prof. ALEXANDER P. POPOV.

Chuvash State Agricultural Academy: 428000 Cheboksary, K. Marksa ul. 29; tel. (8352) 22-23-34; depts: agronomy, mechanization, animal husbandry; library: 83,000 vols; Rector NIKOLAI K. KIRILLOV.

Dagestan State Agricultural Academy: 367032 Makhachkala, M. Gadzhieva ul. 180; tel. (8722) 68-24-70; f. 1932; Rector MAGOMED M. DZHAMBULATOV; library: 200,000 vols; publ. *Works*; fields of study: zootechnics, veterinary, fruit and vegetable growing, accountancy.

Irkutsk State Agricultural Academy: 664038 Irkutsk, pos. Molodozhny; tel. (3952) 39-93-30; e-mail rector@ishi.baikal.ru; internet www.irgsha.narod.ru; f. 1934; depts at main campus: economics, accounting, computer engineering, agronomy, agroecology, soil management, energy engineering, mechanization, zoological engineering, veterinary science, wildlife management; Chita campus: economics, accounting, agronomy, mechanization, zoological engineering; library: 504,814 vols; 357 teachers; 7,736 students; br. in Chita; Rector ALEXANDER A. DOLGOPOLOV.

Ivanovo Agricultural Academy: 153012 Ivanovo, Sovetskaya ul. 45; tel. (0932) 32-81-44; e-mail ivgsha@tpi.ru; f. 1918; depts: agronomy, zootechnics, veterinary medicine, mechanization in agriculture, service and exploitation of farm machines and equipment, land use and land distribution, economics and management in rural production, agroecology; library: 260,364 vols; 211 teachers; 3,328 students; Rector V.F. TSARYOV.

Izhevsk State Agricultural Academy: Udmurt Republic, 426069 Izhevsk, Studencheskaya ul. 11; tel. (3412) 58-99-48; e-mail root@isa.udm.ru; internet isa.udm

.ru; f. 1954; depts: agronomy, animal husbandry, veterinary science, forestry, mechanization, bookkeeping and agricultural analysis, economics, mechanization of the processing of farm produce; library: 500,000 vols; 357 teachers; 6,038 students; extramural faculty; Pres. Prof. V. V. FOKIN.

Kazan State Academy of Veterinary Medicine 'N. E. Bauman': Tatarstan, 420074 Kazan, Sibirsky trakt ul.; tel. (8432) 76-15-05; f. 1873; advanced training of veterinary and animal husbandry specialists; library: 410,000 vols; 230 teachers; 3,700 students; Rector Acad. G. Z. IDRISOV; publ. *Nauchnye Trudy* (4–5 a year).

Kazan State Agricultural Academy: 420015 Kazan, Karla Marksa ul. 65; tel. (8432) 36-65-22; internet www.ksha.ru; fields of study: agronomy, mechanization, economics and management, accounting; library: 135,000 vols; Rector Prof. DZHAUDAT I. FAIZRAKHMANOV.

Kostroma State Agricultural Academy: 156530 Kostroma, p/o Karavaevo; tel. (942) 54-12-63; e-mail mobot@ksaa.edu.ru; internet www.ksaa.edu.ru; f. 1949; depts of agronomy, zootechnics, veterinary science, farm mechanization, automobiles and automobile facilities, service and operation of vehicles and machines, electrification and automation of agricultural production, application of computers, architecture, industrial and civil engineering, economics and management, accountancy and auditing, finance and credit, fundamentals of law in agriculture, agricultural management; library: 510,000 vols; 370 teachers; 5,100 students; Rector V. I. VOROBEV.

Kursk State Agricultural Academy 'I. I. Ivanov': 305034 Kursk, Karla Marksa ul. 70; tel. (0712) 33-06-05; e-mail academy@kgsha.ru; internet www.kgsha.ru; f. 1956; fields of study: agronomy, plant protection, zootechnics, mechanization, economics and management, accounting, agroecology, veterinary medicine, seed processing and storage; library: 130,000 vols; Rector VLADIMIR D. FLOUR.

Moscow Agricultural Academy 'K. A. Timiryazev': 127550 Moscow, Timiryazevskaya ul. 49; tel. (495) 976-04-80; e-mail info@timacad.ru; internet www.timacad.ru; f. 1865; faculties of agricultural chemistry, agronomy, agropedagogy, horticulture, economics, soil science and ecology, zootechnics; 33 attached research stations and 5 experimental and instructional farms; br. in Kaluga; library: 1.5m. vols; 650 teachers; 10,000 students; Rector Prof. VLADIMIR M. BAUTIM; publs *Papers of TSHA* (1 a year), *Proceedings of TSHA* (6 a year).

Moscow State Academy of Veterinary Medicine and Biotechnology 'K. I. Skryabin': 100472 Moscow, Akad. K. I. Skryabina 23 ul.; tel. (495) 377-91-17; f. 1919; faculties: veterinary biological science, animal husbandry, pedagogical, animal products; library: 500,000 vols; 360 teachers; 3,500 students; Rector Acad. A. D. BELOV.

Nizhnii Novgorod State Agricultural Academy: 603078 Nizhnii Novgorod pr. Gagarina 97; tel. (8312) 66-07-30; f. 1930; fields of study: accounting, agrochemistry, agronomy, animal husbandry, mechanization, veterinary medicine; library: 500,000 vols; 5,000 students; Rector ALEZEY GALKIN; publ. *Scientific Works* (1 a year).

Penza State Agricultural Academy: 440014 Penza, Botanicheskaya ul. 30; tel. (841) 259-63-54; e-mail psaca@penza.com.ru; internet pgsha.penza.com.ru; f. 1951; fields of study incl. agronomy, agroecology, animal husbandry, mechanization of agriculture, machine repairing, book-keeping and auditing, economics, administration, farm production technology, motor vehicles and motor vehicle management; library: 264,000 vols; 264 teachers; 3,500 students; Rector Prof. VLADIMIR D. KOROTNEV.

Perm Agricultural Academy 'Acad. D. N. Pryanishnikov': 614600 Perm, Kommunisticheskaya ul. 23; tel. (3422) 12-53-94; e-mail pgsha@permregion.ru; f. 1918; depts: agrochemistry and soil science, agronomy, animal husbandry, mechanization, economics and management, accounting, forestry, food technology, applied informatics; library: 320,000 vols; 380 teachers; 9,000 students; Rector YU. N. ZUBAREV.

Primorsky State Agricultural Academy: 692510 Ussuriisk, pr. Blyukhera 44; tel. (42341) 6-33-91; e-mail agracad@hotbox.ru; internet www.primacad.ru; institutes: land management and farming, animal husbandry and veterinary medicine, forestry, economics and business, farm mechanization, staff upgrading and retraining for the agro-industrial complex; f. 1957; library: 380,000 vols; 500 teachers; 5,000 students; Rector A. A. DYOMIN.

Ryazan State Agricultural Academy: 390044 Ryazan, Kostycheva ul. 1; tel. (0912) 55-35-01; e-mail rsaa@narod.ru; internet www.rsaa.narod.ru; fields of study: agronomy, animal husbandry, mechanization, economics and management, accounting; library: 94,000 vols; Rector GENNADY M. TUNIKOV.

St Petersburg Academy of Forestry Technology: 194018 St Petersburg, Institutsky per. 5; tel. (812) 550-07-00; f. 1803; faculties of chemical technology, engineering economics, forest machinery, forestry, forestry engineering, mechanical technology of timber; br. in Syktyvkar; library: 1.4m. vols; 613 teachers; 9,000 students; Rector Prof. V. I. ONEGIN; publ. *Nauchnye Trudy* (1 a year).

Tyumen State Agricultural Academy: 625003 Tyumen, Respubliki ul. 7; tel. (3452) 46-16-50; e-mail acadagro@tmn.ru; internet www.tgsha.ru; f. 1879; attached institutes of agronomy and ecology, finance and management, veterinary medicine and aquaculture; library: 700,000 vols; 250 teachers; 5,000 students; Rector Dr NIKOLAI V. ABRAMOV.

Ulyanovsk State Agricultural Academy: 432601 Ulyanovsk, bul. Novy Venets 1; tel. (88422) 31-42-72; e-mail academy@mv.ru; internet www.academy.mv.ru; f. 1943; depts of agronomy, animal husbandry, mechanization, veterinary, medicine, economics; library: 452,000 vols; 312 teachers; 4,248 students; Rector B. I. ZOTOV.

Urals State Academy of Veterinary Medicine: 457100 Chelyabinsk oblast, Troitsk, Gagarina ul. 13; tel. (3516) 32-00-10; internet www.ugavm.boom.ru; f. 1929; library: 200,000 vols; 180 teachers; 1,434 students; Rector Prof. V. LAZARENKO.

Urals State Agricultural Academy: 620219 Ekaterinburg, K. Libknekhta ul. 42; tel. (3432) 51-33-63; e-mail academy@usaca.ru; internet www.usaca.ru; f. 1940; library: 450,000 vols; 700 teachers; 2,500 students; Rector ALEXANDER N. SEMIN.

Velikie Luki State Agricultural Academy: 182100 Pskov oblast, Velikie Luki, pl. V. I. Lenina 1; tel. (81153) 3-77-28; e-mail vgsha@mart.ru; f. 1958; depts: agronomy and ecology, economics, animal husbandry, engineering; library: 390,000 vols; 291 teachers; 4,114 students; Rector Prof. V. P. SPASOV; publ. *Works* (1 a year).

Volgograd State Agricultural Academy: 400041 Volgograd, Institutskaya ul. 8; tel. (8442) 43-08-45; f. 1944; depts: agronomy, animal husbandry, farm mechanization,

farm electrification, ecology and land reclamation, accounting; library: 568,000 vols; 4,000 students; Rector Acad. A. M. GAVRILOV; publ. *Scientific Information* (2 a year).

Vologda State Dairy Academy 'N. V. Vereschagin': 160555 Vologda pos. Molochnoe, Shmidta ul. 2; tel. (8172) 76-17-30; e-mail rector@molochnoe.ru; internet www .molochnoe.ru; f. 1911; library: 420,000 vols; 270 teachers; 4,000 students; Rector Dr VLADIMIR N. OSTRETSOV; publ. *Works*.

Voronezh State Academy of Forestry Engineering: 394613 Voronezh, Timiryazeva ul. 8; tel. (0732) 53-74-98; e-mail postmaster@julygb.vsi.ru; internet vglta.vrn .ru; f. 1918; faculties: forest engineering, forestry, wood-processing technology, motor-vehicle engineering, forest industry economics and management, furniture design, forest machinery and equipment, safety traffic regulation, landscape gardening, gamekeeping and national parks management, international wood trade, industrial process automation; library: 568,000 vols; 397 teachers; 5,500 students; Rector Prof. V. K. POPOV.

Vyatka State Agricultural Academy: 610017 Kirov, Oktyabrsky pr. 133; tel. (8332) 62-97-19; e-mail vsaa@vit.kirov.ru; f. 1930; depts: agronomy, biology, economics, veterinary medicine, mechanization; library: 407,000 vols; Rector A. K. BOLOTOV.

ECONOMICS, LAW AND POLITICS

Academy of Social Sciences: 117606 Moscow, pr. Vernadskogo 84; tel. (95) 436-93-30; f. 1946; library: 2m. vols; Rector R. G. YUNOVSKII.

Finance Academy under the Government of the Russian Federation: 125468 Moscow, Leningradsky pr. 49; tel. (495) 943-98-55; e-mail academy@fa.ru; internet www .fa.ru; f. 1918; institutes and depts: finance, credit, financial management, insurance, taxes and taxation, accounting and audit, international economic relations, mathematical methods in economics and crisis management, tax police, evening school, distance learning, short-term re-training and skill development; 21st-Century International Finance University; MBA Business School; 650 teachers; 10,000 students; Rector A. G. GRYAZNOVA.

Irkutsk State Academy of Economics: 664015 Irkutsk, ul. Lenina 11; tel. (3952) 24-10-55; e-mail kvm@cc.isea.baikal.ru; f. 1930; faculties: law, world economics, finance, economics of mining industry and construction, economics of engineering and road transport, accounting, information systems, labour economics, public administration, management, economics of using natural resources; library: 530,000 vols; Rector M. A. VINOKUROV.

Khabarovsk State Academy of Economics and Law: 680042 Khabarovsk, Tikhookeanskaya ul. 134; tel. (4212) 35-87-37; auditing and accounting, finance, management, commerce, law, foreign economic relations; library: 400,000 vols; 220 teachers; 7,000 students; Rector Prof. V. A. LIKHOBABIN.

Polar Academy: 192007 St Petersburg, Voronezhskaya ul. 79, A/Ya 533; tel. (812) 167-04-52; f. 1992; Master-level training of students from native Siberian peoples, who are expected to be appointed to high administrative posts in northern and far eastern Siberia; 60 teachers; 100 students; Rector AZURGET CHAUKENVAEVA; publ. *Polarnaya Akademia* (2 a year).

Russian Academy of Economics 'G. V. Plekhanov': 115998 Moscow M-54, Stremyannyi per. 36; tel. (095) 237-85-17; e-mail inter@rea.ru; internet www.rea.ru; f. 1907;

faculties: general economics, finance, taxation, national economy, trade in commodities, economics and mathematics, economics and engineering, international economic relations; graduate school; library: 815,000 vols; 1,000 teachers; 12,000 students; Rector V. I. VIDYAPIN.

St Petersburg State Academy of Engineering and Economics: 191002 St Petersburg, ul. Marata 27; tel. (812) 112-06-33; e-mail oms@engec.ru; internet www.engec .ru; f. 1930; institutes: industrial economics and management, regional economics and management, transport economics and management, management information systems, general management of business and finance, tourism and hotel management; library: 370,000 vols; 310 teachers; 3,540 students; Rector A. I. MIKHAILUSHKIN; publ. *Scientific Proceedings of the Institute* (1 a year).

Samara State Academy of Economics: 443090 Samara, ul. Sovetskoi Armii 141; tel. (8462) 22-15-42; f. 1931; faculties: finance, industrial economics, commerce and marketing, agribusiness, law, management, accounting; library: 596,000 vols; Rector Prof. A. I. NOSKOV.

Saratov State Academy of Law: 410720 Saratov, GSP, Chernyshevskogo ul. 104; tel. (8452) 25-04-86; e-mail post@sgap.ru; internet www.sgap.ru; f. 1931; library: 500,000 vols; 300 teachers; 3,000 students; Rector FEDOR A. GRIGORYEV; publ. *Vestnik Saratovskoi Gosudarstvennoi Academii Prava.*

Urals State Academy of Law: 620066 Ekaterinburg, Komsomolskaya ul. 21; tel. (3432) 74-43-63; e-mail rektorat@usla.ru; internet www.usla.ru; f. 1931; library: 850,000 vols; 327 teachers; 7,310 students; Rector Prof. VIKTOR D. PEREVALOV; publ. *Russian Law Journal* (4 a year).

Volgograd Academy of Public Administration: 400131 Volgograd Gagarina ul. 8; tel. (8442) 33-58-39; e-mail rector@vags.ru; internet www.vags.ru; f. 1992 to prepare and develop qualified administrators for government and non-profit positions; br. in Astrakhan; 250 teachers; 3,000 students; Rector MIKHAIL A. SUKIASYAN.

ENGINEERING AND INDUSTRY

Ivanovo State Textile Academy: 153000 Ivanovo, pr. F. Engels 21; tel. (0932) 32-85-45; e-mail rector@igta.ru; internet www.igta .ru; f. 1918; Rector Prof. VLADIMIR V. ZRYUKIN; Vice-Rectors Prof. ALEXANDER A. TUVIN (Complementary Education), Prof. ALEXANDER N. SMIRNOV (Information and Int. Relations), Prof. GRIGORY I. CHRISTOBORODOV (Scientific and Industrial Activity), Prof. VLADIMIR V. LYUBIMTSEV (Studies); library 740,911 vols; 388 teachers (incl. 51 professors); 8,488 students; publ. *Technology of Textile Industry* (6 a year).

Moscow State Academy of Light Industry: 113127 Moscow, ul. Osipenko 33; tel. (495) 231-58-01; faculties: chemical technology, sewn goods technology, mechanical, leather goods technology, engineering economics; br. in Novosibirsk; library: 392,000 vols; Rector V. A. FUKIN.

Siberian State Academy of Mining and Metallurgy: 654007 Kemerovo oblast, Novokuznetsk, pr. Kirova 42; tel. (3843) 46-35-02; faculties: mining, metallurgy, electrometallurgy, foundry work, mechanical, technology, construction; library: 1m. vols; 620 teachers; 6,000 students; Rector N. M. KULAGIN.

MEDICINE

Astrakhan State Medical Academy: 414000 Astrakhan, Bakinskaya ul. 121; tel. (8512) 22-70-16; e-mail agma@astranet.ru; internet www.agma.astranet.ru; f. 1918; library: 700,000 vols; 520 teachers; 3,500 students; Rector Prof. VALENTIN M. MIROSHNIKOV.

Blagoveshchensk State Medical Academy: 675006 Blagoveshchensk, Gorkogo ul. 95; tel. (4162) 2-27-13; tel. (4162) 2-28-68; 264 teachers; 1,681 students.

Chelyabinsk State Medical Academy: 454092 Chelyabinsk, Vorovskogo ul. 64; tel. (3512) 34-16-86; internet www.vita.chel.su; library: 500,000 vols; 3,000 students; Rector Prof. YURI S. SHAMUROV.

Chita State Medical Academy: 672090 Chita, Gorkogo ul. 39A; tel. (3022) 23-41-63; e-mail macadem@mail.chita.ru; f. 1953; library: 387,000 vols; 311 teachers; 2,400 students; Rector VLADIMIR N. IVANOV.

Dagestan State Medical Academy: 367025 Dagestan Autonomous Republic, Makhachkala, pl. Lenina 6; tel. (8722) 67-07-94; e-mail dgma@iwt.ru; internet www .dgma.ru; Rector ABDURAKHMAN O. OSMANOV.

Ivanovo State Medical Academy: 153462 Ivanovo, pr. F. Engelsa 8; tel. (0932) 30-17-66; e-mail adm@isma.ivanovo.ru; internet www.isma.ivanovo.ru; f. 1930; library: 545,059 vols; 578 teachers; 2,084 students; Rector Prof. RUDOLF R. SHILYAEV.

Izhevsk State Medical Academy: 426034 Udmurt Republic, Izhevsk, Revolyutsionnaya ul. 199; tel. (3412) 52-62-01; e-mail rector@igma.udm.ru; internet www.igma .udm.ru; f. 1933; library: 402,000 vols; 387 teachers; 2,500 students; Rector Prof. NIKOLAI S. STRELKOV.

Kemerovo State Medical Academy: 650029 Kemerovo, Voroshilova ul. 22A; tel. (3842) 73-48-55; e-mail ksma@ksma.kuzstu .ac.ru; internet ksma.kuzstu.ac.ru; f. 1956; library: 390,681 vols; 461 teachers; 3,573 students; Rector ALEXANDER YA. EVTUSHENKO.

Krasnoyarsk State Medical Academy: 660022 Krasnoyarsk, Partizana Zheleznyaka ul. 1; tel. (3912) 27-49-24; e-mail onmpi@krsk .infotel.ru; internet www.krasgma.ru; f. 1942; library: 472,000 vols; 609 teachers; 3,270 students; Rector Prof. VICTOR I. PROKHORENKOV; publ. *Medical Man* (12 a year).

Kuban State Medical Academy: 350614 Krasnodar, Sedina ul. 4; tel. (8612) 68-34-57; e-mail corpus@ksma.kubannet.ru; internet www.ksma.ru; f. 1920, present name and status 1994; library: 560,000 vols; 600 teachers; 5,000 students; Rector BORIS G. ERMOSHENKO.

Nizhnii Novgorod State Medical Academy: 603005 Nizhnii Novgorod, pl. Minina i Pozharskogo 10/1; tel. (8312) 39-06-43; e-mail nnsma@sandy.ru; internet www.n-nov .mednet.com; f. 1920; library: 480,000 vols; 645 teachers; 3,542 students; Rector Prof. VYACHESLAV V. SHKARIN; publ. *Zhurnal* (4 a year).

North Ossetia State Medical Academy: 362019 N Ossetia, Vladikavkaz, Pushkinskaya ul. 40; tel. (8672) 53-42-21; e-mail nosma@dol.ru; f. 1796; 278 teachers; library: 265,000 vols; Rector Prof. KAZBEK D. SALBIEV.

Novosibirsk State Medical Academy: 630091 Novosibirsk, Krasnyi pr., 52; tel. (3832) 22-32-04; e-mail rector@medin.nsc .ru; internet www.medin.nsc.ru; f. 1935; academic year September to June (2 semesters); faculties of clinical psychology, ecology, international physicians, laboratory medicine, medicine, paediatrics, physicians' and professors' improving and retraining and preparatory studies, nurses' training, pharmaceutical science, social activity, stomatology, traditional medicine; evening lyceum, institute of public health economics and management; library: 400,000 specialized vols and periodicals; 784 teachers; 4,500 students; Rector Prof. ANATOLY V. EFREMOV; publs *Eksperimentalnaya Klinicheskaya Medicina* (Experimental Clinical Medicine, 4 a year), *Meditsinskaya Gazeta* (Medical Newspaper, 26 a year).

Omsk State Medical Academy: 644099 Omsk, Lenina ul. 12; tel. (3812) 23-32-89; e-mail osma@omsk-osma.ru; internet www .omsk-osma.ru; f. 1921; faculties: therapeutic and preventive medicine, paediatrics, stomatology; library: 573,199 vols; Rector Prof. ALEXANDER I. NOVIKOV.

Orenburg State Medical Academy: 460014 Orenburg, Sovetskaya ul. 6; tel. (3532) 77-61-03; library: 160,000 vols; Rector SERGEI A. PAVLOVICHEV.

Perm State Medical Academy: 614600 Perm, Kuybyshevskaya ul. 39; tel. (3422) 90-44-53; e-mail med@psma.ru; internet www.psma.ru; library: 541,000 vols; Rector Prof. VLADIMIR A. CHERKASSOV.

St Petersburg State Academy of Paediatric Medicine: 194100 St Petersburg, Litovskaya ul. 2; tel. (812) 245-06-46; f. 1925; library: 600,000 vols; Rector V. V. LEVANOVICH.

St Petersburg State Chemical-Pharmaceutical Academy: 197376 St Petersburg, ul. Professora Popova 14; tel. (812) 234-57-29; e-mail rector@spcpa.ru; internet www .spcpa.ru; f. 1919; faculties: drug industry technology, pharmacy, further education; library: 334,200 vols; 250 teachers; 2,000 students; Rector G.P. YAKOVLEV.

St Petersburg State Medical Academy 'I. I. Mechnikov': 195067 St Petersburg, Piskarevsky pr. 47; tel. (812) 543-50-14; e-mail mechnik@westcall.net; internet www .mechnik.spb.ru; f. 1907; faculties: pre-medical training, general medical, preventative medicine, advanced nursing, foreign students, further training, advanced training; library: 556,000 vols; 361 teachers; 4,500 students; Rector Prof. ALEXANDER V. SHABROV.

Smolensk State Medical Academy: 214019 Smolensk, Krupskoi ul. 28; tel. (812) 55-26-92; e-mail admsgma@sci.smolensk.ru; internet www.sgma.ru; library: 207,000 vols; Rector Prof. VLADIMIR G. PLESHKOV.

Stavropol State Medical Academy: 355017 Stavropol, Mira ul. 310; tel. (8652) 37-06-92; e-mail postmaster@stgmu.ru; internet www.stgma.ru; f. 1937; faculties of general medicine, stomatology, paediatrics, medical college teaching skills, nursing, postgraduate studies; 2 attached museums; clinics of ophthalmology, neurology and vertebraneurology; library: 345,000 vols; 525 teachers; 3,500 students; Rector Prof. B. D. MINAEV; publ. *South Russia Medical Magazine* (6 a year).

Tver Medical Academy: 170642 Tver, Sovetskaya ul. 4; tel. (0822) 33-17-79; library: 446,000 vols; Rector BORIS N. DAVYDOV.

Tyumen Medical Academy: 625023 Tyumen, Odesskaya ul. 54; tel. (3452) 22-62-00; e-mail tgma@tgma.info; internet www.tgma .info; f. 1963; 515 teachers; 3,256 students.

Urals State Medical Academy: 620219 Ekaterinburg, Repina ul. 3; tel. (3432) 51-14-90; e-mail info@usma.ru; internet www .usma.ru; f. 1931; areas of study: anaesthesiology, dentistry, epidemiology, gynaecology, obstetrics, ophthalmology, otolaryngology, paediatric surgery, pathology, surgery paediatrics, therapeutics;

library: 600,000 vols; Rector Prof. ANATOLY P. YASTREBOV; publ. *Herald* (12 a year).

Voronezh State Medical Academy 'N. N. Burdenko': 394036 Voronezh, Studencheskaya ul. 10; tel. (0732) 53-03-98; e-mail foreign@vsma.ac.ru; internet www.vsma.ac .ru; f. 1918; academic year September to June (2 semesters); library: 500,000 vols; 1,100 teachers; 3,850 students; Rector Prof. Dr I. E. YESAULENKO; publs *Applied Informational Aspects in Medicine* (4 a year), *Medical Staff* (12 a year).

Yaroslavl State Medical Academy: 150000 Yaroslavl, Revolutsionnaya ul. 5; tel. (0852) 30-56-41; e-mail rector@yma.ac .ru; internet www.yma.ac.ru; Rector YURI V. NOVIKOV.

SCIENCE AND TECHNOLOGY

Moscow State Academy of Applied Biotechnology: 109029 Moscow, ul. Talalikhina 33; tel. (495) 276-19-10; f. 1931; faculties: dairy industry technology, meat industry technology, food production, automation, plastics processing, low-temperature technology, veterinary sanitation, book-keeping, management; library: 611,000 vols; Rector IOSIF A. ROGOV.

Moscow State Academy of Food Industry: 125080 Moscow, Volokolamskoe shosse 11; tel. (495) 158-03-71; f. 1931; food technology, chemical engineering and biotechnology, information systems in economics, management and marketing, machinery, informatics, power engineering, agricultural engineering; 500 teaching staff; library: 1m. vols; 6,000 students; Pres. Prof. V. I. TUZHILKIN.

Moscow State Academy of Instrumentation and Informatics: 107076 Moscow, ul. Stromynka 20; tel. (495) 268-01-01; faculties: automation in instrument making, engineering, transport and power machine building; library: 250,000 vols; Rector Prof. BORIS M. MIKHAILOV.

Moscow State Geological Prospecting Academy: 117873 Moscow, ul. Miklukho-Maklaya 23; tel. (495) 433-62-56; faculties: geology, geophysics, hydrogeology, prospecting engineering and mining, economics; library: 410,335 vols; 439 teachers; 3,964 students; Rector L. G. GRABCHAK; publ. *Geology and Prospecting* (6 a year).

Ryazan State Radio Engineering Academy: 390050 Ryazan, ul. Gagarina 59/1; tel. (0912) 72-18-44; f. 1951; faculties: automation and telemechanics, computer technology, electronics, engineering economics, humanities, radio engineering, radio equipment design; library: 720,000 vols; Rector V. K. ZLOBIN.

Rybinsk State Academy of Aviation Technology: 152934 Rybinsk, ul. Pushkina 53; tel. (0855) 52-09-90; e-mail root@rgata .adm.yar.ru; internet www.rgata.yaroslavl .ru; f. 1955; faculties: aerotechnology, informatics, radioelectronics, rocket technology; library: c. 500,000 vols; 230 teachers; 4,000 students; Rector Prof. V. F. BEZYAZICHNY; publs *Scientific Notes* (1 a year), *Vestnik* (1 a year).

St Petersburg Academy of Civil Aviation: 196210 St Petersburg, ul. Pilotov 38; tel. (812) 291-28-43; faculty: air traffic control; Rector P. V. KARTAMYSHEV.

St Petersburg State Academy of Aerospace Instrumentation: 190000 St Petersburg, Bol. Morskaya ul. 67; tel. (812) 117-15-22; e-mail common@aanet.ru; internet www .suai.ru; areas of study: automation, informatics and computer systems, information systems in economics, instrumentation, law, management, radio engineering; Rector Prof. ANATOLY A. OVODENKO; library: 1m. vols; publ. *V polet* (12 a year).

St Petersburg State Academy of Refrigeration and Food Technology: 191002 St Petersburg, ul. Lomonosova 9; tel. (812) 315-36-17; depts of refrigeration engineering, equipment for food manufacturing and commerce, cryogenics and conditioning systems; faculties: refrigeration equipment, equipment for food industry, trade and public catering, cryogenic technology and conditioning; library: 850,000 vols; Rector A. V. BARANENKO.

Siberian State Academy of Geodesy: 630108 Novosibirsk, Plakhotnogo ul. 10; tel. (3832) 43-39-37; e-mail rektorat@ssga.ru; internet www.ssga.ru; f. 1932; faculties: geodesy and economics, aerial phototopography, cadastre and regional planning, management and regulation of land relations, optics and optoelectronic instruments, correspondence, evening, preliminary training; institutes: surveying and management, cadastre and geographic information systems, remote sensing and natural resources management, optics and optical technologies, distance education; library: 267,000 vols; 345 teachers; 9,500 students; Rector Prof. IVAN V. LESNYKH.

Voronezh State Technological Academy: 394000 Voronezh, pr. Revolyutsii 19; tel. (732) 55-42-67; e-mail rector@vgta.vrn.ru; internet www.vgta.vrn.ru; f. 1930, present name and status 1994; faculties: mechanical, automation, chemical, technological, technology of meat and dairy products; library: 850,000 vols; 491 teachers; 4,800 students; Rector VITALY K. BITYUKOV.

TRANSPORT

Admiral Makarov State Maritime Academy: 199026 St Petersburg, Vasilevskii ostrov, Kosaya Liniya 15A; tel. (812) 217-19-34; f. 1876; faculties: arctic, navigation, radio engineering, international transport management, electrical engineering, marine engineering; brs in Arkhangelsk, Murmansk; library: 762,000 vols; 380 teachers; 4,400 students; Pres. IVAN I. KOSTYLEV.

Baltic Fishing Fleet State Academy: 236029 Kaliningrad oblast, Molodezhnaya ul. 6; tel. (0112) 21-72-04; e-mail rector@bga.gazinter.net; f. 1966; faculties: economics, marine engineering, navigation, radio engineering; library: 165,426 vols; 253 teachers; 3,000 students; Dir Prof. A. PIMOSHENKO; publ. *Research Work* (1 a year).

Far-Eastern State Maritime Academy: Vladivostok, Verkhneportovaya ul. 50A; tel. (4232) 22-49-58; fmrly Far Eastern Higher School of Marine Engineering; faculties: navigation, ship engineering, management of marine transport, electrical engineering, practical psychology; library: 360,000 vols; Rector V. I. SEDYKH.

Kamchatka State Fishing Fleet Academy: 683003 Petropavlovsk-Kamchatsky, Klyuchevskaya ul. 35; tel. (41500) 22-45-38; e-mail rektor@marine.kamchatka.su; f. 1987; trains specialists for the fishing industry, navigators, marine engineers, electrical engineers, radio engineers, technologists and refrigeration engineers; library: 70,000 vols; 250 teachers; 2,000 students; Rector BORIS I. OLEINIKOV; publ. *Conference Papers* (1 a year).

Moscow State Academy of Water Transport: 115407 Moscow, ul. Sudostroitelnaya 46; tel. (495) 116-30-88; f. 1980; faculties of marine engineering, operations, navigation, mechanization and automation of ports, hydrotechnical construction, engineering economics, legislation, international economic management for water sports; library: 106,000 vols; 5,000 students; Rector Prof. N. P. GARANIN.

Novorossiisk State Maritime Academy: 353918 Novorossiisk, pr. Lenina 93; tel. (8617) 23-03-93; f. 1975; trains specialists in navigation, ship power plant operation, ship electrical and automated equipment operation, ship radio equipment operation, economics and management for the merchant marine; library: 267,000 vols; Dir VASILY GUTSULYAK.

Novosibirsk State Academy of Water Transport: 630099 Novosibirsk, ul. Shchetinkina 33; tel. (3832) 22-24-28; e-mail vyacheslavh@mail.ru; f. 1951; faculties: hydroengineering for waterways and ports, navigation and operation of water transport, ship engineers, electrical engineering, water transport management and economics; library: 450,000 vols; 380 teachers; 10,000 students; Dir I. A. RAGULIN.

Volga State Academy of Water Transport: 603600 Nizhnii Novgorod, ul. Nesterova 5; tel. (8312) 36-37-80; courses in: transport operation and navigation, shipbuilding and ocean technology, land transport systems, electromechanics, electrical engineering, hydrotechnical construction, economics, business management, law; library: 500,000 vols.

Institutes of Higher Education

ARCHITECTURE AND CIVIL ENGINEERING

Moscow Architectural Institute: 103754 Moscow Centre GSP, ul. Rozhdestvenka 11; tel. (495) 924-79-90; e-mail marhi@marhi.ru; internet www.miarch.ru; f. 1866; library: 400,000 vols; 400 teachers; 2,000 students; Pres. ALEKSANDR P. KUDRYAVTSEV.

Moscow Institute of Municipal Economy and Construction: 109807 Moscow, Srednyaya Kalitnikovskaya ul. 30; tel. (495) 278-32-05; f. 1944; faculties of construction, technology, mechanical engineering, urban construction, ecology and sanitary engineering, engineering, management and economics, commerce; 500 teachers; 13,000 students; library: 600,000 vols; Rector N. V. KOLKUNOV.

Novosibirsk Architectural Institute: 630008 Novosibirsk, Belinskogo 151; tel. (3832) 66-42-64; f. 1989; architecture, design; library: 50,000 vols.

AGRICULTURE AND VETERINARY SCIENCE

All-Russian Extra-Mural Agricultural Institute: 143900 Moscow oblast, Balashikha 8; tel. (095) 521-24-64; f. 1930; depts: agriculture, economics and management, electrification, information technology in economics and law, mechanization, zoological engineering; library: 517,000 vols; Rector L. Y. KISELEV; publ. collections of scientific works of the institute (1 a year).

Azov-Black Sea Institute of Agricultural Mechanization: 347720 Rostov oblast, Zernograd, ul. Lenina 21; tel. (08536) 3-18-31; library: 192,000 vols; Rector B. M. TITOV.

Kabardino-Balkar Land Improvement Institute: 360004 Nalchik, ul. L. Tolstogo 185; tel. (86600) 5-69-43.

Kurgan Agricultural Institute: 641311 Kurgan oblast, Ketovskii raion, selo Lesnikovo; tel. (35222) 9-41-40; f. 1944; depts: agronomy, zootechnics, economics, mechan-

ization, industrial and civil construction; library: 358,600 vols; Rector V. D. PAVLOV.

Omsk Veterinary Institute: 664007 Omsk, Oktyabrskaya ul 92; tel. (3812) 24-15-35; f. 1918; library: 205,000 vols; 230 teachers; 2,600 students; Dir Prof. GENNADY A. KHONIN.

St Petersburg Veterinary Institute: 196006 St Petersburg, Moskovskii pr. 112; tel. (812) 298-36-31; f. 1919; library: 194,000 vols; 140 teachers; 1,340 students; Rector G. S. KUZNETSOV; publ. *Trudy* (Works).

Samara Agricultural Institute: 446400 Kinel, Poselok Ust-Kinelskii; tel. (8462) 4-68-72; f. 1919; depts: agronomy, animal husbandry, mechanization; library: 215,000 vols; 210 teachers; 3,500 students; Rector N. S. SHIBRAEV.

Saratov Animal Husbandry and Veterinary Institute: 410071 Saratov, Bol. Sadovaya 220; tel. (8452) 24-45-32; f. 1918; library: 376,500 vols; 213 teachers; 4,500 students; Rector V. I. VOROBYEV.

Saratov Institute of Agricultural Engineering: 410740 Saratov, Sovetskaya ul. 60; tel. (8452) 24-37-66; f. 1932; library: 550,000 vols; 320 teachers; 3,500 students; Rector A. G. RYBALKO.

Tver Agricultural Institute: 171314 Tver, p/o Sakharovo; tel. (822) 39-92-32.

Yakutsk Agricultural Institute: 677891 Yakutsk, ul. P. Morozova 2; tel. (41122) 2-23-20.

ECONOMICS, LAW AND POLITICS

All-Russian Distance Institute of Finance and Economics: 121807 Moscow, ul. Oleko Dundicha 23; tel. (95) 144-85-19; faculties: finance and credit, accounting, management, marketing; depts and brs in 21 Russian cities; library: 1.5m. vols.

Far Eastern Institute of Trade: 690600 Vladivostok, Okeanskii pr. 19; tel. (4232) 2-50-89; f. 1964; faculties: economics, accounting, foodstuffs and non-foodstuffs sciences, technology, organization of public catering; library: 220,000 vols; 572 teachers; 2,760 students; Rector Prof. L. S. PUZYREVSKY.

Institute of Business Studies: 117571 Moscow, pr. Vernadskogo 82; tel. (495) 434-92-53; e-mail ibs@ane.ru; f. 1989; independent; library: 10,500 vols; 182 teachers (32 full-time, 150 part-time); 1,500 students; Pres. Dr SERGEI MIASOEDEV.

Kazan Finance and Economics Institute: 420012 Tatarstan, Kazan, ul. Butlerova 4; tel. (8432) 36-54-41; e-mail rector@kfei.kcn.ru; internet kfei.kcn.ru; f. 1932; faculties: general economics, business economics, finance and credit, distance learning, advanced training for professionals; 240 teachers; 5,000 students; library: 330,000 vols; Rector N. G. KHAIRULLIN.

Krasnoyarsk Institute of Commerce: 660049 Krasnoyarsk, ul. L. Prushinskoi 14; tel. (3912) 21-93-33; f. 1989; library: 205,835 vols; Chief Officers Y. L. ALEXANDROV, B. K. GUSEV.

Moscow Institute of Economics, Statistics and Informatics: 119501 Moscow, Nezhinskaya ul. 7; tel. (495) 442-65-77; e-mail office@rector.mesi.ru; internet www.mesi.ru; f. 1932; faculties: economics and finance, management, law and humanities, statistics and economics, computer technology, Masters programmes; MBA; Open Education and Distance Learning Systems; Institute of Professional Development; library: 269,000 vols; 6,110 teachers (425 in Moscow, 5,685 in Russian regions); 65,000 students (10,000 in Moscow, 55,000 in Russian regions); Rector Prof. VLADIMIR P. TIKHOMIROV.

Moscow State Institute of International Relations: 117454 Moscow, pr. Vernadskogo 76; tel. (495) 434-91-74; internet www.mgimo.ru; f. 1944; faculties: international relations, international economic relations, international law, international business and business administration, international journalism, political science; library: 750,000 vols; 974 teachers; 2,848 students; Rector A. V. TORKUNOV.

Novosibirsk Institute of Commerce: 630087 Novosibirsk, pr. K. Marksa 26; tel. (3832) 46-58-52; f. 1956; faculties: trade economics, trade, accounting, technology; library: 197,000 vols; 240 teachers; 7,500 students; br. in Chita; Rector N. N. PROTOPOPOV.

Novosibirsk Institute of National Economy: 630070 Novosibirsk, Kamennaya ul. 56; tel. (3832) 24-27-22; f. 1968; faculties of industrial economics, economics and planning of supply, financial economics, accounting and statistics; library: 250,000 vols; 4,800 students; Rector V. N. SHCHUKIN.

St Petersburg Institute of Trade and Economics: 194018 St Petersburg, Novorossiiskaya 50; tel. (812) 247-78-06; f. 1930; faculties: trade economics, accounting, trade in industrial goods, trade in foodstuffs, technology; library: 595,300 vols; br. in Krasnoyarsk; Rector V. A. GULIAEV.

Saratov Institute of Economics: 410760 Saratov, ul. Radishcheva 89; tel. (8452) 26-38-50; f. 1918; faculties: industry, agriculture, credit and economics, accounting; library: 255,000 vols; 160 teachers; 4,000 students; Rector K. I. BABAYTSEV.

ENGINEERING AND INDUSTRY

Grozny State Oil Institute: 364051 Grozny, pl. Ordzhonikidze 100; tel. (8712) 22-31-20; f. 1920; faculties: geology, petroleum technology, mechanical engineering, construction engineering, automation and applied informatics; library: 175,864 vols; 340 teachers; 5,565 students; Rector I. A. KERIMOV.

Moscow Institute of Printing: 127550 Moscow, ul. Pryanishnikova 2A; tel. (495) 216-07-46; faculties: printing equipment, printing technology, engineering economics, book trade, layout; br. in St Petersburg.

Norilsk Industrial Institute: 663310 Norilsk, ul. 50-let Oktyabrya 7; tel. (3919) 42-16-31; f. 1961; faculties: mining, metallurgy, economics, mechanical technology, civil and electrical engineering; library: 300,000 vols; 500 teachers; 3,500 students; Rector A. A. KOLEGOV.

Novocherkassk Institute of Engineering Amelioration: 346409 Novocherkassk, Pushkinskaya 111; tel. (86352) 5-57-56; f. 1907; depts: irrigation and land reclamation, forestry; library: 170,000 vols; 250 teachers; 5,100 students.

Rostov-on-Don Automation and Mechanical Engineering Institute: 344023 Rostov-on-Don, pl. Strany Sovetov 2; tel. (8632) 52-93-51; f. 1960; faculties: agricultural engineering, mechanical engineering, automation and robotics; library: 237,424 vols; 565 teachers; 1,730 students; Rector N. G. CHEREDNICHENKO; publ. *Economics and Industrial Management*.

Rubtsovsk Industrial Institute: 658207 Rubtsovsk, Traktornaya ul. 2/6; tel. (38557) 3-26-29; e-mail rii@inst.rubtsovsk.ru; f. 1946; br. of Altai State Technical University; machine technology, motor car and tractor construction, motor vehicles and vehicle

equipment, foundry machinery and technology, applied mathematics, management, industrial and civil engineering; library: 130,000 vols; 193 teachers; 1,950 students; Rector S. A. GURCHENKOV.

St Petersburg Institute of Engineering (LMZ-VTUZ): 195197 St Petersburg, Polyustrovsky pr. 14; tel. (812) 540-01-54; f. 1930; faculties: mechanical engineering, nuclear power engineering, turbine manufacture, management; library: 185,000 vols; 350 teachers; 5,000 students; Rector Prof. M. A. MARTYNOV.

Ukhta Industrial Institute: 169400 Komi Autonomous Republic, Ukhta, Pervomaiskaya ul. 13; tel. (82147) 6-06-10.

MEDICINE

Khabarovsk State Pharmaceutical Institute: 680000 Khabarovsk, ul. K. Marksa 30; tel. (4210) 34-68-26.

Perm Pharmaceutical Institute: 614600 Perm, GSP-277, ul. Lenina 48; tel. (3422) 12-34-45; e-mail pfa@degacom.ru; f. 1937; library: 80,000 vols; 220 teachers; 3,500 students; Rector Prof. Y. OLESHKO.

Pyatigorsk Pharmaceutical Institute: 357533 Pyatigorsk, pr. Kalinina 11; tel. (8790) 9-44-74; f. 1943; library: 370,000 vols; 308 teachers; 2,300 students; Rector V. G. BELIKOV.

SCIENCE AND TECHNOLOGY

Bryansk Technological Institute: 241037 Bryansk, ul. Stanke Dimitrova 3; tel. (0832) 1-19-12; faculties: forestry engineering, forestry machinery, forestry management, timber technology.

Kemerovo Institute of Food Science and Technology: 650056 Kemerovo, bul. Stroitelei 47; tel. (3842) 73-40-40; e-mail office@kemtipp.ru; internet www.kemtipp.ru; f. 1972; divs of mechanics, refrigeration machines, food products technology, meat and dairy products, technology and organisation of public catering; 480 teachers; 10,000 students; Rector VLADIMIR PETROVITCH YUSTRATOV.

Moscow State Food Institute: 109803 Moscow, Zemlynoi Val 73; tel. (495) 915-03-40; f. 1953; faculties: bread products, fish breeding and biotechnology, industrial economics, mechanical engineering; brs in Krasnoyarsk, Vyazma and Rostov; 211 teachers; library: 380,000 vols; Rector O. K. FILATOV.

Moscow Technological Institute: 141220 Moscow oblast, Pushkinskii raion, pos. Cherkizovo 1, Glavnaya ul. 99; tel. (495) 584-30-86; faculties: art and technology, chemical technology, engineering economics, mechanical and radio engineering; brs in St Petersburg, Ufa and Tolyatti.

Omsk Technological Institute for Service Industries: 644099 Omsk, Krasnogvardeiskaya 9; tel. (3812) 24-16-93; faculties of art and technology, engineering economics.

Penza Technological Institute: 440600 Penza, pr. Baidukova 1A; tel. (8412) 55-60-86; e-mail rector@vmis.pti.ac.ru; faculties: mechanical engineering, computer science, economics; library: 140,000 vols; Rector Prof. V. B. MOISEEV.

Russian Extra-Mural Institute of the Textile and Light Industries: 123298 Moscow, ul. Narodnogo Opolcheniya 38, korp. 2; tel. (095) 943-63-59; f. 1932; faculties: textile industry technology, light industry technology, chemical technology, electrical engineering, engineering economics; brs in Barnaul, Ufa, Kemerovo and Omsk; library:

780,000 vols; 350 teachers; 13,000 students; Rector V. S. STRELYAEV.

Shakhty Technological Institute for Service Industries: 346500 Rostov oblast, Shakhty, ul. Shevchenko 147; tel. (8536) 2-20-37; f. 1969; courses in fields of municipal finance and planning, light industry, service industries; library: 370,000 vols, 250,000 patent documents; 300 teachers; 2,000 full-time students; Rector Prof. VICTOR ROMANOV; publ. *Sbornik Rabot Instituta* (collected works, 1 a year).

TRANSPORT

Irkutsk Institute of Railway Engineers: 664074 Irkutsk, ul. Chernyshevskogo 15; tel. (3952) 28-27-12; faculties: electromechanical, construction, traffic management; library: 116,000 vols; 497 teachers; Rector L. P. SURKOV.

Samara Institute of Railway Engineers: 443066 Samara 9, Pervyi Bezymyannyi per. 18; tel. (8462) 51-75-09; faculties: construction, electromechanical, electrotechnical, operating; library: 260,000 vols; 6,000 students; Rector Prof. V. V. IVANOVICH.

Siberian Motor and Highway Institute: 644080 Omsk, pr. Mira 5; tel. (38112) 65-03-02; e-mail info@sibadi.omsk.ru; internet www.sibadi.omsk.ru; f. 1930; faculties: road-building machinery, highway and airport building, bridges and tunnels, industrial and civil engineering, vehicles and vehicle services, traffic organization and services management, road transport economics and management; library: 747,000 vols; 500 teachers; 5,000 students; Rector V. A. SALNIKOV.

Schools of Art and Music
CONSERVATOIRES AND SCHOOLS OF MUSIC

Astrakhan State Conservatoire: 414000 Astrakhan, Sovetskaya ul. 23; tel. (8510) 2-93-11; f. 1969; courses: choral conducting, orchestral instruments, piano, folk instruments, singing, musicology; 450 students; Rector GEORGI I. SLAVNIKOV.

Kazan State Conservatoire: 420015 Tatarstan, Kazan, Bol. Krasnaya ul. 38; tel. (8432) 36-55-33; f. 1945; piano, organ, orchestral and folk instruments, composition, singing, choral conducting, musicology; library: 223,000 vols; 178 teachers; 659 students; Rector R. K. ABDULLIN.

Moscow State Conservatoire 'P. I. Tchaikovsky': 103871 Moscow, ul. Bolshaya Nikitskaya 13; tel. (495) 229-06-41; internet www.mosconsv.ru; f. 1866; faculties: piano, orchestral instruments, singing, operatic and symphonic conducting, choral conducting, composition, musicology; 386 teachers; 865 students; library: 1,244,412 vols; Rector M. A. OVCHINNIKOV (acting).

Nizhnii Novgorod State Conservatoire 'M. I. Glinka': 603600 Nizhnii Novgorod GSP-30, ul. Piskunova 40; tel. (8312) 36-45-27; f. 1946; piano, orchestral and folk instruments, singing, choral conducting, opera and symphony conducting, composition, musicology; library: 130,000 vols; 170 teachers; 700 students; Rector E. B. FERTELMEISTER.

Novosibirsk State Conservatoire 'M. I. Glinka': 630099 Novosibirsk, Sovetskaya ul. 31; tel. (3832) 22-25-22; f. 1956; piano, orchestral and folk instruments, singing, symphony and choral conducting, composition, musicology; library: 104,000 vols; Rector Prof. Dr E. G. GURENKO.

Rostov State Conservatoire 'S. V. Rakhmaninov': 344008 Rostov-on-Don, Budennovsky pr. 23; tel. (8632) 62-36-14; e-mail rostcons@aaanet.ru; internet www.rostcons .aaanet.ru; f. 1967 (fmrly Rostov Musical Pedagogical Institute, present name 1992); courses: piano, orchestral instruments, folk instruments, singing, choral conducting, orchestral conducting, composition, musicology, jazz; library: 204,000 vols; 124 teachers; 630 students; Prin. Prof. A. S. DANILOV.

Russian State Academy of Music 'Gnesins': 121069 Moscow, Povarskaya ul. 30–36; tel. (495) 291-15-54; f. 1944; 476 teachers; 1,337 students; Prin. Prof. S. M. KOLOBKOV.

St Petersburg State Conservatoire 'N. A. Rimsky-Korsakov': 190000 St Petersburg, Teatralnaya pl. 3; tel. (812) 314-96-93; e-mail info@conservatory.ru; internet www .conservatory.ru; f. 1862; piano, orchestral instruments, singing, operatic, symphonic and choral conducting, composition, musicology, opera and ballet direction, musical comedy, folk instruments; library: 462,000 vols, 2,431 incunabula, 7,000 MSS of Russian and European composers; 266 teachers; 1,000 students; Rector S. P. ROLDUGIN; publ. *Teatralnaya Ploshchad* (6 a year).

Saratov State Conservatoire 'L. V. Sobinov': 410600 Saratov, pr. Kirova 1; tel. (8452) 26-06-38; piano, orchestral and folk instruments, choral conducting, singing, composition, musicology, theatre and cinema acting, musical comedy acting; library: 54,065 vols; Rector Prof. VALERY P. LOMAKO.

Urals State Conservatoire 'M. P. Mussorgsky': 620014 Ekaterinburg, pr. Lenina 26; tel. (343) 271-21-80; e-mail mail@uscon .ru; internet www.uscon.ru; f. 1934; piano, orchestral and folk instruments, singing, choral conducting, composition, musicology, sound production; library: 130,000 vols; 190 teachers; 700 students; Rector Prof. MIKHAIL V. ANDRIANOV.

SCHOOLS OF ARTS AND CULTURE

Altai State Institute of Culture: 656055 Barnaul, ul. Yurina 277; tel. (3852) 44-57-09; tel. (3852) 44-54-57; librarianship, cultural and educational work; br. in Omsk.

Chelyabinsk State Institute of Art and Culture: 454091 Chelyabinsk, ul. Ordzhonikidze 36A; tel. (3512) 33-89-32; f. 1968; training in theatre direction, choreography, ballet, conducting, library science; library: 301,000 vols; 508 teachers; 2,700 students; Rector A. P. GRAI.

Eastern Siberian State Institute of Culture: 670005 Buryat Autonomous Republic, Ulan-Ude, ul. Tereshkovoi 1; tel. (31022) 3-33-22; f. 1960; faculties: library science, bibliography; library: 420,000 vols.

Far-Eastern State Academy of Arts: 690600 Vladivostock, Petr Veliky 3; tel. (4232) 26-49-22; e-mail dvgii@fastmail .vladivostock.ru; f. 1962; piano, orchestral instruments, folk instruments, singing, choral conducting, musicology, drama, painting, directing; library: 102,000 vols; 100 teachers; 450 students.

Kazan State Institute of Culture: 420059 Kazan, Orenburgskii trakt 3A; tel. (8432) 37-31-27; librarianship, cultural and educational work.

Kemerovo State Academy of Culture and Arts: 650029 Kemerovo, ul. Voroshilova 17; tel. (3842) 73-29-67; e-mail kemgaki@ mail.ru; internet www.art.kemerovonet.ru; f. 1969; library sciences, information technology, social education, music, theatre, video art, design, art management, worldwide art studies; library: 249,000 vols; 210 teachers;

3,000 students; Rector Prof. EKATERINA L. KUDRINA.

Khabarovsk State Institute of Culture: 680045 Khabarovsk, Krasnorechenskaya ul. 112; tel. (4210) 36-30-39; dept: library science.

Krasnodar State Institute of Culture and Art: 350072 Krasnodar, ul. 40-letiya Pobedy 33; tel. (8612) 55-30-63; f. 1967; depts: library science, folk culture; library: 152,500 vols; 267 teachers; 2,800 students; Dir IRINA I. GORLOVA.

Krasnoyarsk State Institute of Fine Arts: 660049 Krasnoyarsk, ul. Lenina 22; tel. (3912) 23-35-02; courses: piano, orchestral instruments, folk instruments, singing, choral conducting, musicology, theatre and cinema acting.

Moscow Higher School of Industrial Art: 125080 Moscow A-80, Volokolamskoe shosse 9; tel. (495) 158-01-33; f. 1825; refounded 1945; faculties: industrial arts, decorative and applied art, interior design, monumental art; library: 50,000 vols; 1,300 students; Rector A. S. KVASOV.

Moscow Literary Institute of the Union of Writers 'M. Gorky': 103104 Moscow, Tverskoi bul. 25; tel. (495) 291-22-66; library: 106,000 vols.

Moscow State Art Institute 'V. I. Surikov': 109004 Moscow, Tovarishchesky per. 30; tel. (495) 912-39-32; e-mail artinst@ online.ru; f. 1843; depts: architecture, graphic arts, painting, sculpture, theory and history of art; library: 154,000 vols; 103 teachers; 450 students; Dir A. A. BICHUKOV.

Moscow State Institute of Culture: 141400 Moscow oblast, Khimki 6, Bibliotechnaya ul. 7; tel. (495) 570-31-33; f. 1930; librarianship, bibliography, information science, cultural studies, museum studies; library: 786,814 vols; 6,000 students; Rector L. P. BOGDANOV.

Perm State Institute for Arts and Culture: 614000 Perm, ul. Gazety 'Zvezda' 18; tel. (3422) 12-45-93; f. 1975; educational and cultural work; 150 teachers; 1,800 students; library: 170,000 vols; Rector Y. A. MALYANOV.

St Petersburg Academy of Art and Design: 191028 St Petersburg, Solyanoi per. 13; tel. (812) 273-38-04; f. 1876 (fmrly St Petersburg V. I. Mukhina Higher Industrial Art School, present name 1992); faculties: decorative and applied art, monumental arts, design; library: 140,000 vols; 230 teachers; 1,100 students; Rector Prof. A. Y. TALASCHUK.

St Petersburg Institute of Painting, Sculpture and Architecture 'I. E. Repin': 199034 St Petersburg, Universitetskaya nab. 17; tel. (812) 213-61-89; f. 1757; attached to the Acad. of Arts of Russia; depts: painting, sculpture, graphic art, architecture, theory and history of art; library: 500,000 vols; 160 teachers; 1,370 students; Rector Prof. O. A. YEREMEYEV.

St Petersburg State Institute of Culture: 191065 St Petersburg, Dvortsovaya nab. 4; tel. (812) 314-11-21; f. 1918; librarianship, cultural, musical and theatrical studies, cinema and television; library: 600,000 vols; 492 teachers; 5,000 students; Rector Prof. P. A. PODBOLOTOV; publ. *Trudy Instituta* (Proceedings).

Samara State Institute of Culture: 443010 Samara, ul. Frunze 167; tel. (8462) 32-76-54; f. 1971; librarianship, educational and cultural work; library: 239,100 vols; 200 teachers; Dir Prof. I. M. KUZMIN; publs *Culture, Creative Activity, Humanity*.

Ufa State Institute of Fine Arts: 450025 Bashkortostan, Ufa, ul. Lenina 14; tel. (3472)

23-49-56; depts: piano, orchestral instruments, folk instruments, choral conducting, singing, composition, musicology, theatre and cinema acting, folk theatre, painting; Rector Prof. Z. A. NURGALIN.

Voronezh State Institute of Fine Arts: 394088 Voronezh, ul. Lizyukova 42; tel. (0732) 13-14-81; tel. (0732) 13-08-90; piano, orchestral instruments, folk instruments, singing, choral conducting.

SCHOOLS OF FILM AND THEATRE

Drama School attached to the E. B. Vakhtangov State Theatre 'B. V. Shchukin': 121002 Moscow, ul. Vakhtangova 12a; tel. (495) 241-56-44; theatre and cinema acting.

Drama School attached to the Maly Theatre 'M. S. Shchepkin': 103012 Moscow, Pushechnaya ul. 2/6; tel. (495) 923-18-80; tel. (495) 924-38-89; theatre and cinema acting.

Ekaterinburg State Theatrical Institute: 620151 Ekaterinburg, ul. K. Libknechta 38; tel. (3432) 51-36-90; f. 1985; 350 students; Rector Prof. V. BABENKO.

Moscow Choreographic Institute: 119146 Moscow, 2-ya Frunzenskaya ul. 5; tel. (495) 247-37-80.

Russian Academy of Theatre Arts: 103888 Moscow, Mal. Kislovsky per. 6; tel. (495) 291-91-92; e-mail info@gitis.net; internet www.gitis.net; f. 1878; faculties and depts: acting, directing (directing dramatic theatre, circus direction), musical theatre (musical theatre direction and acting), theatre history and criticism (world theatre history, Russian theatre history), ballet-master faculty (choreography), variety theatre (variety arts), theatre management and production (performing arts management), set design; inter-faculty depts: voice and speech training, vocal training, dance training, movement training, history of the arts, history and theory of music and musical performance, history, philosophy and literature, foreign languages, Russian as a foreign language; Rector Prof. MARINA KHMELNITSKAYA.

St Petersburg State Theatre Arts Academy: 192028 St Petersburg, ul. Mokhovaya 34; tel. (812) 273-15-81; e-mail international@tart.spb.ru; internet www.tart .spb.ru; f. 1779; drama and cinema acting, rock opera acting, puppet theatre, stage directing, theatre planning and organization, theatrical equipment and stage planning; research dept; library: 350,000 vols; 150 teachers; 1,160 students; Rector Prof. Dr L. G. SOUNDSTREM.

State Institute of Cinematography: 129226 Moscow, ul. Vilgelma Pika 3; tel. (495) 181-38-68; f. 1919; direction, shooting, screenplay and script writing, cinema studies, economics of cinematography, arts; library: 300,000 vols; 200 teachers; 1,550 students; Rector ALEXANDER NOVIKOV; publ. *Tvorchestvo Molodykh* (Creations of Young Artists).

Studio-School of the Moscow Arts Theatre 'V. I. Nemirovich-Danchenko': 103009 Moscow, Tverskaya ul. 6, str. 7; tel. (495) 229-39-36; f. 1943; drama and cinema acting, theatre directing, theatre technology, set and costume design, theatre management; library: 20,000 vols; 80 teachers; 230 students; Rector Prof. O. P. TABAKOV.

Yaroslavl State Theatre Institute: 150000 Yaroslavl, Dyepootatskaya, 15/43; tel. (4852) 22-23-11; e-mail admin@ theatrins-yar.ru; internet www.theatrins-yar .ru; f. 1980; theatrical art; library: 25,300 vols; 50 teachers; 400 students; Rector Prof. STANISLAV KLITIN.

RWANDA

The Higher Education System

Rwanda became independent from Belgium in 1962, and in 1963 the Université Nationale du Rwanda, its oldest institution of higher education, was founded. However, the vast majority of higher education institutions were founded after 1994. Three new major institutions were opened in the late 1990s: Institut des Sciences, Technologie et de Gestion de Kigali (Kigali Institute of Science and Technology), Institut Supérieur de Santé de Kigali (Kigali Health Institute) and Institut Supérieur Pédagogique de Kigali (Kigali Institute of Education). In 2010/11 there were 73,674 students enrolled in tertiary education; there are 17 public and 14 private higher education institutions. In 2011 a proposal was put forward to merge all public universities into one coherent higher education system. At the end of 2012 the first meeting was held of the group tasked with creating the University of Rwanda, the product of the merger, and it was expected that the institution would be operational at the beginning of the 2013 academic year. Some students attend universities abroad, particularly in Belgium, France and Germany.

The Ministry of Education is the national coordinating body for higher education. The Minister of Education is the Chairman of the Governing Council of the Université Nationale du Rwanda. The Council's leading officers, including the Rector and Vice-Rectors, are government appointees. The operating environment for all higher education institutions, both public and private, is defined by the Higher Education Act of 2005. From 2007 all programmes have been revised according to the Rwanda National Qualifications Framework For Higher Education, which was introduced at the beginning of that year by the National Council of Higher Education (NCHE). Within the new system, all qualifications, with the exception of Doctorate and some (research-based) Masters degrees, are credit-based.

Accreditation of higher education providers is granted by the Ministry of Education, based on a detailed report submitted by the NCHE, which also serves as the quality assurance agency for higher education.

The Certificat du Cycle Supérieur de l'Enseignement Secondaire (Advanced General Certificate of Secondary Education) is required for admission to higher education. The primary undergraduate qualification is the Bachelors degree, which is generally awarded after three years' study, although some courses are longer in duration (e.g. medicine, which lasts six years). Bachelors degrees with Honours are available, following the successful completion of between four and five years' study; all Honours programmes require the submission of a dissertation. Subsequent to the Bachelors degree, students may undertake a Postgraduate Certificate, which lasts up to one year, or a Postgraduate Diploma, which generally lasts for one year. Masters degrees require a minimum of 18 months' study, and the completion of a dissertation. Master of Philosophy and Master of Letters degrees require a minimum of two years' study, and the completion of a dissertation, which must be presented and defended in front of an examining panel. Doctorate degrees require a minimum of three years' additional study and research and the completion of a thesis, which must demonstrate an independent and original contribution to the studied subject, and which must be presented and defended in front of an examining panel.

The universities and specialist institutes offer post-secondary technical and vocational education. Courses last two to three years and students receive (usually) the Diplôme de Technicien Supérieur, Diplôme d'Ingénieur Technicien or Diplôme d'Ingénieur des Travaux. In 2010 a total of 11,315 students were enrolled in vocational training education courses.

Regulatory Bodies

GOVERNMENT

Ministry of Education: POB 622, Kigali; tel. (250) 583051; e-mail info@mineduc.gov.rw; internet www.mineduc.gov.rw; Minister Dr VINCENT BIRUTA.

Ministry of Sports and Culture: BP 1044, Kigali; tel. (250) 252583531; e-mail info@minispoc.gov.rw; internet www.minispoc.gov.rw; Minister PROTAIS MITALI KABANDA.

NATIONAL BODIES

National Council for Higher Education: 2nd Fl., MINEDUC Bldg, POB 6311, Kigali; e-mail info@hec.gov.rw; internet www.hec.gov.rw; assures maintenance in the quality of higher education; upholds int. standards; ensures access to affordable higher education for capacity building; Exec. Dir Dr INNOCENT MUGISHA.

Learned Society

GENERAL

UNESCO Office Kigali: BP2502, Kigali; MINEDUC Compound, Kigali; e-mail kigali@unesco.org; Programme Specialist CONSTANTINO CONSTATINI.

Research Institutes

GENERAL

Institute for Scientific and Technological Research: BP 227, Butare; tel. (250) 530395; e-mail irst@irst.ac.rw; f. 1989; pharmacology, energy, social sciences; library of 9,500 vols; Dir-Gen. Prof. Dr JEAN BAPTISTE NDUWAYEZU.

AGRICULTURE, FISHERIES AND VETERINARY SCIENCE

Institut des Sciences Agronomiques du Rwanda (ISAR): POB 138, Butare; e-mail info@isar.rw; internet www.isar.rw; f. 1962; attached to Min. of Agriculture; library of 2,500 vols; Dir Dr ELIE MUGUNGA MUHINDA; publ. *Technical Letters*.

Attached Research Stations:

Agricultural Research Institute of Rwanda–Ruhande Station: BP 617, Butare; forestry; Dir ATHANASE MUKURARINDA.

Centre de Sélection Bovine de Songa: BP 138, Butare; stockbreeding (cattle, sheep, poultry); Dir (vacant).

Station ISAR/PNAP: BP 73, Ruhengeri; Dir GERVAIS NGERERO.

Station Karama: BP 121, Kigali; plant breeding (living plants, irrigation), stockbreeding (cattle, goats); Dir Ir LAMBERT MAYALA.

Station Rubona: BP 138, Butare; laboratories (chemistry, technology, phytopathology), environmental studies, phytotechnics (living plants, cash crops: coffee, tobacco), zootechnics.

Station Rwerere: BP 73, Ruhengeri; high-altitude cultures (wheat, peas, potatoes); Dir C. SEHENE.

Station Tamira: BP 69, Gisenyi; high-altitude cultures (pyrethrum); Dir C. NTAMBABAZI.

TECHNOLOGY

Direction des Mines et de la Géologie: Ministre de l'Energie, de l'Eau et des Resources Naturelles, BP 447, Kigali; f. 1962; geological services to the Government and private industry; to prepare a geological map of Rwanda; prospecting; library of 6,000 vols; Dir EMMANUEL BIZIMANA; publ. *Bulletin du Service Géologique* (1 a year).

Libraries and Archives

Butare

Bibliothèque Universitaire: Université Nationale du Rwanda, BP 117, Butare; tel. (250) 530122; e-mail nurlibrary@nur.ac.rw; internet www.lib.nur.ac.rw; f. 1964; 290,000 vols; Dir CHARLES RUGENGAMANZI (acting).

Kigali

Archives Nationales du Rwanda: BP 1044, Kigali; f. 1979; 600 vols; Dir ELIAS KIZARI; publ. *Presidential Speeches* (1 a year).

Bibliothèque Nationale du Rwanda: BP 1044, Kigali; tel. 572730; f. 1989; 6,000 vols; Dir SÉVERIM SEKUBUMBA.

Universities

ADVENTIST UNIVERSITY OF CENTRAL AFRICA

POB 2461, Kigali
E-mail: info@auca.ac.rw
Internet: www.auca.ac.rw
Founded 1978
Private control
Language of instruction: English
Rector: JOZSEF SZILVASI
Vice-Rector for Academic Affairs: Dr EPHREM KANYARUKIGA

DEANS

Faculty of Business Administration: Dr EDISON BUTERA
Faculty of Education: Dr NDAHAYO CLAVER
Faculty of Information Technology: NIYIGENA PAPIAS
Faculty of Theology: JEROME BIRIKUNZIRA

INSTITUT SUPERIEUR PEDAGOGIQUE DE KIGALI
(Kigali Institute of Education)

POB 5039, Remera, Kigali
Telephone: 513710
E-mail: admin@kie.ac.rw
Internet: www.kie.ac.rw
Founded 1999
State control
Rector: Prof. Dr GEORGE K. NJOROGE
Vice-Rector for Academic Affairs: Prof. Dr WENCESLAS NZABALIRWA
Dir for Finance: UMURERWA S. FRANÇOISE
Dir for Library Services: THIERRY T. MBARUBUKEYE
Library of 74,159 vols, 18,054 titles, 100 e-books
Number of teachers: 190
Number of students: 4,600
Publication: *Rwanda Journal of Education*

DEANS

Faculty of Arts and Languages: Dr NSANZABIGA EUGENE
Faculty of Science: Dr JEAN DE DIEU BAZIRUWIHA

KIGALI INSTITUTE OF SCIENCE AND TECHNOLOGY

Ave de l'Armée, POB 3900, Kigali
Telephone: (250) 574696
E-mail: info@kist.ac.rw
Internet: www.kist.ac.rw
Founded 1997
Academic year: February to November
Rector: Prof. Dr MARIE CHRISTINA GASINGIRWA (acting)
Vice-Rector for Academic Affairs: Prof. JOLLY MAZIMHAKA (acting)
Vice-Rector for Finance and Admin.: Dr GATABAZI EMMANUEL THOMAS
Dir for Academic Services: Prof. ELIPHAZ BISANDA
Dir for Admin.: LAURENCE MUKANDINDA
Dir for Finance: CALISTUS OBIERO
Chief Librarian: ALPHONSE NGABONZIZA
Number of teachers: 170
Number of students: 2,500

DEANS

Faculty of Applied Sciences: Dr ANTONIE NSABIMANA

Faculty of Architecture and Environmental Design: Prof. AKINYEMI
Faculty of Engineering: Dr MBEREYAHO LEOPOLD

NATIONAL UNIVERSITY OF RWANDA

POB 56, Butare
Telephone: (250) 530122
E-mail: rector@nur.ac.rw
Internet: www.nur.ac.rw
Founded 1963
State control
Language of instruction: English
Academic year: January to October (2 semesters)
Rector: Dr EMILE RWAMASIRABO
Vice-Rector for Academic Affairs: Prof. SILAS MURERAMANZI
Vice-Rector for Admin. and Finance: CANISIUS KARURANGA
Library: see under Libraries and Archives
Number of teachers: 500
Number of students: 11,040
Publications: *Etudes Rwandaises* (2 a year), *Revue Juridique*

DEANS

Faculty of Agriculture: Dr CANISIUS KANANGIRE
Faculty of Arts, Media and Social Sciences: DÉ O BYANA-FASHE
Faculty of Economics and Management: Dr JEAN BOSCO MUTAJOGIRE
Faculty of Law: Dr NGAGI ALPHONSE
Faculty of Medicine: Dr ALEXIS NYAKAYIRO
Faculty of Science: NDAHAYO FIDELE
School of Journalism: JEAN-PIERRE GATSINZI
School of Modern Languages: DEO HODARI
School of Public Health: Dr JOSEPH NTAGANIRA

Other Higher Educational Institutions

Higher Institute of Agriculture and Animal Husbandry: POB 210 Musanze/POB 3971 Kigali; tel. 255102938; e-mail isaeinfos@isae.ac.rw; internet www.isae.ac.rw; f. 1989; Rector and Vice-Rector for Academic Affairs Dr LAETITIA NYINAWAMWIZA (acting); Vice-Rector for Admin. and Finance PUDENCE RUBINGISA; Librarian ESRON UHAGAZE; 85 teachers; 2,542 students; publ. *Rwanda Journal of Agriculture Sciences* (1 a year).

Independent Institute of Lay Adventists of Kigali: POB 6392, Kigali; tel. 255107311; e-mail ict@inilak.ac.rw; internet www.inilak.ac.rw; f. 1997; faculties of economic sciences and management, environmental sciences and law; Rector Dr JEAN NGAMIJE; Vice-Rector for Academic Affairs Dr NYAMULINDA BIDERI ISHUHERI; Vice-Rector for Admin. and Finance RICHARD NIYONKURU; Dir for Library STANISLAS RUZIBIZA; publ. *East African Journal of Science and Technology* (24 a year).

Institut Catholique de Kabyagi (Catholic Institute of Kabyagi): BP 62, Gitamara; tel. 788580935; internet www.uck.ac.rw; f. 2002; 82 teachers; 1,373 students; Rector VINCENT KAGABO; Vice-Rector for Academic Affairs FIDELE DUSHIMIMANA; Vice-Rector for Admin. and Finance IGNACE NDAGIJIMANA.

Institute of Legal Practice and Development: 49 Ave des Sports, Nyanza; tel. 252533238; e-mail info@ilpd.ac.rw; internet www.ilpd.ac.rw; f. 2008; Rector Prof. NICK JOHNSON.

Institute of Technology, Agriculture and Education of Kibungo: POB 6, Kibungo; tel. 255107054; e-mail info@inatek.ac.rw; internet www.inatek.ac.rw; f. 2003; Rector DOMINIQUE KAREKEZI; Vice-Rector for Admin. and Finance BANAMWANA BERNARD.

Institut Polytechnique de Byumba: POB 25, Byumba; tel. 252564514; e-mail ipbbyumba@yahoo.fr; internet www.ipb.ac.rw; f. 2002; depts of management and devt and social sciences; Rector Prof. Dr FAUSTIN NYOMBAYIRE; Vice-Rector for Academic Affairs Prof. Dr JUVENAL NSHIMIYIMANA; Vice-Rector for Admin. and Finance JUSTINE MBABAZI NIYIBIZI.

Kigali Health Institute: POB 3286, Kigali; tel. (250) 572172; e-mail rector@khi.ac.rw; internet www.khi.ac.rw; f. 1996; 144 teachers; 1,289 students; Rector and Vice-Rector for Academic Affairs and Research Dr CHANTAL KABAGABO (acting); Vice-Rector for Admin. and Finance EUGENE KAZIGE; Dir for Library JEANNE LISE GATERA; publ. *Rwanda Journal of Health Sciences*.

Kigali Independent University: POB 2280, Kigali; tel. (250) 788303667; e-mail info@ulk.ac.rw; internet www.ulk-kigali.net; faculties of economics and business studies, law, science and technology and social sciences; 259 teachers; 2,828 students; Rector Dr SEKIBIBI EZECHIEL; Vice-Rector for Academic Affairs Dr KAAYA SIRAJE; publ. *ULK Magazine*.

Kigali Institute of Education: POB 5039, Kigali; e-mail admin@kie.ac.rw; internet www.kie.ac.rw; f. 1999; faculties of arts and languages, education, science and social sciences and business studies; 187 teachers; 4,598 students; Rector Prof. GEORGE K. NJOROGE.

School of Finance and Banking: POB 1514, Kigali; tel. (250) 574302; e-mail info@sfb.ac.rw; internet www.sfb.ac.rw; f. 2002; 598 students; Rector Prof. REID WHITLOCK.

Umutara Polytechnic: POB 57, Nyagatare; e-mail contact@umutarapolytech.ac.rw; internet www.umutarapolytech.ac.rw; f. 2006; Rector Dr JAMES GASHUMBA; Vice-Rector for Academic Affairs Dr EUGENE NDABAGA; Vice-Rector for Finance EMERY MBUGUJE NGABO.

Colleges

Institut Africain et Mauricien de Statistique et d'Economie Appliquée: BP 109, Kigali; tel. 84989; f. 1975 by the OCAM states; 3-year diploma course; library: 9,184 vols; 7 teachers; 38 students; Dir SÉRIGNE T. DIASSE; publ. *Rapport d'enquête* (1 a year).

Institut Supérieur des Finances Publiques (ISFP): BP 1514, Kigali; tel. 574302; f. 1987; attached to the Ministry of Finance; offers 2-year courses in the financial aspects of public administration; library; Dir JEAN-BAPTISTE BYILINGIRO.

Kicukiro College of Technology: POB 6579, Bugesera Rd, Kicukiro; tel. 788308675; e-mail info@iprckigali.ac.rw; internet www.iprckigali.ac.rw; f. 2008; Prin. DIOGENE MULINDAHABI; Vice-Prin. for Acad. Affairs JOSEPH MFINANGA; Vice-Prin. for Admin. and Finance FATINA MUKARUBIBI.

Tumba College of Technology: POB 6638, Rulindo Northern Province; tel. (250) 784501516; e-mail info@tct.ac.rw; internet www.tct.ac.rw; f. 2007; depts of alternative energy, electronics and telecommunication and information technology; Prin. Eng. GATABAZI PASCAL THOMAS; Dir for Acad. Services ABDUL KAYITABA; Dir for Admin. and Human Resources WILSON NZITATIRA; Dir for Finance JOHN BOSCO MACALI; Chief Librarian JEAN DE DIEU KANYESHEJA.

SAINT CHRISTOPHER AND NEVIS

The Higher Education System

The islands of St Christopher and Nevis were settled by the British in the 1620s and remained under British control until 1983, when they jointly became an independent state and joined the Commonwealth as a full member. The College of Further Education was founded in 1988 as an amalgamation of previously existing institutions and was renamed Clarence Fitzroy Bryant College in 1996. In 2000 a privately financed 'offshore' medical college, the Medical University of the Americas, opened in Nevis. The country is also affiliated to the University of the West Indies, which offers distance learning programmes through its School of Continuing Studies in Basseterre. In 2007/08 there were 859 students in tertiary education. Seven institutions offer a number of degree programmes recognized and accredited by the Accreditation Board of the Ministry of Education.

Admission to Bachelors degree courses requires sufficient passes in the Caribbean Examinations Council Secondary Education Certificate or GCE A-Level examinations. Some professional certificates and diplomas are also acceptable for entry. The Bachelors degree at the University of the West Indies lasts three to four years, although some medical degrees may last five years. The Masters degree takes between one and two years and requires the submission of a thesis. Following completion of the Masters, the Doctorate requires two to four years of further study, culminating in the submission and defence of a thesis; some courses also require students to undertake a period of internship relevant to their chosen field of study.

Clarence Fitzroy Bryant College and other colleges offer post-secondary vocational and technical education, leading to the award of qualifications such as Diplomas, Technician Diplomas and Associate degrees.

Regulatory and Representative Bodies

GOVERNMENT

Ministry of Education and Information: Church St, POB 186, Basseterre; 2nd Fl. Education Bldg, Church St, Basseterre; tel. 467-1112; e-mail education.kn@gmail.com; internet www.moeskn.org; Minister NIGEL ALEXIS CARTY.

Ministry of Social and Community Development, Culture and Gender Affairs: POB 878, Port Zante, Basseterre; Victoria Rd, Basseterre; tel. 467-1020; e-mail deptsdcga@yahoo.com; internet www.gov.kn/?q=moscd; Minister Hon. MARCELLA ALTHEA LIBURD.

ACCREDITATION

Accreditation Board: Min. of Education, POB 333, Lockhart St, Basseterre; tel. 466-8610; e-mail board_acc@hotmail.com; Chair. Dr HERMIA MORTON-ANTHONY; Sec. EVAN HARVEY.

Accreditation Commission on Colleges of Medicine (ACCM): see under Ireland.

Learned Societies

HISTORY, GEOGRAPHY AND ARCHAEOLOGY

Nevis Historical and Conservation Society: POB 563, Charlestown, Nevis; tel. 469-5786; e-mail museums@nevis-nhcs.org; internet www.nevis-nhcs.org; f. 1980; administers Nevis Field Study Centre, Museum of Nevis History (birthplace of Alexander Hamilton), Horatio Nelson Museum; 650 mems; library: materials on history and culture of Nevis, St Kitts and West Indies, Alexander Hamilton, Horatio Nelson, and Amerindians; Archives of Nevis, newspapers, and civil, parish and government records, maps; Pres. HALSTEAD BYRON; Sec. SUZANNE GORDON; Exec. Dir JOHN GUILBERT.

LANGUAGE AND LITERATURE

Alliance Française: 1 Orchid St, Greenlands, POB 93, Basseterre, St Kitts; tel. 465-9415; e-mail allfrskn@caribsurf.com; offers courses and exams in French language and culture and promotes cultural exchange with France.

Library

Charlestown

Nevis Public Library: Prince William St, Charlestown, Nevis; tel. 469-0421; e-mail lhanley@niagov.com; Librarian HAZEL FRANCIS (acting).

Universities and Colleges

Clarence Fitzroy Bryant College: Burdon St Campus, POB 268, Basseterre, St Kitts; tel. 465-2856; e-mail info@cfbc.edu.kn; internet www.cfbc.edu.kn; f. 1988 as College of Further Education by merger of 4 instns; present name 1996; Prin. MARILYN ROGERS (acting); Registrar VENETTA MILLS; Librarians LORREL BRADSHAW, LEAH LIBURD.

Medical University of the Americas: POB 701, Charlestown, Nevis; tel. 469-9177; e-mail admissions@mua.edu; internet www.mua.edu; f. 1998; Private control; library: 2,950 books, 110 periodicals; 80 teachers; 600 students (postgraduate); Pres. Dr DAVID L. FREDRICK; Exec. Dean Dr SEWELL DIXON; Dean, Basic Sciences Dr RAY LASH.

University of the West Indies, School of Continuing Studies: Basseterre; tel. 465-6583; e-mail ewiskn@caribsurf.com; Dir OLIVIA EDGECOMBE-HOWELL.

SAINT LUCIA

The Higher Education System

The island became a British colony in 1814 and remained under British rule until 1979, when it became independent (but remaining within the Commonwealth). Tertiary education is principally offered by the Sir Arthur Lewis Community College (founded 1985) and a branch campus of the University of the West Indies. In 2011 there were 2,621 students enrolled in tertiary education. In 2011/12 there were 1,599 students enrolled at the Sir Arthur Lewis Community College. The Ministry of Education, Human Resource Development and Labour is the government agency responsible for higher education.

Admission to higher education courses at the Sir Arthur Lewis Community College requires sufficient passes in the Caribbean Examinations Council Secondary Education Certificate or GCE A-Level examinations. It offers qualifications at the upper-secondary and tertiary levels. Certificate programmes last between one and two years, while Diploma courses are two years in duration. The Associate degree is a two- or three-year programme of study, depending on the subject. Undergraduate Bachelors and postgraduate Masters degrees are available at the University of the West Indies.

Regulatory Body

GOVERNMENT

Ministry of Education, Human Resource Development and Labour: Francis Compton Bldg, Waterfront, Castries; tel. 468-5203; e-mail mineduc@candw.lc; internet www.education.gov.lc; Minister Dr ROBERT KENNEDY LEWIS.

Ministry of Public Service, Sustainable Development, Energy, Science and Technology: Gresham Louisy Administrative Bldg, 2nd Floor, Waterfront, Castries; tel. 468-2234; e-mail minpet@candw.lc; Minister Dr JAMES FLETCHER.

Learned Societies

EDUCATION

National Research and Development Foundation: La Clery, POB 3067, Castries; tel. 452-4253; e-mail info@nrdf.org.lc; internet www.nrdf.org.lc; f. 1983 to promote research and the expansion of economic devt in St Lucia; provides technical assistance, training and consultancy; offers short courses in business management and admin.; Exec. Dir GERALD MORRIS.

HISTORY, GEOGRAPHY AND ARCHAEOLOGY

St Lucia Archaeological and Historical Society: Vigie, POB 3060, La Clery, Castries; tel. 453-2519; f. 1954; organizes public lectures, exhibitions and educational activities; Pres. FORTUNA ANTHONY; Admin. Sec. ERIC BRANFORD.

LANGUAGE AND LITERATURE

Alliance Française: La Pyramide, Pointe Séraphine, POB 898, Castries; tel. 452-6602; e-mail alliancefrancaise@candw.lc; internet www.af-antilles.org; f. 1994; offers courses and examinations in French language and culture, and promotes cultural exchange with France; library of 3,792 vols; Dir CLAUDE GONIN.

NATURAL SCIENCES

Biological Sciences

St Lucia Naturalists' Society: POB 783, Castries; tel. 451-6957; conservation and educational activities; Chair. CRISPIN D'AUVERGNE.

RELIGION, SOCIOLOGY AND ANTHROPOLOGY

Folk Research Centre: Mount Pleasant, POB 514, Castries; tel. 453-1477; e-mail frc@candw.lc; internet www.stluciafolk.org; f. 1973; preserves and promotes the cultural heritage of St Lucia; Chair. HILARY LA FORCE; Exec. Dir KENTRY D. JN PIERRE.

Libraries and Archives

Castries

Central Library of St Lucia: POB 103, Castries; tel. 452-2875; internet www.educ.gov.lc; f. 1847; dept of Min. of Education, Human Resource Devt and Labour; govt public library; 160,000 vols; Dir of Library Services JOHN ROBERT LEE.

National Archives of St Lucia: POB 3060, La Clery, Castries; tel. 452-1654; e-mail stlunatarch_mt@candw.lc; internet www.stluciaarchives.org; f. 1995; 6,000 vols; unselected govt records; spec. historical collns, multimedia; Archivist MARGOT THOMAS.

Museum

Castries

St Lucia National Trust: POB 595, Castries; tel. 452-5005; internet www.slunatrust.org; f. 1975; responsible for the protected areas of Pigeon Island (history, archaeology, geology, natural history), Fregate Islands Nature Reserve and the proposed Praslin Protected Landscape (archaeology, history, coastal resources, geology, flora and fauna), the Anse Galet Nature Reserve (flora and fauna, history) and several offshore islands (bird nesting sites) and other sites; 600 mems; Dir BISHNU TULSIE; publ. *Conservation News* (4 a year).

College

University of the West Indies, School of Continuing Studies: University Centre, POB 306, The Morne, Castries; tel. 452-3866; e-mail uwislu@candw.lc; f. 1948; continuing education; houses the University's Distance Education Centre (UWIDEC) linking the university campuses with eight university centres; Resident Tutor and Head MATTHEW VERNON ROBERTS.

The Higher Education System

From the 18th century the islands were under British control until they became fully independent, within the Commonwealth, as Saint Vincent and the Grenadines in 1978. The Vincentian education system is modelled on the British system. Post-secondary education is provided through the Kingstown Medical College, a campus of St George's University (Grenada), located near Kingstown. The University maintains affiliations with hospitals in the USA, the United Kingdom and the Caribbean for clinical programmes. There are also teacher-training, technical, nursing and community colleges, with total enrolment in 2000 of 904 students. The Ministry of Education is the national body responsible for higher education. In 2004 the Ministry's division of technical education collaborated with the University of Technology in Jamaica to provide one-year Craft certificates in a number of fields, such as agricultural science, and a two-year Technician certificate in business administration. The establishment and management of higher education institutions is governed by the Education Act of 2005.

Regulatory Bodies

GOVERNMENT

Ministry of Education: Halifax St, Kingstown; tel. 457-1104; e-mail office.education@mail.gov.vc; internet www.education.gov.vc; Minister GIRLYN MIGUEL.

Ministry of Tourism, Sports and Culture: NIS Bldg, Second Fl., Upper Bay St, POB 834, Kingstown; tel. 457-1502; e-mail tourism@vincysurf.com; internet www.tourism.gov.vc; Minister Hon. CECIL McKIE.

Learned Societies

ARCHITECTURE AND TOWN PLANNING

Saint Vincent and the Grenadines National Trust: POB 1538, Heritage Hall, Carnegie Bldg, Kingstown; tel. 451-2921; e-mail svgntrust@vincysurf.com; f. 1969; concerned with the preservation of the architectural, cultural and environmental heritage of St Vincent and the Grenadines; educational workshops on conservation and preservation values and skills; advises govt and private sector on sustainable devt policies and legislation; restores and preserves bldgs and objects of archaeological, architectural, artistic, historic, scientific or traditional merit; lists historical bldgs, sites, flora and fauna; maintains photographic inventories of historical and natural sites; 200 mems; Man. Dir RACHEL MOSES.

FINE AND PERFORMING ARTS

Saint Vincent and the Grenadines Vis- ual Arts Society: POB 2303, Kingstown; tel. 457-4454; f. 2003 to encourage the local devt of the visual arts; organizes exhibitions and other events; Sec. CÉCILE COMBLEN.

LANGUAGE AND LITERATURE

Alliance Française: POB 560, Kingstown; Old Public Library Bldg, Kingstown; tel. 456-2095; e-mail afsvg@vincysurf.com; f. 1969; organizes French classes, confs, exhibitions, seminars, films and lectures; Dir VANESSA DEMIRCIYAN.

Libraries and Archives

Kingstown

Department of Libraries, Archives and Documentation Services: Richmond Hill, Kingstown; tel. 457-2022; e-mail publiclibrary@vincysurf.com; f. 1893; attached to Min. of Education; oversees 20 br. libraries containing 262,000 vols; Dir JOAN L. JOB MOSES (acting); Librarian DANA NEVERSON..

Principal Attached Centres:

Documentation Centre: Richmond Hill, Kingstown; tel. 456-1689; e-mail publiclibrary@vincysurf.com; f. 1982; 15,000 vols; Librarian JEON ADAMS.

National Archives: Richmond Hill, Kingstown; tel. 456-1689; e-mail publiclibrary@vincysurf.com; f. 1990; 15,000 vols; Archivist CORDEL MATTHEWS.

National Public Library: Richmond Hill, Kingstown; tel. 457-2022; e-mail publiclibrary@vincysurf.com; f. 2011; 20 br. libraries; 5,200 vols; Dir MICHELLE KING; Librarian DANA NEVERSON; Librarian DONNA MASON-McLEAN; Librarian TRISHA-ANN MOSES.

Museums and Galleries

Kingstown

Botanical Gardens: New Montrose, Kingstown; tel. 457-1003; f. 1763; the oldest botanical gardens in the western hemisphere; conservation of rare species of plants; aviary containing St Vincent parrots; Dir EMMETT DOYLE.

Dr Cecil Cyrus Museum: Montrose, Kingstown; tel. 457-8981; e-mail cyrusclinic@caribsurf.com; f. 2002; colln of medical exhibits, 1,000 pathological specimens, 3,000 photographs; memorabilia of Vincentian life and history, historical maps; Keeper Dr A. CECIL CYRUS.

Fort Charlotte: Berkshire Hill, Kingstown; f. 1806; contains a museum depicting the history of the Black Caribs.

College

Kingstown Medical College: POB 585, Ratho Mill, Kingstown; tel. 456-4832; e-mail sgu_info@mssl.com; internet www.sgu.edu; f. 1979; pre-clinical school affiliated to St George's Univ., Grenada; Dean Dr EDWARD S. JOHNSON.

SAMOA

The Higher Education System

In 1962 Western Samoa (as it was then known) gained independence, having been governed by New Zealand since 1919, first as a League of Nations mandate and then as a UN Trust Territory. The current name was adopted in 1997. There are two higher education institutions in Samoa: the National University of Samoa (founded 1984, and into which the Samoa Polytechnic—founded 1993—was merged in 2006) and a branch campus of the University of the South Pacific, which specializes in agricultural studies and food technology. The National University of Samoa has five faculties, in which an estimated 2,000 students were enrolled in 2010. In 2011 some 1,665 students began non-university tertiary level education at the Institute of Higher Education (1,062) and the Institute of Technology (603).

Admission to non-university-level higher education is on the basis of the Samoa School Certificate, while admission to university-level higher education requires completion of Senior Secondary school and award of the Pacific Senior Secondary School Certificate. The National University of Samoa and the University of the South Pacific also offer one-year pre-university preparation and foundation courses. Sub-degree level qualifications include one-year Certificates and one- or two-year Diplomas. Undergraduate Bachelors degrees at the National University of Samoa and the University of the South Pacific last three years and qualify students for the postgraduate Masters, which requires an additional two years of study.

Regulatory Body

GOVERNMENT

Ministry of Education, Sports and Culture: POB 1869, Apia; tel. 64601; e-mail education@mesc.gov.ws; internet www.mesc.gov.ws; Minister MAGELE MAUILIU.

Learned Societies

GENERAL

UNESCO Office Apia: POB 615, Mata'utu-Uta, Apia; tel. 24276; e-mail apia@unesco.org; internet www.unesco.org/apia; f. 1984; designated cluster office for Australia, Cook Islands, Fiji, Kiribati, Marshall Islands, Federated States of Micronesia, Nauru, New Zealand, Niue, Palau, Papua New Guinea, Samoa, Solomon Islands, Tonga, Tuvalu and Vanuatu; documentation centre; Dir VISESIO PONGI.

BIBLIOGRAPHY, LIBRARY SCIENCE AND MUSEOLOGY

Library Association of Samoa: POB 1622, Apia; tel. 20072; e-mail libraryassociationofsamoa@gmail.com; internet www.las.org.ws; f. 1986 as Library Assen of Western Samoa (LAWS), present name 1997; promotes libraries, literacy, education, reading for pleasure, internet and computer use across Samoa; provides training for all Samoan librarians; preserves Samoan culture, history and literature; Pres. AVALOGO TOGI TUNUPOPO; Sec. RACHELLE HICKS; Treas. OMAR BURGESS.

Research Institute

AGRICULTURE, FISHERIES AND VETERINARY SCIENCE

Scientific Research Organisation of Samoa: POB 6597, Nafanua, Apia; tel. 20664; e-mail enquiries@sros.org.ws; internet www.sros.org.ws; f. 2006, fmrly Research and Devt Institute of Samoa (RDIS); assists farmers and businesses through scientific and technical research; CEO TILAFONO LEATIOGIE DAVID JOSEPH HUNTER.

Libraries and Archives

Apia

Avele College Library: POB 45, Apia; tel. 20831; 5,000 vols serving 520 students.

Nelson Memorial Public Library: POB 598, Apia; tel. 21208; e-mail jpgodinet@lesamoa.net; f. 1959; 1 br. library on Savaii island; 1 bookmobile; spec. collns: R. L. Stevenson, Samoa and Pacific; 92,000 vols; Sr Librarian JACINTA P. GODINET.

Museums

Apia

Museum of Samoa: POB 1869, Apia; tel. 26036; e-mail saphoe@mesc.gov.ws; attached to Min. of Education, Sports and Culture; displays lifestyles, culture, history and environment of Samoans and the Pacific; photographic colln from early missionaries; traditional forms of art and wildlife; artefacts from other Pacific people, donated during the Arts Festival in Apia.

Robert Louis Stevenson Museum: POB 850, Apia; tel. 20798; e-mail info@rlsm.ws; f. 1990; writer Robert Louis Stevenson's (1850–1894) restored house and estate; library of 400 vols; Gen. Man. LUFILUFI RASMUSSEN.

University

IUNIVESITE AOAO O SAMOA
(National University of Samoa)

POB 1622, Apia

Telephone: 20072

E-mail: secretariat@nus.edu.ws

Internet: www.nus.edu.ws

Founded 1984

Languages of instruction: English, Samoan

Academic year: February to November

Motootua campus incl. faculty of nursing and health sciences

Vice-Chancellor and Pres.: Prof. LE'APAI TU'UA 'ILAOA ASOFOU SO'O

Deputy Vice-Chancellor: Dr EMMA KRUSE VAAI

Registrar: LUAGALAU FOISAGAASINA ETEUATI SHON

Univ. Librarian: AVALOGO TOGI TUNUPOPO

Number of teachers: 140

Number of students: 2,000

Publications: *Jafnus* (1 a year), *Prismcs* (1 a year), *The Journal of Sāmoan Studies*

DEANS

Faculty of Arts: MARIA KERSLAKE

Faculty of Business and Entrepreneurship: Dr WOOD SALELE

Faculty of Education: EPENESA LAFI ESERA

Faculty of Nursing and Health Science: FULISIA PITA-UO AIAVAO

Faculty of Science: Dr IOANA CHAN MOW

Colleges

Avele College: POB 45, Apia; tel. 20831; e-mail avelecollege@lesamoa.net; f. 1924; attached to Min. of Education, Sports and Culture; 5-year courses; 520 students, incl. students from the Tokelau Islands; Prin. LAFAITELE AIGA ESERA.

University of the South Pacific, Alafua Campus: PMB, Apia; tel. 21671; e-mail enquiries@samoa.usp.ac.fj; internet www.usp.ac.fj/soa; f. 1977; school of agriculture and food technology incl. applied sciences and agribusiness (see also Fiji chapter); academic year February to December; library: 15,000 vols, 1,000 periodicals; 19 teachers; 200 students; Head and Campus Dir Dr EKPO MMAH OSSOM (acting); Sr Librarian ANGELA JOWITT; publs *IRETA South Pacific Agriculture News* (12 a year), *Journal of South Pacific Agriculture* (4 a year), *South Pacific Agricultural Teacher* (4 a year).

SAN MARINO

The Higher Education System

San Marino evolved as a city state in the early Middle Ages and is the sole survivor of the numerous independent states that existed in Italy before its unification in the 19th century. A treaty of friendship and cooperation with Italy was signed in 1862, renewed in March 1939 and revised in September 1971. The only institution of higher education is the state-run Università degli Studi della Repubblica di San Marino (founded 1985). In 2010/11 there were 44 students who attended the Università, and another 887 students were attending courses outside San Marino.

The Secretariat of State for Education, Culture and the University is the national body responsible for higher educa-

tion. The university's senior administrative and academic officer is the Rector, who is responsible for its internal affairs and external relations. The Departments, Centres and Schools constitute the university's academic division, while the Administrative Directorate deals with its financial affairs.

Admission to the university requires students to hold the Diploma di Maturità (secondary school leavers' certificate). The university employs a three-tier system of education. The first cycle is the Laurea di Primo Livello (Bachelors), which lasts three years and is followed by the Laurea Magistrale (Masters), which lasts between one and two years. The highest academic qualification is the Dottorato di Ricerca (Doctorate), which requires a minimum of three years' additional study.

Regulatory and Representative Bodies

GOVERNMENT

Secretariat of State for Education, Culture and the University: Via Napoleone Bonaparte 3, 47890 San Marino; tel. 0549-887007; e-mail segreteria.ic@gov.sm; internet www.educazione.sm; Secretary of State GIUSEPPE MARIA MORGANTI.

ACCREDITATION

ENIC/NARIC San Marino: Dipartimento Pubblica Istruzione, Contrada Omerelli 23, 47890 San Marino; tel. 0549-882550; e-mail segr.pub-istr@omniway.sm; Coordinator FILIBERTO BERNARDI.

Learned Society

LANGUAGE AND LITERATURE

Alliance Française: Centro Social Dogana, Piazza Tini, 47891 Dogana, San Marino; e-mail alliancefrsm@yahoo.fr; internet www.alliancefrancaise.sm; offers courses and exams in French language and culture and promotes cultural exchange with France.

Library

San Marino

Biblioteca di Stato: Palazzo Valloni 13, Contrada Omerelli, 47890 San Marino; tel. 0549-882248; e-mail biblioteca@omniway.sm; internet www.bibliotecadistato.sm; f. 1839; 120,000 vols, 77 periodicals, collns of posters, photographs and MSS; Dir ELISABETTA RIGHI IWANEJKO.

Museums

San Marino

Museo delle Curiosità: Salita all Rocca 26, Centro Storico, 47890 San Marino; tel. 0549-992437; e-mail info@museodellecuriosita.sm; internet www.museodellecuriosita.sm; colln of curiosities and highly unusual objects.

Museo di San Francesco: Via Basilicius, 47890 San Marino; tel. 0549-885132; internet www.museidistato.sm/museo_trad/msf; f. 1966; exhibits of the artistic heritage of the monastery and other Franciscan churches; panel paintings, canvases, vestments, furnishings, sculptures.

Museo di Stato: Sede Espositiva, Piazzetta del Titano 1, 47890 San Marino; tel. 0549-882670; e-mail info@museidistato.sm; internet www.museidistato.sm; f. 1899; reorganized as autonomous entity 1982; 5,000 objects; archaeological finds from the Neolithic to early Middle Ages; architectural remains of the ancient Basilica; paintings and objects from the 17th-century convent of the Clarisse; works of art of the Republic; San Marino coins and medals (1865–1938); Egyptian, Etruscan and Roman archaeo-

logical finds donated to the State; Dir Dott. FRANCESCA MICHELOTTI.

University

UNIVERSITÀ DEGLI STUDI DELLA REPUBBLICA DI SAN MARINO

Antico Monastero Santa Chiara, Contrada Omerelli 20, 47890 San Marino

Telephone: 378-882541
E-mail: rettorato@unirsm.sm
Internet: www.unirsm.sm

Founded 1985
State control

Rector: Prof. GIORGIO PETRONI
Admin. Dir: Avv. MARIA SCIARRINO
Librarian: Dott. GABRIELLA LORENZI
Library of 45,000 vols, 500 periodicals
Publication: *L'Ateneo del Citano* (1 a year)

DEANS

Department of Biomedical Studies: Prof. VINCENZO GASBARRO
Department of Communication: Prof. PATRIZIA VIOLI
Department of Economics and Technology: Prof. ANGELO MARCELLO TARANTINO
Department of Education and Training: Prof. LUIGI GUERRA
Department of Historical Studies: Prof. LUCIANO CANFORA
Department of Law Studies: Prof. PIER GIORGIO PERUZZI

SÃO TOMÉ E PRÍNCIPE

The Higher Education System

The Democratic Republic of São Tomé and Príncipe is a group of islands lying in the Gulf of Guinea, off the west coast of Africa. It achieved independence from Portugal in 1975. The Government has made higher education a national priority; however, São Tomé e Príncipe is a small, poor and isolated nation, and consequently faces many challenges in progressing towards its strategic goals. The Instituto Universitario de Contabilidade, Administração e Informatica was founded in 1994; it is a private institution that primarily provides vocational training.

The Instituto Superior Politécnico de São Tomé e Príncipe was founded in 1997 and is administered by the Government; it offers Bachelors degrees, particularly in teacher training, although its curriculum has recently expanded to include areas such as business administration, languages, literature and technology. The country's first university, Universidade Lusíada de São Tomé e Príncipe, was inaugurated in 2006. In 2009/10 there were 766 students enrolled within tertiary education. The higher education sector is administered by the Ministry of Education, Culture and Vocational Training.

Regulatory Body

GOVERNMENT

Ministry of Education, Culture and Vocational Training: Rua Misericórdia, CP 41, São Tomé; tel. 222861; e-mail mineducal@cstome.net; Minister JORGE LOPES BOM JESUS.

Learned Society

LANGUAGE AND LITERATURE

Alliance Française: CP 974, São Tomé; tel. 242300; e-mail alliancefr@cstome.ne.

Libraries and Archives

São Tomé

Arquivo Histórico de São Tomé e Príncipe: CP 87, São Tomé; tel. 222306; e-mail ahstp@cstome.net; f. 1969; 60,000 boxes of documents; 5,000 vols of bibliography; Dir MARIA NAZARÉ DE CEITA.

Biblioteca do Ministério de Agricultura e Pesca: CP 47, São Tomé; tel. 224657; f. 1973; 1,750 vols; Librarian TOMÉ DE SOUSA DA COSTA.

Museum

São Tomé

Museu Nacional de São Tomé e Príncipe: CP 87, São Tomé; tel. 221874; history, ethnography, religious art.

University

UNIVERSIDADE LUSÍADA DE SÃO TOMÉ E PRÍNCIPE

Rua da Caixa, 188, 1031
Telephone: 225209

E-mail: ulstp@lis.ulusiada.pt
Internet: stp.ulusiada.pt

Founded 2006
Academic year: October to July
Private control

Courses in economics and business, foreign languages and informatics

College

Instituto Superior Politécnico de São Tomé e Príncipe: Endereço Ministério da Educação, Quinta de Santo António, CP 41, Príncipe; tel. 223896; e-mail isptsp@cstome.net; internet www.stome.net/educa/isp.htm; f. 1997; Dir LÚCIO LIMA VIEGAS PINTO.

SAUDI ARABIA

The Higher Education System

The Kingdom of Saudi Arabia was proclaimed in 1932 following the unification of the central Najd (Nejd) and western Hedjaz regions of the Arabian peninsula under the rule of Ibn Sa'ud, who also established the current ruling Saudi dynasty. The oldest existing institution of higher education is the Madrasat Ahl Al-Hadith (founded 1933), a school of Islamic studies. King Saud University (founded 1957; current name 1982) was the first university-level institution. Universities mostly consist of colleges, and male and female students are often segregated. In 2010 there were 903,567 students enrolled in tertiary education. Higher education institutions in 2010 included 21 state universities, 24 private universities and colleges, 37 health institutes and colleges, 12 technical colleges, 80 teacher-training colleges for women and 18 teacher-training colleges for men. The Higher Education Council is the supreme national body of post-secondary, non-military education. Quality assurance and accreditation is undertaken by the National Commission for Academic Accreditation and Assessment (founded 2002). In late 2009 the Government announced a 25-year higher education initiative, which was intended, inter alia, to increase women's access to higher education and to improve private and teacher education. As part of the initiative, the Princess Nora bint Abdulrahman University was opened in Riyadh in May 2011; the university was expected eventually to cater for around 50,000 female students, rendering it the largest women's university in the world.

Admission to higher education is based on the award of the Tawjihiyah (General Secondary Education Certificate) and performance in the Qudrat (General Aptitude Test). The Associate degree and undergraduate Diploma are pre-university qualifications offered by community colleges and are four-semester (two-year) programmes of study. Saudi degrees are awarded on a 'credit–semester' system, whereby students are required to accrue a specified number of credits each semester in order to graduate. Both the Associate degree and the undergraduate Diploma require 48–70 credits for graduation. The undergraduate Bachelors degree is often a four-year programme of study, although degrees in professional fields of study such as dentistry, medicine and pharmacy last upwards of five years. The minimum number of credits required for graduation ranges between 128 and 204, depending on the course. Graduates holding the Bachelors degree are eligible for admission to the postgraduate Diploma or Masters degree. The postgraduate Diploma lasts one year (30 credits) and the Masters degree is a two-year course (42 credits), including submission of a dissertation. The highest university degree is the Doctorate, which requires a minimum of three years of study and research, culminating in the public defence of a dissertation.

Post-secondary technical and vocational education is supervised by the Technical and Vocational Training Corporation, and admission is based on the Tawjihiyah. Institutions offering technical and vocational education include Colleges of Technology, Higher Technical Institutes, Pre-Vocational and Vocational Training Centres, Trade Schools and Junior Health Colleges. Colleges of Technology provide two-year courses of education leading to the award of the Technical College Certificate; Higher Technical Institutes offer a Diploma programme; Trade Schools specialize in programmes of study relating to trades and professions; and Junior Health Colleges train technicians for the health services profession. In 2009 a total of 118,707 students attended 153 public technical and vocational institutes and a further 114,018 attended programmes in the private sector.

There are also eight military institutions, which are under the supervision of either the Ministry of Defence, the Ministry of the Interior or the Saudi Arabian National Guard. These institutions do not have degree-awarding powers.

Regulatory and Representative Bodies

GOVERNMENT

Ministry of Culture and Information: Intercontinental Rd, Riyadh 11161; tel. (1) 406-8888; e-mail feedback@moci.gov.sa; internet www.moci.gov.sa; Minister Dr Abd Al-Aziz ibn Mohi el-Din Khoja.

Ministry of Education: POB 1142, Airport Rd, Riyadh 11192; tel. (1) 404-2888; e-mail eportal@moe.gov.sa; internet www.moe.gov.sa; Minister Prince Faisal ibn Abdullah ibn Muhammad Al Sa'ud.

Ministry of Higher Education: POB 225085, Riyadh 11153; tel. (1) 441-5555; e-mail contact@mohe.gov.sa; internet www.mohe.gov.sa; Minister Dr Khalid bin Muhammad bin Abdulaziz Al-Anqari.

ACCREDITATION

National Commission for Academic Accreditation and Assessment: POB 8252, Riyadh 11482; internet www.ncaaa.org.sa; 17 mems; Chair. The Minister of Higher Education.

Learned Societies

BIBLIOGRAPHY, LIBRARY SCIENCE AND MUSEOLOGY

Arab Regional Branch of the International Council on Archives (ARBICA): Institute of Public Administration, POB 205, Riyadh 11141; tel. (1) 476-1600, ext. 462; close collaboration with ICA, UNESCO and other int. orgs; mems: 20 Arab countries; Pres. A. Tamini (Tunisia); Sec.-Gen. Fahd Al-Askar (Saudi Arabia); publ. *Arab Archives Journal* (1 a year).

LANGUAGE AND LITERATURE

British Council: C-14, Third Fl., Al-Fazari Sq., Diplomatic Quarter, POB 58012, Riyadh 11594; tel. (1) 483-1818; e-mail enquiry.riyadh@sa.britishcouncil.org; internet www.britishcouncil.org/saudiarabia; teaching centre (men's and women's sections); offers courses and examinations in English language and British culture and promotes cultural exchange with the UK; attached teaching centres in Jeddah and Dammam; Country Dir Alan Smart; Teaching Centre Man. (Men's section) Malcolm Jardine; Teaching Centre Man. (Women's section) Helen Glenn.

NATURAL SCIENCES

Biological Sciences

Saudi Biological Society: King Saud University, POB 2455, Riyadh 11451; tel. (1) 467-5835; f. 1975; 350 mems; Pres. Dr I. A. Irif; Sec.-Gen. Dr F. Al-Mana; publ. *Journal of the Saudi Biological Society*.

Geographical Sciences

Saudi Geographical Society: POB 2456, Riyadh 11451; tel. (1) 467-8798; e-mail sgs@ksu.edu.sa; internet www.saudigs.org; Chair. Prof. Muhammad Makki; Sec.-Gen. Dr Abdallah H. Al-Solai.

Research Institutes

GENERAL

King Faisal Centre for Research and Islamic Studies: POB 51049, Riyadh 11543; tel. (1) 465-2255; e-mail kfcrisinfo@kff.com; internet www.kfcris.com; f. 1983; part of King Faisal Foundation; research in various fields of Islamic civilization; library of 85,000 books, 2,400 periodicals, 23,833 original MSS, 13,000 microfilm and microfiche; audiovisual library of 10,000 vols; children's library of 17,000 vols; Chair. HRH Prince Turki Al-Faisal; Sec.-Gen. Dr Yahya Mahmoud Al-Junaid; publs *Al-Faisal* (12 a year),

Journal of Linguistic Studies (in Arabic, 6 a year).

ECONOMICS, LAW AND POLITICS

Islamic Research and Training Institute: POB 9201, Jeddah 21413; tel. (2) 636-1400; e-mail irti@isdb.org; internet www.irti.org; f. 1982; part of Islamic Development Bank; research to enable the economic and financial activities of the IDB's mem. countries to conform to the Islamic Shari'a; research into all aspects of mem. countries' economic and financial systems; training of personnel (but no formal teaching courses); language of instruction: Arabic; library of 9,000 vols; Dir Prof. Dr MABID ALI AL-JARHI.

EDUCATION

Centre for Research in Islamic Education: POB 1034, Mecca; tel. (2) 556-5677; f. 1980 by the Organization of the Islamic Conference, affiliated 1982 to Umm Al-Qura University; aims to promote Islamic values in education through research, devt and training; Dir Dr ABDURRAZZAK AHMED ZAFAR.

HISTORY, GEOGRAPHY AND ARCHAEOLOGY

King Abdulaziz Research Centre: POB 2945, Riyadh 11461; tel. (1) 441-2316; e-mail ibnsaud@saudinf.com; f. 1972 in memory of the late King; historical research, preservation of historical documents, photographs and other cultural material; library of 28,480 vols, 200 periodicals; also the private library of the late King (2,000 vols); historical archive incl. documents in various languages, esp. Turkish and English, and Arabic MSS; King Abdulaziz Memorial Hall shows events in the late King's life, esp. his military battles; Sec.-Gen. Dr FAHD AL-SEMMARI.

MEDICINE

Saudi German Institute for Nursing & Allied Health Sciences: POB 2550, Jeddah 21461; e-mail webmaster@sgnursing.com; internet www.sgna-sa.com; Pres. Dr SOBHI IBRAHIM BATTERJEE.

TECHNOLOGY

Bureau de Recherches Géologiques et Minières (BRGM): POB 1492, Jeddah 21431; tel. (2) 665-1104; see main entry under France.

King Abdulaziz City for Science and Technology: POB 6086, Riyadh 11442; tel. (1) 481-4329; e-mail public@kacst.edu.sa; internet www.kacst.edu.sa; nat. science agency; Pres. Dr MUHAMMAD IBN IBRAHIM AL-SUWAIYEL.

Libraries and Archives

Jeddah

Educational Library: General Directorate of Broadcasting, Press and Publications, Jeddah.

Mecca

Abbas Kattan Library: Mecca; 7,800 vols, 200 MSS.

Library of Alharam: Mecca; 6,000 vols.

Madrasat Ahl Al-Hadith Library: Mecca.

Medina

Islamic University Library: POB 170, Medina; tel. (4) 847-4080; f. 1961; consists of a central library and 11 brs; 143,000 vols, 27,772 MSS, 8,761 microfilms, 3,247 theses.

King Abdulaziz Library: Medina; tel. (4) 823-2134; f. 1983; 120,000 vols and MSS; Dir D. ABDULRAHMAN BIN SULIMAN ALMUZINY.

Riyadh

Institute of Public Administration Library: POB 205, Riyadh 11141; tel. (1) 476-8888; e-mail library@ipa.edu.sa; internet www.ipa.edu.sa; f. 1961; 240,000 vols in Arabic, English and French, 1,088 periodical titles, 55,000 Saudi public records, 4,953 official publs., 33,420 microforms, 712 CD-ROMs; Dir-Gen. EN MOSTAFA SADHAN.

King Abdulaziz City for Science and Technology Library: POB 6086, Riyadh 11442; tel. (1) 488-3555; 50,000 vols, 75,000 technical reports; Dir of Information Systems HAMAD AL-SADOUN.

King Abdulaziz Public Library: POB 86486, Riyadh 11622; tel. (1) 434-7805; e-mail hyami@kapl.org.sa; internet www.kapl.org.sa; f. 1985; 1m. vols (Arabic and non-Arabic), 1,100 current periodicals, 2,500 MSS, 53,000 historic documents on microform, 5,000 audiovisual items, doctoral dissertations; equestrian information; Supervisor-Gen. Dr. FAISAL A. AL-MUAAMMAR.

King Fahad National Library: POB 7572, Riyadh 11472; tel. (1) 462-4888; internet www.kfnl.gov.sa; f. 1968; 37,000 vols in Arabic, English, French; 150 MSS; Dir ABDUR RAHMAN AL-SARRA.

King Saud University Libraries: POB 22480, Riyadh 11495; tel. (1) 467-3404; e-mail itlibrary@ksu.edu.sa; internet www.ksu.edu.sa; f. 1957; central library and 11 brs incl. Prince Salman Central Library, Central Library for Girls (Malaz), Univ. Studies Centre for girls (Ulayshah), Faculty of Medicine, King Abdulaziz Univ. Hospital, College of Dentistry, College of Applied Medical Sciences, College of Community Services, Library of Preparatory year, Library of Teachers College; 1.54m. vols, 4,500 periodicals, 22,000 MSS, 150,400 govt publs, 24,000 microfilm items, 4,000 microfiche items, 18,000 audiovisual items; Dean Dr SAUD LEILY AL-ROWAILY; Vice-Dean Dr ABDUL RAHMAN A. AL-SHAMMARI.

Saudi Arabian Standards Organization Information Centre: POB 3437, Riyadh 11471; tel. (1) 452-0000; f. 1972; 10,000 vols, 650,000 nat., int. and foreign standards; Dir MUHAMMAD AL-MESHARI.

Museums

Al-Baha

Al-Baha Museum: Al-Baha; tel. (7) 725-2052; f. 2003; regional archaeological and heritage collns.

Al-Jouf

Al-Jouf Museum: Al-Jouf; tel. (4) 622-2151; f. 2004; regional archaeological collns; next to ancient Mraid Castle.

Dammam

Dammam Regional Museum: Dammam 31158; tel. (3) 826-6056; e-mail offica18@school.adst.net; f. 1985; antiquities and heritage collns.

Jazan

Jazan Museum: Jazan province, Subia; tel. (7) 326-1193; f. 1991; regional archaeological collns; next to Al-Adareisa archaeological site.

Jeddah

Al-Khozam Palace Museum: Jeddah; tel. (2) 636-4271; f. 1995; Saudi history from Stone Age to Islamic Age; folklore colln.

Najran

Najran Museum: Al-Okhdood; f. 1995; housed on archaeological site of ancient city of Najran; regional folklore and archaeological collns; restoration laboratory.

Riyadh

National Museum, Riyadh: POB 3734 Riyadh 11481; tel. (1) 403-0104; f. 1999; Saudi history, archaeology, geology, trade, social life and ethnography, and man's relationship with the universe; Dir-Gen. Dr ALI SALEH AL-MOGHANNAM.

Taif

Shubra Palace Museum: Taif; tel. (2) 732-1033; f. 1995; Saudi history since Stone Age to Islamic Age.

Universities

AL-FAISAL UNIVERSITY

POB 50927, Riyadh 11533

Telephone: (1) 440-2000

E-mail: info@alfaisal.edu

Internet: www.alfaisal.edu

Founded 2004

Private control

Academic year: September to July

Provost: Dr FAISAL AL-MUBARAK (acting)

Vice-Pres. for Advancement: Prof. AHMED AL-OBAID (acting)

Vice-Pres. for Research and Graduate Studies: Dr MATHEUS GOOSEN

Dean for Student Affairs: Dr MUHAMMAD ALOWAYED

Vice-Provost for Accreditation and Quality Assurance: Prof. ALA AL-BAKRI

Librarian: Prof. THOMAS L. WILLIAMS

DEANS

College of Business: Dr BAJIS DODIN

College of Engineering: Dr ABDUL MAJEED MUHAMMAD

College of Medicine: Prof. KHALED AL-KATTAN

College of Science and General Studies: Dr NORMAN SWAZO

AL-IMAM MUHAMMAD IBN SAUD ISLAMIC UNIVERSITY

POB 5701, Riyadh 11432

Telephone: (1) 258-0812

E-mail: admission@imamu.edu.sa

Internet: www.imamu.edu.sa

Founded 1953, Univ. status 1974

State control

Language of instruction: Arabic

Academic year: August to June

Rector: HE Prof. Dr SULIMAN A. ABA AL-KHAIL

Vice-Rector: Dr ABDULLAH ASH-SHETHRY

Vice-Rector for Community Service and Continuing Education: AHMAD Y. A. AD-DRIWEESH (acting)

Vice-Rector for Female Student Affairs: Dr KHALID SAAD AL-MEGREN

Vice-Rector for Higher Studies and Scientific Research: Dr ABDULLAH H. AL-KHALAF

Vice-Rector for Shari'a Institute Affairs: Dr BANDAR F. AS-SUWAILAM

Vice-Rector for Studies, Devt, and Academic Accreditation: Dr ABDUR-RAHMAN H. AD-DAWUD

Dean of Academic Research: Dr ABDULLAH IBN ABDULLRAHMAN AL-RABEE

Dean of Admissions and Registrations: Dr SAAD A. AL-GUSAIBY

Dean of Admissions and Students Affairs in Qassim: Dr MEZAYAD IBN IBRAHIM AL-MEZAYAD

Dean of Admissions and Students Affairs in the South: Dr SAAD IBN HUSAIN OTHMAN

Dean of Higher Studies: Dr KHALID A. AL-MESHAL

Dean of Institute Affairs Abroad: Dr IBRAHIM A. AS-SAADAN

Dean of Libraries: Dr MUSAED S. AT-TAIYAR

Dean of Students: Dr MEGREN S. AL-MEGREN

Dean of Univ. Centre for Community Service and Continuing Education: Dr ABDULLAH M. AR-REZAIN

Number of teachers: 1,650
Number of students: 39,940

DEANS

Arabic Language Teaching Institute (Riyadh): Dr ABDULAZIZ I. AL-ESAILY

College of Arabic and Social Sciences (Qassim): Dr MUHAMMAD IBN SULAIMAN-RAJHI

College of Arabic and Social Sciences (in the South): Dr ALI IBN MUHAMMAD ARISH

College of Arabic Language: Dr MUHAMMAD A. AS-SEHABEAIN

College of Computer and Information: Dr ABDULLAH A. AT-TAMIM (acting)

College of Dawa and Mass Communication: Dr ABDULLAH AL-MAJALY

College of Economics and Administrative Sciences: Dr KHALID AL-MEGREN

College of Fundamentals of Religion: Dr FAHD S. AL-FUHAID

College of Islamic Call Dawa (Medina): Dr MOSTAFA IBN OMAR HALABI

College of Islamic Law and Fundamentals of Religion (Al-Qassim): Dr ABDUL RAHMAN AL-MEZAINI (acting)

College of Islamic Law and Fundamentals of Religion (in the South): Dr ABDULAZIZ IBN ALI AL-GHAMDI

College of Language and Translation: Dr MUHAMMAD S. AL-ALAM

College of Medicine: Prof. Dr KHALID A. AL-ABDUL-RAHMAN

College of Science: Dr MUHAMMAD A. AL-QADI (acting)

College of Shari'a and Islamic Studies (Al-Ihsa): Dr MUHAMMAD A. AL-JABR

College of Social Science: Dr FAWZAN A. AL-FAWAZAN

Female University Study Centre: Dr MUHAMMAD I. AL-AJLAN

Shari'a College: Dr ABDULLAH E. AL-ESA

Supreme Jurisdiction Institute: Dr ABDULLAH AS-SELAMAY (acting)

AL-YAMAMAH UNIVERSITY

POB 45180, Riyadh 11512
Telephone: (1) 224-2222
E-mail: info@alyamamah.edu.sa
Internet: www.yu.edu.sa

Founded 2001 as Al-Yamamah College; Univ. status in 2008

Private control

Colleges of business admin., computing and IT

Pres.: Dr AHMED M. AL-EISA (acting)

Vice-Pres. for Academic Affairs: Dr OWEN F. CARGOL

Dean of Women's College: Dr HESSAH M. AL-SHEIK

Dir for Student Affairs: RAMI AL-SHARAFEEN
Dir for Library: MUHAMMAD ASSIM

ISLAMIC UNIVERSITY IN MEDINA

POB 170, Medina
Telephone: (1) 847-4080
Internet: www.iu.edu.sa

Founded 1961
State control
Language of instruction: Arabic
Chancellor: Dr ABDULLAH bin SALAH AL-ABID
Vice-Rector: ABDUL MUHSIN ben HAMAD AL-ABBAD

Number of teachers: 620
Number of students: 3,140

DEANS

College of Prophet Sayings (Hadith) and Islamic Studies: (vacant)

College of the Holy Koran and Islamic Studies: (vacant)

Faculty of Arabic Language: A. D. ABDUL RAZAK BIN FARRAJ ALSAIDI

Faculty of Dawa and the Fundamentals of Islam: (vacant)

Faculty of Islamic Law (Shari'a): D. AHMED ABDULLAH

JAZAN UNIVERSITY

POB 114, Jazan
Telephone: (7) 321-0869
Internet: www.jazanu.edu.sa

Founded 2006
State control

Faculties of applied medical science, architecture and design, arts and humanities, business administration, computer and information systems, dentistry, education, engineering, health sciences, medicine, pharmacy, science, science and arts (in Al-Darb, Farasan, Samtah); Girls faculty of health sciences, Community college

Pres.: Prof. MUHAMMAD A. AL-HAYAZA (acting)

KING ABDULAZIZ UNIVERSITY

POB 1026, Jeddah 21441
Telephone: (2) 695-1995
E-mail: almodyr@kau.edu.sa
Internet: www.kau.edu.sa

Founded 1967
State control
Languages of instruction: Arabic, English
Academic year: September to June

Pres.: Prof. USAMA SADIQ TAYEB
Vice-Pres.: (vacant)
Vice-Pres. for Graduate Studies and Academic Research: Prof. FOUAD M. GHAZALI
Vice-Pres. for Post-Graduate Studies and Scientific Research: Prof. ABDULLA OMAR BAFAIL
Supervisor-Gen. for Admin. and Financial Affairs: Dr SAMIR A. MURSHID
Librarian: Dr MOFAKHAR H. KHAN

Library of 500,000 vols
Number of teachers: 1,150
Number of students: 30,800

Publication: research publs

DEANS

Faculty of Applied Medical Sciences: Prof. GHAZI DAMANHOURI

Faculty of Arts and Humanities: Dr M. A. ABOZEID

Faculty of Computing and Information Technology: A. D. KHALID BIN ABDULLAH FAKIH

Faculty of Dentistry: Prof. TAREK LOUTFI AL-KHATEEB

Faculty of Earth Sciences: Prof. MUHAMMAD R. MOUFTI

Faculty of Economics and Administration: Prof. HUSSAM A. AL-ANGARI

Faculty of Education: Dr A. I. HAFIZ

Faculty of Engineering: Dr FAISAL ISKANDER-ANI

Faculty of Marine Sciences: Dr O. A. HASHIM

Faculty of Medicine: Dr ADNAN ABDULLA ALMAZROA

Faculty of Meteorology, Environment and Arid Land Agriculture: Dr ABDUL REHMAN KHALAF M. AL-KHALAF

Faculty of Pharmacy: Dr HISHAM A. M. MOSLI

Faculty of Science: Prof. ABDULLAH YOUSIF ABDULLAH OBAID

PROFESSORS

Faculty of Arts and Humanities:

AL-BAGHDADI, M. M., Arabic Literature
AL-DIGS, K. S., Islamic Literature
AL-JERASH, M. A., Climatology and Quantitative Methods
AL-KHERIJI, A. M., Social Development
AL-ZEID, I. M., History
ANQAWI, A. A., Medieval Islamic History
BAGADER, A. A., Social Changes
OMER, M. Z., Modern History
TASHKANDI, A. S., Arabic Manuscripts

Faculty of Dentistry:

ABDULRAHMAN, A., Paediatric Dentistry
AL-JEYAR, I. L., Operative
AL-KHATEB, M. M., Fixed Prosthodontics
AL-SABBAGH, A. M., Oral Surgery
FARGHALY, M. M., Dental Public Health
KAMAR, A. A., Dental Biomaterials
KATALDO, A., Oral Pathology
MASOUD, A. J., Endodontics
MUHAMMAD, M. A., Operative
MOUSTAFA, M. A., Removable Prosthodontics, Partial Dentures
NADA, A. M., Removable Prosthodontics, Partial Dentures
OMAR, T. A., Oral Pathology
SAMAH, A., Paediatric Dentistry
SHARQAWI, M. M., Operative
SHOUKRY, M. M. S., Periodontics

Faculty of Earth Sciences:

ALLOUSH, M. A., Building Materials
AL-MAHDI, O. R., Mineral Resources
AL-NASSER, H. S., Geophysics
AL-SHANTI, A. M., Mineralogy
BASAHEL, A. N., Structural Geology
MARZOUKI, M. H., Petrology and Mineralogy
NASSIEF, A. O., Petrology and Mineralogy
RADEEN, A. A., Petrology and Mineralogy
SHAREEF, F. A., Petroleum and Stratigraphy
SHEHATA, W. M., Engineering Geology

Faculty of Economics and Administration:

AL-AMRI, B. O., Civil Law
ALAKI, M. A., Administration and Management Relations
AL-JEFRI, Y. A., Business Administration
ALSABBAB, A. A., Administration and Management Relations
AL-SOBIANI, A. A., Administration and Management Planning
BAIOUMI, A. M., Cost and Management Accounting
BAMOKHRAMA, A. S., Economics
FADEL, S. Y., International Relations
HASANAIN, O. S., Cost Accounting
MADANI, G. O., Finance and Investment
OMRAN, O. A., Law
SOFI, A. A., Financial Administration
ZA'ED, M. E., Cost Accounting
ZOBAIR, M. O., Monetary Theory

Faculty of Education:

ABDULRADHI, H. M., Physics and Theory
AL-MOJADDADI, M. H. M., Shari'a and Legal System
AL-OQABI, A. H., Modern History
AL-SHATAIRI, B. A., Chemistry
BADAWI, A. A., History
BADAWI, F. A., Ancient History
BAMASHMOOS, S. M., Educational Planning
BEDAIR, A. H. M., Biochemistry
HAMID, M. A. I., Weaving
HASSAN, N. M. A., Psychology
JALLOON, A. D., Archery
KHATIR, K. I. M., Tradition of the Prophet

KHOGALI, M. M., Human Geography
MADBROOK, N. A., Principles of Language
REDWAN, M. N., Wrestling
SHAIKH, A. A., English Language Teaching Methods

Faculty of Engineering:

ABD. EL-LATIF, A. K., Mechanical Design and Stress Analysis
ABDEL RAHMAN, M. M., Aerodynamics
ABDIN, M. F., Metrology and Advanced Manufacturing Technology
ABDUL-MAJID, S., Nuclear Instrumentation
ABOKHASHABA, A., Metal Cutting and Spare Parts
ABOLANIN, G. M., Heat and Energy Transfer
ABOLFARAJ, W. H., Industrial Engineering
ABORAZIZAH, O. S., Civil Engineering
AHMED, K. M., Structure and Construction
AKYURT, M., Mechanisms and Robotics
AL-IDRISI, M. M., Operational Research
AL-NOURY, S. I., Structure
ALP, T. Y., Physical Metallurgy
ALY, S. E., Desalination Technology and Two-Phase Flow
AWAD, A. E., Biotechnology, Floriculture
DARWISH, M. A., Rock Blasting
ELGILLANI, D. A., Mineral Processing and Metallurgy
EL-NAGGAR, M. M., Extractive Metallurgy
FATHALAH, K., Heat and Mass Transfer
FATTAH, A. A., Nuclear Reactor Safety and Nuclear Desalination
FOUAD, A. A., Nuclear Desalination
GHAZALI, F. M., Geotechnics
HAQUE, M. Z., Mine Management and Mining Law
KUTBI, I. I., Nuclear Desalination
MUHAMMAD, S. E., Electrical Power Engineering
MOUSSA, H. A., Electrical Power Engineering
NAHHAS, M. N., Aviation Engineering
NAJJAR, Y., Gas Turbines, Engines and Energy Systems
NAWAIR, M. H., Human Factors
RAIH, M. A., Aviation Engineering
RUSHDI, A. M., Computer Engineering and Electrical Communication
SABBAGH, J. A., Heat and Energy Transfer
WAFA, F. F., Structural Engineering
WANAS, M. A., Electronics
YORULMAZ, Y. K., Petroleum Refining and Petrochemicals

Faculty of Marine Sciences:

AHMAD, F., Residual and Tidal Currents
BEHAIRY, A. K. A., Modern Marine Sediments
EL-NAKKADI, A. N., Biochemistry
KHAFAJI, A. K., Marine Plant Physiology
KHALIL, M. S. M., Fish Anatomy
NIAZ, G. R., Marine Biochemistry

Faculty of Medicine:

ABDULMONAM, N. A., Community Medicine
AHMAD, A. O., Haematology
AJABNOOR, M. A., Biochemistry
AL-ARDAWI, M. S., Biochemistry
AL-AWWAD, A. M., Chemistry
AL-BADWI, A. A., Surgery
AL-JOHARI, K. M., Anatomy
AL-KHATEEB, A. M., Physics
AL-MATRAWI, U. M., Parasitology
AL-QADASI, A. A., Biochemistry
AL-SHAIKH, S. A., Paediatrics
ALI, F. M., Medical Technology
ATTALLAH, A. A., Physiology
BASALAMAH, A. H., Obstetrics and Gynaecology
FATANI, H. H., Medicine
ISLAM, S. I., Pharmacology
KHAN, N. M., Anatomy
MATIX, F. A., Microbiology
MUKHTAR, A. M., Surgery
OSMAN, O. O., Pharmacology

RAFFAH, H. M., Surgery
RAZIK, S. M., Surgery
SAJINEE, S. A., Haematology
SALAMA, H. S., Biology
SALMAN, KH. M., Surgery
SHARIF, M. A., Radiology
SHARIF, M. T., Anatomy
SHOBOKSHI, O. A., Medicine
SIRAJ, A. A., E.N.T.
SOLIMAN, S. A., Chemistry
SUKKAR, M. Y., Physiology
SULAIMAN, N. K., Community Medicine
TAYEB, O. S., Pharmacology
TILMISANY, A. M., Pharmacology
YOUSIF, K. M., Surgery
ZAFAR, M. N., Radiology
ZAHRAN, F. M., E.N.T.

Faculty of Meteorology, Environment and Arid Land Agriculture:

ABDURAZZAK, M. G., Water Resources
ABOHASSAN, A. A., Forest Management
AL-HASHIM, G. M., Environmental Toxicology and Health
AL-HIFNY, A. M., Entomology (Bees)
ARAFA, A. S., Environmental Health
EL-AGAMY, S. A., Horticulture
GOKNIL, M. H., Air Pollution
SAMARRAI, S. M., Genetics and Plant Breeding
SHAHEEN, M. A., Genetics and Fruit Breeding
SHEHATAH, M. N., Entomology

Faculty of Science:

ABOU-ZAID, A. A., Fermentation
AHMAD, I., Theoretical Nuclear Physics
AL-DESSOUKI, T. A., Laser Optics
ALHARBI, M. A., Theoretical Nuclear Physics
AL-SAYAD, G. M., Statistics
BAESHIN, N. A., Genetics
BAGHLAF, A. O., Chemistry
BANAGAH, A. A., Parasitology
BASAHEL, S. N., Chemistry
ELDIN, H. M., Environmental Microbiology
EL-MASHAK, E. M., Biophysics
EZMIRLI, T. S., Chemistry
FARAG, A. A., Vertebrate Zoology
GHANEM, K. M., Biotechnology
KHOJA, S. M., Enzymes and Metabolic Regulation
MAGHRABI, Y. M., Plant Physiology
MELIBARI, A. A., Biology
RAFI, M., Experimental Molecular Physics
SABBAK, O. A., Chemistry
SAHAB, S. M., Mathematics
SEJININ, M. J., Plant Pathology
SHAHAB, F., Theoretical Particle Physics
SOLEIMAN, A. H., Chemistry
TAHER, M. O., Entomology (Bionomics)
TAWFIK, K. A., Plant Pathology

ATTACHED RESEARCH INSTITUTES

Centre for Nanotechnology: POB 80216, Jeddah 21589; tel. (2) 695-1399; e-mail cnt@kau.edu.sa; Dir Dr SAMI S. HABIB.

Centre of Excellence in Environmental Studies: POB 80216, Jeddah 21589; tel. (2) 640-0200; e-mail cees@kau.edu.sa; Dir GHAZI A. JAMJOOM.

Centre of Excellence in Genomic Medicine Research: POB 80216, Jeddah 21589; tel. (2) 640-1000; e-mail cegmr.info@kau.edu.sa; internet www.kau.edu.sa/centers/cegmr; Exec. Dir Dr MUHAMMAD H. ALQAHTANI.

FAH Research Centre: POB 80202, Jeddah 21589; tel. (2) 695-2353; e-mail rca_kaau@hotmail.com; internet www.kau.edu.sa/rca/rca; Pres. Dr AYMAN BIN ABDULLAH HABIS.

Islamic Economics Research Centre: POB 80214, Jeddah 21589; tel. (2) 695-2751; e-mail cn-crie@kau.edu.sa; Dir Dr M. A. ELGARI.

King Fahd Medical Research Centre: POB 80216, Jeddah 21589; tel. (2) 640-0000; e-mail kfmrc@kau.edu.sa; internet www.kau.edu.sa/kfmrc; Dir GHAZI A. JAMJOOM (acting).

Water Research Centre: POB 80160, Jeddah 21589; tel. (2) 695-2507; e-mail wrc@kau.edu.sa; internet wrc.kau.edu.sa; Dir Dr ABDULLAH S. AL-GHAMDI

KING ABDULLAH UNIVERSITY OF SCIENCE AND TECHNOLOGY

POB 55455, 4700 KAUST Thuwal 23955-6900
E-mail: admissions@kaust.edu.sa
Internet: www.kaust.edu.sa

Founded 2009
Pres.: CHOON FONG SHIH
Provost: BRIAN MORAN
Dir of Libraries: JOSEPH J. BRANIN
Library of 25,000 books, 2,000 journals (incl. 1,500 ejournals), 10 online research databases

DEANS

Chemical and Life Sciences and Engineering: KEN MINNEMAN
Mathematical and Computer Sciences and Engineering: DAVID KEYES
Physical Sciences and Engineering: (vacant)

KING FAHD UNIVERSITY OF PETROLEUM AND MINERALS

POB 5082, Dhahran 31261
Telephone: (3) 860-0000
E-mail: registrar@kfupm.edu.sa
Internet: www.kfupm.edu.sa

Founded 1963, Univ. status 1975
State control with semi-autonomous operation under a Board of the Univ.
Languages of instruction: English, Arabic
Academic year: September to June (summer semester: June to August)

Chair. of Board of Trustees: HE The Minister of Higher Education Dr KHALID M. AL-ANGARY
Rector: HE Dr KHALID S. AL-SULTAN
Vice-Rector for Academic Affairs: Dr ABDULAZIZ A. AL-SUWAYAN
Vice-Rector for Applied Research and Scientific Research and Graduate Studies: Dr SALEH N. ABDULJAUWAD
Vice-Rector for Technology Devt and Industrial Relations: Dr FALEH ABDULLAH AL-SULAIMAN
Dean of Admissions and Registration: Dr MAMDOUH M. NAJJAR
Dean of Library Affairs: Dr IBRAHIM M. AL-JABRI
Library of 355,700 vols
Number of teachers: 950
Number of students: 8,200
Publication: *Arabian Journal for Science and Engineering* (6 a year)

DEANS

Computer Science and Engineering: Dr UMAR AL-TURKI
Dammam Community College: TARIQ AL-JUFRI
Educational Services: Dr MUHAMMAD S. AL-MULHEM
Engineering Sciences and Applied Engineering: Dr SAMIR A. AL-BAIYAT
Environmental Design: Dr ABDULAZIZ BUB-SHAIT
Industrial Management: Dr AREF A. AL-ASHBAN
Sciences: Dr WALID S. AL-SABAHI
Scientific Research: Dr OSAMA A. JANNADI
Graduate Studies: Dr OSAMA A. JANNADI

KING FAISAL UNIVERSITY

POB 380, Al-Hassa 31982
and POB 1982, Dammam 31441

Telephone: (Dammam) (3) 587-7000; (Al-Hassa) (3) 850-0000
Internet: www.kfu.edu.sa

Founded 1975

State control

Languages of instruction: Arabic, English

Academic year: September to June

Pres.: Prof. Dr YUSSUF M. AL-GINDAN

Vice-Pres.: Dr ABDULAZIZ AL-SAATI (Dammam)

Vice-Pres. for Academic Affairs: Dr SAAD M. AL-HAREKY (Al-Hassa)

Vice-Pres. for Graduate Studies and Scientific Research: Dr ABDULLAH I. AL-SAADAT (Al-Hassa)

Sec.-Gen.: Dr SAAD MUHAMMAD AL-HAREKY

Librarian: Dr FADEL M. HOUSAWI (Al-Hassa)

Number of teachers: 720

Number of students: 12,900

Publications: *Basic and Applied Sciences* (2 a year), *Humanities and Management Sciences* (2 a year)

DEANS

College of Agricultural and Food Sciences (Al-Hassa): Dr ABDULLAH S. AL-GAMDI

College of Applied and Community Service (Al-Hassa): Dr ADNAN AL-MULHIM

College of Applied Medical Sciences (Dammam): Dr BASIL A. AL-SHIAKH

College of Architecture and Planning (Dammam): Dr MUHAMMAD MASOUD AL-ABDULLAH

College of Clinical Pharmacy (Al-Hassa): Dr AHMED A. AL-SHAOIBY

College of Computer Science and Information Technology (Al-Hassa): Dr BADIR AL-GOHAR

College of Dentistry (Dammam): Dr ABDULSALAM A. AL-SULIAMAN

College of Education (Al-Hassa): Dr MUHAMMAD AL-OMARE

College of Management Sciences and Planning (Al-Hassa): Dr HASSAN AL-HAJHOOJ

College of Medicine (Al-Hassa): Dr ALI AL-SULTAN

College of Medicine (Dammam): Dr ABDULLAH M. AL-ROBIASH

College of Nursing (Dammam): Dr NAIF I. AL-AWAAD

College of Science (Al-Hassa): Dr SHAR A. AL-SHIHRY

College of Veterinary Medicine and Animal Resources (Al-Hassa): Dr ABDULLAH AL-AZRAGY

KING KHALID UNIVERSITY

Abha 418, Asir Province

Telephone: (7) 339-0641
E-mail: kku@kku.edu.sa
Internet: www.kku.edu.sa

Founded 1998

State control

Faculties of Arabic language, computer science, dentistry, engineering, science and Shari'a law; colleges of education, medicine and medicinal science and pharmacy; institute of English and translation

Rector: Dr ABDULLAH AL-RASHID

KING SAUD UNIVERSITY

POB 2454, Riyadh 11451

Telephone: (1) 467-0000
E-mail: rectoroffice@ksu.edu.sa
Internet: www.ksu.edu.sa

Founded 1957 as Riyadh Univ., present name 1982

State control

Language of instruction: Arabic (English in Medicine and Engineering)

Academic year: October to June

Rector: Prof. ABDULLAH A. AL-OTHMAN

Vice-Rector: Prof. ABDULAZIZ SALEM AL-RUWAIS

Dean of Admissions and Registrations: Dr ABDULLAH AL-SALMAN

Dean of Student Affairs: Dr FAHED ABDUL MUHSEN AL-MISNED (acting)

Dean of Library Affairs: Dr SULIMAN SALEH AL-AQLAA

Library: see Libraries and Archives

Number of teachers: 2,800

Number of students: 37,400

Publications: *Journal of King Saud University, Statistical Yearbook*

DEANS

Arabic Language Institute: Dr NASSER A. ALGHALI

Centre of Female Scientific and Medical Colleges: Dr AMAL JAMIL FATANI

College of Administrative Sciences: Dr ABDULLAH BIN MUHAMMAD AL-FAISAL

College of Agriculture and Veterinary Medicine: Dr AHMED BIN ALI AL-RUGEIBAH

College of Applied Medical Sciences: Dr ABDULLAH Z. AL-OTAIBI

College of Applied Studies and Community Service: Dr FAHAD N. AL-FAHAD

College of Architecture and Planning: Prof. ABDUL AZIZ S. H. AL MOGREN

College of Arts: Dr FAHAD M. AL-KOLIBI

College of Arts and Sciences in Wady Addawaser: Dr MUBARAK MUHAMMAD EL HAMAD

College of Business Administration: Dr AHMED BIN SALEM AL AMERI

College of Computer and Information Sciences: Dr SAMI SALEH AL-WAKEEL

College of Dentistry: Prof. ABDULLAH S. AL-YAHYA

College of Education: KAHID BIN FAHAD AL-HUTHAIFI

College of Engineering: Prof. ABDULAZIZ A. AL-HMAID

College of Engineering in Al-Kharj: Dr AWAD KH. AL-ASMARI

College of Food and Agricultural Sciences: Dr HASSAN A. AL-KAHTANI

College of Higher Studies: Dr AHMAD SULAIMAN AL-OBAID

College of Languages: Dr SAAD ALHASHASH

College of Law and Political Science: Dr FAHAD HAMOUD ALANAZI

College of Medicine: Prof. MUSSAAD AL-SALMAN

College of Medicine in Al-Kharj: Prof. ABDULLAH M. AL-BEKAIRI

College of Nursing: Dr MUHAMMAD S. AL-NAIF

College of Pharmacy: Dr YOSEF A. ASIRI

College of Pharmacy in Al-Kharj: Dr SALEH I. ALQASOUMI

College of Science: Prof. AWAD BIN MUTAIRIK AL-JOHANI

College of Science and Humanitarian Studies in Al-Kharj: Dr ABDULRAHMAN AL-KHEDHAIRI

College of Teaching: Prof. ALI ABDULLAH AL-AFNAN

College of Tourism and Archaeology: Prof. SAID AL-SAID

Community College in Al-Afalj: Dr RASHED BEN MUBARAK AL-RUSHOUD

Community College in Al-Majma'ah: Dr ABDULLAH ALDAHASH

Community College of Al-Quawyiyah: Dr NASER OREIFI

Community College in Al-Riyadh: Prof. SAAD M. ALSHEHRI

Olyashah Centre for Girls: Dr JAZI BINT MUHAMMAD BIN FAHD ALCBIKI

KING SAUD UNIVERSITY FOR HEALTH SCIENCES

Riyadh

Telephone: (1) 252-0088
Internet: www.ksau-hs.edu.sa

Founded 2008

Campuses in Jeddah and Al-Hassa

Pres.: Dr BANDAR ABDULMOHSEN AL-KNAWY (acting)

Vice-Pres. for Academic Affairs: Prof. YOUSSEF ABDULLAH AL-EISSA

Vice-Pres. for Postgraduate Education: Prof. RASHED SULAIMAN AL-RASHED

Dean of Student Affairs: Prof. ALI SULAIMAN AL-TUWAIJRI

DEANS

College of Applied Medical Sciences: MUHAMMAD ABDULLAH AL-KHAZIM

College of Medicine (Jeddah): Dr HASSAN SAEED BA'AQEEL

College of Nursing (Al-Hassa): Dr ABDULATIF ABDULLAH AL-FARAID

College of Nursing (Jeddah): Dr WAFIKA ABDULRAHEM SULAIMAN

College of Nursing (Riyadh): Dr HAYA MUHAMMAD AL-FOZAN

College of Public Health and Health Informatics: Dr MAJID MUHAMMAD AL-TUWAIJRI

NAIF ARAB UNIVERSITY FOR SECURITY SCIENCES

POB 6830, Riyadh 11452

Telephone: (1) 246-3444
E-mail: info@nauss.edu.sa
Internet: www.nauss.edu.sa

PRINCE MOHAMMAD BIN FAHD UNIVERSITY

POB 1664, Al-Khobar 31952

E-mail: info@pmu.edu.sa
Internet: www.pmu.edu.sa

Founded 2006

Private control

Bachelors and Masters degree level; colleges of business, engineering, IT

Rector: Dr ISSA AL-ANSARI (acting)

Vice-Rector for Academic Affairs: Dr NASSAR M. SHAIKH

Vice-Rector for Business Devt: Dr MASHARY AL-NAIM

Dir for Libraries: Dr JAMIL AHMAD QURESHY

PRINCE SULTAN UNIVERSITY

POB 66833, Riyadh 11586

Telephone: (1) 494-8000
E-mail: info@psu.edu.sa
Internet: www.psu.edu.sa

Founded 1999 as Prince Sultan Private College; Univ. status in 2003

Private control

Rector: Dr AHMED AL-YAMANI (acting)

Vice-Rector for Academic Affairs: Dr ABDUL HAFEEZ FEDA

Vice-Rector for Admin. and Financial Affairs: Dr SAAD SALEH AL-RWAITA

Dean of College for Women: Dr FADIA SAUD ALSALEH

Dir of Libraries: Prof. Dr FOUAD H. R. FARSUNI

DEANS

College of Business Admin.: Dr YAHYA N. AL-SERHAN

College of Computer and Information Sciences: Dr ELTAYEB SALIH ABUELYAMAN

QASSIM UNIVERSITY

POB 6677, Buraydah, Qassim 51452
Telephone: (6) 380-3373
E-mail: syhya@qec.edu.sa
Internet: www.qu.edu.sa
Founded 2004

Colleges of agricultural and veterinary sciences, applied medical sciences, Arabic and social sciences, computer science, dentistry, economics, engineering, medicine, pharmacy, science, Shari'a; community colleges, girls' education colleges
Number of students: 40,000

TAIBAH UNIVERSITY

Madinah
Telephone: (4) 846-0008
E-mail: dar@taibahu.edu.sa
Internet: www.taibahu.edu.sa

Colleges of applied medical sciences, computer science and engineering, dentistry, education, engineering, finance and admin., medicine, pharmacy, science

Pres.: Prof. MANSOUR BIN MUHAMMAD AL-NOUZHA (acting)
Vice-Pres. for Academic Affairs: Dr OSAMAH BIN ISMAEL ABDULAZIZ
Vice-Pres. for Graduate Studies and Research: Prof. TALA BIN OMAR HALAWANI

UMM AL-QURA UNIVERSITY

POB 715, Mecca
Telephone: (2) 557-4644
E-mail: info@uqu.edu.sa
Internet: www.uqu.edu.sa

Founded 1979 from existing faculties of King Abdulaziz Univ.

Rector: Prof. WALEED HUSSAIN ABULFARAJ
Deputy Rector: Dr HASHIM BAKR MUHAMMAD HARIRI
Deputy Rector for Graduate Studies and Scientific Research: Prof. HASHIM BAKR MUHAMMAD HARIRI
Dean of Admission and Registration: Dr ABDULLAH AHMED ABDULLAH
Dean of Graduate Studies: Dr THAMIR HAMDAN JABIR AL-HARBI
Dean of Libraries Affairs: Dr ADNAN MUHAMMAD FAIZ AL-HARTHI
Dean of Students Affairs: Dr SALIH HASAN AL-MAB'UTH

Library of 450,000 vols
Number of teachers: 1,410
Number of students: 32,000

Publications: *Journal of Arabic Language and Sharia Sciences, Journal of Engineering, Medicine and Applied Sciences, Journal of Social Sciences and Education*

DEANS

Faculty of Applied Sciences: Dr AHMED ALI AL-KHAMMASH
Faculty of Arabic Language and Literature: Dr ABDULLAH NASIR AL-GARNI
Faculty of Dawa: Dr ABDULLAH OMAR AL-DUMEIGI
Faculty of Education (Makkah): Dr ZOHAIR AHMED ALI AL-KADMI
Faculty of Education (Taif): Dr SUBHI ABDULHAFEEZ QADI
Faculty of Engineering and Islamic Architecture: Dr TARIG MUHAMMAD AHMED NAHAAS
Faculty of Medicine and Medical Studies: Prof. ABDUL-RAZZAG MUHAMMAD NUR SULTAN
Faculty of Science (Taif): Dr BAKHIT NAFIE AL-MATRAFI
Faculty of Shari'a and Islamic Studies: Dr SAUD IBRAHIM AL-SHEREAM

Faculty of Social Sciences: Dr AHMED YAHIA AL-GHAMDI
Institute of the Custodian of the Two Holy Mosques for Haj Research: Dr USAMA FADL AL-BAR
Institute of Scientific Research and Revival of Islamic Heritage: MUHAMMAD HAMZA AL-SULEIMANI
Institute of Teaching Arabic for Non-native Speakers: Dr SALIH KHAILD DERRI

ATTACHED CAMPUS

Umm Al-Qura University, Taif Campus

Al-Saddad Rd, Shihar, Taif
Telephone: (2) 749-1917
Founded 1981
Pres.: Dr RASHID BIN RAJIH
Vice-Pres. for Finance and Admin.: Dr SAAD AL-SOBAI
Vice-Pres. for Higher Studies and Research: Dr MUHAMMAD IBRAHIM AHMED ALI
Registrar: ALI F. AL-FAER
Librarian: MOHD ADIL USMANI

Library of 50,000 vols
Number of teachers: 90
Number of students: 2,000

DEANS

Faculty of Education: Dr ABDULLAH ABDUL KARIM AL-ABBADI
Faculty of Library Studies: Dr HAMMAD MUHAMMAD AL-SOMALI

UNIVERSITY OF HA'IL

Ha'il City
Telephone: (6) 531-2500
E-mail: al-ghazi@uoh.edu.sa
Internet: www.uoh.edu.sa

Founded 1998 as Ha'il Community College; Univ. status in 2005

Rector: Dr AHMED M. AL-SAIF (acting)
Vice-Rector for Academic Affairs: Dr MUHAMMAD A. AL-NAAFA
Dir of Admissions: SAUD ABDULLAH AL-GAHZI
Number of students: 16,000

DEANS

College of Computer Science and Engineering: Dr SALAH A. ZUGAIL
College of Engineering: Dr MUHAMMAD A. AL-NAAFA
College of Sciences: Dr ALI A. AL-QARAWI

Institutes of Higher Education

College of Business Administration: POB 110200, Jeddah 21361; tel. (2) 215-9000; e-mail info@cba.edu.sa; internet www.cba.edu.sa; Private control; degree level; Dean Prof. HUSSEIN AL-ALAWI.

Dar Al-Hekma College: POB 34801, Jeddah 21478; tel. (2) 630-3333; e-mail officeofthedean@dah.edu.sa; internet www.daralhekma.edu.sa; Private control; f. 1999; accredited by Accrediting Ccl for Ind. Colleges and Schools; to Bachelor degree level; Dean Dr SUHAIR HASSAN AL-QURASHI.

Dr Soliman Fakeeh College for Nursing and Medical Science: POB 2537, Jeddah 21461; tel. (2) 665-5000; e-mail college@drfakeehhospital.com; internet www.dsf-nursingcollege.com; Private control; f. 2003; women's nursing college to Bachelors degree level; Chair. Dr MAZIN FAKEEH.

Effat College: POB 34689, Jeddah 21478; tel. (2) 636-4300; e-mail admissions@effatcollege.edu.sa; internet www.effatcollege.edu.sa; Private control; degree level; colleges of business, engineering, humanities and social sciences; Dean Dr HAIFA JAMAL AL-LAIL.

English Language Teaching Institute: POB 58012, Al Mousa Bldg, Olaya Main Rd, Riyadh 11594; tel. (1) 462-1818; f. 1969 by Min. of Education and directed by the British Ccl; brs in Jeddah and Dammam; Direct Teaching Operations Man. KEVIN SMITH.

Ibn Sina National College for Medical Studies: Jeddah; tel. (2) 637-4566; internet www.ibnsina.edu.sa; Private control; under supervision of Ministry of Higher Education; MMS, BDS and Pharm-D qualifications; medicine, dentistry, pharmacy; Dean Dr RASHID HASSAN HABIBULLA KASHGARI.

Institute of Public Administration: POB 205, Riyadh 11141; tel. (1) 476-7305; e-mail esl@ipa.edu.sa; internet www.ipa.edu.sa; f. 1961; conducts training courses for govt and private-sector employees; researches into and offers advice on admin. problems; Dir-Gen. HAMAD I. AL-SALLOOM; publ. *PA Journal* (4 a year, in Arabic).

Jeddah College of Technology: King Khaled St, Jeddah 17608; tel. (2) 637-0387; internet www.jct.edu.sa.

Jeddah Health Institute: Jeddah; provides basic medical training; similar Institutes at Riyadh and Hofouf.

Jubail Industrial College: POB 10099, Jubail Industrial City 31961; tel. (3) 340-2000; internet www.jic.edu.sa; f. 1982; Private control; Bachelors degrees in chemical, electrical, mechanical engineering.

King Abdulaziz Military Academy: POB 5969, Riyadh; tel. (1) 465-4244; f. 1955; courses given in modern languages, incl. English, French and Hebrew, science and military subjects; library: 20,000 vols; 1,300 students; publ. *Journal*.

King Fahd Security College: POB 2511, Riyadh 11461; tel. (1) 246-4444; internet www.kfsc.edu.sa.

Madrasat Ahl Al-Hadith: Mecca; f. 1933; the institute provides instruction in the Hadith, Koran, Fiqh, Tawheed and other Islamic religious studies; Prin. Sheikh MUHAMMAD ABDUL RAZZAQ; Sec. MUHAMMAD OMAR ABDULHADI.

Prince Sultan College of Tourism and Business: POB 7307, Jeddah 21462; tel. (2) 667-0110; internet www.pscabha.edu.sa; Private control, King Faisal Foundation; accredited by Ministry of Higher Education; BSc degrees in business admin., hospitality management, management information systems, travel and tourism.

Saad College of Nursing and Allied Health Sciences: POB 30353, Al-Khobar 31952; tel. (3) 801-3555; e-mail college@saad.com.sa; internet www.saadcollege.com; Private control, Saad Group; attached to Univ. of Ulster; BSc nursing degree.

Technical Institute: Riyadh; f. 1964; 1,000 students.

Yanbu Industrial College: POB 30436, Madinat Yanbu Al-Sinaiyah; tel. (4) 394-6111; e-mail yic.dir@rc-ynb.com; internet www.yic.edu.sa; f. 1989; engineering technology; library: 11,570 vols; 127 teachers; 1,400 students; Man. Dir BASSAM ABDULLAH YAMANI; Registrar HAMZA ATIK.

SENEGAL

The Higher Education System

Senegal was a French colony from the 17th century until independence was achieved in 1960. The first institution of higher education, a school of medicine, was founded in 1915; this later became an institute of higher education in 1950 and was incorporated into the new Université Cheikh Anta Diop de Dakar in 1957. Université Cheikh Anta Diop de Dakar is one of the five public universities, the others being Université de Saint-Louis (or Université de Gaston-Berger—founded 1990), Université de Thiès, Université de Bambey and Université de Ziguinchor. In addition in 2011 there were 71 private institutions of higher education. In 2010 there were an estimated 92,106 students enrolled in tertiary education. Higher education is largely state funded, although some funding is provided by major international organizations such as United States Agency for International Development (USAID), the European Union (EU) and the World Bank.

From 2012–16, in partnership with the World Bank, the Government began to pursue a fundamental reform of the higher education system. The Comité de pilotage de la concertation nationale pour l'avenir de l'enseignement supérieur (pilot concertation group on the future of higher education) was put in place in 2012 to address the many difficulties being faced by universities, including lack of funding and infrastructure; its findings were due to be published in April 2013. Under the project of law linking university funding to performance (Projet de gouvernance financière de l'enseignement supérieur axée sur les résultats) an Institut supérieur d'enseignement professionnel was being opened at Thiès, offering two-year intensive courses in a professional environment in order to train qualified technicians capable of immediately integrating the workplace. There were also plans for a second university to open in 2014 at Dakar, an agricultural university at Kaolack, as well as a virtual university for distance learning.

The national body responsible for higher education is the Ministry of Higher Education, Universities and Scientific Research, while technical and vocational education is overseen by the Ministry of Technical and Professional Training.

The secondary school Baccalauréat is the main qualification required for admission to higher education, although applicants without the Baccalauréat can sit an alternative entrance examination. Legislation passed in February 2011 provided for the implementation of a new three-tier LMD (Licence–Master–Doctorat) system of university degrees, bringing the Senegalese system closer in line with the European systems under the Bologna Process in a bid to harmonize degree structures, credit systems and quality assurance procedures in all higher education programmes and institutions in Senegal, as well as in the other seven member states of the West African Economic and Monetary Union, all of which have implemented, or have pledged to implement by 2013, the LMD degree system. Under the new simplified system, the first cycle is the undergraduate Licence (Bachelors) degree, which generally lasts three years. The second cycle leads to award of a Master degree after two years' study. Finally, the third cycle consists of a further three years' study and leads to the conferring of a Doctorat qualification.

The primary qualification for post-secondary technical and vocational education is currently the Brevet de Technicien Supérieur en Maintenance.

Regulatory Bodies

GOVERNMENT

Ministry of Culture and Heritage: Bldg Administratif, Third Fl., ave Léopold Sédar Senghor, BP 4001, Dakar; tel. 33-822-4303; e-mail contact@culture.gouv.sn; internet www.culture.gouv.sn; Minister ABDOUL AZIZ MBAYE.

Ministry of Higher Education, Universities, Regional Academic Centres and Scientific Research: Administrative Bldg, Fifth Fl., Right wing, BP 36005, Dakar; tel. 33-849-7552; e-mail first@recherche.gouv.sn; internet www.recherche.gouv.sn; Minister Prof. MARY TEUW NIANE.

Ministry of National Education: 56 ave Lamine Gueye, Dakar; tel. 33-849-5402; e-mail dpre@yahoo.fr; internet www .education.gouv.sn; Minister Mgr SERIGNE MBAYE THIAM.

Ministry of Professional Training, Apprenticeships and Handicrafts: SICAP Keur Gorgui, immeuble Y1C, Dakar; tel. 33-865-7070; internet www.gouv.sn; Minister MAMADOU TALLA.

Learned Societies

BIBLIOGRAPHY, LIBRARY SCIENCE AND MUSEOLOGY

Association Sénégalaise de Bibliothécaires, Archivistes et Documentalistes: ASBAD, BP 3252, Dakar; tel. 33-864-2773; internet www.ebad.ucad.sn/asbad; f. 1988; 200 mems; Pres. DJIBRIL NDIAYE; Sec. BERNARD DIONE; publ. *Canal I. S. T.* (3 a year).

EDUCATION

UNESCO Regional Office in Dakar: BP 3311, Dakar; 12 ave L. S. Senghor, Dakar; tel. 33-849-2323; e-mail dakar@unesco.org; internet www.unesco.org/dakar; f. 1970; designated Cluster Office for Burkina Faso, Cape Verde, Gambia, Guinea-Bissau, Liberia, Mali, Niger and Senegal; Dir ANN THERESE NDONG-JATTA.

LANGUAGE AND LITERATURE

Alliance Française: 3, Rue Parchappe, BP 1777, Dakar; tel. 33-821-0822; e-mail alliancefg@gamtel.gm; internet www .alliancefr-senegalgambie.org; offers courses and exams in French language and culture and promotes cultural exchange with France; attached teaching centres in Kaolack, St Louis, Tambacounda and Ziguinchor; also responsible for operations in Gambia; Dir of Office and of Operations in Senegal and Gambia SERGE AYASSE.

British Council: Rue AAB-68, Amitié Zone A, BP 6232, Dakar; tel. 33-869-2700; e-mail information@britishcouncil.sn; internet www .britishcouncil.com.sn; teaching centre; offers courses and examinations in English language and British culture and promotes cultural exchange with the UK; library of 3,500 vols; Dir ANDREW PINER.

Goethe-Institut: Rue de Diourbel angle Piscine Olympique, Dakar; tel. 33-869-8880; e-mail info@dakar.goethe.org; internet www .goethe.de/dakar; f. 1978; offers courses and examinations in German language and culture and promotes cultural exchange with Germany; Dir UWE RIEKEN.

Research Institutes

GENERAL

Institut de Recherche pour le Développement, Centre de Dakar (IRD): BP 1386, Route des Pères Maristes, Dakar; tel. 33-832-3480; e-mail senegal@ird.fr; internet www .senegal.ird.fr; f. 1950; soil biology, pedology, medical entomology, hydrology, geology, nematology, demography, economics, zoology, botany, agronomy, geography, sociology, nutrition, marine fisheries, public health, tree viruses, vegetal ecology, geophysics, microbiology; see main entry under France; library of 10,000 vols; Dir YVES DUVAL.

Institut Fondamental d'Afrique Noire Cheikh Anta Diop: BP 206, Université Cheikh Anta Diop de Dakar, Dakar; tel. 33-824-1652; e-mail bifan@ucad.sn; internet www.refer.sn; f. 1936, reconstituted 1959; scientific and humanistic studies on Black Africa; also administers library and museums; Dir DJIBRIL SAMB; publs *Bulletin de l'IFAN, Série A—Sciences Naturelles, Série B—Sciences Humaines, Notes Africaines* (4 a year), *Mémoires de l'IFAN, Initiations et Études Africaines.*

AGRICULTURE, FISHERIES AND VETERINARY SCIENCE

Institut Sénégalais de Recherches Agricoles (ISRA): BP 3120, Route des Hydrocarbures, Bel-Air, Dakar; tel. 33-832-2420; e-mail dgisra@isra.sn; internet www.isra.sn; f. 1974; research in all fields of agriculture, forestry and pisciculture; Dir Dr Moussa Bakhayokhu..

Attached Centres:

Centre de Recherche Agronomique de Djibélor: BP 34, Ziguinchor; tel. 33-991-1205; Dir Samba Sall.

Centre de Recherche Agronomique de Kaolack: BP 199, Kaolack; tel. 33-941-2916; Dir Dr Modou Sene.

Centre de Recherche Agronomique de Saint-Louis: BP 240, Richard-Toll; tel. 33-961-1751; Dir Dr Sidy Seck.

Centre de Recherches Océanographiques de Dakar-Thiaroye (CRODT): BP 2241, Dakar; tel. 33-834-0536; f. 1956 for the study of oceanographic physics and biology; 67 scientists; library of 450 vols and 74 periodicals; Dir Diafara Toure.

Centre de Recherches Zootechniques de Dahra-Djoloff: BP 01, Dahra-Djoloff; tel. 33-968-6111; f. 1950; amelioration of local bovine and ovine breeds, rearing and cross-breeding; Dir Tamsir Diop.

Centre de Recherches Zootechniques de Kolda: BP 53, Kolda; tel. 33-996-1152; f. 1972; amelioration of local bovine and ovine breeds; fodder cultivation; Dir Dr Demba Farba Mbaye.

Centre National de Recherches Agronomiques (CNRA): BP 53, Bambey; tel. 33-973-6050; f. 1921; applied agricultural research; stations at Louga and Thilmakha; 45 research mems; library of 6,700 vols; Dir Dr Dogo Seck; publs *Rapport de synthèse, Annuaire analytique des travaux de l'IRAT au Sénégal.*

Centre pour le Développement de l'Horticulture (CDH): BP 2619, Dakar; tel. 33-835-0610; f. 1972; market garden research; Dir Dr Alain Mbaye.

Direction des Recherches sur les Productions Forestières: BP 2313, Route des Pères Maristes, Dakar-Hann; tel. 33-832-3219; Dir Dr Pape Ndiengou Sall.

ECONOMICS, LAW AND POLITICS

Institut Africain de Développement Economique et de Planification des Nations Unies (United Nations African Institute for Economic Development and Planning): BP 3186, Dakar; tel. 33-823-1020; f. 1962 under the aegis of the Economic Comm. for Africa; financed jointly by African states, the UN, and bilateral and multilateral partners; provides training through the org. of courses, seminars, etc., and undertakes research; library of 25,000 vols, 1,400 periodicals; Dir Dr Jeggan C. Senghor.

MEDICINE

Institut d'Hygiène Sociale: BP 3435, Dakar; tel. 33-822-9045; e-mail sensidacons@sentoo.sn.

Institut Pasteur: BP 220, Dakar; tel. 33-839-9200; e-mail pasteur.dakar@pasteur.sn; internet www.pasteur.sn; f. 1896; medical research, microbiology, virology, immunology; library of 2,030 vols, 88 periodicals; Dir Dr André Spigel; Exec. Sec. Camille Abbey.

Organisme de Recherches sur l'Alimentation et la Nutrition Africaines (ORANA): BP 2089, 39 ave Pasteur, Dakar; tel. 33-822-5892; f. 1953; research into African foods and nutritional values, investigations, documentation, teaching; 30 mems; Dir Dr Amadou Makhtar Ndiaye.

TECHNOLOGY

African Regional Centre for Technology/Centre Régional Africain de Technologie: BP 2435, Dakar; tel. 33-823-7712; e-mail arct@sonatel.senet.net; f. 1977 as an intergovernmental institution under the auspices of the OAU and UNECA; aims to promote the use of technology to improve the socio-economic development of Africa; advises and sets up national institutions, holds training seminars and workshops; activities include food science and technology, energy technology, technological consulting and advisory services, training and information and documentation; 31 mem. states; library of 6,000 vols, patents, microfiches, video cassettes; Exec. Dir Dr Ousmane Kane; publs *African Technodevelopment Bulletin* (2 a year, English and French), *Alert Africa Newsletter* (4 a year), *Infonet* (irregular).

Bureau de Recherches Géologiques et Minières (BRGM): BP 268, Dakar; tel. 33-822-7219; mining, hydrogeology, irrigation; also directs research in Mali and Mauritania; Dir D. Fohlen.

Libraries and Archives

Dakar

Archives du Sénégal: Immeuble administratif, Ave Léopold Sédar Senghor, Dakar; tel. 33-823-5072; e-mail pmarchi@primature.sn; f. 1913; 26,000 vols, 1,500 periodicals, 8,000 official publs, 12 km of documents; Dir Saliou Mbaye; publ. *Bibliographie du Sénégal* (2 a year).

Bibliothèque Centrale, Université Cheikh Anta Diop de Dakar: BP 2006, Dakar; tel. 33-824-6981; e-mail hsene@ucad.sn; internet www.bu.ucad.sn; f. 1952; higher education, human and social sciences, law and economics, medicine and pharmacy, science and technology, veterinary science, information science; 353,000 vols, 5,000 periodicals (of which 1,000 are current); Dir Henri Sene.

Bibliothèque de l'Alliance Française: BP 1777, 2 rue Assane Ndoye, Dakar; tel. 33-821-0822; f. 1948; 12,000 vols; Dir Patrick Mandrilly.

Bibliothèque de l'Institut Fondamental d'Afrique Noire: BP 206, Dakar; tel. 33-825-9890; e-mail bifan@ucad.sn; f. 1936; research in humanities and natural sciences; 62,640 vols, 2,972 periodical titles, 5,784 MSS, 6,200 maps; spec. colln: 750 notebooks of William Ponty; Librarian Gora Dia.

Centre National de Documentation Scientifique et Technique (CNDST): Ministère de la Recherche Scientifique et de la Technologie (MRST), 61 Blvd Djily Mbaye, BP 3218, Dakar; tel. 33-822-9619; f. 1977; maintains a database each of research instns, researchers, research projects and research results, and a socioeconomic databank on Senegal; Dir Mohamed Fadhel Diagne; publs *Répertoire des sources d'information sur l'environnement, Répertoire des organismes de documentation au Sénégal, Répertoire des textes législatifs et réglementaires dans le domaine de l'environnement au Sénégal* (1 a year), *Répertoire des textes législatifs et réglementaires au Sénégal* (1 a year).

Centre Régional de Recherche et de Documentation pour le Développement Culturel (CREDEC) (Regional Research and Documentation Centre for Cultural Development): 13 ave du Pdt Bourguiba, Dakar; tel. 33-827-8059; f. 1976; mems: 20 African states; part of African Cultural Institute (see under International); 3,200 vols, spec. collns on African crafts; Coordinator Falilou Diallo; publ. *ICA-Information* (4 a year).

Museums and Art Galleries

Dakar

Musée d'Art Africain: BP 6167, Dakar-Étoile; e-mail bifan@ucad.sn; f. 1936; administered by Institut Fondamental d'Afrique Noire; ethnography and African art; Curator Dr Tahirou Diaw.

Gorée

Musée de la Mer: Gorée; tel. 33-825-9890; e-mail bifan@ucad.sn; f. 1959; administered by Institut Fondamental d'Afrique Noire; sea sciences, oceanography, fishing; colln of 6,000 species of fish, molluscs, polychaete worms, birds, fishing equipment; Curator Dr Seck.

Musée Historique de Gorée: Gorée; e-mail bifan@ucad.sn; administered by Institut Fondamental d'Afrique Noire; exhibitions covering Senegal from prehistory to the present day; Curator Dr Abdoulaye Camara.

Universities

UNIVERSITÉ CHEIKH ANTA DIOP DE DAKAR

BP 5005, Dakar-Fann

Telephone: 33-825-7528

E-mail: rectorat@ucad.edu.sn

Internet: www.ucad.sn

Founded 1915 as École de Médecine, became Institut des Hautes Études 1950, univ. status 1957

State control

Language of instruction: French

Academic year: October to July

Rector: Abdel Kader Boye

Vice-Pres.: Moustapha Sourang

Sec.-Gen.: Alioune Badara Diagne

Librarian: Henri Sene

Library: see under Libraries and Archives

Number of teachers: 700

Number of students: 22,000

Publications: *Annuaire, Dakar Médical* (3 a year), *Journal de la Faculté des Sciences et Techniques* (2 a year), *Notes Africaines, Revue de l'Ecole Normale Supérieure* (2 a year), *Revue de la Faculté des Lettres*

DEANS

Faculty of Arts and Humanities: Mamadou Kandji

Faculty of Economics and Management: Moustapha Kasse

Faculty of Law and Political Science: Moustapha Sourang

Faculty of Medicine, Pharmacy and Odonto-Stomatology: René Ndoye

Faculty of Science and Technology: Libasse Diop

UNIVERSITÉ DU SAHEL

BP 5355 33, Sotrac-Mermoz, Dakar

Telephone: 33-860-9975

E-mail: unis@refer.sn

Internet: www.unis.sn

Founded 1998

State control
Pres.: Issa Sall
Number of teachers: 80
Number of students: 400
Publications: *Les Annales du Sahel, Le Sahalien* (12 a year)

UNIVERSITÉ GASTON BERGER (Gaston Berger University)

BP 234, Saint-Louis
Telephone: 33-961-1906
E-mail: webmaster@ugb.sn
Internet: www.ugb.sn

Founded 1990 as Université De Saint-Louis, current name adopted 1996
State control
Language of instruction: French
Academic year: October to July

Rector: Prof. Ndiawar Sarr
Sec.-Gen.: Papa Sékou Sonko
Librarian: Mamadou Lamine Ndoye
Library of 80,000 vols
Number of teachers: 230

Number of students: 7,000

Colleges

Ecole Inter-Etats des Sciences et Médecine Vétérinaires (EISMV): BP 5077, Dakar; tel. 33-865-1008; e-mail mariamd@eismv.refer.sn; internet www.refer.sn/sngal_ct/edu/eismv/eismv.htm; f. 1968; representing 13 French-speaking African countries; 36 teachers (17 full-time, 19 part-time); 232 students; Dir Prof. François Adébayo Abiola.

Ecole Nationale d'Administration du Sénégal: BP 5209, Dakar; tel. 33-825-5828; e-mail enadakar@gmail.com; internet www.ena.sn; f. 1959; Dir-Gen. Cheikh Awa Balla.

Ecole Nationale Supérieure d'Agriculture: BP A 296, Thiès; tel. 33-951-1257; e-mail ensath@sentoo.sn; internet www.refer.sn/ensa/accueil.htm; f. 1980; 5-year courses in agricultural engineering; training for mems of the agricultural sector; library:

6,000 vols; 10 full-time teachers; 132 students; Dir Prof. Papa Ibra Samb.

Ecole Supérieure d'Economie Appliquée: Km 6, ave Cheikh Anta Diop, BP 5084, Dakar; tel. 33-824-7928; e-mail esea@ucad.edu.sn; internet esea.ucad.sn; f. 1963; library: 4,500 vols; 150 students; Dir Koumakh Ndour; publ. *Bulletin de Recherche Appliquée.*

Ecole Supérieure Polytechnique: BP 5085, Dakar; tel. 33-825-0879; e-mail esp@ucad.sn; internet www.esp.sn; 2nd campus in Thiès; f. 1994; 5-year diploma courses in engineering; library: 22,378 vols; 116 teachers; 2,105 students, (913 undergraduate, 1,192 postgraduate); Dir Abib Ngoum; Registrar Marie Noëlle Mbengue; Vice-Dean Mamadou Adj; Librarians Philomène Faye, Emmanuel Cabou.

Institut de Technologie Alimentaire: BP 2765, Hann, Dakar; tel. 33-832-0070; e-mail ita@metissacana.sn; internet www.ita.sn; f. 1963; Dir Dr Amadou Tidiane Guiro.

SERBIA

The Higher Education System

Following the dissolution of the Socialist Federal Republic of Yugoslavia in 1992, Serbia became part of the Federal Republic of Yugoslavia, which was renamed the State Union of Serbia and Montenegro in 2003. In 2006 Montenegro declared independence from the State Union of Serbia and Montenegro. There are eight state universities in Serbia, the oldest of which is Univerzitet u Beogradu (University of Belgrade—founded 1808), and 11 private universities. Serbian is the main language of instruction, but Hungarian is also used at Univerzitet u Novum Sadu (University of Novi Sad). In addition to the universities, higher education is offered by university faculties, specialist institutes and high schools. In 2011 some 228,531 students were enrolled in both public and private institutes of higher education.

The Ministry of Education is the national body responsible for higher education. The New University Law (2002) initiated several new reforms, including adoption of the European Credit Transfer System (ECTS) and increased autonomy for universities; additionally, Serbia participates in the Bologna Process to establish a European Higher Education Area, the first phase of which was to adopt a credit-based system of comparable degrees with two main cycles (undergraduate and graduate). Following passage of a new Law on Higher Education in 2005, the practical implementation of the Bologna Process formally began in 2006/07, including changes to quality assurance in higher education and the introduction of a three-cycle structure, which involved a complete redesign of university curricula. The new legislation also established the Commission for Accreditation and Quality Evaluation, and introduced the mandatory use of the ECTS. Universities are autonomous establishments, administered by a rector and a university council; management of university faculties is entrusted to faculty councils and deans, who are elected every two years.

Under the old system, admission to higher education was based on completion of general secondary education and award of the Diploma o Zavrsenoj Srednjoj Skoli (Secondary School Leaving Diploma), or completion of a four-year vocational certificate programme. Universities also set their own entrance examinations. The new undergraduate Bachelors degree (three to four years) replaces the old-style awards of Diplom Višeg Obrazovanje (two to three years) and Diplom Visokog Obrazovanja (four to six years). The Magistarska Nauka (Masters) is a one- to two-year programme of study following the Bachelors. Finally, the Doktorat Nauka (Doctorate) is the highest university-level degree and is awarded after a period of research culminating with defence of a thesis.

Technical and vocational education has also undergone reforms in recent years. The aims of the reforms, started in 2002, included creating a centre to develop occupational standards and profiles, teacher-training initiatives and new qualifications. Previously, two- to three-year post-secondary vocational schools offered vocational qualifications, regarded as final qualifications, with the potential to allow access to second- or third-year university undergraduate education. Through reforms along Bologna lines, post-secondary vocational schools have now been transformed into higher education professional (vocational) colleges, offering higher education courses that combine theoretical knowledge with occupational skills. In 2007/08 there were 214,925 students enrolled in 339 vocational institutions. In 2010 the Council for Vocational Education and Training and Adult Education was formally established to oversee the sector.

Regulatory and Representative Bodies

GOVERNMENT

Ministry of Culture and Information: Vlajkovićeva St, 11000 Belgrade; tel. (11) 339-8172; e-mail kabinet@kultura.gov.rs; internet www.kultura.gov.rs; Minister IVAN TASOVAC.

Ministry of Education, Science and Technological Development: Nemanjina 24, 11000 Belgrade; tel. (11) 361-6489; e-mail kabinet@mpn.gov.rs; internet www.mpn.gov.rs; Minister Dr TOMISLAV JOVANOVIC.

ACCREDITATION

Commission for Accreditation and Quality Assurance (CAQA): 2 Blvd Mihajla Pupina, Palace of Serbia, Eastern Entrance, Room 477, 11070 Belgrade; tel. (11) 313-0948; e-mail akreditacija@mpn.gov.rs; internet www.kapk.org; f. 2006; deals with accreditation, evaluation of study programmes, quality assurance of HEIs; 25 mems; Pres. Prof. Dr ENDRE PAP.

ENIC/NARIC Serbia: ENIC Centre of Serbia, Ministry of Education, Nemanjina 22–26, 1000 Belgrade; tel. (11) 361-6607; e-mail enic@mps.sr.gov.rs; internet www.mps.sr.gov.rs; Contact MILENA DAMJANOVIC.

Learned Societies

GENERAL

Matica srpska (Serbian Cultural and Scientific Association): Matice Srpske 1, 21000 Novi Sad; tel. (21) 527-622; e-mail ms@maticasrpska.org.rs; internet www.maticasrpska.org.rs; f. 1826; literary, scientific, cultural and publishing soc.; 2,830 mems; library: 3m. vols; Pres. Dr DRAGAN STANIĆ; Gen. Sec. Asst Prof. DJORDJE DJURIĆ; publs *Letopis Matice srpske* (literary magazine), *Proceedings* (in the following series: natural sciences, history, social sciences, literature and language, philology and linguistics, art, Slavonic studies, theatre and music, classical studies).

Srpska Akademija Nauka i Umetnosti (Serbian Academy of Sciences and Arts): Knez Mihailova 35, 11001 Belgrade; tel. (11) 2027-200; e-mail sasadir@sanu.ac.rs; internet www.sanu.ac.rs; f. 1886; sections of mathematics, physics and geosciences (Sec. DRAGOŠ CVETKOVIĆ), chemical and biological sciences (Sec. MIROSLAV GAŠIĆ), technical sciences (Sec. PETAR MILJANIĆ), medical sciences (Sec. VESELINKA SUŠIĆ), literature and language (Sec. PREDRAG PALAVESTRA), social sciences (Sec. VOJISLAV STANOVČIĆ), historical sciences (Sec. LJUBOMIR MAKSIMOVIĆ), fine arts and music (Sec. MILAN LOJANICA); 139 mems (89 ordinary, 50 corresp.); library: 1.2m. vols (incl. 650,000 vols of periodicals); Pres. NIKOLA HAJDIN; Gen. Sec. DIMITRIJE STEFANOVIĆ; Exec. Dir BUDIMIR LONČAR; publs *Ekonomski zbornik* (Collection of Economic Works), *Galerija* (Gallery), *Glas* (Review), *Godišnjak* (Yearbook), *Iz teorije prava* (Theory of Law), *Muzička izdanja* (Musical Editions), *Naučni skupovi* (Scientific Conferences), *Posebna izdanja* (Monographs), *Spomenik* (Monument), *Srpski dijalektološki zbornik* (Serbian Dialectology Collection), *Srpski etnografski zbornik* (Serbian Ethnographic Collection).

BIBLIOGRAPHY, LIBRARY SCIENCE AND MUSEOLOGY

Bibliotekarsko društvo Srbije (Serbian Library Association): Skerlićeva 1, 11000 Belgrade; tel. (11) 451-242; e-mail milun67@gmail.com; internet www.bds.rs; f. 1947 as Society of Library Workers of Serbia; 2,000 mems; Pres. Dr ŽELJKO VUČKOVIĆ; Sec. VESNA CRNOGORAC; publ. *Bibliotekar* (The Librarian, 2 a year).

ECONOMICS, LAW AND POLITICS

Association of Jurists of Serbia: Proleterskih brigada 74, Belgrade; f. 1946; Pres. Prof. Dr MIODRAG ORLIĆ; publ. *Pravni život*.

Drustva sudija Srbije (Judges' Association of Serbia): Alekse Nenadovća 24, Belgrade; tel. (11) 344-3132; e-mail jaserbia@verat.net; internet www.sudije.rs; f. 1997; non-govt, non-profit org.; works towards advancement of regulations, strengthening respect, professional ethics; dignity of judges; Pres. DRAGANA BOLJEVIC; Pres. MARKO SARIC; Pres. DUSKO MARTIC; publ. *Informator*.

Economists' Society of Serbia: Nusićeva 6/III, POB 490, Belgrade; f. 1944; Pres. BOGOLJUB STOJANOVIĆ; publ. *Ekonomika preduzeća* (12 a year).

EDUCATION

Pedagoško društvo Srbije (Pedagogical Society of Serbia): Terazije 26, 11000 Belgrade; tel. (11) 268-7749; e-mail drustvo@pedagog.rs; internet www.pedagog.rs; f. 1924, reorganized 1949 and 1977; training programmes; devt and project planning; 2,000 mems; Pres. SONJA ŽARKOVIĆ; Sec. MILENA DJOKIĆ; publs *Nastava i vaspitanje* (Teaching and Education, 5 a year), *Pedagoška Biblioteka* (Pedagogical Library, irregular).

FINE AND PERFORMING ARTS

Akademija umetnosti (Academy of Arts): Nemanjina 28, Belgrade; tel. (11) 361-8715; e-mail info@akademijaumetnosti.edu.rs; internet www.akademijaumetnosti.edu.rs; f. 1998; offers undergraduate, graduate academic, specialist academic and doctoral studies in drama and audiovisual arts, music and performing arts, arts, applied art and design; library of 4,000 vols; Dean Prof. MIRJANA KARANOVIC; Pres. DUŠAN ĐOKOVIĆ.

HISTORY, GEOGRAPHY AND ARCHAEOLOGY

Historical Society of Serbia: Faculty of Philosophy, Čika Ljubina 18–20, Belgrade; tel. (11) 320-6570; e-mail is@f.bg.ac.rs; f. 1948; 1,500 mems; Pres. Prof. Dr LJUBOMIR MAKSIMOVIĆ; publs *Belgrade Historical Review* (1 a year), *Istoriski glasnik* (2 a year).

Srpsko geografsko drustvo (Serbian Geographical Society): Studenski trg 3/III, Belgrade; tel. (11) 2184-065; e-mail info@sgd.org.rs; internet www.sgd.org.rs; f. 1910; 1,500 mems; library of 4,500 vols; Pres. Prof. Dr STEVAN M. STANKOVIĆ; Sec. DUSAN KIĆOVIĆ; publs *Editions Spéciales* (1 or 2 a year), *Géographique Actualité*, *Glasnik* (4 a year), *Globus* (1 a year), *Mémoires*, *Terre et Hommes* (1 a year).

LANGUAGE AND LITERATURE

British Council: Terazije 8/II, 11000 Belgrade; tel. (11) 302-3800; e-mail info@britishcouncil.rs; internet www.britishcouncil.rs; f. 1940 as Yugoslav–British Institute, current name adopted 2001; teaching centre; offers courses and exams in English language and British culture; conducts seminars and workshops; promotes cultural exchange with the UK; attached centres in Priština and Podgorica (Montenegro); library of 9,000 vols, 30 periodicals; Dir ANDREW GLASS.

Društvo za Srpski Jezik i Književnost (Society of Serbian Language and Literature): University, Studenski trg 3, Belgrade; tel. (11) 328-5506; e-mail drustvosj@fil.bg.ac.rs; internet drustvosj.fil.bg.ac.rs; f. 1910; Pres. P. STEVANOVIĆ; Sec. D. PAVLOVIĆ; publ. *Pritozi za Knjizevnost, Jezik, Istorija i Folklor*.

Goethe-Institut: Knez Mihailova 50, POB 491, 11000 Belgrade; tel. (11) 262-2823; e-mail info@belgrad.goethe.org; internet www.goethe.de/belgrad; f. 1970; offers courses and exams in German language and culture; promotes cultural exchange with Germany; organizes exhibitions and seminars; library of 12,000 vols; Dir VOLKER MARWITZ.

Serbian PEN Centre: 29/II Terazije St, 11000 Belgrade; tel. (11) 334-4607; e-mail pencent@bitsyu.net; f. 1926, re-f. 1962; 83 mems; Pres. VIDA OGNJENOVIC; Sec. NEDA BOBIC; publ. *Relations* (4 a year, in English, with Asscn of Serbian Writers).

Srpska književna zadruga (Serbian Literary Association): Kralja Milana 19, 11000 Belgrade; tel. (11) 3230-305; e-mail skz@beotel.rs; internet www.srpskaknjizevnazadruga.com; f. 1892; publishing of literary, historical and other learned works; 2,500 mems; library of 12,000 vols; spec. colln of 19th-century periodicals; Pres. SLOBODAN RAKITIC; Sec.-Gen. RADIVOJE KONSTANTINOVIĆ; publ. *Glasnik* (1 a year).

MEDICINE

Serbian Society for Fight against Cancer: Pasterova 14 St, 11000 Belgrade; tel. (11) 2656-386; e-mail serbca@ncrc.ac.yu; internet www.serbiancancer.org; f. 1927; voluntary non-profit org.; raises awareness; supports health professionals and orgs; 30,000 mems; Chair. Prof. Dr SLOBODAN ČIKARIĆ; Vice-Chair. Dr PREDRAG BRZAKOVIĆ; Sec. Dr ANA JOVICEVIC; Sec. Dr VESNA LUKIC; publ. *Bolje Sprečiti nego Lečiti* (The Best Cure is Prevention, 4 a year).

NATURAL SCIENCES

Mathematical Sciences

Society of Mathematicians of Serbia: Knez Mihailova 35, POB 791, Belgrade; tel. (11) 638-263; f. 1948; Pres. Dr DJORDJE KARAPANDŽIĆ; publ. *Matematički Vesnik* (4 a year).

Physical Sciences

Serbian Chemical Society: Karnegijeva 4, 11120 Belgrade; tel. (11) 337-0467; e-mail shd@shd.org.rs; internet www.shd.org.rs; f. 1897; 800 mems; library of 24,300 vols; Pres. Prof. Dr ŽIVOSLAV TEŠIĆ; Sec. Prof. Dr ALEKSANDRA PERIĆ-GRUJIĆ; Sec. Prof. Dr RADA BAOŠIĆ; publs *Hemijski Pregled* (6 a year, in Serbian), *Journal of the Serbian Chemical Society* (12 a year, in English).

Srpsko Geološko Društvo (Serbian Geological Society): Kamenička 6, POB 227, 11000 Belgrade; e-mail office@sgd.rs; internet www.sgd.rs; f. 1891; sections for history of geology; stratigraphy, palaeontology and tectonics; mineralogy, petrology, geochemistry and sedimentology; hydrogeology; engineering geology; oil geology and geophysics; economic geology and the study of ore deposits; organizes symposia and other scientific and professional meetings; 300 mems (active and inactive); Pres. Prof. Dr ZORAN STEVANOVIC; Vice-Pres. Prof. Dr DRAGAN MILOVANOVIĆ; Sec. Dr TIVADAR GAUDENYI.

TECHNOLOGY

Nikola Tesla Society: POB 359, Belgrade; e-mail boris@tesla-society.org; internet www.tesla-society.org; f. 1936 reorg. 1993; organizes int. festival of scientific and technical films, held every 2 years; conducts study tours and scientific meetings; publishing.

Savez inženjera i tehničara Srbije (Union of Engineers and Technicians of Serbia): Kneza Miloša 7, 11000 Belgrade; tel. (11) 323-0067; e-mail office@sits.rs; internet www.sits.org.rs; f. 1868; voluntary, non-govt, non-profit, professional, scientific org.; 44 mem. orgs; Pres. Prof. Dr CASLAV LAĆNJEVAC; Vice-Pres. Dr IGOR MARIĆ; Sec.-Gen. BRANISLAV VUJINOVIĆ; publ. *Tehnika* (scientific and technical magazine).

Research Institutes

GENERAL

Ethnographic Institute of the Serbian Academy of Sciences and Arts: Knez Mihaila 36 /IV, 11000 Belgrade; tel. (11) 263-6804; e-mail eisanu@ei.sanu.ac.rs; internet www.etno-institut.co.rs; promotes theoretical and methodological knowledge in the field of ethnology; organizes ethnological research, scientific conferences, lectures, study visits; cooperates with related cultural institutions in the country and abroad; Dir DRAGANA RADOJIČIĆ; Sec. NEVENKA SPASOJEVIC; publ. *Proceedings of the EI SASA* (bulletin, 1 a year).

Matematički Institut SANU (Mathematical Institute SANU): Kneza Mihaila 36, 11001 Belgrade; tel. (11) 263-0170; e-mail office@mi.sanu.ac.rs; internet www.mi.sanu.ac.rs; f. 1961; organizes seminars and colloquiums; int. collaborations; Dir Dr ZORAN MARKOVI; Deputy Dir Dr ZORAN OGNJANOVIC; Pres. MILAN BOŽIĆ; publs *Publications de l'Institut Mathematique* (2 a year), *Visual Mathematics* (4 a year, online).

AGRICULTURE, FISHERIES AND VETERINARY SCIENCE

Institute for Agricultural Mechanization: Zemun, POB 41, Belgrade; f. 1947; 30 mems; library of 6,000 vols; Dir DJORDJE DJURDJEVIĆ; publ. *Poljoprivredna Tehnika* (Agricultural Engineering, 1 a year).

Institute for Plant Protection and the Environment: T. Drajzera 9, POB 936, 11000 Belgrade; tel. (11) 266-9860; e-mail izbisfu@beotel.yu; f. 1945; depts of biological control, environmental protection, phytopathology, phytopharmacy, toxicology; library of 7,000 books, 12,650 periodicals; Dir Dr DIMITRIJE MATIJEVIĆ; publ. *Zaštita bilja* (Plant Protection, 4 a year).

BIBLIOGRAPHY, LIBRARY SCIENCE AND MUSEOLOGY

Republički zavod za zaštitu spomenika kulture (Institute for the Protection of Cultural Monuments of Serbia): Božidara Adžije 11, 11118 Belgrade; tel. (11) 454-786; e-mail rzzsk@eunet.yu; f. 1947; research, documentation, conservation and restoration, legal protection and maintenance of central registers of immovable cultural property; specialized training of personnel; publication of books and periodicals; Dir MILETA MILIĆ; Head, Architecture Dept BRANA STOJKOVIĆ PAVELKA; Head, Paintings Dept RADIŠA ŽIKIĆ; Head, Physical and Chemical Laboratory (vacant); Head of Dept of History of Art, Ethnology and Archaeology RADOJKA ZARIĆ; depts of law, documentation, photographic laboratory; library of 21,000 vols; publ. *Saopštenja* (Communications).

ECONOMICS, LAW AND POLITICS

Institute of International Politics and Economics: POB 750, Makedonska 25, 11000 Belgrade; tel. (11) 337-3824; e-mail iipe@diplomacy.bg.ac.yu; internet www.diplomacy.bg.ac.yu; f. 1947; int. relations; world economy; int. law; social, economic and political devt in all countries; library of 150,000 vols; Dir DUŠKO DIMITRIJEVIĆ; publs *International Problems* (4 a year), *Medjunarodna Politika* (4 a year), *Pregled evropskog zakonodavstva* (Survey of European Legislations, 6 a year), *Review of International Affairs* (4 a year).

FINE AND PERFORMING ARTS

Institute of Musicology of the Serbian Academy of Sciences and Arts: Knez

Mihailova 36, 11000 Belgrade; tel. (11) 2639-033; e-mail music_inst@music.sanu.ac.rs; internet www.music.sanu.ac.rs; f. 1948; history of Serbian music, Balkan folk music, medieval and traditional Orthodox church music, music theory and aesthetics; library of 5,500 vols; Dir Dr MELITA MILIN; publs *Musicology* (2 a year), *Sources for the History of Serbian Music* (1 a year).

HISTORY, GEOGRAPHY AND ARCHAEOLOGY

Arheološki Institut (Archaeological Institute): Knez Mihailova 35/IV, Belgrade; tel. (11) 637-191; e-mail institut@ai.sanu.ac.yu; internet www.ai.sanu.ac.rs; f. 1947; study of prehistoric, classical and medieval archaeology in the Central Balkan area; library of 13,000 books, 23,000 vols of periodicals; Dir Dr MILOJE VASIĆ; Admin. Sec. OLIVERA ILIĆ; publs *Djerdapske sveske—Cahiers des Portes de Fer, Singidunum* (irregular), *Starinar* (1 a year).

Geographical Institute 'Jovan Cvijić': Đure Jakšića 9, 11000 Belgrade; tel. (11) 263-6276; e-mail general@gi.sanu.ac.rs; internet www.gi.sanu.ac.rs; f. 1947; physical geography; social geography; regional geography; cartography with GIS; environmental studies; spatial planning; Head Dr MILAN RADOVANOVIĆ; publ. *Journal of the Geographical Institute* (1 a year).

Institute for Balkan Studies Serbian Academy of Sciences and Arts: Knez Mihailova 35/IV, 11000 Belgrade; tel. (11) 263-9830; e-mail balkinst@bi.sanu.ac.rs; internet www.balkaninstitut.com; f. 1934 started as Institut des Etudes Balkaniques; present name 1969; Balkans studies from prehistory to the modern age; incl. archaeology, ethnography, anthropology, history, culture, art, literature, law; multidisciplinary approach; Dir Acad. NIKOLA TASIĆ; Vice-Dir DUŠAN T. BATAKOVIĆ; Librarian VALENTINA BABIC; publ. *Balcanica*.

Institute for Byzantine Studies of the Serbian Academy of Sciences and Arts: Knez-Mihailova 35, 11000 Belgrade; tel. (11) 263-7095; e-mail inst.byz@vi.sanu.ac.rs; internet www.vi.sanu.ac.rs; f. 1948; research in modern Byzantine studies; int. cooperation; library of 21,000 vols; Dir Prof. LJUBOMIR MAKSIMOVIĆ; Deputy Dir BOJANA KRSMANOVIĆ; publ. *Zbornik radova Vizantoloskog instituta* (ZRVI).

LANGUAGE AND LITERATURE

Institute for Serbian Language SASA: Đure Jaksic 9, 11000 Belgrade; tel. (11) 218-1383; e-mail isj@isj.sanu.ac.yu; internet www.isj.sanu.ac.rs; f. 1947, present name 1992; processing old Serbian written monuments; etymological research dialectological research; description and Serbian language standardization; scientific meetings; lectures; Pres. PREDRAG PIPER.

MEDICINE

Institut za javno zdravlje Srbije (Institute of Public Health of Serbia): Dr Subotića 5, 11000 Belgrade; tel. (11) 268-4566; e-mail info@batut.org.rs; internet www.batut.org.rs; f. 1924 as Central Institute of Hygiene, present name 2006; epidemiology, microbiology, hygiene and human ecology, social medicine; health care orgs and services; health education; library of 40,000 vols; Dir Dr TANJA KNEZEVIC; publ. *Glasnik* (2 a year).

NATURAL SCIENCES

Biological Sciences

Botanical Institute and Garden of the University of Belgrade: Takovska 43,

---

11000 Belgrade; tel. (11) 767-988; f. 1874; library of 7,000 vols; Dir Prof. Dr JELENA BLAŽENČIĆ; publ. *Bulletin* (1 a year).

Physical Sciences

Astronomska Opservatorija (Astronomical Observatory): Volgina 7, 11060 Belgrade; tel. (11) 241-9553; e-mail contact@aob.rs; internet www.aob.rs; f. 1887, re-formed 1932; astrometry, astrophysics, astrodynamics, cosmology, astrobiology, astronomy and planetology; library of 15,000 vols; Dir Dr ZORAN KNEŽEVIĆ; Chief Officer SRETEN STEPANOVIĆ; publs *Publications of the Astronomical Observatory of Belgrade* (irregular), *Serbian Astronomical Journal* (2 a year).

Hidrometeorološki Zavod Republike Srbije (Hydrometeorological Service of Serbia): Kneza Višeslava 66, 11000 Belgrade; tel. (11) 3050-923; e-mail office@hidmet.gov.rs; internet www.hidmet.gov.rs; f. 1888; forecasts weather and issues severe weather warnings; Dir MILAN DACIĆ; Deputy Dir. DANICA SPASOVA..

Attached observatory:

Meteorološka opservatorija Beograd (Belgrade Meteorological Observatory): Bul. JNA 8, 11000 Belgrade; tel. (11) 685-770; f. 1887; Chief Officer SLOBODAN HADŽIVUKOVIĆ; publ. *Observations Météorologiques à Belgrade*.

Seismological Institute: Tasmajdanski park bb, POB 16, 11120 Belgrade; tel. (11) 322-7013; e-mail seismo@seismo.sr.gov.yu; internet www.seismo.gov.rs; f. 1906; Dirs Dr B. A. SIKOŠEK, Dr M. N. VUKAŠINOVIĆ; Gen. Man. SLAVITZA RADOVANOVITCH; Sec. SLADYANA MAKSIN-JOKSIMOVITCH; 12 mems; publs *Annuaire macroséismique et microséismique, Bulletin mensuel, Studies*.

TECHNOLOGY

Institut za nuklearne nauke 'Vinča' (Vinča Institute of Nuclear Sciences): Mike Petrovića Alasa 12–14, Belgrade; tel. (11) 243-8906; e-mail office@vin.bg.ac.rs; internet www.vin.bg.ac.rs; f. 1948; multidisciplinary scientific research; basic and applied research in natural, technological and nuclear sciences; consulting and research programmes in physics, chemistry, physical chemistry, biology, technical sciences, nuclear energy, electronics, computing, material sciences; production and application of radio isotopes; information systems and data processing; library of 30,000 vols; Dir Dr JOVAN NEDELJKOVIĆ; Pres. Prof. Dr DRAGAN MITRAKOVIC; Exec. Sec. MAJA MILANOV.

Institut za Tehnologiju Nuklearnih i Drugih Mineralnih Sirovina (Institute for Technology of Nuclear and Other Mineral Raw Materials): Franše D'Epere 86, POB 390, 11000 Belgrade; tel. (11) 3691-581; e-mail itnms@itnms.ac.rs; internet www.itnms.ac.rs; f. 1948; research and application of technology in the field of processing nuclear, metallic and non-metallic mineral raw materials; environmental protection; training; 168 staff; library of 4,000 vols, 40,000 periodicals; Dir-Gen. Prof. ZVONKO GULISIJA.

Institute of Technical Sciences of SASA: Knez-Mihailova 35/IV, POB 377, 11000 Belgrade; tel. (11) 218-5437; e-mail its@itn.sanu.ac.rs; internet www.itn.sanu.ac.rs; f. 1947; centres for fine particles processing and nanotechnologies; metallic constructions in civil engineering; scientific and research programmes; publishing and conferences; int. cooperation; Dir Acad. ZORAN DJURIĆ; Sec. ALEKSANDRA STOJIČIĆ.

Libraries and Archives

Belgrade

Arhiv Jugoslavije: Vase Pelagića 33, POB 65, 11000 Belgrade; tel. (11) 369-0252; e-mail arhivyu@arhivyu.rs; internet www.arhivyu.rs; f. 1950; documents regarding Yugoslav history; offers professional training in archival theory and practice; archival literature; exhibits; 26,621 vols, 18,200 reference books and 8,900 periodicals; Dir MILOŠEVIĆ MILADIN (acting); publ. *Arhiv* (1 a year).

Arhiv Srbije (Archives of Serbia): Karnegijeva 2, 11000 Belgrade; tel. (11) 337-0781; e-mail office@archives.org.rs; internet www.archives.org.rs; f. 1898, present name 1969; history of Serbia; protection of cultural heritage, professional guidance and education; assignment of professional titles; devt and promotion of archival activities; 75,000 vols; Dir Dr MIROSLAV PERIŠIĆ; publ. *Arhivski pregled* (1 a year).

Biblioteka grada Beograda (Belgrade City Library): Knez Mihailova 56, Belgrade; tel. (11) 202-4000; internet www.bgb.rs; f. 1929, present bldg 1986; 2m. vols; depts of arts, children's periodicals, cultural programmes, local history; Dir JOVAN RADULOVIC.

Biblioteka Srpske akademije nauka i umetnosti (Library of the Serbian Academy of Sciences and Arts): Knez Mihailova 35, 11000 Belgrade; tel. (11) 2639-120; e-mail katalog@bib.sanu.ac.rs; internet www.sanu.ac.rs; f. 1842 by the Serbian Learned Society; present name 1960; information service, inter-library loan scheme; prepares bibliographies and edits spec. publs; primarily for mems; 1.2m. vols (incl. 550,000 books and 650,000 vols of periodicals); Dir NIKŠA STIPČEVIĆ; publ. *Izdanja biblioteke*.

Narodna biblioteka Srbije (National Library of Serbia): Skerlićeva 1, 11000 Belgrade; tel. (11) 245-1242; e-mail int_cooperation@nb.rs; internet www.nb.rs; f. 1832; large fed. copyright and deposit library; nat. agency for CIP, ISBN, ISSN, ISMN, DOI numbers; centre for nat. current bibliography; nat. centre for conservation and preservation; nat. digital library centre; 6m. vols, incl. electronic titles; large colln of medieval Cyrillic MSS; Dir DEJAN RISTIĆ (acting); publs *Arheografski prilozi* (1 a year), *Glasnik narodne biblioteke Srbije* (Herald of the Nat. Library of Serbia, 1 a year, print and online), *Mélanges archéographiques* (Archaeographic Supplements, print and online), *Srpska bibliografija* (Serbian nat. bibliography, 17 vols).

Univerzitetska biblioteka 'Svetozar Marković' (University Library 'Svetozar Marković'): Bulvr Kralja Aleksandra 71, 11000 Belgrade; tel. (11) 337-0512; e-mail pitajbibliotekara@unilib.bg.ac.rs; internet www.unilib.bg.ac.rs; f. 1921 as successor to the library of the Serbian Lyceum (1838); centre of the network of univ. libraries in Serbia; exhibits; inter-library loan scheme; 1.45m. vols (books, periodicals, newspapers), 548 Serbian and other MSS 12th–18th century, 5,000 old documents; Dir Dr STELA FILIPI MATUTINOVIĆ; Deputy Dir BOGOLJUB MAZIĆ; publ. *Infoteka* (2 a year).

Čačak

Gradska biblioteka Vladislav Petković Dis (Public library 'Vladislav Petkovic Dis'): Gospodar Jovanova 6, 32000 Čačak; tel. (32) 340-960; e-mail biblioteka@cacak-dis.rs; internet www.cacak-dis.rs; f. 1848 as Asscn for Reading Serbian–Slavonic Newspapers in Čačak, present name 1998; incl. scientific dept; depts for adults, children; inter-library loans; 150,000 vols; Dir DANICA OTAŠEVIĆ.

Kragujevac

Narodna Biblioteka (Public Library): Dr Zorana Djindjica 10, 34000 Kragujevac; e-mail nbkragujevac@gmail.com; internet www.nbkg.rs; f. 1866; 50,000 vols.

Niš

Narodna Biblioteka 'Stevan Sremac' (National Library 'Stevan Sremac'): Borivoje Gojkovic no. 9, 18000 Niš; tel. (18) 511-410; e-mail n.vasic09@yahoo.com; internet www .nbss.rs; f. 1879; collns of the Serbian Acad. of Sciences and Arts and Serbian graphics; depts of ancient and rare books; local history; 250,000 vols, 950 titles, 200 original graphic prints; Dir NEBOJŠA VASIĆ; Sec. SONJA ŠUKOVIĆ; Librarian SLAVICA KRIVOKUĆA.

Novi Sad

Arhiv Vojvodine (Archives of Vojvodina): Dunavska 35, 21000 Novi Sad; tel. (21) 489-1800; e-mail info@arhivvojvodine.org.rs; internet www.arhivvojvodine.org.rs; f. 1926 as State archives in Novi Sad, present name 1970; 30,000 vols; Dir STEVAN RAJČEVIĆ; publs *Izveštaji o naučno-istraživačkom radu u inostranstvu* (Research reports from archives abroad), *Naučno-informativna sredstva o arhivskoj gradji u arhivima Vojvodina* (Scientific information on the Vojvodina archives, 4 a year).

Biblioteka Matice srpske (Matica Srpska Library): Ul. Matice srpske 1, 21000 Novi Sad; tel. (21) 420-199; e-mail bms@bms.ns.ac .rs; internet www.bms.rs; f. 1826 in Pest, opened 1838, present location 1864; copyright and deposit library for Serbia; regional information centre of Science and Technology Information Network; depository library for FAO and UNESCO; 3m. vols (incl. books and periodicals), 17 incunabula, 671 MSS, 500 palaeotype, 35,000 old and rare books, 700,000 units of spec. library material (maps, posters, leaflets, music records, cassettes, etc.); Dir MIRO VUKSANOVIĆ; Deputy Dir NOVKA SOKICA ŠUVAKOVIĆ.

Požarevac

Narodna biblioteka (Public Library): Drinska 2, 12000 Požarevac; tel. (12) 221-957; e-mail bibliotekapo@ptt.yu; f. 1847; 112,000 vols.

Sabac

Narodna biblioteka 'Žika Popovič' (Public Library 'Žika Popovič'): Masarikova 18, 15000 Sabac; f. 1847; 200,000 vols.

Museums and Art Galleries

Belgrade

Etnografski Muzej u Beogradu (Ethnographical Museum of Belgrade): Studentski trg. 13, p.p. 357, Belgrade; tel. (11) 328-1888; e-mail info@etnografskimuzej.rs; internet www.etnografskimuzej.rs; f. 1901; permanent and temporary exhibits; collns incl. nat. costumes, jewellery, embroidery and lace, textile household items, devices and contrivances for productions of textiles, elements of nat. architecture, rural household, urban architecture, urban household, agriculture, crafts, pottery, traffic and transport of goods, hunting and fishing, musical instruments, custom items, folk knowledge and belief, warriors' equipment, measures and tally, glass, tuxedo outfits, children's toys, photographs and negatives, art, video records, items of European and other cultures, archives; library of 60,000 vols; Dir VILMA NIŠKANOVIĆ (acting); Deputy Dir VESNA DUS-

KOVIC; Curator JELENA SAVIC; publ. *Glasnik Etnografskog Muzeja* (1 a year).

Istorijski muzej Srbije (Historical Museum of Serbia): Đure Jaksic 9, Belgrade; tel. (11) 328-7242; e-mail istorijskimuzej@ imus.org.yu; internet www.imus.org.rs; f. 1844 as National Museum, present name and status 1963; Dir Dr ANA STOLIĆ; Sr Curator ANDREJ VUJNOVIĆ; publs *Proceedings of the Historical Museum of Serbia, Zbornik* (1 a year).

Museum of Contemporary Art: Ušće 10, blok 15, 11070 Belgrade; tel. (11) 367-6288; e-mail msub@msub.org.rs; internet www .msub.org.rs; f. 1958; opened 1965, exhibits Serbian and foreign art; library of 5,200 vols, 25,500 catalogues; Dir BRANISLAVA ANDJELKOVIC DIMITRIJEVIC; Exec. Dir SLOBODAN NAKARADA; publ. *World Art Critics* (1 a year).

Muzej afričke umetnosti: zbirka Vede i dr Zdravka Pečara (Museum of African Art: the Veda and Dr Zdravko Pechar Collection): 14, Andre Nikolića St, 11000 Belgrade; tel. (11) 265-1654; e-mail africanmuseum@gmail.com; internet www .museumofafricanart.org; f. 1977; displays traditional arts of W Africa; collns incl. masks, sculptures in wood and bronze, gold weights, ceramics, musical instruments, textiles, jewellery, objects of everyday use; organizes exhibitions, workshops, lectures; holds the following events: Afro Festival (annually) and AFRAM (biannually); Dir and Curator NARCISA KNEŽEVIĆ ŠIJAN; publ. *AFRIKA-Studies in Art and Culture, Journal of the Museum of African Art.*

Muzej grada Beograda (Belgrade City Museum): Zmaj Jovina St 1, 11000 Belgrade; tel. (11) 263-8744; e-mail office@mgb.org.rs; internet www.mgb.org.rs; f. 1903; Belgrade from prehistory to the present; depts of archaeology, art, history, literature, numismatics, science; documentation centre; conservation laboratory; library of 23,091 vols, 305 rare books; Dir TATJANA KORIĆANAC (acting); publ. *Godišnjak Grada Beograda* (1 a year).

Muzej istorije Jugoslavije (Museum of Yugoslav History): Botićeva 6, 11000 Belgrade; tel. (11) 367-1485; e-mail info@mij.rs; internet www.mij.rs; f. 1996 by merger of Josip Broz Tito Memorial Centre and Museum of Revolution of Nations and Nationalities of Yugoslavia; history of the people of the fmr Yugoslavia; the life and work of Josip Tito (1892–1980), Pres. of Yugoslavia 1953–80; research, art and educational programmes; library of 200,000 items; Dir NEDA KNEZEVIC (acting); Curator ANA PANIC.

Muzej Nikole Tesle (Nikola Tesla Museum): Krunska 51, 11000 Belgrade; tel. (11) 243-3886; e-mail info@tesla-museum .org; internet www.tesla-museum.org; f. 1952; preserves legacy of the engineer and inventor, Nikola Tesla (1856–1943); contains biographical and scientific works; library of 786 vols, 323 magazines, 155,000 pages of Nikola Tesla's original documents and 1,000 of his personal items; Dir VLADIMIR JELENKOVIĆ; Curators BRATISLAV STOJILJKOVIĆ, IVANA ZORIĆ.

Muzej Pozorišne Umetnosti Srbije (Serbian Museum of Theatre): Gospodar Jevremova 19, 11000 Belgrade; tel. (11) 262-6630; e-mail office@mpus.org.rs; internet www .mpus.org.rs; f. 1950; documents, photographs, newspaper cuttings on the theatre, costumes, decorations, audiovisual documentation; colln of art and memorial objects, theatrical programmes and posters; archives; library of 7,500 vols; Dir KSENIJA RADULOVIĆ; Sec.-Treas. LJILJANA BANOVIC; Sr Curator

MIRJANA ODAVIĆ; publ. *Teatron* (4 a year, print and online).

Muzej primenjene umetnosti (Museum of Applied Art): Vuka Karadžića 18, 11000 Belgrade; tel. (11) 262-6841; e-mail info@ mpu.rs; internet www.mpu.rs; f. 1950; collects, conserves, studies, publishes works of applied art; exhibits incl. ceramics, porcelain, glass, metalwork, jewellery, period furniture, woodwork, textiles and costume, photography, book layout, modern architecture and design, contemporary applied art, fashion and clothing; library: 2m. books, 960 periodicals; Dir IVANKA ZORIĆ; Sec. SLAĐANA TOMIĆ; Sr Curator MILICA CUKIĆ; publ. *Journal* (1 a year).

Narodni muzej u Beogradu (National Museum in Belgrade): Trg Republike 1A, 11000 Belgrade; tel. (11) 330-6000; e-mail pr@narodnimuzej.rs; internet www .narodnimuzej.rs; f. 1844 as Museum Serbski, current name and bldg 1952; archaeological and historical art collns (medieval, Yugoslav and foreign collns), numismatics; conducts exhibitions; library of 85,000 vols; Dir TATJANA CVJETIĆANIN; publs *Glasnik društva prijatelja Narodnog muzeja*, *Kovčežić*, *Numizmatičar*, *Zbornik Narodnog muzeja.*

Prirodnjački muzej u Beogradu (Natural History Museum Belgrade): Njegoševa 51, POB 401, 11000 Belgrade; tel. (11) 344-2147; e-mail nhmbeo@nhmbeo.rs; internet www .nhmbeo.rs; f. 1895 as Jestastvenički Museum of Serbian Land; botanical, environmental, geological, mineralogical, palaeontological, petrological and zoological studies and collns; library: 21,554 books, 1,183 journal titles, 1,005 maps and 226 MSS; Dir Dr SLAVKO SPASIĆ; Sec. for Admin. and Technical affairs MARIJA VUCETIC; publ. *Bulletin* (separate series on biology and geology).

Vojni Muzej (Military Museum): Kalemegdan bb, 11000 Belgrade; tel. (11) 334-3441; e-mail vojnimuzej@mod.gov.rs; internet www .muzej.mod.gov.rs; f. 1878; military history of Serbia, incl. collns of arms, medals, flags, uniforms; archaeological and art colln; archive of 100,000 photographs; 30,000 objects in 12 collns; library of 15,000 vols, 5,000 magazines; Chief Col MIROSLAV KNEŽEVIĆ; publ. *Vesnik* (1 a year).

Zeljeznicki Muzej (Railway Museum of Serbia): 6 Nemanjina ul., 11000 Belgrade; tel. (11) 361-4811; e-mail medijacentar@ srbrail.rs; internet www.zeleznicesrbije.com; f. 1950; library of 20,000 vols; Dir MILAN RADIVOJEVIĆ.

Novi Sad

Galerija Matica Srpska (Art Gallery of Matica Srpska): Trg Galerija 1, 21000 Novi Sad; tel. (21) 489-9000; e-mail ms@ maticasrpska.org.rs; internet www .maticasrpska.org.rs; f. 1847; fine art; paintings, graphics, sculptures and drawings from the 16th to 20th centuries; Dir LEPOSAVA ŠELMIĆ.

Muzej Vojvodine (Museum of Vojvodina): Dunavska 35–37, 21000 Novi Sad; tel. (21) 420-566; e-mail muzejvojvodine1@nscable .net; internet www.muzejvojvodine.org.rs; f. 1947; sections: archaeology, ethnology, history, applied art; organizes lectures, workshops, exhibits; library of 80,000 vols; Dir Prof. Dr VLADMIR MITROVIĆ; publs *Posebna izdanja* (irregular), *Rad Muzeja Vojvodine* (1 a year).

Subotica

Gradski muzej Subotica—Szabadka Városi Múzeum (Municipal Museum of Subotica): Trg Sinagoge 3, 24000 Subotica; tel. (24) 555-128; e-mail muzejsubotica@open

.telekom.rs; internet www.gradskimuzej .subotica.rs; f. 1892; sections: archaeology, local history, art, ethnology (collns from Africa and SE Asia and Oceania), biology, coins (Hungarian and Roman); library of 12,000 vols; Man. HULLÓ ISTVÁN.

Universities

DRŽAVNI UNIVERZITET U NOVOM PAZARU
(State University in Novi Pazar)

Vuk Karadzic bb, Novi Pazar

Telephone: (20) 317-754
E-mail: rektorat@np.ac.rs
Internet: www.np.ac.rs

Founded 2006
State control

Offers Bachelors, Masters and doctoral courses in depts of arts; biochemical and medical sciences; legal and economic sciences; mathematical, physical and information sciences; philosophical-philological sciences; technical and technological sciences

Rector: Prof. ĆEMAL DOLIĆANIN (acting)

MEGATREND UNIVERZITET
(Megatrend University)

8 Goce Delceva, 11070 Belgrade

Telephone: (11) 220-3029
E-mail: info@megatrend.edu.rs
Internet: www.megatrend-edu.net

Founded 1989
Private control

Rector: Prof. Dr MICA JOVANOVIC
Pres.: WALTER SCHWIMMER
Vice-Rector for Int. Cooperation: Prof. SLOBODAN PAJOVIC
Vice-Rector for Research Work: Prof. DRAGANA GNJATOVIĆ
Vice-Rector for Teaching and Internal Organization: Prof. Dr VESNA MILANOVIC
Number of students: 26,000

Publication: *Megatrend Review* (applied economics)

DEANS

Faculty of Bio-farming in Backa Topola: Prof. JELENA BOŠKOVIĆ
Faculty of Business Studies: Prof. Dr GORDANA KOMAZEC
Faculty of Culture and Media: Prof. Dr MILIVOJE PAVLOVIC
Faculty of Management in Zajecar: Prof. Dr NEDELJKO MAGDALINOVIC
Faculty of Public Administration: Prof. Dr MILOMIR MINIĆ
Geoeconomic Faculty: Prof. Dr BRANISLAV PELEVIĆ
Graduate School of Arts and Design, Belgrade: Prof. MILOS SOBAJIC
Graduate School of Bio-farming, Backa Topola: Prof. JELENA BOSKOVIC
Graduate School of Business Economy, Valjevo: Prof. MILAN GRUJIC
Graduate School of Business Studies, Belgrade: Prof. ANA LANGOVIC
Graduate School of Business Studies, Požarevac: Prof. DRAGAN KOSTIC
Graduate School of Business Studies, Vrsac: Prof. MILAN MILANOVIC
Graduate School of Computer Science, Belgrade: Prof. MILAN TUBA
Graduate School of Culture and Media, Belgrade: Prof. MILIVOJE PAVLOVIC
Graduate School of International Economy, Belgrade: BRANISLAV PELEVIC
Graduate School of Management, Zajecar: Prof. NEDELJKO MAGDALINOVIC

Graduate School of Public Admin.: Prof. MILOMIR MINIC
Management and Business College, Professional Studies, Zajecar: DRAGAN MIHAJLOVIC (Dir)
Megatrend Basketball College Borislav Stankovic: Prof. TOMISLAV OBRADOVIC
Megatrend Business College, Professional Studies, Belgrade: NATASA SIMIC (Dir)
Megatrend Virtual Univ., MTVU: Prof. VELJKO SPASIC

UNIVERZITET SINGIDUNUM
(Singidunum University)

Danijelova 32, Belgrade

Telephone: (11) 309-3209
E-mail: mstanisic@singidunum.ac.rs
Internet: www.singidunum.ac.rs

Founded 2005
Private control
Languages of instruction: English, Serbian

Rector: Prof. Dr MILOVAN STANIŠIĆ
Sec.-Gen.: LJILJANA STANCIC-BUKVIC

Publication: *Singidunum Show* (Journal of Theory and Practice)

DEANS

Faculty of Applied Ecology: Dr GORDANA DRAZIC
Faculty of Business (Belgrade): Dr DANIJEL CVJETICANIN
Faculty of Business (Valjevo): Dr OLIVERA NIKOLIC
Faculty of Economics, Finance and Administration: Prof. Dr MIHAILO CRNOBRNJA
Faculty of European Law, Political Studies: Dr ILIJA BABIC
Faculty of Informatics and Computing: Dr MLADEN VEINOVIĆ
Faculty of Management: Dr DRAGAN CVETKOVIC
Faculty of Media and Communications: NADA POPOVIC-PERISIC
Faculty of Tourism and Hospitality Management: Dr KRUNOSLAV CAČIĆ

UNIVERZITET U BEOGRADU
(University of Belgrade)

Studentski trg 1, 11000 Belgrade 6

Telephone: (11) 263-5153
E-mail: officebu@rect.bg.ac.rs
Internet: www.bg.ac.rs

Founded 1808 as the College of Velika škola, reorganized 1905 and 1954
State control
Academic year: October to September

Rector: Dr BRANKO KOVAČEVIĆ
Vice-Rector for Education: Dr NEDA BOKAN
Vice-Rector for Finances and Organization: Dr NEVENKA ŽARKIĆ-JOKSIMOVIĆ
Vice-Rector for Int. Relations: Dr VOJISLAV LEKOVIĆ
Vice-Rector for Science: Dr MARKO IVETIĆ
Sec.-Gen.: SLAVICA KAPETANOVIĆ
Librarian: DEJAN AJDAČIĆ

Library of 700,000 vols, 10,000 periodicals
Number of teachers: 2,550
Number of students: 92,652 (90,152 undergraduate, 2,500 postgraduate)

Publications: *Acta Veterinaria*, *Annals of the Faculty of Law* (in Serbian), *Annals of the Faculty of Philology*, *Bulletin Astronomique de Belgrade*, *Collection of Works of the Faculty of Mining and Geology* (in Serbian), *Collection of Works of the International Slavistics Centre*, *Contemporary Research in Physics* (in Serbian), *Contributions to Language, Literature and Folklore*, *Economic Annals* (in Serbian, 4 a year), *Education—the Theory and the Practice* (in English, Russian and Serbian), *Gazette of the Faculty of Forestry* (2 a year),

Geological Annals of the Balkan Peninsula (in Serbian), *Germanica Belgradensia*, *Headmaster* (in Serbian), *Information Bulletin* (Faculty of Agriculture, in Serbian, 12 a year), *Innovations in the Field of Instruction* (in Serbian), *Italica Belgradensia*, *Journal of Automatic Control* (in English), *Journal of Mining and Metallurgy* (in Serbian), *Lectures in Physical Sciences, Management, Mathematics* (in Serbian), *Medical Research* (in Serbian), *Medical Students, Miscellaneous Studies of the Faculty of Philosophy* (series A: culture and history; series B: social sciences), *October Symposium of Miners and Metallurgists* (1 a year, colln of works, in Serbian), *Philosophical Yearbook* (in Serbian), *Philosophy and Society* (in Serbian), *Physical Education, Physical Engineering* (in English), *Population, Power Engineering* (in English), *Problems of Ethnology and Anthropology, Psychological Research, Review of Research Work at the Faculty of Agriculture* (in English), *Sociological Review, Studies of Adult Education Topics, The Veterinary Herald* (in Serbian), *Transactions* (mechanical engineering, in Serbian and English, 2 a year), *Transport and Traffic in Cities* (in Serbian), *Underground Works* (in Serbian), *Yugoslav Journal of Operations Research* (in English), *Zograf* (iconography)

DEANS

Faculty of Agriculture: Dr NEBOJŠA RALEVIĆ
Faculty of Architecture: Dr VLADIMIR MAKO
Faculty of Biology: Dr JELENA KNEŽEVIĆ-VUKČEVIĆ
Faculty of Chemistry: Dr BRANIMIR JOVANČIĆEVIĆ
Faculty of Civil Engineering: Dr ĐORĐE VUKSANOVIĆ
Faculty of Defectology: Dr JASMINA KOVAČEVIĆ
Faculty of Economics: Dr MARKO BACKOVIĆ
Faculty of Forestry: Dr MILAN MEDAREVIĆ
Faculty of Geography: Dr SRBOLJUB STAMENKOVIĆ
Faculty of Law: Dr MIRKO VASILJEVIĆ
Faculty of Mathematics: Dr MIODRAG MATELJEVIĆ
Faculty of Mechanical Engineering: Dr MILORAD MILOVANČEVIĆ
Faculty of Mining and Geology: Dr VLADICA CVETKOVIĆ
Faculty of Organizational Sciences: Dr MILAN MARTIĆ
Faculty of Pharmacy: Dr NADA KOVAČEVIĆ
Faculty of Philology: Dr SLOBODAN GRUBAČIĆ
Faculty of Philosophy: Dr VESNA DIMITRIJEVIĆ
Faculty of Physical Chemistry: Dr SĆEPAN SĆEPAN
Faculty of Physics: Dr LJUBIŠA ZEKOVIĆ
Faculty of Political Sciences: Dr ILIJA VUJAČIĆ
Faculty of Security Studies: Dr VLADIMIR CVETKOVIĆ
Faculty of Sports and Physical Education: Dr DUŠAN MITIĆ
Faculty of Stomatology: Dr DRAGOSLAV STAMENKOVIĆ
Faculty of Teacher Training: Dr ALEKSANDAR JOVANOVIĆ
Faculty of Technology and Metallurgy: Dr IVANKA POPOVIĆ
Faculty of Transport and Traffic Engineering: Dr SLOBODAN SLOBODAN
Faculty of Veterinary Medicine: Dr VELIBOR STOJIĆ
School of Electrical Engineering: Dr MIODRAG POPOVIĆ
School of Medicine: Dr VLADIMIR BUMBAŠIREVIĆ
Technical Faculty in Bor: Dr MILAN ANTONIJEVIĆ

PROFESSORS

Faculty of Agriculture (Nemanjina 6, 11080 Belgrade-Zemun; tel. (11) 261-5315; e-mail office@agrif.bg.ac.rs; internet www.agrifaculty.bg.ac.rs):

BLAGOJEVIĆ, S., Agricultural Chemistry
ČANAK, M., Mathematics
ĆOROVIĆ, M., Market and Turnover of Agricultural and Agroindustrial Products
ELEZOVIĆ, I., General Phytopharmacy
ERCEGOVIĆ, Đ., Elements and Agricultural Machinery Mechanics
GLAMOČLIJA, Đ., Crop Farming
GRUBIĆ, G., Ruminant Nutrition
IVANOVIĆ, M., Plant Mycosis
JAKOVLJEVIĆ, M. D., Soil and Water Chemistry
JANKOVIĆ, M., Cooling Technology
JELIĆ, M. P., Mathematics
KOSI, F., Thermodynamics and Thermotechnics
KOSTIĆ, N. M., Agrogeology
KOVAČEVIĆ, D., General Crop Farming
LATINOVIĆ, D., Population Genetics and Fertilization of Domestic Animals
LESKOŠEK ČUKALOVIĆ, I., Malt and Beer Technology
MAČEJ, O., Milk Proficiency and Preparation
MITROVIĆ, S., Zootechnics
MRATINIĆ, E., Special Fruit Growing
NEDIĆ, M. J., Special Crop Farming
OBRADOVIĆ, D. B., Technological Microbiology
OSTOJIĆ, M., Milk Production
PAVASOVIĆ, V. L., Technological Operations
PEKIĆ, S., Botany
PERIĆ, V. T., Meat Proficiency and Preparation
PEŠIĆ, R., Macroeconomic Analysis
PETANOVIĆ, R., Acarology
PETKOVIĆ, S., Hydraulics
PETROVIĆ, M., Cattle Breeding
RADOVANOVIĆ, R. M., Meat Industry Follow-Up Products Technology
RAIČEVIĆ, D., Agricultural Machinery
RALEVIĆ, N., Statistics
RALEVIĆ LJUBANOVIĆ, I., Statistics and Operational Research
RISTIĆ, N., Organic Chemistry
RUDIĆ, D. V., Drainage
ŠESTOVIĆ, M. B., Special Phytopharmacy
ŠEVRALIĆ, M., Field and Cooperative Movement Economics
ŠINŽAR, B. C., Botany
SKALICKI, Z., Zootechnics
SPALEVIĆ, B., Soil and Water Conservation
SPASIĆ, R., Special Entomology
STEVANOVIĆ, Đ., Sociology
STEVANOVIĆ, D. R., Agrochemistry
ŠTIKIĆ, R., Plant Physiology
ŠURLAN MOMIROVIĆ, G., Genetics
TODOROVIĆ, M. S., Thermodynamics
VASIĆ, G., Reclamation Systems Production and Maintenance
VELIČKOVIĆ, M., General Fruit Growing
VEREŠ, M., Plant Products Technology
VITOROVIĆ, S. L., Agricultural Toxicology
VUKIĆ, Đ., Agricultural Electrical Technology
VUKŠA, P., Plant Protection Technology
ŽEŽELJ, M., Wheat and Flour Technology

Faculty of Architecture (Blvr Kralja Aleksandra 73/II, 11000 Belgrade; tel. (11) 322-5254; e-mail fakultet@arh.bg.ac.rs; internet www.arh.bg.ac.rs):

BADOVINC, P., Urban Functions
BAJIĆ BRKOVIĆ, M., Urban and Regional Planning
CAGIĆ, P. R., Architectural Design, Design Studio
ĐORĐEVIĆ, D., Construction Management and Utilities Management in Architecture
JOVANOVIĆ POPOVIĆ, M., Architectural Construction and Principles of Bioclimatic Design
KRUNIĆ, S., Design Studio
KUJUNDŽIĆ, V. B., Wood and Metal Structures
KURTOVIĆ FOLIĆ, N., History of Architecture and Settlements
LAZAREVIĆ BAJEC, N., Urban Structures and Zoning
LOJANICA, M. M., Design Studio, Process in Architectural Design
MARUŠIĆ, D. M., Architectural Design, Design Studio
MIHAJLOVIĆ, M., Physics and Materials in Architectural Building Physics
MIHALJEVIĆ, G. P., Built Environment Economics
MITROVIĆ, B., Architectural Design, Design Studio
NESTOROVIĆ, M., Structural Systems, Spatial Structures
PEROVIĆ, M. R., History of Modern Architecture and Town Planning
RAJIĆ, D., Mechanics and Strength of Materials
RAJOVIĆ, S., Architectural and Urban Design
RAKOČEVIĆ, M., Architectural Design
RIBAR, M., Architectural Design, Specific Design Problems
RISTIĆ, M., Analysis of Metal Structures

Faculty of Biology (Studentski trg 16, 11000 Belgrade; tel. (11) 218-6635; e-mail dekanat@bio.bg.ac.rs; internet www.bio.bg.ac.rs):

ANĐELKOVIĆ, M. L., Population Genetics
ČURČIĆ, B., Pedology and Pedobiology with Soil Protection
CVIJIĆ, G., Experimental Physiology
KALEZIĆ, M., Vertebrate Comparative Morphology
KEKIĆ, V., Behavioural Genetics
KONJEVIĆ, R., Plant Physiology
PETKOVIĆ, B., Plant Morphology, General Botany, Botany with Mycology
RADOVIĆ, I., Principles of Ecology
ROMAC, S., Eucaryote Molecular Biology
SIMIĆ, D., Microbiology, Microbiology and Microbial Ecology Genotoxicology, Water Microbiology
STEVANOVIĆ, B., Plant Ecology and Phytogeography, Plant Ecology, Physiology and Physiological Ecology of Plants, Plant Adaptive Types, Physiological Ecology of Plants, Aquatic Botany
STEVANOVIĆ, V., Plant Ecology and Phytogeography, Principles of Ecology, Biogeography, Biodiversity Protection and Revival, Ecosystems of Yugoslavia and the Balkan Peninsula
TOPISIROVIĆ, LJ., Biochemistry
TUČIĆ, N., Organic Evolution Theory

Faculty of Chemistry (Studentski trg 12–16, 11000 Belgrade; tel. (11) 328-2111; e-mail dekan@chem.bg.ac.rs; internet www.chem.bg.ac.rs):

BOJOVIĆ, S., Chemical Education
DOŠEN-MIĆOVIĆ, L., Organic Chemistry
GRŽETIĆ, I., Applied Chemistry
JANKOV, R., Biochemistry
JOVANČIĆEVIĆ, B., Applied Chemistry
JURANIĆ, I., Organic Chemistry
MARKOVIĆ, R., Organic Chemistry
MILOSAVLJEVIĆ, S., Organic Chemistry
NIKETIĆ, S., Inorganic Chemistry
NIKETIĆ, V., Biochemistry
PAVLOVIĆ, V., Organic Chemistry
ŠAIČIĆ, R., Organic Chemistry
ŠOLAJA, B., Organic Chemistry
SOVILJ, S., Inorganic Chemistry
TEŠIĆ, Ž., Analytical Chemistry
VRVIĆ, M., Biochemistry
VUČKOVIĆ, G., Inorganic Chemistry

Faculty of Civil Engineering (Blvr Kralja Aleksandra 73/I, 11000 Belgrade; tel. (11) 321-8524; e-mail lilja@grf.bg.ac.rs; internet www.grf.bg.ac.rs):

ANĐUS, V., Road Design
BAJIĆ, D., Concrete Structures
BRČIĆ, S., Engineering Mechanics and Strength of Materials
BUĐEVAC, D., Metal Structures
ĆORIĆ, B., Theory of Structures
CVETANOVIĆ, A., Elements of Transportation, Roads
ĐORĐEVIĆ, B., Water Power Engineering, Water Resource Systems
DUNICA, Š., Engineering Mechanics and Strength of Materials
GEORGIJEVIĆ, V., Technical Physics, Building Physics, Introduction to Electronics
IVKOVIĆ, B., Construction Management and Technology, Construction Project Management
JOKSIĆ, D., Geodesy, Geodesy on Roads and Railways, Engineering, Geodesy in City Infrastructure Systems, Photogrammetry, Remote Sensing
JOVANOVIĆ, M., River Engineering, Waterways and Ports
KLEM, N., Automatic Data Processing in Geodesy
KOLUNDŽIJA, B., Structural Theory
LJUBISAVLJEVIĆ, D., Municipal Hydraulic Engineering, Water Quality
MAKSIMOVIĆ, Č., Fluid Mechanics, Hydraulic Measurement, Engineering
MAKSIMOVIĆ, M., Soil Mechanics
MALETIN, M., Urban Streets
MURAVLJOV, M., Building Materials
NADJANOVIĆ, D., Concrete Structures
OPRICOVIĆ, S., Systems Optimization
PEROVIĆ, G., Calculus, Congruence Theory
PRAŠČEVIĆ, Ž., Construction Management and Technology, Special Construction Problems
ŠEKULOVIĆ, M., Structural Theory
ŠUMARAC, D., Engineering Mechanics and Strength of Materials
VRAČARIĆ, K., Geodesy
VUKSANOVIĆ, Đ., Structural Theory

Faculty of Defectology (Visokog Stevana 5, 11000 Belgrade; tel. (11) 218-3036; e-mail info@fasper.bg.ac.rs; internet www.fasper.bg.ac.rs):

ANDREJEVIĆ, I., Professional and Occupational Training of Persons with Mental Retardation, Professional Training of Deaf and Hard of Hearing Persons
ANIČIĆ, L., Pedagogy of Mentally Retarded Persons, Methodology of Preschool Work with Mentally Retarded Persons
GOLOBOVIĆ, S., Clinical Logopaedia
ILANKOVIĆ, V., Basics of Kinesitherapy
ISPANOVIĆ RADOJKOVIĆ, V., Neurology and Psychiatry, Neuropsychiatry with Re-educational Methods
JOVANOVIĆ, T., Medical Psychology with Basics of Anatomy
KAŠIĆ, Z., Phonetics, Linguistics
KRAJGER GUZINA, A., Neurology and Psychiatry
MATEJIĆ ČURIČIĆ, Ž., Developmental Psychology, Psychology of Blind and Low Vision Persons
MILANDINOVIĆ, V., Serbian Language Methodology for Children with Mental Retardation, Mathematical Methodology for Children with Mental Retardation
POPOVIĆ KANDIĆ, Z., Criminal Law
RADOMAN, V., Psychology of Deaf and Hard of Hearing Persons, Psychology of Persons with Speech Disturbances
RADOVANOVIĆ, D., Psychology of Persons with Behavioural Disturbances
RADULOVIĆ, K., Psychology of Persons with Mental Retardation, Psychology of Physically Challenged Persons

RAPAIĆ, D., Clinical Somatopaedia
STANKOV, B., Basics of Strabology with Orthoptics and Pleoptics
TREBJEŠANIN, Ž., General Psychology with Personality Psychology

Faculty of Economics (Kamenička 6, 11000 Belgrade; tel. (11) 302-1240; e-mail ekof@ekof.bg.ac.rs; internet www.ekof.bg.ac.rs):

ANIČIĆ, R. M., Methods of Economic Analysis
ARSENIĆ, Ž., Vehicle Design, Experimental Methods
BABIĆ, S. L., Price Theory, Industrial Organization
BAJEC, J. M., Contemporary Economic Systems, Public Sector Economy
BAKIĆ, O., Tourism Marketing, Tourist Organization Business Operations
BORIČIĆ, B., Mathematics, Program Languages
BOŽIĆ, V. S., Transport Economics, Marketing Logisitics
ČAČIĆ, K. T., Tourism and Catering Business Management, Tourism Economics, Tourism Marketing
CEROVIĆ, B. D., Transition Economics
CVJETIĆANIN, D., Operational Research, Economic and Mathematical Methods and Models
DEVETAKOVIĆ, S. R., National Economy, Technological Development and Policy, Agrarian Policy
ĐOLEVIĆ, V. R., Economic Statistics, Bases of Statistical Analysis
ĐUKIĆ, Đ., Banking, Securities Trading
ĐURIČIN, D., Strategic Management
EREMIĆ, M. B., Market Research, Bases of Statistical Analysis, Theoretical Statistics
ILIĆ, B. B., Political Economy
IVANIŠEVIĆ, M., Business Finance, Business Financial Restructuring
JAKŠIĆ, M. P., Development and Contemporary Economic Thought, Macroeconomic Analysis
JOKSIMOVIĆ, L., Contemporary Economic Systems, Public Sector Economics
JOVANOVIĆ GAVRILOVIĆ, B., National Economy, Development Theory and Planning, Industrial Economics
JOVANOVIĆ GAVRILOVIĆ, P. R., Yugoslav Economic Relations with Foreign Countries, International Business Finance, International Financing
JOVIČIĆ, M. M., Econometry, Times Series Analysis
KOČOVIĆ, J., Financial and Actuary Mathematics, Insurance, Insurance Tariffs
KOVAČ, O., International Finances, Yugoslav Economic Relations with Foreign Countries, European Union Economics
LOVRETA, S. M., Trade and Sales Management, Trade Economics
LOVRIĆ, M., Bases of Statistical Analysis
MALENOVIĆ, N., Business Economics
MARIČIĆ, B. R., Marketing, Consumer Behaviour
MEDOJEVIĆ, B. V., Political Economy
MILOVANOVIĆ, M. R., Price Theory, Macroeconomic Analysis
NIKOLIĆ, M. M., Business Economic, Energy Economics
PAVLIČIĆ, D., Bases of Statistical Analysis, Decision Making Theory
PETKOVIĆ, M., Business Organization, Human Resources Management, Organizational Development
PETKOVIĆ, V. V., Sociology with Labour Sociology, Tourism Sociology
PETROVIĆ, L., Samples Theory and Experiment Planning, Mathematics, Theoretical Statistics
PETROVIĆ, P. D., Econometry, Open Economy Macroeconomics

RIKALOVIĆ, G., National Economy, Agrarian Economics, Transport Economics
ŠKARIĆ JOVANOVIĆ, K. I., Financial Accounting, Balance Theory and Policy, Special Balances
STANIŠIĆ, M., Accounting Information Systems, Auditing Theory, Auditing
STEVANOVIĆ, N., Cost Accounting Systems, Management Accounting
ŠUVAKOVIĆ, DJ. M., Price Theory, Production Theory
TODOROVIĆ, J. B., Marketing Research and Marketing Information Systems, Management Information Systems, Price Theory
ZARIĆ, S., Economic Analysis Methods, Market and Market Institutions

Faculty of Forestry (Kneza Višeslava 1, 11000 Belgrade; tel. (11) 305-3990; e-mail sf.bg@sezampro.rs; internet www.sfb.bg.ac.rs):

BAJIĆ, V., Forest Utilization, Forestry Mechanization
BANKOVIĆ, S. V., Dendrometry, Geodesy
DANON, G., Basics of Mechanical Engineering, Wood Processing Tool Machinery
ĐOROVIĆ, M., Agricultural Field Improvement
ISAJEV, V., Seed Production, Nursery Practice and Afforestation, Genetics with Plant Breeding
JAIĆ, M., Surface Wood Processing
JOKSIMOVIĆ, V., Erosion Control Agroecosystems
KARADŽIĆ, D., Forest Phytopathology, Ornamental Plant Diseases
KOLIN, B., Hydrothermic Wood Processing, Veneers and Composite Boards
KOSTADINOV, S., Torrents and Erosion
KOSTADINOVIĆ, A., Sociology
KRSTIĆ, M., Silviculture, Forest Improvement
LETIĆ, L., Woodland Water Exploitation, Forest Hydrology
MARJANOV, M., Engineering Mechanics
MATIĆ, V., Materials in Erosion Control Works, Ecological Materials
MIHAJLOVIĆ, L., Forest Protection, Forest Entomology
MILJKOVIĆ, J. P., Chipboards, Particle Boards and Wood-Based Materials
NEŠIĆ, M., Wood Processing Production Management, Change Control, Wood Processing Management
PETKOVIĆ, S. D., Hydraulics with Hydrology, Water Management Basics
RANKOVIĆ, N., Forest Economics, Forest Organization and Management, Timber Trade, Forest Economic Geography
SKAKIĆ, D., Final Wood Processing, Timber Construction
SOKOLOVIĆ, S., Design, Furniture Design
SOŠKIĆ, B. M., Wood Properties, Mill Conversion of Wood
STOJANOVIĆ, L., Silviculture, Forest Improvement
ŠULETIĆ, R., Wood Processing Enterprise Design, Project and Investment Management, Enterprise Development Management
TODOROVIĆ, P. S., Wood Industry Control System Technology, Engineering Physics
TODOROVIĆ, T. N., Geotechnics in Flood Control, Geodynamics, Hydrogeology with Geomorphology
TOMIĆ, Z. S., Dendrology, Forest Phytocenology
VOJKOVIĆ, L., Landscape Design, History of Landscape Architecture
VUČKOVIĆ, M., Increment Study
VUKIĆEVIĆ, M., Wood Processing Production Organization, Operational Research

Faculty of Geography (Studentski trg 3/III, 11000 Belgrade; tel. (11) 218-3537; e-mail dekanat@gef.bg.ac.rs; internet www.gef.bg.ac.rs):

DERIĆ, B., Regional Planning
GRČIĆ, M., Political Geography, Industrial and Transport Geography
KUKRIKA, M., Computing, Information Technology
LJEŠEVIĆ, M., Environment
MANOJLOVIĆ, P., Geomorphology, Mathematical Geography
PAVLOVIĆ, M., Yugoslav Geography, Yugoslav Regional Geography
SPASOVSKI, M., Population Geography, Demography
STAMENKOVIĆ, S., Urban Geography, Applied Urban Geography
STANKOVIĆ, S. M., Tourism Geography, World Tourism Geography
STOJKOV, B., Spatial Planning Analysis and Synthesis Methods, Urban and Rural Spatial Planning
ŽIVKOVIĆ, D., Cartography, Topical Mapping

Faculty of Law (Blvr Kralja Aleksandra 67, 11000 Belgrade; tel. (11) 302-7600; e-mail pravni@ius.bg.ac.rs; internet www.ius.bg.ac.rs):

ANTIĆ, O., Succession Law
AVRAMOVIĆ, S. D., General History of Law
BASTA, D. N., Legal Philosophy
BESAROVIĆ, V. M., Commercial Law, Copyright and Intellectual Property Law
BRAJIĆ, V. M., Labour Law
ČAVOŠKI, K. S., Introduction to Law
ĐUKIĆ VELJOVIĆ, Z., Constitutional Law
IGNJATOVIĆ, Đ., Criminology and Penology
JANJIĆ KOMAR, M., Family Law
JEKIĆ, Z. M., Criminal Procedure
KOŠUTIĆ, B. P., Introduction to Law
KREĆA, M. D., International Public Law
LABUS, M. Z., Political Economy
LILIĆ, S., Administrative Law and Governance
MARKOVIĆ, R. Č., Constitutional Law, Administrative Law
MARKOVIĆ, S., Copyright and Intellectual Property Law
MILIĆ, V. B., Sociology
MITROVIĆ, D., Introduction to Law, Autonomy Law
MITROVIĆ, M., Sociology
ORLIĆ, M. V., Introduction to Civil Law, Real Law
POPOVIĆ, D. M., Public Finances and Financial Law
POPOVIĆ, D. M., General History of Law
STOJANOVIĆ, Z., Criminal Law
SUNDEROVIĆ, B., Labour Law
TABOROŠI, S. A., Law of the Economic System
TODOROVIĆ, M., Sociology
TRKULJA, J., Political Systems
VASILJEVIĆ, M. S., Commercial Law and Traffic Law
VUKADIN, E., Economic Policy

Faculty of Mathematics (Studentski trg 16, 11000 Belgrade; tel. (11) 202-7801; e-mail matf@matf.bg.ac.rs; internet www.matf.bg.ac.rs):

ANGELOV, T., Stellar Astronomy, Stellar Structure and Evolution
BOKAN, N., Differential Geometry
JARIĆ, J. P., Continuum Mechanics, Tensor Calculus
JEVTIĆ, M. J., Complex Analysis
JOVANOVIĆ, B. S., Numerical Analysis
KADELBURG, Z. L., Analysis
KNEŽEVIĆ, J., Differential Equations
KUZMANOVSKI, M., Positional Astronomy
LAŽETIĆ, N., Analysis
MATELJEVIĆ, M. S., Complex Analysis
MIJAJLOVIĆ, Ž. D., Algebra, Mathematical Logic

PAVLOVIĆ, M., Complex and Functional Analysis
RADOJČIĆ, M., Algebra, Mathematical Logic
VREĆICA, S., Topology

Faculty of Mechanical Engineering (K. M. Arias Raljić 1, 11120 Belgrade; tel. (11) 337-0266; e-mail dekan@mas.bg.ac.rs; internet www.mas.bg.ac.rs):

ADŽIĆ, M., Fuels, Industrial Water, Lubricants, Combustion
BENIŠEK, M. H., Hydraulic Machinery, Measurement Techniques
BLAGOJEVIĆ, Đ., Rocket Propulsion, Flight Dynamics with Aerodynamics
BOGNER, M. G., Process Equipment Mechanical Design and Selection
BOJANIĆ, P. O., Computer Graphics
BRKIĆ, L. D., Steam Boilers, Thermal Power
ČANTRAK, S., Hydraulics and Pneumatics, Hydromechanics
ČOVIĆ, V. M., Mechanics
DEBELJKOVIĆ, D. L., Linear System Design, Object and Process Dynamics
ĐORĐEVIĆ, S., Mechanism Design
ĐORĐEVIĆ, V. D., Fluid Mechanics
DUBOKA, Č. V., Vehicle Maintenance Technology, Experimental Methods
DUBONJIĆ, R. R., Economy
GAJIĆ, A., Turbomachinery, Hydraulic Torque Converters
GEORGIJEVIĆ, D., Mathematics
GOLUBOVIĆ, Z., Mechanics
HOFMAN, M., Ship Theory, Ship Behaviour in Waves
IVANOVIĆ, G., Theory of Vehicle Motion, Theory of Effectiveness
JAĆIMOVIĆ, B., Process Planning, Heat and Mass Transfer Equipment
JANKES, G., Industrial Furnaces and Boilers, Furnace Design
JANKOVIĆ, J., Aircraft Equipment and Systems
JANKOVIĆ, M., Fundamentals of Machine Design
JARAMAZ, S., Interior Ballistics, Projectile Design
JOJIĆ, B. Ž., Aircraft Propulsion, Rocket Propulsion
KALAJDŽIĆ, M. J., Production Process Automation
KLARIN, M. M., Production Organization, Terotechnology
KORUGA, D., Bioautomatic Control
KOZIĆ, Đ., Thermodynamics, Heat and Mass Transfer
KRIVOŠIĆ, I. N., Aircraft Structure
KUBUROVIĆ, M., Environmental Engineering, Drying Equipment
MAJSTOROVIĆ, V., Quality Management
MARKOSKI, M. J., Cooling Devices, Pipelines
MARKOVIĆ, D., Agricultural Machines
MILINOVIĆ, M., Rocket and Launcher Design, Fire Control Systems
MILOSAAVLJEVIĆ, A., Engineering Materials
MILUTINOVIĆ, D., Manufacturing Technology, Industrial Robots
MLADENOVIĆ, N., Mechanics
NEDELJKOVIĆ, M., Hydraulic Machinery, Pumps and Fans
OGNJANOVIĆ, M., Machine Elements, Machine Design
PAVLOVIĆ, M., Fluid Mechanics, Gas Dynamics
PEŠIĆ, S., Aerodynamics, Propellers and Rotors
PETKOVIĆ, Z., Material Handling Machines, Steel Structures
PETROVIĆ, S. V., Internal Combustion Engine Theory and Design
PETROVIĆ, Z., Computer-Aided Design, Aircraft Armament
PILIPOVIĆ, M., Manufacturing Systems, Production Process Automation

PLAVŠIĆ, N. I., Machine Elements, Fundamentals of Machine Design
POKRAJAC, S., Sociology, Industrial Management
RAC, A. A., Tribology
RADENOVIĆ, S., Mathematics
RADOJČIĆ, D., Resistance, Propulsion Steering of Ships
RADOVANOVIĆ, M. R., Fuels, Industrial Water, Lubricants
RAŠUO, B., Aircraft Maintenance, Flight Mechanics
RIBAR, Z., Pneumoelectric Control Systems, Hydroelectric Control Systems
RUŽIĆ, D. B., Strength of Materials
SAVIĆ, B., Heat Turbomachines, Thermal Power Plants
SEDMAK, A., Engineering Materials
SEKULIĆ, A., Mechanism Design, Technical Drawing with Engineering Design Graphics
ŠIJAČKI ŽERAVČIĆ, V., Engineering Materials
SPASIĆ, Ž., Computer-Integrated Manufacturing
STEFANOVIĆ, Z., Aerodynamic Construction
STUPAR, S., Computer-Aided Design, Aircraft Armament
TANOVIĆ, L., Tools and Tooling, Manufacturing Technology
TOMIĆ, M., Internal Combustion Engines, Internal Combustion Engine Equipment
TOPIĆ, R., Agricultural Machinery Design and Construction
TOŠIĆ, S., Conveyors and Lifting Devices, Material Handling System Design
VELJIĆ, M., Agricultural Machinery Design and Construction
VUKOVIĆ, J. U., Mechanics
ZEKOVIĆ, D., Mechanics
ŽIVANOVIĆ, T., Power Steam Boilers, Plant Boilers

Faculty of Mining and Geology (7 Djušina Str., 11000 Belgrade; tel. (11) 323-8832; e-mail dean@rgf.bg.ac.rs; internet www.rgf.bg.ac.rs):

BABIĆ, D., Genetic Mineralogy, Mineralogy, Technical Mineralogy
BATALOVIĆ, V., Hydraulic and Pneumatic Machines in Mining, Boring Machines and Equipment, Exploitation and Oil and Gas Transport
BLEČIĆ, N., Coal Deposits, Mining Geology
ČALIĆ, N. M., Theoretical Bases of Mineral Processing, Mineral Processing
ČOKORILO, V., Underground Mining Mechanization
ĆORIĆ, S., Geostatic Calculation
CVETKOVIĆ MRKIĆ, S., Ground Improvement Methods and Engineering Geology
ĐAJIĆ, N., Thermodynamics, Heat Engines and Energy Plants, Automation and Process Control
DANGIĆ, A. V., Geochemistry, Mineral Raw Material Deposits, Geology and Environmental Protection
DEUŠIĆ, S., Mineral Processing Machinery and Equipment
DIMITRIJEVIĆ, S., Surveying, Mining Photogrammetry
ĐOKOVIĆ, I. M., Geological Mapping, Environmental Geology
DRAGIŠIĆ, V., Mineral Deposit Hydrogeology, General Hydrogeology
GAGIĆ, D., Methods and Technology for Underground Excavation of Bedded Deposits, Underground Excavation Methods
GRUBOR, D., Physics
GRUJIĆ, M., Mine Transport and Hoisting
GRŽETIĆ, I., Physical Chemistry of Ore Deposits, Geology and Environmental Protection, Laboratory Investigation of Mineral Resources

ILIĆ, M. M., Exploration of Building Material Deposits, Nonmetallic Mineral Deposits
IVIĆ, A. P., Mathematics
IVKOVIĆ, S. Ž., Elements of Machines, Machine Design, Metalworking
JANIĆIĆ, D., Historical Geology, Geology of Yugoslavia
JELENKOVIĆ, R., Metallic Mineral Deposits, Mineral Deposits
JEVREMOVIĆ, D., Engineering Geological Investigation, Geological Construction Materials
KARANOVIĆ, L., X-Ray Structural Analysis, Applied Crystallography
KNEŽEVIĆ, S., Historical Geology, Quaternary Geology, Stratigraphy of Yugoslavia
KOSTIĆ PULEK, A., Chemistry
LAZIĆ, M., Special Hydrogeology, Exploratory Drilling
LILIĆ, N., Mine Ventilation, Mine Safety, Environmental Impact of Surface Drilling
LOGAR, M., Silicate Classification, Industrial Product Mineralogy, Geology and Environmental Protection, Mineral Raw Materials in Technology
LOKIN, P. M., Principles of Geotechnics, Geotechnical Investigation Methods
MARINKOVIĆ, S., Chemistry, Oil Chemistry with Basic Refining
MAROVIĆ, M. S., Neotectonics, Geotectonics, Geology of Yugoslavia
MIHAJLOVIĆ, Đ., Palaeobotany, Palaeoecology, Evolutionary Palaeontology, Fossil Organism Comparative Morphology, Micropalaeontology
MILIČIĆ, M., Mathematics, Numerical Analysis
MILOVANOVIĆ, D. J., Metamorphic Rock Petrology, Technical Petrology, Yugoslav Rock Formation Geology
MITROVIĆ, V., Reservoir Physics, Fluid Mechanics, Oil and Gas Reservoir Engineering
PAVLOVIĆ, V., Open Pit Exploitation Technology, Open Pit Exploration Technology, Removal of Water in Open Pit Mining
PEŠIĆ, L., Essentials of Geology, Principles of Geology
PETKOVIĆ, Z., Basics of Deposit Exploitation, Mineral Resource Deposit Exploitation
POHARAC LOGAR, V., Instrumental Mineralogy, Mineralogy
POPOV, S. R., Physical Chemistry, Fundamentals of Inorganic Chemistry
PROHASKA, S. J., Hydrogeology
PURTIĆ, N. M., Drilling and Blasting
PUŠIĆ, M., Ground Water Dynamics and Hydrology
RABRENOVIĆ, D., Historical Geology, Palaeogeography
RADOJEVIĆ, J. R., Rock Mechanics, Geomechanics, Rock and Soil Mechanics
SIMEUNOVIĆ, D. M., Underground Mine Design, Mine Organization, Underground Excavation Methods
SIMIĆ, R., Surface Mining Methods, Removal of Water in Open Pit Mining
STAJEVIĆ, B., Solid Mineral Deposit Prospecting and Exploration, Geological and Geochemical Prospecting
STARČEVIĆ, M., Gravity Methods for Investigation, Geophysical Investigation Methodology, Seismology, Geophysical Electronic Instruments, Geophysics
STEVANOVIĆ, Z., Hydrogeological Investigation Methods, Hydrogeological Investigation
SUDAR, M., Micropalaeontology, Palaeontological and Biostratigraphic Research Methodology
SUNARIĆ, D., Engineering Geology, Engineering Geodynamics

TANSKOVIĆ, T., Mining Equipment Maintenance, Thermodynamic Machinery
TOMANEC, R., Raw Material Testing Methods for Mineral Processing Technology
TOMIĆ, V., Hydrogeological Mapping
TRIFUNOVIĆ, P., Mining Materials Technology
VUJASINOVIĆ, S. O., Ground Water Protection, Geology and Environmental Protection
VUJIĆ, S. B., Application of Computers in Mining, Programming
ZAJIĆ, B., Hoisting Equipment

Faculty of Organizational Sciences (Jove Ilića 154, 11040 Belgrade; tel. (11) 395-0893; e-mail dekanat@fon.bg.ac.rs; internet www.fon.bg.ac.rs):

ĆAMILOVIĆ, S. V., Human Resources Management
ČANGALOVIĆ, M., Operations Research, Discrete Mathematics
ĆIRIĆ, V. V., Computer Program Design Principles
ČUPIĆ, M. E., Decision Making Theory, Decision Support Systems
DABIĆ, S., Stock Exchanges and Shareholding
DAJOVIĆ, S. V., Mathematics
DRAKULIĆ, M., Information Systems and Law, Business Law
DULANOVIĆ, Ž., Basics of Organization, Organization Projects
FILIPOVIĆ, V., Marketing, Strategic Marketing
JOVANOV, Đ., Mathematics, Numerical Analysis
KOSTIĆ, K., Management Systems
KRČEVINAC, S. B., Operations Research, Econometric Methods
LAZAREVIĆ, B. J., Information System Design
LEVI JAKŠIĆ, M. I., Technology Management
MILIĆEVIĆ, V., Management Economics and Business Planning, International Management
MITROVIĆ, Ž. V., Quality Management, Quality Control
PEŠALJEVIĆ, M., Quality Management, Standardization Systems, Metrology Systems
PETROVIĆ, B. M., Work Studies
PETROVIC, M. M., Manpower Planning
RADENKOVIĆ, B., Simulation and Simulation Languages
RADOVIĆ, M. K., Fundamentals of Production Systems, Production Systems
STARČEVIĆ, D., Distributed Information Systems
TODOROVIĆ, J. M., Production Management
VUČIĆ, V. V., Mathematics, Operations Research
VUJOŠEVIĆ, M., Optimization Methods
VUKOVIĆ, N. A., Probability and Statistics
ŽARKIĆ JOKSIMOVIĆ, N., Financial Management and Accounting, Management Accounting

Faculty of Pharmacy (Vojvode Stepe 450, 11221 Belgrade; tel. (11) 247-3224; e-mail info@pharmacy.bg.ac.rs; internet www.pharmacy.bg.ac.rs):

AGBABA, D., Pharmaceutical Chemistry
DIMITRIJEVIĆ, M., Immunology
ĐURIĆ, Z., Pharmaceutical Technology with Biopharmacy, Industrial Pharmacy with Cosmetology
JANČIĆ, R., Botany
JELIĆ IVANOVIĆ, Z., Medicinal Biochemistry and Clinical Chemistry
JELIKIĆ STANKOV, M., Analytical Chemistry
JOVANOVIĆ, M., Pharmaceutical Technology with Biopharmacy, Industrial Pharmacy with Cosmetology

JOVANOVIĆ, T., General and Inorganic Chemistry
KORIĆANAC, Z, General and Inorganic Chemistry
KRSTIĆ, S., Pharmacology
LEPOSAVIĆ, G., Pathophysiology
MAJKIĆ SINGH, N., Medicinal Biochemistry and Clinical Enzymology
MALEŠEV, D., Physical Chemistry, Instrumental Methods, Chemical Laboratory Methods
MEDENICA, M., Physical Chemistry, Instrumental Methods, Chemical Laboratory Methods
MILETIĆ, I., Bromatology, Quality and Food Safety Control
POKRAJAC, M., Analytical Chemistry
RISTOVSKI, L., Physics
SPASIĆ, S., Medical Biochemistry, Statistics in Pharmacy
SPASOJEVIĆ KALIMANOVSKA, V., Medicinal Biochemistry and Clinical Enzymology
STOJANOV, M., General Biochemistry and Medicinal Biochemistry
STUPAR, M., Pharmaceutical Technology with Biopharmacy, Industrial Pharmacy with Cosmetology
UGREŠIĆ, N., Pharmacology
VLADIMIROV, S., Pharmaceutical Chemistry
VULETA, G., Industrial Pharmacy with Cosmetology
ŽIVANOVIĆ, L., Drugs Analysis

Faculty of Philology (Studentski trg 3, 11000 Belgrade; tel. (11) 263-8622; e-mail info@fil.bg.ac.rs; internet www.fil.bg.ac.rs):

BOGOSAVLJEVIĆ, S., German Literature
BOJOVIĆ, Z., Yugoslav Literature from the Renaissance to Romanticism
BOZOVIĆ, R. N., Arabic Language and Literature
BOZOVIĆ, Z. N., Russian Literature
ĆORIĆ, B., History of the Serbian Language
DERETIĆ, J. R., Serbian and South-Slav Literature
DESIĆ, M. P., Serbo-Croat Language Teaching Methodology
DJINDJIĆ, S. M., Albanian Studies
GRUBAČIĆ, S. K., German Language
HLEBEC, B., English Language
IVANIĆ, D., Modern Serbian Literature
JANIĆIJEVIĆ, J., Cultural Studies
JANKOVIĆ, V. D., Literary Theory
JEREMIĆ, L., World Literature and Literary Theory
JOVANOVIĆ, G. M., Polish Literature
KOJEN, L., Aesthetics and Literary Theory
MAROJEVIĆ, R. N., Russian Literature
NESKOVIĆ, R. R., Philosophical Fundamentals of Marxism
NIKOLIĆ, M., Contemporary Serbian Language
NOVAKOVIĆ, J. R., French Literature
PETKOVIĆ, N. B., Modern Yugoslav Literature, Twentieth Century Literature
PETROVIĆ, S. D., Sociology of Culture and Art
PIPER, P. J., Russian Literature
POLOVINA, V., General Linguistics
RADIĆ DUGONJIĆ, M., Russian Language
SIMIĆ, R. D., Contemporary Serbo-Croatian Language with Stylistics
STANKOVIĆ, B. D., Russian Language
STOJANOVIĆ, D. S., World Literature with Literary Theory
TANASKOVIĆ, D. R., Arabic Language and Literature
TRNAVCI, H. I., Albanian Language and Literature
VUKOBRAT, S., English Literature

Faculty of Philosophy (Čika Ljubina 18–20, 11000 Belgrade; tel. (11) 263-9119; e-mail info@f.bg.ac.rs; internet www.f.bg.ac.rs):

ALIBABIĆ, Š., Theory of Educational Organization

BANDIĆ, D. I., Ethnology of Yugoslavia (Spiritual Culture)
BOGDANOVIĆ, M. I., Social Research Methodology
BOGOSAVLJEVIĆ, S., Statistics in Psychology
BOJANOVIĆ, R. Ž., Psychology of Interpersonal Relations
BOLČIĆ, S. I., Sociology of Work
BULATOVIĆ, R. N., Andragogy of Work
CUPURDIJA, B., Social Anthropology
DENEGRI, J., History of Modern Art
DIMIĆ, L., Yugoslav History
DOŠEN, K., Philosophy
DUŠANIĆ, S. S., Ancient History
ELAKOVIĆ, S., History of Philosophy
HRNJICA, S., General Psychology with Personality Psychology
JELIĆ, V., History of Greek Literature
KAČAVENDA RADIĆ, N., Andragogy of Free Time
KOCIĆ, L. P., General Pedagogy
KOVAČEVIĆ, I., Methodology of Ethnology and Anthropology
KULJIĆ, T., Political Sociology
KUZMANOVIĆ, B., Social Psychology
LAZIĆ, M., Sociology
LJUSIĆ, R., National History of the New Age
LOMA, A., Historical Grammar of the Greek Language
MAKSIMOVIĆ, L. M., Byzantine History
MEDIĆ, S., Family Andragogy
MIKIĆ, Ž. M., Physical Anthropology
MILIĆ, A., Family Sociology
MILIN, M., Introduction to the Classics
MIMICA, A., History of Social Theory
MITROVIĆ, A., General History of the New Age
OPALIĆ, P., Social Pathology
PAJEVIĆ, D., Work Psychology
PEŠIĆ, M., Preschool Pedagogy
RADOŠ, K., Educational Psychology
RICL, M., Ancient History
RISTOVIĆ, M., General Modern History
ŠARANOVIĆ BOŽANOVIĆ, N., General Pedagogy
SPREMIĆ, M. M., General History of the Middle Ages
STANKOVIĆ, Dj. Dj., Yugoslav History
ŠUPUT, M., History of Architecture
TODIĆ, B., Introduction to Art History
TRNAVAC, N., School Pedagogy
VOJVODIĆ, M. S., General History of the New Age
VUJOVIĆ, S., Urban Sociology
ZEC, M., Introduction to Economics
ZUROVAC, M. M., Aesthetics

Faculty of Physical Chemistry (Studentski trg 12–16, 11000 Belgrade; tel. (11) 218-7133; e-mail ffh@ffh.bg.ac.rs; internet www.ffh.bg.ac.rs):

ANIĆ, S., Physical Chemistry
BAČIĆ, G., Physical Chemistry of Fluids, Nuclear Spectrometry
DONDUR, V., Chemical Kinetics, Catalysis
HOLCLAJTNER ANTUNOVIĆ, I., General Physical Chemistry, Plasma Physical Chemistry
JEREMIĆ, M., Physical Chemistry
MARKOVĆ, D., Physical Chemistry, Physical Chemistry in Environmental Protection
MENTUS, S. V., Electrochemistry, Physical Chemistry of Solid Electrolytes
MILJANIĆ, S., Radiochemistry and Nuclear Chemistry
MIOČ, U., Physico-Chemical Analysis, Applied Spectroscopy
PERIĆ, M. N., Quantum Chemistry and Molecular Structures, Spectra and Structures

Faculty of Physics (Studentski trg 12, 11000 Belgrade; tel. (11) 263-0152; e-mail dekanat@ff.bg.ac.rs; internet www.ff.bg.ac.rs):

ANIČIN, I., Nuclear Physics

BELIĆ, D. S., Atomic and Molecular Physics, Applied Physics

ĆURIĆ, M. B., Dynamic Meteorology, Cloud Physics

DAMNJANOVIĆ, M., Quantum and Mathematical Physics, Condensed Matter Physics

ĐENIŽE, S. I., Ionized Gas and Plasma Physics, Atomic and Molecular Physics

DRNDAREVIĆ, S., Nuclear Physics, Particle and Field Physics

JANJIĆ, Z. I., Dynamic Meteorology

KNEŽEVIĆ, M., Statistical Physics

KONJEVIĆ, N., Classical and Quantum Optics, Lasers

KRPIĆ, D., Nuclear Physics, Particle and Field Physics

MILOŠEVIĆ, S., Statistical Physics

PURIĆ, J. M., Ionized Gas and Plasma Physics

SAVIĆ, I., Nuclear Physics, Condensed Matter Physics

SREKOVIĆ, A., Ionized Gas and Plasma Physics

STAMATOVIĆ, A. S., Applied Physics, Atomic and Molecular Physics

ZEKOVIĆ, L., Applied Physics, Condensed Matter Physics

Faculty of Political Sciences (Jove Ilića 165, 11000 Belgrade; tel. (11) 397-6422; e-mail fpn@fpn.bg.ac.rs; internet www.fpn.bg.ac.rs):

DAMJANOVIĆ, M. D., Organization and Management Studies

JEVTIĆ, M., Religious and Political Studies

KECMANOVIĆ, N., Family Sociology

LAKIĆEVIĆ, M., Social Development and Planning

MILOSAVLJEVIĆ, M. V., Social Pathology

PAVLOVIĆ, V. D., Political Sociology of Modern Society

PEŠIĆ, M. D., General Sociology

PODUNAVAC, M. L., Theory of Political Systems

RADOJKOVIĆ, M. J., Communication Studies

SAMARDŽIĆ, S., European Relations and Studies

SIMEUNOVIĆ, D., Foundations of Political Science

SIMIĆ, M., Rehabilitation of Disabled Persons, Public Health

SLAVUJEVIĆ, Z., Political Marketing and Public Relations

SOKIĆ, S. R., Yugoslav Economy, National Economic Studies

ŠTAMBUK, V. Z., Cybernetics and Informatics

TRGOVČEVIĆ, L., Contemporary Political History

VASILJEVIĆ, B., Contemporary Political Economy

VESELINOV, D. S., Political Ecomony

VIDANOVIĆ, I., Social Case Work

VUKOVIĆ, D., Systems of Social Welfare

Faculty of Security Studies (Gospodara Vučića 50, 11000 Belgrade; tel. (11) 645-1843; e-mail dekanat@fb.bg.ac.rs; internet www.fb.bg.ac.rs):

CVETKOVIĆ, M., Contemporary Combat Systems and Devices

KANDIĆ, D., Introduction to Philosophy and Ethics, Ethics

MILAŠINOVIĆ, R., Conflict Theory

MIŠOVIĆ, S., Violent Conflict Theory

PLAVŠIĆ, M., Macroeconomics

Faculty of Sports and Physical Education (Blagoja Parovića 156, 11000 Belgrade; tel. (11) 353-1000; e-mail dekanat@dif.bg.ac.rs; internet www.dif.bg.ac.rs):

ALEXSIĆ, V., Football

BOKAN, B., Physical Culture Theory

ĆIRKOVIĆ, Z., Martial Arts

ILIĆ, N., Physiology

JOVANOVIĆ, S., Martial Arts

KARALEJIĆ, M., Basketball

KUKOLJ, M., General Anthropology

LAZAREVIĆ, L., Psychology

NIKOLIĆ, Z., Physiology

PETROVIĆ, Z., Physical Culture Facilities

RADISAVIJEVIĆ, L., Rhythmic-Sports Gymnastics

RADISAVIJEVIĆ, M., Corrective Gymnastics

RADOJEVIĆ, J., Sports Gymnastics

STAKIĆ, D., General Sociology and Physical Culture Sociology

STEFANOVIĆ, D., Athletics

UGARKOVIĆ, D., Human Development Biology with Elements of Sports Medicine

Faculty of Stomatology (Dr Subotića 8, 11000 Belgrade; tel. (11) 268-5288; e-mail dekan@stomf.bg.ac.rs; internet www.stomf.bg.ac.rs):

BELOICA, D. Ć., Paediatrics, Preventive Dentistry

DAPČEVIĆ, B., Internal Medicine

DERGENC, R, Otorhinolarnygology

DIMITRIJEVIĆ, B. B., Periodontology, Oral Medicine

DIMITRIJEVIĆ, B. R., Maxillofacial Surgery

GAVRIĆ, M. M., Maxillofacial Surgery

IVANOVIĆ, V., Conservation Dentistry Endodontics

JANKOVIĆ, L., Periodontology, Oral Medicine

KONTIĆ, M., General Surgery

LEKOVIĆ, V. M., Periodontology, Oral Mechine

MIJANOVIĆ, B., General Surgery

MIKOVIĆ, M. D., Forensic Medicine

MILENKOVIĆ, P. B., Pathophysiology

NIKODIJEVIĆ, M., General Surgery

NIKOLIĆ, L., Ophthalmology

PAP, K., Conservation Dentistry Endodontics

POTIĆ, J. B., Neurology and Psychiatry

SJEROBABIN, I., Maxillofacial Surgery

STAMENKOVIĆ, D., Prosthodontics

STANIŠIĆ-SINOBAD, D. N., Prosthodontics

STOJIĆ, D., Pharmacology, Toxicology

TODOROVIĆ, L. M., Oral Surgery

URSU MAGIDU, I., Periodontology, Oral Medicine

VRANJEŠ, D., Neurology and Psychiatry

VULOVIĆ, M. D., Paediatric Preventive Dentistry

ZELIĆ, O. B., Periodontology, Oral Medicine

Faculty of Teacher Training (Narodnog frontna 43, 11000 Belgrade; tel. (11) 361-5225; e-mail dekanat@uf.bg.ac.rs; internet www.uf.bg.ac.rs):

BANDJUR, V. B., Didactics

JOVANOVIĆ, A., Literature

KECMANOVIĆ, N., Sociology

Faculty of Technology and Metallurgy (Karnegijeva 4, 11000 Belgrade; tel. (11) 337-0460; e-mail tmf@tmf.bg.ac.rs; internet www.tmf.bg.ac.rs):

IVANIĆ, L., Casting, Theory of Casting

MAGADALINOVIĆ, D., Comminution and Classification

MARKOVIĆ, D., Materials Testing

MILIĆEVIĆ, Ž., Underground Mining Technology

MILJKOVIĆ, M., Mine Ventilation, Technical Safety Precautions

RAJČIĆ VUJASINOVIĆ, M., Hydro- and Electrometallurgical Process Theory

STANKOVIĆ, R., Transport and Haulage, Transport in Mineral Technologies

STANKOVIĆ, V., Metallurgical Operations

STANKOVIĆ, Z., Physical Chemistry

STANOJLOVIĆ, R., Physical Methods of Concentration, Mineral Processing

STAVRIĆ, B. J., Economics and Production Organization

ŽIVKOVIĆ, Ž., Nonferrous Metal and Alloy Metallurgy, Pyrometallurgical Process Theory

Faculty of Transport and Traffic Engineering (Vojvode Stepe 305, 11000 Belgrade; tel. (11) 309-1234; e-mail dean@sf.bg.ac.rs; internet www.sf.bg.ac.rs):

BABIĆ, O., Air Traffic Control, Air Cargo Transport

BAKMAZ, M. R., Telecommunications Switching Technology, Telecommunications Traffic and Networks

BOJKOVIĆ, Z. S., Electrical Engineering, Basic Telecommunications Technology, Telecommunications Traffic Exploitation

BUKUMIROVIĆ, M. M., Cybernetics, Cybernetics in Transport and Traffic, Computer Simulation, System Modelling on Computer, Programming Languages in Postal and Telecommunications Traffic

ČOLIĆ, V., Ships and Vessels, Ship Resistance and Propulsion, Basics of Water Transport

CVETKOVIĆ, P. A., Fluid Mechanics, Mechanics, Materials Strength

KUZMANOVIĆ, D., Mechanics

LAZOVIĆ, S. M., Telecommunication Systems

MANDIĆ, D., Railway Traction, Urban Rail Systems, Rail Traffic Operation, Application of Telematics and Process Automation in Railway Traffic

MILORADOVIĆ, S., Mathematics

PANTELIĆ VUJANIĆ, S., Sociology, Traffic and Transport Engineering Law, Navigable Waterways Law, Air Transport Law, Traffic Law, Postal and Telecommunications Law, Railway Transport Law

PAPIĆ, V., Motor Vehicle Maintenance, Transport Vehicles and Maintenance

POPOVIĆ, J., Probability and Statistics, Operations Research

PUTNIK, N. D., Terminals

RADMILOVIĆ, Z., Port Planning and Design, Fleet Operation and Management, Water Transport Basics

RADOJKOVIĆ, Z., Roads, Civil Engineering Basics

ŠELMIĆ, R. R., Elements of Transport Devices and Installations, Thermodynamics

SRETENOVIĆ, M., Materials Handling, Fundamentals in Materials Handling

TOŠIĆ, V. S., Airports

VEŠOVIĆ, V. B., Transport and Traffic Organization and Management, Transport and Traffic, Transport and Traffic Work Organization, Postal and Telecommunications Organization and Management

VUJANIĆ, M., Traffic Safety, Accident Prevention, Accident Reconstruction

VUKANOVIĆ, S. V., Traffic Management and Control, Intelligent Transport Systems

VUKOBRAT, M. D., Mechanics

ŽEŽELJ, S., Motor Vehicles

Faculty of Veterinary Medicine (Blv Oslobodenja 18, 11000 Belgrade; tel. (11) 361-5436; e-mail podrska@vet.bg.ac.rs; internet www.vet.bg.ac.rs):

ALEKSIĆ, Z., Forensic Veterinary Medicine

AŠANIN, R. M., Microbiology and Immunology

BALGOJEVIĆ, Z., Anatomy

BALTIĆ, M., Fish, Crab and Shellfish Food Quality and Hygiene

BOŽIĆ, T., Pathophysiology

BUNIČIĆ, O., Meat Hygiene and Meat Technology

DJURIČIĆ, B., Infectious Diseases of Domestic Animals

DOBRIĆ, Đ., Infectious Diseases of Domestic Animals

DREKIĆ, D. M., Anatomy

GLEDIĆ, D. S., Histology and Embryology

IVANOV, I., Ruminant and Swine Diseases, Clinical Diagnostics

JEZDIMIROVIĆ, M., Pharmacology and Toxicology
JOVANOVIĆ, M., General Pathology and Pathological Morphology
JOVANOVIĆ, S. J., Animal Breeding
KATIĆ, V., Dairy Product Hygiene
KATIĆ RADIVOJEVIĆ, S., Parasitology
KNEŽEVIĆ, M. A., General Pathology and Pathological Morphology
KULIŠIĆ, Z., Parasitology
LAZAREVIĆ, M., Physiology
MIJAČEVIĆ, Z. M., Dairy Product Technology
NIKOLIĆ, Z., Anatomy
NIKOLOVSKI STEFANOVIĆ, Z., Equine and Small Animal Disease, Clinical Propaedeutics
PALIĆ, T. D., Avian Diseases, Equine and Small Animal Diseases
PAVLOVIĆ, V., Domestic Animal Reproduction, Artificial Insemination
PEJIN, I., Statistics
PETRUJKIĆ, T., Domestic Animal Reproduction, Artificial Insemination
POPOVIĆ, D., Biophysics
POPOVIĆ, N., Wild Animal Diseases, Equine and Small Animal Diseases
RADENKOVIĆ DAMNJANOVIĆ, B., Animal Hygiene and General Hygiene
ŠAMANC, H., Ruminant and Swine Diseases
ŠĆEPANOVIĆ, D., Sociology and Ethics
ŠIMIĆ, M., Histology and Embryology
SINOVEC, Z., Animal Nutrition Physiology and Pathology
SMILJANIĆ, D., Unit Operations
STOJANOVIĆ, L. V., Dairy Product Hygiene
STOJIĆ, V., Physiology
TRAILOVIĆ, D., Cattle Production Economics and Organization, Health Care, Cattle and Food Marketing and Transfer, Equine and Small Animal Diseases, Clinical Propaedeutics
VASIĆ, J., Surgery, Orthopaedics, Ophthalmology
VICKOVIĆ, D., Forensic Veterinary Medicine
VUKOVIĆ, I., Meat Technology

School of Electrical Engineering (Blvr Kralja Aleksandra 73, 11120 Belgrade; tel. (11) 324-8464; e-mail dekanat@etf.rs; internet www.etf.bg.ac.rs):

CVETKOVIĆ, D. M., Mathematics
ĐORDJEVIĆ, A. R., Microwave Technology, Electromagnetics, Fundamentals of Electrical Engineering
DRAJIĆ, D. B., Statistical Telecommunication Theory, Computer Telecommunications, Digital Transfer Techniques, Transfer and Recording Codes
DUKIĆ, M., Signal Processing and Transfer, Telecommunications, Radio Systems
ĐURIĆ, M., Power System Components, Power Engineering System Regulation, Replay Protection, Power Stations and Distribution Plants
KOSTIĆ, M., Electrical Lighting, Electrical Installations with Lighting
KOVAČEVIĆ, B. D., Automatic Control, Stochastic Systems and Estimation
LACKOVIĆ, I. B., Mathematics
LAZIĆ, B., Fundamentals of Computer Technology, Computer Architecture, Operating Systems
MARJANOVIĆ, S. N., Electronics
MATAUŠEK, M. R., Optimal Process Control, Automatic Control Systems, Process Control, Process Identification
MERKELE, M., Mathematics, Probability and Statistics
MIKIČIĆ, D. J., Technical Mechanics with Hydraulics, Fundamentals of Mechanical Engineering
MILANOVIĆ, V., Quantum Mechanics, Electronic Device Components, Solid State

Physical Electronics, Semiconducting Microstructures
MILUTINOVIĆ, V., Microprocessing Systems, Computer VLSI Systems
OSMOKROVIĆ, P., Electrical Engineering Materials, Dosimetry and Radiation Protection, Nuclear Physics
PAUNOVIĆ, Đ., Radio Systems, Telecommunication Electronics, Radio Relay Systems, Design and Simulation Methods, Radiotechnics
PETROVIĆ, D., A.C. Electrical Machinery, Electromechanical Power Conversion
PETROVIĆ, G., Digital Telecommunications, Digital Telephone Exchange Design, Telecommunication Networks, Digital Transfer Technology, Communication System Simulation, Computational Systems
PETROVIĆ, T., Simulation and Modelling, Non-linear Control Systems, Automatic Control Robust Systems Regulation
PETROVIĆ, Z., Satellite Systems, Fundamentals of Telecommunications, Integrated Telecommunications Networks
POPOVIĆ, B. D., Electrical Measurements, Biomedical Engineering, Biomedical Instrumentation
POTKONJAK, V. N., Robots and Automation
PRAVICA, P. B., Telecommunications
RADUNOVIĆ, J. B., Materials Physics, Optoelectronic Devices and Systems, Optoelectronic and Laser Systems, Electro-optics, Statistical Physics
RAJAKOVIĆ, N., Distributive and Industrial Networks, Power Systems Analysis, Power Systems Exploitation, Power Systems Analysis
RAKOVIĆ, D., Materials Physics, Biophysics
RAMOVIĆ, R., Microelectronics, Electronic Device Components, Semiconductor Analysis and Modelling
REIJIN, B., Electrical Circuit Theory, Medical Informatics, Digital Information Processing, Electrical Circuit Theory
SAVIĆ, M. S., High Voltage Technology, High Voltage Equipment
ŠIMIĆ, S. K., Mathematics
ŠKOKLJEV, I., General Power Engineering, Power Engineering System Planning
SREĆKOVIĆ, M., Laser Technics, Quantum Electronics
STANKOVIĆ, D. K., Sensors and Converters, Physico-Technical Measurement, Sensors and Actuators
STANKOVIĆ, S. S., Stochastic Signal Processing, Artificial Intelligence and Neural Networks, Automatic Control Systems, Digital Signal Processing
STOJIĆ, M. R., Automatic Control, Digital Control Systems
VASILJEVIĆ, D. M., Digital System Design
VELAŠEVIĆ, D. M., Programming Compilers, Expert Systems, Digital Programming
ŽIVKOVIĆ, D. B., Computer System Control, Pulse and Digital Electronics
ZLATANOVIĆ, M. D., Sensors and Convertors, Atomic and Molecular Spectroscopy, Fundamentals of Mechanical Engineering

School of Medicine (Dr Subotica 8, 11000 Belgrade; tel. (11) 363-6368; e-mail boca@med.bg.ac.rs; internet www.med.bg.ac.rs):

ALEKSANDRIĆ, B., Forensic Medicine
ANTUNOVIĆ, V., Surgery
APOSTOLSKI, S., Neurology
ARSOV, V. J., Surgery
ASIĆ RADOSAVLJEVIĆ, G., Internal Medicine
AVRAMOVIĆ, D. M., Internal Medicine
BACETIĆ, D., Pathological Anatomy
BANIĆEVIĆ, M., Paediatrics
BLAGOTIĆ, M. Ž., Anatomy
BOGDANOVIĆ, R., Paediatrics
BOŠKOVIĆ, D., Internal Medicine

BOŠNJAK, V. I., Internal Medicine
BOŽANIĆ, M., Internal Medicine
BOŽIĆ, M., Infectious Diseases
BRKIĆ POPOVIĆ, V., Internal Medicine
BULAJIĆ, M., Internal Medicine
BUMBAŠIREVIĆ, V., Histology and Embryology
BUNJEVAČKI, G., Paediatrics
BUTKOVIĆ, I., Surgery
ČEBEŠEK, R., Internal Medicine
ČEMERIKIĆ, D. A., Pathological Physiology
ČOLOVIĆ, M., Internal Medicine
ČOLOVIĆ, R., Surgery
CUCIĆ, V. S., Social Medicine
CVEJIĆ, V., Biochemistry
CVETKOVIĆ, D. H., Pathological Anatomy
CVETKOVIĆ, M., Gynaecology and Obstetrics
DENIĆ DJORDJEVIĆ, G., Pathological Physiology
ĐERIĆ, D., Otolaryngology and Maxillofacial Surgery
DJORDJEVIĆ, L. V., Anatomy
DJURIČIĆ, B., Biochemistry
ĐORĐEVIĆ, M., Surgery
ĐORĐEVIĆ, P., Internal Medicine
DOTLIĆ, R., Statistics and Informatics in Medicine
DRAŠKOVIĆ MAŠIREVIĆ, G., Physiology
DREZGIĆ, M., Internal Medicine
ĐUKIĆ, P., Surgery
ĐUKIĆ, V., Surgery
DUNJIĆ, D., Forensic Medicine
ERIĆ MARINKOVIĆ, J., Statistics and Informatics in Medicine
GANOVIĆ, R., Gynaecology and Obstetrics
GLEDOVIĆ, Z., Epidemiology
GLIŠIĆ, S., Surgery
GOLUBOVIĆ, G., Internal Medicine
GOLUBOVIĆ, S., Ophthalmology
GRBOVIĆ, L. Č., Pharmacology and Toxicology
GRUJIĆ, M., Internal Medicine
HADŽI ĐOKIĆ, J. B., Surgery
HAN, R., Nuclear Medicine
HAVELKA, M., Pathological Anatomy
IGNAJČEV, M., Ophthalmology
ILANKOVIĆ, N., Psychiatry
ILIĆ, A. B., Anatomy
JAKOVIĆ, M., Surgery
JANIĆIJEVIĆ, M., Surgery
JANKOVIĆ, S., Epidemiology
JANOŠEVIĆ, L., Otolaryngology and Maxillofacial Surgery
JANOŠEVIĆ, S., Statistics and Informatics in Medicine
JAREBINSKI, M. S., Epidemiology
JAŠOVIĆ, M., Psychiatry
JEVREMOVIĆ, I., Epidemiology
JORGA, I., Physiology
JORGA, V., Hygiene and Medical Ecology
JOVANOVIĆ, T. M., Physiology
JOVANOVIĆ, T. P., Microbiology and Immunology
KALEZIĆ, V., Surgery
KAŽIĆ, T. M., Pharmacology and Toxicology
KOCIJANČIĆ, M., Internal Medicine
KOCIJANČIĆ, R., Hygiene and Medical Ecology
KONTIĆ, Đ., Ophthalmology
KOSTIĆ, V., Neurology
KOVAČEVIĆ, N., Internal Medicine
KOVAČEVIĆ, S. J., Forensic Medicine
LABAN, A. I., Pathological Anatomy
LAČKOVIĆ, V. B., Histology and Embryology
LASTIĆ, S. S., Anatomical Pathology
LATKOVIĆ, Z., Ophthalmology
LONČAR STEVANOVIĆ, H., Physiology
LOTINA, S., Surgery
LUKIĆ, V. S., Neurology
MAGLAJIĆ, S., Paediatrics
MAKSIMOVIĆ, Ž., Surgery
MANČIĆ, J., Paediatrics
MARIĆ, J., Psychiatry
MARINKOVIĆ, S. V., Anatomy

MARŠEVALSKI, A., Physical Medicine and Rehabilitation
MARTINOVIĆ, Ž., Neurology
MATIĆ, M., Internal Medicine
MICIĆ, D., Internal Medicine
MICIĆ, S., Surgery
MIJAĆ, M., Anatomy
MILENKOVIĆ, S., Ophthalmology
MILIĆEVIĆ, N., Histology and Embryology
MILIĆEVIĆ, R., Surgery
MILIĆEVIĆ, Ž., Histology and Embryology
MILIKIĆ MITIĆ, M., Internal Medicine
MILOVIĆ, I., Surgery
MILUTINOVIĆ, D., Surgery
MIMIĆ OKA, J. I., Biochemistry
MISITA, V., Ophthalmology
MITROVIĆ, M. M., Surgery
MUJOVIĆ, V. M., Physiology
MUNJIZA, M., Psychiatry
NEDELKJOV, V., Pathological Physiology
NEŠIĆ, V., Internal Medicine
NIKOLIĆ, G., Physical Medicine and Rehabilitation
NIKOLIĆ, P. L., Infectious Diseases
NIKOLIĆ, S., Infectious Diseases
OBRADOVIC, M., Forensic Medicine
OBRADOVIĆ, V., Nuclear Medicine
OCIĆ, G., Neurology
OSTOJIĆ, M., Internal Medicine
OŠTRIĆ, V., Internal Medicine
PANTELIĆ ATANACKOVIĆ, M., Pathological Anatomy
PANTIĆ, S., Histology and Embryology
PAOVIĆ STANOJEVIĆ, A., Ophthalmology
POPOVIĆ, R., Biology and Human Genetics
PAUNOVIĆ, V., Psychiatry
PAVLOVIĆ, M. D., Infectious Diseases
PAVLOVIĆ, M. R., Physiology
PAVLOVIĆ, M. Ž., Occupational Medicine
PAVLOVIĆ, S., Nuclear Medicine
PEJOVIĆ, M., Psychiatry
PERIŠIĆ, M., Internal Medicine
PERIŠIĆ, V., Paediatrics
PEŠIĆ, B., Pathological Physiology
PETKOVIĆ, S., Gynaecology and Obstetrics
PILIPOVIĆ, N., Internal Medicine
PLEĆAŠ, D., Hygiene and Medical Ecology
POPOVIĆ, G., Physical Medicine and Rehabilitation
POPOVIĆ, M. R., Surgery
POTIĆ VESOVIĆ, V., Physical Medicine and Rehabilitation
PROSTRAN, M., Anatomy
PROSTRAN, M., Pharmacology and Toxicology
RADEVIĆ, B., Surgery
RADONJIĆ, V., Anatomy
RADULOVIĆ, N., Paediatrics
RADULOVIĆ, R., Otolaryngology and Maxillofacial Surgery
RAMIĆ, Z., Microbiology and Immunology
RANKOVIĆ, A., Anatomy
REBIĆ, P., Internal Medicine
REPAC, R. M., Surgery
RISTIĆ, M., Surgery
RUNIĆ, S., Gynaecology and Obstetrics
SAMARDŽIĆ, M., Surgery
SAMARDŽIĆ, R. G., Pharmacology and Toxicology
ŠAŠIC, M., Infectious Diseases
SAVIČ DJURKOVIĆ, R. M., Biochemistry
ŞEFEROVIĆ, P., Internal Medicine
ŠIKIĆ, B., Pathological Physiology
SIMEUNOVIĆ, S. D., Paediatrics
SIMIĆ, S., Social Medicine
SINĐELIĆ, R., Surgery
SKENDER, M., Pathological Anatomy
SLAVKOVIĆ, S., Surgery
STANIMIROVIĆ, B., Gynaecology and Obstetrics
STARČEVIĆ, V., Physiology
STAROVIĆ, D., Surgery
STEFANOVIĆ, B., Histology and Embryology
STEVOVIĆ, D. M., Surgery
STOJKOVIĆ MOSTARICA, M., Microbiology and Immunology

SUBOTIĆ, S. L., Surgery
SUZIĆ, S., Physiology
TALIĆ, B. S., Surgery
TEOFILOVSKID, G. E., Anatomy
TIMOTIJEVIĆ, I., Psychiatry
TODOROVIĆ, S., Neurology
TRPINAC, D., Histology and Embryology
VASILJEVIĆ, J., Pathological Anatomy
VASILJEVIĆ, Z., Internal Medicine
VELIMIROVIĆ, D., Surgery
VELIMIROVIĆ, D., Pathological Anatomy
VELJKOVIĆ, S. D., Forensic Medicine
VIDAKOVIĆ, A. R., Occupational Medicine
VLAHOVIĆ SVABIĆ, M., Microbiology and Immunology
VLAJINAC, H. D., Epidemiology
VUČKOVIĆ, V., Physiology
VUČOVIĆ, D., Surgery
VULOVIĆ, D. M., Pathological Physiology
VULOVIĆ, Z., Chemistry in Medicine
ZAMAKLAR, D., Surgery
ZEC KRANJČIĆ, I., Microbiology and Immunology
ŽIVKOVIĆ, S., Surgery

Technical Faculty in Bor (Vojske Jugoslavije 12, 19210 Bor; tel. (30) 424-555; e-mail office@tf.bor.ac.rs; internet www.tf.bor.ac.rs):

IVANIĆ, L., Casting, Theory of Casting
MAGDALINOVIĆ, N. M., Comminution and Classification
MARKOVIĆ, D., Metals Testing
MILIĆEVIĆ, Ž. M., Underground Mining Technology
MILJKOVIĆ, M. A., Mine Ventilation, Technical Safety Precautions
RAJČIĆ VUJASINOVIĆ, M., Theory of Hydro- and Electrometallurgical Processes
STANKOVIĆ, R., Transport and Haulage, Transport in Mineral Technologies
STANKOVIĆ, V., Metallurgical Operations
STANKOVIĆ, Z. D., Physical Chemistry
STANOJLOVIĆ, R. D., Physical Concentration Methods, Mineral Processing
ŽIVKOVIĆ, Ž. D., Metallurgy of Non-Ferrous Metals and Alloys, Pyrometallurgical Process Theory

UNIVERZITET U KRAGUJEVCU
(University of Kragujevac)

Jovana Cvijica bb, 34000 Kragujevac

Telephone: (34) 370-270

E-mail: unikg@kg.ac.rs

Internet: www.kg.ac.rs

Founded 1976

State control

Academic year: October to June

Rector: Prof. Dr SLOBODAN ARSENIJEVIC
Vice-Rector for Finance: Prof. Dr BRANISLAV JEREMIC
Vice-Rector for Education: Prof. Dr SNEŽANA SOKOVIĆ
Vice-Rector for Int. Relations: Prof. Dr NENAD FILIPOVIĆ
Vice-Rector for Science and Research: Prof. Dr ZIVADIN BUGARCIC
Gen. Sec.: ZORICA AVRAMOVIC
Librarian: RUŽICA IGNJATOVIĆ

Library of 100,000 vols
Number of teachers: 1,000
Number of students: 14,000

Publication: *LIPAR* (cultural and literary themes, 4 a year)

DEANS

Faculty of Agriculture in Čačak: Prof. Dr VLADETA STEVOVIĆ
Faculty of Economics in Kragujevac: Prof. Dr VERICA BABIĆ
Faculty of Education in Jagodina: Prof. SRETKO DIVLJAN
Faculty of Engineering in Kragujevac: Prof. Dr MIROSLAV BABIĆ

Faculty of Hotel Management and Tourism in Vrnjačka Banja: Prof. Dr DRAGANA GNJATOVIĆ
Faculty of Law in Kragujevac: Prof. Dr PREDRAG STOJANOVIC
Faculty of Mechanical and Civil Engineering in Kraljevo: Prof. Dr MILOMIR GAŠIĆ
Faculty of Medical Sciences in Kragujevac: Prof. Dr PREDRAG ČANOVIĆ
Faculty of Natural Sciences and Mathematics in Kragujevac: Prof. Dr DRAGOSLAV NIKEZIC
Faculty of Philology and Arts in Kragujevac: Prof. Dr IVAN KOLARIĆ
Faculty of Technical Sciences in Čačak: Prof. Dr JEROSLAV ŽIVANIĆ
Teacher-Training Faculty in Užice: Prof. Dr RADMILA NIKOLIĆ

UNIVERZITET U NIŠU
(University of Niš)

Univerzitetski trg 2, 18000 Niš

Telephone: (18) 257-970

E-mail: uniuni@ni.ac.rs

Internet: www.ni.ac.rs

Founded 1965

State control

Rector: Prof. Dr DAGAN ANTIC (acting)
Vice-Rector for Finance: Prof. Dr SLOBODAN ANTIC (acting)
Vice-Rector for International Cooperation: Prof. Dr VESNA LOPICIC (acting)
Vice-Rector for Scientific Work: Prof. Dr DRAGAN DÖNITZ (acting)
Vice-Rector for Teaching: Prof. Dr VLASTIMIR DJOKIC (acting)
Sec.-Gen.: DRAGOSLAV DJOKIĆ

Number of teachers: 1,514
Number of students: 25,844

Publications: *Facta Universitatis* (scientific journal, irregular), *Teme* (journal for social theory and practice, 4 a year)

DEANS

Faculty of Arts: Prof. DRAGOSLAV ACIMOVIC (acting)
Faculty of Civil Engineering and Architecture: Prof. Dr DRAGAN ARANDJELOVIĆ
Faculty of Economics: Dr EVICA PETROVID
Faculty of Electronic Engineering: Prof. Dr DRAGAN ANTIĆ
Faculty of Law: Prof. Dr NEVENA PETRUSIC
Faculty of Mechanical Engineering: Prof. Dr VLASTIMIR NIKOLIĆ
Faculty of Medicine: Prof. Dr MILAN VIŠNJIĆ
Faculty of Occupational Safety: Prof. Dr LJILJANA ŽIVKOVIĆ
Faculty of Philosophy: Prof. Dr MOMCILO STOJKOVIC
Faculty of Science and Mathematics: Prof. Dr DRAGAN S. ĐORDEVIĆ
Faculty of Sports and Physical Education: Prof. Dr DOBRICA ŽIVKOVIČ
Faculty of Technology in Leskovac: Prof. Dr JAKOV STAMENKOVIĆ
Teacher-Training Faculty in Vranje: Prof. Dr STANA SMILJKOVIĆ

PROFESSORS

Faculty of Arts (Knjeginje Ljubice 10, 18000 Niš; tel. (18) 522-396; e-mail info@artf.ni.ac.rs; internet www.artf.ni.ac.rs):

CEKIĆ, N., Forms Design

Faculty of Civil Engineering and Architecture (Aleksandra Medvedeva 14, 18000 Niš; tel. (18) 588-200; e-mail gaf@gaf.ni.ac.rs; internet www.gaf.ni.ac.rs):

ANDJELKOVIĆ, H., Descriptive Geometry
ANDJELKOVIĆ, M., Industrial Facilities Design, Public Facilities Design
ARANDJELOVIĆ, D., Hydraulic Engineering
CEKIĆ, N., Public Facilities Design, Essential Designing

DAMNJANOVIĆ, M., Architectural Structures, Metal Structures, Metal Structures in Buildings

DRENIĆ, D., Structure Testing, Coupled and Special Structures

IGIĆ, T., Strength of Materials, Structure Plasticity and Limitation Analysis

ILIĆ, Č., Railway Engineering, Superstructures and Stations

ILIĆ, D., Housing Design, Project Development

MARKOVIĆ, M., Descriptive Geometry

MARKOVIĆ, V., Dams and Water Potential Utilization

MILENKOVIĆ, S., Urban Water Supply and Sewerage Systems Engineering

MITKOVIĆ, P., Urbanism, Area Planning

PETKOVIĆ, D., Concrete Structures, Concrete Bridges

POPOVIĆ, B., Structure Plasticity and Limitation Analysis, Structure Statics

PROLOVIĆ, V., Foundation Engineering

PROTIĆ, P., Mathematics

RADIVOJEVIĆ, G., Statics of Architectural Structures, Construction Systems

SPASOJEVIĆ, N., Concrete Bridges, Concrete Structures

STOJIĆ, D., Timber Structures and Scaffolds, Timber and Masonry Structures

TRAJKOVIĆ, D., Organization of Construction Works

VELIČKOVIĆ, D., Metal Structures

ZDRAVKOVIĆ, S., Structural Stability and Dynamics, Theory of Surface Girders

ŽIVKOVIĆ, D., Hydrotechnical Structures

ZLATANOVIĆ, M., Organization of Construction Works, Elements of Road Engineering

Faculty of Economics (Trg Kralja Aleksandra Ujedinitelja 11, 18000 Niš; tel. (18) 528-601; e-mail ekonomski@eknfak.ni.ac.rs; internet www.eknfak.ni.ac.rs):

ARANDJELOVIĆ, Z., Yugoslav Economy, Economic Policy

BARAC, N., Business Logistics Management

BOGDANOVIĆ, S., Mathematics

ČUZOVIĆ, S., Trade Economics, Trade Management

CVETANOVIĆ, S., Theory and Policy of Economic Development

DJEKIĆ, S., Agricultural Economics, Agricultural Management

FIGAR, N., Business Economics

GLIGORIJEVIĆ, Ž., Industrial Economics, Industrial Management

GROZDANOVIĆ, D., Business Economics

HAFNER, P., Sociology

JOVANOVIĆ, R., Informatics

KITANOVIĆ, D., Political Economy

KOSTIĆ, V., Russian Language

KRSTIĆ, B., Banking, Banking Management

KRSTIĆ, J., Financial Accounting, Auditing

NIKOLIĆ, S., Business Organization

NOVIĆEVIĆ, B., Managerial Accounting

PREDIĆ, B., Business Planning and Development Policy

SEKULOVIĆ, M., Economic Doctrines, Transition Economics

STANKOVIĆ, L., Marketing, International Marketing

TODOROVIĆ, E., Business Finance

TODOROVIĆ, O., Operations Research, Financial Mathematics

ZDRAVKOVIĆ, D., Theory of Prices and Pricing Policy

Faculty of Electronic Engineering (Aleksandra Medvedeva 14, 18000 Niš; tel. (18) 529-105; e-mail efinfo@elfak.ni.ac.rs; internet www.elfak.ni.ac.rs):

ARSIĆ, M., Measurements in Electronics, Telemetry

DAMNJANOVIĆ, M., VLSI Design, Electronic System Design

DANKOVIĆ, B., Methods of Intelligent Control, Process Control, Process Identification

DELETIĆ, S., Theory of Social Development

DIMITRIJEVIĆ, B., Electrical Measurement, Intelligent Instrumentation, Measurement in Microelectronics

DJORDJEVIĆ, B., Digital Electronics, Electronic Circuits

DJORDJEVIĆ KAJAN, S., Computer Graphics, Systems Software, Data Structures and Databases, Software Engineering

GMITROVIĆ, M., Network Synthesis and Signal Processing

JANKOVIĆ, N., Power Components and Circuits, Sensors and Convertors

KOCIĆ, LJ., Mathematics, Numerical Mathematics

KOVAČEVIĆ, M., Mathematics, Numerical Mathematics

KRSTIĆ, D., Wireless Engineering, High-Frequency Electronics

LITOVSKI, V., Electronics, Neural Networks, Electronic Circuit Design

MARKOVIĆ, V., Microwave Electronics, Satellite Communications

MILOSAVLJEVIĆ, Č., Elements of Automatic Control, EMP Regulation

MILOŠEVIĆ, M., Electroacoustics, Audiotechnics

MILOVANOVIĆ, B., Microwave Technology, Microwave Systems, Mobile Telecommunications

MILOVANOVIĆ, D., Electronics, Analogue Electronics

MILOVANOVIĆ, G., Mathematics, Mathematical Methods, Numerical Mathematics

MILOVANOVIĆ, I., Mathematics, Discrete Mathematics

MITIĆ, D., Elements of Electrical Engineering, Electromagnetics

NAUMOVIĆ, M., SAU Design, Automatic Control Theory, Intelligent Control Methods

NIKOLIĆ, Z., Quality and Reliability

NIKOLIĆ, Z., Mobile Telecommunications, Basic Telecommunications, Telecommunications in Electronic Power Engineering

PEJČIĆ, M., Philosophy and Sociology

PEJOVIĆ, M., Physics

PETKOVIĆ, M., Mathematics

PETKOVIĆ, P., Computer-Aided Design, Electronics Circuit Design, Integrated Circuit Design

RADENKOVIĆ, V., Electrical Measurement, Measurement in Electric Power Engineering

RANČIĆ, P., Electrical Installations and Illumination, Special Electrical Installations

RISTIĆ, S., Electronic Components, Semiconducting Components, Power Components and Circuits

STANKOVIĆ, M., Basic Computer Technology, Programming Languages, Assemblers

STANKOVIĆ, R., Logic Design, Pattern Recognition

STEFANOVIĆ, D., Optoelectronics

STEFANOVIĆ, M., Optic Telecommunications, Telecommunication Theory, Digital Telecommunications, Telecommunication System Design, Radar Systems and Radiolocation

STOJADINOVIĆ, N., Quality and Reliability, Physical Electronics, Failure Physics and Diagnostics, Components Characterization, Basic Microelectronics

STOJANOVIĆ, V., Circuit Theory, Television Systems, Television, Digital Picture Processing

STOJČEV, M., Microprocessing Technology, Microprocessing Systems

STOJILKOVIĆ, S., Low Temperature Electronics

TOKIĆ, T., Microcomputers and Programming, Microcomputer Systems and I/O Devices

VELIČKOVIĆ, D., Electromagnetics, Basic Electrical Engineering

ŽIVKOVIĆ, LJ., Materials for Electronics

Faculty of Law (Trg Kralja Aleksandra 11, 18000 Niš; tel. (18) 500-201; e-mail pravni@prafak.ni.ac.rs; internet www.prafak.ni.ac.rs):

BOŽIĆ, M., Economic Policy

ĆIRIĆ, A., International Trade Law

DJURDJIĆ, V., Criminal Procedural Law with Crime Investigation and Law Enforcement

GORČIĆ, J., Financial Law

KONSTANTINOVIĆ-VILIĆ, S., Criminology, Penology

KOVAČEVIĆ-KUŠTRIMOVIĆ, R., Introduction to Civil and Property Law

MIJAČIĆ, M., Law of Obligation

MILENOVIĆ, D., Trade Law

NIKOLIĆ, D., General Legal History

PETROVIĆ, M., Administrative Law, Management Science with Legal Informatics

RADIVOJEVIĆ, Z., Public International Law

ROČKOMANOVIĆ, M., Private International Law

SERJEVIĆ, V., Political Economy

SIMIĆ, M., Introduction to Law

STANIMIROVIĆ, D., Sociology

STANKOVIĆ, G., Civil Procedural Law, Arbitration Law

STOJANOVIĆ, D., Constitutional Law

STOJIČIĆ, S., National Legal History

Faculty of Mechanical Engineering (ul. Aleksandra Medvedeva 14, 18000 Niš; tel. (18) 588-229; e-mail info@masfak.ni.ac.rs; internet www.masfak.ni.ac.rs):

BLAGOJEVIĆ, B., Aeration and Ventilators, Cooling Techniques

BOGDANOVIĆ, B., Hydro-Power Transmitters, Compressors and Ventilators, Piping

BORIČIĆ, Z., Fluid Mechanics, Hydraulic and Pneumatic Systems of Automatic Control

ĆOJBAŠIĆ, LJ., Basic Processing Technology, Prime Materials

DJOKIĆ, V., Theory and Methods of Mechanical Systems Design, Elements of Construction Theory, Construction Methods, Welded Constructions, Rubber Construction Machines

DJORDJEVIĆ, D., Sociology and Philosophy of Natural Sciences, Basic Labour Sociology and Economics

DJURDJANOVIĆ, M., Welding, Welding Technology, Machine Systems Tribology

DOMAZET, D., Modelling and Optimization of Production Systems, Computer-Aided Production Design

HEDRIH, K., Elastodynamics

ILIĆ, G., Measurement Technology, Thermodynamics

JEVTIĆ, V., Technical Logistics, Mining and Building Machinery, Continuous Transport Machinery, Mining Mechanization, Driving System Dynamics, Fundamentals of Technical Logisitics

JOVANOVIĆ, M., Computer-Aided Design, Information Technologies, Structure Analysis, Geometric Modelling, Metal Construction

LAKOVIĆ, S., Thermal Plants, Thermal Power Plants, Boilers

LAZAREVIĆ, D., Tools, Non-Conventional Methods, Polymer Modelling Tools

MARINKOVIĆ, V., Machining, Processing Tribology

MILENKOVIĆ, D., Turbomachine Theory and Fundamentals, Hydraulic Machines, Special Pumps

MILOVANČEVIĆ, D., Mathematics

MILTENOVIĆ, V., Machine Parts, Reliability of Machine Systems, Integral Product Development, Machine System Supervision and Protection

NIKODIJEVIĆ, D., Fluid Mechanics, Oil Hydraulics and Pneumatics, Hydraulic Components, Hydro-Pneumatic Elements in Mechatronics, Physics

NIKOLIĆ, V., Automatic Control, Automatic Control Discrete Systems, Systems of Control in Mechatronics, Optimal Control, Nonlinear Control Systems, Neural and Fuzzy Modelling and Control

PAVLOVIĆ, N., Mechanisms in Mechatronics, Micromechanics, Elements of Fine Mechanics, Optical Elements in Mechatronics

PAVLOVIĆ, R., Mechanics, Plate and Shell Theory

PETKOVIĆ, LJ., Mathematics, Numerical Mathematics and Programming

PETROVIĆ, T., Measurement Techniques, Basic Mechatronics, Mechanical Elements in Mechatronics, Mechatronic System Design, Special Design Methods

RADOJKOVIĆ, N., Thermodynamics, Thermal and Diffusing Apparatus

STEFANOVIĆ, A., Internal Combustion Engines

STOJILJKOVIĆ, M., Automation of Production, Packing Machines, Pneumatic and Hydraulic Components, Assembling and Packing Technology, Digital Control Techniques

STOJILJKOVIĆ, V., Production Management, Processing by Plastic Deformation, Management in Mechanical Engineering, Production Process Statistical Control

TASIĆ, Ž., Electrical Engineering and Electronics, Basic Mechatronics

TEMELJKOVSKI, D., Machines for Processing by Deformation

VULIĆ, A., Power Conveyors, Quality of Machine Systems, Technical Diagnostics, Special-Purpose Machines, Agricultural Machines

ŽIVKOVIĆ, D., Hydromechanics of Mixtures, Thermal Turbomachines

ŽIVKOVIĆ, Ž., Theory of Machines and Mechanisms, Technical Drawing, Mechatronic System Modelling

Faculty of Medicine (Blvr Dr Zorana Đinđića 81, 18000 Niš; tel. (18) 457-0029; e-mail contact@medfak.ni.ac.rs; internet www.medfak.ni.ac.rs):

ANTIĆ, M., Medical Sociology
BABIĆ, M., Neurosurgery
BAŠIĆ, H., Pathological Anatomy
BJELAKOVIĆ, G., Biochemistry
BOGIĆEVIĆ, M., Nuclear Medicine
BOŠNAKOVIĆ, P., Radiology
BURAZOR, M., Internal Medicine, Cardiology
DAĆIĆ-SIMONOVIĆ, D., Dental Pathology
DENOVIĆ, B., Forensic Medicine
DIMOV, D., Pathological Anatomy
DJORDJEVIĆ, D., Internal Medicine, Pneumophysiology
DJORDJEVIĆ, V., Biochemistry
DJORDJEVIĆ, V., Internal Medicine, Nephrology
FILIPOVIĆ, S., Elements of Clinical Oncology
IGIĆ, A., Prosthodontics
IGIĆ, S., Prosthodontics
ILIĆ, R., Pathological Anatomy
ILIĆ, S., Internal Medicine, Cardiology
ILIĆ, SL., Nuclear Medicine
JEREMIĆ, M., Surgery, General Surgery
JOVANOVIĆ, D., Physiology
JOVČIĆ, S., Paediatric Surgery
KAMENOV, B., Paediatrics
KATIĆ, V., Pathological Anatomy
KOCIĆ, B., Microbiology and Immunology

KOJOVIĆ, Z., Physical Medicine and Rehabilitation
KONSTANTINOVIĆ, LJ., Infectology
KOSTIĆ, V., Infectology
KOSTIĆ, Ž., Hygiene and Medical Ecology
KRSTIĆ, M., Infectology
KUTLEŠIĆ, Ć., Pathological Anatomy
LOVIĆ, B., Internal Medicine, Cardiology
MALOBABIĆ, Z., Pharmacology and Toxicology
MARKOVIĆ, V., Internal Medicine, Cardiology
MARKOVIĆ, Z., Internal Medicine, Rheumatology
MIHAJLOVIĆ, D., Pathological Anatomy
MIHAJLOVIĆ, M., Physiology
MIHAJLOVIĆ, P., Physics
MILADINOVIĆ, P., Gynaecology and Obstetrics
MILATOVIĆ, S., Radiology
MILENKOVIĆ, Z., Surgery, Neurosurgery
MILIĆEVIĆ, R., Paediatric Surgery
MILJKOVIĆ, S., Psychiatry with Medical Psychology
MILOSAVLJEVIĆ, LJ., Otorhinolaryngology
MILOSAVLJEVIĆ, M., Gynaecology and Obstetrics
MIRKOVIĆ, B., Oral and Periodontal Diseases
MITIĆ, N., Dental Pathology
MITIĆ, S., Dental Pathology
MITROVIĆ, M., Surgery, Orthopaedics
MITROVIĆ, R., Hygiene, Medical Ecology
NIKOLIĆ, J., Biochemistry
NOVAK, D., Paediatrics
ORLOV, S., Oral and Periodontal Diseases
PARAVINA, M., Dermatovenereology
PAVLOVIĆ, D., Biochemistry
PEROVIĆ, M., Histology and Embryology
POP-TRAJKOVIĆ, Ž., Gynaecology and Obstetrics
RADENKOVIĆ, S., Pathological Physiology
RADIĆ, S., Pathological Physiology
RAIĆEVIĆ, R., Internal Medicine, Nephrology
RANKOVIĆ, Ž., Infectology
SAVIĆ, M., Paedodontics and Preventive Stomatology
SAVIĆ, V., Pathological Anatomy
SKOĆAJIĆ, S., Dental Pathology
SPALEVIĆ, M., Forensic Medicine
SPASIĆ, M., Epidemiology
STAMENKOVIĆ, I., Internal Medicine, Gastroenterology
STANIŠIĆ, V., Medical Statistics and Informatics
STANKOVIĆ, A., Internal Medicine, Rheumatology
STANKOVIĆ, D., Prosthodontics
STEFANOVIĆ, N., Anatomy
STEFANOVIĆ, V., Internal Medicine, Nephrology
STOJILJKOVIĆ, M., General Surgery
STOJILJKOVIĆ, S., Pathological Physiology
TIODOROVIĆ, B., Epidemiology
VELJKOVIĆ, S., Physiology
VIŠNJIĆ, M., Plastic Surgery
VUĆETIĆ, D., Gynaecology and Obstetrics
VUĆETIĆ, R., Anatomy
VUJIĆIĆ, B., Oral Surgery
ZLATANOVIĆ, G., Opthalmology
ŽIVKOVIĆ, DJ., Internal Medicine, Pneumophysiology

Faculty of Occupational Safety (Čarnojevića 10A, 18000 Niš; tel. (18) 529-701; e-mail dekanat@znrfak.ni.ac.rs; internet www.znrfak.ni.ac.rs):

ANDJELKOVIĆ, B., Protection against Fire in Technical Processes, Introduction to Working and Living Environment Protection, Technological Processes in the Living Environment
CVETKOVIĆ, D., Noise and Vibrations, Noise in the Living Environment
DJORDJEVIĆ, J., Sociology, Social Ecology

IVANJAC, M., Labour Law
JANKOVIĆ, Ž., Safety at Work with Machines and Devices, Fire Extinguishing Processes and Methods
JOVANOVIĆ, D., Protection against Fire and Explosions, Uncontrolled Combustion Processes
MITIĆ, D., Ignition and Combustion Theory, Engineering Materials
NEDELJKOVIĆ, V., Ventilation and Air-Conditioning Systems, Energy and Living Environment
SPASIĆ, D., Economics of Occupational Safety, Economics of Environmental Protection
STANKOVIĆ, M., Mathematics, Mathematical Modelling
ŽIVKOVIĆ, LJ., Safety at Work with Thermal Plants
ŽIVKOVIĆ, N., Systems and Equipment for Industrial Waste Treatment, Air Protection

Faculty of Philosophy (Ćirila i Metodija 2, 18000 Niš; tel. (18) 514-312; internet www.filfak.ni.ac.rs):

BOGDANOVIĆ, N., History of Serbian Language, Dialectology
BUTIGAN, Z., Sociology of Politics
DJORDJEVIĆ, Z., Introduction to History with Methodology
DJUROVIĆ, R., Serbian Language (Phonology with Accentology)
IVKOVIĆ, M., Sociology of Education, Social Sciences Teaching Methods
MAŠOVIĆ, D., Introduction to American Studies, American Literature
MILOSAVLJEVIĆ, LJ., History of Social Theories, Introduction to Philosophy
MITROVIĆ, LJ., General Sociology
NAUMOVIĆ, M., Sociology of Rural Areas, Sociology of Urban Areas
NEŠIĆ, B., Pedagogical Psychology
NEŠIĆ, V., Social Psychology
PETROVIĆ, C., Political Economy with Elements of Economic Systems
RISTIĆ, R., Introduction to Canadian and Australian Studies
STOJADINOVIĆ, M., Yugoslav Literature
STOJANOVIĆ, M., Yugoslav Literature
STOJKOVIĆ, M., Sociology of Morals, Labour Sociology
VELIĆKOVIĆ, D., Russian Language
VIDANOVIĆ, DJ., English Morphology and Teaching Methods
ŽUNIĆ, D., Sociology of Art, Sociology of Culture and Arts with Serbian Cultural History

Faculty of Science and Mathematics (Višegradska 33, 18000 Niš; tel. (18) 223-430; e-mail dragan@pmf.ni.ac.rs; internet www.pmf.ni.ac.rs):

ĆIRIĆ, M., Mathematical Logic, Computer Technology Teaching Methods, Philosophy and History of Mathematics
DIMITRIJEVIĆ, P., Electromagnetism and Optics, Physics
JANKOVIĆ, S., Differential and Integral Equations, Theory of Probability and Random Processes
KOĆINAC, LJ., Linear Algebra and Analytical Geometry, Topology
MILETIĆ, G., Instrumental Analytical Chemistry
MILJKOVIĆ, LJ., Solid State Physics, Physics of Materials
NIKOLIĆ, R., Higher Inorganic Chemistry
NOVAKOVIĆ, N., Physics, Plasma Physics
OBRADOVIĆ, M., Physical Chemistry
PALIĆ, R., Organic Chemistry
PAVLOTIĆ, T., Mechanics and Thermodynamics, Physics of Surfaces and Thin Layers
PECEV, T., Analytical Chemistry
PREMOVIĆ, P., General and Inorganic Chemistry

PURENOVIĆ, M., Industrial Chemistry
RADOVANOVIĆ, B., Instrumental Methods of Structural Analysis, Mechanisms of Organic Reactions
RAKOČEVIĆ, V., Functional Analysis, Theory of Measures and Integrals
STANIMIROVIĆ, P., Programming Languages, Mathematical Programming
URSIĆ-JANKOVIĆ, J., Biochemistry

Faculty of Sports and Physical Education (Čarnojevića 10A, 18000 Niš; tel. (18) 510-900; e-mail info@ffk.ni.ac.rs; e-mail faksfiz@ni.ac.rs):

BUBANJ, R., Biomechanics
DJURAŠKOVIĆ, R., Biology of Human Development with Sports Medicine
JOKSIMOVIĆ, S., Football, Skiing
KOSTIĆ, R., Dancing
KOSTIĆ, R., Volleyball
PETKOVIĆ, D., Sports Gymnastics
POPOVIĆ, R., Rhythmical and Sports Gymnastics
VUČKOVIĆ, S., Recreation Theory and Teaching Methods, Activities in Nature
ŽIVANOVIĆ, N., Theory and History of Physical Education
ŽIVKOVIĆ, D., Theory of Corrective Gymnastics, Corrective Gymnastics Teaching Methods

Faculty of Technology in Leskovac (Blvr oslobodjenja 124, 16000 Leskovac; tel. (16) 247-203; e-mail info@tehfin.tehfak.ni.ac.rs):

CAKIĆ, M., Physical Chemistry, Instrumental Analysis
CVETKOVIĆ, D., Organic Chemistry, Organo-Chemical Technology
CVETKOVIĆ, LJ., Production Management and Basic Marketing, Product Management
DJORDJEVIĆ, G., Mathematics
DJORDJEVIĆ, S., Organic Chemistry
GLIGORIJEVIĆ, V., Planning of Textile Processes, Knitting Technology
ILIĆ, P., General Chemistry
KOCIĆ, M., Physics
MARKOVIĆ, D., Instrumental Analysis, Organic Analysis, Chemical-Engineering Thermodynamics
NOVAKOVIĆ, M., Dyeing and Printing Technology
STANKOVIĆ, M., Biochemistry, Technology of Natural Organic Products
STANKOVIĆ, S., Analytical Chemistry
STOJILJKOVIĆ, D., Elements of Equipment in Processing Industry, Engineering Drawing, Mechanics
STOJILJKOVIĆ, S., Thermodynamics and Thermotechnics, Construction Materials, Process Analysis and Simulation, Chemical-Engineering Thermodynamics
TRAJKOVIĆ, C., Clothing Production Technology, Textile Quality Control and Testing
VELJKOVIĆ, V., Unit Operations in Chemical Engineering

Teacher-Training Faculty in Vranje (Partizanska 14, 17500 Vranje; tel. (17) 431-960; e-mail ucfaxvranje@yahoo.com; internet www.ucfak.ni.ac.rs):

CENIĆ, S., General Pedagogy, History of Pedagogy
MALINOVIĆ, T., Mathematics, Mathematical Teaching Methods

UNIVERZITET U NOVOM PAZARU
(University of Novi Pazar)

Demetrius Tucovića bb, 36300 Novi Pazar
Telephone: (20) 316-634
E-mail: info@uninp.edu.rs
Internet: www.uninp.edu.rs

Founded 2002
Private control

Language of instruction: Bosnian, English, German, Serbian
Academic year: October to July
Pres.: MUFTI MUAMER EF. ZUKORLIĆ
Rector: Prof. Dr MEVLUD DUDIC
Pro-Rector: Dr AMELA LUKAČ
Gen. Man.: Dr NUSRET NICEVIĆ
Man.: ALEKSANDAR IVANOVIĆ

Library of 10,000 vols
Number of teachers: 270
Number of students: 2,500

Publications: *AGROBIZ, Pravni izazovi na početku XXI veka, Univerzitetska misao*

DEANS

Department of Art: Prof. Dr FEHIM HUSKOVIĆ
Department of Economics: Prof. Dr BEĆIR KALAC
Department of Legal Science: Prof. Dr MUAMMER NICEVIĆ
Department of Natural and Technical Sciences: Prof. Dr CAMIL SUKIĆ
Department of Pedagogical and Psychological Science: Dr ADMIR MURATOVIĆ
Department of Philological Sciences: Dr ŠAMINA DAZDAREVIĆ

UNIVERZITET U NOVOM SADU
(University of Novi Sad)

Trg Dositeja Obradovića 5, 21000 Novi Sad
Telephone: (21) 6350-622
E-mail: rektorat@uns.ac.rs
Internet: www.uns.ac.rs

Founded 1960
State control
Languages of instruction: Hungarian, Serbian
Academic year: October to July
Rector: Prof. MIROSLAV VESKOVIĆ
Vice-Rector for Education: Prof. MILAN SIMIĆ
Vice-Rector for Finance: Prof. RADOVAN PEJANOVIĆ
Vice-Rector for International Relations and Science: Prof. PAVLE SEKERUŠ
Vice-Rector for Students: GORAN RADIĆ
Gen. Sec.: ANĐELKA STANOJEVIĆ

Library of 15,000 vols, 450 theses, 400 periodicals
Number of teachers: 3,300
Number of students: 48,415

Publication: *Glas Univerziteta* (newspaper, 12 a year)

DEANS

Academy of Arts: Prof. ZORAN TODOVIĆ
Faculty of Agriculture: Prof. Dr MILAN KRAJINOVIĆ
Faculty of Civil Engineering: Prof. Dr DRAGAN MILAŠINOVIĆ
Faculty of Economics: Prof. Dr NENAD VUNJAK
Faculty of Education: Prof. Dr ALEKSANDAR PETOJEVIĆ
Faculty of Law: Prof. Dr RANKO KEČA
Faculty of Medicine: Prof. Dr NIKOLA GRUJIĆ
Faculty of Natural Sciences and Mathematics: Prof. Dr NEDA MIMICA-DUKIĆ
Faculty of Philosophy: Prof. Dr LJILJANA SUBOTIĆ
Faculty of Sport and Physical Education: Prof. Dr MILENA MIKALAČKI
Faculty of Technical Sciences: Prof. Dr ILIJA ĆOSIĆ
Faculty of Technology: Prof. Dr ZOLTAN ZAVARGO
'Mihajlo Pupin' Technical Faculty: Prof. Dr MILAN PAVLOVIĆ
Teacher Training Faculty in Hungarian: Prof. Dr KATALIN KAIĆ

PROFESSORS

Academy of Arts (Akademija Umetnosti, Djure Jakšića 7, 21000 Novi Sad; tel. (21)

422-177; e-mail aofarts@uns.ac.rs; internet www.akademija.uns.ac.rs):

BLANUŠA, M., Painting and Painting Technology
ČERNOGUBOV, B., Choir
DENKOVIĆ, LJ., Sculpture
DJAK, Ž., Graphics and Graphic Technology
DOBANOVAČKI, B., Poster Arts
DRAŠKOVIĆ, B., Acting, Directing
GILIĆ, V., Directing
HORVAT, L., Viola
JANKETIĆ, M., Acting
JOVANOVIĆ, V., Elements of Vocal Technique
JOVANOVIĆ, Z., Chamber Music
KATUNAC, D., History of Music, History of Performing
KINKA, R., Piano
KLEMENC, I., Stage Movement
KNEŽEVIĆ, S., Graphics and Graphic Technology
LAZIĆ, R., History and Aesthetics of Directing
MARINKOVIĆ, O., Diction
MIŠIĆ, LJ., Dance
OGNJENOVIĆ, V., Acting
OSTOJIĆ, N., Tone Syllable
OSTOJIĆ, T., Conducting
PREDOJEVIĆ-MILOVANOVIĆ, V., Voice Technique
RAKIDŽIĆ, J., Painting and Painting Technology
RNJAK, D., History of World Drama and Theatre
SIMONOVIĆ, M., Voice Technique
SRDIĆ, N., Clarinet
STANOJEV, M., Graphics and Graphic Technology
STAŠEVIĆ, M., Drawing and Drawing Technology
ŠUBOTIĆ, I., History of Art
STATKIĆ, M., Composition
TODOROVIĆ, D., Painting and Painting Technology
UZELAC, M., Aesthetics
VARGA, I., Cello

Faculty of Agriculture (Poljoprivredni Fakultet, Trg Dositeja Obradvića 8, 21000 Novi Sad; tel. (21) 485-3500; e-mail dean@polj.ns.ac.rs; internet polj.uns.ac.rs):

ALMAŠI, R., Special Entomology
ANTOV, G., Cattle Breeding, Animal Husbandry
BABIĆ, LJ., Drying and Storage, Basic Agricultural Engineering
BAJKIN, A., Agricultural Machinery
BALAŽ, F., Mycoses of Plants, Plant Protection
BALAŽ, J., Mycoses and Bacterioses of Plants
BELIĆ, S., Water Management, Irrigation and Drainage Engineeering
BOGDANOVIĆ, D., Agrochemistry
BOŠNJAK, DJ., Crop Irrigation
BOŽIDAREVIĆ, D., Marketing of Agricultural and Food Products
BRKIĆ, M., Elements of Agricultural Technology, Thermotechnology in Agriculture
ČINDRIĆ, P., Fruit Growing and Viticulture
ČOBANOVIĆ, K., Statistics, Statistical Methods
DJUKIĆ, D., Forage Crop Production
DJUKIĆ, NI., Agricultural Machinery
DJUROVKA, M., Vegetable Crop Production
ERIĆ, P., Forage Crops
GOVEDARICA, M., Microbiology
GVOZDENOVIĆ, D., Pomology, Picking and Storage of Fruit
HADŽIĆ, V., Pedology
JARAK, M., Microbiology
JASNIĆ, S., Plant Pathology, Plant Viruses

JOVANOVIĆ, M., Economics of Agricultural Estates, Economics of Agricultural Engineering
KEVREŠAN, S., Chemistry
KNEŽEVIĆ, A., Botany
KONSTANTINOVIĆ, B., Special Phytopharmacy, Control of Weeds
KORAĆ, M., Pomology, Viticulture
KOVČIN, S., Nutrition of Nonruminant Animals
KRAJINOVIĆ, M., Animal Husbandry
KRALJEVIĆ-BALALIĆ, M., Genetics
LAZIĆ, B., Vegetable Crop Production
LAZIĆ, V., Agricultural Machinery
MALETIN, S., Agricultural Zoology
MALINOVIĆ, N., Agricultural Machinery
MARINKOVIĆ, B., Arable Crop Production, Agronomy
MARKOVIĆ, V., Vegetable Crop Production
MIHAILOVIĆ, D., Meteorology
MIHAJLOVIĆ, L., Agricultural Cooperative Economics, Agrarian Policy
MIHALJEV, I., Seed Production
MILIĆ, D., Organization of Fruit and Vine Production, Business Organization and Economics
MOLNAR, I., Agronomy
NIKOLIĆ, R., Agricultural Tractors, Agricultural Machinery
NOVKOVIĆ, N., Planning Theory and Methodology of Organization
OBRENOVIĆ, D., Business Analysis, Bookkeeping
PAPRIĆ, DJ., General Viticulture
PEJANOVIĆ, R., Economy
PEJIĆ, N., Nutrition of Ruminant Animals
PEKANOVIĆ, V., Botany
PETRIĆ, D., General Entomology
PETROVIĆ, N., Plant Physiology, Protection of Ecosystems
PETROVIĆ, S., Genetics
POKRIĆ, V., Land Reclamation
POPOVIĆ, M., Plant Biochemistry, Biochemistry of Farm Animals
POTKONJAK, S., Economics of Melioration and Mechanization, Economics of Water Resources
POTKONJAK, V., Mechanization in Animal Breeding, Means of Transportation in Agriculture
RATAJAC, R., Agricultural Zoology, Ecology
SAVIĆ, S., Fodder, Feeding Technology
SRDJEVIĆ, B., Informatics
STAJNER, D., Chemistry
STANČIĆ, B., Breeding of Farm Animals
STARČEVIĆ, LJ., Arable Crop Production
STEVANOVIĆ, M., Agronomy
STOJANOVIĆ, S., Botany
ŠTRBAC, P., Special Entomology, Plant Protection
SUPIĆ, B., Poultry Production, Animal Husbandry
TEODOROVIĆ, M., Pig Breeding
UBAVIĆ, M., Agrochemistry
VIDOVIĆ, V., Improvement of Farm Animals
ŽIVANOVIĆ, M., Special Phytopharmacy

Faculty of Civil Engineering (Gradjevinski Fakultet, Kozaračka 2A, 24000 Subotica; tel. (24) 554-300; e-mail dekanat@gf.su.ac.rs; internet www.gf.uns.ac.rs):

BENAK, J., Water Refinement and Water Quality
ĆULIBRK, R., Earthworks, Elements of Traffic Arteries
DELEVIĆ, K., Organization in Building
GOSTOVIĆ, M., Engineering Geodesy
KLEIN, R., Architecture
MEŠTER, DJ., Technical Mechanics
MIHAILOVIĆ, V., Concrete Structures
MILAŠINOVIĆ, D., Resistance of Materials, Theory of Surface Bearers
SAM, A., Social Sciences
STOJKOVIĆ, S., Watercourses, Flood Management

VLAJIĆ, LJ., Experimental Analysis of Construction
ZELENHASIĆ, E., Hydrology and Elements of Hydrotechnology

Faculty of Economics (Ekonomski Fakultet, Segedinski put 9–11, 24000 Subotica; tel. (24) 628-000; e-mail dekanat@ef.uns.ac.rs; internet www.ef.uns.ac.rs):

ACIN, DJ., International Economic Relations
ACIN SIGULINSKI, S., International Trade, Management in International Trade
ADŽIĆ, S., Economic System and Economic Policy, National Economy
AHMETAGIĆ, E., Theory of an Organization
ANDRIĆ, M., Accountancy and Revision, Financial Control and Revision
BALABAN, N., Principles of Informatics, Support Systems in Decision Making
BALJ, B., Philosophy
BANDIN, J., Accountancy and Bookkeeping
BANDIN, T., Business Economics
ČILEG, M., Operational Research
DJURKOVIĆ, J., Principles of Informatics, Analysis and Planning of Information Systems
DMITROVIĆ, LJ., Management Accounting
GABRIĆ MOLNAR, I., Sociology
JAKOVČEVIĆ, K., Business Economics
JOSIFIDIS, K., Macroeconomics
KALINIĆ, V., Trade Company Management, Marketing in Trade
KIŠ, T., Econometrics
KONČAR, J., Economics of Domestic Commerce and Commercial Politics
KRMPOTIĆ, T., Agrotechnology
LEKIĆ, T., Development of Technology and Commercial Recognition of Goods
LEKOVIĆ, B., Principles of Management
LJUBOJEVIĆ, Ć., Marketing Services
LOVRE, K., Programming of Agricultural Development
MALEŠEVIĆ, DJ., Analysis of Business Enterprise Operations
MESAROŠ, K., Mathematics for Economists
SAGI, A., Microeconomics
SALAI, S., Marketing of Research, Market Communications
STOJKOVIĆ, M., Statistics
SUŠNJAR, G., Human Resources Management
ŠUVAKOV, T., Microeconomics
TODOSIJEVIĆ, R., Strategic Management, Investments
TOT, A., History of Economic Thought
VASILJEV, S., Marketing
VUGDELIJA, D., Mathematics for Economists
VUNJAK, N., Finance, Banking

Faculty of Education (Pedagoški Fakultet, Podgorička 4, 25000 Sombor; tel. (25) 460-595; e-mail dekanat@pef.uns.ac.rs; internet www.pef.uns.ac.rs):

BERBER, S., School Hygiene with Ecology
DJURIĆ, DJ., Social Psychology, Educational Psychology
ERAKOVIĆ, T., Defectology
GRHOVAC, S., Teaching Methods in Serbian Language and Literature, Performing Arts
JANKOVIĆ, P., General Pedagogy
LIPOVAC, M., Pedagogy, Didactics
LJUBOJEV, P., Mass Communication, Film and Television Culture
MALEŠEVIĆ, J., Elements of Natural Sciences
NENADIĆ, M., General Sociology, Sociology of Education
PETROVIĆ, N., Mathematics and Teaching Methods in Mathematics
PINTER, J., Teaching Methods in Mathematics, Informatics in Education

Faculty of Law (Pravni Fakultet, Trg Dositeja Obradovića 1, 21000 Novi Sad; tel. (21)

485-3040; e-mail dekanat@pf.ns.ac.rs; internet www.pf.uns.ac.rs):

ARSIĆ, Z., Economic Law
BOŠKOVIĆ, M., Criminology, Penology
CARIĆ, S., Economic Law
CVEJIĆ-JANČIĆ, O., Family Law, Inheritance Law
DJURDJEV, A., Constitutional Law
DJURDJEV, D., International Public Law
ETINSKI, R., International Public Law
GRUBAČ, M., Criminal Procedural Law
JOVANOVIĆ, PA., Contemporary Political Systems
JOVANOVIĆ, PR., Labour Law
KEČA, R., Civil Procedural Law
KRKLJUŠ, LJ., History of Yugoslav State and Law
MALENICA, A., Roman Law
MARJANOVIĆ, M., Sociology
MILKOV, D., Administrative Law
PAJVANČIĆ, M., Constitutional Law
PERIĆ, O., Criminal Law
PIHLER, S., Criminal Law
POPOV, DJ., Principles of Economics
POPOVIĆ, M., Theory of State and Law
SALMA, J., Law of Obligation
ŠARKIĆ, S., History of State and Law
ŠOGOROV, S., Economic Law
STANKOVIĆ, F., Principles of Economics
VRANJEŠ, M., Financial Law
VUČKOVIĆ, M., Law of Obligation
VUKADINOVIĆ, G., Theory of State and Law
VUKIĆEVIĆ, M., Introductory Economics

Faculty of Medicine (Medicinski Fakultet, Hajduk Veljkova 3, 21000 Novi Sad; tel. (21) 420-677; e-mail dekanmf@uns.ac.rs; internet www.medical.uns.ac.rs):

ALEKSIĆ, S., Gynaecology and Obstetrics
AVRAMOV, S., Surgery
BABIĆ, LJ., Pathology
BALTIĆ, V., Internal Medicine
BUDAKOV, P., Pathology
BUJAS, M., Gynaecology and Obstetrics
BORIŠEV, V., Surgery
BOROTA, J., Biochemistry
ČIKOŠ, J., Internal Medicine
ĆURIĆ, S., Internal Medicine
CVEJANOV, M., Surgery
DJAKOVIĆ-ŠVARCER, K., Pharmacology and Toxicology
DJILAS-TODOROVIĆ, LJ., Internal Medicine
DOKMANOVIĆ-DJORDJEVIĆ, M., Gynaecology and Obstetrics
DŽOLEV, A., Maxillofacial Surgery
ERI, Ž., Pathology
FILIPOVIĆ, D., Physiology
GEBAUER, E., Paediatrics
GRUJIĆ, N., Physiology
GRUJIĆ, V., Social Medicine
GUDOVIĆ, R., Anatomy
GUDURIĆ, B., Surgery
HADŽIĆ, B., Pathology
HADŽIĆ, M., Pathology
IVETIĆ, V., Physiology
IVKOVIĆ-LAZAR, T., Internal Medicine
JANJIĆ, DJ., Surgery
JERANT-PATIĆ, V., Microbiology with Parasitology and Immunology
JEŠIĆ-VINDIŠ, M., Internal Medicine
JOVANOVIĆ, J., Infectious Diseases
KNEŽEVIĆ, A., Psychiatry and Medical Psychology
KOVAČEVIĆ, Z., Biochemistry
KRISTIFOROVIĆ-ILIĆ, M., Hygiene
KRSTIĆ, A., Paediatrics
KRSTIĆ-BOŽIĆ, V., Biology
KULAUZOV, M., Pathological Physiology
KULAUZOV, M., Microbiology with Parasitology and Immunology
LATINOVIĆ, S., Ophthalmology
LAŽETIĆ, B., Physiology
LUČIĆ, A., Pathological Physiology
LUČIĆ, Z., Radiology
LUKAČ, I., Radiology
MAČVANIN, N., Occupational Medicine

MARTINOV-CVEJIN, M., Social Medicine
MIHALJ, M., Anatomy
MIHALJEV-MARTINOV, J., Neurology
MIKOV, M., Pharmacology and Toxicology
MILIČIĆ, A., Surgery
MIROSAVLJEV, M., Hygiene
MILOŠEVIĆ, D., Otorhinolaryngology
MILUTINOVIĆ, B., Physiology
MIRKOVIĆ, M., Surgery
MIROSAVLJEV, M., Hygiene
OBRADOVIĆ, D., Anatomy
PAVLOV-MIRKOVIĆ, M., Gynaecology and Obstetrics
PAVLOVIĆ, S., Internal Medicine
PEJIN, D., Internal Medicine
PJEVIĆ, M., Gynaecology and Obstetrics
PJEVIĆ, M., Surgery
POLZOVIĆ, A., Anatomy
POPOV, I., Psychiatry, Medical Psychology
POPOVIĆ, D., Forensic Medicine
POPOVIĆ, J., Pharmacology and Toxicology
POPOVIĆ, LJ., Surgery
POPOVIĆ, M., Chemistry
RISTIĆ, J., Maxillofacial Surgery
RONČEVIĆ, N., Paediatrics
SABO, A., Pharmacology and Toxicology
SAVIĆ, K., Medical Rehabilitation
SAVIĆ, M., Occupational Medicine
ŠĆEKIĆ, V., Internal Medicine
SEDLAK-VADOC, V., Pathological Physiology
ŠEGEDI, D., Obstetrics and Gynaecology
ŠEGULJEV, Z., Epidemiology
ŠIMIČ, M., Forensic Medicine
ŠLJAPIĆ, N., Pathology
SOMER, LJ., Histology and Embryology
SOMER, T., Surgery
STANKOVIĆ, S., Biophysics
STANULOVIĆ, M., Pharmacology and Toxicology
STOJANOVIĆ, S., Surgery
STOJKOV, J., Surgery
STOJŠIĆ, DJ., Internal Medicine
TASIĆ, M., Forensic Medicine
TOPALOV, V., Internal Medicine
VADOC-SEDLAK, V., Pathological Physiology
VOJINOVIĆ-MILORADOV, M., Chemistry
VUKADINOVIĆ, S., Surgery
VUKOVIĆ, B., Epidemiology
ŽAMUROVIĆ, A., Medical Rehabilitation
ŽIKIĆ, M., Neurology
ZORIČIĆ, D., Surgery

Faculty of Natural Sciences and Mathematics (Prirodno-Matematički Fakultet, Trg Dositeja Obradovića 3, 21000 Novi Sad; tel. (21) 455-630; e-mail dekanpmf@uns.ac.rs; internet www.pmf.uns.ac.rs):

ABRAMOVIĆ, B., Microanalysis
ACKETA, D., Informatics and Numerical Mathematics
BIKIT, I., Nuclear Physics
BJELICA, L., Physical Chemistry
BOGDANOVIĆ, Ž., Physical Geography
BOŽIĆ-KRSTIĆ, V., Biology with Human Genetics
BUDIMAC, Z., Informatics and Numerical Mathematics
BUDINČEVIĆ, M., Analysis and Geometry
BUGARSKI, D., Geography
ČRVENKOVIĆ, S., Mathematics
ĆURČIĆ, S., Social Geography
CVETKOVIĆ, LJ., Informatics and Numerical Mathematics
DALMACIJA, B., Chemical Technology and Environmental Protection
DAVIDOVIĆ, R., Regional Geography
DIVJAKOVIĆ, V., Physics of Condensed Matter
DJURDJEV, B., Social Geography
DJUROVIĆ, S., Atomic Physics, Physical Electronics
GAAL, F., Analytical Chemistry
GAJIĆ, LJ., Analysis and Probability
GAJIN, S., Microbiology
GRUBOR-LAJŠIĆ, G., Biochemistry, Physiology, Histology

HADŽIĆ, O., Probability and Statistics, Mathematics
HALAŠI, R., Organic Analysis
HERCEG, D., Numerical Mathematics
JANJIĆ, J., Physics
JOVANOVIĆ, LJ., Chemistry
KAPOR, A., Physics of Condensed Matter
KAPOR, D., Theoretical Physics
KARLOVIĆ, E., Chemical Technology and Environmental Protection
KOSANIĆ, M., General Chemistry
KOVAČEVIĆ, R., Biochemistry
KRSTIĆ, B., Plant Physiology
KUHAJDA, K., Chemistry of Natural Products
LEOVAC, V., Inorganic Chemistry
LOZANOV-CRVENKOVIĆ, Z., Analysis and Probability
MADARASZ-SZILAGYI, R., Algebra and Mathematics
MAŠKOVIĆ, LJ., Classical Theoretical Mechanics
MATAVULJ, M., Microbiology
MERKULOV, LJ., Botany, Plant Anatomy and Morphology
MILJKOVIĆ, LJ., Physical Geography
MILJKOVIĆ, N., Physical Geography
NIKOLIĆ, A., Physical Chemistry
OBADOVIĆ, D., Physics, Physics of Liquid Crystals
PAP, E., Mathematics, Analysis and Geometry
PAUNIĆ, DJ., Informatics and Numerical Mathematics
PENOV-GAŠI, O., Organic Chemistry
PERIŠIĆ-JANJIĆ, N., General and Inorganic Chemistry
PETROVIĆ, D., Biophysics, Medical Physics
PETROVIĆ, J., Organic Chemistry
PETROVIĆ, O., Microbiology, Bacteriology
PETROVIĆ, V., Algebra and Mathematics
PILIPOVIĆ, S., Analysis and Probability
POPSAVIN, V., Chemistry of Natural Products
ŠEŠELJA, B., Mathematical Logic and Algebra, Mathematical Elements of Informatics
ŠETRAJČIĆ, J., Theoretical Physics
ŠIMIĆ, S., Biology, Zoology
ŠKRINJAR, M., Theoretical Physics
STANKOVIĆ, Š., Biophysics, Medical Physics
STANKOVIĆ, Ž., Plant Physiology
STEVANOVIĆ, D., Morphology and Taxonomy of Invertebrates
STOJAKOVIĆ, Z., Linear Algebra
STOJANOVIĆ, S., Theoretical Mechanics and Electrodynamics
ŠURANJI, T., Analytical Chemistry
SURLA, D., Computer Science
SURLA, K., Numerical Mathematics
TAKAČI, A., Mathematics
TAKAČI, DJ., Mathematics, Analysis and Geometry
TERZIĆ, M., Atomic and Isotopic Molecular Spectroscopy
TOMIĆ, P., Geography
TOŠIĆ, B., Theoretical Physics
TOŠIĆ, R., Combinatorics
VAPA, LJ., Biochemistry, Physiology, Histology, Genetics
VOJINOVIĆ-MILORADOV, M., General Chemistry
VOJVODIĆ, G., Algebra and Logic
VRBAŠKI, Ž., Chemical Technology
VUČKOVIĆ, M., Botany, Plant Ecology, Ecology of Medicinal Herbs
VUJIČIĆ, B., Physical Electronics
ŽDERIĆ, M., Biology
ŽIGRAI, I., Analytical Chemistry

Faculty of Philosophy (Filozofski Fakultet, Dr Zorana Đinđića 2, 21000 Novi Sad; tel. (21) 450-690; e-mail dekanat@unsff.ns.ac.rs; internet www.ff.uns.ac.rs):

BANJAI, J., Literary Theory
BEKIĆ, T., German Literature

BERIĆ, V., History of German Language
BIRO, M., Elements of Clinical Psychology, Elements of Psychotherapy and Consulting
BOŠNJAK, I., Hungarian Literature
BURZAN, M., Serbian Language
ČAKI, P., Introduction to Expert and Scientific Work, Library Science
ČELOVSKI, S., Slovak Studies
ĆOVIĆ, B., Russian Literature
DINIĆ-KNEŽEVIĆ, D., Medieval History of Yugoslav Nations
DJOŠIĆ, D., Demography with Statistics
DUDOK, D., History of Slovak Language and Literature
EGERIĆ, M., Modern Serbian Literature
GADJANSKI-MARICKI, K., Classical Languages, Ancient History
GENC, L., Genetics and Educational Psychology
GEROLD, L., Hungarian Literature
GORDIĆ, S., Serbian and Yugoslav Literature, Serbian Critics
GRANDIĆ, R., Theory of Education, Family Pedagogy
GRKOVIĆ, M., History of Serbian and Comparative Grammar of Slavic Languages
HARPANJI, M., Slovak Literature, Literary Theory
IGNJATOVIĆ, I., General Psychology, Psychology of Personality
IVANOVIĆ, R., History of Yugoslav Literature
JUKIĆ, S., Elements of Pedagogy, Methodical Bases of Educational Work
JUNG, K., Ethnology, Hungarian Folk Literature
KAIĆ, K., History of Hungarian Culture
KAMENOV, E., Pre-School Education
KAPOR-STANULOVIĆ, P., Development of Psychology, Mental Health
KARANOVIĆ, Z., Serbian Folk Literature
KLEUT, M., Serbian Literature
KOKOVIĆ, D., Sociology and Sociology of Culture
KOSANOVIĆ, B., Russian Literature
KULIĆ, M., Philosophy
LANC, I., Introduction to General and Hungarian Linguistics
MATIĆ, LJ., French Literature
MATIJAŠEVIĆ, J., Modern Russian Language
MILOSAVLJEVIĆ, P., Methodology of Literary Studies
MILOŠEVIĆ, B., Introduction to Sociology, Occupational Sociology
MLADENOVIĆ, U., Pedagogic Psychology, Genetic and Pedagogic Psychology
MOLNAR-ČIKOŠ, L., Syntax of Hungarian Language, Phonetics of Hungarian Language
MOMČILOVIĆ, B., English Literature
OLJAČA, M., Educational System
PEROVIĆ, M., Philosophy
PETROVIĆ, D., Dialectology of Serbian and Standard Serbian Language
PIŽURICA, M., History of Serbian Language
POPOV, Č., Modern History
PUŠIĆ, LJ., Urban Sociology
RADOVANOVIĆ, M., General Linguistics
RADOVIĆ, M., Comparative Literature
RAMAČ, J., Ruthenian Language, Ukrainian Language
REDJEP, J., Medieval Literature
RISTIĆ, Z., Methodology of Psychology
RODIĆ, R., School Education
ROKAI, P., Medieval History
SAVIĆ, S., Sociolinguistics and Discourse Analysis
SIMEUNOVIĆ, V., Philosophy
STEFANOVIĆ, M., Literary Theory, Serbian Literature
STEPANOV, R., Theory of Law and Politics
STOJAKOV, S., Introduction to Education Science
ŠIPKA, M., Statistical Psychology

STRAJNIĆ, N., Comparative Literature
TAMAŠ, J., Ruthenian Literature, Ukrainian Literature
TOČANAC, D., Modern French Language
TRIPKOVIĆ, M., Sociology and Sociological Theories
UTAŠI, Č., History of Hungarian Literature
VUKOVIĆ, G., Modern Serbian Language

Faculty of Sport and Physical Education (Fakultet sporta i fizičkog vaspitanja, Lovćenska 16, 21000 Novi Sad; tel. (21) 450-188; e-mail admin@fsfv.ac.rs; internet www .fsfvns.rs):

BALA, G., Kinesiology of Individual Sports
BJELICA, S., Sociological and Psychological Elements of Kinesiology
DIMOVA, K., Kinesiology of Individual Sports
DUNDJEROVIĆ, R., Kinesiology of Individual Sports
KALAJDŽIĆ, J., Kinesiology of Sports Games
KRSMANOVIĆ, B., Theory and Methods of Physical Education
LUKAĆ, D., Sports Medicine
MALACKO, J., Kinesiology of Sports
NIĆIN, DJ., Kinesiology
RADOSAV, M., Football
RAIČ, A., Economical and Political Elements of Kinesiology
SAVIĆ, M., Martial Sports
TONČEV, I., Kinesiology of Individual Sports
ULIĆ, D., Kinesitherapy

Faculty of Technical Sciences (Fakultet Tehničkih Nauka, Trg Dositeja Obradovića 6, 21000 Novi Sad; tel. (21) 485-2055; e-mail ftndean@uns.ac.rs; internet www.ftn.uns.ac .rs):

ATANACKOVIĆ, T., Material Resistance
BABIN, N., Transport Machines
BAČLIĆ, B., Mechanics and Thermodynamics of Continuum
BANJANIN, M., Theory of Communications
BAŠIĆ, DJ., Thermoprocessing Systems
BOROVAC, B., Industrial Robots
BUKUROV, Ž., Fluid Mechanics
ČASNJI, F., Motor Vehicles
ČIRIĆ, D., Physics
ČOMIĆ, I., Mathematics
COSIĆ, I., Planning of Production Systems
CVETIĆANIN, L., Mechanics
DIMIĆ, M., Mass Transfer, Heat Apparatus
DJORDJEVIĆ, R., Construction Theory
DJORDJEVIĆ, T., Theory of Traffic Flow and Capacity
DJUKIĆ, DJ., Mechanics
DOROSLOVAČKI, R., Discrete Mathematics
DOVNIKOVIĆ, L., Descriptive Geometry
FOLIĆ, R., Concrete Structures and Structural Theory
GAJIĆ, V., Logistics of Enterprise
GALOGAŽA, M., Technology of Prediction, Marketing and Enterprise
GATALO, R., Machine Tools, Flexible Technological Systems
GEORGIJEVIĆ, M., Storage, Equipment and Simulations
GERIĆ, LJ., Distributive Installations
GRKOVIĆ, V., Turbines
GVOZDENAC, D., Thermal Energy and Measurement in Thermal Engineering
HAJDUKOVIĆ, M., Architecture of Computer Systems
HODOLIĆ, J., Productive Engineering Equipment
INIĆ, M., Traffic Safety
KAKAŠ, D., Heat Treatment
KISIN, S., Metal Constructions
KLINAR, I., Motor Equipment
KOPIĆ, DJ., Technology of Railway Transport
KOVAČ, P., Welding
KOVAČ, R., Casting Technology
KOVAČEVIĆ, I., Mathematics

KOVAČEVIĆ, V., Logical Planning of Computing Systems
KOZIMIDIS-LUBURIĆ, U., Physics
KOZIMIDIS-PETROVIĆ, A., Physics
KUZMANOVIĆ, S., Mechanical Elements
LIČEN, H., Automation of Measuring Processes
LUKIĆ, S., Elements of Building Planning
MALBAŠA, V., Electronic Systems and Communication Networks
MALBAŠKI, D., Elements of Computer Programming and Programme Languages
MARIĆ, M., Heat Science, Drying Technology
MARINIĆ, I., Sociology and Economy
MARTINOV, M., Agricultural Machines
MILIDRAG, S., Motor Vehicles
MILIKIĆ, D., Treatment Methods by Material Removal
MILINSKI, N., Physics
MILOŠEVIĆ, V., Digital Telecommunication
MOGIN, P., Databases
NIKIĆ, J., Mathematics
NOVAK, L., Circuit and Systems Theory
OBRADOVIĆ, D., Digital Communications
OBRADOVIĆ, M., Intercomputer Communications
PEKARIĆ-NADJ, N., Principles of Electrical Engineering
PERUNOVIĆ, P., Boilers
PEŠALJEVIĆ, M., Engineering Communications and Logistic Control
PETROVAČKI, D., Automatic Control
PLANČAK, M., Technology of Plasticity and Cold Extrusion
POPOVIĆ, D., Synthesis of Complex Systems in Automatic Control
PRODANOVIĆ, M., City and Spatial Planning
RADIVOJEVIĆ, R., Sociology, Sociology of Work
RADOVIĆ, R., Urban Planning, Contemporary Architecture
SABO, B., Welding Technology
SATARIĆ, M., Physics
ŠAVIĆ, V., Logistic Technical Systems
ŠEŠIĆ, Ž., Internal Combustion Engines
SIDJANIN, L., Materials Science, Engineering Materials
SOVILJ, B., Technoeconomic Optimization
STANIVUKOVIĆ, D., Reliability of Mechanical Systems
STOJAKOVIĆ, M., Mathematics, Statistical Methods in Planning
STREZOSKI, V., Elements of Electroenergetics
TEŠIĆ, M., Agricultural Machinery
TODIĆ, V., Technological Processes
TOROVIĆ, T., Internal Combustion Engine
UZELAC, B., Mathematical Methods
VILOTIĆ, D., Plasticity Technology
VLADIĆ, J., Uninterrupted and Automatic Transport
VLAHOVIĆ, M., Recognition of Goods in Transport
VUKOVIĆ, S., Architectural Construction
VUKOVIĆ, V., Fluid Mechanics
ŽIVANOV, LJ., Microelectronics, Principles of Electronics
ZLOKOLICA, M., Theory of Mechanisms and Machines
ŽUPUNSKI, I., Electrical Measurements

Faculty of Technology (Tehnološki Fakultet, Blvr Cara Lazara 1, 21000 Novi Sad; tel. (21) 485-3600; e-mail deantf@uns.ac.rs; internet www.tf.uns.ac.rs):

CARIĆ, M., Milk and Dairy Technology
CURAKOVIĆ, M., Wrapping and Packaging
DJILAS, S., Organic Chemistry
DJURIĆ, M., Engineering Thermodynamics
DOKIĆ, P., Chemistry and Technology of Emulsions and Cosmetics, Colloid Chemistry
GRUJIĆ-IVKOV, O., Malt and Beer Technology
JAKOVLJEVIĆ, J., Starch Technology

KIŠ, E., Physical Chemistry, Catalysis
LOMIĆ, G., Physical Chemistry, Catalysis
MARINKOVIĆ-NEDUČIN, R., Physical Chemistry, Catalysis
MARJANOVIĆ, N., Food Analysis
PAUNOVIĆ, R., Mathematical Modelling in Industrial Processes
PEJIN, D., Yeast and Alcohol Technology, Industrial Microbiology
PERIČIN, D., Biochemistry, Industrial Enzymology
PERUNIČIĆ, M., Process Dynamics and Control, Process Control Systems
PETROVIĆ, LJ., Meat Processing Technology
POPOV-RALJIĆ, J., Ready-Made Food Technology
PRIBIŠ, V., Meat Processing Technology, Sensory Evaluation of Food
RADONJIĆ, LJ., Construction Materials, Inorganic Materials
RANOGAJEC, J., Ceramics Technology, Inorganic Raw Materials and Products
RAZMOVSKA, R., Yeast and Alcohol Technology
RUŽIĆ, N., Technology of Wine Production
SEĆEROV-SOKOLOVIĆ, R., Industrial Processes Design, Environmental Protection in the Chemical Industry
ŠKRBIĆ, B., Natural Gas Engineering
ŠKRINJAR, M., Food Microbiology
SOKOLOVIĆ, S., Petroleum Refining Technology, Petrochemical Products Applications
SOVILJ, M., Unit Operations, Measurement Techniques
SOVILJ, V., Colloid Chemistry, Physical Chemistry of Macromolecules
STOILJKOVIĆ, D., Physical Chemistry of Polymer Materials, Plastics Materials Technology
TEKIĆ, M., Design of Equipment for the Chemical Industry, Separation Processes
TOJAGIĆ, S., Ready-Made Food Technology

'Mihajlo Pupin' Technical Faculty (Tehnički Fakultet 'Mihajlo Pupin', Djure Djakovića bb, 23000 Zrenjanin; tel. (23) 550-515; e-mail dekanat@tf.zr.ac.rs; internet www.tfzr.uns .ac.rs):

ADAMOVIĆ, Ž., Mechanics, Maintenance, Hydraulics and Pneumatics
ČERNIČEK, I., Theory of Systems, Theory of Management and Decision Making
DJARMATI, Z., Chemistry with Chemical Technology, Chemistry and Biochemistry
HOTOMSKI, P., Informatics
LAMBIĆ, M., Mechanical Engineering, Energetics
MITROVIĆ, Ž., Mathematics
SOTIROVIĆ, V., Informatics
STOJADINOVIĆ, V., Industrial Engineering
ŠUNJKA, S., Textile Technology

There are research institutes attached to each faculty

UNIVERZITET UMETNOSTI U BEOGRADU
(University of Arts in Belgrade)

Kosančićev venac 29, 11000 Belgrade
Telephone: (11) 262-5166
E-mail: rektorat@arts.bg.ac.rs
Internet: www.arts.bg.ac.rs
Founded 1957 as Acad. of Arts, present status 1973
Academic year: October to September
Rector: Prof. Dr LJILJANA MRKIĆ POPOVIĆ
Pres.: Prof. SLAVENKO SALETOVIC
Vice-Pres.: Prof. ANDJELKA BOJOVIĆ
Vice-Pres.: Prof. Dr DIMITRIJE GOLEMOVIĆ
Vice-Pres.: Prof. MARINA NAKIĆENOVIĆ
Sec.-Gen.: OLGA STANKOVIĆ

Library of 200,000 vols

Number of teachers: 500
Number of students: 2,500
Publication: *Bilten INFO* (dramatic arts, 12 a year)

DEANS

Faculty of Applied Arts: Prof. VLADIMIR KOSTIĆ DIVAČ
Faculty of Dramatic Arts: ZORAN S. POPOVIĆ
Faculty of Fine Arts: Prof. SLOBODAN ROKSANDIĆ
Faculty of Music: Prof. Dr DUBRAVKA JOVIČIĆ (acting)

PROFESSORS

Faculty of Applied Arts (Kralja Petra 4, 11000 Belgrade; tel. (11) 218-2047; e-mail fpu@eunet.rs; internet www.fpu.edu.rs):

ANĐELKOVIĆ, M.
BAJIĆ, M.
BLAŽINA, Z.
BOČINA, R.
BOŽOVIĆ, N.
BULAJIĆ, Z.
ĆIRIĆ, R.
ĆIRIĆ-KRSTIĆ, G.
CVIJANOVIĆ, S.
DENIĆ, D.
DIMITRIJEVIĆ, D.
ĐOLIĆ, S.
DRAGOVIĆ, J.
DRAGUTINOVIĆ, A.
DRAGUTINOVIĆ, M.
DRAGUTINOVIĆ-KOMATINA, S.
DRAMIĆANIN, M.
ĐULIZAREVIĆ, S.
ĐURIČKOVIĆ, S.
FULGOSI, D.
GAVRIĆ, Z.
GLOGOVAC, M.
HULJEV, I.
IVANOVIĆ, Z.
IZVONAR, D.
JANKOVIĆ, Z.
JANKOVIĆ-NEDELKOV, T.
KAJTEZ, S.
KARANOVIĆ, B.
KNEŽEVIĆ, I.
KNEŽEVIĆ, N.
KOMAD-ARSENIJEVIĆ, G.
KOSTIĆ, M.
KOSTIĆ, V.
KRSMANOVIĆ, K.
KUZMANOVIĆ, B.
KUZMANOVIĆ-NOVOVIĆ, I.
LAĐUŠIĆ, M.
LALIĆ, R.
LAZIĆ, T.
LAZOVIĆ, M.
LUKOVIĆ, M.
MANOJLOVIĆ, D.
MANOJLOVIĆ, S.
MANOJLOVIĆ, T.
MARCIKIĆ, I.
MIĆANOVIĆ, Z.
MIJATOVIĆ, A.
MILIĆEVIĆ, I.
NAKIĆENOVIĆ, M.
NANOVIĆ, B.
NEŠIĆ, D.
NIKOLIĆ, S.
NINČIĆ, O.
NOVAKOVIĆ, M.
OGNJANOVIĆ, M.
PETKOVIĆ, Z.
PETROVIĆ, G.
PETROVIĆ, L.
PETROVIĆ, M.
POPOVIĆ, Z.
RAKIĆ, I.
RUSALIĆ, D.
SAMARDŽIĆ, R.
ŠAVIĆ, S.
ŠĆEPANOVIĆ, V.
SEKULIĆ, T.
SIMONOVIĆ, J.

STAMENKOVIĆ, M.
STOJADINOVIĆ, O.
STOJANOVIĆ, D.
ŠTRBAC, V.
TATAREVIĆ, V.
TIKVEŠA, L.
TODIĆ, M.
TOMAŠEVIĆ, M.
TRNINIĆ, M.
VELJOVIĆ, I.
VIĆENTIĆ, N.
VLAHOVIĆ, J.
VUČKOVIĆ, M.
VUJOVIĆ-STOJANOVIĆ, M.
VUKIĆEVIĆ, V.
VUKSAN, D.
ZARIĆ, G.
ZEČEVIĆ, S.
ŽIKIĆ, S.
ŽIVKOVIĆ, M.

Faculty of Dramatic Arts (Blvr umetnosti 20, 11070 Belgrade; tel. (11) 214-0419; e-mail fduinfo@eunet.rs; internet www.fdubg.com):

ALEKSIC, B.
BAJIC, D.
BOGOEVA SEDLAR, LJ.
COLAKOVIC, M.
COLIC BILJANOVSKI, D.
DAKOVIC, N.
DAUTOVIC, F.
DEJANOVIC, V.
DESPOT, B.
DIMITRIJEVIC, A.
DJOKIC, J.
DJUKIC, A.
DJUKIC, V.
DRAGICEVIC SESIC, M.
GADJANSKI, M.
GLUSICA, M.
IMAMI, P.
IVANOVIC, S.
JEVTIC, N.
JEVTOVIC, V.
JEZERKIC, V.
JOVANOVIC, D.
JOVIĆEVIC, A.
KARAJICA, F.
KARANOVIC, S.
KNEZEVIC, R.
MANDIC, A.
MANDIC, T.
MARIC, G.
MARICIC, N.
MARKOVIC, G.
MARKOVIC, M.
MILETIN, M.
MRKIC POPOVIC, L.
PAJKIC, N.
PAVLOVIC, M.
PEKOVIC, G.
POPOV, D.
POPOVIC, Z.
PROKIC, N.
RANKOVIC, R.
SALETOVIC, S.
SAVIN, E.
SAVKOVIC, M.
SIJAN, S.
SIMJANOVIC, Z.
TABACKI, M.
TERZIC, G.
TODOROVIC, R.
VESELINOVIC, D.
VOLK, M.
VUJIC, I.

Faculty of Fine Arts (Pariska br. 16, 11000 Belgrade; tel. (11) 263-0635; e-mail dekanat@flu.bg.ac.rs; internet www.flu.bg.ac.rs):

ANTONIJEVIĆ, R.
BAJIĆ, M.
BISENIĆ, D.
BOJOVIĆ, A.
DIMOVSKI, Z.
DRAGOJLOVIĆ, M.
DRAGOJLOVIĆ, M.

GRAOVAC, Z.
GRBA, D.
ILIĆ, D.
JOKSIMOVIĆ, A.
JOKSIMOVIĆ, Z.
JOVANOVIĆ, D.
KAĆIĆ, D.
KALIĆ-KUMANUDI, J.
KNEŽEVIĆ, R.
KNEŽEVIĆ, V.
KRSTIĆ, V.
LALIĆ, V.
MILINKOVIĆ, Z.
MLADENOVIĆ, A.
MLAĐOVIĆ, M.
MOMIROV, D.
NIKOLIĆ, G
NOVAKOVIĆ, Z.
PANTIĆ, A.
PECIĆ, D.
PETROVIĆ, D.
POPTSIS, M.
PRODANOVIĆ, M.
RADOJEV, N.
RAJČEVIĆ, S.
RAKOVIĆ, B
ROKSANDIĆ, S.
SIMEONOVIĆ ČELIĆ, I.
ŠIVAČKI, J.
ŠKORC, B.
SMILJANIĆ, Z.
STANAĆEV, D.
ŠUICA, N.
TODOROVIĆ, J.
TODOROVIĆ, Z.
VASIĆ, C.
VELJAŠEVIĆ, V.
VUKOSAVLJEVIĆ, N.
VUKOVIĆ, B.
VUKOVIĆ, Z.
ZARIĆ, K.
ŽIVKOVIĆ, V.

Faculty of Music (Kralja Milana 50, 11000 Belgrade; tel. (11) 265-9466; e-mail fmuinfo@fmu.bg.ac.rs; internet www.fmu.bg.ac.rs):

BELIĆ, S.
BOŽIĆ, S.
ČETKOVIĆ, Z.
ĐORĐEVIĆ, M.
ERIĆ, Z.
GOLEMOVIĆ, D.
GRGIN, A.
HOFMAN, S.
IGNJATOVIĆ, N.
ISAESKI, M.
JOKANOVIĆ, M.
JOVANOVIĆ, L.
JOVIČIĆ, D.
KARLOVIĆ, M.
KOSANOVIĆ, M.
KRŠIĆ-SEKULIĆ, V.
MAKSIMOVIĆ-VESELINOV, J.
MARINKOVIĆ, S.
MEZEI, L.
MIHAILOVIĆ, J.
MILANKOVIĆ, V.
MLAĐENOVIĆ, D.
NIKOLIĆ, M.
OGRIZOVIĆ, V.
PERIĆ, D.
PETROVIĆ, M.
POPOVIĆ, L.
POPOVIĆ, N.
RAŠKOVIĆ, F.
SERDAR, A.
SINADINOVIĆ, D.
SUĐIĆ, B.
ŠUVAKOVIĆ, M.
TOŠIĆ, S.
TOŠIĆ, V.
TRAJKOVIĆ, V.
VASIĆ, O.
VESELINOVIĆ–HOFMAN, M.
VUJIĆ, A.
ŽIVKOVIĆ, N.

College

Belgrade Business School: Kraljice Marije 73 (27 Marta 149), 11000 Belgrade; tel. (11) 240-1888; e-mail info@bbs.edu.rs; internet www.bbs.edu.rs; f. 1956 as Junior Commer-cial-Business College, present name and status 2002; offers three-year diploma courses in finance, accounting, marketing, foreign and domestic trade, commerce, management, business informatics and computers, banking and insurance, customs, taxes and budget; int. studies programme; distance studies; library: 20,000 vols; 90 teachers (60 full-time, 30 part-time); 2,000 students; Dir Prof. Dr ILIJA SAMARDŽIĆ (acting).

SEYCHELLES

The Higher Education System

The Republic of Seychelles comprises some 115 islands in the western Indian Ocean. Seychelles achieved full independence from Britain, as a sovereign republic within the Commonwealth, in 1976. The University of Seychelles was established in October 2009. In 2010 the National Institute of Education became the university's School of Education offering three and four-year degree programmes in teacher-training. In 2011 there were around 300 students enrolled on 12 degree programmes delivered though the University of London International Programmes. The University, which is governed by the Chancellor, Senate and University Board, was expected eventually to be able to cater for approximately 1,500 students, and a distance education programme was to be introduced. The Seychelles Polytechnic (founded 1983) offers one- to three-year Diploma and Certificate courses, and the National College of the Arts (founded 1997) offers one- and two-year programmes of study. There are several professional institutes of training and an Adult Learning and Distance Education Centre. There were 2,198 students in post-secondary (non-tertiary) education in 2011.

The Ministry of Education is responsible for post-secondary, tertiary and adult education. The Ministry offers scholarships for students wishing to pursue tertiary education overseas. Under the Higher Education Act, the Ministry has instigated reforms in the education system in five priority areas to increase its effectiveness. A number of reforms were carried out during 2009–11. In November 2011 the National Assembly voted unanimously to approve the Tertiary Education Act (2011), which was intended further to develop tertiary and post-secondary education within Seychelles. Upon implementation, the legislation would provide for, inter alia, the establishment of a Tertiary Education Commission and a number of higher education institutions.

Regulatory Bodies

GOVERNMENT

Ministry of Education: POB 48, Mont Fleuri; tel. 283283; e-mail esb@eduhq.edu.sc; internet www.education.gov.sc; Minister MACSUZY MONDON.

Ministry of Tourism and Culture: Victoria; Minister ALAIN ST ANGE.

Learned Societies

LANGUAGE AND LITERATURE

Alliance Française: Ave Bois de Rose, BP 210, Victoria; tel. 282424; e-mail info@allianceseychelles.org; internet www.alliancefr.sc; offers courses and exams in French language and culture and promotes cultural exchange with France.

British Council: see chapter on Mauritius.

Research Institute

GENERAL

National Heritage: POB 573, Victoria, Mahé; tel. 321333; e-mail heritage@seychelles.net; f. 1987; controlled by Culture Division of the Min. of Education; carries out research into the cultural heritage of Seychelles; Advisor MARCEL BARRY ROSALIE.

Libraries and Archives

Victoria

Seychelles National Archives: POB 720, 5th June Ave, Victoria, Mahé; tel. 321333; e-mail archives@seychelles.net; internet www.sna.gov.sc; Dir ALAIN LUCAS.

Seychelles National Library: POB 45, Francis Rachel St, Victoria, Mahé; tel. 321333; e-mail natlib@seychelles.net; internet www.national-library.edu.sc; f. 1910 as Carnegie Library; 75,000 vols (incl. 3 br. libraries & 2 regional reading centres); 3 brs; spec. collns: documents on Indian Ocean region, FAO, UNESCO, IMO and ILO publs; Prin. Librarian ANNE-MARY ROBERT; Sr Librarian CHRISTIANE ADELINE.

Museum

Victoria

National Museum: POB 720, La Bastille, Victoria, Mahé; tel. 321333; e-mail mizenasyonal@gmail.com; f. 1964; Dir CECILLE KALEBI.

Polytechnic

SEYCHELLES POLYTECHNIC

POB 77, Anse Royale, Victoria
Telephone: 371188
E-mail: info@seypoly.edu.sc
Internet: www.seypoly.edu.sc
Founded 1983
State control
Language of instruction: English
Academic year: January to December

Dir: JEAN RASSOOL
Asst Dir for Admin.: HELENE BELMONT
Asst Dir for Studies: AUDREY NANON
Sr Librarian: MARIE-FRANCE LOZÉ

Library of 9,500 vols
Number of teachers: 60
Number of students: 580

School of Music

National College of the Arts: Min. of Community Devt, Youth, Sports and Culture, POB 1383, Mahé; tel. 224777; e-mail acollart@hotmail.com; f. 1997; depts of music, dance, visual arts, drama; 33 teachers (28 full-time, 5 part-time); 720 students (120 full-time, 600 part-time); Dir DAVID CHETTY.

SIERRA LEONE

The Higher Education System

Formerly a British colony and protectorate, Sierra Leone gained independence from the United Kingdom in 1961. Fourah Bay College (founded 1827), a constituent college of the University of Sierra Leone (founded 1967), is the oldest current institution of higher education. Before joining the University, degrees from Fourah Bay College were awarded by the University of Durham (United Kingdom). In 2011 there were three degree-awarding institutions in Sierra Leone—the University of Sierra Leone, Njala University (formerly the Njala University College of the University of Sierra Leone; current status adopted in 2005) and the Milton Margai College of Education and Technology (founded 2000). In 2001/02 a total of 9,041 students were enrolled in tertiary education. The Universities Act of 2005 allows for the creation of private universities.

The Ministry of Education, Science and Technology is responsible for higher education. The Tertiary Education Commission Act, approved in 2001, established a Commission to ensure that higher education academic programmes were effectively monitored, and set regulations for the approval and establishment of new higher education institutions.

Admission to higher education is on the basis of the West African Senior School Certificate examination. One-year Certificate and two- to three-year Diploma courses are available in mostly professional fields of study, such as agriculture, engineering and marine biology. The undergraduate Bachelors is either a three- to four-year 'General' degree or a four- to five-year 'Honours' degree. At postgraduate level, students first take the Masters degree, which is awarded after one year following the Bachelors (Honours) or two years following the Bachelors (General) and requires submission of a dissertation or project. The Master of Philosophy requires an additional two years of study in certain subjects following award of a Masters degree, and also requires submission of a dissertation. The Doctor of Philosophy is the highest university degree, requiring three years of research leading to submission of a thesis.

The evaluation and certification of technical and vocational education is the responsibility of the National Council for Technical, Vocational and other Academic Awards (NCTVA— founded 2001); in 2011 the NCTVA was in the process of establishing a national framework for vocational qualifications. Post-secondary technical and vocational education is available from technical institutes in Kenema and Freetown and the Institute of Public Administration and Management attached to the University of Sierra Leone. The technical institutes offer a range of British-accredited qualifications, including City and Guilds certificates, London Chamber of Commerce and Industry examinations and Royal Society of Arts secretarial examinations, although increasingly these are being replaced by courses certified by the NCTVA. The Institute of Public Administration and Management (founded 1980) specializes in continuing education and workplace-based training.

Regulatory Bodies

GOVERNMENT

Ministry of Education, Science and Technology: New England, Freetown; tel. (22) 240881; Minister Dr MINKAILU BAH.

Ministry of Tourism and Culture: Ministerial Bldg, George St, Freetown; tel. (22) 222588; Minister PETER BAJUKU KONTEH.

Learned Societies

BIBLIOGRAPHY, LIBRARY SCIENCE AND MUSEOLOGY

Sierra Leone Association of Archivists, Librarians and Information Scientists: 7 Percival St, Freetown; f. 1970; 90 mems; Pres. OLATUNGIE CAMPBELL; Sec. AGNES MOROVIA; publ. *SLAALIS Bulletin* (4 a year).

HISTORY, GEOGRAPHY AND ARCHAEOLOGY

Historical Society of Sierra Leone: c/o Dept of History, Fourah Bay College, Univ. of Sierra Leone, Freetown; f. 1975; 30 mems; Pres. G. S. ANTHONY; publ. *Journal* (2 a year).

LANGUAGE AND LITERATURE

Alliance Française: 30 Howe St, POB 510, Freetown; tel. (76) 683523; offers courses and exams in French language and culture and promotes cultural exchange with France.

British Council: Tower Hill, POB 124, Freetown; tel. (76) 290111; e-mail slenquiries@sl.britishcouncil.org; internet www.britishcouncil.org/sierraleone; offers courses and exams in English language and British culture and promotes cultural exchange with the UK; Dir LOUISA WADDINGHAM.

MEDICINE

Sierra Leone Medical and Dental Association: POB 932, Freetown; tel. (22) 220753; e-mail info@mdcsierraleone.org; internet www.mdcsierraleone.org; f. 1961; 220 mems; library of 3,000 vols (shared with main hospital); Pres. Dr ARTHUR C. WILLIAMS; Chief Medical Officer Dr KISITO S. DAOH; Registrar Dr SAMUEL J. THORPE; publ. *Journal* (1 a year).

NATURAL SCIENCES

General

Sierra Leone Science Association: c/o ICT Directorate, Univ. of Sierra Leone, Freetown; tel. 278748034; e-mail ictdirectorate@usl.edu.sl; internet www.usl .edu.sl; f. 1960; Hon. Pres. Prof. Dr ERNEST H. WRIGHT; Dir Dr DANIEL STEVENS.

Research Institutes

GENERAL

Institute of African Studies: c/o Univ. of Sierra Leone, Fourah Bay College, Freetown; f. 1962; undertakes research in sociology, history and culture of Sierra Leone; offers undergraduate and postgraduate courses in cultural studies; Dir Dr ARTHUR ABRAHAM; publ. *Africana Research Bulletin* (2 a year).

NATURAL SCIENCES

Biological Sciences

Institute of Marine Biology and Oceanography: Fourah Bay College, Univ. of Sierra Leone, Freetown; f. 1966; 4-year degree programme in marine science, undergraduate diploma in aquatic biology and fisheries; research and training in oceanography, marine algae and ecology, fishery biology and management, aquaculture, marine pollution, estuarine dynamics, and coastal processes; Dir Dr I. W. O. FINDLAY; publ. *Annual Bulletin*.

Physical Sciences

Geological Survey Division: Min. of Mines, Youyi Bldg, Brookfields, Freetown; internet www.slminerals.org; f. 1918 to locate mineral deposits and to advise on all matters relating to the Earth; library of 16,000 vols incl. periodicals; Dir A. H. GABISI; publs *Bulletin* (1 a year), *Short Papers* (1 a year).

Libraries and Archives

Freetown

Fourah Bay College Library: Univ. of Sierra Leone, Freetown; tel. (22) 227924; e-mail fbclibrary2005@yahoo.com; internet www.fbcusl.8k.com; f. 1827; 200,000 vols, 300 current periodicals; Sr Librarian OLIVER HARDING.

Public Archives of Sierra Leone: c/o Fourah Bay College, Freetown; f. 1965; 63,000 linear ft of records; Sr Archivist ALBERT MOORE.

Sierra Leone Library Board: POB 326, Rokel St, Freetown; e-mail sielib2002@yahoo .com; f. 1959; nationwide public library and information services; also acts as a nat. library (legal deposit); 1 central library (HQ), 3 regional libraries, 14 br. and dist.

libraries; 110,000 vols; Chief Librarian SAL-LIEU TURAY; publs *Children's magazine, Golden Jubilee Souvenir, Sierra Leone Publications* (1 a year).

Museum

Freetown

Sierra Leone National Museum: Cotton Tree Bldg, POB 908, Freetown; e-mail cabnicol70@yahoo.co.uk; internet www .sierraleoneheritage.org/museum; historical, ethnographical and archaeological colln; Curator JOSEPHINE KARGBO (acting).

Universities

NJALA UNIVERSITY

Henry St, Freetown
Telephone: (22) 228788
E-mail: enquire@njalauniversity.sl
Internet: www.njalauniversity.edu.sl
Founded 2005
State control
Vice-Chancellor and Prin.: Prof. ABU SESAY
Vice-Prin.: P. K. SAIDU

DEANS

School of Agriculture: Dr MOHAMED T. LAHAI
School of Community Health Sciences: Dr G. M. T. ROBERT
School of Education: P. K. SAIDU
School of Environmental Sciences: THOMAS R. A. WINNEBAH
School of Forestry and Horticulture: Dr OMIYALE OLUFEMI
School of Social Sciences: Dr BANGURA AMADU
School of Technology: Dr A. BAIMBA ANDREW

PROFESSORS

School of Agriculture:
 KOROMA, J. P. C., Crop Science
 RHODES, E. R., Soil Science
School of Education:
 BOMAH, A. K., Geography and Rural Development

UNIVERSITY OF SIERRA LEONE

A. J. Momoh St, Tower Hill, Freetown
Telephone: (22) 226859
E-mail: aiah_gbakima2000@yahoo.com
Internet: www.tusol.org
Founded 1967
State control
Language of instruction: English
Academic year: October to June

Chancellor: THE PRESIDENT OF THE REPUBLIC OF SIERRA LEONE
Vice-Chancellor: Prof. AIAH A. GBAKIMA
Pro-Chancellor: Prof. V. E. H. STRASSER-KING
Deputy Vice-Chancellor: Prof. J. A. S. RED-WOOD-SAWYERR
Registrar: E. T. NGANDI
Librarian: GLADYS JUSU-SHERIFF
Number of teachers: 300
Number of students: 4,310 (full-time)
Publications: *African Research Bulletin* (2 a year), *Calendar and Prospectus* (1 a year), *Varsity Update* (12 a year)..

CONSTITUENT COLLEGES

Fourah Bay College

POB 87, Mount Aureol, Freetown
Telephone: (22) 227924
Internet: fbcusl.8k.com
Founded 1827, affiliated to the Univ. of Durham in 1876, became a constituent college of the univ. in 1966
State control
Language of instruction: English
Academic year: October to June
Deputy Vice-Chancellor: Prof. S. P. T. GBA-MANJA
College Librarian: Rev. OLIVER L. T. HARDING (acting)
Library of 120,000 vols
Number of students: 5,500
Publications: *Journal of Pure & Applied Sciences, Journal of Social Sciences*

DEANS

Faculty of Arts: Rev. Dr L. A. FOULLAH
Faculty of Basic Medical Sciences: Dr J. K. GEORGE (acting)
Faculty of Clinical Sciences: Dr M. L. BARYOH
Faculty of Engineering and Architecture: Ing. A. B. SAVAGE
Faculty of Law: Prof. H. M. JOKO-SMART
Faculty of Pure and Applied Science: Prof. A. B. KARIM
Faculty of Social Sciences and Law: S. B. WEEKES
Postgraduate Studies: Prof. J. A. D. ALIE

PROFESSORS

Faculty of Arts:
 WYSE, A. J. G., History
Faculty of Economic and Social Sciences:
 ABRAHAM, A., Institute of African Studies
Faculty of Engineering:
 DAVIDSON, O. R., Mechanical Engineering
Faculty of Pure and Applied Science:
 AWUNOR-RENNER, E. R. T., Physics
 COLE, N. H. A., Botany

STRASSER-KING, V. E. H., Geology
WILLIAMS, M. O., Zoology

College of Medicine and Allied Health Sciences

Internet: www.comahs.usl.edu.sl
Founded 1987
Deputy Vice-Chancellor: Prof. S. M. GEVAO

DEANS

Clinical Sciences: Dr M. L. BARYOH
Medical Sciences: Dr J. K. GEORGE (acting)
Nursing: Dr SALLY A. OPALEYE

PROFESSORS

Faculty of Basic Medical Sciences:
 GEORGE, J. K., Anatomy
Faculty of Clinical Sciences:
 TAQI, A. M., Paediatrics
Faculty of Pharmaceutical Sciences:
 AYITEY-SMITH, E., Pharmacology.

OFF-CAMPUS INSTITUTE

Institute of Public Administration and Management: PMB, Tower Hill, Freetown; tel. (22) 224801; e-mail hpynebailey@ipam .edu.sl; internet www.ipam.usl.edu.sl; library of 1,875 vols; 56 teachers (20 full-time, 36 part-time); 2,961 students (2,700 undergraduate, 261 postgraduate); Deputy Vice-Chancellor Prof. EKUNDAYO J. D. THOMPSON (acting); Dean of Campus Dr CLAUDIUS P. BART-WILLIAMS; Head of Library HECTORA PYNE-BAILEY (acting); publ. *Emerald Journals*

Colleges

Milton Margai College of Education and Technology: Goderich, nr Freetown; f. 1960; trains secondary school teachers; library: 23,000 vols; 55 teachers; 624 students; Prin. Dr DENIS KARGBO; Registrar J. U. WRIGHT (acting).

Paramedical School: POB 50, Bo; f. 1979 with funds from the Govt and the EEC; trains primary health workers; Prin. Dr V. O. COLE.

Technical Institute: Congo Cross, Freetown; tel. (76) 617039; f. 1952; 80 teachers; 980 students; City and Guilds Craft and Technical Courses and Commercial Education; certificate, diploma and higher diploma courses in engineering, business, secretarial work and education; focal point for the UNEVOC project; Prin. MOHAMED A. JALLOH.

SINGAPORE

The Higher Education System

In 1826 the East India Company formed the Straits Settlements by the union of Singapore and the dependencies of Penang and Malacca on the Malay Peninsula. They came under British rule in 1867. In 1946 Singapore became a separate crown colony, and in 1959 achieved complete internal self-government. After seceding from the Federation of Malaysia in 1965, Singapore became an independent republic. There are three public universities—National University of Singapore (founded 1980), Nanyang Technological University (founded as Nanyang Technological Institute in 1981; current status 1991) and Singapore Management University (founded 2000). Combined enrolment at the public universities totalled 72,710 students in 2009. In 2005 the Open University Centre (founded 1992), affiliated with the Open University (United Kingdom), was elevated to university status and renamed SIM University; it is a private institution specializing in adult education and correspondence courses. In the late 2000s the number of higher education institutions increased with the opening of, among others, the Singapore University of Technology and Design and the Singapore Institute of Technology. There were also several private institutions operating in conjunction with universities overseas—in particular in Germany and the USA. In 2009 the total number of students enrolled at the country's five polytechnics amounted to 80,635, while a further 24,846 students were enrolled at the Institute of Technical Education (ITE) and 4,934 students were enrolled at the National Institute of Education. In 2012 a total of 243,546 students were enrolled in tertiary level public and private education.

At the higher education level, the Ministry of Education primarily offers policy guidance and quality assurance, as well as providing funding. Under the Private Education Act 2009 all private education institutions offering diploma and degree courses, or full-time post-secondary education leading to the award of a certificate, are required to register with the Council for Private Education. Adult and technical training is the responsibility of the Ministry of Manpower.

Admission to university undergraduate degrees is on the basis of results in A-Level examinations; some institutions also run entrance examinations and interviews. The undergraduate Bachelors degree lasts three years at 'Pass' level and four years at 'Honours' level, although degrees in certain professional fields of study, such as medicine, dentistry, law, engineering and construction, last longer. Both postgraduate Diplomas and Masters degrees are one- or two-year programmes of study, and the Doctor of Philosophy, the highest university degree, requires at least a further three years.

Post-secondary technical and vocational education is offered by the polytechnics and the Institute of Technical Education. The five polytechnics offer three levels of qualification, Certificate, Diploma and Advanced Diploma, in a range of professional fields of study. The ITE (founded 1992) replaced the former Vocational and Industrial Training Board and is under the control of the Ministry of Education. Consisting of 10 centres on two campuses, it specializes in full- and part-time training, workplace-based apprenticeships and continuing education. The two main qualifications offered by the ITE are the National ITE Certificate (NITEC) and the Higher NITEC.

Regulatory Body

GOVERNMENT

Ministry of Culture, Community and Youth: Old Hill St Police Station, 140 Hill St, No 01-01A, Singapore 179369; tel. 63383632; e-mail contact@mccy.gov.sg; internet www.mccy.gov.sg; Minister LAWRENCE WONG (acting).

Ministry of Education: 1 N Buona Vista Dr., MOE Bldg, Singapore 138675; tel. 68722220; e-mail contact@moe.gov.sg; internet www.moe.gov.sg; Minister HENG SWEE KEAT.

Ministry of Manpower: 18 Havelock Rd, 07-01, Singapore 059764; tel. 64385122; e-mail mom_hq@mom.gov.sg; internet www .mom.gov.sg; Minister TAN CHUAN JIN.

Learned Societies

GENERAL

Singapore National Academy of Science: Science Centre Singapore, 15 Science Centre Rd, Singapore 609981; tel. 64255000; e-mail singaporenas@gmail.com; internet www.snas .org.sg; f. 1977; Pres. Prof. ANDREW WEE; Sec. R SUBRAMANIAM; publ. *COSMOS* (irregular, print and online, www.worldscientific.com/ worldscinet/cosmos).

Singapore Society of Asian Studies: Kent Ridge, POB 1076, Singapore 911103; internet www.sgsocietyofasianstudies.wordpress .com; f. 1982; promotes study of Asian culture and heritage, with emphasis on the SE Asian region; 130 mems; Pres. LIM GUAN HOCK; Sec.

Dr YEO MANG THONG; publ. *Asian Culture* (1 a year).

ARCHITECTURE AND TOWN PLANNING

Singapore Institute of Architects: 79 Neil Rd, Singapore 088904; tel. 62262668; e-mail info@sia.org.sg; internet www.sia.org.sg; f. 1923; 1,000 mems; Pres. EDWARD D'SILVA; Hon. Sec. JOHNNY TAN; publs *SIA Year Book*, *Singapore Architect* (4 a year).

BIBLIOGRAPHY, LIBRARY SCIENCE AND MUSEOLOGY

Library Association of Singapore: Bukit Merah Central, POB 0693, Singapore 9115; e-mail lassec@las.org.sg; internet www.las .org.sg; f. 1955; 328 mems; Pres. CHOY FATT CHEONG; Hon. Sec. LIM-YEO PIN PIN; publs *Singapore Libraries* (2 a year), *Singapore Libraries Bulletin* (4 a year).

ECONOMICS, LAW AND POLITICS

Singapore Institute of International Affairs: 2 Nassim Rd, Singapore 258370; tel. 67349600; e-mail research@siiaonline .org; f. 1961; organizes talks, conferences, etc.; commissions research on East Asian economic integration, sustainable development and governance issues, and peace and development in SE Asia; 379 mems; Chair. Assoc. Prof. SIMON TAY; Dir YEO LAY HWEE.

FINE AND PERFORMING ARTS

Singapore Art Society: 10 Kampong Eunos, Singapore 417775; tel. 67430609; e-mail artsocty@signet.com.sg; internet www.singaporeartsociety.com; f. 1949; fosters art appreciation; 325 mems; Pres. TERENCE TEO CHIN KEONG.

LANGUAGE AND LITERATURE

Alliance Française: 1 Sarkies Rd, Singapore 258130; tel. 67378422; e-mail afsing@ alliancefrancaise.org.sg; internet www .alliancefrancaise.org.sg; offers courses and examinations in French language and culture and promotes cultural exchange with France; Exec. Dir YVES CORBEL.

British Council: 30 Napier Rd, Singapore 258509; tel. 64731111; e-mail enquiries@ britishcouncil.org.sg; internet www .britishcouncil.org.sg; f. 1947; teaching centre; offers courses and exams in English language and British culture and promotes cultural exchange with the UK; attached teaching centres in Holland Village, Marsiling and Tampines; Dir LES DANGERFIELD; Dir of Teaching Centre MARTIN HOPE.

Goethe-Institut: 163 Penang Rd 05-01, Winsland House II, Singapore 238463; tel. 67354555; e-mail info@singapore.goethe.org; internet www.goethe.de/so/sin/deindex.htm; offers courses and examinations in German language and culture and promotes cultural exchange with Germany; library of 8,000 vols; Dir Dr ULRICH NOWAK.

MEDICINE

Academy of Medicine, Singapore: 81 Kim Keat Rd, NKF Centre, Singapore 328836; tel. 65937800; e-mail main@ams.edu.sg; internet www.ams.edu.sg; f. 1957; professional corporate body of medical and dental specialists; postgraduate training of doctors; Master Dr LIM SHIH HUI; publ. *Annals* (4 a year).

Singapore Medical Association: Level 2, 2 College Rd, Alumni Medical Centre, Singapore 169850; tel. 62231264; e-mail sma@sma .org.sg; internet www.sma.org.sg; f. 1959; 3,900 mems; Pres. Prof. C. H. Low; Hon. Sec. Dr W. M. Yue; publ. *Singapore Medical Journal* (12 a year).

NATURAL SCIENCES

General

Singapore Association for the Advancement of Science: c/o Science Centre Singapore, Science Centre Rd, Singapore 609081; f. 1976; constituent mem. of the Singapore National Academy of Science; Pres. Lim Tit Meng; Sec. Anne Dhanaraj.

Mathematical Sciences

Singapore Mathematical Society: Mathematics Dept, National University of Singapore, Kent Ridge, Singapore 119260; tel. 68742394; e-mail smsuser@math.nus.edu.sg; internet sms.math.nus.edu.sg; f. 1952; aims to maintain the status and advance the interests of the profession of mathematics, to improve the teaching of mathematics, and to provide means of interaction between students, teachers and others interested in mathematics; 620 mems; Pres. Prof. Tan Eng Chye; Sec. Prof. Tang Wee Kee; publ. *Mathematical Medley* (2 a year).

Physical Sciences

Institute of Physics, Singapore: c/o Dept of Physics, National University of Singapore, Kent Ridge, Singapore 119260; tel. 67722604; e-mail ips@physics.nus.edu.sg; f. 1973; promotes study of and research in physics in Singapore; organizes confs, talks, seminars, exhibitions, visits to industrial and commercial establishments and educational tours abroad; 180 mems; Pres. Prof. Bernard Tan; Sec. Assoc. Prof. Andrew T. S. Wee; publs *Physics Update* (2 a year), *Singapore Journal of Physics* (2 a year).

Research Institutes

ECONOMICS, LAW AND POLITICS

Asian Media Information and Communication Centre: Jurong Point, POB 360, Singapore 916412; tel. 67927570; e-mail enquiries@amic.org.sg; internet www.amic .org.sg; f. 1971; non-profit regional documentation centre; works in cooperation with UNESCO and other int. orgs to promote the understanding and devt of communication and its application in the Asia-Pacific region with regard to economic, social and cultural progress; publishes media journals and books; organizes seminars, capacity building workshops; convenes confs; conducts communication research; library of 35,000 records in databases, 350 journals; regional centre for Japan Prize Circulating Library; Sec.-Gen. Prof. Sundeep R. Muppidi; publs *AMCB* (6 a year), *Asian Communication Handbook* (every 3–4 years), *Asian Journal of Communication* (6 a year), *Media Asia* (4 a year).

Institute of Southeast Asian Studies: Heng Mui Keng Terrace, Pasir Panjang, Singapore 119614; e-mail admin@iseas.edu .sg; f. 1968; undertakes research on SE Asia, esp. problems of devt, modernization, political and social change; library of 400,000 vols; Dir Tan Chin Tiong; Librarian Zaleha Tamby; publs *ASEAN Economic Bulletin* (3 a year), *Contemporary Southeast Asia* (3 a year), *Regional Outlook, Social Issues in Southeast Asia* (2 a year), *SOJOURN, Southeast Asian Affairs* (1 a year).

EDUCATION

East Asian Institute (EAI): 469A Bukit Timah Rd, Tower Block, 06–01, Singapore 259770; tel. 65163715; e-mail eaizyn@nus .edu.sg; internet www.eai.nus.edu.sg; f. 1997; attached to Nat. Univ. of Singapore; promotes both academic and policy-oriented research on East Asian devt; focuses on political, economic and social devt of contemporary China (incl. Hong Kong and Taiwan) and China's growing economic relations with the region and the world, incl. Japan, Korea, ASEAN; library of 27,892 vols, incl. colln of yearbooks and 359 journals, periodicals and newspapers from the People's Republic of China, Hong Kong and Taiwan; Chair. Prof. Gungwu Wang; Dir Prof. Yongnian Zheng; publs *China: An International Journal (CIJ)*, *East Asian Policy (EAP)* (4 a year).

Institute of Technical Education (ITE): 2 Ang Mo Kio Dr., Singapore 567720; tel. 65902578; e-mail itehq@ite.edu.sg; internet www.ite.edu.sg; f. 1992; Dir and CEO Bruce Poh; publ. *The Quality Workforce* (6 a year).

Libraries and Archives

Singapore

National Archives of Singapore: 1 Canning Rise, Singapore 179868; tel. 63327909; e-mail nas@nlb.gov.sg; internet www.nas.gov .sg; f. 1968; 3,400 vols, 43 current periodicals, 1.5m. photographs, 128,200 building plans, 6,630 maps, 66,427 microfilm rolls, 18,000 cassettes of recorded interviews.

National Library Board: 100 Victoria St, 14-01, Nat. Library Bldg, Singapore 188064; tel. 63323133; e-mail helpdesk@library.nlb .gov.sg; internet www.nlb.gov.sg; f. 1995; attached to Min. of Communications and Information; oversees management of Nat. Archives, Nat. Library, network of 24 public libraries and 12 libraries belonging to govt agencies; 8.67m. vols, collns in languages of English, Chinese, Malay, Tamil, incl. books, audiovisuals, microfilm items, serials and other library materials; Chief Exec. Elaine Ng; publs *Index to Singapore Information*, *Singapore National Bibliography* (online).

National University of Singapore Libraries: 12 Kent Ridge Crescent, Singapore 119275; tel. 65162069; e-mail clbsec@ nus.edu.sg; internet www.lib.nus.edu.sg; f. 1905; 2.4m. vols (Central Library 1.1m. vols; Japanese Resources 51,955 vols; Chinese Library 465,644 vols; C. J. Koh Law Library 157,087 vols; Hon Sui Sen Memorial Library 90,992 vols; Medical Library 170,040 vols; Science Library 286,221 vols), 23,844 electronic titles, 27,423 audiovisual items, 24,266 microforms; Dir., NUS Libraries Sylvia Yap; publ. *Guide to NUS Libraries* (1 a year).

Museums and Art Galleries

Singapore

National Heritage Board: 61 Stamford Rd, Singapore 178892; tel. 63361460; e-mail nhb_feedback@nhb.gov.sg; internet www .nhb.gov.sg; f. 1993 by merger of National Archives, National Museum and Oral History Dept; history and oral history archives; consists of Asian Civilizations Museum, Singapore History Museum, Singapore Art Museum, Children's Discovery Gallery; library of 25,000 vols; Chair. Ong Yew Huat; CEO Rosa Daniel.

Singapore Art Museum: 71 Bras Basah Rd, Singapore 189555; tel. 63323222; e-mail feedback@singaporeartmuseum.sg; internet www.singaporeartmuseum.sg; f. 1996; modern and contemporary SE Asian art; Dir Dr Susie Lingham; publ. *The Quarterly*.

Singapore Botanic Gardens: National Parks Board, Cluny Rd, Singapore 259569; tel. 64717361; e-mail nparks_sbg_visitor_services@nparks.gov.sg; internet www.nparks.gov.sg; f. 1859; botanical and horticultural research with particular reference to SE Asia and the tropics; library of 30,000 vols; CEO Poon Hong Yuen; Dir for Gdns Dr Nigel Taylor; Keeper of Herbarium and Library Dr Wong Khoon Meng; publ. *The Gardens Bulletin Singapore* (2 a year).

Universities

NANYANG TECHNOLOGICAL UNIVERSITY

50 Nanyang Ave, Singapore 639798

Telephone: 67911744

E-mail: adm_intnl@ntu.edu.sg

Internet: www.ntu.edu.sg

Founded 1981 as Nanyang Technological Institute; present name and status 1991

Academic year: July to July

Pres.: Dr Su Guaning

Provost: Prof. Bertil Andersson

Sr Assoc. Provost: Prof. Er Meng Hwa

Assoc. Provost for Graduate Education and Special Projects: Prof. Lam Khin Yong

Assoc. Provost for Innovation: Jeffrey Nadison

Assoc. Provost for Research: Prof. Michael Khor

Sec.: Anthony Teo

Chief Financial Officer: Goh Boon Huat

Chief Human Resource Officer: Angela Lim Sau Ting

Chief Planning Officer and Registrar: Chan Kwong Lok

Chief Univ. Advancement Officer: Chew Kheng Chuan

Dir of Corporate Communications: Dr Vivien Chiong

Librarian: Choy Fatt Cheong

Number of teachers: 1,640

Number of students: 33,100

Publications: *Asian Business Law Review* (4 a year), *Asian Journal of Communication* (3 a year), *Asian Mass Communication Bulletin* (6 a year), *Asia Pacific Journal of Education* (2 a year), *Electrical and Electronic Engineering Bulletin* (1 a year), *Mechanical and Aerospace Engineering Research Bulletin* (1 a year), *Media Asia* (4 a year), *Nanyang Business Review* (2 a year), *Pedagogies: An International Journal* (2 a year), *School of Computer Engineering Research Report* (1 a year), *Singteach* (4 a year), *Teaching Education* (4 a year), *Technical Reports* (12 a year)

DEANS

College of Engineering: Prof. Pan Tso-Chien

College of Humanities, Arts and Social Sciences: Prof. Alan Chan Kam-Leung

College of Science: Prof. Mark Featherstone

Cornell-Nanyang Institute of Hospitality Management: Dr Russell Arthur Smith

Nanyang Business School: Prof. Gillian Yeo Hian Heng

School of Art, Design and Media: Prof. Vibeke Sorensen

School of Biological Sciences: Prof. Alex Law Sai Kit (acting)

School of Chemical and Biomedical Engineering: Prof. Ching Chi Bun

School of Civil and Environmental Engineering: Assoc. Prof. EDMOND LO YAT-MAN
School of Computer Engineering: Prof. THAMBIPILLAI SRIKANTHAN
School of Electrical and Electronic Engineering: Prof. KAM CHAN HIN
School of Humanities and Social Sciences: Prof. EUSTON QUAH (acting)
School of Materials Science and Engineering: Prof. FREDDY BOEY YING CHIANG (acting)
School of Mechanical and Aerospace Engineering: Prof. LING SHIH FU (acting)
School of Physical and Mathematical Sciences: Prof. LING SAN
S. Rajaratnam School of Int. Studies: Ambassador BARRY DESKER
Wee Kim Wee School of Communication and Information: Assoc. Prof. BENJAMIN HILL DETENBER

PROFESSORS

College of Engineering (Block S3.2, Level B1, 50 Nanyang Ave, Singapore 639798; tel. 67906706; e-mail d-coe@ntu.edu.sg; internet www.ntu.edu.sg/coe):

LIM, E. N.
LIM, M. K.

Nanyang Business School (Block S3, 50 Nanyang Ave, Singapore 639798; tel. 67904636; e-mail wwwnbs@ntu.edu.sg; internet www.nbs.ntu.edu.sg):

ANG, S., Strategy, Management and Organization
DUFEY, G., Banking and Finance
HONG, H.
NEO, B. S.
SETHI, V., Information Technology and Operations Management
SIGUAW, J. A., Cornell-Nanyang Institute of Hospitality Management
TAN, H. T., Accounting
WEE, C. H., Strategy, Management and Organization
WILLIAMS, J. J., Accounting
YEO, F. H. H., Accounting

National Institute of Education (1 Nanyang Walk, Singapore 637616; tel. 67903888; e-mail niepr@nie.edu.sg; internet www.nie.edu.sg):

CHEW, C. H.
GAN, L. H.
GOH, K. C.
GOPINATHAN, S.
HOGAN, D. J.
LEE, S. K.
LUKE, A. A. J.
MATTHEWS, J. S.
TAN, L. W. H.
XU, S. Y.

School of Biological Sciences (60 Nanyang Dr., SBS-01n-21, Singapore 637551; tel. 63162800; e-mail d-sbs@ntu.edu.sg; internet www.ntu.edu.sg/sbs):

LAW, A. S. K., Molecular and Cell Biology
LUN, K. C., Structural and Computational Biology
NORDENSKLÖLD, L., Structural and Computational Biology
TAM, J. P. K.

School of Chemical and Biomedical Engineering (Block 1 Innovation Centre, 16 Nanying Dr., Unit 100, Level 1, Singapore 637722; tel. 67906743; e-mail cbe@ntu.edu.sg; internet www.ntu.edu.sg/cbme):

CHING, C. B.

School of Civil and Environmental Engineering (Block N1, 50 Nanyang Ave, Singapore 639798; tel. 67905265; e-mail d-cee@ntu.edu.sg; internet www.ntu.edu.sg/cee):

CHIEW, Y. M., Environmental and Water Resources Engineering
CHOA, V. C. E., Geotechnical Engineering

CHOI, E. C. C., Construction Technology and Management
FAN, H. S. L., Transportation Engineering
FAN, S. C., Structures and Mechanics
PAN, T. C., Structures and Mechanics
RAHARDJO, H., Geotechnical and Transportation Engineering
SOH, C. K., Structures and Mechanics
TAY, J. H., Environmental and Water Resources Engineering

Wee Kim Wee School of Communication and Information (31 Nanyang Link, Singapore 637718; tel. 67904577; e-mail wwwsci@ntu.edu.sg; internet www.ntu.edu.sg/sci):

FOO S. B., Information Studies
KUO C. Y. E., Communication Research

School of Computer Engineering (Block N4, 2A-32, Nanyang Ave, Singapore 639798; tel. 67905786; e-mail wwwsce@ntu.edu.sg; internet www.ntu.edu.sg/sce):

GOH, A. E. S., Information Systems

School of Electrical and Electronic Engineering (Block S2.1, 50 Nanyang Ave, Singapore 639798; tel. 67905367; e-mail wwweee@ntu.edu.sg; internet www.ntu.edu.sg/eee):

CHOI, S. S., Power Engineering
DO, M. A., Circuits and Systems
ER, M. H.
GAY, R. K. L., Information Communication Institute of Singapore
KAM, C. H., Microelectronics
KOH, S. N., Communication Engineering
KOT, C. C., Information Engineering
LIM, Y. C., Information Engineering
SOH, Y. C., Control and Instrumentation
SUNDARARAJAN, N., Control and Instrumentation
XIE, L. H., Control and Administration
YOON, S. F., Microelectronics
ZHU, W. G., Microelectronics

School of Humanities and Social Sciences (Block S3.2, Level B2, 50 Nanyang Ave, Singapore 639798; tel. 67906983; e-mail d-hss@ntu.edu.sg; internet www.hss.ntu.edu.sg):

CHEW, S. B., Economics
KOH, T. A., English
KUO, C. O. E., Sociology
LIM, C. Y., Economics
REISMAN, D. A., Economics

School of Materials Science and Engineering (Block N4.1, No 01-30, Nanyang Ave, Singapore 639798; tel. 67904142; e-mail wwwsme@ntu.edu.sg; internet www.ntu.edu.sg/sme):

BOEY, F. Y. C.

School of Mechanical and Aerospace Engineering (Block N3, 50 Nanyang Ave, Singapore 639798; tel. 67905486; e-mail wwwmae@ntu.edu.sg; internet www.ntu.edu.sg/mae):

ASUNDI, A. K., Engineering Mechanics
HELANDER, M. E. G., Systems and Engineering Management
KHOO, L. P., Mechatronics and Design
KHOR, K. A., Manufacturing Engineering
LAM, Y. C., Manufacturing Engineering
LIEW, K. M., Engineering Mechanics
LIM, L. E. N., Manufacturing Engineering
LIM, M. K., Engineering Mechanics
LING, S. F., Engineering Mechanics
LYE, S. W., Manufacturing Engineering
MEGUID, S. A., Engineering Mechanics
SHANG, H. M., Engineering Mechanics
TAM, K. C., Manufacturing Engineering
YUE, C. Y.

School of Physical and Mathematical Sciences (Block 5, Level 3, 1 Nanyang Walk, Singapore 637616; tel. 67903754; e-mail spms-v1@ntu.edu.sg; internet www.ntu.edu.sg/spms/home):

LEE, S. Y.

LEUNG, P. H., Physical and Mathematical Sciences
LING, S., Mathematical Sciences
LOH, T. P., Chemistry and Biological Chemistry

ATTACHED RESEARCH INSTITUTES

Advanced Materials Research Centre: tel. 67904626; e-mail d-amrc@ntu.edu.sg; Dir Assoc. Prof. SUBODH MHAISALKAR.

Bioinformatics Research Centre: tel. 63162957; internet www.ntu.edu.sg; Dir Assoc. Prof. SUBBU S. VENKATRAMAN.

BioMedical Engineering Research Centre: internet www3.ntu.edu.sg/bmerc; Dir Assoc. Prof. LIM CHU SING DANIEL.

Centre for Advanced Numerical Engineering Simulations: Dir Prof. LIEW KIM MEOW.

Centre for Financial Engineering: tel. 67904758; e-mail mfe@ntu.edu.sg; Dir Assoc. Prof. BUEN SIN LOW.

Centre for Graphics and Imaging Technology: Dir Assoc. Prof. WONG KOK CHEONG.

Centre for High-Performance Embedded Systems: tel. 67906638; e-mail chipes@ntu.edu; internet www.chipes.ntu.edu.sg; Dir Prof. THAMBIPILLAI SRIKANTHAN.

Environmental Engineering Research Centre: Dir Assoc. Prof. STEPHEN TAY TIONG LEE.

Maritime Research Centre: tel. 67905321; e-mail d-mrc@ntu.edu.sg; Dir Assoc. Prof. TAN SOON KEAT.

Nanyang Technopreneurship Centre: tel. 67906675; e-mail ntc@ntu.edu.sg; Dir Assoc. Prof. TAN TENG KEE.

Network Technology Research Centre: tel. 67905019; e-mail ntrc@ntu.edu.sg; internet www.ntu.edu.sg/ntrc; Dir Assoc. Prof. PING SHUM.

NTU-BCA Centre for Advanced Construction Studies: Dir Assoc. Prof. TING SENG KIONG.

NTU-MINDEF Protective Technology Research Centre: tel. 67905285; e-mail ptrc@ntu.edu.sg; internet www.ntu.edu.sg/ptrc; Dir Prof. TSO-CHIEN PAN.

Positioning and Wireless Technology Centre: tel. 67917326; e-mail d-pwtc@ntu.edu.sg; internet www.ntu.edu.sg/centre/pwtc; Dir Assoc. Prof. CHOI LOOK LAW.

Robotics Research Centre: tel. 67905568; e-mail d-rrc@ntu.edu.sg; internet www.ntu.edu.sg/mae/centres/rrc; Dir Assoc. Prof. GERALD SEET

NATIONAL UNIVERSITY OF SINGAPORE

21 Lower Kent Ridge Rd, Singapore 119077
Telephone: 65166666
E-mail: webmaster@nus.edu.sg
Internet: www.nus.edu.sg

Founded 1980 by merger of fmr Univ. of Singapore and Nanyang Univ.
State control
Language of instruction: English
Academic year: July to June (2 semesters)

Pres.: Prof. TAN CHORH CHUAN
Deputy Pres. for Acad. Affairs and Provost: Prof. TAN ENG CHYE
Deputy Pres. for Admin.: JOSEPH P. MULLINIX
Deputy Pres. for Research and Technology: Prof. BARRY HALLIWELL
Vice-Pres. for Campus Infrastructure: Prof. YONG KWET YEW
Vice-Pres. for Endowment and Institutional Devt: WEE SIN THO
Vice-Pres. for Human Resources: DANIEL CHO KWONG CHOW

Vice-Pres. for Research Strategy: Prof. SEERAM RAMAKRISHNA

Vice-Pres. for Univ. and Global Relations: Prof. LILY KONG

Vice-Provost for Academic Personnel: Prof. LAI CHOY HENG

Vice-Provost for Education: Prof. TAN THIAM SOON

Vice-Provost for Student Life: Prof. TAN TAI YONG

CEO: Dr LILY CHAN

Registrar: CHRISTINE CHEN (acting)

Librarian: JILL QUAH

Library: see under Libraries and Archives

Number of teachers: 2,200

Number of students: 33,700

Publication: *Knowledge Enterprise* (10 year)

DEANS

Duke-NUS Graduate Medical School Singapore: TONY CHEW (Chair.)

Faculty of Arts and Social Sciences: Prof. BRENDA YEOH

Faculty of Dentistry: Assoc. Prof. GRACE ONG HUI LIAN

Faculty of Engineering: Prof. CHAN ENG SOON

Faculty of Law: Prof. TAN CHENG HAN

Faculty of Science: Prof. SHEN ZUOWEI

Lee Kwan Yew School of Public Policy: Prof. KISHORE MAHBUBANI

NUS Business School: Prof. BERNARD YEUNG

NUS Graduate School for Integrative Sciences and Engineering: Prof. LI BAOWEN (Exec. Dir)

School of Computing: Prof. BENG CHIN OOI

School of Design and Environment: Prof. HENG CHYE KIANG

Yong Loo Lin School of Medicine: Prof. JOHN WONG

Yong Siew Toh Conservatory of Music: Prof. BERNARD LANSKEY (Dir)

PROFESSORS

Faculty of Arts and Social Sciences:

CHAN, H. C., Political Science
KAPUR, B. K., Economics
MOHANAN, K. P., English Language and Literature
MUKUL, A., Public Policy
NG, C. K., History
QUAH, S. T. J., Political Science
SIDLE, R. C., Geography
SINGH, R., Social Work and Psychology
SURYADINATA, L., Political Science
WANG, G. W., East Asian Institute
WONG, K. L. C. A., Sociology
WONG, Y. W., Chinese Studies

Faculty of Business Administration:

KAU, A. K., Marketing
LEONG, S. M., Marketing
TAN, C. H., Management and Organization
WONG, K. A., Finance and Accounting

Faculty of Dentistry:

CHEW, C. L., Restorative Dentistry
LOH, H. S., Oral and Maxillofacial Surgery

Faculty of Engineering:

ANG, B. W., Industrial and Systems Engineering
ARUN, S. M., Mechanical Engineering
CHAN, S. H. D., Electrical and Computer Engineering
CHEONG, H. F., Civil Engineering
CHEW, Y. T., Mechanical Engineering
CHING, C. B., Chemical and Environmental Engineering
CHOW, Y. K., Civil Engineering
CHUA, S. J., Electrical and Computer Engineering
CHUNG, T. S. N., Chemical and Environmental Engineering
FWA, T. F., Civil Engineering
GOH, T. N., Industrial and Systems Engineering

HANG, C. C., Electrical and Computer Engineering
KAM, P. Y., Electrical and Computer Engineering
KANG, E. T., Chemical and Environmental Engineering
KOOI, P. S., Electrical and Computer Engineering
LAM, K. Y., Mechanical Engineering
LEE, T. H., Electrical and Computer Engineering
LEONG, M. S., Electrical and Computer Engineering
LI, M. F., Electrical and Computer Engineering
LIEW, A. C., Electrical and Computer Engineering
LIM, S. C., Mechanical Engineering
LIM, Y. C., Electrical and Computer Engineering
LING, C. H., Electrical and Computer Engineering
LOW, T. S., Electrical and Computer Engineering
LYE, K. M., Electrical and Computer Engineering
NEE, Y. C. A., Mechanical Engineering
NEOH, K. G., Chemical and Environmental Engineering
NG, W. J., Civil Engineering
NHAN, P. T., Mechanical Engineering
PARAMASIVAM, P., Civil Engineering
PHANG, C. H. J., Electrical and Computer Engineering
POO, A. N., Mechanical Engineering
SHANG, H. M., Mechanical Engineering
SHANKAR, N. J., Civil Engineering
SHANMUGAM, N. E., Civil Engineering
SHIH, C. F., Engineering
TAN, T. C., Chemical and Environmental Engineering
TAY, A. O. A., Electrical and Computer Engineering
TOYOAKI, N., Civil Engineering
VISWANADHAM, N., Mechanical Engineering
WIJEYSUNDERA, N. E., Mechanical Engineering
WONG, L., Electrical and Computer Engineering
YAP, M., Chemical and Environmental Engineering
YEO, S. P., Electrical and Computer Engineering
YONG, K. Y., Civil Engineering

Faculty of Law:

JAYAKUMAR, S.
KOH, T. B. T.
PINSLER, J.
SORNARAJAH, M.
TAN, Y. L.
WOON, C. M. W.

Yong Loo Lin School of Medicine:

AW, T. C., Pathology
BOSE, K., Orthopaedic Surgery
CHAN, H. L., Medicine
CHAN, S. H., Microbiology
CHIEW, Y. C., Medicine
GOPALAKRISHNAKONE, P., Anatomy
GWEE, M., Pharmacology
HALLIWELL, B., Biochemistry
HWANG, L. H. P., Physiology
KOH, S. Q. D., Community, Occupational and Family Medicine
KUA, E. H., Psychological Medicine
LEE, E. H., Orthopaedic Surgery
LEE, H. P., Community, Occupational and Family Medicine
LEE, J. D. E., Pharmacology
LEE, T. L., Anaesthesia
LEE, Y. S., Pathology
LIM, P., Medicine
LING, E. A., Anatomy
LIU, E., Medicine
LOW, P. S., Paediatrics
NG, S. C., Obstetrics and Gynaecology

OH, M. S. V., Medicine
ONG, C. N., Community, Occupational and Family Medicine
PHO, W. H. R., Orthopaedic Surgery
PRASAD, R. N. V., Obstetrics and Gynaecology
SATKUNANANTHAM, K., Orthopaedic Surgery
SHAMAL, D. D., Orthopaedic Surgery
SIT, K. H., Anatomy
SIT, K. P., Biochemistry
TAN, C. C., Medicine
TAN, K. A. L., Diagnostic Radiology
TAN, W. C., Medicine
TAN, Y. H., Medicine
WEE, A., Pathology
WONG, E. L. J., Medicine
YAP, H. K., Paediatrics

Faculty of Science:

BAI, Z., Statistics and Applied Probability
BERRICK, A. J., Mathematics
CHAN, S. O. H., Chemistry
CHEN, H. Y. L., Mathematics
CHONG, C. T., Mathematics
CHOU, L. M., Biological Sciences
CHOW, S. N., Mathematics
DING, J. L., Biological Sciences
GOH, S. H., Chemistry
HEW, C. L., Biological Sciences
HOR, T. S. A., Chemistry
IP, Y. K. A., Biological Sciences
KOH, K. M., Mathematics
LAI, C. H., Physics
LAM, T. J., Biological Sciences
LEE, C. K., Chemistry
LEE, S. L., Mathematics
LEE, S. Y., Chemistry
LI, F. Y. S., Chemistry
LIM, C. S., Mathematics
LIM, H., Physics
NIEDERREITER, H., Mathematics
OH, C. H., Physics
ONG, C. K., Physics
ONG, P. P. P., Physics
PHILPOTT, M. R., Materials Science
SY, H. K., Physics
TANG, S. H., Physics
TANG, S. M., Physics
TRUONG, Y. K.-N., Statistics and Applied Probability
WATT, F., Physics

School of Computing:

JAFFAR, J., Computer Science
LING, T. W., Computer Science
LU, H. J., Computer Science
OOI, B. C., Computer Science
PNG, P. L. I., Information Systems
WEI, K. K., Information Systems
YUEN, C. K., Computer Science

School of Design and Environment:

BROWN, G. R., Real Estate
OFORI, G., Building

SIM UNIVERSITY

461 Clementi Rd, Singapore 599491
Telephone: 62489777
E-mail: student_recruitment@unisim.edu.sg
Internet: www.unisim.edu.sg

Founded 1992, present name and status 2005
Private control

Chair.: Prof. CHAM TAO SOON
Pres.: CHEONG HEE KIAT
Registrar: Assoc. Prof YIP WOON KWONG

DEANS

School of Arts and Social Sciences: Dr GENICE NGG (acting)
School of Business: Prof. TAN NGOH TIONG
School of Human Development and Social Services: Prof. TAN NGOH TIONG
School of Science and Technology: Assoc. Prof. PHILIP CHEANG HONG NING (acting)

SINGAPORE INSTITUTE OF TECHNOLOGY

25 N Bridge Rd, EFG Bank Bldg 03–01, Singapore 179104
Telephone: 65921189
E-mail: adm.intl@singaporetech.edu.sg
Internet: www.singaporetech.edu.sg
Founded 2009
State control

Chair.: NG YAT CHUNG
Deputy Chair.: NG CHER PONG
Pres.: Prof. TAN CHIN TIONG
Deputy Pres. for Academics: Dr TING SENG KIONG
Deputy Pres. for Operations: TAN CHEK MING

SINGAPORE MANAGEMENT UNIVERSITY

Tanglin, POB 257, Singapore 912409
Bukit Timah Campus, 469 Bukit Timah Rd, Oei Tiong Ham Bldg, Singapore 259756
Telephone: 68220100
E-mail: enquiry@smu.edu.sg
Internet: www.smu.edu.sg
Founded 2000
Private control

Pres.: HOWARD HUNTER
Provost: Prof. CHIN TIONG TAN
Registrar: TAN LEE CHUAN
Chief Librarian: KOH BEE CHIN

DEANS

Lee Kong Chian School of Business: Prof. DAVID B. MONTGOMERY
School of Accountancy: Assoc. Prof. PANG YANG HOONG
School of Economics and Social Sciences: Prof. ROBERTO S. MARIANO
School of Information Systems: STEVEN MILLER

PROFESSORS

Lee Kong Chian School of Business (Business Bldg, 469 Bukit Timah Rd, Singapore 259756; e-mail dmontgomery@smu.edu.sg; internet www.business.smu.edu.sg):

LIM, K. G.
MONTGOMERY, D.
PANG, E. F.
PHANG, A.
TAN, C. T.
YANG, K. K.

School of Accountancy (Accountancy Bldg, 469 Bukit Timah Rd, Singapore 259756; tel. 68220610; e-mail adelineheng@smu.edu.sg; internet www.accountancy.smu.edu.sg):

TAN, T. M.
YOUNG, K. K.

School of Economics and Social Sciences (The Federal Bldg, 469 Bukit Timah Rd, Singapore 259756; tel. 68220832; e-mail sess@smu.edu.sg; internet www.sess.smu.edu.sg):

KUEN, T. S.
MARIANO, R. S.

School of Information Systems (Raffles Bldg, 469 Bukit Timah Rd, Singapore 259756; tel. 68220903; e-mail sis@smu.edu.sg; internet www.sis.smu.edu.sg):

DENG, R. H.
LEE, J. K.

SINGAPORE UNIVERSITY OF TECHNOLOGY & DESIGN (SUTD)

287 Ghim Moh Rd, 04-00, Singapore 279623
Telephone: 63036600
E-mail: enquiry@sutd.edu.sg
Internet: www.su.edu.sg

Offers courses in architecture and sustainable design, engineering product development, engineering systems and design, information systems technology and design

Chair.: PHILIP NG
Pres.: TOM MAGNANTI
Provost: Prof. CHONG TOW CHONG
Assoc. Provost: Prof. PEY KIN LEONG

Polytechnics

NANYANG POLYTECHNIC

180 Ang Mo Kio Ave 8, Singapore 569830
Telephone: 64515115
E-mail: nyp_registry@nyp.edu.sg
Internet: www.nyp.edu.sg
Founded 1992

Pres.: TAN PHENG HOCK
Prin. and CEO: LIN CHENG TON
Deputy Prin. for Academic Affairs and Registrar: CHAN LEE MUN
Deputy Prin. for Devt: BRUCE POH GEOK HUAT
Deputy Prin. for Technology: EDWARD HO SZE LEUNG
Chief Librarian: WONG CHIEW AUN

NGEE ANN POLYTECHNIC

535 Clementi Rd, Singapore 599489
Telephone: 64666555
E-mail: dept-cc@np.edu.sg
Internet: www.np.edu.sg
Founded 1963
State control
Language of instruction: English
Academic year: April to March

Chair.: KIN FEI TANG
Prin.: BOON WEE, CLARENCE TI
Deputy Prin.: MEI FONG LOOI
Deputy Prin.: KOK WAI, PETER LAM
Deputy Prin.: WEE BENG MAH
Sr Dir: GUEK IM TANG-LIM
Sr Dir: CHEH HOON CHOO-YEO
Library Dir: CAROLINE CHOON KHENG PHUA

Library of 175,000 vols, 460 periodicals, 43,000 ebooks, 50 edatabases and 30,000 audiovisual titles
Number of teachers: 935
Number of students: 17,927 (16,227 full-time, 1,700 part-time)
Publications: NP Tribune (online), NP News (2 or 3 a year, online)

DEANS

Centre of Innovation (Environmental and Water Technology): LI PHIN TAM-LIM
Centre of Innovation (Marine and Offshore Technology): CHANDA SUBRATA
CET Academy: KWAN YEW CHAN
School of Business and Accountancy: SIEW HONG, ANNA YAP-TOO
School of Design and Environment: PECK HONG PANG-ENG
School of Engineering, Electrical Engineering Div.: GEK CHOO LEK-LIM
School of Engineering, Electronic and Computer Engineering Div.: KEE WAN NG
School of Engineering, Mechanical Div.: YEE SIONG, PETER LIANG
School of Film and Media Studies: HWAI MIN, ANITA KUAN
School of Health Sciences: Dr CHIEW HUN PHANG
School of Humanities and Social Sciences: HUI LENG TIEW-TEO
School of InfoComm Technology: LI KWANG, ANGELA WEE
School of Interdisciplinary Studies: ANDREW THURAIRAJA SABARATNAM
School of Life Sciences and Chemical Technology: KIOW LENG, HEDY GOH

Technology Development and Innovation: SEOW HAR LEE-GOH

REPUBLIC POLYTECHNIC

1 Kay Siang Rd, Singapore 248922
Telephone: 63768000
E-mail: gsm@rp.edu.sg
Internet: www.rp.edu.sg
Founded 2002

Prin. and Chief Exec.: Prof. LOW TECK SENG
Deputy Registrar: SEAN TAY
Library Man.: YEE WAI FUN

SINGAPORE POLYTECHNIC

500 Dover Rd, Singapore 139651
Telephone: 67751133
E-mail: ccom@sp.edu.sg
Internet: www.sp.edu.sg
Founded 1954
Language of instruction: English
Academic year: April to February (4 terms)

Chair.: TAN KAY YONG
Prin.: TAN HANG CHEONG
Deputy Prin. for Admin.: EDWARD QUAH KOK WAH
Deputy Prin. for Corporate Devt: HEE JOH LIANG
Registrar: TAN PENG ANN
Librarian: FANG SIN GUEK

Library of 266,000 vols, periodicals and multimedia and 60,000 electronic resources
Number of teachers: 860
Number of students: 17,443 (15,523 full-time, 1,920 part-time)
Publications: fullstop (8 a year), inSPire (1 a year), RIOT (1 a year)

TEMASEK POLYTECHNIC

21 Tampines Ave 1, Singapore 529757
Telephone: 67882000
E-mail: corpcomm@tp.edu.sg
Internet: www.tp.edu.sg
Founded 1990

Prin. and CEO: BOO KHENG HUA
Registrar: SOH ENG KHIM
Library Dir: ESTHER ONG

Library of 218,000 vols, 1,900 periodicals
Number of teachers: 800
Number of students: 16,000
Publications: In Tempo (4 a year, online), Temasek Journal, T's (2 a year)

Institutes of Technical Education

DIGIPEN INSTITUTE OF TECHNOLOGY—SINGAPORE

PIXEL Bldg, 10 Central Exchange Green, 01-01, Singapore 138649
Telephone: 65771900
E-mail: singapore@digipen.edu
Internet: singapore.digipen.edu
Founded 2008
Private control

Bachelors in arts (game design), fine arts (production animation), science (game design, real-time interactive simulation)

GERMAN INSTITUTE OF SCIENCE AND TECHNOLOGY—TUM ASIA (GIST—TUM ASIA)

10 Central Exchange Green, 03-01, Pixel Bldg, Singapore 138649
Telephone: 67777407
E-mail: admin@gist.edu.sg
Internet: www.gist.edu.sg
Private control

Offers Bachelors and Masters programmes in aerospace engineering, electrical engineering and information technology, industrial chemistry, integrated circuit design, microelectronics, transport and logistics; br. of Technische Universität München, Germany

Publication: *GIST—TUM Asia Digest*

INSTITUTE OF TECHNICAL EDUCATION

10 Dover Dr., Singapore 138683
Telephone: 65902288
E-mail: itehq@ite.edu.sg
Internet: www.ite.edu.sg
Founded 1992 as Post-Secondary Technical Education Institution
State control

3 Colleges: ITE College Central, ITE College East, ITE College West; courses in applied and health sciences, automotive engineering, business and services, design and media, electronics and info-comm technology, engineering, machine technology

Chair.: BOB TAN BENG HAI
Deputy Chair.: HENG CHIANG GNEE
Dir and CEO: BRUCE POH GEOK HUAT

Publications: *ignITE* (2 a year), *iLink*, *infin-ITE*, *Transforming Lives—The ITE Story*

Schools of Art and Music

LASALLE College of the Arts: 1 McNally St, Singapore 187940; tel. 64965000; e-mail enquiries@lasalle.edu.sg; internet www.lasalle.edu.sg; f. 1984 as St Patrick's Arts Centre, present status 2004, present name and location 2007; attached to LASALLE Foundation Limited; design, fine art, media, performing arts; 2,300 students; Pres. Prof. ALASTAIR PEARCE; Provost and Chief Academic Officer VENKA PURUSHOTHAMAN; Chair. PETER SEAH.

Nanyang Academy of Fine Arts: 80 Bencoolen St, Singapore 189655; tel. 65124000; e-mail president@nafa.edu.sg; internet www.nafa.edu.sg; f. 1938 as Nanyang Fine Arts College, present name 1990; offers diploma, Bachelors and Masters degrees; depts of 3D design, arts management and education, dance, design and media, fashion studies, fine art, music, theatre; library: 80,000 vols of books and journals; 2,200 students; Chair. Prof. CHAM TAO SOON; Vice-Chair. POH CHOON ANN; Vice-Chair. Prof. PHUA KOK KHOO; Pres. CHOO THIAM SIEW; Vice-Pres. LIEW CHIN CHOY.

New York University Tisch School of Arts Asia: 3 Kay Siang Rd, Singapore 248923; tel. 65001700; e-mail tisch.asia@nyu.edu; internet www.tischasia.nyu.edu.sg; f. 2007; offers Masters degree in animation and digital arts, dramatic writing, film production; Dean and Chair. MARY SCHMIDT CAMPBELL; Artistic Dir OLIVER STONE; Pres. PARI SARA SHIRAZI; Chair. of Graduate Dept of Dramatic Writing RICHARD WESLEY; Chair. of Graduate Dept of Film DAVID K. IRVING; Exec. Dir ANNIE STANTON; Exec. Dir GERARD I. BUENO; Dir of Admin. JASON SETH BECKERMAN; Dir for Graduate Dept of Animation and Digital Arts JEAN-MARC GAUTHIER; Dir of Public Affairs and Marketing TIMOTHY TAN.

Colleges

ESSEC Business School: 100 Victoria St, 13-02, Nat. Library Bldg, Singapore; tel. 68849780; e-mail mailtaxe@nullessec.fr; internet www.essec.edu; f. 2006; offers Bachelors, Masters and PhD; courses in business administration, finance and asset management, financial techniques, hospitality management, information systems and telecommunication networks, international business law and management, international food industry management, international luxury brand management, international supply chain management, logistics and supply chain management, management, management of technological projects, marketing management, strategy and management of international business, urban environmental and services management, executive MBA, executive education; Dean JEAN-MARC XUEREB.

INSEAD: 1 Ayer Rajah Ave, Singapore 138676; tel. 67995388; internet www.insead.edu; f. 2000; offers MBA, Exec. MBA, PhD programmes; Dean FRANK BROWN.

S P Jain Center of Management: 10 Hyderabad Rd, off Alexandra Rd, Singapore 119579; tel. 62704748; e-mail admissionssg@spjain.org; internet www.spjain.org; f. 2006; banking and international finance, business strategy, communications, economics, entrepreneurship, financial management, human resource management, information technology management, international business, international management, leadership, logistics, marketing management, mergers and acquisitions, operations management, organizational behaviour, portfolio management, quantitative methods, services management, supply chain management; Head Prof. SUBBARAMAN IYER; Dean Dr MICHAEL J. BARNES; Deputy Dean Dr PARVINDER ARORA; Dean for Global Bachelor of Business Admin. Programme Dr DAWN DEKLE.

The University of Chicago Booth School of Business: 101 Penang Rd, Singapore 238466; tel. 68356482; e-mail asia.inquiries@chicagobooth.edu; internet www.chicagobooth.edu; f. 2000; offers Exec. MBA programmes; Dean (vacant); publ. *Chicago Booth Magazine* (3 a year).

William F. Harrah College of Hotel Administration: 100 Victoria St, Nat. Library Bldg 11–02, Singapore 188064; tel. 63329538; e-mail admissions@unlv.edu.sg; internet www.unlv.edu.sg; f. 2006; attached to Univ.of Nevada, Las Vegas, USA; Dean STUART H. MANN.

SLOVAKIA

The Higher Education System

Many of Slovakia's higher education institutions predate the foundation of the former Czechoslovakia in 1918, with the oldest being the Univerzita Komenského v Bratislave (Comenius University in Bratislava—founded 1465). The next oldest university is the Univerzita Pavla Jozefa Šafárika v Košiciach (Šafárik University of Košice—the history of which can be traced back to the foundation of Academia Cassoviensis by Benedikt Kishdy, Bishop of Eger, in 1657). In 1990, following the removal of the communist Government which had been in power since 1948, Czechoslovakia was replaced by the Czech and Slovak Federative Republic (CzSFR). In turn, the CzSFR was dissolved in 1993 and the Czech Republic and Slovakia became independent sovereign states. In addition to the universities, higher education is offered by academies of art, military and police academies, technical universities, universities of economics and universities of pedagogy. In 2009 there were 33 institutions of higher education, with a total enrolment of 144,018 students. There has been a marked increase in the number of postgraduate students in recent years; in 2008/09 there were 10,417 Slovak and 754 foreign students studying for a PhD in Slovakia. In 2010 a total of 234,526 students were enrolled in tertiary level education.

The Ministry of Education, Science, Research and Sport is the central body responsible for the education sector. Higher education is administered according to the Higher Education Act (No. 172) of 1990; following ratification of later legislation in 2002, which was further amended in 2011, Slovakia now participates in the Bologna Process to establish a European Higher Education Area, the first phase of which is to adopt a credit-based system of comparable degrees with two main cycles (undergraduate and postgraduate). Since 2005/06 the use of European Credit Transfer and Accumulation System (ECTS) has been obligatory in all higher education institutions, although some had already begun the implementation before then. Since 2008/09 Diploma Supplements have been issued automatically to all graduates. The Accreditation Commission of the Slovak Republic is an independent agency that advises the Government and monitors the quality of higher education in Slovakia through evaluation, accreditation and recognition of quality assurance systems, institutions and study programmes.

The Vysvedcenie o Maturitnej Skúške (Secondary School Leaving Certificate) is the main requirement for admission to higher education; additionally, many institutions administer entrance examinations. The Bakalár (Bachelors) is the undergraduate degree and is awarded after three or four years' study, depending on the subject. Graduates holding the Bakalár are eligible for admission to the first postgraduate degree, the Magister (Masters) or Inzinier (Engineer), which lasts between one and three years. Doctoral-level studies last at least three years, require submission of a dissertation and lead to the award of the Doktor (Doctorate).

The Vocational Education and Training Act (No. 184) of 2009 provides for the establishment of national, regional and sectoral councils to oversee vocational and professional education, and the Lifelong Learning Act (No. 568) of the same year provides for the establishment of a national qualifications framework. The National Lifelong Learning Institute (formerly the Academia Istropolitana), established in 2010, is preparing the way for the establishment and implementation of the National Strategy for Lifelong Learning and Lifelong Guidance, planned for 2015.

Regulatory and Representative Bodies

GOVERNMENT

Ministry of Culture: nám. SNP 33, 813 31 Bratislava; tel. (2) 2048-2111; e-mail mksr@culture.gov.sk; internet www.culture.gov.sk; Minister Mgr MAREK MAĎARIČ.

Ministry of Education, Science, Research and Sport: Stromová 1, 813 30 Bratislava; tel. (2) 5937-4111; e-mail info@minedu.sk; internet www.minedu.sk; Minister Ing. PETER PELLEGRINI.

ACCREDITATION

Akreditačná Komisia (Accreditation Commission): Stromová 1, 813 30 Bratislava 1; tel. (2) 5937-4240; e-mail contact@akredkom.sk; internet www.akredkom.sk; f. 1990; monitors and evaluates the quality of education, research, devt and artistic and other creative activities in Slovak univs; 21 mems; Chair. Prof. Ing. Dr LUBOR FIŠERA.

ENIC/NARIC Slovakia: Centre for the Recognition of Diplomas, Min. of Education, Stromová 1, 813 30 Bratislava 1; tel. (2) 5923-8121; e-mail naric@minedu.sk; Dir Prof. PETER PLAVCAN.

NATIONAL BODIES

Rada Vysokých Škôl (Higher Education Council): Ilkovičova 3, 812 19 Bratislava; tel. (2) 6029-1894; internet www.radavs.sk; addresses issues on activity, organization, financing and management of higher education instns and adopts necessary measures; 140 mems; Pres. Prof. Ing. Dr VIKTOR SMIEŠKO.

Slovenská Akademická Asociácia pre Medzinárodnú Spoluprácu (Slovak Academic Association for International Cooperation): Svoradova 1, 811 03 Bratislava; tel. (2) 2092-2201; e-mail erasmusplus@saaic.sk; internet www.saaic.sk; f. 1992; ind. NGO providing information to univs and other instns about participation in educational and research activities through int. programmes; Pres. Prof. Dr BEATA BRESTENSKÁ; Exec. Dir IRENA FONODOVÁ.

Slovenská Akademická Informačná Agentúra (Slovak Academic Information Agency): Nám. Slobody 23, 812 20 Bratislava 1; tel. (2) 5930-4700; e-mail saia@saia.sk; internet www.saia.sk; f. 1990; ind. NGO assisting in internationalization of education and research in Slovakia; supports the mobility of students, univ. teachers and researchers from public and private research orgs; nat. scholarship programme; Chair. Prof. Ing. MILAN ŽALMAN; Exec. Dir KATARÍNA KOŠŤÁLOVÁ.

Slovenská Rektorská Konferencia (Slovak Rectors' Conference): SRC Institute, Konventná 1, 811 02 Bratislava; tel. (2) 5413-1238; e-mail srk@srk.sk; internet www.srk.sk; f. 1993; coordinates and promotes rectors' activities at univs to create a common higher education policy; Pres. Prof. Dr LIBOR VOZÁR; Sec.-Gen. Mgr MÁRIA ČIKEŠOVÁ; publ. SRC Bulletin (in Slovak).

Learned Societies

GENERAL

Slovenská Akadémia Vied (Slovak Academy of Sciences): Štefánikova 49, 814 38 Bratislava; tel. (2) 5751-0111; e-mail president@savba.sk; internet www.sav.sk; f. 1942 as Slovenska Akademia Vied a Umeni; depts of agriculture and veterinary sciences, culture and art sciences, earth and space sciences, exact and technical sciences, mathematical, physical and computer sciences, medical sciences, natural sciences and chemistry, social sciences and humanities, technical sciences; attached research institutes: see under Research Institutes; library: see under Libraries and Archives; Pres. Prof. Dr JAROMÍR PASTOREK; Scientific Sec. Ing. Dr FEDOR GÖMÖRY; publs Acta Hydrologica Slovaca (2 a year, print and online, www.ih.sav ba.sk/ah), Acta Montanistica Slovaca (4 a year, print and online, actamont.tuke.sk), Acta Physica Slovaca (6 a year, in English, print and online, www.physics.sk/aps), Acta Virologica (4 a year, print and online, www.elis.sk), Activitas Nervosa Superior Rediviva (4 a year, online, www.rediviva .sav.sk), Architektúra a urbanizmus (4 a year, print and online, www.ustarch.sav.sk), ARS (2 a year, in English, French, German, Slovak, print and online), Asian and African

Studies (2 a year, in English, print and online), *AVANS* (online, www.archeol .sav.sk/otiraz.htm), *Biologia* (6 a year, print and online), *Building Research Journal* (4 a year, print and online, www.ustarch.sav.sk), *Chemical Papers* (6 a year, online, www.chempap.org), *Clovek a Spoločnosť* (4 a year, online, www.saske.sk/cas), *Computing and Informatics* (6 a year, print and online, www.cai.sk), *Contributions of the Astronomical Observatory Skalnaté Pleso* (3 a year, print and online, www.astro.sk/ caosp.html), *Contributions to Geophysics and Geodesy* (4 a year, print and online), *Ekológia* (4 a year, print and online, elis.sk), *Ekonomický časopis / Journal of Economics* (10 a year, in Czech, English, Slovak, print and online, www.ec.sav.sk), *Endocrine Regulations* (4 a year, print and online, www .elis.sk), *Entomological Problems* (6 a year, online, www.entomologicalproblems.sav.sk), *Etnologické rozpravy* (2 a year, print and online, www.uet.sav.sk/etnologickerozpravy.htm), *Filozofia* (10 a year, print and online, klemens.sav.sk/fiusav/filozofia), *Folia Oecologica* (2 a year, print and online), *General Physiology and Biophysics* (4 a year, print and online, www.gpb.sav.sk), *Geografický časopis* (4 a year, print and online), *Geographia Slovaca* (2–3 a year, in English and Slovak, print and online), *Geologica Carpathica* (6 a year, in English, print and online, www.geologicacarpathica.sk), *Helminthologia* (4 a year, print and online, www.saske.sk/pau/helminth.htm), *História* (3 a year, print and online, www.historiarevue.sk), *Historický časopis* (4 a year, print and online, www.historickycasopis.sk), *Human Affairs* (2 a year, print and online, www.humanaffairs.sk), *Interdisciplinary Toxicology* (4 a year, print and online, www.intertox.sav.sk), *Jazykovedný časopis* (2 a year, print and online, www.juls.sav.sk), *Journal of Electrical Engineering* (6 a year, print and online, iris.elf.stuba.sk/jeeec), *Journal of Hydrology and Hydromechanics* (4 a year, in Czech, English, Slovak, print and online, www.ih.savba.sk/jhh), *Kartografické listy* (1 a year, in Slovak, print and online, gis.fns.uniba.sk/kartografickelisty), *Kovové materiály-Metallic Materials* (6 a year, print and online, www.kovmat.sav.sk), *Kultúra slova* (6 a year, print and online), *Mathematica Slovaca* (6 a year, print and online, maslo.mat.savba.sk), *Measurement Science Review* (3 a year, print and online, www.measurement.sk), *Musicologica Slovaca* (2 a year, in Czech and Slovak, print and online), *Neoplasma* (6 a year, print and online, www.neoplasma.sk), *Organon F* (4 a year, in Czech, English and Slovak, print and online, klemens.sav.sk/fiusav/organon), *Powder Metallurgy Progress* (4 a year, print and online, www.imr.saske.sk/pmp.htm), *Právny obzor* (6 a year, print and online, www.prav nyobzor.sk), *Pedagogika.sk* (4 a year, print and online), *Slavica Slovaca* (3 a year, print and online, www.slavu.sav.sk/casopisy/slavica.php), *Slovak Review* (3 a year, print and online, www.slovakreview.sav.sk), *Slovenská archeológia* (2 a year, print and online, www.archeol.sav.sk/filtiraz.htm), *Slovenská literatúra* (6 a year, print and online, uslit .sav.sk/slovlit.htm), *Slovenská Numizmatika* (online, www.archeol.sav.sk/numiz.htm), *Slovenská reč* (6 a year, print and online), *Slovenské divadlo* (4 a year, print and online), *Slovenský národopis* (4 a year, print and online, www.uet.sav.sk/slovenskynaro dopis.htm), *Sociológia-Slovak Sociological Review* (6 a year, in English and Slovak, print and online), *Strojnícky časopis* (Journal of Mechanical Engineering, 6 a year, in Czech, English, Slovak, print and online, www.strojcas.sav.sk), *Studia Politica Slovaca* (2 a year, in English and Slovak, print

and online, www.upv.sav.sk), *Studia Psychologica* (4 a year, print and online, psychologia.sav.sk/sp), *Študijné zvesti* (2 a year, print and online, www.archeol.sav.sk/studij ne.htm), *Tatra Mountains—Mathematical Publications* (3 a year, print and online, tatra.mat.savba.sk), *Východoslovenský pravek* (irregular, print and online, www.arch eol.sav.sk/vychpr.htm), *World Literature Studies* (2–3 a year, in Czech, English, German, Slovak, print and online), *Životné prostredie* (6 a year, print and online, uke.sav.sk).

AGRICULTURE, FISHERIES AND VETERINARY SCIENCE

Slovenská spoločnosť pre polnohospodárske, lesnícke a potravinárske a veterinárne vedy (Slovak Society for Agriculture, Forestry, Food and Veterinary Sciences): Radlinskeho 9, 812 37 Bratislava; tel. (2) 5292-6055; f. 1968; 564 mems; Pres. Prof. Dr A. DANDAR; Sec. Dr M. TAKÁCSOVA.

ARCHITECTURE AND TOWN PLANNING

Spolok Architektov Slovenska (Slovak Architects' Society): Panská 15, 811 01 Bratislava; tel. (2) 5443-1078; e-mail director_sas@euroweb.sk; internet www .sasarch.sk; promotes and popularizes architecture education; organizes professional and educational activities; 1,500 mems; library of 2,700 vols; Pres. Prof. Ing. Dr JÁN BAHNA; Dir Dr PETER MIKLOŠ; publs *Fórum architektúry* (6 a year), *Projekt* (Slovak Architectural Review, 6 a year).

EDUCATION

Slovenská Pedagogická Spoločnosť pri SAV (Slovak Education Society): Herdovo nám 2, 917 01 Trnava; internet www.spaeds .org; f. 1965; promotes devt of education as a discipline; organizes confs, discussions, lectures and seminars; 365 mems; Pres. Prof. Mgr LADISLAV MACHÁČEK; Sec. Dr VLADIMÍR MICHALIČKA; publ. *Slovak Journal for Educational Sciences / Slovenský časopis pre pedagogické vedy* (4 a year, print and online, www.casopispedagogika.sk).

FINE AND PERFORMING ARTS

Slovenská Výtvarná Únia (Slovak Union of Visual Arts): Dostojevského rad 2, 811 09 Bratislava; tel. (2) 5296-2402; e-mail office@ svu.sk; internet www.svu.sk; f. 1991; rep. of interests of mems; organizes and coordinates activities and services for mems in visual arts; cooperates with other orgs and artists and theorists; 1,800 mems; Pres. PAVOL KRAL; publs *Profil*, *Výtvarný život* (6 a year, print).

HISTORY, GEOGRAPHY AND ARCHAEOLOGY

Slovenská Archeologická Spoločnosť pri SAV (Slovak Archaeological Society): Akademická 2, 949 21 Nitra; tel. (37) 7335-738; e-mail sas.archeologia@gmail.com; internet www.sas.sav.sk; f. 1956; encourages and develops scientific research work in the field of archaeology; assists in the rescue and protection of archaeological finds and sites; organizes colloquia, seminars, lectures; 320 mems; library of 860 vols; Pres. Dr ELENA MIROŠŠAYOVÁ; Sec. Mgr Dr KLAUDIA DAŇOVÁ; publs *Bibliografia Slovensky Archeologie* (irregular), *Informator* (2 a year).

Slovenská Geografická Spoločnosť pri Slovenskej Akadémii Vied (Slovak Geographical Society at the Slovak Academy of Sciences): Štefánikova 49, 814 73 Bratislava; tel. (2) 5751-0209; e-mail geognovo@savba .sk; internet www.sgs.sav.sk; f. 1946 as Slovak Geographic Soc.; 5 regional sections

in Bratislava, Central Slovak, E Slovak, Košice, W Slovak; 3 specialised sections of applied geography, school geography, theoretical geography; 300 mems; Pres. Prof. RENÉ MATLOVIČ; Sec. Mgr Dr FRANTIŠEK Križan.

Slovenská Historická Spoločnosť pri SAV (Slovak Historical Society): Klemensova 19, POB 198, 814 00 Bratislava; tel. (2) 5292-5753; internet www.shs.sav.sk; f. 1946; sections devoted to modern history, economic history, urban history, military history, gender studies, literature, history of religion; regional divs in Banská Bystrica, Košice, Prešov, Topolčany, Trenčín; 280 mems; Pres. Dr DUŠAN KOVÁČ; Scientific Sec. Mgr Dr GABRIELA DUDEKOVÁ; publ. *Historický časopis* (4 a year, online, www.historickycasopis.sk).

Spoločnosť Slovenských Archivárov (Society of Slovak Archivists): Drotárska cesta 42, 817 01 Bratislava; tel. (2) 6280-1190; internet www.archivari.sk; f. 1989; coordinates to develop archives; provides platform to share knowledge and experience and professional exchanges; organizes confs, excursions, seminars and study visits; protects interests and rights of mems; Pres. Dr RADOSLAV RAGAČ; Sec. Dr ELENA MACHAJDÍKOVÁ; publ. *Fórum archivárov* (4 a year, print and online, www.archivari.sk/3.aspx).

LANGUAGE AND LITERATURE

Alliance Française: Palais Kutscherfeld, Sedlarska 7, 812 83 Bratislava 1; tel. (2) 5934-7105; e-mail culturel@france.sk; internet slovaquie.alliance.free.fr; offers courses and exams in French language and culture; promotes cultural exchange with France; regional cttees in Banská Bystrica, Košice; Dir ROBERT GUILLAUME.

British Council: Panská 17, 811 01 Bratislava; tel. (2) 5443-1074; e-mail info@ britishcouncil.sk; internet www .britishcouncil.org/slovakia; f. 1992; teaching centre; offers courses and exams in English language and British culture; promotes cultural exchange with the UK; attached centres in Banská Bystrica, Košice, Prešov, Nitra and Žilina; Dir ALENA REBROVA.

Goethe-Institut: Panenská 33, 814 82 Bratislava; tel. (2) 5443-3130; e-mail info@ bratislava.goethe.org; internet www.goethe .de/bratislava; offers courses and exams in German language and culture; promotes cultural exchange with Germany; centres in Banská Bystrica and Košice; library of 12,500 vols; Dir WOLFGANG FRANZ; Sec. RENÁTA STRAKOŠOVÁ.

Slovenská Jazykovedná Spoločnosť (Slovak Linguistics Society): Panská 26, 813 64 Bratislava 1; tel. (2) 5433-1761; e-mail vybor_sjs@juls.savba.sk; internet www.juls .sav.sk/sjs; f. 1957; promotes research in fields of general linguistics, phonetics, Slavic and Slavonic studies; organizes nat. and int. confs, discussions, lectures and seminars; 155 mems; Pres. Dr ADRIANA FERENČÍKOVÁ; Sec. Mgr Dr ANNA RAMŠÁKOVÁ; publs *Spisy Slovenskej jazykovednej spoločnost*, *Varia*, *Zápisník slovenského jazykovedca*.

Spoločnosť Učiteľov Nemeckého Jazyka a Germanistov Slovenska (SUNG)/Verband der Deutschlehrer und Germanisten der Slowakei (Union of German Teachers and Germanists of Slovakia): Tomášikova 4, POB 14, 820 09 Bratislava 29; tel. (2) 4342-2253; e-mail sung.kontakt@ gmail.com; internet www.sung.sk; f. 1991; Pres. Prof. Dr NADEŽDA ZEMANÍKOVÁ; Gen. Sec. MICHAL DVORECKÝ; publs *Begegnungen* (1 or 2 a year, print and online), *Slowakische Zeitschrift für Germanistik* (1 or 2 a year, print and online).

Spolok Slovenských Spisovateľov (Slovak Writers' Society): Laurinská 2, 815 84 Bratislava 1; tel. (2) 5441-8670; e-mail spolspis@stonline.sk; internet www.spolokspisovatelov.org; f. 1923; regional brs in Banská Bystrica, Košice, Nitra and Žilina; 350 mems; Pres. Dr Ján Tužinský; Sec.-Gen. Mgr Pavol Janík; publs *Dotyky* (literature by young writers, 4 a year, print and online), *Literárny týždenník* (Literary Weekly, irregular).

MEDICINE

Slovenská Parazitologická Spoločnosť pri SAV (Slovak Society for Parasitology): Hlinkova 3, 040 01 Košice; tel. (55) 6334-455; e-mail sps@saske.sk; internet www.saske.sk/pau/sps.html; f. 1993; promotes and implements scientific research activities to develop parasitology science; organizes scientific workshops, lectures, discussions, workshops, tours; 135 mems; Pres. Dr Ivica Hromadová; Sec. Dr Martina Miterpáková; publ. *Správy slovenskej parazitologickej spoločnosti* (irregular).

NATURAL SCIENCES
General

Rada Slovenských Vedeckých Spoločností (Slovak Council of Scientific Societies): Štefánikova 49, 814 38 Bratislava; tel. (2) 5941-0514; e-mail rsvs@savba.sk; internet www.rsvs.sav.sk; f. 1990; promotes devt of science; coordinates and supports scientific works; organizes confs, seminars and lectures; 55 mem. socs; Pres. Dr Dalibor Krupa.

Biological Sciences

Slovenská Biologická Spoločnosť (Slovak Biological Society): Sasinkova 4, 811 08 Bratislava; f. 1967; 180 mems; Pres. Dr Igor M. Tomo; publ. *Bulletin* (2 a year).

Slovenská Botanická Spoločnosť pri SAV (Slovak Botanical Society SAS): Botanický ústav SAV, Dúbravská cesta 9, 841 01 Bratislava 4; tel. (2) 5942-6164; internet www.sbs.sav.sk; f. 1966; promotes and develops botany by guiding scientific research; protects the professional status of mems; monitors quality of teaching of botany in schools; 390 mems; Pres. Dr Milan Valachovič; Scientific Sec. Dr Pavol Mereďa; publ. *Bulletin Slovenská Botanická Spoločnosť* (2 a year with irregular supplements, in Slovak with English abstracts, print and online, www.sbs.sav.sk/SBS1/indexbulletin.html).

Slovenská Ekologická Spoločnosť (Slovak Ecological Society): c/o Dept of Ecology and Environmental Sciences, Univerzita Konštantína Filozofa v Nitre, Tr. A. Hlinku 1, 949 01 Nitra; tel. (37) 6408-595; e-mail fpetrovic@ukf.sk; internet www.sekos.sav.sk; f. 1992; develops conceptual work in ecology; sections of applied ecology, ecology of mountains, ecosystem ecology, environmental ecology, general and theoretical ecology, landscape ecology, population ecology; 192 mems; Pres. Prof. Dr František Petrovič; publ. *Ekologické Štúdie* (Ecological Studies, 1 a year).

Slovenská Entomologická Spoločnosť (Slovak Entomological Society): c/o Ustav zoológie SAV, Dúbravská ceste 9, 845 06 Bratislava; tel. (2) 6029-6249; internet www.ses.sav.sk; f. 1968; disseminates results of scientific research to develop entomology; organizes scientific confs and lectures; hosts Entomological Day annually; 233 mems; Pres. Prof. Dr Oto Majzlan; Sec. Dr Pavol Prokop; publs *Entomofauna carpathica* (4 a year), *Entomological Problems* (2 a year).

Slovenská Spoločnosť pre Biochémiu a Molekulárnu Biológiu (Slovak Society for Biochemistry and Molecular Biology): Vlárska 3, 833 06 Bratislava 3; internet www.ssbmb.sav.sk; f. 1959; 220 mems; Pres. Prof. Dr Ján Turňa; Scientific Sec. Ing. Dr Albert Breier.

Slovenská Zoologická Spoločnosť pri SAV (Slovak Zoological Society SAS): Mlynská dolina B-2, 842 15 Bratislava; tel. (2) 6029-6680; internet www.szs.sav.sk; f. 1957; promotes scientific research; facilitates exchange of information and results of research; 160 mems; Pres. Mgr Ján Kautman; Sec. Alžbeta Talarovicová; publ. *Správy Slovenskej zoologickej spoločnosti* (1 a year).

Slovenskej Ornitologickej Spoločnosť/ BirdLife Slovensko (Slovak Ornithological Society/BirdLife Slovakia): Mlynské nivy 41, 821 09 Bratislava 2; tel. (2) 5542-2185; e-mail vtaky@vtaky.sk; internet www.vtaky.sk; f. 1985; conducts research on wild birds and their habitats; organizes confs and seminars; facilitates projects to protect species, habitats, areas; 1,007 mems; Chair. Štefan Benko; Vice-Chair. Anton Krištín; publs *Tichodroma* (1 a year, print and online, www.tichodroma.sk), *Vtáky* (Birds, 4 a year).

Mathematical Sciences

Jednota Slovenských Matematikov a Fyzikov (Union of Slovak Mathematicians and Physicists): Faculty of Mathematics, Physics and Informatics, Univerzita Komenského, Mlynská dolina F2, 842 48 Bratislava; tel. (2) 6029-5111; e-mail jsmf@fmph.uniba.sk; internet www.jsmf.eu.sk; f. 1969; promotes devt of mathematics and physics; disseminates results of scientific research; assists schools in teaching of mathematics, physics, computer science; 1,500 mems; Pres. Dr Martin Kalina; Sec. Mgr Dr Marek Hyčko; publ. *Obzory matematiky, fyziky a informatiky* (4 a year).

Physical Sciences

Slovenská Astronomická Spoločnosť pri SAV (Slovak Astronomical Society): c/o Astronomický ústav SAV, 059 60 Tatranská Lomnica; tel. (52) 7879-148; e-mail hric@ta3.sk; internet www.sas.astro.sk; f. 1959; brs in Banská Bystrica, Bratislava, Hurbanovo, Hlohovec, Prešov, Tatranská Lomnica, Žilina; 180 mems; Pres. Dr Ladislav Hric; Scientific Sec. Dr Rudolf Gális.

Slovenská Chemická Spoločnosť (Slovak Chemical Society): Radlinského 9, 812 37 Bratislava; tel. (2) 5249-5205; e-mail schs@chtf.stuba.sk; internet www.schems.sk; f. 1929; 874 mems; Pres. Dr Milan Drábik; Sec. Dr Dalma Gyepesová; publ. *ChemZi* (2 a year).

Slovenská Geologická Spoločnosť (Slovak Geological Society): Mlynská dolina 1, 817 04 Bratislava; tel. (2) 5937-5378; e-mail ladislav.simon@geology.sk; internet www.geologickaspolocnost.sk; f. 1965; brs in Banská Bystrica, Bratislava, Košice; promotes cooperation among mems to develop their technical, pedagogical, practical and popularization activities; 330 mems; Pres. Dr Ladislav Šimon; Scientific Sec. Ing. Dr Zoltán Németh; publ. *Mineralia Slovaca* (4 a year).

Slovenská Meteorologická Spoločnosť (Slovak Meteorological Society): c/o Slovenský hydrometeorologický ústav, Jeséniova 17, 833 15 Bratislava; tel. (2) 5477-2004; f. 1960; attached to Slovak Academy of Sciences; 175 mems; Pres. Pavel Šťastný; Sec. Marian Ostrožlík.

PHILOSOPHY AND PSYCHOLOGY

Slovenské Filozofické Združenie pri SAV (Slovak Philosophical Association): Klemensova 19, 813 64 Bratislava; tel. (2) 5292-6448; e-mail sfz@sfz.sk; internet www.sfz.sk; f. 1990; 292 mems; Pres. Mgr Dr Pavol Sucharek; Exec. Sec. Mgr Dr Simona Wagnerová.

RELIGION, SOCIOLOGY AND ANTHROPOLOGY

Národopisná Spoločnosť Slovenska (Slovak Ethnography Society): Klemensova 19, 813 64 Bratislava; tel. (2) 5296-4707; e-mail nss@savba.sk; internet www.nss.sav.sk; f. 1958; encourages and develops scientific research and theoretical work; organizes and participates in nat. and int. confs, seminars, scientific symposia, lectures; 250 mems; Pres. Dr Hana Hlôšková; Sec. Dr Katarína Nováková; publ. *Etnologické rozpravy* (Ethnological Review, 2 a year).

Slovenská Antropologická Spoločnosť (Slovak Anthropological Society): Mlynská dolina B2, 842 15 Bratislava; e-mail benus@fns.uniba.sk; f. 1965; 117 mems; Pres. Dr Milan Thurzo; Sec. Eva Nescakova; Sec. Silvia Bodorikova; Treas. Dr Radoslav Benus; publ. *Slovenska Antropologia* (2 a year).

Slovenská Orientalistická Spoločnosť (Slovak Society for Oriental Studies): Klemensova 19, 813 64 Bratislava; tel. (2) 5292-6226; e-mail kaorheha@savba.sk; internet www.orient.sav.sk/slovenska-orientalisticka-spolocnost; f. 1960; disseminates results of scientific research; organizes nat. and int. confs, seminars, scientific symposia, lectures; 42 mems; Pres. Dr Viera Pawliková-Vilhanová; Sec. Mgr Dr Henrieta Hatalová; publs *Asian and African Studies* (2 a year), *Human Affairs* (2 a year).

Slovenská Sociologická Spoločnosť pri SAV (Slovak Sociological Association): Klemensova 19, 813 64 Bratislava; tel. (2) 5296-4355; internet www.sociologia.eu.sk; f. 1964; 296 mems; Pres. Prof. Dr Jozef Matulník; Sec. Dr Margita Minichová; publs *Sociologicky Zapisník* (4 a year), *Spravodajca SSS* (2 a year).

TECHNOLOGY

Slovenská Spoločnosť pre Mechaniku pri SAV (Slovak Society for Mechanics): c/o Prof. Milan Sokol, Faculty of Civil Engineering STU in Bratislava, Dept of Structural Mechanics, Radlinského 11, 813 68 Bratislava; tel. (2) 5478-8662; internet web.tuke.sk/svf-ssmsav; f. 1967; 53 mems; Pres. Prof. Ing. Dr Milan Sokol; Sec. Ing. Dr Luboš Hruštinec; publ. *Bulletin*.

Research Institutes
ARCHITECTURE AND TOWN PLANNING

Institute of Construction and Architecture: Dúbravská cesta 9, 845 03 Bratislava 45; tel. (2) 5477-3548; e-mail usarstav@savba.sk; internet www.ustarch.sav.sk; f. 1953; attached to Slovak Acad. of Sciences; develops theoretical, numerical and experimental methods and their applications to mechanics; provides doctoral studies in the scientific fields of architecture and town-planning, engineering structures and transport buildings, applied mechanics; Dir Ing. Peter Matiašovský; Scientific Sec. Ing. Jozef Kriváček; publs *Architektúra a urbanizmus* (4 a year, print and online), *Building Research Journal* (4 a year, print and online).

ECONOMICS, LAW AND POLITICS

Ekonomický Ústav SAV (Institute of Economic Research of Slovak Academy of Sciences): Šancova 56, 811 05 Bratislava; tel. (2) 5249-8214; internet www.ekonom.sav.sk; f. 1953; conducts economic research on nat. issues and utilization and cultivation of potential, ways and resources for devt; research depts of economic modelling and analyses, empirical research, macroeconomics and knowledge economy, socio-economic devt and labour market, world economy; library of 32,000 vols, 1,400 periodicals; Dir Prof. Ing. Dr MILAN ŠIKULA; Scientific Sec. Mgr ĽUBOMIR LAUDAR; publ. *Ekonomický časopis* (Journal of Economics, 10 a year, in Czech, English, Slovak, print and online, ekonom.sav.sk/en/casopis).

Prognostický Ústav Slovenskej Akadémie Vied (Institute for Forecasting of the Slovak Academy of Sciences): Sancová 56, 811 05 Bratislava; tel. (2) 5249-5114; e-mail progasis@savba.sk; internet www.prog.sav.sk; f. 1989; acts as research body and govt think-tank to design policies; conducts interdisciplinary research in theoretical, methodological and conceptual issues of soc. in nat. and int. context, human dimension of global environmental change, co-evolution of institutional and technology change; Dir Ing. Dr MARTINA LUBYOVA; Scientific Sec. Dr STEFAN SABO; publs *Ekonomický časopis* (Economic Magazine), *Prognostické práce* (Forecasting Papers, irregular, print and online).

Ústav Politických Vied SAV (Institute of Political Sciences of Slovak Academy of Sciences): Klemensova 19, 813 64 Bratislava; Dúbravská cesta 9, 813 64 Bratislava; tel. (2) 5478-9724; e-mail polipek@savba.sk; internet www.upv.sav.sk; f. 1990 as Institute of Politology of the Slovak Academy of Sciences, present name and status 2002; conducts basic research into political relations and processes within internal and int. political contexts; Dir Dr MIROSLAV PEKNÍK; Scientific Sec. Dr PETER DINUŠ; publ. *Studia Politica Slovaca* (2 a year, print and online).

Ústav Štátu a Práva SAV (Institute of State and Law of Slovak Academy of Sciences): Klemensova 19, 813 64 Bratislava; tel. (2) 5296-1833; e-mail usapsekr@savba.sk; internet www.usap.sav.sk; f. 1953; conducts research on general theory of state and law, political science, philosophy, law, public admin., govt, constitutional and admin. law, economic and commercial law, civil law, medical law, int. law and int. relations; Dir Prof. Dr JÁN ŠVIDROŇ; Sec. Dr TATIANA WEISSOVÁ; publ. *Právny obzor* (Legal Horizon, 6 a year, print and online, www.pravnyobzor.sk).

EDUCATION

Ústav Informácií a Prognóz Školstva (Institute of Information and Prognoses of Education): Staré Grunty 52, 842 44 Bratislava 4; tel. (2) 6929-5111; e-mail uips@uips.sk; internet www.uips.sk; f. 1976; attached to Min. of Education, Science, Research and Sport; provides information to support and improve management and devt of areas falling within the management responsibilities of the Min.; provides education for teaching and non-teaching staff in the field of information and communication technologies at regional level; library of 4,691 vols; Dir Ing. JURAJ HOMOLA; publs *Academia* (4 a year), *Informatika v škole* (Informatics in Education, 2 a year, print and online), *Mládež a spoločnosť* (Youth and Society, 4 a year), *Prevencia* (Prevention, 4 a year, print and online).

FINE AND PERFORMING ARTS

Ústav Dejín Umenia (Institute of Art History): Dúbravská cesta 9, 841 04 Bratislava 4; tel. (2) 5479-3895; internet www.dejum.sav.sk; f. 1953 as Dept for Theory and History of Art of the Institute of History of the Slovak Acad. of Sciences, current name adopted 1990; attached to Slovak Acad. of Sciences; researches into history of Slovak art and architecture since Middle Ages; Dir Dr IVAN GERÁT; Sec. Mgr ERIKA OKRUHLICOVÁ; publ. *ARS* (2 a year, print and online).

Ústav Divadelnej a Filmovej Vedy SAV (Institute of Theatre and Film Research of Slovak Academy of Sciences): Dúbravská cesta 9, 841 04 Bratislava; tel. (2) 5477-7193; internet www.udfv.sav.sk; f. 1953; conducts research in the theory and history of the theatre, movie, radio and television arts and sciences; provides doctoral studies of history and theory of the theatre art; library of 13,000 vols; Chair. Prof. Dr MILOŠ MISTRÍK; Dir Dr ANNA HLAVÁČOVÁ; publ. *Slovenské divadlo* (Slovak Theatre, 4 a year).

Ústav Hudobnej Vedy SAV (Institute of Musicology, Slovak Academy of Sciences): Dúbravská cesta 9, 841 04 Bratislava 4; tel. (2) 5477-3589; e-mail musicology@savba.sk; internet www.uhv.sav.sk; f. 1943, present name and status 1951; Dir Dr HANA URBANCOVÁ; Sec. Mgr MARCELA KRÚŽEKOVÁ; publs *Musicologica Slovaca et Europaea* (irregular), *Ethnomusicologicum* (irregular).

HISTORY, GEOGRAPHY AND ARCHAEOLOGY

Archeologický Ústav SAV v Nitre (Institute of Archaeology of Slovak Academy of Sciences): Akademická 2, 949 21 Nitra; tel. (37) 6410-051; e-mail nrausekr@savba.sk; internet www.archeol.sav.sk; conducts research in scientific fields of archeology, classical archeology and museology; library of 34,200 vols of monographs and working papers, 30,000 journals; Dir Dr MATEJ RUTTKAY; Scientific Sec. Mgr Dr KLAUDIA DAŇOVÁ; publs *AVANS* (1 a year, print and online), *Slovenská archeológia* (2 a year, print and online), *Slovenská numizmatika* (jtly with Nat. Numismatic Cttee, every 2 years, print and online), *Študijné zvesti AÚ SAV* (Study Rumours, 2 a year, print and online), *Východoslovenský pravek* (Eastern Prehistory, irregular, print and online).

Geografický Ústav SAV (Institute of Geography of Slovak Academy of Sciences): Štefánikova 49, 814 73 Bratislava; tel. (2) 5751-0187; e-mail geogsekr@savba.sk; internet www.geography.sav.sk; f. 1943, current name adopted 1963; basic and strategic applied research in human geography, regional geography, physical geography and geoinformatics; provides doctoral education in physical geography and geoecology, regional geography; library of 17,000 vols, 150 periodicals; Dir Prof. Dr VLADIMÍR IRA; Scientific Sec. Dr DANIEL MICHNIAK; publs *Geografický časopis* (Geographical Journal, 4 a year), *Geographia Slovaca* (2–3 a year, in English and Slovak), *Geomorphologia Slovaca et Bohemica* (2 a year, in English and Slovak), *Kartografické listy* (Yearbook).

Historický Ústav SAV (Institute of History of Slovak Academy of Sciences): Klemensova 19, 813 64 Bratislava; tel. (2) 5292-5753; e-mail histinst@savba.sk; internet www.history.sav.sk; f. 1943; conducts basic research in fields of Slovak history from ancient times to the present, selected issues of gen. history, history of science and technology in Slovakia; library of 75,000 vols; Dir Dr SLAVOMÍR MICHÁLEK; Science Sec. Mgr Dr MAROŠ HERTEL; publs *Forum Historiae* (2 a year, print and online, www.forumhistor-

iae.sk), *Historický časopis* (Historical Journal, 4 a year, print and online, www.historickycasopis.sk), *Historické štúdie* (Historical Studies, 1 a year), *Human Affairs* (2 a year, print and online, www.humanaffairs.sk), *Slovanské štúdie* (Slavic Studies, 2 a year), *Studia Historica Slovaca* (1 a year), *Veda a technika v dejinách* (Science and Technology in History, irregular), *Z dejín vied a techniky* (History of Sciences and Technology in Slovakia, 1 a year).

LANGUAGE AND LITERATURE

Jazykovedný Ústav Ľudovít Štúra SAV (Ľudovít Štúr Institute of Linguistics of Slovak Academy of Sciences): Panská 26, 813 64 Bratislava 1; tel. (2) 5443-1761; e-mail info@juls.savba.sk; internet www.juls.savba.sk; f. 1943, present name 1966; basic research in nat. contemporary system, functioning of language in contemporary communication, theory and practice of language culture, technical terminology, etymology and linguistic geography, history of language, corpus linguistics and natural language-processing; library of 22,000 vols; Dir Prof. Dr PAVOL ŽIGO; Scientific Sec. Dr SIBYLA MISLOVIČOVÁ; publs *Jazykovedný časopis* (Linguistic Journal, 2 a year), *Kultúra slova* (The Culture of the Word, 6 a year), *Slovenská reč* (Slovak Speech, 6 a year).

Ústav Slovenskej Literatúry SAV (Institute of Slovak Literature of Slovak Academy of Sciences): Konventná 13, 813 64 Bratislava; tel. (2) 5441-6025; e-mail usllred@savba.sk; internet www.uslit.sav.sk; f. 1943; library of 50,000 vols; Dir Mgr DANA HUČKOVÁ; Scientific Sec. Mgr OĽGA VANEKOVÁ; publ. *Slovenská literatúra* (6 a year).

Ústav Svetovej Literatúry SAV (Institute of World Literature of Slovak Academy of Sciences): Konventná 13, 813 64 Bratislava; tel. (2) 5443-1995; e-mail usvlust@savba.sk; internet www.usvl.sav.sk; f. 1991, fmrly Institute of World Literature and Languages; basic research of phenomena and processes of world literature in these major fields: developmental tendencies of modern literary movements, theoretical and methodological questions of general literary process, history of literary translation in Slovakia, theoretical and methodological questions of translation, interdisciplinary research of major cultural epochs; library of 54,000 vols (incl. books and journals); Dir Mgr Dr ADAM BŽOCH; Academic Sec. Mgr Dr RÓBERT GÁFRIK; publ. *World Literature Studies* (4 a year).

MEDICINE

Neurobiologický Ústav SAV (Institute of Neurobiology of Slovak Academy of Sciences): Soltésovej 4, 040 01 Košice; tel. (55) 7276-200; internet inb.saske.sk; f. 1977; studies nervous tissue and central nervous system under physiological and pathological conditions; laboratories of neuropathology and neuroprotectivity, electron-microscopy, historadiography, histochemistry and immunohistochemistry, molecular neurobiology, proteosynthesis, lipid metabolism, neurotransmitters and neuromodulators; Dir Dr NADEŽDA LUKÁČOVÁ.

Parazitologický Ústav SAV (Institute of Parasitology of Slovak Academy of Sciences): Hlinkova 3, 040 01 Košice; tel. (55) 6334-455; e-mail pausav@saske.sk; internet www.saske.sk/pau; f. 1953; research topics incl. parasitic zoonoses, tick-borne diseases, systematics, phylogeny and genetic variability and ecology of parasites, anthelmintic resistance, immune response and diagnostics of parasites, devt of new drugs paralyzing neuromuscular system of parasite, ecological aspects of environmental protection and research of plant parasitic nematodes; library of 8,000 vols; Dir Dr BRANISLAV PEŤKO; Scientific Sec. Dr MARTA ŠPAKULOVÁ; publ. *Helminthologia* (4 a year, print and online, www.saske.sk/pau/Helminth.htm).

Ústav Experimentálnej Endokrinológie SAV (Institute of Experimental Endocrinology of Slovak Academy of Sciences): Vlárska 3, 833 06 Bratislava; tel. (2) 5477-2800; e-mail ueensekr@savba.sk; internet www .endo.sav.sk; f. 1954; 10 laboratories; Dir Prof. Dr IWAR KLIMEŠ; Sec. Ing. Dr J. BRTKO; publ. *Endocrine Regulations* (4 a year, in English, print and online).

Ústav Experimentálnej Farmakológie a Toxikológie (Institute of Experimental Pharmacology and Toxicology): Dúbravská cesta 9, 841 04 Bratislava; tel. (2) 5477-3586; e-mail exfasekr@savba.sk; internet www.uef .sav.sk; f. 1969; attached to Slovak Acad. of Sciences; depts of biochemical pharmacology, cardiovascular and smooth muscle pharmacology, cellular pharmacology, neuropharmacology, pharmacology of inflammation, reproductive toxicology, toxicology and laboratory animal breeding (at Dobrá Voda); provides PhD course in the field of pharmacology and biochemistry; Dir Dr MICHAL DUBOVICKÝ; Scientific Sec. Dr TATIANA MAČIČKOVÁ; Scientific Sec. Dr TOMÁŠ PERĚČKO.

Ústav Experimentálnej Onkológie SAV (Cancer Research Institute of Slovak Academy of Sciences): Vlárska 7, 833 91 Bratislava 37; tel. (2) 5932-7255; internet www .exon.sav.sk; f. 1946; research on retrovirus studies, cancer immunology, experimental therapy, chemical carcinogenesis, molecular genetics dealing with DNA repair, molecular biology and biochemistry; incl. laboratories of cancer genetics, molecular genetics, molecular oncology, mutagenesis and carcinogenesis, tumor immunology; Dir Dr JÁN SEDLÁK; Scientific Sec. Dr ALENA GÁBELOVÁ; publ. *Neoplasma* (6 a year, print and online, www.neoplasma.sk).

Ústav Normálnej a Patologickej Fyziológie SAV (Institute of Normal and Pathological Physiology of Slovak Academy of Sciences): Sienkiewiczova 1, 813 71 Bratislava; tel. (2) 3229-6020; internet www.unpf .sav.sk; f. 1953; basic research in experimental medicine focused on cardiovascular and nervous systems; laboratories of cognitive neuroscience, motor control, neuro-cardiovascular interactions, neurohumoral regulation of hemodynamics, vascular disorders etiopathogenesis; Dir Dr OĽGA PECHÁŇOVÁ; Scientific Sec. Dr IVETA BERNÁTOVÁ; publ. *Activitas Nervosa Superior Rediviva* (print and online, www.rediviva.sav.sk).

Ústav pre Výskum Srdca SAV (Institute for Heart Research of Slovak Academy of Sciences): Dúbravská cesta 9, POB 104, 840 05 Bratislava 45; tel. (2) 5477-4405; e-mail usrdsekr@savba.sk; internet www.usrd.sav .sk; f. 1955 as Laboratory for Experimental Surgery of Slovak Acad. of Sciences, present status 1964, present name 1990; basic medical research in the area of cardiovascular system diseases; depts of biochemistry, cardiac physiology and pathophysiology, histochemistry and electron microscopy; laboratory of protein chemistry; Dir Dr MIROSLAV BARANČÍK; Scientific Sec. Ing. Dr MONIKA IVANOVÁ.

Virologický Ústav SAV (Institute of Virology of Slovak Academy of Sciences): Dúbravská cesta 9, 845 05 Bratislava; tel. (2) 5930-2401; e-mail virufcem@savba.savba .sk; internet www.virology.sav.sk; f. 1953; conducts research in the field of virology, molecular biology, oncology, normal and pathological physiology; Dir Dr JURAJ KOPÁ-

ČEK; publ. *Acta Virologia* (4 a year, print and online).

NATURAL SCIENCES
Biological Sciences

Botanický Ústav SAV (Institute of Botany of Slovak Academy of Sciences): Dúbravská cesta 9, 845 23 Bratislava; tel. (2) 5942-6111; e-mail botuinst@savba.sk; internet ibot.sav .sk; f. 1957 by merger of Laboratory of Geobotany and Plant Systematics and Laboratory of Plant Biology; strategic and applied research in biological and ecological sciences; nat. nature protection and environment management; library of 22,500 vols; Dir Dr IVAN JAROLÍMEK; Scientific Sec. Mgr Dr ANNA GUTTOVÁ; publ. *Biologia* (6 a year).

Institute of Experimental Phytopathology and Entomology of Slovak Academy of Sciences: Nádražná 52, 900 28 Ivanka pri Dunaji; tel. (2) 4594-3331; internet www.uefe .sav.sk; f. 1953; depts of entomology, mycology, virology; Dir Ing. ANTON JANITOR; publ. *Entomological Problems* (2 a year).

Institute of Forest Ecology of the Slovak Academy of Sciences: Ludovíta Štúra 2, 960 53 Zvolen; tel. (45) 5330-914; e-mail infodir@sav.savzv.sk; internet www.savzv .sk; f. 1983; research on forest ecosystems in W Carpathians with focus on biology and ecology of organisms associated with successional processes in forest ecosystems; Dir Ing. Dr JOZEF VAĽKA; Scientific Sec. Ing. Dr MIROSLAV BLAŽENEC; publ. *Folia Oecologica*.

Ústav Biochémie a Geneticky Živočíchov SAV (Institute of Animal Biochemistry and Genetics of Slovak Academy of Sciences): Moyzesova 61, 900 28 Ivanka pri Dunaji; tel. (2) 4594-3052; e-mail greksak@ ubgz.savba.sk; internet www.ubgz.sav.sk; f. 1990; research depts of biochemistry of biomembranes, immunogenetics, physiology and ethology; provides doctoral studies in biochemistry, animal physiology; Dir Dr IVAN HAPALA; Scientific Sec. Dr JANA ANTALÍKOVÁ.

Ústav Fyziológie Hospodárskych Zvierat SAV (Institute of Animal Physiology of Slovak Academy of Sciences): Šoltésovej 4, 040 01 Košice; tel. (55) 7287-841; e-mail ufhzsav@saske.sk; internet www2.saske.sk/ iap; f. 1964 as Dept of Animal Physiology of the Institute of Experimental Biology, present status 1969; basic research on physiology of the gastrointestinal tract, molecular diagnostics of the commensal microflora related to healthy food and health protection in animals and humans; provides doctoral studies in animal physiology, biochemistry, microbiology, veterinary anatomy and physiology; Dir Dr ŠTEFAN FAIX; Scientific Sec. Dr VLADIMIR KMET.

Ústav Genetiky a Biotechnológií Rastlín SAV (Institute of Plant Genetics and Biotechnology of Slovak Academy of Sciences): Akademická 2, POB 39A, 950 07 Nitra; tel. (37) 6943-409; internet pribina.savba.sk/ ugbr; f. 1990 as Institute of Plant Genetics, present name 1998; research on plant reproduction and breeding, molecular biology and biotechnology of plant processes; Dir Dr JÁN SALAJ; Scientific Sec. Ing. Dr ANDREA HRICOVÁ.

Ústav Krajinnej Ekológie SAV (Institute of Landscape Ecology of Slovak Academy of Sciences): Štefánikova 3, POB 254, 814 99 Bratislava; tel. (2) 5249-3882; e-mail director@savba.sk; internet www.uke.sav.sk; f. 1983; coordinates and elaborates ecological plans and projects; basic and applied research on environmental assessment areas, habitat-mapping and biomonitoring, landscape knowledge into decision-making, management, planning process and environ-

mental policy; library of 20,000 vols; Dir Dr ZITA IZAKOVIČOVÁ; Scientific Sec. Ing. Dr DAGMAR ŠTEFUNKOVÁ; publs *Ekológia* (Ecology, 4 a year, print and online), *Životné postredie* (Environment, 6 a year).

Ústav Molekulárnej Biológie SAV (Institute of Molecular Biology of Slovak Academy of Sciences): Dúbravská cesta 21, 845 51 Bratislava; tel. (2) 5930-7411; e-mail umbidir@savba.sk; internet www.imb.savba .sk; f. 1976, inc. Institute of Microbiology 2000; research depts of biochemistry and structural biology, gene expression, genomics and biotechnology, microbial genetics, microbiology, molecular apidology, neurobiology, protein evolution; Dir Dr JAN KORMANEC; Scientific Sec. Dr LUBOŠ KĽUČÁR; publ. *Biologia* (4 a year).

Ústav Molekulárnej Fyziológie a Genetiky SAV (Institute of Molecular Physiology and Genetics of Slovak Academy of Sciences): Vlárska 5, 833 34 Bratislava; tel. (2) 5477-5266; e-mail usrdtylo@savba.sk; internet www.umfg.sav.sk; f. 1990; depts of cell physiology and genetics, muscle cell research, transport proteins; 8 laboratories; library of 1,000 vols; Dir Dr Ing. OĽGA KRIŽANOVÁ; publ. *General Physiology and Biophysics* (4 a year, print and online, www.gpb.sav.sk).

Ústav Zoológie SAV (Institute of Zoology of Slovak Academy of Sciences): Dúbravská cesta 9, 845 06 Bratislava; tel. (2) 5930-2602; internet www.zoo.sav.sk; f. 1990; applied and basic research in the fields of conservation, agriculture, forestry and health; Dir Dr MILAN KOZANEK; publs *Biologia* (6 a year, print and online), *Entomological Problems* (2 a year, print and online, www.entomologicalproblems.sav.sk).

Mathematical Sciences

Matematický Ústav SAV (Mathematical Institute of Slovak Academy of Sciences): Štefánikova 49, 814 73 Bratislava; tel. (2) 5249-7316; e-mail mathinst@mat.savba.sk; internet www.mat.savba.sk; f. 1959; research in mathematics, applied mathematics, computer science; cooperates with univs and supports education; science popularization; brs in Košice, Banská Bystrica; library of 26,000 vols; Dir Prof. Dr ANATOLIJ DVURE-ČENSKIJ; Scientific Sec. KAROL NEMOGA; publs *Mathematica Slovaca* (6 a year, print and online, maslo.mat.savba.sk), *Tatra Mountains Mathematical Publications* (3 a year, print and online, tatra.mat.savba.sk), *Uniform Distribution Theory* (2 a year, print and online, udt.mat.savba.sk).

Physical Sciences

Astronomický Ústav SAV (Astronomical Institute of Slovak Academy of Sciences): Slovak Academy of Sciences, 059 60 Tatranská Lomnica; tel. (52) 7879-111; e-mail astrinst@astro.sk; internet www .astro.sk; f. 1943; astronomical and astrophysical research, incl. sun, interplanetary matter, star systems, exoplanets; library of 10,146 vols, 6,150 vols of periodicals; Dir Dr ALEŠ KUČERA; Scientific Sec. Dr MARTIN VANKO; publ. *Contributions of the Astronomical Observatory Skalnate Pleso* (2 a year, print and online, www.ta3.sk/caosp/ index.html).

Chemický Ústav SAV (Institute of Chemistry of Slovak Academy of Sciences): Dúbravská cesta 9, 845 38 Bratislava; tel. (2) 5477-2080; e-mail chemsekr@savba.sk; internet www.chem.sk; f. 1953 as Institute of Chemical Technology of Organic Compounds, current name adopted 1955; facilitates training for organic chemistry, biochemistry, microbiology, physical chemistry, macromolecular chemistry, biotechnologies; Dir Dr MIROSLAV KOÓŠ; Scientific Sec.

Dr DESANA LIŠKOVÁ; publ. *Chemical Papers* (6 a year, in English, print and online, www.chempap.org).

Fyzikálny Ústav SAV (Institute of Physics of Slovak Academy of Sciences): Dúbravská cesta 9, 845 11 Bratislava; tel. (2) 5941-0501; internet www.fu.sav.sk; f. 1955 as Cabinet of Physics of Slovak Acad. of Sciences, current name adopted 1963; depts of complex physical systems, metal physics, multilayers and nanostructures, nuclear physics, theoretical physics, research centre for quantum information; library of 10,000 vols (incl. books and journals); Dir Dr STANISLAV HLAVÁČ; Scientific Sec. Mgr Dr ERIK BARTOŠ; publ. *Acta Physica Slovaca* (6 a year, print and online, www.physics.sk/aps).

Geofyzikálny Ústav SAV (Geophysical Institute of Slovak Academy of Sciences): Dúbravská cesta 9, 845 28 Bratislava; tel. (2) 5941-0626; e-mail geofsekr@savba.sk; internet gpi.savba.sk; f. 1953; depts of atmospheric physics, geomagnetism, gravimetry and geodynamics, seismology; Dir Dr LADISLAV BRIMICH; publ. *Contributions to Geophysics and Geodesy* (4 a year).

Geologický Ústav SAV (Geological Institute of Slovak Academy of Sciences): Dúbravská cesta 9, POB 106, 840 05 Bratislava 45; tel. (2) 3229-3201; e-mail geolinst@savba.sk; internet www.geol.sav.sk; f. 1953, current name adopted 1966; br. in Banská Bystrica; conducts research of geological structure and rock composition of W Carpathians and their devt from the Paleozoic up to the Tertiary; Dir Dr IGOR BROSKA; Scientific Sec. Dr IGOR PETRÍK; publ. *Geologica Carpathica* (6 a year, print and online, www.geologicacarpathica.sk).

Ústav Anorganickej Chémie SAV (Institute of Inorganic Chemistry of Slovak Academy of Sciences): Dúbravská cesta 9, 845 36 Bratislava 45; tel. (2) 5941-0401; e-mail uachsekr@savba.sk; internet www.uach.sav .sk; f. 1953; depts of ceramics, hydrosilicates, molten systems, theoretical chemistry; Dir Prof. Dr PAVOL ŠAJGALÍK.

Ústav Experimentálnej Fyziky SAV (Institute of Experimental Physics of Slovak Academy of Sciences): Watsonova 47, 040 41 Košice; tel. (55) 792-220; e-mail sekr@saske .sk; internet uef.saske.sk; f. 1969; research into the fields of sub-nuclear physics, condensed-matter physics, space physics, theoretical physics and biophysics; Dir Dr KAROL FLACHBART; Scientific Sec. Mgr PAVOL SZABÓ.

Ústav Geotechniký SAV (Institute of Geotechnics of Slovak Academy of Sciences): Watsonova 45, 043 53 Košice; tel. (55) 7922-601; e-mail ugtsekr@saske.sk; internet www .saske.sk/ugt; f. 1954, present name 1993; research depts of destructional and constructional geotechnics, environment and hygiene in mining engineering, physical and physicochemical mineral-processing methods, mechanochemistry, mineral biotechnologies; Dir Prof. Ing. Dr VITÄZOSLAV KRÚPA; Scientific Sec. Prof. Dr PETER BALAZ; publ. *Acta Montanistica Slovaca* (4 a year, print and online (actamont.tuke.sk)).

Ústav Hydrológie SAV (Institute of Hydrology of Slovak Academy of Sciences): Račianská 75, 831 02 Bratislava 3; tel. (2) 4425-9404; e-mail uh@savba.sk; internet www.ih.savba.sk; f. 1953 as Water Management Laboratory; current name adopted 1989; depts of lowland hydrology, mountain hydrology, soil hydrology, surface stream water and groundwater interactions; library of 13,000 vols; Dir Dr PAVLA PEKÁROVÁ; publs *Acta Hydrologica Slovaca* (2 a year, print and online, www.ih.savba.sk/ah), *Journal of Hydrology and Hydromechanics* (produced jtly with the Institute of Hydrodynamics of the Academy of Sciences of the Czech Republic, 6 a year, print and online, www.ih.savba.sk/jhh).

Ústav Materiálového Výskumu SAV (Institute of Materials Research of Slovak Academy of Sciences): Watsonova 47, 040 01 Košice; tel. (55) 7922-402; e-mail imrsas@imr .saske.sk; internet www.imr.saske.sk; f. 1955 as Laboratory of Mechanical Engineering and Metallurgical Technologies at Technical Univ. in Kosice, present status 1970, current name adopted 1992; develops new materials and technologies; conducts research on the nature of transformations and transport processes that occur within the structures of materials of varying chemical character (metals, ceramics, plastics) and internal composition (crystalline, amorphous, composite); also conducts research on mechanical and physical properties of materials; Dir Dr PETER ŠEVC; Deputy Dir Dr JÁN MIHALIK; Deputy Dir Ing. Dr KAREL SAKSL; publs *Acta Metallurgica Slovaca* (4 a year, print and online, www.ams.tuke.sk), *Kovové materiály* (Metallic Materials, print and online, www.kovmat.sav.sk), *Powder Metallurgy Progress* (4 a year, print and online, www.imr.saske.sk/pmp/index.htm).

Ústav Merania SAV (Institute of Measurement Science of Slovak Academy of Sciences): Dúbravská cesta 9, 841 04 Bratislava 4; tel. (2) 5477-4033; e-mail umersekr@savba.sk; internet www.um.savba.sk; f. 1953 as Laboratory for Research and Design of Measuring and Physical Devices, current name adopted 1988; scientific depts of biomeasurements, imaging methods, magnetometry, optoelectronic measuring methods, theoretical methods; library of 8,000 vols; Dir Ing. Dr MILAN TYŠLER; Scientific Sec. Ing. JÁN MÁŇKA; publ. *Measurement Science Review* (online, www.measurement.sk).

Ústav Polymérov SAV (Polymer Institute of the Slovak Academy of Sciences): Dúbravská cesta 9, 845 41 Bratislava 45; tel. (2) 3229-4308; e-mail upolsekr@savba.sk; internet www.polymer.sav.sk; f. 1967; depts of biomaterials research, composite materials, molecular simulations of polymers, synthesis and characterisation of polymers, economical, technical; Dir Ing. Dr IGOR LACÍK; Sec. SIDÓNIA KALINOVÁ.

PHILOSOPHY AND PSYCHOLOGY

Filozofický Ústav SAV (Institute of Philosophy of Slovak Academy of Sciences): Klemensova 19, 811 09 Bratislava; tel. (2) 5292-1215; e-mail filosekr@savba.sk; internet www.klemens.sav.sk/fiusav; f. 1946; conducts research on analytic philosophy and philosophy of science, through social and political philosophy, phenomenology, history of philosophical and political thinking to ethics; Dir Prof. Dr TIBOR PICHLER; Scientific Sec. Dr KAROL KOLLÁR; publs *Filozofia* (10 a year), *Organon F* (4 a year).

Ústav Experimentálnej Psychológie SAV (Institute of Experimental Psychology of Slovak Academy of Sciences): Dúbravska cesta 9, 813 64 Bratislava; tel. (2) 5477-5625; internet www.psychologia.sav.sk; f. 1952 as Dept of Psychology of the Philosophical Institute of Slovak Acad. of Sciences and Arts, current name adopted 1963; conducts basic research of cognitive processes in social context; processes and disseminates scientific findings; Dir Prof. Dr VIERA BAČOVÁ; Scientific Sec. Dr EVA BALLOVÁ MIKUŠKOVÁ; publ. *Studia Psychologica* (4 a year, in English, print and online, www.psychologia.sav.sk/sp).

RELIGION, SOCIOLOGY AND ANTHROPOLOGY

Sociologický Ústav SAV (Institute for Sociology of Slovak Academy of Sciences): Klemensova 19, 813 64 Bratislava; tel. (2) 5296-4355; e-mail sociolog@savba.sk; internet www.sociologia.sav.sk; f. 1965 as Sociological Institute, current name adopted 1990; maintains Slovak Archive of Social Data; library of 13,000 vols; Dir Mgr Dr ROBERT KLOBUCKÝ; Deputy Dir Mgr Ing. Dr MILOSLAV BAHNA; publ. *Sociológia—Slovak Sociological Review* (6 a year, in English and Slovak).

Spoločenskovedný Ústav SAV (Institute of Social Sciences of Slovak Academy of Sciences): Karpatská 5, 040 01 Košice; tel. (55) 6255-856; e-mail gajdosm@saske.sk; internet www.saske.sk/svu; f. 1975; depts of history and psychology; provides doctoral studies; library of 7,000 vols; Dir Mgr Dr MICHAL KENTOŠ; publ. *Človek a Spoločnosť* (4 a year, online, www.saske.sk/cas).

Ústav Etnológie SAV (Institute of Ethnology of Slovak Academy of Sciences): Klemensova 19, 813 64 Bratislava; tel. (2) 5296-4707; e-mail uetnsekr@savba.sk; internet www.uet .sav.sk; f. 1946; conducts theoretically advanced field-based research on long-term effects of modernisation on mundane life in rural and urban areas; library of 10,000 vols, 63 periodicals; Dir Mgr Dr TATIANA PODOLINSKÁ; publs *Etnologické rozpravy* (Ethnological Disputes, 2 a year, print and online, www.uet.sav.sk/etnologickerozpravy.htm), *Slavistická Folkloristika* (Studies of Slavonic Folklore), *Slovenský národopis* (Slovak Ethnology, 5 a year, print and online, www.uet .sav.sk/slovenskynarodopis.htm).

Ústav Orientalistiky SAV (Institute of Oriental Studies of Slovak Academy of Sciences): Klemensova 19, 813 64 Bratislava; tel. (2) 5292-6326; e-mail kaoreast@savba.sk; internet www.orient.sav.sk; f. 1960; conducts research in Oriental history, archaeology, linguistics, literature, religion, ethnography, philosophy; library of 16,186 vols; Dir Mgr Dr DUŠAN MAGDOLEN; Sec. GERTRÚDA BOLYÓOVÁ; publ. *Asian and African Studies* (2 a year, print and online, orient.sav.sk/asian-and-african-studies).

Ústav Výskumu Sociálnej Komunikácie SAV (Institute for Research in Social Communication of Slovak Academy of Sciences): Klemensova 19, 813 64 Bratislava 1; tel. (2) 5477-5683; e-mail kvsbk@savba.sk; internet kvsbk.sav.sk; f. 1990 as Dept of Social and Biological Communication, current name adopted 2010; conducts basic research into complex relations between the biological, social and cultural aspects of human existence; Dir Dr GABRIEL BIANCHI; Sec. and Librarian ANNA HUDECOVÁ; publ. *Human Affairs* (2 a year, print and online, www.humanaffairs.sk).

TECHNOLOGY

Elektrotechnický Ústav SAV (Institute of Electrical Engineering of Slovak Academy of Sciences): Dúbravská cesta 9, 841 04 Bratislava; tel. (2) 5922-2555; e-mail elusav@savba.sk; internet www.elu.sav.sk; f. 1963; conducts research and devt of semiconductor, superconductor, oxide and magnetic materials and devices, incl. theoretical and experimental study of their structural, optical, transport properties and devices for the information technology and power engineering; Dir Ing. Dr KAROL FRÖHLICH; Scientific Sec. Mgr Dr BOHUMÍR ZAŤKO; publ. *Journal of Electrical Engineering* (12 a year, online, iris.elf.stuba.sk/jeeec).

Ústav Informatiky SAV (Institute of Informatics of Slovak Academy of Sciences):

Dúbravská cesta 9, 845 07 Bratislava; tel. (2) 5477-1004; e-mail sekr.ui@savba.sk; internet www.ui.sav.sk; f. 1991 as Institute of Computer Systems, current name adopted 1999; research and education in informatics, nano- and micro-technology, cybernetics; Dir Ing. Dr LADISLAV HLUCHÝ; Scientific Sec. Ing. Dr LADISLAV MATAY; publ. *Computing and Informatics* (6 a year, print and online, www.cai.sk).

Ústav Materiálov a Mechanicky Strojov SAV (Institute of Materials and Machine Mechanics of Slovak Academy of Sciences): Račianska 75, 831 02 Bratislava 3; tel. (2) 4425-4751; e-mail ummssekr@savba.sk; internet www.immm.sav.sk; f. 1980 by merger of Institute of Metallic Materials (f. 1953) and Institute of Machine Mechanics (f. 1956); depts of microstructure of surfaces and interfaces, new materials and technologies, properties of materials and structures; library of 13,000 vols; Dir Ing. Dr KAROL IŽDINSKÝ; Scientific Sec. Ing. Dr JAROSLAV JERZ; publs *Kovové materiály* (Metallic Materials, 6 a year, in English, print and online, www.kovmat.sav.sk), *Strojnícky časopis* (Journal of Mechanical Engineering, 6 a year, print and online, www.strojcas.sav.sk).

Výskumný Ústav Dopravný, a.s. (Transport Research Institute, Inc.): Veľký Diel 3323, 010 08 Žilina; tel. (41) 5652-819; e-mail info@vud.sk; internet www.vud.sk; f. 1954 as Transport Scientific and Research Institute, present status 2002; Man. Dir Ing. ĽUBOMÍR PALČÁK; publ. *Horizonty dopravy* (4 a year).

Libraries and Archives

Banská Bystrica

Štátna Vedecká Knižnica v Banskej Bystrici (State Scientific Library in Banska Bystrica): Lazovná 9, 975 58 Banská Bystrica; tel. (48) 4155-111; e-mail svkbb@svkbb.eu; internet www.svkbb.eu; f. 1926; 2m. vols; Dir Dr OĽGA LAUKOVÁ.

Bratislava

Archív hlavného mesta SR Bratislavy (Archives of the Capital of the Slovak Republic, Bratislava): Markova 1, POB 40, 850 05 Bratislava; tel. (2) 5443-3248; e-mail archiv@samb.vs.sk; f. 13th century; attached to Min. of Interior; closed to public; 95,000 vols; Dir Mgr PETER VIGLAŠ.

Centrum Vedecko-Technických Informácií Slovenskej Republiky (Slovak Centre of Scientific and Technical Information): Lamačská cesta 8/A, 811 04 Bratislava; tel. (2) 6925-3102; e-mail sekretariat@cvtisr.sk; internet www.cvtisr.sk; f. 1938 as Slovak Technical library, present name 1996; 362,000 vols, 144,000 vols of periodicals, 28,000 trade publs, 239,000 patents, 90,000 standards; Dir Prof. Dr JÁN TURŇA; publs *Bulletin Centra VTI SR* (4 a year), *Euro-Info* (10 a year), *Infotrend* (4 a year), *iTlib.Information Technologies and Libraries, Signálne informácie* (12 a year).

Mestská Knižnica v Bratislava (Municipal Library Of Bratislava): Klariská 16, 814 79 Bratislava 1; tel. (2) 5443-3244; e-mail info@mestskakniznica.sk; internet www.mestskakniznica.sk; f. 1900; 280,000 vols; Dir Mgr Dr JURAJ SEBESTA.

Slovenská Ekonomická Knižnica Ekonomickej Univerzity v Bratislave (Slovak Economic Library): Dolnozemská cesta 1/a, 852 35 Bratislava; tel. (2) 6729-1414; e-mail sek@sekba.euba.sk; internet www.sek.euba.sk; f. 1948, current name adopted 1993; specialized material in field of economic sciences and interdisciplinary sciences;

364,757 vols, 297 periodicals; Dir Mgr JITKA KMEŤOVÁ.

Slovenská Pedagogická Knižnica (Slovak Education Library): Hálova 6, 851 01 Bratislava 5; tel. (2) 6820-8612; e-mail riaditel@spgk.sk; internet www.spgk.sk; f. 1956; 296,000 vols; Dir Dr VLADIMÍR GRIGAR.

Univerzitná Knižnica v Bratislave (University Library in Bratislava): Michalská 1, 814 17 Bratislava 1; tel. (2) 5980-4222; e-mail ukb@ulib.sk; internet www.ulib.sk; f. 1919; carries out coordination, statistical, educational and methodological work for libraries in Slovakia; nat. depository library; 2.5m. vols; Dir-Gen. Dr TIBOR TRGIŇA.

Ústredná Knižnica Slovenskej Akadémie Vied (Central Library of the Slovak Academy of Sciences): Klemensova 19, 814 67 Bratislava; tel. (2) 5292-1733; e-mail knizhude@savba.sk; internet www.uk.sav.sk; f. 1953; 520,000 vols; Dir Mgr ANDREA DOKTOROVÁ.

Košice

Štátna Vedecká Knižnica v Košiciach (State Scientific Library in Košiče): Hlavná 10, 042 30 Košice; tel. (55) 2454-126; e-mail sekretariat@svkk.sk; internet www.svkk.sk; f. 1946 as library of Agricultural and Forest Engineering College in Košice; specialization in mining, metallurgy, applied geology and related ecology; 2.5m. vols (incl. 1.2m. vols of books and bound periodicals, 1.2m. vols of spec. documents); Dir Dr JÁN GAŠPAR; publs *Zoznam zahraničných časopisov objednaných na východné Slovensko* (1 a year), *Súpis bibliografií a rešerší vypracovaných v SVK Košice* (1 a year).

Verejná Knižnica Jána Bocatia v Košiciach (Ján Bocatius Public Library): Hlavná 48, 042 61 Košice; tel. (55) 6223-291; e-mail vkjb@vkjb.sk; internet www.vkjb.sk; f. 1924; 300,000 vols; Dir Dr KLÁRA KERNEROVÁ.

Martin

Slovenská Národná Knižnica (Slovak National Library): Námestie J. C. Hronskeho 1, 036 01 Martin; tel. (43) 2451-131; e-mail snk@snk.sk; internet www.snk.sk; f. 2000; literary archives and museum documents, complete Slovak printed production; 4.7m. vols; Gen. Dir Ing. Dr KATARÍNA KRIŠTOFOVÁ; publs *Biografické štúdie* (1 a year), *Genealogicko-heraldický hlas* (2 a year), *Inventar rukopisov ALÚ MS* (1 a year), *Knižnica* (Library, 12 a year), *Slovenská národná bibliografia* (4 a year, CD-ROM; 1 a year, print).

Nitra

Slovenská Poľnohospodárska Knižnica (Slovak Agricultural Library): Stúrova 51, 949 59 Nitra; tel. (37) 6517-743; e-mail slpk@uniag.sk; internet www.slpk.sk; f. 1946; 525,000 vols; Dir Mgr Dr BEÁTA BELLÉROVÁ.

Prešov

Štátna Vedecká Knižnica v Prešove (State Scientific Library in Prešov): Hlavná 99, 081 89 Prešov; tel. (51) 2451-101; e-mail kniznica@svkpo.gov.sk; internet www.svkpo.sk; f. 1952; 450,000 vols; Dir Mgr VALÉRIA ZÁVADSKÁ.

Zvolen

Slovenská Lesnícka a Drevárska Knižnica (Slovak Library of Forestry and Wood Sciences): Masarykova 20, 961 02 Zvolen; tel. (45) 5206-641; e-mail sldk@tuzvo.sk; internet sldk.tuzvo.sk; f. 1952; attached to Technical Univ. in Zvolen; 350,000 vols; Dir Ing. ALENA POLÁČIKOVÁ; publs *Bibliography of the Technical University in Zvolen* (1 a year), *Ecology Bulletin* (6 a year), *Forestry Bulletin* (12 a year), *Wood Sciences Bulletin* (12 a year).

Museums and Art Galleries

Banská Bystrica

Múzeum Slovenského Národného Povstania (Museum of the Slovak National Uprising): Kapitulská 23, 975 59 Banská Bystrica; tel. (48) 2451-101; e-mail muzeumsnp@muzeumsnp.sk; internet www.muzeumsnp.sk; f. 1955; permanent exhibition on anti-fascist struggle of the Slovak people during the Second World War; open air museum of heavy weapons; administers nat. cultural landmark Kalište and exposition in Ráztocká Valley; library of 17,000 vols; Dir STANISLAV MIČEV.

Stredoslovenské Múzeum v Banskej Bystrici (Central Slovakia Museum Banská Bystrica): Nám. Slovenského národného povstania 4, 975 90 Banská Bystrica; tel. (48) 4125-895; e-mail smbb@stonline.sk; internet www.stredoslovenskemuzeum.sk; f. 1889; socio-scientific collns of archaeology, art and history, numismatics, ethnography; natural sciences collns of inorganics, botany, zoology; administers houses of Ján Thurzo, Tihányis, Matej; library of 12,000 vols; Dir Dr ROMAN HRADECKÝ; publs *Katalog chladných zbraní*, *Katalog fajky a fajčiarske potreby*, *Stredné Slovensko* (1 a year).

Banská Štiavnica

Slovenské Banské Múzeum (Slovak Mining Museum): Kammerhofská 2, 969 01 Banská Štiavnica; tel. (45) 6949-422; e-mail sbm@muzeumbs.sk; internet www.muzeumbs.sk; f. 1900, present name 1967; exhibition on history of mining; administers mining museum, old castle, new castle, Jozefa Kollára gallery; library of 21,000 vols; Dir Dr JOZEF LABUDA; publ. *Zborník SBM* (bulletin).

Bratislava

Galéria Mesta Bratislavy (Bratislava City Gallery): Mirbach Palace, Františkánske nám. 11, 815 35 Bratislava; tel. (2) 5443-1556; e-mail gmb@gmb.sk; internet www.gmb.sk; f. 1961; Slovak and Central European art; temporary exhibitions of modern nat. and int. art; library of 12,000 vols; Dir Dr IVAN JANČÁR.

Múzeum Mesta Bratislavy (Bratislava City Museum): Radničná st 1, 815 18 Bratislava; tel. (2) 5910-0812; e-mail mmba@bratislava.sk; internet muzeum.bratislava.sk; f. 1868; colln on applied arts, art history, archaeology, ethnography, history, history of pharmacy, numismatics; library of 21,000 vols; Dir Dr PETER HYROSS; Sec. JARMILA DOMESOVÁ.

Slovenská Národná Galéria (Slovak National Gallery): Riečna 1, 815 13 Bratislava 1; tel. (2) 2047-6226; e-mail info@sng.sk; internet www.sng.sk; f. 1948; permanent colln of gothic art, baroque art, Italian paintings from 16th to 18th century, Dutch art of 17th century, Slovak art of 19th century; administers castle in Zvolen, mansion of Strážky in Spišská Belá, Ludovít Fulla gallery in Ružomberok, Gallery of Naïve Art in Pezinok-Cajla; library of 100,710 vols, 80,000 documents; Gen. Dir Dr ALEXANDRA KUSÁ.

Slovenské Národné Múzeum (Slovak National Museum): Vajanského nábrežie 2, POB 13, 810 06 Bratislava 16; tel. (2) 5934-9111; e-mail riaditel@snm.sk; internet www.snm.sk; f. 1893, present name and status 1961; has 18 specialized museums; serves as coordinating, methodological, professional advisory, statistical, educational and informational centre of the entire museum sector;

3.9m. colln items on archaeology, art, history, natural history; library of 92,000 vols; Dir Dr RASTISLAV PÚDELKA; publs *Bulletin* (2 a year), *Múzeum* (guidance for museum and art gallery workers, 4 a year), *Pamiatky a múzeá* (Sights and Museums, 4 a year).

Košice

Slovenské Technické Múzeum (Slovak Technical Museum): Hlavná 88, 040 01 Košice; tel. (55) 6224-035; e-mail stmke@stm-ke.sk; internet www.stm-ke.sk; f. 1947, current name adopted 1983; 14,000 colln objects on mining, metallurgy, smith's craft, watchmaker's trade, machinery, electrical engineering, geodesy and cartrography, photography and cinematography; administers technological monuments; library of 17,003 vols; Gen. Dir Ing. EUGEN LABANIČ.

Východoslovenské Múzeum v Košiciach (Museum of Eastern Slovakiá in Košice): Hviezdoslavová 3, 041 36 Košice; tel. (55) 6220-309; e-mail info@vsmuzeum.sk; internet www.vsmuzeum.sk; f. 1872; 500,000 colln objects on art, ethnography, history, natural sciences; library of 60,000 vols; Dir Dr RÓBERT POLLÁK; publs *Historica Carpatica* (1 a year), *Natura Carpatica* (1 a year).

Kremnica

NBS—Múzeum Mincí a Medailí (National Bank of Slovakia—Museum of Coins and Medals): Štefánikovo nám. 11/21, 967 01 Kremnica; tel. (45) 6780-301; e-mail muzeum@nbs.sk; internet www.muzeumkremnica.sk; f. 1890; history of mining and money, medals and coins; Dir Mgr MARIANA NOVOTNÁ; Sec. BARBORA ŠVECOVÁ.

Piešťany

Balneologické Múzeum, Piešťany (Museum of Balneology, Piešťany): Beethovenova 5, 921 01 Piešťany; tel. (33) 7722-875; e-mail krupa.vladimir@zupa-tt.sk; internet www.balneomuzeum.sk; f. 1928; history of Slovak spas, regional history; collns on archaeology, history, folklore, history of balneology, fine arts, numismatics, natural sciences; library of 9,500 vols; Dir Dr VLADIMÍR KRUPA.

Prešov

Šarišská Galéria v Prešove (Šariš Gallery in Prešov): Hlavná 51, 080 01 Prešov; tel. (51) 7725-423; e-mail sg.po@centrum.sk; internet sgpresov.sk; f. 1956 as Krajská Galéria v Prešove, present name 1991; 4,124 colln objects of applied arts and crafts, drawings, graphics, paintings, sculptures from 15th to 20th century; spec. collns of icons from 18th century; Dir Dr RUDOLF DUPKALA.

Svidník

Múzeum ukrajinskej kultúry (Museum of Ukrainian Culture): Centrána 258, 089 01 Svidník; tel. (54) 2451-001; e-mail sekretariat-muk@snm.sk; internet www.snm.sk/?muzeum-ukrajinskej-kultury-uvodna-stranka; f. 1956; history and culture of the Ukrainians and Ruthenians in Slovakia; administers ethnographical open air exhibition, art historical exhibition, cultural and historical exhibition; Dezider Milly art gallery; library of 44,354 vols; Dir Dr MIRÓSLAV SOPÓLIGA.

Vojenské Historické Múzeum (Museum of Military History): Bardejovská 14, 089 01 Svidník; tel. (54) 7521-398; f. 1965; history of the military in E Slovakia 1914-1945; br. in Piešťany; library of 3,225 vols; Dir Mgr VLADIMÍR HOSPODÁR.

Tatranská Lomnica

Múzeum Tatranského Národného Parku (Museum of the Tatra National Park): 059 60 Tatranská Lomnica; tel. (52) 4780-365; e-mail muzeum@lesytanap.sk; internet www.lesytanap.sk/en/services/museum.php; f. 1957; colln on the fields of botany, ethnography, geology, history, natural history, zoology; library of 19,520 vols; Dir Ing. MIKULÁŠ MICHELČIK.

Universities

EKONOMICKÁ UNIVERZITA V BRATISLAVE
(University of Economics in Bratislava)

Dolnozemská cesta 1, 852 35 Bratislava

Telephone: (2) 6729-1111

E-mail: komunikacia@euba.sk

Internet: www.euba.sk

Founded 1940 as College of Commerce, present name 1992

State control

Language of instruction: English, French, German, Slovak

Academic year: September to June,

Rector: Prof. Dr RUDOLF SIVÁK

Vice-Rector for Devt: Dr LUBOMÍR STRIEŠKA

Vice-Rector for Education: Prof. Dr FERDINAND DAŇO

Vice-Rector for Int. Relations: Dr JANA LENGHARTOVÁ

Vice-Rector for Management of Academic Projects: Dr JANA MIKOCZIOVÁ

Vice-Rector for Research and Doctoral Studies: Prof. Dr ANETTA ČAPLÁNOVÁ

Librarian: Mgr JITKA KMEŤOVÁ

Number of teachers: 700

Number of students: 12,000

Publications: *Acta oeconomica Cassoviensia* (2 a year, in English), *Almanach: current issues of World Economics and Politics* (2 a year, in Slovak), *Business Review* (2 a year), *Ekonóm* (5 a year), *Ekonomické rozhlady* (4 a year, in English and Slovak), *Ekonomika a informatika* (2 a year, in Czech, English, Slovak), *Ekonomika a manažment* (3 a year, in Slovak), *Ekonomika cestovného ruchu a podnikanie* (4 a year, in Slovak), *Finančné trhy* (12 a year, in Czech, Slovak), *International Relations* (2 a year), *Journal of Innovations and Applied Statistics* (1 a year, in Slovak), *Management Information Systems* (2 a year, in English), *Manažment v teórii a praxi* (4 a year, in Slovak), *Medzinárodné vzťahy* (2 a year, in English, Slovak), *Nová ekonomika* (4 a year, in Czech, English, Slovak), *Podniková revue* (2 a year, in Slovak), *Region Direct* (2 a year, in Czech, English, Slovak), *Studia commercialia Bratislavensia* (4 a year, in English, Slovak)

DEANS

Faculty of Applied Languages: Prof. Dr LÍVIA ADAMCOVÁ

Faculty of Business Economics (in Košice): Prof. Dr MICHAL TKÁČ

Faculty of Business Informatics: Prof. Dr MICHAL FENDEK

Faculty of Business Management: Prof. Dr LUBOSLAV SZABO

Faculty of Commerce: Dr ŠTEFAN ŽÁK

Faculty of International Relations: Prof. Dr LUDMILA LIPKOVÁ

Faculty of National Economy: Prof. Dr JÁN LISÝ

KATOLÍCKA UNIVERZITA V RUŽOMBERKU
(Catholic University in Ružomberok)

Námestie A. Hlinku 60, 034 01 Ružomberok

Telephone: (44) 4304-693

E-mail: info@ku.sk

Internet: www.ku.sk

Founded 2000

Jt control of Slovak state and the Catholic Church

Language of instruction: Slovak

Rector: Prof. Dr TADEUSZ ZASEPA

Vice-Rector for Devt: Prof. Dr PETER OLEKSAK

Vice-Rector for Education: Prof. Dr JANA MORICOVÁ

Vice-Rector for Int. Relations: Dr RÓBERT LAPKO

Vice-Rector for Quality and Complex Accreditation: Dr STEFAN TKÁČÍK

Vice-Rector for Research and Arts: Dr JÁN VEĽBACKÝ

Dir for Univ. Library: Dr SONA HLINKOVA

Library of 124,756 vols

Number of teachers: 430

Number of students: 7,370

Publications: *Disputationes Scientificae Universitatis Catholicae in Ružomberok*, *Kuriér Katolíckej univerzity*, *Rozhladenie*, *Verba Theologica*, *Zdravotnícke Štúdie*

DEANS

Faculty of Arts and Letters: Dr MARIAN KUNA

Faculty of Health Service: Prof. Dr ANTON LACKO

Faculty of Pedagogy: Prof. Dr TOMÁŠ JABLONSKÝ

Faculty of Theology: Prof. Dr CYRIL HIŠEM

PANEURÓPSKA VYSOKÁ ŠKOLA
(Pan-European University)

Tomašikova 20, 821 02 Bratislava

Telephone: (2) 4820-8803

E-mail: rektorat@paneurouni.com

Internet: www.paneurouni.com

Founded 2004 as Bratislavská vysoká škola, present name 2010

Private control

Rector: Prof. Dr JÁN SVÁK

Vice-Rector for Educational Activities: Prof. Ing. Dr KAJETANA HONTYOVÁ

Vice-Rector for Int. Relations: Prof. Dr BEA VERCHRAEGEN

Vice-Rector for Research and Science: Ing. Dr JITKA KLOUDOVÁ

Dir for Libraries: Mgr MELÁNIA BUCHLOVÁ

Library of 13,000 vols, 130 periodicals

Number of students: 5,000

Publications: *Creative and Knowledge Society*, *Economy and Business*, *Notitiae ex Academia Bratislavensi Iurisprudentiae*

DEANS

Faculty of Economics and Business: Prof. Ing. Dr LADISLAV KABÁT

Faculty of Informatics: Ing. Dr MARTIN ŠPERKA

Faculty of Law: Prof. Dr JAROSLAV IVOR

Faculty of Massmedia: Dr SAMUEL BREČKA

Faculty of Psychology: Prof. Dr TEODOR KOLLÁRIK

PREŠOVSKÁ UNIVERZITA V PREŠOVE
(University of Prešov)

ul. 17. novembra 15 080 01 Prešov

Telephone: (51) 7563-100

Internet: www.unipo.sk

Founded 1997

State control

Academic year: September to June

Rector: Prof. Dr RENÉ MATLOVIČ
Vice-Rector for Educational Affairs: Prof. Dr
MILAN PORTIK
Vice-Rector for Int. Relations: Dr IVANA
CIMERMANOVÁ
Vice-Rector for Science, Art and Accredit-
ation: Prof. Dr PETER KÓNYA
Vice-Rector for Univ. Devt, Information
Technologies and Quality Assurance: Ing.
Dr PETER ADAMIŠIN
Dir for Library: Ing. HAĽKO PETER
Library of 300,000 vols
Number of students: 9,000

DEANS

Faculty of Arts: Prof. Dr VASIL GLUCHMAN
Faculty of Education: Dr JANA BURGEROVÁ
Faculty of Greek Catholic Theology: Prof. Dr
PETER ŠTURÁK
Faculty of Health Care: Prof .Dr ANNA
ELIAŠOVÁ
Faculty of Humanities and Natural Sciences:
Dr NADEŽDA KRAJČOVÁ
Faculty of Management: LADISLAV SOJKA
Faculty of Orthodox Theology: Prof. Dr JÁN
ŠAFIN
Faculty of Sports: Dr PAVEL RUŽBARSKÝ

SLOVENSKÁ POĽNOHOSPODÁRSKA
UNIVERZITA V NITRE
(Slovak University of Agriculture in
Nitra)

Trieda A. Hlinku 2, 949 76 Nitra
Telephone: (37) 6415-111
E-mail: verejnost@uniag.sk
Internet: www.uniag.sk
Founded 1946 as Vysoká Škola Poľnohospo-
dárska, current name adopted 1996
State control
Languages of instruction: English, Slovak
Academic year: September to June
Rector: Prof. Dr Ing. PETER BIELIK
Vice-Rector for Education: Prof. Dr ZDENKA
GÁLOVÁ
Vice-Rector for Information and Univ. Devel-
opment: Dr Ing. ZUZANA PALKOVÁ
Vice-Rector for Science and Research: Prof.
Ing. MARIÁN BRESTIČ
Chancellor: Ing. ANNA BOŽIKOVÁ
Bursar: Dr Ing. OĽGA ROHÁČIKOVÁ
Library: see under Libraries and Archives
Number of teachers: 470
Number of students: 10,300
Publications: Acta fytotechnica et zootechnica
(4 a year), Acta Horticulturae et regioec-
turae (4 a year), Acta oeconomica et
informatica (4 a year), Acta regionalia et
enviromentalica (4 a year), Acta Zootech-
nica (1 a year)

DEANS

Faculty of Agrobiology and Food Resources:
Prof. Ing. Dr DANIEL BÍRO
Faculty of Biotechnology and Food Sciences:
Prof. Ing. JÁN TOMÁŠ
Faculty of Economics and Management: Prof.
Dr Ing. IVETA ZENTKOVÁ
Faculty of Engineering: Prof. Dr Ing. ZDENKO
TKÁČ
Faculty of European Studies and Regional
Development: Prof. Dr ANNA BANDLEROVÁ
Horticulture and Landscape Engineering
Faculty: Ing. KLAUDIA HALÁSZOVÁ

PROFESSORS

Faculty of Agronomy (tel. (37) 6511-244;
e-mail dekaf@uniag.sk):

BEŽO, M., Plant Genetics
BULLA, J., Fundamental Zootechnics
FECENKO, J., Special Plant Production
GÁLIK, R., Fundamental Zootechnics
HALAJ, M., Special Zootechnics
HANES, J., Pedology

HOLÚBEK, R., Special Plant Production
KOVÁČ, L., Fundamental Zootechnics
KOVÁČIK, J., General Zootechnics
KÚBEK, A., Fundamental Zootechnics
KULICH, J., Plant Production
LÍŠKA, E., General Plant Production
MICHALÍK, I., Plant Production
MICHALÍKOVÁ, A., Plant Protection
PAJTÁŠ, M., General Zootechnics
PAŠKA, I., Special Zootechnics
PIVKO, J., General Zootechnics
POLÁČEK, Š., Plant Production
PRASLIČKA, J., Plant Protection
ŠŤASTNÝ, P., Fundamental Zootechnics

Faculty of Economics and Management (tel.
(37) 6515-511; e-mail dekfem@uniag.sk):

BANDLEROVÁ, A., Economics and Manage-
ment
BIELIK, P., Food Industry Management
GOZORA, V., Economics and Management
HRONEC, O., Management
HRUBÝ, J., Economics
HUDÁK, J., Sectorial Economics
KABÁT, L., Economics
KUZMA, F., Economics
OKENKA, I., Economics and Management
PODOLÁK, A., Economics
REPKA, I., Economics
ŠIMO, D., Economics
VIŠŇOVSKÝ, J., Economics
ZOBORSKÝ, I. M., Economics

Faculty of Engineering (tel. (37) 6415-301;
e-mail dektf@uniag.sk):

BALLA, J., Agricultural Engineering
JECH, J., Technology and Mechanization of
Agriculture
LOBOTKA, J., Technology and Mechaniza-
tion of Agriculture
PÁLTIK, J., Technology and Mechanization
of Agriculture
PETRANSKÝ, I., Technology and Mechaniza-
tion of Agriculture
SEMETKO, J., Technology and Mechaniza-
tion
ŠESTÁK, J., Technology and Mechanization
of Agriculture
TOLNAI, R., Agricultural Engineering
ŽIKLA, A., Technology and Mechanization

Horticulture and Landscape Engineering
Faculty (Tulipánová 7, 949 76 Nitra; tel.
(37) 6415-410; e-mail dekfzki@uniag.sk):

ANTAL, J., Land Improvement
DEMO, M., Plant Production
HRICOVSKY, I., Plant Production
HRUBÍK, P., Horticulture
HUSKA, D., Land Improvement
MACHOVEC, J., Horticulture
ŠPÁNIK, F., Special Plant Production
STRED'ANSKY, J., Land Improvement
SUPUKA, J., Phytopathology
VREŠTIAK, P., Special Plant Production

SLOVENSKÁ TECHNICKÁ
UNIVERZITA V BRATISLAVE
(Slovak University of Technology in
Bratislava)

Vazovova 5, 812 43 Bratislava 1
Telephone: (2) 5249-7196
E-mail: public@stuba.sk
Internet: www.stuba.sk
Founded 1938 as Technical Univ. of M. R.
Štefánik, current name adopted 1991
State control
Languages of instruction: English, Slovak
Academic year: September to September
Rector: Prof. Ing. Dr ROBERT REDHAMMER
Vice-Rector for Devt: Prof. Ing. MILAN SOKOL
Vice-Rector for Education: Dr Ing. FRANTIŠEK
HORŇÁK
Vice-Rector for Int. Relations: Prof. Ing.
MARIÁN PECIAR

Vice-Rector for Science and Research: Prof.
Ing. Dr STANISLAV BISKUPIČ
Bursar: Ing. Dr DUŠAN FAKTOR
Librarian: VIERA POLČÍKOVÁ
Library of 400,000 vols
Number of teachers: 1,600
Number of students: 19,000

Publications: Acta Chimica Slovaca (4 a year,
in English), ALFA—Architektonické listy
FA STU (4 a year, in Slovak with summary
in English), Almanach Znalca (4 a year, in
Slovak), AT & P Journal (12 a year, in
Slovak with summary in English), Computing and Informatics (4 a year, in Eng-
lish), EE–Journal for Electrical and Power
Engineering (6 a year, in Slovak with
summary in English), Formation Sciences
and Technologies—Bulletin of the ACM
Slovakia (2–4 a year), Journal of Cyber-
netics and Informatics (ejournal for control
community, in English), Journal of Elec-
trical Engineering (6 a year, in English),
Kovové materiály (12 a year, in Slovak),
Mathematical Publications (2–3 a year, in
English), Scientific Proceedings of FME
STU in Bratislava (in English), Slovak
Journal of Civil Engineering (4 a year, in
English), Spektrum (10 a year, in Slovak),
Tatra Mountains

DEANS

Faculty of Architecture: Ing. Dr ĽUBICA
VITKOVÁ
Faculty of Chemical and Food Technology:
Prof. Dr JÁN ŠAJBIDOR
Faculty of Civil Engineering: Prof. Ing. Dr
ALOJZ KOPÁČIK
Faculty of Electrical Engineering and Infor-
mation Technology: Prof. Dr GABRIEL
JUHÁS
Faculty of Informatics and Information Tech-
nologies: Dr Ing. PAVEL ČIČÁK
Faculty of Materials Science and Technology
in Trnava: Prof. Dr OLIVER MORAVČÍK
Faculty of Mechanical Engineering: Prof.
Ing. LUBOMIR ŠOOŠ

PROFESSORS

Faculty of Architecture:

DULLA, M., Architecture
KEPPL, J., Architecture
KOVÁČ, B., Town Planning
PETELEN, I., Industrial Design
PETRÁNSKY, Ľ., Theory and History of Art
Design
ŠPAČEK, R., Architecture
VODRÁŽKA, P., Architecture

Faculty of Chemical and Food Technology:

BAJUS, M., Fuel Technology
BAKOŠ, D., Macromolecular Chemistry and
Engineering
BÁLEŠ, V., Chemical Engineering and Pro-
cess Control
BOČA, R., Inorganic Chemistry
BOSKUPIČ, S., Physical Chemistry and
Chemical Physics
BREZOVA, V., Chemical Physics
BUSTIN, D., Analytical Chemistry
CIK, G., Technology of Macromolecular
Substances
FELLNER, P., Technology of Inorganic
Chemistry
FIŠERA, L., Organic Chemistry
GRACZA, T., Organic Chemistry
HIVES, J., Technology of Inorganic Chem-
istry and Materials
HRONEC, M., Organic Technology
KOMAN, M., Inorganic Chemistry
KRUPČÍK, J., Analytical Chemistry
LABUDA, J., Analytical Chemistry
LEHOTAY, J., Analytical Chemistry
LOKAJ, J., Material Engineering
MALÍK, F., Biochemical Technology
MARCHALIN, S., Organic Chemistry

MARKOS, J., Chemical Engineering and Process Control
MESZAROS, A., Chemical Engineering and Process Control
MIKLEŠ, J., Technical Cybernetics
MOCÁK, J., Analytical Chemistry
MRAVEC, D., Organic Technology and Fuel Technology
ŠAJBIDOR, J., Biochemical Technology
SCHMIDT, S., Food Chemistry and Technology
ŠIMA, J., Inorganic Chemistry
ŠIMON, P., Physical Chemistry
STASKO, A., Physical Chemistry
VALACH, F., Physical Chemistry and Chemical Physics
VALKO, L., Physical Chemistry
VARECKA, L., Biochemistry

Faculty of Civil Engineering:

AGÓCS, Z., Steel and Timber Structures
BAJZA, A., Non-Metallic Materials and Construction Materials
BALÁŽ, L., Construction Engineering
BALIAK, F., Construction Engineering
BANÍK, I., Physics
BARTOŠ, P., Geodesy and Cartography
BEDNÁROVÁ, E., Hydraulic Engineering
BETKO, B., Engineering Theory and Construction Engineering
BEZÁK, B., Transport Engineering
BIELEK, M., Building Construction
BILČÍK, J., Construction Engineering
CHMÚRNY, I., Engineering Theory and Construction Engineering
DUŠIČKA, P., Hydraulic Engineering
FILLO, L., Construction Engineering
GAŠPARÍK, J., Construction Technology
GSCHWENDT, I., Transport Engineering
HEFTY, J., Geodesy and Cartography
HRAŠKA, J., Engineering Theory and Construction Engineering
HULLA, J., Geotechnology
KLEPSATEL, F., Building Construction
KOMORNÍKOVÁ, M., Applied Mathematics
KOPÁČIK, A., Geodesy and Cartography
KRIŠ, J., Construction in Health Care Sector
LAPOS, J., Construction Engineering
LOVÍŠEK, J., Mechanics of Solid and Pliable Bodies
MACURA, V., Landscaping
MAJDÚCH, D., Concrete Structures and Bridges
MELICHER, J., Geodesy and Cartography
MESIAR, R., Applied Mathematics
MIKULA, K., Applied Mathematics
MUDRONČÍK, M., Building Structures and Architecture
OHRABLO, F., Building Construction
OLÁH, J., Building Construction
PETRÁŠ, D., Engineering Theory and Construction Engineering
PUŠKÁR, A., Engineering Theory and Construction Engineering
RAVINGER, J., Applied Mechanics
ROUSEKOVÁ, I., Non-Metallic Materials and Construction Materials
ŠIRÁŇ, J., Applied Mathematics
SOKOL, M., Applied Mechanics
SOKOL, Š., Geodesy and Cartography
SOLTÉSZ, A., Hydraulic Engineering
STANĚK, V., Geodesy and Cartography
ŠUMEC, J., Building Construction
ŠVEDA, M., Non-Metallic Materials and Construction Materials
SZOLGAY, J., Hydrology and Water Management
TOMAŠOVIČ, P., Engineering Theory and Construction Engineering
TURČEK, P., Building Construction
VALÁŠEK, J., Building Construction
ZAJAC, J., Building Construction
ZAPLETAL, I., Technology and Materials Engineering

Faculty of Electrical Engineering and Information Technology:

BALLO, I., Physical Engineering
BAROŇÁK, I., Telecommunication
BOCK, I., Applied Mathematics
BREZA, J., Electronics
CIRÁK, J., Physical Engineering
DONOVAL, D., Electronics
ĎURAČKOVÁ, D., Electronics
DURNÝ, R., Solid-State Physics
FARKAŠ, P., Telecommunication
GROŠEK, O., Applied Informatics
HUBA, M., Automation
JANÍČEK, F., Electrical Energy
JASENEK, J., Theory of Electromagnetism
JURIŠICA, L., Technical Cybernetics
KOVÁČ, J., Electronics
KOZÁK, Š., Automation and Control
MIGLIERINI, M., Solid-State Physics
MURGAŠ, J., Cybernetics
MURÍN, J., Applied Mechanics
NEČAS, V., Nuclear Energy
PODHRADSKÝ, P., Telecommunications
POLEC, J., Telecommunications
SITEK, J., Condensed Matter Physics and Acoustics
SLUGEŇ, V., Nuclear Energy
SMIEŠKO, V., Measurement Engineering
SMOLA, A., Electrical Energy
STOPJAKOVÁ, V., Electronics
TVAROŽEK, V., Electronics
UHEREK, F., Electronics
ŽALMAN, M., Automation and Control

Faculty of Informatics and Information Technologies:

BIELIKOVA, M., Software Engineering
HORVATH, P., Applied Informatics
KOLESAR, M., Computer Engineering
KVASNICKA, V., Artificial Intelligence
MOLNAR, L., Informatics
NAVRAT, P., Information Systems
POSPICHAL, J., Applied Informatics
SAFARIK, J., Informatics

Faculty of Materials Science and Technology in Trnava:

BAČA, J., Mechanical Engineering Technology
BALOG, K., Occupational Health and Safety
BARÁNEK, I., Production Technologies, Machine Technologies and Materials
BLAŠKOVITŠ, P., Mechanical Engineering Technology
BLEHA, T., Materials
ČAMBÁL, M., Industrial Engineering
ČAUS, A., Production Technologies, Machine Technologies and Materials
CYRUS, P., Teacher Training of Vocational Subjects and Practical Training for Didactics
DRIENSKY, D., Engineering Education
DUSZA, J., Materials
GRGAČ, P., Materials Engineering
HRIVŇÁK, I., Physical Metallurgy and Materials Engineering
HRIVŇÁKOVÁ, D., Physical Metallurgy
HUSAR, P., Automation, Applied Informatics
JAHNÁTEK, L., Industrial Engineering
JANAČ, A., Machinery
JANOVEC, J., Materials
JOEHNE, M., Industrial Engineering
KALUŽNÝ, J., Materials Engineering
KIPS, M., Teacher Training of Vocational Subjects and Practical Training
KOLITSCH, A., Materials
KOŠTURIAK, J., Quality of Production
KOVÁČ, J., Physics
KOZIK, T., Teacher Training of Vocational Subjects and Practical Training for Didactics
KUPČA, L., Materials
LINCZÉNYI, A., Quality of Production
LIPA, Z., Production Technologies
LOKAJ, J., Materials

MORAVČÍK, O., Applied Information Science and Automation in Industry
MUDRONČÍK, D., Automation and Applied Information Science
MURGAŠ, M., Industrial Engineering
OŽVOLD, M., Materials
PETERKA, J., Production Technologies, Machine Technologies and Materials
POKUSA, A., Production Technologies
RICHTER, V., Automation
SABLIIK, J., Quality of Production
SAKÁL, P., Industrial Engineering
SCHREIBER, P., Automation and Applied Informatics
ŠVRČEK, D., Production Technology
TURŇA, M., Welding and Welding Machines
ULRICH, K., Production Technologies, Machine Technologies and Materials
URBAN, M., Materials
VELÍŠEK, K., Production Technology
VRBAN, A., Applied Information Science and Automation

Faculty of Mechanical Engineering:

BENKO, B., Production Technology and Materials
BUKOVECZKY, J., Transportation Machines and Equipments
DEDIK, L., Instrumentation, Informatics and Automation Technology
ELESZTOS, P., Applied Mechanics
GODNAR, E., Production Technology and Materials
GULAN, L., Machines and Equipment for Building, Processing and Agriculture
HAVELSKY, V., Thermal Power Engineering and Environmental Technology
HEKELOVA, E., Production Quality and Technological Systems Safety
HULKO, G., Instrumentation, Informatics and Automation Technology
KRESEK, A., Manufacturing Systems with Industrial Robots and Manipulators
MOLNAR, V., Power Engineering
PALENCAR, R., Instrumentation, Informatics and Automation Technology
PECIAR, M., Machines and Equipment for Chemical and Food Industries
ROHLA-ILKIV, B., Instrumentation, Informatics, Mechatronic and Automation Technology
SKAKALA, J., Instrumentation, Informatics and Automation Technology
SLADEK, J., Applied Mechanics
SOOS, L., Production Machines
STAREL, L., Applied Mechanics
TICHY, J., Transport Technology
TOLNAY, M., Mechanical Engineering Technologies
URBAN, J., Transport Technology
VALCUHA, Š., Construction of Manufacturing Machines
VARCHOLA, M., Hydraulic and Pneumatic Machines and Equipment
VAVRO, K., Power Engineering
VERES, M., Machine Parts and Mechanisms
ZAHOREC, O., Applied Mechanics

Institute of Engineering Studies:

MÉSZÁROS, A., Chemical Engineering and Process Control

Institute of Management:

FINKA, M., Spatial Planning
IVANICKA, K., Management
ROCH, I., Spatial Planning
SCHOLICH, D., Spatial Planning

SLOVENSKÁ ZDRAVOTNÍCKA UNIVERZITA V BRATISLAVE (Slovak Medical University in Bratislava)

Limbová 12, 833 03 Bratislava
Telephone: (2) 5937-0111
E-mail: info@szu.sk
Internet: www.szu.sk

Founded 2002
State control
Language of instruction: Slovak
Rector: Prof. Dr DANA FARKAŠOVÁ
First Vice-Rector and Vice-Rector for Further Education: Prof. Dr PETER ŠIMKO
Vice-Rector for Bestowment of Academic and Scientific Titles and Honours: Prof. Dr PETER BUJDÁK
Vice-Rector for Int. Relations: Prof. Dr JÁN SLEZÁK
Vice-Rector for Practical Lectures in Health Care Facilities: Prof. Dr JAROSLAV KRESÁNEK
Vice-Rector for Science and Research: Dr MARTIN GAJDOŠ
Vice-Rector for Undergraduate Studies: Dr VIKTOR MAJTÁN
Bursar: Ing. JOZEF HUDÁK
Library Dir: Mgr ZUZANA ONDEROVÁ
Library of 16,137 vols, 132 periodicals
Number of teachers: 400
Number of students: 16,540

DEANS

Faculty of Health (Banská Bystrica): Prof. Dr SVETOZÁR DLUHOLUCKÝ
Faculty of Medicine: Prof. Dr TIBOR ŠAGÁT
Faculty of Nursing and Professional Health Studies: Dr MÁRIA MUSILOVÁ
Faculty of Public Health: Dr ŠTEFÁNIA MORICOVÁ

PROFESSORS

Faculty of Health (Banská Bystrica):
DLUHOLUCKÝ, S., Paediatrics
KRALINSKÝ, K., Urgent Medical Care

Faculty of Medicine:
BREZA, J., Urology
ČERNÁK, A., Ophthalmology
FISCHER, V., Cardiosurgery
GÚTH, A., Physiology, Balneology, and Medical Rehabilitation
HARUŠTIAK, S., Surgery and Thoracic Surgery
HATALA, R., Cardiology
HOLOMÁŇ, J., Clinical Pharmacology
KOTHAJ, P., Gastroenterological Surgery
KOVÁČ, G., Clinical Biochemistry and Laboratory Medicine
KOZA, I., Clinical Oncology
KRAJČÍK, S., Geriatrics
KRESÁNEK, J., Adolescent Medicine
KRISTÚFEK, P., Functional Diagnostics
KUKUMBERG, P., Neuropsychiatry
LECHTA, V., Logopaedia
LISÝ, L., Neurology
MASARIK, J., Biophysics
PECHAN, J., Surgery
RIEČANSKÝ, I., Cardiology and Angiology
ROVENSKÝ, J., Rheumatology
ŠABÓ, A., Biology
ŠAGÁT, T., Paediatric Anaesthiology and Intensive Medicine
ŠAKALOVÁ, A., Haematology
ŠEFRÁNEK, V., Vascular Surgery
ŠIMKO, P., Injury-related Surgery
ŠTENCL, J., Obstetrics and Gynaecology
ŠTEŇO, J., Neurosurgery
TÓTH, K., Medical Law
VAVREČKA, A., Gastroenterology
VOJTAŠŠÁK, J., Orthopaedics

Faculty of Nursing and Professional Health Studies:
FARKAŠOVÁ, D., Nursing
MALÝ, M., Physiotherapy
ŠVEC, J., Oncology

Faculty of Public Health:
HEGYI, L., Medical Teaching
ŠAJTER, V., Theoretical Science
ŠULCOVÁ, M., Health in the Workplace

STREDOEURÓPSKA VYSOKÁ ŠKOLA V SKALICI
(Central European University in Skalica)

Kráľovská 386/11, 909 01 Skalica
Telephone: (34) 6647-061
E-mail: riaditel@sevs.sk
Internet: www.sevs.sk
Founded 2005
Private control
Depts of ecology and environment sciences, political science, sciences
Chancellor: Ing. Dr HEIDY SCHWARCZOVÁ
Vice-Chancellor for Education: Ing. MICHAELA FERIKOVÁ KREMLOVÁ
Vice-Chancellor for Int. Relations: Dr IVO HLAVÁČEK
Vice-Chancellor for Science and Research: Mgr Dr PETER JANČOVIČ
Number of students: 1,200

TECHNICKÁ UNIVERZITA V KOŠICIACH
(Technical University of Košice)

Letná 9, 042 00 Košice
Telephone: (55) 6021-111
E-mail: rektor@tuke.sk
Internet: www.tuke.sk
Founded 1952 as Košice Technical College, current name adopted 1991
State control
Languages of instruction: English, Slovak
Academic year: September to August
Rector: Prof. Ing. Dr ANTON ČIŽMÁR
Vice-Rector for Devt and Construction: Prof. Ing. EMIL SPIŠÁK
Vice-Rector for Education: Ing. Dr PAVEL RASCHMAN
Vice-Rector for External Relations and Marketing: Prof. Ing. Dr JURAJ SINAY
Vice-Rector for Science and Research: Prof. Ing. STANISLAV KMEŤ
Bursar: Ing. MARCEL BEHÚN
Dir for Library: Ing. Dr ONDREJ LÁTKA
Number of teachers: 850 (820 full-time, 30 part-time)
Number of students: 16,000
Publications: *Acta Electrotechnica et Informatica* (4 a year), *Acta Mechanica Slovaca* (4 a year), *Acta Metallurgica Slovaca* (4 a year), *Acta Montanistica Slovaca* (4 a year), *Halo TU* (12 a year)

DEANS

Faculty of Arts: Dr Ing. JURAJ KOBAN
Faculty of Aeronautics: Dr FRANTIŠEK OLEJNÍK
Faculty of Civil Engineering: Ing. Dr VINCENT KVOČÁK
Faculty of Economics: Prof. Dr VINCENT SOLTÉS
Faculty of Electrical Engineering and Informatics: Prof. Ing. Dr LIBERIOS VOKOROKOS
Faculty of Manufacturing Technologies Prešov: Prof. Ing. Dr JOZEF NOVÁK-MARCINČIN
Faculty of Mechanical Engineering: Prof. Ing. Dr FRANTIŠEK TREBUNA
Faculty of Metallurgy: Dr Ing. PETER HORNAK
Faculty of Mining, Ecology, Process Control and Geotechnology: Prof. Dr GABRIEL WEISS

PROFESSORS

Faculty of Arts (tel. (55) 6022-177; e-mail dekan.fu@tuke.sk; internet www.fu.tuke.sk):
BARTUSZ, J., Fine Art
Faculty of Civil Engineering (Vysokoškolská 4, 042 00 Košice; tel. (55) 6024-003; e-mail sekretariat.svf@tuke.sk; internet www.svf.tuke.sk):

HORNIAKOVÁ, L., Theory of Construction of Overground Buildings
HUDÁK, J., Theory of Construction of Engineering Structures
JUHÁS, P., Theory of Construction of Engineering Structures
KMEŤ, S., Theory of Construction of Engineering Structures
ŠTEVULOVÁ, N., Environmental Studies
TKÁČOVÁ, K., Mineralogy and Ecotechnology

Faculty of Economics (Němcovej 32, 040 01 Košice; tel. (55) 6330-983; e-mail dekanat.ekf@tuke.sk; internet www.ekf.tuke.sk):
ŠAMSON, Š., Economic Theory
ŠOLTÉS, V., Mathematics

Faculty of Electrical Engineering and Informatics (Letná 9, 042 00 Košice; tel. (55) 6022-221):
BANSKÝ, J., Radio Electronics, Electronic Technology
ČIŽMÁR, A., Electronics and Telecommunications Engineering
HUDÁK, Š., Computers and Informatics
JELŠINA, M., Electronic Computers
KOLCUM, M., Energetics, High-Voltage Engineering
KOVÁČ, D., Energetics, High-Voltage Engineering
KROKAVEC, D., Technology and Automation
KROKAVEC, M., Computers and Informatics
LEVICKÝ, D., Radio Electronics
MADARÁSZ, L., Technical Cybernetics
MARCHEVSKÝ, S., Electronics and Telecommunications Engineering
MARTON, K., Energetics, High-Voltage Engineering
MICHAELI, L., Radio Electronics
MIHALÍK, J., Electronics and Telecommunications Engineering
SARNOVSKÝ, J., Technical Cybernetics
SINČÁK, P., Artificial Intelligence
SOMORA, M., Materials Engineering
ŠPÁNY, V., Radio Electronics
TIMKO, J., Electrical Engineering
TURÁN, J., Radio Electronics
ZBORAY, L., Electrical Engineering

Faculty of Manufacturing Technologies Prešov (Bayerova 1, 080 01 Prešov; tel. (51) 7723-012; internet www.tuke.sk/fvtpo):
NOVÁK-MARCINČIN, P., Production Engineering
RAGAN, E., Mechanical Technology
VASILKO, K., Mechanical Technology

Faculty of Mechanical Engineering (Letná 9, 042 00 Košice; tel. (55) 6330-016; e-mail sekretariat@sjf.tuke.sk; internet www.sjf.tuke.sk):
BADIDA, M., Environmental Protection
BIGOŠ, P., Construction of Transport Machinery
ČOP, V., Robots and Manipulators
HAJDUK, M., Manufacturing Systems with Robots and Manipulators
HRIVŇÁK, A., Technology of Mechanical Engineering
IMRIŠ, I., Non-Ferrous Metallurgy
KAŽIMÍR, I., Technology of Mechanical Engineering
KLIMO, V., Machine Parts
KNIEWALD, D., Technology of Mechanical Engineering
KOVÁČ, J., Automation and Management
KOVÁČ, M., Robots and Manipulation Devices
LACHVÁČ, J., Production Machines and Equipment
LIBERKO, I., Industrial Engineering and Management
MAJERNÍK, M., Environmental Studies
POLLÁK, L., Technology of Mechanical Engineering
RITÓK, Z., Machine Parts

SALOKY, T., Automation and Control in Mechanical Engineering
ŠIMŠÍK, D., Automation and Management
SINAY, J., Transport and Manipulation
SMRČEK, J., Manufacturing Systems with Robots and Manipulators
SPIŠÁK, E., Engineering Technology and Materials
TAKÁČ, K., Technology of Mechanical Engineering
TREBUŇA, F., Mechanics

Faculty of Metallurgy (Letná 9, 042 00 Košice; tel. (55) 6022-023; e-mail dekanat .hf@tuke.sk; internet web.tuke.sk/hf):

BURŠÁK, M., Physical Metallurgy and Materials Science
FLÓRIÁN, K., General and Analytical Chemistry
HAVLIK, T., Non-Ferrous Metallurgy
HOLOUBEK, D., Thermal Power Engineering
KRAKOVSKÁ, E., Analytical Chemistry
KVAČKAJ, T., Ferrous Metallurgy
LUKÁČ, I., Physical Metallurgy and Materials Science
MICHEĽ, J., Materials Science
MIHOK, L., Ferrous Metallurgy
ŠTOFKO, M., Non-Ferrous Metallurgy
TOMÁŠEK, K., Non-Ferrous Metallurgy
VARGA, A., Thermal Power Engineering
VIRČÍKOVÁ, E., Non-Ferrous Metallurgy
ZRNÍK, J., Physical Metallurgy and Materials Science

Faculty of Mining, Ecology, Process Control and Geotechnology (Letná 9, 042 00 Košice; tel. (55) 6021-111; e-mail sekrd.fberg@tuke .sk; internet www.fberg.tuke.sk):

BOROŠKA, J., Mining, Mechanization, Transport and Deep Well Drilling
DOJČÁR, O., Mining
FABIÁN, J., Mining
FARYAD, S. W., Mining Geology and Geological Prospecting
JACKO, S., Geological Prospecting, Geological Engineering
KOŠTIAĽ, I., Production Control
KOSTÚR, K., Control of the Acquiring and Processing of Raw Materials
KUNÁK, L., Mining Surveying and Geodesy
LEŠKO, M., Minerals Processing
MALINDŽÁK, D., Control of Acquiring and Processing of Raw Materials
PINKA, J., Mining, Mechanization, Transport and Deep Well Drilling
PODLUBNÝ, I., Control of Acquiring and Processing of Raw Materials
RYBÁR, P., Mining and Geotechnology
SASVÁRI, T., Mining Geology and Geological Prospecting
ŠEKULA, F., Mining
STROFFEK, E., Mining, Mining Mechanization
ŠUTTI, J., Three-Dimensional Geodesy
VODZINSKÝ, V., Economy and Management
WEISS, G., Mining Surveying and Geodesy
ZÁBRANSKÝ, F., Petrology

TECHNICKÁ UNIVERZITA VO ZVOLENE
(Technical University in Zvolen)

ul. T. G. Masaryka 2117/24, 960 53 Zvolen
Telephone: (45) 5206-111
E-mail: info@tuzvo.sk
Internet: www.tuzvo.sk
Founded 1952 as Univ. College of Forestry and Wood Technology, current name adopted 1991
State control
Language of instruction: Czech, English, German, Slovak, Russian
Academic year: September to June
Rector: Prof. Ing. RUDOLF KROPIL
Vice-Rector for Devt: Dr DANICA KAČIKOVÁ

Vice-Rector for Education: Dr ANDREJ JAN-KECH
Vice-Rector for Int. Relations: Mgr Ing. Dr RASTISLAV ŠULEK
Vice-Rector for Science and Research: Ing. Dr JAROSLAV ŠÁLKA
Bursar: Ing. JOSEF DRÁBEK
Dir for Library: Ing. ALENA POLÁČIKOVÁ
Library of 359,000 vols
Number of teachers: 240
Number of students: 5,000
Publications: *Acta Facultatis Forestalis* (1 a year), *Acta Facultatis Xylologiae* (1 a year), *Proceedings of Research Works of the Faculty of Ecology and Environmental Sciences* (1 a year), *Scientific and Pedagogical News* (1 a year)

DEANS

Faculty of Ecology and Environmental Sciences: Ing. Dr BRANKO SLOBODNÍK
Faculty of Environmental and Manufacturing Technology: Dr Ing. MARIÁN KUČERA
Faculty of Forestry: Prof. Ing. Dr VILIAM PICHLER
Faculty of Wood Sciences and Technology: Prof. Ing. Dr MIKULÁŠ SIKLIENKA

PROFESSORS

Faculty of Ecology and Environmental Sciences:

CHRAPAN, J., Radioecology
KOŠTÁLIK, J., Physical Geography
MIDRIAK, R., Landscape Ecology
MIKLOS, L., Landscape Ecology
SUPUKA, J., Landscape Ecology

Faculty of Environmental and Manufacturing Technology:

DANKO, M., Processes and Technology of Forest Production
MIKLEŠ, M., Processes and Technology of Forest Production

Faculty of Forestry:

BUBLINEC, E., Nature and Environment
GARAJ, P., Forest Protection and Game Management
HLADÍK, M., Forest Management
KODRÍK, J., Forest Protection and Game Management
KOLENKA, I., Forest Economics
PAGAN, J., Silviculture
PAULE, L., Forest Genetics
ŠANIGA, M., Silviculture
ŠMELKO, S., Biometry and Forest Management
VALTÝNI, J., Forest Hydrology—Torrent Control
ŽIHLAVNÍK, Š., Geodesy and Photogrammetry

Faculty of Wood Sciences and Technology:

BOROTA, J., Management of Tropical Forests
BUČKO, J., Chemistry and Chemical Technology
DEKRÉT, A., Mathematics
DUBOVSKÁ, R., Metal Processing Technology
HORSKÝ, D., Mechanical Technology of Wood
KURJATKO, S., Wood Science
LIPTÁKOVÁ, E., Wood Products Manufacturing
MARČOK, M., Physics and Applied Mechanics
OSVALD, A., Fire Protection
PETRANSKÝ, L., Design
RAJČAN, E., Physics and Applied Mechanics
REINPRECHT, L., Wood Technology Engineering
ŠUPÍN, M., Forestry Policy, Trade, Marketing
TREBULA, P., Technology of Wood
VINCÚR, P., Economics

TRENČIANSKA UNIVERZITA ALEXANDRA DUBČEKA V TRENČÍNE
(University of Alexander Dubcek in Trencin)

Študentská 2, 911 50 Trenčín
Telephone: (32) 7400-108
E-mail: rektor@tnuni.sk
Internet: www.tnuni.sk
Founded 1997
State control
Academic year: September to June
Rector: Ing. Dr JOZEF HABÁNIK
Pro-Rector for Education: Dr EVA ČERVEŇANOVÁ
Pro-Rector for Science, Research and Int. Relations: Prof. Dr MAREK LIŠKA
Pro-Rector for Strategy and Devt: Ing. Dr VILIAM CIBULKA
Bursar: Ing. Dr LUBICA HARAKAĽOVÁ
Chief Librarian: Mgr MÁRIA REHUŠOVÁ
Library of 13,663 vols
Number of teachers: 250
Number of students: 5,390
Publications: *Kvalita Inovácia Prosperita* (Quality, Innovation, Prosperity, online (www.qip-journal.eu)), *Projektový bulletin TnUAD*, *TnU Trendy* (4 a year), *University Review*

DEANS

Faculty of Health: Dr JÁN BIELIK
Faculty of Industrial Technology: Prof. Ing. Dr JÁN VAVRO
Faculty of Social Economics Relationship: Dr Mgr SERGEJ VOJTOVIČ
Faculty of Special Technologies: Ing. Dr PETER LIPTÁK

PROFESSORS

Faculty of Industrial Technology:

CAPEK, I.
JAMBRICKY, M.
KOPECKY, M.
KOSTIAL, P.
LETKO, I.
MACKO, V.
SLABEYCIUS, J.
STEFANIK, J.
YONA, E.

Faculty of Social Economics Relationship:

ALEXY, J.
BARÁNIK, M.
BARTAK, P.
BENCO, J.
BLAZEJ, A.
CAMPAI, O.
LIPTAK, J.
STRAZOVSKA, H.
VOJTOVIC, S.

Faculty of Special Technologies:

BATORA, B.
DUBOVSKA, R.
VARKOLY, L.

TRNAVSKÁ UNIVERZITA V TRNAVE/ UNIVERSITAS TYRNAVIENSIS
(Trnava University in Trnava)

Hornopotočná 23, 918 43 Trnava
Telephone: (33) 5939-111
E-mail: rektor@truni.sk
Internet: www.truni.sk
Founded 1992
State control
Academic year: October to August
Rector: Prof. Dr MAREK ŠMID
Pro-Rector for Devt: Ing. Dr BLANKA KUDLÁČOVÁ
Pro-Rector for Education and Student Affairs: Dr LUBICA ILIEVOVÁ
Pro-Rector for External Relations and Cooperation: Prof. Dr MILAN KATUNINEC

Pro-Rector for Science, Research and Artistic Activities: Prof. Dr LADISLAV CSONTOS
Bursar: Ing. MILAN HORNÁČEK
Librarian: Ing. ZUZANA MARTINKOVIČOVÁ
Library of 68,073 vols, 241 periodicals
Number of teachers: 350
Number of students: 7,680

DEANS

Faculty of Arts: Dr MARTA DOBROTKOVÁ
Faculty of Education: Prof. Dr RENÉ BÍLIK
Faculty of Health Care and Social Work: Prof. Dr VLADIMÍR BOŠÁK
Faculty of Law: Prof. Dr HELENA BARANCOVÁ
Faculty of Theology: Dr MILOŠ LICHNER

UNIVERZITA J. SELYEHO V KOMÁRNE/SELYE JÁNOS EGYETEM, KOMÁROM
(University of J. Selyeho in Komárno)

Bratislavská cesta 3322, 945 01 Komárno

Telephone: (35) 7733-073
E-mail: info@selyeuni.sk

Founded 2004
State control
Language of instruction: Hungarian

Rector: Dr JÁNOS TÓTH
Vice-Rector: Dr MELINDA NAGY
Vice-Rector: Dr PETER CSIBA
Vice-Rector: Prof. Ing. VERONIKA STOFFOVA

Library of 150,000 vols, 40 periodicals
Number of teachers: 90
Number of students: 3,000

DEANS

Faculty of Economy: Prof. Dr hab. SIKOS T. TAMÁS
Faculty of Pedagogy: Dr MARGITY ERDÉLYI
Faculty of Reformed Theology: Dr JÁNOS MOLNÁR

UNIVERZITA KOMENSKÉHO V BRATISLAVE
(Comenius University in Bratislava)

Šafárikovo nám. 6, 818 06 Bratislava 16

Telephone: (2) 5292-1594
E-mail: kr@rec.uniba.sk
Internet: www.uniba.sk

Founded 1465 as Academia Istropolitana, re-opened with present name 1919
State control
Languages of instruction: English, Slovak
Academic year: October to June

Rector: Prof. Dr KAROL MIČIETA
Vice-Rector for Devt: Dr IVAN OSTROVSKÝ
Vice-Rector for Information Technology: Prof. Dr JÁN TURŇA
Vice-Rector for Int. Relations: Prof. Ing. Dr LUDOMÍR ŠLAHOR
Vice-Rector for Legislation: Prof. Dr MÁRIA PATAKYOVÁ
Vice-Rector for Science and Postgraduate Studies: Prof. Dr DUŠAN MEŠKO
Vice-Rector for Study: Prof. Dr JÁN PEKÁR
Registrar: Ing. MONIKA TARABOVÁ
Dir for Library: Dr DANIELA GONDOVÁ

Number of teachers: 2,100
Number of students: 27,000

Publication: Naša univerzita (12 a year)

DEANS

Evangelical Faculty of Theology: Mgr Dr LUBOMÍR BATKA
Faculty of Education: Prof. Dr ALICA VAN-ČOVÁ
Faculty of Law: Prof. Dr PAVOL KUBÍČEK
Faculty of Management: Prof. Dr JOZEF KOMORNÍK
Faculty of Mathematics, Physics and Informatics: Prof. Dr JOZEF MASARIK

Faculty of Medicine in Bratislava: Prof. Dr PETER LABAŠ
Faculty of Natural Sciences: Dr MILAN TRIZNA
Faculty of Pharmacy: Prof. Dr JÁN KYSELOVIČ
Faculty of Philosophy: Prof. Dr JAROSLAV ŠUŠOL
Faculty of Physical Education and Sports: Dr MIROSLAV HOLIENKA
Faculty of Protestant Theology: Mgr LUBOMÍR BATKA
Faculty of Social and Economic Sciences: Prof. Dr SILVIA MIHÁLIKOVÁ
Jessenius Faculty of Medicine in Martin: Prof. Dr JÁN DANKO
Roman Catholic Faculty of Theology: Dr MARIAN ŠURÁB

PROFESSORS

Faculty of Education (Račianska 59, 813 34 Bratislava; tel. (2) 4425-4960; e-mail sd@fedu.uniba.sk; internet www.fedu.uniba.sk):

BLANÁR, V., Slovak Language
ČIŽMÁR, J., Teaching of Mathematics
CVRKAL, I., Modern Non-Slavonic Philology, German Literature
KAČALA, J., Slovak Language
KOVÁČ, D., Educational Psychology
KUSIN, V., Philosophy
LECHTA, V., Special Education
MAJZLAN, O., Ecology
MARČOK, V., Theory and History of Slovak Literature
MISTRÍK, E., Synthetic Philosophy
OBDRŽÁLEK, Z., Education
ONDREIČKA, K., Graphics
PAŽITKA, M., Modern Non-Slavonic Philology
PIKÁLEK, Š., Social Work
POVCHANIČ, S., Modern Non-Slavonic Philology
POŽÁR, L., Psychology
RANINEC, J., Music Education
REPKA, R., Linguistics of Concrete Language Groups
ŠEDIVÝ, O., Descriptive Geometry
SLIACKY, O., Theory and History of Slovak Literature
ŠTRAUS, F., Theory and History of Slovak Literature
ŠULKA, R., Descriptive Geometry
ŠUPŠÁKOVÁ, B., Arts and Crafts
ŠVEC, M., Mathematics
TRUP, L., Modern Non-Slavonic Philology
VAŠEK, Š., Special Education
VIETOROVÁ, N., Modern Non-Slavonic Philology
ZELINA, M., Education

Faculty of Law (tel. (2) 5924-4104; e-mail sd_prafuk@flaw.uniba.sk; internet www.flaw.uniba.sk):

CÚTH, J., International Law
HUSÁR, E., Penal Law
KLIMKO, J., History of State and Law
MAMOJKA, M., Commercial Law
MATHERN, V., Penal Law
OVEČKOVÁ, O., Economic and Financial Law
PLANKOVÁ, O., Civil Law
POSLUCH, M., State Law
ŠKULTÉTY, P., Administrative Law
STRAKA, J., Czechoslovak History

Faculty of Management (POB 95, Odbojárov 10, 820 05 Bratislava; tel. (2) 5011-7526; e-mail sd@fm.uniba.sk; internet www.fm.uniba.sk):

HLAVATÁ, I., Finance
KOMORNÍK, J., Probability and Mathematical Statistics
KORČEK, L., Economics
PIŠKANIN, A., Economics and Industrial Management
RALBOVSKÝ, M., Finance
RUDY, J., Business Management

ZAPLETAL, V., Economics

Faculty of Mathematics, Physics and Informatics (Mlynská dolina, 842 48 Bratislava; tel. (2) 6542-6720; e-mail sd@fmph.uniba.sk; internet www.fmph.uniba.sk):

BEZÁK, V., Condensed Matter Physics
BRUNOVSKÝ, P., Mathematics
ČHORVÁT, D., Biophysics
ČIŽMÁR, J., Teaching Mathematics
DUBNIČKOVÁ, A., Physics
GRUSKA, J., Informatics
HIANÍK, T., Biophysics
HUBAČ, I., Biophysics
KABÁT, L., Economics
KAČUR, J., Mathematics
KATRIŇÁK, T., Mathematics
KODNÁR, R., Mathematics
KOSTYRKO, P., Mathematics
LUKÁČ, P., Plasma Physics
MASARIK, J., Physics
MEDVEĎ, M., Mathematics
MOCZO, P., Physics
NOGA, M., Theoretical Physics
PÁZMÁN, A., Mathematics
PIŠÚT, J., Theoretical Physics
PLESNÍK, J., Mathematics
POVINEC, P., Physics
PREŠNAJDER, P., Physics
ROVAN, B., Informatics
RUŽIČKA, J., Physics
ŠALÁT, T., Mathematics
ŠÁRO, S., Nuclear Physics
SITÁR, B., Physics
SKALNÝ, J., Physics
ŠTRBA, A., Experimental Physics
TOMLAIN, J., Meteorology and Climatology

Faculty of Medicine in Bratislava (Špitálska 24, 813 72 Bratislava; tel. (2) 5296-1736; e-mail sd@fmed.uniba.sk; internet ww.fmed.uniba.sk):

ÁGHOVÁ, L., Public Health
BADA, V., Internal Medicine
BAKOSS, P., Epidemiology
BALAŽOVJECH, I., Internal Medicine
BÁLINT, O., Infectious Diseases
BENIAK, M., Social Medicine
BEŇUŠKA, J., Normal Anatomy, Histology and Embryology
BERGENDI, L., Biochemistry
BILICKÝ, J., Radiology
BOROVSKÝ, M., Gynaecology and Obstetrics
BREZA, J., Urology
BUC, M., Immunology
BUCHVALD, J., Dermatovenereology
CÁRSKY, J., Medicinal Chemistry and Biochemistry
DANIHEL, L., Pathological Anatomy and Forensic Medicine
ĎURAČKOVÁ, Z., Biochemistry
ĎURIŠ, I., Internal Medicine
FERENČÍK, M., Immunology and Immunochemistry
GERINEC, A., Ophthalmology
HOLOMÁŇ, K., Gynaecology and Obstetrics
HORŇÁK, M., Urology
HULÍN, L., Normal and Pathological Anatomy
JAKUBOVSKÝ, J., Pathological Anatomy and Forensic Medicine
KAPELLEROVÁ, A., Paediatrics
KOTULOVÁ, D., Microbiology
KOVÁCS, L., Paediatrics
KRIŠKA, M., Pharmacology
MAKAI, F., Orthopaedics and Traumatology
MICHALKOVÁ, D., Paediatrics
MIKEŠ, Z., Internal Medicine, Cardiology
MRÁZ, P., Anatomy
OLÁH, Z., Ophthalmology
ONDRUŠ, D., Oncology
PONŤUCH, P., Internal Medicine
PROFANT, M., Otorhinolaryngology
REDHAMMER, R., Internal Medicine
REMKOVÁ, A., Internal Medicine
SATKO, I., Stomatology
SIMAN, J., Surgery

ŠIMKO, F., Normal and Pathological Physiology
ŠTRMEŇ, P., Ophthalmology
ŠTVRTINOVÁ, V., Internal Medicine
ŠUŠKA, P., Gynaecology and Obstetrics
ŠVEC, J., Oncology
TRAUBNER, P., Neurology
TURČÁNI, M., Normal and Pathological Physiology
TURČÁNI, P., Neurology
VARSÍK, P., Neurology
VAŠKO, J., Stomatology
VOJTASSAK, J., Surgery
ZAVIAČIČ, M., Pathological Anatomy and Forensic Medicine
ZLATOŠ, J., Normal Anatomy, Histology and Embryology
ZLATOŠ, L., Normal and Pathological Physiology
ŽUCHA, L., Psychiatry

Faculty of Natural Sciences (Mlynská dolina, 842 15 Bratislava 4; tel. (2) 6029-6111; e-mail www-admin@fns.uniba.sk; internet www.fns.uniba.sk):

ADAMČÍKOVÁ, Ľ., Physical Chemistry and Chemical Physics
EBRINGER, L., Microbiology
GROLMUS, J., Genetics
HENSEL, K., Zoology
HOLBA, V., Physical Chemistry
HOVORKA, D., Petrology
HUDÁK, J., Plant Physiology
JEDLIČKA, L., Zoology
JURÁNI, B., Pedology
KELLÖ, V., Physical Chemistry and Chemical Physics
KETTNER, M., Microbiology
KMINIAK, M., Ecology
KOLAROV, J., Biochemistry
KOLLÁROVÁ, M., Biochemistry and Molecular Biology
KOVÁČ, L., Biochemistry
KOVÁČ, M., Stratum Geology, Geology and Palaeontology, Applied Geophysics
KRAUS, I., Applied Geophysics
KRCHO, J., Cartography
MACÁŠEK, F., Nuclear Chemistry
MASAROVIČOVÁ, E., Plant Physiology
MATYS, M., Engineering Geology
MIADOKOVÁ, E., Genetics
MLÁDEK, J., Human and Regional Geography
ONDRÁŠIK, R., Hydrology and Engineering Geology
ORSZÁGH, L., Zoology
PAULOV, J., Human and Regional Geography
ROJKOVIČ, I., Stratum Geology, Geology and Palaeontology, Applied Geophysics
SCHWENDT, P., Inorganic Chemistry
ŠEFARA, J., Stratum Geology, Geology and Palaeontology, Applied Geophysics
ŠEVČÍK, P., Physical Chemistry
SILNÝ, P., Theory of Teaching Chemistry
ŠOJÁK, L., Analytical Chemistry
ŠOMŠÁK, L., Botany
ŠUBÍK, J., Biochemistry
ŠUCHA, V., Stratum Geology
TOMA, Š., Organic Chemistry
URBAN, M., Chemical Physics
VLČEK, D., Genetics
VOZÁROVÁ, A., Mineralogy, Petrology and Geochemistry
ZAŤKO, M., Geography
ŽÚRKOVÁ, Ľ., Inorganic Chemistry

Faculty of Pharmacy (Odbojárov 10, 832 32 Bratislava; tel. (2) 5557-2022; e-mail sd@fpharm.uniba.sk; internet www.fpharm.uniba.sk):

BALGAVÝ, P., Physics
ČIŽMÁRIK, J., Pharmaceutical Chemistry
DEVÍNSKY, F., Pharmaceutical Chemistry
FOLTÁN, V., Public Health
GRANČAI, D., Pharmacognosis
HAVRÁNEK, E., Pharmaceutical Chemistry

KOVÁCS, P., Biochemistry
MLYNARČÍK, D., Galenic Pharmacy
PŠENÁK, M., Biochemistry
RAK, J., Galenic Pharmacy
REMKO, M., Physical Chemistry and Chemical Physics
SARKA, K., Physical Chemistry and Chemical Physics
ŠPRINGER, V., Social Pharmacy
ŠVEC, P., Pharmacology

Faculty of Philosophy (Gondova 2, POB 32, 814 99 Bratislava; tel. (2) 5292-1078; e-mail sd@fphil.uniba.sk; internet www.fphil.uniba.sk):

BAĎURÍK, J., History
BAJZÍKOVÁ, E., Slovak Language
BAKOŠ, J., Fine Art
CHALUPKA, L., Music
DOLNÍK, J., General Linguistics
DUDOK, M., Slavonic Philology
HERETÍK, A., Psychology
HOLEC, R., History
HRČKOVÁ, N., Music
HVIŠČ, J., Slavonic Philology
KIMLIČKA, S., Librarianship and Information Science
KOLLÁRIK, T., Psychology
KREKOVIČ, E., Archaeology
KUKLICA, P., Classical Philology
KUSÝ, M., Philosophy
MARCELLI, M., Philosophy
MÉSZÁROS, O., Modern Non-Slavonic Philology
MICHÁLEK, J., Ethnography
MIKULA, V., Slovak Literature
MLACEK, J., Slovak Language
PAULÍNY, J., Modern Non-Slavonic Philology
PERHÁCS, J., Pedagogy
POTZLOVÁ-MALIKOVÁ, M., Fine Art
POVCHANIČ, Š., Modern Non-Slavonic Philology
PŠENÁK, J., Pedagogy
SCHENK, J., Sociology
SOKOLOVSKÝ, L., History
SVEC, S., Pedagogy
SZOMOLÁNYIOVÁ, S., Political Science
TANDLICHOVÁ, E., Theory of English Language Teaching
TUŠER, A., Journalism
VOJTEK, J., General History
ZAMBOR, M., Philosophy
ŽIGO, M., Philosophy
ŽIGO, P., Slovak Language
ŽILINEK, M., Pedagogy

Faculty of Physical Education and Sports (Nábrežie arm. generála L. Sobodu, 814 69 Bratislava; tel. (2) 5441-1909; e-mail sd@fsport.uniba.sk; internet www.fsport.uniba.sk):

GREXA, J., History
HAMAR, D., Sport Kinanthropology
HELLEBRANDT, V., Sport Kinanthropology
KAMPMILLER, T., Sport Kinanthropology
KASA, J., Sport Kinanthropology
MORAVEC, R., Sport Kinanthropology
ŠTULRAJTER, V., Physiology

Faculty of Protestant Theology (Bartókova 8, 811 02 Bratislava; tel. (2) 6728-8250; e-mail sd@fevth.uniba.sk; internet www.fevth.uniba.sk):

BÁNDY, J., Protestant Theology
KIŠŠ, L., Protestant Theology

Faculty of Social and Economic Sciences (Mlynské luhy 4, 821 05 Bratislava; tel. (2) 2066-9800; e-mail sd@fses.uniba.sk; internet www.fses.uniba.sk):

KABÁT, L., Economics
KLEIN, F., Therapeutics and Special Education
KOLLÁRIK, T., Psychology
KUSÝ, M., Philosophy
KVASNIČKA, V., Informatics

Jessenius Faculty of Medicine in Martin (Malá Hora 4A, 036 01 Martin; tel. (43) 4133-305; e-mail sdek@jfmed.uniba.sk; internet www.jfmed.uniba.sk):

BÁNOVČIN, P., Paediatrics
BUCHANCOVÁ, J., Internal Medicine
BUCHANEC, J., Paediatrics
DANKO, J., Gynaecology and Obstetrics
DROBNÝ, M., Neurology
HAJTMAN, A., Otorhinolaryngology
HANÁČEK, J., Physiology and Pathophysiology
JAKUŠ, J., Pathophysiology
JAVORKA, K., Physiology and Pathophysiology
JURKO, A., Paediatrics
KLIMENT, J., Urology
KORPÁŠ, J., Pathological Physiology
KUBISZ, P., Internal Medicine
LEHOTSKÝ, J., Biochemistry
MAZÚCH, J., Surgery
MEŠKO, D., Internal Medicine
MÉZEŠ, V., Medicinal Biochemistry
MOKÁŇ, D. M., Internal Medicine
NOSÁĽOVÁ, G., Pharmacology
NOVOMESKÝ, F., Forensic Medicine
PÉČ, J., Dermatovenereology
PLANK, L., Pathological Anatomy
SÁMEL, M., Epidemiology
STRAKA, S., Epidemiology
STRÁNSKY, A., Physiology and Pathophysiology
TATÁR, M., Normal and Pathological Physiology
ZIBOLEN, M., Paediatrics

Roman Catholic Faculty of Theology (Kapitulska 26, 814 58 Bratislava; tel. (2) 5443-5109; e-mail sd@frcth.uniba.sk; internet www.frcth.uniba.sk):

BOŠMÁNSKY, K., Catholic Theology
ĎURICA, M., Catholic Theology
JUDÁK, V., Catholic Theology
KUTARŇA, J., Theology
VRAGAŠ, S., Catholic Theology

UNIVERZITA KONŠTANTÍNA FILOZOFA V NITRE
(Constantine the Philosopher University in Nitra)

Tr. A. Hlinku 1, 949 74 Nitra

Telephone: (37) 6408-001

E-mail: ukf@ukf.sk

Internet: www.ukf.sk

Founded 1959 as Pedagogical Institute, current status 1992, current name adopted 1996

State control

Languages of instruction: English, French, German, Hungarian, Italian, Russian, Slovak, Spanish

Academic year: September to August

Rector: Prof. Dr LIBOR VOZÁR
Vice-Rector for Academic Affairs: Dr RUŽENA ŽILOVÁ
Vice-Rector for Implementation of IT: Mgr Dr JÁN SKALKA
Vice-Rector for Lifelong Learning: Dr MARCELA VEREŠOVÁ
Vice-Rector for Public Relations and Social Affairs: Dr MIROSLAV TVRDOŇ
Vice-Rector for Science and Research: Prof. Dr MÁRIA BAUEROVÁ
Bursar: Ing. ĽUBICA EHRENHOLDOVÁ
Dir for Library: Dr ANEŽKA STRIHOVÁ

Library of 264,378 vols, 334 periodical titles
Number of teachers: 586
Number of students: 10,534

DEANS

Faculty of Arts: Prof. Dr BERNARD GARAJ
Faculty of Central European Studies: Dr ATTILA KOMZSÍK

Faculty of Education: Prof. Dr EVA SZÓR-
ÁDOVÁ
Faculty of Natural Sciences: Prof. Dr ĽUBO-
MÍR ŽELENICKÝ
Faculty of Social Sciences and Health Care:
Prof. Dr EVA SOLLÁROVÁ

PROFESSORS
BAKOŠ, E., Nursing
BAUEROVÁ, M., Botany and Genetics
BEŇUŠKOVÁ, Z., Ethnology
BÍLEK, M., Chemistry
BUJNA, J., Archaeology
CHRENEK, P., Zoology and Anthropology
ČUKAN, J., Culture and Tourism
DIATKA, C., Ethics
DURNÝ, R., Physics
FRANEK, L., Spanish Language
FULIER, J., Mathematics
GABURA, J., Social Work
GADUŠOVÁ, Z., English Language
GARAJ, B., Ethnology
GERO, Š., Mass Media/Marketing
GLOVŇA, J., Slovak Language
GROMOVÁ, E., Translation and Interpreting
HAJKO, D., Culturology
HAŠKOVÁ, A., Technical Education
HEČKOVÁ, J., History
HRAŠKA, Š., Botany and Genetics
HREŠKO, J., Ecology
JOMOVÁ, K., Chemistry
KAPSOVÁ, E., Literary Communication
KÁRPÁTI, A., Teacher Training with Hungar-
ian as a Language of Instruction
KECSKÉS, A., Physics
KERUĽOVÁ, M., Slovak Literature
KLUVANEC, D., Physics
KMEŤ, T., Informatics
KOMLÓSI, L., English Language Teaching
KONEČNÝ, M., Geography
KOPRDA, P., Italian Language
KORINA, N., Russian Language
KOZÍK, T., Technical Education
KRALČÁK, Ľ., Slovak Language
KRAUS, I., Gemology
KRNO, S., Politology/European Studies
KURINCOVÁ, V., Pedagogy
LÁSZLÓ, B., Teacher Training with Hungar-
ian as a language of instruction
LAURINČÍK, J., Zoology and Anthropology
LÍŠKOVÁ, A., Urgent Medicine
LOHNERT, J., Urgent Medicine
LUŽICA, R., Romany Studies
MALÁ, E., English Language Teaching
MARKECHOVÁ, D., Mathematics
MAZUR, S., Romany Studies
MIKULECKÝ, P., Informatics
MIŠŠÍKOVÁ, G., English Language
MLYNČEK, M., Nursing
MÜGLOVÁ, D., Translation and Interpreting
NAGY, G., Hungarian Language
PETROVÁ, G., Pedagogy
PETROVIČ, F., Ecology
PLESNÍK, L., Literary Communication
POKRIVČÁK, A., English Language
POSPÍŠIL, I., Central European Languages
and Cultures
PUSZTAY, J., Hungarian Language
ŘEHULKA, E., Psychology
ROMSAUER, P., Archaeology
RÓZOVÁ, Z., Ecology
RUISEL, I., Psychology
ŠEDIVÝ, O., Mathematics
ŠEIDLER, P., Pedagogy
ŠIMONEK, J., Physical Education
SIROTKIN, A., Zoology and Anthropology
SOKOLOVÁ, J., Russian Language
SOLLÁROVÁ, E., Psychology
SVAČINA, Š., Nursing
SVĚTLÍK, J., Mass Media/Marketing
SWIATKIEWICZ, W., Sociology
SZCZEPANSKI, M., Sociology
SZÓRÁDOVÁ, E., Music Education
TIRPÁKOVÁ, A., Mathematics
TUČNÁ, E., Slovak Literature
TURČÁNI, M., Informatics

VALKO, M., Chemistry
VAŇKO, J., Slovak Language
VOZÁR, L., Physics
WIEDERMANN, E., Museology
ZACHARELLO, M., Italian Language
ZELENICKÁ, E., Russian Language
ZELENICKÝ, L., Physics
ZELENKA, M., Central European Languages
and Cultures
ŽEŇUCH, P., Culturology
ŽILKA, T., Central European Languages and
Cultures
ZOZUĽAK, J., Philosophy

UNIVERZITA MATEJA BEL V BANSKEJ BYSTRICI
(Matej Bel University Banská Bystrica)

Národná 12, 974 01 Banská Bystrica

Telephone: (48) 4461-111
E-mail: rektorka@umb.sk
Internet: www.umb.sk

Founded 1992 by merger of Pedagogic Fac-
ulty and School of Economics
State control
Academic year: September to June

Rector: Prof. Dr. BEATA KOSOVÁ
Vice-Rector for Devt and Informatization:
Prof. Dr STANISLAV HOLEC
Vice-Rector for Int. Cooperation: Dr IGOR
KOSÍR
Vice-Rector for Pedagogic Activities: Prof.
Ing. Dr MILOTA VETRÁKOVÁ
Vice-Rector for Public Relations: Dr ŠTEFAN
PORUBSKÝ
Vice-Rector for Science and Research: Dr
ALEXANDRA BITUŠIKOVÁ
Bursar: Ing. RUŽENA FRAŇOVÁ
Dir for Library: Dr LUDMILA HOMOLOVÁ

Library of 220,000 vols (incl. books, periodicals and documents)
Number of students: 7,500

DEANS
Faculty of Economics: Ing. Dr VLADIMÍR
HIADLOVSKÝ
Faculty of Education: Prof. Dr VOJTECH
KORIM
Faculty of Humanities: Mgr Dr VLADIMÍR
BILOVESKÝ
Faculty of Law: Prof. DR MRÁZ STANISLAV
Faculty of Natural Sciences: Dr ALFONZ
GAJDOŠ
Faculty of Political Sciences and Inter-
national Relations: Prof. Dr JÁN KOPER

UNIVERZITA PAVLA JOZEFA ŠAFÁRIKA V KOŠICIACH
(Pavol Jozef Šafárik University of Košice)

Šrobárova 2, 041 80 Košice

Telephone: (55) 2341-100
E-mail: rektor@upjs.sk
Internet: www.upjs.sk

Founded 1657 as Academia Cassoviensis,
present name and status 1959
State control
Languages of instruction: English, Slovak
Academic year: September to July

Rector: Prof. Dr LADISLAV MIROSSAY
Vice-Rector for Devt: Prof. Dr RUŽENA TKÁ-
ČOVÁ
Vice-Rector for Int. Relations: Mgr Dr SLÁVKA
TOMAŠČÍKOVÁ
Vice-Rector for Science and Research: Prof.
Dr JURAJ ČERNÁK
Vice-Rector for Univ. Education and Infor-
mation Technologies: Prof. Dr PAVOL
SOVÁK
Bursar: Ing. KAROL LÁSZLÓ
Dir for Library: Dr DANIELA DŽUGANOVÁ

Number of teachers: 500
Number of students: 5,700

Publications: *Acta iuridica Cassoviensia*,
*Folia Facultatis Medicae Universitatis
Safarikianae Cassoviensia*, *Thaiszia*

DEANS
Faculty of Arts: Prof. Dr JÁN GBÚR
Faculty of Law: Dr GABRIELA DOBROVIČOVÁ
Faculty of Medicine: Prof. Dr LEONARD
SIEGFRIED
Faculty of Public Administration: Prof. Dr
IGOR PALÚŠ
Faculty of Science: Dr GABRIEL SEMANIŠIN

PROFESSORS
Faculty of Law:
GAŠPAR, M., Administrative Law
PALÚŠ, I., Administrative Law
Faculty of Medicine:
JURKOVIČ, I., Pathology
KAFKA, J., Psychiatry
KALINA, I., General Biology
KOHÚT, A., Pharmacology
MYDLÍK, M., Internal Medicine
PAČIN, J., Gynaecology and Obstetrics
ŠAŠINKA, A., Paediatrics
ŠULLA, I., Neurosurgery
TOMORI, Z., Physiology
VAJÓ, J., Surgery
Faculty of Science:
AHLERS, I., General Biology
AHLERSOVÁ, E., Animal Physiology
BUKOVSKÝ, L., Mathematics
CHALUPKA, S., Theoretical Physics
FEHER, A., Physics
GÁLOVÁ, M., Analytical Chemistry
GYŐRYOVÁ, K., Inorganic Chemistry
HONČARIV, R., Genetics
JENDROĽ, S., Mathematics
KRISTIÁN, F., Organic Chemistry
MIŠUROVÁ, E., General Biology
PODHRADSKÝ, D., Biochemistry
SÍLEŠ, E., Physics
Dept of Languages:
RYBÁK, J., Slavonic Languages

UNIVERZITA SV. CYRILA A METODA V TRNAVA
(University of Saints Cyril and Methodius in Trnava)

Námestie Jozefa Herdu 2, 917 01 Trnava

Telephone: (33) 5565-128
E-mail: info@ucm.sk
Internet: www.ucm.sk

Founded 1997
State control
Academic year: October to June

Rector: Ing. Dr JOZEF MATÚŠ
Vice-Rector for Devt and Social Issues: Prof.
Dr MÁRIA KOVÁROVÁ
Vice-Rector for Educational Activities and
Accreditation: Dr DAGMAR VALENTOVIČOVÁ
Vice-Rector for Int. Relations and Public
Relations: Dr MARTIN KLUS
Vice-Rector for Research and Devt Activities:
Prof. Ing. Dr JOZEF LEHOTAY
Bursar: ROMAN MAREŠ
Dir for Library: Mgr DARINA KRÁĽOVÁ

Number of teachers: 220
Number of students: 3,130

Publications: *Atteliér* (print and online,
www.attelier.sk), *Journal of Applied
Mathematics, Statistics and Informatics
(JAMSI)* (print and online, jamsi.fp-
v.ucm.sk), *Journal of Information Technologies* (print and online, ki.fpv.ucm.sk/
casopis), *Nova Biotechnologica et Chimica*
(print and online, www.nbc-journal
.fpv.ucm.sk), *Slovenská politologická revue*
(Slovak Journal of Political Sciences, print
and online, revue.kpol.ff.ucm.sk), *Societas
Et Res Publica* (4 a year, print and online,
serp.fsv.ucm.sk)

DEANS

Faculty of Arts: Prof. Dr Ján Danek
Faculty of Mass Media Communication: Dr Dana Petranová
Faculty of Natural Sciences: Ing. Dr Stanislav Hostin
Faculty of Social Sciences: Dr Peter Horváth

UNIVERZITA VETERINÁRSKEHO LEKÁRSTVA A FARMÁCIE V KOŠICIACH
(University of Veterinary Medicine and Pharmacy in Košice)

Komenského 73, 041 81 Košice
Telephone: (55) 6325-293
E-mail: sekretariat2@uvlf.sk
Internet: www.uvlf.sk
Founded 1949 as Veterinary College in Košice, current name adopted 2010
State control
Languages of instruction: English, Slovak
Academic year: September to June
Programmes in animal health, cynology, food quality, food safety, hygiene, immunology, neuroscience, pharmacy, virology
Chancellor: Mgr Ľudmila Kundríková
Rector: Prof. Dr Emil Pilipčinec
Vice-Rector for Academic Affairs: Prof. Dr Jana Mojžišová
Vice-Rector for Devt and Quality Assurance: Dr Peter Korim
Vice-Rector for Doctoral Studies: Prof. Ing. Dr Oľga Ondrašovičová
Vice-Rector for Research and Devt Activities and External Relations: Prof. Dr Jaroslav Legáth
Bursar: Dr Silvia Rolfová
Librarian: Dr Libuša Bodnárová
Library of 91,133 vols, 114 periodicals
Number of teachers: 220
Number of students: 2,020
Publications: *Folia Veterinaria* (4 a year), *Slovenský veterinársky časopis* (6 a year)

PROFESSORS

Bajová, V., Infectious Diseases
Bíreš, J., Internal Diseases of Ruminants and Swine
Blahovec, J., Biochemistry
Cabadaj, R., Food Hygiene and Food Technology
Danko, J., Anatomy and Histology
Kačmárik, J., Obstetrics and Gynaecology
Kováč, G., Internal Diseases of Ruminants and Swine
Legáth, J., Toxicology
Lenartová, V., Chemistry and Biophysics
Lešník, F., Biology
Levkut, M., Pathological Anatomy
Maráček, I., Physiology
Maretta, M., Anatomy and Histology
Mesároš, P., Andrology
Mikula, I., Microbiology and Immunology
Paulík, Š., Infectious Diseases
Vajda, V., Nutrition and Veterinary Dietetics
Várady, J., Comparative Physiology
Zibrín, M., Anatomy and Histology

ŽILINSKÁ UNIVERZITA V ŽILINE
(University of Žilina)

Univerzitná 8215/1, 010 26 Žilina
Telephone: (41) 5135-001
E-mail: rektor@uniza.sk
Internet: www.uniza.sk
Founded 1953 as Vysoká Škola Železničná (Railways Higher Education Institute) in Prague, current name adopted 1996
State control
Languages of instruction: English, Slovak
Academic year: September to July

Rector: Prof. Ing. Dr Tatiana Čorejová
Vice-Rector for Devt: Prof. Dr Milan Malcho
Vice-Rector for Education: Dr Milan Trunkvalter
Vice-Rector for Foreign and Public Relations: Ing. Dr Peter Fabián
Vice-Rector for Science and Research: Prof. Ing. Dr Ján Čelko
Bursar: Jana Gjašíková
Dir for Univ. Library: Dr Marta Sakalová
Library of 216,025 vols
Number of teachers: 700
Number of students: 10,150
Publications: *Komunikácie–vedecké listy ŽU* (Communications–Scientific Letters, 4 a year), *Krizový Manažment* (Crisis Management), *Materiálové inžinierstvo* (Materials Engineering, 1 a year), *Pokrok v Elektrickom a Elektromikrom Inžinigrstve* (Advances in Electrical and Electronic Engineering), *Práce a štúdie ŽU* (Works and Studies, 1 a year), *Zborník z konferencie TRANSCOM* (Proceedings of the TRANSCOM Conf., every 2 years), *Zborník z vedeckých konferencií ŽU* (Proceedings of the Scientific Confs, every 5 years), *Znalectvo-Cestná doprava, Elektrotechnika, Strojarstvo* (Expertise in Road Transport, Electrotechnology and Mechanical Engineering, 4 a year), *Znalectvo-Stavebnictvo a Podnikové Hospodárstvo* (Expertise in Civil Engineering and Enterprise Economics, 4 a year)

DEANS

Faculty of Civil Engineering: Prof. Dr Josef Vičan
Faculty of Electrical Engineering: Prof. Ing. Dr Milan Dado
Faculty of Humanities: Dr Vlasta Cabanová
Faculty of Management Science and Informatics: Prof. Ing. Dr Karol Matiaško
Faculty of Mechanical Engineering: Prof. Ing. Dr Milan Sága
Faculty of Operation and Economics of Transport and Communications: Prof. Ing. Anna Križanová
Faculty of Special Engineering: Prof. Ing. Dr Ladislav Šimák

PROFESSORS

Faculty of Civil Engineering (Univerzitna 8215/1, 010 26 Žilina; tel. (41) 5135-501; e-mail info@fstav.uniza.sk; internet svf.uniza.sk):

Benčat, J., Structural Mechanics
Bujnák, J., Theory and Construction of Engineering Structures
Čelko, J., Theory and Construction of Engineering Structures
Čorej, J., Theory and Construction of Engineering Structures
Kovařík, K., Theory and Construction of Engineering Structures
Melcer, J., Structural Mechanics
Mikolaj, J., Theory and Construction of Engineering Structures
Moravčík, M., Applied Mechanics
Schlosser, F., Theory and Construction of Engineering Structures
Vičan, J., Theory and Construction of Engineering Structures

Faculty of Electrical Engineering (Univerzitná 1, 010 26 Žilina; tel. (41) 5132-051; e-mail dean.office@fel.uniza.sk; internet fel.uniza.sk):

Blunár, K., Communications Engineering
Bury, P., Physics of Condensed Matter and Acoustics
Čápová, K., Theoretical Electrotechnology
Dado, M., Telecommunications
Dobrucký, B., Electric Traction and Electric Drives

Hrabovcová, V., Electric Traction and Electric Drives
Neveselý, M., Theoretical Electrotechnology
Trstenský, D., Communications Engineering
Vittek, J., Electric Traction and Electric Drives

Faculty of Humanities (Univerzitná 8215/1, 010 26 Žilina; tel. (41) 5136-101; e-mail zuzana.murarikova@fpv.uniza.sk; internet fhv.uniza.sk):

Baják, I., Physics
Boichuk, O., Mathematics
Čáp, I., Physics
Diblík, J., Applied Mathematics
Konvit, M., Transport and Communications Technology
Kurcz, J., Musicology
Oberuč, J., Education and Psychology
Polonský, D., Education and Psychology
Volf, I., Teaching of Physics

Faculty of Management Science and Informatics (Univerzitná 1, 010 26 Žilina; tel. (41) 5134-050; e-mail dekan@fri.uniza.sk; internet www.fri.uniza.sk):

Alexík, M., Information and Control Systems
Cenek, P., Transport and Communications Technology
Hittmár, S., Management in Transport
Janáček, J., Transport and Communications Technology
Manuliak, I., Information and Control Systems
Marček, D., Management
Skýva, L., Technical Cybernetics

Faculty of Mechanical Engineering (Veľký diel, 010 26 Žilina; tel. (41) 5132-501; e-mail dsjf@fstroj.uniza.sk; internet www.fstroj.uniza.sk):

Bokuvka, O., Materials Engineering
Dzimko, M., Machine Elements and Mechanisms
Gregor, M., Industrial Engineering and Management
Hlavňa, V., Transportation and Handling Technologies
Honner, K., Workplace Arrangement
Konečná, R., Material Engineering
Košturiak, J., Industrial Engineering and Management
Kukuča, P., Transportation and Handling Technologies
Kuric, I., Mechanical Engineering
Málik, L., Machine Elements and Mechanisms
Medvecký, Š., Machine Elements and Mechanisms
Meško, J., Mechanical Engineering
Mičieta, B., Industrial Management
Obmaščík, M., Mechanical Engineering
Palček, P., Materials Engineering
Skočovský, P., Materials Engineering
Sládek, G., Mechanical Engineering
Zvolenský, P., Transport and Handling Technologies

Faculty of Operation and Economics of Transport and Communications (Univerzitná 1, 010 26 Žilina; tel. (41) 5133-050; internet fpedas.uniza.sk):

Cisko, Š., Economics
Čorejová, T., Transport and Communications Technology
Gnap, J., Economics
Havel, K., Transport and Communications Technology
Hollarek, T., Transport Engineering
Kazda, A., Transport and Communications Technology
Kevický, D., Transport and Communications Technology
Královenský, J., Economics

Kříž, J., Transport and Communications Technology

Liščák, Š., Transport and Communications Technology

Nedelka, M., Transport and Communications Technology

Sedláček, B., Economics

Štofková, J., Economics

Surovec, P., Transport and Communications Technology

Voleský, K., Transport and Communications Technology

Faculty of Special Engineering (Ul. 1. mája 32, 011 17 Žilina; tel. (41) 5136-601; e-mail dekanfsi@fsi.uniza.sk; internet fsi.uniza.sk):

Maca, J., Operational Research, Stochastic Dynamics of Systems

Mikolaj, J., Transport Economics

Poledňák, P., Fire Protection

Šeidl, M., Logistics, Transport Technology

Šimák, L., Crisis Management

Colleges

Bratislavská Medzinárodná Škola Liberálnych Stúdií (Bratislava International School of Liberal Arts): Grösslingova 53, 811 09 Bratislava; tel. (2) 5923-4312; e-mail bisla@bisla.sk; internet www.bisla.sk; f. 2006; courses in arts, int. relations, philosophy, political science; Rector Dr Samuel Abrahám; Vice-Rector Prof. Dr František Novosád; publ. *Kritikca a Kontext* (Critics and Context, irregular, print and online, www.kritika.sk).

Dubnický Technologický Inštitút v Dubnici nad Váhom (Dubnica Technology Institute in Dubnica nad Váhom): ul. Sládkovičova 533/20, 018 41 Dubnica nad Váhom; tel. (42) 4424-123; e-mail studijne@dti.sk; internet www.dti.sk; f. 2006; offers Bachelors and Masters degrees in vocational subjects and practical training; Rector Prof. Dr Erich Petlák; Pro-Rector for Devt Dr Lubica Gáborová; Pro-Rector for Education and Marketing Dr Karol Korintuš; Pro-Rector for Research Dr Tomáš Lengyelfalusy; Head of Library Marcela Kopincová; publs *Acta Technologica Dubnicae* (2 a year), *DTIčko*.

Vysoká Škola Bezpečnostného Manažérstva v Košiciach (University of Security Management in Košice): Kukučínova 17, 040 01 Košice; tel. (55) 7204-174; e-mail vsbm@vsbm.sk; internet www.vsbm.sk; f. 2006; undergraduate and engineering degrees in economic and management, juridical specialization, security; Rector Prof. Ing. Dr Marián Mesároš; Vice-Rector for Education and External Relations Ing. Dr Imrich Dufinec; Vice-Rector for Informatics and Devt Ing. Dr Peter Lošonczi; Vice-Rector for Science and Research Prof. Ing. Dr Vladimír Sedlák; Dir for Libraries Ing. Mária Schürgerová; publs *Košická bezpečnostná revue* (2 a year, print and online, www.vsbm.sk/revue.html), *zbor-*

ník vedeckých prác, Zóna 10 (4 a year (print and online, www.vsbm.sk/zona_10.html).

Vysoká Škola Ekonómie a Manažmentu Verejnej Správy v Bratislave (School of Economics and Management in Public Administration in Bratislava): Furdekova 16, 851 04 Bratislava; e-mail sekretariat@vsemvs.sk; internet www.vsemvs.sk; f. 2004; undergraduate and postgraduate degrees in economics, public administration and management of small and medium enterprises; Rector Ing. Dr Viera Cibáková; Vice-Rector for Devt Ing. Dr Viera Sysáková; Vice-Rector for Entrepreneurial Activities Dr Zoltán Rózsa; Vice-Rector for Full-Time Education Ing. Dr Anna Kachaňáková, Vice-Rector for Part-Time Education Ing. Dr Judita Táncoàšová; Vice-Rector for Public Relations and Int. Cooperation Ing. Dr Stanislav Filip; Vice-Rector for Science and Research Prof. Ing. Dr Štefan Slávik; publ. *Verejná správa a regionálny rozvoj*.

Vysoká Škola Manažmentu v Trenčíne (College of Management in Trenčín/City University of Seattle): Bezručova 64, 911 01 Trenčín; tel. (32) 6529-337; e-mail trencin@vsm.sk; internet www.vsm.sk; f. 1999; library: 23,000 vols, 100 periodicals; undergraduate and postgraduate degrees in business admin., knowledge management; br. in Bratislava; Rector Prof. Dr Branislav Lichardus; Dean David Griffin; Library Dir Mgr Lucia Baginová.

Vysoká Škola Medzinárodného Podnikania ISM Slovakia v Prešove (International School of Management Slovakia): Duchnovičovo námestie 1, 080 01 Prešov; tel. (51) 7581-798; e-mail sekretariatrektora@ismpo.sk; internet www.ismpo.sk; f. 2005; depts of economics, management and marketing, social sciences; Rector Prof. Dr Lev Bukovský; Pro-Rector for Devt Dr Eva Dolinská; Pro-Rector for Education Ing. Dr Renáta Madzinová.

Vysoká Škola v Sládkovičove (College in Sládkovičovo): Fučíkova 269, 925 21 Sládkovičovo; tel. (31) 7881-711; e-mail info@vssladkovicovo.sk; internet www.vssladkovicovo.sk; f. 2005; faculties of law, public policy and public administration, social studies; Rector Prof. Ing. Dr Mojmír Mamojka; Pro-Rector for Education Dr Boris Susko; Pro-Rector for Int. Relations, Scientific Research and Publishing Activity Prof. dr Miroslav Daniš.

Vysoká Škola Zdravotníctva a Sociálnej Práce Sv. Alžbety (St. Elizabeth College of Health and Social Work in Bratislava): Palackého č. 1, POB 104, 810 00 Bratislava; tel. (2) 5778-0613; internet www.vssvalzbety.sk; f. 2003; depts of nursing, prenatal and perinatal psychology, medicine and social sciences, psychology, public health and health management, social work, social work with ethnic minorities, refugees and human rights, sociology, theoretical disciplines, laboratory investigation methods and dental technician training, tropical health;

Rector Prof. Dr Vladimír Krčméry; Pro-Rector for Devt Prof. Dr Peter Juriš; Pro-Rector for Education Prof. Dr Stefan Galbavý; Pro-Rector for Research and Devt Activities Prof. Dr Jozef Matulník; Head of Library Mgr Mária Červenková.

Schools of Art and Music

Akadémia umení v Banskej Bystrici (Academy of Arts in Banská Bystrici): ul. Jána Kollára 22, 974 00 Banská Bystrici; tel. (48) 4320-111; e-mail rektor@aku.sk; internet www.aku.sk; f. 1997; faculties of dramatic arts, fine arts and performing arts; 593 students; Rector Mgr Dr Matúš Oľha; Pro-Rector Prof. Ľudovít Hološka; Pro-Rector Mgr Dr Mária Strenáčiková; Pro-Rector Dr Peter Vítko; Dir for Library Ivana Badinská.

Konzervatórium Košice (Conservatory in Košice): Timonova 2, 042 03 Košice; tel. (55) 6222-092; e-mail kon-ke@stonline.sk; internet www.konke.sk; f. 1951; depts of accordion, brass and percussion, dance, dramatic music and arts, music and dramatics art, organ and church music, piano, string instruments, vocals; library: 20,185 vols, 3,079 music records; 103 teachers; 269 students; Dir Mag. Bartolomej Buráš; Deputy Dir Mgr Silvia Sidorová.

Vysoká Škola Múzických Umení v Bratislave (Academy of Performing Arts Bratislava): Ventúrska 3, 813 01 Bratislava; tel. (2) 5930-1421; e-mail rektor@vsmu.sk; internet www.vsmu.sk; f. 1949; faculties of film and television, music and dance, theatre; library: 47,231 vols, 9,966 music records and CDs, 781 video cassettes and DVDs, 5,749 theses; 220 teachers; 1,080 students; Rector Dr Milan Rašla; Pro-Rector for Devt, Research and Artistic Activities Dr Jozef Puškáš; Pro-Rector for Education Mgr Jana Billová; Pro-Rector for Foreign and Public Relations Dr Ida Hledíková; Dir for Library Dr Elena Ružeková.

Vysoká škola výtvarných umení (Academy of Fine Arts and Design): Hviezdoslavovo nám. 18, 814 37 Bratislava; tel. (2) 5942-8500; e-mail rektor@afad.sk; internet www.afad.sk; f. 1949; depts of applied art and division of drawing, architecture, design, intermedia and multimedia, painting and other media, photography and new media, printmaking and other media, restoration, sculpture, textiles, theory and history of art, visual communication; library: 37,300 vols, 62 periodical titles; 108 teachers; 667 students; Rector Prof. Stanislav Stankoci; Pro-Rector for Education Mgr Dr Jozef Kovalčík; Pro-Rector for Foreign Relations Mgr Dr Silvia Seneši Lutherová; Pro-Rector for Grant and Project Activities Mgr Dr Lucia Okoličányova; Pro-Rector for Research and Artistic Activities Prof. Ivan Csudai; Head of Library Dr Oľga Kasajová.

SLOVENIA

The Higher Education System

Slovenia's higher education institutions predate the foundation of the former Yugoslavia in 1918, with the oldest being Univerza v Ljubljani (University of Ljubljana—founded 1595). In 1991 Slovenia declared independence from the Socialist Federal Republic of Yugoslavia. In 2007/08 90,403 undergraduates were enrolled in 89 higher education institutions. In 2010 a total of 114,873 students were enrolled in tertiary-level education. There are four universities (three public and one private), the oldest of which is the Univerza v Ljubljani (founded 1919).

Higher education is organized according to the terms of the Higher Education Act (1994, amended 2004 and 2006). In addition to the universities, other institutions of higher education include fakultet (university faculties), urnetniske akademije (art academies), and professional institutes. The Council for Higher Education was founded in 1993 as the main accreditation body and since 2006 had been responsible for quality assurance. It was superseded in 2010 by the Quality Assurance Agency for Higher Education. A 'credit' system for awarding postgraduate degrees was introduced in 1998 and was extended to undergraduate degrees in 2002. Following amendments to the Higher Education Act in 2004, Slovenia now participates in the Bologna Process to establish a European Higher Education Area, the first phase of which is to adopt a credit-based system of comparable degrees with two main cycles (undergraduate and graduate). Since 2005/06 Diploma Supplements have been issued automatically to all graduates. The Professional and Scientific Titles Act (2006) laid out the new system of degrees and titles to be awarded in accordance with the principles of the Bologna Process; since 2009/10 all offerings have been Bologna-style programmes.

In 2010 the Government announced the National Higher Education Master Plan for the period 2011–20, which was intended significantly to improve the quality of the higher education system. The initiative included, inter alia, plans to establish polytechnics by 2020 (these would be the only institutions at which professional higher education study programmes would be available); an increase in the total levels of funding available for the higher education sector, and the introduction of a performance-related system of financing whereby higher education institutions would be allocated funding on the basis of their quality, development and efficiency, rather than on the basis of the number of students enrolled; and measures to bolster links between higher education institutions and the economic and public sectors. At 2011 an eight-level national qualification framework was under development.

The Matura (secondary school leavers' diploma) is the main requirement for admission to higher education. University places are offered on a quota basis. Higher education degrees are now divided into three cycles. The first cycle consists of either academic or professional undergraduate degrees, equivalent to Bachelors, requiring 180–240 credits during two to four years of study. The second-cycle degree is the Magister (Masters), lasting up to two years and requiring 60–120 credits. The Doctorat (Doctorate) constitutes the third cycle of university degrees and lasts a minimum of three years (180 credits).

Post-secondary technical and vocational education is provided by višje strokovne šole (vocational colleges). The primary qualification is the Post-Secondary Diploma, which usually requires two years' study. Quality standards are set by the national accreditation bodies, but higher vocational education is administered by the Ministry of Education, Science, Culture and Sport and regulated by the Higher Vocational Education Act (2004).

Regulatory and Representative Bodies

GOVERNMENT

Ministry of Culture: Maistrova ul. 10, 1000 Ljubljana; tel. (1) 369-59-00; e-mail gp.mk@gov.si; internet www.mk.gov.si; Minister Dr UROŠ GRILC.

Ministry of Education, Science and Sport: Masarykova 16, 1000 Ljubljana; tel. (1) 400-52-00; e-mail gp.mizs@gov.si; internet www.mizs.gov.si; Minister Dr JERNEJ PIKALO.

ACCREDITATION

ENIC–NARIC Slovenia: Min. of Education, Science and Sport, ENIC-NARIC centre Slovenia, Masarykova cesta 16, 1000 Ljubljana; tel. (1) 478-46-00; e-mail enicnaric-slovenia.mvzt@gov.si; internet www.mizs.gov.si/si/delovna_podrocja/direktorat_za_visoko_solstvo/enicnaric_center; Head Mag. ALENKA LISEC.

Slovenian Quality Assurance Agency for Higher Education—SQAA: Slovenska cesta 9, 1000 Ljubljana; tel. (1) 400-57-71; e-mail info@nakvis.si; internet www.nakvis.si; f. 1993; accredits HEIs; approves higher education study programmes; performs external evaluation of HEIs; Dir TATJANA DEBEVEC (acting).

NATIONAL BODY

Association of Rectors of Slovenia: University of Nova Gorica, 5000 Nova Gorica; tel. (5) 331-52-61; internet www.ung.si; Pres. Prof. Dr DANILO ZAVRTANIK.

Learned Societies

GENERAL

Slavistično društvo Slovenije (The Society for Slavic Studies of Slovenia): Aškerčeva 2/II, 1000 Ljubljana; internet www.ff.uni-lj.si/slovjez/sds/sds.html; f. 1935; a forum for professional Slavists, to provide a link between research and professional practice, to nurture cultural values regarding Slovene language and literature and awareness of Slovene history; to organize support for and publish Slavic research in academic and popular books and periodicals; Chair. IRENA NOVAK POPOV; Sec. MATJAŽ ZAPLOTNIK; publs *Jezik in slovstvo* (Language and Literature, 6 a year), *Kronike Slavističnega Društva* (12 a year, online), *Slavistična revija* (Slavonic Review, 4 a year).

Slovenska Akademija Znanosti in Umetnosti (Slovenian Academy of Sciences and Arts): Novi trg 3, 1000 Ljubljana; tel. (1) 470-61-00; e-mail sazu@sazu.si; internet www.sazu.si; f. 1938; promotes and contributes to the devt of scientific thought and artistic creativity; 70 full mems, 30 assoc. mems; library: see under Libraries and Archives; Pres. Prof. Dr JOŽE TRONTELJ; Sec.-Gen. Prof. Dr ANDREJ KRANJC; publs *Acta Archaeologica, Acta Carsologica, Acta Geographica, Opera, Traditiones*.

BIBLIOGRAPHY, LIBRARY SCIENCE AND MUSEOLOGY

Zveza bibliotekarskih društev Slovenije (Union of Associations of Slovene Librarians): Turjaška 1, 1000 Ljubljana; tel. (1) 200-11-93; e-mail zveza-biblio.ds-nuk@guest.arnes.si; internet www.zbds-zveza.si; f. 1947; 1,000 mems, coordinates activities with 8 regional library assocs; Pres. MELITA AMBROŽIČ; Vice-Pres. MARTINA KEREC; Sec. LILI HUBEJ; Treas. ZDENKA RUDOLF; publ. *Knjižnica* (Library, 4 a year).

FINE AND PERFORMING ARTS

Društvo slovenskih skladateljev (Society of Slovene Composers): trg francoske revolucije 6, 1000 Ljubljana; tel. (1) 241-56-60; e-mail info@dss.si; internet www.dss.si; f. 1945; represents and promotes Slovene composers; promotes the creation of new Slovene music; organizes concerts of contemporary Slovene music; 114 mems; Pres. NENAD FIRST; publ. *Edicije DSS* (printed scores, etc., of its mems).

Slovensko umetnostnozgodovinsko društvo (Slovenian Art History Society):

Aškerčeva cesta 2, 1000 Ljubljana; tel. (1) 241-12-10; e-mail suzd@suzd.si; internet www.suzd.si; f. 1921; excursions, symposia, congresses; 300 mems; library of 22,000 vols; Chair. Dr MARIA IRENE MISLEJ; Vice-Pres. Dr ROBERT PESKAR; Sec. METKA DOLENEC ŠOBA; publs *Bilten SUZD* (5 a year, online), *Zbornik za umetnostno zgodovino* (Art History Journal, 1 a year, print and online).

HISTORY, GEOGRAPHY AND ARCHAEOLOGY

Zveza geografov Slovenije (Association of Slovenian Geographers): Filozofska fakulteta, Aškerčeva 2, 1000 Ljubljana; tel. (1) 241-12-1248; e-mail lucija.mikliccvek@ff .uni-lj.si; internet zgs.zrc-sazu.si; f. 1922; supports professional research, stimulates and directs modernization of teaching; organizes professional confs, lectures, publs and field works; 700 mems; Pres. STANKO PELC; Vice-Pres. VLADIMIR DROZG; Sec. LUCIJA MIKLIČ CVEK; publs *Geografski obzornik* (4 a year), *Geografski vestnik* (2 a year).

Zveza zgodovinskih društev Slovenije (Slovenian Historical Association): Aškerčeva 2, 1000 Ljubljana; tel. (1) 241-12-01; e-mail zzds@ff.uni-lj.si; internet www.ff .uni-lj.si/drustva/zzds; f. 1839; 1,649 mems; library of 5,215 vols; Pres. Dr EGON PELIKAN; Vice-Pres. Dr NEVENKA TROHA; Vice-Pres. BORUT BATAGELJ; publs *Časopis za zgodovino in narodopisje* (2 a year), *Kronika* (3 a year), *Prispevki za novejšo zgodovino* (Contributions to Contemporary History, 1 a year), *Zgodovinski časopis* (Historical Review, 4 a year).

LANGUAGE AND LITERATURE

British Council: Center Tivoli, Tivolska 30, 1000 Ljubljana; tel. (1) 300-20-30; e-mail info@britishcouncil.si; internet www .britishcouncil.si; offers courses and exams in English language and British culture and promotes cultural exchange with the UK; library of 400 vols; Dir STEVE GREEN.

Goethe-Institut: Bleiweisova 30, 1000 Ljubljana; tel. (1) 300-00-11; e-mail info@ ljubljana.goethe.org; internet www.goethe .de/ljubljana; offers courses and exams in German language and culture; promotes cultural exchange with Germany; Dir HENDRIK KLONINGER.

Slovenska Matica (Slovenian Society): Kongresni trg 8, 1000 Ljubljana; tel. (1) 422-43-40; e-mail drago.jancar@siol.net; internet www.slovenska-matica.si; f. 1864; literary and publishing soc.; 2,800 mems; library of 10,000 vols; Pres. Prof. Dr MILČEK KOMELJ; Sec. DRAGO JANČAR.

NATURAL SCIENCES
General

Društvo matematikov, fizikov in astronomov Slovenije (Society of Mathematicians, Physicists and Astronomers of Slovenia): Jadranska ul. 19, 1000 Ljubljana; tel. (1) 476-65-59; e-mail tajnik@dmfa.si; internet www.dmfa.si; f. 1949; 1,010 mems; Chair. Prof. Dr ANDREJ LIKAR; Vice-Pres. NADA RAZPET; Sec. JANEZ KRUSIC; publs *Obzornik mat. fiz.* (6 a year), *Presek* (6 a year).

Prirodoslovno Društvo Slovenije (Natural History Society of Slovenia): Salendrova ul. 4, 1573, 1001 Ljubljana; tel. (1) 252-19-14; e-mail prirodoslovno.drustvo@guest.arnes.si; internet www.proteus.si; f. 1934; 2,500 mems; Pres. RADOVAN KOMEL; Sec.-Gen. JANJA BENEDIK; publ. *Proteus* (10 a year).

Physical Sciences

Jamarska zveza Slovenije (Speleological Association of Slovenia): Lepi pot 6, POB 2544, 1109 Ljubljana; tel. (1) 428 34 44; e-mail predsedstvo@jamarska-zveza.si; internet www.jamarska-zveza.si; f. 1889; 43 caving socs and research groups with a total of 1,000 mems; Pres. VIDKO KREGAR; Sec IRENA STRAŽAR; publs *Jamar* (1 a year), *Naše jame* (2 a year).

Research Institutes
GENERAL

Inštitut za Antropološke in Prostorske Študije ZRC SAZU (Institute of Anthropological and Spatial Studies ZRC SAZU): Novi trg 2, 1000 Ljubljana; tel. (1) 470-64-95; e-mail iaps@zrc-sazu.si; internet iaps .zrc-sazu.si; f. 1994; attached to Scientific Research Centre of SASA (ZRC SAZU); Dir Dr IVAN ŠPRAJC.

Kmetijski inštitut Slovenije (Agricultural Institute of Slovenia): Hacquetova ul. 17, 1000 Ljubljana; tel. (1) 280-52-62; e-mail info@kis.si; internet www.kis.si; f. 1898; library of 32,000 vols; Dir Dr ANDREJ SIMONČIČ; publ. *Raziskave in Studije* (Research and Studies).

Zavod za gradbeništvo Slovenije (Slovenian National Building and Civil Engineering Institute): Dimičeva 12, 1000 Ljubljana; tel. (1) 280-42-50; e-mail info@zag.si; internet www.zag.si; f. 1949; research and devt in the field of building and civil engineering; Dir Dr ANDRAŽ LEGAT.

Znanstvenoraziskovalni Center Slovenske akademije znanosti in umetnosti (ZRC SAZU) (Research Centre of the Slovenian Academy of the Sciences and Arts): Novi trg 2, 1000 Ljubljana; tel. (1) 470-61-00; e-mail zrc@zrc-sazu.si; internet www .zrc-sazu.si; f. 1981 by Slovenian Acad. of Sciences and Arts; network of research institutes (listed individually in this section of Research Institutes) in the humanities and natural sciences; Dir Dr OTO LUTHAR.

BIBLIOGRAPHY, LIBRARY SCIENCE AND MUSEOLOGY

Inštitut za Kulturno zgodovino ZRC SAZU (Institute for Cultural History at ZRC SAZU): Novi trg 5, 1000 Ljubljana; tel. (1) 470-61-00; e-mail ibb@zrc-sazu.si; internet odmev.zrc-sazu.si/instituti/ikz; f. 1999, as Inštitut za Biografiko in Bibliografijo (Institute of Biographical and Bibliographical Studies), current name 2007; attached to Scientific Research Centre of SASA (ZRC SAZU); biographical research and studies; research of modern Slovenian and European history; Head Prof. IGOR GRDINA; publ. *Življenja in dela-Lives and Works* (book series).

FINE AND PERFORMING ARTS

Glasbenonarodopisni Inštitut ZRC SAZU (Institute of Ethnomusicology ZRC SAZU): Novi trg 2, 1000 Ljubljana; tel. (1) 470-62-65; e-mail gni@zrc-sazu.si; internet gni.zrc-sazu.si; f. 1934; attached to Scientific Research Centre of SASA (ZRC SAZU); conducts ethnomusicological and ethnochoreological research; Dir Prof. Dr MARJETKA GOLEŽ KAUČIČ; Sec. ANJA SEREC HODŽAR; publ. *Traditiones* (2 a year).

Muzikološki inštitut ZRC SAZU (Institute of Musicology at ZRC SAZU): Novi trg 2, 1000 Ljubljana; tel. (1) 470-61-96; internet mi.zrc-sazu.si; f. 1972; attached to Scientific Research Centre of SASA (ZRC SAZU);

library of 7,000 vols; Head Dr METODA KOKOLE; publs *De Musica Disserenda* (2 a year), *Monumenta Artis Musicae Sloveniae* (2 a year).

Umetnostnozgodovinski inštitut Franceta Steleta ZRC SAZU (France Stele Institute of Art History at ZRC SAZU): Novi trg 2, POB 306, 1001 Ljubljana; tel. (1) 470-61-00; e-mail umzg@zrc-sazu.si; internet uifs .zrc-sazu.si; f. 1972; attached to Scientific Research Centre of SASA (ZRC SAZU); library of 17,000 vols; Dir Dr BARBARA MUROVEC (acting); Sec. ROMANA ZAJC; publs *Acta historiae artis Slovenica* (2 a year), *Umetnosta Kronika* (4 a year).

HISTORY, GEOGRAPHY AND ARCHAEOLOGY

Geografski inštitut Antona Melika ZRC SAZU (Anton Melik Geographical Institute at ZRC SAZU): 13 Gosposka ul., 1000 Ljubljana; tel. (1) 470-63-54; e-mail gi@ zrc-sazu.si; internet giam2.zrc-sazu.si; f. 1946; attached to Scientific Research Centre of Slovenian Acad. of Sciences and Arts (ZRC SAZU); depts of physical, social, regional geography, natural disasters, geographical information system, thematic cartography, environmental protection; geographical museum and library; also houses a cartographic colln and 3 spec. geographical collns: Landscapes of Slovenia, Settlements of Slovenia and Glaciers of Slovenia; HQ of the Comm. for the Standardization of Geographical Names; library of 42,000 vols and periodicals; Dir Dr DRAGO PERKO; Asst Dir Dr MATIJA ZORN; Asst Dir Dr. MIMI URBANC; publs *Geografija Slovenije* (Geography of Slovenian, book series, in Slovene, 2 a year), *Geografski zbornik* (Acta Geographica Slovenica, scientific journal, in English and Slovenian, 1 to 2 a year), *Georithem* (in Slovenian, 2 to 5 a year), *GIS v Sloveniji* (GIS in Slovenia, book series, in Slovenian, every 2 years), *Naravne nesreče* (Natural Disasters, book series, in Slovene, every 3 years), *Regionalni razvoj* (Regional Devt, book series, in Slovene, every 2 years).

Inštitut za arheologijo ZRC SAZU (Institute of Archaeology at ZRC SAZU): Novi trg 2, 1000 Ljubljana; tel. (1) 470-63-80; e-mail iza@zrc-sazu.si; internet iza.zrc-sazu.si; f. 1947; attached to Scientific Research Centre of SASA (ZRC SAZU); library of 50,000 vols; Dir Dr JANA HORVAT; publs *Arheološki vestnik* (Acta Archaeologica, 1 a year), *Opera Instituti archaeologici Sloveniae*.

Zgodovinski inštitut Milka Kosa ZRC SAZU (Milko Kos Historical Institute at ZRC SAZU): Novi trg 2, 1000 Ljubljana; tel. (1) 470-62-00; e-mail zi@zrc-sazu.si; internet zimk.zrc-sazu.si; f. 1947; attached to Scientific Research Centre of SASA (ZRC SAZU); conducts research on Slovenian history from early Middle Ages to World War I; Head Prof. Dr PETRA SVOLJŠAK.

LANGUAGE AND LITERATURE

Inštitut za slovenski jezik Frana Ramovša ZRC SAZU (Fran Ramovš Institute of the Slovenian Language at ZRC SAZU): Novi trg 2, p.p. 306, 1001 Ljubljana; tel. (1) 470-61-60; e-mail isj@zrc-sazu.si; internet isjfr.zrc-sazu.si; f. 1945; attached to Scientific Research SAZU (ZRC SAZU); Slovenian lexicography; library of 25,000 vols; Head Prof. Dr MARKO SNOJ; Sec. ALENKA LAP; publs *Jezikoslovni zapiski* (2 a year), *Slovenski jezik* (Slovene Linguistic Studies, every 2 years).

Inštitut za slovensko literaturo in literarne vede ZRC SAZU (Institute of Slovenian Literature and Literary Studies at ZRC SAZU): Novi trg 2, 1000 Ljubljana;

tel. (1) 470-63-00; e-mail lit@zrc-sazu.si; internet isllv.zrc-sazu.si/#v; f. 1947; attached to Research Centre of the Slovenian Academy of Sciences and Arts (ZRC SAZU); research on Slovenian literature, comparative literature, literary theory, digital humanities, textual criticism and cultural studies; library of 37,000 vols; Dir Prof. Dr MARKO JUVAN; Sec. ALENKA MAČEK; publs *Studia litteraria*, *Zbrana dela slovenskih pesnikov in pisateljev* (Collected Works of Slovenian Writers and Poets).

MEDICINE

Družbenomedicinski inštitut ZRC SAZU (Sociomedical Institute at ZRC SAZU): Novi trg 2, 1000 Ljubljana; tel. (1) 470-61-00; e-mail imv@zrc-sazu.si; internet dmi .zrc-sazu.si; f. 1981 as Inštitut za medicinske vede; social sciences, humanities and medical sciences; sociological and social-anthropological interpretation of classical demographic models and concepts, social-anthropological theory of ethnicity and nationalism, personality, psychosocial, neuropsychological and neurobiological theories of social behaviour; attached to Scientific Research Centre of SASA (ZRC SAZU); Dir Dr DUŠKA KNEŽEVIĆ HOČEVAR.

NATURAL SCIENCES

Biological Sciences

Biološki inštitut Jovana Hadžija ZRC SAZU (Jovan Hadži Institute of Biology at ZRC SAZU): Novi trg 5, 1000 Ljubljana; tel. (1) 470-63-10; e-mail bio@zrc-sazu.si; internet bijh.zrc-sazu.si; f. 1950; attached to Scientific Research Centre of SASA (ZRC SAZU); Chair. Dr MATJAŽ KUNTNER.

Paleontološki inštitut Ivana Rakovca ZRC SAZU (Ivan Rakovec Institute of Palaeontology at ZRC SAZU): Novi trg 2, p.p. 306, 1001 Ljubljana; tel. (1) 470-63-71; e-mail spela@zrc-sazu.si; internet piir.zrc-sazu.si; f. 1949; attached to Scientific Research Centre of the Slovenian Acad. of Sciences and Arts (ZRC SAZU); Dir Dr ŠPELA GORIČAN.

Physical Sciences

Inštitut za matematiko, fiziko in mehaniko Jezik (Institute of Mathematics, Physics and Mechanics): Jadranska 19, 1000 Ljubljana; tel. (1) 426-71-77; internet www .imfm.si; f. 1960; research and technical activities in fields of mathematics, physics, mechanics and theoretical computer science; Dir Prof. Dr JERNEJ KOZAK; Deputy Dir TANJA CVEK; publ. *Ars Mathematica Contemporanea* (2 a year).

Institut Jožef Stefan (Jožef Stefan Institute): Jamova 39, 1000 Ljubljana; tel. (1) 477-39-00; e-mail info@ijs.si; internet www.ijs.si; f. 1949; basic and applied research in the fields of natural sciences and technology; Dir Prof. Dr JADRAN LENARČIČ.

Geološki Zavod Slovenije (Geological Survey of Slovenia): Dimičeva ul. 14, 1000 Ljubljana; tel. (1) 280-97-00; e-mail www@ geo-zs.si; internet www.geo-zs.si; f. 1946; geology, geotechnology, geophysics, mining, soil and rock mechanics, drilling and blasting, manufacturing and maintenance of drilling equipment; 1,300 mems; library of 15,000 vols, 300 periodicals, 30,000 reports; Dir Dr MARKO KOMAC; publ. *Geologija* (2 a year).

Inštitut za raziskovanje krasa ZRC SAZU (Karst Research Institute at ZRC SAZU): Titov trg 2, 6230 Postojna; tel. (1) 700-19-00; e-mail izrk@zrc-sazu.si; internet kras.zrc-sazu.si; f. 1947; karstology and speleology; attached to Research Centre of SASA (SRC SAZU); Dir Dr TADEJ SLABE; Sec. SONJA STAMENKOVIĆ; publs *Acta Carsologica*

(2–3 a year), *Annotated Bibliography of Karst Publications* (1 a year).

PHILOSOPHY AND PSYCHOLOGY

Filozofski inštitut ZRC SAZU (Institute of Philosophy at ZRC SAZU): Novi trg 2, POB 306, 1001 Ljubljana; tel. (1) 470-64-70; e-mail fi@zrc-sazu.si; internet fi2.zrc-sazu.si/en/ predstavitev#v; f. 1979; attached to Scientific Research Centre at SASA (ZRC SAZU); research into encounters between philosophy and psychoanalysis, science, politics and art; library of 5,000 vols; Head Dr RADO RIHA; Sec. MATEJ AŽMAN; publ. *Filozofski vestnik* (3 a year).

RELIGION, SOCIOLOGY AND ANTHROPOLOGY

Inštitut za narodnostna vprašanja (Institute for Ethnic Studies): Erjavčeva 26, 1000 Ljubljana; tel. (1) 200-18-72; e-mail inv@inv .si; internet www.inv.si; f. 1925; study of inter-ethnic relations in Slovenia and abroad and of Slovene ethnic minorities in neighbouring countries; sociolinguistics, human rights, migration, general ethnic issues; library of 38,000 vols; Pres. ŽARKO BOGUNOVIĆ; Dir SONJA NOVAK LUKANOVIC; publ. *Razprave in gradivo* (Treatises and Documents, 3 a year).

Inštitut za slovensko izseljenstvo in migracije ZRC SAZU (Slovenian Migration Institute ZRC SAZU): Novi trg 2, 1000 Ljubljana; tel. (1) 470-64-85; e-mail izi@ zrc-sazu.si; internet isi.zrc-sazu.si; f. 1986; attached to Scientific Research Centre of SASA (ZRC SAZU); interdisciplinary research into migration processes in Slovenia and in the international environment; Head Dr MARINA LUKŠIČ-HACIN; publs *Bilten* (Newsletter, 1 a year), *Dve Domovini* (Two Homelands, 2 a year).

Inštitut za slovensko narodopisje ZRC SAZU (Institute of Slovenian Ethnology at ZRC SAZU): Novi trg 2, 1000 Ljubljana; tel. (1) 470-42-92; e-mail isn@zrc-sazu.si; internet isn2.zrc-sazu.si; f. 1951; attached to Scientific Research Centre SASA (ZRC SAZU); research in ethnology and folklore studies, audiovisual research and archive; library of 19,000 vols; Head INGRID SLAVEC GRADIŠNIK; Sec. BOŽENA GABRIJELČIČ; publs *Studia Mythologica Slavica* (1 a year), *Traditiones* (2 a year).

Libraries and Archives

Celje

Osrednja knjižnica Celje (Public Library of Celje): Muzejski trg 1A, 3000 Celje; tel. (3) 426-17-10; e-mail sikce@knjiznica-celje.si; internet www.ce.sik.si; f. 1946; 365,000 vols; Dir POLONA RIFELJ.

Koper

Osrednja knjižnica Srečka Vilharja (Srečko Vilhar Public Library): trg Brolo 1, 6000 Koper; tel. (5) 663-26-00; e-mail info@kp .sik.si; internet www.kp.sik.si; f. 1951; 300,000 vols; Librarian Prof. IVAN MARKOVIĆ.

Ljubljana

Arhiv Republike Slovenije (Archives of the Republic of Slovenia): Zvezdarska 1, p.p. 21, 1127 Ljubljana; tel. (1) 241-42-00; e-mail ars@gov.si; internet www.arhiv.gov.si; f. 1887; colln of important archives, esp. those connected with the territory populated by Slovenes since 12th century; archive of Slovene film production since 1905; Dir Dr BOJAN CVELFAR; Librarian ALENKA HREN.

Biblioteka Slovenske akademije znanosti in umetnosti (Library of the Slovenian Academy of Sciences and Arts): Novi trg 3–5, POB 323, 1000 Ljubljana; tel. (1) 470-62-46; e-mail sazu-biblioteka@sazu.si; internet www.sazu.si/biblioteka.html; f. 1938; 520 vols; Librarian MARIJA FABJANČIČ; publs *Kratko poročilo o delu v letu* (1 a year), *Mesečni seznam novosti* (12 a year), *Objave* (irregular).

Centralna ekonomska knjižnica (Central Economic Library): Kardeljeva ploščad 17, 1000 Ljubljana; tel. (1) 589-25-91; e-mail cek@ef.uni-lj.si; internet www.ef.uni-lj.si/ cek; f. 1946; library and information centre for business, economics and related sciences; European documentation centre; 242,000 vols; 301 current periodicals (print), 11,000 ejournals; 9,000 mems; Head IVAN KANIČ; publ. *Mesečni pregled novih knjig* (12 a year).

Centralna medicinska knjižnica, Medicinska fakulteta (Central Medical Library, Faculty of Medicine): Vrazov trg 2, 1000 Ljubljana; tel. (1) 543-77-35; e-mail infocmk@ mf.uni-lj.si; internet www.mf.uni-lj.si/cmk; f. 1945; central library for the Faculty of Medicine, Slovene health-care orgs and biomedical research instns; literature of biomedicine; 210,000 books and periodicals, 1,100 ejournals and 150 ebooks; Dir Dr ANAMARIJA ROŽIĆ-HRISTOVSKI.

Centralna tehniška knjižnica Univerze v Ljubljani (Central Technical Library of the University of Ljubljana): trg republike 3, 1000 Ljubljana; tel. (1) 200-34-00; e-mail post@ctk.uni-lj.si; internet www.ctk.uni-lj.si; f. 1949; central technical library for the university; specialized information centre for engineering, civil engineering and standards; information and referral centre for science and technology; inter-library loan centre; 230,000 vols, research papers, standards, regulations; Dir Dr MIRO PUŠNIK; publ. *New Books Accession List* (4 a year).

Knjižnica Narodnega Muzeja Slovenije (Library of the National Museum of Slovenia): Prešernova 20, POB 1967, 1000 Ljubljana; tel. (1) 241-44-68; e-mail anja.dular@ nms.si; internet www.nms.si/odd/knj/knj .html; f. 1821; 250,000 vols; spec. colln of Slovene prints from 16th century; Librarian Doc. Dr ANJA DULAR; publs *ARGO* (journal on museology), *Viri–monograph series* (Topics in Slovenian Material Culture).

Knjižnica Pravne fakultete v Ljubljani (Library of the Faculty of Law of Ljubljana): Poljanski Nasip 2, 1000 Ljubljana; tel. (1) 420-32-31; e-mail knjiznica@pf.uni-lj.si; internet www.pf.uni-lj.si/ knjiznica-in-zalozba; f. 1920; 131,000 vols; Head Librarian MARIJAN PAVČNIK.

Narodna in univerzitetna knjižnica (National and University Library): Turjaška 1, POB 259, 1000 Ljubljana; tel. (1) 200-11-88; e-mail uprava@nuk.uni-lj.si; internet www.nuk.uni-lj.si; f. 1774; incorporates state copyright and deposit library, Nat. Slovene library, Univ. of Ljubljana library, library promotion and consultancy centre, permanent education centre and library research centre; UNESCO deposit library; Information and Documentation Centre on the Council of Europe, and EU Colln; 2.5m. vols, incl. 1.2m. books, 324,000 serials, 80,000 printed music items, 23,700 sound recordings, 13,800 audiovisual items, 7,400 MSS (incl. 85 parchments and 508 incunabula), 74,000 maps, 170,000 pictorial items, 3,800 microforms; Dir MATEJA KOMEL SNOJ; publs *Knjižničarske novice* (12 a year, print; online), *Signalne informacije* (12 a year, print; online), *Slovenska bibliografija* (4 a year, print; online).

Mestna knjižnica Ljubljana (Ljubljana City Library): Kersnikova ul. 2, 1000 Ljubljana; tel. (1) 600-13-00; e-mail info@mklj.si; internet www.mklj.si; f. 2008 as Slovanska knjižnica Ljubljana (Slavic Library); language, literature, history and culture of the Slavs; 1.6m. vols; Dir Mag. JELKA GAZVODA.

Maribor

Univerzitetna knjižnica Maribor (University of Maribor Library): Gospejna ul. 10, 2000 Maribor; tel. (2) 250-74-00; e-mail ukm-tajnistvo@uni-mb.si; internet www.ukm.si; f. 1903; 960,000 vols; Dir Dr. ZDENKA PETERMANEC (acting); publ. *Casopis za zgodovino in narodopisje* (Journal of History and Ethnology, 1 a year).

Novo Mesto

Knjižnica Mirana Jarca Novo Mesto ('Miran Jarc' Regional Public Library): Rozmanova ul. 28, 8000 Novo Mesto; tel. (7) 393-46-00; e-mail knjiznicanm@nm.sik.si; internet www.nm.sik.si; f. 1946; 600,000 vols; Dir CLAUDIA JERINA MESTNIK.

Museums and Art Galleries

Brežice

Posavski muzej (Regional Museum): Cesta prvih borcev 1, 8250 Brežice; tel. (7) 496-12-71; e-mail ivan.kastelic@guest.arnes.si; internet www.posavski-muzej.si; f. 1949; colln of archaeological exhibits from Neolithic times to the early Middle Ages; also ethnographical colln; historical section: from Slovene-Croat peasants' revolt of 1573 to the present; Baroque festival hall with frescoes (1703) and Baroque gallery; memorial room of painter Franjo Stiplovšek; library of 7,350 vols, 35 periodicals; Dir Dr. TOM TEROPŠIČ; Curator IVAN KASTELIČ.

Celje

Pokrajinski muzej Celje (Celje Regional Museum): trg Celjskih knezov 8, 3000 Celje; tel. (3) 428-09-50; e-mail info@pokmuz-ce.si; internet www.pokmuz-ce.si; f. 1882 as City Museum; present status 1965; collns of archaeology, art and cultural history, ethnography and history; library of 8,456 vols; Dir DARJA PIRKMAJER.

Ljubljana

Mednarodni Grafični Likovni Center (MGLC) (International Centre of Graphic Arts): Grad Tivoli, Pod turnom 3, 1000 Ljubljana; tel. (1) 241-38-00; e-mail lili .sturm@mglc-lj.si; internet www.mglc-lj.si; f. 1986; permanent colln of contemporary int. graphics, artists' books and printed ephemera; organizes the int. Biennial of Graphic Arts; exhibitions of prints, drawings, artists' books and printed ephemera; print workshops; Dir Dr BARBARA SAVENC.

Mestni muzej Ljubljana (City Museum of Ljubljana): Gosposka 15, 1000 Ljubljana; tel. (1) 241-25-00; e-mail info@mgml.si; internet www.mgml.si; f. 1935; cultural history museum of Ljubljana; collns incl. archaeological dept, containing articles from lake dwellings of the chalcolithic period, cemeteries of the Illyrian-Celtic period and of Roman domination (Emona), and from the Old Slavic period; cultural historical colln; modern history; also fine arts exhibitions; information centre about the cultural and natural heritage in the Ljubljana area; publs various guides; library of 9,324 vols; Dir BLAŽ PERŠIN.

Moderna galerija (Museum of Modern Art): Tomšičeva 14, 1000 Ljubljana; tel. (1) 241-68-00; e-mail info@mg-lj.si; internet www.mg-lj .si; f. 1948; incl. Museum of Contemporary Art; permanent colln of modern and contemporary Slovene and int. art from the Impressionists to the present day; organizes regular art exhibitions, lectures and events; library: art library of 52,000 vols; Dir ZDENKA BADOVINAC.

Muzej novejše zgodovine slovenije (National Museum of Contemporary History): Celovška cesta 23, 1001 Ljubljana; tel. (1) 300-96-10; e-mail uprava@muzej-nz .si; internet www.muzej-nz.si; f. 1948; important archives, museum objects and library material of Slovene history since 1914; Dir Dr KAJA ŠIROK.

Narodna galerija (National Gallery): Puharjeva 9, 1000 Ljubljana; tel. (1) 241-54-34; e-mail info@ng-slo.si; internet www .ng-slo.si; f. 1918; colln of Gothic sculptural arts, medieval frescoes and copies of Gothic frescoes from Slovenia; colln of Slovenian Renaissance, Baroque and 19th-century paintings and sculptures; paintings by Slovenian impressionists; European painters since the 14th century; colln of Slovenian graphic arts from the 18th to the early 20th century; photo-documentation of works of art from Slovenia; library of 34,000 vols; Dir Dr BARBARA JAKI.

Narodni muzej Slovenije (National Museum of Slovenia): Prešernova ul. 20, POB 1967, 1000 Ljubljana; tel. (1) 241-44-00; e-mail info@nms.si; internet www.nms.si; f. 1821; depts of archaeology; history and applied arts; coins and medals; graphic arts; conservation and restoration; brs: National Museum of Slovenia (Metelkova); Sneznik Castle Museum; Museum of Bled (mediaval castle); library of 220,000 vols; Dir Prof. Dr PETER KOS; publs *Argo* (2 a year), *Catalogi et Monographiae* (1 a year), *Situla* (1 a year), *Viri* (irregular).

Prirodoslovni muzej Slovenije (Slovenian Museum of Natural History): Prešernova 20, POB 290, 1001 Ljubljana; tel. (1) 241-09-40; e-mail uprava@pms-lj.si; internet www2 .pms-lj.si; f. 1821; zoology, botany, geology; library of 12,500 vols of books and periodicals; Dir BREDA CINC JUHANT; publs *Acta Entomologica Slovenica* (2 a year), *Illiesia–International Journal of Stonefly Research* (1 a year, print and online), *Scopolia* (3 a year).

Slovenski etnografski muzej (Slovenian Ethnographical Museum): Metelkova 2, 1000 Ljubljana; tel. (1) 300-87-00; e-mail etnomuz@etno-muzej.si; internet www .etno-muzej.si; f. 1923; Slovenian and non-European ethnographic collns; library of 30,000 vols; Dir Dr BOJANA ROGELJ ŠKAFAR; publ. *Etnolog* (1 a year).

Slovenski šolski muzej (Slovenian School Museum): trg Plečnikov 1, 1000 Ljubljana; tel. (1) 251-30-24; e-mail solski.muzej@guest .arnes.si; internet www.ssolski-muzej.si; f. 1898; school documents and educational books since 16th century; exhibition about the devt of schools in Slovenia; library of 59,000 vols, 542 fascicules; 17,084 documents for all schools in Slovenia; Dir Mag. STANKO OKOLIŠ; publ. *Solska kronika* (School Chronicle, 2 a year).

Zemljepisni muzej Geografskega inštituta Antona Melika ZRC SAZU (Geographical Museum of the Anton Melik Geographical Institute at ZRC SAZU): Gosposka ul. 13, 1000 Ljubljana; tel. (1) 470-63-58; e-mail zm@zrc-sazu.si; internet giam .zrc-sazu.si; f. 1946; attached to the Anton Melik Geographical Institute at ZRC SAZU; maps and atlases of Slovenia, geographical collns; Head PRIMOŽ GAŠPERIČ; Dir Dr DRAGO PERKO.

Maribor

Pokrajinski muzej Maribor (Regional Museum of Maribor): Grajska ul. 2, 2000 Maribor; tel. (2) 228-35-51; e-mail info@ pmuzej-mb.si; internet www.pmuzej-mb.si; f. 1903 from collns of the Maribor Museum, the historical socs and the Episcopal Museum; archaeological, ethnological, historical, fine and applied art, costume colln exhibits; library of 12,000 vols; Dir MIRJANA KOREN.

Piran

Obalne Galerije Piran (Coastal Galleries of Piran): Tartinijev trg 3, 6330 Piran; tel. (5) 671-20-80; internet www.obalne-galerije.si; f. 1975; group of galleries; displays contemporary art of Slovenian coast; Dir TONI BILOSLAV.

Pomorski Muzej Sergej Mašera (Maritime Museum Sergej Masera): Cankarjevo nabrežje 3 p.p. 103, 6330 Piran; tel. (5) 671-00-40; e-mail muzej@pommuz-pi.si; internet www2.arnes.si/~kppomm; f. 1954 as the Civic Museum of Piran, present name 1967; colln and study of the maritime past of the Slovene coast, Slovene naval history and related economic activities; archaeological, maritime and art-history collns; an anthropological study and colln of items used in salt-making and fishing; library of 14,000 vols; Dir MARTINA GAMBOZ.

Ptuj

Pokrajinski muzej Ptuj (Ptuj Regional Museum): Muzejski trg 1, 2250 Ptuj; tel. (2) 787-92-30; e-mail muzej-ptuj.uprava@siol .net; internet www.pok-muzej-ptuj.si; f. 1893; history, archaeology, art, ethnography, numismatics, musical instruments, lapidary, reconstructions of 4 temples of Mithras; library of 17,000 vols; Dir Prof. ALEŠ ARIH; publs *Archaeologia Poetovionensis, Zbornik*.

Škofja Loka

Loški Muzej (Loški Museum): Grajska pot 13, 4220 Skofja Loka; tel. (4) 517-04-00; e-mail loski.muzej@guest.arnes.si; internet www.loski-muzej.si; f. 1939 by the Museum Asscn of Škofja Loka; special colln of exhibits relating to the Freising dominion (973–1803); ethnographic, topographic, natural history and historical exhibits; records of altars since 17th century, exhibits of medieval guilds; relics of the struggle for national liberation; art gallery; open-air museum; library of 18,000 vols; Pres. JANA MLAKAR; publ. *Loški razgledi*.

Universities

EURO-MEDITERRANEAN UNIVERSITY

Sončna pot 20, 6320 Portorož

Telephone: (5) 925-00-50

E-mail: university@emuni.si

Internet: www.emuni.si

Founded 2008

Private control

Masters in environmental analysis and management, intercultural business communication; PhD courses

Pres. LARIS GAISER (acting)

UNIVERZA NA PRIMORSKEM UNIVERSITA' DEL LITORALE (University of Primorska)

Titov trg 4, 6000 Koper

Telephone: (5) 611-75-00

E-mail: info@upr.si

Internet: www.upr.si

Founded 2003

State control
Languages of instruction: Slovene, English
Academic year: October to September
Rector: Prof. DRAGAN MARUŠIČ
Vice-Rector for Economics and Finance: Assoc. Prof. ROK STRAŠEL
Vice-Rector for Education: Assoc. Prof. NADJA PLAZAR
Vice-Rector for Science and Research: Assoc. Prof. ŠTEFKO MIKLAVIČ
Sec.-Gen.: INGRID KOCJANČIČ
Library of 40,000 vols, 400 periodicals across 5 libraries
Number of teachers: 328
Number of students: 6,499

DEANS

Faculty of Education: Dr MARA COTIČ
Faculty of Health Sciences: Dr ANDREJ CÖR
Faculty of Humanities: Dr GORAZD DREVEN-ŠEK
Faculty of Management: Dr ANITA TRNAVČE-VIČ
Faculty of Mathematics, Science and Information Technology: Dr KLAVDIJA KUTNAR
Faculty of Tourism Studies (Turistica): Dr ANTON GOSAR

UNIVERZA V LJUBLJANI
(University of Ljubljana)

Kongresni trg 12, 1000 Ljubljana
Telephone: (1) 241-85-00
E-mail: rektorat@uni-lj.si
Internet: www.uni-lj.si
Founded 1595, reconstituted 1809, reopened 1919
State control
Languages of instruction: Slovene, English
Academic year: October to September (2 terms)
Rector: Prof. Dr IVAN SVETLIK
Vice-Rector: Prof. Dr MARTIN ČOPIČ
Vice-Rector: Prof. Dr MAJA MAKOVEC BRENČIČ
Vice-Rector: Prof. Dr GORAN TURK
Sec.-Gen.: ANDREJA KERT
Librarian for Central and Technical Library: MIRO PUŠNIK
Librarian for Nat. and Univ. Library: MATEJA KOMEL SNOJ
Library: 3m. vols
Number of teachers: 4,088
Number of students: 66,000
Publications: *Seznam predavanj* (1 a year), *University of Ljubljana*

DEANS

Academy of Fine Arts: Prof. BOJAN GORENC
Academy of Music: Prof. ANDREJ GRAFENAUER
Academy of Theatre, Radio, Film, Television: Prof. ALEŠ VALIČ
Faculty of Architecture: Prof. PETER GABRI-JELČIČ
Faculty of Arts: Prof. Dr VALENTIN BUCIK
Faculty of Biotechnology: Prof. Dr MIHAEL JOŽEF TOMAN
Faculty of Chemistry,Chemical Technology: Prof. Dr ANTON MEDEN
Faculty of Civil and Geodetic Engineering: Prof. Dr MATJAŽ ,, MIKOŠ
Faculty of Computer, Information Science: Prof. Dr NIKOLAI ZIMIC
Faculty of Economics: Prof. DUSAN MRAMOR
Faculty of Education: Prof. JANEZ KREK
Faculty of Electrical Engineering: Prof. Dr JANEZ NASTRAN
Faculty of Health Sciences: Prof. Dr FRANCE SEVŠEK
Faculty of Law: Prof. Dr PETER GRILC
Faculty of Maritime Studies, Transport: Prof. ELEN TWRDY
Faculty of Mathematics, Physics: Prof. ANDREJ LIKAR

Faculty of Mechanical Engineering: Prof. Dr JOŽE DUHOVNIK
Faculty of Medicine: Prof. Dr DUŠAN ŠUPUT
Faculty of Natural Sciences, Engineering: Prof. JAKOB LIKAR
Faculty of Pharmacy: Prof. Dr STANISLAV GOBEC
Faculty of Public Administration: Prof. Dr STANKA SETNIKAR CANKAR
Faculty of Social Sciences: Prof. Dr ANTON GRIZOLD
Faculty of Social Work: Prof. Dr BOGDAN LEŠNIK
Faculty of Sports: Prof. Dr MILAN ŽVAN
Faculty of Theology: Prof. Dr STANKO GER-JOLJ
Faculty of Veterinary Medicine: Prof. Dr MARJAN KOSEC

UNIVERZA V MARIBORU
(University of Maribor)

Slomškov trg 15, 2000 Maribor
Telephone: (2) 235-52-80
E-mail: rektorat@uni-mb.si
Internet: www.uni-mb.si
Founded 1975
State control
Language of instruction: Slovene
Academic year: October to September
Rector: Prof. Dr IVAN ROZMAN
Vice-Rector for Int. and Inter-Univ. Cooperation: Assoc. Prof. Dr MARKO MARHL
Vice-Rector for Legal and General Affairs: Prof. Dr BOJAN SKOF
Vice-Rector for Scientific Research and Business Cooperation: Prof. Dr MILAN MARČIČ
Vice-Rector for Students: DANIEL VUK
Sec.-Gen.: BOŠTJAN BRUMEN
Librarian: Dr ZDENKA PETERMANEC
Number of teachers: 1,800
Number of students: 24,600
Publications: *Časopis za zgodovino in narodopisje*, *Naše gospodarstvo* (6 a year, published by the Faculty of Business and Economics), *Organizacija in Kadri* (10 a year, published by the Faculty of Organizational Sciences), *Univerzitetna revija*, *Znanstvena revija*

DEANS

Faculty of Agricultural Sciences and biosystems: Dr JERNEJ TURK
Faculty of Arts: Prof. Dr MARKO JESENŠEK
Faculty of Business and Economics: Prof. Dr SAMO BOBEK
Faculty of Chemistry and Chemical Engineering: Prof. Dr ŽELJKO KNEZ
Faculty of Civil Engineering: Prof. Dr MIROSLAV PREMROV
Faculty of Criminal Justice: Prof. Dr GORAZD MESKO
Faculty of Education: Prof. Dr SAMO FOŠNA-RIČ
Faculty of Electrical Engineering,Computer Science: Prof. Dr IGOR TIČAR
Faculty of Energy: Prof. Dr ANDREJ PREDIN
Faculty of Health Sciences: Prof. Dr PETER KOKOL
Faculty of Law: Prof. Dr RAJKO KNEZ
Faculty of Logistics: Prof. Dr MARTIN LIPIČ-NIK
Faculty of Mechanical Engineering: Prof. Dr NIKO SAMEC
Faculty of Medicine: Prof. Dr IVAN KRAJNC
Faculty of Natural Sciences and Mathematics: Prof. Dr NATAŠA VAUPOTIČ
Faculty of Organizational Sciences: Dr FERJAN MARKO

PROFESSORS

Faculty of Agriculture (Pivola 10, 2311 Maribor; tel. (2) 320-90-00; e-mail fk@uni-mb.si; internet fk.uni-mb.si):

BAVEC, F., Organic Farming, Crops, Vegetables and Ornamental Plants
CENCIČ, A., Microbiology, Biochemistry, Molecular Biology and Biotechnology
IVANCIC, A., Genetics and Breeding of Plants
KRAJNČIČ, B., Plant Physiology, Biology, Botany
KRAMBERGER, B., Grass and Fodder Production
LAKOTA, M., Engineering biosystems
LEŠNIK, M., Phytomedicine
LEŠNIK, M., Foreign Languages Expert
NEMEC, J., Mathematical Methods, Informatics and Statistics in agriculture
ŠKORJANC, D., Animal Genetics and Breeding
SLEKOVEC, M., Chemistry, Agrochemistry and Pedology
TOJNKO, S., Fruit and Fruit Processing
TURK, J, Agricultural Economics and Rural Devt
VOLK, M., Physiology, Anatomy and Animal Health
VRŠIC, S., Viticulture and Enology

Faculty of Business and Economics (Razlagova 14, 2000 Maribor; tel. (2) 229-00-00; e-mail epf@uni-mb.si; internet www.epf.uni-mb.si):

BOBEK, D., Business Administration in Banking
BELAK, J., Economics
FILIPIČ, D., Finance
GUSEL, L., Yugoslav Import-Export System
HAUC, A., Project Management
INDIHAR, S., Mathematics
KENDA, V., International Trade
KOKOTEC-NOVAK, M., Economics
KOLETNIK, F., Accounting, Auditing
MULEJ, M., Dialectical Theory of Systems
MUSIL, V., Polymeric Materials
OVIN, R., Economic Policy
PAUKO, F., Tourism
PIVKA, H., Business Law
RADONJIČ, D., Market Research
SAVIN, D., Political Economy
SRUK, V., Sociology, Philosophy and Political Science
ŽIŽMOND, E., Economic Policy

Faculty of Chemistry and Chemical Engineering (Smetanova ul. 17, 2000 Maribor; tel. (2) 229-44-01; e-mail fkkt@uni-mb.si; internet www.atom.uni-mb.si):

DOBČNIK, D., Analytical Chemistry
DOLEČEK, V., Physical Chemistry
DROFENIK, M., Inorganic Chemistry
GLAVIČ, P., Inorganic Technology
KNEZ, Ž, Separation Process
KROPE, J., Thermoenergetics

Faculty of Civil Engineering (Smetanova ul. 17, 2000 Maribor; tel. (2) 229-43-02; e-mail fg@uni-mb.si; internet kamen.uni-mb.si):

CVIKL, B., Physics
LEP, J., Mathematics
PŠUNDER, M., Building Economics
ŠKRABL, S., Materials
TRAUNER, L., Soil Mechanics, Geotechnics
UMEK, A., Earthquake Engineering

Faculty of Education (Koroska 160, 2000 Maribor; tel. (2) 229-36-00; internet www.pfmb.uni-mb.si):

BELEC, B., Geography
BOKOR, J., Hungarian Linguistics
BREŠAR, M., Mathematics
BRUMEN, M., Physics
FLERE, S., Sociology
JAUŠOVEC, N., Psychology
JUTRONIĆ-TIHOMIROVIĆ, D., English Linguistics

KLAVŽAR, S., Mathematics
KLEMENČIČ, M., Contemporary History
MIŠČEVIĆ, N., History of Philosophy
MLINARIČ, J., History of Middle Ages
PANDUR, L., Painting Design
ROZMAN, F., History of Southeast Europe
VAUHNIK, J., Special Didactics of Sports Education
VUKMAN, J., Mathematics
ZORKO, Z., History of Language, Dialectology

Faculty of Electrical Engineering and Computer Science (Smetanova ul. 17, 2000 Maribor; tel. (2) 220-70-00; e-mail feri@uni-mb.si; internet www.feri.uni-mb.si):

BREŠAR, F., Mathematics
DOLINAR, D., Electro-Mechanical Control Systems
GRČAR, B., Control and Regulation Systems
GUID, N., Computer Graphics
HORVAT, B., Computing and Microcomputer Systems
JEZERNIK, K., Robotics
KUMPERŠČAK, V., Physics
ROZMAN, I., Information Systems
ZAGRADIŠNIK, I., Electrical Machines
ŽAZULA, D., Systems Software
ŽUMER, V., Programming Languages

Faculty of Law (Mladinska 9, 2000 Maribor; tel. (2) 250-42-00; e-mail info.pf@uni-mb.si; internet www.pf.uni-mb.si):

DEVETAK, S., Public International Law
FLERE, S., Sociology
GEČ-KORQŠEC, M., Family Law
IVANJKO, S., Company Law, Insurance Law
KRANJC, J., Roman Law
OJNIK, S., History of Law
PERNEK, F., Financial Law
RUPNIK, J., Constitutional Law
TOPLAK, L., International Business Law

Faculty of Mechanical Engineering (Smetanova ul. 17, 2000 Maribor; tel. (2) 220-75-00; e-mail fs@uni-mb.si; internet www.fs.uni-mb.si/en):

ALUJEVIĆ, A., Mechanics, Thermodynamics
BALIČ, J., Manufacturing Technologies, Theory of Systems, Computer Integrated Manufacturing, Manufacturing Systems
FLAŠKER, J., Machine Elements II, Mechanical Design of Devices I, Technical Regulations
JEZERNIK, A., CAD/CAM
KRIŽMAN, A., Industrial Engineering, Metal Heat Processing
MAJCEN LE MARECHAL, A., Chemistry, Organic Chemistry I
OBLAK, M., Mechanics and Hydrodynamics
POLAJNAR, A., Work Study and Manufacturing Systems Planning
ŠKERGET, L., Fluid Mechanics and Heat Transfer, Transport Phenomena, Eco-Engineering in Manufacturing
ŠOSTAR, A., Technological Measurements

Faculty of Organizational Sciences (Kidričeva cesta 55A, 4000 Kranj; tel. (4) 237-42-00; e-mail dekanat@fov.uni-mb.si; internet www.fov.uni-mb.si):

FLORJANČIČ, J., Personnel Administration
GRIČAR, J., Analysis and Design of Organizational Systems
JEREB, J., Human Resources Management
JESENKO, J., Quantitative Methods
JUG, J., Andragogy and Human Relations, Human Resources
KLJAJIČ, M., Systems Theory
RAJKOVIČ, V., Management Information Systems
VILA, A., Production Process Management
VRŠEC, E., Production Systems

Faculty of Health Sciences (Zitna 15, 2000 Maribor; tel. (2) 300-47-00; e-mail vzs@uni-mb.si; internet sola.vzdr.uni-mb.si):

BERVAR, M., Surgery
BORKO, E., Gynaecology and Obstetrics
BRUMEC, V., Physiology
GOLOUH, R., Pathology
HREN-VENCELJ, H., Microbiology, Parasitology

KAJZER, Š., Elements of Administration and Management
KRAJNC-SIMONETTI, S., Social Medicine and Statistics in Health Care
MULEJ, M., Anaesthesiology and Reanimatology
POKORN, D., Medical Dietetics
RAIŠP, I., Internal Medicine

UNIVERZA V NOVI GORICI
(University of Nova Gorica)

Vipavska 13, Rožna Dolina, 5000 Nova Gorica

Telephone: (5) 331-53-97
E-mail: info@ung.si
Internet: www.ung.si

Founded 1995
Autonomous
Pres.: Prof. Dr DANILO ZAVRTANIK
Vice-Pres. for Education: Prof. Dr MLADEN FRANKO
Vice-Pres. for Research: Prof. Dr GVIDO BRATINA
Sec.: ERICA GOJKOVIĆ

Library of 10,000 vols, 100 periodicals, 200 non-book materials and e-edition of scientific journals
Number of students: 800

DEANS

Business School of Engineering: Prof. Dr TANJA URBANČIČ
College of Arts: BOŠTJAN POTOKAR
College of Viticulture, Enology: Prof. DANILO ZAVRTANIK
Faculty of Applied Sciences: Prof. Dr GVIDO BRATINA
Faculty of Environmental Sciences: Prof. Dr POLONCA TREBŠE
Faculty of Humanities: Dr FRANC MARUŠIĆ
Faculty of Postgraduate Studies: Prof. IZTOK ARCON

SOLOMON ISLANDS

The Higher Education System

Formerly a British protectorate since 1900, Solomon Islands became independent within the Commonwealth in 1978. The Solomon Islands College of Higher Education (founded 1984) and the University of the South Pacific Solomon Islands Centre (founded 1971) are the principal institutions of higher education. Scholarships are available for higher education at various universities overseas. In October 2010 the Government announced a Strategic Framework for National Distance Education and Flexible Learning, which outlined a range of measures intended to improve and expand the provision of distance education and flexible learning in Solomon Islands, and proposed the eventual development of a national qualifications framework. Higher education is the responsibility of the Ministry of Education and Human Resources Development. It was announced in late 2011 that the University of the South Pacific was to finance and build a new campus in Solomon Islands.

The Pacific Senior Secondary Certificate or the Solomon Islands School Certificate is the main requirement for admission to the University of the South Pacific (and also to the University of Papua New Guinea). Preliminary and Foundation programmes, both of which last for one year, are available to prepare students for admission to degree courses. The Bachelors is the main undergraduate degree, and lasts for three years in most subjects; however, some courses are longer in duration—for example, medicine, which lasts four years and is taught at the Fiji School of Medicine—while the University of Papua New Guinea offers four-year Bachelor degrees, with an additional year for 'Honours' degrees. After the Bachelors, the first postgraduate degree is the one- to two-year Masters, which is followed by the Doctorate, the highest university degree, which requires a minimum of two years' additional study. In addition to Bachelors, Masters and Doctoral degrees, the University of the South Pacific also offers courses leading to professional and in-service qualifications, while the University of Papua New Guinea offers Postgraduate Diploma qualifications.

The Solomon Islands College of Higher Education (comprising seven schools) is an autonomous institution primarily offering technical and vocational education via Certificate and Diploma courses. As with degree-level education, some students intending to enrol on Certificate and Diploma courses first elect to take a preparatory one-year Foundation course.

Regulatory Bodies

GOVERNMENT

Ministry of Culture and Tourism: POB G26, Honiara; tel. 26848; Minister SAMUEL MANETOALI.

Ministry of Education and Human Resources Development: POB G28, Honiara; tel. 28643; e-mail pseducation@pmc.gov.sb; Minister DICKSON HA'AMORI.

Learned Societies

GENERAL

Commonwealth Secretariat: POB 1681, Honiara; tel. 38374; e-mail regionaldirector@cypsp.org.sb; internet www.thecommonwealth.org/cyppacific; provides young citizens of the Commonwealth with knowledge, skills and opportunities; encourages citizens to participate in the devt and governance of their communities and socs; Dir AFU LEAH BILLY.

Libraries and Archives

Honiara

Solomon Islands National Archives: Min. of Education and Human Resources Devt, POB 781, Honiara; tel. 21426; f. 1979; British Solomon Islands Protectorate records 1900–78, Solomon Islands govt records since 1978; colln of records, microfilm, film and sound recordings on Solomon Islands and Western Pacific; Dir JULIAN CHONIGOLO.

Solomon Islands National Library: POB 165, Min. of Education and Human Resources Devt, Watts St, Honiara; tel. 21601; e-mail nls@welkam.solomon.comb.sb; f. 1974; Solomon Islands colln and central reference colln; 2 br. libraries at Solomon Islands Centre of the Univ. of the S Pacific and Solomon Islands Nat. Museum and Cultural Centre; 120,000 vols; Dir EDDIE MARAHARE.

Solomon Islands National University Library: Kukum Campus, Prince Philip Highway, Honiara; tel. 39016; e-mail mul@sinu.edu.sb; internet www.sinu.edu.sb/library.html; f. 2012; 3 brs in Honiara (capital), and 1 in the W Province (Solomon Islands); 90,000 vols, 26 serial titles, 20 current serial titles; Man. NICHOLAS RUBOSA (acting).

Museum

Honiara

Solomon Islands National Museum and Cultural Centre: POB 313, Honiara; tel. 24896; e-mail loafoa@yahoo.com; f. 1969; attached to Min. of Culture and Tourism; colln began in 1950s, permanent site 1969; research into all aspects of Solomon's culture (prehistory, language, oral tradition, music, dance and architecture); promotes traditional crafts, music and dance; art, heritage, photography, archaeology, natural history (animal specimens, wet and dry), contemporary, technology, audiovisual material, books, journals, posters, pamphlets, documents, outdoor sculptures, art, monuments; houses relics of Second World War; Dir LAWRENCE FOANA'OTA; publs *Custom Stories*, *Journal*.

Colleges

Solomon Islands College of Higher Education: POB R113, Honiara; tel. 30111; e-mail siche@solomon.com.sb; internet www.siche.edu.sb; f. 1984; 4 campuses: Kukum, Panatina, Ranadi, Poitete; offers Bachelor of nursing; library: see under Libraries and Archives; 135 teachers; 1,200 students; Dir DONALD MALASA; Dean of Academic Services NORMAN HATIGEVA.

University of the South Pacific Solomon Islands Centre: POB 460, Honiara; tel. 21307; e-mail usuramo_j@usp.ac.fj; internet www.usp.ac.fj; f. 1971; responsible for providing USP courses through extension; developing nat. continuing education courses; promoting research on subjects of nat. interest; library: 15,000 vols; 4 teachers; 600 students (mostly distance-learning); Dir JOHN USURAMO; Librarian TONY DADALO.

SOMALIA

The Higher Education System

The union of former British and Italian Somaliland took effect in 1960, when the independent Somali Republic (Somalia) was proclaimed. In 1954 the Italian Government established institutes of law, economics and social studies, and in 1969 these institutions were incorporated into the National University of Somalia. In 1990 there were an estimated 10,400 students enrolled in higher education and in 1991 there were 4,640 university students. However, in the early 1990s the campus of the National University of Somalia in Mogadishu was largely destroyed during a civil war that effectively brought the higher education sector to a standstill. The University of Qaran was established in 2000, and at 2011 it was the sole operating public university in Somalia; based in Mogadishu, the University has four other branch campuses in the country. A number of private universities have been founded since the mid-1990s, including Amoud University (founded 1996), Mogadishu University (founded 1997), University of Hargeisa (founded 2000), Benadir University (founded 2002), Puntland State University and Burao University (both founded 2004). More recently, Plasma University and University of Somalia were both founded in 2005 and are based in Mogadishu; Kismayo University was founded in 2007 and East Somali University opened its doors in 2010. In 2010/11 a total of 14,370 students were enrolled in the 15 private institutes of higher education. However, the quality of the education offered in these institutions was variable, and in 2011 the Ministry of Education, Culture and Higher Education was in the process of classifying them into four categories: university (four-year college with multiple faculties), community or city college (four-year college with limited faculties), institute (diploma-issuing in a specialized field), and adult education programmes.

Owing to security concerns, the Somali Government was based in Nairobi, Kenya, until mid-2005; hence, there was no direct government control over higher education prior to this. Today, higher education institutions are government-funded, but not all are under the supervision of the Ministry of Education, Culture and Higher Education. In May 2011 the Government announced a National Education Plan, which sought to address ongoing shortcomings within the education sector in the wake of the civil war; inter alia, the initiative included plans to establish a National Education Commission, to implement quality assurance and accreditation schemes, and further to develop and expand the provision of technical and vocational education.

The Secondary School Certificate is the main requirement for admission to higher education; other criteria include two years' national youth service and a competitive entrance examination. The Laurea (Bachelors) is the main undergraduate degree, and lasts four years. There are numerous institutions of professional education offering post-secondary vocational and technical qualifications, which require between one and four years' study.

Regulatory and Representative Bodies

GOVERNMENT

Ministry of Education, Culture and Higher Education: Mogadishu; tel. (61) 8699566; e-mail info@moesomalia.net; internet www.moesomalia.net; Minister Dr MARYAM KASIM.

Research Institutes

NATURAL SCIENCES

Physical Sciences

Geological Survey Department: Ministry of Water Development and Mineral Resources, POB 744, Mogadishu; library of 500 vols; Dir V. N. KOZERENKO.

Libraries and Archives

Mogadishu

National Library of Somalia: POB 1754, Mogadishu; tel. (1) 22758; f. 1970; research, legal deposit; 30,000 vols, 75 periodicals; training in library science; Dir HASSAN NOOR FARAH.

Museum

Mogadishu

Somali National Museum: Corso Republica, POB 6917, Mogadishu; tel. (1) 21041; f. 1934; ethnographical, historical and natural science collections; library of 3,000 vols; Dir AHMED FARAH.

Universities

AMOUD UNIVERSITY

Borama, Awdal
E-mail: registrar@amouduniversity.org
Internet: amouduniversity.org
Private control

Pres.: Prof. SULEIMAN AHMED GULAID
Deputy Pres.: Prof. AHMED ABDULLAHI BOQORE
Deputy Pres.: Prof. OMAR ALI ABDILLAHI
Chief: YURUP ABDIRAHMAN MUUMIN
Librarian: QABUL NUH ALI

Library: main campus library: 65,000 vols, all subjects; Borama City campus: 30,000 vols, all subjects; medical and allied health sciences library of 20,000 vols

DEANS

Faculty of Agriculture and Environmental Sciences: Prof. ABUBAKAR SH. ABDI
Faculty of Business and Public Administration: Prof. ABDISAMAD EGEH HABANEH
Faculty of Computing and ICT: EDWIN OMONDI OKECH
Faculty of Economics and Political Science: MOHYADIN
Faculty of Education: Prof. ABDIRAHMAN AHMED MUHAMMAD
Faculty of Engineering: FARAH
Faculty of Sharia and Law: Dr MUHAMMAD ALI NAGEEYE
School of Dentistry: Dr ABDIRASHID SH. IBRAHIM OMAR
School of Medical Laboratory Technology: Dr MUHAMMAD DAUD QAWDAN
School of Medicine and Surgery: Dr ISMAIL MUHAMMAD AYE
School of Nursing & Midwifery: Dr FADUMA H. ABUBAKAR
School of Pharmacology: ABDIRASHID DAHIR AYE
School of Postgraduate Studies: AHMED
School of Public Health: Dr MUHAMMAD AHMED AARE

NATIONAL UNIVERSITY OF SOMALIA

POB 15, Mogadishu

Telephone: 25035

Founded 1954, univ. status 1969
Languages of instruction: Somali, Arabic, Italian, English

Rector: MUHAMMAD GANNI MUHAMMAD
Vice-Rector for Academic Affairs: MUHAMMAD ELMI BULLALE
Registrar: NUREYN SHEIKH ABRAR
Librarian: Mrs SIRAD YUSUF ISMAIL

Number of teachers: 550
Number of students: 4,640

DEANS

Faculty of Agriculture: MUHAMMAD ALI MUHAMMAD
Faculty of Economics: MUHAMMAD ISMAIL SHEIKH
Faculty of Education: HUSSEIN MUSA ALI
Faculty of Engineering: ABDULLAHI JIMALE MUHAMMAD
Faculty of Geology: MUHAMMAD ABDI ARUSH
Faculty of Industrial Chemistry: AHMED MAYE ABDURAHMAN
Faculty of Islamic and Arabic Studies: SHARIF MUHAMMAD ALI ISAAK
Faculty of Journalism: MUHAMMAD ISMAIL ABDIRAHMAN
Faculty of Languages: (vacant)
Faculty of Law: ABUD MUSAD ABUD
Faculty of Medicine: ABDI AHMED FARAH
Faculty of Political Science: ADEN ABDULLAHI NUR

Faculty of Technical Teacher Education: ABDULLAHI MUHAMMAD WARSAMME
Faculty of Veterinary Medicine: ABDULHAMID HAJI MUHAMMAD
Somali Institute of Development Administration and Management: IBRAHIM MUHAMMAD ABYAN

UNIVERSITY OF HARGEISA

University Ave Rd, Hargeisa

Telephone: (2) 422166
E-mail: contact@hargeisauniversity.net
Internet: www.hargeisauniversity.net
Founded 2000
Private control
Academic year: September to July (2 semesters)

Vice-Pres. for Admin.: MUHAMMAD MUHAMMAD FARAH

Registrar: YUSUF AINAB
Library of 15,000 vols

College

Veterinary College: Mogadishu; 10 teachers; 30 students; Projects Dir Dr J. NEILSEN.

SOUTH AFRICA

The Higher Education System

Higher education institutions predate the formation of the Union of South Africa in 1910, with the oldest being the University of Cape Town (formerly South African College), which was founded in 1829. The development of the higher education system in the 20th century was affected by the 'apartheid' (segregation) laws imposed by the National Party in the period 1948–91, which resulted in the emergence of historically 'white' and 'black' universities and universities of technology (tertiary education institutions offering technological and commercial vocational training, formerly known as technikons). In 1986 the 'quota clause' of the governing Universities Act was abolished and institutions were free to admit students irrespective of race or ethnicity; by 1991 all the apartheid laws had been repealed. In 1999 there were 21 universities and 15 universities of technology. In 2004–05 the number of universities was reduced to 11, while the number of universities of technology was reduced to six, and four comprehensive institutions and two national higher education institutes were created. In 2009 there were 837,779 students enrolled in 23 public institutions of higher education and 420,475 in 49 public institutions of further education and training. In 2012 the Government announced plans to open two new universities at Mpumalanga (at the current site of Lowveld Agricultural College) and Kimberley in the Northern Cape.

Higher education is principally funded by the Government and administered by the Department of Higher Education and Training (formed when the Ministry of Education was controversially split in two in 2009), under the terms of the Higher Education Act (1997; amended 2008). Public higher education institutions operate autonomously with the right to establish their own programmes of study; private institutions must register with the Department of Higher Education and Training and apply for programme accreditation from the South African Qualifications Authority. A constitutional amendment transferring responsibility for further education and training from provincial governments to the Department of Higher Education and Training was approved in September 2011; it was hoped that the amendment would enable the consolidation, alignment and proper coordination of further education and training colleges, and thereby help to address South Africa's ongoing national skills shortage. The government of a University is the duty of the Council, which comprises senior officers, such as the Vice-Chancellor, staff representatives, students, alumni and local government officials, among others. The Senate is the supreme academic body, and is made up of Heads of Department and Professors. Faculty Boards are subordinate to the Senate. The Vice-Chancellor, Rector or Principal is the chief executive officer. The government budget and students' tuition fees are the main sources of higher education funding.

The Senior Certificate was gradually phased out in favour of the National School Certificate as the main criterion for admission to higher education and this process was completed by 2009. Undergraduate admissions are administered by the Matriculation Board of Higher Education South Africa (formed in 2005 from the amalgamation of the South African Universities Vice-Chancellors Association and the Committee of Technikon Principals). The main undergraduate degree is the 'Ordinary' or 'Honours' Bachelors, which is usually a three-year programme of study, although some professionally related fields of study, such as architecture, dentistry, law and medicine, last between four and six years. A Bachelors with 'Honours', or a professional degree, is required for admission to the postgraduate Masters degree, a one- or two-year course of research. The Doctorate is the highest university degree; it requires a minimum research period of two years after the award of the Masters, and students must submit a thesis.

Tertiary-level technical and vocational education is principally offered by the universities of technology. In addition to non-university Certificates and Diplomas, universities of technology offer university-level degrees with a professional or technical focus. The Bachelor of Technology is a four-year undergraduate degree, the Master of Technology is a one- or two-year postgraduate research degree and the Doctor of Technology is a two-year research project following the award of the Master of Technology.

The Council on Higher Education (CHE) was established under the terms of the Higher Education Act (1997) and is responsible for quality assurance in higher education and training by accrediting private providers and programmes. Within the CHE, the Higher Education Quality Committee (HEQC) sets the quality assurance criteria with which both public and private higher education institutions must comply; the HEQC is also responsible for the accreditation (in terms of both institutions and study programmes) of private institutions. In 2008 Act 67 legislated for the establishment of a National Qualifications Framework; this is administered by the South African Qualifications Authority (SAQA).

Regulatory and Representative Bodies

GOVERNMENT

Department of Arts and Culture: Private Bag X897, Pretoria 0001; Kingsley Centre 481 Stanza Bopape, 10th Fl., cnr Steve Biko and Pretorius Sts, Arcadia, Pretoria; tel. (12) 441-3000; e-mail minister@dac.gov.za; internet www.dac.gov.za; Minister PAUL P. MASHATILE.

Department of Higher Education and Training: Private Bag X893, Pretoria 0001; 123 Frances Baard St, Pretoria 0001; tel. (12) 312-5555; e-mail callcentre@dhet.gov.za; internet www.dhet.gov.za; Minister Dr BLADE NZIMANDE.

ACCREDITATION

Council for Quality Assurance in General and Further Education and Training: Post Net Suite 102, Private Bag X1, Queenswood, Pretoria 0121; 37 General Van Ryneveld St, Persequor Techno Park, Pretoria 0020; tel. (12) 349-1510; e-mail info@umalusi.org.za; internet www.umalusi.org.za; monitors and improves the quality of gen. and further education and training in S Africa; Chair. Prof. SISZWE MABIZELA; CEO Dr MAFU RAKOMETSI.

NATIONAL BODIES

Council on Higher Education and Higher Education Committee: POB 94, Persequor Technopark, Brummeria 0020; 1 Quintin Brand St, Persequor Technopark, Brummeria 0020; tel. (12) 349-3840; e-mail info@che.ac.za; internet www.che.ac.za; f. 1998; CEO AHMED ESSOP.

Higher Education South Africa: POB 27392, Sunnyside, Pretoria 0132; UNISA Sunnyside Campus, Bldg 3, Level 1, cnr Rissik and Steve Biko St, Sunnyside, Pretoria; tel. (12) 481-2821; e-mail info@hesa.org.za; internet www.hesa.org.za; f. 2005; works to enhance the role and contribution of higher education in society; aims to contribute to nat. devt goals through critical enquiry, and scholarly and intellectual leadership; 23 mems (public univs and univs of technology); Chair. Dr MAX PRICE; CEO Dr JEFFREY MABELEBELE.

International Education Association of South Africa: POB 27394, Sunnyside, Pretoria 0132; tel. (12) 484-1146; e-mail admin@ieasa.studysa.org; internet www.ieasa.studysa.org; f. 1997; advocates, promotes and supports internationalization of higher education by providing a professional forum for instns and individuals to address challenges and develop opportunities in int. education; Pres. Dr LAVERN SAMUELS; Admin. Man. THILOR MANIKAM.

National Association of Distance Education and Open Learning in South

Africa (NADEOSA): POB 31822, Braamfontein, Johannesburg 2017; tel. (11) 403-2813; e-mail info@saide.org.za; internet www .nadeosa.org.za; f. 1996; provides a forum for S African organizations and individuals who are committed to increasing access to an affordable, cost-effective and quality learning environment in which learners are empowered to become self-sufficient members of society; 55 mem. orgs; Pres. Prof. LOUIS VAN NIEKERK; Sec. Prof. LOUIE SWANEPOEL.

South African Qualifications Authority (SAQA): Postnet Suite 248, Private Bag X06, Waterkloof 0145; 1067 Arcadia St, Hatfield, Pretoria; tel. (86) 010-3188; e-mail saqainfo@ saqa.org.za; internet www.saqa.org.za; f. 1995; incl. 12 mems; enhance quality of education and training in S Africa, create nat. framework for learning achievements, devt and implementation of Nat. Qualifications Framework; CEO JOE SAMUELS; Deputy CEO JULIE REDDY.

Learned Societies

GENERAL

Royal Society of South Africa: 4.17 P. D. Hahn Bldg, Univ. of Cape Town, Rhodes Gift 7700; tel. (21) 650-2543; e-mail royalsociety@ uct.ac.za; internet www.royalsocietysa.org .za; f. 1908; promotes science; research and scholarship; advances all aspects of science; publishes scientific journal; public lectures; organises confs, colloquia; expeditions; 487 mems (212 fellows, 35 hon. fellows, 240 ordinary mems); library of 33,000 vols of scientific periodicals; Pres. Prof. DON A. COWAN; Gen. Sec. Prof. JANNIE HOFMEYR; publ. *Transactions of the Royal Society of South Africa* (3 a year).

Suid-Afrikaanse Akademie vir Wetenskap en Kuns (South African Academy for Science and Arts): Private Bag X11, Arcadia, Pretoria 0007; Engelenburghuis, Ziervogelstraat 574, Arcadia, Pretoria 0083; tel. (12) 328-5082; e-mail akademie@akademie.co.za; internet www.akademie.co.za; f. 1909; promotes science, technology, arts and the Afrikaans language; 800 mems; Chair. Prof. W. A. M. CARSTENS; CEO Dr DIONE PRINSLOO; publs *SA Tydskrif vir Natuurwetenskap en Tegnologie* (4 a year), *Tydskrif vir Geesteswetenskappe* (3 a year).

AGRICULTURE, FISHERIES AND VETERINARY SCIENCE

South African Society for Animal Science: POB 13884, Hatfield, Pretoria 0028; tel. (12) 420-6017; e-mail secretary@sasas.co .za; internet www.sasas.co.za; f. 1961; advances animal science and promotes viable animal production systems; 400 mems; Pres. Dr MICHIEL M. SCHOLTZ; Exec. Sec. Prof. JANNES B. J. VAN RYSSEN; publs *Applied Animal Husbandry & Rural Development* (1 a year, online, www.sasas.co.za/aahrd), *South African Journal of Animal Science* (1 a year, print and online, www.journals.sasas.co.za).

South African Society of Dairy Technology/Suid Afrikaanse Vereniging vir Suiweltegnologie: POB 1853, Silverton 01217; Block C, Old Farm Office Park, 881 Old Farm Rd, Fearie Glen, Pretoria; tel. (12) 991-4164; e-mail info@sasdt.co.za; internet www.sasdt .co.za; f. 1967; promotes and encourages technological and scientific advancement in the dairy industry; 300 mems; Pres. STEPHAN STEYN; Sec. YVONNE STEYN.

Southern African Institute of Forestry: Postnet Suite 329, Private Bag X4, Menlo Park 0102; tel. (82) 523-8733; e-mail saif@ mweb.co.za; internet www.saif.org.za; f. 1968; assists mems to achieve excellence in the practice of forestry, promotes growth and sustainability in the industry, while being responsible as custodians of a sensitive environment; 560 mems; Pres. ROB THOMPSON; Nat. Sec. CORINE VILJOEN; publ. *Southern Forests: A Journal of Forest Science* (4 a year, print and online).

ARCHITECTURE AND TOWN PLANNING

South African Institute of Architects: Private Bag X10063, Randburg 2125; Bouhof (Ground Fl.), 31 Robin Hood Rd, Robindale, Randburg 2104; tel. (11) 782-1315; e-mail admin@saia.org.za; internet www.saia.org .za; f. 1996; professional voluntary association of architects; 2,600 mems; Pres. SINDILE NGONYAMA; Vice-Pres. SIMMY PEERUTIN; publs *Architecture South Africa* (6 a year, print and online, www.saia.org.za/?page_id=714), *Digest of South African Architecture* (1 a year).

BIBLIOGRAPHY, LIBRARY SCIENCE AND MUSEOLOGY

Library and Information Association of South Africa (LIASA): POB 1598, Pretoria 0001; 228 Johannes Ramokhoase St, Pretoria; tel. (12) 323-4912; e-mail liasa@liasa .org.za; internet www.liasa.org.za; f. 1997; advocates, supports and promotes the provision of efficient, user-orientated library and information services; develops library and information services profession; offers networking, education, training and devt and professional recognition opportunities; 1,800 mems; Pres. UJALA SATGOOR; Pres.-Elect SEGAMETSI MOLAWA; Sec. THERESE ELS; publ. *South African Journal of Libraries and Information Science* (2 a year).

South African Museums Association: Flat No 3, 50 Bellair Rd, Vredehoek 8001; tel. (21) 461-2315; e-mail samuseums@gmail .com; internet www.sama.za.net; f. 1936; membership-based professional nat. museums asscn; 400 mems incl. 150 institutional mems; Pres. CATHERINE SNEL; Sec. ISHMAEL MBHOKODO.

ECONOMICS, LAW AND POLITICS

Economic Society of South Africa: POB 73354, Lynnwood Ridge 0040; Tukkiewerf 2/21, Univ. of Pretoria, Lynnwood Rd, Pretoria 0002; tel. (12) 420-3525; e-mail saje@up.ac .za; internet www.essa.org.za; f. 1925; promotes discussion of economic issues, in particular those affecting S Africa; brs in Bloemfontein, Cape Town, Eastern Cape, Johannesburg, Kwazulu-Natal, Limpopo, North-West, Pretoria and Stellenbosch; 900 mems; Pres. PHILIPPE BURGER; Sec. LE ROUX BURROWS; publ. *The South African Journal of Economics* (4 a year, print and online, www.onlinelibrary.wiley.com/journal/10.1111/%28ISSN%291813-6982).

Institute of Bankers in South Africa: Sandown Mews, 2nd Fl., 88 Stella Rd, Sandown, Sandton 2196; tel. (11) 783-4329; e-mail info@iob.co.za; internet www.iob.co .za; f. 1904; 10,000 mems; Chair. JALDA HODGES; publ. *South African Banker* (4 a year).

South African Institute of International Affairs: POB 31596, Braamfontein, Johannesburg 2017; Jan Smuts House, East Campus, Univ. of Witwatersrand, Johannesburg; tel. (11) 339-2021; e-mail info@saiia.org.za; internet www.saiia.org.za; f. 1934; brs in Cape Town, Pietermaritzburg, East London; encourages wider and more informed awareness of the importance of int. affairs; 3,500 mems; library: Jan Smuts House Library; 10,000 books, 2,000 journals; spec. collns incl. UN depository colln, World Bank regional depository library, Martin Edmonds colln; Chair. FRED PHASWANA; Chief Exec. ELIZABETH SIDIROPOULOS; publ. *South African Journal of International Affairs* (3 a year, print and online, www.saiia.org.za/General/south-african-journal-of-international-affairs).

FINE AND PERFORMING ARTS

Federasie van Afrikaanse Kultuurvereninginge (Association of Afrikaans Cultural Societies): POB 2655, Brooklyn Sq. 0075; Gerard Moerdykhuis, Voortrekkermonumentterrein Eeufeesweg, Pretoria; tel. (12) 301-1777; e-mail fak@fak.org.za; internet www.fak.org.za; f. 1929; devt of African language and culture; 2,300 affiliated socs; Man. Dir Dr DANIE LANGNER.

South African National Association for the Visual Arts (SANAVA): POB 2691, Brooklyn Sq., Pretoria 0075; tel. (12) 460-5826; e-mail info@sanava.co.za; internet www.sanava.co.za; f. 1851 as the Cape Fine Arts Soc., current name adopted 1998; encourages visual arts nationally and internationally; devt of visual artists; 25 autonomous brs with individual galleries, management cttees, as well as 29 affiliated orgs; 5,500 mems; Nat. Pres. DIRKIE OFFRINGA; Nat. Exec. Officer ANTON LOUBSER.

HISTORY, GEOGRAPHY AND ARCHAEOLOGY

Genealogical Society of South Africa: Suite 143, Postnet X2600, Houghton 2041; tel. (86) 672-2412; internet www.genza.org .za; f. 1964; promotes and facilitates interest in genealogy and family history; brs in Bloemfontein, Cape Town, Durban, George, Johannesburg, Kimberley, Pietermaritzburg, Port Elizabeth, Potchefstroom and Klerksdorp, Pretoria, Vereeniging, Western Gauteng; 900 mems; Nat. Pres. PETRO COREEJESBRINK; Sec. JUDI MEYER; publ. *Familia* (4 a year, print and online).

Nederlands Cultuurhistorisch Instituut (Dutch Culture Historical Institute): Univ. of Pretoria, Pretoria 0002; tel. (12) 420-2808; internet www.up.ac.za; f. 1931; offers books and information on Dutch culture, history and art; 250 mems; library of 32,000 vols; Dir ROBERT MOROPA.

Society of South African Geographers: POB 339, Univ. of the Free State, Bloemfontein 9300; tel. (51) 401-2184; e-mail britss@ ufs.ac.za; internet www.ssag.co.za; f. 1994; 400 mems; Pres. Prof. SOPHIE OLDFIELD; Admin. Officer SANDRA BRITS; publ. *South African Geographical Journal* (2 a year).

South African Archaeological Society: POB 15700, Vlaeberg 8018; tel. (21) 712-3629; e-mail archsoc@iziko.org.za; internet www.archaeologysa.co.za; f. 1945; 1,000 mems; library of 1,000 vols, 5,000 periodicals; Pres. Dr SIMON HALL; Asst Sec. CAROLE GOEMINNE; publs *Goodwin Series* (irregular), *The Digging Stick* (3 a year).

Van Riebeeck Society: POB 15151, Vlaeberg 8018; Centre for the Book, 62 Queen Victoria St, Cape Town 8000; tel. (21) 423-8424; e-mail vanriebk@mweb.co.za; internet www.vanriebeecksociety.co.za; f. 1918; publishes and republishes original and rare documents, books and pamphlets relating to the history of Southern Africa; 1,075 mems; Chair. Prof. HOWARD PHILLIPS; Sec. PIET E. WESTRA.

LANGUAGE AND LITERATURE

Alliance Française: 17 Lower Park Dr., Cnr Kerry Rd, Johannesburg; tel. (11) 646-

1169; e-mail info@alliance.org.za; internet www.alliance.org.za; f. 1936; offers courses and exams in French language and culture and promotes cultural exchange with France; attached teaching centres in Bloemfontein, Cape Town, Durban, Mitchell's Plain, Pietermaritzburg, Port Elizabeth, Potchefstroom, Pretoria, Somerset West, Soweto, Stellenbosch and Franschoek, Vaal Triangle; also responsible for Alliance Française operations in Botswana, Lesotho and Swaziland.

British Council: POB 655, Parklands 2121; Dunkeld Cnr, 275 Jan Smuts Ave, Dunkeld West, Johannesburg 2196; tel. (11) 560-9300; e-mail ssa.enquiries@britishcouncil.org; internet www.britishcouncil.org.za; offers courses and exams in English language and British culture and promotes cultural exchange with the UK; attached offices in Johannesburg (teaching centre) and Cape Town; responsible for British Council activities in Botswana, Lesotho, Malawi, Mauritius, Mozambique, Namibia, Swaziland, Zambia and Zimbabwe.

Classical Association of South Africa: c/o Secretary, PMB X6001, Potchefstroom 2520; e-mail johan.steenkamp@nwu.ac.za; internet www.casa-kvsa.org.za; f. 1908; promotes the study and appreciation of classical antiquity; organizes various activities both on nat. and regional basis; hosts a biennial conf. on classics, ancient history and related disciplines; 350 mems; Chair. M. LAMBERT; Sec. J. STEENKAMP; publs *Acta Classica* (1 a year), *Akroterion* (1 a year).

English Academy of Southern Africa: Room D23, RW5, Richard Ward Bldg, POB 124, WITS, Johannesburg 2050; tel. (11) 717-9339; e-mail englishacademy@societies.wits .ac.za; internet www.englishacademy.co.za; f. 1961; concerned with all forms and uses of English; promotes education, research and debate; organizes lectures and promotes creative, critical and scholarly talents of users of English in S Africa; awards the English Academy Medal, the Olive Schreiner Prize, the Percy FitzPatrick Prize, the Sol Plaatje Prize for Translation and the Thomas Pringle Awards for translation; 300 mems; Pres. Prof. RAJENDRA CHETTY; Hon. Sec. DAVID E. ROBINSON; publ. *The English Academy Review: Southern African Journal of English Studies* (2 a year).

Goethe-Institut: Private Bag X18, Parkview, Johannesburg 2122; 119 Jan Smuts Ave, Parkwood, Johannesburg 2193; tel. (11) 442-3232; e-mail info@johannesburg.goethe .org; internet www.goethe.de/johannesburg; f. 1995; offers courses and exams in German language and culture and promotes cultural exchange with Germany; attached centre in Cape Town; project space in Johannesburg CBD; regulates the work in the Sub-Saharan countries incl. 11 institutes and 14 Goethe cultural centres; library of 7,600 vols, incl. books, magazines, newspapers, audio and video cassettes and DVDs; Dir Dr NORBERT SPITZ.

South African PEN Centre: POB 732, Constantia, Cape Town 7848; e-mail rudebs@icon.co.za; internet www.sapen.co .za; f. 1960; 213 mems (200 full, 13 assoc.); Pres. ANTHONY FLEISCHER; Sec. DEBORAH HORN-BOTHA.

MEDICINE

Association of Surgeons of South Africa: Postnet Suite 199, Private Bag X2600, Houghton, 2041; ASSA Suite, Wits Donald Gordon Medical Centre, 18 Eton Rd, Parktown 2193; e-mail assa@worldonline.co.za; internet www.surgeon.co.za; f. 1945; 250 mems; Pres. Prof. ROBERT BAIGRIE; Chair.

Prof. MARTIN VELLER; publ. *South African Journal of Surgery*.

Colleges of Medicine of South Africa: 17 Milner Rd, Rondebosch 7700; tel. (21) 689-9533; e-mail administration@colmedsa.co.za; internet www.collegemedsa.ac.za; f. 1954; provides postgraduate examinations in all brs of medicine for all doctors and dentists in S Africa; incl. 28 colleges of medicine and dentistry; small archive and reference library; 12,000 mems; CEO LIZE TROLLIP; Academic Registrar ANN VORSTER; publ. *Transactions* (2 a year, print and online, www.collegemedsa.ac.za/view_document_list. aspx?Keyword=Transactions).

Nutrition Society of Southern Africa: POB 836, Hartbeespoort 0216; tel. (82) 667-4723; e-mail nssa@mweb.co.za; internet www .nutritionsociety.co.za; f. 1955; advances scientific study of nutrition; 323 mems; Pres. Prof. MARIUS SMUTS; Chair. Dr PAUL VAN JAARVELD; Hon. Sec. and Treas. NAZEEIA SAYED; publ. *The South African Journal of Clinical Nutrition* (4 a year, print and online, www.sajcn.com/index.php/SAJCN).

South African Medical Association: POB 74789, Lynnwood Ridge, Pretoria 0040; Block F, Castle Walk Corporate Park, Nossob St, Erasmuskloof Ext. 3, Pretoria 0181; tel. (21) 481-2000; e-mail online@samedical.org; internet www.samedical.org; f. 1998; professional org. for medical practitioners in S Africa; 21 brs; 16,000 mems; Chair. MZUKISI GROOTBOOM; Pres. Prof. ZEPHNE VAN DER SPUY; publ. *South African Medical Journal* (12 a year, print and online, www.samj.org.za/index.php/samj).

South African Society of Basic and Clinical Pharmacology: POB 225, Dept of Pharmacology and Therapeutics, Faculty of Health Sciences, Univ of Limpopo, Medunsa 0204; tel. (12) 521-4145; e-mail office@ sapharmacol.co.za; internet www .sapharmacol.co.za; f. 1966; promotes and develops interest in teaching and research in basic and clinical pharmacology; promotes communication and cooperation between socs and industry representing pharmacology and related disciplines; creates forums to present and exchange ideas with state and provincial depts, local and other authorities; 154 mems; Pres. Prof. CHRISTIAAN BRINK; Vice-Pres. Prof. BERND ROSENKRANZ; Sec. Gen. Prof. VANESSA STEENKAMP.

South African Society of Obstetricians and Gynaecologists: POB 363, Tongaat 4400; tel. (32) 944-1308; e-mail haynes@sun .ac.za; internet www.sasog.co.za; f. 1946; 571 mems; Pres. Prof. B. D. GOOLAB; Hon. Sec. Dr HAYNES VAN DER MERWE.

NATURAL SCIENCES

General

Associated Scientific and Technical Societies of South Africa: POB 93480, Yeoville 2143; 18A Gill St, Observatory 2198; tel. (11) 487-1512; f. 1920; promotes the interests of scientific, professional and technical societies; advances the knowledge of scientific and technical subjects; assists in raising the standard of mathematics and science for underprivileged scholars; raises awareness of career prospects in technology; and provides secretarial, liaison, and meeting facilities, etc., for its mem. societies; 60,000 mems in 51 mem. socs; Pres. A. S. MEYER; Man. ERROL H. VAN ROOY.

Southern Africa Association for the Advancement of Science/Suider-Afrika Genootskap vir die Bevordering van die Wetenskap: POB 366, Irene 0062; e-mail secretary@s2a3.org.za; internet s2a3.org.za;

f. 1902; 83 mems; Nat. Pres. Dr IAN RAPER; Nat. Sec. SHIRLEY A. KORSMAN.

Biological Sciences

BirdLife South Africa: POB 515, Randburg 2125; Lewis House, 239 Barkston Dr., Blairgowrie 2194; tel. (11) 789-1122; e-mail info@birdlife.org.za; internet www.birdlife .org.za; f. 1930 as South African Ornithological Society, current name adopted 1996; promotes the enjoyment, conservation, study and understanding of wild birds and their habitats; prevent extinction of any bird species; conservation and improve habitats and sites of birds; 6,000 mems; Pres. Dr PHOEBE BARNARD; CEO MARK D. ANDERSON; publs *African Birdlife* (6 a year), *Ornithological Observations*, *Ostrich: Journal of African Ornithology* (4 a year).

Botanical Society of South Africa: Private Bag X10, Claremont 7735; tel. (21) 797-2090; e-mail info@botanicalsociety.org.za; internet www.botanicalsociety.org.za; f. 1913; promotes the conservation, cultivation, wise use and study of the indigenous flora of S Africa; 30,000 mems; Chair. MIKE HARPER; Exec. Dir ZAITOON RABANEY; publ. *Veld and Flora* (4 a year).

Herpetological Association of Africa: c/o Buyi Makhubo, Dept of Herpetology, National Museum, POB 266, Bloemfontein 9300; e-mail buyi.makhubo@nasmus.co.za; internet www.africanherpetology.org; f. 1965; promotes the study and conservation of reptiles and amphibians, especially African species; Chair. Prof. LE FRAS MOUTON; Sec. BUYI MAKHUBO; publ. *African Journal of Herpetology*.

South African National Biodiversity Institute (SANBI): Private Bag X101, Silverton 0184; 2 Cussonia Ave, Brummeria, Pretoria; tel. (12) 843-5000; e-mail info@ sanbi.org.za; internet www.sanbi.org; f. 2004; promotes the conservation, sustainable use and appreciation of S Africa's biodiversity; library; libraries at Pretoria and Kirstenbosch with 20,000 vols; Chair. NANA MAGOMOLA (acting); CEO Dr TANYA ABRAHAMSE; publs *African Biodiversity Conservation* (1 a year), *Flowering Plants of Africa* (every 2 years).

South African Society for Biochemistry and Molecular Biology: c/o Dept of Biochemistry, Microbiology and Biotechnology, Rhodes Univ., Grahamstown 6140; tel. (46) 603-8262; e-mail a.edkins@ru.ac.za; internet www.sasbmb.org.za; f. 1973; 450 mems; Pres. Prof. THERESA COETZER; Vice-Pres. DEREK LITTHAUER.

South African Society for Microbiology: Private Bag 3, Univ. of Witwatersrand, Wits 2050; tel. (11) 717-6327; internet sasm.org .za; 600 mems; Pres. KOOS ALBERTYN; Sec. Dr KARL RUMBOLD.

Southern African Society of Aquatic Scientists: c/o Dr Nico Smit, Centre for Aquatic Research, Dept of Zoology, Univ. of Johannesburg, POB 524, Auckland Park 2006; tel. (11) 559-2457; e-mail nicos@uj.ac .za; internet www.riv.co.za/sasaqs; f. 1964 as Limnological Society of South Africa; holds annual congresses and general meetings; 250 mems; Pres. Prof. JANINE ADAMS; Hon. Sec. Dr DENISE SCHAEL; publ. *African Journal of Aquatic Science* (3 a year).

Southern African Wildlife Management Association: POB 217, Bloubergstrand 7436; tel. (21) 554-1297; e-mail elma@mweb .co.za; internet www.sawma.co.za; f. 1970; 400 mems; Pres. Prof. LOUW C. HOFFMAN; Vice-Pres Dr HARRIET DAVIES-MOSTERT; Treas. PIETER NEL; publ. *South African Journal of Wildlife Research* (2 a year, print and online, reference.sabinet.co.za/sa_epublication/wild).

WESSA—Wildlife and Environment Society of South Africa: 1 Karkloof Rd, POB 394, Howick 3290; tel. (33) 330-3931; e-mail marketing@wessa.co.za; internet www.wessa.org.za; f. 1926; 5,500 mems; Chair. Dr RICHARD LEWIS; Vice-Chair. DIANNE PERRET; CEO Dr THOMMIE BURGER; publs *EnviroKids* (4 a year, in English), *Environment* (4 a year, in English).

Physical Sciences

Astronomical Society of Southern Africa: c/o SAAO, POB 9, Observatory, Cape Town 7935; tel. (21) 447-0025; internet assa.saao.ac.za; f. 1922, current name adopted 1956; 250 mems; Pres. MATIE HOFFMAN; Hon. Sec. LERIKA CROSS; publ. *MNASSA-Monthly Notes of the Astronomical Society of Southern Africa* (6 a year, print and online, www.mnassa.org.za/).

Geological Society of South Africa: POB 61809, Marshalltown, Johannesburg 2107; Chamber of Mines Bldg, 5th Fl., 5 Hollard St, Johannesburg; tel. (11) 492-3370; e-mail info@gssa.org.za; internet www.gssa.org.za; f. 1895; promotes the study of the Earth sciences, facilitates the professional devt of its mems, and advances the use of geoscience in the academic, professional, and public sectors; 3,485 mems, incl. 986 student mems; Pres. AVINASH BISNATH; Exec. Man. CRAIG SMITH; publ. *South African Journal of Geology* (4 a year, print and online, sajg .geoscienceworld.org).

South African Chemical Institute: School of Chemistry and Physics, Univ. of KwaZulu-Natal, Westville Campus, Private Bag X54001, Durban 4000; tel. (76) 758-1240; e-mail saci@ukzn.ac.za; internet www.saci.co .za; f. 1912; promotes chemistry, chemists, chemical education and chemical industry in S Africa; 900 mems; Pres. Prof. SIMON LOTZ; Exec. Sec. Dr PATRICIA FORBES; publ. *South African Journal of Chemistry* (4 a year, online, journals.sabinet.co.za/sajchem/).

South African Institute of Physics: Postnet Suite 165, Private Bag X025, Lynnwood Ridge 0040; CSIR Main Campus, Bldg 19A, Offices A149 and A151, Meiring Naude Rd, Brummeria 0184; tel. (12) 841-2627; e-mail info@saip.org.za; internet www.saip.org.za; f. 1955; 490 mems; Pres. Dr IGLE GLEDHILL; Sec. Dr MALEBO TIBANE.

RELIGION, SOCIOLOGY AND ANTHROPOLOGY

South African Institute of Race Relations: POB 291722, Melville 2109; 2 Clamart Rd, Richmond, Johannesburg 2092; tel. (11) 482-7221; e-mail prisca@sairr.org.za; internet www.sairr.org.za; f. 1929; research, policy critiques, risk analysis on S Africa; publishing, bursary admin.; library: J. H. Hofmeyer Library specializing in S African current affairs incl. 120 journals, historical documents, statistics, biographies; Pres. Prof. JONATHAN JANSEN; Chief Exec. JOHN KANE-BERMAN.

TECHNOLOGY

Aeronautical Society of South Africa (AeSSA): POB 11928, Die Hoewes 0163; tel. (12) 662-5113; e-mail admin@aessa.org .za; internet www.aessa.org.za; f. 1911, merged with South African Institute of Aerospace Engineering and the Royal Division of AeSSA in 2001 to form Royal Aeronautical Society of South Africa (RAeSSA); current name adopted 2005; theoretical and practical research; advances the growth and scientific study of aeronautics; offers advice, instruction and facilities for those studying the

subject; organizes meetings, lectures; 20,000 mems; Pres. Prof. LAURENT DALA; Hon. Sec. HEINRICH TORLAGE.

Institution of Certificated Mechanical and Electrical Engineers, South Africa: POB 531, Bruma 2026; Office No 5, Lakeside Two, Ernest Oppenheimer Ave, Bruma; tel. (11) 615-4304; e-mail icmeesa@icmeesa.org .za; internet www.icmeesa.org.za; f. 1912, current name adopted 1957; 1,444 mems; Pres. SAREL JOHANNES KLOPPERS; publ. *Vector Magazine* (12 a year, print and online, z.vector.ee.co.za/).

South African Institute of Electrical Engineers: POB 751253, Gardenview 2047; SAIEE House, 18A Gill St, Observatory, Johannesburg; tel. (11) 487-3003; e-mail info@saiee.org.za; internet www.saiee.org.za; f. 1909; 6,000 mems; Pres. Dr P. NAIDOO; Hon. Vice-Pres. M. BARBOLINI; publs *SAIEE Africa Research Journal* (4 a year), *WATTnow* (12 a year).

South African Institution of Civil Engineering (SAICE): Private Bag X200, Halfway House 1685; SAICE House, Block 19, Thornhill Office Park, Bekker St, Vorna Valley X21, Midrand; tel. (11) 805-5947; e-mail civilinfo@saice.org.za; internet www.saice .org.za; f. 1903; represents the civil engineering profession in S Africa; offers courses in various disciplines of civil engineering; offers career guidance; 10,000 mems; Pres. STANFORD MKHACANE; CEO MANGLIN PILLAY; publs *Civil Engineering* (11 a year, print and online, www.saice.org.za/services/civil-engineering-magazine), *JOURNAL of the South African Institution of Civil Engineering* (4 a year, print and online, www.saice.org.za/services/journal-issues).

South African Institution of Mechanical Engineering (SAIMechE): POB 511, Bruma 2026; Office 5B, Ground Fl., Lakeside Two, 3 Ernest Oppenheimer Ave, Bruma 2198; tel. (11) 615-5660; e-mail info@ saimeche.org.za; internet www.saimeche.org .za; f. 1892; 4,500 mems; Pres. Prof. KUDZAI K. NYANGONI; Vice-Pres. DIRK FINDEIS; publs *R&D Journal* (4 a year, online, www.saimeche.org.za/?page=RDJournal), *SA Mechanical Engineer* (11 a year, print and online, www.promech.co.za/sa-mechanical-engineer-2/).

Southern African Institute of Mining and Metallurgy: POB 61127, Marshalltown 2107; Chamber of Mines Bldg, 5th Fl., 5 Hollard St, cnr Sauer and Marshall St, Johannesburg; tel. (11) 834-1273; internet www.saimm.co.za; f. 1894; brs in Johannesburg, Pretoria, Zululand, Western Cape, Bushveld, Mpumalanga, the Free State, Zambia and Namibia; 3,000 mems; Pres. MAREK DWORZANOWSKI; Man. SAM MOOLLA; publ. *Journal* (6 a year).

Research Institutes

GENERAL

Africa Institute of South Africa: POB 630, Pretoria 0001; Embassy House, 1 Bailey Lane (cnr Edmond St), Arcadia, Pretoria; tel. (12) 304-9700; e-mail ai@ai.org.za; internet www.ai.org.za; f. 1960; applied research and the colln of information in the fields of politics, socio-economics, devt and int. relations on the African continent and its diaspora; Chair. Dr BEKUMUZI HLATSHWAYO; Exec. Dir Dr THANDI SIDZUMO-MAZIBUKO; publ. *Africa Insight* (4 a year, print and online, www.ajol.info/index.php/ai/index).

Council for Scientific and Industrial Research (CSIR): POB 395, Pretoria 0001; Meiring Naudé Rd, Brummeria, Pretoria; tel.

(12) 841-2911; e-mail callcentre@csir.co.za; internet www.csir.co.za; f. 1945; performs multidisciplinary research and technological innovation to contribute to industrial devt and the quality of life of people of S Africa; library: see under Libraries and Archives; Chair. Prof. FRANCIS PETERSEN; Pres. and CEO Dr SIBUSISO SIBISI; publ. *ScienceScope* (4 a year).

AGRICULTURE, FISHERIES AND VETERINARY SCIENCE

Agricultural Research Council: POB 8783, Pretoria 0001; 1134 Park St, Hatfield, Pretoria; tel. (12) 427-9700; e-mail nkami@ arc.agric.za; internet www.arc.agric.za; f. 1990; promotes agriculture and related industries; facilitates and ensures natural resource conservation and alleviates poverty; Pres. and CEO Dr SHADRACK MOEPHULI..

Attached Research Institutes:

Animal Production Institute, Irene: ARC-Animal Production Instn, Private Bag X2, Irene 0062; Old Olifantsfontein Rd, Irene; tel. (12) 672-9111; e-mail ulecuona@arc.agric.za; internet www.arc .agric.za/arc-api/pages/arc-api-homepage .aspx; research and devt in animal breeding and genetics; nutrition and food science; library of 10,000 vols; Dir Dr M. A. MAGADLELA.

ARC Infruitec-Nietvoorbij/Institute for Deciduous Fruit, Vines and Wine: Private Bag X5026, Stellenbosch 7599; Klapmuts Rd R44, Stellenbosch; tel. (21) 809-3100; e-mail infocape@arc.agric.za; internet www.arc.agric.za/ arc-infruitec-nietvoorbij/pages/arc-infrnietv-homepage.aspx; f. 1997; research on the cultivation and post-harvest technology of deciduous fruit, viticulture, alternative crops, indigenous herbal teas; production of wine and brandy; library of 5,000 vols; Research Man. Dr JOHAN VAN ZYL.

ARC Institute for Industrial Crops: Private Bag X82075, Rustenburg 0300; tel. (12) 4279999; e-mail infoiic@arc.agric .za; internet www.arc.agric.za; basic and applied research on tobacco cotton and industrial crops; Sr Man. Dr GRAHAM THOMPSON; Sr Sec. KAREN SMOOK.

ARC Small Grain Institute: Private Bag X29, Bethlehem 9700; Blydskap Rd, Lindley Direction, Bethlehem 9700; tel. (58) 307-3400; e-mail bugere@arc.agric.za; internet www.arc.agric.za/arc-sgi/pages/ arc-sgi-homepage.aspx; f. 1947; research on improvement and cultivation of wheat and small grain crops; Man. Dr COBUS LE ROUX.

Grain Crops Institute: Private Bag X1251, Potchefstroom 2520; 114 Chris Hani St, Agricultural Research Centre, Hendrik Schoeman and JPF Sellschop Bldgs, Potchefstroom; tel. (18) 299-6100; e-mail jamesm@arc.agric.za; internet www .arc.agric.za/arc-gci/pages/arc-gci-home-page.aspx; f. 1981; research on grain crops and oil and protein seeds; Dir Dr P. J. A. VAN DER MERWE.

Institute for Agricultural Engineering: Private Bag X519, Pretoria 0127; 141 Cresswell Rd, Weavindpark; e-mail iaeinfo@arc.agric.za; internet www.arc .agric.za/arc-iae/pages/arc-iae%20home-page.aspx; f. 1961; research on agricultural mechanization, farm structures, irrigation, resource conservation, energy, aquaculture and product processing; Dir Prof. TIMOTHY SIMALONGA.

Institute for Soil, Climate and Water: Private Bag X79, Pretoria 0001; 600 Belvedere St, Arcadia 0083; tel. (12) 310-2500; e-mail iscwinfo@arc.agric.za; internet www.arc.agric.za/arc-iscw/pages/arc-iscw-homepage.aspx; f. 1902; soil science, agrometeorology, water utilization, remote sensing, analytical services; library of 10,000 vols; Research and Technology Man. Dr MPHEKGO MAILA.

Institute of Tropical and Subtropical Crops: Private Bag X11208, Nelspruit 1200; 3 Rivier St, Nelspruit; tel. (13) 753-2071; e-mail infoitsc@arc.agric.za; internet www.arc.agric.za/arc-itsc/pages/arc-itsc-homepage.aspx; f. 1926; provide sustainable and appropriate technologies for production and post-harvest handling of citrus and subtropical crops; Dir Dr JOHANN VAN ZYL.

Onderstepoort Veterinary Institute: Private Bag X5, Onderstepoort 0110; 100 Old Soutpan Rd, Onderstepoort; tel. (12) 529-9111; e-mail ovi-info@arc.agric.za; internet www.arc.agric.za/arc-ovi/pages/arc-ovi-homepage.aspx; f. 1908; research on animal diseases; production of vaccines; diagnostic service; library of 96,000 vols; Dir Dr DAAN VERWOERD; Research Institute Man. Dr MISHECK MULUMBA; publ. *Onderstepoort Journal of Veterinary Research* (4 a year).

Plant Protection Research Institute: Private Bag X134, Pretoria 0001; KwaMhlanga/Moloto Rd R573, Pretoria; tel. (12) 808-8000; e-mail infoppri@arc.agric.za; internet www.arc.agric.za/arc-ppri/pages/arc-ppri-homepage.aspx; f. 1962; promotes economically and environmentally acceptable pest control and sustainable farming; research on invertebrates, fungi, bacteria and viruses; advisory service on aspects of biological control; library of 9,000 vols; Dir MIKE WALTERS.

Range and Forage Institute: Private Bag X05, Lynn East, Pretoria 0039; tel. (12) 841-9611; research on sustainable livestock and rangeland management systems; Head Dr AIMIE AUCAMP.

Roodeplaat Vegetable and Ornamental Plant Institute: Private Bag X293, Pretoria 0001; KwaMhlanga/Moloto Rd (R573), Roodeplaat, Pretoria; tel. (12) 841-9611; e-mail vopiinfo@arc.agric.za; internet www.arc.agric.za/arc-vopi/pages/arc-vopi-homepage.aspx; f. 1949; research on vegetables, and on cut flowers, pot plants and other ornamental plants; Dir Dr SONJA VENTER.

MEDICINE

National Health Laboratory Service: Private Bag X8, Sandringham, Johannesburg 2131; Modderfontein Rd, Sandringham, Johannesburg; tel. (11) 386-6000; e-mail enquiries@nhls.ac.za; internet www.nhls.ac.za; f. 2001; provides laboratory service to all public sector healthcare providers; supports and conducts health research; provides training for health science education; library of 17,500 vols, 250 periodical titles, 5,000 reprint titles of staff papers; Board Chair. Prof. ALGONDA PEREZ; CEO SAGIE PILLAY.

South African Medical Research Council: POB 19070, Tygerberg 7505; Francie van Zijl Dr., Parowvallei, Cape; tel. (21) 938-0911; e-mail info@mrc.ac.za; internet www.mrc.ac.za; f. 1969; nat. research programmes: environment and devt, health systems and policy, infection and immunity, molecules and disease, non-communicable diseases, and women and child health; Chair. Prof. MIKE MACHABA SATHEKGE; Pres. Prof. GLENDA E. GRAY.

NATURAL SCIENCES

Biological Sciences

Durban Botanic Gardens: POB 3740, Durban 4000; 9A John Zikale Berea, Durban, KwaZulu-Natal; tel. (31) 322-4021; e-mail dbginfo@durban.gov.za; internet www.durbanbotanicgardens.org.za; f. 1849; collns of orchids, cycads, palms and bromeliads; herb garden; garden for the blind; water lily pond, fern garden; indigenous medicinal plants; Chair. IVOR DANIEL; Curator MARTIN CLEMENT.

National Zoological Gardens of South Africa: 232 Boom St, Pretoria 0001; tel. (12) 339-2700; e-mail info@nzg.ac.za; internet www.nzg.ac.za; f. 1899; attached to Nat. Research Foundation; library of 4,000 vols, 40 periodicals; Man. Dir Dr CLIFFORD NXOMANI.

Physical Sciences

Council for Geoscience: Private Bag X112, Pretoria 0001; 280 Pretoria St, Silverton, Pretoria 0001; tel. (12) 841-1911; e-mail info@geoscience.org.za; internet www.geoscience.org.za; f. 1912; applied and fundamental geological research, mapping; library of 200,000 books, 10,000 maps; Chair. Prof. PHUTI E. NGOEPE; CEO MXOLISI KOTA.

Hartebeesthoek Radio Astronomy Observatory: POB 443, Krugersdorp 1740; tel. (12) 301-3100; e-mail info@hartrao.ac.za; internet www.hartrao.ac.za; f. 1961; attached to Nat. Research Foundation; radio telescope 26 m in diameter used for observations of Local Galaxy, spectroscopy of interstellar and circumstellar atoms and molecules, masers, pulsars, quasars and active galaxies; collaborates in global VLBI Networks; library of 1,000 vols, 75 periodicals; Man. Dir Dr MICHAEL GAYLARD; Assoc. Dir Prof. LUDWIG COMBRINCK.

NECSA (South African Nuclear Energy Corporation) SOC Ltd.: POB 582, Pretoria 0001; Elias Motsoaledi St (Church St West Extension), R104, Pelindaba, Brits Dist. 0240; tel. (12) 305-4911; e-mail webmaster@necsa.co.za; internet www.necsa.co.za; f. 1948 as Atomic Energy Board, current name adopted 1999; develops, utilizes and manages nuclear technology for nat. and regional socio-economic devt; CEO G. P. TSHELANE.

Satellite Applications Centre: Div. of Microelectronics and Communications Technology, CSIR, POB 395, Pretoria 0001; tel. (12) 334-5003; e-mail callcentre@csir.co.za; f. 1961; since 1975 part of CSIR; receives, archives and processes METEOSAT, LANDSAT, NOAA and SPOT data; online LANDSAT data catalogue; library of 500 vols, 30 periodicals; Operations Man. RAOUL HODGES.

South African Astronomical Observatory: POB 9, Observatory 7935; Observatory Rd, Observatory 7925; tel. (21) 447-0025; e-mail enquiries@saao.ac.za; internet www.saao.ac.za; f. 1972 by merger of Royal Observatory Cape of Good Hope and Republic Observatory, Johannesburg; equipment incl. 11-, 1.9-, 1.0-, 0.75- and 0.5-m reflectors; library of 30,000 vols; Dir Prof. TED WILLIAMS; Librarian SAMANTHA BENNETT.

RELIGION, SOCIOLOGY AND ANTHROPOLOGY

Human Sciences Research Council (HSRC): Private Bag X41, Pretoria 0001; 134 Pretorius St, Pretoria 0002; tel. (12) 302-2000; e-mail info@hsrc.ac.za; internet www.hsrc.ac.za; f. 1969; promotes, supports and coordinates research in the human and social sciences; advises the govt on research priorities; disseminates research findings; promotes the training of people for research work and makes available to all S Africans the full range of disciplines in the human sciences; library of 60,000 vols, 700 current periodicals; Chair. NASIMA BADSHA; Pres. and CEO Dr OLIVE SHISANA; publ. *HSRC Review* (4 a year, print and online, www.hsrc.ac.za/en/review).

Institute for the Study of Mankind in Africa: School of Anatomical Sciences, University of the Witwatersrand Medical School, 7 York Rd, Parktown 2193; tel. (11) 717-2405; e-mail science.pg@wits.ac.za; f. 1960 to perpetuate the work of Prof. Raymond A. Dart on the study of mankind in Africa, past and present, in health and disease; serves as a centre of anthropological and medical field work; functions partly under the auspices of the Univ. of the Witwatersrand; Pres. Prof. J. N. MAINA.

TECHNOLOGY

MINTEK: Private Bag X3015, Randburg 2125; 200 Malibongwe Dr., Strijdom Park, Randburg; tel. (11) 709-4111; internet www.mintek.co.za; f. 1934; research, devt and technology transfer to promote mineral technology and to foster the establishment and expansion of industries in the fields of minerals and mineral products; library of 30,000 vols; Chair. LINDA MAKATINI; Pres. and CEO Dr ABIEL MNGOMEZULU.

South African Bureau of Standards: Private Bag X191, Pretoria 0001; 1 Dr Lategan Rd, Groenkloof; tel. (12) 428-7911; e-mail info@sabs.co.za; internet www.sabs.co.za; f. 1945; draws up nat. standards, administers the SABS mark and listing schemes; Chair. C. B. SIBISI; CEO Dr BONI MEHLOMAKULU (acting).

Libraries and Archives

Alice

University of Fort Hare Library: Private Bag X1314, Alice 5700; tel. (40) 602-2011; e-mail dmc@ufh.ac.za; internet www.ufh.ac.za/library; f. 1916; 165,000 vols; contains the Howard Pim Library of Rare Books, Bisset Berry colln; Univ. Librarian YOLISA SOUL.

Bloemfontein

Free State Libraries and Information Consortium (FRELICO): c/o UFS Library and Information Service, POB 301, Bloemfontein 9300; tel. (51) 401-2745; e-mail sandra@ufs.ac.za; f. 1996; 3m. books; Dir BETSY EISTER; publ. *Free State Libraries* (4 a year).

Mangaung Library: POB 1029, Bloemfontein 9300; Moshoeshoe St, Rocklands, Bloemfontein 9300; tel. (51) 435-2851; f. 1875; legal deposit, nat. drama library and public library; 500,000 vols, 65,000 plays; Man., Education, Library, Arts and Culture N. L. MOHLAODI; publ. *Catalogue of the National Drama Library*.

University of the Free State Library and Information Services: POB 301, Bloemfontein 9300; tel. (51) 401-2745; e-mail eisterkb@ufs.ac.za; internet library.ufs.ac.za; f. 1904; colln incl. rare pamphlets and other early South African publs of Dreyer-Africana Colln and items on South African Boer War; 576,000 vols (3,000 periodicals); Dir KEITUMETSE EISTER.

Cape Town

Education Library and Information Service (EDULIS): Private Bag X9099, Cape Town 8000; 1st Fl., Middestad Mall, Charl Malan St, Bellville; tel. (21) 957-9600; e-mail edulis@westerncape.gov.za; internet edulis .pgwc.gov.za; f. 1859; attached to Western Cape Education Dept; 60,000 vols, 150 current periodicals; Deputy Head ROSE DAMON.

Library of Parliament: POB 18, Cape Town 8000; Ground Fl., NCOP Wing, Parliament St, Cape Town 8000; tel. (21) 403-2140; e-mail library@parliament.gov.za; internet www.parliament.gov.za/live/content.php?category_id=122; f. 1857; provides gen. and legislative reference services and a press-cutting service to mems and officers of Parliament; legal deposit library and depository for UN publs; 120,000 vols in Parliament subject areas; 150 periodicals; 350,000 items incl. spec. collns of rare books, artworks, historical maps, manuscripts, photographs, artefacts, incl. the Mendelssohn or Africana, Jardine and Anglo-Boer War Collns; Librarian ALBERT NTUNJA.

Royal Society of South Africa Library: 4.17 P D Hahn Bldg, c/o Univ. of Cape Town, Rhodes Gift 7700; tel. (21) 650-2543; e-mail royalsociety@uct.ac.za; internet www .royalsocietysa.org.za; f. 1877, Royal Charter 1908; 33,000 vols of scientific periodicals, held by Univ. of Cape Town Library; publ. *Transactions of the Royal Society of South Africa* (3 a year).

University of Cape Town Libraries: Private Bag X3, Rondebosch, Cape Town 7701; tel. (21) 650-3703; e-mail libraries@uct.ac.za; internet www.lib.uct.ac.za; f. 1905; comprises Chancellor Oppenheimer Library, Bolus Herbarium, Brand van Zyl Law Library, Built Environment Library, Health Sciences Library, Hiddingh Hall Library (fine arts and drama), Institute of Child Health Library, Jewish Studies Library, WH Bell Music Library; 1.2m. vols, 105,000 journal titles, 38,000 audio visual items and 203 online databases; spec. collns incl. African language collns, African Studies colln, Bolus colln, Kipling Colln, Bleek and Lloyd Colln; records of the Jewish community in the W Cape; MSS collns of literary figures incl. C. Louis Leipoldt, Pauline Smith, and Olive Schreiner; Exec. Dir GWENDA THOMAS.

Western Cape Provincial Library Service: POB 2108, Cape Town 8000; cnr of Chiappinni and Hospital Sts, Cape Town 8001; tel. (21) 483-2273; e-mail capelib@ westerncape.gov.za; internet www .capegateway.gov.za/library; f. 1945; attached to Dept of Cultural Affairs and Sport, Western Cape; 15 regional libraries; 330 affiliated libraries; library promotion; training of public librarians; 6m. vols; collns of art prints, phonographic records, CDs, audio cassettes, 16mm films, video cassettes, DVDs; Dir NOMAZA DINGAYO; publ. *Cape Librarian/Kaapse Bibliotekaris* (6 a year, print and online, www.westerncape.gov.za/ your_gov/106/documents/mags/1539).

Durban

eThekwini Municipal Library: POB 917, Durban 4000; 99 Umgeni Rd, Durban; tel. (31) 311-2401; e-mail naidookrisen@durban .gov.za; internet www.durban.gov.za/ city_services/parksrecreation/libraries/ pages/default.aspx; f. 1853 as Durban Mechanics Institute, renamed Durban Municipal Library 1911; 90 brs; 1.5m. vols; spec. collns of African Studies and Shakespeare; Dir R. NYONGWANA (acting); Dir TREVOR MASINGA (acting).

University of KwaZulu-Natal Libraries: King George V Ave, Glenwood, Durban 4041; tel. (31) 260-2317; internet library.ukzn.ac .za; f. 2004; 5 main libraries in two centres, four in Durban and one in Pietermaritzburg and several br. libraries; 1,317,144 vols of journals, books, theses, reports, other print media; Dir for Library Services NORA BUCHANAN.

East London

East London Central Library: Gladstone St, POB 652, East London 5201; tel. (43) 722-4991; f. 1876; 225,000 vols; Librarian M. M. DAVIDSON.

Grahamstown

Grahamstown Public Library: POB 180, Grahamstown 6140; 45 Hill St, Grahamstown 6139; tel. (46) 603-6039; f. 1842; 81,053 vols; Asst Dir PATRICIA VUBELA.

Rhodes University Library: POB 184, Grahamstown 6140; tel. (46) 603-8436; e-mail library@ru.ac.za; internet www.ru.ac .za/library; f. 1904; 400,000 vols; Dir for Library Services UJALA SATGOOR (acting).

Johannesburg

City of Johannesburg Library and Information Services: 22 Solomon St, Braamfontein, Johannesburg; tel. (11) 226-0951; f. 1890; 1.9m. vols; Dir NOBUNTU MPENDULO.

Library of the South African Institute of Race Relations: POB 291722, Melville 2109; 2 Clamart Rd Richmond, Johannesburg 2092; tel. (11) 482-7221; e-mail prisca@ sairr.org.za; internet www.sairr.org.za; f. 1929; archival and documentary material; newspaper clippings from 1930 on race relations, politics, labour and economics; bibliographies on race relations; 7,030 vols; Head of Information TAMARA DIMANT.

University of the Witwatersrand Library: Private Bag 3, Wits 2050; 1 Jan Smuts Ave, Braamfontein, Johannesburg 2000; tel. (11) 717-1901; internet www.wits .ac.za/library; f. 1922; 2 central libraries, 14 br. libraries; 1.2m. vols, access to 46,000 ejournal titles; spec. collns incl. Africana, Hebraica and Judaica, Archaeology and Egyptology, early printed books, historical and literary papers (incl. Church of the Province of S Africa), Portuguese; Univ. Librarian FELIX N. UBOGU.

Kimberley

Kimberley Africana Library: POB 627, Kimberley 8300; 63-65 Dutoitspan Rd, Kimberley; tel. (53) 830-6247; e-mail info@ africanalibrary.co.za; internet africanalibrary.co.za; f. 1887 as Kimberley Public Library, renamed 1986; open to researchers; 127,000 vols; Africana Library of 14,000 vols, 640 MSS, 12,000 photographs; photograph colln on North Cape and Diamond Fields and South African War; Judy Scott Library of 43,000 vols; Library Dir SHIRLEY JAMES.

Pietermaritzburg

KwaZulu-Natal Provincial Library Service: Private Bag X9140, Pietermaritzburg 3201; 222 Jabu Ndlovu St, Pietermaritzburg 3200; tel. (33) 264-3400; e-mail nengat@ kzndac.gov.za; f. 1952; consists of central org. and reference library at Pietermaritzburg; 4 regional offices for Coast, S Coast, Midlands and N areas, serving 170 public libraries; 3.4m. vols, 21,000 CDs, 32,000 video cassettes, 6,500 DVDs; Gen. Man. SIBONGILE NZIMANDE; Sr Man. CAROL SLATER; publ. *KZN Librarian* (4 a year).

Msunduzi Municipal Library Services: POB 415, Pietermaritzburg 3200; Churchill Sq., Church St, Pietermaritzburg; tel. (33) 345-2383; internet www.msunduzi.gov.za/ site/library; f. 1851 as Natal Society Library, current name adopted 2004; incl. main library, 10 br. libraries; lending, children's, reference, legal deposit, school assignments, music, map collns, Africana colln; 600,000 vols; Man. MANDLA NTOMBELA; publ. *Natalia* (1 a year).

Port Elizabeth

Nelson Mandela Metropolitan University Library and Information Services: Private Bag X6058, Port Elizabeth 6000; tel. (41) 504-3397; e-mail info@nmmu.ac.za; internet library.nmmu.ac.za; f. 2005; L. C. Steyn Colln of Roman Dutch Law; 556,822 vols; Dir ROBERT PEARCE.

Nelson Mandela Public Library Service: POB 66, Port Elizabeth 6000; tel. (41) 506-5555; e-mail mmajeke@mandelametro.gov .za; f. 1901; incl. 22 libraries; research and orientation workshops for scholars; 500,000 vols; Africana, genealogical and maritime collns; Dir for Libraries, Arts and Culture VELISWA GWINTSA; Sec. MANDY MAJEKE (acting).

Potchefstroom

North-West University Libraries: Private Bag X05, Noordbrug 2522; Hoffman St 11, Ferdinand Postma Library, Bldg E7, Potchefstroom 2531; tel. (18) 299-2000; e-mail fpbinfo@nwu.ac.za; internet www.nwu.ac.za/ library; f. 1869; main library (Ferdinand Postma Library), Education Sciences Library, Music Library, Mafikeng Campus Library, Natural Sciences Library, Theological Library (Jan Lion Cachet Library), Vaal Triangle Campus Library at Vanderbijlpark; 547,035 vols, 120,000 ebooks, 1,694 current periodicals; spec. collns: Carney Africana Colln, Hertzog Law Colln, Colln of the Institute for Research in Children's Literature; Dir ELSA ESTERHUIZEN.

Pretoria

Agricultural Information Centre: Private Bag X388, Pretoria 0001; tel. (12) 319-6872; e-mail daleenk@daff.gov.za; internet www .daff.gov.za/doadev/sidemenu/links/digest5 .htm; f. 1910; attached to Agricultural Information Services; Department of Agriculture, Fisheries and Forestry; library, documentation centre and nat. Agris/Caris centre, resource centre; 40,000 vols, 50 current periodicals, 140,000 pamphlets; Asst Dir DALEEN KOEN.

Council for Scientific and Industrial Research Information Services (CSIRIS): POB 395, Pretoria 0001; tel. (12) 841-2088; e-mail rdomingo@csir.co.za; internet www.csir.co.za/csiris/index.html; f. 1945; provides scientific, technical and business management information services to CSIR research staff and external clients; 90,000 bound vols, 4,000 serial titles and 22,000 pamphlets; Man. Dr MARTIE VAN DEVENTER.

Gauteng Library and Archive Services: Private Bag X33, Johannesburg 2000; tel. (11) 355-2500; e-mail koekie.meyer@gpg.gov .za; f. 1995; consists of head office in Johannesburg, and 4 regional libraries; provides library and information service to 324 public and community libraries and depots in Gauteng province; 3.5m. vols; Dir J. M. MEYER (acting).

Mary Gunn Library: Private Bag X101, Silverton 0184; tel. (12) 843-5042; internet www.sanbi.org/information/libraries/mary-gunn-library; f. 1916; attached to S African Nat. Biodiversity Institute; botanical library; 11,768 vols, 3,000 pamphlets, 1,009 journal titles; spec. colln: Africana and Rare Antiquarian Book Colln; CEO Dr TANYA ABRAHAMSE; Librarian ANNE-LISE FOURIE.

National Archives and Records Service: Private Bag X236, Pretoria 0001; 24 Hamilton St, Arcadia, Pretoria; tel. (12) 441-3200; e-mail archives@dac.gov.za; internet www

.national.archives.gov.za; 140 kms of shelves, incl. textual records, electronic records, audio-visual, photographic and cartographic material; National Archivist Dr GRAHAM A. DOMINY.

National Library of South Africa: Private Bag X990, Pretoria 0001; 228 Johannes Ramokhoase (Proes) St, Pretoria 0001; tel. (12) 401-9700; e-mail infodesk@nlsa.ac.za; internet www.nlsa.ac.za; f. 1999 by amalgamation of South African Library and Staats-Bibliotheek der Zuid-Afrikaansche Republiek; nat. reference and preservation library with legal deposit privileges; MSS collns of Cape and early SA; Africana colln; UN and World Bank depository library; exhibitions of library material; 750,000 vols, 200,000 bound periodicals, 8,000 current periodicals, 45,000 bound newspapers, 300 current newspapers, 20,000 maps, 100,000 iconographic items; spec. collns incl. Grey Colln of 115 medieval MSS, 5,000 vols incl. incunabula and early S African imprints; Dessinian (17th–18th century); Nourse Cromwelliana (17th century); Fairbridge (19th century); Nat. Librarian RACHEL MORE (acting).

University of Pretoria Libraries: Dept of Library Services, University of Pretoria, POB 12411, Hatfield, Pretoria 0028; Dept of Library Services, Univ. of Prestoria, Lynnwood Rd, Hatfield, Pretoria; tel. (12) 420-2235; internet www.ais.up.ac.za; f. 1908; 1.2m. vols, pamphlets, govt publs, 5,698 periodicals, 8,000 gramophone records, 26,000 items of sheet-music, 2,250 CDs; Dir ROBERT MOROPA.

Sovenga

University of Limpopo Libraries and Information Services: Private Bag X1112, Sovenga 0727; tel. (15) 268-2656; internet www.ul.ac.za/index.php?entity=libraries; f. 1960; incl. 2 campus libraries and 2 br. libraries; spec. colln relating to Africa, audio-visual colln, Couper Medical Colln,; 235,000 vols, 80,000 ebooks, 581 periodicals; Exec. Dir MAKGABELA CHUENE; Exec. Sec. DORIS MOKALA MATSHAYA.

Stellenbosch

Stellenbosch University Library and Information Service: Private Bag X5036, Stellenbosch 7599; J. S. Gericke Library, J. S. Marais Sq., c/o Victoria and Ryneveld Sts, Stellenbosch; tel. (21) 808-2486; internet library.sun.ac.za; f. 1895; 5 brs libraries; 1.2m. vols; Sr Dir ELLEN TISE.

Museums and Art Galleries

Bloemfontein

Anglo-Boer War Museum: POB 34061, Faunasig 9325; Monument Rd, Bloemfontein 9301; tel. (51) 447-3447; e-mail museum@anglo-boer.co.za; internet www.anglo-boer.co.za; f. 1931; art colln on Anglo-Boer War, life in concentration and prisoner-of-war camps; research library with Africana colln; Dir TOKKIE PRETORIUS; Deputy Dir JOHANN DU PISANI.

National Museum, Bloemfontein: POB 266, Bloemfontein 9300; 36 Aliwal St, Bloemfontein; tel. (51) 447-9609; e-mail direk@nasmus.co.za; internet www.nasmus.co.za; f. 1877; focuses on natural, cultural history and art; incl. 13 research depts, 4 satellite museums; library of 10,810 vols, 1,731 journals, 11,105 pamphlets; Dir RICK NUTTALL; publs *Culna* (1 a year, print and online, www.nasmus.co.za/museum/library/publica-tions/culna), *Navorsinge van die Nasionale Museum* (print and online, www.nasmus.co.za/museum/library/publications/scientific-journal).

SA Armour Museum: Private Bag X40004, Tempe 9318; tel. (51) 402-1777; e-mail armourschool@mweb.co.za; internet www.saarmourmuseum.co.za; f. 1995; artefacts, objects, books, documents relating to history of S African armoured forces; displays of armoured fighting vehicles, guns, radar, mine rollers, ploughs; research library; Curator WILLEM WILKE.

Cape Town

Gold of Africa Barbier-Mueller Museum: Martin Melck House, 96 Strand St, Cape Town 8001; tel. (21) 405-1540; e-mail museum@goldofafrica.com; internet www.goldofafrica.com; f. 2000; Martin Melck House built in 1783; timeline of gold, trade and history of gold in Africa, displays gold objects recovered from grave sites at Mapungubwe Hill and Thlamela; 350 W African gold artefacts.

Iziko Museums of South Africa: POB 61, Cape Town 8000; 25 Queen Victoria St, Cape Town; tel. (21) 481-3800; e-mail info@iziko.org.za; internet www.iziko.org.za; f. 1999, current name adopted 2012; incl. 11 museums, 1 fossil park; CEO ROOKSANA OMAR..

Art Sites:

Iziko—Michaelis Collection: The Iziko Old Town House, Greenmarket Sq., Cape Town; tel. (21) 481-3933; e-mail hproud@iziko.org.za; f. 1914; Dutch and Flemish paintings, drawings and prints ofrom the 16th century to the early 20th century; Dutch and colonial furniture; library of 1,500 vols; Curator for Historical Collns of Painting and Sculpture HAYDEN PROUD.

Iziko—South African National Gallery: Govt Ave, Company's Garden, Cape Town; tel. (21) 481-3970; e-mail info@iziko.org.za; internet www.iziko.org.za/museums/south-african-national-gallery; f. 1871; collns of South African, African, British, French, Dutch and Flemish art; also photography, sculpture, beadwork, textiles and architecture; library of 15,000 vols, journals and pamphlets; public access by appointment; Dir for Art Collns RAISON NAIDOO.

Natural History Sites:

Iziko—Planetarium: 25 Queen Victoria St, Cape Town; tel. (21) 481-3900; e-mail info@iziko.org.za; internet www.iziko.org.za/museums/planetarium; f. 1987; organizes shows; holiday workshops and astronomy courses; Man. THEO FERREIRA.

Iziko—South African Museum: 25 Queen Victoria St, Cape Town; tel. (21) 481-3800; e-mail info@iziko.org.za; internet www.iziko.org.za/museums/south-african-museum; f. 1825; 1.5m. specimens; collns incl. ethnography, applied arts, philately, transport, weaponry, toys, fossils, stone tools, marine exhibits; library of 12,000 vols, 4,000 periodicals; Dir for Natural History Collns Dr HAMISH ROBERTSON; publ. *African Natural History* (1 a year).

Iziko—West Coast Fossil Park: POB 42, Langebaanweg, Cape Town 7375; R45 Langebaanweg, Cape Town 7375; tel. (22) 766-1606; e-mail info@fossilpark.org.za; f. 1998; Dir for Natural History Collns Dr HAMISH ROBERTSON.

Social History Sites:

Iziko—Bertram House: Hiddingh Campus, Orange St, Cape Town; tel. (21) 481-3972; e-mail info@iziko.org.za; internet www.iziko.org.za/museums/bertram-house; f. 1984; early 19th-century Georgian townhouse; displays of Georgian furniture, Chinese and English porcelain, and English silver and kitchenware; Dir for Social History Collns Dr LALOU MELTZER.

Iziko—Bo-Kaap Museum: 71 Wale St, Cape Town; tel. (21) 481-3938; e-mail info@iziko.org.za; internet www.iziko.org.za/museums/bo-kaap-museum; f. 1978; local Islamic culture and heritage; Dir for Social History Collns Dr LALOU MELTZER.

Iziko—Groot Constantia: Groot Constantia Estate, Constantia, Cape Town; tel. (21) 795-5140; e-mail info@iziko.org.za; internet www.iziko.org.za/museums/groot-constantia-manor-house; f. 1927; 17th-century wine estate and manor house; art colln; wine museum; exhibits furniture, paintings, textiles, ceramics, brass, copperware of 18th to late 19th century Cape farmers; Dir for Social History Collns Dr LALOU MELTZER.

Iziko—Koopmans-De Wet House: 35 Strand St, Cape Town; tel. (21) 481-3935; e-mail info@iziko.org.za; internet www.iziko.org.za/museums/koopmans-de-wet-house; f. 1914; early 18th-century townhouse; colln of Cape furniture, Chinese and Japanese ceramics, Dutch Delftware, paintings, glass and silverware; Dir for Social History Collns Dr LALOU MELTZER.

Iziko—Rust-en-Vreugd: 78 Buitenkant St, Cape Town; tel. (21) 481-3903; e-mail info@iziko.org.za; internet www.iziko.org.za/museums/rust-en-vreugd; f. 1965; 18th-century Cape Dutch house with colln of African watercolours and prints from the William Fehr Colln; Dir for Art Collns RIASON NAIDOO.

Iziko—Slave Lodge: cnr Adderley and Wale Sts, Cape Town; tel. (21) 467-7229; e-mail info@iziko.org.za; internet www.iziko.org.za/museums/slave-lodge; f. 1966 as South African Cultural History Museum, current name adopted 1998; slavery, human rights, nat. and local history, illustrating life in 18th and 19th centuries; library of 14,000 vols; Dir for Social History Collns Dr LALOU MELTZER; Curator for Social History Collns F. H. CLAYTON.

Iziko—Maritime Centre: 1st Fl., Unio-Castle House, Dock Rd, Victoria and Albert Waterfront, Cape Town 8000; tel. (21) 405-2880; e-mail info@iziko.org.za; internet www.iziko.org.za/museums/maritime-centre; f. 1990; focuses on fishing and shipping industry; colln of ships; floating exhibition: SAS Somerset, boom defence vessel built in 1942; Marsh Colln; Dir for Social History Collns Dr LALOU MELTZER.

Iziko—William Fehr Collection: The Castle of Good Hope, Buitenkant St, Cape Town; tel. (21) 467-7223; e-mail info@iziko.org.za; internet www.iziko.org.za/museums/william-fehr-collection-at-the-castle-of-good-hope; f. 1965; colln of paintings and decorative arts of relevance to Cape region; Dir for Social History Collns Dr LALOU MELTZER.

Museum of Coast and Anti-Aircraft Artillery: Fort Wynyard, POB 14068, Green Point 8051; tel. (21) 419-1765; f. 1987; coast and anti-aircraft guns and relics displayed in a restored coast artillery battery.

Durban

Durban Natural Science Museum: POB 4085, Durban 4000; 1st Fl. City Hall, 234 Anton Lembede St, Durban 4001; tel. (31) 311-2256; internet www.durban.gov.za/city_services/parksrecreation/museums/nsm/pages/default.aspx; f. 1989; natural sciences library; Dir ALLISON RUITERS; publ. *Durban Museum Novitates* (1 a year).

Local History Museums: Old Court House Museum, 77 Samora Machel St (previously Aliwal St), Durban; tel. (31) 311-2223; e-mail mnikathib@durban.gov.za; internet www .durban-history.co.za; f. 1966; incl. 7 museums; local and KwaZulu Natal-historical collns, restored Natal colonial public bldg; Dir BHEKI MCHUNU (acting)..

Attached Museums:

Bergtheil Museum: 16 Queens Rd, Westville, Durban; tel. (31) 311-6607; collns related to local communities, particularly early German settlers.

Cato Manor Heritage Centre: Nthuthuko Junction, Francois Rd, Cato Manor, Durban; tel. (31) 261-3216; interpretative centre featuring the history of Cato Manor, incl. aspects related to forced removals and the Apartheid era.

Kwa Muhle Museum: 130 Bram Fischer Rd (previously Ordnance Rd), Durban; tel. (31) 311-2237; f. 1994; urban life in the Apartheid era, with emphasis on the 'Durban System' of administering the African population 1908–1986.

Old Court House Museum: 77 Samora Machel St (previously Aliwal St), Durban; tel. (31) 311-2229; incl. early sugar cane press, Henry Francis Fynn's Cottage, early pharmacy, haberdashery store; photographs and documents on history and heritage of Durban.

Old House Museum: 31 Diakonia St (previously St Andrews St), Durban; tel. (31) 311-2261; f. 1954; a replica of the Robinson Home, a house belonging to the founder of the city's first morning newspaper; contains displays of early domestic life.

Pinetown Museum: Library Complex, cnr Crompton and Main Rds, Pinetown, Durban; tel. (31) 311-6343; collns related to the Pinetown area.

Port Natal Maritime Museum: Maritime Place, Durban; tel. (31) 311-2230; f. 1988; Natal and Durban maritime history, 2 tugs and a minesweeper; Site Supervisor PHILLIP LABUSCHAGNE.

Phansi Museum: 500 Esther Roberts Rd, Glenwood, Durban 4001; tel. (31) 206-2889; e-mail info@phansi.com; internet www .phansi.com; f. 2000; colln of 4,000 artefacts.

East London

East London Museum: POB 11021, Southernwood, East London 5213; 319 Oxford St, Southernwood, East London; tel. (43) 743-0686; e-mail derekh@elmuseum.za.org; internet www.elmuseum.za.org; f. 1921; collns of conchology, ichthyology, ornithology of the Eastern Cape Province, cultural history of the Border region and ethnography of the Southern Nguni peoples; houses specimen of coelacanth (primitive fish) and world's only dodo egg; administers Victorian house museum; library; Curator MCEBISI MAGADLA (acting); publ. *Annals of the Eastern Cape Museums.*

Franschhoek

Huguenot Memorial Museum: POB 37, Franschhoek 7690; tel. (21) 876-2532; e-mail hugenoot@museum.co.za; internet www .museum.co.za; f. 1967; research into Cape Huguenot history, exhibition of over 400 Huguenot artefacts and documents; Chair. L. CYSTER; Curator E. A. JOHANNES.

Graaff-Reinet

Graaff-Reinet Museum: POB 104, Graaff-Reinet 6280; tel. (49) 892-3801; e-mail

graaffreinetmuseum@intekom.co.za; internet www.graaffreinetmuseums.co.za; f. 1956; incl. Military History Museum, Old Library, Old Residency, Reinet House, Urquhart House; 4 old bldgs, fossil and rock art colln, colln of Graaff-Reinet's cultural and natural heritage; Head ANZISKE KAYSTER.

Grahamstown

Albany Museum: Somerset St, Grahamstown; tel. (46) 622-2312; e-mail albanymuseum@ru.ac.za; internet www.ru .ac.za/albanymuseum/; f. 1855; collns incl. anthropology, archaeology, earth science, entomology and arachnology, freshwater invertebrates, genealogy, history, ichthyology, historical artefacts and genealogical archive of 1820 British settlers; Selmar Schonland Herbarium; research institute of Rhodes Univ.; library of 2,000 vols, 1,400 periodicals; Museum Man. BONGANI MGIJIMA; Asst Man. ZONGEZILE MATSHOBA (acting); publs *Annals of the Eastern Cape Provincial Museums* (irregular), *Southern African Field Archaeology* (1 a year).

National English Literary Museum: Private Bag 1019, Grahamstown 6140; 87 Beaufort St, Grahamstown; tel. (46) 622-7042; e-mail nelm@ru.ac.za; internet www .ru.ac.za/static/institutes/nelm; f. 1980; collns of literary MSS, books, photographs, journal articles, academic theses and press cuttings by S African writers; educational programmes, exhibitions, lectures; library of 31,000 vols; Dir BEVERLEY THOMAS; Curator CRYSTAL WARREN.

Johannesburg

Apartheid Museum: POB 82283, Southdale, Johannesburg 2135; Northern Parkway and Gold Reef Rd, Ormonde 2001; tel. (11) 309-4700; e-mail info@apartheidmuseum .org; internet www.apartheidmuseum.org; f. 2001; film footage, photographs and artefacts illustrating the rise and decline of the apartheid system; Dir CHRISTOPHER TILL.

City of Johannesburg Museums and Galleries: POB 517, Newton 2113; 2nd Fl., Newton Bldg, 2 President St, Newton, Johannesburg; tel. (11) 373-7500; Dir for Arts, Culture and Heritage Services STEVEN SHACK..

Branch Museums:

Adler Museum of Medicine: Faculty of Health Sciences, Univ. of the Witwatersrand, 7 York Rd, Parktown, Johannesburg 2193; tel. (11) 717-2081; e-mail adler .museum@wits.ac.za; internet www.wits .ac.za/health/adlermuseum; f. 1962, current name adopted 1999; history of medicine, dentistry and pharmacy; colln of medical, dental and surgical instruments and equipment; reconstructions of early 20th-century pharmacy, doctor's and dentist's surgeries, herbalist shop and traditional medicine display, incl. unani/tibb, ayurveda, western herbal medicine and homoeopathy, traditional healing; library of 5,000 vols; Curator ROCHELLE KEENE; publ. *Adler Museum Bulletin* (2 a year).

Bensusan Museum of Photography and Library: MuseuMAfricA, 121 Bree St, Newtown, Johannesburg; tel. (11) 833-5624; e-mail photographiclibrary@joburg .org.za; f. 1968; colln incl. rare and valuable precision-made photographic equipment, incl. early Daguerre camera bought in 1839; Collector's Gallery; colln of pictures from the earliest wet-plate prints to digital images and experiments in 3 dimensions, such as stereoscopic views and holograms; specializes in preserving the work of S African photographers; Curator DUDU MADONSELA.

Bernberg Fashion Museum: c/o Museum Africa, POB 517, Newtown, Johannesburg 2113; 121 Bree St, Newtown, Johannesburg; tel. (11) 833-5624; e-mail museumafrica@joburg.org.za; f. 1973; costume and accessories since the 17th century; collns housed in Museum Africa.

Hector Pieterson Museum: 8288 Khumalo St, Orlando West 1804; tel. (11) 536-0611; commemorates Soweto march of 16 June 1976, incl. television footage of the uprising and coverage of the anti-apartheid struggle; Curator ALI HLONGWANE.

James Hall Museum of Transport: POB 80, Rosettenville, Johannesburg 2130; Pioneers' Park, Rosettenville Rd, La Rochelle, Johannesburg; tel. (11) 435-9485; e-mail curator@jhmt.org.za; internet www.jhmt.org.za; f. 1964; land transport in all its forms: ox-wagons, coaches and carts, bicycles, motorbikes, tractors, fire engines, buses, trams, trains, and cars from the Model T Ford to electric cars; Curator PETER HALL.

Johannesburg Art Gallery: POB 30951, Braamfontein, Johannesburg 2017; Joubert Park Gardens, King George St, Joubert Park, Johannesburg; tel. (82) 725-3130; e-mail jag@joburg.org.za; internet www.joburg.org.za; f. 1910; colln of 9,000 artworks comprising contemporary S African art; traditional S African art and modern int. art; print colln and historical European paintings and sculptures; extensive public programmes; library of 9,500 vols; Dir ANTOINETTE MURDOCH.

MuseuMAfricA: POB 517, Newtown, Johannesburg; 121 Bree St, Newtown, Johannesburg; tel. (11) 833-5624; e-mail museumafrica@joburg.org.za; internet www.joburg.org/culture; permanent displays show urban life in Johannesburg and its place in S Africa's history; themes incl. the gold miner, life in a shack and township jazz; coverage of Mahatma Gandhi's and Nelson Mandela's time in the city; displays on early man, stone-age and iron-age communities, San rock art in a reconstructed shelter, lifestyle of the first white settlers in the Johannesburg area; Chief Curator ALI HLONGWANE.

Roodepoort Museum: Civic Centre, Christiaan de Wet Rd, Florida Park 1709; tel. (11) 761-0225; e-mail annes@joburg.org .za; f. 1963; permanent displays illustrate the changes brought about by the discovery of gold in the area, incl. reconstructed 19th century farmhouse, late Victorian home, 1920s and 1930s interiors; exhibition of decorative arts; guided tours; curriculum-based school programme; open by appointment only; Curator ANNE SMART.

Kimberley

McGregor Museum: Atlas St, POB 316, Kimberley 8300; tel. (53) 839-2700; e-mail cfortune@museumsnc.co.za; internet www .museumsnc.co.za; f. 1907; archaeology and rock art, history (incl. Anglo-Boer War of 1899–1902), geology, zoology and herbarium of N Cape; ethnological colln housed in Duggan-Cronin Gallery, incorporates Magersfontein Battlefield Museum, Rudd House, Dunluce and Memorial to the Pioneers of Aviation; Dir COLIN FORTUNE.

King William's Town

Amathole Museum: POB 1434, King William's Town 5600; cnr of Albert and Alexandra Rd, King William's Town; tel. (43) 642-4506; e-mail fred.k@museum.za.net; internet www.museum.za.net; f. 1884 as a naturalist soc., current name adopted 1999; Southern Africa mammalogy, Xhosa ethnography, local history, Eastern Cape missionary history and Eastern Cape German settler history; library of 8,200 vols, 150 current periodicals; spec. collns incl. Kitton Colln of Africana; Dir FRED KIGOZI; Deputy Dir SOMINE VAN DER MERWE; publ. *Cape Provincial Museums Annals*.

Attached Museum:

Missionary Museum: POB 1434, King William's Town 5600; Berkeley St, King William's Town; tel. (43) 642-4506; e-mail stephanie.v@museum.za.net; f. 1972; satellite museum; missionary history in E Cape; missionary library; Dir FRED KIGOZI; Curator of History STEPHANIE VICTOR.

Paarl

Afrikaanse Taalmuseum/Afrikaans Language Museum: Gideon Malherbe House, 11 Pastorie Ave, Paarl; tel. (21) 872-3441; e-mail admin@taalmuseum.co.za; internet www.taalmuseum.co.za; f. 1975; printing press of first Afrikaans newspaper; earliest versions of written Afrikaans; Dir JACK LOUW.

Pietermaritzburg

KwaZulu-Natal Museum: Private Bag 9070, Pietermaritzburg 3200; 237 Jabu Ndlovu St, Pietermaritzburg 3021; tel. (33) 345-1404; e-mail info@nmsa.org.za; internet www.nmsa.org.za; f. 1904; collns incl. entomology, mollusca, archaeology, historical anthropology, mammals, arachnology, earthworms, herpetology, palaentology, local history; library of 12,000 books, 2,500 periodicals, 61,000 pamphlets, 8,000 photographs, 900 maps, 8,000 slides; Dir (vacant); Deputy Dir SANDILE MIYA; publs *African Invertebrates and Southern African Humanities* (2 a year, print and online, africaninvertebrates.org), *Southern African Humanities* (print and online, www.sahumanities.org.za).

Tatham Art Gallery: Chief Albert Luthuli (Commercial) Rd, Opposite City Hall, POB 321, Pietermaritzburg 3200; tel. (33) 392-2801; e-mail brendan.bell@msunduzi.gov.za; internet www.tatham.org.za; f. 1903; British and French painting since 19th century, sculpture and graphics, Southern African painting, sculpture, ceramics, prints and ethnic objects and art; Whitwell Colln; library of 2,300 vols; Dir BRENDAN BELL; Asst Dir BRYONY CLARK.

Port Elizabeth

Bayworld: POB 13147, Humewood, Port Elizabeth 6013; Beach Rd, Humewood, Port Elizabeth 6013; tel. (41) 584-0650; e-mail pr@bayworld.co.za; internet www.bayworld.co.za; f. 1856; incl. Port Elizabeth Museum, No 7 Castle Hill Museum, Snake Park; displays on maritime history, marine biology, marine mammalogy, herpetology, marine ornithology, local history, birds, dinosaurs; library of 20,000 vols; Dir SYLVIA VAN ZYL; Asst Dir ISAAC DANIELS.

Nelson Mandela Metropolitan Art Museum: 1 Park Dr., Port Elizabeth 6001; tel. (41) 506-2000; e-mail artmuseum@mandelametro.gov.za; internet www.artmuseum.co.za; f. 1956 as King George VI Art Gallery; municipal art museum; collns of S African and British art, Indian miniatures, int. graphics, Chinese textiles; Dir Dr MELANIE HILLEBRAND.

Pretoria

DITSONG Museums of South Africa: POB 4197, Pretoria 0001; GaMohle Bldg, 70 WF Nkomo (Church) St W, Pretoria; tel. (12) 000-0010; e-mail info@ditsong.org.za;

internet www.ditsong.org.za; f. 1999; incl. 8 nat. museums..

Attached Museums:

Ditsong National Museum of Military History: POB 52090, Saxonwold 2132; tel. (10) 001-3515; e-mail milmus@ditsong.za; internet www.ditsong.org.za/militaryhistory.htm; f. 1947 as S African Nat. War Museum, current name adopted 2009; displays guns, armoured fighting vehicles, aircraft and naval hardware, small arms, orders, decorations, medals, history of medicine at war, history of Umkhonto-we-Sizwe, Anglo Boer War, First World War; library of 70,000 vols; publ. *Military History Journal* (2 a year).

Ditsong National Museum of Natural History: 432 Paul Kruger St, Pretoria 0001; tel. (12) 322-7632; internet www.ditsong.org.za/naturalhistory.htm; f. 1892 as Staatsmuseum; collns of hominid fossils, fossils, skeletons, skins and mounted specimens of amphibians, fish, invertebrates, reptiles, mammals; library: specializing in zoology, palaeontology and faunal history of S Africa; 11,000 monographs, 1,800 periodical titles, 90,000 reprints, newspaper clippings.

Kruger Museum: 60 WF Nkomo St, Pretoria; tel. (12) 000-0010; e-mail krugerm@ditsong.org.za; internet www.ditsong.org.za/kruger.htm; f. 1975; house of S. J. P. Kruger, Pres. of the old Zuid-Afrikaansche Republiek (ZAR).

National Cultural History Museum: 149 Visagie St, Pretoria 0002; tel. (12) 324-6082; internet www.ditsong.org.za/culturalhistory.htm; incl. rock paintings and engravings of the San people; Iron Age figurines from Schroda in the Limpopo province; art gallery on S African culture.

Pioneer Museum: Keunig St, Silverton, Pretoria; tel. (12) 813-8006; e-mail pioneerm@ditsong.org.za; internet www.ditsong.org.za/pioneer.htm; traditional 19th century rural house, herb and vegetable garden, orchard, furnished wagon house, vineyard.

Sammy Marks Museum: Old Bronkhorstspruit Rd, Donkerhoek, Pretoria; tel. (12) 755-9542; e-mail marks@ditsong.org.za; internet www.ditsong.org.za/sammymarks.htm; f. 1986; house of industrialist and entrepreneur Sammy Marks; colln of Victorian silver, porcelain and furniture; original belongings of the Marks family.

Tswaing Meteorite Crater Museum: Onderstepoort Rd (M35), Soshanguve, Pretoria; tel. (76) 945-5911; e-mail tswaing@ditsong.org.za; internet www.ditsong.org.za/tswaing.htm; preserved meteorite impact crater.

Willem Prinsloo Agricultural Museum: POB 677, Rayton 1001; Farm Kaalfontein, Rayton; tel. (12) 736-2035; e-mail prinsloo@ditsong.org.za; internet www.ditsong.org.za/willemprinsloo.htm; history of devt of agriculture in S Africa from the Stone Age until 1945; colln of farming implements, tractors, animal-drawn vehicles; historic farmyard; Man. M. ZDARA.

Museum of Anthropology and Archaeology: Theo van Wijk Bldg, Room 4-160, Muckleneuk Campus, Univ. of S Africa, Preller St, Muckleneuk, Pretoria; tel. (12) 429-6297; e-mail coetzfp@unisa.ac.za; f. 1957; attached to Dept of Anthropology and Archaeology, Univ. of S Africa; displays 27,000 objects; spec collns: anthropology, historical archaeology, Iron Age archaeology, Junod Tsonga, Ndebele, Palaeo-Anthropol-

ogy, pottery, Stone Age archaeology, Xhosa; Curator FRANCOIS COETZEE; Asst Curator ANNELIESE H. MEHNERT.

Pretoria Art Museum: POB 40925, Arcadia, Pretoria 0007; cnr Schoeman and Wessels Sts, Arcadia Park, Arcadia, Pretoria 0083; tel. (12) 344-1807; e-mail art.museum@tshwane.gov.za; internet www.pretoriaartmuseum.co.za; f. 1963; S African art, small colln of int. graphic art, 17th-century Dutch and Flemish art, colln of traditional and contemporary African art; Head DIRK OEGEMA; Curator HANNELIE DU PLESSIS.

Stellenbosch

Stellenbosch Museum: Private Bag X5048, Stellenbosch 7599; Erfurthuis, Ryneveld St 37, Stellenbosch 7600; tel. (21) 887-2948; e-mail stelmus@mweb.co.za; internet www.stelmus.co.za; f. 1962; comprises 18th-century powder magazine (weaponry, Stellenbosch military history); Village Museum (4 houses illustrating life from 1690–1890), Toy and Miniature Museum; reference library; Man. W. SCHOLTZ.

Wellington

Wellington Museum: POB 166, Wellington 7654; Church St, Wellington; tel. (21) 873-4710; e-mail welmus@mweb.co.za; internet media1.mweb.co.za/wellingtonmuseum; incl. Stone Age artefacts, traditional ethnic tools, musical instruments and jewellery of ethnic tribes, colln of Egyptian artefacts from reign of King Akhenaten.

Universities

CAPE PENINSULA UNIVERSITY OF TECHNOLOGY

POB 1906, Belleville 7535

Symphony Way (off Robert Sobukwe Rd), Belleville

Telephone: (21) 959-6767
E-mail: info@cput.ac.za
Internet: www.cput.ac.za

Founded 2005 by merger of Cape Technikon and Peninsula Technikon
public control

Campuses at Athlone, Cape Town, Granger Bay, Mowbray, Wellington

Chancellor: TREVOR MANUEL
Vice-Chancellor and Rector: Dr PRINS NEVHUTALU
Deputy Vice-Chancellor for Academics: Prof. ANTHONY STAAK
Deputy Vice-Chancellor for Research, Technology, Innovation and Partnerships: Dr CHRIS NHLAPO
Registrar: NIKILE NTSABABA
Dean of Students: CORA NJOLI MOTALE
Dir for Libraries: ELISHA CHIWARE

Number of teachers: 765
Number of students: 32,604

DEANS

Faculty of Applied Sciences: Prof. OLALEKAN FATOKI
Faculty of Business: Prof. MZIKAYISE BINZA
Faculty of Education and Social Sciences: Prof. THOBEKA MDA
Faculty of Engineering: Dr NAWAZ MAHOMED
Faculty of Health and Wellness Sciences: Prof. DHIRO GIHWALA
Faculty of Informatics and Design: Prof. JOHANNES CRONJE

RESEARCH CENTRES

Centre for Instrumentation Research: Dept of Electrical Engineering, Faculty of Engineering, POB 652, Cape Town 8000; tel.

(21) 460-4281; e-mail cir@cput.ac.za; research and devt in acoustics, instrumentation, networks and embedded systems, power electronics, signal processing, RF, microwave design; Dir Dr RICHARDT WILKINSON.

Fundani Centre for Higher Education Development: POB 652, Cape Town 8001; tel. (21) 460-3133; e-mail winbergc@cput.ac.za; internet www.cput.ac.za/services/fundani; Dir Prof. CHRISTINE WINBERG

CENTRAL UNIVERSITY OF TECHNOLOGY, FREE STATE

Private Bag X20539, Bloemfontein 9300
Pres. Brand St 20, Westdene, Bloemfontein 9301
Telephone: (51) 507-3911
Internet: www.cut.ac.za
Founded 1981
public control
Academic year: January to December
Vice-Chancellor and Prin.: Prof. THANDWA ZIZWE MTHEMBU
Deputy Vice-Chancellor for Academic and Research: Prof. HENK DE JAGER
Deputy Vice-Chancellor for Resources and Operations: Prof. NEIL GARROD
Registrar: Dr NOTHEMBA MRWETYANA
Welkom Campus Man.: Dr OUPA MAKOLA
Dir for Library: J. M. KABAMBA
Library of 143,354 vols
Number of teachers: 1,582
Number of students: 13,631
Publications: *Interim* (2 a year), *Journal for New Generation Sciences (JNGS)* (2 a year)

DEANS

Faculty of Engineering and Information-Technology: Prof. ALFRED B. NGOWI
Faculty of Health and Environmental Sciences: Prof. SAM MASHELE (acting)
Faculty of Humanities: Prof. DAVID PHATHABANTU NGIDI
Faculty of Management Sciences: Prof. ALBERT STRYDOM

DURBAN UNIVERSITY OF TECHNOLOGY

POB 1334, Durban 4000
Telephone: (31) 373-2000
E-mail: info@dut.ac.za
Internet: www.dut.ac.za
Founded 2002 by merger of M. L. Sultan Technikon and Technikon Natal, current name adopted 2006
public control
Academic year: January to December
Campus at Midlands; incl. Business Studies Unit, Institute for Systems Science, Institute for Water and Wastewater Technology
Vice-Chancellor and Prin.: Prof. AHMED BAWA
Deputy Vice-Chancellor for Academic Affairs: Prof. NOMTHANDAZO GWELE
Deputy Vice-Chancellor for Institutional Support: Prof. NQABOMZI GAWE
Deputy Vice-Chancellor for Technology, Innovation and Partnerships: Prof. FRED OTIENO
Registrar: Dr T. S. PILLAY (acting)
Number of students: 23,000
Publication: *The Edge* (4 a year)

DEANS

Faculty of Accounting and Informatics: Prof. THIRUTHLALL NEPAL
Faculty of Applied Sciences: Prof. SUREN SINGH
Faculty of Arts and Design: Dr RENE SMITH (acting)
Faculty of Engineering and the Built Environment: Prof. THEO ANDREW

Faculty of Health Sciences: Prof. LINA PUCKREE
Faculty of Management Studies: Dr RISHI BALKARAN (acting)

MANGOSUTHU UNIVERSITY OF TECHNOLOGY

POB 12363, Jacobs 4026
511 Mangosuthu Highway, Umlazi, Durban 4031
Telephone: (31) 907-7111
E-mail: webmaster@mut.ac.za
Internet: www.mut.ac.za
Founded 1978 as Mangosuthu Technikon, current name adopted 2007
public control
Academic year: January to December
Vice-Chancellor and Prin.: Prof. MASHUPYE RATALE KGAPHOLA
Deputy Vice-Chancellor. for Academic Affairs: Prof. M. RAMOGALE
Deputy Vice-Chancellor for Resources and Planning: Dr STEPHEN KHEHLA NDLOVU
Registrar: S. NAIDOO
Library of 54,454 vols
Number of teachers: 150
Number of students: 10,000

DEANS

Faculty of Engineering: Prof. S. J. MALINGA
Faculty of Management Sciences: G. GOVENDA
Faculty of Natural Sciences: Prof. N. J. NDLAZI

NELSON MANDELA METROPOLITAN UNIVERSITY

POB 77000, Port Elizabeth 6031
Telephone: (41) 504-1111
E-mail: info@nmmu.ac.za
Internet: www.nmmu.ac.za
Founded 2005 by merger of Univ. of Port Elizabeth, PE Technikon and the Port Elizabeth Campus of Vista Univ.
public control
Language of instruction: English
Academic year: February to November
Vice-Chancellor: Prof. DERRICK SWARTZ
Deputy Vice-Chancellor for Academic Affairs: Prof. PIET NAUDE
Deputy Vice-Chancellor for Institutional Support: Dr SIBONGILE MUTHWA
Deputy Vice-Chancellor for Research and Engagement: Prof. THOKOZILE MAYEKISO
Campus Prin. for George Campus: Prof. CHRISTO FABRICIUS
Campus Prin. for Missionvale Campus: Prof. PHAKAMA NTSHONGWANA
Registrar: Dr FAROON GOOLAM
Dean of Students: KHAYA MATISO
Library: see under Libraries and Archives
Number of teachers: 1,500
Number of students: 27,000

DEANS

Faculty of Arts: Prof. VELILE NOTSHULWANA
Faculty of Business and Economic Sciences: Prof. NIEKIE DORFLING
Faculty of Education: Prof. DENISE ZINN
Faculty of Engineering, Built Environment and Information Technology: Dr OSWALD FRANKS
Faculty of Health Sciences: Prof. VICTOR EXNER
Faculty of Law: Prof. VIVIENNE LAWACK-DAVIDS
Faculty of Science: Prof. ANDREW LEITCH

NORTH-WEST UNIVERSITY/ NOORDWES-UNIVERSITEIT/ YUNIBESITI YA BOKONE-BOPHIRIMA

Institutional Office, Private Bag X1290, Potchefstroom 2520
Bldg C1, 53 Borcherd St, Potchefstroom 2531
Telephone: (18) 299-4897
Internet: www.nwu.ac.za
Founded 2004 by merger of Potchefstroom Univ. for Christian Higher Education and Univ. of the North-West
public control
Languages of instruction: Afrikaans, English
Academic year: February to November
Chancellor: Dr KGOSI LERUO MOLOTEGI
Vice-Chancellor: Dr THEUNS ELOFF
Deputy Vice-Chancellor for Research, Innovation and Technology: Prof. FRIKKIE VAN NIEKERK
Deputy Vice-Chancellor for Teaching-Learning: Prof. MARTIN OOSTHUIZEN
Registrar: Prof. M. M. VERHOEF
Dir for Library: ELSA ESTERHUIZEN
Library: see under Libraries and Archives
Number of teachers: 600
Number of students: 40,800
Publications: *Didaktikom* (4 a year), *Fokus* (4 a year), *In die Skriflig* (4 a year), *Koers* (4 a year), *Literator* (3 a year), *Woord en Daad* (4 a year)

DEANS

Mafikeng Campus:

Faculty of Agriculture, Science and Technology: Dr ENO EBENSO
Faculty of Commerce and Administration: Prof. SONIA SWANEPOEL
Faculty of Education: Prof. DAWID GERICKE
Faculty of Human and Social Sciences: Prof. P. A. BOTHA
Faculty of Law: Prof. MELVIN L. M. MBAO

Potchefstroom Campus:

Faculty of Arts: Prof. JAN SWANEPOEL
Faculty of Economic and Management Sciences: Prof. SUSAN VISSER
Faculty of Education Sciences: Prof. ROBERT BALFOUR
Faculty of Engineering: Prof. L. J. GROBLER
Faculty of Health Sciences: Prof. AWIE KOTZÉ
Faculty of Law: Prof. NICOLA SMIT
Faculty of Natural Sciences: Prof. KOBUS PIENAAR
Faculty of Theology: Prof. FIKA JANSE VAN RENSBURG

Vaal Triangle Campus:

Faculty of Economic Sciences and Information Technology: Prof. HERMAN VAN DER MERWE
Faculty of Humanities: Prof. A. M. C. THERON

PROFESSORS

Mafikeng Campus (PMB X2046, Mmabatho 2745; tel. (18) 389-2111; e-mail travisk@uniwest.ac.za; internet www.uniwest.ac.za):

Faculty of Agriculture, Science and Technology:

BEIGHLE, D. E., Animal Health
FUNNAH, S. M., Plant Production
KHALIQUE, C. M., Mathematical Sciences
TAOLO, S. H., Mathematical Sciences

Faculty of Human and Social Sciences:

CHIKULO, B. C., Development Studies
KALULE-SABITI, I., Population Training and Research Unit
MANSON, A., History
MOGEKWU, M., Communication

Faculty of Law:

MBAO, M. L. M., Public Law and Legal Philosophy

Potchefstroom Campus (PMB X6001, Potchefstroom 2531; tel. (18) 299-1111; internet www.puk.ac.za):

Faculty of Arts:

CARSTENS, W. A. M., School of Languages (Dir)
COMBRINK, A. L., Dean
DE LANGE, A. M., English and Literature
DU PISANI, J. A., History
DU PLESSIS, H. G. W., ATKV Writing School
DU PLOOY, H. J. G., Afrikaans and Dutch
JOOSTE, S. J., Music
MOLLER, P. H., Sociology
SCHUTTE, P. J., Communication Studies
VAN DER WALT, J. L., English and Literature
VAN WYK, W. J., School of Social Studies (Dir)
VENTER, J. J., Philosophy

Faculty of Economic and Management Sciences:

BISSCHOFF, C. A., Potchefstroom Business School
COETSEE, L. D., Potchefstroom Business School
COETZEE, K., Chartered Accountant Training
COETZEE, W. N., Potchefstroom Business School
DE KLERK, G. J., Dean
DU PLESSIS, J. L., Potchefstroom Business School
DU TOIT, A., Chartered Accountant Training
ELOFF, T., School of Accounting Sciences (Dir)
GERICKE, J. S., Chartered Accountant Training
JANSEN VAN RENSBURG, L. R., Entrepreneurship, Marketing and Tourism Management
JORDAAN, K., Chartered Accountant Training
KOTZE, J. G., Potchefstroom Business School
KROON, J., Entrepreneurship, Marketing and Tourism Management
NAUDE, W. A., Decision-making and Management for Economic Development
PRETORIUS, J. P. S., Potchefstroom Business School
RADEMEYER, A., Chartered Accountant Training
ROTHMAN, S., Industrial Psychology
SAAYMAN, M., Tourism
SCHOLTZ, P. E., School of Human Resource Sciences (Dir)
VAN HEERDEN, J. H. P., School of Economics, Risk Management and International Trade (Dir)
VISSER, S. S., Management Accountant Training
VIVIERS, W., Economics, Risk Management and International Trade

Faculty of Educational Sciences:

DREYER, C., Postgraduate School of Education
MENTZ, P. J., Education and Training
MONTEITH, J. L. D. K., Postgraduate School of Education
SPAMER, E. J., Teachers' Centre
STEYN, H. J., Dean
VAN DER WESTHUIZEN, P. C., Postgraduate School of Education

Faculty of Engineering:

DE KOCK, J. A., Electrical and Electronic Engineering
DU TOIT, C. G. D. K., Mechanical and Material Engineering
FICK, J. I. J., Dean
GREYVENSTEIN, G. P., Mechanical and Material Engineering

HELBERG, A. S. J., Electrical and Electronic Engineering
HOFFMAN, A. J., Electrical and Electronic Engineering
MATHEWS, E. H., Centre for Research and Commercialization
ROUSSEAU, P. G., Energy Systems
WAANDERS, F. B., Chemical and Mineral Engineering

Faculty of Health Sciences:

BERGH, J. J., Pharmaceutical Chemistry
BONESCHANS, B., CENQAM
BREYTENBACH, J. C., Pharmaceutical Chemistry
DE RIDDER, J. H., Human Movement Studies
DEKKER, T. G., Industrial Pharmacy
DU PLESSIS, J., Drug Research and Development
GREEF, M., Nursing
HARVEY, B. H., Pharmacy
KOELEMAN, H. A., Dean
KOTZÉ, A. F., Pharmaceutics
KOTZE, G. J., Social Work
LIEBENBERG, W., Institute for Industrial Pharmacy
MALAN, D. D. J., Human Movement Studies
MALAN, N. T., Physiology, Nutrition and Consumer Sciences
OLIVER, D. W., Pharmacy
STRYDOM, H., Social Work
THOMAS, A. J., Pharmacy
VENTER, C. A., Physiology
VENTER, D. P., Pharmacology
WISSING, M. P., Psycho-social Behavioural Science

Faculty of Law:

DU PLESSIS, W., Legal Pluralism and Legal History
FERREIRA, G. M., Public Law and Legal Philosophy
PIENAAR, G. J., Private Law
ROBINSON, J. A., Private Law
STANDER, A. L., Private Law
VENTER, F., Dean

Faculty of Natural Sciences:

BOUWMAN, H., Zoology
BREET, E. L. J., Chemistry
BRUINSMA, O. S. L., Separation Sciences and Technology
BURGER, R. A., Space Physics
DE JAGER, O. C., Physics
DE JONGH, D. C. J., Centre for Business Mathematics and Informatics
DE JONGH, P. J., Centre for Business Mathematics and Informatics
DE KLERK, J. H., Mathematics
DE VILLIERS, A. B., Geography and Environmental Studies
DU TOIT, G. J., Environment Sciences and Management
FOURIE, J. H., Computer, Statistical and Mathematical Sciences
GEYSER, H. S., Town and Regional Planning
GROBLER, J. J., Business Mathematics and Informatics
KOTZÉ, H. F., Biochemistry
MORAAL, H., Physics
PETERSEN, M. A., Mathematics
PIENAAR, J. J., Chemistry and Biochemistry
PIETERSE, A. J. H., Life Sciences
POTGIETER, M. S., Physics
RAUBENHEIMER, B. C., Space Physics
RIEDEL, K. J., Microbiology
STEYN, T., Computer Sciences and Information
STYGER, P., Centre for Business Mathematics and Informatics
SWANEPOEL, J. W. H., Statistics and Operational Research
THERON, P. D., Zoology

VAN DER WALT, D. J., Physics
VAN HAMBURG, H., Environment Sciences and Development
VAN WYK, D. J., Dean
VOSLOO, H. C. M., Chemistry

Faculty of Theology:

DE KLERK, B. J., Practical Theology
DU PLOOY, A. LE R., Dean
JANSE VAN RENSBURG, J. J., New Testament
JORDAAN, G. J. C., New Testament
LOTTER, G. A., Practical Theology
VAN ROOY, H. F., Theology and the Development of the South African Society
VENTER, J. M., Practical Theology
VORSTER, J. M., Ecclesiology

Vaal Triangle Campus (POB 1174, Vanderbijlpark 1900; tel. (16) 910-3111; e-mail dvdamct@puknet.puk.ac.za; internet www.puk.ac.za):

Faculty of the Vaal Triangle:

DE KLERK, P., History
JORDAAN, D. B., Modelling Sciences
LUCOUW, P., Economic Sciences
PRETORIUS, J. B., Business Management
THERON, A. M. C., Dean
VERHOEF, M. M., Languages

RHODES UNIVERSITY

POB 94, Grahamstown 6140

Telephone: (46) 603-8111

E-mail: registrar@ru.ac.za

Internet: www.ru.ac.za

Founded 1904 as Rhodes Univ. College, current name and status 1951

public control

Academic year: February to November (4 terms)

Chancellor: LEX MPATI
Vice-Chancellor: Dr SALEEM BADAT
Deputy Vice-Chancellor for Academic and Student Affairs: Dr SIZWE MABIZELA
Deputy Vice-Chancellor for Research and Devt: Dr PETER CLAYTON
Registrar: Dr STEPHEN FOURIE
Dean of Students: Dr VIVIAN DE KLERK
Dir for Library: UJALA SATGOOR
Library: see under Libraries and Archives
Number of teachers: 310
Number of students: 6,200

Publications: *African Music Journal* (1 a year, print and online, www.ru.ac.za/ilam/publications/africanmusicjournal/), *English in Africa* (1 a year), *Journal of Contemporary African Studies* (3 a year), *New Coin Poetry* (2 a year), *Philosophical Papers* (2 a year), *Rhodes Journalism Review* (irregular, print and online, www.rjr.ru.ac.za)

DEANS

Faculty of Commerce: Prof. DAVID SEWRY
Faculty of Education: Dr DI WILMOT
Faculty of Humanities: Prof. FRED HENDRICKS
Faculty of Law: Prof. JONATHAN CAMPBELL
Faculty of Pharmacy: Prof. R. B. WALKER
Faculty of Science: Prof. RIC BERNARD

PROFESSORS

ADENDORFF, R., English Language and Linguistics
ADESINA, J. O. T., Sociology and Industrial Sociology
ANTROBUS, G. G., Economics
BERGER, G. J. E. G., Journalism and Media Studies
BERNARD, R. T. F., Zoology
BLATCH, G. L., Biochemistry, Microbiology and Biotechnology
BOTHA, C. E. J., Botany
CHARTERIS, J., Human Kinetics and Ergonomics

CLAYTON, P. G., Computer Science
COETZEE, J. K., Sociology and Industrial Sociology
CRAIG, A. T. F., Zoology and Entomology
DAVIES-COLEMAN, M. T., Chemistry
DAYA, S., Pharmacy
DE KLERK, V. A., Linguistics and English Language
DE WET, C. J., Anthropology
DUNCAN, J. R., Biochemistry
EDWARDS, D. J. A., Psychology
EUVRARD, G. J., Education
FABRICIUS, C., Environmental Science
FAURE, P., Economics
FOX, R. C., Geography
GORDON, G. E., Drama
GOUWS, J. S., English
HAIGH, J. M., Pharmacy
HARVEY, N., Management
HENDRICKS, F. T., Sociology and Industrial Sociology
HEPBURN, H. R., Entomology
HODGSON, A. N., Zoology and Entomology
HUGHES, D. A., Water Research
IRWIN, P. R., Education
JACOB, R. E., Geology
JAQUES, F. E., School of Languages
JONAS, J. L., Physics and Electronics
KANFER, I., Pharmaceutics
KAYE, P. T., Organic Chemistry
LEWIS, C. A., Geography
MABIZELA, S. G., Pure and Applied Mathematics
MARSH, J. S., Geology
MAYLAM, P. R., History
McQUAID, C. D., Zoology
MIDGLEY, J. R., Law
MØLLER, V., Social and Economic Research
MOORE, J. M., Exploration Geology
MQEKE, R. B., Law
NEL, E. L., Geography
NEL, H., Economics
NYOKONG, T., Chemistry
RADLOFF, S. E., Statistics
ROSE, P. D., Biotechnology
ROWNTREE, K. M., Geography
SCARR, D. T., Music and Musicology
SCHMAHMANN, B. L., Fine Art
SCOTT, P. A., Human Kinetics and Ergonomics
SEWRY, D. A., Information Systems
SKELTON, P., Aquatic Biodiversity
STACK, E. M., Accounting
STAUDE, G. E., Management
STONES, C. R., Psychology
TERRY, P. D., Computer Science
VALE, P. C. J., Political and International Studies
WALTERS, P. S., English
WEBB, A. C. M., Economics
WENTWORTH, E. P., Computer Science
WRIGHT, L. S., Study of English in Africa

SOL PLAATJE UNIVERSITY

Private Bag X5008, Kimberley 8300
N Campus, Chapel St, Kimberley
Telephone: (53) 807-5300
E-mail: information@spu.ac.za
Internet: www.spu.ac.za
Founded 2013
public control
Chair: JENNIFER GLENNIE
Head: Prof. YUNUS BALLIM
Number of students: 135

STELLENBOSCH UNIVERSITY

Private Bag X1, Matieland 7602
Telephone: (21) 808-9111
E-mail: info@sun.ac.za
Internet: www.sun.ac.za
Founded 1918
public control
Language of instruction: Afrikaans

Academic year: February to December (4 terms)
Chancellor: Prof. JOHANN RUPERT
Rector and Vice-Chancellor: Prof. H. RUSSEL BOTMAN
Vice-Rector for Community Interaction and Personnel: Prof. JULIAN SMITH
Vice-Rector for Learning and Teaching: Prof. ARNOLD SCHOONWINKEL
Vice-Rector for Research and Innovation: Prof. EUGENE CLOETE
Registrar: JOHANN ASPELING
Sr Dir of Library Services: ELLEN TISE
Library: see under Libraries and Archives
Number of teachers: 975
Number of students: 28,156

Publications: *Maatskaplike Werk* (Social Work, 4 a year), *Matieland*

DEANS

Faculty of AgriSciences: Prof. MOHAMMAD KARAAN
Faculty of Arts and Social Sciences: Prof. JOHAN HATTINGH
Faculty of Economic and Management Sciences: STAN DU PLESSIS
Faculty of Education: Prof. MAUREEN ROBINSON
Faculty of Engineering: Prof. HANSIE KNOETZE
Faculty of Law: Prof. SONIA HUMAN
Faculty of Medicine and Health Sciences: Prof. JIMMY VOLMINK
Faculty of Military Science: Prof. SAMUEL TSHEHLA
Faculty of Science: Prof. LOUISE WARNICH
Faculty of Theology: Prof. NICO KOOPMAN

PROFESSORS

Faculty of AgriSciences (tel. (21) 808-4792; e-mail jcr@sun.ac.za; internet www.sun.ac.za/agric):

AGENBAG, G. A., Agronomy and Pastures
BREDENKAMP, B. V., Forestry Science
BRITZ, T., Food Science
FEY, M. V., Soil Science
GOUSSARD, P. G., Oenology and Viticulture
HOLZ, G., Plant Pathology
MARAIS, G. F., Genetics
SAMWAYS, M. J., Entomology
THERON, K. I., Horticulture
VAN HUYSSTEEN, L., Soil Science
VAN WYK, G., Forestry Science
VINK, N., Agricultural Economics
WARNICH, L., Genetics

Faculty of Arts and Social Sciences (tel. (21) 808-2138; e-mail akrit@sun.ac.za; internet www.sun.ac.za/arts):

BEKKER, S. B., Sociology
BOTHA, R. P., Linguistics
CILLIERS, F. P., Philosophy
CORNELIUS, I., Ancient Studies
DU TOIT, P. V. D. P., Political Science
GAGIANO, A. H., English
GOUWS, A., Political Science
GOUWS, R. H., Afrikaans and Dutch
GREEN, S., Social Work
GROVÉ, I. J., Music
GRUNDLINGH, A. M., History
HATTINGH, J. P., Philosophy
HAUPTFLEISCH, T., Drama
KAGEE, S. A., Psychology
KINGHORN, J., Biblical Studies
KLOPPER, D. C., English
KLOPPER, S., Fine Arts
KOTZE, H. J., Political Science
KRITZINGER, A. S., Sociology
MOUTON, J., Sociology
NAIDOO, A. V., Psychology
RABE, L., Journalism
ROOSENSCHOON, H., Music
SWARTZ, L. P., Psychology
THOM, J. C., Ancient Studies
VAN DER MERWE, W. L., Philosophy

VAN DER WAAL, C. S., Sociology
VAN NIEKERK, A. A., Philosophy
VILJOEN, L., Afrikaans and Dutch
VON MALTZAN, C. H., Modern Foreign Languages
ZIETSMAN, H. L., Geography and Environmental Studies
ZULU, N. S., African Languages

Faculty of Economic and Management Sciences (tel. (21) 808-2225; e-mail mm4@sun.ac.za; internet www.sun.ac.za/economy):

AUGUSTYN, J. C. D., Industrial Psychology
BIEKPE, N. B., Business Administration
BROWN, W., Accounting
BURGER, A. P., Public and Development Management
CLOETE, G. S., Public and Development Management
DE VILLIERS, J. U., Business Management
DE WET, T., Statistics and Actuarial Science
GEVERS, W. R., Business Management and Administration
HOUGH, J., Business Management
LEIBOLD, M., Business Management
MOSTERT, F. J., Business Management
OLIVIER, P., Accounting
OOSTHUIZEN, H., Business Administration
PIENAAR, W. J., Logistics
SCHOOMBEE, G. A., Economics
SCHWELLA, E., Public and Development Management
SLATTERY, P. G., Statistics and Actuarial Science
SMIT, B. W., Economics
SMIT, E. VAN DER M., Business Management and Administration
STEEL, S. J., Statistics and Actuarial Science
SWILLING, M., Public and Development Management
TERBLANCHE, N. S., Business Management
VAN DER BERG, S., Economics
VAN SCHALKWYK, C. J., Accounting

Faculty of Education (tel. (21) 808-2258; e-mail jbdb@sun.ac.za; internet www.sun.ac.za/education):

BERKHOUT, S. J., Educational Policy Studies
BITZER, E. M., Didactics
CARL, A. E., Didactics
KAPP, C. A., Centre for Higher and Adult Education
LE GRANGE, L. L. L., Didactics
PARK, J., Didactics
SCHREUDER, D. R., Didactics
SWART, R. E., Educational Psychology
WAGHID, Y., Educational Policy Studies

Faculty of Engineering (tel. (21) 808-4203; e-mail mop@sun.ac.za; internet www.sun.ac.za/eng):

ALDRICH, C., Chemical Engineering
BASSON, A. H., Mechanical Engineering
BASSON, G. R., Civil Engineering
BESTER, C. J., Civil Engineering
BRADSHAW, S. M., Chemical Engineering
BURGER, A. J., Chemical Engineering
CLOETE, J. H., Electrical and Electronic Engineering
DAVIDSON, D. B., Electrical and Electronic Engineering
DUNAISKI, P. E., Civil Engineering
DU PLESSIS, J. P., Applied Mathematics
DU PREEZ, N. D., Industrial Engineering
HERBST, B. M., Applied Mathematics
JENKINS, K. J., Civil Engineering
KAMPER, M. J., Electrical and Electronic Engineering
KNOETZE, J. H., Chemical Engineering
LORENZEN, L., Chemical Engineering
LOURENS, J. G., Electrical and Electronic Engineering
MEYER, P., Electrical and Electronic Engineering

PEROLD, W. J., Electrical and Electronic Engineering
READER, H. C., Electrical and Electronic Engineering
SCHOONWINKEL, A., Electrical and Electronic Engineering
STEYN, W. H., Electrical and Electronic Engineering
VAN NIEKERK, J. L., Mechanical Engineering
VON BACKSTRÖM, T. W., Mechanical Engineering
WEIDEMAN, J. A. C., Applied Mathematics

Faculty of Health Sciences (tel. (21) 938-9200; e-mail wvdmerwe@maties.sun.ac.za; internet www.sun.ac.za/med.fac):

BEYERS, N., Paediatrics and Child Health
BRINK, P. A., Internal Medicine
CHIKTE, U. M. E., Assoc. Dean
COETZEE, A. R., Anaesthesiology
DE VILLIERS, B., Assoc. Dean
DE VILLIERS, M. R., Family Medicine and Primary Care
DE VILLIERS, P. J. T., Family Medicine and Primary Care
DOUBELL, A. F., Internal Medicine
DU TOIT, D., Anatomy and Histology
EMSLEY, R. A., Psychiatry
ERASMUS, R. T., Chemical Pathology
HEYNS, C. F., Urology
HOUGH, F. S., Internal Medicine
KOESLAG, J. H., Medical Physiology and Biochemistry
KRUGER, T. F., Obstetrics and Gynaecology
LABADARIOS, D., Human Nutrition
LIEBOWITZ, L. D., Medical Microbiology
LOOCK, J. W., Otorhinolaryngology
MANSVELT, E. P., Haematology
MEYER, D., Ophthalmology
MOORE, S. W., Surgery
ROSSOUW, G. J., Cardiothoracic Surgery
SCHER, A. T., Radiation Oncology
SCHNEIDER, J. W., Anatomical Pathology
SEEDAT, S., Psychiatry
THERON, G. B., Obstetrics and Gynaecology
VAN DER BIJL, P., Pharmacology
VAN DER MERWE, W. L., Medical Physiology and Biochemistry
VAN HEERDEN, B. B., Head of School of Medicine
VERNIMMEN, F. J. A. I., Radiation Oncology
VLOK, G. J., Orthopaedic Surgery
WARREN, B. L., Surgery
WELMANN, E. B., Nursing Science
WRIGHT, C. A., Anatomical Pathology

Faculty of Law (tel. (21) 808-4853; e-mail yolandi@sun.ac.za; internet www.sun.ac.za/law):

BUTLER, D. W., Mercantile Law
DE VOS, W., Private Law and Roman Law
DE WAAL, M. J., Private Law and Roman Law
DU PLESSIS, J. E., Private Law and Roman Law
DU PLESSIS, L. M., Public Law
ERASMUS, M. G., Public Law
HUGO, C. F., Mercantile Law
HUMAN, C. S., Private Law and Roman Law
LIEBENBERG, S., Public Law
LOUBSER, M. M., Private Law and Roman Law
LUBBE, G. F., Private Law and Roman Law
PIENAAR, J. M., Private Law and Roman Law
SUTHERLAND, P. J., Mercantile Law
VAN DER MERWE, S. E., Public Law
VAN DER WALT, A. J., Public Law

Faculty of Science (tel. (21) 808-3072; e-mail se@sun.ac.za; internet www.sun.ac.za/science):

CHOWN, S. L., Plant and Animal Science
CROUCH, A. M., Chemistry
DE VILLIERS, J. M., Mathematics

DICKS, L. M. T., Microbiology
DILLEN, J. L. M., Chemistry
EGGERS, H. C., Chemistry
GEYER, H. B., Physics
GREEN, B. W., Mathematics
HAPGOOD, J. P., Biochemistry
HOFMEYR, J. H. S., Biochemistry
KOCH, K. R., Chemistry
KOSSMANN, J. M., Zoology
KRZESINSKI, A. E., Computer Science
LAURIE, D. P., Mathematics
MUCINA, L., Plant and Animal Science
MYBURGH, K. H., Physiological Sciences
PRIOR, B. A., Microbiology
PRODINGER, H., Mathematics
RAUBENHEIMER, H. G., Chemistry
RAWLINGS, D. E., Microbiology
REINECKE, A. J., Plant and Animal Science
RICHARDSON, D. M., Plant and Animal Science
ROBINSON, T. J., Plant and Animal Science
ROZENDAAL, A., Geology
SANDERSON, R. D., Polymer Science
SCHOLTZ, F. G., Physics
SMITH, V. R., Plant and Animal Science
SNOEP, J. L., Biochemistry
STEVENS, G., Geology
SWART, P., Biochemistry
VAN JAARSVELD, A. S., Plant and Animal Science
VAN WYK, L., Mathematics
VAN ZYL, W. H., Microbiology
VON BERGMANN, H. M., Physics

Faculty of Theology (tel. (21) 808-3255; e-mail karinl@sun.ac.za; internet www.sun.ac.za/theology):

BOSMAN, H. L., Old and New Testament
HENDRIKS, H. J., Practical Theology and Missiology
MOUTON, A. E. J., Old and New Testament
SMIT, D. J., Systematic Theology

TSHWANE UNIVERSITY OF TECHNOLOGY

Private Bag X680, Pretoria 0001
Telephone: (12) 382-5911
E-mail: general@tut.ac.za
Internet: www.tut.ac.za

Founded 2004 by merger of Technikon Pretoria, Technikon Northern Gauteng and Technikon North West

Vice-Chancellor and Prin.: Prof. NTHABISENG OGUDE
Deputy Vice-Chancellor for Institutional Support: ISAAC TLHABADIRA
Deputy Vice-Chancellor for Post-Graduate Studies Research and Innovation: Prof. LULAMA MAKHUBELA
Deputy Vice-Chancellor for Student Affairs and Extra-Curricular Devt: Dr EZEKIEL MORAKA
Deputy Vice-Chancellor for Teaching, Learning and Technology: Dr STANLEY MUKHOLA (acting)
Registrar: Prof. MATOANE MOTHATA
Library of 70,000 vols
Number of teachers: 855
Number of students: 60,000

DEANS

Faculty of Economics and Finance: Prof. ROBERT RUGIMBANA (acting)
Faculty of Engineering and the Built Environment: Prof. BEN VAN WYK
Faculty of Humanities: Prof. ELSABE COETZEE (acting)
Faculty of Information and Communication Technology: Prof. JOSIAH MUNDA (acting)
Faculty of Management Sciences: Dr EDGAR NESAMVUNI
Faculty of Science: Prof. PIETER MARAIS
Faculty of the Arts: Prof. MZO SIRAYI

UNIVERSITY OF CAPE TOWN

Private Bag X3, Rondebosch 7701
Telephone: (21) 650-9111
E-mail: int-iapo@uct.ac.za
Internet: www.uct.ac.za

Founded 1829 as South African College; current name adopted 1916, current status 1918
public control
Academic year: February to December (2 semesters)

Chancellor: GRAÇA MACHEL
Vice-Chancellor: Dr MAX PRICE
Deputy Vice-Chancellor: Prof. SANDRA KLOPPER
Deputy Vice-Chancellor: Prof. THANDABANTU NHLAPO
Deputy Vice-Chancellor: Prof. CRAIN SOUDIEN
Deputy Vice-Chancellor: Prof. DANIE VISSER
Pro-Vice-Chancellor: Prof. MURRAY LEIBBRANDT
Pro-Vice-Chancellor: Prof. MARK NEW
Registrar: HUGH AMOORE
Exec. Dir for Libraries: GWENDA THOMAS
Library: see under Libraries and Archives
Number of teachers: 2,000
Number of students: 25,500

Publications: *Acta Juridica* (1 a year), *Impact*, *Journal of Energy in Southern Africa* (4 a year, print and online, www.erc.uct.ac.za/jesa/jesa-archives.htm), *Responsa Meridiana* (1 a year), *Yizani*

DEANS

Centre for Higher Education Development: Assoc. Prof. SUELLEN SHAY
Faculty of Commerce: Prof. DON ROSS
Faculty of Engineering and the Built Environment: Prof. FRANCIS WILLIAM PETERSEN
Faculty of Health Sciences: Prof. WILLEM DE VILLIERS (acting)
Faculty of Humanities: Prof. SAKHELA BUHLUNGU
Faculty of Law: Prof. PAMELA JANE SCHWIKKARD
Faculty of Science: Prof. ANTON LE ROEX
Graduate School of Business: Prof. WALTER BAETS (Dir)

PROFESSORS

Faculty of Commerce (tel. (21) 650-4375; e-mail com-faculty@uct.ac.za; internet www.commerce.uct.ac.za):

ABEDIAN, I., Economics
BARR, G. D. I., Statistical Sciences
BRADFIELD, D., Statistical Sciences
DORRINGTON, R. E., Management Studies
EVERINGHAM, G. K., Accounting
FAULL, N. H. B., Graduate School of Business
HORWITZ, F., Graduate School of Business
KAHN, S. B., Economics
KANTOR, B. S., Economics
KAPLAN, D., Economics
LICKER, P. S., Information Systems
NATTRASS, N., Economics
SIMPSON, J. D., Business Science
SMITH, D. C., Information Systems
SULCAS, P., Graduate School of Business
TROSKIE, C. G., Statistical Sciences
UNDERHILL, L. G., Statistical Sciences
WILSON, F. A. H., Economics

Faculty of Engineering and the Built Environment (tel. (21) 650-2699; e-mail ebe-faculty@uct.ac.za; internet www.ebe.uct.ac.za):

ABBOTT, J., Civil Engineering
ALEXANDER, M. G., Civil Engineering
ALLEN, C., Mechanical Engineering
BALL, A., Mechanical Engineering
BENNETT, K. F., Mechanical Engineering
BOWEN, P. A., Construction Economics and Management

BRAAE, M., Electrical Engineering
DE JAGER, G., Electrical Engineering
DEWAR, D., School of Architecture and Planning
DOWNING, B. J., Electrical Engineering
EKAMA, G. A., Civil Engineering
GRYZAGORIDAS, T., Mechanical Engineering
HANSFORD, G. S., Chemical Engineering
NURICK, G. N., Mechanical Engineering
O'CONNOR, C. T., Chemical Engineering
REDDY, B. D., Centre for Research in Computational and Applied Mechanics
REINECK, K. M., Electrical Engineering
RÜTHER, H., Geomatics
STEVENS, A. J., Construction Economics and Management

Faculty of Health Sciences (tel. (21) 406-6346; e-mail medfac@curie.uct.ac.za; internet www.health.uct.ac.za):

BAQWA, D., Primary Health Care
BATEMAN, E. D., Medicine
BEATTY, D. W., Paediatrics and Child Health
BENATAR, S. R., Medicine
BENINGFIELD, S. J., Radiology
BONNICI, F., Medicine
BORNMAN, P. C., Surgery
COMMERFORD, P. J., Medicine
CRUSE, J. P., Anatomical Pathology
DAVIDSON, J., Chemical Pathology
DENT, D. M., Surgery
ELS, W. J., Anatomy and Cell Biology
FOLB, P. I., Pharmacology
GEVERS, W., Medical Biochemistry
HALL, P., Anatomical Pathology
HARLEY, E. H., Chemical Pathology
JACOBS, M. E., Paediatrics and Child Health
JAMES, M. F. M., Anaesthetics
KIRSCH, R. E., Medicine
KNOBEL, G. J., Forensic Medicine and Toxicology
LOUW, J., Medicine
MOLTENO, C. D., Psychiatry
MURRAY, A. D. N., Ophthalmology
MYERS, J. E., Community Health
NOAKES, T. D., Physiology
NOVITZKY, N., Haematology
PADAYACHEE, G. N.
PARKER, M. I., Medical Biochemistry
PETER, J. C., Neurosurgery
POWER, D. J., Paediatrics and Child Health
RAMESAR, R., Human Genetics
ROBERTSON, B. A., Psychiatry
RODE, H., Paediatric Surgery
SEGGIE, J., Medicine
SELLARS, S. L., Otorhinolaryngology
STEYN, L. M., Medical Microbiology
VAN DER SPUY, Z. M., Obstetrics and Gynaecology
VAN NIEKERK, J. P., Medicine
VAUGHAN, C. L., Biomedical Engineering
VILJOEN, J. F., Anaesthesia
VON OPPEL, U., Cardiothoracic Surgery
WALTERS, J., Orthopaedic Surgery
WERNER, I. D., Radiation Oncology
WILSON, E. L., Immunology
ZILLA, P., Cardiovascular Research

Faculty of Humanities (tel. (21) 650-2717; e-mail hum-dean@uct.ac.za; internet www.humanities.uct.ac.za):

BRINK, A., English Language and Literature
BUNTING, I., Philosophy
CHIDESTER, D. S., Religious Studies
COCHRANE, J. R., Religious Studies
COETZEE, J. M., English Language and Literature
COOPER, B., Centre for African Studies
CORNILLE, J.-L., French Language and Literature
DE GRUCHY, J., Religious Studies (Graduate School of Humanities)
DU TOIT, A. B., Political Studies
FOSTER, D. H., Psychology

GITAY, Y., Hebrew and Jewish Studies
GODBY, M. A. P., Historical Studies
HAYNES, D. J., Drama
KLATZOW, P., Music
LASS, R. G., Linguistics
LOUW, J., Psychology
MAMA, A., African Gender Institute
MAREE, J., Sociology
MAY, J., South African College of Music
MESTHRIE, R., Linguistics and Southern African Languages
MULLER, J. P., Education
NASSON, W., History
NOYES, J., German Language and Literature
REYNOLDS, P. F., Social Anthropology
SALAZAR, PH.-J., French Language and Literature (Graduate School of Humanities)
SATYO, S. C., African Languages
SAUNDERS, C. C., Historical Studies
SCHRIRE, R. A., Political Studies
SEEGERS, A., Political Studies
SHAIN, M., Hebrew and Jewish Studies
SKOTNES, P., Fine Art
SNYMAN, H. J., Afrikaans and Netherlandic Studies (Graduate School of Humanities)
TAYOB, A. I., Religious Studies
UNDERWOOD, P. G., School of Librarianship
VAN HEERDEN, E. R., Afrikaans and Netherlandic Studies
WEST, M., Social Anthropology
WHITAKER, R. A., Classics
WORDEN, N. A., Historical Studies
YOUNG, D. N., Education
YOUNGE, G., Fine Art

Faculty of Law (tel. (21) 650-3086; e-mail lawnv@law.uct.ac.za; internet www.law.uct.ac.za):

BENNETT, T. W., Public Law
BLACKMAN, M. S., Commercial Law
BURMAN, S. B., Private Law
CHEADLE, M. H., Public Law
CORDER, H. M., Public Law
DEVINE, D. J., Public Law
HUTCHISON, D. B., Private Law
JOOSTE, R. D., Commercial Law
MALUWA, T., Public Law
MURRAY, C. M., Public Law
VAN BUEREN, G., Law
VISSER, D. P., Private Law

Faculty of Science (tel. (21) 650-2712; e-mail sci-science@uct.ac.za; internet www.science.uct.ac.za):

ASCHMAN, D. G., Physics
BARR, G. D. I., Statistical Sciences
BECKER, R. I., Mathematics and Applied Mathematics
BOND, W., Botany
BRADFIELD, D., Statistical Sciences
BRANCH, G. M., Zoology
BRUNDRIT, G. B., Oceanography
BULL, J., Chemistry
BUTTERWORTH, D. S., Mathematics and Applied Mathematics
CLEYMANS, J. W. A., Physics
DE WIT, M. J., Geological Sciences
DOMINGUEZ, C. A., Physics
DU PLESSIS, M., Zoology
ELLIS, G. F. R., Mathematics and Applied Mathematics
FAIRALL, A. P., Astronomy
FIELD, J. G., Zoology
FUGGLE, R. F., Environmental and Geographical Science
GÄDE, G., Zoology
GURNEY, J. J., Geological Sciences
HALL, M. J., Archaeology
KHAM, M. J., Mathematics, Science and Technology Education
KLUMP, H. H., Biochemistry
KRITZINGER, P. S., Computer Science
KURTZ, D. W., Astronomy
LE ROEX, A. P., Geological Sciences
LUTJEHARMS, J. R. E., Oceanography

MACGREGOR, K. J., Computer Science
MOSS, J. R., Chemistry
NASSIMBENI, L. R., Chemistry
PARKINGTON, J. E., Archaeology
PEREZ, S. M., Physics
REDDY, B. D., Mathematics and Applied Mathematics
SILLEN, A., Archaeology
STEWART, T. J., Statistical Sciences
THOMSON, J. A., Microbiology
TROSKIE, C. G., Statistical Sciences
UNDERHILL, L. G., Statistical Sciences
VAN DER MERWE, N. J., Archaeology
VIOLLIER, R. D., Physics
WARNER, B., Astronomy
WEBB, J. H., Mathematics and Applied Mathematics

UNIVERSITY OF FORT HARE

Private Bag X1314, Alice 5700
1 King Williams Town Rd, Alice 5700
Telephone: (40) 602-2011
E-mail: registrar@ufh.ac.za
Internet: www.ufh.ac.za

Founded 1916 as South African Native College, current name adopted 1970
public control
Academic year: February to December
Campuses in Bisho, East London
Chancellor: THEMBILE SKWEYIYA
Vice-Chancellor: Dr MVUYO TOM
Deputy Vice-Chancellor for Academic Affairs: Prof. L. OBI
Deputy Vice-Chancellor for Institutional Support: Dr JABULANI MJWARA
Registrar: (vacant)
Dean for Research and Devt: Prof. G. DE WET
Dean of Students: B. GALLANT
Univ. Librarian: YOLI SOUL
Library: see under Libraries and Archives
Number of teachers: 240
Number of students: 2,900

Publications: *Fort Hare Papers*, *The Fort Harian*

DEANS

Faculty of Education: Prof. G. MOYO (acting)
Faculty of Management and Commerce: Prof. T. MJOLI
Faculty of Science and Agriculture: Prof. FARHAD AGHDASI
Faculty of Social Sciences and Humanities: Prof. M. M. SOMNISO
Nelson R. Mandela School of Law: Prof. OBENG MIREKU

UNIVERSITY OF JOHANNESBURG

POB 524, Auckland Park 2006
Telephone: (11) 559-4555
E-mail: myfuture@uj.ac.za
Internet: www.uj.ac.za

Founded 2005 by merger of Rand Afrikaans Univ., Technikon Witwatersrand and Soweto and East Rand campuses of Vista Univ.
public control
Languages of instruction: Afrikaans, English
Academic year: January to November
Chancellor: Prof. NJABULO S. NDEBELE
Vice-Chancellor: Prof. IHRON RENSBURG
Deputy Vice-Chancellor for Academic Affairs: Prof. ANGINA PAREKH
Deputy Vice-Chancellor for Finance: Prof. JACO VAN SCHOOR
Deputy Vice-Chancellor for Internationalization, Advancement and Student Affairs: Prof. TINYIKO MALULEKE
Deputy Vice-Chancellor for Research, Postgraduate Studies and the Library: Prof. TSHILIDZI MARWALA
Deputy Vice-Chancellor for Strategic Services: Prof. DEREK VAN DER MERWE

Registrar: Prof. KINTA BURGER
Exec. Dir for Library and Information Centre: Dr ROOKAYA BAWA

Library of 452,273 vols
Number of teachers: 350
Number of students: 49,000

DEANS

Faculty of Art, Design and Architecture: Prof. FEDERICO FRESCHI
Faculty of Economic and Financial Science: Prof. AMANDA DEMPSEY
Faculty of Education: Prof. SARAH GRAVETT
Faculty of Engineering and the Built Environment: Prof. SAURABH SINHA
Faculty of Health Sciences: Prof. ANDRÉ SWART
Faculty of Humanities: Prof. R. LIONEL POSTHUMUS (acting)
Faculty of Law: Prof. PATRICK O'BRIEN
Faculty of Management: Prof. DANEEL VAN LILL
Faculty of Science: Dr ANNAH MOTEETEE

PROFESSORS

ABRAHAMSE, H., Biomedical Technology
ALBERTS, V., Physics
ALEXANDER, P., Centre for Sociological Research
AMORY, A., Mathematics, Science, Technology and Computer Education
ANKIEWICZ, P., Mathematics, Science, Technology and Computer Education
ANNEGARN, H., Geography and Environmental Management and Energy Studies
AURIACOMBE, C., Public Governance
BERNDT, A., Marketing Management
BEUKES, N., Geology
BOESSENKOOL, A., Business Management
BROERE, I., Mathematics
BUHLUNGU, S., Sociology
BURGER, W., Afrikaans
BURNETT-LOUW, C., Sport and Movement Studies
CAIRNCROSS, B., Geology
CASE, M., Power and Control Engineering Technology
CHABELI, M., Professional Nursing Practice
CLOETE, G., Public Governance
COETSEE, D., Accountancy
COETZEE, J., Biblical and Religious Studies
COETZEE, J., Industrial Psychology and People Management
COETZEE, P., Chemistry
CONNELL, S., Geography and Environmental Management and Energy Studies
CONRADIE, C., Afrikaans
CONRADIE, W., APB Entrepreneurship
CORNELIUS, S., Private Law
CROUS, F., Industrial Psychology and People Management
DARKWA, J., Chemistry
DE BRUIN, G., Industrial Psychology and People Management
DE BRUYN, H., Business Management
DE KLERK, N., Communication
DE VILLIERS, D., Criminal Law and Procedure
DE WET, D., Humanities Dean's Office
DEMPSEY, A., Economic and Financial Sciences Dean's Office
DU RAND, J., Biblical and Religious Studies
DU TOIT, A., Information and Knowledge Management
DU TOIT, S., Mercantile Law
DUBERY, I., Biochemistry
EHLERS, E., Academy for Information Technology
ESACK, F., Psychology
FERREIRA, H., Electrical and Electronic Engineering Science
FERREIRA, J., Optometry
FRANGOS, C., Statistics
GELDENHUYS, D., Politics
GREYLING, L., Economics and Econometrics
GRUNDLINGH, L., Historical Studies

HAARHOFF, J., Civil Engineering Science
HAMILTON, L., Politics
HARRIS, W., Optometry
HOLLANDER, W., Sport
JACOBS, G., Division for Institutional Planning and Quality Promotions
JANSE VAN RENSBURG, J., Semitic Languages
JANSE VAN VUREN, J., Zoology
JOHL, C., Linguistics and Literary Theory
JOOSTE, C., Marketing Management
JOOSTE, K., Professional Nursing Practice
KATZ, Z., Mechanical Engineering Science
KRUGER, G., Chemistry
KRUGER, S., Management Dean's Office
LANDSBERG, C., Politics
LOMBARD, F., Statistics
LOTTER, H., Philosophy
MACKENZIE, C., English
MAINA, J., SWC Chemistry
MALHERBE, E., Public Law
MANS, K., Accountancy
MARWALA, T., Engineering and the Built Environment Dean's Office
MARX, B., Accountancy
METZ, T., Philosophy
MOORE, D., Anthropology and Development Studies
MYBURGH, C., Educational Psychology
NEELS, J., Private Law
NEL, A., Mechanical Engineering Science
NIEUWENHUIZEN, C., Business Management
NOLTE, A., Maternal and Child Nursing
NURICK, A., Mechanical Engineering Science
O'BRIEN, P., Law Dean's Office
OLDEWAGE, A., Zoology
OLIVIER, L., Accountancy
OTTO, J., Private Law
PATEL, L., Social Work
PIENAAR, M., Afrikaans
PILLAY, J., Educational Psychology
POGGENPOEL, M., Psychiatric Nursing
POSTHUMUS, L., African Languages
PRETORIUS, J., Electrical and Electronic Engineering Science
PRINSLOO, G., Transport and Supply Chain Management
RAUBENHEIMER, H., Mathematics
RAUTENBACH, I., Law Dean's Office
RENSLEIGH, C., Information and Knowledge Management
ROODT, G., Industrial Psychology and People Management
RUTTKAMP, E., Philosophy
SADIE, A., Politics
SAUTHOFF, M., APB Art, Design and Architecture Dean's Office
SCHERZINGER, K., English
SMIT, N., Mercantile Law
SMITH, D., Industrial Psychology and People Management
SNYMAN, J., Philosophy
SONNEKUS, J., Private Law
STEEB, W., Applied Mathematics
STONES, C., Psychology
STRYDOM, A., Physics
STRYDOM, H., Public Law
THOMAS, A., Business Management
TRIEGAARDT, J., Social Work
UYS, J., Industrial Psychology and People Management
UYS, J., Sociology
VAN DER BANK, F., Zoology
VAN DER LINDE, K., Mercantile Law
VAN DER WESTHUIZEN, D., Mathematics, Science, Technology and Computer Education
VAN LILL, D., Tourism and Hospitality Management
VAN ROOYEN, H., Curriculum and Instruction
VAN TONDER, C., Industrial Psychology and People Management
VAN VUUREN, L., Industrial Psychology and People Management
VAN WYK, B., Botany and Plant Biotechnology
VAN ZYL, G., Economics and Econometrics

VELDSMAN, T., Industrial Psychology and People Management
VENTER, A., Politics
VERHOEF, G., Accountancy
VERWEY, S., Communication
VILJOEN, K., Geology
VILLET, C., Applied Mathematics
VIVIERS, H., Biblical and Religious Studies
VON SOLMS, S., Academy for Information Technology
VOOGT, T., Accountancy
WALTERS, J., Transport and Supply Chain Management
WATNEY, M., Criminal Law and Procedure
WEPENER, V., Zoology
WHITEHEAD, C., Botany and Plant Biotechnology
WILLIAMS, D., Chemistry
WINKLER, H., Physics
WOLMARANS, J., Greek and Latin Studies
ZIMPER, A., Economics and Econometrics

UNIVERSITY OF KWAZULU-NATAL

Westville Campus, PMB X54001, Durban 4000
Univ. Rd, Westville

Telephone: (31) 260-8596
E-mail: enquiries@ukzn.ac.za
Internet: www.ukzn.ac.za

Founded 2004 by merger of Univ. of Natal and Univ. of Durban-Westville
Language of instruction: English
public control
Academic year: February to December (4 terms)

Chancellor: Dr ZWELI MKHIZE
Vice-Chancellor and Prin.: Prof. MALEGAPURU WILLIAM MAKGOBA
Deputy Vice-Chancellor and Head of College of Agriculture, Engineering and Science: Prof DEO JAGANYI (acting)
Deputy Vice-Chancellor and Head of College of Health Sciences: Prof. ROB SLOTOW
Deputy Vice-Chancellor and Head of College of Humanities: Prof. CHERYL POTGIETER
Deputy Vice-Chancellor and Head of College of Law and Management Studies: Prof. JOHN CANTIUS MUBANGIZI
Deputy Vice-Chancellor for Research: (vacant)
Deputy Vice-Chancellor for Teaching and Learning: Prof. RENUKA VITHAL
Registrar: Prof. CONVY BALOYI

Library: 1.4m. vols of journals, books, theses, reports and other print media..

BRANCH CAMPUSES

Edgewood Campus: Private Bag X03, Ashwood 3605;cnr Richmond and Marionhill Rd, Pinetown; tel. (31) 260-8596; e-mail education@ukzn.ac.za.

Howard College Campus: Univ. of Kwa-Zulu-Natal, Durban 4041;Mazisi Kunene Rd, Glenwood, Durban; tel. (31) 260-8596; e-mail enquiries@ukzn.ac.za.

Medical School Campus: Private Bag 7, Congella 4013;Umbilo Rd, Durban; tel. (31) 260-8596; e-mail undergrad@ukzn.ac.za.

Pietermaritzburg Campus: Private Bag X01, Scottsville 3209;King Edward Ave, Scottsville, Pietermaritzburg; tel. (31) 260-8596; e-mail enquiries@ukzn.ac.za

UNIVERSITY OF LIMPOPO

Turfloop Campus, Private Bag X1106, Sovenga 0727

Telephone: (15) 268-2435
Internet: www.ul.ac.za

Founded 2005 by merger of Medical Univ. of Southern Africa and Univ. of the North
Academic year: January to December

Campus in Medunsa

Chancellor: Dr REUEL JETHRO KHOZA
Vice-Chancellor and Prin.: Prof. NEHEMIA
MASHOMANYE MAHLO MOKGALONG (acting)
Deputy Vice-Chancellor for Academic Affairs
and Research: Prof. M. M. SIBARA (acting)
Deputy Vice-Chancellor for Medunsa Campus: Prof. T. S. GUGUSHE
Registrar: K. NHLANE
Dean of Students: MOKGADI JOHANNA
MKHONZA
Exec. Dir for Library: M. M. CHUENE
Library: see under Libraries and Archives
Number of teachers: 400
Number of students: 12,000

DEANS

Faculty of Health Sciences: Prof. ERROL A.
HOLLAND
Faculty of Humanities: Dr MAKGWANA
ARNAUS RAMPEDI
Faculty of Management and Law: Prof.
PUMELA MSWELI
Faculty of Science and Agriculture: Prof.
HLENGANI SIWEYA

UNIVERSITY OF MPUMALANGA

Private Bag X11283, Nelspruit 1200
c/o Lowveld College of Agriculture, cnr R40
White River Rd and Fredenheim Rd,
Riverside, Mbombela 1200
Telephone: (13) 753-3065
E-mail: studentapplications@ump.ac.za
Internet: www.ump.ac.za
Founded 2013
public control
Chair: Dr MADODA DAVID MABUNDA
Head: RAMARANKA ANDY MOGOTLANE

UNIVERSITY OF PRETORIA

Private Bag X20, Hatfield 0028
cnr Lynnwood Rd and Roper St, Hatfield
Telephone: (12) 420-3111
E-mail: csc@up.ac.za
Internet: www.up.ac.za
Founded 1908 as Transvaal Univ. College;
current name adopted 1930
public control
Languages of instruction: Afrikaans, English
Academic year: February to December (2
semesters)
Campuses in Groenkloof, Mamelodi, Prinshof, Onderstepoort, Sandton, Hammanskraal
Chancellor: Prof. WISEMAN NKUHLU
Vice-Chancellor and Prin.: Prof. CHERYL DE
LA REY
Sr Vice-Prin.: Prof. C. R. DE BEER (acting)
Vice-Prin. for Academic Affairs: Prof. TYRONE
PRETORIUS
Vice-Prin. for Research and Postgraduate
Education: Prof. STEPHANIE BURTON
Vice-Prin. for Student Affairs and Residences: Prof. THEMBA MOSIA (acting)
Registrar: Prof. NIEK GROVÉ
Dir for Library: ROBERT MOROPA
Library: see under Libraries and Archives
Number of teachers: 1,400
Number of students: 50,000
Publication: *Tukkie* (2 a year)

DEANS

Faculty of Economic and Management Sciences: Prof. ELSABÉ LOOTS
Faculty of Education: Prof. IRMA ELOFF
Faculty of Engineering, the Built Environment and Information Technology: Prof. R.
F. SANDENBERGH
Faculty of Health Sciences: Prof. ERIC BUCH
Faculty of Humanities: Prof. NORMAN T. F.
DUNCAN

Faculty of Law: Prof. ANDRÉ BORAINE
Faculty of Natural and Agricultural Sciences: Prof. ANTON STRÖH
Faculty of Theology: Prof. JOHAN BUITENDAG
Faculty of Veterinary Science: Prof. GERRY
SWAN
Gordon Institute of Business Science: Prof.
NICK BINEDELL

PROFESSORS

Faculty of Economic and Management Sciences:

ALBERTS, N. F., Tourism Management
BASSON, J. S., Human Resources Management
BLIGNAUT, J. N., Economics
BRAND, H. E., Human Resources Management
BRYNARD, P. A., School of Public Management and Administration
DE BEER, J. J., Human Resources Management
DE JAGER, H., Auditing
DE LA REY, J. H., Financial Management
DE VILLIERS, C. J., Financial Management
DE WET, J. M., Marketing and Communication Management
DE WIT, P. W. C., Business Management
DU PLESSIS, P. J., Marketing and Communication Management
FOURIE, D. J., School of Public Management and Administration
GLOECK, J. D., Auditing
GOUWS, D. G., Financial Management
HALL, J. H., Financial Management
HARMSE, C., Economics
HEATH, E. T., Tourism Management
HOOLE, C. R., Human Resources Management
KOORNHOFF, C., Accounting
KUYE, J. O., School of Public Management and Administration
LAMBRECHTS, H. A., Financial Management
MAASDORP, E. F. DE V., Business Management
MARX, A. E., Business Management
OOST, E. J., Financial Management
SCHOEMAN, N. J., Economics
STEYN, F. G., Economics
THORNHILL, C., School of Public Management and Administration
VAN DER SCHYF, D. B., Auditing
VAN HEERDEN, J. H., Economics
VERMEULEN, L. P., Human Resources Management

Faculty of Education:

ALANT, E., Augmentative and Alternative Communication
BECKMANN, J. L., Education Management and Policy Studies
BOUWER, A. C., Educational Psychology
CRONJÉ, J. C., Curriculum Studies
FRASER, W. J., Curriculum Studies
MAREE, J. G., Curriculum Studies
NKOMO, M., Educational Management and Policy Studies
ONWU, G. O. M., Science, Mathematics and Technology Education
VAN ROOYEN, L., Curriculum Studies

Faculty of Engineering, Built Environment and Information Technology (University of Pretoria, Pretoria 0002; tel. (12) 420-2005; e-mail dean@eng.up.ac.za; internet www.up.ac.za/ebit):

BOTHMA, T. J. D., Information Science
BRÜMMER, D. G., Construction Economics
CLAASEN, S. J., Industrial and Systems Engineering
CRIMSEHL, U. H. J., Chemical Engineering
DE VILLIERS, C., Informatics
ELOFF, J. H. P., Computer Science
FISHER, R. C., Architecture
GRIMSEHL, U. H. J., Chemical Engineering

HORAK, E., Civil and Biosystems Engineering
LEUSCHNER, F. W., Electrical, Electronic and Computer Engineering
MEYER, J. P., Mechanical and Aeronautical Engineering
ORANJE, M. C., Town and Regional Planning
PISTORIUS, P. C., Materials Science and Metallurgical Engineering
POURIS, A., Institute for Technological Innovation
PRETORIUS, M. W., Engineering and Technology Management
VAN DER MERWE, J. N., Mining Engineering

Faculty of Health Sciences:

ANDERSON, R., Immunology
BARTEL, P. R., Neurology
BECKER, J. H. R., Surgery
BLITZ-LINDEQUE, J. J., Family Medicine
BUCH, E., School of Health Systems and Public Health
DIPPENAAR, N. G., Physiology
DREYER, L., Anatomical Pathology
DU PLESSIS, D. J., Cardiothoracic Surgery
GREY, S. V., Health Sciences General
KER, J. A., Internal Medicine
KRUGER, M., Paediatrics
LEVINSON, I. P., Urology
LINDEQUE, B. G., Obstetrics and Gynaecology
MAFOJANE, N. A., Neurology
MARITZ, N. G. J., Orthopaedics
MATHIVHA, T. M., Cardiology
MEDLEN, C. E., Pharmacology
MEIRING, J. H., Anatomy
MEYER, H. P., Internal Medicine
MOKOENA, T. R., Surgery
MULDER, A. A. H., Ear, Nose and Throat Medicine
MWANTEMBE, O., Internal Medicine
PATTINSON, R. C., Obstetrics and Gynaecology
RANTLOANE, J. L. A., Anaesthesiology
REIF, S., Urology
RHEEDER, P., Clinical Epidemiology
ROOS, J. L., Psychiatry
ROUX, P., Ophthalmology
SAAYMAN, G., Forensic Medicine
SCHOLTZ, M. E., Radiology
SCHUTTE, C.-M., Neurology
SNYMAN, J. R., Pharmacology
STEYN, M., Anatomy
SWART, J. G., Otorhinolaryngology
VAN GELDER, A. L., Internal Medicine
VAN PAPENDORP, D. H., Physiology
VAN WYK, N. C., Nursing Science
VERMAAK, W. J. H., Chemical Pathology
VILJOEN, M., Physiology
WITTENBERG, D. F., Paediatrics

Faculty of Humanities:

ANTONITES, A., Philosophy
BERGH, J. S., Historical and Heritage Studies
BOTHA, P. J., Ancient Languages
CARSTENS, A., Afrikaans
DU PLESSIS, A., Political Sciences
FOURIE, E., Music
GOSLIN, A. E., Biokinetics
GRAY, R. A., English
GROBBELAAR, J., Sociology
HAGEMANN, F. R., Drama
HARRIS, K. L., Historical and Heritage Studies
HOUGH, M., Political Sciences
KRUGER, P. E., Biokinetics, Sport and Leisure Sciences
LOMBARD, A., Social Work
LOUW, B., Communication Pathology
MARCHETTI-MERCER, M. C., Psychology
MAREE, D. J. F., Psychology
MEDALIE, D., English
MITI, K. N., Political Science
MLAMBO, A. S., Historical and Heritage Studies

NEOCOSMOS, M., Sociology
NIEHAUS, I. A., Anthropology and Archaeology
NZEWI, M. E., Music
OHLHOFF, C. H. F., Afrikaans
PEETERS, L. F. H. M. C., Modern European Languages
POTGIETER, J. H., Ancient Languages
PRETORIUS, F., Historical and Heritage Studies
PRETORIUS, R., Criminology
PRINSLOO, D. J., African Languages
PRINSLOO, G. T. M., Ancient Languages
ROODT, P. H., Afrikaans
SAUTHOFF, M. D., Visual Arts
SCHOEMAN, J. B., Psychology
SCHOEMAN, M. M. E., Political Sciences
SHARP, J. S., Anthropology and Archaeology
STANDER, H. F., Ancient Languages
STANFORD, H. J., Music
STEYN, B. J. M., Biokinetics
VAN DER MERWE, A., Communication Pathology
VAN DER MESCHT, H., Music
VAN NIEKERK, C., Music
VAN WYK, G. J., Biokinetics, Sport and Leisure Sciences
VILJOEN, W. D., Music
WALTON, C. R., Music
WEBB, V. N., Afrikaans
WEIDEMAN, A. J., Unit for Language Skills Development
WESSELS, J. A., English
WILLEMSE, H. S. S., Afrikaans

Faculty of Law (tel. (12) 420-2412; e-mail duard.kleyn@up.ac.za):

BORAINE, A., Procedural Law
BOTHA, C. J., Public Law
BURDETTE, D. A., Centre for Practical and Continuing Legal Education
CARSTENS, P. A., Public Law
DAVEL, C. J., Private Law and Centre for Child Law
DELPORT, P. A., Mercantile and Labour Law
HANSUNQULE, K. M., Centre for Human Rights
HAUPT, F. S., Law Clinic
HEYNS, C. H., Centre for Human Rights
KLOPPER, H. B., Mercantile and Labour Law
KOTZE, D. J. L., Procedural Law
LOTZ, D. J., Mercantile Law
MAITHUFI, I. P., Private Law
NAGEL, C. J., Mercantile Law
NICHOLSON, C. M. A., Legal History, Comparative Law and Legal Philosophy
SCHOEMAN, M. C., Private Law
SCOTT, T. J., Private Law
THOMAS, P. J., Legal History, Comparative Law and Legal Philosophy
VAN ECK, B. P. S., Mercantile Law
VAN JAARSVELD, S. R., Mercantile Law
VAN MARLE, K., Legal History, Comparative Law and Legal Philosophy
VAN SCHALKWYK, L. N., Private Law
VILJOEN, F. J., Legal History, Comparative Law and Legal Philosophy
VISSER, P. J., Private Law

Faculty of Natural and Agricultural Sciences (Room 2-32, Agricultural Sciences Building, University of Pretoria, Pretoria 0002; tel. (12) 420-3201; internet www.up.ac.za/science):

ALBERTS, H. W., Physics
AURET, F. D., Physics
BEAVON, K. S. O., Geography and Geoinformatics
BENNETT, N. C., Zoology and Entomology
BESTER, M. N., Zoology and Entomology
BRAUN, M. W. H., Physics
BREDENKAMP, G. J., Botany
BRINK, D. J., Physics
CASEY, N. H., Animal and Wildlife Sciences

CLOETE, T. E., Microbiology and Plant Pathology
COUTINHO, T. A., Microbiology and Plant Pathology
CROWTHER, N. A. S., Statistics
DE KLERK, H. M., Consumer Science
DE WAAL, S. A., Geology
HUISMANS, H., Genetics
KIRSTEN, J. F., Agricultural Economics, Extension and Rural Development
KUNERT, K. J., Botany
LOTZ, S., Chemistry
LOUW, A. I., Biochemistry
MALHERBE, J. B., Physics
MEYER, J. J. M., Botany
MILLER, H. G., Physics
MINNAAR, A., Food Sciences
NEITZ, A. W. H., Biochemistry
NICOLSON, S. W., Zoology and Entomology
PLASTINO, A. R., Physics
REINHARDT, C. F., Plant Production and Soil Science
ROHWER, E. R., Chemistry
SCHOLTZ, C. H., Zoology and Entomology
STRÖH, A., Mathematics and Applied Mathematics
VAN AARDE, R. J., Zoology and Entomology
VAN ROOYEN, C. J., Agricultural Economics, Extension and Rural Development
VAN WYK, A. E., Botany
VERSCHOOR, J. A., Biochemistry
VLEGGAAR, R., Chemistry

Faculty of Theology:

DE VILLIERS, D. E., Dogmatics and Christian Ethics
DREYER, Y., Practical Theology
HOFMEYR, J. W., Church History and Church Policy
HUMAN, D. J., Old Testament Studies
LE ROUX, J. H., Old Testament Studies
MEIRING, P. G. J., Science of Religion and Missiology
MÜLLER, J. C., Practical Theology
VAN AARDE, A. G., New Testament
VAN DER MERWE, P. J., Science of Religion and Missiology
VAN DER WATT, J. G., New Testament Studies
VENTER, P. M., Old Testament Studies
WETHMAR, C. J., Dogmatics and Christian Ethics

Faculty of Veterinary Science (Private Bag X04, Ondestepoort 0110; tel. (12) 529-8000; e-mail dean@op.up.ac.za; internet www.up.ac.za/academic/veterinary):

BERTSCHINGER, H. J., Wildlife Unit
BOOMKER, J. D. F., Veterinary Tropical Diseases
BOOTH, K. K., Anatomy and Physiology
COETZER, J. A. W., Veterinary Tropical Diseases
GROENEWALD, H. B., Anatomy and Physiology
GUTHRIE, A. J., Centre for Equine Research
KIRBERGER, R. M., Companion Animal Clinical Studies
LOURENS, D. C., Production Animal Studies
McCRINDLE, C. M., Paraclinical Sciences
PENZHORN, B. L., Veterinary Tropical Diseases
RAUTENBACH, G. H., Production Animal Studies
STADLER, P., Companion Animal Clinical Studies
SWAN, G. E., Paraclinical Sciences
TERBLANCHE, W. M., Deputy Dean

School of Dentistry:

BOTHA, S. J., Centre for Stomatological Research
BUCH, B., Diagnostics and Röntgenology
BÜTOW, K. W., Maxillofacial and Oral Surgery
DE WET, F. A., Prosthetics and Dental Mechanics

JACOBS, F. J. (acting), Maxillofacial and Oral Surgery
KEMP, P. L., Prosthetics and Dental Mechanics
VAN HEERDEN, W. F. P., Oral Pathology and Oral Biology
VAN WYK, P. J., Community Dentistry
VERWAYEN, F. D., Periodontics and Oral Medicine

UNIVERSITY OF SOUTH AFRICA

POB 392, Unisa 0003
Telephone: (12) 429-3111
E-mail: artes@unisa.ac.za
Internet: www.unisa.ac.za

Founded 1873, Royal Charter 1877; merged with Technikon Southern Africa and inc. Vista Univ. 2004

Languages of instruction: Afrikaans, English

Academic year: February to November

Chancellor: Justice BERNARD MAKGABO NGOEPE
Prin. and Vice-Chancellor: Prof. M. S. MAKHANYA
Chair. of the Ccl: Dr MATTHEWS PHOSA
Pro-Vice-Chancellor: Prof. N. BAIJNATH
Vice-Prin. for Academic Affairs, Teaching and Learning: Prof. M. C. MARÉ
Vice-Prin. for Advisory and Assurance Services: Prof. DIVYA SINGH
Vice-Prin. for Finance and Univ. Estates: ADRIAN T. ROBINSON
Vice-Prin. for Institutional Devt: Prof. M. QHOBELA
Vice-Prin. for Operations: Prof. B. J. ERASMUS
Vice-Prin. for Research and Innovation: Prof. M. PHAKENG
Univ. Registrar: Prof. MOGEGE MOSIMEGE
Librarian: Dr B. MBAMBO-THATA

Number of teachers: 1,790
Number of students: 321,890

Publications: *Africanus* (2 a year), *Ars Nova* (1 a year), *Codicillus* (2 a year), *Communicatio* (2 a year), *De Arte* (2 a year), *Educare* (1 a year), *Kleio* (1 a year), *Language Matters* (1 a year), *Mousaion* (2 a year), *Musicus* (3 a year), *Politeia* (3 a year), *Scrutiny²* (2 a year), *Unisa Psychologia* (2 a year)

DEANS

College of Agriculture and Environment Sciences: Prof. M. J. LININGTON
College of Economics and Management Sciences: Prof. V. A. CLAPPER
College of Education: Prof. K. P. DZVIMBO
College of Graduate Studies: Prof. GREG CUTHBERTSON
College of Human Sciences: Prof. R. M. H. MOEKETSI
College of Law: Prof. R. SONGCA
College of Science, Engineering and Technology: Prof. G. MOCHE

PROFESSORS

ABRIE, A., Accounting
ACKERMANN, P. L. S., Graduate School of Business Leadership
ADLEM, W. L. J., Public Administration
AILOLA, D. A., Mercantile Law
BADENHORST, J. A., Business Management
BARROW, J. E., Computer Science
BEATY, D. T., Graduate School of Business Leadership
BECKER, H. M. R., Applied Accountancy
BEGEMANN, E., Business Management
BEKKER, P. M., Criminal and Procedural Law
BESTER, G., Educational Studies
BEYERS, E., Psychology
BISHOP, N. T., Mathematics, Applied Mathematics and Astronomy
BODENSTEIN, H. C. A., Educational Studies

BOOT, G., Accounting
BOOYENS, S. W., Advanced Nursing Sciences
BOOYSE, J. J., Further Teacher Training
BOOYSEN, H., Constitutional and International Law
BORNMAN, C. H., Computer Science
BOTHA, J. E., New Testament
BOTHA, N. J., Constitutional and International Law
BOTHA, P. J. J., New Testament
BRITS, J. P., History
BRYNARD, D. J., Public Administration
BURNS, Y. M., Constitutional and International Law
CALITZ, E., Economics
CANT, M. C., Business Management
CARPENTER, G., Constitutional and International Law
CHURCH, J., Jurisprudence
CILLIERS, C. H., Criminology
CILLIERS, F. VAN N., Industrial Psychology
COETZER, I. A., Educational Studies
CONRADIE, H., Criminology
CRONJE, D. S. P., Private Law
CRONJE, G. J. DE J., Business Management
CRONJE, P. M., Accounting
CROUS, S. F. M., Educational Studies
DADOO, Y., Semitics
DE BEER, C. S., Information Science
DE BEER, F. C., Anthropology and Archaeology
DE BEER, F. C., Development Administration
DE JONGH, M., Anthropology and Archaeology
DEMBETEMBE, N. C., African Languages
DICK, A. L., Information Science
DREECKMEYER, M., Secondary School Education
DREYER, J. M., Advanced Nursing Sciences
DU PISANIE, J. A., Economics
DU PLESSIS, I. J., New Testament
DU PLESSIS, P. J., Graduate School of Business Leadership
DU TOIT, C. W., Research Institute for Theology and Religion
DU TOIT, G. S., Business Management
ENGELBRECHT, J., New Testament
ERASMUS, B. J., Business Management
FARIS, J. A., Criminal and Procedural Law
FAURE, A. M., Political Sciences
FINLAYSON, R., African Languages
FOURIE, D. P., Psychology
FOURIE, L. J., Economics
FOURIE, P. J., Communication
FRANZSEN, R. C. D., Mercantile Law
GELDENHUYS, D. G., Musicology
GHYOOT, V. G., Business Management
GRÄBE, R. C., Theory of Literature
GROBBELAAR, A. F., Accounting
GROBBELAAR, J. I., Sociology
GROBLER, G. M. M., African Languages
GROBLER, P. A., Business Management
GRUNDLINGH, A. M., History
HAVENGA, M. K., Mercantile Law
HAVENGA, P. H., Mercantile Law
HAWTHORNE, L., Private Law
HEIDEMA, J., Mathematics, Applied Mathematics and Astronomy
HENDRIKSE, A. P., Linguistics
HIGGS, P., Educational Studies
HOFMEYR, K. B., Graduate School of Business Leadership
HOUGH, J., Business Management
HUBBARD, E. H., Linguistics
HUGO, P. J., Political Sciences
HUGO, W. M. J., Graduate School of Business Leadership
JANSE VAN RENSBURG, J. B., Applied Accountancy
JORDAAN, W. J., Psychology
JOUBERT, J. J., Criminal and Procedural Law
JULYAN, F. W., Accounting
KATKOVNIK, V., Statistics
KLERCK, W. G., Graduate School of Business Leadership
KRIEK, D. J., Political Science

KRITZINGER, J. N. J., Missiology
KRUGER, E. G., Secondary School Teacher Education
KRÜGER, J. S., Religious Studies
LANDMAN, A. A., Mercantile Law
LEMMER, E. M., Further Teacher Training
LESSING, A. C., Educational Studies
LIEBENBERG, E. C., Geography
LIGTHELM, A. A., Bureau for Market Research
LOMBARD, D. B., Classics
LÖTTER, S., Criminal and Procedural Law
LOUWRENS, L. J., African Languages
LÜBBE, J. C., Semitics
LUCAS, G. H. A., Business Management
McKAY, V. I., Institute for Adult Basic Education and Training
McLEARY, F., Graduate School of Business Leadership
MADER, G. J., Classics
MARAIS, A. DE K., Business Management
MARÉ, E. A., History of Art, Fine Art
MARÉ, M. C., Criminal and Procedural Law
MAREE, M. C., Romance Languages
MARKHAM, R., Statistics
MARTINS, J. A., Bureau for Market Research
MARX, J., Business Management
MISCH, M. K. E., German
MOHR, P. J., Economics
MOTLHABI, M. B. G., Systematic Theology and Theological Ethics
MSIMANG, C. T., African Languages
MYNHARDT, C. M., Mathematics, Applied Mathematics and Astronomy
NAUDE, C. M. B., Criminology
NELL, V., Social and Health Sciences
NESER, J. J., Criminology
NTULI, D. B., African Languages
OBERHOLZER, M. O., Educational Studies
OLIVIER, A., Primary School Education
ORR, M. A., English
PALMER, P. N., Business Management
PAUL, S. O., Chemistry
PAUW, J. C., Public Administration
PELSER, G. P. J., Graduate School of Business Leadership
PIETERSE, H. J. C., Practical Theology
PLUG, C., Psychology
POTGIETER, C., Further Teacher Education
POTGIETER, J. M., Private Law
POTGIETER, T. J. E., Graduate School of Business Leadership
POULOS, G., African Languages
PRETORIUS, E. A. C., New Testament
PRETORIUS, J. T., Mercantile Law
PRETORIUS, L., Sociology
PRINSLOO, E. D., Philosophy
RABINOWITZ, I. A., English
RADEMEYER, G., Psychology
REYNHARDT, E. C., Physics
ROELOFSE, J. J., Communication
ROOS, H. M., Afrikaans
RUTHERFORD, B. R., Mercantile Law
RYAN, P. D., English
SADLER, E., Applied Accountancy
SALBANY, S. DE O., Applied Mathematics, Mathematics and Astronomy
SCHEFFLER, E. H., Old Testament
SCOTT, S. J., Private Law
SEBOTHOMA, W. A., New Testament
SERUDU, S. M., African Languages
SHAHIA, M., Transport Economics and Logistics
SMIT, B. F., Criminology
SMIT, P. J., Business Management
SMITH, J. DU P., Economics
SMITH, K. W., History
SMUTS, C. A., Transport Economics and Logistics
SNYDERS, F. J. A., Psychology
SNYMAN, C. R., Criminal and Procedural Law
SNYMAN, J. W., African Languages
SOFIANOS, S. A., Physics
SÖHNGE, W. F., Educational Studies
STEENEKAMP, T. J., Economics
STEFFENS, F. E., Statistics
STEYN, B. L., Accounting

STRIKE, W. N., Romance Languages
STRYDOM, J. W., Business Management
SUMMERS, G. J., Chemistry
SWANEPOEL, C. F., African Languages
SWANEPOEL, C. H., Institute for Educational Research
SWANEPOEL, C. J., Quantitative Management
SWANEPOEL, F. A., C. B. Powell Bible Centre
SWANEPOEL, P. H., Afrikaans
SWANEVELDER, J. J., Accounting
SWART, G. J., Mercantile Law
SWEMMER, P. N., Auditing
TERBLANCHE, S. S., Criminal and Procedural Law
THOMASHAUSEN, A. E. A. M., Institute for Foreign and Comparative Law
TORR, C. S. W., Economics
TROSKIE, R., Advanced Nursing Sciences
VAKALISA, N. C. G., Secondary School Education
VAN ASWEGEN, A., Private Law
VAN BILJON, R. C. W., Social Work
VAN BLERK, A. E., Jurisprudence
VAN DELFT, W. F., Social Work
VAN DEN BERG, P. H., Graduate School of Business Leadership
VAN DER MERWE, C. A., Quantitative Management
VAN DER MERWE, D. P., Criminal and Procedural Law
VAN DER WALT, A. J., Private Law
VAN DYK, P. J., Old Testament
VAN HEERDEN, B., Auditing
VAN NIEKERK, E., Systematic Theology, Theological Ethics
VAN NIEKERK, J. P., Mercantile Law
VAN ROOY, M. P., Educational Studies
VAN WYK, A. M. A., Private Law
VAN WYK, C. W., Jurisprudence
VAN WYK, D. H., Constitutional and International Law
VAN WYK, H. DE J., Bureau for Market Research
VAN ZYL, A. E., Educational Studies
VILJOEN, H. G., Psychology
VISSER, C. J., Mercantile Law
VISSER, P. S., Educational Studies
VORSTER, H. J. S., Auditing
VORSTER, J. N., New Testament
VORSTER, L. P., Indigenous Law
VORSTER, S. J. R., Mathematics, Applied Mathematics and Astronomy
WATKINS, M. L., Industrial Psychology
WEINBERG, A. M., English
WESSELS, W. J., Old Testament
WHELPTON, F. P. VAN R., Indigenous Law
WIECHERS, E., Educational Studies
WIECHERS, N. J., Private Law
WILLIAMS, G., Applied Accountancy
WOLFAARDT, J. A., Practical Theology
WOLFAARDT, J. B., Industrial Psychology
WOLVAARDT, J. S., Quantitative Management
YADAVALLI, V. S. S., Statistics

UNIVERSITY OF THE FREE STATE

POB 339, Bloemfontein 9300
205 Nelson Mandela Dr., Park West, Bloemfontein

Telephone: (51) 401-9111
E-mail: info@ufs.ac.za
Internet: www.ufs.ac.za

Founded 1904 as Grey Univ. College, current name adopted 2001
public control
Languages of instruction: Afrikaans, English
Academic year: February to November

Campus in Qwaqwa

Chancellor: Dr KHOTSO MOKHELE
Vice-Chancellor and Rector: Prof. JONATHAN D. JANSEN
Vice-Rector for Academic Affairs: Prof. DRIEKIE HAY
Vice-Rector for External Relations: Dr KELEBOGILE CHOICE MAKHETHA

Vice-Rector for Operations: Dr N. I. MORGAN
Vice-Rector for Research: Prof. CORLI WIT-
THUHN
Dean of Student Affairs: B. R. BUYS
Registrar: Dr DEREK SWEMMER
Dir for Library and Information Services:
KEITUMETSE EISTER
Library of 650,000 vols, 14,000 ebooks
Number of teachers: 480
Number of students: 33,000

DEANS

Faculty of Economic and Management Sci-
ences: Prof. H. J. KROUKAMP
Faculty of Education: Prof. D. FRANCIS
Faculty of Health Sciences: Prof. G. J. VAN
ZYL
Faculty of Humanities: Prof. L. J. S. BOTES
Faculty of Law: Prof. J. J. HENNING
Faculty of Natural and Agricultural Sci-
ences: Prof. N. J. L. HEIDEMAN
Faculty of Theology: Prof. S. D. SNYMAN

UNIVERSITY OF THE WESTERN CAPE

Private Bag X17, Bellville 7535
Robert Sobukwe Rd, Bellville 7535
Telephone: (21) 959-2911
E-mail: info@uwc.ac.za
Internet: www.uwc.ac.za
Founded 1959 as Univ. College of the West-
ern Cape, current name adopted 1970
public control
Languages of instruction: Afrikaans, English
Academic year: February to December

Rector: Prof. BRIAN O'CONNELL
Deputy Vice-Chancellor for Academic
Affairs: Prof. RAMESH BHARUTHRAM
Deputy Vice-Chancellor for Student Devt
and Support Services: Prof. LULLU TSHI-
WULA
Pro-Vice-Chancellor: PATRICIA LAWRENCE
Registrar: Dr INGRID MILLER
Librarian: PATEKA NTSHUNTSHE-MATSHAYA
Library of 297,756 vols, 1,280 journals,
41,333 electronic journals
Number of teachers: 910
Number of students: 18,000
Publications: *Journal of Community Health*
(1 a year), *Journal of Student Affairs in
Africa* (2 a year), *KRONOS: Journal of
Cape History, Law, Democracy and Devel-
opment* (4 a year, print and online,
ldd.org.za), *Multilingual Margins*

DEANS

Faculty of Arts: Prof. DUNCAN BROWN
Faculty of Community and Health Sciences:
Prof. JOSÈ FRANTZ
Faculty of Dentistry: Prof. YUSUF OSMAN
Faculty of Economics and Management Sci-
ences: Prof. KOBUS VISSER
Faculty of Education: Prof. ZUBEIDA DESAI
Faculty of Law: Prof. JULIA SLOTH-NIELSEN
Faculty of Natural Science: Prof. MICHAEL
DAVIES-COLEMAN

UNIVERSITY OF THE WITWATERSRAND, JOHANNESBURG

Private Bag 3, Wits 2050
1 Jan Smuts Ave, Braamfontein 2000
Telephone: (11) 717-1000
E-mail: studysa.international@wits.ac.za
Internet: www.wits.ac.za
Founded 1922
public control
Academic year: February to November

Chancellor: DIKGANG MOSENEKE
Vice-Chancellor and Prin.: Prof. ADAM HABIB
Vice-Prin. and Deputy Vice-Chancellor for
Academic: Prof. ANDREW CROUCH

Deputy Vice-Chancellor for Advancement
and Partnerships: Prof. ROB MOORE
Deputy Vice-Chancellor for Finance, Human
Resources and Transformation: Prof.
TAWANA KUPE
Deputy Vice-Chancellor for Knowledge,
Information Management and Infrastruc-
ture: Prof. BEATRYS LACQUET
Deputy Vice-Chancellor for Research and
Postgraduate Affairs: Dr ZEBLON VILAKAZI
Registrar: NITA LAWTON-MISRA (acting)
Univ. Librarian: FELIX N. UBOGU
Library: see under Libraries and Archives
Number of teachers: 1,800
Number of students: 30,833
Publications: *Industrial Law Journal* (12 a
year), *Palaeontologia Africana* (1 a year),
South African Journal On Human Rights
(3 a year, print and online, www.wit-
s.ac.za/academic/clm/law/11088/southafri-
canjournalonhumanrights.html), *The
African Journal of Information and Com-
munication* (1 a year, online, www.wit-
s.ac.za/linkcentre/ajic/17669/the_african_-
journal_of_information_amp;_communica-
tion.html)

DEANS

Faculty of Commerce, Law and Management:
Prof. IMRAAN VALODIA
Faculty of Engineering and the Built Envir-
onment: Prof. IAN R. JANDRELL
Faculty of Health Sciences: Prof. MKHULULI
LUKHELE (acting)
Faculty of Humanities: Prof. RUKSANA OSMAN
Faculty of Science: Prof. HELDER MARQUES

PROFESSORS

Faculty of Education:

ENSLIN, P. A.
PENDLEBURY, S. A.
SKUY, M. S.

Faculty of Engineering:

BRYSON, A. W., Chemical Engineering
ERIC, R. H., Metallurgy and Materials
Engineering
FOURIE, A., Civil Engineering
GLASSER, D., Chemical Engineering
HANRAHAN, H. E., Electrical Engineering
HILDEBRANDT, D., Process and Materials
Engineering
IWANKIEWICZ, R. M., Applied Mathematics
LANDY, C. F., Electrical Engineering
MACLEOD, I. M., Control Engineering
MCCUTCHEON, R. T., Project and Construc-
tion Management
ONSONGO, W. M., Undergraduate Engin-
eering Education
PHILLIPS, H. R., Mining Engineering
REYNDERS, J. P., Electrical Engineering
SHEER, T. J., Mechanical Engineering
SKEWS, B. W., Mechanical Engineering
STEPHENSON, D., Hydraulic Engineering

Faculty of Engineering and the Built Environment:

BREMNER, L., Architecture
MULLER, J. G., Town and Regional Planning
SCHLOSS, R. I., Construction Economics
and Management

Faculty of Health Sciences:

ALLWOOD, C., Psychiatry
ALTINI, M., Oral Pathology
CARMICHAEL, T., Ophthalmology
CARR, L., Prosthetic Dentistry
CLEATON-JONES, P. E., Experimental Odon-
tology
COOPER, P. A., Paediatrics
CREWE-BROWN, H., Medical Microbiology
CRONJE, S. L., Cardiothoracic Surgery
DAVIES, M. R. Q., Paediatric Surgery
ERKEN, E. H. W., Orthopaedic Surgery
EVANS, W. G., Orthodontics

FELDMAN, C., Medicine
FRITZ, V. U., Neurology
GEORGE, J. A., Orthopaedic Surgery
GRAY, I. P., Chemical Pathology
HAVLIK, I., Pharmacology
HOFMEYR, G. J., Obstetrics and Gynaecol-
ogy
HUDDLE, K., Medicine
JOFFE, B. I., Medicine
KALK, W. J., Clinical Endocrinology
KEW, M. C., Medicine
KLUGMAN, K. P., Clinical Microbiology
KRAMER, B., Anatomical Sciences
LABURN, H. P., Physiology
LOWNIE, J. F., Maxillofacial and Oral Sur-
gery
MACPHAIL, A. P., Medicine
MAINA, J. N., Anatomical Sciences
MANGA, P., Cardiology
MCINTOSH, W., Ear, Nose and Throat Sur-
gery
MEYERS, A. M., Nephrology
MILNE, F. J., Medicine
MITCHELL, D., Physiology
MITCHELL, G., Physiology
OWEN, P., Prosthetic Dentistry
PANTANOWITZ, D., Surgery
PATERSON, A. C., Anatomical Pathology
PETIT, J.-C., Oral Medicine and Period-
ontology
PETTIFOR, J. M., Paediatrics
PICK, W., Community Health
RAMSAY, M., Human Genetics
REES, D., Occupational Health
RUDOLPH, M. J., Community Medicine
SARELI, P., Cardiology
SCHOUB, B. D., Virology
SHIPTON, E. A., Anaesthesia
SPARKS, B. L. W., Family Health
SUR, R., Radiation Oncology
VAN GELDEREN, C. J., Obstetrics and
Gynaecology
VILJOEN, D., Human Genetics
WADEE, A. A., Immunology

Faculty of Humanities and Faculty of Science:

ADLER, J., Mathematics Education Devel-
opment
ALEXANDER, J. J., Microbiology
ANHAEUSSER, C. R., Geology
ASHER, A., Statistics and Actuarial Science
BEICHELT, F., Statistics and Actuarial Sci-
ence
BONNER, P. L., History
BOZZOLI, B., Sociology
BRADLEY, J. D., Chemistry
BUNN, D., History of Art
CAWTHORN, R. G., Geology
COCK, J., Sociology
COMINS, J. D., Physics
COPLAN, D. B., Social Anthropology
COVILLE, N. J., Organo-Metallic Chemistry
CRUMP, A., Fine Arts
DABBS, E., Genetics
DELIUS, P. S., History
DIRR, H. W., Biochemistry
DRIVER, K., Mathematics
DU PLESSIS, P., Physics
EVERY, A. G., Physics
FABIAN, B. C., Zoology
FATTI, L. P., Statistics
FISHER, J., Psychology
GLASSER, L., Physical Chemistry
HEISS, W. D., Theoretical Physics
HOCH, M. J. R., Solid State Physics
HOFMEYR, I., African Literature
HUFFMAN, T. N., Archaeology
HUNT, J. H. V., Mathematics
LODGE, T., Political Studies
LOWTHER, J. E., Physics
LUBINSKY, D. S., Mathematics
MAAKE, N. P., African Languages
MCCARTHY, T. S., Geology
MCKENDRICK, B. W., Social Work

McLACHLAN, D. S., Electronic Properties of Solids
MARQUES, H., Chemistry
MASON, D. P., Applied Mathematics
MICHAEL, J. P., Organic Chemistry
MOYS, M., School of Process and Materials Engineering
MURRAY, B. K., Edwardian British History
OLIVIER, G., Afrikaans and Dutch
OWEN-SMITH, N., Zoology
PENDLEBURY, M., Philosophy
PENN, C., Speech Pathology and Audiology
PIENAAR, R. N., Botany
PRODINGER, H., Mathematics
ROBB, L. J., Geology
RODRIGUES, J. A. P., Physics
ROGERS, K. H., Botany
ROGERSON, C. M., Geography
ROLLNICK, M., College of Science
RUBIDGE, B. S., Palaeontology
SCURRELL, M. S., Chemistry
STADLER, A. W., Political Studies
STREMLAU, J. J., International Relations
TAYLOR, J., Dramatic Art
TYSON, P. D., Climatology
VILJOEN, M. J., Mining Geology
VON HOLY, A., Microbiology
WEBSTER, E. C., Sociology
WRIGHT, C., Geophysics
WRIGHT, C. J., Computational and Applied Mathematics

UNIVERSITY OF VENDA

Private Bag X5050, Thohoyandou 0950
Univ. Rd, Thohoyandou 0950
Telephone: (15) 962-8000
E-mail: info@univen.ac.za
Internet: www.univen.ac.za

Founded 1982
public control

Vice-Chancellor and Prin.: Prof. PETER MBATI
Deputy Vice-Chancellor for Academic Affairs: Prof. J. E. CRAFFORD
Deputy Vice-Chancellor for Operations: Dr J. J. ZAAIMAN
Registrar: Prof. A. E. NESAMVUNI
Dir for Library: MUSHONI MULAUDZI

Library of 90,871 vols, 823 periodicals
Number of teachers: 310
Number of students: 9,500

Publication: *Journal of Educational Studies* (2 a year)

DEANS

School of Agriculture: Prof. GODWIN AINA-MENSA MCHAU
School of Education: Dr PETER MULAUDZI
School of Environmental Sciences: Prof. J. O. ODIYO
School of Health Sciences: Prof. LUNIC BASE KHOZA
School of Human and Social Sciences: Prof. MOKGALE MAKGOPA
School of Law: ANNETTE LANSINK
School of Management Sciences: Prof. AGYA-PONG B. GYEKYE
School of Mathematical and Natural Sciences: Prof. JAN CRAFFORD

PROFESSORS

Faculty of Human and Social Sciences, Management Sciences and Law:
AKINNUSI, D. M.
AYURU, R. N.
BAYONA, E. L. M.
GYEKE, A. B.
LUKHAIMANE, E. K.
MIREKU, O.
SIMUKONDA, H. P. M.
SPENCER, J. P.
STEYN, J. N.
Faculty of Natural and Applied Sciences:
AGBONJINMI, A. P.

AMUSA, L. O.
DU TOIT, P. J.
KHOZA, L. B.
KIRUNDA, E. F.
MAKINDE, M. O.
MBHENYANE, X. G.
OGOLA, J. S.
OLE-MEILUDI, R. E.
OLORUNDA, A. O.
OMARA-OJUNGU, P. H.
ONI, S. A.
SHAI-MAHOKO, N. S.
SIMALENGA, T. E.
VAN DER WAAL, B. C. W.
VAN REE, T.

UNIVERSITY OF ZULULAND

Private Bag X1001, KwaDlangezwa 3886
1 Main Rd, Vulindlela, KwaDlangezwa 3886
Telephone: (35) 902-6000
E-mail: admissions@unizulu.ac.za
Internet: www.unizulu.ac.za

Founded 1960 as Univ. College of Zululand, current name adopted 1970
public control

Academic year: February to December

Chancellor: JOEL SIBUSISO NDEBELE
Vice-Chancellor: Prof. N. M. MAZIBUKO
Deputy Vice-Chancellor for Research and Innovation: Prof. ROB MIDGLEY
Deputy Vice-Chancellor for Teaching and Learning: Prof. XOLISWA MTOSE
Registrar: Dr M. G. VINGER
Dean of Students: Dr Z. MKHIZE (acting)
Librarian: L. VAHED

Number of teachers: 300
Number of students: 16,118

Publication: *Paidonomia*

DEANS

Faculty of Arts: Prof. J. D. THWALA
Faculty of Commerce, Administration and Law: Prof. D. TEWARI
Faculty of Education: Prof. X. MTOSE
Faculty of Science and Agriculture: Prof. O. M. NDWANDWE

PROFESSORS

Faculty of Arts (tel. (35) 902-6087):
BUIJS, G. C. U., Anthropology
DALRYMPLE, L. I., Drama
DE VILLIERS, J., History
EDWARDS, S. D., Psychology
GLASS, H. G. L., Sociology
GUMBI, T. A. P., Social Work
HOOPER, M. J., English
KHUMALO, L. Z. M., African Languages
KLOPPER, R. M., Afrikaans
LOUBSER, J. A., Bibliological Studies
MAKHANYA, E. M., Geography
MEIHUIZEN, N. C. T., English
MERSHAM, G. M., Communication Science
NZIMAKWE, D. P., Nursing Science
OCHOLLA, D. N., Library and Information Science
POTGIETER, P. J., Criminal Justice
SONG, A., Missiology, Religious Studies and Practical Theology
WAIT, E. C., Philosophy
ZUNGU, B. M., Nursing Science
Faculty of Commerce, Administration and Law (tel. (35) 902-6123):
CLOETE, J., Business Management
LIVINGSTONE, M., Accountancy and Auditing
NAIDOO, I. U., Accountancy and Auditing
SABELA, T. R., Public Administration and Political Science
SHRESTHA, B. C., Economics
SONI, R., Constitutional Law
Faculty of Education (tel. (35) 902-6348):
COETSEE, M. F., Human Movement Science

DLAMINI, E. T., History of Education and Comparative Education
GABELA, R. V., Educational Planning and Administration
JACOBS, M., Didactics
SIBAYA, P. T., Educational Psychology
URBANI, G., Educational Psychology
Faculty of Science and Agriculture (tel. (35) 902-6649):
BEESHAM, A., Mathematical Sciences
BERMANSEDER, N., Engineering
COETSEE, M. F., Human Movement Science
CYRUS, D. P., Zoology
DAVIDSON, A. T., Physics
DJAVOVA, T., Biochemistry
FERREIRA, D. P., Botany
JURY, M. R., Geography
KELBE, B. E. M.-L., Hydrology
KOLAWOLE, G. A., Chemistry
NDWANDWE, M. O., Physics

VAAL UNIVERSITY OF TECHNOLOGY

Private Bag X021, Vanderbijlpark 1900
Andries Potgieter Blvd, Vanderbijlpark 1900
Telephone: (16) 950-9000
E-mail: international@vut.ac.za
Internet: www.vut.ac.za

Founded 1966 as College of Advanced Technical Education, current name adopted 2004
public control

Campuses in Daveyton, Kempton Park, Secunda, Upington

Chancellor: P. D. F. TLAKULA
Vice-Chancellor and Prin.: Prof. I. N. MOU-TLANA (acting)
Deputy Vice-Chancellor for Operations and Resources: Prof. G. N. ZIDE
Deputy Vice-Chancellor for Teaching and Learning: (vacant)
Deputy Vice-Chancellor for Technology, Innovation and Advancement: Prof. H. A. LOUW
Registrar: Dr T. D. MOKOENA
Exec. Dir for Library and Information Services: NORMA ROBERTS

Library of 42,000 vols, 4,480 periodicals
Number of teachers: 320
Number of students: 21,000

Publications: *Sediba sa Thuto* (academic journal, 1 a year), *Tempo* (communications journal, 2 a year)

DEANS

Faculty of Applied and Computer Science: Prof. B. R. MABUZA
Faculty of Engineering and Technology: Prof. M. NDEGE
Faculty of Human Sciences: Prof. RIANA VAN DER BANK
Faculty of Management Sciences: Prof. M. DHURUP

WALTER SISULU UNIVERSITY

Private Bag X1, Unitra 5117
Telephone: (47) 502-2844
Internet: www.wsu.ac.za

Founded 2005 by merger of Eastern Cape Technikon, Border Technikon and Univ. of Transkei
public control

Academic year: January to December

Campuses in Butterworth, Buffalo City, Queenstown

Chancellor: Dr BRIGALIA NTOMBEMHLOPE BAM
Administrator: Prof. LOURENS VAN STADEN
Vice-Chancellor and Prin.: Prof. KHAYA MFE-NYANA
Deputy Vice-Chancellor for Academic Affairs and Research: Prof. SANDILE PHINDA SONGCA (acting)

Deputy Vice-Chancellor for Planning, Quality Assurance and Devt: Prof. J. JADEZWENI
Registrar: KHAYA MAPHINDA
Dir for Library and Information Services: W. DANSTER

Number of teachers: 360
Number of students: 4,600

DEANS

Faculty of Business, Management Sciences and Law: Prof. C. ANYANGWE (acting)
Faculty of Education: Prof. A. COETSER (acting)
Faculty of Health Sciences: Prof. N. E. SOKHELA (acting)
Faculty of Science, Engineering and Technology: F. GERBER (acting)

Other Higher Education Institutions

AAA School of Advertising: POB 3423, Cape Town 8000; 4th Fl., Manhattan Place, 130 Bree St, Cape Town 8001; tel. (21) 422-1800; e-mail info@aaaschool.co.za; internet www.aaaschool.co.za; f. 1986; campus in Johannesburg; CEO Dr LUDI KOEKEMOER.

Auckland Park Theological Seminary: Private Bag X75, Auckland Park 2006; 55 Richmond Ave, Auckland Park, Johannesburg 2092; tel. (11) 726-7029; e-mail admin@afmtc.org; internet www.afmtc.org; f. 1956, current name adopted 1997; Prin. Prof. W. J. HATTINGH; Vice-Prin. Prof. F. P. MÖLLER.

Baptist Theological College of Southern Africa: POB 50710, Randburg 2125; 260 Oak Ave, Randburg, Johannesburg; tel. (11) 886-0421; e-mail info@btc.co.za; internet www.btc.co.za; f. 1951; library: 12,000 vols; Prin. Dr MARTIN POHLMANN; Registrar GLENN TALBOT.

Belgium Campus: POB 60782, Karenpark 0118; 138, Sixth Ave, Heatherdale, Pretoria, tel. (12) 542-3114; e-mail info@belgiumcampus.ac.za; internet www.belgiumcampus.co.za; f. 1999; Dir ENRICO M. JACOBS.

Boston City Campus and Business College: Postnet Norwood, Suite 287, POB X5, Norwood 2117; 1st Fl., 130 Main St (Opposite Carlton Centre), Johannesburg; tel. (11) 331-2455; e-mail info@boston.co.za; internet www.boston.co.za; f. 1991; over 40 centres in S Africa; 25,000 students; CEO ARI KATZ; Man. Dir SUE DE ROOS..

Attached Institute:

Boston Media House: Postnet Norwood, Suite 287, POB X5, Norwood 2117;137 Eleventh St, Parkmore; tel. (11) 883-0933; e-mail info@boston.co.za; internet www.boston.co.za/media-house/; brs in Pretoria Arcadia, Umhlanga; CEO ARI KATZ; Registrar CARIKE VERBOOY.

Cape Town Baptist Seminary: POB 38473, Gatesville, Cape Town 7766; 64 Tarentaal Rd, Cape Town 7769; tel. (21) 637-9020; e-mail info@ctbs.org.za; internet www.ctbs.org.za; f. 1974, current name adopted 1993; Prin. Dr LINZAY RINQUEST; Librarian JANINE AYRTON; publ. *SA Baptist Journal of Theology* (print and online, www.ctbs.org.za/sa-baptist-journal-of-theology/).

Centre for Creative Education: POB 280, Plumstead 7801; McGregor House, 4 Victoria Rd, Plumstead; tel. (21) 797-6802; e-mail info@cfce.org.za; internet www.cfce.org.za/cfce/; f. 1993; Man. Dir HELEN STOTKO; Academic Head WILLEM VAN DER VELDEN.

**Christelike Gereformeerde Teologiese Seminarium/Christian Reformed Theo-

logical Seminary:** POB 784, Bronkhorstspruit 1020; Holding 3, Von Willich St, Verster Park, Bronkhorstspruit; tel. (13) 932-2562; e-mail admin@cgts.co.za; internet www.cgts.co.za; f. 1953; Prin. Rev. F. C. BODENSTEIN; Admin. Registrar Rev. L. J. VISSER.

CIDA City Campus: POB 890341, Lyndhurst 2106; tel. (11) 887-4495; e-mail info@cida.co.za; internet www.cidacitycampus.co.za; f. 2000; Exec. Dir M. M. NJAH.

CityVarsity: POB 37180, Overport, Durban 4067; 32 Kloof St, Cape Town; tel. (11) 242-6360; e-mail info@cityvarsity.co.za; internet www.cityvarsity.co.za; Nat. Gen. Man. MICHELLE YOUNG; Academic Man. PAUL LENSEN.

Cornerstone Christian College: POB 13434, Observatory 7705; cnr Durham and Victoria Rds, Observatory 7705; tel. (87) 755-7755; e-mail info@cornerstone.ac.za; internet www.cornerstone.ac.za; f. 1970, current name adopted 2001; Prin. Dr WAYNE HERMAN (acting); Registrar CAROLINE DE WET.

Cranefield College: POB 70591, The Willows (Wilgers) 0041; Cranefield House, 569 Rossouw St, The Willows, Pretoria 0184; tel. (12) 807-3990; e-mail admin@cranefield.ac.za; internet www.cranefield.ac.za; Prin. Prof. PIETER STEYN; Registrar Dr PIETER VAN DYK.

CTI Education Group: Bldg 1, Fourways Manor Office Park, cnr. Roos and Macbeth Sts, Fourways 2191; tel. (11) 467-8422; e-mail info@cti.ac.za; internet www.cti.co.za; f. 1979; faculties of creative arts and communication, commerce, information technology, law and social sciences; CEO Dr TOM BROWN.

Da Vinci Institute: POB 185, Moddertein 1645; Da Vinci House, 16 Park Rd, Modderfontein; tel. (11) 608-1331; e-mail info@davinci.ac.za; internet www.davinci.ac.za; f. 1992; CEO Prof. BENNIE ANDERSON; Registrar Dr LINDA CHIPUNZA.

Damelin: 57 Underwood Rd, Pinetown 3610; tel. (86) 053-2887; e-mail academics@damelin.co.za; internet www.damelin.co.za; f. 1943; faculties of creative arts, commerce, leisure and information technology, management science and communication; CEO ROB KATZ.

FEDISA: POB 503, Sea Point, Cape Town 8060; 81 Church St, Cape Town CBD 8001; tel. (21) 424-0975; e-mail info@fedisa.co.za; internet www.fedisa.co.za; f. 2005; CEO ALLEN LEROUX; Dir for Admissions GERALD BIRD.

George Whitefield College: POB 64, Muizenberg 7950; 34 Beach Rd, Muizenberg, Cape Town 7950; tel. (21) 788-1652; e-mail info@gwc.ac.za; internet www.gwc.ac.za; f. 1989; Prin. MARK DICKSON; Academic Registrar ALAN BECKMAN.

Global School of Theology Western Cape: POB 952, Roodepoort 1725; tel. (11) 760-1549; e-mail globalinfo@iafrica.com; internet www.gstwc.org.za; f. 1986 as Cape College of Theology; Nat. Dir Dr T. HOSCH.

Greenside Design Center College of Design: POB 84190, Greenside 2034; 118 Greenway, Greenside, Johannesburg; tel. (11) 646-1984; e-mail info@designcenter.co.za; internet designcenter.co.za; f. 1987; Dir Prof. DES LAUBSCHER; Dir INGRID TEMPLER.

Hebron Theological College: POB 11118, Rynfield 1514; 7 Sports Rd, Slaterville, Benoni; tel. (11) 965-1252; e-mail info@hebroncollege.co.za; internet www.hebroncollege.co.za; f. 1989 by merger of All Africa School of Theology and Hebron Bible College, current name adopted 2000; Dir and Prin. Dr J. R. FAWCETT; Asst Prin. Rev. C. F. J. KOTZÉ; publ. *The Africa Journal of Pentecostal Studies*.

Helderberg College: POB 22, Somerset West 7129; Annandale Dr., Somerset West 7130; tel. (21) 850-7500; e-mail info@hbc.ac.za; internet www.hbc.ac.za; f. 1893, current name adopted 1928; faculties of arts, business, theology; library: 72,870 vols; Pres. VINCENT RICHARD INJETY; Registrar PIETER STEYN.

Henley Business School: Kirstenhof Park, cnr of Milcliff and Witkoppen Rds, Paulshof 2191; tel. (11) 808-0860; e-mail fremponga@henleysa.ac.za; internet www.henleysa.ac.za; f. 1992; Dean and Dir JONATHAN FOSTER-PEDLEY; Academic Dir FREMPONG ACHEAMPONG.

Independent Institute of Education (IIE): POB 2369, Randburg 2125; ADvTECH House, Inanda Greens, 54 Wierda Rd W, Wierda Valley, Sandton 2196; tel. (11) 676-8021; e-mail info@iie.ac.za; internet www.iie.ac.za; f. 2005; incl. Design School Southern Africa (DSSA), Forbes Lever Baker, Rosebank College, Vega School, Varsity College; 23 tertiary campuses; faculties of applied humanities, business, information technology; Dir Dr FELICITY COUGHLAN; Academic Man. Dr ANNE-KA VAN DEN HOEK.

Inscape Education Group: Post Net Suite 104, Private Bag X19, Menlo Park 0102; 431 Atterbury Rd, Menlo Park; tel. (12) 346-2189; e-mail admin@inscape.co.za; internet www.inscape.co.za; f. 1981; campuses in Cape Town, Durban, Johannesburg, Pretoria; Dir R. EDMONDS.

International College of Bible and Missions: POB 2214, Roodepoort 1725; 16 Mare St, Roodepoort 1724; tel. (11) 760-4681; e-mail info@icbm.ac.za; internet www.icbm.ac.za; f. 2000; CEO and Prin. Dr FRANK SHAYI; Registrar ANNE FORSYTH.

LISOF/Leaders in the Science of Fashion: POB 1284, Parklands 2121; cnr Eileen and Geneva Rd, Blairgowrie, Johannesburg; tel. (86) 115-4763; e-mail info@lisof.co.za; internet www.lisof.co.za; f. 1993; campus in Hatfield; Academic Head F. SOMERVILLE.

Lyceum College: Private Bag X32074, Braamfontein 2017; 1st Fl., Success House, cnr Smit and Melle Sts, Braamfontein 2017; tel. (11) 712-2000; e-mail info.lyceum@icg.edu.za; internet www.lyceum.co.za; f. 1917 as Lyceum Advancement College, current name adopted 2003; schools of business studies, education, fleet management, public safety; Academic Dir Prof. P. BEARD; Academic Man. BENJAMIN VAN ROOYEN.

Management College of Southern Africa (MANCOSA): POB 49494, East End 4018; 26 Samora Machel St, Durban 4001; tel. (31) 300-7200; e-mail undergrad@mancosa.co.za; internet www.mancosa.co.za; f. 1995; 8,000 students; Prin. Prof. YUSUF KARODIA.

Midrand Graduate Institute: POB 2986, Halfway House, Midrand 1685; 44 Alsatian Rd, Glen Austin Extension 3, Midrand; tel. (11) 690-1700; e-mail info@mgi.ac.za; internet www.mgi.ac.za; f. 1989; faculties of commerce, creative arts, information technology, law, science and engineering, social science; campuses in Bedfordview, Bloemfontein, Cape Town, Durban, Durbanville, East London, Nelspruit, Port Elizabeth, Potchefstroom, Pretoria, Randburg; Prin. and Man. Dir Dr DOLF STEYN.

Milpark Education (Pty) Ltd.: POB 44235, Claremont, Cape Town 7735; 2nd Fl., Sunclare Bldg, cnr Protea and Dreyer Rds, Claremont, Cape Town 7708; tel. (21) 673-9100; e-mail info@milpark.ac.za; internet www.milpark.ac.za; f. 1997 as Milpark Business School (Pty) Ltd., current name adopted 2013; campus in Johannesburg; schools of business, commerce, financial planning and insurance, investment and banking; CEO JULIAN VAN DER WESTHUIZEN; Registrar MELANIE ORTON.

Monash South Africa: Private Bag X60, Roodepoort 1725; 144 Peter Rd, Ruimsig, Johannesburg; tel. (11) 950-4000; e-mail inquiries@monash.ac.za; internet www .monash.ac.za; f. 2001; campus of Monash Univ., Australia; schools of business and economics, health sciences, information technology, social science; 2,617 students; CEO ESTHER BENJAMIN; Library Man. NTHABISENG KOTSOKOANE.

Mukhanyo Theological College: POB 594, KwaMhlanga 1022; Plot 1 Solomon Mahlangu Dr., KwaMhlanga 1022; tel. (13) 947-2179; e-mail academicsmtc@gmail.com; internet www.mukhanyo.co.za; f. 1994; Prin. Dr BRIAN A. DEVRIES; Registrar RYAN MITCHELL.

Open Window School of Visual Communication: POB 68371, Highveld 0169; John Vorster Dr. Extension E, Southdowns, Irene; tel. (12) 648-9200; e-mail info@openwindow .co.za; internet www.openwindow.co.za; f. 1992; depts of film arts, visual communication; Vice-Chancellor and Academic Registrar Dr SIMONIA MAGARDIE.

Oval International: POB 2671, Umhlanga 4320; 31 Joe Slovo St (Field St), Durban 4000; tel. (31) 305-3072; e-mail registrar@ oval.co.za; internet www.myoval.co.za; f. 1989; faculties of commerce and management, hospitality and tourism, information technology; Prin. PRAVIN MAHARAJ.

PC Training and Business College: Private Bag X23, Umhlanga Rocks, Durban 4320; 292 Anton Lembede (Smith) St, Durban 4000; tel. (31) 304-9340; e-mail info@ gopctraining.co.za; internet www.pctbc.co.za; f. 1998; campuses in Benoni, Bloemfontein, Braamfontein, Cape Town, Johannesburg, Kempton Park, Krugersdorp, Midrand, Pietermaritzburg, Polokwane, Pretoria, Randburg, Vereeniging; faculties of business economics, management and sciences, media, information and communications technology; library: 107,000 vols; CEO JAY RAMNUNDLALL; Registrar Dr MUNI KOOBLALL.

Prestige Academy: POB 2220, Bellville 7535; Bellville Business Park, D. J. Wood Way, Bellville 7530; tel. (21) 949-5036; e-mail info@prestigeacademy.co.za; internet www .prestigeacademy.co.za; f. 1994; campus in Centurion; faculties of art design and infor-

mation technology, business; Prin. S. DE JONGH; Dir THEO SCHOEMAN.

Production Management Institute of Southern Africa (PMI): POB 211089, Bluff 4036; The Lodge, 305 Musgrave Rd, Strathmore Park, Durban 4001; tel. (31) 201-1260; internet www.pmi-sa.co.za; f. 1976; brs in Bloemfontein, Cape Town, East London, Johannesburg, Mothibiestad, Port Elizabeth; Man. Dir TIM SMEETON; Academic Dir Dr SENOELO NKHASE LELOKA.

Regenesys Business School: Postnet Suite No 71, Private Bag X9976, Sandton City 2146; Regenesys Campus, 4 Pybus Rd (cnr Katherine St), Sandton, Johannesburg; tel. (11) 669-5000; e-mail info@regenesys.co.za; internet www.regenesys.co.za; f. 1999; Chair. Dr MARKO SARAVANJA; CEO and Dir SIEGIE BROWNLEE.

Regent Business School: POB 10686, Marine Parade 4056; 35 Samora Machel (Aliwal St), Durban 4001; tel. (31) 304-4626; e-mail study@regent.ac.za; internet www.regent.ac .za; f. 1998; campuses in East London, Johannesburg, Swaziland; Prin. Prof. MARVIN M. KAMBUWA.

South African College of Applied Psychology: POB 97, Claremont 7708; 1st Fl. Sun Clare Bldg, 21 Dreyer St, Claremont, Cape Town; tel. (86) 077-1111; e-mail info@sacap .edu.za; internet www.sacap.edu.za; f. 1997; campus at Johannesburg; Chair. Prof. TONY NAIDOO; Academic Dean Dr ASHLEY SMYTH.

South African Theological Seminary: POB 258, Rivonia 2128; 61 Wessels Rd, Rivonia; tel. (11) 234-4440; e-mail info@sats .edu.za; internet www.sats.edu.za; f. 1996; Prin. Dr REUBEN VAN RENSBURG; Vice-Prin. Dr KEVIN SMITH.

Southern Africa Bible College: POB 11165, Rynfield, Benoni 1514; Plot 14, Van Ryn Small Holdings, Cloverdene Rd, Benoni; tel. (11) 969-4497; e-mail sabcinfo@iburst.co .za; internet www.southernafricabiblecollege .org; f. 1966; library: 10,000 vols; Pres. AL J. HORNE; CEO and Dir FRED BERGH.

Southern Business School: Private Bag X03, Helderkruin 1733; Plot 10, R28 Service Rd, Diswilmar, Krugersdorp 1739; tel. (11) 662-1444; e-mail info@sbs.ac.za; internet www.sbs.ac.za; f. 1996; Prin. C. P. W. VORSTER.

St Augustine College of South Africa: POB 44782, Linden 2104; 53 Ley Rd, Victory

Park, Johannesburg; tel. (11) 380-9000; e-mail admin@staugustine.ac.za; internet www.staugustine.ac.za; f. 1999; depts of applied ethics, theology; library: 35,000 vols; Pres. Dr MADGE KARECKI; Registrar MARILISE SMURTHWAITE (acting).

St John Vianney Seminary NPC: POB 17128, Groenkloof, Pretoria 0027; 179 Main St, Waterkloof, Pretoria 0181; tel. (12) 460-2039; e-mail info@sjv.ac.za; internet www.sjv .ac.za; f. 1948; 133 students; Pres. Rev. Fr MOLEWE SIMON MACHINGOANE; Vice-Pres. Rev. Fr MASILO JOHN SELEMELA.

St Joseph's Theological Institute: Private Bag 6004, Hilton 3245; Dist Rd D546, Cedara; tel. (87) 353-8940; e-mail dean@sjti .ac.za; internet www.sjti.ac.za; f. 1990; depts of developmental studies, philosophy, religious studies, theology; library: 40,221 vols, 108 periodicals, 51 DVDs, 48 CDs, 5 CDROMs, 259 audio cassettes, 299 videos; 210 students; Pres. Fr SYLVESTER DAVID; Registrar MANDLA NDABA.

Stellenbosch Academy of Design and Photography: POB 762, Stellenbosch 7599; 41 Tegno Rd, Techno Park, Stellenbosch 7600; tel. (21) 880-2623; e-mail info@ stellenboschacademy.co.za; internet www .stellenboschacademy.co.za; f. 2002; Institutional Dir BARBARA FASSLER; Registrar ALTA SCHOEMAN.

Stenden South Africa: POB 2821, Port Alfred 6170; tel. (46) 604-2200; e-mail info@ stenden.ac.za; internet www.stenden.ac.za; f. 2003, current name adopted 2008; schools of disaster management and hospitality management; Academic Dean and Gen. Man. Dr WOUTER HENSENS; Deputy Gen. Man. ALROY TAAI.

Tertiary School in Business Administration (TSiBA): POB 13071, Mowbray 7705; Mupine College, 307 Forest Dr. Extension, Pinelands 7405; tel. (21) 532-2750; e-mail info@tsiba.org.za; internet www.tsiba.org.za; f. 2004; campus in Eden; CEO ADRI MARAIS; Dean NOLAN BEUDEKER.

Theological Education by Extension College: POB 74257, Turffontein 2140; 20 Gantner St, Haddon, Johannesburg 2190; tel. (11) 683-3284; e-mail admin@tee.co.za; internet www.tee.co.za; f. 1976; 3,400 students; Exec. Dir and CEO M. D. BAXTER; Exec. Dir Rev. C. V. DUNSMUIR.

SOUTH SUDAN

The Higher Education System

South Sudan gained its independence in July 2011, after a six-year post-war political transition that had entailed semi-autonomy from Sudan's government. Both the transition and independence have had huge implications for South Sudan's higher education sector. On the positive side, the end of the 22-year north–south civil war in 2005 and the achievement of semi-autonomous status catalyzed significant donor support, much of it centred on state-building, including the establishment of a Ministry of Higher Education, Science and Technology. However, independence has also brought substantial negative implications, most notably the end of any prospect of financial support for higher education institutions by Sudan's government.

The two prolonged periods of civil war in pre-secession Sudan (in 1953–72 and 1983–2005), during which a significant number of higher education institutions in the south and west were badly damaged or destroyed, prompted a number of southern universities to relocate to the north. In late 2010 such institutions were returned to the south during a five-day repatriation exercise orchestrated by Sudan's Ministry of Higher Education and Scientific Research.

Less than a year after independence, South Sudan found itself in a financial crisis arising from a dispute over a post-secession sharing of oil revenues with Sudan. South Sudan's public universities too were in a state of crisis. The University of Northern Bahr el Ghazal, in Aweil, was unable to open its doors to students. The Government acknowledged in March 2012 that it simply did not have enough money to support the two-year-old institution, despite its public status. Also in March 2012, staff at the University of Bahr el Ghazal, which is located in Wau and opened in the early 1990s, announced that they were going on strike, claiming that the Government was three months behind in paying wages.

The University of Juba, the country's principal institution of higher learning, has also been hampered by financial problems. Underlining the extent of internal ethnic tensions in the new country, the Juba campus was also affected by inter-group tensions in the year after independence. In late March 2012, the university was temporarily closed down, after pitched battles between students from the dominant Dinka community and various other ethnic groups. Earlier that month, Juba had become the second public institution of higher learning in South Sudan to ban tribal associations, following the lead of the Doctor John Garang de Mabior Memorial University of Science and Technology. The latter institution is based in Bor, the capital of Jonglei State, where hundreds of people were killed in clashes between the Lou Nuer and Murle communities in late 2011 and early 2012.

Given the financial constraints faced by the public sector and the relative freedom generated by the end of Sudan's harsh Islamist rule, private universities have begun to spring up in South Sudan, competing with their public counterparts for students and non-government funding. However, in March 2012, Minister of Higher Education, Science and Technology Dr Peter Adwok Nyaba gave notice of his department's intention to reform universities, in a drive that would target both public and private institutions. He claimed that some new private centres of learning were masquerading as universities and lacked accreditation by the Government. In 2012, despite protestations from the Association of Private Universities, the Ministry closed down 22 private higher education institutions. According to a policy framework document published by the Ministry soon after independence, there had been, at that stage, over 35 private institutions. Meanwhile, with regard to public sector reform, the Ministry was overseeing a commission to rationalize the universities of Juba, Upper Nile, Bahr el Ghazal, Rumbek and the Dr. John Garang de Mabior Memorial University of Science and Technology. The closure and merger of departments were some of the ideas being considered, in a context of the ongoing funding crisis. A National Council of Higher Education was set up in 2012 tasked with introducing strategies and policies to reform higher education in both the public and private sector.

In order to qualify for an undergraduate position in public sector universities in South Sudan, a four-year secondary school education is required. One of the main private institutions—The Bridge University, in Juba—requires at least seven passes in the country's Secondary School Certificate for relevant subjects, while for diplomas at least five passes are required, together with 'proficiency in written and spoken English'.

Only a miniscule proportion of South Sudan's population receives a university education, owing largely to the effect of more than two decades of north–south civil war on its territories' infrastructure and school system. During the 1983–2005 civil war (and the preceding conflict that lasted from 1956 to 1972), hundreds of thousands of people missed out on primary and secondary school education. As independence dawned, the legacy of the conflict—together with a tendency among some cattle-herding communities to eschew formal education—was an adult literacy rate of just 27%, according to the United Nations Development Programme. The literacy rate for women was just 16%, while 42% of civil servants lacked a secondary school education, according to the same source. For the 2011/12 academic year, the four main public universities—Juba, Bahr el Ghazal, Upper Nile and Rumbek—approved a total intake of 2,722 students, out of just over 4,500 applications, according to the Ministry of Higher Education, Science and Technology. By contrast, there were over 215,000 applicants to Sudan's universities for the same period.

In the final intake (2011/12) before South Sudan achieved independence from Sudan in July 2011, the number of approved applicants for the main public universities were as follows: University of Juba, 1,310; University of Bahr el Ghazal, 599; Upper Nile, 441; Rumbek, 372.

The John Garang De Mabior Memorial University of Science and Technology and the University of Northern Bahr el Ghazal were missing from the list. With regard to the former, Vice-Chancellor Prof. Aggrey Ayuen Majok told the press that his institution was ready to host 160 students (40 in each of its four faculties), but South Sudan's Ministry of Higher Education, Science and Technology had not notified the admissions board in Khartoum, Sudan. Meanwhile, the University of Northern Bahr el Ghazal had yet to receive any funding, from either Khartoum or Juba, despite having been bestowed university status by Sudan's President Omar al-Bashir in 2010. South Sudan's President Salva Kiir officially cut the ribbon to open this institution in March 2012. Even at that late stage, Kiir underlined that the university was still 'not budgeted for' in the national accounts, although he pledged that his government would attempt to secure a funding avenue.

Regulatory Bodies

GOVERNMENT

Ministry of Culture, Youth and Sports: Juba; tel. (54) 722875037; Minister Hon. NADIA AROP DUDI.

Ministry of Education, Science and Technology: Juba; tel. (955) 107417; e-mail datjoel@yahoo.com; internet www .moest.gov.sd; Minister Hon. JOHN GAI YOAH.

Library

Juba

University of Juba Library: POB 82, Juba; tel. (155) 888489; f. 1977; 38,700 vols, 664 periodicals; depository library for UN, UNESCO, WHO, FAO and World Bank; Librarian OKENY A. ADALA (acting).

Universities

DOCTOR JOHN GARANG DE MABIOR MEMORIAL UNIVERSITY OF SCIENCE AND TECHNOLOGY

POB, Bor, Jonglei State
Telephone: (955) 363752
E-mail: info@jgmust-edu.org
Internet: jgmust-edu.org
Founded 2007 as an institute, univ. status 2010
State control
Faculties of agriculture, economics and management sciences, education, environmental studies, humanities, law and science and technology
Vice-Chancellor: Prof. AGGREY AYUEN MAJOK
Deputy Vice-Chancellor: Dr MELHA ROUT BIEL

RUMBEK UNIVERSITY

c/o Rumbek Secondary School, Rumbek, Rumbek Central County, Lakes State
Founded 2010
State control
Faculties of education and economic and social sciences
Vice-Chancellor: Prof. MICHAEL MAKER MANGONY (acting)
Number of teachers: 40
Number of students: 500

SAINT MARY'S UNIVERSITY IN JUBA

Juba, Central Equatoria State
Founded 2009
Private control
Faculties of arts, education, science and computer studies, social studies
Vice-Chancellor: PAULINO LUKUDU LORO

THE BRIDGE UNIVERSITY

POB 434, Juba
Telephone: (955) 235665
E-mail: magijude@yahoo.com
Internet: www.thebridgeuniversity.com
Founded 2009
Private control
Language of instruction: English
Faculties of business admin. and management, education, humanities and social sciences and science
Vice-Chancellor: Dr ANDREW ANTHONY CULA
Univ. Secretary: JUDE MAGINOT
Academic Registrar: MOSES OKWII
Bursar: PHILEMON BWANGA
Administrator: IVAN FRED TABAN
Dean of Students: PADDY TUMUHIMBISE
Number of teachers: 65
Number of students: 3,000

UNIVERSITY OF BAHR EL-GHAZAL

Wau, Wau County, Western Bahr Al-Ghazal State
E-mail: ubgzal@sudanmail.net
Founded 1991
State Control
Languages of instruction: Arabic, English
Faculties of economics, education, medicine and health sciences, veterinary sciences; institute of public health
Vice-Chancellor: TIMOTHY TELAR
Number of students: 1,000

UNIVERSITY OF JUBA

POB 82, Juba
Telephone: (155) 888405
E-mail: info@juba.edu.sd
Internet: www.juba.edu.sd
Founded 1975 with financial help from the EEC; first student admission 1977
State control
Language of instruction: English
Academic year: March to December (2 semesters)
Vice-Chancellor: Prof. AGGREY ABATE
Principal: WANI SULE
Sec.-Gen.: Prof. MOSES MACAR KACUOL
Librarian: ALFRED D. LADO (acting)
Number of teachers: 220
Number of students: 16,565
Publications: *Juvarsity* (12 a year), *Library News* (12 a year)

DEANS

College of Applied and Industrial Sciences: Prof. TARIG OSMAN KHIDIR
College of Arts and Humanities: Prof. ABDEL-RAHIM MUHAMMAD KHABIR
College of Arts, Music and Drama: Prof. MUHAMMAD EL-AMIN ALI
College of Community Studies and Rural Development: SHADIA MUHAMMAD IDRIS
College of Computer Science and Information Technology: Dr MUHAMMAD HASSAN MUDAWI
College of Education: Dr AMIRA MUHAMMAD FADALALLA
College of Engineering and Architecture: Dr IBRAHIM AHMED MUHAMMAD KHALID
College of Law: DENG AWUR WANYIN
College of Medicine: Dr ABDELAYE KUNNA MAJOUB
College of Natural Resources and Environmental Studies: (vacant)
College of Social and Economic Studies: SAMSON SAMUEL WASSARA

UNIVERSITY OF NORTHERN BAHR EL-GHAZAL

Mathiang, Aweil
Telephone: (123) 106510
E-mail: info@unbeg.edu.sd
Internet: www.unbeg.edu.sd
Founded 2010
State control
Language of instruction: English
Academic year: December to August
Chancellor: PRES. OF THE REPUBLIC OF SOUTH SUDAN
Vice-Chancellor: Prof. JOHN APURUOT AKEC
Prin.: Prof. KARLO AYUEL KUCGOR
Academic Sec.: Dr SALIM GIBRIL AHMED (acting)

DEANS

Faculty of Architecture and Physical Planning: Prof. ADIL MUSTAFA AHMAD (acting)
Faculty of Health Sciences and Medical Technology: Dr ROSE AJACK KOSTA (acting)
Faculty of Petroleum, Engineering and Earth Sciences: Dr ABDALLA KODI (acting)
Faculty of Preparatory, Human Resource Development and Vocational Studies: BEDA DIING AMOI (acting)

UPPER NILE UNIVERSITY

Malakal, Upper Nile State
Telephone: (183) 220825
Founded 1991
State control
Language of instruction: Arabic
Academic year: November to June
Faculties of agriculture, animal production, arts and humanities, computer science, education, forestry, medicine and public health, nursing, science, social science, veterinary medicine and vocational medicine
Vice-Chancellor: Prof. BOL DENG CHOL
Library of 23,000 vols

SPAIN

The Higher Education System

Institutions of higher education pre-date the consolidation of the Kingdom of Spain within the Iberian peninsula in the early 16th century, with the oldest being Universidad Pontificia de Salamanca, which was founded in 1134. Spain participates in the Bologna Process to establish a European Higher Education Area, the first phase of which is to adopt a credit-based system of comparable degrees with two main cycles (undergraduate and graduate). Little progress was made until 2005, when a royal decree was passed establishing the new degree structure. Higher education is provided by public and private universities, higher technical colleges (escuelas técnicas superiores), university colleges (colegios universitarios), university faculties (facultades universitarias) and university schools (escuelas universitarias). In 2005/06 there were 72 universities, including the open university (UNED—founded 1972). In 2010/11 there were 1,546,355 students enrolled in universities including to Masters level; a further 8,747 were preparing doctoral theses. By 2012 there were 79 universities of which 50 were public and 29 private.

The Ministry of Education, Culture and Sport has overall responsibility for higher education, although much of the administration has been devolved to the 17 Autonomous Communities. Universities were granted the right to become autonomous under the law on University Reform (1983), although very few have chosen to do so. The 1983 legislation was supplemented by further reforms enacted under the terms of the Spanish Universities Act (2001; modified in 2007), covering university governance, entrance examinations, quality assurance, accreditation and staff recruitment. The 2007 law called into existence two governing bodies, the Conference of University Policy (la Conferencia General de Política Universitaria), which is presided over by the Minister of Education, Culture and Sport, and the Universities Council (el Consejo de Universidades), which brings together the university rectors. At 2012 a national qualifications framework was under development.

The main requirements for admission to higher education are the Bachillerato (secondary school certificate) and the Prueba de Acceso Universidad (university entrance examination). Under the new system, university degrees are divided into three cycles. The first cycle, Título de Grado (Bachelors degree), lasts four years, following which students may progress to the second cycle, the Título de Máster (Masters degree), which lasts between one and two years. The third cycle, the Doctorado (Doctorate), constitutes the highest level of university degree and requires an additional three or four years of classwork and research, culminating with the submission and defence of a thesis. Pre-Bologna qualifications (which included the Diplomado, Diplomatura, Licenciado, Licenciatura and professional titles) are in the process of being phased out, with new students no longer being admitted onto such courses and the final existing students enrolled on such programmes due to graduate in 2014.

The main qualification offered in vocational and technical education is the Técnico Superior (higher certificate), awarded after one-and-a-half to two years of study. Occupational training is also available; students are awarded the Certificados de Profesionalidad (vocational certificate).

The Agencia Nacional de Evaluación de la Calidad y Acreditación (National Agency for Quality Assessment and Accreditation), which was founded in 2002 following the Spanish Universities Act, is responsible for accrediting programmes of study, providing quality assurance and acting as the inter-agency coordinating body for Spanish higher education.

Regulatory and Representative Bodies

GOVERNMENT

Ministry of Education, Culture and Sport: Calle Alcalá 34, 28071 Madrid; tel. 917018000; e-mail prensa.cultura@mecd.es; internet www.mecd.gob.es; Minister JOSÉ IGNACIO WERT ORTEGA.

ACCREDITATION

Agencia Nacional de Evaluación de la Calidad y Acreditación (National Agency for Quality Assessment and Accreditation): Calle Orense 11, Seventh Fl., 28020 Madrid; tel. 914178230; e-mail informacion@aneca.es; internet www.aneca.es; f. 2002; contributes to the quality improvement of the higher education system through the assessment, certification and accreditation of univ. degrees, programmes, teaching staff and instns; Dir RAFAEL VAN GRIEKEN SALVADOR.

NARIC España (Spanish NARIC): Ministerio de Educación, Cultura y Deporte, Subdirección General de Títulos y Reconocimiento de Cualificaciones, Paseo del Prado 28, 28014 Madrid; tel. 915065593; e-mail naric@mecd.es; internet www.mecd.gob.es/educacion-mecd/areas-educacion/universidades/educacion-superior-universitaria/titulos/naric.html; provides information about processes of academic and professional recognition of qualifications in Spain and in other countries; Technical Adviser BELÉN HERNÁNDEZ.

NATIONAL BODIES

Asociación Iberoamericana de Educación Superior a Distancia (Ibero-American Association of Distance Higher Education): Bravo Murillo 38, 28015 Madrid; tel. 913986549; e-mail aiesad@adm.uned.es; internet www.aiesad.org; f. 1981; network for the devt of distance education in Spanish-speaking Latin America; teacher-training; provides information, cooperation and coordination of mem. instns through jt projects; promotes research and application of new methods in distance higher education; 43 mems; library of 50 vols; Pres. Dr JUAN A. GIMENO ULLASTRES; Permanent Sec. and Treas. Dra MARÍA TERESA AGUADO ODINA; publ. *Revista Iberoamericana de Educación a Distancia (RIED)* (Ibero-American Review of Distance Education, 2 a year, print and online, www.utpl.edu.ec/ried).

Conferencia de Rectores de las Universidades Españolas (CRUE) (Conference of Rectors of Spanish Universities): Plaza de las Cortes 2, Seventh Fl., 28014 Madrid; tel. 913601200; e-mail info@crue.org; internet www.crue.org; f. 1994; fosters links between univs and public authorities; promotes improvement of higher education through cooperation and dialogue between univs; 75 mem. univs (50 public, 25 private); Pres. ADELAIDA DE LA CALLE MARTÍN; Sec.-Gen. MARÍA TERESA LOZANO MELLADO.

Conferencia General de Política Universitaria (National Conference of University Policy): c/o Alcalá 36, 28071 Madrid; f. 2007; coordinating, cooperative and consultative body for matters concerning higher education policy; chaired by the Min. of Education, Culture and Sport; Dir JORGE SÁINZ GONZÁLEZ.

Consejo de Universidades (University Council): c/o Alcalá 36, 28071 Madrid; tel. 917018000; f. 2007; advises and promotes coordination in the univ. system; chaired by the Min. of Education, Culture and Sport; mems incl. (among others) the Rectors of the state univs; Pres. JOSÉ IGNACIO WERT ORTEGA.

Consejo General de los Colegios Oficiales de Doctores y Licenciados en Filosofía y Letras y en Ciencias (National Council of Official Colleges of Doctors and Licentiates in Arts and Science): Bolsa 11, 28012 Madrid; tel. 915224597; e-mail secretaria@consejogeneralcdl.es; internet www.consejogeneralcdl.es; f. 1945; protects and represents education professionals; seeks to promote initiatives that contribute to improving the quality of education in Spain; 60,000 mems; Pres. JOSEFINA CAMBRA GINÉ; Sec.-Gen. JESÚS BONALS CODINA; publ. *Trivium* (4 a year).

Learned Societies

GENERAL

Agencia Española de Cooperación Internacional para el Desarrollo (AECID) (Spanish Agency of International Cooperation for Development): Avda Reyes Católicos 4, 28040 Madrid; tel. 915838100; e-mail centro.informacion@aecid.es; internet www.aecid.es; f. 1998; attached to Min. of Foreign Affairs and Cooperation; contributes to peace, freedom, human security and the eradication of poverty; promotes respect for human rights and devt of democratic systems; promotes the role of culture and knowledge in devt; library of 600,000 vols; Pres. JESÚS MANUEL GRACIA ALDAZ; Dir JUAN LÓPEZ-DÓRIGA PÉREZ; publs Awraq, Cooperación Española (4 a year), Cuadernos Hispanoamericanos, Pensamiento Iberoamericano.

Attached Institutes:

Dirección General de Cooperación con África y Asia (Department for Cooperation with Africa, Asia and Eastern Europe): Avda Reyes Católicos 4, Ciudad Universitaria, 28040 Madrid; tel. 915838565; technical assistance, economic cooperation, cultural activities, research grants, scholarships; library of 65,000 vols, 800 periodicals; Dir ALBERTO VIRELLA GOMES.

Instituto de Cooperación Iberoamericana (Institute for Ibero-American Cooperation): Avda Reyes Católicos 4, Ciudad Universitaria, 28040 Madrid; tel. 915838100; f. 1946; promotes cultural understanding between Spain and the USA by organizing confs, congresses, cultural exhibitions and univ. exchanges, scholarships for students; finances programmes of cultural, scientific, economic and technical cooperation; information dept; Centre for Advanced Hispanic Studies; organizes programmes to diffuse the Spanish language and culture in the USA; radio, cinema and theatre unit; library: see under Libraries and Archives; Pres. FERNANDO VILLALONGA; Dir-Gen. JESÚS MANUEL GRACIA ALDAZ; publs Cuadernos Hispanoamericanos (12 a year), Pensamiento Iberoamericano (2 a year).

Casa de Velázquez: Calle de Paul Guinard 3, Ciudad Universitaria, 28040 Madrid; tel. 914551580; e-mail info@casadevelazquez.org; internet www.casadevelazquez.org; f. 1928 as Escuela de Altos Estudios Hispánicos; run by the Min. of Higher Education and Research; French school for research relating to arts, languages, literatures and socs of Spain, Iberian and Ibero-American countries; grants sr fellowships to French artists or scholars to work in Spain; training of artists, researchers, teachers in devt of artistic and scientific exchanges between France and other countries concerned; 34 mems; library of 104,000 vols, 1,700 periodicals; Dir JEAN-PIERRE ÉTIENVRE; publ. Mélanges de la Casa de Velázquez (4 a year).

Dirección de Relaciones Culturales y Científicas (Cultural and Scientific Relations Department): Avda Reyes Católicos 4, Agencia Española de Cooperación Internacional, 28040 Madrid; tel. 915838100; internet www.maec.es; f. 1926; promotes Spanish culture and science in foreign countries; int. cultural and scientific agreements, exchange of professors and lecturers, scholarships; Dir ITZIAR TABOADA AQUERRETA.

Fundación Instituto d'Estudis Nord-Americans (Institute of North American Studies): Vía Augusta 123, 08006 Barcelona; tel. 932405110; e-mail ien@ien.es; internet www.ien.es; f. 1951; organizes cultural exchange programmes, lectures, discussions, musical events, theatre, cinema, art exhibitions, seminars; courses in English and in American Studies; runs an academic counselling service and is the official centre for examinations for students entering the US univs; 400 mems; library of 10,000 vols, 100 periodicals; Pres. ROBERT M. MANSON; Exec. Dir CARLES DOMINGO.

Fundación Juan March: Castelló 77, 28006 Madrid; tel. 914354240; e-mail direccion@march.es; internet www.march.es; f. 1955; organizes art exhibitions, concerts, lecture series, seminars; administers the Spanish Library of Contemporary Music and Theatre; directs museums of Arte Abstracto Español (Cuenca) and Fundación Juan March (Palma de Mallorca); operates Instituto Juan March de Estudios e Investigaciones through which it promotes specialized research in areas of political science and sociology; Pres. JUAN MARCH DELGADO; Dir JAVIER GOMÁ LANZÓN; publ. Revista de la Fundación Juan March (9 a year).

Institut d'Estudis Catalans (Institute of Catalan Studies): Carrer del Carme 47, 08001 Barcelona; tel. 932701620; e-mail informacio@iec.cat; internet www.iec.cat; f. 1907; sections on biological sciences, history and archaeology, philology, philosophy and social sciences, science and technology; 183 mems (125 ordinary, 58 corresp.), 28 affiliated scientific mem. socs; Pres. SALVADOR GINER DE SAN JULIÁN; Sec.-Gen. ROMÀ ESCALAS I LLIMONA; publs Acta Numismàtica, Actes d'Història de la Ciència i de la Tècnica, Anuari de la Societat Catalana d'Economia, Anuari de la Societat Catalana de Filosofia, Anuari de la Societat Catalana d'Estudis Jurídics, Arxiu de Textos Catalans Antics, Butlletí de la Institució Catalana d'Història Natural, Butlletí de la Societat Catalana d'Estudis Històrics, Butlletí de la Societat Catalana de Matemàtiques, Butlletí de la Societat Catalana de Musicologia, Butlletí de la Societat Catalana de Pedagogia, Catalan Historical Review, Catalan Social Sciences Review, Cinematògraf, Comunicació. Revista de recerca i d'anàlisi Continuació de Treballs de Comunicació, Contributions to Science, Dossiers Agraris, Educació i Història: Revista d'Història de l'Educació, Educació Química, Estudis Romànics, Gazeta, Itaca: Quaderns Catalans de Cultura Clàssica, Journal of Catalan Intellectual History, Lambard: Estudis d'Art Medieval, Llengua & Literatura, Memòria, Miscel·lània Litúrgica Catalana, Notícies de la Societat Catalana de Matemàtiques, Noubiaix, Quaderns Agraris, Periodística, Recursos de Física, Revista Catalan de Dret Privat, Revista Catalan de Física, Revista Catalana de Micologia, Revista Catalana de Musicologia, Revista Catalan de Pedagogia, Revista Catalana de Sociologia, Revista de Dret Històric Català, Revista de Física, Revista de la Societat Catalana de Química, Revista de Tecnologia, Sessió Conjunta d'Entomologia, Tamid, TECA: Tecnologia i Ciència dels Aliments, Terminàlia, Trabades d'Història de la Ciència i la Tècnica, Treballs de Comunicació, Treballs de Física, Treballs de la Societat Catalana de Biologia, Treballs de la Societat Catalana de Geografia, Treballs de Sociolingüística Catalana.

Instituto Cervantes: Alcalá 49, 28014 Madrid; tel. 914367600; e-mail informa@cervantes.es; internet www.cervantes.es; f. 1991; promotes Spanish language and the culture of Spain and Spanish-speaking Latin and Central America globally; operates in 26 countries; maintains teaching centres in Sofia (Bulgaria), Zagreb (Croatia), Belgrade (Serbia), Hanoi (Viet Nam); Dir CARMEN CAFFAREL SERRA; Gen. Sec. CARMEN PÉREZ-FRAGERO RODRÍGUEZ DE TEMBLEQUE.

Instituto Complutense de Ciencia de la Administración (Complutense Institute of Administrative Science): Facultad de Políticas y Sociología, Planta 2ª, despacho 2609, Campus de Somosaguas, 28223 Madrid; tel. 913942893; e-mail icca@pas.ucm.es; internet www.incca.es; f. 1986; attached to Universidad Complutense de Madrid; promotes basic and applied research in the field of nat. and foreign public admin.; develops training and technical assistance on the various areas of govt interest; Dir RAFAEL BAÑÓN I MARTÍNEZ; Sec.-Gen. GEMA PASTOR ALBALADEJO; publ. Cuadernos de Gobierno y Administración Pública.

Instituto de España (Institute of Spain): C/ San Bernardo 49, 28015 Madrid; tel. 915224885; e-mail secretaria@insde.es; internet www.insde.es; f. 1938; the Institute's constituent academies form a 'Senado de la Cultura Española'; Pres. ALBERTO GALINDO TIXAIRE; Sec.-Gen. PEDRO GARCÍA BARRENO..

Constituent Academies:

Real Academia de Bellas Artes de San Fernando (San Fernando Royal Academy of Fine Arts): Calle Alcalá 13, 28014 Madrid; tel. 915240864; e-mail director@rabasf.org; internet rabasf.insde.es; f. 1752; attached museum: see under Museums and Art Galleries; 57 mems; library of 40,000 vols, 1,100 periodicals; Dir ANTONIO BONET CORREA; Sec.-Gen. FERNANDO DE TERÁN TROYANO.

Real Academia de Ciencias Exactas, Físicas y Naturales (Royal Academy of Exact, Physical and Natural Sciences): Valverde 22 y 24, 28004 Madrid; tel. 917014230; e-mail secretaria@rac.es; internet www.rac.es; f. 1847; sections of exact sciences, natural sciences, physical and chemical sciences; 43 mems, 90 Spanish corresp. mems; Pres. MIGUEL ÁNGEL ALARIO FRANCO; publs Revista (4 a year), Serie A: Matemáticas (4 a year).

Real Academia de Ciencias Morales y Políticas (Royal Academy of Moral and Political Sciences): Plaza de la Villa 2, 28005 Madrid; tel. 915481330; e-mail biblioteca@racmyp.es; internet www.racmyp.es; f. 1857; 93 mems (44 ordinary, 14 Spanish corresp., 35 foreign corresp.); library of 125,000 vols, 340 periodicals; Pres. MARCELINO OREJA AGUIRRE; Sec. JULIO IGLESIAS DE USSEL; publs Anales (1 a year), Papeles y Memorias (4 a year).

Real Academia de Jurisprudencia y Legislación (Royal Academy of Jurisprudence and Law): Calle Marqués de Cubas 13, 28014 Madrid; tel. 915222069; e-mail secretaria.rajyl@insde.es; internet rajyl.insde.es; f. 1730; 38 mems; library of 40,000 vols; Pres. LANDELINO LAVILLA ALSINA; Sec.-Gen. RAFAEL NAVARRO-VALLS; publ. Anales.

Real Academia de la Historia (Royal Academy of History): Calle León 21, 28014 Madrid; tel. 914290611; e-mail direccion@rah.es; internet www.rah.es; f. 1738; 33 mems, 370 corresp. mems; library of 350,000 vols, 180,000 MSS; Dir GONZALO ANES Y ÁLVAREZ DE CASTRILLÓN; Permanent Sec. ELOY BENITO RUANO.

Real Academia Española (Royal Spanish Academy): Calle de Felipe IV 4, 28014 Madrid; tel. 914201478; e-mail secretaria@rae.es; internet www.rae.es; f. 1713; 40 ordinary mems, 3 elected mems; Dir VICTOR GARCÍA DE LA CONCHA; Sec. DARÍO VILLANUEVA.

Real Academia Nacional de Farmacia (Royal National Academy of Pharmacy): Calle de la Farmacia 9–11, 28004 Madrid;

tel. 915310307; e-mail secretaria@ranf
.com; internet www.ranf.com; f. 1589; 44
mems; library of 30,000 vols; Pres. MARÍA
TERESA MIRAS PORTUGAL; Permanent Sec.
LUIS ANTONIO DOADRIO VILLAREJO; publ.
Anales (4 a year).

Real Academia Nacional de Medicina
(Royal National Academy of Medicine):
Calle Arrieta 12, 28013 Madrid; tel.
915470318; internet www.ranm.es; f.
1733; 46 mems, 81 Spanish corresp.
mems, 82 foreign corresp. mems; library
of 100,000 vols; Pres. MANUEL DÍAZ-RUBIO
GARCÍA; Sec.-Gen. MIGUEL LUCAS TOMÁS;
publ. *Anales* (4 a year).

Instituto Egipcio de Estudios Islámicos
(Egyptian Institute of Islamic Studies): Calle
Francisco de Asís Méndez Casariego 1, 28002
Madrid; tel. 915639468; e-mail secretaria@
institutoegipcio.com; internet www
.institutoegipcio.com; f. 1950 as Instituto
Faruk I de Estudios Islámicos, present
name 1952; promotes scientific research and
cooperation between Egyptian and Spanish
univs; establishes relations between the Arab
community and Latin American univs; holds
Arabic and Spanish classes, Egyptology
courses; art exhibitions of Egyptian and
Spanish works; 14 mems; library of 38,000
vols, 1,200 periodicals; Dir Dr ELSAYED
IBRAHIM SOHEIM; Sec. ALMUDENA GARCÍA;
publ. *Las Ciudades de Al-Andalus: Zaragoza*
(1 a year).

**Real Academia de Bellas Artes y Cien-
cias Históricas de Toledo** (Royal Academy
of Fine Arts and Historical Sciences of
Toledo): Calle de Esteban Illán 9, 45001
Toledo; tel. 925214322; e-mail
realacademiatoledo@telefonica.net; internet
www.realacademiatoledo.es; f. 1916; 25
mems, 26 corresp. mems; library of 4,000
vols; Dir RAMÓN SÁNCHEZ GONZÁLEZ; Sec.
JOSÉ LUIS ISABEL SÁNCHEZ; publ. *Toletum*.

**Real Academia de Ciencias, Bellas
Letras y Nobles Artes de Córdoba** (Royal
Academy of Science, Literature and Fine
Arts in Córdoba): Ambrosio de Morales 9,
14003 Córdoba; tel. 957413168; e-mail
racordoba@insde.es; internet www.racordoba
.es; f. 1810; promotes research and stimulates public awareness of all kinds of knowledge, scientific, historical, literary and
artistic; institutes of Califales studies, genealogical and heraldic studies, Gongorino studies, studies of performing arts; 35 mems;
library of 30,000 vols, 700 periodicals; Dir Dr
JOAQUÍN CRIADO COSTA; Sec. Dra MARÍA JOSÉ
PORRO HERRERA.

**Reial Acadèmia de Ciències i Arts de
Barcelona** (Royal Academy of Science and
Arts of Barcelona): Rambla dels Estudis 115,
08002 Barcelona; tel. 933170536; e-mail
secretaria@racab.es; internet www.racab.es;
f. 1764 as Conferencia Physycomatemática
Experimental, present name 1887; asscn of
investigators of science and its applications;
promotes culture of Catalan soc. relevant to
the applied arts; 75 mems; library of 150,000
vols; Pres. Dr RAMON PASCUAL DE SANS; Gen.
Sec. Dr JOAN JOFRE I TORROELLA; publ.
*Memorias de la Real Academia de Ciencias
y Artes de Barcelona*.

Real Academia de Doctores de Espana
(Spanish Royal Academy of Doctors): San
Bernardo 49, 28015 Madrid; tel. 915319522;
e-mail rad@radoctores.es; internet www
.radoctores.es; f. 1922 as Academia de Doctores de Madrid, current name adopted 1984;
sections of architecture and fine arts, engineering, experimental sciences, humanities,
law, medicine, pharmacy, philosophy, political science and economics, theology, veterinary science; 304 mems (incl. 4 hon. mems,
100 mems, 110 national corresp., 90 foreign

corresp. mems); Pres. Dr LUIS MARDONES
SEVILLA; Sec.-Gen. Dra ROSA MARÍA GAR-
CERÁN PIQUERAS; publs *Anales* (irregular),
Anuario.

**Real Academia Hispano-Americana de
Ciencias, Artes y Letras** (Royal Spanish-
American Academy of Sciences, Arts and
Letters): Paseo Carlos III 9–1A, 11003 Cadiz;
tel. 956221680; e-mail raha@raha.es;
internet www.raha.es; f. 1909; 25 mems, 6
hon. mems; library of 120,000 vols; Dir MARÍA
DEL CARMEN CÓZAR NAVARRO; Sec.-Gen. FER-
NANDO SÁNCHEZ GARCÍA; publs *Anuario*,
Revista Hispanoamericana (1 a year, online).

AGRICULTURE, FISHERIES AND
VETERINARY SCIENCE

Institut Agrícola (Agricultural Institute):
Plaça Sant Josep Oriol 4, 08002 Barcelona;
tel. 933011636; e-mail info@institutagricola
.org; internet www.institutagricola.org; f.
1851; training courses in environmental
laws and regulations, farming, food safety
and food handlers, pest control, phytosanitary applicator; 2,000 mems; library of
16,000 vols, 200 periodicals; Pres. BALDIRI
ROS I PRAT; Sec. MATEU COMALRENA DE
SOBREGRAU; publ. *La Drecera* (6 a year).

Real Academia de Ciencias Veterinarias
(Royal Academy of Veterinary Sciences): c/o
Prof. Dr Mariano Illera Martín, Maestro
Ripoll 8, 28006 Madrid; tel. 915611799;
e-mail info@racve.es; internet www.racve
.es; f. 1975; 38 mems, 5 hon. mems, 32
corresp. mems in Spain, 81 corresp. mems
abroad; Pres. Prof. ARTURO RAMÓN ANADÓN
NAVARRO; Sec.-Gen. SALVIO JIMÉNEZ PÉREZ;
publ. *Anales* (1 a year).

ARCHITECTURE AND TOWN PLANNING

Col·legi d'Arquitectes de Catalunya
(Association of Architects of Catalonia): Plaça
Nova 5, 08002 Barcelona; tel. 933015000;
e-mail coac@coac.net; internet www.coac.net;
f. 1931; 9,000 mems; library of 80,000 vols;
Dean LLUÍS-XAVIER COMERÓN I GRAUPERA;
Sec. ASSUMPCIÓ PUIG I HORS; publ. *Quaderns
d'Arquitectura i Urbanisme*.

BIBLIOGRAPHY, LIBRARY SCIENCE
AND MUSEOLOGY

Amics dels Museus de Catalunya
(Friends of the Museums of Catalonia): Palau
de la Virreina, La Rambla 99, 08002 Barcelona; tel. 933014379; e-mail amics@
amicsdelsmuseus.org; internet www
.amicsdelsmuseus.org; f. 1933; promotes and
disseminates culture through collaboration
with museums and other instns; 800 mems, 6
hon. mems, 81 assoc. mems, 52 other mems;
Pres. FAUSTO SERRA DE DALMASES; Sec.-Gen.
MARINA GÓMEZ CASAS.

**Federación Española de Asociaciones
de Archiveros, Bibliotecarios, Arqueólogos, Museólogos y Documentalistas**
(Spanish Federation of Associations of Archivists, Librarians, Archaeologists, Museum
Curators and Documentalists): Calle de las
Huertas 37, 28014 Madrid; tel. 915751727;
e-mail anabad@anabad.org; internet www
.anabad.org; f. 1999; works to conserve archaeological and artistic heritage of Spain;
promotes training of professionals of archives, libraries, museums, documentation and
information centres, archaeological parks,
visitor centres; 1,500 mems; Pres. BEATRIZ
GARCÍA GÓMEZ.

ECONOMICS, LAW AND POLITICS

**Centro de Estudios Políticos y Consti-
tucionales** (Centre for Political and Constitutional Studies): Plaza de la Marina
Española 9, 28071 Madrid; tel. 915401950;

e-mail cepc@cepc.es; internet www.cepc.gob
.es; f. 1977 by merger with Instituto de
Estudios Políticos; promotes analysis, study
and research of legal and sociopolitical reality on nat. and int. level; organizes courses
and seminars; 100 mems; library of 85,400
vols, 1,869 periodicals; Dir Dra BENIGNO
PENDÁS GARCÍA; Man. ISRAEL PASTOR SAINZ-
PARDO; publs *Anuario Iberoamericano de
Justicia Constitucional* (1 a year, online),
Derecho Privado y Constitución (1 a year,
online), *Historia y Politica* (2 a year, online),
Memoria (1 a year), *Revista de Administración Pública* (3 a year, online), *Revista de
Derecho Comunitario Europeo* (3 a year,
online), *Revista de Estudios Políticos* (4 a
year, online), *Revista Española de Derecho
Constitucional* (3 a year, online).

Col·legi de Notaris de Catalunya (Notarial College of Catalonia): Carrer Notariat 4,
08001 Barcelona; tel. 933174800; e-mail
info@catalunya.notariado.org; internet www
.colnotcat.es; f. 1932; 500 mems; Dir ÁNGEL
SERRANO DE NICOLÁS; Sec. ESTEBAN CUYAS
HENCHE; publ. *La Notaría*.

**Il·lustre Col·legi d'Advocats de Barce-
lona** (Illustrious Bar Association of Barcelona): Calle Mallorca 283, 08037 Barcelona;
tel. 934961880; e-mail icab@icab.es; internet
www.icab.es; f. 1833; works to defend legal
practice; promotes legal profession within
soc.; offers professional training and devt;
20,000 mems; library: see under Libraries
and Archives; Dean PEDRO L. YÚFERA SALES;
Sec. LUIS ANTONIO SALES CAMPRODON; publs
Món Jurídic (10 a year), *Revista Jurídica de
Catalunya* (Law Journal of Catalonia, 4 a
year).

**Instituto Nacional de Administración
Pública** (National Institute of Public Administration): Calle Atocha 106, 28012 Madrid;
tel. 912739100; e-mail direccion@inap.es;
internet www.inap.map.es; f. 1940; library
of 150,000 vols, 3,000 periodicals; Dir MAN-
UEL ARENILLA SÁEZ; Man. ENRIQUE SILVESTRE
CATALÁN; publs *Cuadernos de Derecho Público* (3 a year), *Documentación Administra-
tiva* (3 a year), *Gestión y Análisis de Políticas
Públicas* (3 a year), *Revista de Estudios de
Administración Local* (3 a year), *Revista
Internacional de Administrativas* (4 a year).

Instituto Nacional de Estadística
(National Statistics Institute): Paseo de la
Castellana 183, 28071 Madrid; tel.
915839100; e-mail biblioteca@ine.es;
internet www.ine.es; f. 1945; conducts large
scale statistical operations incl. demographic
and economic censuses, nat. accounts, demographic and social statistics, economic and
social indicators, coordination and maintenance of company directories Electoral Census
training; library of 40,000 vols, 80,000 microfiches; Pres. GREGORIO IZQUIERDO LLANES;
Sec.-Gen. NATIVIDAD DOMÍNGUEZ CALAVERAS;
publs *Anuario Estadístico de España* (Statistical Yearbook of Spain, 1 a year), *Boletín
Mensual de Estadística* (Monthly Statistical
Bulletin, 12 a year), *Boletín Trimestral de
Coyuntura* (4 a year), *Censos de Población y
Viviendas* (Population and Housing Census,
every 10 years), *Directorio Central de Empre-
sas (Dirce)* (Central Companies Directory, 1 a
year), *Encuesta Anual de Comercio* (Annual
Trade Survey, 1 a year), *Encuesta de Pobla-
ción Activa (EPA)* (Economically Active
Population Survey, 4 a year), *España en
Cifras* (Spain in Figures, in Spanish or
English), *Estadística Española* (Spanish
Statistical Magazine, 3 a year), *Estadística
Industrial* (1 a year), *Indice* (6 a year),
Nomenclaturas y Metodología.

**Real Sociedad Económica de Amigos del
País de Tenerife** (Royal Economic Society
of Friends of Tenerife): Calle San Agustín 23,

38201 San Cristóbal de La Laguna; tel. 922250010; e-mail secretaria@rseapt.com; internet www.rseapt.com; f. 1777; 500 mems; library of 12,000 vols; Dir ANDRÉS MANUEL DE SOUZA IGLESIAS; Sec. Dr JOSE MANUEL DIAS YANES.

EDUCATION

Instituto Universitario Investigación José Ortega y Gasset: Calle Fortuny 53, 28010 Madrid; tel. 917004100; e-mail jefatura.estudios@fog.es; internet www.ortegaygasset.edu; f. 1986; organizes cultural activities and undertakes debate and research in the fields of the social sciences and humanities; attached institute in Toledo offers courses in Hispanic, Latin American and European Studies (incl. anthropology, archaeology, politics, economics, geography, history, art, Spanish language, literature), designed specifically for foreign students; library of 50,000 vols, 300 periodicals; Dir FERNANDO VALLESPÍN OÑA; publs Revista de Estudios Orteguianos (2 a year), Revista de Occidente (12 a year).

FINE AND PERFORMING ARTS

Asociación Española de Pintores y Escultores (Association of Spanish Artists and Sculptors): Calle Infantas 30, Second Fl., 28004 Madrid; tel. 915224961; e-mail administracion@apintoresyescultores.es; internet www.apintoresyescultores.es; f. 1910; develops cultural activities; fosters devt of visual arts; 1,000 mems; Pres. JOSÉ GABRIEL ASTUDILLO LÓPEZ; Sec. DOLORES BARREDA PÉREZ; publ. Gaceta de Bellas Artes (12 a year).

Ateneo Científico, Literario y Artístico de Madrid (Scientific, Literary and Artistic Athenaeum in Madrid): Calle Prado 21, 28014 Madrid; tel. 914291750; e-mail biblioteca@ateneodemadrid.es; internet www.ateneodemadrid.com; f. 1835; 7,000 mems; library of 350,000 vols, 2,800 newspaper collns and periodicals, 150,000 monographs, 27,000 pamphlets; Pres. CARLOS PARÍS AMADOR; Librarian FRANCISCO JOSÉ CASTAÑÓN BLANCO; publ. El Atenneo (1 a year).

Ateneu Barcelonès (Barcelona Athenaeum): Calle de la Canuda 6, 08002 Barcelona; tel. 933436121; e-mail info@ateneubcn.org; internet www.ateneubcn.org; f. 1860; thematic sections of arts, chess, cinema, economy, history, language and literature, music, philosophy, political, legal and social studies; 4,000 mems; library: see under Libraries and Archives; Pres. FRANCESC CABANA; Sec. MAX ARIAS.

Ateneu Científic, Literari i Artístic de Mao: Sa Rovellada de Dalt 25, 07703 Mahón; tel. 971360553; e-mail ateneu@ateneumao.org; internet www.ateneumao.org; f. 1905; administers natural history museum; library of 15,000 vols; 630 mems; Pres. MARGARITA ORFILA PONS; Sec. JOSÉ M. PUIG MARTÍN; Sec. OSCAR SBERT LOZANO; publ. Revista de Menorca (4 a year).

Consejo General de la Música (General Council on Music): Calle de la Davallada 12, 08870 Sitges; tel. 938949990; e-mail consejo@musicae.org; Pres. MANUEL VALLRIBERA I MIR.

Institut Amatller d'Art Hispànic (Amatller Institute of Hispanic Art): Passeig de Gràcia 41, 08007 Barcelona; tel. 932160175; e-mail amatller@amatller.org; internet www.amatller.org; f. 1941; preserves photographs and index to digitized system; promotes research into the history of Hispanic Art; library of 26,000 vols, 350,000 photographs; Pres. FRANCESC FONTBONA I DE VALLESCAR; Sec. JACINT BERENGUER I. CASAL.

Institut del Teatre (Theatrical Institute): Plaça Margarida Xirgu s/n, 08004 Barcelona; tel. 932273900; e-mail i.teatre@institutdelteatre.cat; internet www.institutdelteatre.org; f. 1913 as Catalan School of Dramatic Arts; drama and dance school; documentation and research information centre; library of 150,000 vols; Dir-Gen. JORDI FONT I CARDONA; Man. RAMON JOVELLS I. ARGELICH.

Real Academia de Bellas Artes de la Purísima Concepción (Royal Academy of Fine Arts): Casa de Cervantes, Calle del Rastro s/n, 47001 Valladolid; tel. 983398004; e-mail info@realacademiaconcepcion.net; internet www.realacademiaconcepcion.net; f. 1779; 32 mems; Pres. JESÚS URREA FERNÁNDEZ; Sec. MANUEL ARIAS MARTINEZ.

Real Academia de Bellas Artes de Santa Isabel de Hungría (Royal Academy of Fine Arts, Santa Isabel de Hungría): Abades 14, Casa de los Pinelo, 41004 Seville; tel. 954221198; e-mail rabasih@insacan.org; internet www.insacan.org/rabasih/rabasihsede.html; f. 1660; research, courses and exhibitions; 40 mems; library of 3,900 vols; Pres. ISABEL DE LEÓN BORRERO; Sec.-Gen. FERNANDO FERNÁNDEZ GÓMEZ; publs Boletín de Bellas Artes (1 a year), Temas de Estética y Arte (1 a year).

Real Academia de Bellas Artes de San Telmo (Royal Academy of Fine Arts of San Telmo): Málaga; internet www.realacademiasantelmo.org; f. 1849 as Academia de Bellas Artes de Málaga, present name 1883; 34 mems; Pres. MANUEL DEL CAMPO Y DEL CAMPO; Sec. FRANCISCO CABRERA PABLOS; publ. Anuario.

Real Academia de Nobles y Bellas Artes de San Luis (Royal Academy of Noble and Fine Arts of San Luis): Plaza de los Sitios 6, 50001 Zaragoza; tel. 976217969; e-mail rasanluis@rasanluis.es; internet www.rasanluis.es; f. 1792; comprises 5 sections: architecture, sculpture, painting, music, literature and 3 permanent cttees; 38 mems; library of 5,500 vols; Pres. Dr DOMINGO JESÚS BUESA CONDE; Sec.-Gen. JAVIER SAURAS VIÑUALES.

Real Sociedad Fotográfica (Royal Photographic Society): Calle de los Tres Peces 2, 28012 Madrid; tel. 915397579; e-mail info@rsf.es; internet www.rsf.es; f. 1899; 1,400 mems; library of 3,800 vols; Pres. ENRIQUE SANZ RAMÍREZ; Sec.-Gen. MARÍA ANTONIA GARCÍA DE LA VEGA; publ. Boletín (4 a year).

HISTORY, GEOGRAPHY AND ARCHAEOLOGY

Arxiu Històric de la Ciutat de Barcelona: Carrer Santa Llúcia 1, 08002 Barcelona; tel. 932562255; e-mail arxiuhistoric@bcn.cat; internet www.bcn.es/arxiu/arxiuhistoric; f. 1917; archives of municipal records and local press; undertakes historical research on Barcelona; organizes courses, lectures, exhibitions; library: see under Libraries and Archives; Dir XAVIER TARRAUBELLA MIRABET; publs Barcelona Quaderns d'Història (2 a year), Història, Antropología, y Fuentes Orales (2 a year), Quaderns del Seminari d'Història de Barcelona (irregular).

Deutsches Archaeologisches Institut (German Archaeological Institute): Serrano 159, 28002 Madrid; tel. 915610904; e-mail sekretariat@madrid.dainst.org; internet www.dainst.org; f. 1943; studies archaeology of the Iberian Peninsula and Morocco from prehistory to the early Christian and Islamic Middle Ages; library of 65,000 vols; Dir Prof. Dr DIRCE MARZOLI; Scientific Dir Prof. Dr THOMAS G. SCHATTNER; publs Hispania Antiqua, Iberia Archaeologica, Madrider Beiträge, Madrider Forschungen, Madrider

Mitteilungen (1 a year), Studien über frühe Tierknochenfunde von der Iberischen Halbinsel.

Instituto de Historia y Cultura Naval (History and Naval Culture Institute): Calle Juan de Mena 1, 28014 Madrid; tel. 913795050; e-mail ihcn@fn.mde.es; internet www.armada.mde.es; f. 1976; promotes study of Spanish naval history; facilitates research and publishes the results; associated with the Consejo Superior de Investigaciones Científicas; library: see under Libraries and Archives; Dir TEODORO DE LESTE CONTRERAS.

Instituto Geográfico Nacional (National Geographical Institute): Calle del General Ibáñez de Ibero 3, 28003 Madrid; tel. 915979422; e-mail ign@fomento.es; internet www.ign.es; f. 1870; geodesy and geophysics, cartography, map printing, seismology, astronomy, runs the Nat. Astronomical Observatory (see under Research Institutes); 1,200 mems; library of 28,000 vols; Dir-Gen. ALBERTO SERENO ÁLVAREZ; publs Anuario de Geomagnetismo, Anuario del Observatorio Astronómico, Boletín Astronómico, Boletines Sísmicos.

Real Sociedad Geográfica (Royal Geographic Society): Calle Monte Esquinza 41, 28010 Madrid; tel. 913082477; e-mail secretaria@realsociedadgeografica.com; internet www.realsociedadgeografica.com; f. 1876 as Sociedad Geográfica de Madrid, present name 1901; promotes geographical knowledge in all its aspects; participates in state-funded research projects; 450 mems; library of 11,000 vols, 12,700 booklets, 110 periodicals; Pres. JUAN VELARDE FUERTES; Sec.-Gen. Dr JOAQUÍN BOSQUE MAUREL; publ. Boletín de la Real Sociedad Geográfica.

Reial Societat Arqueològica Tarraconense (Royal Archaeological Society in Tarragona): POB 573, 43080 Tarragona; Carrer Major 35, 43003 Tarragona; tel. 977233789; e-mail informacio@arqueologica.org; internet www.arqueologica.org; f. 1844; Iberian, Roman and early Christian archaeology; ancient, medieval, modern and contemporary history of Tarragona; 550 mems; library of 3,000 vols, 20,000 periodicals; Pres. RAFAEL GABRIEL COSTA; Sec. ÒSCAR MARTIN VIELBA; publ. Butlletí Arqueològic (4 a year).

Servicio de Investigación Prehistórica de la Excelentísima Diputación Provincial (Prehistoric Research Society of the Province of Valencia): Calle de la Corona 36, 46003 Valencia; tel. 963883565; e-mail sip@dival.es; internet www.museoprehistoriavalencia.es; f. 1927; palaeolithic, neolithic, Bronze and Iron Ages, Iberian and colonial exhibits, prehistoric Americana; 30 mems; library of 60,000 vols, 1,429 periodicals; Curator MARÍA JESÚS DE PEDRO MICHÓ; publs Archivo de Prehistoria Levantina, Serie Trabajos Varios del SIP.

Societat Arqueològica Lul·liana (Lulliana Archaeological Society): Calle Montisión 9, 07001 Palma; tel. 971713912; e-mail arqueologicaluliana@gmail.com; internet www.arqueologicaluliana.com; f. 1880; represents Mallorcan culture; collns of paintings and sculptures, archaeology, ceramics, epigraphs, inscriptions, decorative arts, furniture, ivory, glass, fans, clothing, weights and measures, earthenware cooking pots, architectural fragments; 600 mems; library of 20,000 vols; Pres. ANTONIO PLANAS ROSSELLÓ; Sec. MARIA CARME COLL FONT; publ. Bolletí de la Societat Arqueològica Lul·liana (1 a year).

LANGUAGE AND LITERATURE

Alliance Française de Madrid: Cuesta de Santo Domingo 13, 28013 Madrid; tel.

914351532; e-mail informacion2@
alliancefrancaisemadrid.net; internet www
.alliancefrancaisemadrid.net; offers courses
and exams in French language and culture
and promotes cultural exchange with France;
attached offices in Alicante, Burgos, Cartagena, Gijon, Girona, Granada, Granollers, La
Coruña, Las Palmas, Lerida, Lleida, Málaga,
Oviedo, Palma de Mallorca, Sabadell, Sama
de Langreo, Santa Cruz de Tenerife, Santander, Santiago de Compostela, Valladolid,
Vigo, Vitoria; Pres. JUAN J. LUNA; Sec. JULIAN
OCAÑA; Dir-Gen. ELISABETH RANEDO.

**Asociación de Escritores y Artistas
Españoles** (Spanish Writers' and Artists'
Association): Calle de Leganitos 10, First Fl.
Derecha, 28013 Madrid; tel. 915599067;
e-mail secretaria@aeae.es; internet www
.aeae.es; f. 1871; 527 mems; library of 3,000
vols; Pres. JUAN VAN-HALEN; Dir and Sec.-
Gen. JOSÉ LÓPEZ MARTÍNEZ.

British Council: Paseo del General Martínez, Campos 31, 28010 Madrid; tel.
913373593; e-mail prensa@britishcouncil.es;
internet www.britishcouncil.org/spain/
madrid; offers courses and examinations in
English language and British culture and
promotes cultural exchange with the UK in
13 centres across Spain (7 in Madrid, 2 in
Barcelona, and 1 each in Bilbao, Valencia,
Segovia and Palma de Mallorca); library of
26,000 vols; Dir ROD PRYDE.

**Euskaltzaindia/Real Academia de la
Lengua Vasca** (Royal Academy of the
Basque Language): Plaza Barria 15, 48005
Bilbao; tel. 944158155; e-mail info@
euskaltzaindia.net; internet www
.euskaltzaindia.net; f. 1918; research into
and conservation of the Basque language;
197 mems (incl. 29 full mems, 33 hon. mems,
135 assoc. academic mems); library of 70,000
vols; Pres. ANDRÉS URRUTIA BADIOLA; Sec.
XABIER KINTANA URTIAGA; Treas. SAGRARIO
ALEMAN; publs *Erlea*, *Euskaltzaindiaren Ara-
uak* (3 a year), *Euskaltzainak Bilduma*
(irregular), *Euskararen Lekukoak*, *Euskera*
(3 a year), *Iker*, *Jagon*, *Mendaur bilduma*
(irregular), *Onomasticon Vasconiae*, *Plaza-
berri* (irregular).

Goethe-Institut: Calle Zurbarán 21, 28010
Madrid; tel. 913913944; e-mail info@madrid
.goethe.org; internet www.goethe.de/madrid;
offers courses and exams in German language and culture and promotes cultural
exchange with Germany; attached centres in
Alcalá de Henares, Colmenarejo, Colmenar
Viejo, Getafe, Leganés, Villanueva de la
Cañada, Granada and San Sebastián; library
of 15,000 vols; Dir MARGARETA HAUSCHILD;
Sec. MARIANGELES MARTÍNEZ.

Real Academia Galega (Royal Galician
Academy): Tabernas 11, 15001 Coruña; tel.
981207308; e-mail secretaria@
realacademiagalega.org; internet www
.realacademiagalega.org; f. 1906; protects
and promotes the Galician language and
literature; 30 mems; library of 60,000 vols;
Pres. XOSÉ LUÍS MÉNDEZ FERRÍN; Sec. XOSÉ
LUÍS AXEITOS AGRELO; publs *Boletín da Real
Academia Galega*, *Cadernos de Lingua*.

**Real Academia Sevillana de Buenas
Letras** (Seville Royal Academy of Fine
Arts): Calle Abades 14, 41004 Seville; tel.
954225200; e-mail academia@
academiasevillanadebuenasletras.org; internet www.academiasevillanadebuenasletras
.org; f. 1751; 29 mems, 7 hon., 100 corresp.;
library of 7,000 vols, 150 periodicals; Dir
ENRIQUETA VILA VILAR; Sec. JOSE ANTONIO
GÓMEZ MARÍN; Sec. RAFAEL VALENCIA RODRI-
GUEZ; publ. *Boletín* (1 a year).

Reial Acadèmia de Bones Lletres (Royal
Academy of Belles Lettres): Carrer del Bisbe
Caçador 3, 08002 Barcelona; tel. 933102349;

e-mail bones-lletres@boneslletres.cat;
internet www.boneslletres.cat; f. 1700; 36
mems; Pres. PERE MOLAS RIBALTA; Sec. JOSEP
MASSOT I MUNTANER; publ. *Boletín*.

Sociedad General de Autores y Editores
(General Society of Authors and Publishers):
Fernando VI 4, 28004 Madrid; tel.
913499550; internet www.sgae.es; f. 1899;
dedicated to the defence and collective management of the intellectual property rights of
its mems who are authors, music editors and
heirs; 103,000 mems; library of 25,000 vols;
Pres. ANTÓN REXA; publ. *Boletín* (4 a year).

MEDICINE

**Academia de Ciencias Médicas de Bil-
bao** (Academy of Medical Sciences of Bilbao):
Lersundi 9, Fifth Fl., 48009 Bilbao; tel.
944233768; e-mail info@docorcomunicacion
.com; internet www.acmbilbao.org; f. 1895;
organizes courses, workshops, symposiums,
confs and scientific meetings; promotes studies of pharmacy, biology, veterinary medicine
and odontology; promotes and strengthens
the humanistic side attached to medical
practice; 1,200 mems; library of 10,000 vols;
Pres. Dr JUAN IGNACIO GOIRIA ORMAZABAL;
Sec.-Gen. Prof. Dr RICARDO FRANCO VICARIO;
publ. *Gaceta Médica de Bilbao* (4 a year).

**Acadèmia de Ciències Mèdiques de Cat-
alunya i de Balears** (Academy of Medical
Sciences and Health of Catalonia and the
Balearic Islands): Calle Major de Can Car-
alleu 1–7, 08017 Barcelona; tel. 932031050;
e-mail academia@academia.cat; internet
www.acmcb.es; f. 1872; serves as forum for
health care professionals from Catalonia, the
Balearic Islands, Valencia, Andorra; fosters
continuing education and study and the
cultivating of health science in human, technical, social, civic aspects; 20,000 mems;
Pres. ALVAR NET CASTEL; publs *Annals de
Medicina* (4 a year), *Informatiu*, *Memòries*.

**Academia Española de Dermatología y
Venereología** (Spanish Academy of Derma-
tology and Venereology): Calle Ferraz 100,
First Fl. izq, 28080 Madrid; tel. 915446284;
e-mail secretaria@aedv.es; internet www
.aedv.es; f. 1909; brs: Andalusia, Asturias,
Cantabria and Castille Leon, Balearic
Islands, Canary Islands, Catalonia, Centro,
Euskadi, Navarre, La Rioja and Aragon,
Galicia, Murcia, Valencia; 450 mems, 50
hon. mems, 3 corresp. mems; library of
1,000 vols; Pres. Dr JOSÉ CARLOS MORENO
GIMÉNEZ; Sec. Dr HUGO ALBERTO VÁZQUEZ
VEIGA; publs *Actas Dermosifiliográficas* (12
a year), *Revista Dermactual* (12 a year).

Academia Médico-Quirúrgica Española
(Spanish Academy of Medicine and Surgery):
Calle Villanueva 11, 28001 Madrid; f. 1844;
500 mems; Pres. Prof. LUIS ORTIZ QUINTANA;
Sec. Dr BARTOLOMÉ BELTRÁN; publ. *Anales*.

**Consejo General de Colegios Oficiales
de Farmacéuticos** (General Council of
Spanish Pharmacists): Calle Villanueva 11,
Seventh Fl., 28001 Madrid; tel. 914324100;
e-mail congral@redfarma.org; internet www
.portalfarma.com; f. 1942; 65,472 mems;
Pres. PEÑA LÓPEZ CARMEN; publs *Farmacéuticos* (12 a year), *Panorama Actual del
Medicamento* (11 a year).

**Consejo General de Colegios Oficiales
de Médicos de España** (Spanish General
Council of Official Medical Colleges): Plaza
de las Cortes 11, 28014 Madrid; tel.
914317780; internet www.cgcom.org; f. 1930;
52 mems; Pres. Dr SONIA LÓPEZ ARRIBAS;
publs *Europa al Día* (26 a year), *Periódico
OMC* (12 a year), *Revista de la OMC* (4 a
year).

**Real Academia de Medicina y Cirugía de
Palma de Mallorca** (Royal Academy of

Medicine and Surgery, Palma de Mallorca):
Calle Morey 8, 07001 Palma de Mallorca; tel.
971721230; f. 1831; 19 mems; Pres. JOSÉ
TOMÁS MONSERRAT; Sec. SANTIAGO FORTEZA
FORTEZA.

**Sociedad de Pediatría de Madrid y
Castilla—La Mancha** (Paediatrics Society
of Madrid and Castilla La Mancha): Calle
Cea Bermúdez 39, Bajo, 28003 Madrid; tel.
914358031; e-mail spmycm@mcmpediatria
.org; internet www.mcmpediatria.org; f.
1913; 1,000 mems; Pres. Dr JOSÉ GARCÍA-
SICILIA LÓPEZ; Sec.-Gen. Dr JUAN JOSÉ JIMÉ-
NEZ GARCÍA; publ. *MCM—Pediatría* (3 a
year).

**Sociedad Española de Patología Diges-
tiva** (Society of Digestive Diseases): Francisco Silvela 69, 2° C, 28028 Madrid; tel.
914021353; e-mail sepd@sepd.es; internet
www.sepd.es; f. 1933; 800 mems; Pres. Dr
MIGUEL MUÑOZ-NAVAS; Sec. Dr FEDERICO
ARGÜELLES ARIAS; publs *G. I. & Hepatology
News*, *Revista Española de las Enfermedades
Digestivas* (12 a year).

**Sociedad Española de Radiología Méd-
ica** (Spanish Society of Medical Radiology):
Gran Vía 1, 28013 Madrid; tel. 915752613;
e-mail secretaria@seram.es; internet seram
.es; f. 1946; teaching, devt, advocacy and
research on all aspects related to diagnostic
and therapeutic medical imaging; 3,500
mems; Pres. Dra CARMEN AYUSO COLELLA;
Sec.-Gen. Dra FÁTIMA MATUTE TERESA; publs
Diagnóstico por la Imagen (4 a year), *Radiología* (6 a year).

NATURAL SCIENCES
General

**Real Academia de Ciencias Exactas,
Físicas, Químicas y Naturales de Zaragoza** (Royal Academy of Exact, Physical,
Chemical and Natural Sciences in Zaragoza):
Facultad de Ciencias, Universidad de Zaragoza, Calle Pedro Cerbuna, 50009 Zaragoza;
tel. 976761255; e-mail racz@unizar.es;
internet acz.unizar.es; f. 1916; comprises
sections on exact sciences, physics and chemistry, natural sciences; 40 mems, 44 corresp.
mems; Pres. LUIS JOAQUÍN BOYA BALET; Sec.
JOSÉ F. CARIÑENA MARZO; publ. *Revista* (1 a
year).

**Sociedad de Ciencias 'Aranzadi'/'Ara-
nzadi' Societe de Sciences** ('Aranzadi'
Society of Sciences): Calle Zorroagagaina
11, 20014 San Sebastián; tel. 943466142;
e-mail idazkaritza@aranzadi-zientziak.org;
internet www.aranzadi-zientziak.org; f.
1947; encourages interest in various brs of
natural science, prehistory and ethnology,
biodiversity, anthropology; 1,540 mems;
library of 28,000 vols, 2,181 periodicals;
Pres. FRANCISCO ETXEBERRIA; Sec.-Gen.
JUANTXO AGIRRE MAULEON; publs *Aranzadiana* (1 a year), *Aranzadi Berriak*, *Boletín de
Astronomía* (4 a year), *Munibe Antropologia—Arkeologia* (1 a year), *Munibe Ciencias
Naturales—Natur Zientziak* (1 a year).

Biological Sciences

Asociación Española de Entomología
(Spanish Entomological Association): Centro
Iberoamericano de Biodiversidad, Universidad de Alicante, Apdo 99, 03080 Alicante;
e-mail galante@ua.es; internet www
.entomologica.es; f. 1977; promotes and popu-
larises entomological studies, with particular
interest in wildlife and Macaronesian Iber-
obalearic through meetings and publs;
spreads awareness of arthropods; promotes
conservation of wildlife and natural areas;
Pres. Dr EDUARDO GALANTE PATIÑO; Sec. Dr
JOSÉ MARÍA HERNÁNDEZ DE MIGUEL; publ.
Boletín de la AeE (2 a year).

Real Sociedad Española de Historia Natural (Royal Spanish Natural History Society): Facultades de Biología y Geología, Universidad Complutense de Madrid, 28040 Madrid; tel. 913945000; e-mail rsehno@bio.ucm.es; internet rshn.geo.ucm.es; f. 1871; biological and geological sciences; 800 mems; library of 10,000 vols, 2,500 current periodicals; Pres. ISABEL RÁBANO GUTIÉRREZ ARROYO; Sec. Dr LUIS ALFREDO BARATAS DÍAZ; publs *Boletín de la RSEHN: Actas*, *Boletín de la RSEHN: Sección Biológica* (4 a year), *Boletín de la RSEHN: Sección Geológica* (4 a year), *Memorias de la RSEHN*.

Sociedad Española de Etología (Spanish Ethological Society): Museu Ciències Naturals de Barcelona, Pº Picasso s/n, Parc Ciutadella, 08003 Barcelona; tel. 932562217; e-mail larroyo@bcn.cat; internet www.etologia.org; f. 1984; promotes, collaborates and communicates among Spanish-speaking ethologists; ethology; disseminates knowledge through publs, confs, lectures and teaching of ethology in various curricula; 350 mems; Pres. ADOLFO CORDERO RIVERA; Sec. JUAN CARLOS SENAR; publs *Acta Etohologica* (2 a year), *EtoloGUÍA* (2 a year).

Mathematical Sciences

Real Sociedad Matemática Española (Royal Spanish Mathematical Society): Despacho 525, Facultad de Matemáticas, Universidad Complutense de Madrid, Plaza de las Ciencias 3, 28040 Madrid; tel. 913944937; e-mail secretaria@rsme.es; internet www.rsme.es; f. 1911; 1,500 mems; Pres. ANTONIO CAMPILLO LÓPEZ; Sec. HENAR HERRERO SANZ; publs *Boletín de la RSME*, *Gaceta de la RSME* (3 a year), *Gaceta Digital*, *Revista Matemática Iberoamericana* (4 a year).

Physical Sciences

Asociación Nacional de Químicos de España (Spanish National Association of Chemists): Calle Lagasca 27, 28001 Madrid; tel. 914310703; e-mail anquejg@anque.es; internet www.anque.es; f. 1945; attached to Consejo General de Colegios Oficiales de Químicos de España; mem. of the int. Fed. of Mediterranean Asscns and of the European Fed. of Chemical Engineering; 11,000 mems; Pres. CARLOS NEGRO ALVAREZ; Sec. MARIA DEL CARMEN LOBO BEDMAR; publ. *Química e Industria* (12 a year).

Real Sociedad Española de Física (Royal Spanish Society of Physics): Facultad de Ciencias Físicas, Universidad Complutense de Madrid, Ciudad Universitaria s/n, 28040 Madrid; tel. 913944350; e-mail rsef@fis.ucm.es; f. 1903; collective org. of specialized groups covering different areas of physics; 800 mems; Pres. Prof. MARÍA DEL ROSARIO HERAS CELEMÍN; Sec.-Gen. Prof. CARMEN MARÍA PEREÑA FERNÁNDEZ; publs *Revista Española de Física* (4 a year), *Revista Iberoamericana de Física* (1 a year).

Real Sociedad Española de Química (Royal Spanish Society of Chemistry): Facultad de Ciencias Químicas, Universidad Complutense de Madrid, Ciudad Universitaria s/n, 28040 Madrid; tel. 913944361; e-mail secretario.general@rseq.org; internet www.rseq.org; f. 1903; 3,578 mems; Pres. JESÚS JIMÉNEZ BARBERO; Sec.-Gen. PEDRO J. PÉREZ ROMERO; publ. *Anales* (4 a year).

Sociedad Española de Astronomía (Spanish Society of Astronomy): Universitat de Barcelona, Facultad de Física, Avda Martí Franquès 1, 08028 Barcelona; tel. 934034986; e-mail contacto@sea-astronomia.es; internet www.sea-astronomia.es; f. 1992; promotes devt of astronomy; organizes lectures and courses; 500 mems; library of 3,000 vols; Pres. JAVIER GORGAS; Sec. MARIA ANGELES GOMEZ FLECHOSO.

Sociedad Geológica de España (Geological Society of Spain): Facultad de Ciencias, Universidad de Salamanca, Plaza de la Merced s/n, 37008 Salamanca; tel. 923294752; e-mail sge@usal.es; internet www.sociedadgeologica.es; f. 1985; promotes, encourages and disseminates knowledge, progress and applications of geology; 1,000 mems; Pres. MARCOS AURELL CARDONA; Sec. JOSÉ EUGENIO ORTIZ MENÉNDEZ; publs *Geogaceta* (2 a year), *Geo-Temas* (irregular), *Revista de la Sociedad Geológica de España* (2 a year).

RELIGION, SOCIOLOGY AND ANTHROPOLOGY

Federación Española de Religiosos de Enseñanza—Centres Catholiques (FERE-CECA)/Escuelas Católicas (Spanish Federation of Religious Institutions in Education—Catholic Centres): Calle Hacienda de Pavones 5, 1°, 28030 Madrid; tel. 913288000; e-mail escuelascatolicas@escuelascatolicas.es; internet www.escuelascatolicas.es; f. 1957 as Federación Española de Religiosos de Enseñanza (FERE); groups all the centres of elementary, secondary and higher education of the Catholic Church; 2,635 centres; library of 7,000 vols, 150 periodicals; Pres. INMACULADA TUSET GARÍN; Sec.-Gen. JUAN ANTONIO OJEDA ORTIZ; publs *Revista EC* (6 a year), *Revista Educadores* (Teachers' Review, 4 a year).

Institución 'Fernando el Católico', Excma Diputación Provincial de Zaragoza (Institution of Ferdinand the Catholic): Plaza de España 2, 50071 Zaragoza; tel. 976288878; e-mail ifc@dpz.es; internet ifc.dpz.es; f. 1943 as Institución 'Fernando el Católico', current name adopted 2006; attached to Consejo Superior de Investigaciones Científicas (CSIC); sections: linguistics and literature, Aragonese art, history, geography and ecology, economic and social studies, law, music for young people, ancient music; Ccl of 12 representing the univ. and municipality; library of 100,000 vols; Dir ÇARLOS FORCADELL ÁLVAREZ; Academic Sec. ALVARO CAPALVO LIESA; publs *Anuario Aragonés del Gobierno Local*, *Archivo de Filología Aragonesa*, *Caesaraugusta: Revista de Arqueología, Prehistoria e Historia Antigua*, *Ciencia Forense: Revista Aragonesa de Medicina Legal*, *Cuadernos de Aragón*, *Emblemata, Ius Fugit: Revista de Estudios Histórico-Jurídicos de la Corona de Aragón*, *Nassarre: Revista Aragonesa de Musicología*, *Palaeohispanica: Revista sobre Lenguas y Culturas de la Hispania Antigua*, *Revista de Derecho Civil Aragonés*, *Revista de Historia Jerónimo Zurita*, *Seminario de Arte Aragonés*.

Real Instituto de Estudios Asturianos (Institute of Asturian Studies): Palacio Conde de Toreno, Plaza Porlier 9, 1°, 33003 Oviedo; tel. 984182801; e-mail ridea@asturias.org; internet ridea.org; f. 1945; 50 mems, 4 hon. mems, 77 corresp. mems; library of 6,203 vols, 250 periodicals, 3,000 photographs; Dir JUAN IGNACIO RUIZ DE LA PEÑA SOLAR; Sec.-Gen. Dra INÉS IBÁÑEZ DE LA CUESTA; publs *Boletín de Ciencias de la Naturaleza* (1 a year), *Boletín de Letras del Real Instituto de Estudios Asturianos* (2 a year).

Real Sociedad Bascongada de los Amigos del País Euskalerriaren Adiskideen Elkartea (Royal Society of Friends of the Basque Country): Peña y Goñi 5–2° izda, 20002 San Sebastián; tel. 943285577; e-mail comisiongipuzkoa@bascongada.e.telefonica.net; internet www.bascongada.org; f. 1763; promotes inclination towards Bascongada sciences, fine arts and letters; 25 mems; Dir ASUNCIÓN URZAINKI MIKELEIZ; publs *Anuario de Eusko-Folklore Aranzadiana Orria*, *Boletín* (4 a year), *Boletín de Estudios Históricos sobre San Sebastián* (1 a year), *Boletín de la Cofradía Vasca de Gastronomía*, *Egan*, *Munibe*.

TECHNOLOGY

Col·legi Oficial d'Enginyers Industrials de Catalunya: Via Laietana 39, 08003 Barcelona; tel. 933192300; e-mail atencioeic@eic.cat; internet www.eic.cat; f. 1950; asscn of engineering graduates of the Schools of Industrial Engineers of Spain; 8,000 mems; library of 22,000 vols; Dean JOAN VALLVÉ I RIBERA; Sec. MANUEL CASAS I VILELLA; publs *Agenda Dels Enginyers* (24 a year), *Full Dels Enginyers* (12 a year).

Instituto de la Ingeniería de España (Spanish Institute of Engineering): Calle General Arrando 38, 28010 Madrid; tel. 913197417; e-mail iie@iies.es; internet www.iies.es; f. 1905; comprises 10 asscns of higher engineers and the *Aula de Ingeniería* (training centre), offering courses, seminars, etc. for postgraduate students; 100,000 mems; Pres. MANUEL MOREU MUNAIZ; Gen. Sec. ASIS MARTÍN-OAR FERNÁNDEZ DE HEREDIA.

Sociedad Española de Cerámica y Vidrio (Spanish Ceramic and Glass Society): Calle Kelsen 5, 28049 Madrid; tel. 91735860; e-mail secv@icv.csic.es; internet www.secv.es; f. 1960; promotes technical progress in ceramic and glass work and disseminates information about manufacture and devts within the field; 750 mems; library of 500 vols; Pres. MIGUEL CAMPOS VILANOVA; Sec.-Gen. CARMEN BAUDIN; publ. *Boletín* (6 a year).

Research Institutes

GENERAL

Centro de Estudios Avanzados en Ciencias Sociales (Center for Advanced Study in the Social Sciences): Fundación Juan March, Castelló 77, 28006 Madrid; tel. 914354240; e-mail direccion@march.es; internet www.march.es/ceacs; f. 1986; attached to Instituto Juan March de Estudios e Investigaciones; research in sociology and political science; PhD programmes; Research Dir IGNACIO SÁNCHEZ-CUENCA.

Consejo Superior de Investigaciones Científicas (CSIC) (National Research Council): Serrano 117, 28006 Madrid; tel. 915681400; internet www.csic.es; f. 1940; serves cultural and technological devt; acts as a creative instrument and forum for Spanish science; has 100 research centres, incl. institutes directly governed by CSIC, those operated jtly by CSIC and univs, and others in asscn with regional govt or other instns; maintains office for transfer of technology in cooperation with Spanish supervisory agencies for technological devt; journals published by the institutes, scientific and cultural dissemination, scientific publishing house, technical facilities and installations; library of 100,000 vols, 70,000 periodicals; Pres. EMILIO LORA-TAMAYO D'OCON; publ. *Arbor* (6 a year).

Attached Research Institutes in the Field of Humanities and Social Sciences:

Centro de Ciencias Humanas y Sociales (Centre for Humanities and Social Sciences): Calle Albasanz 26–28, 28037 Madrid; tel. 916022300; e-mail direccion.cchs@csic.es; internet www.cchs.csic.es; f. 2006; research on field of humanities and social sciences; library: 1m. vols; Dir JOSÉ ANTONIO BERENGUER SÁNCHEZ;

publs *Al-Qantara* (2 a year), *Anales Cervantinos* (1 a year), *Archivo Español de Arqueología* (1 a year), *Archivo Español de Arte* (4 a year), *Asclepio* (2 a year), *Emerita* (2 a year), *Estudios Geográficos* (2 a year), *Gladius* (1 a year), *Hispania* (3 a year), *Hispania Sacra* (2 a year), *Isegoría* (2 a year), *Revista de Dialectología y Tradiciones Populares* (2 a year), *Revista de Filología Española* (2 a year), *Revista de Indias* (3 a year), *Revista de Literatura* (2 a year), *Revista Española de Documentación Científica* (4 a year), *Sefarad* (2 a year), *Trabajos de Prehistoria* (1 a year).

Escuela de Estudios Árabes (School of Arabic Studies): Cuesta del Chapiz 22, 18010 Granada; tel. 958222290; e-mail director.eeh@csic.es; internet www.eea.csic.es; research on history and culture of al-Andalus through written documents and Islamic archaeology and architecture; library of 17,000 vols of monographs; Dir JUAN CASTILLA BRAZALES.

Escuela de Estudios Hispano Americanos (School of Hispanic-American Studies): Calle Alfonso XII 16, 41002 Seville; tel. 954501120; e-mail director.eeha@csic.es; internet www.eeha.csic.es; Dir ANTONIO GUTIÉRREZ ESCUDERO; publ. *Anuario de Estudios Americanos* (2 a year).

Escuela Española de Historia y Arqueología en Roma (CSIC) (Spanish School of History and Archeology in Rome): Via di Torre Argentina 18, 00186 Rome RM, Italy; tel. 66810001; e-mail escuela@csic.it; internet www.eehar.csic.es; f. 1910; research on historical relations between Spain and Italy, from Antiquity to Modern times; library of 22,000 vols; Dir FERNANDO GARCÍA SANZ.

Institución Milá y Fontanals: Calle Egipcíaques 15, 08001 Barcelona; tel. 934423489; e-mail imf@imf.csic.es; internet www.imf.csic.es; f. 1968; research activities: anthropology, archaeology, medieval studies, ethnography, history of science, musicology and sociology; library of 80,000 vols of monographs, 2,200 periodicals; Dir LUIS CALVO CALVO; publs *Anuario de Estudios Medievales* (2 a year), *Anuario Musical* (12 a year).

Instituto de Análisis Económico (Institute of Economic Analysis): Universitat Autònoma, 08193 Bellaterra (Barcelona); tel. 935806612; e-mail director.iae@csic.es; internet www.iae.csic.es; f. 1985; research areas of econometrics, experimental economics, game theory, industrial org. and regulation, growth and devt, macroeconomics; monetary economics, political economics and public economics; Dir Dr CLARA PONSATI OBIOLS.

Instituto de Economía, Geografía y Demografía: Calle Albasanz 26–28, 28037 Madrid; tel. 916022300; e-mail direccion.iegd@csic.es; f. 1986; Dir Dr GLORIA FERNANDEZ-MAYORALAS; publ. *Estudios Geográficos* (4 a year).

Instituto de Estudios Documentales sobre Ciencia y Tecnología: Calle Albasanz 26–28, 28037 Madrid; tel. 916022300; e-mail director.cindoc@csic.es; internet www.cindoc.csic.es; f. 1992 as Centro de Información y Documentación Científica (CINDOC), following merger between Instituto de Información y Documentación en Ciencia y Tecnología (ICYT) and Instituto de Información y Documentación en Ciencias Sociales y Humanidades (ISOC); mainly devoted to the analysis of science, technology and knowledge transfer; Dir Dr LUIS MANUEL PLAZA GÓMEZ; publ. *Revista Española de Documentación Científica* (4 a year).

Instituto de Estudios Gallegos 'Padre Sarmiento': Rua de San Roque 2, 15704 Santiago de Compostela (La Coruña); tel. 981540220; e-mail direccion.iegps@csic.es; internet www.iegps.csic.es; f. 1943; library of 35,000 vols; Dir Prof. EDUARDO J. PARDO DE GUEVARA Y VALDÉS; publs *Cuadernos de Estudios Gallegos* (1 a year), *Serie de 'Anejos' de Cuadernos de Estudios Gallegos* (1 a year).

Instituto de Estudios Sociales Avanzados: Calle Campo Santo de los Mártires 7, 14004 Córdoba; tel. 957760625; e-mail contacto@iesa.csic.es; internet www.iesa.csic.es; Dir EDUARDO MOYANO ESTRADA; publ. *Revista Internacional de Sociología* (3 a year).

Instituto de Filosofía (Institute of Philosophy): Calle Pinar 25, 28006 Madrid; tel. 914117005; e-mail director.ifs@csic.es; internet www.ifs.csic.es; library of 50,000 vols; Dir JOSÉ MARÍA GONZÁLEZ GARCÍA; publs *Isegoría* (2 a year), *SORITES: Electronic Magazine of Analytical Philosophy* (online).

Instituto de Historia (Institute for History): Calle Albasanz 26–28, 28037 Madrid; tel. 916022300; e-mail mercedes.aguilar@cchs.csic.es; internet www.ih.csic.es; Dir Dr CONSUELO NARANJO OROVIO; publs *Archivo Español de Arqueología* (1 a year), *Archivo Español de Arte* (4 a year), *Asclepio* (2 a year), *Gladius* (1 a year), *Hispania* (3 a year), *Hispania Sacra* (2 a year), *Revista de Indias* (3 a year), *Trabajos de Prehistoria* (2 a year).

Instituto de Historia de la Medicina y de la Ciencia López Piñero (López Piñero Institute for the History of Medicine and Science): Palacio de Cerveró, Plaza Cisneros 4, 46003 Valencia; tel. 963926229; e-mail iu.historia.ciencia.doc@uv.es; internet www.ihmc.uv-csic.es; f. 1985; develops and fosters research activity related to historical and social studies on medicine and science; preserves, studies and propagates Spanish historico-medical and historico-scientific heritage by digitalising printed texts, cataloguing and studying the colln of medical and scientific instruments and disseminating its bibliographical and documentary holdings; library of 40,000 vols, incl. 10,000 monographs, 1,000 reference titles, 3,000 medical books from 16th–18th centuries and 15,000 vols from 19th and 20th centuries; spec. collns of journals from the 18th and 19th centuries; Dir MARÍA LUZ LÓPEZ TERRADA; publs *Boletín del Instituto Médico Valenciano* (Bulletin of the Valencian Medical Institute), *Cuadernos Valencianos de Historia de la Medicina y de la Ciencia*.

Instituto de Lengua, Literatura y Antropología: Calle Albasanz 26–28, 28037 Madrid; tel. 916022817; e-mail direccion.illa@csic.es; f. 2007; Dir VIOLETA M. DEMONTE BARRETO; publs *Anales Cervantinos* (1 a year), *Revista de Dialectología y Tradiciones Populares* (2 a year), *Revista de Filología Española* (2 a year), *Revista de Literatura* (2 a year).

Instituto de Lenguas y Culturas del Mediterráneo y Oriente Próximo: Calle Albasanz 26–28, 28037 Madrid; tel. 916022430; e-mail maite.ortega@cchs.csic.es; internet www.ilc.csic.es; f. 1984 as Instituto de Filologia, integrated within Centro de Ciencias Humanas y Sociales (CCHS) 2008; studies and edns of texts in ancient languages: Arabic, Hebrew, MSS in oriental languages (Arabic, Coptic, Greek, Hebrew and Latin); library: 1m. vols; Research Prof. Dr MARÍA TERESA ORTEGA MONASTERIO; publs *Al-Qantara* (2

a year), *Emerita* (2 a year), *Sefarad* (2 a year).

Instituto de Politicas y Bienes Publicos (Institute of Public Goods and Policies): c/o Albasanz 26–28, 3D, 28037 Madrid; tel. 916022534; e-mail direccion.ipp@csic.es; internet www.ipp.csic.es; f. 2007; advances knowledge in domain of relationship between the society, the market and the state; Dir LUIS SANZ MENÉNDEZ; publs *Energy*, *Energy Policy*, *Environmental and Resource Economics*, *Journal of the American Society for Information Science and Technology*, *Party Politics*, *Politics & Society*, *Research Policy*, *Scientometrics*, *West European Politics*.

Instituto Histórico Hoffmeyer: Avda de la Constitución 114, 10400 Jaraiz de la Vera (Cáceres); tel. 927170646; e-mail hoffmeyer@iam.csic.es; internet www.hoffmeyer.iam.csic.es; Dir PEDRO MATEOS CRUZ; publ. *Gladius* (1 a year).

Attached Research Institutes in the Field of Biology and Biomedicine:

Centro Andaluz de Biología del Desarrollo: CSIC-Universidad Pablo de Olavide, Carretera de Utrera, Km 1, 41013 Seville; tel. 954349399; internet www.cabd.es; Dir Prof. EDUARDO SANTERO.

Centro Biológica Molecular Severo Ochoa: Calle Nicolás Cabrera 1, Campus de la Universidad Autónoma, 28049 Madrid; tel. 911964401; e-mail institucional@cbm.uam.es; internet www.cbm.uam.es; Dir SANTIAGO LAMAS PELÁEZ.

Centro de Investigación del Cáncer: Campus Miguel de Unamuno, Univ. de Salamanca, 37007 Salamanca; tel. 923294720; e-mail cicancer@usal.es; internet www.cicancer.org; f. 1997; basic, clinical and translational cancer research; Dir Dr EUGENIO SANTOS.

Centro de Investigaciones Biológicas: Ramiro de Maeztu 9, 28040 Madrid; tel. 918373112; e-mail vlarraga@cib.csic.es; internet www.cib.csic.es; Dir MARÍA JESÚS MARTÍNEZ HERNÁNDEZ.

Centro de Investigaciones Científicas Isla de la Cartuja: Avda Americo Vespucio 49, Isla de la Cartuja, 41092 Seville; tel. 954489500; e-mail ciccartuja@ciccartuja.es; internet www.ciccartuja.es; Dir MIGUEL ANGEL DE LA ROSA ACOSTA.

Centro de Investigación y Desarrollo: Carrer de Jordi Girona 18–26, 08034 Barcelona; tel. 934006100; e-mail director@cid.csic.es; internet www.cid.csic.es; f. 1967; library of 30,000 vols; Dir ANGEL MESSEGUER PEYPOCH.

Centro Nacional de Biotecnología (Spanish National Centre for Biotechnology): UAM, Campus del Cantoblanco, 28049 Cantoblanco (Madrid); tel. 915854500; e-mail director.cnb@csic.es; internet www.cnb.uam.es; f. 1992; Dir JOSÉ MARÍA VALPUESTA.

Instituto Biomedicina de Valencia (Institute of Biomedicine of Valencia): Calle Jaime Roig 11, 46010 Valencia; tel. 963391760; e-mail director.ibv@csic.es; internet www.ibv.csic.es; f. 1998; research into structural biology (X-ray crystallography), human molecular genetics, molecular/cell biology related to human disease, venomics, inborn errors of urea cycle, signalling cascades related to AMP kinase and to esteroids, molecular biology, genetics and signalling in type-2 diabetes; Dir Prof. PASCUAL SANZ BIGORRA.

Instituto Cajal: Avda Dr Arce 37, 28002 Madrid; tel. 915854750; e-mail director.incr@csic.es; internet www.cajal.csic.es; f.

1906; neurobiological research; library of 36,000 vols; Dir Ignacio Torres Alemán.

Instituto de Biología Molecular 'Eladio Viñuela': c/o Nicolás Cabrera 1, 28049 Cantoblanco (Madrid); tel. 911964401; e-mail director.ibm@csic.es; f. 1975; Dir César de Haro Castella.

Instituto de Biología Molecular de Barcelona (Molecular Biology Institute of Barcelona): Calle Baldiri Reixac 10–12, 08028 Barcelona; tel. 934034668; e-mail contact@ibmb.csic.es; internet www.ibmb.csic.es; Dir Martí Aldea Malo.

Instituto de Biología Molecular y Celular de Plantas 'Eduardo Primo Yúfera': Ingeniero Fausto Elio s/n, 46022 Valencia; tel. 963877856; e-mail director .ibmcp@csic.es; internet www.ibmcp.upv .es; f. 1994; Dir Prof. Vicente Pallás Benet.

Instituto de Biología y Genética Molecular: Calle Sanz y Fores, s/n, esq. Real de Burgos, 47003 Valladolid; tel. 983184801; e-mail director.ibgm@csic.es; internet www.ibgm.med.uva.es; f. 1998; Dir Jesús Balsinde Rodríguez.

Instituto de Bioquímica Vegetal y Fotosíntesis (Institute of Plant Biochemistry and Photosynthesis): Avda Americo Vespucio s/n, Isla de la Cartuja, 41092 Seville; tel. 954489506; e-mail ibvf@ibvf .csic.es; internet www.ibvf.csic.es; Dir Luis Carlos Romero González.

Instituto de Investigaciones Biomédicas 'Alberto Sols': Calle Arturo Duperier 4, 28029 Madrid; tel. 915854400; e-mail director@iib.uam.es; internet www.iib.uam .es; f. 1973; Dir Jaime Renart.

Instituto de Investigaciones Biomédicas de Barcelona: Calle Rosselló 161, 6–7°, 08036 Barcelona; tel. 933638300; e-mail direccion.iibb@csic.es; internet www.iibb.csic.es; f. 1995; multidisciplinary biomedical research in biochemistry, cell biology, neurosciences, pathophysiology with spec. emphasis on translational research; Dir Dr Cristina Suñol Esquirol.

Instituto de Microbiología Bioquímica: Campus Miguel de Unamuno, Universidad de Salamanca, Edif. Departmental, Avda Campo Charro s/n, 37007 Salamanca; tel. 923294900; e-mail directorimb@usal.es; internet www.imb .usal-csic.es; Dir Dr Angel Durán Bravo.

Instituto de Neurociencias: Apdo de Correos 18, 03550 San Juan (Alicante); tel. 965233700; e-mail in@umh.es; internet in.umh.es; f. 1990, present name and status 1999; Dir Juan Lerma Gómez.

Instituto de Parasitología y Biomedicina 'López Neyra' (Institute of Parasitology and Biomedicine 'López-Neyra'): Parque Tecnológico de Ciencias de la Salud, Avda del Conocimiento s/n, 18100 Armilla (Granada); tel. 958181621; e-mail director.ipbln@csic.es; internet www.ipb .csic.es; Dir Alfredo Berzal Herranz.

Unidad de Biofísica: Apdo 644, 48080 Bilbao; tel. 946012625; e-mail biofisica@lg .ehu.es; internet www.unidaddebiofisica .org; f. 1999; joint centre of the CSIC and the Univ. of the Basque Country; basic research and graduate teaching in biophysics; Head Félix M. Goñi.

Attached Research Institutes in the Field of Natural Resources:

Centro de Ciencias Medioambientales: Calle Serrano 115 bis, 28006 Madrid; tel. 917452500; e-mail director .ccma@csic.es; Dir Alberto Fereres Castiel.

Centro de Edafología y Biología Aplicada del Segura: Campus Universitario de Espinardo, 30100 Murcia; tel. 968396200; e-mail gerente@cebas.csic.es; internet www.cebas.csic.es; Dir Dr Juan José Alarcón Cabañero.

Centro de Estudios Avanzados de Blanes: Cala St Francesc 14, 17300 Blanes (Gerona); tel. 972336101; e-mail info@ceab .csic.es; internet www.ceab.csic.es; Dir Daniel Martín Sintes.

Centro de Investigaciones sobre Desertificación (CIDE) (Desertification Research Centre (CIDE)): Carretera Moncada-Náquera, Km 4, 5 Apdo Oficial 46113 Moncada Valencia; tel. 963424162; e-mail cide@uv.es; internet www.uv.es/cide; f. 1996; Dir Dr Vicente Andreu.

Estación Biológica de Doñana (Doñana Biological Station): Apdo 1056, 41013 Seville; tel. 954232340; e-mail informacion@ebd.csic.es; internet www .ebd.csic.es; f. 1964; wetland ecology, evolutionary and molecular ecology, ecological synthesis, conservation biology (incl. biological invasions) and plant–animal interactions; library of 10,000 vols; Dir Prof. Juan José Negro Balmaseda; publ. *Doñana. Acta Vertebrata* (2 a year).

Estación Experimental de Zonas Áridas: Cuetra de Sacramento s/n, La Cañada de San Urbano, 04120 Almería; tel. 950281045; e-mail director.eeza@csic.es; internet www.eeza.csic.es; f. 1947 as Instituto de Aclimatacion de Almeria, present name 1975; Dir Francisco Valera Hernández.

Instituto Andaluz de Ciencias de la Tierra: Avda de Las Palmeras 4, 18100 Armilla; tel. 958230000; e-mail director .iact@csic.es; internet www.iact.csic.es; f. 1994; devt and support for research activity in the field of earth sciences; strengthens research links with other centres in Spain and abroad; participates in training programmes for postgraduate and postdoctoral research assistants; Dir Dr Alberto López Galindo.

Instituto Botánico de Barcelona (Botanical Institute of Barcelona): Passeig del Migdia, Parque de Monjuïc, 08038 Barcelona; tel. 932890611; e-mail biblioteca@ibb.csic.es; internet www.ibb .bcn-csic.es/institut_cas.html; f. 1917; affiliated to the Botanic Garden of Barcelona, Montjuïc Park; library of 11,000 vols, 80,000 herbarium sheets; Man. Joan Lambea Castro; Head Librarian Karina Barros Ferradás; publ. *Collectanea Botanica* (1 a year).

Instituto de Acuicultura de Torre de la Sal: Calle Ribera de Cabanes s/n, Cabanes, 12595 Castellón; tel. 964319500; e-mail director.iats@csic.es; internet www .iats.csic.es; Dir Juan Carlos Navarro Tárrega.

Instituto de Agroquímica y Tecnología de Alimentos: Avda Agustín Escardino 7, 46980 Paterna (Valencia); tel. 963900022; e-mail info@iata.csic.es; internet www.iata.csic.es; Dir Dra Amparo M. Querol Simón; publ. *Food Science and Technology International* (6 a year).

Instituto de Ciencias de la Tierra 'Jaume Almera' (Institute of Earth Sciences 'Jaume Almera'): Calle Lluis Solé Sabarís, s/n, Apdo 30102, 08028 Barcelona; tel. 934095410; e-mail director.ictja@csic .es; internet www.ija.csic.es; library of 16,500 vols, 1,050 periodicals; Dir Montserrat Torne i Escasany.

Instituto de Ciencias del Mar (Institute of Marine Sciences): Passeig Marítim de la Barceloneta 37–49, 08003 Barcelona; tel. 932309500; e-mail icmdir@icm.csic.es; internet www.icm.csic.es; Dir Albert Palanques Monteys; publ. *Scientia Marina* (4 a year).

Instituto de Ciencias Marinas de Andalucía: Calle República Saharaui 2, Campus Universitario Río San Pedro, 11519 Puerto Real (Cádiz); tel. 956832612; e-mail director.icman@csic.es; internet www.icman.csic.es; f. 1955; Dir María del Carmen Sarasquete Reiriz.

Instituto de Geociencias (Geosciences Institute): Facultad de Ciencias Geológicas, Universidad Complutense, Calle José Antonio Novais, 2, 3ª 28040 Madrid; tel. 913944813; e-mail info@igeo.ucm-csic.es; internet www.igeo.ucm-csic.es; f. 2011 by merger of Instituto de Geología Económica with Instituto de Astronomía y Geodesia; Man. María Isabel Sevillano Navarro; publs *Estudios Geológicos* (online (estudiosgeol.revistas.csic.es/index.php/estudiosgeol)), *Journal of Iberian Geology* (online (www.ucm.es/info/estratig/journal.htm)).

Instituto de Investigación en Recursos Cinegéticos: Ronda de Toledo s/n, 13071 Ciudad Real; tel. 926295450; e-mail irec@irec.uclm.es; internet www.uclm.es/irec; Dir Jorge Cassinello Roldán.

Instituto de Investigaciones Marinas de Vigo: Calle Eduardo Cabello 6, 36208 Vigo (Pontevedra); tel. 986231930; e-mail direccion@iim.csic.es; internet www.iim .csic.es; f. 1951 as Instituto de Investigaciones Pesqueras de Barcelona, present name 1986; Dir Carmen González Sotelo.

Instituto de Productos Naturales y Agrobiología: Avda Astrofísico Francisco Sánchez 3, 38206 La Laguna (Tenerife); tel. 922256847; e-mail info@ipna.csic.es; internet www.ipna.csic.es; f. 1956 as Centro de Edafología y Biología Aplicada de Tenerife, present name 1990; agrobiology, ecology, organic chemistry, volcanology; Dir Dr Cosme García Francisco.

Instituto de Recursos Naturales y Agrobiología de Salamanca: Apdo 257, 37071 Salamanca; Cordel de Merinas 40–52, 37008 Salamanca; tel. 923219606; e-mail divulgacion@irnasa.csic.es; internet www.irnasa.csic.es; f. 1957 as Centro de Edafología y Biología Aplicada de Salamanca, present name 1988; scientific research on agriculture and natural resources; incl. sustainable devt of agriforest systems, animal pathology, environmental degradation and recovery, and plant abiotic stress; Dir Juan Bautista Arellano Martínez.

Instituto de Recursos Naturales y Agrobiología de Sevilla (Institute for Natural Resources and Agrobiology): Apdo 1052, 41080 Seville; Avda Reina Mercedes 10, 41012 Seville; tel. 954624711; e-mail director.irnas@csic.es; internet www .irnase.csic.es; Dir José Manuel Pardo Prieto.

Instituto Mediterraneo de Estudios Avanzados (Mediterranean Institute for Advanced Studies): Calle Miquel Marquès 21, 07190 Esporles, Mallorca; tel. 971611716; e-mail director.imdea@csic.es; internet www.imedea.uib-csic.es; Dir Joaquín Tintoré Subirana.

Instituto Pirenaico de Ecología: Campus de Aula Dei, Avda Montañana 1005, 50059 Zaragoza; tel. 976369393; e-mail director.ipe@csic.es; internet www.ipe.csic .es; f. 1983; Dir Blas Lorenzo Valero Garcés; publ. *Pirineos* (1 a year).

Museo Nacional de Ciencias Naturales: see under Museums and Art Galleries.

Real Jardín Botánico: see under Museums and Art Galleries.

Attached Research Institutes in the Field of Agricultural Sciences:

Estación Experimental de Aula Dei: Avda Montañana 1005, 50059 Zaragoza; tel. 976716100; e-mail director.eead@csic .es; internet www.eead.csic.es; f. 1944; library of 9,802 vols of book titles, 190,000 e-books, 1,804 journals, 13,000 electronic journals; Dir Jesús Val Falcón.

Estación Experimental del Zaidín: Apdo 419, 18008 Granada; Calle Professor Albareda 1, 18008 Granada; tel. 958181600; e-mail director.eez@csic.es; internet www.eez.csic.es; library of 4,000 vols, 300 periodicals; Dir Nicolás Toro García.

Estación Experimental 'La Mayora': 29760 Algarrobo-Costa, (Málaga); tel. 952548990; e-mail director.eelm@csic.es; internet www.eelm.csic.es; f. 1968; agronomy, horticulture, pomology, virology, mycology, plant tissue culture; library of 3,000 vols; Dir Enrique Moriones Alonso.

Instituto de Agricultura Sostenible (Institute for Sustainable Agriculture): Alameda del Obispo, s/n, Apdo 4084, 14080 Córdoba; tel. 957499200; e-mail gerente.ias@csic.es; internet www.ias.csic .es; f. 1992; Dir José Alfonso Gómez Calero.

Instituto de Agrobiotecnología: Universidad Pública de Navarra, Campus de Arrosadia, 31192 Navarra; tel. 948168000; e-mail info@agrobiotecnologia.es; internet www.agrobiotecnologia.es; f. 1999 as Instituto de Agrobiotecnología y Recursos Naturales, present name 2004; Dir Iñigo Lasa.

Instituto de Ganadería de Montaña: Finca Marzanas s/n, 24346 Grulleros, (León); tel. 987317064; e-mail director .eae@csic.es; internet www.igm.ule-csic.es; Dir Dr Francisco Javier Giráldez García.

Instituto de Investigaciones Agrobiológicas de Galicia: Avda de Vigo s/n, Apdo 122, 15780 Santiago de Compostela (La Coruña); tel. 981590958; e-mail direccion.mbg@csic.es; internet www.iiag .csic.es; library of 3,000 vols, 279 periodicals; Dir María Tarsy Carballas Fernández.

Misión Biológica de Galicia: Apdo 28, 36080 Pontevedra; El Palacio, Salcedo, 36143 Pontevedra; tel. 986854800; e-mail director.mbg@csic.es; internet www.mbg .csic.es; Dir Dr Pedro Revilla Temiño.

Attached Research Institutes in the Field of Physical Science and Technology:

Centro de Tecnologías Físicas 'Leonardo Torres Quevedo': Calle Serrano 144, 28006 Madrid; tel. 915618806; e-mail director.cetef@csic.es; internet www.cetef .csic.es; Dir Dra Alicia Pons Aglio.

Centro Física 'Miguel Antonio Catalán': Calle Serrano 121, 28006 Madrid; tel. 915616800; e-mail informatica@cfmac.csic .es; internet www.cfmac.csic.es; f. 1994; Dir Joaquín Campos Acosta.

Centro Nacional de Microelectrónica (National Microelectronics Center): Campus Universidad Autónoma, 08193 Bellaterra (Barcelona); tel. 935947700; e-mail info@cnm.es; internet www.cnm.es; f. 1986; research and devt of micro- and nanoelectronics; Dir Francisco Serra Mestres.

Centro Técnico de Informática: Calle Pinar 19, 28006 Madrid; tel. 915642963;

e-mail director.cti@csic.es; internet www .cti.csic.es; Dir José Carrero Vivas.

Instituto de Astrofísica de Andalucía: Apdo 3004, 18008 Granada; Glorieta de la Astronomía s/n, 18008 Granada; tel. 958121311; e-mail director.iaa@csic.es; internet www.iaa.es; Dir José Manuel Vílchez Medina; Librarian M. Angeles Arco Sarmiento.

Instituto de Estructura de la Materia: Calle Serrano 121, 28006 Madrid; tel. 915616800; e-mail director.iem@csic.es; internet www.iem.csic.es; f. 1976; Dir Dr Guillermo Antonio Mena Marugán.

Instituto de Física Corpuscular: Edificio Institutos de Investigación, Apdo 22085, 46071 Valencia; tel. 963543473; e-mail director.ific@csic.es; internet ific.uv .es; Dir Francisco J. Botella Olcina.

Instituto de Física de Cantabria: Edificio Juan Jorda, Avda de los Castros s/n, 39005 Santander; tel. 942201459; e-mail info@ifca.unican.es; internet www.ifca.es; Dir Enrique Martinez Gonzalez.

Instituto de Física Fundamental: Calle Serrano 113–123, 28006 Madrid; tel. 915616800; e-mail director.iff@csic.es; internet www.iff.csic.es; f. 1992, present name 2009; scientific research in basic physics: theoretical physics of molecules, cluster and extended media, quantum information, dark energy, probabilistic logical inference, physical modelling and entropy, radiation–matter interactions; Dir Dr Gerardo Delgado Barrio.

Instituto de Investigación de Inteligencia Artificial (Artificial Intelligence Research Institute): Campus UAB, 08193 Bellaterra (Barcelona); tel. 935809570; e-mail director.iiia@csic.es; internet www .iiia.csic.es; f. 1991; research and devt in Artificial Intelligence (multiagent systems, machine learning, case-based reasoning, data privacy, logic foundations of ai, automated reasoning, search, constraints satisfaction; models of trust and reputation, negotiation algorithms, autonomous and developmental robotics); library of 3,000 vols; Dir Prof. Ramon López de Mántaras; publ. *Transactions on Data Privacy* (online (www.tdp.cat)).

Instituto de Microelectrónica de Barcelona: Campus Universidad Autónoma de Barcelona, 08193 Cerdanyola del Valles, (Barcelona); tel. 935947700; e-mail director .imb-cnm@csic.es; internet www.imb-cnm .csic.es; f. 1985; Dir Prof. Carles Cane.

Instituto de Microelectrónica de Madrid: Calle Isaac Newton 8, Tres Cantos, 28760 Madrid; tel. 918060700; e-mail director.imm-cnm@csic.es; internet www.imm-cnm.csic.es; Dir Prof. Luis González Sotos.

Instituto de Microelectrónica de Sevilla: Calle Américo Vespucio s/n, 41092 Seville; tel. 954466666; e-mail direccion.ims-cnm@csic.es; internet www .imse-cnm.csic.es; f. 1996; Dir Dr Santiago Sánchez Solano.

Instituto de Óptica 'Daza de Valdés': Calle Serrano 121, 28006 Madrid; tel. 915616800; e-mail director.io@csic.es; internet www.io.csic.es; f. 1946; research in visual optics, biophotonics, image science, non-linear dynamics, fibre optics, nanophotonics, plasmonics, photonics with high energy ions, photonics and nanostructures and ultrafast science, thin-films optics, radiometry and photometry; Dir Joaquin Campos Acosta.

Instituto de Robótica e Informática Industrial: Calle Llorens i Artiges 4–6, 2°, Parc Tecnològic de Barcelona, 08028 Bar-

celona; tel. 934015751; e-mail admin-iri@ iri.upc.edu; internet www.iri.upc.edu; Dir Alberto Sanfeliu.

Instituto de Seguridad de la Información (Information Security Institute): Calle Serrano 144, 28006 Madrid; tel. 915618806; e-mail info@isi.csic.es; internet www.ifa.csic.es; f. 2011; Dir Luis Hernández Encinas.

Observatorio Física Cósmica de l'Ebro: Horta Alta 38, Apdo 10, 43520 Roquetas (Tarragona); tel. 977500511; e-mail biblioteca@obsebre.es; internet www.obsebre.es; f. 1904; sections: geomagnetism, ionosphere, seismology, meteorology, climate and solar activity; library of 50,000 vols, 2,100 periodicals; Dir Dr Juan José Curto.

Attached Research Institutes in the Field of Materials Science and Technology:

Centro de Física de Materiales (Center of Materials Physics): P. Manuel de Lardizabal 5, 20018 Donostia, San Sebastián; tel. 943018786; e-mail rdm@ehu.es; internet cfm.ehu.es; Dir Ricardo Díez Muiño.

Centro Nacional de Investigaciones Metalúrgicas (National Center for Metallurgical Research): Avda Gregorio del Amo 8, 28040 Madrid; tel. 915538900; e-mail director.cenim@csic.es; internet www .cenim.csic.es; f. 1964; metallurgical research, steel research, new materials, composites, recycling of metals; library of 20,000 vols; Dir Manuel Carsí Cebrián; publ. *Revista de Metalurgia* (6 a year).

Instituto de Cerámica y Vidrio: Calle Kelsen 5, 28049 Madrid; tel. 917355840; e-mail director.icv@csic.es; internet www .icv.csic.es; Dir Dr Antonio Javier Sánchez-Herencia.

Instituto de Ciencia de Materiales de Aragón: Facultad San Ciencias, CSIC—Universidad de Zaragoza, Pl. de San Francisco s/n, 50009 Zaragoza; tel. 976761231; e-mail direccion.icma@csic.es; internet www.icma.unizar-csic.es; f. 1985; Dir Jesús Javier Campo Ruiz.

Instituto de Ciencia de Materiales de Barcelona: Campus Universidad Autónoma, 08193 Cerdanyola del Valles, (Barcelona); tel. 935801853; e-mail info@icmab .es; internet www.icmab.es; Dir Xavier Obradors Berenguer.

Instituto de Ciencia de Materiales de Madrid: Sor Juana Inés de la Cruz 3, 28049 Madrid; tel. 913349000; e-mail direccion.icmm@csic.es; internet www .icmm.csic.es; f. 1986 by merger of 3 centres: Institute of Materials Physics, Solid State Physics Institute and Mineral Physics-Chemistry Institute; personnel from the Inorganic Chemistry 'Elhuyar' Institute joined the ICMM 1987; research in material science, aiming at multidisciplinary character and covering theoretical and experimental, basic and applied aspects; Dir Prof. Federico Jesús Soria Gallego.

Instituto de Ciencia de Materiales de Sevilla: CSIC—Universidad de Sevilla, Americo Vespucio s/n, Isla de la Cartuja, 41092 Seville; tel. 954489527; e-mail buzon@icmse.csic.es; internet www.icms .us-csic.es; Dir Alfonso Caballero Martínez.

Instituto de Ciencia y Tecnología de Polímeros: Calle Juan de la Cierva 3, 28006 Madrid; tel. 915622900; e-mail director.ictp@csic.es; internet www.ictp .csic.es; library of 2,000 vols, 40 periodicals; Dir Dr Daniel López García.

Instituto de Ciencias de la Construccíon 'Eduardo Torroja' (Eduardo Torroja Institute for Construction Science): Calle Serrano Galvache 4, 28033 Madrid; tel. 913020440; e-mail director.ietcc@csic .es; internet www.ietcc.csic.es; Dir ÁNGEL ARTEAGA; publs *Informes de la Construcción* (6 a year), *Materiales de la Construcción* (4 a year).

Attached Research Institutes in the Field of Food Science and Technology:

Instituto de Fermentaciones Industriales: Calle Juan de la Cierva 3, 28006 Madrid; tel. 915622900; e-mail director .ifi@csic.es; internet www.ifi.csic.es; f. 1967; research in food science and technology; participation in research projects and contracts with companies, nat. and int. confs, scientific symposia; teaching doctorate courses in univs, undergraduate and dipl. courses, masters courses and training teachers for technical college; Dir Dra LOURDES AMIGO GARRIDO.

Instituto de la Grasa: Avda Padre García Tejero 4, 41012 Seville; tel. 954611550; e-mail director.ig@csic.es; internet www.ig .csic.es; Dir Dr RAFAEL GARCÉS; publ. *Grasas y Aceites* (6 a year).

Instituto de Nutrición y Bromatología: CSIC—Universidad Complutense, Facultad de Farmacia, Cdad Universitaria, 28040 Madrid; tel. 915490038; e-mail director.inb@csic.es; Dir ASCENSIÓN MARCOS SÁNCHEZ.

Instituto de Productos Lácteos de Asturias: Ctra de Infiesto s/n, 33300 Villaviciosa (Oviedo); tel. 985892131; e-mail direccion.ipla@csic.es; internet www.ipla.csic.es; Dir CLARA GONZÁLEZ DE LOS REYES-GAVILÁN.

Instituto del Frío: Calle José Antonio Novais 10, 28040 Madrid; tel. 915492300; e-mail director.if@csic.es; internet www.if .csic.es; Dir M. P. MONTERO GARCÍA.

Attached Research Institutes in the Field of Chemical Science and Technology:

Centro de Química Orgánica 'Lora Tamayo': Juan de la Cierva 3, 28006 Madrid; tel. 915622900; e-mail director .cenquior@csic.es; internet www.cenquior .csic.es; Dir MARÍ JESÚS PÉREZ PÉREZ.

Instituto de Carboquímica: Miguel Luesma Castán 5, 50018 Zaragoza; tel. 976733977; e-mail director@icb.csic.es; internet www.icb.csic.es; Dir RAFAEL MOLINER ALVAREZ; publ. *Memoria Científica* (every 2 years).

Instituto de Catálisis y Petroleoquímica (Institute of Catalysis and Petrochemistry): Calle Marie Curie 2, 28049 Cantoblanco (Madrid); tel. 915854800; e-mail director.icp@csic.es; internet www .icp.csic.es; Dir JOAQUÍN PÉREZ PARIENTE.

Instituto de Investigaciones Químicas: Calle Americo Vespucio 49, Isla de la Cartuaja, 41092 Seville; tel. 954489553; e-mail director.iiq@csic.es; internet www.iiq.cartuja.csic.es; Dir JOSÉ MANUEL GARCÍA FERNÁNDEZ.

Institut de Química Avançada de Catalunya (Institute of Advanced Chemistry of Catalonia): Calle Jordi Girona 18–26, 08034 Barcelona; tel. 934006100; e-mail director.cid@csic.es; internet www.iqac .csic.es; Dir RAMON ERITJA CASADELLÀ.

Instituto de Química Física 'Rocasolano' (Institute of Physical Chemistry 'Rocasolano'): Calle Serrano 119, 28006 Madrid; tel. 915619400; e-mail director .iqfr@csic.es; internet www.iqfr.csic.es; f. 1946; research in structural biology, functional biophysics, chemical kinetics and

reactivity, computational chemistry and physics, laser design and applications, surface structure and chemistry, materials science and nanotechnology, molecular basis of biological processes; Dir JUAN DE LA FIGUERA BAYÓN.

Instituto de Química Médica: Calle Juan de la Cierva 3, 28006 Madrid; tel. 915622900; e-mail direccion.iqm@csic.es; internet www.iqm.csic.es; f. 1973; design and synthesis of potential new drugs in different therapuetic areas; new chemical entities as tools for the identification of novel therapeutic targets; computational chemistry and molecular modeling; training of postgraduate students; Dir Dra MARIA-JESUS PEREZ-PEREZ.

Instituto de Química Orgánica General (Institute of General Organic Chemistry): Calle Juan de la Cierva 3, 28006 Madrid; tel. 915622900; e-mail director .iqog@csic.es; internet www.iqog.csic.es; f. 1966; research in organic chemistry and related fields, incl. organic synthesis, physical organic chemistry, environmental chemistry, analytical chemistry of organic compounds, carbohydrate chemistry, bioorganic chemistry, biocatalysis, enzyme technology, peptides, proteins, computational chemistry, computational toxicology; library of 3,000 vols; Dir Dr EDUARDO GARCÍA-JUNCEDA.

Instituto de Tecnología Química: CSIC-Universidad Politécnica, Avda de los Naranjos s/n, 46022 Valencia; tel. 963877800; e-mail itq@itq.upv.es; internet itq.upv-csic.es; Dir Prof. MIGUEL ÁNGEL MIRANDA ALONSO.

Instituto Nacional del Carbón: Calle Francisco Pintado Fe 26, 33080 Oviedo; tel. 985119090; e-mail director.incar@csic.es; internet www.incar.csic.es; f. 1947; Dir Dr JUAN MANUEL DÍEZ TASCÓN.

Laboratorio de Investigación en Fluidodinámica y Tecnologías de la Combustión (Laboratory for Research in Fluid Dynamics and Combustion Technologies): Calle María de Luna 10, 50018 Zaragoza; tel. 976506520; e-mail litec@litec.csic.es; internet www.litec.csic.es; f. 1991; research in combustion and fluid mechanics; Dir Dr LUIS VALIÑO GARCÍA.

Fundació Catalana per a la Recerca i la Innovació (FCRI) (Catalan Foundation for Research and Innovation): Pg Lluís Companys 23, 08010 Barcelona; tel. 932687700; e-mail info@fundaciorecerca.cat; internet www.fundaciorecerca.cat; f. 1986; promotes social recognition of scientific and technological research; Pres. ANTONI ESTEVE I CRUELLA; Dir ENRIC CLAVEROL TINTURÉ; publ. *Tecno 2000* (12 a year).

Institut d'Estudis Internacionals i Interculturals (Institute for International and Intercultural Studies): Edifici E1, 08193 Bellaterra, Barcelona; tel. 935812111; e-mail ce.internacionals@uab.es; attached to Universitat Autònoma de Barcelona; Dir SEÁN GOLDEN.

Instituto CEU de Humanidades Ángel Ayala: Calle Juan XXIII 8, 28040 Madrid; tel. 914568406; e-mail ihuman@ceu.es; internet www.angelayala.ceu.es; attached to Fundación Universitaria San Pablo CEU; research within the field of the humanities, specifically in the areas of art, history, literature, social doctrine of the Church, thought and philosophy, humanistic aspects of the natural sciences; Dir JOSÉ PEÑA GONZÁLEZ; publ. *Nuntium*.

Instituto de Relaciones Europeo-Latinoamericanas (IRELA) (Institute for European-Latin American Relations): Apdo

2600, 28002 Madrid; Calle Pedro de Valdivia 10, 28006 Madrid; tel. 915617200; e-mail info@irela.org; f. 1984; organizes confs for European and Latin American officials, diplomats, journalists, politicians, businessmen, trade unionists; academics on different aspects of European-Latin American relations; specific research, collection and systematization of information on relations between the 2 regions; advisory activities for regional instns in Europe and Latin America; Dir WOLF GRABENDORFF.

Instituto Interuniversitario de Estudios de Iberoamérica y Portugal (Inter-University Institute of Latin American and Portuguese Studies): Casa del Tratado, 47100 Tordesillas; tel. 983771806; e-mail ieip@uva.es; attached to Universidad de Valladolid; Dir FELIPE CANO TORRES.

Instituto Universitario de Desarrollo Regional (Regional Development Institute): Universidad de Granada, Edificio Centro de Documentación Científica, c/o Rector López Argüeta s/n, 18071 Granada; tel. 958243083; e-mail idr@ugr.es; internet fccee2.ugr.es/ desarrollo_regional; attached to Universidad de Granada; organizes specialized teaching; research on issues related to regional and local devt; Dir YOLANDA JIMÉNEZ OLIVENCIA; Sec. JOSÉ ANTONIO CAMACHO BALLESTA.

AGRICULTURE, FISHERIES AND VETERINARY SCIENCE

Centro de Investigación Ecológica y Aplicaciones Forestales (Centre for Ecological Research and Forestry Applications): Edifici C, Campus de Bellaterra (UAB), 08193 Cerdanyola del Vallès Barcelona; tel. 935811312; e-mail ibec0@uab.es; internet www.creaf.uab.es; f. 1987; attached to Universidad de Barcelona; basic and applied research in territorial ecology to improve environmental planning and management in rural and urban areas; Dir JAVIER RETANA.

Instituto Nacional de Investigación y Tecnología Agraria y Alimentaria (INIA) (National Institute for Agricultural and Food Research and Technology): Carretera de la Coruña, Km 7.5, 28040 Madrid; tel. 913473900; e-mail direccion@inia.es; internet www.inia.es; f. 1971 as Nat. Institute for Agricultural Research, present name 1991; research on animal production and health, environment, food quality and safety, forestry, plant production and protection; library of 40,000 vols, 5,000 periodicals; Dir Dr MANUEL LAINEZ-ANDRÉS; Sec.-Gen. PILAR GAITÓN-ESTEBAN; publs *Forest Systems* (3 a year, in English), *Spanish Journal of Agricultural Research* (4 a year, in English).

ECONOMICS, LAW AND POLITICS

Centro de Investigaciones Sociológicas: Montalbán 8, 28014 Madrid; tel. 915807600; e-mail cis@cis.es; internet www.cis.es; f. 1977; assigned to govt Min. of the Presidency; promotes research in social sciences, arranges courses and seminars, collaborates with similar nat. and int. orgs, creates databases for relevant material; library of 30,000 vols, 720 periodicals; Pres. FÉLIX REQUENA SANTOS; publs *Clásicos Contemporáneos, Clásicos del Pensamiento Social, Cuadernos Metodológicos* (4 a year), *Revista Española de Investigaciones Sociológicas* (4 a year).

Escuela Superior de Gestión Comercial y Marketing (ESIC) (Business and Marketing School (ESIC)): Avda Valdenigrales, 28223 Madrid; tel. 914524100; e-mail info .madrid@esic.es; internet www.esic.es; f. 1965; attached to Universidad Rey Juan Carlos; scientific and technical research on business management and marketing; training of professionals at any level, focusing on the field of marketing both domestically and internationally; library of 16,000 vols, 150 periodicals; Dir-Gen. SIMÓN REYES MARTÍNEZ CÓRDOVA; publ. *Revista Española de Investigación de Marketing ESIC* (2 a year).

Instituto Andaluz Interuniversitario de Criminología (Interuniversity Andalusian Institute of Criminology): Sección Universidad de Granada, Edificio Centro de Documentación Científica, Calle Rector López Argüeta s/n, 18071 Granada; tel. 958243150; e-mail criminol@ugr.es; internet www.ugr.es/~criminol; attached to Universidad de Granada; coordinates, conducts and promotes scientific research in criminology; organizes postgraduate teaching programmes; Dir Prof. Dr LORENZO MORILLAS CUEVA; Sec. Prof. Dr JESÚS BARQUÍN SANZ.

Instituto Complutense de Análisis Económico (Complutense Institute of Economic Analysis): Facultad de Ciencias Económicas, Campus de Somosaguas, 28223 Madrid; tel. 913942611; e-mail icaesec@ccee.ucm.es; internet www.ucm.es/icae; attached to Universidad Complutense de Madrid; basic and applied research; situation analysis; doctoral programmes in economics, quantitative finance; Masters in economic analysis and financial economics; organizes courses and confs; Dir JESÚS RUIZ ANDÚJAR; Sec. JUAN ÁNGEL JIMÉNEZ MARTÍN.

Instituto de Análisis Industrial y Financiero (Institute of Industrial and Financial Analysis): Facultad de Ciencias Económicas y Empresariales, Pabellón Central, 1ª Planta, Campus de Somosaguas, 28223 Madrid; tel. 913942456; e-mail infocom@ucm.es; internet www.ucm.es/bucm/cee/iaif; f. 1990; attached to Universidad Complutense de Madrid; manages and promotes applied research in the fields of industrial economics and financial economics; industrial devt, internationalization of production activities, technological change; Dir JOZEF JOHANES HENDRIKUS HEIJS; Sec. ELENA GALLEGO ABAROA.

Instituto de Derecho Público (Institute of Public Law): Campus de Vicálvaro, Edificio Departamental, Despacho 109, Paseo de los Artilleros, 28032 Madrid; tel. 914887872; e-mail instituto.dp@urjc.es; internet www .idp-urjc.com; f. 2001; attached to Universidad Rey Juan Carlos; centre for research and teaching; arbitration, comparative law, comparative local, urban and metropolitan politics, constitutional jurisdiction, constitutional and statutory reform, financial regulation and supervision, fundamental right to education, gender, history of constitutionalism, immigration, labour law, legal tax, terrorism and rule of law; Dir Prof. ENRIQUE ÁLVAREZ CONDE; publs *Boletín de Derecho Deportivo, Revista Europea de Derechos Fundamentales, Revista General de Derecho Público Comparado.*

Instituto de Estudios de la Democracia (Institute of Democratic Studies): Calle Julián Romea 23, 28003 Madrid; tel. 914566311; e-mail id@ceu.es; internet www .uspceu.com/cntbnr/sitio_id/id_index.htm; attached to Universidad CEU San Pablo; promotes research in the field of social sciences, postgraduate training and research; centres of int. observatory of victims of terrorism, political economy and regulation, religious information studies, Spanish democratic transition studies; Pres. JOSÉ MANUEL OTERO NOVAS; Dir Dr LUIS NÚÑEZ LADEVÉZE; publ. *Revista DOXA.*

Instituto de Estudios Europeos y Derechos Humanos (Institute of European Studies and Human Rights): Universidad Pontificia de Salamanca, Calle Compañía 5, 37002 Salamanca; tel. 923277142; e-mail

europa@upsa.es; internet www.upsa.es/ facultades/facultadesycentros/europeos/ficha .php; f. 1981; research, discussion and teaching on EU and human rights; multidisciplinary training; organizes confs and seminars; Dir Dr ANGEL LOSADA VÁZQUEZ.

Instituto de Estudios Fiscales (Institute of Fiscal Studies): Avda Cardenal Herrera Oria 378, 28035 Madrid; tel. 913398800; e-mail informacion@ief.minhap.es; internet www.ief.es; f. 2000; attached to Min. of the Economy; research, economic and legal study and consultation in matters relating to public income and expenditure, impact on the economic and social system, analysis and exploitation of tax statistics; library of 80,000 vols; Dir-Gen. JOSÉ ANTONIO MARTÍNEZ ÁLVAREZ; publs *Crónica Tributaria* (4 a year), *Cuadernos de Formación, Foro Fiscal Iberoamericano, Hacienda Pública Española* (Review of Public Economics, 4 a year), *Presupuesto y Gasto Público* (3 a year).

Instituto García Oviedo: Facultad de Derecho, Avda Enramadilla 18–20, 41018 Seville; tel. 954551226; e-mail instgarciaov@ us.es; internet iugo.us.es; f. 1954; attached to Universidad de Sevilla; applied research in the field of public law, with focus on admin. law; organizes training; Dir CONCEPCIÓN BARRERO RODRÍGUEZ; Sec. ROBERTO GALÁN VIOQUE.

Instituto Universitario de Estudios Europeos: Instituto del Valle 21, 28003 Madrid; tel. 915140422; e-mail idee@ceu.es; internet www.idee.ceu.es; f. 1999; attached to Universidad CEU San Pablo; research within the field of European integration and other areas pertaining to int. relations; Dir Dr JOSÉ MARÍA BENEYTO PÉREZ.

Instituto Valenciano de Investigaciones Económicas (Valencian Institute of Economic Research): Calle Guardia Civil 22 esc. 2 1º, 46020 Valencia; tel. 963190050; e-mail ivie@ivie.es; internet www.ivie.es; f. 1990; develops, fosters and projects economic research at nat. and int. level; creates databases; promotes devt of collaboration networks; Man. Dir GERMÁN MOLINA PARDO; Research Dir FRANCISCO PÉREZ GARCÍA.

L. R. Klein—Centro Stone: Facultad de CC. EE. y EE, Módulo E-XIV, 28049 Madrid; tel. 914978670; e-mail klein.stone@uam.es; internet www.uam.es/klein/stone; f. 1999 as 'Lawrence R. Klein' Instituto de Predicción Económica, present name 2002; attached to Universidad Autónoma de Madrid; analysis, assessment and prediction of the Spanish economy; Dir ANTONIO PULIDO SAN ROMÁN; publ. *Hispalink* (online).

EDUCATION

Centro Nacional de Innovación e Investigación Educativa (National Centre for Educational Research and Innovation): Calle General Oraá 55, 28006 Madrid; tel. 917459400; e-mail ifiie@educacion.es; internet www.educacion.gob.es/cniie; f. 1983; attached to Min. of Education, Culture and Sport; conducts and coordinates educational research on improving school success, guidance and support to schools, qualifications framework, basic skills, intercultural education, education and gender, education and media, innovation programmes; organizes teacher-training activities; library of 85,000 vols; Dir MARÍA RODRIGUEZ; publs *Boletín, Revista de Educación.*

Institut de Ciències de l'Educació (Institute of Education Sciences): Edifici A, Bellaterra, 08193 Barcelona; tel. 935811708; e-mail ga.ice@uab.cat; internet www.uab .cat/ice; attached to Universitat Autònoma de Barcelona; Dir NEUS SANMARTÍ PUIG.

Institut de Ciències de l'Educació (Institute of Education Sciences): Carretera de Valls, 43007 Tarragona; tel. 977558071; e-mail gesice@urv.cat; internet www.ice.urv .cat; f. 1991; attached to Universitat Rovira i Virgili; promotes and conducts educational research to assist the technical staff and structure of the univ.; organizes courses for training teachers; Dir ANGEL-PÍO GONZÁLEZ SOTO.

Institut de Ciències de l'Educació Josep Pallach (Josep Pallach Institute of Education Sciences): Castell de Peralada 14 Baixos, 17071 Girona; tel. 972418702; e-mail ice@udg .edu; internet www.udg.edu/ice; f. 2002; attached to Universitat de Girona; trains academic staff at all levels in order to improve quality of education at univ. level; Dir RAFAEL GARCÍA CAMPOS.

Institut de Creativitat i Innovació Educatives (Institute of Creativity and Educational Innovation): Avda Blasco Ibáñez 32, 46010 Valencia; tel. 963864031; e-mail iucie@ uv.es; internet www.uv.es/icie; f. 1978; attached to Universidad de Valencia; basic and applied research in the field of education and aesthetics; promotes scientific partnerships with other orgs and instns to meet social demands in research and academic activity; Dir RICARD RAMON HUERTA; publ. *EARI* (print and online, www.revistaeari.org).

Instituto de Ciencias de la Educación (Institute of Education Sciences): Universidad Pontificia de Salamanca, Calle Compañía 5, 37002 Salamanca; tel. 923277140; e-mail ice@upsa.es; internet www.upsa.es/ facultades/facultadesycentros/ice/ficha.php; f. 1974; attached to Universidad Pontificia de Salamanca; trains teachers at all levels and in all contexts; technical research; promotes education and generates innovation and excellence in teaching; Dir Dr JESÚS GARCÍA ARROYO.

HISTORY, GEOGRAPHY AND ARCHAEOLOGY

Centre d'Estudis del Patrimoni Arqueològic de La Prehistòria (Centre for the Study of the Archaeological Heritage of Prehistory): Edifici B, Bellaterra, 08193 Barcelona; tel. 935813705; e-mail cepap@uab.cat; internet cepap.uab.cat; attached to Universitat Autònoma de Barcelona; Dir Prof. RAFAEL MORA TORCAL; publ. *Treballs d'Arqueologia* (1 a year, in Catalan, English, French and Spanish).

Centro de Documentación y Estudios para la Historia de Madrid (Centre of Documentation and Studies on the History of Madrid): Facultad de Formación del Profesorado, Despacho 215, Campus de Cantoblanco, 28049 Madrid; tel. 914974201; e-mail director.cdhm@uam.es; internet www.uam .es/otroscentros/historiamadrid; f. 1989; attached to Universidad Autónoma de Madrid; Dir VIRGILIO PINTO CRESPO.

Instituto del Patrimonio Cultural de España (Institute of Cultural Heritage of Spain): Calle Pintor El Greco 4, Ciudad Universitaria, 28040 Madrid; tel. 915504400; e-mail subdireccion.ipce@mecd .es; internet ipce.mcu.es; f. 1985 as Instituto de Conservación y Restauración de Bienes Culturales, present name 2008; attached to Min. of Education, Culture and Sport; researches, conserves and restores cultural heritage; research work in areas of applied sciences, archaeology, art history, ethnology, literature, restoration; photographic archive of 500,000 images; library of 40,000 vols, 1,600 periodicals; Dir-Gen. ALFONSO MUÑOS; publs *Informes y Trabajos* (2 a year), *Patrimonio Cultural de España* (in English and

Spanish), *Revista Bienes Culturales, Revista Patrimonio Cultural de España*.

Instituto Feijoo del Siglo XVIII (Feijoo Institute of Eighteenth-Century Studies): Calle Teniente Alfonso Martínez, Campus de Humanidades, Universidad de Oviedo, 33011 Oviedo; tel. 985104671; e-mail admifes@uniovi.es; internet www.ifesxviii.es; f. 1972 as Centro de Estudios del Siglo XVIII, present name 1987; attached to Universidad de Oviedo; develops research programmes related to Spain and Latin America in the 18th century; organizes related courses, confs, seminars, symposia; promotes scientific publs; library of 10,000 vols, 110 periodicals; Dir Prof. ÁLVARO RUIZ DE LA PEÑA SOLAR; publs *Bibliografía Dieciochista, Boletín del Centro de Estudios del Siglo XVIII* (1 a year), *Cuadernos de Estudios del Siglo XVIII* (1 a year), *Cuadernos de la Cátedra Feijoo*.

Instituto Universitario de Historia Simancas (Simancas Institute of History): Real de Burgos, Casa del Alcaide, 47011 Valladolid; tel. 983423527; e-mail simancas@uva.es; internet www.uva.es/simancas; f. 1988; attached to Universidad de Valladolid; promotes research and specialized teaching of history; areas of economic history, medieval history, modern history; postgraduate programmes; organizes confs, seminars, panel discussions, debates; training for researchers and archivists; library of 291,385 vols, 1,634 journals; Dir Dr MARÍA ISABEL DEL VAL VALDIVIESO; Sec. Dr HILARIO CASADO ALONSO.

LANGUAGE AND LITERATURE

Centro de Investigaciones Lingüísticas (Centre of Linguistics Research): Paseo Rector Esperabé 47, 37008 Salamanca; tel. 923294400; e-mail cilus@usal.es; internet www.usal.es/cilus; f. 1995; attached to Universidad de Salamanca; promotes and disseminates research on Spanish language; training and devt of qualified professionals; Dir JESÚS MARIA MANCHO DUQUE.

Institut de Llengua i Cultura Catalanes (Institute of Catalan Language and Culture): Plaça Ferrater Mora 1, 17071 Girona; tel. 972418231; e-mail ilcc@udg.edu; internet www.udg.edu/ilcc; f. 1986; attached to Universitat de Girona; conducts research on history of Catalan language, medieval, modern and contemporary literature, works of Francesc Eiximenis, Occitan language and literature, literary journalism, humanism and literature; library of 7,000 vols; Dir Dr SADURNÍ MARTÍ; Sec. Dr NARCÍS IGLÉSIAS; publs *Editorial collections, Mot so razo, Qüern*.

MEDICINE

Centro Público de Educación Especial María Soriano (Public Centre For Special Educational Needs): Avda de la Peseta 30, 28054 Madrid; tel. 914624600; e-mail cpee.mariasoriano.madrid@educa.madrid.org; internet www.educa.madrid.org/cpee.mariasoriano.madrid; f. 1922; Dir JULIÁN PALACIOS SÁNCHEZ.

Escuela Nacional de Medicina del Trabajo (National School of Occupational Medicine): Pabellón 8, Facultad de Medicina, Ciudad Universitaria, 28040 Madrid; tel. 918224012; e-mail secretaria.enmt@isciii.es; internet www.isciii.es/isciii/es/contenidos/fd-formacion/escuela-nacional-medicina-trabajo.shtml; f. 1948; attached to Insituto de Salud Carlos III; Dir JERÓNIMO MAQUEDA BLASCO; publ. *Medicina y Seguridad del Trabajo* (4 a year, print and online).

Institut de Recerca Biomèdica de Lleida (Biomedical Research Institute of Lleida): Avda Alcalde Rovira Roure 80, 25198 Lleida; tel. 973702201; e-mail info@irblleida.cat; internet www.irblleida.org; f. 2004; attached to Univ. of Lleida; advances biomedical research to improve and facilitate optimal health care activity and coverage; Dir Dr XAVIER MATIAS-GUIU.

Institut Universitari d'Investigació en Ciències de la Salut (University Institute of Research in Health Sciences): Km Carretera de Valldemossa, Universitat de les Illes Balears, 07122 Palma de Mallorca; tel. 971173257; internet www.iunics.es; attached to Universitat de les Illes Balears; promotes scientific and technological research in health sciences in the Balearic Islands; Dir Dr FELIX GRASES.

Instituto de Bioingeniería (Institute of Bioengineering): Universidad Miguel Hernández de Elche, Avda de la Universidad, 03202 Elche; tel. 966658817; e-mail bioingenieria@umh.es; internet bioingenieria.umh.es; attached to Universidad Miguel Hernández; research in biochemistry and cell therapy, biomaterials, cells and tissues engineering, cellular physiology and nutrition, chemical safety and toxicology, genetics, molecular design and synthesis, pharmacology and clinical trial, visual rehabilitation and neuroprotesis; Dir EUGENIO VILANOVA GISBERT.

Instituto de Biología Molecular y Celular (Institute of Molecular and Cellular Biology): Edificio Torregaitán, Universidad Miguel Hernández de Elche, Avda de la Universidad, 03202 Alicante; tel. 966658759; e-mail biomolcel@umh.es; internet ibmc.umh.es; f. 2002 as Instituto Universitario de Investigación; attached to Universidad Miguel Hernández de Elche; basic and applied research in molecular and cellular design, molecular diagnosis and therapies; promotes scientific collaborations; doctoral programmes; Dir ANTONIO FERRER MONTIEL.

Instituto de Neurociencias (Institute of Neurosciences): Campus de San Juan, Universidad Miguel Hernández de Elche, 03550 Alicante; tel. 965233700; e-mail in@umh.es; internet in.umh.es; f. 1990 as a unit of Univ. of Alicante, present location 1996; attached to Universidad Miguel Hernández de Elche; provides laboratories, equipment and technical personnel for neurobiological research; cellular and systems neurobiology, developmental neurobiology, molecular neurobiology; Dir JUAN LERMA GÓMEZ.

NATURAL SCIENCES

General

Instituto de Energía Solar (Solar Energy Institute): Avda Complutense s/n, 28040 Madrid; tel. 915441060; e-mail info@ies-def.upm.es; internet www.ies.upm.es; attached to Universidad Politécnica de Madrid; conducts research in the fields of quantum calculation, fundamental studies, semiconductors, silicon technology, system and instruments integration, photovoltaic systems; Dir CARLOS DE CAÑIZO NADAL.

Instituto Español de Oceanografía (Spanish Institute of Oceanography): Avda de Brasil 31, 28020 Madrid; tel. 915974443; e-mail ieo@md.ieo.es; internet www.ieo.es; f. 1914; sections of physics, chemistry, pollution, geology, fishery biology and marine biology; coastal laboratories at Cádiz, Gijón, La Coruña, Málaga, Palma de Mallorca, San Pedro del Pinatar, Santa Cruz de Tenerife, Santander and Vigo; 6 research vessels; library of 18,500 vols, 3,900 periodicals; Dir EDUARDO BALGUERÍAS GUERRA; publs *IEO* (4 a year, online), *Temas Oceanográficos*.

Biological Sciences

Centro de Biotecnología Marina (Marine Biotechnology Centre): Muelle de Taliarte, s/n, 35214 Telde, Las Palmas de Gran Canaria; tel. 928133290; e-mail info@marinebiotechnology.com; internet marinebiotechnology.org; attached to University of Las Palmas de Gran Canaria; comprises applied algology and biological oceanography research groups; Dir Prof. GUILLERMO GARCÍA REINA.

Instituto de Neurociencias 'Federico Olóriz' ('Federico Oloriz' Institute of Neurosciences): Avda de Madrid s/n, Facultad de Medicina, Universidad de Granada, 18012 Granada; tel. 958244033; e-mail ineurociencias@ugr.es; internet ineurociencias.ugr.es; f. 1955; attached to Universidad de Granada; multidisciplinary study of neuroscience, anatomical and anthropological studies; Dir Dr FRANCISCO VIVES MONTERO; Sec. MILAGROS GALLO TORRE.

Mathematical Sciences

Instituto Carlos I de Física Teórica y Computacional ('Carlos I' Institute of Theoretical and Computational Physics): Facultad de Ciencias, Universidad de Granada, Campus de Fuentenueva, 18071 Granada; tel. 958242860; e-mail carlos1@ugr.es; internet ic1.ugr.es; attached to Universidad de Granada; works for improved infrastructure, new resources, optimization of available resources; Dir PEDRO L. GARRIDO GALERA; Sec. ELVIRA ROMERA GUTIÉRREZ.

Physical Sciences

Agencia Estatal de Meteorología (State Meteorological Agency): Calle Leonardo Prieto Castro 8, Ciudad Universitaria, 28071 Madrid; tel. 915819810; internet www.aemet.es; f. 2006; under Min. of Agriculture, Food and Environment; 17 meteorological centres, 4,500 stations, 90 observatories; library of 20,000 vols.

Centro de Estudios Ambientales del Mediterráneo (Mediterranean Center for Environmental Studies): Parque Tecnológico, Universidad Miguel Hernández, Calle Charles R. Darwin 14, 46980 Valencia; tel. 961318227; e-mail info@ceam.es; internet portales.gva.es/ceam; f. 1991; attached to Universidad Miguel Hernández de Elche; research programmes incl. atmospheric pollution, air pollutant effects, forest management, meteorology and climatology; Exec. Dir MANUEL ESCOLANO PUIG.

Centro de Investigación Operativa (Center of Operations Research University Institute): Edificio Torretamarit, Universidad Miguel Hernández de Elche, Avda. de la Universidad, 03202 Elche; tel. 966658572; e-mail cio@umh.es; internet cio.umh.es; f. 2005; analysis of efficiency and productivity, computational statistics, computer interaction and pattern recognition, dynamic systems and applications, knowledge-engineering and data analysis, linear systems, code theory and applications, marketing research, optimization and stability, resource management and optimization, statistical applications in modeling and forecasting; organizes doctoral programmes and confs; Dir FEDERICO BOTELLA BEVIÁ; Sec. JAVIER ALCARAZ SORIA.

Fundación Galileo Galilei (Galileo Galilei Foundation): Rambla José Ana Fernández Pérez 7, 38712 Breña Baja; tel. 922433666; e-mail secretary@tng.iac.es; internet www.tng.iac.es; f. 1979; attached to Istituto Nazionale di Astrofisica, Italy; promotes astrophysical research by managing and running the Telescopio Nazionale Galileo

(TNG), nat. facility of the Italian astronomical community; Dir EMILIO MOLINARI.

Instituto Andaluz de Geofísica y Prevención de Desastres Sísmicos (Andalusian Institute of Geophysics and Prevention of Seismic Disasters): Calle Profesor Clavera Nº 12, Campus Universitario de Cartuja s/n, 18071 Granada; tel. 958243556; e-mail morales@iag.ugr.es; internet www.ugr.es/~iag; attached to Universidad de Granada; research on seismology, seismic instrumentation, seismic and seismic risk prevention, historical seismicity and geophysical prospecting; maintains the Andalusian Seismic Network; Dir JOSÉ MORALES SOTO.

Instituto de Astrofísica de Canarias (IAC): Calle Vía Láctea, 38205 La Laguna, Tenerife, Canary Islands; tel. 922605200; e-mail director@iac.es; internet www.iac.es; f. 1982; astrophysical research and technical projects; library of 13,000 vols, 360 periodicals; Dir Prof. FRANCISCO SÁNCHEZ MARTÍNEZ.

Attached Observatories:

Observatorio del Roque de los Muchachos: Apdo 50, Calle Cuesta de San José s/n, 38712 Breña Baja, La Palma, Canary Islands; tel. 922405500; e-mail adminorm@iac.es; f. 1985; European Northern Observatory; Site Man. Dr JUAN CARLOS PÉREZ ARENCIBIA.

Observatorio del Teide: Calle Vía Láctea s/n, 38205 La Laguna, Tenerife, Canary Islands; tel. 922329100; e-mail teide@iac.es; f. 1985; European Northern Observatory; Site Man. Dr MIQUEL SERRA RICART.

Observatori Fabra: Camí de l'Observatori, s/n, 08035 Barcelona; tel. 934175736; e-mail secretaria@racab.com; internet www.fabra.cat; f. 1904; attached to Reial Acadèmia de Ciències i Arts de Barcelona; sections of astronomy, meteorology, seismology; Dir Dr JOSEP MARIA CODINA I VIDAL.

Observatorio Astronómico Nacional (National Astronomical Observatory): Campus de la Universidad de Alcalá, 28801 Madrid; tel. 915270107; f. 1790; attached to Instituto Geográfico Nacional; library of 12,000 vols; Dir Dr RAFAEL BACHILLER; publ. *Anuario* (1 a year).

Real Instituto y Observatorio de la Armada (Royal Naval Institute and Observatory): Cecilio Pujazón, s/n, 11110 Cadiz; tel. 956545099; e-mail secretaria@roa.es; internet www.roa.es; f. 1753; positional astronomy, ephemerides, time, geophysics and satellite geodesy; collaborates with the British and the American Nautical Almanac Offices, Centre Nat. d'Etudes Spatiales, Le Bureau des Longitudes and Das Astronomische Rechen Institut; library of 29,900 vols, 3,500 maps; Dir Dr FERNANDO BELIZÓN RODRÍGUEZ; publs *Almanaque Náutico* (1 a year), *Anales, Observaciones Meteorológicas, Magnéticas y Sísmicas, Efemérides Astronómicas* (1 a year), *Fenómenos Astronómicos* (2 a year).

PHILOSOPHY AND PSYCHOLOGY

Instituto de Investigación de Drogodependencias (Institute of Drug Addiction Research): Campus de Sant Joan, Universidad Miguel Hernández de Elche, Crta. Nacional 332, s/n, 03202 Alicante; tel. 965919319; e-mail inid@umh.es; internet inid.umh.es; f. 1997; research, devt and training in the field of drug addiction; coping strategies and drug use, design and devt of drug prevention programmes, devt of multivariate model drug prevention, psychosocial study of advertising in the field of drug addiction, study of addicted behaviour and attitudes; Dir JOSÉ A. GARCÍA DEL CASTILLO RODRÍGUEZ.

Instituto de Pensamiento Iberoamericano (Institute of Iberoamerican Thought): Universidad Pontificia de Salamanca, Calle Compañía 5, 37002 Salamanca; tel. 923277143; e-mail ipi@upsa.es; internet www.upsa.es/facultades/facultadesycentros/ipi/ficha.php; f. 1981; attached to Universidad Pontificia de Salamanca; explores Latin-American Baroque and its relationship to European Modernity; Dir Dr ILDEFONSO MURILLO MURILLO.

RELIGION, SOCIOLOGY AND ANTHROPOLOGY

Centro de Investigación en Contabilidad Social y Medioambiental (Centre for Social and Environmental Accounting Research): Edificio 44, 'Josefa Amar', Universidad Pablo de Olavide, Ctra de Utrera, Km 1, 41013 Seville; tel. 954349280; e-mail cicsma@upo.es; internet www.upo.es/cicsma; f. 2003; attached to Universidad Pablo de Olavide; Dir Prof. Dr FRANCISCO CARRASCO FENECH.

Instituto de Ciencias de la Familia (Institute of Family Sciences): Universidad Pontificia de Salamanca, C/ Compañía 5, 37002 Salamanca; tel. 923277141; e-mail cc.familia@upsa.es; internet www.ccfamilia.upsa.es; f. 1972; attached to Universidad Pontificia de Salamanca; science and current issues related to marriage; creates awareness and promotes various family services through research and teaching; Dir Dr ALFONSO SALGADO.

Instituto Español Bíblico y Arqueológico. Casa de Santiago (Spanish Institute of Biblical Archaeology): Sheyah St, POB 19030, 91190 Jerusalem; tel. (02) 6274942; e-mail casadesantiago@upsa.es; internet www.ieba.upsa.es; f. 1955; attached to Universidad Pontificia de Salamanca; research and postgraduate studies in biblical literature and archaeology; Bible courses for priests and theology students; library of 3,000 vols; Dir Prof. Dr JOSÉ MANUEL SÁNCHEZ CARO.

Instituto Universitario de Estudios de la Mujer (University Institute of Women's Studies): Calle Francisco Tomás y Valiente 5, Edificio de Ciencias Económicas y Empresariales, Módulo VI, Planta Baja, Campus Cantoblanco, 28049 Madrid; tel. 914974595; e-mail secretaria.iuem@uam.es; f. 1993; attached to Universidad Autónoma de Madrid; performs, promotes and coordinates research on feminism, women and gender; training of professionals in feminism and gender; Dir YOLANDA GUERRERO NAVARRETE.

Instituto Universitario de Investigación Ortega y Gasset (Ortega y Gasset University Research Institute): Calle Fortuny 53, 28010, Madrid; tel. 917004100; e-mail comunicacion@fog.es; f. 1986; attached to Fundación José Ortega y Gasset; affiliated to Universidad Complutense de Madrid; graduate degree programmes and research in social sciences and humanities; library of 50,000 vols, 300 periodicals; Dir FERNANDO VALLESPÍN OÑA.

TECHNOLOGY

Centro de Estudios e Investigaciones Técnicas de Gipuzkoa (Centre for Technical Studies and Research, Gipuzkoa): Paseo de Manuel Lardizabal 15, 20018 San Sebastián; tel. 943212800; e-mail comunicacion@ceit.es; internet www.ceit.es; f. 1982; attached to Universidad de Navarra; areas of research incl. applied mechanics, electronics and communications, environmental engineering, materials, microelectronics and microsystems; Gen. Dir ALEJO AVELLO ITURRIAGAGOITIA.

Centro de Innovación Para la Sociedad de la Información (Innovation Centre for the Information Society): Edificio Central del Parque Científico y Tecnológico, Campus Universitario de Tafira, 35017 Las Palmas de Gran Canaria; tel. 928451045; e-mail info@cicei.ulpgc.es; internet www.cicei.com; attached to Universidad de Las Palmas de Gran Canaria; research and devt of information technologies in the areas of training and learning, business, management; Dir Prof. Dr ENRIQUE RUBIO ROYO.

Centro de Investigaciones Energéticas, Medioambientales y Tecnológicas (Centre for Energy, Environmental and Technological Research): Avda Complutense 40, 28040 Madrid; tel. 913466000; e-mail contacto@ciemat.es; internet www.ciemat.es; f. 1951; controls and directs research and study of nuclear and new and renewable energies, environmental policy and several advanced technologies; library of 32,000 vols, 300,000 reports, 750,000 microcards, 2,000 periodicals; Dir-Gen. CAYETANO LÓPEZ MARTÍNEZ.

Centro Láser of Universidad Politécnica de Madrid (Laser Centre of Technical University of Madrid): Edif. Tecnológico 'La Arboleda', Campus Sur UPM, Carretera de Valencia Km 7300, 28031 Madrid; tel. 913324280; internet www.upmlaser.upm.es; f. 1998; promotes research, devt and diffusion of laser technology; Dir JOSÉ LUIS OCAÑA MORENO.

Centro Nacional de Aceleradores (National Accelerators Center): Calle thomas Alva Edison Nº 7, 41092 Seville; tel. 954460553; e-mail cna@us.es; internet centro.us.es/cna; f. 1997; research in the field of particle accelerators and its applications; Dir JOAQUÍN JOSÉ GÓMEZ CAMACHO.

Instituto Científico y Tecnológico de Navarra (Scientific and Technological Institute, Navarre): Avda Pío XII 53, 31008 Pamplona; tel. 948176748; e-mail ict@unav.es; internet www.unav.es/centro/ict; f. 1986; attached to Universidad de Navarra; Dir GUILLERMO GARCÍA DEL BARRIO.

Instituto de Biocomputación y Física de Sistemas Complejos (Institute of Biocomputation and Physics of Complex Systems): Edif. I+D, Calle Mariano Esquillor, 50018 Zaragoza; tel. 976762989; e-mail info@bifi.es; internet bifi.es; attached to Universidad de Zaragoza; research in the areas of computing applied to the physics of complex systems and biological models; Dir ALFONSO TARANCÓN LAFITA.

Instituto de Nutrición y Tecnología de los Alimentos 'José Mataix Verdú' (Institute of Nutrition and Food Technology 'José Mataix Verdú'): Centro de Investigación Biomédica, Parque Tecnológico de Ciencias de la Salud, Avda del Conocimiento s/n, 18100 Granada; tel. 958241000; internet winyta.ugr.es; f. 1989; applied research studies of the nutritional status of population and groups; provides education and training; Dir EMILIO MARTÍNEZ DE VICTORIA MUÑOZ; Sec. JESÚS FRANCISCO RODRÍGUEZ HUERTAS; publ. *NutrINYTA*.

Instituto de Robótica (Institute of Robotics): Avda 2085, 46071 Valencia; Polígono de La Coma s/n, 46980 Paterna; tel. 9663543567; internet smagris3.uv.es/irtic; f. 1991; attached to Universitat de València; research within the fields of transport and traffic telematics, computer graphics and virtual reality simulation of civil equipment, network services and computer security, control of robotic devices and digital image processing; Dir Prof. Dr JOSE JAVIER SAMPER ZAPATER.

Instituto de Sistemas Optoelectrónicos y Microtecnología (Institute for Systems based on Optoelectronics and Microtechnology): ETSI Telecomunicación (UPM), Ciudad Universitaria s/n, 28040 Madrid; tel. 915495700; e-mail montse.isom@die.upm.es; internet www.isom.upm.es; f. 2000; attached to Universidad Politécnica de Madrid; graduate research and education in electrical engineering; conducts research in the fields of detection, processing, transmission and recording of information by means of opto- and micro-electronics; Dir ENRIQUE CALLEJA PARDO.

Instituto Geológico y Minero de España (Spanish Geological and Mining Institute): Calle Ríos Rosas 23, 28003 Madrid; tel. 913495700; e-mail igme@igme.es; internet www.igme.es; f. 1849 as Comisión para la Carta Geológica de Madrid y General del Reino; attached to Min. of Science and Innovation; documentation centre of 20,000 items in microfilm; sections of geology, geophysics, mineral resources, subterranean hydrology, laboratories, museum; library of 30,000 vols, 2,750 periodicals; Dir JORGE CIVIS LLOVERA; publs *Boletín Geológico y Minero* (4 a year), *Revista Española de Micropaleontología* (3 a year).

Instituto Universitario de Ciencias y Tecnologías Cibernéticas (Institute for Cybernetic Science and Technology): Campus Universitario de Tafira, 35017 Las Palmas de Gran Canaria; tel. 928457100; e-mail ciber@ciber.ulpgc.es; internet www.iuctc.ulpgc.es; basic and applied research in science and technology of computers and computing, systems theory, cognitive science, artificial perception, computational biomedicine, computational neuroscience, computational economics, information technology, robotics.

Instituto Universitario de Investigación del Automóvil (University Institute for Automobile Research): Ctra de Valencia Km 7, Campus Sur UPM, 28031 Madrid; tel. 913365300; e-mail insia@insia.upm.es; internet www.insia.upm.es; attached to Universidad Politécnica de Madrid; research, devt and innovation on safety and environmental impact of vehicles; provides specialized postgraduate training; Dir FRANCISCO APARICIO IZQUIERDO.

Instituto Universitario de Investigación en Ingeniería de Aragón (Aragón Engineering Research Institute): I3A Edif. I+D+I, Calle Mariano Esquillor s/n, 50018 Zaragoza; tel. 976762707; e-mail i3a@unizar.es; internet i3a.unizar.es; f. 2002; attached to Univ. of Zaragoza; research in biomedical engineering, industrial technologies, information and communication technologies, processing and recycling; Dir JUAN IGNACIO GARCÉS GREGORIO.

Instituto Universitario de Microelectrónica Aplicada (Institute for Applied Microelectronics): Edificio de Electrónica y Telecomunicación, Campus Universitario de Tafira, 35017 Las Palmas de Gran Canaria; tel. 928451233; e-mail iuma@iuma.ulpgc.es; internet www.iuma.ulpgc.es; f. 1990; attached to University of Las Palmas de Gran Canaria; promotes, organizes and plans research objectives in fields of microelectronic technology and its applications; organizes confs, seminars, congresses, talks, meetings; Dir Prof. ANTONIO NÚÑEZ ORDÓÑEZ; Sec. Prof. P. PÉREZ-CARBALLO.

Instituto Universitario de Micrograve-dad 'Ignacio Da Riva' (Institute of Microgravity 'Ignacio Da Riva'): Plaza Cardenal Cisneros 3, 28040 Madrid; tel. 913366353; e-mail idr@idr.upm.es; internet www.idr

.upm.es; attached to Universidad Politécnica de Madrid; conducts research and devt in field of space science, microgravity and engineering; Dir JOSÉ MESEGUER RUÍZ; Sec. SEBASTIÁN FRANCHINI.

Libraries and Archives

Barcelona

Archivo Capitular de la Catedral de Barcelona (Archive of the Holy Church of the Cathedral of Barcelona): Catedral de Barcelona, Pla de la Seu s/n, 08002 Barcelona; tel. 933100669; f. 9th century; documents since 9th century; treatises on Holy Scripture, ecclesiastical history and law; religious and economic history; 255 MSS, 200 incunabula and various printed books from the original Biblioteca Capitular; 41,000 parchment documents, 20,000 vols; Archives Prefect JOSEP BAUCELLS REIG.

Archivo de la Corona de Aragón (Archive of the Crown of Aragon): Calle Almogávers 77, 08018 Barcelona; tel. 934854285; e-mail aca@mecd.es; internet www.mcu.es/archivos/mc/aca; f. 1318; managed by Min. of Education, Culture and Sport; safeguards, preserves, organizes and disseminates documentation accumulated over 7 centuries from various instns belonging to the Spanish Historical Heritage; 26,500 vols, 168 periodicals; Dir CARLOS LÓPEZ RODRÍGUEZ.

Arxiu Diocesà de Barcelona (Diocesan Archives, Barcelona): Carrer del Bisbe 5, 08002 Barcelona; tel. 932701017; e-mail dpcarqbcn@filnet.es; f. 11th century; registers (1,200) from 1302; Diocesan Archivist Dr JOSÉ MA MARTI BONET; publ. *El Archivo Diocesano d' Barcelona*.

Biblioteca Balmes (Balmes Library): Duran y Bas 9, 08002 Barcelona; tel. 933177284; e-mail biblioteca@balmesiana .org; internet www.balmesiana.org; f. 1923; collns of ecclesiastical history, numerous treatises of dogmatic and moral theology, sacred scriptures, patristic, scholastic, philosophical; specializes in church studies; 40,000 vols, 345 periodicals; Dir Dr RAMÓN CORTS BLAY.

Biblioteca de l'Arxiu Històric de la Ciutat de Barcelona: Carrer Santa Llúcia 1, 08002 Barcelona; tel. 933181195; e-mail bibliotecaarxiuhistoric@bcn.cat; internet www.bcn.cat/arxiu/arxiuhistoric; f. 1921; colln of books published in Barcelona since the 15th century; the Massana Library containing works on iconography and the history of costume; other libraries donated by private donors; 150,000 vols; Dir XAVIER TARRAU-BELLA MIRABET.

Biblioteca de l'Associació d'Enginyers Industrials de Catalunya (Library of the Association of Industrial Engineers of Catalonia): Via Laietana 39, 08003 Barcelona; tel. 933192366; e-mail biblioteca@infocentre.eic .cat; f. 1863; 21,200 vols; Librarian FERRAN PUERTA I SALES.

Biblioteca de la Universitat de Barcelona (Barcelona University Library): Baldiri Reixac 2, 08028 Barcelona; tel. 934035715; e-mail pi@bib.ub.es; internet www.bib.ub .edu; f. 1835; network of 18 libraries attached to the univ.; 1.2m. vols, 1,000 incunabula, 2,500 MSS; Dir DOLORS LAMARCA MORELL.

Biblioteca del Centre Excursionista de Catalunya (Library of the Catalan Alpin Club): Calle Paradís 10, 08002 Barcelona; tel. 933152311; e-mail biblioteca@cec.cat; internet biblioteca.cec.cat; f. 1876; 39,000 vols, 7,000 maps, 300 periodicals; Dir CRISTINA FERRER; publs *Espeleòleg* (irregular), *Muntanya* (6 a year).

Biblioteca del Collegi de Notaris i Arxiu Històric de Protocols de Barcelona: Notariat 4, 08001 Barcelona; tel. 933174800; e-mail info@catalunya.notariado .org; f. 1862; specializes in law and the medieval history of Catalonia; 40,000 vols; Archivist LAUREA PAGAROLAS SABATÉ; Librarian MONTSERRAT GÓMEZ; publs *Estudios Històrics i Documents dels Arxius de Protocols*, *La Notaría* (3 a year).

Biblioteca del Foment del Treball Nacional (Library of Department of Trade Development): Vía Laietana 32, 08003 Barcelona; tel. 934841257; e-mail biblioteca@foment .com; internet www.foment.com; f. 1889; 90,000 vols, 2,500 periodicals; Librarian NURIA SARDÁ; publ. *Horizonte Empresarial* (12 a year).

Il·lustre Col·legi d'Advocats de Barcelona, Biblioteca (Barcelona Bar Association Library): Mallorca 283, 08037 Barcelona; tel. 936011260; e-mail direcciobiblioteca@icab .cat; internet www.icab.cat; f. 1833; reference and research services; digital library; 300,000 vols, 1,500 periodicals; Co-Head PATRICIA SANPERA; Co-Head ISABEL JUNCOSA; publs *Revista Jurídica de Catalunya* (4 a year), *Món Jurídic* (10 a year).

Reial Acadèmia Catalana de Belles Arts de Sant Jordi (Royal Catalan Academy of Fine Arts, Sant Jordi): Casa Llotja, 2°, Passeig d'Isabel II 1, 08003 Barcelona; tel. 933192432; e-mail secretaria@racba.org; internet www.racba.org; f. 1849; 10,000 vols; Pres. JOAN ANTONI SOLANS HUGUET; Sec. LEOPOLDO GIL NEBOT; publs *Annuari* (every 2 years), *Butlleti* (1 a year).

Bilbao

Biblioteca Universitaria de Deusto (University of Deusto Library): Ramón Rubial 1, 48009 Bilbao; tel. 944139415; e-mail biblioteca@deusto.es; internet www .biblioteca.deusto.es; f. 1886; 1m. vols, 10,000 periodicals; Dir NIEVES TARANCO DEL BARRIO.

Granada

Archivo de la Real Chancillería de Granada (Archives of the Royal Chancery of Granada): Plaza del Padre Suárez 1, 18009 Granada; tel. 958575757; e-mail informacion .arch.gr.ccd@juntadeandalucia.es; internet www.juntadeandalucia.es/cultura/archivos/realchancilleria; f. 1904; collects, preserves, organizes and promotes documentary heritage from legal bodies; 6,500 vols, 200 periodicals; Dir DAVID TORRES IBÁÑEZ.

Jerez de la Frontera

Biblioteca del Campus de Jerez: Avda. de la Universidad s/n, 11405 Jerez de la Frontera Cádiz; tel. 956037015; e-mail biblioteca .campusjerez@uca.es; internet biblioteca.uca .es/sbuca/bibcjer.htm; f. 1921; 75,000 vols, 1,500 periodicals; Dir ROSA MARÍA TORIBIO RUIZ.

Biblioteca del Museo Arqueológico Municipal de Jerez (Jerez Archaeological Museum Town Library): Plaza del Mercado s/n, 11408 Jerez de la Frontera; tel. 956149560; e-mail museoarq@aytojerez.es; f. 1873; incunabula, important collns from 17th to 18th centuries, local collns on horses, bullfighting, flamenco; documents dating back to the reconquest of Jerez by Alfonso El Sabio, documents on the discovery of America; 100,000 vols; Dir RAMÓN CLAVIJO PROVENCIO.

La Coruña

Arquivo do Reino de Galicia (Archive of the Kingdom of Galicia): Xardín de San Carlos s/n, 15001 La Coruña; tel. 981209251; e-mail arq.reino.galicia@xunta .es; internet arquivosdegalicia.xunta.es/

portal/arquivo-do-reino-de-galicia; f. 1775; comprises a total of 150,926 bundles of documents dating back to AD 867, concerning disputes and lawsuits of the 'Real Audiencia de Galicia' and the 'Audiencia Territorial' relative to the clergy, the nobility, villages and private persons; 18th- and 19th-century documents of 'Real Intendencia', concerning govt and admin. of Galicia; documents 1808–14 of the 'Junta Superior de Armamento y Defensa' relative to the Peninsular War; documents of Provincial Admin. of La Coruña since the 19th century, concerning the govt, police, education, economy, tourism, finance, health; records of families, labour unions and churches since the 12th century; colln of parchment 867–1586; 7,686 maps, plans and drawings since the 16th century; 101,847 photographs and postcards, 1,298 microforms; 25,475 vols, 1,551 periodicals (incl. 23 current) and 929 pamphlets closely related to the archives and of special interest for research; Dir María Carmen Prieto Ramos.

Lérida (Lleida)

Arxiu Històric de Lleida (Historical Archive of Lleida): Carrer Governador Montcada s/n, 25002 Lleida; tel. 973288250; e-mail ahll .cultura@gencat.cat; internet cultura.gencat .cat/arxius/ahl; f. 1952; organizes courses and dissemination of archive sessions for training users and researchers; 10,336 linear m of documents dating from 14th to 21st century; incl. records from Administració de la Generalitat de Catalunya; Dir Joan Farré Viladrich; publ. *Arxius. Butlletí de la Subdirecció general d'Arxius* (4 a year).

Madrid

Archivo Central del Ministerio de Empleo y Seguridad Social (Central Archive of the Ministry of Employment and Social Security): Calle Agustín de Bethencourt 4, 28003 Madrid; tel. 913630921; e-mail archivocentral@meyss.es; internet www .mtin.es; f. 1920; Head Carmen Concepción Saiz Gómez; publ. *Revista del Ministerio de Trabajo e Inmigración* (12 a year).

Archivo General de la Administración: Paseo de Aguadores 2, 28871 Alcalá de Henares, Madrid; tel. 918892950; e-mail aga@mecd.es; internet www.mcu.es/archivos/mc/aga; f. 1969; preserves and makes available information or scientific research documents of public admin. that are no longer of current admin. relevance; 3,000 vols; Dir Alfonso Dávila Oliveda.

Archivo Histórico Nacional (National Historical Archives): Calle Serrano 115, 28006 Madrid; tel. 917688500; e-mail ahn@ mcu.es; internet www.mcu.es/archivos/mc/ ahn; f. 1866; preserves and protects historical documents; 400,000 archival items and 30,000 library items, 4,000 ancient monographs, 400 periodicals; Dir Carmen Sierra Bárcena.

Biblioteca Central del Ministerio de Hacienda y Administraciones Públicas (Central Library of the Ministry of Finance and Public Administration): Calle Alcalá 9, Planta Baja, 28071 Madrid; tel. 915958342; e-mail biblioteca.alcala@minhac.es; internet www.minhap.gob.es/es-es/publicaciones/bibliotecas; f. 1852; 82,000 vols, 200 MSS; Librarian Esperanza Salán Paniagua.

Biblioteca Central de Marina (Central Naval Library): Calle Montalbán 2, 28014 Madrid; tel. 913796024; e-mail bca@fn.mde .es; internet www.portalcultura.mde.es/ cultural/bibliotecas/madrid/biblioteca_121 .html; f. 1874; subject areas of architecture and shipbuilding, discovery and exploration, geography, legislation, naval history, scientific expeditions; 90,000 vols; Dir María Eugenia Moreu Aboal.

Biblioteca Central Militar (Central Military Library): Paseo de Moret 3, 28008 Madrid; tel. 917808700; e-mail bcm@et.mde .es; internet www.portalcultura.mde.es/ cultural/bibliotecas/madrid/biblioteca_107 .html; f. 1932; attached to Instituto de Historia y Cultura Militar del Ejército de Tierra; specializes in all matters relating to art, science and military history; 200,000 vols, 1,000 periodicals, 1,700 MSS; Dir Inocencia Soria González.

Biblioteca de la Escuela Técnica Superior de Ingenieros de Caminos, Canales y Puertos de Madrid (Library of the Higher School for Road, Canal and Port Engineers of Madrid): Ciudad Universitaria, 28040 Madrid; tel. 913366739; f. 1834; 64,912 vols, 1,407 periodicals, 3,510 maps, 13,779 microfiches, 587 theses; Dir Concepción García Viñuela.

Biblioteca de la Universidad Complutense de Madrid (Complutense University of Madrid Library): Ciudad Universitaria, 28040 Madrid; tel. 913947985; e-mail bucweb@buc.ucm.es; internet www.ucm.es/ bucm; f. 1499; 2.85m. vols, 72,879 MSS, 49,000 periodicals, 24,000 DVDs, 7,400 microforms, 12,800 CD-ROMs, 9,400 CDs, 40,000 maps; Dir Manuela Palafox Parejo.

Biblioteca del Ministerio de Asuntos Exteriores y de Cooperación (Library of the Ministry of Foreign Affairs and Cooperation): Escuela Diplomatica, Paseo de Juan XXIII 5, 28040 Madrid; tel. 913796928; e-mail escuela.biblioteca@maec.es; f. 1943; works on diplomatic and consular law, int. economics, history, geography, int. law, modern history, political and civil law and int. relations; 60,000 vols, 300 periodicals; Head Helena del Barrio Alvarellos.

Biblioteca Hispánica (Hispanic Library): Avda de los Reyes Católicos 4, Ciudad Universitaria, 28040 Madrid; tel. 915838175; e-mail biblioteca.hispanica@ aecid.es; f. 1941; attached to Agencia Española de Cooperación Internacional para el Desarrollo; 348,142 vols, 13,167 periodicals; spec. colln: Latin American incunabula; Dir Dra Carmen Díez Hoyo.

Biblioteca 'María Moliner' de la ETSI Industriales: Calle José Gutiérrez Abascal 2, 28006 Madrid; tel. 913363076; e-mail biblioteca.industriales@upm.es; internet www.etsii.upm.es/biblioteca; f. 1850; 40,000 vols; Dir Isabel Inés Mendoza García.

Biblioteca Nacional de España (National Library of Spain): Paseo de Recoletos 20–22, 28071 Madrid; tel. 915807800; e-mail info@ bne.es; internet www.bne.es; f. 1712 as Biblioteca Pública de Palacio; deposit library; ISSN nat. centre; 4m. vols, 2.7m. monographs, 160,545 periodicals, 188,981 drawings and photographs, 331,280 audio recordings, 186,681 musical scores, 104,768 audiovisual, 84,421 maps and charts, 40,795 MSS; Dir Ana Santos Aramburo.

Biblioteca San Dámaso: Calle San Buenaventura 9, 28005 Madrid; tel. 913644010; e-mail biblioteca@sandamaso.es; internet www.sandamaso.es/biblioteca.php; f. 1929; sections corresponding to the Bible, systematic theology, philosophy, religious studies, catechetics and liturgy; works related to German culture, theology and philosophy; auxiliary libraries incl. Biblioteca Alemana Görres (studies on German-Spanish cultural relations); 165,000 vols, 672 periodicals; Dir Prof. Dr Nicolás Álvarez de las Asturias.

Centro de Información Documental de Archivos: Paseo de Aguadores 2, 28804 Madrid; tel. 918838539; e-mail biblioteca .cida@mecd.es; internet www.mcu.es/ archivos/mc/cida/index.html; f. 1977; attached to Subdirección General de los Archivos Estatales/Office of the Nat. Archives; disseminates and publicizes Spanish Documentary Heritage, produces annual statistical information about Nat. Archives, coordinates the Nat. Archives Libraries Network and standardizes archival descriptions; 11,066 vols, 691 periodicals, 236 CDs and DVDs, 4,588 pamphlets, 11,843 monographs; Dir Josefa Villanueva Toledo; publ. *Boletín de Información Bibliográfica* (online, www.mcu.es/ccbae/es/inicio/inicio.cmd).

Hemeroteca Municipal de Madrid (Periodicals Library of the Corporation of Madrid): Calle Conde Duque 9–11, 28015 Madrid; tel. 915133164; e-mail infohemeroteca@madrid.es; internet www .madrid.es/hemeroteca; f. 1918; 250,000 vols; Dir Inmaculada Zaragoza Garcia.

Real Biblioteca (Royal Library): Palacio Real, Calle Bailén s/n, 28071 Madrid; tel. 914548700; e-mail realbiblioteca@ patrimonionacional.es; internet www .realbiblioteca.es; f. early 18th century; collns of MSS, incunabula, music, rare editions since 16th century, maps, engravings and drawings; colln of book-bindings; research library; 250,000 vols; Dir Dr María Luisa López-Vidriero; publ. *Avisos: Noticias de la Real Biblioteca* (4 a year).

Palma de Mallorca

Arxiu del Regne de Mallorca (Archives of the Kingdom of Mallorca): Cuerta de Valldemossa, km 7, Edifici Adduno, Calle de Blaise Pascal, Parc Bit, 07121 Palma de Mallorca; tel. 971725999; e-mail arm@arxregne.caib.es; internet arxregne.caib.es/web/default.htm; f. 1851; 11,000 linear m of documents; public and private archives since 13th century; 15,000 vols, 200 periodicals; Dir Ricard Urgell Hernández.

Peralada

Biblioteca del Palacio de Peralada (Palace of Peralada Library): Plaça del Carmen s/n, 17491 Peralada Girona; tel. 972538125; e-mail inespadrosa@castilloperalada.com; f. 1889; organizes confs, exhibitions; 100,000 vols, 1,200 MSS, 195 incunabula, 10,000 photographs, 20,000 pamphlets and parchments; Librarian Inés Padrosa Gorgot.

Sabadell

Arxiu Històric de Sabadell (Historical Archives of Sabadell): Carrer Indústria 32–34, 08202 Sabadell; tel. 937268777; e-mail ahs@ajsabadell.cat; internet www.sabadell .net/websajsab/arxiu; f. 14th century; documents, preserves, distributes documentary heritage since 1111; MSS of *Arxius Privats* (private records) since 1247, *Fons eclesiàstic* (ecclesiastical archives) since 1334, *Corts Senyorials* (Court of Justice) since 1347, *Escrivania* (notarial archives) since 1400, *Actes* (Proceedings of local council meetings) since 1449, *Hemeroteca oficial* since 1570, *Fons d'empresa* (records of 30 companies) from 19th century; colln of local journals and reviews since 1855; 14,000 vols, 2,000 periodicals, 100,000 photographs, 625 audiovisual records; Dir Joan Comasòlivas i Font; publ. *Arraona* (1 a year).

San Lorenzo de El Escorial

Real Biblioteca del Monasterio de San Lorenzo de El Escorial (Royal Library of the Monastery of San Lorenzo de El Escorial): Avda D. Juan de Borbón y Battenberg 1, 28200 San Lorenzo de El Escorial, Madrid; tel. 918903889; e-mail real.biblioteca@ctv.es; internet rbme.patrimonionacional.es; f. 1563; 75,000 vols, 600 incunabula, 7,000 engravings, 923 drawings, 10,608 printed books of the 16th century, MSS: 2,000 Arabic, 1,308 Latin, 765 vernacular, 76 Hebrew, 580 Greek; complete copy of the *Biblia Poliglota Complutensis* and of the *Biblia Poliglota* of Antwerp on parchment, and the *Epítome de Anatomía*, by Vesalius, also on parchment; Dir Dr P. JOSÉ LUIS DEL VALLE MERINO.

Santander

Biblioteca Central de Cantabria (Central Library of Cantabria): Ruiz de Alda 19, 39009 Santander; tel. 942241550; e-mail bcc@gobcantabria.es; internet bcc.cantabria.es; f. 1839 as Biblioteca del Instituto Cántabro para la Enseñanza de la Náutica y el Comercio, present name 1999, present site 2010; promotes reading, training and research; collects, catalogues, preserves and disseminates the bibliographic and print, sound and visual production of Cantabria; 2,000 vols; Dir JUAN JOSÉ AMADO FERNÁNDEZ.

Biblioteca de Menéndez Pelayo (Menéndez Pelayo Library): Calle Rubio 6, 39001 Santander; tel. 942234534; e-mail biblioteca-mp@ayto-santander.es; internet www.bibliotecademenendezpelayo.org; f. 1915; the private library of this writer left by him to the town; 45,000 vols; Dir ROSA FERNÁNDEZ-LERA; publ. *De re Bibliographica* (1 a year).

Seville

Archivo Ducal de Medinaceli (Medinaceli Archives): Plaza de Pilatos 1, Seville; tel. 954225298; e-mail direccion@fundacionmedinaceli.org; internet www.fundacionmedinaceli.org/archivo; archives of 9th to 20th century; 5,000 vols; Dir-Gen. JUAN MANUEL ALBENDEA SOLÍS; publ. *Histórica*.

Archivo General de Indias (Archives of the Indies): Edificio de La Cilla, Avda de la Constitución 3, Calle Santo Tomás 5, 41071 Seville; tel. 954500528; internet www.mcu.es/archivos/mc/agi; f. 1785; documents relating to Spanish colonial admin. in America and the Philippines; 36,000 vols, 43,000 files; Dir ISABEL SIMÓ RODRIGUEZ; publs *Catálogos de Pasajeros a Indias*, *Catálogos de Mapas y Planos*, *CD-ROM Tesoros del Archivo General de Indias*.

Biblioteca Capitular y Colombina: Institución Colombina, Calle Alemanes s/n, 41004 Seville; tel. 954560769; e-mail bibliotecas@icolombina.es; internet www.icolombina.es; f. 1509; 60,000 vols; Dir NURIA CASQUETE DE PRADO SAGRERA.

Simancas

Archivo General de Simancas (Simancas General Archives): Calle Miravete 8, 47130 Simancas, Valladolid; tel. 983590750; e-mail eduardo.pedruelo@mcu.es; internet www.mcu.es/archivos/mc/ags; f. 1540; 70,000 filed documents and 5,000 vols of documents, 20,000 vols; Dir EDUARDO PEDRUELO MARTIN.

Toledo

Archivo y Biblioteca Capitulares (Archives and Library of the Cathedral Chapter): Catedral de Toledo, Calle Hombre de Palo 2, Apdo 295, 45001 Toledo; tel. 925212423; e-mail archivocapitular@catedralprimada.es; internet www.catedralprimada.es/archivo_capitular_informacion; f. 1085; the *Archivo Capitular* contains c. 6,000 catalogued documents (mostly medieval) since 1085; 127 vols of Chapter's Records (1466–present); the library (f. 1383); 903 vols, 2,521 MSS; Dir Dr ANGEL FERNÁNDEZ COLLADO.

Biblioteca de Castilla—La Mancha (Library of Castilla—La Mancha): Cuesta de Carlos V s/n, 45001 Toledo; tel. 925256680; e-mail biblioclm@jccm.es;

internet www.jccm.es/biblioclm; f. 1998; under the Min. of Education, Culture and Sport; 380,000 vols, 4,000 periodicals; spec. collns incl. Borbón-Lorenzana (more than 100,000 vols 16th–19th centuries, 700 MSS, 414 incunabula), Fondo Regional; Dir CARMEN MORALES MATEO; Dir JUAN SÁNCHEZ SÁNCHEZ.

Valencia

Archivo del Reino (Archive of United Kingdom): Paseo de la Alameda 22, 46010 Valencia; tel. 963184550; e-mail arv@gva.es; internet dglab.cult.gva.es/arxiuregne; f. 1419; 13,500 vols, 4,190 flyers, 250 periodicals; Dir FRANCESC TORRES FAUS.

Zaragoza

Biblioteca Ibercaja 'José Sinues' (José Sinues Ibercaja Library): Fernando el Católico 1–3, 50006 Zaragoza; tel. 976359887; e-mail bjsinues@ibercajaobrasocial.org; f. 1975; owned by the Ibercaja credit company; open only to mems; 64,152 vols, 50 periodicals, 250 audiovisual items; spec. colln: Biblioteca Moncayo of 15,000 vols by Aragonese authors or on the subject of Aragón.

Museums and Art Galleries

Barcelona

Museu d'Arqueologia de Catalunya (Archaeological Museum of Catalonia): Passeig de Santa Madrona 39–41, Parc de Montjuïc, 08038 Barcelona; tel. 934232149; e-mail mac.cultura@gencat.cat; internet www.mac.cat; f. 1990; collns of prehistoric, Greek, Phoenician, Visigothic and Roman art; comprises Barcelona and Girona Archaeological Museums, the Greco-Roman city Empúries, the historical complex Olèrdola, the Iberian settlement Ullastret, Underwater Archaeology Centre of Catalonia, Iberian settlements Molí d'Espígol (Tornabous), Castell (Palamós), Coll del Moro (Gandesa) and Castellet de Banyoles (Tivissa), Roca dels Moros (El Cogul), Roman city of Iesso (Guissona); library of 40,000 vols; Dir XAVIER LLOVERA MASSANA; publs *Cypsela* (2 a year), *Empúries* (2 a year).

Museu d'Art Contemporani de Barcelona (MACBA) (Barcelona Museum of Contemporary Art): Plaça dels Angels 1, 08001 Barcelona; tel. 934120810; e-mail pei@macba.cat; internet www.macba.es; f. 1995; modern Catalan and int. art; library: 1,900 periodicals; Dir BARTOMEU MARÍ RIBAS.

Museu de Ciències Naturals de Barcelona (Natural Sciences Museum of Barcelona): Passeig Picasso s/n, 08003 Barcelona; tel. 932562200; e-mail aomedes@bcn.cat; internet www.bcn.es/museuciencies; f. 1878; permanent exhibitions of 3m. items in the fields of mineralogy, petrology, palaeontology, zoology, botany; research areas incl. biodiversity and molecular biology, bioestratigraphy and paleobiogeography of the Tethys Sea, evolutionary and behavioural ecology, geological structure of Catalonia, history of the natural sciences; library of 20,150 vols, 3,000 periodicals, 3,600 maps; Dir Dr. ANNA OMEDES; Man. JOAN CIRILO; publs *Animal Biodiversity and Conservation* (2 a year, in English), *Arxius de Miscelània Zoològica* (online), *Collectanea Botanica* (1 a year), *Monografies del Museu de Ciències Naturals*, *Treballs del Museu de Geologia de Barcelona* (1 a year).

Museu de la Música (Museum of Music): L'Auditori, Calle Lepant 150, 08013 Barcelona; tel. 932563650; e-mail museumusica@

bcn.cat; internet www.museumusica.bcn.cat; f. 1946; valuable collns of antique instruments; phonographs and gramophones, historical early recordings; archives of Albéniz, Granados and other Catalan composers; library of 12,000 vols; Dir JAUME AYATS.

Museu d'Història de Barcelona: Plaça del Rei, 08002 Barcelona; tel. 932562100; e-mail museuhistoria@bcn.cat; internet www.museuhistoria.bcn.es; f. 1943; 15th-century mansion containing Roman remains in situ (1st- to 4th-century Roman wall), 11th- to 15th-century Royal Palace; documentation centre, information service; library of 7,000 vols, 200 periodicals; Dir ANTONI NICOLAU MARTÍ; publ. *Quaderns d'Arqueologia i Història de la Ciutat de Barcelona*.

Subordinate institutions:

Casa Museu Verdaguer: Carrer Major 7, 08519 Folgueroles; tel. 938122157; e-mail info@verdaguer.cat; internet www.verdaguer.cat; 18th-century farmhouse, former home of the poet Jacint Verdaguer; Dir CARME TORRENTS I BUXÓ.

MUHBA Park Güell: Casa del Guarda, Park Güell, Carrer Olot s/n, 08024 Barcelona; tel. 932562122; e-mail museuhistoria@bcn.cat; internet www.bcn.cat/museuhistoriaciutat/ca/muhba_park_guell.html; information centre; incl. maps, models, photographs and audiovisual items on relationships between Gaudí, Güell (the patron) and city of Barcelona; Dir Dr JOAN ROCA.

MUHBA Plaça del Rei: Plaça del Rei s/n, 08002 Barcelona; tel. 932562100; e-mail museuhistoria@bcn.cat; internet www.bcn.cat/museuhistoriaciutat/es/muhba_placa_del_rei.html; 11th-century Count's Palace, later the residence of the kings of Catalonia and Aragón; Padellàs House, a Gothic palace; Roman remains in situ (1st century BC to 8th century AD); Chief Curator JULIA BELTRÁN DE HEREDIA.

MUHBA Santa Caterina: c. Joan Capri, 08003 Barcelona; tel. 932562122; e-mail museuhistoria@bcn.cat; internet www.bcn.cat/museuhistoriaciutat/ca/muhba_santa_caterina.html; f. 1943; depicts the archaeological history of the city of Barcelona through archaeological sites, medieval monuments, Gaudí work at Park Güell, Spanish civil war defences and industrial bldgs, from the Bronze Age to the latest examples of contemporary architecture; 12 centres; library of 10,000 vols; Dir Dr JOAN ROCA; publ. *QUARHIS. Quaderns d'Arqueologia i Història de la Ciutat de Barcelona*.

Reial Monestir de Santa Maria de Pedralbes: Baixada del Monestir 9, 08034 Barcelona; tel. 932563434; e-mail monestirpedralbes@bcn.cat; internet www.bcn.cat/monestirpedralbes; f. 1326, opened to public 1983; Gothic church and monastery; Gothic mural paintings, art colln on the history of the monastery medicinal garden; Chief Curator Dr ANNA CASTELLANO I TRESSERRA.

Museu Etnològic (Ethnological Museum): Passeig de Santa Madrona 16–22, Parc de Montjuïc, 08038 Barcelona; tel. 932563484; e-mail museuetnologic@bcn.es; internet www.museuetnologic.bcn.es; f. 1948; more than 70,000 artefacts pertaining to African, Asiatic, American, Oceanic and Spanish ethnography and American archaeology; library of 45,000 vols, 1,152 periodicals; Dir JOSEP FORNÉS I GARCÍA.

Museu Geològic del Seminari de Barcelona (Geological Museum of the Seminary of Barcelona): Calle Diputació 231, 08007 Barcelona; tel. 934541600; e-mail almeracomas@

hotmail.com; f. 1847; palaeontology of invertebrates, colln of nearly 70,000 fossils; library of 14,000 vols; Dir Dr SEBASTIÀ CALZADA; publs *Batalleria* (1 a year), *Butlletí de l'Associació d'Amics de l'MGSB* (4 a year), *Pagurus* (online (www.telefonica.net/web2/pa-ko/pagurus)), *Scripta Musei Geologici Seminarii Barcinonensis* (irregular).

Museu Marítim de Barcelona (Barcelona Maritime Museum): Avda de les Drassanes s/n, 08001 Barcelona; tel. 933429920; e-mail m.maritim@diba.cat; internet www.mmb.cat; f. 1929; 75 years of maritime culture and history; preserves, studies and disseminates colln of maritime heritage of the Mediterranean; photographic, cartographic and documental archives; colln of 158 objects of weaponry; restoration workshop; library of 15,000 vols; Dir-Gen. ROGER MARCET I BARBÉ.

Museu Nacional d'Art de Catalunya (National Art Museum of Catalonia): Palau Nacional, Parc de Montjuïc, 08038 Barcelona; tel. 936220360; e-mail mnac@mnac.cat; internet www.mnac.cat; f. 1934; history of Catalan art from the Romanesque period to the mid-20th century; colln of sculpture, painting, objets d'art, drawing, engraving, posters, photography and coinage; organizes educational programmes, debates, lectures and seminars; library of 105,000 vols, 3,000 periodicals; Pres. MIQUEL ROCA I JUNYENT; Dir PEPE SERRA VILLALBA; publs *Butlletí*, *Revista*.

Museu Picasso (Picasso Museum): Carrer Montcada 15–23, 08003 Barcelona; tel. 932563000; e-mail museupicasso@bcn.cat; internet www.museupicasso.bcn.cat; f. 1963; comprises more than 3,800 paintings, pottery, drawings and engravings by Pablo Picasso (1881–1973), incl. the series 'Las Meninas' and the artist's donation, in 1970, of 940 works of art; library of 4,000 vols, 80 periodicals; Dir BERNARDO LANIADO-ROMERO.

Bilbao

Guggenheim Bilbao Museo (Guggenheim Museum Bilbao): Abandoibarra 2, 48001 Bilbao; tel. 944359080; e-mail informacion@guggenheim-bilbao.es; internet www.guggenheim-bilbao.es; f. 1997; modern American and European art; Dir JUAN IGNACIO VIDARTE.

Museo de Bellas Artes de Bilbao/Bilboko Arte Ederren Museoa (Bilbao Fine Arts Museum): Museo Plaza 2, 48009 Bilbao; tel. 944396060; e-mail info@museobilbao.com; internet www.museobilbao.com; f. 1908, opened 1914; more than 8,000 works of old, modern and contemporary art incl. paintings, sculptures, works on paper, applied arts; library of 33,000 vols, 300 periodicals; Dir JAVIER VIAR.

Burgos

Museo de Burgos: Calle Miranda 13, 09002 Burgos; tel. 947265875; e-mail museo.burgos@jcyl.es; internet www.museodeburgos.com; f. 1871; Casa Miranda: archaeological collns (from Palaeolithic to Visigothic); Casa Angulo: fine arts collns (from Mozarabic to contemporary painting), enamels, ivories, tomb of Juan de Padilla, Tablas Flamencas (Ecce Homo) and 15th- to 20th-century painting, sculpture, altarpieces; library of 3,000 vols; Dir Dr JUAN CARLOS ELORZA Y GUINEA; publ. *Anales*.

Cartagena

Museo Arqueológico Municipal (Archaeological Museum): Calle Ramón y Cajal 45, 30204 Cartagena; tel. 968128968; e-mail informacionmuseo@ayto-cartagena.es; internet www.museoarqueologicocartagena.es; f. 1943; collns of Roman remains found in the area, incl. mining, architecture, sculpture, industrial arts exhibits; model sites; Dir Dr MARÍA COMAS GABARRÓN; publ. *MASTIA*.

Chipiona

Museo Misional de Nuestra Señora de Regla: Colegio de Misioneros Franciscanos, 11550 Chipiona; f. 1939; 600 exhibits of early Roman Christian relics, ancient Egyptian and other N African objects, antique coins; Dir RECTOR DEL COLEGIO.

Córdoba

Museo Arqueológico de Córdoba (Archaeological Museum of Cordoba): Plaza de Jerónimo Páez 7, 14003 Córdoba; tel. 957355517; e-mail museoarqueologicocordoba.ccul@juntadeandalucia.es; f. 1868; 33,500 exhibits; archaeological, prehistoric and local finds, Roman and medieval collns; library of 13,500 vols; Dir MARÍA DOLORES BAENA ALCANTARA.

Figueres

Teatre-Museu Dalí (Dali Theatre Museum): Plaça Gala-Salvador Dalí 5, 17600 Figueres; tel. 972677500; e-mail t-mgrups@dali-estate.org; internet www.salvador-dali.org/museus/figueres/dali-nit.html; f. 1974; comprises 1,500 paintings, sculptures and other works by Salvador Dalí, his private colln of works by other artists; Dir ANTONI PITXOT I SOLER.

Granada

Museo de Bellas Artes (Museum of Fine Arts): Palacio de Carlos V, 18009 Granada; tel. 958575450; e-mail museobellasartesgranada.ccul@juntadeandalucia.es; f. 1839; paintings and sculpture by local artists from 16th century to mid-20th century; library of 5,000 vols; Dir RICARDO TENORIO VERA.

Ibiza

Museo Arqueologico de Ibiza/Museu Arqueológic d'Eivissa: Calle Via Romana 31, 07800 Espanya; tel. 971301771; e-mail maef@telefonica.net; internet www.maef.es; f. 1907; preserves, researches and exhibits material remains of history of the islands of Ibiza and Formentera; Phoenician, Carthaginian and Roman remains from the necropolis of Puig des Molins (nat. monument and World Heritage Property); Pres. JOSE MANUEL VÁZQUEZ CORA; publ. *Treballs del Museu Arqueológic d'Eivissa I Formentera* (2 a year).

Attached Museum:

Museu Monogràfic del Puig des Molins: Via Romana 31, Eivissa (Ibiza); tel. 971301771; e-mail mmpm@telefonica.net; f. 1966; Phoenician, Punic and Roman remains from the nat. monument of Puig des Molins, declared as a World Heritage Site by UNESCO in 1999; organizes lectures, courses about archaeology and Phoenician-Punic archaeology; library of 21,586 vols; Dir and Curator JORGE H. FERNÁNDEZ GÓMEZ; publ. *Treballs del Museu Arqueológic d'Eivissa I Formentera*.

La Escala

Museu d'Arqueologia de Cataluyna—Empúries: Calle Puig i Cadafalch s/n, 17130 L'Escala; tel. 972770208; e-mail macempuries.cultura@gencat.cat; internet www.mac.cat/eng/branches/empuries; f. 1908; colln of excavations of Graeco-Roman city Empúries; library of 11,000 vols; Dir MARTA SANTOS.

Las Palmas

Museo Canario (Canarian Museum): Dr Verneu 2, Vegueta, 35001 Las Palmas de Gran Canaria; tel. 928336800; e-mail info@elmuseocanario.com; internet www.elmuseocanario.com; f. 1879; local archaeology and anthropology, ethnography and natural sciences; library of 40,000 vols; Dir-Gen. DIEGO LÓPEZ DÍAZ; publ. *El Museo Canario* (1 a year).

Lérida (Lleida)

Gabinet Numismàtic: Institut d'Estudis Ilerdencs, Plaça de la Catedral s/n, 25002 Lérida; tel. 973271500; e-mail gabinumi@diputaciolleida.es; f. 1976; Roman, Iberian, Ibero-Roman, medieval and modern exhibits.

Museo de la Paeria: Plaça Paeria 1, 25007 Lérida; tel. 973700394; e-mail cultura@paeria.cat; f. 1963; historical documents and objects belonging to the municipality; archaeological finds of Lérida.

Museu d'Art Jaume Morera (Jaume Morera Art Museum): Carrer Major 31, Avinguda de Blondel 38–40, Edif. Casino Principal, 25007 Lérida; tel. 973700419; e-mail mmorera@paeria.cat; internet mmorera.paeria.es; f. opened 1917; modern paintings mainly by Catalan artists, incl. works by Morera, C. Haes and others; Dir JESÚS NAVARRO I GUITART.

Museu de Lleida Diocesà i Comarcal: Carrer Sant Crist 1, 25002 Lleida; tel. 973283075; e-mail museu@museudelleida.cat; internet www.museudelleida.cat; f. 1893; medieval sculptures; sub-section at Rambla de Aragón containing religious paintings, metalwork and vestments; Dir CÈSAR CARRERAS.

Servei d'Arqueologia de la Fundació Pública Institut d'Estudis Ilerdencs (Archaeological Services of the Public Foundation the Institute of Lleida Studies): Plaça Catedral s/n, 25002 Lérida; tel. 973271500; e-mail arqueolo@diputaciolleida.cat; internet www.fpiei.cat/ca/serveis/arqueologia.asp; f. 1954; archaeology, excavation; first Trinitarian house of Iberian Peninsula; Bronze Age to Medieval Age; Dir JOAN RAMON GONZÁLEZ PÉREZ.

Madrid

Instituto de Valencia de Don Juan (Don Juan Institute of Valencia): Calle Fortuny 43, 28010 Madrid; tel. 913081848; f. 1916; historical archives; museum of ancient Spanish industrial arts; illuminated MS *Les Statuts de la Toison d'Or* with miniatures; library of 10,000 vols; Dir BALBINA MARTÍNEZ CAVIRO.

Museo Arqueológico Nacional (National Archaeological Museum): Calle Serrano 13, 28001 Madrid; tel. 915777912; e-mail info.man@mecd.es; internet man.mcu.es; f. 1867; 16th-century miniatures; collns relating to Egyptian, Cypriot, Greek and Etruscan antiquities and to nat. prehistory, Iron Age, Iberian and Hispano-Roman art; from medieval and modern times: ivory carvings, Spanish pottery, Islamic pottery, brocades, tapestries, porcelain, furniture, textiles, numismatic colln; temporarily closed for renovation; library of 140,000 vols, 3,000 serial titles; medieval MSS incl. Huesca Bible of 12th century, *Beato de Liébana, Comentarios al Apocalipsis* (12th–13th century), *Martirologio y Regla de S. Benito* (13th century), *Cantorales* (15th century); Dir ROSA CHUMILLAS ZAMORA; publ. *Boletín* (irregular).

Museo Cerralbo: Calle Ventura Rodríguez 17, 28008 Madrid; tel. 915473646; e-mail museo.cerralbo@mcu.es; internet museocerralbo.mcu.es; f. 1924; the 17th Marquis of Cerralbo left his house to the nation as a museum, together with his colln of 50,000 paintings, drawings, engravings, porcelain, arms, carpets, coins, furniture; incl.

paintings by El Greco, Ribera, Titian, Van Dyck, Tintoretto; library of 13,000 vols; Dir LURDES VAQUERO ARGÜELLES.

Museo de Historia de Madrid (Historical Museum of Madrid): Calle Fuencarral 78, 28004 Madrid; tel. 917011863; e-mail smuseosm@madrid.es; internet www.madrid.es/museodehistoria; f. 1929, fmrly Museo Municipal de Madrid; historical and artistic evolution of Madrid since 16th century; portraits, paintings, designs, engravings, sculptures, plans, silversmiths' work, coins, ceramics, porcelain; paintings by Berruguete, Maella, Luca Giordano, Bayeu, Castillo, Goya and other contemporary artists, 1830 Madrid scale model, Ramón de Mesonero Romanos and Ramón Gómez de la Serna studies; Dir EDUARDO SALAS VÁZQUEZ.

Museo de la Farmacia Hispana (Museum of Spanish Medicine): Facultad de Farmacia, Universidad Complutense Madrid, Plaza de Ramón y Cajal s/n, 28040 Madrid; tel. 913941797; e-mail museofar@farm.ucm.es; internet www.ucm.es/info/mhfarhis; f. 1951; attached to Universidad Complutense de Madrid; colln of balances and granatarios, boxes and cabinets, drug colln, glass and crystal, mortars, old pharmacy, pottery and porcelain, scientific instrumentation; library of 10,000 vols; Dir FRANCISCO JAVIER PUERTO SARMIENTO.

Museo de la Real Academia de Bellas Artes de San Fernando (Royal Academy of Fine Arts of San Fernando): Calle de Alcalá 13, 28014 Madrid; tel. 915240864; e-mail museo@rabasf.org; internet www.realacademiabellasartessanfernando.com; f. 1752; 1,400 paintings, 600 sculptures, 15,000 drawings and prints, furniture, silverware and jewellery, porcelain, decorative arts; Spanish paintings since 16th century, European paintings from 16th–18th centuries, Spanish sculpture since 17th century; Dir for Academy ANTONIO BONET CORREA.

Museo del Ferrocarril de Madrid (Madrid Railway Museum): Paseo de las Delicias 61, 28045 Madrid; tel. 902228822; e-mail museodelicias@ffe.es; internet www.museodelferrocarril.org; f. 1984; 4,800 pieces explaining the history of Spanish railways; steam, diesel and electric trains, models, exhibitions; photographic archive; library of 31,000 vols, 200 periodicals; Dir CARLOS ABELLÁN RUIZ; publ *Colección de Historia Ferroviaria, Cuadernos del Archivo Histórico Ferroviario, Cuadernos del Museo* (12 a year), *Didactic Handbooks, Railway Museum Bulletin, Monographs, TST* (2 a year).

Museo del Romanticismo (Museum of Romanticism): Calle San Mateo 13, 28004 Madrid; tel. 914481045; e-mail informacion.romanticismo@mcu.es; internet museoromantico.mcu.es; f. 1921 as Museo Romántico, closed 2001, reopened under present name 2009; supervised by Min. of Education, Culture and Sport; paintings, furniture, books and decorations of Spanish romantic period; concerts, meetings, family and school programmes, lectures; library of 13,000 vols, 300 periodicals; Dir Dra ASUNCIÓN CARDONA.

Museo de San Isidro. Los Orígenes de Madrid (Museum of St Isidro, Origins of Madrid): Plaza San Andrés 2, 28005 Madrid; tel. 913667415; e-mail museosanisidro@madrid.es; internet www.madrid.es/museosanisidro; f. 2000, fmrly Museo de San Isidro; colln of models and artistic works related to the tradition of San Isidro and Santa Maria de la Cabeza; 600 archaeological pieces related to history of Madrid and environs; library of 12,000 vols; Dir EDUARDO SALAS VÁZQUEZ; publ *Estudios de Prehistoria y Arqueología Madrileñas* (1 a year).

Museo Nacional Centro de Arte Reina Sofía: Calle Santa Isabel 52, 28012 Madrid; tel. 917741000; e-mail info@museoreinasofia.es; internet www.museoreinasofia.es; f. 1990; Spanish and int. modern and contemporary art; library of 184,202 vols, 131,786 monographs, 1,960 periodical publs, 204 MSS, 1,863 audiovisual documents, 1,400 graphic documents and 336 electronic documents; Dir MANUEL J. BORJA-VILLEL; publ. *Carta* (2 a year).

Museo Nacional de Antropología (National Museum of Anthropology): Calle Alfonso XII 68, 28014 Madrid; tel. 915306418; e-mail antropologico@mecd.es; internet mnantropologia.mcu.es; f. 1910, fmrly a section of the Nat. Museum of Natural Science; colln of 30,000 objects and documents from Europe, Asia, the Philippines, Micronesia, Melanesia, Central and S America, the Sahara, Morocco, W and Central Africa, the fmr Spanish Guinea; library of 14,000 vols and anthropological periodicals; Dir PILAR ROMERO DE TEJADA Y PICATOSTE; publ. *Anales of National Museum of Anthropology* (1 a year).

Museo Nacional de Artes Decorativas (National Museum of Decorative Arts): Calle Montalbán 12, 28014 Madrid; tel. 915326499; e-mail mnad@mnad.mcu.es; internet mnartesdecorativas.mcu.es; f. 1912; supervised by Min. of Education, Culture and Sport; collns of interior decorative arts, especially Spanish from 15th–19th centuries, incl. carpets, furniture, leatherwork, jewellery, tapestries, ceramics, glass, porcelain, textiles; library of 20,000 vols, 500 periodicals; Dir SOFIA RODRIGUEZ BERNIS.

Museo Nacional de Ciencias Naturales (National Museum of Natural Sciences): José Gutiérrez Abascal 2, 28006 Madrid; tel. 914111328; e-mail director.mncn@csic.es; internet www.mncn.csic.es; f. 1771 as Real Gabinete de Historia Natural; attached to Consejo Superior de Investigaciones Científicas; natural history and scientific collns, mainly from Iberia, Central and S America, the Philippines, N Africa; library of 63,000 vols, 4,300 periodicals; Dir SANTIAGO MERINO RODRIGUEZ; publs *Graellsia* (1 a year), *Estudios Geológicos* (2 a year).

Museo Nacional de Ciencia y Tecnología (National Museum of Science and Technology): Paseo de las Delicias 61, 28045 Madrid; tel. 916037400; e-mail infomuseo@muncyt.es; internet www.muncyt.es; f. 1880; 15,000 objects from scientific, technological devices, vehicles, machine tools and industrial tools; library of 13,400 vols, 1,100 periodicals; Dir RAMÓN NÚÑEZ CENTELLA.

Museo Nacional del Prado (National Prado Museum): Paseo del Prado s/n, 28014 Madrid; tel. 913302800; e-mail museo.nacional@museodelprado.es; internet www.museodelprado.es; f. 1819; paintings of British, Dutch, Flemish, French, German, Italian and Spanish origins; sculptures of the 16th–19th century, Medieval Age, Greek and Roman origin; prints and drawings; library of 70,000 vols, 1,000 periodicals; Dir MIGUEL ZUGAZA; publ. *Boletín* (1 a year).

Museo Nacional de Reproducciones Artísticas (National Museum of Art Reproductions): Avda Juan de Herrera 2, 28040 Madrid; tel. 915497150; f. 1877; more than 3,000 reproductions of Oriental, Greek, Roman and Hispano-Roman statuary, medieval and Renaissance art, classical and medieval sculpture and decorative arts; library of 10,000 vols; Dir MARÍA JOSÉ ALMAGRO GORBEA.

Museo Naval (Naval Museum): Paseo del Prado 5, 28014 Madrid; tel. 915238789; e-mail museonavalmadrid@fn.mde.es;

internet www.armada.mde.es/museonaval; f. 1843, current location 1932; attached to Min. of the Navy; engravings of sea battles, portraits, nautical instruments and armaments; models of ships since 14th century; more than 6,000 original maps, charts, prints and drawings of many countries since 1600; 70,000 photographs; library of 20,000 vols, 350 periodicals; Dir GONZALO RODRÍGUEZ GONZÁLEZ-ALLER; publ. *Revista de Historia Naval* (4 a year).

Museo Sorolla (Sorolla Museum): General Martínez Campos 37, 28010 Madrid; tel. 913101584; e-mail museo@msorolla.mcu.es; internet museosorolla.mcu.es; f. 1931; permanent exhibition of 350 of the artist's works; temporary exhibitions; library of 7,000 vols; Dir CONSUELO LUCA DE TENA NAVARRO.

Museo Thyssen-Bornemisza: Palacio de Villahermosa, Paseo del Prado 8, 28014 Madrid; tel. 913690151; e-mail mtb@museothyssen.org; internet www.museothyssen.org; f. 1988; paintings and sculpture from 13th–20th centuries; Man. Dir TOMÀS LLORENS.

Museu Lázaro Galdiano (Lázaro Galdiano Foundation): Calle Serrano 122, 28006 Madrid; tel. 915616084; e-mail secretaria.fundacion@flg.es; internet www.flg.es; f. 1951; attached to Fundación Lázaro Galdiano; 12,500 items: Italian, Spanish and Flemish Renaissance paintings; Primitives; Golden Age, 18th- and 19th-century Spanish paintings; 16th- and 17th-century Dutch paintings; English 18th- and 19th-century colln; collns of ivory, medals and coins, furniture, enamels, watches, jewellery, furniture, weapons and armour, oriental and Spanish tapestries and cloth; library of 35,000 vols, 1,000 periodicals; Dir ELENA HERNANDO GONZALO; publ. *Goya. Revista de Arte* (3 a year).

Patrimonio Nacional (National Heritage): Palacio Real, Calle Bailen s/n, 28071 Madrid; tel. 914548700; e-mail info@patrimonionacional.es; internet www.patrimonionacional.es; f. 1940; state instn responsible for all the museums situated in royal palaces and properties; governed by Admin. Council; Dir ALICIA PASTOR MOR; publ. *Reales Sitios* (4 a year).

Subordinate Institutions:

Abadía Benedictina de la Santa Cruz del Valle de los Caídos: Carretera de Guadarrama-El Escorial, 28209 Valle de Cuelgamuros, (Madrid); tel. 918905611; f. 1957; monument to the fallen, commissioned by Gen. Franco.

Monasterio de las Descalzas Reales: Plaza de las Descalzas s/n, 28013 Madrid; tel. 914548800; f. 1557; combined museum and enclosed convent; 16th- and 17th-century paintings and artefacts.

Monasterio de Santa Maria la Real de las Huelgas: Calle Los Compases s/n, 09001 Burgos; tel. 947201630; f. 1187.

Monasterio de Yuste: 10430 Cuacos de Yuste, (Cáceres); tel. 927172197; f. 1402.

Palacio Real de Aranjuez: Plaza de Parejas, 28300 Aranjuez, (Madrid); tel. 918910740; former royal palace rich in 18th-century art.

Palacio Real de la Almudaina: Palau Reial s/n, 07001 Palma de Mallorca, Balearic Islands; tel. 971214134; built in the middle ages; royal palace; Gothic chapel of St Anne; Arab baths.

Palacio Real de La Granja de San Ildefonso: Plaza de España 17, 40100 La Granja de San Ildefonso (Segovia); tel. 921470019; f. 18th century; built for Philip V; gardens and fountains; colln of furniture and artefacts from the 18th and 19th centuries; tapestry museum.

Palacio Real de Madrid: Calle Bailen s/n, 28071 Madrid; tel. 914548800; f. 18th century; rooms devoted to 16th- to 18th-century tapestries, clocks, painting and porcelain from the royal palaces and pharmacy; Royal Armoury; rooms with original 18th-century decor; colln of furniture, paintings and porcelain from the 18th and 19th centuries; archives since the 12th century; library: see under Libraries and Archives.

Palacio Real de Riofrío: Bosque de Riofrío, 40420 Navas de Riofrío (Segovia); tel. 921470020; built in 1752.

Palacio Sitio de El Pardo: Calle Manuel Alonso s/n, 28048 El Pardo (Madrid); tel. 913761500; built for Henry IV in 15th century, rebuilt for Carlos I in 1553 and enlarged in the 18th century by Sabatini; 18th-century tapestries, some by Goya.

Real Monasterio de la Encarnación: Plaza de la Encarnación 1, 28013 Madrid; tel. 914548800; f. 1611; combined museum and enclosed convent; 17th- and 18th-century paintings and sculptures; colln of 700 bronze, coral, ivory and fine timber artefacts from Spain, Germany, Italy, Netherlands.

Real Monasterio de Santa Clara de Tordesillas: 47100 Tordesillas (Valladolid); tel. 983770071; f. 1363.

Real Monasterio de Santa Isabel: Calle de Santa Isabel 48, 28012 Madrid; f. 16th century; 17th- and 18th-century paintings.

Planetario de Madrid (Planetarium of Madrid): Avda del Planetario 16, 28045 Madrid; tel. 914673461; e-mail buzon@planetmad.es; internet www.planetmad.es; f. 1986; promotes and disseminates astronomical knowledge and sciences; Dir ASUNCIÓN SÁNCHEZ JUSTEL.

Mérida

Museo Nacional de Arte Romano (National Museum of Roman Art): Calle José Ramón Mélida s/n, 06800 Mérida; tel. 924311690; e-mail mnar@mnar.es; internet museoarteromano.mcu.es; f. 1838, present site since 1986; 37,000 artefacts; Roman, Visigoth archaeology; library of 16,000 vols, 695 periodicals; Dir Dr JOSÉ MARÍA ÁLVAREZ MARTÍNEZ; publs Anas (1 a year), Cuadernos Emeritenses (irregular), Studia Lusitana.

Palma de Mallorca

Museo de Mallorca: Calle de Portella 5, 07001 Palma; tel. 971717540; internet www.museudemallorca.es; f. 1961; collns on history, ethnology, fine arts, prehistory; Dir JOANA MARIA PALOU.

Pontevedra

Museo de Pontevedra: Calle Pasantería 2–12, 36002 Pontevedra; tel. 986804100; internet www.museo.depo.es; f. 1927; pottery and ancient industrial and naval history of Galicia; prehistoric jewellery and jet ornaments; Spanish paintings since 15th century; library of 150,000 vols, 6,000 periodicals, 500 maps; Dir LEOPOLDO NÓVOA; publ. El Museo de Pontevedra (1 a year).

Sabadell

Museu d'Art de Sabadell: Carrer Doctor Puig 16, 08202 Sabadell; tel. 937257144; e-mail mas@ajsabadell.cat; f. 1981; colln of paintings, ceramics, photography from early 19th century to 1960s; Dir JOSEP SERRANO; publ. Arraona.

Museu d'Història de Sabadell: Carrer Sant Antoni 13, 08201 Sabadell; tel. 937278555; e-mail mhs@ajsabadell.cat; f.

1931 as Museu de la Ciutat, present name 1970; prehistoric archaeological, numismatic collns, native handicrafts; Iberico-Roman section; textiles and mineralogy; Dir GENÍS RIBÉ MONGÉ; publ. Arraona (1 a year).

Sabiñánigo

Museo de Dibujo 'Castillo de Larrés': Apdo 25, 22612 Huesca; tel. 9744482981; e-mail serrablo@serrablo.org; internet www.serrablo.org/museodibujo; f. 1991; Pres. ALFREDO GAVÍN.

San Roque

Museo Monográfico Municipal de Carteia: Palacio de los Gobernadores, Calle Rubín de Celis 1, 11360 Cadiz; tel. 956781587; e-mail prensasanroque@airtel.net; internet cpd.sanroque.es/fmc/museo_carteia.htm; f. 2001; explains the history of excavations in the town and the historical devt of the ancient settlement of Carteia; Dir RAFAEL CALDELA LÓPEZ.

San Sebastián

Palacio del Mar—Aquarium (Sea Museum and Aquarium): Plaza Carlos Blasco de Imaz, 20003 Donostia, San Sebastián; tel. 943440099; e-mail sog@aquariumss.com; internet www.aquariumss.com; f. 1928; history of seafaring since 13th century, models of historical ships, portraits of navigators and local fishing tackle; oceanographic museum and marine laboratory; aquarium with Atlantic and tropical fishes; Dir CARMEN ARRAZOLA.

San Telmo Museoa: Plaza Zuloaga 1, 20003 San Sebastián; tel. 943481580; e-mail santelmo@donostia.org; internet www.santelmomuseoa.com; f. 1900, inaugurated 1902; colln of paintings, sculptures, drawings, etchings, Egyptian figures, weapons, medals, ceramics, musical instruments, steles, maps, photographs, farming equipment or agizaiolas; 26,000 pieces on archaeology, fine art, ethnography, photography, history; library of 11,000 vols; Dir SUSANA SOTO.

Santander

Museo de Prehistoria y Arqueología de Cantabria (Prehistoric and Archaeological Museum): Avda Los Castros 65–67, 39005 Santander; tel. 942209922; e-mail mupac@gobcantabria.es; f. 1926; palaeolithic to Middle Ages in Cantabria; library of 62,000 vols; Dir ROBERTO ONTAÑÓN.

Santiago de Compostela

Museo das Peregrinacións de Santiago (Pilgrimage Museum of Santiago): Rue de San Miguel 4, 15704 Santiago de Compostela; tel. 981581558; e-mail difusion.mdperegrinacions@xunta.es; internet www.mdperegrinacions.com; f. 1951, inaugurated 1965; relics and items related to St James and the Pilgrimages; medieval art and history of the 'Camino de Santiago'; library of 8,246 vols, 350 periodicals; Dir BIEITO PÉREZ OUTEIRIÑO.

Seville

Museo Arqueológico de Sevilla (Archaeological Museum of Seville): Plaza de América s/n, 41013 Seville; tel. 955120632; e-mail museoarqueologicosevilla.ccd@juntadeandalucia.es; internet www.juntadeandalucia.es/culturaydeporte/museos/mase; f. 1867; 60,000 exhibits; Roman statues, mosaics; incorporates municipal collns; treasures of Tarshish; Dir ANA DOLORES NAVARRO ORTEGA.

Museo de Bellas Artes de Sevilla (Museum of Fine Arts of Seville): Plaza del Museo 9, 41001 Seville; tel. 955542942;

e-mail museobellasartessevilla.ccud@juntadeandalucia.es; f. 1835; paintings by local artists from 15th to 20th centuries; Baroque art (esp. Murillo, Zurbarán and Valdés Leal); library of 12,000 vols, 562 periodicals; Dir MARÍA DEL VALME MUÑOZ RUBIO.

Sitges

Museu Cau Ferrat: Carrer Davallada 12, Third Fl., Miramar Bldg, 08870 Sitges; tel. 938940364; e-mail m.sitges@diba.es; f. 1933; closed for renovations from 2010; house and studio of the painter and writer Santiago Rusiñol; contains drawings and paintings by Rusiñol and his friends and contemporaries, (Casas, Picasso, Utrillo); woodcarving, sculpture, paintings (El Greco), ceramics (since 14th century), furniture, ironwork (13th–19th centuries), glass (16th–19th centuries); Dir MARIA-NADAL SAU I GIRALT.

Soria

Museo Numantino: Paseo del Espolón 8, 42001 Soria; tel. 975221397; e-mail museo.soria@jcyl.es; f. 1913; prehistoric, ethnological, Roman and medieval archaeological collections, comprising 180,000 objects; library of 10,000 vols; Dir ELÍAS TERÉS NAVARRO.

Tarragona

Museu i Necròpolis Paleocristians: Avda de Ramón y Cajal 84, 43005 Tarragona; tel. 977211175; e-mail mnat@mnat.cat; f. 1930; objects discovered during excavation of the Roman-Christian necropolis; Dir FRANCESC TARRATS-BOU.

Museu Nacional Arqueològic de Tarragona (National Museum of Archaeology of Tarragona): Plaça del Rei 5, 43003 Tarragona; tel. 977236209; e-mail mnat@mnat.es; internet www.mnat.es; f. 1834; archaeological, historical, local Roman exhibits; library of 14,000 vols, 785 periodicals; Dir FRANCESC TARRATS-BOU.

Toledo

Museo del Greco (El Greco Museum): Paseo del Tránsito s/n, 45002 Toledo; tel. 925216967; e-mail museodelgreco@mcu.es; internet museodelgreco.mcu.es; f. 1911; the artist's house; later works by El Greco; works from the Spanish schools of the 17th century; furniture of the 16th–17th century and ceramics from the Talaverana factory; colln of paintings by Spanish artists incl. Francisco de Zurbarán and Bartolomé Esteban Murillo; Dir CONSOLACIÓN PASTOR PASTOR.

Museo de Santa Cruz: Calle Miguel de Cervantes 3, 45001 Toledo; tel. 925221036; e-mail museodesantacruz@jccm.es; f. 1961; archaeology, fine arts, industrial and decorative arts; library of 13,000 vols; Dir ALFONSO CABALLERO; publ. Memoria del Museo de Santa Cruz (irregular).

Affiliated Museums:

Museo Casa de Dulcinea en El Toboso: Calle Don Quijote 1, 45820 El Toboso; tel. 925197288; f. 1967; ethnography of La Mancha area and period reconstruction in the 17th-century Casa Solariega.

Museo de Arte Contemporáneo: Calle de las Bulas s/n, 45002 Toledo; tel. 925227871; f. 1973.

Museo de Cerámica 'Ruíz de Luna': Plaça de San Agustín s/n, 45600 Talavera de la Reina; tel. 925800149; f. 1963; local ceramics.

Museo de los Concilios y de la Cultura Visigoda: Calle San Román s/n, 45002 Toledo; tel. 925227872; f. 1969; Visigothic art and archaeology.

Museo Taller del Moro: Calle Taller del Moro 4, 45002 Toledo; tel. 925224500; f. 1961; Mudejar art and archaeology.

Museo Sefardi-Sinagoga del Tránsito: Calle Samuel Leví s/n, 45002 Toledo; tel. 925223665; e-mail museo.msefardi@mcu.es; internet museosefardi.mcu.es; f. 1964; Jewish synagogue built in the 14th century by Samuel Ha-Levi, treas. to King Don Pedro I, 'The Cruel'; given to the Military Order of Calatrava in 1494 by Ferdinand and Isabella; in 18th century became church of Sta María del Tránsito; nat. monument; created Sephardic Museum 1964; archaeology, life and costumes of Sephardic Jews; colln of documentary books, MSS; library of 16,000 vols; Dir SANTIAGO PALOMERO PLAZA.

Valencia

Museo de Bellas Artes de Valencia (Museum of Fine Arts of Valencia): Calle de San Pío V 9, 46010 Valencia; tel. 963870300; e-mail museobellasartesvalencia@gva.es; internet www.museobellasartesvalencia.gva.es; f. 1839; 3,000 paintings; sculpture, archaeology, drawing and print sections; library of 23,964 vols, 843 periodicals, 7,892 photographs, 614 CDs, 72,000 press clippings; Dir PAZ OLMOS PERIS.

Museo Nacional de Cerámica y Artes Suntuarias 'González Marti': Poeta Querol 2, 46002 Valencia; tel. 963516392; e-mail difusion.mceramica@mcu.es; internet mnceramica.mcu.es; f. 1947; 26,209 exhibits; colln of ceramics and decorative arts, set in the Palace of the Marquis of Dos Aguas; library of 25,000 vols, 1,100 periodicals; Dir Dr JAUME COLL CONESA; publ. *Materiales y Documentos*.

Museu de Prehistòria de València: Calle Corona 36, 46003 Valencia; tel. 963883565; e-mail sip@dival.es; internet www.museuprehistoriavalencia.es; f. 1927; prehistoric art and culture; Roman era; Iberian culture and coin collns; Valencian archaeology; intense field work in archaeological sites; organizes educational activities, workshops, temporary exhibits, courses, confs; library of 60,000 vols, 1,429 periodicals; Dir HELENA BONET ROSADO; publs *Archivo de Prehistoria Levantina*, *Serie de Trabajos Varios del S.I.P.*

Valladolid

Museo Casa de Cervantes, Valladolid (Cervantes' House Museum, Valladolid): Calle del Rastro s/n, 47001 Valladolid; tel. 983308810; e-mail informacion@mcervantes.mcu.es; internet museocasacervantes.mcu.es; f. 1948; furniture and possessions of the writer; library of 10,000 vols; Dir JESÚS URREA FERNÁNDEZ.

Museo de Valladolid (Valladolid Museum): Palacio de Fabio Nelli, Plaza de Fabio Nelli s/n, 47003 Valladolid; tel. 983351389; e-mail museo.valladolid@jcyl.es; f. 1879; archaeology and fine art; articles from palaeolithic times to the 18th century; library of 15,000 vols; Dir ELOISA WATTENBERG GARCÍA.

Museo Nacional Colegio de San Gregorio: Cadenas de San Gregorio 1–3, 47011 Valladolid; tel. 983250375; e-mail direccion.museoescultura@mecd.es; internet museosangregorio.mcu.es; f. 1933 as Museo Nacional de Escultura, present name 2008; housed in the old Colegio de San Gregorio, since late 15th century; works by Alonso Berruguete, Juan de Juni, Gregorio Fernández, Alonso Cano, Felipe Vigarny and others; library of 20,000 vols; Dir MARÍA BOLAÑOS ATIENZA; publ. *Boletín*.

Vic

Museu Episcopal de Vic (Episcopal Museum of Vic): Plaça Bisbe Oliba 3, 08500 Vic; tel. 938869360; e-mail informacio@museuepiscopalvic.com; internet www.museuepiscopalvic.com; f. 1891; medieval arts, provincial Romanesque, Gothic precious metalwork, textiles, embroideries, liturgical vestments, forged iron; Dir JOSEP MARIA RIBA FARRÉS.

Zamora

Museo de Zamora (Museum of Zamora): Plaza de Santa Lucía 2, 49002 Zamora; tel. 980516150; e-mail museo.zamora@jcyl.es; internet www.museoscastillayleon.jcyl.es/museodezamora; f. 1911; housed in 16th-century palace; colln of 300,000 artefacts of palaeontology, prehistory and archaeology, fine arts, ethnography; library of 9,254 vols, 241 periodicals; Dir ROSARIO GARCÍA ROZAS.

Zaragoza

Museo de Zaragoza (Museum of Zaragoza): Plaza de los Sitios 6, 50001 Zaragoza; tel. 976222181; e-mail museoza@aragob.es; f. 1848; archaeology, prehistory, Roman, Arab, Gothic, Moorish, Romanesque and Renaissance exhibits; primitive arts and crafts, paintings from 14th–19th centuries, contemporary Aragonese artists; ethnology and ceramics sections are located at Parque Primo de Rivera; library of 31,000 vols; Dir Dr MIGUEL BELTRÁN LLORIS; publs *Boletín* (1 a year), *Catálogos Exposiciones*, *Guías Didácticas* (2 or 3 a year).

Museo Pablo Gargallo: Plaza de San Felipe 3, 50003 Zaragoza; tel. 976724922; e-mail museogargallo-oficinas@ayto-zaragoza.es; internet www.zaragoza.es/ciudad/museos/es/gargallo; f. 1982; collns of sculpture, designs and cartoons by Gargallo; research on his life and works and modern art in gen.; library of 9,000 vols; Dir MARÍA CRISTINA GIL IMAZ; publ. *Revista de Arte*.

Universities

ASOCIACIÓN UNIVERSITARIA IBEROAMERICANA DE POSTGRADO

Colegio Arzobispo Fonseca, Calle Fonseca 4, 37002 Salamanca
Telephone: 923210039
E-mail: auip@auip.org
Internet: www.auip.org
Private control
Consists of 170 instns of higher education in Spain, Portugal, Latin America, the Caribbean
Pres.: FRANCISCO GONZÁLEZ LODEIRO
First Vice-Pres.: IVÁN RAMOS CALDERÓN
Vice-Pres.: DANIEL HERNÁNDEZ RUIPÉREZ
Vice-Pres.: DÍDAC RAMÍREZ I SARRIÓ
Vice-Pres.: JULIO CEZAR DURIGAN
Vice-Pres.: VÍCTOR ANTONIO CORRALES BURGUEÑO
Dir-Gen.: VÍCTOR E. CRUZ CARDONA

I. E. UNIVERSIDAD
(I.E. University)

Calle Cardenal Zúñiga 12, 40003 Segovia
Telephone: 921412410
E-mail: university@ie.edu
Internet: www.ie.edu
Founded 1973 as a Business School, present name and status 2008
Private control
Language of instruction: Spanish
Academic year: September to June (2 semesters)

Schools of architecture and design, art and humanities, biology, business, communication, law, social and behavioural sciences; also has campus in Madrid
Pres.: Dr SANTIAGO ÍÑIGUEZ DE ONZOÑO
Rector: Dr SALVADOR CARMONA MORENO
Assoc. Vice-Rector: Dr ISABEL SÁNCHEZ GARCÍA
Vice-Rector for Coordination and Research: Dr MARCO TROMBETTA
Vice-Rector for Planning: Dr SAMUEL GONZÁLEZ MANCEBO
Vice-Rector for Students: Dr MARCO TROMBETTA (acting)
Dean for Graduate Studies: MANUEL FERNÁNDEZ VILLALTA
Dean for Undergraduate Studies: ANTONIO DE CASTRO CARPEÑO
Gen. Sec.: Dr ROBERTO RUIZ SALCES
Library Dir: AMADA MARCOS BLÁZQUEZ
Library of 36,000 vols, 4,500 ejournals and periodicals, 11,000 ebooks
Number of teachers: 190
Number of students: 1,400

MONDRAGON UNIBERTSITATEA

Apdo 23, Loramendi 4, 20500 Mondragón
Telephone: 943712185
E-mail: info@mondragon.edu
Internet: www.mondragon.edu
Founded 1997
Private control
Languages of instruction: Basque, English, Spanish
Academic year: September to July (2 semesters)

Rector: IOSU ZABALA
Vice-Rector: JOSE MARI AIZEGA ZUBILLAGA
Academic Vice-Rector: JON ALTUNA
Gen. Sec. and Admin. Dir: IDOIA PEÑACOBA ETXEBARRIA
Librarian: OBDULIA VELEZ

Library of 85,000 vols, 950 periodicals
Number of teachers: 250
Number of students: 3,100

Publications: *Irakur Gida* (1 a year), *Jakingarriak*, *Mendeberriak* (3 a year), *MUniversitas*

DEANS

Faculty of Business Studies: LANDER BELOKI MENDIZABAL
Faculty of Engineering: VICENTE ATXA URIBE (Dir)
Faculty of Gastronomic Sciences: JOSE MARI AIZEGA (Dir)
Faculty of Humanities and Education: NEKANE ARRATIBEL INTXAUSTI

NEBRIJA UNIVERSIDAD
(Nebrija University)

Campus de la Berzosa, Hoyo de Manzanares, 28249 Madrid
Telephone: 914521101
E-mail: informa@nebrija.es
Internet: www.nebrija.com
Founded 1995
Private control
Language of instruction: Spanish
Academic year: September to June (2 semesters)

Rector: Prof. Dra MARIA PILAR VÉLEZ MELÓN
Vice-Rector for Academic Affairs: ALBERTO LÓPEZ ROSADO
Vice-Rector for Research: JUAN ANTONIO MAESTRO DE LA CUERDA

Library of 44,000 vols, 300 periodicals
Number of students: 2,800

DEANS

Faculty of Arts and Letters: MARTA BARALO OTTONELLO

Faculty of Communications Sciences: Dra MARTA PERLADO LAMO DE ESPINOSA

Faculty of Social Sciences: Prof. CARLOS CUERVO-ARANGO MARTÍNEZ

Health Sciences: CARLOS CALLEJA DE FRUTOS (Dir)

Nebrija Business School: ANTONIO DIAZ MORALES (Dir)

UNIVERSIDAD ALFONSO X EL SABIO
(Alfonso X el Sabio University)

Avda Universidad 1, 28691, Madrid

Telephone: 918109200

E-mail: info@uax.es

Internet: www.uax.es

Founded 1993

Private control

Language of instruction: Spanish

Academic year: October to June (2 semesters)

Faculties of applied languages, education, engineering and architecture, health and sports sciences, social and legal studies

Pres.: JESÚS NÚÑEZ VELÁZQUEZ

Rector: JOSÉ DOMÍNGUEZ DE POSADA

Library of 68,200 vols, 380 periodicals

Number of teachers: 1,000

Number of students: 12,500

Publications: *A x A* (online), *Linguax* (online), *Revista Electrónica Biociencias* (1 a year, online), *Saberes* (online), *Tecnologí@ y Desarrollo* (online)

UNIVERSIDAD AUTÓNOMA DE MADRID

Ciudad Universitaria de Cantoblanco, 28049 Madrid

Telephone: 914975000

E-mail: informacion.general@uam.es

Internet: www.uam.es

Founded 1968

State control

Language of instruction: Spanish

Academic year: October to June

Rector: JOSÉ MARÍA SANZ MARTÍNEZ

Vice-Rector for Campus and Community Care: MARÍA ÁNGELES ESPINOSA BAYAL

Vice-Rector for Cooperation and Univ. Extension: MARGARITA ALFARO AMIEIRO

Vice-Rector for Graduate Studies: JUAN ANTONIO HUERTAS MARTÍNEZ

Vice-Rector for Innovation, Transfer and Technology: JOSÉ RAMÓN DORRONSORO IBERO

Vice-Rector for Int. Relations: ASUNCIÓN MARTÍNEZ CEBRIÁN

Vice-Rector for Postgraduate Studies: ÁNGEL RODRÍGUEZ GARCÍA-BRAZALES

Vice-Rector for Research: NURIA FERNÁNDEZ MONSALVE

Vice-Rector for Scientific Policy and Research Infrastructures: RAFAEL GARESSE ALARCÓN

Vice-Rector for Students and Continuing Education: ANTONIO ÁLVAREZ-OSSORIO ALVARIÑO

Vice-Rector for Teaching and Research Staff: CARLOS GARCÍA DE LA VEGA

Sec.-Gen.: MARIA PILAR CÁMARA ÁGUILA

Librarian: MIGUEL JIMÉNEZ ALEIXANDRE

Library of 906,048 vols, 17,262 periodicals

Number of teachers: 2,250

Number of students: 35,000

Publications: *Al Sur* (4 a year), *Anuario de la Facultad de Derecho* (1 a year), *Anuario del Departamento de Filosofía* (4 a year), *Anuario del Departamento de Historia de la Filosofía* (1 a year), *Anuario del Departamento de Historia y Teoría del Arte* (1 a year), *Apuntes de la Autónoma* (irregular),

Boletín del Instituto de Ciencias de la Educación (irregular), *Boletín Geográfico* (3 a year), *Coyuntura Trimestral* (4 a year, journal of the Laurence R. Klein Institute of Economic Forecasting), *Cuaderno Gris* (3 a year), *Cuadernos de Prehistoria y Arqueología* (1 a year), *Edad de Oro* (1 a year), *Encuentros Multidisciplinares* (Multidisciplinary Research and Debate, 3 a year), *Journal of Human Ecology* (irregular), *La Ecoalternativa* (4 a year), *Manuscrit. CAO* (1 a year), *Narria* (4 a year), *Relaciones Internacionales*, *Revista de Cantoblanco* (12 a year), *Revista de Lengua y Literatura Catalana, Gallega y Vasca* (1 a year), *Revista internacional de Estudios de Derecho y Arbitraje*, *Revista Jurídica de la UAM* (2 a year), *Tarbiya* (educational research and innovation, 3 a year)

DEANS

Faculty of Economics and Business Sciences: ANA MARÍA LÓPEZ GARCÍA

Faculty of Law: Dr FERNANDO MOLINA FERNÁNDEZ

Faculty of Medicine: JUAN ANTONIO VARGAS NÚÑEZ

Faculty of Philosophy and Letters: ANTONIO CASCÓN DORADO

Faculty of Psychology: ÁNGELA LOECHES ALONSO

Faculty of Sciences: ISABEL CASTRO PARGA

Faculty of Teacher Training and Education: ROSALÍA ARANDA REDRUELLO

UNIVERSIDAD CAMILO JOSÉ CELA

Calle Castillo de Alarcón, 49 Urb. Villafranca del Castillo, 28692 Madrid

Telephone: 918153131

E-mail: info@ucjc.edu

Internet: www.ucjc.edu

Founded 1999

Private control

Language of instruction: Spanish

Pres.: FELIPE SEGOVIA OLMO

Vice-Rector for Academic Affairs and Faculty: ENRIQUE FERNÁNDEZ REDONDO

Vice-Rector for Innovation: AINARA ZUBILLAGA DEL RIO

Vice-Rector for Research and Doctoral Affairs: ADOLFO SÁNCHEZ BURÓN

Sec.-Gen.: JOSÉ LUIS DELSO MARTÍNEZ-TREVIJANO

Library Dir: ANNA MARIA ALONSO

Library of 23,000 vols, 278 periodicals

Number of students: 5,000

Publications: *EduPsykhé* (1 a year), *Revista digital Intenciones* (2 a year, online (www.revistaintenciones.com))

DEANS

Faculty of Communication Sciences: Dr JULIO CÉSAR PÉREZ HERRERO

Faculty of Health Sciences: Dr MIGUEL ÁNGEL PÉREZ NIETO

Faculty of Law and Economics: Dr JESÚS GRACIA SANZ

Faculty of Social Sciences and Education: ESTHER ROBLES SASTRE

UNIVERSIDAD CARLOS III DE MADRID

Calle Madrid 126–128, Getafe, 28903 Madrid

Telephone: 916246000

E-mail: rector@uc3m.es

Internet: www.uc3m.es

Founded 1989

State control

Languages of instruction: English, Spanish

Academic year: September to June (2 semesters)

Rector: Prof. DANIEL PEÑA SANCHEZ DE RIVERA

Vice-Rector for Colmenarejo Campus: MARÍA PALOMA DÍAZ PÉREZ

Vice-Rector for Communication, Culture and Sports and Continuing Education: MIGUEL SATRÚSTEGUI GILI-DELGADO

Vice-Rector for Equality and Cooperation: Prof. ROSARIO RUIZ FRANCO

Vice-Rector for Infrastructure and Environmental Affairs: Prof. CARLOS DELGADO KLOOS

Vice-Rector for Int. Relations: Prof. ÁLVARO ESCRIBANO SÁEZ

Vice-Rector for Postgraduate Studies and Campus Madrid-Puerta Toledo: Prof. ISABEL GUTIÉRREZ CALDERÓN

Vice-Rector for Research: CARLOS BALAGUER BERNALDO DE QUIRÓS

Vice-Rector for Student Affairs and Residence Halls: MARÍA LUISA GONZÁLEZ-CUÉLLAR SERRANO

Vice-Rector for Teaching Staff and Depts: JUAN JOSÉ ROMO URROZ

Vice-Rector for Undergraduate Studies: Dr LUIS RAÚL SÁNCHEZ FERNÁNDEZ

Gen. Sec.: JESÚS RAFAEL MERCADER UGUINA

Head Librarian: MARÍA TERESA DE MOLINA MARTÍN-MONTALVO

Number of teachers: 1,423

Number of students: 17,711

Publications: *CIAN, Derechos y Libertades, Eunomía, Forinf@ Online, Hispania Nova, LITTERAE* (1 a year), *Revista de Historia Económica* (in English and Spanish), *Revista de Historiografía, Semanal 3, Spanish Labour Law and Employment Relations Journal, Universitas*

DEANS

Higher Polytechnic School: Prof. DANIEL SEGOVIA VARGAS

School of Humanities, Communications, and Documentation: JOSÉ MANUEL PALACIO ARRANZ

School of Social Sciences and Law: Prof. MANUEL ÁNGEL BERMEJO CASTRILLO

UNIVERSIDAD CATÓLICA DE VALENCIA 'SAN VICENTE MÁRTIR'
(San Vicente Martir Catholic University of Valencia)

Calle Guillem de Castro 65, 46008 Valencia

Telephone: 963924643

E-mail: ucv@ucv.es

Internet: www.ucv.es

Founded 2003

Private control

Language of instruction: Spanish

Academic year: September to May (2 semesters)

Rector: Dr JOSÉ ALFREDO PERIS CANCIO

Vice-Rector for Academic Org. and Employment: Dr JOSÉ MANUEL PAGÁN AGULLÓ

Vice-Rector for Faculty and Continuing Education: Dr JOSÉ IGNACIO PRATS MORA

Vice-Rector for Int. Relations and Sports: Dr PABLO VIDAL GONZÁLEZ

Vice-Rector for Research, Devt and Innovation: Dr FRANCISCO JAVIER ROMERO GÓMEZ

Vice-Rector for Strategic Planning and Quality: Dr JUAN MOROTE SARRION

Vice-Rector for Student Affairs and Social Action: Dr YOLANDA RUIZ ORDÓÑEZ

Vice-Rector for Univ. Extension and Cultural Chaplain: Dr JOSÉ LUÍS SÁNCHEZ GARCÍA

Sec.-Gen.: ANTONIO ORERO CLAVERO

Library of 62,000 vols

DEANS

Faculty of Economic and Business Sciences: Dr JUAN SAPENA BOLUFER

Faculty of Law: Dr JOSÉ VICENTE MOROTE SARRIÓN

Faculty of Medicine and Dentistry: Dr GERMÁN CERDÁ OLMEDO
Faculty of Nursing: Dr GERMÁN CERDÁ OLMEDO
Faculty of Philosophy, Anthropology and Social Work: Dr GINÉS MARCO PERLES
Faculty of Physical Activity and Sport Sciences: Dra AMPARO BARGUES BONET
Faculty of Physiotherapy and Podology: Dr IGNACIO GÓMEZ PÉREZ
Faculty of Psychology, Teaching and Education Sciences: Dr GABRIEL MARTÍNEZ RICO
Faculty of Veterinary and Experimental Sciences: Dr JOSÉ TENA MEDIALDEA

UNIVERSIDAD CATÓLICA SAN ANTONIO
(Saint Anthony Catholic University)

Campus de Los Jerónimos nº 135, 30107 Guadalupe, Murcia
Telephone: 902182181
E-mail: info@ucam.edu
Internet: www.ucam.edu
Founded 1996
Private control
Language of instruction: Spanish
Academic year: September to June (2 semesters)

Rector: Dra JOSEFINA GARCÍA LOZANO
Vice-Rector for Int. Relations and Communication: PABLO BLESA ALEDO
Vice-Rector for Religious Affairs: JOSÉ ALBERTO CÁNOVAS SÁNCHEZ
Vice-Rector for Research: ESTRELLA NÚÑEZ DELICADO
Vice-Rector for Univ. Extension: ANTONIO ALCARAZ LÓPEZ
Sec.-Gen.: JOSÉ ALARCÓN TERUEL
Library Dir: MARÍA DOLORES RÍOS ALMAZÁN
Library of 120,604 vols, 8,631 periodicals
Number of teachers: 888
Number of students: 10,300

Publications: *Cultura, Ciencia y Deporte*, *Fisioterapia* (2 a year, print and online), *Sphera Publica*

DEANS

Faculty of Health Sciences: ANDRÉS MARTÍNEZ-ALMAGRO ANDREO
Faculty of Legal Sciences and Business: (vacant)
Faculty of Nursing: PALOMA ECHEVARRÍA PÉREZ
Faculty of Physical Activity and Sport Sciences: ANTONIO SÁNCHEZ PATO
Faculty of Social and Communication Sciences: PABLO BLESA ALEDO

UNIVERSIDAD CATÓLICA SANTA TERESA DE JESÚS DE ÁVILA

Calle Los Canteros s/n, 05005 Ávila
Telephone: 920251020
E-mail: info@ucavila.es
Internet: www.ucavila.es
Founded 1996
Private control
Language of instruction: Spanish
Academic year: September to June (2 semesters)

Grand Chancellor: HE JESÚS GARCÍA BURILLO
Chancellor: HE Dr MARÍA DEL ROSARIO SÁEZ YUGUERO
Vice-Chancellor for Academic Org. and Innovation: Dr CONCEPCIÓN ALBARRÁN FERNÁNDEZ
Vice-Chancellor for Research and Postgraduate Studies: Dr TOMÁS SANTAMARÍA PATO
Vice-Chancellor for Teaching Staff and Quality: BEGOÑA LAFUENTE NAFRÍA
Gen. Sec.: Dr FRANCISCO TRULLÉN GALVE
Library Dir: MARIA SONSOLES RODRÍGUEZ CRESPO

DEANS
Faculty of Sciences and Arts: Dr PEDRO MÁS ALIQUE
Faculty of Social and Legal Sciences: Dr ÁLVARO MENDO ESTRELLA

UNIVERSIDAD CEU CARDENAL HERRERA
(CEU Cardenal Herrera University)

Calle Luis Vives 1, 46115 Valencia
Telephone: 961369000
E-mail: informa@uch.ceu.es
Internet: www.uchceu.es
Founded 1971
Private control
Academic year: September to June (2 semesters)

Rector: ROSA MARÍA VISIEDO CLAVEROL
Vice-Rector for Academic Affairs and Faculty: FRANCISCO BOSCH MORELL
Vice-Rector for Centre at Elche: CÉSAR CASIMIRO ELENA
Vice-Rector for Research and Int. Relations: IÑAKI BILBAO ESTRADA
Vice-Rector for Student Affairs and Univ. Extension: MARÍA JOSÉ GONZÁLEZ SOLAZ
Sec.-Gen.: JOSE MANUEL AMIGUET ESTEBAN
Library Dir: ELENA SAURÍ RODRIGO
Library of 90,000 vols, 2,019 periodicals

DEANS

Faculty of Health Sciences: ALICIA LÓPEZ CASTELLANO
Faculty of Humanities and Communication Sciences: ELÍAS DURÁN DE PORRAS
Faculty of Law, Business and Political Science: ROSA PASCUAL SERRATS
Faculty of Veterinary Science: SANTIAGO VEGA GARCÍA

UNIVERSIDAD CEU SAN PABLO

Julián Romea 23, 28003 Madrid
Telephone: 914566300
E-mail: ceu.sec.vrrii@ceu.es
Internet: www.uspceu.com
Founded 1993
Private control
Language of instruction: Spanish
Academic year: September to July (2 semesters)

Rector: JUAN CARLOS DOMÍNGUEZ NAFRÍA
Vice-Rector for Academic Affairs and Postgraduate Studies: JAVIER ITURRIOZ DEL CAMPO
Vice-Rector for Faculty: FEDERICO MARTÍNEZ RODA
Vice-Rector for Int. Relations: JOSÉ LUIS PIÑAR MAÑAS
Vice-Rector for Research: MARIA CORAL BARBAS ARRIBAS
Vice-Rector for Student Affairs: LEOPOLDO ABAD ALCALÁ
Sec.-Gen.: ALBERTO DÍAZ-ROMERAL GÓMEZ
Library Dir: JOSÉ MORILLO-VELARDE SERRANO
Library of 230,000 vols
Number of teachers: 890
Number of students: 7,000

DEANS

Faculty of Economic and Business Sciences: Dr RICARDO JAVIER PALOMO ZURDO
Faculty of Humanities and Communication Sciences: Dr JOSÉ FRANCISCO SERRANO OCEJA
Faculty of Law: Dra AMPARO LOZANO MANEIRO
Faculty of Medicine: Dr TOMÁS CHIVATO PÉREZ
Faculty of Pharmacy: BEATRIZ DE PASCUAL-TERESA FERNÁNDEZ
Higher Polytechnic School: DAVID SANTOS MEJÍA (Dir)

UNIVERSIDAD COMPLUTENSE DE MADRID

Ciudad Universitaria, Avda de Seneca 2, 28040 Madrid
Telephone: 914520400
E-mail: infocom@ucm.es
Internet: www.ucm.es
Founded 1499
State control
Language of instruction: Spanish
Academic year: October to July (2 semesters)

Rector: Prof. JOSÉ CARRILLO MENÉNDEZ
Vice-Rector for Academic Affairs: EUMENIO ANCOCHEA SOTO
Vice-Rector for Graduate Studies: SILVIA IGLESIAS RECUERO
Vice-Rector for Innovation: MANUEL MAÑAS BAENA
Vice-Rector for Institutional and Int. Relations: JUAN FERRERA CUESTA
Vice-Rector for Org.: JOAQUÍN GOYACHE GOÑI
Vice-Rector for Postgraduate and Continuing Education: JOSÉ MARÍA ALUNDA RODRÍGUEZ
Vice-Rector for Quality Assessment: ELENA GALLEGO ABAROA
Vice-Rector for Research: JOAQUÍN PLUMET ORTEGA
Vice-Rector for Students: MARÍA ENCINA GONZÁLEZ MARTÍNEZ
Vice-Rector for Transfer: MERCEDES MOLINA IBÁÑEZ
Vice-Rector for Univ. Community Care: CRISTINA VELÁZQUEZ VIDAL
Sec.-Gen.: MATILDE CARLÓN RUIZ
Library: see under Libraries and Archives
Number of teachers: 6,206
Number of students: 75,601

Publications: *Memoria de la UCM, Gaceta Complutense, Tribuna Complutense*

DEANS

Faculty of Biological Sciences: ANTONIO TORMO GARRIDO
Faculty of Chemical Sciences: REYES JIMÉNEZ APARICIO
Faculty of Commerce and Tourism: MIGUEL ÁNGEL SASTRE CASTILLO
Faculty of Computer Science: DANIEL MOZOS MUÑOZ
Faculty of Dentistry: JOSÉ CARLOS DE LA MACORRA GARCÍA
Faculty of Documentation Science: JOSÉ MARÍA DE FRANCISCO OLMOS
Faculty of Economic and Business Sciences: MARÍA BEGOÑA GARCÍA GRECIANO
Faculty of Education (Teacher Training Centre): MARÍA JOSÉ FERNÁNDEZ DÍAZ
Faculty of Fine Arts: JOSU LARRAÑAGA ALTUNA
Faculty of Geography and History: LUIS ENRIQUE OTERO CARVAJAL
Faculty of Geological Sciences: JOSÉ RAMÓN MAS MAYORAL
Faculty of Information Science: MARÍA DEL CARMEN PÉREZ DE ARMIÑÁN GARCÍA-FRESCA
Faculty of Law: RAÚL LEOPOLDO CANOSA USERA
Faculty of Mathematical Science: FRANCISCO JAVIER MONTERO DE JUAN
Faculty of Medicine: JOSÉ LUIS ÁLVAREZ-SALA WALTHER
Faculty of Nursing, Physiotherapy and Podiatry: ENRIQUE PACHECO DEL CERRO
Faculty of Optometry: FRANCISCO JAVIER ALDA SERRANO
Faculty of Pharmacy: RAFAEL LOZANO FERNÁNDEZ
Faculty of Philology: DÁMASO LÓPEZ GARCÍA
Faculty of Philosophy: RAFAEL VALERIANO ORDEN JIMÉNEZ
Faculty of Physical Sciences: MARÍA LUISA LUCÍA MULAS
Faculty of Political and Sociological Sciences: HERIBERTO CAIRO CAROU

Faculty of Psychology: CARLOS GALLEGO LÓPEZ
Faculty of Social Work: ANDRÉS ARIAS ASTRAY
Faculty of Statistical Studies: CARMEN NIETO ZAYAS
Faculty of Veterinary Science: PEDRO LUIS LORENZO GONZÁLEZ

UNIVERSIDAD DE ALCALÁ
(University of Alcalá)

Plaza de San Diego s/n, Alcalá de Henares, 28801 Madrid
Telephone: 918854000
E-mail: ciu@uah.es
Internet: www.uah.es
Founded 1499
State control
Language of instruction: Spanish
Academic year: September to May (2 semesters)

Rector: FERNANDO GALVÁN REULA
Vice-Rector for Academic Planning and Faculty: Prof. Dr JOSÉ VICENTE SAZ PÉREZ
Vice-Rector for Coordination and Communication: Prof. Dr JOSÉ SANTIAGO FERNÁNDEZ VÁZQUEZ
Vice-Rector for Guadalajara Campus and Students: Dra NAZARETH PÉREZ DE CASTRO
Vice-Rector for Innovation and New Technology: Prof. Dr JOSÉ ANTONIO GUTIÉRREZ DE MESA
Vice-Rector for Int. Relations: Prof. Dra ELENA LÓPEZ DÍAZ-DELGADO
Vice-Rector for Postgraduate and Continuing Education: Dr JUAN RAMÓN VELASCO PÉREZ
Vice-Rector for Research: Dra MARÍA LUISA MARINA ALEGRE
Vice-Rector for Teaching Quality and Innovation: Dra LEONOR MARGALEF GARCÍA
Vice-Rector for Univ. Extension and Institutional Relations: Dr JAVIER RIVERA BLANCO
Sec.-Gen.: Dr MIGUEL RODRÍGUEZ BLANCO
Library Dir: MARÍA DEL CARMEN FERNÁNDEZ-GALIANO PEYROLÓN
Library of 500,000 vols, 7,000 periodicals
Number of teachers: 1,762 (947 full-time, 815 part-time)
Number of students: 29,000

Publications: *Anuario Facultad De Derecho*, *Astrágalo* (2 a year), *Barataria* (1 a year), *Barbastella* (1 a year), *Cairón* (1 a year), *Camino Real* (2 a year), *Cuadernos Didácticos De Medio Ambiente* (24 a year), *Encuentro* (1 a year), *Estudios de Historia Social y Económica de América* (2 a year), *Fisioterapia* (2 a year), *Henares*, *Idagación* (1 a year), *Las Comarcas Agrarias de España*, *Lecciones Inagurales*, *Lengua Y Migración* (2 a year), *Literatura Medieval* (1 a year), *Poética Medieval*, *Polis* (1 a year), *Quodlibet* (4 a year), *Quórum Revista de Pensamiento Iberoamericano*, *Reale* (2 a year), *Reden* (2 a year), *Revista*, *Serie Geográfica*, *Signo* (irregular), *Teatro* (2 a year)

DEANS

Faculty of Biology (Científico-Tecnológico Campus): CARMEN BARTOLOMÉ ESTEBAN
Faculty of Chemistry (Científico-Tecnológico Campus): M. MELIA RODRIGO LÓPEZ
Faculty of Economics and Business (Histórico Campus): EMMA T. CASTELLÓ TALIANI
Faculty of Environmental Sciences (Científico-Tecnológico Campus): ROSA VICENTE LAPUENTE
Faculty of Information (Histórico Campus): M. PILAR LACASA DÍAZ
Faculty of Law (Histórico Campus): JOSÉ M. ESPINAR VICENTE
Faculty of Medicine (Científico-Tecnológico Campus): M. JULIA BUJÁN VARELA

Faculty of Nursing and Physiotherapy (Científico-Tecnológico Campus): ÁNGEL L. ASENJO ESTEVE
Faculty of Nursing (Guadalajara Campus): M. ANGELES MEDRANO FERNÁNDEZ
Faculty of Pharmacy (Científico-Tecnológico Campus): FIDEL ORTEGA ORTIZ-APODACA
Faculty of Philosophy and Letters (Histórico Campus): M. LUISA JUÁREZ HERVÁS
Faculty of Tourism (Guadalajara Campus): SILVIA GIRALT ESCOBAR

UNIVERSIDAD DE ALICANTE/ UNIVERSITAT D'ALACANT

Carretera San Vicente del Raspeig s/n, 03690 Alicante
Telephone: 965903400
E-mail: informacio@ua.es
Internet: www.ua.es
Founded 1979
State control
Languages of instruction: Spanish, Valenciano
Academic year: September to May (2 semesters)

Pres.: MANUEL PALOMAR SANZ
Vice-Pres. for Academic Affairs and Faculty: JOSÉ VICENTE CABEZUELO PLIEGO
Vice-Pres. for Campus Facilities and Sustainability: RAFAEL MUÑOZ GUILLENA
Vice-Pres. for Culture, Sports and Language Policies: CARLES CORTES ORTS
Vice-Pres. for Economic Planning: MONICA MARTI SEMPERE
Vice-Pres. for Information Technologies: FRANCISCO MACIÁ PÉREZ
Vice-Pres. for Int. Relations: JUAN LLOPIS TAVERNER
Vice-Pres. for Research, Devt and Innovation: AMPARO NAVARRO FAURE
Vice-Pres. for Students: NURIA GRANÉ TERUEL
Vice-Pres. for Studies, Training and Quality: MARIA CECILIA GÓMEZ LUCAS
Gen. Sec.: ARÁNZAZU CALZADA GONZÁLEZ
Library Dir: REMEDIOS BLANES
Number of teachers: 1,600
Number of students: 30,000

Publications: *Anales de literatura española* (online), *Mediterranea Series de estudios biológicos* (online)

DEANS

Faculty of Arts: JORGE OLCINA CANTOS
Faculty of Economics and Business Sciences: MARIA JESÚS SANTA MARÍA BENEYTO
Faculty of Education: MARÍA ÁNGLES MARTÍNEZ RUIZ
Faculty of Health Sciences: ANA MARIA LAGUNA PÉREZ
Faculty of Law: PEDRO J. FEMENÍA LÓPEZ
Faculty of Sciences: DAVID GUIJARRO ESPÍ (acting)

UNIVERSIDAD DE ALMERÍA

Ctra Sacramento s/n, La Cañada de San Urbano, 04120 Almería
Telephone: 9500015000
E-mail: sgeneral@ual.es
Internet: www.ual.es
Founded 1993
State control
Language of instruction: Spanish
Academic year: September to June (2 semesters)

Rector: PEDRO ROQUE MOLINA GARCÍA
Vice-Rector for Infrastructure, Campus and Sustainability: ISABEL MARÍA ROMÁN SÁNCHEZ
Vice-Rector for Int. Relations and Cooperation for Devt: MARÍA SAGRARIO SALABERRI RAMIRO

Vice-Rector for Research, Devt and Innovation: JOSÉ LUÍS MARTÍNEZ VIDAL
Vice-Rector for Students, Univ. Extension and Sports: JOSÉ ANTONIO GUERRERO VILLALBA
Vice-Rector for Teachers and Academic Org.: JOSÉ JUAN CARRIÓN MARTÍNEZ
Sec.-Gen.: MARÍA LUISA TRINIDAD GARCÍA
Library Dir: ENCARNACIÓN FUENTES MELERO
Publications: *Nimbus* (2 a year), *Odisea* (1 a year), *Revista de Estudios Regionales* (4 a year)

DEANS

College of Law: FERNANDO FERNÁNDEZ MARÍN
Economics and Business Studies College: JOSÉ JOAQUÍN CÉSPEDES LORENTE
Faculty of Education Science, Nursing and Physiotherapy: DOLORES RODRÍGUEZ MARTÍNEZ
Faculty of Humanities and Psychology: FRANCISCO JAVIER GARCÍA GONZÁLEZ
Higher Polytechnic School and Experimental Science College: ANTONIO GIMÉNEZ FERNÁNDEZ

UNIVERSIDAD DE BURGOS
(University of Burgos)

Hospital del Rey s/n, 09001 Burgos
Telephone: 947258736
E-mail: intl@ubu.es
Internet: www.ubu.es
Founded 1994
State control
Language of instruction: Spanish
Academic year: September to June (2 semesters)

Rector: ALFONSO MURILLO VILLAR
Vice-Rector for Academic Affairs and Quality: MANUEL PÉREZ MATEOS
Vice-Rector for Admin. and Services: ALFREDO BOL ARREBA
Vice-Rector for Economics and Business Relations: JOSÉ LUIS PEÑA ALONSO
Vice-Rector for Infrastructure and New Technologies: JUAN MANUEL MANSO VILLALAÍN
Vice-Rector for Int. Relations and Cooperation: ELENA VICENTE DOMINGO
Vice-Rector for Research: JORDI ROVIRA CARBALLIDO
Vice-Rector for Student Affairs and Univ. Extension: RENÉ JESÚS PAYO HERNANZ
Sec.-Gen.: JOSÉ MARÍA GARCÍA-MORENO GONZALO
Library Dir: FERNANDO MARTÍN RODRÍGUEZ
Library of 100,000 vols, 1,500 periodicals
Number of teachers: 700
Number of students: 10,000

DEANS

Faculty of Economics and Business Sciences: ÓSCAR LÓPEZ DE FORONDA PÉREZ
Faculty of Humanities and Education: IGNACIO FERNÁNDEZ DE MATA
Faculty of Law: Profa Dra MARÍA TERESA CARRANCHO HERRERO
Faculty of Sciences: GONZALO SALAZAR MARDONES

UNIVERSIDAD DE CÁDIZ
(University of Cádiz)

Calle Ancha 16, 11001 Cádiz
Telephone: 956015027
E-mail: rector@uca.es
Internet: www.uca.es
Founded 1979
State control
Language of instruction: Spanish
Academic year: October to June (2 semesters)

Rector: EDUARDO GONZÁLEZ MAZO

Vice-Rector for Academic Affairs and Faculty: PALOMA BRAZA LLORET

Vice-Rector for Planning and Quality: MARÍA JOSÉ MUÑOZ CUETO

Vice-Rector for Research and Transfer: MANUEL BETHENCOURT NÚÑEZ

Vice-Rector for Social, Cultural and Int. Projection: MARINA GUTIÉRREZ PEINADO

Vice-Rector for Students: DAVID ALMORZA GOMAR

Vice-Rector for Teaching and Training: MIGUEL ÁNGEL PENDÓN MELÉNDEZ

Sec.-Gen.: FRANCISCA FUENTES RODRÍGUEZ

Library Dir: RICARDO CHAMORRO RODRÍGUEZ

Number of teachers: 1,052
Number of students: 22,000

DEANS

Faculty of Economics and Business: MANUEL LARRÁN JORGE

Faculty of Educational Sciences: JOSÉ MARÍA MARISCAL CHICANO

Faculty of Labour Sciences: EVA GARRIDO PÉREZ

Faculty of Law: JESÚS SÁEZ GONZÁLEZ

Faculty of Marine and Environmental Sciences: JOSÉ MARÍA QUIROGA ALONSO

Faculty of Medicine: ANTONIO MANUEL LORENZO PEÑUELAS

Faculty of Nursing: MARIA ÁNGELES MARTELO BARO

Faculty of Nursing and Physiotherapy: ANA GARCÍA BAÑÓN

Faculty of Philosophy and Letters: MANUEL ARCILA GARRIDO

Faculty of Sciences: MARÍA DOLORES GALINDO RIAÑO

Faculty of Social Sciences and Communication: PALOMA LÓPEZ ZURITA

UNIVERSIDAD DE CANTABRIA
(University of Cantabria)

Avda de los Castros, 39005 Santander

Telephone: 942201500

E-mail: informacion.general@unican.es

Internet: www.unican.es

Founded 1972
State control
Languages of instruction: English, Spanish
Academic year: September to July

Rector: JOSÉ CARLOS GÓMEZ SAL

Vice-Rector for Academic Affairs: FERNANDO ETAYO GORDEJUELA

Vice-Rector for Culture, Participation and Dissemination: ELENA MARTÍN LATORRE

Vice-Rector for Faculty: FERNANDO CAÑIZAL BERINI

Vice-Rector for Institutional Relations and Coordination of Cantabria Campus: JUAN ENRIQUE VARONA ALABERN

Vice-Rector for Int. Relations: CONCEPCIÓN LÓPEZ FERNÁNDEZ

Vice-Rector for Research and Knowledge Transfer: ÁNGEL PAZOS CARRO

Vice-Rector for Spaces, Services and Sustainability: ÁNGELA DE MEER

Vice-Rector for Student Affairs, Employment and Entrepreneurship: RAFAEL TORRES JIMÉNEZ

Registrar and Sec.-Gen.: JOSÉ IGNACIO SOLAR CAYÓN

Library Dir: MARÍA JESÚS SÁIZ

Library of 399,372 vols, 8,794 journals, 15,065 online magazines, 77,995 ebooks, 26,559 audiovisual materials, 463 databases

Number of teachers: 1,297
Number of students: 12,736

Publication: *Campus Life*

DEANS

Faculty of Economics and Business Sciences: BEGOÑA TORRE OLMO

Faculty of Education: JOSÉ MANUEL OSORO SIERRA

Faculty of Law: JUAN BARÓ PAZOS

Faculty of Medicine: FRANCISCO JAVIER LLORCA DÍAZ

Faculty of Philosophy and Letters: JESÚS A. SOLÓRZANO TELECHEA

Faculty of Sciences: ERNESTO ANABITARTE CANO

UNIVERSIDAD DE CASTILLA—LA MANCHA
(University of Castilla—La Mancha)

Calle Altagracia 50, 13071 Ciudad Real

Telephone: 902204100

E-mail: informacion@uclm.es

Internet: www.uclm.es

Founded 1982
State control
Language of instruction: Spanish
Academic year: September to May (2 semesters)

Rector: Prof. Dr MIGUEL ÁNGEL COLLADO YURRITA

Vice-Rector for Academic Affairs and Int. Programmes: Profa Dra FÁTIMA GUADAMILLA GÓMEZ

Vice-Rector for Culture and Univ. Extension: Profa. Dra MARÍA ÁNGELES ZURILLA CARIÑANA

Vice-Rector for Economy and Planification: Prof. Dr MANUEL VILLASALERO DÍAZ

Vice-Rector for Research and Scientific Affairs: Prof. Dr JOSÉ JULIÁN GARDE LÓPEZ-BREA

Vice-Rector for Students: Profa Dra BEATRIZ CABAÑAS GALÁN

Vice-Rector for Teaching: Prof. Dr JUAN JOSÉ LÓPEZ CELA

Vice-Rector for Transference and Relationships with Enterprises: Prof. Dr PEDRO ANTONIO CARRIÓN PÉREZ

Gen. Sec.: Profa Dra NURIA GARRIDO CUENCA

Registrar: Profa Dra MARÍA CÁNDIDA GUTIÉRREZ GARCÍA

Man. Dir: TOMÁS LÓPEZ MORAGA

Librarian: FRANCISCO ALIA MIRANDA

Library of 952,268 vols, 22,252 periodicals, 3,000 journals

Number of teachers: 2,312

Number of students: 30,523 (28,289 undergraduate, 2,234 postgraduate and doctoral)

Publications: *Ensayos*, *Equis*, *Infocampus* (12 a year, print and online, infocampus.uclm.es), *lamusa—digital* (in English, French, German, Italian, Spanish, online), *Multiárea Revista de Didacta*, *ólobo* (online), *Praxis Sociológica* (online), *Revista de Docencia e Investigación* (Journal of Education and Research), *Revista Digital El Recreo* (online, www.uclm.es/profesorado/ricardo/Periodico.htm), *Revista DO2* (DO2 Magazine), *Revista de Enfermería*, *Revista Estudios de Filología Moderna* (1 a year), *Sin Título* (Untitled, 1 a year)

DEANS

Faculty of Arts (Ciudad Real): Dr MATÍAS BARCHINO PÉREZ

Faculty of Business Relations and Human Resources (Albacete): Prof. Dr JOAQUÍN APARICIO TOVAR

Faculty of Chemical Sciences and Technology (Ciudad Real): ÁNGEL RÍOS CASTRO

Faculty of Economic and Business Sciences (Albacete): Dr ÁNGEL TEJADA PONCE

Faculty of Education (Albacete): Prof. Dr PEDRO LOSA SERRANO

Faculty of Education (Ciudad Real): Prof. Dr EMILIO NIETO LÓPEZ

Faculty of Education (Cuenca): MARTÍN MUELAS HERRAIZ

Faculty of Education (Toledo): ERNESTO GARCÍA SANZ

Faculty of Educational Sciences and Humanities (Cuenca): Dr SANTIAGO YUBERO JIMÉNEZ

Faculty of Environmental Sciences and Biochemistry (Toledo): FRANCISCO J. TAPIADOR

Faculty of Fine Arts (Cuenca): ANA NAVARRETE TUDELA

Faculty of Humanities (Albacete): FRANCISCO CEBRIÁN ABELLÁN

Faculty of Humanities (Toledo): Prof. Dr RICARDO IZQUIERDO BENITO

Faculty of Journalism: ANTONIO LAGUNA PLATERO

Faculty of Labour Relations and Human Resources (Albacete): JOAQUÍN APARICIO TOVAR

Faculty of Law (Albacete): Prof. Dr DIEGO JOSÉ GÓMEZ INIESTA

Faculty of Law and Social Sciences (Ciudad Real): JUAN RAMÓN DE PÁRAMO ARGÜELLES

Faculty of Law and Social Sciences (Toledo): PEDRO JOSÉ CARRASCO PARRILLA

Faculty of Medicine (Albacete): Dr JOSÉ MARTÍNEZ PÉREZ

Faculty of Medicine (Ciudad Real): Dr JUAN EMILIO FELIU ALBIÑANA

Faculty of Nursing (Albacete): RIOBERTO LÓPEZ HONRUBIA

Faculty of Nursing (Ciudad Real): CARMEN PRADO LAGUNA

Faculty of Nursing (Cuenca): MARÍA ROSARIO OLMO GASCÓN

Faculty of Occupational Therapy, Speech Therapy and Nursing (Talavera de la Reina): Dr BEGOÑA POLONIO LÓPEZ

Faculty of Pharmacy (Albacete): MARÍA DEL MAR ARROYO JIMÉNEZ

Faculty of Social Sciences (Cuenca): Prof. Dr JOSÉ MONDÉJAR JIMÉNEZ

Faculty of Social Sciences (Talavera de la Reina): Dr PEDRO JIMÉNEZ ESTÉVEZ

Faculty of Social Work (Cuenca): ELISA LARRAÑAGA RUBIO

Faculty of Sport Sciences (Toledo): Dr JOSÉ MANUEL GARCÍA GARCÍA

UNIVERSIDAD DE CÓRDOBA
(University of Cordoba)

Avda Medina Azahara 5, 14071 Córdoba

Telephone: 957218000

E-mail: rector@uco.es

Internet: www.uco.es

Founded 1972
State control
Language of instruction: Spanish
Academic year: September to June (2 semesters)

Rector: JOSÉ MANUEL ROLDÁN NOGUERAS

Vice-Rector for Academic Affairs and Teaching Staff: JOSÉ NARANJO RAMÍREZ

Vice-Rector for Coordination, Students and Culture: MANUEL TORRES AGUILAR

Vice-Rector for Information Technology and Communications: JUAN ANTONIO CABALLERO MOLINA

Vice-Rector for Int. Relations and Cooperation: CARMEN GALÁN SOLDEVILLA

Vice-Rector for Postgraduate Studies and Continuing Education: JOSE CARLOS GÓMEZ VILLAMANDOS

Vice-Rector for Regulatory Devt: PEDRO GÓMEZ CABALLERO

Vice-Rector for Science Policy and Campus of Excellence: JUSTO P. CASTAÑO FUENTES

Sec.-Gen.: JULIA ANGULO ROMERO

Librarian: MARÍA DEL CARMEN LIÑÁN MAZA

Library of 460,000 vols, 10,000 periodicals

Number of teachers: 1,577

Number of students: 19,520 (17,000 undergraduate, 1,250 postgraduate, 1,270 doctoral)

DEANS

Faculty of Educational Science: FRANCISCO VILLAMANDOS DE LA TORRE
Faculty of Labour Sciences: Prof. Dr FEDERICO NAVARRO NIETO
Faculty of Law, Economics and Business: Prof. Dr MIGUEL J. AGUDO ZAMORA
Faculty of Medicine: Prof. Dr RAFAEL SOLANA LARA
Faculty of Nursing: CARMEN VACAS DÍAZ
Faculty of Philosophy and Letters: Prof. Dr EULALIO FERNÁNDEZ SÁNCHEZ
Faculty of Sciences: Prof. Dr MANUEL BLÁZQUEZ RUIZ
Faculty of Veterinary Science: Prof. Dr LIBRADO CARRASCO OTERO

UNIVERSIDAD DE DEUSTO
(University of Deusto)

Apdo 1, 48080 Bilbao
Avda de las Universidades 24, 48007 Bilbao
Telephone: 944139000
E-mail: secretaria.general@deusto.es
Internet: www.deusto.es

Founded 1886
Private control
Languages of instruction: English, Spanish
Academic year: September to May (2 semesters)

Chancellor: ADOLFO NICOLÁS PACHÓN
Rector: JOSÉ MARÍA GUIBERT UCÍN
Vice-Rector for Academic Org.: MARÍA BEGOÑA ARRIETA HERAS
Vice-Rector for Communication, Language Policy and Student Affairs: ROBERTO SAN SALVADOR DEL VALLE DOISTUA
Vice-Rector for Identity and Mission: JOSÉ JAVIER PARDO IZAL
Vice-Rector for Int. Relations and Students: ÁLVARO DE LA RICA ASPIUNZA
Vice-Rector for Research: CRISTINA ITURRIOZ LANDART
Vice-Rector for San Sebastián Campus and Univ. Community: JOSÉ JAVIER PARDO IZAL
Gen. Sec.: MARÍA BEGOÑA ARRIETA HERAS
Library Dir: NIEVES TARANCO DEL BARRIO

Library: 1m. vols, 10,000 periodicals
Number of teachers: 2,800
Number of students: 9,560

Publications: *ADOZ Boletín del Centro de Documentación en Ocio* (4 a year), *ADOZ Revista de Estudios de Ocio Aisiazko Ikaskuntzen Aldizkaria* (Journal of Leisure Studies, 4 a year), *Anuario de Acción Humanitaria y Derechos Humanos* (Yearbook on Humanitarian Action and Human Rights), *Anuario de Estudios Cooperativos* (1 a year), *Anuario del Instituto Ignacio de Loyola* (1 a year), *Boletín de Estudios Económicos* (3 a year), *Boletín de la Asociación Internacional de Derecho Cooperativo* (International Association of Cooperative Law Journal, 2 a year), *Cuadernos Europeos de Deusto* (2 a year), *Deusto* (4 a year), *Deusto Ingeniería* (1 a year), *Enseiukarrean* (1 a year), *ESIDE* (1 a year), *Estudios de Deusto* (3 a year), *Estudios Empresariales* (3 a year), *Letras de Deusto* (4 a year), *Mundaiz* (2 a year), *RAS* (2 a year), *Revista de Derecho y Genoma Humano* (2 a year), *Revista Noticias UD Berriak* (4 a year)

DEANS

Faculty of Economics and Business Administration: GUILLERMO DORRONSORO ARTABE
Faculty of Engineering: INES MAGDALENA JACOB TAQUET
Faculty of Humanities: JOSÉ ÁNGEL ACHÓN INSAUSTI
Faculty of Law: JOSÉ LUIS ÁVILA ORIVE
Faculty of Philosophy and Education Sciences: JOSU SOLABARRIETA EIZAGUIRRE

Faculty of Psychology and Education: JOSU SOLABARRIETA EIZAGUIRRE
Faculty of Social and Human Sciences: JOSÉ ANTONIO RODRÍGUEZ RANZ
Faculty of Theology: VICENTE VIDE RODRÍGUEZ

UNIVERSIDAD DE EXTREMADURA
(University of Extremadura)

Avda de Elvas s/n, 06006 Badajoz
Telephone: 924289369
E-mail: uexba@unex.es
Internet: www.unex.es

Founded 1973
State control
Language of instruction: Spanish
Academic year: September to July (2 semesters)

Rector: Prof. Dr SEGUNDO PÍRIZ DURÁN
Vice-Rector for Digital Univ.: Prof. Dr CARMEN GARCÍA GONZÁLEZ
Vice-Rector for Int. Relations: Prof. Dr MARIA DEL MAR GUERRERO MANZANO
Vice-Rector for Quality and Infrastructure: Prof. Dr ANTONIO DÍAZ PARRALEJO
Vice-Rector for Research, Transfer of Results and Innovation: Prof. Dr MANUEL ADOLFO GONZÁLEZ LENA
Vice-Rector for Student Affairs and Employment: Prof. Dr CIRO PÉREZ GIRALDO
Vice-Rector for Teaching and Institutional Relations: Prof. Dr JOSÉ LUIS GURRÍA GASCÓN
Vice-Rector for Teaching Staff: Prof. Dr SERGIO JOSÉ IBÁÑEZ GODOY
Vice-Rector for Univ. Extension: Prof. Dr MARÍA ISABEL LÓPEZ MARTÍNEZ
Registrar: Prof. Dr INMACULADA DOMÍNGUEZ FABIÁN
Library Dir: ÁNGELES FERRER GUTIÉRREZ

Library of 473,490 vols, 20,261 ebooks, 17,437 ejournals
Number of teachers: 1,827
Number of students: 24,721

DEANS

Faculty of Business Studies and Tourism (Cáceres): VICENTE MANUEL PÉREZ GUTIÉRREZ
Faculty of Documentation and Communication Sciences (Badajoz): AGUSTÍN VIVAS MORENO
Faculty of Economics and Business Sciences (Badajoz): FRANCISCO MANUEL PEDRAJA CHAPARRO
Faculty of Education (Badajoz): ZACARÍAS CALZADO ALMODÓVAR
Faculty of Law (Cáceres): JAIME ROSSELL GRANADOS
Faculty of Medicine (Badajoz): JUAN MANUEL MORENO VÁZQUEZ
Faculty of Nursing and Occupational Therapy (Cáceres): ROSA MARÍA ROJO DURÁN
Faculty of Philosophy and Letters (Cáceres): JOSÉ LUIS BERNAL SALGADO
Faculty of Sciences (Badajoz): LUCÍA RODRÍGUEZ GALLARDO
Faculty of Sport Sciences (Cáceres): Prof. Dr GUILLERMO JOSÉ OLCINA CAMACHO
Faculty of Teacher Training (Cáceres): VÍCTOR MARÍA LÓPEZ RAMOS
Faculty of Veterinary Sciences (Cáceres): MARGARITA MARTÍNEZ TRANCÓN

UNIVERSIDAD DE GRANADA
(University of Granada)

Avda del Hospicio s/n, 18071 Granada
Telephone: 958243000
E-mail: informa@ugr.es
Internet: www.ugr.es

Founded 1531
State control
Languages of instruction: English, Spanish

Academic year: October to September

Rector: FRANCISCO GONZÁLEZ LODEIRO
Vice-Rector for Academic Org. and Teaching Staff: LUIS M. JIMÉNEZ DEL BARCO JALDO
Vice-Rector for Health Science Technological Park: IGNACIO JESÚS MOLINA PINEDA DE LAS INFANTAS
Vice-Rector for Infrastructure and Campuses: BEGOÑA MORENO ESCOBAR
Vice-Rector for Int. Relations and Devt Cooperation: DOROTHY KELLY
Vice-Rector for Quality Assurance: MARÍA JOSÉ LEÓN GUERRERO
Vice-Rector for Scientific Policy and Research: MARÍA DOLORES SUÁREZ ORTEGA
Vice-Rector for Student Affairs: ROSA MARIA GARCÍA PÉREZ
Vice-Rector for Undergraduate and Postgraduate Teaching: LOLA FERRE CANO
Vice-Rector for Univ. Extension and Sports: MARÍA ELENA MARTÍN-VIVALDI CABALLERO
Sec.-Gen.: ROSSANA GONZÁLEZ GONZÁLEZ
Library Dir: MARÍA JOSÉ ARIZA RUBIO

Library of 686,300 vols, 15,338 periodicals, 35 incunabula
Number of teachers: 3,650
Number of students: 80,000

Publications: *Anales de la Cátedra Francisco Suarez, Arenal: Revista de Historia de Mujeres, Chronica Nova: Revista de Historia Moderna* (1 a year), *Cuadernos de Arte* (1 a year), *Cuadernos de Estudios Medievales, Cuadernos de Estudios Medievales y de Ciencias y Técnicas Historiográficas, Cuadernos de Prehistoria, Cuadernos de Prehistoria y Arqueología, Cuadernos Geográficos* (2 a year, print and online, www.ugr.es/local/cuadgeo), *Dynamis: Acta Hispanica ad Medicinae: Scientiarumque Historiam Ilustrandam* (2 a year), *Florentia Iliberritana Revista De Estudios De La Antigüedad Clásica, Miscelánea de Estudios Arabes y Hebraicos* (1 a year), *Revista de Educación* (1 a year), *Revista de la Facultad de Derecho de la Universidad de Granada, Sendebar: Boletín de la Facultad de Traducción e Interpretación* (1 a year), *Zoologica Baetica*

DEANS

Faculty of Communication and Documentation: ANTONIO ÁNGEL RUIZ RODRÍGUEZ
Faculty of Dentistry: Dr ALBERTO RODRÍGUEZ ARCHILLA
Faculty of Economic and Business Sciences: Dr MARÍA DEL MAR HOLGADO MOLINA
Faculty of Educational Sciences: Dr JOSÉ ANTONIO NARANJO RODRÍGUEZ
Faculty of Education and Humanities (Ceuta): Dr RAMÓN GALINDO MORALES
Faculty of Education and Humanities (Melilla): CARMEN ENRIQUE MIRÓN
Faculty of Fine Arts: Dr VÍCTOR MEDINA FLÓREZ
Faculty of Health Sciences: Prof. ANTONIO MUÑOZ VINUESA
Faculty of Health Sciences (Ceuta): Dr RAFAEL GUISADO BARRILAO
Faculty of Labour Sciences: Prof. PEDRO ANTONIO GARCÍA LÓPEZ
Faculty of Law: Dr MIGUEL OLMEDO CARDENETE
Faculty of Medicine: Prof. Dr INDALECIO SÁNCHEZ-MONTESINOS GARCÍA
Faculty of Nursing (Melilla): Dra BIBINHA BENBUNAN BENTATA
Faculty of Pharmacy: LUÍS RECALDE MANRIQUE
Faculty of Philosophy and Literature: JOSÉ ANTONIO PÉREZ TAPIAS
Faculty of Political Science and Sociology: Dr SUSANA CORZO FERNÁNDEZ
Faculty of Psychology: Dr FRANCISCA EXPÓSITO JIMÉNEZ
Faculty of Science: Dr ANTONIO RÍOS GUADIX

Faculty of Social Sciences (Melilla): JUAN ANTONIO MARMOLEJO MARTÍN
Faculty of Social Work: ÁNGEL RODRÍGUEZ MONGE
Faculty of Sports Sciences: AURELIO UREÑA ESPA
Faculty of Translation and Interpretating: Dr ÁNGELA COLLADO AIS

UNIVERSIDAD DE HUELVA
(University of Huelva)

Calle Dr Cantero Cuadrado 6, 21071 Huelva
Telephone: 959218000
E-mail: rector@uhu.es
Internet: www.uhu.es
Founded 1993
State control
Language of instruction: Spanish
Academic year: September to June (2 semesters)

Rector: Prof. Dr FRANCISCO JOSÉ MARTÍNEZ LÓPEZ
Vice-Rector for Academic Org. and Faculty: Prof. Dr JUAN JOSÉ GARCÍA DEL HOYO
Vice-Rector for Infrastructure, Technology and Quality: Prof. Dr ÁNGEL ISIDRO MENA NIETO
Vice-Rector for Research: Prof. Dr JESÚS DAMIÁN DE LA ROSA DÍAZ
Vice-Rector for Student Affairs, Employment and Business Admin.: Prof. Dra ISABEL MARÍA RODRÍGUEZ GARCÍA
Vice-Rector for Univ. Extension and Int. Relations: Prof. Dr MANUEL JOSÉ DE LARA RÓDENAS
Sec.-Gen.: Prof. Dr JOSÉ LUIS LÁZARO SÁNCHEZ
Librarian: ROSA ALAMILLO GRANADOS
Library of 249,994 vols, 4,893 periodicals
Number of teachers: 700
Number of students: 12,000

Publications: *XXI. Revista de Educación, Análisis y Modificación de Conducta, Arys, Enlightening Tourism: A Pathmaking Journal* (2 a year, print and online), *Exemplaria Classica, Geogaceta, Huelva en su Historia, International Journal of Digital Accounting Research, Portularia Revista de Trabajo Social* (in Spanish), *Revista de Economía Mundial, Sociedad Geológica de España, Trabajo* (2 a year)

DEANS

Faculty of Business Studies: Prof Dra MARÍA ASUNCIÓN GRÁVALOS GASTAMINZA
Faculty of Educational Science: Prof. FRANCISCO JOSÉ MORALES GIL
Faculty of Experimental Sciences: Prof. Dr RAFAEL TORRONTERAS SANTIAGO
Faculty of Humanities: Prof. Dr JUAN MANUEL CAMPOS CARRASCO
Faculty of Law: Prof. Dra AURORA MARIA LÓPEZ MEDINA
Faculty of Nursing: Prof. Dra ANA ABREU SÁNCHEZ
Faculty of Social Work: Prof. Dr IVÁN RODRÍGUEZ PASCUAL
Faculty of Work Sciences: Prof. Dr AGUSTÍN GALÁN GARCÍA

UNIVERSIDAD DE JAÉN
(University of Jaén)

Campus Las Lagunillas, 23071 Jaén
Telephone: 953212121
E-mail: info@ujaen.es
Internet: www.ujaen.es
Founded 1993
State control
Language of instruction: Spanish
Academic year: September to May (2 semesters)

Rector: MANUEL PARRAS ROSA

Vice-Rector for Information and Communication Technology: JESÚS CARLOS MARTÍNEZ BAZÁN
Vice-Rector for Infrastructure, Campus Devt and Sustainability: NICOLÁS RUÍZ REYEZ
Vice-Rector for Int. Relations: MARIA VICTORIA LÓPEZ RAMÓN
Vice-Rector for Planning, Quality, Social Responsibility and Communication: JORGE DELGADO GARCÍA
Vice-Rector for Research, Technological Devt and Innovation: MARÍA ANGELES PEINADO HERREROS
Vice-Rector for Students and Employment: ADORACIÓN MOZAS MORAL
Vice-Rector for Teaching and Faculty: JUAN CARLOS CASTILLO ARMENTEROS
Vice-Rector for Univ. Extension, Sports and Institution Planning: ANA MARIA ORTIZ COLÓN
Sec.-Gen.: NICOLÁS PÉREZ SOLA
Library Dir: SEBASTIÁN JARILLO CALVARRO
Library of 265,780 vols, 4,356 periodicals
Number of teachers: 1,000
Number of students: 16,000

Publications: *Arqueología y Territorio Medieval, Arte y Movimiento, Boletín de Literatura Oral* (1 a year), *Iniciación a la Investigación, Jaén Journal on Approximation, Journal of Nematode Morphology and Systematics, Revista de Estudios Empresariales, Revista Estudios Jurídicos, Revista Paraiso, The Grove. Working Papers on English Studies*

DEANS

Faculty of Experimental Sciences: FERMÍN ARANDA HARO
Faculty of Health Sciences: ALFONSO JESÚS CRUZ LENDÍNEZ
Faculty of Humanities and Educational Science: MARÍA DE LA VILLA CARPIO FERNÁNDEZ
Faculty of Social Sciences and Law: LUIS JAVIER GUTIERREZ JEREZ
Faculty of Social Work: JOSÉ LUIS SOLANA RUIZ

UNIVERSIDAD DE LA LAGUNA

Pabellón de Gobierno, Calle Molinos de Agua s/n, 38200 La Laguna
Telephone: 922319000
E-mail: sioinfo@ull.es
Internet: www.ull.es
Founded 1792, opened 1817
State control
Language of instruction: Spanish
Academic year: September to May (2 semesters)

Rector: EDUARDO DOMÉNECH MARTÍNEZ
Vice-Rector for Internationalisation and Excellence: RODRIGO TRUJILLO GONZÁLEZ
Vice-Rector for Investigation and Transfer of Knowledge: CATALINA RUIZ PÉREZ
Vice-Rector for Planning and Facilities: MARÍA GRACIA RODRÍGUEZ BRITO
Vice-Rector for Students: MIRIAM C. GONZÁLEZ AFONSO
Vice-Rector for Study Plans and Postgraduate Degrees: JOSÉ MARÍA PALAZÓN LÓPEZ
Vice-Rector for Univ. and Society Relations: MARÍA NÉLIDA RANCEL TORRES
Vice-Rector for Technologies of the Information and Communications: ROSA MARIA AGUILAR CHINEA
Vice-Rector for Univ. Services: JUSTO ROBERTO PÉREZ CRUZ
Registrar: JUAN M. RODRÍGUEZ CALERO
Librarian: LUIS GONZALO REY PINZÓN
Library of 700,000 vols, 12,000 periodicals
Number of teachers: 1,764
Number of students: 25,103

Publications: *Anales de la Facultad de Derecho* (1 a year), *Clepsidra* (1 a year),

Cuadernos del Cemyr (1 a year), *Fortunatae: Revista Canaria de Filología, Cultura y Humanidades Clásicas* (1 a year), *Latente* (1 a year), *Revista Canaria de Estudios Ingleses* (2 a year), *Revista de Bellas Artes* (1 a year), *Revista de Filología* (1 a year), *Revista de Historia Canaria* (1 a year), *Revista Laguna* (2 a year), *Tempora* (1 a year)

DEANS

Faculty of Art: ALFONSO RUIZ RALLO
Faculty of Biology: NÉSTOR TORRES DARIAS
Faculty of Chemistry: JOSÉ MANUEL GARCÍA FRAGA
Faculty of Economic and Business Sciences: JOSÉ ANTONIO ÁLVAREZ GONZÁLEZ
Faculty of Education: OLGA ALEGRE DE LA ROSA
Faculty of Geography and History: JOSÉ ASCENCIÓN DELGADO DELGADO
Faculty of Information Sciences: CARMEN RODRÍGUEZ WANGÜEMERT
Faculty of Law: MARCEL MANUEL BONNET ESCUELA
Faculty of Mathematics: ANTONIO MARTINÓN CEJAS
Faculty of Medicine: EMILIO SANZ ÁLVAREZ
Faculty of Pharmacy: ENRIQUE MARTÍNEZ CARRETERO
Faculty of Philology: JUAN IGNACIO OLIVA CRUZ
Faculty of Philosophy: ÁNGELA SIERRA GONZÁLEZ
Faculty of Physics: CECILIO HERNÁNDEZ RODRÍGUEZ
Faculty of Political and Social Sciences: CARMEN MARINA BARRETO VARGAS
Faculty of Psychology: PEDRO AVERO DELGADO

UNIVERSIDAD DE LA RIOJA

Avda de La Paz 93, 26006 Logroño
Telephone: 941299100
E-mail: informacion@unirioja.es
Internet: www.unirioja.es
Founded 1992
State control
Language of instruction: Spanish
Academic year: September to May (2 semesters)

Rector: JOSÉ ARNÁEZ VADILLO
Vice-Rector for Faculty, Planning and Teaching Innovation: JOSÉ ANTONIO CABALLERO LÓPEZ
Vice-Rector for Research and Knowledge Transfer: JAVIER TARDÁGUILA LASO
Vice-Rector for Student Affairs and Employment: MARÍA CRUZ NAVARRO PÉREZ
Sec.-Gen. for Institutional and Int. Relations: MARIOLA URREA CORRES
Library Dir: MARTA MAGRIÑA
Library of 250,000 vols, 6,000 electronic periodicals
Number of teachers: 430
Number of students: 7,500

Publications: *Anuario Jurídico de La Rioja* (1 a year), *Boletín Europeo de la Universidad de La Rioja* (irregular), *Brocar: Cuadernos de Investigación Histórica* (1 a year), *Contextos Educativos: Revista de Educación* (1 a year), *Cuadernos de Gestión* (2 a year), *Cuadernos de Investigación Filológica* (1 a year), *Cuadernos de Investigación Geográfica* (1 a year), *Documentos de Trabajo del Dpto. de Economía y Empresa* (irregular), *Fábula. Revista Literaria* (2 a year), *Iberia: Revista de la Antigüedad* (1 a year), *Journal of English Studies* (1 a year)

DEANS

Faculty of Business Sciences: JUAN CARLOS AYALA CALVO

Faculty of Law and Social Sciences: MARIA RONCESVALLES BARBER CÁRCAMO

Faculty of Literature and Education: JORGE FERNÁNDEZ LÓPEZ

Faculty of Sciences, Agriculture Studies and Information: SUSANA CABREDO PINILLOS

Technical School of Industrial Engineering: JAVIER BRETÓN RODRÍGUEZ (Dir)

Univ. School of Nursing: ROSARIO ARÉJULA BENITO (Dir)

UNIVERSIDAD DE LAS PALMAS DE GRAN CANARIA

Calle Juan de Quesada 30, 35001, Las Palmas de Gran Canaria, Canary Islands

Telephone: 928457443

E-mail: relint@ulpgc.es

Internet: www.ulpgc.es

Founded 1989

State control

Language of instruction: Spanish

Academic year: September to May (2 semesters)

Rector: Dr JOSÉ REGIDOR GARCÍA

Vice-Rector for Communication, Quality and Institutional Coordination: Dra TRINIDAD ARCOS PEREIRA

Vice-Rector for Culture, Sport and Comprehensive Care: Dra ISABEL PASCUA FEBLES

Vice-Rector for Degrees and Doctoral Degrees: Dr RAFAEL ROBAINA ROMERO

Vice-Rector for Faculty and Academic Planning: Dr GUSTAVO MONTERO GARCÍA

Vice-Rector for Int. Relations and Cooperation: Dra ROSARIO BERRIEL MARTÍNEZ

Vice-Rector for Research, Devt and Innovation: Dr ANTONIO FALCÓN MARTEL

Vice-Rector for Student Affairs and Employabililty: Dr NICOLÁS DÍAZ DE LEZCANO SEVILLANO

Sec.-Gen.: CARMEN SALINERO ALONSO

Registrar: CARMEN SALINERO ALONSO

Library Dir: MARÍA DEL CARMEN MARTÍN MARICHAL

Library of 661,175 vols, 7,634 periodicals

Number of teachers: 1,500

Number of students: 24,057

DEANS

Faculty of Economics, Business and Tourism: JUAN MANUEL BENÍTEZ DEL ROSARIO

Faculty of Geography and History: Dr GERARDO DELGADO AGUIAR

Faculty of Health Sciences: Dr FELIPE RODRÍGUEZ DE CASTRO

Faculty of Law and Social Sciences: IGNACIO DÍAZ DE LEZCANO SEVILLANO

Faculty of Marine Sciences: MELCHOR GONZÁLEZ DÁVILA

Faculty of Philology: Dr ANTONIO MARIA MARTÍN RODRÍGUEZ

Faculty of Sport Sciences and Physical Activity: Dr ANTONIO GONZÁLEZ MOLINA

Faculty of Teacher Training: MARINO ALDUÁN GUERRA

Faculty of Translation and Interpretation: Dr RICHARD CLOUET

Faculty of Veterinary Science: JORGE ORÓS MONTÓN

UNIVERSIDAD DEL PAÍS VASCO/ EUSKAL HERRIKO UNIBERTSITATEA
(University of the Basque Country)

Barrio Sarriena s/n, 48940 Bilbao

Telephone: 946012000

E-mail: comunicacion@ehu.es

Internet: www.ehu.es

Founded 1968 as Universidad de Bilbao, present name 1980

State control

Languages of instruction: Basque, Spanish

Academic year: September to July (2 semesters)

Rector: Dr IÑAKI GOIRIZELAIA ORDORIKA

Vice-Rector for Álava Campus: JAVIER GARAIZAR CANDINA

Vice-Rector for Bizkaia Campus: CARMELO GARITAONANDIA

Vice-Rector for Faculty and Research: FRANCISCO JAVIER GIL GOIKOURIA

Vice-Rector for Gipuzkoa Campus: ANA ARRIETA AYESTARAN

Vice-Rector for Graduate Studies and Innovation: AMAYA ZARRAGA CASTRO

Vice-Rector for Postgraduate Studies and Int. Relations: NEKANE BALLUERKA LASA

Vice-Rector for Projection and Transfers: AMAIA MASEDA

Vice-Rector for Research: FERNANDO PLAZAOLA MUGURUZA

Vice-Rector for Students, Employability and Social Responsibility: MAITE ZELAIA GARAGARZA

Sec.-Gen.: JOSÉ LUIS MARTÍN GONZÁLEZ

Librarian: CARMEN GUERRA BLASCO

Library of 873,116 vols, 17,008 periodicals

Number of teachers: 5,000

Number of students: 44,000

Publications: *Acto de Investidura* (1 a year), *Anuario del Seminario de Filología Vasca 'Julio de Urquijo'* (International Journal of Basque Linguistics and Philology, 1 a year), *Memoria de Actividades* (1 a year), *Memoria Estadística* (1 a year), *Psicodidactics* (The International Journal of Development Biology, 8–10 a year), *Recursos Científicos y Líneas de Investigación* (1 a year), *Resúmenes de Tesis Doctorales* (1 a year)

DEANS

Faculty of Arts (Alava): IÑAKI BAZAN DIAZ

Faculty of Chemistry (Gipuzkoa): IÑIGO LEGORBURU FAUS

Faculty of Computer Science (Gipuzkoa): AGUSTÍN ARRUABARRENA

Faculty of Economic and Business Studies (Bizkaia): Dr ARTURO RODRÍGUEZ CASTELLANOS

Faculty of Fine Arts (Bizkaia): JOSU REKALDE IZAGIRRE

Faculty of Law (Bizkaia): DEMETRIO LOPERENA ROTA

Faculty of Law (Gipuzkoa): FRANCISCO JAVIER QUEL LÓPEZ

Faculty of Medicine and Dentistry (Bizkaia): Prof. AGUSTÍN MARTÍNEZ IBARGÜEN

Faculty of Pharmacy (Alava): MAILO VIRTO LEKUONA

Faculty of Philosophy and Educational Science (Gipuzkoa): XABIER ETXAGUE ALCALDE

Faculty of Physical Activities and Sport Sciences (Alava): MAITE FUENTES AZPIROZ

Faculty of Psychology (Gipuzkoa): ANA ISABEL VERGARA IRAETA

Faculty of Science and Technology (Bizkaia): ESTHER DOMÍNGUEZ PÉREZ

Faculty of Social and Communication Sciences (Bizkaia): ALFONSO UNCETA SATRÚSTEGUI

UNIVERSIDAD DE LEÓN

Avda de la Facultad 25, 24004 León

Telephone: 987291000

E-mail: rectorado@unileon.es

Internet: www.unileon.es

Founded 1979

State control

Language of instruction: Spanish

Academic year: September to June (2 semesters)

Rector: JOSÉ ÁNGEL HERMIDA ALONSO

Vice-Rector for Academic Org.: MATILDE SIERRA VEGA

Vice-Rector for Campus Infrastructure: MARÍA VICTORIA SECO FERNÁNDEZ

Vice-Rector for Faculty: JOSÉ LUIS FANJUL SUÁREZ

Vice-Rector for Int. and Institutional Relations: JOSÉ LUIS CHAMOSA GONZÁLEZ

Vice-Rector for Research: ALBERTO JOSÉ VILLENA CORTÉS

Vice-Rector for Student Affairs: JOSÉ MANUEL GONZALO ORDEN

Sec.-Gen.: SUSANA RODRÍGUEZ ESCANCIANO

Registrar: PIEDAD GONZÁLEZ GRANDA

Library Dir: MARÍA MARSÁ VILA

Library of 458,170 vols, 13,815 periodicals

Number of teachers: 898

Number of students: 15,072

Publications: *AmbioCiencias*, *Artes Marciales* (2 a year), *Contextos*, *Cuestiones de género*, *De Arte*, *Estudios Humanísticos: Filología*, *Estudios Humanísticos: Historia*, *Interculturalidad y Traducción*, *Lancia*, *Lectura y Signo*, *Pecvnia*, *Polígonos*, *Silva: Estudios de Humanismo y Tradición Clásica*

DEANS

Faculty of Arts: MARIA VICTORIA HERRÁEZ ORTEGA

Faculty of Biological and Environmental Sciences: BLANCA RAZQUÍN PERALTA

Faculty of Economic and Business Administration: JOSÉ MIGUEL FERNÁNDEZ FERNÁNDEZ

Faculty of Education: JOSÉ MARÍA SANTAMARTA LUENGOS

Faculty of Law: Dr JUAN JOSÉ FERNÁNDEZ DOMÍNGUEZ

Faculty of Sciences of Physical Activity and Sport: Dr JULIÁN ESPARTERO CASADO

Faculty of Veterinary Science: JOSÉ GABRIEL FERNÁNDEZ ÁLVAREZ

Faculty of Work Studies: MARIA DE LOS REYES MARTÍNEZ BARROSO

UNIVERSIDAD DE MÁLAGA
(University of Malaga)

Avda Cervantes 2, 29071 Málaga

Telephone: 952131000

E-mail: informacion@uma.es

Internet: www.uma.es

Founded 1972

State control

Language of instruction: Spanish

Academic year: October to July

Rector: ADELAIDA DE LA CALLE MARTÍN

Vice-Rector for Academic Affairs: MARÍA JOSÉ BLANCA MENA

Vice-Rector for Campus: RAQUEL BARCO MORENO

Vice-Rector for Communication and Int. Relations: PEDRO FARIAS BATLLE

Vice-Rector for Coordination: JOSE ÁNGEL NARVÁEZ BUENO

Vice-Rector for Cultural Affairs: MARÍA ISABEL CALERO SEGALL

Vice-Rector for Institutional Relations and Pres. Cabinet: CARLOS DE LAS HERAS PEDROSA

Vice-Rector for Research: MARÍA VALPUESTA FERNÁNDEZ

Vice-Rector for Student Affairs: JUAN ANTONIO PERLES ROCHEL

Sec.-Gen.: MIGUEL PORRAS FERNÁNDEZ

Library Coordinator: GREGORIO GARCÍA RECHE

Library of 979,851 vols, 24,983 periodicals

Number of teachers: 1,600

Number of students: 36,000

Publications: *Boletín de Arte* (1 a year), *Filosofía Malacitana* (1 a year), *Histología Médica* (2 a year), *Revista Unión de Editoriales Universitarias Españolas (UNE)* (2 a year)

DEANS

Faculty of Commerce and Management: FRANCISCO CANTALEJO GARCÍA

Faculty of Communication Science: JUAN ANTONIO GARCÍA GALINDO

Faculty of Economic and Business Studies: Dr EUGENIO JOSÉ LUQUE DOMÍNGUEZ

Faculty of Education Science: JOSÉ FRANCISCO MURILLO MAS

Faculty of Fine Arts: SALVADOR HARO GONZÁLEZ

Faculty of Health Sciences: MARIA TERESA LABAJOS MANZANARES

Faculty of Law: JUAN JOSÉ HINOJOSA TORRALVO

Faculty of Medicine: JOSÉ PABLO LARA MUÑOZ

Faculty of Philosophy and Letters: SEBASTIÁN FERNÁNDEZ LÓPEZ

Faculty of Psychology: JULIÁN ALMARAZ CARRETERO

Faculty of Sciences: FRANCISCO JOSÉ PALMA MOLINA

Faculty of Social and Work Studies: ANA ROSA DEL ÁGUILA OBRA

Faculty of Tourism: ANTONIO J. GUEVARA PLAZA

PROFESSORS

Faculty of Economic and Business Studies:

AGUIRRE SADABA, A., Economics and Business Administration

GARCÍA LIZANA, A., Applied Economics (Political)

GONZÁLEZ PAREJA, A., Applied Economics (Mathematics)

MOCHON MORCILLO, F., Economic Analysis

OTERO MORENO, J. M., Applied Economics (Statistics and Econometrics)

PINO ARTACHO, J., State Law and Sociology

REQUENA RODRÍGUEZ, J. M., Financial Economics and Accountancy

SÁNCHEZ MALDONADO, J., Applied Economics (Structure and Public Finance)

Faculty of Law:

AURIOLES MARTIN, A., Private Law

CARRETERO LESTON, J. L., Public Law

ORTEGA CARILLO DE ALBÓRNOZ, A., Civil, Ecclesiastical and State Law

ROBLES GARZÓN, J. A., Political Science, International Law

Faculty of Medicine:

BROTAT ESTER, M., Radiology, Physical and Psychiatric Medicine

CASTILLA GONZALO, J., Normal and Pathological Morphology

FERNÁNDEZ-CREHUET NAVAJAS, J., Preventative Medicine and Public Health

OCAÑA SIERRA, J., Medicine

SÁNCHEZ DE LA CUESTA Y ALARCÓN, F., Physiology, Pharmacology and Paediatrics

SÁNCHEZ DEL CURA, G., Surgery, Obstetrics and Gynaecology

Faculty of Philosophy and Letters:

ALVAR EZQUERRA, M., Spanish and Romance Philology

CUEVAS GARCÍA, C., Spanish Philology and Theory of Literature

ESTEVE ZARAZAGA, J. M., Theory and History of Education

GARCÍA DE LA FUENTE, O., Classical Philology and Arabic and Islamic Studies

LAVIN CAMACHO, E., English and French Philology

MARTINEZ FREIRE, P., Philosophy

MORALES FOLGUERAS, J. M., History of Art

NADAL SÁNCHEZ, A., Modern History

OCANA OCANA, M. C., Geography

PÉREZ GÓMEZ, A., Didactics

RODRIGUEZ OLIVA, P., Prehistory and Science of Antiquity and Middle Ages

TRAINES TORRES, M. V., Psychology

Faculty of Science:

ARENAS ROSADO, J. F., Physical Chemistry

CABEZUDO ARTERO, B., Plant Biology

CANO PAVÓN, J. M., Analytical Chemistry

CUENCA MIRA, J. A., Algebra, Geometry and Topology

FERNÁNDEZ-FIGARES PÉREZ, J. M., Cellular and Genetic Biology

FERNÁNDEZ JIMÉNEZ, C., Applied Physics

GARCÍA RASO, E., Animal Biology

JIMÉNEZ LÓPEZ, A., Inorganic Chemistry, Crystallography and Mineralogy

RODRÍGUEZ JIMÉNEZ, J. J., Chemical Engineering

RODRÍGUEZ ORTIZ, C., Applied Mathematics and Statistics

SERRANO LOZANO, L., Ecology and Geology

SUAU SUÁREZ, R., Biochemistry, Molecular Biology and Organic Chemistry

University School of Teacher Training:

DEL CAMPO Y DEL CAMPO, M., Didactics of Expression, Music

GARCÍA ESPAÑA, J., Didactics, Social Science, Experimental Science

MANTECON RAMÍREZ, B., Didactics of Language and Literature

University Polytechnic:

OLLERO BATURONE, A., Systems Engineering, Information Science, Electronics

RUIZ MUNOZ, J. M., Electrical Engineering, Electronic Technology

SIMON MATA, A., Mechanical Engineering, Engineering Graphics

TROYA LINERO, J. M., Language and Science of Computing

UNIVERSIDAD DE MURCIA

Avda Teniente Flomesta 5, 30003 Murcia

Telephone: 868883000

E-mail: rector@um.es

Internet: www.um.es

Founded 1915

State control

Language of instruction: Spanish

Academic year: September to May (2 semesters)

Rector: JOSÉ ANTONIO COBACHO GÓMEZ

Vice-Rector for Academic Staff: JOSÉ MARÍA RUIZ GÓMEZ

Vice Rector for Coordination and Communication: MARÍA ANGELES ESTEBAN ABAD

Vice-Rector for Finance and Infrastructure: ANTONIO CALVO-FLORES SEGURA

Vice-Rector for Institutional Relations and Health Sciences: MANUEL VIDAL SANZ

Vice Rector for Research and Int. Relations: GASPAR ROS BERRUEZO

Vice Rector for Strategic Devt and Training: FERNANDO MARTÍN RUBIO

Vice-Rector for Students and Employment: MARÍA ISABEL SÁNCHEZ-MORA MOLINA

Vice-Rector for Studies: CONCEPCIÓN ROSARIO PALACIOS BERNAL

Vice Rector for Univ. Extension and Electronic Admin.: MERCEDES FARIAS BATLLE

Sec.-Gen.: JOAQUÍN LOMBA MAURANDI

Library Dir: LOURDES COBACHO GÓMEZ

Library of 718,276 vols, 9,416 periodicals

Number of teachers: 2,101

Number of students: 34,483

Publications: *Agroecología* (1 a year), *Anales de Biología* (1 a year), *Anales de Derecho* (1 a year), *Anales de Documentación*, *Anales de Filología Francesa* (1 a year), *Anales de Psicología* (4 a year), *Anales de Veterinaria* (1 a year), *Antigüedad y Cristianismo* (1 a year), *Anuario de Hojas de Warmi*, *Areas. Revista Internacional de Ciencias Sociales*, *Arte y Políticas de Identidad* (1 a year), *Cartaphilus* (2 a year), *Cuadernos de Psicología del Deporte* (2 a year), *Cuadernos de Turismo* (2 a year), *Daimon* (2 a year), *Documentos de Trabajo de Sociología Aplicada*, *Educatio Siglo XXI*, *Enfermería Global* (4 a year), *Estudios Románicos*, *Historia Agraria* (4 a year), *International Journal of English Studies*, *Medievalismo*, *Miscelánea Medieval Murciana*, *Myrtia* (2 a year), *Naveg@mérica* (2 a year), *Papeles de Geografía* (2 a year), *Revista de Investigación Educativa*, *Revista de Investigación Lingüística*, *Revista de Investigación sobre Flamenco*, *Sociología Histórica*, *Tonos Digital* (online (www.um.es/tonosdigital))

DEANS

Faculty of Arts: JOSÉ MARÍA JIMÉNEZ CANO

Faculty of Biology: Dr JOSÉ MESEGUER PEÑALVER

Faculty of Chemistry: GREGORIO SÁNCHEZ GÓMEZ

Faculty of Communication and Documentation: FRANCISCO JAVIER MARTÍNEZ MÉNDEZ

Faculty of Computer Science: PEDRO MIGUEL RUIZ MARTÍNEZ

Faculty of Economics and Business Studies: MARÍA PILAR MONTANER SALAS

Faculty of Education: CONCEPCIÓN MARTÍN SÁNCHEZ

Faculty of Fine Arts: JUAN ROMERA AGULLÓ

Faculty of Law: FAUSTINO CAVAS MARTÍNEZ

Faculty of Mathematics: Prof. Dr FRANCISCO ESQUEMBRE MARTÍNEZ

Faculty of Medicine: JOAQUÍN GARCÍA-ESTAÑ LÓPEZ

Faculty of Nursing: Prof. DAVID ARMERO BARRANCO

Faculty of Optometry: PALOMA SOBRADO CALVO

Faculty of Philosophy: ANTONIO CAMPILLO MESEGUER

Faculty of Psychology: JUAN JOSÉ LÓPEZ GARCÍA

Faculty of Social and Health Sciences (Lorca): JESÚS GÓMEZ AMOR

Faculty of Social Work: ENRIQUE PASTOR SELLER

Faculty of Sport Sciences: MIGUEL LÓPEZ BACHERO

Faculty of Veterinary Studies: ANTONIO JOSÉ ROUCO YÁNEZ

Faculty of Work Sciences: DOMINGO ANTONIO MANZANARES MARTÍNEZ

UNIVERSIDAD DE NAVARRA
(University of Navarra)

Campus Universitario, 31080 Navarra

Telephone: 948425600

E-mail: relint@unav.es

Internet: www.unav.es

Founded 1952

Private control

Languages of instruction: English, Spanish

Academic year: September to June (2 semesters)

Chancellor: Mgr JAVIER ECHEVARRÍA

Vice-Chancellor: Mgr RAMÓN HERRANDO

Rector: Prof. Dr ALFONSO SÁNCHEZ-TABERNERO

Vice-Rector for Academic Programmes: Dr BORJA LÓPEZ-JURADO

Vice-Rector for Communications: Prof. JUAN MANUEL MORA

Vice-Rector for Faculty: Prof. MARÍA IRABURU

Vice-Rector for Int. Relations: Prof. PILAR LOSTAO

Vice-Rector for Research: Dr ICIAR ASTIASARÁN

Vice-Rector for Student Affairs: Prof. TOMÁS GÓMEZ-ACEBO

Sec.-Gen.: Dr GONZALO ROBLES GONZÁLEZ

Library Dir: VÍCTOR SANZ SANTACRUZ

Library: 1.2m. vols, 60,000 journals

Number of teachers: 1,791 (900 full-time, 891 part-time)

Number of students: 13,197 (11,198 full-time, 1,999 part-time)

Publications: *Anuario de Derecho Internacional* (1 a year), *Anuario Filosófico* (3 a year), *Comunicación y Sociedad* (2 a year), *Ius Canonicum* (2 a year), *Nuestro Tiempo* (12 a year), *Persona y Derecho* (2 a year), *Redacción* (4 a year), *Revista de Arquitectura*, *Revista de Edificación* (4 a year), *Revista de Medicina* (4 a year), *RILCE* (2 a year), *Scripta Theologica* (4 a year)

DEANS

Faculty of Canon Law: ANTONIO VIANA
Faculty of Communication: MONICA HERRERO SUBÍAS
Faculty of Ecclesiastical Philosophy: Dr JOSÉ ÁNGEL GARCÍA CUADRADO
Faculty of Economics and Business Administration: Dra REYES CALDERÓN
Faculty of Humanities and Social Sciences: JAUME AURELL
Faculty of Law: Prof. Dr PABLO SÁNCHEZ-OSTIZ
Faculty of Medicine: Dr JORGE IRIARTE FRANCO
Faculty of Nursing: Dra MARÍA ISABEL SARACÍBAR RAZQUIN
Faculty of Pharmacy: Dra ADELA LÓPEZ DE CERAIN SALSAMENDI
Faculty of Philosophy and Letters: Dr ROSALIA BAENA
Faculty of Sciences: Dr IGNACIO LÓPEZ GOÑI
Faculty of Theology: Dr JUAN CHAPA
IESE Business School: Prof. JORDI CANALS
ISEM Fashion Business School: TERESA SÁDABA GARRAZA (Dir)
School of Architecture: Dr JOSÉ ÁNGEL MEDINA (Dir)
School of Engineering (San Sebastián): Dr IÑIGO PUENTE URRUZMENDI
School of Management Assistants ISSA (San Sebastián): MARÍA JESÚS ÁLVAREZ (Dir)

PROFESSORS

Faculty of Canon Law:

BAÑARES PARERA, J. I., Family Law
CALVO-ÁLVAREZ, J., Administrative Canon Law
FUENTES ALSONSO, J. A., Administrative Canon Law
GÓMEZ-IGLESIAS, V., Constitutional Canon Law
MIRAS POUSO, J. M., Administrative Canon Law
MOLANO GRAGERA, E., Constitutional Canon Law
OTADUY, J., Ecclesiastical Law
OTADUY GUERIN, J., General and Personal Law
RINCÓN, T., Administrative Canon Law
RODRÍGUEZ-OCAÑA, R., Procedural Canon Law
VIANA TOMÉ, A., Ecclesiastical Organization
VILADRICH BATALLER, P. J., Canon Law

Faculty of Communication:

AMOEDO CASAIS, A., Journalistic Projects
ARRESE RECA, A., Media Business
ARTÁZCOZ LÓPEZ, M. A., Journalistic Projects
AZURMENDI ADARRAGA, A., Public Communication
BARRERA DEL BARRIO, C., Public Communication
BRINGUÉ SALA, J., Media Business
CODINA BLASCO, M., Public Communication
CUEVAS ÁLVAREZ, E., Audiovisual Communication
DE LA RICA ARANGUREN, A., Audiovisual Communication
DE LOS ÁNGELES VILLENA, J., Media Business
ECHART ORÚS, P., Audiovisual Communication

ETAYO PÉREZ, C., Media Business
FAUS BELAU, A., Audiovisual Communication
GARCÍA AVILÉS, J. A., Journalistic Projects
GARCÍA-NOBLEJAS LINIERS, J. J., Audiovisual Communication
JIMENO LÓPEZ, M. A., Journalistic Projects
LA PORTE FERNÁNDEZ-ALFARO, M. T., Public Communication
LATORRE IZQUIERDO, J., Audiovisual Communication
LEÓN ANGUIANO, B., Journalistic Projects
LÓPEZ-ESCOBAR FERNÁNDEZ, E., Public Communication
LÓPEZ PAN, F., Journalistic Projects
LOZANO BARTOLOZZI, P., Public Communication
MARTÍNEZ COSTA, M. P., Journalistic Projects
MEDINA, M., Media Business
MONTERO DÍAZ, M., Public Communication
MORENO MORENO, E., Journalistic Projects
NAVAS GARCÍA, A., Public Communication
ORIHUELA COLLIVA, J. L., Audiovisual Communication
PARDO FERNÁNDEZ, A., Audiovisual Communication
PÉREZ LATRE, F. J., Media Business
PIQUE I FERNÁNDEZ, A. M., Journalistic Projects
PORTILLA MANJÓN, I., Media Business
REDONDO GÁLVEZ, G., History
SÁDABA CHALEZQUER, R., Media Business
SÁDABA GARRAZA, M. T., Public Communication
SALAVERRÍA ALIAGA, R., Journalistic Projects
SÁNCHEZ ARANDA, J. J., Public Communication
SÁNCHEZ-TABERNERO SÁNCHEZ, A., Media Business
VARA MIGUEL, A., Media Business
VERDERA ALBIÑANA, F., Public Communication
ZORRILLA RUIZ, J., Journalistic Projects

Faculty of Economics and Business:

ABBRITTI, M., Economics
ALFARO TANCO, J. A., Business Admin.
ALVAREZ ARCE, J. L., Economics
ARANDA LEÓN, C., Business Admin.
ARELLANO GIL, J., Business Admin.
BLANCO, B., Business Economics and Quantitative Methods
BLAZSEK, S., Economics
CALDERÓN CUADRADO, R., Business Admin.
CORGNET, B., Economics
CUÑADO EIZAGUIRRE, J., Applied Economics
ELIZALDE, J., Applied Economics
GALERA PERAL, F., Applied Economics
GAVLE, S., Business Economics and Quantitative Methods
GIL ALAÑA, L., Economics
GONZÁLEZ ENCISO, A., Economics
KINATEDEE, M., Economics
LEIVA, R., Business
MARTÍNEZ-ECHEVARRÍA, M. A., Economics
MATEO DUEÑAS, R., Business
MATHEW, A. J., Economics
MENDI GÜEMES, P., Economics
MOLERO GARCÍA, J. C., Applied Economics
MORENO ALMÁRCEGUI, A., Economics
MORENO IBÁNEZ, A., Economics
PÉREZ DE GRACIA HIDALGO, F., Applied Economics
PUJOL TORRAS, F., Economics
RÁBADE Y HERRERO, L. A., Business
RAVINA BOHORQUEZ, L., Economics
RODRÍGUEZ CARREÑO, I., Economics
RODRÍGUEZ CHACÓN, V., Business
SALVATIERRA, S. M., Quantitative Methods
SAN MARTÍN ECHAURI, C., Quantitative Methods
SEBREK, S., Business
TOLSA MAJÓS, A., Applied Economics
TORRES SÁNCHEZ, R., Economics

ZARATIEGUI LAVIANO, J. M., Economics
ZARCO JASSO, H., Business Admin.

Faculty of Law:

APARISI MIRALLES, A., Philosophy of Law
ARECHEDERRA ARANZADI, L., Civil Law
BLANCO FERNÁNDEZ, M., Canon Law
DOMINGO OSLÉ, R., Roman Law
GÓMEZ MONTORO, A., Constitutional Law
LÓPEZ-JURADO, B., Administrative Law
LÓPEZ SÁNCHEZ, M. A., Commercial Law
MUERZA ESPARZA, J., Procedural Law
SÁNCHEZ-OSTIZ GUTIÉRREZ, P., Criminal Law
SIMÓN ACOSTA, E., Financial Law
VALPUESTA GASTAMINZA, E., Commercial Law

Faculty of Medicine:

ALBEROLA GÓMEZ-ESCOLAR, I., Internal Medicine
ALCÁZAR ZAMBRANO, J. L., Obstetrics and Gynaecology
ALEGRÍA EZQUERRA, E., Cardiology
ÁLVAREZ-CIENFUEGOS SUÁREZ, J., General Surgery
ALZINA DE AGUILAR, V., Paediatrics
AMILLO GARAYOA, S., Orthopaedics Surgery
AQUERRETA BEOLA, A., Radiology
ARTIEDA GONZÁLEZ-GRANDA, J., Neurology
AYMERICH SOLER, M. S., Neurology
AZANZA PEREA, J. R., Pharmacology
AZCONA SAN JULIÁN, C., Paediatrics
BARBA COSIALS, J., Cardiology
BAZÁN ALVAREZ, A., Plastic Surgery
BEGUIRISTAIN GÚRPIDE, J. L., Orthopaedics Surgery
BELOQUI RUIZ, Ó., Internal Medicine
BERIÁN POLO, J. M., Urology
BILBAO JAUREGUIZAR, I., Radiology
BODEGAS FRÍAS, M. E., Histology
BORRÁS CUESTA, F., Biochemistry
BURRELL BUSTOS, M. A., Pathological Anatomy
CALABUIG NOGUÉS, J., Cardiology
CALVO GONZÁLEZ, A., Histology
CARRASCOSA MORENO, F., Anaesthesiology and Resuscitation
CASADO CASADO, M., Radiology
CENARRUZBEITIA SAGARMINAGA, E., Physiology
CERVERA ENGUIX, S., Psychiatry
CIVEIRA MURILLO, M. P., Medical Secretaryship
COLINA LORDA, I., Internal Medicine
COMA CANELLA, I., Cardiology
CORRALES IZQUIERDO, J., Internal Medicine
CUESTA PALOMERA, B., Haematology
DE CASTRO, P., Neurology
DEL POZO LEÓN, J. L., Microbiology
DE MIGUEL VÁZQUEZ, C., Biochemistry
DÍAZ GARCÍA, R., Microbiology
DIÉGUEZ LÓPEZ, I., Allergology
DIEZ GOÑI, N., Physiology
DÍEZ MARTÍNEZ, J., Internal Medicine
ECHARTE ALONSO, L., Biomedicine
FERNÁNDEZ ALONSO, M., Microbiology
FORRIOL CAMPOS, F., Laboratory Medicine
FRECHILLA MANSO, D., Pharmacology
GARCÍA-MORATO, J. R., Anthropology
GIL SOTRES, P., Biomedicine
HONORATO PÉREZ, J., Pharmacology
HONTANILLA CATALAY, B., Plastic Surgery
IDOATE GASTEARENA, M., Pathological Anatomy
IRABURU ELIZALDE, M., Biochemistry
IRALA ESTEVEZ, J., Preventive Medicine
LAHORTIGA RAMOS, F., Psychiatry
LASHERAS ALDAZ, B., Pharmacology
LÁZARO CANTERO, R., Anthropology
LEÓN SANZ, M. P., Biomedicine
LÓPEZ GARACÍA, M. P., Psychiatry
LOZANO ESCARIO, M. D., Pathological Anatomy
LUCAS ROS, I., Internal Medicine
LUQUIN PULIDO, M. R., Neurology
MALDONADO LÓPEZ, M., Ophthalmology

Manrique Rodríguez, M., Otolaryngology
Manrique Smela, M., Neurology
Martín Algarra, S., Oncology
Martínez de Tejada de Garaizabal, G., Microbiology
Martínez González, M. A., Epidemiology and Public Health
Martínez Irujo, J. J., Biochemistry
Martínez Lage, M., Neurology
Martínez Monge, R., Radiology
Martínez Regueira, F., General Surgery
Martínez Vila, E., Neurology
Martín Trenor, A., General Surgery
Masdeu Puche, J., Neurology
Medina Cabrera, J. F., Internal Medicine
Melero Bermejo, I., Immunology
Mengual Poza, E., Anatomy
Merino Roncal, J., Immunology
Monedero Rodríguez, P., Anaesthesiology and Resuscitation
Montuenga Badia, L., Histology
Moreno Montañés, J., Ophthalmology
Moriyón Uría, I., Microbiology
Muñoz Navas, M. A., General Surgery
Narbona García, J., Paediatrics
Novo Villaverde, J., Genetics
Obeso Inchausti, J., Neurology
Odero de Dios, L., Genetics
Olavide Goya, I., Anaesthesiology
Páramo Fernández, J. A., Haematology
Pardo Caballos, A., Biomedicine
Pardo Mindán, J., Pathological Anatomy
Pastor Muñoz, M. A., Neurology
Peñuelas Sánchez, I., Biochemistry
Pérez Fernández, N., Otolaryngology
Pérez Mediavilla, L. A., Biochemistry
Prensa Sepúlveda, L., Anatomy
Prieto Valtueña, J., Internal Medicine
Prósper, F., Haematology
Purroy Unanua, A., Nephrology
Qian, C., Internal Medicine
Quiroga Vilas, J., Internal Medicine
Redondo, P., Dermatology
Richter Echevarría, J. A., Nuclear Medicine
Rio Zambrana, J., Pharmacology
Robles García, J. E., Urology
Rocha Hernando, E., Haematology
Rodríguez Ortigosa, C., Biochemistry
Rosell Costa, D., Urology
Rouzaut Subirá, A., Biochemistry
Rubio Vallejo, M., Microbiology
Ruiz-Canela López, M., Biomedicine
Salvador Rodríguez, F. J., Endocrinology
Sánchez Ibarrola, A., Immunology
Sangro Gómez-Acebo, B., Internal Medicine
Santidrian Alegre, S., Physiology
Sanz Larruga, M. L., Allergology
Seguí Gómez, M., Internal Medicine
Serrano Martínez, M., Internal Medicine
Sesma Egozcue, P., Pathological Anatomy
Sierrasesúmaga Ariznavarreta, L., Paediatrics
Sola Gallego, J. J., Pathological Anatomy
Torre Buxalleu, W., General Surgery
Ullán Serrano, J., Anatomy
Valentí Nin, J. R., Orthopaedic Surgery
Velayos Jorge, J. L., Anatomy
Villaro Gumpert, A. C., Histology
Villas Tomé, C., Orthopaedic Surgery
Viteri Torres, C., Neurology
Zapata García, R., Psychiatry
Zornoza Celaya, G., General Surgery
Zubieta Zarraga, J. L., Radiology
Zudaire Bergara, J. J., Urology

Faculty of Pharmacy
(Some professors also serve in the Faculty of Sciences)

Aguirre García, N., Pharmacology
Aldana Moraza, I., Organic Chemistry
Aldaz Pastor, A., Pharmacy and Pharmaceutical Technology
Ansorena, D., Bromatology and Toxicology
Aquerreta González, I., Pharmacy and Pharmaceutical Technology
Astiasarán Anchía, I., Bromatology and Toxicology
Barber Cárcamo, A., Physiology and Nutrition
Beitia Berrotarán, G.
Berjón San Juan, A., Physiology and Nutrition
Blanco, M. J., Pharmacy and Pharmaceutical Technology
Calvo, I., Pharmacy and Pharmaceutical Technology
Cid Canda, C., Bromatology and Toxicology
de Peña Fariza, M. P., Bromatology
Díaz García, J. M., Pharmacy and Pharmaceutical Technology
Dios Viéitez, C., Pharmacy and Pharmaceutical Technology
Espuelas, S., Pharmacy and Pharmaceutical Technology
Idoate García, A., Pharmacy and Pharmaceutical Technology
Fernández de Trocóniz, I., Pharmacy and Pharmaceutical Technology
Font Arellano, M., Organic Chemistry
García del Barrio, G., Pharmacy and Pharmaceutical Technology
Garrido, M. J., Pharmacy and Pharmaceutical Technology
Gil Royo, A. G., Bromatology and Toxicology
Giráldez Deiró, J., Pharmacy and Pharmaceutical Technology
Goñi Leza, M. del M., Pharmacy and Pharmaceutical Technology
Lacasa Arregui, C., Pharmacy and Pharmaceutical Technology
Lasheras Aldaz, B., Pharmacology
Lizarraga Pérez, E., Organic Chemistry
Lobo, J. M., Pharmacy and Pharmaceutical Technology
López de Ceráin, A., Bromatology and Toxicology
López Guzmán, J., Biomedicine
Lostao Crespo, P., Physiology and Nutrition
Manuel Irache Garreta, J. M., Pharmacy and Pharmaceutical Technology
Martí del Moral, A., Physiology and Nutrition
Martínez Hernández, A., Physiology and Nutrition
Mohino Sánchez, A., Bromatology and Toxicology
Monge Vega, A., Organic Chemistry
Moreno Aliaga, M. J., Physiology and Nutrition
Muñoz Hornillos, M., Physiology and Nutrition
Ortega Eslava, A., Pharmacy and Pharmaceutical Technology
Palop Cubillo, J. A., Organic Chemistry
Ramírez Gil, M. J., Pharmacology
Recarte Flamarique, F., Pharmacy and Pharmaceutical Technology
Renedo Omaechevarría, M. J., Pharmacy and Pharmaceutical Technology
Romero Cuevas, M., Organic Chemistry
Ruiz de la Heras, A., Bromatology and Toxicology
Sanmartín Grijalba, C., Organic Chemistry
Tros de Ilarduya, C., Pharmacy and Pharmaceutical Technology
Ygartua Ayerra, P., Pharmacy and Pharmaceutical Technology
Zamarreño Arregui, A. M., Pharmacy and Pharmaceutical Technology
Zapelena Íñiguez, M. J., Bromatology and Toxicology
Zulet Alzórriz, M. A., Physiology

Faculty of Sciences:

Aguirreola Morales, J., Plant Physiology
Alvarez Calviño, R., Botany
Alvarez Galindo, J. I., Chemistry and Pedology
Álvarez Jaurrieta, M. L., Chemistry and Edaphology
Antolín Bellver, C., Plant Physiology
Aquerreta Molina, S., Botany
Ardanza-Trevijano, S., Physics and Applied Mathematics
Ariño Plana, A., Zoology and Ecology
Azcárate Iriarte, R., Chemistry and Edaphology
Baquero Martín, E., Zoology and Ecology
Bragard, J., Physics and Applied Mathematics
Burguete Más, F. J., Physics and Applied Mathematics
Calasanz Abinzano, M. J., Genetics
Cavero, Y., Chemistry and Pedology
Chasco Ugarte, M. J., Physics and Applied Mathematics
Clavería Iracheta, V., Botany
de Miguel Velasco, A., Botany
Díaz Calavia, E. J., Physics
Ederra Indurain, A., Botany
Escala Urdapilleta, C., Zoology and Ecology
Fernández Alvarez, J. M., Chemistry and Pedology
Fernández Asenjo, L., Chemistry and Pedology
Garayoa Poyo, R., Economy
García Casado, P., Chemistry and Pedology
García Delgado, M., Genetics
García Unciti, M. S., Dietetics
García Zamora, J. M., Chemistry and Pedology
García-Mina Freire, J. M., Chemistry and Pedology
Garcimartín, A., Physics and Applied Mathematics
Garde Garde, J. M., Zoology and Ecology
Garrigó i Reixach, J., Chemistry and Pedology
Goicoechea Preboste, N., Plant Physiology
González, W., Physics and Applied Mathematics
González Gaitano, G., Chemistry and Pedology
Guerrero Setas, D., Edaphology
Hernández Minguillón, M. A., Zoology and Ecology
Herrera Mesa, L., Zoology and Ecology
Ibáñez Gastón, R., Botany
Irigoyen Iparrea, J. J., Plant Physiology
Isasi Allica, J. R., Chemistry and Pedology
Jordana Butticaz, R., Zoology and Ecology
Juaristi Iranzu, R., Botany
Labat Ayerra, A., Chemistry and Pedology
Larraz Azcárate, M., Zoology and Ecology
López Fernández, M. L., Botany
López Goñi, I., Microbiology
López Moratalla, N., Biochemistry
López Zabalza, M. J., Biochemistry
Mancini, H., Physics and Applied Mathematics
Martín Bachiller, C., Chemistry and Pedology
Martínez Oharriz, C., Chemistry and Pedology
Martínez Remírez, M., Physiology
Maza Ozcoidi, D., Physics and Applied Mathematics
Miranda Ferreiro, R., Zoology and Ecology
Moraza Zorrilla, L., Zoology and Ecology
Navarro Blasco, I., Chemistry and Pedology
Novo Villaverde, J., Genetics
Odero de Dios, M. D., Genetics

PALACIOS, C., Physics and Applied Mathematics

PELAEZ LÓPEZ, A., Physics and Applied Mathematics

PEÑAS, F. J., Chemistry and Pedology

PÉREZ GARCÍA, C., Physics and Applied Mathematics

PIUDO AINZINENA, M. J., Botany

PUIG BAGUER, J., Zoology and Ecology

RODÉS NAVARRO, D., Zoology and Ecology

RODRÍGUEZ GARCÍA, J. A., Genetics

RUILOPE PINEDA, R., Chemistry and Pedology

SÁNCHEZ CARPINTERO, I., Chemistry and Pedology

SÁNCHEZ DÍAZ, M., Plant Physiology

SÁNCHEZ GONZÁLEZ, M., Chemistry and Pedology

SÁNCHEZ MONGE, J. M., Chemistry and Pedology

SANTAMARÍA ELOLA, C., Chemistry and Pedology

SANTAMARÍA ULECIA, J. M., Chemistry and Pedology

SERRANO MARTÍNEZ, M., Zoology and Ecology

SIRERA BEJARANO, R., Chemistry and Pedology

VELAZ RIVAS, I., Chemistry and Pedology

VIZMANOS, J. L., Genetics

ZORNOZA CEBEIRO, A., Chemistry and Pedology

ZUDAIRE RIPA, I., Genetics

Faculty of Theology:

ARANDA LOMEÑA, A., Dogmatic Theology

ARANDA PÉREZ, G., Sacred Scripture: New Testament

BASTERO ELEIZALDE, J. L., Dogmatic Theology

IZQUIERDO URBINA, C., Fundamental Theology

MERINO RODRÍGUEZ, M., Patristics

SARANYANA CLOSA, J. I., History of Theology

SARMIENTO FRANCO, A., Moral Theology

VARO PINEDA, F., Sacred Scripture: New Testament

School of Engineering:

ALVAREZ SÁNCHEZ-ARJONA, M. J., Industrial Organization

ARCELUS ALONSO, M., Organization

ARIZTI URQUIJO, F., Fundamental Electronics

AVELLO ITURRIAGAGOITIA, A., Theory of Machines

BAGUER ALCALÁ, A., Organization of Work

BASTERO DE ELEIZALDE, C., Mathematical Methods

BASTERO DE ELEIZALDE, J. M., Mechanics

BERENGUER PÉREZ, R., Electronics

BISTUÉ GARCÍA, G., Electricity

BLANCO DEL PRADO, C., Calculus

BUSTAMENTE MERINO, P., Informatics

CAMPOS CAPELASTEGUI, J., Mechanics

CELIGÜETA LIZARZA, J. T., Computational Mechanics

DE LOS MOZOS VILLAR, L., Mechanics

DE MIGUEL SICILIA, J. J., Anthropology

DE NO LENGARÁN, J., Electricity

FERNÁNDEZ DÍEZ, J., Mechanical Technology

FLAQUER FUSTER, J., Linear Algebra

FLÓREZ ESNAL, J., Robotics

FONTAN AGORRETA, L., Fundamentals of Electronics

FUENTES PÉREZ, M., Metallurgy

GARCÍA-ALONSO MONTOYA, A., Electrical Engineering

GARCÍA RICO, A., Electrical Machines

GARCÍA-ROSALES VÁZQUEZ, C., Materials

GIL NOBAJAS, J. J., Electricity and Electronics

GIL SEVILLANO, J., Metallurgy

GIMÉNEZ ORTIZ, G., Mechanical Technology

GÓMEZ-ACEBO TEMES, T., Thermodynamics

GRACIA GAUDÓ, J., Electronics

GURRUCHAGA VÁZQUEZ, J. M., Technical Drawing

IZU BELLOSO, P., Materials

JIMÉNEZ CONDE, M., General Physics

LÓPEZ DE ARANCIBIA, A., Mechanics

LÓPEZ SORIA, B., Materials

MARTÍN ABREU, F., Mechanics

MARTÍNEZ ESNAOLA, J. M., Mechanics of Continua

MUÑOZ EMPARAN, A., Telecommunications

PARGADA GIL, M., Advanced Mathematics

PÉREZ TOCA, M., Electricity

PUENTE URRUZMENDI, I., Mechanics

RAMOS GONZÁLEZ, J. C., Mechanics

RIVAS NIETO, A., Fluids

RODRÍGUEZ IBABE, J. M., Materials

RUBIO DÍAZ-CORDOVÉS, A. R., Electricity

SANCHO SEUMA, J. I., Electricity

SANTOS GARCÍA, J., Organization

SARRIEGUI DOMÍNGUEZ, J. M., Organization

SERNA OLIVEIRA, M. A., Mechanics

SERRANO BÁRCENA, N., Organization

VERA RODRÍGUEZ, E., Steel Structures

VILES DÍEZ, E., Statistics

VIÑOLAS PRAT, J., Mechanics

UNIVERSIDAD DE OVIEDO

Calle San Francisco 3, 33003 Oviedo

Telephone: 985102901

E-mail: rector@uniovi.es

Internet: www.uniovi.es

Founded 1608

State control

Languages of instruction: English, Spanish

Academic year: September to May (2 semesters)

Rector: Prof. VICENTE GOTOR SANTAMARÍA

Vice-Rector for Campuses, Centres and Depts: JOSÉ CARLOS RICO FERNÁNDEZ

Vice-Rector for Economic Planning, Agreements and Contracts: SANTIAGO ALVAREZ GARCÍA

Vice-Rector for Internationalization and Postgraduate Studies: COVADONGA BETEGÓN BIEMPICA

Vice-Rector for IT: Prof. VÍCTOR GUILLERMO GARCÍA GARCÍA

Vice-Rector for Research and Campus of Int. Excellence: MARÍA PAZ SUÁREZ RENDUELES

Vice-Rector for Students: LUIS J. RODRÍGUEZ MUÑIZ

Vice-Rector for Teaching Staff and Academic Org.: Prof. JULIO ANTONIO GONZÁLEZ GARCÍA

Vice-Rector for Univ. Extension and Communication: Prof. VICENTE JESÚS DOMÍNGUEZ GARCÍA

Gen. Sec.: IGNACIO GONZÁLEZ DEL REY RODRÍGUEZ

Librarian: Dr. RAMÓN RODRÍGUEZ ÁLVAREZ

Library of 850,000 vols, 14,000 periodicals

Number of teachers: 2,154

Number of students: 29,000

Publications: *Aljamía, Archivos de la Facultad de Medicina, Archivum, Asturiensía Medievalía, Brevoria Geológica Astúrica, Ería, Revista de Geografía, Liño, Revista de Arte, Magister, Memorias de Historia Antigua, Revista de Biología, Revista de Ciencias, Revista de Minas, Sociedad y Poder, Trabajos de Geología*

DEANS

Faculty of Biology: TOMÁS EMILIO DÍAZ GONZÁLEZ

Faculty of Chemistry: JOSÉ MANUEL FERNÁNDEZ COLINAS

Faculty of Economics and Business: Prof. MANUEL GONZÁLEZ DÍAZ

Faculty of Geology: LOPE CALLEJA ESCUDERO

Faculty of Law: BENJAMÍN RIVAYA GARCÍA

Faculty of Medicine and Science of Health: ALFONSO LÓPEZ MUÑIZ

Faculty of Philosophy and Letters: CRISTINA VALDÉS RODRÍGUEZ

Faculty of Psychology: MARCELINO CUESTA IZQUIERDO

Faculty of Science: NORBERTO CORRAL BLANCO

Faculty of Teacher Training and Education: JUAN CARLOS SAN PEDRO VELEDO

Jovellanos Faculty of Commerce, Tourism and Social Sciences: EUGENIA SUÁREZ SERRANO

UNIVERSIDAD DE SALAMANCA

Patio de Escuelas Mayores 1, 37008 Salamanca

Telephone: 923294400

E-mail: informacion@usal.es

Internet: www.usal.es

Founded 1218 by Alfonso IX of León, reorganized by Alfonso X of Castile 1254

State control

Language of instruction: Spanish

Academic year: September to June (2 semesters)

Rector: DANIEL HERNÁNDEZ RUIPÉREZ

Vice-Rector for Academic Policy: JOSÉ ÁNGEL DOMÍNGUEZ PÉREZ

Vice-Rector for Economics and Management: RICARDO LÓPEZ FERNÁNDEZ

Vice-Rector for Faculty: MARIANO ESTEBAN DE VEGA

Vice-Rector for Innovation and Infrastructure: PASTORA VEGA CRUZ

Vice-Rector for Int. and Institutional Relations: NOEMÍ DOMÍNGUEZ GARCÍA

Vice-Rector for Research: MARÍA DE LOS ÁNGELES SERRANO GARCÍA

Vice-Rector for Student Affairs and Professional Integration: CRISTINA PITA YAÑEZ

Vice-Rector for Teaching: MARÍA LUISA MARTÍN CALVO

Sec.-Gen.: ANA CUEVAS BADALLO

Library Dir: MARGARITA BECEDAS GONZÁLEZ

Library: 1.5m. vols, 22,706 periodicals

Number of teachers: 2,200

Number of students: 32,000

DEANS

Faculty of Agricultural and Environmental Sciences: CARMELO ÁVILA ZARZA

Faculty of Biology: MANUEL ANTONIO MANSO MARTÍN

Faculty of Chemical Science: CARMEN MARÍA DEL HOYO MARTÍNEZ

Faculty of Economics and Business: JAVIER GONZÁLEZ BENITO

Faculty of Education: MARÍA ESPERANZA HERRERA GARCÍA

Faculty of Fine Arts: JOSÉ MANUEL PRADA VEGA

Faculty of Geography and History: VALENTÍN CABERO DIÉGUEZ

Faculty of Law: RAFAEL DE AGAPITO SERRANO

Faculty of Medicine: FRANCISCO JAVIER GARCÍA CRIADO

Faculty of Pharmacy: ANTONIO MURO ÁLVAREZ

Faculty of Philology: VICENTE GONZÁLEZ MARTÍN

Faculty of Philosophy: RICARDO ISIDRO PIÑERO MORAL

Faculty of Psychology: JOSÉ CARLOS SÁNCHEZ GARCÍA

Faculty of Sciences: JUAN MANUEL CORCHADO RODRÍGUEZ

Faculty of Social Sciences: JOSÉ MANUEL DEL BARRIO ALISTE

Faculty of Translation and Documentation: MARIA TERESA FUENTES MORÁN

UNIVERSIDAD DE SEVILLA
(University of Seville)

Calle San Fernando 4, 41004 Seville
Telephone: 954551000
E-mail: rector@us.es
Internet: www.us.es

Founded 1505
State control
Language of instruction: Spanish
Academic year: September to July (2 semesters)

Rector: Dr ANTONIO RAMÍREZ DE ARELLANO LÓPEZ
Vice-Rector for Academic Affairs: Prof. Dr MIGUEL ÁNGEL CASTRO ARROYO
Vice-Rector for Infrastructure: Dr MARÍA PASTORA REVUELTA MARCHENA
Vice-Rector for Institutional Relations: Prof. Dr TERESA GARCÍA GUTIÉRREZ
Vice-Rector for Internationalization: Dr CARMEN BARROSO CASTRO
Vice-Rector for Postgraduate Studies: Dr CARMEN VARGAS MACIAS
Vice-Rector for Research: Dr MANUEL GARCÍA LEÓN
Vice-Rector for Student Affairs: Dr JULIA DE LA FUENTE FERIA
Vice-Rector for Teaching Staff: Dr MARIA ELENA CANO BAZAGA
Vice-Rector for Technology Transfer: Dr RAMÓN GONZÁLEZ CARVAJAL
Gen. Sec.: Prof. Dra CONCEPCIÓN HORGUÉ BAENA
Library Dir: SONSOLES CELESTINO ANGULO

Number of teachers: 4,400
Number of students: 70,000

Publications: *Ambitos. Revista Internacional de Comunicación* (1 a year), *Anales de la Universidad Hispalense* (1 a year), *Anduli. Revista Andaluza de Ciencias Sociales* (1 a year), *Argumentos de Razón Técnica* (1 a year), *Comunicación* (2 a year), *Cuestiones de fisioterapia* (4 a year), *eDap* (irregular), *Elia* (1 a year), *Espacio y Tiempo* (1 a year), *Fedro* (2 a year), *Fragmentos de Filosofía* (1 a year), *Frame* (irregular), *Fuentes* (1 a year), *Habis* (1 a year), *Habitat y Sociedad* (irregular), *I/C Revista Científica de Información y Comunicación* (1 a year), *Laboratorio de Arte* (1 a year), *Philologia hispalensis* (1 a year), *Pixel-Bit* (2 a year), *Proyecto, Progreso, Arquitectura* (2 a year), *Questiones Publicitarias* (1 a year), *Revista de Estudios Norteamericanos* (1 a year), *Revista de Estudios Regionales* (4 a year), *Rhythmica* (1 a year)

DEANS

Faculty of Biology: ANTONIO ILDEFONSO TORRES RUEDA
Faculty of Chemistry: MARÍA PILAR MALET MAENNER
Faculty of Communication: ANTONIO CHECA GODOY
Faculty of Dentistry: PEDRO BULLON FERNANDEZ
Faculty of Economics and Business Sciences: CARMEN NUÑEZ GARCÍA
Faculty of Education Sciences: JUAN DE PABLOS PONS
Faculty of Fine Arts: MARÍA TERESA CARRASCO GIMENA
Faculty of Geography and History: ANTONIO GARCIA GOMEZ
Faculty of Law: ANTONIO MERCHAN ALVAREZ
Faculty of Mathematics: ANTONIO BEATO MORENO
Faculty of Medicine: JUAN RAMÓN LACALLE REMIGIO
Faculty of Nursing, Physiotherapy and Podology: JUAN PABLO SOBRINO TOBO
Faculty of Pharmacy: JOSÉ MANUEL VEGA PÉREZ
Faculty of Philology: RAFAEL DE LA CRUZ LOPEZ-CAMPOS BODINEAU
Faculty of Philosophy: MANUEL BARRIOS CASARES
Faculty of Physics: JOSÉ GÓMEZ ORDÓÑEZ
Faculty of Psychology: JESUS GARCIA MARTINEZ
Faculty of Tourism and Finance: JOSÉ LUIS CABALLERO JIMÉNEZ
Faculty of Work Sciences: MARIA MILAGRO MARTIN LOPEZ
University School of Nursing 'Cruz Roja Española': FELIX JULIO JARA FERNANDEZ (Dir)
University School of Nursing 'Virgen del Rocío': MERCEDES BUENO FERRAN (Dir)

UNIVERSIDAD DE VALLADOLID
(University of Valladolid)

Calle Plaza de Santa Cruz 8, 47002 Valladolid
Telephone: 983423000
E-mail: servicio.alumno@uva.es
Internet: www.uva.es

Founded 1241
State control
Language of instruction: Spanish
Academic year: September to June (2 semesters)

Rector: MARCOS SACRISTÁN REPRESA
Vice-Rector for Academic Affairs: LUIS MIGUEL NIETO CALZADA
Vice-Rector for Culture and Infrastructure: ANTONIO ORDUÑA DOMINGO
Vice-Rector for Economy: GUIOMAR MARTÍN HERRÁN
Vice-Rector for Equity and Infrastructure: ANTONIO ORDUÑA DOMINGO
Vice-Rector for Faculty: LUIS MIGUEL NIETO CALZADA
Vice-Rector for Int. Relations and Univ. Extension: JOSÉ MARÍA MARBÁN PRIETO
Vice-Rector for Palencia Campus: PEDRO ANTONIO CABALLERO CALVO
Vice-Rector for Research and Scientific Policy: JOSÉ MANUEL LÓPEZ RODRÍGUEZ
Vice-Rector for Segovia Campus: JOSÉ VICENTE ÁLVAREZ BRAVO
Vice-Rector for Soria Campus: AMELIA RUTH MOYANO GARDINI
Vice-Rector for Teaching and Students: ROCÍO ANGUITA MARTÍNEZ
Vice-Rector for Teaching Staff: LUIS MIGUEL NIETO CALZADA
Sec.-Gen.: LUIS ANTONIO SANTOS DOMÍNGUEZ
Library Dir: MERCEDES ARRANZ SOMBRÍA

Library of 815,517 vols, 15,725 periodicals
Number of teachers: 2,589
Number of students: 28,028

DEANS

Faculty of Economic and Business Sciences (Valladolid): JOSÉ ANTONIO SANZ GÓMEZ
Faculty of Education and Social Work (Valladolid): CARLOS HERMINIO MORIYÓN MOJICA
Faculty of Law: ANDRÉS AUGUSTO DOMÍNGUEZ LUELMO
Faculty of Medicine: RICARDO JAIME RIGUAL BONASTRE
Faculty of Philosophy and Letters: ESTILITA MILAGROS ALARIO TRIGUEROS
Faculty of Sciences (Valladolid): FERNANDO VILLAFAÑE GONZÁLEZ
Faculty of Social, Legal and Communication Sciences (Segovia): AGUSTÍN GARCÍA MATILLA
Faculty of Translation and Interpretation (Soria): ANTONIO BUENO GARCÍA
Faculty of Work Sciences (Palencia): JOSÉ ANTONIO OREJAS CASAS

UNIVERSIDAD DE ZARAGOZA

Calle Pedro Cerbuna 12, 50009 Zaragoza
Telephone: 976761000
E-mail: ciur@unizar.es
Internet: www.unizar.es

Founded 1542
State control
Language of instruction: Spanish
Academic year: September to July (2 semesters)

Rector: MANUEL JOSÉ LÓPEZ PÉREZ
Vice-Rector for Academic Policy: MARÍA DEL MAR LÁZARO LÓPEZ
Vice-Rector for Culture and Social Policy: PILAR FERNÁNDEZ SOTORRIO
Vice-Rector for Economic Affairs: BLANCA IBORRA MUÑOZ
Vice-Rector for Huesca Campus: MARÍA DEL CARMEN NAVAL MAIRAL
Vice-Rector for Int. Relations and Devt Cooperation: JUAN MANUEL GARCÍA TENÍAS
Vice-Rector for Scientific Policy: MARÍA JESÚS SANZ FONZ
Vice-Rector for Students and Employment: ÁGUEDA OLIVA CASADO
Vice-Rector for Teaching Staff: MARÍA ROSA IZQUIERDO POZUELO
Vice-Rector for Technological Transfer and Innovation: SONIA BORDALLO CAMPOS
Vice-Rector for Teruel Campus: MERCEDES RABADÁN HONTANGAS
Sec.-Gen.: JUAN F. HERRERO PEREZAGUA
Librarian: RAMÓN ABAD HIRALDO

Library: 1m. vols, 20,000 periodicals
Number of teachers: 3,803
Number of students: 35,649

Publications: *Ager: Revista de Estudios sobre Despoblación Rural* (1 a year), *Anales de la Facultad de Veterinaria*, *Antigrama: Revista del Departamento de Historia del Arte* (1 a year), *Anuario de pedagogía* (1 a year), *Aragón en la Edad Media* (1 a year), *Archivos de la Facultad de Medicina*, *Arqueología Espacial: Revista del Seminario de Arqueología y Etnología Turolense*, *Boletín de la Asociación de Demografía Histórica* (2 a year), *Boletín Informativo*, *Cuadernos Aragoneses de Economía* (2 a year), *Cuadernos de Bioestadística y sus Aplicaciones Informáticas* (2 a year), *El Gnomo: Boletín de Estudios Becquerianos*, *European Journal of Psychiatry* (4 a year), *Geographicalia* (4 a year), *Geórgica* (irregular), *Guía*, *Kalathos: Revista del Seminario de Arqueología y Etnología Turolense* (1 a year), *Llull: Revista de la Sociedad Española de Historia de la Ciencia y de las Técnicas* (3 a year), *Medicina Naturista: Revista Internacional de Difusión Biomédica* (4 a year), *Miscelánea* (2 a year), *Naturaleza Aragonesa: Revista de la Sociedad de Amigos del Museo Paleontológico* (2 a year), *Organización del Conocimiento en Sistemas de Información y Documentación* (2 a year), *Resúmenes de Tesis Doctorales*, *Revista Aquatic*, *Revista de Demografía Histórica* (2 a year), *Revista de Desarrollo Rural y Cooperativismo Agrario*, *Revista de Gestión Pública y Privada* (1 a year), *Revista Española de Filosofía Medieval* (1 a year), *Revista Interuniversitaria de Formación del Profesorado* (3 a year), *Revista Universidad*, *Riff-Raff: Revista de Pensamiento y Cultura* (3 a year), *Saldvie: Estudios de Prehistoria y Archeología* (1 a year), *Scire: Representación y Organización del Conocimiento* (2 a year), *Stvdivm: Revista de Humanidades* (2 a year), *Tropelías: Revista de Teoría de la Literatura y Literatura Comparada* (1 a year), *Temas*

DEANS

Faculty of Business and Public Administration: Dr CARLOS JAVIER RUBIO POMAR

Faculty of Economics and Business: Dr JOSÉ ALBERTO MOLINA CHUECA

Faculty of Education: Dr ENRIQUE GARCÍA PASCUAL

Faculty of Health Sciences: Dr JUAN FRANCISCO LEÓN PUY

Faculty of Health and Sport Sciences (Huesca): Prof. Dra FRANCESCA MONTICELLI

Faculty of Humanities and Education Sciences (Huesca): Dra MARTA LIESA ORUS

Faculty of Law: Dr JUAN GARCÍA BLASCO

Faculty of Medicine: Dr FRANCISCO JAVIER CASTILLO GARCÌA

Faculty of Philosophy and Letters: Dr ELISEO SERRANO MARTIN

Faculty of Sciences: Dra ANA ISABEL ELDUQUE PALOMO

Faculty of Social Sciences and Humanities (Teruel): Dr MARÍA LUISA ESTEBAN SALVADOR

Faculty of Veterinary Science: Prof. Dr JESÚS GARCÍA SÁNCHEZ

Faculty of Work and Social Sciences: Dr MIGUEL MIRANDA ARANDA

UNIVERSIDAD EUROPEA DE MADRID (CEES)

Calle Tajo s/n, Urbanización El Bosque, Villaviciosa de Odón, 28670 Madrid

Telephone: 902232350
E-mail: uem@uem.es
Internet: www.uem.es
Founded 1995
Private control
Languages of instruction: English, Spanish
Academic year: September to June (2 semesters)

Rector: Dra ÁGUEDA BENITO

Vice-Rector for Academic Quality and Innovation: Dr PEDRO JOSÉ LARA

Vice-Rector for Students and Career Placement: Dr MARTA ARROYO

Gen. Sec.: Dra ELENA DE LA FUENTE

Library Dir: ISABEL RICO RODRÍGUEZ

Library of 90,000 vols, 1,300 periodicals

DEANS

School of Art and Communication: Dr LUIS CALANDRE

School of Biomedical Sciences: Dra ELENA GAZAPO

School of Health Sciences: Dra ADELAIDA PORTELA

School of Social Sciences: Dr JOSÉ RAMOS

School of Sports Science: Dr JUAN MAYORGA

UNIVERSIDAD EUROPEA MIGUEL DE CERVANTES

Calle Padre Julio Chevalier 2, 47012 Valladolid

Telephone: 983001000
E-mail: info@uemc.es
Internet: www.uemc.es
Founded 2002
Private control
Language of instruction: Spanish

Rector: MARTÍN J. FERNÁNDEZ ANTOLÍN

Vice-Rector for Academic Affairs, Quality and Employment: JUAN VICENTE GARCÍA MANJÓN

Vice-Rector for Research and Int. Relations: ESTEFANÍA JERÓNIMO SÁNCHEZ-BEATO

Vice-Rector for Student Affairs and Univ. Extension: JOAQUÍN ESTEBAN ORTEGA

Sec.-Gen.: JOSÉ ANTONIO OTERO PARRA

Number of teachers: 150
Number of students: 1,500

DEANS

Faculty of Health Sciences: DAVID GARCÍA LÓPEZ

Faculty of Humanities and Information Sciences: BEATRIZ RANCAÑO PÉREZ

Faculty of Legal and Economic Sciences: CARLOS BELLOSO MARTÍN

UNIVERSIDAD FRANCISCO DE VITORIA

Ctra Pozuelo-Majadahonda Km. 1.800, 28223 Madrid

Telephone: 913510303
E-mail: info@ufv.es
Internet: www.ufv.es
Founded 1993
Private control
Language of instruction: Spanish
Academic year: October to June (2 semesters)

Rector: Dr DANIEL SADA CASTAÑO

Vice-Rector for Academic Org. and Quality: Dr VICENTE LOZANO DÍAZ

Vice-Rector for Faculty and Research: Dr CLEMENTE LÓPEZ GONZÁLEZ

Vice-Rector for Int. Relations: Dr JUAN PÉREZ MIRANDA

Sec.-Gen.: JOSÉ ANTONIO VERDEJO DELGADO

Library Dir: ROSA SALORD BERTRÁN

Library of 75,000 vols

Publication: *Comunicación y Hombre* (1 a year)

DEANS

Faculty of Health Sciences: Dr MAITE IGLESIAS BADIOLA

Faculty of Legal and Social Sciences: Dr JOSÉ MARIA ORTIZ IBARZ

UNIVERSIDAD INTERNACIONAL DE ANDALUCÍA (International University of Andalucia)

Rectorado de la Universidad, Sede de la Cartuja, Monasterio Santa María de las Cuevas, Calle Americo Vespucio 2, Isla de la Cartuja, 41092 Seville

Telephone: 954462299
E-mail: sevilla@unia.es
Internet: www.unia.es
Founded 1994
State control

Offers postgraduate and specialist courses; campuses in Baeza, Malaga, Rabida

Rector: Dr JUAN MANUEL SUÁREZ JAPÓN

Vice-Rector for Academic Affairs and Postgraduate Studies: Dr PLÁCIDO NAVAS LLORET

Vice-Rector for Innovation and Communication Technologies: Prof. Dr LLANOS MORA LÓPEZ

Vice-Rector for Int. Relations and Cooperation: Prof. Dr MARÍA ANTONIA PEÑA GUERRERO

Vice-Rector for Planning and Quality: Prof. Dr JULIO TERRADOS CEPEDA

Vice-Rector for Univ. Extension and Participation: Prof. Dr MARÍA DEL ROSARIO GARCÍA-DONCEL HERNÁNDEZ

Sec.-Gen.: Prof. MARÍA JESÚS GUERRERO LEBRÓN

UNIVERSIDAD INTERNACIONAL MENÉNDEZ PELAYO (Menéndez Pelayo International University)

Isaac Peral 23, 28040 Madrid

Telephone: 915920600
E-mail: rector@uimp.es
Internet: www.uimp.es
Founded 1932
State control

Languages of instruction: English, Spanish

Masters in arts, education and cultural management, banking and finance, climacteric and menopause, constitutional law, crystallography and crystallization, economics and finance, high specialization in plastics and rubber, international business management, phonetics and phonology, professional English, public management of housing and land, psychology, renewable energy, fuel cells and hydrogen, safety and durability of structures and materials, teaching Spanish as a foreign language, translation and new technologies, tropical biodiversity and conservation areas; int. Masters in maritime and port administration, mastology

Rector: CÉSAR NOMBELA CANO

Vice-Rector for Innovation and Devt Projects: RODRIGO MARTÍNEZ-VAL PEÑALOSA

Vice-Rector for Int. Relations and Campus Llamas: SEBASTIÁN COLL MARTÍN

Vice-Rector for Postgraduate Studies and Research: MARIA PILAR CANO DOLADO

Vice-Rector for Univ. Extension and Language Courses: IGNACIO AHUMADA LARA

Sec.-Gen.: MIRYAM DE LA CONCEPCIÓN GONZÁLEZ RABANAL

UNIVERSIDAD JAUME I DE CASTELLÓ

Avda de Vicent Sos Baynat s/n, 12071 Castelló de la Plana

Telephone: 964728000
E-mail: info@uji.es
Internet: www.uji.es
Founded 1991
State control
Language of instruction: Spanish
Academic year: September to May (2 semesters)

Rector: Dr VICENT CLIMENT JORDÀ

Vice-Rector for Academic Affairs and Teaching Staff: Prof. FRANCISCO LÓPEZ BENET

Vice-Rector for Campus, New Technology and PAS: Prof. JUAN PABLO AIBAR AUSINA

Vice-Rector for Cooperation, Int. and Institutional Relations and Multilingualism: Prof. INMACULADA FORTANET GÓMEZ

Vice-Rector for Culture and Univ. Extension: WENCESLAO RAMBLA ZARAGOZÁ

Vice-Rector for Foundations and Social Responsibility: Prof. MARÍA ÁNGELES FERNÁNDEZ IZQUIERDO

Vice-Rector for Research and Postgraduate Studies: Prof. ANTONIO BARBA JUAN

Vice-Rector for Strategic Planning, Quality and Communication: Prof. MIGUEL ANGEL MOLINER TENA

Vice-Rector for Students, Employment and Educational Innovation: Prof. PILAR GARCÍA AGUSTÍN

Sec.-Gen.: Prof. MARIA VICTORIA PETIT LAVALL

Library Dir: VICENT FALOMIR DEL CAMPO

Library of 274,444 vols
Number of teachers: 1,022
Number of students: 13,500

Publications: *Cultura, Lenguaje y Representación* (Culture, Language and Representation), *Language Values*, *Potestas. Grupo Europeo de Investigación Histórica* (1 a year), *Recerca. Revista de pensament i anàlisi* (1 a year)

DEANS

Faculty of Health Sciences: RAFAEL BALLESTER ARNAL

Faculty of Humanities and Social Sciences: ROSA MARÍA AGOST CANÓS

Faculty of Law and Economics: CRISTINA PAUNER CHULVI

UNIVERSIDAD MIGUEL HERNÁNDEZ DE ELCHE

Avda de la Universidad s/n, 03202 Elche
Telephone: 966658610
E-mail: info@umh.es
Internet: www.umh.es
State control
Language of instruction: Spanish
Academic year: September to June (2 semesters)

Rector: Prof. Dr JESÚS TADEO PASTOR CIURANA
Vice-Rector for Academic Affairs: Dra MARÍA JOSÉ ALARCÓN GARCÍA
Vice-Rector for Culture and Univ. Extension: Dr ESTHER SITGES MACIÁ
Vice-Rector for Economics and Business: Dr FERNANDO VIDAL GIMÉNEZ
Vice-Rector for Human Resources: Dr EVA ALIAGA AGULLÓ
Vice-Rector for Institutional Relations: Dra MARÍA TERESA PÉREZ VÁZQUEZ
Vice-Rector for Int. Relations: Dr MANUEL MIGUEL JORDÁN VIDAL
Vice-Rector for Material Resources: Dr ÓSCAR REINOSO GARCÍA
Vice-Rector for Research and Innovation: Dr FERNANDO BORRÁS ROCHER
Vice-Rector for Student Affairs and Athletics: Dr FRANCISCO JAVIER MORENO HERNÁNDEZ
Sec.-Gen.: Prof. Dra MARÍA MERCEDES SÁNCHEZ CASTILLO
Library Dir: JOSE PABLO GALLO LEON

Library: 8,500 periodicals
Number of teachers: 1,024
Number of students: 14,500

DEANS

Faculty of Experimental Sciences: JOSÉ LUIS RUIZ GÓMEZ
Faculty of Fine Arts: JOSÉ VICENTE MARTÍN MARTÍNEZ
Faculty of Medicine: ANTONIO F. COMPAÑ ROSIQUE
Faculty of Pharmacy: JORGE MANZANARES ROBLES
Faculty of Social and Health Sciences: EDUARDO MANUEL CERVELLÓ GIMENO
Faculty of Social and Legal Sciences (Elche): FERNANDO MIRÓ LLINARES
Faculty of Social and Legal Sciences (Orihuela): JOSÉ ANTONIO CAVERO RUBIO
Polytechnic School of Elche: GERMAN TORREGROSA PENALVA
Polytechnic School of Orihuela: JUAN JOSE RUIZ MARTINEZ

UNIVERSIDAD NACIONAL DE EDUCACIÓN A DISTANCIA (National Distance Education University)

Cl de Juan del Rosal, Ciudad Universitaria, 28040 Madrid
Telephone: 913986600
E-mail: infouned@adm.uned.es
Internet: www.uned.es
Founded 1972
State control
Language of instruction: Spanish
Academic year: October to July (2 semesters)

Rector: JUAN A. GIMENO ULLASTRES
Vice-Rector for Academic Affairs: ENCARNACIÓN SARRIÁ SÁNCHEZ
Vice-Rector for Associated Centres: ANTONIO FERNÁNDEZ FERNÁNDEZ
Vice-Rector for Coordination, Quality and Innovation: MIGUEL SANTAMARÍA LANCHO
Vice-Rector for Faculty: MIGUEL ÁNGEL ÁLVAREZ RUBIO
Vice-Rector for Internationalization and Cooperation: MARÍA TERESA AGUADO ODINA
Vice-Rector for Lifelong Learning: JULIO BORDAS MARTINEZ

Vice-Rector for Management: JORDI MONTSERRAT GARROCHO
Vice-Rector for Planning and Economic Affairs: MARTA DE LA CUESTA GONZÁLEZ
Vice-Rector for Research: PALOMA COLLADO GUIRAO
Vice-Rector for Students, Employment and Culture: ALVARO JARILLO ALDEANUEVA
Vice-Rector for Technology: COVADONGA RODRIGO SAN JUAN
Sec.-Gen.: ANA MARÍA MARCOS DEL CANO
Library: 1.2m. vols
Number of teachers: 1,496
Number of students: 260,079

DEANS

Faculty of Economics and Business Sciences: AMELIA PÉREZ ZABALETA
Faculty of Education: Dr JOSÉ LUIS GARCÍA LLAMAS
Faculty of Geography and History: Dr MARÍA J. PERÉX AGORRETA
Faculty of Law: MERCEDES GÓMEZ ADANERO
Faculty of Philology: Dr ANTONIO MORENO HERNÁNDEZ
Faculty of Philosophy: Dr JACINTO RIVERA DE ROSALES CHACÓN
Faculty of Political Science and Sociology: JOSÉ ANTONIO OLMEDA GÓMEZ
Faculty of Psychology: Dr MIGUEL ÁNGEL SANTED GERMÁN
Faculty of Sciences: Dr ANTONIO ZAPARDIEL PALENZUELA

UNIVERSIDAD PABLO DE OLAVIDE

Carretera de Utrera Km 1, 41013 Sevilla
Telephone: 954349200
E-mail: rector@upo.es
Internet: www.upo.es
Founded 1997
State control
Language of instruction: Spanish
Academic year: September to July (2 semesters)

Rector: VICENTE C. GUZMÁN FLUJA
Vice-Rector for Culture, Participation and Social Commitment: ELODIA HERNANDEZ LEÓN
Vice-Rector for Educational Planning and Teaching: JOSÉ ANTONIO SÁNCHEZ MEDINA
Vice-Rector for Int. Relations and Communication: PILAR RODRÍGUEZ REINA
Vice-Rector for Postgraduate Studies, Education and Employment: MIGUEL ÁNGEL GUAL FONT
Vice-Rector for Research and Technology Transfer: BRUNO MARTÍNEZ HAYA
Vice-Rector for Student Affairs, Sports and Environment: MODESTO LUCEÑO GARCÉS
Vice-Rector for TIC, Quality and Innovation: ALICIA TRONCOSO LORA
Sec.-Gen.: JOSÉ ANTONIO COLMENERO GUERRA
Library Dir: CARMEN BAENA DÍAZ

Library of 347,577 vols, 25,284 periodicals
Number of teachers: 1,042
Number of students: 11,500

DEANS

Faculty of Business: Prof. Dr FRANCISCO CARRASCO FENECH
Faculty of Experimental Sciences: Dr ANTONIO GALLARDO CORREA
Faculty of Humanities: Prof. Dr JOSÉ MIGUEL MARTÍN MARTÍN
Faculty of Law: Prof. Dr ANDRÉS RODRÍGUEZ BENOT
Faculty of Social Sciences: Prof. Dr GUILLERMO FERNÁNDEZ DOMÍNGUEZ
Faculty of Sports: Prof. Dr ANTONIO JOSÉ FERNÁNDEZ MARTÍNEZ
Polytechnic School: Dr JESÚS SALVADOR AGUILAR RUIZ (Dir)

UNIVERSIDAD PONTIFICIA 'COMILLAS'

Calle Alberto Aguilera 23, 28015 Madrid
Telephone: 915422800
E-mail: oia@oia.upcomillas.es
Internet: www.upcomillas.es
Founded 1890, present status 1904
Private control
Language of instruction: Spanish
Academic year: October to June

Rector: Dr JULIO LUIS MARTÍNEZ MARTÍNEZ
Vice-Rector for Academic Affairs and Teaching Staff: Dr ANTONIO OBREGÓN GARCÍA
Vice-Rector for Economic Affairs: Dr CECILIO MORAL BELLO
Vice-Rector for Research and Int. Relations: Dr PEDRO LINARES LLAMAS
Vice-Rector for Services to the Univ. Community and Student Affairs: Dra ANA GARCÍA-MINA FREIRE
Sec.-Gen.: Dra CLARA MARTÍNEZ GARCÍA
Librarian: EUSEBIO GIL CORIA

Library of 550,000 vols
Number of teachers: 962
Number of students: 9,804

Publications: *Estudios Eclesiásticos* (4 a year), *ICADE* (4 a year), *Migraciones* (2 a year), *Miscelánea Comillas* (3 a year), *Pensamiento* (3 a year)

DEANS

Faculty of Canon Law: Dr GABINO URÍBARRI BILBAO
Faculty of Economics and Business Sciences: Dra ALFREDO ARAHUETES GARCÍA
Faculty of Human and Social Sciences: Dra BELÉN MERCEDES UROSA SANZ
Faculty of Law: IÑIGO A. NAVARRO MENDIZÁBAL
Faculty of Theology: GABINO URÍBARRI BILBAO

ASSOCIATED INSTITUTIONS

There are other Theological and Philosophical Faculties in Spain conferring degrees, which are partly associated with the Pontifical Universities, as follows:

Facultad de Teología de Granada (Institución Universitaria de la Compañía de Jesús)

Profesor Vicente Callao, 15 18011 Granada
Telephone: 958185252
E-mail: info@teol-granada.com
Internet: www.teol-granada.com
Founded 1939
Academic year: October to July

Grand Chancellor: RP ADOLFO NICOLÁS PACHÓN
Rector: Prof. DIEGO M. MOLINA MOLINA
Vice-Rector for Academic Affairs: Prof. IGNACIO ROJAS GÁLVEZ
Vice-Rector for Institutional Relations and Univ Extension: MIREN JUNKAL GUEVARA LLAGUNO
Sec.: CARLOS JAVIER PALOMEQUE BAENA
Librarian: RP ILDEFONSO CAMACHO LARAÑA

Library of 350,000 vols
Number of teachers: 27
Number of students: 327

Publications: *Archivo Teológico Granadino* (Post-Tridentine theology, 1 a year), *Proyección* (4 a year)

PROFESSORS

ALARCOS MARTÍNEZ, F., Moral Theology
BÉJAR BACAS, J. S., Dogmatic Theology
BERDUGO VILLENA, T., Latin
CAMACHO LARAÑA, I., Moral Theology
CASTÓN BOYER, P., Sociology
DOMÍNGUEZ MORANO, C., Psychology
GRANADO BELLIDO, C., Patrology and Dogmatic Theology

GUEVARA LLAGUNO, M., Scripture
HERNÁNDEZ MARTÍNEZ, J., Dogmatic Theology
JIMÉNEZ ORTIZ, A., Fundamental Theology
LÓPEZ AZPITARTE, E., Moral Theology
LÓPEZ CUERVO, T., Greek
MARTÍNEZ MEDINA, J., Ecclesiastical Art
MARTÍN MORILLAS, A., Philosophy
MOLINA MOLINA, D., Dogmatic Theology
NAVAS GUTIÉRREZ, A., Ecclesiastical History
RODRÍGUEZ CARMONA, A., Scripture
RODRÍGUEZ IZQUIERDO GAVALA, J. M., Liturgy
ROJAS GÁLVEZ, I., Scripture
ROMÁN MARTÍNEZ, M. C., Scripture
RUIZ LOZANO, P., Philosophy
SÁNCHEZ NOGALES, J. L., Philosophy
SICRE DÍAZ, J. L., Scripture
VOLO PÉREZ, R., Scripture
YUBERO SOTO, J., Dogmatic Theology

Institut de Teologia Fonamental

Calle Llaceres 30, Sant Cugat del Vallés Barcelona

Telephone: 936741150
E-mail: itf@jesuites.net

Founded 1964

Jesuit College forming part of the Faculty of Theology of Cataluña; open to non-Jesuit students

Chancellor: Dr LLUÍS MARÍA SISTACH (Archbishop of Barcelona)
General Moderator: LLUÍS MAGRIÑÀ VECIANA
Dir: JOAN CARRERA
Librarian: ORIOL TUÑI

Library of 350,000 vols, 800 periodicals
Number of teachers: 14
Number of students: 150

Publications: *Actualidad Bibliográfica, Cuadernos de Teología Fundamental, Selecciones de Teología*

PROFESSORS

ALEGRE, X., New Testament Scripture
BOADA, J., Fundamental Theology
CARRERA, J., Fundamental Moral Theology
COLL, J. Ma., Fundamental Theology
FLAQUER, J., Fundamental Theology
GARCÍA DONCEL, M., Philosophy of Sciences
GIMÉNEZ, J., Fundamental Theology
GONZÁLEZ FAUS, J. I., Systematic Theology
LATORRE, J., New Testament Scripture
MÀRIA, J., Ethical Issues
MELLONI, X., Fundamental Theology
PUIG, LL., Fundamental Theology
RAMBLA, J. Ma., Spiritual Theology
TUÑÍ, O., New Testament Scripture
VALL, H., Ecumenical Theology

UNIVERSIDAD PONTIFICIA DE SALAMANCA

Calle Compañía 5, 37002 Salamanca
Telephone: 923277100
E-mail: info.alumno@upsa.es
Internet: www.upsa.es

Founded 1219, present name and status 1940
Private control
Language of instruction: Spanish
Academic year: September to June

Rector: Dr ÁNGEL GALINDO GARCÍA
Vice-Rector for Academic Planning and Quality: Dr JOSÉ MANUEL ALFONSO SÁNCHEZ
Vice-Rector for Economy: Dr VIDAL ALONSO SECADES
Vice-Rector for Research, Innovation and New Technologies: Dr ANTONIO SÁNCHEZ CABACO
Sec.-Gen.: Dr MIGUEL ÁNGEL HERNÁNDEZ ROBLEDO
Dir of Library: Dr ANTONIO GARCÍA MADRID

Library of 500,000 vols
Number of teachers: 351
Number of students: 8,500

Publications: *Comunicación y Pluralismo, Cuadernos Salmantinos de Filosofía, Diálogo Ecuménico, Familia, Helmántica, Papeles Salmantinos de Educación, Revista Española de Derecho Canónico, Salmanticensis, Sociedad y Utopía*

DEANS

Faculty of Canon Law: Dr JOSÉ SAN JOSÉ PRISCO
Faculty of Communication: Dr FERNANDO MARTÍNEZ VALLVEY
Faculty of Computer Sciences: Dr ALBERTO PEDRERO ESTEBAN
Faculty of Education: Dra JESÚS GARCÍA ARROYO
Faculty of Health Sciences: Dra ROSA SÁNCHEZ BARBERO
Faculty of Human and Social Sciences: Dr MARIA JESÚS GARCÍA ARROYO
Faculty of Philosophy: Dr ILDEFONSO MURILLO MURILLO
Faculty of Psychology: Dr JOSÉ RAMÓN YELA BERNABÉ
Faculty of Theology: Dr JACINTO NÚÑEZ REGODÓN

UNIVERSIDAD PÚBLICA DE NAVARRA/NAFARROAKO UNIBERTSITATE PUBLIKOA
(Public University of Navarre)

Campus de Arrosadía, 31006 Pamplona Navarre
Telephone: 948169000
E-mail: infoweb@unavarra.es
Internet: www.unavarra.es

Founded 1987
State control
Languages of instruction: Basque, English, Spanish
Academic year: September to June (2 semesters)

Rector: Dr JULIO LAFUENTE LÓPEZ
Vice-Rector for Academic Policy: Prof. Dr JESÚS MARÍA PINTOR BOROBIA
Vice-Rector for Economy, Planning and Quality: Prof. Dr MANUEL RAPÚN GÁRATE
Vice-Rector for Int. Relations: Dr JAVIER CASALÍ SARASÍBAR
Vice-Rector for Research: Dr ALFONSO CARLOSENA GARCÍA
Vice-Rector for Students and Employment: Dr PALOMA VÍRSEDA CHAMORRO
Vice-Rector for Tudela Campus: JOSÉ RAMON ALFARO LÓPEZ
Vice-Rector for Univ. Awareness: Prof. ELOÍSA RAMÍREZ VAQUERO
Univ. Sec.: JAVIER ECHEVERRIA MARTORELL
Library Dir: GUILLERMO SÁNCHEZ MARTÍNEZ

Library of 410,788 vols, 9,309 periodicals
Number of teachers: 932
Number of students: 8,635

Publications: *Anales de Derecho* (1 a year), *Arrosadia* (4 a year), *Comunicaciones, Documentos de Trabajo* (Irregular), *Huarte de San Juan. Filología y Didáctica de la Lengua* (1 a year), *Huarte de San Juan. Geografía e Historia* (1 a year), *Huarte de San Juan. Psicología y Pedagogía* (1 a year)

DEANS

Faculty of Economic and Business Sciences: PABLO AROCENA GARRO
Faculty of Humanities and Social Sciences: EDUARDO LACASTA ZABALZA
Faculty of Legal Sciences: JOSÉ FRANCISCO ALENZA GARCÍA
Graduate School for Health Sciences: PALOMA TORRE HERNÁNDEZ (Dir)
Technical School for Agricultural Engineering: ALBERTO ENRIQUE MARTÍN (Dir)

Technical School for Industrial Engineering and Telecommunications: IGNACIO R. MATÍAS MAESTRO (Dir)

UNIVERSIDAD REY JUAN CARLOS

Calle Tulipán s/n, 28933 Móstoles, Madrid
Telephone: 916655060
E-mail: info@urjc.es
Internet: www.urjc.es

Founded 1997
State control
Language of instruction: Spanish
Academic year: October to June
Campuses in Alcorcón, Fuenlabrada, Móstoles, Vicálvaro

Rector: Prof. PEDRO GONZÁLEZ-TREVIJANO SÁNCHEZ
Vice-Rector for Academic Affairs, Teaching Staff and Campus Coordination: Dr FERNANDO SUÁREZ BILBAO
Vice-Rector for European Harmonization and Alignment: JOSÉ MARÍA ÁLVAREZ MONZONCILLO
Vice-Rector for Information and Communication: FRANCISCO JOSÉ BLANCO JIMÉNEZ
Vice-Rector for Int. Relations, Institutes, Univ. Centres, Policy Guidance, Employment and Devt Cooperation: ANA MARÍA SALAZAR DE LA GUERRA
Vice-Rector for Research: RAFAEL ÁNGEL GARCÍA MUÑOZ
Vice-Rector for Social Policy, Environmental Quality and Health Univ.: CARMEN GALLARDO PINO
Vice-Rector for Student Affairs, Diplomas and Postgraduate Studies: MARÍA ANGUSTIAS PALOMAR GALLEGO
Vice-Rector for Univ. Clinic Institutional Hospital Relations: JUAN CARLOS MIANGOLARRA PAGE
Vice-Rector for Univ. Extension and Affiliated Centres: JOSÉ MANUEL VERA SANTOS
Sec.-Gen.: ANDRÉS GAMBRA GUTIÉRREZ
Library Dir: RICARDO GONZÁLEZ CASTRILLO

Number of teachers: 900
Number of students: 15,000

DEANS

Faculty of Communication Sciences (Fuenlabrada): Prof. ANTONIO GARCÍA JIMÉNEZ
Faculty of Health Sciences (Alcorcón): Prof. ÁNGEL GIL DE MIGUEL
Faculty of Social Sciences and Law (Vicálvaro): Prof. PILAR LAGUNA SÁNCHEZ
Faculty of Tourism Sciences (Fuenlabrada): Prof. CATALINA VACAS GUERRERO
School of Experimental Sciences (Mostoles): Prof. JOSÉ ANTONIO CALLES (Dir)
School of Informatics (Mostoles): Prof. LUIS PASTOR PÉREZ (Dir)
School of Telecommunications Engineering (Fuenlabrada): Prof. FRANCISCO JAVIER RAMOS LÓPEZ

UNIVERSIDADE DA CORUÑA
(University of A Coruña)

Rúa da Maestranza 9, 15001 A Coruña
Telephone: 981167000
E-mail: reitor@udc.es
Internet: www.udc.es

Founded 1989
State control
Languages of instruction: Galician, Spanish
Academic year: September to May (2 semesters)

Rector: Dr XOSÉ LUÍS ARMESTO BARBEITO
Vice-Rector for Degrees, Quality and New Technologies: Prof. JULIO ABALDE ALONSO
Vice-Rector for Economic Planning and Infrastructure: Prof. AMALIA BLANCO LOURO

Vice-Rector for Ferrol Campus and Social Responsibility: Prof. ARACELI TORRES MIÑO
Vice-Rector for Int. Relations and Cooperation: NATALIA ÁLVAREZ LATA
Vice-Rector for Research and Transfer: RICARDO CAO ABAD
Vice-Rector for Students, Sports and Culture: MARÍA JOSÉ MARTÍNEZ LÓPEZ
Vice-Rector for Teaching Staff and Planning: Prof. GUSTAVO REGO VEIGA
Gen. Sec.: CARLOS AMOEDO SOUTO
Head Librarian: ANGELES CAMPOS RODRÍGUEZ
Library of 670,000 vols, 7,600 periodicals
Number of teachers: 1,500
Number of students: 25,000

DEANS

Faculty of Business and Economics: GUSTAVO REGO VEIGA
Faculty of Communication Science: JOSÉ JUAN VIDELA RODRÍGUEZ
Faculty of Computing: ALBERTO VALDERRUTEN VIDAL
Faculty of Economics and Business: ANXO CALVO SILVOSA
Faculty of Educational Science: ANA IGLESIAS GALDO
Faculty of Health Sciences: SERGIO EDUARDO SANTOS DEL RIEGO
Faculty of Humanities and Documentation: JOSÉ MANUEL RECUERO ASTRAY
Faculty of Labour Sciences: MOISÉS ALBERTO GARCÍA NÚÑEZ
Faculty of Law: ELOY MIGUEL GAYÁN RODRÍGUEZ
Faculty of Philology: MARÍA TERESA LÓPEZ FERNÁNDEZ
Faculty of Sciences: HORACIO NAVEIRA FACHAL
Faculty of Sociology: ANTÓN ÁLVAREZ SOUSA
Faculty of Sport Sciences and Physical Education: RAFAEL MARTÍN ACERO

UNIVERSIDADE DE SANTIAGO DE COMPOSTELA
(University of Santiago de Compostela)

Praza do Obradoiro s/n, 15782 Santiago de Compostela
Telephone: 881811001
E-mail: reitor@usc.es
Internet: www.usc.es

Founded 1495
State control
Languages of instruction: Galician, Spanish
Academic year: September to July (2 semesters)

Rector: JUAN CASARES LONG
Vice-Rector: BENITA SILVA
Vice-Rector: FRANCISCO GONZÁLEZ
Vice-Rector: FRANCISCO DURÁN
Vice-Rector: JESÚS LÓPEZ
Vice-Rector: PABLO RAMIL
Vice-Rector: PEDRO GARCÍA
Vice-Rector: SARA CANTORNA
Vice-Rector: VICTOR MILLET
Registrar: LOURDES NOYA
Librarian: MARÍA ISABEL CASAL REYES

Library: 1.5m. vols, 140 incunabula
Number of teachers: 2,262
Number of students: 27,795

Publications: *Actas de Derecho Industrial y Derecho de Autor* (1 a year), *Agora* (2 a year), *Anejos de la revista Verba, Anuario Gallego de Filología, Boletín Galego de Literatura* (2 a year), *Cursos y Congresos de la Universidad de Santiago de Compostela, Dereito* (2 a year), *Dorna* (1 a year), *ERAS. European Review of Artistic Studies* (1 a year), *Estudios Penales y Criminológicos, Estudos de Lingüística Galega* (1 a year), *Gallaecia* (1 a year), *Innovación educativa* (1 a year), *Memoria, Moenia* (1 a year), *Nova Acta Científica Composte-*

lana (1 a year), *Quintana* (1 a year), *Recursos Rurais* (1 a year), *Revista Galega de Economía* (2 a year), *RIPS: Revista de investigaciones políticas y sociológicas* (2 a year), *Sarmiento* (1 a year), *Semata* (1 a year), *Trabajos Compostelanos de Biología, Troianalexandrina* (1 a year), *Verba* (1 a year)

DEANS

Faculty of Biology: MARIA LUZ GONZALEZ CAAMAÑO
Faculty of Business Administration and Management (Lugo): LUIS E. GAGO
Faculty of Chemistry: JOSÉ RAMON ESTÉVEZ
Faculty of Communication Sciences: JOSÉ PEREIRA
Faculty of Economics and Business Science: EMILIA VÁZQUEZ
Faculty of Education (Lugo): FRANCISCO RODRÍGUEZ
Faculty of Education Sciences: LUIS FERRADÁS
Faculty of Geography and History: JUAN MONTERROSO
Faculty of Humanities (Lugo): MARIA ISABEL GONZALEZ REY
Faculty of Labour Relations: JUAN JOSÉ ARES FERNÁNDEZ
Faculty of Law: LUIS MIGUEZ MACHO
Faculty of Mathematics: VICTORIA M. OTERO ESPINAR
Faculty of Medicine and Dentistry: JUAN GESTAL OTERO
Faculty of Nursing: JESÚS NÚÑEZ IGLESIAS
Faculty of Optics and Optometry: LUZ MARIA GIGIREY PRIETO
Faculty of Pharmacy: ISABEL M. SANDEZ MACHO
Faculty of Philology: MARÍA JOSÉ LÓPEZ COUSO
Faculty of Philosophy: LUIS MODESTO GARCIA
Faculty of Physics: LUIS MIGUEL VARELA CABO
Faculty of Political Sciences: MARÍA NIEVES LAGARES DÍEZ
Faculty of Psychology: CAROLINA TINAJERO VACAS
Faculty of Sciences (Lugo): JOSÉ MANUEL MARTÍNEZ AGEITOS
Faculty of Veterinary Medicine (Lugo): GERMÁN SANTAMARINA PERNAS
School of Agriculture and Forestry (Lugo): JAVIER BUENO
School of Engineering: ANTONIO MOSQUERA

UNIVERSIDADE DE VIGO

Campus as Lagoas, Marcosende, 36310 Vigo
Telephone: 986812000
E-mail: informacion@uvigo.es
Internet: www.uvigo.es

Founded 1990
State control
Language of instruction: Spanish
Academic year: September to July (2 semesters)

Rector: Prof. SALUSTIANO MATO DE LA IGLESIA
Vice-Rector for Academic Org., Teaching Staff and Degrees: Profa MARGARITA ESTÉVEZ TORANZO
Vice-Rector for Economy and Planning: Prof. JOSÉ MANUEL GARCÍA VÁZQUEZ
Vice-Rector for Int. Relations: Prof. MANUEL FERNÁNDEZ IGLESIAS
Vice-Rector for Knowledge Transfer: Prof. JOSÉ ANTONIO VILÁN VILÁN
Vice-Rector for Ourense Campus: Profa MARÍA LAMEIRAS FERNÁNDEZ
Vice-Rector for Pontevedra Campus: Profa ANTONIA BLANCO PESQUEIRA
Vice-Rector for Research: Profa MARÍA ASUNCIÓN LONGO GONZÁLEZ
Vice-Rector for Student Affairs, Teaching and Quality: Prof. IGNACIO BARCIA RODRÍGUEZ

Vice-Rector for Univ. Extension: Prof. XOSÉ HENRIQUE COSTAS GONZÁLEZ
Sec.-Gen.: Prof. INMACULADA VALEIJE ÁLVAREZ
Librarian: MARÍA DEL CARMEN PÉREZ PAIS
Library of 180,000 vols
Number of teachers: 1,200
Number of students: 30,000

Publications: *Anuario de Investigación en Literatura Infantil y Juvenil, Aspectos de Filoloxía Inglesa e Alemá, HesperiaAnuario de filología hispánica* (1 a year), *La Tabla Redondaanuario de estudios torrentinos* (1 a year), *Lingua e Dereito, Sarmiento* (1 a year), *Thalassas. An International Journal of Marine Sciences* (2 a year), *VIAL, Vigo international journal of applied linguistics* (1 a year)

DEANS

Ourense Campus:

Faculty of Business Sciences and Tourism: Profa MARÍA ELISA ALÉN GONZÁLEZ
Faculty of Education Sciences: Profa MERCEDES SUÁREZ PAZOS
Faculty of History: Profa BEATRIZ COMENDADOR REY
Faculty of Law: ROBERTO ORLANDO BUSTILLO BOLADO
Faculty of Science: Prof. PEDRO A. ARAÚJO NESPEREIRA
University School of Nursing: ESTRELLA PORTELA ATRIO (Dir)

Pontevedra Campus:

Faculty of Education Sciences and Sports: Prof. FRANCISCA FARIÑA RIVERA
Faculty of Fine Arts: Prof. JUAN CARLOS MEANA MARTÍNEZ
Faculty of Physiotherapy: MANUEL GUTIÉRREZ NIETO
Faculty of Social Sciences and Communication: Prof. JUAN MANUEL CORBACHO VALENCIA (acting)
University School of Nursing: MIGUEL ÁNGEL PIÑÓN CIMADEVILA (Dir)

Vigo Campus:

Faculty of Biology: Profa JESÚS M. MÍGUEZ MIRAMONTES
Faculty of Chemistry: SOLEDAD GARCÍA FONTÁN
Faculty of Economic and Business Sciences: SANTIAGO GOMEZ FRAIZ
Faculty of Legal and Labour Sciences: ANA MARÍA PITA GRANDAL
Faculty of Marine Sciences: JESÚS SOUZA TRONCOSO
Faculty of Philology and Translation: MARÍA ROSA PÉREZ RODRÍGUEZ
Meixoeiro University School of Nursing: VICTORIA LOJO VICENTE (Dir)
Povisa University School of Nursing: ALFONSO GARCÍA SUÁREZ (Dir)
University College of Business Studies: PATRICIO SÁNCHEZ BELLO

UNIVERSITAT ABAT OLIBA CEU
(Abat Oliba CEU University)

Bellesguard 30, 08022 Barcelona
Telephone: 932540900
E-mail: info@uao.es
Internet: www.uao.es

Founded 2003
Private control
Language of instruction: Spanish
Academic year: September to June (2 semesters)

Depts of communication sciences, economics and business, humanities and education, law and political science, psychology

Rector: Dr CARLOS PÉREZ DEL VALLE
Vice-Rector for Academic Affairs: Dr ENRIQUE MARTÍNEZ

Vice-Rector for Quality and Research: Dr JAVIER BARRAYCOA
Vice-Rector for Student Affairs: Dr MARCIN KAZMIERCZAK
Sec.-Gen.: Dra CARMEN PARRA
Librarian: ELENA VILLATORO BOAN
Library of 20,000 vols, 100 periodicals
Number of students: 2,000

UNIVERSITAT AUTÒNOMA DE BARCELONA

Plaça Cívica, Campus Universitari, 08193 Barcelona
Telephone: 935811111
E-mail: informacio@uab.es
Internet: www.uab.es
Founded 1968
State control
Languages of instruction: Catalan, Spanish
Academic year: September to July (2 semesters)

Rector: FERRAN SANCHO PIFARRÉ
Vice-Rector for Economic Policy and Org.: MONTSERRAT FARELL FERRER
Vice-Rector for Institutional Relations and Environment: MANEL SABÉS XAMANÍ
Vice-Rector for Int. Relations: LLUÍS QUINTANA TRIAS
Vice-Rector for Quality, Teaching and Employability: GLORIA GONZÁLEZ ANADÓN
Vice-Rector for Research: PILAR DELLUNDE CLAVÉ
Vice-Rector for Strategic Projects and Planification: LLUÍS TORT BARDOLET
Vice-Rector for Student Affairs and Cooperation: SÍLVIA CARRASCO PONS
Vice-Rector for Teaching Staff and Academic Programming: JUAN JESÚS DONAIRE BENITO
Sec.-Gen.: JUDITH SOLÉ RESINA
Librarian: JOAN RAMÓN GÓMEZ ESCOFET

Library of 1,114,509 vols, 39,000 periodicals
Number of teachers: 3,615
Number of students: 29,018

Publications: *Anàlisi: Quaderns de Comunicació i Cultura, Anuari d'Anglès, Cuadernos de Psicología, Cuadernos de Traducción e Interpretación, Documents d'Anàlisi Geogràfica, Educar, Enrahonar: Quaderns de Filosofia, Estudios de la Antigüedad, Faventia, Medievalia, Orsis: Organismes i Sistemes, Papers: Revista de Sociologia, Quaderns de Música Històrica Catalana, Quaderns de Treball, Recerca Musicològica, Revistas de Historia Moderna y Contemporánea del Departamento* (1 a year)

DEANS

Faculty of Biosciences: Dr JOSEP VENDRELL ROCA
Faculty of Communications Studies: JOSEP MARIA CATALÀ DOMENECH
Faculty of Economics and Business Studies: JORDI MASSÓ CARRERAS
Faculty of Education: NÚRIA GORGORIÓ
Faculty of Law: Dr JOSEP M. DE DIOS MARCER
Faculty of Medicine: MANEL ARMENGOL I CARRASCO
Faculty of Philosophy and Arts: TERESA CABRÉ MONNÉ
Faculty of Political Science and Sociology: Dr JOAN BOTELLA CORRAL
Faculty of Psychology: MAITE MARTÍNEZ GONZÁLEZ
Faculty of Sciences: JORDI BARBÉ GARCÍA
Faculty of Translation and Interpreting: LAURA SANTAMARIA
Faculty of Veterinary Medicine: REYES PLA SOLER

UNIVERSITAT DE BARCELONA
(University of Barcelona)

Gran Via de les Corts Catalanes 585, 08007 Barcelona
Telephone: 934021100
E-mail: rectorat@ub.edu
Internet: www.ub.edu
Founded 1450
State control
Languages of instruction: Catalan, English, Spanish
Academic year: September to June (2 semesters)

Rector: Dr DÍDAC RAMÍREZ I SARRIÓ
Vice-Rector for Academic Policy and Quality: Dr GASPAR ROSSELLÓ NICOLAU
Vice-Rector for Admin. and Org.: Dra CARME PANCHÓN IGLESIAS
Vice-Rector for Communication and Projection: Dr PERE J. QUETGLAS NICOLAU
Vice-Rector for Institutional Relations and Culture: Dra LOURDES CIRLOT VALENZUELA
Vice-Rector for Int. Policy: MARIA CALLEJÓN FORNIELES
Vice-Rector for Research, Innovation and Knowledge Transfer: Dr JORDI ALBERCH VIÉ
Vice-Rector for Science Policy: Dr ENRIC I. CANELA CAMPOS
Vice-Rector for Students and Language Policy: Dra GEMMA FONRODONA BALDAJOS
Vice-Rector for Teaching Staff: Dr MANUEL VILADEVALL SOLÉ
Sec.-Gen.: Dr ISABEL MIRALLES GONZALEZ
Library Dir: ADELAIDA FERRER TORRENS

Library of 1,484,794 vols
Number of teachers: 5,312
Number of students: 84,484

DEANS

Faculty of Biology: Dr JOAQUÍM GUTIÉRREZ FRUITÓS
Faculty of Chemistry: Dr PERE LLUÍS CABOT JULIÀ
Faculty of Dentistry: Prof. Dra SÍLVIA SÁNCHEZ GONZÁLEZ (acting)
Faculty of Economics and Business: Dra ELISENDA PALUZIE I HERNÁNDEZ
Faculty of Education: ANA MARÍA ESCOFET ROIG
Faculty of Fine Arts: Dr SALVADOR GARCÍA FORTES
Faculty of Geography and History: FRANCESC XAVIER ROIGÉ VENTURA
Faculty of Geology: Dr LUIS CABRERA PÉREZ
Faculty of Law: Dr ENOCH ALBERTÍ ROVIRA
Faculty of Library and Information Science: ERNEST ABADAL FALGUERAS
Faculty of Mathematics: MARIA CARMEN CASCANTE CANUT
Faculty of Medicine: Dr FRANCESC CARDELLACH LÓPEZ
Faculty of Pharmacy: Dr JOAN ESTEVA DE SAGRERA
Faculty of Philology: Dr ADOLFO SOTELO VÁZQUEZ
Faculty of Philosophy: NORBERT BILBENY I GARCIA
Faculty of Physics: Dr ATILÀ HERMS I BERENGUER
Faculty of Psychology: Dr MANEL VIADER JUNYENT
Faculty of Teacher Training: ALBERT BATALLA FLORES
University School of Nursing: ANA MARIA PULPON SEGURA (Dir)

UNIVERSITAT DE GIRONA
(University of Girona)

Pl Sant Domènec 3, Les Àligues Bldg, 17071 Girona
Telephone: 972418041
E-mail: informacio@udg.edu

Internet: www.udg.edu
Founded 1991
State control
Language of instruction: Catalan
Academic year: September to June (2 semesters)

Rector: Dra ANA MARIA GELI DE CIURANA
Vice-Rector for Academic Policy: Dr FRANCESC FELIU TORRENT
Vice-Rector for Campus and Infrastructure: LLUÍS ALBÓ RIGAU
Vice-Rector for Implementing Regulations: Dra SUSANA OROMI VALL-LLOVERA
Vice-Rector for Institutional Relations, Society and Culture: Dr JOAQUIM MARIA PUIGVERT SOLA
Vice-Rector for Int. Policy: Dra MARIA LUISA PEREZ CABANI
Vice-Rector for Personnel and Social Policy: Dr TEODOR MARIA JOVÉ LAGUNAS
Vice-Rector for Planning and Quality: Dr MARTÍ CASADESÚS FA
Vice-Rector for Research and Knowledge Transfer: Dr JOSEP CALBÓ ANGRILL
Vice-Rector for Strategic Projects and Economics: Dr LIBRADO JESÚS GARCÍA GIL
Vice-Rector for Student Cooperation and Equality: MARIA ROSA TERRADELLAS PIFERRER
Sec.-Gen.: Dr CARLES ABELLA AMETLLER
Librarian: ANTÒNIA BOIX

Library of 372,144 vols, 6,793 periodicals
Number of teachers: 804
Number of students: 12,952

Publication: *Engega*

DEANS

Faculty of Arts: Dr JOSE LUIS VILLANOVA VALERO
Faculty of Business and Economic Sciences: Dr MARIA CARMEN SAURINA CANALS
Faculty of Education and Psychology: Dr JOSEP MARIA SERRA BONET
Faculty of Law: Dr GUILLERMO ORMAZABAL SÁNCHEZ
Faculty of Medicine: Dr RAMON BRUGADA
Faculty of Nursing: JOSEFINA PATIÑO MASO
Faculty of Science: Dr VICTORIA DE LOS ANGELES SALVADO MARTIN
Faculty of Tourism: Dr MARIA DOLORS VIDAL CASELLAS
Polytechnic School: Dr QUIM SALVI MAS (Dir)

UNIVERSITAT DE LES ILLES BALEARS
(University of the Balearic Islands)

Carretera de Valldemossa, Km 7.5, 07122 Palma
Telephone: 971173000
E-mail: informacio@uib.es
Internet: www.uib.es
Founded 1978
State control
Languages of instruction: Catalan, English, Spanish
Academic year: September to June (2 semesters)

Rector: Dra MONTSERRAT CASAS AMETLLER
Vice-Rector for Academic Affairs: Dr JUAN JOSÉ MONTAÑO MORENO
Vice-Rector for Economic and Univ. Venues: Dr DAVID PONS FLORIT
Vice-Rector for Faculty and Postgraduate Studies: Dr JAUME JESÚS CAROT GINER
Vice-Rector for Information Technology: Dr CARLOS JUIZ GARCÍA
Vice-Rector for Infrastructure and Environment: Dra RAQUEL HERRANZ BASCONES
Vice-Rector for Int. Relations and Cooperation: Dra CATALINA NATIVITAT JUANEDA SAMPOL
Vice-Rector for Research: Dra GEMMA ISABEL TURNES PALOMINO

Vice-Rector for Scientific Policy and Innovation: Dr VICTOR CERDÀ MARTÍN

Vice-Rector for Student Affairs: Dra MARIA JUAN GARAU

Vice-Rector for Univ. Affairs: Dra PATRÍCIA TRAPERO LLOBERA

Sec.-Gen.: Dr ANTONI GILI PASCUAL

Library Dir: MIQUEL PASTOR TOUS

Number of teachers: 1,202

Number of students: 14,739

Publications: *Annals of Tourism Research* (2 a year), *Educació i Cultura*, *Mayurqa* (1 a year), *Revista de Psicología del Deporte*, *Taula* (2 a year), *Treballs de Geografia*

DEANS

Faculty of Economics and Business: Prof. MARGARITA PAYERAS LLODRÀ

Faculty of Education: Prof. JOSÉ LUIS OLIVER TORELLÓ

Faculty of Law: SANTIAGO JOSÉ CAVANILLAS MÚJICA

Faculty of Nursing and Physiotherapy: Prof. JOAN ERNEST DE PEDRO GÓMEZ

Faculty of Philosophy and Letters: Prof. NICOLAU DOLS SALAS

Faculty of Psychology: Prof. ALBERT JOSÉ SESÉ ABAD

Faculty of Science: Prof. ANTONIO AMENGUAL COLOM

Faculty of Tourism: Prof. BARTOLOMÉ DEYÁ TORTELLA

Higher Polytechnic University School: YOLANDA GONZÁLEZ CID

UNIVERSITAT DE LLEIDA
(University of Lleida)

Plaça de Víctor Siurana 1, 25003 Lleida

Telephone: 973702000

E-mail: bustia@rectorat.udl.cat

Internet: www.udl.cat

Founded 1991

State control

Languages of instruction: Catalan, English, Spanish

Academic year: September to July (2 semesters)

Rector: ROBERTO FERNÁNDEZ DÍAZ

Vice-Rector for Campus: JESÚS AVILLA HERNÁNDEZ

Vice-Rector for Cultural Activities and Univ. Outreach: JOAN BISCARRI GASSIÓ

Vice-Rector for Int. Relations and Cooperation: ASTRID BALLESTA REMY

Vice-Rector for Planning, Innovation and Companies: FERRAN BADIA PASCUAL

Vice-Rector for Research: JAUME PUY LLORENS

Vice-Rector for Scientific and Technological Policy: ALBERT SORRIBAS TELLO

Vice-Rector for Students, Postgraduate and Continuing Education: NEUS VILA RUBIO

Vice-Rector for Teaching: FRANCISCO GARCÍA PASCUAL

Vice-Rector for Teaching Staff: CARLES CAPDEVILA MARQUÉS

Registrar: Dra ANA MARÍA ROMERO BURILLO

Gen. Sec.: TERESA ARECES PIÑOL

Library Dir: LOLI MANCIÑEIRAS VAZ-ROMERO

Library of 320,341 vols, 4,861 periodicals

Number of teachers: 966

Number of students: 9,582

Publications: *Arrabal* (1 a year), *Qualitative Theory of Dynamical Systems* (2 a year), *Revista d'Arqueologia de Ponent* (1 a year), *Sintagma* (1 a year), *Ull Crític* (1 a year)

DEANS

Faculty of Arts: Dr JOAN J. BUSQUETA RIU

Faculty of Educational Sciences: MARI-PAU CORNADÓ TEIXIDÓ

Faculty of Law and Economics: Dr JOAN PERE ENCISO RODRÍGUEZ

Faculty of Medicine: Dr JOAN RIBERA CALVET

Faculty of Nursing: M. LUISA GUITARD SEIN-ECHALUCE

Polytechnic School: FRANCESC GINÉ DE SOLA (Dir)

UNIVERSITAT DE VALÈNCIA
(University of Valencia)

Avda Blasco Ibáñez 13, 46010 Valencia

Telephone: 963864100

E-mail: rectorat@uv.es

Internet: www.uv.es

Founded 1499

State control

Language of instruction: Spanish

Academic year: September to July (2 semesters)

Rector: Prof. Dr ESTEBAN MORCILLO SÁNCHEZ

Vice-Rector for Academic Org.: Dra MARÍA VICENTA MESTRE ESCRIVÁ

Vice-Rector for Arts, Culture and Heritage: Dr ANTONIO ARIÑO VILLARROYA

Vice-Rector for Communication and Institutional Relations: SILVIA BARONA VILAR

Vice-Rector for Community Participation and Outreach: Dr JORGE HERMOSILLA PLA

Vice-Rector for Continuing Education: (vacant)

Vice-Rector for Economics: MÁXIMO FERRANDO BOLADO

Vice-Rector for Infrastructure and Sustainability: Dra CLARA MARTÍNEZ FUENTES

Vice-Rector for Int. Relations and Cooperation: Dr OLGA GIL MEDRANO

Vice-Rector for Planning and Equality: ANTONIO ARIÑO VILLARROYA

Vice-Rector for Postgraduate Studies: Dr ROSA MARÍN SÁEZ

Vice-Rector for Research and Science Policy: Dr PEDRO M. CARRASCO SORLI

Vice-Rector for Studies and Language Policy: Dr ISABEL VÁZQUEZ NAVARRO

Registrar: MARÍA JOSÉ AÑÓN ROIG

Library Dir: JOSEP LLUÍS SIRERA TURÓ

Library of 1,484,000 vols, 17,600 periodicals

Number of teachers: 3,300

Number of students: 58,500 (46,000 undergraduate, 12,500 postgraduate)

Publications: *Caràcters* (12 a year), *Celestinesca* (1 a year), *Imago* (1 a year), *L'Espill* (4 a year), *Mètode* (4 a year), *Pasajes* (4 a year), *Recerques*

DEANS

Faculty of Biological Sciences: JAVIER LLUCH TARAZONA

Faculty of Chemistry: PILAR CAMPINS FALCÓ

Faculty of Economics: VICENT SOLER I MARCO

Faculty of Geography and History: ESTER ALBA PAGÁN

Faculty of Law: MARÍA ELENA OLMOS ORTEGA

Faculty of Mathematics: RAFAEL CRESPO GARCÍA

Faculty of Medicine and Odontology: FEDERICO V. PALLARDO CALATAYUD

Faculty of Nursing and Chiropody: JULIO FERNÁNDEZ GARRIDO

Faculty of Pharmacy: MARÍA TERESA BARBER SANCHIS

Faculty of Philology, Translation and Communication: CARLOS PADILLA CARMONA

Faculty of Philosophy and Educational Sciences: JESÚS ALCOLEA BANEGAS

Faculty of Physical Activity and Sport Sciences: VICENTE AÑÓ SANZ

Faculty of Physics: SOLEDAD GANDIA FRANCO

Faculty of Physiotherapy: CELEDONIA IGUAL CAMACHO

Faculty of Psychology: ALICIA SALVADOR FERNANDEZ-MONTEJO

Faculty of Social Sciences: ERNEST CANO CANO

Faculty of Teaching: MANUEL MONFORT PAÑEGO

School of Engineering: VICENTE CERVERÓN LLEÓ (Dir)

UNIVERSITAT DE VIC

Calle Sagrada Família 7, 08500 Barcelona

Telephone: 938861222

E-mail: relin@uvic.es

Internet: www.uvic.es

Founded 1997

Private control

Languages of instruction: Catalan, English, Spanish

Academic year: September to June (2 semesters)

Rector and Pres.: JORDI MONTAÑA I MATOSAS

Vice-Rector for Academic Org. and Teaching Staff: Dr PERE QUER

Vice-Rector for Research and Knowledge Transfer: Drs MARTA OTERO

Registrar: Drs CARME SANMARTÍ I ROSET

Gen. Man.: JORDI CODINA

Library Dir: ANNA ANDREU MOLINA

Library of 63,284 vols, 1,484 periodicals

Number of teachers: 471

Number of students: 5,500

DEANS

BAU Design School: Prof. ELISABET PLANTADA (Dir)

Faculty of Business and Communication Studies: Dr XAVIER FERRÀS

Faculty of Education, Translation and Humanities: FRANCESC CODINA

Faculty of Health Sciences and Welfare: MARGARIDA PLA

Polytechnic School: Dr JORDI VILLÀ (Dir)

UNIVERSITAT INTERNACIONAL DE CATALUNYA
(International University of Catalonia)

Carrer Immaculada 22, 08017 Barcelona

Telephone: 932541800

E-mail: info@uic.es

Internet: www.uic.es

Founded 1997

Private control

Languages of instruction: Catalan, Spanish

Academic year: October to July (2 semesters)

Rector: Dr PERE ALAVEDRA RIBOT

Vice-Rector for Academic Org. and Teaching Staff: Dra MARÍA FERNÁNDEZ CAPO

Vice-Rector for Research: Dr FREDERIC MARIMÓN VIADIU

Vice-Rector for Univ. Community: Dr BELÉN ZÁRATE RIVERO

Sec.-Gen.: BELÉN CASTRO BAÑERES

Library Man.: EVA MARÍA DEL RÍO PÉREZ

DEANS

Faculty of Communication Sciences: Dr IVÁN LACASA MAS

Faculty of Dentistry: Dr LUÍS GINER TARRIDA

Faculty of Economic and Social Sciences: Dr MIQUEL BASTONS PRAT

Faculty of Education: Dr ALBERT ARBOS BERTRAN

Faculty of Humanities: Dra TERESA VALLÈS BOTEY

Faculty of Legal and Political Studies: Dr JAVIER JUNCEDA MORENO

Faculty of Medicine and Health Sciences: Dr ALBERT BALAGUER SANTAMARIA

UNIVERSITAT OBERTA DE CATALUNYA
(Open University of Catalonia)

Avda Tibidabo 39–43, 08035 Barcelona

Telephone: 932532300

E-mail: queries@uoc.edu

Internet: www.uoc.edu
Founded 1995
Language of instruction: Catalan

Schools of cooperation, languages; depts of arts and humanities, economics and business studies, health sciences, information and communication sciences, information technology, multimedia and telecommunications, law and political science, psychology and educational sciences

Pres.: Dr IMMA TUBELLA I CASADEVALL
Vice-Pres. for Faculty and Academic Organisation: Dr PERE FABRA ABAT
Vice-Pres. for Postgraduate Studies and Lifelong Learning: Dr JOSEP MARIA DUART I MONTOLIU
Vice-Pres. for Research and Innovation: Dr TERESA SANCHO VINUESA
Vice-Pres. for Technology: Dr LLORENÇ VALVERDE I GARCIA
Gen. Sec.: Dr LLORENÇ VALVERDE I GARCIA
Library Dir: PEP TORN POCH

Library of 18,000 vols
Number of teachers: 3,720
Number of students: 60,096

Publications: *Anàlisi. Quaderns de Cultura*, *artnodes* (online (artnodes.uoc.edu)), *COMeIN* (online (comein.uoc.edu)), *Digithum* (online (digithum.uoc.edu)), *EcoUniversitat* (in Catalan), *eLC Research Paper Series* (2 a year, online (elcrps.uoc.edu)), *IDP. Revista de Internet, Derecho y Política* (online (idp.uoc.edu)), *IN3 Working Paper Series* (3 a year), *Journal of Conflictology* (2 a year), *Mosaic* (online (mosaic.uoc.edu)), *RUSC. Revista de Universidad y Sociedad del Conocimiento* (online (rusc.uoc.edu)), *UOC Papers* (online (www.uoc.edu/uocpapers)), *Walk In* (print and online (walkin.uoc.edu/divulgacio/walkin/en/numero07/index.html))

UNIVERSITAT POMPEU FABRA

Plaça de la Mercè 10–12, 08002 Barcelona
Telephone: 935422000
E-mail: rector@upf.edu
Internet: www.upf.edu

Founded 1990
State control
Languages of instruction: Catalan, Spanish
Academic year: September to June (2 semesters)

Rector: Dr JAUME CASALS PONS
Vice-Rector for Economy, Information Resources and Institutional Relations: Dr ANTONI BOSCH DOMÈNECH
Vice-Rector for Institutional Planning and Evaluation: CARLES RAMIÓ MATAS
Vice-Rector for Int. Relations: Dr JOSEP FERRER RIBA
Vice-Rector for Research: Dr ANGEL LOZANO SOLSONA
Vice-Rector for Social Responsibility and Promotion: Dr MÒNICA FIGUERAS MAZ
Vice-Rector for Science Policy: Dr FRANCESC POSAS GARRIGA
Vice-Rector for Teaching and Academic Planning: Dra MIREIA TRENCHS PARERA
Vice-Rector for Teaching Staff: LOUISE ELIZABETH McNALLY SEIFERT
Sec.-Gen.: PELEGRÍ VIADER CANALS

Library of 600,000 vols, 12,800 periodicals
Number of teachers: 876
Number of students: 11,235 (9,115 undergraduate, 2,120 postgraduate)

Publication: *upf.edu* (2 a year, in Catalan)

DEANS

Faculty of Communication: Dr FRANCISCO JAVIER RUIZ COLLANTES
Faculty of Economic and Business Sciences: Dr VICENTE ORTUN RUBIO
Faculty of Health and Life Sciences: Dr JOAQUIN GEA GUIRAL
Faculty of Humanities: Dr JOSEP MARIA CASTELLA LIDON
Faculty of Law: Dr JOSEP MARIA VILAJOSANA RUBIO
Faculty of Political and Social Sciences: Dr DAVID SANCHO ROYO
Faculty of Translation and Interpretation: Dra MARIA DOLORES CAÑADA PUJOLS
Polytechnic School (ESUP): ENRIC PEIG OLIVE (Dir)

UNIVERSITAT RAMON LLULL

Claravall 1–3, 08022 Barcelona
Telephone: 936022200
E-mail: info@url.edu
Internet: www.url.edu

Founded 1990
Private control
Languages of instruction: Catalan, English, Spanish
Academic year: September to June (2 semesters)

Rector: Dr JOSEP M. GARRELL I GUIU
Vice-Rector for Academic Policy: Dr JORDI RIERA ROMANÍ
Vice-Rector for Int. Relations and Student Affairs: Dr CARLO MARIA GALLUCCI CALABRESE
Vice-Rector for Research and Innovation: Dr LLUÍS COMELLAS RIERA
Sec.-Gen.: Dra ANNA BERGA TIMONEDA
Library Dir: MERCÈ YLL

Library: 1.27m. vols, 15.000 periodicals
Number of teachers: 1,110
Number of students: 17,576

Publications: *ConsCIÈNCIAurl* (online (recerca.url.edu)), *La URL Informa*, *Ramon Llull Journal of Applied Ethics* (print and online (www.rljae.org)), *Signes*

DEANS

Blanquerna Faculty of Communication Sciences: Dr JOSEP M. CARBONELL ABELLÓ
Blanquerna Faculty of Health Sciences: Dr MÀRIUS DURAN HORTOLÀ
Blanquerna Faculty of Psychology, Education Sciences and Sport: Dr JOSEP GALLIFA ROCA
ESADE Business School: Dr ALFONS SAUQUET ROVIRA
ESADE Law School: Dr ENRIC BARTLETT CASTELLA
Faculty of Philosophy: Dr JAUME AYMAR I RAGOLTA
IQS School of Engineering: Dra ROSA NOMEN RIBÉ
IQS School of Management: Dr JESÚS TRICÁS PRECKLER
La Salle School of Architecture: ROBERT TERRADAS MUNTAÑOLA (Dir)
La Salle School of Electronics and Computer Engineering: Dr FRANCESC MIRALLES TORNER (Dir)
La Salle School of Telecommunications Engineering: XAVIER SENMARTÍ (Dir)
Pere Tarrés Faculty of Social Education and Social Work: Dr FRANCISCO JOSÉ LÓPEZ JIMÉNEZ
Vidal i Barraquer University School of Mental Health: Dr CARLES PÉREZ TESTOR (Dir)

UNIVERSITAT ROVIRA I VIRGILI

Carrer de l'Escorxador s/n, 43003 Tarragona
Telephone: 9022337878
E-mail: contacteu@urv.cat
Internet: www.urv.cat

Founded 1991
State control
Languages of instruction: Catalan, English, Spanish

Academic year: September to June

Rector: Prof. Dr JOSEP ANTON FERRÉ VIDAL
Vice-Rector for Academic Policy and Research Staff: Dr JOSEP PALLARÈS MARZAL
Vice-Rector for Institutional Evaluation: Dra MONTSERRAT GIRALT BATISTA
Vice-Rector for Int. Relations: Dra MAR GUTIÉRREZ-COLON PLANA
Vice-Rector for Science Policy and Research Management: Dr JOSEP MANEL RICART PLA
Vice-Rector for Teaching, Students and Univ. Community: Dra ARANTXA CAPDEVILA GÓMEZ
Vice-Rector for Transference and Innovation: Dr MIQUEL ÀNGEL BOVÉ SANS
Vice-Rector for Univ. and Soc.: Dr JORDI TOUS PALLARÈS
Gen. Sec.: Dr MARIO RUIZ SANZ

Library of 576,202 vols, 11,152 magazines
Number of teachers: 893
Number of students: 13,874 (11,689 undergraduate, 2,185 postgraduate)

Publications: *Revista Catalana de Dret Ambiental* (2 a year), *Revista Internacional de Organizaciones* (print and online, www.rcda.cat), *URV Magazine* (4 a year), *URV Publications* (4 a year)

DEANS

Faculty of Arts: Dr JOSEP SÁNCHEZ CERVELLÓ
Faculty of Business and Economics: Dr GLÒRIA BARBERÀ MARINÉ
Faculty of Chemistry: Dr JOAN IGUAL RIPOLLÈS
Faculty of Educational Sciences and Psychology: Dra PALOMA VICENS CALDERÓN
Faculty of Legal Sciences: Dr ALFONSO GONZÁLEZ BONDIA
Faculty of Medicine and Health Sciences: Dr ANTONI CASTRO SALOMÓ
Faculty of Nursing: Dr ROSER RICOMÀ MUNTANÉ
Faculty of Oenology: Dr JOAN MIQUEL CANALS BOSCH
Faculty of Tourism and Geography: Dr SALVADOR ANTON CLAVÉ
School of Architecture: Dr JOSEP BERTRAN ILARI
School of Chemical Engineering: Dr JOSEP BONET ÀVALOS
School of Engineering: Dr DOMÈNEC SAVI PUIG VALLS (Dir)

Polytechnics

UNIVERSIDAD POLITÉCNICA DE CARTAGENA
(Technical University of Cartagena)

Plaza del Cronista Isidoro Valverde, Edif. La Milagrosa, 30202 Cartagena, Murcia
Telephone: 968325400
E-mail: gestion.academica@upct.es
Internet: www.upct.es

Founded 1998
State control
Language of instruction: Spanish
Academic year: September to June (2 semesters)

Depts of agricultural science and technology, applied mathematics and statistics, applied physics, architecture and building technology, business economics, chemical and environmental engineering, economics, electrical engineering, electronics, computer technology and projects, electronic technology, financial economics and accounting, food engineering and agricultural equipment, graphic expression, information technologies and communications, legal science, materials and manufacturing engineering, mechanical engineering, mining, geological and cartographic engineering, naval architecture technology, plant production, quantitative methods and computing, structures and construction, systems and automation engineering, thermal and fluids engineering

Rector: JOSÉ ANTONIO FRANCO LEEMHUIS
Vice-Rector for Academic Affairs: JOSÉ LUIS MUÑOZ LOZANO
Vice-Rector for Academic Staff: ÁNGEL RAFAEL MARTÍNEZ LORENTE
Vice-Rector for Economic and Strategic Planning: EMILIO TRIGUEROS TORNERO
Vice-Rector for Information Technologies and Communication: JUAN LUIS PEDREÑO MOLINA
Vice-Rector for Infrastructure and Sustainability: JOSÉ PÉREZ GARCÍA
Vice-Rector for Int. Relations and Devt Cooperation: JOSÉ MANUEL FERRÁNDEZ VICENTE
Vice-Rector for Planning and Coordination: JOSÉ ANTONIO CASCALES PUJALTE
Vice-Rector for Research and Innovation: PABLO SALVADOR FERNÁNDEZ ESCÁMEZ
Vice-Rector for Student Affairs and Univ. Extension: FRANCISCO MARTÍNEZ GONZÁLEZ
Registrar: MARÍA DEL CARMEN PASTOR ALVAREZ
Librarian: MA. ÁNGELES GARCÍA DEL TORO

Library of 50,000 vols, 2,528 periodicals
Number of teachers: 500
Number of students: 7,210

UNIVERSIDAD POLITÉCNICA DE MADRID
(Technical University of Madrid)

Calle Ramiro de Maeztu 7, 28040 Madrid
Telephone: 913366000
Internet: www.upm.es
Founded 1971
State control
Language of instruction: Spanish
Academic year: September to June (2 semesters)

Rector: CARLOS CONDE LÁZARO
Vice-Rector for Academic Planning and Doctoral Studies: D. EMILIO MINGUEZ TORRES
Vice-Rector for Academic Staff: JOSÉ LUÍS MONTAÑES GARCÍA
Vice-Rector for Economic Affairs: LINAREJOS GÁMEZ MEJÍAS
Vice-Rector for Information and Communication Services: JUAN JOSÉ MORENO NAVARRO
Vice-Rector for Int. Relations: JOSÉ MANUEL PÁEZ BORRALLO
Vice-Rector for Quality and Organizational Structure: SARA GÓMEZ MARTÍN
Vice-Rector for Research: GONZALO LEÓN SERRANO
Vice-Rector for Student Affairs: JOSE LUÍS GARCÍA GRINDA
Sec.-Gen.: CRISTINA PÉREZ GARCÍA
Dir for Univ. Library: MARÍA BOYER LAGOS

Library of 775,000 vols of monographs, 11,800 periodicals, 2,000 units of audiovisual material, 20,000 e-titles
Number of teachers: 3,414
Number of students: 41,374
Publication: *Urban*

DEANS

Faculty of Computer Sciences (Madrid): VICTOR ROBLES FORCADA
Faculty of Physical Activity and Sport Sciences: JAVIER SAMPEDRO MOLINEUV

UNIVERSIDAD POLITÉCNICA DE VALENCIA

Camino de Vera s/n, 46022 Valencia
Telephone: 963877000
E-mail: informacion@upv.es
Internet: www.upv.es

Founded 1968
State control
Languages of instruction: Spanish, Valencian
Academic year: September to June (2 semesters)

Schools of agricultural engineering and environment, architecture, building engineering, civil engineering, design engineering, engineering in computer science, engineering in geodesy, cartography and surveying, industrial engineering, telecommunications engineering

Rector: FRANCISCO JOSÉ MORA MÁS
Vice-Rector for Campus and Sustainability: CARMEN JORDÁ SUCH
Vice-Rector for Digital Resources and Online Formation: VINCENT BOTTI NAVARRO
Vice-Rector for Economic Affairs and Planning: MIGUEL A. MARTÍNEZ IRANZO
Vice-Rector for Faculty and Academic Planning: ISMAEL MOYA CLEMENTE
Vice-Rector for Research, Innovation and Transfer: JOSÉ ESTEBAN CAPILLA ROMÁ
Vice-Rector for Social Responsibility and Cooperation: ROSA PUCHADES PLA
Vice-Rector for Studies and Univ. Extension: MARIA VICTORIA VIVANCOS RAMÓN
Vice-Rector for Studies, Quality and Accreditation: MIGUEL ÁNGEL FERNÁNDEZ PRADA

Library of 558,311 vols, 18,722 digital periodicals
Number of teachers: 2,672
Number of students: 38,027
Publication: *Butlletí Oficial de la Universitat Politècnica de València*

DEANS

Faculty of Business Administration and Management: ISMAEL MOYA CLEMENTE
Faculty of Fine Arts: JOSÉ LUIS CUETO LOMINCHAR

UNIVERSITAT POLITÈCNICA DE CATALUNYA BARCELONATECH
(Polytechnic University of Catalonia)

Calle Jordi Girona 31, 08034 Barcelona
Telephone: 934016200
E-mail: international@barcelonatech.upc.edu
Internet: www.upc.edu
Founded 1971
State control
Languages of instruction: Spanish, Catalan
Academic year: September to June (2 semesters)

Rector: ENRIC FOSSAS COLET
Vice-Rector for Architecture: JOSEP PARCERISA BUNDÓ
Vice-Rector for Community, Social Action and Sustainability: JOAN PUIGDOMÈNECH FRANQUESA
Vice-Rector for Research Policy: FERNANDO OREJAS VALDÉS
Vice-Rector for Studies and Planning: ANTONI RAS SABIDÓ
Vice-Rector for Teaching Policy: MARIBEL ROSSELLÓ NICOLAU
Vice-Rector for Teaching and Research Staff: MIQUEL SORIANO IBÁÑEZ
Vice-Rector for Univ. Policy: SISCO VALLVERDÚ BAYÉS
Sec.-Gen.: FRANCISCO JAVIER NAVALLAS RAMOS

Number of teachers: 2,634
Number of students: 37,783
Publications: *Informacions* (12 a year, in Catalan, print and online, www.upc.edu/revistainformacions), *The Mag* (4 a year, in English, print and online, www.upc.edu/themag)

DEANS

Barcelona School of Informatics: NÚRIA CASTELL ARIÑO
Barcelona School of Nautical Studies: SANTIAGO ORDÁS JIMÉNEZ (Dir)
Faculty of Mathematics and Statistics: JORDI QUER BOSOR
Terrassa School of Optics and Optometry: ESTER GUAUS GUERRERO (Dir)

Colleges
GENERAL

Schiller International University: Calle Joaquín Costa 20, 28002 Madrid; tel. 914482488; e-mail mad_admissions@schiller.edu; internet www.schillermadrid.edu; f. 1964; Bachelors degrees in interdisciplinary studies, international business, international relations and diplomacy; Masters degrees in business administration, international business; library: 10,000 vols; Dir Dr MANUEL ALONSO-PUIG; Registrar and Head of Studies DUNCAN SHAW; Librarian BEATRIZ OVEJERO.

ECONOMICS AND LAW

ESADE (Escuela Superior de Administración y Dirección de Empresas) (Higher School of Administration and Business Management): Avda Pedralbes 60–62, 08034 Barcelona; tel. 932806162; e-mail info@esade.edu; internet www.esade.edu; f. 1958; attached to Ramon Llull Univ.; campuses in Argentina, Madrid, Pedralbes (Barcelona), Sant Cugat (Barcelona); Dir-Gen. EUGENIA BIETO; Sec.-Gen. FRANCISCO LONGO; publs *ESADE Alumni*, *ESADE Knowledge Bulletin*.

EuroArab Management School (EAMS): Calle Cárcel Baja 3, 18001 Granada; tel. 958805050; e-mail info@eams.fundea.es; f. 1995; degree and education programmes on management devt; Dir-Gen. JOAQUÍN ABÓS.

Institut Universitari d'Estudis Europeus (University Institute of European Studies): Universitat Autonoma de Barcelona, Bldg E1, 08193 Barcelona; tel. 935812016; internet www.iuee.eu; f. 1985; attached to Universitat Autònoma de Barcelona; Masters in European integration, European policies on international cooperation for development; Doctorate in international relations and European integration; participates in confs on European issues throughout Spain; Dir Prof. Dr BLANCA VILÀ.

Real Centro Universitario Escorial—María Cristina: Paseo de los Alamillos 2, 28200 Madrid; tel. 918904545; e-mail contacto@rcumariacristina.com; internet www.rcumariacristina.com; f. 1892; attached to Universidad Complutense de Madrid; courses in administration and management, law, chiropractic; Masters in counselling and consulting information technology; Masters online of European School of Management and Business; library: 57,000 vols, 500 periodicals; 60 teachers; 1,200 students; Rector EDELMIRO MATEOS MATEOS; Dir SIXTO ÁLVAREZ MELCÓN; Sec. CARLOS J. SÁNCHEZ DÍAZ; publs *Anuario Jurídico y Económico* (1 a year), *La Ciudad de Dios* (4 a year), *Nueva Etapa* (1 a year).

MEDICINE

Escuela Andaluza de Salud Pública (Andalusian School of Public Health): Campus Universitario de Cartuja, Cuesta del Observatorio 4, Apdo de correos 2.070, 18080 Granada; tel. 958027400; e-mail comunicacion.easp@juntadeandalucia.es;

internet www.easp.es; f. 1985; courses in public health management and services; library: 59,000 vols, 2,500 periodicals; 50 teachers; 2,000 students; Dir ISABEL RUIS PÉREZ; publ. *Hablemos de Europa*.

MILITARY SCIENCE

Escuela de Guerra del Ejército (Army War College): Santa Cruz de Marcenado 25, 28015 Madrid; tel. 915242000; f. 1842; library: 45,000 vols; 60 teachers; 180 students; Dir Brig.-Gen. RICARDO MARTÍNEZ ISIDORO.

TECHNOLOGY

ETEA Loyola—Facultad de Ciencias Económicas y Empresariales (Faculty of Business and Economics—Loyola (ETEA)): Escritor Castilla Aguayo 4, Apdo 439, 14004 Córdoba; tel. 957222100; e-mail comunica@etea.com; internet www.etea.com; f. 1963; attached to Universidad de Córdoba; undergraduate and postgraduate courses in business administration, finance and accounting; extension courses in management; management consultancy services; 150 teachers; library: 50,000 vols; Dir GABRIEL MARIA PÉREZ ALCALÁ.

Institut Químic de Sarrià (Sarrià Institute of Chemistry): Universitat Ramon Llull, Calle Via Augusta 390, 08017 Barcelona; tel. 932672000; e-mail secre@iqs.edu; internet www.iqs.edu; f. 1905 as Laboratorio Químico del Ebro in Roquetes (Tarragona), present name and location 1916; attached to Universitat Ramon Llull; library: 55,000 vols, 780 periodicals; 125 teachers; 1,500 students; Prin. Dr PERE REGULL CLIMENT; Dir of Admin. SONIA AMORÓS RAMOS; Sec.-Gen. Dr XAVIER TOMÀS MORER; publs *Afinidad* (6 a year), *IQS* (1 a year).

Schools of Art and Music

Conservatori Municipal de Música de Barcelona: Bruc 110–112, 08009 Barcelona; tel. 934584302; e-mail conservatori@cmmb.cat; internet www.cmmb.cat; f. 1886; library: 27,400 vols and scores; 102 teachers; 1,815 students; Dir ALBERT LLANAS; Head of Studies M. LLUÏSA IBÁÑEZ; Academic Sec. SÍLVIA LLANAS.

Conservatorio Superior de Música de Málaga: Plaza Maestro Artola 2, 29013 Málaga; tel. 951298340; e-mail info@conserv-sup-malaga.com; internet www.conserv-sup-malaga.com; f. 1880; depts of bowed strings, conducting and composition, didactics of music and singing, musicology, keyboard instruments, plucked strings, wind and percussion; Dir MARIANO TRIVIÑO ARREBOLA; Sec. MIGUEL ÁNGEL LEIVA VERA; Dir for Studies MANUEL GIL PÉREZ; publ. *Hoquet* (1 a year).

Conservatorio Superior de Música de Murcia: Paseo del Malecón 9, 30004 Murcia; tel. 968294758; e-mail info@csmmurcia.com; internet www.csmmurcia.com; f. 1917; library: 1,546 vols, 52 periodicals; 85 teachers; 3,000 students; Dir MIGUEL ÁNGEL CENTENERO GALLEGO; Vice-Dir ROSARIO JÓDAR GARCÍA; Sec. EMILIO GRANADOS PARRILLA; publ. *Cadencia* (3 a year).

Conservatorio Superior de Música de Valencia 'Joaquin Rodrigo': Calle Cinesta Ricardo Muñoz Suay, 46013 Valencia; tel. 963605316; e-mail info@csmvalencia.es; internet www.csmvalencia.es; f. 1879; depts of bass percussion and jazz, composition, singing and direction, education and musicology, polyphonic instruments, woodwinds; library: 12,000 vols; 40 teachers; 900 students; Dir EDUARDO MONTESINOS COMAS; Vice-Dir ADOLFO BUESO CASASÚS; Dir for Studies JUAN IZNARDO COLOM; Dir for Studies VICENTE PASTOR GARCÍA; Sec. JOSÉ MANUEL MIÑANA JUAN; publ. *Memoria* (1 a year).

Conservatorio Superior de Música 'Manuel Castillo': Calle Baños 48, 41002 Seville; tel. 954915630; e-mail secretaria@consev.es; internet consev.es; f. 1933; library: 30,000 vols; 120 teachers; 2,400 students; Dir LUIS IGNACIO MARÍN GARCÍA; Sec. KATALIN SZEKELY; publ. *Diferencias*.

Conservatorio Superior de Música 'Rafael Orozco' de Córdoba: Calle Angel Saavedra 1, 14003 Córdoba; tel. 957379647; e-mail oficina@csmcordoba.com; internet www.csmcordoba.com; f. 1902; depts of composition, musicology, keys, string instruments, wind percussion; library: 15,000 vols; 95 teachers; 3,000 students; Dir JUAN DE DIOS GARCÍA AGUILERA; Dir for Studies ANTONIO CANTERO MAZARIEGOS; Sec. ÁNGELES GALLARDO LORENZO; publ. *Musicalia*.

Escuela Superior de Arte Dramático de Murcia: Plaza de los Apóstoles, 30001 Murcia; tel. 968214628; e-mail secretaria@esadmurcia.es; internet www.esadmurcia.es; f. 1918 as Conservatorio Provincial de Música y Declamación, present name 1993; depts of interpretation, body movements, plastic theatre, speech and language, stage management, writing and theatre studies; Dir ALBERTO ALFARO.

Escuela Superior de Bellas Artes de San Carlos (San Carlos School of Fine Arts): Calle San Pio V 9, 46010 Valencia; f. 1756; library: 5,100 vols; 30 teachers; 300 students; Dir DANIEL DE NUEDA LLISIONA.

Escuela Superior de Música Reina Sofía (Reina Sofía Higher School of Music): Plaza de Oriente s/n, 28013 Madrid; tel. 915230419; e-mail esmrs@albeniz.com; internet www.escuelasuperiordemusicareinasofia.es; f. 1991; depts of academic studies, artistic studies, complementary training, performance; library: 1,200 vols; Dir PALOMA O'SHEA; Academic Sec. BEATRIZ ECHEVERRÍA-TORRES; Dir for Library ÁLVARO GUIBERT.

Musikene—Euskal Herriko Goi-Mailako Musika Ikastegia/Centro Superior de Música del País Vasco (Musikene—Higher School of Music of the Basque Country): Palacio Miramar, Mirakontxa 48, 20007 San Sebastián; tel. 943316778; e-mail info@musikene.net; internet www.musikene.net; f. 2001; depts of analysis, composition and technology, jazz, keyboard instruments and voice, pedagogy, culture, thought and body techniques, strings, woodwind and percussion; 150 teachers; Academic Sec. IZASKUN ETXEBESTE GUTIÉRREZ; publ. *Ahaire*.

Real Conservatorio Profesional de Música 'Manuel de Falla' de Cadiz: Casa de las Artes, Ave de las Cortes de Cádiz 3, 11012 Cádiz; tel. 956243106; e-mail secretarioconservatorio@gmail.com; internet www.conservatoriomanueldefalla.es; f. 1860 as Academia Santa Cecilia; 60 teachers; 1,000 students; Dir MIGUEL GARRIDO ALDOMAR; publ. *Mina 3*.

Real Conservatorio Superior de Música de Madrid (Royal Academy of Music, Madrid): Calle Doctor Mata 2, 28012 Madrid; tel. 915392901; e-mail info@rcsmm.eu; internet www.educa.madrid.org/web/csm.realconservatorio.madrid; f. 1830; depts of brass and percussion, complementary piano, composition, early music, key, musicology, pedagogy, piano repertoire, sets, string, woodwind; library: 135,000 vols; 150 teachers; 700 students; Dir ANA GUIJARRO MALAGÓN; Academic Sec. ANTONIO MORENO TITOS; Head of Library ELENA MAGALLANES LATAS; publ. *Musica* (1 a year).

Real Escuela Superior de Arte Dramático (Royal School of Dramatic Art): Avda de Nazaret 2, 28009 Madrid; tel. 915042151; e-mail director@resad.es; internet www.resad.es; f. 1831; library: 22,300 vols; 60 teachers; 350 students; Dir ÁNGEL MARTÍNEZ ROGER; Academic Sec. ANA ISABEL FERNÁNDEZ VALBUENA; publ. *Acotaciones* (2 a year).

SRI LANKA

The Higher Education System

Institutions of higher education pre-date the independence of Sri Lanka (formerly Ceylon) from the United Kingdom in 1948, with the oldest being the University of Colombo, which was founded in 1921 (present name 1979). In 1978 an Act of Parliament created the current university system, following which several existing colleges were promoted to university status. In 2010 there were a total of 97,864 students enrolled at 15 universities under the jurisdiction of the University Grants Commission, which supervises and administers all aspects of higher education, and a total of 252,949 students were enrolled in public and private tertiary level education. There are also two universities under the jurisdiction of the Ministry of Higher Education (Buddhist and Pali University, Buddhasravaka Bhikku University) as well as the Sri Lanka Institute of Advanced Technological Education (SLIATE). The universities are mostly government funded, and although students do not pay tuition fees, they are required to pay registration and examination fees. However, students at the Open University (founded 1980) and postgraduate students at private higher education institutions are required to pay tuition fees. Private higher education institutions are not recognized by the state in Sri Lanka. They are not quality assured by the University Grants Commission or other Sri Lankan authorities as they are not considered to offer legal degrees. Consequently, they cannot issue Sri Lankan degrees but operate in conjunction with overseas universities, including British institutions. There are private colleges that award post-secondary qualifications but not degrees. In 2011 the Higher Education for the Twenty First Century Project was launched. It was funded by a US $40m. credit from the International Development Association (part of the World Bank) to be spread over five years. Among the aims of the project were to put in place a national qualifications framework, create a quality assurance and accreditation system for higher education, and develop the SLIATE as a centre of excellence. The Ministry of Higher Education also announced plans to upgrade six universities, in Colombo, Peradeniya, Moratuwa, Kelaniya, Ruhuna and Sri Jayewardenepura, with $6m. to be disbursed with a view to improving standards of teaching, research and infrastructure at each of the institutions in a bid to bolster their international reputation.

New regulations regarding university entrance requirements came into effect in 2000, as a result of which students are now required to complete a minimum of three subjects at GCE A-Level in addition to sitting a Common General Paper and a General English Paper, although the Open University (founded 1980) does not have formal entrance requirements. A quota system is in force, whereby 40% of places are awarded on a merit-basis, 55% are divided between the 25 administrative districts according to population size, and 5% are reserved for students from educationally underprivileged districts (primarily in the north, east and south-east of the country). In 2011 the Government introduced a controversial compulsory leadership-training programme, which requires all students selected for undergraduate courses at state universities to undergo a three-week period of training at military and police bases managed by the Ministry of Defence and Urban Development. The undergraduate Bachelors degree is classified as either 'General' or 'Special': the former lasts three years and covers three subjects in equal depth, while the latter lasts four years and is a subject-specific programme of study, culminating in a dissertation. Professional degrees, which are offered in technical or practical disciplines such as medicine, engineering and architecture, last four years (or, in the case of medicine, five years plus an additional internship year). Graduates with the Bachelors degree are eligible for the one-year Postgraduate Diploma or the two-year Masters degree, with the latter usually requiring completion of theory examinations and submission of a dissertation. Finally, the Doctorate (mostly PhD) is awarded after a two- or three-year period of research following award of the Masters, culminating in submission of a thesis.

Post-secondary technical and vocational education comprises: short-term training courses of between six and 10 months offered to all school-leavers by various institutions under the control of the Ministry of Education; and courses of two to four years leading to the award of, variously, the National Certificate, National Diploma and Higher National Diploma. City and Guilds qualifications are also available at various institutions and are very popular. The National Vocational Qualifications Framework of Sri Lanka was introduced in 2005 in a bid to unify Technical and Vocational Education and Training (TVET). The framework and skill standards are based on the New Zealand Qualifications Framework. The Tertiary and Vocational Education Commission is the national lead body for the implementation of TVET in Sri Lanka.

Regulatory and Representative Bodies

GOVERNMENT

Ministry of Culture and the Arts: Eighth Fl., Sethsiripaya, Battaramulla, Colombo; tel. (11) 2861147; e-mail minister@cultural.gov.lk; internet www.cultural.gov.lk; Minister T. B. EKANAYAKE.

Ministry of Education: 'Isurupaya', Pelawatta, Battaramulla, Colombo; tel. (11) 2785141; e-mail info@moe.gov.lk; internet www.moe.gov.lk; Minister BANDULA GUNAWARDHANA.

Ministry of Higher Education: 18 Ward Place, Colombo 7; tel. (11) 2694486; e-mail info@mohe.gov.lk; internet www.mohe.gov.lk; Minister S. B. DISSANAYAKE.

Ministry of Technology and Research: POB 1571, 408 Galle Rd, Colombo 3; tel. (11) 2374700; e-mail mstsasad@sltnet.lk; internet www.motr.gov.lk; Minister PATALI CHAMPIKA RANAWAKA.

ACCREDITATION

Quality Assurance and Accreditation Council of the University Grants Commission: 65/4 Kirula Rd, Colombo; tel. (11) 2368794; e-mail colinpeiris@qaacouncil.lk; internet www.qaacouncil.lk; f. 2004; ensures quality, continuous devt, accreditation, efficient performance of Sri Lankan higher education instns; Chair. Prof. M. T. M. JIFFRY; Dir Prof. COLIN N. PEIRIS (acting).

FUNDING

University Grants Commission: 20 Ward Pl., Colombo 7; tel. (11) 2695301; e-mail secretary@ugc.ac.lk; internet www.ugc.ac.lk; f. 1978; allocates funds to univs and univ. institutes, serves as the central admissions agency for undergraduate studies; plans, coordinates and monitors activities of the univ. system to maintain academic standards; 8 mems; Chair. Prof. KSHANIKA HIRIBUREGAMA; Sec. TISSA NANDASENA.

NATIONAL BODY

Tertiary and Vocational Education Commission: 'Nipunatha Piyasa', 354/2 Elvitigala Mw Narahenpita, Colombo; tel. (11) 5849291; e-mail info@tvec.gov.lk; internet www.tvec.gov.lk; f. 1991; apex body for accreditation, policy formulation, planning, quality assurance, coordination, devt of tertiary and vocational education; Chair. Prof. DAYANTHA WIJEYESEKERA; Dir-Gen. Dr T. A. PIYASIRI.

Learned Societies

GENERAL

Institute of Sinhala Culture: 'Sudarshi' 375 Bauddhaloka Mawatha, Colombo 7; tel. (11) 4687979; e-mail instituteofsinhalaculture.sl@gmail.com; internet instituteofsinhalaculture.lk; f. 1954; preservation and devt of Sinhala culture: art and architecture, drama, dance, music, folklore, arts and crafts, film, research, traditional embroidery, puppetry; presents cultural programmes; holds seminars and workshops; 680 mems; Pres. JEEVAN KUMARANATHUNGA; Sec. Prof. MUDIYANSE DISSANAYAKE.

National Academy of Sciences of Sri Lanka: 120/10 Vidya Mawatha, Colombo 7; tel. (11) 2585038; e-mail nassl@sltnet.lk; internet www.nassl.org; f. 1976; promotes advancement and dissemination of scientific knowledge; acts as consultative body to govt of Sri Lanka on matters and activities related to application of science and technology in nat. devt; 110 mems; Pres. Dr KINGSLEY DE ALWIS; Gen. Sec. Prof. NILANTHI DE SILVA.

Royal Asiatic Society of Sri Lanka: Royal Asiatic Society Bldg, 96 Ananda Coomaraswamy Mawatha, Colombo 7; tel. (11) 2699249; e-mail info@royalasiaticsociety.lk; internet www.royalasiaticsociety.lk; f. 1845; promotes inquiries into history, religions, languages, literature, arts, sciences and social conditions of the present and fmr inhabitants of Sri Lanka, and connected cultures; library contains one of the largest collns of books on Sri Lanka, and others on Indian and Eastern culture in gen.; 950 mems; library of 11,000 vols, 350 titles; Pres. Dr SUSANTHA GOONATILAKE; Hon. Jt Sec. Prof. A. W. D. RATNASIRI; Hon. Jt Sec. W. STERLING PERERA; publ. *Journal of the Royal Asiatic Society of Sri Lanka* (1 a year).

BIBLIOGRAPHY, LIBRARY SCIENCE AND MUSEOLOGY

Sri Lanka Library Association: Sri Lanka Professional Centre, 275/75 Stanely Wijesundara Mawatha, Colombo 7; tel. (11) 2589103; e-mail slla@sltnet.lk; internet www.slla.org .lk; f. 1960; acts as pivotal professional body for library, documentation and information services in Sri Lanka; provides library education programmes; sets professional standards; fosters cooperation between all individuals and orgs interested in the welfare of libraries; acts as a forum for exchange of ideas among mems; safeguards and promotes rights, privileges and status of librarians and information scientists; 415 mems; Pres. M. S. U. AMARASIRI; Gen. Sec. INDRANI PONNAMPERUMA; publ. *Sri Lanka Library Review* (1 a year).

University Librarians Association of Sri Lanka: c/o Library, Open Univ. of Sri Lanka, Nawala, Nugegoda; e-mail editor.jula@gmail .com; internet www.ulasl.org; protects and maintains professional status, interests and welfare of univ. librarianship; 100 mems; Pres. Dr PRADEEPA WIJJETUNGE; Gen. Sec. R. MAHESWARAN; publ. *Journal of University Librarians Association* (1 a year).

ECONOMICS, LAW AND POLITICS

Ceylon Institute of World Affairs: c/o Mervyn de Silva, 82B Ward Pl., Colombo 7; f. 1957; Pres. ANTON MUTTUKUMARU.

EDUCATION

National Education Society of Sri Lanka: Faculty of Education, Univ. of Colombo, Colombo 3; 75 mems; publ. *Education*.

FINE AND PERFORMING ARTS

Arts Council of Sri Lanka: 12/1 Polduwa Rd, Battaramulla, Colombo; tel. (11) 2884027; e-mail artscouncilsl@yahoo.com; internet www.artscouncil.lk; f. 1952; promotes art projects in Sri Lanka; carries out projects in all fields of arts, incl. painting, drama, music, literature, ballet, dancing, folk song, folklore; aims to develop quality of fine art of Sri Lanka; Chair. Prof. MUDIYANSE DISSANAYAKE; Gen. Sec. and Exec. Officer P. M. S. BANDARA; publ. *Kala Magazine* (4 a year).

Ceylon Society of Arts: Art Gallery, Ananda Coomarassamy Mawatha, Colombo 7; tel. (11) 4693067; f. 1887; Pres. KALAPATHI-P. SUNIL; Hon. Gen. Sec. M. D. S. GUNATHILAKE.

HISTORY, GEOGRAPHY AND ARCHAEOLOGY

Archaeological Society of Sri Lanka: c/o Dept of Archaeology, Sir Marcus Fernando Mawatha, Colombo 7; f. 1966; Pres. Prof. CHANDRA WIKKRAMAGAMAGE; Co-Sec. S. LAKDUSINGHE; Co-Sec. W. H. WIJAYAPALA.

Ceylon Geographical Society: 61 Abdul Caffoor Mawatha, Colombo 3; f. 1938; 100 mems; Pres. Prof. K. KULARATNAM; Sec. Dr K. U. SIRINANDA; Sec. Dr W. P. T. SILVA; publ. *The Ceylon Geographer* (1 a year).

LANGUAGE AND LITERATURE

Alliance Française de Colombo: 11 Barnes Pl., Colombo 7; tel. (11) 2693467; e-mail secr@alliancefr.lk; internet www .alliancefr.lk; f. 1954 as Sri Lankan Association, present status 1955; offers courses and exams in French language and culture and promotes cultural exchange with France; attached teaching centres in Kandy and Matara; 600 mems; library of 12,000 vols; Dir KAUSHALYA DIAS; publ. *Rendez-vous* (12 a year).

British Council: 49 Alfred House Gardens, POB 753, Colombo 3; tel. (11) 7521521; e-mail info.lk@britishcouncil.org; internet www.britishcouncil.org/srilanka; teaching centre; offers courses and exams in English language and British culture and promotes cultural exchange with the UK; responsible for British Council work in the Maldives; attached teaching centre in Kandy; library of 45,000 vols; Dir TONY REILLY O'BRIEN; Teaching Centre Man. PAUL HILDER.

English Speaking Union of Sri Lanka: 14A, 16K Lane Galle Rd, Colombo 3; tel. (11) 4575843; e-mail upali_iccs@sltnet.lk; f. 1981; library of 3,000 vols; incls an English Language School; Pres. Dr UPALI RATNAYAKE; publ. *Open Mind* (4 a year).

Goethe-Institut: 39 Gregory's Rd, Colombo 7; tel. (11) 2694562; e-mail info@colombo .goethe.org; internet www.goethe.de/ colombo; f. 1957; offers courses and examinations in German language and culture and promotes cultural exchange with Germany; library of 6,000 vols; Dir RICHARD LANG.

MEDICINE

Sri Lanka Medical Association: Wijerama House, 6 Wijerama Mawatha, Colombo 7; tel. (11) 2693324; e-mail slma@eureka.lk; internet www.slma.sharedcarevault.info; f. 1887 as Ceylon Branch of the British Medical Association, present name and status 1972; provides a forum for medical practitioners; 1,200 mems; Pres. Prof. VAJIRA H. W. DISSANAYAKE; Hon. Sec. Dr LASANTHA MALAWIGE; publs *Abstracts of Anniversary Academic Sessions* (1 a year), *Ceylon Medical Journal* (4 a year).

NATURAL SCIENCES

General

Sri Lanka Association for the Advancement of Science: 'Vidya Mandiraya', 120/10 Wijerama Rd, Colombo 7; tel. (11) 2688740; e-mail hqslaas@gmail.com; internet www .slaas.org; f. 1944; provides systematic direction of scientific enquiry; promotes contact among scientific workers; disseminates scientific knowledge; holds annual session; 7 secs; 6,000 mems; Gen. Pres. Prof. S. W. KOTAGAMA; Gen. Sec. Dr M. M. M. NAJIM; Gen. Sec Prof. NILANTHI BANDARA; publs *Proceedings*, *Vidya Viyapthi*, *Vingnana Murusu*.

PHILOSOPHY AND PSYCHOLOGY

Ceylon Humanist Society: Rutnam Inst. Bldg, Univ. Lane, Jaffna; Pres. J. T. RUTNAM; Sec. O. M. DE ALWIS.

RELIGION, SOCIOLOGY AND ANTHROPOLOGY

Buddhist Academy of Ceylon: 109 Rosmead Pl., Colombo.

Maha Bodhi Society of Sri Lanka: 130 Rev. Hikkaduwe Sri Sumangala Nahimi Mawatha, Colombo 10; tel. (11) 2677626; e-mail banagalaupatissa@gmail.com; f. 1891; propagates Buddhism throughout the world; 900 mems; Pres. BANAGALA UPATISSA NAYAKA THERO; Hon. Sec. B. H. M. RATNASIRI; publ. *Sinhala Bauddhaya* (12 a year).

TECHNOLOGY

Institution of Engineers, Sri Lanka: 120/ 15 Wijerama Mawatha, Colombo 7; tel. (11) 2698426; e-mail es@iesl.lk; internet www.iesl .lk; f. 1956; provides a forum for engineers of all disciplines; promotes advancement of science and practice of engineering; 7,273 mems; library of 12,000 vols; Pres. ANANDA RANASINGHE; Exec. Sec. ARUNDHATI WIMALASURIYA; publs *Engineer* (3 a year), *Sri Lanka Engineering News* (12 a year), *Transactions* (1 a year).

Research Institutes

AGRICULTURE, FISHERIES AND VETERINARY SCIENCE

Coconut Research Institute: Bandirippuwa Estate, Lunuwila 61150; tel. (31) 2255300; e-mail director@cri.lk; internet www.cri.lk; f. 1929; quasi-governmental research institute serving coconut industry of Sri Lanka; library: see Libraries and Archives; Chair. Dr NIMAL WEERASINGHE; Dir Dr C. JAYASEKARE; publs *COCOS* (4 a year), *Coco News* (3 a year).

Hector Kobbekaduwa Agrarian Research and Training Institute: 114 Wijerama Mawatha, POB 1522, Colombo 7; tel. (11) 2696981; e-mail hartilib@sltnet.lk; internet www.harti.lk; f. 1972; attached to Min. of Agriculture; research into and policy analysis on agrarian structures and the economic, social and institutional aspects of agricultural devt; operates training programmes; library: see Libraries and Archives; Dir Prof. PREMALAL DE SILVA; publ. *Sri Lanka Journal of Agrarian Studies* (2 a year, in English and Sinhala).

Horticultural Research and Development Institute: Gannoruwa, Peradeniya; tel. (81) 2288011; e-mail directorhordi@ gmail.com; internet www.agridep.gov.lk; f. 1965; research on fruit, vegetables, roots and tubers, other horticultural crops, ornamental flowers and soya-processing; library of 10,854 vols; Dir W. M. K. B. WAHUNDENIYA; publ. *Tropical Agriculturist* (1 a year).

National Aquatic Resources Research and Development Agency: Crow Island, Colombo 15; tel. (11) 2521000; e-mail dg@ nara.ac.lk; internet www.nara.ac.lk; f. 1981;

research in fisheries and aquatic resources; library of 350 vols; Chair. Dr S. G. SAMAR-ASUNDARA; Dir-Gen. M. D. I. B. GAMAGE; publ. *NARA Journal* (1 a year).

Rice Research and Development Institute: Batalagoda, Ibbagamuwa; tel. (37) 2222681; e-mail rice@rrdi.ac.lk; f. 1994; Dir S. ABEYSIRIWARDENE.

Rubber Research Institute of Sri Lanka Library: Dartonfield, Agalawatta 12200; tel. (34) 2247426; internet www.rrisl.lk; f. 1953; Colombo office and laboratories: Telawala Rd, Ratmalana, Mt Lavinia; research and advisory services on rubber-planting and manufacture; comprises 10 research depts, biometry section, adaptive research unit, extension dept and economic research unit, specification unit and estate dept; library of 10,500 vols, 275 periodical titles; Dir Dr W. M. G. SENEVIRATNA; publs *Journal* (1 a year), *Rubber Puwath* (1 a year).

Tea Research Institute of Sri Lanka: St Coombs, Talawakelle; tel. (52) 2258201; e-mail info@tri.lk; internet www.tri.lk; f. 1925; generates and disseminates new technologies related to tea cultivation and processing; library: see under Libraries and Archives; Dir I. SARATH B. ABESINGHE; publs *Sri Lanka Journal of Tea Science* (2 a year), *Tea Quarterly*, *TRI Update* (2 a year).

Veterinary Research Institute: POB 28, Gannoruwa, Peradeniya; tel. (81) 22388312; e-mail info@vri.lk; internet www.vri.lk; f. 1911 as Veterinary diagnostic laboratory, present name and status 1967; concerned with research and investigations into health and production problems of livestock and poultry; veterinary vaccine production; Dir Dr B. D. R. WIJEWARDHANA; publ. *Sri Lanka Veterinary Journal* (4 a year).

ECONOMICS, LAW AND POLITICS

Economic Research Unit: Business Intelligence Dept, Bank of Ceylon, Colombo; Business Intelligence Officer S. E. A. JAYA-WICKREMA.

Institute of Policy Studies of Sri Lanka: 100/20 Independence Ave, Colombo; tel. (11) 2143100; e-mail ips@ips.lk; internet www.ips .lk; f. 1988; conducts policy-oriented economic research; Exec. Dir SAMAN KELEGAMA; publ. *Sri Lanka State of the Economy Report* (1 a year).

Marga Institute Centre for Development Studies: 941/1 Jayanthi Mawatha, Kotte Rd, Ethul Kotte 1; tel. (11) 2888790; e-mail library@margasrilanka.org; internet www .margasrilanka.org; f. 1972; non-profit multidisciplinary research org. undertaking critical, non-partisan study of devt issues in Sri Lanka and the wider Asian region; library of 24,800 vols, 50 periodicals; Chair. MANGALA MOONESINGHE; Chair. Emeritus Dr GODFREY GUNATILLEKE; Vice-Chair. MYRTLE PERERA; Head of Library and Information Services DEEPALI TALAGALA; publs *Marga Monograph Series on Ethnic Reconciliation*, *The Marga Quarterly Journal*.

Wiros Lokh Institute: 81-1A Isipatana Mawatha, Colombo 5; tel. (11) 2580817; e-mail wiroshermes@yahoo.com; internet www.socialreit.org; f. 1981, operationally merged with Capital Markets for the Marginalized Inc. (USA) and Capital for the Marginalized Ltd (Singapore); private research and training foundation; promotes awareness of globalization in the region; spec. projects: innovation in social housing and financing, urban regeneration and sports recreation for urban areas; capital markets, spices, silks and other traditional crafts; 75 mems; library of 20,000 vols; Chair. Dr DARIN GUNESEKERA;

Dir of Child Rights Div. CHANDRIKA GUNESE-KERA; Gen. Exec. ABHEYAPALA DE SILVA.

EDUCATION

National Institute of Education: POB 21, High Level Rd, Maharagama; tel. (11) 7601601; e-mail info@nie.lk; internet www .nie.lk; f. 1986; conducts policy research on education; designs and develops curricula for general and teacher education; provides professional devt of educational community; Dir-Gen. Prof. W. M. ABEYRATNE BANDARA.

HISTORY, GEOGRAPHY AND ARCHAEOLOGY

Archaeological Survey Department of Sri Lanka: Sir Marcus Fernando Rd, Colombo 7; tel. (11) 4694727; e-mail arch@ diamond.lanka.net; f. 1890; library of 15,000 vols; Dir-Gen. Dr SENARATH DISSANAYAKE; publs *Administration Report* (1 a year), *Ancient Ceylon* (1 a year), *Memoirs*.

MEDICINE

Institute of Indigenous Medicine: Univ. of Colombo, Rajagiriya; tel. (11) 2692385; e-mail director@iim.cmb.ac.lk; internet iim .cmb.ac.lk; f. 1977; attached to Univ. of Colombo; research areas incl. Ayurveda, Unani, indigenous system of medicine; library of 28,000 vols; Dir Dr M. W. S. J. KUMARI (acting).

Medical Research Institute: POB 527, Colombo 8; tel. (11) 2693532; e-mail director@mri.gov.lk; internet www.mri.gov .lk; f. 1900; research in animal studies, bacteriology, biochemistry, entomology, haematology, histo-pathology, immunology, molecular biology, mycology, nutrition, parasitology, pharmacology, rabies, virology; Dir Dr ANIL SAMARANAYAKE.

NATURAL SCIENCES

Biological Sciences

Department of Wildlife Conservation: 811A, Jayanthipura Rd, Battatamula, Colombo 7; tel. (11) 2888585; e-mail dg@dwc .gov.lk; internet www.dwc.gov.lk; f. 1950; promotes scientific research relevant to management of wildlife resources in Sri Lanka; library of 1,962 vols; Dir-Gen. H. D. RATNAYAKE; publs *Sri Lanka WildLife*, *Vana Divi* (1 a year), *National Parks of Sri Lanka*.

Physical Sciences

Department of Meteorology: 383 Bauddhaloka, Mawatha, Colombo 7; tel. (11) 2694846; e-mail meteo@slt.lk; internet www .meteo.gov.lk; f. 1948; climatological data for Sri Lanka; time service; astronomical service; weather-forecasting; agrometeorological service; weather services to gen. public, the agricultural, aviation, energy sectors, fisheries, shipping sectors; research in meteorology, climatology, climate change and allied subjects; library of 18,000 vols; Dir Dr G. B. SAMARASINGHE; publs *Agrometeorological Bulletin* (4 a year), *Monthly Weather Review* (12 a year), *Report of the Department of Meteorology* (1 a year).

TECHNOLOGY

Geological Survey and Mines Bureau: Senanayake Bldg, 4 Galle Rd, Dehiwala; tel. (11) 2739307; internet www.gsmb.sit.lk; f. 1903; systematic geological mapping of Sri Lanka; identification and assessment of its mineral resources; issues licences to regulate exploration, mining, processing, transport, trading in and export of minerals; Chair. Dr N. P. WIJAYANANDA (acting); Dir-Gen. B. A. PEIRIS; publs *Memoirs*, *Mineral Year Book*.

Industrial Technology Institute: 363 Bauddhaloka Mawatha, Colombo 7; tel. (11) 2379800; e-mail info@iti.lk; internet iti.lk; f. 1955 as Ceylon Institute of Scientific and Industrial Research; current name adopted 1998; attached to Min. of Technology and Research; applied technical research in several industrial sectors for government agencies and the public; process research, resource studies, waste material utilization, product testing, standards, calibration and repair of instruments, technical consultation; industrial devt; information services centre; library: see under Libraries and Archives; Chair Prof. VIJAYA KUMAR; Dir Dr A. M. MUBARAK.

National Science Foundation: 47/5 Maitland Pl., Colombo 7; tel. (11) 2696771; e-mail dir@nsf.ac.lk; internet www.nsf.ac.lk; f. 1968 as Nat. Science Ccl, present name and status 1998; attached to Min. of Technology and Research; initiates, facilitates and supports basic and applied scientific research by univs, scientific and technological instns and scientists; fosters the interchange of scientific information among scientists in Sri Lanka and foreign countries; awards scholarships and fellowships for scientific study or work at appropriate instns; provides a central clearing house for the colln and analysis of data on the scientific and technical resources in Sri Lanka; provides information for policy formulation on science and technology; promotes popularization of science; documentation and publs unit; acts as nat. research reports depository on science and technology; library of 7,250 vols; Chair. Prof. SIRIMALI FERNANDO; Exec. Dir SUNETHRA PERERA (acting); publs *Journal of the National Science Foundation* (4 a year), *Sri Lanka Journal of Social Sciences* (2 a year).

Sri Lanka Water Resources Board: 2A Hector Kobbekaduwa Ave, Colombo 7; tel. (11) 2697050; e-mail wrbmiwm@sltnet.lk; f. 1966; advises the Govt on all matters concerning conservation and utilization of water resources; undertakes hydro geological investigation and groundwater devt projects; library of 4,620 vols, 60 periodicals; Chair. K. YOGANATHAN.

Libraries and Archives

Agalawatta

Rubber Research Institute of Sri Lanka Library: Dartonfield, Agalawatta; br. library: Telawala Rd, Ratmalana; tel. (34) 2247426; e-mail dirrri@sltnet.lk; internet www.rrisl.lk; f. 1953; collects and disseminates information on natural rubber and related areas; 10,000 vols, 255 periodical titles; Librarian S. U. AMARASINGHE; publs *Journal of the Rubber Research Institute of Sri Lanka* (1 a year), *Rubber Puwath* (1 a year).

Colombo

Centre for Development Information: National Planning Dept, Min. of Finance and Planning, POB 1547, Galleface Secretariat, Colombo 1; tel. (11) 2484609; e-mail cdi@npd.treasury.gov.lk; internet www .treasury.gov.lk/epprm/npd/cdinew.htm; f. 1979; participates in regional information networks, and maintains an int. exchange programme; nat. focal point for SAARC Documentation Centre, New Delhi, India; coordinates and collates socio-economic information; 25,000 vols, unpublished report colln; Sr Librarian I. HENDAVITHARANA; publs *Bibliography of Economic and Social Development in Sri Lanka*, *Current Acquisitions* (4 a year), *Guide to Current Periodical Litera-*

ture in Economic and Social Development (4 a year), *Register of Development Research in Sri Lanka.*

Colombo National Museum Library: POB 854, Colombo 7; tel. (11) 2693314; f. 1877 (incorporating colln of Govt Oriental Library, f. 1870); depository for Sri Lanka publns since 1885; 12m. vols (incl. 141,703 monographs, 4,500 periodical titles, 3,772 palm leaf MSS in Sinhala, Sanskrit, Pali, Burmese and Cambodian); Chief Librarian I. P. K. KUMARASIRI; publs *Sri Lanka Periodicals Index*, *Sri Lanka Periodicals Directory*, *Bibliographical Series.*

Colombo Public Library: 15 Sir Marcus Fernando Mawatha, Colombo 7; tel. (11) 2691968; e-mail colombopublibrary@yahoo .com; internet www.colombopubliclibrary .org; f. 1925; 15 brs; 2 mobile libraries; spec. collns: Sri Lanka, Buddhism, FAO Depository, fine arts, Braille, Japan, Theo Auer colln; 10m. vols, 2,000 periodical titles; Chief Librarian VARUNI GANGABADAARACHCHI; publ. *Administration Report* (1 a year).

Department of National Archives: POB 1414, 7 Philip Gunawardena Mawatha, Colombo 7; tel. (11) 4694523; e-mail narchive@slt.lk; internet www.archives.gov .lk; f. 1902; contains official records of the Dutch admin. from 1640 to 1796, British admin. from 1796 to 1948; official records of ind. Sri Lanka since 1948; codices of Portuguese admin. prior to 1656 and some documents in Dutch, English, Sinhalese and Tamil; operates a Presidential Archival Depository and a Reference Service; deals with documents in private possession; legal depository for all printed material in the country, effects the registration of printing presses, printed publs, newspapers; holds copies of books printed since 1885 and newspapers since 1832; Dir Dr SAROJA WETTA-SINGHE; publs *Administration Report of The National Archives*, *Catalogue of Newspapers* (1 a year), *Catalogue of Printing Presses* (1 a year), *Quarterly Statement of Books printed in Sri Lanka*, *Sri Lanka Archives* (1 a year).

Hector Kobbekaduwa Agrarian Research and Training Institute Library: POB 1522, 114 Wijerama Mawatha, Colombo 7; tel. (11) 4696981; e-mail hartilib@sltnet.lk; internet www .harti.lk/en/divisions/library; f. 1972; several hundred reports and reprints; spec. colln on Sri Lanka; part of Nat. Centre for Information on Agrarian Devt; 21,000 vols, 20,000 journals; Librarian S. L. KATUGAMPOLA.

Industrial Technology Institute Information Services Centre: 363 Bauddhaloka Mawatha, Colombo 7; tel. (11) 2379807; e-mail info@iti.lk; internet iti.lk/ information; f. 1955; several thousand reports, reprints, standards; information service to scientists, industrialists and engineers; computer database of books and articles in periodicals; nat. centre of Asian and Pacific Information Network on medicinal and aromatic plants; 35,000 vols, 300 journals; Head of Information Services Centre SURANEE M. SAMARASEKERA; publs *Bibliographical Services*, *State of the Art surveys on spices and essential oilbearing plants*, *News Digest*, *Food Digest*, *S & T News*, *Management Thought.*

Law Library: Hultsdorp, Colombo 12; tel. (11) 4324676; f. 1855; Dir A. COOREY.

National Library and Documentation Centre: 14 Independence Ave, Colombo 7; tel. (11) 2685203; e-mail libservice@mail .natlib.lk; internet www.natlib.lk; f. 1990; spec. collns: Ola Leaf colln, drama MS colln, library and information science colln, Martin Wickramasinghe colln, folklore colln; ISBN, ISMN and ISSN nat. centres; compiles Nat.

Union Catalogue and Online Public Access Catalogue (OPAC); 300,000 vols (incl. govt publs), 500 periodical titles, 6,000 microforms, 1,800 maps, audiovisual items, electronic media; Dir-Gen. N. H. M. CHITHRANANDA (acting); Dir of Documentation Services Div. G. D. AMARASIRI; Dir of Library Services Div. N. MALLAWA ARACHCHI; publs *Directory of Government Publications*, *Devolution of Power and Ethnic Problems* (database), *Library News* (4 a year), *Index to Postgraduate Theses*, *ISBN Publishers Directory*, *Natnet Lanka Newsletter*, *Periodical Article Index* (4 a year), *Sri Lanka National Bibliography* (12 a year), *Sri Lanka Newspaper Index.*

University of Colombo Library: POB 1698, Colombo 7; tel. (11) 2583043; e-mail sumanaj@lib.cmb.ac.lk; internet www.lib .cmb.ac.lk; f. 1942; 400,000 vols, 970 periodicals; Librarian D. C. KURUPPU (acting); publs *Ceylon Journal of Medical Science* (2 a year), *Colombo Law Review* (1 a year), *Sri Lanka Journal of International Law* (1 a year), *University of Colombo Review* (1 a year).

Lunuwila

Coconut Research Institute Library: Lunuwila; tel. (31) 2253795; e-mail library@ cri.lk; internet www.cri.lk; f. 1929; houses Int. Coconut Information Centre; spec. colln of world literature on the coconut available in hard copy; microfiches, diskettes; 35,000 vols; Librarian P. D. U. C. DHARMAPALA (acting); publ. *Cocos.*

Moratuwa

Centre for Entrepreneurship Development and Consultancy Services: I. D. B., 615 Galle Rd, Katubedda, Moratuwa 10400; tel. (11) 2605372; e-mail idb@sltnet.lk; internet www.idb.gov.lk; f. 1969; acquisition, processing of library materials, dissemination of industrial information, reference and enquiry services, consultancy services; 20,000 vols, 25 current periodicals; Librarian SWARNA WIJEKOON (acting); publ. *New Arrivals* (12 a year).

Peradeniya

University of Peradeniya Library: POB 35, Peradeniya; Univ. of Peradeniya, Peradeniya 20400; tel. (81) 2392470; e-mail librarian@pdn.ac.lk; internet www.lib.pdn.ac .lk; f. 1921; collns incl. deposit materials obtained under printers' and publishers' ordinance since 1955, reference colln on Sri Lanka, palm-leaf MSS and rare materials on Sri Lanka, and collns on environmental and religious studies; 1m. vols; Librarian Dr P. WIJETUNGE; publs *Ceylon Journal of Science—Biological Sciences*, *Ceylon Journal of Science—Physical Sciences*, *Sri Lanka Journal of the Humanities*, *Modern Sri Lanka Studies.*

Talawakele

Tea Research Institute Library: St Coombs, Talawakelle; tel. (52) 2258201; e-mail info@tri.lk; internet www.tri.lk; f. 1925; collects and disseminates information on tea and allied subjects; 25,000 vols and 250 periodicals for reference and loan, incl. spec. reference section; Librarian (vacant); publ. *Sri Lanka Journal of Tea Science* (2 a year).

Museums and Art Galleries

Anuradhapura

Anuradhapura Folk Museum: Old Town, Anuradhapura; tel. (25) 2234624; f. 1971; regional museum for North Central Province; Curator L. H. D. M. HETTIARCHCHI.

Colombo

Dutch Museum: Prince St, Colombo 1; tel. (11) 2448466; f. 1982; 3,000 objects related to the Dutch rule 1658–1796.

Colombo National Museum: POB 854, Sir Marcus Fernando Mawatha, Colombo 7; tel. (11) 2694366; e-mail ranjith.s.hewage@yahoo .com; f. 1877 as Colombo Museum; nat. colln of art, antiquities and folk culture; research centre; Museum Keeper S. H. RANJITH.

National Museum of Natural History: Ananda Coomaraswamy Mawatha, Colombo 7; tel. (11) 2691399; e-mail nmnh_dnm@ yahoo.com; f. 1986; nat. colln of natural sciences; Museum Keeper K. A. NAYANA DARSHANI PERERA.

Galle

Galle National Museum: Church St, Galle; tel. (91) 2232051; f. 1986; collns incl. traditional masks, ornamental objects made from turtle shells, ancient wooden carvings; large water vessels, porcelain objects, arms and weapons used by Dutch soldiers.

Kandy

Kandy National Museum: Dharmapala Mawatha, Kandy; tel. (81) 2223867; f. 1942; regional museum for the Central Province; 17th- to 18th-century Kandyan history; Museum Keeper K. D. V. CHANDIMAL.

Peradeniya

Royal Botanic Gardens: Peradeniya; tel. (81) 2388088; e-mail royalbotanicgardens@ yahoo.com; internet www.botanicgardens .gov.lk/peradeniya; f. 1821; botanical survey of Sri Lanka, floriculture research and devt; education and training; Deputy Dir ACHALA ATTANAYAKE; Curator P. D. S. WIJERATNE.

Ratnapura

Ratnapura National Museum: Ehelapola Walauwa, Colombo Rd, Ratnapura; tel. (45) 2252451; e-mail pradeep_t@yahoo.com; f. 1988; regional museum for the Sabaragamuwa Province; prehistoric archaeological inventions, natural heritage, geological, anthropological, zoological artefacts and models; Museum Keeper KUMARASIRI THEN-NEGEDARA.

Universities

EASTERN UNIVERSITY

Vantharumoolai, Chenkaladi

Telephone: (65) 2240490
E-mail: aradmin@esn.ac.lk
Internet: www.esn.ac.lk

Founded 1981 as Batticaloa Univ. College, current name adopted 1986
State control
Languages of instruction: English, Tamil
Academic year: January to December
Chancellor: Dr T. VARAGUNAM
Vice-Chancellor: Prof. M. S. MOOKIAH
Registrar: A. D. HARRIS (acting)
Sr Asst Librarian: T. ARULNANDHY
Library of 60,000 vols
Number of teachers: 100
Number of students: 2,420 (1,513 internal, 907 external)

DEANS

Faculty of Agriculture: S. RAVEENDRANATH
Faculty of Arts and Culture: A. MURUGATHAS (acting)
Faculty of Commerce and Management: S. SENTHILNATHAN
Faculty of Science: Dr J. C. N. RAJENDRA

GENERAL SIR JOHN KOTELAWALA DEFENCE UNIVERSITY

Kandawala Estate, Rathmalana
Telephone: (11) 2635268
E-mail: kdudefence@kdu.ac.lk
Internet: www.kdu.ac.lk
Founded 1980, fmrly Gen. Sir John Kotelawala Defence Acad., present name and status 2008
State control
Chancellor: ROHAN DE SILVA DALUWATTE
Vice-Chancellor: MILINDA PEIRIS
Deputy Vice-Chancellor for Academic Affairs: Prof. Dr RAVINDRA LAL WEERARATNE KOGGALAGE
Registrar: H. G. U. KARIYAWASAM
Librarian: T. C. RANAWELLA (acting)
Offers bachelor degree courses in engineering, law, logistic management, management and technical sciences, medicine and surgery

OPEN UNIVERSITY OF SRI LANKA

POB 21, Nawala, Nugegoda 10250
Telephone: (11) 2881000
E-mail: pio@ou.ac.lk
Internet: www.ou.ac.lk
Founded 1980
State control
Languages of instruction: English, Sinhala, Tamil
Chancellor: SAM S. WIJESINGHE
Vice-Chancellor: Prof. UPALI VIDANAPATHIRANA
Deputy Vice-Chancellor: Dr JANAKA LIYANAGAMA
Registrar: VINDHYA JAYASENA
Librarian: Dr WATHMANEL SENEVIRATNE
Library of 92,000 vols
Number of teachers: 300
Number of students: 19,300
Publication: *Open University Review of Engineering Technology*

DEANS

Faculty of Education: Prof. G. DAYALATHA LEKAMGE
Faculty of Engineering Technology: Prof. W. A. WIMALAWEERA
Faculty of Humanities and Social Sciences: Dr MAHIM MENDIS
Faculty of Natural Sciences: Dr GAYA RANAWAKA

RAJARATA UNIVERSITY OF SRI LANKA

Mihintale
Telephone: (25) 2266650
E-mail: rajalib@sltnet.lk
Internet: www.rjt.ac.lk
Founded 1996
State control
Languages of instruction: Sinhala, English
Chancellor: Prof. A. V. SURAWEERA
Vice-Chancellor: Prof. K. A. NANDASENA
Registrar: A. G. KARUNARATHNE
Librarian: A. S. SIRIWARDHANE
Library of 43,000 vols
Number of teachers: 150
Number of students: 2,500

DEANS

Faculty of Agriculture: Prof. P. A. WEERASINGHE
Faculty of Applied Sciences: Dr M. M. GOONASEKARA
Faculty of Management Studies: Prof. RANJITH WIJEYAWARDANE
Faculty of Social Sciences and Humanities: Prof. A. LAGAMUWA

SABARAGAMUWA UNIVERSITY OF SRI LANKA

POB 02, Belihuloya 70140
Telephone: (45) 2280014
E-mail: ccs@sab.ac.lk
Internet: www.sab.ac.lk
Founded 1996
State control
Language of instruction: English
Chancellor: Prof. KUBURUGAMUWE VAJIRA THERO
Vice-Chancellor: Prof. MAHINDA S. RUPASINGHE
Registrar: K. M. NAVARATHNE BANDA (acting)
Librarian: T. N. NEIGHSOOREI
Library of 116,070 vols, 262 periodical titles
Publications: *Journal of Agricultural Sciences* (3 a year), *Sabaragamuwa University Journal* (1 a year), *Sinhala Journal*

DEANS

Faculty of Agricultural Sciences: Dr ASANGA D. AMPITIYAWATTA
Faculty of Applied Sciences: Dr M. NIRMALI WICKRAMARATHNE
Faculty of Geomatics: Dr K. R. M. U. BANDARA
Faculty of Management Studies: R. M. WASANTHA RATHNAYAKE
Faculty of Social Sciences and Languages: Prof. M. SUNIL SHANTHA

SOUTH EASTERN UNIVERSITY OF SRI LANKA

Univ. Park, Oluvil 32360
Telephone: (67) 2255138
E-mail: vcoffice@seu.ac.lk
Internet: www.seu.ac.lk
Founded 1995 at Addalaichenai as South Eastern Univ. College; present name, status and location 1996
State control
Languages of instruction: English, Tamil
Chancellor: Prof. ACHI M. ISHAQ
Vice-Chancellor: Dr S. M. MOHAMED ISMAIL
Registrar: H. ABDUL SATHTHAR
Librarian: M. M. RIFAUDEEN (acting)
Library of 45,000 books, 20 periodicals
Number of teachers: 120
Number of students: 1,270
Publication: *Journal of Management* (1 a year)

DEANS

Faculty of Applied Sciences: Dr M. I. S. SAFEENA
Faculty of Arts and Culture: S. M. ALIFF
Faculty of Islamic Studies and Arabic Language: M. S. M. JALALDEEN
Faculty of Management and Commerce: M. B. M. AMJATH

UNIVERSITY OF COLOMBO

94 Cumaratunga Munidasa Mawatha, Colombo 3
Telephone: (11) 2581835
E-mail: registrar@admin.cmb.ac.lk
Internet: www.cmb.ac.lk
Founded 1921, current name adopted 1979
State control

Languages of instruction: English, Sinhala, Tamil
Academic year: October to September
Chancellor: Rev. Dr OSWALD GOMIS
Vice-Chancellor: Prof. KSHANIKA HIRIMBUREGAMA
Registrar: T. L. R. SILVA (acting)
Rector of Sripalee Campus: Dr TUDOR WEERASINGHE
Librarian: D. C. KURUPPU (acting)
Library: see under Libraries and Archives
Number of teachers: 450
Number of students: 9,160
Publications: *The Ceylon Journal of Medical Science* (2 a year), *University of Colombo Review* (1 a year), *University Calendar* (every 3 years)

DEANS

Faculty of Arts: Prof. INDRALAL DE SILVA
Faculty of Education: Prof. MARIE E. S. PERERA
Faculty of Law: N. SELVAKKUMARAN
Faculty of Management and Finance: H. D. KARUNARATHNE
Faculty of Medicine: Prof. ROHAN JAYASEKARA
Faculty of Science: Prof. T. R. ARIYARATNE
Faculty of Graduate Studies: Prof. SUNIL CHANDRASIRI

UNIVERSITY OF JAFFNA

POB 57, Thirunelvely, Jaffna
Telephone: (21) 2222483
E-mail: ujvc@mail.ewisl.net
Internet: www.jfn.ac.lk
Founded 1974, current name adopted 1978
State control
Languages of instruction: English, Tamil
Academic year: October to July
Chancellor: Prof. M. SIVASURIYA
Vice-Chancellor: Prof. VASANTHY ARASARATNAM
Registrar: VISVANATHAN KANDEEPAN
Librarian: SRIKANTHALUXMY ARULANANTHAM (acting)
Library of 198,960 vols
Number of teachers: 450
Number of students: 5,150
Publications: *Cintanai* (4 a year), *Jaffna Dry Zone Agriculture* (2 a year), *Journal of Business Studies* (2 a year), *Journal of Science and Management* (1 a year), *Journal of South Asian Studies* (1 a year), *Vingnanam*

DEANS

Faculty of Agriculture: Dr G. MIHINTHAN
Faculty of Applied Science (Vavuniya Campus): Dr S. KRISHNAKUMAR
Faculty of Arts: Prof. V. P. SIVANATHAN
Faculty of Business Studies (Vavuniya Campus): Dr T. MANGALESWARAN
Faculty of Graduate Studies: Prof. S. SATHIASEELAN
Faculty of Management Studies and Commerce: Prof. T. VELNAMBY
Faculty of Medicine: Dr S. BALAKUMAR
Faculty of Science: Prof. K. KANDASAMY

PROFESSORS

ARASARATNAM, V., Biochemistry
GNANAKUMARAN, N., Philosophy
KANDASAMY, K., Physics
KRISHNARAJAH, S., History
KUGABALAN, K., Geography
KUMARAVADIVEL, R., Physics
MANIVASAKAR, A. V., Political Science
MIKUNTHAN, G., Agricultural Biology
PILENDRAN, G., Christian Civilization
PUSHPARATNAM, P., History
RAGUNATHAN, M., Tamil
RAMANATHAN, K., Hindu Civilization
RAVIRAJAN, P., Physics

SATHIASEELAN, S., History
SHANMUGALINGAM, N., Sociology
SINNATHAMBY, M., Education
SRISATKUNARAJAH, S., Mathematics
VELNAMBY, T., Accounting
VETHANATHAN, M., Hindu Civilization
VISAKARUBAN, K., Tamil

UNIVERSITY OF KELANIYA

Kelaniya 11600
Telephone: (11) 2903903
E-mail: vcoffice@kln.ac.lk
Internet: www.kln.ac.lk

Founded 1875 as Vidayalankara Pirivena; Univ. status 1959; reorganized 1972 as a campus of Univ. of Sri Lanka; current name adopted 1978
State control
Languages of instruction: English, Sinhala
Chancellor: KUSALA DHAMMA THERO
Vice-Chancellor: Prof. SARATH AMUNUGAMA
Registrar: W. M. KARUNARATHNE
Librarian: Dr L. A. JAYATISSA
Library of 210,000 vols
Number of teachers: 525
Number of students: 8,696

Publications: *Journal of the Faculty of Humanities* (1 a year), *Journal of the Faculty of Social Science* (1 a year), *Kalyani* (1 a year)

DEANS

Faculty of Commerce And Management Studies: Dr D. M. SEMASINGHE
Faculty of Graduate Studies: Prof. M. GUNESEKERA
Faculty of Humanities: Prof. LAKSHMAN SENEVIRATHNE
Faculty of Medicine: Prof. N. R. DE SILVA
Faculty of Science: Prof. D. D. S. KULATHUNGA
Faculty of Social Science: Prof. A. H. M. H. ABAYARATHNE

PROFESSORS

ARIYARATNE, M. H. J., Surgery
DEEN, K. I., Surgery
DE SILVA, D. G. H., Paediatrics
DE SILVA, H. J., Medicine
DE SILVA, N. R., Parasitology
EDIRISINGHE, D., Philosophy
GUNASEKERA, M., English
HEWAVISENTHI, S. J., Pathology
JAYASEKARA, L. R., Botany
KUMARASINGHE, K., Sinhala
KURUPPUARACHCHI, K. A. L. A., Psychiatry
PARANAGAMA, P. A., Chemistry
RAJAPAKSHA, R. M. W.
SIRIPALA, W. P., Physics
SUGATHARATHANA, V. K., Sanskrit
SUMANAPALA, G. D., Pali and Buddhist Studies
SUNILCHANDRA, N. P., Microbiology
TENNAKOON, K. U. A., Economics
WICKRAMASINGHE, A. R., Public Health
WIJESINGHE, P. S., Obstetrics and Gynaecology
WIJEYARATNE, M. J. S., Zoology

UNIVERSITY OF MORATUWA

Katubedda, Moratuwa
Telephone: (11) 2650441
E-mail: info@mrt.ac.lk
Internet: www.mrt.ac.lk

Founded 1893 as Government Technical School, current name adopted 1978
State control
Language of instruction: English
Academic year: October to September
Chancellor: Dr ROLAND SILVA
Vice-Chancellor: Prof. K. A. K. W. JAYAWARDANE

Deputy Vice-Chancellor: Prof. R. A. ATTALAGE
Registrar: A. L. JOUFER SADIQUE
Librarian: R. C. KODIKARA
Library of 85,000 vols, 300 journals
Number of teachers: 280
Number of students: 5,450

Publications: *Ambalama*, *Development Planning Review* (4 a year), *Tampitavihara*

DEANS

Faculty of Architecture: Prof. P. K. S. MAHANAMA
Faculty of Engineering: Prof. U. G. A. PUSWEWALA
Faculty of Information Technology: Prof. A. S. KARUNANANDA (acting)

UNIVERSITY OF PERADENIYA

Univ. Park, Peradeniya 20400
Telephone: (81) 2388301
E-mail: vc@pdn.ac.lk
Internet: www.pdn.ac.lk

Founded 1942 by incorporation of Ceylon Medical College (f. 1870) and Ceylon Univ. College (f. 1921); reorganized 1972, current name adopted 1978
State control
Languages of instruction: English, Sinhala, Tamil
Academic year: October to September
Chancellor: Dr PREMADASA UDAGAMA
Vice-Chancellor: Prof. S. B. S. ABAYAKOON
Deputy Vice-Chancellor: Prof. K. PREMARATNE
Registrar: U. D. DODANWELA (acting)
Librarian: Dr P. WIJETUNGE
Library: see under Libraries and Archives
Number of teachers: 750
Number of students: 9,500

Publications: *Ceylon Journal of Science*, *Modern Sri Lanka Studies*, *Sri Lanka Journal of Biological Science*, *Sri Lanka Journal of Humanities*, *Sri Lanka Journal of Physical Science*

DEANS

Faculty of Agriculture: Dr K. SAMARASINGHE
Faculty of Allied Health Sciences: Dr D. B. M. WICKRAMARATNE
Faculty of Arts: Dr A. ABHAYARATNE
Faculty of Dental Sciences: Dr U. B. DISSANAYAKE
Faculty of Engineering: Prof. S. B. WEERAKOON
Faculty of Medicine: Dr G. BUTHPITIYA
Faculty of Science: Prof. S. H. P. P. KARUNARATNE
Faculty of Veterinary Medicine and Animal Science: Prof. P. ABEYNAYAKE

PROFESSORS

Faculty of Agriculture (tel. (81) 2395010; e-mail deanagri@pdn.ac.lk; internet www.pdn.ac.lk/agri):

BANDARA, J. M. R. S., Agricultural Biology
BOGAHAWATTA, C., Agricultural Economics
CYRIL, H. W., Animal Science
DE COSTA, W. A. J. M., Crop Science
GOONASEKERE, K. G. A., Agricultural Engineering
GUNATHILAKA, H. M., Agricultural Economics
GUNAWARDENA, E. R. N., Agricultural Engineering
IBRAHIM, M. N. M., Animal Science
ILLEPERUMA, D. C. K., Food Science and Technology
JAYAKODY, A. N., Agricultural Soil Science
KUMARAGAMAGE, D., Agricultural Soil Science
MAPA, R. B., Soil Science
PEIRIS, B. C. N., Agricultural Crop Science

PERERA, A. L. T., Agricultural Biology
PERERA, A. N. F., Animal Science
PERERA, E. R. K., Animal Science
SAMARAJEEWA, U., Food Science and Technology
SANGAKKARA, U. R., Agricultural Crop Science
SIVAYOGANATHAN, C., Agricultural Extension
THATTIL, R. O., Crop Science

Faculty of Arts (tel. (81) 2392500; e-mail deanarts@pdn.ac.lk; internet www.pdn.ac.lk/arts):

AMARASINGHE, Y. R., Political Science
DE SILVA, M. W. A., Sociology
GUNATHILAKE, W. M., Sinhala
HENNAYAKE, H. M. S. K., Geography
KARUNATILAKE, P. V. B., History
LIYANAGE, K., Political Science
MADDEGAMA, U. P., Sinhala
MADDUMA BANDARA, C. M., Geography
NUHUMAN, M. A. M., Tamil
PATHMANATHAN, S., History
PERERA, S. W., English
PREMASIRI, P. D., Pali and Buddhist Studies
SAMARANAYAKE, S. V. D. G., Political Science
SENADHEERA, S., Education
SENEVIRATNE, S. D. S., Archaeology
SILVA, K. T., Sociology
SIRISENA, W. M., Sociology
SIRIWEERA, W. S., History
SIVARAJAH, A., Political Science
WEERAKKODY, D. P. M., Classical Languages
WICKRAMASINGHE, A., Geography

Faculty of Dental Sciences (tel. (81) 2387500; e-mail deandental@pdn.ac.lk; internet www.pdn.ac.lk/dental):

AMARATUNGE, N. A. DE S., Oral Surgery
EKANAYAKE, A. N. I., Community Dentistry
EKANAYAKE, S. L., Community Dentistry
MENDIS, B. R. R. N., Oral Pathology
NANAYAKKARA, C. D., Basic Science
WIJEYEWEERA, R. L., Community Dentistry

Faculty of Engineering (tel. (81) 2393000; e-mail deaneng@pdn.ac.lk; internet www.pdn.ac.lk/eng):

AMIRTHANATHAM, G. E., Chemical Engineering
EKANAYAKE, E. M. N., Electrical and Electronic Engineering
HOOLE, S. R. H., Electrical and Electronic Engineering
RANAWEERA, M. P., Civil Engineering
SAMUEL, T. D. M. A., Engineering Mathematics
SENEVIRATNE, K. G. H. C. N., Civil Engineering
SIVASEGARAM, S., Mechanical Engineering

Faculty of Medicine (tel. (81) 2388840; e-mail deanmed@pdn.ac.lk; internet www.med.pdn.ac.lk):

AMARASINGHE, W. I., Obstetrics and Gynaecology
CHANDRASEKERA, M. S., Anatomy
EDIRISINGHE, J. S., Parasitology
NUGEGODA, D. B., Community Medicine
PERERA, P. A. J., Biochemistry
RATNATUNGE, N. V. I., Pathology
RATNARUNGE, P. C. A., Surgery
SENANAYAKE, N., Medicine
THEVANESAN, V., Microbiology
UDUPIHILLE, M., Physiology
WELGAMA, D. J., Parasitology
WIJESUNDARA, M. K. DE S., Parasitology

Faculty of Science (tel. (81) 2388693; e-mail deansci@pdn.ac.lk; internet www.pdn.ac.lk/sci):

ADIKARAM, N. K. B., Botany
BANDARA, B. M. R., Chemistry
BANDARA, H. M. N., Chemistry

CAREEM, M. A., Physics
DAHANAYAKE, K. G. A., Geology
DE SILVA, K. H. G. M., Zoology
DE SILVA, P. K., Chemistry
DISSANAYAKE, C. B., Geology
DISSANAYAKE, M. A. K. L., Physics
EDIRISINGHE, J. P., Zoology
GUNATILLAKE, C. V. S., Botany
GUNATILLAKE, I. A. U. N., Botany
GUNAWARDANA, R. P., Chemistry
ILLEPERUMA, O. A., Chemistry
KARUNARATHN, N. L. V. V., Chemistry
KARUNARATNE, B. S. B., Physics
KARUNARATNE, S. H. P. P., Zoology
KULASOORIYA, S. A., Botany
KUMAR, N. S., Chemistry
KUMAR, V., Chemistry
NAMAL PRIYANTHA, Chemistry
RAJAPAKSHE, R. M. G., Chemistry
SENEVIRATNE, H. H. G., Mathematics
TENNAKOON, D. T. B., Chemistry

Faculty of Veterinary Medicine and Animal Science (tel. (81) 2388205; e-mail deanvet@pdn.ac.lk; internet www.pdn.ac.lk/vet):

ABEYGUNAWARDENA, H., Farm Animal Production and Health
ABEYNAYAKE, P., Veterinary Pathological Biology
GUNAWARDENA, V. K., Veterinary Basic Science
KURUWITA, V. Y., Veterinary Clinical Science
SILVA, I. D., Veterinary Clinical Science

UNIVERSITY OF RUHUNA

Matara
Telephone: (41) 2222681
E-mail: vcsm@admin.ruh.ac.lk
Internet: www.ruh.ac.lk
Founded 1978 as Ruhuna Univ. College, present name 1984
State control
Languages of instruction: Sinhala, English
Academic year: October to September
Chancellor: PALLATHTHARA SUMANAJOTHI NAYAKA THERO
Vice-Chancellor: Prof. SUSIRITH MENDIS
Deputy Vice-Chancellor: Prof. GAMINI SENANAYAKE
Registrar: P. S. KALUGAMA
Librarian: ANANDA KARUNARATNE
Library of 140,000 vols
Number of teachers: 550
Number of students: 5,500
Publication: *Rohana Research Journal*

DEANS

Faculty of Agriculture: Prof. MANGALA DE ZOYSA
Faculty of Engineering: Dr A. M. N. ALAGIYAWANNA
Faculty of Fisheries and Marine Science and Technology: Dr TILAK P. D. GAMAGE
Faculty of Graduate Studies: Prof. L. P. JAYATISSA
Faculty of Humanities and Social Sciences: Prof. P. HEWAGE
Faculty of Management and Finance: Dr P. A. P. SAMANTHA KUMARA
Faculty of Medicine: Dr SAMPATH GUNAWARDENE
Faculty of Science: Prof. W. G. D. DHARMARATNE

UNIVERSITY OF SRI JAYEWARDENEPURA

Gangodawila, Nugegoda
Telephone: (11) 2802022
E-mail: info@sjp.ac.lk
Internet: www.sjp.ac.lk

Founded 1959 as Vidyodaya Univ. of Ceylon; reorganized 1972 as campus of Univ. of Sri Lanka; present name and status 1978
State control
Languages of instruction: Sinhala, English
Chancellor: Rev. Prof. BELLANWILA WIMALARATNE THERO
Vice-Chancellor: Dr N. L. A. KARUNARATNE
Registrar: K. GNANASIRI BRITTO
Librarian: NAYANA WIJAYASUNDARA
Library of 200,000 vols
Number of teachers: 410
Number of students: 8,400
Publications: *Vidyodaya Journal of Sciences*, *Vidyodaya Journal of Social Sciences*

DEANS

Faculty of Applied Sciences: Prof. SUDANTHA LIYANAGE
Faculty of Humanities and Social Sciences: Prof. P. ATHUKORALE
Faculty of Management Studies: Prof. SAMPATH AMARATUNGA
Faculty of Medical Sciences: Prof. MOHAN DE SILVA
Faculty of Graduate Studies: Prof. SWARNA PIYASIRI

PROFESSORS

ABEYSEKARA, A. M., Chemistry
ARIYARATNE, S., Sinhala
BAMUNUARACHCHI, A., Chemistry
DAYANANDA, R. A., Statistics
DE SILVA, W. M. M., Surgery
DERANIYAGALA, S. P., Chemistry
ENDAGAMA, M., History and Archaeology
FERNANDO, D. J. S., Medicine
FERNANDO, D. P. A., Surgery
FERNANDO, G. H., Pharmacology
FERNANDO, S., Microbiology
FERNANDO, W. S., Chemistry
HETTIARATCHI, S. B., History and Archaeology
JANSZ, E. R., Biochemistry
JAYATISSA, W. A., Social Statistics
JAYAWARDENA, M. A. J., Obstetrics and Gynaecology
JIFFRY, M. T. M., Physiology
JINADASA, J., Zoology
KARIYAWASAM, T., Sinhala
KARUNANAYAKE, M. M., Geography
NANDADASA, H. G., Botany
PERERA, B. A. T., Sociology and Anthropology
PERERA, G. A., Pali and Buddhist Studies
PIYASIRI, S., Zoology
RANASINGHE, D. M. S. H. K., Forestry and Environmental Science
TANTRIGODA, D. A., Physics
WARNASOORIYA, N. D., Paediatrics
WEERAKOON, S., Mathematics
WEERASEKARA, D. S., Obstetrics and Gynaecology
WICKRAMASINGHE, S. M. D. N., Biochemistry
WIJAYARATNE, M. W. W., Sinhla
WIJEBANDARA, W. D. C., Pali and Buddhist Studies
WIJEWARDENA, K. A. K. K., Community Medicine and Family Medicine
WITHANA, R. J., Pathology
YAPA, P. A. J., Botany

UNIVERSITY OF THE VISUAL & PERFORMING ARTS

21 Albert Crescent, Colombo 7
Telephone: (11) 2690240
E-mail: vcuvpa@sltnet.lk
Internet: www.vpa.ac.lk
Founded 2005, fmrly Institute of Aesthetic Studies affiliated to Univ. of Kelaniya (f. 1974)
State control
Vice-Chancellor: Prof. JAYASENA KOTTEGODA
Registrar: B. M. DAYAWANSA
Number of teachers: 82

Number of students: 3,085

DEANS
Faculty of Dance and Drama: R. K. ARIYARATHNA
Faculty of Music: B. R. DASSANAYAKA
Faculty of Visual Arts: SARATH CHANDRAJEEWA

UVA WELLASSA UNIVERSITY

Badulla 90000
Telephone: (55) 2226400
E-mail: info@uwu.ac.lk
Internet: www.uwu.ac.lk
Founded 2005
State control
Language of instruction: English
Academic year: October to September
Chancellor: BENGAMUWE DHAMMADINNA THERO
Vice-Chancellor: Prof. RANJITH PREMALAL DE SILVA
Registrar: NILMINI DIYABEDANAGE
Number of teachers: 150
Number of students: 1,950

DEANS
Faculty of Animal Science and Export Agriculture: Dr G. CHANDRASENA
Faculty of Management: Dr O. G. DAYARATNE BANDA
Faculty of Science and Technology: Dr A. M. A. N. B. ATTANAYAKE

WAYAMBA UNIVERSITY OF SRI LANKA

Lional Jayathilake Mawatha, Kanadulla, Kuliyapitiya
Telephone: (37) 2281412
E-mail: vc@wyb.ac.lk
Internet: www.wyb.ac.lk
Founded 1999
State control
Languages of instruction: English, Sinhala
Chancellor: Prof. C. L. V. JAYATHILAKE
Vice-Chancellor: Prof. S. J. B. A. JAYASEKERA
Registrar: E. M. G. EKANAYAKE
Librarian: W. G. P. GAMLATH
Library of 50,171 vols
Number of teachers: 130
Number of students: 2,870

DEANS
Faculty of Agriculture and Plantation Management: Prof. D. P. S. T. G. ATTANAYAKE
Faculty of Applied Sciences: Dr E. M. P. EKANAYAKE
Faculty of Business Studies and Finance: E. S. WICKRAMASINGHE
Faculty of Livestock, Fisheries and Nutrition: Dr M. S. W. DE SILVA

Other Higher Education Institutes

Aquinas University College: 990 Gnanartha Pradeepa Mawatha, Maradana Rd, Colombo 8; tel. (11) 2694014; e-mail rector@aquinas.lk; internet www.aquinas.lk; f. 1954 as Aquinas College of Higher Studies, present name and status 2004; faculties of agriculture, business and financial management, engineering, hospitality management, information technology, linguistics, marketing and management, nursing, professional studies, theology, undergraduate studies; library: 43,000 vols; 150 teachers; 7,500 students; Rector Rev. Dr PLACIDUS DE SILVA; Vice-Rector Rev. Fr NAMAL FERNANDO; Registrar M. L. FERNANDO; publ. *Aquinas Journal* (1 a year).

Ceylon College of Physicians: 341/1 Kotte Rd, Rajagiriya; tel. (11) 2888146; e-mail ccp@eureka.lk; internet ceycollphysicians.org; f. 1967; Pres. Prof. SARATH LEKAMWASAM; Joint Sec Dr C. NIRMALA WIJEKOON; Joint Sec. Dr D. U. S. BULUGAHAPITIYA; publ. *Journal of the Ceylon College of Physicians* (1 a year).

Gampaha Wickramarachchi Ayurveda Institute: Univ. of Kelaniya, Kandy Rd, Yakkala; tel. (33) 2222748; e-mail ayurgmp@sltnet.lk; internet www.kln.ac.lk/institutes/wickramarachchi; f. 1929; attached to Univ. of Kelaniya; offers Bachelors of Ayurveda medicine and surgery; library: 20,000 vols; Dir Prof. JANITHA A. LIYANAGE.

In-Service Training Institute: Gannoruwa, POB 21, Peradeniya; tel. (81) 2288146; f. 1965; agricultural education and training; Dir HENRY GAMAGE.

Institute of Biochemistry, Molecular Biology and Biotechnology: 90 Cumaratunga Munidasa Mawatha, Colombo 3; tel. (11) 2552528; e-mail info@ibmbb.cmb.ac.lk; internet www.ibmbb.lk; f. 2004; attached to Univ. of Colombo; offers courses in molecular life sciences; Dir Prof. KAMANI H. TENNEKOON.

Institute of Human Resource Advancement: Bauddhaloka Mawatha, Colombo; tel. (11) 2503393; e-mail info@ihrauoc.org; internet www.ihra.cmb.ac.lk; attached to Univ. of Colombo; courses offered incl. computer applications in business, driving and road safety instructor training, counselling psychology, geoinformatics, int. business, video-editing and media; Dir Dr W. K. HIRIMBUREGAMA.

Institute of Technology: Katubedda, Moratuwa; tel. (11) 2650064; e-mail tag@civil.mrt.ac.lk; attached to Univ. of Moratuwa; Dir Dr T. A. G. GUNASEKARA.

Jaffna College: Vaddukoddai; tel. (70) 2212531; f. 1823, current name adopted 1872; provides primary, secondary, tertiary and technical education; library: 60,000 vols; 50 teachers; 1,170 students; Prin. ANTHONY A. PAUL; publ. *Jaffna College Miscellany*.

Attached Institutes:

Christian Institute for the Study of Religion and Society: c/o Christian Theological Seminary, Maruthanarmadam, Chunnakam; Dir C. V. SELLIAH.

Evelyn Rutnam Institute for Inter-Cultural Studies: University Lane, Thirunelvely, Jaffna; Dir Rev. ANTHONY A. PAUL.

Institute of Agriculture: Maruthanamadam; 5 teachers; 40 students; Prin. T. KUGATHASAN.

Institute of Technology: Vaddukoddai; 10 teachers; 150 students; Dir H. R. G. HOOLE (acting).

National Centre for Advanced Studies in Humanities & Social Sciences: 6A Sukhastan Gardens, Ward Pl., Colombo 7; tel. (11) 2693974; e-mail info@ncas.lk; internet www.ncas.lk; f. 2005; offers advanced studies in humanities and social sciences; Dir Dr R. M. K. RATNAYAKE; publ. *Sri Lanka Journal of Advanced Social Studies* (2 a year).

National Institute of Library and Information Science: Univ. of Colombo, Colombo 3; tel. (11) 2507148; e-mail director@nilis.cmb.ac.lk; internet www.cmb.ac.lk/academic/institutes/nilis; f. 1999; attached to Univ. of Colombo; postgraduate and general training facilities in the field of library and information science; Dir UPALI AMARASIRI.

Postgraduate Institute of Agriculture: POB 55, Old Galaha Rd, Peradeniya; tel. (81) 2386542; e-mail info@pgia.ac.lk; internet www.pgia.ac.lk; f. 1975; attached to Univ. of Peradeniya; agricultural biology, agricultural economics, agricultural engineering, agricultural extension, animal science, biostatistics, business admin., crop science, food science and technology, plant protection, soil science; Dir Prof. B. COLIN N. PEIRIS.

Postgraduate Institute of Archaeology: 407 Bauddhaloka Mawatha, Colombo 7; tel. (11) 2694151; e-mail info@pgiar.lk; internet www.pgiar.lk; f. 1986; attached to Univ. of Kelaniya; postgraduate education, professional training, research in archaeology and related subjects; Dir Prof. JAGATH WEERASINGHE.

Postgraduate Institute of English: POB 21, Nawala, Nugegoda 10250; tel. (11) 2825804; e-mail pgiedir@gmail.com; internet www.ou.ac.lk/pgie; f. 2005; attached to Open Univ. of Sri Lanka; offers Masters degree and courses related to English and teaching of English; Dir Dr H. RATWATTE (acting).

Postgraduate Institute of Management: 28 Lesley Ranagala Mawatha, Colombo 8; tel. (11) 2689639; e-mail admin@pim.lk; internet www.pim.lk; f. 1986; attached to Univ. of Sri Jayewardenepura; faculties of arts, applied sciences, graduate studies, management studies and commerce, medical sciences; 4,500 students; Dir Prof. UDITHA LIYANAGE.

Postgraduate Institute of Medicine: 160 Norris Canal Rd, Colombo 7; tel. (11) 2688649; e-mail pgim_dir@sltnet.lk; internet www.cmb.ac.lk/pgim; f. 1980;

attached to Univ. of Colombo; provides specialist training of medical doctors; Dir Prof. JAYANTHA JAYAWARDANA.

Postgraduate Institute of Pali & Buddhist Studies: Sunethra Mahadevi Piriven Vidyayathana Premises, Pepiliyana, Boralesgamuwa, Colombo; tel. (11) 2809321; e-mail pgipbs@sltnet.lk; internet www.kln.ac.lk/institutes/pgipbs; f. 1975; attached to Univ. of Kelaniya; postgraduate studies in Pali and Buddhist studies; library: 15,000 vols; Dir Prof. Dr G. D. SUMANAPALA.

Postgraduate Institute of Science: POB 25, Peradeniya; tel. (81) 2385660; e-mail info@pgis.lk; internet www.pgis.lk; f. 1996; Univ. of Peradeniya; offers postgraduate programmes; library: 15,200 vols, 576 journals; Dir Prof. B. S. B. KARUNARATNE.

School of Agriculture: Kundasale; tel. (81) 2420485; f. 1916; library: 5,500 vols; 20 teachers; 250 students; Prin. P. K. K. R. PERERA; publ. *Progress Report* (1 a year).

South Asian Institute of Technology and Medicine: POB 11, Millennium Dr., off Chandrika Kumaratunga Mawatha, Malabe; tel. (11) 2413351; e-mail info@saitm.edu.lk; internet www.saitm.edu.lk; faculties of engineering, information communications technology, management and finance, medicine; Chair. Prof. NEVILLE FERNANDO.

Sri Lanka College of Technology: POB 542, Olcot Mawatha, Colombo 10; e-mail tdt@sltnet.lk; internet www.srilankatech.net; f. 1893; courses in commerce, trade and engineering; 4,530 students; Dir-Gen. K. A. A. WIJERATHNE.

Sri Lanka Institute of Information Technology: New Kandy Rd, Malabe; tel. (11) 2413900; e-mail info@sliit.lk; internet www.sliit.lk; f. 1999; offers degrees in the field of information technology; campuses in Colombo, Jaffna, Kandy, Matara; Dir of Academics CHANDRA DE SILVA; Dir of Administration G. L. J. HEWAWASAM.

Sri Lanka Law College: POB 1501, Colombo; 244 Hulftsdorp St, Colombo 12; tel. (11) 2323759; e-mail locwal@slt.lk; internet www.sllc.ac.lk; f. 1874; run by Ccl of Legal Education; prepares students for admission to the Bar and conducts examinations; library: 11,462 vols; 1,500 students; Prin. Dr W. D. RODRIGO.

University of Colombo School of Computing: UCSC Bldg Complex, 35 Reid Ave, Colombo 7; tel. (11) 2581245; e-mail info@ucsc.cmb.ac.lk; internet www.ucsc.cmb.ac.lk; attached to Univ. of Colombo; offers undergraduate and postgraduate degree courses in computer science; Dir Prof. G. N. WIKRAMANAYAKE; Deputy Dir Dr D. N. RANASINGHE.

SUDAN

The Higher Education System

Higher education institutions pre-date the independence of Sudan (formerly The Sudan) from the United Kingdom in 1956, with the oldest being Omdurman Islamic University, which was founded in 1912. Gordon Memorial College (founded 1902) has offered degrees since 1945, under the supervision of University of London (United Kingdom), and from 1956 became known as University of Khartoum. The higher education system was severely affected by two protracted civil wars following independence (in 1955–72 and 1983–2005), during which many educational institutions were badly damaged or completely destroyed in the southern and western parts of the country. In 2000 there were an estimated 200,538 students enrolled in universities (of which 26 were public) and other institutions of higher education. In the 2000s there was a significant increase in the number of public institutions, while a more positive government view of private institutions also led to expansion in this sector. Following a public referendum, South Sudan formally seceded from Sudan in July 2011; higher education statistics for post-secession Sudan were not immediately available.

Higher education is the responsibility of the Ministry of Higher Education and Scientific Research, and is governed by the Higher Education Act (1990) and the Higher Education Regulatory Act (2005). The National Council for Higher Education, which is chaired by the Minister of Higher Education and Scientific Research and which comprises university vice-chancellors and prominent academic figures, is responsible for planning, coordinating, financing and implementing government policies on higher education; this body is also responsible for quality assurance. In 2007 the Arab Network for Quality Assurance in Higher Education was established as a non-profit non-governmental organization, working with the International Network of Quality Assurance Agencies in Higher Education and the Association of Arab Universities. Its member organizations include the Evaluation and Accreditation Commission, part of the Sudanese Ministry of Higher Education and Scientific Research. The President of Sudan is the Chancellor of every university and is also responsible for appointing most of the other senior officers. Each university is operated by a University Council.

Results in the Sudan School Certificate are the main criterion for admission to higher education: students are required to achieve a pass-mark of 50% or higher in seven subjects to be admitted to university, and 50% or higher in five subjects to be admitted to non-university courses. Non-university courses consist principally of Intermediate or General Diplomas and are offered by several public and private institutions. Courses last for three years. The Bachelors is the undergraduate qualification, and may be awarded as either a 'General' (four years) or an 'Honours' (five years) degree. Professional areas of study, such as medicine, dentistry and engineering, may last longer (up to six years). Graduates with either of the Bachelors degrees may be admitted to programmes of study leading to the award of the Postgraduate Diploma, a one- or two-year course. The postgraduate Masters degree is a two- to three-year programme of study open to students holding a Bachelors (Honours) degree. However, students with a Bachelors (General) degree may gain access to the Masters by completing a Postgraduate Diploma. Some Masters programmes also require applicants to sit an entrance examination. The highest university-level degree is the Doctor of Philosophy, a research degree requiring a minimum of an additional three years' study and culminating in submission of a thesis.

Technical and vocational education is principally offered at secondary level, but the Sudan University of Science and Technology and the Sudan Open University (founded 2002) provide correspondence courses and continuing education. In 2005 the National Council for Technical and Technological Education was established to consolidate all programmes under one accreditation body.

Regulatory Bodies

GOVERNMENT

Ministry of Culture and Information: Khartoum; internet www.krt.gov.sd/cul.php; Minister Dr TAYEB HASSAN BADAWI.

Ministry of Higher Education and Scientific Research: POB 2081, Khartoum; tel. (183) 772515; e-mail info@mohe.gov.sd; internet www.mohe.gov.sd; Minister Dr SAMIYAH MUHAMMAD AHMED ABU-KISHWAH.

Ministry of Public Education: Khartoum; tel. (183) 772808; e-mail moe-sd@moe-sd.com; Minister SU'AD ABDEL RAZIQ MUHAMMAD SAEED.

Ministry of Science and Communications: POB 2904, Communications Tower-Mansheya, Khartoum; tel. (187) 173701; e-mail info@msc.gov.sd; internet www.msc.gov.sd; Minister Dr TAHANI ABDULLAH ATIYA.

ACCREDITATION

Evaluation and Accreditation Commission: Ministry of Higher Education and Scientific Research, POB 2081, Khartoum; tel. (91) 23126; e-mail evacsud@yahoo.com; f. 2003; Pres. ISAM M. MOHAMED.

Learned Societies

LANGUAGE AND LITERATURE

Alliance Française: POB 465, El Obeid; tel. (183) 23617; e-mail haidaro2000@yahoo.fr; offers courses and exams in French language and culture and promotes cultural exchange with France; attached teaching centre in Wad Medani.

British Council: 14 Abu Sin St, POB 1253, Central Khartoum; tel. (183) 780817; e-mail info@sd.britishcouncil.org; internet www.britishcouncil.org/sudan; offers courses and exams in English language and British culture and promotes cultural exchange with the UK; library of 10,000 vols, 90 periodicals; Dir DAVID CODLING.

Research Institutes

GENERAL

National Centre for Research: POB 2404, Khartoum; tel. (183) 779040; e-mail profsalih@hotmail.com; f. 1991; conducts pure and applied scientific research for the realization of Sudan's economic and social devt; incorporates research institutes in renewable energy, environment and natural resources, technology, tropical medicine, medicinal and aromatic plants, economic and social studies, remote sensing, biotechnology and biological engineering; Dir Prof. ABDEL KARIM MUHAMMAD SALIH.

AGRICULTURE, FISHERIES AND VETERINARY SCIENCE

Agricultural Research Corporation: POB 126, Wad Medani; tel. (511) 842226; e-mail arcdg@sudanmail.net; internet www.arcsudan.sd; f. 1904; part of Ministry of Science and Technology; research centres: Food Research Centre, Land and Water Research Centre, Crop Protection Research Centre, Forestry Research Centre, Date Palm Research Centre; 16 research stations; library: see Libraries; Dir-Gen. Prof. AZHARI ABDELAZIM HAMADA; publ. *Sudan Journal of Agricultural Research* (2 a year).

Animal Production Corporation, Research Division: POB 624, Khartoum; Dir of Research Dr MUHAMMAD EL TAHIR ABDEL RAZIG; Senior Veterinary Research Officer Dr AMIN MAHMOUD EISA.

Forestry Research Centre: POB 7089, Khartoum; f. 1962; Dir Prof. HASSAN A. MUSNAD.

ECONOMICS, LAW AND POLITICS

Sudan Academy for Administrative Sciences: POB 2003, Khartoum; f. 1980; provides post-service training for government officials; conducts studies on current administrative problems; Dir-Gen. Dr OSMAN ELZUBERI AHMED; publ. *Journal of Administration and Development*.

MEDICINE

Sudan Medical Research Laboratories: POB 287, Khartoum; f. 1935; Dir MAHMOUD ABDEL RAHMAN ZIADA.

NATURAL SCIENCES

Physical Sciences

Geological Research Authority: POB 410, Khartoum; tel. (183) 777939; e-mail gras@sudanmail.net; internet www.gras-sd.com; f. 1905; attached to Min. of Energy and Mining; applied research and surveys; library: see Libraries and Archives; Dir-Gen. Dr ABDELRAZIG O. M. AHMED.

TECHNOLOGY

Industrial Research and Consultancy Centre: POB 268, Khartoum; tel. (183) 613225; f. 1965 by the Government with assistance from the UN Development Programme; performs tests, investigations, analysis, research and surveys; offers advice and consultation services to industry; General Dir Dr IBRAHIM HASSAN M. EL AMIN.

Libraries and Archives

Khartoum

Antiquities Service Library: POB 178, Khartoum; tel. (183) 780935; f. 1946; 7,200 vols excluding periodicals; Librarian AWATIF AMIN BEDAWI.

Educational Documentation Centre: POB 2490, Khartoum; tel. (183) 71898; f. 1967; 20,000 vols; Dir IBRAHIM M. S. SHATIR; publ. *Al-Tawitheq El Tarbawi* (Educational Documentation, 2 a year).

Flinders Petrie Library: Sudan Antiquities Service, POB 178, Khartoum; tel. (183) 780935; f. 1946; 6,000 vols.

Geological Research Authority of the Sudan Library: POB 410, Khartoum; tel. (183) 770934; f. 1904; 2,200 vols, 63 periodicals; spec. colln: geology of the Sudan; Chief Librarian SALAH ABDEL GADIR MUHAMMAD; publ. *Bulletin*.

Library of the Sudan University of Science and Technology: POB 407, Khartoum; tel. (183) 778922; e-mail library@sustech.edu; f. 1950; 14 libraries on 9 sites; 55,000 vols; Chief Librarian GAWAHIR SIDAHMED EL HASSAN.

National Chemical Laboratories Library: National Chemical Laboratories, Ministry of Health, POB 287, Khartoum; f. 1904; 2,500 vols, 1,600 pamphlets.

National Records Office: POB 1914, Khartoum; f. 1953; 20m. documents covering Sudanese history since 1870; 12,820 vols; Sec.-Gen. Dr M. I. ABU SALEEM; publ. *Majallatal Wathaiq* (Archives Magazine).

Sudan Medical Research Laboratories Library: POB 287, Khartoum; f. 1904 (as part of Wellcome Tropical Research Laboratories); 7,000 pamphlets, 6,000 vols.

University of Khartoum Library: POB 321, Khartoum 11115; tel. (11) 770022; e-mail library@uofk.edu; internet lib.uofk.edu; f. 1945; depository library for UN, FAO, ILO, WHO and UNESCO publs; 333,000 vols, 4,200 periodicals; incl. spec.

Sudan and African colln; Chief Librarian Prof. AHMED HASSAN FAHAL.

Omdurman

Omdurman Central Public Library: Omdurman; f. 1951; 17,650 vols.

Wad Medani

Agricultural Research Corporation, Central Library: POB 126, Wad Medani; tel. (511) 842226; e-mail arc.library@arcsudan.sd; internet www.arcsudan.sd; f. 1930; 15,000 vols, 20,000 pamphlets, 250 periodicals, set of *The Essential Electronic Agricultural Library* (TEEAL) on CD-ROM and LAN version (LanTEEAL); Head Librarian AHLAM ISMAIL MUSA; publs *Sudan Journal of Agricultural Research (SJAR)* (online), *Annual Reports of the ARC research programmes*, *Proceedings of the ARC research programmes*.

Gezira Research Station Library: Wad Medani; 6,500 vols on agricultural topics.

Museums and Art Galleries

Khartoum

Sudan National Museum: POB 178, Khartoum; tel. (183) 70680; f. 1971; depts of antiquities, ethnology and Sudanese modern history; Dir HASSAN HUSSEIN IDRIS; Curator SIDDIG M. GASM AL-SID; publ. *Report on the Antiquities Service and Museums, Kush* (1 a year).

Attached Museums:

Ethnographical Museum: POB 178, Khartoum; tel. (183) 77052; f. 1956; collection and preservation of ethnographical objects; Curator MUHAMMAD HAMED.

Khalifa's House: Omdurman.

Merowe Museum: Merowe, Northern Province; antiquities and general.

Sheikan Museum: el Obeid; archaeological and ethnographic museum.

Sultan Ali Dinar Museum: el Fasher.

Sudan Natural History Museum: Univ. of Khartoum, POB 321, Khartoum 11115; e-mail nhm@uofk.edu; f. 1906; attached to Univ. of Khartoum; Keeper Dr ABUALGASIM IBRAHIM ABDELHALIM.

Universities

AL-FASHIR UNIVERSITY

POB 125, Al-Fashir, N Darfur

Telephone: (527) 43394

E-mail: director@fashir.edu.sd

Internet: www.fashir.edu.sd

Founded 1975

State control

Faculties of arts, education, health sciences, human development, natural resources, Sharia law

Vice-Chancellor: Prof. ABDALLAH ABEL HAI ABU BAKER

Publication: *Journal of Al-Fashir University for Applied Sciences* (2 a year)

AL-NEELAIN UNIVERSITY

POB 12702, Khartoum 12702

Telephone: 777-441

E-mail: prinfo@neelain.edu.sd

Internet: www.neelain.edu.sd

Founded 1955 as Khartoum br. of Cairo Univ.; ind. status and present name 1993

State control

Language of instruction: Arabic

Vice-Chancellor: AWAD HAJ ALI AHMED

Faculties of agriculture, animal production and fisheries, arts, commerce and socio-economic studies, engineering, graduate studies, law, medicine, optometry and visual sciences, science and technology and statistics, population studies and information technology; Nile Basin Studies Research Centre

Number of teachers: 270

Number of students: 36,000

AL-ZAIEM AL-AZHARI UNIVERSITY

POB 1933, Omdurman

Telephone: (15) 560501

E-mail: qurashi@sudanmail.net

Founded 1993

State control

Number of teachers: 350

Number of students: 5,100

BAKHET EL-RUDDA UNIVERSITY

POB 1311, Khartoum, Eldewaym

Telephone: (531) 22440

Founded 1997

State control

Languages of instruction: Arabic, English

Vice-Chancellor: ANAAS A. EL-HAFEEZ

Number of teachers: 200

Number of students: 4,030

DEANS

Faculty of Agriculture and Natural Resources: GHANIM SABIH

Faculty of Economics and Administration: ILHAM SAADALLAH

Faculty of Education: SALIH NOURIN

Faculty of Medicine: YOUSIF SULTAN

Faculty of Postgraduate Studies: MAHMOUD HASSAN

BLUE NILE UNIVERSITY

POB 143, Damazeen, Blue Nile

Telephone: (183) 785614

Vice-Chancellor: MUHAMMAD EL-HASSAN ABDUL EL-RAHMAN

Founded 1995

Faculties of education and engineering; centres of extramural studies and continuing education

EL-DALANG UNIVERSITY

El-Dalang, S Kordofan

Telephone: (183) 785614

E-mail: info@dalanjuniversity.net

Internet: www.dalanjuniversity.edu.sd

Founded 1990

State control

Faculties of agriculture, education, social development, teacher training; centres of computer science, peace studies

Vice-Chancellor: KAMESS KAGO KUNDA

EL-GADARIF UNIVERSITY

POB 449, el-Gadarif 32211

Telephone: (441) 43668

E-mail: unged@sudanmail.net

Founded 1990; univ. status 1994

State control

Languages of instruction: Arabic, English

Vice-Chancellor: OMER KURDI

Number of teachers: 150

Number of students: 3,840

DEANS

Faculty of Agricultural and Environmental Sciences: ABDEL-AZIZA TAHA
Faculty of Economics and Administrative Science: EL-GUZOLI MUHAMMAD
Faculty of Education: SULTAN NOUR
Faculty of Medicine and Medical Sciences: EL-DIRDIRY SALAH

EL-IMAM EL-MAHDI UNIVERSITY

POB 209, Kosti 11588
Telephone: (571) 22545
E-mail: abdosm@sudanmail.net
Internet: www.elmahdi.edu.sd

Founded 1993
State control

Faculties of Arabic and Islamic sciences, arts, engineering and technical studies, law and Islamic law, medicine and health sciences; centres for computer studies, extramural studies

Vice-Chancellor: ABDELRAHIM OSMAN MUHAMMAD

KASSALA UNIVERSITY

Kassala 266
Telephone: (411) 22095
E-mail: vc@kassalauni.edu.sd
Internet: kassalauni.edu.sd

Founded 1990
State control

Faculties of agriculture, computer science and IT, economics, education, engineering, medicine; community college and college of higher education; tuberculosis research centre

Vice-Chancellor: Prof. AZHAR OMAR ABDEL-BAGI

NILE VALLEY UNIVERSITY

POB 1843, Khartoum
E-mail: info@nilevalley.edu.sd
Internet: www.nilevalley.edu.sd

Founded 1990
State control
Language of instruction: Arabic
Academic year: October to June

Vice-Chancellor: Prof. FASIAL A. EL-HAG
Prin.: Dr ATTA A. FADLALLA
Academic Sec.: Prof. MAHMOUD Y. OSMAN
Library of 31,143 books, 76 periodicals
Number of teachers: 240
Number of students: 6,890 (6,798 undergraduate, 92 postgraduate)

DEANS

Faculty of Agriculture: Dr SAIFELDIN M. AL-AMIN
Faculty of Commerce and Business Administration: HAMZA A. HAMZA
Faculty of Education: Dr MUHAMMAD A. MUHAMMAD
Faculty of Engineering and Technology: IZZELDIN A. ABDALLA
Faculty of Islamic and Arabic Studies: ABDELNABI A. EL-TAYEB
Faculty of Medicine: (vacant)
Teaching-Training College: ABDELGADIR S. HAMAD

NYALA UNIVERSITY

POB 155, Nyala, SS Darfur
Telephone: (711) 33122
E-mail: nyalauni@yahoo.com
Internet: www.nyalauniversity.net

Founded 1994
State control
Academic year: April to December

Faculties of community devt, economics and commerce, education, engineering, law, nursing, technology, veterinary science; Centre for Peace Studies

Vice-Chancellor

Number of teachers: 150
Number of students: 6,300

OMDURMAN ISLAMIC UNIVERSITY

POB 382, Omdurman
Telephone: (187) 511525
E-mail: info@oiu.edu.sd
Internet: www.oiu.edu.sd

Founded 1912, univ. status 1965
State control
Language of instruction: Arabic
Academic year: October to June

Chair. of Univ. Ccl: Sheikh M. M. SADIQ AL-KAMMOURI
Vice-Chancellor: Prof. MOHAMMED OSMAN SALIH
Sec.-Gen.: Dr HASSAN AHMED HASSAN
Academy Sec.: Prof. HASSAN AHMED el-HASSAN
Librarian: ABDUL SEED OSMAN
Library of 172,858 vols
Number of teachers: 850
Number of students: 51,640 (47,638 undergraduate, 4,002 postgraduate)
Publications: Faculty of Arts Magazine, Faculty of Islamic Studies Magazine

DEANS

Faculty of Agriculture: Dr M. AL-H. SIDDEEG
Faculty of Arabic Language: Prof. BABEKIR AL-ZACOULT
Faculty of Arts: Prof. H. ABDUL-RAHMAN
Faculty of Basic Medical Sciences: Dr M. SALAH ELDIN
Faculty of Computer Sciences: M. S. MUHAMMAD
Faculty of Economics: Dr S. M. MUHAMMAD
Faculty of Education: Prof. AL-H. OMER HAJ
Faculty of Engineering: Dr H. AL-TAYEB
Faculty of Higher Studies: Dr H. AL-ABBASSI
Faculty of Human Development: Dr IBRAHEEM A. M. AHMED
Faculty of Management Science: Dr A. ABDELRAIID
Faculty of Medicine: Prof. A. I. YOUSSIF
Faculty of Pharmacy: Dr M. AL-H. ABDULLAH
Faculty of Shari'a and Law: Dr A. IBRAHEEM

RED SEA UNIVERSITY

POB 24, Port Sudan
Telephone: (311) 27878
E-mail: info@rsu.edu.sd
Internet: rsu.edu.sd

Founded 1994
State control

Faculties of applied sciences, arts, earth sciences, economics and administration, education, engineering, marine science and fisheries, medicine and health sciences, technical studies; centre for the study of the Beja culture; marine research institute

Vice-Chancellor: Prof. ABDEL RAOUF ABBAS AHMAD BADAWI

Number of teachers: 80
Number of students: 800

SHENDI UNIVERSITY

POB 142/143, Shendi
Telephone: (261) 5662100
E-mail: info@ush.sd
Internet: www.ush.sd

Founded 1990 as Faculty of Nile Valley Univ., present status and title 1994
State control

Language of instruction: Arabic
Academic year: October to August

Vice-Chancellor and Pres.: Prof. TALAAT ELTAHIR
Vice-Pres.: Assoc. Prof. AHMED IBRAHIM
Prin.: Assoc. Prof. SALAH ELHADIA
Dean for Graduate Studies and Scientific Research Faculty: Assoc. Prof. YOUSIF YOUSIF
Dean for Student Affairs: Asst Prof. NADIR SIR ELKHATIM
Dir for Information Technology Centre: ABUBAKER ELRAZI AHMED

Number of teachers: 280
Number of students: 5,800

Publication: Journal of Shendi University (scientific, cultural and social topics, 2 a year)

DEANS

Arts Faculty: Assoc. Prof. HASSAN AWAD ELKARIM
Community Development Faculty: Asst Prof. ELYAS ASHWAL
Community Faculty: Assoc. Prof. M. ELHASSAN ELHAFIAN
Economics, Commerce and Business Administration Faculty: Assoc. Prof. WIJDAN MAHADI
Education Faculty: Assoc. Prof. YASSIR OSMAN
Health Faculty: Asst Prof. ABD ELSALM DAOOD
Medical Laboratory Science Faculty: Asst Prof. MUHAMMAD OSMAN
Medicine and Surgery Faculty: Assoc. Prof. MASOOD ELKHALIFA
Nursing Faculty: Assoc. Prof. NABILA ABD ELALLA
Science and Technology Faculty: Asst Prof. HASSAN ELKHADIR

UNIVERSITY OF SINNAR

Sinnar
Telephone: (561) 785614
Internet: www.sinnaruniv.edu.sd

Founded 1994

Colleges of agriculture, economics and administration science, education, engineering, Islamic and Arabic sciences, medicine and health sciences, Sharia law; community college

Vice-Chancellor: Prof. MUHAMMAD WARRAG OMER

Publication: Sinnar University Journal (2 a year)

SUDAN UNIVERSITY OF SCIENCE AND TECHNOLOGY

POB 407, Khartoum
Telephone: (183) 772508
E-mail: sust@sudanet.net
Internet: www.sustech.edu

Founded 1950
State control
Academic year: September to May

Vice-Chancellor: Prof. Dr AHMED ELTAYEB AHMED
Deputy Vice-Chancellor: Prof. Dr GADALLA ABDALLA ELHASSAN
Sec.-Gen.: Dr HASHIM ALI SALIM
Number of teachers: 980
Number of students: 55,920

Publication: Science and Technology (2 a year)

DEANS

College of Agricultural Studies: Dr YOUSIF MUHAMMAD AHMED
College of Animal Production Science and Technology: Dr HASSAN MUHAMMAD ADAM

SUDAN

College of Business Studies: Dr MUSA HASAB ELRASOUL KHIER ELSIED
College of Communication Science: Prof. MUKHTAR OSMAN ELSIDDIQ
College of Computer Science and Information Technology: Dr MUHAMMAD ELHAFIZ MUSTAFA
College of Education: Dr ABDEL RAZEG ABDALLAH ELBONI
College of Engineering: Prof. SHAMBUOL ADLAN MUHAMMAD
College of Fine and Applied Arts: Dr OMER MUHAMMAD ELHASSAN
College of Forestry and Range Science: Dr ALI KHALID ALI
College of Graduate Studies: Prof. Dr OSMAN SAAD ALI
College of Languages: Dr SAADIA MOSA OMER
College of Medical Laboratory Science: Dr HUMODI AHMED SAEED
College of Music and Drama: Dr SAAD YOUSIF OBEID
College of Petroleum Engineering and Technology: Dr RASHID AHMED MOHAMMED
College of Physical Education and Sports: Dr HAMID ELSAYED DAFALLAH
College of Medical Radiologic Sciences: Dr ALSAFI AHMED ABD ALLA
College of Sciences: Dr ELFATIH AHMED HASSAN
College of Technology: Dr MUBARAK EL MAHAL AHMED
College of Veterinary Medicine: Prof. Dr AMEL OMER BAKHEIT
College of Water and Environmental Engineering: Dr YOUSIF ALI YOUSIF

UNIVERSITY OF DONGOLA

POB 47, Dongola
Telephone: (241) 21515
Internet: www.uofd.edu.sd
Founded 1994
State control
Faculties of agriculture, arts, education, law and Islamic law, medicine, mining and earth sciences
Vice-Chancellor: MUHAMMAD OSMAN AHMED
Number of teachers: 256

UNIVERSITY OF GEZIRA

POB 20, Wad Medani, 2667 Khartoum
Telephone: 5118-43174
E-mail: principal@uofg.edu.sd
Internet: www.uofg.edu.sd
Founded 1975
Language of instruction: English
Vice-Chancellor: (vacant)
Sec.-Gen.: Dr MAHMOUD ABDALLA IBRAHIM
Librarian: ABUEL GAITH SANHOURI
Number of teachers: 140
Number of students: 1,000

DEANS

Faculty of Agriculture: Dr OSMAN ALI SID AHMED
Faculty of Economics and Rural Development: Dr EL TAHIR MOHAMED NUR
Faculty of Education: Prof. ABDEL SALAM MAHMOUD ABDALLA
Faculty of Medicine: Prof. SALAH ELDIN TAHA SALIH
Faculty of Science and Technology: Dr ELNUR KAMAL EL DIN ABU SABAH
Graduate Studies and Academic Affairs: ISAM ABDEL RAHMAN AHMED
Preparatory College: Prof. FAYSAL AWAD
Dean of Students: Dr ABD EL-MUTAAL GIRSHAB

UNIVERSITY OF HOLY QU'RAN AND ISLAMIC SCIENCES

POB 1459, Omdurman
Telephone: (18) 7559012
E-mail: quranunv@quran-unv.edu.sd
Internet: www.quran-unv.edu.sd
Founded 1990 by merger of Holy Qu'ran College and Omdurman Higher Institute
State control
Faculties of Arabic language, community, Da'wa and information, economics and administrative sciences, education, the Holy Koran, Sharia law, social sciences; centre for women's studies
Vice-Chancellor: Prof. EBRAHIM NORIN EBRAHIM
Deputy Vice-Chancellor: Prof. AHMED SAEED SALMAN
Library of 50,600 vols
Number of teachers: 560
Number of students: 11,890
Publication: *Nour Al-Mathani Journal*

UNIVERSITY OF KHARTOUM

POB 321, 11115 Khartoum
Telephone: (83) 772601
E-mail: vc@uofk.edu
Internet: www.uofk.edu
Founded 1956, fmrly Univ. College of Khartoum
State control
Languages of instruction: Arabic, English
Academic year: July to April
Vice-Chancellor: Prof. ELSIDDIG AHMED ELMUSTAFA EL SHEIKH
Deputy Vice-Chancellor: Dr SUMIA MUHAMMAD AHMED ABU KASHAWA
Prin.: Dr MOHSIN HASSAN ABDALL HASHIM
Academic Sec.: Dr MUSTAFA MUHAMMAD ALI EL BALLA
Personnel Sec.: Ustaz ABDELRAZIG HASSAN OBEID
Librarian: Prof. AHMED HASSAN FAHAL
Library: see under Libraries and Archives
Number of teachers: 1,670
Number of students: 26,090

DEANS

Faculty of Agriculture: Prof. ELAMIN ABDELMAGID EL AMIN
Faculty of Animal Production: Dr IBRAHIM ABDELSALAM YOUSIF
Faculty of Arts: Dr INTISAR SEIGIROUN ELZAIN
Faculty of Dentistry: Dr NADIA AHMED YAHIA
Faculty of Economic and Social Studies: Dr HASSAN ELHAG ALI
Faculty of Education: Prof. ELTYEB AHMED ELMUSTAFA EL SHEIKH
Faculty of Engineering and Architecture: Prof. MUHAMMAD OSMAN AKODE
Faculty of Forestry: Dr ABDALLA MIRGANI ELTYEB
Faculty of Geography and Environment: Dr AHMED ELFAIEQ
Faculty of Law: Dr ELRASHID HASSAN SAED
Faculty of Mathematical Sciences: Dr MOHSIN HASSAN ABDALLA HASHIM
Faculty of Medical Laboratory Sciences: Prof. NASRELDIN BILAL AHMED
Faculty of Medicine: Prof. AMMAR ELTAHIR AHMED
Faculty of Nursing Sciences: Dr BASHIR ELGAILY
Faculty of Pharmacy: Dr ABUBAKR OSMAN MUHAMMAD NOOR
Faculty of Public Health and Environmental Hygiene: Dr KAMIL MIRGHANI SHAABAN
Faculty of Science: Dr SALAH BASHIR ABDALLA
Faculty of Technological and Developmental Studies: Dr ABDALLA GUMAA FRWA

Faculty of Veterinary Medicine: Prof. ELGAILANI ALI ELAMIN
Graduate College: Prof. MUHAMMAD MUHAMMAD AHMED ELNOUR
School of Management Studies: Prof. ABDELGADIR MUHAMMAD AHMED

UNIVERSITY OF KORDOFAN

POB 160, El Obeid, N Kordofan 517
Telephone: (611) 23119
E-mail: info@kordofan.edu.sd
Internet: www.kordofan.edu.sd
Founded 1990
State control
Faculties of arts, commercial studies, community, computer studies and statistics, education, engineering and technical science, medicine and health sciences, natural resources and environmental studies, science; Centre of Peace Studies and Development, Gum Arabic Research Centre
Vice-Chancellor: Prof. AHMED ABDALLA AGABELDOUR
Publication: *Journal of Natural Resources and Environmental Studies*

UNIVERSITY OF WESTERN KORDOFAN

POB 2081, Khartoum
Telephone: (183) 785614
E-mail: evac@sudanmail.net
Internet: www.uwkordofan.net
Founded 1997
State control
Faculties of agriculture, economics and community development, education, Islamic studies and Arabic, medicine and health sciences, natural resources and environmental studies, petroleum and underground water, Sharia law; Centre for Peace Studies; Institute of Rehabilitation and Training of Imams and Preachers
Vice-Chancellor: Prof. NOURAL-DAIM OSMAN

UNIVERSITY OF ZALENGEI

Zalengei, West Darfur 6
Telephone: (713) 22013
E-mail: uzal@student.net
Founded 1994
State control
Language of instruction: Arabic
Faculties of agriculture, education, Holy Koran and Islamic studies
Vice-Chancellor: AHMED MUHAMMAD ABAKER
Number of teachers: 100
Number of students: 1,250

Colleges and Institutes

Faculty of Hygiene and Environmental Studies: POB 205, Khartoum; tel. 72690; f. 1933; 26 staff; 4 depts; awards BSc and MSc in environmental health; Librarian M. MUHD. SALIH; Dean B. M. EL-HASSAN.

Khartoum Nursing College: POB 1063, Khartoum; 3-year diploma course; Prin. A. M. OSMAN.

Yambio Institute of Agriculture: Sud 82/002, c/o UNDP POB 913, Khartoum; f. 1972; library: 5,000 vols; 15 staff; 130 students; 2-year diploma courses; Prin. CHRISTOPHER LADO GALE.

SURINAME

The Higher Education System

Higher education institutions predate the independence of Suriname (formerly Dutch Guiana) from the Netherlands in 1975, with the oldest being Anton de Kom Universiteit van Suriname, which was founded in 1968 and is the sole university in the country. It has three faculties, in medical sciences, social sciences and technological sciences, and nine research institutes. In addition to the university, higher education is offered by six technical and vocational schools, including two teacher training institutes, a nursing college, a dental care foundation, an arts academy and a polytechnic college. In 2011/12 there were 3,840 students enrolled at the university, with a further estimated 2,000 students enrolled in other institutions of higher education.

The Ministry of Education and Community Development is the government agency responsible for higher education.

The Dutch-style Voorbereidend Wetenschappelijk Onderwijs (university preparatory education examination) is the main criterion for admission to higher education. Students holding the Hoger Algemeen Vormend Onderwijs (higher general secondary education examination) may also gain entrance to higher education, via a bridging year of study. The Bachelor of Science degree courses are offered at the University lasting for four years, with the exception of business administration, which lasts three years. Bachelor of Arts degree courses in art, journalism and socio-cultural studies are offered at the Academie voor Hoger Kunst en Cultuuronderwijs (Academy for Higher Arts and Cultural Education). The University does not offer Masters degrees. The other five technical and vocational institutions offer post-secondary certificates and diplomas in specific professional fields.

In the mid-2000s the Government identified quality assurance in higher education as a priority, and in 2007 approved legislation that created an interim national accreditation body. This organization subsequently undertook a pilot project in which three Surinamese and two Dutch experts considered the eligibility of the country's various higher education institutions for formal accreditation. A permanent national accreditation agency, the Nationaal Orgaan voor Accreditatie (NOVA), was established following the completion of the project, with the aim of improving standards in higher education in Suriname and ensuring regional and international comparability of its higher education programmes.

Regulatory Bodies

GOVERNMENT

Ministry of Education and Community Development: Dr Samuel Kafiluddistraat 117–123, Paramaribo; tel. 498850; e-mail minond@sr.net; internet www.gov.sr/sr/ministerie-van-onderwijs-en-volksontwikkeling.aspx; Minister ASHWIN ADHIN.

ACCREDITATION

Nationaal Orgaan voor Accreditatie (NOVA) (National Agency for Accreditation): Costerstraat 16, Paramaribo; tel. 521508; e-mail info@novasur.org; internet www.novasur.org; f. 2012; Dir ASTRID RUNS.

Learned Societies

ECONOMICS, LAW AND POLITICS

Surinaamse Veerniging van Accountants (Suriname Institute of Chartered Accountants): Mr. Jagernath Lachmonstraat 160-162, Paramaribo; tel. 6801335; e-mail info@suva.sr; internet www.suva.sr; 32 mems; Chair. RUDIE TJONG A HUNG; Sec. MICHAEL LUTCHMAN.

LANGUAGE AND LITERATURE

Alliance Française: Henck Arronstraat 116, Paramaribo; tel. 422206; e-mail alliance597@live.com; offers courses and exams in French language and culture and promotes cultural exchange with France.

Research Institutes

AGRICULTURE, FISHERIES AND VETERINARY SCIENCE

Centre for Agricultural Research in Suriname: Leysweg 14, POB 1914, Paramaribo; tel. 490128; e-mail directie@celos.sr.org; internet www.celos.sr.org; f. 1967; attached to Anton de Kom Univ. of Suriname; research in tropical agriculture, application of new technologies in agriculture; Dir MEVR. S. SILOS; publ. *Bos en Natuur*.

ECONOMICS, LAW AND POLITICS

Algemeen Bureau voor de Statistiek in Suriname (General Bureau of Statistics in Suriname): Klipstenenstraat 5, Paramaribo; tel. 473737; e-mail info@statistics-suriname.org; internet www.statistics-suriname.org; f. 1947; national data colln, survey and research on economy of Suriname; Dir Drs IWAN A. SNO.

NATURAL SCIENCES

Foundation for Nature Conservation in Suriname (STINASU): Cornelis Jongbawstraat 14, POB 12252, Paramaribo; tel. 476597; e-mail stinasu@sr.net; internet www.stinasu.com; f. 1969; conducts scientific research and provides nature education; Dir Ir MARIE DJOSETRO (acting).

TECHNOLOGY

Geologisch Mijnbouwkundige Dienst (Geological Mining Service): Mr. Jagernath Lachmanstraat 181, Paramaribo; tel. 434331; f. 1943; attached to Min. of Natural Resources; library of 20,000 vols; Head M. AUTAR (acting); publ. geological maps.

Libraries

Paramaribo

Bibliotheek Anton de Kom Universiteit van Suriname (Library Anton de Kom University of Suriname): University Campus, Building I; tel. 464547; e-mail adekbib@uvs.edu; internet ub.uvs.edu; f. 1968; consists of Central Library and a medical library; Dir JANE W.F. SMITH.

Bibliotheek van het Cultureel Centrum Suriname (Library of the Suriname Cultural Centre): Henck Arronstraat 112–114, POB 1241, Paramaribo; tel. 473309; e-mail stgccs@yahoo.com; f. 1948; 7 brs, 2 bookmobiles; Book Reading Club; movie screenings; 50,000 vols; Librarian MARCELLA AUGUSTUSZOON; Dir Dr NADIÀ BECKER.

Museums

Commewijne

Openluchtmuseum Fort Nieuw Amsterdam (Open Air Museum Fort Nieuw Amsterdam): Wilhelminastraat, Nieuw Amsterdam, Commewijne; tel. 322225; e-mail info@fortnieuwamsterdam.sr; internet www.fortnieuwamsterdam.sr; cannons, guns, monuments from 18th century; Chair. Drs R. BURGOS; Sec. Ir R. VAN ESSEN.

Paramaribo

Stichting Surinaams Museum: Abraham Crijnssenweg 1, Fort Zeelandia, POB 2306, Paramaribo; tel. 425871; e-mail museum@cq-link.sr; internet www.surinaamsmuseum.net; f. 1947; archaeology, art, history, ethnology; library of 35,000 vols; Dir Drs J. H. J. VAN PUTTEN; publ. *Libri Musei Surinamensis*.

University

ANTON DE KOM UNIVERSITEIT VAN SURINAME
(Anton de Kom University of Suriname)

Leysweg 86, POB 9212, Paramaribo
Telephone: 465558
E-mail: info@uvs.edu
Internet: adekus.uvs.edu

Founded 1968, renamed in 1983
Language of instruction: Dutch
Academic year: October to September

Pres.: Dr RYAN SIDIN
Sec.: K. GOENOPAWIRO
Library: see under Libraries and Archives
Number of teachers: 387
Number of students: 4,496

Publications: *Journal of Social Sciences* (2 a
year), *Suriname Medical Bulletin* (4 a
year)

DEANS

Faculty of Medicine: Dr JERRY TOELSIE
Faculty of Social Sciences: L. MONSELS

Faculty of Technology: ROBERT TJIEN FOOH
Institute for Graduate Studies and Research:
M. SCHALKWIJK (Dir)

Colleges

Academie voor Hoger Kunst-en Cultuur-onderwijs (Academy for Higher Arts and
Cultural Education): Waterkant 14, Para-maribo; tel. 477749; internet www.ahkco.net;

f. 1981; offers bachelors degrees in visual
arts, journalism and socio-cultural educa-tion.

**Polytechnic College/Instituut voor
Hoger Beroepsonderwijs in Suriname:**
Kinderdorpstraat 2–4, Doekhieweg-Oost,
Paramaribo; tel. 490328; e-mail info@ptc
.edu.sr; internet www.ptc.edu.sr; offers bach-elors degrees in engineering and information
technology, and masters degree in business
administration.

SWAZILAND

The Higher Education System

Higher education institutions pre-date the independence of Swaziland from the United Kingdom in 1968, with the oldest being the University of Swaziland (formerly the University of Botswana, Lesotho and Swaziland), which was founded in 1964. In 2011/12 some 5,416 students were enrolled at the University of Swaziland, which has its main campus at Kwaluseni and two further campuses at Luyengo (which houses the Faculty of Agriculture and Research Centre) and Mbabane (where nursing and environmental health programmes are offered at the Faculty of Health Sciences); there are also a number of other institutions of higher education. Plans to establish the Swaziland Christian Medical University, which would become the country's first medical institution, were at an advanced stage in 2011; construction of the university, which was expected to take three years to complete, was to be funded by investors from the Republic of Korea (South Korea).

GCE A-Levels, the Cambridge Overseas School Certificate or the Cambridge Overseas Higher School Certificate can be used to gain admission to undergraduate courses at the University. The undergraduate Bachelors degree last fours years (five for law), divided into two cycles, each lasting two years. Postgraduate Masters degrees are awarded in a restricted number of fields, including arts, sciences and education, and require between one and two years' study.

Post-secondary technical and vocational education is offered by a number of institutions, including Swaziland College of Technology and Swaziland Institute of Management and Public Administration. Swaziland College of Technology offers craft, technician and diploma courses, which generally last between three and five years.

Regulatory Body

GOVERNMENT

Ministry of Education and Training: POB 39, Mbabane; tel. (268) 24042491; e-mail ps_education@gov.sz; internet www .gov.sz; Minister Hon. PHINEAS MAGAGULA.

Ministry of Sports, Culture and Youth Affairs: POB 4843, Mbabane; 4th Fl., Swazi Bank Bldg next to DPM offices, Gwamile St, Mbabane; tel. (268) 24045053; internet www .gov.sz; Minister Hon. DAVID CRUISER NGCAM-PHALALA.

Learned Societies

BIBLIOGRAPHY, LIBRARY SCIENCE AND MUSEOLOGY

Swaziland Library Association: POB 2309, Mbabane H100; Elwatini Bldg, cnr Market and Warner Sts, Mbabane; tel. (265) 24042633; e-mail fmkhonta@uniswacc .uniswa.sz; internet www.swala.sz; f. 1984; 120 mems; Chair. FAITH MKHONTA; Sec. JABULILE DLAMINI; publ. *SWALA Journal* (2 a year).

Research Institutes

AGRICULTURE, FISHERIES AND VETERINARY SCIENCE

Lowveld Experiment Station: POB 11, L312 Matata; tel. (268) 3636311; f. 1964; agricultural research, cotton-breeding, cotton entomology; Chief Research Officer P. D. MKHATSHWA.

Malkerns Research Station: POB 4, Malkerns; tel. (268) 5283306; f. 1959; general research on crops, vegetables, fruits and farming systems; 14 research sections; library of 5,000 vols; Chief Research Officer P. D. MKHATSHWA.

Mpisi Cattle Breeding Experimental Station: Mpisi; aims to improve indigenous Nguni cattle; provides multiplication studs of Brahman, Simmentaler and Friesland cattle for beef, milk and cross-breeding; Dir R. A. JOHN; Man. I. A. MORLEY HEWITT.

TECHNOLOGY

Geological Survey and Mines Department: POB 57, Mbabane; tel. (268) 24044330; e-mail geo.director@swazi.net; f. 1944; activities: mapping of the territory (published at a scale of 1:25,000 and 1:50,000), the investigation of mineral occurrences by prospecting, detailed mapping and diamond-drilling, mine and quarry inspections, control of explosives and prospecting; 18 mems; small library; Dir SIMON MAPHANGA LALA; publ. *Bulletins*.

Libraries and Archives

Mbabane

Swaziland National Archives: POB 946, Mbabane; e-mail director_archives@gov.sz; f. 1970; govt records since 1880s; colln of historical photographs, newspapers, maps, reports; oral history and biographies of prominent Swazis; 5,600 vols; Dir KHOLEKILE MTHETHWA.

Swaziland National Library Service: POB 1461, Mbabane; tel. (268) 24042633; e-mail director_snls@gov.sz; internet www .gov.sz; f. 1971; operates a public library service throughout the country with br. libraries at Manzini, Mpaka, Lomahasha, Nhlangano, Siteki, Pigg's Peak, Big Bend, Bhunya, Tshaneni, Mankayana, Lavumisa, Hlatikulu and Mhlume; mobile library visits; libraries at secondary schools; 80,000 vols, 150 periodicals; Dir NOMSA MKHWANAZI; publs *Accessions List* (irregular), *Index to Swaziland Collection* (irregular).

Museum

Lobamba

Swaziland National Museum: POB 100, Lobamba; tel. (268) 24161178; f. 1972 under the patronage of the Swaziland National Trust Commission; museum with extramural functions, giving information about Swazi culture as well as other Southern African Bantu groups; reference library; Curator ROSEMARY ANDRADE; publ. *Museum Occasional Paper*.

University

UNIVERSITY OF SWAZILAND

Private Bag 4, M201 Kwaluseni

Telephone: (268) 25170000

Internet: www.uniswa.sz

Founded 1964 as part of Univ. of Botswana, Lesotho and Swaziland, present name 1982

Language of instruction: English

Academic year: August to May

Provides distance education

Chancellor: HM KING MSWATI III
Vice-Chancellor: Prof. C. M. MAGAGULA
Pro-Vice-Chancellor: Prof. V. S. B. MTETWA
Registrar: S. S. VILAKATI
Librarian: M. R. MAVUSO

Library of 178,000 vols, 1,500 periodicals
Number of teachers: 300
Number of students: 4,200

Publications: *UNISWA Journal of Agriculture, Science and Health Sciences* (2 a year), *UNISWA Journal of Social Science, Humanities and Education* (2 a year)

DEANS

Faculty of Agriculture: Prof. B. M. DLAMINI
Faculty of Commerce: Prof. P. N. JOUBERT
Faculty of Education: Dr B. T. DLAMINI
Faculty of Health Sciences: Prof. N. A. SUKARTI
Faculty of Humanities: Prof. C. H. HARFORD
Faculty of Science: Prof. M. D. DLAMINI
Faculty of Social Sciences: Prof. A. M. ZAMBERIA

Colleges

Mananga Agricultural Management Centre: Mananga Center, POB 5100, Mbabane; Ezulwini Rd, Ezulwini; tel. (268) 24163156; e-mail info@mananga.sz; internet www.mananga.sz; f. 1972; offers management devt training programs, tailor-made programmes, residential and outreach courses in management devt, rural livelihoods, poverty reduction and sustainable devt, integrated environment management and health management related courses; Dir

Dr R. P. TARUVINGA; Registrar S. HLATSH-
WAYO.

**Nazarene Higher Education Consor-
tium:** POB 6800, M200 Manzini; f. 2007 by
merger of the Nazarene College of Theology,
the Nazarene College of Nursing and the
Nazarene College of Education; offers diploma and degree level qualifications, the
latter through affiliation with the Univ. of
Swaziland; Rector and Prin. of Nazarene
College of Nursing Dr WINNIE NHLENGETHWA;
Prin. of Nazarene College of Theology Rev.

COLLEN S. MAGAGULA; Prin. of Nazarene
College of Education SAMARIA MBINGO.

Swaziland College of Technology: POB
69, H100 Mbabane; tel. (268) 24042681;
e-mail scot@africaonline.co.sz; internet www
.scot.co.sz; f. 1946 as Trade School, present
name 1968; faculties of business admin.,
building and civil engineering, education,
engineering and science and information
and communications technology; courses are
offered at Diploma and Bachelor of Technology levels; library: 18,000 vols; 60 teachers;

700 students; Prin. CASPER MFANA DUBE;
Registrar PHEPHILE SIMELANE-NDLANGAMAN-
DIA.

**Swaziland Institute of Management and
Public Administration:** POB 495, Mbabane; tel. (268) 25186600; internet www
.simpa.ac.sz; f. 1965; short courses in aspects
of business practice are offered; 21 teachers
(15 full-time, 6 part-time); 900 students;
Prin. NHLANHLA NXUMALO; Dean for Studies
ERIC MKHONZA.

SWEDEN

The Higher Education System

The oldest institution of higher education is Uppsala Universitet (Uppsala University), which was founded in 1477; the next oldest is Lunds Universitet (Lund University), which was founded in 1666. Several institutions date from the 19th century, among them Kungliga Tekniska Högskolan (Royal Institute of Technology—founded 1827), Stockholms Universitet (Stockholm University—founded 1878) and Göteborgs Universitet (Gothenburg University—founded 1891). Higher education is offered by universities (universitet), university colleges or institutes of higher education (högskola). In 2012 there were 14 public universities and 20 public university colleges; a further three independent higher education institutions—Chalmers University of Technology, Stockholm School of Economics, Jönköping University Foundation—were entitled to award doctoral-level qualifications. In addition 10 independent institutions were accredited to offer qualifications to Masters level and a further four specialized in psychotherapy awards. In 2010/11 there were some 363,000 students enrolled at undergraduate and Masters level, and a further 18,900 enrolled at doctoral level.

Higher education formerly was administered by the Högskoleverket (Swedish National Agency for Higher Education). In 2013 three government agencies—the Högskoleverket, Internationella programkontoret (International Programme Office for Education and Training) and the Verket för högskoleservice (Swedish Agency for Higher Education Services)—ceased to exist and their areas of responsibility were moved to the Universitetskanslersämbetet (Swedish Higher Education Authority) and the Universitets- och högskolerådet (Swedish Council for Higher Education). In 1977 the Higher Education Act classified 100 programmes of undergraduate education by five subject areas (administrative, economic and social science; health; information, communication and fine arts; teacher training; and technical); however, in 1989 responsibility for curriculum-planning was handed over to the universities, and further reforms in 1993 delineated undergraduate programmes into general or professional fields of study. Also in 1993 higher education was decentralized and a new degree system was introduced. Sweden participates in the Bologna Process to establish a European Higher Education Area, the first phase of which is to adopt a credit-based system of comparable degrees with two main cycles (undergraduate and graduate). In 2002 the Ministry of Education and Research established a working group to assess the feasibility of introducing a new degree system to correspond with the criteria of the Bologna Process, and subsequently a new system (see below) was fully implemented in 2007. The Högskoleverket quality-assured all professional degree programmes in the period 2001–06. The new six-year cycle of programme evaluations started in 2007, covering all degrees at first, second and third level. Tuition for domestic and European Union (EU) students is free. However, at the beginning of the 2011/12 academic year Sweden introduced tuition fees for non-EU students; as a result, the number of foreign student applicants declined by 64 per cent.

The main requirement for admission to higher education is completion of secondary education and award of the Avgångsbetyg or Slutbetyg från Gymnasieskola (upper secondary school leaving certificate). Alternatively, applicants can be admitted upon completion of komvux (adult secondary school), completion of folkhögskola (folk high school) or at least four years of professional experience before the age of 25, as well as knowledge of Swedish and English. Specialist programmes of study may have additional criteria. Furthermore, applicants sit either the Högskoleprov (special aptitude test) or Högskoleprovet (national university aptitude test). The newly established university degree system comprises three cycles, each subdivided into two parts; degrees are awarded on a 'credit' basis, and Sweden has adopted the European Credit Transfer System (ECTS). The undergraduate Bachelors degrees is the Kandidatexamen, which lasts three years (180 credits). Yrkesexamen (professional degrees) may last longer. The Masters-equivalent degrees are the Magisterexamen, lasting one year (60 credits), and the Masterexamen, which lasts two years (120 credits). Both the Magisterexamen and the Masterexamen allow access to doctoral-level studies, which consist of the Licentiatexamen, a two-year research degree (120 credits), and the Doktorsexamen, a research degree culminating with submission and defence of a thesis; while it is possible to complete the Doktorsexamen in four years (240 credits), most students take six years.

The Kvalificerad Yrkesutbildning (Advanced Vocational Education—AVE), which was introduced in 1996 on a trial basis and enacted as law in 2002, primarily consists of programmes of study jointly organized by employers and institutions of tertiary education, and lasts between one and three years. The main government provider is the Myndigheten för Yrkeshögskolan (Swedish National Agency for Higher Vocational Education). Yrkeshögskoleutbildning (Higher Vocational Education Courses—HVECs) were introduced in 2009 and will gradually replace the AVE, which is to be phased out by 2013. HVECs last a minimum of six months. HVECs lasting at least one year and including a minimum of 25% workplace-based training as well as submission of a dissertation lead to award of the Yrkeshögskoleexamen (Higher Vocational Education Examination Certificate).

Regulatory and Representative Bodies

GOVERNMENT

Ministry of Culture: Drottninggatan 16, SE-103 33 Stockholm; tel. (8) 405-10-00; e-mail registrator@culture.ministry.se; internet www.sweden.gov.se/sb/d/8371; Minister for Culture and Sport LENA ADELSOHN LILJEROTH.

Ministry of Education and Research: Drottninggatan 16, SE-103 33 Stockholm; tel. (8) 405-10-00; e-mail registrator@education.ministry.se; internet www.sweden.gov.se/sb/d/2063; Minister JAN BJÖRKLUND.

ACCREDITATION

ENIC/NARIC Sweden: c/o Universitets- och högskolerådet, POB 45093, SE-104 30 Stockholm; tel. (10) 470-03-00; e-mail registrator@uhr.se; internet www.uhr.se/sv/bedomning-av-utlandsk-utbildning/utlandsk-utbildning/arbeta-i-sverige/sok-tidigare-utlatanden; f. 1995, present status 2013; assesses and recognizes foreign higher education; Head LARS PETERSSON.

NATIONAL BODIES

Folkhögskolornas informationstjänst (Information Service of the Swedish Folk High Schools): POB 380 74, SE-100 64 Stockholm; Rosenlundsgatan 50, Stockholm; tel. (8) 796-00-50; e-mail info@folkhogskola .nu; internet www.folkhogskola.nu; Coordinator AGNETA WALLIN.

Myndigheten för Yrkeshögskolan (Swedish National Agency for Higher Vocational Education): POB 145, SE-721 05 Västerås; Ingenjör Bååths gata 19, SE-722 12 Västerås; tel. (10) 209-01-00; e-mail info@myh .se; internet www.myh.se; f. 2009; Gen. Dir PIA ENOCHSSON.

Rådet för högre utbildning (Council for the Renewal of Higher Education): POB 7285, SE-103 89 Stockholm; Luntmakargatan 13, Stockholm; tel. (8) 56-30-88-61; e-mail rhu@rhu.se; f. 1990; Chair. Prof. LARS HAIKOLA.

Skolverket (Swedish National Agency for Education): SE-106 20 Stockholm; Fleminggatan 14, Stockholm; tel. (8) 52-73-32-00; e-mail registrator@skolverket.se; internet www.skolverket.se; sets out the goals and guidelines for pre-schools and schools through the Education Act and the Curricula; Dir-Gen. ANNA EKSTRÖM.

Styrelsen för Internationellt Utvecklingssamarbete (Swedish International Development Cooperation Agency): Valhallavägen 199, SE-105 25 Stockholm; tel. (8) 698-50-00; e-mail sida@sida.se; internet www.sida.se; attached to Min. for Foreign Affairs; carries out devt cooperation with 33 countries in Africa, Asia, Europe and Latin America; allocates aid and funding; Dir-Gen. CHARLOTTE PETRI GORNITZKA (acting).

Svenska institutet (Swedish Institute): Slottsbacken 10, POB 7434, SE-103 91 Stockholm; tel. (8) 453-78-00; e-mail si@si.se; internet www.si.se; f. 1945; promotes int. exchange within the areas of culture, education, research, society; Dir-Gen. ANNIKA REMBE.

Sveriges universitets- och högskoleförbund (SUHF) (Association of Swedish Higher Education): Tryckerigatan 8, SE-111 28 Stockholm; tel. (8) 32-13-88; internet www.suhf.se; f. 1995; provides forum for exchange of views and cooperation among its mem. instns and safeguards their interests; 40 mems (incl. 16 univs, 18 univ. colleges, 6 univ. art colleges); Chair. PAM FREDMAN; Sec.-Gen. MARIANNE GRANFELT.

Learned Societies
GENERAL

Finlandsinstitutet (Finnish Cultural Centre): POB 1355, SE-111 83 Stockholm; Snickarbacken 2–4 (vid Birger Jarlsgatan 35), SE-111 39, Stockholm; tel. (8) 54-52-12-00; e-mail info@finlandsinstitutet.se; internet www.finlandsinstitutet.se; f. 1995; 1 of 16 Finnish cultural instns worldwide; organizes cultural events, seminars, concerts, art exhibitions, language courses; library of 16,000 vols, audio books, CDs, video cassettes; Dir ANDERS ERIKSSON.

Kungl. Humanistiska Vetenskaps-Samfundet i Uppsala (Royal Society of Humanities at Uppsala): c/o Prof. Staffan Fridell, Dept of Scandinavian Languages, POB 527, SE-751 20 Uppsala; tel. (18) 471-12-94; e-mail info@khvsu.se; internet www.khvsu.se; f. 1889; promotes study of humanities; 5 meetings a year, with lectures and discussion; distributes awards and scholarships; 120 mems (100 Swedish, 20 foreign); Pres. Prof. MARIA ÅGREN; Gen. Sec. Prof. STAFFAN FRIDELL; publs *Acta Westiniana*, *Årsböcker* (Yearbook), *Skrifter* (Proceedings, irregular), *Uppländska domböcker*.

Kungl. Vetenskapsakademien (Royal Swedish Academy of Sciences): POB 50005, SE-104 05 Stockholm; Lilla Frescativägen 4A, SE-114 18 Stockholm; tel. (8) 673-95-00; e-mail info@kva.se; internet kva.se; f. 1739; acts as a forum where researchers can meet across subject borders; supports young researchers; rewards prominent contributions to research; arranges int. scientific contacts; acts as a voice of science and influences research policy priorities; stimulates interest in mathematics and natural sciences in schools; disseminates scientific and popular-scientific information in various forms; 615 mems (440 Swedish, 175 foreign); Pres. Prof. BARBARA CANNON; Permanent Sec. Prof. STAFFAN NORMARK; publs *Acta Mathematica*, *Acta Zoologica*, *Ambio*, *Arkiv för Matematik*, *ETAI*, *Physica Scripta*, *Zoologica Scripta*.

Kungl. Vetenskaps- och Vitterhets-Samhället i Göteborg (KVVS) (Royal Society of Arts and Sciences in Gothenburg): POB 222, SE-405 30 Gothenburg; tel. (31) 786-14-00; e-mail info@kvvs.se; internet www.kvvs.se; f. 1778; scientific lectures, confs, symposia, cooperation with other scientific academies, domestic and foreign support to long-term scientific research programmes; publs, exchange of publs nationally and internationally; 366 mems (276 Swedish, 90 foreign); Chair. Prof. KRISTER HOLMBERG; Sec. Gen. Prof. BIRGER KARLSSON; Treas. Prof. MARTIN FRITZ; publ. *Årsbok* (Yearbook).

Kungl. Vetenskaps-Societeten i Uppsala (Royal Society of Sciences at Uppsala): St Lars St 1, SE-753 10 Uppsala; tel. (18) 13-12-70; e-mail kansli@vetenskapssocietetenuppsala.se; internet www.vetenskapssocietetenuppsala.se; f. 1710, charter 1728; promotes research principally in mathematics, natural sciences, medicine, Swedish antiquities and topography by publishing scholarly works, awarding grants, collecting and making available relevant publs, lectures; 230 mems (130 full mems, 100 foreign mems); library of 600 periodicals; Pres. HM KING CARL XVI GUSTAF; Chair. Prof. MATS ALMGREN; Sec. Prof. LARS-OLOF SUNDELÖF; publs *Årsbok* (1 a year), *Matrikel* (1 a year), *Nova Acta Regia Societatis Scientiarum Upsaliensis* (irregular).

Kungl. Vitterhets Historie och Antikvitets Akademien (Royal Swedish Academy of Letters, History and Antiquities): Kungl. Vitterhetsakademien, POB 5622, SE-114 86 Stockholm; Villagatan 3, SE-114 86 Stockholm; tel. (8) 440-42-80; e-mail kansli@vitterhetsakad.se; internet www.vitterhetsakad.se; f. 1753, current name adopted 1786; promotes research and other activities in the fields of humanities, social sciences, religion, law; 166 mems (121 Swedish, 39 foreign, 6 hon.); library: see under Libraries and Archives; Pres. Prof. GUNNEL ENGWALL; Sec. Gen. Dr ERIK NORBERG; publs *Arkiv* (archives), *Fornvännen* (journal), *Handlingar* (proceedings).

AGRICULTURE, FISHERIES AND VETERINARY SCIENCE

Kungl. Skogs- och Lantbruksakademien (Royal Swedish Academy of Agriculture and Forestry): POB 6806, SE-113 86 Stockholm; Drottninggatan 95B, SE-113 86 Stockholm; tel. (8) 545-477-00; e-mail akademien@ksla.se; internet www.ksla.se; f. 1813; promotes sustainable devt, agriculture, forestry, horticulture, animal husbandry, hunting, fishing and water management; 635 mems (482 working, 153 foreign); library: see under Libraries and Archives; Pres. Dr KERSTIN NIBLAEUS; Sec.-Gen. Dr CARL-ANDERS HELANDER; publs *Freja* (6 a year), *KSLA Nytt & Noterat* (4 a year, online), *Kungl. Skogs och Lantbruksakademiens Tidskrift (KSLAT)* (4 a year).

ARCHITECTURE AND TOWN PLANNING

Svenska Teknik & Designföretagen (Swedish Federation of Consulting Engineers and Architects): POB 55545, SE-102 04 Stockholm; Sturegatan 11, SE-102 04 Stockholm; tel. (8) 762-67-00; e-mail std@std.se; internet www.std.se; f. 2001; focuses on improving the environment for mem. companies that operate both as a commercial party and employer; 700 mem. companies; Chair. INGER LINDBERG BRUCE; Man. Dir LENA WÄSTFELT; publ. *Sector Review* (1 a year).

ECONOMICS, LAW AND POLITICS

Centre for the Study of International Relations: Hagtornsvägen 9, Enebyberg, SE-182 47 Stockholm; tel. (8) 612-33-62; e-mail info@cintrel.org; f. 1971; studies social sciences, int. politics, law and economy; ind. of any political party; organizes lectures and confs, research seminars; library; Pres. CLÄES PALME; Vice-Pres. and Dir Prof. Dr RICHARD K. T. HSIEH; publ. *Review*.

International Law Association, Swedish Branch: c/o Atty John Kadelburger AB, Engelbrektsgatan 9–11, SE-114 32 Stockholm; tel. (8) 120-661-32; e-mail sekretariat@ilasweden.se; internet www.ilasweden.se; f. 1922; studies and develops int. law (private and procedural); promotes studies in comparative law; draws up proposals for conflict resolution and unification of measures in int. law; fosters int. understanding and goodwill; Pres. Prof. OVE BRING; Sec. and Treas. JOHN KADELBURGER.

Kungl Krigsvetenskapsakademien (Royal Swedish Academy of War Sciences): Teatergatan 3, 1 tr, SE-111 48 Stockholm; tel. (76) 760-96-40; e-mail info@kkrva.se; internet www.kkrva.se; f. 1796 as Swedish Military Asscn, present status 1805; promotes military sciences, incl. civil defence, economic defence and psychological defence, security and defence policy; 400 mems; Pres. Prof. BO HULDT; Sec. BJÖRN ANDERSON; publ. *Kungl Krigsvetenskapsakademiens Handlingar och Tidskrift* (4 a year).

Nationalekonomiska Föreningen (Swedish Economic Association): c/o SOFI, Stockholm Univ., SE-106 91 Stockholm; tel. (8) 16-34-54; e-mail susan.niknami@sofi.su.se; internet www.nationalekonomi.se; f. 1877; study of economics; 1,200 mems; Chair. Prof. MÅRTEN PALME; Sec. Dr SUSAN NIKNAMI; publ. *Ekonomisk Debatt* (8 a year).

Utrikespolitiska Institutet (Swedish Institute of International Affairs): POB 27035, SE-102 51 Stockholm; Drottning Kristinas väg 37, SE-102 51 Stockholm; tel. (8) 511-768-00; e-mail info@ui.se; internet www.ui.se; f. 1938; research on int. affairs; enhances public understanding of current int. affairs; confs, seminars and other events; 250 mems; library of 40,000 vols, 400 periodicals; Dir ANNA JARDFELT; Head of Research Dr JOHAN ERIKSSON; publs *Internationella studier*, *Länder i fickformat*, *Research Report*, *UI Papers*, *Världens Fakta*, *Världspolitikens dagsfrågor*.

FINE AND PERFORMING ARTS

Föreningen Svenska Tonsättare (Society of Swedish Composers): POB 17092, SE-104 62 Stockholm; Hornsgatan 103, 13 tr, SE-117 28 Stockholm; tel. (8) 783-88-43; internet www.fst.se; f. 1918; promotes contemporary classical music composition; promotes artistic, financial and social interests of its mems; 366 mems; Pres. MARTIN Q. LARSSON; Vice-Pres. ERIK PETERS.

Fylkingen (Society of Contemporary Music and Intermedia Art): Söder Mälarstrand 27, SE-118 25 Stockholm; Münchenbryggeriet, Torkel Knutssonsgatan 2, Münchenbryggeriet, Stockholm; tel. (8) 84-54-43; e-mail intermedia@fylkingen.se; internet www.fylkingen.se; f. 1933 as a chamber music soc.; promotes new music and intermedia art; 250 mems; Chair. SUSANNE SKOG; Sec. INGRID OLTERMAN; publ. *Hz* (2 a year, online (www.hz-journal.org)).

Kulturrådet (Swedish Arts Council): POB 27215, SE-102 53 Stockholm; tel. (8) 519-264-00; e-mail kulturradet@kulturradet.se; internet www.kulturradet.se; f. 1974; attached to Min. of Culture; funding, advisory and investigatory body responsible for implementing nat. cultural policy; covers theatre, dance, music, literature, cultural journals; public libraries, art, museums and exhibitions; Chair. KERSTIN BRUNNBERG; Dir-Gen. KENNET JOHANSSON; publ. *Kulturrådet*.

Kungliga Akademien för de fria Konsterna (Konstakademien) (Royal Swedish Academy of Fine Arts): POB 16317, SE-103 26 Stockholm; Fredsgatan 12, Jakobsgatan 27C, SE-103 26 Stockholm; tel. (8) 23-29-25; internet www.konstakademien.se; f. 1735; promotes devt of painting, sculpture, architecture and allied arts; 145 mems (102 Swedish, 24 foreign, 19 hon.); library of 60,000 vols; Pres. ULLA FRIES; Permanent Sec. SUSANNA SLÖÖR.

Kungl. Musikaliska Akademien (Royal Swedish Academy of Music): Blasieholmstorg 8, SE-111 48 Stockholm; tel. (8) 407-18-00; e-mail adm@musakad.se; internet www .musakad.se; f. 1771; promotes and protects the art and science of music; awards Rolf Schock Prize, Christ Johnson Prize and Royal Swedish Acad. of Music Jazz Prize; 230 mems (170 Swedish, 60 foreign); Pres. Prof. GUSTAF SJOKVIST; Permanent Sec. TOMAS LÖNDAHL; publs *Arsskrift* (yearbook), *Musica Sveciae* (record anthology).

Musikaliska Konstföreningen (Swedish Art Music Society): Sveavägen 12, Saltsjöbaden, SE-133 34 Stockholm; tel. (709) 20-61-96; e-mail noter@ musikaliskakonstforeningen.se; internet www.musikaliskakonstforeningen.se; f. 1859; publishes and sells works of ancient and contemporary composers; promotes Swedish music; Chair. ERIK LUNDKVIST; Sec. HANS ENFLO; Treas. ALF WESTELIUS.

Svensk Form (Swedish Society of Crafts and Design): POB 204, SE-101 24 Stockholm; Svensksundsvägen, 13 Skeppsholmen, SE-111 49 Stockholm; tel. (8) 463-31-30; e-mail info@svenskform.se; internet svenskform.se; f. 1845 as Swedish Soc. for Industrial Design; promotes Swedish designs and handicraft; incl. 11 regional asscns; 8,000 mems; Man. Dir EWA KUMLIN; publ. *Form* (6 a year).

Svenska Samfundet för Musikforskning (Swedish Society for Musicology): POB 7448, SE-103 91 Stockholm; tel. (46) 12-10-27; internet musikforskning.se; f. 1919; unifying forum for musicologists; disseminates knowledge of musicological research in and about Sweden; 87 mems; Chair. JACOB DERKERT; Sec. MATTIAS LUNDBERG; Treas. EVA KJEL-LANDER; publs *Monumenta Musicae Sveciae*, *Svensk Tidskrift för Musikforskning* (Swedish Journal of Musicology, 1 a year).

Sveriges Allmänna Konstförening (Swedish Association for Art): POB 5343, SE-102 47 Stockholm; Slupskjulsvägen 34, Skeppsholmen, Stockholm; tel. (8) 10-46-77; e-mail info@konstforeningen.se; internet www.konstforeningen.se; f. 1832; promotes Swedish contemporary art; organizes exhibitions; 5,000 mems; Pres. EVA SCHÖLD; Dir JENNIE FAHLSTRÖM; Treas. JAN-ERIK SÖDER-HIELM; publ. *Sveriges Allmänna Konstförenings årspublikation* (Swedish General Art Association's annual publication).

HISTORY, GEOGRAPHY AND ARCHAEOLOGY

Karolinska Förbundet: Riksarkivet, POB 12541, SE-102 29 Stockholm; tel. (8) 727-02-15; e-mail info@karolinskaforbundet.se; internet www.karolinskaforbundet.se; f. 1910; promotes research and dissemination of knowledge on the Caroline era; 1,000 mems; Pres. Dr ÅSA KARLSSON; Sec. Dr PETER NORDSTRÖM; publ. *Karolinska Förbundets Arsbok* (Yearbook).

Kartografiska Sällskapet (Swedish Cartographic Society): c/o Lantmäteriet, SE-801 82 Gävle; tel. (26) 63-32-37; e-mail ks@ kartografiska.se; internet www .kartografiska.se; f. 1908; promotes and develops cartography and other topics related to mapping or use of maps in Sweden in areas such as photogrammetry, remote sensing, geodesy, geographical information systems, geographic information technology, historical cartography; 2,073 mems; Pres. PETER WASSTRÖM; Sec. KARIN GRÅNÄS; publs *Kart & Bildteknik* (4 a year), *National Report* (mapping activities, every 4 years, in English), *Sveriges Kartläggning* (mapping of Sweden, every 10 years).

Riksförbundet Sveriges Museer (RSM) (Association of Swedish Museums): Kyrkogatan 16A, SE-371 32 Karlskrona; tel. (708) 11-60-40; internet www.sverigesmuseer.se; f. 1906; works to safeguard and promote communal interests of the museum sector; 175 mem. museums; Pres. ROBERT OLSSON; Sec.-Gen. MATS PERSSON; publ. *Svenska Museer* (5 a year).

Svenska Sällskapet för Antropologi och Geografi (Swedish Society for Anthropology and Geography): c/o Madeleine Bonow, School of Natural Sciences, Technology and Environmental Studies, Södertörn Univ., SE-141 89 Huddinge; tel. (8) 608-47-08; e-mail ssagmail@yahoo.se; internet www.ssag.se; f. 1873 as Asscn for Anthropology, current name adopted 1877; advances the devt of anthropology and geography in Sweden; communicates with foreign socs with the same objectives; supports research into anthropology and geography; 900 mems; library of 10,000 vols; Pres. Prof. STEN HAGBERG; Sec. Dr MADELEINE BONOW; Treas. Dr THOMAS BORÉN; publs *Arsboken Ymer* (1 a year), *Geografiska Annaler A—Physical Geography* (4 a year), *Geografiska Annaler B—Human Geography* (4 a year), *Ymir* (1 a year).

LANGUAGE AND LITERATURE

Alliance Française: c/o Diana Schwarcz, Sandhamnsgatan 12, SE-11 540 Stockholm; tel. (8) 29-08-33; e-mail info@afstockholm .com; internet www.afstockholm.com; f. 1889; offers courses and exams in French language and culture and promotes cultural exchange with France; attached offices in Borås, Falun, Gothenburg, Halmstad, Helsingborg, Höglandet, Jönköping, Kalmar, Kristianstad, Linköping, Lund, Norrköping, Nyköping, Örebro, Örnsköldsvik, Östersund, Skaraborg, Skelleftea and Uppsala; Pres. JOHAN STENBERG; Sec. DIANA SCHWARCZ; Treas. ÅKE NILSSON.

British Council: c/o Hub Stockholm Riddargatan 17D, 3tr, SE-114 57 Stockholm; tel. (61) 957-77-55; e-mail sweden.enquiries@ britishcouncil.org; internet www .britishcouncil.org; offers courses and exams in English language and British culture and promotes cultural exchange with the UK; Country Dir ELIN SVENSSON.

Goethe-Institut: Bryggargatan 12A, SE-111 21 Stockholm; tel. (8) 459-12-00; e-mail info@ stockholm.goethe.org; internet www.goethe .de/stockholm; offers courses and exams in German language and culture and promotes cultural exchange with Germany; attached teaching centre in Gothenburg; library of 3,500 vols, 45 periodicals; Dir and Head of Programme Work HEIKE FRIESEL; Dir and Head of Programme Work RAINER HAUS-WIRTH; Deputy Dir and Head of Language Dept KARIN THELEMANN.

Instituto Cervantes: Bryggargatan 12A, SE-111 21 Stockholm; tel. (8) 440-17-60; e-mail info.stockholm@cervantes.es; internet estocolmo.cervantes.es/se; f. 2005; offers courses and exams in Spanish language and culture and promotes cultural exchange with Spain and Spanish-speaking Latin and Central America; library of 13,000 vols incl. books, magazines, CDs and DVDs; Dir JOAN M. ALVAREZ VALENCIA; Librarian JOHNNY PETTERSSON.

Samfundet de Nio (Academy of the Nine): Villagatan 14, SE-114 32 Stockholm; tel. (70) 573-44-08; internet www.samfundetdenio.se; f. 1913; awards literary prizes; Pres. Prof. INGE JONSSON; Sec. and Treas. ANDERS R. ÖHMAN; publ. *De Nios litterära kalender* (1 a year).

Språkrådet (Language Council of Sweden): POB 20057, SE-104 60 Stockholm; Alsnögatan 7, 7 tr, Stockholm; tel. (8) 442-42-00; e-mail sprakradet@sprakradet.se; internet www.sprakradet.se; f. 2006 by merger of Swedish Language Ccl, Sweden Finnish Language Ccl and Plain group in the Cabinet Office; attached to Institute for Language and Folklore; official language planning agency; provides advice on language issues and follows language devt in Sweden; engaged in linguistic research and promotes Swedish and Nordic language cooperation; Head LENA EKBERG; publs *Kieliviesti* (4 a year), *Klarspråk–bulletin från Språkrådet* (4 a year).

Svenska Akademien (Swedish Academy): POB 2118, SE-103 13 Stockholm; Källargränd 4, Gamla Stan, Stockholm; tel. (8) 555-125-00; e-mail sekretariat@ svenskaakademien.se; internet www .svenskaakademien.se; f. 1786; Swedish language and literature; awards Nobel Prize for Literature; 18 mems; library: see under Libraries and Archives; Permanent Sec. Prof. PETER ENGLUND; Treas. CARINA LINDQVIST; publ. *Svenska Akademiens Handlingar* (1 a year).

Svenska PEN (Swedish PEN): Johannesgränd 1, SE-111 30 Stockholm; tel. (70) 272-57-33; e-mail info@svenskapen.se; internet www.svenskapen.se; f. 1922; promotes literature; discussion, debates, communication among writers; 900 mems; Chair. OLA LARSMO; Sec. PETER KARLSSON; Treas. JESPER MONTHÁN.

Svenska Vitterhetssamfundet: Mariatorget 1C, SE-118 48 Stockholm; tel. (8) 10-19-69; e-mail vitterhet@gmail.com; internet www.svenskavitterhetssamfundet.se; f. 1907; publishes critical edns by Swedish authors; 311 mems; Sec. PETRA SÖDERLUND.

Sveriges Författarförbund (Swedish Writers' Union): POB 3157, SE-103 63 Stockholm; Drottninggatan 88B, Stockholm; tel. (8) 545-132-00; e-mail sff@sff.info; internet www.forfattarforbundet.se; f. 1893 as Swedish Asscn of Authors, present name and status 1970; protects intellectual and economic interests of writers and translators; 2,835 mems; Pres. GUNNAR ARDELIUS; Dir LOUISE HEDBERG; publ. *Författaren* (6 a year).

MEDICINE

Socialstyrelsen (National Board of Health and Welfare): SE-106 30 Stockholm; Rålambsvägen 3, Stockholm; tel. (75) 247-30-00; e-mail socialstyrelsen@socialstyrelsen .se; internet www.socialstyrelsen.se; f. 1968 by merger of Royal Medical Board and Royal Board of Social Affairs; attached to Min. of Health and Social Affairs; collects, compiles, analyses and disseminates relevant data; develops and implements standards based on legislation and data collected; maintains health data registers and official statistics; Dir-Gen. LARS-ERIK HOLM.

Svenska Läkaresällskapet (Swedish Society of Medicine): POB 738, SE-101 35 Stockholm; Klara Östra Kyrkogata 10, SE-101 35 Stockholm; tel. (8) 440-88-60; e-mail sls@sls.se; internet www.sls.se; f. 1808, present bldg 1906; promotes research, education and devt in health care sector; 16,000 mems; Chair. PETER FRIBERG; Sec. PER TORNVALL; publ. *Svenska Läkaresällskapets Handlingar Hygiea.*

NATURAL SCIENCES

General

Kungl. Skytteanska Samfundet (Royal Skytte Society): Humanisthuset, SE-901 87 Umeå; tel. (90) 14-14-28; e-mail skytteanska@adm.umu.se; internet www.skytteanskasamfundet.se; f. 1956; promotes and supports scientific research, particularly that of Norrland interest; Pres. LARS-ERIK EDLUND; Sec. ULF WIBERG; publs *Journal of Northern Studies* (2 a year), *Kungl. Skytteanska Samfundets årsbok* (Yearbook), *THULE* (1 a year).

Svenska Linnésällskapet (Swedish Linnaeus Society): POB 15093, SE-750 15 Uppsala; tel. (18) 471-62-71; e-mail info@linnaeus.se; internet www.linnaeus.se; f. 1917; expands knowledge about Carl Linnaeus and his work; encourages interest in nature and scientific culture; publishes writings by and about Carl Linnaeus and his disciples; attached museum; Pres. BIRGITTA JOHANSSON-HEDBERG; Sec. MIKAEL STRANDANGER; Treas. LARS-OLOF LINDELL; publ. *Swedish Linnaeus Society Yearbook (SLA).*

Wenner-Gren Stiftelserna (Wenner-Gren Foundations): Sveavägen 166, 23rd Fl., SE-113 46 Stockholm; tel. (8) 736-98-11; internet www.swgc.org; f. 1962; residence and meeting place for foreign and visiting scientists; Chair. Prof. DAN BRÄNDSTRÖM; Scientific Sec. Prof. BRITT-MARIE SJÖBERG.

Biological Sciences

Kungl. Fysiografiska Sällskapet i Lund (Royal Physiographic Society of Lund): Stortorget 6, SE-222 23 Lund; tel. (46) 13-25-28; e-mail kansli@fysiografen.se; internet www.fysiografen.se; f. 1772 as Acad. of Natural Sciences, Medicine and Technology, present name and status 1778; science, medicine and technology; 500 mems, 100 foreign corresps; Pres. Prof. ROLAND VON BOTHMER; Sec. and Treas. PER ALM; publ. *Arsbok* (Biennial Yearbook, every 2 years).

Naturskyddsföreningen (Swedish Society for Nature Conservation): POB 4625, Asögatan 115, 2 tr, SE-116 91 Stockholm; tel. (8) 702-65-00; e-mail medlem@naturskyddsforeningen.se; internet www.naturskyddsforeningen.se; f. 1909; deals with environmental issues; areas of work incl. climate, oceans, forests, pollution, agriculture; mem. of IUCN; 192,000 mems; Pres. MIKAEL KARLSSON; Dir CATHARINA LIHNELL IRON HESTER; publ. *Sveriges Natur* (6 a year).

Svenska Bioenergiföreningen (Svebio) (Swedish Bioenergy Association (Svebio)): Holländargatan 17, SE-111 60 Stockholm; tel. (8) 441-70-80; e-mail info@svebio.se; internet www.svebio.se; f. 1980; devt of bioenergy in Sweden; 300 mems; Chair. GUNNAR OLOFSSON; Man. Dir GUSTAV MELIN.

Mathematical Sciences

Lunds Matematiska Sällskap (Lund Mathematical Society): c/o Matematiska Institutionen, POB 118, SE-221 00 Lund; internet www.matematik.lu.se/lms; f. 1923; promotes greater interest in mathematics and related subjects, both among the gen. public and students; 150 mems; Pres. Prof.

NILS DENCKER; Sec. and Treas. FREDRIK EKSTRÖM.

Svenska Matematikersamfundet (Swedish Mathematical Society): c/o Mats Andersson, Dept of Mathematics, Chalmers Univ. of Technology and Univ. of Gothenburg, SE-412 96 Goteborg; tel. (31) 772-35-71; e-mail president@swe-math-soc.se; internet www.swe-math-soc.se; f. 1950; meetings, journals, education of mathematics teachers, mathematics competition for students, travel grants for PhD students, research prizes for young mathematicians; 540 mems; Chair. Prof. MATS ANDERSSON; Sec. ELIZABETH WULCAN; publs *Mathematica Scandinavia* (with other Scandinavian mathematical socs), *Nordisk Matematisk Tidskrift* (with other Scandinavian mathematical socs).

Svenska Statistikfrämjandet (Swedish Statistics Promotion): Arenavägen 7, SE-121 88 Stockholm; tel. (8) 688-76-66; e-mail sekrfram@gmail.com; internet www.statistikframjandet.se; f. 2008 by merger of Statistical Soc. and Swedish Statistician Community; promotes research, devt, education in statistics; provides a forum for its mems; Pres. BO WALLENTIN; Sec. THORBJÖRN GUDMUNDSSON.

Physical Sciences

Geologiska Föreningen (Geological Society of Sweden): c/o Insitutionen för geo- och ekosystemsvetenskaper, Lunds Univ., Sölvegatan 12, SE-223 62 Lund; tel. (46) 222-46-35; e-mail info@geologiskaforeningen.se; internet geologiskaforeningen.se; f. 1871; promotes geology and Earth science; 600 mems; Chair. MARK JOHNSON (acting); Sec. ANNA KIM-ANDERSSON; publs *Geologiskt forum* (4 a year, in Swedish), *GFF* (4 a year, in English).

Kungl. Örlogsmannasällskapet (Royal Swedish Society of Naval Sciences): Teatergatan 3, 5 tr, SE-111 48 Stockholm; tel. (8) 664-70-18; e-mail akademien@koms.se; internet www.koms.se; f. 1771, reorganized 1777; promotes devts in naval sciences and maritime sciences; library of 15,000 vols, maps, charts, archival records; 400 mems; Pres. THOMAS ENGEVALL; Sec.-Gen. BO RASK; publ. *Tidskrift i Sjöväsendet (TiS)* (4 a year).

Svenska Fysikersamfundet (Swedish Physical Society): Dept of Physics and Astronomy, POB 516, SE-751 20 Uppsala; tel. (13) 28-12-03; e-mail kansliet@fysikersamfundet.se; internet www.fysikersamfundet.se; f. 1920; promotes physics research and applications; spreads knowledge about physics and physics education; stimulates public interest in physics and natural sciences in gen.; 800 mems; Chair. ANNE-SOFIE MÅRTENSSON; Sec. Dr RAIMUND FEIFEL; publs *Fysikaktuellt* (4 a year), *Kosmos* (1 a year).

RELIGION, SOCIOLOGY AND ANTHROPOLOGY

Kungl. Gustav Adolfs Akademien för svensk folkkultur (Royal Gustavus Adolphus Academy for Swedish Folk Culture): Klostergatan 2, SE-753 21 Uppsala; tel. (18) 71-16-38; e-mail info@kgaa.nu; internet www.kgaa.nu; f. 1932; 218 mems (incl. honorary); Pres. Prof. LENNART ELMEVIK; Sec. Dr MAJ REINHAMMAR; Treas. INGEMAR ANDERSÉN; publs *Acta Academiae Regiae Gustavi Adolphi* (irregular), *Arv. Nordic Yearbook of Folklore* (1 a year), *Ethnologia Scandinavica* (1 a year), *Namn och bygd* (1 a year), *Saga och Sed* (1 a year), *Studia Anthroponymica Scandinavica* (1 a year), *Svenska landsmål och svenskt folkliv* (1 a year).

TECHNOLOGY

Kungl. Ingenjörsvetenskapsakademien—IVA (Royal Swedish Academy of Engineering Sciences): POB 5073, SE-102 42 Stockholm; Grev Turegatan 16, SE-102 42 Stockholm; tel. (8) 791-29-00; e-mail info@iva.se; internet www.iva.se; f. 1919; promotes engineering and economic science; acts as a clearing house for scientific information; establishes contacts with foreign research orgs by means of lectures and confs, trade research orgs and research agreements with East European countries, China and the Republic of Korea; 1,000 Swedish and foreign mems; library of 10,000 vols; Pres. Prof. BJÖRN O. NILSSON; Sec. JOHAN WEIGELT; publs *IVA-Aktuellt, Meddelanden, Rapporter.*

Svenska Geotekniska Föreningen (Swedish Geotechnical Society): c/o Minocta Ekonomi Tellusvägen 43, SE-186 36 Vallentuna; tel. (13) 20-18-00; e-mail info@sgf.net; internet www.sgf.net; f. 1950; 1,000 individual mems, 25 corporate mems; Chair. GUNILLA FRANZÉN; Sec. HÅKAN KARLSSON.

Sveriges Ingenjörer (Swedish Association of Graduate Engineers): POB 1419, SE-111 84 Stockholm; Malmskillnadsgatan 48, Stockholm; tel. (8) 613-80-00; e-mail info@sverigesingenjorer.se; internet www.sverigesingenjorer.se; f. 2007, merger of Civil Engineers and Professional Engineers; safeguards and promotes interests of its mems; 135,000 mems; Pres. ULF BENGTSSON; Man. Dir RICHARD MALMBORG; publs *Ingenjören* (5 a year), *Ny Teknik-Teknisk Tidskrift* (52 a year).

Research Institutes

GENERAL

Forskningsrådet Formas (Swedish Research Council Formas): POB 1206, SE-111 82 Stockholm; Kungsbron 21, Stockholm; tel. (8) 775-40-00; e-mail registrator@formas.se; internet www.formas.se; f. 2001; govt research funding agency; encourages and supports research related to sustainable devt; programme areas incl. environment, agriculture (incl. horticulture, fisheries and reindeer husbandry), forestry and the natural environment, the built environment, urban and regional planning; Dir-Gen. ROLF ANNERBERG; Sec.-Gen. Prof. Dr ANNA LEDIN; publs *Miljöforskning* (6 a year, print and online), *Sustainability* (4 a year, in English, online).

Life & Peace Institute: Sabygatan 4, SE-753 23 Uppsala; tel. (18) 66-01-30; e-mail info@life-peace.org; internet www.life-peace.org; f. 1985; deals with non-violent conflict transformation and research about role of religion in peace and conflict as well as traditional conflict resolution mechanisms; regional offices in Nairobi (Kenya), Bukavu (Democratic Republic of the Congo), Khartoum (Sudan); Pres. Rev. GUSTAF ODQVIST; Exec. Dir PETER KARLSSON SJÖGREN; publs *Horn of Africa Bulletin* (6 a year), *New Routes* (4 a year).

Stockholm International Water Institute: Drottninggatan 33, SE-111 51 Stockholm; tel. (8) 121-360-00; e-mail siwi@siwi.org; internet www.siwi.org; f. 1991; generates and promotes knowledge, solutions and tools related to water for sustainable devt on 5 thematic areas: water governance, transboundary water management, climate change and water, the water, food and energy nexus, water economics; organizes World Water Week; Chair. PETER FORSSMAN; Exec. Dir TORGNY HOLMGREN.

Stockholm Resilience Centre: Stockholm Univ., Kräftriket 2B, SE-106 91 Stockholm; tel. (8) 674-70-70; e-mail info@stockholmresilience.su.se; internet www.stockholmresilience.org; f. 2007; transdisciplinary research of social-ecological systems; jt initiative between Stockholm Univ., Stockholm Environment Institute, Beijer Int. Institute of Ecological Economics; Exec. Dir Prof. JOHAN ROCKSTRÖM; Science Dir Prof. CARL FOLKE.

Vetenskapsrådet (Swedish Research Council): POB 1035, SE-101 38 Stockholm; Västra Järnvägsgatan 3, Stockholm; tel. (8) 546-440-00; e-mail vr@vr.se; internet www.vr.se; f. 2001; attached to Min. of Education and Research; provides support for basic research of highest academic quality in all areas of knowledge; assumed duties of fmr Swedish Ccl for Planning and Co-ordination of Research, Swedish Ccl for Research in the Humanities and Social Sciences, Swedish Medical Research Ccl, and Swedish Natural Science Research Ccl, and Swedish Research Ccl for Engineering Sciences; cttees for Culture and the Social Sciences; Dir-Gen. Prof. Dr MILLE MILLNERT; Exec. Dir GÖRAN ENANDER.

AGRICULTURE, FISHERIES AND VETERINARY SCIENCE

AgriFood Economics Centre: POB 730, Scheelevägen 15D, SE-220 07 Lund; e-mail info@agrifood.lu.se; internet www.agrifood.se; f. 2009; cooperative venture between Swedish Univ. of Agricultural Sciences (SLU) and Lund Univ.; economic analysis of food, agriculture, fishing and rural devt; Research Dir Dr EWA RABINOWICZ.

JTI–Institutet för jordbruks- och miljöteknik (JTI—Swedish Institute of Agricultural and Environmental Engineering): POB 7033, SE-750 07 Uppsala; tel. (10) 516-69-00; e-mail info@jti.se; internet www.jti.se; f. 1945, present status 2009; attached to SP Technical Research Institute of Sweden; focuses on research, devt and information in areas of agricultural engineering and environmental technology; Exec. Dir MONICA AXELL (acting); publ. DRIV.

Skogforsk (Forestry Research Institute of Sweden): Dag Hammarskjölds Väg 36A, Uppsala Science Park, SE-751 83 Uppsala; tel. (18) 18-85-00; e-mail skogforsk@skogforsk.se; internet www.skogforsk.se; central research body for the Swedish forestry sector; research programmes on wood utilization, technology, logistics and forest bioenergy, forest tree breeding, silviculture and environment; Man. Dir. JAN FRYK; Deputy Dir. KAJ ROSÉN; publ. Skogforsks Redogörelser (6 a year).

Statens Veterinärmedicinska Anstalt (National Veterinary Institute): Ulls Väg 2B, SE-751 89 Uppsala; tel. (18) 67-40-00; e-mail sva@sva.se; internet www.sva.se; f. 1911; attached to Min. for Rural Affairs; research, diagnostic work, consultative work concerning control and prophylaxis of animal diseases; nat. veterinary laboratory; incl. central laboratory, epizootiology unit, animal diseases specialist unit; library of 27,000 vols; Dir-Gen. JENS MATTSSON; Sec. GUNILLA LINDGREN; publ. SVA Vet (irregular).

Wallenberg Wood Science Centre: Teknikringen 56–58, SE-100 44 Stockholm; Chalmers, Kemigården 4, SE-412 96 Gothenburg; tel. (8) 790-81-18; e-mail blund@kth.se; internet wwsc.se; f. 2009; jt research centre at KTH and Chalmers; focus on building material research programme to develop new products using forests; Chair. Prof. BJÖRN HÄGGLUND; Dir Prof. LARS BERGLUND.

ARCHITECTURE AND TOWN PLANNING

Nordregio (Nordic Centre for Spatial Development): POB 1658, SE-111 86 Stockholm; Skeppsholmen, Holmamiralens väg 10, Stockholm; tel. (8) 463-54-00; e-mail nordregio@nordregio.se; internet www.nordregio.se; f. 1997, present status 2000; administered by Nordic Ccl of Mins; demography, global climate change and local adaptation, governance and gender, innovation and knowledge, int. energy policy, regional devt, urban and rural systems; Dir Dr KJELL NILSSON; publs European Journal of Spatial Development (online (www.nordregio.se/ejsd)), Journal of Nordregio (4 a year).

ECONOMICS, LAW AND POLITICS

Beijerinstitutet för Ekologisk Ekonomi (Beijer Institute of Ecological Economics): POB 50005, SE-104 05 Stockholm; Lilla Frescativägen 4A, Stockholm; tel. (8) 673-95-00; e-mail beijer@beijer.kva.se; internet www.beijer.kva.se; f. 1977, reorganized 1991; attached to Royal Swedish Acad. of Sciences; collaborative research between economists and ecologists and related disciplines; Chair. SCOTT BARRETT; Dir Prof. CARL FOLKE; publs Ecology and Society (e-journals, 2 a year), Environment and Development Economics (e-journal).

Ekonomiska Forskningsinstitutet (Economic Research Institute): Stockholm School of Economics, POB 6501, SE-113 83 Stockholm; tel. (8) 736-90-00; e-mail efi@hhs.se; internet www.hhs.se/efi; f. 1929; attached to Stockholm School of Economics; research in economics, business administration, finance and law; 20 centres; library of 150,000 vols, 15,000 e-journals, 60 databases; Dir Prof. FILIP WIJKSTRÖM; publ. Forskning i Fickformat (4 a year).

Entrepreneurship and Small Business Research Institute: Saltmätargatan 9, SE-113 59 Stockholm; tel. (8) 458-78-00; e-mail info@esbri.se; internet www.esbri.se; f. 1996; research on entrepreneurship and small and medium-sized enterprises; founded award for entrepreneurship; Chair. Prof. ANDERS FLODSTRÖM; Man. Dir MAGNUS ARONSSON.

Institute for International Economic Studies: c/o Stockholm Univ., SE-106 91 Stockholm; A-bldg, Eighth Floor, Södra Huset, Stockholm Univ., SE-104 05 Stockholm; tel. (8) 16-20-00; internet www.iies.su.se; f. 1962; research in fields of political economy, macroeconomics, climate change and the economy, economic development, mass media, labour market; Dir HARRY FLAM; Deputy Dir JAKOB SVENSSON; publ. The Review of Economic Studies (4 a year).

Institute for Security and Development Policy: Västra Finnbodavägen 2, SE-131 30 Nacka; tel. (8) 410-569-60; e-mail info@isdp.eu; internet www.isdp.eu; f. 2007; research into int. conflict, security and devt, esp. Eurasia; Dir Dr SVANTE CORNELL; Deputy Dir JOHANNA POPJANEVSKI; publs The Central Asia-Caucasus Analyst (web journal), The China and Eurasia Forum Quarterly (4 a year), The Turkey Analyst (52 a week).

Institutet för Näringslivsforskning (Research Institute of Industrial Economics): POB 55665, SE-102 15 Stockholm; Grevgatan 34, Stockholm; tel. (8) 665-45-00; e-mail info@ifn.se; internet www.ifn.se; f. 1939 as Industrial Institute for Economic and Social Research, current name adopted 2006; conducts research in the field of economics; Chair. MICHAEL TRESCHOW; Dir Prof. Dr MAGNUS HENREKSON; publ. Årsbok (Yearbook).

Institution för Spanska, Portugisiska och Latinamerikastudier: Stockholms Univ., Universitetsvägen 10B, SE-106 91 Stockholm; tel. (8) 16-34-36; internet www.ispla.su.se; f. 2000; research on Spanish, Portuguese, Latin American economic, social and political devt; information, seminars, courses; library of 40,000 vols; Head Prof. LARS FANT.

Nordiska Afrikainstitutet (Nordic Africa Institute): POB 1703, SE-751 47 Uppsala; Villavägen 6, SE-752 36 Uppsala; tel. (18) 471-52-00; e-mail nai@nai.uu.se; internet www.nai.uu.se; f. 1962; documentation, information and research centre for current African affairs; publ. work, lectures and seminars; library of 70,000 vols, 400 periodicals, 127 online databases; Dir IINA SOIRI (acting); Chief Librarian ÅSA LUND MOBERG; publs Africa Now, Current African Issues, Policy Notes.

Raoul Wallenberg Institute of Human Rights and Humanitarian Law: Stora Gråbrödersg. 17B, POB 1155, SE-221 05 Lund; tel. (46) 222-12-00; internet rwi.lu.se; f. 1984; ind. academic instn for human rights promotion through research, training and education; library of 30,000 vols; Chair. LENNART SVENSÄTER; Dir MARIE TUMA; publs Baltic Yearbook of International Law, Chinese Yearbook of Human Rights, International Journal on Minority and Group Rights (4 a year), Nordic Journal of International Law (4 a year).

Ratio Institute: Sveavägen 59, 4 tr., POB 3203, SE-103 64 Stockholm; tel. (8) 441-59-00; e-mail info@ratio.se; internet www.ratio.se; f. 2002; researches enterprise and entrepreneurship; conducts research-seminar series; Pres. and CEO NILS KARLSON; Vice-Pres. NICLAS BERGGREN.

Statistiska Centralbyrån (Statistics Sweden): POB 24300, SE-104 51 Stockholm; Karlavägen 100, Stockholm; tel. (8) 506-940-00; e-mail scb@scb.se; internet www.scb.se; f. 1858; supplies customers (govt and private sector) with statistics for decision making, debate and research; br. in Örebro; library: see under Libraries and Archives; Dir.-Gen. STEFAN LUNDGREN; publs Företag—Tidning för Uppgiftslämnare (1 a year), Journal of Official Statistics, SCB—Kundtidning (4 a year), Statistical Abstract of Sweden, Statistical Reports, Statistical Yearbook of Sweden, Survey of Living Conditions.

Stockholm Institute for Scandinavian Law: Faculty of Law, Univ. of Stockholm, SE-106 91 Stockholm; tel. (8) 16-25-48; e-mail sisl@juridicum.su.se; internet www.scandinavianlaw.se; f. 1956; attached to Faculty of Law, Stockholm Univ.; spreads knowledge about Scandinavian law and jurisprudence abroad.

Stockholm Institute of Transition Economics: POB 6501, SE-113 83 Stockholm; Sveavägen 65, Ninth Floor, A, Stockholm; tel. (8) 736-96-70; e-mail site@hhs.se; internet www.hhs.se/site; f. 1989; attached to Stockholm School of Economics; research and policy centre on transition in former USSR and E Europe; Chair. FINN RAUSING; Dir Dr TORBJÖRN BECKER.

Stockholm International Peace Research Institute: Signalistgatan 9, SE-169 70 Solna; tel. (8) 655-97-51; e-mail sipri@sipri.org; internet www.sipri.org; f. 1966; research in conflict, armaments, arms control and disarmament; library of 52,000 vols, 550 journals; Chair. GÖRAN LENNMARKER; Dir Prof. Dr TILMAN BRUECK; publ. SIPRI Yearbook.

Swedish Collegium for Advanced Study (SCAS): Linneanum, Thunbergsvägen 2, SE-752 38 Uppsala; tel. (18) 55-70-85; e-mail info@swedishcollegium.se; internet www.swedishcollegium.se; f. 1985; offers 14 fellowships for study at the Collegium each semester; Chair. Prof. LARS MAGNUSSON; Prin. Prof. BJÖRN WITTROCK.

LANGUAGE AND LITERATURE

Institutet för Språk och Folkminnen (Institute for Language and Folklore): POB 135, SE-751 04 Uppsala; von Kraemers allé 2, Arkivcentrum, Uppsala; tel. (18) 65-21-60; e-mail registrator@sofi.se; internet www.sofi .se; f. 2006; collects, preserves and researches on dialects, place names, personal names and folklore; works on language planning and language policy; Gen.-Dir INGRID JOHANSSON LIND.

MEDICINE

Laboratory for Molecular Infection Medicine Sweden: University of Umeå, SE-901 87 Umeå; tel. (90) 785-67-60; internet www.mims.umu.se; f. 2007; promotes research in the field of molecular medicine by promoting the career opportunities for young scientists; Dir Prof. Dr BERNT ERIC UHLIN; Sec. Prof. Dr ÅKE FORSBERG.

Livsmedelsverket (National Food Agency): POB 622, SE-751 26 Uppsala; Hamnesplanaden 5, Uppsala; tel. (18) 17-55-00; e-mail livsmedelsverket@slv.se; internet www.slv .se; f. 1972; attached to Min. of Rural Affairs, Food and Fisheries; central admin. authority for matters concerning food; protects interests of the consumer by working for safe food, fair practices in the food trade, healthy eating habits; library of 11,000 vols; Dir-Gen. INGER ANDERSSON; publs Livsmedelsverkets författningar (The National Food Administration's Regulations), Vår Föda (popular scientific).

Ludwig Institute for Cancer Research Ltd: POB 595, SE-751 24 Uppsala; Biomedical Centre, Husargatan 3, Entrance C11, Third Floor, Uppsala; tel. (18) 16-04-00; e-mail ludwig@licr.uu.se; internet www.licr .uu.se; f. 1972; research to elucidate the signalling pathways that control cell growth; Dir Prof. Dr CARL-HENRIK HELDIN.

Statens Folkhälsoinstitut (Swedish National Institute of Public Health): Forskarens väg 3, SE-831 40 Östersund; tel. (63) 19-96-00; e-mail info@fhi.se; internet www.fhi .se; attached to Min. of Health and Social Affairs; monitors and coordinates implementation of nat. public health policy; acts as nat. expert agency for devt and dissemination of methods and strategies in the field of public health, based on scientific evidence; exercises supervision in the areas of alcohol and tobacco; Dir-Gen. Dr SARAH WAMALA.

Stockholm Brain Institute: Karolinska Institutet, Retzius väg 8, SE-171 76 Stockholm; tel. (70) 745-97-61; e-mail none-marie .kemp@ki.se; internet www.stockholmbrain .se; research on neuroscience; consortium of Karolinska Institutet, Royal Institute of Technology, Stockholm Univ.; Dir Dr EDWIN C. JOHNSON; Sec. LOUISE VON ESSEN.

NATURAL SCIENCES
General

Abisko naturvetenskapliga station (Abisko Scientific Research Station): Vetenskapens väg 38, SE-981 07 Abisko; tel. (980) 400-21; e-mail ans@ans.polar.se; internet www.polar.se/en/abisko; f. 1903, present status 1935; attached to Swedish Polar Research Secretariat; researches mainly on sub-arctic biology and Earth sciences; hosts the Climate Impacts Research Centre (CIRC); Head Dr CHRISTER JONASSON.

Stockholm Environment Institute: Linnégatan 87D, POB 24218, SE-104 51 Stockholm; tel. (8) 30-80-44; e-mail info@

sei-international.org; internet www .sei-international.org; f. 1989; policy-related research on int. environmental technology and management issues, incl. acidic deposition coordinated abatement strategies, climatic change assessment, energy futures, economics and environmental value, water, sanitation and integrated waste-management, urban environment, common property, energy and devt, biotechnology, risk assessment, atmospheric environment, cleaner production, sustainable devt planning and computer tools for integrated management risk and vulnerability; centres in Stockholm, Tallinn (Estonia), Dar es Salaam (Tanzania), Bangkok (Thailand), York (UK), Oxford (UK), Boston (USA); Chair. KERSTIN NIBLAEUS; Exec. Dir Prof. JOHAN L. KUYLENSTIERNA; publ. Renewable Energy for Development (4 a year).

Sven Lovén Centrum för Marina Vetenskaper (Sven Lovén Centre for Marine Sciences): Kristineberg 566, SE-451 78 Fiskebäckskil; tel. (31) 786-00-00; internet www.loven.gu.se; f. 1877 as Kristineberg Marine Research Station, present name and status 2008; attached to Univ. of Gothenburg; marine ecology, taxonomic, systematics and biodiversity, morphological, molecular and physiological research into marine animals and plants; laboratory at Tjärnö; Dir MICHAEL KLAGES.

Biological Sciences

Bergianska stiftelsen (Bergius Foundation): Stockholm Univ., SE-106 91 Stockholm; tel. (8) 545-917-00; e-mail prefekt@ bergianska.se; internet www.bergianska.se/ english/research; f. 1791; attached to Royal Swedish Acad. of Sciences; botanical and horticultural research; biodiversity projects: Rubiaceae, Rosaleae; Dir Prof. BIRGITTA BREMER.

IVL Svenska Miljöinstitutet (IVL Swedish Environmental Research Institute): POB 21060, SE-100 31 Stockholm; Valhallavägen 81, SE-114 27 Stockholm; tel. (8) 598-563-00; e-mail info@ivl.se; internet www.ivl.se; f. 1966; undertakes research projects and contract assignments for ecologically, economically, socially sustainable growth within business and soc.; Chair. ANNIKA HELKER LUNDSTRÖM; Pres. and CEO TORD SVEDBERG.

Science for Life Laboratory: POB 1031, SE-171 21 Solna; Karolinska Institutet Science Park, Tomtebodavägen 23A, SE-171 65 Solna; tel. (70) 326-29-11; internet www .scilifelab.se; f. 2010; nat. resource centre; research in molecular biosciences and medicine; org. divided into SciLifeLab Stockholm and SciLifeLab Uppsala; collaboration between 4 univs: Stockholm Univ., Karolinska Institutet, Royal Institute of Technology, Uppsala Univ.; Dir (Stockholm) Prof. Dr MATHIAS UHLÉN; Dir (Uppsala) Prof. Dr KERSTIN LINDBLAD-TOH.

Mathematical Sciences

Institut Mittag-Leffler (Mittag-Leffler Institute): Auravägen 17, SE-182 60 Djursholm; tel. (8) 622-05-60; e-mail info@ mittag-leffler.se; internet www.mittag-leffler .se; f. 1916, present status 1919; attached to Royal Swedish Acad. of Sciences; research and postdoctoral training in mathematical sciences; library of 60,000 vols; Dir Prof. ARI LAPTEV; publs Acta Mathematica (4 a year), Arkiv för matematik (2 a year).

Physical Sciences

Institutet för rymdfysik (Swedish Institute of Space Physics): POB 812, SE-981 28 Kiruna; Rymdcampus 1, SE-981 92 Kiruna; tel. (980) 790-00; e-mail irf@irf.se; internet www.irf.se; f. 1957 as Kiruna Geophysical

Observatory, current status 1973, current name adopted 1987; research, education and associated observatory activities in space physics, space technology and atmospheric physics; library of 7,000 vols, 200 journals; Dir Dr LARS ELIASSON; publs IRF Scientific Report (irregular), Kiruna Geophysical Data (4 a year).

Manne Siegbahnlaboratoriet (MSL) (Manne Siegbahn Laboratory (MSL)): Frescativägen 26, SE-114 18 Stockholm; tel. (8) 16-20-00; internet www.msi.se; f. 1937 as Nobel Institute of Physics, present name 1993, present status 2004; attached to Stockholm Univ.; research in atomic, molecular and surface physics; low-energy ion accelerators (ion sources), accelerator-storage ring for highly charged ions; computer, electronics, mechanical workshop divs; library of 10,000 vols; Dir SVEN MANNERVIK.

Nordiska Institutet För Teoretisk Fysik (Nordic Institute for Theoretical Physics): see under International.

Stockholms Observatorium (Stockholm Observatory): SE-106 91 Stockholm; Roslagstullsbacken 21, Stockholm; tel. (8) 553-785-00; internet www.astro.su.se; f. 1753; attached to Institutionen för Astronomi, Stockholm Univ.; Dir Prof. GÖRAN ÖSTLIN.

Stockholms universitets Institut för Solfysik (Institute for Solar Physics of Stockholm University): AlbaNova Univ. Centre, Roslagstullsbacken 21, SE-106 91 Stockholm; tel. (8) 16-20-00; e-mail scharmer@astro.su .se; internet www.solarphysics.kva.se; f. 1951 as Research Station for Astrophysics in Italy under the Royal Swedish Acad. of Sciences, reorganized 2013; attached to Stockholm Univ. and Swedish Research Ccl; solar research; operates Swedish 1-m Solar Telescope (SST) at La Palma (Canary Islands); Dir Prof. GÖRAN SCHARMER.

Sveriges Geologiska Undersökning (Geological Survey of Sweden): POB 670, SE-751 28 Uppsala; Villavägen 18, Uppsala; tel. (18) 17-90-00; e-mail sgu@sgu.se; internet www .sgu.se; f. 1858; attached to Min. of Enterprise, Energy and Communications; nat. authority responsible for matters relating to Sweden's geological characteristics and mineral resources management; library of 100,000 vols, 200 journals; Dir.-Gen. JAN MAGNUSSON.

Swedish Meteorological and Hydrological Institute: Folkborgsvägen 1, SE-601 76 Norrköping; tel. (11) 495-80-00; e-mail smhi@ smhi.se; internet www.smhi.se; under Min. of Environment; manages and develops information on weather, water and climate; Dir-Gen. LENA HÄLL ERIKSSON.

RELIGION, SOCIOLOGY AND ANTHROPOLOGY

Institutet för Social Forskning (Swedish Institute for Social Research): Universitetsvägen 10F, Univ. of Stockholm, SE-106 91 Stockholm; Universitetsvägen 10F, eighth and ninth fl., Frescati, Stockholm; tel. (8) 16-20-00; internet www.sofi.su.se; f. 1972; attached to Stockholm Univ.; research into social policy, welfare, inequality and labour market; Chair. KÅRE BREMER; Dir ANDERS BJÖRKLUND.

International Institute of Sociology: c/o The Swedish Collegium for Advanced Study, Linneanum, Thunbergsvägen 2, SE-752 38 Uppsala; tel. (18) 55-70-85; e-mail info@iisoc .org; internet www.iisoc.org; f. 1893; organizes world congress in sociology; Pres. BJÖRN WITTROCK; Sec.-Gen. PETER HEDSTRÖM; publs Annals of the International Institute of Sociology, International Review of Sociology (3 a year).

TECHNOLOGY

CBI Betonginstitutet AB (Swedish Cement and Concrete Research Institute): SE-100 44 Stockholm; Drottning Kristinas väg 26, SE-114 28 Stockholm; tel. (10) 516-68-00; e-mail cbi@cbi.se; internet www.cbi.se; f. 1942, present status 2008; research and devt; material testing; consulting and training in concrete and rock material field; library of 10,000 vols; Dir Prof. JOHAN SILFWERBRAND; Chair. FREDRIK WINBERG; publs *CBI-nytt* (2 a year), *CBI rapporter* (CBI report).

FOI Totalförsvarets Forskningsinstitut (FOI Swedish Defence Research Agency): SE-164 90 Stockholm; Gullfossgatan 6, Stockholm; tel. (8) 555-030-00; e-mail registrator@foi.se; internet www.foi.se; f. 2001; attached to Min. of Defence; conducts research into security-policy studies and analyses of defence and security; systems for control and management of crises; protection against and management of hazardous substances, IT security; brs in Grindsjön, Linköping, Umeå; Chair. EVA LINDENCRONA (acting); Dir-Gen. JAN-OLOF LIND.

Glafo (Swedish Glass Research Institute): PG Vejdes väg 15, SE-351 96 Växjö; Vejdes Plats 3, SE-352 52 Växjö; tel. (10) 516-63-50; e-mail info@glafo.se; internet www.glafo.se; attached to Technical Research Institute of Sweden; conducts research for the glass industry; Man. Dir MARIANNE GRAUERS.

Innventia AB: POB 5604, SE-114 86 Stockholm; Drottning Kristinas väg 61, Stockholm; tel. (8) 676-70-00; e-mail info@innventia.com; internet www.innventia.com; f. 1942 as STFI-Packforsk, present name 2009; research into pulp, paper, graphic media, packaging and logistics; activities range from basic research to projects into packaging, graphic media and environmentally friendly energy and chemicals; library of 15,000 vols, 500 periodicals; Pres. BIRGITTA SUNDBLAD; Exec. Vice-Pres. ANDERS ENGSTRÖM; publ. *Beyond* (4 a year).

Mobile VINN Excellence Centre: c/o SICS, POB 1263, SE-164 29 Kista; Electrum Bldg, Sixth Fl., Kistagången 16/Isafjordsgatan 22, SE-164 26 Kista; tel. (703) 79-39-64; e-mail oskar@mobilelifecentre.org; internet www.mobilelifecentre.org; f. 2007; research into mobile services and ubiquitous computing; Dir OSKAR JUHLIN.

SIK—Institutet för Livsmedel och Bioteknik AB (SIK—Swedish Institute for Food and Biotechnology): POB 5401, SE-402 29 Gothenburg; Frans Perssons väg 6, Delsjömotet; tel. (10) 516-66-00; e-mail info@sik.se; internet www.sik.se; f. 1946; research and devt, documentation and education on production, preservation, food safety, biotechnology, structure and rheology, packaging, information and marketing; library of 7,000 vols; Pres. KLAS HESSELMAN; Research Dir ULF SONESSON; Sec. TINA PETERSSON; publs *SIK-Dokument*, *SIK-Report*.

SP Kemi, Material och Ytor (SP Chemistry, Materials and Surfaces): POB 5607, SE-114 86 Stockholm; Drottning Kristinas väg 45, SE-114 28 Stockholm; tel. (10) 516-60-00; e-mail info@yki.se; internet www.yki.se; f. 2013 by merger of YKI, Institute for Surface Chemistry and SP Technical Research Institute of Sweden; research into applied surface and colloid chemistry; library of 5,500 vols; Research Dir AGNE SWERIN; Research Dir JUKKA LAUSMAA.

Stålbyggnadinstitutet (Swedish Institute of Steel Construction): Vasagatan 52, Fourth Floor, SE-111 20 Stockholm; tel. (8) 661-02-80; e-mail info@sbi.se; internet www.sbi.se; f. 1967; steel construction research; organizes annual steel construction conf.; instituted steel industry award; Chair. JOHAN ANDERSSON; publ. *Stålbyggnad* (4 a year).

Statens Geotekniska Institut (Swedish Geotechnical Institute): Olaus Magnus Väg 35, SE-581 93 Linköping; tel. (13) 20-18-00; e-mail sgi@swedgeo.se; internet www .swedgeo.se; f. 1944; govt agency responsible for safety issues relating to landslides and coastal erosion; research, information and consulting work in soil mechanics and foundation engineering, environment and energy geotechnology; computerized library retrieval system; brs in Gothenburg, Malmö, Stockholm; library of 100,000 bibliographic records, 10,000 books, 1,600 journals; Dir-Gen. ÅSA-BRITT KARLSSON; Sec. KERSTIN CARLSSON; publ. *SGI Publication*.

Swedish ICT: Electrum 233, Isafjordsgatan 22/Kistagången 16, SE-164 40 Kista; tel. (8) 632-78-90; e-mail info@swedishict.se; internet www.swedishict.se; research and devt on information, communication, technology; group of instns incl. Acreo, SICS, Interactive Institute, Imego, Viktoria Institute, Santa Anna IT Research Institute; Chair. ULF WAHLBERG; CEO HANS HENTZELL.

Swerea IVF AB: POB 104, SE-431 22 Mölndal; Argongatan 30, SE-431 53 Mölndal; tel. (31) 706-60-00; e-mail ivf@swerea.se; attached to Swerea Group; production engineering, materials applications, textiles, polymers, ceramics; CEO MATS LUNDIN; Sec. INGRID CHRISTOFFERSON; publ. *Teknik & Tillväxt* (Technology & Growth, 6 a year).

Swerea KIMAB AB (Swerea Corrosion and Metals Research Institute AB): POB 7047, SE-164 07 Kista; Isafjordsgatan 28A, SE-164 40 Kista; tel. (8) 440-48-00; e-mail kimab@swerea.se; f. 1921, present status 2005; attached to Swerea Group; develops, improves solutions for materials research; areas of research incl. application of instrumental methods for chemical analysis, welding, brazing and soldering; hot working, cold forming and microscopy; the relationship between microstructure and properties; solidification processes and their industrial applications; continuous casting; powder metallurgy; corrosion problems in connection with microstructure with a special interest in stainless steels; library of 2,000 vols of books, 50 periodicals; Man. Dir STAFFAN SÖDERBERG.

Swerea MEFOS AB: POB 812, SE-971 25 Luleå; tel. (920) 20-19-00; e-mail mefos@swerea.se; internet www.swerea.se/mefos; research in process metallurgy, heating, metalworking and energy technology; Man. Dir GÖRAN CARLSSON.

Swerea SICOMP: POB 271, SE-941 26 Piteå; Fibervägen 2, SE-943 33 Öjebyn; tel. (911) 744-00; e-mail sicomp@swerea.se; internet www.swerea.se/sicomp; research in polymer fibre composites; Man. Dir HANS HANSSON.

Swerea SWECAST: POB 2033, SE-550 02 Jönköping; Tullportsgatan 3, SE-553 22 Jönköping; tel. (36) 30-12-00; e-mail swecast@swerea.se; internet www.swerea.se/swecast; conducts research and provides consulting in foundry-related matters, incl. materials technology, casting simulation, process technology, energy use and environmental concerns; CEO MATS HOLMGREN; Exec. Sec. CARINA JONSHEIM.

Libraries and Archives
Alvesta

Alvesta Bibliotek (Alvesta Library): Allbogatan 17, SE-342 80 Alvesta; tel. (472) 152-69; e-mail biblioteket@alvesta.se; internet bibliotek.alvesta.se; 4 br. libraries, 1 mobile library; Chief Librarian ANN-KATRIN URSBERG.

Borås

Bibliotek & läranderesurser, Högskolan i Borås (Library & Learning Resources, University of Borås): SE-501 90 Borås; Järnvägsgatan 1, Borås; tel. (33) 435-40-50; e-mail biblioteket@hb.se; internet www.hb .se/biblioteket; f. 1972; 114,000 vols, 1m. ebooks, 36,000 ejournals; Dir SVANTE KRISTENSSON.

Borås stadsbibliotek (Borås City Library): SE-501 80 Borås; tel. (33) 35-76-20; e-mail boras.stadsbibliotek@boras.se; f. 1931, present location 1974; 300,000 vols; Chief Librarian ÅSA HEDBERG-KARLSSON.

Eskilstuna

Eskilstuna stads bibliotek (Eskilstuna Municipal Library): Kriebsensgatan 4, SE-632 20 Eskilstuna; tel. (16) 710-51-10; f. 1925; 3 brs in Lagersberg, Torshälla and Årby; 425,000 vols; Head KARIN ZETTERBERG.

Gävle

Gävle stadsbibliotek (Gävle City Library): POB 801, SE-801 30 Gävle; Slottstorget 1, Gävle; tel. (26) 17-96-00; e-mail stadsbiblioteket@gavle.se; internet www .gavle.se/uppleva-gora/bibliotek; f. 1907; 700,000 vols; Dir for Libraries LISBETH FORSLUND.

Gothenburg

Chalmers Bibliotek (Chalmers Library): Chalmers Tvärgata 1, SE-412 96 Gothenburg; tel. (31) 772-37-37; e-mail support.lib@chalmers.se; internet www.lib.chalmers.se; f. 1829; attached to Chalmers Univ. of Technology; 530,000 vols, 620 journals, 7,650 ejournals; Library Dir DANIEL FORSMAN..

Attached Libraries:

Arkitekturbiblioteket (Architecture library): Sven Hultins gata 6, SE-412 96 Gothenburg; tel. (31) 772-24-13; e-mail arch.lib@chalmers.se; Head Librarian ELISABETH KIHLÉN.

Lindholmenbiblioteket: Forskningsgången 6, SE-412 96 Gothenburg; tel. (31) 772-57-84.

Göteborgs stadsbibliotek (Gothenburg City Library): Götaplatsen 3, POB 5404, SE-402 29 Gothenburg; tel. (31) 368-33-00; e-mail info.stadsbiblioteket@kultur.goteborg .se; f. 1861; 405,807 vols, incl. 290,000 books; Chief Librarian CHRISTINA PERSSON.

Göteborgs universitetsbibliotek (Gothenburg University Library): POB 222, SE-405 30 Gothenburg; Renströmsgatan 4, Gothenburg; tel. (31) 786-17-49; e-mail universitetsbiblioteket@ub.gu.se; internet www.ub.gu.se; f. 1861; legal deposit library for Swedish publs; 2.7m. vols, 5,636 journals, 13,068 ejournals; spec. collns incl. MSS colln, women's history colln, Snoilsky colln (early Swedish literature), EDC colln, UN colln, Ibero-American colln; Dir MARGARET HEMMED; Head Librarian EVA HUNTINGTON; publs *Acta*, *Qupea*.

Halmstad

Halmstads Stadsbibliotek (Halmstad City Library): POB 4083, SE-300 04 Halmstad; Axel Olsons Gata 1, SE-302 27 Halmstad; tel. (35) 13-71-81; e-mail stadsbiblioteket@halmstad.se; internet www.halmstad.se/bibliotek; f. 2006; 209,000 vols; Chief Librarian ANETTE HAGBERG; Librarian BENEDICTE SÖDERGREN.

Jönköping

Högskolebiblioteket i Jönköping: Högskoleområdet, House C, Gjuterigatan 5, SE-553 18 Jönköping; tel. (36) 10-10-10; internet hj.se/bibl; f. 1914; attached to Jönköping Univ.; 200,000 vols of books, 60,000 ebooks, 19,000 journals; Library Dir BERNT KARLSSON.

Stadsbibliotek Jönköpings (Jönköping Public Library): POB 1029, SE-551 11 Jönköping; Dag Hammarskjölds plats 1, Jönköping; tel. (36) 10-55-75; e-mail stadsbibl@jonkoping.se; internet bibliotek.jonkoping.se; f. 1916; 600,000 vols (incl. 700 newspapers and magazines, CDs, DVDs, audio books); Librarian ULF MOBERG.

Kalmar

Kalmar Stadsbibliotek (Kalmar Public Library): Huvudbiblioteket, POB 610, SE-391 26 Kalmar; Tullslätten 4, Kalmar; tel. (480) 45-06-37; e-mail stadsbiblioteket@kalmar.se; internet www.kalmar.se/invanare/fritid-och-kultur/biblioteken/bibliotek/huvudbibliotek; f. 1922; 130,000 vols, 300 Swedish periodicals, 25 journals; Chief Librarian SUZANNE HAMMARGREN.

Linnéuniversitetets Bibliotek (Linnaeus University Library): SE-391 82 Växjö; Nygatan 18A, Kalmar; tel. (480) 44-61-00; e-mail kalmar.ub@lnu.se; internet lnu.se/ub; 360,000 vols; Library Dir CATTA TORHELL.

Karlskrona

Blekinge Tekniska Högskola Library (Blekinge Institute of Technology Library): Library Gräsvik, SE-371 79 Karlskrona; Library Gräsvik, Vallhallavägen 1, Karlskrona; tel. (455) 38-51-01; e-mail biblioteket@bth.se; internet www.bth.se/bib; 2 units: Library Gräsvik, Karlskrona; Library Piren, Karlshamn; incl. learning lab and educational devt; Dir ANNIKA ANNEMARK.

Köpings

Köpings Stadsbibliotek (Köpings City Library): Folkets Hus, SE-731 41 Köpings; tel. (221) 251-82; e-mail stadsbiblioteket@koping.se; internet www.koping.se/bibliotek; Chief Librarian INGER FELLDIN.

Kristianstad

Högskolan Kristianstad Biblioteket (Kristianstad University Library): SE-291 88 Kristianstad; Elmetorpsvägen 15, House 7, Kristianstad; tel. (44) 20-30-59; e-mail biblioteket@hkr.se; internet www.hkr.se/sv/lrc/biblioteket; Librarian HANNA DEHLIN.

Linköping

Linköpings Stadsbibliotek (Linköping City Library): POB 1984, SE-581 19 Linköping; Östgötagatan 5, Linköping; tel. (13) 20-66-01; e-mail stadsbiblioteket@linkoping.se; internet www.linkoping.se/bibliotek; f. 1926; 666,000 vols; Chief Librarian LENA AXELSSON.

Linköpings Universitetsbibliotek (Linköping University Library): SE-581 83 Linköping; tel. (13) 28-19-10; e-mail hb@bibl.liu.se; internet www.bibl.liu.se; f. 1969; 5 campus libraries; 825,256 vols of books, 2,000 journals, 14,333 ejournals, 102,288 ebooks; Library Dir MARGARETHA GRAHN; publ. *Publikation*.

Luleå

Luleå Stadsbiblioteket (Luleå City Library): Skeppsbrogatan 17, SE-971 79 Luleå; tel. (920) 45-59-51; e-mail biblioteket@kulturen.lulea.se; Chief Librarian LENA LUNDBERG VESTERLUND.

Luleå Universitetsbibliotek (Luleå University library): SE-971 87 Luleå; Betahouse, Univ. campus, Porsön, Luleå; tel. (920) 49-15-20; e-mail lulelibrary@ltu.se; internet www.ltu.se/ltu/lib; campus libraries at Luleå, Piteå, Skellefteå; research library for Norrbotten County Council; 200,000 vols, 15,000 ejournals, 50,000 ebooks; Library Dir JENNY SAMUELSSON.

Lund

Landsarkivet i Lund (Lund Regional Archives): POB 2016, SE-220 02 Lund; Porfyrvägen 20, Lund; tel. (10) 476-82-00; e-mail landsarkivet.lla@riksarkivet.se; f. 1903; holds records of govt bodies in S Sweden (counties of Halland, Skåne, Blekinge); 44,000 linear m of paper, 62,800 maps and drawings, 210,000 photographs, small portfolio of microfilm, motion picture and videocassettes, 520,000 microfiche; spec. collns: estate archives; Chief Archivist JAN DAHLIN.

Universitetsbiblioteket, Lunds Universitet (Lund University Library): POB 3, Helgonabacken, SE-221 00 Lund; tel. (46) 222-00-00; internet www.ub.lu.se; f. 1671; legal deposit library and nat. lending library; MSS incl. *Necrologium Lundense*, the oldest Scandinavian MS; 5m. vols, 129,000 MSS, 120,000 items of microforms; spec. collns: *Bibliotheca Gripenhielmiana* (6,000 vols of 16th- and 17th-century prints), Taussig colln of Schubert MSS, Broman colln of Elsevier prints, De La Gardie colln of prints and MSS; Dir CHRISTINA FRISTRÖM.

Malmö

Malmö Stadsbibliotek (Malmö City Library): SE-205 81 Malmö; Kung Oscars väg 11, SE-211 33 Malmö; tel. (40) 660-85-00; e-mail info.stadsbiblioteket@malmo.se; internet www.malmo.se/bibliotek; f. 1905; 490,000 vols; Librarian TORBJÖRN NILSSON.

Norrköping

Archives for UFO Research Foundation: POB 11027, SE-600 11 Norrköping; tel. (703) 68-32-21; e-mail afu@ufo.se; internet www.afu.info; f. 1973; repositories for UFO data and UFO-related folklore; colln of 1,200 m; 23,000 vols; Chair. HÅKAN BLOMQVIST.

Norrköpings Stadsbibliotek (Norrköping City Library): POB 2113, SE-600 02 Norrköping; Södra Promenaden 105, Norrköping; tel. (11) 15-26-65; e-mail stadsbiblioteket@norrkoping.se; internet www.nsb.norrkoping.se; f. 1913; 7 br. libraries, 3 bookmobiles; 472,785 vols; Chief Librarian BIRGITTA HJERPE.

Örebro

Örebro stadsbibliotek (City Library and County Library of Örebro län): POB 325 10, SE-701 35 Örebro; Näbbtorgsgatan 12, Örebro; tel. (19) 21-61-10; e-mail biblinfo@orebro.se; f. 1862; 780,000 vols; Chief Librarian CHRISTER KLINGBERG; publ. *Samfundet Örebro Stads- och Länsbiblioteks vänner. Meddelande 1929*.

Östersund

Östersunds Bibliotek (Östersund's Library): SE-831 80 Östersund; Rådhusgatan 25–27, SE-831 80 Östersund; tel. (63) 14-30-50; e-mail biblioteket@ostersund.se; internet www.bibliotekmitt.se; f. 1816, present location 1958; 1 main library, 3 area libraries, 1 mobile library, 2 hospital libraries; 478,000 vols; Chief Librarian MAJ ERIKSSON.

Skara

Stifts- och Landsbiblioteket i Skara (State County and City Library of Skaraborgs Län): POB 194, SE-532 23 Skara; Prubbatorget 1, Skara; tel. (511) 32-060; e-mail skarabibliotek@skara.se; f. 1938; 400,000 vols, 200 running m MSS; Chief Librarian PEMA MALMGREN; publ. *Acta*.

Skövde

Högskolebiblioteket i Skövde (University of Skövde Library): POB 408, SE-541 28 Skövde; tel. (500) 44-80-60; e-mail biblioteket@his.se; internet www.his.se/biblioteket; 120,000 vols, 8,000 journals, 14,600 ejournals; Library Dir ULF-GÖRAN NILSSON.

Stockholm

Antikvarisk-topografiska arkivet (Antiquarian Topographic Archives): POB 5405, SE-114 84 Stockholm; Östra stallet, Storgatan 41, Stockholm; tel. (8) 519-180-50; e-mail ata@raa.se; f. 1786; archives of the Collegium Antiquitatum and the Royal Archives of Antiquities (1666–1786), archives and collns of the Royal Academy of Letters, History and Antiquities (1786–1975) and of the Central Board of Antiquities and Nat. Historical Museums, archives of the office of monuments (1918–67) of the Nat. Board of Public Bldgs; 300 private archives; 120,000 maps and drawings; 1.1m. negatives and photographs; Dir Dr MIKAEL JAKOBSSON.

Handelshögskolans i Stockholm—Bibliotek (Stockholm School of Economics Library): POB 6501, SE-113 83 Stockholm; tel. (8) 736-97-02; e-mail library@hhs.se; internet www.hhs.se/library; f. 1909; provides access to information within the fields of business, economics and the social sciences that is relevant to the teaching and research carried out at Stockholm School of Economics; 30,000 electronic journals and 4,500 m of shelf space containing printed materials; Dir MARIE-LOUISE FENDIN.

Karolinska Institutet, Universitetsbiblioteket (Karolinska Institute University Library): POB 200, SE-171 77 Stockholm; Berzelius väg 7B, Stockholm; tel. (8) 524-840-00; e-mail ub@ki.se; internet ki.se/lib; f. 1810; Library Dir CHRISTER BJÖRKLUND.

Konstbiblioteket, Nationalmuseum och Moderna Museet (Joint Art Library of the Nationalmuseum and the Museum of Modern Art): POB 16 176, SE-103 24 Stockholm; Holmamiralens väg 2, Skeppsholmen, Stockholm; tel. (8) 519-543-52; e-mail konstbiblioteket@nationalmuseum.se; internet www.nationalmuseum.se/sv/english-startpage/research/art-library; f. late 19th century; literature on Western art since the Renaissance; 330,000 vols, 247 serials, 2,390,000 cuttings, 900 journal titles; Librarian MARIA SYLVÉN.

Kungliga biblioteket—Sveriges nationalbibliotek (National Library of Sweden): POB 5039, SE-102 41 Stockholm; Humlegården, Stockholm; tel. (10) 709-30-00; e-mail kungl.biblioteket@kb.se; internet www.kb.se; f. early 16th century; responsible for the union catalogue *LIBRIS* and for cooperation among scientific libraries (Nat. Cooperation Dept); 4m. vols; spec. collns incl. incunabula, Elzevirs, maps, portraits, heraldry, Old Swedish and Icelandic MSS; Nat. Librarian GUNILLA HERDENBERG; publ. *Acta Bibliothecæ regiæ Stockholmiensis*.

Kungl. Skogs- och Lantbruksakademiens Bibliotek (Royal Swedish Academy of Agriculture and Forestry Library): POB 6806, SE-113 86 Stockholm; Drottninggatan 95B, Stockholm; tel. (8) 54-54-77-00; e-mail kslab@ksla.se; internet www.ksla.se/anh; f. 1813; colln of books on rural and agricultural history, horticulture, forestry and related fields; 90,000 vols, 450 periodicals; Librarian PER ERIKSSON; publs *Miscellanea*, *Skogs- och Lantbrukshistoriska Meddelanden* (irregular).

Kungliga Tekniska Högskolans Bibliotek (Royal Institute of Technology Library): Osquars Backe 25, SE-100 44 Stockholm; Osquars Backe 31, Stockholm; tel. (8) 790-70-88; e-mail sekr@lib.kth.se; internet www.kth.se/kthb; f. 1827; centre for computerized information and documentation services in science and technology; 848,249 vols, 161,742 ebooks, 9,083 ejournals (incl. br. libraries); Chief Librarian MATS HERDER; publ. *Stockholm Papers in History and Philosophy of Science and Technology*.

Kurdiska Biblioteket (Kurdish Library): Gustavslundsvägen 170, SE-167 51 Bromma; tel. (8) 679-88-03; e-mail info@kurdlib.org; internet www.kurdlib.org; f. 1997; collects, preserves and makes available all printed works written by Kurds or that have relationship with the Kurds and Kurdistan; 13,000 vols of books, 700 journals; Dir NEWZAD HIRORI.

Musik- och teaterbiblioteket vid Statens musikverk (Music and Theatre Library of Sweden): POB 16326, SE-103 26 Stockholm; Torsgatan 19, SE-113 21 Stockholm; tel. (8) 519-554-12; e-mail exp@muslib.se; internet statensmusikverk.se/musikochteaterbiblioteket; f. 1771, present name and status 2010, merger of Theatre Library of Sweden (f. 1935); attached to Statens musikverk; large colln of 18th-century music and 19th-century theatre material; about 300 archives and collns; incl. a documentation centre for Swedish music; 120,000 vols of books, 378,000 notes, 5,000 play scripts, 200 journals, CDs and DVDs; Chief Librarian Prof. DAN LUNDBERG; publ. *Dokumenterat: bulletin från Musik- och teaterbiblioteket* (online, www.muslib.se/publ/bulletin.html).

Östasiatiska Biblioteket (Far Eastern Library—Library of the Museum of Far Eastern Antiquities): POB 16381, SE-103 27 Stockholm; Tyghusplan, Skeppsholmen, Stockholm; tel. (8) 519-557-77; e-mail helena.rundkrantz@ostasiatiska.se; internet www.varldskulturmuseerna.se/en/ostasiatiskamuseet/research-collections/the-far-eastern-library/; f. 1986; colln of Chinese periodicals, Japanese colln of A. E. Nordenskiöld, colln of Chinese congshu, colln of Western-language books on Asia; library is administered within the MFEA Unit for Research and Devt; 100,000 vols; Librarian HELENA RUNDKRANTZ.

Regeringskansliet Utrikesdepartementets Bibliotek (Library of the Swedish Ministry for Foreign Affairs): SE-103 33 Stockholm; tel. (8) 405-10-00; internet www.regeringen.se; not open to the public; Librarian GRETA QUESADA.

Riksarkivet (National Archives of Sweden): POB 12541, SE-102 29 Stockholm; Fyrverkarbacken 13, Stockholm; tel. (10) 476-70-00; e-mail riksarkivet@riksarkivet.ra.se; internet www.riksarkivet.se; f. 1618, present status 2010; regional archives at Gothenburg, Härnösand, Lund, Östersund, Uppsala, Vadstena, Visby; Military archives and Research Center SVAR are also attached; 670,000 m of archival holdings; Dir-Gen. BJÖRN JORDEL; publs *Arsbok för Riksarkivet och landsarkiven* (1 a year), *Glossarium till medeltidslatinet i Sverige*, *Skrifter utgivna av Riksarkivet*, *Svenskt diplomatarium*.

Riksdagsbiblioteket (Library of the Swedish Parliament): SE-100 12 Stockholm; Storkyrkobrinken 7A Stockholm; tel. (8) 786-40-00; e-mail biblioteket@riksdagen.se; internet www.riksdagen.se/sv/start/bibliotek-startsida; f. 1851; serves the Riksdag, the admin. services and research; chiefly devoted to political science, administration, social science and law; 700,000 vols, 4,000 printed and eperiodicals; Chief Librarian GUNILLA LILIE

BAUER; publ. *Fakta om folkvalda: Riksdagen 1985* (biographical handbook, every 4 years).

Statistiska Centralbyråns Bibliotek (Statistics Sweden Library): POB 24300, SE-104 51 Stockholm; tel. (8) 506-950-66; e-mail library@scb.se; internet www.scb.se; f. 1858; research library for official Swedish statistics; all statistics published by Statistics Sweden; literature on statistical theories and methodology; colln of statistical results from most of the countries of the world and from 50 int. orgs and the EU's statistical office Eurostat till 2008; 230,000 vols, 1,400 periodicals; Chief Librarian CHRISTINA CRONSIOE; publ. *Statistics from International Organizations and other Issuing Bodies* (1 a year).

Stockholms Stadsarkiv (Stockholm City Archives): POB 22063, SE-104 22 Stockholm; Kungsklippan 6, Stockholm; tel. (8) 508-283-00; e-mail stadsarkivet@stockholm.se; internet www.ssa.stockholm.se; f. 1930; provincial archives for Stockholm; documents from regional authorities and the municipal govt of Stockholm; archives on urban history of Stockholm; 130,000 vols, 68,000 shelf m of archives; City Archivist LENNART PLOOM; publs *Stadsarkivets småtryck* (irregular), *Stockholms stadsarkiv. Årsberättelse* (1 a year), *Stockholms tänkeböcker från år 1592* (irregular).

Stockholms stadsbibliotek (Stockholm Public Library): SE-113 80 Stockholm; Odengatan 63, Spelbomskan, Stockholm; tel. (8) 508-311-00; e-mail stadsbiblioteket@stockholm.se; internet biblioteket.stockholm.se; f. 1928; 40 libraries; 3,237,490 vols; Chief Librarian INGA LUNDÉN.

Stockholms universitetsbibliotek (Stockholm University Library): SE-106 91 Stockholm; Universitetsvägen 14D, Stockholm; tel. (8) 16-28-00; internet www.sub.su.se; f. 1877; 8 brs; 2.5m. printed vols, 500 database and 35,000 ejournals; Library Dir WILHELM WIDMARK.

Svenska Akademiens Nobelbibliotek (Nobel Library of the Swedish Academy): POB 2118, SE-103 13 Stockholm; Källargränd 4, Gamla Stan, Stockholm; tel. (8) 555-125-52; e-mail info@nobelbiblioteket.se; internet www.nobelbiblioteket.se; f. 1901; recent works of literature, literary criticism and linguistics; assists the Swedish Acad. in evaluations required for the Nobel Prize in Literature; 200,000 vols, 150 journals; Chief Librarian LARS RYDQUIST.

Svenskt Visarkiv (Centre for Swedish Folk Music and Jazz Research): POB 16326, SE-103 26 Stockholm; Torsgatan 19, Stockholm; tel. (8) 519-554-88; e-mail info@visarkiv.se; internet www.visarkiv.se; f. 1951; attached to Swedish Nat. Collns of Music; collects, preserves, publishes material concerning instrumental folk music, folk songs, jazz and traditional music since end of the 16th century till present; Dir DAN LUNDBERG.

Sveriges Radio Förvaltings AB (Resources of the Swedish Broadcasting Corporation): Oxenstiernsgatan 20, SE-105 10 Stockholm; tel. (8) 784-54-00; internet www.srf.se; f. 1925; documents relating to Swedish public service broadcasting and television; Archivist BJÖRN BLOMBERG.

Vitterhetsakademiens Bibliotek (Library of the Royal Swedish Academy of Letters, History and Antiquities): POB 5405, SE-114 84 Stockholm; Storgatan 41, Stockholm; tel. (8) 519-183-26; e-mail bibl@raa.se; internet www.raa.se/bibliotek; f. 1753, current name adopted 1786; attached to Swedish Nat. Heritage Board; spec. collns on archaeology, medieval art and architecture, numismatics, preservation of cultural heritage; open to the public; affiliated library incl. Colln of Numis-

matic Books; 445,000 vols; Head of Dept of Archives and Library MIKAEL JAKOBSSON; publ. *Fornvännen*.

Sundsvall

Universitetsbiblioteket, Mittuniversitet (Mid Sweden University Library): SE-851 70 Sundsvall; Holmgatan 10, Hus N, Sundsvall; tel. (60) 14-87-50; e-mail bibsvl@miun.se; internet www.bib.miun.se; campus libraries in Härnösand, Östersund; 22,475 vols, 20,000 ejournals, 60 electronic databases; Dir for Libraries MORGAN PALMQVIST.

Umeå

Umeå stadsbibliotek (Umeå City Library): Rådhusesplanaden 6A, SE-901 78 Umeå; tel. (90) 16-33-00; e-mail stadsbiblioteket@umea.se; internet www.minabibliotek.se; f. 1903; 25 brs in Bjurholm, Nordmaling, Roberts, Umeå, Vindeln and Vannas municipalities; 770,000 vols; Chief Librarian INGER EDEBRO SIKSTRÖM.

Umeå Universitetsbibliotek (Umeå University Library): SE-901 74 Umeå; Social Sciences Bldg, Umeå Univ., Umeå; tel. (90) 786-56-93; e-mail umub@ub.umu.se; internet www.ub.umu.se; f. 1950 as Scientific Library in Umeå, present name and status 1964; 1.5m. vols, 18,000 journals, 12,000 ejournals; Library Dir MIKAEL SJÖGREN.

Uppsala

SLU-Biblioteket, Sveriges Lantbruksuniversitet (SLU University Library, Swedish University of Agricultural Sciences): POB 7071, SE-750 07 Uppsala; Almas Allé 12, Uppsala; tel. (18) 67-11-03; e-mail biblioteket@slu.se; internet www.slu.se/sv/bibliotek; f. 1977; consists of Ultunabiblioteket (main library, in Uppsala) and 8 brs; Dir SNORRE RUFELT.

Uppsala stadsbibliotek (Uppsala City Library): POB 643, SE-751 27 Uppsala; Svartbäcksgatan 17, SE-753 75 Uppsala; tel. (18) 727-17-00; e-mail stadsbibli.inf@uppsala.se; internet www.uppsala.se/kulturfritid/bibliotek; f. 1906; 800,000 vols; Chief Librarian MARIE-LOUISE RITON.

Uppsala universitetsbibliotek (Uppsala University Library): POB 510, SE-751 20 Uppsala; Carolina Rediviva, Dag Hammarskjölds väg 1, Uppsala; tel. (18) 471-00-00; e-mail info@ub.uu.se; internet www.ub.uu.se; f. 1620; consists of 10 subject libraries and cultural heritage collns; 5.5m. vols, 18,000 eperiodicals, 400,000 ebooks, 200 databases, 30 encyclopaedias and 62,000 MSS, incl. *Codex argenteus*, the 'Silver Bible' from the 6th century, a translation of the Gospels into the Gothic language, Swedish and Icelandic medieval MSS, the Bibliotheca Walleriana (medical books), a colln of old music books and MSS, a colln of old maps, engravings and drawings, incl. the *Carta Marina* of 1539 by Olaus Magnus (earliest accurate map of Scandinavia); Dir Prof. LARS BURMAN; publs *Acta Bibliothecae R. Universitatis Upsaliensis*, *Scripta Minora Bibliothecae R. Universitatis Upsaliensis*, *Uppsala University Library's exhibition catalogues*.

Varberg

Campusbiblioteket i Varberg (Campus Library in Varberg): Otto Torells gata 18, SE-432 44 Varberg; tel. (340) 69-74-46; e-mail varberg@bib.hh.se; internet www.campusbiblioteket.se; f. 2003; operated jtly by Varberg Kommun and Halmstad Univ.'s Varberg Campus; Librarian CHRISTINA GABRIELSSON; Librarian LENNART ERLING; Librarian VERONICA AASHEIM KVIST.

Varberg Bibliotek: Engelbrektsgatan 7, SE-432 80 Varberg; tel. (340) 886-01; e-mail biblioteket@varberg.se; 6 br. libraries, 1 mobile library; 250,000 titles; Chief Librarian PER FALK.

Värmland

Värmlandsarkiv (Värmland Archives): POB 475, SE-651 11 Karlstad; Hööksgatan 2, SE-651 11 Karlstad; tel. (54) 701-11-50; e-mail varmlandsarkiv@regionvarmland.se; internet varmlandsarkiv.regionvarmland.se; f. 1970, present status 2001; attached to Nat. Archives of Sweden; colln of 25,000 linear m; 25,000 vols.

Västerås

Mälardalens Högskolebibliotek (Mälardalens University Library): POB 832, SE-721 22 Västerås; Högskoleplan 1, Västerås; tel. (21) 10-13-36; e-mail biblioteket@mdh.se; internet www.mdh.se/library; 110,000 vols, 80,000 ebooks, 240 journals, 13,000 ejournals; Library Dir ANNSOFIE OSCARSSON.

Västerås stadsbibliotek (Västerås City Library): Biskopsgatan 2, SE-721 87 Västerås; tel. (21) 39-46-01; e-mail stadsbibliotek@vasteras.se; internet www .bibliotek.vasteras.se; f. 1952; 6 associated libraries and a mobile library; 571,000 vols; Chief Librarian EVA MATSSON.

Växjö

Smålands Musikarkiv (Småland's Music Archive): Västergatan 13, SE-352 31 Växjö; tel. (470) 70-03-00; internet www .smalandsmusikarkiv.nu; f. 1992; attached to Musik i Syd; colln incl. music from Småland and adjacent landscape; 2,000 vols; Head MAGNUS GUSTAFSSON.

Växjö Bibliotek (City and County Library, Kronobergs län): POB 1202, SE-351 12 Växjö; Västra Esplanaden 7, SE-351 12 Växjö; tel. (470) 4-14-44; e-mail stadsbiblioteket@vaxjo.se; internet www .vaxjo.se/bibliotek; f. 1666, present bldg 2003; 8 brs; 400,000 vols; Library Dir ANNA-KARIN AXELSSON.

Visby

Almedalsbiblioteket (Almedals Library): POB 1121, SE-621 22 Visby; Cramérgatan 3–5, SE-621 57 Visby; tel. (498) 29-90-00; e-mail almedalsbiblioteket@hgo.se; internet www.almedalsbiblioteket.se; f. 1865; 502,000 vols; Head of Library KERSTIN SIMBERG.

Museums and Art Galleries

Falun

Dalarnas Museum: POB 22, SE-791 21 Falun; Stigaregatan 2–4, Falun; tel. (23) 76-55-00; e-mail info@dalarnasmuseum.se; internet www.dalarnasmuseum.se; f. 1962; shows cultural heritage from the Stone Age to present time; exhibits Archaeological Society collection activities from 1862; colln of costume and textiles, folk art, folk music, graphics, Selma Lagerlof's library; Dir JAN RAIHLE.

Gävle

Länsmuseet Gävleborgs (Gävleborg County Museum): POB 746, SE-801 28 Gävle; Södrastrandgatan 20, Gävle; tel. (26) 65-56-00; e-mail lansmuseetgavleborg@xlm .se; internet www.lansmuseetgavleborg.se; f. 1978 as Gävle Museum; exhibits art, silver and gold metal work, representations of circus life, archaeology of Gävle, selection from Hedvig Ulfsparre's private colln of textiles, devt of modern mass production; Museum Dir ANDERS JOHNSSON.

Sveriges Järnvägsmuseum (Swedish Railway Museum): POB 407, SE-801 05 Gävle; Rälsgatan 1, Gävle; tel. (10) 123-21-00; e-mail museumgavle@trafikverket.se; internet www.trafikverket.se/museer/ sveriges-jarnvagsmuseum-gavle; f. 1915; colln of locomotives, carriages, wagons, other railway items; photographs, pictures, historic film material, railway literature, archival material; br. in Ängelholm; Dir ROBERT SJÖÖ.

Gothenburg

Aeroseum: Holmvägen 100, SE-417 46 Gothenburg; Säve Depå, Holmvägen, Gothenburg; tel. (31) 55-83-00; e-mail info@ aeroseum.se; internet www.aeroseum.se; f. 1999, present status 2008; history and devt of aviation; preserves ex-military subterranean aircraft hangars; Chair. ROGER ELIASSON; Sec. LENA TYBRANDT-STRAND.

Göteborgs Konsthall: Gotaplatsen, SE-412 56 Gothenborg; tel. (31) 368-34-50; e-mail goteborgs.konsthall@kultur.goteborg.se; internet www.konsthallen.goteborg.se; f. 1923; exhibits contemporary art; organizes artist talks, tours, seminars and classes; presents group and solo exhibitions of nat. and int. artists; Dir. MIKAEL NANFELDT.

Göteborgs Naturhistoriska Museet (Gothenburg Museum of Natural History): POB 7283, SE-402 35 Gothenburg; Slottsskogen Östra, Museivägen 10, SE-413 11 Göteborg; tel. (10) 441-44-00; e-mail gnm@ vgregion.se; internet www.gnm.se; f. 1833, present location 1923; exhibits Swedish animal world and animals from around the world; themes incl. Earth's structure and life history, marine life, environmental problems, humans as biological beings and ecological concepts; specimens date from 18th century; zoological colln of 10m. animals, vertebrate colln of 100,000 specimens; library of 80,000 vols; Dir Dr ANN STRÖMBERG; publ. *Arstryck*.

Göteborgs Stads Kulturförvaltning (Gothenburg Arts and Culture): Norra Hamngatan 8, SE-411 14 Gothenburg; tel. (31) 365-00-00; e-mail info@kultur.goteborg .se; internet www.goteborg.se/kultur; f. 1993; Chair. of Trustees HELENA NYHUS; Vice-Chair. of Trustees LENNART S. WIDING..

Attached Museums:

> **Göteborgs Konstmuseum** (Gothenburg Museum of Art): Götaplatsen, SE-412 56 Gothenburg; tel. (31) 368-35-00; e-mail info .konstmuseum@kultur.goteborg.se; internet konstmuseum.goteborg.se; f. 1925; European paintings, sculpture, prints and drawings from 1400; spec. collns of French art since 1820 and Scandinavian art incl. works by Monet, Picasso, Rembrandt, Van Gogh; art library; Dir ISABELLA NILSSON.

> **Göteborgs Stadsmuseum** (Gothenburg City Museum): Norra Hamngatan 12, SE-411 14 Gothenburg; tel. (31) 368-36-00; e-mail stadsmuseum@kultur.goteborg.se; internet www.stadsmuseum.goteborg.se; f. 1861, present status 1993; archaeology since prehistoric times, industrial heritage; Dir CORNELIA LÖNNROTH.

> **Röhsska Museet** (Röhss Museum of Applied Art and Design): POB 53178, SE-400 15 Gothenburg; Vasagatan 37–39, SE-400 15 Gothenburg; tel. (31) 368-31-50; e-mail info@rohsska.se; internet rohsska .se; f. 1916, present status 1961; colln incl. 50,000 objects of crafts, applied arts and industrial design; Swedish and European decorative art, Greek and Roman antiquities, material from Japan and China; library of 30,000 vols; Dir TED HESSELBOM; publ. *Röhsska Konstslöjdmuseets årsbok* (Röhsska Museum Yearbook).

Sjöfartsmuseet Akvariet (Maritime Museum and Aquarium): Karl Johansgatan 1–3, SE-414 59 Gothenburg; tel. (31) 368-35-50; e-mail info.sjofartsmuseum@ kultur.goteborg.se; internet www .sjofartsmuseum.goteborg.se; f. 1913; permanent exhibitions on world shipping significant for Gothenburg and W Sweden; themes incl. pirates, life at sea; temporary exhibitions and programme activities; library of 20,000 vols; Dir ANNA ROSENGREN; publ. *Unda Maris*.

Kvibergs Museum: Lilla Regementsvägen 33, SE-415 28 Gothenburg; tel. (31) 48-06-02; e-mail kvibergsmuseum@telia.com; internet www.kvibergsmuseum.se; f. 1895; highlights military action in Kviberg area; Dir TORGNY ALLVIN.

Världskulturmuseet (Museum of World Culture): POB 5303, SE-402 27 Gothenburg; Södra vägen 54, Gothenburg; tel. (10) 456-12-00; e-mail info@varldskulturmuseet.se; internet www.varldskulturmuseet.se; f. 2004; exhibitions and programmes on contemporary issues about the world; library of 30,000 titles, 900 journals and yearbooks; Dir MARGARETA ALIN.

Hässleholms

Bjärnum Museum och Hembygdssamlingar (Bjärnum Museum and Local Historical Collections): Parkgatan, SE-280 20 Hässleholms; tel. (451) 200-91; e-mail info@ bjarnumsmuseum.se; internet www .bjarnumsmuseum.se; f. 1952; 100,000 articles describing the lifestyle of ancestors; objects covering a period of approx. 11,000 years; Chair. ARNE WIGHAGEN; Sec. ANDERS SVENSSON.

Helsingborg

Dunkers Kulturhus (Arts Centre): Kungsgatan 11, SE-252 21 Helsingborg; tel. (42) 10-74-00; e-mail dunkerskulturhus@helsingborg .se; internet www.dunkerskulturhus.se; f. 2002; exhibitions with town history, cultural history; contemporary art exhibitions; theatre, ballet, modern dance, jazz, chamber music and world music concerts; Dir ELISABETH ALSHEIMER.

Grafiska Museet Helsingborg (Helsingborg Printing Museum): c/o Fredriksdal Museums and Gardens, Gisela Trapps väg 5, SE-254 37 Helsingborg; tel. (42) 10-45-24; e-mail info@grafiskamuseet.se; internet www.grafiskamuseet.se; f. 1990; working printing museum; Chair. GÖRAN PALM.

Höganäs

Höganäs Museum och Konsthall: Polhemsgatan 1, SE-263 37 Höganäs; tel. (42) 34-13-35; e-mail hoganas.museum@telia .com; internet www.hoganasmuseum.se; f. 1924, present status 1997; exhibits historical industrial period; art gallery; Chair. SIMON ARNE.

Karlskoga

Nobelmuseet i Karlskoga: Björkbornsvägen 10, SE-691 33 Karlskoga; tel. (46) 586-834-94; e-mail info@nobelkarlskoga.se; internet nobelmuseetikarlskoga.se; exhibits on Alfred Nobel and his home, laboratory on Björkborn Manor; Dir and Curator HANS JOHANSSON.

Karlskrona

Blekinge Museum: Borgmästaregatan 21, SE-371 35 Karlskrona; tel. (455) 30-49-60; e-mail blekingemuseum@karlskrona.se; internet www.blekingemuseum.se; f. 1899 as preservation soc., present status 1983; exhibits history of Blekinge; Dir MARCUS SANDEKJER.

Museum—The Kulenovic Collection: Stortorget 5, Karlskrona; tel. (455) 25573; e-mail rizah.kulenovic@telia.com; internet www.kulenoviccollection.se; f. 1997, as Museum Lionardo da Vinci Ideale; exhibition of paintings, drawings, etchings and prints, sculptures, artefacts, ceramics; Raphael, da Vinci, Rembrandt, Caravaggio, van Gogh and Picasso and others; art objects in the form of figurines, vases and figurines dating from around 3000 BC onwards; Dir RIZAH KULE-NOVIC.

Köpings

Köpings Museum: SE-731 85 Köpings; tel. (221) 253-51; e-mail museum@koping.se; internet www.koping.se/uppleva-och-gora/museum/kopings-museum; f. 1887; shows Köpings history over 10,000 years; 4,000 glass plates, approx. 8,000 photographs since 1860s; 25,000 magazines; Dir ROY CASSÉ.

Kristianstad

Regionmuseet Kristianstad (Regional Museum in Kristianstad): POB 134, SE-291 22 Kristianstad; Stora Torg, Kristianstad; tel. (44) 13-58-00; e-mail info@regionmuseet.se; internet www.regionmuseet.se; has 3 br. museums: Film Museum, Railway Museum, Åhus Museum; archive and photographic archive; colln incl. archaeological material, natural history colln of rocks, fossils, animals, military equipment, railway historical stock, movie historical stock, school and teaching materials; agricultural lot, textiles and clothing, business interiors, crafts, furniture, utensils, glass, porcelain, ceramic arts, crafts, toys, musical instruments; art colln by Scanian artists, oils, watercolours, prints and sculptures; Dir BARBRO MELLAN-DER.

Kristinehamn

Kristinehamns Konstmuseum: Dr Enwalls väg 13C, SE-681 84 Kristinehamn; tel. (550) 882-00; e-mail info.konstmuseum@kristinehamn.se; internet www.kristinehamnskonstmuseum.com; f. 1997; modern and contemporary art; colln of works created by artists connected to Värmland; works of artists Bengt Olson and Stig Olson; Dir ANNA SVENSSON.

Jokkmokk

Ájtte Svenskt Fjäll- och Samemuseum (Ájtte Swedish Mountain and Sami Museum): POB 116, SE-962 23 Jokkmokk; Kyrkogatan 3, SE-962 31 Jokkmokk; tel. (971) 170-70; e-mail info@ajtte.com; internet www.ajtte.com; exhibits Sami culture; spec. museum of mountain chains, natural and cultural resources, information centre for mountain tourists; Dir KJELL-ÅKE ARONSSON.

Jönköping

Radiomuseet (Radio Museum): Tändsticksgränd 16, SE-553 15 Jönköping; tel. (36) 71-39-59; e-mail radiomuseet@telia.com; internet www.radiomuseet.com; f. 1988; exhibits loudspeaker equipment and microphones, historical radio broadcasting equipment, sound recording devices from Edison's wax cylinders to modern CD.

Landskrona

Tycho Brahe museet (Tycho Brahe Museum): Landsvägen 182, SE-260 13 St Ibb; tel. (418) 725-30; e-mail tychob@landskrona.se; internet www.tychobrahe.com; f. 2005; colln of films, archaeological finds from field, reconstructed instruments, models, pictures and multimedia; incl. Tycho Brahe's underground observatory Stjärneborg, a reconstructed Renaissance Garden, Tycho Brahe museum, and science centre; Dir GÖRAN NYSTRÖM.

Lidingö

Millesgården: Carl Milles väg 2, SE-181 34 Lidingö; Herserudsvägen 32, Lidingö; tel. (8) 446-75-90; e-mail info@millesgarden.se; internet www.millesgarden.se; f. 1936; 4 rooms for exhibition: art gallery, artist home and small studio; colln of sculptures made by artists; Dir ONITA WASS.

Linköping

Linköpings Slotts- och Domkyrkomuseum: Borggården, SE-582 28 Linköping; tel. (13) 12-23-80; e-mail info@lsdm.se; internet lsdm.se; displays aspects of medieval times, such as episode of bubonic plague, medical practices, status and regalia, pests, family banners; Dir MARKUS LINDBERG.

Lund

Botaniska Museet (Botanical Museum): POB 117, SE-221 00 Lund; tel. (46) 222-89-66; e-mail museichef@biol.lu.se; internet www.biomus.lu.se/botaniska-museet; attached to Lund Univ.; colln incl. about 2.5m. specimens of plants; fungi, lichens, mosses, vascular plants; Dir Prof. ULF ARUP.

Kulturen in Lund (Cultural History Museum in Lund): POB 1095, SE-221 04 Lund; Tegnérsplatsen, SE-223 50 Lund; tel. (46) 35-04-00; e-mail info@kulturen.com; internet www.kulturen.com; f. 1882; ethnography, cultural history, medieval archaeology; open-air museum, town and country houses; applied arts (ceramics, textiles, silver, glass); weapons and uniforms; musical instruments; furniture and fittings; trades; commerce and crafts; fishery; farming; folk art; archaeological finds from medieval Lund; holds more than 30 historical bldgs, around 125,000 items and 1m. archaeological finds from 3000 BC to present; Östarp, old farm with inn, 30 km from Lund; library of 35,000 vols; Dir ANKI DAHLIN; publ. *Kulturen* (yearbook).

Lund konsthall: Mårtenstorget 3, SE-223 51 Lund; tel. (46) 35-52-95; e-mail lundskonsthall@lund.se; internet www.lundskonsthall.se; f. 1957; nat. and int. art exhibition; visual and spatial articulation of exhibitions, catalogues, public talks, lectures and discussion events; in charge of producing public art projects for new bldgs financed by the City of Lund; Dir ÅSA NACKING.

Lunds Universitets Historiska museet (Lund University Historical museum): Krafts torg 1, SE-223 50 Lund; tel. (46) 252-20-73; e-mail info@luhm.lu.se; internet www.luhm.lu.se; f. 1805; exhibits Kilian Stobaeus Cabinet of Curiosities from the 18th century, finds from excavations of the Iron Age city of Uppåkra and artefacts from the Scanian Stone, Bronze and Iron Ages; coin colln; dept of Medieval church art and Antique artefacts; Dir PER KARSTEN.

Skissernas Museum (Museum of Sketches): Finngatan 2, SE-223 62 Lund; tel. (46) 222-72-83; e-mail adk@adk.lu.se; internet www.adk.lu.se; f. 1934; Swedish, Nordic and int. collns; colln of sketches and models; sculpture colln; Dir PATRICK AMSELLEM.

Zoologiska Museet (Zoological Museum): Ecology bldg, Sölvegatan 37, SE-223 62 Lund; tel. (46) 222-93-34; e-mail museichef@zool.lu.se; internet www.biomus.lu.se/zoologiska-museet; attached to Lund Univ.; scientific colln; contains approx. 10m species, mostly insects and other invertebrates; Dir Dr LARS LUNDQVIST; publ. *Entomologica scandinavica* (Scandinavian Entomology).

Lycksele

Skogsmuseet i Lycksele (Forestry Museum in Lycksele): POB 176, SE-921 23 Lycksele; Lapland, SE-921 23 Lycksele; tel. (950) 379-45; internet www.skogsmuseet.se; f. 1983; exhibitions on the manual logging era and the mechanized logging era showing woodland population; Birger Nordin Sami colln of art objects and books; Dir BJÖRN ÅSTRÖM.

Malmö

Idrottsmuseet (Sports Museum): Fritidsförvaltningen, POB 8111, SE-200 41 Malmö; Eric Perssons väg, Malmö; tel. (40) 34-26-88; e-mail idrottsmuseet@malmo.se; internet www.malmo.se/idrottsmuseet; material on people who have devoted their lives to sport; active athletes, managers and spectators; publ. *Skånsk Idrotts Historia*.

Malmö Konsthall: St Johannesgatan 7, SE-205 80 Malmö; tel. (40) 34-60-00; e-mail info.konsthall@malmo.se; internet www.konsthall.malmo.se; f. 1975; exhibits int. and nat. art ranging from the classics of modernism to current experiments; organizes theatre, film, poetry, video installations, multimedia, music, lectures and debates; Chief Curator ANNA HOLMBOM.

Malmö Konstmuseum (Malmö Art Museum): POB 406, SE-201 24 Malmö; Malmöhusvägen 6, SE-211 18 Malmö; tel. (40) 34-44-37; e-mail malmokonstmuseum@malmo.se; internet www.malmo.se/konstmuseum; f. 1841 as Malmö Museum, reorganized 1932; collns incl. primarily Nordic art, European art, decorative art and design objects since 1500s; 40,000 works of art; Dir CECILIA WIDENHEIM.

Malmö Museer (Malmö Museums): POB 406, SE-201 24 Malmö; Malmöhusvägen 6, Malmö; tel. (40) 34-44-00; e-mail malmomuseer@malmo.se; internet www.malmo.se/museer; f. 1841; incl. cmdr's house, Ebba's house on Snapperupsgatan, Slottsmöllan at Mölleplatsen, Slottsholmen (with hus Castle), Technology & Maritime House, Wowragården in Southern Sallerup; Dir GÖRAN LARSSON.

Teatermuseet (Theatre Museum): Kalendegatan 5C, SE-211 35 Malmö; tel. (40) 12-48-83; e-mail info@teatermuseet.com; internet www.teatermuseet.com; preserves, documents history and traditions of theatre and the performing world; colln incl. Artillery Photographs from Hippodromteatern in Malmö dating from 1924 until closure in 1949, personal letters and photographs of Swedish actors, large colln of press clippings from Swedish newspapers on theatre activities since 1930s, MSS from Skåne theatre history.

Mariefred

Swedish National Portrait Gallery: c/o Collections and Swedish National Portrait Gallery, Nationalmuseum, POB 16176, SE-103 24 Stockholm; Gripsholm Castle, Mariefred; tel. (8) 519-543-00; e-mail info@nationalmuseum.se; internet www.nationalmuseum.se; f. 1822; colln of Swedish portraits since 16th century; Dir Dr MAGNUS OLAUSSON.

Mora

Zornmuseet (Zorn Museum): Vasagatan 36, POB 32, SE-792 21 Mora; tel. (250) 59-23-10; e-mail info@zorn.se; internet www.zorn.se; f. 1939; 4 divs: Zorn Museum, Zorn House, open-air museum Zorn's Gammelgård and Gopsmor; incl. Textile Museum; permanent exhibition: 'Midnight' (1891), 'Dairy Maid' (1908), 'Dance in the Gopsmor Cottage' (1913) as well as the 2 self-portraits in red and in a wolfskin (both 1915); 'Mormor' (1883) and 'The Misses Salomon' (1888) and water studies; Zorn's etchings and silver colln; Dir JOHAN CEDERLUND.

Norrköping

Norrköpings Konstmuseum (Norrköping Art Museum): Kristinaplatsen, SE-602 34 Norrköping; tel. (11) 15-26-00; e-mail konstmuseet@norrkoping.se; internet www.norrkoping.se/kultur-fritid/museer/konst-museum; Swedish art since 1600s; int. and nat. graphic colln; print colln consists of works from artists incl. Dürer, Rembrandt and Goya; sculpture park incl. works of Carl Milles, Bror Hjorth and Arne Jones; creative workshops, music, lectures, further training for teachers, corporate events.

Nyköping

Sörmlands museum: POB 314, SE-611 26 Nyköping; tel. (155) 24-57-00; e-mail info.museet@dll.se; internet www.sormlandsmuseum.se; archive of letters, diaries, records, maps, drawings, reports, stories; collns of wedding dresses from the 1700s, home furnishing, textiles; archipelago colln and archaeological colln; organizes courses, lectures, walks, field trips, travelling exhibitions; publishes books; Dir KARIN LINDVALL.

Örebro

Örebro Läns Museum: Engelbrektsgatan 3, SE-702 12 Örebro; tel. (19) 602-87-00; e-mail info@olm.se; internet www.orebrolansmuseum.se; art colln ranges in time since late 1700s; painting; archaeological colln; preserves local history, handicraft, artwork, and cultural heritage sites; organizes lectures, workshops, tours and children's activities; colln of antiques, fine jewellery and clothing, replica of a medieval church interior with altar paintings and shrines; Dir MIKAEL EIVERGÅRD.

Rattvik

Folkmusikens hus (Folk Music House): Dalagatan 7, SE-795 31 Rattvik; tel. (48) 79-70-50; e-mail kontakt@folkmusikenshus.se; internet www.folkmusikenshus.se; f. 1994; folk music centre; colln of CDs, sheet music and literature; serves as information hub for folk music and dance; organizes exhibitions, concerts, dances, education, archival services; Pres. LARS-ERIK KALLES; Vice-Pres. MATS HULANDER.

Simrishamn

Österlens Museum: Storgatan 24, SE-272 31 Simrishamn; tel. (414) 81-96-70; e-mail osterlens.museum@simrishamn.se; internet www.simrishamn.se/sv/kultur_fritid/oster-lens_museum; f. 1917; colln relating to life in Swedish countryside; exhibits native plants, local agriculture, handicraft e.g. lace-making and metal work, fossils and archaeological objects, tools, furniture, clothing and nautical equipment from Eastern Skåne; colln of coins and historical jewellery; Gislövs Forging Museum; Dir LENA ALEBO.

Skara

Västergötlands Museum: POB 253, SE-532 23 Skara; Stadsträdgården, SE-532 31 Skara; tel. (511) 260-00; e-mail vastergotlandsmuseum@vgregion.se; internet www.vastergotlandsmuseum.se; f. 1863; 3 permanent exhibitions: prehistoric colln of 17 bronze shields buried under water 3,000 years ago, Skara in the Middle Ages, and exposé on 19th century artist Agnes de Frumerie; exhibits local handicrafts and design, traditional games, energy conservation, school projects; Dir MARIE-LOUISE FASTH.

Skurup

Johanna Museet: POB 85, SE-274 22 Skurup; Sandåkra 6, Skurup; tel. (411) 427-80; e-mail info@johannamuseet.se; internet www.johannamuseet.se; f. 1983; objects exhibiting technological devts during the 1900s.

Svaneholms Slottsmuseum (Svaneholm Castle Museum): Svaneholms Slott, SE-274 91 Skurup; tel. (411) 400-12; e-mail svaneholm.museum@telia.com; f. 1935; textile collns of both upper-class and peasant class; colln incl. archaeological finds from the area, works of art, old toys, furniture, photographs and archives; Pres. SVEN ROSENGREN.

Stockholm

Aquaria Vattenmuseum (Aquaria Water Museum): Djurgården, Falkenbergsgatan 2, SE-115 21 Stockholm; tel. (8) 708-72-00; e-mail info@aquaria.se; internet www.aquaria.se; f. 1991; presents physical view of different climates and environments around the world with aquariums and indoor vegetation; centred on 3 themes: the Amazon rain forest, tropical seas, and Nordic waters.

Arkitektur- och designcentrum (Swedish Centre for Architecture and Design): Skeppsholmen, SE-111 49 Stockholm; tel. (8) 587-270-00; e-mail info@arkitekturmuseet.se; internet www.arkdes.se; f. 1962; collects drawings, sketches and items associated with the history of Swedish bldg, Swedish architects, foreign architects working in Sweden; 2m. drawings and sketches, 600,000 photographs and 2,000 models and other items; library of 25,000 vols; Dir LENA RAHOULT.

Biologiska Museet (Biological Museum): POB 27807, SE-115 93 Stockholm; Hazeliusporten, Djurgården, Stockholm; tel. (8) 442-82-15; e-mail bokning@skansen.se; internet www.biologiskamuseet.com; f. 1893; colln of Scandinavian mammals and birds in their natural, ecological habitat; use of dioramas to present natural habitat.

Dansmuseet (Dance Museum): Gustav Adolfs torg 22–24, SE-111 52 Stockholm; tel. (8) 441-76-50; e-mail info@dansmuseet.se; internet www.dansmuseet.se; f. 1933 in Paris as Archives Internationales de la Danse, 1953 in Sweden; performing arts museum; exhibitions of dance, theatre, visual art and photography; art works from all over the world, notably Ballets Suédois; videotheque, folk dance dept; Rolf de Maré archive; Dir Dr ERIK NÄSLUND.

Etnografiska Museet (Museum of Ethnography): POB 27140, SE-102 52 Stockholm; Djurgårdsbrunnsvägen 34, SE-102 52 Stockholm; tel. (8) 519-550-00; e-mail info@etnografiska.se; internet www.varldskulturmuseerna.se/etnografiskamuseet; f. 1880; colln of 150,000 artefacts from Africa, America, Asia, Australia and the Pacific; also houses the Sven Hedin Foundation; library of 45,000 vols incl. books and journals; Dir ANDERS BJÖRKLUND; Librarian ZSUZSANNA MÜLLER; publ. *Ethnos* (4 a year).

Färgfabriken Contemporary Art Gallery: Lövholmsbrinken 1, SE-117 43 Stockholm; tel. (8) 645-07-07; e-mail info@fargfabriken.se; internet www.fargfabriken.se; f. 1995; exhibits contemporary works of art; Man. Dir PERNILLA LESSE; Creative Dir JOACHIM GRANIT.

Fotografiska: Stadsgårdshamnen 22, SE-116 45 Stockholm; tel. (8) 50-90-05-00; e-mail info@fotografiska.eu; internet en.fotografiska.eu; f. 1940; exhibits contemporary photography; organizes seminars and courses; Dir CATRINE RIVEDAL.

Galleri Kontrast: Hornsgatan 8, SE-118 20 Stockholm; tel. (8) 641-49-99; e-mail gkv@gallerikontrast.se; internet www.gallerikontrast.se; f. 1996; documentary photography; exhibits Swedish picture of the year, World Press Photo and work from Nordens Fotoskola; Chair. ROLF ADLERCREUTZ; Curator MIA KLINTEWALL.

Gustav III's Antikmuseum (Gustav III's Museum of Antiquities): Kungliga Slottet, SE-111 30 Stockholm; tel. (8) 402-61-30; internet www.royalcourt.se/royalcourt/royalpalaces/theroyalpalace/gustaviiismuseumofantiquities; f. 1794; art colln; private sculpture colln of Gustav III; sculptures and artefacts from late 18th century and belonging to Scandinavian region.

Historiska Museet (National Historical Museum): POB 5428, SE-114 84 Stockholm; Narvavägen 13–17, Stockholm; tel. (8) 519-556-00; e-mail info@historiska.se; internet www.historiska.se; comprises Museum of Nat. Antiquities and Royal Cabinet of Coins and Medals; collns comprise archaeological artefacts from Sweden and Swedish ecclesiastical art; Dir.-Gen. MARIA JANSÉN.

Judiska Museet (Jewish Museum): POB 6299, SE-102 34 Stockholm; Hälsingegatan 2, Stockholm; tel. (8) 557-735-60; e-mail info@judiska-museet.se; internet www.judiska-museet.se; f. 1987; adaptation of Jews to Swedish soc. and their contribution to culture, art, literature, trade, industry etc.; culture and religion of Jews, their manners and customs, in the synagogue and in their homes; history of the Swedish Jews; Dir YVONNE JACOBSSON; Project Man. YAEL FRIED.

Konstnärshuset: Smålandsgatan 7, SE-111 46 Stockholm; tel. (8) 611-10-09; e-mail info.konstnarshuset@telia.com; internet www.konstnarshuset.com; f. 1899; exhibits architectural works and contemporary art; Sec. BO L. JOHANSSON.

Kulturhuset: POB 16414, SE-103 27 Stockholm; 7, Sergels torg, SE-103 72 Stockholm; tel. (50) 83-15-08; e-mail info.kulturhuset@stockholm.se; internet www.kulturhuset.stockholm.se; f. 1974; organizes photographic exhibitions, stories for children, concerts, literary discussions, films, debates, theatre; 2 libraries; Dir ERIC SJÖSTRÖM.

Kungl. Myntkabinettet—Sveriges Ekonomiska Museum (Royal Coin Cabinet—National Museum of Economy): Slottsbacken 6, POB 5428, SE-114 84 Stockholm; tel. (8) 519-553-04; e-mail info@myntkabinettet.se; internet www.myntkabinettet.se; f. 1630; coin colln representing all ages; exhibition displays coins, banknotes, tokens, stock certificates, bank materials, wallets, piggy banks and other objects related to economic history; exhibits medals' history and devt; Musuem Dir EVA RAMBERG.

Lars Bohman Gallery: Karlavägen 16, SE-114 24 Stockholm; tel. (8) 20-78-07; e-mail info@larsbohmangallery.com; internet www.larsbohmangallery.com; f. 1982; exhibits works of int. contemporary artists that incl. painting, drawing, sculpture, video and photography; Man. MALIN LEVÉN; Man. PELLE HÖGLUND.

Liljevalchs Konsthall: Djurgårdsvägen 60, SE-115 21 Stockholm; tel. (8) 508-313-30; e-mail info.liljevalchs@stockholm.se; internet www.liljevalchs.se; f. 1916; ind. and public art gallery for contemporary art; Head MARTEN CASTENFORS.

Livrustkammaren (Royal Armoury): Royal Palace, Slottsbacken 3, SE-111 30 Stockholm; tel. (8) 402-30-30; e-mail registrator@lsh.se; internet www.livrustkammaren.se; f. 1628; attached to Min. of Culture; houses items once in the possession of Swedish monarchs and their families; artefacts in the colln reflect official occasions such as state ceremonies, weddings, coronations and funerals; historical collns dating from mid-

16th century; Swedish royal arms, costumes, jewels, coaches; library of 43,000 vols; Dir MALIN GRUNDBERG; publ. *Livrustkammaren: the Journal of Royal Armoury* (1 a year).

Component Sites:

Hallwylska Museet: Hamngatan 4, SE-111 47 Stockholm; tel. (8) 402-30-99; e-mail registrator@lsh.se; internet www.hallwylskamuseet.se; f. 1900; private residence of Hallwyl family; colln of furniture, paintings, applied art; Dir HELI HAAPA-SALO; publ. *Hallwyliana*.

Skoklosters Slott: SE-746 96 Skokloster; tel. (8) 402-30-70; e-mail registrator@lsh.se; internet www.skoklostersslott.se; baroque castle built in 1654 by Count C. G. Wrangel; contains mainly 17th-century furniture, paintings, applied art and armour; library; library of 20,000 vols; Admin. Dir REBECKA ENHÖRNING; publ. *Skokloster Studies*.

Magasin 3 Konsthall: Frihamnen, SE-115 56 Stockholm; tel. (8) 54-56-80-40; e-mail art@magasin3.com; internet www.magasin3.com; f. 1987; colln of contemporary art; 3-dimensional works, drawings, photographic works and video cassettes; 'Dawning' by James Turrell; Dir DAVID NEUMAN; Chief Curator RICHARD JULIN.

Medelhavsmuseet (Museum of Mediterranean and Near Eastern Antiquities): POB 16008, SE-103 21 Stockholm; Fredsgatan 2, Stockholm; tel. (8) 519-550-50; e-mail info@medelhavsmuseet.se; internet www.varldskulturmuseerna.se/medelhavsmuseet; f. 1954 by merger of Egyptian Museum and Cyprus colln, present location 1982; archaeological collns of ancient and historical relics from Mediterranean countries; Dir SANNE HOUBY-NIELSEN.

Moderna Museet (Museum of Modern Art): POB 16382, SE-103 27 Stockholm; Skeppsholmen, Stockholm; tel. (8) 520-235-00; e-mail mmv@modernamuseet.se; internet www.modernamuseet.se; f. 1958; contemporary paintings and sculptures by Swedish and foreign artists, also photographs and drawings; colln since 1900; br. at Malmö; 5,000 paintings, sculptures and installations, 25,000 watercolours, drawings and prints, 100,000 photographs; Dir DANIEL BIRNBAUM.

Museum Tre Kronor: Kungliga Slottet, SE-107 70 Stockholm; tel. (8) 402-61-00; internet www.royalcourt.se/kungligaslotten/kungligaslottet/museumtrekronor; f. 1999; colln of objects rescued from fire of 1697 and newly created models; depicts the Tre Kronor Palace's devt from defence fort to the Renaissance palace of today.

Nationalmuseum: POB 16176, SE-103 24 Stockholm; Södra Blasieholmshamnen, Stockholm; tel. (8) 519-543-00; e-mail info@nationalmuseum.se; internet www.nationalmuseum.se; f. 1792; 16,000 paintings, sculptures and other objects, 500,000 drawings and prints, 30,000 items of applied art; also administers collns of several royal castles with 23,000 works of art; library: see under Libraries and Archives; Dir-Gen. Prof. BERNDT ARELL; publs *Art Bulletin of Nationalmuseum Stockholm* (1 a year), *Nationalmuseums skriftserie. N. S.*

Naturhistoriska Riksmuseet (Swedish Museum of Natural History): POB 50007, SE-104 05 Stockholm; Frescativägen 40, SE-114 18 Stockholm; tel. (8) 519-540-40; e-mail info@nrm.se; internet www.nrm.se; f. 1739; attached to Min. of Culture; collns and research units: vertebrates, entomology, invertebrates, palaeozoology, phanerogamic botany, cryptogamic botany, palaeobotany, mineralogy, isotope geology, DNA laboratory, contaminants; Dir JAN OLOV WESTERBERG.

Nobelmuseet (Nobel Museum): POB 2245, SE-103 16 Stockholm; Stortorget 2, Gamla Stan, Stockholm; tel. (8) 53-48-18-00; e-mail info@nobelmuseum.se; internet www.nobelmuseum.se; honours Nobel Prize winners by highlighting their achievements and displaying some of their work; organizes lectures, group discussions, games, interactive exhibitions; permanent colln incl. children's room educating about the Nobel Prizes in physics, chemistry, medicine, literature, peace, and economics; library of 5,000 vols; Dir Dr OLOV AMELIN.

Nordiska museet (Nordic Museum): POB 27820, SE-115 93 Stockholm; Djurgårdsvägen 6–16, Stockholm; tel. (8) 519-546-00; e-mail nordiska@nordiskamuseet.se; internet www.nordiskamuseet.se; f. 1873, present name and status 1907; nat. museum of cultural history since 16th century, ethnological and industrial art collns; 10m. archive and photographic items; library of 250,000 vols; Dir LARS O. GRÖNSTEDT.

Observatoriemuseet (Observatory museum): Drottninggatan 120, SE-113 60 Stockholm; tel. (8) 545-483-90; e-mail observatoriet@kva.se; internet www.observatoriet.kva.se; f. 1991; organizes seminars, visits and excursions; exhibition on history of bldg; exhibits photographic work; Dir MIRJA HAGAR LAUSSON.

Östasiatiska Museet (Museum of Far Eastern Antiquities): POB 16381, SE-103 27 Stockholm; Tyghusplan, Skeppsholmen, Stockholm; tel. (8) 519-557-50; e-mail info@ostasiatiska.se; internet www.varldskulturmuseerna.se/ostasiatiskamuseet; f. 1926, present status 1999; Chinese paintings, sculptures and ceramics; Chinese pottery and bronze objects; Japanese, Korean, SE Asian and Indian collns; library of 100,000 vols of books; Dir ANDERS BJÖRKLUND (acting); publ. *Bulletin* (1 a year).

Postmuseum: POB 2002, SE-103 11 Stockholm; Lilla Nygatan 6, T-Gamla Stan, Stockholm; tel. (8) 781-17-55; e-mail postmuseum@posten.se; internet www.postmuseum.posten.se; f. 1906; exhibits items connected with the Swedish Post Office and its history; colln of stamps, letterboxes and signs, postal art, furniture, cars, bicycles, stamp cancelling machines, uniforms, postal horns, emblems, mailmen's bags; collns of pictures and documents; philatelic collns; library of 60,000 vols, 180 journals; Dir OLLE SYNNERHOLM.

Prins Eugens Waldemarsudde: POB 16176, SE-103 24 Stockholm; Prins Eugens väg 6, Djurgården, Stockholm; tel. (8) 54-58-37-00; e-mail info@waldemarsudde.se; internet www.waldemarsudde.se; f. 1947; colln of artwork by Carl Larsson, Anders Zorn, Karl Nordström, Prince Eugen; sculptures by Carl Eldh, Per Hasselberg, Auguste Rodin, Carl Milles; exhibits sculpture, hand drawing, graphics and art medals; Museum Dir and Curator KARIN SIDÉN.

Scenkonstmuseet (Swedish Museum of Performing Arts): POB 16326, SE-103 26 Stockholm; Sibyllegatan 2, Stockholm; tel. (8) 519-554-90; e-mail info-mtm@musikverk.se; internet statensmusikverk.se/musikochteatermuseet; f. 1899 as Musikhistoriska Museet, present location 1979; attached to Music Devt and Heritage Sweden; 50,000 objects brought to life through exhibitions and educational activities; Dir STINA WESTERBERG; Head Curator and Deputy Dir LARS ANNERSTEN.

Skansen: POB 27807, SE-115 93 Stockholm; Djurgårdsslätten 49–51, SE-115 93 Stockholm; tel. (8) 442-80-00; e-mail info@skansen.se; internet www.skansen.se; f. 1891, present status 1963; open-air museum and zoological garden; Dir JOHN BRATTMYHR.

Spritmuseum (Museum of Spirits): Djurgårdsvägen 38 SE-115 21 Stockholm; tel. (8) 121-313-00; internet spritmuseum.se; f. 2012; collns of objects, images, tags since late 1800s; alcohol historical archives; colln of wine and liquor bottles; library of 4,500 vols, 150 journal titles; Dir INGRID LEFFLER; Curator EVA LENNEMAN.

Statens försvarshistoriska museer (National Swedish Museums of Military History): POB 14095, SE-104 41 Stockholm; Riddargatan 13, Stockholm; tel. (8) 519-563-10; e-mail info@sfhm.se; internet www.sfhm.se; f. 1976, merger of Army Museum in Stockholm, Navy Museum in Karlskrona, Air Force Museum in Linköping and Board of Military Traditions; attached to Min. of Culture; promotes knowledge about Swedish armed forces through the ages and their role in devt of soc.; Dir-Gen. STAFFAN BENGTSSON.

Statens Maritima Museer (National Maritime Museums): POB 27131, SE-102 52 Stockholm; Linnégatan 64, SE-114 54 Stockholm; tel. (8) 519-549-00; e-mail registrator@maritima.se; internet www.maritima.se; attached to Min. of Culture; responsible for museums in Swedish state care that have maritime profile; Dir ROBERT OLSEN..

Component Museums:

Marinmuseum (Naval Museum): POB 48, SE-371 32 Karlskrona; Stumholmen, Karlskrona; tel. (455) 35-93-00; e-mail registrator@maritima.se; internet www.marinmuseum.se; f. 1752; 55,000 exhibits since 17th century; library of 20,000 vols; Dir RICKARD BAUER; publ. *Aktuellt-Marinmuseum* (yearbook).

Sjöhistoriska museet (Maritime Museum): POB 27131, SE-102 52; Djurgårdsbrunnsvägen 24, Stockholm; tel. (8) 519-549-00; e-mail sjohistoriska@maritima.se; internet www.sjohistoriska.se; f. 1938; collns of Swedish naval and merchant history; history of Swedish shipbuilding; archive of drawings and photographs; colln comprises 100,000 objects, incl. over 1,500 models of ships and boats; library of 60,000 vols; Dir HANS-LENNART OHLSSON; publ. *Sjöhistorisk årsbok* (every 2 years).

Vasamuseet (Vasa Museum): POB 27131, SE-102 52 Stockholm; Galärvarvsvägen 14, Djurgården, Stockholm; tel. (8) 519-548-00; e-mail vasamuseet@maritima.se; internet www.vasamuseet.se; f. 1987; exhibits associated with Swedish warship and a steam icebreaker; Dir MARIKA HEDIN.

Stiftelsen Musikkulturens Främjande (Nydahl Collection): Riddargatan 35–37, SE-114 57 Stockholm; tel. (8) 661-71-71; e-mail smf@nydahlcoll.se; internet www.nydahlcoll.se; f. 1920; colln of old music instruments; arranges concerts and lectures; music MSS colln incl. works of composers Beethoven, Chopin, Donizetti, Mozart, Rossini, Schubert and Schumann, and Swedish and Scandinavian composers; colln of iconographic material, drawings, paintings and photos; a library of scores; colln of music literature belonging to Prof. Ingmar Bengtsson; Curator GÖRAN GRAHN.

Stockholms läns museum (Stockholm County Museum): Sickla Industriväg 5B, SE-131 54 Nacka; tel. (8) 586-194-00; e-mail museet@stockholmslansmuseum.se; internet www.stockholmslansmuseum.se; f. 1982; prehistoric finds; architectural and cultural history; library of 10,000 vols; Dir PETER BRATT.

Stockholms Stadsmuseum (Stockholm City Museum): POB 15025, SE-104 65 Stockholm; Ryssgården, Slussen; tel. (8) 508-316-00; e-mail info@stadsmuseum.stockholm.se;

internet www.stadsmuseum.stockholm.se; f. 1937; history and devt of Stockholm; archaeology and cultural heritage; colln of photographs, maps, art and artefacts; incl. library and archives; preserves 300,000 items of historical interest; 20,000 works of art, 3,000 oil paintings, 3m. photographs; library of 40,000 vols; Dir ANN-CHARLOTTE BACKLUND; publs *Blick* (articles covering the activity of the admin.), *Sankt Eriks årsbok* (yearbook).

Affiliated Museum:

Stockholms Medeltidsmuseum (Museum of Medieval Stockholm): POB 2343, SE-103 18 Stockholm; Strömparterren, Norrbro, Stockholm; tel. (8) 508-317-90; e-mail info.medeltidsmuseet@stockholm.se; internet www.medeltidsmuseet.stockholm.se; f. 1986; archaeological remains of Stockholm, reflecting its foundation and history from c. 1250–1550; Head TINA RODHE; Curator LIN ANNERBÄCK.

Strindbergsmuseet (Strindberg Museum): Drottninggatan 85, SE-111 60 Stockholm; tel. (8) 411-53-54; internet www.strindbergsmuseet.se; colln of objects related to Strindberg; collns divided into 7 categories: cultural history, art, theatre, photographs, press clippings, library, audiovisual media; photographic archive with 2,500 photographs; library of 5,000 vols; Dir STEFAN BOHMAN; Sr Curator ERIK HÖÖK.

Tekniska Museet (National Museum of Science and Technology): POB 27842, SE-115 93 Stockholm; Museivägen 7, SE-115 93 Stockholm; tel. (8) 450-56-00; e-mail info@tekniskamuseet.se; internet www.tekniskamuseet.se; f. 1924; history of science and technology; devt of Swedish industry and engineering; mining, iron and steel, steam power and machines, cars and aircraft, history of electricity, chemistry, computers, Polhem's colln of engineering models, mechanical workshop and model railway; Teknorama science centre; Cino4 special effects 3D films, archives of drawings and photographs; library of 50,000 vols, 200,000 maps, drawings and sketches of industrial installations, machines, tools and products; Dir ANN FOLLIN; publ. *Daedalus* (1 a year).

Thielska Gallery: Sjötullsbacken 8, SE-115 25 Stockholm; tel. (8) 662-58-84; e-mail info@thielska-galleriet.se; internet www.thielska-galleriet.se; f. 1926; colln of Nordic Heirloom Art; works of artists Edvard Munch, Carl Larsson, Bruno Liljefors and Eugène Jansson; Dir ANDREAS BRÄNDSTRÖM.

Svalöv

Galleri Tapper-Popermajer (Tapper-Popermajer Art Gallery): Bantorget 2, SE-268 71 Teckomatorp; e-mail info@tapper-popermajer.com; internet www.tapper-popermajer.com; f. 1999; exhibits nat. and int. artists' work; organizes lecturers and musical events; Owner HANS TAPPER.

Svedala

Statarmuseet i Skåne: Torupsvägen 606–59, SE-233 64 Bara; tel. (40) 44-70-90; e-mail brevladan@statarmuseet.com; internet www.statarmuseet.com; f. 1995; organizes training courses, seminars, theme days and events with the starting point of the seasons; has archive; exhibits kitchen commons, sleeping accommodation, and tiny garden plot of bonded labourers of the time; Dir BARBRO FRANCKIE.

Tjörn

Nordiska Akvarellmuseet (Nordic Watercolour Museum): Södra hamnen 6, SE-471 32 Skärhamn; tel. (304) 60-00-80; e-mail info@akvarellmuseet.org; internet www.akvarellmuseet.org; f. 1989; Nordic centre for contemporary art, research and training; exhibits works of contemporary int. watercolourists; organizes lectures, theatrical performance, dance, music and discussions; Dir BERA NORDAL.

Umeå

Bildmuseet (Image Museum): c/o Umeå Univ., SE-901 87 Umeå; Konstnärligt campus, Östra Strandgatan 30B, SE-903 33 Umeå; tel. (90) 786-52-27; e-mail info@bildmuseet.umu.se; internet www.bildmuseet.umu.se; f. 1981; exhibits int. contemporary art and visual culture: photography, design, architecture; combines contemporary perspective with historical flashbacks; Dir KATARINA PIERRE (acting).

Pengsjö nybyggarmuseum (Pengsjö settler's museum): c/o Sven-Eric Nyman, Rönnbärsstigen 17, SE-903 46 Umeå; tel. (90) 13-05-33; e-mail sven-eric.nyman@pengsjomuseum.se; internet www.pengsjomuseum.se; exhibits bldgs from 17th, 18th and 19th centuries; colln from peasant and Sami culture; Head SVEN-ERIC NYMAN.

Västerbottens museum: POB 3183, SE-903 40 Umeå; tel. (90) 16-39-00; e-mail info@vbm.se; internet www.vbm.se; f. 1886; collns of Sami culture with its gear and clothing; incl. photo archive; Chair. ANDERS LIDSTRÖM; Dir ULRICA GRUBBSTRÖM; publ. *Västerbotten* (4 a year).

Attached Museums:

Svenska Skidmuseet (Swedish Ski Museum): f. 1928; colln of hand-made skis, snowshoes for both man and horse, prehistoric skis, ski equipment, world's oldest surviving pods, Kalvträsk scabbard.

Fiske- och sjöfartsmuseet (Fishing and Maritime Museum): f. 1975; colln of pictures, models and objects related to boats, ships and maritime industries.

Uppsala

Evolutionsmuseet (Museum of Evolution): Norbyvägen 16, SE-752 36 Uppsala; tel. (18) 471-27-39; e-mail info@em.uu.se; internet www.evolutionsmuseet.uu.se; f. 1999; attached to Uppsala Univ.; 3.1m. botany specimens, palaeontology collns, zoology collns; Dir MATS ERIKSSON.

Museum Gustavianum: Akademigatan 3, SE-753 10 Uppsala; tel. (18) 471-75-71; e-mail museum@gustavianum.uu.se; internet www.gustavianum.uu.se; f. 1997; exhibits Anatomical Theatre, the Augsburg Art Cabinet and objects from Valsgärde; the Antique colln; the Egyptian colln; the Nordic archaeology colln; the physical cabinet; art collns; coin cabinet; Dir ING-MARIE MUNKTELL.

Upplandsmuseet (Upplands Museum): Fyristorg 2, SE-753 10 Uppsala; tel. (18) 16-91-00; e-mail info@upplandsmuseet.se; internet www.upplandsmuseet.se; f. 1959; provincial cultural history; collns of 750,000 objects and nearly 1.5m. glass negatives, film negatives and prints, extensive archive of topographic data, measurements, records and maps; Dir BENT SYSE; Dir HÅKAN LIBY; publ. *Uppland*.

Varberg

Hallands Kulturhistoriska Museum: Varbergs Fästning, SE-432 44 Varberg; tel. (340) 828-30; e-mail info@hkm.varberg.se; internet www.lansmuseet.varberg.se; f. 1916, present name 2011; 50,000 historical items; 20,000 archaeological finds; 200,000 photographs; library of 20,000 vols; Dir CURRY HEIMANN.

Växjö

Kulturparken Småland AB: POB 102, SE-351 04 Växjö; Södra Järnvägsgatan 2, SE-351 04 Växjö; tel. (470) 70-42-00; e-mail info@kulturparkensmaland.se; internet www.kulturparkensmaland.se; Swedish glass colln; collns incl. objects of cultural historical significance, visual art, textiles, church furnishings, archaeological finds and agricultural history; permanent exhibits on 2 themes: Småland's rural industrial landscape and 5 centuries of Swedish glass; castle ruins of Kronoberg; Kronoberg agricultural museum; numismatic colln; incl. Smålands Museum, The Swedish Glass Museum, The House of Emigrants, Kronoberg Castle Ruins, Kronoberg Agriculture Museum, Centre for Cultural Heritage, Kronoberg Archive; Dir ERICA MÅNSSON.

Viken

Beredskapsmuseet: Djuramossavägen 160, SE-260 40 Viken; tel. (42) 22-40-39; e-mail info@beredskapsmuseet.com; internet www.beredskapsmuseet.com; f. 1997; located in a Second World War underground military facility; exhibits Sweden's defences during the Second World War through equipment, photography etc.; Dir JOHAN ANDRÉE.

Universities

GÖTEBORGS UNIVERSITET
(Gothenburg University)

POB 100, SE-405 30 Gothenburg

Telephone: (31) 786-00-00
E-mail: registrator@gu.se
Internet: www.gu.se

Founded 1891, became state univ. 1954
Academic year: September to June

Vice-Chancellor: PAM FREDMAN
Pro-Vice-Chancellor: HELENA LINDHOLM SCHULZ
Deputy Vice-Chancellor for Education: METTE SANDOFF
Deputy Vice-Chancellor for External Relations and Innovation: Prof. MARGARETA WALLIN PETERSON
Deputy Vice-Chancellor for Quality Management: BENGT-OVE BOSTRÖM
Deputy Vice-Chancellor for Research: STAFFAN EDÉN
Head of Admin. and Registrar: PER-OLOF REHNQUIST
Chief Librarian: MARGARETA HEMMED
Library: see under Libraries and Archives
Number of teachers: 2,700
Number of students: 38,000

Publication: *Acta Universitatis Gothoburgensis*

DEANS

Faculty of Arts: Prof. MARGARETA HALLBEERG
Faculty of Education: Prof. ROGER SÄLJÖ
Faculty of Fine, Applied and Performing Arts: Prof. INGRID ELAM
Faculty of Science: Prof. ELISABET AHLBERG
Faculty of Social Sciences: Prof. BIRGER SIMONSON
IT Faculty: Prof. JAN SMITH
Sahlgrenska Academy: Prof. OLLE LARKÖ
School of Business, Economics and Law: INGRID ELAM
Teacher Training: Prof. ELISABETH HESSLE-FORS-ARKTOFT

PROFESSORS

Faculty of Arts (POB 200, SE-405 30 Gothenburg; tel. (31) 786-00-00; internet www.hum.gu.se):

AGRELL, B., Comparative Literature

AHLBERGER, C., History
AHLSÉN, E., Neurolinguistics
AIJMER, K., English
ALLWOOD, J., General Linguistics
ANDERSSON, L.-G., Modern Swedish
ANDERSSON, S.-G., German
BÄRMARK, J., Theory of Science
BENSON, K., Spanish
BERGH, G., English
BJÖRNBERG, A., Musicology
BORIN, L., Natural Language Processing
BOYD, S., General Linguistics
BYRSKOG, S., New Testament Exegesis
COOPER, R., Computational Linguistics
DAHL, E.-L., History of Science and Ideas
EDSTRÖM, K.-O., Musicology
ENGDAHL, E., Swedish
EKLUND, B.-L., Modern Greek
ERIKSSON, A., Phonetics
FLORBY, G., English Literature
FORSER, T., Comparative Literature
HAGLUND, D., Religious Studies
HALLBERG, M., Theory of Science
HANSSON, S., Comparative Literature
HELDNER, C., French
HOLMQUIST, I., Women Studies
JOHANNESSON, L., History of Art
KRISTIANSEN, K., Archaeology
LAGER, T., Computational Linguistics
LARSSON, L., Comparative Literature
LEGÈRE, K., African Languages
LIEDMAN, S.-E., History of Science and Ideas
LILJA, E., Comparative Literature
LILLIESTAM, L., Musicology
LINDBERG, B., History of Science and Ideas
LINDBERG, I., Swedish as a Second Language
LINDKVIST, T., Medieval History
LJUNGGREN, M., Russian Literature
MALM, M., Comparative Literature
MALMGREN, H., Theoretical Philosophy
MALMGREN, S.-G., Swedish
MALMSTEDT, G., History
MUNTHE, C., Practical Philosophy
NÄSSTRÖM, B.-M., History of Religion
NILSSON, B., History of Christianity
NILSSON, I., History of Science and Ideas
NORDBLADH, J., Archaeology
OHLANDER, S., English
OLAUSSON, L., Conditions in Science and Humanities
OLOFSSON, A., English
OLOFSSON, S., Old Testament Exegesis
PANKOW, C., German
PERSSON, I., Practical Philosophy
PERSSON, L., History
PLATEN, E., German Literature
RALPH, B., Northern Languages
RETSÖ, J., Arabic
SANDBERG, B., German
SJÖGREN, O., Film Studies
SKARIN-FRYKMAN, B., Ethnology
STÅLHAMMAR, M., English Terminology
STRANDBERG-OLOFSSON, M., Classical Archaeology and Ancient History
THUNMAN, N., Japanese
WESTERSTÅHL, D., Theoretical Philosophy
WINBERG, C., History
WISTRAND, M., Latin

Faculty of Education (POB 300, SE-405 30 Gothenburg; tel. (31) 786-00-00; e-mail kansli.ufn@ped.gu.se; internet www.ufn.gu.se):

AHLBERG, A., Special Education and Educational Research
ALEXANDERSSON, M., Education and Educational Research—Didactics
ANDERSSON, B., Education and Educational Research—Didactics
BENGTSSON, J., Philosophy of Education
GUNNARSSON, L., Education and Educational Research
GUSTAFSSON, J.-E., Education and Educational Research
HOLMER, J., Work Science

LANDER, R., Education and Educational Research
LASSBO, G., Education and Educational Research
LINDBLAD, S., Education and Educational Research
LINDSTRÖM, B., Education and Educational Research
MARTON, F., Education and Educational Research
MUNCK, J., Education and Educational Research
NILSSON, L., Education and Educational Research
OHLSSON, S., English
OSCARSON, M., Education and Educational Research
OTT, A., Science Education
PATRIKSSON, G., Education and Educational Research
PRAMLING-SAMUELSSON, I., Education and Educational Research
SÄLJÖ, R., Education and Educational Science
SHANAHAN, H., Home Economics
SIMONSON, B., History
THÅNG, P.-O., Education and Educational Research
WENESTAM, C.-G., Education and Educational Research
WERNERSSON, I., Education and Educational Research

Faculty of Fine, Applied and Performing Arts (POB 141, SE-405 30 Gothenburg; tel. (31) 786-00-00; internet www.konst.gu.se):

DAVIDSSON, H., Organ
du RÉES, G., Film Directing
EKLUND, B., Trumpet
ELDENIUS, M., Music Theory
FOLKESTAD, G., Research in Music Education
GÅRDFELDT, G., Communication and Performance Skills, Drama
HYBBINETTE, P., Fine Arts in Design
JORMIN, A., Contrabass and Improvisation
LÜTZOW-HOLM, O., Composition
NÄSSEN, E., Voice
NIELSEN, E., Percussion and Contemporary Music
OLSSON, B., Research in Music Education
THORSÉN, S.-M., Music and Society
WASKO, R., Fine Arts
WIKLUND, A., Music Drama

Faculty of Science (POB 460, SE-405 30 Gothenburg; tel. (31) 786-00-00; e-mail info@science.gu.se; internet www.science.gu.se):

ÅBERG, P., Marine Ecology
ABRAMOWICZ, M., Astrophysics
ADLER, L., Marine Microbiology
AHLBERG, E., Inorganic Chemistry
AHLBERG, P., Organic Chemistry
ANDERSSON, L., Hydrosphere Science
ANDERSSON, M., Zooecology
ANDERSSON, S., Animal Ecology
ANDERSSON, S., Physics
ANDREASSON, L.-E., Molecular Biophysics
ARKERYD, L., Applied Mathematics
AXELSSON, M., Comparative Integrative Zoology
BADEN, S. P., Marine Ecology
BILLETER, M., Molecular Biophysics
BJÖRK, G., Polar Oceanography
BJÖRNSSON, B. T., Zoophysiology
BJURSELL, G., Molecular Biology
BLANCK, H., Plant Physiology
BLOMBERG, A., Functional Genomics
BOHLIN, T., Animal Ecology
BRZEZINSKI, J., Mathematics
CAMPBELL, E., Atomic and Molecular Physics
CARLSSON, P., Genetics
CEDERWALL, M., Theoretical Physics
CHEN, D., Physical Meteorology
CLARKE, A., Plant Molecular Biology

CORNELL, D., Geochemistry
DAVE, G., Environmental Protection
ELWING, H., Surface Biophysics
ERSÉUS, C., Evolutionary Morphology and Systematics
FÖRLIN, L., Zoophysiology
FRANZÉN, L., Physical Geography
GÖTMARK, F., Zooecology
HÅKANSSON, M., Organometallic Chemistry
HALL, P., Marine Sediment Diagenesis
HALLENBERG, N., Systematic Biology
HANSTORP, D., Experimental Physics
HELLSING, B., Physics
HERMANSSON, M., Marine Microbiology
HOHMANN, S., Molecular Microbial Physiology
HOLMGREN, S., Zoophysiology
HOLMLID, L., Physical Chemistry, especially Energy-related Basic Research
JAGNER, D., Analytical Chemistry
JOHANNESSON, H., Theoretical Physics
JOHANNESSON, K., Biology, Marine Ecology
JONSON, M., Condensed Matter Physics
JONSSON, P., Marine Ecology
KARLBERG, A.-T., Dermatochemistry and Skin Allergy
KJELLANDER, R., Physical Chemistry
KOMITOV, L., Physics
LARSON, S. A., Geology
LARSSON, A., Environmental Protection
LEVAN, G., Genetics
LINDHE, U., Zoology (Structural and Animal)
LINDQVIST, O., Inorganic Chemistry
LINDQVIST, S., Physical Geography
LINDVALL, T., Mathematical Statistics
LJUNGSTRÖM, E., Atmospheric Science
LUTHMAN, K., Medicinal Chemistry
MALMGREN, B., Marine Geology
MEHLIG, B., Physics
MOLAU, U., Plant Ecology
NILSSON, S., Zoophysiology
NORDBERG, K., Palaeoceanography
NORDHOLM, S., Physical Chemistry
NYMAN, G., Physical Chemistry
NYSTRÖM, T., Scientific Microbiology
OLSSON, O., Developmental Biology of Plants
OMSTEDT, A., Geosphere Dynamics
ÖSTLIN, S., Solid-State Physics
PEDERSEN, K., Biology, Microbiology
PENDRILL, A.-M., Physics
PETTERSSON, J., Environmental Atmospheric Sciences
PIHL, L., Marine Fish Ecology
PLEIJEL, H., Environmental Protection
RODHE, J., Oceanography
ROSEN, A., Molecular Physics
ROSENBERG, R., Marine Ecology
RYDBERG, L., Oceanography
RYDSTRÖM, J., Biochemistry
SANDELIUS, A.-S., Plant Physiology
SELLDÉN, G., Tree Physiology, Influence of Air Pollution
SHCHERBINA, N., Mathematics
SHEKTER, R., Theoretical Physics
SILVERIN, B., Zoology (Structural and Animal)
SJÖGREN, P., Mathematics
SJÖLIN, L., Inorganic Chemistry
STENSON, J., Biology, Aquatic Ecology
STEVENS, R., Environmental and Quaternary Geology
STIGEBRANDT, A., Oceanography
STIGH, J., Bedrock Geology
STOLIN, A., Mathematics
SUNDBÄCK, K., Biology, Marine Botany
SUNDBERG, P., Zoomorphology
SUNDELL, K., Animal Zoophysiology
SUNDQVIST, CH., Plant Physiology
SUNNERHAGEN, P., Eucaryotic Molecular Biology
SVANSTEDT, N., Mathematics
TISELIUS, P., Marine Ecology
TURNER, D. R., Marine Chemistry
WALLENTINUS, I., Marine Botany

WALLIN PETERSSON, M., Zoophysiology
WEDBORG, M., Marine Analytical Chemistry
WERMUTH, N. E., Biostatistics
WETTERBERG, O., Conservation, specializing in integrated conservation of the built environment
WILLANDER, M., Experimental Physics
ZHUKOV, M., Theoretical Physics

Faculty of Social Sciences (POB 720, SE-405 30 Gothenburg; tel. (31) 786-10-00; e-mail lars-olof.karlsson@gu.se; internet www.samfak.gu.se):

ARCHER, T., Psychology
ÅRHEM, K., Social Anthropology
ASP, K., Journalism
BJERELD, U., Political Science
BJÖRNBERG, U., Sociology
BOHOLM, Å., Social Anthropology
BROBERG, A., Psychology
BRORSTRÖM, B., Management Economics
BÄCK, H., Public Administration
BÄCK-WIKLUND, M., Social Work
DEMKER, M., Political Science
ESAIASSON, P., Political Science
FURÅKER, B., Sociology
GÄRLING, T., Psychology
GILLJAM, M., Political Science
GLIMELL, H., Science and Technology Studies
GUSTAFSSON, B., Social Work
HANSEN, S., Psychology
HETTNE, B., Peace and Conflict Research
HJELMQUIST, E., Behavioural Studies of Disabilities and Handicap
HÖGLUND, L., Library and Information Science
HOLMBERG, S., Political Science
HWANG, P., Psychology
JOHANSSON, B., Psychology
JONSSON, D., Sociology
LINDAHL, R., Political Science
LUNDQVIST, L. J., Political Science
OLSSON, S., Social Work
PETERSON, A., Sociology
PIERRE, J., Political Science
ROMBACH, B., Management Economics
ROTHSTEIN, B., Political Science
SVENSSON, L. G., Sociology
WEIBULL, L., Mass Communication

IT Faculty (Forskningsgången 6, SE-412 96 Gothenburg; tel. (31) 786-00-00; e-mail jan.smith@chalmers.se; internet www.itufak.gu.se):

BRENNER, P., Mathematics
COQUAND, T., Computer Science
DAHLBOM, B., Informatics

Sahlgrenska Academy (POB 400, SE-405 30 Gothenburg; tel. (31) 786-00-00; e-mail registrator@sahlgrenska.gu.se; internet www.sahlgrenska.gu.se):

AHLMAN, H., Endocrine Surgery
ALBERTSSON-WIKLAND, K., Paediatric Growth Research
ALBREKTSSON, T., Handicap Research
ALLEBECK, P., Social and Preventive Medicine
ÅMAN, P., Tumour Biology
ANDERSSON, O., Medicine
ASHTON, M., Biopharmacy
AXELSSON, G., Hygiene
AXELSSON, R., Psychiatry
BAGGE, U., Anatomy
BARREGÅRD, L., Clinical Environmental Medicine
BENGTSSON, B.-Å, Clinical Endocrinology
BERGBOM, I., Nursing
BERGFELDT, L., Cardiology
BERGGREN, U., Odontological Psychology
BERGLUNDH, T., Parodontology
BERGSTRÖM, T., Clinical Microbiology
BETSHOLTZ, Ch., Medical Biochemistry
BIBER, B., Anaesthesiology and Intensive Care

BILLIG, B., Cellular Aging and Apoptosis
BIRKHED, D., Cariology
BJÖRKELUND, C., General Medicine
BLENNOW, K., Clinical Neurochemistry
BLOMSTRAND, C., Neurology
BONDJERS, G., Cardiological Research
BORÉN, J., Cardiovascular Research
BRAIDE, M., Anatomy
BRÄNNSTRÖM, M., Obstetrics and Gynaecology
BREIMER, M., Clinical Molecular Genetics
BRY, K., Paediatrics, especially Neonatology
CARLSSON, J., Physiotherapy
CARLSSON, L., Clinical Metabolic Research
CARLSTEN, H., Rheumatology
DAHLÉN, G., Oral Microbiology
DAHLGREN, C., Medical Microbiology
DAHLGREN, U., Oral Immunology
DAHLSTRÖM, A., Histology
DAMBER, J.-E., Urology
DICKSON, S., Psychology, especially Neuroendocrinology
EDÉN, S., Physiology, especially Endocrinology
EDENBRANDT, L., Clinical Physiology, especially Nuclear Medicine
EKROTH, R., Thoracic Surgery
EKSTRÖM, J., Pharmacology
ELAM, M., Clinical Neurophysiology
ELIAS, P., Medicinal Biochemistry
EMILSON, C.-G., Cardiology
ENERBÄCK, S., Medical Genetics
ENGEL, J., Pharmacology
ERICSON, L., Anatomy
ERIKSSON, E., Pharmacology
ERIKSSON, P., Neurobiology, especially Stem Cell Research
FÄNDRIKS, L., Integrative Physiology and Pharmacology
FASTH, A., Paediatric Immunology and Rheumatology
FOSSELL-ARONSSON, E., Radiophysics
FREDMAN, P., Neurochemistry
FRIBERG, P., Clinical Physiology
FUNA, K., Medical Cell Biology
GASTON-JOHANSSON, F., Nursing Sciences
GILLBERG, C., Child and Youth Psychiatry and Handicap Research
GRANSTRÖM, G., Otorhinolaryngology
GRÖNDAHL, H.-G., Oral Diagnostic Radiology
GRÖNDAHL, K., Oral Diagnostic Radiology
GUSTAFSSON, B., Neurophysiology
HAGBERG, H., Obstetrics and Gynaecology, especially Periodontology
HAGBERG, M., Occupational Medicine
HAGLID, K., Histology
HAMBERGER, L., Obstetrics and Gynaecology
HANSSON, G., Biochemistry, especially Gastrointestinal Glycobiology
HANSSON, H.-A., Histology
HANSSON, T., Occupational Orthopaedics
HANSSON RÖNNBÄCK, E., Glia Cell Research
HARALDSSON, B., Kidney Medicine with Experimental Alignment
HÅRD, T., Structural Biology, especially Protein Chemistry
HEDNER, T., Clinical Pharmacology
HELLSTRAND, K., Immune Therapy
HELLSTRÖM, A., Paediatric Ophthalmology, especially Growth Factors
HELLSTRÖM, M., Diagnostic Radiology
HJALMARSSON, O., Paediatrics
HOLM, S., Experimental Surgery
HOLMÄNG, A., Laboratory Medicine
HOLMGREN, J., Medical Microbiology
HOLMSTRÖM, H., Plastic Surgery
HULTBORN, R., Oncology
HULTHÉN, L., Clinical Nutrition, especially Human Trace Element Research
ISAKSSON, O., Endocrinology
ISGAARD, J., Hormonal Regulation of the Heart, especially Growth and Repair Processes

IWARSON, S., Infectious Diseases
JACOBSSON, L., Medical Radiophysics
JANSON, P.-O., Obstetrics and Gynaecology
JANSSON, J.-O., Tissue Regeneration
JANSSON, T., Physiology, especially Perinatal Physiology
JERN, C., Neurology, especially Vascular Diseases and Vascular Genetics
JERN, S., Cardiovascular Physiology
JOHANSSON, B. R., Anatomy
JONASON, J., Pharmacology
JONTELL, M., Endocrinology with Oral Diagnostics
KAHNBERG, K.-E., Dental Surgery
KARLSSON, A., Experimental Rheumatology
KARLSSON, J.-O., Histology
KARLSSON, S., Prosthetic Dentistry
KÄRRHOLM, J., Orthopaedic Surgery
KINDBLOM, L.-G., Pathology
LAGERGÅRD, T., Vaccine Research
LARKÖ, O., Dermatology and Venereal Disease
LARSON, G., Laboratory Medicine, especially Glycobiology
LARSSON, S., Pneumology
LEKHOLM, U., Oral Implant Surgery
LINDAHL, A., Cartilage Tissue Regeneration
LINDBLOM, B., Eye Diseases
LINDE, A., Oral Biochemistry
LISSNER, L., Epidemiology
LÖTVALL, J., Clinical Allergology
LUNDHOLM, K., Surgery
LYCKE, N., Clinical Immunology
MAGNUSSON, B., Oral Pathology
MATTSSON, B., General Medicine
MEIS-KINDBLOM, J., Pathology
MELLANDER, L., International Medicine
MILSOM, I., Gynaecology and Obstetrics
MOHLIN, B., Orthodontics
MÖLLER, C., Audiology
NILSSON, O., Pathology
NILSSON, T., Functional Morphology
NISSBRANDT, H., Pharmacology
NORDGREN, S., Surgery
NORÉN, J., Paedodontics
NYGREN, H., Histology
NYSTRÖM, E., Medicine
OHLSSON, C., Hormonal Regulation of Bone Metabolism and Growth
OLAUSSON, M., Clinical Transplantation Surgery
OLDFORS, A., Pathology
OLMARKER, K., Experimental Spinal Pain Research, especially Neuropathic Pain Mechanism
OLOFSSON, S.-O., Medical Biochemistry
OLSSON, J., Odontological Technology
ÖSTMAN-SMITH, I., Paediatric Cardiology
PILHAMMAR-ANDERSSON, E., Nursing Pedagogics
REIT, C., Endodontology
RIDELL, M., Medical Microbiology
RISBERG, B., Surgery
RÖNNBÄCK, L., Neurology
ROSENGREN, A., Epidemiology
ROUPE, G., Dermatology and Venereal Diseases
RYDEVIK, B., Orthopaedic Surgery
RYMO, L., Clinical Chemistry
SAMUELSSON, B., Transfusion Medicine
SANDBERG, M., Biochemistry
SEMB, H., Evolutionary Biology
SENNERBY, L., Handicap Research, especially Experimental and Clinical
SILLÉN, U., Paediatric Surgery
SJÖBERG, B., Medical Biochemistry
SJÖSTRÖM, L., Clinical Research
SJÖVALL, H., Physiology and Pathophysiology of the Digestive and Intestinal Channel
SKOOG, I., Psychiatry, especially Social Psychiatry and Epidemiology
SMITH, U., Medicine
SOUSSI, B., Experimental Medicine, especially NMR Spectroscopy

STEINECK, G., Cancer Epidemiology
STENEVI, U., Ophthalmology
STENMAN, G., Pathology
STRANDVIK, B., Paediatrics
SULLIVAN, M., Psychology
SVENNERHOLM, A.-M., Infectious Diseases and Immunology
SWEDBERG, K., Medicine
TARKOWSKI, A., Rheumatology
THELLE, D., Cardiovascular Epidemiology and Prevention
THOMSEN, P., Medical Biomaterials Research
TYLÉN, U., X-Ray Diagnostics
WAHLSTRÖM, J., Clinical Genetics
WALLERSTEDT, S., Medicine
WALLGREN, A., Radio Therapeutics
WALLIN, A., Geriatric Neuropsychiatry
WENNERBERG, A., Oral Prosthetics
WENNERGREN, G., Paediatrics
WENNSTRÖM, J., Parodontology
WICK, M. J., Clinical and Experimental Immunology
WIGSTRÖM, H., Medical Physics
WIKKELSÖ, C., Neurology
WIKLUND, O., Medicine
WIKSTRÖM, M., Oral Microbiology

School of Business, Economics and Law (POB 600, SE-405 30 Gothenburg; tel. (31) 786-49-48; e-mail info@handels.gu.se; internet www .handels.gu.se):

ALVSTAM, C.-G., International Economic Geography
ANDERSSON, D. T., Marketing
BERGENDAHL, G., Managerial Economics
BIGSTEN, A., Economics
CRAMÉR, P., International Law, European Integration Law
CZARNIAWSKA, B., Business Administration
DOTEVALL, R., Commercial Law
FLOOD, L., Econometrics
FRISÉN, M., Statistics
GADD, C.-J., Economic History
HIBBS, D., Economics
HJALMARSSON, L., Economics
JENSEN, A., Transport Management
JOHANSSON STENMAN, O., Economics
JÖNSSON, S., Business Administration
JONSSON, S., Economic History
LINDBLOM, T., Business Administration
MÅRTENSSON, R., Business Administration
NORBÄCK, L.-E., Business Administration
NORDSTRÖM, L., Human Geography
OLSON, O., Accounting and Finance
OLSSON, U., Economic History
PÅHLSSON, R., Tax Law
POLESIE, T., Accounting and Finance
RAMBERG, C., Commercial Law
SANDELIN, B., Economics
SOLLI, R., Business Administration
STERNER, T., Environmental Economics
STJERNBERG, T., Management and Organization
TÖLLBORG, D., Legal Science
TÖRNQVIST, U., Business Administration
VILHELMSON, B., Human Geography
WESTERHÄLL, V. L., Public Law

KARLSTADS UNIVERSITET
(Karlstad University)

SE-651 88 Karlstad
Universitetsgatan 2, Karlstad
Telephone: (54) 700-10-00
E-mail: information@kau.se
Internet: www.kau.se
Founded 1967 as Universitetsfilialen, became Högskolan i Karlstad 1977, current name adopted 1999
State control
Languages of instruction: English, Swedish
Academic year: August to June
Vice-Chancellor: ÅSA BERGENHEIM
Pro-Vice-Chancellor: THOMAS BLOM

Univ. Dir: ANNE-CHRISTINE LARSSON
Library Dir: JAKOB HARNESK
Library of 180,000 vols
Number of teachers: 700
Number of students: 11,500
Publications: *Anslaget* (26 a year), *Utbilder* (6 a year)

DEANS

Faculty of Arts and Social Science: PATRIK LARSSON
Faculty of Education: BJÖRN ÅRSTRAND
Faculty of Health, Science and Technology: Prof. BJÖRN ARVIDSSON

LINKÖPINGS UNIVERSITET
(Linköping University)

SE-581 83 Linköping
Telephone: (13) 28-10-00
E-mail: liu@liu.se
Internet: www.liu.se
Founded 1970
Academic year: September to June
Vice-Chancellor: Prof. Dr HELEN DANNETUN
Deputy Vice-Chancellor: Prof. Dr KARIN FÄLTH-MAGNUSSON
Deputy Vice-Chancellor for External Relation: PETER VÄRBRAND
Univ. Dir: KENT WALTERSSON
Library: see under Libraries and Archives
Number of teachers: 1,800
Number of students: 27,300 (incl. 18,120 full-time students)

DEANS

Faculty of Arts and Sciences: Prof. BO HELLGREN
Faculty of Educational Sciences: Prof. KARIN MÅRDSJÖ BLUME
Faculty of Health Sciences: Prof. JOHAN DABROSIN SÖDERHOLM
Institute of Technology: Dr ULF NILSSON

PROFESSORS

Faculty of Arts and Sciences:

ADELSWÄRD, V., Communication Studies
AHLUND, A, Ethnicity Studies
ALLARD, B., Water and Environmental Studies
ANSELM, J., Technology and Social Change
ANWARD, J., Language and Culture Studies
ARNESDOTTER, I., Business Law
ARONSSON OTTOSSON, K., Child Studies
BECKMAN, S., Technology and Social Change
BERNER, B., Technology and Social Change
BORGQUIST, L., Health and Society
CARLGREN, I., Education
CARSTENSEN, J., Health and Society
COLLSTE, G., Applied Ethics
DAHLGREN, L.-O., Education
EDQUIST, C., Technology and Social Change
ELLEGÅRD, K., Technology and Social Change
ELLSTÖM, P.-E., Education
ERIKSSON, B. E., Health and Society
FRODI, A., Psychology
GOLDKUHL, G., Information Systems
GRANSTÖM, K., Education
GRIMWALL, A., Statistics
HALLDÉN, G., Child Studies
HELLGREN, B., Management
HJORT AF ORNÄS, A., Water and Environmental Studies
HULTMAN, G., Education
HYDÉN, L.-C., Communication Studies
INGELSTAM, L., Technology and Social Change
JANSSON, J., Transport Economics
JOHANSSON, R., Ethnicity Studies
KYLHAMMER, J., Communication Studies
LINDKVIST, L., Management
LINELL, P., Communication Studies

LOHM, U., Water and Environmental Studies
LUNDQVIST, J., Water and Environmental Studies
LYKKE, N., Gender Studies
LYXELL, B., Psychology
MYRBERG, M., Education
NÄSMAN, E., Society and Cultural Studies
NELSON, M. C., History
NILSSON, G. B., Technology and Social Change
NORDENFELT, L., Health and Society
NORDIN, I., Health and Society
PETERSON, B., Philosophy
ÖBERG, G., Water and Environmental Studies
QVARSELL, R., Health and Society
RAHM, L., Water and Environmental Studies
RÖNNBERG, J., Psychology
SANDELL, R., Clinical Psychology
SANDIN, B., Child Studies
SJÖGREN, H., Technology and Social Change
SKOGH, G., Economics
SUNDIN, E., Technology and Social Change
SUNDIN, J., Health and Society
SVENSSON, B., Water and Environmental Studies

Faculty of Health Sciences:

ALM-CARLSSON, G., Medical Radiation Physics
ANDERSSON, R., Pharmacology
ARNQVIST, H., Medical Cell Biology
ASPENBERG, P., Orthopaedic Surgery
AXELSON, O., Occupational and Environmental Medicine
BERGDAHL, B., Medicine
BLOMQVIST, A., Pain Research
BORCH, K., Surgery
BRUNK, U., Pathology
CARLSSON, P., Health Technology Assessment
EK, A.-C., Caring Science
EKBERG, K., Work and Rehabilitation
FAGERHOLM, P., Ophthalmology
FORSBERG, P., Infectious Diseases
FORSUM, U., Clinical Microbiology
GERDLE, B., Rehabilitation Medicine
GRANERUS, A.-K., Geriatric Medicine
HAMMAR, M., Obstetrics and Gynaecology
HAMMARSTRÖM, S., Medical Cell Biology
HILDEBRAND, C., Medical Cell Biology
HULTMAN, P., Pathology
KÅGEDAL, B., Clinical Chemistry
KARLBERG, B., Medicine
KINLSTRÖM, E., Clinical Microbiology
LARSSON, S.-E., Orthopaedic Surgery
LENNQUIST, S., Disaster Medicine and Traumatology
LINDSTRÖM, S., Medical Cell Biology
LISANDER, B., Anaesthesiology
LUDVIGSSON, J., Paediatrics
LUNDBLAD, A., Clinical Chemistry
LUNDQUIST, P.-G., Otorhinolaryngology
MAGNUSSON, K.-E., Medical Microbiology
MARAISSON, J., Geriatrics
MÅRDH, S., Cell Biology
MESSNER, K., Skeletal Biology
NILSSON, L., Microbiology
NORDENSKJÖLD, B., Oncology
NORDIN, C., Psychiatry
ÖBERG, Å., Medical Engineering (Instrumentation)
ÖBERG, B., Physiotherapy
OLIN, C., Cardiothoracic Surgery
OLSSON, A. G., Internal Medicine
OLSSON, J.-E., Neurology
ÖSTRUP, L., Plastic Surgery
PAULETTE-HULTCRANTZ, E., Otorhinolaryngology
PETERSSON, C., Clinical Pharmacology
RAMMER, L., Forensic Science and Medicine
ROSDAHL, I., Dermatology and Venereology

ROSÉN, A., Inflammation and Tumour Biology
SERUP, J., Dermatology and Venereology
SJÖBERG, F., Critical Care, especially Burn Intensive Care
SMEDBY, Ö., Diagnostic Radiology
SMEDS, S., Surgery
SÖDERFELT, B., Neurology
SÖDERKVIST, P., Cell Biology, especially Medical Genetics
STENDAHL, O., Medical Microbiology
STENMAN, G., Medical Genetics
STRÅLFORS, P., Medical Cell Biology
STRANG, P., Palliative Medicine
SUNDQUIST, T., Medical Microbiology, especially Inflammation
SVANBORG, E., Clinical Neuropsychology
SVANVIK, J., Surgery
TAGESSON, C., Experimental Medicine
THEODORSSON, E., Neurochemistry
TIMPKA, T., Social Medicine and Public Health Sciences
TRELL, E., Primary Health Care and General Practice
WÅLINDER, J., Psychiatry
WASTESON, A., Medical Cell Biology
WIGERTZ, O., Medical Engineering (Medical Information Processing)
WIJMA, B., Women's Health
WRANNE, B., Clinical Physiology

Institute of Technology:
ABRAHAMSSON, M., Logistics Management
AHRENBERG, L., Computational Linguistics
ANDERSSON, L.-E., Applied Mathematics
ARONSSON, G., Applied Mathematics
ARWIN, H., Applied Optics
ASK, P., Biomedical Engineering
BALTZER, L., Organic Chemistry
BERGGREN, C., Production Management
BERGGREN, K.-F., Theoretical Physics
BORÉN, H., Organic Chemistry
BRANDES, O., Industrial Marketing
BREGE, S., Industrial Marketing
CARLSSON, U., Biochemistry
CHEN, W., Materials Science
DADFAR, H., International Marketing
DAHLBERG, T., Solid Mechanics and Strength of Materials
DAHLGAARD, J. J., Quality Technology and Management
DOHERTY, P., Computer Science
EDGAR, B., Applied Mathematics
EKEDAHL, L.-G., Applied Physics, Catalytic Reactions
EKLUND, J., Industrial Ergonomics
ELDÉN, L., Numerical Analysis
ERICSON, T., Data Transmission
ERICSSON, T., Engineering Materials
FAHLMAN, A., Physics
FRITZSON, P., Computer Science
GLAD, T., Automatic Control
GRANLUND, G., Computer Vision
GRUBBSTRÖM, R. W., Production Economics
GUSTAFSSON, F., Communication Systems
HÄGGLUND, S., Computer Science
HANSSON, G., Experimental Semiconductor Physics
HELMERSSON, U., Thin Film Physics
HOLLNAGEL, E., Industrial Ergonomics
HOLMBERG, K., Optimization
HOLTZ, P.-O., Materials Science
HULTMAN, L., Thin Film Physics
INGANÄS, O., Biomolecular and Organic Electronics
INGEMARSSON, I., Information Theory
JANZÉN, E., Semiconductor Physics
JOHANSSON, L., Materials Science
JONSSON, B. H., Biochemistry
KAMKAR, M., Software Engineering
KARLSSON, B., Energy Systems
KARLSSON, J. M., Telecommunications
KLARBRING, A., Optimization Models in Structural Mechanics
KNUTSSON, H., Medical Informatics
KOSKI, T., Mathematical Statistics

KRUS, P., Fluid Power Technology
KRUSE, B., Digital Images and Media Technology
KVARNSTRÖM, I., Organic Chemistry
LIEDBERG, B., Sensor Science
LINDBERG, P.-O., Optimization
LINUSSON, S., Applied Mathematics
LIU, D., Computer Engineering
LJUNG, L., Automatic Control
LOYD, D., Applied Thermodynamics and Fluid Mechanics
LUND, A., Chemical Physics
LUNDGREN, J., Traffic Systems
LUNDSTRÖM, I., Applied Physics
MALUSZYNSKI, J., Programming Theory
MANDENIUS, C.-F., Biotechnology
MAZ'YA, V., Applied Mathematics
MILLNERT, M., Automatic Control
MONEMAR, B., Condensed Matter Physics
MOSFEGH, B., Energy Systems
MUKHERJEE, S. D., Electronic Production
NIELSEN, L., Vehicle Systems
NILSSON, G., Biomedical Instrumentation
NILSSON, L., Solid Mechanics
NOVAK, A., Production Engineering
ÖBERG, Å., Biomedical Engineering
OHLSSON, K., Industrial Ergonomics
PALMBERG, J.-O., Fluid Power Technology
PENG, Z., Computer Systems
PERSSON, J., Medical Technology Assessment
RAPP, B., Economic Information Systems
RAUCH, W., Applied Mathematics
RIKLUND, R., Theoretical Physics
RÖNNQVIST, M., Optimization
RYDBERG, K.-E., Fluid Power Technology
SALANECK, W., Surface Physics and Chemistry
SANDAHL, K., Software Engineering
SANDEWALL, E., Computer Science
SANDKULL, B., Industrial Organization
SERNELIUS, B., Theoretical Physics
SHAHMEHRI, N., Computer Science
SJÖLANDER, S., Zoology
STAFSTRÖM, S., Computational Physics
STRANDBERG, L., Traffic Safety and Environment
SVENSSON, C., Electronic Devices
TENGVALL, P., Applied Physics
UHRBERG, R., Surface and Semiconductor Physics
VÅRBRAND, P., Optimization
WANHAMMAR, L., Electronic Systems
WIGERTZ, O., Medical Informatics

LINNÉUNIVERSITETET
(Linnaeus University)

SE-391 82 Kalmar
SE-351 95 Växjö

Telephone: (772) 28-80-00
E-mail: info@lnu.se
Internet: lnu.se

Founded 2010, following merger of Växjö Universitet (f. 1967 as a br. of Lund Univ.) and Högskolan i Kalmar (f. 1977)
State control
Languages of instruction: English, swedish
Academic year: September to June

Faculties of arts and humanities, business and economics, health and life sciences, social sciences, technology

Rector: STEPHEN HWANG
Pro-Rector: BO BERGBÄCK
Pro-Rector: LENA FRITZÉN
Pro-Rector: NILS NILSSON
Univ. Dir: PER BROLIN
Library Dir: CATTA TORHELL

Library: see under Libraries and Archives
Number of teachers: 2,000
Number of students: 42,000 (15,600 full-time)

LULEÅ TEKNISKA UNIVERSITET
(Luleå University of Technology)

SE-971 87 Luleå

Telephone: (920) 49-10-00
E-mail: registrator@ltu.se
Internet: www.ltu.se

Founded 1971
State control
Language of instruction: Swedish

Vice-Chancellor: JOHAN STERTE
Deputy Vice-Chancellor: ERIK HÖGLUND
Deputy Vice-Chancellor: BIRGITTA BERGVALL-KÅREBORN
Head for Univ. Admin.: STAFFAN SARBÄCK
Univ. Librarian: TERJE HÖISETH

Library of 240,932 vols, 15,663 periodicals
Number of teachers: 730 (incl. researchers)
Number of students: 12,000

PROFESSORS

Department of Applied Physics and Mechanical Engineering:

FREDRIKSSON, S., Physics
GUSTAVSSON, H., Fluid Mechanics
HÖGLUND, E., Machine Elements
JINYUE, Y., Energy Engineering
KAPLAN, A., Systems Engineering
KARLSSON, L., Computer Aided Design
MOLIN, N. E., Experimental Mechanics
ODÉN, M., Engineering Materials
OLDENBURG, M., Solid Mechanics
VARNA, J., Polymer Engineering

Department of Business Administration and Social Sciences:

BERGSTRÖM, I., Management Control
DE RAADT, D., Informatics and Systems Sciences
HÄGERFORS, A., Computer and Systems Sciences
HANSSON, S., Political Science, History and Geography
HÖRTE, S.-Å., Industrial Organization
KLEFSJÖ, B.
LUNDGREN, N.-G., Political Science, History and Geography
MICHANEK, G., Jurisprudence
RADETZKI, M., Economics
SALEHI-SANGARI, E., Industrial Marketing
WIKLUND, H., Quality and Environmental Management

Department of Chemical and Metallurgical Engineering:

BERGLUND, K. A., Biochemical and Chemical Process Engineering
BJÖRKMAN, B., Process Metallurgy
FORSLING, W., Chemistry
FORSSBERG, E., Mineral Processing
STERTE, J., Chemical Technology

Department of Civil and Mining Engineering:

BORGBRANT, J., Construction Management
ELFGREN, L., Structural Engineering
JOHANSSON, B., Steel Structures
KLISINSKI, M., Structural Mechanics
KNUTSSON, S., Soil Mechanics and Foundation Engineering
KUMAR, U., Operation and Maintenance Engineering
LAGERQVIST, O., Steel Structures
LINDQVIST, P.-A., Rock Engineering
NORDLUND, E., Rock Mechanics
OLOFSSON, T., Structural Engineering

Department of Communication and Languages:

MAGNUSSON, U., English
PERSSON, G., English

Department of Computer Science and Electrical Engineering:

DELSING, J., Embedded Internet Systems Laboratory (EISLAB)
MEDVEDEV, A., Automatic Control

WERNERSSON, Å., Embedded Internet Systems Laboratory (EISLAB)

Department of Environmental Engineering:
ELMING, S.-Å., Applied Geophysics
HANAEUS, J., Sanitary Engineering
LAGERKVIST, A., Water Science and Technology
NORDELL, B., Renewable Energy
ÖHLANDER, B., Applied Geology
ÖSTMAN, A., Geographical Information Technology
SELLGREN, A., Water Resources Engineering

Department of Human Work Sciences:
ÅGREN, A., Sound and Vibration
ALM, H., Engineering Psychology
JOHANSSON, J., Industrial Work Environment
PETTERSSON, D., Industrial Design

Department of Mathematics:
EULER, M., Applied Mathematics
HEABERG, T., Applied Mathematics
PERSSON, L.-E., Applied Mathematics
STRAESSER, R., Applied Mathematics

Department of Wood Technology:
GRÖNLUND, A., Wood Technology
MORÉN, T., Wood Physics
WESTERMARK, U., Wood Material Science

School of Education:
ALEXANDERSSON, M., Pedagogics

School of Music:
BRÄNDSTRÖM, S., Education and Teaching Methods in Music
ERICSSON, H.-O., Organ
SANDSTRÖM, J., Composition
WESTBERG, E., Choir Singing and Choir Conducting

LUNDS UNIVERSITET
(Lund University)

POB 117, SE-221 00 Lund
Telephone: (46) 222-00-00
E-mail: lu@lu.se
Internet: www.lu.se
Founded 1666
State control
Languages of instruction: English, Swedish
Academic year: September to June (2 semesters)

Vice-Chancellor: Dr PER ERIKSSON
Pro-Vice-Chancellor: Prof. Dr EVA ÅKESSON
Asst Vice-Chancellor for Innovation: Prof. CARL BORREBAECK
Asst Vice-Chancellor for Internationalisation: KRISTINA ENEROTH
Asst Vice-Chancellor for Leadership: Prof. NILS DANIELSEN
Asst Vice-Chancellor for Research and Int. Issues: Prof. SVEN STRÖMQVIST
Univ. Dir: SUSANNE KRISTENSSON
Library: see under Libraries and Archives
Number of teachers: 640
Number of students: 47,000
Publication: *LUM* (9 a year)

DEANS
Faculty of Engineering: Prof. ANDERS AXELSSON
Faculty of Fine and Performing Arts: SOLFRID SÖDERLIND
Faculty of Humanities and Theology: Prof. LYNN ÅKESSON
Faculty of Law: Prof. CHRISTINA MOËLL
Faculty of Medicine: Prof. GUNILLA WESTERGREN-THORSSON
Faculty of Science: Prof. OLOV STERNER
Faculty of Social Sciences: Prof. ANN-KATRIN BÄCKLUND
School of Economics and Management: Prof. FREDRIK ANDERSSON

PROFESSORS

Faculty of Humanities and Theology:
ANDERSSON, G., Musicology
ANDRÉN, A., Medieval Archaeology
BJÖRLING, F., Slavic Languages
BLOMQVIST, J., Greek Language and Literature
BROBERG, G., History of Ideas and Sciences
BRUCE, G., Phonetics
EDLUND, B., Musicology
EINARSSON, J., Scandinavian Languages
ENÉVIST, I., Spanish
FLORBY, G., English Literature
FRYKMAN, J., European Ethnology
GÄRDENFORS, P., Cognitive Science
GREATREX, R., Chinese
GUSTAFSSON, H., History
HAETTNER-AURELIUS, E., Literature
HÅKANSSON, G., General Linguistics
HANSSON, B., Theoretical Philosophy
HÅRDH, B., Archaeology
HEDLING, E., Film
HOADLEY, M., Southeast Asian History and Bahasa Indonesia
HOLMBERG, B., Semitic Languages
HORNBORG, A., Human Ecology
IREGREN, E., Historical Osteology
KARLSSON, K.-G., History
LARSSON, B., French
LARSSON, L., Archaeology
LARSSON, L., Literature
LÖFGREN, O., European Ethnology
LÖVKRONA, I., European Ethnology
MOLNÁR, V., German
NORDIN, S., History of Ideas and Science
OLAUSSON, D., Archaeology
OREDSSON, S., History
ÖSTERBERG, E., History
PALM, A., Literature
PERSSON, I., Practical Philosophy
PILTZ, A., Latin
PLATZACK, C., Scandinavian Languages
RABINOWICZ, W., Practical Philosophy
RAGVALD, L., Chinese
RIDDERSTAD, P. S., Book and Library History
RYDÉN, P., Literature
RYSTEDT, E., Classical Archaeology and Ancient History
SAHLIN, N.-E., Theoretical Philosophy
SALOMON, K., International History
SALOMOUSSON, A., European Ethnology
SANDQVIST, S., French
SCHLYTER, S., Romance Languages
SJÖBLAD, C., Literature
SJÖLIN, J.-G., History of Contemporary Art
SONESSON, G., Cultural Semiotics
STEENSLAND, L., Slavic Languages
STRÖMQVIST, S., Language Acquisition
SVANTESSON, J.-O., General Linguistics
SVENSSON, J., Swedish
SVENSSON, L.-H., English Literature
THORMÄHLEN, M., English Literature
VIBERG, Å., General Linguistics
WARREN, B., English
WEIMARCK, T., History of Contemporary Art
WIÉANDER, Ö., Classical Archaeology
WIENBERG, J., Medieval Archaeology

Faculty of Law:
BERGHOLTZ, G., Legal Procedure
BERGSTRÖM, S., Tax Law
BOGDAN, M., Comparative and Private International Law
FAHLBECK, R., Labour Law
GORTON, L., Banking Law
MELANDER, G., Public International Law
MODÉER, K. A., Legal History
NUMHAUSER-HENNING, A., Private Law
NYSTRÖM, B., Private Law
PECZENIK, A., Jurisprudence
TRÄSKMAN, P. O., Criminal Law
VOGEL, H.-H., Public Law
WESTBERG, P., Legal Procedure

Faculty of Medicine:
ABRAHAMSSON, P.-A., Oncological Urology
ÅHRÉN, B., Clinical Metabolic Research
ÅKERLUND, M., Obstetrics and Gynaecology
ÅKERSTROM, B., Medical Chemistry
ALLING, CH., Medical Neurochemistry
ALM, P., Pathology
ANDERSSON, K.-E., Clinical Pharmacology
ANDERSSON, R., Surgery
ANDERSSON, T., Experimental Pathology
ARNER, A., Physiology
BÄCK, O., Dermatology
BELFRAGE, P., Medical Biochemistry
BERGLUND, G., Internal Medicine
BERGLUND, M., Clinical Alcohol Research
BJÖRCK, L., Medical Biochemistry
BJÖRKLUND, A., Histology
BJURSTEN, L.-M., Bio-implant Research
BORGSTRÖM, A., Surgery
BRUNDIN, P., Neuroscience
CARLSTEDT, I., Mucosal Biology
DAHLBÄCK, B., Coagulation Research
DEGERMAN, E., Experimental Diabetes Research
DEHLIN, O., Geriatric Medicine
DILLNER, J., Virology
EHINGER, B., Ophthalmology
EKBLOM, P., Molecular Cell Biology
EKDAHL, C., Physiotherapy
EKHBERG, O., Diagnostic Radiology
ELMESTÅHL, S., Geriatrics
ERLANSON-ALBERTSSON, C.
FÄSSLER, R., Experimental Pathology
FENYÖ, E.-M., Virology
FORSGREN, A., Clinical Bacteriology
FRANSSON, L.-Å., Cell Biology
GERDTHAM, U., Public Health Science
GRÄNDE, P.-O., Anaesthesia and Intensive Care
GROOP, L., Endocrinology
GRUBB, A., Clinical Biochemistry
GULLBERG, U., Haematology
GUSTAFSON, L., Geriatric Psychiatry
HAGANDER, B., Medicine
HAGMAR, L., Environmental Medicine
HÅKANSSON, R., Experimental Endocrinology
HEIJL, A., Ophthalmology
HEINEGÅRD, D., Medical Biochemistry
HELLSTRAND, P., Muscle Research
HERMERÉN, G., Medical Ethics
HESSLOW, G., Neuroscience
HÖGESTÄTT, E., Clinical Pharmacology
HOLMBERG, L., Paediatrics
HOLMDAHL, R., Medical Inflammation Research
HOLMER, N.-G., Biomedical Engineering
HOLM WALLENBERG, C., Molecular Cell Biology
HOLTÅS, S., Neuroradiology
HOVELIUS, B., General Practice
IHSE, I., Surgery
JACOBSEN, S. E., Stem Cell Biology
JANZON, L., Epidemiology
JEPPSSON, B., Surgery
JOHNELL, O., Orthopaedic Surgery
JONSON, B., Clinical Physiology
KARLSSON, S., Gene Therapy in Molecular Medicine
KILLANDER, D., Oncology
LANDBERG, G., Pathology
LEANDERSON, T., Immunology
LEED-LUNDBERG, F., Cellular and Molecular Physiology
LERNMARK, Å., Experimental Diabetes Research
LEVANDER, S., Psychiatry
LIDGREN, L., Orthopaedics
LINDAHL, G., Medical Microbiology and Immunology
LINDGREN, B., Health Economics
LINDGREN, S., Medicine
LINDVALL, O., Restorative Neurology
LJUNGGREN, B., Dermatology and Venereology

LÖFDAHL, C.-G., Lung Disease
LÖFQVIST, A., Logopaedic Phonetics
LOHMANDER, S., Orthopaedics
LÖWENHIELM, P., Forensic Medicine
LUNDBERG, D., Anaesthesiology
LUNDBORG, G., Hand Surgery
LUNDQUIST, I., Pharmacology
LUTHMAN, H., Genetic Epidemiology
MCNEIL, T., Medical Behavioural Research
MAGNUSSON, M., Otorhinolaryngology
MALMSTRÖM, A., Medical and Physiological
  Chemistry
MARSAL, K., Obstetrics and Gynaecology
MATTIASSON, A., Urology
MATTSON, R., Reproduction Immunology
MATTSSON, S., Medical Radiation Physics
MITELMAN, F., Clinical Genetics
NETTELBLADT, U., Logopaedics
NILSSON, Å., Internal Medicine
NILSSON, J., Experimental Cardiovascular
  Research
NILSSON-EHLE, P., Clinical Chemistry
NORRBY, R., Infectious Diseases
NORRVING, B., Neurology
ÖHMAN, R. L., Psychiatry
OLBRANT, K., Cell Biology
OLOFSSON, T., Haematology
OLSSON, B., Cardiology
OLSSON, H., Oncology
OLSSON, I., Haematology
OWMAN, CH., Histology
PÅHLMAN, S., Molecular Medicine
PERSSON, B., Medical Radiation Physics
PERSSON, C. G. A., Experimental Clinical
  Pharmacology
PESONEN, E., Child Cardiology
PETTERSSON, H., Diagnostic Radiology
PRELLNER, K., Otorhinolaryngology
RAHM-HALLBERG, I., Caring Sciences
RÅSTAM, L., Applied Public Health
RENCK, H., Anaesthesiology
RIPPE, B., Nephrology
RISBERG, J., Neuropsychology
RORSMAN, P., Membrane Physiology
ROSÉN, I., Clinical Neurophysiology
SALFORD, L., Neurosurgery
SCHOUENBORG, J., Physiology
SJÖBERG, N.-O., Obstetrics and Gynaecol-
  ogy
SKERFVING, S., Occupational Medicine
STEEN, S., Thoracic Surgery
STENFLO, J., Clinical Chemistry
SUNDLER, F., Histology
SUNDLER, R., Cell Biology
SVANBORG, C., Clinical Immunology
THORNGREN, K.-G., Orthopaedics
TRÄSKMAN BENDZ, L., Psychiatry
WADSTRÖM, T., Bacteriology
WIELOCH, T., Neurobiology
WINGSTRAND, H., Orthopaedics
WOLLMER, P., Clinical Physiology

Faculty of Science:
ADLER, J.-O., Nuclear Physics
AHLBERG, P., Historical Geology and Palae-
  ontology
ÅKESSON, T., Elementary Particle Physics
ALERSTAM, T., Animal Ecology
ALLEN, J. F., Plant Cell Biology
ALMBLADH, C.-O., Physics
ANDERSEN, T., Astronomy
ANDERSSON, B., Theoretical Physics
ANDERSSON, C., Inorganic Chemistry
ANDRÉASSON, P.-G., Mineralogy and Pet-
  rology
ARDEBERG, A., Astronomy
ARNASON, U., Evolutionary Genetics
ASMUSSEN, S., Mathematical Statistics
BÅÅTH, E., Microbial Ecology
BENGTSSON, B. O., Genetics
BENGTSSON, G., Chemical Ecology and
  Ecotoxicology
BENGTSSON, S.-A., Systematic Zoology
BERG, U., Organic Chemistry
BJÖRCK, S., Quaternary Geology
BJÖRN, L. O., Plant Physiology

BRÖNMARK, C., Limnology
CHAO, K., Theoretical Physics
CONSTANTIN, A., Mathematics
DRAVINS, D., Astronomy
EDSTRÖM, A., Zoophysiology
EEROLA, P., Experimental Particle Physics
ELDING, L. I., Inorganic Chemistry
ERIKSSON, M., Physics
EVERITT, E., Microbiology
FAGERSTRÖM, T., Theoretical Ecology
FAHLANDER, C., Physics
FALKENGRENGRERUP, U., Plant Ecology
FREJD, T., Organic Chemistry
GORTON, L., Analytical Chemistry
GRANELI, W., Limnology
GUSTAFSON, G., Theoretical Physics
GUSTAFSSON, H.-Å., High-Energy Heavy
  Ion Physics
HANSSON, B., Chemical Ecology and Eco-
  toxicology
HANSSON, L.-A., Limnology
HEBERT, H., Molecular Biophysics
HEDENMALM, H., Mathematics
HELLBORG, R., Nuclear Physics
HELLDÉN, U., Physical Geography
HOLM, E., Radiation Physics
HOLMBERG, B., Inorganic Chemistry
HÖSSJER, O., Mathematical Studies
JAKOBSSON, B., Subatomic Physics
JANSSON, H.-B., Microbial Ecology
JARLSKOG, G., Physics
JEPPSSON, L., Historical Geology and Palae-
  ontology
JERGIL, B., Biochemistry
JOHANSSON, S., Atomic Spectroscopy
JÖNSSON, B., Physical Chemistry
JÖNSSON, J.-Å., Analytical Chemistry
JÖNSSON, L., Elementary Particle Physics
KANJE, M., Zoological Cell Biology
KANTOR, I., Mathematics
KARLSTRÖM, G., Theoretical Physics
KJELLBOM, P., Plant Biochemistry
KÄRNEFELT, I., Systematic Botany
LARSSON, C., Plant Biochemistry
LARSSON, K., Historical Geology and Palae-
  ontology
LARSSON, P., Chemical Ecology and Ecotox-
  icology
LARSSON, R., Zoology
LILJAS, A., Molecular Biophysics
LINDAU, I., Synchrotron Light Research
LINDEGREN, L., Astronomy
LINDH, A., Mineralogy and Petrology
LINDMAN, B., Physical Chemistry
LINDROTH, A., Physical Geography
LINGAS, A., Computer Sciences
LINSE, P., Macromolecular Chemistry
LITZÉN, U., Atomic Spectroscopy
LOFSTEDT, C., Ecology, Chemical Commu-
  nication
LÖRSTAD, B., Elementary Particle Physics
LUNDBERG, P., Theoretical Ecology
MARTINSON, I., Atomic Physics
MATHIASSON, L., Analytical Chemistry
MAX MØLLER, I., Plant Physiology
MELIN, A., Mathematics
MEURMAN, A., Mathematics
NIHLGÅRD, B., Plant Ecology
NILSSON, D. E., Zoology
NILSSON, J.-A., Animal Ecology
NILSSON, N., Mathematics
NILSSON, S. G., Animal Ecology
NYHOLM, R., Synchrotron Radiation Instru-
  mentation
OLSSON, U., Physical Chemistry
OREDSSON, S., Animal Physiology
OSCARSSON, A., Inorganic Chemistry
PEETRE, J., Mathematics
PETERSON, C., Theoretical Physics
PETTERSON, G., Biochemistry
PICULELL, L., Physical Chemistry
PRENTICE, H., Systematic Botany
ROOS, B., Theoretical Chemistry
RUTBERG, B., Microbiology
RUTBERG, L., Microbiology
SANDGREN, P., Quaternary Geology

SCHRÖDER, B., Nuclear Physics
SJÖSTRAND, T., Theoretical Physics
SMITH, H., Animal Ecology
SÖDERGREN, A., Chemical Ecology and
  Ecotoxicology
SÖDERLIND, G., Numerical Mathematics
SÖDERMAN, O., Physical Chemistry
SÖDERSTRÖM, B., Microbial Ecology
SOMMARIN, M., Plant Biochemistry
STÅHLBERG, F., Magnetic Resonance
STENLUND, E., Cosmic and Subatomic
  Physics
STRAND, S.-E., Radiation Physics
STYRING, S., Biochemistry
SUNDSTRÖM, V., Chemical Dynamics
SVENSSON, B. E. Y., Theoretical Physics
SYKES, M., Plant Ecology
TJERNELD, F., Biochemistry
TUNLID, A., Microbial Ecology
TYLER, G., Plant Ecology
VON BARTH, U., Physics
VON SCHANTZ, T., Animal Ecology
WENNERSTRÖM, H., Physical Chemistry
WESTRÖM, B., Animal Physiology
WIDELL, S., Plant Physiology

Faculty of Social Sciences:
AGNÉR SIGBO, G., Informatics
ÅKERSTRÖM, M., Sociology
ALLWOOD, C.-M., Psychology
ALVESSON, M., Business Administration
ANDERSSON, G., Social Work
ANDERSSON, S. I., Psychology
ARWIDI, O., Business Administration
ÅSHEIM, B. T., Economic Geography
ÅSTRÖM, K., Sociology of Law
BENGTSSON, T., Economic History
BERONIUS, M., Sociology
BORGLIN, A., Public Sector Economics
BRANTE, T., Sociology
CARLSSON, S., Informatics
CARLSSON WETTERBERG, C., Gender Studies
CLARK, E., Social Geography
DAHL, G., Sociology
DAHLGREN, P., Sociology of Communication
DJURFELDT, G., Sociology
EDEBALK, P.-G., Social Work
EDGERTON, D., Econometrics
EHN, P., Information and Computer Sci-
  ences
EKHOLM FRIEDMAN, K., Social Anthropology
ELGSTRÖM, O., Political Science
ELIASSON, R.-M., Social Work
ESSEVELD, J., Sociology
FLODGREN, B., Business Law
FRIEDMAN, J., Social Anthropology
GUNNARSSON, CHR., Economic History
HANSSON, B., Economics
HANSSON, G., International Economics
HETZLER, A., Social Policy
HOLMQUIST, B., Statistics
HYDÉN, H., Sociology of Law
JACOBSSON, B., Business Administration
JERNECK, M., Political Science
JOHANSSON, C. R., Industrial and Organi-
  zational Psychology
JÖNSSON, CHR., Political Science
LAGNEVIK, M., Business Administration
LANDSTRÖM, H., Entrepreneurship and
  Small Business
LARSSON, R., Business Administration
LINDBERG, S., Sociology
LINDÉN, A.-L., Sociology
LUNDQUIST, L., Political Science, especially
  Public Administration
LYTTKENS, C. H., Economics
MALM, A., Business Administration
NORBERG, C., Corporate Law and Tax Law
OHLSSON, R., Modern Economic and Social
  History
OLANDER, L.-O., Social and Economic Geog-
  raphy
OLERUP, A., Informatics
OLSSON, C.-A., Economic History
OXELHEIM, L., International Business

PERSSON, I., Economics, especially Women's Studies

ROSENBECK, B., Gender Studies

RUNDQUIST, F.-M., Social and Economic Geography

RYDÉN, O., Personality Psychology

SALONEN, T., Social Work

SAMUELSSON, P., Corporate Law and Capital Market Law

SCHÖN, L., Economic History

SELLERBERG, A.-M., Sociology

SÖDERSTRÖM, L., Economics, especially Social Policy

STENELO, L.-G., Political Science

STÅHL, I., Economics

STANKIEWICZ, R., Science and Technology Policy

SUNESSON, S., Social Work

SVENSSON, C., Business Administration

SVENSSON, L., Pedagogy

SVENSSON, L.-G., Economics

SWÄRD, H., Social Work

Faculty of Technology:

ÅBERG, S., Mathematical Physics

ADLERCREUTZ, P., Biotechnology

ÅKESSON, B., Applied Nutrition

AKSELSSON, R., Ergonomics

ALAKÜLA, M., Industrial Electrical Engineering

ALDÉN, M., Laser-Based Combustion Diagnostics

ALY, G., Chemical Engineering

ANDERSON, J. B., Digital Communications

ANDERSSON, A., Chemical Engineering, especially Heterogenous Catalysis

ANDERSSON-ENGELS, S., Experimental Physics

ÅRZÉN, K.-E., Automatic Control

ASP, N.-G., Applied Nutrition

ÅSTRÖM, K. J., Mathematics

AXELSSON, A., Chemical Engineering

AXSÄTER, S., Production Management

BARUP, K., Architectural Conservation and Restoration

BENGTSSON, L., Water Resources Engineering

BENGTSSON, P.-E., Laser-Based Combustion Diagnostics

BENGTSSON, R., Mathematical Physics

BERGENSTÅHL, B., Food Technology

BERNDTSSON, R., Water Resources Engineering

BERNHARDSSON, B., Automatic Control

BJELM, L., Engineering Geology

BJÖRK, I., Applied Nutrition and Food Chemistry

BOHGARD, M., Ergonomics and Aerosol Technology

BOLMSJÖ, G., Robotics

BÖRJESSON, P.-O., Signal Processing

BORREBAECK, C., Immunotechnology

BOVIN, J.-O., Materials Chemistry and High-Resolution Electron Microscopy

BÜLOW, L., Biochemistry

DAHLBLOM, O., Structural Mechanics

DAMS, M., Computer Science

DEJMEK, P., Food Engineering

ECKHARDT, C.-C., Industrial Design

EDFORS, O., Radio Communications

EDSTRÖM, M., Architectural Conservation and Restoration

EKHOLM, A., Computer Aided Architectural Design

ELIASSON, A.-C., Cereal Technology

ELMROTH, A., Building Physics

ENGSTRÖM, L., Experimental Physics, especially Atomic Physics and Optics

FAGERLUND, G., Building Materials

FREDLUND, B., Building Science

FUCHS, L., Fluid Mechanics

GONZALEZ, A., Theoretical and Applied Aesthetics

GUSTAFSSON, P. J., Structural Mechanics

HAGANDER, P., Automatic Control

HÄGGLUND, T., Automatic Control

HAHN-HÄGERDAL, B., Applied Microbiology

HALLE, B., Physical Chemistry

HANSON, H., Water Resources Engineering

HANSSON, B., Construction Management

HELSING, J., Scientific Computing

HEYDEN, A., Mathematics

HOLMBERG, B., Traffic Planning

HOLMSTEDT, G., Fire Safety Engineering

HOLST, J., Mathematical Statistics

HOLST, O., Biotechnology

HOLST, U., Mathematical Statistics

HYDÉN, C., Traffic Engineering

JACOBSON, B., Machine Elements

JAMES, P., Proteomics

JARLSKOG, C., Theoretical Particle Physics

JENSEN, L. H., Building Services

JENSEN, U., Real Estate Management

JOHANNESSON, R., Information Theory

JOHANNESSON, T., Materials Engineering

JOHANSSON, B., Combustion Engines

JOHANSSON, G., Ergonomics and Aerosol Technology

JOHANSSON, R., Automatic Control

JOHANSSON, T., Information Theory

JOHANSSON, T.-B., Energy Systems Analysis

JÖNSON, G., Packaging Logistics

JÖNSSON, A. S., Chemical Engineering

JÖNSSON, B., Physical Chemistry

JÖNSSON, B., Rehabilitation Engineering

KARLSSON, A., Electromagnetic Theory

KARLSSON, H., Chemical Engineering, Process Chemistry and Catalysis

KARLSSON, J. M., Communication Systems

KRISTENSSON, G., Electromagnetic Theory

KRÖLL, S., Atomic Physics

KUCHINSKI, K., Computer Science

KÜLLER, R., Environmental Psychology

KÖRNER, U., Communication Systems

L'HUILLIER, A., Atomic Physics

LA COUR JANSEN, J., Water and Waste Water Engineering

LARSON, M., Water Resources Engineering

LARSSON, P.-O., Applied Biochemistry

LAURELL, T., Electrical Measurements

LIDÉN, G., Chemical Reaction Engineering

LIDGREN, L., Environmental Economics

LINDGREN, G., Mathematical Statistics

LINDSTRÖM, K., Electrical Measurements

LUNDHOLM, G., Combustion Engines

MAGNUSSON, B., Software Technology

MAGNUSSON, S.-E., Fire Safety Engineering

MALMQVIST, K., Nuclear Physics

MARTINSSON, B., Aerosol Physics

MATTIASSON, B., Biotechnology

MAURER, F., Polymer Technology

MOLIN, G., Food Hygiene

MOLISCH, A., Radio Communications

MONTELIUS, L., Solid State Physics

NILSSON, S., Technical Analysis Chemistry, especially Microanalytical Chemistry

NYMAN, M., Food Chemistry

ODENBRAND, I., Chemical Engineering, especially Environmental Catalysis

OLSSON, G., Industrial Automation

OMLING, P., Solid State Physics

PAULSSON, M., Dairy Technology

PERSSON, H. W., Electrical Measurements

PETERSON, H., Structural Mechanics

PHILIPSON, L., Computer Systems

PIÓRO, M., Communication Systems

PISTOL, M.-E., Solid State Physics

RÅDBERG, J., Urban Planning

RÅDSTRÖM, P., Applied Microbiology, especially Genetic Applications

RAGNARSSON, I., Mathematical Physics

RANTZER, A., Automatic Control

REUTERSWÄRD, L., Architecture and Development Studies

RISTINMAA, M., Solid Mechanics

RYCHLIK, I., Mathematical Statistics

RYDÉN, T., Mathematical Statistics

SAABYE OTTOSEN, N., Solid Mechanics

SAMUELSSON, L., Solid-State Physics

SANDBERG, G., Structural Mechanics

SCHMELING, J., Mathematics

SEIFERT, W., Solid-State Physics

SENTLER, L., Structural Engineering

SMEETS, B., Information Theory

SÖDERBERG, J., Construction Management

SÖRNMO, L., Biomedical Signals Processing

SPARR, G., Mathematics

STÅHL, A., Traffic Planning

STÅHL, J.-E., Production and Materials Engineering

STENSTRÖM, S., Chemical Engineering

STERNER, O., Bio-organic Chemistry

SUNDÉN, B., Heat Transfer

SVANBERG, S., Atomic Physics

SVERDRUP, H., Biogeochemistry

SÄRNER, E., Water and Environmental Engineering

THAM, K., Architecture

THELANDERSSON, S., Structural Engineering

THÖRNQVIST, L., Energy Economics and Planning

TORISSON, T., Thermal Power Engineering

TORNBERG, E., Food Engineering

TRÄGÅRDH, C., Food Engineering

TRÄGÅRDH, G., Food Engineering, especially Membrane Technology

WAHLUND, K.-G., Technical Analytical Chemistry

WAHSTRÖM, C.-G., Experimental Physics

WALLENBERG, R., Solid-State Chemistry

WANDEL, S., Engineering Logistics

WARFVINGE, P., Biogeochemistry

WERNE, F., Building Functions Analysis

WHITLOW, H. J., Nuclear Physics, especially Ion Physics

WIMMERSTEDT, R., Chemical Engineering

WITTENMARK, B., Automatic Control

WOHLIN, C., Software Systems Engineering

YUAN, J., Circuit Design

ZACCHI, G., Chemical Engineering

ZIGANGIROW, K. S., Telecommunications Theory

MITTUNIVERSITETET (Mid Sweden University)

SE-851 70 Sundsvall

Telephone: (771) 97-50-00

E-mail: info@miun.se

Internet: www.miun.se

Founded 1993 by merger of Univ. Colleges of Sundsvall/Härnösand and Östersund, merger of Sundsvall/Örnsköldsvik and Sundsvall Colleges of Health Sciences 1995, present status 2005

State control

Languages of instruction: English, Swedish

3 Campuses

Vice-Chancellor: ANDERS SÖDERHOLM

Pro-Vice-Chancellor: MATS TINNSTEN

Univ. Dir: YASMINE LINDSTRÖM

Dir for Libraries: MORGAN PALMQVIST

Library: see under Libraries and Archives

Number of teachers: 560

Number of students: 16,000

DEANS

Faculty of Human Sciences: SUSANNA ÖHMAN

Faculty of Science, Technology and Media: HANS-ERIK NILSSON

ÖREBRO UNIVERSITET (University of Örebro)

SE-701 82 Örebro

Telephone: (19) 30-30-00

E-mail: registrator@oru.se

Internet: www.oru.se

Founded 1967 as Högskolan i Örebro, present name and status 1999

State control

Academic year: September to June

Schools of business, health and medical sciences, hospitality, culinary arts and meal science, humanities, education and social sciences, law, psychology and social work, medicine, music, theatre and art, science and technology

Vice-Chancellor: JENS SCHOLLINS
Pro-Vice-Chancellor: GUNILLA LINDSTRÖM
Head Librarian: MARIE DANIELSEN

Library of 325,000 vols, 10,000 periodicals
Number of teachers: 670
Number of students: 17,000

STOCKHOLMS UNIVERSITET
(Stockholm University)

SE-106 91 Stockholm
Bloms hus, Universitetsvägen 10A, Stockholm
Telephone: (8) 16-20-00
E-mail: registrator@su.se
Internet: www.su.se

Founded 1878, became State Univ. 1960
State control
Language of instruction: Swedish
Academic year: August to June

Vice-Chancellor: Prof. Dr ASTRID SÖDERBERGH WIDDING
Pro-Vice-Chancellor: Prof. LENA GERHOLM
Deputy Vice-Chancellor for Humanities and Social Sciences: Prof. KARIN BERGMARK
Deputy Vice-Chancellor for Science: Prof. ANDERS KARLHEDE
Univ. Dir: ANN-CAROLINE NORDSTRÖM

Library: see under Libraries and Archives
Number of teachers: 4,350
Number of students: 29,100

Publication: *Acta Universitatis Stockholmiensis*

DEANS

Faculty of Humanities: Prof. BENGT NOVÉN
Faculty of Law: Prof. JONAS EBESSON
Faculty of Science: Prof. ANDERS KARLHEDE
Faculty of Social Sciences: Prof. MATS DANIELSON

PROFESSORS

Faculty of Humanities:

ÅMARK, K., History
AILI, H., Latin
ALBERG-JENSEN, P., Slavic Languages
ANDRÉN, A., Archaeology
BARTNING, I., French
BECKER, K., Journalism
BERGLIE, Q., Religion
BERGMAN, B., Sign Language
BILY, M., Slavic Languages
BODIN, P.-A., Slavic Languages
BOLTON, K., English
CARLSHAMRE, S., Theoretical Philosophy
CULLHED, A., Literary History
DAHL, Ö., General Linguistics
DAHLBÄCK, G., History of the Middle Ages
EKECRANTZ, J., Media and Communication
ENGSTRAND, O., Phonetics
FALK, C., Swedish Language
FALK, J., Spanish
FANT, L., Ibero-Romance Languages
FAWKNER, H., English
FERM, O., History
FORSGREN, M., French
GERHOLM, L., Ethnology
GERÖ, E.-C., Greek
GLETE, J., History
HALL, T., Scandinavian and Comparative Art History
HEED, S.-Å., Theatre Studies
HELANDER, K., Theatre Studies
HELLBERG, S., Scandinavian Languages
HVITFELT, H., Journalism
HYLTENSTAM, K., Bilingualism
INGDAHL KAZMIERA, A., Slavic Languages
IVERSEN, H., Latin
JARRICK, A., History
JOHANNESSON, N.-L., English

KANGERE, B., Baltic Languages
KÖLL, A. M., Baltic Studies
KOPTJEVSKAJA TAMM, M., General Linguistics
KOSKINEN, M., Film Studies
LACERDA, F., Phonetics
LANGE, S., Scandinavian Languages
LARSEN, H., Musicology
LEANDER-TOUATI, A.-M., Ancient Culture
LIDÉN, K., Archaeology
LILJA, S., History
LINDBERG-WADA, G., Japanology
LINDROTH, J., History of Athletics
LJUNGGREN, A., Russian
LODÉN, T., Language and Culture of China
LYSELL, R., History of Literature
MALMNÄS, P.-E., Theoretical Philosophy
MOLIN, K., History
MURDOCH, D., Theoretical Philosophy
NEEDHAM, P., Theoretical Philosophy
NEUGER, L., Polish
NIKOLAJEVA, M., History of Literature
NILSSON, L., History of Municipality
NYSTEDT, J., Italian
OETKE, C., Language and Culture of India
OHLSSON, R., Practical Philosophy
OLSSON, J., Film Studies
PAGIN, P., Theoretical Philosophy
RIAD, T., Scandinavian Languages
RÖHL, M., History of Literature
ROSÉN, S., Language and Culture of Korea
ROSENBERG, T., Gender Studies
ROSENDAHL, M., Latin American Studies
ROSSHOLM, G., History of Literature
ROSSHOLM LAGERLÖF, M., Art History
SAUTER, W., Theatre Studies
SCHEFFER, C., Ancient Culture
SJØVOLD, T., Historical Osteology
SMITH, W., Indology
SÖDERBERGH WIDDING, A., Film Studies
STRAND, H., Swedish
STROUD, C., Bilingualism
SVARTHOLM, K., Swedish as a Second Language for the Deaf
SVENSSON, G., Theoretical Philosophy
TÄNNSJÖ, T., Practical Philosophy
TEODOROWICZ-HELLMAN, E., Polish
TERSMAN, F., Practical Philosophy
TRAUNMÜLLER, H., Auditative Phonetics
VOLK, M., Computer Linguistics
WÅGHALL NIVRE, E., German
WANDE, E., Finnish
WARDINI, E., Arabic
WESTIN, B., History of Literature

Faculty of Law:

BJARUP, J., Jurisprudence
BOHLIN, A., Public Law
BRING, O., International Law
DIESEN, C., Procedure
EBBESSON, J., Environmental Law
EDELSTAM, H., Procedure
EKLUND, R., Private Law, Labour Law
HEUMAN, L., Procedure
KÄLLSTRÖM, K., Private Law
KLEINEMAN, J., Civil Law
LEIJONHUFVUD, M., Penal Law
LEVIN, M., Private Law
MAGNUSSON SJÖBERG, C., Law and Informatics
MAHMOUDI, S., International Law
MELZ, P., Financial Law
PEHRSON, L., Economics and Economic Law
PETERSON, C., Legal History
ROSÉN, J., Civil Law
SANDGREN, C., Civil Law
SANDSTRÖM, M., History of Law
SCHIRATSKY, D., Theoretical Philosophy
SEIPEL, P., Law and Informatics
SILFVERBERG, C., Financial Law
VOGEL, H.-H., Public Law
WAHL, N., European Law
WAHLGREN, P., Law and Informatics
WARNLING-NEREP, W., Public Law
WENNBERG, S., Penal Law

Faculty of Science

Biology Section:

BERGMAN, B., Physiological Botany
BORG, H., Aquatic Environmental Chemistry
BROMAN, D., Aquatic Ecotoxicology
CANNON, B., Animal Physiology
ELMGREN, R., Marine Ecology
ERIKSSON, O., Plant Ecology
FOLKE, C., Management of Natural Resources
GRÄSLUND, A., Biophysics
HAGGÅRD, E., Genetics
ISAKSSON, L., Microbiology
KAUTSKY, N., Marine Ecotoxicology
LINDBERG, U., Zoological Cell Biology
MÖLLER, G., Immunology
NÄSSEL, D., Functional Zoomorphology
RADESÄTER, T., Ethology
RANNUG, U., Toxicological Genetics
SJÖBERG, B.-M., Molecular Biology
WALLES, B., Morphological Botany
WIESLANDER, L., Molecular Genome Research
WIKLUND, C., Ecological Zoology
WULFF, F., Marine Systems Ecology

Chemistry Section:

ANDERSSON, B., Biochemistry
BÄCKVALL, J.-E., Organic Chemistry
BARTFAI, T., Neurochemistry
BERGMAN, Å., Environmental Chemistry
BRZEZINSKI, P., Biochemistry, esp. Molecular Energy Research
DEPIERRE, J., Biochemistry, especially Enzymological Toxicology
HULTH, P.-O., Experimental Physics
JANSSON, B., Chemical Environmental Analysis
JOSEFSSON, B., Analytical Chemistry
KOWALEWSKI, J., Physical Chemistry
LEVITT, M., Chemical Spectroscopy
LIDIN, S., Inorganic Chemistry
NELSON, D., Biochemistry
NORDLUND, P., Structural Biochemistry
NORRESTAM, R., Structural Chemistry
NYGREN, M., Material Chemistry, Electroceramics
ODHAM, G., Analytical Environmental Chemistry
SONNHAMMER, E., Bioinformatics
VON HEIJNE, G., Theoretical Chemistry

Earth and Environmental Studies Section:

BACKMAN, J., General and Historical Geology
HALLBERG, R., Microbial Chemistry
HOLMGREN, K., Physical Geography
IHSE, M., Ecological Geography
INGRI, J., Geochemistry and Petrology
KARLÉN, W., Physical Geography
LUNDÉN, B., Remote Sensing
RINGBERG, B., Quaternary Geology
ROSSWALL, T., Water and Environmental Studies
WASTENSON, L., Remote Sensing

Mathematics–Physics Section:

BARGHOLTZ, C., Nuclear Physics
BJÖRK, J.-E., Mathematics
BOHM, C., Technology of Physical Systems
EKEDAHL, T., Mathematics
FRANSSON, C., Astrophysics
HANSSON, H., Theoretical Physics
HANSSON, H.-C., Air Pollution
HOLMGREN, S.-O., High-Energy Physics
KÄLLEN, E., Dynamic Meteorology
LARSSON, M., Experimental Molecular Physics
MARTIN-LÖF, A., Actuarial Mathematics and Mathematical Statistics
OLOFSSON, H., Astronomy
PALMGREN, J., Biostatistics
PASSARE, M., Mathematics
RODHE, H., Chemical Meteorology
ROOS, J. E., Mathematics
SCHUCH, R., Atomic Physics

SIEGBAHN, P., Theoretical Physics
SUNDQVIST, H., Meteorology
SVENSSON, R., Astrophysics with Cosmology

Faculty of Social Sciences:
AGELL, J., Economics
AHRNE, G., Sociology
ALMKVIST, O., Psychology
ARAI, M., Economics
BACKENROTH-OHSAKO, G., Psychology
BERG, P.-O., Business Administration
BERGLUND, B., Perception and Psychophysics
BERGMARK, A., Social Work
BERNHARDT, E., Demography
BJÖRKUND, A., Economics
CALMFORS, L., International Economics
CHINAPAH, V., International Education
CHRISTIANSSON, S.-Å., Psychology
DAHL, G., Social Anthropology, Development Research
DAHLERUP, O., Political Science
DAUN, H., International Education
EDWARDS, M., Political Science
EKBERG, J., Economics
EKENBERG, L., Computer and Systems Science
ERIKSON, R., Sociology
FÄGERLIND, I., International and Comparative Education
FLAM, H., International Economics
FLYGHED, J., Criminology
FORSBERG, G., Human Geography
FRANK, O., Statistics
GOLDMANN, K., Political Science
GUILLET DE MONTHOUX, P., Business Administration
GUMMESSON, E., Business Administration
HANNERZ, U., Social Anthropology
HART, T., Asia-Pacific Studies
HEDBERG, B., Business Administration
HEDSTRÖM, P., Sociology, Population Processes
HESSLE, S., Social Work
HOEM, J., Demography
HORN AF RANTZIEN, H., International Economics
JOHANSSON, G., Working Life Psychology
JONSSON, E., Business Administration, Administrative Economics
KORPI, W., Social Politics
KÜHLHORN, E., Sociological Alcoholic Research
LENNTORP, B., Human and Economic Geography
LUNDBERG, B., Information Administration
LUNDBERG, U., Human Biological Psychology
MONTGOMERY, H., Cognitive Psychology
NILSSON, L.-G., Psychology
NORSTRÖM, T., Sociology, Social Politics
NYSTEDT, L., Psychology, Social Perception
ÖST, L.-G., Clinical Psychology
OVARSELL, B., Education
PALME, J., Computer and Systems Sciences
PALME, M., Social Security
PERSSON, M., International Economics
PERSSON, T., International Economics
PREMFORS, R., Political Science
SAHLIN-ANDERSON, K., Public Organization
SARNECKI, J., Criminology
SIVEN, C.-H., Economics, especially Economic Politics
SKÖLDBERG, K., Business Administration
SÖDERBERG, J., Economic History
SPORRONG, U., Geography, especially Human Geography
SVEDBERG, P., Development Economics
SVENSON, O., Nuclear Power Safety (Psychology)
SVENSSON, L., International Economics
SWEDBERG, R., Economic Sociology
TÅHLIN, M., Sociology
TARSCHYS, D., Political Science, especially Planning and Administration

THAM, H., Criminology
THORBURN, D., Statistics
THORSLUND, M., Social Work
VÅGERÖ, D., Medical Sociology
WADENSJÖ, E., Employment Policy
WESTIN, C., Immigration Research
WIJKANDER, H., International Economics
WIKANDER, U., Economic History
WITTROCK, B., Political Science

SVERIGES LANTBRUKSUNIVERSITET (Swedish University of Agricultural Sciences)

POB 7070, SE-750 07 Uppsala
Telephone: (18) 67-10-00
E-mail: registrator@slu.se
Internet: www.slu.se

Founded 1977 by merger of fmr Lantbrukshögskolan, Skogshögskolan and Veterinärhögskolan
Academic year: September to May
Vice-Chancellor: LISA SENNERBY FORSSE
Deputy Vice-Chancellor: TORBJÖRN VON SCHANTZ
Pro-Vice-Chancellor for Cooperation: JOHAN SCHNÜRER
Pro-Vice-Chancellor for Education: LENA ANDERSSON-EKLUND
Pro-Vice-Chancellor for Environmental Monitoring and Assessment: GÖRAN STÅHL
Library Dir: SNORRE RUFELT
Library: see under Libraries and Archives
Number of teachers: 500
Number of students: 3,800 full-time, 720 postgraduate

DEANS

Faculty of Forest Sciences: PETER HÖGBERG
Faculty of Landscape Planning, Horticulture and Agricultural Science: HÅKAN SCHRÖDER
Faculty of Natural Resources and Agricultural Science: BARBARA EKBOM
Faculty of Veterinary Medicine and Animal Science: KARIN ÖSTENSSON

PROFESSORS

(Some professors serve in more than 1 faculty)
Faculty of Forest Sciences:
ÅGREN, G., Systems Ecology
ANDRÉN, H., Conservation Biology
ARNOLD, S. VON, Forest Cell Biology
BERGSTEN, U., Reforestation
BISHOP, K., Environmental Assessment
BORGEFORS, G., Remote Sensing and Image Analysis
CLARHOLM, M., Soil Ecology
DANELL, K., Wildlife Ecology
DANIEL, G., Wood Products
ELFVING, B., Forest Yield Research
ELOWSON, T., Wood Technology
ERICSSON, A., Forest Plant Physiology
ERIKSSON, L.-O., Aquaculture
ERIKSSON, L. O., Forest Planning
FINLAY, R., Forest Microbiology
GEMMEL, P., Forestry
GOBRAN, G., Ecology, Soil Science
GUSTAVSSON, L., Conservation Biology
HÄLLGREN, J.-E., Forest Plant Physiology
HANSSON, L., Population Ecology
HÅNELL, B., Silviculture
HÖGBERG, P., Soil Science
JEGLUM, J., Forest Peatland Science
JOHANSSON, M.-B., Forest Soil Science
JOHANSSON, T., Forest Management
JOHNSSON, R., Aquatic Ecology
KRISTRÖM, B., Natural Resources Economics
LÅNGSTROM, B., Forest Protection from Insects
LARSSON, S., Forest Entomology
LINDER, S., Forest Ecology
LINDGREN, D., Forest Genetics

LOHMANDER, P., Forest Management
LÖNNSTEDT, L., Business Economics
LUNDKVIST, H., Soil Ecology
LUNDQVIST, H., Fish Biology
MAGNHAGEN, C., Aquaculture
MORITZ, T., Forest Plant Physiology
NÄSHOLM, T., Forest Plant Physiology
NILSSON, M.-C., Forest Vegetation Ecology
NILSSON, P.-O., Energy System in Forestry
NILSSON, T., Ultrastructure and Disintegration of Wood
NILSSON, U., Reforestation
NYLINDER, M., Wood Measurement and Cross-Cutting
NYLUND, J.-E., Forest Microbiology
ODÉN, P. C., Forestry Seed Research
OLSSON, H., Remote Sensing applied to Forestry
OLSSON, M., Forest Soil Chemistry
PERSSON, H., Root Ecology
PERSSON, T., Biology of Forest Soils
RANNEBY, B., Forest Survey
ROSEN, K., Forest Soils
SALLNÄS, O., Forest Operations
SANDBERG, G., Morphogenesis of Trees
STÅHL, G., Forest Survey
STENLID, J., Pathology of Forest Trees
SUNDBERG, B., Forest Plant Physiology
VERWIJST, T., Forestry
WÄSTERLUND, I., Forestry Technology
WIBE, S., Forest Economics
WINGSLE, G., Forest Plant Physiology
ZACKRISSON, O., Forest Vegetation Ecology

Faculty of Natural Resources and Agriculture Science:
ÅMAN, P., Plant Products
ANDERSSON, G., Molecular Genetics
ANDERSSON, H., Agricultural Economics
ANDERSSON, I., Plant Biochemistry
ANDRÉN, O., Soil Biology and Agriculture
BENGTSSON, B., International Crop Production Science
BENGTSSON, J., Environmental Science and Conservation
BERGSTRÖM, L., Water Quality Management
BJÖRCK, L., Dairy Products Science
BJÖRNHAG, G., Animal Physiology
BOLIN, O., Economics of Agriculture, International Trade
BOTHMER, R. VON, Genetics and Breeding of Cultivated Plants
BRYNGELSSON, T., Molecular Plant Biology
BUCHT, E., Landscape Planning
BYLUND, A.-C., Meat Science
DANELL, B., Animal Breeding
DANELL, Ö., Reindeer Husbandry
EBBERSTEN, S., Organic Farming/Ecological Farming
EKBOM, B., Entomology
EKLUND, H., Structural Molecular Biology
EMMELIN, L., Environmental Impact Assessment
FLORGÅRD, C., Landscape Architecture
GEBRESENBET, G., Agricultural Engineering
GERHARDSON, B., Plant Pathology
GLIMELIUS, K., Genetics and Plant Breeding
GREN, J.-M., Natural Resource and Environmental Economics
GULLBERG, U., Plant Breeding
GUSTAFSON, A., Water Quality Management
GUSTAFSSON, L., Systems Analysis
GUSTAFSSON, M., Plant Disease Resistance
GUSTAFSSON, P., Landscape Architecture
GUSTAVSSON, R., Planting Design and Management
HANSSON, B. S., Plant Protection Sciences
HAVNEVIK, K., Rural Development
HUSS-DANELL, K., Crop Science
JÄGERSTAD, M., Food Chemistry
JANSSON, C., Molecular Cell Biology
JARVIS, N., Biogeophysics

JENSÉN, P., Horticultural Science
JILAR, T., Horticultural Building and Climate Technology
KENNE, L., Organic Chemistry
KIRCHMANN, H., Soil Fertility
KNIGHT, S., Biochemistry
LARSEN, R., Greenhouse Production, Horticultural Crops
LARSSON, L.-G., Molecular Genetics
LILJENSTRÖM, H., Biometry
LINDBERG, J.-E., Animal Nutrition and Management
LUNDQVIST, P., Work Science
LUNDSTRÖM, K., Meat Science
MÅRTENSSON, A., Soil Fertility
MEIJER, J., Molecular Cell Biology
MERKER, A., Plant Breeding
MOWBRAY, S., Biochemistry
MYRDAL, J., History of Agriculture
NILSSON, C., Building Science
NILSSON, I., Soil Chemistry and Pedology
NILSSON, J., Cooperation
NITSCH, U., Agricultural Communication
NORBERG, T., Inorganic Chemistry
NYBOM, H., Horticultural Genetics and Plant Breeding
NYBRANT, T., Agricultural Control Engineering
ÖBERG, K., Ergonomics
ÖHLMER, B., Agricultural Business Administration
OLOFSSON, C., Entrepreneurial Studies
OLSSON, K., Animal Physiology
OLWIG, K. R., Landscape Planning
PERSSON, I., Inorganic and Physical Chemistry
PETTERSSON, J., Applied Entomology
RABINOWICZ, E., Economic Analysis of Food and Agricultural Systems
RIDDERSTRÅLE, Y., Animal Physiology
RONNE, H., Molecular Genetics
ROSSWALL, T., Water and Environmental Studies
SÄLLVIK, K., Agricultural Building Functions Analysis
SCHNÜRER, J., Food Microbiology
SKÄRBÄCK, E., Comprehensive Landscape Planning
SORTE, G., Landscape Architecture
STYMNE, S., Plant Breeding, Biochemistry
TORSTENSSON, L., Soil Microbiology
UVNÄS-MOBERG, K., Animal Physiology
VALKONEN, J., Virology comprising Plant Viruses
VON ROSEN, D., Statistics
WELANDER, M., Horticultural Science
WIKTORSSON, H., Animal Nutrition and Management
YUEN, J., Plant Pathology

Faculty of Veterinary Medicine and Animal Science:

ALENIUS, S., Medicine for Ruminants
ALGERS, B., Animal Hygiene
ALM, G., Immunology
ANDERSSON, L., Genetics
BELAK, S., Virology
BJÖRK, I., Medical and Physiological Chemistry
DANIELSSON-THAM, M.-L., Food Hygiene
DREVEMO, S., Anatomy and Histology
EINARSSON, S., Obstetrics and Gynaecology
ENGSTRÖM, W., Pathology
ERIKSSON, S., Medical and Physiological Chemistry
FELLSTRÖM, C., Swine Diseases
FORSBERG, M., Veterinary Diagnostic Endocrinology
GUSTAVSSON, I., Genetics
HEDHAMMAR, H., Small Animal Medicine
JENSEN, P., Ethology
JENSEN-WAERN, M., Comparative Medicine
JONES, B., Clinical Chemistry
JÖNSSON, L., Pathology
KINDAHL, H., Obstetrics and Gynaecology
KVART, C., Clinical Physiology

LINDE-FORSBERG, C., Small Animal Reproduction
LINNÉ, T., Virology
LORD, P., Clinical Radiology
LUTHMAN, J., Medicine for Ruminants
MORENO-LOPEZ, J., Virology
NORRGREN, L., Aquatic Ecotoxicology
OSKARSSON, A., Food Hygiene
PLÖEN, L., Anatomy and Histology
PRINGLE, J., Equine Medicine
RODRÍGUEZ-MARTÍNEZ, H., Reproduction Biotechnology
SVENSSON, C., Production Diseases of Farm Animals
SVENSSON, S., Bacteriology
TJÄLVE, H., Toxicology
UGGLA, A., Parasitology

UMEÅ UNIVERSITET
(Umeå University)

SE-901 87 Umeå
Telephone: (90) 786-50-00
E-mail: umea.universitet@umu.se
Internet: www.umu.se
Founded 1965
State control
Languages of instruction: English, Swedish
Academic year: September to June
Vice-Chancellor: Dr LENA GUSTAFSON
Pro-Vice-Chancellor: Prof. KJELL JONSSON
Deputy Vice-Chancellor for Education: ANDERS FÄLLSTRÖM
Deputy Vice-Chancellor for External Relations and Innovation: Prof. AGNETA MARELL
Deputy Vice-Chancellor for Research: Prof. Dr MARIANNE SOMMARIN
Univ. Dir: LARS LUSTIG
Head of Admin.: SIV OLOFSSON
Library: see under Libraries and Archives
Number of teachers: 2,130
Number of students: 36,100 (incl. 1,300 postgraduate)

DEANS

Faculty of Arts: Prof. PER-OLOF ERIXON
Faculty of Medicine: Prof. ANDERS BERGH
Faculty of Science and Technology: Prof. ÅSA RASMUSON-LESTANDER
Faculty of Social Sciences: DIETER MÜLLER

PROFESSORS

Faculty of Arts (internet www.humfak.umu.se):

ANDERSSON, G., Science of Science
BANNERT, R., Phonetics
BRÄNDSTRÖM, A., Historical Demography
EDLUND, L.-E., Scandinavian Languages
EDMAN, M., Philosophy and Science of Humanities
EHN, B., Ethnology
ERICSSON, T., History
FORSGREN, K.-Å., German Language
GENRUP, K., Ethnology
GRANQVIST, R., English Language
GROUNDSTROEM, A., Finnish Language
HATJE, A.-K., History
HENE, B., Swedish Language
JOHANSSON, I., Theoretical Philosophy
JONSSON, K., History of Science and Ideas
LARSSON, T., Archaeology
LILIEQUIST, M., Ethnology
LINDBLAD, I.-B., Media and Communications
LINDSTRÖM, S., Theoretical Philosophy
LUNDGREN, B., Ethnology
PETTERSSON, A., Comparative Literature
POUSSA, P., English Language
RAMQVIST, P., Archaeology
RINGBY, P., Comparative Literature
SJÖBERG TAUSSI, M., History in a Social Historic Perspective
SKÖLD, P., History, Lapp Culture
SMEDS, K., Museology

SÖRLIN, S., Environmental History
SPOLANDER, R., History of Art
STRAARUP, J., Religious Studies
STRANGERT, E., Phonetics
SUNDIN, B., History of Science and Ideas
SVONNI, M., Lapp Language and Culture
WERBART, B., Archaeology
WIKSTRÖM, E., Fine Arts

Faculty of Medicine (internet www.medfak.umu.se):

ADOLFSSON, R., Psychiatry
ÅHLSTRÖM, K., X-Ray and Diagnostics
ALFREDSSON, H., Sports Medicine
ALSTERMARK, B., Physiology, especially Neurology
ASIKAINEN, S., Oral Microbiology
BÄCKSTRÖM, T., Obstetrics and Gynaecology
BERGENHEIM, T., Neurosurgery
BERGH, A., Pathology
BERGSTRÖM, S., Microbiology
BERNSPÅNG, B., Occupational Therapy
BJÖRNSTIG, U., Surgery, especially Trauma and Civil Defence Medicine
BOMAN, K., Medicine
BORÉN, T., Medical Chemistry
BROSTRÖM, L.-A., Orthopaedics
BUCHT, G., Geriatrics
DAHLQUIST, G., Paediatrics, especially Diabetes
DAHLQVIST, S., Rheumatology
DANIELSSON, A., Gastroenterology
DIJKEN, J. VAN, Cariology
DOORN, J. VAN, Logopedics
EDLUND, H., Molecular Development Biology
EDLUND, T., Molecular Genetics
EGELRUD, T., Dermatology and Venereology
EMDIN, S., Surgery
ERIKSSON, A., Forensic Medicine
ERIKSSON, J., Medicine
ERIKSSON, P.-O., Clinical Oral Physiology
FÄLLMAN, M., Medical Microbiology
FISHER, A., Occupational Therapy
FORSGREN, L., Neurology
FOWLER, C., Pharmacology
GOTHEFORS, L., Paediatrics
GRANKVIST, K., Clinical Chemistry, especially Experimental Toxicology
GRÖNBERG, H., Oncology
GROTH, S., Clinical Physiology
GRUNDSTRÖM, T., Tumour Biology
GUNNE, J., Prosthetic Dentistry
GUSTAFSON, Y., Geriatric Medicine
HÄGGLÖF, B., Child and Youth Psychiatry
HALLMANS, G., Nutrition Research
HAMMARSTRÖM, A., Public Health (Gender Perspective)
HAMMARSTRÖM, M.-L., Immunology
HAMMARSTRÖM, S., Immunology
HENRIKSSON, R., Experimental Oncology
HERNELL, O., Paediatrics, especially Nutrition Research
HÖGBERG, U., Obstetrics and Gynaecology
HOLMBERG, D., Molecular Genetics
HULTMARK, D., Medical Molecular Biology
JACOBSSON, L., Psychiatry
JANLERT, U., Public Health
JÄRVHOLM, B., Occupational and Environmental Medicine
JOHANSSON, I., Cariology
JOHANSSON, R., Physiology
JOHANSSON, S., Physiology
KARLSSON, M., Medical Radiation Physics
KELLERTH, J.-O., Anatomy
KULLGREN, G., Psychiatric Epidemiology
LALOS, A., Public Health (Gender Perspective)
LARSÉN, K., Sports Medicine
LERNER, U., Oral Cell Biology
LIBELIUS, R., Clinical Neurophysiology
LINDHOLM, L., Family Medicine
LINDSTRÖM, P., Histology and Cell Biology
LJUNGBERG, B., Urology

LORENTZON, R., Sports Medicine
LUNDGREN, E., Applied Cell Biology
LUNDGREN, S., Oral and Maxillofacial Surgery
LUNDMAN, B., Nursing
MARKLUND, S., Clinical Chemistry
MOLIN, M., Prosthetic Dentistry
NAREDI, P., Surgery
NILSSON, E., Surgery
NORBERG, A., Advanced Nursing
NORDBERG, G., Health and Hygiene
NORGREN, M., Biomedical Laboratory Sciences
NY, T., Medical and Physiological Chemistry
OLIVECRONA, G., Medical Chemistry
OLOFSSON, B.-O., Medicine
OLSSON, K., Physiology
OLSSON, T., Medicine
ROOS, G., Pathology
SANDMAN, P.-O., Advanced Nursing
SANDSTRÖM, T., Pulmonary Medicine
SCHLEUCHER, J., Medical Biophysics
SEHLIN, J., Histology and Cell Biology
SELSTAM, G., Physiology
SJÖLUND, B. H., Rehabilitation Medicine
SJÖSTEDT, A., Clinical Bacteriology
STENLING, R., Pathology
STIGBRAND, T., Immunochemistry
STRÖMBERG, I., Histology and Cell Biology
STRÖMBERG, N., Cardiology
SUNDELIN, G., Advanced Nursing
SUNDVIST, K. G., Clinical Immunology
SVENSSON, O., Orthopaedics
TÄLJEDAL, I.-B., Histology
TÄRNVIK, A., Infectious Diseases
THELANDER, L., Medical and Physiological Chemistry
THORNELL, L.-E., Anatomy
TWETMAN, S., Paedodontics
UHLIN, B. E., Medical Microbiology
WACHTMEISTER, L., Ophthalmology
WADELL, G., Virology
WALDENSTRÖM, A., Cardiology
WALL, S., Epidemiology and Public Health
WESTER, P., Medicine
WESTMAN, G., Family Medicine
WIBERG, M., Anatomy
WIDMARK, A., Oncology
WINKVIST, A., Epidemiology

Faculty of Science and Technology (internet www.teknat.umu.se):

ANDERSSON, B., Environmental Chemistry
AVONDOGLIO, P., Industrial Design
AXNER, O., Physics
BÅMSTEDT, U., Marine Sciences
BJÖRK, G., Microbiology
BONDESSON, L., Mathematical Statistics
BRODIN, G., Physics
BYSTRÖM, A., Microbiology
CEDERGREN, A., Analytical Chemistry
CEGRELL, U., Mathematics (Complete Analysis)
EDLUND, U., Organic Chemistry
EKLUND, P., Computer Science
ERICSON, L., Plant Ecology
ERIKSSON, E. S., Structural Biology
FRECH, W., Analytical Chemistry
GARDESTRÖM, P., Plant Physiology
GILLBRO, T., Biophysical Chemistry
GUSTAFSSON, P., Plant Molecular Biology
HÄGGKVIST, R., Discrete Mathematics
HEBY, O., Cellular and Developmental Biology
IRGUM, K., Analytical Chemistry
JANLERT, L.-E., Computing Science
JANSSON, M., Physical Geography
JANSSON, S., Plant Biology
JOHANSSON, L., Physical Chemistry
JOHNELS, D., Organic Chemistry
KÅGSTRÖM, B., Numerical Analysis and Parallel Computing
KASTBERG, A., Experimental Optical Physics
KIHLBERG, J., Organic Chemistry

KIRKWOOD, S., Atmospheric Physics
KLECZKOWSKI, L., Plant Physiology
KULLMAN, L., Physical Geography
LARSON, M., Applied Mathematics
LARSSON, J., Plasma Physics
LESTANDER, A., Genetics
LI, H., Signal Processing
LINDAHL, O., Medical Technology
LINDBLOM, G., Physical Chemistry
LUNDIN, R., Space Physics
MALMQVIST, B., Ecology
MARKLUND, S., Environmental Chemistry
MINNHAGEN, P., Theoretical Physics
NILSSON, C., Landscape Ecology, especially Running Waters
NORDIN, A., Energy Technology
ÖHMAN, L.-O., Inorganic Chemistry
OKSANEN, L., Ecology
OLIVEBERG, M., Biochemistry
ÖQUIST, G., Plant Physiology
OTTO, CH., Animal Ecology
PALMGREN, B., Design
PERSSON, L., Aquatic Ecology
PERSSON, P., Chemistry, Molecular Chemistry
PETTERSSON, L., Inorganic Chemistry
RAMMER, J., Condensed Matter Theory
RENBERG, I., Ecological and Environmental Impact Assessment
RÖNNMARK, K., Theoretical Space Physics
SAMUELSSON, G., Plant Physiology
SANDAHL, I., Space Physics
SAURA, A., Genetics
SCHRÖDER, W., Biochemistry
SELLSTEDT, A., Plant Physiology
SHELANKOV, A., Condensed Matter Physics
SHINGLER, V., Microbiology
SHIRIAEV, A., Automatic Control Engineering
SJÖBERG, S., Inorganic Chemistry
SJÖSTRÖM, M., Inorganic Chemistry
STENFLO, L., Theoretical Plasma Physics
STOTT, M., Interaction Design
SUNDQVIST, B., Condensed Matter Physics
TYSKLIND, M., Environmental Chemistry
WEDIN, P.-Å., Numerical Analysis
WESTLUND, P.-O., Theoretical Chemistry
WOLD, S., Chemometrics
WOLF-WATZ, H., Applied Molecular Biology

Faculty of Social Sciences (internet www.samfak.umu.se):

ÅBERG, R., Sociology
ARMELIUS, B.-Å., Clinical Psychology
ARMELIUS, K., Clinical Psychology
ARONSSON, T., Environmental and Natural Resources Economics
BACKMAN, J., Pedagogics and Educational Psychology
BENGTSSON, M., Business Administration and Economics
BOTER, H., Business Administration and Economics
BRÄNNÄS, K., Econometrics
BRÄNNLUND, R., Economics
BROSTRÖM, G., Statistics
DAHLGREN, L., Medical Sociology
ECKERBERG, K., Political Science
EDSTRÖM, Ö., Legal Science
FRANKE, S., Pedagogics
GUNNARSSON, Å, Legal Science
GUSTAFSSON, G., Political Science
HALLERÖD, B., Sociology
HALLSTRÖM, P., Legal Science
HAMILTON, D., Pedagogics
HENRIKSSON, W., Pedagogics
HOLM, E., Social and Economic Geography, especially Social Community Planning and Financial Control
JOHANSSON, G., Nutritional Studies
JOHANSSON, M., Pedagogics (Sports)
JOHANSSON, O., Political Science
JOHANSSON, S., Social Work
JOHANSSON, U., Pedagogics
KAPTELININ, V., Informatics
LINDQVIST, R., Social Work

LÖFGREN, K.-G., Economics, especially Evaluating Labour Market Research
MALMBERG, G., Social and Economic Geography
MÄNTYLÄ, T., Psychology (Cognitive Science)
MOLANDER, B., Psychology
NIEMI-KIESILÄINEN, J., Legal Science
NILSSON, I., Pedagogics
NYBERG, L., Psychology
NYGREN, L., Social Work
PERSSON, O., Library and Information Science
RÄTHZEL, N., Sociology
SKÖG, L. A., Business Administration
SÖDERHOLM, A., Informatics
STAGE, C., Pedagogics
STOLTERMAN, E., Informatics
SUNDBOM, E., Clinical Psychology
SVALLFORS, S., Sociology
TESAR, G., Business Administration and Economics (Marketing and International Business Administration)
WATERWORTH, J., Informatics
WIBERG, U., Economic Geography, especially the Structural Issues of Sparsely Populated Areas

UPPSALA UNIVERSITET
(Uppsala University)

POB 256, SE-751 05 Uppsala
Telephone: (18) 471-00-00
E-mail: info@uadm.uu.se
Internet: www.uu.se
Founded 1477
Academic year: September to June
Vice-Chancellor: Prof. Dr EVA ÅKESSON
Deputy Vice-Chancellor: Prof. ANDERS MALMBERG
Vice-Rector for Arts and Social Sciences: Prof. MARGARETHA FAHLGREN
Vice-Rector for Medicine and Pharmacy: Prof. BRITT SKOGSEID
Vice-Rector for Science and Technology: Prof. ULF DANIELSSON
Univ. Dir: ANN FUST
Chief Librarian: LARS BURMAN
Library: see under Libraries and Archives
Number of teachers: 3,600
Number of students: 20,000
Publications: *Acta Universitatis Upsaliensis*, *Multiethnica*, *Universen* (12 a year)

DEANS

Faculty of Arts: Prof. JAN LINDEGREN
Faculty of Educational Sciences: Prof. PETER WAARA
Faculty of Languages: Prof. BJÖRN MELANDER
Faculty of Law: Prof. TORBJÖRN ANDERSSON
Faculty of Medicine: Prof. STELLAN SANDLER
Faculty of Pharmacy: Prof. GÖRAN ALDERBORN
Faculty of Science and Technology: Prof. ULF DANIELSSON
Faculty of Social Sciences: Prof. LARS MAGNUSSON
Faculty of Theology: Prof. MIKAEL STENMARK

PROFESSORS

Faculty of History and Philosophy
   I. Historical-Philosophical Division:

ÅHLBERG, L.-O., Aesthetics and Cultural Studies
ALANEN, L., History of Philosophy
ARVASTSON, G., Ethnology
BEACH, H., Cultural Anthropology
BURMAN, L., Rhetoric
DANIELSSON, S. O., Practical Philosophy
FAHLGREN, M., Literature
FRÄNGSMYR, T., History of Science
HERSCHEND, F., Archaeology
IVARSDOTTER, A., Musicology
JANSSON, T., History

JOHANNISSON, K. M., History of Science and Ideas
KJELLBERG, E., Musicology
KYHLBERG, O., Archaeology
LANDGREN, B., Literature
LINDEGREN, J., History
PARKMAN, S., Musicology
PETTERSSON, T., Literature
RUNBLOM, H., History
SANTILLO FRIZELL, B., Archaeology
SINCLAIR, P., African Archaeology
SKUNCKE, M.-C., Literature
SÖDERLIND, S., Art History
SVEDJEDAL, J. O., Literature
TROY, L., Archaeology

II. Linguistic Division:

EKLUND, S. I., Latin
FRYCKSTEDT, M., English Literature
GREN-EKLUND, G., Indology
GUSTAVSSON, S. R., Slavic Languages
HELANDER, H. O., Latin
ISAKSSON, B., Semitic Languages
JONASSON, K., French Language
KINDSTRAND, J. F., Greek Language and Literature
KROHN, D., German Language
KRONNING, H., French Language
KYTÖ, M., English Language
LARSSON, L.-G., Finno-Ugric Languages
LUNDÉN, R., American Literature
MAIER, I., Russian Language
MELANDER, B., Swedish Language
MULLER, G., German Language and Literature
NORDBERG, B., Sociolinguistics
PACKALEN, A. M., Polish Language
PALM MEISTER, C., German Language
PEDERSEN, O., Assyriology
PETERSON, L., Scandinavian Languages
RAAG, R., Finno-Ugric Languages
ROSENQVIST, J.-O., Byzantine Studies
SÅGVALL-HEIN, A., Computational Linguistics
STRANDBERG, S., Scandinavian Onomastics
SUNDELL, L.-G., French Language
SVANE, B., French Literature
THELANDER, M., Swedish Language
UTAS, B., Iranian Studies
VIBERG, Å, Linguistics
WILLIAMS, H., Swedish Language
WOLLIN, L., Scandinavian Languages

Faculty of Law:

ANDERSSON, H., Private Law
ANDERSSON, T., Private Law
CAMERON, I., International Law
ERIKSSON, M., International Law
FRÄNDBERG, A., History of Law
JÄNTERÄ-JAREBORG, M., International Law
JAREBORG, N., Penal Law
LEHRBERG, B., Penal Law
LINDBLOM, P. H., Judicial Procedure
LINDELL, B., Judicial Procedure
LYSEN, G., International Law
MARCUSSON, L. M., Administrative Law
MATTSSON, N. G., Taxation
MÖLLER, M., Private Law
NYGREN, R. O., History of Law
ÖSTERDAHL, I., International Law
SALDEEN, A., Private Law
THORELL, P. H., Business Law
WESTERLUND, S., Environmental Law

Faculty of Medicine:

ÅKERMAN, K., Cell Physiology
ÅKERSTRÖM, G., Endocrinological Surgery
AKUSJÄRVI, G., Microbiology
ALDSKOGIUS, H., Medical Structural Biology
ALM, A., Ophthalmology
ANDERSSON, A. E. V., Diabetes Research
ANDERSSON, J. H., Immunology
ANNIKO, M., Otorhinolaryngology
AQUILONIUS, S.-M., Neurology
ARNETZ, B., Social Medicine

AXELSSON, O. L., Women's and Children's Health
BERGQVIST, D., Vascular Surgery
BERNE, CH., Medicine
BLOMBERG, J., Clinical Virology
BOBERG, M., Social Medicine
BOMAN, G., Pulmonary Medicine
CARLSSON, J., Biomedical Radiation Science
CLAESSON-WELSH, L., Genetics and Pathology
DAHL, M.-L., Medicine
DAHL, N., Clinical Genetics
DUMANSKI, J., Genetics and Pathology
EBENDAL, T., Developmental Biology
EDLING, C., Occupational Medicine
ERIKSSON, U., Histology
FLEMSTRÖM, G. F., Physiology
FRIES, E., Cell Biology
FRIMAN, G., Infectious Diseases
GEBRE-MEDHIN, M., International Child Care
GERDIN, B., Intensive and Burns Care
GLIMELIUS, B., Oncology
GUSTAFSSON, J., Women's and Children's Health
GYLFE, E., Secretion Research
GYLLENSTEN, U., Medical Molecular Genetics
HAGLUND, U., Surgery
HÄLLGREN, R., Medicine
HAU, J., Comparative Medicine
HEDENSTIERNA, G., Medicine
HEYMAN, B., Genetics and Pathology
HILLERED, L., Clinical Neurochemistry
HOLMBERG, L., Surgery
JOHANSSON, S., Cell Biology
KÄMPE, O., Molecular Medicine
KARLSSON, A., Experimental Endocrinology
KJELLEN, L., Medical Biochemistry and Microbiology
LANDEGREN, U., Molecular Medicine
LARHAMMAR, D. S., Molecular Cell Biology
LARSSON, R., Medicine
LINDAHL, U., Medical Chemistry
LINDGREN, P. G., X-ray Diagnosis
LINDHOLM, D., Neurobiology
LINDMARK, G., International Mother and Child Health
LITHELL, H., Geriatrics
LJUNGHALL, S., Medicine
LÖNNERHOLM, G., Women's and Children's Health
LUNDQVIST, H., Oncology
MAGNUSSON, A., Oncology
MAGNUSSON, G., Molecular Virology
MÅRDH, P.-A., Medicine
NILSSON, K., Cell Pathology
NILSSON, O., Orthopaedics
NISTÉR, M., Experimental Pathology
NORLÉN, B. J., Urology
ÖBERG, K., Oncological Endocrinology
ORELAND, L. A. M., Pharmacology
PÅHLMAN, L., Surgery
PERSSON, E., Physiology
PERSSON, L., Physiology
PETTERSSON, U. G., Medical Genetics
RAININKO, R., Neuroradiology
RASK, L., Medical Biochemistry
RASK-ANDERSEN, H., Surgery
RASTAD, J., Surgery
RAUSCHNING, W., Surgery
ROOMANS, G. M., Medical Ultrastructure
ROSENQVIST, U., Health Services Research
RUBIN, K., Connective Tissue Biochemistry
SALDEEN, T., Forensic Medicine
SANDLER, S., Medical Cell Biology
SCHWARTZ, S., Medical Biochemistry and Microbiology
SEDIN, G., Perinatal Medicine
SIEGBAHN, A., Medicine
SJÖDEN, P.-O., Nursing and Health Care
SJÖQVIST, M. I. J., Physiology
STJERNSCHANTZ, J., Pharmacology
SVÄRDSUDD, K., Family Medicine
SYVÄNEN, A.-C., Medicine

TOREBJÖRK, E., Pain Research
TÖTTERMAN, T., Clinical Immunology
TURESSON, I., Oncology
TUVEMO, T., Paediatrics
ULMSTEN, U., Obstetrics and Gynaecology
VAHLQUIST, A., Dermatology and Venereology
VENGE, P., Clinical Chemistry
VON KNORRING, A.-L., Child Psychiatry
VON KNORRING, L., Psychiatry
WADELIUS, C., Genetics and Pathology
WALLENTIN, L., Cardiology
WESTERMARK, B. A., Tumour Biology
WESTERMARK, P., Pathology
WESTMAN, J. O., Anatomy
WIESEL, F.-A., Psychiatry
WIKLUND, L., Anaesthesiology

Faculty of Pharmacy:

ALDERBORN, G., Pharmacy
ARTURSSON, P., Pharmacy
BOHLIN, L., Pharmacognosy
BRITTEBO, E. B., Toxicology
DENCKER, L., Toxicology
ENGSTRÖM, S. O. A., Pharmacy
HALLBERG, A., Organic Pharmaceutical Chemistry
HAMMARLUND-UDENAES, M., Pharmacokinetics
ISACSON, D., Pharmacy
KARLSSON, M., Pharmacokinetics
LANG, M., Biochemistry
LENNERNÄS, H., Pharmacy
NYBERG, F., Pharmacological and Biological Research on Drug Dependence
NYSTRÖM, L.-CHR., Pharmacy
OLIW, E., Pharmacological and Biological Research on Drug Dependence
PETTERSSON, C., Analytical Pharmaceutical Chemistry
WESTERLUND, D., Analytical Pharmaceutical Chemistry
WIKBERG, J., Pharmacological and Biological Research on Drug Dependence
WIKVALL, K., Biochemistry

Faculty of Science and Technology:

ÅGREN, J., Ecological Botany
AHLÉN, A., Signal Processing
ALEKLETT, K., Nuclear Physics
ALEXEEV, A., Theoretical Physics
ALMGREN, M., Biochemistry
ANDERSSON, A., Computer Science
ANDERSSON, P., Organic Chemistry
ANDERSSON, S., Evolutionary Biology
ANNERSTEN, H. S., Mineral Chemistry and Petrology
ÅQVIST, J., Evolutionary Biology
ARNESEN, A., Physics
BADELEK, B., Experimental Physics
BENGTSSON, E., Computerized Image Analysis
BENNETT, K. D., Quaternary Geology
BERG, O., Molecular Evolution
BERG, S., Solid State Electronics
BERGER, R., Inorganic Chemistry
BERGLUND, A., Animal Ecology
BERGSTRÖM, Y., Materials Science
BJÖRKLUND, M., Animal Ecology
BOHMAN, O., Organic Chemistry
BOTNER, O., High-Energy Physics
BRÄNDAS, E., Quantum Chemistry
BRANDT, I., Ecotoxicology
BRANDT ANDERSSON, Y., Inorganic Chemistry
BREMER, B., Systematic Botany
BREMER, K., Systematic Botany
BRUNSTRÖM, B. O., Ecotoxicology
CARLSSON, B., Systems and Control
CARLSSON, J.-O., Inorganic Chemistry
CHATTOPADHYAYA, J., Bio-organic Chemistry
COORAY, V., Electricity and Lightning
DAHLGREN CALDWELL, K., Surface Biotechnology
DANIELSSON, U., Theoretical Physics
EDWARDS, K., Physical Chemistry

EHRENBERG, M., Molecular Biology with Kinetics
EKELÖF, T., Experimental Elementary Particle Physics
EKMAN, J., Population Biology
ELLEGREN, H., Evolutionary Biology
ENGMAN, L., Organic Chemistry
ENGSTRÖM, P., Physiological Botany
ERICSSON, T., Materials Physics
ERIKSSON, O., Condensed Matter Physics
FÄLDT, G. L., Theoretical Physics
FROELICH, P., Quantum Chemistry
GEE, D. G., Orogenic Dynamics
GELIUS, U., Physics
GESTBLOM, B., Physics
GOSCINSKI, O., Quantum Chemistry
GRANQVIST, C.-G., Solid-State Physics
GUNNINGBERG, P., Computer Communication
GUSTAFSSON, B., Numerical Analysis
GUSTAFSSON, B., Theoretical Astrophysics
GUSTAFSSON, L., Animal Ecology
GUT, A., Mathematical Statistics
HAGERSTEN, E., Computer Architecture
HAJDU, J., Biochemistry
HÅKANSSON, L., Sedimentology
HÅKANSSON, P., Ion Physics
HALLDIN, S., Hydrology
HALLGREN, A., Experimental Physics
HEJHAL, D. A., Mathematics
HELLMAN, L., Molecular and Comparative Immunology
HERMANSSON, K. G., Inorganic Chemistry
HILBORN, J., Polymer Chemistry
HÖGLUND, J., Population Biology
HOGMARK, S., Materials Science
HÖISTAD, B., Nuclear Physics
HOLMER, L., Historical Geology and Palaeontology
HUGHES, D., Evolutionary Biology
INGELMANN, G., High-Energy Physics
ISRAELSSON, S. O., Meteorology
JACOBSON, S., Materials Science
JANSON, S., Mathematics
JANSSON, U., Inorganic Chemistry
JOHANSSON, B., Condensed Matter Theory
JOHANSSON, S., Materials Science
JOHANSSON, T., Nuclear Physics
JONES, A., Structural Molecular Biology
JONSSON, B., Computer Systems
JUHL-JÖRICKE, B., Mathematics
KAISER, S. G., Mathematics
KÄLLNE, J., Neutron Physics
KARLSSON, L., Experimental Physics
KIRSEBOM, L., Evolutionary Biology
KISELMAN, C. O., Mathematics
KOLSTRUP, E., Physical Geography
LÅNGSTROM, B., Radiopharmaceutical Organic Chemistry
LANSHAMMER, H., Systems and Control
LEIJON, M., Electricity
LIBERMAN, M., Theoretical Statistical Physics
LILJAS, L., Evolutionary Biology
LINDBLAD, P., Evolutionary Biology
LINDER, C., Physical Didactics
LINDGREN, J. B. R., Inorganic Chemistry
LÖTSTEDT, P., Numerical Analysis
LUNDAHL, P., Biochemistry
LUNDBERG, A., Evolutionary Biology
LUNDBERG, B., Solid Mechanics
LUNELL, S. G., Applied Quantum Chemistry
MANNERVIK, B., Biochemistry
MARKIDES, K., Analytical Chemistry
MÅRTENSSON, N., Physics of Metals and Metal Surfaces
MATTSSON, O. L., Organic Chemistry
McGREEVY, R. L., Neutron Research
MILBRINK, G., Animal Ecology
MOLLER, F., Computing Science
NIEMI, A., Theoretical Physics
NIKLASSON, G., Materials Science and Solar Energy
NILSSON, A., Chemical Physics
NILSSON, A., Systematic Botany

NORDBLAD, P., Solid-State Physics
NORDGREN, J., Soft X-ray Physics
NYHOLM, L., Analytical Chemistry
OHLSSON, R., Developmental Zoology
OLSSON, E., Experimental Physics
PAMILO, P., Conservation Biology
PAROSH, A., Computer Systems
PAVLENKO, V. P., Astronomy
PEDERSEN, L. B., Solid Earth Physics
PEEL, J. S., Historical Geology and Palaeontology
PETTERSSON, K. I., Evolutionary Biology
PILSTRÖM, L. H., Immunology
PISKOUNOV, N., Astronomy
POSSNERT, G., Accelerator Mass Spectrometry
RIBBING, C.-G., Solid-State Physics
RICKMAN, H., Astronomy
ROBERTS, R., Solid Earth Physics
RODHE, A., Hydrology
RONQUIST, F., Systematic Zoology
ROOS, A., Solid-State Physics
RYDIN, H., Plant Ecology
SAXENA, S., Theoretical Geochemistry
SCHWEITZ, J.-A., Materials Science
SIEGBAHN, H., Atomic and Molecular Physics
SJÖBERG, S., Organic Chemistry
SKÖLD, K., Neutron Research
SMEDMAN, A.-S., Meteorology
SÖDERHÄLL, K. T., Physiological Mycology
SÖDERSTRÖM, T., Automatic Control
STERNAD, M., Signals and Systems
STOICA, P., Systems Modelling
STOLTENBERG-HANSEN, V., Logic of Mathematics
STRÖMQUIST, L., Applied Environmental Impact Analysis
SUNDQVIST, B. U. R., Ion Physics
SVEDLINDH, P., Solid-State Physics
SVENSSON, B. W., Animal Ecology
SVENSSON, S., Physics
TALBOT, C. J., Geodynamics and Tectonics
TAPIA-OLIVARES, O., Physical Chemistry
TÄRNLUND, S. A., Computer Science
TEGELSTRÖM, H., Conservation Biology and Genetics
TEGENFELT, J. S., Inorganic Chemistry
THOMAS, J. O., Solid-State Electro-chemistry
THOTTAPPILLIL, R., Electricity
THULIN, M., Systematic Botany
THUNE, M., Scientific Computing
TIBELL, L. B., Systematic Botany
TINTAREV, K., Mathematics
TOTTMAR, O., Comparative Physiology
TRANVIK, L., Limnology
VIRO, O., Mathematics
VIRTANEN, A., Molecular Cell Biology
WAGNER, G., Microbiology
WAHLBERG, C., Astronomy
WANG, Y., Computer Systems
WÄPPLING, R., Physics
ZILITINKEVICH, S., Meteorology

Faculty of Social Sciences:

AGELL, J., Economics
ANDERSSON, R. K. G., Housing and Urban Research
BÄCK, L., Urban Geography
BÄCKMAN, L., Cognitive Psychology
BLOMQUIST, S., Local Public Economics
BOHLIN, G., Developmental Psychology
BORGEGÅRD, L.-E., Urban Geography
BÖRJESSON, E. A., Psychology
BROADY, D., Education
BURNS, T., Sociology
CARLSNAES, W., Political Science
CHRISTOFFERSSON, A. L., Statistics
DIMBERG, U., Psychology
EDIN, P.-A., Labour Market Relations
EKEHAMMAR, B., Psychology
ENGWALL, L., Business Studies
EYERMAN, R., Sociology
FOGELKLOU, A., East European Studies

FORSGREN, M. O., International Business Studies
FREDRIKSON, M., Clinical Psychology
GERNER, K., East European Studies
GOTTFRIES, N., Economics
GUSTAFSSON, C., Education
HADENIUS, A., Political Science
HAGEKULL, B., Developmental Psychology
HÅKANSSON, K. G., Sociology
HALLEN, L., Business Studies
HAMFELT, A., Computer Science
HAMMARSTRÖM, G., Sociology
HANSSON, A., Computer Science
HEDLUND, S., East European Studies
HEDMAN, L., Media and Communication
HERMANSSON, B. J., Political Science
HOLMLUND, B., Economics
HOPPE, G., Economic Geography
ISACSON, M., Economic History
KEMENY, P. J., Urban Sociology
KLEVMARKEN, A., Econometrics
LEWIN, L., Political Science
LINDBLAD, S., Education
LINDH, T., Economics
LUNDGREN, E., Sociology
LUNDGREN, U. P., Education
MAGNUSSON, L., Economic History
MALMBERG, A., Economic Geography
MELIN, L. G., Clinical Psychology
ÖBERG, S., Social and Economic Geography
OHLSON, H., Economics
PETERSSOHN, E., Business Administration
RIIS, U., Education
RISCH, T., Computer Science
SAHLIN-ANDERSSON, K., Business Studies
SÖDER, M., Sociology
SÖDERSTEN, J., Economics
SOMMESTAD, L., Economic History
TORNSTAM, L., Sociology
TURNER, B., Housing Economics
VEDUNG, E., Housing Policy
VON HOFSTEN, C., Perceptional Psychology
WALLENSTEEN, P. N., Peace and Conflict
WIGREN, R., Economics
WITTROCK, B., Advanced Study in the Social Sciences

Faculty of Theology:

BÄCKSTRÖM, A., Sociology of Religion
BEXELL, O., Ecclesiology
BRÅKENHIELM, C.-R., Studies of Faiths and Ideologies
BRODD, S.-E., Studies of Churches and Religious Denominations
DE MARINIES, VALERIE, Psychology of Religion
FRANZÉN, R., Church History
GRENHOLM, C.-H., Ethics
HERRMANN, E., Philosophy of Religions
HULTGÅRD, A., History of Religions
NORIN, S., Old Testament Exegesis
PETTERSSON, T., Sociology of Religion
SCHALK, P., History of Religions
SYREENI, K., New Testament Exegesis
WIKSTRÖM, O., Psychology of Religion

University Colleges

Ersta Sköndal Högskola (Ersta Sköndal University College): Stigbergsgatan 30, POB 11189, SE-100 61 Stockholm; tel. (8) 555-050-00; e-mail info@esh.se; internet www.esh.se; f. 1998; depts of diaconal studies, church music and theology, health care sciences, social sciences and St Lukas Educational Institute; 1,400 students; Vice-Chancellor JAN-HÅKAN HANSSON; Sec. ANN-MARGRET BERGMAN; Chief Librarian ANN-KRISTIN FORSBERG.

Högskolan Dalarna (Dalarna University College): SE-791 88 Falun; tel. (23) 77-80-00; e-mail ioffice@du.se; internet www.du.se; f. 1977; schools of health and social sciences, humanities and media studies, technology and business studies; 800 teachers; 18,000 students; Vice-Chancellor Prof. MARITA HILLIGES; Library Dir MARGARETA MALMGREN.

Högskolan i Borås (University College of Borås): SE-501 90 Borås; Allégatan 1, Borås; tel. (33) 435-40-00; e-mail registrator@hb.se; internet www.hb.se; f. 1977; schools of business and informatics, education and behavioural sciences, engineering, health sciences, library and information science, textiles; library: see under Libraries and Archives; 650 teachers; 13,820 students; Rector Prof. BJÖRN BRORSTRÖM; Pro-Rector MARTIN HELLSTRÖM; Head of Library SVANTE KRISTENSSON.

Högskolan i Gävle (Gävle University College): SE-801 76 Gävle; Kungsbackavägen 47, Gävle; tel. (26) 64-85-00; e-mail registrator@hig.se; internet www.hig.se; f. 1977; faculties of education and business, engineering and sustainable development, health and occupational studies; library: 90,000 vols, 550 periodicals; 700 teachers; 14,500 students; Vice-Chancellor Prof. Dr MAJ-BRITT JOHANSSON; Pro-Vice-Chancellor and Head of the Education and Research Office Dr SVANTE BRUNÅKER; Chief Admin. Officer ELISABETH DAUNELIUS; Head of Library MAIVOR HALLÉN.

Högskolan i Halmstad (Halmstad University): POB 823, SE-301 18 Halmstad; Kristian IV:s väg 3, Halmstad; tel. (35) 16-71-00; e-mail registrator@hh.se; internet www.hh .se; f. 1973; schools of business and engineering, humanities, information science, computer and electrical engineering, social and health sciences, teacher education; library: 130,000 vols, 50,000 ebooks, 10,000 ejournals, 5000 printed journals; 260 teachers; 10,100 students; Vice-Chancellor Dr MIKAEL ALEXANDERSSON; Pro-Vice-Chancellor Dr CARINA IHLSTRÖM ERIKSSON; Univ. Director and Registrar INGER M. JOHANSSON.

Högskolan i Jönköping (Jönköping University): POB 1026, SE-551 11 Jönköping; Gjuterigatan 5, SE-553 18 Jönköping; tel. (36) 10-10-00; e-mail info@hj.se; internet www.hj.se; f. 1977; schools of business, education and communication, engineering, health sciences; library: see under Libraries and Archives; 500 teachers; 8,600 students; Rector Dr ANITA HANSBO.

Högskolan i Skövde (University of Skövde): POB 408, SE-541 28 Skövde; Högskolevägen, Skövde; tel. (500) 44-80-00; e-mail registrator@his.se; internet www.his.se; f. 1977, present status 1983; schools of humanities and informatics, life sciences, technology and society; library: see under Libraries and Archives; 320 teachers; 4,500 full-time students; Rector and Vice-Chancellor Prof. Dr SIGBRITT KARLSSON; Pro-Rector LARS NIKLASSON; Vice-Rector for Education ANITA KJELLSTRÖM; Vice-Rector for Internationalization AFROUZ BEHOUDI; Dir JOHAN ALMER.

Högskolan Kristianstad (Kristianstad University): SE-291 88 Kristianstad; Elmetorpsvägen 15, SE-291 88 Kristianstad; tel. (44) 20-30-00; e-mail info@hkr.se; internet www.hkr.se; f. 1977; depts of behavioural sciences, business studies, humanities and social sciences, health sciences and mathematics and science; school of engineering; 2 campuses: Campus Kristianstad and Campus Hässleholm; library: see under Libraries and Archives; 500 teachers; 14,000 students; Rector SANIMIR RESIC.

Högskolan på Gotland (Gotland University): Cramérgatan 3, SE-621 67 Visby; tel. (498) 29-99-00; e-mail info@hgo.se; internet www.hgo.se; f. 1998; primarily business administration and international management and coastal zone management, secondary subjects incl. archaeology, osteology,

information technology and business administration, international business relations, technology, art and new media, building restoration, Russian, history, human geography, ethnology, ecology, art history and cross-cultural communication; 110 teachers; 2,500 students; Rector Dr ERIKA SANDSTRÖM; Pro-Rector OLLE JANSSON.

Högskolan Väst (University West): SE-461 86 Trollhättan; Gustava Melins gata 2, Trollhättan; tel. (520) 22-30-00; e-mail registrator@hv.se; internet www.hv.se; f. 1990 as Högskolan Trollhättan/Uddevalla, present name 2006; depts of economics and IT, engineering science, nursing, health and culture, social and behavioural studies; 500 teachers; 11,000 students; Rector and Vice-Chancellor Prof. KERSTIN NORÉN; Pro-Rector JAN THELIANDER; Vice-Rector for Innovation Prof. STEFAN CHRISTIERNIN; Dir MARITA JOHANSON (acting).

Mälardalens Högskola (Mälardalen University): POB 883, SE-721 23 Västerås; tel. (21) 10-13-00; e-mail info@mdh.se; internet www.mdh.se; f. 1977; schools of business, society and engineering, education, culture and communication, health, care and social welfare, innovation, design and engineering; library: see under Libraries and Archives; 460 teachers; 12,000 students; Vice-Chancellor KARIN RÖDING; Pro-Vice-Chancellor Prof. PAUL PETTERSSON; Deputy-Vice-Chancellor KARIN AXELSSON; Univ. Dir MARIE ERIKSSON.

Malmö Högskola (Malmö University): SE-205 06 Malmö; tel. (40) 665-70-00; e-mail intsek@mah.se; internet www.mah.se; f. 1998; faculties of health and society, culture and society, education and society, odontology, technology and society; 1,440 teachers; 25,000 students (full-time and part-time); Vice-Chancellor Prof. STEFAN BENGTSSON; Deputy Vice-Chancellor CECILIA CHRISTERSSON; Pro-Vice-Chancellor EVA ENGQUIST; Pro-Vice-Chancellor Prof. HANS LINDQUIST.

Södertörns Högskola (Sodertorn University): SE-141 89 Huddinge; Alfred Nobels allé 7, SE-141 52 Huddinge; tel. (8) 608-40-00; e-mail international@sh.se; internet www.sh .se; f. 1996; schools of culture and education, historical and contemporary studies, natural sciences, technology and environmental studies, social sciences; library: 119,313 vols; 450 teachers; 13,500 students; Vice-Chancellor Prof. MOIRA VON WRIGHT; Pro-Vice-Chancellor Dr NILS EKEDAHL; Pro-Vice-Chancellor Dr REBECKA LETTEVALL; Chief Administrative Officer BJÖRN SANDAHL (acting); Library Dir KARIN GRÖNVALL.

Sophiahemmet Högskola (Sophiahemmet University): POB 5605, SE-114 86 Stockholm; Lindstedtsvägen 8, Solhemmet, Stockholm; tel. (8) 406-20-00; e-mail info@ sophiahemmethogskola.se; internet www .sophiahemmethogskola.se; f. 1884 as Drottningens Sjuksköterskeskola (Queen's School of Nursing); Bachelors and Masters degree courses in nursing science; library: 20,000 vols, 100 periodicals; 1,300 students; Rector JAN ÅKE LINDGREN; Library Dir WAHLFRIDSSON EVA UNEMO.

Other Institutes of University Standing

Blekinge Tekniska Högskola (Blekinge Institute of Technology): SE-371 79 Karlskrona; Campus Gräsvik (Valhallavägen 1), Karlskrona; tel. (455) 38-50-00; e-mail info@ bth.se; internet www.bth.se; f. 1989, present name adopted 2000; schools of computing, engineering, health science, management,

planning and media design; 140 teachers; 8,800 students; Vice-Chancellor ANDERS HEDERSTIERNA; Pro-Vice-Chancellor HENRIC JOHNSON; Head of Admin. HENRICK GYLLBERG.

Chalmers Tekniska Högskola (Chalmers University of Technology): SE-412 96 Gothenburg; tel. (31) 772-10-00; e-mail info@adm.chalmers.se; internet www .chalmers.se; f. 1829; depts of applied information technology, applied mechanics, applied physics, architecture, chemical and biological engineering, civil and environmental engineering, computer science and engineering, Earth and space sciences, energy and environment, fundamental physics, materials and manufacturing technology, mathematical sciences, microtechnology and nanoscience, product and production devt, shipping and marine technology, signals and systems, technology management and economics; maintains 44 attached centres; library: see under Libraries and Archives; 1,600 teachers; 11,000 students; Pres. and CEO Prof. Dr KARIN MARKIDES; First Vice-Pres. Prof. MATS VIBERG; Dean. JOHAN CARLSTEN; Vice-Pres. for Advancement LARS BORJESSON; Vice-Pres. for Research and Research Education Prof. ALF-ERIK ALMSTEDT; Vice-Pres. for Strategy and Sustainable Devt Prof. JOHN HOLMBERG; Vice-Pres. for Undergraduate and Master Programmes Prof. Dr MARIA KNUTSON WEDEL; Libraries Dir L. NELLDE.

Gymnastik- och Idrottshögskolan (Swedish School of Sport and Health Sciences): POB 5626, SE-114 86 Stockholm; Lidingövägen 1, SE-114 33 Stockholm; tel. (8) 120-537-00; e-mail registrator@gih.se; internet www .gih.se; f. 1813, fmrly Stockholm Univ. College of Physical Education and Sports, present name 2005; programmes incl. physical education teaching, sports science and coaching, sports science and health science; library: 60,000 vols, 6,000 periodicals; 60 teachers; 650 students; Rector Prof. KARIN HENRIKSSON-LARSEN; Pro-Rector Dr KARIN REDELIUS; Vice-Rector Dr HANS ROSDAHL; Vice-Rector TAGE STERNER; Registrar and Sec. AMANDA WEBRINK; Head of Library LOTTA HAGLUND.

Handelshögskolan i Stockholm (Stockholm School of Economics): POB 6501, SE-113 83 Stockholm; Sveavägen 65, Stockholm; tel. (8) 736-90-00; e-mail info@hhs.se; internet www.hhs.se; f. 1909; depts of accounting, economics, finance, law, languages and economic statistics, management and organization, marketing and strategy; library: see under Libraries and Archives; 170 teachers; 2,000 students; Pres. ROLF WOLFF; Sr Exec. Vice-Pres. for Administration LARS AGREN; Vice-Pres. for Internationalization LARS STRANNEGÅRD; Dir for Academic Affairs LENA HILDEBY; Dir for Student Services CHRISTINA ZANDER; Library Dir MARIE-LOUISE FENDIN.

Högskolan för Design och Konsthantverk (School of Design and Crafts): POB 131, SE-405 30 Gothenburg; Kristinelundsgatan 6–8, SE-405 30 Gothenburg; tel. (31) 786-00-00; e-mail info@hdk.gu.se; internet www.hdk .gu.se; f. 1848, merger of School of Craft and Design, Dals Långed 2012; attached to Gothenburg Univ.; product design, interior and graphic design, ceramic art, textile art, jewellery design, film scenography; library: 20,000 vols; 40 teachers; 250 students; Head BITTE NYGREN; Deputy Head JEFF KALLER; Head of Admin. JEANETTE JOHANSSON; Librarian KARIN SUNDÉN.

Högskolan för Scen och Musik (Academy of Music and Drama): POB 210, SE-405 30 Gothenburg; Fågelsången 1, Gothenburg; tel.

(31) 786-40-20; e-mail information@hsm.gu
.se; internet www.hsm.gu.se; f. 1916, present
status 2005; attached to Göteborgs Univ.;
courses and programmes in music, musical
theatre, opera and theatre; 150 teachers; 700
students; Head STAFFAN RYDÉN; Deputy
Head for Internationalization ANNA MARIA
KOZIOMTZIS; Deputy Head for Education EVA
NISTE; Chief Librarian PIA SHEKHTER.

Internationella Handelshögskolan (Jönköping International Business School): POB
1026, SE-551 11 Jönköping; Gjuterigatan 5,
Jönköping; tel. (36) 10-10-00; e-mail info@jibs
.hj.se; internet hj.se/jibs.html; f. 1994;
attached to Jonkoping Univ.; business
administration, economics, political science,
business informatics and commercial law;
220 teachers; 2,100 students; Man. Dir and
Dean Prof. Dr JOHAN ROOS; Dir for Administration NILS-OLE EHRSTEDT; Assoc. Dean for
Education PAUL MCGURR; Assoc. Dean for
Research Prof. Dr VIVIAN VIMARLUND.

Karolinska Institutet: SE-171 77 Stockholm; Solna Br.: Solnavägen 1, Solna, Stockholm; Huddinge Br.: Alfred Nobels Allé 8,
Huddinge, Stockholm; tel. (8) 524-800-00;
e-mail registrator@ki.se; internet ki.se; f.
1810; medical univ.; library: see under Libraries and Archives; 480 teachers; 6,000 students; Pres. Prof. Dr ANDERS HAMSTEN; Vice-
Pres. Prof. KERSTIN THAM; Univ. Dir BENGT
NORRVING; Chief Librarian CHRISTER BJÖRK-
LUND; publs *Computerized Publication Register* (information on all publs issued by the
Institute), *Curriculum*, *Students' Handbook*.

Konstfack (University College of Arts,
Crafts and Design): POB 3601, SE-126 27
Stockholm; LM Ericssons väg 14, SE-126 26
Stockholm; tel. (8) 450-41-00; e-mail
registrator@konstfack.se; internet www
.konstfack.se; f. 1844, present bldg 2004;
depts of design, crafts and arts, fine art,
visual arts education; library: 110,000 vols;
135 teachers; 920 students; Vice-Chancellor
MARIA LANTZ; Pro-Vice-Chancellor ANN CATH-
RINE ANDERSSON; Chief Librarian LISA MAR-
TLING PALMGREN.

Kungliga Konsthögskolan (Royal Institute of Art): POB 16315, SE-103 26 Stockholm; Flaggmansvägen 1, SE-111 49
Stockholm; tel. (8) 614-40-00; e-mail info@
kkh.se; internet www.kkh.se; f. 1735, present
location 1995, present name 2010; attached
to Min. of Education and Research; offers
Bachelors and Masters courses in fine arts;
library: 60,000 vols; 40 teachers; 210 students; Vice-Chancellor MÅNS WRANGE; Pro-
Vice-Chancellor MILOU ALLERHOLM; Pro-Vice-
Chancellor EBERHARD HÖLL; Head for Admin.
LARS-ERIK OLSSON; Librarian ANNAKARIN
LINDBERG; Librarian ULF NORDQVIST; publs
*Konsthögskolan Elevkatalog, Konsthögsko-
lans Broschyr*.

Kungl. Musikhögskolan i Stockholm
(Royal College of Music in Stockholm): POB
27711, SE-115 91 Stockholm; Valhallavägen
105, Stockholm; tel. (8) 16-18-00; e-mail
info@kmh.se; internet www.kmh.se; f. 1771;
depts of classical music, composition, conducting and music theory, folk music, jazz,
music and media production, music education; 320 teachers; 1,000 students; Prin.
CECILIA RYDINGER ALIN (acting); Vice-Prin.
STAFFAN SCHEJA; Library Man. NORDGREN
KARIN.

Kungliga Tekniska Högskolan (Royal
Institute of Technology): SE-100 44 Stockholm; Brinellvägen 8, Stockholm; tel. (8) 790-
60-00; e-mail info@kth.se; internet www.kth
.se; f. 1827, present location 1917; schools of
architecture and built environment, biotechnology, chemical science and engineering,
computer science and communication, electrical engineering, information and communication technology, industrial engineering
and management, engineering sciences, technology and health, education and communication in engineering science, innovation
engineering; library: see under Libraries
and Archives; 480 professors; 14,000 students; Pres. Prof. Dr PETER GUDMUNDSON;
Deputy Pres. EVA MALMSTRÖM JONSSON; Vice-
Pres. for Faculty Devt and Gender Equity
GUSTAV AMBERG; Vice-Pres. for Faculty of
Innovative Engineering MARGARETA NORELL
BERGENDAHL; Vice-Pres. for Int. Affairs
RAMON WYSS; Vice-Pres. for Research BJÖRN
BIRGISSON; Vice-Pres. for Sustainable Devt
GÖRAN FINNVEDEN; Univ. Dir ANDERS LUNDG-
REN; Chief Librarian G. LAGER; publs *Cata-
logue, Study Handbook* (1 a year).

Stockholms Dramatiska Högskola
(Stockholm Academy of Dramatic Arts):
POB 27095, SE-102 51 Stockholm; Valhallavägen 189, SE-115 53 Stockholm; tel. (8) 120-
531-00; e-mail info@stdh.se; internet www
.stdh.se; f. 2011 after merger of Theatre
Academy in Stockholm and Dramatic Institute; depts of acting, film and media, performing arts; 280 students; Rector BO-ERIK
GYBERG; Pro-Rector FREDRIK OLDSJÖ.

Umeå Institute of Design: SE-901 87
Umeå; Östra Strandgatan 30, Umeå; tel.
(90) 786-69-96; e-mail info@dh.umu.se;
internet www.dh.umu.se; f. 1989; attached
to Umeå Univ.; BA, MA and Doctoral programmes in industrial design and related
specializations; 16 teachers; Rector Prof.
ANNA VALTONEN; Head of Dept MARIA GÖR-
ANSDOTTER.

SWITZERLAND

The Higher Education System

Higher education institutions predate the proclamation of the Helvetic Republic in 1798, with the oldest being the Universität Basel, which was founded in 1460. Other long-standing institutions include the Université de Lausanne (founded 1537), the Université de Genève (founded 1559) and the Universität Luzern (founded 1574; current status since 2000). There are 10 cantonal universities, and the main languages of instruction are French, German or Italian, depending on the canton. However, in 2007 the Swiss Conference of Cantonal Ministers of Education designed an inter-cantonal reform system (HarmoS) that endeavoured to unify the different education systems in the different cantons. At 2012 the agreement had been ratified by 15 cantons (in which it is now legally binding); a decision was to be reached in 2015 whether sufficient concordance had been achieved, with those cantons that had not ratified the agreement being invited to make their positions known by the end of 2014. Other institutions of higher education include two federal institutes of technology, and universities of applied sciences (known as Fachhochoshulen, Hautes Ecoles Spécialisées or Scuole Universitarie Professionale). Switzerland participates in the Bologna Process to establish a European Higher Education Area, the first phase of which is to adopt a credit-based system of comparable degrees with two main cycles (undergraduate and graduate). In 2010/11 there were 258,623 students enrolled in tertiary level education, of which 131,494 were enrolled at universities, 75,035 were enrolled at universities of applied sciences and 52,094 were enrolled at vocational institutions.

There is no federal agency for higher education, responsibility for which is divided between the Confederation and the cantons. The cantons are responsible for the universities and are their primary source of funding; they also supervise the universities of applied sciences and many vocational and training institutions. The Confederation supervises and funds the federal institutes of technology; legislates on vocational education and training and the universities of applied sciences; and funds vocational education and training, as well as providing additional funding for the cantonal universities. The Confederation and cantons cooperate through the Swiss University Conference (SUC), which was established to coordinate the management of the universities. At the end of 2012 a public consultation was under way on the revision of the law on funding of tertiary level education.

Either the Federal Maturity Certificate (Maturitätszeugnis, Certificat de Maturité, Baccalauréat or Attestato di Maturità) or the Federally Recognized Cantonal Maturity Certificate (Eidgenössisch anerkanntes kantonales Maturitätszeugnis, Certificat de Maturité cantonal reconnu par la Confédération or Attestato di Maturità cantonale riconosciuto dalla Confederazione) is the main requirement for admission to university. Cantonal Maturity Certificates that do not have federal recognition (Kantonale Maturität, Maturité Cantonale or Maturità Cantonale) give limited access to higher education, while the Vocational Maturity Certificate (Eidgenössisches Berufsmaturitätszeugnis, Certificat fédéral de maturité professionelle or Attestato federale di maturità professionale) is required for admission to the Fachhochoshulen, Hautes Ecoles Spécialisées or Scuole Universitarie Professionale, and also allows access to universities when taken in combination with an additional examination (Passarellenprüfung Berufsmaturität, Ergänzungsprüfung, Passerelle maturité professionnelle, examen complémentaire, Passerella maturità professionale or esami complementari). The new Bologna-style degree system, comprising the Bachelors, Masters and Doctorate, had been fully implemented by 2008. The Bachelors is a three-year degree, equivalent to the old four-year Diplom, Diplôme, Licence or Lizentiat. The first postgraduate degree is the Masters, a one-and-a-half- to two-year programme following the Bachelors. Finally, the highest university degree is the Doctorate (Doktorat, Doctorat), which is only offered by the universities and is awarded after between two and five years of research, culminating with defence of a thesis.

Technical and vocational education is regulated by federal law and implemented by cantonal authorities. Students split their time between the workplace and the classroom, and the primary qualification is the Federal Apprenticeship Certificate or Certificate of Proficiency (Fähigkeitszeugnis, Certificate de Capacité or Attestato di Capacità). There are also Advanced Vocational Schools (Ecoles Professionnelles Supérieures or Scuole Medie Professionale) offering advanced programmes in technical and vocational education.

The Centre of Accreditation and Quality Assurance of the Swiss Universities (OAQ) is an independent body that defines quality assurance requirements and regularly checks compliance with these and prepares guidelines for the national accreditation procedures. In addition, it conducts accreditation procedures as well as other quality assessments such as evaluations and audits on behalf of the Swiss University Conference and the Confederation. The political authorities have mandated the OAQ to undertake quality audits of the universities and federal institutes of technology every four years to determine whether their quality assurance systems are compatible with internationally accepted standards. A system of accreditation has been in place since 2002. It is a voluntary procedure open to academic institutions and their study programmes, both from the public and private sectors. It consists of a three-step procedure comprising self-evaluation, external evaluation and finally decision on accreditation. The accreditation is based on an assessment of compliance with predefined, internationally accepted quality standards as mentioned above. The accreditation decision is made by the Swiss University Conference. An unconditional positive decision is granted for seven years.

Regulatory and Representative Bodies

GOVERNMENT

State Secretariat for Education, Research and Innovation: Effingerstrasse 27, 3003 Bern; tel. 313222129; e-mail info@sbfi.admin.ch; internet www.sbfi.admin.ch; Head JOHANN N. SCHNEIDER-AMMANN.

ACCREDITATION

Organ für Akkreditierung und Qualitätssicherung der Schweizerischen Hochschulen/Organe d'accréditation et d'assurance de qualité des hautes écoles suisses (Swiss Center of Accreditation and Quality Assurance in Higher Education): Falkenplatz 9, POB 7456, 3001 Bern; tel. 313801150; e-mail info@oaq.ch; internet www.oaq.ch; f. 2001; promotes quality of teaching and research at univs; develops guidelines and quality standards for academic accreditation and carries out accreditation procedures on basis of guidelines introduced by Schweizerische Universitätskonferenz/Conférence universitaire suisse (SUK/CUS); Dir Dr CHRISTOPH GROLIMUND.

Schweizerische Universitätskonferenz/ Conférence universitaire suisse (Swiss University Conference): Sennweg 2, POB 576, 3012 Bern 9; tel. 313066060; e-mail cus@cus.ch; internet www.cus.ch; f. 1969, present status 2001; coordination of Swiss univs and institutes of higher education; empowered to accredit public or private academic instns and programmes; awards project-specific grants; issues directives on evaluation of teaching and research; 18

mems, representing cantons, univs, Nat. Union of Students, etc.; Pres. Dr BERNHARD PULVER; Sec.-Gen. Dr MARTINA WEISS; Deputy Sec.-Gen. VALÉRIE CLERC BOREL; publ. *SUK Info* (4 a year).

Swiss ENIC—Naric: Rectors' Conf. of the Swiss Univs, POB 607, 3000 Bern 9; tel. 313066042; e-mail christine.gehrig@crus.ch; internet www.enic.ch; provides information on Swiss and foreign higher education systems and on recognition of qualifications; Head CHRISTINE GEHRIG.

FUNDING

Rat der Eidgenössischen Technischen Hochschulen/Conseil des Ecoles polytechniques fédérales (Board of the Swiss Federal Institutes of Technology): Häldeliweg 15, 8092 Zürich; tel. 446322367; internet www.ethrat.ch; appointed by Swiss Fed. Council; allocates funds to Swiss Fed. Institutes of Technology in Zurich and Lausanne, the Paul Scherrer Institut, the Swiss Fed. Institute for Forest, Snow and Landscape Research, Materials Science and Technology Research Instn and Swiss Fed. Institute of Aquatic Science and Technology; centre in Bern; Pres. Dr FRITZ SCHIESSER; Vice-Pres. Prof. Dr PAUL L. HERRLING; Exec. Dir Dr MICHAEL KÄPPELI.

Schweizerischer Nationalfonds zur Förderung der wissenschaftlichen Forschung/Fonds national suisse de la Recherche scientifique (Swiss National Science Foundation): Wildhainweg 3, POB 8232, 3001 Bern; tel. 313082222; e-mail com@snf.ch; internet www.snf.ch; f. 1952; promotes ind. scientific research; supports basic research in all disciplines; supports applied research through Nat. Research Programmes; facilitates and promotes int. engagement for Swiss research community and provides funding opportunities; Pres., Foundation Council GABRIELE GENDOTTI; Dir DANIEL HÖCHLI; publ. *Horizons* (4 a year).

NATIONAL BODIES

EDK/IDES (IDES Information and Documentation Centre): Speichergasse 6, POB 660, 3000 Bern 7; tel. 313095100; e-mail ides@edk.ch; internet www.edk.ch; f. 1962 (with partial integration of CESDOC 1994); collects information and documents about Swiss education system and makes them accessible; serves cantonal education and training depts; library of 50,000 vols; Pres. ISABELLE CHASSOT; Dir ANNEMARIE STREIT.

Rektorenkonferenz der Schweizer Universitäten (CRUS)/Conférence des Recteurs des Universités Suisses (CRUS) (Rectors' Conference of the Swiss Universities): Sennweg 2, 3012 Bern; tel. 313066036; e-mail crus@crus.ch; internet www.crus.ch; f. 1904, present status 2001; 12 mem univs; represents Swiss univs in relation with govt and other bodies; responsible for strategic planning and cooperation between univs; coordinates the implementation of the Bologna reform at the doctoral degree awarding univs; provides information service on Swiss and foreign univs; administers bilateral govt scholarships for Swiss students; nat. information service on questions of academic recognition (Swiss ENIC); EURAXESS bridgehead in Switzerland; administers Scientific Exchange Programme between Switzerland and the New Member States of EU (Sciex-NMSch); library of 4,000 vols; Pres. Prof. Dr ANTONIO LOPRIENO; Sec.-Gen. Dr MATHIAS STAUFFACHER; publs *proff.ch* (online), *Studying in Switzerland: Universities*.

Schweizerische Konferenz der kantonalen Erziehungsdirektoren (EDK)/Con-
férence suisse des directeurs cantonaux de l'instruction publique (Swiss Conference of Cantonal Ministers of Education): Speichergasse 6, POB 660, 3000 Bern 7; tel. 313095111; e-mail edk@edk.ch; internet www.edk.ch; assembly of the 26 cantonal govt ministers responsible for education, training, culture and sport; negotiating partner of federal govt for jt responsibility of education (high school, vocational education, univs) and represents cantons in foreign countries in educational and cultural affairs; centre in Bern; Pres. ISABELLE CHASSOT; Gen. Sec. HANS AMBÜHL.

Schweizerischer Wissenschafts- und Innovationsrat/Conseil Suisse de la Science et de l'innovation (Swiss Science and Innovation Council): Hallwylstrasse 15, 3003 Bern; tel. 313230048; e-mail swir@swir.admin.ch; internet www.swir.ch; advisory body to govt on all matters relating to science policy; provides and evaluates fundamentals of nat. policy on education, research and technology; Pres. Prof. ASTRID EPINEY; Head of Secretariat Prof. CHRISTIAN SIMON.

Vereinigung der Schweizerischen Hochschuldozierenden/Association Suisse des Enseignant-e-s d'Université (Swiss University Teachers' Association): Buchhalden 5, 8127 Forch; tel. 446333399; e-mail vsh-sekretariat@ethz.ch; internet www.hsl.ethz.ch; f. 1971; promotes public understanding of univ. matters and univ. professions; represents interests of univ. lecturers; maintains int. ties among univ. teachers; Pres. Prof. Dr CHRISTIAN BOCHET; Gen. Sec. Prof. Dr GERNOT KOSTORZ.

Learned Societies

GENERAL

Akademie der Naturwissenschaften Schweiz SCNAT/Académie des sciences naturelles SCNAT (Swiss Academy of Sciences SCNAT): Schwarztorstrasse 9, 3007 Bern; tel. 313104020; e-mail info@scnat.ch; internet www.scnat.ch; f. 1815, present name 2004; promotes scientific integrity and ethically considered treatment of scientific knowledge and its application; promotes active exchange of opinion between science and society through information and promotional events on new areas of research, support of regional projects and awarding of prizes for outstanding communication of scientific content; 74 mems incl. expert asscns and cantonal and regional asscns; Pres. Prof. THIERRY J. L. COURVOISIER; Sec.-Gen. Dr JÜRG PFISTER; Treas. Prof. HELMUT WEISSERT; publ. *SCNATinfo*.

Institut National Genevois: Promenade du Pin 1, 1204 Geneva; tel. 223104188; internet www.inge.ch; f. 1853; divided into 4 sections: economics, moral and political sciences, fine arts, music and letters and science; encourages advancement and dissemination of science, literature, fine arts, industry, commerce and agriculture; 750 mems; Pres. PIERRE KUNZ; Sec.-Gen. MICHELLE SAUDIN; Treas. JEAN-CLAUDE MEYER; publ. *Mémoires*.

Schweizerische Akademie der Geistes- und Sozialwissenschaften/Académie Suisse des Sciences Humaines et Sociales (Swiss Academy of Humanities and Social Sciences): Hirschengraben 11, POB 8160, 3011 Bern; tel. 313131440; e-mail sagw@sagw.ch; internet www.sagw.ch; f. 1946; represents concerns of humanities and social sciences to decision makers and authorities and to media and public; provides infrastructure for humanities and
social science research; organizes confs and meetings of nat. and int. mem. orgs; 60 mem. socs; Pres. Prof. Dr HEINZ GUTSCHER; Vice-Pres. Prof. Dr BEATRICE SCHMID; Sec.-Gen. Dr MARKUS ZÜRCHER.

Schweizerische Akademie der Technischen Wissenschaften/Académie Suisse des Sciences Techniques (Swiss Academy of Engineering Sciences): Gerbergasse 5, 8001 Zürich; tel. 442265011; e-mail info@satw.ch; internet www.satw.ch; f. 1981; co-operation with similar socs; acts in advisory capacity to govt; promotes utilization and devt of technology for benefit of society; 290 individual mems, 50 mem. orgs; Pres. Prof. Dr ULRICH W. SUTER; Vice-Pres. Dr ARTHUR RUF; Vice-Pres. Dr IRENE AEGERTER; Man. Dir Dr ROLF HÜGLI; publ. *Technoscope* (3 a year).

AGRICULTURE, FISHERIES AND VETERINARY SCIENCE

Association des Groupements et Organisations Romands de l'Agriculture—AGORA: Ave des Jordils 5, POB 128, 1000 Lausanne 6; tel. 216140477; e-mail info@agora-romandie.ch; internet www.agora-romandie.ch; f. 1881, as Fédération des Sociétés d'Agriculture de Suisse Romande (FSASR), present name and status 1996; defends professional interests of Romande agriculture; promotes vocational training and devt of service activities; 21 corporate mems; library of 200 vols; Pres. FRANÇOIS HALDEMANN; Dir WALTER WILLENER; publs *d'arboriculture et d'horticulture* (6 a year), *Revue suisse d'agriculture* (6 a year), *Revue suisse de viticulture*.

Gesellschaft Schweizer Tierärztinnen und Tierärzte/Société des Vétérinaires Suisses: Brunnmattstr. 13, POB 45, 3174 Thörishaus; tel. 313073535; e-mail info@gstsvs.ch; internet www.gstsvs.ch; f. 1813; represents professional interests of ind. and employed veterinarians; 2,700 mems; Pres. CHARLES TROLLIET; Man. Dir RUEDI HELFER-DÖLKER; publ. *Schweizer Archiv für Tierheilkunde* (12 a year).

ARCHITECTURE AND TOWN PLANNING

Bund Schweizer Architekten/Fédération des Architectes Suisses: Pfluggässlein 3, POB 907, 4001 Basel; tel. 612621010; e-mail mail@bsa-fas.ch; internet www.architects-fsa.ch; f. 1908; represents professional interests of architects; provides information on architecture profession and its role in soc.; supports education, training and research of architecture; 858 mems; Pres. PAUL KNILL; Vice-Pres. ALDO NOLLI; Vice-Pres. ELISABETH BOESCH; Vice-Pres. ROLF SEILER; Treas. YVO THALMANN; publ. *Werk, Bauen und Wohnen* (12 a year).

Schweizer Heimatschutz (Swiss Heritage Society): Seefeldstr. 5A, POB 1122, 8032 Zürich; tel. 442545700; e-mail info@heimatschutz.ch; internet www.heimatschutz.ch; f. 1905; promotes advancement of Switzerland's architectural heritage; preserves important landmarks, develops structural environment, and promotes good architectural design; 27,000 mems; Pres. PHILIPPE BIÉLER; Vice-Pres. RUTH GISI-WILLISEGGER; Vice-Pres. SEVERIN LENEL; Sec.-Gen. ADRIAN SCHMID; publ. *Heimatschutz/Patrimoine* (French and German, 4 a year).

Société Suisse des Ingénieurs et des Architectes/Schweizerischer Ingenieur- und Architektenverein: POB, 8027 Zürich; Selnaustr. 16, 8001 Zürich; tel. 442831515; e-mail contact@sia.ch; internet www.sia.ch; f. 1837; promotes sustainable devt and quality of natural and built environment; guards professional interests of its mems; 14,683 mems; Pres. DANIEL KÜNDIG;

Vice-Pres. ANDREAS BERNASCONI; Vice-Pres. LAURENT VULLIET; Sec-Gen. HANS-GEORG BÄCHTOLD; publs *TEC21*, *TRACÉS* (24 a year).

BIBLIOGRAPHY, LIBRARY SCIENCE AND MUSEOLOGY

Bibliothek Information Schweiz/Bibliothèque Information Suisse (Swiss National Association of Libraries and Librarians): Bleichemattstr. 42, 5000 Aarau; tel. 628231938; e-mail info@bis.ch; internet www.bis.ch; f. 1987, by merger of Bibliotheken und der Bibliothekarinnen/Bibliothekare der Schweiz (BBS) and Schweizerische Vereinigung für Dokumentation (SVD) 2008; rep. of mems in politics and public; lobbying of decision makers from education, science and culture in fields of library policy and devt, intellectual, cultural promotion, professional training; 1,650 mems incl. instns and professionals; Pres. HERBERT STAUB; Gen. Sec. HALO LOCHER; publ. *ARBIDO* (4 a year).

Genossenschaft der Urheber und Verleger von Musik/Coopérative des auteurs et éditeurs de musique (Cooperative Society of Music Authors and Publishers): Bellariastr. 82, POB 782, 8038 Zürich; tel. 444856666; e-mail suisa@suisa.ch; internet www.suisa.ch; f. 1923; issues licences authorising its clients to perform, broadcast, disseminate and reproduce music; collects royalties of its members for public use of their works in Switzerland and Liechtenstein; centres in Lausanne and Lugano; 29,000 mems; Pres. HANS ULRICH LEHMANN; Vice-Pres. MARCO ZANOTTA; CEO and Gen. Dir ANDREAS WEGELIN.

Schweizer Diplombibliothekare/innen/Bibliothécaires Diplôme(e)s Suisses (Association of Swiss Graduate Librarians): POB 607, 3000 Bern 7; Sekretariat, c/o Martin Rohde, Sportweg 15, 3097 Liebefeld; tel. 40248542; e-mail info@sdb-bds.ch; internet www.sdb-bds.ch; f. 1988; promotes professional interests of qualified librarians; regional groups in Aarau, Basel, Bern, Lausanne, Zentralschweiz and Zürich; 500 mems; publ. *SDB/BDS News* (3 a year).

Schweizerische Bibliophilen Gesellschaft/Société Suisse des Bibliophiles (Swiss Bibliophile Society): Alte Landstr. 95, POB 40, 8804 Au; e-mail erfueter@gmx.ch; f. 1921; 600 mems; Pres. Dr AGLAJA HUBER; Hon. Treas. EDUARD R. FUETER; publs *Librarium 58* (3 a year), *Stultifera Navis 44–57*.

Verband der Museen der Schweiz/Association des Musées Suisses: c/o Landesmuseum Zürich, POB, 8021 Zürich; tel. 442186588; e-mail info@museums.ch; internet www.museums.ch; f. 1966; asscn of Swiss museums and zoological and botanical gardens, to represent their interests; forms a link between Swiss museums and Int. Council of Museums (see International Organizations chapter); organizes annual conf. and work sessions on museology, conservation, restoration and other related topics; jt projects with univs, training; basic program for new museum professionals, spec. courses for guides, security and technical staff, academic museology courses in cooperation with univs; Int. Museum Day; 670 institutional mems; Pres. GIANNA A. MINA; Gen. Sec. DAVID VUILLAUME; publs *Revue museums.ch* (1 a year), *Schweizer Museumsführer/Guide des musées suisses* (irregular).

Verein Schweizerischer Archivarinnen und Archivare/Association des archivistes suisses (Association of Swiss Archivists): c/o Büro Pontri GmbH, Solothurnstr. 13, POB, 3322 Urtenen-Schönbühl; tel. 313122666; e-mail info@vsa-aas.org;

internet www.vsa-aas.org; f. 1922; ensures professionalization of archives; encourages establishment of coordinated archival heritage; represents interests of mems; advanced professional training, confs, lobbying, collaboration and coordination within and for Swiss archival community; 713 mems; Pres. Dr ANNA PIA MAISSEN; Vice-Pres. GREGOR EGLOFF; Sec. DANIEL KRESS; Treas. PHILIPPE KÜNZLER; publ. *ARBIDO* (4 a year).

ECONOMICS, LAW AND POLITICS

Bundesamt für Statistik/Office Fédéral de la Statistique (Federal Statistical Office): Espace de l'Europe 10, 2010 Neuchâtel; tel. 327136011; e-mail info@bfs.admin.ch; internet www.statistik.ch; f. 1860; nat. centre for public statistics; production and publication of statistics; Dir-Gen. Dr JÜRG MARTI; publ. *Statistical Yearbook* (1 a year).

Gottlieb Duttweiler Institute: Langhaldenstr. 21, POB 531, 8803 Rüschlikon/Zürich; tel. 447246111; e-mail info@gdi.ch; internet www.gdi.ch; f. 1963; conducts scientific research in social and economic fields; monitoring of social change; organizes confs, seminars and workshops; 35 mems; CEO Dr DAVID BOSSHART; Asst CEO INGRID SCHMID; publ. *GDI Impuls*.

Schweizerische Gesellschaft für Aussenpolitik/L'Association Suisse de Politique Extérieure: c/o Karin Büchli, Netzwerk Müllerhaus, Bleicherain 7, 5600 Lenzburg 1; tel. 628880120; e-mail info@sga-aspe.ch; internet www.sga-aspe.ch; f. 1968; deals with matters of foreign, int. trade, integration and security policy; organizes lectures, confs and seminars on current foreign policy issues; 800 mems; Pres. HADORN ADRIAN; Sec.-Gen. Dr ULRICH E. GUT.

Schweizerische Gesellschaft für Volkswirtschaft und Statistik/Société Suisse d'Economie et de Statistique (Swiss Society of Economics and Statistics): c/o SNB/BNS, Börsenstr. 15, 8022 Zürich; tel. 446313785; e-mail mail@sgvs.ch; internet www.sgvs.ch; f. 1864; promotes and advances economic research and improves collaboration between domestic and int. research community, promotes young economists by providing appropriate platform to present their scientific work; awards SSES Young Economist Awards; 600 mems; library: see entry for Schweiz. Wirtschaftsarchiv; Pres. PHILIPPE BACCHETTA; Sec. and Treas. FABIENNE SCHÜRMANN; publ. *Swiss Journal of Economics and Statistics/Schweizerische Zeitschrift für Volkswirtschaft und Statistik/Revue suisse d'économie et de statistique* (4 a year).

Schweizerische Vereinigung für Internationales Recht/Société Suisse de Droit International: c/o Dr Stefan Breitenstein, Lenz & Staehelin, Bleicherweg 58, 8027 Zürich; tel. 442041212; e-mail stefan.breitenstein@lenzstaehelin.com; internet www.svir-ssdi.ch; f. 1914; promotes qualitative implementation of int. law; promotes lawyers working in field of int. and European law; organizes Swiss conf. of int. law; 300 mems; Pres. Prof. CHRISTINE KADDOUS; Vice-Pres. Prof. DANIEL GIRSBERGER; Sec. Dr STEFAN BREITENSTEIN; Treas. Dr MONIQUE JAMETTI GREINER; publs *Schweizerische Zeitschrift für internationales und europäisches Recht* (5 a year), *Swiss Studies in International Law*.

Schweizerischer Anwaltsverband/Fédération Suisse des Avocats (Swiss Bar Association): Marktgasse 4, POB 8321, 3011 Bern; tel. 313130606; e-mail info@swisslawyers.com; internet www.swisslawyers.com; f. 1898; preserves and defends independent legal profession in

Switzerland and abroad; represents Swiss law as against federal authorities and int. orgs; fosters relations among cantonal bar asscns; 8,620 mems; Pres. Avv. BRENNO BRUNONI; Vice-Pres. Dr BEAT VON RECHENBERG; Vice-Pres. PIERRE-DOMINIQUE SCHUPP; Gen. Sec. Lic. RENÉ RALL; publs *Anwaltsrevue/Revue de l'Avocat* (12 a year), *Schriftenreihe*.

Schweizerischer Notarenverband/Fédération Suisse des Notaires: Tavelweg 2, 3074 Muri; tel. 313105840; e-mail info@schweizernotare.ch; internet www.schweizernotare.ch; f. 1920; safeguards interests of freelance notary; rep. of professional notary to authorities and opinion on federal issues associated with exercise of notary in context; maintains relationships and follow notary feds of other countries and int. orgs notary; 1,500 mems; Pres. Me PHILIPPE BOSSET; Sec. Me ANDREAS B. NOTTER.

FINE AND PERFORMING ARTS

Berufsverband Visuelle Kunst/Société Des Artistes Visuels (Visual Arts Asscociation): Räffelstrasse 32, 8045 Zürich; tel. 444621030; e-mail office@visarte.ch; internet www.visarte.ch; f. 1865, present name and status 2001; defends visual artists' interests on political and social levels; seeks to ensure favourable conditions for artistic production and provides counsel to artists; 3,300 mems incl. 2,600 active mems; Pres. HEINRICH GARTENTOR; Vice-Pres. NATALIA SCHMUKI; Man. REGINE HELBLING; publs *Arte Svizzera, Art Suisse, Schweizer Kunst* (2 a year).

Gesellschaft für Schweizerische Kunstgeschichte/Société d'histoire de l'art en Suisse: Pavillonweg 2, 3012 Bern; tel. 313083838; e-mail gsk@gsk.ch; internet www.gsk.ch; f. 1880; studies and publicizes cultural heritage and diversity of Switzerland dating back to antiquity; 9,500 mems; Pres. Dr BENNO SCHUBIGER; Vice-Pres. Dr JACQUES BUJARD; Sec. Dr MATTHIAS EPPENBERGER; Treas. ERICH WEBER; publs *Beiträge zur Kunstgeschichte der Schweiz, Die Kunstdenkmäler der Schweiz, Inventar der neueren Schweizer Architektur, k+a* (4 a year), *Kunst Architektur in der Schweiz* (4 a year), *Kunstführer durch die Schweiz, Schweiz. Kunstführer* (20 a year).

Hindemith Stiftung (Hindemith Foundation): Champ Belluet 41, 1807 Blonay; tel. 219430528; e-mail administration@hindemith.org; internet www.hindemith.org; f. 1968; promotes and cultivates music, in particular contemporary music; maintains musical and literary heritage of Paul Hindemith; encourages research in field of music and diffusion of research results; awards prizes; Pres. Prof. Dr ANDREAS ECKHARDT; Man. and Vice-Pres. FRANÇOIS MARGOT; publs *Frankfurter Studien, Hindemith General Original Edition, Les Annales Hindemith* (1 a year).

Attached Institutions:

Centre de Musique Hindemith (Hindemith Centre for Music): Chemin Lacuez 3, 1807 Blonay; tel. 219430520; e-mail centre.de.musique@hindemith.org; internet www.hindemith.org; f. 1978; chamber music master classes; Dir MARCEL LACHAT.

Hindemith-Institut Frankfurt (Hindemith-Institute Frankfurt): Eschersheimer Landstrasse 29–39, 60322 Frankfurt-am-Main, Germany; tel. (69) 5970362; e-mail institut@hindemith.org; internet www.paul-hindemith.org; archives of Hindemith's autograph scores and sketches, manuscript versions of musico-theoretical writings, autobiographical catalogues of works and extensive correspondence; Dir Dr SUSANNE SCHAAL-GOTTHARDT.

Kunstverein St Gallen: Museumstr. 32, 9000 St Gallen; tel. 712420687; e-mail kunstverein@kunstmuseumsg.ch; internet www.kunstmuseumsg.ch; f. 1827; promotes int. contemporary art exhibitions; 2,000 mems; Pres. LORENZ BÜHLER; Man. Dir NADIA VERONESE.

Pro Helvetia (Swiss Arts Council): Hirschengraben 22, 8024 Zürich; tel. 442677171; e-mail info@prohelvetia.ch; internet www.prohelvetia.ch; f. 1939; promotes artistic creation, fosters cultural outreach and facilitates cultural exchange with int. artists; offices in Warsaw, Cairo, Cape Town, New Delhi, Shanghai and Paris; Pres. MARIO ANNONI; Dir PIUS KNÜSEL; publ. *Passagen / Passages* (3 a year).

Schweizer Blasmusikverband/Association Suisse des Musiques (Swiss Windband Association): Gönhardweg 32, POB, 5001 Aarau; tel. 628228111; e-mail info@windband.ch; internet www.windband.ch; f. 1862; 76,000 mems, 32 associated mem. orgs; Chair. VALENTIN BISCHOF; publ. *Unisono* (26 a year).

Schweizer Musikrat/Conseil Suisse de la Musique (Swiss Music Council): Haus der Musik, Gönhardweg 32, POB 3839, 5001 Aarau; tel. 628229423; e-mail info@musikrat.ch; internet www.musikrat.ch; f. 1964; mem. of CIM (UNESCO); mem. of various musical orgs; rep. of interests of music creators to public and political bodies at fed. level and in educational and cultural issues; 50 mem. orgs; Pres. MARKUS FLURY; Dir STEFANO KUNZ; publs *Guide for Musical Studies in Switzerland*, *Schweizer Muzikzeitung* (irregular).

Schweizerische Musikforschende Gesellschaft/Société Suisse de Musicologie: Universität Bern, Institut für Musikwissenschaft, Hallerstr. 5, 3012 Bern; tel. 316318396; e-mail info@smg-ssm.ch; internet www.smg-ssm.ch; f. 1915, present name 1934; supports music research; organizes lectures, confs and congresses; country rep. of RILM (Répertoire Int. de Littérature Musicale); 7 sections in Basel, Bern, Luzern, St. Gallen-Zürich, Suisse Romande, Svizzera Italiana, Zürich; awards Glarean Prize for musical research and Jacques-Handschin Prize; 600 mems; Pres. Prof. Dr CRISTINA URCHUEGUÍA; Vice-Pres. Prof. Dr LUCA ZOPPELLI; Treas. Lic. CHRISTOPH BALLMER; publs *Editionen der Schweizerischen Musikforschenden Gesellschaft, Musik aus Schweizer Klöstern, Publikationen der Schweizerischen Musikforschenden Gesellschaft. Serie II, Schweizer Jahrbuch für Musikwissenschaft* (1 a year).

Schweizerischer Kunstverein/Société Suisse des Beaux-Arts (Swiss Art Association): Zeughausstr. 55, 8026 Zürich; tel. 442983035; e-mail info@kunstverein.ch; internet www.kunstverein.ch; f. 1806, present name 1839; promotes and protects interests of art assocs and art lovers on fed. level; lobbies and advocacies of mem. sections on nat. level; 44,000 individual mems of 34 local and regional art asscns; Pres. PETER STUDER (acting); publ. *Kunstbulletin* (10 a year).

Schweizerischer Tonkünstlerverein/Association Suisse des Musiciens: Ave du Grammont 11 bis, 1007 Lausanne 13; tel. 216143290; e-mail info@asm-stv.ch; internet www.asm-stv.ch; f. 1900; advocates and promotes interests of composers, soloists, improvisers, conductors and chorus, musicologists and music dirs; 950 mems; Pres. WILLIAM BLANK; Treas.

SIMONA RYSER; Dir CSABA KÉZÉR; publ. *dissonanz / dissonance* (4 a year).

Schweizerischer Werkbund/Werkbund Suisse: Limmatstr. 118, POB, 8031 Zürich; tel. 442727176; e-mail swb@werkbund.ch; internet www.werkbund.ch; f. 1913; organized into regional groups: Argovie, Bâle, Berne, Grisons, Suisse centrale, Suisse orientale, Romandie and Zurich; supports professionals from fields of creation, art and culture; organizes nationwide debates regarding design creation; 900 mems; Pres. IWAN RASCHLE; Treas. ALEXANDER ZOANNI; Sec.-Gen. BERND ZOCHER; publs *SWB-Dokumente*, *SWB-Information* (4 a year).

Schweizerisches Institut für Kunstwissenschaft/Institut Suisse pour l'Etude de l'Art (Swiss Institute for Art Research): Zollikerstr. 32, POB 1124, 8032 Zürich; tel. 443885151; e-mail sik@sik-isea.ch; internet www.sik-isea.ch; f. 1951; registration of Swiss works of art and Swiss artists; studies in art and technology; research, documentation, dissemination of knowledge and information in fields of fine art, art business and art technology; 1,700 mems; library of 114,000 vols; Pres. ANNE KELLER-DUBACH; Vice-Pres. and CEO Dr TONI SCHÖNENBERGER; Treas. Dr ERICH HUNZIKER; Dir Dr ROGER FAYET; publs *Kataloge Schweizer Museen und Sammlungen*, *KUNSTmaterial*, *Museen der Schweiz, Oeuvrekataloge Schweizer Künstler*, outlines.

SGD Swiss Graphic Designers: Bahnhofstr. 11, POB 157, 9230 Flawil; tel. 713934535; internet www.sgd.ch; f. 1972 by merger of VSG (Verband Schweizer Grafiker) and BGG (Bund Gestalter Grafische/Graphic Designers Asscn of AGC), present name 1993; protects and advances economic and professional interests of its members and offers advice and assistance; cooperates with nat. and int. orgs and with partners from economic and scientific worlds; 600 mems; Pres. DANILO SILVESTRI; Vice-Pres. MICHAELA VARIN; Sec.-Gen. ERIKA REMUND; publ. *SGD Information* (4 a year).

Société Suisse de Pédagogie Musicale/Società Svizzera di Pedagogia Musicale (Swiss Society of Music Education): Bollstr. 43, 3076 Worb, Bern; tel. 313522266; e-mail zentralsekretariat@smpv.ch; internet www .smpv.ch; f. 1893; 15 regional asscns; promotes musical education and research; 5,000 mems; Pres. BRIGITTE SCHOLL; Sec. LISA BUCHI; publ. *Agenda du musicien*.

HISTORY, GEOGRAPHY AND ARCHAEOLOGY

Antiquarische Gesellschaft in Zürich: c/o Staatsarchiv des Kantons Zürich, POB, 8057 Zürich; tel. 16356911; e-mail sekretariat@ antiquarische.ch; internet www .antiquarische.ch; f. 1832; concerned with history of Zürich and Swiss history in gen.; organizes lectures, meetings, field trips and guided tours; 550 mems; Pres. Dr ROLAND BÖHMER; publs *Mitteilungen der Antiquarischen Gesellschaft in Zürich* (1 a year), *Neujahrsblatt* (1 a year).

Archäologie Schweiz/Archéologie Suisse (Swiss Archaeology): Petersgraben 51, POB 116, 4003 Basel; tel. 612613078; e-mail info@archaeologie-schweiz.ch; internet www.archaeologie-schweiz.ch; f. 1907, current name adopted 2005; supports research on archaeological heritage and disseminates knowledge; 2,200 mems; library of 30,000 vols; Pres. PETER-ANDREW SCHWARZ; Sec. URS NIFFELER; Treas. WERNER H. GRAF; publ. *Archäologie Schweiz / Archéologie Suisse* (4 a year).

Geographisch-Ethnographische Gesellschaft Zürich: Geographisches Institut der Universität Zürich, Winterthurerstr. 190, 8057 Zürich; tel. 16355111; e-mail gegz@ geo.unizh.ch; internet www.geo.unizh.ch/ gegz; f. 1889, by merger of Ethnographic Society (f. 1888) and Geographical Society (f. 1897); promotes geographical and ethnographic knowledge and sustainable use of resources; understanding of foreign cultures and global connections; 450 individual and corporate mems; Pres. Prof. Dr MAX MAISCH; Vice-Pres. Prof. Dr ULRIKE MÜLLER-BÖKER; Sec. and Treas. Dr REGULA VOLKART; publ. *Geographica Helvetica* (4 a year).

Geographisch-Ethnologische Gesellschaft Basel/Société de Géographie et d'Ethnologie de Bâle: c/o Geographisches Institut, Klingelbergstr. 27, 4056 Basel; tel. 612673660; e-mail info@gegbasel .ch; internet www.gegbasel.ch; f. 1923; provides knowledge on topics in geography and anthropology; maintains contact with univs and cultural instns for research and training; 428 mems; Pres. Prof. Dr HARTMUT LESER; Hon. Pres. Dr GEORG BIENZ; Treas. HANSPETER MEIER; publs *Basler Beiträge zur Geographie* (irregular), *Basler Beiträge zur Physiogeographie* (irregular), *Regio Basiliensis* (3 a year).

Geographische Gesellschaft Bern (Geographical Society Bern): Hallerstr. 12, 3012 Bern; tel. 316318816; e-mail gb@giub.unibe .ch; internet www.swissgeography.ch/de/ members/ggb.php; f. 1873; attached to Verband Geographie Schweiz; organizes lectures, excursions; 300 mems; Pres. LEKTORIN ELISABETH BÄSCHLIN; Sec. MONIKA WÄLTI; publ. *Berner Geographische Mitteilungen* (1 a year), *Jahrbuch* (irregular).

Historische und Antiquarische Gesellschaft zu Basel: St. Alban-Vorstadt 5, 4002 Basel; tel. 612058605; e-mail a .salvisberg@merianstiftung.ch; internet pages.unibas.ch/hag; f. 1836; aims to revive intellectual life in Basel; promotes historical studies and knowledge; organizes lectures, seminars and excursions for mems; 450 mems; library of 30,000 vols; Pres. Lic. ANDRÉ SALVISBERG; publ. *Basler Zeitschrift für Geschichte und Altertumskunde* (1 a year).

Historischer Verein des Kantons Bern: c/o Universitätsbibliothek Bern, Münstergasse 61, 3000 Bern 8; tel. 316319203; e-mail christian.luethi@ub.unibe.ch; internet www.hvbe.ch; f. 1846; promotes studies, dissemination of information and discussions on history of Bern among its mems; organizes lectures, publs and excursions for mems; 1,000 mems; Pres. Lic. CHRISTIAN LÜTHI; Treas. SASCHA M. BURKHALTER; publs *Archiv des Historischen Vereins* (1 a year), *Berner Zeitschrift für Geschichte* (4 a year).

Historischer Verein des Kantons St Gallen: c/o Kantonsbibliothek Vadiana, Notkerstr. 22, 9000 St Gallen; e-mail info@hvsg .ch; internet www.hvsg.ch; f. 1859; supports projects on preservation and study of heritage; promotes dialogues on topical issues related to history; demonstrates diversity of cultural history to life through meetings, study tours and film clips; 500 mems; Pres. Dr CORNEL DORA; publs *Neujahrsblatt (NJBL)* (1 a year), *St Galler Kultur und Geschichte* (jtly with the Archives of Canton St Gallen).

Historischer Verein Obwalden: POB 1314, 6061 Sarnen; tel. 416606522; e-mail info@hvow.ch; internet www.hvow.ch; f. 1877, as Historisch-antiquarischer Verein von Obwalden; promotes understanding and interest in historical issues; preserves historic and ethnographic heritage in Canton; organizes publs, excursions and lectures;

Pres. VICTOR BIERI; Vice-Pres. NOTKER DILLIER; Treas. ANNELIS ROHRER; publ. *Obwaldner Geschichtsblätter*.

Schweizerische Gesellschaft für Geschichte/Société Suisse d'Histoire: Villettemattstr. 9, 3007 Bern; tel. 313813821; e-mail generalsekretariat@ sgg-ssh.ch; internet www.sgg-ssh.ch; f. 1841; promotes studies and training related to history; divided in 4 depts; defends professional interests of historians; rep. of historical br. to int. orgs; 1,400 mems; Pres. Prof. Dr REGINA WECKER; Vice-Pres. SACHA ZALA; Vice-Pres. MAURO CERUTTI; Gen. Sec. Dr ERIKA FLÜCKIGER STREBEL; Treas. MAX HAUCK; publs *ITINERA* (irregular), *Quellen zur Schweizergeschichte*, *Schweizerische Zeitschrift für Geschichte* (1 a year).

Schweizerische Gesellschaft für Kartographie/Société Suisse de Cartographie (Swiss Society of Cartography): Wolfgang-Pauli-Str. 15, 8093 Zürich; tel. 446333031; e-mail sgk@kartografie.ch; internet www .kartographie.ch; f. 1969; promotes training of theoretical and practical cartography; acts as platform for int. relations with cartographic instns; represents interests of mems; organizes workshops, professional internal training courses, exhibitions and confs; 310 mems; Pres. STEFAN ARN; Sec. STEFAN RÄBER; Treas. MARTIN PROBST; publs *Cartographica Helvetica* (2 a year), *Topographic Maps–Map Graphic and Generalization*.

Schweizerische Numismatische Gesellschaft/Société Suisse de Numismatique (Swiss Numismatic Society): c/o J.-P. Righetti, Route de Fribourg 54, 1724 Ferpicloz; tel. 264130216; e-mail schachernicole@gmx.ch; internet www .numisuisse.ch; f. 1879; promotes all branches of numismatic science through its publs dealing with classical, medieval and modern coins, paper money and medals; organizes annual numismatic days; 650 mems; Pres. Lic. HORTENSIA VON ROTEN; Vice-Pres. Dr MARKUS PETER; Sec. NICOLE SCHACHER; Treas. JEAN-PIERRE RIGHETTI; publs *Schweizerische Numismatische Rundschau* (1 a year), *Schweizer Münzblätter* (4 a year), *Schweizer Münzkatalog*, *Schweizer Studien zur Numismatik*, *Typos*.

Schweizerische Vereinigung für Altertumswissenschaft/Association Suisse pour l'Étude de l'Antiquité: Univ. Bern, Historisches Institut, Länggassstr. 49, 3000 Bern 9; tel. 313012326; e-mail thomas .spaeth@cgs.unibe.ch; internet www.sagw .ch/svaw.html; f. 1943; promotes research and teaching in all areas of classical studies; fosters int. relations with corresp. asscns; 200 mems; Pres. Prof. Dr THOMAS SPÄTH; Treas. Prof. Dr PIERRE SANCHEZ; publs *Museum Helveticum* (2 a year, online, www.sagw.ch/publikationen/museumhelveticum.html), *Schweizerische Beiträge zur Altertumswissenschaft* (online, www.sagw.ch/publikationen/beitraege-altertumswissenschaft.html).

Società Storica Locarnese: POB 1119, 6601 Locarno; e-mail info@ societastoricalocarnese.ch; internet www .societastoricalocarnese.ch; f. 1954; colln and conservation of documents relating to history of Locarno area; promotes study of history and art of ancient church in the region of Locarno (Locarno and Maggia); organizes exhibitions, confs, and lectures; 150 mems; Pres. RODOLFO HUBER; Vice-Pres. DAMIJANA GRAMIGNA; Sec. ERICA BARLOCCHI; Treas. EMMY FERRARI.

Société d'Egyptologie, Genève: POB 26, 1218 Grand-Saconnex; tel. 227910974; e-mail info@segweb.ch; internet www.segweb.ch; f.

1978; promotes study of Egyptology and related disciplines (coptology, Islamic studies, etc.); organizes confs, seminars and courses; supports research; 400 mems; library of 2,000 vols; Pres. Dr PHILIPPE GERMOND; Vice-Pres. Dr RODOLPHE KASSER; Vice-Pres. JEAN-LUC CHAPPAZ; Sec. SANDRA GUARNORI NICOLLIN; Treas. DANIEL NICOLLIN; publ. *Cahiers* (irregular).

Société d'Histoire de la Suisse Romande: Chemin du Cerisier 1, 1004 Lausanne; e-mail mail@shsr.ch; internet www.shsr.ch; f. 1837; supports historical and archaeological research; organizes seminars and visits; tries to foster interest in history of W Switzerland in public; 530 mems; library: see Bibliothèque Cantonale et Universitaire de Lausanne; Pres. ALAIN CLAVIEN; Vice-Pres. FRANÇOISE DUBOSSON.

Société d'Histoire et d'Archéologie de Genève: c/o Bibliothèque de Genève, 1211 Geneva 4; e-mail info@shag-geneve.ch; internet www.shag-geneve.ch; f. 1838; preserves historical and archaeological past of Geneva; promotes research and disseminates results through publs; 440 mems; library of 10,000 vols, 1,000 MSS; Pres. Dr. MATTHIEU DE LA CORBIÈRE; Pres. FRANÇOIS JACOB; Sec. MARTINE PIGUET; Treas. ANDRÉ WAGNIÈRE; publs *Bibliographie genevoise* (1 a year), *Cahiers, Mémoires et Documents*.

Société de Géographie de Genève: Route de Malagnou 1, CP 6434, 1211 Geneva 6; tel. 223798347; e-mail ruggero.crivelli@unige.ch; internet www.geographie-geneve.ch; f. 1858; promotes study, advancement and dissemination of geographical science in all its brs; 250 mems; Pres. CHRISTIAN MOSER; Vice-Pres. RENÉ ZWAHLEN; Sec. Dr RUGGERO CRIVELLI; Treas. CHRISTIANE OLSZEWSKI; publ. *Le Globe* (1 a year).

Société Vaudoise d'Histoire et d'Archéologie (Waldensian Society of History and Archaeology): 32, rue de la Mouline, 1022 Chavannes-près-Renens; tel. 213163711; e-mail info@svha-vd.ch; internet www .svha-vd.ch; f. 1902; preserves historic monuments in Canton of Vaud; encourages genealogical research; organizes confs, visits to monuments and exhibitions, excursions and study circles; 800 mems; Pres. LISE FAVRE; Treas. and Sec. RUTH LINIGER; publ. *Revue historique vaudoise* (1 a year).

Verband Geographie Schweiz/Association Suisse de Géographie (Association of Swiss Geographers): Geographisches Institut der Univ. Bern, Erlachstr. 9A, 3012 Bern; tel. 316318567; e-mail pbachmann@giub .unibe.ch; internet www.swissgeography.ch; f. 1990; coordinates 6 regional and 5 thematic socs, 8 univ. institutes; Central Cttee acts as nat. cttee of IGU; Pres. Prof. HANS-RUDOLF EGLI; Sec. Dr PHILIPP BACHMANN; publ. *GeoAgenda (Mitteilungsblatt der ASG)* (5 a year).

Vereinigung der Freunde Antiker Kunst/Association des Amis de l'Art Antique (Association of Friends of Classical Art): c/o Archäologisches Seminar der Universität, Schönbeinstr. 20, 4056 Basel; tel. 612673068; e-mail editor@antikekunst.ch; internet www.antikekunst.ch; f. 1956; promotes interest in classical archaeology; offers lectures, guided visits to exhibitions, trips to Classical sites; 6 regional groups in Basel, Berne-Bienne-Solothurn, Fribourg, Geneva, Lausanne and Zurich; 1,050 mems; Pres. Prof. Dr MARTIN GUGGISBERG; publ. *Antike Kunst* (1 a year).

LANGUAGE AND LITERATURE

Alliance Française de Zurich: Merkurstr. 34, 8032 Zürich; tel. 442619306; e-mail info@ afz.ch; internet www.afz.ch; f. 1883; offers

courses and exams in French language and culture and promotes cultural exchange with France; organizes confs, guided tours, lectures, cultural meetings; attached offices in Basel, Berne, Fribourg, Hermance, Locarno, Lucerne, Lugano, Lugnasco and St Gallen.

Autorinnen und Autoren der Schweiz AdS (Swiss Society of Writers): Konradstr. 61, 8031 Zürich; tel. 443500460; e-mail sekretariat@a-d-s.ch; internet www.a-d-s.ch; f. 2003; supports professional interests of writers in field of political, literary, linguistic and cultural asscn, in respect of copyright; creates relationships between AUTRIC, authors, translators, language regions and countries; 940 mems; Pres. RAPHAEL URWEIDER; Dir-Gen. NICOLE PFISTER FETZ.

British Council: Sennweg 2, POB 532, 3000 Bern 9; tel. 315603794; e-mail britishcouncil@britishcouncil.ch; internet www.britishcouncil.org/switzerland; offers courses and examinations in English language and British culture; promotes cultural exchange with the UK; Dir CAROLINE MORRISSEY; Deputy Dir SIMON BRIMBLECOMBE.

Centre PEN Suisse Romand (PEN Club of French-speaking Cantons of Switzerland): Ave Krieg 26, 1208 Grand Saconnex; tel. 227882231; e-mail ckrul@bluewin.ch; internet www.penromand.ch; f. 1949; defends freedom of expression and promotes int. cultural exchanges; promotes peace according to the PEN Charter; 70 mems; Pres. CLAUDE KRUL; Sec.-Gen. ZEKI ERGAS; Treas. ALFRED DE ZAYAS; publ. *Pages littéraires*.

Collegium Romanicum: c/o Yasmina Foehr-Janssens, Univ. de Genève, 5, rue de-Candolle, 1211 Genève; e-mail yasmina .foehr@lettres.unige.ch; internet www.sagw .ch/collegium-romanicum; f. 1947; study of Romance languages and literature; 200 mems; Pres. Prof. Dr YASMINA FOEHR-JANSSENS; Vice-Pres. Prof. Dr ANGELA FERRARI; Sec. Prof. Dr ALAIN CORBELLARI; publs *Romanica Helvetica*, *Versants* (2 a year), *Vox Romanica* (1 a year).

Deutschschweizer PEN-Zentrum: c/o Adi Blum, Burgunderstrasse 13A, 3018 Bern; tel. 796577771; e-mail office@pen-dschweiz.ch; internet www.pen-dschweiz.ch; f. 1979; promotes literature and freedom of expression; works by int. PEN charter; 80 mems; Pres. MICHAEL GUGGENHEIMER; Sec. ADI BLUM; publ. *Briefzeitung* (2 a year).

Gesellschaft für deutsche Sprache und Literatur in Zürich: c/o Deutsches Seminar, Schönberggasse 9, 8001 Zürich; e-mail gfdsl@ds.uzh.ch; internet www.ds.uzh.ch/ gfdsl; f. 1894; promotes research of linguistics and literary studies; offers courses and lectures; 230 mems; Pres. ZELJKO MEDVED.

Institut dal Dicziunari Rumantsch Grischun: Ringstr. 34, 7000 Chur; tel. 812846642; e-mail info@drg.ch; internet www.drg.ch; f. 1885; conservation and research into Romansh language; publ. of documented vocabulary of Romansh-speaking people of Switzerland; 1,000 mems; library of 18,000 vols; Pres. Dr CHRISTIAN COLLENBERG; Vice-Pres. CHASPER PULT; publs *Annalas* (1 a year), *Dicziunari Rumantsch Grischun* (2 a year).

Institut et Musée Voltaire: 25 rue des Délices, 1203 Geneva; tel. 224189560; e-mail institut.voltaire@ville-ge.ch; internet www .ville-ge.ch/imv; f. 1954; research centre, exhibitions, confs; library of 22,000 vols and MSS, 2,500 printed editions of Voltaire's writings; Curator FRANÇOIS JACOB; publs *La Gazette des Délices* (4 a year), *La Ligne d'ombre* (irregular).

Schweizerische Sprachwissenschaftliche Gesellschaft/Société Suisse de Linguistique: c/o Dr Britta Juska-Bacher Deutsches Seminar Universität Basel Nadelberg 4, 4051 Basel; e-mail britta .juska-bacher@unibas.ch; f. 1947; 207 mems; Pres. Prof. JACQUES MOESCHLER; Sec. Dr BRITTA JUSKA-BACHER; publs *Bulletin Vals-Asla* (2 a year), *Cahiers Ferdinand de Saussure.*

MEDICINE

Académie Suisse des Sciences Médicales/Schweizerische Akademie der Medizinischen Wissenschaften (Swiss Academy of Medical Sciences): Peterspl. 13, 4051 Basel; tel. 612699030; e-mail mail@ samw.ch; internet www.samw.ch; f. 1943; promotes professional training of scientists, esp. in clinical research; supports research in biomedical and clinical research; clarifies ethical questions in connection with medical devts and their effects on society; 160 mems; Pres. Prof. PETER SUTER; Vice-Pres. Prof. PETER MEIER-ABT; Vice-Pres. Prof. WALTER REINHARD; Gen. Sec. Dr HERMAN AMSTAD; Treas. Dr DIETER SCHOLER.

Schweizerische Gesellschaft für Chirurgie/Société Suisse de Chirurgie: Bahnhofstr. 55, 5001 Aarau; tel. 628362098; e-mail info@sgc-ssc.ch; internet www.sgc-ssc .ch; f. 1913; promotes scientific activity and generation of academics in field of surgery; rep. of professional interests of mems; 1,202 mems; Pres. Prof. Dr PHILIPPE MOREL; Vice-Pres. Prof. Dr RALPH A. SCHMID; Gen. Sec. Dr FRÉDÉRIC DUBAS; publ. *Swiss Surgery.*

Schweizerische Gesellschaft für Geschichte der Medizin und der Naturwissenschaften/Société Suisse d'Histoire de la Médecine et des Sciences Naturelles (Swiss Society for the History of Medicine and Sciences): c/o Prof. Hans Konrad Schmutz, Naturmuseum Winterthur, Museumstr. 52, 8400 Winterthur; tel. 522675166; e-mail hubert.steinke@mhi .unibe.ch; internet www.sggmn.ch; f. 1921; promotes history of medicine and sciences; supports young scientists and confers Henry E. Sigerist Prize for promotion of young scholars; 300 mems; Pres. Prof. Dr phil. HANS KONRAD SCHMUTZ; Vice-Pres. Dr Lic. IRIS RITZMANN; Sec. Dr HUBERT STEINKE; publ. *Gesnerus* (4 a year).

Schweizerische Gesellschaft für Innere Medizin/Société Suisse de Médecine Interne (Swiss Society of General Internal Medicine): POB 422, 4008 Bâle; Solothurnerstr. 68, 4053 Bâle; tel. 612259330; e-mail info@sgim.ch; internet www.sgim.ch; f. 1932; supports professional and economic interests of Swiss postgraduate internees of management, economics, communication and medical humanities; promotes internal medical research; encourages networking partnership of hospital and ambulatory medicine; 2,100 mems; Pres. Prof. VERENA BRINER; Sec.-Gen. Dr REGULA SIEVERS-FREY.

Schweizerische Gesellschaft für Orthopädie und Traumatologie/Société Suisse d'Orthopédie et de Traumatologie: 15 Ave des Planches, 1820 Montreux; tel. 219632139; e-mail office@cpconsulting.ch; internet www.sgosso.ch; f. 1942; present name 2006; promotes professional and economic interests of orthopaedic surgeons; promotes specialization in orthopaedics within field of research and teaching; 11 regional groups; 839 mems; Pres. Prof. Dr CHRISTIAN GERBER; Vice-Pres. Prof. Dr BERNHARD CHRISTEN; Sec. Dr THOMAS KEHL; Treas. Dr ANDREAS EGLI.

Schweizerischer Apothekerverband/ Société Suisse des Pharmaciens: Sta-tionsstr. 12, POB, 3097 Bern-Liebefeld; tel. 319785858; e-mail info@pharmasuisse.org; internet www.pharmasuisse.org; f. 1843; promotes interests of pharmacy in areas of teaching, research, policy and practice; 5,528 mems; Pres. DOMINIQUE JORDAN; Vice-Pres. PETER BURKARD; Vice-Pres. CHRISTIAN ROUVINEZ; publs *Apotheken-Handbuch* (1 a year), *Index Nominum, Pharmactuel* (6 a year), *Schweizer Apothekerzeitung* (24 a year).

NATURAL SCIENCES

General

Naturforschende Gesellschaft in Basel: c/o Nunzio Putrino, Gartenst. 2, 6300 Zug; tel. 797223913; e-mail sekretariat@ngib.ch; internet www.ngib.ch; f. 1817; promotes natural history; organizes lectures for semester programme; 600 mems; library of 74,000 vols; Pres. Prof. Dr ORESTE GHISALBA; Vice-Pres. Prof. Dr RETO BRUN; Sec. PUTRINO NUNZIO; Treas. Dr HANS-PETER SCHÄR; publ. *Mitteilungen der Naturforschenden Gesellschaften beider Basel.*

Naturforschende Gesellschaft in Bern: Universitätsbibliothek, Münstergasse 61, Postfach, 3000 Bern 8; tel. 313203231; e-mail info@ngbe.ch; internet www.ngbe.ch; f. 1786; attached to Universität Bern; spreads scientific thought and new knowledge from various fields of natural sciences; organizes lecture cycles, field trips; 300 mems; Pres. Dr MARCO HERWEGH; Vice-Pres. Prof. Dr GÜNTER BAARS; Sec. Dr KURT GROSSENBACHER; Treas. MATTHIAS HAUPT; publ. *Mitteilungen* (1 a year).

Naturwissenschaftliche Gesellschaft Winterthur: c/o Peter Lippuner, Geiselweidstr. 6, 8400 Winterthur; internet www .ngw.ch; f. 1884; lectures, field trips, publs of scientific articles to foster understanding of natural sciences; 660 mems; Pres. PETER LIPPUNER; Vice-Pres. Dr HANS KONRAD SCHMUTZ; Sec. Dr SABINE OERTLI; Treas. Dr URS BLUMER; publ. *Mitteilungen* (every 3 years).

Schweizerische Energie-Stiftung/Fondation Suisse pour l'Energie (Swiss Energy Foundation): Sihlquai 67, 8005 Zürich; tel. 442715464; e-mail info@ energiestiftung.ch; internet www .energiestiftung.ch; f. 1976; promotes energy policy suitable for human beings and environment and control of energy consumption; promotes alternative sources of energy and practice of conservation; 3,000 mems; Pres. GERI MÜLLER; Vice-Pres. DIETER KUHN; publs *Energie Umwelt* (4 a year), *SES-Reports* (irregular).

Schweizerische Stiftung für Alpine Forschungen/Fondation Suisse pour Recherches Alpines (Swiss Foundation for Alpine Research): Stadelhoferstr. 42, 8001 Zürich; tel. 442531200; e-mail mail@ alpinfo.ch; internet www.alpinfo.ch; f. 1939; supports scientific studies in field of mountains, mountain people and mountain sports; 11 mems; Pres. ETIENNE GROSS; Man. Dir THOMAS WEBER.

Società Ticinese di Scienze Naturali: c/o Museo cantonale di Storia naturale, viale Cattaneo 4, 6900 Lugano; tel. (91) 8154761; e-mail stsn-info@scnatweb.ch; internet stsn .ch; f. 1903; promotion and advancement of natural sciences; organizes confs, assembly, courses, exhibitions, excursions; promotes and supports activities of Cantonal Museum of Natural History and Biology Centre Alpine Piora; 400 mems; Pres. Dr M. TONOLLA; Sec. SIMONA CASATI; publ. *Memorie.*

Société de Physique et d'Histoire Naturelle de Genève: POB 6434, Route de Malagnou, 1211 Geneva 6; tel. 224186300; internet www.unige.ch/sphn; f. 1790; natural and exact sciences; organizes confs and excursions for mems; 195 mems; Pres. Dr MICHEL GRENON; Sec. ETIENNE CHAROLLAIS; publ. *Archives des sciences* (2 a year).

Société Vaudoise des Sciences Naturelles (Waldensian Society of Natural Sciences): Palais de Rumine, 1005 Lausanne; tel. 213124334; e-mail svsn@unil.ch; internet www.unil.ch/svsn; f. 1819; study, advancement and dissemination of natural sciences and related sciences; publ. of research in biology, geology, chemistry, physics, mathematics, and history and methodology of science; 600 mems; library: 1,000 periodicals in library reading-room: see also Bibliothèque Cantonale et Univ. de Lausanne; Pres. JACQUES SESIANO; Treas. JEAN-LUC EPARD; publ. *Mémoires* (irregular).

Biological Sciences

Bernische Botanische Gesellschaft (Bernese Botanical Society): Altenbergrain 21, 3013 Bern; tel. 316314938; e-mail steffen .boch@ips.unibe.ch; internet homepage .hispeed.ch/bebege; f. 1918; promotes private and business interest in vegetation science, plant ecology and floristics; organizes lectures on floristic, geobotanical and ecophysiological issues; 380 mems; Pres. STEFFEN BOCH; Sec. RITA GERBER; Treas. REGINE BLÄNKNER; publ. *Sitzungsberichte* (1 a year).

Schweizerische Botanische Gesellschaft/Société Botanique Suisse: Institute of Plant Sciences, University of Bern, Altenbergrain 21, 3013 Bern; tel. 316314928; internet www.botanica-helvetica .ch; f. 1889; encourages plant sciences and initiatives aimed at protecting flora, and conservation of its living environment; cultivates exchange of ideas and experiences and friendly relations between Swiss botanists; 700 mems; Pres. Prof. Dr MARKUS FISCHER; Vice-Pres. Prof. Dr PETER LINDER; Sec. CHRISTOPHE BORNAND; Treas. Dr STEFAN EGGENBERG; publ. *Alpine Botany* (2 a year).

Schweizerische Entomologische Gesellschaft/Société Entomologique Suisse: c/o Hannes Baur, Naturhistorisches Museum, Bernastr. 15, 3005 Bern; tel. 313507264; e-mail hannes.baur@nmbe.ch; internet seg.scnatweb.ch; f. 1858; studies Swiss entomological fauna; develops entomological knowledge; mems are professional or amateur entomologists; 10 local sections Alpstein, Basel, Bern, Freiburg, Geneva, Lucerne, Neuenburg, Waadt, Wallis and Zürich; 293 mems; library of 18,000 vols; Pres. Dr DENISE WYNIGER; Vice-Pres. Dr DANIEL BURCKHARDT; Sec. HANNES BAUR; publ. *Insecta Helvetica/Fauna Helvetica.*

Mathematical Sciences

Schweizerische Mathematische Gesellschaft/Société Mathématique Suisse (Swiss Mathematical Society): Mathematisches Institut, Universität Bern, Sidlerstr. 5, 3012 Bern; tel. 316318834; e-mail nicolas.monod@epfl.ch; internet www .math.ch; f. 1910; organizes confs and courses of mathematics at schools; 480 mems; Pres. BRUNO COLBOIS; Vice-Pres. CHRISTINE RIEDTMANN; Sec. and Treas. NICOLAS MONOD; publs *Commentarii Mathematici Helvetici* (4 a year), *Elemente der Mathematik* (4 a year).

Physical Sciences

Bundesamt für Meteorologie und Klimatologie (MeteoSchweiz) (Federal Office of Meteorology and Climatology (MeteoSwiss)): Krähbühlstr. 58, 8044 Zürich; tel. 442590111; internet www.meteoschweiz.ch; f. 1880, present name 1996; meteorological and climatological services; rep. of Switzerland in World Meteorological Org.; 3 regional centres, in Zurich, Geneva and Locarno; 296 mems; library of 40,000 vols; Dir DANIEL K. KEUERLEBER; Librarian GREGOR STORK; publs *Annalen, Arbeitsberichte der MeteoSchweiz, Veröffentlichung der MeteoSchweiz.*

Schweizerische Astronomische Gesellschaft/Société Astronomique Suisse (Swiss Astronomical Society): c/o Geri Hildebrandt, Mittlere Gstückstr. 14D, 8180 Bülach; tel. 448601221; e-mail ghildebrandt@hispeed.ch; internet www .astronomie.ch/sag; f. 1938; promotes exchanges of information related to astronomy between mems and gen. public; 2,400 mems; Pres. Dr WALTER KREIN; Vice-Pres. BEAT MÜLLER; Vice-Pres. RAOUL BEHREND; Sec. GERI HILDEBRANDT; publ. *Orion* (6 a year).

Schweizerische Chemische Gesellschaft/Societe Suisse de Chimie (Swiss Chemical Society): Schwarztorstr. 9, 3007 Bern; tel. 313104090; e-mail info@scg .ch; internet www.scg.ch; f. 1881 as Neue Schweizerische Chemische Gesellschaft, present name 2001; represents chemists and scientists of chemistry related fields in Switzerland and in int. orgs; 2,600 mems; Pres. Prof E. PETER KÜNDIG; Exec. Dir DAVID SPICHIGER; publ. *Chimia* (online (www.chimia.ch)).

Schweizerische Geologische Gesellschaft/Société Géologique Suisse (Swiss Geological Society): c/o Dr Gilles Borel, Musée cantonal de géologie, UNIL-L'Anthropole, 1015 Lausanne; tel. 216924474; e-mail gilles.borel@unil.ch; internet www.geolsoc.ch; f. 1882; promotes advancement of earth sciences by organizing meetings supported by SCNAT, and by annual reunions of spec. interest groups; 1,000 mems; Pres. Dr GILLES BOREL; Vice-Pres. Dr NEIL MANKTELOW; Treas. Dr ROGERR RÜTTI; Sec. Dr STEPHAN DELL'AGNOLO; publ. *Eclogae geologicae Helvetiae* (Swiss Journal of Geosciences, 3 a year).

Schweizerische Paläontologische Gesellschaft/Société Paléontologique Suisse (Swiss Palaeontological Society): Naturmuseum Solothurn Klosterpl. 2, 4500 Solothurn; tel. 326227021; e-mail sps@ scnatweb.ch; internet spg.scnatweb.ch; f. 1921; attached to Swiss Acad. of Sciences (SCNAT); organizes scientific symposia (Swiss Geoscience Meeting), short courses and guided excursions, annual assembly, awards Amanz Gressly-Award for outstanding contributions to Swiss palaeontology; addresses palaeontological questions from geological and biological points of view; 170 mems; Pres. Dr LIONEL CAVIN; Sec. SILVAN THÜRING; publ. *Swiss Journal of Geosciences* (jtly with Swiss Geological and Mineralogical Socs).

Schweizerische Physikalische Gesellschaft/Société Suisse de Physique (Swiss Physical Society): Dept. Physik, Klingelbergstr. 82, 4056 Basel; e-mail sps@unibas .ch; internet www.sps.ch; f. 1908; supports exchange of ideas within research community by offering workshops; SPS awards for outstanding achievements of young scientists; offers forum at interface of basic research and applied physics; 1,200 mems; Pres. Dr CHRISTOPHE ROSSEL; Vice-Pres. Dr ANDREAS SCHOPPER; Sec. Dr ANTOINE POCHELON; Treas. Dr PIERANGELO GRÖNING.

PHILOSOPHY AND PSYCHOLOGY

Schweizerische Gesellschaft für Psychologie/Société Suisse de Psychologie: Univ. of Bern, Dept of Psychology, Berne 9, Muesmattstr., 3000 Bern; tel. 789022695; e-mail sekretariat@ssp-sgp.ch; internet

www.ssp-sgp.ch; f. 1943; promotes scientific psychology in education, research and practice; protects professional interests of its mems; 560 mems; Pres. Prof. Dr SABINE SCZESNY (acting); Sec. HEIDI RUPRECHT; publ. *Swiss Journal of Psychology* (4 a year).

Schweizerische Philosophische Gesellschaft/Société Suisse de Philosophie: c/o Christophe Calame, 53 ave de Rumine, 1005 Lausanne; e-mail christophe .calame@bluewin.ch; internet www.sagw.ch/ philosophie; f. 1940; study and discussion of philosophical problems; organizes meetings; 800 mems; Pres. CHRISTOPHE CALAME; Vice-Pres. LEA BÄHLER; Sec. JULIA SCHEIDEGGER; Treas. Lic. HUBERT SCHNÜRIGER; publs *Studia philosophica* (1 a year), *Supplementa* (irregular).

Schweizerischer Berufsverband für Angewandte Psychologie/Association Professionnelle Suisse de Psychologie Appliquée: Vogelsangstr. 15, 8006 Zürich; tel. 432680405; e-mail info@sbap.ch; internet www.sbap.ch; f. 1952; rep. of professional interests of its members and interests of applied psychology; 1,000 mems; Pres. HEIDI AESCHLIMANN; Sec. MANUELA LISIBACH.

RELIGION, SOCIOLOGY AND ANTHROPOLOGY

Schweizerische Gesellschaft für Afrikastudien/Société Suisse d'Etudes Africaines: Postfach 8212, 3001 Bern; tel. 612672742; internet www.sagw.ch/africa; f. 1974; 200 mems; Co-Pres. Dr DANIEL KÜNZLER; Co-Pres. ANNE MAYOR; Sec. Dr VEIT ARLT.

Schweizerische Gesellschaft für Soziologie/Société Suisse de Sociologie (Swiss Sociological Association): c/o Marie-Eve Zufferey, Département de Sociologie, Université de Genève, Blvd du Pont d'Arve 40, 1211 Geneva; tel. 223798309; e-mail sss@unige.ch; internet www.sgs-sss.ch; f. 1955; represents interests of Swiss sociology in relation to scientific and political instns; 600 mems; Pres. Prof. ERIC D. WIDMER; Vice-Pres. Prof. Dr KURT IMHOF; Gen. Sec. Prof. Dr CHRISTOPH MAEDER; publ. *Schweizerische Zeitschrift für Soziologie/Revue suisse de sociologie/Swiss Journal of Sociology* (3 a year).

Schweizerische Gesellschaft für Volkskunde/Société Suisse des Traditions Populaires (Swiss Folklore Society): Spalenvorstadt 2, 4001 Basel; tel. 612671163; e-mail sgv-sstp@volkskunde.ch; internet www.volkskunde.ch; f. 1896; documents Swiss popular culture in its historical and current forms; supports and promotes ethnographic research; 740 mems; library of 63,545 vols; Pres. Dr MARIUS RISI; Sec. ERNST J. HUBER; Treas. HANS-ULRICH VOLLENWEIDER; publs *Schweizer Volkskunde* (3 a year), *Schweizerisches Archiv für Volkskunde* (2 a year).

Schweizerische Theologische Gesellschaft/Société Suisse de Théologie: c/o Prof. Dr Wolfgang Müller, Theologische Fakultät der Universiät Luzern, Gibraltarstr. 3, POB 7763, 6000 Luzern 7; tel. 412286635; e-mail wolfgang.mueller@ unilu.ch; internet www.sagw.ch/sthg; f. 1965; promotes technical and theological debate and scientific research; organizes theological seminars and confs; 272 mems; Pres. Prof. Dr WOLFGANG W. MÜLLER; Vice-Pres. Prof. Dr DENIS MÜLLER; Treas. Prof. Dr PIERRE BÜHLER; Sec. KATHERINE SIEGENTHALER.

Schweizerische Trachtenvereinigung/Fédération Nationale des Costumes Suisses (Swiss National Costume Association): Rosswiesstr. 29, POB 8608 Bubikon; tel. 552631563; e-mail info@ trachtenvereinigung.ch; internet www

.trachtenvereinigung.ch; f. 1926; maintains and renews different Swiss costumes, folk dance records and descriptions, folk songs, folk music and folk theatre and dialects; organizes projects and courses; 23,400 mems; Pres. ROLAND MEYER-IMBODEN; Vice-Pres. FRITZ BRAND; Vice-Pres. GÉRARD QUELOZ; publ. *Tracht und Brauch/Costumes et Coutumes* (4 a year).

TECHNOLOGY

Fachleute Geomatik Schweiz/Professionnels Geomatique Suisse (Swiss Association of Geomatics): c/o André Franziska, Flühlistr. 30B, 3612 Steffisburg; tel. 334381462; e-mail admin@pro-geo.ch; internet www.pro-geo.ch; f. 1929 as Verband Schweizerische Vermessungsfachleute, current name adopted 2005; supports interests of mems professionally and socially; provides apprenticeship training; 11 regional sections, in Aargau, Basel, Bern, Fribourg, E Switzerland, Rätia, Ticino, Valais, W Switzerland, Central Switzerland, Zürich; 1,318 mems; Pres. CATHY EUGSTER; Sec. and Treas. FRANZISKA ANDRÉ-HUBER; publ. *Geomatik Schweiz* (12 a year).

Schweizerische Gesellschaft für Automatik/Association Suisse pour l'Automatique (Swiss Federation of Automatic Control): SGA Sekretariat, Christl Vogel, Eggwilstr. 16A, 9552 Bronschhofen; tel. 719118416; e-mail sekretariat@sga-asspa.ch; internet www.sga-asspa.ch; f. 1956; promotes and develops knowledge of techniques of measurement, control and calculation, and their application in field of automation; 200 individual mems, 17 corporate mems; Pres. Dr JÜRG KELLER; Sec. CHRISTL VOGEL; publ. *Lernmodule* (4 a year).

Schweizerische Gesellschaft für Mikrotechnik/Association Suisse de Microtechnique: c/o FRSM, Ruelle DuPeyrou 4, CP 2353, 2001 Neuchâtel; tel. 327200900; e-mail asmt@fsrm.ch; internet www .sgmt-asmt.ch; f. 1962; promotes working in Swiss microtechnology enterprises and instns; offers engineering education in univs, engineering schools; organizes confs, lectures, courses and study tours; 73 mems; Pres. PHILIPP FISCHER; Sec. SUZANNE SCHWENDENER.

Schweizerischer Verband der Ingenieur-Agronomen und der Lebensmittel-Ingenieure/Association suisse des ingénieurs agronomes et des ingénieurs en technologie alimentaire: Länggasse 79, 3052 Zollikofen; tel. 319105075; e-mail svial@svial.ch; internet www.svial.ch; f. 1901; active in 5 areas: agricultural production and environment, food and nutrition, management of agricultural and food industry, training and consulting, govt and politics; promotes professional interests of its mems; 2,000 mems; Pres. NICOLAS FELLAY; Sec. ERNST BAUMANN; publ. *Journal* (4 a year).

Swiss Engineering-STV (Association of Engineers and Architects): Weinbergstr. 41, 8006 Zürich; tel. 442683711; e-mail info@ swissengineering.ch; internet www .swissengineering.ch; f. 1905; supports professional interests of mems; encourages engineering education and training and protection of traditional titles; 15,000 mems; Pres. MAURO PELLEGRINI; Sec.-Gen. STEFAN ARQUINT; publs *Revue Technique Suisse, Schweizerische Technische Zeitschrift, Swiss Engineering STZ/Swiss Engineering rts* (10 a year).

Verband Schweizer Abwasser- und Gewässerschutzfachleute/Association suisse des professionnels de la protection des eaux (Swiss Water Association):

Europastr. 3, Glattbrugg; tel. 433437070; e-mail sekretariat@vsa.ch; internet www.vsa.ch; f. 1944; promotes waste-water technology and water pollution control through advanced technical training for its mems through confs, courses and on-the-job exchanges; publication of standards and guidelines; 1,350 mems, 2,400 reps; Pres. WÜRSTEN MARTIN; Vice-Pres. CHAIX OLIVIER.

Research Institutes

GENERAL

European Journalism Observatory: Via G. Buffi 13, 6904 Lugano; tel. 586664126; e-mail ejo@lu.unisi.ch; internet it.ejo.ch; f. 2004; attached to Univ. della Svizzera italiana; promotes links between newsrooms and communications research by aiding media managers, analysts, editors and journalists; analyzes research and trends in media industry; Dir Dr STEPHAN RUSS-MOHL; Co-Dir MARCELLO FOA.

Institute of Management: Via G. Buffi 13, 6904 Lugano; internet www.ima.eco.unisi.ch; attached to Univ. della Svizzera italiana; research in different fields of management studies: strategic management, clusters and regional competitiveness, entrepreneurship and family business, public administration and health care management; programmes at undergraduate and postgraduate levels.

Istituto di Marketing e Comunicazione Aziendale (Institute of Marketing and Communication Management): Via G. Buffi 13, 6904 Lugano; tel. 586664756; e-mail ivan.snehota@usi.ch; internet www.imca.com.usi.ch; attached to Univ. della Svizzera italiana; scientific and applied research and teaching in field of corporate communication, information and communication management, marketing and organizational communication; Dir Prof. IVAN SNEHOTA.

Istituto Media e Giornalismo (Institute for Media and Journalism): Via G. Buffi 13, 6904 Lugano; tel. 586664738; e-mail imeg.com@usi.ch; internet www.imeg.com.usi.ch; attached to Univ. della Svizzera italiana; research and teaching activities on two constituent parts of communication: content (text) and their containers (media); main characteristics of media in historical, economic and social context; forms of access and use of media and methods of use content from a variety of audiences; strategies of instns and companies dealing with nat. and int. media; Dir GIUSEPPE RICHERI; Co-Dir STEPHAN RUSS-MOHL.

Laboratorio di Storia delle Alpi (Laboratory of History of the Alps): Largo Bernasconi 2, 6850 Mendrisio; tel. 586665819; e-mail labisalp.arc@usi.ch; internet www.arc.usi.ch/labisalp; f. 2000; attached to Univ. della Svizzera italiana; research on alpine space, in its cultural, demographic, economic, social and political aspects; Head LUIGI LORENZETTI; Sec. MONICA BANCALÀ; publ. *Histoire des Alpes / Storia delle Alpi / Geschichte der Alpen* (1 a year).

AGRICULTURE, FISHERIES AND VETERINARY SCIENCE

Office Fédéral de l'Agriculture/Bundesamt für Landwirtschaft (Federal Office for Agriculture): Ministry of Public Economy, Mattenhofstr. 5, 3003 Bern; tel. 313222511; e-mail info@blw.admin.ch; internet www.blw.admin.ch; centre for federal agricultural research; promotes multifunctional agriculture; implements decisions taken by electorate, Swiss parliament and govt and plays active role in formulating agricultural policy;

Dir-Gen. Dr MANFRED BÖTSCH; Deputy Dir Dr JACQUES CHAVAZ; publs *Agrarforschung* (12 a year), *Revue suisse d'agriculture* (12 a year).

Federal Agricultural Research Stations:

Agroscope: Route de Duillier, POB 1012, 1260 Nyon 1; tel. 223634444; e-mail info@faw.admin.ch; internet www.agroscope.admin.ch; agricultural research for sustained economic activity in agricultural, nutritional and environmental sectors; develops scientific knowledge and technical principles for agricultural and environmental policy decisions and their legal implementation; Dir of Agroscope Changins-Wädenswil Dr JEAN-PHILIPPE MAYOR; Dir of Agroscope Liebefeld-Posieux-Haras Dr MICHAEL GYSI; Dir of Agroscope Reckenholz-Tänikon Dr PAUL STEFFEN; publs *Agrarforschung Schweiz / Recherche Agronomique Suisse*, *ALP aktuell*, *Revue suisse de viticulture arboriculture horticulture*, *Schweizer Zeitschrift für Obst- und Weinbau*.

ARCHITECTURE AND TOWN PLANNING

Fondazione Archivio del Moderno (Archive of the Modern): Largo Bernasconi 2, 6850 Mendrisio; tel. 586665500; e-mail archivio.arc@usi.ch; internet www.arc.usi.ch/archivio.htm; f. 1996; ind. research institute supporting Acad. of Architecture of Mendrisio, reinforcing its teaching and scholarly activities; acquisition, protection, preservation and exploitation of archives of architecture, urban planning, engineering, design, art and photography; promotes scientific research in fields of history of modern and contemporary architecture, art, design, territory and civil engineering, recognizing their leading role in current state of society; Dir LETIZIA TEDESCHI; Deputy Dir NICOLA NAVONE.

Istituto di Ricerca per il Progetto Urbano Contemporaneo (Institute for the Contemporary Urban Project): Largo Bernasconi 2, 6850 Mendrisio; e-mail i.cup@arch.unisi.ch; internet www.arch.unisi.ch/ris_ist_icup; f. 2004; attached to Univ. della Svizzera italiana; research studies on grounds of quantitative parameters: economic capacity of territory, effect of new infrastructures, energetic consumption, mobility, re-use of existing architectures, sustainability, transport; Dir Prof. JOSEP ACEBILLO.

ECONOMICS, LAW AND POLITICS

Center for Comparative and International Studies (CIS) Zürich: Haldeneggsteig 4, 8092 Zürich; tel. 446326385; e-mail cispostmaster@gess.ethz.ch; internet www.cis.ethz.ch; f. 1997; research centre for comparative politics and int. relations; fosters cooperation in research and education; organizes research seminars, workshops and public events with leading academics and political practitioners; topics of research: democracy, political violence, markets and politics, and sustainable devt; Dir Prof. LARS-ERIK CEDERMAN; Vice-Dir Prof. MARCO STEENBERGEN.

Institut Suisse de Droit Comparé/Schweizerisches Institut für Rechtsvergleichung (Swiss Institute of Comparative Law): 1015 Lausanne; tel. 216924911; e-mail info@isdc.ch; internet www.isdc.ch; f. 1982; attached to Federal Dept of Justice and Police; provides Fed. Govt with documents and studies necessary for legislation and for conclusion of int. conventions; participates in int. efforts towards unification of law; gives information and consultations to courts, admins, attorneys and interested persons; conducts its own scientific research, pro-

motes and coordinates studies in Swiss univs and provides researchers in Switzerland with appropriate centre for study; library: see under Libraries and Archives; Dir Prof. Dr CHRISTINA SCHMID (acting); Vice-Dir Dr LUKAS HECKENDORN URSCHELER.

Institute of Economics: Via G. Buffi 13, 6904 Lugano; tel. 586664783; e-mail marisa.clemenz@usi.ch; internet www.idep.eco.usi.ch; f. 1998; attached to Univ. della Svizzera italiana; research in fields of public economics and public management; offers graduate and postgraduate courses; Dir MASSIMO FILIPPINI.

Institute of Finance: Via G. Buffi 13, 6904 Lugano; tel. 586664752; e-mail abf.istfin.eco@usi.ch; internet www.istfin.eco.usi.ch; f. 1999; attached to Univ. della Svizzera italiana; research about quantitative and institutional themes of financial markets; offers postgraduate studies; Dir GIOVANNI BARONE-ADESI.

Istituto di Diritto (Institute of Law): Via G. Buffi 13, 6904 Lugano; tel. 586664627; e-mail marco.borghi@usi.ch; internet www.idusi.eco.usi.ch; attached to Univ. della Svizzera italiana; offers postgraduate training and interdisciplinary activities; research in field law in Ticino; organizes exhibitions; Dir MARCO BORGHI.

Istituto di Ricerche Economiche (Institute for Economic Research): Via Maderno 24, CP 4361, 6904 Lugano; tel. 586664661; e-mail ire.eco@usi.ch; internet www.ire.eco.usi.ch; attached to Univ. della Svizzera italiana; research on various aspects of regional and urban economics, ranging from regional growth and devt to competitiveness and innovation and from labour market issues to transportation and mobility; Dir RICO MAGGI; Vice-Dir SIEGFRIED ALBERTON.

Schweizerisches Institut für Auslandforschung/Institut Suisse de Recherches Internationales (Swiss Institute of International Studies): Frau Anja Spring Augustinerhof 1, 8001 Zürich; tel. 442121313; e-mail info@siaf.ch; internet www.siaf.ch; f. 1943; attached to Univ. Zürich; deals with current issues in the fields of politics, economy, society, science and culture and selects qualified and internationally renowned speakers; gives SIAF Award for outstanding theses, Licentiate and Masters theses at Univ. and ETH Zurich; Pres. KASPAR VILLIGER; Vice-Pres. Dr MARTIN MEYER; Treas. JOSEF MEIER; publ. *Sozialwissenschaftliche Studien* (1 a year).

EDUCATION

Institut de Recherche et de Documentation Pédagogique: Faubourg de l'Hôpital 43–45, CP 556, 2002 Neuchâtel; tel. 328898600; e-mail secretariat@irdp.ch; internet www.irdp.ch; f. 1970; research in French-speaking Switzerland, into educational methods, organization and administration; creation and analysis of teaching aids; document; library of 10,000 vols; Dir MATTHIS BEHRENS; publ. *Le point sur la recherche* (irregular).

Institut Européen de l'Université de Genève: rue Jean-Daniel Colladon 2, 1204 Genève; tel. 223797850; internet www.unige.ch/ieug; f. 1963; directs, coordinates and promotes educational programmes in European studies and research on Europe in interdisciplinary perspective; organizes symposia, seminars, workshops and confs; library of 18,000 vols, 25,000 monographs, 92 periodicals; Dir Prof. NICOLAS LEVRAT; Librarian JEAN-MARC MEMBREZ; publ. *Euryopa*.

Istituto di Studi Italiani: Via Lambertenghi 10A, 6904 Lugano; tel. 586664700; e-mail ism.com@usi.ch; internet www.isi.com.usi .ch; f. 2007; attached to Univ. della Svizzera italiana; offers graduate, postgraduate, doctoral studies in language, Italian literature and culture; scientific research projects in tradition of Italian studies; Dir Prof. CARLO OSSOLA.

HISTORY, GEOGRAPHY AND ARCHAEOLOGY

Institut d'Histoire de la Réformation: rue de-Candolle 5, 1211 Geneva 4; tel. 223797128; e-mail marlene.jaouich@unige .ch; internet www.unige.ch/ihr; f. 1969; attached to Univ. de Genève; promotes research and postgraduate studies in history of ideas, instns and practices of reformation; Dir Prof. MARIA-CRISTINA PITASSI; Sec. MARLÈNE JAOUICH; Sec. LORRAINE DUBUIS.

LANGUAGE AND LITERATURE

Institut de langue et civilisation françaises (Institute of French Language and Civilization): Faubourg de l'Hôpital 61–63, 2000 Neuchâtel; tel. 327181800; e-mail ilcf .ce@unine.ch; internet www2.unine.ch/ilcf; f. 1892; attached to Univ. of Neuchâtel; research centre specialized in teaching French; Dir PHILIPPE TERRIER; Sec. BRIGITTE STEINER.

Istituto di Argomentazione, Linguistica e Semiotica (Institute of Argumentation, Linguistics and Semiotics): Via G. Buffi 13, 6904 Lugano; tel. 586664791; e-mail ials .com@usi.ch; internet www.ials.com.usi.ch; attached to Univ. della Svizzera italiana; research related to argumentation, argumentation in context (esp. in finance, media and advertising), speech communication, pragmatics of discourse and dialogue, intercultural communication, linguistic structures and processes of interpretation of texts, multimodality; Dir Prof. Dr ANDREA ROCCI.

MEDICINE

Centre Interfacultaire de Gérontologie (Interfaculty Centre for Gerontology): route de Acacias 54, 1227 Acacias; tel. 223793790; e-mail cig@unige.ch; internet cig.unige.ch; f. 1992; attached to Univ. de Genève; research on various aspects of ageing, vulnerability and life course; Dir Prof. MICHEL ORIS.

Institut für Bio- und Medizinethik (IBMB) (Institute for Biomedical Ethics): Universität Basel, Bernoullistr. 28, 4056 Basel; tel. 612671786; e-mail admin-ibmb@ unibas.ch; internet ibmb.unibas.ch; f. 2011; attached to Univ. of Basel; areas of research: biobanking and data-sharing, clinical ethics support, confidentiality and disclosure of information, dual-use research, neuroethics, open disclosure, research ethics, tobacco use in Swiss prisons; library of 3,000 vols; Head of Institute Prof. Dr BERNICE SIMONE ELGER.

Institute of Communication and Health: Via G. Buffi 6, 6904 Lugano; tel. 586664487; e-mail teresa.cafaro@usi.ch; internet www .ich.com.usi.ch; attached to Univ. of Lugano; theoretical and applied researches for preservation and improvement of individual health; organizes social and organizational programmes for promotion of health, wellness and health policy; offers postgraduate educational programmes in health communication and management; Dir Dr PETER J. SCHULZ; Admin. Man. TERESA CAFARO.

ISGF–Schweizer Institut für Sucht- und Gesundheits- forschung Zürich (Swiss Research Institute for Public Health and Addiction): Konradstr. 32, POB, 8031 Zürich; tel. 444481160; e-mail isgf@isgf.uzh.ch;

internet www.isgf.uzh.ch; f. 1993; attached to Univ. of Zurich; research and service sectors, covering legal and illegal drugs, non substance-related addictive behaviour, health-planning and economics, consulting and assessments and transfer of knowledge through training; Scientific Dir Dr MICHAEL SCHAUB; Man. Dir CLAUDIA ZWEIFEL.

Schweizerisches Institut für Allergie- und Asthmaforschung (Swiss Institute of Allergy and Asthma Research): Obere Str. 22, 7270 Davos; tel. 814100848; e-mail siaf@ siaf.uzh.ch; internet www.siaf.uzh.ch; f. 1988; attached to Univ. of Zurich; applied and basic research in field of allergies and asthma; Dir Prof. Dr CEZMI A. AKDIS.

Schweizerisches Tropen- und Public Health-institut (Swiss TPH)/Institut Tropical et de Santé Publique Suisse (Swiss Tropical and Public Health Institute): Socinstr. 57, 4051 Basel; Socinstr. 55a, Eulerstr. 54, 68, 77 4051 Basel; tel. 612848111; e-mail library-tph@unibas.ch; internet www.swisstph.ch; f. 1943, present name 2010; provides teaching, research and services in field of int. health devt; library of 7,000 vols, 80 journals, 9,000 monographs, annual reports, reprints, course programs and theses; Pres. Prof. Dr FELIX GUTZWILLER; Vice-Dir JÖRG H. SCHWARZENBACH; Dir Prof. Dr MARCEL TANNER; Deputy Dir NICOLAUS LORENZ; Deputy Dir NINO KÜNZLI.

NATURAL SCIENCES

General

Collegium Basilea (Institute of Advanced Study): Hochstr. 51, 4053 Basel; tel. 765245846; e-mail info@colbas.org; internet www.colbas.org; f. 1999; supports interdisciplinary postdoctoral research, mainly in biological, physical and chemical sciences, with emphasis on physico-chemical foundations of living systems and in applications of complexity theory; library of 7,000 vols; Pres. Prof. Dr JEREMY J. RAMSDEN; publs *Journal of Biological Physics and Chemistry* (4 a year), *Nanotechnology Perceptions* (3 a year).

High Altitude Research Stations Jungfraujoch & Gornergrat Int: Sidlerstr. 5, 3012 Bern; tel. 316314052; e-mail louise .wilson@space.unibe.ch; internet www .ifjungo.ch; f. 1930; high-altitude research in solar astronomy, astrophysics, environmental sciences, atmospheric physics, atmospheric chemistry, glaciology, meteorology, physics and biology; international foundation run by scientific organizations of Austria, Belgium, Germany, Italy, Switzerland and the UK; Hon. Pres. Prof. Dr HANS BALSIGER; Pres. Prof. Dr ERWIN O. FLÜCKIGER; Treas. KARL MARTIN WYSS; Dir Prof. Dr MARKUS LEUENBERGER; publ. *Review on Activity*.

Space Center: Station 11, 1015 Lausanne; tel. 216936948; e-mail space.center@epfl.ch; internet space.epfl.ch; attached to Ecole Polytechnique Fédérale de Lausanne; promotes space technology across science, education and industry; Dir Prof. HERBERT SHEA.

Staatssekretariat für Bildung und Forschung SBF/Secretariat d'Etat à l'education et à la recherche SER (State Secretariat for Education and Research SER): Hallwylstr. 4, 3003 Bern; tel. 313229691; e-mail info@sbf.admin.ch; internet www.sbf.admin.ch; f. 1969; prepares policy decisions for education and science and executes scientific policy; coordinates activities of Fed. bodies concerned with research and education; supports univs and other institutes of higher education and contributes to grants; is responsible for encouragement and general coordination of research and higher education; with other depts deals with int. scientific affairs; Dir

MAURO DELL'AMBROGIO; Deputy Dir JÜRG BURRI.

Stiftung für Humanwissenschaftliche Grundlagenforschung/Fondation pour la Recherche de Base dans les Sciences de l'Homme: Kirchgasse 42, 8001 Zürich; tel. 443830922; e-mail info@ academia-engelberg.ch; f. 1970; basic research in human sciences; Pres. Prof. JULES ANGST; Dir Dr WALTER BODMER.

Biological Sciences

Centre d'Imagerie BioMedicale (Centre for Biomedical Imaging): Station 6, 1015 Lausanne; tel. 216934467; e-mail info@cibm .ch; internet www.cibm.ch; attached to Ecole Polytechnique Fédérale de Lausanne; research on understanding of biomedical processes in health and disease, focusing on mechanisms of normal functioning, pathogenic mechanisms, characterization of disease onset prior to structural damage, metabolic and functional consequences of gene expression, and non-invasive insights into disease processes under treatment; Dir Prof. ROLF GRUETTER.

Conservatoire et Jardin botaniques de la Ville de Genève: POB 60, 1292 Chambésy; tel. 224185100; e-mail periodiques.cjb@ ville-ge.ch; internet www.ville-ge.ch/cjb; f. 1817; systematic botany, taxonomy, floristics, ecology, phytogeography; research in plant systematics, floristics, and population genetics; library of 100,000 vols, 4,429 periodicals (1,495 current); Dir Prof. PIERRE-ANDRÉ LOIZEAU; publs *Boissiera*, *Candollea*.

Universität Bern Institut für Pflanzenwissenschaften (Institute of Plant Sciences (IPS)): Altenbergrain 21, 3013 Bern; tel. 316314911; e-mail ipsinfo@ips.unibe.ch; internet www.ips.unibe.ch; f. 1862; attached to Univ. of Bern; consists of 6 ind. research sections; research covers vegetation ecology, plant ecology, paleoecology, molecular ecology and plant devt, plant breeding, plant nutrition, molecular physiology; teaching at all academic levels; receives c. one-third of budget from the Swiss Nat. Science Foundation, EU and other orgs; Dir Prof. Dr MARKUS FISCHER; Sec. HELGA RODRÍGUEZ..

Botanic Garden:

    Botanischer Garten Bern: Altenbergrain 21, 3013 Bern; tel. 316314945; e-mail info@botanischergarten.ch; internet boga.unibe.ch; f. 1859; Dir Prof. Dr MARKUS FISCHER.

Mathematical Sciences

Centre Interfacultaire Bernoulli (Bernoulli Interfaculty Centre of Mathematics): Station 15, 1015 Lausanne; tel. 216932583; internet cib.epfl.ch; attached to Ecole Polytechnique Fédérale de Lausanne; organizes programmes and symposiums related to research in field of mathematics; Dir TUDOR RATIU.

Physical Sciences

Centre Universitaire d'Ecologie Humaine et des Sciences de l'Environnement: route de Drize 7, 1227 Carouge; tel. 223790875; internet www.unige.ch/ecohum; f. 1976, present status 2008; attached to Univ. de Genève; research and teaching in natural and social sciences; Dir B. BÜRGENMEIER; publ. *journées du cuepe*.

Eidgenössische Forschungsanstalt für Wald, Schnee und Landschaft (Swiss Federal Institute for Forest, Snow and Landscape Research): Zürcherstr. 111, 8903 Birmensdorf; tel. 447392111; e-mail wslinfo@wsl .ch; internet www.wsl.ch; attached to ETH Zurich; concerned with use, devt and protection of natural and urban spaces; maintains experimental and research plots for studying rock fall or debris flow, study areas for monitoring effects of climate change on forests and sites damaged by storms or fires for investigating impact of natural hazards; library of 16,000 vols, 4,000 maps of Switzerland, 1,500 journals, 3,000 ejournals; Dir Prof. Dr JAMES KIRCHNER; Deputy Dir Dr CHRISTOPH HEGG.

Institut für Astronomie: ETH Zürich, Wolfgang-Pauli-Str. 27, 8093 Zürich; tel. 446337608; e-mail marcella@phys.ethz.ch; internet www.astro.phys.ethz.ch; f. 1864; attached to ETH Zürich; research on astronomy and astrophysics; Chair. Prof. Dr MARCELLA CAROLLO; Vice-Chair. Prof. MICHAEL MEYER.

Observatoire Astronomique de l'Université de Genève: 51 Ch. des Maillettes, 1290 Geneva; tel. 223792200; e-mail gilbert .burki@obs.unige.ch; internet www.unige.ch/ sciences/astro; f. 1772; attached to Univ. de Genève; astronomy, astrophysics research; 115 mems; library of 6,000 vols, 500 periodicals; Dir Prof. STÉPHANE UDRY; Librarian CLAUDE GUIDI.

Schweizerische Gesellschaft für Astrophysik und Astronomie/Société Suisse d'Astrophysique et d'Astronomie (Swiss Society for Astrophysics and Astronomy): Observatoire de Genève 51, Ch. des Maillettes, 1290 Geneva; e-mail georges.meynet@ unige.ch; internet obswww.unige.ch/ssaa; f. 1968; research in astrophysics and astronomy; training of researchers through courses; Pres. Prof. DANIEL SCHAERER; Vice-Pres. MICHAEL MEYER; Treas. Dr YANN ALIBERT; Sec. Prof. GEORGES MEYNET.

Specola Solare Ticinese, Locarno (Solar Observatory Ticinese, Locarno): Via ai Monti 146, CP 71, 6605 Locarno 5; tel. 917562379; e-mail cagnotti@gmail.com; internet www .specola.ch; f. 1957; solar observation; determination of Wolf number; data collected sent regularly to SIDC; library of 600 vols; Pres. Prof. Dr PHILIPPE JETZER; Dir Dr MARCO CAGNOTTI (acting); publ. *MERIDIANA* (6 a year).

WSL-Institut für Schnee- und Lawinenforschung (SLF) (WSL Institute for Snow and Avalanche Research): Flüelastr. 11, 7260 Davos Dorf; tel. 814170111; e-mail contact@ slf.ch; internet www.slf.ch; f. 1936; attached to Swiss Federal Institute for Forest, Snow and Landscape Research; research on physics and mechanics of snow and snow pack, avalanche formation and mechanics, protective structure, snow and avalanche interaction with forests, and an avalanche warning service; library of 20,000 vols; Dir Prof. Dr JAMES KIRCHNER; Deputy Dir Dr CHRISTOPH HEGG; publs *Mitteilungen, Unfallberichte, Winterbericht* (1 a year).

Libraries and Archives

Aarau

Aargauer Kantonsbibliothek (Aargau Cantonal Library): Aargauerplatz, 5000 Aarau; tel. 628352362; e-mail kantonsbibliothek@ag.ch; internet www.ag .ch/kantonsbibliothek; f. 1803; oldest document is written parchment from early 9th century; specializes in designed humanities; spec. collns: Zurlaubiana (history of Switzerland and Europe), Frank Wedekind archive; 727,000 vols, 2,000 periodicals, 850 incunabula, 1,500 MSS; Dir Dr RUTH WÜST.

Staatsarchiv Aargau (State Archives of Aargau): Entfelderstr. 22, 5001 Aarau; tel. 628351290; e-mail staatsarchiv@ag.ch; internet www.ag.ch/staatsarchiv; f. 1803;

records of 1027 to 1803 and systematic documentation of the admin. since the founding of Canton; divided into dept; 130,000 entries; 70,000 records in Govt Council resolutions from 1971 to 1996, consisting of title and description; State Archivist Lic. ANDREA VOELLMIN; Sec. ANITA MÜLLER.

Basel

Allgemeine Bibliotheken der Gesellschaft für das Gute und Gemeinnützige: Im Schmiedenhof 10, 4051 Basel; tel. 612641111; e-mail info@ stadtbibliothekbasel.ch; internet www .stadtbibliothekbasel.ch; f. 1807; 290,000 vols; central library and 8 br. libraries; Dir KLAUS EGLI; Vice-Dir MARIE-THÉRÈSE BANDERA.

Archiv für Schweizerische Kunstgeschichte: Im Laurenz-Bau, St. Alban-Graben 8, Postfach, 4010 Basel; tel. 612066292; e-mail info-kunsthist@unibas .ch; internet kunsthist.unibas.ch/seminar/ archiv-fuer-schweizerische-kunstgeschichte; attached to Universitätsgut; illustrations of monuments, works of painting, sculpture and ancient and modern decorative arts, literature on Swiss art history as reference library, projection images; 6,000 vols; Dir NIKLAUS MEIER.

Bibliothek des Museums der Kulturen Basel (Library of the Museum of Basel Culture): Münsterplatz 20, 4051 Basel; tel. 612665630; e-mail mkb.biblio@bs.ch; internet www.mkb.ch; f. 1901; specialized literature on ethnology in areas dealt with by museum's collns, and scientific history of ethnology; 96,000 vols, 320 journals; Chief Librarian ANGELIKA KUTTER; Librarian JAGODA DESPOTOVIC.

Schweizerisches Wirtschaftsarchiv/ Archives Economiques Suisses (Swiss Economic Archives): Peter Merian-Weg 6, 4002 Basel; tel. 612673219; e-mail info@ wwzb.unibas.ch; internet www.ub.unibas.ch/ wwz-bibliothek-swa; f. 1910; nat. centre for economic information and economic history; open to gen. public; 650,000 vols, incl. business reports, periodicals, statistical publs, reports on social instns and professional socs; 2.5m. newspaper cuttings; Dir IRENE AMSTUTZ; Sec. BARBARA DÜRR.

Staatsarchiv Basel-Stadt: Martinsgasse 2, 4001 Basel; tel. 612678601; e-mail stabs@bs .ch; internet www.staatsarchiv.bs.ch; history of canton of Basel and its communities; Dir Lic. ESTHER BAUR; publ. *Quellen und Forschungen zur Basler Geschichte*.

Universitätsbibliothek Basel (University Library of Basel): Schönbeinstr. 18–20, 4056 Basel; tel. 612673100; e-mail info-ub@unibas .ch; internet www.ub.unibas.ch; f. 1460; 3.3m. vols, scientific works, 10,000 musical MSS, 3,000 incunabula, 35,000 topographic maps, 100,000 reproductions of portraits; Dir HANNES HUG; Vice-Dir FELIX WINTER; publs *Die Amerbachkorrespondenz, Die Matrikel der Universität Basel, Die mittelalterlichen Handschriften der Universitätsbibliothek Basel*.

Bern

Bibliothek des Musikschule Konservatorium Bern: Kramgasse 36, 3011 Bern; e-mail office@konsibern.ch; internet www .konsibern.ch; f. 1917; 50,000 vols; Pres. ANNAMARIE ZINSLI.

Burgerbibliothek Bern/Bibliothèque de la Bourgeoisie de Berne (Burger Library Bern): Hallwylstr. 15, Postfach 135, 3000 Bern 6; tel. 313203333; e-mail bbb@ burgerbib.ch; internet www.burgerbib.ch; f. 1951; medieval MSS, Bongarsiana-Codices, documents concerning Swiss and Bernese

history and bequests of Albrecht von Haller and Jeremias Gotthelf; acts as archival capacity for Burgergemeinde (civic community), guilds and Burgers' socs; 15,000 vols, 50 periodicals, 2,700 m of historical MSS, of which 50 m medieval MSS; Dir Dr CLAUDIA ENGLER; Sec. ANNELIES HÜSSY; publs *Passepartout, Schriften der Burgerbibliothek Bern*.

Schweizerische Nationalbibliothek/Bibliothèque Nationale Suisse (Swiss National Library): Hallwylstr. 15, 3003 Bern; tel. 584628935; e-mail info@nb.admin .ch; internet www.nb.admin.ch; f. 1895; contains all publs issued in Switzerland and foreign publs by Swiss authors or concerning Switzerland; Swiss union catalogue, SwissInfoDesk, Swiss Literary Archives, Prints and Drawings Dept, Swiss ISSN Centre, Centre Dürrenmatt Neuchâtel; 5.6m. vols, incl. 2.9m. books, 836,251 bound vols of periodicals, 475,864 engravings, photos and maps, 77,448 musical publs, 20,437 microforms and CD-ROMs, 20,428 audiovisual items, 24,111 online publs, 326 collns in the Swiss Literary Archives, 78 collns in the Prints and Drawings Dept; Dir MARIE-CHRISTINE DOFFEY; Vice-Dir ELENA BALZARDI; publs *Bibliographie der Schweizergeschichte/Bibliographie de l'histoire Suisse/Bibliografia Della Storia Svizzera, The Swiss Book/Le Livre Suisse/Das Schweizer Buch/Il Libro Svizzero* (24 a year), *Quarto (Zeitschrift des Schweizerischen Literaturarchivs/Revue des Archives Littéraires Suisses/Rivista dell'Archivio Svizzero di Letteratura/Revista da l'Archiv Svizzer da Litteratura)*.

Schweizerisches Bundesarchiv (Swiss Federal Archives): Archivstr. 24, 3003 Bern; tel. 313228989; e-mail bundesarchiv@bar .admin.ch; internet www.bar.admin.ch; f. 1798; appraises, secures, describes and provides access to archive-worthy records of Swiss Confederation; Dir ANDREAS KELLERHALS; Deputy Dir P. KUNZLER.

Staatsarchiv des Kantons Bern: Falkenpl. 4, POB 8424, 3001 Bern; tel. 316335101; e-mail info.stab@sta.be.ch; internet www.sta.be.ch/staatsarchiv; collects, registers and preserves canton's archival heritage; microfilms of parish registers; State Archivist Dr PETER MARTIG; Sec. MADLEN TANNER; publ. *Das Staatsarchiv des Kantons Bern*.

Universitätsbibliothek Bern: Münstergasse 61, 3000 Bern 8; tel. 316319211; e-mail info@ub.unibe.ch; internet www.ub .unibe.ch; f. 1528; 50 br. libraries; 4.6m. vols, 17,000 online journals; Chief Librarian MARIANNE RUBLI SUPERSAXO.

Bubendorf

Fondation Bibliotheca Afghanica (Afghanistan Institute in Switzerland): Bruehlstr. 2, 4416 Bubendorf; tel. 619339877; e-mail info@afghanistan-institut .ch; internet www.phototheca-afghanica.ch; f. 1975; research institute and archive; Afghani nature, culture and contemporary history; material on Afghan history, geography, ethnography, religion and politics; German newspaper clippings; Mujahideen and Communist govt publs; 19,000 vols, 60,000 photographs; Dir PAUL BUCHERER-DIETSCHI.

Chur

Staatsarchiv Graubünden: Karlihofpl., 7001 Chur; tel. 812572803; e-mail info@sag .gr.ch; internet www.sag.gr.ch; f. 1803; written works on history of Graubünden; records of the Canton of Graubünden and its predecessors (Freistaat der drei Bünde); Dir Lic. RETO WEISS; publ. *Quellen und Forschungen zur Bündner Geschichte QBG*.

Cologny

Bibliotheca Bodmeriana (Fondation Martin Bodmer): 19–21 route du Guignard, 1223 Cologny; tel. 227074433; e-mail info@fondationbodmer.ch; internet www.fondationbodmer.org; f. 1972; 160,000 vols; spec. collns of papyrus, MSS, autographs, incunabula, music MSS, drawings; Dir Prof. CHARLES MÉLA.

Fribourg

Bibliothèque Cantonale et Universitaire de Fribourg/Kantons-und Universitätsbibliothek Freiburg: rue Joseph-Piller 2, 1701 Fribourg; tel. 263051333; e-mail bcu@fr.ch; internet www.fr.ch/bcuf; f. 1848; spec. colln of MSS and incunabula of Middle Ages to present; Heritage Fribourg colln; organizes cultural activities; 3.55m. vols; Dir Dr MARTIN GOOD.

Geneva

Archives d'etat de Genève (State Archives of Geneva): 1 rue de l'Hôtel de Ville, 1211 Geneva 3; tel. 223279320; e-mail archives@etat.ge.ch; internet www.ge.ch/archives; material on history of Geneva; Dir PIERRE FLÜCKIGER.

Bibliothèque d'Art et d'Archéologie des Musées d'art et d'histoire: 5 Promenade du Pin, 1204 Geneva; tel. 224182700; e-mail info.baa@ville-ge.ch; internet www.ville-ge.ch/baa; f. 1911; library of Musées d'Art et d'Histoire de la Ville de Genève and public art library; 400,000 vols, 6,200 periodicals, 140,000 exhibition and auction catalogues, CD-ROMs, databases, microforms, video cassettes, iconography; Chief Curator VÉRONIQUE GONCERUT ESTÈBE; publ. *Geneva* (1 a year).

Bibliothèque de Genève: Promenade des Bastions, 1211 Geneva 4; tel. 224182800; e-mail info.bge@ville-ge.ch; internet www.ville-ge.ch/bge; f. 1562; 2.2m. vols and pamphlets, 70,000 posters, 23,000 maps, 45,000 engravings, 400 painted portraits, 15,000 MSS; Dir JEAN-CHARLES GIROUD.

Bibliothèque de l'ONUG (United Nations Office at Geneva Library): Palais des Nations, 1211 Geneva 10; tel. 229174181; e-mail library@unog.ch; internet www.unog.ch/library; f. 1919; manages cultural activities at Palais des Nations; organizes c. 70 annual events (concerts, exhibitions, film festivals) in cooperation with Permanent Mission of the UN Member State; 1.1m. vols, 4m. documents and publs of UN and its specialized agencies, 500,000 govt documents, 9,000 periodicals; archives of the League of Nations; Chief Librarian (vacant); publ. *Bibliographie Mensuelle* (12 a year).

Bibliothèques de l'Université de Genève (Libraries of University of Geneva): Rue De-Candolle 5, 1205 Geneva; internet www.unige.ch/biblio/index.html; incl. 4 libraries..

Attached Libraries:

Bibliothèques Uni Arve: Quai Ernest-Ansermet 30, 1211 Geneva 4; tel. 223796506; e-mail biblio-sciences2@unige.ch; internet www.unige.ch/biblio/sciences; incl. collns on anthropology, astronomy, biology, chemistry, computer sciences, earth science and environment, environmental sciences, mathematics, physics, pharmaceutical sciences; 100,000 vols of monographs and periodicals, 4,700 microforms; Man. ANNABEL CHANTERAUD.

Bibliothèque Uni Bastions: Rue De-Candolle 5, 1205 Geneva; tel. 223797368; e-mail biblio-bastions-unil@unige.ch; internet www.unige.ch/biblio/bastions; collns on comparative literature, foreign languages, history, linguistics, philosophy, theology; Librarian HÉLÈNE VINCENT.

Bibliothèque Uni CMU: Rue Michel-Servet 1, 1211 Geneva 4; tel. 223795100; e-mail biblio-medecine@unige.ch; internet www.unige.ch/medecine/bibliotheque; incl. 200,000 vols of periodicals, 770 journals, 2,200 ejournals, ebooks; Man. TAMARA MORCILLO.

Bibliothèque Uni Mail: Blvd du Pont-d'Arve 40, 1205 Geneva; tel. 223799299; e-mail bib-unimail@unige.ch; internet www.unige.ch/biblio/unimail; collns on economics and social sciences, international relations, musicology, psychology and educational sciences; Asst Man. ANNE-CATHERINE MOUCHET.

Bibliothèques Municipales: 10 rue de la Tour-de-Boël, CP 3930, 1211 Geneva 3; tel. 224183250; e-mail webbmu@ville-ge.ch; internet www.ville-ge.ch/bmu; f. 1931; 7 br. libraries, sports library, bookmobile service; 800,000 vols; Dir VÉRONIQUE PÜRRO; publ. *AgendaBM*.

International Labour Office Library: 4 route des Morillons, 1211 Geneva 22; tel. 227998675; e-mail inform@ilo.org; internet www.ilo.org/inform; f. 1919; core repository of ILO publs produced in Geneva and in ILO's offices around world; open to public on request; 2m. vols and pamphlets, 3,000 current periodicals (incl. annuals and official gazettes); computerized database (LABOR-DOC), containing 210,000 abstracts, available for online searching worldwide through facilities of ESA-IRS and Questel-ORBIT and on CD-ROM; Dir L. DRYDEN; publ. *ILO Thesaurus: Labour*.

World Health Organization Library and Information Networks for Knowledge: 20 Ave Appia, 1211 Geneva 27; tel. 227912062; e-mail library@who.int; internet www.who.int/library; f. 1948; WHO permanent colln, int. public health literature, journals and databases, historical colln, govt statistical reports, WHOLIS database; Librarian TOMAS ALLEN.

Grand Saint-Bernard

Bibliothèque de l'Hospice du Grand Saint-Bernard: 1946 Bourg-Saint-Pierre; tel. 277871236; e-mail hospicestbernard@gsbernard.ch; internet www.gsbernard.ch; library of Austin Canons monastery; works on history, theology, Catholic literature, natural sciences (botany, entomology, zoology, ornithology, mineralogy), applied sciences (physics, arithmetic, chemistry, astronomy), geography and travel, philosophy, law (civil and canon) liturgy and numismatics, ancient MSS and maps; 32,500 vols, 8,000 periodicals.

Lausanne

Bibliothèque & Archives de la Ville de Lausanne: 11 pl. Chauderon, 1003 Lausanne; tel. 213156915; e-mail bml@lausanne.ch; internet www.lausanne.ch/bibliotheque; f. 1934; 2 main libraries; 4 brs in Chailly, Entre-Bois, Montriond, Grand-Vennes; 4 linear km of municipal archives of admin. and private regional records from 1142 to present; books in French and foreign languages; multimedia collns; 5,000 items of original artwork; 358,000 vols, 150,000 comics research colln; Dir FRÉDÉRIC SARDET.

Bibliothèque cantonale et universitaire–Lausanne: 6, Place de la Riponne, 1014 Lausanne; tel. 213167863; e-mail info-riponne@bcu.unil.ch; internet www.bcu-lausanne.ch; f. 1537; br. in Dorigny; legal deposit library of Vaud Canton; regional documentation; 2.4m. vols, 170 incunabula; 29,500 CDs, 33,000 musical scores, 10,000 audiovisual materials and 2,500 LP records; Dir JEANNETTE FREY; publs

Catalogues des fonds de manuscrits, Catalogues des manuscrits musicaux.

Bibliothèque de l'EPFL—Rolex Learning Centre: Rolex Learning Centre, Station 20, 1015 Lausanne; tel. 216932156; e-mail questions.bib@epfl.ch; internet library.epfl.ch; f. 1945; attached to École Polytechnique Fédérale de Lausanne; open to public; specializes in fields of study and research at EPFL; organizes confs and publs; science and technology; 550,000 vols, 11,000 ejournals, 100 databases, 48,000 ebooks; Dir ISABELLE KRATZ.

Bibliothèque de l'Institut Suisse de Droit Comparé: Dorigny, 1015 Lausanne; tel. 216924911; internet www.isdc.ch; f. 1982; collects legal material from all countries in all fields of law, incl. int. law; European Documentation Centre; 360,000 vols, 2,000 periodicals, 900 electronic resources; Head SADRI SAIEB.

Bibliothèque Universitaire de Médecine (University Library of Medicine): Centre Hospitalier Universitaire Vaudois, 1011 Lausanne; tel. 213145082; e-mail bdfm@chuv.ch; internet www.chuv.ch/bdfm; f. 1968; colln on different areas of health and medicine; 60,000 vols, 2,000 periodicals, 12,000 ejournals, microcomputer facilities, audiovisual library; Head Librarian ISABELLE DE KAENEL.

Lucerne

Staatsarchiv des Kantons Luzern: Schützenstr. 9, POB 7853, 6000 Lucerne 7; tel. 412035365; e-mail staatsarchiv@lu.ch; internet www.staatsarchiv.lu.ch; f. 1803; Siegel colln, seal stamp colln, Cliché-sammlung, autograph colln, copy colln, photo and copy colln, photo negative and microfilm colln, newspapers; 25,000 vols; Archivist Dr JÜRG SCHMUTZ; publ. *Luzerner Historische Veröffentlichungen* (irregular).

Zentral- und Hochschulbibliothek Luzern: Sempacherstr. 10, 6002 Lucerne; tel. 412285312; e-mail info@zhbluzern.ch; internet www.zhbluzern.ch; f. 1951; incl. Burghers' library, canton library and library of Univ. of Lucerne; Lucerne Documentary Heritage Colln; differentiated spectrum of technical, factual and entertainment media; 960,893 vols, 2,736 MSS, 136,285 engravings, photos and maps, 37,117 microforms; colln of Swiss publs up to 1848; Dir Dr ULRICH NIEDERER; Deputy Dir Dr WILFRIED LOCHBÜHLER.

Lugano

Biblioteca Cantonale: Lugano, Ticino: Viale C. Cattaneo 6, 6901 Lugano; tel. 918154611; e-mail bclu-segr.sbt@ti.ch; internet www.sbt.ti.ch/bclugano; f. 1852; colln on religion, theology, art, language, philology, linguistics, literature, with particular reference to Italian culture; inc. *Libreria Patria*, special colln of 'Ticinensia', 40,000 vols; Archivio Prezzolini and collns on contemporary culture; 300,000 vols, 1,300 periodicals, 198 incunabula; Dir Prof. GERARDO RIGOZZI.

Neuchâtel

Archives de l'Etat de Neuchâtel: Le Château, 12 rue de la Collégiale, 2000 Neuchâtel; tel. 328896040; e-mail service.archivesetat@ne.ch; internet www.ne.ch/archives; f. 1898; stores and manages documents of State and private documents relating to history of Canton of Neuchâtel; maintains historical library and administrative library; State Archivist LIONEL BARTOLINI; Librarian GÉRALDINE GALFETTI.

Bibliothèque des Pasteurs: Fbg de l'Hôpital 41, 2000 Neuchâtel; tel. 327254666; e-mail carmen.burkhalter@unine.ch; f. 1538;

theological library of 90,000 vols, 80,000 monographs; Librarian CECILIA GRIENER HURLEY.

Bibliothèque Publique et Universitaire: 3 pl. Numa-Droz, CP 1916, 2000 Neuchâtel; tel. 327177302; e-mail secretariat.bpu@unine .ch; internet bpun.unine.ch; f. 1788; 600,000 vols, 1,900 periodicals, 8,000 posters, 40,000 books of information and general knowledge and multimedia documents (DVDs, CD-ROMs and audio books); Dir THIERRY CHÂTELAIN; publs *Bibliothèques et musées*, *Revue historique neuchâteloise*, and bulletins of chronometry, geography, and natural sciences.

St Gallen

Kantonsbibliothek Vadiana St Gallen: Notkerstr. 22, 9000 St Gallen; tel. 582292321; e-mail kb.vadiana@sg.ch; internet www.kb.sg.ch; f. 1551; colln point for St Gallische literature; 3 specialty divs: Vadian colln, collns of county Library and St Gallen centre for books (Zebu); 800,000 vols; Dir Dr CORNEL DORA; publ. *Veröffentlichungen der Gesellschaft Pro Vadiana*.

Stiftsbibliothek St Gallen (Stifts Library of St Gallen): Klosterhof 6D, Postfach, 9004 St Gallen; tel. 712273416; e-mail stibi@stibi .ch; internet www.stiftsbibliothek.ch; f. 719; library of fmr Benedictine Abbey of St Gall; important colln of MSS from Carolingian and Ottonian periods (8th–11th centuries); colln shows depth of European culture and documents cultural achievements of Abbey of St Gall from 8th century to dissolution of monastery in 1805; 170,000 vols; Dir Dr CORNEL DORA.

Sion

Médiathèque Valais (Bibliothèque Cantonale)/Mediathek Wallis (Kantonsbibliothek): 18 Ave de Pratifori, CP 182, 1951 Sion; tel. 276064550; e-mail mv.sion@ mediatheque.ch; internet www.mediatheque .ch; f. 1853; 4 brs: Brig, Sion, Martigny, Saint-Maurice; spec. collns on Alps; 840,000 vols; Dir DAMIAN ELSIG.

Solothurn

Bibliomedia Schweiz Suisse Svizzera: Rosenweg 2, 4500 Solothurn; tel. 326249020; e-mail solothurn@bibliomedia .ch; internet www.buchstart.ch; f. 1920; promotes devt of libraries and promotion of reading; brs at Solothurn, Lausanne and Biasca; 500,000 vols; Dir Dr PETER WILLE; Sec. BÉATRICE AEGERTER; publ. *Le Cri du Hibou* (irregular).

Zentralbibliothek (Central Library): Bielstr. 39, 4502 Solothurn; tel. 326276262; e-mail info@zbsolothurn.ch; internet www .zbsolothurn.ch; f. 1930; 1m. vols, 30,000 children's books, 100 cultural nachlasse, 550 current periodicals and series, 7,000 illustrations and graphics, 900 incunabula, 13,200 MSS, 42,000 music records, 18,000 music scores; Dir for Admin. PETER PROBST; Dir for Collns Lic. VERENA BIDER; publs *Musik aus der Sammlung der Zentralbibliothek Solothurn* (edns of regional compositions), *Veröffentlichungen der Zentralbibliothek Solothurn*, *Veröffentlichungen der Zentralbibliothek Solothurn: Kleine Reihe*.

Winterthur

Stadtbibliothek: Obere Kirchgasse 6, POB 132, 8402 Winterthur; tel. 522675148; e-mail stadtbibliothek@win.ch; internet www .winbib.ch; f. 1660; spec. collns of local history, numismatics, music, African languages, MSS, letters and literature; non-lending library book collns, incl. books, music notes and cards from 1465 to 1900; open to public; 6 brs; 900,000 vols; Dir Dr HERMANN ROMER; publ. *Neujahrsblatt* (1 a year).

Zürich

ETH-Bibliothek (Library of the Swiss Federal Institute of Technology (ETH Zurich)): Rämistrasse 101, 8092 Zürich; tel. 446322135; e-mail info@library.ethz.ch; internet www.library.ethz.ch; f. 1855; specializes in science and technology; colln of architecture, civil engineering, engineering sciences, natural sciences and mathematics, system-oriented natural sciences, management and social sciences; 7.8m. vols and documents. 2.88m. monographs and bound journals, 2.2m. microforms, 4,574,000 digital documents, 2m. images, 334,000 maps, 15,500 ejournals, 5,400 subscribed journals, 144 databases, 121,000 ebooks, 176,000 abstracts and indices; Dir Dr WOLFRAM NEUBAUER; Deputy Dir ANDREAS KIRSTEIN.

Schweizerisches Sozialarchiv/Archives sociales suisses: Stadelhoferstr. 12, 8001 Zürich; tel. 432688740; e-mail kontakt@ sozialarchiv.ch; internet www.sozialarchiv .ch; f. 1906; centre of social documentation; open to public; collects corporate archives of traditional and new social movements and private documents of activists during such movements; 160,000 vols, 1,500 current periodicals, 160,000 brochures and pamphlets, 1.2m. newspaper cuttings, 32,000 archival documents, 102,500 iconic documents, 150 ejournals; Dir Dr ANITA ULRICH; Deputy Dir Dr URS KÄLIN.

Staatsarchiv des Kantons Zürich: Winterthurerstr. 170, 8057 Zürich; tel. 446356911; e-mail staatsarchivzh@ji.zh.ch; internet www.staatsarchiv.zh.ch; f. 1837; archives of canton of Zürich and specialized library (local publs) and collns of statutes and numerous pamphlets); archives: 30,000 m, 92,000 vols; Dir Dr BEAT GNÄDINGER.

Zentralbibliothek Zürich: Zähringerpl. 6, 8001 Zürich; tel. 442683100; e-mail zb@zb .uzh.ch; internet www.zb.uzh.ch; f. 1914; city, cantonal and univ. library, inc. libraries of Naturforschende Gesellschaft in Zürich, Antiquarische Gesellschaft in Zürich, Geographisch-Ethnographische Gesellschaft Zürich, Schweizerischer Alpenclub, Allgemeine MusikGesellschaft Zürich, Bibliotheca Fennica; 5.25m. vols, 106,000 MSS and autographs, 11,260 incunabula, 249,000 maps, and spec. collns of graphic arts (222,000 items), 35,000 records and audio cassettes; 8,700 current print periodicals, 45,000 electronic periodicals, 190 newspapers; Dir Prof. SUSANNA BLIGGENSTORFER.

Zentrale für Betriebswirtschaft & Zentrale für Wirtschaftsdokumentation, Universität Zürich: Plattenstr. 14, 8032 Zürich; tel. 446343911; e-mail bfb@business .uzh.ch; internet www.business.uzh.ch/ libraries/libraryba.html; f. 1910, present status 1990; attached to Univ. of Zurich; large worldwide colln of annual reports of major companies; periodicals, OECD colln, online library catalogues in fields of business studies and economics, daily newspapers, magazines and statistical material available; 36,000 vols, 122 periodicals; Dir KATHARINA HERTZBERG-SCHILLING.

Museums and Art Galleries

Aarau

Aargauer Kunsthaus: Aargauerplatz, 5001 Aarau; tel. 628352330; e-mail kunsthaus@ag .ch; internet www.aargauerkunsthaus.ch; f. 1959; Swiss painting and sculpture since 1750; colln of paintings by Caspar Wolf, Johann Heinrich Füssli, Ferdinand Hodler, Cuno Amiet, Louis Soutter, Félix Vallotton, Max Bill, Sophie Taeuber-Arp; temporary exhibitions; Dir MADELEINE SCHUPPLI; Deputy Dir and Curator THOMAS SCHMUTZ.

Avenches

Musée Romain Avenches: 1580 Avenches; tel. 265573300; e-mail musee.romain@vd.ch; internet www.aventicum.org; f. 1824; situated at 2nd century AD Roman amphitheatre; mosaics, funerary stelae and sculptures; excavations of Aventicum; temporary exhibitions; library of 18,000 vols; Pres. Prof. P. DUCREY; Dir Dr MARIE-FRANCE MEYLAN KRAUSE; publ. *Aventicum* (2 a year).

Basel

Antikenmuseum Basel und Sammlung Ludwig: St Alban Graben 5, 4010 Basel; tel. 612011212; e-mail info@ antikenmuseumbasel.ch; internet www .antikenmuseumbasel.ch; f. 1961; exhibition of art and culture of the Mediterranean area; collns of Greek art (2500–100 BC), Roman art (100 BC–AD 300), Etruscan art and Egyptian art, spec. exhibitions; Dir Dr ANDREA BIGNASCA.

Historisches Museum Basel: Verwaltung, Steinenberg 4, 4051 Basel; tel. 612058600; e-mail historisches.museum@bs.ch; internet www.hmb.ch; f. 1894; 4 brs containing colln of objects from Middle Ages to 20th century, civic culture of Basel in 18th and 19th centuries and colln of old musical instruments, numismatics, coaches and sleighs; library of 21,000 vols, 38 journals, 183 periodicals; Dir Dr MARIE-PAULE JUNGBLUT; Librarian DANIEL SUTER; publ. *Basler Kostbarkeiten* (1 a year).

Kunstmuseum Basel: St Albangraben 16, 4010 Basel; tel. 612066262; internet www .kunstmuseumbasel.ch; f. 1662; pictures from 15th century to present day, notably by Witz, Holbein and contemporary painters; colln incl. Grünewald, Rembrandt, 16th- and 17th-century Dutch painting, Cézanne, Gauguin and Van Gogh; colln of Cubist art; sculptures by Rodin and 20th-century artists; American art since 1950; dept of prints and drawings with old Upper Rhine, German and Swiss masters and 20th-century works; library of 150,000 vols, 200 periodicals; Dir Dr BERNHARD MENDES BÜRGI; Man. Dir FAUSTO DE LORENZO; Head of Library RAINER BAUM..

Attached Museum:

Museum für Gegenwartskunst (Museum of Contemporary Art): St Alban-Rheinweg 60, 4010 Basel; tel. 612066262; internet www.kunstmuseumbasel.ch/en/ museum-fuer-gegenwartskunst; f. 1980; contemporary art from collns of Emanuel Hoffmann Foundation and Kunstmuseum; Dir Dr BERNHARD MENDES BÜRGI; Curator NIKOLA DIETRICH.

Museum der Kulturen Basel: Muensterpl. 20, 4051 Basel; tel. 612665600; e-mail info@ mkb.ch; internet www.mkb.ch; f. 1849; ethnographical collns from all parts of the world, esp. from Oceania, Indonesia, S America and Europe; textiles; historic photographs, incl. stocks of fmr Swiss Museum of Ethnology; 300,000 objects; temporary exhibitions; library: see under Libraries and Archives; Dir Dr ANNA SCHMID; Vice-Dir Lic. DOMINIK WUNDERLIN; publs *Basler Beiträge zur Ethnologie*, guides.

Bern

Bernisches Historisches Museum: Helvetiapl. 5, 3005 Bern; tel. 313507711; e-mail info@bhm.ch; internet www.bhm.ch; f. 1894;

Burgundian tapestries, Königsfeld Diptych, Bern's silver treasure, Stone Age, Celts and Romans, art from Asia and Oceania, bronze hydria from Grächwil and series of ethnographic and numismatic collns; colln from early Middle Ages to Ancien Régime; Einstein museum; temporary exhibitions; Dir Dr JAKOB MESSERLI; Vice-Dir Prof. Dr FELIX MÜLLER.

Kunstmuseum (Museum of Fine Arts Bern): Hodlerstr. 8–12, 3000 Bern 7; tel. 313280944; e-mail info@kunstmuseumbern .ch; internet www.kunstmuseumbern.ch; f. 1879; colln of 3,000 paintings and sculptures incl. Italian paintings from 14th to 16th centuries; works by Swiss masters from 15th to 19th centuries; works illustrating devt of art since 19th century by Manet, Cézanne, Monet, Pissaro, Renoir, Van Gogh, members of 'Blaue Ritter', 'Brücke', and Bauhaus movements, Rothko and Pollock, and other modern works by Hodler and other Swiss, French and German artists; Hermann and Margrit Rupf Foundation, incl. paintings by Picasso, Braque, Léger, Gris and Kandinsky; Adolf Wölfli Foundation; graphic art colln of more than 48,000 drawings, engravings, photographs, video cassettes and films; library of 110,000 vols; Dir Dr MATTHIAS FREHNER; Curator Dr THERESE BHATTACHARYA-STETTLER; Curator Dr KATHLEEN BÜHLER; publ. *Berner Kunstmitteilungen* (4 a year).

Naturhistorisches Museum: Bernastr. 15, 3005 Bern; tel. 313507111; e-mail contact@ nmbe.ch; internet www.nmbe.ch; f. 1832; colln incl. 220 dioramas of Swiss mammals and birds, big game (esp. African), Swiss fish, amphibians and reptiles, minerals of Swiss Alps, invertebrates, hall of skeletons; Earth science exhibition; 3 depts: Earth sciences, mineralogy and palaeontology, invertebrates and vertebrates; promotes research in Univ. of Bern; Dir Dr CHRISTOPH BEER; publ. *Contributions to Natural History* (2 a year).

Zentrum Paul Klee Bern: Monument im Fruchtland 3, 3000 Bern 31; tel. 313590101; e-mail kontakt@zpk.org; internet www.zpk .org; f. 2005; 4,000 works of art by Paul Klee (1879–1940) and colln of biographical material; exhibition space for contemporary artists; children's museum 'Creaviva'; organizes concerts and theatre; Dir PETER FISCHER.

Biel

Museum Schwab: Seevorstadt 50, 2502 Biel; tel. 323227603; e-mail info@muschwab .ch; internet www.bielbienne.ch/ww/de/pub/ aktiv/kultur/museen/schwab.cfm; f. 1873; contains prehistoric exhibits, esp. of lakedwelling culture, New Stone Age, Bronze Age, and 2nd Iron Age; colln of items from Roman period (Petinesca); temporary exhibitions; Dir MADELEINE BETSCHAVT.

Chur

Bündner Kunstmuseum: Postplatz, 7000 Chur; tel. 812572868; e-mail info@bkm.gr.ch; internet www.buendner-kunstmuseum.ch; f. 1900; colln of works by Swiss artists, Segantini, Hodler, Alberto, Augusto and G. Giacometti, E. L. Kirchner and Angelica Kauffmann; exhibitions of Swiss and foreign art; Dir STEPHAN KUNZ; Curator Dr KATHARINA AMMANN.

Fribourg

Musée d'Art et d'Histoire: 12 rue de Morat, 1700 Fribourg; tel. 263055140; e-mail mahf@fr.ch; internet www.fr.ch/ mahf; f. 1823; housed in Hotel Ratzé (16th century); collns of prehistoric, Roman and medieval exhibits; important collns of Swiss sculpture and painting since 11th century;

works from Marcello Foundation; monumental pieces by Jean Tinguely; stained glass gallery; works of art in Freiburg in 19th and 20th centuries; Dir VERENA VILLIGER STEINAUER; Curator STEPHAN GASSER.

Geneva

Fondation Baur, Musée des Arts d'Extrême-Orient (Baur Foundation-Museum of Far Eastern Art): 8 rue Munier Romilly, 1206 Geneva; tel. 227043282; e-mail musee@fondationbaur.ch; internet fondation-baur.ch; f. 1964; 9,000 Chinese and Japanese art objects; Chinese imperial ceramic ware, jades and snuff bottles from 10th to 19th centuries and Japanese prints, lacquer, netsuke, and sword fittings, Chinese lacquer ware and export ceramics; temporary exhibitions related to Chinese and Japanese artwork; library of 5,500 vols; Dir MONIQUE CRICK; Curator HELEN LOVEDAY.

Musée Ariana: 10 Ave de la Paix, 1202 Geneva; tel. 224185450; e-mail ariana@ ville-ge.ch; internet www.ville-geneve.ch/ ariana; f. 1884; 25,000 objects on European and Eastern ceramics and glass; Dir ISABELLE NAEF GALUBA; Curator ANNE-CLAIRE SCHUMACHER; publ. *La Gazette de l'Ariana* (2 a year).

Musée d'art et d'histoire: 2 rue Charles-Galland, 1206 Geneva; tel. 224182600; e-mail mah@ville-ge.ch; internet www.ville-ge.ch/ mah; f. 1910; contains local prehistory section; Mediterranean, Egyptian, Near Eastern, Byzantine and Coptic archaeology; Italian, Dutch, Flemish, German, French, English and Swiss (esp. Genevese) paintings, paintings since beginning of 20th century, European sculpture, applied art and numismatic colln; library of 300,000 vols, 5,900 periodicals, 70,000 auction catalogues from 1857 to present; Dir JEAN-YVES MARIN; publs *Genava* (1 a year), *Journal des Musées d'art et d'histoire* (3 a year).

Attached Museums:

Cabinet d'Arts Graphiques: 5 promenade du Pin, 1204 Geneva; tel. 224182770; e-mail cde@ville-ge.ch; f. 1886, as separate institution, part of Musées d'art et d'histoire 1910; 350,000 items covering 5 centuries of printmaking; multiples and 20th and 21st century artist's books; Keeper Dr CHRISTIAN RÜMELIN.

Maison Tavel: 6 rue du Puits Saint-Pierre, 1204 Geneva; tel. 224183700; e-mail mah@ville-ge.ch; f. 1986; history of city; exhibits of artefacts and images from 14th to 19th century; Dir JEAN-YVES MARIN.

Musée Rath: Pl. Neuve, 1204 Geneva; tel. 224183340; e-mail mah@ville-ge.ch; f. 1828; temporary exhibitions; Dir JEAN-YVES MARIN.

Musée d'Art Moderne et Contemporain (Museum of Modern and Contemporary Art): 10 rue des Vieux-Grenadiers, 1205 Geneva; tel. 223206122; internet www.mamco.ch; f. 1994; specializes in works since 1960; temporary exhibitions; archives of works of art; Dir CHRISTIAN BERNARD; Deputy Dir and Chief Curator FRANÇOISE NINGHETTO; Sec.-Gen. VALÉRIE MALLET.

Musée d'ethnographie de Genève: CP 1549, 1211 Geneva 26; tel. 224184550; e-mail musee.ethno@ville-ge.ch; internet www.ville-ge.ch/meg; f. 1901; African colln; American colln; Asian colln; European colln; Oceanic colln; musical instruments; colln of 400 films; colln of 130,000 historical photographs; also houses Archives Internationales de Musique Populaire; library of 45,000 vols, 1,500 periodicals; Dir Dr BORIS WASTIAU; publ. *Totem* (3 a year).

Musée d'Histoire des Sciences: 128 rue de Lausanne, 1202 Geneva; tel. 224815060; e-mail mhs@ville-ge.ch; internet www .ville-ge.ch/mhs; f. 1964; scientific instruments; Dir JACQUES AYER.

Muséum d'Histoire Naturelle: Route de Malagnou 1, 1208 Geneva; tel. 224186300; e-mail info.mhn@ville-ge.ch; internet www .ville-ge.ch/mhng; f. 1820; depts of mammalogy and ornithology, herpetology and ichthyology, invertebrates, arthropods and insects, entomology, archaeozoology, geology and palaeontology, mineralogy; library of 200,000 vols, 40,000 monographs, 4,000 geological and topographical maps, 2,000 periodicals (800 current), also manages Bibliothèque de l'Association Nos Oiseaux and Bibliothèque du Centre de Coordination Ouest pour l'Étude et la Protection des Chauves-souris; Dir JACQUES AYER; Librarian CHRISTELLE MOUGIN; publs *Catalogue des Invertébrés de la Suisse*, *Le Rhinolophe* (1 a year), *Revue suisse de Zoologie* (4 a year), *Revue de Paléobiologie* (2 a year).

Glarus

Kunsthaus Glarus: Im Volksgarten, POB 665, 8750 Glarus; tel. 556402535; e-mail office@kunsthausglarus.ch; internet www .kunsthausglarus.ch; f. 1870; 19th and 20th century Swiss art, Swiss and foreign contemporary art; temporary exhibitions; Pres. KASPAR MARTI; Vice-Pres. THOMAS ASCHMANN; Dir SABINE RUSTERHOLZ.

La Chaux-de-Fonds

Musée des Beaux-Arts: 33 rue des Musées, 2300 La Chaux-de-Fonds; tel. 329676077; e-mail mba.vch@ne.ch; internet cdf-mba.ne .ch; f. 1864; colln of paintings, sculptures, video cassettes and prints from 19th century (Matisse, Renoir, Van Gogh, Constable, Rouault) to present; works of Swiss artists (Anker, Vallotton, Bailly, Hodler), particularly of Neuchâtel district (Robert, Kaiser, l'Eplattenier, Perrin, Humbert, Le Corbusier, etc.); colln of European and American artists; temporary exhibitions; Dir LADA UMSTÄTTER.

Musée International d'Horlogerie: 29 rue des Musées, 2301 La Chaux-de-Fonds; tel. 329676861; e-mail mih.vch@ne.ch; internet www.mih.ch; f. 1902; artistic and technical collns of watches, clocks, instruments and objects connected with measurement of time; time research dept; modern carillon; library of 3,000 vols; Curator M. LUDWIG OECHSLIN.

Lausanne

Musée Cantonal des Beaux-Arts: Palais de Rumine, pl. Riponne 6, 1014 Lausanne; tel. 213163445; e-mail info.beaux-arts@vd.ch; internet www.musees.vd.ch/fr/ musee-des-beaux-arts; f. 1841; colln of works since 18th century mainly by artists often related to the Canton de Vaud; int. exhibitions of classical, modern and contemporary art; Dir BERNARD FIBICHER; Chief Curator CATHERINE LEPDOR; Curator NICOLE SCHWEIZER; Curator CAMILLE LÉVÊQUE-CLAUDET.

Musée Historique de Lausanne: 4 pl. de la Cathédrale, 1005 Lausanne; tel. 213154101; e-mail musee.historique@lausanne.ch; internet www.lausanne.ch/mhl; f. 1918; model of 17th century Lausanne, collns relating to local and regional history: silver, furniture, paintings and drawings, plans of the town, musical instruments; library; history of city from medieval times to 19th century; colln in 3 depts: paintings and graphic arts, objects, photographic collns; organizes interactive workshops, meetings, performances and concerts; Dir LAURENT GOLAY; publ. *Mémoire vive* (1 a year).

The Olympic Museum/Le Musée Olympique: 1 Quai d'Ouchy, 1006, Lausanne; tel. 216216511; internet www.olympic.org/museum; f. 1993; attached to Int. Olympic Cttee; themed exhibitions; philatelic and numismatic exhibition; works of Arnoldi, Berrocal, Botero, Calder, Chillida, Folon, Graham, Niki de Saint Phalle, Tàpies, Mitoraj in bronze, marble and steel to offer their interpretation of sport, athlete and Olympic ideals; library of 23,000 monograph vols, 420 journals, 20,000 historical archival files, 9,500 films, 35,000 hours of film footage, 6,500 hours of sound files, 610,000 photographic documents (120,000 digitized); Dir of the IOC Information Management Dept PHILIPPE BLANCHARD; publ. *Symposium on Olympism—Proceedings* (1 a year).

Ligornetto

Museo Vincenzo Vela: 6853 Ligornetto; tel. 916407044; e-mail museo.vela@bak.admin.ch; internet www.bundesmuseen.ch/museo_vela; f. 1898; bequests of sculptor Lorenzo Vela and painter Spartaco Vela; colln of 19th-century Lombard and Piemontese paintings, autograph drawings and private collns of photographs; portraits of leading figures of the Risorgimento; landscaped garden; temporary exhibitions; Dir Dr GIANNA A. MINA; Sec. MARIANGELA ROSIELLO-AGNOLA.

Locarno

Museo Civico e Archeologico: Servizi Culturali, Via B. Rusca 5, 6600 Locarno; tel. 917563180; e-mail servizi.culturali@locarno.ch; f. 1970; 14th century fortress housing archaeological colln and historical museum; Dir Prof. RICCARDO CARAZZETTI.

Pinacoteca Casa Rusca: Servizi Culturali, Via B. Rusca 5, 6600 Locarno; tel. 917563185; e-mail servizi.culturali@locarno.ch; f. 1987; restored 17th century building housing municipal art gallery; incl. Jean Arp colln, and works by Calder, Hans Richter, Van Doesburg, etc.; Dir Prof RICCARDO CARAZZETTI.

Lucerne

Historisches Museum (Museum of History): Altes Zeughaus, Pfistergasse 24, POB 7437, 6000 Lucerne 7; tel. 412285424; e-mail historischesmuseum@lu.ch; internet www.historischesmuseum.lu.ch; f. 1986; colln of coat of mail worn by Leopold III at battle of Sempach 1386, Milanese round shields from battle of Giornico 1478, column on Weinmarkt fountain by Conrad Lux 1481, gothic altarpieces, baroque sleigh owned by Amrhyn-Göldlin family 1673, pewter vessels, Swiss costumes, coats of arms in stained glass, industrial products; organizes theatre tours and temporary exhibitions; Dir Dr HEINZ HORAT; Asst Dir and Curator Lic. ALEXANDRA STROBEL; Curator KURT LUSSI; publs *Jahrbuch der Historischen Gesellschaft Luzern, Jahresbericht des Historischen Museums.*

Kunstmuseum Luzern (Museum of Art Lucerne): Europapl. 1, 6002 Lucerne; tel. 412267800; e-mail info@kunstmuseumluzern.ch; internet www.kunstmuseumluzern.ch; f. 1925; 18th- to 20th-century Swiss landscape painting and portraiture, Swiss art after 1945, foreign contemporary art; temporary exhibitions of contemporary works of art; Dir PETER FISCHER; Curator CHRISTOPH LICHTIN.

Richard Wagner-Museum: Richard Wagner-Weg 27, 6005 Lucerne; tel. 413602370; e-mail info@richard-wagner-museum.ch; internet www.richard-wagner-museum.ch; f. 1933; home of Richard Wagner from 1866 to 1872; contains original scores of *Siegfried-Idyll, Schuster-* lied (*Meistersinger*), etchings, paintings, busts and Erard grand piano which accompanied Wagner throughout Europe; maintains image archive; lectures and presentations; Dir KATJA FLEISCHER.

Verkehrshaus der Schweiz (Swiss Transport Museum): Lidostr. 5, 6006 Lucerne; tel. 413704444; e-mail mail@verkehrshaus.org; internet www.verkehrshaus.org; f. 1959; transport by land, water and air, communication and tourism; transportation archives; IMAX theatre; planetarium; Dir DANIEL SUTER.

Lugano

Museo Civico di Belle Arti: Villa Ciani, Parco Civico, 6900 Lugano; tel. 588667201; e-mail museodibellearti@lugano.ch; f. 1903; works by artists of Ticino since 17th century, and by French and Italian artists.

Neuchâtel

Musée d'Art et d'Histoire: Esplanade Léopold Robert 1, 2000 Neuchâtel; tel. 327177920; e-mail mahn@ne.ch; internet www.mahn.ch; f. 1885; pictures, drawings, prints and sculptures by local and other Swiss artists; French 18th and 19th century works (Courbet, Corot, and others); French Impressionists; furniture, coins and medals; colln of 18th-century automata by Jaquet-Droz; has art library; Curator of Dept of Applied Arts CAROLINE JUNIER; Curator of Numismatic Cabinet GILLES PERRET; Curator of Visual Arts WALTER TSCHOPP..

Attached Gallery:

    Galeries de l'Histoire: Ave Du Peyrou 7, 2000 Neuchâtel; tel. 327177920; e-mail mahn@ne.ch; internet www.mahn.ch; f. 2003; Curator CHANTAL LAFONTANT VALLOTTON.

Musée d'Ethnographie (Museum of Ethnography): 4 rue St-Nicolas, 2000 Neuchâtel; tel. 327178560; e-mail secretariat.men@ne.ch; internet www.men.ch; f. 1795; collns incl. Africa, Ancient Egypt, Arctic, Asia, Europe, South Sea Islands, USA; musical instruments; library of 25,000 vols, 300 periodicals; music archives of original recordings; Curator MARC-OLIVIER GONSETH.

Muséum d'Histoire Naturelle: Rue des Terreaux 14, 2000 Neuchâtel; tel. 327177960; e-mail info.museum@unine.ch; internet www.museum-neuchatel.ch; f. 1835; zoological, entomological, geological and botanical collns; Curator CHRISTOPHE DUFOUR; publ. *Ville de Neuchâtel, Bibliothèques et Musées* (1 a year).

Olten

Kunstmuseum Olten: Kirchgasse 8, 4603 Olten; tel. 622128676; e-mail info@kunstmuseumolten.ch; internet www.kunstmuseumolten.ch; f. 1845; drawings and paintings by Martin Disteli (1802–1844); paintings, drawings and sculptures by Swiss artists; organizes school workshops and temporary exhibitions; library of 500 vols; Curator PATRICIA NUSSBAUM.

St Gallen

Historisches und Völkerkundemuseum: Museumstr. 50, 9000 St Gallen; tel. 712420642; e-mail info@hmsg.ch; internet www.hmsg.ch; f. 1877, as Historisches Museum; present name 2004 following merger with Völkerkundemuseum; historical-archeological section: prehistoric and early history, history of St Gall; period rooms from 16th to 19th century, glass paintings, furniture, pewter art, Swiss folk art, porcelain, costumes, fire and light, kitchen, pharmacy, religious art, flags, weapons and uniforms; ethnological section: culture of ancient Egypt, masks and sculptures of Africa, cult objects from Oceania, Inuit cultures of N America, native Indian tribes of N, Central and S America; Islamic cultural area from N Africa to Central Asia; cultural areas of India incl. Sri Lanka, Indochina, Indonesia, China and Japan; children's museum; Dir Dr DANIEL STUDER.

Kunstmuseum: Museumstr. 32, 9000 St Gallen; tel. 712420671; e-mail info@kunstmuseumsg.ch; internet www.kunstmuseumsg.ch; f. 1877; works by 19th and 20th century masters, post-war sculpture, contemporary art; Dir Lic. ROLAND WÄSPE; Deputy Dir and Curator Lic. KONRAD BITTERLI; Curator Lic. MATTHIAS WOHLGEMUTH.

Museum Kirchhoferhaus: Museumstr. 27, 9000 St Gallen; tel. 712447521; e-mail info@hmsg.ch; prehistoric and historic exhibits; 17th–19th century paintings by Graff, Diogg, Stäbli, Hodler, Corot, Renoir and others; peasant art of eastern Switzerland; furniture, silverware; closed to public; Dir Dr DANIEL STUDER.

Naturmuseum St Gallen: Museumstr. 32, 9000 St Gallen; tel. 712420670; e-mail info@naturmuseumsg.ch; internet www.naturmuseumsg.ch; f. 1846; 19th-century exhibits incl. birds, plants and insects; Nile crocodile from 1623 and skeleton of Anatosaurus; colln available for scientific research; library of 2,000 vols; Curator Dr TONI BÜRGIN; publ. *Museumsbriefe.*

Textilmuseum mit Textilbibliothek: Vadianstr. 2, 9000 St Gallen; tel. 712221744; e-mail info@textilmuseum.ch; internet www.textilmuseum.ch; f. 1886; colln of tissues of Egyptian graves, historical embroideries from 14th century, handmade lace from major European centres of excellence, ethnographic textiles, historic fabrics and costumes, handmade utensils and objects of contemporary textile art; library of 20,000 vols; special colln of 2m. textile samples; Dir HANSPETER SCHMID; Curator URSULA KARBACHER; Librarian REGULA LÜSCHER.

Schaffhausen

Museum zu Allerheiligen: Baumgartenstr. 6, 8200 Schaffhausen; tel. 526330777; e-mail admin.allerheiligen@stsh.ch; internet www.allerheiligen.ch; f. 1938; archaeology, history, natural history, numismatic and graphics colln; art of City and Canton of Schaffhausen and of Switzerland; Dir Dr PETER JEZLER.

Solothurn

Kunstmuseum Solothurn: Werkhofstr. 30, 4500 Solothurn; tel. 326244000; e-mail kunstmuseum@solothurn.ch; internet www.kunstmuseum-so.ch; f. 1902; colln of works by Hans Holbein the Younger; int. colln, incl. works by Van Gogh, Klimt, Matisse, Picasso and Braque; Swiss art colln from 1850 to 1990, incl. works by Hodler; paintings, drawings, watercolours; primitive art section; Curator Dr CHRISTOPH VÖGELE; Sec. CHRISTINE KOBEL.

Vevey

Musée Jenisch Vevey: 2 ave de la Gare, 1800 Vevey; tel. 219253520; e-mail info@museejenisch.ch; internet www.museejenisch.ch; f. 1898; comprises Fine Arts Museum (19th- and 20th-century Swiss and foreign artists, old master drawings, Oskar Kokoschka Foundation, Balthus Foundation) and Cantonal Museum of Prints (16th–20th century prints); Dir DOMINIQUE RODRIZZANI.

Winterthur

Kunstmuseum Winterthur (Art museum Winterthur): Museumstr. 52, POB 235, 8402 Winterthur; Museumstr. 52, 8400 Winterthur; tel. 522675162; e-mail info@kmw .ch; internet www.kmw.ch; f. 1848; painting and sculpture from late 19th century to present, incl. works by Arp, Bishop, Bonnard, Brancusi, D. Rabinowitch, de Staël, Degas, Fabro, Fontana, Giacometti, Gris, Guston, Léger, Lehmbruck, Kandinsky, Klee, Kounellis, M. Rosso, Magritte, Maillol, Manzoni, Marden, Merz, Monet, Morandi, Paolini, Picasso, Richter, Rodin, Schlemmer, Van Gogh; drawings and prints; administered by Kunstverein Winterthur; Pres. Dr JÜRG SPILLER; Dir Dr DIETER SCHWARZ; publ. *Jahresbericht Kunstvereins Winterthur*.

Museum Oskar Reinhart am Stadtgarten: Stadthausstr. 6, 8400 Winterthur; tel. 522675172; e-mail museum.oskarreinhart@ win.ch; internet www.museumoskarreinhart .ch; f. 1951; public art gallery; exhibits paintings and drawings of Swiss, German and Austrian schools from the 18th to the 20th century; Curator Dr MARC FEHLMANN; Curator PETER WEGMANN.

Zürich

Botanischer Garten und Museum der Universität Zürich: Zollikerstr. 107, 8008 Zürich; tel. 446348461; e-mail botanischer .garten@systbot.uzh.ch; internet www.bg .uzh.ch; f. 1837; worldwide herbarium, esp. of African and New Caledonian flora; exhibitions on plants; organizes guided tours for public and schools; courses, exhibitions; library of 100,000 vols; Dir Prof. Dr ELENA CONTI; Head Curator PETER ENZ.

Graphische Sammlung der ETH Zürich (Collection of Prints and Drawings of ETH Zurich): Rämistr. 101, 8092 Zürich; tel. 446324046; e-mail info@gs.ethz.ch; internet www.gs.ethz.ch; f. 1867; 150,000 prints and drawings from 15th century to present, with spec. reference to devt of graphic art in Switzerland; Chief Curator PAUL TANNER; Curator Dr MICHAEL MATILE.

Kunsthaus Zürich: Postfach, 8024 Zürich; Heimpl. 1, 8001 Zürich; tel. 442538484; e-mail info@kunsthaus.ch; internet www .kunsthaus.ch; f. 1910; chiefly paintings and sculptures since 19th century by Swiss and foreign artists; selection of old masters; extensive colln covering all brs of graphic art since 16th century; unique Giacometti colln; Monet, Cézanne, van Gogh, Picasso and Chagall; contemporary artists incl. Baselitz, Beuys and Twombly; video colln; library of 250,000 vols, 320 journals; Dir Dr CHRISTOPH BECKER; Curator Dr PHILIPPE BUETTNER; Curator Dr TOBIA BEZZOLA; Curator BICE CURIGER; Curator BERNHARD VON WALDKIRCH; Curator MIRJAM VARADINIS; publ. *Kunsthaus-Magazin* (4 a year).

Musée Suisse/Schweizerisches Landesmuseum (Swiss National Museum): Museumstr. 2, 8021 Zürich; tel. 442186511; e-mail kanzlei@snm.admin.ch; internet www .landesmuseen.ch; f. 1898; incl. Castle of Prangins, Forum of Swiss History Schwyz and collns centre in Affoltern and Albis; Switzerland's largest colln of objects regarding cultural history of Switzerland; permanent and spec. exhibitions cover all periods from prehistory to the 21st century; library of 90,000 vols, 2,000 periodicals; Pres. MARKUS NOTTER; Dir Dr ANDREAS SPILLMAN; Deputy Dir MARKUS LEUTHARD; publs *Kulturmagazin* (in German and French, 4 a year), *Zeitschrift für Schweizerische Archäologie und Kunstgeschichte* (4 a year).

Museum für Gestaltung Zürich (Museum of Design Zürich): Postfach, 8031 Zürich;

Ausstellungsstr. 60, 8005 Zürich; tel. 434466767; e-mail welcome@ museum-gestaltung.ch; internet www .museum-gestaltung.ch; f. 1875; attached to Zurich Univ. of the Arts; design colln, graphic art colln, poster colln; temporary exhibitions, research, education and publishing; library: public library of 90,000 vols; Dir CHRISTIAN BRÄNDLE..

Affiliated Museum:

Museum Bellerive: Höschgasse 3, 8008 Zürich; tel. 434464469; e-mail welcome@ museum-gestaltung.ch; internet www .museum-bellerive.ch; f. 1968; colln of applied and fine arts in glass, ceramics, textiles, marionettes, musical instruments; 2 or 3 exhibitions annually exploring art and design, modern classics and recent trends; Man. JACQUELINE GREENSPAN; Asst Curator TANJA TRAMPE.

Museum Rietberg Zürich: Gablerstr. 15, 8002 Zürich; tel. 442063131; e-mail museum .rietberg@zuerich.ch; internet www .stadt-zuerich.ch/kultur/de/index/institutionen/museum_rietberg.html; f. 1952; works of art from Asia, Africa, Oceania and Americas; E. von der Heydt colln; organizes tours and educational programmes; Dir Dr ALBERT LUTZ; Deputy Dir KATHARINA EPPRECHT; Chief Curator JOHANNES BELTZ.

Paläontologisches Institut und Museum der Universität: Karl Schmid-Str. 4, 8006 Zürich; tel. 446342339; internet www.pim .uzh.ch; f. 1991; attached to Univ. Zürich; Triassic reptiles and fishes, Triassic and Jurassic invertebrates, Tertiary mammals; library of 5,500 vols, 30,000 publs; Curator Dr HEINZ FURRER.

Zoologisches Museum der Universität Zürich (Zoological Museum of the University of Zurich): Karl Schmid-str. 4, 8006 Zürich; tel. 446343838; e-mail zminfo@zm .uzh.ch; internet www.zm.uzh.ch; f. 1833; permanent exhibition of 1,500 animals; scientific collns of 800 mammals, 3,300 birds, 1,900 reptiles and amphibians, 3,000 insects and 24,000 mollusc species; spec. collns: fruit fly colln and the Mousson colln; slide shows and film screenings; library of 7,000 vols; Dir Prof. Dr LUKAS KELLER.

Universities

ÉCOLE POLYTECHNIQUE FÉDÉRALE DE LAUSANNE

1015 Lausanne
Telephone: 216931111
E-mail: mediacom@epfl.ch
Internet: www.epfl.ch

Founded 1853, present status 1969
Language of instruction: French
Federal State control
Academic year: October to July

Pres.: Prof. PATRICK AEBISCHER
Vice-Pres. for Academic Affairs: Prof. PHILIPPE GILLET
Vice-Pres. for Innovation and Technology Transfer: Prof. ADRIENNE CORBOUD FUMAGALLI
Vice-Pres. for Institutional Affairs: Prof. MARIN VETTERLI
Vice-Pres. for Planning and Logistics: Prof. FRANCIS-LUC PERRET
Gen. Sec.: JEAN-FRANÇOIS RICCI (acting)
Library Dir: DAVID AYMONIN
Library: see under Libraries and Archives
Number of teachers: 275
Number of students: 6,000

DEANS

College of Human Sciences: Prof. FRANCESCO PANESE (acting)
College of Management of Technology: Dr MARTIN VETTERLI (acting)
School of Architecture, Civil and Environmental Engineering: Prof. MARC PARLANGE
School of Basic Sciences: Prof. THOMAS RIZZO
School of Computer and Communication Sciences: Dr MARTIN VETTERLI
School of Engineering: Prof. DEMETRI PSALTIS
School of Life Sciences: DIDIER TRONO

PROFESSORS

Department of Architecture:

ABOU-JAOUDÉ, G., Computer-Aided Design
BERGER, P., Architecture
CANTAFORA, A., Architecture
CHUARD, P., Building Techniques
DUTRY, G.
LAMUNIÈRE, I., History and Theory of Architecture
LUCAN, J., Architectural Theory
MANGEAT, V., Architecture
MARCHAND, B., History and Theory of Architecture
MESTELAN, P., Architecture
MOREL, C., Building Techniques
ORTELLI, L., Architectural Theory
SCARTEZZINI, J.-L., Solar Energy Research Building
STEINMANN, M., Architecture
THALMANN, P., Economics

Department of Biomedical Engineering:

EBRAHIMI, T., Visual Information Processing
LASSER, T., Biomedical Optics
SALATHE, R., Applied Optics
STERGIOPULOS, N., Cardiovascular Technology
UNSER, M., Biomedical Imaging
ZUPPIROLI, L., Optoelectronics

Department of Chemistry and Chemical Engineering:

BODENHAUSEN, G.
BÜNZLI, J.-C.
DYSON, P.
FREITAG, R., Laboratory of Cellular Biotechnology
GIRAULT, H., Institute of Physical Chemistry
GRAETZEL, M., Institute of Physical Chemistry
JOHNSSON, K.
KROSSING, I.
MERBACH, A.
MUTTER, M.
PITSCH, S.
RENKEN, A., Institute of Chemical Engineering III
RIZZO, T., Institute of Physical Chemistry
RÖTHLISBERGER, U.
ROULET, R.
SEVERIN, K.
VOGEL, H., Laboratory of Polymer Chemistry
VOGEL, P.
VON STOCKAR, U.

Department of Civil Engineering:

BADOUX, M., Institute of Reinforced and Prestressed Concrete
BOVY, P., Institute of Transportation and Planning
BRUEHWILER, E., Maintenance, Construction and Safety of Structures
DESCOEUDRES, F., Road Mechanics
DUMONT, A.-G., Institute of Soils, Rocks and Foundations
FAVRE, R., Institute of Structural Engineering
FREY, FR., Laboratory of Structural and Continuum Mechanics
GRAF, W.-H., Hydraulic Research
HIRT, M., Institute of Steel Structures

JACQUOT, P., Stress Analysis and Measurement

LAFITTE, R., Institute of Hydraulics and Energy

MARCHAND, J.-D., Economics of Infrastructure

NATTERER, J., Timber Construction

PARRIAUX, A., Geology

PERRET, F.-L., Construction Management

PFLUG, L., Optical Stress Analysis Laboratory

RIVIER, R., Institute of Transportation and Planning

SANDOZ, J.-L., Timber Construction

SARLOS, G., Institute of Hydraulics and Energy

SCHLEISS, A., Institute of Hydraulics and Energy

SMITH, I., Institute of Reinforced and Prestressed Concrete

VULLIET, L., Soil Mechanics

Department of Communications Systems:

HUBAUX, J.-P.

KUNT, M.

LE BOUDEC, J.-Y.

NUSSBAUMER, H.

PETITPIERRE, C.

VETTERLI, M.

Department of Computer Science:

BOURLARD, H., Artificial Intelligence Laboratory

CORAY, G., Dir, Theoretical Computer Science Laboratory

DE COULON, F., Dir, Computer-Aided-Learning Laboratory

FALTINGS, B., Dir, Artificial Intelligence Laboratory

GERSTNER, W., Mini- and Micro-Computer Laboratory

HERSCH, R.-D., Dir, Peripheral Systems Laboratory

LE BOUDEC, J.-Y., Dir, Communication Network Laboratory

MANGE, D., Dir, Logic Systems Laboratory

NICOUD, J.-D., Dir, Mini- and Micro-Computer Laboratory

PETITPIERRE, C., Dir, Data Communication Laboratory

SANCHEZ, E., Logic Systems Laboratory

SCHIPER, A., Dir, Operating Systems Laboratory

SPACCAPIETRA, S., Dir, Databases Laboratory

STROHMEIER, A., Dir, Software Engineering Laboratory

THALMANN, D., Dir, Computer Graphics Laboratory

THIRAN, P., Institute of Data Communication

WEGMANN, A., Industrial Computer Engineering Laboratory

ZAHND, J., Dir, Logic Systems Laboratory

Department of Electrical Engineering:

DECLERCQ, M., Electronics Laboratory

ENZ, C., General Electronics

FAZAN, P., Electronics Laboratory

GERMOND, A., Electrical Installations Laboratory

IONESCU, M.-A., General Engineering

JUFER, M., Electromechanics Laboratory

KAYAL, M., General Electronics

KUNT, M., Signal Processing Laboratory

MLYNEK, D., Electronics Laboratory

MOSIG, J., Electromagnetism and Acoustics

ROBERT, PH., Metrology Laboratory

ROSSI, M., Electromagnetism and Microwaves Laboratory

RUFER, A.-C., Electronics Laboratory

SIMOND, J.-J., Electromechanics and Electrical Machines Laboratory

SKRIVERVIK, A., Electromagnetism and Acoustics

WAVRE, N., Electromechanics and Electrical Machines Laboratory

Department of Environmental Engineering:

BEY, I., Atmospheric Chemistry Modelling

HARMS, H., Pedology

HOLLIGER, C., Environmental Biotechnology

JOLLIET, O., Ecosystem Management

MERMOUD, A., Institute of Development of Earth and Water

MUSY, A., Institute of Agricultural Engineering

PÉRINGER, P., Institute of Environmental Engineering

SCHLAEPFER, R., Soils and Water

TARRADELLAS, J., Institute of Environmental Engineering

VAN DEN BERGH, H., Institute of Environmental Engineering

VÉDY, J.-C., Institute of Agricultural Engineering

Department of Materials Science and Engineering:

HOFMANN, H., Powder Technology Laboratory

JACQUOT, P., Meteorology and Photonics

KURZ, W., Metallurgy

LANDOLT, D., Chemical Metallurgy

MÅNSON, J.-A., Polymer Composite Technology

MATHIEU, H. J., Chemical Metallurgy Laboratory

MORTENSEN, A., Mechanical Metallurgy Laboratory

RAPPAZ, M., Physical Metallurgy Laboratory

SCRIVENER, K., Construction Materials

SETTER, N., Ceramics Laboratory

Department of Mathematics:

BARTHOLDI, L.

BAYER-FLUCKIGER, E.

BEN AROUS, G., Probability Theory

BUSER, P., Geometry

DACAROGNA, B., Analysis

DALANG, R., Probability Theory

DAVISON, A.

DERIGHETTI, A.

JORIS, H.

LIEBLING, T., Operational Research

MADDOCKS, J., Analysis

MORGENTHALER, S., Statistics

MOUNTFORD, T.

OJANGUREN, M., Mathematical Methodology

QUARTERONI, A.

RAPPAZ, J.

RATIU, T. S.

SHOKROLLAHI, A.

STUART, C., Numerical Analysis and Simulation

THÉVENAZ, J.

WERRA, D. DE, Operational Research

Department of Mechanical Engineering:

AVELLAN, F., Institute of Hydraulic Machinery and Fluid Mechanics

BÖLCS, A., Institute of Thermal Engineering

BONVIN, D., Institute of Automatic Control

BOTSIS, J., Applied Mechanics

CURNIER, A., Laboratory of Applied Mechanics

DEVILLE, M., Institute of Hydraulic Machinery and Fluid Mechanics

FAVRAT, D., Laboratory of Industrial Energy Systems

GIOVANOLA, J., Laboratory of Mechanical Systems Design

GLARDON, R., Applied Mechanics and Institute of Machine Design

LONGCHAMP, R., Institute of Automatics

MONKEWITZ, P., Institute of Hydraulic Machinery and Fluid Mechanics

OWEN, R., Fluid Mechanics

THOME, J., Laboratory of Applied Thermodynamics

XIROUCHAKIS, P., Applied Mechanics and Institute of Machine Design

ZYSSET, P., Laboratory of Applied Mechanics

Department of Microengineering:

BLEULER, H., Institute of Microtechnology

CLAVEL, R., Institute of Microtechnology

GIJS, M., Microsystems

HONGLER, M.-O., Microtechnology

JACOT-DESCOMBES, J., Institute of Microtechnology

LEBLEBICI, Y., Microelectronics

NICOLLIER, C., Institute of Microtechnology

PFLUGER, P., Institute of Microtechnology

POPOVIC, R., Institute of Microtechnology

RENAUD, P., Institute of Microtechnology

RYSER, P., Microtechnology

SIEGWART, R., Institute of Microtechnology

Department of Physics:

ANSERMET, J.-P., Experimental Physics Institute

BALDERESCHI, A., Applied Physics Institute

BARÈS, P.-A., Theoretical Physics

BENOIT, W., Nuclear Engineering Institute

BRÜESCH, P., General Physics of Solids

BUTTET, J., Experimental Physics Institute

CHÂTELAIN, A., Experimental Physics Institute

CHAWLA, R., Nuclear Engineering Institute

DEVEAUD-PLEDRAN, B., Micro- and Opto-electronics Institute

FIVAZ, R., Dir, Applied Physics Institute

GRUBER, C., Theoretical Physics Institute

ILEGEMS, M., Dir, Micro- and Opto-electronics Institute

KAPON, E., Micro- and Opto-electronics Institute

KERN, K., Experimental Physics Institute

KUNZ, H., Theoretical Physics Institute

LÉVY, F., Applied Physics Institute

MARGARITONDO, G., Applied Physics Institute

MARTIN, J.-L., Dir, Nuclear Engineering Institute

MARTIN, PH., Theoretical Physics Institute

MEISTER, J.-J., Applied Physics Institute

MONOT, R., Experimental Physics Institute

QUATTROPANI, A., Theoretical Physics Institute

REINHART, F. K., Micro- and Opto-electronics Institute

STERGIOPOULOS, N., Medical Engineering

ZUPPIROLI, L., Nuclear Engineering Institute

EIDGENÖSSISCHE TECHNISCHE HOCHSCHULE ZÜRICH (ETH) (Swiss Federal Institute of Technology)

8092 Zürich

HG, Rämistr. 101, 8092 Zürich

Telephone: 446321111

E-mail: praesidium@sl.ethz.ch

Internet: www.ethz.ch

Founded 1855

Languages of instruction: French, German

Federal State control

Academic year: October to July (two semesters)

Pres.: Prof. Dr RALPH EICHLER

Rector: Prof. HEIDI WUNDERLI-ALLENSPACH

Vice-Pres. for Research and Corporate Relations: Prof. Dr ROLAND Y. SIEGWART

Vice-Pres. for Finance and Control: Dr ROBERT PERICH

Vice-Pres. for Human Resources and Infrastructure: Prof. Dr ROMAN BOUTELLIER

Sec.-Gen.: HUGO BRETSCHER

Library: see under Libraries and Archives

Number of teachers: 400

Number of students: 16,000

Publications: *ETH Globe* (4 a year), *ETH Life* (online magazine), *ETH Life Print* (9 a year)

PROFESSORS

Agriculture and Food Science (D-Agrl, ETH Zentrum, 8092 Zürich; tel. 446323887; e-mail rutz@agrl.ethz.ch; internet www.agrl.ethz.ch/):

ABDULAI, A., Economics of Nutrition
AMADÒ, R., Food Chemistry
AMRHEIN, N., Plant Science
APEL, K., Plant Science
DORN, S., Applied Entomology
ESCHER, F., Food Technology
FROSSARD, E., Plant Nutrition
GRUISSEM, W., Plant Biotechnology
HURRELL, R. F., Human Nutrition
KREUZER, M., Animal Nutrition
KÜNZI, N., Animal Breeding
LANGHANS, W., Physiology and Animal Husbandry
LEHMANN, B., Farm and Agrobusiness Management
MCDONALD, B., Phytopathology
PUHAN, Z., Dairy Science
RIEDER, P., Agricultural Market and Policy
STAMP, P., Agronomy and Plant Breeding
STRANZINGER, G., Breeding Biology
TEUBER, M., Food Microbiology
WENK, C., Biology of Nutrition
WINDHAB, E., Food Engineering

Applied Biosciences (D-Anbi, Uni Irchel, Winterthurerstr. 110, 8057 Zürich; tel. 446356042; e-mail wyrsck@anbi.ethz.ch; internet www.pharma.ethz.ch):

BOUTELLIER, U., Exercise Physiology
FOLKERS, G., Pharmaceutical Chemistry
MERKLE, H. P., Galenic Pharmacy
MÖHLER, H., Pharmacology
MÜNTENER, M., Anatomy
MURER, K.
NERI, D., Protein Engineering
SCHUBIGER, P. A., Radiopharmacy
STICHER, O., Pharmacognosy and Phytochemistry
WUNDERLI-ALLENSPACH, H., Biopharmacy

Architecture (D-Arch, ETH Honggerberg, 8093 Zürich; tel. 446332885; e-mail michel@arch.ethz.ch; internet www.arch.ethz.ch):

ANGÉLIL, M., Architecture and Design
CAMINADA, G. A., Architecture and Design
CAMPI, M., Architecture and Design
DANIELS, K., Building Systems
DE MEURON, P., Architecture and Design
DEPLAZES, A., Architecture and Technology
DIENER, R., Architecture and Design
EBERLE, D., Architecture and Design
ENGELI, M., Architecture and Computer-Aided Architectural Design
FLÜCKIGER, H., Spatial Development
HERZOG, J., Architecture and Design
HOVESTADT, L., Computer-Aided Architectural Design
JENNY, P., Visual Design
KELLER, B., Building Physics
KÖHLER, B., History and Theory of Architecture
KOLLHOFF, H., Architecture and Technology
KRAMEL, H. E., Architecture and Technology
KRUCKER, B., Architecture and Design
KÜNZLE, O., Building Structures
LYNN, G., Spatial Conception and Exploration
MAGNAGO LAMPUGNANI, V., History of Urbanism
MEILI, M., Architecture and Design
MEYER, A., Architecture and Design
MEYER, P., Architecture and Building Realization
MÖRSCH, G., Preservation of Historical Monuments and Sites

OECHSLIN, W., History of Art and Architecture
OSWALD, F., Architecture and Urbanism
RUCHAT-RONCATI, F., Architecture and Design
RÜEGG, A., Architecture and Design
SCHETT, W., Architecture and Design
SCHMID, W. A., Regional Planning and Methodology
SCHMITT, G., Computer-Aided Architectural Design
SIK, M., Architecture and Design
THIERSTEIN, A., Spatial Development

Biology (D-Biol, ETH Zentrum, 8092 Zürich; tel. 446325942; e-mail ulrich@biol.ethz.ch; internet www.biol.ethz.ch):

AEBI, M., Microbiology
BAILEY, J. E., Biotechnology
BARRAL, Y., Biochemistry
DIMROTH, P., Microbiology
EPPENBERGER, H. M., Cell Biology
FELDON, J., Behavioural Neurobiology
GLOCKSHUBER, R., Molecular Biology and Biophysics
HELENIUS, A., Biochemistry
HENGARTNER, H., Experimental Immunology
HENNECKE, H., Microbiology
KUTAY, U., Biochemistry
LEISINGER, TH., Microbiology
MANSUY, I., Neurobiology
MARTIN, K. A. C., Systematic Neurophysiology
RICHMOND, T. J., Molecular Biology and Biophysics
SCHWAB, M. E., Neuroscience
SUTER, U., Cell Biology
THÖNY-MEYER, L., Molecular Microbiology
WERNER, S., Cell Biology
WINKLER, F. K., Structural Biology
WITHOLT, B., Biotechnology
WÜRGLER, F. E., Genetics
WÜTHRICH, K., Molecular Biology and Biophysics

Chemistry (D-Chem, ETH Zentrum, 8093 Zürich; tel. 446323055; e-mail hauser@chem.ethz.ch; internet www.chem.ethz.ch):

BAIKER, A., Chemical Engineering and Catalysis
CARREIRA, E. M., Organic Chemistry
CHEN, P., Physical-organic Chemistry
DIEDERICH, F., Organic Chemistry
GRÜTZMACHER, H., Inorganic Chemistry
GÜNTHER, D., Analytical Chemistry
HILVERT, D., Organic Chemistry
HÜNENBERGER, PH. H., Physical Chemistry
HUNGERBÜHLER, K., Safety and Environmental Protection
KOPPENOL, W. H., Bioinorganic Chemistry
MEIER, B. H., Physical Chemistry
MERKT, F., Physical Chemistry
MORBIDELLI, M., Chemical Reaction Engineering
NESPER, R., Inorganic Chemistry
PRINS, R., Industrial Chemistry
QUACK, M., Physical Chemistry
RÖTHLISBERGER, U., Computer-Aided Inorganic Chemistry
RYS, P., Technical Chemistry
SCHWEIGER, A., Physical Chemistry
SEEBACH, D., Organic Chemistry
TOGNI, A., Organometallic Chemistry
VAN GUNSTEREN, W. F., Computer-Aided Chemistry
VASELLA, A. T., Organic Chemistry
WILD, U. P., Physical Chemistry
WOKAUN, A., Chemistry
ZENOBI, R., Analytical Chemistry

Civil, Environmental and Geomatics Engineering (D-Baug, ETH Honggerberg, 8093 Zürich; tel. 446332691; e-mail altenburger@baug.ethz.ch; internet www.baum.ethz.ch):

AMANN, P., Soil Engineering and Soil Mechanics

ANDERHEGGEN, E., Applied Computer Science
AXHAUSEN, K. W., Traffic Engineering
BACCINI, P., Material Flux and Waste Management
BÖHNI, H., Materials Science
BRÄNDLI, H., Traffic Engineering
BURLAND, P., Hydrology and Water Resource Management
CAROSIO, A., Geodesy
FABER, M., Structural Engineering
FONTANA, M., Structural Engineering
GIGER, CH., Geographic Information Systems
GIRMSCHEID, G., Construction Management and Process Technology
GRÜN, A., Photogrammetry
GUJER, W., Sanitary Engineering
HERMANNS STENGELE, R., Geotechnics
HURNI, L., Cartography
INGENSAND, H., Geodesy
KAHLE, H.-G., Geodesy
KINZELBACH, W., Hydromechanics
KOVARI, K., Tunnelling
MARTI, P., Structural Engineering
MINOR, H.-E., Hydraulic Structures
SCHALCHER, H.-R., Planning and Construction Management
SCHMID, W. A., Rural Engineering and Planning
SPRINGMAN, S., Geotechnical Engineering
VIRTANEN, S., Metallic High-Performance Materials
VOGEL, TH., Structural Engineering
WITTMANN, F. H., Materials Science

Computer Science (D-Infk, ETH Zentrum, 8092 Zürich; tel. 446327220; e-mail haeni@inf.ethz.ch; internet www.inf.ethz.ch):

ALONSO, G., Information Systems
BIERE, A., Computer Systems
GANDER, W., Scientific Computing
GONNET, G. H., Scientific Computing
GROSS, M., Computer Graphics
GROSS, TH., Computer Systems
GUTKNECHT, J., Computer Systems
MATTERN, F., Information Systems
MAURER, U., Theoretical Computer Science
NAGEL, K., Scientific Computing
NIEVERGELT, J., Theoretical Computer Science
NORRIE, M., Information Systems
RICHTER-GEBERT, J., Theoretical Computer Science
SCHEK, H.-J., Information Systems
SCHIELE, B., Scientific Computing
STÄRK, R., Theoretical Computer Science
STRICKER, TH. M., Computer Systems
WELZL, E., Theoretical Computer Science
WIDMAYER, P., Theoretical Computer Science
ZEHNDER, C. A., Information Systems

Earth Sciences (D-Erdw, ETH Zentrum, 8092 Zürich; tel. 446325647; e-mail bonadurer@erdw.ethz.ch; internet www.erdw.ethz.ch):

BURG, J.-P., Structural Geology
GIARDINI, D., Seismology and Geodynamics
GREEN, A. G., Applied Geophysics
HALLIDAY, A. N., Isotope Geochemistry
HEINRICH, CH. A., Mineral Resources and Processes of the Earth's Interior
KUNZ, M., Crystallography
LÖW, S., Engineering Geology
LOWRIE, W., Geophysics
MCKENZIE, J., Earth System Sciences
SEWARD, T. M., Geochemistry
STEUER, W., Crystallography
THIERSTEIN, H. R., Micropalaeontology
THOMPSON, A. B., Petrology
TROMMSDORFF, V., Petrography

Electrical Engineering (D-Elek, ETH Zentrum, 8092 Zürich; tel. 446325002; e-mail marcel.kreuzer@ee.ethz.ch; internet www.itet.ethz.ch):

ANDERSSON, G., Electrical Energy Systems and Processes
BÄCHTOLD, W., Electromagnetic Fields and Microwaves
DAHLHAUS, D., Mobile Radio Communication
EGGIMANN, F., Signal and Information Processing
ERLEBACH, TH., Theory of Communication Networks
FICHTNER, W., Integrated Systems
FRÖHLICH, K., Electric Power Transmission and High Voltage Technology
GUT, J., Military Security Technology
HUANG, Q., Integrated Systems
HUBBELL, J. A., Biomedical Engineering and Medical Informatics
HUGEL, J., Electrical Engineering Design
JÄCKEL, H., Electronics
KÜNDIG, A., Computer Engineering and Communication Networks
LAPIDOTH, A., Information Theory
LEUTHOLD, P., Communication Technology
LOELIGER, H.-A., Signals Processing
MORARI, M., Automatic Control
NIEDERER, P., Biomedical Engineering and Medical Informatics
PLATTNER, B., Computer Engineering and Communications Networks
SCHAUFELBERGER, W., Automatic Control
STILLER, B., Communication Systems
THIELE, L., Computer Engineering
TRÖSTER, G., Electronics
VAHLDIECK, R., Field Theory
VAN GOOL, L., Computer Vision

Environmental Sciences (D-Umnw, ETH Zentrum, 8092 Zürich; tel. 446322523; e-mail secretariat@umnw.ethz.ch; internet www.env.ethz.ch):

DAVIES, H. C., Atmospheric Physics, Dynamic Meteorology
EDWARDS, P., Plant Ecology
EWALD, K., Nature and Landscape Protection
FLÜHLER, H., Soil Physics
IMBODEN, D., Environmental Physics
KAISER, F. G., Human Environmental Relations
KRETZSCHMAR, R., Soil Chemistry
MIEG, H. A., Human–Environmental Relations
OHMURA, A., Climatology
PETER, TH., Atmospheric Chemistry
ROY, B. A., Plant Biodiversity
SCHÄR, C., Hydrology and Climatology
SCHMID-HEMPEL, P., Experimental Ecology
SCHOLZ, R. W., Environmental Sciences
SCHULIN, R., Soil Protection
SCHWARZENBACH, R., Organic Environmental Chemistry
WALDVOGEL, A., Atmospheric Physics
WARD, J. V., Aquatic Ecology
WEHRLI, B., Aquatic Chemistry
ZEHNDER, A. J. B, Environmental Biotechnology
ZEYER, J., Soil Biology

Forest Sciences (D-Fowi, ETH Zentrum, 8092 Zürich; tel. 446326194; e-mail benz@fowi .ethz.ch; internet www.fowi.ethz.ch):

BACHMANN, P., Forest Inventory and Planning
BUGMANN, H., Mountain Forest Ecology
HEINIMANN, H. R., Forestry Engineering
HOLDENRIEDER, O., Forest Pathology and Dendrology
KISSLING-NÄF, I., Forest Resource Economics
SCHMITHÜSEN, F., Forestry Policy and Economics
SCHÜTZ, J.-PH., Silviculture

Humanities, Social and Political Sciences (D-Gess, ETH Zentrum, 8092 Zürich; tel. 446322308; e-mail margelisch@gess.ethz.ch; internet www.gess.ethz.ch):

BERNAUER, T., International Relations
BESOMI, O., Italian Language and Literature
BUCHMANN, M., Sociology
DÄLLENBACH, L., French Language and Literature
EISNER, M., Sociology
FREY, K., Education
GABRIEL, J. M., International Relations
GUGERLI, D., History of Technology
HERTIG, R., Law
HOLENSTEIN, E., Philosophy
KAPPEL, R., Problems of Developing Countries
NEF, U. CH., Law
NOWOTNY, H., Philosophy and Social Studies
RIS, R., German Language and Literature
RUCH, A., Law
SCHIPS, B., Economics
SCHUBERT, R., Economics
SPILLMAN, K. R., Security Studies and Conflict Research
SUTER, CH., Sociology
TOBLER, H. W., General History
VICKERS, B., English Language and Literature
WENGER, A., Swiss and International Security Policy

Industrial Management and Manufacturing Engineering (D-Bepr, ETH Zentrum, 8092 Zürich; tel. 446325718; e-mail wismer@bepr .ethz.ch; internet www.bepr.ethz.ch/main .htm):

ABELL, D. F., Technology and Management
FAHRNI, F., Technology Management
GROTE, G., Work Psychology
HUBER, F., Industrial Engineering and Management
KOLLER, TH., Hygiene and Applied Physiology
KRUEGER, H., Ergonomics
MEYER, U., Textile Machinery
REISSNER, J., Forming Technology
SCHÖNSLEBEN, P., Industrial Engineering and Management
TSCHIRKY, H., Industrial Engineering and Management
WEHNER, T., Work and Organizational Psychology

Materials Science (D-Werk, ETH Zentrum, 8092 Zürich; tel. 446322520; e-mail krombach@ifp.mat.ethz.ch; internet www .mat.ethz.ch):

GAUCKLER, L. J., Non-metallic Materials
LUISI, P. L., Macromolecular Chemistry
ÖTTINGER, H. CH., Polymer Physics
SMITH, P., Polymer Technology
SPEIDEL, M. O., Metals and Metallurgy
SPENCER, N. D., Surface Technology
STÜSSI, E., Biomechanics
SUTER, U. W., Macromolecular Chemistry
WINTERMANTEL, E., Biocompatible Materials

Mathematics (D-Math, ETH Zentrum, 8092 Zürich; tel. 446325615; e-mail mathdept@ math.ethz.ch; internet www.math.ethz.ch):

BÜHLMANN, P. L., Mathematics
BURGER, M., Mathematics
DELBAEN, F., Financial Mathematics
EMBRECHTS, P., Mathematics
FEICHTNER, E. M., Mathematics
FELDER, G., Mathematics
GROTE, M. J., Mathematics
HAMPEL, F., Statistics
ILMANEN, T., Mathematics
JELTSCH, R., Applied Mathematics
KIRCHGRABER, U., Mathematics
KNÖRRER, H., Mathematics
KNUS, M. A., Mathematics
KÜNSCH, H. R., Mathematics
LANFORD, O. E., III, Mathematics
LANG, U., Mathematics
LÜTHI, H.-J., Operations Research

MISLIN, G., Mathematics
NUCINKIS, B. E. A., Mathematics
OSTERWALDER, K., Mathematics
PINK, R., Mathematics
SALAMON, D. A., Mathematics
SALMHOFER, M., Mathematics
SCHWAB, CH., Applied Mathematics
STAMMBACH, U., Mathematics
STRUWE, M., Mathematics
SZNITMAN, A.-S., Mathematics
TRUBOWITZ, E., Mathematics
WÜSTHOLZ, G., Mathematics
ZEHNDER, E., Mathematics

Mechanical and Process Engineering (D-Mavt, ETH Zentrum, 8092 Zürich; tel. 446322596; e-mail vonrohr@mavt.ethz.ch; internet www.mavt.ethz.ch):

ABHARI, R., Turbomachinery
DUAL, J., Mechanics
EBERLE, M., Internal Combustion Engines and Combustion Technology
ERMANNI, P., Composites and Structures
FILIPPINI, M., Economics and Energy Policy
GEERING, H. P., Measurement and Control
GUZZELLA, L., Internal Combustion Engines
JOCHEM, E., Economics and Energy Policy
KLEISER, L., Fluid Dynamics
KOUMOUTSAKOS, P., Fluid Dynamics
KRÖGER, W., Safety Technology
MAZZOTTI, M., Process Engineering
MEIER, M., Product Development
MEYER-PIENING, H.-R., Lightweight Structures and Ropeways
POULIKAKOS, D., Thermodynamics in Emerging Technology
PRATSINIS, S. E., Process Engineering
RÖSGEN, TH., Fluid Dynamics
RUDOLF VON ROHR, PH., Process Engineering
SAYIR, M., Mechanics
SCHWEITZER, G., Robotics
SEILER, A., Engineering and Management
STEINER, M., Control Systems
STEINFELD, Renewable Energy Carriers
STEMMER, A., Nanotechnology
YADIGAROGLU, G., Nuclear Engineering

Physics (D-Phys, ETH Hönggerberg, 8093 Zürich; tel. 446332585; e-mail rafailidis@ phys.ethz.ch; internet www.phys.ethz.ch):

BALTES, H., Quantum Electronics
BATLOGG, B., Solid State Physics
BLATTER, J. W., Theoretical Physics
DEGIORGI, L., Solid State Physics
DOUGLAS, R. J., Theoretical Neuroinformatics
EICHLER, R., Experimental Particle Physics
ENSSLIN, K., Solid State Physics
FRÖHLICH, J., Theoretical and Mathematical Physics
GRAF, G. M., Theoretical Physics
GÜNTER, P., Quantum Electronics
HEPP, K., Theoretical Physics
HOFER, H., Experimental Particle Physics
HUNZIKER, W., Theoretical Physics
KELLER, U., Quantum Electronics
KOSTORZ, G., Applied Physics
LANDOLT, M., Solid State Physics
LANG, J., Experimental Particle Physics
MARTIN, K. A. C., Systematic Neurophysiology
OTT, H. R., Solid State Physics
PAUSS, F., Experimental Particle Physics
PESCIA, D., Solid State Physics
RICE, TH. M., Theoretical Physics
RUBBIA, A., Experimental Particle Physics
SCHMID, CH., Theoretical Physics
STENFLO, J. O., Astrophysics
VAN ER VEEN, J. F., Experimental Particle Physics

UNIVERSITÀ DELLA SVIZZERA ITALIANA
(University of Lugano)

Via Lambertenghi 10, 6904 Lugano
Telephone: 586664000
E-mail: info@usi.ch
Internet: www.usi.ch

Founded 1996
State control
Languages of instruction: English, Italian
Academic year: September to June

2 Campuses at Lugano and Mendrisio

Pres.: PIERO MARTINOLI
Gen. Sec.: Lic. phil. ALBINO ZGRAGGEN
Head Librarian for Lugano Campus: Dr GIUSEPPE ORIGGI
Head Librarian for Mendrisio Campus: SERGIO STEFFEN

Library of 70,000 vols
Number of teachers: 795
Number of students: 2,919

DEANS

Academy of Architecture: MARIO BOTTA
Faculty of Communication Sciences: Prof. Dr LORENZO CANTONI
Faculty of Economics: Prof. RICO MAGGI
Faculty of Informatics: MAURO PEZZÈ

UNIVERSITÄT BASEL

Peterspl. 1, 4003 Basel
Telephone: 612671298
E-mail: studienberatung@unibas.ch
Internet: www.unibas.ch

Founded 1460
Languages of instruction: German, English
Academic year: August to July

Rector: Prof. ANTONIO LOPRIENO
Vice-Rector for Devt: Prof. Dr ALEX N. EBERLE
Vice-Rector for Research and Professional Devt: Prof. Dr PETER MEIER-ABT
Vice-Rector for Teaching: Prof. Dr HEDWIG J. KAISER
Exec. Dir: CHRISTOPH TSCHUMI
Librarian: H. HUG

Library: see under Libraries and Archives
Number of teachers: 1,300
Number of students: 11,360

DEANS

Faculty of Business and Economics: Prof. Dr. MANFRED BRUHN
Faculty of Humanities: Prof. Dr C. OPITZ-BELAKHAL
Faculty of Law: Prof. Dr PETER JUNG
Faculty of Medicine: Prof. Dr ALBERT URWYLER
Faculty of Psychology: Prof. Dr MICHAELA WÄNKE
Faculty of Science: Prof. Dr MARTIN SPIESS
Faculty of Theology: Prof. Dr ALFRED BODENHEIMER

PROFESSORS

Faculty of Economics (Wirtschaftswissenschaftliches Zentrum (WWZ), Petersgraben 51, 4003 Basel):

BORNER, S., Political Economics
BRUHN, M., Marketing and Management
KUGLER, P., Monetary Macroeconomics
MÜLLER, W. R., Business Administration
SCHIERENBECK, H., Business Administration
WEDER, R., Economics
ZIMMERMANN, H., Finance Theory

Faculty of Humanities:

HOLL, U., Media Sciences
MAASEN, SABINE, Social Studies of Science

Faculty of Law (Peter Merian-Weg 8, 4056 Basel; tel. 612672531; e-mail dekanat-ius@unibas.ch; internet www.ius.unibas.ch):

BEHNISCH, U., Public Law
GLESS, S., Criminal Law
HANDSCHIN, L., Private Law
KRAMER, E. A., Civil Law
NADAKAVUKAREN SCHEFER, K., Public Law
PETERS, A., Public Law, Swiss National Law
PIETH, M., Penal Law
RIVA, E., Public Law
SCHEFER, M., Swiss National Law
SCHWENZER, I., Civil Law
SEELMANN, K., Penal Law, Philosophy of Law
STÖCKLI, F., Private Law
SUTTER-SOMM, T., Civil Law and Civil Procedural Law
THURNHERR, D., Public Law
TOBLER, C., Public Law

Faculty of Medicine (Klingelbergstr. 61, 4056 Basel; tel. 612652050; internet www.medizin.unibas.ch):

ACKERMANN-LIEBRICH, U., Social and Prophylactic Medicine
BETTLER, B., Physiology
BÜHLER, F. R., Pharmaceutical Medicine
CHRISTOFORI, G., Biochemistry and Genetics
DE GEEST, S., Nursing
DICK, W., Orthopaedics
DITTMANN, V., Legal Medicine
ECKSTEIN, F., Cardiology
FLAMMER, J., Ophthalmology
GASSER, TH., Urology
GRATWOHL, A., Internal Medicine
HESS, C., Ambulant Internal Medicine
HOLLÄNDER, G., Paediatric Molecular Medicine
ITIN, P., Dermatology and Venereology
KAPPOS, L., Neurology
KRAPF, R., Internal Medicine
KÜNZLE, N., Social and Preventive Medicine
LAMBRECHT, J. TH., Dentistry
LUIGI, M., Neurosurgery
MARINELLO, C. P., Dentistry
MIHATSCH, M. J., General and Special Pathology
MORONI, CHR., Medical Microbiology
MÜLLER, V., Internal Medicine
MÜLLER-SPAHN, F. S., Adult Psychiatry
OERTLI, D., General Surgery
OSSWALD, S., Cardiology
PALMER, E., Experimental Transplantation Immunology and Nephrology
PFISTERER, M., Cardiology
PÜHSE, U., Science of Sports Medicine
QUERVAIN, D., Cognitive Neurosciences
RIECHER-RÖSSLER, Adult Psychiatry
ROLINK, A., Immunology
SCHAAD, U. B., Paediatrics
SCHEIDEGGER, D. H., Anaesthetics
SCHIFFERLI, J., Internal Medicine
SCHMIDT-TRUCKSÄSS, A., Sports Medicine
SKODA, R., Molecular Medicine
STEIGER, J., Internal Medicine
STEINBRICH, W., Medical Radiology
TOLNAY, M., Pathology
TYNDALL, L. A., Rheumatology
WEIGER, R., Dentistry
ZEILHOFER, H.-F., Reconstructive Surgery
ZELLER, R., Anatomy and Embryology
ZIMMERLI, W., Internal Medicine

Faculty of Philosophy and History (Bernoulistr. 28, 4056 Basel):

ANGEHRN, E., Philosophy
ARLT, W., Musicology
BERGMAN, M., Sociology
BEYER, A., Modern History of Art
BIERL, A., General Philology
BOEHM, G., History of Art

BURGHARTZ, S., History of the 14th–16th centuries
ENGLER, B., English Philology
FÖRSTER, T., Ethnology
GLAUSER, J., Nordic Philology
GUSKI, A., Slavonic Philology
HÄCKI BUHOFER, A., German Philology
HARICH-SCHWARZBAUER, H., Latin Philology
HAUMANN, H., History of Eastern Europe
HONOLD, A., Modern German Literature
KOPP, R., Romance Philology
KREBS, G., Philosophy
KREIS, G., Modern General History and Swiss History
LEIMGRUBER, W., Folklore, European Ethnology
LOPRIENO, A., Egyptology
LÜDI, G., Romance Philology
MÄDER, U., Sociology
MILLET, O., French Philology
MOOSER, J., History of the 20th Century
OPITZ-BELAKHAL, C., History of the 17th and 18th Centuries
PILLER, I., Sociolinguistics and Sociology of English as a Global Language
SCHAFFNER, M., Swiss History and Recent General History
SCHELLEWALD, B., History of Art
SCHMID, B., Ibero-Romance Philology
SCHNELL, R., German Philology
SCHOELER, G., Islamic Studies
SIEGMUND, F., Prehistory and Early History
SIMON, R., German Literary Studies
STÄHELI, U., Sociology
STUCKY, R., Classical Archaeology
TERZOLI, M. A., Romance Philology
THOLEN, G. C., Media Science
VON GREYERZ, K., Recent General History and Swiss History
VON MÜLLER, A, Medieval History
VON UNGERN-STERNBERG, J, Ancient History

Faculty of Psychology (Missionsstr. 60–62, 4055 Basel; tel. 612673528; e-mail info-psycho@unibas.ch; internet www.unibas.ch/psycho):

GROB, A., Developmental Psychology
MARGRAF, J., Clinical Psychology
OPWIS, K., General Psychology and Methodology
WÄNKE, M., Social and Business Psychology

Faculty of Science (Pharmazentrum, Klingelbergstr. 50, 4056 Basel; tel. 612673053; internet www.unibas.ch/philnat):

A'CAMPO, N., Mathematics
AEBI, U., Structural Biology
AFFOLTER, M., Neurobiology and Developmental Biology
ALEWELL, CH., Environmental Earth Sciences
BARDE, Y. A., Neurobiology
BICKLE, T. A., Microbiology
BOLLER, TH., Botany
BRUDER, C., Theoretical Physics
CONSTABLE, E., Inorganic Chemistry
CORNELIS, G., Microbiology
EBERT, D., Zoology
ENGEL, A., Structural Biology
ERNST, B., Molecular Pharmaceutics
FOLKERS, G., Pharmaceutical Chemistry
GASSER, S., Molecular Biology
GEHRING, W. J., Physiology of Development and Genetics
GIESE, B., Organic Chemistry
GROTE, M. S., Mathematics
GRZESIEK, S., Structural Biology
GÜNTHERODT, H.-J., Experimental Physics
HALL, M., Biochemistry
HAMBURGER, M. O., Pharmacy
HAURI, H., Cell Biology
IM HOF, H.-CHR., Mathematics
KELLER, W., Cell Biology
KÖRNER, CHR., Botany

KRAFT, H., Mathematics
LESER, H., Physical Geography
LE TENSORER, J.-M., Pre- and Early History
LEUENBERGER, H., Pharmaceutical Technology
LOSS, D., Theoretical Physics
MAIER, J. P., Physical Chemistry
MASSER, D., Mathematics
MEIER, W., Chemistry
PARLOW, E., Meteorology and Climatology
PFALTZ, A., Organic Chemistry
PHILIPPSEN, P., Applied Microbiology
REICHERT, H., Zoology
RÜEGG, M., Neurobiology
SCHMID, S. M., Geology and Palaeontology
SCHNEIDER-SLIWA, R., Human Geography
SCHÖNENBERGER, CH., Experimental Physics
SEELIG, J., Structural Biology
SPIESS, M., Biochemistry
TANNES, M., Epidemiology and Medical Parasitology
THIELEMANN, F. K., Theoretical Physics
TSCHUDIN, CH., Applied Information Technology
VETTER, T., Applied Information Technology
WIEMKEN, A. M., Botany
ZUBERBÜHLER, A., Inorganic Chemistry

Faculty of Theology (Nadelberg 10, 4051 Basel; tel. 612672901; internet theolrel.unibas.ch):

BERNHARDT, R., Systematic Theology, Dogmatics
BRÄNDLE, R., New Testament, History of the Early Church
GÄBLER, U., Ecclesiastical and Dogmatic History
GRÖZINGER, A., Practical Theology
LIENEMANN, CH., Ecumenical Movement and Mission
MATHYS, H.-P., Old Testament and Semitic Languages
MOHN, J., Science of Religion
PFLEIDERER, G., Systematic Theology, Ethics
STEGEMANN, E., New Testament
WALRAFF, M., History of the Church and of Theology

Institute for Jewish Studies (Leimenstr. 48, 4051 Basel; tel. 612051636; e-mail institut-judaistik@unibas.ch; internet www.jewishstudies.unibas.ch):

BODENHEIMER, A., Jewish Literature and History
PICARD, J., Modern Jewish History and Culture

UNIVERSITÄT BERN

Hochschulstr. 4, 3012 Bern
Telephone: 316318111
E-mail: info@imd.unibe.ch
Internet: www.unibe.ch
Founded 1834, (inc. Theological School, f. 1528)
State control
Language of instruction: German
Academic year: September to August
Rector: Prof. Dr URS WÜRGLER
Vice-Rector for Research: Prof. Dr MARTIN TÄUBER
Vice-Rector for Univ. Education: Prof. Dr GUNTER STEPHAN
Admin. Dir: Dr DANIEL ODERMATT
Chief Librarian: Prof. Dr ROBERT BARTH
Number of teachers: 3,552
Number of students: 14,300
Publications: *uniaktuell* (online magazine), *UniPress–Forschung und Wissenschaft*

DEANS
Faculty of Economics and Social Science: Prof. Dr HARLEY KROHMER
Faculty of Humanities: Prof. Dr HEINZPETER ZNOJ
Faculty of Human Sciences: Prof. Dr ROLAND SEILER
Faculty of Law: Prof. Dr STEPHAN WOLF
Faculty of Medicine: Prof. Dr PETER EGGLI
Faculty of Science: Prof. Dr SILVIO DECURTINS
Faculty of Theology: Prof. Dr SILVIA SCHROER
Vetsuisse Faculty: Prof. Dr ANDREAS ZURBRIGGEN

UNIVERSITÄT LUZERN
(University of Lucerne)

Frohburgstr. 3, 6002 Lucerne
Telephone: 412295000
E-mail: international@unilu.ch
Internet: www.unilu.ch
Founded 1574, present status 2000
Languages of instruction: English, French, German
Academic year: August to July
Rector: Prof. Dr PAUL RICHLI
Vice-Rector for Research: Prof. Dr MARTIN BAUMANN
Vice-Rector for Teaching and Int. Relations: Prof. Dr MARKUS RIES
Admin. Sec.: JUSTINA SCHMIDLIN
Number of teachers: 325
Number of students: 2,700

DEANS
Faculty of Humanities and Social Sciences: Prof. Dr CHRISTOPH A. SCHALTEGGER
Faculty of Theology: Prof. Dr MARKUS RIES
School of Law: Prof. Dr FELIX BOMMER

UNIVERSITÄT ST GALLEN
(University of St Gallen)

Dufourstr. 50, 9000 St Gallen
Telephone: 712242111
E-mail: info@unisg.ch
Internet: www.unisg.ch
Founded 1898, present name 2011
State control
Languages of instruction: German, English
Academic year: April to March
Pres.: Prof. Dr THOMAS BIEGER
Vice-Pres.: Lic. WERNER GÄCHTER
Exec. Dir: Lic. MARKUS BRÖNNIMANN
Library Dir: Dr XAVER BAUMGARTNER
Number of teachers: 927
Number of students: 6,726
Publications: *Aussenwirtschaft* (6 a year), *Electronic Markets* (4 a year), *Thexis* (6 a year)

DEANS
Law School: Prof. LUKAS GSCHWEND
School of Economics and Political Science: Prof. MONIKA BÜTLER
School of Finance: Prof. Dr KARL FRAUENDORFER
School of Humanities and Social Sciences: Prof. ULRICH SCHMID
School of Management: Prof. WALTER BRENNER

PROFESSORS
ANDEREGG, J., German Language and Literature
BACK, A., Information Processing
BAUDENBACHER, C., Private, Commercial and Economic Law
BAUMER, J.-M., Development Policy
BEHR, G., Business Administration
BELZ, C., Marketing
BERNET, B., Business Administration, Banking
BIEGER, T., Business Administration, Tourism
BOURQUI, C., Business Administration
BURMEISTER, K. H., History of Law
CHONG, L., Business Administration
DACHLER, P., Psychology
DOPFER, K., Foreign Trade and Development Theory
DRUEY, J. N., Civil and Commercial Law
DUBS, R., Business Pedagogy
DYLLICK, T., Business Administration
EHRENZELLER, B., Public Law
FICKERT, R., Business Administration
FISCHER, G., Economics
FRAUENDORFER, K., Operations Research
GÄRTNER, M., Economics
GEISER, T., Civil and Commercial Law
GOMEZ, P., Business Administration
GROSS, P., Sociology
GRÜNBICHLER, A., Finance
HALLER, M., Insurance and Business Administration, Risk Management
HAUSER, H., Foreign Trade Theory and Policy
HILB, M., Business Administration
INGOLD, F. P., Russian Language and Literature
JAEGER, F., Economic Policy
KAUFMANN, V., French Language and Literature
KEEL, A., Statistics
KIRCHGÄSSNER, G., Economics
KLEY, R., Political Science
KOLLER, A., Civil and Commercial Law
LECHNER, M., Empirical Economic Research and Econometrics
LEUENBERGER, T., Modern History
MANELLA, J., Business Administration
MARTINONI, R., Italian Language and Literature
MASTRONARDI, P., Public Law
MEIER, A., Economics
MEIER-SCHATZ, C., Civil and Commercial Law
METZGER, CH., Business Administration
MOHR, E., Economics
MÜLLER, H., Mathematics
MÜLLER-STEWENS, G., Business Administration
NOBEL, P., Private, Commercial and Economic Law
OESTERLE, H., Information Processing
PLEITNER, H. J., Business Administration
REETZ, N., Economics
RIKLIN, A., Political Science
ROBERTO, V., Private, Commercial and Economic Law
ROBINSON, A. D., English Language and Literature
RUIGROK, W., International Management
RUUD, F., Accounting
SCHEDLER, K., Public Management
SCHMID, B., Information Processing
SCHMID, H., Economics
SCHUH, G., Technology
SCHWANDER, I., Civil Law
SCHWEIZER, R., Public Law
SILES, J. R., Spanish Language and Literature
SPREMANN, K., Business Administration
STÄHLY, P., Operations Research
STIER, W., Empirical Social Research and Applied Statistics
TOMCZAK, T., Business Administration
TRECHSEL, ST., Criminal Law and Criminal Case Law
ULRICH, P., Economic Ethics
VALLENDER, C., Public Law and Law of Taxation
VON KROGH, F., Business Administration
WALDBURGER, R., Taxation Law
WINTER, R., Information Processing
WUNDERER, R., Business Administration
ZIMMERMANN, H., Financial Market Analysis

UNIVERSITÄT ZÜRICH

Rämistr. 71, 8006 Zürich
Telephone: 446341111
Internet: www.uzh.ch
Founded 1833, as Universitas Turicensis, univ. status 1912
State control
Language of instruction: German
Academic year: October to July (2 semesters)
Pres.: Prof. Dr ANDREAS FISCHER
Vice-Pres. for Arts and Social Sciences: Prof. Dr OTTFRIED JARREN
Vice-Pres. for Law and Economics: Prof. Dr EGON FRANCK
Vice-Pres. for Medicine and Natural Sciences: Prof. Dr DANIEL WYLER
Admin. Dir. and Dir of Finance: Dipl.-Ing. STEFAN SCHNYDER
Sec.-Gen.: Dr KURT REIMANN
Librarian: Dr HEINZ DICKENMANN

Number of teachers: 512
Number of students: 25,854

Publications: *unijournal* (6 a year), *unimagazin* (4 a year), *unireport* (1 a year)

DEANS

Faculty of Arts: Prof. Dr BERND ROECK
Faculty of Economics: Prof. Dr JOSEF FALKINGER
Faculty of Law: Prof. Dr WOLFGANG WOHLERS
Faculty of Medicine: Prof. Dr KLAUS GRÄTZ
Faculty of Science: Prof. Dr MICHAEL HENGARTNER
Faculty of Theology: Prof. Dr CHRISTOPH UEHLINGER
Vetsuisse Faculty: Prof. Dr FELIX R. ALTHAUS

PROFESSORS

Centre for Dentistry, Oral and Maxillary Medicine (Plattenstr. 11, 8028 Zürich; tel. 446343203):

GRÄTZ, K., Oral Surgery
HÄMMERLE, C., Crowns and Bridges
IMFELD, T., Preventive Dentistry, Periodontology, Cardiology
PALLA, S., Dental Prosthesis
PELTOMÄKI, T., Children's Dentistry

Faculty of Economics (tel. 446342314; e-mail dekanatww@zuv.uzh.ch; internet www.oec.uzh.ch):

BACKES-GELLNER, U., Business Admin.
BERNSTEIN, A., Dynamic and Distributed Application Systems
CHESNEY, M., Quantitative Finance
DIETL, H., Service and Operation Management
DITTRICH, K. R., Computer Science
EWERHART, C., Information Economy
FALKINGER, J., Finance and Macroeconomics
FEHR, E., Economics
FRANCK, E., Business Admin.
GALL, H. C., Software Engineering
GEIGER, H., Banking and Finance
GIBSON-ASNER, R., Financial Economics
GLINZ, M., Informatics
HABIB, M., Corporate Finance Theory
HENS, T., Financial Economics
HOFFMANN, M., Int. Trade and Finance
HOTZ-HART, B., Economics
JANSSEN, M., Financial Economics
KLATTE, D., Mathematics and Economics
MEYER, C., Accountancy and Financial Control
OSTERLOH, M., Business Admin.
PAJAROLA, R., Multimedia
PAOLELLA, M., Empirical Finance
PFAFF, D., Accountancy and Financial Control
PFEIFER, R., Computer Science
RUUD, F., Accountancy and Financial Control
SAEZ-MARTI, F., Microeconomics

SCHAUER, H., Computer Science
SCHENKER-WICKI, A., Business Management
SCHERER, A. G., Business Admin.
SCHMUTZLER, A., Economics
SCHWABE, G., Information Management
STAFFELBACH, B., Business Admin.
STILLER, B., Systems and Communication
VOLKART, R., Banking and Finance
WEHRLI, H. P., Business Admin.
WINKELMANN, R., Empirical Economics
WOITEK, U., History of Economics and National Economy
ZILIBOTTI, F., National Economics
ZWEIFEL, P., Political Economy
ZWEIMÜLLER, J., Macroeconomics

Faculty of Law (tel. 446342233; e-mail dekrwf@ius.uzh.ch; internet www.jur.uzh.ch):

BIAGGINI, G., State, Administrative and European Law
BREITSCHMID, P., Private Law
BÜCHLER, A., Private Law
DONATSCH, A., Criminal Law
ERNST, W., Roman Law
FÖGEN, M. T., Roman Law and Comparative Law
FORSTMOSER, P., Trade Law
GÄCHTER, TH., State, Administrative and Securities Law
GRIFFEL, A., State and Administrative Law
HEINEMANN, A., Economic Law
HILTY, R., Private Law
HONSELL, H., Swiss and European Civil Law, Roman Law
HUGUENIN, C., Private Economic Law and European Law
JAAG, T., State and Administrative Law
JOSITSCH, D., Criminal Law
KAUFMANN, C., State and Administrative Law, Law of Nations
KELLER, H., State Law
KILLIAS, M., Criminal Law
KLEY, A., State Law
MEIER, I., Civil Case Law, Bankruptcy Law
NOBEL, P. J., Swiss and European Trading and Economic Law
OBERHAMMER, P., Civil Case Law
OTT, W., Philosophical and Swiss Civil Law
PORTMANN, W., Private and Industrial Law
RAUSCH, H., Environmental and Administrative Law
REICH, M., Tax, Fiscal and Administrative Law
REY, H., Swiss Civil Law
SCHNYDER, A., Private Economic Law
SENN, M., Philosophical Law
TAG, B., Criminal Law
THIER, A., History of Law
THÜRER, D., Law of Nations, State and Administrative Law
UHLMANN, F., State and Administrative Law
VON DER CRONE, H. C., Private and Business Law
WEBER, R., European Law
WEBER-DÜRLER, B., State and Administrative Law
WOHLERS, P., Private, Economic and European Law
ZOBL, D., Civil Law, Banking and Securities Law

Faculty of Medicine (Zürichbergstr. 14, 8091 Zürich; tel. 446341071; e-mail renate.gay@usz.ch; internet www.med.uzh.ch):

AGUZZI, A., Neuropathology
AKDIS, C., Immunology
ARAND, M., Pharmacology
ATTIN, TH., Preventive Dentistry
BÄR, W., Forensic Medicine
BASSETTI, C., Neurology
BERGER, E. G., Physiology
BERGER, W., Medical Molecular Genetics
BILLER-ANDORNO, N., Biomedical Ethics
BOLTSHAUSER, E., Paediatrics

BORGEAT, A., Anaesthesiology
BÖSIGER, P., Biomedical Technology
BÖTTGER, E. C., Medical Microbiology
BOUTELLIER, U., Physiology
BUCHER, H. U., Neonatology
BUCK, A., Nuclear Medicine
BUDDEBERG, C., Social Psychology
CLAVIEN, P. A., Abdominal Surgery
DIETZ, V., Paraplegology
FEHR, J., Haematology
FINK, D. A., Gynaecology
FONTANA, A., Clinical Immunology
FRENCH, L., Dermatology
FRIED, M., Gastroenterology
FRITSCHY, J. M., Neuropharmacology
GAY, S., Experimental Rheumatology
GENONI, M., Heart Surgery
GERBER, C., Orthopaedics
GIOVANOLI, P., Surgery
GRÄTZ, K., Pathology
GROSCURTH, P., Anatomy
GRÜTTER, M. G., Biochemistry, Macromolecular Crystallography
GUTZWILLER, F., Social and Preventive Medicine
HÄMMERLE, CH., Dentistry
HELD, L., Biostatics
HELL, D., Clinical Psychiatry
HELMCHEN, F., Neurology
HENGARTNER, H., Experimental Pathology
HENNET, TH., Human Biology
HOCK, C., Biological Pharmacology
HODLER, J., Radiology
HUG, E., Radiology
IMFELD, TH., Preventive Dentistry
IMTHURN, B., Gynaecological Endocrinology
JENNI, R., Cardiology
JIRICNY, J., Molecular Radiology
KAISSLING, B., Anatomy
KNUTH, A., Oncology
KOLLIAS, S., Radiology
KULLAK-UBLICK, G. A., Clinical Pharmacology
LANDAU, K., Ophthalmology
LIPP, H. P., Anatomy
LOFFING, J., Anatomy
LÜSCHER, T. F., Cardiology
LÜTOLF, U. M., Radiotherapy
MANSUY, I., Neurology
MARINCEK, B., Diagnostic Radiology
MEULI, M., Surgery
MICHEL, B., Rheumatology
MITSIADIS, TH., Oral Biology
MOCH, H., Pathology
MODESTIN, J., Clinical Psychiatry
MÖLLING, K., Virology
MURER, H., Physiology
NADAL, D., Paediatrics
NEUHASS, S., Neurobiology
NITSCH, R. M., Psychiatry
NOLL, G., Molecular Biology
PALLA, S., Prosthetics
PELTOMÄKI, T., Maxillary Orthopaedics
PLÜCKTHUN, A., Biochemistry
PRÊTRE, R., Children's Cardiac Surgery
PROBST, R. R., Otorhinolaryngology
PRUSCHY, M., Molecular Biology
REINECKE, M., Anatomy
ROGLER, G., Internal Medicine
RÖSSLER, W., Clinical Psychiatry
ROTH, J., Cell Molecular Pathology
RUDIN, M., Pharmacology
RUSSI, E., Internal Medicine
RÜTTIMANN, B., History of Medicine
SALLER, R., Naturopathy
SCHINZEL, A., Medical Genetics
SCHMID, E., Anaesthesia
SCHMID, S., Otorhinolaryngology
SCHNYDER, U., Psychiatry
SCHÖNLE, E., Paediatrics
SCHWAB, M. E., Neurology and Anatomy
SEGER, R., Children's Medicine, Immunology and Haematology
SENNHAUSER, F. H., Paediatrics
SONDEREGGER, P., Biochemistry
SPAHN, D. R., Anaesthesiology

SPINAS, G. A., Endocrinology, Diabetology and Pathophysiology
STEINHAUSEN, H.-C., Child and Youth Psychiatry
STEINMANN, B. U., Paediatrics
STEURER, J., Internal Medicine
SULSER, T., Urology
TRENTZ, O., Accident Surgery
VALAVANIS, A., Neuroradiology
VERREY, F., Physiology
VETTER, W., Internal Medicine
VON ECKARDSTEIN, A., Clinical Chemistry
VON SCHULTHESS, G. K., Nuclear Medicine
WAGNER, A., Bioinformatics
WEBER, R., Clinical Infectology
WEDER, W., Thorax Surgery
WENGER, R. H., Physiology
WIESER, H.-G., Neurology, Special Epileptology
WOGGON, B., Pharmacotherapy
WOLFER, D., Anatomy
WÜTHRICH, B., Dermatology and Venereology
ZEILHOFER, H. U., Pharmacology
ZIMMERMANN, R., Obstetrics and Gynaecology
ZINKERNAGEL, R. M., Experimental Pathology
ZÜND, G., Surgery

Faculty of Philosophy (tel. 446342234; e-mail heidi.moor@access.unizh.ch; internet www.uzh.ch/fakultaet/phil):

BONFADELLI, H., Journalism
BOOTHE, B., Clinical Psychology
BORNSCHIER, V., Economic Sociology
BOSKOVSKA, N., History of Eastern Europe
BOSSONG, G., Romance Philology
BRANDSTÄTTER, V., General Psychology
BRONFEN, E., English and American Literature
BUCHMANN, M., Sociology
CLAUSSEN, P. C., Art History of the Middle Ages
CRIVELLI, T., Special Romance Literature
DELLA CASA, PH., History of Medieval Art
DESCOEDRES, G., History of Medieval Art
DUNKEL, G. E., Comparative Indo-German Linguistics
DURSCHEID, CH., German Language
EBERLE, F., Pedagogy
EBERT, K. H., General German Philology
EHLERT, U., Psychology
EIGLER, U., Classical Philology
ESSER, F., Journalism
ESTERHAMMER, A., English Literature
FATKE, R., Pedagogy, Special Social Pedagogics
FINKE, P., Ethnology
FISCH, J., General Modern History
FISCHER, A., English Philology
FREUD, A., Applied Psychology
FRIES, U., English Philology
FRÖHLICHER, P., History of French Literature
GASSMANN, R. H., Sinology
GESER, H., Sociology
GILOMEN, H. J., General Economic and Social History, Swiss History
GLASER, E., German Philology
GLAUSER, J., Nordic Philology
GLESSGEN, M.-D., Romance Philology
GLOCK, H.-J., Philosophy
GONON, P., Pedagogy
GRODDECK, W., New German Literature
GÜNTHER, H., History of Modern Art
GUTSCHER, H., Social Psychology
GYR, U., Folklore
HAUG, H.-J., Psychiatry
HAUSENDORF, H., German Language
HELBLING, J., Ethnology
HESS, M., Computer Linguistics
HEUSSER, M., English Literature
HINRICHSEN, H.-J., Musicology
HIRSIG, R., Psychological Methods
HORNUNG, R., Social Psychology

HUG, S., Political Science
IMHOF, K., Journalism
JÄNCKE, L., Neuropsychology
JARREN, O., Publicity Science
JONAS, K., Social Psychology
JUCKER, A., English Philology
KELLNER, B., Old German Literature
KIENING, C., German Literature
KLEINMANN, M., Psychology
KOHLER, G., Philosophy, Political Philosophy
KOLB, G., Ancient History
KRIESI, H., Political Science
KRÜGER, G., Modern History
KYBURZ-GRABER, R., Pedagogy
LABARTHE, P., Romance Literature
LA FAUCI, N., Romance Philology, Italian Linguistics
LEIST, A., Ethics
LIENHARD, M., Spanish
LINKE, W. A., German Literature
LOETZ, F., History
LOPEZ GUIL, I., Iberoromanic Literature
LOPORCARO, M., Romance Philology, History of Italian
LÜTTEKEN, L., Musicology
MAERCKER, A., Psychopathology
MAREK, CH., Ancient History
MARTIN, M., Gerontology
MARX, W., General Psychology
MICHAELOWA, K., Politology
MICHEL, P., Ancient German Literature
MOOS, C., General and Swiss Modern History
MÜLLER NIELABA, D., German Literature
NÄF, B., Ancient History
NAUMANN, B., German Literature
OELKERS, J., Pedagogy
OPPITZ, M., Ethnology
PETERS, J.-U., Slavic Philology
PICONE, M., Italian Literature
RANDERIA, S., Ethnology
REDDICK, A., English Literature
REUSSER, K., Pedagogy
RIATSCH, C., Romance Literature
RIEDWEG, C., Classical Philology, Ancient Greek Studies
RIEMENSCHNITTER, A., Chinese Philology
ROECK, B., General and Swiss History
ROSSI, L., Romance Literature
RUCH, W., Psychology
RUDOLPH, U., Islamic Sciences
RUF, U., Pedagogy
RULOFF, D., Political Science
SAPORITI, K., Philosophy
SARASIN, P., General and Swiss Modern History
SCHABER, P., Philosophy
SCHNEIDER, S., German Literature
SCHREIER, D., English Language
SCHREINER, P., Indology
SCHULTHESS, P., Philosophical Theory
SIEGERT, G., Journalism
STOTZ, P., Middle Latin Philology
SZYDLIK, M., Sociology
TANNER, J., General and Swiss Modern History
TEUSCHER, S., Medieval Studies
TRÖHLER, M., Cinema Studies
URSPRUNG, PH., Modern Art
WAGNER, K., German Literature
WEISS, D., Slavonic Languages
WILKENING, F., General Psychology
WIRTH, W., Publicity Science
ZEY, C., History

Faculty of Science (Winterthurerstr. 190, 8057 Zürich; tel. 446344002; e-mail dekanat@mnf.uzh.ch; internet www.mnf.uzh.ch):

ACBERSOLD, R., Functional Genomics
ALBERTO, R., Inorganic Chemistry
AMSLER, C., Experimental Physics
BALDRIDGE, K., Computer-supported Chemistry
BARBOUR, A. D., Biomathematics

BASLER, K., Zoology, Molecular Development Genetics
BERKE, H. G. H., Inorganic Chemistry
BOLTHAUSEN, E., Mathematics, esp. Applied Mathematics
BRODMANN, M., Mathematics
BUCHER, H. F. R., Palaeontology
BURG, J.-P., Geology
CAFLISCH, A., Computer-supported Structural Biology
CATTANEO, A. S., Mathematics
CHIPOT, M. M., Mathematics
CONTI, E., Systematic Biology
DE LELLIS, C., Pure Mathematics
DOUGLAS, R., Neuroinformatics
EBERL, L., Microbiology
ENDRESS, P. K., Systematic Botany
FABRIKANT, S. I., Geography, esp. Geographical Information Science
FINK, H.-W., Experimental Physics
GEHRMANN, T., Theoretical Physics
GREBER, U., Zoology
GROSSNIKLAUS, U., Biology
HAEBERLI, W., Geography
HAHNLOSER, R., Neuroinformatics
HAMM, P., Physical Chemistry
HEINRICH, C. A., Crystallography and Petrography
HENGARTNER, M. O., Molecular Biology
HUTTER, J., Physical Chemistry
ITTEN, K. I., Geography
KAPPELER, T., Mathematics
KELLER, B., Plant Molecular Biology
KELLER, H., Physics of Condensed Matter
KÖNIG, B., Zoology, Behavioural Biology
KRESCH, A., Pure Mathematics
LAKE, G., Theoretical Physics
LEHNER, C. F., Developmental Biology
LINDER, H. P., Systematic Biology
MARTIN, K. A., Neurophysiology Systems
MARTINOIA, E., Plant Biology
MOORE, B., Theoretical Physics
MÜLLER-BÖKER, U., Anthropogeography
NOLL, M., Molecular Biology
OKONEK, CH., Mathematics
OSTERWALDER, J., Experimental Physics
REYER, H.-U., Zoology
ROBINSON, J. A., Organic Chemistry
ROSENTHAL, J. J., Mathematics
SAUTER, S. A., Mathematics
SCHAFFNER, W., Molecular Biology
SCHILLING, A., Experimental Physics
SCHMID, B., Environmental Science
SCHMIDT, M., Physical Geography
SCHMIDT, M. W., Crystalline Geology
SCHROEDER, V., Mathematics
SEEGER, S., Physical Chemistry
SELJAK, U., Theoretical Physics
SIEGEL, J. S., Organic Chemistry
STEINMANN-ZWICKY, M., Zoology
STENFLO, J. O., Astronomy
STEURER, W., Crystallography
STOECKLI, E., Neurobiology
STRAUMANN, U., Physics
THIERSTEIN, H. R., Micro-Palaeontology
THOMPSON, A. B., Petrology
VAN SCHAIK, C. P., Anthropology
VON MERING, CH., Bioinformatics
WARD, P., Zoology, Ecology
WEIBEL, R., Geography
WYLER, D., Theoretical Physics
ZOLLIKOFER, CH., Zoology

Faculty of Theology (Kirchgasse 9, 8001 Zürich; tel. 446344721; e-mail dekanat@theol.uzh.ch):

BERGIAN, S., History of Church and Dogma
BÜHLER, P., Systematic Theology
CAMPI, E., History of Church and Dogma
DALFERTH, I. U., Systematic Theology
FISCHER, J., Theological Ethics
KRÜGER, T., Old Testament
KUNZ, R., Practical Theology
SCHMID, K., Old Testament
UEHLINGER, C., History and Science of Religions

VOLLENWEIDER, S., New Testament
ZUMSTEIN, J., New Testament

Faculty of Veterinary Medicine (Winterthurerstr. 252, 8057 Zürich; tel. 446358121; e-mail dekanat@vetadm.uzh.ch; internet www.vet.uzh.ch):

ACKERMANN, M., Virology
ALTHAUS, F., Pharmacology and Toxicology
AUER, J. A., Veterinary Surgery
BRAUN, U., Internal Medicine of Ruminants
BÜRKI, K., Laboratory Animal Science
DEPLAZES, P., Parasitology
EHRENSPERGER, F., Immunopathology
GASSMAN, M., Veterinary Physiology
HATT, J. M., Small Animals
HOTTIGER, M., Molecular Biology
HÜBSCHER, U., Biochemistry
KÄHN, W., Reproductive Medicine
LUTZ, H., Internal Medicine
LUTZ, TH., Physiology
MONTAVON, P. M., Surgery of Small Domestic Animals
NAEGELI, H. P., Toxicology
POSPISCHIL, A., Pathology
REUSCH, C., Internal Medicine (Small Animals)
SPIESS, B., Veterinary Ophthalmology
STEPHAN, R., Foodstuff Security
WANNER, M., Animal Nutrition
WITTENBRINK, M. M., Veterinary Bacteriology

UNIVERSITÉ DE FRIBOURG/UNIVERSITÄT FREIBURG

1700 Fribourg
Telephone: 263007111
E-mail: rectorat@unifr.ch
Internet: www.unifr.ch
Founded 1889
State control
Languages of instruction: English, French, German
Academic year: August to July

Rector: Prof. GUIDO VERGAUWEN
Vice-Rector: Prof. THOMAS HUNKELER
Vice-Rector: Prof. TITUS JENNY
Vice-Rector: Prof. JACQUES PASQUIER
Vice-Rector: Prof. ALEXANDRA RUMO-JUNGO
Librarian: MARTIN GOOD

Library: 3.46m. vols
Number of teachers: 240
Number of students: 10,000

Publication: *Universitas Friburgensis* (4 a year)

DEANS

Faculty of Arts: Prof. MARC-HENRY SOULET
Faculty of Economics and Social Sciences: Prof. STEPHANIE TEUFEL
Faculty of Law: Prof. MARCEL ALEXANDER NIGGLI
Faculty of Sciences: Prof. FRITZ MULLER
Faculty of Theology: Prof. FRANZ MALI

PROFESSORS

Faculty of Arts (Ave Europe 20, 1700 Fribourg; tel. 263007500; e-mail lettres@unifr.ch; internet www.unifr.ch/lettres):

AUSTENFELD, T., American Literature
BACCI, M., History of Arts and Archaeology
BEISE, A., Germanic Literature and History of Literature
BERRENDONNER, A., Modern French Linguistics
BERTHELE, R., Multilingualism
BILLERBECK, M., Classical Philology
BIZZARRI, H., Spanish Philology and History of the Spanish Language
BLESS, G., Therapeutic Pedagogy
BOURQUI, C., Modern French Literature
BUDOWSKI, M., Social Policy
CALDARA, R., Psychology

CAMOS, V., Psychology
CASASUS, G., Contemporary History
CHARLIER, B., University Didactics
CHRISTEN, H., Germanic Linguistics
CLAVIEN, A., General and Swiss Contemporary History
DAPHINOFF, D., English Literature
DASEN, V., Archaeology
DORSCH, ST., Philosophy
DUCHENE, A., Multilingualism and Language Didactics
DUTTON, E., English Medieval Language and Literature
FORSTER, E., Science of Education
FUMAGALLI, E., Italian Literature
GAUTHIER, F., Sociology of Religions
GENETELLI, C., Italian Philology
GHOSE, I., English Literature
GIORDANO, C., Ethnology
GOHARD, A., French as a Foreign Language
GONZALEZ MARTINEZ, E., Sociology
GURTNER, J.-L., General Pedagogy
HARTMANN, E., Speech Therapy
HAUSER, C., Contemporary History
HAYOZ, N., Political Science
HERLTH, J., Slavistic Studies
HUNKELER, T., French Literature
KARFIK, P., Philosophy of Antiquity
KLUMB, P., Cognitive Psychology
KRONIG, W., Special Education
KRUGER, O., Religious Studies
LUTZ, E., German Philology
MAILLAT, D., English Language
MANSER, T., Psychology
MARTIN SOLCH, C., Clinical Psychology
MOTTA, U., Italian Literature
MULLER, R., German Literature
MUNSCH, S., Psychology
NIDA-RUMELIN, M., Philosophy
NOLLERT, M., Social Policy
OGAY BARKA, T., Anthropology of Education
PAULI, C., General Didactics
PEÑATE RIVERO, J., Spanish Literature
PETITPIERRE, G., Special Education
PIÉRART, M., Ancient History
POGLIA MILETI, FR., General Sociology
PRAZ, A.-F., Contemporary, General and Swiss History
RASCH, B., Cognitive Psychology
REINHARDT, V., Early Modern History of Europe and Switzerland
REVAZ, F., French Linguistics
ROSSARI, C., French Linguistics
RUEGG, F., Social Anthropology
SAUER, J., Psychology
SCHMIDLIN, R., German
SCHMIDT, H.-J., Medieval History of Europe and Switzerland
SCHMIDT, T., Classical Philology
SCHOBI, D., Clinical Psychology
SKENDEROVIC, D., Contemporary History
SOLDATI, G., Modern and Contemporary Philosophy
SOULET, M., Social Work
STOICHITA, V., History of Art
STUDER, TH., German as a Foreign Language
SUAREZ-NANI, T., Medieval Philosophy, Ontology
SURDEZ, M., Sociology
SWIDERSKI, E., Philosophy
VERNAY, P., Roman Philology
VIEGNES, M., French Literature
WALTER-LAAGER, C., Educational Sciences
WEICHLEIN, S., Contemporary History
WILD, M., Philosophy
WOLF, J.-C., Ethical and Political Philosophy
ZOPPELLI, L., History of Music

Faculty of Economics and Social Sciences (Blvd de Pérolles 90, 1700 Fribourg; tel. 263008200; e-mail decanat-ses@unifr.ch; internet www.unifr.ch/economics):

BAMBAUER-SACHSE, S., Marketing

BORTIS, H., History of Economic Theory
BOURGEOIS, D., Media and Communication
DAVOINE, E., Administration of Human Resources
DEMBINSKI, P., Business and International Management
DONZE, L., Statistics
EICHENBERGER, R., Public Finance
FAHR, A., Media and Communication
FRIBOULET, J.-J., Economic History
GMÜR, M., Management, NPO–Management
GRÖFLIN, H., Information Systems
GROSSMANN, V., Macro Economy
GRÜNIG, R., Management
GUGLER, P., Social and Political Economy
HANGGLI, R., Media and Communication
INGENHOFF, D., Media and Communication
ISAKOV, D., Financial Management
MADIES, T., Political Economy
MEIER, A., Informatics
MORSCHETT, D., International Management
PASQUIER, J., Informatics
PUPPIS, M., Media and Communication
ROSSI, S., Macro Economy
SCHÖNHAGEN, P., Media and Communication
TEUFEL, S., International Telecommunications Management
WALLMEIER, M., Financial Management
WIDMER, M., Decision Support Systems
WOLFF, R., Economic Theory and Empirical Research

Faculty of Law (Ave Europe 20, 1700 Fribourg; tel. 263008000; e-mail droit-decanat@unifr.ch; internet www.unifr.ch/droit):

AMSTUTZ, M., Private Law
BELSER WYSS, M., Private Law
BESSON, S., International Public Law, European Law
BORS, M., Roman Law
CARDINAUX, B., National Insurance and Labour Law
DUBEY, J., Public Law and Private Construction Law
EPINEY, A., Constitutional Law, International Public Law, European Law
FIOLKA, G., International Criminal Law
FOUNTOULAKIS MASCH, C., Private Law
GRISEL RAPIN, C., Public Law
HÄNNI, P., Constitutional and Administrative Law
HEINZMANN, M., Civil Procedure and Foundations of Law
HINNY, P., Tax Law
HÜRLIMANN-KAUP, B., Private Law
LE ROY, Y., History of Law, Canon Law
NIGGLI, M., Criminal Law
PAHUD DE MORTANGES, R., History of Law
PERRIN, B., Criminal Law
PICHONNAZ, P., Private Law
PREVITALI, A., Social Insurance Law
PROBST, T., Private Law
PROGIN-THEUERKAUF, S., European Migration Law
QUELOZ, N., Criminal Law
RIEDO, C., Criminal Law and Criminal Procedure
ROMY, I., International Private Law
RUMO-JUNGO, A., Private Law
STEINAUER, P.-H., Civil Law
STÖCKLI, H., Civil Law, Trade Law
STOFFEL, W., International Private Law, Trade Law
TORRIONE, H., Tax Law and Philosophy of Law
WALDMANN, B., Public Law
WERRO, F., Private Law
ZUFFEREY, J. B., Public Law

Faculty of Science (Ch. du Musée 9, Pérolles, 1700 Fribourg; tel. 263008111; e-mail science@unifr.ch; internet www.unifr.ch/sciences):

AEBI, P., Physics

ALBRECHT, U., Biochemistry
ALLAN, M., Physical Chemistry
ANNONI, J.-M., Neurology
BALLY, T., Physical Chemistry
BELSER, P., Inorganic Chemistry
BERNHARD, C., Experimental Physics
BERRUT, J.-P., Mathematics
BERSIER, L.-F., Ecology and Evolution
BOCHET, C., Organic Chemistry
BOURQUIN STROHER, C., Pharmacology
BRADER, J., Physics
BRESCIANI, J.-P., Movement Sciences
CELIO, M., Histology
CONZELMANN, A., Biochemistry
COOK, S., Cardiology
CUDRE-MAUROUX, PH., Computer Science
DAUL, C. A., Inorganic Chemistry
DELALOYE, R., Geomorphology and Physical Geography
DESSAI, A., Mathematics
DE VIRGILIO, C., Biochemistry
DOUSSE, J.-C., Experimental Physics
FILGUEIRA, L., Anatomy
FINK, A., Biochemistry of Nanoparticles
FOUBERT, A., Sedimentology
FROMM, K., Inorganic Chemistry
GABRIEL, J.-P., Mathematics
GRAEFE, O., Human Geography
GRITSEV, V., Physics
GROBETY, B. H., Mineralogy
HAUCK, C., Physical Geography
HIRSBRUNNER, B., Computer Science
HÖLZLE, M., Physical Geography
HUGHES, K., Microbiology
INGOLD, R., Computer Science
JACOB, C., Biology
JAZWINSKA MULLER, A., Biology
JENNY, T., Organic Chemistry
JOYCE, W., Palaeontology
KELLERHALS, R., Mathematics
KILBINGER, A., Chemistry
KRESSLER, D. A.
KRETZ, R., Anatomy
LATTUADA, M., Biochemistry of Nanoparticles
LAUBER, A., Endocrinology
LEXER, C., Evolutionary Biology
MAUCH, F., Plant Biology
MAZZA, C., Statistics and Theory of Probability
MERLO, M., Clinical Medicine
MÉTRAUX, J.-P., Plant Biology
MONTANI, J.-P., Physiology
MÜLLER, F., Zoology
MÜLLER-SCHÄRER, H., Ecology and Evolution
NAIQUE DESSAI, A., Mathematics
NITSCHE, U., Computer Science
NORDMANN, P., Microbiology
PARLIER, H., Mathematics
RAINER, G., Neuroscience
ROTHEN-RUTISHAUSER, B., Bio-Nanomaterials
ROUILLER, E., Physiology
RÜEGG, C., Pathology
SCHEFFOLD, F., Experimental Physics
SCHNEITER, R., Biochemistry
SCHWALLER, B., Anatomy
SERNEELS, V., General Geology
SPRECHER, S. G., Neurobiology
STEINER, U., Soft Matter Physics
TAUBE, W., Movement and Sport Science
THEILIG, F., Anatomy
TOGNI, M., Cardiology
ULTES-NITSCHE, U., Computer Science
WEDER, C., Polymer Chemistry
WEGMANN, D., Biochemistry
WEIS, A., Experimental Physics
WENGER, A., Medicine and Society
WENGER, S., Mathematics
WERNER, P., Theoretical Physics
YANG, Z., Physiology
ZHANG, Y.-C., Theoretical Physics
ZUMBÜHL, A., Chemistry

Faculty of Theology (Ave Europe 20, 1700 Fribourg; tel. 263007370; e-mail decanat-theol@unifr.ch; internet www.unifr.ch/theo):

AMHERDT, F.-X., Pastoral Theology
BAUER, T. J., New Testament
COLLAUD, T., Moral Theology
DE LA SOUJEOLE, B.-D., Dogmatic Theology
DELGADO, M., Church History
DEVILLERS, L., New Testament
EMERY, G., Dogmatic Theology
HALLENSLEBEN, B., Dogmatic Theology
HODEL, B., Church History
KAPTIJN, A., Canon Law
KLOCKENER, M., Moral Theology
LEFEBVRE, P., Exegesis and Old Testament
MALI, F., Patristic and History of Ancient Church
SHERWIN, M., Fundamental Moral Theology
STEYMANS, H. U., Old Testament
VERGAUWEN, G., Ecumenism
ZANDER, H., History of Religion

UNIVERSITÉ DE GENÈVE

Rue du Général-Dufour 24, 1211 Geneva 4
Telephone: 223797111
E-mail: secretariat-rectorat@unige.ch
Internet: www.unige.ch
Founded 1559, univ. status 1873
Language of instruction: French
Academic year: October to July

Rector: Prof. JEAN-DOMINIQUE VASSALLI
Vice-Rector: Prof. ANIK DE RIBAUPIERRE
Vice-Rector: Prof. YVES FLÜCKIGER
Vice-Rector: Prof. PIERRE SPIERER
Sec.-Gen.: Dr STÉPHANE BERTHET

Library: see under Libraries and Archives
Number of teachers: 3,569
Number of students: 14,500

Publication: *Campus*

DEANS

Faculty of Arts: Prof. ERIC WEHRLI
Faculty of Economics and Social Science: Prof. BERNARD MORARD
Faculty of Law: Prof. CHRISTIAN BOVET
Faculty of Medicine: Prof. JEAN-LOUIS CARPENTIER
Faculty of Psychology and Educational Sciences: Prof. JEAN-PAUL BRONCKART
Faculty of Science: Prof. JEAN-MARC TRISCONE
Faculty of Theology: ANDREAS DETTWILER
School of Translation and Interpretation: LANCE HEWSON

PROFESSORS

Faculty of Arts (3 rue de Candolle, 1211 Geneva 4; tel. 223797111; internet www.unige.ch/lettres):

ADAMZIK-BEVAND, K., German Literature and Civilization
ALVAR, C., Spanish Language and Literature
BARDAZZI, G., Romance Literature
BERELOWITCH, W., History
BOCCADORO, B., Musicology
BOLENS-JEANNERET, G., English Language and Literature
BORGEAUD, P., History of Ancient Religions
CAVIGNEAUX, A., Oriental Languages
CERUTTI, M., General History
CONRAD, C., History
DARBELLAY, E., Musicology
DE LIBERA, A., Philosophy
DESCOEUDRES, J.-P., Archaeology
FOEHR-JANSSENS, Y., Medieval French Literature
GAJO, G., Romance Literature
GAMBONI, L., Linguistics
GENEQUAND, C., Muslim and Arab Civilization

GROSRICHARD, A., French Literature
HAEBERLI, E., English Literature
HELG, A., General History
HURST, A., Classical Greek
JACCARD, J.-P., Russian Language
JENNY, L., French Literature
KOT, S., General History
LASSITHIOTAKIS, M., Modern Greek
LOMBARDO, P., French Literature
MADSEN, D., English Language and Literature
MANZOTTI, E., Italian Linguistics
MÉLA, CH., Medieval Romance Languages and Literature
MOESCHLER, J., General Linguistics
MORENZONI, F., History
MULLIGAN, K., Philosophy
NAEF, S., Arabic Language
NATALE, M., History of Art
NELIS, D., Latin Literature
PERUGI, M., Medieval Latin Language and Literature
PONT, J.-C., History of Sciences
PORRET, M., Modern History
POT, O., French Literature
RIGOLI, J., French Literature
SCHRADER, H. J., German Literature and Civilization
SCHUBERT, P., Modern Greek
SHLONSKY, UR., Linguistics
SOUYRI, P.-F., Japanese
SPURR, D. A., Modern English Literature
TALENS, C. J., Spanish Language and Literature
TILLIETTE, J.-Y., Medieval Latin Language and Literature
VALLOGGIA, M., Egyptology
WALTER, F., General History
WEHRLI, E., French Linguistics and Computer Science
WETZEL, R., German Literature and Civilization
WINKLER, M., German Literature and Civilization
WIRTH, J., History of Art in the Middle Ages
ZUFFEREY, Chinese Studies

Faculty of Economics and Social Science (40 blvd du Pont-d'Arve, 1211 Geneva 4; tel. 223797111; internet www.unige.ch/ses):

ALLAN, P., Political Science
ANTILLE GAILLARD, G., Economics and Social Science
BALLMER-CAO, T.-H., Political Science
BENDER, A., Industrial Organization
BERGADAA DELMAS, M., Marketing
BRAILLARD, P., European Globalization
BURGENMEIER, B., Political Economy
CARLEVARO, F., Econometrics
CASSIS, Y., Economic History
CATTACIN, S., Sociology
CURZON-PRICE, V., Economics
DE BLASIS, J. P., Industrial Organization
DE LA GRANDVILLE, O., Political Economy
DE MELO, J., Political Economy
DEBARBIEUX, B., Geography
DENIS, J. E., Industrial Organization
DUMONT, P.-A., Industrial Organization
DUMONTIER, P., Accountancy
FLUECKIGER, Y., Political Economy
GILLI, M., Computer Science, Econometrics
HOESLI, M. E. R., Real Estate Financing
HORBER, E., Sociology
HUSSY, C., Geography
JARILLO, J.-C., Economic Strategy
KELLERHALS, J., Sociology
KONSTANTAS, D., Information Systems
KRISHNAKUMAR, J., Econometrics
LANE, J. E., Political Science
LAWRENCE, R. J., Human Ecology
LEFOLL, J., Industrial Organization
LEONARD, M., Computer Science applied to Business
LOUBERGÉ, H., Political Economy

MAGNENAT THALMANN, N., Information Systems
MIRONESCO, C., Political Science
MORARD, B., Accountancy
MÜLLER, T., Econometrics
ORIS, M., Economic History
OSSIPOW, W., Political Science
PROBST, G., Industrial Organization
RAFFOURNIER, B., Accountancy
RECORDON, P. A., Contracts
RITSCHARD, G., Econometrics
RONCHETTI, E., Industrial Organization
ROYER, D., Statistics
SAUVAIN, C., Demography
SCAILLET, O., Statistics and Probability
SCHMITT, N., Political Economy
SCHNEIDER, S. C., Industrial Organization
SCHULTHEISS, F., Sociology
SCIARINI, P., Political Science
THOENIG, M., Political Economy
VERLEY, P., Economic History
VERNEX, J. C., Geography
VIAL, J.-PH., Industrial Organization
VIALLON, P., Sociology
VICTORIA FESER, M.-P., Statistics and Probability
WEBER, L., Political Economy
WINDISCH, U., Sociology

Faculty of Law (40 blvd du Pont-d'Arve, 1211 Geneva 4; tel. 223797111; internet www .unige.ch/droit):

AUBERT, G., Administrative Law
AUER, A., Constitutional Law
BADDELEY, M., Civil Law
BELLANGER, F., Fiscal Law
BOISSON DE CHAZOURNES, L., Public International Law
BOVET, C., Fiscal Law
BUCHER, A., Civil Law
CASSANI, U., Penal Law
CHAPPUIS, C., Business Law
DELLEY, J.-D., Constitutional Law
FLUECKIGER, A., Constitutional Law
FOEX, B., Civil Law
GREBER, P. Y., Administrative Law
HOTTELIER, M., Constitutional Law
JEANDIN, N., Civil Law
KADDOUS, C., Public International Law
KADNER, T., Civil Law
KAUFMANN-KOHLER, G., Private International Law
KELLER, A., History of Institutions and Law
LEVRAT, N., Public International Law
MALINVERNI, G., Constitutional Law, Introduction to the Science of Law
MANAÏ-WEHRLI, D., Civil Law
MONNIER, V., History of Institutions and Law
OBERSON, X. B., Fiscal Law
PETER, H., Civil Law
PETITPIERRE-SAUVAIN, A., Commercial Law
ROBERT, C. N., Penal Law, Criminology
ROTH, R., Penal Law
SASSOLI, M., Public International Law
STAUDER, B., German Commercial Law
STETTLER, M., Civil Law
TANQUEREL, T., Constitutional Law
THÉVENOZ, L., Civil Law
TRIGO TRINDADE, R. M., Business and Commercial Law
WINIGER, B., European and Civil Law

Faculty of Medicine (C.M.U., 1 rue Michel-Servet, 1211 Geneva 4; tel. 223795111; internet www.unige.ch/medecine):

ANTONORAKIS, S., Genetics and Microbiology
ASSIMACOPOULOS, F., Medical Biochemistry
BADER, C., Oto-neuro-ophthalmology
BAEHNI, P., Dentistry
BAERTSCHI, A. J., Physiology
BAIROCH, A., Medical Biochemistry
BARRAZZONE, C., Paediatrics
BECKER, C., Radiology
BEGHETTI, M., Paediatrics

BELIN, D., Pathology
BELLI, D. C., Paediatrics
BELSER, U., Dentistry
BERNER, M., Paediatrics
BERNHEIM, L., Physiology
BERTRAND, D., Physiology
BERTSCHY, G., Psychiatry
BISCHOF, P. A., Gynaecology and Obstetrics
BORISCH, B., Pathology
BOUNAMEAUX, H., Medicine
CAPPONI, A., Endocrinology
CARPENTIER, J.-L., Morphology
CAVERZASIO, J., Medicine
CHARDOT, C., Paediatrics
CHEVROLET, J.-C., Medicine
CLERGUE, F., Cardiology
COLLART BUCKHARD, M., Medical Biochemistry
COSSON, P., Morphology
DAYER, J.-M., Medicine
DAYER, P., Pharmacology
DEMAUREX, N., Physiology
DE TRIBOLET, N., Oto-neuro-ophthalmology
DUBUISSON, J.-S., Gynaecology and Obstetrics
FANTINI, B., Medicine
FASEL, J., Morphology
FERRERO, F., Pharmacology
FRENCH, L., Oto-neuro-ophthalmology
GABAY, C., Medicine
GEISSBUHLER, A., Radiology
GENTA, R., Pathology
GEORGOPOULOS, C. P., Medical Biochemistry
GIANNAKOPOULOS, P., Psychiatry
GIRARDIN, E., Paediatrics
GOLAY, A., Medicine
GUYOT, J., Oto-neuro-ophthalmology
HADENGUE, A., Medicine
HALBAN, PH., Medicine
HARDING, T., Legal Medicine
HOCHSTRASSER, D., Medical Biochemistry
HOESSLI, D., Pathology
HOFFMEYER, P., Surgery
HUEPPI, P., Paediatrics
IMHOF, B., Pathology
ISELIN, C., Surgery
IZUI, S., Pathology
KATO, A. C., Oto-neuro-ophthalmology
KAYSER BENGT, E. J., Sports Medicine
KILIARIDIS, S., Orthodontics
KISS, J. Z., Morphology
KOLAKOFSKY, D., Microbiology
KRAUSE, K. H., Medicine
KREJCI, I., Dentistry
LANDIS, T., Oto-neuro-ophthalmology
LE COULTRE, C., Surgery
LERCH, R., Medicine
LEW, D. P., Microbiology
LINDER, P., Medical Biochemistry
LÜSCHER, C., Oto-neuro-ophthalmology
MAGISTRETTI, P., Psychiatry
MALAFOSSE, A., Psychiatry
MARTIN, P.-Y., Nephrology
MAURON, A., Clinical Ethics
MEDA, P., Morphology
MENTHA, G., Surgery
MICHEL, C., Oto-neuro-ophthalmology
MICHEL, J.-P., Geriatrics
MOMBELLI, A., Orthodontics
MONTESANO, R., Morphology
MORABIA, A., Social Medicine
MOREL, D., Cardiology
MOREL, PH., Surgery
MUHLETHALER, M., Neurophysiology
MÜLLER, D., Pharmacology
MÜLLER, F., Dental Prosthesis
PALACIO-ESPASA, F., Psychiatry
PANIZZON, R., Oto-neuro-ophthalmology
PELIZZONE, M., Oto-neuro-ophthalmology
PERNEGER, T., Social Medicine
PERRIER, A., Medicine
PETER, R., Surgery
PHILIPPE, J., Medicine
PITTET, D., Medicine
PITTET-CUENOD, B., Surgery

PRALONG, F., Medicine
RAPIN, CH.-H., Gerontology
RATIB, O., Radiology
REITH, W., Genetics, Microbiology
RICHTER, M. W., Surgery
ROCHAT, T., Medicine
ROSE, K., Medical Biochemistry
ROUGEMONT, A., Social Medicine
ROUX, L., Genetics, Microbiology
RUEFENACHT, D., Radiology
RUIZ-ALTABA, A., Stem Cells
SAFRAN, A.-B., Oto-neuro-ophthalmology
SAMSON, J., Dentistry
SAPPINO, P., Oncology
SAURAT, J.-H., Dermatology
SCHLEGEL, W., Medicine
SCHNIDER, A., Oto-neuro-ophthalmology
SIEGRIST, C.-A., Paediatrics
SIGWART, U., Medicine
SOLDATI-FAVRE, D., Genetics, Microbiology
STALDER, J., Medicine
STRUBIN, M., Genetics, Microbiology
SUTER, P., Surgery
SUTER, S., Paediatrics
VAN DER GOOT GRUNBERG, F., Genetics, Microbiology
VASSALLI, J.-D., Morphology
VILLEMURE, J.-G., Oto-neuro-ophthalmology
VU, NU. V., Medicine
WOLLHEIM, C., Medicine
ZUBLER, R., Medicine

Faculty of Protestant Theology (3 rue de Candolle, 1211 Geneva 4; tel. 223797111; e-mail info@theologie.unige.ch; internet www.unige.ch/theologie):

BACKUS, I., History of the Reformation
BENEDICT, J., History of the Reformation
DERMANGE, F., Ethics
DETTWILER, A., New Testament Exegesis
GRANDJEAN, M., History of Christianity
NORELLI, E., New Testament Exegesis
PITASSI, M. C., History of the Reformation

Faculty of Psychology and Educational Sciences (40 blvd du Pont-d'Arve, 1211 Geneva 4; tel. 223797111; internet www.unige.ch/fapse):

Section of Psychology:

BARISUKOV, K., Psychology of Mental Deficiency
BETRANCOURT, M., Training Technologies
CASPAR, F., Psychology
DE RIBAUPIERRE, A., Differential Psychology
EID, M., Data Analysis
FRAUENFELDER, U. H., Psycholinguistics
GENDOLLA, G., Psychology
GILLIÈRON-PALÉOLOGUE, C., Psychology, Epistemology
HAUERT, C.-A., Psychology of Development
KAISER, S., Verbal and Non-Verbal Communication
KERZEL, D., Cognitive Psychology
LORENZI-CIOLDI, F., Social Psychology
MOUNOUD, P., Psychology of Personality Development
MUGNY, G., Social Psychology
ROBERT-TISSOT, C., Child Psychotherapy
SCHERER, K., Social Psychology
VAN DER LINDEN, M., Psychopathology
VANHULLE, S., Psychology
VIVIANI, P., Statistics and Modelling in Psychology
ZESIGER, P. E., Language Disorders

Section of Educational Sciences:

ALLAL, L., Pedagogical Evaluation
AUDIGIER, F., Teaching of Social Science and Humanities
BAYER, E., Research Techniques in Education
BELLIER, S., Educational Sciences
BRONCKART, J.-P., Introduction to Language Theories
BUCHEL, F., Cognitive Education

CHATELANAT, G., Educational Sciences
CIFALI, M., Psycho-pedagogy
CRAHAY, M., Educational Sciences
DASEN, P., Introduction to Educational Sciences
DOLZ-MESTRE, J., Educational Sciences
DURAND, M., Adult Education
GIORDAN, A., Psycho-pedagogy in Sciences
HANHART, S., Education
HOFSTETTER-ROSET, R., Educational Sciences
JOBERT, G., Adult Education
MAGNIN, C. F., History of Education
PAYET, J. P., Sociology of Education
PERAYA, D., Educational Sciences
PERREGAUX, C., Cultural and Linguistic Diversity at School
PERRENOUD, P., General Pedagogy
SAADA-ROBERT, M., Learning Process
SCHNEUWLY, B., Introduction to Language Theories
SCHUBAUER, M.-L., Social Psychology
SCHURMANS BRONCKART, M. N., Social Construction of Knowledge

Faculty of Science (30 quai Ernest-Ansermet, 1211 Geneva 4; tel. 223796111; internet www .unige.ch/sciences):

ALEXAKIS, A, Organic Chemistry
ALEXEEV, A., Mathematics
AUGUSTYNSKI, J., Applied Mineral Chemistry
BALLIVET, M., Biochemistry
BENY, J.-L., Animal Biology
BESSE, M., Anthropology, Ecology
BLECHA, A., Astronomy
BLONDEL, A., Nuclear Physics
BORKOVEC, M., Applied Mineral Chemistry
BOURQUIN, M., Nuclear Physics
BROUGHTON, W. J., Botany
BUCHS, D., Electronic Computing
BUETTIKER, M., Theoretical Physics
BUFFLE, J., Mineral Chemistry
BURKI, G., Astronomy
CARRUPT, P. A., Pharmacy
CHOPARD, B., Electronic Computing
CLARK, A. G., Nuclear Physics
CORAY, D., Mathematics
COURVOISIER, TH., Astronomy
DAVAUD, E. J., Geology
DE LA HARPE, P., Mathematics
DOELKER, E., Pharmacy
DOMINIK, J., History and Philosophy of Science
DROZ, M., Theoretical Physics
DUBOULE, D., Animal Biology
DUNGAN, M., Mineralogy
DURRER, R., Theoretical Physics
ECKMANN, J. P., Theoretical Physics and Mathematics
EDELSTEIN, S., Biochemistry
FISCHER, Ø., Physics
FONTBOTÉ, L., Mineralogy
GANDER, M.-J., Mathematics
GEOFFROY, M., Physical Chemistry
GIAMARCHI, T., Solid State Physics
GISIN, N., Theoretical Physics
GORIN, G. E., Geology
GRENON, M., Astronomy
GRUENBERG, J., Biochemistry
GULAÇAR, F., Physical Chemistry
GURNY, R., Pharmacy
HAIRER, E., Mathematics
HAUSER, A., Physical Chemistry
HOCHSTRASSER, D., Pharmacy
HOPFGARTNER, G., Pharmacy
HOSTETTMANN, K., Pharmacy
IZZAURRALDE, E., Molecular Biology
JEAN-PETIT-MATILE, S., Organic Chemistry
KIENZLE, M.-N., Solid State Physics
KINDLER, P., Geology and Palaeontology
KRAEMER BILBE, A., Cell Biology
KUNDIG, E. P., Organic Chemistry
LACHAL, B. M., Problems of Energy
LACHAVANNE, J.-B., Anthropology
LACOUR, J., Organic Chemistry

LANGANEY, A., Anthropology
LELUC, C., Nuclear Physics
MAEDER, A., Astronomy
MAGGIORE, M., Theoretical Physics
MARTINOU, J.-C., Cell Biology
MAYOR, M., Astronomy
MONOD, N., Mathematics
PALAZZO ROLIM, J., Electronic Computing
PASZKOWSKI, J., Vegetal Biology
PELLEGRINI, CH., Computer Science
PENEL, C., Botany
PFENNIGER, D., Astronomy
PICARD, D., Biology
PIGUET, C., Mineral Chemistry
POHL, M., Nuclear Physics
PONT, J.-C., History and Philosophy of Science
PUN, T., Computer Science
RAPIN, D., Nuclear Physics
RIEZMAN, H., Biochemistry
ROCHAIX, J.-D., Biology
RODRIGUEZ, I., Animal Biology
RONGA, F., Mathematics
RUEGG, U.-T., Pharmacy
SANCHEZ-MAZAS DE ABREU, A., Anthropology
SCAPPOZZA, L., Pharmacy
SCHALTEGGER, U., Mineralogy
SCHIBLER, U., Molecular Biology
SHORE, D., Molecular Biology
SMIRNOV, S., Mathematics
SPIERER, P., Animal Biology
STRASSER, R., Botany
STREIT, F., Mathematics
TRISCONE, J.-M., Solid State Physics
van der MAREL, D., Solid State Physics
VAUTHEY, E., Physical Chemistry
VEUTHEY, J.-L., Pharmaceutical Chemistry
WANNER, G., Mathematics
WERNLI, R., Micropalaeontology
WILDI, W., Geology
WILLIAMS, A. F., Applied Mineral Chemistry
WITTWER, P., Theoretical Physics
WOLF, J.-P., Physics
WOLFENDER, J. L., Pharmacy
YVON, K., Structural Crystallography
ZANINETTI, L., Zoology and Palaeontology

Institute of Architecture (7 route de Drize, 1227 Carouge; tel. 223790799; e-mail info@ archi.unige.ch; internet www.unige.ch/ia):

CÊTRE, J.-P., Materials and Structures
MARIANI, R., Urban History
REICHLIN, B., Theory of Architecture
SCHEIWILLER, A., Architectural Design and Arts and Crafts
SIMONNET, C., Culture and History of Architecture and Arts and Crafts
WEBER, W., Architecture

School of Translation and Interpretation (40 blvd du Pont-d'Arve, 1211 Geneva 4; tel. 223797111; internet www.unige.ch/eti):

ABDEL HADI, M., Arabic
ARMSTRONG, S., Use of Computers
BOCQUET, C.-Y., French
DANIEL, M., Translation with Computer Assistance
DE BESSÉ, B., Terminology
FANTUZZI, M., Italian
GEMAR, J.-C., French
GRIN, F., French
HEWSON LANCE, S. F., English
LEE-JAHNKE, H., German
MARCHESINI, G., Italian
MOSER-MERCER, B., German
SETTON, R. A. M., Interpretation
WEIBEL, L., French

ATTACHED SCHOOLS

École d'Education Physique et de Sport (School of Physical Education and Sport): tel. 223797722; attached to Faculty of Medicine; Dir P. HOLENSTEIN.

École de Langue et de Civilisation Françaises (School of French Language and Culture): tel. 223797111; e-mail elcf@ unige.ch; internet www.unige.ch/lettres/elcf; attached to Faculty of Arts; teaching activities, research and services in areas of French language (FLE), applied linguistics and multilingualism; Dir Prof. LAURENT GAJO.

ASSOCIATED INSTITUTES

Institut Oecuménique de Bossey (Ecumenical Institute): Château de Bossey, POB 1000, 1299 Crans-près-Céligny;Château de Bossey, Chemin Chenevière 2, Bogis-Bossey; tel. 229607300; e-mail bossey@wcc-coe.org; internet www.wcc-coe.org/bossey; f. 1946; Dir IOAN SAUCA

UNIVERSITÉ DE LAUSANNE

1015 Lausanne
Telephone: 216921111
E-mail: uniscope@unil.ch
Internet: www.unil.ch

Founded 1537, present name and status 1890
State control
Languages of instruction: English, French
Academic year: September to July

Rector: Prof. DOMINIQUE ARLETTAZ
Vice-Rector for Junior Faculty Devt and Diversity: Prof. FRANCISKA KRINGS
Vice-Rector for Quality and Human Resources: Dr JACQUES LANARÈS
Vice-Rector for Research and Int. Relations: Prof. PHILIPPE MOREILLON
Vice-Rector for Sustainability and Campus: BENOÎT FRUND
Vice-Rector for Teaching and Student Affairs: Prof. DANIELLE CHAPERON
Gen. Sec.: MARC DE PERROT

Library: 2.4m. vols
Number of teachers: 1,346
Number of students: 13,646

Publications: *Allez Savoir!*, *Uniscope*

DEANS

Faculty of Arts: Prof. FRANÇOIS ROSSET
Faculty of Biology and Medicine: Prof. BÉATRICE DESVERGNE
Faculty of Business and Economics: Prof. THOMAS VON UNGERN-STERNBERG
Faculty of Geosciences and Environment: Prof. FRANÇOIS BUSSY
Faculty of Law and Criminal Justice: Prof. BETTINA KAHIL-WOLFF
Faculty of Social and Political Science: Prof. FABIEN OHL
Faculty of Theology and Religious Studies: Prof. JÖRG STOLZ

PROFESSORS

Faculty of Arts (Anthropole, 1015 Lausanne; tel. 216922900; internet www.unil.ch/ lettres):

ALBERA, F., History and Aesthetics of Cinema
ALBONICO, S., Italian Literature
ANDENMATTEN, B., Medieval History
BARILIER, E., Modern French Literature
BARONI, R., Teaching French as a Foreign Language
BAVAUD, F., Mathematical and Statistical Methods
BERTHOUD, A.-C., Applied Linguistics
BIELMAN, A., Ancient History
BOILLAT, A., History and Aesthetics of Cinema
BOUVIER, D., Greek Language and Literature
BURGER, M., Indian Studies and Comparative History of Religions
CHAPERON, D., French Language and Literature

CORBELLARI, A., French Literature of the Middle Ages
COSSY, V., English
CÉLIS, R., Philosophy
ERISMANN, C., Medieval Philosophy
ESCOLA, M., Modern French Literature
ESFELD, M.-A., Philosophy
FALCONER, R., Modern and Contemporary English literature
FORQUENOT DE LA FORTELLE, A., Russian Literature and Culture
FUCHS, M., Roman Provincial Archaeology
GUEX, S., Contemporary History
GUIDO, L., History and Aesthetics of Cinema
HEIDMANN, U., Comparative Literature
IMESCH OECHSLIN, K., History of Art
JEANNERET, T., Teaching French as a Foreign Language
JOLIVET, R., Theoretical and Experimental Linguistics
KAENEL, P., History of Art
KAPOSSY, B., Modern History
KILANI SCHOCH, M., French as a Foreign Language
KUNZ, E., German
KUNZ, M., Spanish Language and Literature
KUNZ WESTERHOFF, D., French Literature
LUGINBÜHL, T., Roman Provincial Archaeology
LUGON, O., Image Aesthetics
LÜTHI, D., Modern Art, Introduction—Architecture and Heritage
MAGGETTI, D., French Swiss Literature
MICHEL, C., History of Modern Art
MICHEL, L., Modern French Literature
MÜHLETHALER, J.-C., Medieval French Literature
OSTORERO, M., Medieval History
PHILIPPE, G., French Linguistics
REBER, K., Classical Archaeology
RENEVEY, D., Medieval English Literature
RODRIGUEZ, A., Modern and Contemporary French Literature
ROMANO GOSETTI DI STURMECK, S., History of Medieval Art
ROSSET, F., Literature and Culture (18th–21st century)
SCAFFAI, N., Italian Literature
SCHERRER-SCHAUB, C., Tibetan and Buddhist Studies
SCHNIEWIND, A., Philosophy of Antiquity
SCHNYDER, A., Medieval German Language and Literature
SCHWARZ, A., German Linguistics
SCHWYTER, J. R., English Linguistics
SERIOT, P., Russian Linguistics and Philology
SOLTYSIK MONNET, A., American Literature
STAROBINSKI, G., Musicology
STRAUCH, I., Buddhist Studies
TOMASIN, L., History of Italian
TORTAJADA, M., History and Aesthetics of Cinema
TOSATO-RIGO, D., Modern History
UTZ, P., German Language and Literature
VALLOTTON, F., Contemporary History
VALSANGIACOMO, N., Contemporary History
VAN MAL-MAEDER, D., Latin Language and Literature
VON ARBURG, H.-G., German Language and Literature
WACHTER, R., Indo-European Historical Linguistics
WEBER HENKING, I., German Language and Literature
ZUFFEREY, F., Medieval French
ZURBUCHEN PITTLIK, S., Modern and Contemporary Philosophy

Faculty of Biology and Medicine (Rue du Bugnon 21, 1005 Lausanne; tel. 216925000; e-mail info.fbm@unil.ch; internet www.unil.ch/fbm):

ACHA-ORBEA, H., Biochemistry

ANGELILLO-SCHERRER, A., Haematology
ANSERMET, F., Psychiatry
ARSENIJEVIC, Y., Ophthalmology
AUBERT, J. D., Lung Transplantation
BARRANDON, Y., Experimental Surgery
BARRAS, V., History of Medicine and Health
BART, P. A., Internal Medicine
BAUMGARTNER, J. D., Infectious Diseases
BENAROYO, L., Medical Ethics
BENTON, R., Genomics
BERGER, M., Surgical Intensive Care
BERGMANN, S., Medical Genetics
BESSON, J., Psychiatry
BETTSCHART, V., Surgery
BISCHOFF, T., General Medicine
BOCHUD, F., Applied Radiophysics
BOCHUD, M., Epidemiology
BONNY, O.
BONVIN, E., Psychiatry
BORASIO, G. D., Palliative Care
BORRUAT, F. X., Neuro-Ophthalmology
BOURHIS, J., Radiation Oncology
BOVET, P., Social and Preventive Medicine
BUCHSER, E., Anaesthesiology
BUCLIN, T., Clinical Pharmacology and Toxicology
BÜLA, C., Geriatrics
BURNAND, B., Clinical Epidemiology
BURNIER, M., Nephrology
CALANDRA, T., Infectious Diseases
CLARKE HOSEK, S., Neuropsychology
COLLIER CLOSE, J., Microbiology
COMETTA, A., Infectious Diseases
CONUS, P., Psychiatry
CORNUZ, J., Preventive Medicine
CORPATAUX, J. M., Thoracic and Vascular Surgery
COTECCHIA, S., Pharmacology
COUKOS, G., Oncology
DAEPPEN, J. B., Alcohology
DANUSER, B., Occupational Medicine
DÉCOSTERD, I., Anaesthesiology
DÉGLON, N., Cellular and Molecular Neurotherapies
DELALOYE, J. F., Gynaecology
DE LEVAL, L., Pathology
DEMARTINES, N., Visceral Surgery
DÉMONET, J. F., Dementia and Memory Disorders
DENYS, A., Interventional Radiology
DESPLAND, J. N., Psychiatry
DESVERGNE, B., Genomics
DIVIANI, D., Pharmacology and Toxicology
DO CUENOD, K. Q., Translational Research
DORTA, G., Gastroenterology
DOTTO, G. P., Biochemistry
DRAGANSKI, B., Neurological Electrophysiology
DUBOIS-ARBER, F., Social and Preventive Medicine
DUCHOSAL, M., Haematology
DU PASQUIER, R., Neurology
EAP, B., Psychopharmacology
EECKHOUT, E., Cardiology
FAJAS COLL, L., Physiology
FANCONI, S., Paediatrics
FANKHAUSER, C.
FARMER, E., Plant Biology
FARRON, A., Orthopaedics and Traumatology
FASEL, N., Biochemistry
FASSHAUER, D., Neurosciences
FEIHL, F., Clinical Pathophysiology
FITTING, J. W., Pneumonology
FITZE, P. S., Ecology and Evolution
FLATT, T., Ecology and Evolution
FRACKOWIAK, R., Neurology
FREY, P., Paediatric Surgery
FROMER, M., Cardiology
GABUTTI, L., Nephrology
GASSER, J., Psychiatry
GATFIELD, D., Genomics
GAUTIER, E., Orthopaedics and Traumatology
GELDNER, N.
GENTON, B., Travel Medicine

GHIKA, J., Neurology
GILLIET, M. F., Dermatology
GIRARDIN, E., Paediatric Nephrology
GMEL, G., Alcohology
GOLOUBINOFF, P., Plant Biology
GOUDET, J., Evolution
GRAVIER, B., Psychiatry
GREUB, G., Microbiology
GUARDA, G., Biochemistry
GUDINCHET, F., Sports Science
GUISAN, A., Plant Ecology
HAEFLIGER, J.-A., Internal Medicine
HAHNLOSER, D., Visceral Surgery
HALFON, O., Paediatric Psychiatry
HANS, D., Locomotor System, Bone Diseases
HARDTKE, C., Plant Biology
HAYOZ, D., Angiology
HEGI, M., Biology of Brain Tumours
HELD, W., Cancer Research
HERNANDEZ, N., Genomics
HERR, W., Genomics
HIRT, L., Neurology
HOHL, D., Dermatology
HOHLFELD, P., Obstetrics
HORNUNG, J.-P., Cell Biology and Morphology
HULLIN, R., Heart Failure and Transplantation
JICHLINSKI, P., Urology
JOLLES-HAEBERLI, B., Orthopaedics
JOLLIET, P., Intensive Care Medicine
JONGENEEL, C. V., Bioinformatics
KAESSMANN, H., Genomics
KATANAEV, V., Pharmacology and Toxicology
KAWECKI, T., Zoology
KELLER, L., Basic Evolutionary Ecology
KERN, C., Anaesthesiology
KRIEG, M.-A., Bone Diseases
KUNTZER, T., Neurology
KUNZ, S., Basic Virology
LAPOUGE, K., Basic Microbiology
LAUNOIS, P., Biochemistry
LAURENT-APPLEGATE, L., Foetal Cell Therapy
LA VECCHIA, C., Epidemiology
LEHMANN, L., Ecology and Evolution
LEVI, F. G., Epidemiology
LEVIVIER, M., Neurosurgery
LÉVY, F., Onco-Immunology
LEYVRAZ, P.-F., Orthopaedics and Traumatology of the Locomotor System
LEYVRAZ, S., Oncology
LIAUDET, L., Intensive Care Medicine
LUTHER, S., Biochemistry
LÜTHI, A., Neurosciences
MAEDER, P., Radiodiagnostics
MANGIN, P., Forensic Medicine
MARCHETTI, O., Infectious Diseases
MARSLAND, B., Pneumonology
MARTIN, S., Basic Microbiology
MARTINON, F., Biochemistry
MAYER, A., Biochemistry
MAZZOLAI, L., Angiology
MEIER, P., Nephrology
MERMOD, N., Molecular Genetics
MEULI, R., Diagnostic and Interventional Radiology
MEUWLY, J. Y., Diagnostic and Interventional Radiology
MEYLAN, P., Microbiology
MICHAUD, P. A., Adolescent Health
MICHIELIN, O., Translational Oncology
MILLET, G., Sports Science
MONOD, M., Dermatology
MOOSER, V., Biomedecine
MORADPOUR, D., Gastroenterology and Hepatology
MOREILLON, P., Basic Microbiology
MORIN, D., Care Training and Research
MUNIER, M., Ophthalmology
MURRAY, M., Neuropsychology and Neurorehabilitation, Radiology
MURRAY, M., Biomedical Imaging
NICOD, L., Pneumonology

OZSAHIN, E. M., Radiation Oncology

PACCAUD, F. M., Social and Preventive Medicine

PANESE, F., Ethics, Communication and Security

PANNELL, J. R., Evolutionary Botany

PANTALEO, G., Allergology and Clinical Immunology

PASCHE, P., Reconstructive Surgery in Oncology

PASCUAL, M. A., Surgery and Medicine

PEDRAZZINI, T., Hypertension and Vascular Medicine

PELET, S., Basic Microbiology

PELLERIN, L., Physiology

PERRIN, N., Basic Ecology

PETROVA, T.

PITTELOUD, N., Endocrinology

POIRIER, Y., Plant Molecular Biology

PRALONG, F., Endocrinology

PREISIG, M., Psychiatry

PRIOR, J., Nuclear Medicine

PRÊTRE, R., Cardiovascular Surgery

QANADLI, S. D., Diagnostic and Interventional Radiology

RADDATZ, E., Physiology

RAFFOUL, W., Plastic and Reconstructive Surgery

RAMELET, A. S., Care Training and Research

RAVUSSIN, P., Anaesthesiology

REGAZZI, R., Cell Biology and Morphology

REINBERG, O., Paediatric Surgery

REYMOND, A, Genomics

RIS, H. B., Thoracic Surgery

ROBINSON-RECHAVI, M., Ecology and Evolution

ROMERO, P., Clinical Onco-Immunology

ROULET PEREZ, E., Neuropaediatrics

ROULIN, A., Ecology and Evolution

ROUSSON, V. C., Statistical Methodology

RUEGG, C., Oncology

SALAMIN, N., Phylogeny and Computational Biology

SANDERS, I., Ecology and Evolution

SANGLARD, D., Microbiology

SANTOS-EGGIMANN, B., Social and Preventive Medicine

SCHALLER, M. D., Intensive Care Medicine

SCHILD, L., Pharmacology and Toxicology

SCHIZAS, C., Orthopaedics and Traumatology of the Locomotor System

SCHORDERET, D., Human Molecular Genetics

SCHOUMANS POUW, J., Cytogenetics

SCHWITTER, J., Cardiac MRI

SCHÜRCH, B., Neuropsychology and Neurorehabilitation

SIMON, C. H., Otorhinolaryngology

SINGY, P., Psychiatry

SO ALEXANDER, A. K., Rheumatology

SPEISER, D., Clinical Tumour Immune-Biology

SPERTINI, F., Immunology and Allergology

SPERTINI, O., Haematology

STAMENKOVIC, I., Experimental Pathology

STAUB, O., Pharmacology & Toxicology

STAUFFER, J. C., Cardiology

STIEFEL, F., Psychiatry

STUBER, M., Diagnostic and Interventional Radiology

STUPP, R., Oncology

SUPERTI-FURGA, A., Molecular Paediatrics

SUTER, M., Visceral Surgery

TACCHINI-COTTIER, F., Biochemistry

TAFTI, M., Genomics

TAPPY, L., Physiology

TELENTI, A., Medical Virology

THIRAN, J. P., Medical Radiology

THOME MIAZZA, M., Biochemistry

THORENS, B., Physiology

TISSOT, J. D., Haematology

TOLSA, J. F., Neonatology

TONI, N., Cell Biology and Morphology

TONIOLO, P., Social and Preventive Medicine

TROILLET, N., Preventive Medicine

VADER, J. P., Social and Preventive Medicine

VAN DER MEER, J. R., Basic Microbiology

VAN LINTHOUDT, D., Rheumatology

VASSALLI, G., Cardiology

VERDUN, F., Radiophysics

VINGERHOETS, F., Neurology

VOGT, P., Cardiology

VOLLENWEIDER, P., Internal Medicine

VOLTERRA, A., Cell Biology and Morphology

VON GUNTEN, A., Psychiatry of Old Age

WAEBER, B., Clinical Pathophysiology

WAEBER, G., Internal Medicine

WEDEKIND, C., Conservation Biology

WELKER, E., Cell Biology and Morphology

WIDMANN, C., Physiology

WOLFENSBERGER, T. J., Ophthalmology

XENARIOS, I., Computational Biology

YERSIN, B., Emergency Medicine

ZAMBELLI, P. Y., Orthopaedics and Child Traumatology

ZANETTI, G., Preventive Medicine

ZEHN, D., Immunology and Allergology

ZOGRAFOS, L., Ophthalmology

Faculty of Business and Economics (Internef, 1015 Lausanne; tel. 216923300; internet www.hec.unil.ch):

ALBRECHER, H., Mathematics

AMAND, M., Macroeconomics

ANTONAKIS, J., Organizational Behaviour

BACCHETTA, P., Economics

BENHIMA, K., Macroeconomics

BONARDI, J.-P., Strategy

BRUHIN, A., Empirical Methods

BRÜLHART, M., Applied Econometrics and Microeconomics

BURKERT, M., Accounting and Control

CADOT, O., International Economics

CASTANER, X.

CESTRE, G., Marketing

CHAVEZ, V., Empirical Methods

CZELLAR, S., Marketing

DANON, R., Taxation

DE TREVILLE, S., Operations Management

DIETZ, J., Organizational Behaviour

DIMOPOULOS, T., Finance

DONG, M., Financial Accounting

DOUKAKIS, L., Financial Accounting

DUFRESNE, F., Mathematics for Economists and Actuarial Mathematics

DUPARC, J., Formal Logic

EBERLE, R., Financial Accounting

GAILLE, S., Actuarial Science

GARBINATO, B., Programming Methods, Architectures and Systems

GARELLI, S., International Business Management

GHERNAOUTI HÉLIE, S., Information Technology

GLAUSER, P.-M., Taxation

GOETTE, L., Microeconomics

GOYAL, A., Finance

GRASSI, S., Management and Strategy of Health Institutions

HAMERI, A.-P., Operations Management

HASHORVA, E., Operations Management

HOFFRAGE, U., Decision Theory

JONDEAU, E., Business Finance—General Finance

JUNOD, V., Business Law

KLAUS, B., Economics

KOCHER, B., Marketing

KRINGS, F., Organizational Behaviour

LAJOS, J., Marketing

LALIVE, R., Econometrics

LEGNER, C.

MAEDER, P., Actuarial Science

MAREWSKI, J., Organizational Behaviour

MAURER, J., Health Economics

MISSONIER, S., Information Systems

MORHART, F., Marketing

MORRICONE, S., Financial Accounting

MUSTAKI, G., Business Law/Law of Obligations

NEUENSCHWANDER, D.

OYON, D., Business Management

PALAZZO, G., Business Ethics

PELGRIN, F., Econometrics

PHILIPPE, D., Strategy

PIGNEUR, Y., Management

POILLY, C., Macroeconomics

RICHA, A., Business Law

ROCKINGER, M., Finance

ROHNER, D., Microeconomics

ST-AMOUR, P., Macroeconomics focusing on Public Finance

SANTOS PINTO, L. P., Economics

SATO, Y., Finance

SCHUERHOFF, N., Finance

STEINMANN, T., Tax System

THOENIG, M., Macroeconomics

TOMASSINI, M., Information Technology

USUNIER, J.-C., Marketing

VAN ACKERE, A., Decision Science

VILLA, A., Information Systems

VON UNGERN-STERNBERG, T., Political Economy and Analysis of Industrial Structures

WASSERFALLEN, J.-B., Health Economics

WENTLAND FORTE, M., Information Technologies

ZEHNDER, C., Organisational Behaviour

ZHDANOV, A., Business Finance

Faculty of Geosciences and Environment (Géopolis, 1015 Lausanne; tel. 216923500; internet www.unil.ch/gse):

ARLETTAZ, D., Mathematics

BAUMGARTNER, L., Mineralogy and Petrography

BAUMGARTNER, P., Sedimentology and Study of the History of the Earth

BOISVERT, V., Environmental Economics and Natural Resources

BOURG, D., Social Sciences of Nature and the Environment

BUSSY, F., Petrology

DA CUNHA, A., Human Geography

EPARD, J. L., Geology

ERKMAN, S., Human Ecology

FÖLLMI, K., Sedimentary Geology and Geochemistry

HERMAN, F., Geophysics and Thermochronology

HOLLIGER, K., Geophysics

JABOYEDOFF, M., Alpine Geological Hazards and Geomatics

JAUBERT, R., Geography

KANEVSKI, M., Geomatics

LANE, S.

LINDE, N., Geophysics

LUNATI, I., Geophysics

MAIGNAN, M., Geostatistics

MARILLIER, F., Geophysics for Seismic Exploration

MÜNTENER, O., Mineralogy and Petrography

PENA, J., Environmental Mineralogy

PFEIFER, H. R., Mineral Analysis

PINI, G., Transport and Ecology

PODLADCHIKOV, Y., Mathematics and Applied Physics for Geosciences

REYNARD, E., Physical Geography

ROZENBLAT, C., Human Geography

RUEGG, J., Territorial Planning and Environmental Policies

SCHMALHOLZ, S., Tectonics and Geodynamics

VENNEMANN, T., Stable Isotope Geochemistry

VÉRON, R., Human Geography

VERRECCHIA, E., Biogeochemistry

Faculty of Law and Criminal Justice (Internef, 1015 Lausanne; tel. 216922740; internet www.unil.ch/droit):

AEBI, M., Criminology—Forensic Psychology

BARANZINI, R., Political Economy

BAUME, S., State Theory, History of Political Ideas

BIANCHI, F., Real Estate Law
BIERI, L., Law of Obligations
BOILLET, V., Constitutional Law
BONOMI, A., Comparative Law and Private International Law
BOVAY, B., Administrative Procedures
BRIDEL, P., Political Economy
BRULHART, V., Private Insurance Law
CHAMPOD, C., Chemical Criminalistics
CHENAUX, J. L., Commercial Law
CHERPILLOD, I., Intellectual Property
COTTIER, B., Multimedia Law
DELÉMONT, O., Forensic Science
ESSEIVA, P., Forensic Science, Drugs, Chemometrics
FAVRE, A. C., Environmental Law and Administrative Law
GILLIÉRON, P., Private Law of New Technologies
HAHN, M., European Law
HALDY, J., Judicial Organization and Procedures
JAQUET-CHIFFELLE, D. O., Digital Traces
KAHIL-WOLFF, B., German Social Law and Legal Language
KUHN, A., Criminology
MACALUSO, A., Criminal Law, Mutual Judicial Assistance and Criminal Procedure
MARGOT, P., Forensic Photography
MARTENET, V., Swiss and Comparative Constitutional Law, Competition Law
MASSONNET, G., Forensic Science—Microtraces—Transfer Traces
MEIER, P., Civil Law and Data Protection
MOREILLON, L., Criminal Law and Criminal Procedure
MORIN, A., Law of Obligations
NGUYEN, M. S., Aliens Law
NOËL, Y., Tax Law
PAPAUX, A., Introduction to Law/Methodology
PETER, H., Roman Law
PHILIPPIN, E., Commercial Law
PIOTET, D., Civil Law
POLTIER, E., Administrative Law
RAPP, J. M., Law of Obligations, Special Part, Commercial Law
RIBAUX, O., Security, Intelligence and Crime Analysis
SCHNEIDER, J. A., Occupational Pension Schemes
TAPPY, D., History of Law and Civil Procedure
TARONI, F., Interpretation and Evaluation of Scientific Evidence
THOENI, C., Law and Economics
WEYERMANN, C., Aging of Forensic Traces
WILSON, B., Public International Law
WYLER, R., Labour Law
ZIEGLER, A., International Public Law and Economics

Faculty of Social and Political Science (Géopolis, 1015 Lausanne; tel. 216923120; internet www.unil.ch/ssp):

BANCEL, N., Social Sciences of Sport and Physical Education
BATOU, J., Political and Social History of Europe in the 20th Century
BAYLE, E., Sport Management
BENNANI-CHRAÏBI, M., Comparative Political Systems, Third World
BERCHTOLD, A., Statistics
BERNARDI, L., Sociology
BRANDNER, C., Methodology in Psychology
BRAUN, D., Basic Concepts in Political Science, Political Systems
BÜHLMANN, F., Sociology of the Life
BUTERA, F., Social Psychology
CLÉMENCE, A., Social Psychology
DAVID, T., Economic and Social History
DOUDIN, P.-A., Developmental Psychology/ Social Psychology
ETEMAD, B., Extra-European History
FARAGO, P., Management
FASSA RECROSIO, F., Sociology of Education

FILLIEULE, O., Political Sociology
FONTANA, B., History of Political Ideas
GIAUQUE, D., Organizational Sociology and Public Administration
GRAZ, J.-C., Political Science—International Relations
GROSSEN, M., Clinical Psycho-Psychology
HAUW, D., Sport Psychology
HAVER, G., Sociology of the Image
HIRSCHI, A., Counselling Psychology
JOYE, D., Methodology in Social Sciences
KAUFMANN, L., General Sociology, Sociology of Communication
KILANI, M., Cultural and Social Anthropology
KNÜSEL, R., Sociology of Political and Social Action
LANARÈS, J., University Teaching
LAVENEX, P., Neurosciences
LE FEUVRE, N., Sociology of Work
LERESCHE, J.-P., Comparative Public Policies and Actions and Governance Analysis
LUTZ, G., Political Analysis
MAFFI, I., Cultural and Social Anthropology
MERRIEN, F. X., Theories of Change and Social Field—Evaluative Research
MOHR, C, Cognitive Psychology
MORO, C., General Psychology, Experimental Pedagogy
MOTTIER, V., Methodology in Social Sciences
NAHRATH, S., Public Policies
OESCH, D., Life Course and Social Policy
OHL, F., Sport and Physical Education Science
PANESE, F., Social Studies of Medicine and Science
PAPADOPOULOS, I., Public Policies, Swiss Policies
PASSY, F., Quantitative Data Analysis in Political Science
POMINI, V., Adult Clinical Psychology
PREZIOSO, S., Political and Social History of Europe
ROMAN, P., Clinical Psychology, Psychopathology and Psychoanalysis
ROSSI, I., Health Anthropology
ROSSIER, J., Counselling and Career Guidance Psychology
ROUX, P., Gender Studies
SANTIAGO, M., Health Psychology
SCHAUFELBUEHL, J., History of International Relations after 1945
SPINI, D., Social Psychology in the Life Course
STAERKLÉ, C., Social Psychology
VINCK, D., Social Studies of Science and Technology
VOUTAT, B., Political Sociology
ZIMMERMANN, G., Developmental Psychology: Adolescence and Socialisation

Faculty of Theology and Religious Studies (Anthropole, 1015 Lausanne; tel. 216922700; e-mail secretariattheologie@unil.ch; internet www.unil.ch/ftsr):

AMSLER, F., History of Christianity
BECCI TERRIER, I., Social Sciences of Contemporary Religions
BRANDT, P.-Y., Psychology of Religion
CLIVAZ, C., New Testament and Ancient Christian Literature
EHRENFREUND, J., Judaism
GROSSE, C., Sciences of Contemporary Religions
HAMIDOVIC, D., Jewish Apocryphal Literature and History of Judaism in Antiquity
MANCINI, S., Religious Studies: Marginalized Religious Traditions
MÜLLER, D., Fundamental and Special Ethics
NIHAN, C., Hebrew Bible
RÖMER, T., Old Testament

ROUSSELEAU, R., History of Modern Politico-Religious Processes
SALZBRUNN, M., Religions, Migration and Diaspora
STOLZ, J., Sociology of Religion

UNIVERSITÉ DE NEUCHÂTEL

Ave du 1er-Mars 26, 2000 Neuchâtel

Telephone: 327181000

E-mail: contact@unine.ch

Internet: www.unine.ch

Founded 1838

State control

Languages of instruction: French, English

Academic year: September to June

Chancellor: Dr MARTINE RAHIER

Vice-Chancellor for Education: Dr JEAN-JACQUES AUBERT

Vice-Chancellor for Governance and Legal Affairs: Dr PASCAL MAHON

Vice-Chancellor for Research Devt and Quality: Dr SIMONA PEKAREK

Sec.-Gen.: PHILIPPE JEANNERET

Librarian: LAURENT GOBAT

Number of teachers: 181

Number of students: 4,358

DEANS

Faculty of Economics: JEAN-MARIE GRETHER
Faculty of Humanities: GENEVIÈVE DE WECK
Faculty of Law: FLORENCE GUILLAUME
Faculty of Science: Prof. PETER KROPF
Faculty of Theology: Prof. FÉLIX MOSER

PROFESSORS

Faculty of Economics (Ave du 1er-Mars 26, 2000 Neuchâtel; tel. 327181500; e-mail secretariat.seco@unine.ch; internet www.unine.ch/seco):

BANGERTER, A.
BARANZINI, R.
BELKONIENE, A.
BLILI, S.
CADOT, O.
DAL ZOTTO, C.
DE BOND, W.
DUBOIS, M.
FARSI, M.
GRETHER, J.
KOSTECKI, M.
MELFI, G.
RAMACIOTTI, D.
REINER, G.
SALVA LOPEZ, C.
SCHATT, A.
SCHMID MAST, M.
SCHOENENBERGER, A.
STANOEVSKA-SLABEVA, K.
STARICA, C.
STOFFEL, K.
TILLE, Y.
TSCHAN SEMMER, F.
ZARIN-NEJADAN, M.

Faculty of Humanities (1 Espace Louis-Agassiz, 2000 Neuchâtel; tel. 327181700; internet www.unine.ch/lettres):

ACHERMANN, C.
ANDRES-SUAREZ, I.
AUBERT, J.
BANDELIER, A.
BEGUELIN, M.
BONNEFOIT, R.
CHAPPUIS SANDOZ, L.
CHRISTIN, O.
CLÉMENT, F.
CORBELLARI, A.
COTELLI, S.
CREVOISIER, O.
DAHINDEN, J.
D'AMATO, G.
DEBARY, O.
DE SAUSSURE, L.
DE WECK, G.

DIEMOZ, F.
DRIDI, H.
DUBOIS, M.
FILLIEULE, O.
FOSSARD, M.
FRESIA, M.
GASSER, P.
GESLIN, P.
GHASARIAN, C.
GILOMEN, H.
GLAUSER, R.
GREMAUD, G.
GRIENER, P.
HAINARD, F.
HERMAN, T.
HERTZ WERRO, E.
HONEGGER, M.
IANNACCONE, A.
JAQUIER KAEMPFER, C.
KAESER, M.
KAMBER, A.
KLAUSER, F.
KRISTOL, A.
LUESCHER, J.
LUGINBUEHL, M.
MCINTYRE, A.
MAILLAT, D.
MARIAUX, P.
MARRO, P.
MERONI, B.
MIEVILLE, D.
MOREROD, J.
MOSER, L.
NEDELCU, M.
NÄF, A.
PEKAREK DOEHLER, S.
PERRET, J.
PERRET-CLERMONT, A.
PETER, P.
PETRIS, L.
PIGUET, E.
REBETEZ, M.
RUPP, K.
RYTZ, F.
SÁNCHEZ MÉNDEZ, J.
SANGSUE, D.
SCHNYDER, P.
SCHRAMM, T.
SCHULTHESS, D.
SCHWEIZER, V.
SKUPIEN DEKENS, C.
SOUGY, N.
SUTER, C.
SÖDERSTRÖM, O.
TERRIER, P.
TISSOT, L.
TUDEAU-CLAYTON, M.
VAN ELSLANDE, J.
VIBERT, D.
VINCENT, P.
VUILLEMIN, N.
WERLY, S.
ZITTOUN, T.

Faculty of Law (26 Ave du 1er-Mars, 2000 Neuchâtel; tel. 327181200; e-mail secretariat.droit@unine.ch; internet www.unine.ch/droit):

AMARELLE, C.
BOHNET, F.
CARRON, B.
CHENAUX, J.
CLERC, E.
DANON, R.
DISTEFANO, G.
DUNAND, J.
GUILLAUME, F.
GUILLOD, O.
GUY-ECABERT, C.
JEANNERET, Y.
JONGE, F.
KRAUS, D.
KUHN, A.
MAHON, P.
MARCHAND, S.
MAVROIDIS, P.

MUELLER, C.
NGUYEN, M.
OSWALD, D.
RIGOZZI, A.
RUMLEY, P.
SALVADE, V.
SPRUMONT, D.
TISSOT, N.

Faculty of Science (11 rue Emile-Argand, 2000 Neuchâtel; tel. 327182100; e-mail secretariat.sciences@unine.ch; internet www.unine.ch/sciences):

AEBI, P.
BALLIF, C.
BELBAHRI, L.
BENAIM, M.
BESSON, O.
BETSCHART, B.
BLAU, M.
BSHARY, R.
COLBOIS, B.
DERENDINGER, J.
DE ROOIJ, N.
DESCHENAUX, R.
FARINE, P.
FELBER, F.
FELBER, P.
FOELLMI, K.
FREI HALLER, B.
GERMOND, J.
GERN, L.
GOBAT, J.
GROEBLI, Y.
GUERIN, P.
HERZIG, H.
HUNKELER, D.
JOB, D.
JOLISSAINT, P.
JUNIER, P.
KALT, A.
KESSLER, F.
KRAUS, D.
KROPF, P.
LE BAYON, R.
MAUCH-MANI, B.
MILETI, G.
MITCHELL, E.
MONTANDON, P.
MONTANI, J.
NEIER, R.
NEUHAUS, J.
PERROCHET, P.
PFISTER, K.
RAEBER, P.
RENARD, P.
ROUILLER, E.
SAVOY, J.
SCHILL, E.
SCHIRMER, M.
SCHLENK, F.
SIEGRIST, H.
SÜDMEYER, T.
SUESS-FINK, G.
THERRIEN, B.
TURLINGS, T.
VALETTE, A.
VANNOTTI, M.
VERRECCHIA, E.
VOORDOUW, M.
VUATAZ, F.
VUILLEUMIER, J.
WILLI, Y.
ZUBER, M.
ZUBERBUEHLER, K.
ZWAHLEN, F.

Faculty of Theology (41 Faubourg de l'Hôpital, 2000 Neuchâtel; tel. 327181900; e-mail secretariat.factheol@unine.ch; internet www.unine.ch/theol):

BASSET, L.
MOSER, F.
ROSE, M.

Other Institutes of Higher Education

INSTITUT DE HAUTES ÉTUDES EN ADMINISTRATION PUBLIQUE (IDHEAP)
(Swiss Graduate School of Public Administration)

Quartier UNIL Mouline, 1015 Lausanne
rue de la Mouline 28, 1022 Chavannes-près-Renens

Telephone: 215574000
E-mail: idheap@idheap.unil.ch
Internet: www.idheap.ch

Founded 1981

Pres.: Dr BARBARA HAERING
Dir: Prof. JEAN-LOUP CHAPPELET
Gen. Sec.: JACQUES-ANDRÉ VULLIET

Library of 10,000 vols and 100 periodicals
Number of teachers: 12
Number of students: 384

INSTITUT DE HAUTES ÉTUDES INTERNATIONALES ET DU DÉVELOPPEMENT
(Graduate Institute of International and Development Studies)

rue de Lausanne 132, CP 136, 1211 Geneva 21

Telephone: 229085700
E-mail: prospective@graduateinstitute.ch
Internet: graduateinstitute.ch

Founded 2008 by merger of Institut universitaire de hautes études internationales (f. 1927) and Institut universitaire d'études du développement (f. 1961)
Private control
Languages of instruction: English, French
Academic year: September to June

Dir: Prof. PHILIPPE BURRIN
Deputy Dir: Prof. ELISABETH PRÜGL
Dean of Studies: Prof. BRUNO ARCIDIACONO

Library of 300,000 vols, 850 journals, 5,500 DVDs and video cassettes
Number of teachers: 50
Number of students: 810

Publications: *Journal International Relations* (in French), *International Development Policy* (in English and French)

INSTITUT UNIVERSITAIRE KURT BÖSCH
(Kurt Bösch University Institute)

CP 4176, 1950 Sion 4
Chemin de l'Institut 18, 1967 Bramois

Telephone: 272057300
E-mail: institut@iukb.ch
Internet: www.iukb.ch

Founded 1989, present status 1992
Language of instruction: French
Academic year: September to June

Dir: Prof. PHILIP D. JAFFÉ
Vice-Dir: Prof. STÉPHANE NAHRATH

UNIVERSITÄRE FERNSTUDIEN SCHWEIZ/FORMATION UNIVERSITAIRE À DISTANCE
(Distance Learning University)

Überlandstr. 12, POB 265, 3900 Brig

Telephone: 279223180
E-mail: admin@fernuni.ch
Internet: www.fernuni.ch

Founded 2005, by merger of three regional study centres: Brig Study Centre of the Distance Learning Univ. Switzerland, Brig VS, Pfäffikon Study Centre of the Distance Learning Univ. Switzerland, Pfäffikon SZ

and French-Swiss Distance Learning Centre CRED, Sierre VS
State control
Languages of instruction: French, German
Rector: Prof. Dr PAUL VOLKEN
Dir for Planning, Cooperation and e-Learning: Dr KURT GRÜNWALD
Dir for Service Centre and Coordination: STÉPHANE PANNATIER
Number of students: 2,190

Universities of Applied Sciences

BERNER FACHHOCHSCHULE/HAUTE ÉCOLE SPÉCIALISÉE BERNOISE
(Bern University of Applied Sciences)

Hallerstr. 10, 3012 Berne
Telephone: 318483300
E-mail: office@bfh.ch
Internet: www.bfh.ch
Founded 1997
Languages of instruction: English, French, German
Pres.: Dr RUDOLF GERBER
Number of teachers: 1,945 f.t.e.
Number of students: 5,673

FACHHOCHSCHULE NORDWESTSCHWEIZ
(University of Applied Sciences of Northwestern Switzerland)

Schulthess-Allee 1, POB 235, 5200 Brugg
Telephone: 564624911
E-mail: info.hgk@fhnw.ch
Internet: www.fhnw.ch
Founded 2006, by merger of three Univs of applied sciences (Aargau, Basel-Stadt and Basel-Landschaft, and Solothurn), School of Education of Solothurn and School of Education and Social Sciences of Basel-Stadt and Basel-Landschaft and Acad. of Music Basel
State control
Languages of instruction: English, German
Pres.: PETER SCHMID-SCHEIBLER
Vice-Pres.: PETER KOFMEL
Number of teachers: 1,265
Number of students: 9,231

FACHHOCHSCHULE OSTSCHWEIZ/ HAUTE ÉCOLE SPÉCIALISÉE DE LA SUISSE ORIENTALE
(University of Applied Sciences of Eastern Switzerland)

Bogenstr. 7, 9000 St. Gallen
Telephone: 712808383
E-mail: info@fho.ch
Internet: www.fho.ch
Founded 1999
State control
Languages of instruction: English, German
Pres.: STEFAN KÖLLIKER
Vice-Pres.: MARTIN JÄGER
Head of Library: CRISTINA CARLINO
Number of students: 3,300
Publication: Zeitschrift der Fachhochschule Ostschweiz (2 a year)

HAUTE ÉCOLE SPÉCIALISÉE DE SUISSE OCCIDENTALE/ FACHHOCHSCHULE WESTSCHWEIZ
(University of Applied Sciences Western Switzerland)

Rue de la Jeunesse 1, CP 452, 2800 Delémont 1
Telephone: 324244900
E-mail: info@hes-so.ch
Internet: www.hes-so.ch
Founded 1997
State control
Languages of instruction: English, French
Pres.: MARC-ANDRÉ BERCLAZ
Vice-Pres.: MARTIN KASSER
Number of students: 15,500

HOCHSCHULE LUZERN
(Lucerne University of Applied Sciences and Arts)

Frankenstr. 9, POB 2969, 6002 Lucerne
Telephone: 412284242
E-mail: info@hslu.ch
Internet: www.hslu.ch
Founded 1997
State control
Rector: Prof. SABINE JAGGY
Exec. Dir: ANDREAS KALLMANN
Number of teachers: 661
Number of students: 8,438
Publication: Hochschule Luzern—Das Magazin (3 a year)

KALAIDOS FACHHOCHSCHULE

Wirtschaft AG, Hohlstr. 535, 8048 Zürich
Telephone: 442001919
E-mail: info@kalaidos-fh.ch
Internet: www.kalaidos-fh.ch
Founded 1995
Private control
Rector: Lic. JÜRG EGGENBERGER
Number of teachers: 75
Number of students: 1,729
Publication: Kalaidoskop

LES ROCHES-GRUYÈRE UNIVERSITY OF APPLIED SCIENCES

rue du Lac 118, 1815 Clarens
Telephone: 219892600
E-mail: info@lrguas.ch
Internet: www.lrguas.ch/les_roches_gruyere
Founded 2008, by merger of Les Roches Int. School of Hotel Management and Glion Institute of Higher Education
Private control
Dir-Gen.: Dr DEBORAH PRINCE

SCUOLA UNIVERSITARIA PROFESSIONALE DELLA SVIZZERA ITALIANA
(University of Applied Sciences and Arts of Southern Switzerland)

Le Gerre, 6928 Manno
Telephone: 586666000
E-mail: info@supsi.ch
Internet: www.supsi.ch
Founded 1997
State control
Pres.: ALBERTO COTTI
Dir: FRANCO GERVASON
Number of teachers: 652
Number of students: 5,000

ZÜRCHER FACHHOCHSCHULE

Walchepl. 2, POB, 8090 Zürich
Telephone: 432592348

E-mail: info@zfh.ch
Internet: www.zfh.ch
State control
Languages of instruction: English, German
Gen. Sec.: Dr RETO THALER
Number of teachers: 1,322
Number of students: 14,000

Colleges

C. G. Jung Institute Zürich: Hornweg 28, 8700 Küsnacht; tel. 449141040; e-mail cg@junginstitut.ch; internet wwww.junginstitut.ch; f. 1948; private teaching and research institute for analytical psychology as conceived by psychoanalyst, Carl Gustav Jung (1875–1961); clinical and professional training programme leading to Diploma; courses and seminars in German and English for qualified auditors; spec. training in child psychotherapy (for German-speaking students); several further education programmes; counselling centre; int. picture archive and library; library: 15,000 vols; 100 teachers; 150 students; Pres. Dipl. DANIEL BAUMANN; Dir of Studies Lic. URSULA WEISS.

Eidgenössische Hochschulinstitut für Berufsbildung/Institut Fédéral des Hautes Études en Formation Professionnelle (Swiss Federal Institute for Vocational Education and Training): Kirchlindachstr. 79, 3052 Zollikofen; tel. 319103700; internet www.ehb-schweiz.ch; f. 1972, present name 2007; regional campuses in Lugano, Lausanne and Zurich; teaching and research in areas of vocational pedagogy, vocational and professional education and training and career devt; Chair. Prof. Dr STEFAN C. WOLTER; Dir Dr DALIA SCHIPPER; Deputy Dir Dr ALEXANDER ETIENNE.

Facoltà Di Teologia Di Lugano: Via G. Buffi 13, CP 4663, 6904 Lugano; tel. 586664555; e-mail info@teologialugano.ch; internet www.teologialugano.ch; f. 1993; research and teaching in liberal arts, particularly in fields of theology, canon law and philosophy; Rector AZZOLINO CHIAPPINI; Sec.-Gen. and Treas. LUCA MATTIOLO; publ. Rivista Teologica di Lugano (RTLu) (in French, German and Italian).

Franklin College Switzerland: Via Ponte Tresa 29, 6924 Sorengo (Lugano); tel. 919852260; e-mail info@fc.edu; internet www.fc.edu; f. 1969; language of instruction: English; academic year September to May; mem. of Asscn of American Int. Colleges and Univs, Ccl of Ind. Colleges; accredited by Middle States Asscn; 11 accredited undergraduate degree courses; library: 36,000 vols, 150 periodicals; 50 teachers; 450 students; Pres. ERIK O. NIELSEN.

Haute Ecole Pédagogique des Cantons de Berne, du Jura et de Neuchâtel— BEJUNE: Rue du Banné 23, 2900 Porrentruy; tel. 844886996; e-mail info@hep-bejune.ch; internet www.hep-bejune.ch; f. 2001; campuses at Bienne and La Chaux-de-Fonds; courses in teaching at pre-school, primary, secondary and further education level; Rector JEAN-PIERRE FAIVRE; publ. Revue Académique Electronique (1 a year).

Pädagogische Hochschule: Baslerstr. 43, 5201 Brugg; tel. 848012210; e-mail info.ph@fhnw.ch; internet www.fhnw.ch/ph; courses in pre-school, primary and secondary teaching, special psychology and pedagogy and research and development in applied pedagogy; 2,000 students; Dir Prof. Dr HERMANN FORNECK; Exec. Sec. KATJA MINI.

Pädagogische Hochschule Bern: Weltistr. 40, 3006 Bern; tel. 313092711; e-mail

iinfo-iwb@phbern.ch; internet www.phbern
.ch; f. 2005; institutes of pre-school and
primary-level teaching, secondary-level
teaching I and II, remedial pedagogy, further
training and of educational media; 2,000
students; Rector Prof. Dr MARTIN SCHÄFER;
Sec. ERICH SCHMID; Gen. Sec. Dr MONIKA
PÄTZMANN.

**Pädagogische Hochschule des Cantons
St Gallen:** Notkerstr. 27, 9000 St Gallen; tel.
712439400; e-mail phs_sekretariat@unisg.ch;
internet www.phsg.ch; f. 1983; campus at
Gossau; courses in secondary-level teaching;
210 teachers; 810 students; Rector Prof. Dr
ERWIN BECK; Exec. Dir MARKUS SEITZ.

**Schiller International University—Swit-
zerland:** (For general information, see entry
for Schiller International University in Germany chapter).

Campuses:

**Schiller International University—
American College of Switzerland:**
1854 Leysin; tel. 244930309; e-mail
siuacsadmissions@bluewin.ch; internet
www.american-college.com; f. 1963; degree
courses in liberal arts and business administration; French and English Language
Institute for EFL/ESL students (programme certificate); library of 48,000
vols; Pres. WALTER LEIBRECHT.

**Schiller International University—
Engelberg:** Dorfstr. 40, 6390 Engelberg;
tel. 416397474; e-mail info@
schiller-university.ch; internet www
.schiller-university.ch; f. 1978; Dir
ROBERTA LO.

**Staatsunabhängige Theologische
Hochschule Basel** (Basel Theological Seminary (State Independent)): Mühlestiegrain
50, 4125 Riehen BS; tel. 616468080; e-mail
info@sthbasel.ch; internet www.sthbasel.ch;
f. 1970; Masters and doctoral degree programmes in theology; distance-learning
courses in Hebrew and Greek; excavation
project in Israel; Rector Prof. Dr JACOB
THIESSEN.

Theologische Hochschule Chur: Alte
Schanfiggerstr. 7, 7000 Chur; tel.
812549999; e-mail sekretariat@
priesterseminar-thc.ch; internet www.thchur
.ch; f. 1807, present status 2006; courses in
philosophy and theology; library: 50,000 vols;
Rector Prof. Dr EVA-MARIA FABER; Head of
Library Prof. Dr MICHAEL DURST.

Schools of Art and Music

ART

**Centre de Formation Professionnelle
Arts Appliqués:** 2 rue Necker, 1201 Geneva;
tel. 223885000; internet edu.ge.ch/cfpaa; f.
1876 as École des Arts Industriels; jewellery,
ceramics, stylism, interior architecture,
dressmaking, graphic art, art expression; 7
bldgs; library: 11,000 vols, 70 periodicals; 125
teachers; 600 students; Dir GUY MÉRAT.

**École Cantonale d'Art de Lausanne/
Haute École d'Art et de Design** (University of Art and Design Lausanne): ave du
Temple 5, CP 555, 1001 Lausanne; ave du
Temple 5, 1020 Lausanne; tel. 213169933;
e-mail ecal@ecal.ch; internet www.ecal.ch; f.
1821; depts of fine arts, audiovisual studies,
graphic design, multimedia and industrial
design, film studies; 227 teachers; 574 students incl. exchange students; Dir PIERRE
KELLER.

École Cantonale d'Art du Valais: rue
Bonne-Eau 16, 3960 Sierre; tel. 274565511;
e-mail ecav@ecav.ch; internet www.ecav.ch;
f. 1948, present name 1997; courses in
graphic design and visual arts; organizes
summer acad. and workshops; library: 12,000
vols, 40 periodicals, 900 DVDs, video cassettes, CD-ROMs and music CDs; 200 students; Dir SIBYLLE OMLIN.

Haute École d'Art et de Design-Genève
(Geneva University of Art and Design): 15
blvd James-Fazy, 1201 Geneva; tel.
223885100; e-mail info.head@hesge.ch;
internet head.hesge.ch; f. 2006, by merger
of École Supérieure des Beaux-arts (f. 1748)
and Haute École d'Arts Appliqués (HEAA);
courses in fine arts, cinema specialization
and design; library: 7,000 vols, 2,500 CDs
and DVDs, 50 periodicals, 4,500 exhibition
catalogues; 97 teachers; 670 students; Dir
JEAN-PIERRE GREFF; Deputy Dir MARC PIC-
CAND; Exec. Sec. DIANE CHRISTINAZ.

MUSIC

Conservatoire de Fribourg: 8 route Louis
Braille, CP 88, 1763 Granges-Paccot; tel.
263059940; e-mail conservatoire@fr.ch;
internet www.fr.ch/cof; f. 1904; attached to
Dept of Culture, Directorate of Education,
Culture and Sport (SCID); vocal and instrumental music, dance and drama; library:
12,000 vols, 20,000 printed music; 207 teachers; 5,000 students; Dir GIANCARLO GEROSA;
Librarian CHRISTIANE ANTONIAZZA-TORCHE.

Conservatoire de Musique: 12 rue de
l'Arquebuse, CP 5155, 1211 Geneva; tel.
223196060; e-mail cmg@cmusge.ch; internet
www.cmusge.ch; f. 1835; 7 educational
centres; all brs of music, dramatic art and
classical ballet; library: 70,000 vols, music
scores; 144 teachers; 2,400 (full-time) students; Dir EVA AROUTUNIAN; Librarian JAC-
QUES TCHAMKERTEN.

**Conservatoire de Musique de Neuchâ-
tel:** 21 Espace de l'Europe, 2000 Neuchâtel;
tel. 328896912; e-mail conservatoire.ne@
cmne.ch; internet www.cmne.ch; f. 1918; pre-
vocational courses, courses in all fields of
music; library: 2,000 vols, 800 CDs, 20,000
scores; 2,100 students; Dir FRANÇOIS HOTZ;
Librarian JOËLLE EICHENBERGER; publ. *Le
Journal* (2 a year).

HEMU Lausanne (High School of Music in
Lausanne): 2 rue de la Grotte, CP 5700, 1002
Lausanne; tel. 213213535; e-mail info@
hemu-cl.ch; internet www.hemu.ch; f. 1861;
research and courses in classical and jazz;
library: 20,000 scores and 4,000 reference
books; 120 teachers; 1,400 students; Dir-Gen.
HERVÉ KLOPFENSTEIN.

Konservatorium Winterthur: Tösserto-
belstr. 1, 8400 Winterthur; tel. 522681580;
e-mail info@konservatorium.ch; internet
www.konservatorium.ch; f. 1873; courses
and workshops related to music and musical
instruments; lessons for children, adolescents and adults with disabilities; 105 teachers; 224 students; Dir HANS-ULRICH
MUNZINGER.

Musik Akademie Basel: 6 Leonhardsstr.,
4003 Basel; tel. 612645757; e-mail info@
mab-bs.ch; internet www.musik-akademie
.ch; f. 1867; comprises 3 institutes: music
school providing non-professional musical
education, conservatory providing professional musical education, Schola Cantorum
Basiliensis providing specialized education
in early music; library: 100,000 vols; 430
staff; 9,000 students; Rector Dr ANDRÉ
BALTENSPERGER; Exec. Dir MARC DE HALLER.

Musikschule Konservatorium Bern:
Kramgasse 36, 3000 Bern 8; tel. 313265353;
e-mail office@konsibern.ch; internet www
.konsibern.ch; f. 1858; library: 50,000 vols;
140 teachers; Dir GERHARD MÜLLER; Deputy
Dir MARKUS PLATTNER.

**Zürich Konservatorium Klassik und
Jazz:** Hirschengraben 1, 8001 Zürich; tel.
442504600; e-mail info@konsi.ch; internet
www.konsi.ch; f. 1875; 125 teachers; 2,700
students; Man. DANIEL KNECHT; Admin. Dir
CHRISTINE GISLER.

SYRIA

The Higher Education System

Higher education institutions predate Syria's independence from France in 1946, with the oldest being the University of Damascus, which was founded in 1903 (when Syria was part of the Ottoman Turkish Empire). There were 279,614 students enrolled in higher education (excluding private universities) in 2006/07, with another 6,000 at private universities. A further 2,500 were enrolled at the Syrian Virtual University (established in 2002, offering degree courses via the internet). Before extensive civil unrest broke out across the country in March 2011, government figures showed that there were six public universities, 20 licensed private universities and four higher institutes operating. In 2012 a memorandum of understanding was signed with the universities of Tehran and Shiraz, Iran, to train medical and nursing students in cooperation with Al-Assad University and the Children's Hospital.

The Ministry of Higher Education is responsible for the universities, intermediate institutes (also attached to other ministries) and higher institutes, and the Council of Higher Education is the coordinating body. Higher education policy is planned centrally but implementation is decentralized. The intermediate institutes, of which there are around 190, are supervised by the Supreme Council of Intermediate Institutes. Legislative Decree No. 36 (2001) authorized the establishment of private institutions of higher education. The Ministry of Higher Education is, in theory, the agency responsible for quality assurance in Syria, although in practice there are no formal procedures in place and the Ministry does not often directly intervene. Higher Council Decision 154 (2005) established the legal basis for quality assurance, and plans for a quality assurance and accreditation agency were under discussion in 2011.

Applicants are legally required to possess the General Secondary Certificate to be admitted to university. The specific grade requirements for admission to programmes are determined by the Council of Higher Education. The Bachelors (*Licence*—French, or *Ijâza fi*—Arabic) is often a four-year degree, although some disciplines are longer in duration, such as architecture, dentistry, engineering, pharmacy and veterinary medicine (all five years) and medicine (six years). The first postgraduate degree is the Diploma of Higher Studies or Postgraduate Diploma, a full-time course of a professional nature lasting one or two years. Additionally, there is a Diploma of Qualification and Specialization, which is a professional qualification in commerce, medicine and teacher-training. Following the award of the Diploma of Higher Studies, the Masters degree is a two-year course consisting of both taught and research elements. Finally, the highest university degree is the Doctor of Philosophy (PhD), which usually requires an additional three years' study, comprises both taught and research elements, and culminates in submission and defence of a thesis.

The intermediate institutes are the main institutions for the provision of post-secondary technical and vocational education. Courses last two years and are administered either by the Ministry of Higher Education or one of the relevant ministries. Upon completion of the course, students are awarded the Certificate of Assistant Bachelor.

Regulatory and Representative Bodies

GOVERNMENT

Ministry of Culture: rue George Haddad, Rawda, Damascus; tel. (11) 3331556; e-mail info@moc.gov.sy; internet www.moc.gov.sy; Minister Dr LUBANAH MSHAWEH.

Ministry of Education: rue Shahbander, al-Masraa, Damascus; tel. (11) 3313206; e-mail info@syrianeducation.org.sy; internet www.syrianeducation.org.sy; Minister Dr HAZWAN AL-WAZZ.

Ministry of Higher Education: BP 9251, pl. Mezzeh Gamarik, Damascus; tel. (11) 2119865; e-mail dep.adminstration@mohe .gov.sy; internet www.mohe.gov.sy; Minister Dr MALIK ALI.

NATIONAL BODY

Council of Higher Education: BP 9355, Damascus; tel. (11) 2126336; e-mail dep .adminstration@mohe.gov.sy; regulates and oversees the higher education system; Minister GHIATH BARAKAT; Sec.-Gen. RIAD AL-AJLANI.

Learned Societies

GENERAL

Arabic Language Academy of Damascus: BP 327, Damascus; tel. (11) 3713103; e-mail mla@net.sy; f. 1919; Arabic Islamic legacy and linguistic studies and terminology; 20 mems; Chair. Dr MARWAN AL-MAHASINI; Sec.-Gen. Dr A. WASSEK CHAHID; publ. *Majallat Majmaa al-Lughah al-Arabiyyah bi-Dimashq* (4 a year, review).

LANGUAGE AND LITERATURE

British Council: Maysaloun St, Shalaan, BP 33105, Damascus; tel. (11) 3310631; e-mail info@sy.britishcouncil.org; internet www.britishcouncil.org/syria; f. 1974; information services; Education UK teaching centre; offers courses and exams in English language and British culture and promotes cultural exchange with the UK; library of 7,000 vols; additional electronic resources and audiovisual materials; Dir PAUL DOUBLEDAY; Teaching Centre Man. AMIR RAMZAN.

Goethe-Institut: Adnan Malki St 8, BP 6100, Damascus; tel. (11) 3719435; e-mail info@damascus.goethe.org; internet www .goethe.de/damaskus; offers courses and exams in German language and culture and promotes cultural exchange with Germany; library of 5,200 vols; Dir MANFRED EWEL; Librarian REGINA ABBOUD.

Instituto Cervantes: 10 Malek Abdel Aziz al Saud St, Sebki, Damascus; tel. (11) 3737061; e-mail cendam@cervantes.es; internet damasco.cervantes.es; offers courses and exams in Spanish language and culture and promotes cultural exchange with Spain and Spanish-speaking Latin and Central America; library of 10,000 vols; Dir PABLO MARTIN ASUERO.

Research Institutes

GENERAL

Institut Français du Proche-Orient: BP 344, Damascus; tel. (11) 3330214; e-mail f .burgat@ifporient.org; internet www .ifporient.org; f. 1922 as Institut Français d'études Arabes de Damas (Ifead); 2003 merged with Centre d'études et de recherches sur le Moyen-Orient contemporain (Cermoc) and L'Institut français d'archéologie de Beyrouth; archaeological research, study of the classical Arab world, Islamic civilization, and history and studies of modern Syria; library of 100,000 vols, 1,500 periodicals; Dir FRANÇOIS BURGAT; Gen. Sec. EMMANUEL RATTIN; Librarian MARTINE GILLET; publ. *Bulletin d'Etudes Orientales* (1 a year).

AGRICULTURE, FISHERIES AND VETERINARY SCIENCE

Arab Centre for the Study of Arid Zones and Dry Lands: BP 2440, Damascus; tel. (11) 5743087; e-mail email@acsad.org; internet www.acsad.org; f. 1968 by the Arab League; studies problems of management conservation and devt of agricultural resources, incl. water, soil, plant and animal resources; emphasis on resources survey and assessment, causes of degradation and desertification, processes of conservation and devt, economic evaluation and social implications, proper management through appropriate technologies, technical training, processing and dissemination of pertinent scientific and technical knowledge and information; mems: 16 Arab states; library of 1,500 vols, 152 periodicals, 65,000 references;

Dir-Gen. Dr HASSAN SEOUD; publs *Agriculture and Water in Arid Regions of the Arab World* (2 a year), *The Camel Newsletter* (2 a year).

EDUCATION

Arab Centre for Arabization, Translation, Authorship and Publication: Al-Afif St, 2 Senbul Jadet, BP 3752, Damascus; tel. (11) 3334876; e-mail acatap@net.sy; internet www.acatap.org; f. 1991; attached to the Arab League Educational, Cultural and Scientific Organization (ALECSO); translates and prints recent educational, medical and scientific titles in Arabic; organizes seminars and workshops; library of 3,500 items; Dir Prof. Dr ZAID IBRAHEEM AL ASSAF; publ. *Arabization* (2 a year).

Libraries and Archives

Aleppo

Al Maktabah Al Wataniah: Bab El-Faradj, Aleppo; tel. (21) 236130; f. 1924; Librarian YOUNIS ROSHDI.

Damascus

Al Zahiriah (Public Library): Bab el Barid, Damascus; f. 1919; main subjects are sciences, literature and language, history, biography, religion; 100,000 vols, 50,000 periodicals; spec. colln: rare pre-1900 Arabic books; Librarian SAMA EL MAHASSINI.

Assad National Library: Malki St, BP 3639, Damascus; tel. (11) 3320803; e-mail anl@alassad-library.gov.sy; internet www .alassad-library.gov.sy; f. 1984; nat. deposit library; publishes National Bibliography, trains librarians; 280 staff; 147,124 vols, 19,000 Arabic MSS; Gen. Dir GHASSAN LAHHAM; publs *Analytical Index of Syrian Periodicals*, *Index of Syrian University Theses*, *National Bibliography* (1 a year).

University of Damascus Library: BP 3003, Damascus; tel. (11) 33924406; e-mail library@damasuniv.edu.sy; internet www .damascusuniversity.edu.sy/library; f. 1903; 32 brs; 250,000 vols, 2,700 periodicals; Library Dir Dr MUHAMMAD ZUHEIR BAKLEH.

Museums and Art Galleries

Aleppo

Aleppo National Museum: BP 6581, Aleppo; tel. (21) 212400; f. 1931; archaeology and modern art; spec. colln of Iron Age artefacts; library of 4,000 vols; Head Curator Dr SHAWQI SHAATH.

Busra

Busra Museum: Busra; tel. (15) 790105; traditional arts and crafts; Dir of Archaeological Research Dr SULEIMAN MOGHDAD.

Damascus

Adnan Malki Museum: Adnan Malki Sq., Damascus; dedicated to Lt Col Malki, assassinated in 1955 failed Syrian Socialist Nationalist Party coup.

Agricultural Museum: Halbouni, Damascus; colln of agricultural tools; paintings of rural life.

Military Museum: Takeih Suleimanieh, Damascus; depictions of famous battles; colln of weapons.

Museum of Arabic Epigraphy: Jakmakieh Madressa, Damascus; tel. (11) 2219746; f. 1974; examples of calligraphy from different periods and colln of tools used in writing Arabic script; Dir FAYEZ HOMSI.

National Museum: Syrian University St, Damascus 4; tel. (11) 2219148; f. 1919; Sections: Prehistory; Ancient Oriental; Greek, Roman and Byzantine; Arab and Islamic; Modern Art; of special interest is the reconstruction of the Palmyrene Hypogeum of Yarhai (2nd century AD), of the Dura Synagogue (3rd century AD), of the Umayyad Qasr El-Hair El-Gharbi (8th century AD) and of the Damascus Hall (18th century AD); houses the Directorate-General of Antiquities and Museums, established by decree in 1947 to conserve Syrian antiquities and to supervise archaeological museums and excavations; Dir-Gen. of Antiquities and Museums ALI AL-KAYYEM; publs *Les Annales Archéologiques Arabes Syriennes*, *Les Chroniques Archéologiques en Syrie*.

Popular Traditions Museum Qasrelazem: Bzourieh St, Damascus; tel. (11) 2261650; f. 1954; library of 3,000 vols; Curator HASSAN KAMAL.

Deir ez-Zor

Deir ez-Zor Museum: Pl. du Président, Deir ez-Zor; tel. (51) 222530; f. 1974; archaeology; library of 1,000 vols; Dir ASSAD MUHAMMAD; publ. *Les Annales Archéologiques de Syrie*.

Hama

Hama Museum: rue Abou al-Fida'a Hama; tel. (33) 224550; f. 1956; history and folklore; Dir ABDEL RAZZAQ ZAGZOUQ.

Homs

Homs Museum: rue al-Koutli, Homs dar Al-Thakafa; tel. (31) 220002; f. 1974; archaeology, folk and modern art; Curator MAJED EL MOUSSLI.

Palmyra

Palmyra National Museum: Palmyra; tel. (31) 910573; f. 1961; archaeological findings from prehistory to 16th century; attached museum of Syrian desert folklore, traditional handicraft industry and agriculture; Dir KHALED AL AS'AD.

Sweida

Sweida Museum: rue de Qanawat, Sweida; tel. (16) 232035; artefacts from Roman, Nabatean and Islamic periods; Curator M. HOUSSEIN ZEIN EL-DIN.

Tartos

Tartos Museum: Tartos; tel. (43) 220541; Islamic history; Curator RAMIZ HOUCHE.

Universities

AL-BAATH UNIVERSITY

BP 77, Homs
Telephone: (31) 431847
E-mail: baath-univ@net.sy
Internet: www.albaath-univ.edu.sy
Founded 1979
State control
Language of instruction: Arabic
Academic year: September to June
Pres.: Prof. Dr YASSER HOURI
Vice-Pres. for Admin. and Student Affairs: Prof. Dr HOUSAM BARAKAT
Vice-Pres. for Scientific Affairs: Prof. Dr AUODI SALHA
Admin. Officer: KASSEM HAMMOUD
Dir of Int. Relations: ABDUL ILAH AL-ABDOU
Librarian: LINA MAASRANI
Library of 63,000 vols
Number of teachers: 800

Number of students: 26,730

DEANS

Faculty of Agriculture: Dr ABDULA AL-ISA
Faculty of Chemical and Petroleum Engineering: Dr SHARIF SADIQ
Faculty of Civil Engineering and Architecture: Dr MUHAMMAD HAKEMI (Architecture)
Faculty of Civil Engineering and Architecture: Dr BASSAM IBRAHIM (Civil Engineering)
Faculty of Dentistry: Dr MUHAMMAD SABEH ARAB
Faculty of Education: Dr IBRAHIM KHADOUR
Faculty of Informatics: Dr MUHAMMAD AL-RAJAB
Faculty of Literature: Dr AHMAD DAHMAN
Faculty of Mechanical and Electrical Engineering: Dr RADWAN AL-MASRI
Faculty of Medicine: Dr ISA TUMI
Faculty of Pharmacy: Dr IMAD HADAD
Faculty of Sciences: Dr MALEK ALI
Faculty of Veterinary Science (in Hama): Dr MUHAMMAD ALI AL-IMADI
Intermediate Institute of Computer Engineering: Dr MUHAMMAD AL-HAG YOUNES
Intermediate Institute of Engineering: Dr MOUFAK FAKHOURI
Intermediate Institute of Industry: Dr HASSAN FARAH
Intermediate Institute of Veterinary Medicine: Dr ASAD AL-ABID

TISHREEN UNIVERSITY
(University of October)

POB 2230, Latakia
Telephone: (41) 445290
E-mail: president@tishreen.edu.sy
Internet: www.tishreen.edu.sy
Founded 1971 as univ. of Latakia
State control
Language of instruction: Arabic
Academic year: September to June
Rector: Prof. Dr HANI SHAABAN
Vice-Rector for Academic Affairs: Prof. Dr IBRAHEEM SULAIMAN
Vice-Rector for Admin. and Students Affairs: Prof. Dr AHMAD KELZIEYEH
Vice-Rector for Open Learning: Prof. Dr RAFIK JIBLAWI
Vice-Rector for Scientific Research and Postgraduate Studies: Prof. Dr BASSAM HASSAN
Provost: SALAH SHABAAN
Dir for Libraries and Cultural Activities: ABDUL RAHMAN RAIEYS AL MENA
Library of 60,214 vols, 468 periodicals
Number of teachers: 1,280
Number of students: 100,400

Publications: *Journal of Agriculture, Journal of Arts and Humanities, Journal of Basic Science, Journal of Law and Economics, Journal of Medical Science, Journal of Studies and Scientific Research*

DEANS

Faculty of Agriculture: Dr RIYAD ZEIDAN
Faculty of Architecture: Dr RAMZI AL-SHEIKH
Faculty of Arts and Humanities: Dr SADEEK GHAREEB
Faculty of Civil Engineering: Dr GHATFAN AMMAR
Faculty of Dentistry: Dr AMMAR LAIKAH
Faculty of Economics: Dr YOUSEF MUHAMMAD
Faculty of Education: Dr ELYAS AL-KHOURI NAMEH
Faculty of Electrical and Mechanical Engineering: Dr ALAA AL DEEN HOUSAM AL DEEN
Faculty of Fine Arts: Dr RAMZI AL-SHEIKH
Faculty of Informatics Engineering: Dr RADWAN DANDAH
Faculty of Law: Dr SALMAN OUTHMAN
Faculty of Medicine: Dr LOAY NADAF
Faculty of Nursing: MARWAN ISSA

Faculty of Pharmacology: Dr TAMEEM HASHEM HAMMAD

Faculty of Physical Education: Dr ALI SALMAN

Faculty of Science: Dr MUHAMMAD ISSA

UNIVERSITY OF ALEPPO

Aleppo

Telephone: (21) 2671200

E-mail: alepuniv@alepuniv.edu.sy

Internet: www.alepuniv.edu.sy

Founded 1958

State control

Languages of instruction: Arabic, English, French

Academic year: September to June

Pres.: Dr KHDER OURFALI

Vice-Pres. for Academic Affairs: Dr RIYAD ALMOUSTAFA

Vice-Pres. for Admin. and Student Affairs: Dr MUSTAFA AFYOUNI

Vice-Pres. for Open Education: Dr MUHAMMAD GHASSAN DAHHAN

Vice-Pres. for Research and Postgraduate Studies: Dr NAJAH TANNOUS

Sec.: Dr ABDUL KADER HABBACHE

Registrar: AHMAD BAZAR

Librarian: MARWAN ABSI

Number of teachers: 4,180

Number of students: 131,950

Publications: *Aleppo's Adiyat, Journal for the History of Arabic Science, Medical Scholarly Journal Magazine, Research Journal of Aleppo University* (comprises the following series: Arts and Humanities; Medical Sciences; Agricultural Sciences; Basic Sciences; Engineering Sciences; *Adiyat Halab*)

DEANS

Faculty of Administration Sciences (Idleb): Dr KAMAL DISHLI

Faculty of Agriculture: Dr AHMAD ALSHEIKH KADDOUR

Faculty of Agriculture II (Idleb): Dr ABBAS ALSHEIKH

Faculty of Applied Fine Arts: Dr GEORGE TOUMA

Faculty of Architecture: Dr LAMIS HERBLE

Faculty of Arts and Humanities: Dr AHMED KADDOUR

Faculty of Arts and Humanities II (Idleb): BASEM JABBOUR

Faculty of Civil Engineering: Dr MUHAMMAD AMIN CHAGHALE

Faculty of Dentistry: Dr MUHAMMAD SULTAN

Faculty of Economics: Dr ALAA EDDIN JABAL

Faculty of Education: Dr MUHAMMAD ABDULLAH KASIM

Faculty of Education II (Idleb): Dr AHMAD ABORASS

Faculty of Electrical and Electronic Engineering: Dr LOUAY CHACHATI

Faculty of Informatics: Dr SOUHAIL KHAWATMI

Faculty of Law: Dr OMAR FARESS

Faculty of Law II (Idleb): Dr IMAD KMINASSI

Faculty of Mechanical Engineering: Dr NABHAN KHYATTA

Faculty of Medicine: Dr RIAD NOR EDDIN ELASFARI

Faculty of Nursing: Dr NIZAR HAMMAD

Faculty of Pharmacy: Dr AHMAD KHALIL

Faculty of Sciences: Dr TAREK ZAAROURI

Faculty of Sciences II (Idleb): Dr NAWRAS HASSOUN

Faculty of Shariaa: Dr AHMAD ALOMAR

Faculty of Technological Engineering: Dr NABIL SHEIKH KOROSH

Faculty of Veterinary Medicine (Idleb): Dr FAHED SAHYOUNI

Higher Institute for the History of Arabic Sciences: Dr SAKHER OLABI

Higher Institute of Languages: Dr ABDUL JABBAR OUAYED

UNIVERSITY OF DAMASCUS

Damascus

Telephone: (11) 2232152

E-mail: w-mualla@scs-net.org

Internet: www.damascusuniversity.edu.sy

Founded 1903

State control

Language of instruction: Arabic

Academic year: September to June

Pres.: Dr WAEL MUALLA

Vice-Pres. for Academic Affairs: Dr MUHAMMAD SALEM AL-RIKAB

Vice-Pres. for Admin. and Student Affairs: Prof. Dr TAREK al-KHAIR

Vice-Pres. for Postgraduate Studies and Scientific Research: Dr RAKAN RAZOUK

Registrar: YOUSEF KAHELEH

Librarian: KAIS SHAHEEN

Library of 51,500 vols, 70,000 vols in libraries of faculties

Number of teachers: 2,700

Number of students: 120,000 (60,000 distant learning)

Publications: *Dirasat Tarikhiyyah* (historical review, 4 a year), *Journal for Agricultural Studies* (4 a year), *Journal for Basic and Applied Sciences* (4 a year), *Journal for the Arts, Humanities and Sciences* (4 a year), *Journal for the Economic and Legal Sciences* (4 a year), *Journal for the Medical Sciences* (4 a year), *Statistical Collections* (1 a year), *University Journal* (4 a year)

DEANS

Faculty of Agriculture: Prof. Dr HAMZEH BLAL

Faculty of Architecture: Dr PIERRE NANO

Faculty of Arts and Humanities: Prof. Dr WAHAB ROUMIEH

Faculty of Civil Engineering: Prof. Dr AMJAD ZENO

Faculty of Computer Science: Dr AMMAR KHEIR-BEK

Faculty of Dentistry: Prof. Dr M. HASAN YOUSEF

Faculty of Economics: Prof. Dr MUSTAFA AL-KAFRI

Faculty of Fine Arts: Prof. Dr MUHAMMAD SHAHEEN

Faculty of Law: Prof. Dr MUHAMMAD AL-HUSEIN

Faculty of Mechanical and Electrical Engineering: (vacant)

Faculty of Medicine: Prof. Dr NEZAR ASSAD

Faculty of Pharmacy: Prof. Dr ANTOIN LAHHAM

Faculty of Political Science: Prof. Dr OMAR ABDULLAH

Faculty of Science: Prof. Dr ESSAM KASSEM

Faculty of Sharia: Prof. MUHAMMAD al-HASAN al-BOGHAA

Faculty of Tourism: Dr REEM RAMADAN

Colleges

Higher Institute of Applied Sciences and Technology: BP 31983, Barzeh, Damascus; tel. (11) 5140520; e-mail info@hiast.edu.sy; internet www.hiast.edu.sy; f. 1983; awards BSc, MSc, PhD; depts of informatics, systems engineering, mathematics, physics, electronics, management, mechanics; language of instruction: Arabic; 120 teachers; 400 students; Dir Prof. Dr OMRAN KOUBA.

Higher Institute of Political Science: Al-Tall, Damascus; tel. (11) 5911704; f. 1976; depts of administration and public relations, international relations and political studies; library: 15,000 vols; 25 teachers; 434 students; Dean HUSEIN AL-SAYED HUSEIN.

TAIWAN

The Higher Education System

In 1945, following Japan's defeat in the Second World War, Taiwan became one of the provinces of the Republic of China, which was then ruled by the Kuomintang (KMT, Nationalist Party). However, having been defeated on the mainland by the Communist revolution (which led to the proclamation of the People's Republic of China), in 1949 the KMT Government was forced to remove itself to Taipei, the capital of Taiwan, where it established a KMT regime and declared itself to be the rightful Chinese Government, as well as its intention ultimately to recover control of the mainland from the Communists. The population is mainly Chinese in origin, and the official language is Mandarin (Guoyu); Taiwanese, Hakka and English are also spoken. Most universities in Taiwan have been founded since 1949, but some were formerly mainland institutions that either relocated during the Communist takeover or were refounded; these include Fu-Jen Catholic University (founded in 1925 in Beijing), National Central University (originally based in Nanking), National Chiao Tung University (founded in 1896 in Shanghai), National Tsing Hua University (founded in 1911 in Beijing), and Soochow University (founded in 1900 in the mainland province of Jiangsu). In 1987 the nine teachers' junior colleges were upgraded to teachers' colleges. These admit senior secondary graduates for a four-year course. High-school teachers are trained at normal universities. In 2010/11 there were 116 universities, 15 junior colleges and 32 independent colleges, most of which offer postgraduate facilities; total enrolment in higher education in that year was 1,352,084 students. Higher education is highly centralized and the Constitution places great emphasis on the importance of education. The higher education system is based on the US model.

The Ministry of Education supervises the Universities and Colleges Joint Entrance Examination, which is required for admission to higher education. However, students may also gain admission through two other methods, either by applying directly to the institution in question and meeting that institution's entry requirements, or through recommendation on grounds of academic excellence.

Junior colleges, which provide two- or five-year Junior College Diploma programmes, are the first level of higher education. Two-year junior colleges admit graduates from Senior and Senior Vocational High Schools, while five-year junior colleges accept students from Junior High Schools. The majority of junior colleges are privately run. Institutes of technology operate on a similar basis: two-year institutes admit junior college graduates and four-year institutes admit senior vocational school graduates. There are also 'Open' universities, which specialize in adult education.

The Bachelors degree is the main university undergraduate qualification, and usually lasts four years, although some specialist programmes are longer in duration, including civil engineering, dentistry, law and medicine, which take between five and seven years. At postgraduate level, the Masters degree requires one to four years' study, while the final qualification, the Doctorate, requires two to seven years' study following the Masters. Technical and vocational education and training is provided by senior vocational schools and junior colleges. Periods of study vary between two to five years.

Legislative amendments allowing mainland Chinese students to enrol at Taiwanese universities for the first time since 1949 were approved by the Taiwanese parliament in August 2010; however, mainland Chinese would remain unable to enrol at university departments related to Taiwan's national security. The first mainland students were admitted in 2011.

Regulatory Bodies

GOVERNMENT

Ministry of Culture: No 30-1 Beiping E Rd, Zhongzheng Dist., Taipei, 10049; tel. (2) 2343-4000; internet www.moc.gov.tw; Minister LUNG YINGTAI.

Ministry of Education: No 5 Zhongshan S Rd., Zhongzheng Dist., Taipei 10051; tel. (2) 77366666; internet www.moe.gov.tw; Minister Dr CHIANG WEI-LING.

Research, Development and Evaluation Commission: 6/F, 2-2 Chi Nan Rd, Sec. 1, Taipei 10051; tel. (2) 23419066; e-mail service@rdec.gov.tw; internet www.rdec.gov.tw; f. 1969; Minister SUNG YU-HSIEH.

NATIONAL BODIES

Bureau of International Cultural and Educational Relations: Min. of Education, No 5 Jhongshan S. Rd, Jhongjheng Dist., Taipei 10051; Min. of Education, 13F, No 5 Syujhou Rd, Jhongjheng Dist., Taipei 100; tel. (2) 77365608; e-mail cschang@mail.moe.gov.tw; internet english.moe.gov.tw; f. 1947; assists colleges and univs to enter into academic cooperation with foreign instns of higher learning; sponsors int. scholar exchange programmes; organizes bilateral confs on higher education; encourages Taiwan specialists, academics and doctoral students to participate in int. academic confs abroad; provides Taiwan Scholarships to encourage exceptional foreign students to pursue degrees in Taiwan; works with govts,

cultural and educational instns and commercial enterprises to obtain scholarships for Taiwan students; Dir-Gen. Dr CHIN-SHENG CHANG.

Learned Societies

GENERAL

Academia Sinica: 128 Academia Rd, Section 2, Nankang, Taipei 11529; tel. (2) 27822120; e-mail aspublic@gate.sinica.edu.tw; internet www.sinica.edu.tw; f. 1928; 220 mems; attached research institutes: see under Research Institutes; library of 2,236,000 vols; Pres. Dr YUAN-TSEH LEE; Dir-Gen. Dr YIH-HSIUNG YEH; Chief of Secretariat Dr CHI-CHIUNG LO; publs *Academia Economic* (papers), *Academia Sinica* (2 a year), *Asia-Major* (2 a year), *Asia-Pacific Forum* (4 a year), *Botanical Bulletin* (4 a year), *Bulletin of the Institute of Ethnology*, *Bulletin of the Institute of History and Philosophy*, *Bulletin of the Institute of Mathematics*, *Bulletin of the Institute of Modern History* (4 a year), *Disquisitions of the Past and Present* (2 a year), *EurAmerica Quarterly*, *Journal of Social Sciences and Philosophy*, *Language and Linguistics* (4 a year), *Mathmedia* (4 a year), *Research on Women in Chinese History* (1 a year), *Statistica Sinica* (4 a year), *Taiwan Economic Forecasts and Policies Academia Economic Papers*, *Taiwan Historical Research* (2 a year), *Taiwan Journal of Anthropology* (2 a year), *Taiwanese*

Sociological Review (2 a year), *Zoological Studies* (4 a year).

China Academy: Hwa Kang, Yang Ming Shan; f. 1966; private instn for sinological studies, consisting of 20 academic asscns and research institutions and Chinese and foreign mems; 591 acads, 312 hon. acads, 1,815 fellows; library of 450,000 vols; Pres. CHANG CHI-YUN; Sec.-Gen. PAN WEI-HO; publs *Beautiful China Pictorial Monthly* (bilingual Chinese and English), *Chinese Culture* (in English, 4 a year), *Renaissance Monthly* (in Chinese), *Sino-American Relations* (in English, 4 a year), *Sinological Monthly* (in Chinese), *Sinological Quarterly* (in Chinese).

China National Association of Literature and the Arts: 4 Lane 22, Nuigpo St W, Taipei.

China Society: 7 Lane 52, Wenchow St, Taipei; f. 1960; centre for Chinese studies; 100 mems; Pres. Dr CHEN CHI-LU; publ. *Journal* (1 a year).

AGRICULTURE, FISHERIES AND VETERINARY SCIENCE

Agricultural Association of China: 14 Wenchow St, Taipei; tel. (2) 23636681; f. 1917; mems: 159 instns, 2,554 individuals; Pres. TSONG-SHIEN WU; publ. *Journal* (4 a year).

Chinese Forestry Association: 2 Sec. 1, Hang-chow S Rd, Taipei 100; tel. (2) 33221299; e-mail cfa@forest.gov.tw; internet www.forestry.org.tw; f. 1967; 1,219 mems;

Chair. JEN-TEH YEN; publ. *Quarterly Journal of Chinese Forestry*.

BIBLIOGRAPHY, LIBRARY SCIENCE AND MUSEOLOGY

Library Association of the Republic of China (Taiwan): 20 Chungshan S Rd, Taipei 10001; tel. (2) 23312475; e-mail lac@ncl.edu.tw; internet www.lac.org.tw; f. 1953; 1,977 mems; Pres. LI-KUEI HSUEH; Sec. Gen. CHIAO-MIN LIN; publ. *Journal of Library and Information Science Research* (2 a year).

ECONOMICS, LAW AND POLITICS

Chinese National Foreign Relations Association: Third Fl., 94 Nanchang St, Sec. 1, Taipei; Pres. HUANG KUO-SHU.

Taipei Bar Association: 7 Roosevelt Rd, Taipei; internet www.tba.org.tw; f. 1947.

HISTORY, GEOGRAPHY AND ARCHAEOLOGY

Academia Historica (Academy of History): 406 Sec. 2, Pei Yi Rd, Hsintien, Taipei; tel. (2) 22175500; internet www.drnh.gov.tw; f. 1947; responsible for researching and compiling material on Taiwanese national history; 175 mems; library of 10,000,000 items (nat. archives, books, documents); Pres. CHANG YEN HSIEN; Sec.-Gen. Prof. LI CHUNG KUANG; publs *Bulletin* (2 a year), *Journal* (2 a year).

LANGUAGE AND LITERATURE

British Council: 2F-A2, 106 XinYi Rd, Section 5, Taipei 11047; tel. (2) 87221000; e-mail enquiries@britishcouncil.org.tw; internet www.britishcouncil.org/taiwan; teaching centre; offers courses and exams in English language and British culture and promotes cultural exchange with the UK; Dir ALISON DEVINE.

World Chinese Language Association: 1 Ningbo E St, Zhongzheng Dist., Taipei 10093; tel. (2) 23511385; e-mail wcla.cec@msa.hinet.net; internet www.wcla.org.tw; f. 1972; promotes research on Chinese and in teaching Chinese as a second language; encourages academic exchange of Chinese language in the world; Chair. WAN-LI CHENG; CEO PENG-CHENG DONG; publ. *Journal of Chinese Language Teaching* (4 a year, in Chinese and English).

MEDICINE

Chinese Medical Association: 201 Shih-Pai Rd, Sec. II, Beitou Dist., Taipei; tel. (2) 28757358; e-mail cma@vghtpe.gov.tw; internet www.taipei-cma.org; f. 1915; Dir FANG-YUE LIN; publ. *Journal of the Chinese Medical Association* (12 a year, print and online, www.jcma-online.com).

NATURAL SCIENCES

Mathematical Sciences

Chinese Statistical Association: 1 Nan Chung Rd, Sec. 1, Taipei; f. 1941; 1,082 mems; Pres. C. C. LEE; publ. *Chinese Statistical Journal*.

Mathematical Society of the Republic of China: Dept of Mathematics, Nat. Cheng Kung Univ., 1 Roosevelt Rd, Taipei 10617; tel. (2) 23677625; e-mail tms@math.ntu.edu.tw; internet www.taiwanmathsoc.org.tw; f. 1935; Pres. GERARD JENNHWA CHANG; Gen. Sec. KUO-CHING HUANG; Treas. HUI-WEN LIN; publ. *Taiwanese Journal of Mathematics* (6 a year, print and online, journal.taiwanmathsoc.org.tw).

Physical Sciences

Chemical Society: POB 1-18, Nankang, Taipei 115; tel. (2) 27898574; e-mail ccswww@gate.sinica.edu.tw; internet www.chemistry.org.tw; f. 1932; 3,000 mems; Sec.-Gen. LING-KANG LIU; publs *Hua Hsueh* (in Chinese, 4 a year), *Journal of the Chinese Chemical Society* (in English, 12 a year).

Committee on the Promotion of the Peaceful Uses of Atomic Energy: 110 Yenping S Rd, Taipei; Pres. MILTON J. T. SHIEH.

Physical Society of Republic of China: POB 23–30, Taipei 106; tel. (2) 23634923; e-mail cjp@psroc.phys.ntu.edu.tw; internet psroc.phys.ntu.edu.tw; f. 1958; Pres. YEE HSIUNG; Gen. Sec. CHAO-MING FU; publs *Physics Bimonthly* (6 a year, in Chinese, print and online, psroc.phys.ntu.edu.tw/bimonth), *Chinese Journal of Physics* (6 a year, in English, print and online, psroc.phys.ntu.edu.tw/cjp).

PHILOSOPHY AND PSYCHOLOGY

Confucius-Mencius Society of the Republic of China: 45 Nanhai Rd, Taipei; f. 1960; spreads knowledge about Confucius and Mencius, seeks the improvement of public morals and the creation of a better society; 3,900 mems; Chair. Dr CHEN LI-FU; Sec. HUA CHUNG-LIN; publ. *Confucius-Mencius Monthly*, *Journal of Confucius-Mencius Society*.

RELIGION, SOCIOLOGY AND ANTHROPOLOGY

Chinese Association for Folklore: 422 Fulin Rd, POB 68-1292, Shihlin, Taipei; f. 1932; Chinese and Asian folklore; 47 mems; library of 1,000 vols and MSS; Chair. Prof. LOU TSU-KUANG; Sec. AMY LOU.

TECHNOLOGY

Chinese Institute of Civil and Hydraulic Engineering: 4th Fl., 1 Jen Ai Rd, Sec. 2 Taipei; tel. (2) 23926325; e-mail ciche@ciche.org.tw; internet www.ciche.org.tw; f. 1973; 7,500 mems; Pres. YU CHENG; publs *Journal of Civil and Hydraulic Engineering* (4 a year), *Journal of the Chinese Institute of Civil and Hydraulic Engineering* (4 a year).

Chinese Institute of Engineers: Fl. 3, No. 1 Ren-ai Rd, Sec. 2, Taipei 10055; tel. (2) 23925128; e-mail secretariat@cie.org.tw; internet www.cie.org.tw; f. 1912; 18,125 individual mems and 78 group mems; library of 7,500 vols, 60 periodicals; Sec. FENZA CHIANG; publs *Journal of the Chinese Institute of Engineers* (8 a year), *Newsletter* (4 a year), *Transactions* (6 a year).

Research Institutes

GENERAL

National Institute for Compilation and Translation: 179 Heping E Rd, Sector 1, Da-An District, Taipei City 10644; tel. (2) 33225558; e-mail trcnews@mail.nict.gov.tw; internet www.nict.gov.tw; f. 1932; translates foreign books, examines and approves textbooks, standardizes scientific and technical terms; 75 mems; library of 100,000 vols; Dir-Gen. PAN WEN-CHUNG; publs *Compilation and Translation Review* (print and online), *Journal of Textbook Research* (print and online).

AGRICULTURE, FISHERIES AND VETERINARY SCIENCE

Council of Agriculture: 37 Nanhai Rd, Taipei; tel. (2) 23812991; internet www.coa.gov.tw; f. 1984; govt agency under the Exec. Yuan, with ministerial status; administers nat. agriculture, forestry, fisheries, livestock farming and food; library of 18,000 vols; Min. Dr PAO-CHI CHEN.

Taiwan Agricultural Research Institute: 189 Zhongzheng Rd, Wufeng, Taichung 41362; tel. (4) 23302301; e-mail mwf-doc@wufeng.tari.gov.tw; internet www.tari.gov.tw; f. 1895; insect colln; Dir JUNNE-JIH CHEN; publ. *Journal of Taiwan Agricultural Research* (4 a year).

Taiwan Fisheries Research Institute: 199 Hou-Ih Rd, Keelung 220; tel. (2) 24622101; internet www.tfrin.gov.tw; f. 1933, current name adopted 2003; attached to Ccl of Agriculture; library of 16,000 vols; Dir-Gen. Dr CHIN-LAU KUO; publs *Journal of Taiwan Fisheries Research*, *Mariculture Research*.

Taiwan Forestry Research Institute: 53 Nan-Hai Rd, Taipei 10066; tel. (2) 23039978; e-mail service@serv.tfri.gov.tw; internet www.tfri.gov.tw; f. 1896; library of 33,000 vols; Dir-Gen. STAR HUANG; Sec.-Gen. CHIN-SHIEN WU; publ. *Taiwan Journal of Forest Science* (4 a year).

Taiwan Sugar Research Institute: 54 Sheng Chan Rd, Tainan; tel. (6) 2671911; e-mail tsc02@taisugar.com.tw; f. 1902; supported by Taiwan Sugar Corpn; library of 46,800 vols; Dir LONG-HUEI WANG; publs *Extension Bulletin*, *Report* (in Chinese, 4 a year, English summary), *Technical Bulletin*.

ECONOMICS, LAW AND POLITICS

Co-operative League of the Republic of China: 11-2 Fu Chow St, Taipei; tel. (2) 23219343; f. 1940; cooperative business research and education; Chair. YANG CHIA-LIN; Exec. Dir and Sec.-Gen. HSU WEN-FU; publs *CLC Co-operative News* (1 a year), *Co-operative Economics* (4 a year).

Institute of Economics: c/o Academia Sinica, Nankang, Taipei 11529; tel. (2) 27822791; internet www.sinica.edu.tw/~econ; f. 1962; attached to Academia Sinica; Dir Dr CHUNG-MING KUAN; publs *Academia Economic Papers* (4 a year), *Taiwan Economic Forecast and Policy* (2 a year).

FINE AND PERFORMING ARTS

National Taiwan Arts Education Centre: 47 Nan Hai Rd, Taipei; tel. (2) 23110574; internet www.arte.gov.tw; f. 1957; in charge of the research, extension and guidance of art education in Taiwan; Dir JOSEPH TSU-SHENG WU; publs *Journal of Aesthetic Education* (6 a year), *Newsletter of Arts Education* (12 a year), *The International Journal of Arts Education* (2 a year).

HISTORY, GEOGRAPHY AND ARCHAEOLOGY

Institute of History and Philology: c/o Academia Sinica, Nankang, Taipei 11529; tel. (2) 27829555; internet www.ihp.sinica.edu.tw/english; attached to Academia Sinica; Dir Prof. TUNG-KUEI KUAN.

Institute of Modern History: c/o Academia Sinica, Nankang, Taipei 11529; tel. (2) 27824166; attached to Academia Sinica; Dir Prof. KO-WU HUANG; Sec. SHU-LING CHIANG.

MEDICINE

Institute of Biomedical Sciences, Preparatory Office: c/o Academia Sinica, Nankang, Taipei 11529; attached to Academia Sinica; Dir Dr CHENG-WEN WU.

NATURAL SCIENCES

General

National Science Council: 106 Ho-ping E Rd, Section 2, Taipei 106; tel. (2) 27377981; e-mail klchou@nsc.gov.tw; internet www.nsc.gov.tw; f. 1959; br. of central govt; promotes nat. science and technology devt, supports academic research and establishes industrial parks; Minister CYPRUS C. Y. CHU; Sr Systems Coordinator K. L. CHOU; publs *East Asian Science, Technology and Society* (in English, 4 a year), *Indicators of Science and Technology* (in Chinese and English, 1 a year), *International Journal of Science and Mathematics Education* (in English, 4 a year), *Journal of Biomedical Science* (in English, 6 a year, open access journal since January 2009), *National Science Council Review* (in English and Chinese, 1 a year), *Science Development* (in Chinese, 12 a year).

Biological Sciences

Institute of Biological Chemistry: 128 Academia Rd Section 2, Nankang, Taipei 115; tel. (2) 27855696; e-mail ibc@gate.sinica.edu.tw; internet www.ibc.sinica.edu.tw; f. 1970; attached to Academia Sinica; research areas incl. glycosciences, mechanism-based drug discovery, membrane dynamics, post-translational modifications in physiology and diseases; Dir Dr MING-DAW TSAI (acting).

Institute of Molecular Biology: Academia Sinica, Nankang, Taipei 11529; tel. (2) 27899175; e-mail imbwww@imb.sinica.edu.tw; internet www.imb.sinica.edu.tw; f. 1982; attached to Academia Sinica; research groups incl. biotechnology devt, cellular communication and signal transduction, genetics and devt, molecular virology, nuclear structure and function, structure-function relationship in biological systems; Dir Dr SOO-CHEN CHENG.

Institute of Plant and Microbial Biology: 128 Academia Rd, Section 2, Nankang, Taipei 11529; tel. (2) 27899590; e-mail hsiaoyun@gate.sinica.edu.tw; internet ipmb.sinica.edu.tw; f. 1929; attached to Academia Sinica; Dir LONG-FANG CHEN (acting); publ. *Botanical Studies* (in English, print and online, www.as-botanicalstudies.com).

Institute of Zoology: c/o Academia Sinica, Nankang, Taipei 11529; attached to Academia Sinica; Dir Dr JEN-LEIH WU.

Mathematical Sciences

Institute of Mathematics: POB 23–216, Taipei 10699; Academia Sinica, 6F, Astronomy-Mathematics Bldg, No 1, Section 4, Roosevelt Rd, Taipei 10617; tel. (2) 23685999; e-mail mathas@math.sinica.edu.tw; internet www.math.sinica.edu.tw; f. 1947; attached to Academia Sinica; research activities incl. mathematical analysis, number theory and algebra, geometry, probability, combinatorial mathematics and applications, fluid mechanics and computational mathematics; library of 48,000 vols, 1,100 int. periodicals, 250 Chinese and Japanese periodical titles, 500 ejournals, 110 cassettes; Dir Dr SHUN-JEN CHENG (acting).

Institute of Statistical Science: c/o Academia Sinica, 128 Academia Rd Sec. 2, Taipei 11529; tel. (2) 27835611; internet www.stat.sinica.edu.tw; f. 1982; attached to Academia Sinica; Dir Dr KER-CHAU LI; publ. *Statistica Sinica* (4 a year).

Physical Sciences

Atomic Energy Council: No 80, Section 1, Chenggong Rd, Yunghe Dist., Taipei 23452; tel. (2) 82317919; e-mail public@aec.gov.tw; internet www.aec.gov.tw; f. 1955; govt agency for peaceful application of atomic energy; library of 11,000 vols, deposit library at the Nat. Tsing Hua Univ. of 36,000 vols and 424,000 microcards; Chair. Dr CHUEN-HORNG TSAI; Chief Exec. Sec. SYH-TSONG CHIOU; publs *Nuclear Climate* (12 a year), *Nuclear Science Journal* (6 a year).

Central Geological Survey: POB 968, Taipei 100; tel. (2) 29462793; e-mail cgs@linx.moeacgs.gov.tw; internet www.moeacgs.gov.tw; f. 1946; maps; library of 50,000 vols and periodicals; Dir CHAO-CHUNG LIN; publs *Bulletin, Ti-Chih* (geology, 2 a year).

Institute of Atomic and Molecular Sciences: POB 23–166, Taipei 10617; Academia Sinica, No 1, Section 4, Roosevelt Rd, Taipei 10617; tel. (2) 23620212; e-mail office@po.iams.sinica.edu.tw; internet www.iams.sinica.edu.tw; f. 1982; attached to Academia Sinica; research activities incl. advanced materials and surface science, atomic physics and optical science, biophysics and bioanalytical technology, chemical dynamics and spectroscopy; library of 19,000 vols, 200 journals; Dir Dr MEI-YIN CHOU.

Institute of Chemistry: 128 Academia Rd, Section 2, Nankang, Taipei 115; tel. (2) 27821889; internet www.chem.sinica.edu.tw; f. 1928; attached to Academia Sinica; research areas incl. catalysis, chemical biology, materials chemistry; library of 27,000 vols, 110 journal subscriptions; Dir Dr YU-JU CHEN.

Institute of Earth Sciences: Academia Sinica, Nankang, Taipei 11529; tel. (2) 27839910; attached to Academia Sinica; Dir LOU-CHUANG LEE.

Institute of Information Science: 128 Academia Rd, Section 2, Nankang, Taipei 11529; tel. (2) 27883799; e-mail secretary@iis.sinica.edu.tw; internet www.iis.sinica.edu.tw; f. 1982; attached to Academia Sinica; research groups incl. bioinformatics, computation theory and algorithms, data management and information discovery, programming languages and formal methods; library of 21,000 vols, 300 journals; Dir Dr WEN-LIAN HSU (acting); publ. *IIS Technical Report* (1 a year).

Institute of Nuclear Energy Research: 1000 Wenhua Rd, Jiaan Village, Lung-Tan 32546; tel. (3) 4711400; e-mail iner@iner.gov.tw; internet www.iner.gov.tw; f. 1968; research in peaceful uses of atomic energy; Dir-Gen. Dr YIN-PANG MA (acting).

Institute of Physics: 128 Academia Rd, Section 2, Nankang, Taipei 11529; tel. (2) 27880058; internet www.phys.sinica.edu.tw; f. 1928 in Shanghai, est. in Taiwan 1962; attached to Academia Sinica; research areas incl. nanoscience, complexity, medium and high-energy physics; library of 30,000 vols, incl. 15,000 bound vols of journals, 300 periodicals, 4 CD-ROM databases; Dir Dr TING-KUO LEE (acting).

PHILOSOPHY AND PSYCHOLOGY

Sun Yat-sen Institute for Social Sciences and Philosophy: c/o Academia Sinica, Nankang, Taipei 11529; tel. (2) 27821693; e-mail issp@www.issp.sinica.edu.tw; internet www.issp.sinica.edu.tw; f. 1981; attached to Academia Sinica; Dir Dr ANGELA KI CHE LEUNG; publ. *Journal of Social Sciences and Philosophy* (4 a year).

RELIGION, SOCIOLOGY AND ANTHROPOLOGY

Institute of Ethnology: c/o Academia Sinica, Nankang, Taipei 11529; tel. (2) 26523321; e-mail tja@gate.sinica.edu.tw; internet www.sinica.edu.tw/ioe; f. 1955; attached to Academia Sinica; main field of research: social and cultural anthropology; Dir Prof. HUANG SHU-MIN; publs *Field Materials* (irregular), *Taiwan Journal of Anthropology* (2 a year).

Institute of European and American Studies: Academia Sinica, Nankang, Taipei 11529; e-mail euram@gate.sinica.edu.tw; attached to Academia Sinica; Dir Dr WEN-CHING HO; publ. *EurAmerica* (4 a year).

TECHNOLOGY

Bureau of Standards, Metrology and Inspection: No 4 Jinan Rd., Section 1, Taipei 100; tel. (2) 23431700; e-mail b01p1@bsmi.gov.tw; internet www.bsmi.gov.tw; f. 1947; attached to Min. of Economic Affairs; devt of nat. standards, verification of weights and measuring instruments, inspection of commodities and provision of other certification or testing services; library of 20,000 vols, 500 periodicals; Dir-Gen. JAY-SAN CHEN; publs *Catalogue of Chinese National Standards* (1 a year), *Chinese National Standards* (irregular), *Official Gazette for Patents* (36 a year), *Official Gazette for Standards* (12 a year), *Official Gazette for Trademarks* (24 a year).

Industrial Technology Research Institute: 195 Chung Hsing Rd, Section 4, Chu-Tung, Hsinchu 31040; tel. (3) 5820100; internet www.itri.org.tw; f. 1973; library of 130,000 vols; Chair. Dr CHING-YEN TSAY; Pres. Dr JYUO-MIN SHYU; Gen. Dir Dr TA-HSIEN LO; publs *Chemical Industry Notes*, *Electro-optics Development Journal*, *Energy-Resources and Environment* (4 a year, in Chinese), *Materials and Society*, *Mechatronics Journal*, *Metrology Information* (6 a year, in Chinese), *Mining Technology*, *MRL Bulletin of Research and Development* (2 a year, in English), *Opto-Electronics and Systems*, *Reports of Center for Measurement Standards* (12 a year, in Chinese), *Superconductor Applications News*, *UCL Chemical Information Digest*.

Research Laboratories:

Centre for Aviation and Aerospace: Hsinchu; Dir Dr RICHARD Y. H. LIN.

Centre for Industrial Safety and Health Technology: Hsinchu; Dir Dr ADA W. S. MA.

Centre for Measurement Standards: Hsinchu; Dir Dr CHANG HSU.

Centre for Pollution Control Technology: Hsinchu; Dir Dr LING-YUAN CHEN.

Computer and Communication Research Laboratories: Hsinchu; Dir Dr STEVEN CHENG.

Electronics Research and Service Organization: Hsinchu; Dir Dr DAVID C. T. HSING.

Energy and Resources Laboratories: Bldg 64, 195 Chung Hsing Rd., Section 4 Chutung, Hsinchu; tel. (35) 915497; e-mail gene@itri.org.tw; Dir Dr ROBERT J. YANG.

Materials Research Laboratories: Hsinchu and Kaohsiung; Dir Dr LI-CHUNG LEE.

Mechanical Industry Research Laboratories: Hsinchu; Dir Dr C. RICHARD LIU.

Opto-Electronics and Systems Laboratories: Hsinchu; Dir Dr MIN-SHYONG LIN.

Union Chemical Laboratories: Hsinchu; Dir Dr JOHN-SEE LEE.

Libraries and Archives

Tainan

National Cheng Kung University Library: 1 Ta Hsueh Rd, Tainan 70101;

tel. (6) 2757575; e-mail em65790@email.ncku .edu.tw; internet www.lib.ncku.edu.tw; f. 1927; 1,685,049 vols, 12,676 periodicals; Dir MING-TZONG YANG; publ. *Bulletin* (4 a year).

Taipei

Agricultural Science Information Centre: POB 7-636, Taipei 106; tel. (2) 23626222; internet www.asic.org.tw; f. 1977; 11,000 vols, 638 periodicals, databases; Dir WAN-JIUN WU.

Dr Sun Yat-sen Library: National Dr Sun Yat-sen Memorial Hall, 505 Ren-ai Rd, Section 4, Taipei 110; tel. (2) 27588008; e-mail sun@yatsen.gov.tw; internet www.yatsen .gov.tw; f. 1929; 299,345 vols on Dr Sun Yat-sen's writings and studies on San Min Chu Yih and modern Chinese history; Curator SHAW MING-HUANG; publ. *Modern China* (6 a year).

Fu Ssu-nien Library, Institute of History and Philology: 130 Yen Chiu Yuan Rd, Sec. 2, Nankang, Taipei 11521; tel. (2) 27829555; f. 1928; 420,000 vols, 3,000 periodicals; spec. collns incl. 33,889 stone and bronze rubbings, 13,100 folk plays, 310,000 cabinet records of Ming and Ch'ing dynasties; Dir JUEI-HSIU WU.

National Central Library: 20 Chung Shan S Rd, Taipei 100; tel. (2) 23619132; e-mail iechief@ncl.edu.tw; internet www.ncl.edu.tw; f. 1933; 4,198,475 vols, incl. 190,000 rare books, stone rubbings and historical material; Dir-Gen. Dr TSENG SHU-HSIEN; publs *Chinese National Bibliography* (12 a year), *Index to Chinese Periodicals* (4 a year), *NCL Bulletin* (2 a year), *NCL News Bulletin* (4 a year).

Branch Library:

Taiwan Branch Library, National Central Library: 1 Hsinshen S Rd, Sec. 1, Taipei; tel. (2) 27724724; internet www .ncltb.edu.tw; f. 1915; 592,023 vols; spec. collns incl. Taiwan and S Asia; Dir LIN WEI-JEI; publs *Catalogue of Materials for the Blind, Catalogue of NCL Taiwan Branch Collection on Southeast Asia, Catalogue on China in Japanese Languages, Catalogue on China in Western Languages, Index to Taiwan-Related Periodical Literature Collected in NCL Taiwan Branch, List of Non-Chinese Serials in NCL Taiwan Branch, The Annotative Catalogue of Taiwan Documents, Union Catalogue of Taiwan-Related Bibliographies.*

National War College Library: Yangmingshan, Taipei; 156,639 vols on political subjects; Librarian LO MOU-PIN.

Parliamentary Library, Legislative Yuan: 1 Chung Shan S Rd, Taipei 10051; tel. (2) 23585278; e-mail npl@ly.gov.tw; internet npl.ly.gov.tw; f. 1947; gen. reference, govt publs, legal documents; 259,963 vols; Dir Dr SHOW-RONG WANG; publs *Chinese legislative news review index* (12 a year), *Chinese legislative news reviews series* (irregular), *Code Amendment Cyclopedia* (irregular), *Code and reference book catalogue* (irregular), *Code resource pathfinder* (6 a year), *Collection of Interpellation Records* (irregular), *Gazette, Index to Chinese Legislative Literature* (6 a year), *Index to Legal Periodicals* (irregular), *Index of Legislative Records* (every 3 years), *LEGISIS thesaurus* (irregular), *Legislative Decision Support Service* (12 a year), *Legislative Microform Catalogue* (irregular), *Library Communications Quarterly, Proceedings and Serials Catalogue* (irregular), *Selective Abstracts of US Congressional Records* (irregular), *Selected Dissemination of Information Series* (6 a year), *Subject Guide to Chinese Code* (irregular), *The Legislative Yuan Library Catalogue* (irregular).

Taipei Public Library: No 125 Jianguo Rd, Section 2, Taipei 10659; tel. (2) 27552823; internet www.tpml.edu.tw; f. 1952; 1 main library, 43 brs and 11 reading rooms; Dir SHIHCHANG HORNG.

Museums and Art Galleries

Kaohsiung

Kaohsiung Museum of Fine Arts: 80 Meishukuan Rd, Kaohsiung; tel. (7) 5550331; internet www.kmfa.gov.tw; f. 1994; Dir PEI-NI BEATRICE HSIEH.

Taichung

National Taiwan Museum of Fine Arts: 2, Sec. 1, Wu Chuan West Rd, Taichung 403; tel. (4) 23723552; e-mail artnet@art.ntmofa .gov.tw; internet www.ntmofa.gov.tw; f. 1986; mostly works of Taiwan artists; library of 70,000 vols; Dir TSAI-LANG HUANG; publ. *Journal of National Taiwan Museum of Fine Arts* (4 a year).

Taipei

Chinese Postal Museum: 45 Chungking South Rd, Sec. 2, Taipei 100; tel. (2) 23945185; e-mail musol@mail.post.gov.tw; internet www.post.gov.tw/museum.htm; f. 1966; library of 27,000 vols; Dir SUSAN TENG-KUEI YU.

Hwa Kang Museum: 55 Hwa Kang Rd, Chinese Culture Univ., Yang Ming Shan, Taipei 111; tel. (2) 28610511; e-mail cuch@ staff.pccu.edu.tw; internet www2.pccu.edu .tw/cuch; f. 1971; Chinese folk arts, pottery, porcelain, calligraphy and paintings; Dir MARGARET CHEN LEE.

National Museum of History: 49 Nan Hai Rd, Taipei 10066; tel. (2) 23610270; internet www.nmh.gov.tw; f. 1955; Chinese and Taiwanese historical and archaeological artefacts; library of 30,000 vols; Dir YUNG-CHUAN HUANG; publs *Bulletin of the National Museum of History* (in Chinese, 12 a year), *Journal of the National Museum of History* (in Chinese, 2 a year).

National Palace Museum: Wai-shuang-hsi, Shih-lin, Taipei; tel. (2) 28812021; internet www.npm.gov.tw; f. 1925; colln consists chiefly of historic and archaeological treasures brought from mainland China; library of 155,136 vols, 624 periodical titles, 200,907 rare books, 395,335 Ch'ing documents; Dir SHIH SHOU-CHIEN; publs *National Palace Museum Monthly of Chinese Art* (12 a year), *Research Quarterly* (4 a year).

National Taiwan Museum: 2 Xiang-yang Rd, Taipei 100; tel. (2) 23822566; internet www.ntm.gov.tw; f. 1908; anthropology, earth sciences, zoology and botany; Dir CHI-MING CHEN; publs *Journal of Taiwan Museum* (in English), *Taiwan Natural Science*.

National Taiwan Science Education Center: 189 Shihshang Rd, Shihlin Dist., Taipei 111; tel. (2) 66101234; internet www .ntsec.gov.tw; f. 1956; planetarium, science exhibitions, lectures and films; Dir-Gen. NAN-SHYAN CHU; publ. *Science Study Monthly* (in Chinese).

Shung Ye Museum of Formosan Aborigines: 282 Chishan Rd Section 2, Shi-Lin Dist, Taipei 11143; tel. (2) 28412611; e-mail shungye@gate.sinica.edu.tw; internet www .museum.org.tw; f. 1994; holds a colln of artefacts of Taiwan's indigenous peoples; promotes understanding between ethnic groups and undertakes research and preservation of Aboriginal cultural works; Museum Curator and Dir ERIC H. Y. YU.

Taipei Astronomical Museum: 363 Kee-Ho Rd, Taipei 111; tel. (2) 28314551; e-mail tam001@tam.gov.tw; internet www.tam.gov .tw; f. 1996; exhibits hall, cosmic adventure, IMAX and 3D theatre, observation area; organizes lectures, astronomer workshops and programmes, teacher training; Pres. GUO-GUANG CIOU; Gen. Sec. CHING-HSIUNG WANG; publs *Astronomical Almanac* (1 a year), *Journal Taipei Astronomical Museum, Report on Sunspot Observations* (1 a year), *Taipei Skylight* (4 a year).

Taipei Fine Arts Museum: 181, Sec. 3, Zhong Shan N Rd, Taipei 10461; tel. (2) 25957656; e-mail info@tfam.gov.tw; internet www.tfam.gov.tw; f. 1983; modern art; Dir TSAI-LANG HSIAO (acting); publs *Journal* (2 a year), *Modern Art* (6 a year).

Universities

CHINESE CULTURE UNIVERSITY

55 Hwa Kang Rd, Yang Ming Shan, Taipei

Telephone: (2) 28610511
E-mail: president@staff.pccu.edu.tw
Internet: www.pccu.edu.tw

Founded 1962
Private control

Colleges of agriculture, arts, business administration, education, engineering, environmental design, foreign languages, journalism and mass communications, law, liberal arts, science, social sciences

Pres.: Dr WU WANN-YIH

Library: 1m. vols, 5,000 periodicals

CHUNG YUAN CHRISTIAN UNIVERSITY

200 Chung Pei Rd, Chung Li 32023

Telephone: (3) 2651703
E-mail: oia@cycu.edu.tw
Internet: www.cycu.edu.tw

Founded 1955, present name and status 1980
Private control
Academic year: August to July

Colleges of business, design, electrical engineering and computer science, engineering, humanities and education, law, science

Pres.: Dr SAMUEL K. C. CHANG
Vice-Pres.: Prof. CHEN SHIA-CHUNG

Library of 800,000 vols
Number of teachers: 800
Number of students: 15,000

Publication: *Chung Yuan Journal*

FENG CHIA UNIVERSITY

100 Wenhwa Rd, Seatwen, Taichung 40724

Telephone: (4) 24517250
E-mail: linkages@fcu.edu.tw
Internet: www.fcu.edu.tw

Founded 1961
Private control
Languages of instruction: Chinese, English
Academic year: September to June

Pres.: AN-CHI LIU
Vice-Pres.: YUAN-TONG LEE
Sec.-Gen.: HAI-PING HSIEH
Chief Librarian: HSIANG-HOO CHING

Library of 590,000 vols
Number of teachers: 1,107
Number of students: 19,124 (17,517 undergraduate, 1,607 postgraduate)

Publications: *Accounting Journal, Architecture Quarterly, Banking and Insurance, Civil Engineering Journal, Computer Sci-*

ence, *Co-operative Research, FCU Weekly, Finance Research, Industrial Engineering, International Trade, Mechanical Engineering, Statistics Journal, Textile Science*

DEANS

College of Business: PAO-LONG CHANG
College of Construction and Devt: BING-JEAN LEE
College of Continuing Education: YOU-REN SHIAU
College of Engineering: TONG-MIIN LIOU
College of Humanities and Social Studies: YEN CHU
College of Information and Electrical Engineering: CHUANG-CHIEN CHIU
College of Sciences: TAI-LEE HU

FU-JEN CATHOLIC UNIVERSITY

510 Chungcheng Rd, Hsin-Chuang, Taipei
Telephone: (2) 29031111
E-mail: fjuweb@mails.fju.edu.tw
Internet: www.fju.edu.tw
Founded 1925 in Beijing; re-opened in Taiwan 1961
Academic year: August to July
Pres.: Dr JOHN NING-YUEAN LEE
Vice-Pres: Dr PERRY C. CHIU, Dr PETER SHANG-SHING CHOU, Rev. LOUIS GENDRON
Sec.-Gen.: JOHN SHIANG-YANG HWANG
Dean of Academic Affairs: Dr YIU-LUNG CHEN
Dean of Gen. Affairs: Prof. ZERMAN HU
Dean of Research and Devt: Dr SHIH-MING KO
Dean of Student Affairs: Dr HUNG YAN CHEN
Registrar: TZU-CHI LI
Librarian: Dr H. H. CHENG
Library of 828,000 vols
Number of teachers: 1,591
Number of students: 23,658
Publications: *Catholic Observer, Fu Jen Philosophical Studies, Fu Jen Studies* (4 a year)

DEANS

College of Fine Arts: Dr MING-JIAN FANG
College of Foreign Languages: Dr NICHOLAS KOSS
College of Human Ecology: Dr SHAU-YEN HUANG
College of Law: Dr AH-YEE LEE
College of Liberal Arts: Dr THOMAS FU-BEING CHEN
College of Management: Dr DENG-YUAN HUANG
College of Medicine: Dr VINCENT HAN-SUN CHIANG
College of Science and Engineering: Dr JOSEPH L. G. HWA
Holistic Education Centre: Dr DAMIANUS JEN-LUNGKAO
School of Continuing Education: Dr CAJUS CHI-CHI LIN

NATIONAL CENTRAL UNIVERSITY

300 Jhongda Rd, Chung-Li 32001
Telephone: (3) 4227151
E-mail: ncu7300@ncu.edu.tw
Internet: www.ncu.edu.tw
Founded 1968 as re-establishment of Nat. Central Univ. (Nanking)
Academic year: August to July
Pres.: Dr JING-YANG JOU
Vice-Pres.: Dr KWANG-HWA LII
Vice-Pres.: Dr GIN-RONG LIU
Dean for Academic Affairs: Prof. JYH-CHEN CHEN
Dean for Gen. Affairs: EDMOND LIU-WU HOURNG
Dean for Research and Devt: SHANG-YAO YAN
Dean for Student Affairs: LIN-NI HAU
Sec. Gen.: KUO-KAI SHYU
Librarian: Prof. FAN YIWEN

Publications: *Bulletin of Geophysics* (2 a year), *Journal of Humanities East/West* (2 a year)

DEANS

College of Earth Sciences: Prof. YEN-HSYANG CHU
College of Engineering: Prof. JYH-CHEN CHEN
College of Hakka Studies: SEO-GIM LO
College of Information Technology and Electrical Engineering: Prof. WEN-JUNE WANG
College of Liberal Arts: CHO-HON YANG
College of Management: Dr GWO-JI SHEEN
College of Science: Prof. CHENG-CHUNG LEE

NATIONAL CHENG KUNG UNIVERSITY

1 Ta-Hsueh Rd, Tainan 70101
Telephone: (6) 2757575
E-mail: em50000@mail.ncku.edu.tw
Internet: www.ncku.edu.tw
Founded 1931 as Tainan Technical College, renamed Taiwan Provincial College of Engineering 1946, present name 1971
State control
Language of instruction: Chinese, some English
Academic year: September to June
Pres.: Dr CHIANG KAO
Dean of Academic Affairs: Dr YAN-KUIN SU
Registrar: SHIN-FU HUANG
Librarian: Dr JEN-FA MIN
Number of teachers: 1,200
Number of students: 19,000
Publications: *Bulletin of National Cheng Kung University* (1 a year), *Journal of National Cheng Kung University* (1 a year)

DEANS

College of Design: Dr MING-FU HSU
College of Electrical Engineering and Computer Science: Dr CHING-TING LI
College of Engineering: Dr WEN-TENG WU
College of Liberal Arts: Dr KAO-PING CHANG
College of Management Science: Dr WANN-YIH WU
College of Medicine: Dr RUEY-JEN SUNG
College of Sciences: Dr SHU-CHENG YU
College of Social Sciences: Dr JENN-YEU CHEN

Graduate institutes are attached to the College of Engineering, the College of Liberal Arts, the College of Management Science, the College of Medicine, the College of Sciences and the College of Social Sciences

NATIONAL CHENGCHI UNIVERSITY

64 Zhinan Rd Sec. 2, Wenshan 116, Taipei
Telephone: (2) 29393091
E-mail: oic@nccu.edu.tw
Internet: www.nccu.edu.tw
Founded 1927, univ. status 1946; state-funded
State control
Languages of instruction: Chinese, English
Academic year: September to June (2 semesters)
Pres.: SE-HWA WU
Vice-Pres. and Dean of Academic Affairs: LIEN-KONG TSAI
Dean of General Affairs: TAI-MING BEN
Dean of Student Affairs: MEI-LIE CHU
Dir of Library: JYI-SHANE LIU
Library of 2,106,128 vols
Number of teachers: 684 (full- and part-time)
Number of students: 16,038

DEANS

College of Commerce: CHUEN-LUNG CHEN
College of Communication: CHIH-YU CHAN
College of Education: WEI-WEN CHUNG

College of Foreign Languages: NAI-MING YU
College of Int. Affairs: CHUNG-CHIAN TENG
College of Law: KAI-LIN FAUNG
College of Liberal Arts: WHEI-MING CHOU
College of Science: ARBEE CHEN
College of Social Sciences: SONG-LING YANG

NATIONAL CHIAO TUNG UNIVERSITY

1001 University Rd, Hsinchu 300
Telephone: (35) 712121
E-mail: president@mail.nctu.edu.tw
Internet: www.nctu.edu.tw
Founded 1896, re-established in Hsinchu 1958
public control
Languages of instruction: Chinese, English
Academic year: August to July (2 semesters)
Pres.: Prof. YAN-HWA WU LEE
Dean for Academic Affairs: Prof. CHIN-TENG LIN
Dean for Int. Affairs: SHYH-JYE JOU
Dean for Research and Devt: Dr EDWARD-YI CHANG
Dean for Student Affairs: Prof. MEI-LING HUANG
Library Dir: SHYAN-MING YUAN
Library of 820,186 vols, 2,713 periodicals
Number of teachers: 712
Number of students: 14,021

DEANS

College of Biological Science and Technology: Prof. JONG YUH-JYH
College of Computer Science: YU-CHEE TSENG
College of Electrical and Computer Engineering: (vacant): Prof. HSUEH-MING HANG
College of Engineering: Prof. CHIUN-HSUN CHEN
College of Hakka Studies: Assoc. Prof. WEI AN CHANG
College of Humanities and Social Sciences: Prof. C. DAVID TSENG
College of Management: Prof. HSIN-LI CHANG
College of Photonics: Dr MORRIS (MING-DOU) KER
College of Science: Prof. HENRY HORNG-SHING LU

NATIONAL CHUNG HSING UNIVERSITY

250 Kuo-kuang Rd, Taichung 402
Telephone: (4) 22873181
E-mail: presid@nchu.edu.tw
Internet: www.nchu.edu.tw
Founded 1919 as Advanced Acad. of Agronomy and Forestry, current name and status 1971
State control
Languages of instruction: Chinese, English
Academic year: August to July
Pres.: Dr DER-TSAI LEE
Vice-Pres.: YAU-HEIU HSU
Vice-Pres.: CHUN-LIANG LIN
Dean for Academic Affairs: FU-HSING LU
Dean for Gen. Affairs: FUH-MIN FANG
Dean for Research and Devt: CHUAN-MU CHEN
Dean for Student Affairs: SHENG-JUNG OU
Library Dir: DA-JHIH GUAN
Library: 1.7m. vols
Number of teachers: 804
Number of students: 16,889

DEANS

College of Agriculture and Natural Resources: SU-CHIN CHEN
College of Engineering: FRANK F. S. SHIEU
College of Law and Politics: BERNARD Y. KAO
College of Liberal Arts: SHU-CHING CHEN
College of Life Science: HONG-CHEN CHEN
College of Management: BING-HUEI LIN

College of Science: MAW-RONG LEE
College of Veterinary Medicine: MAO FRANK CHIAHUNG

NATIONAL OPEN UNIVERSITY

172 Chung Cheng Rd, Lu Chow, Taipei 24702

Telephone: (2) 22829355
E-mail: elec007@mail.nou.edu.tw
Internet: www.nou.edu.tw

Founded 1986
Language of instruction: Chinese
Academic year: September to June

Pres.: Dr SHENG-SHIUNG HUANG
Registrar: LI-CHI HSIEH
Dean of Academic Affairs: Dr CHIA-SHING YANG

Number of teachers: 2,037 (88 full-time, 1,949 part-time)
Number of students: 40,000

Publication: *National Open University Learning Journal* (24 a year)

NATIONAL PINGTUNG UNIVERSITY OF SCIENCE AND TECHNOLOGY

1 Hseuh-Fu Rd, Nei Pu Hsiang, Pingtung Hsien 912

Telephone: (8) 7703660
E-mail: choumasa@mail.npust.edu.tw
Internet: www.npust.edu.tw

Founded 1954 as Taiwan Provincial Institute of Agriculture; became National Pingtung Institute of Agriculture 1981 and National Pingtung Polytechnic Institute 1991; present name and status 1997

Colleges of agriculture, engineering, management and humanities, social sciences

Pres.: CHANG-HUNG CHOU

Library of 227,198 vols
Number of teachers: 324
Number of students: 9,000

Publication: *Bulletin* (1 a year)

NATIONAL TAIWAN NORMAL UNIVERSITY

162 East Ho Ping Rd, Sec. 1, Taipei 10610
Telephone: (2) 23625101
E-mail: scr@deps.ntnu.edu.tw
Internet: www.ntnu.edu.tw

Founded 1946
Language of instruction: Chinese
State control
Academic year: August to July (2 semesters)

Pres.: MAW-FA CHIEN
Vice-Pres.: CHUNG-YANG TSAI
Sec.-Gen.: HSI-PING WANG
Dean of General Affairs: DAR-CHIN RAU
Dean of Internship Supervision and Placement: (vacant)
Dean of Research and Devt: LILLIAN MEEI-JIN HUANG
Dean of Students: HU-HSIUNG LI
Dean of Studies: C. H. GEORGE KAO
Registrar: AN-PAN LIN
Library Dir: HARRY LIANG

Number of teachers: 1,131
Number of students: 9,716

Publications: *A-V Education* (6 a year), *Bulletin, NTNU Alumni* (12 a year), *Secondary Education* (6 a year), graduate institutional and departmental journals

DEANS

College of Education: WU-TIEN WU
College of Fine and Applied Arts: CHING-LANG CHANG
College of Liberal Arts: WEN-HSING WU
College of Sciences: CHU-NAN CHANG

College of Sports and Recreation: YAO-HUI CHIEN
College of Technology: LUNG-SHERN LEE
Extension Division: SUZ-WEI YANG

NATIONAL TAIWAN OCEAN UNIVERSITY

2 Pei-Ning Rd, Keelung
Telephone: (2) 24622192
Internet: www.ntou.edu.tw

Founded 1953 (fmrly Nat. Taiwan College of Marine Science and Technology)
Language of instruction: Mandarin
Academic year: August to July

Pres.: KUO-TIEN LEE
Vice-Pres.: SAN-SHYAN LIN
Vice-Pres.: CHING-FONG CHANG
Dean of Academic Affairs: KUO-KAO LEE
Dean of General Affairs: KUO-CHENG YANG
Dean of Research and Devt: HSUAN-HSIH LEE
Dean of Student Affairs: TAN-KIN WANG
Librarian: YIN-HWANG LIN

Library of 423,000 vols, 3,000 periodicals
Number of teachers: 325
Number of students: 7,731

Publication: *Journal of Marine Science and Technology* (4 a year)

DEANS

Electrical Engineering and Computer Science: CHUNG-CHENG CHANG
Engineering: JIAHN-HORNG CHEN
Life and Resource Science: DENG-FWU HWANG
Maritime Science and Management: CHIH-CHING CHANG
Ocean Science and Resource: MING-AN LEE

NATIONAL TAIWAN UNIVERSITY

1 Roosevelt Rd, Section 4, Taipei 10617
Telephone: (2) 3366-3366
E-mail: secretor@ntu.edu.tw
Internet: www.ntu.edu.tw

Founded 1928 during the Japanese occupation as the Taihoku Imperial Univ.; taken over and renamed by Chinese Govt in 1945
Language of instruction: Chinese
Academic year: August to July (2 semesters)

Pres.: Dr SI-CHEN LEE
Vice-Pres. for Academic Affairs: Dr TAI-JEN GEORGE CHEN
Vice-Pres. for Admin. Affairs: TZONG-HO BAU
Vice-Pres. for Financial Affairs: MING-JE TANG
Dean of Academic Affairs: BEEN-HUANG CHIANG
Dean of Gen. Affairs: Dr HONG-KI HONG
Dean of Int. Affairs: TUNG SHEN
Dean of Research and Devt: JI-WANG CHERN
Dean of Student Affairs: JOYCE YEN FENG
Library Dir: SHIUE-HUA CHEN

Library of 3,000,000 vols
Number of teachers: 3,509
Number of students: 33,416

Publications: *Acta Botanica Taiwania, Acta Geologica Taiwanica, Acta Oceanographica Taiwanica*

DEANS

College of Bio-Resources and Agriculture: BAO-JI CHEN
College of Electrical Engineering and Computer Science: SOO-CHANG PEI
College of Engineering: HUAN-JANG KEH
College of Law: MING-CHEN TSAI
College of Liberal Arts: KUO-LIANG YEH
College of Life Science: GRACE CHU-FANG LO
College of Management: MAO-WEI HUNG
College of Medicine: PAN-CHYR YANG
College of Public Health: DUNG-LIANG JIANG
College of Science: CHING-HUA LO
College of Social Sciences: YUNG-MAU CHAO

School of Dentistry: CHUN-PIN LIN
School of Professional and Continuing Studies: RUEI-SHIANG GUO
School of Veterinary Medicine: CHEN-HSUAN LIU (Chair.)

NATIONAL TAIWAN UNIVERSITY OF SCIENCE AND TECHNOLOGY

43 Keelung Rd, Sec. 4, Taipei
Telephone: (2) 27376101
E-mail: president@mail.ntust.edu.tw
Internet: www.ntust.edu.tw

Founded 1974
Academic year: August to July (2 semesters)

Pres.: SHUN-TYAN CHEN
Dean of Studies: CHENG-SEEN HO

Library of 279,326 vols
Number of teachers: 315
Number of students: 8,106

NATIONAL TSING HUA UNIVERSITY

101, Sec. 2, Kuang Fu Rd, Hsinchu 30013
Telephone: (3) 5715131
E-mail: presid@my.nthu.edu.tw
Internet: www.nthu.edu.tw

Founded 1911, re-established in Hsinchu 1956
Language of instruction: Chinese
Academic year: August to July

Pres.: Dr LIH J. CHEN
Librarian: HSIAO-CHIN HSIEH

Number of teachers: 635
Number of students: 12,050

Publication: *Tsing Hua Journal of Chinese Studies* (Sinology, Literature and History and Philosophy, 4 a year)

DEANS

College of Electrical Engineering and Computer Science: KEH-YUNG CHENG
College of Engineering: NYAN-HWA TAI
College of Humanities and Social Sciences: Dr WEI-AN CHANG
College of Life Science: YEN-CHUNG CHANG
College of Nuclear Science: RUEY-AN DOONG
College of Science: HUAN-CHIU KU
College of Technology Management: CHAO-HSI HUANG
Commission of General Education: HSIAO-CHIN HSIEH

SOOCHOW UNIVERSITY

70 Linhsi Rd, Shihlin, Taipei 111
Telephone: (2) 28819471
E-mail: secretary@scu.edu.tw
Internet: www.scu.edu.tw

Founded 1900
Private control
Languages of instruction: Chinese, English
Academic year: September to June (2 semesters)

Pres.: CHAO-SHUIAN LIU
Vice-Pres.: CHUN-MEI MA
Vice-Pres. for Academic Affairs: MAO-TING CHIEN
Registrar: CHENG-TSUN LIN
Librarian: YUAN-JEE DING

Library of 692,767 vols
Number of teachers: 1,149 (incl. part-time teachers)
Number of students: 15,085

Publications: *Journal of Chinese Studies* (1 a year), *Journal of Economics and Business* (4 a year), *Journal of Foreign Languages and Cultures* (1 a year), *Journal of History* (1 a year), *Journal of Japanese Language Teaching* (1 a year), *Journal of Mathematics* (1 a year), *Journal of Philosophical Studies* (2 a year), *Journal of Political*

Science (2 a year), Journal of Sociology (2 a year), Law Review (2 a year)

TAIPEI NATIONAL UNIVERSITY OF THE ARTS

1 Hsueh Yuan Rd, Kuan-Tu, Taipei 112

Telephone: (2) 28961000
E-mail: www@www.tnua.edu.tw
Internet: www.tnua.edu.tw

Founded 1982 as National Institute of the Arts, current name adopted 2001

Pres.: Prof. YANG CHYI-WEN
Vice-Pres.: Prof. CHUNG-SHIUAN CHANG
Dean of Academic Affairs: Prof. HSI-CHUAN LIU
Dean of General Affairs: YUE-HUNG CHEN
Dean of Research and Devt: Assoc. Prof. SHAW-REN LIN
Dean of Student Affairs: Assoc. Prof. HUEI-TENG CHAN

Library of 453,147 vols
Number of teachers: 151
Number of students: 3,160

Publications: Arts Review (2 a year), Guandu Music Journal (2 a year), Journal of Cultural Resources (1 a year), Journal of Fine Arts (1 a year), Kuandu General Education Journal (1 a year), Taipei Theatre Journal (2 a year)

DEANS

Faculty of Cultural Resources: HUI-CHENG LIN
Faculty of Dance: MING-SHEN KU
Faculty of Fine Art: KAI-HUANG CHEN
Faculty of Film and New Media: SU-CHU HSU
Faculty of Music: HWEI-JIN LIU
Faculty of Theatre: LEE-ZEN CHIEN

TAMKANG UNIVERSITY

151 Ying-Chuan Rd, Tamsui, Taipei 25137

Telephone: (2) 26215656
Internet: www.tku.edu.tw

Founded 1950 (formerly Tamkang College of Arts and Sciences)
Private control
Languages of instruction: Chinese, English
Academic year: August to July

Pres.: Dr HORNG-JINH CHANG
Vice-Pres. for Academic Affairs: Dr CHAO-KANG FENG
Vice-Pres. for Admin.: Dr FLORA CHIA-I CHANG
Sec. Gen.: Dr TUN-LI CHEN
Dean of Academic Affairs: Dr HIS-JEN FU
Dean of General Affairs: Prof. CHING-JEN HUNG
Dean of Student Affairs: Dr HUAN-CHAO KEH
Librarian: Prof. HONG-CHU HUANG

Library of 753,911 vols, 6,901 periodicals
Number of teachers: 2,033
Number of students: 26,600

Publications: Educational Media and Library Science, International Journal of Information and Management Science, Journal of Future Studies, Tamkang Journal, Tamkang Journal of International Affairs, Tamkang Mathematics, Tamkang Review

DEANS

Business: Dr JONG-RONG CHIOU
Engineering: Dr SHI-CHIH CHU
Extension Education Centre: Prof. YAO-LUNG HAN
Foreign Languages and Literature: Dr YAOFU LIN
International Studies: Dr WOU WEI
Liberal Arts: Dr SHIH-HSION HUANG
Management: Dr LIANG-YU OUYANG
Science: Dr KAN-NAN CHEN
Technocracy: Prof. HSIN-FU TSAI

TUNGHAI UNIVERSITY

181 Taichung Harbour Rd, Sec. 3, Taichung 40704

Telephone: (4) 23590200
E-mail: kpwang@mail.thu.edu.tw
Internet: www.thu.edu.tw

Founded 1955 under the auspices of the United Board for Christian Higher Education in Asia
Languages of instruction: Chinese, English
Academic year: September to July (2 semesters)

Pres.: KANG-PEI WANG
Dean of Academic Affairs: CHENG-TUNG LIN
Dean of General Affairs: I-CHAO HSIAO
Dean of Student Affairs: HUNG-DER FU
Librarian: CHUNG-LIN LU

Number of teachers: 826
Number of students: 14,500

Publications: The Vineyard, Tunghai Bulletin, Tunghai Journal, Tunghai News

DEANS

College of Agriculture: TSUN-CHUNG TSAI
College of Arts: HAI-YUN HUANG
College of Engineering: JEN-TENG TSAI
College of Management: TSAI-DING LIN
College of Science: CHING-SHENG CHEN
College of Social Sciences: JENN-HWAN WANG

Colleges and Institutes

China Medical College: 91 Hseuh Shih Rd, Taichung 404; tel. (4) 2057153; f. 1958; Private control; 2 campuses (in Taichung and Peikang), 6 graduate institutes, 12 undergraduate schools, Chiang Kai-shek Medical Center, 2 teaching hospitals; 4,666 students; Pres. MASON CHEN.

Kaohsiung Medical University: 100 Shih Chuan 1st Rd, Kaohsiung 807; tel. (7) 3117820; internet www.kmu.edu.tw; f. 1954; Private control; colleges of medicine, dental medicine, pharmacy, nursing, health sciences, life sciences; undergraduate division of 19 schools; 12 postgraduate institutes; 7 research centres: health and social services, industrial hygiene, gender studies, tropical medicine, orthopaedics, genomics, proteomics; 428 teachers; 6,106 students; library: 175,802 vols, 2,970 periodicals; Pres. Dr GWO-JAW WANG; publ. Kaohsiung Journal of Medical Sciences (12 a year).

National Kaohsiung University of Applied Sciences: 415 Chien-Kung Rd, Kaohsiung 807; tel. (7) 3814526; f. 1963; depts of accounting, applied foreign languages, business administration, chemical, civil, cultural industries development, electrical, electronic, finance, human resource development, industrial management, information management, international trade, mechanical, mould- and die-making engineering, taxation and finance, tourism; graduate institutes of civil engineering and disaster prevention, commerce, electrical energy and control, electronic and information engineering, finance and information, mechanical and precision engineering, tourism management; library: 171,674 vols; 415 teachers; 10,727 students; Pres. Dr REN-YIH LIN; publ. Journal (1 a year).

Taipei Institute of Technology: 3, Sec. 1, Shin-sheng S Rd, Taipei; f. 1912; 8,973 students; library: 112,000 vols; Pres. Dr CHIH TANG.

Taipei Medical University: 250 Wu Hsing St, Taipei, 110; tel. (2) 27361661; f. 1960; Private control; undergraduate and graduate programmes; 1,000 teachers incl. full-time and part-time; 6,000 students; library: 132,015 vols, 650 periodicals; Pres. Prof. WEN-TA CHIU; Vice-Pres. Prof. TA-LIANG CHEN; publ. Journal (2 a year).

Tatung University: 40 Chungshan N Rd, Sec. 3, Taipei; tel. (2) 25925252; e-mail registrar@ttu.edu.tw; internet www.ttu.edu.tw; f. 1956; Private control; depts of applied mathematics, bioengineering, business management, chemical engineering, computer science and engineering, electrical engineering, industrial design, information management, materials engineering, mechanical engineering; graduate institutes in electro-optical engineering and communications engineering; 200 teachers; 2,500 students; library: 159,683 vols; Pres. T. S. LIN; Dean of Studies JAN-CHEN HONG.

School of Art and Music

National Taiwan College of Arts: Panchiao, Taipei; tel. (2) 22722181; internet www.ntca.edu.tw; f. 1955; Chinese music, cinema, dance, drama, fine arts, graphic arts, industrial arts, music, painting, radio and television, sculpture; 364 teachers; 2,300 students; library: 104,000 vols; Pres. MING-SHEAN WANG.

TAJIKISTAN

The Higher Education System

Higher education institutions predate the independence of Tajikistan (formerly Tajik SSR) from the USSR in 1991, with the oldest being Tajik State Pedagogical University S. Aini, and Tajik Agricultural University, both of which were founded in 1931. In 2000 the Presidents of Kazakhstan, Kyrgyzstan and Tajikistan co-signed a charter of foundation for a new University of Central Asia, which was to be established in Khorog (in Kuhistoni Badakhshon Autonomous Viloyat) and administered by the Aga Khan Development Network, based in Geneva, Switzerland; this began admitting students in 2006. Higher education is provided by three types of higher education institutions; as well as the universities (donishgoh), there are also academies (akademiya) and institutes (donishkada). In 2003 constitutional amendments abolished free higher education. In 2011 there were 153,286 students enrolled at 30 institutes of higher education.

The National Strategy for Education Development for the period 2006–15 was initiated by the Government in August 2005 with a view to improving and reforming a number of key issues in educational management, finance and quality assurance. The Office for the Attestation of Education Institutions, which comprises representatives of the Ministry of Education together with teachers and researchers, is the agency responsible for accreditation and quality assurance in the higher education sector.

The Certificate of Completed Secondary Education or the Diploma of Completed Vocational Education are the main requirements for admission to higher education. Most universities and academies have adopted a three-cycle system of Bakalavr (Bachelor), Magister (Masters) and Doctorontura (Doctorate) degrees, but the Darajai Mutakhassis (Specialist Diploma)—a Soviet-style undergraduate degree lasting five or six years and allowing students to enter directly into doctoral-level studies upon successful completion—is still offered in professional fields such as engineering, medicine and pharmacy. The Bakalavr degree is a four-year programme of study, after which a graduate may study for the Magister, the first postgraduate degree. The Magister is a two-year course culminating in the submission of a thesis; students who have successfully completed the Magister may undertake doctoral-level studies. As well as the European-style Doctorontura (which is the highest academic qualification available), the Soviet-style Kandidat Nauk (Candidate of Science) is also available; both are awarded after two to three years of independent research. The Doctorontura is a purely academic degree, aimed at students who wish to pursue a career in academia or research, and must be completed within a maximum of three years.

As part of the higher education reform, there were plans to introduce the European Credit Transfer System for degrees on a national level; the system had already been piloted in 2007 at the Technological University of Tajikistan and the Tajik University of Commerce. Although Tajikistan is not a signatory country, moves were under way to comply with the Bologna Process. A National Testing System for admission to higher education was due to be put in place from 2014 onwards.

Technical and vocational education at the post-secondary level consists of two-year programmes of study, which are open to holders of the Certificate of Completed Secondary Education or the Diploma of Completed Vocational Education and lead to the title of Junior Specialist.

Regulatory and Representative Bodies

GOVERNMENT

Ministry of Culture: Xiyoboni Rudaki 34, 734025 Dushanbe; tel. (372) 210305; Minister SHAMSIDDIN ORUMBEKOV.

Ministry of Education and Science: Kuchai Nosirmuhammad St 13A 734024 Dushanbe; tel. (372) 214605; e-mail malumot@netrt.org; Minister NURUDDIN SAIDOV.

Learned Societies

GENERAL

Academy of Science of the Republic of Tajikistan: 33 Rudaki Ave, 734025 Dushanbe; tel. (372) 215083; e-mail info@anrt.tj; internet anrt.tj; f. 1951; divs of Physical-Mathematical, Chemical and Geological Sciences (Chair. S. ODINAEV, Scientific Sec. R. I. KOSTOVA), Biological and Medical Sciences (Chair. M. YAKUBOVA, Scientific Sec. M. QURBANOVA), Social Sciences (Chair. K.OLIMOV, Scientific Sec. SH. UMAROVA); attached research institutes: see Research Institutes; 79 mems (36 full, 43 corresp.); library: see Libraries and Archives; Pres. Prof. MAMADSHO ILOLOV; Vice-Pres. Prof. KAROMATULLO OLIMOV; Vice-Pres. Prof. SAIDMUHAMMAD ODINAEV; Vice-Pres. Prof. MUHIBA YAKUBOVA; Gen. Sec. Dr KHAKIM AHMEDOV; publs Proceedings (each div. publishes its own edn, 4 a year), Doklady (Reports), Problemy gastroenterologii, Izvestiya (bulletins: Physical-Engineering and Geological Sciences, Biological Sciences, History and Philology, Philosophy, Economics and Law).

LANGUAGE AND LITERATURE

British Council: see chapter on Uzbekistan.

RELIGION, SOCIOLOGY AND ANTHROPOLOGY

Red Crescent Society of Tajikistan: 120 Umar Khayom str., 734017 Dushanbe; tel. (372) 240374; e-mail zmuhabbatov@redcrescent.tj; prevents and mitigates human suffering in compliance with complete impartiality and non-discrimination based on ethnicity, race, age, gender, religious beliefs, class and political views; promotes mutual understanding and friendship among people; contributes to peace all over the world; Pres. GHIESIDDIN MEROJEV; Sec-Gen. ZAFAR MUHABBATOV.

Tajikistan Association of Professional Social Workers: 137 Rudaki St, Fifth Fl., Ste 50, 734003, Dushanbe; tel. (372) 243461; e-mail info@tapsw.org.tj; internet www.tapsw.org.tj; f. 2009; promotes and enhances social work education; assists in devt of social work knowledge, practice, services; develops social work standards in Tajikistan.

Research Institutes

GENERAL

Khatlon Scientific Centre: Kulob; tel. (332) 223636; f. 1985; attached to Acad. of Sciences of the Republic of Tajikistan; Dir TILLO BOBOEV.

Khujand Scientific Centre: ul. Syrdarinskaya 26, 735714 Khudzhand; tel. (379) 251774; attached to Acad. of Sciences of the Republic of Tajikistan; Chair. M. R. DZHALILOV; Scientific Sec. M. SUBKHONOV.

ARCHITECTURE AND TOWN PLANNING

Institute of Geology, Earthquake Engineering and Seismology: ul. Aini 121, 734029 Dushanbe; tel. (372) 250669; e-mail tisss@iscuk.td.silk.org; f. 1951; attached to Acad. of Sciences of the Republic of Tajikistan; library of 6,000 vols, 40 periodicals; Dir SOBIT KH. NEGMATULLAEV; Sec. PULAT A. YASUNOV; publs Prognoz zemletryasenii (1 a year, in Russian), Zemletryaseniya Sredney Azii i Kazakhstana (1 a year, in Russian).

BIBLIOGRAPHY, LIBRARY SCIENCE AND MUSEOLOGY

Institute of Language, Literature, Oriental Studies and Written Heritage named after Rudaki: Kirov 35, 734025 Dushanbe; tel. (372) 273404; attached to Acad. of Sciences of the Republic of Tajikistan; Dir D. NAZRIYEV.

ECONOMICS, LAW AND POLITICS

Institute of Economy and Demography: ul. Aini 44, 734000 Dushanbe; tel. (372) 216750; f. 1951; attached to Acad. of Sciences of the Republic of Tajikistan; Dir R. K. RAKHIMOV.

Institute of State and Law: Pr. Rudaki 19, 734025 Dushanbe; tel. (372) 216572; e-mail isalanrt@rambler.ru; f. 2005; attached to Acad. of Sciences of the Republic of Tajikistan; library of 5,000 vols; Dir SAITUMBAR ADINAEVICH RAJABOV; publ. *Izvestiya Akademii Nauk RT, seriya Philosophiya i Pravo*.

HISTORY, GEOGRAPHY AND ARCHAEOLOGY

Institute of History, Archaeology and Ethnography named after A. Donish: Pr. Rudaki 33, 734025 Dushanbe; tel. (372) 223742; f. 1932; attached to Acad. of Sciences of the Republic of Tajikistan; Dir R. M. MASOV.

LANGUAGE AND LITERATURE

Institute of Language, Literature, Oriental Studies and Written Heritage named after Rudaki: Pr. Rudaki 21, 734025 Dushanbe; tel. (372) 216011; f. 1932; attached to Acad. of Sciences of the Republic of Tajikistan; Dir A. M. MANIYAZOV.

MEDICINE

Institute of Gastroenterology: Parvin 12, 734002 Dushanbe; tel. (372) 217782; e-mail mansurov@academy.td.silk.org; f. 1959; attached to Acad. of Sciences of Republic of Tajikistan; library of 5,000 vols; Dir Prof. G. MIRODJEV; publ. *Problems of Gastroenterology* (4 a year).

NATURAL SCIENCES

Biological Sciences

Institute of Botany, Physiology and Genetics: Ul. Karamova 27, 734017 Dushanbe; tel. (372) 247188; f. 1941; attached to Acad. of Sciences of the Republic of Tajikistan; Dir U. I. ISMOILOV.

Institute of Plant Physiology and Genetics: Ul. Aini 299/2, 734063 Dushanbe; tel. (372) 252644; e-mail akotibbm@ac.tajik.net; f. 1964; attached to Acad. of Sciences of the Republic of Tajikistan; Dir Prof. KHURSHED KARIMOV.

Institute of Zoology and Parasitology named after E. N. Pavlovskii: Post Office 70, 734025 Dushanbe; tel. (372) 255871; f. 1941; attached to Acad. of Sciences of the Republic of Tajikistan; Dir A. K. GAFUROV.

Pamir Biological Institute: Kholdorov St 1, 736002 Khorog; tel. (352) 204182; e-mail pamir@eco.khorugh.td.silk.org; internet pbi .narod.ru; f. 1969; attached to Acad. of Sciences of the Republic of Tajikistan; Dir Dr OGONAZAR AKNAZAROV.

Mathematical Sciences

Institute of Mathematics: Ul. Aini 299/1, 734063 Dushanbe; tel. (372) 258089; e-mail usmanov@ac.tajik.net; f. 1973; attached to Acad. of Sciences of the Republic of Tajikistan; Dir Z. D. USMANOV.

Physical Sciences

Institute of Astrophysics: Ul. Bukhoro 22, 734042 Dushanbe; tel. (372) 274614; e-mail astro@ac.tajik.net; f. 1958; attached to Acad. of Sciences of the Republic of Tajikistan; Dir KHURSAND I. IBADINOV; publ. *Bulletin* (2 a year).

Institute of Chemistry named after V. I. Nikitin: Ul. Aini 299/2, 734063 Dushanbe; tel. (372) 252604; e-mail sarvar@ac.tajik.net;

f. 1946; attached to Acad. of Sciences of the Republic of; Dir U. M. MIRSAYIDOV.

Institute of Geology: Ul. Aini 267, 734063 Dushanbe; tel. (372) 253267; f. 1941; attached to Acad. of Sciences of the Republic of Tajikistan; Dir M. R. DHALILOV.

Institute of Water Problems, Hydropower and Ecology: Parvin 12, 734002 Dushanbe; tel. (372) 245231; e-mail kobuliev@mail.ru; f. 2002; attached to Acad. of Sciences of the Republic of Tajikistan; Dir Prof. ZAINALOBUDIN KOBULIEV.

PHILOSOPHY AND PSYCHOLOGY

Institute of Philosophy, Political Sciences and Law named after A. M. Bahovaddinov: Pr. Rudaki 33, 734025 Dushanbe; tel. (372) 237796; e-mail noibprez@ac.tajik .net; attached to Acad. of Sciences of the Republic of Tajikistan; f. 1991; Dir M. DINORSHOYEV.

RELIGION, SOCIOLOGY AND ANTHROPOLOGY

Institute of Economics and Demographics: Ayni 44, 734024 Dushanbe; tel. (90) 1080481; e-mail inst.demography.tj@ gmail.com; internet www.demography.tj; f. 2003 as Institute of Demography, present name and status 2011; attached to Acad. of Sciences of the Republic of Tajikistan; population, fertility, mortality, family issues, internal and external migration processes, policy-making; library of 100 vols; Dir Prof. BOBOEV OLIMJON BOBOEVICH.

Institute of Humanities: Lenin 35, 736000 Khorog; tel. (352) 226755; f. 1991; attached to Acad. of Sciences of the Republic of Tajikistan; Dir SHODIKHON YUSUFBEKOV.

Institute of Oriental Studies and Written Heritage: Kiroka 35, 734025 Dushanbe; tel. (372) 272336; e-mail ogonazar@ac.tajik .net; f. 1958; attached to Acad. of Sciences of the Republic of Tajikistan.

TECHNOLOGY

Nuclear and Radiation Safety Agency: 17A Khamza Khakimzoda St, 734003 Dushanbe; tel. (372) 2247797; e-mail info@nrsa.tj; internet www.nrsa.tj; f. 2003; attached to Acad. of Sciences of the Republic of Tajikistan; Dir ULMAS MIRSAIDOV.

S. U. Umarov Physical-Technical Institute of Academy of Sciences of Rebublic of Tajikistan: Aini Ave 299/1, 734063 Dushanbe; tel. (37) 2258092; e-mail muminov@phti.tj; internet www.phti.tj; f. 1964; attached to Acad. of Sciences of the Republic of Tajikistan; theoretical and mathematical physics (classical and quantum statistics, field theory, non-linear science); materials science (crystal physics, polymer science); nanoscience and nanotechnology; lasers and infrared spectroscopy; cryophysics; mathematical modelling of climate and climate change; application of nuclear physics methods; instrumentation and detectors; radiation safety and ecology; renewable energy sources; Dir Prof. Dr KHIKMAT KH. MUMINOV; Vice-Dir Dr ALIMAHMAD KHOLOV.

Libraries and Archives

Dushanbe

Indira Gandhi Central Scientific Library of the Academy of Sciences of the Republic of Tajikistan: Pr. Rudaki 33, 734025 Dushanbe; tel. (37) 2214302; f. 1933; 1.5m. vols; Dir Dr A. A. ASLITDINOVA.

Firdavsi Tajik National Library: Pr. Rudaki 36, 734025 Dushanbe; tel. (372) 274726; 3m. vols; Dir SH. TOSHEW.

State Patent and Technical Library of Republic of Tajikistan: Ul. Aini 14A, 734042 Dushanbe; tel. (372) 279705; e-mail gptb.tj@mail.ru; internet www.gptb.tj; f. 1965; 150m. vols (incl. 14m. patents); Dir BOYMUROD BOEV.

Tajik State University Library: Pr. Rudaki 17, 734016 Dushanbe; tel. (372) 233981; f. 1948; 1m. vols; Dir R. YARBABAYEV; publ. *Vestnik* (1 a year).

Museum

Dushanbe

Tajik State Historical Museum: Ul. Aini 31, 734012 Dushanbe; tel. (372) 231544; history, culture, art; library of 14,000 vols; Dir M. MAKHMUDOV.

Universities

AVICENNA TAJIK STATE MEDICAL UNIVERSITY

139 Rudaki Ave, 734003 Dushanbe

Telephone: (372) 244583

E-mail: tajmedun@rambler.ru

Internet: www.tajmedun.tj

Founded 1939 as Tajik Medical Institute, fmrly Tajik Abu-Ali Ibn-Cina State Medical Institute, present name 2009

State control

Languages of instruction: English, Russian, Tajik

Academic year: September to July

Rector: Prof. Dr UBAIDULLO KURBANOV

Library of 701,498 vols

Number of teachers: 800

Number of students: 7,450

DEANS

Faculty of Dentistry: SHARORA DZHURAEVA

Faculty of Medicine: MUHIDDIN TABAROV

Faculty of Pharmaceutical Science: ERAHMAD KHOLOV

Faculty of Public Health: SHAROFIDDIN MATINOV

BOBOJON GAFUROV KHUJAND STATE UNIVERSITY

B. Mavlonbekova 1, 735700 Khujand

Telephone: (342) 265273

E-mail: hgu-rector@khujandi.com

Internet: www.hgu.tj

Founded 1932

State control

Language of instruction: English, Russian, Tajik, Uzbek

Rector: VAHOB NABIEV

Library of 500,000 vols

Number of teachers: 465

Number of students: 10,600

DEANS

Art: G. JURAYEV

Cybernetics and World Economics: A. ABDULLOYEV

Drawing and Graphics: S. OLOV

Eastern Languages (Arabic and Persian): U. GAFFOROVA

Economics: A. ABDULLOYEV

Finance and Marketing: A. MAJIDOV

Foreign Languages: M. AZIMOVA

History: U. GAFFOROV

Law: IKROM KASIMOV

Mathematics: A. KASHIDOV

Natural Sciences: S. KARIMOV
Pedagogy: S. SHAROPOV
Physics and Technology: S. YAKUBOV
Russian and Literature: A. AZIZOV
Tajik Philology: N. F. FAIZULLAYEV
Uzbek Language: I. MAVLONBERDIYEV

CENTRAL INSTITUTE OF ADVANCED QUALIFICATION OF TEACHERS

Chechova 13, 734013 Dushanbe
Telephone: (372) 215457
Founded 1935
State control
Faculties of economics, educational administration, foreign languages education, pedagogy, psychology, science education and teacher-training
Rector: ABUNAZAR A. SOIBOV
Vice-Rector: ABDUHALIM GAFFAROV
Number of students: 2,000

FISCAL—LEGAL INSTITUTE

Drujby Narodov 96, 734013 Dushanbe
Telephone: (3772) 215948
State control
Faculties of economics and law
Rector: D. G. GULMIRZOYEV

HIGHER SCHOOL OF THE MINISTRY OF THE INTERIOR

Vose 123, 734025 Dushanbe
Telephone: (372) 270607
State control
Faculties of history, law

INSTITUTE OF ENTREPRENEURSHIP AND SERVICE OF TAJIKISTAN

Borbad Ave 48/5, 734055 Dushanbe
Telephone: (372) 348800
E-mail: dsx_ips@mail.ru
Internet: www.dsx.tj
Founded 1991
State control
Languages of instruction: Russian, Tajik
Academic year: September to June
Rector: Prof. Dr DILOVAR QODIROV
Deputy Rector for Education: BAHRIDDIN B. JABBOROV
Deputy Rector for Science and Int. Relations: Prof. Dr SAID A. AHMADOV
Deputy Rector for Teaching: SHERMAHMAD B. JONMAMMADOV
Librarian: JAMILA PULODOVNA KHOLOVA
Library of 34,877 vols
Number of teachers: 170
Number of students: 3,250
Publications: Payom (1 a year), Sohibkor (12 a year)

DEANS
Accounting and Management: IZATULLO NASIRDINOV
Entrepreneurship and Management: ZOIRJON RAHMONOV
Financial Services: ISLOMBEK KHORKASHEV
Information Services and Marketing: ABDURAHIM ISMOILOV
Tourism and Custom Services: FAIZIDDIN QODIROV

KHOROG INSTITUTE OF SOCIAL SCIENCES

Khorog
Telephone: (352) 225886
E-mail: jangibekov@land.ru
State control
Languages of instruction: English, Russian

Academic year: September to June
Rector: SH. YUSUFBEKOV
Number of teachers: 280
Number of students: 5,000

KHOROG STATE UNIVERSITY

736000 Khorog
Telephone: (342) 202218
Founded 1992
State control
Languages of instruction: English, Russian, Tajik
Academic year: September to June
Faculties of economics, history, mathematics, natural sciences and philology
Rector: IMOMYORBEK QALANDARBEKOV
Vice-Rector for Int. Relations: Doc. OLGA SAYFULLOEVA
Number of teachers: 320
Number of students: 4,000

DEANS
Foreign Languages: Doc. MUNIRA IMATSHOEVA

KULYAB STATE UNIVERSITY

Safarov 26, 735360 Kulyab
Telephone: (332) 223507
E-mail: kgu@mail.tj
State control
Faculties of economics, history, mathematics, pedagogy, philology and physics

MODERN HUMANITARIAN UNIVERSITY

Microraion 17, 735700 Khujand
Telephone: (342) 221958
Founded 1998
State control
Language of instruction: Russian
Rector: M. I. BAKIYEV
Number of teachers: 40
Number of students: 380

DEANS
Faculty of Computer Science: U. V. SIT
Faculty of Languages: SH. D. KHODJAYEV
Faculty of Law: N. T. RAKHIMOV
Faculty of Management: G. A. USUPOVA

REPUBLICAN INSTITUTE OF ADVANCED TEACHERS' STUDIES

Chehova 13, 734013 Dushanbe
Telephone: (372) 216467
State control

RUSSIAN-TAJIK SLAVONIC UNIVERSITY

M. Tursunzade 30, 734032 Dushanbe
Telephone: (372) 223550
E-mail: rtsu_slavistica@mail.ru
Internet: www.rtsu-slavist.tj
Founded 1996
State control
Faculties of economics, history, international relations, law and philology
Rector: Prof. MAHMADUSUF S. IMOMOV
Library of 42,208 vols

TAJIK AGRARIAN UNIVERSITY NAMED AFTER SHIRINSHO SHOTEMUR

Pr. Rudaki 146, 734003 Dushanbe
Telephone: (372) 247207
E-mail: rectortau31@mail.ru

Internet: www.tajagroun.tj
Founded 1931
State control
Languages of instruction: Tajik, Russian
Academic year: September to June
Rector: Dr SATTORI IZZATULLO
Pro-Rector for Culture: Doc. HASANOV NAHTULLO RAHMATOVICH
Pro-Rector for Economy: KAMOLJON MAHMUDOV
Pro-Rector for Education: Prof. SALIMOV AMONULLO FAIZULLOEVICH
Pro-Rector for Int. Relations: KODIROV TURA ABDULLOEVICH
Pro-Rector for Science: Prof. Dr SARDOROV MAHMADIYOR NAIMOVICH
Head of Educational Dept: MAKSATULLO ISMOILOV
Dir for Library: ODINA DAVLATOV
Library of 356,434 vols, 63 periodicals
Number of teachers: 540
Number of students: 8,130
Publication: Kishovarz

DEANS
Faculty of Accounting and Finance: Prof. Dr SAMANDAROV ISKANDAR HUSEINOVICH
Faculty of Agrobusiness: Prof. Dr NOROV MASTIBEK SAMADOVICH
Faculty of Agronomy: HAYDAROV ZIKRIYOKHON YOKUBOVICH
Faculty of Animal Science: KOSIMOV RAJABEK BOBORAJABOVICH
Faculty of Economy: BAEVA NODIRA KHOLMURADOVNA
Faculty of Horticulture and Agricultural Biotechnology: Prof. Dr KARIMOV MUZAFFAR KARIMOVICH
Faculty of Hydromeliorative Science: ABDUGAFFOR AKRAMOV
Faculty of Mechanization of Agriculture: AHMADOV BAHROM RAJABOVICH
Faculty of Veterinary Medicine: Prof. Dr HABIBOV ABDUJALIL KHALILOVICH

TAJIK INSTITUTE OF MANAGEMENT

Kairakkum
Telephone: (344) 322485
State control
Faculties of management and marketing
Rector: YU. MADJIDOV

TAJIK ISLAMIC UNIVERSITY

Shodmoni 58, 734001 Dushanbe
Telephone: (372) 249261
State control
Faculties of general studies, Islamic law and religious studies
Rector: ABDUJALOL ALIZODA

TAJIK OPEN UNIVERSITY

Rudaki 108, 735500 Penjikent
Telephone: (347) 555309
E-mail: tou@pnjk.tajik.net
Founded 1991
State control
Languages of instruction: Russian, Tajik
Divs of computing and programming, law and management
Prin.: AHMADJON HOTAMOV
Number of teachers: 140 (full-time)
Number of students: 410

TAJIK STATE INSTITUTE OF FINE ARTS

Ul. Borbada 73A, 734032 Dushanbe
Telephone: (372) 314545
Founded 1967

Faculties of cultural science, performing arts, library science and information, musical-pedagogical studies and theatre

Rector: Prof. TALABKHUJA SATTOROV

Library of 70,000 vols

Number of students: 1,500

TAJIK STATE INSTITUTE OF LANGUAGES

F. Muhammadiyeva 13, 734064 Dushanbe

Telephone: (372) 329529

E-mail: mabdullaeva@yandex.ru

Founded 1980

State control

Languages of instruction: Tajik, Russian

Rector: MAVLUDA ABDULLAYEVA

Vice-Rector: KHURSHED ZIYOYEV

Library of 113,000 vols

Number of teachers: 65

Number of students: 760

DEANS

Faculty of Foreign Languages: KHALIDA ASTANOVA

Faculty of Philology: KAHHOR AVAZOV

TAJIK STATE NATIONAL UNIVERSITY

Pr. Rudaki 17, 734025 Dushanbe

Telephone: (372) 217711

E-mail: tgnu@mail.ru

Internet: www.tgnu.tarena.tj

Founded 1948, present status 1997

State control

Languages of instruction: Tajik, Russian

Academic year: September to July

Rector: Prof. KH. S. SAFIEV

Vice-Rector for Educational Affairs: Prof. D. KH. SAFAROV

Vice-Rector for Int. Relations: N. N. JUMAEV

Vice-Rector for Scientific Affairs: A. A. AMINJANOV

Librarian: R. I. YARBABAEV

Number of teachers: 1,230

Number of students: 13,100

Publications: *Guli Murod* (4 a year), *Science* (1 a year), *Vestnik* (4 a year)

DEANS

Faculty of Accounting: D. U. UROKOV

Faculty of Biology: Dr M. GIYOSOV

Faculty of Chemistry: L. KUDRATOVA

Faculty of Economics and Management: Prof. T. B. GANIEV

Faculty of Finance and Credit: SH. D. DUSTBOEV

Faculty of History: Prof. N. M. MIRZOEV

Faculty of Journalism and Translation Studies: Prof. A. SAIDULLOEV (acting)

Faculty of Law: M. A. MAKHMUDOV

Faculty of Mechanics and Mathematics: Dr R. M. MUSTAFOKULOV

Faculty of Mountain Geology: M. M. PHOZILOV

Faculty of Oriental Languages: S. SH. SHUKROEVA

Faculty of Philosophy: Prof. A. MUKHABATOV (acting)

Faculty of Physics: K. K. KOMILOV

Faculty of Tajik Philology: M. S. IMOMOV

TAJIK STATE PEDAGOGICAL UNIVERSITY NAMED AFTER S. AINI

Pr. Rudaki 121, 734001 Dushanbe

Telephone: (37) 2248993

E-mail: info@tgpu.tj

Internet: www.tgpu.tj

Founded 1931

State control

Faculties of economics and management, finance and accountancy, history, law, mechanics and mathematics, pedagogics, philology

Rector: NURIDDIN ABDUJABBOR RAHMONOV

TAJIK STATE UNIVERSITY OF COMMERCE

Dehoti 1/2, 734055 Dushanbe

Telephone: (372) 348546

E-mail: kaa77@tajik.net

Internet: www.tguk.tj

Founded 1991

State control

Languages of instruction: Russian, Tajik

Academic year: September to June

Rector: MUMIN SHARIPOV

Vice-Rector for Academic Affairs: TOLIBOV KOBIL KOSIMOVICH

Vice-Rector for Int. Affairs: ZARRINA HALIMOVNA KADIROVA

Library of 107,000 vols

Number of teachers: 170

Number of students: 2,400

DEANS

Faculty of Customs: KHAMID MADJIDOV

Faculty of Distance Education: MUKHIDDIN KHOMIDOV

Faculty of Economics and Management: SAFIULLO HABIBOV

Faculty of World Economics and Financing: ZUYORATSHO AKOBIROV

TAJIK STATE UNIVERSITY OF LAW, BUSINESS AND POLITICS

17 micro region, Bldg 1, Sugd, 735700 Khujand

Telephone: (342) 223811

E-mail: tsulbp-dia@rambler.ru

Internet: www.tsulbp.tj

State control

Faculties of business and management, computer technology and accounting, finance, innovation and commercial technology, law, political science and international relations

Rector: H. R. PULATOV

TAJIK TECHNICAL UNIVERSITY NAMED AFTER ACADEMICIAN M. OSIMI

Pr. Acad Rajabovs 10, 734042 Dushanbe

Telephone: (372) 213511

E-mail: ttu@ttu.tj

Internet: www.ttu.tj

Founded 1956

State control

Languages of instruction: Tajik, Russian

Number of teachers: 530

Number of students: 6,000

Rector: ABDURASULOV ANVAR

DEANS

Business Engineering: S. KAMOLIDDINOV

Chemical Technology and Metallurgy: A. SHARIFOV

Construction and Architecture: A. FAZILOV

Energy Engineering: R. JALILOV

Mechanical Technology: S. ZULFANOV

Transport and Road Engineering: A. TURSUNOV

TECHNOLOGICAL UNIVERSITY OF TAJIKISTAN

N. Narabayev 63/3, 734061 Dushanbe

Telephone: (372) 347987

E-mail: rektorat@tat.tajik.net

Founded 1992

State control

Languages of instruction: Tajik, Russian, English

Academic year: September to June

Rector: AMIR H. KATAYEV

Vice-Rector: NURALI N. SHOYEV

Library of 70,000 vols

Number of teachers: 160

Number of students: 1,050

Publications: *Collection of Scientific Works* (2 a year), *Herald of Ecology* (12 a year)

DEANS

Faculty of Industrial Informatics: MIRZO YUSUPOV

Faculty of International Studies: NASRULLO HOJAYOROV

Faculty of Textile Technology and Mechanical Engineering: VALIJON M. MIRAKILOV

TANZANIA

The Higher Education System

Higher education institutions predate the formation of the United Republic of Tanzania (by a merger of the independent states of Tanganyika and Zanzibar) in 1964, with the oldest being St Augustine University of Tanzania (formerly Nyegezi Social Training Centre), which was founded in 1960. In 2008 there were 64,664 students enrolled in 71 public institutions of higher education (which comprised 34 teacher-training colleges, 16 technical colleges, eight full universities, three constituent universities and 10 other higher institutions), with a further 17,865 students enrolled at 51 private institutions (which comprised 40 teacher-training colleges and 11 universities). In 2010 a total of 85,113 students were enrolled in tertiary level education. Higher education is administered by the Ministry of Education and Vocational Training. Quality assurance within university-level education is overseen by the Tanzania Commission for Universities (formerly the Higher Education Accreditation Council; current name adopted in 2005). In late 2012 accredited institutions numbered 27 full universities, of which 11 were public universities, 17 university colleges (3 public) and one private university centre of Agriculture and Technology at Arusha. The regulatory authority for non-university higher education institutions is the National Council for Technical Education. A 10-stage Tanzanian Qualifications Framework was still under development at 2012, and was expected to include the introduction of a credit-based degree system.

Students are required to gain three passes in the Advanced Certificate of Secondary Education and five passes at Certificate of Secondary Education level in order to gain admission to higher education. Examinations are administered by the National Examinations Council of Tanzania. Undergraduate Certificate and Diploma courses are available in a number of study areas and last between one and two years. Undergraduate Bachelors degrees usually last three years, although programmes in mainly professional fields of study last longer, such as engineering, nursing, pharmacy (four years) and medicine (five years). Following the award of the Bachelors, graduates may take the one-year Postgraduate Diploma or the Masters degree, which lasts one to three years and requires submission of a thesis. The highest university degree is the Doctor of Philosophy (PhD), which requires a minimum of two years research, culminating with the submission of a thesis.

The National Council for Technical Education was established in 1997 to create a national system of post-secondary, non-university education. Post-secondary technical and vocational education is organized within the Framework of Technical and Vocational Education and Training Qualifications (also known as the National Technical Awards Framework), and qualifications include the Technician Certificate, the Diploma and the Higher Diploma. There are also a number of institutions offering semi-professional training, in fields such as accountancy, agricultural studies and nursing; such institutions are administered by the relevant government ministry.

Regulatory Bodies

GOVERNMENT

Ministry of Communication, Science and Technology: Plot 1168/19, Jamhuri St, POB 2645, Dar es Salaam; tel. (22) 2111254; e-mail mst@mst.go.tz; internet www.mst.go.tz; Minister Prof. MAKAME MNYAA MBARAWA.

Ministry of Education and Vocational Training: Kivukoni Front, POB 9121, Dar es Salaam; tel. (22) 2120403; e-mail psmoevt@moe.go.tz; internet www.moe.go.tz; Minister Dr SHUKURU JUMANNE KAWAMBWA.

Ministry of Information, Youth, Culture and Sports: POB 8031, Dar es Salaam; Golden Jubilee Tower, Ohio St, Dar es Salaam; tel. (22) 2123947; e-mail km@hum .go.tz; internet www.hum.go.tz; Minister Hon. Dr FENELLA E. MUKANGARA.

Learned Societies

GENERAL

UNESCO Dar es Salaam Cluster Office: POB 31473, Dar es Salaam; Plot 127C, Mafinga St (off Kinondoni Rd), Dar es Salaam; tel. (22) 2666623; e-mail dar-es-salaam@unesco.org; designated Cluster Office for Comoros, Madagascar, Mauritius, Seychelles and Tanzania; library of 2,500 vols; Dir and Rep. VIBEKE JENSEN.

AGRICULTURE, FISHERIES AND VETERINARY SCIENCE

Tanzania Veterinary Association: POB 3174, Chuo Kikuu Morogoro; tel. (23) 2604979; e-mail deanfvm@suanet.ac.tz; f.

1968; 350 mems; Chair. Prof. D. M. KAMBARAGE; publs *Annual Proceedings of the Tanzania Veterinary Association Scientific Conferences, Tanzania Veterinary Journal*.

BIBLIOGRAPHY, LIBRARY SCIENCE AND MUSEOLOGY

Tanzania Library Association: POB 33433, Dar es Salaam; tel. \(22) 2775411; e-mail tla_tanzania@yahoo.com; internet www.tlatz.org; f. 1965 as a br. of the East African Library Association, reorganized 1973 as an independent body; 200 mems; Chair. Dr ALLI MCHARAZO; Sec. P. MUNUBHI; publ. *Matukio* (Newsletter, irregular).

ECONOMICS, LAW AND POLITICS

East Africa Law Society: POB 6240, Arusha; 6 Corridor Area, Off Jandu Rd, Arusha; tel. (27) 2543226; e-mail info@ealawsociety.org; internet www.ealawsociety .org; f. 1996; 10,000 mems; CEO TITO BYENKYA; publs *The East African Human Rights Report* (1 a year), *The East African Lawyer* (4 a year).

HISTORY, GEOGRAPHY AND ARCHAEOLOGY

Historical Association of Tanzania: c/o Department of History, University of Dar es Salaam, POB 35050, Dar es Salaam; tel. (22) 2410397; f. 1966; 2,000 mems; Chair. Prof. K. I. TAMBILA; Sec. Dr E. P. A. N. MIHANJO; publ. *Tanzania Zamani*.

LANGUAGE AND LITERATURE

Alliance Française: Ali Hassan Mwinyi Rd (behind Las Vegas Casino), Upanga, POB 2566, Dar es Salaam; tel. (22) 2111331; e-mail info@afdar.com; internet www

.ambafrance-tz.org; offers courses and exams in French language and culture and promotes cultural exchange with France; attached teaching centre in Arusha.

British Council: Samora Ave/Ohio St, POB 9100, Dar es Salaam; tel. (22) 2116574; e-mail info@britishcouncil.or.tz; internet www.britishcouncil.org/tanzania; teaching centre; offers courses and exams in English language and British culture and promotes cultural exchange with the UK; Dir TOM COWIN.

Research Institutes

GENERAL

Tanzania Commission for Science and Technology: POB 4302, Dar es Salaam; tel. (22) 2700745; e-mail costech@costech.or.tz; internet www.costech.or.tz; f. 1986; 73 mems; library of 8,000 vols; Dir-Gen. Dr HASSAN MSHINDA; publ. *Tanzania Science and Technology Newsletter* (4 a year).

AGRICULTURE, FISHERIES AND VETERINARY SCIENCE

Agricultural Research Institute (Mlingano): ARI Mlingano, POB 5088, Tanga; tel. (27) 2647647; e-mail mlingano@iwayafrica .com; internet www.kilimo.go.tz/ research-training/mlingano.htm; f. 1934; research on cultivation of sisal and other crops, soils, resourcing of efficient farming methods, horticulture; germplasm collection of tropical and subtropical fruits, spices and essential oils; Dir SHABANI HAMISI.

Forestry and Beekeeping Division: c/o Ministry of Natural Resources and Tourism, POB 426, Dar es Salaam; tel. (22) 2864249; e-mail dfob@mnrt.go.tz; internet www.nfp.co

.tz; forest-surveying, mapping, industrial development, economics, management and education as part of the National Forest Policy and National Beekeeping Policy (both adopted 1998); library of 2,500 vols; Dir Dr FELICIAN KILAHAMA.

Mikocheni Agricultural Research Institute: POB 6226, Kinondoni District, Dar es Salaam; tel. (22) 2700552; e-mail mari@mari .or.tz; integrated pest management, with emphasis on biological control of coconut pests; Dir Dr ALOIS KULLAYA.

National Livestock Research Institute: POB 202, Mpwapwa, Dodoma; tel. (26) 2320853; f. 1905; research in dairy science, breeding and nutrition of livestock, Mpwapwa cattle and Malya goats, pastural agronomy and multidisciplinary research; Nat. Livestock Research Institute; research information documentation and dissemination; library of 4,000 vols, 40 periodicals; Dir Dr REGINALD P. MBWILE; publ. *Progressive Stockman* (4 a year).

Tanzania Forestry Research Institute: POB 1854, Morogoro; tel. (023) 2613725; internet www.tafori.org; library of 3,000 vols; Dir-Gen. L. NSHUBEMUKI; publ. *Tanzania Silviculture Research Notes* (4 a year).

Tanzania Wildlife Research Institute: POB 661, Arusha; tel. (27) 2509871; e-mail info@tawiri.org; internet www.tawiri.org; research into wildlife, with the objective of providing scientific information and advice to the Govt of Tanzania and local wildlife management authorities on the sustainable conservation of wildlife; Chair Prof. PETER MSOLLA.

Tropical Pesticides Research Institute: POB 3024, Arusha; tel. (27) 2548813; e-mail tpri@habari.co.tz; internet www.habari.co.tz/ tpri; f. 1962; research into all aspects of pesticide application and behaviour; library of 5,000 vols; Dir Dr GRATIAN BAMWENDA.

HISTORY, GEOGRAPHY AND ARCHAEOLOGY

Geological Survey of Tanzania: c/o Min. of Energy and Minerals, POB 903, Dodoma; tel. (26) 2324943; e-mail madini-do@gst.go.tz; internet www.gst.go.tz; f. 1925; attached to Min. of Energy and Minerals; regional mapping, mineral exploration and assessment; supporting laboratory facilities; reprints, bulletins, memoirs, books and maps; library of 4,000 books; Chief Exec., Geological Survey of Tanzania Prof. A. H. MRUMA (acting); Librarian/Information Officer E. LUHOKO; publs *Bulletins*, *Records of the Geological Survey of Tanzania*.

LANGUAGE AND LITERATURE

Eastern African Centre for Research on Oral Traditions and African National Languages (EACROTANAL): POB 600, Zanzibar; f. 1979 as a regional and intergovernmental organization to encourage research and develop means of collection, analysis, conservation and diffusion of oral traditions and promotion of national languages; provides short-term training courses on these subjects; library of 3,000 vols (incl. 148 old Arabic MSS from Zanzibar); one of 3 African regional centres, set up by Burundi, Comoros, Ethiopia, Madagascar, Mauritius, Mozambique, Somalia, Sudan, Tanzania; Exec. Dir KHATIB MAKAME OMAR (acting); publs annotated bibliography of the Arabic MSS (every 2 years), *Paukwa Pakawa* (traditional tales, 1 a year).

Institute of Kiswahili Research: POB 35110, Dar es Salaam; tel. (22) 2410757; e-mail tuki@ikr.udsm.ac.tz; internet www .udsm.ac.tz/ikr/; f. 1970; initiates and con-

ducts fundamental research in all aspects of Kiswahili language; cooperates with local public authorities and int. organizations; promotes the standardization of orthography and the development of language generally; preparing new standard dictionary, technical dictionaries, grammars, monographs on oral literature; library of 3,000 vols; Dir Prof. M. M. MULOKOZI; publs *Kiswahili* (1 a year), *Mulika* (1 a year).

MEDICINE

National Institute for Medical Research (NIMR): Headquarters, Ocean Rd, POB 9653, Dar es Salaam; tel. (22) 2121400; e-mail headquarters@nimr.or.tz; internet www.nimr.or.tz; f. 1949 at Muheza as the Malaria Unit; investigation into human vector-borne diseases, especially malaria, bancroftian filariasis, and onchocerciasis; Dir Dr ANDREW KITUA.

National Institute for Medical Research, Mwanza Centre: POB 1462, Mwanza; tel. (28) 250189; f. 1949; investigations into various tropical diseases with emphasis on bilharziasis, and other soil-transmitted helminths, bacterial diseases, sanitation and water, diarrhoeal diseases, sexually transmitted diseases, HIV/AIDS; library of 2,300 vols; Dir Dr R. M. GABONE; publs *NIMR Bulletin*, *Proceedings of the Annual NIMR Joint Scientific Conference*.

Libraries and Archives

Dar es Salaam

Tanzania Information Services Department: POB 9142, Dar es Salaam; tel. (22) 2122771; e-mail maelezo@pmo.go.tz; reference books on Tanzania, journalism, photography, social sciences, geography and history; newspapers and periodicals.

Tanzania Library Services Board: Bibi Titi Mohamed Rd, POB 9283, Dar es Salaam; tel. (22) 2150048; e-mail tlsb@africaonline.co .tz; internet www.tlsb.or.tz; f. 1964; 16 brs; Dir-Gen. ELIEZER A. MWINYIMVUA.

Tanzania National Archives: Vijibweni St, POB 2006, Dar es Salaam; tel. (22) 2151279; e-mail dram@intafrica.com; internet www.tanzania.go.tz/psrp/record1 .html; f. 1963; German and British colonial archives, post-independence archives; Dir J. M. KARUGILA; publ. *Guide to Archives*.

University of Dar es Salaam Library: POB 35092, Dar es Salaam; tel. (22) 2410241; e-mail general@libis.udsm.ac.tz; internet www.library.udsm.ac.tz; f. 1961; legal deposit library; 600,000 vols, 280 journals, spec. collns: E Africana Colln, UN Colln, Law Colln; 8,000 periodicals; Dir JANGAWE MSUYA.

Morogoro

Sokoine National Agricultural Library: POB 3022, Morogoro; tel. (23) 2604639; e-mail library@suanet.ac.tz; internet www .suanet.ac.tz; f. 1964 as library for the College of Agriculture, library for Faculty of Agriculture, Forestry and Veterinary Medicine of the Univ. of Dar es Salaam 1972, Sokoine Univ. of Agriculture Library 1984, present name and status 1991; attached to Sokoine Univ. of Agriculture; learning, teaching, research, consultancy and outreach services; 75,000 vols, 100 periodicals; Library Dir Dr DORIS. S. MATOVELO.

Mwanza

Ladha Meghji Indian Public Library: POB 70, Mwanza; tel. (28) 2500482; e-mail desaitz@yahoo.com; f. 1935; 11,130 vols; runs English, French, oriental language and computer classes; Librarian RAMAN DESAI.

Zanzibar

Museum Research Library: c/o Dept of Antiquities, Archives and Museum, Zanzibar National Archives, POB 116, Zanzibar; tel. (22) 30342; e-mail dama@zitec.org; f. 1930; reference library; 15,000 vols and 1,000 periodicals; Head of the Library SULEIMAN SEIF.

Zanzibar National Archives: POB 116, Zanzibar; tel. (22) 35241; e-mail dama@zitec .org; f. 1956; history and administration; 3,500 vols; Archivist HAMAD OMAR.

Museums and Art Galleries

Dar es Salaam

National Museums of Tanzania: POB 511, Dar es Salaam; tel. (22) 2122030; internet www.museum.or.tz; f. 1937 as King George V Memorial Museum, name changed 1963; ethnography, palaeoanthropology, history and marine biology; houses the *Zinjanthropus* skull and other material from Olduvai Gorge and other Palaeolithic sites; also houses reference library; Dir-Gen. Dr N. A. KAYOMBO..

Branch Museums:

Arusha Declaration Museum: POB 7423, Arusha; tel. (27) 2507800; e-mail adm-arusha@habari.co.tz; internet www .arushamuseum.ac.tz; f. 1977; preservation and exhibition of political, social and economic history; Director ELIZABETH SOLOMON.

Arusha Natural History Museum: POB 2160, Arusha; tel. (27) 2507540; e-mail nnhm@habari.co.tz; internet www .museum.or.tz; Curator FELISTA MANGALU.

Village Museum: POB 511, Dar es Salaam; tel. (22) 2700437; e-mail villagemuseum@raha.com; f. 1967; traditional house styles and crafts; Curator JACKSON M. KIHIYO.

Zanzibar

Zanzibar Government Museum: POB 116, Zanzibar; tel. (24) 2230342; e-mail dama@zitec.org; internet www.museum.com/ jb/museum?id=24191; f. 1925; operates House of Wonders Museum at Forodhani (history and culture of Zanzibar and Swahili Coast civilization, f. 2001), Palace Museum at Mizingani (history of the Zanzibar sultans, f. 1994), Peace Memorial Museum at Mnazi Minoja (history, ethnography, natural history and archaeology of Zanzibar, f. 1925), Pemba Museum at Chake (history of Pemba Island, f. 2000); Dir H. H. OMAR.

Universities

HUBERT KARIUKI MEMORIAL UNIVERSITY

POB 65300, 322 Regent Estate, Dar es Salaam

Telephone: (22) 2700021
E-mail: secvc@hkmu.ac.tz
Internet: www.hkmu.ac.tz

Founded 1997; univ. status 2000
Language of instruction: English
Academic year: September to August

Vice-Chancellor: Prof. KETO E. MSHIGENI
Deputy Vice-Chancellor for Finance, Planning and Admin.: Prof. PASCHALIS RUGARABAMU
Dir of Postgraduate Studies and Research Institute: Prof. SYLVESTER L. B. KAJUNA
Dean of Students: Dr ALPHAGE LIWA
Sr Librarian: STANSLAUS NGADAYA

DEANS

Faculty of Medicine: Dr FELICIAN RUTACHUN-ZIBWA
Faculty of Nursing: Prof. PAULINE P. MELLA

PROFESSORS

LUTAHOIRE, S., Medicine
MELLA, P., Nursing
MSAMATI, B. C., Medicine
MWAIKAMBO, E., Medicine

INTERNATIONAL MEDICAL AND TECHNOLOGICAL UNIVERSITY

Mbeze Beach area, New Bagamoyo Rd, POB 77594, Dar es Salaam

Telephone: (22) 2647036
E-mail: imtu@costech.or.tz
Internet: www.imtu.edu

Founded 1995 by Vignan Educational Foundation (India) and Tanzanian Govt
Number of teachers: 23
Vice-Chancellor: Dr V. P. KIMATI
Deputy Vice-Chancellor for Academic Affairs: V. S. RAKESH
Dir of Finance: P. B. KUMAR
Dean of Students: Dr RENJU THOMAS

MZUMBE UNIVERSITY
(Chuo Kikuu Mzumbe)

POB 1, Mzumbe, Morogoro

Telephone: (23) 2604380
E-mail: mu@mzumbe.ac.tz
Internet: www.mzumbe.ac.tz

Founded 1972 as Institute of Devt Management; present name and univ. status 2001
State control
Language of instruction: English
Academic year: October to June
Chancellor: Hon. Judge (retd) BARNABAS SAMATTA
Vice-Chancellor: Prof. JOSEPH ANDREW KUZILWA
Deputy Vice-Chancellor for Academic Affairs: Prof. MAGISHI NKWABI MGASA
Deputy Vice-Chancellor for Admin. and Finance: Prof. FAUSTIN KAMUZORA
Dir of Information and Communications Technology: ALMAS MAGUYE
Dir of MU Mbeya campus: ROSS KINEMO
Dir of Research and Postgraduate Studies: Dr AGGREY KIHOMBO
Registrar: Prof. HAMISI I. MAHIGI
Dir of Library and Technical Services: MATILDA KUZILWA
Library of 50,000 books, 900 current periodicals
Number of teachers: 270
Number of students: 3,551
Publications: *Economics and Development Papers, Journal of Public Policy and Administration, Uongozi Journal of Management and Development Dynamics* (4 a year)

DEANS

Dar es Salaam Business School: Dr ANDREW MBWAMBO
Faculty of Commerce: Dr JOSEPH A. KIMEME
Faculty of Law: ELEUTER G. MUSHI
Faculty of Public Administration and Management: Prof. JOSEPHAT ITIKA
Faculty of Science and Technology: Prof. Dr PHILBERT NDUNGURU
Faculty of Social Science: Prof. Dr EULALIA I. TEMBA

ATTACHED RESEARCH INSTITUTES

Institute of Continuing Studies: POB, Mzumbe; tel. (23) 2604380; e-mail ics@mzumbe.ac.tz; Dir ALOYCE MAZIKU.

Institute of Development Studies: POB 83, Mzumbe; tel. (23) 2604380; e-mail ids@mzumbe.ac.tz; Dir Prof. AURELIA KAMUZORA.
Institute of Public Administration: POB 2, Mzumbe; tel. (23) 2604380; e-mail ipa@mzumbe.ac.tz; Dir Dr EMMANUEL MATIKU

OPEN UNIVERSITY OF TANZANIA

Kawawa Rd, Kinondoni Municipality, POB 23409, Dar es Salaam

Telephone: (22) 2668992
E-mail: vc@out.ac.tz
Internet: www.out.ac.tz

Founded 1992
State control
Languages of instruction: English, Kiswahili
Academic year: January to December

Chancellor: Dr JOHN SAMWEL MALECELA
Vice-Chancellor: Prof. TOLLY S. A. MBWETTE
Deputy Vice-Chancellor for Academic Affairs: Prof. DONATUS A. KOMBA
Registrar: Prof. USWEGE M. MINGA
Librarian: A. S. SAMZUGI
Library of 5,000 vols
Number of teachers: 113 (33 full-time, 80 part-time)
Number of students: 12,945
Publication: *HURIA Journal*

PROFESSORS

AMAA, K. O., Business Management
KIWANGA, C. A., Science, Technology and Environmental Studies
KOMBA, D. A., Education
MASENGE, R. W. P., Science, Technology and Environmental Studies
MUKOYOGO, M. C., Law
TEMU, A. J., Arts and Social Sciences

23 regional centres and 69 study centres

ST AUGUSTINE UNIVERSITY OF TANZANIA

POB 307, Mwanza

Telephone: (28) 2552725
E-mail: saut@saut.ac.tz
Internet: www.saut.ac.tz

Founded 1960 as Nyegezi Social Training Centre; present status and name 1998
Private control (Catholic Church)
Language of instruction: English
Academic year: October to June

Vice-Chancellor: Prof. CHARLES KITIMA

Library of 15,000 vols, 30 periodicals
Number of teachers: 44
Number of students: 404

DEANS

Faculty of Business Administration: ILDE-FONS CHONYA (acting)
Faculty of Humanities and Mass Communication: JOSEPH MLACHA (acting)

SOKOINE UNIVERSITY OF AGRICULTURE

POB 3000, Chuo Kikuu, Morogoro

Telephone: (23) 2603511
E-mail: sua@suanet.ac.tz
Internet: www.suanet.ac.tz

Founded 1984, previously a faculty of Univ. of Dar es Salaam
State control
Language of instruction: English
Academic year: September to June

Chancellor: AL NOOR KASSUM
Vice-Chancellor: Prof. G. C. MONELA
Deputy Vice-Chancellor for Academic Affairs: Prof. D. M. KAMBARAGE
Deputy Vice-Chancellor for Admin. and Finance: Prof. A. E. PEREKA
Dir, Solomon Mahlangu Campus: Assoc. Prof. N. D. URIO

Registrar: Assoc. Prof. H. O. DIHENGA
Librarian: D. S. MATOVELO
Library: see Libraries and Archives
Number of teachers: 452
Number of students: 3,619 (2,925 undergraduate, 694 postgraduate)

DEANS

Faculty of Agriculture: Prof. B. P. TIISEKWA
Faculty of Forestry and Nature Conservation: Prof. P. R. GILLAH
Faculty of Science: Dr Y. C. MUZANILA
Faculty of Veterinary Medicine: Assoc. Prof. P. N. WAMBURA

PROFESSORS

ABELI, W., Forest Engineering
ASSEY, R., Veterinary Anatomy
BALTHAZARY, S., Physiology, Biochemistry, Pharmacology and Toxicology
BATAMUZI, E., Surgery and Theriogenology
BITEGEKO, S., Surgery and Theriogenology
CHAMSHAMA, S., Forest Biology
GWAKISA, P., Microbiology and Parasitology
HAMZA, K., Wood Utilization
ISHENGOMA, R., Wood Utilization
KAJEMBE, G., Forest Mensuration and Management
KAMBARAGE, D., Veterinary Medicine and Public Health
KASSUKU, A., Veterinary Microbiology and Parasitology
KAZWALA, R., Veterinary Medicine and Public Health
KESSY, B., Veterinary Surgery and Theriogenology
KIFARO, G., Animal Science
KILONZO, B., Veterinary Microbiology and Parasitology
KIMAMBO, A., Animal Science
KINABO, L., Veterinary Physiology, Biochemistry, Pharmacology and Toxicology
KURWIJILA, R., Animal Science
LASWAI, G., Animal Science
LASWAI, H., Food Science and Production
LEKULE, F., Animal Science
LULANDALA, L., Forest Biology
LWOGA, A., Crop Science and Production
MABAGALA, R., Crop Science and Production
MACHANG'U, R., Veterinary Microbiology and Parasitology
MADOFE, S., Forest Biology
MALIMBWI, R., Forest Mensuration
MALIONDO, S., Forest Biology
MASELLE, R., Veterinary Pathology
MATOVELO, J., Veterinary Pathology
MBASSA, G., Veterinary Anatomy
MDOE, N., Agricultural Economics and Agribusiness
MGASA, M., Veterinary Surgery and Theriogenology
MGONGO, F., Veterinary Surgery and Theriogenology
MISANGU, R., Crop Science and Production
MLAMBITI, M., Agricultural Economics and Agribusiness
MLANGWA, J., Veterinary Medicine and Public Health
MLOZI, M., Agricultural Education and Extension
MONELA, G., Forest Economics
MOSHA, R., Veterinary Physiology, Biochemistry, Pharmacology and Toxicology
MSANYA, B., Soil Science
MTAMBO, M., Veterinary Medicine and Public Health
MTENGA, L., Animal Science
MUHIKAMBELE, V., Animal Science
MUNISHI, P., Forest Biology
MUTAYOBA, B., Veterinary Physiology, Biochemistry, Pharmacology and Toxicology
NGOMUO, A., Veterinary Physiology, Biochemistry, Pharmacology and Toxicology
NYARUHUCHA, C., Food Science

PEREKA, A., Veterinary Physiology, Biochemistry, Pharmacology and Toxicology
REUBEN, S., Crop Science and Production
RUTATORA, D., Agricultural Education and Extension
SEMOKA, J., Soil Science
SEMUGURUKA, W., Veterinary Pathology
SENKONDO, E., Agricultural Economics and Agribusiness
SHAYO, N., Food Science and Production
SHEM, M., Animal Science
SIBUGA, K., Crop Science and Production
SILAYO, R., Veterinary Microbiology and Parasitology
TARIMO, A., Agricultural Engineering and Land Planning
TIISEKWA, B., Food Science and Production

ATTACHED CENTRES

Computer Centre: POB 3218, Chuo Kikuu, Morogoro; e-mail ccentre@suanet.ac.tz; Dir Prof. S. D. TUMBO.

Development Studies Institute: POB 3024, Chuo Kikuu, Morogoro; e-mail dsi@suanet.ac.tz; Dir Prof. A. Z. MATTEE.

Directorate of Research and Postgraduate Studies: POB 3151, Morogoro; tel. (23) 2604388; e-mail drpgs@suanet.ac.tz; Dir Prof. J. A. MATOVELO.

Institute of Continuing Education: POB 3044, Morogoro; tel. (23) 2604549; e-mail ice@suanet.ac.tz; Dir Assoc. Prof. G. G. KIMBI.

SUA Centre for Sustainable Rural Development: POB 3035, Morogoro; tel. (23) 2604360; e-mail suajica@suanet.ac.tz; Dir Prof. D. F. RUTATORA.

SUA Pest Management Centre: POB 3110, Morogoro; tel. (23) 2604621; e-mail pestman@suanet.ac.tz; Dir Prof. R. H. MAKUNDI

TUMAINI UNIVERSITY

POB 55, Usa River, Arusha
Telephone: (27) 2541144
E-mail: tu@kilinet.co.tz
Internet: www.tumainiuniversity.ac.tz
Founded 1996, present status 2001
Private control (Evangelical Lutheran Church in Tanzania)
Language of instruction: English
Vice-Chancellor: Prof. JOHN F. SHAO
Number of teachers: 400
Number of students: 9,000
Publication: *Tumaini Hill* (newsletter, 4 a year)..

CONSTITUENT COLLEGES

Iringa University College

POB 200, Iringa
Telephone: (26) 2720900
Founded 1993
Provost: NICOLAS BANGU
Deputy Provost for Academic Affairs: Rev. Dr RICHARD LUBAWA

DEANS

Faculty of Arts and Social Sciences: EGIDIO Y. CHAULA
Faculty of Business and Economics: EMMANUEL LUVANDA
Faculty of Law: THOMAS MWAHOMBELA
Faculty of Theology: PETER FUE

Kilimanjaro Christian Medical University College

POB 2240, Moshi
Telephone: (27) 2754377
E-mail: info@kcmuco.ac.tz
Internet: www.kcmuco.ac.tz
Founded 1997

Provost: EGBERT M. KESSI
Deputy Provost for Academic Affairs: Prof. NOEL SAM

DEANS

Faculty of Medicine: KIEN MTETA
Faculty of Nursing: MARCELINA H. MSUYA
Faculty of Rehabilitative Science: HAROLD G. SHANGALI

Makumira University College

POB 55, Usa River, Arusha
Telephone: (27) 2541034
E-mail: provost@makumira.ac.tz
Internet: www.makumira.ac.tz
Founded 1954
Provost: Rev. Prof. JOSEPH W. PARSALAW
Deputy Provost for Academic Affairs: Prof. ISMAEL R. MBISE
Dean of Students: ZAKARIA MATINDA
Dean of Students: Rev. Dr E. A. MUNGURE

DEANS

Faculty of Humanity and Social Sciences: APOLO A. MUGYENYI
Faculty of Law: DANIEL PALLANGYO
Faculty of Theology: Rev. HABAKUKI LWENDO

Sebastian Kolowa University College

POB 370, Lushoto
Telephone: (27) 2640114
E-mail: admin@sekuco.org
Internet: www.sekuco.org
Provost: Rev. Dr ANNETH MUNGA

DEANS

Faculty of Education: PAUL O. NWAOGU
Faculty of Law: MUTABAZI LUGAZIYA (acting)
Faculty of Science: NATHAN MUNYIAMBA (acting)

Stefano Moshi Memorial University College

POB 881, Moshi
Telephone: (27) 2757070
E-mail: smmuco@smmuco.ac.tz
Provost: ARNOLD TEMU (acting)
Deputy Provost for Academic Affairs: Prof. PETER CHONJO (acting)

DEANS

Faculty of Business and Management: Dr GASPER MPEHONGWA
Faculty of Education: ISMAIL NKYA (acting)
Faculty of Science and Technology: TABUSIA GODSON (acting)

Tumaini University Dar es Salaam College

POB 77588, Dar es Salaam
Telephone: (22) 2701316
E-mail: provost@tumainidsm.ac.tz
Internet: www.tumainidsm.ac.tz
Private control
Language of instruction: English
Academic year: September to July
Provost: Prof. USWEGE MINGA
Library of 15,000 vols, 20,000 CDs
Number of teachers: 69
Number of students: 2,300
Publication: *Law and Management Journal*

DEANS

Faculty of Arts and Social Sciences: JAMES KAZOKA
Faculty of Business Administration: GILLIARD LOTH
Faculty of Law: SOST MRAMBA

UNIVERSITY OF BUKOBA

POB 1725, Bukoba
Telephone: (28) 2220691
E-mail: uobtz@yahoo.com
Internet: uobtz.tripod.com
Founded 1999
State control
Language of instruction: English
Academic year: October to June
Chancellor: C. G. KAHAMA
Vice-Chancellor: Prof. M. HODD
Deputy Vice-Chancellor: Prof. ISRAEL KATOKE
Registrar: SAMUEL MUTASA
Library of 1,000 vols
Number of teachers: 20
Number of students: 50

DEANS

Faculty of Commerce and Management: JOSEPH MWABUKI
Faculty of Social and Natural Science: CHRISTOPHER RWIZA (acting)

UNIVERSITY OF DAR ES SALAAM

POB 35091, Dar es Salaam
Telephone: (22) 2410500
E-mail: vc@admin.udsm.ac.tz
Internet: www.udsm.ac.tz
Founded 1961; univ. status 1970
Language of instruction: English
Academic year: October to June (two semesters)
Chancellor: Ambassador F. KAZAURA
Vice-Chancellor: Prof. RWEKAZA MUKANDALA
Deputy Vice-Chancellor for Academic Affairs: Prof. M. A. H. MABOKO
Deputy Vice-Chancellor for Admin.: Prof. Y. D. MGAYA
Dir for Postgraduate Studies: Prof. B. M. MWINYIWIWA
Dir for Research: Prof. J. V. TESHA
Library: see Libraries and Archives
Number of teachers: 1,172
Number of students: 19,650
Publication: *Research Bulletin* (2 a year)

DEANS

College of Arts and Social Sciences: B. B. MAPUNDA
College of Engineering Technology: J. H. Y. KATIMA
College of Natural and Applied Sciences: Prof. F. S. S. MAGINGO
Dar es Salaam University College of Education: Prof. S. B. MISANA
Mkwawa University College of Education: Prof. P. A. K. MUSHI
School of Education: Prof. E. P. BHALALUSESA
School of Informatics and Communication Technologies: Prof. J. R. IKINGURA
School of Journalism and Mass Communication: Dr B. KILLIAN
School of Law: P. J. KABUDI

PROFESSORS

CHAMBEGA, D., Electrical Power Engineering
CHAMI, F., History and Archaeology
FIMBO, G., Economic Law
GALABAWA, J., Educational Planning and Administration
ISHUMI, A., Educational, Management, Foundations and Lifelong Studies
JOHN, G., Energy Engineering
KIMAMBO, I., History and Archaeology
LUHANGA, M., Electrical and Computer Systems Engineering
MAGHIMBI, S., Sociology and Anthropology
MASANJA, V., Mathematics
MASSAMBA, D., Institute of Kiswahili Research
MBAGO, M., Statistics

MBUNDA, F., Educational Psychology and Curriculum Studies

MLAWA, H., Institute of Development Studies

MOSHA, H., Educational Management, Foundations and Learning

MPANGALA, G., Institute of Development Studies

MSAKI, P., Physics

MSAMBICHAKA, L., Economics

MTALO, F., Water Resources Engineering

MUHONGO, S., Geology

MUNISHI, G., Political Science and Public Administration

MUSHI, P., Adult Education and Extension

MUSHI, S., Political Science and Public Administration

MUTAHABA, G., Political Science and Public Administration

MUTAKYAHWA, M., Geology

NGANA, J., Institute of Resource Assessment

NGWARE, S., Institute of Development Studies

NJAU, E., Physics

NYICHOMBA, B., Design and Production Engineering

OMARI, I., Curriculum and Teaching

OSORO, E., Economic Development

PETER, C., Private Law

RUGUMAMU, S., Institute of Development Studies

RUGUMAMU, W., Geography

RUTASHOBYA, L., Marketing

SHISHIRA, E., Institute of Resource Assessment

SHIVJI, I., Chairs

ZANZIBAR UNIVERSITY

POB 2440, Zanzibar

Telephone: (77) 3901217

E-mail: info@zanvarsity.ac.tz

Internet: www.zanvarsity.ac.tz

Founded 1998

State control

Language of instruction: English

Vice-Chancellor: Prof. MUSTAFA A. A. ROSHASH (acting)

Library of 4,000 vols, 1,000 ebooks

Number of teachers: 32

Number of students: 1,977

DEANS

Faculty of Arts and Social Sciences: MUHAMMAD JIDDAWY

Faculty of Business Administration: AHMAD MAJID ALI

Faculty of Law and Shariah: SOWED JUMA MAYANJA

Colleges

College of African Wildlife Management, Mweka: POB 3031, Moshi; tel. (27) 2756451; e-mail mweka@mwekawildlife.org; internet www.mwekawildlife.org; f. 1963; professional and technical training, research and consultancy services in African wildlife management; qualifications awarded include certificate, diploma, advanced diploma and postgraduate diploma in wildlife management; library: 10,000 vols; 16 teachers; 150 students; Prin. DEO-GRATIAS M. GAMASSA.

College of Business Education: POB 1968, Dar es Salaam; tel. (22) 2150177; e-mail principalcbe@yahoo.com; f. 1965; 55 teachers; 1,300 students; two- and three-year diploma courses in business administration and metrology; certificate course in business administration; postgraduate course in business administration; Prin. S. M. HYERA.

Dar es Salaam Institute of Technology: Private Bag 2958, Dar es Salaam; tel. (22) 2150174; e-mail principaldit@intafrica.com; internet www.dit.ac.tz; f. 1957; civil, mechanical, electrical, electronics and telecommunications engineering courses; science and laboratory technology and computing studies courses; library: 27,000 vols; 180 teachers; 3,600 students (1,200 full-time, 2,400 part-time); Prin. Prof. J. W. A. KONDORO.

Eastern and Southern African Management Institute: POB 3030, Arusha; tel. (27) 2508384; e-mail esamihq@esamihq.ac.tz; internet www.esami-africa.org; f. 1974, reconstituted 1980; country offices in Kenya, Malawi, Mozambique, Namibia, Swaziland, Tanzania, Uganda, Zambia, Zimbabwe; conducts management devt programmes; programmes in corporate entrepreneurship, energy and environment management, finance and banking, gender devt and management, governance and public sector management, human resource management, information technology, transport and infrastructure devt, health services management and admin; also Executive MBA and MBA in Transport Economics and Logistics Management; 44 teachers (24 full-time, 20 assoc.); library: 12,000 vols, 15,000 pamphlets; Dir-Gen. Dr BONARD MWAPE; publs *African Management Development Forum* (2 a year), *ESAMI Newsletter* (4 a year).

Institute of Finance Management: Shaaban Robert St, POB 3918, Dar es Salaam; tel. (22) 2112931; e-mail principal@africaonline .co.tz; internet www.ifm.ac.tz; f. 1972; courses incl. certificates in insurance, social security administration, information technology and computer science; library: 32,000 vols, 100 periodicals; 80 teachers; 1,710 students; Chief Exec. Prof. JOSHUA DORIYE (acting); Dir of Studies Dr ISAYA JAIRO (acting); publ. *African Journal of Finance and Management* (2 a year).

Kivukoni Academy of Social Sciences: POB 9193, Dar es Salaam; tel. (22) 2820041; e-mail kass@kasstz.org; internet www.kasstz .org; f. 1961; two-year diploma courses in social sciences, economic development and gender issues in development; one-year certificate in youth work; library: 27,000 vols; 30 teachers; 250 students; Prin. Dr JOHN M. J. MAGOTTI.

Moshi University College of Cooperative and Business Studies: POB 474, Sokoine Rd, Moshi; tel. (27) 2751183; e-mail moshiuniversity@yahoo.com; internet www.muccobs.ac.tz; f. 1963; library: 37,000 vols; Gender Documentation Centre on cooperatives and development; Health Information Centre; 90 teachers; 900 students; Prin. Prof. S. A. CHAMBO; publs *Journal of Cooperative and Business Studies* (2 a year), *Research Abstracts* (every 3 years), *Research Report Series*.

National Social Welfare Training Institute: POB 3375, Dar es Salaam; tel. (22) 2700918; f. 1974; 20 teachers; 180 students; library: 7,172 vols; Prin. T. F. NGALULA; publ. *Jamii Journal.*

University College of Lands and Architectural Studies: POB 35176, Dar es Salaam; tel. (22) 2775004; e-mail uclas@uclas.ac .tz; internet www.uclas.ac.tz; f. 1996; architecture, building economics, land management and valuation, land-surveying, geomatics, environmental engineering, urban and rural planning; Centre for Information Communication Technology (geographic information systems, remote sensing and ICT Studies); Institute of Human Settlements Studies (applied research and documentation services in housing, building, planning and environmental management); library: 20,000 vols; spec. collns of UN publications, theses and masterplans; 111 teachers; 1,060 students; Prin. Prof. IDRIS KIKULA; publ. *Journal of Building and Land Development* (3 a year).

THAILAND

The Higher Education System

The oldest institution of higher education is Chulalongkorn University, which was founded in 1917. In 2005 there were 1,950,892 students enrolled in 156 institutions under the authority of the Office of the Higher Education Commission, and a further 615,548 students enrolled in 408 institutions under the authority of the Office of the Vocational Education Commission. In 2011 a total of 2,497,323 students were enrolled in tertiary level education.

Following the National Education Act (1999; amended 2002) and the Act for Streamlining of Ministries and Government Agencies (2003), the Ministry of Education, the Ministry of University Affairs and the Office of the National Education Commission were incorporated into a supra-Ministry of Education. Higher education is the responsibility of the Ministry of Education's Higher Education Commission. The University Personnel Act (2004; amended 2008) allowed for the decentralization of authority within the university sector, enabling universities to formulate their own rules and procedures. A roadmap for higher education quality development was launched for the period 2005–08, following which a six-level, credit-based National Qualifications Framework for Higher Education was established in 2009. A 15-Year Long Range Plan on Higher Education covering the period 2008–22 was instigated with a view to bolstering quality standards within the Thai higher education sector by, inter alia, reforming university-level education and financing so as to enhance efficiency, and strengthening university governance. In 2009 the Ministry of Education chose nine 'flagship' public universities that would be upgraded to national research universities, and would be provided with additional funding. An initiative to create centres of excellence in research and development was also launched. Private higher education institutions are governed by the Private Higher Education Institution Act of 2003 (revised in 2007).

The main requirements for admission to higher education are 12 years of secondary school education and the MAW 6 (M6) certificate. Applicants to state institutions must sit the Written Entrance Examination, and private institutions may also require applicants to fulfil additional criteria for admission. A two-year Advanced Diploma course often leads onto the Bachelors, which is the principal undergraduate degree and is a four-year programme of study, although degrees in mainly professional fields of study may last longer, such as architecture, dentistry, pharmacy (all five years) and medicine (six years). The one-year Graduate Diploma offers a further level of specialization after the Bachelors and is generally offered in professional fields. The main postgraduate degree is the Masters, which usually lasts two years (although can take up to five years to complete) and may be either a taught or a research degree. Following the Masters, some students go on to take the Higher Graduate Diploma, which is a one-year course that aims to develop professional expertise in the chosen subject of study. The highest university degree is the Doctor of Philosophy (PhD), which requires a minimum of three years and a maximum of eight years of classwork and research.

Post-secondary vocational and technical education is overseen by the Ministry of Education's Office of the Vocational Education Commission. Qualifications offered include the Diploma in Vocational Education, Higher Certificate (Technician Level) and Higher Diploma of Technical Education (all two years). Private vocational institutes exist, some of which follow curricula devised by the Ministry of Education and some of which devise their own syllabus; qualifications awarded by the latter are not recognized by the Ministry, but are recognized by some employers.

Regulatory and Representative Bodies

GOVERNMENT

Ministry of Culture: 666 Thanon Borommaratchachonnani Rd, Bang Plad, Bang Bamru, Bangkok 10700; tel. (2) 422-8888; e-mail webmaster@m-culture.go.th; internet www.m-culture.go.th; Minister SONTAYA KHUNPLOEM.

Ministry of Education: Wang Chankasem, Thanon Ratchadamnoen Nok, Dusit, Bangkok 10300; tel. (2) 281-9281; e-mail website@moe.go.th; internet www.moe.go.th; Minister Prof. Dr CHATURON CHAISANG.

Ministry of Science and Technology: RAMA 6 Rd, Thung-Phyathai, Ratchathewee, Bangkok 10400; tel. (2) 333-3700; e-mail info@most.go.th; internet www.most.go.th; Minister PIRAPAN PALUSUK.

NATIONAL BODIES

Association of Private Higher Education Institutions of Thailand: Siam Univ., 235 Petchkasem Rd, Phasi-charoen, Bangkok 10160; tel. (2) 354-5689; internet www.apheit.com; f. 1976; Pres. Assoc. Prof. Dr CHIRADET OUSAWAT.

Council of University Presidents of Thailand (CUPT): 333 Moo 1, Muang Dist., Chiangrai 57100; tel. (53) 706-175; e-mail cupt@chula.ac.th; internet www.cupt-thailand.net; f. 1972; 24 mem. univs and institutes of higher learning; Pres. Assoc. Prof. Dr WANCHAI SIRICHANA.

Higher Education Commission: 328 Si Ayutthay Rd, Ratchathewi, Bangkok 10400; tel. (2) 610-5200; e-mail info@mua.go.th; internet www.mua.go.th; part of Min. of Education; makes policy recommendations, sets standards and plans devt in higher education; devises criteria and guidelines for the allocation of resources; tests and assesses academic and professional standards for purposes of quality assurance; coordinates and promotes research activities; Chair. THE MIN. OF EDUCATION; Sec.-Gen. Dr SUMATE YAMNOON; publ. *Thai Higher Education Review* (4 a year).

Learned Societies

GENERAL

Office of the National Culture Commission: Ratchadapisek Rd, Huay Khwang, Bangkok 10320; tel. (2) 247-0013; e-mail it_onc@culture.mail.go.th; internet www.culture.go.th; f. 1979; advises the Ministerial Council on cultural policy, and promotes coordination and cooperation in cultural activities (e.g. ASEAN projects, UNESCO programmes, intraregional music workshop, cultural exchanges, varied research); 300 mems; library of 30,000 vols; Sec.-Gen. ARTORN CHANDAVIMOL; publ. *Thai Culture Magazine* (52 a year).

Royal Institute: Sanam Seua Pa, Dusit, Bangkok 10300; tel. (2) 356-0477; e-mail ripub@royin.go.th; internet www.royin.go.th; f. 1933; promotes investigation and encouragement of all brs of knowledge, the exchange of knowledge and advises the Govt; incl. 60 academic cttees; 160 mems; library of 25,000 vols; Pres. Prof. Dr PRAYOON KANCHANADUL; Sec.-Gen. CHAMNONG TONGPRASERT.

Siam Society under Royal Patronage: 131 Soi 21 (Asoke), Asokemontri Rd, Wattana, Bangkok 10110; tel. (2) 661-6470; e-mail info@siam-society.org; internet www.siam-society.org; f. 1904; promotes the preservation of Thai heritage, culture, art, flora and fauna; 2,000 mems; library of 35,000 vols; Pres. M. R. CHAKRAROT CHITRABONGS; Hon. Sec. MONITA SINGHAKOWIN; publs *Journal, Natural History Bulletin* (2 a year).

BIBLIOGRAPHY, LIBRARY SCIENCE AND MUSEOLOGY

Thai Library Association: 1346 Akhan Songkhro 5 Rd, Klongjan, Bangkapi, Bangkok 10240; tel. (2) 734-9022; e-mail tla2497@yahoo.com; internet www.tla.or.th; f. 1954; 1,600 mems; Pres. M. CHAVALIT; Sec. K. SUCKCHAROEN; publ. *The World of Books*.

EDUCATION

UNESCO Office Bangkok and Asia and Pacific Regional Bureau for Education: Prakanong Post Office, POB 10110, Bangkok; located at: 920 Sukhumvit Rd, Bangkok 10110; tel. (2) 391-0577; e-mail bangkok@ unesco.org; internet www.unesco.org/ bangkok; f. 1961; designated Cluster Office for Cambodia, Laos, Myanmar, Thailand and Viet Nam; Dir SHELDON SHAEFFER.

LANGUAGE AND LITERATURE

Alliance Française: 29 Thanon Sathorn Tai, Bangkok 10120; tel. (2) 670-4200; e-mail bangkok@alliance-francaise.or.th; internet www.alliance-francaise.or.th; offers courses and exams in French language and culture and promotes cultural exchange with France; attached teaching centres in Chiang Mai, Chiang Rai and Phuket; Dir of Operations, Thailand ANDRÉ SCHMITT.

British Council: 254 Chulalongkorn Soi 64, Siam Sq., Phayathai Rd, Pathumwan, Bangkok 10330; tel. (2) 652-5480; e-mail info@ britishcouncil.or.th; internet www .britishcouncil.or.th; teaching centre; offers courses and exams in English language and British culture and promotes cultural exchange with the UK; attached teaching centres in Chiang Mai, Ladprao, Pinklao and Srinakarin; Dir PETER UPTON.

Goethe-Institut: 18/1 Soi Goethe, Sathorn 1 Rd, Bangkok 10120; tel. (2) 287-0942; e-mail info@bangkok.goethe.org; internet www .goethe.de/bangkok; f. 1960; offers courses and exams in German language and culture and promotes cultural exchange with Germany; library of 8,000 vols; Dir Dr NORBERT SPITZ.

MEDICINE

Medical Association of Thailand: 4th Fl., Royal Golden Jubilee Bldg, 2 Soi Soonvijai, New Petchburi Rd,, Bangkok 10310; tel. (2) 314-4333; e-mail info@mat.or.th; internet www.mat.or.th; f. 1921; 3,057 mems; Pres. Dr WONCHAT SUBHACHATURAS; Sec.-Gen. Prof. Dr SARANATRA WAIKAKUL; publ. *Journal*.

NATURAL SCIENCES

General

Science Society of Thailand: Faculty of Science, Chulalongkorn Univ., Phyathai Rd, Bangkok 10330; tel. (2) 252-4516; e-mail scisoc.thailand@gmail.com; internet www .scisoc.or.th; f. 1948; 2,500 mems; Pres. Prof. Dr SUPHOT HANNONGBUA; Sec.-Gen. Dr PIAMSOOK PONGSAWASDI; publs *ScienceAsia* (6 a year, print and online, www.scienceasia.org), *Scientific Journal* (12 a year).

Research Institutes

AGRICULTURE, FISHERIES AND VETERINARY SCIENCE

Fishery Technological Development Division: Dept of Fisheries, Plodprasop Bldg, Kaset-Klang, Chatuchak, Bangkok 10900; tel. (2) 940-6130; internet www .fisheries.go.th/industry/eng-home.html; f. 1956, current status 1992; fish handling, processing and utilization; analytical and sanitary certificate for export; Dir UDOM SUNDRARAVIPAT.

Forest Products Research and Development Division: Royal Forest Dept, Min. of Agriculture and Co-operatives, 61 Paholyothin Rd, Jatujak, Bangkok 10900; tel. (662) 579-4844; f. 1935; wood and non-wood products research and utilization; library of 20,000 vols; Dir of Div. WANIDA SUBANSENEE.

Rubber Research Institute of Thailand: Phaholyothin Rd, Chatuchak, Dept of Agriculture, Ministry of Agriculture and Co-operatives, Bangkok 10900; tel. (2) 579-

4184; e-mail irubber2005@yahoo.com; internet www.rubberthai.com; Dir SUKHUM WONG-EK; Deputy Dir for Admin. POLCHIT BUAKAEW; publ. *Rubber Thai Journal* (online, www.rubberthai.com/en/index.php/rub-berthai-journal).

NATURAL SCIENCES

Biological Sciences

Phuket Marine Biological Center: POB 60, Phuket 83000; 51 Moo, 8 Sakdided Rd, Tambon Wichit Amphoe Muang, Phuket 83000; tel. (7) 639-1128; e-mail pmbc@dmcr .mail.go.th; internet www.pmbc.go.th; f. 1966; research and training of marine biologists; Dir DEB MENASWETA.

RELIGION, SOCIOLOGY AND ANTHROPOLOGY

Buddhist Research Centre: Wat Benchamabopitr, Bangkok; f. 1961; sponsored by Department of Religious Affairs, Ministry of Education; publs *Pali-Thai-English Dictionary, vol. 1.*

TECHNOLOGY

Department of Alternative Energy Development and Efficiency: Kasatsuk Bridge, Rama I Rd, Bangkok 10330; tel. (2) 223-0021; e-mail dede@dede.go.th; internet www.dede.go.th; f. 1953; conducts research and inspection, surveys and gathers data on energy resources; lays down safety regulations, sets up standards for the sale of energy, promotes the use of energy to improve the economy; library of 13,000 vols; Dir-Gen. SIRIPORN SAILASUTA; publs *Electric Power in Thailand* (1 a year), *Oil and Thailand* (1 a year), *Thailand Alternative Energy Situation* (1 a year), *Thailand Energy Situation* (1 a year).

Department of Mineral Resources: Min. of Natural Resources and Environment, 75/ 10 Rama VI Rd, Ratchatewi, Bangkok 10400; internet www.dmr.go.th; f. 1891; attached to Min. of Natural Resources and Environment; geological mapping, mineral-prospecting, mining, mineral-dressing and metallurgical research; 5 museums, library; Dir-Gen. NITAT POOVATANAKUL.

Department of Science Service: Rama VI Rd, Ratchathewim, Bangkok 10400; tel. (2) 201-7000; e-mail pr@dss.go.th; internet www .dss.go.th; f. 1891; attached to Min. of Science and Technology; testing, calibration and analysis services; research in food technology, industrial fermentation, pulp and paper raw materials, chemical engineering processes, air and water pollution control; research in ceramics; scientific and technological information service; library: see under Libraries and Archives; Dir-Gen. SAOWANEE MUSIDANG; Sec. UMAPORN SUKMOUNG; publ. *Journal* (3 a year).

Office of Atoms for Peace: 16 Vibhavadi Rangsit Rd, Bangkok 10900; tel. (2) 596-7600; e-mail icop@oaep.go.th; internet www .oaep.go.th; f. 1961, previously Office of Atomic Energy for Peace; library of 11,000 vols, 265 periodicals; Sec.-Gen. SUPHAN SAENGTHONG; Deputy Sec.-Gen. VICHIAN VONGSAMAN.

Thailand Institute of Scientific and Technological Research: Technopolis Klong 5, Klong Luang, Pathumthani, Bangkok 10120; tel. (2) 577-4157; e-mail tistr@ tistr.or.th; internet www.tistr.or.th; f. 1963; principal govt research agency; research depts: pharmaceuticals and natural products, food industry, chemical industry, biotechnology, building technology, electronics industry, engineering industry, materials technology, agricultural technology, energy

technology, environmental and resources management, ecological research, Thai packaging centre; 690 staff; Governor Dr SURAPOL VATANAWONG (acting).

Libraries and Archives

Bangkok

Asian Institute of Technology Library: POB 4, Klong-Luang, Pathumthani 12120; tel. (2) 524-5853; e-mail ref@ait.ac.th; internet www.library.ait.ac.th; f. 1959; provides services and training in library and information services; 250,000 vols, 900 periodicals; Head of Library BOONTHAREE PHOONCHAI.

Bureau of Science and Technology Information: Library Science and Technology Bldg, 75/7 Rama 6 Rd, Ratchathewi Dist., Bangkok 10400; tel. (2) 201-7250; e-mail info@dss.go.th; internet www.dss.go.th/ ewdss/index.php/sti-bg; f. 1918, formerly Library of Dept of Science Service, current name 2002; spec. library and technical information services incl. patents, standards and trade literature; 450,000 vols; Dir BENJAPHAT JATURONRUSMI.

Chulalongkorn University, Center of Academic Resources: Phyathai Rd, Bangkok 10330; tel. (2) 218-2905; internet www .car.chula.ac.th; f. 1910; Central Library (995,264 vols), Thailand Information Center (73,400 vols), Audio Visual Center (14,269 vols), International Information Center (20,147 vols), Academic Development and Service Center; Dir Dr KAMALES SANTIVEJKUL (acting).

Kasetsart University, Main Library: Bangkok 10900; tel. (2) 940-5834; e-mail lib@ku.ac.th; internet www.lib.ku.ac.th; f. 1943; 279,465 vols, 647 periodicals, 48,218 theses, 107,631 jackets, 9,408 titles of audiovisual materials; Dir Mrs AREE THUNKIJJANUKIJ; publ. *Buffalo Bulletin* (4 a year).

Knowledge Centre: 35 Mu 3 Tambon Klong Ha, Amphoe Khlong Luang, Pathum Thani 12120; tel. (2) 577-9294; e-mail klc@tistr.or .th; internet klc.tistr.or.th; f. 1961; documentation services to science and technology; 55,443 vols of monographs in Thai, 19,287 vols of monographs in English, 37,156 vols of periodicals; Dir Dr NARUMOL RUENWAI; Librarian SAIVAROON KLOMJAI.

National Archives of Thailand: Fine Arts Dept, Samsen Rd, Dusit Bangkok 10300; tel. (2) 281-1599; e-mail taweta2001@yahoo.com; f. 1952; historical and research resources services for official agencies, scholars and public; 5 major classes of documentary material: textual (10,274 ft), audiovisual (24,508 glass plates, 442,149 photographs, 808,693 film negatives and slides, 19,840 maps, drawings and blueprints, 2,496 posters, 4,427 calendars, 4,467 audio tapes, 3,941 video cassettes, 962 microfilm rolls, 734 CDs, 34 digital tapes), bound vols, govt publs and rare books (42,418 titles), documents, memory records and contemporary records (1,867 titles), clippings and news items (677,112 titles); Dir THIPWANNA CHUMPENGPAN (acting).

National Library of Thailand: Samsen Rd, Bangkok 10300; tel. (2) 281-7927; e-mail nlt@nlt.go.th; internet www.nlt.go.th; f. 1905; nat. research library; depository for UN publs and UNESCO documents and collns; controls Int. Standard Serial Number (ISSN–Thailand), ISSN Regional Centre for Southeast Asia (ISSN-SEA); 2.5m. vols, unique and rare collns: 163,607 rare books, 355,172 MSS, 132,239 indexes, 336,000 bibliographies; digitized materials: 53,655 rare books, 26,420 MSS, 221,839 microfilms; depository colln: 263,878 books, 325,246 periodicals, 738,449 newspapers, 11 nat. and spec. databases; Dir WILAWAN SAPPHANSAEN; publs *ISSN-SEA Bulletin, Thai National Bibliography.*

Neilson Hays Library: 195 Suriwongse Rd, Bangkok; tel. (2) 233-1731; e-mail neilson@ loxinfo.co.th; internet www.neilsonhays.com; f. 1869; Librarian PRAPHEN CHITRAKDI.

Siriraj Medical Library: Faculty of Medicine Siriraj Hospital, Mahidol Univ., 2 Wang Lang Rd, Bangkoknoi, Bangkok 10700; tel. (2) 411-3112; e-mail silib@mahidol.ac.th; internet www.medlib.si.mahidol.ac.th/siriraj/index.php; f. 1897; 118,624 vols, 14,320 theses, 2,084 audiovisual materials; Chief Librarian LURIYA MANASAI; publs *Journal of the Medical Association of Thailand, Siriraj Hospital Gazette.*

Srinakharinwirot University, Central Library: Sukhumvit 23, Wattana, Bangkok 10110; tel. 258-4002; e-mail library@swu.ac.th; internet lib.swu.ac.th; f. 1954; audiovisual centre; campus in Ongkarak, Nakornnayok; 492,123 vols, 78,600 theses and dissertations, 14,910 periodicals; Dir Asst Prof. NONGNATH CHAIRAT; publ. *New Books of the Month—A Bibliography.*

Thammasat University Libraries: 2 Prachand Rd, Bangkok 10200; tel. (2) 623-5171; e-mail tulib@tu.ac.th; internet www.library.tu.ac.th; f. 1934; 11 br. libraries; 2.1m. vols (social sciences and humanities, medical science, science and technology), 4,782 periodicals, 63 databases, 75,538 audiovisual items; Dir SRICHAN CHANCHEEWA.

United Nations Economic and Social Commission for Asia and the Pacific Library: United Nations Bldg, Rajdamnern Ave, Bangkok 10200; tel. (2) 288-1360; e-mail escap_libref.unescap@un.org; internet www.unescap.org/unis/library/weblib.htm; economic and social development; 150,000 vols; Chief Librarian EVELYN DOMINGO-BARKER; publs *Asian and Pacific Bibliography* (1 a year), *ESCAP Documents and Publications* (1 a year).

Museum

Bangkok

National Museum Bangkok: Na Phra That Rd, Phra Borom Maha Ratchawang, Phra Nakhon, Bangkok 10200; tel. (2) 224-1396; internet www.bangkok-museum.go.th; f. 1874; permanent exhibitions on Thai history, archaeology and art history of Thailand from the prehistoric period to the Bangkok period, decorative arts and ethnology; prehistoric artefacts, bronze and stone sculptures, costumes, textiles, ancient weapons, coins, wood-carvings, ceramics, royal regalia, theatrical masks and dresses, marionettes, shadow-play figures, funeral chariots, illustrated books, musical instruments, monuments, historic bldgs; lectures on Thai art and culture; library; Dir SOMCHAI NA NAKHONPANOM; publs *Guide to Old Sukhothai, Guide to the National Museum, Official Guide to Ayutthaya and Bang Pa-in, Thai Cultural Series.*

Universities and Technical Institutes

ASIAN INSTITUTE OF TECHNOLOGY

POB 4, Klong Luang, Pathumthani 12120
Telephone: (2) 516-0110

E-mail: provost@ait.ac.th
Internet: www.ait.ac.th
Founded 1959
Language of instruction: English
Academic year: January to December
Ind. graduate institute, open to graduates from all countries; 2 semesters per year leading to Diploma; 4-semester (2-year) course leading to a Masters degree; further 3 years leading to Doctoral degree
Pres.: Prof. MARIO T. TABUCANON (acting)
Provost: Prof. MARIO T. TABUCANON
Dir of Promotion Activities: SANJEEV JAYA-SINGHE
Sec.: KARMA RANA
Library: see under Libraries and Archives
Number of teachers: 110
Number of students: 2,000

DEANS

School of Advanced Technologies: Prof. M. T. TABUCANON (acting)
School of Civil Engineering: Prof. CHONGRAK POLPRASERT (acting)
School of Environment, Resources and Development: Prof. CHONGRAK POLPRASERT
School of Management: Dr NAZRUL ISLAM (acting)

ASIAN UNIVERSITY

POB 15, Baan Amphur Post Office, Baan Amphur, Chonburi 20250
89 Moo 1, Highway 331 Rd, Huayyai, Banglamung, Chonburi 20260
Telephone: (38) 253-700
E-mail: admissions@asianust.ac.th
Internet: www.asianust.ac.th
Founded 1997
Private control
Language of instruction: English
Academic year: August to April (2 semesters)
Pres.: Dr VIPHANDH ROENGPITHYA
Vice-Pres. for Admin.: PANIT NILUBOL
Registrar: LADDA THIRAPORN
Librarian: SARANYA MANEEWAN
Library of 14,015 vols, 12,735 in English and 1,280 vols in Thai
Number of teachers: 40
Number of students: 130

DEANS

Faculty of Business: Dr SAROJ AUNGSUMALIN
Faculty of Engineering: Asst. Prof. Dr APICHAT TUNGTHANGTHUM
Faculty of Liberal Arts: CHARURAT TANTRAPORN

ASSUMPTION UNIVERSITY

Hua Mak Campus, 682 Ramkhamhaeng 24 Rd, Hua Mak, Bangkapi, Bangkok 10240
Bang Na Campus, 88 Moo 8, K. M. 26 Bang Na-Trad Rd, Samutprakarn 10540
Telephone: (2) 300-4543
E-mail: abac@au.edu
Internet: www.au.edu
Founded 1969, became university in 1990, formerly Assumption Business Administration College
Private control (Catholic: Brothers of St Gabriel)
Language of instruction: English
Academic year: June to March
Pres.: Rev. Bro. BANCHA SAENGHIRAN
Vice-Pres. for Academic Affairs: Rev. Bro. VISITH SRIVICHAIRATANA
Vice-Pres. for Admin. Affairs: Dr CHAVALIT MEENNUCH
Vice-Pres. for Financial Affairs: Rev. Bro. ANUPATT P. YUTTACHAI
Vice-Pres. for Information Technology: Prof. Dr SRISAKDI CHARMONMAN

Vice-Pres. for Research Affairs: Asst Prof. Dr JIRAWAT WONGSWADIWAT
Vice-Pres. for Student Affairs: Rev. Bro. LOECHAI LAVASUT
Registrar: KAMOL KITSAWAD
Dir of Central Library: SUPRATA SINCHAISUK
Library of 500,000 vols
Number of teachers: 1,230
Number of students: 20,000
Publications: *ABAC Journal, ABAC Today, AU Journal of Technology, English Teacher, Galaxy, International Journal of Computer and Engineering Management (IJCEM), Journal of Risk Management and Insurance, Prajna-Vihara (The Journal of Philosophy and Religion)*

DEANS

Graduate School of Business: Rev. Bro. VINAI VIRIYADIDHAYAVONGS
Graduate School of Computer Engineering Management (MS Programme): Dr CHAMNONG JUNGTHIRAPANICH
Graduate School of Computer Information Systems (MS Programme): Air Marshal Dr CHULIT MEESAJJEE
Graduate School of Computer Information Systems (PhD Programme): Asst Prof. Dr VICHIT AVATCHANAKORN
Graduate School of Counselling Psychology: Dr DOLORES DE LEON
Graduate School of Education: Assoc. Prof. Dr METHI PILANTHANANOND
Graduate School of Internet and E-Commerce Technology: Rear Admiral PRASART SRIBHADUNG
Graduate School of Philosophy and Religion: Asst Prof. Dr WARAYUTH SRIWARAKUEL
School of Architecture: PISIT VIRIYAVADHANA
School of Arts: Dr PIMPORN CHANDEE
School of Biotechnology: Dr CHURDCHAI CHEOWTIRAKUL
School of Business: Dr CHERDPONG SIBANRUANG
School of Communication Arts: CHALIT LIMPANAVECH
School of Engineering: Dr SUDHIPORN PATUMTAEWAPIBAL
School of Law: Assoc. Prof. PORNCHAI SOONTHORNPAN
School of Nursing Science: Dr NANTHAPHAN CHINLUMPRASERT
School of Risk Management and Industrial Services: BANCHA THEERASATIANKUL (acting)
School of Science and Technology: Asst Prof. SUPAVADEE NONTAKAO

BANGKOK UNIVERSITY

Rama 4 Rd, Klong-Toey, Bangkok 10110
Telephone: (2) 350-3500
E-mail: buiao@bu.ac.th
Internet: www.bu.ac.th
Founded 1962 as Thai Polytechnic Institute, present status 1984
Private control
Languages of instruction: English, Thai
Academic year: August to March (2 semesters)
Pres.: Asst Prof. Dr MATHANA SANTIWAT
Advisor to the Pres.: Prof. Dr POTE SAPIANCHAI
Vice-Pres. for Academic Affairs: Asst Prof. Dr TIPARATANA WONGCHAROEN
Vice-Pres. for Admin. Affairs: Assoc. Prof. LAKSANA SATAWEDIN
Vice-Pres. for External Affairs: Dr SUPONG LIMTHANAKOOL
Vice-Pres. for Financial Affairs: NARUMON OSATHANUGRAH
Vice-Pres. for Int. Affairs: Dr UTTAMA SAVANAYANA

Vice-Pres. for Information Resources and Technology: SOMCHIT LIKHITTAWORN

Vice-Pres. for Student Affairs: SOMMAI DOKMAI

Dir of Library: Dr SHANANA RODSOODTHI

Library of 400,000 vols

Number of teachers: 1,100

Number of students: 26,880

Publications: *BU Academic Journal* (2 a year), *Executive Journal* (4 a year)

DEANS

Graduate School: Asst Prof. Dr SIVAPORN WANGPIPATWONG

International College: Assoc. Prof. Dr TIPCHAN WONGCHANTA

School of Accounting: Dr SUTHA JIARANAIKULVANICH

School of Business Administration: Asst Prof. Dr VEERAPONG MALAI

School of Communication Arts: Asst Prof. Dr PEERAYA HANPONGPANDH

School of Economics: Dr UKRIST TUCHINDA

School of Engineering: Dr NATTHAPHOB NIMPITIWAN

School of Fine and Applied Arts: Asst Prof. SANSERN MILINDASUTA

School of Humanities: Asst. Prof. Dr SOMYOT WATTANAKAMOLCHAI

School of Law: Asst Prof. Dr AUNYA SINGSANGOB

School of Science and Technology: Dr WUTNIPONG WARAKRAISAWAT

BURAPHA UNIVERSITY

169 Saen Sook, Muang Chonburi 20131

Telephone: (38) 745-900

Internet: www.adm.buu.ac.th

Founded 1955

State control

Language of instruction: Thai

Academic year: June to March

Pres.: Prof. Dr SUCHART UPATHAM

Vice-Pres. for Academic Affairs: Assoc. Prof. Dr RENA PONRUENGPHANT

Vice-Pres. for Admin.: Assoc. Prof. BOONSERM POOHSANGUAN

Vice-Pres. for Finance and Property Affairs: Assoc. Prof. SUDA SUWANNAPIROM

Vice-Pres. for Int. Relations: Asst Prof. PICHAN SAWANGWONG

Vice-Pres. for Planning and Devt: VIRAT KARAVAPITTAYAKULA

Vice-Pres. for Research Affairs: Prof. Dr SOMSAK PHANTUWATTANA

Vice-Pres. for Student Affairs: Asst Prof. BOOMKA THAIKRA

Librarian: Dr KWANCHADIL PHISALPHONG

Library of 231,635 vols

Number of teachers: 660

Number of students: 10,000 (8,000 undergraduate, 2,000 postgraduate)

Publication: *Journal of Science, Technology and Humanity*

DEANS

Faculty of Education: Assoc. Prof. Dr CHALONG TUBSEE

Faculty of Engineering: Asst Prof. Dr WIRONGA RUENGPHRATHUENGSUKA

Faculty of Fine and Applied Arts: Prof. THESAKAI THONANOPKONG

Faculty of Humanities and Social Sciences: Assoc. Prof. Dr CHARAN CHAKANDANG

Faculty of Marine Technology: Dr PINCHAI SONCHAENG

Faculty of Nursing: Asst Prof. Dr SUNTHARAWADEE THEMPICHET

Faculty of Public Health: Assoc. Prof. Dr SASTRI SAOWAKONTHA

Faculty of Science: Assoc. Prof. Dr KASHANE CHALERMWAT

Faculty of Science and Art: Asst. Prof. RANOP PRAVATNGAM

Graduate School: Assoc. Prof. Dr PRATOOM MUONGMEE

CHIANG MAI UNIVERSITY

239 Huay Keaw Rd, Muang Dist., Chiang Mai 50200

Telephone: (53) 943-661

E-mail: irdcmu@chiangmai.ac.th

Internet: www.cmu.ac.th

Founded 1964

Private control

Languages of instruction: Thai, English

Academic year: June to May (3 semesters)

Pres.: Prof. Dr PONGSAK ANGKASITH

Vice-Pres. for Academic and Educational Quality Affairs: Prof. WIPADA KUNIVIKTIKUL

Vice-Pres. for Gen. Admin., Human Resource Management and Univ. Council Affairs: Asst Prof. SUPHACHAI CHUARATANAPHONG

Vice-Pres. for Int. Relations and Alumni Affairs: Asst Prof. Dr NAT SIRITHUNYALUG

Vice-Pres. for Physical and Campus Management: Asst Prof. Dr PRAYOTE OUNCHANUM

Vice-Pres. for Planning, Financial and Property Management: Assoc. Prof. Dr PAIROTE WIRIYACHAREE

Vice-Pres. for Research and Academic Services: Asstn Prof. JAKKAPAN VORAYOS

Vice-Pres. for Student Devt and Spec. Affairs: Assoc. Prof. Dr AMNAT YOUSUKH

Vice-Pres. for Univ. Ccl Affairs and Information Technology: Asst Prof. SUPHACHAI CHUARATANAPHONG

Registrar: Asst Prof. TODSAPORN PICHAIYA

Librarian: WARARAK PATTANAKIATPONG

Number of teachers: 2,200

Number of students: 39,400 (623 int. students)

Publications: *Arts Journal* (2 a year), *Chiang Mai Journal of Science* (4 a year), *Chiang Mai Medical Journal* (4 a year), *Chiang Mai University Journal of Natural Sciences* (2 a year), *Chiang Mai University Journal of Social Sciences and Humanities* (1 a year), *Chiang Mai Veterinary Journal* (2 a year), *CM Dental Journal* (2 a year), *Determination* (1 a year), *Educational Research Journal* (1 a year), *Engineering Journal Chiang Mai University* (3 a year), *Graduate Research Conference Proceeding*, *Journal of Agriculture* (3 a year), *Journal of East Review* (1 a year), *Journal of Economics* (3 a year), *Journal of Education* (2 a year), *Journal of Human Sciences* (1 a year), *Journal of Social Sciences* (1 a year), *Nursing Journal* (4 a year), *The Thai Feminist Review* (1 a year)

DEANS

Chiang Mai Univ. Int. College: Assoc. Prof. Dr ANNOP PONGWAT

College of Arts, Media and Technology: Dr PITIPONG YODMONKON

Faculty of Agriculture: Assoc. Prof. THEERA VISITPANICH

Faculty of Agro-Industry: Asst Prof. Dr CHARIN TECHAPUN

Faculty of Architecture: Dr EKKACHAI MAHAEK

Faculty of Associated Medical Sciences: Asst Prof. Dr WASNA SIRIRUNGSI

Faculty of Business Administration: BOONSAWART PRUGSIGANONT

Faculty of Dentistry: Assoc. Prof. THONGNARD KUMCHAI

Faculty of Economics: Dr PISIT LEEAHTAM

Faculty of Education: Assoc. Prof. Dr PONGSAK PANKAEW

Faculty of Engineering: Assoc. Prof. Dr SERMKIAT JOMJUNYONG

Faculty of Fine Arts: Assoc. Prof. PONGDEJ CHAIYAKUT

Faculty of Humanities: Assoc. Prof. Dr SUMALEE SAWATDIRAKPONG

Faculty of Law: Dr CHATREE RUENGDETNARONG

Faculty of Mass Communications: Assoc. Prof. JIRAPORN WITAYASAKPUN

Faculty of Medicine: Assoc. Prof. NIWES NANTACHIT

Faculty of Nursing: Assoc. Prof. Dr THANARUK SUWANPRAPISA

Faculty of Pharmacy: Assoc. Prof. WANDEE TAESOTIKUL

Faculty of Political Science and Public Admin.: Assoc. Prof. PAIRAT TRAKARNSIRINONT

Faculty of Social Sciences: Dr SIDTHINAT PRABUDHANITISARN

Faculty of Veterinary Medicine: Assoc. Prof. Dr LERTRAK SRIKITJAKARN

Graduate School: Assoc. Prof. Dr SURASAK WATANESK

CHULALONGKORN UNIVERSITY

254 Phayathai Rd, Pathumwan, Bangkok 10330

Telephone: (662) 215-0871

E-mail: info@chula.ac.th

Internet: www.chula.ac.th

Founded 1917

State control

Language of instruction: Thai

Academic year: June to March

Pres.: Prof. PIROM KAMOLRATANAKUL

Vice-Pres. for Academic Affairs: Asst Prof. M. R. KALAYA TINGSABADH

Vice-Pres. for Admin.: Assoc. Prof. CHESADA SANGSUBHAN

Vice-Pres. for Finance: Assoc. Prof. DUNUJA KUNPANITCHAKIT

Vice-Pres. for Information Technology: Asst Prof. BOONCHAI SOWANWANICHCHAKUL

Vice-Pres. for Int. Relations: Prof. KUA WONGBOONSIN

Vice-Pres. for Physical Resources Management: Assoc. Prof. LERSOM STHAPITANONDA

Vice-Pres. for Property Management: Assoc. Prof. Gr. Capt. PERMYOT KESOLBHAND

Vice-Pres. for Research and Innovations: Prof. KUA WONGBOONSIN

Vice-Pres. for Strategy and Planning: Assoc. Prof. Dr SITTICHAI TUDSRI

Vice-Pres. for Student Affairs: Assoc. Prof. TANIT TONGTHONG

Registrar: Assoc. Prof. PRADISTHA INTARAKOSIT

Library: see under Libraries and Archives

Number of teachers: 2,430

Number of students: 31,900 (20,420 undergraduate, 11,480 postgraduate)

Publications: *Chula Samphan* (26 a year), *Data on Freshmen Entering Chulalongkorn University*, *Fact Book* (1 a year), *'Pra Keaw' Students' Handbook* (1 a year), *Research Journal* (1 a year)

DEANS

College of Population Studies: Assoc. Prof. VIPAN PRACHUABMOH

College of Public Health Science: Prof. Dr SURASAK TANEEPANICHSKUL

Faculty of Allied Health Sciences: Asst Prof. Dr VANIDA NOPPONPUNTH

Faculty of Architecture: Prof. Dr BUNDIT CHULASAI

Faculty of Arts: Asst Prof. Dr PRAPOD ASSAVAVIRULHAKARN

Faculty of Commerce and Accountancy: Assoc. Prof. Dr ANNOP TANLAMAI

Faculty of Communication Arts: Assoc. Prof. Dr YUBOL BENJARONGKIJ

Faculty of Dentistry: Assoc. Prof. WACHARAPORN TASACHAN

Faculty of Economics: Prof. Dr TEERANA PONGMAKAPAT

Faculty of Education: Prof. Dr SIRICHAI KANJANAWASEE

Faculty of Engineering: Assoc. Prof. Dr BOONSOM LERDHIRUNWONG

Faculty of Fine and Applied Arts: Assoc. Prof. Dr SUPPAKORN DISATAPUNDHU

Faculty of Law: Assoc. Prof. SAKDA THANITCUL

Faculty of Medicine: Prof. Dr ADISORN PATRADUL

Faculty of Nursing: Asst Prof. Capt. YUPIN AUNGSUROCH

Faculty of Pharmaceutical Sciences: Assoc. Prof. PINTIP PONGPECH

Faculty of Political Science: Prof. Dr CHARAS SUWANMALA

Faculty of Psychology: Asst Prof. Dr KAKANANG MANEESRI

Faculty of Science: Prof. Dr SUPOT HANNONGBUA

Faculty of Veterinary Science: Prof. Dr MONGKOL TECHAKUMPHU

Graduate School: Assoc. Prof. Dr PORNPOTE PIUMSOMBOON

Petroleum and Petrochemical College: Asst Prof. POMTHONG MALAKUL

School of Sport Science: Assoc. Prof. Dr VIJIT KANUNGSUKKASEM

DHURAKIJPUNDIT UNIVERSITY

110/1-4 Prachacheun Rd, Laksi, Bangkok 10210

Telephone: (2) 954-7300
E-mail: dpuic@dpu.ac.th
Internet: www.dpu.ac.th

Founded 1968
Private control
Languages of instruction: Chinese, English, Thai
Academic year: June to February (2 semesters)
Pres.: Assoc. Prof. Dr VARAKORN SAMAKOSES
Registrar: BUPHA ANUNTARASIRICHAI
Librarian: SUWAKHON SIRIWONGWORAWAT
Library of 220,304 vols
Number of teachers: 530
Number of students: 29,000
Publication: *Sudhiparidhasna* (Univ. journal)

DEANS

Faculty of Accounting: Dr PATTANAN PETCHCHERDCHOO

Faculty of Arts and Sciences: Assoc. Prof. PREEYA UNARATANA

Faculty of Business Administration: Assoc. Prof. Dr UPATHAM SAISANGJAN

Faculty of Communication Arts: Asst Prof. Dr THANTAKARN DUANGRAT

Faculty of Economics: THAMMARAK KARNPISIT

Faculty of Engineering: Dr CHAIYAPORN KHAMAPATAPHAN

Faculty of Fine and Applied Arts: Assoc. Prof. Dr SULUCK SRIBURI

Faculty of Information Technology: Assoc. Prof. Dr NUTCHAREE PREMCHAISAWADI

Faculty of Law: Prof. Dr PRASIT EKABUTRA

Faculty of Public Admin.: POONSAK PRANOOTNARAPARN

Int. College: Asst Prof. Dr HARALD KRAUS

Language Institute: Asst Prof. Dr PEANSIRI EKNIYOM

HUACHIEW CHALERMPRAKIET UNIVERSITY

18/18 Bangna-Trad Rd, Bangplee Dist., Samutprakarn 10540

Telephone: (2) 312-6300

E-mail: regist@hcu.ac.th
Internet: www.hcu.ac.th

Founded 1942 as Midwifery School; became a college 1981; present name and status 1992
Private control
Language of instruction: Thai
Academic year: June to May
Pres.: Assoc. Prof. Dr PRACHAK POOMVISES
Vice-Pres.: PISANU RIENMAHASARN
Vice-Pres.: SANGUANSRI KENGKIJKOSOL
Vice Pres.: Assoc. Prof. Dr CHANTRA SHAIPANICH (acting)
Vice-Pres. for Academic Affairs: Asst. Prof. Dr URAIPAN JANVANICHYANONT
Vice-Pres. for Planning and Devt: Assoc. Prof. Dr CHIRADET OUSAWAT
Vice-Pres. for Student Affairs: KANOGWAN CHANTHANAMONGKOL
Dir of Library and Information Centre: SUCHANYA CHIRABANDHU
Library of 209,803 books, 1,157 periodicals
Number of teachers: 480
Number of students: 8,934 (8,620 undergraduate, 226 postgraduate, 88 certificate)

DEANS

Faculty of Business Administration: Prof. Lt.-Gen. PISANU RIENMAHASARN

Faculty of Communication Arts: Asst. Prof. Dr URAIPAN JANVANICHYANONT

Faculty of Law: Lt.-Gen. SUPHOT NA BANGCHANG

Faculty of Liberal Arts: Assoc. Prof. Dr SUREERAT MARAPO

Faculty of Medical Technology: Asst Prof. ISAYA JANWITHYANUCHIT

Faculty of Nursing: Assoc. Prof. Dr JARIYAWAT KOMPAYAK

Faculty of Pharmaceutical Science: Assoc. Prof. Dr CHANTRA SHAIPANICH

Faculty of Physical Therapy: BOONRAT NGOWTRAKUL

Faculty of Public and Environmental Health: Asst. Prof. Dr SAOVALUG LUKSAMIJARULKUL

Faculty of Science and Technology: Assoc. Prof. RACHNEE RUKVEERADHUM

Faculty of Social Work and Social Welfare: NUANYAI WATTANAKOON

Faculty of Traditional Chinese Medicine: UDOM CHANTHARAKSRI

Graduate School: Asst Prof. PANNARAI SANGVICHIEN

KASETSART UNIVERSITY

Bangkhen Campus: 50 Ngamwongwan Rd, Chatuchak, Bangkok 10900

Chalermprakiat Sakon Nakhon Province Campus: 59 Moo 1, Sakhon Nakhon–Nakhonphranom Rd, Amphur Moung, Sakonnakhon 47000

Kamphaeng Saen Campus: 1 Moo 6, Tambon Kamphaeng Saen, Amphur Kamphaeng Saen, Nakhon Pathom 73140

Si Racha Campus: 199 Moo 6, Sukhumvit Rd, Tambon Tungsukla, Amphur Si Racha, Changwat Chon Buri 20230

Telephone: (2) 942-8171
E-mail: fro@ku.ac.th
Internet: www.ku.ac.th

Founded 1943
State control
Languages of instruction: English, Thai
Academic year: June to March (2 semesters)
Pres.: Assoc Prof. VUDTECHAI KAPILAKANCHANA
Vice-Pres. for Academic Affairs: Assoc. Prof. Dr SIREE CHAISERI
Vice-Pres. for Academic Service: Dr DAMRONG SRIPRARAM
Vice-Pres. for Central Management: Assoc. Prof. Dr UTSANEE LEERAWAT

Vice-Pres. for Chalermprakiat Sakon Nakorn Campus: Assoc. Prof. Dr PONGSAK SURIYAVANAGUL

Vice-Pres. for Financial and Property Management: Asst Prof. Dr RANGSAN PITIPUNYA

Vice-Pres. for Information Technology: Assoc Prof. SURASAK SANGUANPONG

Vice-Pres. for Int. Relations: Assoc. Prof. Dr POONPIPOPE KASEMSAP

Vice-Pres. for Kamphaeng Saen Campus: Assoc. Prof. Dr SOMBAT CHINAWONG

Vice-Pres. for Quality Assurance: Assoc. Prof. NONGLAK NGAMJAREON

Vice-Pres. for Research: Assoc. Prof. Dr SORNPRACH THANISAWANYANGKURA

Vice-Pres. for Si Racha Campus: Assoc. Prof. Dr CHAIWAT CHAIKUL

Vice-Pres. for Spec. Projects: Asst Prof. Dr THANWA JITSANGUAN

Vice-Pres. for Student Affairs and Physical Devt: NIPHON LIMLEAMTHONG

Registrar: Assoc. Prof. SAHAT PATARATHITINANT

Librarian: Dr AREE THUNKIJJANUKIJ

Library: see under Libraries and Archives
Number of teachers: 3,600
Number of students: 68,900 (55,200 undergraduate, 13,700 postgraduate)

Publications: *Kasetsart Journal* (4 a year, natural sciences edn; 3 a year, social sciences edn), *Knowledge of the Land* (1 a year, university's academic affairs, in English)

DEANS

Faculty of Agriculture: VICHAN VICHUKIT

Faculty of Agriculture (Kamphaeng Saen): SEKSOM ATTAMANGKUNE

Faculty of Agro-Industry: TANABOON SAJJAANANTAKUL

Faculty of Architecture: RATCHOT CHOMPUNICH

Faculty of Business Administration: BODIN RASSAMEETHES

Faculty of Economics: NUCHANATA MUNGKUNG

Faculty of Economics (Si Racha): SRI-ON SOMBOONSUP

Faculty of Education: SURACHAI JEWCHAREONSAKUL

Faculty of Education and Development Sciences: BUNJOB PIROMKAM

Faculty of Engineering: THANYA KIATIWAT

Faculty of Engineering (Kamphaeng Saen): BANCHA KWANYUEN

Faculty of Engineering (Si Racha): KIATYUTH KVEEYARN

Faculty of Environment: DAMRONG SRIPRARAM (acting)

Faculty of Fisheries: SURIYAN TUNKIJJANUKIJ

Faculty of Forestry: WANCHAI ARUNPRAPARUT

Faculty of Humanities: PUTTACHART POTIBUL

Faculty of Liberal Arts and Management Science: ORASA ARAMRATTANA

Faculty of Liberal Arts and Science: CHANAN SUDSUKH

Faculty of Management Sciences: AMNART THEERAVANICH

Faculty of Natural Resources and Agro-Industry: ONANONG TAPANAPUNNITIKUL

Faculty of Resources and Environment: RUJA ARUNBANJERDKUL

Faculty of Science: SURAPOL PATHARAKORN

Faculty of Science and Engineering: SIRIVAT POONVASIN

Faculty of Science (Si Racha): SUCHAI TANAIADCHAWOOT

Faculty of Social Sciences: MANITPOL URABUNNUALCHAT

Faculty of Sport Science: RATREE RUANGTHAI

Faculty of Veterinary Medicine: APINUN SUPRASERT

Faculty of Veterinary Technology: WORAWUT RERKAMNUAYCHOKE

Graduate School: GUNJANA THEERAGOOL

International Maritime College: SUPIT UMNUAY

PROFESSORS

ATTATHOM, S., Plant Pathology
ATTATHOM, T., Entomology
CHANDRAPATYA, A., Entomology
CHAREONVIRIYAPHAP, T., Entomology
KANCHANALAI, T., Civil Engineering
LAOHAKOSOL, V., Mathematics
LIMTONG, S., Microbiology
LIMTRAKUL, J., Chemistry
MAKARABHIROM, K., English Literature
NAIVIKUL, O., Food Science and Technology
NA-NAKORN, U., Aquaculture
PANICHSAKPATANA, S., Soil Science
ROONGTANAKIAT, N., Applied Radiation and Isotopes
RUJOPAKARN, W., Transportation Engineering
SALAKIJ, C., Pathology
SIRIPHANICH, J., Horticulture
SRINIVES, P., Agronomy
SUPRASERT, A., Anatomy
TRISURAT, Y., Forest Biology
YINGJAJAVAL, S., Soil Physics

KHON KAEN UNIVERSITY

123 Mitraparb Rd, Amphur Muang, Khon Kaen 40002

Telephone: (4) 300-9700
E-mail: vpinter@kku.ac.th
Internet: www.kku.ac.th

Founded 1964
State control
Language of instruction: Thai
Academic year: June to March (2 semesters)

Pres.: Assoc. Prof. Dr SUMON SAKOLCHAI
Vice-Pres. for Academic and Int. Affairs: Assoc. Prof. Dr KUTHILDA TUAMSUK
Vice-Pres. for Admin. Affairs: Assoc. Prof. DUMRONG HORMDEE
Vice-Pres. for Planning and IT: Asst Prof. AROM TATAWASART
Vice-Pres. for Research: Asst Prof. PUSAN SIRITHORN
Vice-Pres. for Spec. Affairs: Asst Prof. WICHAI NEERATANAPHAN
Vice-Pres. for Student Affairs: Asst Prof. Dr ANAN HIRANSALEE
Vice-Pres. for Student Devt: Assoc. Prof. LIKHIT AMARTTAYAKONG
Vice-Pres. for Univ. Facilities: SURACHET MANGMEESRI

Library of 339,614 vols
Number of teachers: 1,810
Number of students: 18,457

Publications: *Architecture Journal* (4 a year), *Bulletin of Medical Technology and Physical Therapy* (4 a year), *Humanities and Social Sciences Journal* (4 a year), *Information* (2 a year), *I-San Journal of International Medicine* (4 a year), *Journal of Learning and Teaching Competency* (4 a year), *Journal of Learning and Teaching Innovation* (4 a year), *Journal of Library and Information Science* (4 a year), *Journal of Medical Technology and Physical Therapy* (4 a year), *Journal of Mekong Societies* (4 a year), *Journal of Nursing* (4 a year), *Kaen Kaset* (4 a year), *Khon Kaen Agriculture Journal* (6 a year), *KKU Dental Journal* (2 a year), *KKU Engineering Journal* (4 a year), *KKU Engineering Quarterly*, *KKU Health Sciences Center Bulletin* (6 a year), *KKU Journal of Education* (4 a year), *KKU Journal of Management Science* (1 a year), *KKU Quality Assurance Journal* (2 a year), *KKU VET Journal* (2 a year), *Science Journal* (4 a year), *Srinagarind Medical Journal* (4 a year)

DEANS

Faculty of Agriculture: Asst Prof. ASSANEE PRACHINBURAVAN
Faculty of Architecture: Asst. Prof. TANOO POLWAT
Faculty of Associated Medical Sciences: Assoc. Prof. YUPA UAVIJTIAROON
Faculty of Dentistry: Asst Prof. Dr NIWUT JUNTAVEE
Faculty of Education: Assoc. Prof. Dr SAMPAN PANPURK
Faculty of Engineering: Assoc. Prof. Dr WINIT CHINSUWAN
Faculty of Fine and Applied Arts: Assoc. Prof. Dr CHALERMSAK PIKULSRI
Faculty of Humanities and Social Sciences: Assoc. Prof. SRIPANYA CHAIYAI
Faculty of Management Sciences: Assoc. Prof. SUMETH KAENMANEE
Faculty of Medicine: Asst Prof. SUCHART AREEMITR
Faculty of Nursing: Asst Prof. Dr WANAPA SRITANYARAT
Faculty of Pharmaceutical Sciences: Assoc. Prof. SUMON SAKOLCHAI
Faculty of Public Health: Assoc. Prof. AROON JIRAWATKUL
Faculty of Sciences: Asst Prof. Dr WANCHAI SOOMLEG
Faculty of Technology: Asst Prof. Dr KRIENGSAK SRISUK
Faculty of Veterinary Medicine: Assoc. Prof. PRACKAK PUAPERMPOONSRI
Graduate School: Assoc. Prof. Dr SOMMAI PRIPREM

KING MONGKUT'S INSTITUTE OF TECHNOLOGY LADKRABANG

Chalongkrung Rd, Ladkrabang Dist., Bangkok 10520

Telephone: (2) 329-8000
E-mail: ic@kmitl.ac.th
Internet: www.kmitl.ac.th

Founded 1960
State control
Academic year: June to March

Nanotechnology research centre, data storage technology and applications research centre

Chancellor: SURAYUD CHULANONT
Vice-Chancellor: Prof. Dr POTE SAPIANCHAI
Pres.: Prof. Dr TAWIL PAUNGMA
Vice-Pres. for Academic Affairs: SUCHEEP SUKSUPATH
Vice-Pres. for Admin.: KITTI TIRASESTH
Vice-Pres. for Chumporn Campus: SURAPOL SETHABUTR
Vice-Pres. for Devt: AMNOUY PANITKULPONG
Vice-Pres. for Finance and Property: WILAIWAN WONYODPUN
Vice-Pres. for Int. Affairs: DUSANEE THANABORIPAT
Vice-Pres. for Planning: KULTHORN LUERNSHAVEE
Vice-Pres. for Student Affairs: PACHERNCHAI CHAIYASITH
Admin. Officer: RUAMPORN INTARAPRASONG
Dir of Central Library: GASAMAPONG PONGCHOMPORN

Library of 67,000 vols
Number of teachers: 810
Number of students: 15,100

Publications: *IT Journal* (2 a year), *Journal* (2 a year), *Journal of Science—Ladkrabang* (2 a year), *Ladkrabang Engin* (4 a year), *Research Abstracts* (irregular)

DEANS

Administration and Management College: Prof. Dr JIRASEK TRIMETSOONTORN
College of Data Storage Innovation: Prof. Dr SIRIDECH BOONSANG

College of Nanotechnology: Prof. Dr JITI NUKEAW
Faculty of Agricultural Technology: SAKCHAI CHOOCHOTE
Faculty of Agro- Industry: Prof. Dr PRAPHAN PINSIRODOM
Faculty of Architecture: PICHATE SOVITTAYASAKUL
Faculty of Engineering: Prof. Dr SUCHAVEE SUWANSAWAT
Faculty of Industrial Education: PEERAWUT SUWANJAN
Faculty of Information Technology: Prof. Dr CHANBOON SATHITWIRIYAWONG
Faculty of Science: Prof. Dr DUSANEE THANABORIPAT
Graduate School: MANAS SANGWORASIL
International College: Prof. Dr SUPAT KITTIRATSATCHA

KING MONGKUT'S INSTITUTE OF TECHNOLOGY NORTH BANGKOK

1518 Pibulsongkram Rd, Bangsue, Bangkok 10800

Telephone: (2) 913-2500
E-mail: iro@kmitnb.ac.th
Internet: www.kmitnb.ac.th

Founded 1959
State control
Languages of instruction: Thai, English
Academic year: June to March

Pres.: Prof. Dr TERAVUTI BOONYASOPON
Vice-Pres. for Academic Affairs: Assoc. Prof. Dr CHANASAK BAITIANG
Vice-Pres. for Admin. and Int. Affairs: Asst Prof. WATANA PINSEM
Vice-Pres. for Finance: Asst Prof. ACHARA SUNGSUWAN
Vice-Pres. for Prachinburi Campus: Asst Prof. WORAWIT CHATURAPANICH
Vice-Pres. for Research and Quality Assurance: Assoc. Prof. CHARN THANADNGARN
Vice-Pres. for Student Affairs: Asst Prof. WITTAYA WIPAWIWAT
Vice-Pres. for Univ. Devt and Promotion: ARUN PUTHAYANGKURA
Registrar: SANGOB KONGKA
Dir of Central Library: MONTREE KHEMRACH

Number of teachers: 630
Number of students: 16,400

Publications: *Journal of King Mongkut's Institute of Technology North Bangkok* (in Thai, 6 a year), *Technical Education Development* (in Thai, 4 a year)

DEANS

College of Industrial Technology: Asst Prof. PREECHA ONG-AREE
Faculty of Agro-Industry: Asst Prof. MALEE SIMSRISAKUL (acting)
Faculty of Applied Arts: Assoc. Prof. SURAPHI TONSIENGSOM (acting)
Faculty of Applied Science: Asst Prof. WICHAI SURACHERDKIATI
Faculty of Engineering: Asst Prof. Dr SIRISAK HARNCHOOWONG
Faculty of Information Technology: Assoc. Prof. Dr MONCHAI TIANTONG (acting)
Faculty of Technical Education: Asst Prof. Dr PISIT METHAPATARA
Faculty of Technology and Industrial Management: PEERASAK SAREKUL
Graduate College: Asst Prof. Dr VIBOON CHUNKAG

KING MONGKUT'S UNIVERSITY OF TECHNOLOGY THONBURI

126 Pracha-utit Rd, Bangmod, Thungkruh, Bangkok 10140

Telephone: (2) 470-8000
E-mail: int.off@kmutt.ac.th
Internet: www.kmutt.ac.th

Founded 1960 as Thonburi Technical Institute, combined with two other Institutes to form King Mongkut's Institute of Technology 1971, but regained autonomy as King Mongkut's Institute of Technology Thonburi 1986, present name and status 1998

State control

Languages of instruction: Thai, English

Academic year: June to March

Pres.: Assoc. Prof. Dr SAKARINDR BHUMIRATANA

Senior Vice-Pres. for Academic Affairs: Assoc. Prof. Dr SUVIT TIA

Senior Vice-Pres. for Admin. Affairs: Assoc. Prof. PRASERT KANTHAMANON

Vice-Pres. for Human Resources: Asst Prof. SUPANEE LERTTRILUCK

Vice-Pres. for Planning and Information: THANITSORN CHIRAPORNCHAI

Vice-Pres. for Property and Finance: Asst Prof. Dr TIPPAWAN PINANICHKUL

Vice-Pres. for Research: Asst Prof. Dr BUNDIT FUNGTAMMASAN

Vice-Pres. for Student Devt: Assoc. Prof. Dr CHAOWALIT LIMMANEEVICHITR

Registrar: APAKORN PADUNGSATAYAWONG

Library of 120,000 books, 2,200 periodicals, 2,000 CD-ROMs, 14 online databases

Number of teachers: 580

Number of students: 12,450

Publication: *Research and Development Journal* (4 a year)

DEANS

Faculty of Engineering: Assoc. Prof. Dr BUNCHAREON SIRINAOWAKUL

Faculty of Science: Assoc. Prof. Dr WORANUJ KIRDSINCHAI

Graduate School of Management and Innovation: Asst. Prof. Dr PASIT LORTERAPONG

Joint Graduate School of Energy and Environment: Assoc. Prof. Dr BUNDIT FUNGTHAMMASAN

School of Architecture and Design: MICHAEL PAIRPOL

School of Bioresources and Technology: Assoc. Prof. NARUMON JEYASHOKE

School of Energy, Environment and Materials: Dr PATTANA RAKKAWAMSUK

School of Industrial Education and Technology: Assoc. Prof. Dr SITTICHAI KAEWKUEKOOL

School of Information Technology: Asst Prof. Dr BORWORN PAPASRATORN

School of Liberal Arts: Asst Prof. Dr PORNAPIT DARASAWANG

PROFESSORS

CHUCHEEPSAKUL, S., Civil Engineering

CHULLABODHI, C., Energy Management Technology

JIRARATANANON, R., Chemical Engineering

SOPONRONNARIT, S., Energy Technology

WONGWISES, S., Mechanical Engineering

KRIRK UNIVERSITY

3 Ram-Indra Rd, Bangkhem, Bangkok 10220

Telephone: (2) 552-3500

E-mail: info@krirk.ac.th

Internet: www.krirk.ac.th

Founded 1952, current name 1995

Private control

Academic year: June to May

Pres.: NAPAT MANGALABRUKS

Vice-Pres. for Academic Affairs: SUPHAT THIRAWETCHACHAROENCHAI

Library of 68,000 vols, 419 periodicals

Number of teachers: 130

Number of students: 3,500

DEANS

Faculty of Business Administration: KUNTHON SISOEMPHOK

Faculty of Communication Arts: Prof. Major-Gen. SANITPONG KHEMTONG

Faculty of Economics: SUTHEP CHANDAWAN

Faculty of Law: Dr AMONRAT KUNSUTCHARIT

Faculty of Liberal Arts: Dr PHENPRAPHA PHATRANUKROM

Political Communication College: Dr NANTHANA NANTHAWAROPHAT

MAE FAH LUANG UNIVERSITY

333 Moo 1, Muang Dist., Chiangrai 57100

Telephone: (53) 916-000

E-mail: inter@mfu.ac.th

Internet: www.mfu.ac.th

Founded 1998

Public Autonomous University

Academic year: June to March (2 semesters)

Schools of agricultural technology, biotechnology, information technology, liberal arts, management science and science.

Pres.: Assoc. Prof. Dr VANCHAI SIRICHANA (acting)

Vice.-Pres.: Assoc. Prof. GANNAGA SATITTADA

Vice.-Pres.: Assoc. Prof. NAREEWAN CHINTAKANOND

Vice.-Pres.: PORNTHIP PHUTIYOTHIN

Vice.-Pres.: Asst Prof. PRITANA PRADIPASEAN

Vice.-Pres.: Assoc. Prof. Dr TED TESPRATEEP

Vice.-Pres.: Assoc. Prof. Group Capt. YUTANA TRA-NGARN

Library Dir: Dr PATHA SUWANNARAT

Library of 200,000 vols

Number of teachers: 350

Number of students: 9,200 (60 diploma, 8,190 undergraduate, 950 postgraduate)

DEANS

School of Agro-Industry: Assoc. Prof. Dr ORAPIN BHUMIBHAMON

School of Anti-Ageing and Regenerative Medicine: Prof. Dr THAMTHIWAT NARARATWANCHAI

School of Cosmetic Science: Assoc. Prof. Dr PANVIPA KRISDAPHONG

School of Health Science: Dr SAMRUENG KANJANAMETHAKUL

School of Information Technology: Group Capt. Dr THONGCHAI YOOYATIVONG

School of Law: Assoc. Prof. Dr CHALOR WONGWATTANAPHIKULA

School of Liberal Arts: Assoc. Prof. CHAKRAPAND WONGBURANAVART

School of Management: Assoc. Prof. Dr CHUTA MANUSPHAIBOON

School of Nursing: Assoc. Prof. SUPRANEE ATHASERI

School of Science: Prof. Dr SIRIWAT WONGSIRI

MAEJO UNIVERSITY

Sansai, Chiang Mai 50290

Telephone: (53) 873-000

Internet: www.mju.ac.th

Founded 1934, present name 1992 (fmrly Maejo Institute of Agricultural Technology)

State control

Language of instruction: Thai

Academic year: June to March

Pres.: Prof. Dr THEP PHONGPARNICH

Vice-Pres. for Admin.: Prof. ARKORN KANJANAPHACHOT

Vice-Pres. for Admin.: Asst. Prof. Dr CHAMNIAN YOSRAJ

Vice-Pres. for Assets and Spec. Affairs: PRAMOTE KLIBNGERN

Vice-Pres. for Education Quality Standards: Asst. Prof. PRASAN WONGMANEERUNG

Vice-Pres. for Information Technology and Communications: Asst. Prof. Dr. SIRICHAI UNSRISONG

Vice-Pres. for Planning and Int. Affairs: Prof. Dr NUMCHAI THANUPON

Vice-Pres. for Research and Academic Affairs: Assoc. Prof. Dr CHALERMCHAI PUNYADEE

Vice-Pres. for Student Devt and Alumni Relations: Prof. MANAS GUMPUKUL (acting)

Vice-Pres. for Student Devt and Alumni Relations: Assoc. Prof. ARKOM KANJANAPHACHOTE (acting)

Registrar: KRISSADA BHACKDEE

Librarian: WASSANA PHONGPAL

Library of 1,357 vols, 1,032 periodicals

Number of teachers: 1,190

Number of students: 12,920

Publications: *Journal of Agricultural Research and Extension* (6 a year, in Thai, with English summaries), *Maejo International Journal of Science and Technology*, *Maejo Journal* (6 a year, in Thai)

DEANS

Faculty of Agricultural Business: Asst. Prof. Dr PRAPHANT OSATHAPHANT

Faculty of Architecture and Environmental Design: SIRICHAI HONGVITYAKORN

Faculty of Business Admin.: BOONSOM SUKHAJIT

Faculty of Economics: Asst Prof. THANARUG MECKHAYAI

Faculty of Engineering and Agro-Industry: RACHATA CHEUVIROJ

Faculty of Fisheries Technology and Aquatic Resources: Assoc. Prof. Dr KRIANGSAK MENG-AMPAN

Faculty of Information and Communication: Assoc. Prof. Dr WITTAYA DAMRONGKIATTISAK

Faculty of Liberal Arts: Asst Prof. Dr SAOWALUCK CHAYTAWEEP

Faculty of Science: Asst Prof. PHUENGPORN NIUMSUP

School of Admin. Science: PRADTANA YOSSUCK

School of Tourism Devt: Assoc. Prof. Dr WEERAPON THONGMA

MAHANAKORN UNIVERSITY OF TECHNOLOGY

51 Cheum Sampan Rd, Nong Chok, Bangkok 10530

Telephone: (2) 988-3655

E-mail: pr@mut.ac.th

Internet: www.mut.ac.th

Founded 1990 as Mahanakorn College

Faculties of administration, engineering, graduate studies, science, science and information technology, veterinary science

Chancellor: Prof. Dr YONGYUT SATJAVANIT

Vice-Chancellor: YOUNGSAK KANATANAVANIT

Pres.: Assoc. Prof. Dr SITTHICHAI POOKAIYAUDOM

Vice-Pres. for Academic Affairs: CHIRAYUT MAHATTHONKUN

Vice-Pres. for Student Affairs: ATHIKHOM RUEKASABUT

Publication: *Engineering Transactions* (3 a year)

MAHASARAKHAM UNIVERSITY

Khamriang, Kantarawichai Dist., Maha Sarakham 44150

Telephone: (43) 75-4241

E-mail: iroffice@msu.ac.th

Internet: www.inter.msu.ac.th

Founded 1968 as Mahasarakham College of Education, became Mahasarakham campus of Srinakharinwirot Univ. in 1974, present name and status 1994

State control

Academic year: June to March

Languages of instruction: Thai, English

Pres.: Assoc. Prof. Dr SUPACHAI SAMAPPITO (acting)

Vice-Pres. for Academic Affairs and Research: Prof. Dr PREECHA PRATHEPHA
Vice-Pres. for Admin.: Dr RUMPAI GAENSAKOO
Vice-Pres. for Personnel Devt and Univ. Council Affairs: Asst Prof. THIENSAK MAK-KAPAN-OPAS
Dir for Academic Resource Centre: PORNPI-MOND MANOCHAI

Library of 1,539,936 books, 3,279 periodicals
Number of teachers: 990
Number of students: 39,120

DEANS

College of Graduate Studies: Assoc. Prof. Dr SUNAN SAIKRUSUN
College of Music: Dr PRAMOTE DANPRADIT
College of Politics and Governance: Assoc. Prof. SIDA SORNSRI
Faculty of Accounting and Management: Assoc. Prof. PHAPRUKEBARAMEE USSAHAWA-NITCHAKIT
Faculty of Architecture, Urban Design and Creative Arts: TARAWUT BOONLUA
Faculty of Education: Assoc. Prof. PRAWIT ERAWAN
Faculty of Engineering: Dr SAMPAN RITTI-DECH
Faculty of Environment and Resource Studies: Assoc. Prof. Dr SAMPAN RITTIDECH (acting)
Faculty of Fine and Applied Arts: PEERAPONG SENSAI
Faculty of Humanities and Social Sciences: Dr THAVEESILP SUBWATTANA
Faculty of Informatics: Dr SUJIN BUTDISUWAN
Faculty of Medicine: Prof. Dr REON SOMANA
Faculty of Nursing: Assoc. Prof. Dr DARUNEE RUJKORAKARN
Faculty of Pharmacy: Dr JUNTIP KANJANASILP
Faculty of Public Health: Dr SONGKRAMCHAI LEETHONGDEE
Faculty of Science: Assoc. Prof. THIENSAK MAKKAPAN-OPAS (acting)
Faculty of Technology: Assoc. Prof. Dr ANU-CHITA MOONGNGARM
Faculty of Tourism and Management: Dr SOMKIET POOPATWIBOON
Faculty of Veterinary Sciences: Assoc. Prof. Dr WORAPHON ENGWANICH

MAHIDOL UNIVERSITY

999 Phuttamonthon 4 Rd, Salaya, Phutta-monthon, Nakorn Pathom 73170

Telephone: (2) 849-6230
E-mail: opinter@mahidol.ac.th
Internet: www.mahidol.ac.th

Founded 1888, as Siriraj Medical School; present name 1969
State control

Pres.: Prof. PIYASAKOL SAKOLSATAYADORN
Vice-Pres.: Prof. NAPATAWN BANCHUIN
Vice-Pres. for Academic Infrastructures Devt: Assoc. Prof. SUPACHAI TANGWONGSAN
Vice-Pres. for Admin. and Univ. Ccl Sec.: Prof. PASSIRI NISALAK
Vice-Pres. for Amnaj Charoen Campus: BOONSANONG BOONMEE
Vice-Pres. for Campus Devt: Asst Prof. NAKORN HAMAH
Vice-Pres. for Collaboration and Networking: Assoc. Prof. CHURNRURTAI KANCHANACHITRA
Vice-Pres. for Education: Assoc. Prof. SUNANTA VIBULJAN
Vice-Pres. for Finance and Assets: Assoc. Prof. SATIT HOTRAKITYA
Vice Pres. for Human Resources and Quality Devt: Prof. PRASIT WATANAPA
Vice Pres. for Int. Relations: Assoc. Prof. EMORN WASANTWISUT
Vice-Pres. for Law and Regulation Devt: Asst Prof. SINGHAPAN TONGSAWAS
Vice-Pres. for Nakhon Sawan Campus: Dr SOMPONG YOONGTONG

Vice-Pres. for Policy and Informatics Technology: Assoc. Prof. SORANIT SILTHARM
Vice-Pres. for Research and Academic Affairs: Prof. SANSANEE CHAIYAROJ
Vice-Pres. for Student and Univ. Affairs: Assoc. Prof. PREECHA SOONTRANAN

Library of 540,118 vols, 186,663 bound periodicals, 4,247 current periodicals, 15,961 audiovisual units, 97,786 theses, 79 online databases; 38,193 ejournals and 65,976 ebooks, 21 libraries
Number of teachers: 3,600 (170 full profs, 791 assoc. profs, 822 asst profs and 1,817 lecturers)
Number of students: 25,130

Publications: *Environment and Natural Resources Journal* (2 a year), *Journal of Applied Animal Science* (3 a year), *Journal of Health Education* (3 a year), *Journal of Language and Culture* (2 a year), *Journal of Nursing Science* (3 a year), *Journal of Population and Social Studies* (2 a year), *Journal of Public Health* (3 a year), *Journal of Public Health Admin.* (2 a year), *Journal of Public Health and Devt* (3 a year), *Journal of Public Health Nursing* (3 a year), *Journal of Ratchasuda College for Research and Development of Persons with Disabilities* (2 a year), *Journal of Religion and Culture* (2 a year), *Journal of Sahasat* (2 a year), *Journal of Tropical Medicine and Parasitology* (2 a year), *Mahidol Journal* (2 a year), *Mahidol Dental Journal* (3 a year), *Mahidol University Journal of Pharmaceutical Sciences* (4 a year), *MUMJ-Mahidol University Music Journal* (2 a year), *Music Journal* (12 a year), *Quality of Life and Law Journal* (2 a year), *Pacific Journal of Allergy and Immunology* (4 a year), *Ramathibodi Medical Journal* (4 a year), *Ramathibodi Nursing Journal* (4 a year), *ScienceAsia—Journal of the Science Society of Thailand* (4 a year), *Siriraj Medical Journal* (12 a year), *Southeast Asian Journal of Tropical Medicine and Public Health* (4 a year), *The Journal: Journal of the Faculty of Arts* (2 a year), *Thai Journal of Phytopharmacy* (2 a year)

DEANS

Faculty of Dentistry: Assoc. Prof. THEERA-LAKSNA SUDDHASTHIRA
Faculty of Engineering: Asst Prof. RAWIN RAVIWONGSE
Faculty of Environmental and Resource Studies: Asst Prof. SITTIPONG DILOKWANICH
Faculty of Graduate Studies: Prof. BANCHONG MAHAISAVARIYA
Faculty of Information and Communication Technology: Assoc. Prof. JARERNSRI MITR-PANONT
Faculty of Liberal Arts: Prof. PRASIT WATA-NAPA (acting)
Faculty of Medical Technology: Prof. VIRA-PONG PRACHAYASITTIKUL
Faculty of Medicine, Ramathibodi Hospital: Prof. RAJATA RAJATANAVIN
Faculty of Medicine, Siriraj Hospital: Clinical Prof. TEERAWAT KULTHANAN
Faculty of Nursing: Assoc. Prof. FONGCUM TILOKSKULCHAI
Faculty of Pharmacy: Assoc. Prof. CHUTHA-MANEE SUTHISISANG (acting)
Faculty of Physical Therapy: Assoc. Prof. ROONGTIWA VACHALATHITI
Faculty of Public Health: Assoc. Prof. PHI-TAYA CHARUPOONPHOL
Faculty of Science: Prof. SKORN MONGKOLSUK
Faculty of Social Sciences and Humanities: Assoc. Prof. WARIYA CHINWANNO
Faculty of Tropical Medicine: Assoc. Prof. PRATAP SINGHASIVANON
Faculty of Veterinary Science: Assoc. Prof. PARNTEP RATANAKORN

NARESUAN UNIVERSITY

Phitsanulok 65000

Telephone: (55) 261-000
E-mail: international@nu.ac.th
Internet: www.nu.ac.th

Founded 1990
State control
Academic year: June to March

Library of 120,000 vols
Number of teachers: 870
Number of students: 21,400

Publication: *Naresuan University Journal*

NATIONAL INSTITUTE OF DEVELOPMENT ADMINISTRATION

118 Seri Thai Rd, Klongchan, Bangkapi, Bangkok 10240

Telephone: (2) 377-7400
E-mail: nisnida@nida.nida.ac.th
Internet: www.nida.ac.th

Founded 1966
State control
Languages of instruction: Thai, English
Academic year: June to May (3 semesters)

Pres.: Assoc. Prof. Dr PREECHA JARUNGIDANAN
Vice-Pres. for Academic Affairs: Assoc. Prof. Dr SAGOL JARIYAVIDYANONT
Vice-Pres. for Admin.: Assoc. Prof. CHAMAI-PORN KUNAKEMAKORN
Vice-Pres. for Planning: Prof. Dr CHARTCHAI NA CHIANGMAI

Library of 233,000 vols
Number of teachers: 160
Number of students: 10,400

Publications: *NIDA Bulletin* (6 a year), *Thai Journal of Development Administration* (4 a year)

DEANS

School of Applied Statistics: Assoc. Prof. Dr JIRAWAN JITHAVECH
School of Business Administration: Dr THA-KOL NUNTHIRAPAKORN
School of Development Economics: Asst Prof. Dr WISARN PUPPHAVESA
School of Language and Communication: Assoc. Prof. Dr PATCHAREE POKASAMRIT
School of Public Administration: Prof. Dr SOMBAT THAMRONGTHANYAWONG
School of Social Development: Asst Prof. Dr TONG-ON MUNJAITON

PROFESSORS

School of Applied Statistics (tel. (2) 375-8944; e-mail jirawan@nida.nida.ac.th):

SUWATTEE, P., Statistics

School of Business Administration (tel. (622) 375-8874; e-mail thakol@nida.nida.ac.th):

CHAMNONG, V., Organizational Behaviour

School of Public Administration (tel. (662) 375-1296; e-mail sombat@nida.nida.ac.th):

CHANGRIEN, P., Political Science
PERMANJIT, G., City and Regional Planning
THAMRONGTHANYAWONG, S., Public Policy and Planning

School of Social Development (tel. (662) 375-9111; e-mail tangon@nida.nida.ac.th):

BHANTHUMNAVIN, D., Social Psychology
NORANITPADUNGKARN, C., Social Sciences
SMUCKARN, S., Social Psychology

PAYAP UNIVERSITY

Amphur Muang, Chiang Mai 50000

Telephone: (53) 851-478
E-mail: intexch@payap.ac.th
Internet: www.payap.ac.th

Founded 1974
Private control
Languages of instruction: English, Thai

Academic year: June to March (Thai Programme),September to April (English Programme)

Pres.: Dr PENPILAI RITHAKANANONE

Vice-Pres. for Academic Affairs: Dr YUWALAK CHIVAKIDAKARN

Vice-Pres. for Finance: Dr RUX PROHMPALIT

Vice-Pres. for Int. Affairs: MARTHA G. BUTT

Vice-Pres. for Planning and Devt: Dr TAWEE-SAK SUPASA

Vice-Pres. for Religious Affairs: Dr ESTHER WAKEMAN

Librarian: SUNTREE RATAYA-ANANT

Library of 125,100 vols

Number of teachers: 390

Number of students: 7,000

Publication: *Payap Journal* (1 a year)

DEANS

College of Music: Dr CHAIPRUCK MEKARA

Faculty of Accountancy, Finance and Banking: SUPREEYA MANEESAI

Faculty of Arts: MALEE KONGWANNIT

Faculty of Business Administration: Dr TATIKUN CHAIWAN

Faculty of Communication Arts: NARUMOL VANTANEE

Faculty of Economics: Dr KITJA TOPAIBOON

Faculty of Law: Dr SANYALUX PANWATTANALIKIT

Faculty of Nursing: KAMOLWAN DISABUT

Faculty of Science: Dr PISAMAI KIJKUOKOOL

Faculty of Social Sciences and Humanities: CHULEEPORN WIMUKTANON

International College: Dr SOMBOON PANYAKOM

McCormick Faculty of Nursing: Dr. PANIDA SENANANT

McGilvary College of Divinity: Dr SATANUN BOONYAKIET

PRINCE OF SONGKLA UNIVERSITY

15 Karnjanavanich Rd, Hat Yai, Songkhla 90110

Telephone: (74) 446824

E-mail: psu-international@psu.ac.th

Internet: www.psu.ac.th

Founded 1967

State control

Languages of instruction: English, Thai

Academic year: June to March (2 semesters)

4 Campuses in Pattani, Phuket, Surat, Trang

Pres.: Assoc. Prof. Dr CHUSAK LIMSAKUL

Vice-Pres. for Academic Affairs (Hat-Yai Campus): Assoc. Prof. Dr CHUTAMAS SATASOOK

Vice-Pres. for Academic and International Affairs (Pattani Campus): Asst Prof. Dr YUPADEE CHAISUKSANT

Vice-Pres. for Assets and Outreach: PUTTISAK PUTTAWIBUL

Vice-Pres. for Hat-Yai Campus: PHICHIT RERNGSANGVATANA

Vice-Pres. for Int. Affairs: Prof. Dr AMORNRAT PHONGDARA

Vice-Pres. for IT and Physical Structure: Assoc. Prof. Dr KRERKCHAI THONGNOO

Vice-Pres. for Pattani Campus: Asst Prof. SOMPONG THONGPONG

Vice-Pres. for Phuket Campus: Assoc. Prof. PUWADON BOOTRAT

Vice-Pres. for Planning and Finance (Hat Yai Campus): Asst Prof. Dr NIWAT KEAWPRADUB

Vice-Pres. for Planning and System Devt (Pattani Campus): Asst Prof. NOPPORN RIENTHONG

Vice-Pres. for Research System and Graduate Studies: Assoc. Prof. Dr PERAPONG TEKASAKUL

Vice-Pres. for Student and Cultural Devt (Pattani Campus): Asst Prof. NIFARID RADEN-AHMAD

Vice-Pres. for Student Devt and Alumni Affairs (Hat Yai Campus): Assoc. Prof. Dr WORAWUT WISUTMETHANGOON

Vice-Pres. for Surat Thani Campus: Assoc. Prof. Dr CHAROEN NAKASON

Vice-Pres. for Trang Campus: Asst. Prof. PAKTRA KOOBURAT

Number of teachers: 1,500

Number of students: 13,100

Publication: *PSU Arts and Culture*

DEANS

Faculty of Agro-Industry: Prof. Dr SOOTTAWAT BENJAKUL (acting)

Faculty of Arts and Management Sciences: Dr SUTHIJIT CHOENGTHONG

Faculty of Communication Sciences: Asst Prof. WALAKKAMOL CHANGKAMOL

Faculty of Dentistry: Assoc. Prof. Dr CHAIRAT CHAROEMRATROTE

Faculty of Economics: Asst Prof. Dr BUSSABONG CHAICHAROENWATANA (acting)

Faculty of Education: Asst Prof. Dr NATHAVIT PORTJANATANTI

Faculty of Engineering: Assoc. Prof. Dr UDOMPHON PUETPAIBOON

Faculty of Environmental Management: Asst Prof. Dr ROTCHANATCH DARNSAWASD

Faculty of Fine and Applied Arts: Assoc. Prof. RAWEWAN CHAUMPLUK

Faculty of Hospitality and Tourism: Assoc. Prof. Dr PRATHANA KUNNAOVAKUN

Faculty of Humanities and Social Sciences: Assoc. Prof. AWANG LANUI

Faculty of International Studies: Asst Prof. Dr SONTAYA ANAKASIRI

Faculty of Law: WASIN SUWANNARAT

Faculty of Liberal Arts: Assoc. Prof. Dr ADISA TEO

Faculty of Management Science: Asst Prof. JONGPID SIRIRAT

Faculty of Medicine: Assoc. Prof. SUTHAM PINJAROEN

Faculty of Medical Technology: Assoc. Prof. Dr SIROJ JITSURONG

Faculty of Natural Resources: Asst Prof. TAWEESAK NIYOMBANDITH

Faculty of Nursing: Assoc. Prof. Dr ARANYA CHAOWALIT

Faculty of Pharmaceutical Science: Asst Prof. Dr SIRIRAT PINSUWAN

Faculty of Political Science: Asst Prof. CHITCHANOK RAHIMMULA

Faculty of Science: Assoc. Prof. Dr WILAIWAN CHOTIGEAT

Faculty of Sciences and Industrial Technology: Assoc. Prof. Dr OPART PIMPA

Faculty of Technology and Environment: Assoc. Prof. Dr PUN THONGCHUMNUM

Faculty of Traditional Thai Medicine: Assoc. Prof. Dr SANAN SUBHADHIRASAKUL (acting)

Faculty of Veterinary Science: Assoc. Prof. Dr USA CHETHANOND (Dir)

Graduate School: Asst Prof. Dr TEERAPON SRICHANA

RAMKHAMHAENG UNIVERSITY

Ramkhamhaeng Rd, Huamark, Bangkok 10240

Telephone: (2) 310-8000

E-mail: admin@ram1.ru.ac.th

Internet: www.ru.ac.th

Founded 1971

State control

Languages of instruction: Thai, English

Academic year: June to March (2 semesters)

Campus in Bang Na and 23 regional campuses; also faculties of fine and applied arts, hospitality management, human resource development, mass communication technology, public health; graduate school; institute of international studies

Pres.: Asst Prof. WUTISAK LARPCHAROENSAP

Rector: Prof. RANGSAN SAENGSOOK

Vice-Rector for Academic Affairs and Research: Prof. Dr CHUTA THIANTHAI

Vice-Rector for Admin.: Assoc. Prof. PRASAT SANGASILP

Vice-Rector for Amnartcharoen Province Regional Campus: Asst Prof. CHALERMCHAI PIWRUANGNNONT

Vice-Rector for Campus Affairs: Assoc. Prof. KIM CHAISANSOOK

Vice-Rector for Cultural Affairs: Dr WICHAI SUNGPRAPAI

Vice-Rector for Devt: Assoc. Prof. WIRAT SANGUANWONWAN

Vice-Rector for Educational Technology: Asst Prof. Dr PANYA SIRIROJ

Vice-Rector for Finance: Assoc. Prof. SOMCHINTANA SIVALI

Vice-Rector for Gen. Affairs: Assoc. Prof. ARUNTAVADEE PHATNIBUL

Vice-Rector for Int. Affairs: Assoc. Prof. RAMPAI SIRIMANAKUL

Vice-Rector for Khon Kaen Province Regional Campus: Assoc. Prof. VICHAI THARANONT

Vice-Rector for Legal Affairs and Property: Prof. SURACHAI SUWANPREECHA

Vice-Rector for Nakhornpanom Province Regional Campus: Asst Prof. VIBOON TOVANABOOT

Vice-Rector for Nakhornratsrima Province Regional Campus: Assoc. Prof. VISIT TAWEESET

Vice-Rector for Nakhornsrithammarat Province Regional Campus: Assoc. Prof. Dr AROM CHANUANCHIT

Vice-Rector for Policy and Planning: Assoc. Prof. MANOP PRAMANACHOTE

Vice-Rector for Prachinburi Province Regional Campus: Asst Prof. CHAMNAN TEMMUANGPUK

Vice-Rector for Prae Province Regional Campus: Assoc. Prof. KULYANEE TARASUEB

Vice-Rector for Public Relations: Assoc. Prof. Dr WISANU SUWANA-PERM

Vice-Rector of the Rector's Office: Assoc. Prof. Dr KHOSIT INTAWONGSE

Vice-Rector for Sri Sa Ket Province Regional Campus: WICHIAN CHUENCHOB

Vice-Rector for Student Affairs: Assoc. Prof. SUMETH KAEWPRAG

Vice-Rector for Sukhothai Province Regional Campus: Asst Prof. SAMRAN SOMBOONPHOL

Vice-Rector for Trang Regional Campus: Assoc. Prof. PETJARAPORN JANTARASUT

Vice-Rector for Univ. Affairs: Assoc. Prof SITTIPAN BUDDHAHUN

Vice-Rector for Uthaithani Province Regional Campus: Asst Prof. ROENGRAK JAMPANGOEN

Vice-Rector for Welfare: Assoc. Prof. NOPPAKUN KUNACHEVA

Number of teachers: 860

Number of students: 340,300

DEANS

Faculty of Business Administration: Prof. RANGSAN SAENGSOOK (acting)

Faculty of Economics: Assoc. Prof. VANCHAI RIMVITAGAYORN

Faculty of Education: Assoc. Prof. RAVIWAN SRIKRAMKRAN

Faculty of Engineering: Asst Prof. SUVAT SRIVITHAYARAKS

Faculty of Humanities: Assoc. Prof. Dr PIT SOMPONG

Faculty of Law: Assoc. Prof. JARAL LENGVITTAYA

Faculty of Political Science: Assoc. Prof. PRONCHAI DHEBPANYA

Faculty of Science: Assoc. Prof. SUPOTE CHAITIUMVONG

RANGSIT UNIVERSITY

52/347, Muang Ake, Phaholyothin Rd, Tambon-Lakhok, 12000 Pathum Thani

Telephone: (2) 997-2200
E-mail: info@rangsit.rsu.ac.th
Internet: www.rsu.ac.th

Founded 1985
Private control
Languages of instruction: English, Thai
Academic year: May to April

Pres.: Dr ARTHIT OURAIRAT
Vice-Pres. for Academic Affairs: Asst Prof. Dr NARES PANTARATORN
Vice-Pres. for Admin.: AUMNOUVUT SARASALIN
Vice-Pres. for Planning and Quality Devt: Dr ARTAWIT OURAIRAT
Vice-Pres. for Student Affairs: Dr PHONGPAT ANUMUTRATHCHAKIJ
Library Dir: Dr MALIRAN PRADITTEERA

Library of 106,895 vols
Number of teachers: 2,000
Number of students: 30,000

SIAM UNIVERSITY

235 Petchkasem Rd, Phasi-Charoen, Bangkok 10160

Telephone: (2) 867-8088
E-mail: siam@siam.edu
Internet: www.siam.edu

Founded 1973
Private control
Academic year: June to March

Pres.: Dr PORNCHAI MONGKHONVANIT
Vice-Pres. for Academic Affairs: Prof. Dr NIMNUAN SRICHAD
Vice-Pres. for Planning and Devt: Dr PAYUNGSAK JANTRASURIN
Vice-Pres. for Public Affairs and Cooperative Education: THANAVADEE BOONLUE
Vice-Pres. for Research: Prof. Dr NIPONE SOOKPREEDEE
Registrar: SURADEJ PRUGSAMATZ
Librarian: JIRAPAT HARNNUSSORN

Library of 161,561 vols
Number of teachers: 530
Number of students: 14,300
Publications: *Cultural Approach* (2 a year), *Engineering Journal of Siam University* (2 a year), *Journal of Nursing, Siam University* (2 a year), *Siam Business Review* (3 a year), *Siam University Law Journal* (1 a year), *Siam University Review* (6 a year)

DEANS

Graduate School of Business: Dr VICHIT SUPINIT
Graduate School of Communication Arts: Assoc. Prof. Dr THANAVADEE BOONLUE
Graduate School of Education: Assoc. Prof. Dr AMORNCHAI TANTIMEDH
Graduate School of Engineering: Dr VANCHAI RIJIRAVANICH
Graduate School of Information Technology: Assoc. Prof. Dr WICHIAN PREMCHAISWADI
Graduate School of Public Administration: Assoc. Prof. Dr SURAPOL KANCHANACHITRA
School of Business Administration: Dr SUMRIT TIANDUM
School of Communication Arts: Assoc. Prof. Dr SIRICHAI SIRIKAYA
School of Engineering: Assoc. Prof. SARAVUTH VORASUMANTA
School of Law: Dr SOMMAI CHANRUANG
School of Liberal Arts: Dr SUBORDAS WARMSINGH
School of Nursing Science: Assoc. Prof. ORNTIPA SONGSIRI
School of Science: Dr KANJANA MAHATTANATAWEE

SILPAKORN UNIVERSITY

22 Boromrachachonnani Rd, Taling-Chan, Bangkok 10170

Telephone: (2) 880-7374
E-mail: webmaster@su.ac.th
Internet: www.su.ac.th

Founded 1943
State control
Language of instruction: Thai
Academic year: June to March (2 semesters)

Pres.: Dr UTHAI DULYAKASEM
Vice-Pres. for Academic and Research Affairs: Assoc. Prof. Dr MANEE LUANGTANA-ANAN
Vice-Pres. for Admin. Affairs: Asst Prof. RAPEEPUN CHALONGSUK
Vice-Pres. for Art and Culture: Asst Prof. YANAWIT KUNCHAETHONG
Vice-Pres. for Planning and Devt: Assoc. Prof. CHARUNPAT PUVANANT
Vice-Pres. for Student Affairs: PORNSAWAN AMARANONTA
Vice-Pres. for Quality Assurance in Education: Asst Prof. Dr RENU VEJARATPIMOL
Registrar: SAICHON SAJJANIT
Librarian: KANCHANA SUKONTHAMANEE

Library of 552,330 vols
Number of teachers: 1,020
Number of students: 22,340

DEANS

Faculty of Music: THANATORN JIARAKUN
Graduate School: Assoc. Prof. Dr SIRICHAI CHINATANKUL
Silpakorn University International College (SUIC): Assoc. Prof. Dr SOMPID KATTIYAPIKUL (Dir)

CONSTITUENT CAMPUSES

Phetchaburi Information Technology Campus: 1 Moo 3, Cha-am, Pranburi Rd, Samphraya, Amphoe Cha Am, Phetchaburi 76120; tel. (3) 259-4043

DEANS

Faculty of Animal Sciences and Agricultural Technology: Assoc. Prof. Dr KRIENGSAK POONSUK
Faculty of Information and Communication Technology: Asst Prof. CHAICHARN THAVARAVEJ
Faculty of Management Sciences: Asst Prof. Dr WANCHAO SUTANANTA

Sanamchand Palace Campus: 6 Rajamaka Nai Rd, Mueang Dist., Nakhon Pathom 73000; tel. (34) 253-910; Vice-Pres. Dr CHACORN VIPUSANAVANISH; Asst Pres. for Student Affairs Asst Prof. Dr BUSARAKORN MAHAYOTHEE; Librarian KANCHANA SUKONTHAMANEE

DEANS

Faculty of Arts: Asst Prof. Dr MANEEPIN PHROMSUTHIRAK
Faculty of Education: Assoc. Prof. Dr KANIT KHEOVICHAI
Faculty of Engineering and Industrial Technology: Asst Prof. Dr JESDAWAN WICHITWECHKARN
Faculty of Pharmacy: Assoc. Prof. Dr JURAIRAT NANTANIT
Faculty of Science: Asst Prof. Dr JARUNGSAENG LAKSANABOONSONG

Wang Thapra Palace Campus: 31 Na-Phra Lan Rd, Phra Nakhon Dist., Bangkok 10200; tel. (2) 623-6115; Vice-Pres. Asst Prof. SOMCHAI EKPANYAKUL; Asst Pres. for Student Affairs Assoc. Prof. TINNAKORN KASORNSUWAN

DEANS

Faculty of Archaeology: Assoc. Prof. SAYAN PRAICHARNJIT (acting)
Faculty of Architecture: Assoc. Prof. CHINASAK TANDIKUL

Faculty of Decorative Arts: Assoc. Prof. EAKACHART JONEURAIRATANA
Faculty of Painting, Sculpture and Graphic Arts: Assoc. Prof. PARINYA TANTISUK

SOUTH-EAST ASIA UNIVERSITY

19/1 Phetkasem Rd, Nona Khaem, Bangkok 10160

Telephone: (2) 807-4500
E-mail: webmaster@sau.ac.th
Internet: www.sau.ac.th

Pres.: Assoc. Prof. Dr NARONG SINSAWASDI

Founded 1973 as South-East Asia College, univ. status 1992

Faculties of arts and sciences, business administration, engineering, law; graduate school; language institute

Library of 68,000 vols, 650 journals
Number of students: 5,190

SRINAKHARINWIROT UNIVERSITY

114 Sukhumvit 23, Bangkok 10110

Telephone: (2) 664-1000
E-mail: ird@swu.ac.th
Internet: www.swu.ac.th

Founded 1954, univ. status 1974
State control
Language of instruction: Thai
Academic year: June to May

Pres.: Assoc. Prof. Dr SUMONTHA PROMBOON
Vice-Pres. for Academic Affairs: Assoc. Prof. Dr SAKCHAI NIRUNTHAWEE
Vice-Pres. for Admin. Affairs: Assoc. Prof. Dr PAISAL WANGPHANICH
Vice-Pres. for Arts and Culture: VINAI BHURAHONGSE
Vice-Pres. for Finance and Personnel: Assoc. Prof. Dr PINITI RATANANUKUL
Vice-Pres. for Int. Relations: Dr SUTASSI SMUTHKOCHORN
Vice-Pres. for Planning and Devt: Asst Prof. Dr CHAVANEE TONGROACH
Vice-Pres. for Research: Prof. Dr SERMSAK WISALAPORN
Vice-Pres. for Student Affairs: Asst Prof. MANEE THONGGOOM
Registrar: ORAPIN KAEWLAI
Dir of Central Library: Asst Prof. NONGNATH CHAIRAT

Library: see under Libraries and Archives
Number of teachers: 1,520
Number of students: 16,900

Publication: journals in humanities, nursing, pharmaceutical science, physical education and science, each 2 a year

DEANS

Faculty of Dentistry: Assoc. Prof. Dr TIPAPORN VONGSURASIT
Faculty of Education: Assoc. Prof. Dr KHOMPET CHATSUPAKUL
Faculty of Engineering: AREE HANSUEBSAI
Faculty of Fine Arts: Prof. Dr WIROON TUNGCHAROEN
Faculty of Health Science: Assoc. Prof. Dr WITTAYA TONSUWONNONT
Faculty of Humanities: Asst Prof. SUPA PANCHAROEN
Faculty of Medicine: Assoc. Prof. ARUNWONG THEPCHATRI
Faculty of Nursing: Assoc. Prof. Dr TASSANA BOONTHONG
Faculty of Pharmaceutical Sciences: Lt-Col Dr NOPDOL THONGNOPNUA
Faculty of Physical Education: Asst Prof. PHAN JIARANAI
Faculty of Science: Dr YUVADEE NAKAPADUNGRUT
Faculty of Social Sciences: Asst Prof. KAWEE WORRAKAWIN

Graduate School: Assoc. Prof. Dr NAPAPORN HAWANONDHA

SRIPATUM UNIVERSITY

Bangkhen Campus, 61 Phaholyotin Rd, Jatujak, Bangkok 10900

Telephone: (2) 579-1111
E-mail: webspu@spu.ac.th
Internet: www.spu.ac.th

Founded 1970
Languages of instruction: Thai, English
Academic year: August to April

Pres.: RUTCHANEEPORN POOKAYAPORN PHUK-KAMARN
Vice-Pres. for Academic Affairs: Asst Prof. Dr NIMNUAN SRICHAD
Vice-Pres. for Admin.: CHUA MAICHAROEN
Vice-Pres. for Student Affairs: SOPIT PANOMAI
Vice-Pres. for Technology: Assoc. Prof. Dr SUCHAI THANAWASTIEN
Library Dir: Asst Prof. Dr NAMTIP VIPAWIN

Library of 104,000 vols
Number of teachers: 490
Number of students: 16,440 (16,000 under-graduate, 440 postgraduate)

DEANS

Faculty of Accounting: KALAYAPORN BANMARUNG BURKE
Faculty of Architecture: Asst Prof. SUTHON VIRIYASOMBOON
Faculty of Business Administration: Dr KAMOL CHAIYAWAT
Faculty of Communication Arts: Assoc. Prof. ARUNEEPRAPA HOMSETHI
Faculty of Economics: SOMNUEK TANGEHAROEN
Faculty of Engineering: Assoc. Prof. NARONG U-THANOM
Faculty of Informatics: AMNUAY MUTHITAJAROEN
Faculty of Law: PARINYA PATHUMPONG
Faculty of Liberal Arts: Asst Prof. Dr GLORIA VIDHEECHAROEN
Graduate School: Dr NITINAI BUNNAG

SUKHOTHAI THAMMATHIRAT OPEN UNIVERSITY

Muang Thong Thani, Chaengwattana Rd, Bangpood, Pakkret, Nonthaburi 11120

Telephone: (2) 504-7777
E-mail: if.proffice@stou.ac.th
Internet: www.stou.ac.th

Founded 1978
State control
Language of instruction: Thai
Academic year: July to April (2 semesters)

Pres.: Assoc. Prof. Dr CHAILERD PICHIT-PORNCHAI
Vice-Pres. for Academic Affairs: Prof. Dr SIRIWAN SRIPAHOL
Vice-Pres. for Admin. and Univ. Ccl Affairs: Assoc. Prof. VORAVUTH THEPTHONG
Vice-Pres. for Corporate Communications and Int. Affairs: Asst Prof. ORASA PANKHAO
Vice-Pres. for Educational Services: Assoc. Prof. NUTTAPORN PIMPARYON
Vice-Pres. for Financial Affairs: Assoc. Prof. Dr GALLAYANEE PARKATT
Vice-Pres. for Human Resources and Systems Devt: Asst Prof. CHERNCHOK SOANKWAN
Vice-Pres. for IT: Assoc. Prof. Dr VIPA JAROENPUNTARUK
Vice-Pres. for Planning and Research: Assoc. Prof. Dr JAKKRIS SIVADECHATHEP (acting)
Vice-Pres. for Univ. Assets: Assoc. Prof. Dr BOONSRI PROMMAPUN

Library of 651,000 vols, 1,930 periodicals
Number of teachers: 400
Number of students: 221,300

DEANS

School of Agricultural Cooperatives: Asst Prof. Dr PONGPHAN THIENHIRUN
School of Communication Arts: Assoc. Prof. SUMON YUESIN
School of Economics: Asst Prof. Dr SOMCHIN SUNTAVARUK
School of Educational Studies: Assoc. Prof. Dr SOMPRASONG WITTAYAGIAT
School of Health Science: Asst Prof. Dr ADISAK SATTAM
School of Home Economics: Assoc. Prof. Dr JUMPOL NIMPANICH (acting)
School of Law: THIENCHAI NA NAKORN
School of Liberal Arts: Assoc. Prof. Dr PAITOON MIKUSOL
School of Management Science: Assoc. Prof. SUNA SITHILERTPRASIT
School of Political Science: Assoc. Prof. ROSALIN SIRIYAPHAN
School of Science and Technology: Assoc. Prof. Dr JUMPOL NIMPANICH

SURANAREE UNIVERSITY OF TECHNOLOGY

111 University Ave, Muang Dist., Nakhon Ratchasima 30000

Telephone: (44) 224-141
E-mail: cenintaf@sut.ac.th
Internet: www.sut.ac.th

Founded 1990
State control
Languages of instruction: English, Thai
Academic year: May to April

Rector: Prof. Dr PRASART SUEBKA
Vice-Rector for Academic Affairs: Prof. Dr SUKIT LIMPIJUMNONG
Vice-Rector for Admin. Affairs: Dr WUT DANKITTIKUL
Vice-Rector for Devt: Assoc. Prof. Dr RANGSAN WONGSAN
Vice-Rector for Gen. Affairs: Asst Prof. Dr ARAK TIRA-UMPHON
Vice-Rector for Planning: Assoc. Prof. Dr SITTICHAI SEANGATITH
Vice-Rector for Student Affairs: Dr GUNTIMA SIRIJEERACHAI
Registrar: Asst Prof. Dr AIM-ORN TASSANASORN
Librarian: Assoc. Prof. Dr PRAPAVADEE SUEBSONTHI

Library of 118,149 books, 415 periodicals
Number of teachers: 360
Number of students: 12,960 (11,260 under-graduate, 1,700 postgraduate)

DEANS

Institute of Agricultural Technology: Assoc. Prof. Dr SUWAYD NINGSANOND
Institute of Engineering: Asst Prof. Dr KONTORN CHAMNIPRASART
Institute of Medicine: Prof. Dr VANICH VANAPRUKS
Institute of Nursing: SRIKIAT ANANSAWAS
Institute of Science: Assoc. Prof. Dr PRAPAN MANYUM
Institute of Social Technology: Dr PEERASAK SIRIYOTIN

THAKSIN UNIVERSITY

140 Moo 4 Tambon Khao Roop Chang, Muang Dist., Song Khla 90000

Telephone: (74) 311-885
E-mail: tsuinter@tsu.ac.th
Internet: www.tsu.ac.th

Founded 1996

Pres.: SOMBOON CHITPONG

Faculties of education, humanities and social sciences, science; institute of Southern Thai studies

THAMMASAT UNIVERSITY

2 Prachand Rd, Bangkok 10200

Telephone: (2) 221-6111
E-mail: inter@tu.ac.th
Internet: www.tu.ac.th

Founded 1934
State control
Languages of instruction: Thai, English
Academic year: June to February (2 semesters), summer sessionMarch to May

Rector: Prof. Dr SURAPON NITIKRAIPOT
Vice-Rector for Academic Affairs: Prof. Dr SIRILUCK ROTCHANAKITUMNUAI
Vice-Rector for Devt Planning and Technology: Asst Prof. Dr PRODPRAN SIRITHEERASAS
Vice-Rector for Financial Admin.: Asst Prof. SURASAK LIKASITWATANAKUL
Vice-Rector for Gen. Admin. (Lampang Center): Asst Prof. KAMONTHIP CHAMKRAJANG
Vice-Rector for Gen. Admin. (Rangsit Center): Assoc. Prof. GASINEE WITOONCHART
Vice-Rector for Gen. Admin. (Tha Prachan Center): Assoc. Prof. Dr UDOM RATHAMARIT
Vice-Rector for Int. Affairs: Assoc. Prof. Dr CHULACHEEP CHINWANNO
Vice-Rector for Personnel: Assoc. Prof. HARIRAK SUTABUTRA
Vice-Rector for Research Devt: Assoc. Prof. Dr PREECHA WANICHSETAKUL
Vice-Rector for Student Affairs: Asst Prof. Dr PARINYA THEWANARUEMITKUL
Registration Office Dir: Asst Prof. Dr VIRAVAT CHANTACHOTE
Librarian: SRICHAN CHANCHEEWA

Library: see under Libraries and Archives
Number of teachers: 1,620
Number of students: 32,500

Publications: *Faculty Bulletin*, *Journal of Business Administration*, *Journal of Political Science*, *Social Work Journal*, *Thammasat Law Journal*, *Thammasat University Journal*

DEANS

College of Innovative Education: Assoc. Prof. M. R. PONGSVAS SVASTI
College of Interdisciplinary Studies: Assoc. Prof. Dr NANTANA RONAKIAT
Faculty of Allied Health Science: Prof. Dr VITHOON VIYANANT
Faculty of Architecture and Planning: Prof. Dr SANTIRAK PRASERTSUK
Faculty of Commerce and Accountancy: Assoc. Prof. Dr KULPATRA SIRODOM
Faculty of Dentistry: YUVABOON CHANCHAMCHAROON
Faculty of Economics: Assoc. Prof. Dr PATAMAWADEE SUZUKI
Faculty of Engineering: Assoc. Prof. Dr URUYA WEESAKUL
Faculty of Fine and Applied Arts: SUTHIDA KALAYANAROOJ
Faculty of Journalism and Mass Communication: Asst Prof. Dr PORNCHIT SOMBUTPHANICH
Faculty of Law: Prof. Dr SOMKIT LERTPAITHOON
Faculty of Liberal Arts: Assoc. Prof. Dr CHATCHAWADEE SARALAMBA
Faculty of Medicine: Assoc. Prof. CHITTINAD HAVANOND
Faculty of Nursing: Asst Prof. Dr SIRIPORN KHAMPALIKIT
Faculty of Political Science: Assoc. Prof. Dr SIRIPORN WAJJWALKU
Faculty of Public Health: Assoc. Prof. Dr NUNTAVARN VICHIT-VADAKAN
Faculty of Science and Technology: Assoc. Prof. SAITONG AMORNWICHET
Faculty of Social Administration: Asst Prof. Dr DECHA SUNGKAWAN
Faculty of Sociology and Anthropology: Asst Prof. PORNCHAI TRAKULWARANONT

Graduate School: Assoc. Prof. MANOON PAHIRAH

Pridi Banomyong International College: Assoc. Prof. Dr PIMPAN VESSAKOSOL

Sirindhon International Institute of Technology: Prof. Dr CHONGRAK POLPRASERT

UBON RATCHATHANI UNIVERSITY

85 Sathonlamark Rd, Warin Chamrap, Ubon Ratchathani 34190

Telephone: (45) 353-052

E-mail: intercoop@ubu.ac.th

Internet: www.ubu.ac.th

Founded 1987

State control

Languages of instruction: Englsih, Thai

Academic year: June to May

Pres.: Prof. Dr NONGNIT TEERAWATANASUK

Vice-Pres. for Academic Affairs: Dr UTITH INPRASIT

Vice-Pres. for Admin. and Community Relations: MANOON SRIVIRAT

Vice-Pres. for Facilities: NITISAK KAEWSENA

Vice President for Research and Innovations: Dr INTHIRA SAHEE

Vice-Pres. for Int. Relations: Prof. Dr PATAREEYA WISAIJORN

Vice-Pres. for Planning and Devt: Dr JUTHAMAS JITCHAROEN

Vice-Pres. for Research and Academic Services: Asst. Prof. Dr KUNGWAN THUMMASAENG

Vice-Pres. for Student Devt: Dr NARINTORN BOONBRAHM

Vice-Pres. for Student Affairs: THAI SANGTHEAN

Librarian: SUOACHAI HATHONGKHAM

Library of 221,483 vols of books, 53,618 periodicals, 17,561 audio visuals, 13 databases

Number of teachers: 650

Number of students: 13,700 (13,000 undergraduate, 600 masters, 100 doctoral)

DEANS

College of Medicine and Public Health: PUAN SUTHIPINITTHARM

Faculty of Agriculture: Assoc. Prof. Dr WATCHARAPONG WATTANAKUL

Faculty of Applied Arts and Design: Asst. Prof. Dr WANWALAI ATHIWASPONG (acting)

Faculty of Engineering: Prof. Dr NOTE SANGTIAN

Faculty of Law: BUNLEU KONGCHAN

Faculty of Liberal Arts: Asst. Prof. Dr KANOKWAN MANOROM (acting)

Faculty of Management Science: Dr WIROTE MANOPIMOKE

Faculty of Nursing: Dr SUREE TRUMIKABORWORN

Faculty of Pharmaceutical Science: Assoc. Prof. CHUTINUN PRASITPURIPRECHA

Faculty of Political Science: Assoc. Prof. Dr CHAIYAN RATCHAKUL

Faculty of Science: Asst Prof. JANPEN INTARAPRASERT

UNIVERSITY OF THE THAI CHAMBER OF COMMERCE

10/F Bldg 7, 126/1 Vibhavadi Rangsit Rd, Din Daeng, Bangkok 10400

Telephone: (2) 697-6000

E-mail: icutcc@gmail.com

Internet: www.utcc.ac.th

Founded 1940 as College of Commerce; current name and status 1984

Pres.: SAUWANEE THAIRUNGROJ

Dean: JAKARIN SRIMOON

Assoc. Dean for Academic Affairs: PORNPAN BOONPATTANAPORN

Assoc. Dean for Admin. Affairs: RATIRAT MAHASAP

Assoc. Dean for Student Affairs: PREEYANUCH CHANPRASERT

Library of 100,000 vols, 6,000 periodicals

WALAILAK UNIVERSITY

222 Thaiburi, Thasala Dist., Nakhon Si Thammarat 80160

Telephone: (75) 384-000

E-mail: wu@praduu.wu.ac.th

Internet: www.wu.ac.th

Pres.: Dr SUPAT POOPAKA

Founded 1992

State control

Institutes of agricultural technology, allied health sciences and public health, engineering and resources management, information science, liberal arts, management, nursing and science

Colleges and Institutes
AGRICULTURE

Rajamangola Institute of Technology, Surin Campus: Surin; tel. (44) 511-022; internet www.surin.rit.ac.th; f. 2001, fmrly Surin Agricultural College; 143 teachers; 2,289 students; Dir Asst Prof. Dr WIEHIEN OUNRUEN.

TIMOR-LESTE

The Higher Education System

Universidade Nacional Timór Lorosa'e (formerly Universitas Timor Timur), which was founded in 2000, predates Timor-Leste's (formerly East Timor) independence from Indonesia in 2002. It is Timor-Leste's principal institution of higher education. It was largely destroyed during civil unrest in 1999, but reopened in November 2000. In 2001 there were an estimated 6,349 students enrolled in tertiary education. Since 2000 there has been significant growth in the higher education sector and the number of institutions grew from six in 1999 to over 20 in 2007. By 2011 the number of higher education institutions had fallen to 11 (of which nine were accredited) with a total enrolment of 27,010 students. The Ministry of Education is responsible for the provision of higher education. The National Agency for Academic Assessment and Accreditation was established in 2010 to take full responsibility for defining standards and criteria for academic accreditation and assessment and for accrediting higher education institutions and their programmes.

Responsibility for vocational education and training is divided between the Ministry of Education and the Office of the Secretary of State for Labour and Solidarity. In 2005 there were seven technical vocational schools operated by the Government and an estimated 40 further private providers, with a total student enrolment of approximately 6,000. In the same year a National Development Plan was adopted to identify training needs and address skill shortages in order to restructure the sector.

Regulatory Body

GOVERNMENT

Ministry of Education: Rua de Vila Verde, Díli; tel. 3339-654; e-mail education@gov .east-timor.org; Minister BENDITO DOS SANTOS FREITAS.

Research Institutes

LANGUAGE AND LITERATURE

Instituto Nacional de Linguística (National Institute of Linguistics): Liceu 'Dr Francisco Macado', Avda Cidade de Lisboa, Díli; tel. 3313-142; e-mail indldili@yahoo .com; internet www.shlrc.mq.edu.au/ ~leccles; f. 2001 to study, protect and foster the official languages of Timor-Leste, Tetum and Portuguese; official govt body with the charter of coordinating and overseeing all indigenous language research and development projects; attached to National University of East Timor; Dir-Gen. Prof. Dr BENJAMIM DE ARAÚJO E CORTE-REAL; Dir of Research and Publications Prof. Dr GEOF-FREY HULL; publ. *Research Bulletin* (electronic, 2 a year).

NATURAL SCIENCES

Centro Nacional de Investigação Científica (National Centre of Scientific Research): Liceu Dr Francisco Machado, Avda Cidade de Lisboa, Díli; tel. 3332-705; e-mail cnic_timor@yahoo.com; f. 2001; research in agriculture, business and economics, education, political and social sciences, technology; Dir Prof. AFONSO DE ALMEIDA.

Libraries and Archives

Díli

National University of Timor Lorosa'e Library: Avda Cidade de Lisboa, Díli; fmrly library of Universitas Timor Timur; large part of its colln removed or destroyed during civil unrest in 1999; Univ. Librarian ALEX-ANDRINO DE ARAUJO.

Xanana Gusmão Reading Room: Rua Belarmina Lobo Lecidere, POB 3, Díli; tel. 3322-831; e-mail xgrroom@mail .timortelecom.tp; internet www.xgrroom.org; f. 2000; Dir KIRSTY SWORD GUSMÃO.

University

UNIVERSIDADE NACIONAL TIMÓR LOROSA'E
(National University of East Timor)

Avda Cidade de Lisboa, Díli

Telephone: 3321-251

E-mail: webmaster@untl.edu.tl

Internet: www.untl.edu.tl

Founded 2000 by merger of Universitas Timor Timur (f. 1986, under Indonesian control) and Politeknik Dili (f. 1990)

State control

Faculties of agriculture; education, arts and humanities; economics and management; engineering, sciences and technology; law; medicine and health sciences; social sciences

Rector: Prof. Dr AURÉLIO GUTERRES
Univ. Librarian: VENCESLAU DO REGO
Number of students: 7,000

TOGO

The Higher Education System

The principal institution of higher education is the Université de Lomé (formerly University of Benin), which was founded in 1965 as the Institut Supérieur de Bénin (Advanced Institute of Benin) in conjunction with the neighbouring state of Benin. The Université de Lomé had about 14,000 students in the early 2000s, and scholarships to French universities are also available. A second university opened in Kara, in the north of Togo, in early 2004. There are also several private higher education institutions, such as the Institut Universitaire d'Agoénzivé which offers undergraduate courses, and the Insititut Superieur de Philosophie et Sciences Humaines which offers Masters courses in philosophy and human sciences. In 2006/07 there were 32,502 students enrolled in tertiary education; this figure had risen to 63,496 by 2011.

Higher education is the responsibility of the Ministère de l'Enseignement Supérieur et de la Recherche (Ministry of Higher Education and Research). The funding of higher education is administered by the Grand Conseil des Universités (General Higher Education Council), which determines institutional budgets following consultation with the institutions. Students' tuition fees account for approximately 5% of income.

The secondary school Baccalauréat is the main requirement for admission to higher education. Applicants without the Baccalauréat are required to sit an entrance examination. A three-tier, credit-based Licence–Master–Doctorat (LMD) degree system was introduced in 2006, thus bringing Togo's system closer into line with the Bologna-style European model. The new system, which reduced the number of semesters in each academic year from three to two, begins with a three-year first cycle of undergraduate study leading to award of the Licence. Following the Licence, students may proceed to a two-year postgraduate Masters degree. The third and final cycle is the Doctorat, which requires a minimum of three years' additional study. The LMD reform will lead to the eventual abolishment of the old university degree system, which was based on the old French system of three cycles. The first cycle typically lasted two years and led to the award of the undergraduate Diplôme Universitaire d'Études Générales, Diplôme Universitaire d'Études Littéraires, Diplôme Universitaire de Techniques Juridiques or Diplôme Universitaire d'Études Scientifiques, or, in professional fields, the Diplôme de Technicien Supérieur. The second cycle consisted of one year of study leading to the award of the Licence (Bachelors), followed by a further year leading to the award of the Maîtrise (Masters). Finally, the third cycle comprised firstly a one- to two-year period of study leading to the award of the Diplôme d'Études Supérieures Specialisées or Diplôme d'Études Approfondies, and secondly a two-year period of study culminating with the award of the Doctorat (Doctorate). Professional degrees lasting longer than four years were offered by faculties of the university and specialist schools, such as the Diplôme d'Ingénieur Agronome (five years), Diplôme d'Ingénieur de Conception (five years) and Doctorat de Médecine (seven years).

The technical and vocational education system has also been undergoing a period of reform. A Baccalauréat is required for entry to the Brevet de Technicien Supérieur, which requires three years of study and qualifies the holder to access professional training or to work in their chosen field of study. The introduction of a two-year Diplôme Universitaire de Technologie is under development.

Regulatory Bodies

GOVERNMENT

Ministry of Arts and Culture: Lomé; Minister KOUMÉALO ANATÉ.

Ministry of Higher Education and Research: rue Colonel de Roux, BP 12175, Lomé; tel. 22-22-09-83; internet www.republicoftogo.com/toutes-les-rubriques/education; Minister OCTAVE NICOUÉ BROOHM.

Ministry of Primary and Secondary Education and Literacy: BP 398, Lomé; tel. 22-21-20-97; Minister FLORENT BADJAM MANGANAWOÉ.

Ministry of Technical Education and Professional Training: Lomé; Minister HAMADOU BRIM BOURAÏMA-DIABACTE.

Learned Societies

LANGUAGE AND LITERATURE

Goethe-Institut: 25, Rue Kokéti, angle Rue de l'Eglise, BP 914, Lomé; tel. 2210894; e-mail info@lome.goethe.org; internet www.goethe.de/lome; offers courses and exams in German language and culture and promotes cultural exchange with Germany; Dir TORSTEN OERTEL.

Research Institutes

AGRICULTURE, FISHERIES AND VETERINARY SCIENCE

Institut de Recherches du Café, du Cacao et Autres Plantes Stimulantes (IRCC): BP 90, Kpalimé; tel. 441-00-34; f. 1967; research to improve quality and production of coffee, cocoa and other stimulants; experimental unit at Tové; Dir K. EDEM DJIEKPOR.

Institut Togolais de Recherche Agronomique/Centre de Recherche Agronomique de la Savane Humide: BP 01, Kolokopé Anié; tel. 444-30-00; e-mail crash@laposte.tg; f. 1948; see main entry under France; Dir M. BONFOH BEDIBETE; publ. *Coton et Fibres Tropicales*.

NATURAL SCIENCES

General

Institut National de la Recherche Scientifique: BP 2240, Lomé; tel. 221-01-39; f. 1965; initiation of national scientific research; rural development research; 12 permanent staff; library of 5,000 vols; publ. *Études Togolaises* (2 a year).

Libraries and Archives

Lomé

Archives Nationales du Togo: POB 1002, 41 ave Sarakauva, Lomé; tel. 221-63-67; f. 1976; attached to Min. of Higher Education and Research; 2,500 vols, specializing in colonial history, tropical agronomy, stock breeding, health; Curator SENGHOR MOUSSA.

Bibliothèque Nationale: BP 1002, Lomé; tel. 221-04-10; e-mail dban@tg.refer.org; German and French archives; 18,050 vols, 400 periodicals (incl. 74 current); Dir WENMI-AGORE M. COULIBALEY.

Universities

UNIVERSITÉ DE KARA

BP 43, Kara
Telephone: 661-02-85
Internet: www.univkara.org
Founded 1999
State control
Pres.: KOMI P. TCHAKPELE
Number of teachers: 30
Number of students: 1,480

DEAN'S LIST

Faculty of Arts and Humanities: BADAMELI KOSSI SIMVÉILÉ

Faculty of Economics and Management: JOHNSON KUAWO-ASSANE

Faculty of Law and Political Sciences: COULIBALEY BABAKANE DJOBO

Faculty of Science and Technology: BABA GNON

UNIVERSITÉ DE LOMÉ

BP 1515, Lomé
Telephone: 221-35-00
E-mail: ngayiber@tg.refer.org
Internet: www.ub.tg
Founded 1965 as a Higher Institute; univ. status 1970
State control
Language of instruction: French
Academic year: October to June (3 terms)
Incl. all the instns of higher education in the country
Pres.: Prof. NICOUÉ L. GAYIBOR
Vice-Pres.: THIOU T. K. TCHAMIE
Sec.-Gen.: ABALO KODJO TABO
Librarian: A. B. F. GBIKPI-BENISSAN

Library of 70,000 vols
Number of teachers: 650
Number of students: 14,200

Publications: *Livret de l'Etudiant, Annales (Lettres, Sciences, Médecine, Droit-Economie), Actes des Journées Scientifiques, Annuaire statistique, Journal de la Recherche Scientifique, Campus Actualités*

DEANS AND DIRECTORS

Faculty of Economics and Business Management: K. AYASSOU
Faculty of Law: Prof. PEDRO AKUETE SANTOS
Faculty of Letters and Humanities: Prof. KOMLA M. F. NUBUKPO
Faculty of Medicine: Prof. KOFFI N'DAKENA
Faculty of Sciences: Prof. M. GBEASSOR
CIC-CAFMICRO (Computer Centre): TSATSOU FIADJOE
Distance Learning Centre: MARYSE A. QUASHIE
Higher School of Agriculture: K. AGBEKO
Higher Secretarial School: A. MAGNAN
Medical Training School: Prof. BATOMA SOSSOU
National Higher School of Engineering: E. K.-S. BEDJA
National Institute of Education: A. KOMLAN

University Technical Institute of Food and Biological Sciences: Prof. COMLAN A. DE SOUZA
University Technical Institute of Management: N. BIGOU-LARE

Colleges

Ecole Africaine des Métiers d'Architecture et d'Urbanisme: 422, rue des Balises, Lomé; tel. 221-62-53; internet www.eamau.org; f. 1975; courses in architecture and town-planning; in-service courses for trained architects; library: 4,775 vols; 23 teachers; 102 students; Dir-Gen. TCHINI KODJO MAWUENA.

Ecole Nationale d'Administration: Ave de la Libération, Lomé; tel. 221-21-30; f. 1958; provides training for Togolese civil servants; 100 teachers; 500 students; library: 1,000 vols; Dir DAGO YABRE; Sec.-Gen. KOMIKUMA DOGBEVI.

TONGA

The Higher Education System

Institutions of higher education pre-date the independence of Tonga from the United Kingdom in 1970, with the oldest being the 'Atenisi Institute, which was founded in 1966. The University of the South Pacific has a campus in Tonga. Some degree courses are also offered at the university division of the 'Atenisi Institute, which received accreditation in 2011. An establishment offering higher education, the 'Unuaki-'o-Tonga Royal Institute, opened in 2004. In 2003 there were an estimated 668 students enrolled in tertiary level education.

Higher Education is overseen by the Tonga National Qualifications and Accreditation Board (TNQAB). The Board was created by the TNQAB Bill, which was approved in 2004 and enacted in 2007.

Among the qualifications required for admission to higher education are the Higher Leaving Certificate, New Zealand University Entrance Certificate and Pacific Secondary Certificate. There is also a one-year Foundation Programme for applicants to the University of the South Pacific. The Bachelors is the undergraduate degree and typically lasts three years, although some courses may last longer; the Bachelors in medicine at the Fiji School of Medicine, for example, is a four-year degree. Following completion of the Bachelors, graduates may study for the Masters, which is a one- or two-year course of study. The highest university degree is the Doctorate, requiring a minimum of a further two years' study following award of the Masters.

The Government provides over one-half of all facilities and training for post-secondary vocational and technical education. Institutions providing such education include the Community Development Training Centre, the Tonga Institute of Science and Technology, the Civil Service Training Centre and the Royal School of Science and Technology.

Regulatory Bodies

GOVERNMENT

Ministry of Education, Women's Affairs and Culture: POB 61, Vuna Rd, Kolofo'ou, Nuku'alofa; tel. 23511; e-mail ivakauta@foi.gov.to; internet www.mewac.gov.to; Minister Dr ANA MAUI TAUFE'ULUNGAKI.

ACCREDITATION

Tonga National Qualifications and Accreditation Board (TNQAB): New City Bldg, Nuku'alofa; tel. 28136; internet www.tnqab.to; f. 2007; attached to Min. of Education and Training; reviews and approves qualifications for schools and public and private post-secondary education; informs learners, education providers, employers and others on the status and standard of awards provided.

Learned Societies

BIBLIOGRAPHY, LIBRARY SCIENCE AND MUSEOLOGY

Tonga Library Association: c/o USP Tonga Centre, POB 278, Nuku'alofa; tel. 29055; e-mail taufui_l@usp.ac.fj; f. 1981; training courses and library-related activities; provides support for both govt and non-govt libraries incl. academic, schools and spec. libraries; 40 mems; Pres. LOSALINE TAUFU'I.

NATURAL SCIENCES

Tonga Wildlife Centre: PMB 52, Nuku'alofa; tel. 29449; e-mail birdpark@kalianet.to; internet www.tongaturismo.info/twc.htm; protects rare and endangered birds; educates people; collects information on birds and their needs.

Libraries and Archives

Nuku'alofa

Ministry of Education, Women Affairs and Culture Library: POB 123, Nuku'alofa; tel. 21588; f. 1976; provides supplementary reading and text books for students; public library service; 12,432 vols; 1,515 vols of Pacific spec. colln; Librarian TU'ILOKAMANA TUITA.

University of the South Pacific, Tonga Campus Library: POB 278, Nuku'alofa; tel. 29240; 15,000 vols; Library Officer LOSALINE TAUFU'I.

Museum

Nuku'alofa

Tupou College Museum: POB 25, Nuku'alofa; tel. 32240; f. 1866; artefacts from Tonga's history; Prin. Rev. SIOSAIA PELE.

Universities

'ATENISI UNIVERSITY

POB 90, Nuku'alofa

Telephone: 24819

E-mail: thedean@atenisi.edu.to

Internet: www.atenisi.edu.to

Founded 1975; attached to 'Atenisi Institute

Private control

Academic year: February to December

Schools of arts, humanities, natural sciences, social sciences

Dean: Dr MICHAEL G. HOROWITZ

Assoc. Dean: FIRITIA VELT

Library Coordinator: ROBERT H. BECK

'UNUAKI'-O-TONGA ROYAL INSTITUTE

POB 2936, Taufa'ahau Rd, Haveluloto, Nuku'alofa,

Telephone: 25663

E-mail: info@utri.to

Internet: www.utri.to

Founded 2004

Chair.: HRH Princess SALOTE MAFILE'O PILOLEVU TUITA

Pres. and Vice-Chair.: Prof. 'ETUATE LAVULAVU

Vice-Pres. for Academic Affairs and Chief Exec. Dir: Prof. Dr MICHAEL FAIA

Exec. Vice-Pres.: SIONE TUALAU VIMAHI

Vice-Pres.: Prof. VINOD TRIVEDI

Dir for Admin. and Int. Relations: MELE LUPEHA'AMOA 'ILAIU

Dir for Admissions: KALOLAINE KOLUSE

Dir for Finance: MEHTA BHAVIK

Dir for Research and Deputy Dir of Admissions: SIONA TALANOA FIFITA

Dir for Student Services: TELESIA LAVULAVU

Dir for Technical and Vocational Training: PITA LIKILIKI PUA

Colleges

'Atenisi Institute: POB 90, Nuku'alofa; tel. 24819; e-mail director1@atenisi.edu.to; internet www.atenisi.edu.to; f. 1966; anthropology, astronomy, chemistry, economics, global history, languages, life science, literature, mathematics, music and art, philosophy, physics, politics, psychology, sociology; comprises univ. (q.v.) and performing arts centre; Private control; library: 5,000 vols; Dir SISI'UNO HELU; Library Coordinator ROBERT H. BECK.

Hango Agricultural College: POB 16, Ohonua, Eua; tel. 50044; f. 1968; attached to Free Wesleyan Church Education System; 1-year diploma course in para-veterinary studies, 1-year diploma course in horticulture/cropping, 2-year certificate course; library: 1,200 vols; 7 teachers; 55 students.

Tonga Institute of Science and Technology: POB 485, Nuku'alofa; tel. 22667; e-mail tist1uf@kalianet.to; f. 1985; offers training in maritime studies and technical trades; library: 300 vols; 20 teachers; 160 students; Prin. Dr 'UHILA-MOE-LANGI FASI.

University of the South Pacific, Tonga Centre: POB 278, Nuku'alofa; tel. 29055; f. 1971, present location 1987; extension centre with responsibilities for distance education, adult non-formal education; interests in village and community devt and technology; 2 centres: Vava'u and Ha'apai; library: see under Libraries and Archives; Dir Dr 'ANA HAU'ALOFA'IA KOLOTO.

TRINIDAD AND TOBAGO

The Higher Education System

The Trinidad campus of the University of the West Indies (UWI) at St Augustine offers undergraduate and postgraduate programmes. The UWI Arthur Lok Jack Graduate School of Business (founded 1989; current name 2005) offers postgraduate courses, and develops programmes for local companies. The University of Trinidad and Tobago (founded in 2004) has ten campuses and received accreditation in 2010 for a range of qualifications from certificate to PhD level; in 2009 it had a student population of 7,484. The University of London also offers a number of accredited, mainly law and business, programmes at six registered and affiliated centres; in 2012 its student population numbered 2,700. A Tertiary Qualifications Framework was awaiting approval at 2011; upon approval, the Framework would formally implement a six-tier qualifications system, comprising Certificate, Diploma, Associate degree, Bachelors degree, Masters degree and Doctorate qualifications.

The Ministry of Tertiary Education and Skills Training is the national agency with overall responsibility for higher education in Trinidad and Tobago. The National Training Agency is the body responsible for coordinating, monitoring and evaluating technical and vocational education, while the Accreditation Council of Trinidad and Tobago is the governing body for the assurance of quality in post-secondary and tertiary education. However, the need for the coordination and rationalization of technical and vocational education, and the move to establish a Caribbean Single Market and Economy including proposals for the free movement of certified skilled labour, have prompted National Training Agencies in the region to exploit the benefits of joint and concerted efforts by establishing among themselves the Caribbean Association of National Training Agencies.

Applicants are required to have a minimum of two GCE A-Levels for admission to undergraduate courses, and either the Caribbean Examinations Council Secondary Education Certificate or GCE O-Levels for admission to preliminary science, evening or part-time courses. Undergraduate Certificate programmes typically last one year, while Diploma programmes generally require two years' study. Two-year Associate degrees are awarded by institutions such as the College of Nursing and the National Institute of Higher Education, and the undergraduate Bachelors degree is a three- or four-year programme of study at the University of the West Indies. The postgraduate degrees are the Masters, which lasts two years, and Doctorate programmes, which must be completed within five years and culminate in submission of a thesis.

Post-secondary technical and vocational education is administered according to a framework of national vocational qualifications (TTNVQs). There are five levels: Pre-Craft, Craft, Technician, Professional, and Chartered or Advanced Professional. TTNVQs are offered by a range of professional institutes and centres. However, there are plans to replace TTNVQs with Caribbean Vocational Qualifications (CVQs), a competency-based qualification intended to introduce greater portability of qualifications across the Caribbean region. As with TTNVQs, there are five levels of CVQs: Semi-Skilled Worker, Skilled or Independent Worker, Supervisor or Technician or Instructor, Manager or Entrepeneur and Executive Professional.

Regulatory and Representative Bodies

GOVERNMENT

Ministry of Education: 18 Alexandra St, St Clair; tel. 622-2181; e-mail mined@tstt.net.tt; internet www.moe.gov.tt; Minister Dr TIM GOPEESINGH.

Ministry of Science and Technology: International Water Front Center, Level 19, Tower D, 1A Wrightson Rd, Port of Spain; tel. 627-0588; e-mail communicationstte@gov.tt; Minister Dr RUBERT GRIFFITH.

Ministry of Tertiary Education and Skills Training: The International Waterfront Centre, 16th–18th Fl., Tower C, 1A Wrightson Rd, Port-of-Spain; tel. 623-9922; e-mail mtestcommunications@gov.tt; internet www.stte.gov.tt; Minister FAZAL KARIM.

Ministry of the Arts and Multiculturalism: JOBCO Bldg, 51–55 Frederick St, Port-of-Spain; tel. 625-8519; e-mail culturedivision.tt@gmail.com; internet www.culture.gov.tt; Minister Dr LINCOLN DOUGLAS.

ACCREDITATION

Accreditation Council of Trinidad and Tobago (ACTT): Level 3, Bldg B, ALGICO Plaza, 91–93 St Vincent St, Port-of-Spain; tel. 623-2500; e-mail info@actt.org.tt; internet www.actt.org.tt; f. 2004; assures the quality and integrity of higher education through the recognition, registration and accreditation of instns and programmes;

board of 10 mems; Chair. Dr MICHAEL DOWLATH; Exec. Dir MICHAEL BRADSHAW.

Learned Societies

AGRICULTURE, FISHERIES AND VETERINARY SCIENCE

Agricultural Society of Trinidad and Tobago: 52 Penco St, Penco Court, Lange Park, Chaguanas; tel. 672-8995; e-mail agrisoctt@yahoo.com; internet www.agriculture.gov.tt; f. 1894; 528 mems; Pres. WENDY LEE YUEN; publ. *Journal* (1 a year).

Tobago District Agricultural Society: Main St, Scarborough; Pres. Capt. R. H. HARROWER; Sec. S. A. DAVIES.

ARCHITECTURE AND TOWN PLANNING

Trinidad and Tobago Institute of Architects: POB 585, Port-of-Spain; tel. 624-8842; e-mail administration@ttia-architects.org; internet www.ttia-architects.org; f. 1954; current name adopted 1982; 90 mems (incl. overseas); Pres. MARK RAYMOND; Sec. STEVE JAMESON; publ. *Journal* (1 a year).

BIBLIOGRAPHY, LIBRARY SCIENCE AND MUSEOLOGY

Library Association of Trinidad and Tobago: POB 1275, Port-of-Spain; e-mail lat46@gmail.com; internet www.latt.org.tt; f. 1960; Pres. SELWYN RODULFO; Exec. Sec. DANIELLE FRASER; publ. *Bulletin*.

ECONOMICS, LAW AND POLITICS

Law Association of Trinidad and Tobago: POB 534, Port-of-Spain; tel. 625-9350; e-mail lawassociationtt@gmail.com; internet www.lawassociationtt.com; f. 1986; 750 mems; Pres. MARTIN G. DALY; Sec. PATRICIA DINDYAL; publ. *The Lawyer* (2 a year).

FINE AND PERFORMING ARTS

Trinidad Music Association: 51–55 Frederick St, Port-of-Spain; f. 1941; 102 mems; Pres. ROBERT JOHNSTONE; Hon. Sec. VELMA JARDINE.

LANGUAGE AND LITERATURE

Alliance Française: 17 Alcazar St, Clair, POB 1288, Port-of-Spain; tel. 622-6726; e-mail info@alliancetnt.com; internet www.alliancetnt.com; offers courses and exams in French language and culture, and promotes cultural exchange with France.

British Council: c/o British High Commission, 19 St Clair Ave, St Clair, POB 778, Port-of-Spain; tel. 628-0565; e-mail information@britishcouncil.org.tt; internet www.britishcouncil.org/tt; offers courses and exams in English language and British culture, and promotes cultural exchange with the UK; Man. HARRIET MASSINGBERD.

MEDICINE

Pharmacy Board of Trinidad and Tobago: Professional Centre Building, Wrightson Rd Extension, Port-of-Spain; tel.

627-6731; e-mail pboftt@tstt.net.tt; f. 1899; 300 mems; Pres. ANDREW RAHAMAN; Hon. Sec. NORMA INNISS.

NATURAL SCIENCES

Physical Sciences

Geological Society of Trinidad and Tobago: POB 3524, La Romaine, Trinidad; tel. 679-6064; e-mail gstt@tstt.net.tt; internet www.gstt.org; f. 1976; 250 mems; library of 2,000 vols; Pres. Dr FAZAL HOSEIN; Pres.-Elect CURTIS ARCHIE.

Research Institute

AGRICULTURE, FISHERIES AND VETERINARY SCIENCE

Caribbean Agricultural Research and Development Institute (CARDI): University Campus, St Augustine, Trinidad; tel. 645-1205; e-mail infocentre@cardi.org; internet www.cardi.org; f. 1975; sites in 13 Caribbean countries; Exec. Dir FRANK B. LAUCKNER.

Libraries and Archives

Port-of-Spain

National Archives: The Government Archivist, POB 763, 105 St Vincent St, Port-of-Spain; tel. 626-2874; e-mail nattenquires@moi.gov.tt; internet www.natt.gov.tt; f. 1960; records from 1797; govt and private archives; microfilm copies of Trinidad and Tobago records in other countries; Govt Archivist SHERYL LEE KIM; publ. *Select Documents.*

National Library and Information System Authority: National Library of Trinidad and Tobago, cnr Hart and Abercromby Sts, Port-of-Spain; tel. 624-4496; e-mail nalis@nalis.gov.tt; internet www2.nalis.gov.tt; f. 1998; 23 public libraries; heritage library; 124 school libraries; 29 spec. libraries; 24 br. libraries; colln of 729,715 items; Exec. Dir ANNETTE WALLACE.

St Augustine

University of the West Indies, Main Library: St Augustine; tel. 662-2002; e-mail mainlib@sta.uwi.tt; internet www.mainlib.uwi.tt; f. 1960; 403,503 vols, 49,455 bound serials, 22,783 microfilms, 27,000 other non-book items, 1,418 maps, 4,054 multimedia items, 5,804 photographs, 10,721 vertical files, 816 video cassettes, 1,323 audio cassettes, 1,610 vinyl records; spec. collns: W Indiana, Oral and Pictorial Records Collns Index, journal articles on the W Indies or by W Indians; Campus Librarian JENNIFER JOSEPH.

San Fernando

San Fernando Carnegie Free Library: Harris Promenade, San Fernando; tel. 652-2921; f. 1919; 36,109 vols; spec. colln: West Indies, Carnival; Librarian REYNOLD BASSANT.

Museum and Art Gallery

Port-of-Spain

National Museum and Art Gallery of Trinidad & Tobago: 117 Frederick St, Port-of-Spain; tel. 623-5941; e-mail nationalmuseum117@gmail.com; internet www.nmag.gov.tt; f. 1892; archaeology, art, Carnival, history, natural history, petroleum technology; Curator LORRAINE JOHNSON (acting).

Universities

UNIVERSITY OF THE WEST INDIES, ST AUGUSTINE CAMPUS

St Augustine, Trinidad

Telephone: 662-2002

Internet: www.sta.uwi.edu

Founded 1948 by the Govts of the Caribbean Commonwealth Territories with the cooperation of the British Govt

autonomous

Language of instruction: English

Academic year: August to July

Serves Jamaica, Trinidad and Tobago, Barbados and the Commonwealth Territories in the Caribbean

Chancellor: Sir GEORGE ALLEYNE

Vice-Chancellor: Prof. E. NIGEL HARRIS

Pro-Vice-Chancellor and Campus Prin.: Prof. CLEMENT SANKAT

Deputy Prin.: Prof. RHODA REDDOCK

Registrar: JEREMY CALLAGHAN

Librarian: JENNIFER JOSEPH

Library of 403,503 vols, 49,455 bound serials, 10,047 periodicals, 22,783 microforms, 5,804 photographs, 1,418 maps, 1,323 CDs, 816 video cassettes, 811 audio cassettes

Number of teachers: 730

Number of students: 16,410

Publications: *Caribbean Agro Economic Society* (conf. proceedings), *Caribbean Dialogue* (policy bulletin of Caribbean affairs), *Caribbean Review of Gender Studies* (online), *Creating Language Links*, *History in Action* (online), *Journal of Business, Finance and Economics in Emerging Economies*, *Journal of Caribbean Curriculum*, *Journal of Caribbean History*, *Journal of Tropical Agriculture*, *Journal of West Indian Literature*, *St Augustine News*, *UWI Today Newspaper*, *West Indian Journal of Engineering*

DEANS

Faculty of Engineering: Prof. BRIAN COPELAND

Faculty of Humanities and Education: Dr FUNSO AIYEJINA

Faculty of Medical Sciences: Prof. SAMUEL RAMSEWAK

Faculty of Science and Agriculture: Prof. DYER NARINESINGH

Faculty of Social Sciences: Dr H. GHANY

PROFESSORS

ADESIYUN, A., Public Health

ADDAE, J., Physiology

ADOGWA, A., Anatomy

AGARD, J., Life Sciences

AGOZINO, O., Criminology

AIYEJINA, F., Literature

AKINGBALA, J., Chemical Engineering

ALI, Z., School of Medicine

BERTRAND, W., Chemical Engineering

BHATT, B., Mathematics and Computer Science

BISSESSAR, A., Public Management

BRATHWAITE, R., Food Production

CHADWICK, A., Civil Engineering

COOPER, J., Pathology

COPELAND, B., Electrical and Computer Engineering

DAISLEY, H., Anatomical Pathology

DAWE, R., Chemical Engineering

EKWUE, E., Mechanical Engineering

EZENWAKA, C., Para-Clinical Science

EZEOKOLI, C., Veterinary Surgery

GIFT, S., Electrical Engineering

GIRVAN, N., International Relations

HUTCHINSON, G., Clinical Medical Science

IMBERT, C., Mechanical Engineering

KOCHHAR, G., Mechanical Engineering

LALLA, B., Linguistics

LAWRENCE, A., Environmental Biology

LEWIS, T., Civil Engineering

LEWIS, W., Mechanical Engineering

MAHARAJH, H., Clinical Medical Science

MCRAE, A., Human Anatomy

MOHAMMED, P., Centre for Gender and Development Studies

MONTEIL, M., Para-Clinical Science

MURTI, P., Histopathology

NARAYNSINGH, V., Surgery

NARINESINGH, D., Chemistry

OPADEYI, J., Land and Surveying

PANTIN, D., Economics

PINTO PEREIRA, L., Basic Health Science

PITT-MILLER, P., Anaesthetics

POSTHOFF, C., Mathematics and Computer Science

PUN, K., Mechanical Engineering

RAMDATH, D., Basic Health Science

RAMNARINE, I., Life Sciences

RAMSARAN, R., International Relations

RAMSEWAK, S., Obstetrics and Gynaecology

REDDOCK, R., Gender, Social Change and Development

ROBERTSON, I., Linguistics

SAHAI, A., Math and Computer Science

SAUNDERS, R., Physics

SEEMUNGAL, T., School of Medicine

SHARMA, C., Electrical and Computer Engineering

SHAW, P., Food Production

SINGH, G., Chemistry

STEVENSON, A., Centre for Medical Science Education

SURYA RAO, D., Civil Engineering

SYAN, C., Mechanical Engineering

TEELUCKSINGH, S., School of Medicine

THEODORE, K., Economics

TYLER, B., Chemical Engineering

UMAHARAN, P., Life Sciences

YOUSSEF, V., Linguistics

UNIVERSITY OF TRINIDAD AND TOBAGO (UTT)

74–98 O'Meara Industrial Park, Arima

Telephone: 642-8888

E-mail: utt.marketing@utt.edu.tt

Internet: utt.edu.tt

Founded 2004

State control

Language of instruction: English

Academic year: September to July

Pres.: Prof. KENNETH RAMCHAND

Provost: Dr FAZAL ALI

Vice-Provost for Postgraduate Studies: Prof. ADEL SHARAF

Assoc. Provost for Humanities, Soc. Sciences and the Academies: JEANETTE MORRIS

Assoc. Provost for Science, Engineering and Technology: Prof. PRAKASH PERSAD

Vice-Pres. for Finance and Admin.: VISHWANATH MAHARAJH

Vice-Pres. for Quality Assurance and Institutional Effectiveness: Dr RUBY S. ALLEYNE

Asst Vice-Pres. for Human Resources: CEDRIC CONNOR

Asst Vice-Pres. for Student Support Services: STEPHEN SHEPPARD

Registrar and Corporate Sec.: DEBBIE SIRJU-SINGH

Chief Univ. Librarian: Dr MARTHA PREDDIE

Library of 60,103 vols, 677 print journals, 2,253 multimedia items

Number of teachers: 437

Number of students: 6,838

Publications: *Caribbean Journal of Criminology and Public Safety, Caribbean Journal of Teacher Education and Pedagogy, Talkaree*

PROFESSORS

ATHRE, K., Mechanical Engineering

BHATTACHARYA, A., Business Development and Marketing

BLAIR, P., Sports and Leisure Studies

LIVERPOOL, H., Carnival Studies

OSUJI, P., Biosciences, Agriculture and Food Technologies

PERSAD, C., Design and Manufacturing

PERSAD, P., Undergraduate Studies, Design and Manufacturing

RAMBALLY, R., Information, Computing and Telecommunications and Digital Media Studies

RAUCH, U., Educational Technology

STOUTE, V., Graduate Studies and Research

SUITE, W., Civil Engineering

TUNISIA

The Higher Education System

The University of Tunisia was founded in 1960, and divided in 1986 into three universities: Tunis, Centre and Sfax-South. In 1987 the university at Tunis was divided into four subject-based institutions, which in turn were later reorganized into multidisciplinary institutions. Several private universities have received accreditation since 2000. A distance-learning university, Université Virtuelle de Tunis, was established in 2002. Inadequacies within the higher education system and high youth unemployment levels, even among high-calibre university graduates, were among a number of grievances that led to the outpouring of widespread popular discontent in December 2010 that ultimately resulted in the ousting of President Zine al-Abidine Ben Ali in January 2011; however, it remains to be seen whether the revolution will engender real opportunities for meaningful higher education reform in Tunisia.

Higher education is funded from the national budget. Institutions of higher education are accredited by the Ministère de l'Enseignement Supérieur et de la Recherche Scientifique (MESRS—Ministry of Higher Education and Scientific Research). Private higher education institutions operate on the basis of a licence granted by the Ministry. This licence enables them to offer specific courses in specific fields. Licences are reviewed periodically in order to maintain standards of quality. At the beginning of 2012 there were 13 universities and 151 higher education and research institutions (of which 24 Instituts Supérieurs des Études Technologiques) under the MESRS, and 44 private higher education institutions. A total of 339,619 students were enrolled in higher education in the 2011–12 academic year.

The secondary school Baccalauréat is the main requirement for admission to higher education. Tunisia has traditionally followed the French system of higher education but is currently undergoing reform. It aims to introduce a three-tier system of Licence–Master–Doctorat (LMD) and bring Tunisian education into line with the European Bologna Process. The implementation of the LMD started in 2006 with the aim of enrolling all students onto these new programmes by 2009; the system was thus to be fully implemented by 2012, following which traditional qualifications would still be available but only upon request. The traditional university degrees are divided into three cycles: the first cycle ends with the award of the Diplôme Universitaire d'Études Scientifiques or Diplôme Universitaire d'Études Littéraires; the second cycle comprises the Licence or a Maîtrise; and the third cycle the doctoral-level degrees, specifically Diplôme d'Études Approfondies and Doctorat d'État. The professional title Diplôme d'Ingénieur is a second-cycle degree awarded after three years and the Docteur en Médecine is awarded after seven years. The new LMD system comprises three awards. The Licence is an undergraduate degree awarded three years after the Baccalauréat de l'Enseignement Secondaire. There are two types of Licence available, namely the Licence Fondamentale and the Licence Appliquée. The Master is a postgraduate degree awarded two years after the Licence. There are two types of Masters available, namely the Master Recherché and the Master Professionnel. The first year is classroom-based, the second year contains independent research or professional training, including project work. The Doctorat is a postgraduate research degree awarded three years after the Master degree. Studies are organized in credit points (60 credit points correspond to one year of study) similar to the European Credit Transfer System within the Bologna System.

Technical and vocational programmes are administered by the Ministry of Vocational Training and Employment. The leading qualification of post-secondary technical and vocational education is the Brevet de Technicien Supérieur (BTS), which requires the Baccalauréat or Brevet de Technicien Professionnel and comprises 65% practical training and 35% classroom-based learning. The BTS allows access to Tunisia's private, but not public, universities.

Regulatory Bodies

GOVERNMENT

Ministry of Culture: 8 rue 2 mars 1934, la Kasbah, 1006 Tunis; tel. (71) 56-30-06; e-mail minculture.info@email.ati.tn; internet www.culture.tn; Minister MEHDI MABROUK.

Ministry of Education: Blvd Bab Benat, 1030 Tunis; tel. (71) 56-87-68; e-mail ministere@minedu.edunet.tn; internet www.education.gov.tn; Minister SALEM LABYADH.

Ministry of Higher Education and Scientific Research (MESRS): ave Ouled Haffouz, 1030 Tunis; tel. (71) 78-63-00; e-mail mes@mes.rnu.tn; internet www.mes.tn; Minister MONCEF BEN SALEM.

Learned Societies

GENERAL

Comité Culturel National: 105 ave de la Liberté, 1002 Tunis; tel. (71) 28-81-54; f. 1968; central body co-ordinating national and international cultural activities, sponsored by the Min. of Culture and by foreign embassies; regional and local cultural committees throughout the country; 16 mems; Pres. MUHAMMAD TALBI; Sec.-Gen. SAMIR BELHAJ YAHIA.

BIBLIOGRAPHY, LIBRARY SCIENCE AND MUSEOLOGY

Association Tunisienne des Bibliothécaires, Documentalistes et Archivistes: BP 380, 1015 Tunis; f. 1965; information sciences; 250 mems; Pres. ABDELBAKI DALY; publ. *Rassid* (multilingual, 4 a year).

Comité National des Musées: Musée National du Bardo, Tunis; f. 1961; Pres. HABIB BEN YOUNES; publ. *Les musées de Tunisie*.

EDUCATION

Arab League Educational, Cultural and Scientific Organization (ALECSO) (Organisation Arabe pour l'Education, la Culture et la Science): POB 1120, ave Muhammad V, Tunis; tel. (71) 90-62-36; e-mail alecso@alecso.org.tn; internet www.alecso.org.tn; f. 1970; regional units: Arab Centre for Arabization, Translation, Authorship and Publication (Damascus, Syria), Institute of Arab Manuscripts (Cairo, Egypt), Institute of Arab Research and Studies (Cairo, Egypt), Khartoum International Institute for Arabic Language (Khartoum, Sudan), Arabization Coordination Bureau (Rabat, Morocco); promotes devt of education, culture and sciences in Arab countries; 22 Arab countries; library of 8,200 vols, 110 periodicals; Dir-Gen. MUHAMMAD AL AZIZ BEN ACHOUR; Deputy Dir-Gen. MUHAMMAD AL KADASI; publs *Arab Journal of Culture* (2 a year), *Arab Journal of Education* (2 a year), *Arab Journal of Sciences and Information* (2 a year), *Journal of Mass Education* (2 a year).

FINE AND PERFORMING ARTS

Union Nationale des Arts Plastiques: Musée du Belvédère, Tunis.

LANGUAGE AND LITERATURE

British Council: 87 Ave Mohamed V, 1002 Tunis; tel. (71) 14-53-00; e-mail info@tn.britishcouncil.org; internet www.britishcouncil.org/tunisia; offers courses and exams in English language and British culture, and promotes cultural exchange with the UK; library of 8,000 vols; Dir NIGEL BELLINGHAM (acting)..

Teaching Centre:

> **Teaching Centre:** 2nd/3rd Fl., 47 Ave Habib Bourguiba, Tunis 1001; tel. (71) 35-35-68; Man. TANIA PUGLIESE (acting).

Goethe-Institut: Sprachabteilung: 14 rue Ibn el Jazzar, 1002 Tunis; tel. (71) 84-82-66; e-mail info@tunis.goethe.org; internet www.goethe.de/wm/tun/deindex.htm; offers courses and examinations in German language and culture, and promotes cultural exchange with Germany; Dir CHRISTIANE BOHRER.

Institut des Belles Lettres Arabes: 12 rue Jamâa al Haoua, 1008 Tunis Bab Menara; tel. (71) 56-01-33; e-mail ibla@gnet.tn; internet www.iblatunis.org; f. 1930; cultural centre; library of 32,000 vols on Tunisian studies and Arabic literature; Dir Dr JEAN FONTAINE; publ. *IBLA* (2 a year).

Instituto Cervantes: 120 ave de la Liberté, 1002 Tunis Belvédère; tel. (71) 78-88-47; e-mail centun@cervantes.es; internet tunez .cervantes.es; offers courses and examinations in Spanish language and culture, and promotes cultural exchange with Spain and Spanish-speaking Latin and Central America; library of 16,000 vols; Dir FRANCISCO CORRAL SÁNCHEZ-CABEZUDO.

Union des Écrivains Tunisiens: 20 ave de Paris, 1000 Tunis; tel. (71) 25-78-07; e-mail uniondesecrivains@yahoo.fr; internet www .uet.c.la; f. 1970; 560 mems; Pres. D. SHAHEDDINNE BOUJAH; Sec.-Gen. SLAHEDDINNE LAHMADI; publ. *El Massar*.

Research Institutes

GENERAL

Centre d'Études Maghrébines à Tunis: 19 bis rue d'Angleterre, Impasse Menabrea, BP 404, 1049 Tunis-Hached; tel. (71) 32-62-19; e-mail cemat@planet.tn; internet www.la .utexas.edu/research/mena/cemat; f. 1985; operated by American Institute for Maghreb Studies, Univ. of Arizona, Tucson; sponsors research by scholars of all nationalities and in all disciplines; gives research grants to Americans and Maghribis; facilitates liaison with N African scholars; holds annual research conf. and frequent lectures; library of 2,300 vols, 1,000 dissertations; Dir Dr LAURENCE MICHALAK.

Institut de Recherche pour le Développement (IRD): 5 impasse Chahrazed, BP 434, 1004 Tunis El Menzah; tel. (71) 75-00-09; e-mail tunisie@ird.fr; f. 1958; pedology, hydrology, microbiology, medical entomology, agricultural economics, archaeology, desertification, remote detection; library; see main entry under France; Dir J. CLAUDE.

Institut National de Recherche Scientifique et Technique (INRST) (National Institute of Scientific and Technical Research): BP 95, Hammam-Lif 2050; tel. (71) 43-00-44; e-mail webmaster@inrst.rnrt .tn; internet www.semide.tn/english/inrst .htm; f. 1969; applied physics, biology, chemistry, biotechnology, earth sciences, devt of the use of domestic and industrial waste.

AGRICULTURE, FISHERIES AND VETERINARY SCIENCE

Institut National de Recherche en Génie Rural, Eaux et Forêts (National Research Institute of Water, Forests and Rural Engineering): BP 10, Ariana 2080; tel. (71) 70-90-33; e-mail inrgref@iresa.agrinet.tn; internet www.inrgref.agrinet.tn; f. 1959, current name adopted 1995; agricultural machinery, agronomy, ecology, irrigation, new and renewable energy, soil and water conservation.; Dir MUHAMMAD NEJIB REJEB.

Institut de la Recherche Vétérinaire de Tunisie: rue Djebel Lakhdhar La Rabta, 1006 Tunis; tel. (71) 56-26-02; e-mail hammami.salah@iresa.agrinet.tn; f. 1887; veterinary research, laboratory disease diagnosis, food hygiene; library of 3,000 vols; Dir-Gen. Prof. Dr HAMMAMI SALAH; publ. *Bulletin of Epidemiology*.

Institut National de la Recherche Agronomique de Tunisie (INRAT): rue Hédi Karray 2049, Ariana; tel. (71) 23-00-24; e-mail netij.benmechlia@iresa.agrinet.tn; f. 1914; improvement of vegetable and livestock production through the use of appropriate agroecological and socio-economic methods; 7 research laboratories, 2 research units, 13 regional experimental stations; library of 8,000 vols, 1,500 periodicals; Dir Dr N. BEN MECHLIA; publ. *Annales* (1 a year).

Institut National de Recherches Forestières de Tunisie: BP 2-2080, Ariana; f. 1967 under present title; research in all aspects of forestry; library: Documentation Centre comprises 2,981 vols and 3,144 documents; Dir M. DAHMAN; publs *Bulletin d'Information* (2 or 3 a year), *Annales*, *Notes de Recherches*.

Institut National des Sciences et Technologies de la Mer: 28 rue 2 mars 1934, 2025 Salammbô; tel. (71) 73-04-20; e-mail messaoudi.saida@instm.rnrt.tn; internet www.instm.rnrt.tn; f. 1924; fisheries research, aquaculture, fishing technology, marine environment, toxicology, algology; marine museum; library of 40,000 vols; Dir-Gen. Prof. RIDHA MRABET; Librarian SAIDA MESSAOUDI; publs *Bulletin, INSTM* (1 a year), *Notes* (3 a year).

BIBLIOGRAPHY, LIBRARY SCIENCE AND MUSEOLOGY

Institut National du Patrimoine (National Heritage Institute): 4 place du Château, 1008 Tunis; tel. (71) 56-16-22; e-mail dginp@inp.rnrt.tn; internet www.inp .rnrt.tn; f. 1957; attached to Min. of Culture; archaeology, museography, ethnography, research, protection and evaluation of the nat. heritage; library of 25,000 vols; Dir ABDELAZIZ DAOULATLI; publ. *Africa*.

EDUCATION

Institut National des Sciences de l'Éducation: 17 rue d'Irak, 1002 Tunis-Belvédère; tel. (71) 28-77-22; f. 1969; conducts research, undertakes assessment of curricula, books, students and teaching techniques, develops the use of audiovisual aids in education, organizes seminars and conferences; library of 30,000 vols; Dir NEJIB AYED; publs *Bulletin pédagogique*, *Cahiers de l'INSE*, *Revue Tunisienne des Sciences de l'Education*.

MEDICINE

Institut Pasteur de Tunis: BP 74, 13 place Pasteur, 1002 Tunis Belvédère; tel. (71) 84-37-55; e-mail contact@pasteur.rns.tn; internet www.pasteur.tn; f. 1893; research in health sciences; library of 4,000 vols, 250 periodicals; Pres. HECHMI LOUZIR; Librarian M. ABDELHAKIM BEN HASSINE; publ. *Archives* (4 a year).

TECHNOLOGY

Centre National de l'Informatique: 17 rue Belhassen ben Chaâbane, al-Omrane, 1005 Tunis; tel. (71) 78-30-55; e-mail contact .info@cni.tn; internet www.cni.nat.tn; f. 1976; assistance, training, devt of computer applications and software, management of processing centres; library of 4,000 vols; Dir MONGI MILED.

Office National des Mines: BP 215, 1080 Tunis Cedex; premises at: 24 rue 8601, La Charguia, 2035 Tunis; tel. (71) 78-88-42; e-mail contact@onm.nat.tn; f. 1962; geological research and map-making; bibliographic database on geology of Tunisia; library of 15,000 vols, 450 periodicals; Pres. and Dir-Gen. MUHAMMAD FADHEL ZERELLI; publs *Annales des Mines et de la Géologie*, *Notes du service géologique*.

Libraries and Archives

Tunis

Archives Nationales de Tunisie (National Archives of Tunisia): 122 Blvd 9 avril 1938, 1030 Tunis; tel. (71) 57-68-00; e-mail archives.nationales@email.ati.tn; internet www.archives.nat.tn; f. 1874; 5,000 vols, MSS in Arabic, Turkish, French, Italian and English; Dir-Gen. HÉDI JALLEB; publ. *Inventaires des Documents d'Archives Conservés*.

Bibliothèque Nationale: BP 42, 1000 Tunis; tel. (71) 57-27-06; e-mail bibliothequenationale@email.at.tn; internet www.bnt.nat.tn; f. 1885; depository of books published in Tunisia (mostly in Arabic); documentation and information dept; 1.5m. vols in 12 languages; 15,000 periodicals; 40,000 Arabic and Oriental MSS; Curator SAMIA KAMARTI; publs *Catalogue général des manuscrits* (1 a year), *Le Livre Tunisien* (1 a year).

Bibliothèques Publiques: Head Office: 39 rue Asdrubal, Lafayette, 1002 Tunis; tel. (71) 78-25-52; f. 1965; 293 public libraries throughout the country, notably at Tunis, Béja, Bizerte, Gabès, Gafsa, Jendouba, Kairouan, Kasserine, El Kef, Medenine, Monastir, Nabeul, Sfax, Sousse, Siliana, Mahdia, Ariana, ben Arous, Zagnouan, Sidi Bouzid, Tozeur, Kébili and Tetaouine; 233 children's libraries, 266 local and community libraries and 27 mobile libraries; 2.75m. vols; Chief Curator ALI MARZOUKI; publs *Bulletin* (1 a year), *Répertoire*, *Statistics of Public Libraries*.

Centre de Documentation Nationale: blvd 7 Novembre, 1004 Tunis-El Menzah; tel. (71) 70-49-60; e-mail csi.cdn@email.ati .tn; f. 1966; 13,500 monographs, 2,400 periodicals, 210,000 press articles, 30,000 photographs; Dir-Gen. SAHRAOURI GAMAOUN.

Museums and Art Galleries

Carthage

Musée National de Carthage: BP 3, 2016 Carthage; tel. (71) 73-00-36; f. 1964; library of 5,000 vols on archaeology (spec. colln: antiquity); Dir ABDELMAJID ENNABLI.

El Jem

Musée Archéologique d'El Jem: al Jem; tel. (73) 63-00-93; e-mail ibenjerbania@yahoo .fr; Archaeologist in Charge of Research BEN JERBANIA IMED.

Kairouan

Musée National d'Art Islamique de Raqqâda (Raqqada National Museum of Islamic Art): Kairouan; model of Great Mosque of Kairouan, coin colln, ceramics from 9th and 10th century; Koran room.

Makthar

Musée Archéologique de Makthar: Makthar; Punic and Roman artefacts.

Monastir

Musée d'Art Islamique du Ribat: Monastir.

Sbeïtla

Musée de Sbeïtla: Sbeïtla; Roman antiquities.

Sfax

Musée Archéologique de Sfax: Sfax.

Sousse

Musée Archéologique de Sousse (Kasbah): Sousse.

Tunis

Maison des Arts: Parc du Belvédère, 1002 Tunis; tel. (71) 28-37-49; e-mail maisondesarts.tn@gmail.com; internet www .maisondesarts.tn; f. 1992; art exhibition, musical and cultural activities; library of 6,000 vols; Dir ALI LOUATI.

Musée National du Bardo (National Bardo Museum): 2000 Le Bardo, Tunis; tel. (71) 51-36-50; internet www.bardomuseum.tn; f. 1888; contains prehistoric collns, relics of Punic, Greek and Roman art, and ancient and modern Islamic arts, large colln of Roman mosaics; library of 4,700 vols; Chief Curator TAHER GHALIA; publ. *Les Nécropoles Puniques de Tunisie.*

Universities

UNIVERSITÉ DU 7 NOVEMBRE À CARTHAGE

29 rue Asdrubal, 1002 Tunis

Telephone: (71) 78-75-02

E-mail: pu7nc@univ7nc.rnu.tn

Internet: www.univ7nc.rnu.tn/fr/indexfr.htm

Founded 1988 as Université de Droit, d'Économie et de Gestion; current name adopted 2000

Pres.: Prof. TAÏEB HADHRI

Sec.-Gen.: MOHAMED AMEUR ISMAÏL

Number of teachers: 2,000

Number of students: 30,590

DEANS

Faculty of Economics and Management (Nabeul): EZZEDDINE ZOUARI

Faculty of Law, Political and Social Sciences (Tunis): (vacant)

Faculty of Sciences (Bizerte): CHAABANE CHEFI

UNIVERSITÉ EZZITOUNA

21 rue Sidi Jelizi, place Maakel Ezzaïm, 1008 Tunis

Telephone: (71) 57-55-14

Internet: www.uz.rnu.tn

Founded 1988 from existing faculties

State control

Faculties of theology and religious studies

Pres.: SALEM BOUYAHIA

Publications: *Al-Miskat* (1 a year), *Ettanwir* (1 a year)

UNIVERSITÉ DE LA MANOUBA

Campus Universitaire de la Manouba, la Manouba 2010

Telephone: (71) 60-14-99

E-mail: mail@uma.rnu.tn

Internet: www.uma.rnu.tn

Founded 2001

State control

Pres.: SLAHEDDINE GHERISSI

Vice-Pres.: MUHAMMAD AL KADHI

Sec.-Gen.: SAÏD GHRAB

Number of students: 30,560 ..

ATTACHED RESEARCH INSTITUTES

Faculty of Letters: tel. (71) 60-10-45; Dean CHOKRI MABKHOUT; Sec.-Gen. AHMED AL BOUKHARI CHETOUI.

Higher Institute for the Promotion of the Handicapped: IPH, 2 rue Jabrane Khalil Jabrane, la Manouba 2010; tel. (70) 60-40-91; e-mail directeur.iph@iph.org.tn;

internet www.iph.nat.tn; Dir LOFTI BELLALEHOM; Sec.-Gen. MOUNIRA CHAABOUNI.

Higher Institute of Accounting and Business Administration: tel. (71) 60-18-90; Dir SAMIR AL GHAZOUANI; Sec.-Gen. LOTFI CHABBI.

Higher Institute of Documentation: tel. (71) 60-16-50; Dir KHALED MILED; Sec.-Gen. ABDERRAOUF BOUBAKAR.

Higher Institute of Multimedia Arts: ISAMM, Charguia 1; tel. (70) 83-72-06; Dir CHIRAZ LAATIRI.

Higher Institute of Sport and Physical Education: ISSEP, Kssar Essaid, la Manouba 2010; tel. (71) 54-84-32; e-mail crd@ issep-ks.rnu.tn; internet www.issep-ks.rnu .tn; Dir MOURAD JALEL MAAOUI; Sec.-Gen. ALI NCIRI.

Higher Institute of the History of the National Movement: Dir MUHAMMAD LOFTI CHAIBI.

Higher School of Commerce: tel. (71) 60-27-60; e-mail contact@esct.rnu.tn; internet www.esct.rnu.tn; Dir HAFEDH BEN ABDENNEBI; Sec.-Gen. HAMDA YAAKOUBI.

Higher School of Sciences and Design Technology: ESSTD, ave de l'Indépendance, Denden 2011; tel. (71) 61-07-00; Dir RAIF MALEK; Sec.-Gen. ADEL HENID.

Institute of Press and Communications Science (IPSI): tel. (71) 60-03-55; e-mail ipsi@ipsi.rnu.tn; internet www.ipsi.rnu.tn; Dir MUHAMMAD HAMDANE; Sec.-Gen. AHMED HADJI.

National School of Computer Sciences: tel. (71) 60-04-44; internet www.ensi.rnu.tn; Dir KHALID GHEDIRA.

School of e-Commerce: tel. (71) 60-29-19; Dir MALEK GHANIMA.

School of Veterinary Medicine: Dir MUHAMMAD HABIB JEMLI.

Sidi Thabet Higher Institute of Biotechnology: ISB, Sidi Thabet 2020; tel. (71) 52-05-88; e-mail info.isbst@isbst.rnu.tn; Dir RAFIKA CHEKIR; Sec.-Gen. HAYET MANSOURI.

UNIVERSITÉ DE SFAX

route de l'Áeroport, 3029 Sfax

Telephone: (74) 24-09-86

E-mail: universite@uss.rnu.tn

Internet: www.uss.rnu.tn

Founded 1986 from existing faculties; campus at Gafsa

State control

Languages of instruction: Arabic, French

Academic year: September to June

Pres.: EZZEDDINE BOUASSIDA

Sec.-Gen.: LOTFI SELLAMI

Number of teachers: 2,800

Number of students: 39,660

DEANS

Faculty of Arts and Humanities: MABROUK AL BEHI

Faculty of Economics and Administration: BORHEN TRIGUI

Faculty of Law: MUHAMMAD MAHFOUDH

Faculty of Medicine: KHALED ZGHAL

Faculty of Sciences: MAHER MNIF BEN SALAH

CONSTITUENT INSTITUTES

Higher Institute of Applied Humanities Studies, Gafsa: Dir IBRAHIM JADLA.

Higher Institute of Business Administration: Dir ABDELWAHEB REBAI.

Higher Institute of Business Administration, Gafsa: Dir MALEK OURIMI.

Higher Institute of Crafts and Technical Training: Dir NOURREDINE ELHENI.

Higher Institute of Electronics and Telecommunications Technology: Dir LOFTI KAMOUN.

Higher Institute of Industrial Management: Dir HABIB CHABCHOUB.

Higher Institute of Information Technology and Media Studies: Dir ABDELMAJID BEN HAMADOU.

Higher Institute of Management Training, Gafsa: Dir AMMAR AKRIMI.

Higher Institute of Music: Dir MOURAD SIALA.

Higher Institute of Sport and Physical Education: Dir JALEL MILADI.

Higher Institute of Technology, Gafsa: Dir JALEL KHDIRI.

Higher Institute of Technology, Sfax: Dir SLIMÈNE GABSI.

Institute of Advanced Business Studies: Dir FAIKA SCANDER CHARFI.

National School of Commerce: Dir ABDELKADER CHAABANE.

National School of Engineering: Dir BOUBAKER AL EUCH.

National School of Health Science and Technology: Dir MONGIA HACHICHA.

Olivier Institute: Dir TAÏ MILADI.

Preparatory Institute for Engineers: Dir FATHI LAADHAR.

RESEARCH CENTRE

Biotechnology Centre: Dir HAMADI AYADI

UNIVERSITÉ DE SOUSSE/ UNIVERSITY OF SOUSSE

Ave Khelifa Karooui, Sahloul IV, POB 526, Sousse

Telephone: (73) 36-81-29

E-mail: universite.centre@uc.rnu.tn

Internet: www.uc.rnu.tn

Founded 1986

State control

Languages of instruction: Arabic, French

Academic year: September to July

Pres.: Prof. FAYSAL MANSOURI

Vice-Pres.: BECHIR BEL HAJ ALI

Vice-Pres.: MUHAMMAD SAID

Library of 277,010 vols

Number of teachers: 2,100

Number of students: 31,500

DEANS

Faculty of Arts and Humanities: MONCEF BEN ABDELJALIL

Faculty of Economic Sciences and Management: Dr AMINE HAMMAS

Faculty of Law and Political Sciences: LOTFI TARCHOUNA

Faculty of Medicine: ALI MTIRAOUI

High School of Sciences and Technology of Hammam Sousse: NAJEH FARHAT

Institute of Agronomy of Chott Meriem: ABDELHAMID BOUJELBEN

Institute of Applied Sciences and Technology: NABIL BELKAHLA

Institute of Computer Sciences and Communication Techniques of Hammam Sousse: OUAJDI KORBAA

Institute of Finance and Fiscality: SANA MANSOURI

Institute of Fine Arts: MONGI SOYAD

Institute of Higher Commercial Studies: LASSAD LAKHAL

Institute of Management: MUHAMMAD CHOURI

Institute of Music: KHALED SLAMA

Institute of Nursing Sciences: SOUAD CHALBI

Institute of Science and Health Technics: MUHAMMAD BEN DHIEB

Institute of Transport and Logistics: KHALIFA SELLIMI

National School of Engineers: ZOUBEIR TOURKI

UNIVERSITÉ DE TUNIS

92 blvd du 9 avril 1938, 1007 Tunis

Telephone: (71) 56-73-22

E-mail: universite.tunis@utunis.rnu.tn

Internet: www.utunis.rnu.tn

Founded 1988 as Université des Lettres, des Arts et des Sciences Humaines (Tunis I) from existing faculties, present name 2001

Pres.: ABDERRAOUF MAHBOULI

Sec.-Gen.: LAMJED MESSOUSSI

Library of 186,000 vols

Number of teachers: 1,280

Number of students: 32,000

Publications: *Les Annales de l'Université* (in Arabic), *Les Cahiers de Tunisie* (multilingual), *La Revue des Langues* (multilingual), *La Revue Tunisienne des Sciences de la Communication*, *Revue Géographique* (multilingual)

DEANS AND DIRECTORS

Centre for Economic and Social Studies and Research: HACHMI LABAÏED

Faculty of Humanities and Social Sciences: HABIB DLALA

Faculty of Law, Economics and Management: CHOKRI MAMOGHLI

Faculty of Letters: (vacant)

Higher Documentation Institute: HENDA HAJAMI BEN GHZALA

Higher Institute of Applied Studies in Humanities: JAMEL BEN TAHAR

Higher Institute of Cultural Studies and Heritage Professions of Tunis: HABIB BAKLOUTI

Higher Institute of Drama: MUHAMMAD MESSAOUD DRISS

Higher Institute of Education and Training: MALIKA TRABELSI

Higher Institute of Management: ABDELWAHED TRABELSI

Higher Institute of Music: MUSTAPHA ALOULOU

Higher Institute for Youth and Cultural Activity: MONCEF JAZZAR

Higher Teacher Training School: MABROUK EL MANNAÏ

National Institute of Heritage: BÉJI BEN MAMI

Preparatory Institute for Engineering Studies: MUHAMMAD ABEDELMANAF BEN ABDRABOU

Tunis College of Science and Technology: JILANI LAMLOUMI

Tunis Higher Institute of Fine Arts: MUHAMMAD BEN TAHER GUIGA

UNIVERSITÉ DE TUNIS EL MANAR

Campus Universitaire, Manar II, 2092 Tunis

Telephone: (71) 87-33-66

E-mail: unitumanar@tun2.rnu.tn

Founded 1988 as Université des Sciences, des Techniques et de Médecine de Tunis (Tunis II) from existing faculties, present name 2001

Pres.: Prof. YOUSSEF ALOUANE

Sec.-Gen.: ISMAIL KHALIL

Number of teachers: 2,740

Number of students: 23,490

Publication: *Revue de l'Université* (6 a year)

DEANS

Bourguiba Institute of Modern Languages: ABED EL MAJID EL BEDOUI

El Khawarizmi Computer Centre: HENDA HADJAMI BEN GHEZELA

El Manar Preparatory School of Engineering: MUHAMMAD EL ABAAD

Faculties of Economics and Management: MUHAMMAD HADDAR

Faculty of Mathematics, Physics and Natural Sciences: CHEDLI TOUBLI

Faculty of Medicine: RACHID MECHMECH

Faculty of Law and Political Science: CHAFIK SAÏED

Higher Institute of Computer Science: SAMIR BEN AHMED

Higher Institute of Humanities: MUHAMMAD MAHJOUB

Higher Institute of Medical Technology: FATMA SLIM EL HILA

Higher Institute for Sport and Physical Education: ABDELAZIZ SFAR

Higher School of Food Technology: ABDELKADER CHERIF

Higher School of Health Sciences and Technology: MUHAMMAD HABIB JAAFOURA

Higher School of Post and Telecommunication: NACEUR AMMAR

Higher School of Science and Technology: SLAHEDDINE EL-GHRISSI

Institute for the Advancement of Disabled People: RAOUF BEN AMMAR

Kef Higher School of Agriculture: BOUZID NASRAOUI

Kef Institute for Sport and Physical Education: YOUSSEF FEKIH

Mateur Higher School of Agriculture: HEDI ABDOULI

Mateur Preparatory School of Engineering: MUHAMMAD BEJAOUI

Medjez el Bab Higher School of Rural Engineering: ABDERRAZEK SUISSI

Mograne Higher School of Agriculture: TIJANI MAHOUACHI

Nabeul Preparatory Institute of Engineering: MONCEF HADDED

National Agricultural Research Institute: SALAH MEKNI

National Institute of Agronomy: MONCEF EL-HARRABI

National Research Institute of Rural Engineering for Water and Forests: NEJI RAJEB

National Research Institute of Sciences and Technology: MUHAMMAD NOBIL

National School of Computer Science: FAROUK KAMMOUN

National School of Engineering: KHALIFA MAÂLEL

National University Centre for Scientific and Technical Documentation: FATMA CHAMMAM BEN ABDALLAH

Pasteur Institute: KOUSSAI EDALAJI

Polytechnic Institute: TAIEB HADHRI

Preparatory Institute of Scientific Studies and Technology: FAOUZIA CHARFI

School of Civil Aviation and Meterorlogy: MUHAMMAD TOUIL

Sidi Thabet National School of Veterinary Medicine: ATEF MALEK

Tabarka Forestry School: HAMDA SAOUDI

Veterinary Research Institute: MALEK ZRELLI

Other Institutions of Higher Education

Centre Culturel International d'Hammamet: ave des Nations Unies, 8050 Hammamet; tel. (72) 28-04-10; f. 1962; theatrical techniques, history and sociology of the theatre and video; Dir TAOUFIK BESBÈS.

Conservatoire National de Musique, de Danse et d'Arts Populaires: 20 ave de Paris, Tunis.

École Nationale d'Administration: 24 ave du Docteur Calmette, Mutuelleville, Tunis; tel. (71) 28-83-00; f. 1964; library: 53,000 vols; 1,050 students; Dir MAHER KAMOUN; publ. *Revue Tunisienne d'Administration Publique* (3 a year).

École Nationale de la Statistique: BP 65, Tunis; f. 1969; 1- and 2-year diploma courses.

Institut d'Économie Quantitative: 27 rue de Liban, 1002 Tunis; tel. (71) 28-36-33; f. 1964; methodological research in planning and documentation in social and economic fields; library: 7,500 vols, 300 periodicals; Dir-Gen. GHORBEL HÉDI.

Institut National du Travail et des Études Sociales: Z. I. Charguia II, BP 692, 1080 Tunis; tel. (71) 70-62-07; e-mail intes@intes.rnu.tn; internet www.intes.rnu.tn; language of instruction: Arabic; library: 5,000 vols; 110 teachers (34 full-time, 76 part-time); 2,200 students; Dir Prof. MUSTAPHA NASRAOUI; publ. *Travail et Développement* (2 a year).

TURKEY

The Higher Education System

Institutions of higher education include universities, faculties, institutes, colleges, conservatories, vocational colleges and research centres. Turkey joined the Bologna Process in 2001; however, reforms to the degree structure were not required since the Turkish higher education system was already based on three cycles. The Lisbon Convention was signed in 2004 and came into force in 2007. In 2005/06 some 2,181,217 students attended 1,306 higher education institutes, including 69 universities of various types, although a large number of new institutes have been established in subsequent years. In 2005/06 there were 73,061 students enrolled at Istanbul Üniversitesi (founded 1453, reorganized 1933). In 2012 there were 103 public universities, 65 private universities and seven vocational schools of higher education. In 2010 a total of 3,529,334 students were enrolled in tertiary level education in both the public and private sector. Quality assurance remains based on internal institutional evaluation, with some degree programmes assessed by specialized agencies, but full implementation of a national quality assurance system is planned. The National Qualifications Framework was approved in January 2010 and pilot implementation commenced in June 2011, with full implementation scheduled to be effected by December 2012.

The Yükseköğretim Kurulu (YöK—Council of Higher Education), which operates within the provisions set forth in the Constitution (Articles 130 and 131) and the 1981 Higher Education Law (No. 2547), is a fully autonomous public body responsible for the planning, coordination, governance and supervision of higher education in Turkey, and sets institutional budgets and defines criteria for the award of degrees. In accordance with the Higher Education Law, the rectors of all the public universities are appointed jointly by the faculty, the YöK and the President of Turkey, although the Turkish Government has in recent years mooted proposals to eliminate the YöK and the system of political influence within the higher education system.

The main criteria for admission to higher education is the Ögrenci Secme Sinavi (ÖSS—State University Entrance Examination), administered by the Öğrenci Seçme ve Yerleştirme Sistemi (ÖSYS—Student Selection and Placement Centre). Universities set their own entrance requirements based on scores in the ÖSS. In mid-2009 the YöK voted to reform the admissions system in order to end discrimination against graduates of vocational high schools, including religious schools; under the new system, the value of the points achieved by graduates of vocational high schools would no longer be lowered if they sought to study new subjects, as had been the case under the old system. Since 2002 the two-year Ön Lisans Diplomasi (Associate Degree) has been broadened to encompass technical and vocational education. The Lisans Diplomasi (Bachelors) is mostly a four-year programme of study, although some disciplines require longer periods of study, such as dentistry, architecture, veterinary medicine (five years) and medicine (six years). The first postgraduate degree is the two-year Yüsek Lisans Diplomasi (Masters), admission to which is on the basis of a competitive examination administered by the ÖSYM. The final university degree is the Doctor of Philosophy (Doktora); again, admission, which is open to holders of a Masters degree, or equivalent qualification, is on the basis of a competitive examination administered by the ÖSYM, and students are required to complete a four-year period of study and research, culminating in submission of a thesis.

As determined by the Law on Apprenticeship and Vocational Training (1986), technical and vocational education is provided by one of the three following methods: formal vocational education, apprenticeship training, or vocational courses. Since 2002 students have been allowed to enter vocational higher education without taking an entrance examination. In terms of formal vocational training, the main institutions are specialist vocational schools attached to universities, in addition to two-year colleges of technology and commercial colleges. Students who successfully complete the course of study are awarded the Ön Lisans (followed by subject name) and title of Tekniker (Technician). Apprenticeship training is offered largely at the secondary level, while vocational courses (where the highest available qualification is the Usta Ögreticilik Belgesi—Master Trainer Certificate) are aimed at adults who have left formal education.

Regulatory and Representative Bodies

GOVERNMENT

Ministry of Culture and Tourism: Kültür ve Turizm Bakanlığı, Atatürk Bul. 29, 06050 Opera, Ankara; tel. (312) 309-08-50; e-mail info@kulturturizm.gov.tr; internet www.kultur.gov.tr; Minister ÖMER ÇELİK.

Ministry of National Education: Milli Eğitim Bakanlığı, Atatürk Bul., Bakanlıklar, Ankara; tel. (312) 419-14-10; e-mail sgb@meb.gov.tr; internet www.meb.gov.tr; Minister NABI AVCI.

ACCREDITATION

ENIC/NARIC Turkey: EU and Int. Relations Office, Yükseköğretim Kurulu Baskanligi (YÖK), 06539 Bilkent, Ankara; tel. (312) 298-72-43; e-mail naric@yok.gov.tr; Head DENIZ ATES.

NATIONAL BODIES

Türk Üniversite Rektörleri Komitesi (Turkish University Rectors' Committee): Yükseköğretim Kurulu, Bilkent, Ankara; tel. (312) 266-47-25; f. 1967; rectors of all Turkish univs, with 5 former rectors; advises the Higher Education Ccl and the Interuniversity Board on university affairs, promotes cooperation between univs; Pres. Prof. Dr KEMAL GÜRÜZ; Sec. Prof. Dr UĞUR BÜGET.

Yükseköğretim Kurulu (Council of Higher Education): 06539 Bilkent, Ankara; tel. (312) 298-70-00; e-mail webadmin@yok.gov.tr; internet www.yok.gov.tr; f. 1981; NGO responsible for the organization and governance of the higher education instns, and for the teaching and research carried out; 22 mems; Pres. Prof. Dr YUSUF ZİYA ÖZCAN; Gen. Sec. TURGUT KILIÇ.

Learned Societies

AGRICULTURE, FISHERIES AND VETERINARY SCIENCE

Türk Veteriner Hekimleri Birliği (Turkish Veterinary Medical Association): Ehlibeyt Mah. Ceyhun Atıf Kansu Cad. Aktas Apt. 1/2-3 Balgat/Cankaya, Ankara; tel. (312) 435-54-15; e-mail merkezkonseyi@tvhb.org.tr; internet www.tvhb.org.tr; f. 1954; 20,000 mems; Pres. TALAT GÖZET; Vice-Pres. ALI KOÇ; Gen. Sec. TAHIR GONCAGÜL; publ. *Turkish Veterinary Medical Association/Turk Veteriner Hekimleri Birligi Dergisi* (irregular).

BIBLIOGRAPHY, LIBRARY SCIENCE AND MUSEOLOGY

Türk Kütüphaneciler Derneği (Turkish Librarians' Association): Necatibey Cad. Elgün Sok. 8/8, 06440 Kızılay, Ankara; tel. (312) 230-13-25; e-mail tkd.dernek@gmail.com; internet www.kutuphaneci.org.tr; f. 1949; 2,000 mems; Pres. ALI FUAT KARTAL; Sec.-Gen. EMRE HASAN AKBAYRAK; publ. *Türk Kütüphaneciliği* (4 a year).

ECONOMICS, LAW AND POLITICS

Türk Hukuk Kurumu (Turkish Law Association): Adakale Sokak No 28 Daire 3 Yenişehir, 06420 Ankara; tel. (312) 431-26-90; e-mail thk@turkhukukkurumu.org.tr; internet www.turkhukukkurumu.org.tr; f. 1934; Pres. SABIH KANADOĞLU; Sec. TÜLAY YILMAZ; publs *La Turquie*, *Türk Hukuk Lûgati*.

HISTORY, GEOGRAPHY AND ARCHAEOLOGY

Türk Tarih Kurumu (Turkish Historical Society): Kızılay Sok. 1, 06100 Sıhhıye Ankara; tel. (312) 310-23-68; e-mail ttkinfo@ttk.org.tr; internet www.ttk.org.tr; f. 1931; 40 mems; library of 228,577 vols; Pres. Prof. Dr YUSUF HALAÇOĞLU; publs *Belgeler* (1 a year), *Belleten* (3 a year).

LANGUAGE AND LITERATURE

British Council: Posta Kutusu 34, Çankaya, Ankara; tel. (312) 455-36-00; internet www.britishcouncil.org/turkey; f. 1940; offers courses and exams in English language and British culture and promotes cultural exchange with the UK; attached offices in Istanbul (teaching centre) and Izmir; Dir of Operations, Turkey JEFF STREETER.

Goethe-Institut: Atatürk Bulvarı 131, Bakanlıklar, 06640 Ankara; tel. (312) 419-52-83; e-mail il@ankara.goethe.org; internet www.goethe.de/om/ank; offers courses and exams in German language and culture and promotes cultural exchange with Germany; attached centres in Istanbul and Izmir; library of 15,000 vols; Dir Dr THOMAS LIER.

Instituto Cervantes: Tarlabasi Bulvarı, Zambak Sokak 33, 80080 Istanbul; tel. (212) 292-65-36; e-mail cenest@cervantes.es; internet estambul.cervantes.es; offers courses and exams in Spanish language and culture and promotes cultural exchange with Spain and Spanish-speaking Latin and Central America; library of 7,500 vols; Dir PABLO MARTÍN ASUERO.

PEN Yazarlar Derneği (Turkish PEN Centre): Istiklal Cad., 225, Beyoglu is Merkezi, B Blok, Kat 2, 143, Beyoglu, Istanbul; e-mail pprtr@superonline.com; f. 1989; 200 mems; Pres. VECDI SAYAR; publ. *Turkish PEN Reader* (in English, 2 a year).

Türk Dil Kurumu (Turkish Language Institute): Atatürk Bulvarı 217, Kavaklıdere, 06680 Ankara; tel. (312) 428-61-00; e-mail bim@tdk.org.tr; internet www.tdk.org.tr; f. 1932; 40 mems; library of 35,000 vols on Turkish studies; Pres. Prof. Dr ŞÜKRÜ HALUK AKALIN; Sec.-Gen. ALI KARAÇALI; publs *Tercüme Yıllığı* (Yearbook of Translation), *Türk Dili Araştırmaları Yıllığı* (Yearbook of Turkic Studies), *Türk Dili Dergisi* (Journal of Turkish Language, 12 a year), *Türk Dünyası Dergisi* (Journal of Turkish World, 2 a year).

MEDICINE

Türk Cerrahi Derneği (Turkish Surgical Society): Koru Mah. Ihlamur Cad. 26, 06810 Çayyolu, Ankara; tel. (312) 241-99-90; e-mail turkcer@turkcer.org.tr; internet www.turkcer.org.tr; f. 1929.

Türk Mikrobiyoloji Cemiyeti (Turkish Microbiological Society): PK 57, 34492 Beyazit, Istanbul; tel. (212) 531-70-89; e-mail tmc@tmc-online.org; internet www.tmc-online.org; f. 1931; 350 mems; Pres. Prof. Dr NEHAZAT GÜRLER; Sec.-Gen. Doc. Dr ORHAN CERN AKTEPE; publ. *Türk Mikrobiyoloji Cemiyeti Dergisi* (Journal, 4 a year).

Türk Nöropsikiyatri Derneği (Turkish Neuropsychiatric Society): Op. Dr. Raif Bey Sok. 31/2, 34360 Sisli, Istanbul; tel. (212) 219-97-77; e-mail bilgi@turknoropsikiyatri.org; f. 1914; meetings to discuss aspects of psychiatry and neurology; 1,200 mems; Pres. Prof. PEYKAN GÖKOLP; publ. *Nöropsikiyatri Arşivi* (Archives of Neuropsychiatry, 4 a year).

Türk Ortopedi ve Travmatoloji Birliği Derneği (Turkish Association of Orthopaedics and Traumatology): Bayraktar Mahallesi Ikizdere Sok. 21/12, Kat 2 GOP, Ankara; tel.

(312) 436-11-40; internet www.totbid.org.tr; Pres. Prof. Dr BÜLEIT ALPARSLAN.

Türk Oto-Rino-Larengoloji Cemiyeti (Turkish Otorhinolaryngological and Head and Neck Surgery Society): Buyudere Cad. Tankaya 18/1 Kat 1, Şişli, 80260 Istanbul; tel. (212) 233-11-26; e-mail kbb@kbb.org.tr; internet www.kbb.org.tr; f. 1930; 2,500 mems; Pres. Prof. Dr ASIM KAYTAZ; Gen. Sec. Prof. Dr FERHAN ÖZ; publ. *Turkish Archives of Otolaryngology* (3 a year).

Türk Tabipleri Birliği (Turkish Medical Association): GMK Bul. Şehit Daniş Tunalıgil Sok. 2 Kat 4, Maltepe, 06570 Ankara; tel. (312) 231-31-79; e-mail ttb@ttb.org.tr; internet www.ttb.org.tr; f. 1953; 98,500 mems; Pres. Prof. Dr ERIŞ BILALOĞLU; Gen. Sec. Dr FERIDE AKSU TANIK.

Türk Tibbi Elektro Radyografi Cemiyeti (Turkish Electro-Radiographical Society): Valikonagi Cad. 10, Harbiye, Istanbul; f. 1924.

Türk Tıp Tarihi Kurumu (Turkish Medical History Society): c/o Uludağ Üniversitesi, Tıp Fakültesi, Deontoloji ve Tıp Tarihi Anabilim Dalı, Bursa; tel. (532) 452-94-37; e-mail ademirer@yahoo.com; f. 1938; 120 mems; library of 70,000 vols; Pres. Prof. Dr AYŞEGÜL ERDEMIR DEMIRHAN.

Türk Tüberküloz ve Toraks Derneği (Turkish Association of Tuberculosis and Thorax): Ankara Üniversitesi, Tıp Fakültesi, Göğüs Hastalıkları Anabilim Dalı, 06100 Cebeci- Ankara; tel. (312) 319-00-27; e-mail akaya@medicine.ankara.edu.tr; internet www.tubtoraks.org; Dir Dr ÖZLEM ÖZDEMIR KUMBASAR; publ. *Journal* (4 a year).

Türk Üroloji Derneği (Turkish Urological Society): c/o Prof. Nurettin Öktem Sokak, Lale Palas Apt. 18/2, 34382 Şişli, Istanbul; tel. (212) 232-46-89; e-mail uroturk@uroturk.org.tr; internet www.uroturk.org.tr; f. 1933; 1,093 mems; Pres. Prof. VURAL SOLOK; publ. *Türk Üroloji Dergisi* (Turkish Journal of Urology, 4 a year).

NATURAL SCIENCES

Mathematical Sciences

Türkiye Matematik Derneği (Mathematical Society of Turkey): Sabancı Üniversitesi, Karaköy İletişim Merkezi, Bankalar Cad. 2, 80020 Karaköy, Istanbul; tel. (212) 292-49-39; e-mail emrah@su.sabanciuniv.edu; internet www.tmd.org.tr; f. 1948; development of mathematics among young people; 509 mems; Pres. Prof. Dr TOSUN TERZIOĞLU; Gen. Sec. Prof. Dr HÜLYA ŞENKON; publ. *Matematik Dünyası* (2 a year).

Physical Sciences

Türkiye Kimya Derneği (Chemical Society of Turkey): Halaskârgazi Cad. 53, D. 8 Uzay Apt, Harbiye, Istanbul; tel. (212) 240-73-31; e-mail tkd@turchemsoc.org; internet www.turchemsoc.org; f. 1919; 1,500 mems; Pres. Prof. Dr OSMAN YAVUZ ATAMAN'IN; publ. *Kimya ve Sanayi* (Chemistry and Industry).

PHILOSOPHY AND PSYCHOLOGY

Türkiye Felsefe Kurumu (Philosophical Society of Turkey): Ahmet Rasim Sok. 8/2, Çankaya, 06550 Ankara; tel. (312) 440-74-08; e-mail toc@tfk.org.tr; internet www.tfk.org.tr; f. 1974; promotes philosophy and philosophical education in Turkey; encourages philosophical thinking in public life and secures int. cooperation through seminars, symposia and courses; 175 individual mems; Pres. IOANNA KUÇURADI; Sec.-Gen. GULRIZ UYGUR; publ. *Bülten* (3 a year).

Yeni Felsefe Cemiyeti (New Philosophical Society): Işık Lisesi, Nişantaşı, Istanbul; f. 1943.

TECHNOLOGY

TMMOB Jeoloji Mühendisleri Odası (Chamber of Geological Engineers of Turkey): PK 464, Yenişehir, 06444 Ankara; tel. (312) 434-36-01; e-mail jmo@jmo.org.tr; internet www.jmo.org.tr; f. 1974; 9,780 mems; library of 17,000 vols; Pres. AYDÝN CELEBI; Sec.-Gen. BAHATTIN MURAT DEMIR; publs *Abstracts of the Geological Congress of Turkey* (1 a year), *Abstracts of Geological Research in Turkey* (1 a year), *Blue Planet* (2 a year), *Bulletin News* (4 a year), *Geological Bulletin of Turkey* (2 a year), *Journal of Geological Engineering* (2 a year).

Research Institutes

GENERAL

Research Centre for Islamic History, Art and Culture (IRCICA): POB 24, Beşiktaş, 80692 Istanbul; Yildiz Sarayi, Seyir Kosku Barbaros Bulvarı, Besiktas, 34349 Istanbul; tel. (212) 259-17-42; e-mail ircica@ircica.org; internet www.ircica.org; f. 1979; a subsidiary of the Organization of Islamic Cooperation; activities relating to research, publishing, documentation and information on subjects concerning Islamic civilisation and Muslim cultures incl. history of Muslim nations, history of science, archaeology, architecture and urbanism, fine arts and handicrafts, preservation of cultural heritage, and cultural devt issues; organizes confs, symposia, exhibitions, workshops, training courses and competitions; publishes books in various languages; library of 720,000 vols, 1,764 periodicals, 70,000 historical photographs, 1,500 historical maps, 1,150 microfilms, 200 CDs and DVDs, 1,860 audio cassettes, 6,150 archive documents, 4,000 calligraphy plates; Dir-Gen. Dr HALIT EREN.

Türk Kültürünü Araştırma Enstitüsü (Turkish Cultural Research Institute): Bahçelievler 7.Cad. 17 Sok. No 38, 06490 Ankara; tel. (312) 213-31-00; e-mail bilgi@turkkulturu.org.tr; internet www.turkkulturu.org.tr; f. 1961; scholarly research into all aspects of Turkish culture; Dir Dr ŞÜKRÜ ELÇIN; publs *Cultura Turcica* (1 a year), *Türk Kültürü Araştırmaları Dergisi* (2 a year, print and online, www.tkaed.org).

Türkiye Bilimsel ve Teknik Araştırma Kurumu (Scientific and Technical Research Council of Turkey): Tunus Cad. 80, 06100 Kavaklıdere, Ankara; tel. (312) 468-53-00; e-mail www-adm@tubitak.gov.tr; internet www.tubitak.gov.tr; f. 1963; govt body which carries out, sponsors, promotes and coordinates research activities in pure and applied sciences; library of 19,000 vols, 426 periodicals; Pres. Prof. Dr NÜKET YETIS; Sec.-Gen. IBRAHIM BERBEROGLU (acting); publs *Bilim ve Teknik* (Science and Technology, 12 a year), *Turkish Journal of Agriculture and Forestry Sciences* (6 a year), *Turkish Journal of Biology* (6 a year), *Turkish Journal of Botany* (6 a year), *Turkish Journal of Chemistry* (6 a year), *Turkish Journal of Earth Sciences* (6 a year), *Turkish Journal of Electrical Engineering and Computer Sciences* (3 a year), *Turkish Journal of Engineering and Environmental Sciences* (6 a year), *Turkish Journal of Mathematics* (6 a year), *Turkish Journal of Medical Sciences* (6 a year), *Turkish Journal of Physics* (6 a year), *Turkish Journal of Veterinary and Animal Sciences* (6 a year), *Turkish Journal of Zoology* (6 a year).

Attached Institutes:

Defence Research and Development Institute: PK 16 Mamak, 06261 Ankara;

tel. (312) 399-03-38; Dir Prof. Dr ERES SÖYLEMEZ.

Marmara Araştırma Merkezi (Marmara Research Centre): PK 21, 41470 Gebze, Kocaeli; tel. (262) 677-20-00; e-mail mam .bilgi@tubitak.gov.tr; internet www.mam .gov.tr; f. 1972; materials science, optoelectronics, Earth sciences, food science, nutrition, information technology, chemistry, chemical technology, environmental technology and energy; library of 30,000 vols, 90,000 bound periodicals; Dir (vacant).

TÜBİTAK Marmara Araştırma Merkezi Gen Mühendisliği ve Biyoteknoloji Araştırma Enstitüsü (TÜBİTAK Marmara Research Centre Genetic Engineering and Biotechnology Institute): Anibal Cad. Barış Mah., PK 21, 41470 Gebze, Kocaeli; tel. (262) 677-20-00; e-mail gmbe .web@mam.gov.tr; internet www.rigeb.gov .tr; f. 1983; Dir Asst Prof. AYNUR BASALP.

TÜBİTAK Uzay Teknolojileri Araştırma Enstitüsü (TUBITAK Space Technologies Research Institute): Middle East Technical Univ. (ODTÜ) Campus, 06531 Ankara; tel. (312) 210-13-10; e-mail uzay .bilgi@tubitak.gov.tr; internet www.uzay .tubitak.gov.tr; f. 1985; research and devt in space technologies, electronics, software; Dir TAMER BEŞER.

Ulusal Elektronik ve Kriptoloji Araştırma Enstitüsü (National Electronics and Cryptology Research Institute): PK 74, 41470 Gebze, Kocaeli; tel. (262) 648-10-00; e-mail uekae@uekae.tubitak.gov.tr; internet www.uekae.tubitak.gov.tr; library of 2,700 vols, 70 periodicals; Dir Prof. Dr AYHAN TÜRELI.

AGRICULTURE, FISHERIES AND VETERINARY SCIENCE

Kavak ve Hızlı Gelişen Tür Orman Ağaçları Araştırma Müdürlüğü (Poplar and Fast-Growing Forest Trees Research Institute): PK 93, 41001 Izmit, Kocaeli; tel. (262) 311-69-64; e-mail kavak@kavak.gov.tr; internet www.kavak.gov.tr; f. 1962; attached to Ministry of Forests; development of forest nursery and reafforestation techniques, introduction of new forest tree species, increase of wood production, research into poplar cultivation and management techniques; library of 3,700 vols; Dir Dr FARUK Ş. ÖZAY; publs *Annual Bulletin*, *Magazine*, *Technical Bulletin*.

Tarım ve Köyişleri Bakanlığı, Zirai Mücadele Araştırma Enstitüsü (Ministry of Agricultural and Rural Affairs, Plant Protection Research Institute): Yenimahalle, Gayret Mahallesi Fatih Sultan Mehmet Bulv. 66, 06172 Ankara; tel. (312) 344-74-30; internet www.zmmae.gov.tr; f. 1934; depts dealing with research into combating plant diseases, pests and weeds; engaged in phytopathology, entomology, insect taxonomy and toxicology, nematology; analyzes pesticides and crop pesticide residues; library of 5,000 vols; Dir Dr ALI TAMER; publ. *Bitki Koruma Bülteni* (Plant Protection Bulletin, English, French or German summary, irregular).

HISTORY, GEOGRAPHY AND ARCHAEOLOGY

British Institute at Ankara: Tahran Cad. 24, 06700 Kavaklidere, Ankara; tel. (312) 428-03-30; e-mail library@biaatr.org; internet www.biaa.ac.uk *London Office:* c/o Claire McCafferty, British Institute at Ankara, British Academy, 10 Carlton House Terrace, London, SW1Y 5AH, UK; f. 1947; supports, promotes and publishes British research focused on Turkey and the Black Sea littoral, in all academic disciplines

within the arts, humanities and social sciences; maintains centre of excellence in Ankara, focused on the archaeology and related subjects of Turkey; library of 50,000 vols; Dir Dr LUTGARDE VANDEPUT; Admin. CLAIRE MCCAFFERTY; publs *Anatolian Studies* (1 a year), *Heritage Turkey*.

Deutsches Archäologisches Institut İstanbul Şubesi (Deutsches Archäologisches Institut Istanbul Branch): Gümüşsuyu/Inönü Caddesi 10, 34437 Istanbul; tel. (212) 393-76-00; e-mail sekretariat.istanbul@ dainst.de; internet www.dainst.de; f. 1929; research into archaeology and cultural history in Turkey from prehistory to the Ottoman period; library of 60,000 vols; Dir Prof. Dr F. PIRSON; publs *Byzas*, *Istanbuler Beihefte*, *Istanbuler Forschungen*, *Istanbuler Mitteilungen des DAI* (1 a year).

Hollanda Araştırma Enstitüsü (Netherlands Institute in Turkey): Istiklâl Caddesi 181, Beyoğlu, Istanbul; tel. (212) 293-92-83; e-mail nit@nit-istanbul.org; internet www .nit-istanbul.org; f. 1958; library of 15,000 vols; Dir Dr FOKKE GERRITSEN; Librarian GÜLTEN YILDIZ; publ. *Anatolica* (1 a year).

Institut Français d'Etudes Anatoliennes d'Istanbul (Fransız Anadolu Araştırmaları Enstitüsü/French Institute of Anatolian Studies, Istanbul): PK 54, Palais de France, Nuru Ziya Sok, 80072 Beyoğlu-Istanbul; tel. (212) 244-17-17; e-mail ifea@ifea-istanbul .net; internet www.ifea-istanbul.net; f. 1930; Anatolian studies from prehistory to contemporary period; 15 mems; library of 24,000 vols; Dir PIERRE CHUVIN; publs *Anatolia antiqua* (1 a year), *Anatolia moderna* (1 a year).

Orient-Institut Istanbul/Deutsche Gesellschaft Geisteswissenschaftlicher Institute im Ausland/Orient Enstitüsü, İstanbul (Orient Institute Istanbul): Susam Sokak 16, D.8, 34433 Cihangir, Istanbul; tel. (212) 293-60-67; e-mail oiist@oidmg.org; internet www.oidmg.org; f. 1987; Turkish, Ottoman and central Asian Studies; library of 40,000 vols, 1,388 periodicals; Dir Prof. Dr RAOUL MOTIKA; Asst Dir Dr RICHARD WITTMANN.

MEDICINE

Çocuk Sağlığı Enstitüsü, Hacettepe Üniversitesi İhsan Doğramacı Çocuk Hastanesi (Institute of Child Health at Hacettepe University Children's Hospital): İhsan Doğramacı Çocuk Hastanesi 2, Blok 3, 06100 Yenisehir-Ankara; tel. (312) 324-42-91; e-mail tkutluk@hacettepe.edu.tr; internet www.cocuk.hacettepe.edu.tr; f. 1958; Masters and PhD training in paediatric sub-specialties; Dir Prof. Dr TEZER KUTLUK; publs *Çocuk Sağlığı ve Hastalıkları Dergisi* (abstracts in English, 4 a year), *Turkish Journal of Paediatrics* (4 a year).

NATURAL SCIENCES

General

Türk Bilim Tarihi Kurumu (Turkish Society for History of Science): POB 24, 34349 Beşiktaş, Istanbul; tel. (212) 259-17-42; e-mail ircica@superonline.com; f. 1989; research and publications on history of science with emphasis on Ottoman history of science; organization of symposia; Pres. Prof. Dr EKMELEDDIN İHSANOĞLU.

Türkiye Deniz Araştırmaları Vakfı (TUDAV) (Turkish Marine Research Foundation): POB 10, Beykoz, 81650 Istanbul; tel. (216) 424-07-72; e-mail kcguven@yahoo.com .tr; internet www.tudav.org; f. 1993; marine sciences; library of 11,243 vols; Dir Prof. Dr KASIM CEMAL GUVEN; publ. *Journal of The*

Black Sea Mediterranean Environment (4 a year).

Physical Sciences

Maden Tetkik ve Arama Genel Müdürlüğü (MTA) (General Directorate of Mineral Research and Exploration): İsmet Inönü Bulvarı, Ankara; tel. (312) 287-34-30; e-mail mta@mta.gov.tr; internet www.mta.gov.tr; f. 1935; conducts the Geological Survey of Turkey and evaluates mineral resources; library: see Libraries and Archives; Dir-Gen. A. KEMAL ISIKER; publs *Bulletin of Mineral Research and Exploration* (2 a year, in English), annual reports and maps.

RELIGION, SOCIOLOGY AND ANTHROPOLOGY

Islâm Araştyrmalarý Merkezi (Centre for Islamic Studies): Ycadiye Baðlarbaþý Caddesi, Number 40, 34660 Üsküdar, Istanbul; tel. (216) 474-08-50; e-mail isam@isam.org.tr; internet www.isam.org.tr; f. 1988; library of 225,000 vols, 3,300 periodical titles; Chair. Prof. Dr M. AKIF AYDIN; publ. *Turkish Journal of Islamic Studies*.

TECHNOLOGY

Afet İşleri Genel Müdürlüğü Deprem Araştırma Dairesi (General Directorate of Disaster Affairs Earthquake Research Department): Yüksel Cad. 7/B, Yenişehir, Ankara; tel. (312) 287-36-45; e-mail zemin@ deprem.gov.tr; internet www.deprem.gov.tr; f. 1969; attached to Ministry of Public Works and Resettlement; establishment, operation and maintenance of nationwide strong ground motion recorder network; earthquake prediction; preparation of codes and regulations for earthquake-resistant design and construction; research into earthquake hazard minimization; education and information for the public; comprises Earthquake Engineering, Seismology and Laboratory Divisions; Dir MUSTAFA TAYMAZ; publ. *Bulletin* (4 a year).

Araştırma Dairesi Başkanlığı (Demiryollar, Limanlar ve Hava Meydanları İnşaatı Genel Müdürlüğünün) (Department of Research and Materials (General Directorate of Railways, Harbour and Airport Construction)): Macun mah. Serpme Sok 3, 06338 Yenimahalle, Ankara; tel. (312) 397-33-50; e-mail dlharastirma1@ttnet.net.tr; internet www.dlh.gov.tr/arastirma; f. 1948; road materials testing, pavement design, soil and rock mechanics and geotechnical investigations; 60 staff; library of 2,467 vols; Dir YUSUF ZIYA BOYACI; publ. *Research Bulletin*.

Devlet Su İşleri, Teknik Araştırma ve Kalite Kontrol Dairesi (State Hydraulic Works, Technical Research and Quality Control Department): Ismet Inonu Bul., 06100 Yücetepe, Ankara; tel. (312) 417-83-00; e-mail takk@dsi.gov.tr; internet www.dsi .gov.tr; f. 1958; research and laboratory work on hydraulic engineering, soil mechanics, construction materials and concrete, chemistry, isotopes for hydrology; *in situ* research on water works; library; Dir HAYDAR KOÇAKER; publ. *DSI Teknik Bülteni* (original papers, some in foreign languages).

Marmara Research Centre: POB 21, 41470 Gebze, Kocaeli; tel. (262) 641-23-00; e-mail bilgi@mam.gov.tr; internet www.mam .gov.tr; f. 1972; research into basic and applied sciences, and industrial research; library of 90,000 vols, 746 periodicals; Dir Prof. ÖMER KAYMAKÇALAN.

Sarayköy Nükleer Araştırma ve Eğitim Merkezi (Sarayköy Nuclear Research and Training Centre): Saray Mahallesi, Atom Caddesi, 27 Kazan, 06983 Ankara; tel. (312) 815-43-00; internet www.anaem.gov.tr; f.

1967; attached to the Turkish Atomic Energy Authority; applied research in radiation chemistry and physics, electronics, nuclear agriculture, materials sciences and plasma physics; library of periodicals and technical reports; Dir I. TUKENMEZ; publ. *Turkish Journal of Nuclear Sciences* (2 a year).

Libraries and Archives

Afyon

Gedik Ahmed Paşa Library: Dumlupınar Mah. Şeyh Mehmet, Cad. 1, Afyon; tel. (272) 213-54-33; f. 1785; 30,000 vols.

Ankara

Ankara Üniversitesi, Kütüphane ve Dokümantasyon Daire Başkanlığı (Ankara University Libraries and Documentation Centre): Şevket Aziz Kansu Bldg, İncitaşı Sok, Beşevler, Ankara; tel. (312) 223-57-61; e-mail atilgan@ankara.edu.tr; internet www.ankara.edu.tr; f. 1946; 722,309 vols, 33,000 ebooks, 621 printed periodicals, 11,000 ejournals, 4,308 audiovisual materials, 17,872 MSS and 29,029 dissertations and theses; Library Dir Dr DOGAN ATILGAN; publs *Ankara Avrupa Çalışmaları Dergisi, Ankara Üniversitesi Dil ve Tarih-Coğrafya Fakültesi Dergisi, Ankara Üniversitesi Hukuk Fakültesi Dergisi, Ankara Üniversitesi Siyasal Bilgiler Fakültesi Dergisi, Ankara Üniversitesi Tıp Fakültesi Mecmuası, Ankara Üniversitesi Veteriner Fakültesi Dergisi, Ankara Üniversitesi Ziraat Fakültesi Tarım Bilimleri Dergisi.*

Library of National Defence: Ankara; f. 1877; 8,678 vols in Turkish, 5,820 vols in other languages; state-governed.

Maden Tetkik ve Arama Genel Müdürlüğü Kütüphanesi (General Directorate of Mineral Research and Exploration Library): Uzaktan Algılama Merkezi, Söğütözü, 06520 Ankara; tel. (312) 287-34-30; e-mail uzak1@mta.gov.tr; internet www.mta.gov.tr; f. 1935; 48,000 vols, 2,321 serial titles.

Middle East Technical University Library: Universiteler Mahallesi, Dumlupına Bulvarı Number 1, Cankaya, 06800 Ankara; tel. (312) 210-27-80; e-mail lib-hot-line@metu.edu.tr; internet www.lib.metu.edu.tr; f. 1956; maintains custody of the univ.'s recording, microfilm and projection equipment; 663,882 vols, 461,323 books, 183,259 bound periodicals, 1,317 journal subscriptions, 51,298 ejournals, 132,638 ebooks in 150 databases, 19,300 master and doctoral theses; Dir CEVAT GÜVEN.

Milli Kütüphane (National Library of Turkey): Bahçelievler, Ankara 06940; tel. (312) 222-38-12; e-mail info@mkutup.gov.tr; internet www.mkutup.gov.tr; f. 1946; 1,136,997 vols, 911,675 vols of periodicals, 35,024 MSS, 197,577 non-book items; Pres. TUNCEL ACAR; publs *Türkiye Bibliyografyası* (Turkish National Bibliography, 12 a year), *Türkiye Makaleler Bibliyografyası* (Bibliography of articles in Turkish periodicals, 12 a year).

Public Library: Ankara; f. 1922; 21,000 vols in Turkish, 10,200 vols in European languages, over 1,200 MSS in Arabic and Persian.

Türkiye Büyük Millet Meclisi Kütüphane ve Arşiv Hizmetleri Başkanlığı (Turkish Grand National Assembly Library and Archives Services Department): TBMM Kütüphane ve Arşiv Hizmetleri Başkanlığı, 06543 Bakanlıklar, Ankara; tel. (312) 420-68-35; e-mail kutuphane@tbmm.gov.tr; internet www.tbmm.gov.tr/kutuphane; f. 1920; 271,298 vols in social sciences incl. 243,606

in Turkish, 12,578 in Ottoman Turkish language, 34,349 in English, 17,090 in French, 1,000 in Arabic and Persian, 60 MSS, 59,134 vols of periodicals; Chair. MEHMET TOPRAK; publ. *Bilgi* (4 a year).

Antalya

Antalya Tekelioğlu İl Halk Kütüphanesi (Tekelioğlu Library): Ucgen Mah. 96. Sok. 54, Antalya; tel. (242) 344-51-37; f. 1924; 5,000 vols, nearly 2,000 MSS in Persian, Arabic and Turkish; Dir AYŞE D. SAVGUN.

Balıkeşir

Il Halk Kütüphanesi, Balıkeşir (Provincial Public Library, Balıkeşir): Bahçelievler Mah Kıralı Sok., Balıkeşir; tel. (266) 241-32-33; f. 1901; 1,286 MSS in Turkish, Arabic and Persian, 49,000 vols in Turkish, Arabic and English, 766 in other languages, 5,088 periodicals; Dir A. ERCAN TIĞ.

Darende

Mehmet Paşa Library: Darende; f. 1776; 4,000 vols, 800 MSS.

Edirne

Selimiye Library: Edirne; f. 1575; 36,113 vols (incl. 3,172 MSS and 3,894 vols in Arabic); Librarian OZLEM AĞIRGAN.

Isparta

Halil Hamit Paşa Library: Isparta; f. 1783; 20,200 vols, over 850 MSS; Dir MAHMUT KAYICI.

Istanbul

Atatürk Kitaplığı (Ataturk Library): Mete Caddesi 45, Taksim, Istanbul; tel. (212) 249-56-83; f. 1929; public library; 184,000 vols.

Beyazıt Devlet Kütüphanesi (Beyazit State Library): Turan Emeksiz Sok 6, 344450 Beyazıt, Istanbul; tel. (212) 522-31-67; f. 1882; legal deposit library; 500,000 vols in various languages, 11,120 MSS, 32,992 photographs, 21,616 periodicals; Dir YUSUF TAVACI.

Boğaziçi University Library: Bebek, 80815 Istanbul; tel. (212) 257-50-16; e-mail bulib@boun.edu.tr; internet www.library.boun.edu.tr; f. 1863; 375,000 vols in English and other languages, incl. a special colln of over 30,332 vols on the Near East, 10,000 rare books and MSS; 220 periodicals, 2,500 records and 200 CDs; Librarian HATICE ÜN.

Ecumenical Patriarchate Library: İstanbul Rum Patrikliği, Sadrazam Ali Paşa Caddesi 35, 34220 Fener, Istanbul; internet www.patriarchate.org; foundation dates from beginning of Patriarchate, reorganization 1890; 25,000 vols in main library, 1,500 MSS, 45,000 vols in br. library at Orthodox Seminary of Heybeliada; Dir Rev. PANAĞHIOTIS THEODORIDIS (under the jurisdiction of the Holy Synod).

Institute of Turkology Library: Istanbul University, 34452 Beyazıt, Istanbul; f. 1924; 50,000 vols relating to Turkish language, literature, history and culture.

Istanbul Teknik Üniversitesi Kütüphane ve Dokümantasyon Daire (Istanbul Technical University Library and Documentation Division): Ayazağa Kampüsü, Maslak 34469, Istanbul; tel. (212) 285-39-96; e-mail kutuphane@itu.edu.tr; internet www.library.itu.edu.tr; f. 1795; six separate libraries on five university campuses; 372,000 vols; Dir of Libraries AYHAN KAYGUSUZ.

Istanbul University Library and Documentation Centre: University PTT 34452, Beyazıt, Istanbul; tel. (212) 455-57-83; e-mail uko@istanbul.edu.tr; internet www.kutuphane.istanbul.edu.tr; f. 1925; com-

prises the central university library and 17 faculty libraries; 500,000 vols, 18,606 MSS, 18,000 periodicals (3,100 current), 35,000 theses; Dir Doç. Dr ÜMIT KONYA.

Köprülü Yazma Eser Kütüphanesi (Köprülü Library): Divan Yolu Cad. 29, Cemberlitas-Eminonu, Istanbul; tel. (212) 516-83-13; f. 1677; 3,000 vols, 2,755 MSS, of which 193 are from early Ottoman presses, and 42 handwritten works from before the 10th century.

Millet Kütüphanesi (Public Library): Macar Kardeşler Cad. 85, 34260 Fatih, Istanbul; tel. (212) 631-36-07; f. 1916; 33,980 vols, 8,844 MSS.

Nuruosmaniye Library: Camii Avlusu, Cagaloglu, Istanbul; tel. (212) 527-20-04; f. 1755; 6,000 vols, 5,000 MSS.

Süleymaniye Kütüphanesi (Süleymaniye Library): Aysekadin Hamami Sok. 35, Beyazıt, Istanbul; tel. (212) 520-64-60; f. 1557; 113,068 vols and 66,117 MSS in Turkish, Uyghur, Arabic and Persian; 109 different collections incl. those from Ayasofya, Fatih and Husrev Pasha; MS restoration service; brs at Atif Efendi, Hacı Selim Ağa, Köprülü, Nuru-Osmaniye, Ragıppaşa; Dir Dr NEVZAT KAYA.

Women's Library and Information Center Foundation: Fener Mahallesi, Fener Vapur Iskelesi Karşısı, Fener Haliç, 34220 Istanbul; tel. (212) 534-95-50; 6,500 vols; Dir BEKIR KEMAL ATAMAN.

Izmir

National Library of Izmir: Milli Kütüphane Cad. 39, Konak- Izmir; f. 1912; 299,000 vols in Turkish, 40,000 vols in European languages, 19,000 vols in Oriental scripts, 4,000 MSS, 4,843 periodicals; Dir ALI RIZA ATAY.

Konya

Public Library: Purcuklu Mah., Turbe Cad. 23, Karatoy, Konya; f. 1947; 20,000 vols, 6,000 MSS.

Nevşehir

Damat Ibrahim Paşa Library: Nevşehir; f. 1727; 5,500 vols, 600 MSS.

Museums and Art Galleries

Adana

Adana Bölge Müzesi (Adana Regional Museum): Adana; f. 1926; depts of archaeology and ethnography; conference hall, laboratories, library and administrative sections; more than 107,000 items from the Neolithic to Roman and Byzantine periods; unique statue of a god made from natural crystal dating from Hittite Empire.

Amasya

Amasya Müzesi: Atatürk Cad. 91 Amasya; tel. (358) 218-45-13; f. 1926; moved 1961 to the Gök Medrese Mosque; archaeological finds from the early Bronze Age to Ottoman period; includes mummies dating from the Imperial period.

Ankara

Anadolu Medeniyetleri Müzesi (Museum of Anatolian Civilizations): Samanpazarı, Ankara; tel. (312) 324-31-60; e-mail anmedmuz@gmail.com; internet www.anadolumedeniyetlerimuzesi.gov.tr; f. 1921; exhibits cover the Palaeolithic, Neolithic, Chalcolithic, Early Bronze Age, Hittite, Phrygian, Urartian and Classical periods;

Hittite reliefs from Alaca, Carchemish, Sakcagözü and Aslantepe and Ankara regions; collns represent excavations at Karain, Çatal Hüyük, Hacılar, Can Hasan, Alacahöyük, Ahlatlıbel, Karaz, Alişar, Karaoğlan, Karayavşan, Oymaağaç, Merzifon, Beycesultan, Kültepe, Acemhöyük, İnandık, Boğazköy, Eskiyapar, Patnos, Adilcevaz, Uşak-İkiztepe, Pazarlı, Gordion (now Yassihoyuk), Altıntepe, with spec. sections for cuneiform tablets and coins; library of 6,567 vols; Dir MELIH ARSLAN; publs *Museum Annual*, *Museum Conference Annual*, *Museum Lectures* (1 a year), *Museum News* (2 a year), *The Anatolian Civilizations Museum Periodical*.

Anıtkabir Atatürk Müzesi (Atatürk's Mausoleum and Museum): Anıt Caddesi, Tandoğan, Ankara; tel. (312) 231-79-75; internet www.tsk.mil.tr./anitkabir; f. 1953; official and civil possessions of Mustafa Kemal Atatürk (1881–1938), founder of the Turkish Republic and its first Pres.; colln incl. documents, medals, plaques and albums; panoramas and paintings of battles of the founding of the Turkish republic; library of 3,123 vols from the private library of Atatürk; Museum Cmdr Lt-Col HALIM KURT.

Ethnographical Museum: Talatpasa Bulvarı, Ankara; tel. (312) 311-95-56; f. 1930; specimens of Turkish and Islamic art, archives and Islamic seals; library of 6,245 vols; Dir SEMA KOÇ.

Kurtuluş Savaşı ve Cumhuriyet Müzeleri (Museums of the Turkish Independence War and Turkish Republic): Cumhuriyet Bulvarı No. 14–22, Ulus, Ankara; f. 1961; located in former Grand National Assembly buildings; library of 60,000 vols and 20,000 documents; Dir MUSTAFA SÜEL.

Natural History Museum: MTA, Genel Müdürlüğü, Eskişehir Yolu Balgat, 06520 Ankara; tel. (312) 201-23-96; e-mail muze1@mta.gov.tr; internet www.mta.gov.tr; f. 1968; attached to General Directorate of Mineral Research and Exploration; Dir Dr GONCA NALCIOGLU.

Antakya

Hatay Museum: Gündüz Cad. 1, Antakya, Hatay; tel. (326) 214-61-68; f. 1934; collection of mosaics from Roman Antioch, also finds from Al-Mina, Atchana, Çatal Hüyük, Judeidah and Tainat excavations; Dir MEHMET ERDEM.

Antalya

Antalya Müzesi (Antalya Museum): Konyaaltı Caddesi, Antalya; tel. (242) 238-56-88; f. 1922; prehistory, archaeology, numismatics, ethnography, children's section and garden exhibition; library of 7,500 vols; Dir SELAHATTIN EYÜP AKSU.

Aydın

Aydın Müzesi: Hasan Efendi Mahallesi, Kapalı Spor Salonu yanı Aydın; tel. (256) 225-22-59; f. 1959; archaeology, ethnography, historical coins.

Bergama

Pergamon Museum: Cumhurıyet Cadd. 10, 35700 Bergama-Izmir; tel. (232) 631-28-83; f. 1936; houses the historical relics discovered as the result of excavations conducted at Pergamon; Dir ADNAN SARIOĞLU.

Bodrum

Bodrum Sualtı Arkeoloji Müzesi (Bodrum Museum of Underwater Archaeology): 48000 Bodrum; tel. (252) 316-25-16; e-mail bodrum-museum@yahoo.com; internet www.bodrum-museum.com; f. 1964 in the castle of Bodrum (built 15th century, by the Knights of St John from Rhodes); finds from land and underwater, incl. ceramics, metal, stone, gold and glass, from the Mycenaean, Attic, Hellenic, Roman, Byzantine and Ottoman eras; remains of late Bronze age ship; Dir (vacant).

Bursa

Bursa Arkeoloji Müzesi: Kültürpark, Bursa; tel. (224) 234-49-18; f. 1902; archaeological finds from Bursa, Balıkesir and Bilecik; prehistoric, Roman and Byzantine finds, stone, ceramic, glass and metal objects, coins; library of 3,824 vols; Chief Officer SALIH KÜTÜK.

Bursa Türk ve Islâm Eserleri Müzesi (Bursa Turkish and Islamic Art Museum): Yeşil, Bursa; tel. (224) 327-75-39; f. 1975 in the Yeşil Medrese, built by the Ottoman Sultan Mehmet I Çelebi; items from 12th century to late Ottoman period; illuminated MSS, samples of calligraphy, woodwork, metalwork, embroidery, costumes, ceramics; open-air museum of gravestones.

Çanakkale

Truva Müzesi (Troy Museum): Çanakkale; at the entrance to the ruins of Troy in Çanakkale; small exhibitions of pottery, figurines, statues and glass objects.

Eskişehir

Eskişehir Arkeoloji Müzesi: Akarbaşı Mahallesi, Hasan Polatkan Bul. 64, Eskişehir; tel. (222) 230-13-71; e-mail muze2603@kultur.gov.tr; f. 1935; plant and animal fossils; prehistory (ceramics, idols, stone and bone objects); the walls are decorated with late Roman mosaics found in excavations at Doryleum; Museum Head M. DURSUN ÇAĞLAR.

Istanbul

Âsiyan Museum: Aşiyan Yokuşu, 80810 Bebek, Istanbul; tel. (212) 263-69-86; home of Turkish poet and artist T. Fikret (1867–1915).

Askeri Müze ve Kültür Sitesi Komutanlığı (Military Museum and Cultural Centre): Harbiye, Istanbul; tel. (212) 233-27-20; f. 1846; military uniforms, weapons, tents, trophies, flags and standards from ancient times; library of 26,000 vols; Dir Col ZAFER KILIÇ.

Ayasofya (Hagia Sophia—Saint Sophia) Museum: Sultanahmet, Fatih, 34122 Istanbul; tel. (212) 522-09-89; e-mail ayasofyamuzesi@kultur.gov.tr; internet www.kultur.gov.tr; f. 1935; built as an East Roman Basilica by Justinian and dedicated in AD 537, it was a church until 1453, after which it became a mosque; in 1935 it was made a state museum; contains East Roman and Turkish antiquities; Pres. Assoc. Prof. A. HALUK DURSUN; Dir HAYRULLAH CENGIZ; publ. *The Annual of St Sophia*.

Istanbul Arkeoloji Müzeleri (Archaeological Museums of Istanbul): Gülhane, 34400 Istanbul; tel. (212) 520-77-40; f. 1891; includes Archaeological, Turkish Tiles and Ancient Orient museums, with Sumerian, Akkadian, Hittite, Assyrian, Egyptian, Urartu, Phrygian, Greek, Roman and Byzantine works of art; more than 1m. exhibits; library of 80,000 vols; Dir HALIL ÖZEKNLI.

İstanbul Deniz Müzesi (Istanbul Naval Museum): Deniz Müzesi Komutanlığı, Beşiktaş, İstanbul; tel. (212) 327-43-45; e-mail muze.istanbul.iletisim@dzkk.tsk.tr; internet www.denizmuzeleri.tsk.tr; f. 1897, current location 1961; colln of 20,000 objects incl. amphoras, Atatürk's belongings, bells, certificates, clocks and furniture, coins, escutcheons and coat-of-arms, figureheads, firmans, flags and ensigns, historical caiques, lights, lithographic limestone, maps, MSS, navigational instruments, orders (decorations) and medals, paintings, photographs, plates, seals, ship models, ship riggings, stamps, stone inscription tablet, tombstones, tughras of sultans, uniforms, weapons; library of 20,000 vols, 20m. documents, 15 catalogues, 863 maps, 41 atlases and photographs consisting of 30,000 pieces; Dir Capt. FATIH ERBAŞ.

Istanbul Resim ve Heykel Müzesi (Museum of Painting and Sculpture): Beşiktaş, Istanbul; tel. (212) 261-42-98; f. 1937; Turkish paintings and sculptures since 19th century; international art exhibitions; Dir Prof. KEMAL İSKENDER.

Sabancı Üniversitesi Sakıp Sabancı Müzesi (Sabancı University Sakıp Sabancı Museum): Sakıp Sabancı Cad. 42, Emirgan 34467, Istanbul; tel. (212) 277-22-00; e-mail muze@sabanciuniv.edu; internet muze.sabanciuniv.edu; f. 2002; permanent colln of calligraphic items since 15th century, paintings since 19th century; temporary exhibitions; Dir Dr NAZAN ÖLÇER.

Tanzimat Müzesi (Tanzimat Museum): Gülhane Parkı, 94400 Sirkeci, Istanbul; tel. (212) 512-63-04; f. 1952 in Ihlamur Pavilion, current site since 1983; operated by Istanbul Metropolitan Municipality; documents, paintings and objects pertaining to the Tanzimat period of reform 1839–76; Curator FADIME GELEŞ.

Topkapı Palace Museum: Sultanahmet 34400, Istanbul; tel. (212) 522-44-22; internet www.kultur.gov.tr; palace built by Mehmed II; collns of Turkish armour, cloth, embroidery, glass and porcelain, copper- and silver-ware, treasure, paintings, miniatures, illuminated MSS, royal coaches, collns of Sèvres and Bohemian crystal and porcelain, clocks, important colln of Chinese and Japanese porcelain amassed by the Sultans, colln of MSS, Ottoman tent; Audience Hall, Council Hall of Viziers, Baghdad and Revan Köşks, Harem; library of 18,000 MSS and 200,000 archive documents; Dir FILIZ ÇAĞMAN.

Türk ve Islam Eserleri Müzesi (Museum of Turkish and Islamic Art): Ibrahim Paşa Sarayı, At Meydani 46, Sultanahmet, Istanbul 34400; tel. (212) 518-18-05; internet www.tiem.org; f. 1914; Turkish and Islamic rugs, illuminated MSS, sculpture in stone and stucco, woodcarvings, metalwork and ceramics, traditional crafts and ethnographical material, all gathered from Turkish mosques and tombs; library: 4,142 MSS and 3,279 vols; Dir NAZAN ÖLCER.

Izmir

Izmir Arkeoloji Müzesi: Halit Rıfat Paşa Cad. 4, Konak, Izmir; tel. (232) 489-07-96; e-mail izmirmuze@ttnet.net.tr; f. 1927; works from the Archaic, Classical and Hellenistic periods of the Ionian civilization; Dir MEHMET TUNA.

Konya

Konya Museums: Il Kültür Müdürlüğü, Müze Müdürlüğü, Konya Valiliği; Dir for Museums Dr ERDOĞAN EROL..

Attached Museums:

   Atatürk Museum: colln of documents and objects connected with Atatürk, also Konya clothing and other ethnographic exhibits.

   Classical Museum: collns of Neolithic, early Bronze Age, Hittite, Phrygian, Greek, Roman and Byzantine monuments.

   Mevlâna Museum: f. in Mevlâna Turbe; Seljuk, Ottoman and Turkish collections, clothing, carpets, coins, library.

Seljuk Museum: f. in Ince Minare; contains stone and wooden works of the Seljuk period.

Sirçali Medresseh: sarcophagus and inscription, collections of Seljuk and Ottoman period.

Turkish Ceramics Museum: f. in Karatay Medresseh; contains ceramics from 13th–18th centuries.

Polatlı

Gordion Museum: Polatlı, Ankara; tel. (312) 638-21-88; e-mail anmedmuz@marketweb.net.tr; f. 1965; built near the Great Tumulus believed to be that of the Phrygian king Midas; archaeological items found during excavations at Gordion (now Yassıhöyük); Dir ILHAN TEMIZSOY.

Selçuk

Efes Müzesi Müdürlügü (Ephesus Museum): Kusadasi Cad., 35920 Selçuk-Izmir; tel. (232) 892-60-10; f. 1929; art (mostly statues and reliefs) excavated from Ephesus; library of 3,200 vols; Dir SELAHATTIN ERDEMGIL; publ. *Efes Müzesi Yıllıgı* (1 a year).

Selimiye

Side Müzesi: Manavgat-Antalya, Side (Selimiye); tel. (242) 753-10-06; f. 1962; museum is located in a Late Roman bath; statues and busts of Roman gods, goddesses and emperors; library of 985 vols; Dir ORHAN ATVUR.

Van

Van Müzesi: Şerefiye Mahallesi, Hacıosman Sokak 9, Van; tel. (432) 216-11-39; f. 1947; archaeological finds from the Urartu Civilization.

Universities

ABANT IZZET BAYSAL ÜNİVERSİTESİ

Gölköy Kampüsü, 14280 Bolu
Telephone: (374) 254-10-00
Internet: www.ibu.edu.tr
Founded 1992
State control
Languages of instruction: Turkish, English
Academic year: September to June

Pres.: Prof. Dr HAYRI COSKUN
Vice-Pres.: Prof. Dr AKCAHAN GEPDIREMEN
Vice-Pres.: Prof. Dr MEHMET BAHAR
Vice-Rector: Prof. Dr RESUL ERYIGIT

Number of teachers: 930
Number of students: 17,400

DEANS

Faculty of Arts and Sciences: Prof. Dr AHMET VARILCI
Faculty of Dentistry: Prof. Dr ISMET DURAN
Faculty of Economics and Admin. Sciences: Prof. Dr RAMAZAN GOZEN
Faculty of Education: Prof. Dr CANAN CETIN-KANAT
Faculty of Engineering: Prof. Dr MAHMUT ACIMIS
Faculty of Fine Arts: Prof. Dr HAYRI COSKUN (acting)
Faculty of Medicine: Prof. Dr HASAN KOCOGLU

ADNAN MENDERES ÜNİVERSİTESİ

Aytepe Mevkii, Merkez Kampus, 09010 Aydin
Telephone: (256) 218-20-37
E-mail: erasmus@adu.edu.tr
Internet: www.adu.edu.tr

Founded 1992
State control
Language of instruction: Turkish
Academic year: September to June

Rector: Prof. Dr MUSTAFA BIRINCIOĞLU
Vice-Rector: Dr ALI BELGE
Vice-Rector: Prof. Dr A. SEDA SARACALOĞLU
Vice-Rector: Prof. Dr CAVIT BIRCAN
Sec.-Gen.: YUSUF KÖK (acting)

Number of teachers: 1,240
Number of students: 28,100

Publications: *Bulletin* (4 a year), *Journal of Medical Faculty*

DEANS

Faculty of Agriculture: Prof. Dr ÖMER FARUK DURDU
Faculty of Economics and Administration: Prof. Dr MUSTAFA BIRINCIOĞLU
Faculty of Education: Prof. Dr A. SEDA SARACALOĞLU
Faculty of Medicine: Prof. Dr ABDULVAHIT YÜKSELEN
Faculty of Science and Letters: Prof. Dr ADNAN ERDAĞ
Faculty of Veterinary Science: Prof. Dr HASAN EREN

AFYON KOCATEPE ÜNİVERSİTESİ

Ahmet Necdet Sezer Kampüsü, Gazligol Yolu, 03200 Afyonkarahisar
Telephone: (272) 444-03-03
E-mail: rektor@aku.edu.tr
Internet: www.aku.edu.tr

Founded 1992
State control

Rector: Prof. Dr ALI ALTUNTAŞ
Vice-Rector: Prof. Dr BELKIS ÖZKARA
Vice-Rector: Prof. Dr KEMALETTIN ÇONKAR
Vice-Rector: Prof. Dr NECAT İMIRZALIOĞLU
Gen. Sec.: İSMET DOĞAN
Librarian: ABDULLAH KÜNDEYİ

Library of 127,592 print vols and ebooks, 840 periodicals
Number of teachers: 1,030
Number of students: 28,849 (27,339 undergraduate, 1,510 graduate)

DEANS

Faculty of Arts and Sciences: Prof. Dr BELKIS ÖZKARA
Faculty of Arts and Sciences (Uşak): Prof. Dr LÜTFI ÖZAV
Faculty of Economics and Administrative Sciences (Uşak): Prof. Dr H. HÜSEYIN BAYRAKLI
Faculty of Economics and Management Science: Prof. Dr KEMALETTIN ÇONKAR
Faculty of Education: Prof. Dr MUSTAFA ERGÜN
Faculty of Education (Uşak): Prof. Dr ADNAN ŞİSMAN
Faculty of Engineering: Prof. Dr RAMAZAN ŞEVIK
Faculty of Engineering (Uşak): Prof. Dr FIKRI ŞENOL
Faculty of Fine Arts: Prof. Dr RIZA AŞIKOĞLU
Faculty of Medicine: Prof. Dr NECAT İMIRZA-LIĞOLU
Faculty of Technical Education: Prof. Dr GALIP SAİD
Faculty of Veterinary Medicine: Prof. Dr HIFZI OĞUZ SARIMEHMETOĞLU

AKDENIZ ÜNİVERSİTESİ

Dumlupınar Bulvarı Kampus, 07058 Antalya
Telephone: (242) 227-59-83
E-mail: international@akdeniz.edu.tr
Internet: www.akdeniz.edu.tr

Founded 1982; previously affiliated to Ankara Univ.
State control

Language of instruction: Turkish
Academic year: October to June

Rector: Prof. Dr MUSTAFA AKAYDIN
Vice-Rector: Prof. Dr MEHMET RIFKI AKTEKIN
Vice-Rector: Prof. Dr SADIK ÇAKMAKÇI
Vice-Rector: Prof. Dr MUSTAFA PEKMEZCI
Gen. Sec.: NUSRET ÇELIK
Librarian: NEVZAT ŞABAN

Number of teachers: 1,600
Number of students: 19,100

Publications: *Journal of the Faculty of Agriculture*, *Journal of the Faculty of Medicine* (4 a year), *University Bulletin*

DEANS

Faculty of Agribusiness: Prof. Dr AHMET AKTAŞ
Faculty of Agriculture: Prof. Dr HALIL İBRAHIM UZUN
Faculty of Arts and Sciences: Prof. Dr MUSTAFA GÖKÇEOĞLU
Faculty of Communications: Prof. Dr ÜMIT ATABEK
Faculty of Economics and Administrative Sciences: Prof. Dr FULYA SARVAN
Faculty of Education: Prof. Dr MEHMET YALÇIN
Faculty of Engineering: Prof. Dr HIKMET RENDE
Faculty of Fine Arts: Prof. Dr ABDULLAH UZ
Faculty of Fisheries: Prof. Dr RAMAZAN İKIZ
Faculty of Law: Prof. Dr MERAL SAĞIR ÖZTOPRAK
Faculty of Medicine: Prof. Dr MUSTAFA MELIKOĞLU
Faculty of Veterinary Science: Prof. Dr BAYRAM ALI YUKARI

ANADOLU ÜNİVERSİTESİ
(Anadolu University)

Yunus Emre Kampüsü, 26470 Eskişehir
Telephone: (222) 335-05-80
E-mail: gensek@anadolu.edu.tr
Internet: www.anadolu.edu.tr

Founded 1958
State control
Languages of instruction: Turkish, English
Academic year: September to June

Rector: Prof. Dr DAVUT AYDIN
Vice-Rector: Prof. Dr AYDIN ZIYA OZGUR
Vice-Rector: Prof. Dr MERYEM AKOGLAN KOZAK
Vice-Rector: Prof. Dr MUSTAFA CAVCAR
Vice-Rector: Prof. Dr ENDER SUVACI
Vice-Rector: Prof. Dr NACI GUNDOGAN
Registrar and Sec.-Gen.: CETIN KAYA
Librarian: ADNAN YILMAZ

Library of 200,000 vols
Number of teachers: 1,800
Number of students: 1,387,729 (incl. open-education students)

Publications: *Journal of Sciences and Technology* (2 a year), *Journal of Social Sciences* (2 a year), *Online International Journal of Communication Studies* (2 a year), *Turkish Online Journal of Distance Education* (2 a year)

DEANS

Faculty of Architecture and Design: Prof. Dr SEVIN AKSOYLU
Faculty of Communication Sciences: Prof. Dr E. NEZIH ORHON
Faculty of Economics: Prof. Dr SADIK RIDVAN KARLUK
Faculty of Economic and Administrative Sciences: Prof. Dr RECAI DONMAZ
Faculty of Education: Prof. Dr GUL DURMUSOGLU KOSE
Faculty of Engineering and Architecture: Prof. Dr TUNCAY DOGEROGLU
Faculty of Fine Arts: Prof. Dr BILGIHAN UZUNER

Faculty of Humanities: Prof. Dr MUHSIN MACIT

Faculty of Law: Prof. Dr UFUK AYDIN

Faculty of Management: Prof. Dr MELIH ERDOGAN

Faculty of Open Education: Prof. Dr KERIM BANAR

Faculty of Pharmacy: Prof. Dr YASEMIN YAZAN

Faculty of Science: Prof. ERTUGRUL YORUKO-GULLARI

ATTACHED SCHOOLS

College for the Handicapped: e-mail engyo@anadolu.edu.tr; Dir Prof. Dr AHMET KONROT.

School of Civil Aviation: Dir Prof. Dr MUSTAFA KARA.

School of Drama and Music: Dir NAZLI GÜLMEZ.

School of Foreign Languages: Dir Assoc. Prof. HANDAN YAVUZ.

School of Industrial Arts: Dir Prof. Dr YAŞAR HOŞCAN.

School of Physical Education and Sports: Dir Prof. Dr COŞKUN BAYRAK.

School of Tourism and Hotel Management: e-mail turizm@anadolu.edu.tr; Dir Prof. Dr DENIZ BÜLER.

GRADUATE SCHOOLS

Graduate School of Health Sciences: Dir Prof. Dr YUSUF ÖZTÜRK.

Graduate School of Science: e-mail fenens@anadolu.edu.tr; internet www .fenbilens.anadolu.edu.tr; Dir Prof. Dr ORHAN ÖZER.

Graduate School of Social Sciences: Prof. Dr ALTUĞ İFTAR.

Handicapped Research Institute: Eskisehir; tel. (222) 335-29-14; internet eae .anadolu.edu.tr; Dir Prof. Dr ELIF TEKIN IFTAR.

Institute of Communication Sciences: Dir (vacant).

Institute of Educational Sciences: e-mail ensegty@anadolu.edu.tr; internet www.ebe .anadolu.edu.tr; Dir Prof. Dr İLKNUR KEÇIK.

Institute of Fine Arts: Dir Prof. Dr ATILLA ATAR.

Institute of Satellite and Space Sciences: Dir Assoc. Prof. Dr CAN AYDAY.

Institute of Transport Economics: Dir Prof. Dr NEZIH VARCAN

ANKARA ÜNİVERSİTESİ

06100 Tandoğan, Ankara
Telephone: (312) 212-60-40
E-mail: koyuncu@ankara.edu.tr
Internet: www.ankara.edu.tr
Founded 1946
State control
Language of instruction: Turkish
Academic year: October to June

Rector: Prof. Dr CEMAL TALUĞ
Vice-Rector: Prof. Dr NILGÜN HALLORAN
Vice-Rector: Prof. Dr N. YASEMIN YALIM
Vice-Rector: Prof. Dr ARGUN KARACABEY
Gen. Sec.: SERPIL GÜNER
Registrar: Prof. Dr S. TUNA KARAHAN
Registrar: SINEM ÖZKARA
Librarian: Prof. Dr DOĞAN ATILGAN
Library of 800,000 vols and 7,984 periodicals
Number of teachers: 3,550 44500

Publications: Ankara Üniversitesi Yıllığı (Annals of the University), Turkish Journal of Geographical Sciences, and faculty and research institute publications

DEANS

Çankırı Faculty of Forestry: Prof. Dr İLHAMI KÖKSAL

Faculty of Agriculture: Prof. Dr AHMET ÇOLAK

Faculty of Communication: Prof. Dr ESER KÖKER

Faculty of Dentistry: Prof. Dr ADNAN ÖZTÜRK
Faculty of Divinity: Prof. Dr NESIMI YAZICI
Faculty of Education: Prof. Dr GÖNÜL AKÇA-METE

Faculty of Engineering: Prof. Dr ALI ULVI YILMAZER

Faculty of Health Education: Prof. Dr ŞEN-GÜL HABLEMITOĞLU

Faculty of Humanities: Prof. Dr RAHMI ER
Faculty of Law: Prof. Dr MUSTAFA AKKAYA
Faculty of Medicine: Prof. Dr İLKER ÖKTEN
Faculty of Natural and Applied Science: Prof. Dr MUAMMER CANEL

Faculty of Pharmacy: Prof. Dr MAKSUT COŞKUN

Faculty of Political Science: Prof. Dr CELAL GÖLE

Faculty of Veterinary Medicine: Prof. Dr İBRAHIM BURGU

ATTACHED INSTITUTES

Graduate Institute of Biotechnology: Dir Prof. Dr NEJAT AKAR.

Graduate Institute of Education: Dir Prof. Dr MERAL UYSAL.

Graduate Institute of Hepatology: Dir Prof. Dr S. CIHAN YURDAYDIN.

Graduate Institute of the History of the Turkish Revolution: e-mail tite@ankara .edu.tr; Dir Prof. Dr YAVUZ ERCAN.

Graduate Institute of Medical Jurisprudence: Dir Prof. Dr HALIL GÜMÜŞ.

Graduate Institute of Medical Sciences: e-mail eabayrak@ankara.edu.tr; Dir Prof. Dr RIFAT VURAL.

Graduate Institute of Science: Dir Prof. Dr METIN OLGUN.

Graduate Institute of Social Sciences: e-mail bsosbil@ankara.edu.tr; Dir Prof. Dr CAN HAMAMCI.

ATTACHED SCHOOLS AND COLLEGES

Çankırı School of Health: Dir Prof. Dr MEHMET KIYAN.

School of Başkent: Dir Prof. Dr HANDE K. ERSOY.

School of Beypazarı: Dir Prof. Dr İLHAN KARAÇAL.

School of Çankırı: Dir Prof. Dr SABAHATTIN BALCI.

School of Cebeci Health Services: Dir Doç. Dr TÜLIN BEDÜK.

School of Dikimevi Health Services: Dir Prof. Dr AHMET DERYA AYSEV.

School of Foreign Languages: Dir Prof. Dr ERSIN ONULDURAN.

School of Home Economics (Faculty of Agriculture): Dir Prof. Dr EMINE GÖNEN.

School of Justice (Faculty of Law): Dir Doç. Dr HALUK KONURALP.

School of Kalecik: Dir Prof. Dr DOĞAN ERDOĞAN.

School of Kastamonu: Dir Prof. Dr BAHRI GÖKÇEBAY.

School of Physical Education and Sports: Dir Prof. Dr EMIN ERGEN.

State Conservatory: e-mail devkons@ ankara.edu.tr; Dir Prof. Dr NURHAN KARADAĞ

ATATÜRK ÜNİVERSİTESİ

Rektörlüğü, 25240 Erzurum
Telephone: (442) 231-10-30

E-mail: ata@atauni.edu.tr
Internet: www.atauni.edu.tr
Founded 1957, reorganized 1982 following the Higher Education Reform
State control
Language of instruction: Turkish
Academic year: October to June

Pres.: HIKMET KOÇAK
Sec.-Gen.: USTUN OZEN
Head of Int. Affairs Office: FAHRI YAVUZ
Library of 300,000 vols
Number of teachers: 2,530 (incl. teaching assts)
Number of students: 40,200

Publications: Atatürk Dergisi (2 a year), Atatürk Üniversitesi Diş Hekimliği Fakültesi Dergisi (4 a year), Atatürk Üniversitesi Erzincan Hukuk Fakültesi Dergisi (2 a year), Atatürk Üniversitesi İlahiyat Fakültesi Dergisi (2 a year), Atatürk Üniversitesi Tıp Dergisi (4 a year), Erzincan Eğitim Fakültesi Dergisi (2 a year), Güzel Sanatlar Enstitüsü Dergisi (2 a year), Güzel Sanatlar Fakültesi Sanat Dergisi (2 a year), İktisadi ve İdari Bilimler Dergisi (2 a year), Kazım Karabekir Eğitim Fakültesi Dergisi (2 a year), Sosyal Bilimler Dergisi (2 a year), Sosyal Bilimler Enstitüsü Dergisi (2 a year), Türkiyat Araştırmaları Enstitüsü Dergisi (2 a year), Ziraat Fakültesi Dergisi (4 a year)

DEANS

Faculty of Agriculture: MUSTAFA YILDIRIM CANBOLAT

Faculty of Arts: Prof. Dr YILMAZ ÖZBEK
Faculty of Arts and Sciences (Erzincan): Prof. Dr MUHARREM GÜLERYÜZ

Faculty of Communication and Journalism: Prof. Dr ÖNDER BARLI

Faculty of Dentistry: Prof. Dr ABUBEKIR HARORLI

Faculty of Economics and Administrative Sciences: Prof. Dr SUPHI ORHAN

Faculty of Education: Prof. Dr SAMIH BAYR-AKÇEKEN

Faculty of Education (Ağrı): Prof. Dr BILGE SEYİDOĞLU

Faculty of Education (Bayburt): Prof. Dr AHMET GÜRSES

Faculty of Education (Erzincan): Prof. Dr ERDOĞAN BÜYÜKKASAP

Faculty of Engineering: Prof. Dr CAFER ÇELIK

Faculty of Fine Arts: Prof. Dr KEMALETTIN YİĞİTER

Faculty of Law School (Erzincan): Prof. Dr AHMET NEZIH KÖK

Faculty of Medicine: Prof. Dr M. SELÇUK ATAMANALP

Faculty of Pharmacy: Prof. Dr FATIH AKÇAY
Faculty of Science: O. IRFAN KÜFREVIOĞLU
Faculty of Theology: Prof. Dr BAHATTIN KÖK
Faculty of Veterinary Sciences: Prof. Dr MUSTAFA ATASEVER

ATILIM ÜNİVERSİTESİ

Kızılcaşar Mah. Köyü, 06836 İncek Gölbası, Ankara
Telephone: (312) 586-80-00
E-mail: iro@atilim.edu.tr
Internet: www.atilim.edu.tr
Private control

Pres.: Prof. Dr ABDURRAHIM ÖZGENOĞLU
Gen. Sec.: Prof. Dr ABDÜLAZIZ ŞEREN
Vice-Pres.: Prof. Dr İSMAIL BIRCAN
Vice-Pres.: Prof. Dr İHSAN TARAKÇIOĞLU

DEANS

Faculty of Arts and Sciences: Prof. Dr OYA BATUM MENTEŞE

Faculty of Engineering: Prof. Dr KAMIL İBRAHIM AKMAN

Faculty of Law: Prof. Dr NAMI ÇAĞAN

Faculty of Management: Prof. Dr HALIL İBRAHIM ÜLKER

BAHÇEŞEHİR ÜNİVERSİTESI

34538 Bahçeşehir, Istanbul
Telephone: (212) 669-65-23
E-mail: info@bahcesehir.edu.tr
Internet: www.bahcesehir.edu.tr

Founded 1998

Rector: Prof. Dr SÜHEYL BATUM
Vice-Pres.: Prof. Dr NURBAY GÜLTEKIN
Vice-Pres.: Prof. Dr ESER KARAKAŞ
Library of 43,095 vols, 22,000 ebooks, 472 periodicals and 3,106 ejournals
Number of teachers: 150
Number of students: 1,200

DEANS

Faculty of Architecture: Prof. Dr ERHAN A. BALKAN
Faculty of Arts and Science: Prof. Dr ÖMER ASIM SAÇLI
Faculty of Engineering: Prof. Dr ŞENAY YALÇIN
Faculty of Law: Prof. Dr CUMHUR ÖZAKMAN
Faculty of Management: Prof. Dr İLKAY SUNAR

BALIKESIR ÜNİVERSITESI

Soma Cad, 10100 Balikesir
Telephone: (266) 245-96-50
E-mail: hacioglu@balikesir.edu.tr
Internet: www.balikesir.edu.tr
State control
Academic year: September to July

Rector: Prof. Dr NECDET HACIOĞLU
Gen. Sec.: Prof. Dr FAIZ TÜRKAN
Library of 14,520 vols, 294 periodical subscriptions, 17 databases
Number of teachers: 610
Number of students: 22,141 full-time, 9,108 evening

DEANS

Faculty of Arts and Sciences: OKTAY ARSLAN
Faculty of Economics and Administration: ADEM ÇABUK
Faculty of Education: BEDRIYE TUNÇSIPER
Faculty of Engineering and Architecture: ŞERIF SAYLAN

BAŞKENT ÜNİVERSITESI

Baglica Kampusu Eskisehir Yolu 20 km, Baglica, 06530 Etimesgut, Ankara
Telephone: (312) 234-10-10
E-mail: webmaster@baskent.edu.tr
Internet: www.baskent.edu.tr

Founded 1993
Private control

Rector: Prof. Dr MEHMET HABERAL
Library of 117,044 vols, 1,041 periodicals
Number of teachers: 950
Number of students: 9,360 (8500 undergraduate, 860 postgraduate)

DEANS

Faculty of Commercial Sciences: Prof. Dr DOĞAN YAŞAR AYHAN
Faculty of Communications: Prof. Dr AHMET NEDIM TULUNGÜÇ
Faculty of Dentistry: Prof. Dr KENAN ARAZ
Faculty of Economic and Administrative Sciences: Prof. Dr ABDULKADIR VAROĞLU
Faculty of Education: Prof. Dr ŞEREF MIRASYEDIOĞLU
Faculty of Engineering: Prof. Dr BERNA DENGIZ
Faculty of Fine Arts, Design and Architecture: Prof. Dr ADNAN TEPECIK

Faculty of Health Sciences: Prof. Dr KORKUT ERSOY
Faculty of Law: Prof. Dr KUDRET GÜVEN
Faculty of Medicine: Prof. Dr HALDUN MÜDERRISOĞLU
Faculty of Science and Letters: Prof. Dr RAHMI YAĞBASAN

BEYKENT ÜNİVERSITESI

34900 Beykent, Istanbul
Telephone: (212) 872-64-32
E-mail: info@beykent.edu.tr
Internet: www.beykent.edu.tr

Founded 1997
Language of instruction: English
Academic year: October to June

Rector: Prof. Dr MEHMET FIKRET GEZGIN
Vice-Rector: Prof. Dr MUSTAFA DELICAN
Vice-Rector: Prof. Dr ÜNSAL OSKAY
Gen. Sec.: Prof. Dr NURETTIN ERDEM
Library and Learning Centre Man.: UĞUR BULGAN
Library of 27,500 vols, 165 periodicals, 2,000 CDs, 850 audio cassettes
Number of teachers: 200
Number of students: 2,500

DEANS

Faculty of Arts and Science: ZAFER ASLAN
Faculty of Economics and Administrative Sciences: Prof. Dr MEHMET ZELKA
Faculty of Engineering and Architecture: Prof. Dr ERTAN ÖZKAN
Faculty of Fine Arts: Prof. Dr ÜNSAL OSKAY
Preparatory School: MUSTAFA MELEK (Dir)

BILKENT ÜNİVERSITESI
(Bilkent University)

Bilkent, 06800 Ankara
Telephone: (312) 266-41-25
E-mail: contact@bilkent.edu.tr
Internet: www.bilkent.edu.tr

Founded 1984
Private control (educational foundation)
Language of instruction: English
Academic year: September to June

Pres., Bd of Trustees: Prof. ALI DOĞRAMACI
Rector: Prof. ABDULLAH ATALAR
Vice-Rector for Academic Affairs and Provost: Prof. METIN HEPER
Vice-Rector for Admin. and Financial Affairs and Gen. Sec.: Prof. KÜRŞAT AYDOĞAN
Vice-Rector for Student Affairs: Prof. ORHAN AYTÜR
Vice-Rector and Librarian: Dr PHYLLIS L. ERDOĞAN
Number of teachers: 1,100
Number of students: 12,000

DEANS

Faculty of Art, Design and Architecture: Prof. BÜLENT ÖZGÜÇ
Faculty of Business Administration: Prof. ERDAL EREL
Faculty of Economic, Administrative and Social Sciences: Prof. DILEK ÖNKAL
Faculty of Education: Prof. MEHMET BARAY
Faculty of Engineering: Prof. LEVENT ONURAL
Faculty of Humanities and Letters: Prof. TALAT HALMAN
Faculty of Law: Prof. OSMAN BERAT GÜRZUMAR
Faculty of Music and Performing Arts: Assoc. Prof. IŞIN METIN
Faculty of Science: Prof. HASAN ERTEN
School of Applied Languages: TANJU İNAL
School of English Language: JOHN O'DWYER
Vocational School of Computer Technology and Office Management: KAMER RODOPLU
Vocational School of Tourism and Hotel Services: KAMER RODOPLU

BOĞAZIÇI ÜNİVERSITESI
(Boğaziçi University)

34342 Bebek, Istanbul
Telephone: (212) 358-15-00
E-mail: halkilis@boun.edu.tr
Internet: www.boun.edu.tr

Founded 1863; fmrly Robert College
State control
Languages of instruction: English, Turkish
Academic year: September to July

Rector: Dr AYSE SOYSAL
Vice-Rector: Prof. Dr CEM BEHAR
Vice-Rector: Prof. Dr GULEN AKTAS GREENWOOD
Vice-Rector: Prof. Dr TURAN ÖZTURAN
Dean of Students: Prof. Dr ALI IZZET TEKCAN
Sec.-Gen.: MINE KALENDEROĞLU
Registrar: ZELIHA BALKAN
Librarian: HATICE ÜN
Number of teachers: 980
Number of students: 10,000

Publications: *Boğaziçi University Journal* (1 a year), *Biomedical Engineering Bulletin* (4 a year), *Education Bulletin* (2 a year)

DEANS

Faculty of Arts and Sciences: Prof. Dr OMER OGUZ
Faculty of Economics and Administrative Sciences: Prof. Dr ESER BORAK
Faculty of Education: Prof. Dr CEM ALPTEKIN
Faculty of Engineering: Prof. Dr ALI RIZA KAYLAN

ATTACHED SCHOOLS AND COLLEGES

School of Applied Disciplines: Dir Prof. Dr MELTEM ÖZTURAN.
School of Foreign Languages: Dir Prof. Dr ESER TAYLAN.
School of Vocational Education: Dir Prof. Dr MELTEM ÖZTURAN

BÜLENT ECEVIT ÜNİVERSITESI

67100 Zonguldak
Telephone: (372) 257-41-30
Internet: w3.beun.edu.tr

Founded 1992
State control
Languages of instruction: English, Turkish
Academic year: September to July

Rector: Prof. Dr MAHMUT ÖZER
Vice-Rector: Prof. Dr M. HALUK GÜVEN
Vice-Rector: Prof. Dr MUHLIS BAĞDIGEN
Vice-Rector: Prof. Dr ORHAN UZUN
Chief Librarian: GÜLBEY ÜNAL
Library of 35,000 vols, 12,000 periodicals
Number of teachers: 1,000
Number of students: 21,610

Publications: *Journal of the Faculty of Engineering* (4 a year), *Journal of the Faculty of Forestry* (2 a year)

DEANS

Faculty of Arts and Sciences: Prof. Dr KEMAL BÜYÜKGÜZEL
Faculty of Communication: Prof. Dr MUHLIS BAĞDIGEN
Faculty of Dentistry: Prof. Dr MEHMET SELÇUK ORUÇ
Faculty of Economics and Administration: Prof. Dr HASAN VERGIL
Faculty of Education: Prof. Dr ALI AZAR
Faculty of Engineering: Prof. Dr MUSTAFA AYDIN
Faculty of Fine Arts: Prof. Dr ŞÜKRÜ OĞUZ ÖZDAMAR
Faculty of Medicine: Prof. Dr GAMZE MOÇAN KUZEY
Faculty of Pharmacy: Prof. Dr H. TUĞRUL ATASOY
Faculty of Theology: Prof. Dr HASAN VERGIL

CAG UNIVERSITY

Adana-Mersin, Karayolu uzeri, 33800 Yenice/Mersin
Telephone: (324) 651-48-00
E-mail: cag@cag.edu.tr
Internet: www.cag.edu.tr
Founded 1997
Private control
Languages of instruction: English, Turkish
Academic year: September to June
Rector: Prof. Dr H. ÇETIN BEDESTENCI
Librarian: ELIF ALAYBEYOGLU

Library of 100,000 vols
Number of teachers: 220
Number of students: 3,500
Publication: *Journal of Social Sciences* (2 a year)

DEANS

Faculty of Arts and Sciences: Prof. Dr DENIZ AYNUR GULER
Faculty of Economics and Administration Science: Prof. Dr MUSTAFA BASARAN
Faculty of Law: Prof. Dr YUCEL ERTEKIN
Higher Vocational School: Assoc. Prof. Dr ILHAN OZTURK
Institute of Social Sciences: Asst Prof. Dr MURAT KOC

ÇANAKKALE ONSEKIZ MART ÜNIVERSITESI

Terzioḍlu Kampüsü, 17020 Çanakkale
Telephone: (286) 218-00-18
E-mail: ozelkalem@comu.edu.tr
Internet: www.comu.edu.tr
Founded 1992
State control
Language of instruction: Turkish
Academic year: September to June
Rector: Prof. Dr RAMAZAN LACINER
Vice-Rector: Prof. Dr HUSEYIN OZDEMIR
Vice-Rector: Prof. Dr RAMAZAN GULENDAM
Vice-Rector: Prof. Dr SUKRIYE ARAS HISAR

Library of 350,000 vols, 200,000 ebooks
Number of teachers: 1,450
Number of students: 33,500

DEANS

Faculty of Architecture and Design: Prof. Dr ABDULLAH KELKIT
Faculty of Agriculture: Prof. Dr FEVZI UGUR
Faculty of Communication: Prof. Dr RAMAZAN GULENDAM
Faculty of Economics and Administrative Studies: Prof. Dr HAMIT PALABIYIK
Faculty of Economics and Administrative Sciences in Canakkale: Prof. Dr MEHMET TEKKOYUN
Faculty of Education: Prof. Dr KEMAL YUCE
Faculty of Engineering: Prof. Dr CENGIZ CANER
Faculty of Fine Arts: Prof. Dr ABDULLAH KELKIT
Faculty of Marine Sciences and Technology: Prof. Dr OLCAY HISAR
Faculty of Medicine: Prof. Dr HUSEYIN OZDE-MIR
Faculty of Sciences and Arts: Prof. Dr AHMET ERDEM
Faculty of Theology: Prof. Dr ABDURRAHMAN KURT

PROFESSORS

Faculty of Agriculture (Terzioḍlu Kampüsü, 17020 Çanakkale):

ALTAY, H., Soil
ATASOGLU, C., Animal Feeding
BAYTEKIN, H., Field Crop
CELIK, K., Animal Feeding
EKINCI, H., Soil
GENC, L., Agricultural Structures
GOKKUS, A., Field Crop

KAVDIR, İ., Agriculture Machinery
KAYNAS, K., Plants
KORKMAZ, S., Phytopathology
KUMUK, T., Agriculture Politics
MENDES, M., Biometry
MUFTUOGLU, M., Soil
OZCAN, H., Soil
OZPINAR, A., Entomology
SAVAS, T., Animal Husbandry
TURHAN, H., Agriculture Biotechnology
UGUR, F., Animal Husbandry
YURTMAN, İ., Animal Feeding

Faculty of Economics and Administrative Studies (Biga, Çanakkale):

ACER, Y., International Law
ENER, M., Economics
ERDOGAN, E., Economics
KASIMOGLU, M., Management and Organization
LACINER, S., International Relations
PALABIYIK, H., Environment and Urbanization
TEKKOYUN, M., Operations

Faculty of Education (Terzioḍlu Kampüsü, 17020 Çanakkale):

BAYSAL, H., Physics
KILINC, A., Turkish
KOKSAL, D., Foreign Languages
YASAR, O., Geography
YILDIZ, R., Computer and Technology
YUCE, K., Turkish

Faculty of Engineering (Terzioḍlu Kampüsü, 17020 Çanakkale):

CANER, C., Food Sciences
HISAR, Ş., Food Technology
KOKSAL, H., Structure
OZDEN, S., Geology
PERINCEK, D., Geology
TUTKUN, S., Geology
YIGITBAS, E., Geology

Faculty of Fine Arts (Terzioḍlu Kampüsü, 17020 Çanakkale):

AKTUG, C. A., Art

Faculty of Marine Sciences and Technology (Terzioḍlu Kampüsü, 17020 Çanakkale):

COLAKOGLU, F., Management Technology
GOKSAN, T., Aquaculture
HISAR, O., Sea Biology
ISMEN, A., Fishing Technology
OZEKINCI, U., Fishing Technology
TUNCER, S., Sea Biology
YIGIT, M., Aquaculture

Faculty of Medicine:

AKGUN, Y., Surgery
AKSULU, H., Pharmacology
ARSLAN, E., Plastic Surgery
COSKUN, M., Medical Biology
DEREKOY, F., Nose, Ears and Throat
EDREMITOGLU, M., Physiology
ERDOGAN, A., Anatomy
ERSAY, A., Urology
KARAAYVAZ, M., Surgery
KARAMAN, H., Neurology
MIRICI, A., Chest
OTKUN, A., Infectious Diseases
OZDEMIR, H., Radioodiagnostics
OZDEMIR, Ö., Medical Genetics
SILAN, F., Medical Genetics
UZUN, M., Physiology

Faculty of Sciences and Arts (Terzioḍlu Kampüsü, 17020 Çanakkale):

AKGUL, C., Biochemistry
ARSLAN, N., Archaeology
AYDIN, M., Chemistry
AYDIN, N., Algebra and Number Theory
BUDDING, E., Astrophysics
CICEK, C., Physics
DEMIRCAN, O., Space Sciences and Technology
DILGIN, Y., Chemistry
ERDEM, A., Astrophysics
GONUZ, A., Biology

GULENDAM, R., Turkish Literature
GUNDUZ, B., Biology
GUVEN, B., Mathematics
HACI, Y., Analysis and Functions
IBRAHIMOV, A., Geography
KAYA, İ., Physics and Chemistry
KOC, T., Geography
OZDEMIR, E., Physics and Chemistry
OZDER, S., Physics
OZER, S., English Language and Literature
OZLER, Z., Turkish
TAKAOGLU, T., History
TARHAN, İ., Physics
TOK, C., Zoology
UYSAL, A., Art History
UYSAL, İ., Botanic
YILMAZ, İ., Space Sciences and Technology
YILMAZ, S., Chemistry

Faculty of Theology (Terzioḍlu Kampüsü, 17020 Çanakkale):

AKBAS, M., Philosophy of Religions
AYENGIN, T., Islam Law
ISIK, H., History of Religions
KESLER, F., Religious Studies

ATTACHED SCHOOLS AND INSTITUTES

Natural and Applied Sciences Institute: Terzioḍlu Kampüsü, 17020 Çanakkale; Dir Prof. Dr MEHMET EMIN ÖZEL.

School of Health Services: Saglik Yukse-kokulu, Onsekiz Mart Univs, 17100 Canak-kale; tel. (286) 217-10-01; internet www.syo .comu.edu.tr; Dir Prof. GUNHAM ERDEM.

School of Tourism and Health Management: Terzioḍlu Kampüsü, 17020 Çanak-kale; e-mail turotel@comu.edu.tr.

Social Studies Institute: Terzioḍlu Kampüsü, 17020 Çanakkale; Dir Assoc. Prof. R. CENGIZ AKÇAY

ÇANKAYA ÜNIVERSITESI

Öğretmenler Cad. 14, Yüzüncü Yil, 06530 Balgat, Ankara
Telephone: (312) 284-45-00
E-mail: webadmin@cankaya.edu.tr
Internet: www.cankaya.edu.tr
Founded 1997
Private control
Languages of instruction: English, Turkish
Academic year: September to June
Pres.: SITKI ALP
Vice-Pres.: İSMAIL AKINALTUĞ
Vice-Pres.: YUSUF GUNGOR
Rector: Prof. Dr ZIYA AKTAŞ
Vice-Rector: Prof. Dr KENAN TAS
Sec.-Gen.: LÜTFI ÖNSOY
Dir for Library: FATIH KUMSEL

Library of 9,278 vols, 140 periodicals
Number of teachers: 210
Number of students: 3,200 (3,000 undergraduate, 200 postgraduate)

DEANS

Faculty of Arts and Sciences: Prof. Dr EMEL DOGRAMACI
Faculty of Economics and Administrative Sciences: Prof. Dr AHMED YALNIZ
Faculty of Engineering and Architecture: Prof. Dr ZIYA AKTAŞ
Faculty of Law: Prof. Dr TURGUT ÖNEN

CELAL BAYAR ÜNIVERSITESI

45000 Manisa
Telephone: (236) 237-28-86
E-mail: kutuphane@bayar.edu.tr
Internet: www.bayar.edu.tr
Founded 1992
State control
Rector: Prof. Dr CEMIL ÖZCAN
Vice-Rector: Prof. Dr ÜLGEN OK
Vice-Rector: Prof. Dr CENGIZ YILMAZ

Number of teachers: 1,100
Number of students: 21,400

Publications: *Journal of Management and Economics* (2 a year), *Journal of Social Sciences* (2 a year)

DEANS

Faculty of Arts and Sciences: Prof. ŞULE AYCAN

Faculty of Economic and Administrative Sciences: Prof. SEMRA ÖNCÜ

Faculty of Education: Prof. NAZMI TOPÇU

Faculty of Engineering: Prof. ERGUN KÖSE

Faculty of Medicine: Prof. EROL ÖZMEN

ÇUKUROVA ÜNİVERSİTESİ

Balcalı Kampüsü, 01330 Balcalı, Adana

Telephone: (322) 338-60-84
E-mail: international@cu.edu.tr
Internet: www.cu.edu.tr

Founded 1973
State control
Language of instruction: Turkish
Academic year: September to July

Rector: Prof. Dr ALPER AKINOĞLU
Vice-Rector: Prof. Dr BANU İNANÇ
Vice-Rector: Prof. Dr M. RIFAT ULUSOY
Vice-Rector: Prof. Dr SÜLEYMAN GÜNGÖR
Sec.-Gen.: NAZAN KARATAŞ
Librarian: TURHAN YILMAZ

Library of 140,000 vols
Number of teachers: 1,900
Number of students: 36,100

Publications: *University Bulletin* (2 a year), faculty journals (all 3 a year)

DEANS

Faculty of Agriculture: Prof. Dr AYZIN B. KÜDEN

Faculty of Arts and Sciences: Prof. Dr SADULLAH SAKALLIOĞLU

Faculty of Communication: Prof. Dr VEDAT PEŞTEMALCI

Faculty of Dentistry: Prof. Dr İLTER UZEL

Faculty of Divinity: Prof. Dr ALI OSMAN ATEŞ

Faculty of Economics and Admin. Sciences: Prof. Dr MUAMMER TEKEOĞLU

Faculty of Education: Prof. Dr A. NECMI YAŞAR

Faculty of Engineering and Architecture: Prof. Dr BEŞIR ŞAHIN

Faculty of Fine Arts: Prof. Dr YUSUF GÜRÇI-NAR

Faculty of Fisheries: Prof. Dr OYA IŞIK

Faculty of Law: Prof. Dr ALPER AKINOĞLU

Faculty of Medicine: Prof. Dr BEHNAN ALPER

CUMHURIYET ÜNİVERSİTESİ
(Republic University)

58140 Campus-Sivas

Telephone: (346) 219-11-58
E-mail: rektor@cumhuriyet.edu.tr
Internet: www.cumhuriyet.edu.tr

Founded 1974, reorganized 1982
State control
Language of instruction: Turkish
Academic year: October to June

Rector: Prof. Dr FERIT KOÇOĞLU
Vice-Rector: Prof. Dr ZAFER KARS
Vice-Rector: Prof. Dr HALDUN SÜMER
Vice-Rector: Prof. Dr ORHAN TATAR
Sec.-Gen.: Dr EROL ŞANLI
Librarian: AYGÜL ÜNAL

Number of teachers: 1,300
Number of students: 20,000

DEANS

Faculty of Arts and Sciences: Prof. Dr RAIF GÜLER

Faculty of Dentistry: Prof. Dr TIMUR ESENER

Faculty of Economic and Administrative Sciences: Prof. Dr M. ALI AKPINAR

Faculty of Education: Prof. Dr NEVZAT BATTAL

Faculty of Engineering: Prof. Dr ALI ÖZTÜRK

Faculty of Fine Arts: Prof. Dr KADIR KARKIN

Faculty of Medicine: Prof. Dr REYHAN EĞIL-MEZ

Faculty of Theological Studies: Prof. Dr N. YAŞAR AŞIKOĞLU YILMAZ

DICLE ÜNİVERSİTESİ
(Tigris University)

21280 Diyarbakır

Telephone: (412) 248-82-02
E-mail: fcan@dicle.edu.tr
Internet: www.dicle.edu.tr

Founded 1966 as branch of Ankara Univ., ind. 1973
State control
Academic year: October to June

Rector: Prof. Dr FIKRI CANORUÇ
Vice-Rector: Prof. Dr ERALP ARIKAN
Vice-Rector: Prof. Dr ZÜLKÜF GÜLSÜN
Gen. Sec.: MEHMET TEKDÖŞ
Librarian: SEVGI EKMEKÇILER
Academic year: October to May

Library of 72,000 books, 6,000 periodicals, 1,350 theses and 3 CD databases
Number of teachers: 700
Number of students: 9,000

Publications: *Medical Faculty Journal, University Annual*

DEANS

Faculty of Agriculture: Prof. Dr DOĞAN ŞAKAR

Faculty of Dentistry: Prof. Dr FATMA ATAKUL

Faculty of Education: Prof. Dr ÖMER SAYA

Faculty of Education (Siirt): Assoc. Prof. YÜKSEL COŞKUN

Faculty of Engineering and Architecture: Assoc. Prof. FIKRI KAHRAMAN

Faculty of Law: Assoc. Prof. Dr FAZIL HÜSNÜ ERDEM

Faculty of Medicine: Assoc. Prof. Dr RECEP IŞIK

Faculty of Science and Letters: Prof. Dr HALIL HOŞGÖREN

Faculty of Technical Education (Batman): Prof. Dr O. ZEKI HEKIMOĞLU

Faculty of Theology: Assoc. Prof. ABDULKERIM ÜNALAN

Faculty of Veterinary Medicine: Prof. Dr SAVAŞ HATIPOĞLU

PROFESSORS

Faculty of Arts and Sciences:
BAŞARAN, D., Botany
BILGIN, F. H., Zoology
GÜLSÜN, Z., Atomic and Molecular Physics
GÜMGÜM, B., Inorganic Chemistry
GÜNIGÜNI, B., Inorganic Chemistry
TEZ, Z., Physical Chemistry
YILMAZ, A., General Physics

Faculty of Education:
ASLAN, E., Turkish Language and Literature
SÖNMEZ, A., Physics

Faculty of Medicine:
ARIKAN, E., Microbiology
AYDINOL, B., Biochemistry
BAHÇECI, M., Internal Diseases
BAYHAN, N., Anaesthesiology
BUDAK, T., Medical Biology
CANORUÇ, F., Internal Diseases
ÇELIK, S., Biophysics
DEĞERTEKIN, H., Internal Diseases
DERICI, M., Dermatology
ERDOĞAN, F., Physical Rehabilitation
GÜL, T., Gynaecology and Obstetrics
GÜRGEN, F., Psychiatry
İLÇIN, E., Public Health

IŞIKOĞLU, B., Internal Diseases
KELLE, A., Medical Biology
METE, Ö., Microbiology
MÜFTÜOĞLU, E., Internal Diseases
NERGIS, Y., Histology
ÖZAYDIN, M., Pathology
ÖZGEN, G., Cardiovascular and Thoracic Surgery
TAŞ, M. A., Public Health
TOPCU, I., Otorhinolaryngology
TOPRAK, N., Internal Diseases
YILMAZ, N., Gynaecology and Obstetrics

DOGUS UNIVERSITY

Acıbadem, Zeamet Sok 21, 34722 Kadıköy, Istanbul

Telephone: (216) 544-55-55
E-mail: info@dogus.edu.tr
Internet: www.dogus.edu.tr

Founded 1997
Private control
Languages of instruction: Turkish, English
Academic year: September to June

Rector: Prof. Dr MITAT UYSAL
Gen. Sec.: MINE KALENDEROGLU
Library and Documentation Centre: SÖNMEZ ÇELIK

Library of 107,200 vols, 300 print journals, 23,700 electronic journals
Number of teachers: 460
Number of students: 4,187 (3,940 undergraduate, 247 postgraduate)

Publication: *Dogus University Journal*

DEANS

Faculty of Arts and Sciences: Prof. Dr DILEK DOLTAŞ

Faculty of Economic and Administrative Sciences: Prof. Dr ERTAN OKTAY

Faculty of Engineering: Prof. Dr FÜSUN ÜLENGIN

Faculty of Fine Arts and Design: Prof. Dr RIFAT ÇELEBI

Faculty of Law: Prof. Dr HASAN FEHIM ÜÇIŞIK

Institute of Science and Technology: Prof. Dr AHMET NURI CERANOGLU

Institute of Social Sciences: Prof. Dr ELIF ÇEPNI

Vocational School: MEHMET EEMEK

DOKUZ EYLUL UNIVERSITY
(Ninth September University)

Cumhuriyet Bul. 144, 35210 Alsancak, Izmir

Telephone: (232) 412-1212
E-mail: gen.sek@deu.edu.tr
Internet: www.deu.edu.tr

Founded 1982
State control
Languages of instruction: English, Turkish
Academic year: September to June

Rector: Prof. Dr MEHMET FUZUN
Vice-Rector: Prof. Dr ALP TIMUR
Vice-Rector: Prof. Dr HALIL KOSE
Vice-Rector: Prof. Dr İSMAIL HAKKI BAHAR
Sec.-Gen.: Prof. Dr CAN KARACA
Librarian: HALE BALTEPE

Library of 300,000 vols, 70 databases, 130,000 ebooks, 26,000 e-periodicals
Number of teachers: 3,000
Number of students: 50,000

Publications: *Arpa Boyu Dergisi, Sosyal Bilimler Enstitüsü Dergisi* (Social Sciences Institute Review, 2 a year), *Tip Fakültesi Dergisi* (Faculty of Medicine Review), *Yedi Dergisi* (Faculty of Theology Review)

DEANS

Faculty of Architecture: Prof. Dr ORCAN GÜNDÜZ

Faculty of Arts and Sciences: Prof. Dr NILGÜN MORALI

Faculty of Business Administration: Prof. Dr ORHAN İAÖZ

Faculty of Economics and Administrative Sciences: Prof. Dr ŞENAY ÜÇDOĞRUK

Faculty of Education: Prof. Dr FERDA AYSAN

Faculty of Engineering: Prof. Dr CÜNEYT GÜZELIŞ

Faculty of Fine Arts: Prof. Dr SELÄHATTIN PARLADIR

Faculty of Law: Prof. Dr ŞEREF ERTAŞ

Faculty of Medicine: Prof. Dr ŞEBNEM ÖZKAN

DUMLUPINAR ÜNİVERSİTESİ

M. Kampüs Rektörlük Binası Tavşanlı, Yolu 10 km, 43100 Kütahya

Telephone: (274) 265-20-31

E-mail: ssevim@dumlupinar.edu.tr

Internet: www.dumlupinar.edu.tr

Founded 1992

State control

Academic year: November to July

Rector: Prof. Dr GÜNER ÖNCE

Vice-Rector: Prof. Dr BAHRI ÖTEYAKA

Vice-Rector: Prof. Dr ALI SARIKOYUNCU

Sec.-Gen.: YALÇIN KALAY

Registrar: MIKTAT BEKTAŞ

Head of Library: İSMAIL BAYRAM

Library of 28,000 books, 168 periodicals

Number of teachers: 520

Number of students: 19,000

DEANS

Faculty of Arts and Sciences: Prof. ALI SARIKOYUNCU

Faculty of Economic and Administrative Sciences (Bilecik): Prof. BAHRI ÖTEYAKA

Faculty of Education: Prof. Dr AHMET YAMIK

Faculty of Engineering: Prof. CEM ŞENSÖĞÜT

Faculty of Fine Arts: Prof. Dr ADNAN TEPECIK

Faculty of Technical Education (Simav): Prof. GÜNER ÖNCE

Graduate School of Science and Engineering: Assoc. Prof. İSKENDER IŞIK

Graduate School of Social Sciences: Prof. AHMET KARAASLAN

EGE ÜNİVERSİTESİ
(Aegean University)

Bornova, Izmir

Telephone: (232) 388-01-10

E-mail: ulkubay@med.ege.edu.tr

Internet: www.ege.edu.tr

Founded 1955

State control

Language of instruction: Turlish

Academic year: October to June

Rector: Prof. Dr ÜLKÜ BAYINDIR

Vice-Rector: Prof. Dr HALUK BAYLAS

Vice-Rector: Prof. Dr FIKRET İKIZ

Vice-Rector: Prof. Dr MUSTAFA METIN

Gen. Sec.: CIHANGIR SOYGÜL

Librarian: NURCAN ESLIK BAYKAL

Number of students: 30,900

Publications: *Aegean Medical Journal, Fen Dergisi, Tıp Fakültesi Mecmuası, Ziraat Fakültesi Dergisi*, and faculty publications

DEANS

Faculty of Agriculture: Prof. Dr SEMIH ERKAN

Faculty of Communications: Prof. Dr AHMET BÜLENT GÖKSEL

Faculty of Dentistry: Prof. Dr SELDA ERTÜRK

Faculty of Economics and Administrative Sciences: Prof. Dr REZAN TATLIDIL

Faculty of Education: Prof. Dr KADIR ASLAN

Faculty of Engineering: Prof. Dr MUSTAFA TÜRKSEVER

Faculty of Fisheries: Prof. Dr AHMET KOCATAŞ

Faculty of Medicine: Prof. Dr ATA ERDENER

Faculty of Pharmacy: Prof. Dr ERÇIN ERCIYAS

Faculty of Science: Prof. Dr BEKIR ÇETINKAYA

Faculty of Science and Letters: Prof. Dr KASIM EĞIT

RESEARCH CENTRES

Agricultural Research Center: Dir Prof. Dr TAYFUN ÖZKAYA.

Botanical Garden and Herbarium Research Center: Dir Prof. Dr ÖZCAN SEÇMEN.

Cancer Surveillance and Research Center: Dir Prof. Dr AYFER HAYDAROĞLU.

Centre for Strategic Studies.

Environmental Studies Research Center: Dir Prof. Dr ÜMIT ERDEM.

European Languages and Cultures Research Center (ADIKAM): Dir Prof. Dr GERTRUDE DURUSOY.

Family Planning and Infertility Research Center.

Genetic Disease Research Center: Dir Prof. Dr CIHANGIR ÖZKINAY.

Health Research Center (University Hospital).

Information and Communication Technologies Research Center: Dir Prof. Dr FAZIL APAYDIN.

Izmir Research Center: Dir Prof. Dr IŞIK TARAKÇIOĞLU.

Natural History Research Center (The Museum of Natural History): Dir Prof. Dr NIMET ÖKTEM.

Organ Transplantation Research Centre: Dir Prof. Dr ÖZDEMIR YARARBAŞ.

Poison Research Center.

Principles of Atatürk and Recent Turkish History Research Center: Dir Prof. Dr FAZILET VARDAR-SUKAN.

Science and Technology Research Center: Dir Prof. Dr S. ŞUHA SUKAN.

Seed Technology Research Center: Dir Prof. Dr BENIAN ESER.

Submarine Research Center.

Textile and Apparel Manufacturing Research Center: Dir Prof. Dr IŞIK TARAKÇIOGLU.

Women's Studies Research Center.

ERCİYES ÜNİVERSİTESİ

38039 Kayseri

Telephone: (352) 437-49-22

E-mail: info@erciyes.edu.tr

Internet: www.erciyes.edu.tr

Founded 1978

State control

Language of instruction: Turkish

Academic year: October to June

Rector: Prof. Dr FAHRETTIN KELEŞTEMUR

Vice-Rector: Prof. Dr IBRAHIM UZMAY

Vice-Rector: Prof. Dr METIN HÜLAGÜ

Vice-Rector: Prof. Dr MUSTAFA ÇETIN

Registrar: SEMA ASLAN

Librarian: GÜLNUR YAKAN

Library of 265,950 vols, 87,000 books, 71,000 journals, 67,400 ebooks, 40,550 ejournals

Number of teachers: 2,200

Number of students: 45,500

Publications: *Journal of the Faculty of Economics and Administrative Sciences, Journal of the Medical School, Journal of the Graduate School of Health Sciences, Journal of the Graduate School of Sciences, Journal of the Graduate School of Social Sciences, Journal of the Theology Faculty, Journal of the Veterinary Medicine Faculty*

DEANS

Faculty of Agriculture: Prof. Dr HALIL KIRNAK

Faculty of Architecture: Prof. Dr FAHRETTIN KELEŞTEMUR UZMAY

Faculty of Arts: Prof. Dr ÜMIT TOKATLI

Faculty of Aviation and Space Science: Prof. Dr KEMAL APALAK

Faculty of Communication: Prof. Dr HAMZA ÇAKIR

Faculty of Dentistry: Prof. Dr ALPER ALKAN

Faculty of Economics and Administrative Sciences: Prof. Dr EKREM ERDEM

Faculty of Education: Prof. Dr ABDULLAH SAYDAM

Faculty of Engineering: Prof. Dr MUSTAFA ALÇI

Faculty of Fine Arts: Prof. Dr FAHRETTIN KELEŞTEMUR

Faculty of Health Science: Prof. Dr ÜMIT SEVIĞ

Faculty of Law: Doç. Dr İSMAIL KAYAR

Faculty of Medicine: Prof. Dr MUHAMMET GÜVEN

Faculty of Pharmacy: Prof. Dr MÜBERRA KOŞAR

Faculty of Science: Prof. Dr HÜSEYIN ALTINDIŞ

Faculty of Theology: Prof. Dr M. ZEKI DUMAN

Faculty of Veterinary Medicine: Prof. Dr HALIT CANATAN

PROFESSORS

Faculty of Agriculture:

CANHILAL, R., Plant Protection
ILBAŞ, A., Field Crops
KIRNAK, H., Biosystem Engineering
SERIN, Y., Field Crops
SILICI, S., Agricultural Biotechnology
TIRYAKI, O., Plant Protection
YETIŞIR, H., Garden Plants

Faculty of Arts:

AKTAN, A., History
ARGUNŞAH, H., Turkish Language and Literature
ARGUNŞAH, M., Turkish Language and Literature
ASMA, B., Russian Language and Literature
DEMIRCI, S., History
DIKEÇLIGIL, F., Sociology
GÖRKEM, I., Turkish Language and Literature
HÜLAGÜ, M., History
INBAŞI, M., History
KESKIN, M., History
KILIÇ, A., Turkish Language and Literature
ÖZKAN, N., Turkish Language and Literature
TOKATLI, S., Turkish Language and Literature
TOKATLI, Ü., Turkish Language and Literature
TÜRKMEN, K., Art History
ÜÇGÜL, S., Russian Language and Literature
YUVALI, A., History

Faculty of Communication:

ÇAKIR, H., Journalism

Faculty of Dentistry:

ALKAN, A., Clinical Sciences
GÜRGAN, C. A., Clinical Sciences
KESIM, B., Clinical Sciences
KESIM, I., Clinical Sciences

Faculty of Economics and Administrative Sciences:

AKDOĞAN, A., Administrative Sciences
AKDOĞAN, M., Administrative Sciences
ALKAN, H., Politics and Public Administration
ATIK, H., Economics
BILGILI, F., Economics
BILGINOĞLU, M., Economics
ÇALIŞKAN, F., Administrative Sciences
DURSUN, Y., Administrative Sciences

ERDEM, E., Economics
KILAVUZ, E., Economics
NAKIP, M., Administrative Sciences
ÖZDEVECIOĞLU, M., Administrative Sciences
ÖZKAN, A., Administrative Sciences
SÖNMEZ, I., Administrative Sciences
UNUTULMAZ, O., Administrative Sciences
UZAY, N., Economics
UZAY, Ş., Administrative Sciences
VARINLI, I., Administrative Sciences
YILDIZ, R., Economics

Faculty of Education:

ALTAN, M. Z., Foreign Languages Education
ÇELIKTEN, M., Educational Sciences
KAYA, H.
ŞAHIN, A., Secondary School Physics and Mathematics Education
SARAÇOĞLU, S., Primary School Education
SAYDAM, A., Primary School Education

Faculty of Engineering:

AKANSU, S., Machine Engineering
ALÇI, M., Electrical and Electronic Engineering
ALTUNTOP, N., Machine Engineering
APALAK, M., Machine Engineering
ARDIÇLIOĞLU, M., Civil Engineering
ATIŞ, C., Civil Engineering
BEŞDOK, E., Geomatics Engineering
BILIŞIK, A., Textile Engineering
DANIŞMAN, K., Electrical and Electronic Engineering
GÜNEY, K., Electrical and Electronic Engineering
HAKTANIR, T., Civil Engineering
HAYTA, M., Food Engineering
KARABOĞA, N., Electrical and Electronic Engineering
KARABOĞA, D., Computer Engineering
KARACAN, I., Textile Engineering
KARAMIŞ, M., Machine Engineering
KAYACIER, A., Food Engineering
KILIÇ, R., Electrical and Electronic Engineering
KILIK, R., Machine Engineering
ÖZCEYHAN, V., Machine Engineering
ÖZDEN, S., Machine Engineering
ÖZKAN, C., Geomatics Engineering
SINANOĞLU, C., Industrial Design Engineering
TAŞPINAR, N., Electrical and Electronic Engineering
ÜNALAN, S., Machine Engineering
UZMAY, I., Machine Engineering
YAPICI, H., Energy Systems Engineering
YETIM, H., Food Engineering
YILDIRIM, Ş., Mecatronics Engineering
YILDIZ, C., Electrical and Electronic Engineering
YÜKSEL, M., Biomedical Engineering

Faculty of Fine Arts:

GÖKÇE, N., Painting
LEVENDOĞLU ÖNER, N. O., Music

Faculty of Health Science:

SEVIĞ, E. U., Nursing

Faculty of Law:

DOĞAN, M., Private Law
KAYAR, I., Private Law

Faculty of Medicine:

AKÇALI, Y., Surgical Medicine
AKSU, M., Internal Medicine
AKTAŞ, E., Internal Medicine
ALP MEŞE, E., Internal Medicine
ALTUNTAŞ, H., Basic Medical Sciences
ARGÜN, M., Surgical Medicine
ARSLAN, D., Internal Medicine
AŞCIOĞLU, M., Basic Medical Sciences
AVŞAROĞULLARI, Ö., Internal Medicine
AYCAN, K., Basic Medical Sciences
AYDOĞAN, S., Basic Medical Sciences
AYGEN, E., Surgical Medicine
AYGEN, B., Internal Medicine

AYKUT, M., Internal Medicine
BALKANLI, S., Surgical Medicine
BAŞBUĞ, M., Surgical Medicine
BAŞKOL, M., Internal Medicine
BAŞKOL, G., Basic Medical Sciences
BAŞTÜRK, M., Internal Medicine
BAYRAM, F., Internal Medicine
BILGEN, M., Basic Medical Sciences
BILGIN, M., Surgical Medicine
BORLU, M., Internal Medicine
BOYACI, A., Surgical Medicine
ÇALIŞ, M., Internal Medicine
ÇANATAN, H., Basic Medical Sciences
CANER, Y., Clinical Sciences
CANÖZ, Ö., Basic Medical Sciences
ÇETIN, M., Internal Medicine
ÇETINKAYA, F., Internal Medicine
CEYHAN, O., Internal Medicine
ÇOKSEVIM, B., Basic Medical Sciences
ÇORUH, A., Surgical Medicine
ÇORUH, A., Surgical Medicine
COŞKUN, A., Internal Medicine
CÜCER, N., Basic Medical Sciences
DEMIR, R., Internal Medicine
DEMIR, H., Internal Medicine
DEMIRCI, D., Surgical Medicine
DOĞAN, H., Surgical Medicine
DOĞANAY, M., Internal Medicine
DOLU, N., Basic Medical Sciences
DÜNDAR, M., Internal Medicine
DURAK, A., Internal Medicine
DURSUN, N., Basic Medical Sciences
DÜŞÜNSEL, R., Internal Medicine
DUYGULU, F., Surgical Medicine
EKMEKÇIOĞLU, O., Surgical Medicine
EMIROĞULLARI, Ö., Surgical Medicine
ERDEM, Ş., Surgical Medicine
ERDOĞAN, F., Internal Medicine
ERENMEMIŞOĞLU, A., Internal Medicine
ERGIN, A., Internal Medicine
ERKAN, M., Surgical Medicine
ERKILIÇ, K., Surgical Medicine
ERSOY, A., Internal Medicine
ERYOL, N., Internal Medicine
EŞEL, E., Internal Medicine
ESER, B., Internal Medicine
EVEREKLIOĞLU, C., Surgical Medicine
FERAHBAŞ, A., Internal Medicine
GÖKAHMETOĞLU, S., Basic Medical Sciences
GÖLGELI, A., Basic Medical Sciences
GÜLER, G., Surgical Medicine
GÜLMEZ, I., Surgical Medicine
GÜLMEZ, I., Internal Medicine
GÜNAY, G., Surgical Medicine
GÜNAY, O., Internal Medicine
GÜNDÜZ, Z., Internal Medicine
GÜNEŞ, T., Internal Medicine
GÜNEY, E., Surgical Medicine
GÜRSOY, Ş., Internal Medicine
GÜVEN, M., Internal Medicine
GÜVEN, K., Internal Medicine
HALICI, M., Surgical Medicine
KAHRAMAN, H., Surgical Medicine
KAPLAN, B., Internal Medicine
KARAHAN, Ö., Internal Medicine
KARAKÜÇÜK, M., Surgical Medicine
KARAYOL AKIN, A., Surgical Medicine
KELEŞTEMUR, H., Internal Medicine
KENDIRCI, M., Internal Medicine
KILIÇ, E., Basic Medical Sciences
KILIÇ, H., Basic Medical Sciences
KIRNAP, M., Internal Medicine
KOÇ, R., Surgical Medicine
KOÇ, A., Basic Medical Sciences
KONTAŞ, O., Surgical Medicine
KÖSE, S., Basic Medical Sciences
KÖSEOĞLU, E., Internal Medicine
KÜÇÜKAYDIN, M., Surgical Medicine
KUK, S., Basic Medical Sciences
KULA, M., Internal Medicine
KÜLAHLI, I., Surgical Medicine
KUMANDAŞ, S., Internal Medicine
KURTOĞLU, S., Internal Medicine
KURTSOY, A., Surgical Medicine
MADENOĞLU, H., Surgical Medicine
MENKÜ, A., Surgical Medicine

MIRZA, G., Surgical Medicine
MIRZA, M., Internal Medicine
MISTIK, S., Internal Medicine
MÜDERRIS, I., Surgical Medicine
MUHTAROĞLU, S., Basic Medical Sciences
MUTLU, M., Surgical Medicine
NARIN, N., Internal Medicine
NARIN, F., Basic Medical Sciences
OĞUZHAN, A., Internal Medicine
OĞUZKAYA, F., Surgical Medicine
OK, E., Surgical Medicine
ÖKTEM, I., Surgical Medicine
ÖKTEN, T., Surgical Medicine
ÖNER, A., Surgical Medicine
OYMAK, F., Internal Medicine
OYMAK, O., Internal Medicine
ÖZBAKIR, Ö., Internal Medicine
ÖZCAN, N., Internal Medicine
ÖZÇELIK, B., Surgical Medicine
ÖZDAMAR, S., Basic Medical Sciences
ÖZDARENDELI, A., Basic Medical Sciences
ÖZDEMIR, M., Internal Medicine
ÖZGÖÇMEN, S., Internal Medicine
ÖZKAN, M., Internal Medicine
ÖZKUL, Y., Internal Medicine
ÖZTÜRK, A., Internal Medicine
ÖZTÜRK, F., Surgical Medicine
ÖZTÜRK, M., Internal Medicine
ÖZYAZGAN, I., Surgical Medicine
PATIROĞLU, T., Internal Medicine
PATIROĞLU, T., Surgical Medicine
PERÇIN RENDERS, D., Basic Medical Sciences
POYRAZOĞLU, M., Internal Medicine
ŞAHIN, Y., Surgical Medicine
ŞAHIN, I., Basic Medical Sciences
SELÇUKLU, A., Surgical Medicine
SERIN, I., Surgical Medicine
SOYUER, S., Internal Medicine
SÖZÜER, E., Surgical Medicine
SÜER, C., Basic Medical Sciences
SUNGUR, M., Internal Medicine
TAHAN, F., Internal Medicine
TALASLIOĞLU, A., Internal Medicine
TAŞDEMIR, H., Surgical Medicine
TATLIŞEN, A., Surgical Medicine
TAYYAR, M., Surgical Medicine
TOKGÖZ, B., Internal Medicine
TOPSAKAL, R., Internal Medicine
TOSUN, Z., Surgical Medicine
TRUE, K., Surgical Medicine
TURAN, C., Surgical Medicine
TURAN, M., Internal Medicine
TÜRK, C., Surgical Medicine
TUTUŞ, A., Internal Medicine
ÜLGER, H., Basic Medical Sciences
ÜNAL, A., Internal Medicine
ÜNLÜ, Y., Surgical Medicine
ÜNLÜHIZARCI, K., Internal Medicine
UNUR, E., Basic Medical Sciences
ÜSTÜNBAŞ, H., Internal Medicine
ÜZÜM, K., Internal Medicine
YAKAN, B., Basic Medical Sciences
YAZAR, S., Basic Medical Sciences
YILDIZ, K., Surgical Medicine
YILMAZ, A., Surgical Medicine
YÜCESOY, M., Internal Medicine

Faculty of Pharmacy:

DEMIRHAN, I., Basic Pharmaceutical Sciences
KOŞAR, M., Pharmaceutical Profession Sciences
NARIN, I., Basic Pharmaceutical Sciences
ÖZBILGE, H., Basic Pharmaceutical Sciences

Faculty of Science:

AKKURT, M., Physics
AKSOY, A., Biology
ALBAYRAK, E., Physics
ALTINDIŞ, H., Mathematics
AYYILDIZ, E., Physics
AYYILDIZ, N., Biology
BARAN, M., Mathematics
BÜYÜKMUMCU, Z., Chemistry
CAN, H., Mathematics

ÇOBAN, A., Chemistry
DAĞDEMIR, Y., Physics
GENÇASLAN, M., Physics
GÜLDESTE, A., Physics
GÜNDÜZ, M., Physics
GÜRCAN, F., Mathematics
GÜZEL, Y., Chemistry
ILHAN, I., Chemistry
KARTAL, Ş., Chemistry
KESKIN, M., Physics
KEŞLIOĞLU, K., Physics
KÖK, T., Chemistry
KÜÇÜK, I., Astronomy and Space Sciences
MARAŞLI, N., Physics
MUCUK, O., Mathematics
ÖNEM, Ş., Physics
ÖZARSLAN, H., Mathematics
ÖZPOZAN, N., Chemistry
ÖZPOZAN, T., Chemistry
ÖZSOY, S., Physics
ÖZTÜRK, I., Mathematics
PATAT, Ş., Chemistry
SARIPINAR, E., Chemistry
SOYLAK, M., Chemistry
TEZ, C., Biology
TOKALIOĞLU, Ş., Chemistry
TUNÇBILEK, A., Biology
TÜRKOĞLU, O., Chemistry
ÜLGEN, A., Chemistry
YAŞUK, F., Physics
YILDIRIM, I., Chemistry
YILDIRIM, S., Physics

Faculty of Theology:

APAYDIN, H., Basic Islamic Sciences
AYDIN, M., Philosophy and Religious Sciences
BAKTIR, M., Primary School Religion and Moral Education
BENLI, Y., Basic Islamic Sciences
CEBECI, L., Primary School Religion and Moral Education
ÇELIK, C., Philosophy and Religious Sciences
CIHAN, A., Philosophy and Religious Sciences
DUMAN, M., Basic Islamic Sciences
ERTÜRK, R., Philosophy and Religious Sciences
GÖRENER, I., Basic Islamic Sciences
GÜNGÖR, H., Philosophy and Religious Sciences
KAYACIK, A., Philosophy and Religious Sciences
PAZARBAŞI, E., Basic Islamic Sciences
POLAT, S., Basic Islamic Sciences
ŞAHIN, H., Philosophy and Religious Sciences
SAMUR, S., Islamic History and Arts
SEVERCAN, Ş., Islamic History and Arts
TAŞTAN, A., Philosophy and Religious Sciences
TOKSARI, A., Basic Islamic Sciences
ÜNAL, M., Philosophy and Religious Sciences
YEŞILYURT, T., Basic Islamic Sciences

Faculty of Veterinary Medicine:

ATALAN, G., Clinical Sciences
ATASEVER, A., Preclinical Sciences
AYDIN, F., Preclinical Sciences
BAYTOK, E., Zootechny and Animal Feeding
BEKYÜREK, T., Clinical Sciences
ÇETIN, N., Basic Sciences
EREN, M., Basic Sciences
GÖNÜLALAN, Z., Food Hygiene and Technology
GÜNEŞ, V., Clinical Sciences
GÜRBULAK, K., Clinical Sciences
INCI, A., Preclinical Sciences
IŞCAN, K., Zootechny and Animal Feeding
KELEŞ, I., Clinical Sciences
KOCAOĞLU GÜÇLÜ, B., Zootechny and Animal Feeding
KÜÇÜK, O., Zootechny and Animal Feeding
KÜÇÜK BAYRAM, G., Basic Sciences
LIMAN, B., Preclinical Sciences

LIMAN, N., Basic Sciences
NUR, I., Basic Sciences

FATİH ÜNİVERSİTESİ

34500 Büyükçekmece, Istanbul
Telephone: (212) 866-33-00
E-mail: info@fatih.edu.tr
Internet: www.fatih.edu.tr
Founded 1996
Private control
Language of instruction: English (in faculties)
Language of instruction: Turkish (in Vocational Schools)
Academic year: September to June
Rector: Prof. Dr SERIF ALI TEKALAN
Vice-Rector: Prof. Dr FAHRETTIN GUCIN (acting)
Vice-Rector: Prof. Dr AYHAN BOZKURT (acting)
Vice-Rector: Prof. Dr MUHAMMET RAMAZAN YIGITOGLU (acting)
Sec.-Gen.: ERTUGRUL MESCIOGLU
Dir for Financial Affairs: MUTTALIP YILMAZ
Dir for Int. Programs Office: FERHAT ARSLAN
Dir for Int. Students Office: ERDOGAN TUZEN
Dir for Library and Documentation: ERCUMENT DEMIRBOZAN
Dir for Student Affairs Office: CUNEYT UMUTLU
Librarian: ERCÜMENT DEMIRBOZAN
Library of 69,760 vols, 47,092 ebooks, 7,651 journals, 979 theses, 70,000 e-theses, 40 periodicals, 882 CDs
Number of teachers: 340
Number of students: 11,800
Publications: *Civilacademy: Journal of Social Sciences* (3 a year), *EJEPS, European Journal of Economic and Political Studies*, *Fatih Bulletin*, *Genc Kariyer*, *Journal of Economic and Social Research* (2 a year), *Kariyer Penceresi*, *Peers (Student Journal)* (2 a year), *Politics, Reflections (Student Journal)* (2 a year), *Text (Student Journal)* (3 a year)

DEANS

Ankara Vocational School: YUKSEL NIZAMOGLU
Ankara Vocational School of Medical Sciences: YUKSEL NIZAMOGLU
Faculty of Arts and Sciences: Prof. Dr CEVDET NERGIZ
Faculty of Economics and Admin. Sciences: Prof. Dr MURAT KARAGOZ
Faculty of Education: Prof. Dr FAHRETTIN GUCIN
Faculty of Engineering: Prof. Dr CEVDE MERIC
Faculty of Law: Prof. OSMAN KASIKCI
Faculty of Medicine: Prof. Dr MUHAMMET RAMAZAN YIGITOGLU (acting)
Faculty of Theology: Prof. Dr MUHIT MERT
Graduate School of Biomedical Engineering: Prof. SADIK KARA
Graduate School of Sciences and Engineering: Assoc. Prof. NURULLAH ARSLAN
Graduate School of Social Sciences: Assoc. Prof. MEHMET KARAKUYU
Istanbul Vocational School: Assoc. Prof. OSMAN NURI ARAS
School of Nursing: Prof. SENOL DANE
Vocational School of Justice: Prof. OSMAN KASIKCI

FİRAT ÜNİVERSİTESİ
(Euphrates University)

23119 Elazığ
Telephone: (424) 212-85-10
E-mail: okalem@firat.edu.tr
Internet: www.firat.edu.tr
Founded 1975
Language of instruction: Turkish

Academic year: October to June
Rector: Prof. Dr MEHMET HAMDI MUZ
Vice-Rector: Prof. Dr A. Y. ERKIN OĞUR
Vice-Rector: Prof. Dr HARUN ÖZER
Gen. Sec.: GAZI ÖZCAN
Librarian: Prof. Dr FAHRETTIN GÖKTAŞ
Number of teachers: 1,560
Number of students: 15,900
Publications: *Journal of Health Sciences* (2 a year), *Journal of Science and Engineering* (2 a year), *Journal of Social Sciences* (2 a year)

DEANS

Faculty of Agriculture (Bingöl): (vacant)
Faculty of Aquatic Sciences: Prof. Dr BÜLENT ŞEN
Faculty of Arts and Sciences: Prof. Dr İBRAHIM YILMAZÇELIK
Faculty of Communication: Prof. Dr ASAF VAROL
Faculty of Economic and Management Sciences (Tunceli): (vacant)
Faculty of Education: Prof. Dr MEHMET AYDOĞDU
Faculty of Education (Muş): (vacant)
Faculty of Engineering: Prof. Dr DURSUN PEHLIVAN
Faculty of Medicine: Prof. Dr ÖZGE ARDIÇOĞLU
Faculty of Technical Education: Prof. Dr ALI İNAN
Faculty of Theology: Doç. Dr MUSTAFA ÖZTÜRK
Faculty of Veterinary Medicine: Prof. Dr H. BASRI GÜLCÜ

ATTACHED SCHOOLS AND COLLEGES

College of Health Sciences: Dir Prof. Dr EMINE ÜNSALDI.

College of Health Sciences (Elazig): Dir Prof. Dr ZÜLAL AŞCI TORAMAN.

College of Physical and Sports Education (Elazig): Dir Prof. Dr MEHMET ÜLKER.

College of Social Sciences (Elazig): Dir Doç. Dr ORHAN KILIÇ.

College of Technical Sciences (Elazig): Dir Doç. Dr NECATI KULOĞLU.

College of Vocational Education (Bingöl): Dir Prof. Dr MÜKREMIN APAYDIN.

College of Vocational Education (Maden): Dir Doç. Dr ALI İNAN.

College of Vocational Education (Malazgirt): Dir Prof. Dr KADIR SERVI.

College of Vocational Education (Muş): Dir Doç. Dr KADIR SERVİ.

College of Vocational Education (Sivrice): Dir Prof. Dr HARUN ÖZER.

College of Vocational Education (Tunceli): Dir Prof. Dr SALIH ÖZÇELIK.

Fine Arts–Music: Dir Assoc. Prof. Dr GÜLDENIZ EKMEN AGİŞ.

Keban Sleyman Demırel College of Vocational Education: Dir Assoc. Prof. Dr HÜSAMETTIN KAYA.

Kemaliye Hacı Ali Akin College of Vocational Education: Dir Prof. Dr MEHMET CEBECI

GALATASARAY ÜNİVERSİTESİ

Ciragan Cad. 36, 34357 Ortaköy, Istanbul
Telephone: (212) 227-44-80
E-mail: dyarsuvat@gsu.edu.tr
Internet: www.gsu.edu.tr
Founded 1992
Academic year: October to June
State control
Rector: Prof. Dr DUYGUN YARSUVAT
Vice-Rector: Prof. Dr SEYFETTIN GÜRSEL
Vice-Rector: Prof. Dr PIERRE LE MIRE

Vice-Rector: Prof. Dr ETHEM TOLGA
Vice-Rector: Prof. Dr NECMI YÜZBAŞIOĞLU
Gen. Sec.: Prof. Dr İSMAIL ÖZTÜRK

Library of 42,000 vols
Number of teachers: 140
Number of students: 1,670

DEANS

Faculty of Communications: Prof. Dr E.
ÖZDEN CANKAYA
Faculty of Engineering and Technology: Prof.
Dr ETHEM TOLGA
Faculty of Law: Prof. Dr HAMDI YASAMAN
Faculty of Science and Letters: Prof. Dr
KENAN GÜRSOY

GAZİ ÜNİVERSİTESİ

06500 Teknikokullar, Ankara
Telephone: (312) 202-22-22
E-mail: rektor@gazi.edu.tr
Internet: www.gazi.edu.tr
Founded 1982
State control
Language of instruction: Turkish
Academic year: September to June

Rector: Prof. Dr RIZA AYHAN
Vice-Rector: Prof. Dr METIN AKTAS
Vice-Rector: Prof. Dr CUMHUR SAHIN
Vice-Rector: Prof. Dr DURAN ALTIPARMARK
Sec.-Gen.: Prof. Dr BAHTIYAR AKYILMAZ
Librarian: TÜNSEL CANATALI

Library of 308,723 vols
Number of teachers: 3,760
Number of students: 64,663 (55,068 under-
graduate, 9,595 postgraduate)

Publication: *Gazi Üniversitesi Bülteni* (6 a
year)

DEANS

Faculty of Architecture: Prof. Dr HÜSNU CAN
Faculty of Arts and Design: Prof. Dr FATMA
ALI SINANOGLU
Faculty of Commerce and Tourism: Prof. Dr
NEVZAT AYPEK
Faculty of Communication: Prof. Dr NACI
BOSTANCI
Faculty of Dentistry: Prof. Dr DERVIS YILMAZ
Faculty of Economic and Administrative Sci-
ences: Prof. Dr KADIR ARIKI
Faculty of Economics and Administrative
Sciences (Çorum): Prof. Dr HASAN KAVAL
Faculty of Education (Gazi): Prof. Dr MUS-
TAFA SAFRAN
Faculty of Education (Kastamonu): Prof. Dr
ALEMI YETIM
Faculty of Education (Kırşehir): Prof. Dr
SELAHATTİN SALMAN
Faculty of Engineering (Çorum): Prof. Dr
NAIL UNSAL
Faculty of Forestry (Kastamonu): Prof. Dr
HASAN VURDU
Faculty of Fine Arts: Prof. Dr ALEV CAKMAO-
GLU KURU
Faculty of Health Sciences: Prof. Dr A.
GULSAN TURKOZSUCAK
Faculty of Industrial Arts Education: Prof.
Dr İRFAN SÜER
Faculty of Law: Prof. Dr IHSAN ERDOGAN
Faculty of Medicine: Prof. Dr PEYAM CINAZ
Faculty of Pharmacy: Prof. Dr TURHAN
BAYKAL
Faculty of Sciences (Kırşehir): Prof. Dr İRFAN
AKGÜN
Faculty of Technical Education: Prof. Dr
CEMIL CETINKAYA
Faculty of Theology (Çorum): Prof. Dr HASAN
ONAT
Faculty of Vocational Education: Prof. Dr
FATMA ALI SINANOGLU

GRADUATE SCHOOLS

**Graduate School of Accident Research
and Prevention:** e-mail
kazalariarastirma@gazi.edu.tr; internet kaza
.gazi.edu.tr; Dir Prof. Dr ALI BUMIN.

**Graduate School of Educational Sci-
ences:** e-mail egtbil@gazi.edu.tr; internet
www.egtbil.gazi.edu.tr; Dir Prof. Dr SEMIH
YALÇIN.

Graduate School of Health Sciences:
e-mail saglikb@gazi.edu.tr; internet www
.saglikb.gazi.edu.tr; Dir OKTAY ÜNER.

Graduate School of Natural Sciences:
Maltepe, Ankara; e-mail fenbil@gazi.edu.tr;
internet www.fbe.gazi.edu.tr; Dir Prof. Dr
AHMET BIGER.

Graduate School of Social Sciences:
e-mail sbe@gazi.edu.tr; internet sbe.gazi
.edu.trKavaklıdere, Ankara; Dir Prof. Dr
İHSON ERDOĞAN

GAZİANTEP ÜNİVERSİTESİ

POB 300, 27310 Gaziantep
Telephone: (342) 360-10-10
E-mail: gensek@gantep.edu.tr
Internet: www.gantep.edu.tr
Founded 1987
Academic year: October to June

Rector: Prof. Dr ERHAN EKINCI

Number of teachers: 2,800
Number of students: 49,250

Publications: *Sosyal Bilimler Dergisi* (social
sciences, 1 a year), *Tıp Fakültesi Dergisi*
(medicine, 2 a year)

DEANS

Faculty of Arts and Science: IHSAN ÜNVER
Faculty of Arts and Science (Kilis): ÖMER
BAKKALOGLU
Faculty of Economics and Business Admin-
istration: ISMAIL H. ÖZSABUNCUOĞLU
Faculty of Education: MUHSIN MACIT
Faculty of Education (Adiyaman): HACI
DURAN
Faculty of Education (Kilis): ALI RIZA TEKIN
Faculty of Engineering: MUSTAFA ÖZAKÇA
Faculty of Medicine: ABDURAHMAN KADAYIFÇI

GAZİOSMANPAŞA ÜNİVERSİTESİ

60150 Tokat
Telephone: (356) 252-14-52
E-mail: tokat@gop.edu.tr
Internet: www.gop.edu.tr
Founded 1992
State control
Academic year: October to June

Rector: Prof. Dr ZEHRA SEYFIKLI
Vice-Rector: Prof. Dr MEHMET ARSLAN
Vice-Rector: Prof. Dr MEHMET TEKIN
Librarian: ERDAL ŞAHINI

Library of 60,063 vols, 1,425 theses, 375
periodicals, 48 musical notes, 40 diskettes,
295 CD-ROMs, 19 electronic databases
Number of teachers: 840
Number of students: 13,300 (12,500 undergraduate, 810 postgraduate)

DEANS

Faculty of Agriculture: Prof. Dr GÜNGÖR
YILMAZ
Faculty of Arts and Sciences: Prof. Dr HANEFI
VURAL
Faculty of Economic and Administrative Sci-
ences: Prof. Dr OSMAN KARAKACIER
Faculty of Education: Prof. Dr MUSTAFA
BALOĞLU
Faculty of Medicine: Prof. Dr MURAT FIRAT
Faculty of Natural Sciences and Engineer-
ing: (vacant)

GEBZE YÜKSEK TEKNOLOJİ ENSTİTÜSÜ

PK 141, 41400, Gebze Kocaeli
Telephone: (262) 605-15-01
E-mail: okalem@gyte.edu.tr
Internet: www.gyte.edu.tr
Founded 1992
Language of instruction: Turkish
State control
Academic year: September to June

Rector: Prof. Dr ORHAN ŞAHIN
Vice-Rector: ARIF ERGIN
Vice-Rector: Prof. Dr MUAMMER KALYON
Vice-Rector: Prof. Dr TAŞKIN KAVZOĞLU

Library of 14,000 vols, 49 edatabases, 60,000
online periodicals, 27 printed periodicals
Number of teachers: 480
Number of students: 4,835 (1,987 undergraduate 2,226 graduate, 622 PhD)

DEANS

Faculty of Architecture: Prof. Dr TÜLAY ESIN
TIKANSAK
Faculty of Business Administration: Prof. Dr
HALIT KESKIN
Faculty of Engineering: Prof. Dr M. ALAITTIN
HASTAOGLU
Faculty of Science: Prof. Dr ADEM KILIÇ

HACETTEPE ÜNİVERSİTESİ

Hacettepe Üniversitesi, 06100 Ankara
Telephone: (312) 305-5000
E-mail: information@hacettepe.edu.tr
Internet: www.hacettepe.edu.tr
Founded 1967
State control
Language of instruction: English, French,
German, Turkish
Academic year: September to August

Rector: Prof. Dr UĞUR ERDENER
Vice-Rector: Prof. Dr HASAN KAZDAĞLI
Vice-Rector: Prof. Dr HÜSEYIN SELÇUK GEÇIM
Vice-Rector: Prof. Dr SEVIL GÜRGAN
Sec.-Gen.: TURHAN MENTEŞ
Registrar: A. RIFKI GÖKMEN (Deputy Regis-
trar)
Dir for Libraries: AYŞEN KÜYÜK (Deputy Dir)

Library: Beytepe campus library of 185,554
vols, 34,940 journals, 1,216,181 theses,
1,996 CDs, 1,071 record albums
Number of teachers: 3,600
Number of students: 30,000

Publications: *Hacettepe Tıp/Cerrahi Bülteni*
(4 a year), and several faculty bulletins

DEANS

Beytepe Campus:

Faculty of Communication: Prof. Dr SUAVI
AYDIN
Faculty of Economics and Adminstrative
Sciences: Prof. Dr AHMET BURÇIN YERELI
Faculty of Education: Prof. Dr BUKET
AKKOYUNLU
Faculty of Engineering: Prof. Dr HAYRI
YILMAZ KAPTAN
Faculty of Fine Arts: Prof. Dr UĞURCAN
AKYÜZ
Faculty of Law: Prof. Dr SELMA ÇETINER
Faculty of Letters: Prof. Dr MUSA YAŞAR
SAĞLAM
Faculty of Science: Prof. Dr MEHMET AŞKIN
TÜMER

Hacettepe Campus:

Faculty of Dentistry: Prof. Dr CELAL TÜMER
Faculty of Health Sciences: Prof. Dr HALIT
TANJU BESLER
Faculty of Medicine: Prof. Dr SARP SARAÇ
Faculty of Pharmacy: Prof. Dr A. AHMET
BAŞARAN

Sihhiye Campus:

Faculty of Pharmacy: Prof. Dr LÜTFIYE ÖMÜR DEMIREZER

Kastamonu Faculty of Medicine: Prof. Dr SÜLEYMAN SIRRI KES

PROFESSORS

Faculty of Dentistry:

ALPARSLAN, M. G., Oral and Dental Therapeutics
ALTAY, A., Paediatric Dentistry
ANIL (GAZI), N., Prosthesis
ASLAN, Y., Prosthesis
AVCI, M., Prosthesis
BAŞEREN, N. M., Oral and Dental Therapeutics
BERKER, A. E., Periodontics
BOLAY (SARIOĞLU), Ş., Oral and Dental Therapeutics
CANAY (OLGUN), R. Ş., Prosthesis
ÇAĞLAYAN, F., Periodontics
ÇAĞLAYAN, G., Periodontics
ÇALT, T., Endodontics
CIĞER, S., Orthodontics
DAYANGAÇ, B., Oral and Dental Therapeutics
DAYANGAÇ, B., Prosthesis
DEMIREL (USLU), F., Prosthesis
DURMAZ, V., Oral and Dental Therapeutics
ERATALAY, Y. K., Periodontics
GÖKALP, S., Oral and Dental Therapeutics
GÖRDUYSUS, M., Endodontics
GÖRÜCÜ, J., Oral and Dental Therapeutics
GÜRGAN, S., Oral and Dental Therapeutics
HERSEK, N. E., Prosthesis
KANSU, A. Ö., Oral and Dental Therapeutics
KANSU, H., Oral and Dental Therapeutics
KEYF (HAMARAT), F., Prosthesis
KOCADERELI, I., Orthodontics
KÖPRÜLÜ, H., Oral and Dental Therapeutics
KÖSEOĞLU, O. T., Dental Surgery
KURANER, T., Oral and Dental Therapeutics
NAZLIEL, H., Periodontics
NOHUTÇU, R. M., Periodontics
ÖKTEMER, M., Prosthesis
ÖLMEZ, M. S., Paediatric Dentistry
ÖNEN, A., Oral and Dental Therapeutics
ÖZÇELIK, B., Oral and Dental Therapeutics
ÖZGÜNALTAY, H. G., Oral and Dental Therapeutics
ŞAHIN, E., Prosthesis
ŞAHIN (SÖKMEN), S., Prosthesis
ŞAHMALI, S., Prosthesis
SAYGILI, G., Prosthesis
ŞENGÜN, F. D., Periodontics
SERPER, A., Endodontics
TAŞAR, F., Dental Surgery
TAŞMAN, F., Endodontics
TUNCER, M., Periodontics
URAN, N., Oral Surgery
YAMALIK, N., Periodontology
YENIGÜL, M., Prosthesis

Faculty of Economics and Administrative Sciences:

AKALIN, G., Public Finance
AKTAN, O. H., Economics
BILICI, N., Public Finance
ÇAĞLAR, A., Public Administration
CAN, H., Economics
ERDOĞAN, M., Public Administration
IPÇI, M. Ö., Accounting and Finance
KARAN, M., Business Administration
KAZDAĞLI, H., Economics
MORGIL, O., Economics
ŞAHINÖZ, A., Economics
ŞIŞIK, Ü., Economics
TANYERI, I., Economics
TELATAR, M. E., Economics
TIMUR, H., Economics
TOKAT, M., Economics
UYGUN, H., Economics

Faculty of Education:

ABAK, M., Physics
ACAR, N., Counselling and Guidance
AKKOYUNLU, B., Computer Education and Instructional Technologies
AKMAN, B., Pre-School Teaching
AŞKAR, P., Computer Education and Instructional Technologies
BAŞAR, H., Education
BAŞKAN, A. G., Educational Administration, Supervision, Planning and Economics
BÜLBÜL, A., Mathematics Teaching
DEMIREL, Ö., Education
DEMIREZEN, M., Language Studies
ERATALAY, N., French
ERÇETIN, Ş. Ş., Educational Administration, Supervision, Planning and Economics
EREN, A., Physics
ERSEVER, O. G., Counselling and Guidance
ERTEM, C., Language and Literature
GENÇ, A., German Language Teaching
HAMAN, S., Physics Teaching
KAVAK, Y., Education
KESKIL, G., English Language Teaching
KIRAN, A., Language Studies
KIZIROĞLU, I, Biology
MORGIL, I., Analytical Chemistry
ÖNALP, B., Biology
ÖNSOY, R., Education
ÖZ, H., English Language Teaching
PATIR, S., Chemistry
SAĞLAM, N., Biology
SALIHOĞLU, H., Language Studies
SENEMOĞLU, N., Education
SIPAHILER, F., Biology
SÖNMEZ, V., Education
SORAN, H., Biology
TUĞRUL, B., Pre-School Teaching

Faculty of Engineering:

ACAR, J., Food
AKSU, Z., Process and Reactor Design
ALPER, E., Chemistry
APAYDIN, F., Physics
ARIKAN, A., Hydrogeology
AYDAR, E., Mineralogy, Petrography
AYTAÇ, S., Food Sciences
BAYARI, S. C., Hydrogeology
BAYHAN, H., Geology
BEŞKARDEŞ, O., Chemistry
BIRGÜL, O., Nuclear Physics
BOZDEMIR, M. T., Unit Operations and Thermodynamics
ÇADIRCI, I., Electrical Engineering
ÇAĞLAR, A., Chemistry
CANKURTARAN, M., Physics
ÇELELBI, S. S., Chemistry
ÇELIK, H., Physics
ÇELIK, S., Food Sciences
ÇELIK, T., Physics
ÇINER, T. A., Geology
ÇOLAK, Ü., Nuclear Physics
DEMIRCIOĞLU, H., Electrical Engineering
DEMIREL, H., Mining Engineering
DURUBOY, H. Z., Physics
DURUSOY (DÖRTER), B. T., Mining Engineering
ERAY, A., Solid State Physics
ERCAN, B., Electrical Engineering
ERKAN, Y., Geology
FIRAT, T., Physics
GEÇIM, S., Electrical Engineering
GIRGIN, I, Mining Engineering
GÜMÜŞDERELIOĞLU, M., Chemistry
GÜNDÜC, Y., Electrical Engineering
HÖKELEK, T., Physics
IDE, S., General Physics
INAN, I. D., Physics
KAPTAN, Y., Physics
KARAKAŞ, M. Ü., Computer Science Engineering
KARAYIĞIT, A., Mineral Deposits, Geochemistry
KASAPOĞLU, K. E., Geology

KAYHAN, S., Telecommunications
KENDI, E., General Physics
KÖKSAL, A., Electromagnetic Waves and Microwaves
KÖKSEL, H., Food
KORKMAZ, M., Physics
KULAKSIZ, S., Mining and Mineral Processing
KUTSAL, T., Chemistry
MUTLU, M., Food
ÖKTÜ, Ö., General Physics
ÖNDER, M., Physics
ÖNER, M., Mining Engineering
ÖNER, M., Mining and Mineral Processing
ORAL, B., Physics
ÖZBAŞ, Y., Food Technology
ÖZBAY (DANACI), S., General Physics
ÖZBEY, T., Physics
ÖZDURAL, A. R., Chemistry
ÖZTECIN, E., Physics
PIŞKIN, E., Chemistry
SAATÇI, A., Computer Science Engineering
ŞAFAK, M., Electrical Engineering
SAĞ, Y., Process and Reactor Design
SALDAMLI, I., Food
SARAÇ, C., Mineral Deposits, Geochemistry
SAYDAM, A., Environmental Engineering
ŞENYUR, M. G., Mining and Mineral Processing
ŞIMŞEK, S., Hydrogeology
SUNGAR, R., General Physics
SÜNNETÇIOĞLU, M., Physics
TABAK, F., Physics
TANYOLAÇ, A., Chemistry
TEMEL, A., Mineral Deposits, Geochemistry
TEMIZ, A., Food
TERCAN, A., Mining and Mineral Processing
TOLUNAY, H., Solid State Physics
TOPAÇLI, C., Physics
TOPAÇLI(SUNGUR), A., Atomic and Molecular Physics
TÖRECI, E., Computer Science Engineering
TUNCEL, S. A., Process and Reactor Design
TUNOĞLU, C., General Geology
ÜLKÜ, D., Physics
ULUSAY, R., Applied Geology
ÜNVER, B., Mining and Mineral Processing
US, F., Food
VURAL, H., Food Sciences
YARIMAĞAN, Ü., Computer Science Engineering
YAZGAN, E., Electrical Engineering

Faculty of Fine Arts:

AKYÜZ, U., Graphic Art
AYDINÖZ, A. A., Art
DAKAK, H., Painting
GENCAYDIN, Z., Fine Arts
KAYA, I., Graphic Art
MISMAN, H. A., Painting
PEKMEZCI, H., Painting
PEKTAŞ, H., Graphic Art
SAVAŞ, R., Sculpture

Faculty of Letters:

AKAN, A. V., Sociology
AKKOYUNLU, Z., Folklore Studies
AKSOY, B. M., English Translation and Interpretation
AKSOY, E., Western Language and Literature
ALTAY (AKANSEL), A., English Translation and Interpretation
ARIKAN (GÜRER), G., Sociology
AYDIN, O., Experimental Psychology
BAĞCI, S., History of Art
BAYDUR, K. G., Librarianship
BAYKAN, F., Philosophy
BOZBEYOĞLU, S., French Language and Literature
BOZER, A. D., English Language and Literature
ÇAKIN, I., Librarianship
ÇELIK, A., Librarianship
ÇELIK-ŞAVK, Ü., Turkish Language and Literature

DİKEÇLİGİL, F. B., Sociometry
DOĞAN, Ş., German Language and Literature
ERCİLASUN, B., Literature
ERGAN, N., Sociology
ERKENAL, A., History of Art
ERLAT, J., French Studies
EROL, B., English Language and Literature
HORATA, O., Turkish Language and Literature
İÇLİ, T., Sociology
İNAL, T., French Studies
İZGI, Ö., General Turkish History
KARAKAŞ, S., Experimental Psychology
KIRAN, Z., French Studies
KÖNİG, G., Linguistics
KULA, O., German Language and Literature
KURBANOĞLU, S. S., Librarianship
OCAK, A. Y., History
OCAK, F. T., History
OPPERMANN (TUNÇ), S., English Language and Literature
ÖTÜKEN, S. Y., Archaeology
ÖZ, M., History
ÖZBEK, M., Social Anthropology
ÖZGEN, E., Archaeology
ÖZMEN, K., French Studies
ÖZÖNDER, M. C., Sociology
ÖZYER, N., German Language and Literature
SAĞLAM, M. Y., German Language and Literature
TEPE, H., Philosophy
TONTA, Y., Librarianship
UMUNÇ, H., English Language and Literature
UNAN, F., History
YILDIRIM, D., Literature
YILDIZ, S., German Studies
YIMAZ, E., Turkish Language and Literature

Faculty of Medicine:

ABBASOĞLU, O., Internal Medicine
AÇAN, L., Biochemistry
ACAROĞLU, R.E., Orthopaedics
ADALAR, N., Internal Medicine
ADALIOĞLU, G., Paediatrics
AKALAN, N., Neurosurgery
AKALIN, N., Neurosurgery
AKAN, H. T., Dermatology
AKATA, D., Radiology
AKHAN, H. M. O., Radiology
AKIN, A., Community Health
AKINCI, F.A., Physical Therapy and Rehabilitation
AKOVA, M., Internal Medicine
AKŞIT, D., Anatomy
AKSÖYEK, S., Cardiology
AKSU, A. T., Obstetrics and Gynaecology
AKYOL, F. H., Oncology
AKYOL, Ö., Biochemistry
AKYOL, U. M., Otorhinolaryngology
AKYÜZ (CELEPOĞLU), C., Oncology
ALAÇAM, R., Microbiology
ALEHAN, D., Paediatrics
ALPAR, C., Biostatistics
ALPARSLAN, M., Orthopaedics
ANLAR, B. F., Paediatrics
ARAN, Ö., Surgery
ARAS (SULHUN), T., Nuclear Medicine
ARIKAN, S., Microbiology
ARIOĞLU, S., Internal Medicine
ARİYÜREK, O. M., Radiology
ARSLAN, S., Internal Medicine
AŞAN, E., Morphology
ATAHAN, İ. L., Oncology
ATAKAN, Z. N., Dermatology
AYAS, K., Ear, Nose and Throat Surgery
AYDIN, E., Medical Ethics and History
AYDİNGÖZ, Ü., Radiology
AYHAN, A., Obstetrics and Gynaecology
AYPAR, Ü., Anaesthesiology
AYSUN, S., Paediatrics
AYTAR, Ş., Medical Biology

BAKKALOĞLU, A., Paediatrics
BAKKALOĞLU, A. M., Urology
BALCI, S., Paediatrics
BALKANCI, F., Radiology
BARIŞTA, İ., Internal Medicine
BAŞAR, R., Anatomy
BAŞGÖZE, O., Physical Therapy and Rehabilitation
BATMAN, F., Internal Medicine
BAYRAKTAR, M., Internal Medicine
BAYRAKTAR, Y., Internal Medicine
BEKSAÇ, S., Obstetrics and Gynaecology
BELGİN, E., Ear, Nose and Throat Surgery
BENLİ, K., Neurosurgery
BEŞBAŞ, N., Paediatrics
BESİM, A., Radiology
BİLGİÇ, S., Ophthalmology
BİLİR, N., Community Health
BÖKE, E., Cardiovascular and Thoracic Surgery
BOZKURT, A., Pharmacology
BÜLBÜL, F. F., Plastic and Reconstructive Surgery
BÜYÜKPAMUKÇU, M., Oncology
BÜYÜKPAMUKÇU, N., Paediatric Surgery
ÇAĞLAR, M., Nuclear Medicine
ÇAĞLAR, M., Paediatrics
ÇAKAR, A. N., Morphology
ÇAKMAK, F., Urology
ÇALGÜNERİ, M., Internal Medicine
ÇANER, B. E., Nuclear Medicine
ÇEKIRGE, H., Radiology
ÇEKIRGE, I. S., Radiology
ÇELEBİOĞLU, B., Anaesthesiology
ÇELİK, H. H., Anatomy
ÇELİKER, A., Paediatrics
ÇELİKER, A. R., Physical Therapy and Rehabilitation
ÇELİKER, V., Anaesthesiology and Reanimation
ÇETIN, M., Paediatrics
ÇEYHAN, M., Paediatrics
ÇIFTÇI, A., Paediatrics
ÇİGER, A., Institute of Neurological Sciences
CILA, A., Radiodiagnostics
ÇOKUĞRAŞ, N. A., Biochemistry
ÇÖPLÜ, L., Thoracic Diseases
COSKUN, T., Paediatrics
ÇUHADAROĞLU, F., Psychiatry
CUMHUR, M., Morphology
DAĞDEVIREN, A., Histology and Embryology
DALKARA, N. E. T., Institute of Neurological Sciences
DEMIRCIN, M., Cardiovascular and Thoracic Surgery
DEMIRKAZIK, F., Radiology
DEMIRPENÇE (TANSEL), E., Biochemistry
DİNÇER, F., Physical Therapy and Rehabilitation
DİNÇER, P. R., Medical Biology
DOĞAN, P., Biochemistry
DOĞAN, R., Cardiovascular and Thoracic Surgery
DORAL, M. N., Orthopaedics
DUMAN, O., Physiology
DÜNDAR, S., Internal Medicine
DURUKAN, T., Obstetrics and Gynaecology
ELDEM, M. B., Ophthalmology
ELİBOL, B., Neurology
EMRE (DÖKMECI), S., Internal Medicine
ERBAŞ, A. T., Internal Medicine
ERBAŞ, B. H., Nuclear Medicine
ERDEM, Y., Internal Medicine
ERDENER, U., Ophthalmology
ERGEN, A., Urology
ERGÜVEN (DİKEL), S., Microbiology
ERK, Y., Plastic Surgery
ERKAN, İ., Urology
ERSOY, F. N., Paediatrics
ERSOY, Ü., Cardiovascular and Thoracic Surgery
ERTENLİ, A. İ., Internal Medicine
GEDİK, O., Internal Medicine
GEDIKOĞLU, G., Pathology
GÖKLER, B., Psychiatry

GÖKÖZ, A., Pathology
GÜÇ, D., Oncology
GÜÇ, M. O., Pharmacology
GÜLER, Ç., Community Health
GÜLER, E. N., Internal Medicine
GÜLLÜ, İ., Oncology
GÜMRÜK, F., Paediatrics
GÜNALP, G. S., Obstetrics and Gynaecology
GÜNGEN, Y. Y., Pathology
GÜR (AKMAN), D., Paediatrics
GÜRAKAN, H., Paediatrics
GÜRGAN, T., Obstetrics and Gynaecology
GÜRGERY, A., Paediatrics
GÜRKANYNAK, H. M., Oncology
GÜRLEK, Ö. A., Internal Medicine
GÜRSEL, B., Ear, Nose and Throat Surgery
HALILOĞLU, M., Radiology
HAMALOĞLU, E., General Surgery
HASÇELİK, A. G., Microbiology
HASÇELİK, H. Z., Physical Therapy and Rehabilitation
HAZNEDAROĞLU, C., Internal Medicine
HOSAL, A., Otorhinology
İLGİ, N. S., Morphology
İLHAN, M., Pharmacology
İRKEÇ, M., Ophthalmology
KABAKÇI, M.G., Cardiology
KALAYCI, C., Paediatrics
KALE, G., Paediatrics
KALYONCU, A. F., Thoracic Diseases
KANBAK (SOYLU), M., Anaesthesiology and Reanimation
KANDEMIR, N., Paediatrics
KANSU, E., Oncology
KANSU, T., Institute of Neurological Sciences
KARAAĞAOĞLU, A. E., Medical Biology
KARABUDAK, R., Neurology
KARADUMAN, A., Dermatology
KARS, S. A., Internal Medicine
KART, A., Medical Biology
KAYA, S., Ear, Nose and Throat Surgery
KAYNAROLĞU, Z. V., Surgery
KEÇİK, A., Plastic Surgery
KENDİ, S., Urology
KES, S., Internal Medicine
KILINÇ, K., Biochemistry
KİPER, E. N., Childhood Health and Diseases
KIRATLI, H., Ophthalmology
KÖLEMEN, F., Dermatology
KÜÇÜKALİ, T., Pathology
KUŞ, M. S., Biochemistry
KUTLUK, M. T., Paediatrics
KUTSAL, F. Y., Physical Therapy and Rehabilitation
MAVILİ, M. E., Plastic and Reconstructive Surgery
MOCAN, G., Pathology
MÜFTÜOĞLU, S., Histology and Embryology
MUŞDAL, Y., Orthopaedics and Traumatology
NAZLI, N., Internal Medicine, Cardiology
NURLU (ÖZGÜR), G., Neurology
ÖCAL, M. T., Anaesthesiology
ÖĞRETMENOĞLU, O., Otorhinology
ÖĞÜŞ, İ. H., Biochemistry
ÖKTEM (BONCUK), F., Psychiatry
ONAT, D., Surgery
ÖNDEROĞLU, L. S., Obstetrics and Gynaecology
ÖNDEROĞLU, S., Anatomy
ÖNER, Z. N., Surgery
ÖNERCİ, T. M., Ear, Nose and Throat Surgery
ONUR, E. R., Pharmacology
ORAN, M. B., Radiology
ORER, H., Pharmacology
ORHAN, M., Ophthalmology
OTO, M. A., Internal Medicine
ÖVÜNÇ, K., Cardiology
ÖZCAN, E. O., Neurosurgery
ÖZCEBE, L. H., Community Health
ÖZCEBE, O. İ., Internal Medicine
ÖZÇELİK, H., Paediatrics
ÖZDEMIR, A., Surgery

ÖZDEN, A. K., Medical Biology
ÖZEN, H., Paediatrics
ÖZEN, H. A., Urology
ÖZEN, S., Paediatrics
ÖZENÇ, A. M., Surgery
ÖZER, E. S., Paediatrics
ÖZER, N., Biochemistry
ÖZGEN, T., Institute of Neurological Sciences
ÖZGEN (ULUPİNAR), S., Anaesthesiology
ÖZGÜÇ, M., Medical Biology
ÖZGÜNEŞ, N., Biochemistry
ÖZIŞIK, Y. Y., Oncology
ÖZKAN, S., Ear, Nose and Throat Surgery
ÖZKARA (ŞAHİN), A., Biochemistry
ÖZKUTLU, H., Internal Medicine
ÖZKUTLU, S., Paediatrics
ÖZKUYUMCU, C., Microbiology
ÖZMEN, F., Internal Medicine
ÖZMEN, M. N., Radiology
ÖZMERT, E., Paediatrics
ÖZTEK, A. Z., Community Medicine
ÖZTÜRK, N., Biophysics
ÖZYAR, E., Radiation Oncology
ÖZYAZICI, A., Morphology
PALAOĞLU, Ö. S., Institute of Neurological Sciences
PEKCAN, H., Community Health
PURALİ, N., Biophysics
ŞAFAK, T., Plastic and Reconstructive Surgery
ŞAHİN, A., Urology
ŞAHİN, A. A., Internal Medicine
ŞAHİN, S., Dermatology
ŞANAÇ, A. Ş., Ophthalmology
SANAL, S. Ö., Paediatrics
SARGON, M. F., Anatomy
SAYEK, İ., Surgery
SAYGI (SÜTÇÜ), S., Neurology
SEÇMEER, G., Paediatrics
ŞEFTALIOĞLU, A., Histology
ŞEKEREL, B., Paediatrics
ŞELÇUK, Z., Chest Diseases
SELEKLER, K., Neurology
ŞENER, B., Microbiology
ŞENER, E. C., Ophthalmology
ŞENNAROĞLU, L., Ear Nose and Throat Surgery
ŞENOCAK, M. E., Paediatric Surgery
ŞİMŞEK, H., Internal Medicine
SİVRİ, B., Internal Medicine
SÖYLEMEZOĞLU, F., Pathology
SÖZEN, T., Internal Medicine
SÖZER, A. B., Ear, Nose and Throat Surgery
SUNGUR, A. A., Oncology
SURAT, A., Orthopaedics
TAN, M. E., Neurology
TANYEL, F. C., Paediatric Surgery
TASAR, C., Oncology
TATAR, G., Internal Medicine
TEKGÜL, S., Urology
TEKİNALP, G., Paediatrics
TEKUZMAN, G., Oncology
TEZCAN, F., Biochemistry
TEZCAN, F. İ., Paediatrics
TEZCAN, S., Community Medicine
TOKATLI, A., Paediatrics
TOKGÖZOĞLU, M., Orthopaedics and Traumatology
TOKGÖZOĞLU, S. L., Internal Medicine
TOPALOĞLU, H., Paediatrics
TOPALOĞLU, R., Paediatrics
TOPÇU, M., Institute of Neurological Sciences
TUNCEL, H. M., Anatomy
TUNÇBİLEK, E., Paediatrics
TUNCER, A., Paediatrics
TUNCER, A. M., Paediatrics
TUNCER, M., Pharmacology
TUNCER, Z. S., Obstetrics and Gynaecology
TUNÇKANAT, F. F., Microbiology
TURAN, E., Ear, Nose and Throat Surgery
TURGAN, Ç., Internal Medicine
UĞUR, Ö., Nuclear Medicine
ULUĞ, B., Psychiatry

ULUŞAHIN, N. A., Psychiatry
ÜNAL, M. F., Child Psychiatry
ÜNAL, S., Internal Medicine
UNGAN, P., Biophysics
ÜNSAL, M., Radiology
US (ERSÖZ), A. D., Microbiology
USMAN, A., Internal Medicine
USTAÇELEBİ, S., Microbiology
UZUN (ÖZMEN), Ö., Internal Medicine
VARLI, K., Neurology
YALÇIN, Ş., Internal Medicine
YALÇINRIDVANAĞAOĞLU, A., Physiology
YARALİ, H., Obstetrics and Gynaecology
YASAVUL, Ü., Internal Medicine
YAZICI, M., Orthopaedics
YAZICI, M. K., Psychiatry
YETKİN, S., Paediatrics
YİĞİT, Ş., Paediatrics
YILMAZ, E., Medical Biology
YORDAM, N., Paediatrics
YÖRÜKAN, S., Physiology
YÜCE, A., Childhood Health and Diseases
YÜCE, K., Obstetrics and Gynaecology
YURDAKÖK, K., Paediatrics
YURDAKÖK, M., Paediatrics
YURTER (ERDEM), H., Medical Biology
ZORLU, A. F., Radiation Oncology

Faculty of Pharmacy:
ALTİNÖZ SARİSOY, S., Analytical Chemistry
BALKAN (TAYHAN), A., Pharmaceutical Chemistry
BAŞARAN, A. A., Pharmacognosy
BAŞARAN (GÜNDÜZ), N., Pharmaceutical Toxicology
BAŞÇİ, N., Analytical Chemistry
BİLGİN, A., Pharmaceutical Chemistry
ÇALIŞ, İ., Pharmacognosy
ÇALIŞ, Ü., Pharmaceutical Chemistry
ÇALIŞ, Y. S., Pharmaceutical Technology
ÇAPAN, Y., Pharmaceutical Technology
DALKARA, S., Pharmaceutical Chemistry
DEMİRDAMAR, S. R., Pharmacy
DEMİREZEN, L. Ö., Pharmacognosy
DEMİREZER, L. Ö., Pharmacognosy
ELDEM (ER), T., Pharmaceutical Biotechnology
ERDEMLİ(ŞAHİN), İ., Pharmaceutical Toxicology
ERDOĞAN, H., Pharmaceutical Chemistry
ERSÖZ, T., Pharmacognosy
ERTAN, M., Pharmaceutical Chemistry
EZER, N., Pharmaceutical Botanics
HEKİMOĞLU (KONUR), S., Pharmaceutical Chemistry
HINCAL, A., Galenic Pharmacy
HINCAL, F., Pharmaceutical Toxicology
KIR (KOT), S., Analytical Chemistry
ÖNER, A. F., Pharmaceutical Chemistry
ÖNER, L., Pharmaceutical Chemistry
ÖZALTIN (LEBLEBİC), N., Analytical Chemistry
ÖZER, A. Y., Pharmaceutical Chemistry
ÖZER, İ., Biochemistry
ÖZGÜNES, H., Pharmaceutical Toxicology
PALASKA, E., Pharmaceutical Chemistry
PEKINER, C., Pharmacology
ŞAFAK, C., Pharmaceutical Toxicology
ŞAHİN, G., Pharmaceutical Toxicology
SAKAR, M. K., Pharmaceutical Chemistry
SARAÇ, S., Pharmaceutical Chemistry
SARAÇOĞLU, İ., Pharmacognosy
ŞENEL, S., Pharmaceutical Technology
SÜMER (İLKİZ), N. A., Biochemistry
ŞUMLU, M., Pharmaceutical Technology
TEMİZER, A., Analytical Chemistry
UMA, S., Pharmaceutical Toxicology
ÜNLÜ (KARABABA), N., Pharmaceutical Technology
YEŞIADA, A., Pharmacy

Faculty of Science:
AKAY, M. T., Zoology
AKGÜN, A., Molecular Biology
AKSÖZ, E., Molecular Biology
AKSÖZ, N., General Biology
BALCIOĞLU, N., Organic Chemistry

BARLAS (EMIR), N., Zoology
BEKTAŞ, F. S., Analytical Chemistry
BOŞGELMEZ, A., Zoology
BOZCUK, A. N., Biology
BOZCUK, S., Biology
BROWN, L. M., Mathematics
ÇAĞATAY, N., Zoology
ÇAĞLAR, P., Analytical Chemistry
CANSUNAR, E., General Biology
CIHANGIR, N., Biotechnology
ÇİNGİ, H., Statistics
ÇIRAKOĞLU, Ç., Molecular Biology
DEMİREZEN, Ş., General Biology
DEMIRSOY, A., Zoology
DENİZLİ, A., Biochemistry
DİRİL, N., Molecular Biology
DOĞAN, M., Analytical Chemistry
DURUSOY, M., Molecular Biology
DÜZ, S. F., Chemistry
EKMEKÇİ, F. G., Hydrobiology
ERIK, S., Botany
ERK, A. F., Hydrobiology
EŞ, A. H., Mathematics
ESENSOY, Ö., Statistics
GÖKOĞLU, E., Analytical Chemistry
GÜNAY, S., Statistics
GÜNDÜZ, E., Hydrobiology
GÜNER, A., Polymer and Theoretical Chemistry
GÜVEN, O., Physical Chemistry
HARMANCI, A., Mathematics
İMAMOĞLU, Y., Analytical Chemistry
İNAL, C., Statistics
KALAYCIOĞLU, A., Molecular Biology
KARAN (ZÜMREOĞLU), B., Inorganic Chemistry
KAZANCI, N., Hydrobiology
KESKIN (ELDEM), N., Applied Biology
KILBARER, A. G., Physical Chemistry
KIŞ, M., Physical Chemistry
KOLANKAYA, D., Zoology
KOLANKAYA, N., General Biology
OKAY, G., Organic Chemistry
ORAL (HOCAOĞLU), G., Statistics
ÖNER, C., Molecular Biology
ÖNER (ÖZDÖNMEZ), R., Biotechnology
ÖZÇAĞ, E., Mathematics
PEKMEZ, K., Analytical Chemistry
PEKMEZ (ÖZÇIÇEK), N., Analytical Chemistry
RZAYEV, Z. M. O., Chemistry
SALİH, B., Physical Chemistry
ŞENEL (UYANIK), S., Physical Chemistry
SOLTANOV, K. N., Mathematics
SORKUN, K., Applied Biology
SÖZER, T., Statistics
TATLIDİL, H., Statistics
TERCAN, A., Algebra and Theory of Numbers
TERZİOĞLU, S., Botany
TIRAŞ, Y., Algebra and Theory of Numbers
TOKTAMIŞ, Ö., Statistics
TÜMER, M. A., General Biology
TÜNOĞLU, N., Organic Chemistry
ÜNALEROĞLU, C., Organic Chemistry
ÜNLÜ, H., General Biology
YALVAÇ, T., Mathematics, Geometry and Topology
YERLİ, S. V., Hydrobiology
YILDIRIMLI, Ş., Botany
YILDIZ, A., Analytical Chemistry

HALİÇ ÜNİVERSİTESİ
(Haliç University)

Büyükdere Cad. 101, 34394 Mecidiyeköy, İstanbul

Telephone: (212) 275-20-20
E-mail: info@halic.edu.tr
Internet: www.halic.edu.tr

Founded 1998

Faculties of arts and science, business administration, engineering and medicine.

Pres.: Prof. Dr GÜNDÜZ GEDIKOĞLU

Library of 11,000 vols
Number of teachers: 200
Number of students: 1,200

HARRAN ÜNİVERSİTESİ

Sanlıurfa

Telephone: (414) 312-84-56
E-mail: rektor@harran.edu.tr
Internet: www.harran.edu.tr

Founded 1992
State control

Pres.: Prof. Dr UGUR BUYUKBURC
Vice-Pres.: Prof. Dr URAL DINÇ
Vice-Pres.: Prof. Dr I. HALIL MUTLU
Vice-Pres.: Prof. Dr SELCUK YUCESAN

Number of teachers: 790
Number of students: 5,900

DEANS

Faculty of Agriculture: Prof. Dr MEHMET AKTAS
Faculty of Arts and Sciences: Prof. Dr GÖKSENIN ESELLER
Faculty of Economics: Prof. Dr MUSTAFA PIRILI
Faculty of Engineering: Prof. Dr BILGE ERDILLER
Faculty of Medicine: Prof. Dr SELCUK YUCE-SAN
Faculty of Theology: Prof. Dr IBRAHIM DUZEN
Faculty of Veterinary Sciences: Prof. Dr NAFIZ YURDAYDIN

İNÖNÜ ÜNİVERSİTESİ

Rektörlüğü, 44280 Malatya

Telephone: (422) 377-30-00
E-mail: rektor@inonu.edu.tr
Internet: www.inonu.edu.tr

Founded 1975
State control
Language of instruction: Turkish (English in Faculty of Medicine)
Academic year: October to July

Rector: Prof. Dr CEMIL ÇELIK
Vice-Rector: Prof. Dr ISMAIL ÖZDEMIR
Vice-Rector: Prof. Dr YUSUF TÜRKÖZ
Vice-Rector: Prof. Dr ASIM KÜNKÜL
Sec. Gen.: Dr KADIR KARTALCI

Library of 160,000 vols
Number of teachers: 2,100
Number of students: 19,100

DEANS

Faculty of Agriculture: Prof. BAYRAM MURAT ASMA
Faculty of Communications: Prof. SELMA KARATEPE
Faculty of Dentistry: Prof. Dr SERKAN POLAT
Faculty of Economics and Administrative Sciences: Prof. Dr MEHMET TIKICI
Faculty of Education: Prof. BURHANETTIN DÖNMEZ
Faculty of Engineering: Prof. KADIM CEYLAN
Faculty of Fine Arts: Prof. TURAN SAĞER
Faculty of Fisheries: Prof. Dr KAZIM ŞAHIN
Faculty of Law: Prof. Dr KEMAL ŞENOCAK
Faculty of Medicine: GÜNGÖR GÖKÇEK (Sec.)
Faculty of Pharmacy: Prof. ISMAIL ÖZDEMIR
Faculty of Science and Literature: Prof. Dr RIFAT GÜNEŞ
Faculty of Theology: Prof. HULUSI ARSLAN

IŞIK ÜNİVERSİTESİ

Kumbaba Mevkii, 34980 Sile, Istanbul

Telephone: (216) 528-70-45
E-mail: isikun@isikun.edu.tr
Internet: www.isikun.edu.tr

Founded 1885, present status 1996
Private control
Academic year: October to June

Pres.: Prof. Dr NAFIYE GÜNEÇ KIYAK

DEANS

Faculty of Arts and Sciences: Prof. Dr SABRI ARIK
Faculty of Economics and Administrative Sciences: Prof. Dr MEHMET KAYTAZ
Faculty of Engineering: Prof. YORGO İSTEFA-NOPULOS
Institute of Science and Engineering: Prof. Dr MUSTAFA KARAMAN
Institute of Social Sciences: Prof. Dr MURAT FERMAN

İSTANBUL ÜNİVERSİTESİ

Beyazıt, 34052 Istanbul

Telephone: (212) 440-00-00
E-mail: postmaster@istanbul.edu.tr
Internet: www.istanbul.edu.tr

Founded 1453, reorganized 1933
State control
Languages of instruction: Turkish, English
Academic year: October to February, March to July

Rector: Prof. Dr MESUT PARLAK
Vice-Rector: Prof. Dr NUR SERTER
Vice-Rector: Prof. Dr OSMAN ÖZDEMIR
Vice-Rector: Prof. Dr TAYLAN AKKAYAN
Admin. Officer: NURETTIN ERDEM
Number of students: 49,000

DEANS

Faculty of Communication: Prof. Dr SUAT GEZGIN
Faculty of Dentistry: Prof. Dr BETÜL TUN-CELLI
Faculty of Economics: Prof. Dr MITHAT ZEKI DINÇER
Faculty of Engineering: Prof. Dr CUMA BAYAT
Faculty of Fisheries and Aquatic Science: Prof. Dr MEHMET SALIH ÇELIKKALE
Faculty of Forestry: Prof. Dr BÜLENT SEÇKIN
Faculty of Law: Prof. Dr TANKUT CENTEL
Faculty of Letters: Prof. Dr TANER TARHAN
Faculty of Management: Prof. Dr HAYRI ÜLGEN
Faculty of Medicine: Prof. Dr FARUK ERZEN-GIN
Faculty of Medicine (Cerrahpaşa): Prof. Dr FIKRET SIPAHIOĞLU
Faculty of Pharmacy: Prof. Dr AYSEL GÜRSOY
Faculty of Political Science: Prof. Dr FERYAL ORHON BASIK
Faculty of Science: Prof. Dr NURETTIN MERIÇ
Faculty of Theology: Prof. Dr EMRULLAH YÜKSEL
Faculty of Veterinary Science: Prof. Dr AHMET ALTINEL

İSTANBUL BİLGİ ÜNİVERSİTESİ
(Istanbul Bilgi University)

İnönü Cad. 28, Kuştepe, 34387 Şişli, Istanbul

Telephone: (212) 311-50-00
E-mail: bilgi@bilgi.edu.tr
Internet: www.bilgi.edu.tr

Founded 1994, as Istanbul School of International Studies; present name and status 1996
Private control
Language of instruction: English
Academic year: October to July

Rector: Prof. Dr HALIL GÜVEN
Vice-Rector: Prof. Dr REMZI SANVER
Sec.-Gen.: ÇAĞRI BAĞCIOĞLU
Registrar: MICHEL PAUS

Library of 68,000 vols
Number of teachers: 570
Number of students: 8,640

Publications: Bilgi Bellek, Foreign Policy (6 a year)

DEANS

European Institute: Prof. Dr AYHAN KAYA
Faculty of Architecture: Prof. Dr İHSAN BILGIN
Faculty of Arts and Sciences: Prof. Dr DIANE SUNAR
Faculty of Communication: Prof. Dr HALIL NALÇAOĞLU
Faculty of Economics and Administrative Sciences: Dr EGE YAZGAN
Faculty of Engineering: Prof. Dr LALE DURUIZ
Faculty of Law: Prof. Dr TURGUT TARHANLI
Institute of Natural and Applied Sciences (Graduate School): Prof. Dr DOĞAN GÜNEŞ
Social Science Institute (Graduate School): Dr GÖKSEL AŞAN

İSTANBUL KÜLTÜR ÜNİVERSİTESİ

E5 Karayolu Üzeri, 22 Ataköy Metro Ista-syonu Karsısı, Sirinevler, 34510 Istanbul

Telephone: (212) 639-30-24
E-mail: kultur@iku.edu.tr
Internet: www.iku.edu.tr

Founded 1997
Private control
Languages of instruction: Turkish, English
Academic year: October to May

Rector: Prof. Dr DURSUN KOÇER
Vice-Rector: Prof. Dr GETIN BOLCAL
Vice-Rector: Prof. Dr TAMER KOÇEL
Registrar: Asst Prof. Dr METIN BOLCAL

Library of 6,800 books
Number of teachers: 100
Number of students: 2,100 (2,060 undergraduate, 40 postgraduate)

Publication: Journal (4 a year)

DEANS

Faculty of Arts: Prof. Dr NÜKET GÜZ
Faculty of Business Administration: Prof. Dr TAMER KOÇEL
Faculty of Engineering and Architecture: Prof. Dr OKAY EROSKAY
Faculty of Law: Prof. Dr TAYFUN AKGÜNER
Faculty of Science and Letters: Prof. Dr LATIF TOPAKTAŞ
Vocational School: Prof. Dr TANER BULAT

İSTANBUL TEKNİK ÜNİVERSİTESİ

İTÜ Ayazağa Kampüsü, 34469 İstanbul

Telephone: (212) 285-34-00
E-mail: intoffice@itu.edu.tr
Internet: www.itu.edu.tr

Founded 1773
State control
Languages of instruction: English, Turkish
Academic year: October to July (2 semesters)

Rector: Prof. FARUK KARUDOGAN
Vice-Rector: Prof. A. FUAT ANDAY
Vice-Rector: Prof. Dr HALUK KARADOĞAN
Vice-Rector: Prof. S. ERKIN NASUF
Provost: NEVZAT ÖZKÖK
Librarian: AYHAN KAYGUSUZ

Library: see under Libraries and Archives
Number of teachers: 1,860
Number of students: 17,500

Publications: ARI (Physical and Engineering Sciences, 4 a year), Catalog (every 2 years), ITU'den Haberler (4 a year)

DEANS

Faculty of Aeronautics and Astronautics: Prof. FEVZI ÜNAL
Faculty of Architecture: Prof. CENGIZ GIR-ITLIOĞLU
Faculty of Chemical and Metallurgical Engineering: Prof. HASAN CAN OKUTAN
Faculty of Civil Engineering: Prof. DERIN ORHON
Faculty of Electrical and Electronic Engineering: Prof. HAKAN KUNTMAN

Faculty of Management: Prof. AHMET FAHRI ÖZOK
Faculty of Mechanical Engineering: Prof. TANER DERBENTLI
Faculty of Mines: Prof. MAHIR VARDAR
Faculty of Naval Architecture and Ocean Engineering: Prof. ÖMER GÖREN
Faculty of Science and Letters: Prof. FIGEN KADIRGAN (Deputy)
Faculty of Textile Technologies and Design: Prof. BÜLENT ÖZIPEK
Maritime Faculty: Prof. SAMI AYDIN ŞALCI
Turkish Music Conservatory: Prof. CAN ETILI ÖKTEM

ATTACHED CONSERVATORY AND DEPARTMENTS

Department of Fine Arts: Dir AYLA ÖDEKAN.

Department of Languages and History: e-mail ituydy@itu.edu.tr; Dir ÖNER GÜNÇAVDI.

Department of Physical Education and Sports: Dir EMIN TACER.

Turkish Music Conservatory: internet www.tmdk.itu.edu.tr; Dir CAN ETILI ÖKTEM.

ATTACHED GRADUATE INSTITUTES

Institute of Energy: internet www.energy.itu.edu.tr; Dir HASAN SAYGIN.

Institute of Eurasia Earth Sciences: e-mail alper.unal@itu.edu.tr; Dir OKAN TÜYSÜZ.

Institute of Informatics: Dir NÜZHET DALFES.

Institute of Science and Technology: Dir MEHMET KARACA.

Institute of Social Sciences: e-mail sbe@itu.edu.tr; internet www.sbe.itu.edu.tr; Dir NURAN ZEREN GÜLERSOY

İSTANBUL TİCARET ÜNİVERSİTESİ
(Istanbul Commerce University)

Ragıp Gümüşpala Cad. 84, 34378 Eminönü, Istanbul
Telephone: (212) 511-41-50
E-mail: rektorluk@iticu.edu.tr
Internet: www.iticu.edu.tr
Academic year: September to August

Pres.: Prof. Dr NAZIM EKREN
Library Dir: YASIN DEMIRBAŞ

Library of 40,000 vols
Number of teachers: 250
Number of students: 5,000

DEANS

Faculty of Commercial Science: Prof. Dr AHMET KARA
Faculty of Communications: Prof. Dr CUNEYT BINATLI
Faculty of Engineering: Prof. Dr OĞUZ BORAT
Faculty of Law: Prof. Dr MUSTAFA ERDOĞAN
Faculty of Science: Prof. Dr EKREM SAVAS

İZMİR EKONOMI ÜNİVERSİTESİ
(Izmir University of Economics)

Sakarya Caddesi 156, 35330 Balçova, İzmir
Telephone: (232) 279-25-25
E-mail: oia@ieu.edu.tr
Internet: www.ieu.edu.tr
Founded 2001
Private control
Language of instruction: English
Academic year: September to June

Rector: Prof. Dr TUNCDAN BALTACIOGLU
Vice-Rector: Prof. Dr MURAT ADIVAR
Provost: Prof. Dr M. CEMALI DİNÇER
Sec. Gen: LEVENT GÖKÇEER
Dean of Students: MINE KAYICAN
Dir for Int. Affairs: ERTAN KOYUNCU
Librarian: ALI TUTAL

Number of teachers: 440
Number of students: 6,200

DEANS

Faculty of Arts and Sciences: Prof. Dr İSMIHAN BAYRAMOĞLU
Faculty of Communication: Prof. Dr SEVDA ALANKUŞ
Faculty of Economics and Administrative Sciences: Prof. Dr TUNCDAN BALTACIOGLU
Faculty of Engineering and Computer Science: Prof. Dr TURHAN TUNALI
Faculty of Fine Arts and Design: Prof. Dr ENDER YAZGAN BULGUN

İZMİR YÜKSEK TEKNOLOJİ ENSTİTÜSÜ
(İzmir Institute of Technology)

Gülbahçe Köyü, 35430 Urla, İzmir
Telephone: (232) 750-60-01
E-mail: mustafaguden@iyte.edu.tr
Internet: www.iyte.edu.tr
Founded 1992
public control
Languages of instruction: English, Turkish
Academic year: October to June

Rector: Prof. Dr MUSTAFA GUDEN
Vice-Rector: Prof. Dr MURAT GÜNAYDIN
Vice-Rector: Prof. Dr SEDAT AKKURT
Librarian: GÜLTEKIN GÜRDAL

Library of 21,492 books, 96 periodicals, 6,443 online scientific periodicals
Number of teachers: 420
Number of students: 1,730 (1,200 undergraduate, 530 postgraduate)

DEANS

Faculty of Architecture: Prof. Dr AHMET E. EROĞLU
Faculty of Engineering: Prof. Dr FUNDA TIHMINLIOĞLU
Faculty of Science: Prof. Dr SERDAR ÖZÇELIK
Graduate School of Engineering and Sciences: Prof. Dr TUĞRUL RAMAZAN SENGER

KADİR HAS ÜNİVERSİTESİ

Cibali Merkez Kampüsü, Hisarattı Cad., 34230-01 Cibali-Fatih, Istanbul
Telephone: (212) 533-65-32
E-mail: info@khas.edu.tr
Internet: www.khas.edu.tr
Founded 1997
Private control
Languages of instruction: Turkish, English
Academic year: October to June

Pres.: Prof. Dr YÜCEL YILMAZ
Vice-Pres.: Prof. Dr NÜKHET TAN
Gen. Sec.: Dr AHMET B. SÖĞÜTLÜOĞLU
Registrar: SELMA DÖNMEZ
Head Librarian: ERTUĞRUL ÇIMEN

Library of 13,857 vols
Number of teachers: 140
Number of students: 1,500

DEANS

Faculty of Arts and Sciences: Prof. Dr KEMAL YELEKÇI
Faculty of Communications: Prof. Dr DENIZ BAYRAKDAR SEVGEN
Faculty of Economics and Business Administration: Prof. Dr EROL ÜÇDAL
Faculty of Engineering: Prof. Dr TUNCAY SAYDAM
Faculty of Fine Arts: Prof. Dr FATMA OYA BOYLA (acting)
Faculty of Law: Prof. Dr SELÇUK ÖZTEK

KAFKAS ÜNİVERSİTESİ

Rektörlüğü, Pasacayiri Mh., 36040 Kars
Telephone: (474) 242-68-00
E-mail: bidab@kafkas.edu.tr

Internet: www.kafkas.edu.tr
Founded 1992
State control

Rector: Prof. Dr NECATI KAYA
Number of teachers: 480
Number of students: 10,000

Publications: *University Bulletin* (1 a year), *University Gazette* (4 a year)

KAHRAMANMARAŞ SÜTÇÜ IMAM ÜNİVERSİTESİ

KSÜ Rektörlüğü, Avşar Kampüsü, 46100 Kahramanmaraş
Telephone: (344) 219-10-00
E-mail: baytorun@ksu.edu.tr
Internet: www.ksu.edu.tr
Founded 1992
State control
Academic year: October to June

Rector: Prof. Dr A. NAFI BAYTORUN
Vice-Rector: Prof. Dr ORHAN DOĞAN
Vice-Rector: Prof. Dr CAFER MART
Vice-Rector: Prof. Dr CEMAL TUNCER
Sec.-Gen.: RÜŞTÜ ERTUĞRUL
Librarian: ŞEREF AKBEN

Library of 25,000 books and periodicals
Number of teachers: 700
Number of students: 11,000

DEANS

Faculty of Agriculture: Prof. Dr ERFAN EFE
Faculty of Economics and Administrative Sciences: Prof. Dr AHMET HAMDI AYDIN
Faculty of Education: Prof. Dr ADNAN KÜÇÜKÖNDER
Faculty of Engineering and Architecture: Prof. Dr MEHMET NURI BODUR
Faculty of Forestry: Prof. Dr ORHAN ERDAŞ
Faculty of Medicine: Prof. Dr İLHAMI TANER KALE
Faculty of Sciences and Literature: Prof. Dr ALI DOĞAN
Faculty of Theology: Prof. Dr M. KAMAL ATIK

KARADENİZ TEKNİK ÜNİVERSİTESİ
(Karadeniz Technical University)

61080 Trabzon
Telephone: (462) 377-30-00
E-mail: head@ktu.edu.tr
Internet: www.ktu.edu.tr
Founded 1955
State control
Languages of instruction: English, Turkish
Academic year: October to August

Rector: Prof. Dr İBRAHIM ÖZEN
Vice-Rector: Prof. Dr SELAHATTIN KÖSE
Vice-Rector: Prof. Dr NECATI TÜYSÜZ
Vice-Rector: Prof. Dr ORHAN AYDIN
Gen. Sec.: Assoc. Prof. CÜNEYT ŞEN
Librarian: Prof. Dr MEHMET ARSLAN

Library of 220,000 vols
Number of teachers: 1,570
Number of students: 38,000

Publications: *KTÜ Bülteni* (bulletin, 2 a year), *KTÜ Education Activities* (1 a year)

DEANS

Faculty of Agriculture (Ordu): Prof. Dr Y. NURETTIN İSMAILÇELEBIOĞLU
Faculty of Architecture: Prof. Dr AYŞE SAĞSÖZ
Faculty of Arts and Sciences (Rize): Prof. Dr NAZMI TURAN OKUMUŞOĞLU
Faculty of Communication: Prof. Dr MUSTAFA EMIR
Faculty of Dentistry: Prof. Dr MEHMET TOSUN
Faculty of Economics and Administrative Sciences: Prof. Dr KAMIL YAZICI
Faculty of Economics and Administrative Sciences (Giresun): Prof. Dr METIN BERBER

Faculty of Education (Artvin): Prof. Dr OKTAY TORUL

Faculty of Education (Fatih): Prof. Dr ALI-PAŞA AYAS

Faculty of Education (Giresun): Prof. Dr MEHMET TÜFEKÇI

Faculty of Education (Rize): Prof. Dr MEHMET AKBAŞ

Faculty of Engineering: Prof. Dr MUSTAFA AYTEKIN

Faculty of Engineering (Gümüşhane): Prof. Dr FIKRI BULUT

Faculty of Fine Arts: Prof. Dr MUSTAFA KANDIL

Faculty of Forestry: Prof. Dr ZAFER CEMAL ÖZKAN

Faculty of Law: Prof. Dr OSMAN PEHLIVAN

Faculty of Marine Sciences: Prof. Dr İBRAHIM OKUMUŞ

Faculty of Marine Sciences (Sürmene): Prof. Dr ERTUĞ DÜZGÜNEŞ

Faculty of Medicine: Prof. Dr SÜLEYMAN BAYKAL

Faculty of Pharmaceutical Sciences: Prof. Dr RASIN ÖZYAVUZ

Faculty of Science and Literature: Prof. Dr KENAN İNAN

Faculty of Science and Literature (Giresun): Prof. Dr ZIYA YAPAR

Faculty of Technology: Prof. Dr KENAN GELIŞI

Faculty of Theology: Prof. Dr S. KEMAL SANDIKÇI

PROFESSORS

Faculty of Agriculture (Ordu) (Ordu; tel. (452) 225-05-77; e-mail ziraat@ktu.edu.tr):

İSMAILÇELEBIOĞLU, Y. N., Soil Science
ŞILBIR, Y., Field Crops

Faculty of Architecture (Kanuni Kampüsü, 61080 Trabzon; tel. (462) 377-26-70):

ÇEVIK, S., Architecture
GÜR, Ş., Architecture
KANDIL, M., Architecture
PEHLEVAN, A., Architecture
SAĞSÖZ, A., Architecture
USTA, G., Architecture
YAŞAR, Y., Architecture

Faculty of Arts and Sciences (Giresun) (Gazi Cad. Kışla Hamam Sok., Giresun; tel. (454) 216-25-20):

YANMAZ, E., Physics

Faculty of Arts and Sciences (Rize) (Engindere Mah., Köy Hizmetleri Yanı, 53100 Rize; tel. (464) 223-53-75):

OKUMUŞOĞLU, N. T., Physics

Faculty of Economics and Administrative Sciences (Kanuni Kampüsü, 61080 Trabzon; tel. (462) 325-32-12; e-mail iibf@ktu.edu.tr):

ACUNER, T., Business Administration
AKSAR, Y., International Relations
AKTAŞ, H., International Relations
AKYAZI, H., Economics
ARAFAT, M., International Relations
BOCUTOĞLU, E., Economics
ÇELIK, K., Economics
ÇIFTÇI, O., Labour Economics and Industrial Relations
ÇIKRIKÇI, M., Management
DAĞLI, H., Business Administration
EMIR, M., Business Administration
KARAMUSTAFA, O., Business Administration
KESIM, A., Economics
KOÇER, G., International Relations
KÜÇÜKKALE, Y., Economics
ÖZYURT, H., Economics
SÜRMEN, Y., Business Administration
TANDOĞAN, A., Economics
TERZI, H., Economics
TÜREDI, H., Management
YAMAK, N., Economics
YAZICI, K., Business Administration
YAZICI, K., Management
ZENGIN, H., Econometrics

Faculty of Economics and Administrative Sciences (Giresun) (Giresun):

BERBER, M., Economics

Faculty of Education (Artvin) (Artvin):

TORUL, O., Chemistry

Faculty of Education (Fatih) (Söğütlü, Trabzon; tel. (462) 248-23-05):

AKDENIZ, A., Secondary Science and Mathematics Education
AYAS, A., Secondary Science and Mathematics Education
BAĞIROV, N., Fine Arts Education
BAKI, A., Secondary Science and Mathematics Education
ÇAPA, M., Secondary Social Science Education
ÇEPNI, S., Primary Education
KARANIS, N., Turkish Education
ŞAHIN, B., Secondary Science and Mathematics Education
SESLI, E., Secondary Science and Mathematics Education

Faculty of Education (Giresun) (Giresun; tel. (454) 215-53-72; e-mail gef@ktu.edu.tr):

TÜFEKÇI, M., Chemistry

Faculty of Education (Rize) (Rize; tel. (464) 532-67-92; e-mail ktu.cayeli@superonline.com):

TORUL, O., Chemistry

Faculty of Engineering (Gümüşhane) (Gümüşhane; tel. (456) 233-74-27):

BULUT, F., Geology
DURMUŞ, A., Civil Engineering
UZMAN, Ü., Civil Engineering

Faculty of Engineering (Kanuni Kampüsü, 61080 Trabzon; tel. (462) 325-31-72):

AKÇAY, M., Geological Engineering
AKPINAR, A., Electrical and Electronics Engineering
AKYOL, N., Geomatics Engineering
ALTAŞ, İ., Electrical and Electronics Engineering
ARICI, M., Mechanical Engineering
ARSLAN, F., Metallurgical and Materials Engineering
ARSLAN, M., Geological Engineering
AYDIN, O., Mechanical Engineering
AYTEKIN, M., Civil Engineering
AYVAZ, Y., Civil Engineering
BAYDAR, E., Mechanical Engineering
BAYRAKTAR, A., Civil Engineering
BEKTAŞ, O., Geological Engineering
BERKÜN, M., Civil Engineering
BILGIN, A., Mechanical Engineering
BIYIK, C., Geomatics Engineering
BIYIKLIOĞLU, A., Mechanical Engineering
BULUT, F., Geological Engineering
ÇAKIROĞLU, A.O., Civil Engineering
ÇAPKINOĞLU, Ş., Geological Engineering
ÇELIK, F., Civil Engineering
ÇUHADAROĞLU, B., Mechanical Engineering
DALOĞLU, A., Civil Engineering
DALOĞLU, A., Mechanical Engineering
DILAVER, A., Geomatics Engineering
DOĞAN, M., Mechanical Engineering
DUMANOĞLU, A., Civil Engineering
DURGUN, O., Mechanical Engineering
DURMUŞ, A., Civil Engineering
ERDOĞDU, Ş., Civil Engineering
ERDÖL, R., Civil Engineering
ERTAŞ, B., Civil Engineering
GELIŞLI, K., Geophysical Engineering
GENÇ, S., Geological Engineering
GÖKALP, E., Geomatics Engineering
GÜRÜNLÜ, C., Electrical and Electronics Engineering
HÜSEM, M., Civil Engineering
KARADENIZ, S., Mechanical Engineering
KARALI, C., Geomatics Engineering
KAYA, S., Geomatics Engineering
KESIMAL, A., Mining Engineering
KORKMAZ, S., Geological Engineering

NABIYEV, V., Computer Engineering
ÖNSOY, H., Civil Engineering
SADIKLAR, M., Geological Engineering
SAVAŞKAN, T., Mechanical Engineering
ŞEN, K., Geomatics Engineering
SOFUOĞLU, H., Mechanical Engineering
TÜYSÜZ, N., Geological Engineering
ÜNAL, A., Mechanical Engineering
UZMAN, Ü., Civil Engineering
UZUNER, B., Civil Engineering
YAZICI, R., Computer Engineering
YILMAZ, C., Geological Engineering
YÜKSEK, Ö., Civil Engineering

Faculty of Fine Arts (İnönü Cad. 53, 61300 Akçaabat, Trabzon; tel. (462) 228-12-02):

ALESKEROV, A., Painting

Faculty of Forestry (Kanuni Kampüsü, 61080 Trabzon; tel. (462) 377-28-28):

ACAR, C., Landspace Architecture
ACAR, H., Forestry Engineering
ALTUN, L., Forestry Engineering
AY, N., Forest Industrial Engineering
BAŞKENT, E., Forestry Engineering
BILGILI, E., Forestry Engineering
ÇOLAKOĞLU, G., Forest Industrial Engineering
DEMIRCI, A., Forestry Engineering
DEMIREL, Ö., Landspace Architecture
DENIZ, İ., Forest Industrial Engineering
EROĞLU, M., Forestry Engineering
GERÇEK, Z., Forestry Engineering
GÜMÜŞ, C., Forestry Engineering
KALAYCIOĞLU, H., Forest Industrial Engineering
KIRCI, H., Forest Industrial Engineering
KÖSE, S., Forestry Engineering
NEMLI, G., Forest Industrial Engineering
ÖZBILEN, A., Landspace Architecture
ÖZKAN, Z., Forestry Engineering
TERZIOĞLU, S., Forestry Engineering
TÜRKER, M., Forestry Engineering
TURNA, İ., Forestry Engineering
ÜÇLER, A., Forestry Engineering
USTA, M., Forest Industrial Engineering
YAHYAOĞLU, Z., Forestry Engineering
YAVUZ, H., Forestry Engineering
YILDIZ, Ü., Forest Industrial Engineering

Faculty of Marine Sciences (Sürmene) (Çamburnu, Trabzon; tel. (462) 752-28-05):

BORAN, H., Fisheries Technology Engineering
DINÇER, H., Fisheries Technology Engineering
KÖSE, H., Naval Architecture & Marine Engineering
DÜZGÜNEŞ, E., Fisheries Technology Engineering
KARAÇAM, H., Fisheries Technology Engineering
SEYHAN, H., Fisheries Technology Engineering

Faculty of Medicine (Kanuni Kampüsü, 61080 Trabzon; tel. (462) 377-54-05):

AĞAOĞLU, N., General Surgery
AK, İ., Psychiatry
AKGÜN, A., Physiology
AKYOL, N., Opthalmology
ALHAN, E., General Surgery
ALIOĞLU, Z., Neurology
ARSLAN, M., General Surgery
ARSLAN, M., Internal Medicine
ASLAN, Y., Paediatrics
AYAR, A., Physiology
AYDIN, F., Internal Medicine
AYNACI, O., Orthopaedics and Traumatology
BAHADIR, S., Dermatology
BAKI, A., Paediatrics
BAKI, C., Orthopaedics and Traumatology
BAYKAL, S., Neurosurgery
BOZKAYA, H., Obstetrics and Gynaecology
ÇAN, G., Public Health
ÇALIK, A., General Surgery
ÇIMŞIT, G., Dermatology

ÇINEL, A., General Surgery
ÇIVELEK, A., Cardiovascular Surgery
DEĞER, O., Biochemistry
DILBER, E., Paediatrics
DINÇ, H., Radiodiagnostics
ERCEYES, H., Anaesthesiology and Reanimation
ERDURAN, E., Paediatrics
EREM, C., Internal Medicine
ERSÖZ, H., Internal Medicine
ERTÜRK, M., Microbiology
GEDIK, Y., Paediatrics
GÖKÇE, M., Cardiology
GÖR, A., Urology
GÜLER, M., Physical Medicine and Rehabilitation
GÜMELE, H., Radiodiagnostics
İMAMOĞLU, H., Opthalmology
İMAMOĞLU, M., Otorhinolaryngology
IŞIK, A., Otorhinolaryngology
KALAYCIOĞLU, A., Anatomy
KALKAN, A., Infectious Diseases
KALYONCU, N., Pharmacology
KANDIL, S., Paediatric Psychiatry
KARAGÜZEL, A., Medical Biology
KARAHAN, S., Biochemistry
KEHA, E., Biochemistry
KÖKSAL, İ., Infectious Diseases
KUTLU, M., Cardiology
KUZEYLI, K., Neurosurgery
ODACI, E., Histology and Embriology
ÖKTEN, A., Paediatrics
OMAY, S., Internal Medicine
ÖNCÜ, M., General Surgery
ÖNDER, Ç., Orthopaedics and Traumatology
ÖNDER, E., Biochemistry
ÖREM, A., Biochemistry
ORHAN, F., Paediatrics
OVALI, E., Internal Medicine
ÖZCAN, F., Cardiovascular Surgery
ÖZEN, I., Anaesthesiology and Reanimation
ÖZGÜR, G., Urology
ÖZGÜR, O., Internal Medicine
ÖZLÜ, T., Chest Disease
ÖZMENOĞLU, M., Neurology
ÖZORAN, Y., Pathology
ÖZTÜRK, M., Radiodiagnostic
ÖZYAVUZ, R., Urology
REIS, A., Pathology
SARI, A., Radiodiagnostics
SARI, R., Internal Medicine
SARIHAN, H., Paediatric Surgery
SÖNMEZ, F., Paediatrics
TESTERECI, H., Biochemistry
TOSUN, M., Physical Medicine and Rehabilitation
TURGUTALP, H., Pathology
TURHAN, A., Orthopaedics and Traumatology
ULUSOY, Ş., Internal Medicine
UZUN, D., Internal Medicine
VELIOĞLU, S., Neurology
YANDI, M., General Surgery
YARIŞ, E., Pharmacology
YENILMEZ, E., Histology and Embryology
YILDIZ, K., Pathology
YILDIZ, M., Orthopaedics and Traumatology

Faculty of Science and Literature (Kanuni Kampüsü, 61080 Trabzon; tel. (462) 325-31-41):

ABBASOV, R., Chemistry
AHMET AYAZ, F., Biology
AKBAŞ, M., Mathematics
ALAADDIN YALÇINKAYA, M., History
ALTUNBAŞ, M., Physics
AYAZ, S., Biology
BEYAZOĞLU, O., Biology
ÇAVUŞ, A., Mathematics
ÇELEBI, S., Physics
ÇELIK, A., Turkish Language and Literature
ÇEVIK, U., Physics
ÇIÇEK, K., History

COŞKUN, E., Mathematics
DEMIRBAĞLU, Z., Biology
DOĞAN, A., Turkish Language and Literature
HINTISTAN, S., Nursing
İHSAN KOBYA, A., Physics
İNAN, K., History
İSMAYILOV, Z., Mathematics
KADIOĞLU, A., Biology
KANTEKIN, H., Chemistry
KARABÖCEK, S., Chemistry
KARAL, F., Physics
KARSLIOĞLU, S., Chemistry
KAYGUSUZ, K., Chemistry
KEMAL KAYRA, O., Turkish Language and Literature
KHADJIEV, D., Mathematics
KÜÇÜKÖMEROĞLU, B., Physics
ÖKSÜZ, H., History
OSMAN BELDÜZ, A., Biology
ŞENTÜRK, H., Chemistry
SÖKMEN, A., Chemistry
SÖKMEN, M., Biology
TIRAŞOĞLU, E., Physics
TÜFEKÇI, M., Chemistry
ÜNVER, İ., Mathematics
YALÇINKAYA, M., History
YANMAZ, E., Physics
YAPAR, Z., Mathematics
YAYLI, N., Chemistry
YEREBAKAN, İ., English Language and Literature
YEŞILÇIÇEK ÇALIK, K., Midwifery
YILMAZ, S., Chemistry

Faculty of Theology (Rize) (Atatürk Cad., Piri Çelebi Mah., Rize; tel. (464) 214-11-20; e-mail ilahiyat@ktu.edu.tr):

SANDIKÇI, S. K., Islamic Education

Faculty of Water Resource Sciences (Rize) (İyidere, Rize; tel. (464) 223-52-39):

KADIOĞLU, A., Biology

GRADUATE SCHOOLS

Graduate School of Health Sciences: Dir Prof. Dr ORHAN DEĞER.
Graduate School of Natural and Applied Sciences: Dir Prof. Dr SALIH TERZIOĞLU.
Graduate School of Social Sciences: Dir Prof. Dr HAYDAR AKYAZI

KIRIKKALE ÜNİVERSİTESİ
(Kirikkale University)

Ankara Karayolu 7 km, 71450 Kırıkkale
Telephone: (318) 357-42-42
E-mail: rektorluk@kku.edu.tr
Internet: www.kku.edu.tr
Founded 1992
public control
Academic year: September to July (2 semesters)

Rector: Prof. Dr EKREM YILDIZ
Vice-Rector: Prof. Dr ADNAN KARAISMAILOGLU
Vice-Rector: Prof. Dr HAKAN KOCAMIS
Vice-Rector: Prof. Dr OSMAN CAGLAYAN
Library of 85,704 vols, 46 periodicals, 55 databases
Number of teachers: 1,000
Number of students: 26,710

DEANS

Faculty of Arts and Sciences: Prof. Dr SAFFET NEZIR
Faculty of Dentistry: Prof. Dr ABDULKADIR SENGUL
Faculty of Economic and Administrative Sciences: Prof. Dr NASUH USLU
Faculty of Education: Prof. Dr MEHMET KUTLU
Faculty of Engineering: Prof. Dr VELI ÇELIK
Faculty of Fine Arts: Prof. Dr HASAN ARAPGIRLIOGLU
Faculty of Law: Prof. Dr AHMET BILGIN

Faculty of Medicine: Prof. Dr OSMAN GULER
Faculty of Veterinary Medicine: Prof. Dr SEVKET ARIKAN
School of Health Sciences: Prof. Dr YURDAGUL ERDEM

KOÇ UNIVERSITY

Rumelifeneri Yolu, 34450 Sarıyer, Istanbul
Telephone: (212) 338-10-00
E-mail: information@ku.edu.tr
Internet: www.ku.edu.tr
Founded 1993
Private control
Language of instruction: English
Academic year: September to June

Pres.: Prof. Dr UMRAN İNAN
Vice-Pres. for Academic Affairs: Prof. Dr SELÇUK KARABATI
Vice-Pres. for Research and Devt: Prof. Dr İRŞADI AKSUN
Gen. Sec.: MURAT HALIMOĞLU
Librarian: TUBA AKBAYTÜRK ÇANAK
Library of 211,779 vols
Number of teachers: 450
Number of students: 4,910

DEANS

College of Administrative Sciences and Economics: Prof. Dr BARIŞ TAN
College of Sciences: Prof. Dr ALPHAN SENNAROĞLU
College of Social Sciences and Humanities: Prof. Dr SAMI GÜLGÖZ
Law School: Prof. Dr BERTIL EMRAH ODER
School of Medicine: Prof. Dr ŞEVKET RUACAN

KOCAELI ÜNİVERSİTESİ

Umuttepe Yerleskesi, 41380 Umuttepe, Izmit/Kocaeli
Telephone: (262) 303-13-21
E-mail: kutuphane@kocaeli.edu.tr
Internet: www.kocaeli.edu.tr
Founded 1992
State control
Academic year: September to June

Rector: Prof. Dr SEZER SENER KOMSUOGLU
Vice-Rector for Academic Services: Prof. Dr AYSE SEVIM GOKALP
Vice-Rector for Admin. Services: Prof. Dr HASRET COMAK
Vice-Rector for Financial Services: Prof. Dr ALI DEMIRCI
Chief Librarian: PERIHAN SEMERCI
Library of 80,000 vols incl. books, 115,103 ebooks, 67 online databases, 41,168 ejournals
Number of teachers: 1,950
Number of students: 65,800

Publications: *Ilke Journal* (2 a year), *Journal of Applied Earth Sciences* (2 a year), *Journal of Social Sciences Institute* (2 a year), *Kocaeli University Communication Faculty Research Journal* (2 a year), *Kocaeli University Law Faculty Journal* (2 a year), *Sinecine Sinema Araştırmaları Dergisi* (Journal of Film Studies, 2 a year)

DEANS

Faculty of Architecture and Interior Design: Prof. Dr KAMURAN OZTEKIN
Faculty of Arts: Prof. Dr M. REŞAT BAŞAR
Faculty of Communication: Prof. Dr HASAN AKBULUT
Faculty of Dentistry: Prof. Dr ALI İHYA KARAMAN
Faculty of Economics: Prof. Dr ABDURRAHMAN FETTAHOGLU
Faculty of Education: Prof. Dr CEVAT CELEP
Faculty of Engineering: Prof. Dr SARP ERTURK
Faculty of Law: Prof. Dr N. İLKER COLAK
Faculty of Medicine: Prof. Dr ALI DEMIRCI

Faculty of Science: Prof. Dr HALIS AYGUN
Faculty of Technical Education: Prof. Dr MUSTAFA CANAKCI
Faculty of Technology: Prof. Dr MUSTAFA CANAKCI

MALTEPE ÜNİVERSİTESİ

Marmara Eğitim Köyü, 34857 Maltepe, Istanbul

Telephone: (216) 626-10-50
E-mail: maltepe@maltepe.edu.tr
Internet: www.maltepe.edu.tr

Founded 1997
State control
Languages of instruction: English, Turkish
Academic year: October to June

Rector: Prof. Dr MESUT RAZBONYAH
Librarian: ARZU ACAR
Librarian: BURCU ESENER
Librarian: NAZAN KARAKAŞ

Library of 17,230 vols, 531 periodicals
Number of teachers: 240
Number of students: 2,220

Publications: *Fen-Edebiyat Fakültesi Dergisi* (Science and Letters Faculty Journal, 2 a year), *Hukuk Fakültesi Dergisi* (Law Faculty Journal, 2 a year), *İktisadi ve İdari Bilimler Fakültesi Dergisi* (Economics and Business Administration Faculty Journal, 2 a year), *İletişim Fakültesi Dergisi* (Communication Faculty Journal, 2 a year)

DEANS

Faculty of Architecture: Prof. Dr ERKUT ÖZEL
Faculty of Communication: Prof. Dr SABRI ÖZAYDIN
Faculty of Economics and Business Administration: Prof. Dr ERTAN OKTAY
Faculty of Education: Prof. Dr İSA EŞME
Faculty of Engineering: Prof. Dr MESUT RAZBONYALI
Faculty of Law: Prof. Dr AYDIN AYBAY
Faculty of Medicine: Prof. Dr ŞEFIK GÜNEY
Faculty of Science and Letters: Prof. Dr MÜCELLA ULUĞ

MARMARA ÜNİVERSİTESİ

Göztepe Kampüsü Kadıköy, 34722 Istanbul
Telephone: (216) 414-05-45
Internet: www.marmara.edu.tr

Founded 1883, reorganized 1982
State control
Language of instruction: Arabic, English, French, German, Turkish
Academic year: September to July

Rector: Prof. Dr ZAFER GÜL
Deputy Rector: Prof. Dr HAMZA KANDUR
Deputy Rector: Prof. Dr HASAN SELÇUK
Deputy Rector: Prof. Dr M. EMIN ARAT
Sec.-Gen.: Dr MAHMUT DOĞAN
Librarian: SEVINC KAZAZ

Library of 193,630 vols
Number of teachers: 2,800
Number of students: 68,200

Publications: *Argumentum, Din Eğitimi Araştırmaları Dergisi, Finansal Araştırmalar ve Çalışmalar Dergisi, İktisadi İdari bilimler Fakültesi Dergisi, Journal of Marmara University Dental Faculty, Marmara İletişim Dergisi, Marmara Medical Journal, Marmara'nın Sesi, Marmara Pharmaceutical Journal, Marmara sosyal Araştırmalar Dergisi, Marmara Üniversitesi Atatürk Eğitim Fakültesi Eğitim Bilimleri Dergisi, Marmara Üniversitesi Avrupa Topluluğu Enstitüsü Avrupa Araştırmaları Dergisi, Marmara Üniversitesi Bankacılık ve Sigortacılık Enstitüsü e-Dergisi, Marmara Üniversitesi Fen Bilimleri Dergisi, Marmara Üniversitesi Hukuk Fakültesi Hukuk Araştırmaları Dergisi, Marmara Üniversitesi*

İlahiyat Fakültesi Dergisi, Marmara Üniversitesi Sağlık bilimleri Enstitüsü Dergisi, Marmara Üniversitesi Tıp Fakültesi Dergisi, Öneri, Sanat-Tasarım Dergisi, Türklük Araştırmaları Dergisi

DEANS

Atatürk Faculty of Education: Prof. Dr CEMIL ÖZTÜRK
Faculty of Arts and Sciences: Prof. Dr NIHAT ÖZTOPRAK
Faculty of Communication: Prof. Dr YUSUF DEVRAN
Faculty of Dentistry: Prof. Dr MAHIR GÜNDAY
Faculty of Economic and Administrative Sciences: Prof. Dr ERCAN GEGEZ
Faculty of Engineering: Prof. Dr ERTURUL TAÇGIN
Faculty of Fine Arts: Prof. Dr İNCI DENIZ ILGIN
Faculty of Health Sciences: Prof. Dr GÜLDEN POLAT
Faculty of Law: Prof. Dr M. EMIN ARTUK
Faculty of Medicine: Prof. Dr HASAN FEVZI BATIREL
Faculty of Pharmacy: Prof. Dr GÜLDEN Z. OMURTAG
Faculty of Technical Education: Prof. Dr OSMAN KILIÇ
Faculty of Technology: Prof. Dr AHMET KORHAN BINARK
Faculty of Theology: Prof. Dr ALI KÖSE

MERSİN ÜNİVERSİTESİ

Çiftlik Köyü Kampüsü, 33343 Mersin
Telephone: (324) 361-00-22
E-mail: webadmin@mersin.edu.tr
Internet: www.mersin.edu.tr

Founded 1992
State control

Rector: Prof. Dr UĞUR ORAL
Librarian: HÜSEYIN GÖLALMIŞ

Number of teachers: 100
Number of students: 18,000

DEANS

Faculty of Architecture: Prof. Dr TAMER GÖK
Faculty of Communication: Prof. Dr SELIM AKSÖYEK
Faculty of Economics and Administrative Sciences: Prof. Dr TAYFUR ÖZŞEN
Faculty of Education: Prof. Dr ZAFER GÖKÇAKAN
Faculty of Engineering: Prof. Dr CEMIL CENGIZ ARCASOY
Faculty of Fine Arts: Prof. Dr E. BERIKA İPEKBAYRAK
Faculty of Fisheries: Prof. Dr GÜRKAN EKINGEN
Faculty of Medicine: Prof. Dr ESAT YILGÖR
Faculty of Pharmacy: Prof. Dr ATILLA YALÇIN
Faculty of Science and Letters: Prof. Dr AYHAN SEZER
Faculty of Technical Education (Tarsus): Prof. Dr ÖZDEN BAŞTÜRK

MİMAR SİNAN GÜZEL SANATLAR ÜNİVERSİTESİ
(Mimar Sinan Fine Arts University)

Fındıklı, 80040 Istanbul
Telephone: (212) 145-00-00
E-mail: ulik@msu.edu.tr
Internet: www.msu.edu.tr

Founded 1883, univ. status 1982
State control
Language of instruction: Turkish
Rector: Prof. Dr ÝSMET VILDAN ALPTEKIN
Chief Admin. Officer: ERDAL KÜPELI
Librarian: ASIYE ALAGÖZOĞLU

Library of 51,200 vols
Number of teachers: 420
Number of students: 3,510

DEANS

Faculty of Architecture: Prof. ÝLGI YÜCE AŞKÝN
Faculty of Fine Arts: Prof. RAHMI AKSUNGUR
Faculty of Sciences and Literature: Prof. Dr GÜLAY BAŞARÝR KÝROĞLU

MUĞLA ÜNİVERSİTESİ

48000 Mugla Üniversitesi Rektörlüğü, Kötekli Yerleşkesi, Muğla

Telephone: (252) 211-19-60
E-mail: intoffice@mu.edu.tr
Internet: www.mugla.edu.tr

Founded 1992; present status 2012
State control
Languages of instruction: English, Turkish
Academic year: September to June

Rector: Prof. Dr MANSUR HARMANDAR
Vice-Rector: Prof. Dr ALI OSMAN GÜNDOĞAN
Vice-Rector: MUSTAFA IŞILOĞLU
Vice-Rector: Prof. Dr YUSUF ZIYA ERDIL
Sec.-Gen.: Prof. Dr TUNCER ASUNAKUTLU

Library of 100,000 vols, 500 printed periodicals
Number of teachers: 1,030
Number of students: 26,400

DEANS

Faculty of Economics and Administrative Sciences: Prof. Dr TURGAY UZUN
Faculty of Education: Prof. Dr MUSTAFA VOLKAN COŞKUN
Faculty of Engineering: Prof. Dr TUĞRUL YILMAZ
Faculty of Fine Arts: Prof. Dr MUSTAFA VOLKAN COŞKUN (Deputy)
Faculty of Fisheries: Prof. Dr TAÇNUR BAYGAR
Faculty of Letters and Humanities: Prof. Dr PERVIN ÇAPAN
Faculty of Medicine: Prof. Dr İRFAN ALTUNTAŞ
Faculty of Science: Prof. Dr BEDRETTIN MERCIMEK
Faculty of Technical Education: Prof. Dr TUNCER ASUNAKUTLU
Faculty of Technology: Prof. Dr OSMAN GÖKTAŞ

MUSTAFA KEMAL UNIVERSITY

31040 Antakya, Hatay
Telephone: (326) 221-5815
E-mail: erasmus@mku.edu.tr
Internet: www.mku.edu.tr

Founded 1992
State control
Languages of instruction: English, Turkish
Academic year: September to July

Rector: Prof. Dr HÜSNÜ SALIH GÜDER
Vice-Rector: Prof. Dr ALI KOÇ
Vice-Rector: Prof. Dr MEHMET DALKIZ
Vice-Rector: Prof. Dr M. FATIH CAN

Number of teachers: 1,020
Number of students: 29,260

DEANS

Agriculture: Prof. Dr EMINE ÖZDEMIR
Economics and Administrative Sciences: Prof. Dr YAKUP BULUT
Engineering: Prof. Dr ERTUĞRUL BALTACIOĞLU
Fisheries: Prof. Dr AYŞE BAHAR YILMAZ
Veterinary Sciences: Prof. Dr SUAT ERDOĞAN

NİĞDE ÜNİVERSİTESİ

Niğde Üniversitesi Rektörlüğü, 51100 Niğde
Telephone: (388) 225-26-04
E-mail: ozelkalem@nigde.edu.tr
Internet: www.nigde.edu.tr

Founded 1992
State control
Academic year: September to June

Rector: Prof. Dr ADNAN GÖRÜR
Vice-Rector: Prof. Dr MEHMET ŞENER
Vice-Rector: Prof. Dr MURAT ALP
Sec.-Gen.: Assoc. Prof. Dr MUSTAFA BAYRAK
Dir of the Library and Documentation Dept:
MAZLUME VURAN

Library of 13,000 books, 100 periodicals
Number of teachers: 650
Number of students: 13,900 (13,130 under-
graduate, 770 postgraduate)
Publications: *Natural Sciences, Social Sci-
ences*

DEANS

Faculty of Architecture: MEHMET ŞENER
Faculty of Arts and Science: MUSA ŞAŞMAZ
Faculty of Economics and Business Admin-
istration: ZEKI DOĞAN
Faculty of Education: MURAT ALP
Faculty of Engineering: SAIR KAHRAMAN

OKAN ÜNİVERSİTESİ

Hasanpaşa Uzunçayır Cad. 6, Kadıköy,
Istanbul

Telephone: (216) 325-48-18
E-mail: okan@okan.edu.tr
Internet: www.okan.edu.tr

Founded 2003

Rector: Prof. Dr SADIK KIRBAŞ
Vice-Rector: Prof. Dr CEVDET ÖĞÜT
Librarian: KENAN ÖZTOP
Number of students: 450

DEANS

Faculty of Arts and Sciences: Prof. Dr HASAN
ÖZEKES
Faculty of Economics and Administrative
Sciences: Prof. Dr SADIK KIRBAŞ
Faculty of Engineering: Asst Prof. Dr CEVDET
ÖĞÜT

ONDOKUZ MAYIS ÜNİVERSİTESİ
(Ondokuz Mayis University)

Kurupelit, 55139 Samsun

Telephone: (362) 312-19-19
E-mail: inter@omu.edu.tr
Internet: www.omu.edu.tr

Founded 1975
State control
Language of instruction: Turkish
Academic year: September to June

Rector: Prof. Dr HÜSEYIN AKAN
Vice-Rector: Prof. AHMET BULUT
Vice-Rector: FERŞAT KOLBAKIR
Vice-Rector: Prof. Dr SAIT BILGIÇ
Sec.-Gen.: Asst Prof. SELAHATTIN ÖZYURT
Registrar: NURIYE GÜRKANLI
Librarian: ÖMER BOZKURT

Number of teachers: 1,940
Number of students: 36,100

Publication: *Faculty Journals* (12 a year)

DEANS

Faculty of Aeronautics and Space Sciences:
Prof. Dr ERDEM KOÇ
Faculty of Agriculture: Prof. Dr MEHMET
KURAN
Faculty of Arts and Sciences: Prof. Dr ŞENOL
EREN
Faculty of Communication: Prof. Dr ZEKERIYA
ULUDAĞ
Faculty of Dentistry: Prof. Dr SELIM ARICI
Faculty of Economics and Administrative
Sciences: Prof. Dr FATIH YÜKSEL
Faculty of Education: Prof. Dr CEVDET YIL-
MAZ
Faculty of Engineering: Prof. Dr FEHMI
YAZICI
Faculty of Law: Prof. Dr HAKAN HAKERI
Faculty of Medicine: Prof. Dr HAYDAR ŞAHI-
NOĞLU

Faculty of Theology: Prof. Dr YAVUZ ÜNAL
Faculty of Veterinary Medicine: Prof. Dr
MUSTAFA ALISARI

PROFESSORS

Faculty of Agriculture (Kurupelit 55139
Samsun; tel. (362) 457-60-86; e-mail
iac-agric@omu.edu.tr; internet www.omu
.edu.tr/a/en/academics/faculties/agriculture):

ACAR, Z., Agronomy
APAN, M., Agricultural Structures and
Irrigation
BILGENER, Ş., Horticulture
CINEMRE, H. A., Agricultural Economics
DEMIR, Y., Agricultural Structures and
Irrigation
ECEVIT, O., Plant Protection
ERENER, G., Feeds and Animal Nutrition
GÜLÜMSER, A., Agronomy
KEVSEROĞLU, K., Agronomy
KORKMAZ, A., Soil Science
KURAN, M., Agricultural Biotechnology
MEYDAN, M. A., Agricultural Machinery
MENNAN, H., Plant Protection
ODABAŞ, F., Horticulture
OKUMUS, A., Biometry-Genetics
ÖZCAN, M., Horticulture
ÖZDEMIR, N., Soil Science
ÖZTÜRK, T., Agricultural Structures and
Irrigation
PINAR, Y., Agricultural Machinery
SARICA, M., Animal Science
SARIÇIÇEK, B. Z., Animal Science
TUNCER, C., Entomology
TUNALI, B., Phytopathology

Faculty of Arts and Sciences (Ordu) (Ordu
Fen-Edebiyat Fakültesi, Perşembe, 52750
Ordu; tel. (452) 517-43-70; internet www
.ome.edu.tr/akad/fklt/ordufen/index.html):

AKÇIN, Ö. E., Biology
EKINCI, I., History
MAĞDEN, S., Mathematics
YAPAR, C., Mathematics

Faculty of Arts and Sciences (Samsun)
(Kurupelit 55139 Samsun; tel. (362) 457-60-
80; internet www.omu.edu.tr/a/en/
academics/faculties/science-art):

AFŞIN, B., Chemistry
ALPASLAN, F., Statistics
BATI, B., Chemistry
BIÇER, ENDER, Physical Chemistry
BILGENER, M., Biology
BÜYÜKGÜNGÖR, O., Physics
ÇALIŞKAN, M., Mathematics
ÇALIŞKAN, N., Physics
ÇELIK, F., Physics
DINÇER, M., Physics
DEMIR, H., Applied Mathematics
EDINSEL, K., Psychology
ERDÖNMEZ, A., Physics
EREN, Z., Biology
ERLER, M. Y., History
GÖNÜLOL, A., Biology
GÜLEL, A., Biology
GÜMRÜKÇÜOĞLU, I. E., Chemistry
GÜMÜŞ, H., Physics
GÜRKANLI, A. T., Mathematics
IPEK, N., Born Modern
IŞILDAK, I., Chemistry
KARACAN, T., Turkish
KARTAL, I., General Physics
KARTAL, V., Biology
KEFELIOĞLU, H., Biology
KILINÇ, M., Biology
KÖKSAL, F., Physics
KORKMAZ, H., Chemistry
KUTBAY, H. G., Biology
MENEK, N., Chemistry
NIŞANCI, A., Geography
OKUMUŞOĞLU, N. T., Physics
ÖLMEZ, H., Chemistry
ONAR, A. N., Chemistry
ÖZBALCI, M., Turkish
ÖZKANCA, R., Biology

ÖZKAPLAN, H., Physics
ÖZKOÇ, I., Biology
PANCAR, A., Mathematics
POLAT, N., Biology
SAĞLIK, S., New Turkish Language
ŞENEL, G., Biology
ŞENEL, I., Physics
TAPRAMAZ, R., Physics
TARAKÇI, C., Turkish
USTA, N., Sociology
UZUN, A., Physical Geography
YAVUZ, M., Physics
YILMAZ, M., Mathematics
YILMAZ, V. T., Chemistry
ZEYBEKOĞLU, Ü., Biology

Faculty of Arts and Sciences (Sinop) (Sinop
Fen-Edebiyat Fakültesi, Sinop; tel. (368) 271-
55-20; e-mail sinopfenedebiyat@yahoo.com;
internet www.omu.edu.tr/akad/sinopfen):

ÇANKAYA, E., Statistics
DEMIRCI, K., Mathematics
SIVACI, R., Biology

Faculty of Dentistry (Dişhekimliği Fakültesi,
Kurupelit, 55139 Samsun; tel. (362) 457-60-
30; e-mail dentistry@omu.edu.tr; internet
www.omu.edu.tr/a/en/academics/faculties/
dentistry/index.php):

AYDEMIR, H., Endodontics
AÇIKGÖZ, G., Periodontology
ALKAN, A., Oral and Maxillofacial Surgery
ÇELENK, P., Oral Diagnosis and Radiology
CEYLAN, G., Prosthodontics
KÖPRÜLÜ, H., Dental Diseases and Treat-
ment
KOYUTÜRK, A. E., Pedodontics
TOLLER, M. O., Oral and Maxillofacial
Surgery
TÜRK, T., Orthodontics

Faculty of Economics and Administrative
Sciences (Samsun) (İktisadi ve İdari Bilimler
Fakültesi, Kurupelit Kampüsü, 55139 Sam-
sun; tel. (362) 312-19-19):

GÜZEL, H. A., Economics
KÖKTAŞ, M. E., Political Science and Social
Science

Faculty of Economics and Administrative
Sciences (Ünye) (Ünye İktisadi ve İdari
Bilimler Fakültesi, Ünye; tel. (452) 323-86-
96; e-mail gurolo@omu.edu.tr):

ÖZCÜRE, G., Economics

Faculty of Education (Amasya) (Amasya
Eğitim Fakültesi, Amasya; tel. (358) 252-62-
30; e-mail amasyaeg@omu.edu.tr; internet
www.omu.edu.tr/akad/fklt/aegt/amsegtgiris
.htm):

KARAMUSTAFAOĞLU, O., Computers and
Teaching Technology
ORBAY, M., Primary Education
ÜSTÜN, A., Education
YIĞIT, M., Turkish
ZIYAGIL, M. A., Physical Education and
Sport

Faculty of Education (Samsun) (Eğitim
Fakültesi, Kurupelit, 55139 Samsun; tel.
(362) 312-19-19; internet www.omu.edu.tr/a/
en/academics/faculties/education):

AKBULUT, D. A., History
AYDIN, M., Turkish Language
BARUT, Y., Special Education
BAŞAR, E., Primary Education
BAYRAKTARKATAL, E., Music
BOLAT, H., Foreign Languages
ÇOLAK, M., Foreign Languages
ÇORUH, U., Computer Education and Edu-
cational Technology
DINDAR, B., Education
ENGIN, A., Natural Sciences and Math-
ematics
ERSANLI, K., Education
KIRCI, M., Turkish
KOYUNCU, S., Fine Arts

Faculty of Education (Sinop) (Sinop Eğitim Fakültesi, Sinop; tel. (368) 271-55-35; e-mail sinopegit@omu.edu.tr; internet www.ome .edu.tr/akad/sinop-egt):

AYDIN, H., Computers and Teaching Technology
BAŞAR, E., Primary Education
BOSTANCI, B. A., Foreign Languages
MENTEŞE, S., Education
ÖZDEMIR, O., Primary Education

Faculty of Engineering (Kurupelit, 55139 Samsun; tel. (362) 457-60-36; e-mail onergun@omu.edu.tr; internet www.omu.edu .tr/a/en/academics/faculties/engineering):

BAYRAKLI, F., Environmental Engineering
BEKTAŞ, S., Geodesy and Photogrammetric Engineering
BÜYÜKGÜNGÖR, H., Environmental Engineering
ÇAKIRCIOĞLU, M., Civil Engineering
ÉFENDÍYEV, Ç., Telecommunications
ELEVLİ, B., Industrial Engineering
ERGUN, O. N., Environmental Engineering
HURŞİT, A., Food Engineering
KASIMZADE, A., Civil Engineering
KOCA, F., Food Engineering
ÖNBİLGİN, G., Electrical and Electronic Engineering
TOPALOĞLU, B., Machine Engineering
ULUTAŞ, M., Computer Engineering

Faculty of Fisheries (Sinop) (Su Ürünleri Fakültesi, Akliman Kampüsü, 57000 Sinop; tel. (368) 287-62-62; internet www.omu.edu .tr/akad/fklt/ssu/anamenu.html):

BAT, L., Basic Fisheries Sciences
BİRCAN, R., Fish Breeding
BÜYÜKHATİPOĞLU, Ş., Fish Breeding
ERDEM, M., Fish Breeding
ERKOYUNCU, İ., Fishing and Fish Processing Technology
KALMA, M., Fish Breeding
SAMSUN, O., Fishing and Fish Processing Technology

Faculty of Medicine (Kurupelit 55139 Samsun; tel. (362) 457-60-70; internet www.omu .edu.tr/akad/fklt/tip/anamenu.htm):

ACAR, S., Paediatric Oncology
AĞAR, E., Physiology
AKAN, H., Radiodiagnostics
AKBAŞ, S., Child Psychiatry
AKPOLAT, İ., Pathology
AKPOLAT, M. T., Nephrology
ALBAYRAK, D., Paediatric Haematology
ALPER, T., Obstetrics and Gynaecology
ALVUR, M., Biochemistry
ANLAR, F. Y., Paediatrics
ARIK, A. C., Psychiatry
ARIK, N., Nephrology
ARITÜRK, E., Paediatric Surgery
AŞÇI, R., Urology
AYDIN, M., Paediatric Endocrinology
BAĞCI, H., Medical Biology
BAKIR, T., Gastroenterology
BARIŞ, S., Pathology
BAŞOĞLU, A., Thoracic Surgery
BAŞOĞLU, T., Nuclear Medicine
BAYSAL, M. K., Paediatrics
BEDİR, A., Biochemistry
BEK, Y., Bio-statistics
BERNAY, R. F., Paediatric Surgery
BİLGİÇ, S., Anatomy
BİRİNCİ, Ophthalmology
BÜYÜKALPELLİ, R., Urology
CANTÜRK, F., Physical Medicine and Rehabilitation
CANTÜRK, T., Dermatology
ÇELİK, F., Neurosurgery
ÇELİK, S., Pharmacology
CENGİZ, K., Nephrology
ÇİFTÇİ, N., Histology and Embryology
DABAK, N., Orthopaedics and Traumatology
DİKİCİ, M. F., Family Practice
DİREN, H. B., Radiodiagnostics

DURU, F., Paediatrics
DURUPINAR, B., Microbiology
ELBİSTAN, M., Medical Biology
ERKAN, D., Ophthalmology
ERKAN, L., Thoracic Diseases
ERZURUMLU, K., General Surgery
GEPTİREMEN, A., Pharmacology
GÖKÇE, Ş. Ç., Radiation Oncology
GÜLDOĞUŞ, F., Anaesthesiology
GÜLMAN, B., Orthopaedics and Traumatology
GÜNAL, N., Paediatrics
GÜNAYDIN, M., Microbiology
GÜRMEN, N., Radiodiagnostics
GÜVEN, H., First Aid and Emergency Aid
İÇTEN, N., Anatomy
İNCESU, L., Radiodiagnostics
İŞLEK, İ., Paediatrics
İYİGÜN, O., Neurosurgery
KAHRAMAN, H., Endocrinology
KALAYCI, A. G., Paediatrics
KANDEMİR, B., Pathology
KAPLAN, S., Histology and Embryology
KARACALAR, A., Plastic and Reconstructive Surgery
KARAGÖZ, F., Pathology
KARAİSMAİLOĞLU, N., Orthopaedics and Traumatology
KEÇELİGİL, H. T., Cardiovascular Surgery
KESIM, M., General Surgery
KESİM, Y., Pharmacology
KOCAKAVAK, C., Cardiology
KÖKÇÜ, A., Obstetrics and Gynaecology
KOLBAKIR, F., Cardiovascular Surgery
KOPUZ, C., Anatomy
KORKMAZ, A., Histology and Embryology
KOYUNCU, M., Otorhinolaryngology
KÜÇÜKÖDÜK, Ş., Paediatrics
KURU, O., Physical Medicine and Rehabilitation
LEBLEBİCİOĞLU, H., Clinical Bacteriology and Infectious Diseases
MALATYALIOĞLU, E., Obstetrics and Gynaecology
MALAZGİRT, Z., General Surgery
MARANGOZ, C., Physiology
ÖGE, İ., Ophthalmology
OĞUR, M. G., Paediatrics
ÖKTEN, G., Medical Biology
ONAR, M. K., Neurology
ÖZBENLİ, T., Neurology
ÖZEN, N., General Surgery
ÖZKAN, K., General Surgery
ÖZTÜRK, F., Paediatrics
PEKŞEN, Y., Public Health
RAKUNT, C., Neurosurgery
RIZALAR, R., Paediatric Surgery
ŞAHİN, A. R., Psychiatry
ŞAHİN, M., Cardiology
ŞAHİN, M., Nuclear Medicine
ŞAHİNOĞLU, H., Anaesthesiology
SANIÇ, A., Microbiology
SARIHASAN, B., Anaesthesiology and Reanimation
SARIKAYA, Ş., Urology
SELÇUK, M. B., Radiodiagnostics
ŞEŞEN, T., Otolaryngology
TANYERİ, F., Internal Medicine (Endocrinology)
TANYERİ, Y., Otorhinolaryngology
TAŞCI, N., Physiology
TAŞDEMİR, H. A., Paediatrics
TEKAT, A., Otorhinolaryngology
TÜLEK, N., Clinical Bacteriology and Infectious Diseases
TUNALI, G., Neurology
TÜR, A., Anaesthesiology
TURANLI, A. Y., Dermatology
TÜRE, U., Neurosurgery
TURLA, A., Forensic Medicine
ULUSOY, A. N., General Surgery
ÜNAL, R., Otorhinolaryngology
ÜSTÜN, C., Obstetrics and Gynaecology
ÜSTÜN, F. E., Anaesthesiology
YEŞİLDAĞ, O., Cardiology
YILMAZ, A. F., Urology

YILMAZ, Ö, Cardiology
YÜCEL, İ., Internal Medicine (Oncology)

Faculty of Theology (Kurupelit 55139 Samsun; tel. (362) 457-60-84; e-mail ilhdek@omu .edu.tr; internet www.omu.edu.tr/a/en/ academics/faculties/divinity):

CAN, Y., Islamic History and Arts
DOĞAN, İ., Basic Islamic Sciences
GÜNER, O., Basic Islamic Sciences
KAYA, M., Teaching Ethics and Religious Culture in Primary Education
KOÇAK, M., Basic Islamic Sciences
KÖYLÜ, M., Philosophy and Religious Sciences
PEKER, H., Philosophy and Religion
TERZİ, M. Z., Islamic History and Art
TURAN, A., Basic Islamic Sciences
YAZICI, İ., Basic Islamic Sciences
YETİK, E., Basic Islamic Sciences
ZÜMRÜT, O., Islamic History and Art

Faculty of Veterinary Medicine (Kurupelit, 55139 Samsun; tel. (362) (362) 312-19-19):

AKSOY, A., Pharmacology And Toxicology
ALISARLI, M., Food Hygiene and Technology
CELEBI, M., Reproduction And Artificial Insemination
FINDIK, M., Obstetrics And Gynecology
GULBAHAR, M. Y., Pathology
MUĞLALI, H., Animal Science and Animal Nutrition
UMUR, Ş., Parasitology
YURDUSEV, N., Microbiology

ORTA DOGU TEKNIK ÜNIVERSITESI (Middle East Technical University)

Universiteler Mahallesi Dumlupinar Bulvari Cankaya, 06800 Ankara

Telephone: (312) 210-20-00
E-mail: rektor@metu.edu.tr
Internet: www.metu.edu.tr

Founded 1956
State control
Languages of instruction: English, Turkish
Academic year: October to June (2 semesters)

Pres.: Prof. Dr AHMET ACAR
Vice-Pres.: Prof. Dr ÇİĞDEM ERÇELEBI
Vice-Pres.: Prof. Dr H. NEVZAT ÖZGÜVEN
Vice-Pres.: Prof. Dr VOLKAN ATALAY
Gen. Sec.: Prof. Dr HAMI ALPAS (acting)
Registrar: NESRIN ÜNSAL
Librarian: CEVAT GÜVEN (acting)

Library: see under Libraries and Archives
Number of teachers: 2,550
Number of students: 24,100

Publications: Makina Tasarim ve Imalat Dergisi—MATiM (2 a year), METU Journal of Faculty of Architecture (2 a year), METU Studies in Development (3 a year)

DEANS

Faculty of Architecture: Prof. Dr ALI CENGIZKAN
Faculty of Arts and Sciences: Prof. Dr ERSAN AKYILDIZ
Faculty of Economic and Administrative Sciences: Prof. Dr YAŞAR EYÜP ÖZVEREN
Faculty of Education: Prof. Dr GÖLGE SEFEROĞLU
Faculty of Engineering: Prof. Dr UĞURHAN AKYÜZ

PROFESSORS

Faculty of Architecture (tel. (312) 210-22-01; e-mail archdean@metu.edu.tr; internet www .arch.metu.edu.tr):

BALAMIR, A., Architecture
BAYKAN, A. C., Architecture
BILSEL, F. C., Architecture
CENGIZKAN, A., Architecture
ERAYDIN, A., City and Regional Planning
ERKILIÇ, M., Architecture

ERSOY, M., City and Regional Planning
GÜVEN, S. N., Architecture
GÜZER, C. A., Architecture
HASDOĞAN, G. F., Industrial Design
IŞIK, O., City and Regional Planning
MENNAN, Z., Architecture
ÖZKAYA, A. B., Architecture
PAMIR, A., Architecture
PEKER, A. U., Architecture
PINARCIOĞLU, M. M., City and Regional Planning
SARGIN, G. A., Architecture
SAVAŞ SARGIN, A., Architecture
TUNA, N., City and Regional Planning
TÜREL, A., City and Regional Planning

Faculty of Arts and Sciences (tel. (312) 210-31-01; e-mail fefd@metu.edu.tr; internet www.fef.metu.edu.tr):

ADALI, O., Biology
AKGÜN, S. S., History
AKINOĞLU, B. G., Physics
AKKAYA, A., Sociology
AKKAYA, M., Chemistry
AKYILDIZ, E., Mathematics
ALPAY, Ö., Mathematics
ATAMAN, O. Y., Chemistry
AYVAŞIK, H. B., Psychology
BALCI, M., Chemistry
BALMAN, Ş., Physics
BATMAZ, İ., Sociology
BAYKAL, A., Physics
BAYKAL, Z. S., Physics
BAYRAMLI, E., Chemistry
BEKLIOĞLU YERLI, M., Biology
BILGIÇ, R., Psychology
BILIKMEN, K. S., Physics
BOZTEMUR, R., History
BULUR, E., Physics
CAN, C., Physics
CEYLAN, Y., Philosophy
CIVELEK, F. R., Physics
DOĞAN, M., Biology
DOĞAN, Ö., Chemistry
ECEVIT, F. Y., Sociology
ECEVIT, M., Sociology
ERCAN, G., Mathematics
ERÇELEBI, A., Physics
ERKOÇ, Ş., Physics
FIŞILOĞLU, H., Psychology
GENÇÖZ, T., Psychology
GENÇÖZ, F., Psychology
GÖKAĞAŞ ARSLAN, G., Chemistry
GÖKMEN, A., Chemistry
GÖKMEN, G. I., Chemistry
GÖKTÜRK, E., Chemistry
GRÜNBERG, D., Philosophy
GÜLER, A. M., Physics
GÜNAL, İ., Physics
GÜNDÜZ, U., Biology
GÜRAY, N. T., Biology
HACALOĞLU, J., Chemistry
HASIRCI, V. N., Biology
HASIRCI, N., Chemistry
HOŞGÖR, H. A., Sociology
İLTAN, E. O., Physics
İNAM, A., Philosophy
İZGÜ, K. F., Biology
KARANCI, A. N., Psychology
KARASÖZEN, B., Mathematics
KARASU, A., Physics
KARASU, E. A., Physics
KATIRCIOĞLU, Ş., Physics
KAYA, Z., Biology
KAYRAN, C., Chemistry
KAZAK BERUMENT, S., Psychology
KENCE, A., Biology
KIZILOĞLU, G. N., Physics
KIZILOĞLU, Ü., Physics
KOCABIYIK, S., Biology
KORKMAZ, M., Mathematics
KUZUCUOĞLU, M., Mathematics
NURLU, M. Z., Mathematics
ÖKTEM, H. A., Biology
ÖNAL, A. M., Chemistry
ÖNAL, S., Mathematics

ÖNDER, M. T., Mathematics
ÖNER ÖZKAN, B., Psychology
ÖNSIPER, M. H., Mathematics
ÖZAN, Y., Mathematics
ÖZBUDAK, F., Mathematics
ÖZCENGIZ, G., Biology
ÖZDEMIR, S., Physics
ÖZKAN, İ., Chemistry
ÖZKAR, S., Chemistry
ÖZPINECI, A., Physics
PAK, N. K., Physics
PARLAK, M., Physics
PEYNIRCIOĞLU, N. B., Chemistry
SAKALLI UĞURLU, N., Psychology
SAKTANBER MARDIN, A. N., Sociology
SARIOĞLU, B. O., Physics
SAVCI, M., Physics
SERIN, M., Physics
SEVER, R., Physics
SEVERCAN, F., Biology
SOL, A., Philosophy
SOYKUT, M., History
SÜMER, H. C., Psychology
SÜMER, N., Psychology
TANYELI, C., Chemistry
TAŞELI, H., Mathematics
TEKIN, B., Physics
TEZER, M., Mathematics
TEZER, C., Mathematics
TINCER, İ. T., Chemistry
TOGAN, İ. Z., Biology
TOPPARE, L. K., Chemistry
TUNCEL, S., Chemistry
TURAN, G., Physics
TURAN, Ö., History
TURAN, R., Physics
TURAN, Ş. H., Philosophy
TÜRKER, B. L., Chemistry
VOLKAN, M., Chemistry
YILMAZ, O., Physics
YÜCEL, A. M., Biology
YURDAKUL, M. H., Mathematics
YURTSEVEN, H. H., Physics
ZAFER, A., Mathematics
ZEYREK, M. T., Physics
ZORA, M., Chemistry

Faculty of Economic and Administrative Sciences (tel. (312) 210-30-02; e-mail feas@feas.metu.edu.tr; internet www.feas.metu.edu.tr):

ACAR, A., Business Administration
ACAR, A., Political Science and Public Administration
AKDER, A., Economics
ALTUNIŞIK, M., International Relations
AŞCIGIL, S., Business Administration
AYATA, A., Political Science and Public Administration
BAĞCI, H., International Relations
BÖLÜKBAŞIOĞLU, S., International Relations
DAĞI, İ., International Relations
ERALP, Y., International Relations
ERDIL, E., Economics
ERLAT, G., Economics
GAZIOĞLU, Ş., Economics
GÜNER, Z., Business Administration
KAYA, A., Political Science and Public Administration
ÖCAL, N., Economics
ÖZMEN, E., Economics
ÖZVEREN, Y., Economics
POLAT, N., International Relations
SARI, R., Business Administration
ŞENSES, F., Economics
SOYTAŞ, U., Business Administration
TAYMAZ, E., Economics
TÜRKEŞ, M., International Relations
WASTI PAMUKSUZ, S., Business Administration
YILDIRIM, O., Economics
YILMAZ, Ç., Business Administration
YILMAZ, Ö., Business Administration
YURDUSEV, A., International Relations

Faculty of Education (tel. (312) 210-40-01; e-mail fedu@metu.edu.tr; internet www.fedu.metu.edu.tr):

AKSU, M., Educational Sciences
BERBEROĞLU, H. G., Secondary Science and Mathematics Education
BULUT, S., Secondary Science and Mathematics Education
ÇAĞILTAY, K., Computer Education and Instructional Technology
ÇAKIROĞLU, J., Elementary Education
DALOĞLU, A., Foreign Language Education
DEMIR, A. G., Educational Sciences
ENGINARLAR, H., Foreign Language Education
GEBAN, Ö., Secondary Science and Mathematics Education
KIRAZ, E., Educational Sciences
KOÇAK, M. S., Physical Education and Sports
ÖZDEN, M. Y., Computer Education and Instructional Technology
ÖZTEKIN, C., Elementary Education
SEFEROĞLU, G., Foreign Language Education
TEZER, E., Educational Sciences
UBUZ, B., Secondary Science and Mathematics Education
YILDIRIM, A., Educational Sciences
YILDIRIM, İ. S., Computer Education and Instructional Technology
YILDIRIM, Z., Computer Education and Instructional Technology

Faculty of Engineering (tel. (312) 210-25-02; e-mail muhfd@metu.edu.tr; internet muhfd.metu.edu.tr):

AKAR, G., Electrical and Electronics Engineering
AKDENIZ, M. V., Metallurgical and Materials Engineering
AKGÜN, H., Geological Engineering
AKIN, T., Electrical and Electronics Engineering
AKIN, S., Petroleum and Natural Gas Engineering
AKKAR, D. S., Civil Engineering
AKKÖK, M., Mechanical Engineering
AKMANDOR, İ. S., Aerospace Engineering
AKSEL, M. H., Mechanical Engineering
AKYÜREK, S. Z., Civil Engineering
AKYÜZ, U., Civil Engineering
ALATAN, A. A., Electrical and Electronics Engineering
ALBAYRAK, K., Mechanical Engineering
ALEMDAROĞLU, H. N., Aerospace Engineering
ALPAS, H., Food Engineering
ALPASLAN, F., Computer Engineering
ALTINER, D., Geological Engineering
ALTINER, S., Geological Engineering
ARIKAN, M. A. S., Mechanical Engineering
AROL, A. I., Mining Engineering
AŞIK, M. Z., Engineering Sciences
ATALAY, M. V., Computer Engineering
ATALAY, M. U., Mining Engineering
AYDIN, İ., Civil Engineering
AYDIN ÇIVI, H. O., Electrical and Electronics Engineering
AYDINOL, M., Metallurgical and Materials Engineering
AZIZOĞLU, M., Industrial Engineering
BAKIR, B. S., Civil Engineering
BALKAN, R. T., Mechanical Engineering
BAYINDIRLI, A., Food Engineering
BAYKAL, B., Electrical and Electronics Engineering
BAYRAM, G., Chemical Engineering
BEŞIKCI, C., Electrical and Electronics Engineering
BILGEN, S., Electrical and Electronics Engineering
BINICI, B., Civil Engineering
BIRGÖNÜL, M. T., Civil Engineering
BIRLIK, G. A., Engineering Sciences
BÖLÜKBAŞI, U., Chemical Engineering

BOR, A., Metallurgical and Materials Engineering
BOZKURT, E., Geological Engineering
BOZOĞLU, T. F., Food Engineering
ÇALIŞK, P., Chemical Engineering
ÇALIŞKAN, M., Mechanical Engineering
ÇAMUR, M. Z., Geological Engineering
ÇANATAN, F., Electrical and Electronics Engineering
ÇELENLIGIL, M. C., Aerospace Engineering
ÇETIN, K. O., Civil Engineering
ÇIÇEKLI, F. N., Computer Engineering
ÇILINGIR, F. C., Industrial Engineering
ÇILOĞLU, T., Electrical and Electronics Engineering
ÇOKÇA, E., Civil Engineering
DARENDELILER, H., Mechanical Engineering
DEMIR, Ş., Electrical and Electronics Engineering
DEMIRBAŞ, K., Electrical and Electronics Engineering
DEMIREKLER, M., Electrical and Electronics Engineering
DEMIRER, G. N., Environmental Engineering
DICLELI, M., Engineering Sciences
DIKMEN TOKER, I., Civil Engineering
DILEK, F. B., Environmental Engineering
DOĞRU, A. H., Computer Engineering
DOĞU, T., Chemical Engineering
DOYUM, A. B., Mechanical Engineering
DURAL ÜNVER, M. G., Electrical and Electronics Engineering
DURSUNKAYA, Z., Mechanical Engineering
DÜZGÜN, H. Ş., Mining Engineering
ERASLAN, A. N., Engineering Sciences
ERGUN, M. U., Civil Engineering
ERKMEN, A. M., Electrical and Electronics Engineering
ERKMEN, I., Electrical and Electronics Engineering
ERMIŞ, M., Electrical and Electronics Engineering
EROĞLU, I., Chemical Engineering
EROL, A. O., Civil Engineering
ERTAN, H. B., Electrical and Electronics Engineering
ERTAŞ, A., Electrical and Electronics Engineering
EYÜBOĞLU, B. M., Electrical and Electronics Engineering
GENÇ, F. P., Computer Engineering
GENÇER, N. G., Electrical and Electronics Engineering
GÖĞÜŞ, M., Civil Engineering
GÖKÇAY, C. F., Environmental Engineering
GÖKLER, M. I., Mechanical Engineering
GÖNCÜOĞLU, M. C., Geological Engineering
GÜLEÇ, N. T., Geological Engineering
GÜLTEKIN, G. C., Food Engineering
GÜNAL TÜRKMENOĞLU, A., Geological Engineering
GÜNALP, N., Electrical and Electronics Engineering
GÜNDÜZ, M., Civil Engineering
GÜR, C. H., Metallurgical and Materials Engineering
GÜRBÜZ, R., Metallurgical and Materials Engineering
GÜRKAN, T., Chemical Engineering
GÜVEN, A. N., Electrical and Electronics Engineering
HALICI, U., Electrical and Electronics Engineering
HAMAMCI, H., Food Engineering
HOŞTEN, Ç., Mining Engineering
IDER, S. K., Mechanical Engineering
IŞLER, V., Computer Engineering
KADIOĞLU, F. S., Mechanical Engineering
KALKANLI, A., Metallurgical and Materials Engineering
KARAHANOĞLU, N., Geological Engineering
KARAKAŞ, G., Chemical Engineering
KARAKAYA, I., Metallurgical and Materials Engineering

KARPUZ, C., Mining Engineering
KARSLIOĞLU, M. O., Civil Engineering
KAYALIGIL, M. S., Industrial Engineering
KAYMAKCI, A. H., Geological Engineering
KAYNAK, C., Metallurgical and Materials Engineering
KAYRAN, A., Aerospace Engineering
KILIÇ, S. E., Mechanical Engineering
KIRCA, O., Industrial Engineering
KOÇ, S. S., Electrical and Electronics Engineering
KOCAOĞLAN, E., Electrical and Electronics Engineering
KÖK, M. V., Petroleum and Natural Gas Engineering
KÖKSAL, G., Industrial Engineering
KÖKSALAN, M. M., Industrial Engineering
KUZUOĞLU, M., Electrical and Electronics Engineering
LEBLEBICIOĞLU, M. K., Electrical and Electronics Engineering
MEHMETOĞLU, M. T., Petroleum and Natural Gas Engineering
ÖGEL, B., Metallurgical and Materials Engineering
OKANDAN, E., Petroleum and Natural Gas Engineering
ÖNAL, I., Chemical Engineering
ORAL, S., Mechanical Engineering
ÖSKAY, R., Mechanical Engineering
ÖZCEBE, G., Civil Engineering
ÖZDEMIREL, N. E., Industrial Engineering
ÖZENBAŞ, A. M., Metallurgical and Materials Engineering
ÖZGEN, S., Aerospace Engineering
ÖZGEN, C., Chemical Engineering
ÖZGÖREN, M. K., Mechanical Engineering
ÖZGÜVEN, H. N., Mechanical Engineering
ÖZTÜRK, T., Metallurgical and Materials Engineering
ÖZTÜRK, A., Metallurgical and Materials Engineering
ÖZYÖRÜK, Y., Aerospace Engineering
PARLAKTUNA, M., Petroleum and Natural Gas Engineering
PARNAS, K. L., Mechanical Engineering
PLATIN, B. E., Mechanical Engineering
POLAT, F., Computer Engineering
ŞAHIN, S., Food Engineering
ŞANIN, F. D., Environmental Engineering
SAYAN, G., Electrical and Electronics Engineering
SELÇUK, N., Chemical Engineering
SEVAIOĞLU, O., Electrical and Electronics Engineering
SEVERCAN, M., Electrical and Electronics Engineering
SÖYLEMEZ, E., Mechanical Engineering
SOYLU, R., Mechanical Engineering
SUCUOĞLU, H., Civil Engineering
ŞÜMNÜ, S. G., Food Engineering
SÜZEN, M. L., Geological Engineering
TANIK, Y., Electrical and Electronics Engineering
TARI, Z. S., Computer Engineering
TARMAN, I. H., Engineering Sciences
TEKINALP, O., Aerospace Engineering
TOKDEMIR, T., Engineering Sciences
TOKYAY, M., Civil Engineering
TOKYAY, N., Civil Engineering
TOPAL, T., Geological Engineering
TOPKAYA, C., Civil Engineering
TOPKAYA, Y. A., Metallurgical and Materials Engineering
TOROSLU, I. H., Computer Engineering
TOSUN, I., Chemical Engineering
TÜMER, S. T., Mechanical Engineering
TUNCEL, S. G., Environmental Engineering
TUNCER, I. H., Aerospace Engineering
TUNCER, T. E., Electrical and Electronics Engineering
ÜÇOLUK, G., Computer Engineering
ULAŞ, A., Mechanical Engineering
ÜNER, D., Chemical Engineering
UNGAN, S., Food Engineering
ÜNLÜ, K., Environmental Engineering

ÜNLÜSOY, Y. S., Mechanical Engineering
ÜNVER, B. Z., Electrical and Electronics Engineering
UTKU, M., Civil Engineering
VURAL, H., Mechanical Engineering
YAKUT, A., Civil Engineering
YALÇINER, A. C., Civil Engineering
YAMAN, I. O., Civil Engineering
YAMAN, Y., Aerospace Engineering
YANMAZ, A. M., Civil Engineering
YARMAN VURAL, F. T., Computer Engineering
YAZICI, A., Computer Engineering
YAZICIGIL, H., Geological Engineering
YENER, M. E., Food Engineering
YETIŞ, Ü., Environmental Engineering
YILDIRIM, R. O., Mechanical Engineering
YILDIZ, F., Food Engineering
YILMAZ, L., Chemical Engineering
YILMAZ, Ç., Civil Engineering
YILMAZER, Ü., Chemical Engineering
YÜCEL, H., Chemical Engineering
YÜCEMEN, M. S., Civil Engineering
YÜNCÜ, H., Mechanical Engineering

Graduate School of Marine Sciences (33731 Erdemli; tel. (324) 521-21-50; e-mail ilkay@imf.metu.edu.tr; internet www.ims.metu.edu.tr):

KIDEYŞ, A., Graduate School of Marine Sciences
ÖZSOY, E., Graduate School of Marine Sciences
TUĞRUL, S., Graduate School of Marine Sciences
UYSAL, Z., Graduate School of Marine Sciences
YEMENICIOĞLU, S., Graduate School of Marine Sciences

OSMANGAZİ ÜNİVERSİTESİ

Meşelik Kampüsü, 26480 Eskişehir
Telephone: (222) 239-49-37
E-mail: ogubim@ogu.edu.tr
Internet: www.ogu.edu.tr

Founded 1970
State control
Languages of instruction: Turkish, English
Academic year: October to September

Chancellor: (vacant)
Vice-Chancellor: (vacant)
Rector: Prof. Dr NECAT A. AKGUN
Vice-Rector: Prof. Dr MACIT YAMAN
Vice-Rector: Prof. Dr ATİLLA YILDIRIM
Registrar: ESAT ÇELİK

Library of 33,883 books, 7,521 periodicals
Number of teachers: 870
Number of students: 8,790 (7,930 undergraduate, 860 postgraduate)

Publications: *Journal of the Faculty of Engineering and Architecture* (2 a year), *Journal of the Faculty of Medicine* (2 a year)

DEANS

Faculty of Agriculture: Prof. Dr YAŞAR PANCAR
Faculty of Arts and Sciences: Prof. Dr YALÇIN ŞAHİN
Faculty of Economic and Administrative Sciences: Prof. Dr FAZIL TEKİN
Faculty of Education: Prof. Dr NACI EKEM
Faculty of Engineering and Architecture: Prof. Dr ERCENGİZ YILDIRIM
Faculty of Medicine: Prof. Dr EROL GÖKTÜRK
Faculty of Theology: Prof. Dr MEHMET MAKSUDOĞLU

PAMUKKALE ÜNİVERSİTESİ

Kinikli Campus, 20070 Denizli
Telephone: (258) 296-23-56
E-mail: internationaloffice@pau.edu.tr
Internet: pau.edu.tr/pau

State control
Languages of instruction: English, Turkish
Rector: Prof. Dr HUSEYIN BAGCI
Vice-Rector: Prof. Dr ALI KESKIN
Vice-Rector: Prof. Dr SEBAHATTIN NAS
Number of teachers: 700
Number of students: 31,580

DEANS

Faculty of Arts and Sciences: Prof. Dr HALIL
  CETISLI
Faculty of Economic and Administrative Sci-
  ences: Prof. Dr ALI İHSAN KARAALP
Faculty of Education: Prof. Dr SELAHITTIN
  OZCELIK
Faculty of Engineering: Prof. Dr MUZAFFER
  TOPCU
Faculty of Medicine: Prof. Dr MUSTAFA KILIC
Faculty of Technical Education: Prof. Dr
  RASIM KARABACAK

SABANCİ ÜNİVERSİTESİ

Orhanli, 34956 Tuzla, Istanbul
Telephone: (216) 483-90-00
E-mail: db@sabanciuniv.edu
Internet: www.sabanciuniv.edu

Founded 1994
Private control
Languages of instruction: English, Turkish
Academic year: October to July

Rector: Prof. TOSUN TERZIOĞLU
Gen. Sec.: HALUK BAL
Librarian: HILMI ÇELIK

Library of 60,000 vols, 56 databases
Number of teachers: 410
Number of students: 2,010

DEANS

Faculty of Arts and Social Sciences: Prof.
  AHMET ALKAN
Faculty of Engineering and Natural Sci-
  ences: Prof. KEMAL İNAN
Graduate School of Management: Prof.
  NAKIYE AVDAN BOYACIGILLER

SAKARYA ÜNİVERSİTESİ

Esentepe Kampüsü, 54187 Sakarya
Telephone: (264) 295-54-54
E-mail: basin@sakarya.edu.tr
Internet: www.sakarya.edu.tr

Founded 1992
State control
Languages of instruction: Turkish, English
Academic year: September to June

Rector: Prof. Dr MEHMET DURMAN
Vice-Rector: Prof. Dr MUZAFFER ELMAS
Vice-Rector: Prof. Dr H. RIZA GÜVEN
Vice-Rector: Prof. Dr H. BINNAZ BAYTEKIN
Sec.-Gen.: Dr ZAFER DEMIR
Dir for Library: MUSTAFA ESMELI

Library of 100,008 vols
Number of teachers: 1,240
Number of students: 45,600

Publications: *Adapazarı Meslek Yüksekokulu
  Dergisi Akademik İncelemeler, Saü Bulletin, TOJET: The Turkish Online Journal
  of Educational Technology*

DEANS

Faculty of Arts and Humanities: Prof. Dr
  MURAT TUTUNCU
Faculty of Economic and Administrative Sci-
  ences: Prof. Dr ENGIN YILDIRIM
Faculty of Education: Prof. VAHDETTIN
  SEVINÇ
Faculty of Engineering: Prof. Dr MEHMET ALI
  YALÇIN
Faculty of Fine Arts: Prof. Dr NILGÜN BILGE
Faculty of Technical Education: Prof. Dr
  HÜSEYIN EKIZ
Faculty of Theology: Prof. Dr ALI ERBAŞI

School of Health Sciences: Prof. Dr SEVIN
  ALTINKAYNAK
School of Physical Education and Sports:
  Asst. Prof. Dr ERTUĞRUL GELEN

SELÇUK ÜNİVERSİTESİ

Vali Izzet Bey Cad., Karatay Müzesi Karşisi,
42151 Konya
Telephone: (332) 350-70-05
Internet: www.selcuk.edu.tr

Founded 1975
State control
Language of instruction: Turkish
Academic year: October to May

Rector: Prof. Dr SÜLEYMAN OKUDAN
Vice-Rector: Prof. Dr DINÇER BEDÜK
Vice-Rector: Prof. Dr ŞEFIK BILIR
Vice-Rector: Prof. Dr KÜRŞAT TURGUT
Librarian: Dr CENGIZI KORKMAZ

Number of teachers: 3,260
Number of students: 75,000

Publications: *Journal of Faculty of Engineering and Architecture* (2 a year), *Journal of
  the Faculty of Medicine* (4 a year), *Journal
  of Veterinary Science* (4 a year)

DEANS

Faculty of Agriculture: Prof. Dr MUSTAFA
  ONDER
Faculty of Communication: Prof. Dr HALUK
  HADI SUMER
Faculty of Dentistry: Prof. Dr TAMER ATAO-
  GLU
Faculty of Economics and Administrative
  Sciences: Prof. Dr SERIF SIMSEK
Faculty of Economics and Administrative
  Sciences (Konya): Prof. Dr ORHAN GÖKÇE
Faculty of Education: Prof. Dr MUSA GURSEL
Faculty of Engineering and Architecture:
  Prof. Dr CEVAT INAL
Faculty of Fine Arts: Prof. Dr FEVZI GUNUC
Faculty of Law: Prof. Dr MEHMET AYAN
Faculty of Literature: Prof. Dr AHMET TIRPAN
Faculty of Medicine (Meram): Prof. Dr AHMET
  OZKAGNICI
Faculty of Medicine (Selcuklu): Prof. Dr
  KAGAN KARABULUT
Faculty of Science: Prof. Dr İSMET UCAN
Faculty of Technical Education: Prof. Dr ALI
  UNUVAR
Faculty of Theology: Prof. Dr AHMET ONKAL
Faculty of Veterinary Sciences: Prof. Dr
  ZAFER DURGUN
Faculty of Vocational Education: Prof. Dr
  KADIRCAN OZKAN

SÜLEYMAN DEMIREL ÜNİVERSİTESİ

Merkez Kampüs, Çünür, 32260 Isparta
Telephone: (246) 211-10-00
E-mail: ozelkalem@sdu.edu.tr
Internet: www.sdu.edu.tr

Founded 1992
State control
Languages of instruction: English, Turkish
Academic year: September to July

Rector: Prof. Dr HASAN İBICIOĞLU
Vice-Rector: Prof. Dr İSKENDER AKKURT
Vice-Rector: Prof. Dr HÜSEYIN AKYILDIZ
Vice-Rector: Prof. Dr MEHMET NUMAN TAMER
Vice-Rector: Prof. Dr SÜLEYMAN SEYDI
Gen. Sec.: MUSTAFA DIRI
Library Dir: UĞUR BULGAN

Library of 227,000 vols, 40,000 eperiodicals
Number of teachers: 3,200
Number of students: 55,000

Publications: *Cell Membranes and Free Radical Research* (1 a year), *European Journal
  of Mineral Processing and Environmental
  Protection* (3 a year), *International Journal
  of Technological Sciences* (2 a year, in
  Turkish), *Journal of Engineering Science*

of Design (2 a year, in Turkish), *Journal of
  Natural and Applied Sciences* (1 a year, in
  Turkish), *Journal of SDU Faculty of Den-
  tistry* (2 a year, in Turkish), *Journal of
  Sleep Health* (2 a year, in Turkish), *Jour-
  nal of the Faculty of Administrative Sci-
  ences and Education* (2 a year, in Turkish),
  Journal of the Faculty of Agriculture (2 a
  year, in Turkish), *Journal of the Faculty of
  Forestry* (2 a year, in Turkish), *Medical
  Journal* (4 a year, in Turkish), *Medical
  Journal of Suleyman Demirel University* (4
  a year, in Turkish), *SDÜ Art-e* (2 a year, in
  Turkish), *SDÜ Eğirdir Su Ürünleri Fakültesi Dergisi* (1 a year, in Turkish), *SDÜ
  Egzersiz Dergisi* (1 a year, in Turkish),
  SDÜ Fen Bilimleri Enstitüsü Dergisi (3 a
  year, in Turkish), *SDU Journal of Science*
  (2 a year, in Turkish), *SDÜ Sağlık Bilimleri Enstitüsü Dergisi* (2 a year, in Turkish), *SDÜ Teknik Bilimler Dergisi* (2 a
  year, in Turkish), *SDÜ Vizyoner Dergisi* (2
  a year, in Turkish), *SDÜ Yaşam Dergisi* (2
  a year, in Turkish), *SDÜ Yekarum Dergisi*
  (2 a year, in Turkish)

DEANS

Faculty of Agriculture: Prof. Dr ZEKERIYA
  AKMAN
Faculty of Architecture: Prof. Dr ZIYA GENÇEL
Faculty of Arts and Sciences: Prof. Dr ALI
  KÖKCE
Faculty of Communication: Prof. Dr İLKER
  HÜSEYIN ÇARIKÇI
Faculty of Dentistry: Prof. Dr MUHAMMED
  HAKAN TÜRKKAHRAMAN
Faculty of Economic and Administrative Sci-
  ences: Prof. Dr ABDULLAH EROĞLU
Faculty of Education: Prof. Dr MENDERES
  COŞKUN
Faculty of Engineering: Prof. Dr ERDOĞAN
  KÜÇÜKÖNER
Faculty of Fine Arts: Prof. Dr ŞABAN SITEM-
  BÖLÜKBAŞI
Faculty of Fisheries: Prof. Dr OSMAN ÇETIN-
  KAYA
Faculty of Forestry: Prof. Dr CAHIT BALA-
  BANLI
Faculty of Health: Prof. Dr HALIS KÖYLÜ
Faculty of Law: Prof. Dr FARUK TURHAN
Faculty of Medicine: Prof. Dr HÜSEYIN YOR-
  GANCIGIL
Faculty of Technical Education: Prof. Dr ALI
  KEMAL YAKUT
Faculty of Technology: Prof. Dr OSMAN İPEK
Faculty of Theology: Prof. Dr TALIP TÜRCAN
Graduate School of Fine Arts: Doç. Dr
  ABDULLAH ŞEVKI DUYMAZ
Graduate School of Health Sciences: Prof. Dr
  MEHMET FEHMI ÖZGÜNER
Graduate School of Natural and Applied
  Sciences: Prof. Dr MEHMET CENGIZ KAYA-
  CAN
Graduate School of Social Sciences: Prof. Dr
  SÜLEYMAN SEYDI
Graduate School of Water: Prof. Doç Dr
  İBRAHIM DILER

TRAKYA ÜNİVERSİTESİ

22050 Karaağaç, Edirne
Telephone: (284) 223-40-04
E-mail: rectorsoffice@trakya.edu.tr
Internet: www.trakya.edu.tr

Founded 1982 from existing faculties in
Edirne
Academic year: October to June

Rector: Prof. Dr ENVER DURAN
Vice-Rector: Prof. Dr BEYHAN KARAMANLIO-
  GLU
Vice-Rector: Prof. Dr TIMUR KIRGIZ
Vice-Rector: Prof. Dr ALI KEMAL KUTLU
Librarian: ENDER BILAR

Number of teachers: 1,240
Number of students: 20,300

Publications: *Journal of the Faculty of Agriculture* (2 a year), *Journal of the Faculty of Medicine* (4 a year), *Medical Journal Of Trakya University* (3 a year), *Trakya University Journal of Scientific Research* (2 a year)

DEANS

Faculty of Arts and Sciences: Prof. Dr BÜNYAMIN ÖZGÜLTEKIN
Faculty of Economics and Administrative Sciences: Prof. Dr DERMAN KÜÇÜKALTAN
Faculty of Education: Prof. Dr HILMI İBAR
Faculty of Engineering and Architecture: Prof. Dr AHMET CAN
Faculty of Health Sciences: Prof. Dr FERDA ÖZDEMIR
Faculty of Medicine: Prof. Dr MURAT DIKMENGIL
Faculty of Science and Letters: Prof. Dr ŞEVKET EROL OKAN

UFUK ÜNİVERSİTESİ

Mevlana Bulvarı (Konya Yolu) 86-88, 06520 Balgat, Ankara

Telephone: (312) 284-77-77
E-mail: ufukuni@ufuk.edu.tr
Internet: www.ufuk.edu.tr

Founded 1972; present name and status 1999

Faculties of arts and science, economics and administration, education, law and medicine

Rector: Prof. Dr A. ERGÜN ERTUĞ
Gen. Sec.: İSMET ATIK

Number of teachers: 23
Number of students: 66

ULUDAĞ ÜNİVERSİTESİ

Görükle Kampüsü, Rektörlük Uluslararası İlişkiler Ofisi, 16059 Bursa

Telephone: (224) 294-00-72
E-mail: intoffice@uludag.edu.tr
Internet: www.uludag.edu.tr

Founded 1975 as Bursa Üniversitesi; present name and structure 1982
State control
Language of instruction: Turkish
Academic year: September to June

Rector: Prof. Dr KAMIL DILEK
Vice-Rector: Prof. Dr A. SAIM KILAVUZ
Vice-Rector: Prof. Dr İRFAN KARAGÖZ
Vice-Rector: Prof. Dr MÜFIT PARLAK
Sec.-Gen.: ÖZGÜR AKGÜN KARABULUT
Head of Libraries and Documentation Centre: CANAN KORKMAZ

Library of 67,493 vols
Number of teachers: 2,100
Number of students: 41,100

Publications: *Agriculture* (1 a year), *Education* (1 a year), *Engineering* (1 a year), *Medicine* (1 a year), *Science and Literature* (1 a year), *Theology* (1 a year), *Veterinary Science* (1 a year)

DEANS

Faculty of Agriculture: Prof. Dr İSMAIL FILYA
Faculty of Economics and Administrative Sciences: Prof. Dr İSMAIL EFIL
Faculty of Education: Prof. Dr MURAT ALTUN
Faculty of Engineering and Architecture: Prof. Dr ABDULVAHAP YIĞIT
Faculty of Medicine: Prof. Dr MUSTAFA GÜLLÜLÜ
Faculty of Science and Letters: Prof. Dr İSMAIL NACI CANGÜL
Faculty of Theology: Prof. Dr YAŞAR AYDINLI
Faculty of Veterinary Medicine: Prof. Dr ENGIN KENNERMAN

YAŞAR ÜNİVERSİTESİ

Şehitler Cad. 1522, Sok 6, 35230 Alsancak, Izmir

Telephone: (232) 463-33-44
E-mail: info@yasar.edu.tr
Internet: www.yasar.edu.tr

Founded 1998; present status 2001

Rector: Prof. Dr NECATI SEN
Gen. Sec.: DIDEM ÖKTEM

DEANS

Faculty of Business Economics and Administration: Prof. Dr CENGIZ PINAR
Faculty of Communications: Prof. Dr CENGIZ PINAR (Deputy)
Faculty of Engineering and Architecture: Prof. Dr DEMIR ASLAN
Faculty of Law: Prof. Dr DEMIR ASLAN (Deputy)
Faculty of Science and Letters: Prof. Dr COŞKUN IŞÇI

YEDİTEPE ÜNİVERSİTESİ

26 Agustos Yerlesimi, Kayışdağı Caddesi, 34755 Ataşehir, Istanbul

Telephone: (216) 578-00-00
E-mail: halklailiskiler@yeditepe.edu.tr
Internet: www.yeditepe.edu.tr

Founded 1996
Private control

Rector: Prof. Dr NURCAN BAÇ
Vice-Rector: Prof. Dr MELIH BORAL
Vice-Rector: Prof. Dr NEDRET KURAN BURÇOĞLU
Sec.-Gen.: LEYLA YEŞILADA (acting)
Number of students: 17,380

DEANS

Faculty of Architecture and Engineering: Prof. Dr İBRAHIM FAHIR BORAK
Faculty of Arts and Sciences: Prof. Dr AHMET İNCE
Faculty of Commercial Sciences: Prof. Dr ÖMER GÖKAY
Faculty of Communication: Prof. Dr SUAT ANAR
Faculty of Dentistry: Prof. Dr TURKER SANDALLI
Faculty of Economics and Administrative Sciences: Prof. Dr KADIR AYKUT TOP
Faculty of Education: AYŞE SEMRA AKYEL
Faculty of Fine Arts: Prof. Dr BIKE KOCAOĞLU
Faculty of Law: Prof. Dr HALUK KABAALIOĞLU
Faculty of Medicine: Prof. Dr AYÇA VITRINEL
Faculty of Pharmacy: Prof. Dr DILEK EROL

YILDIZ TEKNİK ÜNİVERSİTESİ

80750 Beşiktaş, Istanbul

Telephone: (212) 259-70-70
E-mail: uerden@yildiz.edu.tr
Internet: www.yildiz.edu.tr

Founded 1911; reorganized 1982 (fmrly State Acad. of Engineering and Architecture)
Academic year: October to July

Rector: Prof. Dr DURUL ÖREN
Vice-Rector for Admin.: Prof. Dr SALIH DURER
Vice-Rector for Education: Prof. Dr ZEKERIYA POLAT
Vice-Rector for Research and Planning: Prof. Dr GÖRÜN ARUN
Sec.-Gen.: ÜMIT ERDEN

Number of teachers: 1,100
Number of students: 17,000

Publication: *Periodical* (4 a year)

DEANS

Faculty of Architecture: Prof. Dr EMRE AYSU
Faculty of Art and Design: Prof. Dr TOMUR ATAGÖK
Faculty of Arts and Sciences: Prof. Dr DURUL ÖREN

Faculty of Chemical and Metallurgical Engineering: Prof. Dr SABRIYE PIŞKIN
Faculty of Civil Engineering: Prof. Dr YALÇIN YÜKSEL
Faculty of Economic and Administrative Sciences: Prof. Dr AYKUT POLATOĞLU
Faculty of Electrical and Electronic Engineering: Prof. Dr GALIP CANSEVER
Faculty of Mechanical Engineering: Prof. Dr HASAN HEPERKAN

ATTACHED COLLEGES

School of Foreign Languages: Dir Prof. Dr NÜKET ÖCAL.

School of Vocational Studies: Dir Assoc. Prof. Dr MUSTAFA SUNU

YÜZÜNCÜ YIL ÜNİVERSİTESİ
(Centennial University)

65080 Van

Telephone: (432) 225-10-10
E-mail: bbaum@yyu.edu.tr
Internet: www.yyu.edu.tr

Founded 1982
State control
Language of instruction: Turkish
Academic year: October to July

Rector: Prof. Dr YÜCEL AŞKIN
Vice-Rector: Prof. Dr ALI FAUT DOĞU
Vice-Rector: Prof. Dr AYŞE YÜKSEL
Vice-Rector: Prof. Dr HASAN CEYLAN
Gen. Sec.: Dr IŞIK TEPE
Librarian: (vacant)

Library of 31,000 vols
Number of teachers: 300
Number of students: 6,100

Publications: *Artos* (Universities and Colleges in Literature, 1 a year), *Eastern Journal of Physical Medicine and Rehabilitation* (12 a year), *Journal of Agricultural Sciences* (1 a year), *Journal of the Faculty of Arts and Sciences-Sciences* (irregular), *Journal of the Faculty of Education-Sciences* (12 a year), *Journal of the Faculty of Education-Social Sciences* (12 a year), *Journal of the Faculty of Theology* (12 a year), *Journal of the Faculty of Veterinary Science* (12 a year), *Journal of the Graduate School of Sciences* (irregular), *Journal of Health Sciences* (12 a year), *Journal of the Institute of Social Sciences* (irregular), *Rahva* (education, 12 a year), *University Bulletin* (12 a year), *Van Medical Journal* (12 a year), *Yeldegirmeni* (Arts, 12 a year)

DEANS

Faculty of Agriculture: Prof. Dr FIRAT CENGIZ
Faculty of Arts and Sciences: Prof. Dr ERKSIN GÜLEÇ
Faculty of Economic and Administrative Sciences: Prof. Dr BÜLENT KARAKAŞ
Faculty of Education: Prof. Dr RAUF YILDIZ
Faculty of Education (Hakkari): Prof. Dr RECAI KARAHAN
Faculty of Engineering: Prof. Dr A. ÜMIT TOLLUOĞLU
Faculty of Fine Arts: Prof. Dr ZÜHRE ŞENTÜRK
Faculty of Medicine: Prof. Dr MANSUR KAMACI
Faculty of Theology: Prof. Dr SELAHATTIN KIYICI
Faculty of Veterinary Science: Prof. Dr NIHAT MERT

PROFESSORS

Faculty of Agriculture:

AKYUZ, N.
ASKIN, Y.
COKSOYLER, N.
ŞEN, S. M.
YASAR, B.

Faculty of Arts and Science:
  AMİRALİ, G.
  CEYLAN, H.
  KARAKAS, B.
  ONLER, Z.
  OZTURK, A.
  RASİMGİL, R.
  TİLEKLİOĞLU, B.
  ULUCAM, A.
  YİLMAZ, A.

Faculty of Education:
  SAVAS, E.

TOZLU, N.
Faculty of Engineering:
  ORCEN, S.
  TOLLUOĞLU, A. U.
Faculty of Medicine:
  AKSOY, H.
  ATAY, G.
  BURDURLU, Y.
  CEYLAN, A.
  DALKİLİC, A. E.
  DEMİRORS, A. P.
  GOKSOY, T.

KAMACİ, M.
ODABAS, D.
TURAN, F.
YAKUT, C.
YETKİN, Y.
YUKSEL, A.

Faculty of Veterinary Science:
  AGAOĞLU, Z. T.
  BOLAT, D.
  BOYNUKARA, B.
  KARADAG, H.
  MERT, N.

TURKMENISTAN

The Higher Education System

Institutions of higher education pre-date the independence of Turkmenistan (formerly Turkmen SSR) from the USSR in 1991, with the oldest being the Turkmen State Medical Institute, which was founded in 1931. Following independence, a policy of bilim (education) was initiated, aimed at distancing Turkmenistan from its Soviet (and hence, Russian) past; a key element in this policy was the reformation of the Turkmen language, primarily through the substitution of the Latin for the Cyrillic alphabet. Free education at Turkmenistan's universities was reported to have been abolished in 2003, while it was reported that the number of places for students in educational establishments had been sharply reduced since the mid-1990s. In 2004 a presidential decree invalidating all higher education degrees received abroad came into effect; all teachers with such degrees were to be dismissed. In 2007 the new President, Gurbanguly Berdymuhamedov, extended the period of higher education from two to five years, effective from the beginning of the 2007/08 school year; in that academic year 13,800 students were enrolled at the country's 18 institutions of higher education. Students were no longer required to complete two years of practical work experience before applying to universities and recognition of foreign degrees was restored. In addition, postgraduate education was introduced for the first time, effective from the beginning of the 2008/09 academic year. President Berdymuhamedov also announced that the Academy of Sciences of Turkmenistan, which had been closed in 1993, was to reopen; a presidential decree re-establishing the Academy, which was to be fully funded by the state budget, was signed in June 2009.

Higher education, which is overseen by the Ministry of Education, is governed according to the Law on Education (2009). The implementation of the new law, inter alia, resurrected degrees for higher and professional education through evening and correspondence courses, which had been abolished during the previous administration of the late President Gen. Saparmyrat Niyazov. Accreditation is the responsibility of the Council of Ministers.

The main requirements for admission to higher education are the Attestat o Srednem Obrazovanji (Certificate of General Secondary Education) and results in competitive entrance examinations, which comprise both written and oral tests. The main undergraduate qualification is the Specialist Diploma (equivalent to the Bachelors degree), which typically lasts five years, although some programmes, including medicine, take six years to complete. From 2008/09 postgraduate courses are available in academic and professional subjects and are open to holders of the Specialist Diploma who also have relevant work experience in their chosen field of study. For admission to doctoral studies, candidates are required to pass two entrance examinations, one testing knowledge of the chosen subject and the other testing proficiency in a foreign language; the doctoral cycle culminates with submission and public defence of a thesis and leads to the award of the Doctorate of Science.

Post-secondary technical and vocational education consists of short-term courses of up to one-and-a-half years open to students who have completed nine years of secondary education. Qualifications include certificates and diplomas, and are intended to prepare students for employment; they do not grant access to higher education.

Regulatory Bodies

GOVERNMENT

Ministry of Culture, Television and Radio Broadcasting: 744000 Ashgabat, ul. Pushkin köç 14; tel. (12) 35-41-05; internet www.culture.gov.tm/site_eng.html; Minister GUNÇA MAMMEDOVA.

Ministry of Education: 744000 Ashgabat, Gerogly köç 2; tel. (12) 35-58-03; Minister GULSHAT MAMMEDOVA.

Learned Society

GENERAL

Academy of Sciences of Turkmenistan: 744000 Ashgabat, ul. Gogolia 15; tel. (12) 25-44-74; internet science.gov.tm; f. 1951; ensures practical realization of scientific and technical policy; Pres. GURBANMYRAT MEZILOV; Deputy Pres. P. KOUWANDYK.

Research Institutes

GENERAL

National Institute of Deserts, Flora and Fauna: 744000 Ashgabat, Bitarap Turkmenistan str. 15; tel. (12) 39-54-27; e-mail desert@online.tm; internet science.gov.tm/en/organisations/desert_institute; f. 1962; attached to Min. of Nature Protection; fundamental and applied research on problems of biology, ecology, the human environment; rational use of nature with regard to func-tional peculiarities of arid ecosystems; Dir Prof. Dr PALTAMET ESENOV (acting); publ. *Problems of Desert Development* (4 a year).

AGRICULTURE, FISHERIES AND VETERINARY SCIENCE

Gara-Kala Experimental Station for Plant Genetic Resources: Balkan Province, Gara-Kala; tel. (48) 3-17-99; f. 1900; Dir ASHIRMUKHAMET SAPARMURADOV.

Research Institute of Cotton Growing of the MAWR: 746423 Maryiskiy velayat, Eloten Region, Institutskiy v.; tel. (560) 2-26-02; Dir Prof. SEITBARDY KURBANGELDIEV; Deputy Dir Dr AKMUKHAMMET CHAPAU.

Research Institute of Livestock and Veterinary Science: 744012 Ashgabat, ul. Gerogly 70; tel. (12) 34-82-97; Chair. NURMURAT ATAEV.

Scientific Research Institute of Farming: 744000 Ashgabat, ul. Ostrovskiy 30; tel. (12) 34-74-35; f. 1900; attached to Min. of Agriculture; Dir ORAZ SOUNOV.

Scientific Research Institute of Grain Crops: 744205 Akhal, Esnev Village, ul. O. Jumaev 1; tel. (13) 73-64-76; f. 1900; Head KHUDAYBERDI KADJIEV.

Turkmen Research Institute of Grain: 744012 Ashgabat, ul. Ostrovskiy 1; tel. (12) 34-74-35; Dir Dr AKMUKHAMMED DURDIEV.

HISTORY, GEOGRAPHY AND ARCHAEOLOGY

Institute of History: 744000 Ashgabat, 2001 Azady St 61,; tel. (12) 35-31-38; e-mail history@online.tm; f. 1936, present name and status 2009; attached to Acad. of Sciences of Turkmenistan; research on the history of Turkmenistan and the Turkmen people from prehistory to present; Dir GULSHAT ORAZMUHAMMEDOVA.

MEDICINE

Scientific Clinical Centre of Cardiology: 744006 Ashgabat, ul. Gerogly 31; tel. (12) 39-04-90; e-mail kykmh@mail.ru; attached to Min. of Health and Medical Industry.

Scientific Clinical Center of Eye Disease named after S. Karanov: Seidi St 32, 744000 Ashgabat; tel. (12) 35-48-70; f. 1932; Dir A. SHAMURAT.

Turkmenistan Scientific-Clinical Centre of Oncology: 744020 Ashgabat, ul. Gorogly 53; tel. (12) 34-48-03; improves methods of medical treatment of cancer in Turkmenistan.

NATURAL SCIENCES

Biological Sciences

Institute of Botany: 744000 Ashgabat, ul. 2033 79; tel. (12) 25-37-58; Dir NURJAMAL ORAZOVNA ORAZMUHAMMEDOVA.

Physical Sciences

Institute of Chemistry: 744012 Ashgabat, Esgerler str. 92; tel. (12) 34-05-08; e-mail chem@online.tm; f. 1957, present status 2007; Dir GELDYEV OTUZBAY ANNABAEVICH.

Institute of Oil and Gas: Ashgabat, ul. Tehran 6; tel. (12) 39-18-46; f. 1970 as Institute 'Turkmen Gas Technology', present name 1993; Dir Dr KHOSHGELDY BABAEV.

Research Institute of Seismology: 744000 Ashgabat, ul. Acad T. Berdyev 20; tel. (12) 39-06-92; e-mail gaip@icctm.org; f. 1998; attached to Min. of Construction; Dir MYRAT MERETLIEVICH CHARYEV; publ. *Seismological Report* (2 a year).

Turkmensuvylymtaslama Institute: 744000 Ashgabat, ul. Beki Seytakov 1; tel. (12) 35-18-35; e-mail tgvh@online.tm; water economy of Turkmenistan; Dir Dr MOSES SARKISOV; Deputy Dir USMAN SAPAROV.

TECHNOLOGY

Biotechnology Scientific Technological Centre: 744000, Ashgabat, ul. Bitarap 15; tel. (3632) 35-14-39; attached to Acad. of Sciences; Head Dr TACHDURDY GEDEMOV.

Institute of Mathematics and Mechanics: 744000 Ashgabat, ul. Gogolia 15; tel. (12) 29-87-13; Dir M. B. ORAZOV.

Libraries and Archives

Ashgabat

Central Scientific Library: 744007 Ashgabat, ul. 2002 15A; tel. (12) 35-65-71; internet library.science.gov.tm; f. 1941, present status 1957; attached to High Ccl for Science and Technology; colln of rare and valuable edns of valuable stock CSL Turkmen books with various graphics (Arabic, Latin, Cyrillic) for the period up to 1917 and subsequent years; publishes scientific-support bibliographical aids; received books on all brs of science from the Central Reservoir libraries of Russia (Moscow); 2.1m. vols; Dir A. B. YAZBERDIYEV.

Magtymguly Turkmen State University Library: 744005 Ashgabat, Sapamurat Turkmenbashi shayely 31; tel. (12) 5-39-22; f. 1950; provides scientific information; participates in educational process; promotes culture; 542,000 vols; Dir. A. T. VOROBEVA.

National Library of Turkmenistan: 744000 Ashgabat, pl. 2001, Berzengi, Nat. Cultural Centre; tel. (12) 35-74-89; f. 1895; 5.5m. vols; Dir OGULGOZEL MUHAMMETGU-LYEVA.

Museums and Art Galleries

Ashgabat

Carpet Museum: 744000 Ashgabat, ul. Gorogly 5; f. 1994; colln of more than 8,000 Turkmen carpets from 17th to 20th century; museum workshop shows weaving of carpets; Dir TUVAKBIBI K. DURDYEVA.

Central Botanical Garden: 744012 Ashgabat, ul. Timiryazeva 17; tel. (12) 24-18-57; f. 1929; spec. collns of native flora, tropical and subtropical plants, Crataegus, Astragalus, Lonicera, Cotoneaster, Quercus, Juniperus, Pinus, Rosa, Allium; Dir Dr B. B. KERBABAEV.

National Museum of Turkmenistan: 744000 Ashgabat, ul. Novofiruzinskoye 30; tel. (12) 51-90-20; e-mail vip@online.tm; f. 1998 by merger of Nat. Museum of History and Ethnography of Turkmenistan, State Museum of History of Turkmenistan and Turkmen State Museum of Fine Art; over 500,000 unique exhibits depicting history, ethnography, fine art; library of 8,830 vols; Dir OVEZMUHAMED MAMETNUROV.

Turkmen History Museum: Ashgabat, 1 Shevchenko St; tel. (12) 35-45-54; displays archeological finds, Ivory ritons; Dir AGABAI ATAGARRYEV.

Charjou

Charjou Historical and Ethnographical Museum: Charjou, ul. Shaidjanov 35; tel. (422) 4-80-79; colln of artefacts from the Lebab velayat; Dir MAYA AKMAMEDOVA.

Universities

INTERNATIONAL TURKMEN–TURKISH UNIVERSITY

744012 Ashgabat, ul. Gyorogly 84

Telephone: (12) 90-84-26

E-mail: ikez@mail.ru

Internet: www.ittu.edu.tm

Founded 1994

Faculties of economics, education, engineering

Rector: GELDYEV REJEPMUHAMED

Vice-Chancellor: RAHMANKULOV FAYZULLA

TURKMEN AGRICULTURAL UNIVERSITY NAMED AFTER S. A. NIYAZOV

744012 Ashgabat, Gyorogly str. 62

Telephone: (12) 34-26-52

Founded 1930

State control

Depts of accounting, agrochemistry, animal husbandry, fruit and vegetable growing, mechanization, veterinary science, viticulture

Rector: MAMEDKULIEV GURBANDURDY

Library of 136,000 vols

Number of teachers: 220

Number of students: 2,000

TURKMEN STATE UNIVERSITY NAMED AFTER MAGTYMGULY

744000 Ashgabat, Saparmurat Turkembashi shayoly 31

Telephone: (12) 35-11-59

E-mail: math3@online.tm

Founded 1931 as Ashgabat Pedagogical Institute, present status and name 1950

State control

Faculties of biology, chemistry, foreign languages, geography, history, humanities and social sciences, law and int. relations, management and int. trade, mathematics and applied maths, physics, Russian philology, theology, Turkmen philology

Rector: Prof. TUGIEV CHARYYAR

Pro-Rector: Prof. ATDAYEV SAPARGELDY ATDAYEVICH

Number of teachers: 550

Number of students: 11,000

Other Higher Educational Institutes

State Academy of Arts of Turkmenistan: 744012 Ashgabat, ul. A. Navoi 90; tel. (12) 39-38-02; f. 1994; attached to Min. of Culture, Television and Radio Broadcasting; painting (miniature painting of Turkmens, machine-tool painting, theatre-decorational painting, figurative expression of the film, monumental painting); graphics (printing graphics, book graphics, placard); national art (carpets, ceramics, jewellery); sculpture; architecture; design; art criticism; Rector BEGMYRADOV GULNAZAR; Vice-Rector TADJY-MOVA JEREN.

Turkmen Institute of National Economy: 744027 Ashgabat, Atamurad Nyyazov shayely 46; tel. (12) 41-90-36; faculties of accounting, economic planning, trade economics; Rector MAKHAMMETGELDI ANNAAMA-NOV.

Turkmen Medical Institute: 744001 Ashgabat, ul. 2028 58; tel. (12) 35-19-53; e-mail medins@online.tm; f. 1931; attached to Acad. of Sciences of Turkmenistan; faculties of medical science, paediatrics, stomatology, pharmaceutical, medico-prophylactic; library: 191,000 vols; Rector GURBANGULY M. BERDYMUKHAMMEDOV (acting).

Turkmen National Institute of Sport and Tourism: 744001 Ashgabat, Atamyrad Nyyazov Shayoly 15A; tel. (12) 36-25-40; faculties of hotel business, tourism business, sport, physical training; Rector ATALYEV YALKAPBERDY.

Turkmen National Institute of World Languages named after D. Azadi: 744011 Ashgabat, ul. Ostrovskogo 47; tel. (12) 34-54-24; f. 1984; European languages: English, French, German, Russian language and literature; Eastern languages: Arabic, Persian, Turkish, Turkmen language and literature; 117 teachers; 805 students; Rector CHARYEV SAPARBERDY; Vice-Rector TAGANDUR-DYEV TAGANDURY.

Turkmen Polytechnic Institute: 744025 Ashgabat, B. Annanova str. 62; tel. (12) 41-18-00; faculties of construction, oil and gas, chemical technology, energy, economics, computer technology and sanitation technology; managing of production; Rector YAZ MOVLYA-MOV.

Turkmen State Institute of Culture: 744000 Ashgabat, Magtymguly Shayoly 4; tel. (12) 27-21-27; e-mail miras@cpart.org; theatrical art, production; archives; Rector SAPARMUHAMEDOV ANNAMURAD; Vice-Rector GOSHAYEV DADEBAY.

Turkmen State Institute of Energy: 745400 Mary, ul. Bayramali 62; tel. (52) 26-04-12; electrical systems and networks; manual and automatic management of technical systems; production of electronics; work up and technology of metals and machines; apparatus of chemical industry; chemical technology of inorganic matters; Rector JUMAGYLYJOV ANNAGULY; Vice-Rector KAKA-BAYEV SAPAR.

Turkmen State Institute of Transport and Communications: 744028 Ashgabat, ul. Oguzhana 13; tel. (12) 27-26-79; e-mail durdyev@online.tm; Rector MERED ASHIR-BAYEV.

Turkmen State Pedagogical Institute named after S. Seydi: 746100 Türkmena-bat, ul. Shabende 7; tel. (42) 23-36-72; languages, teacher-training; Chancellor G. MEZILOV; Rector YAZYLEV CHARY.

TUVALU

The Higher Education System

There was no higher education in Tuvalu before 1979. In that year the University of the South Pacific (Fiji) established an extension centre at Funafuti; the centre offers diploma and vocational courses and the first two years of degree courses (the latter requiring completion in Suva). The only other tertiary institution is the Tuvalu Maritime Training Institute at Amatuku on Funafuti, which was also founded in 1979 (as the Tuvalu Maritime School); about 60 people graduate from the school annually. A project to upgrade infrastructure and facilities at the Institute, in order to meet International Maritime Organization training standards, was undertaken during the 2000s; the project was funded by a US $2m. assistance package granted by the Asian Development Bank. Plans were under discussion for the establishment of a technical education centre that would offer training in a range of technical and vocational fields, including carpentry, engineering, plumbing and secretarial work. The Ministry of Education, Sports and Culture in Funafuti is responsible for higher education.

Regulatory Body

GOVERNMENT

Ministry of Education, Sports and Culture: POB 37, Vaiaku, Funafuti; tel. 20405; e-mail ses@tuvalu.tv; Minister FAUOA MAANI.

Libraries and Archives

Funafuti

National Library and Archives: PMB, Vaiaku, Funafuti; tel. 20711; archive depositary for all govt documents; 19,500 vols, 150 periodicals; Chief Librarian and Archivist ANE TEILAUEA.

Parliamentary Library: Tuvalu Parliament, Vaiaku, Funafuti; tel. 20739; f. 1984; 600 vols; Librarian PAULSON PANAPA.

University

UNIVERSITY OF THE SOUTH PACIFIC, TUVALU CENTRE

POB 21, Funafuti
Telephone: 20811
E-mail: manuella_d@usp.ac.fj
Internet: www.usp.ac.fj/index.php?id=4502#tuvalu
Founded 1979
Dir: DAVID MANUELLA
Library Officer: TOGIOLA FUNAFUTI
Library of 3,000 vols

UGANDA

The Higher Education System

Institutions of higher education pre-date Uganda's independence from the United Kingdom in 1962, the oldest being Makerere University in Kampala, which was founded in 1922 as a technical college for students from British East Africa. After 1949 it was affiliated to the University of London (United Kingdom), and in 1970 it was declared an independent university. In 2012 there were six public universities, 29 private universities, nine public and two private university colleges and two other recognized degree-awarding institutions (The Uganda Management Institute and the Team Institute of Business Management). In addition, there were 89 private and public institutions of tertiary education. In 2011 the number of students enrolled at Uganda's universities and tertiary education institutes totalled 289,545. Public institutions of higher education receive funding from the Ministry of Education and Sports and from the Public Sector Commission.

The National Council for Higher Education (NCHE) is responsible for accreditation and quality assurance, and institutions seeking to award degrees or other programmes of higher education must fulfil a number of requirements. Once an institution has been awarded a provisional licence by the Council it then has three years to apply for chartered status. In mid-2011 the NCHE announced a new tuition fees structure for public universities, which, if approved by the Government, would lead to an increase in fees of more than 300% for most study programmes.

Two passes in the Uganda Advanced Certificate of Education and five passes in the Uganda Certificate of Education are the main requirements for admission to undergraduate degrees. Sub-degree Certificate and Diploma courses lasting one or two years are offered in a range of subjects, often relating to professional fields of study. The principal undergraduate degree is the Bachelors, which requires completion of a final-year project and is usually a three-year programme of study, although degrees in agriculture, engineering, forestry, technology and veterinary science last four years, and degrees in architecture, medicine and pharmacy last five years. The Bachelors is required for admission to a Masters degree programme. Postgraduate Certificate and Diploma courses, which generally last one year, are open to holders of a Bachelors degree and are available primarily in professional disciplines such as education and medicine. Masters degrees last between 18 months and three years, although two years is increasingly becoming the norm. Following the Masters is the Doctorate, the highest university degree, which is awarded after a minimum of three years' study; depending on the subject, doctoral programmes may consist exclusively of research or may comprise a mixture of research and coursework. Higher Doctorates in arts and science are awarded on the basis of published work.

Post-secondary technical and vocational education is offered by a range of institutions, including technical colleges, colleges of commerce, vocational training institutes and cooperative colleges. Awards are broadly classified as Craft, Technician or Higher Technician. The Directorate of Industrial Training (DIT), under the Ministry of Education and Sports, was mandated to develop the Uganda Vocational Qualifications Framework, which is intended to incorporate all nationally recognized vocational qualifications. The DIT is responsible for developing occupational standards, and training modules, and for compiling and distributing assessment and training packages that have an occupational basis. In 2014 this was still under development.

Regulatory and Representative Bodies

GOVERNMENT

Ministry of Education and Sports: Embassy House and Devt Bldg, Plot 9/11, Parliament Ave, POB 7063, Kampala; tel. (41) 234451; e-mail pro@education.go.ug; internet www.education.go.ug; Minister JESSICA ROSE EPEL ALUPO.

ACCREDITATION

National Council for Higher Education (NCHE): POB 7634, Cavers Crescent, Kyambogo, Kampala; tel. (31) 2262140; e-mail nche@infocom.co.ug; internet www.unche.or.ug; f. 2001; statutory agency regulating the management of higher education instns and the quality of higher education; accredits public and private tertiary instns and licenses private tertiary instns; Exec. Dir Prof. A. B. K. KASOZI.

NATIONAL BODIES

Association for Teacher Education in Africa: c/o Assoc. Prof. J. C. B. Bigala, Makerere University, POB 7062, Kampala; e-mail afriate@gmail.com; f. 1970; develops and coordinates syllabuses and materials to be used in teacher education instns; 50 mem. instns in anglophone Africa; Pres. Prof. M. MOHAPELOA; Sec. Assoc. Prof. J. C. B. BIGALA; publs *Education in Eastern Africa*, *Journal of West African Education*.

Inter-University Council for East Africa: POB 7110, Kampala; tel. (41) 4256251; e-mail info@iucea.org; internet www.iucea.org; f. 1980 as a corporate body to succeed the Inter-University Committee for East Africa; aims to facilitate contact and cooperation between the univs of Kenya, Tanzania and Uganda, to provide a forum for discussion on academic matters, and to maintain comparable academic standards; also provides secretariat for the Asscn of Eastern and Southern African Universities (see under International); 36 mem. univs and colleges; Chair. Prof. F. I. B. KAYANJA (Vice-Chancellor, Mbarara University of Science and Technology); Exec. Sec. Prof. MAYUNGA H. H. NKUNYA.

Learned Societies

GENERAL

Uganda Society: POB 4980, Kampala; internet www.africa.upenn.edu/ugandasoc/ugandasociety.htm; f. 1923, present name 1933; premises in the Uganda Museum, Kira Rd, Kampala; membership open to persons of all nationalities and instns, to promote interest in literary, historic, scientific and general cultural matters, discovering and recording facts about the country, arranging lectures and establishing contacts; library of 1,600 vols and periodicals; Pres. Prof. E. H. K. NSUBUGA; Sec. NANNY CARDER; publ. *The Uganda Journal* (2 a year).

BIBLIOGRAPHY, LIBRARY SCIENCE AND MUSEOLOGY

Uganda Library and Information Association: POB 40227, Kampala; f. 1972; 356 mems; Chair. MAGARA ELISAM; Sec. C. BATAMBUZE; publ. *Uganda Library and Information Science Journal* (2 a year).

LANGUAGE AND LITERATURE

Alliance Française: National Theatre, 1st Fl., POB 4314, Kampala; offers courses and exams in French language and culture and promotes cultural exchange with France.

British Council: Plot 4, Windsor Loop, Kira Rd, Kamwokya, Kampala; tel. (41) 4560800; e-mail info@britishcouncil.or.ug; internet www.britishcouncil.org/uganda; offers courses and examinations in English language and British culture; promotes cultural exchange with the UK; library of 5,000 vols, 40 periodicals; Dir KATE EWART-BIGGS.

MEDICINE

Uganda Medical Association: Plot 8, 41–43 Circular Rd, POB 2243, Kampala.

Research Institutes

AGRICULTURE, FISHERIES AND VETERINARY SCIENCE

Animal Health Research Centre: POB 24, Entebbe; f. 1926; research and field work in animal diseases, husbandry and nutrition;

herbarium; library of 13,950 vols; Dir for Veterinary Research Services Prof. O. BWANGAMOI; Librarian H. R. KIBOOLE; publ. *Research Index* (irregular).

Kawanda Agricultural Research Institute: POB 7065, Kampala; e-mail karidir@imul.com; f. 1937; research on bananas and coffee, horticulture, post-harvest soil and soil fertility management, integrated pest management, biometrics, plant breeding, plant pathology; plant herbarium; insect museum; 9 research staff; library of 2,600 vols; Dir for Research Dr MATTHIAS MAGUNDA.

Nakawa Forestry Research Centre: POB 8668, Kampala; f. 1952; logging, milling and building research; preservation and seasoning tests; small specialized library.

ECONOMICS, LAW AND POLITICS

Centre for Basic Research: 15 Baskerville Ave, Kololo, POB 9863, Kampala; tel. (41) 2342987; f. 1988; NGO active in social research; library of 14,000 vols; Exec. Dir Dr SIMON RUTABAJUUKA.

Makerere University Institute of Social Research: POB 16022, Kampala; tel. (41) 2554582; e-mail misronlinetoday@gmail.com; internet misr.mak.ac.ug; f. 1948; conducts ind. research into economic, political and social problems of East Africa; 6 research fellows and Univ. staff in depts of economics, environmental studies, political science, rural economy and extension, social administration, social work, sociology, women's studies; library of 10,000 vols, 70 current periodicals; Dir Prof. MAHMOOD MAMDANI; Dir Dr ADAM BRANCH; Librarian IRENE MBAWAKI; publs *East African Studies* (irregular), *East Africa Linguistic Studies* (irregular), *Mawazo Journal* (2 a year), *Policy Abstracts and Research Newsletter*, USSC Conference papers (1 a year), working papers.

MEDICINE

Uganda Virus Research Institute: Entebbe; e-mail information@iavi.or.ug; internet www.mrcuganda.org; f. 1936 as Yellow Fever Research Institute; renamed East African Virus Research Institute 1950; present name 1977; attached to Uganda Nat. Health Research Org., under the Min. of Health; carries out scientific research concerning communicable diseases, especially viral diseases threatening to public health, and advises the Govt on strategies for disease control and prevention; Communications Officer DAVID WALUGEMBE.

NATURAL SCIENCES

Physical Sciences

Geological Survey and Mines Department: POB 9, Entebbe; tel. (41) 4233910; e-mail dgsm@minerals.go.ug; internet www.uganda-mining.go.ug; f. 1919; library of 22,900 vols; Commr J. T. TUHUMWIRE.

Government Chemist Department: POB 2174, Kampala; forensic chemical examination, bacteriological examination of foods and water, chemical analysis of water, food and drugs, pollution control, identification and assay of drugs, general chemical analysis of soils and ores, isolation and identification of active principles of medicinal plants; Dir GEOFFREY ONEN.

Libraries and Archives

Kampala

Cabinet Office Library: POB 7168, Kampala; tel. 6776590034; e-mail jsokiror@cabinetsecretariat.go.ug; f. 1920; for govt

officials and for research workers; 10,000 vols; Librarian JOHN STEPHEN OKIROR; publ. *Catalogue.*

Forestry Department Library: POB 7124, Kampala; tel. (41) 2347085; f. 1904; specialized library (open to students by spec. arrangement with the Commr for Forestry); literature on forestry and related sciences; 20,000 vols; Librarian W. M. BWIRUKA.

Makerere University, Albert Cook Library: Makerere Univ., College of Health Sciences, POB 7072, Kampala; tel. (41) 4534149; e-mail cooklib@chs.mak.ac.ug; f. 1946; 60,000 vols, 500 periodicals, covering all medical subjects, especially East African and tropical medicine, spec. collns: history of medicine, Mengo Notes, WHO publs, database of Ugandan health literature; Head and Sr Librarian RACHEL NAKALEMBE (acting); publ. *Uganda Health Information Digest* (3 a year).

Makerere University Library Service: POB 16002, Kampala; e-mail universitylibrarian@mulib.mak.ac.ug; internet mak.ac.ug/services/university-library; f. 1940; consists of a Main Library, functioning as Nat. Reference Library, with 7 sub-libraries: 5 located on the main campus: East African School of Library and Information Science Library, Education Library, Institute of Adult and Continuing Education Library, Makerere Institute of Social Research Library and the Veterinary Library; and 2 off-campus: Albert Cook Library at the Medical School, Mulago, and Makerere University Agricultural Research Institute Library at the Agricultural Institute, Kabayoro; 384,000 vols, 330 current periodicals, spec. collns on East Africa, Uganda legal deposit, and private archives; book-bank system of basic textbooks kept in departmental libraries, comprising 182,000 vols; Librarian Prof. MARIA G. N. MUSOKE; publs *East African Studies, Makerere Law Journal, Makerere Political Review, Mawazo.*

National Library of Uganda: Buganda Rd, POB 4262, Kampala; tel. (41) 233633; e-mail library@infocom.co.ug; internet www.nlu.go.ug; f. 1964 as Public Libraries Board, present name 2003; organizes the colln and management of the nation's documented heritage, for current and future use; assists local govts in the management of public libraries; provides bibliographic control and aims to promote a reading culture among Ugandans, through reading tents and book donations to schools; provides an information referral service on Uganda; 157,000 vols, 200 serial titles; Dir GERTRUDE KAYAGA MULINDWA; publ. *National Bibliography of Uganda.*

Museums and Art Galleries

Entebbe

Entebbe Botanical Gardens: Lugard Rd, POB 295, Entebbe; tel. (41) 2320638; e-mail curator@infocom.co.ug; f. 1898; conservation and devt of native and exotic plants, colln and planting of local medicinal plants; Curator JOHN MULUMBA-WASSWA; publ. *Index Seminum* (1 a year).

Game and Fisheries Museum, Aquarium and Library: Johnstone Rd, POB 4, Entebbe; collns of heads of game animals, reptiles, fish and butterflies, hunting and fishing implements, and weapons; library of 1,100 vols; Commr for Fisheries CHRISTOPHER DHATEMWA; Commr for Wildlife MOSES OKUA.

Uganda Wildlife Education Centre: 56–57 Lugard Ave, POB 369, Entebbe; tel. (41) 4320520; e-mail info@uwec.ug; internet www.uweczoo.org; f. 1952, present name and status 1994; conservation, education, rescue and rehabilitation of orphaned, injured and/or confiscated wildlife; captive breeding of endangered wildlife species; Exec. Dir Dr JAMES MUSINGUZI.

Kampala

Uganda Museum: 5–7 Kira Rd, POB 365, Kampala; e-mail info@ugandatourism.org; f. 1908; natural history, geology, ethnology, archaeology, palaeontology; science and industry pavilion; spec. colln of African musical instruments; centre for archaeological research in Uganda; library of 4,000 vols; Curator Dr E. KAMUHANGIRE.

Universities

BISHOP STUART UNIVERSITY

POB 9, Mbarara

Telephone: (485) 4433222
E-mail: info@bsu.ac.ug
Internet: www.bsu.ac.ug

Founded 2002
Private control
Languages of instruction: English, Kiswahili
Academic year: August to June

Vice-Chancellor: Assoc. Prof. MAUDE KAMATENESI MUGISHA
Deputy Vice-Chancellor: Dr SOLOMON NKESIIGA
Dean for Students: JOHN TUHAIRWE
Univ. Sec.: PEACE TINDYEBWA
Academic Registrar: ALFRED BANGIRANA RUPIIHA

Library of 22,800 vols, incl. books, dissertations, periodicals, CD-ROMs, ejournals
Number of teachers: 177
Number of students: 4,580

Publication: *Journal of Development Issues*

DEANS

Faculty of Applied Sciences: Dr JACQUILINE KYOMUHENDO
Faculty of Business and Development Studies: Dr GEORGE MUGANGA
Faculty of Education: DAVID KABANZA
Faculty of Law: Dr GEORGE KASOZI

BUGEMA UNIVERSITY

POB 6529, Kampala
E-mail: registrar@bugemauniv.ac.ug
Internet: www.bugemauniv.ac.ug

Founded 1997
Language of instruction: English
Vice-Chancellor: Prof. PATRICK MANU

DEANS

Graduate School: Dr PAUL KATAMBA
School of Business: Dr KIBIRANGO MOSES
School of Education: Dr KISUNZU KAKULE ISSE NDAMBI
School of Social Sciences: Dr TABITHA SIGUE
School of Theology: Dr GEBRE WORANCHA

BUSITEMA UNIVERSITY

POB 236, Tororo
Telephone: (454) 448813
E-mail: us@adm.busitema.ac.ug
Internet: www.busitema.ac.ug

Founded 2007
State control
Language of instruction: English
Chancellor: FRANCIS GERVASE OMASWA
Vice-Chancellor: Prof. MARY J. N. OKWAKOL

Academic Registrar: ELISHA OBELLA
Dean for Students: AGATHA WOLWA
Univ. Librarian: ABDUL KARIM ISALA

DEANS

Faculty of Agriculture and Animal Sciences:
  Prof. OLILA DEO
Faculty of Engineering: SAMUEL BAKER
  KUCEL
Faculty of Natural Resources and Environ-
  mental Sciences: (vacant)
Faculty of Science and Education: MUWOOYA
  AMOS KISAALE

CAVENDISH UNIVERSITY, UGANDA

Nsambya Plot 1469, Ggaba Rd, POB 33145,
  Kampala

Telephone: (414) 531700
E-mail: info@cavendish.ac.ug
Internet: www.cavendish.ac.ug

Founded 2008
Private control

Chancellor: KENNETH KAUNDA
Vice-Chancellor: DAVID GAME
Vice-Rector for Finance: SAMUEL EPEDUNO
Librarian: ESERI NAMUSWE

Number of teachers: 160
Number of students: 5,000

DEANS

Business Management: BILL NKEETO
Law: DAMAS FRANCISCO
Postgraduate Studies and Research: Prof.
  JAMES MULIRA
Science and Technology: MOSES BALIRWA
Socio-economic Sciences: JOSEPH NYAKANA

GULU UNIVERSITY

POB 166, Gulu

Telephone: (47) 1432095
Internet: www.gu.ac.ug

Founded 2002
State control
Language of instruction: English
Academic year: August to May

Rector: JACK H. PEN-MOGI NYOKI
Univ. Sec.: VINCENT M. OKOTH-OGOLA
Academic Registrar: GEOFFREY LAMTOO
Librarian: AREGU RAPHAEL

Library of 23,000 vols, 33 periodicals
Number of teachers: 188
Number of students: 3,831

DEANS

Faculty of Agriculture and Environment:
  Prof. CALLISTUS W. BALIDDAWA
Faculty of Business and Development Stud-
  ies: UWONDA GILBERT
Faculty of Education and Humanities:
  OKUMU CHARLES
Faculty of Medicine: Prof. EMILIO OVUGA
Faculty of Science: Dr ANDOGAH GEOFFREY

ISLAMIC UNIVERSITY IN UGANDA

POB 2555, Mbale

Telephone: (35) 2512100
E-mail: info@iuiu.ac.ug
Internet: www.iuiu.ac.ug

Founded 1988
Private control
Languages of instruction: Arabic, English
Academic year: August to July

Rector: Dr AHMAD KAWESA SENGENDO
Vice-Rector for Academic Affairs: Dr MPEZA-
  MIHIGO MOUHAMAD
Vice-Rector for Finance: Dr KAZIBA ABDUL
  MPAATA
Univ. Sec.: SSENTONGO ABUBAKAR
Academic Registrar: KASIITA MUSA
Librarian: Dr SESSANGA IDRIS

Library of 42,617 vols, 41,423 books, 1,490
  serial titles, 570 online bibliographic items,
  570 ebooks, 170 reference books, 152 print
  journals, 3,205 research reports, theses
  and dissertations
Number of teachers: 358
Number of students: 6,738
Publications: *Islamic University Journal* (2 a
  year), *IUIU Law Journal* (1 a year)

DEANS

Faculty of Arts and Social Sciences: Dr
  MWANGA MOSES
Faculty of Education: Dr NIMULORA MAIMUNA
Faculty of Islamic Studies and Arabic Lan-
  guage: Dr HUSSEIN MUHAMMAD BOWA
Faculty of Law: SAIDAT NAKITTO
Faculty of Management Studies: KITAKULE
  MUBI HUSSEIN
Faculty of Science: ADAM ALI

KABALE UNIVERSITY

POB 317, Kabale

Telephone: (486) 22803
E-mail: info@kabaleuniversity.ac.ug
Internet: www.kabaleuniversity.ac.ug
Private control
Language of instruction: English
Academic year: August to July (2 semesters)

Vice-Chancellor: Prof. JOY C. KWESIGA
Academic Registrar: Rev. JAMES KARIBWIJE
Univ. Sec.: KENNEDY RWABOONA
Head of Library Services: HELEN MUSANA-
  BERA BYAMUGISHA

KAMPALA INTERNATIONAL UNIVERSITY

POB 20000, Kansanga, Kampala

Telephone: (414) 663813
E-mail: admin@kiu.ac.ug
Internet: www.kiu.ac.ug

Founded 2003
Private control
Language of instruction: English

Chief Univ. Librarian: Dr PRISCA K. G.
  TIBENDERANÀ

KAMPALA UNIVERSITY

POB 25454, Kampala

Telephone: (41) 2258219
E-mail: ar@ku.ac.ug
Internet: www.ku.ac.ug
Private control
Academic year: August to July (2 semesters)

Vice-Chancellor: Prof. BADRU KATEREGGA
Deputy Vice-Chancellor for Academics: Prof.
  A. B. T. BYARUHANGA-AKIIKI
Academic Registrar: Dr EVANS KEROSI
Dean for Students: HANEEM KATEREGGA
Univ. Librarian: EVELYN BUTUNDU

DEANS

School of Arts and Social Sciences: Dr
  SULAYIMAN KATENDE
School of Business and Management Studies:
  AMAAL KINENE NSEREKO
School of Computer Sciences and Informa-
  tion Technology: Dr NAZIL AHMAD SUHAIL
School of Education: KITAGAANA ZAID
School of Industrial Art and Design: Prof.
  MUGUMBYA GAMALIEL SSENYONGA
School of Nursing and Health Sciences:
  JULIET M. KOBUSINGE (Prin.)

KUMI UNIVERSITY

POB 178, Kumi
E-mail: sykim@cnu.ac.kr
Internet: www.kumiuniversity.ac.ug

Founded 1996, present status 2004
Private control

Faculties of computing and information technology, education and languages, social sciences and management studies
Vice-Chancellor: Dr SUN Y KIM

KYAMBOGO UNIVERSITY

POB 1, Kyambogo

Telephone: (41) 4285001
E-mail: uskyu@kyu.ac.ug
Internet: www.kyu.ac.ug

Founded 1954 as Uganda Polytechnic Kyambogo; univ. status 2001 following merger
  with Institute of Teacher Education Kyambogo and Uganda Nat. Institute for Spec.
  Education
State control

Chancellor: Dr ERIC TIYO SSEKEBUGA ADRIKO
Ccl Chair.: JAMES KALEBO
Vice-Chancellor: Prof. ISAIAH OMOLO NDIEGE
Univ. Sec.: PATRICK MADAYA (acting)
Dean for Students: CYRIACO KABAGAMBE
Registrar: ANDREW CULA (acting)
Librarian: BERNARD BAZIRAKE BAMUHIIGA

Library of 150,000 vols, 12,000 periodicals
Number of students: 25,000

DEANS

Faculty of Arts and Social Sciences: Dr FILDA
  L. OJOK (acting)
Faculty of Education: Dr JOKSHAN KAHEERU-
  KATIGO
Faculty of Engineering: DAUDI MUGISA
Faculty of Science: AARON WANYAMA
Faculty of Special Needs and Rehabilitation:
  Dr JOHN B. OKECH
Faculty of Vocational Studies: Dr WILLIAM
  EPEJU
School of Management and Entrepreneur-
  ship: JOCOB OYUGI

MAKERERE UNIVERSITY

POB 7062, Kampala

Telephone: (41) 4533332
E-mail: pro@admin.mak.ac.ug
Internet: mak.ac.ug

Founded 1922 as technical school; became
  univ. college 1949, attained univ. status
  1970
State control
Language of instruction: English
Academic year: October to June

Chancellor: HE THE PRES. OF UGANDA
Vice-Chancellor: Prof. JOHN DDUMBA-SSEN-
  TAMU
Deputy Vice-Chancellor for Academic
  Affairs: Prof. LILLIAN TIBATEMWA-EKIRIKU-
  BINZA
Deputy Vice-Chancellor for Finance and
  Admin.: Prof. SANDY STEVENS TICKODRI-
  TOGBOA
Univ. Sec.: DAVID KAHUNDHA MUHWEZI
Academic Registrar: ALFRED MASIKYE
  NAMOAH
Dean for Students: CYRIACO MBOHERWA KABA-
  GAMBE
Univ. Librarian: Prof. MARIA MUSOKE

Number of teachers: 1,089
Number of students: 27,976
Publication: *Mawazo*

PROFESSORS

College of Agricultural and Environmental
Sciences (tel. (41) 2542277; e-mail pr@caes
.mak.ac.ug; internet caes.mak.ac.ug):

  BAREEBA, F. B., Animal Science
  EKWAMU, A., Crop Science
  KITUNGULU-ZAKE, Y. J., Soil Science
  KIWUWA, G. H., Animal Science
  OSIRU, D. O., Crop Science
  RUBAIHAYO, P. R.
  RUYOOKA, D., Forestry

College of Humanities and Social Sciences (tel. (41) 2542241; e-mail faculty@arts.mak.ac.ug; internet chuss.mak.ac.ug):

AKIIKI-MUJAJU, A. B., Political Science
BYARUHANGA-AKIIKI, A. B. T., Religious Studies and Philosophy
DALFOVO, A. T., Philosophy
GINGYERA-PINYCWA, A. C. G., Political Science
MUKAMA, R.
MWAKA, V. M.
TIBENDERANA, P. K., History

Faculty of Law (tel. (41) 2542284; e-mail lawdean@muklaw.ac.ug):

BAKIBINGA, D. J., Commercial Law
KAKOOZA, J. M. N., Law and Jurisprudence

Faculty of Medicine (tel. (41) 2530020; e-mail sewankam@infocom.co.ug):

ANOKBONGGO, W. W., Pharmacology and Therapeutics
BULWA, F. M., Obstetrics and Gynaecology
MMIRO, F. A., Obstetrics and Gynaecology
MUGERWA, J. W., Pathology
MUNUBE, J., Microbiology
NDUGWA, C. M., Paediatrics and Child Health
ODOI-ADOME, R., Pharmacy
OTIM, M. A., Medicine
OWOR, R., Pathology
SWEANKAMBO, N. K., Medicine

Faculty of Science (tel. (41) 2541258; e-mail deansci@mak.ac.ug):

BANAGE, W. B., Zoology
BANDA, E. K. J., Physics
ILUKOR, J. O., Physics
KAHWA, Y., Physics
KAKONGE, E., Biochemistry
LUBOOBI, L. S., Mathematics
MUGAMBE, P. E., Physics
MUGAMBI, P. E., Mathematics
OKWAKOL, M. N., Zoology
OLWA-ODYEK, Chemistry
POMEROY, D. E., Zoology
SEKAALO, H., Chemistry
TALIGOOLA, H. K., Botany
TUKAHIRWA, E., Environmental Science

Institute of Statistics and Applied Economics (tel. (41) 2534224):

NTOZI, S. P. N.
TULYA-MUHIKA

School of Education (tel. (41) 2540733; e-mail deaneduc@mak.ac.ug):

MUSAAZI, J. S., Higher Education
OCITTI, J., Geography
ODAET, C. F., Educational Foundations and Management
OPOLOT, J. A., Psychology

ATTACHED INSTITUTES

East African School of Library and Information Science: c/o Makerere Univ., POB 7062, Kampala; e-mail administration@easlis.mak.ac.ug; internet www.easlis.mak.ac.ug; f. 1963 to train librarians for all parts of East Africa; 3-year course leads to degree in Library and Information Science; Dir S. A. H. ABIDI.

Institute of Adult and Continuing Education: Kampala; f. 1953; 3 divisions: Adult Education and Communication Studies, Community Education and Extra-Mural Studies, Distance Education; one-year post-secondary school courses; shorter courses are also arranged both at the centre and in surrounding rural areas; Dir NUWA SENTONGO.

Institute of Statistics and Applied Economics: internet statistics.mak.ac.ug; a joint enterprise of the Government of Uganda and the United Nations Development Programme; depts of Planning and Applied Statistics, Population Studies, and Statistical

Methods; 3-year degree courses; Dir Dr X. R. MUGISHA.

Makerere Institute of Social Research: see under Research Institutes

MAKERERE UNIVERSITY BUSINESS SCHOOL

POB 1337, Kampala
Telephone: (41) 4338120
Internet: www.mubs.ac.ug
Founded 2000 as a distinct entity from Makerere University
State control
Language of instruction: English
Academic year: August to July
Prin.: Prof. WASWA BALUNYWA
Deputy Prin.: Assoc. Prof. Dr SAMUEL SSEJAAKA
School Registrar: ANNIE BEGUMISA
Dean for Students: EVACE NYAKOOJO
Library of 50,000 vols

DEANS

Faculty of Commerce: Dr ARTHUR SSERWANGA
Faculty of Computing and Management Science: Prof. JOSEPH M. NTAYI
Faculty of Entrepreneurship and Business Administration: Dr MOSES MUHWEZI
Faculty of Management: ANNET NABATANZI MUYIMBA
Faculty of Marketing and Hospitality Management: Assoc. Prof. GEOFFREY BAKUNDA
Faculty of Vocational and Distance Education: CHARLES OMAGOR
Graduate and Research Centre: Dr MUHAMMED NGOMA

MBARARA UNIVERSITY OF SCIENCE AND TECHNOLOGY

POB 1410, Mbarara
Telephone: (485) 420785
E-mail: ar@must.ac.ug
Internet: www.must.ac.ug
Founded 1989
State control
Language of instruction: English
Academic year: August to May
Chancellor: Prof. PETER N. MUGYENYI
Vice-Chancellor: Prof. FREDERICK I. B. KAYANJA
Deputy Vice-Chancellor: Assoc. Prof. PAMELA MBABAZI
Academic Registrar: STEPHEN BAZIRAKE BABIGUMIRA
Dean for Students: EMMANUEL KYAGABA
Univ. Librarian: ANNE GAKIBAYO
Library of 30,000 vols, 50,000 bound serials
Number of teachers: 144
Number of students: 3,163 (3,001 undergraduate, 62 postgraduate)
Publications: *Medical Journal* (1 a year), *Science Journal* (1 a year)

DEANS

Faculty of Development Studies: Prof. ROBERT MURIISA
Faculty of Medicine: Assoc. Prof. JEROME K. KABAKYENGA
Faculty of Science and Education: Prof. SIMON K. ANGUMA

PROFESSORS

BARANGA, J., Biology
BEGUMYA, Y. R., Physiology
JAEGER, B., Dermatology
KAYANJA, F. I. B., Histology
PEPPER, L., Medicine

ATTACHED INSTITUTE

Institute of Tropical Forest Conservation: POB 44, Kabale; tel. (39) 2709753;

e-mail info@itfc.org; internet www.itfc.org; Dir Dr DOUGLAS SHEIL

MOUNTAINS OF THE MOON UNIVERSITY

POB 837, Fort Portal
Telephone: (483) 22522
E-mail: info@mmu.ac.ug
Internet: www.mmu.ac.ug
Founded 2001
Private control
Language of instruction: English
Academic year: September to August (2 semesters)
Rector: Prof. JOHN KASENENE
Deputy Vice-Chancellor: Dr EDMOND KAGAMBE
Academic Registrar: Dr CHRISTOPHER MUKIDI
Finance Registrar: KAKUNGULU YUNUS
Librarian: MARGARET KATUUTU

NDEJJE UNIVERSITY

POB 7088, Kampala
Telephone: (392) 730327
E-mail: library@ndejjeuniversity.ac.ug
Internet: www.ndejjeuniversity.ac.ug
Founded 1992
Private control
Language of instruction: English
Academic year: August to June
Faculties of arts, basic sciences and information technology, business administration, education, engineering and survey, forest science and environmental management, social sciences
Vice-Chancellor: Prof. Dr ERIABU LUGUJJO
Academic Registrar: BARNABAS M. SEKABEMBE
Librarian: CLEMENT LUTAAYA NABUTTO
Library of 47,083 vols
Number of teachers: 148
Number of students: 7,500

NKUMBA UNIVERSITY

POB 237, Entebbe
Telephone: (414) 321448
E-mail: ar@nkumbauni.ac.ug
Internet: www.nkumbauniversity.ac.ug
Founded 2006
Private control
Language of instruction: English
Academic Registrar: Prof. WILSON MUYINDA MANDE

DEANS

Business Administration: F. M. NGOBO
Commercial and Industrial Art and Design: JOSEPHINE MUKASA WANYANA
Education, Humanities and Sciences: Prof. J. C. SSEKAMWA
Law: Prof. JOSEPH KAKOOZA
Sciences: FAUSTINO ORACH MEZA
Social Sciences: GEORGE MUGISHA BARENZI

ST LAWRENCE UNIVERSITY

POB 24930, Kampala
E-mail: info@slau.ac.ug
Internet: www.slau.ac.ug
Private control
Language of instruction: English
Faculties of art, business, computing and information technology, education, humanities
Vice-Chancellor: Dr FRANK MBAAGA KAKINDA

UGANDA CHRISTIAN UNIVERSITY

POB 4, Mukono
E-mail: ucu@ucu.ac.ug

Internet: www.ucu.ac.ug
Founded 1913 as Bishop Tucker Theological College, present name and status 1997
Private control
Language of instruction: English
Academic year: September to August
Chancellor: HENRY LUKE OROMBI
Vice-Chancellor: Dr JOHN MUSISI SENYONYI
Deputy Vice-Chancellor for Academic Affairs: Dr ALEX KAGUME
Deputy Vice-Chancellor for Devt and External Relations: DOUG FOUNTAIN
Deputy Vice-Chancellor for Finance and Admin.: Dr FLORENCE BAKIBINGA SAJJABI
Dir for Student Affairs: MILTON TWEHEYO
Univ. Librarian: Dr FREDRICK NATHANIEL MUKUNGU
Library of 150,000 vols, 70 periodicals
Number of teachers: 175
Number of students: 11,000 (5 campuses)

DEANS

Bishop Barham Univ. College: Prof. MANUEL MURANGA
Bishop Tucker School of Divinity and Theology: Dr OLIVIA NASSAKA BANJA
Faculty of Business and Admin.: VINCENT KISENYI
Faculty of Education and Arts: Dr MEDARD RUGYENDO
Faculty of Law: Dr PAMELA TIBIHIKIIRA-KALYEGIRA
Faculty of Science and Technology: Dr FABIAN NABUGOOMU
Faculty of Social Sciences: Dr ELIZABETH BACWAYO KUKUNDA
School of Research and Post Graduate Studies: Prof. CHRISTOPHER BYARUHANGA
UCU Mbale Campus: Dr STEPHEN MUNGOMA

UGANDA MARTYRS UNIVERSITY

POB 5498, Kampala
Telephone: (38) 2410611
E-mail: umu@umu.ac.ug
Internet: www.umu.ac.ug
Founded 1993
Private control

Academic year: August to September
Chancellor: Rt Rev. Bishop MATTHIAS SSEKAMANYA
Vice-Chancellor: Prof. Dr CHARLES OLWENY
Deputy Vice-Chancellor for Academic Affairs: Asst Prof. Dr JOSEPH KISEKKA
Deputy Vice-Chancellor for Finance and Admin.: Asst Prof. Dr SIMEON WANYAMA
Registrar: INNOCENT BYUMA
Librarian: JUDITH NANNOZI
Library of 38,435 vols
Number of teachers: 240
Number of students: 4,697
Publications: *Health Policy Journal, Journal of Science, Mtafiti Mwafrika* (African Researcher, 3 a year)

DEANS

Centre for Distance Learning: Dr GUDULA NAIGA BASAZA
Centre for Extra-Mural Studies: Dr MARTIN O'REILLY (Head)
Dept of Good Governance and Peace Studies: Dr MAXIMIANO NGABIRANO (Head)
Dept of Information and Communications Technology: CYPRIAN LWANGA (Head)
Dept of Information Systems: Prof. Dr PETER KALEMA (Head)
East African School of Diplomacy, Governance and International Studies: SAMUEL BALIGIDDE (Dir)
Faculty of Agriculture: Dr JULIUS MWINE
Faculty of Built Environment: CONNIE NSHEMEREIRWE
Faculty of Business Administration and Management: Dr ALEX IJO
Faculty of Education: Prof. ALOYSIUS BYARUHANGA
Faculty of Health Sciences: Dr JOHN FRANCIS MUGISHA
Faculty of Humanities and Social Sciences: Prof. LAURA ARIKO OTAALA
Faculty of Sciences: WILLIAM KAGGWA
Institute of Ethics and Development Studies: Dr JUDE SSEBUWUFU (Dir)
School of Postgraduate Studies: Prof. Dr PETER KANYANDAGO (Dir)

VICTORIA UNIVERSITY

Telephone: (417) 727000
E-mail: info@vu.ac.ug
Internet: www.vu.ac.ug
Private control
Language of instruction: English
Academic year: September to July
Chancellor: Prof. APOLLO NSIBAMBI

DEANS

Faculty of Business: (vacant)
Faculty of Engineering: Prof. DAWOUD SHENOUDA
Faculty of Nursing and Health Science: BARBIE ROSS

Other Higher Educational Institutes

Team Institute of Business Management: POB 8126, Kampala; Plot 446, Kabaka A'njagala Rd, Mengo-Rubaga, Kampala; e-mail info@teamibm.ac.ug; internet www.teamibm.ac.ug; f. 2010; Bachelors in accounting and finance, administrative and secretarial practice, business administration, information technology, management; Masters in finance, human resources and management, procurement and logistics; Chancellor Prof. TARSIS KABWEGYERE; Prin. Prof. A. J. LUTALO-BOSA; Institute Registrar Dr KATO HABIB; Dean for Students MUTEKANGA ESAU.

Uganda Management Institute: Plot 44–52, Jinja Rd, POB 20131, Kampala; tel. (41) 4259722; internet www.umi.ac.ug; f. 1992; schools of business, productivity and competitiveness; civil service, public administration and governance; distance learning and information technology; Dir-Gen. Dr JAMES L. NKATA.

UKRAINE

The Higher Education System

Institutions of higher education pre-date the independence of Ukraine (formerly the Ukrainian SSR) from the USSR in 1991, the oldest being the National University of Kyiv-Mohyla Academy, which was founded in 1615. The next oldest institution is the National University of Lviv 'Ivan Franko', which was founded in 1661. During the period of Soviet rule (1920–91) over 60 universities, academies and institutions of higher education were founded.

The Ministry of Education and Science is the central body supervising and managing the education sector; certain institutions may also fall under other ministries, for example health, agriculture or culture. Ukraine signed up for the Bologna Process in 2005, the first phase of which was to adopt a credit-based system of comparable degrees with two main cycles (undergraduate and graduate). Since 2006/07 the European Credit Transfer and Accumulation System (ECTS) has been introduced for all programmes of the first and second cycles, directly corresponding with the national system of credits. Specialists in the fields of medicine and veterinary medicine, however, still follow a long integrated cycle. Higher education is classified into four levels, in ascending order: technical colleges (Level I), colleges (Level II), institutes (Level III) and universities, academies and institutes (Level IV). In 2010/11 there were 2,491,300 students enrolled in 854 higher education institutions. Proposals to reduce the number of institutions via closures and mergers in a bid to strengthen and consolidate the higher education system were under discussion in 2011. A draft national qualification framework was approved in October of that year and was awaiting approval by the Cabinet of Ministers. In late 2012 a new Law on Higher Education was adopted that delegated some of the powers of the then Ministry of Education and Science, and Youth and Sport to the Ukrainian Center for Educational Quality Assessment (UCEQA) and extended the autonomy of higher education institutions. A working group was also in place to develop criteria for evaluating higher education establishments.

The main requirements for admission to higher education are award of the Atestat pro Povnu Zagal'nu Sersdniu Osvitu (General Secondary Education Certificate) and satisfactory performance in university entrance examinations. Admission to universities from 2013 onwards was to be based on external independent testing, a system implemented since 2010 by the Ukrainian Standardized External Testing Initiative in alliance with, and funded by, the United States Agency for International Development. The UCEQA is responsible for the system that will replace examinations administered by individual universities in order to ensure a uniform entry standard that also meets international standards. In 1996 Ukraine introduced a two-tier Bachelors and Masters degree system. More recently, further reforms have been effected, including the introduction in 2006/07 of the ECTS, in accordance with the principles of the Bologna Process; however, the old-style degrees are still available. The Dyplom Bakalavra (Bachelors) is an undergraduate degree of four years, and is offered parallel to the Dyplom Spetsialista (Specialist Diploma), an integrated five-year programme of study mostly offered by institutes. The first postgraduate degree under the new system is the Dyplom Magistra (Masters), which lasts for one or two years after the award of the Dyplom Bakalavra or Dyplom Spetsialista. Finally, doctoral-level studies consist of two awards, both lasting three years: the Dyplom pro Prysudzhenia Naukovogo Stupenia Kandydata Nauk (Diploma of Candidate of Sciences) and Dyplom pro Prysudzhenia Naukovogo Stupenia Doktora Nauk (Diploma of Doctor of Sciences).

Vocational education is provided by technical and vocational schools, which offer Qualification Certificates and Junior Specialist Diplomas. According to the State Statistics Committee, in 2009/10 there were 975 vocational education and training institutions with some 424,300 students enrolled.

Regulatory and Representative Bodies

GOVERNMENT

Ministry of Culture: 01601 Kyiv, vul. Ivana Franka Str. 19; tel. (44) 235-23-78; e-mail info@mincult.gov.ua; internet mincult.kmu.gov.ua; Minister LEONID M. NOVOKHATKO.

Ministry of Education and Science: 01135 Kyiv, pr. Peremohi 10; tel. (44) 486-32-21; e-mail ministry@mon.gov.ua; internet www.mon.gov.ua; Minister DMYTRO VOLODYMYROVYCH TABACHNYK.

ACCREDITATION

ENIC/NARIC Ukraine: Dept for Licensing and Accreditation, Min. of Education and Science, 10 Ave Pobedy, 01135 Kyiv; tel. (44) 486-74-09; e-mail dlan@mon.gov.ua; internet www.mon.gov.ua; attached to Dept for Scientific Research and Licensing, Min. of Education and Science; recognizes academic foreign qualifications; verifies educational documents issued in Ukraine (apostille); int. academic mobility; Dir MICHAEL GONCHARENKO.

NATIONAL BODIES

Academy of Pedagogical Sciences of Ukraine: 04053 Kyiv, Artema vul. 52A; tel. (44) 211-94-01; e-mail info@apsu.org.ua; internet www.apsu.org.ua; f. 1992; Pres. Prof. VASYL H. KREMEN; publs *Biolohiya i Khimiya v Shkoli* (Biology and Chemistry at School, 4 a year), *Compyuter v Shkoli i Simyi* (Computer at School and at Home, 4 a year), *Defektolohiya* (Defectology, 4 a year), *Fizyka i Astronomiya v Shkoli* (Physics and Astronomy at School, 4 a year), *Heohrafiya i Osnovy Ekonomiky v Shkoli* (Geography and Fundamentals of Economics at School, 4 a year), *Istoriya v Shkolakh Ukrainy* (History in Ukrainian Schools, 4 a year), *Matemmatyka v Shkoli* (Mathematics at School, 4 a year), *Mystetstvo i Osvita* (Arts and Education, 4 a year), *Nauka i Osvita* (Science and Education, 2 a year), *Obdarovana Dytyna* (Gifted Child, 6 a year), *Pedahohichna Hazeta* (Pedagogical Newspaper, 12 a year), *Pedahohika i Psykholohiya* (Pedagogy and Psychology, 4 a year), *Praktychna Psykholohiya i Sotsialna Robota* (Applied Psychology and Social Work, 12 a year), *Profesiyno-Tekhnichna Osvita* (Vocational and Technical Education, 4 a year), *Shlyakh Osvity* (A Way of Education, 4 a year), *Ukrainska Literatura v Zahalnoosvitniy Shkoli* (Ukrainian Literature at Secondary School, 6 a year), *Ukrainska Mova i Literatura v Shkoli* (Ukrainian Language and Literature at School, 4 a year), *Vyshcha Osvita Ukrainy* (Higher Education in Ukraine, 4 a year), *Zarubizhna Literatura v Navchalnykh Zakladakh* (Foreign Literature at Educational Institutions, 12 a year).

Association of Non-State-Owned Educational Institutions of Ukraine: 252115 Kyiv, 16-v Vernadsky Ave; tel. (44) 452-76-55; e-mail assoc@ufimb.kiev.ua; internet www.ambernet.kiev.ua/~tlc/aeiunfp/index_e.htm; f. 1993; aims to improve the educational system in Ukraine; 68 mem. instns; Head Prof. IVAN TIMOSCHENKO.

Union of Rectors of Higher Educational Institutions of Ukraine: 01601 Kyiv, vul. Volodymyrska 60, of. 200; tel. (44) 239-31-52; e-mail uni_rect@univ.kiev.ua; internet www.vnz.univ.kiev.ua; f. 1993; drafts recommendations regarding solutions for higher education and advances them to the Govt; represents and protects the interests of its mems; Pres. Prof. Dr LEONID V. HUBERSKY.

Learned Societies

GENERAL

National Academy of Sciences of Ukraine: 01601 Kyiv, Volodymyrska 54; tel. (44) 225-22-39; e-mail prez@nas.gov.ua; internet www.nas.gov.ua; f. 1918; sections of chemical and biological sciences, physical-technical and mathematical sciences, social sciences and humanities; depts of chemistry, earth sciences, economics, general biology, history, philosophy and law, informatics, literature, language and art criticism, mathematics, mechanics, molecular biology, biochemistry and experimental and clinical physiology, physical and technical problems of materials science, physical and technical problems of power engineering, physics and astronomy; attached research institutes: see under Research Institutes; 708 mems (207 full, 378 corresp., 123 foreign); library: see under Libraries and Archives; Pres. Acad. BORIS PATON; Vice-Pres. Acad. ANATOLIY SHPAK; Chief Scientific Sec. ANATOLIY ZAGORODNY; publs in Ukrainian and English: *Dopovidi NAN Ukrainy, Ekonomika Ukrainy* (Economy of Ukraine, 12 a year), *Kosmichna Nauka i Tekhnologiya* (Space Science and Engineering, 6 a year), *Kyivska Starovyna* (Kyiv Antiquities, 6 a year), *Visnyk NAN Ukrainy* (Journal of the National Academy of Sciences of Ukraine,12 a year, in Ukrainian and English).

Shevchenko Scientific Society: 290013 Lviv, vul. hen. Chuprynka 21; tel. (322) 34-51-63; e-mail ntsh@ipm.lviv.ua; internet www.ntsh.org; f. 1873; broad range of arts and sciences; library of 30,000 vols; Chair. OLEG KUPCHINSKY; publ. *Memoires* (2 a year).

AGRICULTURE, FISHERIES AND VETERINARY SCIENCE

Ukrainian Academy of Agrarian Sciences: 01010 Kyiv, vul. Suvorova 9; tel. (44) 226-32-84; e-mail uaas@aginukraine .com; internet www.aginukraine.com/uaas; f. 1990; 4,900 mems; attached research institutes: see Research Institutes; publ. *Visnyk Agrarnoi Nauky* (12 a year).

ARCHITECTURE AND TOWN PLANNING

National Union of Architects of Ukraine: 01001 Kyiv, vul. Hrychenka 7; tel. (44) 279-98-09; Pres. IHOR SHPARA.

BIBLIOGRAPHY, LIBRARY SCIENCE AND MUSEOLOGY

Association of Libraries of Ukraine: 03039 Kyiv, pr. Richchya Zhovtnya 3; tel. (44) 265-81-04; e-mail nlu@csl.freenet.kiev .ua; internet www.nbuv.gov.ua; Pres. OLEKSIY S. ONYSCHENKO.

ECONOMICS, LAW AND POLITICS

Academy of Legal Sciences of Ukraine: 61024 Kharkiv, vul. Pushkinska 70; tel. (57) 704-19-01; e-mail aprnu@online.kharkiv .com; internet www.aprnu.kharkiv.org; f. 1993; Pres. Acad. VASIL YA. TATSIY.

FINE AND PERFORMING ARTS

National Artists' Union of Ukraine: 04053 Kyiv, vul. Sichovykh Striltsiv 1–5; tel. (44) 212-01-33; e-mail spilka@nbi.com.ua; internet www.nshu.org.ua; f. 1938; 33 regional constituent orgs; 4,330 mems; Head VOLODYMYR A. CHEPELNIK.

National Union of Cinematographers of Ukraine: 01033 Kyiv, vul. Saksahanskoho 6; tel. (44) 287-75-57; e-mail ukrkino@ln.ua; internet www.ukrkino.com.ua; f. 1958; 1,251 mems; Head BORIS I. SAVCHENKO.

National Writers' Union of Ukraine: 01024 Kyiv, vul. Bankova 2; tel. (44) 293-45-86; e-mail nspu@i.kiev.ua; internet www .nspu.kiev.ua; f. 1934 as part of the Writers' Union of the former USSR; 1,600 mems; Head VOLODYMYR O. YAVORIVSKY.

HISTORY, GEOGRAPHY AND ARCHAEOLOGY

Ukrainian Geographical Society: 03022 Kyiv, vul. Vasilkivska 90; e-mail vpsh@icchq .univ.kiev.ua; Head PETRO H. SHISHCHENKO.

LANGUAGE AND LITERATURE

British Council: 04070 Kyiv, 4/12 vul. Hryhoriya Skovorody; tel. (44) 490-56-00; e-mail enquiry@britishcouncil.org.ua; internet www.britishcouncil.org/ukraine; teaching centre; offers courses and exams in English language and British culture; promotes cultural exchange with the UK; attached offices in Donetsk, Kharkiv, Lviv and Odessa; training and professional development centre; Dir TERRY SANDELL; Teaching Centre Man. TONY HUBBARD.

Goethe-Institut: 04655 Kyiv, vul. Voloska, 12/4; tel. (44) 496-97-85; e-mail info@kiew .goethe.org; internet www.goethe.de/ ukraine; f. 1994; offers courses and exams in German language and culture; promotes cultural exchange with Germany; Dir VERA BAGALIANTZ; Deputy Dir PETRA KÖPPEL MEYER.

Institut Français d'Ukraine: 01054 Kiev, 84, rue Hontchara; tel. (44) 482-23-71; e-mail standard@ifu.kiev.ua; internet www .institutfrancais-ukraine.com; f. 1994; offers courses and exams in French language and culture; promotes cultural exchange with France; attached Institut Français in Kharkiv; works in cooperation with the chain of Alliances Françaises in Ukraine: Dnepropetrovsk, Donetsk, Kharkiv, Lougansk, Lviv, Odessa, Rivne, Sebastopol, Simferopol and Zaporijjia.

MEDICINE

Gerontology and Geriatrics Society: Institute of Gerontology, 252655 Kyiv 114, Vyshgorodska vul. 67; tel. (44) 430-40-68; e-mail admin@geront.kiev.ua; f. 1963; 250 mems; library of 72,000 vols; Chair. V. V. BEZRUKOV; Chief Learned Sec. O. K. KULTCHITSKY; publ. *Problems of Ageing and Longevity* (4 a year).

National Academy of Medical Sciences of Ukraine: 04050 Kyiv, vul. Gertsena 12; tel. (44) 483-34-11; e-mail drbut@ukr.net; internet www.amnu.kiev.ua; f. 1993; attached research institutes: see under Research Institutes; 132 mems (incl. 77 corresp. mems and 19 foreign mems); Pres. ANDRII SERDYUK; Chief Scientific Sec. VOLODYMYR A. MIKHNOV; publ. *Journal* (4 a year).

Ukrainian Association of Radiologists: 03022 Kyiv, vul. Lomonsova 33/43; tel. (44) 258-97-86; e-mail aru-kiev@ukr.net; internet www.aruk.org; f. 1992; 6,000 mems; Chair. Prof. VLADIMIR E. MEDVEDEV; publ. *Radiodiagnostics and Radiotherapy* (4 a year).

Ukrainian Physiological Society: 01024 Kyiv, vul. Bohomoltsya 4; tel. (44) 253-29-09; e-mail pkostyuk@biph.kiev.ua; internet uaphsoc.biph.kiev.ua; Head Acad. PLATON H. KOSTYUK; publ. *Fiziologichnyi Zhurnal* (Physiological Journal, 6 a year).

Ukrainian Scientific Society of Cardiologists: c/o Institute of Cardiology 'M. D. Strazhevska', 03151 Kyiv, vul. Narodnogo Opolcheniya 5; tel. (44) 449-70-03; internet www.ukrcardio.org; Pres. VOLODYMYR KOVALENKO.

Ukrainian Scientific Society of Hygienists: 02660 Kyiv, vul. Popudrenka 50; tel. (44) 559-90-90; e-mail regina@usch.kiev.ua; f. 1953; Head ANDRIY M. SERDYUK.

Ukrainian Society of Allergology and Clinical Immunology: c/o Dept of Immunology and Allergy, National Medical University 'O. Bohomolets', 04053 Kyiv, vul. Kotsyubinskoho 9A; tel. (44) 216-54-03; Chair. Prof. H. DRANNIK.

Ukrainian Society of Ophthalmologists: c/o Institute of Eye Diseases and Tissue Therapy, 'V. P. Filatov', 65061 Odessa, bul. Frantsuzsky 49/51; tel. (48) 60-34-46; e-mail iryna.ods@gmail.com; f. 1936; 1,200 mems.

NATURAL SCIENCES

General

Union of Scientific and Engineering Associations of Ukraine: 04053 Kyiv, vul. Artema 21; tel. (44) 212-42-85.

Biological Sciences

Ukrainian Biochemical Society: c/o Palladin Institute of Biochemistry, 01601 Kyiv, vul. Leontovicha 9; tel. (44) 234-59-74; e-mail secretar@biochem.kiev.ua; internet www .biochemistry.org.ua; f. 1928; organizes congresses, seminars and confs; 680 mems; library of 86,000 vols; Chair. Prof. SERHIY V. KOMISARENKO; publs *Biotechnologia* (Biotechnology, 6 a year, in Ukrainian, English and Russian), *Ukrainskyi Biokhimichnyi Zhurnal* (Ukrainian Biochemical Journal, 6 a year, in Ukrainian, English and Russian).

Physical Sciences

Ukrainian Physical Society: 03680 Kyiv, pr. Glushkova 4; tel. (44) 526-40-36; e-mail krav@univ.kiev.ua; internet www.ups.kiev .ua; f. 1990; 425 mems; Pres. Prof. VOLODYMYR G. LITOVCHENKO.

Ukrainian Society of Geodesy, Aerospace Surveying and Cartography: c/o Ministry of Ecology and Natural Resources of Ukraine, 02094 Kyiv, vul. Popudrenka 54; tel. (44) 268-21-09; e-mail ssavchuk@polynet .lviv.ua; Pres. IHOR TREVOHO.

PHILOSOPHY AND PSYCHOLOGY

Ukrainian Psychological Society: 01032 Kyiv, bul. T. Shevchenka 27A, Office 305; tel. (44) 246-54-59; e-mail ucap@ukr.net; Dir Dr VITALIY PANOK.

RELIGION, SOCIOLOGY AND ANTHROPOLOGY

Sociological Association of Ukraine: 01021 Kyiv, vul. Shovkovychna 12; tel. (44) 291-52-46; e-mail rector@univer.kharkov.ua; internet www.sau.kiev.ua; Dir Dr N. SHULGA.

TECHNOLOGY

Chornobyl Center for Nuclear Safety, Radioactive Waste and Radioecology: 07100 Kyiv, Slavutych, vul. Hvardeyskoi Divizii 77, 7/1; tel. (44) 792-30-16; e-mail center@chornobyl.net; internet www .chornobyl.net; f. 1996; Coordinating Dir Prof. YEVGEN V. GARIN.

Ukrainian Society for Non-Destructive Testing: 03680 Kyiv, vul. Bozhenko 11; tel. (44) 287-26-66; e-mail usndt@ukr.net; internet www.usndt.com.ua; f. 1990; 200 mems; Pres. Prof. VOLODYMYR TROITSKIY.

Ukrainian Society for Soil Mechanics, Geotechnicas and Foundation Engineering: 03680 Kyiv, Ivana Klimenka 5/2; tel. (44) 248-89-42; e-mail adm-inst@ndibk .kiev.ua; f. 2001; promotes theory and practice of stabilization of weak soils in bases; interaction of upper structure and soil; devt of new technologies for bases preparation; other practical issues in the field of building; 138 mems; Pres. Prof. PETRO KRYVOSHEIEV; publ. *Geotechnic World*.

Ukrainian Society of Mechanical Engineers: c/o Br. of Mechanics of the Nat. Acad. of Sciences of Ukraine, 49600 Dnipropetrovsk, vul. Leshko-Popelya 15; tel. (56) 745-12-38; e-mail itm@pvv.dp.ua; internet www.itm.dp .ua; Pres. Acad. VIKTOR PYLYPENKO.

Research Institutes

AGRICULTURE, FISHERIES AND VETERINARY SCIENCE

Dairy and Meat Technology Institute: M. Raskovoi 4A, Kyiv 02660; tel. (44) 517-17-37; e-mail verb@timm.kiev.ua; internet www .timm.kiev.ua; f. 1959; attached to Ukrainian Acad. of Agricultural Sciences; library of 27,000 vols; Dir G. A. ERESKO; publ. *Meat and Milk* (6 a year).

Institute of Agricultural Economics: 03680 Kyiv, vul. Geroev Oborony 10; tel. (44) 261-43-21; e-mail info@iae.com.ua; f. 1956; attached to Ukrainian Acad. of Agricultural Sciences; Dir PETRO SABLUK; publ. *Economics of AIC* (12 a year).

Institute of Agriculture: 08162 Kievska oblast, Kyevo-Svyatoshinsky raion, Chabani; tel. (44) 526-23-27; e-mail selection@ukrpack .net; internet www.zemlerobstvo.com; f. 1900; attached to Ukrainian Acad. of Agrarian Sciences; agriculture, crop-growing technologies, agricultural crops selection; library of 35,900 vols in scientific library; 100,000 in total; publs *Agriculture* (1 a year), *Proceedings of the International and All-Ukrainian Congresses.*

Institute of Beekeeping, P. I. Prokopovych: 03143 Kyiv, vul. Zabolotnogo 19; tel. (44) 266-67-98; e-mail prokopovych@ukr.net; f. 1989; attached to Ukrainian Acad. of Agrarian Sciences; library of 4,000 vols; Dir LEONID BODNARCHUK; publs *Apiary* (12 a year), *Beekeeping* (1 a year), *Ukrainian Beekeeper.*

Institute of Cereals: 49600 Dnipropetrovsk, vul. Dzerzhinskogo 14; tel. (56) 244-45-49; e-mail grain@online.alkar.net; f. 1930; attached to Ukrainian Acad. of Agrarian Sciences; maize, winter wheat, other cereals and leguminous plants; library of 110,000 vols; Dir Dr YEVGEN LEBID; publ. *Bulletin* (2 a year).

Institute of Fisheries: 03164 Kyiv, vul. Obukhivska 165; tel. (44) 423-74-61; e-mail vitbekh@online.com.ua; attached to Ukrainian Acad. of Agrarian Sciences; research and devt into the exploitation of aquatic living resources in inland waters; fish genetics and selection; environmental safety; stock conservation and rehabilitation of rare and endangered species; and economic efficiency of Ukrainian fisheries; library of 50,000 vols; Dir OLEKSANDR TRETYAK; publ. *Rybne Gospodarstvo* (1 a year).

Institute of Mechanization of Animal Husbandry: 69097 Zaporizhzya, Island Khortitca; tel. (612) 289-81-44; e-mail imtuaan@ukr.net; internet www.imt.zp.ua; f. 1930; attached to Nat. Acad. of Agrarian Sciences of Ukraine; research centre for electrification of agriculture; library of 45,000 vols; Dir Dr Hab. IGOR ARKADIEVICH SHEVCHENKO; publ. *Mechanization, Ecology, Conversion of Bioresources in Animal Husbandry* (4 a year).

Institute of Plant Protection: 03022 Kyiv, 33 Vasilkovskaya; tel. (44) 257-11-24; e-mail plant_prot@ukr.net; internet ippuaan.by.ru; f. 1946; attached to Ukrainian Acad. of Agrarian Sciences; Dir Acad. Prof. Dr VITALIY FEDORENKO; publs *Karantyn i Zahyst Roslyn* (Plant Quarantine and Protection, 12 a year), *Ukrainian Entomological Journal* (2 a year), *Zahayst i Karantyn Roslyn* (Plant Protection and Quarantine, 2 a year).

Institute of Veterinary Research of the Ukrainian Academy of Agricultural Sciences: 03151 Kyiv, vul. Donetska 30; tel. (44) 245-78-05; e-mail vet@ivm.kiev.ua; internet www.ivm.kiev.ua; attached to Ukrainian Acad. of Agricultural Sciences; Dir ANATOLIY OBRAZHEV; publ. *Veterinary Biotechnology* (2 a year).

Land Use Research Institute: 03151 Kyiv, Narodnogo Opolcheniya 3; tel. (44) 275-73-88; f. 1961; attached to Ukrainian Acad. of Agrarian Sciences; Dir DMITRO S. DOBRYAK; publ. *Land-Use Systems* (4 a year).

Magarach Institute of the Vine and Wine: 334200 the Autonomous Republic of Crimea, Yalta, ul. Kirova 31; tel. (65) 432-55-91; e-mail magarach@yalita.yalta.iuf.net; f. 1828; Dir A. M. AVIDZBA; publs *Magarach–Vinogradarstvo i Vinodelie* (4 a year, in Russian, also English summaries), *Proceedings of the Magarach Institute for Vine and Wine* (2 a year, in Russian), *Proceedings of the Scientific Centre of Viticulture and Oenology* (2 a year, in Russian).

Pig Breeding Institute 'O. V. Kvasnitsky': 36006 Poltava, Shvedska Mogila 1; tel. (53) 252-74-19; e-mail slsvin@e-mail.pl .ua; internet web.poltava.ua/firms/slsvin; f. 1930; library of 60,000 vols; Dir Prof. VALENTIN P. RYBALKO; publ. *Pig Breeding* (1 a year).

Plant Breeding and Genetics Institute—National Center of Seed and Cultivar Investigation: 65036 Odessa, Ovidiopolska doroga 3; tel. (482) 39-54-01; e-mail sgi-uaan@ukr.net; internet www.sgi.od.ua; f. 1912; attached to National Acad. of Agricultural Sciences of Ukraine; devt of breeding and seed production theory, as well as new varieties and hybrids of winter bread and durum wheat, spring and winter barley, maize, sunflower, soybean, alfalfa, sorghum; genetic and genomic research, biotechnology; operates 4 experimental farms for seed production; holds confs and workshops on genetic and plant breeding topics; courses for agronomists and seed-growers; 3-year postdoctoral courses; library of 186,754 vols; Dir Dr VIACHESLAV SOKOLOV; publ. *Collected Scientific Papers* (2 a year).

Institute of Bioenergy Crops and Sugar Beet: 03141 Kyiv, Klinichna vul. 25; tel. (44) 275-50-00; e-mail sugarbeet@ukr.net; internet www.sugarbeet.gov.ua; f. 1922; attached to Ukrainian Acad. of Agrarian Sciences; library of 28,000 vols, 30,000 periodicals; Dir M. V. ROIK; publ. *Tsukrovi buryaky* (Sugar Beet, 6 a year).

Ukrainian Research Institute of Water Management and Ecological Problems: 252010 Kyiv, Inzhenerny prov. 4B; tel. (44) 280-03-02; e-mail undiwep@ukrwecol.kiev .ua; internet www.nbuv.gov.ua/undiwep; f. 1974; library of 10,000 vols; Dir Prof. A. V. YATSYK.

Ukrainian Scientific Research Institute of Ecological Problems: 61166 Kharkiv, vul. Bakulina 6; tel. (57) 702-15-92; e-mail director@niiep.kharkov.ua; internet www .niiep.kharkov.ua; f. 1971 as the All-Union Scientific Research Institute for Protection of Water; Dir Dr GRIGORY D. KOVALENKO (acting).

'V. M. Remeslo' Mironovka Institute of Wheat: 08853 Kievska oblast, P/o Tsentralne Mironovka; tel. (45) 747-41-35; e-mail mwheats@ukr.net; f. 1911; attached to Nat. Acad. of Agrarian Sciences of Ukraine; wheat and barley breeding, seed production and plant growing; library of 40,000 vols; Dir VALENTYN KOCHMARSKYI; publ. *Annual Collected Papers.*

Zakarpatsky Institute of Agroindustrial Production: 90252 Zakarpatska oblast,

Beregovo raion, Selo V. Bakhta; tel. (3141) 2-34-04; f. 1989; 114 mems; library of 40,000 vols; Dir A. V. BAYLAN; publ. *Problems of Agroindustrial Complex of Karpaty* (every 2 years).

ARCHITECTURE AND TOWN PLANNING

Research Institute of Automated Systems in Construction: 03037 Kyiv, vul. M. Krivonosa 2A; tel. (44) 249-72-30; e-mail office@ndiasb.kiev.ua; internet www.ndiasb .kiev.ua; Dir BORIS A. VOLOBOEV.

State Research Institute of Building Constructions: 03680 Kyiv, Ivan Klimenko 5/2; tel. (44) 249-72-34; e-mail adm-inst@ ndibk.kiev.ua; internet www.niisk.com; f. 1943; bldg structures: modelling, designing, testing; 500 mems; library of 49,000 vols, 72,000 patents; Dir Dr GENNEDIY FARENYUK (acting); publs *Building Construction* (2 a year), *World of Geotechnics* (3 a year).

Ukrainian Zonal Scientific and Research Design Institute of Civil Engineering: 01133 Kyiv, bul. L. Ukrainki 26; tel. (44) 286-36-72; e-mail zniiep@adam .kiev.ua; internet www.zniiep.com.ua; f. 1963; library of 125,000 vols; Dir VLADIMIR B. SHEVELEV.

ECONOMICS, LAW AND POLITICS

Council for the Study of Productive Forces of Ukraine: 01032 Kyiv 32, bul. Taras Shevchenka 60; tel. (44) 486-90-66; e-mail komisar@bigmir.net; f. 1934; attached to Nat. Acad. of Sciences of Ukraine; 6 attached scientific schools; Chair. Dr A. A. KOVALENKO.

Institute for Economic Research and Policy Consulting: 01034 Kyiv, Reytarska 8/5-A; tel. (44) 278-63-42; e-mail institute@ier .kiev.ua; internet www.ier.kiev.ua; Dir IGOR BURAKOVSKY.

Institute of Economics: 01011 Kyiv, vul. Panasa Mirnogo 26; tel. (44) 290-84-44; e-mail instecon@ln.ua; f. 1936; attached to Nat. Acad. of Sciences of Ukraine; Dir I. I. LUKINOV.

Institute of Industrial Economics: 83048 Donetsk, Universitetska vul. 77; tel. (62) 55-78-44; e-mail admin@iep.donetsk.ua; f. 1969; attached to Nat. Acad. of Sciences of Ukraine; Dir A. I. AMOSHA; publ. *Ekonomika Promyslovosti* (Economics of Industry, 4 a year, in Ukrainian and Russian).

Institute of State and Law 'V. M. Koretsky': 01601 Kyiv, vul. Tryokhsviatitelskai 4; tel. (44) 278-51-55; e-mail jus@ukrpack .net; f. 1948; attached to Nat. Acad. of Sciences of Ukraine; research into the theory and practice of law and state-bldg; Dir YU. S. SHEMSHUCHENKO; publs *Lawful State* (1 a year), *Pravo Ukrainy* (Law of Ukraine, 12 a year, in Ukrainian and English).

Institute of World Economy and International Relations: 01030 Kyiv, vul. Leontovicha 5; tel. (44) 235-70-22; e-mail iweir_nas@iweir.org.ua; internet www.iweir .org.ua; f. 1992; attached to Nat. Acad. of Sciences of Ukraine; Dir Y. M. PAKHOMOV.

HISTORY, GEOGRAPHY AND ARCHAEOLOGY

Institute of Archaeology: 04210 Kyiv, Heroyiv Stalingrada 12; tel. (44) 418-27-75; e-mail sekretar@iananu.kiev.ua; internet www.iananu.kiev.ua; attached to Nat. Acad. of Sciences of Ukraine; Dir P. P. TOLOCHKO; publ. *Arkheologia* (Archaeology, 4 a year, in Ukrainian and English).

Krypiakevych, I., Institute of Ukrainian Studies: 79026 Lviv, Kozelnytska vul. 4; tel. (32) 270-70-22; e-mail inukr@inst-ukr.lviv

.ua; internet www.inst-ukr.lviv.ua; f. 1951; attached to Nat. Acad. of Sciences of Ukraine; archaeology, history, philology, political science; library of 10,000 vols; Dir YAROSLAV D. ISAIEVYCH; publs *Istorychni ta kulturolohichni studii* (4 a year), *Shashkevychiana* (1 a year), *Ukraina: kulturna spadshchyna, natsionalna svidomist, derzhavnist* (2 a year), *Ukrainska dialektna ta istorychna leksyka* (1 a year).

Ukrainian Institute of History: 01001 Kyiv, vul. Hrushevsky 4; tel. (44) 229-63-62; e-mail institute@history.org.ua; internet www.history.org.ua; attached to Nat. Acad. of Sciences of Ukraine; Dir V. A. SMOLIY; publ. *Ukrainsky Istorychny Zhurnal* (Ukrainian Historical Journal, 6 a year, in Ukrainian and English).

LANGUAGE AND LITERATURE

Institute of Linguistics 'O. O. Potebni': 01001 Kyiv, vul. Hrushevsky 4; tel. (44) 229-02-92; attached to Nat. Acad. of Sciences of Ukraine; Dir V. H. SKLIARENKO; publ. *Movoznavstvo* (Linguistics, 6 a year, in Ukrainian and English).

Institute of Literature 'Shevchenko, T. G.': 01001 Kyiv 1, Hrushevskoho 4; tel. (44) 279-10-84; e-mail admin@ilnan.gov.ua; internet www.ilnan.gov.ua; f. 1926; attached to Nat. Acad. of Sciences of Ukraine; history of Ukrainian literature; source and textual researches of Ukrainian literature; Shevchenko studies; history of foreign literatures; theory of literature and methodology of literary researches; comparative literature; literature bibliography; library of 150,000 vols; Dir MYKOLA ZHULYNSKY; publ. *Slovo i Chas* (Word and Time, 12 a year, in Ukrainian).

MEDICINE

Donetsk Scientific Research Institute of Traumatology and Orthopaedics: 83048 Donetsk, vul. Artema 106; tel. (62) 311-05-08; e-mail info@dniito.org.ua; internet www.dniito.org.ua; f. 1953; Dir Prof. Dr VOLODYMYR KLYMOVYTSKYY; publ. *Trauma* (4 a year).

Filatov Institute for Eye Diseases and Tissue Therapy: 65061 Odessa, vul. Frantsi 49–51; tel. (48) 268-62-18; e-mail filatovorg@ukr.net; internet www.filatovinstitut.com.ua; f. 1936; library of 81,000 vols; Dir Prof. IVAN M. LOGAI; publ. *Ophthalmological Journal* (8 a year).

Grigoriev Institute of Medical Radiology: 61024 Kharkiv, vul. Pushkinska 82; tel. (57) 704-10-65; e-mail imr@ukr.net; internet www.medradiologia.kharkov.ua; f. 1920; attached to Nat. Academy of Medical Science of Ukraine; research, clinical and educational centre; 5 depts: cancer surgery, chemotherapy, nuclear medicine, radiation pathology, radiotherapy; investigates radiation lesions, radiation cytognetics and biodosimetry, immunology, endocrinology, radioprotectors, radiation hygiene and dosimetry; library of 70,000 vols; Dir Prof. Dr MYKOLA I. PYLYPENKO; publ. *Ukrainian Journal of Radiology* (4 a year).

Institute for Occupational Health: 01033 Kyiv, vul. Saksakanskogo 75; tel. (44) 284-34-27; e-mail yik@nanu.kiev.ua; f. 1928; attached to Nat. Acad. of Medical Sciences of Ukraine; occupational health, toxicology of pesticides, industrial toxicology, physiology of mental work and nanotoxicology; library of 50,000 vols; Dir Prof. Y. I. KUNDIEV; publ. *Ukrainian Journal of Occupational Health* (4 a year).

Institute for Problems of Cryobiology and Cryomedicine: 61015 Kharkiv, Pereyaslavskaya St 23; tel. (57) 373-41-43;

e-mail cryo@online.kharkov.ua; internet www.cryo.org.ua; f. 1972; attached to Nat. Acad. of Sciences of Ukraine; library of 54,011 vols; Dir Acad. Prof. Dr ANATOLIY N. GOLTSEV (acting); publ. *Problemy Kriobiologii* (Problems of Cryobiology, 4 a year, in Ukrainian, Russian and English).

Institute of Cardiovascular Surgery, M. Amosov: 03110 Kiev, M. Amosova vul. 6; tel. (44) 275-43-22; e-mail gvknyshov@ukr.net; f. 1983; 980 mems; Dir Prof. GENNADY V. KNYSHOV; Deputy Dir Prof. VITALY B. MAKSYMENKO; publ. *Annual of Cardiovascular Surgery* (1 a year).

Institute of Clinical Radiology: 04075 Kyiv, Pushcha-Voditsa, vul. Gamarnikova 42; attached to Ukrainian Acad. of Medical Sciences; Dir VOLODYMYR BEBESHKO.

Institute of Dermatology and Venereology: 61057 Kharkiv, Chernyshevskogo vul. 7/9; tel. (57) 706-32-00; e-mail idvamnu@mail.ru; internet www.idvamnu.com.ua; f. 1924; attached to Acad. of Medical Sciences of Ukraine; library of 40,000 vols; Dir Prof. IVAN I. MAVROV; publ. *Journal of Dermatology and Venereology* (4 a year).

Institute of Epidemiology and Infectious Diseases 'L. V. Gromashevsky': 01601 Kyiv, vul. S. Razina 4; tel. (44) 277-37-11; Dir A. F. FROLOV.

Institute of Gerontology: 04114 Kyiv, Vyshgorodska vul. 67; tel. (44) 430-40-68; e-mail ig@geront.kiev.ua; internet www.geront.kiev.ua; f. 1963; attached to Ukrainian Acad. of Medical Sciences; library of 72,000 vols; Dir VLADISLAV V. BEZRUKOV; Sec. O. K. KULTCHITSKY; publ. *Problemy stareniya i dolgoletiya* (Problems of Ageing and Longevity, 4 a year).

Institute of Otolaryngology named after Prof. O. S. Kolomiychenko of National Academy of Medical Sciences of Ukraine: 03057 Kyiv, Zoologichna 3; tel. (44) 483-22-02; e-mail amtc@kndio.kiev.ua; internet iol.com.ua; f. 1960; diagnostics, conservative and surgical treatment of patients with ENT-diseases; library of 33,000 vols; Dir Prof. DMYTRO ZABOLOTNYI; publs *Journal of Ear, Nose and Throat Diseases* (6 a year), *Rhinology* (4 a year).

Institute of Pediatrics, Obstetrics and Gynaecology: 04050 Kyiv, Platona Mayborody 8; tel. (44) 483-80-67; e-mail ipag@ukr.net.

Institute of Surgery and Transplantology: 03680 Kyiv, vul. Geroev Sevastopolya 30; tel. (44) 488-13-74; e-mail surgery@i.com.ua; internet www.surgery.org.ua; f. 1972; library of 25,000 vols; Dir Prof. VALERY SAYENKO; publ. *Clinical Surgery* (12 a year).

Kyiv 'N. D. Strazhesko' Research Institute of Cardiology: 03151 Kyiv, vul. Narodnogo Opolchenia 5; tel. (44) 277-66-22; f. 1936; 650 mems; library of 65,000 vols; Dir Prof. V. A. BOBROV.

Kyiv Research Institute of Oncology: Kyiv, vul. Lomonosova 33/43; tel. (44) 266-75-67; f. 1920; library of 27,000 vols; Dir V. L. GANUL.

L. I. Medved's Institute of Ecohygiene and Toxicology: 03680 Kyiv, Heroiv Oborony St 6; tel. (44) 526-97-00; e-mail office@medved.kiev.ua; internet www.medved.kiev.ua; f. 1964; library of 42,000 vols; Dir Prof. Dr MYKOLA PRODANCHUK; publs *Modern Problems of Toxicology* (4 a year), *Preventive Medicine* (4 a year), *Problems of Nutrition* (4 a year).

Lviv Scientific Research Institute of Hereditary Pathology: 79000 Lviv, vul. Lysenko 31A; tel. (32) 276-54-99; f. 1940; library of 28,000 vols; Dir O. Z. HNATEIKO; publ. *Medychna Genetyka* (every 2 years, in

Ukrainian with Russian and English abstracts).

National Research Centre for Radiation Medicine: 04050 Kyiv, 53, Melnikova str.; tel. (44) 483-06-37; e-mail bazyka@yahoo.com; internet www.national.rcrm.net.ua; f. 1986; attached to Nat. Academy of Medical Sciences of Ukraine; radiation biology and hygiene, physical and biological dosimetry, radiation protection; studies of low-dose exposure health effects; library of 32,000 vols; Dir-Gen. Prof. DIMITRY BAZYKA; publ. *Problems of Radiation Medicine* (2 a year).

Phthisiology and Pulmonology Research Institute: vul. M. Amosova 10, 03680 Kyiv; tel. (44) 275-04-02; e-mail admin@ifp.kiev.ua; internet www.ifp.kiev.ua; f. 1922; Dir YURI I. FESCHENKO; publs *Asthma and Allergy* (4 a year), *Ukrainian Chemotherapeutic Journal* (4 a year), *Ukrainian Journal of Pulmonology* (4 a year).

R. E. Kavetsky Institute of Experimental Pathology, Oncology and Radiobiology: 03022 Kyiv, Vasylkivska str. 45; tel. (44) 259-01-83; e-mail iepor@onconet.kiev.ua; internet www.iepor.org.ua; f. 1960; attached to Nat. Acad. of Sciences of Ukraine; investigation of tumour cell biology and its microenvironment in devt of molecular and cellular mechanisms of oncogenesis; evaluation of molecular and cellular markers of initiation, promotion, progression and devt of methods for diagnostics of malignant tumours; determination of molecular aspects of pharmacological correction of carcinogenesis and drug resistance formation of malignant cell and epigenetic approaches; investigation of nanoparticles and nanocomposite's influence on normal and tumour cells' metabolism; devt of approaches to target therapy and sorption detoxification; library of 71,203 vols, 373 periodicals; Dir Prof. Acad. VASYL F. CHEKHUN; publs *Experimental Oncology* (4 a year, in English), *Oncologia* (4 a year, in Ukrainian and Russian).

Research Institute of Physical Methods of Treatment and Medical Climatology 'I. M. Sechenov': 98603 Yalta, Polikurovska vul. 25; tel. (65) 432-75-91; f. 1914; non-medical treatment and prophylaxis of lung diseases and diseases of the cardiovascular and nervous systems; Dir Prof. SERGEI SOLDATCHENKO.

Research Institute of Psychology 'G. S. Kostyuk': 03037 Kyiv, vul. Pankivska 2; tel. (44) 224-19-63; attached to Nat. Acad. of Pedagogical Sciences of Ukraine.

Romodanov, A., Institute of Neurosurgery: 04050 Kyiv, vul. Mayborody 32; tel. (44) 483-95-73; e-mail neuro.kiev@gmail.com; internet www.neuro.kiev.ua; f. 1950; diagnosis, surgical and combined treatment of cerebral and spinal tumors, pathogenesis, diagnosis and treatment of CNS damage and its after-effects, surgical treatment of the most complex cerebrovascular pathologies, study of immune responses in patients with neurological CNS pathology; library of 79,000 vols; Dir Prof. EUGENE PEDACHENKO; publ. *Ukrainian Neurosurgical Journal* (4 a year).

State Scientific Centre of Drugs: Kharkiv 310085, Astronomicheska vul. 33; tel. (57) 744-10-33; e-mail samatov@phukr.kharkov.ua; internet farmacomua.narod.ru; f. 1920; production and devt of finished drugs and technologies for preparation of phytochemicals; library of 28,000 vols; Dir Prof. V. P. GEORGIEVSKY; publ. *Pharmacom* (4 a year, in Ukrainian and Russian).

Sytenko Institute of Spine and Joint Pathology: 61024 Kharkiv, Pushkinska vul. 80; tel. (57) 715-75-06; e-mail post@sytenko

.org.ua; internet www.sytenko.org.ua; f. 1907; attached to Acad. of Medical Sciences of Ukraine; library of 40,500 vols; Dir Prof. MYKOLA O. KORZH; publ. *Orthopaedics, Traumatology and Prosthetics* (4 a year).

Ukrainian Institute of Public Health: 01601 Kyiv, vul. Dymytrova 5, korp. 10A, 7th Fl.; tel. (44) 284-39-38; e-mail health@ uiph.kiev.ua; internet www.uiph.kiev.ua; f. 1997; attached to Ukrainian Min. of Health; Dir Prof. V. M. PONOMARENKO; publ. *Bulletin of the Social Hygiene and Health Protection Organization of Ukraine* (4 a year).

Ukrainian Research Institute of Traumatology and Orthopaedics: 01601 Kyiv, vul. Vorovskogo 27; tel. (44) 216-42-49; e-mail travma@rql.net.ua; f. 1919; library of 57,000 vols; Dir G. V. GAIKO; publs *Statistical Data Report on Traumatological and Orthopaedic Aid to Ukrainians* (1 a year), *Vestnik Ortopedii, Travmatologii i Protezirovaniia* (Orthopaedics, Traumatology and Prosthesis, 4 a year).

Ukrainian Scientific Centre of Hygiene: 02094 Kyiv, vul. Popudrenko 50; tel. (44) 559-73-73; e-mail usch@usch.kiev.ua; f. 1931; incl. Institute of General and Communal Hygiene, and Institute of Medical Genetics; library of 102,213 vols; Dir Dr ANDRIY SERDIUK; publ. *Environment and Health* (4 a year).

NATURAL SCIENCES

Biological Sciences

Institute of Biology of Southern Seas: Pr. Nakhimov 2, 99011 Sevastopol; tel. (69) 254-41-10; e-mail ibss@ibss.iuf.net; internet www.ibss.iuf.net; f. 1871; attached to Nat. Acad. of Sciences of Ukraine; library of 150,000 vols; 350 mems; Dir Dr V. N. EREMEEV; publs *Ekologiya Morya* (Ecology of the Sea, 4 a year), *Morskoj Ekologicheskij Zhurnal* (Marine Ecological Journal, 3 a year).

Institute of Botany 'M. G. Kholodny': 01601 Kyiv, Tereshchenkivska vul. 2; tel. (44) 224-40-41; e-mail inst@botan.kiev.ua; f. 1921; attached to Nat. Acad. of Sciences of Ukraine; library of 106,000 vols; Dir K. M. SYTNIK; publs *Algologiya* (Algology, 4 a year, in Ukrainian and English), *Ukrainsky Botanichny Zhurnal* (Ukrainian Botanical Journal, 6 a year, in Ukrainian and English).

Institute of Cellular Biology and Genetic Engineering: 03143 Kyiv, vul. Zabolotnogo 148; tel. (44) 526-71-09; e-mail cytogen@iicb.kiev.ua; internet www.cytgen .com; f. 1967; attached to Nat. Acad. of Sciences of Ukraine; Dir YA. B. BLUME; Exec. Sec. MARY FEDYUK; publ. *Tsitologia i Genetika* (Cytology and Genetics, 6 a year, in Ukrainian and English).

Institute of Hydrobiology: 04210 Kyiv-210, pr. Geroyiv Stalingrada 12; tel. (44) 419-39-81; internet www.gbiologe.narod.ru/index .htm; attached to Nat. Acad. of Sciences of Ukraine; Dir VIKTOR D. ROMANENKO; publ. *Gidrobiologichesky Zhurnal* (Hydrobiological Journal, 6 a year, in Ukrainian and English).

Institute of Molecular Biology and Genetics: 03680 Kyiv, vul. Acad. Zabolotnoho 150; tel. (44) 526-11-69; e-mail inform@imbg .org.ua; internet www.imbg.org.ua; f. 1973; attached to Nat. Acad. of Sciences of Ukraine; central trends of molecular biology, genetics and biotechnology: structural and functional genomics; proteomics and protein engineering; regulatory systems and signal transduction mechanisms; bioinformatics and computational modelling; gene and cell biotechnologies, gene therapy and diagnostics; library of 90,000 vols; Dir Prof. Dr ANNA V. EL'SKAYA; Scientific Sec. Dr YANINA R.

MISHCHUK; publ. *Biopolymers and Cell* (6 a year, in Ukrainian and English).

Institute of Plant Physiology and Genetics: 03022 Kyiv, Vasylkivska vul. 31/17; tel. (44) 257-51-50; e-mail plant@ifrg.kiev.ua; internet www.ifrg.kiev.ua; f. 1946; attached to Nat. Acad. of Sciences of Ukraine; plant physiology, genetics; Dir Dr VLADIMIR V. MORGUN; Scientific Sec. PAVLO MAJOR; publ. *Fiziologia i Biokhimiia Kulturnykh Rastenii* (Physiology and Biochemistry of Cultivated Plants, 6 a year, in Ukrainian, Russian and English).

Institute of Sorption and Endoecology Problems: 03164 Kyiv, pr. Naumova 13; tel. (44) 452-93-28; e-mail ispe@ispe.kiev.ua; f. 1991; attached to Nat. Acad. of Sciences of Ukraine; Dir V. V. STRELKO.

'O. O. Bohomolets' Institute of Physiology: 01601 Kyiv, vul. Bohomoltsa 4; tel. (44) 293-20-13; e-mail pkostyuk@serv.biph .kiev.ua; attached to Nat. Acad. of Sciences of Ukraine; Dir P. H. KOSTYUK; publs *Fiziologichny Zhurnal* (Physiological Journal, 6 a year, in Ukrainian and English), *Neirofiziologia* (Neurophysiology, 6 a year, in Ukrainian and English).

Palladin Institute of Biochemistry: 01601 Kyiv 30, vul. Leontovicha 9; tel. (44) 234-59-74; e-mail secretar@biochem.kiev.ua; internet www.biochemistry.org.ua; f. 1925; attached to Nat. Acad. of Sciences of Ukraine; 360 mems; library of 82,000 vols; Dir Prof. SERHIY KOMISARENKO; publs *Biotechnologia* (Biotechnology, 6 a year, in Ukrainian, Russian and English), *Ukrainsky Biokhimichny Zhurnal* (Ukrainian Biochemical Journal, 6 a year, in Ukrainian, Russian and English).

Schmalhausen Institute of Zoology: 01601 Kyiv, vul. B. Khmelnytskoho 15; tel. (44) 235-10-70; e-mail iz@izan.kiev.ua; internet www.izan.kiev.ua; f. 1930; attached to Nat. Acad. of Sciences of Ukraine; zoological collns; zoological scientific research; library of 161,947 vols; Dir Prof. IGOR A. AKIMOV; Scientific Dir Dr VITALIY KHARCHENKO; Scientific Dir Prof. IGOR DOVGAL; publ. *Vestnik Zoologii* (Zoological Journal, 6 a year, in Ukrainian and English, online).

Zabolotny Institute of Microbiology and Virology: 03680 Kyiv, Akad. Zabolotny str. 154; tel. (44) 266-11-79; e-mail secretar@serv .imv.kiev.ua; internet www.imv.kiev.ua; f. 1928; attached to Nat. Acad. of Sciences of Ukraine; microbiology, virology, genetics of microorganisms and viruses, physiology and biochemistry of bacteria and micromycetes, microbial biotechnologies; library of 121,000 vols; Dir V. S. PIDGORSKYI; publ. *Mikrobiolohichny Zhurnal* (Microbiology Journal, 6 a year, in Ukrainian, Russian and English).

Mathematical Sciences

Institute of Mathematics: 01601 Kyiv, Tereshchenkivska Str. 3; tel. (44) 234-53-16; e-mail institute@imath.kiev.ua; internet www.imath.kiev.ua; attached to Nat. Acad. of Sciences of Ukraine; Dir A. M. SAMOILENKO; publ. *Ukrainsky Matematychny Zhurnal* (Ukrainian Mathematical Journal, 12 a year, in Ukrainian and English).

Physical Sciences

A. V. Bogatsky Physico-Chemical Institute of the National Academy of Sciences of Ukraine: 65080 Odessa, Lustdorfskaya doroga 86; tel. (48) 766-20-44; e-mail medchem_department@ukr.net; internet physchemin-nas.od.ua/index.php; f. 1977; attached to Nat. Acad. of Sciences of Ukraine; 198 mems; Dir SERGEI ANDRONATI.

Bogolyubov Institute for Theoretical Physics: 03680 Kyiv, vul. Metrologichna

14B; tel. (44) 526-53-62; e-mail itp@bitp.kiev .ua; internet www.bitp.kiev.ua; f. 1966; attached to Nat. Acad. of Sciences of Ukraine; Dir Prof. A. G. ZAGORODNY; publ. *Ukrainian Journal of Physics* (12 a year).

Chuiko Institute of Surface Chemistry: 03164 Kyiv, vul. Naumova, 17; tel. (44) 422-96-04; e-mail info@isc.gov.ua; internet www .isc.gov.ua; f. 1986; attached to Nat. Acad. of Sciences of Ukraine; library of 20,000 vols; Dir Prof. M. T. KARTEL; publs *Chemistry, Physics and Technology of Surface* (4 a year), *Surface*.

Gas Institute: 03113 Kyiv, Degtiarivksa vul. 39; tel. (44) 456-44-71; e-mail ig-secr@i .com.ua; internet ingas.org.ua; f. 1949; attached to Nat. Acad. of Sciences of Ukraine; library of 110,000 vols; Dir Prof. B. I. BONDARENKO; publ. *Ekotekhnologia i Resursosberezheniye* (Energy Technologies and Resource Saving, 6 a year, in Russian with summaries in Ukrainian and English).

G. V. Kurdyumov Institute for Metal Physics: 03680 Kyiv, Acad. Vernadsky Blvd 36; tel. (44) 424-10-05; e-mail metall@ imp.kiev.ua; internet www.imp.kiev.ua; f. 1945; attached to Nat. Acad. of Sciences of Ukraine; research and technologies based on the investigations of electronic structure, electrical, magnetic, optical, structural, thermal and mechanical properties of condensed matter; library of 129,000 vols; Dir Acad. OREST M. IVASISHIN; Academic Sec. Dr EUGENIA V. KOCHELAB; publs *Metallofizika i Noveishie Tekhnologii* (Metal Physics and Advanced Technology, 12 a year, in English, Russian and Ukrainian), *Nanosistemi, Nanomateriali, Nanotehnologii* (Nanosystems, Nanomaterials, Nanotechnologies, 4 a year, in English, Russian and Ukrainian), *Uspehi Fiziki Metallov* (Progress in Physics of Metals, 4 a year, in English, Russian and Ukrainian).

Institute of Bio-organic Chemistry and Petrochemistry: 02660 Kyiv, vul. Murmanska 1; tel. (44) 558-53-88; e-mail users@ bpci.kiev.ua; f. 1987; attached to Nat. Acad. of Sciences of Ukraine; Dir Prof. V. P. KUKHAR; publ. *Katalys i Neftekhimiya* (Catalysis and Petrochemistry, 4 a year).

Institute of Colloid Chemistry and Water Chemistry 'A. V. Dumansky': 03680 Kyiv 142, Vernadsky pr. 42; tel. (44) 424-01-96; e-mail honch@iccw.kiev.ua; f. 1968; attached to Nat. Acad. of Sciences of Ukraine; Dir V. V. GONCHARUK; publ. *Khimiya i Tekhnologiya Vody* (Water Chemistry and Engineering, 6 a year, in Russian and English).

Institute of General and Inorganic Chemistry 'V. I. Vernadsky': 03680 Kyiv, pr. Akademika Palladina 32/34; tel. (44) 444-34-61; e-mail office@ionc.kiev.ua; internet www.ionc.kar.net; f. 1918; attached to Nat. Acad. of Sciences of Ukraine; fundamental and applied research in inorganic chemistry, coordination chemistry, chemistry of solids, nanochemistry, electrochemistry and physical chemistry of melts, aqueous and non-aqueous solutions, processing of original and recycled metal-containing materials; study of structure and properties of ionic melts, solid electrolytes, inorganic sorbents, coordination compounds of rare, rare-earth and other metals, liquid ionic crystals, membrane materials; research in priority directions of inorganic and physico-inorganic chemistry in the brs of high-temperature coordination chemistry in the melts, gas phases and plasma; synthesis and characterization of novel dielectric, semiconductive, optical, ultrapure oxide materials, superconductors and high-temperature ceramics; Dir Prof. Dr SERGIY V. VOLKOV; Dir Prof. Dr VASILY

PEKHNYO; publ. *Ukrainsky Khimichesky Zhurnal* (Ukrainian Chemistry Journal, 12 a year, in Russian, Ukrainian and English).

Institute of Geochemistry, Mineralogy and Ore Formation: 03680 Kyiv-142, pr. Palladina 34; tel. (44) 424-01-05; e-mail pavlenko@igmr.relc.com; f. 1969; attached to Nat. Acad. of Sciences of Ukraine; library of 30,000 vols, 35 periodicals; Dir MYKOLA P. SHCHERBAK; publ. *Mineralogichesky Zhurnal* (Mineralogical Journal, 6 a year, in Ukrainian and English).

Institute of Geological Sciences: 01054 Kyiv, vul. Honchar 55B; tel. (44) 216-94-46; e-mail info@igs-nas.org.ua; f. 1926; attached to Nat. Acad. of Sciences of Ukraine; Dir Prof. PETRO F. HOZHYK; publ. *Geolohichny Zhurnal* (Geological Journal, 4 a year, in Ukrainian and English).

Institute of Geology and Geochemistry of Combustible Minerals: 79060 Lviv, Naukova vul. 3A; tel. (32) 263-25-41; e-mail igggk@mail.lviv.ua; f. 1951; attached to Nat. Acad. of Sciences of Ukraine; Dir V. E. ZABIGAILO; publ. *Geologia i Geokhimia Horiuchykh Kopalyn* (Geology and Geochemistry of Mineral Fuels, 4 a year, in Ukrainian and English).

Institute of Geophysics: 03680 Kyiv, pr. Akademika Palladina 32; tel. (44) 424-01-12; e-mail earth@igph.kiev.ua; internet www.igph.kiev.ua; f. 1960; attached to Nat. Acad. of Sciences of Ukraine; studies of tectonics, structure, geodynamics and evolution of the continental and oceanic lithosphere; compilation of 3-dimensional complex geophysical and petrophysical models of geological structures for the purpose of useful minerals forecast; elaboration of technological automated systems of processing and interpretation of geophysical information; geophysical studies of the environment aimed at the forecast of seismic hazards and other hazardous natural phenomena; Dir V. I. STAROSTENKO; publ. *Geofizichesky Zhurnal* (Geophysical Journal, 6 a year, in Russian, Ukrainian and English).

Institute of Ionosphere: 61002 Kharkiv, Krasnoznamennaya str. 16; tel. (57) 706-22-87; e-mail iion@kpi.kharkov.ua; internet www.iion.org.ua; f. 1991; attached to Nat. Acad. of Sciences of Ukraine and Min. of Education and Science of Ukraine; incoherent scatter method, geophysics, geospace plasma, ionosphere, radio physics; Dir Prof. IGOR DOMNIN.

Institute of Nuclear Research: 03680 Kyiv, pr. Nauky 47; tel. (44) 265-23-49; e-mail interdep@kinr.kiev.ua; internet www.kinr.kiev.ua; f. 1970; attached to Nat. Acad. of Sciences of Ukraine; nuclear physics, atomic energy, radiation physics and radiation material science, physics of plasma, radiation ecology and biology; Dir IVAN M. VYSHNYEVSKIY; Deputy Dir VOLODYMYR OSTASHKO; publ. *Scientific Papers* (irregular).

Institute of Organic Chemistry: 02660 Kyiv, Murmanska vul. 5; tel. (44) 552-71-50; f. 1939; Dir MYRON O. LOZYNSKIY.

Institute of Physical-Organic Chemistry and Coal Chemistry 'L. M. Litvinenko': 83114 Donetsk, vul. R. Lyuksemburg 70; tel. (62) 311-68-30; e-mail postmaster@infou.donetsk.ua; f. 1975; attached to Nat. Acad. of Sciences of Ukraine; coal and products of its processing; synthesis and investigation of the structure and properties of heterocyclic compounds, incl. biologically active ones; library of 110,000 vols, 13 periodicals; Dir Acad. ANATOLY F. POPOV.

Institute of Physics: 03028 Kyiv, pr. Nauky 46; tel. (44) 525-12-20; e-mail fizyka@iop.kiev.ua; internet www.iop.kiev

.ua; f. 1929; attached to Nat. Acad. of Sciences of Ukraine; Dir M. S. BRODYN; publ. *Ukrainsky Fizychny Zhurnal* (Ukrainian Physics Journal, 12 a year, in Ukrainian and English).

Institute of Radio Astronomy: 61002 Kharkiv, Chervonopraporna vul. 4; tel. (57) 706-14-10; e-mail rai@rian.kharkov.ua; internet www.ri.kharkov.ua; f. 1985; attached to Nat. Acad. of Sciences of Ukraine; Dir Dr LEONID M. LYTVYNENKO; publ. *Radiofizyka i Radioastronomiya* (Radio Physics and Radio Astronomy, 4 a year, in Ukrainian, Russian and English).

Institute of Single Crystals: 61001 Kharkiv, pr. Lenina 60; tel. (57) 341-01-66; e-mail info@isc.kharkov.com; internet www.isc.kharkov.com; f. 1961; attached to Nat. Acad. of Sciences of Ukraine; Dir Dr VYACHESLAV M. PUZIKOV; publ. *Functional Materials* (4 a year, in English).

L. V. Pisarzhevsky Institute of Physical Chemistry: 03028 Kyiv, Pr. Nauki 31; tel. (44) 525-11-90; e-mail admini@inphyschem-nas.kiev.ua; internet www.inphyschem-nas.kiev.ua; f. 1927; attached to Nat. Acad. of Sciences of Ukraine; theory of chemical structure; kinetics and reactivity; catalysis; adsorption and adsorbents; chemistry of high energies; physico-inorganic chemistry; library of 135,000 vols (incl. books, brochures and periodic issues); Dir Acad. V. G. KOSHECHKO; publ. *Teoreticheskaya i Eksperimentalnaya Khimiya* (Theoretical and Experimental Chemistry, 6 a year, in Russian and English).

Main Astronomical Observatory: 03680 Kyiv, vul. Akademika Zabolotnogo 27; tel. (44) 526-31-10; e-mail director@mao.kiev.ua; internet www.mao.kiev.ua; f. 1944; attached to Nat. Acad. of Sciences of Ukraine; Dir YA. S. YATSKIV; publs *Kinematika i Fizika Nebesnykh Tel* (Kinematics and Physics of Celestial Bodies, 6 a year, in Ukrainian and English), *Space Science and Technology* (6 a year).

Marine Hydrophysical Institute: 99011 Sevastopol, vul. Kapitanska 2; tel. (69) 254-04-52; e-mail vaivanov@alpha.mhi.iuf.net; internet www.mhi.iuf.net; attached to Nat. Acad. of Sciences of Ukraine; Dir Prof. VITALY A. IVANOV; publs *Morskoy Gidrofizichesky Zhurnal* (Marine Hydrophysical Journal, in Ukrainian, Russian and English), *Physical Oceanography* (6 a year).

Research and Design Institute of Basic Chemistry: 61002 Kharkiv, Mironositska vul. 25; tel. (57) 700-01-23; e-mail office@niochim.kharkov.ua; internet www.niochim.kharkov.ua/niochim1.htm; f. 1923; library of 185,000 vols; Dir E. I. VELIEV.

Ukrainian State Geological Research Institute: 04114 Kyiv, vul. Avtozavodska 78; tel. (44) 430-70-24; e-mail ukrdgri@ukrdgri.gov.ua; internet www.ukrdgri.gov.ua; f. 1953; brs in Chirnigiv, Dnipropetrovsk, Lviv, Poltava and Simferopol; Dir MYKHAYLO D. KRASNOZHON.

V. Lashkaryov Institute of Semiconductor Physics: 03028 Kyiv, pr. Nauky 41; tel. (44) 525-40-20; e-mail info@isp.kiev.ua; internet www.isp.kiev.ua; f. 1960; attached to Nat. Acad. of Sciences of Ukraine; scientific investigations; library of 173,106 vols, 24,509 books; Dir Acad. V. F. MACHULIN; Exec. Dir Prof. VASYL TOMASHYK; publs *Optoelektronika i Poluprovodnikovaya Tekhnika* (Optoelectronics and Semiconductor Technology, 1 a year), *Semiconductor Physics, Quantum Electronics and Optoelectronics* (4 a year, in English).

PHILOSOPHY AND PSYCHOLOGY

'H. S. Skovoroda' Institute of Philosophy: 01001 Kyiv, vul. Tryokhsviatytelska 4; tel. (44) 278-06-05; e-mail if-ukr@i.kiev.ua; internet www.filosof.com.ua; f. 1946; attached to Nat. Acad. of Sciences of Ukraine; research in different areas of philosophy; library of 65,000 vols; Dir Prof MYROSLAV V. POPOVYCH; publs *Filosofska Dumka* (Philosophical Thought, 6 a year, in Ukrainian), *Filosofski Obryi* (Philosophical Horizons, 2 a year, in Ukrainian), *Praktychna Filosofia* (Practical Philosophy, 4 a year), *Religiyna Panorama* (Religious Panorama, 12 a year).

RELIGION, SOCIOLOGY AND ANTHROPOLOGY

Institute of Art, Folklore Studies and Ethnography 'M. T. Rylsky': 01001 Kyiv, vul. Kirova 4; tel. (44) 266-20-08; e-mail etnolog@etnolog.kiev.ua; internet www.etnolog.kiev.ua; f. 1936; attached to Nat. Acad. of Sciences of Ukraine; Dir Prof. Dr H. A. SKRYPNYK; publ. *Folklore Studies.*

Institute of Sociology: 01021 Kyiv, Shovkovychna 12; tel. (44) 255-74-09; e-mail i-soc@i-soc.org.ua; internet www.i-soc.com.ua; f. 1990; attached to Nat. Acad. of Sciences of Ukraine; Dir Prof. VALERIY M. VORONA; publ. *Sotsiolohiya: Teoriya, Metody, Marketing* (Sociology: Theory, Methods, Marketing, 6 a year, in Ukrainian and English).

TECHNOLOGY

B. Verkin Institute of Low Temperature Physics and Engineering: 61103 Kharkiv, pr. Lenina 47; tel. (57) 340-22-23; e-mail ilt@ilt.kharkov.ua; internet www.ilt.kharkov.ua; f. 1960; attached to Nat. Acad. of Sciences of Ukraine; low and ultra low temperature physics; solid state physics; nanophysics and nanotechnologies, incl. nanobiophysics; mathematical physics, analysis and geometry; physical and engineering problems of materials science; library of 40,000 vols; Dir Prof. SERGEI LEONIDOVICH GNATCHENKO; Deputy Dir Dr NIKOLAY IVANOVICH GLUSHCHUK; Deputy Dir Prof. Dr VLADIMIR NIKOLAEVICH SAMOVAROV; Science Sec. Dr ALEXANDER NIKOLAEVICH KALINENKO; publs *Fizika Nizkikh Temperatur* (Low-temperature Physics, 12 a year, in Ukrainian, Russian and English), *Matematicheskaya Fizika, Analiz, Geometria* (Mathematical Physics, Analysis, Geometry, 4 a year, in Ukrainian, Russian and English).

Donetsk Institute for Physics and Engineering 'O. O. Galkin': 83114 Donetsk, 72 R. Lyuksemburg St; tel. (62) 311-52-27; e-mail scsecr@fti.dn.ua; internet www.fti.dn.ua; f. 1965; attached to Nat. Acad. of Sciences of Ukraine; 12 scientific depts, 3 scientific-auxiliary depts, 12 auxiliary subdivs, centre for collective use of devices; electronic and kinetic properties of solids, physics of magnetic phenomena, phase transitions, spectroscopy of solids, physics of strength and plasticity, physical material science, pressure treatment of materials, high-pressure equipment, experimental technique; library of 150,000 vols; Dir Prof. Dr VIKTOR M. VARYUKHIN; Deputy Dir VIKTOR A. BELOSHENKO; Scientific Sec. Dr IRINA YU. RESHIDOVA; publ. *Fizika i Tekhnika Vysokikh Davleniy* (High-pressure Physics and Technology, 4 a year, in Russian and English).

Frantsevich, I. N., Institute of Problems of Materials Science: 03142 Kyiv, vul. Krzhizhanovskoho 3; tel. (44) 424-01-02; e-mail dir@materials.kiev.ua; f. 1952; attached to Nat. Acad. of Sciences of Ukraine; Dir V. V. SKOROHOD; publ. *Porosh-*

kovaya Metallurgia (Powder Metallurgy, 12 a year, in Ukrainian and English).

G. E. Pukhov Institute for Modelling in Energy Engineering: 03164 Kyiv, vul. Generala Naumova 15; tel. (44) 424-10-63; e-mail em@ipme.kiev.ua; internet www.ipme.kiev.ua; f. 1981; attached to Nat. Acad. of Sciences of Ukraine; 150 mems; Dir V. F. EVDOKIMOV; publ. *Elektronnoe Modelirovanie* (Electronic Modelling, 6 a year, in Russian and English).

G. S. Pisarenko Institute for Problems of Strength: 01014 Kyiv, vul. Timiryazevska 2; tel. (44) 285-16-87; e-mail ips@ipp.kiev.ua; internet www.ipp.kiev.ua; f. 1966; attached to Nat. Acad. of Sciences of Ukraine; Dir V. T. TROSHCHENKO; publ. *Problemy Prochnosti* (Strength of Materials, 6 a year, in Russian and English).

Institute of Applied Mathematics and Mechanics: 83114 Donetsk, Roza Luksemburg St 74; tel. (623) 11-03-91; e-mail math@iamm.ac.donetsk.ua; internet www.iamm.ac.donetsk.ua; f. 1965; attached to Nat. Acad. of Sciences of Ukraine; library of 89,415 vols; Dir ALEKSANDR M. KOVALEV; publs *Mekhanika Tverdogo Tela* (1 a year), *Nelineinye Granichnye Zadachi* (1 a year), *Trudy Instituta Prikladnoi Matematiki i Mehaniki NAN Ukrainy* (1 a year), *Ukrains'kyi Matematychnyi Visnyk* (Ukrainian Mathematical Bulletin, 4 issues in 1 vol, 1 a year).

Institute of Cybernetics 'V. M. Hlushkov': 03680 Kyiv MSP, Glushkova 20; tel. (44) 266-20-08; e-mail aik@public.icyb.kiev.ua; internet www.icyb.kiev.ua; attached to Nat. Acad. of Sciences of Ukraine; Dir I. K. SERHIENKO; publs *Kibernetika i Sistemny Analiz* (Cybernetics and Systems Analysis, 6 a year, in Ukrainian and English), *Problemy Upravlenia i Informatiki* (Problems of Control and Informatics, 6 a year, in Ukrainian and English), *Upravlyauschie Sistemy i Mashiny* (Control Systems and Computers, 6 a year, in Ukrainian and English).

Institute of Electrodynamics: 03680 Kyiv, Peremohy 56; tel. (44) 456-01-51; e-mail ied@ied.org.ua; internet www.ied.org.ua; f. 1947; attached to Nat. Acad. of Sciences of Ukraine; Dir O. V. KYRYLENKO; publs *Tekhnichna Elektrodynamika* (Technical Electrodynamics, 6 a year, in Ukrainian, Russian and English), *Works of Institute of Electrodynamics* (3 a year, in Ukrainian and Russian).

Institute of Engineering Mechanics 'A. M. Pidhorny': 61046 Kharkiv, vul. Pozharskoho 2/10; tel. (57) 294-55-14; e-mail root@ipmach.kharkov.ua; internet www.ipmach.kharkov.ua; attached to Nat. Acad. of Sciences of Ukraine; Dir YURI M. MATSEVITIY; publ. *Problemy Mashinostroenia* (Problems of Mechanical Engineering, 4 a year, in Ukrainian and English).

Institute of Engineering Thermophysics: 03057 Kyiv, vul. Zhelyabova 2A, kv 102; tel. (44) 456-62-82; e-mail admin@ittf.kiev.ua; internet www.ittf.kiev.ua; attached to Nat. Acad. of Sciences of Ukraine; Dir ANATOLIY A. DOLINSKIY; publ. *Promyshlennaya Teplotekhnika* (Industrial Thermal Engineering, 6 a year, in Ukrainian and English).

Institute of Geotechnical Mechanics: 320095 Dnipropetrovsk, Simferopolska vul. 2A; tel. (56) 246-01-51; e-mail nanu@igtm.dp.ua; internet www.igtm.narod.ru; f. 1962; attached to Nat. Acad. of Sciences of Ukraine; library of 109,000 vols; Dir A. F. BULAT; publ. *Geotechnical Mechanics* (4 a year).

Institute of Hydromechanics: 03057 Kyiv, vul. Zhelyabova 8/4; tel. (44) 456-43-13;

e-mail office@hydromech.com.ua; internet www.hydromech.kiev.ua; f. 1926; attached to Nat. Acad. of Sciences of Ukraine; library of 84,727 vols; Dir VIKTOR T. GRINCHENKO; publs *Acoustics Bulletin* (4 a year), *Applied Hydromechanics* (4 a year).

Institute of Information Recording: 03113 Kyiv, vul. Shpaka 2; tel. (44) 446-83-89; e-mail petrov@ipri.kiev.ua; internet www.ipri.kiev.ua; f. 1987; attached to Nat. Acad. of Sciences of Ukraine; optical storage, information-analytical systems, information security, digital transfer of Edison cylinders with audio-cultural heritage, expert decision-making support systems; 210 mems; Dir V. V. PETROV; publs *Reestracia Zberezenna i Obrobka Danih* (Data Recording, Storage and Processing, 4 a year, in Ukrainian, Russian and English), *Ukrainsky Referatyvny Zhurnal 'Dzherelo'* (Ukrainian Journal of Abstracts 'Dzherelo', 6 a year, in Ukrainian and English).

Institute of Mining and the Chemical Industry: 79026 Lviv, Striiska vul. 98; tel. (32) 297-13-77; e-mail ghp@ghp.lviv.ua; internet www.glrhimprom.narod.ru; f. 1956; Chair. I. I. ZOZULIA.

Institute of Pulse Processes and Technologies: 54018 Mykolayiv, Zhovtnevy Ave 43A; tel. (51) 222-41-13; e-mail iipt@iipt.com.ua; internet www.iipt.com.ua; f. 1962; attached to Nat. Acad. of Sciences of Ukraine; library of 140,000 vols; Dir O. I. VOVCHENKO.

Institute of Superhard Materials: 04074 Kyiv, Avtozavodska vul. 2; tel. (44) 468-86-32; e-mail almaz@ism.kiev.ua; internet www.ism.ua; f. 1961; attached to Nat. Acad. of Sciences of Ukraine; Dir Prof. N. V. NOVIKOV; publs *Instumentalnyi Swit* (World of Tools, 6 a year), *Sverkhtviordye Materialy* (Superhard Materials, 6 a year, in Russian and English).

Iron and Steel Institute 'Z. I. Nekrasov': 49050 Dnipropetrovsk, pl. Akademika Starodubova 1; tel. (56) 776-53-15; e-mail office.isi@nas.gov.ua; f. 1939; attached to Nat. Acad. of Sciences of Ukraine; Dir Prof. Dr VADIM I. BOLSHAKOV; publ. *Fundamental and Applied Problems of the Steel Industry* (proceedings, 1 a year).

Karpenko Physico–Mechanical Institute of the National Academy of Sciences of Ukraine: 79060 Lviv, Naukova str. 5; tel. (32) 263-30-88; e-mail pminasu@ipm.lviv.ua; internet www.ipm.lviv.ua; f. 1951; problems of modern materials science, physicochemical fracture mechanics of materials and strength of structures; library of 100,000 vols; Dir Acad. V. V. PANASYUK; Scientific Sec. DMYTRO DOSYN; publs *Fizyko-Khimichna Mekhanika Materialiv* (Physical and Chemical Mechanics of Materials, 6 a year, in Ukrainian and English), *Vidbir i Obrobka Informatsii* (Information Extraction and Processing, 2 a year, in Ukrainian).

Pidstryhach Institute of Applied Problems of Mechanics and Mathematics: 79060 Lviv, Naukova str. 3B; tel. (32) 263-83-77; e-mail adm@iapmm.lviv.ua; internet www.iapmm.lviv.ua; f. 1973; attached to Nat. Acad. of Sciences of Ukraine; library of 15,000 vols; Dir Prof. ROMAN M. KUSHNIR; Deputy Dir VOLODYMYR PELYKH; publs *Applied Problems of Mechanics and Mathematics* (1 a year), *Mathematical Methods and Physicomechanical Fields* (4 a year).

Research and Development Institute of the Merchant Marine of Ukraine: 65026 Odessa, Lanzheronovska vul. 15A; tel. (48) 741-17-04; e-mail unii@paco.net; internet www.unii.odessa.ua; f. 1947; Dir ALEXANDER LESNIK.

Research Institute of the Sewn Goods Industry: 03680 Kyiv, vul. P. Lyubchenko 15; tel. (44) 528-55-41; e-mail legprom@i.kiev.ua; internet www.iptelecom.net.ua/~legprom/; f. 1961; library of 22,500 vols; Dir V. P. KRYSKO.

State Research and Design Institute of Chemical Engineering 'Khimtekhnologiya': 93400 Luhansk oblast, Severodonetsk, vul. Vilesova 1; tel. (64) 523-42-20; internet www.ixt.lg.ua; f. 1950; library of 130,000 vols; Dir PETR P. BORISOV; publ. *Collected Research Papers* (12 a year).

State Titanium Research and Design Institute: 69035 Zaporizhia, Lenina 180; tel. (61) 233-23-23; e-mail common@timag.org; internet www.timag.org; f. 1956; design and devt of non-ferrous metallurgical processes, production of semiconductors and carbon-graphite materials; Dir-Gen. Dr IGOR V. ZABELIN.

Timoshenko, S. P., Institute of Mechanics: 03057 Kyiv, vul. Nesterova 3; tel. (44) 456-93-51; e-mail ang@imech.freenet.kiev.ua; internet www.inmech.kiev.ua; library of 20,000 vols; f. 1918; mechanics of composite and inhomogenous materials; structural mechanics; mechanics of coupled fields in materials and structures; mechanics of fracture and fatigue; dynamics and stability of mechanical system motion; attached to Nat. Acad. of Sciences of Ukraine; Dir Prof. Dr ALEXANDER N. GUZ; publs *International Applied Mechanics* (12 a year, in English), *Prikladnaya Mekhanika* (12 a year, in Russian).

Ukrainian State Research and Design Institute of Mining Geology, Rock Mechanics and Mine Surveying (UkrNIMI): 83121 Donetsk, vul. Chelyuskintsev 291; tel. (62) 348-16-48; e-mail ukrnimi@ukrnimi.donetsk.ua; internet www.ukrnimi.donetsk.ua; f. 1929; attached to Nat. Acad. of Sciences of Ukraine; Dir Dr A. V. ANTSIFEROV.

Usikov Institute of Radiophysics and Electronics: 61085 Kharkiv, Ac. Proskura St 12; tel. (57) 720-33-19; e-mail secretar@ire.kharkov.ua; internet www.ire.kharkov.ua; f. 1955; attached to Nat. Acad. of Sciences of Ukraine; interaction between electromagnetic waves and solids as well as biological objects; radio wave propagation in the environment; radiophysical sensing of man-made and natural objects; library of 135,000 vols; Dir Prof. VLADIMIR M. YAKOVENKO; Deputy Dir Dr ALEKSANDR KOGUT; Deputy Dir PETER MELEZHIK; publ. *Radiophysics and Electronics* (4 a year).

Vniichimprojekt Institute: 02002 Kyiv-2, vul. M. Raskovoi 11; tel. (44) 517-05-81; e-mail vniichim@nbi.com.ua; internet www.himpro.com.ua; f. 1970; develops synthetic detergents, personal care products and packaging materials; library of 38,800 vols; Pres. VALERY N. KRIVOSHEI; publs *Khimichna Promyslovist Ukrainy* (6 a year), *Upakovka* (6 a year).

Yuzhniigiprogaz Institute OJSC: 83121 Donetsk, vul. Artema 169G; tel. (62) 305-76-61; e-mail ex@yuzh-gaz.donetsk.ua; internet www.ungg.org; f. 1933; library of 38,000 vols; Dir V. D. BONDARTSOV.

Libraries and Archives

Chernivtsi

Scientific Library Yuriy Fedkovych Chernivtsi National University: 58000 Chernivtsi, vul. Lesi Ukrainki 23; tel. (37) 258-47-60; e-mail biblio@chnu.cv.ua; internet www.library.chnu.edu.ua; f. 1852; 2.6m. vols; Dir MYKHAILO B. ZUSHMAN.

Dnipropetrovsk

Dnipropetrovsk National University Library 'O. Gonchar': 49050 Dnipropetrovsk, vul. Kozakova 8; tel. (56) 246-61-95; e-mail librarydnu@gmail.com; internet www.dsu.dp.ua/lib.html; 1,417,000 vols; Dir S. V. KUBYSHKINA.

Donetsk

Scientific Library of Donetsk National University: 83001 Donetsk, Universitetska vul. 24; tel. (62) 302-92-73; e-mail library.div@donnu.edu.ua; internet library.donnu.edu.ua; f. 1937; 1,172,929 vols; Dir N. A. KARIAGINA; Deputy Dir MAKHNO IRINA.

Kharkiv

Kharkiv V. N. Karazin National University Central Scientific Library: 61022 Kharkiv, m. Svobody 4; tel. (57) 707-52-86; e-mail cnb@univer.kharkov.ua; internet www-library.univer.kharkov.ua; f. 1804; 3.4m. vols, incl. 85,000 rare editions, 19 incunabula, more than 1,000 MSS, books by classical writers and scholars published in their lifetimes; Dir IRINA ZHURAVLYOVA (acting).

Kyiv

Archives of Ukraine.

Attached Archives:

Central State Archive and Museum of Literature and Art of Ukraine: 01601 Kyiv, Volodymyrska vul. 22a; tel. (44) 278-44-81; e-mail cdamlm@bigmir.net; internet csam.archives.gov.ua; f. 1966; Dir OLENA KULCHIY.

Central State Archive of Public Organizations of Ukraine: Kyiv 01011, 8 Kutuzova vul.; tel. (44) 285-55-16; e-mail archiv@cdago.org.ua; internet www.cdago.gov.ua.

Central State Archive of Supreme Bodies of Power and Government of Ukraine: tel. (44) 275-36-66; e-mail tsdavo@archives.gov.ua.

Central State CinePhotoFono Archive of Ukraine 'H. S. Pshenychniy': 03110 Kyiv, Solomyanska str. 24; tel. (44) 275-37-77; e-mail tsdkffa@archives.gov.ua; internet www.tsdkffa.archives.gov.ua; Dir NINA TOPISHKO.

Central State Historical Archive of Ukraine in Kyiv: 03110 Kyiv, Solomyanska vul. 24; tel. (44) 275-30-02; e-mail mail@cdiak.archives.gov.ua; internet www.archives.gov.ua; f. 1852; Dir IVAN KISIL.

State Archive of Kyiv Oblast: 04119 Kyiv, Melnykova vul. 38; tel. (44) 213-75-72.

State Archive of the City of Kyiv: 04060 Kyiv, Oleny Telihy vul. 23; tel. (44) 440-54-16; e-mail archiv@archiv.kyiv-city.gov.ua.

State Committee on Archives of Ukraine: 03110 Kyiv, Solomyanska vul. 24; tel. (44) 275-27-77; e-mail mail@archives.gov.ua; internet www.archives.gov.ua; f. 1919; Dir-Gen. OLHA HINZBURH.

Kyiv National University 'Taras Shevchenko' Library: 01601 Kyiv, vul. Volodymyrska 58; tel. (44) 235-70-98; e-mail info@libcc.univ.kiev.ua; internet www.library.univ.kiev.ua; f. 1834; 3,559,000 vols; Dir VALENTINA G. NESTERENKO.

National Historical Library of Ukraine: 01601 Kyiv, vul. Lavrska 9; tel. (44) 280-46-17; e-mail nibu.kiev@ukr.net; internet dibu.kiev.ua; f. 1939; Dir ALLA SKOROKHVATOVA.

National Parliamentary Library of Ukraine: 01001 Kyiv, vul. M. Hrushevskoho 1; tel. (44) 228-85-12; e-mail office@nplu.org; internet www.nplu.org; f. 1866; 4.5m. vols; Dir TAMARA VYLEHZHANINA; publs *Bibliotechna Planeta* (4 a year), *Kalendar znamennikh i pamyatnikh dat* (4 a year).

National Scientific Medical Library: 01033 Kyiv, vul. L. Tolstogo 7; tel. (44) 234-51-97; e-mail medlib@library.gov.ua; internet www.library.gov.ua; f. 1930; 1.5m. vols; Gen. Dir RAISA I. PAVLENKO.

State Archival Service of Ukraine: 03110 Kyiv, Solomanska St 24; tel. (44) 275-27-77; e-mail mail@archives.gov.ua; internet www.archives.gov.ua; f. 1919; Head OLHA HINZBURH.

State Scientific Agricultural Library of Ukrainian Academy of Agricultural Sciences: 03680 Kyiv, vul. Heroyiv Oborony 10; tel. (44) 527-80-75; e-mail cnsgb@faust.kiev.ua; internet dnsgb.kiev.ua; f. 1921; 1,017,323 vols; Dir Dr VIKTOR A. VERGUNOV; publs *Agropromysloviy Complex Ukraiiny* (abstract journal, 4 a year), *Akademiky Ukraiinskoi Akademii Agrarnykh Nauk* (bibliographic series, 6–7 a year), *Silskohospodarki Knyhy* (4 a year).

State Scientific and Technical Library of Ukraine: 03650 Kyiv, vul. Antonovicha 180; tel. (44) 528-21-85; e-mail alex@gntb.gov.ua; internet gntb.gov.ua; f. 1935; 20m. vols, incl. books, documents and patents related to science and technology; Dir V. H. DRYGAYLO.

Ukrainian Institute for Scientific, Technical and Economic Information: 03680 Kyiv, vul. Horkogo 180; tel. (44) 528-25-22; e-mail uintei@uintei.kiev.ua; internet www.uintei.kiev.ua; Dir ANATOLIY YAMCHUK.

Vernadsky National Library of Ukraine: 03039 Kyiv, pr. 40 Richja Zhovtnja 3; tel. (44) 265-81-04; e-mail nlu@csl.freenet.kiev.ua; internet www.nbuv.go.ua; f. 1919; over 14m. vols; colln incl. books, newspapers, magazines, serials, maps, music scores, fine arts materials, MSS, old and rare books, incunabula, documents; colln of Slavic writings; archives of outstanding Ukrainian and foreign scientists; archives of the Nat. Academy of Sciences of Ukraine; 40 depts and centres of preservation and restoration, culture and education, computer technologies, and publishing; Dir-Gen. O. S. ONYSHCHENKO; publs *Bibliotechnyi Visnyk* (Library Journal, 6 a year, in Ukrainian and English), *Naukovi Pratsi* (Scientific Works, 2 or 3 a year).

Lviv

Lviv Ivan Franko State University Library: 79601 Lviv, vul. Dragomanova 5; tel. (32) 275-60-01; e-mail info@nb.lviv.ua; internet library.franko.lviv.ua; 2.5m. vols; Dir VASILY FEDOROVICH KMET.

Lviv National Stefanyk Scientific Library of Ukraine: 79000 Lviv, vul. Stefanyka 2; tel. (32) 274-43-72; e-mail library@lsl.lviv.ua; internet www.lsl.lviv.ua; f. 1940; 6m. vols; Dir MIROSLAV. M. ROMANYUK.

Odessa

Scientific Library of the Odessa National I. I. Mechnikov University: 65082 Odessa, str. Preobrazhenskaya 24; tel. (48) 726-04-01; e-mail library@onu.edu.ua; internet www.lib.onu.edu.ua; f. 1817; 3.9m. vols; Dir MARINA A. PODREZOVA; Deputy Dir and IT Man. ZAYCHENKO ALLA; publ. *Odessa National University Herald. Series: Library studies, Bibliography studies, Bibliology.*

Simferopol

Taurida National University 'V. I. Vernadsky', Library: 95007 Simferopol, pr. Vernaskogo 4; tel. (65) 251-69-98; e-mail library@crimea.edu; 776,000 vols; Librarian V. I. SPIROVA.

Uzhgorod

Uzhgorod National University Library: Uzhgorod, Kapytulna vul. 9; tel. (31) 223-72-29; internet www.univ.uzhgorod.ua/~library; 1.5m. vols; Dir OLENA I. POCHEKUTOVA.

Museums and Art Galleries

Alupka

Alupka State Palace and Park Preserve: Alupka, Dvortsove shosse 10; tel. (654) 72-22-81; e-mail direction.dvorec@gmail.com; internet worontsovpalace.com.ua; f. 1921; Russian noble culture and way of life in 19th century; spec. colln of 17th-century maps of Europe and America; library of 10,000 vols; Dir K. K. KASPEROVICH.

Alushta

Alushta Literary Memorial Museum of S. M. Sergeev-Tsensky: Alushta, vul. Sergeeva-Tsenskogo 15; tel. (65) 603-06-64; house where the author lived; Dir T. A. FEFYUZA.

Bakhchisarai

Bakhchisarai Historical and Cultural State Preserve: 98405 Crimea, Bakhchisarai, vul. Richna 133; tel. (65) 544-28-81; e-mail hansaray@crimeastar.net; internet www.hansaray.org.ua; f. 1917; works of art, architectural monuments, the Khan Palace of Bakhchisarai (built 1532), cave towns; archaeological sites; archaeology and ethnographic collns; library of 12,000 vols; Dir-Gen. EUGENY PETROV; Deputy Dir OLEKSA HAIWORONSKI.

Chernihiv

Chernihiv Literary Museum 'Mikhailo Kotsyubinsky': 14000 Chernihiv, vul. Kotsyubinskogo 3; tel. (46) 224-04-59; f. 1934; life and work of Kotsyubinsky; library of 11,000 books; Dir IGOR KOTSYUBINSKY; publ. *Collections* (every 5 years).

Chernivtsi

Chernivtsi Memorial Museum 'Yu. A. Fedkovych': Chernivtsi, vul. Pushkina 17; tel. (37) 22-56-78; f. 1945; life and work of the writer A. Fedkovich; Dir D. FYLYPCHUK.

Dniprodzerzhynsk

Dniprodzerzhynsk Museum of Town History: 51931 Dniprodzerzhynsk; tel. (56) 923-11-10; f. 1931; library of 10,000 vols; Dir NATALIA BULANOVA.

Dnipropetrovsk

Dnipropetrovsk Historical Museum 'D. I. Yavornystkiy': Dnipropetrovsk, vul. K. Marksa 16; tel. (56) 246-24-28; e-mail muzeum@a-teleport.com; internet www.museum.dp.ua; Dir NADEZHDA KAPUSTINA.

Dnipropetrovsk State Art Museum: 49044 Dnipropetrovsk, vul. Shevchenko 21; tel. (56) 247-32-65; e-mail info@globe.dp.ua; internet www.artmuseum.dp.ua; Dir VLADIMIR KULICHIKHIN.

Donetsk

Donetsk Art Museum: 83055 Donetsk, Pushkina 35; tel. (62) 304-83-03; e-mail artmuseum@mail.ints.net.

Donetsk Botanical Gardens: 83059 Donetsk, pr. Ilicha 110; tel. (62) 294-12-80; e-mail herb@herb.dn.ua; f. 1964; attached to Nat. Acad. of Sciences of Ukraine; Dir A. Z. GLUKHOV.

Kamyanets-Podilsky

Kamyanets-Podilsky State Historical Museum-Preserve: 32300 Khmelnitska oblast, Kamyanets-Podilsky, vul. Ioanno-Predtechenska 2; tel. (38) 492-37-84; f. 1890; Dir L. P. STANISLAVSKA.

Kerch

Kerch State Archaeological Museum: 98300 Crimea, Kerch, Sverdlova 7; tel. (65) 2-04-75; e-mail museum@kerch.com.ua; f. 1826; library of 20,000 vols; Dir P. I. IVANENKO; publ. *Arkheologiya i istoriya Bospora* (irregular).

Kharkiv

Kharkiv State Art Museum: 61002 Kharkiv, Sovnarkomivska vul. 11; tel. (57) 706-33-95; e-mail artmuseum_kharkiv@i.ua; internet artmuseum.kharkov.ua; f. 1920; Ukrainian, Russian and foreign art from 15th–21st centuries; 24,000 exhibits; library of 19,000 vols; Dir V. V. MYZGINA.

Kharkiv State Historical Museum: 61003 Kharkiv, Universitetska vul. 10; tel. (57) 223-20-94; Dir N. A. VOEVODIN.

Khomutovo

Ukrainian Steppe Nature Reserve: 87620 Donetsk oblast, Novoazov raion, Khomutovo; tel. (62) 792-73-25; e-mail zapovednik@novoazovsk.net; f. 1961; attached to Nat. Acad. of Sciences of Ukraine; Dir Dr ANATOLIY P. GENOV.

Kolomiya

Kolomiya State Museum of Folk Art: Ivano-Frankivska oblast, Kolomiya, Teatralna vul. 25; tel. (34) 332-39-12; e-mail jatkachuk@hutsul.museum; internet hutsul.museum; f. 1926; exhibitions, confs, festivals, scientific work; 87 mems; library of 6,000 vols; Dir Y. TKACHUK; publ. *People's House* (6 a year).

Kyiv

Bohdan and Varvara Khanenko Museum of Arts: 01004 Kyiv, Tereshchenkivska 15–17; tel. (44) 235-02-25; e-mail khanenkomuseum@ukr.net; f. 1919; holds more than 20,000 items of western European, Oriental and ancient art; Dir VIRA VYNOHRADOVA; publ. *Khanenko Readings* (1 a year).

Kyiv Museum of Russian Art: 01004 Kyiv, Tereshchenkivska vul. 9; tel. (44) 451-40-27; e-mail museumru@ukr.net; f. 1922; library of 17,000 vols; Dir IURII VAKULENKO.

Kyiv State Literary Museum 'Lessya Ukrainka': 01032 Kyiv, vul. Saksaganskogo 97; tel. (44) 220-57-52; f. 1962; life and work of the Ukrainian poets and artists of the 19th and early 20th centuries; library of 5,000 vols; Dir IRINA L. VEREMEYEVA.

Museum of Theatrical, Musical and Cinematographic Art of Ukraine: 01015 Kyiv, str. Lavrska 9/24; tel. (44) 280-16-22; e-mail tmf-museum@ukr.net; internet www.tmf-museum.kiev.ua; f. 1923; library of 30,000 vols; Dir IRYNA DROBOT.

National Art Museum of Ukraine: 01001 Kyiv, M. Hrushevskoho str. 6; tel. (44) 278-13-57; e-mail pr@namu.kiev.ua; f. 1899; colln of Ukrainian figurative art; 40,000 exhibits, incl. masterpieces of Ukrainian painting, sculpture and graphics from Kyiv Rus age to present day; Dir A. I. MELNIK.

National Botanical Gardens 'M. M. Gryshko': 01014 Kyiv, Timiryazevska vul. 1; tel. (44) 285-41-05; e-mail nbg@nbg.kiev.ua; f. 1935; attached to Nat. Acad. of Sciences of Ukraine; library of 39,041 vols; Dir Prof. Dr N. V. ZAIMENKO.

National Kyiv-Pechersk Lavra Museum: 01015 Kyiv, vul. Sichnevogo Povstannya 25; tel. (44) 254-22-57; e-mail lavra@lavra.kiev.ua; internet www.lavra.kiev.ua; ancient monastery, icons.

National Museum of the History of Ukraine: 01034 Kyiv, vul. Volodymyrska 2; tel. (44) 228-65-45; e-mail mhistory@i.com.ua; f. 1899; history, archaeology, religion, ethnography, 600,000 exhibits; Dir SERHIY CHAIKOVSKYI.

National Taras Shevchenko Museum: 01004 Kyiv, 12 Taras Shevchenko bulv.; tel. (44) 234-25-23; e-mail shevchenko-museum@ukr.net; f. 1940; life and work of the poet T. G. Shevchenko; Dir CHRISTINA KLIMENKO.

St Sophia of Kiev National Conservation Area: 01034 Kyiv, Volodymyrska vul. 24; tel. (44) 278-26-20; e-mail stsophia@i.kiev.ua; internet www.sophia.org.ua; f. 1934; comprises 11th-century St Sofia cathedral (with early frescoes and mosaics) and other, 18th-century bldgs; attached museums incl. St Cyril Church Museum, St Andrew Church Museum, Golden Gates Museum (11th-century town gatehouse) and, in the Crimea, 6th–15th-century Sudak fortress; Dir-Gen. NELYA M. KUKOVALSKA.

Ukrainian Museum of Folk and Decorative Art: 01015 Kyiv, vul. Sichnevoho Povstannya 21; tel. (44) 290-13-43; f. 1954; library of 3,180 vols; Dir V. G. NAGAI; publ. *Folk Creative Work and Ethnography*.

Lviv

Lviv Historical Museum: 79008 Lviv, pl. Rynok 4/6/24; tel. (322) 74-33-04; f. 1893; Dir BOGDAN CHAYKOVSKIY.

Lviv State Picture Gallery: 79000 Lviv, vul. Stefanika 3; tel. (32) 272-39-48; f. 1907; West European and Ukrainian contemporary art; library of 34,276 vols; Dir BORIS VOZNITSKY.

Andrey Sheptytsky National Museum in Lviv: 79008 Lviv, Svobody 20; tel. (32) 2235-88-46; e-mail nml_shept@ukr.net; f. 1905; colln of over 170,000 artworks; preservation, devt, study and promotion of 11th–21st century Ukrainian art; library of 30,000 scientific vols; Dir IHOR KOZHAN; Academic Sec. ANGELINA ZABYTIVSKA; publ. *Litopys* (Chronicle of the Andrey Sheptytsky National Museum in Lviv, 1 a year).

State Museum of Ethnography, Arts and Crafts: Lviv, pr. Svoboda 15; tel. (32) 297-01-57; f. 1951; attached to Nat. Acad. of Sciences of Ukraine.

State Natural History Museum: 79008 Lviv, Teatralna vul. 18; tel. (32) 274-23-07; e-mail museum@museum.lviv.net; internet museum.lviv.net; f. 1870; attached to Nat. Acad. of Sciences of Ukraine; library of 69,000 vols; Dir Prof. YURIY M. CHORNOBAY; publ. *Proceedings* (1 a year).

Odessa

Odessa Archaeological Museum: 65026 Odessa, vul. Lanzheronovska 4; tel. 722-01-71; e-mail archaeology@farlep.net; internet www.archaeology.farlep.odessa.ua; f. 1825; history of the Northern Black Sea coast area; library of 28,000 vols; Dir V. P. VANCHUGOV; Librarian H. P. UKRAINSKA.

Odessa Fine Arts Museum: 65082 Odessa, Sofievska vul. 5A; tel. (48) 223-82-72; e-mail ofam@tm.odessa.ua; internet www.museum-finearts.odessa.ua; f. 1899; Ukrainian and Russian art since 15th century; library of 15,000 vols; Dir NATALYA S. POLISHCHUK.

Odessa Museum of Western and Eastern Art: 270026 Odessa, Pushkinska vul. 9; tel. (482) 22-48-15; e-mail oweamuseum@hotbox.ru; internet www.oweamuseum.odessa.ua; f. 1920; library of 14,000 vols; Dir VICTOR S. NIKIFOROV.

Poltava

Poltava Art Museum: 36020 Poltava, Frunze 5; tel. (53) 256-35-40; e-mail gallery.poltava@gmail.com; f. 1919; library of 4,000 vols; Curator OLGA KURCHAKOVA.

Poltava State Museum: Poltava, Lenina 2; life and work of the writers P. Mirnyi, J. Kotlyarevsky, V. G. Korolenko, N. V. Gogol; library of 80,000 vols; Dir GALINA P. BELOUS.

Sevastopol

National Preserve of Tauric Chersonesos: 299045 Crimea, Sevastopol, vul. Drevnyaya 1; tel. (69) 255-02-78; e-mail info@chersonesos.org; internet www.chersonesos.org; f. 1892; archaeological park incorporating museum and ruins of Greek colony and Byzantine city of Tauric Chersonesos; library of 30,000 vols; Gen. Dir LEONID ZHUNKO; publ. *Khersonesskyi Sbornik* (Chersonesos Collected Articles, 1 a year).

Sumy

Sumy Art Museum 'Nukanor Onatsky': 40030 Sumy, Krasnaya pl. 1; tel. (54) 222-04-81; internet www.city.sumy.ua/artgallery; f. 1920; Dir GALINA V. AREFEVA.

Yalta

Nikita Botanical Gardens: 98648 Crimea, Yalta, Nikita; tel. (65) 433-55-30; e-mail nbs1812@gmail.com; internet www.nbg.crimea.ua; f. 1812; attached to Ukrainian Acad. of Agrarian Sciences; library of 213,000 vols; 50,000 species and hybrids of flowers, fruits, and woody, subtropical, industrial, oil-bearing and medical plants; Dir Prof. Dr V. N. EZHOV; publs *Bulletin* (3 a year), *Collected Scientific Works* (3 a year).

Universities

AGRARIAN UNIVERSITIES

BILA TSERKVA STATE AGRARIAN UNIVERSITY

09117 Kyivska obl., Bila Tserkva, bul. 50-Richchya Perermoti 96

Telephone: (44) 633-11-01
E-mail: rector@btsau.kiev.ua
Internet: www.btsau.kiev.ua

Founded 1750, present name and status 1995

Faculties of agronomy, biotechnology, culture and art, economics, external studies, languages, law, physical education, qualification improvement, veterinary medicine

Rector: Dr MYKHAILO M. BARANOVSKIY
First Pro-Rector: Prof. Dr VITALIY P. NOVAK
Pro-Rector for Distance Studies: Prof. Dr SVETLANA I. TSEKHMISTRENKO
Pro-Rector for Finance: Dr TATYANA V. ARBUZOVA
Pro-Rector for Research: Prof. Dr IHOR L. YAKIMENKO
Pro-Rector for Studies: Prof. Dr LYLIYA V. BARANOVSKAYA
Publication: *Vestnik BSGAU* (Bila Tserkva State Agrarian University Bulletin)

CRIMEAN AGROTECHNOLOGICAL UNIVERSITY

95492 Simferopol, Agrarnoye
Telephone: (65) 226-33-52
E-mail: rectorat@csau.crimea-ua.com
Internet: www.csau.crimea-ua.com
Founded 1922
State control
Languages of instruction: Russian, Ukrainian
Academic year: September to July
Dir: Prof. MYKHAYLO M. MELNIKOV
Library of 542,425 vols
Number of teachers: 380
Number of students: 4,047

DEANS

Faculty of Agronomy: Dr VALERIY F. VIL'-CHINSKIY
Faculty of Economics and Management: Dr VITALIY M. DYATEL
Faculty of Land Planning and Geodesy: Dr VOLODYMYR M. GORBATYUK
Faculty of Mechanization of Producing and Technology of Processing of Agricultural Production: Dr YURI B. GERBER
Faculty of Veterinary Medicine: Dr VIKTOR I. SKRIPNIK

DNIPROPETROVS'K STATE AGRARIAN UNIVERSITY

49600 Dnipropetrovsk, vul. Voroshylov 25
Telephone: (56) 744-81-32
E-mail: interdsau@gmail.com
Internet: www.dsau.dp.ua
Founded 1922
State control
Language of instruction: Ukrainian
Academic year: September to June
Rector: Prof. ANATOLIY S. I. KOBETS
Vice-Rector for Education: Prof. Dr DMYTRO M. ONOPRIYENKO
Vice-Rector for Research: Prof. YURIY I. GRYTSAN
Dir for Library: ANTONINA G. BRATCHYK
Library of 400,000 vols
Number of teachers: 488
Number of students: 6,314 (3,653 full-time, 2,661 external)
Publication: *Agrosvit* (2 a year)

DEANS

Faculty of Accounting and Finance: Prof. GALYNA Y. PAVLOVA
Faculty of Agricultural Mechanization: Prof. Dr SERHII P. SOKOL
Faculty of Agronomy: Prof. Dr OLEXANDR O. MYTSYK
Faculty of Biotechnology: Prof. Dr STANISLAV G. PISHCHAN
Faculty of Ecology and Irrigation: Prof. Dr ANDRIY V. TKACHUK
Faculty of Marketing and Management: LARYSA M. KURBATS'KA
Faculty of Veterinary Medicine: Prof. Dr IVAN A. BIBEN

KHARKIV PETRO VASYLENKO NATIONAL TECHNICAL UNIVERSITY OF AGRICULTURE

61002 Kharkiv, vul. Artema 44
Telephone: (57) 700-38-88
E-mail: khstua@lin.com.ua
Internet: www.khntusg.com.ua
Founded 1930 as Kharkiv Institute of Agricultural Mechanization and Electrification; current name adopted 2004
public control
Rector: LEONID M. TISHCHENKO (acting)
Counsellor: DMYTRO I. MAZORENKO

Vice-Rector of Distance and Correspondence Education: MYKOLA M. TROYANOV
Vice-Rector for Teaching and Educational Work: VIKTOR I. ZHYLA
Vice-Rector for Teaching and Educational Work and Admin. Affairs: ANATOLIY P. LUTCENKO
Vice-Rector for Scientific Work: VIKTOR A. VOYTOV

Library of 150,000 vols
Number of teachers: 370
Number of students: 7,000

KHARKIV STATE AGRARIAN UNIVERSITY 'V. V. DOKUCHAYEV'

62483 Kharkiv, P/O 'Komunist-1', vul. Mazepy 10
Telephone: (57) 293-71-46
E-mail: cau@kharkov.com
Internet: www.hgau.narod.ru
Founded 1816
Rector: Prof. MYKOLA D. YEVTUSHENKO
Library of 600,000 vols
Number of teachers: 258
Number of students: 5,195

Publications: *Agrochemistry, Common Agriculture, Forestry, Plant Growing and Vegetable Production, Series on Crop Production, Series on Economics and Natural Sciences, Series on Soil Science*

DEANS

Faculty of Agrochemistry and Soil Science: VASYL DEKHTYARYOV
Faculty of Agronomy: YEVGEN OGURTSOV
Faculty of Continuing Education: VOLODYMYR PUZIK
Faculty of Correspondence Studies: VOLODYMYR BILIUSKO
Faculty of Economics: OLEKSANDR ULYAN-CHENKO
Faculty of Forestry: ANATOLIY POLYVYANIY
Faculty of Land Management: VASYL BALA-KYRSKY
Faculty of Plant Protection: VOLODYMYR TURENKO

LVIV NATIONAL AGRARIAN UNIVERSITY

80381 Lviv, V. Velikogo Str. 1
Telephone: (32) 224-23-35
E-mail: lnau@mail.lviv.ua
Internet: www.lnau.lviv.ua
Founded 1856
State control
Academic year: September to June
Depts of agronomy, architecture, ecology, economics, energetics, farm building, land surveying and mechanics
Rector: Prof. Dr VOLODYMYR V. SNITYNSKYY
Library of 600,000 vols
Number of teachers: 370
Number of students: 11,000
Publication: *Transactions*

NATIONAL AGRICULTURAL UNIVERSITY OF UKRAINE

03041 Kyiv, vul. Heroyiv Oborony 15
Telephone: (44) 267-81-19
E-mail: inter@nauu.kiev.ua
Internet: www.nauu.kiev.ua
Founded 1898
Brs in Berezhany, Boyarka, Irpin, Nemishayiv, Nizhyn, Zalishchiky
Rector: DYMTRO O. MELNYCHUK
Library: 1m. vols
Number of teachers: 2,827
Number of students: 22,034

Publication: *For Agricultural Specialists* (6 a year)

DEANS

Faculty of Agricultural Biology: ANATOLIY V. BYKIN
Faculty of Agricultural Management: KOVTUN O. ANATOLIVNA
Faculty of Agricultural Mechanical Engineering: YAROSLAV M. MYKHAYLOVYCH
Faculty of Animal Health: VITALIY Y. LUBETS-KIY
Faculty of Animal Husbandry, Output Production and Processing Technology: YURIY V. ZASUKHA
Faculty of Construction and Design: KONSTYANTYN H. LOPATKO
Faculty of Ecology and Biotechnology: NATALYA M. RIDEY
Faculty of Economics: SERHIY M. KVASHA
Faculty of Electrification and Automation of Agriculture: IVAN P. RADKO
Faculty of Forestry: SERHIY B. KOVALEVSKY
Faculty of Land Management: BOHDAN I. NOVAK
Faculty of Landscape Engineering: ANATOLIY I. KUSHNIR
Faculty of Law: VOLODYMYR I. KURILO
Faculty of Quality and Safety of Agricultural Production: OLGA M. YAKUBCHAK
Faculty of Small Animal Health: OLEG F. PETRENKO
Faculty of Social Pedagogy: PETRO H. LUZAN
Faculty of Water Resources and Aquaculture: PETRO H. SHEVCHENKO

UKRAINIAN NATIONAL FORESTRY UNIVERSITY

79057 Lviv, vul. Gen. Chuprynka 103
Telephone: (32) 237-80-94
E-mail: nltu@ukr.net
Rector: YURIY YU. TUNYTSYA
Vice-Rector: HRYHORIY T. KRYNYTSKYY
Library of 450,000 vols
Number of teachers: 310
Number of students: 3,600

Publications: *Naukovyy visnyk* (Scientific bulletin), *Ukrainski lis* (Ukrainian Forest)

DEANS

Extramural Faculty: Dr YAROSLAV LYKO
Faculty of Economy: Dr YAROSLAV KULCHYTS-KYY
Faculty of Forest Mechanics: Prof. Dr MYKOLA KIRYK
Faculty of Forestry: Prof. Dr STEPAN MYK-LUSH
Faculty of Technology: Prof. Dr VOLODYMYR MAKSYMIV
Institute of Ecological Economics: Dir: Dr LYUDMYLA MAKSYMIV

ZHYTOMYR NATIONAL AGROECOLOGICAL UNIVERSITY

10008 Zhytomyr, Stary bul. 7
Telephone: (41) 237-49-31
E-mail: ecos@znau.edu.ua
Internet: www.znau.edu.ua
Founded 1922
State control
Academic year: September to July
Rector: Dr V. M. MYKYTIUK
Library of 370,000 vols
Number of teachers: 533
Number of students: 8,300

DEANS

Faculty of Accounting and Finance: MAKSYM O. STEPURA
Faculty of Agronomy: PETRO I. TROFYMENKO
Faculty of Animal Husbandry: MYKHAILO M. KRYVYI

Faculty of Ecology: BORYS V. BORYSIUK

Faculty of Economics and Management: OLEKSANDR A. OPALOV

Faculty of Engineering: OLEKSANDR D. MULIAR

Faculty of Forestry: VASYL M. TURKO

Faculty of Veterinary Medicine: ANATOLII S. REVUNETS

HUMANITIES AND SCIENCES UNIVERSITIES

CHERNIVTSI NATIONAL UNIVERSITY 'YURIY FEDKOVYCH'

58012 Chernivtsi, vul. Kotsyubinskoho 2

Telephone: (37) 222-62-35

E-mail: rector@chnu.cv.ua

Internet: www.chnu.cv.ua

Founded 1875

State control

Language of instruction: Ukrainian

Academic year: September to June

Rector: STEPAN V. MELNYCHUK

First Pro-Rector, Pro-Rector for Research: S. V. MELNYCHUK

Pro-Rector for Academic Affairs: ROMAN I. PETRYSHYN

Pro-Rector for Academic Devt: TAMARA V. MARUSYK

Librarian: OLEG I. SHLYUK

Library: see Libraries and Archives

Number of teachers: 786

Number of students: 14,103 (7,421 full-time, 6,682 part-time)

Publications: *Scientific University Annual*, *Universitetsky Visnyk* (12 a year)

DEANS

Faculty of Applied Mathematics: R. I. PETRYSHYN

Faculty of Biology: M. M. MARCHENKO

Faculty of Chemistry: O. S. LYAVYNETS

Faculty of Computer Science: (vacant)

Faculty of Economics: L. S. BILYK

Faculty of Engineering and Technology: Prof. O. V. ANGELSKIY

Faculty of Foreign Languages: R. V. VATSEBA

Faculty of Geography: V. P. RUDENKO

Faculty of History, Politology and International Relations: O. V. DOBRZHANSKIY

Faculty of Law: P. S. PATSURKIVSKIY

Faculty of Pedagogy: I. M. ZVARYCH

Faculty of Philology: B. I. BUNCHUK

Faculty of Philosophy and Theology: V. O. BALUKH

Faculty of Physics: I. V. GUTSUL

DNIPROPETROVSK NATIONAL UNIVERSITY

49050 Dnipropetrovsk, vul. Naukova 13

Telephone: (56) 246-00-95

E-mail: admin@dsu.dp.ua

Internet: www.dsu.dp.ua

Founded 1918

Languages of instruction: Russian, Ukrainian

Academic year: September to July

Pres.: MYKOLA POLYAKOV

Vice-Pres. and President's Deputy: O. O. KOCHUBEY

Vice-Pres. for Academic Affairs: V. G. MUSIYAKA

Vice-Pres. for Foreign Affairs: V. V. KOSTYRKO

Vice-Pres. for Research: M. M. DRON

Librarian: L. S. KUBISHKINA

Library: see Libraries and Archives

Number of teachers: 1,233

Number of students: 13,260

Publication: *Dnipropetrovsk University Newspaper* (12 a year)

DEANS

Faculty of Applied Mathematics: S. V. CHERNYSHENKO

Faculty of Biology and Ecology: O. Y. PAKHOMOV

Faculty of Chemistry: V. F. VARGALYUK

Faculty of Geology and Geography: V. V. BOGDANOVICH

Faculty of History: S. I. SVITLENKO

Faculty of International Economics: N. Y. BOYTSUN

Faculty of Law: P. I. GNATENKO

Faculty of Mass Media: V. D. DEMCHENKO

Faculty of Mechanics and Mathematics: V. O. SYASEV

Faculty of Medicine: J. S. SAPA

Faculty of Philology: O. V. RODNY

Faculty of Physics: R. S. TUTIK

Faculty of Psychology and Pedagogics: I. V. RASPOPOV

Faculty of Radio Physics: V. M. DOLGOV

Faculty of Ukrainian Philology and Art History: I. S. POPOVA

Institute of Economics: S. O. SMIRNOV

Institute of Physics and Technology: Y. A. DZUR

DONETSK NATIONAL UNIVERSITY

83001 Donetsk, vul. Universytetska St 24

Telephone: (62) 337-19-45

E-mail: postmaster@univ.donetsk.ua

Internet: www.donnu.edu.ua

Founded 1965, Donetsk State Univ. until 2000

State control

Languages of instruction: Russian, Ukrainian

Academic year: September to July

Rector: Prof. V. P. SHEVCHENKO

Deputy Rector: Prof. P. V. YEGOROV

Vice-Rector: Prof. N. P. IVANITSYN

Librarian: N. O. KORYAGINA

Library: see under Libraries and Archives

Number of teachers: 900 .

Number of students: 17,500

Publications: *Bulletin* (1 a year), *Donetsk Archaeological Bulletin* (1 a year), *Eastern Ukraine Linguistic Collected Articles* (2 a year), *Economical Cybernetics* (4 a year), *Finance, Accounting, Banks* (2 a year), *Historical and Political Studies* (4 a year), *Juridical Studies* (4 a year), *Management Models in Market Economy* (2 a year), *New Pages in the History of Donbass* (2 a year), *Philological Studies* (2 a year), *Theoretical and Applied Mechanics* (1 a year)

DONETSK NATIONAL UNIVERSITY OF ECONOMICS AND TRADE 'M. TUHAN-BARANOVSKIY'

83050 Donetsk, vul. Shchorsa 31

Telephone: (62) 335-10-29

E-mail: info@donduet.edu.ua

Internet: www.donduet.edu.ua

Founded 1920

State control

Academic year: September to June

Languages of instruction: English, Russian, Ukrainian

Rector: O. O. SHUBIN

First Vice-Rector: L. O. OMELYANOVYCH

Vice-Rector for Economic and Technical Provisions: A. B. ROMANOV

Vice-Rector for Scientific Affairs: A. A. SADEKOV

Vice-Rector for Scientific-Pedagogical Activity and Int. Relations: V. G. POGREBNYAK

Vice-Rector for Social and Educational Affairs: S. V. DROZHZHINA

Librarian: T. P. TKACHENKO

Library of 67,000 vols, 75,000 periodicals

Number of teachers: 450

Number of students: 14,876

DEANS

Institute of Accounting and Finance: V. A. ORLOVA

Institute of Economics and Management: L. V. FROLOVA

Institute of Foodstuff Industries: V. A. SUKMANOV

Faculty of Marketing, Trade and Customs Activity: Prof. I. KH. BASHYROV

Faculty of Restaurant and Hotel Business: Prof. T. V. NUZHNA

International Faculty of Foreign Specialist Training: V. E. VOYLOSHNIKOVA

KHARKIV NATIONAL UNIVERSITY OF ECONOMICS

61001 Kharkiv, pr. Lenina 9A

Telephone: (57) 702-03-04

E-mail: mail@hneu.edu.ua

Internet: www.hdeu.edu.ua

Founded 1930

State control

Languages of instruction: English, Russian, Ukrainian

Academic year: September to June

Rector: Prof. Dr VOLODYMYR PONOMARENKO

Vice-Rector for Int. Relations: Prof. VOLODYMYR YERMACHENKO

Librarian: NATALYA BOZHKO

Library of 864,329 vols, 13,679 periodicals, 2,070 copies of theses and thesis abstracts

Number of teachers: 712

Number of students: 14,000 (incl. 205 postgraduate and doctoral)

Publications: *Business Inform*, *Development Management*, *Economy of Development*

DEANS

Correspondence Faculty: Prof. Dr SERGIJ LUKASHOV

Faculty of Accounting and Audit: Prof. Dr GRIGORY AZARENKOV

Faculty of Economic Informatics: Prof. Dr VOLODYMYR GRACHOV

Faculty of Economy and Law: Prof. Dr TETYANA SERIKOVA

Faculty of Int. Economic Relations: Prof. Dr IVAN PIDDUBNY

Faculty of Management and Marketing: Prof. Dr OLEKSANDR TIMONIN

Finance Faculty: Prof. Dr PAVLO PRONOZA

KHMELNYTSKY STATE UNIVERSITY

29016 Khmelnytsky, vul. Instytutska 11

Telephone: (38) 272-80-76

E-mail: centr@mailhub.tub.km.ua

Internet: www.tup.km.ua

Founded 1962

Rector: MYKOLA SKYBA

Deputy Rector for Academic Work: SERGIY KOSTOGRYZ

Deputy Rector for Academic Work: MYKHAYLO VOYNARENKO

Deputy Rector for Admin. Work: ANATOLIY FOMOV

Deputy Rector for Finance and Economic Activity: VIKTOR NYZHNYK

Deputy Rector for Int. Relations: MYKOLA YOKHNA

Deputy Rector for Scientific Work: VITALIY KAPLUN

Number of teachers: 637

Number of students: 12,976

Publications: *Measuring and Computing Devices in Technological Processes* (2 a year), *Problems of Trybology International*

Scientific Journal (2 a year), *University Herald* (6 a year)

DEANS

Faculty of Applied Mathematics and Computer Technologies: SERGIY KOVALCHUK

Faculty of Business: LIDIYA TORGOVA

Faculty of Correspondence Studies 1: VITALIY KARAZEY

Faculty of Correspondence Studies 2: VIRA BEGNYAK

Faculty of Distance Studies: MYKOLA MAZUR

Faculty of Economics: MYKOLA BONDARENKO

Faculty of Engineering Mechanics: GEORGIY DRAPAK

Faculty of Humanities and Pedagogics: LYUDMYLA STANISLAVOVA

Faculty of International Relations: VITALIY TRETKO

Faculty of Management: LYUDMYLA LYUBOKHYNETS

Faculty of Pre-University and Post-University Training: MYKOLA BABYCH

Faculty of Radio Electronics and Computer Engineering: VOLODYMYR KOSENKOV

Faculty of Technology and Design: A. B. DOMBROVSKIY

KYIV NATIONAL ECONOMIC UNIVERSITY NAMED AFTER VADYM HETMAN

03680 Kyiv, pr. Peremogy 54/1

Telephone: (44) 371-61-12

E-mail: rector@kneu.kiev.ua

Internet: www.kneu.edu.ua

Founded 1906

State control

Language of instruction: Ukrainian

Academic year: September to June

Rector: Prof. Dr ANATOLII PAVLENKO

Librarian: TETIANA KYRYLENKO

Library of 1,366,000 vols, 331 journals

Number of teachers: 1,512 (incl. full-time and part-time)

Number of students: 24,870

Publications: *International Economic Policy*, *Marketing in Ukraine*

DEANS

Faculty of Accounting: Prof. VASYL IEFIMENKO

Faculty of Crediting: Prof. Dr MYKHAILO DYBA

Faculty of Economics and Management: Assoc. Prof. Dr OLEKSANDR VOSTRIAKOV

Faculty of Economy of Agroindustrial Complex: Prof. MYKHAILO KOTSUPATRYI

Faculty of Finance: Prof. VOLODYMYR KHLIVNYY

Faculty of Information Systems and Technologies: Prof. OLEKSANDR SHARAPOV

Faculty of International Economics and Management: Assoc. Prof. IURII SOLODKOVSKYY

Faculty of Law: Prof. Dr VITALII OPRYSHKO

Faculty of Personnel Management and Marketing: Prof. Dr OLEKSANDR SHAFALIUK

KYIV NATIONAL LINGUISTIC UNIVERSITY

03680 Kyiv GSP 150, vul. Chervonoarmiyska 73

Telephone: (44) 227-33-72

E-mail: knlu@knlu.kiev.ua

Internet: www.knlu.kiev.ua

Founded 1948

State control

Academic year: September to June

Rector: Dr ROMAN V. VASKO

Library: 1m. vols

Number of teachers: 605

Number of students: 6,230

Publications: *Methods in Foreign Language Teaching* (4 a year, in Ukrainian and other languages), *Philology of Foreign Languages* (4 a year, in Ukrainian and other languages)

DEANS

Faculty of Economics and Law: MYKOLA HAMZYUK

Faculty of German Philology: IRYNA MOYSEYENKO

Faculty of Oriental Studies: SERGUY SOROKIN

Faculty of Romance Philology: ANATOLIY CHERNUKHA

Faculty of Slavic Philology: ALLA KENDYUSHENKO

Faculty of Translation: OKSANA FRANKO

KYIV NATIONAL UNIVERSITY OF TRADE AND ECONOMICS

02156 Kyiv, vul. Kioto 19

Telephone: (44) 531-47-73

E-mail: rio@knteu.kiev.ua

Internet: www.knteu.kiev.ua

Rector: Prof. Dr ANATOLII A. MAZARAKI

Vice-Rector for Admin. and Economic Work: Prof. Dr LEONID G. SHAPOVAL

Vice-Rector for Scientific-Educational and Methodological Work: Prof. Dr NATALIA V. PRYTULSKA

Vice-Rector for Scientific and Pedagogical Work and Int. Relations: Prof. Dr VALERII M. SAI

Vice-Rector for Scientific-Pedagogic Work: Prof. Dr SVITLANA L. SHAPOVAL

Library: 2m. vols

Number of students: 39,000

DEANS

Commodity Science Faculty: Prof. VICTOR OSYKA

Faculty of Accounting and Economics: Prof. Dr OLEKSANDR A. KHARCHENKO

Faculty of Economics, Management and Law: Dr NATALIYA M. HULYAYEVA

Faculty of Finance and Banking: Dr IGOR V. SMOLIN

Faculty of the Restaurant, Hotel and Tourist Industry: Prof. Dr MYKHAILO I. PERESICHNYY

NATIONAL UNIVERSITY OF KYIV-MOHYLA ACADEMY

04070 Kyiv, vul. Skovorody 2

Telephone: (44) 416-45-15

E-mail: rec@ukma.kiev.ua

Internet: www.ukma.kiev.ua

Founded 1615, closed 1817, re-established 1991, nat. univ. 1994

State control

Languages of instruction: Ukrainian, English

Academic year: September to June

Pres.: VYACHESLAV BRYUKHOVETSKY

First Vice-Pres. and Vice-Pres. for Research and Devt: MYKHAILO BRYK

Vice-Pres. for Academic Affairs: VADYM ZUBKO

Vice-Pres. for Devt: NATALYA SHUMKOVA

Vice-Pres. for Finance and Admin.: LYUDMYLA DYACHENKO

Vice-Pres. for Foreign Cooperation: VOLODYMYR PANCHENKO

Vice-Pres. for Graduate and Postgraduate Studies: LYUDMYLA DYACHENKO

Dean of Students: OLENA TRETYAKOVA

Registrar: NATALIA HRYBCHUK

Librarian: TETYANA YAROSHENKO

Library of 300,000 vols

Number of teachers: 157

Number of students: 2,300

Publications: *Magisterium* (4 a year), *Mandrivets* (Traveller, 6 a year), *Naukovi Zapysky* (Scientific Notes, 13 a year)

DEANS

Faculty of Computer Science: MYKOLA HLYBOVETS

Faculty of Economics: Prof. YURIY BAZHAL

Faculty of Humanities: Prof. VITALIY SCHERBAK

Faculty of Legal Sciences: Dr ANDRIY A. MELESHEVICH

Faculty of Natural Sciences: Dr IRYNA VYSHENSKA

Faculty of Social Sciences and Technology: Prof. SERHIY M. KVIT

Kyiv-Mohyla Business School: PAVLO M. SHEREMETA

NATIONAL UNIVERSITY OF LVIV 'IVAN FRANKO'

79000 Lviv, Universytetska vul. 1

Telephone: (32) 274-12-62

E-mail: kyrylych@franko.lviv.ua

Internet: www.franko.lviv.ua

Founded 1661

Language of instruction: Ukrainian

Academic year: September to June

Rector: Prof. V. VYSOCHANSKY

Vice-Rector for Admin. Affairs: V. VLASEVYCH

Vice-Rector for Economic and Financial Affairs: M. LOZYNSKY

Vice-Rector for Int. Affairs: V. KYRYLYCH

Vice-Rector for Research: B. KOTUR

Vice-Rector for Student Affairs: ZVENISLAVA MAMCHUR

Vice-Rector for Teaching and Educational Affairs: M. ZUBRYTSKA

Provost: V. VYSOCHANSKY

Librarian: VASYL KMET

Library: see under Libraries and Archives

Number of teachers: 1,709

Number of students: 31,000

Publications: *Filolohiya* (Philology), *Inozemna Filologiya* (Foreign Philology), *Matematychni Studii* (Mathematical Studies), *Mineralogichniy Zbirnyk* (Proceedings on Mineralogy), *Paleontologichniy Zbirnyk* (Proceedings on Palaeontology), *Teoretychna Elektrotekhnika* (Theoretical Electrical Engineering), *Ukraina Moderna* (Modern Ukraine), *Ukrainske Literaturoznavstvo* (Ukrainian Literature Studies), *Zhurnal Fizychnykh Doslidzhen* (Journal of Physical Research)

DEANS

Dept of Life Safety: Prof. ZYNOVIY YAREMKO

Dept of Pedagogy: Prof. DMYTRO HERTSYUK

Dept of Physical Culture and Sport: Dr ROMANNA SIRENKO

Faculty of Applied Mathematics and Informatics: Prof. YAREMA G. SAVULA

Faculty of Biology: Assoc. Prof. SVITLANA HNATUSH

Faculty of Chemistry: Prof. MYKHAYLO KALYCHAK

Faculty of Economics: Prof. STEPAN PANCHYSHYN

Faculty of Electronics: Prof. IHOR POLOVINKO

Faculty of Foreign Languages: Assoc. Prof. VOLODYMYR SULYM

Faculty of Geography: Assoc. Prof. YAROSLAV KHOMYN

Faculty of Geology: Prof. MYKOLA PAVLUN

Faculty of History: Assoc. Prof. POMAN SHUST

Faculty of International Relations: MARKIAN MALSKY

Faculty of Journalism: Assoc. Prof. MYKHAYLO PRYSIAZHNY

Faculty of Law: Prof. ANDRIY BOYKO

Faculty of Mechanics and Mathematics: MYKAILO ZARICHNY

Faculty of Philosophy: VOLODYMYR MELNYK
Faculty of Physics: PETRO YAKYBCHUK
Faculty of Pre-University Training: Assoc. Prof. ROMAN O. KROKHMALNY

ODESSA NATIONAL UNIVERSITY 'I. I. MECHNIKOV'

65082 Odessa, vul. Dvoryanska 2
Telephone: (48) 723-52-54
E-mail: rector@onu.edu.ua
Internet: www.onu.edu.ua
Founded 1865
State control
Languages of instruction: Russian, Ukrainian
Academic year: September to July
Rector: Prof. Dr IGOR KOVAL
Pro-Rector for Academic Affairs: Assoc. Prof. ALEXANDR ZAPOROZHCENKO
Pro-Rector for Academic and Methodological Work: Prof. EVGENIY STRELTSOV
Pro-Rector for Admin. Work: VYACHESLAV IGNATENKO
Pro-Rector for Int. Relations: Assoc. Prof. SERGEY SKOROKHOD
Pro-Rector for Scientific Research: Prof. VLADIMIR IVANITSA
Librarian: MARINA PODREZOVA
Library: see under Libraries and Archives
Number of teachers: 1,700
Number of students: 13,000

Publications: *Fisika aerodispersnikh sistem* (1 a year), *Fotoelektronika* (1 a year), *Odessa State University Herald* (1 a year), *Studies in Literature* (1 a year)

DEANS

Faculty of Biology: Assoc. Prof. VENIAMIN ZAMOROV
Faculty of Chemistry: Assoc. Prof. VASILIY MENCHUK
Faculty of Economics and Law: Assoc. Prof. VYACHESLAV TRUBA
Faculty of Geology and Geography: Prof. EVGENIY CHERKEZ
Faculty of History: Assoc. Prof. VYACHESLAV KUSHNIR
Faculty of Philology: Prof. EVGENIY CHERNOIVANENKO
Faculty of Philosophy: Assoc. Prof. ALEXANDR CHAYKOVSKY
Faculty of Physics: Prof. YURY VAKSMAN
Faculty of Romance and Germanic Philology: Assoc. Prof. LIDIYA GOLUBENKO
Illiychevsk Institute of ONU: Prof. GRIGORIY DRAGAN
Institute of Innovation and Postgraduate Education: Prof. L. DUNAEVA
Institute of Mathematics, Economics and Mechanics: Prof. VIKTOR KRUGLOV
Institute of Social Studies: Prof. VIKTOR GLEBOV
Pervomaysk Educational Centre of Science: Assoc. Prof. NATALIA MIKHAL'CHENKO
Preparatory Faculty: Assoc. Prof. NIKOLAY PASCHENKO
Preparatory Faculty for Foreign Citizens: Assoc. Prof. SERGEY FEDORKO

ODESSA STATE ECONOMIC UNIVERSITY

65082 Odessa, Preobrazhenska vul. 8
Telephone: (48) 723-61-58
E-mail: rector@oseu.edu.ua
Internet: www.oseu.edu.ua
Founded 1921
State control
Rector: M. I. ZVERYAKOV
Vice-Rector: GEORGE SHUBARTOVSKIY
Library of 423,000 vols
Number of teachers: 455
Number of students: 6,355

POLTAVA UNIVERSITY OF ECONOMICS AND TRADE

36014 Poltava, Koval str. 3
Telephone: (532) 50-91-70
E-mail: rector@uccu.org.ua
Internet: www.pusku.edu.ua
Founded 1974, fmrly known as Poltava Univ. of Consumer Cooperatives in Ukraine, present name 2010
State control
Languages of instruction: English, Russian, Ukrainian
Academic year: September to June
Rector: Prof. OLEKSIY O. NESTULYA
Vice-Rector: Prof. MYKOLA G. ROGOZA
Vice-Rector for Research and Int. Relations: Prof. OLGA V. KARPENKO
Dir of Library: S. SADOVA
Library of 365,645 vols, 9,464 periodical titles
Number of teachers: 484
Number of students: 10,000

Publication: *PUET Scientific Bulletin*

DEANS

Dept of Economics and Management: P. VORONA
Dept of Finance and Accounting: N. PEDCHENKO
Dept of Food Technology, Hotel, Restaurant and Tourism Business: V. SHKARUPA
Dept of Merchandise and Commerce: N. TYAGUNOVA
Extramural Dept: U. STROCHIHIN

ATTACHED INSTITUTE

Institute of Continuing and Transition Education: courses in accounting and auditing, business, corporate economics, finance, marketing and international management

'TARAS SHEVCHENKO' NATIONAL UNIVERSITY OF KYIV

01601 Kyiv, Volodymyrska St 64/13
Telephone: (44) 239-33-33
E-mail: office.chief@univ.net.ua
Internet: www.univ.kiev.ua
Founded 1834
State control
Languages of instruction: English, Ukrainian
Rector: Prof. Dr LEONID V. HUBERSKY
First Vice-Rector: Prof. Dr OLEG K. ZAKUSYLO
Vice-Rector for Int. Relations: Prof. Dr PETRO O. BEKH
Vice-Rector for Science and Educational Work: Assoc. Prof. Dr VOLODYMYR P. BUGROV
Vice-Rector for Scientific Work: Prof. Dr SERHIY A. VYZHVA
Librarian: VALENTYNA G. NESTERENKO
Library: see under Libraries and Archives
Number of teachers: 2,813
Number of students: 22,500

Publication: *Vestnik Kievskogo Universiteta*

DEANS

Faculty of Chemistry: Prof. Dr YULIAN M. VOLOVENKO
Faculty of Cybernetics: Prof. Dr ANATOLIY V. ANISIMOV
Faculty of Economics: Prof. Dr VIKTOR D. BAZYLEVICH
Faculty of Geography: Prof. Dr YAROSLAV B. OLIYNYK
Faculty of Geology: Prof. Dr VOLODYMYR A. MYKHAILOV
Faculty of History: Prof. Dr VIKTOR F. KOLESNYK
Faculty of Law: Dr IVAN S. HRYTSENKO

Faculty of Mechanics and Mathematics: Prof. Dr MYKHAILO F. HORODNIY
Faculty of Philosophy: Prof. Dr ANATOLIY YE. KONVERSKYI
Faculty of Physics: Prof. Dr MYKOLA V. MAKARETS
Faculty of Psychology: Prof. Dr IVAN V. DANYLUK
Faculty of Radiophysics: Prof. Dr IHOR O. ANISIMOV
Faculty of Social Sciences: Assoc. Prof. ANDRIY P. HORBACHYK
Faculty for International Students: Assoc. Prof. YURIY V. NOSYK
Preparatory Faculty: Prof. TETIANA V. TABENSKA

ATTACHED INSTITUTES

Astronomical Observatory: 01033 Kyiv, Observatorna St 3; tel. (44) 486-26-91; e-mail director@observ.univ.kiev.ua; internet www.observ.univ.kiev.ua/mainu.htm; Dir B. I. HNATYK.

Centre for Ukrainian Studies: 01033 Kyiv, Volodymyrska St 60, Rm 105; tel. (44) 239-31-84; e-mail uaznavstvo@mail.univ.kiev.ua; internet uaznavstvo.univ.kiev.ua; Dir Prof. MYKOLA I. OBUSHNYI.

Information and Computer Centre: 01033 Kyiv, Academician Glushkov Ave 2, Bldg 6; tel. (44) 521-35-14; e-mail admin@univ.kiev.ua; internet www.icc.univ.kiev.ua; Dir Dr YURIY V. BOYKO.

Institute of International Relations: 01033 Kyiv, Melnykova St 36/1; tel. (44) 481-44-37; e-mail decanat_relat@univ.kiev.ua; internet www.iir.kiev.ua; Dir Prof. VALERIY V. KOPIYKA.

Institute of Journalism: 01033 Kyiv, Melnykova St 36/1; tel. (44) 481-44-01; e-mail inst@journ.univ.kiev.ua; internet www.journ.univ.kiev.ua; Dir Prof. VOLODYMYR V. RIZUN.

Institute of Management and Finance: 01033 Kyiv, Vasylkivska St 90A; tel. (44) 521-33-37; e-mail kiembi@econom.univ.kiev.ua; internet www.imf.kiev.ua; Dir DMYTRO M. CHERVANOV.

Institute of Philology: tel. (44) 239-33-02; e-mail philolog@univ.kiev.ua; internet www.philology.kiev.ua; Dir HRIHORIY F. SEMENIUK.

Institute of Postgraduate Education: 03022 Kyiv, Vasilkovskaya St 36; tel. (44) 521-35-51; e-mail admin-ipe@mail.univ.kiev.ua; internet www.ipe.univ.kiev.ua; 139 teachers; 1,646 students; Dir Prof. VALERIY M. PERESEKIN.

Military Institute: 01033 Kyiv, Academician Glushkov Ave 2, Bldg 8; tel. (44) 521-32-92; e-mail balabin@mil.univ.kiev.ua; internet www.mil.univ.kiev.ua; Dir Col VIKTOR V. BALABIN.

Scientific and Research Department: 01033 Kyiv, Lev Tolstoj St 14A, Rm 17; tel. (44) 289-85-80; e-mail ndchinfo@univ.kiev.ua; internet science.univ.kiev.ua; Vice-Rector Prof. Dr VALERIY I. HRYHORUK.

Ukrainian Humanitarian Lyceum: 01024 Kyiv, Kozlovskyi Lane 3; tel. (44) 253-07-89; e-mail uhl-edu@ukr.net; internet www.uhl-edu.kiev.ua; Dir Prof. HALYNA S. SAZONENKO.

Ukrainian Physico–Mathematical Lyceum: 01033 Kyiv, Academician Glushkov Ave 6; tel. (44) 259-03-94; e-mail fizmat_dir@ukr.net; internet www.upml.univ.kiev.ua; Dir OLEH M. KHOMIAKOV.

TAURIDA NATIONAL 'V. I. VERNADSKY UNIVERSITY'

95007 Simferopol, pr. Vernadskoho 4
Telephone: (65) 251-64-98

E-mail: rector@tnu.crimea.ua
Internet: www.tnu.crimea.ua

Founded 1918, present name 1999
State control
Language of instruction: Russian
Academic year: September to July

Rector: NIKOLAY V. BAGROV
Vice-Rector: ALEXANDER M. TIMOHIN
Vice-Rector: ELENA N. CHUJAN
Vice-Rector: VIKTOR F. SHULGIN
Registrar: NIKOLAY V. PRAVDIN
Librarian: VIKTORIA I. SPIROVA

Library: see under Libraries and Archives
Number of teachers: 800
Number of students: 15,000

Publications: *Dynamic Systems* (1 a year), *Ecological Aspects of Nature Protection in the Crimea* (1 a year), *Ecological Study of the Mountainous Crimea* (1 a year), *Ecosystems of the Mountainous Crimea in Studies of Nature Protection* (1 a year), *Notes of Geologists, Pontida: Journal of The Association for the Support of Biological and Landscape Diversity* (1 a year), *Scientific Notes* (1 a year), *The Black Sea Peoples' Culture* (1 a year)

DEANS

Faculty of Biology: SERGEY F. KOTOV
Faculty of Chemistry: VLADIMIR O. KURJANOV
Faculty of Crimean Tatar and Oriental Philology: AIDER M. MEMETOV
Faculty of Economics: SVETLANA V. KLIMCHUK
Faculty of Foreign Languages: ALEXANDER D. PETRENKO
Faculty of Geography: BORIS A. VAKHRUSHEV
Faculty of History: ALEXANDER G. GERTSEN
Faculty of Jurisprudence: LUDMILA D. DONSKAYA
Faculty of Management: VLADIMIR A. PODSOLONKO
Faculty of Mathematics: ALEXANDER I. RUDSKOY
Faculty of Philosophy: YURI A. KATUNIN
Faculty of Physical Training: VLADIMIR F. KROVYAKOV
Faculty of Physics: MARINA V. GLUMOVA
Faculty of Psychology: EVGENIY V. CHERNY
Faculty of Slavic Philology and Journalism: GALINA YU BOGDANOVICH
Faculty of Ukrainian Philology and Ukrainian Studies: YRIY F. PRADID

PROFESSORS

AKULOV, M. R., History of Ukraine
APATOVA, N. V., Information Systems in Economics
ARIFOV, L. YA, Theoretical Physics
BERESTOVSKAYA, D. S., History of World Culture
BERZHANSKY, V. N., Experimental Physics
BOKOV, V. A., Geography
BUROV, G. M., Ancient and Medieval History
CHEKHOV, V. N., Theoretical and Applied Mechanics
CHIRVA, V. YA, Organic and Analytical Chemistry
DEMENTIEV, N. E., History of Russia
DONSKOY, V. I., Informatics
EMIROVA, A. M., Russian Language
FEDORENKO, A. M., Chemistry
FILIMONOV, S. B., History of Ukraine
GABRIELYAN, O. A., Political Science and Sociology
GUBANOV, I. G., Geography
GUBAR, A. I., Ukrainian Language
KALIN, V. K., General Psychology, History of Psychology
KALNOY, I. I., Social Philosophy
KASHENKO, S. G., History of Russian Law
KAZARIN, V. P., Russian and General Literature
KIRICHENKO, A. A., Law
KOPACHEVSKY, N. D., Mathematical Analysis

KORENYUK, I. I., Human and Animal Physiology
KOZLOV, A. S., Greek Language
KRAMARENKO, V. I., Management
KRICHEK, P. M., Ukrainian Literature
KRYUCHKOV, I. V., Economics
KUDRYASHOV, A. P., Political Economy
KUZHEL, A. V., Theory of Functions and Functional Analysis
LAZAREV, F. V., Philosophy
LYSENKO, N. I., General Land Science
MANAKOV, M. K., Physiology of Plants
MARTYNYUK, YU. N., Philosophy
MEMETOV, A. A., Philosophy
MISHNEV, V. G., Botany
NAGORSKAYA, M. N., Management
NIKOLKO, V. N., Philosophy
NOVIKOVA, M. A., Russian and General Literature
OLIFEROV, A. N., Oceanology
OREKHOVA, L. A., Russian Literature
PERSIDSKY, S. K., Differential and Integral Equations
PETRENKO, A. D., German Language
PODSOLONKO, V. A., Economics
POMERANETS, V. N., Economics
POPOV, V. K., Law
REGUSHEVSKY, E. S., Linguistics
RUDYAKOV, A. N., Linguistics
SHARAPA, V. F., History
SHEVLYAKOV, YU. M., Applied Mathematics
SHULGIN, V. F., Chemistry
SIDYAKIN, V. G., Human and Animal Physiology
SOKOLOVSKAYA, ZH. P., Philology
STADNIK, I. P., Theoretical Physics
STASHKOV, A. M., Animal Biophysics
TEMURYANTS, N. A., Human and Animal Physiology
TEREZ, E. K., Astronomy and Teaching Methods of Physics
UNKOVSKAYA, T. E., Management
URSU, D. P., Modern and Contemporary History
VOLYAR, A. V., Physics
YEFIMENKO, A. M., Theoretical Foundations of Physical CultureYENA, V. G., Geography
YURAKHNO, M. V., Zoology

TERNOPIL NATIONAL ECONOMIC UNIVERSITY

46020 Ternopil, vul. Lvivska 11
Telephone: (35) 247-50-51
E-mail: rector@tneu.edu.ua
Internet: www.tneu.edu.ua

Founded 1966
State control
Languages of instruction: English, German, Polish, Ukrainian
Academic year: September to July

Rector: Prof. Dr SERHIY I. YURIY
Vice-Rector for Educational Research and Int. Relations: Dr BOHDAN LUTSIV
Vice-Rector for Educational Research and Organizational Work: Prof. ANDRII KRYSOVATYI
Vice-Rector for Educational Research and Teaching: Dr MYKOLA SHYNKARYK
Vice-Rector for Educational Research and Territory, Distant Structural Subdivisons, Accreditation, Licensing: Prof. HRYHORII ZHURAVEL
Vice-Rector for Humanities and Extra-Curricular Activities: Dr BOHDAN ADAMYK
Vice-Rector for Research: Prof. ZENOVIY ZADOROZHNY
Vice-Rector for Social and Economic Devt: VASYL BULAVYNETS
Librarian: KAZYMYR VOZNIY

Library of 481,493 vols
Number of teachers: 986
Number of students: 18,184

Publications: *Computing, Economic Analysis, Journal of European Economy* (in English, Russian, Ukrainian), *Psycholohiya I Suspilstvo* (Psychology and Society), *Regional Aspects of The Development and Placement of Productive Forces in Ukraine, Svit Finaciv* (World of Finances), *TNEU Herald, Ukrainian Science: Past, Nowadays and Future* (collns of research papers), *Young Science*

DEANS

Faculty of Accounting and Audit: Prof. YAROSLAV D. KRUPKA
Faculty of Agrarian Economics and Management: Prof. ROMAN HEVKO
Faculty of Computer and Information Technologies: Prof. MYKOLA P. DYVAK
Faculty of Economics and Management: Prof. YEVHEN KACHAN
Faculty of Finances: Prof. IHOR HUTSAL
Faculty of International Business and Management: Prof. ANATOLIY M. TYBIN
Faculty of Law: Dr VOLODYMYR VOZNIY
Faculty of Pre-University, Postgraduate Education and Masters Training: Prof. OLEH IVASHCHUK
Faculty of the Banking Business: Dr VASYL TKACHUK
Ukrainian-Dutch Faculty of Economics and Investment Management: Dr LYUDMILA GAVRILYUK-JENSEN
Ukrainian-German Economic Faculty: Dr YURIY HAIDA

UZHHOROD NATIONAL UNIVERSITY

88000 Uzhhorod, vul. Pidhirna 46
Telephone: (31) 223-33-41
E-mail: admin@univ.uzhgorod.ua
Internet: www.univ.uzhgorod.ua

Founded 1945
State control
Language of instruction: Ukrainian
Academic year: September to July

Rector: Prof. Dr MYKOLA M. VEHESH
Pro-Rector for Academic Affairs: OLEXANDR H. SLYVKA
Pro-Rector for Admin. and Economic Affairs: VOLODYMYR V. SHETELYA
Pro-Rector for Research: IHOR P. STUDENJAK
Pro-Rector for Social Devt and Capital Construction: YAROSLAV S. HUK
Registrar: ROSTISLAV. V. ROMANYUK
Librarian: OLENA I. POCHEKUTOVA

Library: see under Libraries and Archives
Number of teachers: 600
Number of students: 8,000

Publication: *Bulletin* (series: Biology, Chemistry, Mathematics, Medicine, Philology, Physics, Romance and Germanic Philology, 1 a year)

DEANS

Faculty of Biology: Asst Prof. V. I. NIKOLAYCHUK
Faculty of Chemistry: Asst Prof. VASYL LENDYEL
Faculty of Economics: Prof. VASIL MIKLOVDA
Faculty of Engineering: Asst Prof. IVAN TURYANYTSYA
Faculty of History: Asst Prof. VOLODYMYR FENYCH
Faculty of International Relations: Prof. M. A. LENDYEL
Faculty of Law: Prof. VASIL YAREMA
Faculty of Mathematics: Asst Prof. MYKHAYLO PAHYRYA
Faculty of Medicine: Asst Prof. BOLDIZHAR BOLDIZHAR
Faculty of Philology: Asst Prof. IVAN SABADOSH
Faculty of Physical Education and Sport: Asst Prof. STEPAN LASUR

Faculty of Physics: Prof. Dr VOLODYMYR LASUR

Faculty of Postgraduate Studies: Prof. IVAN MIKHAYLOVYCH

Faculty of Romance and Germanic Philology: Asst Prof. STEPAN BOBYNETS

VASYL STEFANYK PRECARPATHIAN NATIONAL UNIVERSITY

76025 Ivano-Frankivsk, vul. Shevchenka 57
E-mail: inst@pu.if.ua
Internet: www.pu.if.ua

Founded 1940

Rector: Prof. Dr Hab. IHOR TSEPENDA
Vice-Rector: Prof. Dr Hab. VASYL MARCHUK

V. N. KARAZIN KHARKIV NATIONAL UNIVERSITY

61022 Kharkiv, Maidan Svobody 4
Telephone: (57) 705-12-47
E-mail: univer@karazin.ua
Internet: www.univer.kharkov.ua

Founded 1804
State control
Languages of instruction: Russian, Ukrainian
Academic year: September to June
Rector: Acad. V. S. BAKIROV
Vice-Rector: Asst Prof. A. M. UDOD
Vice-Rector: Prof. M. O. AZARENKOV
Vice-Rector: V. M. RYSHKOV
Vice-Rector: Prof. V. O. KATRYCH
Vice-Rector: Prof. V. V. ALEKSANDROV
Vice-Rector: Prof. YU. V. KHOLIN
Vice-Rector: Prof. Z. F. NAZYROV
Librarian: I. K. ZHURAVLYOVA
Library: 3.5m. vols
Number of teachers: 1,500
Number of students: 15,000
Publication: *Visnyk*

DEANS

International Students Education Centre: (vacant)
School of Biology: Asst Prof. L. I. VOROBYOVA
School of Chemistry: Asst Prof. O. M. KALUGIN
School of Computer Science: Prof. V. T. LAZURYK
School of Ecology: Asst Prof. G. V. TITENKO
School of Economics: Asst Prof. O. I. DAVYDOV
School of Foreign Languages: Prof. V. G. PASYNOK
School of Geology and Geography: Prof. V. A. PERESADKO
School of History: Prof. S. I. POSOKHOV
School of International Economic Relations and Tourist Industry: Prof. V. I. SIDOROV
School of Law: Asst Prof. T. YE. KAGANOVSKA
School of Mathematics and Mechanical Engineering: Prof. G. M. ZHOLTKEVYCH
School of Medicine: Prof. V. M. SAVCHENKO
School of Philology: Prof. YU. M. BEZKHUTRIY
School of Philosophy: Prof. I. V. KARPENKO
School of Physics: Prof. R. V. VOVK
School of Physics and Energy: Prof. K. E. NYEMCHENKO
School of Physics and Technology: Prof. I. O. GIRKA
School of Psychology: Prof. N. P. KREYDUN
School of Radiophysics: Prof. S. M. SHULGA
School of Sociology: Asst Prof. V. I. LUKASCHUK

VOLODYMYR DAHL EAST UKRAINIAN NATIONAL UNIVERSITY

91034 Luhansk, Kvartal Molodezhnyi 20A
Telephone: (64) 241-70-22
E-mail: uni@snu.edu.ua
Internet: www.snu.edu.ua

Founded 1920

State control
Languages of instruction: English, Russian, Ukrainian
Academic year: September to June
Rector: Prof. Dr OLEKSANDR L. GOLUBENKO (acting)
First Vice-Rector: Prof. Dr MYKHAILO F. SMYRNY (acting)
Vice-Rector for International Affairs: Prof. Dr VALERIY DYADYCHEV (acting)
Library: 1m. vols
Number of teachers: 2,750
Number of students: 36,000
Publications: *Actual Issues of Law: Theory and Practice, Applied Ecology, Economics. Management. Enterpreneurship, Historical Notes: Collection of Scientific Papers, Information Security, Marketing: Theory and Practice, Materials and Investigation on Archeology of East of Ukraine, Philosophical Investigations, Political Science Notes, Project Management and Development of Production, Scientific Conducts of Dahl University* (online), *Scientific Media Notes, Scientific Works of Lugansk Branch of International Academy of Informatization, Spiritual Identity: Methodology, Theory and Practice, Theoretical and Practical Problems of Psychology, Visnyk of Volodymyr Dahl East Ukrainian National University on-Technic-Economics-History-Chemical-Physics and Mathematics*

DEANS

Economics Management Department: Prof. MARYNA A. MELNYK
Educational and Scientific Institute of Housing and Communal Services and Building: Prof. MYKOLA D. ANDIYCHUK
Faculty of Applied Mechanics and Material Science: Prof. VLADYMYR I. SOKOLOV
Faculty of Computer Sciences and Technologies: Prof. LARYSA O. GUBACHEVA
Faculty of Electrotechnical Systems: Prof. OLEKSANDR S. ZAKHARCHUK
Faculty of Financial Management: Asst Prof. OLEKSANDR M. ROZMYSLOV
Faculty of Foreign Citizens Training: Asst Prof. EVGEN I. KHARCHENKO
Faculty of Innovation Economics and Cybernetics: Prof. SULTAN K. RAMAZANOV
Faculty of Law: Prof. LIDIA I. LAZOR
Faculty of Management: Prof. VITALIY M. DANICH
Faculty of Mass Communications: Asst Prof. TETYANA A. MIRONOVA
Faculty of Mathematics And Informatics: Asst Prof. YURIY I. STATYVKO
Faculty of Nanoelectronics and Nanotechnologies: Prof. OLEKSANDR P. KRAVCHENKO
Faculty of Natural Sciences: Prof. SERGIY D. KRYVONOSOV
Faculty of Philology: Asst Prof. OLGA E. KRSEK
Faculty of Philosophy: Prof. VIKTORIA K. SUKHANTSEVA
Faculty of Rail Communications Systems: Prof. VALENTYN I. MOGYLA
Faculty of Transport Systems and Logistics: Prof. GRYGORIY I. NECHAEV

ZAPORIZHZHYA NATIONAL UNIVERSITY

69063 Zaporizhia, vul. Zhukovskoho 66
Telephone: (61) 264-45-46
E-mail: rektor@zsu.zp.ua
Internet: www.zsu.edu.ua

Founded 1985
State control
Languages of instruction: Russian, Ukrainian
Academic year: September to July
Rector: Prof. V. A. TOLOK

Pro-Rector for Admin.: I. G. YAKUSHEV
Pro-Rector for Curriculum: V. V. HIRZHON
Pro-Rector for Research and Int. Cooperation: V. Z. HRYSTCHAK
Pro-Rector for Social Devt: V. G. TKACHENKO
Registrar: S. A. EVSTAFENKO
Librarian: V. A. HERASYMOVA
Number of teachers: 541
Number of students: 8,200
Publications: *Antiquities of the Steppe, Black Sea Region and Crimea, Bulletin, Cultural Bulletin* (scientific-theoretical annual of the Lower Dnieper region), *New Paradigm, New Philology, Notes of the Scientific Research Laboratory of the Southern Ukraine, Problems of Bioindication, Renaissance Studies, Zaporizhzhya Legacy* (history of the Southern Ukraine in the 18th century)

DEANS

Faculty of Biology: Dr V. I. DOMNICH
Faculty of Economics: Prof. V. V. KIRICHEVSKIY
Faculty of Foreign Philology: Prof. V. I. SKIBINA
Faculty of History: Prof. F. G. TURCHENKO
Faculty of Law: Dr T. A. DENISOVA
Faculty of Management: Dr I. G. SHAVKUN
Faculty of Mathematics: Prof. N. G. TAMUROV
Faculty of Philology: Prof. O. D. TURGAN
Faculty of Physical Training: Dr V. N. ZAYTSEVA
Faculty of Physics: Dr A. Y. OSIPOV
Faculty of Postgraduate Education: Dr L. D. KRIVEGA
Faculty of Social Pedagogics: Prof. L. I. MISCHIK
Faculty of Sociology and Administration: Prof. V. P. BEKH

PROFESSORS

BAYKINA, N. G., Sports
BEKH, V. P., Politics and Theory of Administration
BESSONOVA, V. P., Biology
BOVT, V. D., Biology
BYLOUSENKO, P. I., Ukrainian Language
CHABANENKO, V. A., General Linguistics
FROLOV, A. K., Human Physiology
GRISTCHAK, V. Z., Applied Mathematics
IVANENKO, V. K., Methods of Teaching Philological Disciplines
KARAGODIN, A. I., History
KIRICHEVSKIY, V. V., Applied Mathematics
LYAKH, S. R., History of Ukraine
MISCHIK, L. I., Pedagogics and Psychology
MOROZOV, L. V., Finance and Credit
NAUMENKO, A. M., German Philology
NOVIKOV, Y. F., Theory and Practice of Management
PAKHOMOVA, T. A., Methods of Teaching Philological Disciplines
PROZOROVA, N. S., History and Theory of State and Law
PRYKHODKO, N. I., Problems of Administration and Social Pedagogics
PRYVARNIKOV, A. K., Algebra and Geometry
PSARYOV, V. I., Physics
SERGEYEV, A. V., Physics
TAMUROV, N. G., Applied Mathematics
TOLOK, V. A., Applied Mathematics
TURCHENKO, F. G., History of the Ukraine
TURGAN, O. D., Theory of Literature and Journalism
TYKHOMIROV, V. N., Foreign Literature
TYMCHENKO, S. M., History of the Ukraine
YESHENKO, V. A., Physiology and Civil Defence
ZATSNIY, Y. A., Theory and Practice of Translation

MEDICAL UNIVERSITIES

BUKOVINIAN STATE MEDICAL UNIVERSITY

58000 Chernivtsi, Teatralna pl. 2
Telephone: (372) 55-37-54
E-mail: bma@bsmu.edu.ua
Internet: www.bsmu.edu.ua

Founded 1944 as Chernivtsi State Medical Institute; as Bukovinian State Medical Acad. 1997; present name and Univ. status 2005
State control
Language of instruction: English
Academic year: September to June

Rector: Prof. TARAS M. BOYCHUK
Vice-Rector for Medical Work: Prof. ANDRIIAN G. IFTODII
Vice-Rector for Science and Int. Relations: Prof. OLEKSANDR I. IVASHCHUK
Vice-Rector for Scientific and Pedagogical Work: Assoc. Prof. IGOR V. GERUSH
Vice-Rector for Scientific-Pedagogical and Educational Work: Assoc. Prof. NINA I. ZORII
Vice-Rector for Univ. Development: Prof. OLEKSANDR M. YUZKO

Library of 394,397 vols
Number of teachers: 611
Number of students: 4,000

Publications: *Bukovinian Medical Herald* (4 a year), *Clinical Anatomy and Operative Surgery* (4 a year), *Clinical and Experimental Pathology* (4 a year)

CRIMEAN STATE MEDICAL UNIVERSITY 'S. I. GEORGIEVSKY'

95006 Simferopol, bul. Lenina 5/7
Telephone: (65) 227-44-62
E-mail: office@crsmu.com
Internet: www.crsmu.com

Founded 1931

Rector: Prof. A. A. BABANIN

Library of 634,371 vols
Number of teachers: 629
Number of students: 4,556

Publications: *Bulletin of Physiotherapy and Balneology* (4 a year), *Problems, Achievements and Perspectives of the Development of Biomedical Sciences and Practical Public Health of Ukraine* (colln of scientific works, 4 a year), *Tavrian Biomedical Bulletin* (4 a year), *Tavrian Journal of Psychiatry* (4 a year)

DEANS

Faculty of Stomatology: Prof. L. I. AVDONINA
First Medical Faculty: Prof. A. I. KRADINOV
International Faculty: Prof. M. N. GRISHIN
Postgraduate Faculty: Prof. N. P. BUGLAK
Second Medical Faculty: Prof. S. N. KRUTIKOV

I. HORBACHEVSKY TERNOPIL STATE MEDICAL UNIVERSITY

46001 Ternopil, Maydan Voli 1
Telephone: (35) 252-44-92
E-mail: university@tdmu.edu.te.ua
Internet: www.tdmu.edu.te.ua

Founded 1957
State control
Languages of instruction: English, Russian, Ukrainian
Academic year: September to July

Rector: Prof. LEONID Y. KOVALCHUK

Library of 500,000 vols
Number of teachers: 560
Number of students: 4,000

Publications: *Achievements of Clinical and Experimental Medicine* (2 a year), *Hospital Surgery* (4 a year), *Infectious Diseases* (4 a

year), *Medical Chemistry* (4 a year), *Medical Education* (4 a year), *Scientific Research Newsletter* (4 a year)

DEANS

Faculty of Dentistry: Prof. YAROSLAV NAGIRNY
Faculty of Foreign Students: Prof. MYKHAYLO KORDA
Faculty of Medicine: Prof. ARKADIY SHULGAY
Faculty of Pharmacy: Prof. LIUDMYLA SOKOLOVA
Faculty of Postgraduate Education: Prof. MARYAN GREBENYK

KHARKIV NATIONAL MEDICAL UNIVERSITY

61022 Kharkiv, 4 Lenin Ave
Telephone: (57) 705-07-11
E-mail: meduniver@knmu.kharkov.ua
Internet: www.knmu.kharkov.ua

Founded 1805, present name and status 2007
State control
Languages of instruction: English, Russian, Ukrainian
Academic year: September to June

Rector: Prof. VLADIMIR LESOVOY
First Vice-Rector for Research and Education: Prof. VALERY KAPUSTNYK
Vice-Rector for Medical Research and Education: Assoc. Prof. YURI REZUNENKO
Vice-Rector for Research: Prof. VALERIY MYASOEDOV
Vice-Rector for Research and Education: Prof. IVAN LETIK
Vice-Rector for Research and Education: Prof. VLADIMIR MARKOVSKYI
Head of Library: IRINA KIRICHOK

Library of 1,016,000 vols, 237 periodicals
Number of teachers: 861
Number of students: 6,371

Publications: *Experimental Clinical Medicine* (4 a year), *Medicine Today and Tomorrow* (4 a year)

DEANS

Academic and Research Institute for Postgraduate Education: Assoc. Prof. VALERIY VYUN
Medical Faculty I: Prof. ANATOLIY TERESHCHENKO
Medical Faculty II: Prof. VASYL OLKHOVSKIY
Medical Faculty III: Prof. MYKOLA PANCHENKO
Medical Faculty IV: Prof. VALERIY MINUKHIN
Medical Faculty V for Training of Foreign Students: Assoc. Prof. DMYTRO MARAKUSHYN
Medical Faculty VI for Training of Foreign Students: Assoc. Prof. VALERIY VYUN

LUHANSK STATE MEDICAL UNIVERSITY

91045 Luhansk, Kvartal 50-richchya Oborony Luhanska 1
Telephone: (64) 254-84-03
E-mail: kanc@lsmu.edu.ua
Internet: www.lsmu.edu.ua

Founded 1956, present name and status 1994

Faculties of dentistry, health care, nursing, paediatrics and pharmacy

Rector: Prof. VALERIY K. IVCHENKO

Library of 420,000 vols
Number of teachers: 394
Number of students: 2,815

LVIV NATIONAL MEDICAL UNIVERSITY 'DANYLO HALYTSKIY'

79010 Lviv, Pekarska Str. 69
Telephone: (32) 272-26-60
E-mail: zimenkovsky@meduniv.lviv.ua

Internet: www.meduniv.lviv.ua
Founded 1784
Rector: Prof. Dr BORYS ZIMENKOVSKY
Library of 520,000 vols
Number of teachers: 1,200
Number of students: 4,977

DEANS

External Faculty: ROMAN EU. DARMOGRAIY
Faculty of Dentistry: ROSTYSLAV M. STUPNYTSKYI
Faculty of Nursing: VIRA I. PIROGOVA
Faculty of Pharmacy: ROMAN B. LESYK
Faculty of Postgraduate Education: OREST YE. SICHKORIZ
Faculty of Stomatology: IVAN M. HOT
First Medical Faculty: BOGDAN V. DYBAS
International Faculty: EUGENE VARYVODA
Second Medical Faculty: YURI YA. KRYVKO

NATIONAL O. BOHOMOLETS MEDICAL UNIVERSITY

01601 Kyiv, T. Shevchenko blvd 13
Telephone: (44) 234-92-76
E-mail: nmu@nmu.edu.ua
Internet: www.nmu.edu.ua

Founded 1841
State control
Languages of instruction: English, Russian, Ukrainian
Academic year: September to June

Rector: Prof. Dr VITALIY MOSKALENKO
Vice-Rector for Int. Affairs, Research and Education: Prof. Dr OLESYA HULCHIY

Library of 750,000 vols
Number of teachers: 1,200
Number of students: 10,000

Publications: *East European Journal of Public Health, Health Care in Ukraine, Scientific Journal of National O. Bohomolets Medical University*

DEANS

Faculty for Int. Students: Prof. ALEXANDER SAVYCHUK
Medical Faculty I (General Medicine): Prof. VICTOR CHERKASOV
Medical Faculty II (General Medicine): Prof. VASYL NETYAZHENKO
Medical Faculty III (Paediatrics): Prof. VASYL PETRENKO
Medical Faculty IV (Preventive Care): Prof. SERHIY OMELCHUK
School for Continuing Education for Trainers: Prof. YURIY MARUSHKO
School of Dentistry: Prof. VALERIY NESPRYADKO
School of Medical Engineering: Prof. VALENTYN YATSENKO
School of Medical Psychology: Prof. SERHIY MAKSYMENKO
School of Military Medicine: Col OLEG VLASENKO
School of Pharmacy: Prof. IRYNA NIZHENKIVSKA

NATIONAL UNIVERSITY OF PHARMACY

61002 Kharkiv, 53 Pushkinskaya Str.
Telephone: (57) 706-35-81
E-mail: mail@ukrfa.kharkov.ua
Internet: www.nuph.edu.ua

Founded 1805
State control
Languages of instruction: English, Russian, Ukrainian
Academic year: September to June (10 semesters)

Rector: Prof. Dr VALENTIN P. CHERNYKH
Vice-Rector for Scientific, Educational Work and Int. Affairs: Prof. Dr SERGEY B. POPOV

Librarian: NATALIYA B. GAVRISH

Library: 1m. vols

Number of teachers: 830

Number of students: 17,500 (incl. 1,600 int. students)

Publications: *Clinical Pharmacy* (4 a year), *Fisiologichno-Aktivni Rechovini* (Physiologically Active Substances, 2 a year), *Klinichna Farmatsiya* (Clinical Pharmacy, 4 a year), *Organic and Pharmaceutical Chemistry* (4 a year), *Visnik Farmatsii* (Pharmacy Bulletin, 4 a year), *Zdorovya Cheloveky* (Health to Mankind, 4 a year)

DEANS

Faculty of Correspondence and Distance Learning: Assoc. Prof. SVETLANA G. KALAYCHEVA

Faculty of Economics and Management: Assoc. Prof. VOLODYMYR V. MALYI

Faculty of Foreign Citizens' Education: Assoc. Prof. VLADIMIR D. GORYACHIY

Faculty of Industrial Pharmacy: Assoc. Prof. TATYANA KRUTSKIKH

Faculty of Medicine and Pharmacy: Assoc. Prof. OLGA I. NABOKA

Faculty of Pharmacy: Assoc. Prof. LILIYA I. VISHNEVSKAYA

Preparatory Faculty for Foreign Citizens: ZOYA I. KOVALENKO

NATIONAL UNIVERSITY OF PHYSICAL EDUCATION AND SPORTS OF UKRAINE

03680 Kyiv, vul. Fizkultury 1

Telephone: (44) 227-54-52

E-mail: rectorat@uni-sport.edu.ua

Internet: www.uni-sport.edu.ua

Founded 1930

Faculties of Olympic and professional sport, physical rehabilitation and sports medicine, physical education, recreation and health-related physical culture; faculty of external studies

Rector: Prof. Dr VOLODYMYR M. PLATONOV

First Pro-Rector for Education: Prof. Dr YURIY M. SHKREBTIY

Pro-Rector for Research: Dr TETYANA YU. KRUTSEVICH

VINNITSA NATIONAL MEDICAL UNIVERSITY 'M. I. PYROHOV'

21018 Vinnytsya, pr. Lenina 9

Telephone: (432) 32-06-85

E-mail: admission@vsmu.vinnica.ua

Internet: www.vnmu.vn.ua

Founded 1921

Rector: Prof. Dr VASYL M. MOROZ

Library of 500,000 vols

Number of teachers: 554

Number of students: 3,600

PEDAGOGICAL UNIVERSITIES

KHARKIV NATIONAL PEDAGOGICAL UNIVERSITY 'H. S. SKOVORODA'

61168 Kharkiv, vul. Blyukhera 2

Telephone: (57) 700-69-09

E-mail: rector@pu.ac.kharkov.ua

Internet: pu.ac.kharkov.ua

Founded 1804

Rector: Prof. Dr IVAN F. PROKOPENKO

Library of 714,689 vols

DEANS

External Faculty: Assoc. Prof. VIKTORIYA M. TYKHONOVICH

Faculty of Art and Design: Prof. Dr NADEZDA V. SHYLOVTSEVA

Faculty of Economics: Prof. Dr HANNA M. GUZENKO

Faculty of Elementary Education: Prof. Dr NATALIYA M. YAKUSHKO

Faculty of Foreign Languages: Dr NATALIYA V. TUCHYNA

Faculty of History: Assoc. Prof. SVETLANA V. BEREZNAYA

Faculty of Law: Prof. Dr VIKTOR O. PROTSEVSKYY

Faculty of Music Education: Assoc. Prof. TETYANA A. SMIRNOVA

Faculty of Natural Sciences: Prof. Dr IGOR IONOV

Faculty of Physical Education: Prof. Dr MYKOLA I. GORODYSKYY

Faculty of Physics and Mathematics: Prof. Dr OLEKSANDR I. GONCHAROV

Faculty of Pre-School Education: Prof. Dr TETYANA P. TANKO

Faculty of Psychology and Sociology: Prof. Dr OKSANA G. VOLKOVA

Faculty of Russian Language and World Literature: Prof. Dr TAMARA P. STAKANKOVA

Faculty of Ukrainian Language and Literature: Prof. Dr IRYNA V. TYMCHENKO

DIRECTORS

Institute of Post-Diploma Education: Prof. Dr MYKOLA V. GADETSKYY

Institute of World Languages: Prof. Dr TAMARA P. STAKANKOVA

NATIONAL PEDAGOGICAL DRAGOMANOV UNIVERSITY

01601 Kyiv, vul. Pyrogova 9

Telephone: (44) 234-11-08

E-mail: shef-npu@ukr.net

Internet: www.npu.edu.ua

Founded 1834 as Gorky Kiev Pedagogical Institute, present name and status 1997

State control

Languages of instruction: English, Russian, Ukrainian

Academic year: September to May

Rector: Acad. Prof. Dr VIKTOR ANDRUSHCHENKO

Vice-Rector: Prof. Dr ANATOLYI AVDIEVSKIY

First Vice-Rector: Dr VOLODYMYR BEKH

First Vice-Rector for Economics and Educational Work: Dr OLEG PADALKA

Vice-Rector for Distance Learning and Innovational Technologies of Learning: Prof. ANATOLYI P. KUDIN

Vice-Rector for Educational and Methodological Work of Humanitarian Institutes: Prof. BOGDAN ANDRUSYSHYN

Vice-Rector for Int. Relations: Prof. VOLODYMYR LAVRYNENKO

Vice-Rector for Methodological Work: Prof. ROMAN VERNYDUB

Vice-Rector for Scientific Work: Prof. HRIHORIY VOLYNKA

Dir for Library: LYUDMYLA SAVENKOVA

Library of 1,233,252 vols, 863,673 books, 150,351 periodicals, 7,149 foreign edns, 125 magnetic tapes and discs, 2,563 theses and dissertations defended within the Univ.

Number of teachers: 1,500

Number of students: 30,000

DEANS

Institute of Foreign Philology: Prof. VOLODYMYR GONCHAROV

Institute of Philosophical Education and Science: Prof. IVAN DROBOT

Institute of Physical Education and Sport: Prof. OLEKSIY TYMOSHENKO

Institute of Physics and Mathematics: Prof. MYKOLA PRATSYOVYTYI

Institute of Sociology, Psychology and Management: Prof. VOLODYMYR YEVTUKH

TECHNICAL UNIVERSITIES

DNIPRODZERZHYNSK STATE TECHNICAL UNIVERSITY

51948 Dnipropetrovska oblast, Dniprodzerzhynsk, vul. Dniprobudivska

Telephone: (56) 955-13-89

E-mail: science@dstu.dp.ua

Internet: www.dstu.dp.ua

Founded 1920, present name and status 1994

Rector: Prof. IHOR O. PAVLYUCHENKOV

First Pro-Rector: Dr VITALIY M. HULYAYEV

DEANS

External Faculty: Prof. YEVHEN B. LEYKO

Faculty of Chemical Technology: Dr OLEH I. POLYANCHYKOV

Faculty of Economics and Management: Dr SERHIY H. DRONOV

Faculty of Electronics and Computer Technology: Prof. OLEKSANDR M. SYANOV

Faculty of Mechanical Engineering: Dr VOLODYMYR SOLOD

Faculty of Metallurgy: Dr OLEKSANDR V. HRESS

Faculty of Post-Diploma Education: Prof. I. V. HUBARYEV

Faculty of Power Engineering: Prof. ANATOLIY M. PAVLENKO

Faculty of Sociology and Philology: Prof. MYKOLA S. KONOKH

DNIPROPETROVSK NATIONAL TECHNICAL UNIVERSITY OF RAILWAY TRANSPORT 'V. LAZARYAN'

49700 Dnipropetrovsk-10, vul. Lazaryana 2

Telephone: (56) 776-59-47

E-mail: dnuzt@diit.edu.ua

Internet: www.diit.edu.ua

Founded 1930

Specialist faculties incl. bridges and tunnels, economics and management in transport, industrial and civil engineering, management of transport processes in railway transport, mechanics, organization of railway construction and track maintenance, technical cybernetics and military training

Rector: Prof. Dr ALEXANDER N. PSHINKO

First Pro-Rector for Education: Prof. Dr BORIS E. BODNAR

Pro-Rector for Research: Dr SERHEY MYAMLYN

Library of 800,000 vols

Number of students: 4,200

DONBASS STATE TECHNICAL UNIVERSITY

94204 Alchevsk, pr. Lenina 16

Telephone: (64) 422-31-23

E-mail: info@dmmi.edu.ua

Internet: www.dmmi.edu.ua

State control

Languages of instruction: English, Russian, Ukrainian

Academic year: September to July

Rector: Prof. Dr NIKOLAY ANTOSCHENKO

Vice-Rector for Academic Affairs: Dr NIKOLAY N. ZABLODSKIY

Vice-Rector for Research: Dr SERGEY V. SEMIRIAGIN

Library of 700,000 vols

Number of teachers: 470

Number of students: 14,000

Publication: *Impulse* (52 a year)

DEANS

Civil Engineering Dept: Dr VLADIMIR BONDARCHUK

Economics and Finances Dept: Dr VALERIY BIELOZERTSEV

Management Dept: Dr LEONID RIABENKO

Mechanical Engineering Dept: Dr ANDREY ZINCHENKO

Metallurgy Dept: Prof. Dr ALEXANDER NOVO-KHATSKIY

Mining Engineering Dept: Dr ALEXANDER MELEZHYK

DONETSK NATIONAL TECHNICAL UNIVERSITY

83000 Donetsk, Artema 58

Telephone: (62) 337-17-33

E-mail: info@dgtu.donetsk.ua

Internet: www.donntu.edu.ua

Founded 1921

Rector: Prof. Dr ALEKSANDR A. MINAEV

First Pro-Rector: Prof. Dr ALEKSANDR A. TROYANSKIY

Pro-Rector for Academic Affairs: Dr ALEKSANDR V. LEVSHOV

Pro-Rector for Admin.: HEORHIY A. ROMANKO

Pro-Rector for Internal Communications and Economic Affairs: ILYA P. NAVKA

Pro-Rector for Research: Prof. Dr EVGENIY A. BASHKOV

Librarian: ANNA A. PETROVA

Library: 1.5m. vols

Number of teachers: 1,500

Number of students: 23,000

Publications: *Development of Mining Minerals* (2 a year), *Problems of Ecology* (1 a year)

Campuses in Gorlovka and Krasnoarmeysk

DEANS

English-Language Technical Faculty: Dr SERGEY A. KOVALEV

Faculty of Computing Technology and Information Science: Dr ALEKSANDR ANOPRIENKO

Faculty of Ecology and Chemical Technology: Dr ALEKSANDR S. PARFENYUK

Faculty of Economics and Management: Prof. VYACHESLAV V. DEMENTYEV

Faculty of Electrotechnical Engineering: Prof. NILOLAY GREBCHENKO

Faculty of Geotechnology and Management in Manufacturing: Prof. YURI F. BULGAKOV

Faculty of Information Technologies and Automation: Dr ALEKSANDR V. KHORKHORDIN

Faculty of Mechanical Engineering: Dr SERGEY A. SELIVRA

Faculty of Mining and Geology: Prof. OLEG I. KALINICHENKO

Faculty of Physics and Metallurgy: Prof. SERGEY SAFYANTS

Faculty of Power Mechanics and Automation: Dr SERGEY A. SELIVRA

Faculty of Radiotechnology: Prof. PAVEL V. STEFANENKO

Foreign Students: Dr SERGEY F. SUKOV

French-Language Faculty of Engineering: Prof. GENNADIY S. KLYAGIN

German-Language Technical Faculty: Dr VIKTOR I. KALASHNIKOV

Polish-Language Technical Faculty: Dr ALEKSANDR YU. MAKEYEV

IVANO-FRANKIVSK NATIONAL TECHNICAL UNIVERSITY OF OIL AND GAS

76019 Ivano-Frankivsk, vul. Karpatska 15

Telephone: (34) 224-22-64

E-mail: admin@nung.edu.ua

Internet: www.ifdtung.if.ua

Founded 1967

Faculties of automation and electrification, economics and management, engineering ecology, gas and oil industry, gas and oil pipelines, geological prospecting, mechanical, mechanics and technology

Rector: Y. I. KRYZHANIVSKY

Library of 790,000 vols

Number of teachers: 413

Number of students: 4,453

KHARKIV NATIONAL AUTOMOBILE AND HIGHWAYS UNIVERSITY

61002 Kharkiv, vul. Petrovskoho 25

Telephone: (57) 700-38-65

E-mail: admin@khadi.kharkov.ua

Internet: www.khadi.kharkov.ua

Founded 1930

State control

Languages of instruction: Russian, Ukrainian

Academic year: September to June

Rector: Prof. Dr ANATOLIY N. TURENKO

First Pro-Rector: Prof. Dr IVAN P. GLADKIY

Vice-Rector for Research and Pedagogy: Prof. SERGIY Y. KHODYREV

Vice-Rector for Research and Pedagogy and Int. Contacts: Prof. GEORGIY I. TOKHTAR

Vice-Rector for Scientific Research: Prof. Dr VIKTOR A. BOGOMOLOV

Vice-Rector for Social, Economic and Admin. Affairs: VICTOR V. BEZRODNY

Library of 450,000 vols

Number of teachers: 573

Number of students: 10,956 full-time, 7,042 external

DEANS

Automobile Faculty: NIKOLAY ALEKSA

Faculty for Foreign Citizens: VLADIMIR BONDARENKO

Faculty of Business and Management: ILYA DMITRIEV

Faculty of Mechatronics: ANDREY LEVTEROV

Faculty of Transport Systems: YURI BEKETOV

Mechanical Faculty: IGOR KIRICHENKO

Road-Construction Faculty: VLADIMIR PSYURNIK

KHARKIV NATIONAL UNIVERSITY OF RADIOELECTRONICS

61166 Kharkiv, pr. Lenina 14

Telephone: (57) 702-18-07

E-mail: info@kture.kharkov.ua

Internet: www.kture.kharkov.ua

Founded 1930

Rector: Prof. Dr MYKHAYLO F. BONDARENKO

Library of 750,000 vols

Number of students: 8,500

DEANS

Faculty of Applied Mathematics and Management: LEONID I. SHKLYAROV

Faculty of Computer Engineering and Management: GENNADIY F. KRIVULYA

Faculty of Computer Sciences: VLADIMIR P. MASHTALIR

Faculty of Electronic Devices: VLADIMIR A. STOROZHENKO

Faculty of Electronic Technology: YURI N. ALEKSANDROV

Faculty of Radiotechnology: SERGEY N. SAKALO

Faculty of Telecommunications and Electronics: IGOR N. PRESNYAKOV

Foreign Students' Preparatory Faculty: VLADIMIR P. NEMCHENKO

Postgraduate Faculty: ZOYA V. DUDAR

KHARKIV STATE TECHNICAL UNIVERSITY OF CIVIL ENGINEERING AND ARCHITECTURE

61002 Kharkiv, Sumska vul. 40

Telephone: (57) 700-10-66

E-mail: office@kstuca.kharkov.ua

Internet: www.kstuca.kharkov.ua

Founded 1930

Rector: Prof. Dr YURIY SHKODOVSKIY

Library of 683,000 vols

Number of teachers: 590

Number of students: 6,500

DEANS

Faculty of Architecture: Prof. OLEKSANDR VASILENKO

Faculty of Construction: Dr YEVGEN YAKOVLEV

Faculty of Economics and Management: Dr OLEKSANDR SYROVATSKIY

Faculty of External Education: Dr OLEKSANDR F. PUGACHOV

Faculty of Mechanical-Technical Engineering: Dr YURIY ZHURAVLEV

Faculty of Postgraduate Education: Dr GENNADIY SUKHORUKOV

Faculty of Pre-University Preparation: Dr IGOR EMETS

Faculty of Sanitary Engineering: Dr VIKTOR SHYLIN

KHERSON NATIONAL TECHNICAL UNIVERSITY

73008 Kherson, Beryslavske shose 24

Telephone: (55) 255-40-11

E-mail: kstu@tlc.kherson.ua

Internet: www.kstu.edu.ua

Founded 1957

Rector: FRANTS B. ROHALSKIY

Library of 400,000 vols

Publication: *Proceedings* (2 a year)

DEANS

Faculty of Cybernetics: Prof. NADIYA A. SOKOLOVA

Faculty of Distance Education: Prof. N. A. PUSTOVAYA

Faculty of Economics: Prof. VOLODYMYR. E. TURSH

Faculty of International Economics: Prof. V. V. KRYUCHOVSKIY

Faculty of Machine Building: Prof. HRIHORIY DYNEVICH

Faculty of Technology and Design: Prof. N. I. VALKO

Preparatory Faculty: Prof. N. S. MYKOLAYCHUK

KIROVOHRAD NATIONAL TECHNICAL UNIVERSITY

25030 Kirovohrad, Prospekt Universytetskyy 8

Telephone: (52) 255-93-59

E-mail: rector@kntu.kr.ua

Internet: www.kntu.kr.ua

Founded 1929

Rector: Prof. Dr MYKHAILO I. CHERNOVOL

Pro-Rector for Education: Prof. MYKOLA M. PETRENKO

Pro-Rector for Science and Research: Dr VOLODYMYR M. KROPIVNIY

Library of 406,021 vols

Number of teachers: 414

Number of students: 4,839

DEANS

Faculty of Agricultural Mechanics: Prof. VASYL M. SALO

Faculty of Auditing and Finance: Prof. HRYHORIY M. DAVYDOV

Faculty of Automation, Power Engineering and Programming: Prof. LARYSA H. VIKHROVA

Faculty of Economy and Management: Prof. OLEXANDR M. LEVCHENKO

Faculty of Machine Design and Development: Dr VOLODYMYR V. YATSUN

Faculty of Mechanics and Technology: Prof. MYKOLA O. KOVRYSHKIN

Preparatory and Specialists' Retraining Faculty: Prof. YEVGEN K. SOLOVYKH

Preparatory Faculty for Foreign Specialists: Prof. IHOR V. SHEPELENKO

KYIV NATIONAL UNIVERSITY OF CONSTRUCTION AND ARCHITECTURE

03037 Kyiv, Vozdukhoflotskii pr. 31

Telephone: (44) 248-49-05
E-mail: knuba@knuba.edu.ua
Internet: www.knuba.edu.ua

Founded 1930
Academic year: September to July

Rector: A. M. TUGAY

Library of 1,213,000 vols
Number of teachers: 850
Number of students: 6,800

'KYIV POLYTECHNIC INSTITUTE' NATIONAL TECHNICAL UNIVERSITY OF UKRAINE

03056 Kyiv, pr. Peremohy 37

Telephone: (44) 236-69-13
E-mail: zgur@zgurov.kiev.ua
Internet: www.ntu-kpi.kiev.ua

Founded 1898
Languages of instruction: English, Russian, Ukrainian
Academic year: September to June

19 Educational depts, 10 educational research institutes, 13 research institutes and 17 other scientific subdivisions (incl. design bureaux, engineering centres)

Rector: Acad. MYKHAYLO Z. ZGUROVSKIY

Library: 3m. vols
Number of students: 40,000

Publications: *Kyivsky Politekhnik* (newspaper, 48 a year), *Vesti* (2 a year)

DEANS

Faculty of Aircraft and Space Systems: Prof. OLEKSANDR V. ZBRUTSKIY

Faculty of Applied Mathematics: Prof. OLEKSANDR A. MOLCHANOV

Faculty of Biotechnology and Bioengineering: Prof. OLEKSIY M. DUGAN

Faculty of Chemical Engineering: Prof. YEVGEN M. PANOV

Faculty of Chemical Technology: Prof. IHOR M. ASTRELIN

Faculty of Electric Power Engineering and Automation: Prof. OLEKSANDR S. YANDULSKIY

Faculty of Electronics: Prof. VALERIY YA. ZHUYKOV

Faculty of Heat Power Engineering: Prof. YEVGEN M. PISMENNIY

Faculty of Informatics and Computer Science: Prof. OLEKSANDR A. PAVLOV

Faculty of Instrument Design and Engineering: Prof. HRIHORIY S. TYMCHYK

Faculty of Law and Sociology: Prof. ANATOLIY P. TUZOV

Faculty of Linguistics: Prof. NATALYA S. SAYENKO

Faculty of Management and Marketing: Prof. VASYL H. HERASIMCHUK

Faculty of Physics and Engineering: Prof. PETRO I. LOBODA

Faculty of Physics and Mathematics: Acad. Prof. VIKTOR H. BARYAKHTER

Faculty of Radio Engineering: Prof. OLEKSANDR I. RYBIN

Faculty of Welding: SERHIY K. FOMICHOV

Intercollegiate Faculty of Medical Engineering: Prof. V. P. YATSENKO

'LVIV POLYTECHNIC' NATIONAL UNIVERSITY

79013 Lviv, vul. St Bandery 12

Telephone: (32) 272-47-33
E-mail: rudavsky@polynet.lviv.ua
Internet: www.lp.edu.ua

Founded 1844

Rector: Prof. Dr YURIY K. RUDAVSKIY
First Pro-Rector: Prof. Dr PETRO P. KOSTROBIY
Pro-Rector for Education and Foreign Affairs: Prof. Dr YURIY M. RASHKEVYCH
Pro-Rector for Research: Prof. Dr YURIY YA. BOBALO

Library: 3m. vols
Number of teachers: 2,000
Number of students: 17,000

Publication: *Journal* (1 a year, 15 series)

NATIONAL AEROSPACE UNIVERSITY KHARKIV AVIATION INSTITUTE

61070 Kharkiv, Chkalova vul. 17

Telephone: (57) 315-10-56
E-mail: khai@khai.edu
Internet: www.khai.edu

Founded 1930
State control
Languages of instruction: English, Russian
Academic year: September to June

Rector: Prof. VLADIMIR S. KRIVTSOV

Library: 1m. vols
Number of teachers: 850
Number of students: 9,500

DEANS

Faculty of Aircraft Control Systems: ANATOLIY S. KULIK

Faculty of Aircraft Design: VITALIY N. KOBRIN

Faculty of Aircraft Radio-Electronic Systems: VIKTOR I. ILYUSHKO

Faculty of Aviation Engine-Building and Power Systems: ANATOLIY I. DOLMATOV

Faculty of Distance Education: YAKOV V. SAFRONOV

Faculty of Economics and Management: IGOR V. CHUMACHENKO

Faculty of Humanities: VOLODYMYR A. KOPILOV

Faculty of International Education: SERGIY I. PLANKOVSKIY

Faculty of Pre-University Training and Professional Skills Improvement: VLADYSLAV F. DEMENKO

Faculty of Rocket Engineering: OLEKSIY G. NIKOLAEV

NATIONAL AVIATION UNIVERSITY

03680 Kyiv, Kosmonavta Komarova Ave 1

Telephone: (44) 406-72-08
E-mail: interdep@nau.edu.ua
Internet: www.nau.edu.ua

Founded 1933
State control
Languages of instruction: English, Russian, Ukrainian
Academic year: September to June

Incl. Institute of Advanced Technologies, Institute of Extramural and Distance Education, Institute of Continuing Education, Preparatory Institute

Rector: Prof. Dr MYKOLA KULYK
Vice-Rector for Admin.-Economic Work: MYKOLA MYKHALKO
Vice-Rector for Correspondence Courses and Distance Studies: PAVLO BORSUK
Vice-Rector for Educational Issues: ANATOLII POLUKHIN
Vice-Rector for Int. Affairs: Prof. Dr IRYNA ZARUBINSKA

Vice-Rector for Scientific-Research Work: Prof. Dr VOLODYMYR KHARCHENKO
Vice-Rector for Student Issues: Prof. YAROSLAV KOZACHOK

Library: 3m. vols

Publications: *Aviator, Biplan, Business and Management, Development Strategy of Ukraine: Sociology, Economics, Law, Science and Youth, Information Security Scientific and Technical Magazine, Economics, Electronics and Control Systems, Higher Institution Establishments, Humanities Education in Engineering, Metrology and Quality Management, Problems of Improving Effectiveness and Infrastructure, Problems of Informatization and Management, Problems of Systems Approach in Economics, Security of Information*

DEANS

Aerospace Institute: VALERII SHMAROV
Humanities Institute: ARTHUR HUDMANYAN
ICAO Institute: GALYNA SUSLOVA
Institute of Air Navigation: VOLODYMYR VASILIEV
Institute of Airports: OKTIABRYNA CHEMAKINA
Institute of Ecological Safety: ALEXANDER ZAPOROZHETS
Institute of Economics and Management: VYACHESLAV MATVEEV
Institute of Information and Diagnostic Systems: SERGIJ FILONENKO
Institute of International Relations: ALLA FOMENKO
Law Institute: IRYNA SOPILKA

NATIONAL MINING UNIVERSITY OF UKRAINE

49027 Dnipropetrovsk, pr. K. Marksa 19

Telephone: (56) 247-07-66
E-mail: dfr@nmuu.dp.ua
Internet: www.nmuu.dp.ua

Founded 1899

Faculties of construction electrical engineering, construction of mines, economics, engineering, geotechnology, law, mining and prospecting

Rector: Prof. GENNADIY PIVNYAK

Library: 1.3m. vols
Number of teachers: 708
Number of students: 10,897

Publications: *University Monthly, University Newspaper* (52 a year)

NATIONAL SHIPBUILDING UNIVERSITY 'ADMIRAL MAKAROV'

54025 Kyiv, Mikolaiv, pr. Heroiv Stalinhrada

Telephone: (51) 235-91-48
E-mail: vc@usmtu.edu.ua
Internet: www.usmtu.edu.ua

Founded 1929

Rector: Prof. Dr HEORHIY F. ROMANOVSKIY
First Pro-Rector: Prof. Dr OLEKSANDR M. DUBOVIY
Pro-Rector for Research: Prof. Dr VYACHESLAV F. KVASNITSKIY

DEANS

Faculty of Engineering Economics: Prof. OLEKSANDR YU. YEGANOV
Preparatory Faculty: Prof. V. I. KONDRATENKO

NATIONAL TECHNICAL UNIVERSITY 'KHARKIV POLYTECHNIC INSTITUTE'

61002 Kharkiv, Frunze Str. 21

Telephone: (57) 706-32-16
E-mail: omsroot@kpi.kharkov.ua

Internet: www.kpi.kharkov.ua

Founded 1885

Rector: LEONID L. TOVAZHNYANSKY

Pro-Rector for Education and Int. Relations: VALERIY O. KRAVETS

Pro-Rector for Research: ANDRIY P. MARCHENKO

Number of teachers: 1,700
Number of students: 26,000

DEANS

Centre of Distance and Pre-University Training: Dr MYKOLA M. SIRENKO

Centre of Extramural Courses: Prof. EDUARD I. ZAIKA

Faculty of Automation and Instrument Making: Prof. ANATOLIY I. HAPON

Faculty of Business Administration: Prof. VIKTOR YA. ZARUBA

Faculty of Business and Finance: Prof. OLEKSANDR M. HAVRIS

Faculty of Chemical Engineering: Dr OLEKSIY M. PASSOKHA

Faculty of Computing and Information Technologies: Prof. MYKOLA I. ZAPOLOVSKIY

Faculty of Economics: Prof. PETRO H. PERERVA

Faculty of Electrical Engineering: Prof. VOLODYMYR V. VOINOV

Faculty of Electric Power: Prof. OLEKSANDR P. LASURENKO

Faculty of Engineering: Dr MIKHAILO S. STEPANOV

Faculty of Engineering Physics: Dr DMITRO V. BRESKLAVSKIY

Faculty of Information Science and Management: Prof. IHOR P. GAMAJUN

Faculty of Inorganic Substances Technology: Prof. SERGIY A. LESHCHENKO

Faculty of Integrated Training: Prof. ANDRIY V. KIPENSKIY

Faculty of Mechanics and Technology: Dr MYKOLA POHRIBNIY

Faculty of Organic Substances Technology: Prof. OLEKSANDR P. NEKRASOV

Faculty of Physics and Technology: Prof. SERHIY M. KOSMACHOV

Faculty of Power Engineering: Prof. MYKOLA O. TARASENKO

Faculty of Transport Engineering: Dr VITALIY V. YEPIFANOV

German Technical Faculty: Dr VIRA M. SHAMARDINA

NATIONAL TRANSPORT UNIVERSITY

01010 Kyiv, vul. Suvorova 1

Telephone: (44) 280-82-03

E-mail: general@ntu.edu.ua

Internet: www.ntu.edu.ua

Founded 1944

Rector: Prof. Dr MYKOLA F. DMYTRYCHENKO

First Pro-Rector: Prof. Dr MYKOLA O. BILYAKOVYCH

Pro-Rector for Research: Prof. Dr MYKOLA M. DYMYTRIEV

Library of 440,000 vols
Number of teachers: 909
Number of students: 15,000

DEANS

Faculty of Economics, Management and Law: LYUDMILA KOZAK

Faculty of Motor Mechanics: YURIY HUTAREVICH

Faculty of Road Building: VYACHESLAV SAVENKO

Faculty of Transport and Information Technologies: Prof. VICTOR DANCHUK

NATIONAL UNIVERSITY OF FOOD TECHNOLOGIES

01601 Kyiv, Volodymrska vul. 68

Telephone: (44) 220-95-55

E-mail: indepart@nuft.edu.ua

Internet: www.nuft.edu.ua

Founded 1930 as Kyiv Institute of Sugar Refinery Production, present name and status 2002

State control

Languages of instruction: Russian, Ukrainian

Academic year: September to June

Rector: Prof. SERGII IVANOV

Library of 1,163,050 vols, 120 periodicals
Number of teachers: 742
Number of students: 13,019

Publications: *Food Industry* (4 a year), *Latest Achievements in the Food Industry and Scientific Research*, *Research Papers of the National University of Food Technologies* (4 a year), *Scientific Works*

DEANS

Faculty of Accounting, Finance and Business: OLEG SHEREMET

Faculty of Automation and Computer Systems: LIUDMILA MANOHA

Faculty of Biotechnology and Food Products Examination: ANDRIY CHAGAIDA

Faculty of Economics and Management: TATIANA MOSTENSKA

Faculty of Fermentation and Baking Industry: PETRO SHIYAN

Faculty of Hotel-Restaurant Business and Tourism: GALINA SEMAKHINA

Faculty of Mechanical Engineering and Packing Technologies: SERGIY BLAZHENKO

Faculty of Power Engineering: MYKHAILO MASLIKOV

Faculty of Sugar, Meat and Dairy Products: OKSANA KOCHUBEY-LITVINENKO

Preparatory Dept: VALENTINA KUDINA

NATIONAL UNIVERSITY OF WATER MANAGEMENT AND NATURE RESOURCES USE

33028 Rivne, vul. Soborna 11

Telephone: (36) 222-10-86

Internet: www.nuwm.rv.ua

Founded 1922

State control

Rector: VASYL A. HURYN

Vice-Rector of Admin. and Social Affairs: VOLODYMYR M. YAKYMCHUK (acting)

Vice-Rector of Research: MYKOLA HIROL

Vice-Rector of Science and Academic Affairs: OLEKSANDR TKACHUK (acting)

Vice-Rector of Science and Int. Relations: HRYHORIY SAPSAY

Vice-Rector of Science and Teaching Methods: ANATOLIY BILESTSKIY

Library of 900,000 vols
Number of teachers: 715
Number of students: 14,000

Publications: *Bulletin* (4 a year), *Hydroamelioration and Hydrotechnical Engineering* (1 a year), *Resource Saving Materials, Construction, Buildings and Structures* (4 a year)

DEANS

Faculty of Applied Mathematics and Computer-Integrated Systems: ANATOLIY P. VLASIUK

Faculty of Building and Architecture: HRYHORIY H. MASIUK

Faculty of Ecology and Natural Resource Application: MYKOLA O. KLYMENKO

Faculty of Economy and Business: SVITLANA O. LEVYTSKA

Faculty of Hydrotechnical Engineering and Hydroenergetics: ANATOLIY M. MAKOVSKIY

Faculty of Land Management and Geoinformation: PETRO H. CHERNIAGA

Faculty of Management: VITALIY P. OKORSKIY

Faculty of Mechanical and Power Engineering: MYKOLA M. MARCHUK

Faculty of Water Management: VASYL TURCHENIUK

ODESSA NATIONAL POLYTECHNIC UNIVERSITY

65044 Odessa, pr. Shevchenko 1

Telephone: (48) 222-34-74

E-mail: ospu@ospu.odessa.ua

Internet: www.ospu.odessa.ua

Founded 1918

Faculties of automation and computer technology, automation and electrification of industry, chemical technology, engineering economics, mechanical technology, nuclear power, radio engineering, robot systems, thermal power

Rector: Prof. Dr VALERIY P. MALAKHOV

Pro-Rector for Studies and Education: Prof. Dr YURIY S. YAMOLSKY

Pro-Rector for Studies and Research: Prof. Dr VALERIY P. MALAKHOV

Library: 1.5m. vols
Number of teachers: 4,000
Number of students: 20,000

ODESSA STATE ENVIRONMENTAL UNIVERSITY

65016 Odessa, vul. Lvivska 15

Telephone: (48) 232-67-35

E-mail: info@odeku.edu.ua

Internet: www.odeku.edu.ua

Founded 1932

State control

Languages of instruction: English, Russian, Ukrainian

Academic year: September to June

Rector: Prof. SERGIY STEPANENKO

Vice-Rector: Dr MYKOLA SERBOV

Chief of Int. Dept: Dr OLEG SHABLIY

Dean for Continuing Education and Training: Dr LARISA POLETAEVA

Library of 50,600 vols
Number of teachers: 274
Number of students: 4,960

Publications: *Meteorology, Climatology and Hydrology* (4 a year), *Ukrainian Hydrometeorological Journal* (4 a year)

DEANS

College of Computer Technology: VOLODYMIR KOVALCHUK

College of Hydrometeorology: SERGIY AVGAYTIS

Faculty of Computer Science: Dr LUDMILA KOVALENKO

Faculty of Distance Learning: Dr OLENA VOLOSHINA

Faculty of Environmental Economics: Dr OLENA VOLODYMYROVA

Faculty of Environmental Studies: Dr ANGELINA CHUGAY

Faculty of Magister's Programmes: GALINA BOROVSKA

Hydrometeorological Institute: LERA OVCHARUK (Dir)

PROFESSORS

Faculty of Computer Science:
KORBAN, V. KH.
KRUGLYAK, Y. M.
PREPELIZHA, G. P.

Faculty of Environmental Studies:
GERASIMOV, O. I.
LOEVA, I. D.

MINICHEVA, G. G.
SAFRANOV, T. A.
SOKOLOV, Y. M.
ZHYKALO, A. N.

Hydrometeorological Institute:
EFIMOV, V. A.
GOPCHENKO, E. D.
LOBODA, N. S.
MICHAYLOV, V. I.
MISCHENKO, Z. A.
POLEVOY, A. M.
SHKOLNY, E. P.
STEPANENKO, S. N.
TUCHKOVENKO, Y. S.

POLTAVA NATIONAL TECHNICAL UNIVERSITY 'YU. KONDRATYUKA'

36601 Poltava, Pershotravnevyy pr. 24

Telephone: (53) 222-28-50
E-mail: v57@pntu.edu.ua
Internet: www.pntu.edu.ua

Founded 1930, present name and status 2002
State control

Rector: Prof. Dr VOLODYMYR O. ONYSHCHENKO
First Vice-Rector: Dr BOGDAN O. KOROBKO
Vice-Rector for Academic Work: Dr BOGDAN KOROBKO
Vice-Rector for Science and Innovations: Prof. Dr hab. VICTOR PASHYNSKY
Vice-Rector for Corporative Management: ANATOLIY MARTYNENKO
Vice-Rector for Social and Int. Affairs: YURI BEREZA
Chief Librarian: VELENTINA SIDORENKO
Library of 500,000 vols, 116 periodicals
Number of teachers: 540
Number of students: 10,000

DEANS

External Faculty: Dr I. O. IVANYTSKA
Faculty of Architecture: Prof. Dr hab. VASYL SHULYK
Faculty of Civil Engineering: Dr LEONID SHCHERBININ
Faculty of Electro-Mechanical Engineering: Dr MYKOLA SHPYLKA
Faculty of Finance and Economics: Dr RAYISA V. SHYNKARENKO
Faculty of Information, Telecommunication Technologies and Systems: Dr OLEG ODARUSHCHENKO
Faculty of Management and Business: Dr VOLODYMYR PENTS
Faculty of Sanitary Engineering: Dr STANISLAV POPOV
Postgraduate Study Centre: GENNADIY GOLOVKO

SEVASTOPOL NATIONAL TECHNICAL UNIVERSITY

99053 Sevastopol, Streletsky Bay, Studgorodok, vul. Mazepy 10

Telephone: (69) 223-50-08
E-mail: root@sevgtu.sebastopol.ua
Internet: sevntu.com.ua

Founded 1963

Rector: M. Z. LAVRINENKO

Library: 1.2m. vols, spec. collns on machine-building and environmental monitoring
Number of teachers: 550
Number of students: 7,000

UKRAINIAN STATE UNIVERSITY OF CHEMICAL TECHNOLOGY

49005 Dnipropetrovsk, Gagarin Ave. 8

Telephone: (56) 247-08-13
E-mail: ughtu@dicht.dp.ua
Internet: www.udhtu.com.ua

Founded 1930
State control

Academic year: July to September
Languages of instruction: Russian, Ukrainian

Rector: Prof. Dr MYKHAYLO V. BURMISTR
First Vice-Rector: Prof. Dr MYKOLA NIKOLENKO
Vice-Rector of Science: Prof. Dr OLEG GIRIN
Vice-Rector of Science and Education: Prof. Dr VIKTOR GOLEUS

Library of 800,000 vols
Number of teachers: 484
Number of students: 7,813

Publications: *Chemistry and Chemical Technology Questions* (4 a year), *Scientific-Technological Digest* (4 a year), *Voprosy himii i himicheskoi tehnologii* (6 a year)

DEANS

Advanced Technologies: ANGELA VACULICH
Faculty of Economics: NATALIA CHUPRINA
Faculty of High-Molecular Compounds Technology: SVETLANA VOLKOVA
Faculty of Inorganic Technology: OLEXANDER PIVOVAROV
Faculty of Organic Technology: NATALYA EVDOKIMENKO
Faculty of Silicate Technology: OLGA RYZHOVA
Mechanical Faculty: ILLYA NACHOVNYY

VINNYTSIA NATIONAL TECHNICAL UNIVERSITY

21036 Vinnytsia, Khmelnitske shose 95

Telephone: (43) 232-57-18
E-mail: vstu@vstu.vinnica.ua
Internet: www.vstu.edu.ua

Founded 1960

Rector: Prof. BORIS I. MOKIN
First Pro-Rector for Research, Int. Relations and Economic and Political Affairs: VOLODYMYR V. HRABKO

Library of 820,000 vols
Number of teachers: 542
Number of students: 7,492

Publications: *Proceedings* (6 a year), *University News* (12 a year)

ZAPORIZHZHYA NATIONAL TECHNICAL UNIVERSITY

69063 Zaporizhzhya, vul. Zhukovskoho 64

Telephone: (61) 764-25-06
E-mail: rector@zntu.edu.ua
Internet: www.zntu.edu.ua

Founded 1900
State control
Languages of instruction: Russian, Ukrainian
Academic year: September to June

Rector: Prof. SERHIY B. BYELIKOV
First Pro-Rector for Education: Dr VOLODYMYR G. PRUSHKIVSKY
Pro-Rector for Education: Dr SERHIY T. YARYMBASH
Librarian: RAISA I. KUCHERUK

Library: 1m. vols
Number of teachers: 770
Number of students: 13,000

Publications: *Electrotechnics and Electroenergetics* (2 a year), *New Materials and Technology in Metallurgy and Machine Construction* (2 a year), *Radio Electronics*, *Radio Electronics, Computer Science and Control* (2 a year)

Academies

Dnipropetrovsk State Medical Academy: 49044 Dnipropetrovsk, vul. Dzerzhinskoho 9; tel. (56) 245-15-65; e-mail dsma@ dsma.dp.ua; internet www.dsma.dp.ua; f. 1916; main specialities: clinical pharmacology, dentistry, general practice, paediatrics, sanitary hygiene; library: 656,600 vols; 598 teachers; 4,045 students; Rector Dr GEORGY V. DZYAK; publs *Dermatology, Cosmetics and Sexual Pathology* (4 a year), *Medical Perspectives* (4 a year), *Urology* (4 a year).

Donbass State Academy of Civil Engineering and Architecture: 86123 Donetsk obl., Makeyevka vul. Derzhavina 2; tel. (62) 290-29-38; e-mail mailbox@dgasa.dn.ua; internet www.dgasa.dn.ua; f. 1972; faculties: architecture, basic and general engineering training, civil engineering, economics, environmental engineering, mechanical engineering, marketing and management; extramural preparatory dept for foreign students, humanities; library: 400,000 vols; 399 teachers; 5,769 students; Rector YEVHEN V. HOROKHOV; publs *Academy News* (12 a year), *Bulletin* (6 a year), *Metal Construction* (4 a year).

Donbass State Engineering Academy: 84313 Kramatorsk, bul. Mashinostroiteley, 39; tel. (62) 641-69-38; e-mail pk@dgma .donetsk.ua; internet www.dgma.donetsk.ua; faculties of automation, automation of metal-shaping processes, economics, engineering and economics, humanities, machine-building.

Ivano-Frankivsk State Medical Academy: 76000 Ivano-Frankivsk, Halytska 2; tel. (34) 222-42-95; e-mail ma@ifdma.if.ua; internet www.ifdma.if.ua; f. 1945; library: 319,000 vols; 389 teachers; 4,994 students; Rector Dr YE. NEIKO.

Kharkiv State Academy of Railway Transport: 61003 Kharkiv, pl. Feierbakha 7; tel. (57) 732-20-67; e-mail info@kart .kharkov.com; internet www.kart.edu.ua; f. 1930; faculties: automation, construction, economics, mechanics, telemechanics and communication, traffic management; brs in Donetsk, Kyiv; library: 700,000 vols; Rector NIKOLAY I. DANKO.

Kharkiv State Academy of Zooveterinary Science: 62341 Kharkiv obl., Dergachevskiy raion, P/O Malaya Danilovka; tel. (57) 635-74-65; e-mail zoovet@zoovet .kharkov.ua; f. 1851; library: 250,000 vols; 190 teachers; 2,500 students; Rector VALERY GOLOVKO.

Kharkiv State Municipal Academy: 61002 Kharkiv, vul. Revolyutsii 12; tel. (57) 247-15-85; e-mail rectorat@ksame.kharkov .com; f. 1930; faculties of accounting and auditing, architecture, economics of civil engineering enterprises, economics of municipal economy enterprises, electric and underground transport, engineering ecology, landscape architecture, management in hotel business and tourism, management of public services and municipal finances, retraining, technical maintenance of buildings, urban electric power supply and lighting, urban planning and development; Electromechanical College, Municipal Economy College; library: 890,000 vols; 1,000 teachers; 12,000 students; Rector Prof. L. N. SHUTENKO.

Lviv Academy of Veterinary Medicine: 79301 Lviv, vul. Pekarska 50; tel. (32) 275-67-84; e-mail vetacademy@hotmail.com; internet www.vetacad.lviv.ua; f. 1784; faculties: biology and technology, economics and management, extramural studies, food technology, veterinary medicine; library: 333,000 vols; 292 teachers; 4,500 students; Rector Prof. Dr R. J. KRAVTSIV.

Lviv Commercial Academy: 79005 Lviv, vul. Tuhan-Baranovskoho 10; tel. (32) 275-65-50; e-mail academy@lac.lviv.ua; internet www.lac.lviv.ua; f. 1899; faculties of commodity science, commerce, economics, international economic relations, law, management; 300 teachers; 5,740 students; library: 600,000 vols; Rector Prof. I. M. KOPYCH.

National Metallurgical Academy of Ukraine: 49600 Dnipropetrovsk, pr. Gagarina 4; tel. (56) 245-31-56; e-mail dmeti@dmeti.dp.ua; internet dmeti.dp.ua; f. 1899; faculties: computing systems and automation, ecology and chemical technologies, economic cybernetics, economics, electrometallurgy, energy and electromechanics, humanities, management, materials sciences and metal forming, mechanics and machine building, metallurgy; library: 524,327 vols; 732 teachers; 12,199 students; Rector OLEKSANDR H. VELYCHKO; publ. *Theory and Practice of Metallurgy* (4 a year).

Odessa National Academy of Food Technologies: 65039 Odessa, vul. Kanatna 112; tel. (482) 29-11-40; e-mail fedosov@optima.com.ua; internet www.osaft.odessa.ua; f. 1902; academic year September to June; faculties: automation of technological processes; economics, management and business; food preserving technology and winemaking; grain and grain products technology; meat and dairy products technology and ecology; mechanical engineering; technology of bread, confectionery and nutrition; 566 teachers (incl. 53 full professors); 10,400 students; library: 600,000 vols; Rector Prof. BOGDAN YEGOROV; publs *Collection of Scientific Works* (2 a year), *Grain Products and Mixed Fodders* (4 a year).

Odessa National Maritime Academy: 65029 Odessa, Didrikhson 8; tel. (48) 777-57-74; e-mail info@ma.odessa.ua; internet www.ma.odessa.ua; f. 1944; faculties: automation, electrical engineering, marine engineering, maritime law, navigation, radio electronics; brs in Mariupol, Izmail, correspondence depts and the maritime college of the technical fleet; library: 578,000 vols; 401 teachers; 7,134 students; Rector Prof. MYKHAYLO V. MIYUSOV; publs *Automization of Ship's Technical Devices* (2 a year), *Marine Transportation and Transport Complexes* (1 a year), *Navigation* (2 a year), *Sea Review* (4 a year), *Ship's Power Plants* (2 a year).

Odessa State Academy of Civil Engineering and Architecture: 65029 Odessa, Didrikhson 4; tel. (482) 20-41-82; e-mail rektorat@gs.org.ua; internet www.ogasa.odessa.ua; f. 1930; faculties: architecture, construction engineering, power engineering, industrial and civil construction, technical engineering, sanitary engineering; library: 600,000 vols; Rector Prof. VITALIY S. DOROFEEV.

Odessa State Academy of Refrigeration: 65026 Odessa, vul. Dvoryanska 1/3; tel. (48) 223-22-20; e-mail admin@osar.odessa.ua; internet www.osar.odessa.ua; f. 1922; faculties: automation and robot engineering, cryogenic engineering, environmental protection and rational use of natural resources, heat technology, mechanical engineering, refrigeration engineering, systems of automatized projection, thermophysics; library: 487,173 vols; 288 teachers; 3,500 students; Rector V. V. PRITULA; publ. *Refrigeration Engineering and Technology* (2 a year).

Poltava State Agrarian Academy: 314003 Poltava, vul. Skovorody 1/3; tel. (5322) 2-26-10; e-mail antonov@agroak.poltava.ua; internet agroak.poltava.ua; f. 1920; depts: accounting and auditing, agronomy, economy of enterprises, farm mechanization, finance, management of organizations, veterinary medicine, zoological engineering; library: 315,000 vols; 247 teachers; 7,000 students; Rector Dr V. N. PISARENKO; publ. *Poltava Agrarian News* (4 a year).

Prydniprovska State Academy of Civil Engineering and Architecture: 49600 Dnipropetrovsk, Chernyshevskeho 24A; tel. (562) 47-16-88; e-mail dik@pgasa.dp.ua; internet www.pgasa.dp.ua; f. 1930; faculties: architecture, building technology, civil engineering, construction, correspondence, economics, mechanics; library: 662,000 vols; 467 teachers; 6,392 students; Rector Prof. V. I. BOLSHAKOV.

State Academy of Food Technology and Trade: 61051 Kharkiv, Klochkivska 333; tel. (57) 336-89-79; e-mail inter-dep62@mail.ru; internet www.hduht.edu.ua; f. 1967; faculties of accountancy and auditing, economics, food industry machines and equipment, food science and food trade, food technology, industrial management, marketing, services management; 350 teachers; 5,000 students; library: 380,000 vols; Rector OLEKSANDR I. CHEREVKO; publ. *Zbirnyk Naukovykh Prats* (1 a year).

Ukrainian Engineering Pedagogics Academy: 61003 Kharkiv, Department of Foreign Relations, vul. Universytetska 16; tel. (572) 731-28-62; e-mail docents@vl.kharkov.ua; f. 1958; faculties: electrical and technological, electromechanics and computer systems, machine-building, mechanical and technological, mining engineering, power engineering, radioelectronics, social-economical; training centres for foreign citizens and engineering educators; library: 1m. vols; 350 teachers; 11,000 students; Rector ELENA KOVALENKO.

Yaroslav Mudry National Law Academy of Ukraine: 61024 Kharkiv, Pushkinskaya ul. 77; tel. (57) 704-11-20; e-mail uracad@bestnet.kharkov.ua; internet www.uracad.kharkiv.edu; f. 1804; library: 1m. vols, 1,000 dissertations, 29,000 rare books and MSS; 600 teachers; 15,000 students; Rector VASYL YA. TATSIY.

Zaporizhzhya State Engineering Academy: 69006 Zaporizhia, pr. Lenina 226; tel. (612) 15-90-34; e-mail admin@zgia.zp.ua; internet www.zgia.zp.ua; f. 1959; faculties: building and water resources, economics of enterprises, electronics and electronic technologies, information technologies, management and finance, mechanics and technology, metallurgy, postgraduate studies, power engineering and energy-saving; library: 501,777 vols; 350 teachers; 10,000 students; Rector Dr V. I. POZHUEV.

Institutes of Higher Education

Donetsk Musical-Pedagogical Institute: 340086 Donetsk, vul. Artema 44; tel. (622) 93-81-22; depts: choral conducting, composition, folk instruments, musicology, orchestral instruments, piano, singing.

Kherson A. D. Tsuryupa Agricultural Institute: 325006 Kherson, vul. Rozy Lyuksemburga 23; tel. (5500) 2-64-71; f. 1874; faculties of agricultural construction and hydromelioration, agronomy, animal husbandry, economics and agrobusiness jurisdiction; library: 300,000 vols; Rector V. A. USHKARENKO.

Krivoi Rog Ore Mining Institute: 324027 Krivoi Rog, vul. 22 Partsezda 11; tel. (564) 23-22-30; f. 1922; faculties: construction, electrical engineering, engineering, geology and ore dressing, mine surveying and geodesy, open-cast mining, underground mining; geological museum; 4,500 students; library of 1.2m. vols; Rector V. F. BIZOV; publ. *Collection of Works* (2 a year).

Lugansk Agricultural Institute: 348008 Lugansk Luhansk 8; tel. (522) 55-92-43; depts of accounting, agronomy, economics, mechanization.

Odessa Agricultural Institute: 270039 Odessa vul. Sverdlova 112; tel. (48) 229-11-80; f. 1918; depts of accounting, agronomy, animal husbandry, economics and management, fruit and vegetable growing, land management, mechanization, veterinary medicine, viticulture; br. in Nikolaev; 1,000 teachers; 5,200 students; library: 280,000 vols; Rector YU. S. TSUKANOV.

Poltava Medical Stomatological Institute: 36024 Poltava, vul. Shevchenko 23; tel. (66) 961-96-26; e-mail study@umsa.com.ua; internet www.umsa.com.ua; f. 1921; Rector V. M. ZHDAN.

Ukrainian Institute of Printing: 79020 Lviv, vul. Podholosko 19; tel. (32) 242-23-40; e-mail uad@uad.lviv.ua; internet www.uad.lviv.ua; faculties of publishing, printing and information technologies; economics and book trade business; printing equipment; preparatory training; library: 384,000 vols; Rector Prof. Dr BOHDAN DURNIAK; Vice-Rector YAROSLAV UHRYN; Vice-Rector VOLODYMYR MAIK; publ. *Journal of Printing and Publishing.*

Schools of Art and Music

Kharkiv Institute of Industrial and Applied Arts: 310002 Kharkiv, vul. Krasnoznamennaya 8; tel. (57) 243-10-56; e-mail root@design.kharkov.ua; f. 1927, renamed 1963; faculties of industrial design, interior design; library: 88,000 vols; 160 teachers; 580 students; Rector V. DANYLENKO.

Kharkiv State Academy of Culture: 61003 Kharkiv, Bursatski Uzviz 4; tel. (57) 712-81-05; e-mail sheiko@ic.ac.kharkov.ua; internet www.ic.ac.kharkov.ua; f. 1929; depts of library and information science, cultural studies, documentation and information work, art, music, theatre, cinema and television; library: 400,000 vols; 257 teachers; 3,393 students; Rector Prof. VASYL M. SHEYKO; publs *Journal* (1 a year), *Kultura Ukrainy* (12 a year).

Kyiv State Institute of Culture: 01133 Kyiv, vul. Shchorsa 36; tel. (44) 269-98-44; departments: folk culture, library science.

Lviv Academy of Arts: 79011 Lviv, vul. Kubiyovycha 38; tel. (32) 276-14-82; e-mail artacademy@mail.lviv.ua; internet www.artacademy.lviv.ua; f. 1946; faculties: decorative and applied arts, design, fine art and restoration, history and theory of art; library: 90,000 vols; 250 teachers; 1,000 students; Rector Prof. ANDRIY BOKOTEY; Vice-Rectors Prof. IGOR GOLOD, Prof. OREST HOLUBETZ; publ. *Scientific Messenger* (1 a year).

National Academy of Fine Arts and Architecture: 04053 Kyiv, vul. Smirnova-Lastochkina 20; tel. (44) 272-15-40; e-mail naoma@ukr.net; internet www.naoma.edu.ua; f. 1917; faculties of architecture, art history, arts management, graphic art, painting, restoration, sculpture, theatrical decorative art; 130 teachers; 800 students; library: 130,000 vols; Rector Prof. ANDREI V. CHEBYKIN.

Odessa State Conservatoire 'A. V. Nezhdanova': 65021 Odessa, vul. Ostrovidova 63; tel. (48) 226-78-76; f. 1913; choral conducting, composition, musicology, orchestral and folk instruments, piano, singing; 140 teachers; 680 students; library: 100,000 vols; Rector OLEKSANDR V. SOKOL.

State Academy of Music 'Mykola Lysenko': 79005 Lviv, vul. Nyzhankivsky 5; tel. (32) 274-31-06; e-mail musinst@lviv.gu.net; internet musicacademy.lviv.ua; f. 1852; faculties: choral conducting, composition, folk instruments, musicology, operatic and symphonic conducting, orchestral instruments, piano, singing; library: 200,000 vols; 175 teachers; 550 students; Rector IHOR PYLATIUK.

Ukrainian National Academy of Music 'P. Tchaikovsky': 01001 Kyiv, Gorodetska vul. 1–3/11; tel. (44) 279-07-92; e-mail rozhok@knmau.com.ua; f. 1913; faculties of choral conducting, composition, folk instruments, music production, music education, opera and symphony orchestra conducting, orchestral instruments, piano, singing, theory and history of music; 310 teachers; 1,200 students; library: 355,000 vols; Rector OLEG TIMOSHENKO; publ. *Ukrainian Musicology* (1 a year).

UNITED ARAB EMIRATES

The Higher Education System

The United Arab Emirates (UAE) universities include the United Arab Emirates University (founded 1976), Ajman University of Science and Technology (founded 1988), University of Sharjah (founded 1997), Zayed University (founded 1998, with two campuses in Abu Dhabi and two in Dubai) and Abu Dhabi University (founded 2003). A branch of the Sorbonne University, based in Paris, France, opened in Abu Dhabi in 2006, and American universities are in operation in Dubai, Ras al-Khaimah and Sharjah. In September 1988 four higher colleges of technology (two for male and two for female students) opened, admitting a total of 1,150 students in 1992/93, all of whom were citizens of the UAE. The total number of higher colleges of technology had increased to 13 by the end of the 2000s. In 2008/09 a total of 87,006 students were enrolled in university and other higher education institutions. By 2011 there were 52 higher education institutions in Dubai alone, with a total enrolment of 43,212 students. Many other students receive higher education abroad.

The Ministry of Higher Education and Scientific Research, founded in 1992, is responsible for all post-secondary education. It is also responsible for the regulation of private institutions in higher education. The Commission for Academic Accreditation (CAA), a department within the Ministry, licenses institutions and accredits degree programmes. The Commission introduced new, more stringent accreditation standards at the beginning of the 2011/12 academic year in a bid to improve the quality of higher education in the UAE; the standards also require institutions to make their facilities and expertise available to the community at large. In 2006 the Knowledge and Human Development Authority (KHDA) was set up by the Government in Dubai to regulate private education in Dubai Free Zones. The KHDA in turn established the University Quality Assurance Board in 2008 to assess and license private universities operating in the free zones, where 60% of higher education institutions in Dubai are based, such as the Manchester Business School operating in the Dubai Knowledge Village. The CAA remains the federal body responsible for tertiary programmes throughout the UAE.

Admission to higher education is on the basis of an average score of at least 70% in the Tawjihiyya examinations (although, as entrance is so competitive, an average of at least 80% is typically required); many institutions also require a score in excess of 150 in the Common Educational Proficiency Assessment (CEPA) English examination. Degrees are awarded on a credit basis. The undergraduate Bachelors degree is a four-year programme of study (medicine lasts seven years). The Masters degree is a one- or two-year course following the Bachelors degree; some programmes follow the US model and include both coursework and thesis, while others are based on the British, research-based model and include only a small number of taught modules. Doctoral programmes were introduced at the United Arab Emirates University from the beginning of the 2009/10 academic year and have subsequently become available at a number of the country's other higher education institutions; such programmes, which typically last between three and four years, follow the US model, comprising one year of coursework and between two and three years of research, culminating in submission of a thesis.

Post-secondary technical and vocational education is offered by higher colleges of technology and other colleges. Higher colleges of technology, which are funded by the Ministry of Finance, provide training for professional and technology careers in the public and private sectors. Admission is on the basis of a score of at least 60% in the Tawjihiyya and performance in the CEPA English examination, and most candidates undertake a one-year preparatory Foundation programme. Among the qualifications offered by the higher colleges of technology are Certificates (two years), Diplomas (one to three years) and Higher Diplomas (three years). Bachelors degree programmes are also available at some higher colleges of technology, in conjunction with other higher education institutions; such programmes require a minimum period of four weeks' work placement. In 2006 the National Institute for Vocational Education (NIVE) was established as an autonomous organization of quality and standard assurance affiliated to the KHDA; qualifications offered by the NIVE are accredited by the KHDA.

Regulatory Bodies

GOVERNMENT

Ministry of Culture, Youth and Community Development: POB 17, Abu Dhabi; tel. (2) 4466145; e-mail info@mcycd.gov.ae; internet www.mcycd.ae; Minister Sheikh NAHYAN BIN MUBARAK AL NAHYAN.

Ministry of Education: POB 3962, Abu Dhabi; tel. (2) 4089999; e-mail ccc.moe@moe .gov.ae; internet www.moe.gov.ae; Minister HUMAID MOH'D OBAID AL-QATTAMI.

Ministry of Higher Education & Scientific Research: POB 45253, Al Najda St, Abu Dhabi; tel. (2) 6428000; e-mail mohe@ uae.gov.ae; internet www.mohesr.ae; Minister Sheikh HAMDAN BIN MUBARAK AL NAHAYAN.

ACCREDITATION

Commission for Academic Accreditation: Min. of Higher Education and Scientific Research, Al Najdah St, POB 45133, Abu Dhabi; tel. (2) 6951461; e-mail badr .aboulela@mohesr.ae; internet www.caa.ae; f. 2000; 4 mems; Dir MUHAMMAD BADR ELDIN ABOUL-ELA.

Learned Societies

LANGUAGE AND LITERATURE

Alliance Française: POB 2646, Abu Dhabi; tel. (2) 6666232; e-mail alliancefrancaise@ af-aboudabi.net; internet www.af-aboudabi .net; offers courses and exams in French language and culture and promotes cultural exchange with France; attached teaching centre in Dubai.

British Council: Villa No 7, Al Nasr St, Khalidya, Abu Dhabi, POB 46523; tel. (2) 6659300; e-mail information@ae .britishcouncil.org; internet www .britishcouncil.org/uae; teaching centre; offers courses and exams in English language and British culture; promotes cultural exchange with the UK; attached teaching centres in Dubai and Sharjah; Dir, United Arab Emirates JO MAHER; Deputy Dir PAUL MASON.

Research Institutes

GENERAL

Centre for Documentation and Research: POB 5884, Abu Dhabi; tel. (2) 4183333; e-mail dg@cdr.gov.ae; internet www.cdr.gov.ae; f. 1968; attached to Ministry of Presidential Affairs; documents, books, maps and articles relating to the Arabian Gulf and the Arabian Peninsula; publishes specialized research studies; convenes nat., regional and int. seminars and confs; organizes exhibitions relating to the UAE; library of 32,000 vols in many languages, 6,481 microfiches, 7m. documents; Pres. Sheikh MANSOUR BIN ZAYED AL NAHYAN.

AGRICULTURE, FISHERIES AND VETERINARY SCIENCE

Agricultural Information Centre: POB 176, Ras al-Khaimah; tel. (2) 4495100; e-mail info@moew.gov.ae; f. 1975 as a UNDP-FAO assisted project, present name 1984; run by Min. of Environment and Water; conducts research into irrigation, plant protection, vegetable varieties, vegetables under plastic houses, soil fertility; library of 500 vols; Research Dir MUHAMMAD HASSAN AL-SHAMSI.

Libraries and Archives

Abu Dhabi

National Archives: POB 2380, Abu Dhabi; tel. (2) 4447797; internet www.cultural.org .ae; f. 1985; attached to the Cultural Foundation, an independent government body; cares for current and historical public records; Dir Dr NASSIR ALI AL-HIMIRI.

National Library: POB 2380, Abu Dhabi; tel. (2) 6515411; e-mail national-library@ tcaabudhabi.ae; internet www.adach.ae; f. 1981; UN Deposit Centre; brs: Emirates and Gulf Library, Batten Children's Library, Al Nahyan Public Library, Al Ain Mall Public Library, Mezayad Mall Public Library, Al Rahah Mall Public Library; 500,000 vols, 3,000 periodical titles, 12,000 audiovisual items; 45000 MSS; Exec. Dir JUMAA AL QUBAISI; publs *National Bibliography* (in Arabic and English), *Union Catalogue of Periodicals in the UAE* (in Arabic and English).

Dubai

Dubai Municipality Public Libraries: POB 67, Dubai; tel. (4) 2262788; e-mail info@dm.gov.ae; internet login.dm.gov.ae; f. 1963; 205,970 vols, 1,707 periodicals; spec. colln of Arab Islamic art books; Head MUHAMMAD JASSIM AL-ERIADI.

Museums and Art Galleries

Al-Ain

Al-Ain Museum: POB 15715, Al-Ain; tel. (3) 764559; e-mail antigan@emirates.net.ae; internet www.aam.gov.ae; f. 1971; archaeology and ethnography; library of 200 vols; archaeological sites at Al-Ain and Umm al-Nar island; Dirs SAIF BIN ALI AL-DARMAKI, Dr WALID YASIN.

Sharjah

Sharjah Museums: POB 39939, Sharjah; tel. (6) 5566002; e-mail info@ sharjahmuseums.ae; internet www .sharjahmuseums.ae; f. 1995; Dir Shiekha HOOR AL-QASIMI.

Universities

ABU DHABI UNIVERSITY

POB 59911, Abu Dhabi
Internet: www.adu.ac.ae
Founded 2003
Private control
Accredited by Min. of Higher Education and Scientific Research
Chancellor: Prof. Dr NABIL IBRAHIM
Librarian: OMAR ABBAS
Number of students: 4,000

DEANS

College of Arts and Sciences: Dr RADWAN AL-JARRAH (acting)
College of Business Administration: Dr MUHAMMAD KHALIFA
College of Engineering and Computer Science: Dr ALY S. NAZMY
University College: Dr JEHAN ZITAWI

AL-AIN UNIVERSITY OF SCIENCE AND TECHNOLOGY

POB 64141, Al-Ain
Telephone: (3) 7024888
E-mail: chancellor@aau.ac.ae

Internet: www.aau.ac.ae
Founded 2005
Private control
Academic year: September to July
Pres.: Prof. FUAD SHEIKH SALEM
Chancellor: Dr NOOR ELDEEN ATATREH
Number of teachers: 150
Number of students: 3,800

DEANS

College of Business: Dr SOBHY EL KHATIB
College of Education: Dr OMAR KHASAWNEH
College of Engineering and IT: Dr NAYEF ABU AGEEL
College of Law: Dr HUSSEIN EL MOUGY
College of Pharmacy: Dr KHAIRI MUSTAFA

AL-GHURAIR UNIVERSITY

POB 37374, Dubai
Telephone: (4) 4200223
E-mail: admissions@agu.ac.ae
Internet: www.agu.ae
Founded 1999
Private control
Accredited by Ministry of Higher Education and Scientific Research; colleges of business studies, computing, engineering and applied sciences; school of design
Pres.: Dr ABDURAHEM MUHAMMAD AL-AMEEN

AL-HOSN UNIVERSITY

POB 38772, Abu Dhabi
Telephone: (2) 4070700
E-mail: info@alhosnu.ae
Internet: www.alhosnu.ae
Founded 2003
Private control
Accredited by Ministry of Higher Education and Scientific Research
Vice-Chancellor: Prof. ABDUL RAHIM SABOUNI
Provost: Dr HAMDI SHEIBANI
Library Dir: Dr ALHAJ SALIM MUSTAFA
Publication: *Journal of Engineering and Applied Sciences* (every 2 years)

DEANS

Faculty of Arts and Social Sciences: Prof. HASSAN MUSTAPHA
Faculty of Business: Prof. AHMAD ZOHDI
Faculty of Engineering and Applied Sciences: Dr HAMDI SHEIBANI

AJMAN UNIVERSITY OF SCIENCE AND TECHNOLOGY (AUST)

POB 346, Ajman
Telephone: (6) 7482222
E-mail: info@ajman.ac.ae
Internet: www.ajman.ac.ae
Founded 1988
Private control
Pres.: Dr SAEED ABDULLAH SALMAN
Vice-Pres. for Admin. and Financial Affairs: THAMER SAEED ABDULLA ALI SALMAN
Vice-Pres. for External Relations and Cultural Affairs: AHMED ANKIT

DEANS

Faculty of Business Administration: Dr YAHYA HADDAD
Faculty of Computer Science: Dr MAHMOUD ABO-NAAJ
Faculty of Dentistry: Prof. SALEM HASSAN ABU FANAS
Faculty of Education and Basic Science: Dr SALEH AWADH OMAR ARAM
Faculty of Engineering: Prof. FAHAR HAYATI
Faculty of Foreign Languages: Dr THARWAT SAKRAN

Faculty of Information, Mass Communication and Public Relations: Dr KHALID AL-KHAJAH
Faculty of Pharmacy and Health Sciences: Dr SAMIR ISSA BLOUKH

AMERICAN UNIVERSITY IN DUBAI

POB 28282, Dubai
Telephone: (4) 3999000
Internet: www.aud.edu
Founded 1995
Private control
Accredited by Ministry of Higher Education and Scientific Research
Pres.: Dr LANCE DE MASI
Exec. Vice-Pres.: ELIAS BOU SAAB
Provost: Dr JIHAD S. NADER
Library Dir: LIZ OESLEBY
Library of 77,334 vols, 345 periodicals

DEANS

School of Business and Administration: Dr DWAYNE A. BANKS
School of Communication and Information Studies: (vacant)
School of Engineering: Dr ALAA K. ASHMAWY

AMERICAN UNIVERSITY IN THE EMIRATES

Dubai International Academic City, POB 503000, Dubai
Telephone: (4) 4499000
E-mail: info@aue.ae
Internet: www.aue.ae
Private control
Colleges of business admin., computer information technology, fine arts and design, media and mass communication

AMERICAN UNIVERSITY OF SHARJAH

POB 26666, Sharjah
Telephone: (6) 5155555
E-mail: info@aus.edu
Internet: www.aus.edu
Founded 1997
Private control
Accredited by Ministry of Higher Education and Scientific Research
Chancellor: Dr PETER HEATH

DEANS

College of Arts and Sciences: WILLIAM HEIDCAMP
College of Engineering: YOUSEF AL-ASSAF
School of Architecture and Design: FATIH RIFKI
School of Business and Management: R. MALCOLM RICHARDS

BRITISH UNIVERSITY IN DUBAI

POB 502216, Dubai
Telephone: (4) 3913626
E-mail: info@buid.ac.ae
Internet: www.buid.ac.ae
Founded 1997
Private control
Accredited by Ministry of Higher Education and Scientific Research; faculties of business, education, engineering, informatics
Vice-Chancellor: Dr ABDULLAH M. ALSHAMSI

CANADIAN UNIVERSITY OF DUBAI

POB 117781, Dubai
Telephone: (4) 3218866
E-mail: info@cud.ac.ae
Internet: www.cud.ac.ae

Founded 2006
Private control
Accredited by Ministry of Higher Education and Scientific Research; schools of applied science and technology, architectural studies and interior design, business, engineering, environment and health
Pres.: ANN BULLER

GULF MEDICAL UNIVERSITY

POB 4184, Ajman
Telephone: (4) 7431333
E-mail: admissions@gmu.ac.ae
Internet: www.gmu.ac.ae
Founded 1998 as Gulf Medical College; univ. status 2008
Private control; Thumbay Group
Accredited by Ministry of Higher Education and Scientific Research; Bachelors and Masters degree programmes
Dir: MOIDEEN THUMBAY

HAMDAN BIN MOHAMMED E-UNIVERSITY

POB 71400, Dubai
Telephone: (4) 4241111
E-mail: hbmeu@hbmeu.ac.ae
Internet: www.hbmeu.ac.ae
Private control
Fmrly Electronic Total Quality Management (E-TQM College)
Chancellor: Dr MANSOOR MUHAMMAD AQIL AL-AWAR
Vice-Chancellor: Dr IBRAHIM MAHMOOD BIN ABDULRAHMAN

DEANS

e-School of Business and Quality Management: Dr KHALID SARTAWI
e-School of Health and Environmental Studies: Dr SAMER HAMIDI (acting)
School of e-Education: Prof. ALAIN R. SENTENI

ITTIHAD UNIVERSITY

POB 2286, Ras al-Khaimah
Telephone: (7) 2059999
E-mail: info@ittihad.ac.ae
Internet: www.ittihad.ac.ae
Founded 1999
Private control
Chancellor: Prof. ABDUL SATTAR AL-ALUSI

KHALIFA UNIVERSITY OF SCIENCE, TECHNOLOGY AND RESEARCH

POB 573, Sharjah
Telephone: (6) 5611333
E-mail: info@kustar.ac.ae
Internet: www.ku.ac.ae
Founded 2007 incorporating the former Etisalat Univ. College as the Sharjah branch campus
Abu Dhabi campus is under devt
Private control
Accredited by Ministry of Higher Education and Scientific Research
Undergraduate and postgraduate degrees in engineering
Pres.: Dr ARIF SULTAN AL-HAMMADI

MIDDLESEX UNIVERSITY DUBAI

POB 500697, Dubai
Telephone: (4) 3678100
E-mail: info@mdx.ac
Internet: www.mdx.ac
Founded 2005

Private control; Middlesex University, London (UK)
Schools of arts and education, business, engineering and information sciences, health and social science
Dir: Prof. RAED AWAMLEH
Number of students: 1,200

NYU ABU DHABI

POB 113100, Abu Dhabi
Telephone: (2) 4069677
E-mail: nyuad@nyu.edu
Internet: nyuad.nyu.edu
Founded 2009
Private control; New York Univ. (USA)
Provost: MARIËT WESTERMANN

PARIS-SORBONNE UNIVERSITY ABU DHABI

POB 38044, Abu Dhabi
Telephone: (2) 5090555
E-mail: admissions@psuad.ac.ae
Internet: www.paris-sorbonne-abudhabi.ae
Founded 2006
Private control

RAS AL-KHAIMAH MEDICAL AND HEALTH SCIENCES UNIVERSITY

POB 11172, Ras al-Khaimah
Telephone: (7) 2269999
E-mail: admissions@rakmhsu.ae
Internet: www.rakmhsu.com
Founded 1993
Jointly controlled by Ras Al-Khaimah Govt, Al Ghurair Investments and ETA Ascon Group, Dubai
Accredited by Ministry of Higher Education and Scientific Research; colleges of dental sciences, medical sciences, nursing, pharmaceutical sciences
Vice-Chancellor: Dr S. GURUMADHVA RAO

UNITED ARAB EMIRATES UNIVERSITY

POB 15551, Al-Ain
Telephone: (3) 7555557
E-mail: vice_chancellor@uaeu.ac.ae
Internet: www.uaeu.ac.ae
Founded 1976
State control
Languages of instruction: Arabic, English
Academic year: September to June
Chancellor: HH Sheikh NAHYAN MUBARAK AL NAHYAN
Vice-Chancellor: Dr ABDULLA AL-KHANBASHI
Provost, Chief Academic Officer and CEO: Dr WYATT R. HUME
Sec.-Gen.: Dr FATIMA AL-SHAMSI
Assoc. Provost for Academic Affairs: Prof. DONALD E. BOWEN
Asst Provost and Dean of Students: Dr COURTNEY STRYKER
Asst Provost for IT and Chief Information Officer: NICK MITCHELL CHOBAN
Asst Provost for Research: Dr MAITHA S. AL-SHAMSI
Library of 439,651 vols, 929 periodicals
Number of teachers: 670
Number of students: 17,000
Publication: individual faculty journals published annually

DEANS

College of Education: Dr GARY M. INGERSOLL
College of Engineering: Prof. REYADH ALMEHAIDEB
College of Food and Agriculture: Prof. GHALEB ALHADRAMI

College of Humanities and Social Sciences: Prof. DONALD BAKER
College of Information Technology: Dr BOUMEDIENE BELKHOUCHE
College of Law: Prof. JASSIM ALI SALEM ALSHAMSI
College of Science: Prof. M. NAIM ANWAR
Faculty of Business and Economics: Prof. DAVID GRAF
Faculty of Medicine and Health Sciences: Prof. GEORGE CARRUTHERS

UNIVERSITY OF ATLANTA—GULF REGION

41st Fl., Jumeirah Emirates Tower, Dubai
E-mail: dubai@uofa.edu
Internet: www.uofa.edu
Private control
Dir: Dr STEVE HERMES

UNIVERSITY OF DUBAI

POB 14143, Dubai
Telephone: (4) 2072600
E-mail: info@ud.ac.ae
Internet: www.ud.ac.ae
Founded 1997 as Dubai Univ. College; present status 2006
Accredited by UAE Ministry of Higher Education and Scientific Research; member of the Association to Advance Collegiate Schools of Business (AACSB), the Accrediting Board for Engineering and Technology (ABET) and the European Foundation for Management Development (EFMD)
Under the control of the state-funded Dubai Chamber of Commerce and Industry
Languages of instruction: Arabic, English
Pres.: M. OMAR HEFNI
Number of teachers: 50
Number of students: 630

DEANS

College of Business Administration: Assoc. Prof. ANANTH RAO
College of Information Technology: Dr FAOUZI KAMOUN

UNIVERSITY OF SHARJAH

POB 27272, Sharjah
Telephone: (6) 5585000
E-mail: info@sharjah.ac.ae
Internet: www.sharjah.ac.ae
Founded 1997
Private control
Chancellor: Prof. SAMY A. MAHMOUD
Vice-Chancellor for Academic Affairs: Prof. SALIM SABRI
Vice-Chancellor for Admin. and Financial Affairs: Dr MUHAMMAD ISMAIL
Vice-Chancellor for Medical Colleges: Prof. MUHAMMAD HUSAM AL-DIN HAMDI
Dir of Libraries: QASIM MUHAMMAD AL-KHALIDI

DEANS

College of Arts, Humanities and Social Sciences: Prof. HAMID M. AL-NAIMIY
College of Business Admin.: Prof. MAHENDRA RAJ
College of Communication: Prof. MUHAMMAD KIRAT
College of Dentistry: Prof. RANI SHAMSUDIN
College of Engineering: Prof. BOUALEM BOASHASH
College of Fine Arts and Design: Dr HASSAN ABDALLA
College of Health Sciences: Prof. BASSAMAT OMAR
College of Law: Prof. ADNAN SIRHAN
College of Medicine: Prof. MUHAMMAD HUSAM AL-DIN HAMDI

College of Pharmacy: Prof. MAZEN KHALIL AL-QATO

College of Sciences: Prof. HAMID M. AL-NAIMIY

College of Shari'a and Islamic Studies: Prof. EL-GURASHI EL-BASHIR (acting)

UNIVERSITY OF WOLLONGONG IN DUBAI

POB 20183, Dubai

Telephone: (4) 3672400

E-mail: info@uowdubai.ac.ae

Internet: www.uowdubai.ac.ae

Founded 1993

Private control

Accredited by Ministry of Higher Education and Scientific Research; faculties of business and management, computer science and engineering, finance and accounting

Pres.: Prof. ROB WHELAN

Number of students: 3,500

ZAYED UNIVERSITY

POB 19282, Dubai

Telephone: (4) 4021111

E-mail: info@zu.ac.ae

Internet: www.zu.ac.ae

Founded 1998

State control

Pres.: HH Sheikh NAHYAN MUBARAK AL NAHYAN

Vice-Pres.: Dr SULAIMAN AL-JASSIM

Provost: DAN JOHNSON

Assoc. Provost for Academic and Int. Affairs: BOB CRYAN

Chief Admin. and Finance Officer: ANDRÉ RACETTE

Dean of Libraries: PATRICIA WAND

DEANS

College of Arts and Sciences: MICHAEL ALLEN

College of Business Sciences: MICHAEL OWEN

College of Communication and Media Sciences: MARILYN ROBERTS

College of Education: PEGGY BLACKWELL

College of Information Technology: LEON JOLOLIAN

Colleges

Al-Khawarizmi International College: POB 25669, Abu Dhabi; tel. (2) 6789700; e-mail ceo@khawarizmi.com; internet www .khawarizmi.com; f. 1985; accredited by Min. of Higher Education and Scientific Research; affiliated to Liverpool John Moores Univ., UK; campus in Al-Ain; BSc in computer technology; Pres. NAEEM RADI.

American College of Dubai: POB 12867, Dubai; tel. (4) 2829992; e-mail info@acd.ae; internet www.centamed.com; accredited by Min. of Higher Education and Scientific Research; business, IT, liberal arts; library: 30,000 vols; Pres. WILLIAM J. O'BRIEN; Provost Dr NIGEL THORPE; Dean of Academic and Faculty Affairs Dr POONAN SINGH; Dean of Business Dr ZAFAR QUERESHI; Dean of Student Affairs S. SHARMA; Registrar CHRISTINE MASCARENHAS; Librarian RANI MANI.

Birla Institute of Technology and Science, Pilani—Dubai: POB 345055, Dubai; tel. (4) 4200700; internet www.bitsdubai .com.

Boston University Institute for Dental Research and Education: POB 505097, Dubai; tel. (4) 4248787; e-mail info@budubai .ae; internet www.budubai.ae; CEO Dr STEVEN MORGANO.

Computer College: Dubai; tel. (4) 2826880; e-mail sales@computer-centre.ae; internet www.cc-uae.com; f. 1993; accredited by Min. of Higher Education and Scientific Research; business administration and IT.

Dubai Aerospace Enterprise Flight Academy: POB 10227, Ras al-Khaimah; tel. (7) 2043524; e-mail admissions@ daeflightacademy.com; internet www .daeflightacademy.com; f. 2006; Man. Dir Capt RICHARD MORRIS.

Dubai Medical College for Girls: POB 20170, Dubai; tel. (4) 2646465; internet www .dmcg.edu; accredited by Min. of Higher Education and Scientific Research; BSc in medicine and surgery; Dean Prof. MUHAMMAD GALAL EL-DIN.

Dubai Pharmacy College: POB 19099, Dubai; tel. (4) 2646968; internet www.dpc .edu; f. 1999; accredited by Min. of Higher Education and Scientific Research; Dean Dr SAEED AHMED KHAN.

Dubai Police Academy: POB 53900 Dubai; tel. (4) 3482255; e-mail college@dubaipolice .gov.ae; internet www.dubaipolice.gov.ae; f. 1989; accredited by Min. of Higher Education and Scientific Research; Dean Dr MUHAMMAD AHMED BIN FAHAD.

Dubai School of Government: POB 72229, Dubai; tel. (4) 3293290; e-mail info@dsg.ae; internet www.dsg.ae; f. 2005; masters degrees in public administration, public policy; Dean TARIK YOUSEF.

Emirates Academy of Hospitality Management: POB 29662, Dubai; tel. (4) 3155555; e-mail info@emiratesacademy.edu; internet www.jumeirah.com/en/ jumeirah-group/the-emirates-academy; f. 2001; accredited by Min. of Higher Education and Scientific Research; 400 students; Man. Dir RON HILVERT.

Emirates Aviation College—Aerospace and Academic Studies: POB 53044, Dubai; tel. (4) 2824000; internet www .emiratesaviationcollege.com; f. 1991 by Dept of Civil Aviation; accredited by Min. of Higher Education and Scientific Research; bachelors degrees in aeronautical engineering, business administration (air transport management); Vice-Pres. Dr AHMED AL-ALI.

Emirates College for Management and Information Technology: POB 39292, Dubai; tel. (4) 2675016; e-mail admissions@ ecmit.ac.ae; internet www.ecmit.ac.ae; f. 1998; accredited by Min. of Higher Education and Scientific Research; British Accreditation Council for Ind. Further and Higher Education; Assoc. Science degrees in business and information technology; Pres. and CEO SUDHIR KARTHA; Librarian SEENA SHAHAN.

Emirates College of Advanced Education: POB 126662, Abu Dhabi; tel. (2) 6964300; e-mail info@ecae.ac.ae; internet www.ecae.ac.ae; Vice-Chancellor IAN HASLAM.

Emirates College of Technology: POB 41009, Abu Dhabi; tel. (2) 6266010; e-mail ectuae@emirates.net.ae; internet www .ectuae.com; f. 1993 as Emirates Institute of Technology; accredited by Min. of Higher Education and Scientific Research; diplomas in accounting, banking and finance, business administration and computer information systems, computer graphic design and animation, e-commerce and marketing, human resource management; Pres. MUHAMMAD AL-MAZROUI.

Emirates Institute for Banking and Financial Studies: POB 4166, Sharjah; tel. (6) 5728880; e-mail info@eibfs.com; internet www.eibfs.com; f. 1983; diploma and short courses; br. in Abu Dhabi; Chair.

AHMAD HUMAID AL-TAYER; Gen. Man. JAMAL AL-JASSMI.

European University College Brussels: POB 500691, Dubai; tel. (4) 3672323; e-mail admissions@ehsal-dubai.net; internet www .ehsal-dubai.net; f. 2003; Dir-Gen. Dr KIRK DE CEULAER.

Falcon College of Hotel Management and Tourism: POB 43319, Abu Dhabi; tel. (2) 4491450; e-mail fchmuae@emirates.net .ae; f. 2007; accredited by Min. of Higher Education and Scientific Research; affiliated to Cesar Ritz Colleges, Switzerland; Chair. ABDULLA ABDULJALIL AL-FAHIM; Dean Dr OSKAR R. SYKORA.

Fujairah College: POB 1207, Fujairah; tel. (2) 2244499; e-mail info@fc.ac.ae; internet www.fc.ac.ae; f. 2006; accredited by Min. of Higher Education and Scientific Research; Assoc. degrees in business administration and information technology; Exec. Dir Prof. GHASSAN AL-QAIMIRI.

Heriot Watt University—Dubai: Dubai International Academic City, Dubai; tel. (4) 3616999; e-mail dubaienquiries@hw.ac.uk; internet www.hw.ac.uk/dubai; undergraduate degrees in construction, engineering, management, quantity surveying, textiles and fashion design; masters programmes in construction, energy, information technology, management, petroleum engineering.

Higher Colleges of Technology: POB 32092, Abu Dhabi; tel. (2) 6815654; e-mail enquiries@hct.ac.ae; internet www.hct.ac.ae; f. 1988; divs of applied communications, business, education, engineering technology, general education, graduate studies, health sciences, information technology; campuses at Al-Ain, Dubai, Fujairah, Ras al-Khaimah, Sharjah; library: 160,000 vols; 950 teachers; 16,000 students; Chancellor HE Sheikh NAHYAN MUBARAK AL NAHYAN; Vice-Chancellor Dr TAYEB KAMALI.

Institute of Management Technology: POB 345006, Dubai; tel. (2) 3604844; e-mail info@imtdubai.ac.ae; internet imtdubai.ac .ae; f. 2006; accredited by Min. of Higher Education and Scientific Research; MBA programmes; Dir Dr FARHAD RAD-SERECHT.

Islamic and Arabic Studies College: Dubai; tel. (2) 3604844; e-mail iasc@ emirates.net.ae; internet www .islamic-college.co.ae; f. 1986; accredited by Min. of Higher Education and Scientific Research; Bachelors, Masters and PhDs in Arabic language, Arabic literature, Islamic Fiqh, Islamic studies, Shariah; 3,489 students.

Mahatma Gandhi University Off Campus Centre: Block 3, Dubai Knowledge Village, Dubai; tel. (4) 3902981; e-mail contact@mgudxboc.com; internet www .mgudxboc.com; f. 2003; BSc in computer science, bachelors in fashion technology, BTS in tourism studies; 700 students.

Manipal University, Dubai Campus: Block 7, Academic City, Dubai; tel. (4) 4291214; e-mail admissions@mahedubai .com; internet www.mahedubai.com; programmes in civil engineering, electronics and communication engineering, instrumentation and control engineering, mechanical engineering, mechatronics engineering.

Masdar Institute of Science and Technology: POB 54115, Abu Dhabi; tel. (2) 6988133; e-mail rorfali@masdar.ae; internet www.mist.ac.ae; f. 2006; masters and PhD programmes in science and engineering disciplines.

Michigan State University—Dubai: POB 345001, Dubai; tel. (4) 5015314; e-mail dubai@msu.edu; internet www.dubai.msu .edu; bachelors and masters degrees.

Murdoch University International Study Center: POB 345005, Dubai; tel. (4) 4355700; e-mail info@murdochdubai.ac.ae; internet www.murdochdubai.com; Dir Prof. JOHN GRAINGER.

Naval College: POB 800, Abu Dhabi; tel. (2) 6157600; f. 1997; accredited by Min. of Higher Education and Scientific Research; bachelors degree in naval studies.

New York Institute of Technology: POB 5464, Abu Dhabi; tel. (2) 4048611; internet www.nyit.edu/nyit_worldwide/united_arab_emirates; f. 2005; initial accreditation by the Min. of Higher Education and Scientific Research for Bachelor of Fine Arts in interior design programme.

Petroleum Institute: POB 2533, Abu Dhabi; tel. (2) 6075100; e-mail enquiries@pi.ac.ae; internet www.pi.ac.ae; f. 2001; accredited by Min. of Higher Education and Scientific Research; BSc degrees in chemical engineering, electrical engineering, mechanical engineering, petroleum engineering, petroleum geosciences; masters of engineering in chemical engineering, electrical engineering, mechanical engineering, petroleum engineering; Provost and Pres. Dr MICHAEL OHADI (acting).

Police College: POB 163, Abu Dhabi; tel. (2) 4447700; e-mail general-manager@policecollege.ac.ae; internet www.policecollege.ac.ae; f. 1985; accredited by Min. of Higher Education and Scientific Research; bachelors degree in law and policing sciences; Dir-Gen. MUSTAFA SHIHAB AL-HASHMI.

Police Sciences Academy Sharjah: POB 1510, Sharjah; tel. (6) 5585888; e-mail info@psa.ac.ae; internet www.psa.ac.ae; f. 1995; accredited by Min. of Higher Education and Scientific Research; bachelors in police sciences.

Rochester Institute of Technology—Dubai: POB 341055, Dubai; tel. (4) 5015314; e-mail dubai@rit.edu; internet www.rit.edu/dubai; graduate degrees in business administration, finance, electrical engineering, mechanical engineering, networking and systems administration, service leadership and innovation; Pres. Dr MUSTAFA ABUSHAGUR.

Royal College of Applied Science and Technology: POB 10141, Ras al-Khaima; tel. (7) 2359080; e-mail bitic-uae@rcast.org; internet www.rcast.org; f. 2004; 2-year MBA programmes in finance, human resource management, marketing and IT; Pres. Prof. Dr PRAVEEN DHYANI.

SAE Institute Dubai: POB 500648, Dubai; tel. (4) 3616173; e-mail infodubai@sae.edu; internet www.sae-dubai.com.

Shaheed Zulfikar Ali Bhutto Institute of Science and Technology: POB 345004, Dubai; tel. (4) 3664601; e-mail info@szabist.ac.ae; internet www.szabist.ac.ae.

Skyline University College: POB 1797, Sharjah; tel. (6) 5441155; e-mail admissions@skylineuniversity.com; internet www.skylinecollege.info; f. 1990; accredited by Min. of Higher Education and Scientific Research; bachelors and masters in business administration; Pres. KAMAL PURI.

Syscoms College: POB 72574, Abu Dhabi; tel. (2) 6760800; e-mail info@syscomscollege.com; internet www.syscomscollege.com; f. 1990; accredited by Min. of Higher Education and Scientific Research; Assoc. of Science degree in information technology.

Troy University ITS Sharjah Campus: POB 5398, Sharjah; tel. (6) 5313111; e-mail info@shjcollege.ac.ae; internet www.shjcollege.ac.ae; f. 1990; assoc. and Bachelors degrees in business administration, computer science; Pres. Dr E. M. S. EDIRISINGHE.

Universal Empire Institute of Medical Sciences: POB 500332, Dubai; tel. (4) 4332773; e-mail administration@ueims.com; internet www.ueims.com; Chair. and Man. Dir SUDHIR GOPI.

UNITED KINGDOM

The Higher Education System

Institutions of higher education date from the 13th century, with the oldest being the University of Oxford, the oldest college of which was founded in 1249; the next oldest university is the University of Cambridge, the oldest college of which was founded in 1284. The oldest Scottish universities are the University of St Andrews and the University of Aberdeen, which were both founded in the 15th century. The 19th century saw a great expansion of the higher education system, with the foundation of over 90 universities, colleges and institutes in the United Kingdom. In 2010/11 there were 164 publicly funded higher education institutions, together with the privately funded University of Buckingham. In that year there were 1,677,345 full-time and 823,955 part-time students (including from overseas) taking higher education courses. Institutions of higher education include universities, university colleges, colleges of higher education and some further education colleges. The United Kingdom joined the Bologna Process in 1999. However, since the United Kingdom already had a three-cycle degree structure based on Bachelors, Masters and doctorate-level qualifications, no structural changes were necessary. Higher education institutions are autonomous bodies and so implementation of Bologna reforms such as the use of the European Credit Transfer and Accumulation System and the issuing of the Diploma Supplement remains at institutional discretion.

Notable legislation pertaining to higher education includes the Further and Higher Education Act 1992, which brought to an end the binary system by which universities and polytechnics were treated separately and enabled former polytechnics to achieve university status, and the Higher Education Act 2004, which brought in changes to the funding of higher education by introducing a scheme whereby students contributed towards their tuition. Institutions of higher education are established by a Royal Charter and most receive some funding from the Government. However, they are autonomous bodies in which admissions, staffing and teaching are administered independently of the Government. Until 2007 the Secretary of State for Education and Skills was responsible, in principle, for all sectors of education in England. In that year some of these responsibilities, as well as some of those from the Department of Trade and Industry, were transferred to a newly created Department for Innovation, Universities and Skills, subsequently reorganized as the Department for Business, Innovation and Skills. In practice the individual Local Education Authorities (LEAs) have substantial autonomy over the education system in their area. The Secretary of State for Wales is responsible for all non-university education in Wales and, since April 1993, for the University of Wales College, Newport. Government finance for publicly funded higher education institutions is distributed by the Higher Education Funding Council (HEFC) in England, the Scottish Funding Council in Scotland, the Department for Education, Culture and Welsh Language in Wales, and the Department for Employment and Learning in Northern Ireland. Student loans are the main form of support for assistance with living costs for higher education students. The amount of loan depends on where a student lives or studies, the length of the academic year, the course of study, the year of the course and the student's and their family's income. Since the academic year 2000/01 eligible full-time Scottish-domiciled or non-British EU students studying in Scotland no longer pay tuition fees. Publicly funded universities in England, Wales and Northern Ireland may charge domestic students tuition fees for undergraduate courses, subject to a state-imposed limit; for the 2010/11 academic year the cap was set at £3,290. In a highly controversial development that provoked violent popular protests in London, in December 2010 Parliament voted significantly to increase the cap on tuition fees, to £9,000 annually, effective from the 2012/13 academic year. Additional forms of student support include dependant's allowances, young and mature student bursaries, hardship funds, disabled students' allowances and care leavers' grants, and the Student Grant Scheme, which was introduced at the beginning of the 2011/12 academic year in place of the Higher Education Grants Scheme. In early 2012 the Government announced that it would cut funding for teaching in universities by 18% and that for the 2012/13 academic year there would be a reduction of 15,000 in the total number of student places available. At the same time it was reported that plans to increase competition in the higher education sector by allowing students applying to private institutions to be eligible for government-backed loans had been abandoned. However, plans to lower the qualifying threshold for university status from 4,000 to 1,000 full-time equivalent students were being pursued.

The Quality Assurance Agency for Higher Education (founded 1997) is an independent body responsible for the accreditation and quality assurance of higher education in the United Kingdom. The review process in Wales is slightly different from that in England and Northern Ireland, reflecting the new framework for quality assurance that is being developed by the Higher Education Funding Council for Wales.

Students in England, Wales and Northern Ireland enter university upon completion of 13 years of education. Universities set their own standards for admission, which are usually based on a student's performance in their A-Level examinations. However, other awards at Level 3 of the National Qualifications Framework (NQF) may also be accepted—for example, the BTEC National Diploma. All undergraduate admissions in the UK (including Scotland) are dealt with by the University and College Admissions Service (UCAS). This organization does not set admission standards, which are established by each individual institution, but it oversees the process of university admission and provides information to students on entry requirements for specific courses. The principal undergraduate degrees are the Bachelor of Arts (BA Hons) and Bachelor of Science (BSc Hons). These are usually full-time, three-year courses but can also be taken as longer part-time courses and may be available through distance learning. In Scotland, where students usually start a year earlier, a full-time first degree generally takes four years for Honours and three years for the broad-based Ordinary degree. The Foundation degree is a new higher education qualification (since 2001) of one year, with a vocational focus. It aims to increase the number of people qualified at higher technician and associate professional level (e.g. legal executives, engineering technicians, personnel officers, laboratory technicians, teaching assistants). Both full- and part-time courses are offered in a variety of work-related subjects and offer progression to a full Honours degree. The Higher National Diploma (HND) or Diploma of Higher Education (Dip HE) are two-year, full-time programmes, and there is the option of turning them into an Honours degree by studying for a further year. Some students go on to do postgraduate studies, usually leading to a Masters degree, such as a Master of Arts (MA), or Master of Science (MSc), or to a Doctorate (PhD). A Masters degree usually lasts one year full-time or two years part-time. A PhD usually lasts three years full-time or six years part-time. In 2003 a four-year PhD was introduced.

The Learning and Skills Act 2000 integrated all planning and funding for post-compulsory learning below higher education, including that provided in schools, into one overarching sector under the auspices of the Learning and Skills Council (LSC), which consists of a network of 10 regional directors and local branches. From 1986 onwards the National Council for Vocational Qualifications (NCVQ) established a framework on

National Vocational Qualifications (NVQs) in England, Wales and Northern Ireland. In 1997 the Council's work was taken over by the Qualifications and Curriculum Authority. The framework is based on five defined levels of achievement, ranging from Level 1, broadly equating to foundation skills in semi-skilled occupations, to Level 5, equating to professional/ senior management occupations. The competence-based system has also been extended in Scotland through a system of Scottish Vocational Qualifications (SVQs) along similar lines to the NVQs. General National Vocational Qualifications (GNVQs), along with General Scottish Vocational Qualifications (GSVQs) have also been introduced. The work of the Qualifications, Curriculum and Assessment Authority for Wales has been taken over by the Welsh Assembly Government.

The principal vocational qualifications now awarded in England, Wales and Northern Ireland are Vocational A-levels, introduced in September 2000, and the new A-Levels in applied subjects. These were designed to replace the Advanced GNVQ, with the aim of improving the standing of vocational qualifications and increasing flexibility within the system. Since September 2002 the Vocational GCSE has also replaced the Foundation, Intermediate and Part One GNVQs. Since September 2008 the new 14–19 Diploma has been offered to students aged 14–19 years who wish to combine their studies within the national curriculum with applied learning and relevant work experience. The LSC is responsible for funding the further education sector in England. It is also responsible for funding provision for non-prescribed higher education in further education sector colleges and further education provided by LEA-maintained and other institutions, referred to as 'external institutions'. In Wales, the Department for Education, Culture and Welsh Language funds further education provision made by further education institutions via a third party or sponsored arrangements. The Scottish Funding Council funds further education colleges in Scotland, while the Department for Employment and Learning funds further education colleges in Northern Ireland. Further and higher education may be pursued through vocational or academic courses, on a full-time, part-time or 'sandwich' basis.

Regulatory and Representative Bodies

In the following section entries whose activities cover the whole of the United Kingdom are listed under the General subheading. Those active in specific nations, for example devolved government departments, are then listed separately under the relevant subheadings which appear in alphabetical order.

GOVERNMENT

England

Department for Business, Innovation and Skills: 1 Victoria St, London, SW1H 0ET; Kingsgate House, 66–74 Victoria St, London, SW1E 6SW; tel. (20) 7215-5000; e-mail enquiries@bis.gsi.gov.uk; internet www.bis.gov.uk; Sec. of State Dr VINCE CABLE; Minister of State for Univs and Science GREG CLARK; Minister of State for Skills and Equalities NICK BOLES; Permanent Sec. MARTIN DONNELLY.

Department for Culture, Media and Sport: 100 Parliament St, London, SW1A 2BQ; tel. (20) 7211-6000; e-mail enquiries@ culture.gov.uk; internet www.culture.gov.uk; Sec. of State for Culture, Media and Sport SAJID JAVID; Permanent Sec. SUE OWEN.

Department for Education: Piccadilly Gate, Store St, Manchester, M1 2WD; tel. (370) 000-2288; internet www.education.gov .uk; Sec. of State for Education NICKY MORGAN; Minister of State for Schools DAVID LAWS; Minister of State for Skills Equalities NICK BOLES; Permanent Sec. CHRIS WORMALD.

Northern Ireland

Department of Culture, Arts and Leisure: Causeway Exchange, 1–7 Bedford St, Belfast, BT2 7EG; tel. (28) 9025-8825; e-mail communications@dcalni.gov.uk; internet www.dcalni.gov.uk; Minister CARÁL NÍ CHUILÍN; Permanent Sec. PETER MAY.

Department of Education: Rathgael House, Balloo Rd, Bangor, BT19 7PR; tel. (28) 9127-9279; e-mail mail@deni.gov.uk; internet www.deni.gov.uk; Minister JOHN O'DOWD; Permanent Sec. PAUL SWEENEY.

Department for Employment and Learning: Adelaide House, 39–49 Adelaide St, Belfast, BT2 8FD; tel. (28) 9025-7777; e-mail info@delni.gov.uk; internet www

.delni.gov.uk; Minister STEPHEN FARRY; Permanent Sec. DEREK BAKER.

Wales

Department for Education and Skills: Welsh Assembly Govt, Cathays Park, Cardiff, CF10 3NQ; e-mail wag-en@mailuk .custhelp.com; internet new.wales.gov.uk; Minister HUW LEWIS; Deputy Minister for Skills and Technology KEN SKATES.

ACCREDITATION

General

Accreditation Service for International Colleges (ASIC): 13 Yarm Rd, Stockton-on-Tees, TS18 3NJ; tel. (1740) 617-920; e-mail info@asic.org.uk; internet www.asic.org.uk; Chair. MAURICE DIMMOCK; CEO LEE HAMMOND.

British Accreditation Council (BAC): Fleet House, Fifth Fl., 8–12 New Bridge St, London, EC4V 6AL; tel. (30) 0330-1400; e-mail info@the-bac.org; internet www .the-bac.org; f. 1984; acts as nat. accrediting body for private post-16 education in the UK; Chair. PETER WILLIAMS; Deputy Chair. DOMINIC SCOTT.

British Council Accreditation Unit: Bridgewater House, 58 Whitworth St, Manchester, M1 6BB; tel. (161) 957-7692; e-mail accreditation.unit@britishcouncil.org; internet www.britishcouncil.org/accreditation .htm; develops, establishes and maintains quality standards for English language provision for int. students delivered by UK providers; Man. ELIZABETH MCLAREN.

ENIC/NARIC United Kingdom: UK NARIC, Oriel House, Oriel Rd, Cheltenham, GL50 1XP; tel. (871) 330-7033; e-mail communications@naric.org.uk; internet www .naric.org.uk; provides information on academic, vocational and professional education and qualifications from across the world; Head Dr CLOUD BAI-YUN.

Open and Distance Learning Quality Council: 79 Barnfield Wood Rd, Beckenham, BR3 6ST; tel. (20) 8658-8337; e-mail info@ odlqc.org.uk; internet www.odlqc.org.uk; f. 1969 as Ccl for the Accreditation of Correspondence Colleges, current name adopted 1995; enhances quality in education and training; accredits open and distance learning providers; Chair. JOHN AINSWORTH; Chief Assessor TONY HOPWOOD; Sec. to Ccl JULIE FOX.

Scotland

Scottish Qualifications Authority (SQA): The Optima Bldg, 58 Robertson St, Glasgow, G2 8DQ; tel. (345) 279-1000; e-mail customer@sqa.org.uk; internet www.sqa.org .uk; sponsored by the Scottish Government's Learning Directorate; nat. body in Scotland responsible for the devt, accreditation, assessment and certification of qualifications other than degrees; SQA qualifications incl. Higher Nat. Certificates and Diplomas, and Scottish Vocational Qualifications; Chief Exec. JANET BROWN; Head of Accreditation GEORGE BROWN.

FUNDING

General

Arts and Humanities Research Council (AHRC): Polaris House, North Star Ave, Swindon, SN2 1FL; tel. (1793) 416-000; e-mail enquiries@ahrc.ac.uk; internet www .ahrc.ac.uk; f. 2005 as successor to the Arts and Humanities Research Board (f. 1998); operates programmes throughout the UK to support research and postgraduate training in the arts and humanities; provides research awards and postgraduate scholarships; CEO Prof. RICK RYLANCE.

Skills Funding Agency: Cheylesmore House, Quinton Rd, Coventry, CV1 2WT; tel. (345) 377-5000; e-mail info@ skillsfundingagency.bis.gov.uk; internet skillsfundingagency.bis.gov.uk; partner org. of the Department for Business, Innovation and Skills; funds and regulates adult further education and skills training; Chair. PAUL DRECHSLER.

UK Commission for Employment and Skills: Renaissance House, Adwick Park, Wath-upon-Dearne, S63 5NB; tel. (1709) 774-800; e-mail info@ukces.org.uk; internet www.ukces.org.uk; f. 2008; publicly funded org. providing strategic leadership on skills and employment issues in the 4 nations of the UK; 29 commissioners; Chair. Sir CHARLIE MAYFIELD.

England

Higher Education Funding Council for England (HEFCE): Northavon House, Coldharbour Lane, Bristol, BS16 1QD; tel. (117) 931-7317; e-mail hefce@hefce.ac.uk; internet www.hefce.ac.uk; f. 1992; promotes and funds teaching and research; meets the needs of students, economy and the soc.; Chair. TIM MELVILLE-ROSS; Chief Exec. Prof. MADELEINE ATKINS.

Scotland

Scottish Funding Council: Apex 2, 97 Haymarket Terrace, Edinburgh, EH12 5HD; tel. (131) 313-6500; e-mail info@sfc.ac.uk; internet www.sfc.ac.uk; f. 2005; nat. strategic body responsible for funding teaching and learning provision, research and other activities in Scotland's colleges and univs; Chair. ALICE BROWN; Chief Exec. LAURENCE HOWELLS.

Wales

Higher Education Funding Council for Wales (HEFCW): Linden Court, Ilex Close, Llanishen, Cardiff, CF14 5DZ; tel. (29) 2076-1861; e-mail info@hefcw.ac.uk; internet www.hefcw.ac.uk; f. 1992; distribution of funds for higher education in 11 institutions in Wales; Dir of Skills, Education and Funding CELIA HUNT; Chief Exec. Dr DAVID BLANEY.

NATIONAL BODIES

General

Alliance Sector Skills Councils (SSCs): Unit 50D, St Olav's Court, London, SE16 2XB; e-mail info@sscalliance.org; internet www.sscallianceextranet.org/home-public/homepage.aspx; f. 2008; 21 mems; works in partnership with the UK Commission for Employment and Skills (UKCES); represents, promotes and supports the work of 21 Sector Skills Councils (SSCs) across the UK; offices in London, Edinburgh, Cardiff and Belfast; Dir JEN TEULON.

City & Guilds: 1 Giltspur St, London, EC1A 9DD; tel. (207) 294-2468; e-mail intcg@cityandguilds.com; internet www.cityandguilds.com; f. 1878; develops relevant qualifications, services and solutions; supports colleges and training providers; CEO and Dir-Gen. CHRIS JONES; Man. Dir KRISTIE DONNELLY.

College of Teachers: Institute of Education, 20 Bedford Way, London, WC1H 0AL; tel. (20) 7911-5536; e-mail enquiries@cot.ac.uk; internet www.collegeofteachers.ac.uk; f. 1849, current name adopted 1998; offers membership to educationists, awards internationally recognized qualifications by examination to teachers and others working in the field of education; 1,630 mems; Patron HRH THE DUKE OF EDINBURGH; Pres. Dr RAPHAEL WILKINS; Exec. Dir and Registrar Prof. IAN CRAIG; publ. *Education Today* (4 a year).

Council for the Curriculum, Examinations and Assessment: 29 Clarendon Rd, Clarendon Dock, Belfast, BT1 3BG; tel. (28) 9026-1200; e-mail info@ccea.org.uk; internet www.ccea.org.uk; f. 1994; non-departmental public body reporting to the Dept of Education in N Ireland; ensures quality and standard in the qualifications and examinations offered by awarding bodies in N Ireland; awards qualifications incl. GCSEs and GCE A- and AS-levels; Chief Exec. RICHARD HANNA.

GuildHE: Woburn House, 20 Tavistock Sq., London, WC1H 9HB; tel. (20) 3393-6132; e-mail info@guildhe.ac.uk; internet www.guildhe.ac.uk; f. 1967 as SCOP (the Standing Conference of Principals Ltd); current name adopted 2006; acts as the rep. org. for higher education colleges, specialist instns and some univs; CEO ANDY WESTWOOD.

Learning and Skills Improvement Service (LSIS): Friars House, Manor House Dr., Coventry, CV1 2TE; tel. (24) 7662-7900; e-mail enquiries@lsis.org.uk; internet www.lsis.org.uk; f. 2008 by merger of the Quality Improvement Agency (QIA) and the Centre for Excellence (CEL); accelerates quality improvement in learning and skills sector;

Chair. DAME RUTH SILVER; Chief Exec. ROB WYE.

National Conference of University Professors: 36 Great Oaks Park, Surrey, GU4 7JG; tel. (7587) 282-627; e-mail editor@ncup.org.uk; internet www.reading.ac.uk/ncup; f. 1989; supports univ. profs in carrying out their responsibilities for the maintenance of academic standards; provides seminars on matters of concern to the nation's univ. system; 640 univ. profs; Pres. Prof. JAWED SIDDIQI; Vice-Pres. Prof. MARGARET COX; Sec. HELEN SPENCE.

National Institute of Adult Continuing Education (England and Wales): Chetwynd House, 21 De Montfort St, Leicester, LE1 7GE; tel. (116) 204-4200; e-mail enquiries@niace.org.uk; internet www.niace.org.uk; f. 1921 as the British Institute for Adult Education; promotes adult learning; provides personalized training courses; 151 individual mems, 426 corporate mems; 45 hon. life mems; library of 20,000 vols; Pres. NICK STUART; Chair. MAGGIE GALLIERS; publs *Adults Learning* (12 a year), *CONCEPT— Journal of Contemporary Community Education Practice Theory* (3 a year), *Convergence* (4 a year), *Journal of Access Policy and Practice* (2 a year), *Journal of Adult and Continuing Education* (2 a year), *Studies in the Education of Adults* (2 a year).

National Society for Education in Art and Design: 3 Mason's Wharf, Potley Lane Corsham, SN13 9FY; tel. (1225) 810134; e-mail info@nsead.org; internet www.nsead.org; f. 1888 as the Society of Art Masters; promotes the interests of art, craft and design education through a democratically elected council; 2,500 mems; Pres. SUSAN COLES; Vice-Pres. MARLENE WYLIE; publs *AD* (3 a year), *International Journal of Art and Design Education* (3 a year).

Nord Anglia Education: Prama House, 267 Banbury Rd, Oxford, OX2 7HT; tel. (1865) 339464; e-mail enquiries@nordanglia.com; internet www.nordangliaeducation.com; f. 1972; works with government depts, education authorities, schools and other public sector orgs to deliver a wide range of education, training and learning support in the UK and the Middle East; inspects and assesses schools, further and vocational educational providers; CEO ANDREW FITZMAURICE.

Office for Fair Access: Northavon House, Coldharbour Lane, Bristol, BS16 1QD; tel. (117) 931-7171; e-mail enquiries@offa.org.uk; internet www.offa.org.uk; f. 2004; safeguards and promotes fair access to higher education by approving and monitoring access agreements; Dir Prof. LES EBDON.

Office for Standards in Education, Children's Services and Skills (Ofsted): Piccadilly Gate, Store St, Manchester, M1 2WD; tel. (300) 123-1231; e-mail enquiries@ofsted.gov.uk; internet www.ofsted.gov.uk; f. 2007 by merger of the Office for Standards in Education (Ofsted) and the Adult Learning Inspectorate; inspects and regulates care for children and young people and those providing education and skills for learners of all ages; reports directly to Parliament; has offices in Bristol, London, Manchester and Nottingham; Chair. Baroness MORGAN OF HUYTON; Chief Inspector MICHAEL WILSHAW; publ. *Ofsted News* (online).

Quality Assurance Agency for Higher Education: Southgate House, Southgate St, Gloucester, GL1 1UB; tel. (1452) 557-000; e-mail enquiries@qaa.ac.uk; internet www.qaa.ac.uk; f. 1997; ind. body funded by subscriptions from univs and colleges of higher education; encourages continuous improvement in the management of the

quality of higher education; Chair. Sir RODNEY BROOKE; Chief Exec. ANTHONY McCLARAN; publ. *QAA News* (24 a year, online).

UK Council for Graduate Education: Lichfield Centre, The Friary, Lichfield, WS13 6QG; tel. (1543) 308-602; e-mail ukcge@ukcge.ac.uk; internet www.ukcge.ac.uk; f. 1994; provides leadership and support to its members to promote a strong and sustainable postgraduate education sector; 125 full institutional mems, 8 assoc. institutional mems, 9 individual mems; Chair Prof. MICK FULLER; Principal Officer CAROLYN WYNNE.

Universities and Colleges Admissions Service (UCAS): POB 28, Cheltenham, GL52 3LZ; Rosehill, New Barn Lane, Cheltenham, GL52 3LZ; tel. (330) 333-0235; e-mail enquiries@ucas.ac.uk; internet www.ucas.com; manages applications to higher education courses in the UK; Chair. PAUL JAGGER; Chief Exec. MARY CURNOCK COOK.

Universities UK: Woburn House, 20 Tavistock Sq., London, WC1H 9HQ; tel. (20) 7419-4111; e-mail info@universitiesuk.ac.uk; internet www.universitiesuk.ac.uk; f. 2000, fmrly Cttee of Vice-Chancellors and Principals of the Univs of the UK (CVCP, f. 1918); promotes, encourages and develops British univs; ensures diversity and autonomy of the UK's higher education sector; 132 exec. heads of British univs; Pres. Prof. Sir CHRISTOPHER SNOWDEN; Chief Exec. NICOLA DANDRIDGE.

University and College Union: Carlow St, London, NW1 7LH; tel. (20) 7756-2500; e-mail hq@ucu.org.uk; internet www.ucu.org.uk; f. 2006; formed by merger of Association of University Teachers and the University and College Lecturers' Union; Pres. SIMON RENTON; Vice-Pres. LIZ LAWRENCE; publs *Environmental news* (online, irregular), *Equality News* (6 a year), *FE news* (online), *HE news* (online), *Health and safety news* (online, 12 a year), *The Journal of Further and Higher Education* (6 a year), *UC* (4 a year).

England

Independent Schools Inspectorate: CAP House, 9–12 Long Lane, London, EC1A 9HA; tel. (20) 7600-0100; e-mail info@isi.net; internet www.isi.net; responsible under Statute for inspecting 1,200 ind. schools in England; inspects British curriculum schools worldwide and maintains operational information systems and a database of the latest reports; Chief Inspector and CEO CHRISTINE RYAN; Chair. PETER WILLIAMSON.

Northern Ireland

Colleges Northern Ireland: 39A Stockman's Way, Belfast, BT9 7ET; tel. (28) 9068-2296; e-mail info@collegesni.ac.uk; internet www.anic.ac.uk; f. 1998 as Association of Northern Ireland's Colleges; liaison with Northern Ireland Assembly, govt depts; Chair. BERTIE FAULKNER.

Education and Training Inspectorate: Inspection Services Br., Dept of Education, Room F29, Rathgael House, 43 Balloo Rd, Bangor, BT19 7PR; tel. (28) 9127-9726; e-mail inspectionservices@deni.gov.uk; internet www.etini.gov.uk; provides inspection services for and information about the quality of education in N Ireland to the Dept of Education, Dept of Culture, Arts and Leisure, and Dept for Employment and Learning; promotes highest possible standards of learning, teaching and achievement throughout education, training and youth sectors; Chief Inspector NOELLE BUICK.

Scotland

Colleges Scotland: Argyll Court, Castle Business Park, Stirling, FK9 4TY; tel. (1786) 892-100; e-mail policy@ collegesscotland.ac.uk; internet www .collegesscotland.ac.uk; f. 2009; supports, represents and promotes the Scottish college sector; Chair. Hon. HENRY McLEISH; Chief Exec. JOHN HENDERSON.

Educational Institute of Scotland: 46 Moray Pl., Edinburgh, EH3 6BH; tel. (131) 225-6244; e-mail enquiries@eis.org.uk; internet www.eis.org.uk; f. 1847; 60,000 mems; Pres. PHIL JACKSON; Gen. Sec. LARRY FLANAGAN; publ. *Scottish Educational Journal* (6 a year).

Education Scotland: Denholm House, Almondvale Business Park, Almondvale Way, Livingston, EH54 6GA; tel. (141) 282-5000; e-mail enquiries@educationscotland .gov.uk; internet www.educationscotland .uk; f. 2011 by merger of Her Majesty's Inspectorate of Education (an exec. agency of the Scottish Government) and Learning and Teaching Scotland; promotes and contributes to sustainable improvements in standards, quality and achievements for all learners in a Scottish education system that is inclusive; Chief Exec. BILL MAXWELL.

Universities Scotland: Holyrood Park House, 106 Holyrood Rd, Edinburgh, EH8 8AS; tel. (131) 226-1111; e-mail info@ universities-scotland.ac.uk; internet www .universities-scotland.ac.uk; 20 mem. univs and other instns; Convener Prof. PETE DOWNES (acting); Dir ALASTAIR SIM.

Wales

Estyn: Anchor Court, Keen Rd, Cardiff, CF24 5JW; tel. (29) 2044-6446; e-mail enquiries@estyn.gov.uk; internet www.estyn .gov.uk; office of HM's Inspectorate for Education and Training in Wales; Chief Inspector ANN KEANE.

Higher Education Wales: 2 Caspian Point, Caspian Way, Cardiff Bay, Cardiff, CF10 4DQ; tel. (29) 2044-8020; e-mail hew@hew.ac .uk; internet www.hew.ac.uk; f. 1996; represents interests of univs in Wales; resources on all aspects of higher education in Wales; Chair. Prof. COLIN RIORDAN; Dir AMANDA WILKINSON.

Learned Societies

GENERAL

Academy of Social Sciences: 30 Tabernacle St, London, EC2A 4UE; tel. (20) 7330-9280; e-mail administrator@acss.org.uk; internet www.acss.org.uk; f. 1999; responds to govt and other consultations on behalf of the social science community; sponsors schemes to promote social sciences, incl. the Campaign for Social Science; 900 acads, 46 mem. learned socs; Pres. Prof. Sir IVOR CREWE; Chair. Prof. CARY COOPER; publ. *Contemporary Social Science* (4 a year).

British Academy: 10–11 Carlton House Terrace, London, SW1Y 5AH; tel. (20) 7969-5200; e-mail chiefexec@britac.ac.uk; internet www.britac.ac.uk; f. 1902; ind. nat. acad. of fellows elected for their eminence in research and publ.; sections: Classical Antiquity, African and Oriental Studies, Theology and Religious Studies, Linguistics and Philology, Early Modern Languages and Literature, Modern Languages, Literature and Other Media, Archaeology, Medieval Studies: History and Literature, Early Modern History to 1800, Modern History since 1800, History of Art and Music, Philosophy, Law, Economics and Economic History, Social Anthropology and Geography, Sociology, Demography and Social Statistics, Political Studies: Political Theory, Govt and Int. Relations, Psychology; 900 mems; Pres. NICHOLAS STERN; Chief Exec. Dr ROBIN JACKSON; publs *British Academy Review* (2 a year), *Journal of the British Academy* (1 a year).

British Council: Bridgewater House, 58 Whitworth St, Manchester, M1 6BB; tel. (161) 957-7755; e-mail general.enquiries@ britishcouncil.org; internet www .britishcouncil.org; f. 1934; promotes knowledge of the United Kingdom and the English language abroad and develops closer cultural relations with other countries; operates in 109 countries; offers English language courses and examinations to test English-language proficiency of foreign students seeking admission to British instns; grants scholarships and other awards to overseas scholars and research workers; promotes liaison between scientists in the United Kingdom and abroad and provides information on British science, medicine and technology; promotes British writers, actors and other artists abroad; organizes overseas exhibitions of British books and periodicals; Chair. VERNON ELLIS; Chief Exec. MARTIN DAVIDSON.

Commonwealth Institute: 6th Fl., New Zealand House, 80 Haymarket, London, SW1Y 4TE; tel. (20) 7024-9822; e-mail information@commonwealth-institute.org; internet www.commonwealth.org.uk; aims to advance primary and secondary education across the Commonwealth; Company Sec. JUDY CURRY..

Attached Centre:

> **Centre for Commonwealth Education:** Faculty of Education, Univ. of Cambridge, 184 Hills Rd, Cambridge, CB2 8PQ; internet www.educ.cam.ac.uk/centres/cce; jt venture between the Commonwealth Institute and the Faculty of Education at the University of Cambridge; Dir MIKE YOUNGER.

English-Speaking Union (of the Commonwealth): Dartmouth House, 37 Charles St, Berkeley Sq., London, W1J 5ED; tel. (20) 7529-1550; e-mail esu@esu.org; internet www.esu.org; f. 1918; int. voluntary org.; runs educational and cultural programmes; offers scholarships for school leavers, teachers and professionals; 60 offices worldwide; 35,000 mems worldwide; library of 3,000 vols; Pres. HRH THE PRINCESS ROYAL; Chair. MARY RICHARDSON; Dir-Gen. (vacant); publ. *Dialogue* (4 a year).

Northern Ireland Foundation: Carnegie Bldg, 121 Donegall Rd, Belfast, BT12 5JL; tel. (28) 9089-1799; e-mail info@nifoundation .net; internet nifoundation.net; f. 2008; ind. non-profit non-govt org.; addresses the legacy of conflict in Northern Ireland by developing leadership programmes and promoting relevant int. research; Chair. JAMES HOLMES; Dir ALLAN LEONARD; Sec. QUINTIN OLIVER.

Royal Society: 6–9 Carlton House Terrace, London, SW1Y 5AG; tel. (20) 7451-2500; e-mail info@royalsoc.ac.uk; internet www .royalsoc.ac.uk; f. 1660; science, technology and engineering; 1,410 mems (1,280 fellows, 130 foreign mems); library: see Libraries and Archives; Pres. Sir PAUL NURSE; Exec. Dir Dr JULIE MAXTON; Biological Sec. Sir JOHN SKEHEL; Foreign Sec. Prof. MARTYN POLIAK-OFF; Physical Sec. Prof. JOHN PETHICA; publs *Biology Letters* (4 a year), *Journal of the Royal Society Interface* (4 a year), *Notes and Records* (4 a year), *Philosophical Transactions* (24 a year), *Proceedings* (24 a year).

Royal Society for the Encouragement of Arts, Manufactures and Commerce (RSA): 8 John Adam St, London, WC2N 6EZ; tel. (20) 7930-5115; e-mail general@rsa .org.uk; internet www.thersa.org; f. 1754; promotes arts, manufactures and commerce; 27,000 fellows; library of 8,000 vols, 11,000 MSS; Pres. HRH Prince PHILIP, DUKE OF EDINBURGH; Chair. VIKKI HEYWOOD; publ. *Journal* (4 a year).

Royal Society of Edinburgh: 22–26 George St, Edinburgh, EH2 2PQ; tel. (131) 240-5000; e-mail rse@royalsoced.org.uk; internet www.royalsoced.org.uk; f. 1783; educational charity; fellowships in science and technology, arts, humanities, social science, business and public service; policy advice to govts; young peoples' programme; 1,571 fellows (1,443 ordinary, 64 hon., 64 corresp.); Pres. Sir JOHN PEEBLES ARBUTH-NOTT; Gen. Sec. Prof. ALAN ALEXANDER; Chief Exec. Dr WILLIAM DUNCAN; publs *Earth and Environmental Science Transactions of the Royal Society of Edinburgh* (4 a year), *Proceedings of the Royal Society of Edinburgh, Section A: Mathematics* (6 a year).

Saltire Society: 9 Fountain Close, 22 High St, Edinburgh, EH1 1TF; tel. (131) 556-1836; e-mail saltire@saltiresociety.org.uk; internet www.saltiresociety.org.uk; f. 1936; conserves and fosters Scottish way of life through arts and crafts, architecture, education, literature; 8 brs throughout Scotland; 1,000 mems; Pres. MAGNUS LINKLATER; Convener DAVID WARD.

Sport and Recreation Alliance: Burwood House, 14 Caxton St, London, SW1H 0QT; tel. (20) 7976-3900; e-mail info@ sportandrecreation.org.uk; internet www .sportandrecreation.org.uk; f. 1935; fmrly Central Ccl of Recreative Physical Training; promotes, protects and provides for sport and recreation sector; 320 nat. governing and rep. bodies; Pres. HRH PRINCE EDWARD, EARL OF WESSEX; Chair., Board of Dirs ANDY REED; Chief Exec. TIM LAMB.

AGRICULTURE, FISHERIES AND VETERINARY SCIENCE

Agricultural Economics Society: AES Secretariat, Holtwood, Red Lion St, Cropredy, Banbury, OX17 1PD; tel. (1295) 750182; e-mail secretariat@aes.ac.uk; internet www.aes.ac.uk; f. 1926; promotes study and teaching of all agricultural economics disciplines; 500 mems; Pres. ROB FRASER; publs *EuroChoices* (3 a year), *Journal of Agricultural Economics* (3 a year).

British Society of Animal Science: POB 3, Penicuik, EH26 0RZ; tel. (131) 650-8784; e-mail bsas@bsas.org.uk; internet www.bsas .org.uk; f. 1944; UK mem. org. of the European Asscn for Animal Production; 1,000 mems; Pres. Dr PETER WILLIAMS; Chief Exec. MIKE STEELE; publs *Advances in Animal Biosciences* (1 a year), *ANIMAL* (12 a year).

British Society of Soil Science: BSSS Administrative Centre, Bldg 53, Cranfield University, Cranfield MK43 0AL; tel. (1234) 752983; e-mail admin@soils.org.uk; internet www.soils.org.uk; f. 1947; merged with the Institute of Professional Soil Scientists 2010; advances the study of soil and its management in agriculture, forestry, environmental matters and other fields; 950 mems; Exec. Officer Dr KATHRYN ALLTON; publs *European Journal of Soil Science* (4 a year), *Soil Use and Management* (4 a year).

British Veterinary Association: 7 Mansfield St, London, W1G 9NQ; tel. (20) 7636-6541; e-mail bvahq@bva.co.uk; internet www .bva.co.uk; f. 1881; promotes and supports the interests of its mems, and the animals under their care; 14,000 mems; Pres. ROBIN HARGREAVES; publs *In Practice* (10 a year),

Off The Record (10 a year), *The Veterinary Record* (52 a year).

Institute of Chartered Foresters: 59 George St, Edinburgh, EH2 2JG; tel. (131) 240-1425; e-mail icf@charteredforesters.org; internet www.charteredforesters.org; f. 1925 as the Society of Foresters of Great Britain; current name adopted 1982; maintains and improves the standards of practice and understanding of forestry and arboriculture; awards chartered forester status (MICFor and FICFor); 1,300 mems; Exec. and Technical Dir SHIREEN CHAMBERS; Pres. Prof. JULIAN EVANS; publs *Chartered Forester* (4 a year), *Forestry* (5 a year).

Institution of Agricultural Engineers (IAgrE): Bullock Bldg (Bldg 53), Univ. Way, Cranfield, Bedford, MK43 0GH; tel. (1234) 750876; e-mail secretary@iagre.org; internet www.iagre.org; f. 1938; professional body for engineers, scientists, technologists and managers in agricultural and allied land-based industries; awards professional qualifications; administers the Land Based Technician Accreditation Scheme (LTA); 2,100 mems; Pres. A. C. NEWBOLD; Chief Exec. and Sec. ALASTAIR J. TAYLOR; publs *Biosystems Engineering* (12 a year), *Landwards* (4 a year).

Royal Agricultural Society of England: Stoneleigh Park, Kenilworth, CV8 2LZ; tel. (24) 7669-2470; e-mail info@rase.org.uk; internet www.rase.org.uk; f. granted Royal Charter 1840; organizes the Royal Show; arranges regular courses, confs; library of archives and collns of artefacts; 11,000 mems; Chief Exec. DAVID GARDNER; publ. *RASE Journal* (1 a year).

Royal College of Veterinary Surgeons: Belgravia House, 62–64 Horseferry Rd, London, SW1P 2AF; tel. (20) 7222-2001; e-mail info@rcvs.org.uk; internet www.rcvs.org.uk; f. 1844; keeps register of veterinary surgeons eligible to practise in the UK, sets standards for veterinary education, awards fellowships, diplomas and certificates to veterinary professionals; veterinary library; 38,500 mems; library of 25,000 vols; spec. colln of 3,000 vols tracing devt of veterinary art and science since 1514; Pres. Col NEIL SMITH; Chief Exec. and Sec. NICK STACE; Registrar GORDON HOCKEY.

Royal Forestry Society: The Hay Barn, Home Farm Dr., Upton Estate, Banbury, OX15 6HU; tel. (1295) 678588; e-mail rfshq@rfs.org.uk; internet www.rfs.org.uk; f. 1882; 4,000 mems; library of 1,500 vols; Pres. Sir JACK WHITAKER; publs *E-news* (24 a year), *Quarterly Journal of Forestry*.

Royal Highland and Agricultural Society of Scotland: Royal Highland Centre, Ingliston, Edinburgh, EH28 8NF; tel. (131) 335-6200; e-mail info@rhass.org.uk; internet www.rhass.org.uk; f. 1784; promotes agriculture and related industries and education; 14,000 mems; library of 6,000 vols; Chief Exec. STEPHEN HUTT; Sec. ADELE THOMSON; publ. *The Review* (3 a year).

Royal Horticultural Society: 80 Vincent Sq., London, SW1P 2PE; tel. (854) 260-5000; e-mail qualifications@rhs.org.uk; internet www.rhs.org.uk; f. 1804; promotes horticulture and gardening; conducts flower shows; offers accredited qualifications in horticulture incl. Master of Horticulture; Lindley Library; 230,000 mems; library of 80,000 vols on gardening, horticulture and cultivated plants in the world and botanical art; Chair. Sir NICHOLAS BACON; Dir-Gen. SUE BIGGS; Sec. JAN NIX; publs *Growing Communities* (4 a year), *Hanburyana* (1 a year), *The Garden* (12 a year), *The Orchid Review* (4 a year), *The Plantsman* (4 a year), etc..

Royal Scottish Forestry Society: St Leonards, Maxwell Lane, Kelso, TD5 7BB; tel. (1573) 223174; e-mail director@rsfs.org; internet www.rsfs.org; f. 1854 as Scottish Arboricultural Society, renamed Royal Scottish Arboricultural Soc. in 1887, current name adopted 1930; meetings; seminars; forest visits; discussion groups; aids in setting standards and associated exams; 1,400 mems; Pres. WILLIAM CRAWFORD; Dir ALASTAIR HARDING; publ. *Scottish Forestry* (4 a year).

Royal Welsh Agricultural Society: Royal Welsh Showground, Llanelwedd, Builth-Wells, LD2 3SY; tel. (1982) 553683; e-mail requests@rwas.co.uk; internet www.rwas.co.uk; f. 1904; promotes agriculture, horticulture, forestry and conservation; organizes Royal Welsh Show, Royal Welsh Agricultural Winter Fair and Royal Welsh Smallholder and Garden Festival; holds demonstrations of modern agricultural methods and processes; 18,000 mems; Chief Exec. STEVE HUGHSON; publ. *Royal Welsh Journal* (1 a year).

Society of Dairy Technology: Larnick Park, Higher Larrick, Trebullett, Launceston, PL15 9QH; tel. (845) 528-0418; e-mail execdirector@sdt.org; internet www.sdt.org; f. 1943; recognised professional body fostering scientific and technological developments in the dairy industries UK and Ireland; supports advancement of dairy science and technology; organizes confs. and seminars; publishes multi-author technical series; 400 mems; Pres. Dr KEN BURGESS; Exec. Dir LIZ WHITLEY; publ. *International Journal of Dairy Technology* (4 a year).

ARCHITECTURE AND TOWN PLANNING

Architectural Association (Inc.): 34–36 Bedford Sq., London, WC1B 3ES; tel. (20) 7887-4000; e-mail graduateadmissions@aaschool.ac.uk; internet www.aaschool.ac.uk; f. 1847; serves the AA School of Architecture, offers facilities for architectural studies to undergraduates and graduates; professional courses; research programmes; publishes books and journals as AA Publications; conducts exhibitions, lectures, symposia, seminars and conversations; 4,500 mems worldwide; library of 46,000 150 rchitectural, art and technical journals titles; incl. photolibrary and archives; Dir BRETT STEELE; Registrar MARILYN DYER; publs *AA Files* (3 a year), *Projects Review* (1 a year).

Association of Building Engineers: Lutyens House, Billing Brook Rd, Weston Favell, Northampton, NN3 8NW; tel. (1604) 404121; e-mail info@abe.org.uk; internet www.abe.org.uk; f. 1925 as the Incorporated Association of Architects and Surveyors, received Royal Charter in 2013; professional body for those specializing in the technology of building; 7,000 mems; Patron LORD LYTTON; Chief Exec. Dr JOHN HOOPER; Pres. STAN BARKER-MCGUIRE; publ. *Building Engineer* (12 a year).

Campaign to Protect Rural England (CPRE): 5-11 Lavington St, London, SE1 0NZ; tel. (20) 7981-2800; e-mail info@cpre.org.uk; internet www.cpre.org.uk; f. 1926; nat. charity that helps people protect, promote and enhance their towns and local countryside; 60,000 mems; Chief Exec. SHAUN SPIERS; publ. *Countryside Voice* (3 a year).

Church Buildings Council: Church House, 27 Great Smith St, London, SW1P 3AZ; tel. (20) 7898-1863; e-mail churchcare@churchofengland.org; internet www.churchcare.co.uk; f. 1921; advises 16,000 parish churches and 42 cathedrals on preserving and restoring their buildings; library

of 12,000 vols; Chair. ANNE SLOMAN; Sec. JANET GOUGH.

Civic Voice: 60 Duke St, Liverpool, L1 5AA; tel. (151) 707-4319; e-mail info@civicvoice.org.uk; internet www.civicvoice.org.uk; f. 2009 as Civic Society Initiative following closure of the Civic Trust (f. in 1957); current name adopted 2010; nat. charity for the civic movement in England; supports over 1,000 local amenity societies; Chair FREDDIE GICK; Treas. MARTIN MEREDITH.

Landscape Institute: Charles Darwin House, 12 Roger St, London, WC1N 2JU; tel. (20) 7685-2640; e-mail mail@landscapeinstitute.org; internet www.landscapeinstitute.org; f. 1929; promotes advancement of the art of landscape architecture; works with government to improve the planning, design and management of urban and rural landscape; 5,194 mems (comprising students, assocs, mems and fellows); library of 15,313 vols, journal articles and landscape drawings; visits to library and archive by non-members by appointment; Pres. SUE ILLMAN; Chief Exec. PHIL MULLIGAN; publs *Landscape* (4 a year), *Landscape Journal Online* (24 a year).

London Society: Mortimer Wheeler House, 46 Eagle Wharf Rd, London, N1 7ED; tel. (20) 7253-9400; e-mail info@londonsociety.org.uk; internet www.londonsociety.org.uk; f. 1912; reviews strategic planning proposals to encourage development of London and preserve its amenities and buildings; library of 3,500 vols; colln of books and MSS incl. journals since 1912; 848 mems; Pres. HRH THE DUKE OF GLOUCESTER; Hon. Sec. PATRICK GASKELL-TAYLOR; publ. *Journal* (2 a year).

National Trust for Places of Historic Interest or Natural Beauty: POB 574, Manvers, Rotherham, S63 3FH; tel. (844) 800-1895; e-mail enquiries@nationaltrust.org.uk; internet www.nationaltrust.org.uk; f. 1895; 2.3m. mems; Pres. PRINCE CHARLES; Chair. Sir SIMON JENKINS; Dir-Gen. Dame HELEN GHOSH; publ. *National Trust Magazine* (3 a year).

National Trust for Scotland: Hermiston Quay, 5 Cultins Rd, Edinburgh, EH11 4DF; tel. (844) 493-2100; e-mail information@nts.org.uk; internet www.nts.org.uk; f. 1931; promotes the preservation of places of historical or architectural interest or natural beauty in Scotland; 310,000 mems; Chair. Sir KENNETH CALMAN; Chief Exec. KATE MAVOR.

Open Spaces Society: 25a Bell St, Henley-on-Thames, RG9 2BA; tel. (1491) 573535; e-mail hq@oss.org.uk; internet www.oss.org.uk; f. 1865 as the Commons Preservation Soc.; campaigns to protect common land, village greens, open spaces and public paths; assists local communities to preserve their surroundings; 2,300 mems; Chair. TIM CROWTHER; Gen. Sec. KATE ASHBROOK; publ. *Open Space* (3 a year).

Oxford Preservation Trust: 10 Turn Again Lane, St Ebbes, Oxford, OX1 1QL; tel. (1865) 242918; e-mail info@oxfordpreservation.org.uk; internet www.oxfordpreservation.org.uk; f. 1926; preserves and enhances for the benefit of public the amenities of Oxford and its surroundings; awards scheme; involved in Oxford's planning process; 1,000 mems; Chair. Prof. ROGER AINSWORTH; Dir DEBORAH DANCE.

Royal Incorporation of Architects in Scotland: 15 Rutland Sq., Edinburgh, EH1 2BE; tel. (131) 229-7545; e-mail info@rias.org.uk; internet www.rias.org.uk; f. 1916 as the professional body for chartered architects in Scotland; 4,000 mems; Pres. IAIN CONNELLY; Sec. and Treas. NEIL BAXTER; publ. *Practice Information* (4 a year).

Royal Institute of British Architects: 66 Portland Pl., London, W1B 1AD; tel. (20) 7580-5533; e-mail info@riba.org; internet www.architecture.com; f. 1834; 28,000 chartered mems; library: see entry for British Architectural Library; Pres. STEPHEN HODDER; Chief Exec. HARRY RICH; publs *Directory of Practices* (1 a year), *RIBA Journal* (12 a year).

Royal Institution of Chartered Surveyors: 12 Great George St, Parliament Sq., London, SW1P 3AD; tel. (20) 7686-8555; e-mail contactrics@rics.org; internet www .rics.org; f. 1868; 140,000 mems; library of 35,000 vols; Pres. MICHAEL NEWEY; Chair. JIM CARTER; publ. *RICS Business* (12 a year).

Royal Town Planning Institute: 41 Botolph Lane, London, EC3R 8DL; tel. (20) 7929-9494; e-mail contact@rtpi.org.uk; internet www.rtpi.org.uk; f. 1914; promotes spatial, sustainable and inclusive planning; runs Planning Aid England and RTPI Services Ltd.; 23,000 mems; library of 10,000 vols; Pres. CATH RANSON; Chief Exec. TRUDI ELLIOTT; publs *Planning Theory and Practice* (4 a year), *RTPI News* (52 a year).

Society for the Protection of Ancient Buildings: 37 Spital Sq., London, E1 6DY; tel. (20) 7377-1644; e-mail info@spab.org.uk; internet www.spab.org.uk; f. 1877; campaigns for conservation of old buildings of historical interest; c. 8,500 mems; Pres. THE DUKE OF GRAFTON; Dir MATTHEW SLOCOMBE; publ. *SPAB Magazine* (4 a year).

Town and Country Planning Association: 17 Carlton House Terrace, London, SW1Y 5AS; tel. (20) 7930-8903; e-mail tcpa@ tcpa.org.uk; internet www.tcpa.org.uk; f. 1899; works to provide housing; promotes sustainable devt through planning policies; 1,000 mems; Chair. LEE SHOSTAK; Chief Exec. KATE HENDERSON; publ. *Town and Country Planning* (11 a year).

Victorian Society: 1 Priory Gdns, Bedford Park, London, W4 1TT; tel. (20) 8994-1019; e-mail admin@victoriansociety.org.uk; internet www.victoriansociety.org.uk; f. 1958; works towards promoting and preserving Victorian and Edwardian buildings in England and Wales; 3,500 mems; Pres. LORD BRIGGS OF LEWES; Dir CHRISTOPHER COSTELLOE; publs *The Victorian Society Journal* (irregular), *The Victorian Magazine* (3 a year).

BIBLIOGRAPHY, LIBRARY SCIENCE AND MUSEOLOGY

Arlis UK and Ireland/Art Libraries Society of United Kingdom and Ireland: Nat. Art Library, Victoria and Albert Museum, Cromwell Rd, S Kensington, London, SW7 2RL; tel. (20) 7942-2317; e-mail arlis@vam.ac .uk; internet www.arlis.org.uk; f. 1969; professional org. for people involved in providing library and information services and documenting resources in the visual arts; 700 mems; Chair. CHRIS FOWLER; Business Man. LORRAINE BLACKMAN; publs *Art Libraries Journal* (4 a year), *Directory* (1 a year).

Aslib (The Association for Information Management): Howard House, Wagon Lane, Bingley, BD16 1WA; tel. (1274) 777-700; e-mail support@aslib.com; internet www .aslib.com; f. 1924 as the Association of Special Libraries and Information Bureaux; serves information professionals and librarians across all sectors by offering comprehensive resources, specialist training, advice and int. networking; organizes nat. and int. confs and meetings; 600 corporate mems and subscriber orgs; library: see under Libraries and Archives; Dir REBECCA MARSH; publs *Aslib Book Guide* (12 a year), *Aslib Proceedings* (10 a year), *Current Awareness*

Abstracts (10 a year), *Library Hi Tech News incorporating Online and CD Notes* (10 a year), *Managing Information* (10 a year, print and online), *Performance, Measurement and Metrics* (3 a year), *Privacy and Data Protection: Managing Information Matters* (4 a year, print and online), *Program* (4 a year), *Records Management Journal* (12 a year), *The Journal of Documentation* (5 a year).

Association of Independent Libraries: c/o The Leeds Library, 18 Commercial St, Leeds, LS1 6AL; tel. (113) 245-3071; e-mail independent.libraries@gmail.com; internet www.independentlibraries.co.uk; f. 1989; develops links between its constituent mems by means of cooperative agreements, newsletters, social gatherings, seminars, workshops and meetings; 30 mems; Pres. ROBERT ANDERSON.

Bibliographical Society: c/o Institute of English Studies, Univ. of London, Senate House, Malet St, London, WC1E 7HU; tel. (20) 7862-8679; e-mail admin@bibsoc.org.uk; internet www.bibsoc.org.uk; f. 1892; promotes study and research in the fields of historical, analytical, descriptive and textual bibliography and the history of printing, publishing, bookselling, bookbinding and collecting; supports bibliographical research by awarding grants and bursaries; 1,000 mems; Pres. CHRISTINE FERDINAND; Hon. Sec. MARGARET L. FORD; publ. *The Library* (4 a year).

Booktrust: Book House, 45 East Hill, London, SW18 2QZ; tel. (20) 8516-2977; e-mail query@booktrust.org.uk; internet www .booktrust.org.uk; f. 1924 as The Nat. Book Council; works to engage people with reading by providing book lists and information service; administers literary prizes; 1,000 mems; Pres. MICHAEL MORPURGO; Chief Exec. VIV BIRD.

Cambridge Bibliographical Society: Univ. Library, West Rd, Cambridge, CB3 9DR; tel. (1223) 333-123; e-mail cbs@lib.cam .ac.uk; internet www.lib.cam.ac.uk/ cambibsoc; f. 1949; publishes occasional monographs and the annual, peer -reviewed Transactions of the Cambridge Bibliographical Society and papers; 450 mems; Pres. DAVID MCKITTERICK; Hon. Sec. Dr TIM EGGINGTON; publs *Monographs* (irregular), *Transactions of the Cambridge Bibliographical Society* (1 a year).

Chartered Institute of Library and Information Professionals (CILIP): 7 Ridgmount St, London, WC1E 7AE; tel. (20) 7255-0500; e-mail info@cilip.org.uk; internet www.cilip.org.uk; f. 2002, merger of Library Asscn and Institute of Information Scientists; charity and professional body for librarians, information specialists and knowledge managers; provides practical career support for mems; 18,000 mems; Pres. BARBARA BAND; Chief Exec. ANNIE MAUGER; publ. *CILIP Update with Gazette* (12 a year).

Chartered Institute of Library and Information Professionals Scotland (CILIPS): 126 West Regent St, Glasgow, G2 2RQ; tel. (141) 228-4790; e-mail admin@ cilips.org.uk; internet www.cilips.org.uk; f. 2002, fmrly Scottish Library Association; attached to CILIP; professional body for librarians and information professionals in Scotland; 2,200 mems; Pres. ROBERT RUTHVEN; Dir CATHERINE KEARNEY.

Chartered Institute of Library and Information Professionals Wales (CILIP Wales): Bute Library, Cardiff Univ., POB 430, Cardiff CF24 0DE; tel. (7837) 032536; e-mail wales@cilip.org.uk; internet www.cilip .org.uk/wales; f. 1931; supports devt of mems through confs, events and training; offers awards and bursaries; 850 mems; Chair. MARLIZE PALMER (acting); publs *Wales Cur-*

rent Awareness (24 a year), *Y Ddolen* (3 a year).

Edinburgh Bibliographical Society: c/o Dr Joseph Marshall, Centre for Research Collections, Edinburgh Univ. Library, George Sq., Edinburgh, EH8 9LJ; tel. (131) 623-3894; e-mail joseph.marshall@ed.ac.uk; internet www .edinburghbibliographicalsociety.org.uk; f. 1890; discusses and elucidates questions connected with books, printed or MSS; promotes and encourages bibliographical studies; publishes papers related to Scottish interests, bibliography, the book trade, history of books and libraries, book collecting; 150 mems; Pres. Prof. PETER GARSIDE; Hon. Sec. HELEN VINCENT; publ. *Journal of the Edinburgh Bibliographical Society* (1 a year), *Transactions*.

Friends of the National Libraries: c/o Dept of Manuscripts, The British Library, 96 Euston Rd, London, NW1 2DB; tel. (20) 7412-7559; e-mail secretary@fnlmail.org.uk; internet www.friendsofnationallibraries.org .uk; f. 1931; promotes acquisition of printed books, MSS and archives of historical, literary or artistic significance; offers grants; 800 mems; Chair. Lord EGREMONT; Hon. Sec. Dr FRANCES HARRIS; publ. *Friends of the National Libraries*.

Museums Association: 42 Clerkenwell Close, London, EC1R 0AZ; tel. (20) 7566-7800; e-mail info@museumsassociation.org; internet www.museumsassociation.org; f. 1889; promotes and improves museums and galleries; trains museum staff; 6,011 mems; Dir MARK TAYLOR; publs *Museum Journal* (11 a year), *Museums and Galleries Yearbook*, *Museums Practice* (4 a year, online).

Museums, Libraries and Archives Council (MLA): Grosvenor House 14 Bennetts Hill, Birmingham, B2 5RS; tel. (121) 667-4326 Wellcome Wolfson Building, 165 Queen's Gate, London, SW7 5HD; tel. (20) 7273-1444; e-mail info@mla.gov.uk; internet www.mla.gov.uk; f. 2000; works with govt, local govt, key agencies and orgs; advises on museum, library and archive affairs; 15 mems; Chair. ANDREW MOTION.

Society of College, National and University Libraries (SCONUL): 94 Euston St, London, NW1 2HA; tel. (20) 7387-0317; e-mail info@sconul.ac.uk; internet www .sconul.ac.uk; f. 1950 as the Standing Conference of National and University Libraries; engages in policy devt, lobbying, coordination and support; 178 mem. institutions; Exec. Dir ANN ROSSITER; publs *SCONUL Annual Library Statistics*, *SCONUL Focus*.

ECONOMICS, LAW AND POLITICS

Association of Chartered Certified Accountants: 29 Lincoln's Inn Fields, London, WC2A 3EE; tel. (20) 7059-5000; e-mail info@accaglobal.com; internet www .accaglobal.com; f. 1904; 162,000 mems; Pres. MARTIN TURNER; Chief Exec. HELEN BRAND; publs *Accounting and Business* (12 a year), *Accountants' Guide*, *Student Accountant* (12 a year), *Teach Accounting* (4 a year).

British Academy of Forensic Sciences: Academic Haematology, Blizard Institute, Barts and the London, 4 Newark St, London, E1 2AT; tel. (20) 7848-4130; e-mail lesley@ bafsadmin.org; internet www.bafs.org.uk; f. 1959; works to improve practice, disseminate information, and advance knowledge in forensic science and forensic medicine; educational meetings and seminars; 400 mems; Chair. Prof. ROBERT FLANAGAN; Sec. Gen. Dr DENISE SYNDERCOMBE COURT; publ. *Medicine, Science and the Law* (4 a year).

British Institute of International and Comparative Law: Charles Clore House, 17 Russell Sq., London, WC1B 5JP; tel. (20) 7862-5151; e-mail contact@biicl.org; internet www.biicl.org; f. 1958 by the amalgamation of the Grotius Society and the Society of Comparative Legislation and Int. Law; organizes the Commonwealth Legal Advisory Service and research in comparative law, int. law, and law of the European Communities; 800 mems; Chair. Dame ROSALYN HIGGINS; Dir Prof. ROBERT MCCORQUODALE; publs *Bulletin of International Legal Developments* (26 a year), *International and Comparative Law Quarterly* (4 a year), and other monographs on int. and comparative law.

Chartered Banker Institute: Drumsheugh House, 38B Drumsheugh Gardens, Edinburgh, EH3 7SW; tel. (131) 473-7777; e-mail info@charteredbanker.com; internet www.charteredbanker.com; f. 1875; develops and promotes professional standards for bankers in the UK and overseas; offers Professional Banker and Chartered Banker qualifications, and regulatory qualifications for mortgage and investment advisers; 10,000 mems; Pres. JOHN NEEDHAM; Chief Exec. SIMON THOMPSON; publ. *Chartered Banker* (6 a year).

Chartered Institute of Management Accountants (CIMA): 26 Chapter St, London, SW1P 4NP; tel. (20) 8849-2251; e-mail cima.contact@cimaglobal.com; internet www.cimaglobal.com; f. 1919, Royal Charter granted 1975; professional examining and membership body for chartered management accountants throughout the world; offers full-time and part-time professional courses; 195,000 mems and students in 176 countries; Pres. M. FURBER; publs *CIMA Insight* (12 a year), *Excellence in Leadership* (4 a year), *Financial Management* (12 a year).

Chartered Institute of Public Finance and Accountancy: 3 Robert St, London, WC2N 6RL; tel. (20) 7543-5600; e-mail corporate@cipfa.org; internet www.cipfa.org.uk; f. 1885 as the Corporate Treasurers and Accountants Institute; current name adopted 1973; professional accountancy body for public services; provides education and training in accountancy and financial management, and monitors professional standards; finances teams, develops new skills, provides advice; 14,000 mems; 3,000 students; Chief Exec. ROB WHITEMAN; publs *PMPA* (4 a year), *Public Finance* (52 a year).

Chartered Insurance Institute: 42–48 High Rd, S Woodford, London, E18 2JP; tel. (20) 8989-8464; e-mail customer.serv@cii.co.uk; internet www.cii.co.uk; f. 1897; inc. by Royal Charter 1912; central org. for the promotion of professionalism and progress among insurance and financial services employees; offers courses; 110,000 mems; library of 15,000 vols; Dir-Gen. D. E. BLAND; Librarian R. L. CUNNEW; publ. *Journal* (6 a year).

Confederation of British Industry (CBI): Centre Point, 103 New Oxford St, London, WC1A 1DU; tel. (20) 7379-7400; e-mail enquiries@cbi.org.uk; internet www.cbi.org.uk; f. 1965; represents interests of private enterprise and industry on nat. and int. level, and seeks to influence govt policymaking; Pres. Sir MICHAEL RAKE; Dir-Gen. JOHN CRIDLAND; publs *Business Voice* (12 a year), *CBI Distributive Trades Survey* (12 a year), *Economic Situation Report* (12 a year), *Industrial Trends Survey* (4 a year).

David Davies Memorial Institute of International Studies: c/o Dept of International Politics, Aberystwyth Univ., Aberystwyth, SY23 3FE; tel. (1970) 622708; e-mail interpol@aber.ac.uk; internet www.aber.ac.uk/ddmi; f. 1951 to commemorate and continue the work of Lord Davies (1880–1944), on the means of establishing a viable world order; provides a forum for policymakers, officials, NGOs, academics and the wider public for sharing perspectives on challenges in contemporary world politics; 2,500 mems; Pres. Prof. KEN BOOTH; Dir JAN RUZICKA.

Economics, Business and Enterprise Association: Adur Business Centre, Little High St, Shoreham-by-Sea, BN43 5EG; tel. (1273) 467542; e-mail office@ebea.org.uk; internet www.ebea.org.uk; f. 1948; promotes and extends the study of economics, business studies, enterprise and related subjects by encouraging curriculum devt; provides mems with professional support; 1,300 mems; Chair. GUY DURDEN; Sec. PAUL WIDDOWSON; publ. *Teaching Business and Economics* (3 a year).

Electoral Reform Society: 6 Chancel St, Blackfriars, London, SE1 0UU; tel. (20) 7928-1622; e-mail ers@electoral-reform.org.uk; internet www.electoral-reform.org.uk; f. 1884 as Proportional Representation Society; ind. campaigning org. working for rights of voters and building a better democracy in Britain; reference library and archive; 2,000 mems; Chair. AMY DODD; Chief Exec. KATIE GHOSE.

European Movement: Southbank House, Black Prince Rd, London, SE1 7SJ; tel. (20) 3176-0543; e-mail emoffice@euromove.org.uk; internet www.euromove.org.uk; f. 1948; promotes European integration and unity at nat. and int. level; Pres. CHARLES KENNEDY; Chair. PETROS FASSOULAS.

Fabian Society: 61 Petty France, Westminster, London, SW1H 9EU; tel. (20) 7227-4900; e-mail info@fabians.org.u; internet www.fabians.org.uk; f. 1884; develops political ideas and public policy on the left; conducts research, organizes confs and seminars; 7,000 mems; Gen. Sec. ANDREW HARROP; publs *Fabian Pamphlets* (4 a year), *Fabian Review* (4 a year).

Institute and Faculty of Actuaries: MacLaurin House, 18 Dublin St, Edinburgh, EH1 3PP; tel. (131) 240-1300; e-mail info@actuaries.org.uk; internet www.actuaries.org.uk; f. 1856; current name adopted 2010; 1,220 (1,174 fellows, 11 hon. fellows, 35 affiliates); library of 6,000 vols, 1,300 vols of historical colln; Pres. DAVID HARE; Chief Exec. DEREK CRIBB; Librarian DAVID RAYMONT; publs *Annals of Actuarial Science* (2 a year), *British Actuarial Journal* (3 a year).

Faculty of Advocates: Parliament House, Edinburgh, EH1 1RF; tel. (131) 226-5071; e-mail clerkoffaculty@advocates.org.uk; internet www.advocates.org.uk; f. 1532; sole professional body for advocates (barristers) in Scotland; conducts talks, seminars and confs; training courses; 739 mems; library: copyright library in respect of legal works of 100,000 law books associated with Nat. Library of Scotland; Dean RICHARD KEEN; Clerk CALUM S. WILSON; Keeper of the Library MUNGO BOVEY.

Federal Trust for Education and Research: 31 Jewry St, London, EC3N 2EY; tel. (20) 7320-3045; e-mail info@fedtrust.co.uk; internet www.fedtrust.co.uk; f. 1945; promotes and carries out research and education into federal solutions to nat., European and global problems, in particular the EU; contributes to the study of federalism and federal systems; 500 mems; Dir BRENDAN DONNELLY.

General Council of the Bar: 289–293 High Holborn, London, WC1V 7HZ; tel. (20) 7242-0082; e-mail contactus@barcouncil.org.uk; internet www.barcouncil.org.uk; f. 1894; represents barristers in England and Wales; provides regulatory functions through the ind. Bar Standards Board; Bar Council Library; Chief Exec. STEPHEN CROWNE; publs *Code of Conduct, Counsel* (incorporating *Bar News*) (12 a year).

Hansard Society: 5th Fl., 9 King St, London, EC2V 8EA; tel. (20) 7710-6070; e-mail contact@hansardsociety.org.uk; internet www.hansardsociety.org.uk; f. 1944; promotes parliamentary democracy, political education, political research and informed discussion of all aspects of modern parliamentary govt; delivers accredited undergraduate and postgraduate modules on British politics and public policy; 400 mems; Chair. LORD GROCOTT; Dir RUTH FOX; publ. *Parliamentary Affairs* (4 a year).

IFS University College: IFS House, 4–9 Burgate Lane, Canterbury, CT1 2XJ; tel. (1227) 818609; e-mail customerservices@ifslearning.ac.uk; internet www.ifslearning.ac.uk; f. 1879; provides qualifications for the financial services industry; 41,000 mems; library of 30,000 vols; Chair Dr PAUL FISHER; Prin. GAVIN SHREEVE; publs *Eclectic* (4 a year), *Financial World* (12 a year), *IFS News* (12 a year).

Institute for Fiscal Studies: 3rd Fl., 7 Ridgmount St, London, WC1E 7AE; tel. (20) 7291-4800; e-mail mailbox@ifs.org.uk; internet www.ifs.org.uk; f. 1969; promotes effective economic and social policies; produces briefing notes and working papers and organizes confs, seminars and briefings; c. 650 individual mems; 100 corporate and institutional mems; Pres. RACHEL LOMAX; Exec. Committee Chair. FRANCES CAIRNCROSS; publ. *Fiscal Studies* (4 a year).

Institute of Chartered Accountants in England and Wales: Chartered Accountants' Hall, Moorgate Pl., London, EC2R 6EA; tel. (20) 7920-8100; e-mail generalenquiries@icaew.com; internet www.icaew.co.uk; f. 1880 by Royal Charter; provides qualifications and professional devt, shares knowledge, insight and technical expertise, and protects the quality and integrity of the accountancy and finance profession; 140,000 mems; library of 45,000 vols, 60,000 articles; Pres. MARTYN JONES; Chief Exec. MICHAEL IZZA; publ. *Accountancy* (12 a year).

Institute of Chartered Accountants of Scotland: CA House, 21 Haymarket Yards, Edinburgh, EH12 5BH; tel. (131) 347-0100; e-mail enquiries@icas.org.uk; internet www.icas.org.uk; f. 1854; deals with professional matters concerning its mems and the public in matters of chartered accountancy; offers qualifications in chartered accountancy; library of 3,000 vols, 140 periodicals, 100 ebooks; 20,000 mems; Pres. BRENDAN NELSON; Chief Exec. ANTON COLELLA; publ. *CA Magazine* (12 a year).

Institute of Chartered Secretaries and Administrators: 16 Park Crescent, London, W1B 1AH; tel. (20) 7580-4741; e-mail info@icsa.org.uk; internet www.icsa.org.uk; f. 1891; chartered membership and qualifying body for professionals in governance, risk and compliance, incl. company secretaries and in-house lawyers; 47,000 mems and students; Chief Exec. SIMON OSBORNE; publs *Chartered Secretary* (12 a year), *Company Secretarial Practice* (4 a year), *The Company Secretary* (12 a year).

Institute of Economic Affairs: 2 Lord North St, Westminster, London, SW1P 3LB; tel. (20) 7799-8900; e-mail iea@iea.org.uk; internet www.iea.org.uk; f. 1955; to improve understanding of economics and its application to business and public policy; Dir-Gen. MARK LITTLEWOOD; publs *Economic Affairs* (3 a year), produces reports, books and papers on all areas of economic policy.

Law Society: 113 Chancery Lane, London, WC2A 1PL; tel. (20) 7242-1222; e-mail info .services@lawsociety.org.uk; internet www .lawsociety.org.uk; f. 1825; regulator and representative body for solicitors in England and Wales; 93,000 mems; library: see Libraries and Archives; Pres. NICK FLUCK; Chief Exec. DES HUDSON; publ. *Gazette* (52 a year).

Political Studies Association of the United Kingdom: 30 Tabernacle St, London, EC2A 4UE; tel. (20) 7330-9289; e-mail psa@ncl.ac.uk; internet www.psa.ac.uk; f. 1950; promotes the study of politics; 1,600 mems; Chair. Prof. CHARLIE JEFFERY; Hon. Sec. Prof. PAUL CARMICHAEL; publs *British Journal of Politics and International Relations* (4 a year), *Political Insight* (4 a year), *Political Studies* (4 a year), *Political Studies Review* (3 a year), *Politics* (3 a year).

Royal Economic Society: Office of the Sec.-Gen., School of Economics and Finance, Univ. of St Andrews, St Andrews, KY16 9AL; tel. (1334) 462479; e-mail royaleconsoc@ st-andrews.ac.uk; internet www.res.org.uk; f. 1890 as British Economic Association, current name adopted 1902; promotes economic research and the advancement of economic knowledge and understanding; cooperates with int. assns of economists; promotes study of economic science in academics, govt service, banking, industry and public affairs; 3,000 mems; Pres. CHARLES R. BEAN; Sec.-Gen. Prof. JOHN BEATH; publs *The Econometrics Journal* (1 a year, online, www.res.org.uk/view/econometricshome.html), *The Economic Journal* (8 a year, online, www.res.org.uk/view/economichome.html).

Royal Faculty of Procurators in Glasgow: 12 Nelson Mandela Pl., Glasgow, G2 1BT; e-mail library@rfpg.org; internet www .rfpg.org; f. 1668 inc. prior to 1668, granted Royal Charter 1796; rep. body for solicitors practising in Glasgow; 1,500 mems; library of 25,000 vols; Dean BRIAN CAMERON.

Royal Institute of International Affairs: Chatham House, 10 St James's Sq., London, SW1Y 4LE; tel. (20) 7957-5700; e-mail contact@chathamhouse.org; internet www .chathamhouse.org; f. 1920 as British Institute of International Affairs; current name adopted 1926; facilitates the study of int. affairs; studies economic, political and security trends in int. relations; researches into Middle East, Asia-Pacific, Africa, Europe, Russia and Central Asia, and into energy and the environment, int. economics, law, security and health; org. debates on international affairs; 5,000 mems (all categories); library: see under Libraries and Archives; Pres Sir JOHN MAJOR; Pres. BARONESS OF SCOTLAND; Pres. Lord ASHDOWN OF NORTON-SUB-HAMDON; Dir Dr ROBIN NIBLETT; publs *International Affairs* (6 a year), *The World Today* (6 a year).

Royal Statistical Society: 12 Errol St, London, EC1Y 8LX; tel. (20) 7638-8998; e-mail rss@rss.org.uk; internet www.rss.org .uk; f. 1834 as the Statistical Society of London; current name adopted 1887; encourages growth, devt and application of statistics; awards for statistical excellence; accrediting univ. courses and holding examinations; 6,000 mems; Pres. JOHN PULLINGER; Exec. Dir HETAN SHAH; publs *Applied Statistics* (4 a year), *Statistical Methodology* (4 a year), *Statistics in Society* (3 a year), *The Statistician* (4 a year).

Selden Society: c/o School of Law, Queen Mary, Univ. of London, Mile End Rd, London, E1 4NS; tel. (20) 7882-3968; e-mail selden-society@qmul.ac.uk; internet www

.selden-society.qmul.ac.uk; f. 1887; encourages the study and advances knowledge of English legal history mainly by publ. of original records of law and legal instns; publishes more than 150 vols on sources and other aspects of English legal history; 1,700 mems; Pres. Rt Hon. Lord IGOR JUDGE; Hon. Treas. CHRISTOPHER WRIGHT; Literary Dir Sir JOHN BAKER; publs *Selden Society Main Series* (1 a year), *Selden Society Supplementary Series* (irregular).

Stair Society: c/o Thomas H Drysdale, 6 The Glebe, Manse Rd, Dirleton East Lothian, EH39 5FB; e-mail stairsecretary@btinternet .com; internet www.stairsociety.org; f. 1934; encourages study and advances knowledge of history of Scots Law by publishing original documents and reprinting and editing works of rarity or importance; 400 mems; Pres. LORD STEWART; Sec. THOMAS H. DRYSDALE.

EDUCATION

ACE Education: 36 Nicholay Rd, London, N19 3EZ; tel. (20) 8407-5142; e-mail enquiries@ace-ed.org.uk; internet www .ace-ed.org.uk; f. 1960 as The Advisory Centre for Education; current name adopted 2010; aims to encourage close home-school relationships, and build discussion on education issues; publ. *Stop Press* (12 a year).

British Educational Leadership Management and Administration Society: Suite 20, Northchurch Business Centre, 84 Queen St, Sheffield, S1 2DW; tel. (114) 279-9926; e-mail info@belmas.org.uk; internet www.belmas.org.uk; f. 1971; promotes quality education through effective leadership and management; advances the practice of and research into educational admin.; maintains close contact with nat. and int. orgs and encourages the foundation of local groups; 850 mems; Chair. Dr PHILIP A. WOODS; Pres. RON GLATTER; Treas. Dr ALISON TAYSUM; publs *Educational Management Administration and Leadership* (6 a year), *Management in Education* (4 a year), *Networks*.

Council for Education in World Citizenship/Cyngor Addysg Mewn Oinasyddiaeth Byd: Welsh Centre for International Affairs, Temple of Peace, King Edward VII Ave, Cathays Park, Cardiff, CF10 3AP; tel. (29) 2022-8549; e-mail centre@wcia.org.uk; internet www.wcia.org .uk/cewc; f. 1939; attached to Welsh Centre For Int. Affairs; provides training and resources for teachers and specializes in the Philosophy for Children method; org. educational events for children; Chief Exec. MARTIN POLLARD.

University Association for Contemporary European Studies: School of Public Policy, Univ. College London, 29–30 Tavistock Sq., London, WC1H 9QU; tel. (20) 7679-4975; e-mail admin@uaces.org; internet www.uaces.org; f. 1968; academic association for Contemporary European Studies; organizes events and confs; funds mems research activities, supports collaborative research networks; 1,200 mems; Exec. Dir LUKE FOSTER; publs *JCMS: Journal of Common Market Studies*, *JCER: Journal of Contemporary European Research* (online, www.jcer.net).

Workers' Educational Association (WEA): 96-100 Clifton St, London, EC2A 4TP; tel. (20) 7426-1950; e-mail london@wea .org.uk; internet www.wea.org.uk; f. 1903; provider of adult education, delivering 9,500 part-time courses; 400 local brs; cooperates with univs and other voluntary asscns through all English regions and in Scotland for the provision of classes; 65,000 mems; 80,000 students; Chief Exec. and Sec.-Gen. RUTH SPELLMAN.

FINE AND PERFORMING ARTS

Arts Council of England: 14 Great Peter St, London, SW1P 3NQ; tel. (845) 300-6200; e-mail chiefexecutive@artscouncil.org.uk; internet www.artscouncil.org.uk; f. 1940 as the Council for the Encouragement of Music and the Arts (CEMA), renamed Arts Council of Great Britain 1945, current name adopted 1994; nat. ind. and non-political body working to develop, sustain and promote the arts; invests public money from govt and National Lottery in arts and culture; Chief Exec. ALAN DAVEY; publ. *Development Funds*.

Arts Council of Northern Ireland: Mac-Neice House, 77 Malone Rd, Belfast, BT9 6AQ; tel. (28) 9038-5200; e-mail info@ artscouncil-ni.org; internet www .artscouncil-ni.org; f. 1943; devt and funding agency for arts; Chair. BOB COLLINS; Chief Exec. ROISÍN McDONOUGH; publ. *Article* (2 a year).

Arts Council of Wales: Bute Pl., Cardiff, CF10 5AL; tel. (29) 2044-1300; e-mail information@artscouncilofwales.org.uk; internet www.artswales.org.uk; f. 1994; funded by the Welsh Assembly Government and distributor of National Lottery funding; supports and encourages the arts; 18 mems; Chair. Prof. DAI SMITH; Chief Exec. NICK CAPALDI.

BFI Southbank: Belvedere Rd, S Bank, Waterloo, London, SE1 8XT; tel. (20) 7928-3535; internet www.bfi.org.uk; f. 1933; nat. agency; encourages and conserves film and television arts; divisions and activities: BFI Nat. Archive (*q.v.*), the Nat. Film Theatre, the London Film Festival, the London Lesbian and Gay Film Festival; education and library services, DVD and book publishing; 24,000 mems; library of 800,000 film titles; Chief Exec. AMANDA NEVILL; publ. *Sight and Sound* (12 a year, illustrated).

British Academy of Songwriters, Composers and Authors: 2nd Fl., British Music House, 26 Berners St, London, W1T 3LR; tel. (20) 7636-2929; e-mail info@basca.org.uk; internet www.basca.org.uk; f. 1999 by merger of Asscn of Professional Composers, British Academy of Songwriters, Composers and Authors, and Composers' Guild of Great Britain; represents the interests of composers and songwriters; holds music awards events; 2,000 mems; Chief Exec. VICK BAIN.

British and International Federation of Festivals: Festivals House, 198 Park Lane, Macclesfield, SK11 6UD; tel. (1625) 428297; e-mail info@federationoffestivals.org.uk; internet www.federationoffestivals.org.uk; f. 1904 as Association of Competition Festivals; current name adopted 1921; member body for amateur competitive festivals of performing arts; HQ of the Amateur Festival Movement; 700 mems; Patron HM THE QUEEN; Chair. MICHAEL SHELTON.

British Institute of Professional Photography: The Coach House, The Firs, High St, Whitchurch, Aylesbury, HP22 4SJ; tel. (1296) 642020; e-mail info@bipp.com; internet www.bipp.com; f. 1901; professional qualifying body; awards the designatory letters FBIPP, ABIPP and LBIPP; represents professional photographers and photographic technicians; trains, qualifies and supports professional photographers; 3,200 mems; Chief Exec. CHRIS HARPER; publ. *The Photographer* (4 a year).

British Society of Painters: 13 Manor Orchards, Knaresborough, North Yorkshire, HG5 0BW; tel. (1423) 540603; e-mail info@ britpaint.co.uk; internet www.britpaint.co .uk; f. 1981; holds 2 exhibitions annually; awards prizes; promotes and preserves crafts of the traditional artist; 62 mems (12 fellows,

50 mems); Pres. DAVID SHEPHERD; Dir LESLIE SIMPSON..

Attached Societies:

British Watercolour Society: 13 Manor Orchards, Knaresborough, N Yorkshire, HG5 0BW; tel. (1423) 540603; e-mail info@britpaint.co.uk; internet www.britpaint.co.uk; f. 1911; holds 2 exhibitions annually; awards prizes; 150 mems; Pres. KENNETH ELMSLEY; Dir MARGARET SIMPSON.

Society of Miniaturists: 13 Manor Orchards, Knaresborough, North Yorkshire, HG5 0BW; tel. (1423) 540603; e-mail info@britpaint.co.uk; internet www.britpaint.co.uk; f. 1895; 35 mems; holds 2 exhibitions annually; awards prizes.

Contemporary Art Society: 59 Central St, London, EC1V 3AF; tel. (20) 7017-8400; e-mail info@contemporaryartsociety.org; internet www.contemporaryartsociety.org; f. 1910; nat. non-profit agency; supports visual arts in the UK; 1,500 mems; Chair. MARK STEPHENS; Dir CAROLINE DOUGLAS.

Crafts Council: 44A Pentonville Rd, London, N1 9BY; tel. (20) 7806-2500; e-mail reference@craftscouncil.org.uk; internet www.craftscouncil.org.uk; f. 1971 as the Crafts Advisory Cttee, current name adopted 1979; directly funded by Arts Council England; nat. org. for contemporary crafts in Great Britain, offering exhibition and education programmes; collaborates with museums; research library; library of 7,200 vols, 190 periodicals; Chair. GEOFFREY CROSSICK; Exec. Dir ROSY GREENLEES; publ. *Crafts* (6 a year).

English Folk Dance and Song Society: Cecil Sharp House, 2 Regent's Park Rd, London, NW1 7AY; tel. (20) 7485-2206; e-mail info@efdss.org; internet www.efdss.org; f. 1932 formed by merger of English Folk Dance Society (EFDS) 1898 and Folk Song Society (FSS) 1911; collects, studies and preserves English folk dances and songs and other folk music; 5,000 mems; library: see under Libraries and Archives; Pres. SHIRLEY COLLINS; Chief Exec. KATY SPICER; publs *English Dance and Song* (4 a year), *Folk Music Journal* (1 a year).

Federation of British Artists: 17 Carlton House Terrace, London, SW1Y 5BD; tel. (20) 7930-6844; e-mail info@mallgalleries.com; internet www.mallgalleries.org.uk; f. 1961; consists of 8 art societies, holds art exhibitions; 650 mems; Dir LEWIS McNAUGHT..

Member Societies:

Hesketh Hubbard Art Society: 17 Carlton House Terrace, London, SW1Y 5BD; tel. (20) 7930-6844; e-mail info@mallgalleries.com; internet www.mallgalleries.org.uk; f. 1930 by the Royal Soc. of British Artists; weekly drawing sessions in Mall Galleries from life models; 200 mems; Pres. SIMON WHITTLE.

New English Art Club: 17 Carlton House Terrace, London, SW1Y 5BD; tel. (20) 7930-6844; e-mail info@mallgalleries.com; internet www.newenglishartclub.co.uk; f. 1886; exhibition held in autumn, open to all artists to submit work for selection; 87 mems; Pres. RICHARD PIKESLEY.

Pastel Society: Jack Beck House, Keasden, Clapham near Lancaster, LA2 8EY; tel. (20) 7930-6844; e-mail jack.beck@btinternet.com; internet www.thepastelsociety.org.uk; f. 1898; annual open exhibition; 65 mems; Pres. CHERYL CULVER.

Royal Institute of Oil Painters: 17 Carlton House Terrace, London, SW1Y 5BD; tel. (20) 7930-6844; e-mail enquiries@theroi.org.uk; internet www.theroi.org.uk; f. 1882 as the Institute of Painters in Oil Colours; current name adopted 1909; annual exhibition; 69 mems; Pres. IAN CRYER.

Royal Institute of Painters in Water Colours: 17 Carlton House Terrace, London, SW1Y 5BD; tel. (20) 7930-6844; e-mail honsec@royalinstituteofpaintersinwatercolours.org; internet www.royalinstituteofpaintersinwatercolours.org; f. 1831; annual exhibition; 70 mems; Pres. RONALD MADDOX.

Royal Society of British Artists: 17 Carlton House Terrace, London, SW1Y 5BD; tel. (20) 7930-6844; e-mail info@mallgalleries.com; internet www.royalsocietyofbritishartists.org.uk; f. 1823; promotes visuals arts; annual open exhibition; 110 mems (incl. 11 hon.); Pres. JAMES HORTON.

Royal Society of Marine Artists: 17 Carlton House Terrace, London, SW1Y 5BD; tel. (20) 7930-6844; e-mail info@mallgalleries.com; internet www.rsma-web.co.uk; f. 1939; annual open exhibition; 51 mems; Pres. ELIZABETH SMITH.

Royal Society of Portrait Painters: 17 Carlton House Terrace, London, SW1Y 5BD; tel. (20) 7930-6844; e-mail info@mallgalleries.com; internet www.therp.co.uk; f. 1891; annual exhibition (May); 54 mems; Pres. ALASTAIR ADAMS.

Society of Wildlife Artists: 17 Carlton House Terrace, London, SW1Y 5BD; tel. (20) 7930-6844; e-mail info@mallgalleries.com; internet www.swla.co.uk; f. 1963; annual open exhibition (September); 77 mems; Pres. HARRIET MEAD.

Guild of Church Musicians: St Katharine Cree, 86 Leadenhall St, London, EC3A 3DH; tel. (1883) 743168; e-mail johnmusicsure@orbixmail.co.uk; internet www.churchmusicians.org; f. 1888; runs courses and seminars, conducts examinations for the Archbishops' Certificate in Church Music and the Archbishops' Certificate in Public Worship, and runs a Fellowship Programme (FGCM) at postgraduate diploma level; 800 mems; Pres. Dr MARY ARCHER; Warden Rev. CANON JEREMY HASELOCK; Gen. Sec. JOHN EWINGTON; publs *Laudate* (2 or 3 a year), *Year Book*.

Heritage Crafts Association: 36 Albemarle Rd, York, YO23 1ER; tel. (19) 0454 1411; e-mail info@heritagecrafts.org.uk; internet www.heritagecrafts.org.uk; f. 2009; supports and promotes UK's heritage crafts; researches status of heritage crafts; 400 mems; Chair. ROBIN WOOD; Treas. CATHERINE DYSON.

Incorporated Association of Organists: 17 Woodland Rd, Northfield, B31 2HU; tel. (121) 475-4408; e-mail w.j.stormont@btinternet.com; internet iao.org.uk; f. 1913; 90 affiliated associations with 6,000 mems worldwide; provides education and training to organists; residential and day courses, master-classes, recitals and lectures; administers a Benevolent Fund for organists; Pres. JAMES LANCELOT; Gen Sec. MALCOLM HAWKE; publ. *Organists' Review* (4 a year).

Incorporated Society of Musicians: 10 Stratford Pl., London, W1C 1AA; tel. (20) 7629-4413; e-mail membership@ism.org; internet www.ism.org; f. 1882; professional asscn for all musicians (performers, teachers and composers); protects rights of those in the music industry; 5,000 mems; Pres. RICHARD HALLAM; Chief Exec. DEBORAH ANNETTS; publs *Yearbook and Register of Members*, *Music Journal* (6 a year).

Institute of Contemporary Arts: 12 Carlton House Terrace, London, SW1Y 5AH; tel. (20) 7930-3647; e-mail sales@ica.org.uk; internet www.ica.org.uk; f. 1946; contemporary cultural centre; supports radical art and culture; organizes exhibitions, lecture series, films, performances and musical events, etc.; 6,000 mems; Exec. Dir GREGOR MUIR; Chair. ALISON MYNERS; publ. *ICA Documents*.

Oriental Ceramic Society: POB 517, Cambridge, CB21 5BE; tel. (1223) 881328; e-mail ocs.london@btinternet.com; internet www.ocs-london.com; f. 1921; 750 mems worldwide; supports understanding of the arts of Asia; monthly lectures, discussions and handling sessions; visits to collns in the UK and abroad; Pres. ROSEMARY SCOTT; Admin. MARY PAINTER; publ. *Transactions of the Oriental Ceramic Society* (1 a year).

Plainsong and Medieval Music Society: Bangor Univ., School of Music, College Rd, Bangor, LL57 2DG Gwynedd; tel. (1248) 383895; e-mail admin@plainsong.org.uk; internet www.plainsong.org.uk; f. 1888; promotes public education in art and science of music, plainsong and medieval music, especially by pubs and performances; organizes annual conf.; 110 mems; Chair. Dr EMMA HORNBY; Sec. Prof. THOMAS SCHMIDT; publ. *Plainsong and Medieval Music* (2 a year).

Professional Photographers Association of Northern Ireland: 142 Bridge St, Portadown, BT63 5AP; tel. (28) 3835-1055; e-mail honsec@ppani.co.uk; internet www.ppani.co.uk; f. 1966; helps improve the standard of photography in the community; Pres. SIMON O'NEILL; Vice-Pres. CIARAN O'NEILL.

Royal Academy of Arts in London: Burlington House, Piccadilly, London, W1J 0BD; tel. (20) 7300-8000; e-mail webmaster@royalacademy.org.uk; internet www.royalacademy.org.uk; f. 1768; fine arts; runs art school; organizes exhibitions; 80 acads; Pres. CHRISTOPHER LE BRUN; and Chief Exec. Dr CHARLES SAUMAREZ SMITH; publs *RA Illustrated* (1 a year), *RA Magazine* (4 a year).

Royal British Society of Sculptors: 108 Old Brompton Rd, London, SW7 3RA; tel. (20) 7373-8615; e-mail info@rbs.org.uk; internet www.rbs.org.uk; f. 1905; ind. artist led org.; promotes and advances the art of sculpture; Pres. TERRY NEW; Dir ANNE RAWCLIFFE-KING; publ. *Sculpture97*.

Royal Cambrian Academy of Art: Crown Lane, Conwy, LL32 8AN; tel. (1492) 593413; e-mail rca@rcaconwy.org; internet www.rcaconwy.org; f. 1882; promotes painting, engraving, sculpture and other forms of art in Wales; 125 mems; Exhibition Officer DAVID HUNTINGTON; Gallery Admin. JOAN HALLIDAY.

Royal Musical Association: 4 Chandos Rd, Chorlton-cum-Hardy, Manchester, M21 0ST; tel. (161) 861-7542; e-mail exec@rma.ac.uk; internet www.rma.ac.uk; f. 1874, inc. 1904; dedicated to the study of music; promotes investigation and discussion of subjects connected with the art, science and history of music; 1,000 mems; Pres. Prof. MARK EVERIST; Hon. Treas. DAVID ROBERTS-JONES; publs *Journal of the Royal Musical Association* (2 a year), *Royal Musical Association Monographs* (1 a year), *Royal Musical Association Research Chronicle* (1 a year).

Royal Photographic Society of Great Britain: Fenton House, 122 Wells Rd, Bath, BA2 3AH; tel. (1225) 325733; e-mail reception@rps.org; internet www.rps.org; f. 1853; promotes photography and image-making and supports photographers; holds exhibitions and competitions for mems and non-mems; organises practical workshops and lectures; 11,000 mems; library of 20,000 vols and periodicals, permanent colln of 250,000 photographs and 8,000 items of photographic equipment; Pres. DEREK BIRCH;

publs *RPS Journal* (12 a year), *The Imaging Science Journal* (8 a year).

Royal Scottish Academy of Art and Architecture: The Mound, Edinburgh, EH2 2EL; tel. (131) 225-6671; e-mail info@royalscottishacademy.org; internet www.royalscottishacademy.org; f. 1826; encourages and supports emerging artists and architects; ind. privately funded instn; 129 mems (98 acads, 31 hon. acads); Dir COLIN R. GREENSLADE; Collns Curator SANDY WOOD.

Royal Television Society: Kildare House, 3 Dorset Rise, London, EC4Y 8EN; tel. (20) 7822-2810; e-mail info@rts.org.uk; internet www.rts.org.uk; f. 1927; advances the art of television; annual awards; 14 regional centres; over 3,000 mems; Pres. Sir PETER BAZALGETTE; Chief Exec. THERESA WISE; publ. *Television* (10 a year).

Royal Watercolour Society: Bankside Gallery, 48 Hopton St, Blackfriars, London, SE1 9JH; tel. (20) 7928-7521; e-mail info@banksidegallery.com; internet www.banksidegallery.com; f. 1804 as the Society of Painter Etchers and Engravers; rep. of watercolour painting in Britain; small archive and diploma collection; 75 mems; Pres. THOMAS PLUNKETT.

Royal West of England Academy: Queen's Rd, Clifton, Bristol, BS8 1PX; tel. (117) 973-5129; e-mail info@rwa.org.uk; internet www.rwa.org.uk; f. 1844; encourages, advances and promotes the appreciation of the fine arts by exhibitions, events and education; library of exhibition catalogues; 160 acads; Dir ALISON BEVAN.

Society for Theatre Research: c/o National Theatre Archive, 83–101 The Cut, London, SE1 8LL; e-mail contact@str.org.uk; internet www.str.org.uk; f. 1948; encourages research into the history and technique of British theatre; holds monthly lectures in winter; distributes research grants; annual theatre book prize and new scholars prize; campaigns for British theatre; 700 individual and corporate mems; Pres. TIMOTHY WEST; Chair. Prof. RICHARD FOULKES; publ. *Theatre Notebook* (3 a year).

Society of Architectural Illustration: Rosemary Cottage, Bletchinglye Lane, Rotherfield, TN6 3NN; tel. (1892) 852578; e-mail info@sai.org.uk; internet www.sai.org.uk; f. 1975; provides architects, developers and designers with high-quality visual representations for use in concept design, presentations and marketing; confers SAI (Member), FSAI (Fellow), Hon. FSAI (Hon. Fellow); 359 mems; Chair. DON COE; Admin. and Treasurer HEATHER COE.

Society of Designer Craftsmen: 24 Rivington St, London, EC2A 3DU; tel. (7531) 798983; e-mail info@societyofdesignercraftsmen.org.uk; internet www.societyofdesignercraftsmen.org.uk; f. 1887 as Arts and Crafts Exhibition Society, current name adopted 1960; annual exhibitions for mems and invited guests; 650 mems; Pres. Prof. CHRISTOPHER FRAYLING; Chair. CHRISTINE DOVE.

Society of Scribes & Illuminators: 6 Queen Sq., London, WC1N 3AT; tel. (1212) 448006; e-mail honsec@calligraphyonline.org; internet www.calligraphyonline.org; f. 1921; promotes the tradition of craftsmanship, calligraphy and fine lettering; advanced training scheme; reference library; 500 mems; Chair. ANGELA DALLEYWATER; Hon. Sec. NICHOLAS CAULKIN; publ. *The Scribe* (2 a year).

HISTORY, GEOGRAPHY AND ARCHAEOLOGY

Ancient Monuments Society: St Ann's Vestry Hall, 2 Church Entry, London, EC4V 5HB; tel. (20) 7236-3934; e-mail office@ancientmonumentssociety.org.uk; internet www.ancientmonumentssociety.org.uk; f. 1924; studies and conserves ancient monuments, historic bldgs and old craftsmanship; in partnership with the Friends of Friendless Churches; 2,200 mems; Pres. EARL OF LEICESTER; Sec. MATTHEW J. SAUNDERS; publ. *Transactions* (1 a year).

Archives and Records Association UK and Ireland: Prioryfield House, 20 Canon St, Taunton, TA1 1SW; tel. (1823) 327077; e-mail ara@archives.org.uk; internet www.archives.org.uk; f. 1947; professional body for archivists, archive conservators and records managers in UK; 2,000 mems; Chair. MARTIN TAYLOR; Chief Exec. JOHN CHAMBERS; publs *ARC Magazine* (12 a year), *Journal* (2 a year).

Baptist Historical Society: Baptist House, POB 44, 129 Broadway, Didcot, OX11 8RT; internet www.baptisthistory.org.uk; f. 1908; promotes the study of and records the history of the Baptists; assists researchers, and gives advice to churches on care and preservation of records; library administered jtly with Angus Library, Regent's Park College, Oxford; 400 mems; Pres. Rev. Dr K. G. JONES; Sec. Rev. S. L. COPSON; publ. *The Baptist Quarterly*.

British Agricultural History Society: Dept of History, Univ. of Exeter, Amory Bldg, Rennes Dr., Exeter, EX4 4RJ; tel. (1392) 263284; e-mail bahs@exeter.ac.uk; internet www.bahs.org.uk; f. 1952; promotes conservation of historically significant landscapes; holds conf.; 800 mems; Pres. Prof. MARK OVERTON; Sec. Dr NICOLA VERDON; Treas. Dr H. CROWE; publ. *Agricultural History Review* (2 a year).

British Archaeological Association: c/o John McNeill, 18 Stanley Rd, Oxford, OX4 1QZ; e-mail secretary@thebaa.org; internet www.britarch.ac.uk/baa; f. 1843; promotes archeology, art and architectural history and related disciplines; 700 mems; Hon. Pres. Dr RICHARD HALSEY; Hon. Sec. JOHN McNEILL; publs *Conference Transactions* (1 a year), *Journal* (1 a year).

British Cartographic Society: c/o Royal Geographic Soc., 1 Kensington Gore, London, SW7 2AR; tel. (115) 932-8684; e-mail admin@cartography.org.uk; internet www.cartography.org.uk; f. 1963; promotes art and science of cartography; holds meetings and publishes periodicals; 700 mems; Pres. PETER JONES; Hon. Sec. Dr TIM RIDEOUT; publs *Cartographic Journal* (4 a year), *Maplines* (3 a year).

British Numismatic Society: c/o Warburg Institute, Woburn Sq., London, WC1H 0AB; tel. (20) 7016-1802; e-mail secretary@britnumsoc.org; internet www.britnumsoc.org; f. 1903; engages in study of all forms of coinage, tokens, banknotes and medals relating to the British Isles and former British colonies; 620 mems; Pres. Dr ROGER BLAND; Sec. PETER J. PRESTON-MORLEY; publ. *British Numismatic Journal* (1 a year).

British Records Association: c/o Finsbury Library, 245 St John St, London, EC1V 4NB; tel. (20) 7833-0428; e-mail info@britishrecordsassociation.org.uk; internet www.britishrecordsassociation.org.uk; f. 1932; encourages and assists preservation, care, use and publication of historical records; annual conf., training day; 1,000 mems; Pres. RT HON. THE LORD NEUBERGER

OF ABBOTSBURY; Chair. Dr A. SMITH; publ. *Archives* (2 a year).

Cambrian Archaeological Association/ Cymdeithas Hynafiaethau Cymru: c/o Heather James, Braemar, Llangunnor Rd, Carmarthen, SA31 2PB; tel. (1267) 231793; internet www.orchardweb.co.uk/cambrians; f. 1846; examines, preserves and illustrates the ancient monuments, and remains of the history, language, manners, customs, arts and industries of Wales; 544 mems incl. 132 corporate, 47 corresp. socs; Pres. Dr SIAN REES; Gen. Sec. HEATHER JAMES; publ. *Archaeologia Cambrensis* (1 a year).

Canterbury and York Society: c/o Borthwick Institute for Archives, Univ. of York, York, YO10 5DD; e-mail cf13@york.ac.uk; internet www.canterburyandyork.org; f. 1904; publishes medieval bishops' registers and other ecclesiastical records; 249 mems; Pres. HIS GRACE THE ARCHBISHOP OF CANTERBURY; Pres. HIS GRACE THE ARCHBISHOP OF YORK; Sec. Dr C. FONGE; publ. *Medieval Bishops' Registers and other Ecclesiastical Records*.

Catholic Record Society: c/o Hon. Sec., 12 Melbourne Pl., Wolsingham, DL13 3EH; tel. (1388) 527747; e-mail membership@catholicrecordsociety.co.uk; internet catholicrecordsociety.co.uk; f. 1904; publishes documentary material on Catholic history in England and Wales since the Reformation; int. membership; holds annual conf.; Hon. Sec. Dr LEO GOOCH; publ. records and monographs.

Council for British Archaeology: St Mary's House, 66 Bootham, York, YO30 7BZ; tel. (1904) 671417; e-mail info@britarch.ac.uk; internet www.britarch.ac.uk; f. 1944; preserves historic buildings, monuments and antiquities; provides a forum for archaeological opinion; improves public knowledge of Britain's past; 600 institutional mems, 5,600 individual mems; Dir Dr MIKE HEYWORTH; publ. *British Archaeology* (6 a year).

Council of British Geography: c/o Royal Geographical Society (with the Institute of British Geographers), 1 Kensington Gore, London, SW7 2AR; tel. (20) 7591-3000; f. 1988; provides a formal org. linking all British geographical socs for the advancement of British geography; coordinates policies of mem. socs, and takes initiatives in educational, academic, research and policy matters; Chair. Prof. M. ROBERTS; Hon. Sec. Prof. P. WOOD.

Ecclesiastical History Society: Dr Sheridan Gilley, Dept of Theology and Religion, Univ. of Durham, Abbey House, Palace Green, Durham, DH1 3RS; e-mail sheridan.gilley@talktalk.net; internet www.history.ac.uk/ehsoc; f. 1961; advances the study of ecclesiastical history and maintains relations between British ecclesiastical historians and scholars abroad; organizes conf.; 960 mems; Pres. Prof. JOHN WOLFEE; Sec. STELLA FLETCHER; publs *Studies in Church History* (1 a year), *Subsidia* (irregular).

Economic History Society: John Wiley & Sons Ltd, PO Box 739, Chichester, PO19 9QH; tel. (1865) 778171; e-mail cs-membership@wiley.com; internet www.ehs.org.uk; f. 1927; supports research and teaching in economic and social history; holds annual conf.; provides fellowships; training course for postgraduate students; 1,300 mems; Pres. Sir RICHARD TRAINOR; Hon. Sec. Dr PETER W. HOWLETT; publ. *Economic History Review* (4 a year).

Egypt Exploration Society: 3 Doughty Mews, London, WC1N 2PG; tel. (20) 7242-1880; e-mail contact@ees.ac.uk; internet www.ees.ac.uk; f. 1882 as the Egypt Exploration Fund; excavation in Egypt and publ. of work, lectures and study days; office in Cairo; 3,000 mems; library of 25,000 vols, journals and pamphlets; Pres. Prof. ALAN B LLOYD; Chair. Dr AIDAN DODSON; publs *Archaeological Survey* (irregular), *Egyptian Archaeology* (2 a year), *Excavation Memoirs* (irregular), *Graeco-Roman Memoirs* (1 a year), *Journal of Egyptian Archaeology* (1 a year).

English Place-Name Society: Institute for Name-Studies, School of English, University of Nottingham, University Park, Nottingham, NG7 2RD; tel. (115) 951-5919; e-mail name-studies@nottingham.ac.uk; internet www.nottingham.ac.uk/english/ins; f. 1923; attached to Univ. of Nottingham; engages in research of place-names and personal names; 500 mems; Hon. Dir JAYNE CARROLL; publ. *Journal* (1 a year).

Friends Historical Society: c/o the library, Friends House, 173 Euston Rd, London, NW1 2BJ; e-mail secretary@f-h-s.org.uk; internet www.f-h-s.org.uk; f. 1903; engages in research of Quaker history; 400 mems; Membership Sec. GIL SKIDMORE; publ. *Journal* (1 a year).

Geographical Association: 160 Solly St, Sheffield, S1 4BF; tel. (114) 296-0088; e-mail info@geography.org.uk; internet www .geography.org.uk; f. 1893; advances geographical knowledge and understanding through education; holds conf. and publishes professional journals; 6,000 mems; Pres. BOB DIGBY; publs *Geography* (3 a year), *Teaching Geography* (3 a year), *Primary Geographer* (3 a year).

Hakluyt Society: c/o Map Library, British Library, 96 Euston Rd, London, NW1 2DB; tel. (1428) 641850; e-mail office@hakluyt .com; internet www.hakluyt.com; f. 1846; promotes world travel history; publishes primary source material of early exploratory voyages, travel and other geographical records; 1,500 mems; Pres. MICHAEL K. BARRITT.

Harleian Society: c/o College of Arms, Queen Victoria St, London, EC4V 4BT; tel. (20) 7236-7728; e-mail info@harleian.org.uk; internet harleian.org.uk; f. 1869, inc. 1902; transcribes, prints and publishes Heraldic Visitations of Counties, Parish Registers and MSS relating to genealogy, family history and heraldry; known for its publications; 300 subscribers; Chair. T. WOODCOCK; Hon. Sec. and Treas. TIMOTHY DUKE (Chester Herald of Arms).

Heraldry Society: 53 Hitchin St, Baldock, SG7 6AQ; tel. (1869) 246188; e-mail honsec@ theheraldrysociety.com; internet www .theheraldrysociety.com; f. 1947; promotes and advances knowledge of heraldry, armoury, chivalry, genealogy and allied subjects; provides forum for research and lectures; 700 mems; Chair. Dr PAUL FOX; publs *The Coat of Arms* (2 a year), *The Heraldry Gazette* (4 a year).

Historic Buildings and Monuments Commission for England (English Heritage): 1 Waterhouse Sq., 138 - 142 Holborn, London, EC1N 2ST; tel. (870) 333-1181; e-mail customers@english-heritage.org.uk; internet www.english-heritage.org.uk; f. 1983; executive non-departmental public body; protects and promotes historic buildings and landscapes throughout England; library of 60,000 vols, journals and reports; Chair. Sir LAURIE MAGNUS; Chief Exec. SIMON THURLEY; publs *Buildings at Risk Register* (1 a year), *Conservation Bulletin* (4 a year), *Register of Parks and Gardens*.

Attached Organizations:

Centre for Archaeology: Fort Cumberland, Fort Cumberland Rd, Eastney, Portsmouth, PO4 9LD; tel. (23) 9285-6700; e-mail cfa@english-heritage.org.uk; provides a resource for English archaeology; publishes books, periodicals and monographs.

English Heritage Archives: The Engine House, Fire Fly Ave, Swindon, SN2 2EH; tel. (1793) 414700; e-mail archive@ english-heritage.org.uk; internet www .english-heritage.org.uk/nmr; f. 1908; over 12m. photographs, drawings, reports and publications; library of 60,000 vols, 400 current journals.

Historical Association: 59A Kennington Park Rd, London, SE11 4JH; tel. (20) 7735-3901; e-mail enquiries@history.org.uk; internet www.history.org.uk; f. 1906; advances the study and teaching of history; colln of history textbooks; 60 brs nationally; 6,500 mems; Pres. Prof. JACKIE EALES; Chief Exec. REBECCA SULLIVAN; publs *History* (4 a year), *Primary History* (3 a year), *Teaching History* (4 a year), *The Historian* (4 a year).

Honourable Society of Cymmrodorion: POB 55178, London, N12 2AY; tel. (20) 7631-0502; e-mail membership@cymmrodorion .org; internet www.cymmrodorian.org; f. 1751, Royal Charter 1951; promotes the practice and devt of Wales-related literature, arts and sciences; 900 mems; Patron HRH THE PRINCE OF WALES; Pres. Prof. PRYS MORGAN; Hon. Sec. PETER JEFFREYS; publs *Dictionary of Welsh Biography*, *Transactions* (1 a year).

Huguenot Society of Great Britain and Ireland: The Huguenot Society, POB 444, Ruislip, Middlesex, HA4 4GU; tel. (20) 6795-199; e-mail president@huguenotsociety.org .uk; internet www.huguenotsociety.org.uk; f. 1885; promotes the publication and exchange of knowledge about the Huguenots in the UK and Ireland; 1,385 mems (9 hon. fellows, 1,376 ordinary fellows); library of 5,500 vols, colln of MSS and rare books, genealogical material; The Huguenot Archive; Pres. MICHAEL COURAGE; Hon. Sec. ANNE NUGENT; Librarian LUCY GWYNN; publs *Huguenot Society Journal* (1 a year), *Quarto Series* (irregular), *Proceedings* (1 a year).

Institute of Heraldic and Genealogical Studies: 79–82 Northgate, Canterbury CT1 1BA; tel. (1227) 768664; e-mail admin@ihgs .ac.uk; internet www.ihgs.ac.uk; f. 1961; provides courses in family history and related subjects; academic facilities for training and research in the study of the history and structure of the family; spec. collns; 250 mems; library of 35,000 vols, 20,000 case studies; Pres. Rt Hon. THE EARL OF LYTTON; Prin. Dr R. C. F. BAKER; publs *Atlas and Index of Parishes*, *Family History* (4 a year), *Syllabus of Study*, *Teacher's Aids*.

Jewish Historical Society of England: 33 Seymour Pl., London, W1H 5AP; tel. (20) 7723-5852; e-mail info@jhse.org; internet www.jhse.org; f. 1893; Jewish Studies Library, University College, London; holds monthly meetings with lectures on Anglo-Jewish history; 800 mems; Pres. Dr PIET VAN BOXEL; Chair. DAVID JACOBS; publ. *Transactions* (1 a year).

London and Middlesex Archaeological Society: c/o Museum of London, London Wall, London, EC2Y 5HN; tel. (20) 7410-2228; e-mail kthomas@mola.org.uk; internet www.lamas.org.uk; f. 1855; promotes research into London's archaeology, local history and historic buildings; 644 mems; Pres. Prof. MARTIN BIDDLE; Hon. Sec. KAREN THOMAS; publ. *Transactions* (1 a year).

London Record Society: c/o The Membership Secretary, Hewton Farmhouse, Bere Alston, Yelverton, Devon, PL20 7BW; e-mail londonrecordsoc@btinternet.com; internet www.londonrecordsociety.org.uk; f. 1964; publishes transcripts, abstracts and lists of the primary sources for the history of London; encourages public interest in archives relating to London; 239 mems; Pres. The Rt. Hon. THE LORD MAYOR OF LONDON; Hon. Sec. Dr HELEN BRADLEY.

London Topographical Society: 103 Harestone Valley Rd, Caterham, CR3 6HR; tel. (1883) 337813; e-mail mike.wicksteed@ btinternet.com; internet www.topsoc.org; f. 1880; publishes material to assist in the study and appreciation of London's history, growth and topography, incl. reproductions of historic maps and views of London; 1,200 mems; Patron HRH THE DUKE OF EDINBURGH; Hon. Sec. MIKE WICKSTEED; publs *London Topographical Record* (every 5 years), maps, views and books.

Manchester Geographical Society: Meadowbank, Ringley Rd, Radcliffe, Manchester, M26 1FW; tel. (161) 723-1433; e-mail secretary@mangeogsoc.org.uk; internet www .mangeogsoc.org.uk; f. 1884; encourages geographical research on NW England; lecture programme, funding research, publishing; 100 mems; library of 4,500 vols (now on permanent loan to the Univ. of Manchester); Chair. COLIN HARRISON; Hon. Sec. Dr PAUL HINDLE; publ. *North West Geography* (2 a year, online).

Monumental Brass Society: c/o Rear-Admiral Michael Harris, King's Lodge, Church St, Whitchurch, RG28 7AS; e-mail mgtharris@btinternet.com; internet www .mbs-brasses.co.uk; f. 1887 preserves and records monumental brasses; compiles and publishes a list of all extant and lost brasses, English and foreign; Pres. H. M. STUCHFIELD; Hon. Sec. C. O. STEER; publs *Portfolio* (irregular), *Transactions* (1 a year).

Palestine Exploration Fund: 2 Hinde Mews, Marylebone Lane, London, W1U 2AA; tel. (20) 7935-5379; e-mail execsec@pef .org.uk; internet www.pef.org.uk; f. 1865; engages in study of Palestine and the Levant (modern-day Syria, Lebanon, Jordan and Israel); annual grants to scholars; 900 subscribers; library of 5,000 vols; 40,000 photographs of Palestine, Jordan and Syria since 1850; Chair. JOHN R. BARTLETT; Exec. and Curator FELICITY COBBING; Librarian ADAM FRAZER; publ. *Palestine Exploration Quarterly* (4 a year).

Prehistoric Society: c/o Institute of Archaeology, University College London, 31–34 Gordon Sq., London, WC1H 0PY; e-mail prehistoric@ucl.ac.uk; internet www .prehistoricsociety.org; f. 1935; promotes prehistoric research; awards and grants; 1,500 mems; Pres. Dr ALISON SHERIDAN; Hon. Sec. Dr JOSH POLLARD; publs *Past* (3 a year), *Proceedings of the Prehistoric Society* (1 a year).

Regional Studies Association: 25 Clinton Pl., Seaford, BN25 1NP; tel. (1323) 899698; e-mail info@rsa-ls.ac.uk; internet www .regionalstudies.org; f. 1965; an interdisciplinary group; research on economic devt and growth, governance and problems of equity and injustice; holds meetings, confs and seminars; organizes study groups; 6 brs; 7 int. sections and present in more than 40 countries; 850 individual, 200 corporate mems, including govt depts, ministries, local authorities, educational institutions, etc.; Chair. JAMIE PECK; Hon. Sec. DANIELA CARL; publs *Regional Insights* (1 a year), *Regional Studies* (10 a year), *Regions* (4 a year), *Special Economic Analysis* (4 a year).

Royal Geographical Society (with the Institute of British Geographers): 1 Kensington Gore, London, SW7 2AR; tel. (20) 7591-3000; e-mail info@rgs.org; internet www.rgs.org; f. 1830; advances geography and supports its practitioners in the UK and across the world; 14,000 mems; library of 150,000 books, 1m. maps and charts, 4,500 atlases, 500,000 mid-19th-century to contemporary pictures and photographs; Pres. HRH THE DUKE OF KENT; Pres. Prof. Dame JUDITH REES; publs *Area* (4 a year), *Geographical* (12 a year), *Geographical Journal* (4 a year), *Transactions* (4 a year).

Royal Historical Society: Univ. College London, Gower St, London, WC1E 6BT; tel. (20) 7387-7532; e-mail royalhistsoc@ucl.ac.uk; internet www.royalhistoricalsociety.org; f. 1868; researches and presents history; archives, libraries, museums; 3,000 mems; library of 3,000 vols; 534,000 records; Pres. Prof. PETER MANDLER; Hon. Sec. Dr ADAM SMITH; publs *Transactions* (1 a year), *Camden*.

Royal Numismatic Society: c/o Dept of Coins and Medals, British Museum, Great Russell St, London, WC1B 3DG; tel. (20) 7323-8272; e-mail rns_webeditor@hotmail.co.uk; internet www.numismatics.org.uk; f. 1836; lectures and publs on classical, Asian, medieval and modern coins, paper money, tokens and medals; 1,000 mems; library of 7,000 vols; Pres. ANDREW BURNETT; Librarian ROBERT THOMPSON; publ. *Numismatic Chronicle* (1 a year).

Royal Philatelic Society London: 41 Devonshire Pl., London, W1G 6JY; tel. (20) 7486-1044; e-mail secretary@rpsl.org.uk; internet www.rpsl.org.uk; f. 1869; 2,055 mems; library of 10,000 vols, 300 periodicals, 2,250 stamp catalogues, 11,000 auction catalogues, monograms and handbooks; Pres. CHRISTOPHER KING; Hon. Sec. WILLIAM HEDLEY; publ. *The London Philatelist* (10 a year).

Royal Scottish Geographical Society: Lord John Murray House, 15–19 North Port, Blackfriars, Perth, PH1 5LU; tel. (1738) 455050; e-mail enquiries@rsgs.org; internet www.rsgs.org; f. 1884; provides research grants and support to scientific expeditions; 14 regional centres; library of 25,000 vols, 20,000 journals, 100,000 35mm colour slides of geographical subjects, over 8,000 antique glass lantern slides, 100,000 maps; 2,200 mems; Chief Exec. MIKE ROBINSON; Chair. J. BARRIE BROWN; publ. *The Scottish Geographical Journal* (4 a year).

Scottish History Society: c/o Dr Annie Tindley, Dept of History, Univ. of Dundee Dundee, DD1 4HN; e-mail siobhan.talbott@manchester.ac.uk; internet www.scottishhistorysociety.com; f. 1886; prints unpublished documents illustrating the history of Scotland; 800 mems; Pres. Prof. ROGER MASON; Hon. Sec. Dr SIOBHAN TALBOTT.

Society for Army Historical Research: c/o Lt Col David Saunders, Wychwood, Scotland Lane, Haslemere, GU27 3AB; internet www.sahr.co.uk; f. 1921; studies British Army history and traditions; awards Templer Medal Book Prize; 1,000 mems; Pres. Field Marshal Sir JOHN CHAPPLE; Hon. Sec. GEORGE EVELYN; publ. *Journal* (4 a year).

Society for Medieval Archaeology: c/o Dept of Archaeology, Univ. of Sheffield, Northgate House, W St, Sheffield, S1 4ET; tel. (114) 222-2920; e-mail d.m.hadley@sheffield.ac.uk; internet www.medievalarchaeology.org; f. 1957; studies archaeology of the post-Roman period; organizes regular confs; offers funds for research; 1,500 mems; library of 57 vols; Pres. MARK GARDINER; Hon. Sec. Prof. DAWN HADLEY;

Hon. Treas. Prof. STEPHEN RIPPON; Hon. Editor Dr OLIVER CREIGHTON; publs *Medieval Archaeology* (1 a year), *Monograph Series* (irregular).

Society for Nautical Research: 14 Milton Place, Gravesend, Kent, DA12 2BT; tel. (1482) 465183; e-mail honsec@snr.org.uk; internet www.snr.org.uk; f. 1910; encourages research into matters relating to seafaring and shipbuilding; 1,600 mems; Pres. HRH THE DUKE OF YORK; Chair. Sir KENNETH EATON; Sec. Dr A. BYRNE MCLEOD; publ. *The Mariners' Mirror* (4 a year).

Society for Post-Medieval Archaeology Ltd: c/o David Cranstone, 267 Kells Lane, Low Fell, Gateshead, NE9 5HU; tel. (191) 482-1037; e-mail cranconsult@btinternet.com; internet www.spma.org.uk; f. 1966; 400 mems; Pres. Dr DAVID CALDWELL; Sec. Dr CHRIS KING; publ. *Post-Medieval Archaeology* (3 a year).

Society for Renaissance Studies: c/o Michelle O'Malley, Centre for Research in the History of Art, University of Sussex, Falmer, Brighton, BN1 9RQ; e-mail m.o-malley@sussex.ac.uk; internet www.rensoc.org.uk; f. 1967; 550 mems; Hon. Chair. Prof. PETER MACK; Hon. Sec. Dr GABRIELE NEHER; publ. *Renaissance Studies* (4 a year).

Society of Antiquaries of London: Burlington House, Piccadilly, London, W1J 0BE; tel. (20) 7479-7080; e-mail admin@sal.org.uk; internet www.sal.org.uk; f. 1707; 2,900 mems; library: see Libraries and Archives; Gen. Sec. JOHN LEWIS; publs *Archaeologia* (1 a year), *The Antiquaries Journal* (1 a year).

Society of Antiquaries of Scotland: c/o National Museums Scotland, Chambers St, Edinburgh, EH1 1JF; tel. (131) 247-4133; e-mail admin@socantscot.org; internet www.socantscot.org; f. 1780; pursues the study of antiquities and history of Scotland through publications, lectures, conferences, workshops and seminars; offers grants and awards; 3,000 mems; Dir Dr SIMON GILMOUR; publs *Proceedings of the Society of Antiquaries of Scotland* (1 a year), *Scottish Archaeological Internet Reports* (online).

Society of Genealogists: 14 Charterhouse Bldgs, Goswell Rd, London, EC1M 7BA; tel. (20) 7251-8799; e-mail librarian@sog.org.uk; internet www.sog.org.uk; f. 1911; promotes the study, science and knowledge of genealogy and family history; genealogical library and education centre in Clerkenwell, London; 11,000 mems; library of 134,000 vols (incl. MSS collns, microforms and digital media); Chair. WILLIAM BORTRICK; Head of Library Services TIM LAWRENCE; publ. *Genealogists' Magazine* (4 a year).

Ulster Archaeological Society: c/o School of Geography, Archaeology and Palaeoecology, Queen's Univ. Belfast, Belfast, BT7 1NN; e-mail ulsterarchaeolsoc@gmail.com; internet www.uas.society.qub.ac.uk; f. 1853; promotes education in archaeology and history of Ulster; organizes public lectures and field trips; survey group; 300 mems; Pres. BARRIE HARTWELL; Hon. Sec. KEN PULLIN; publ. *Ulster Journal of Archaeology* (1 a year).

United Reformed Church History Society: Westminster College, Madingley Rd, Cambridge, CB3 0AA; tel. (1223) 730620; e-mail admin@westminster.cam.ac.uk; internet www.westminster.cam.ac.uk/index.php/urc-history-society; f. 1972; incorporates the Congregational Historical Soc. (f. 1899), the Presbyterian Historical Soc. of England (f. 1913) and the Churches of Christ Historical Soc. (f. 1981); promotes history of the denominations; 250 mems; library of 5,000

vols; Sec. MARGARET THOMPSON; publ. *Journal* (2 a year).

Wesley Historical Society: c/o Dr John A. Hargreaves, 7 Haugh Shaw Rd, Halifax, HX1 3AH; tel. (1422) 250780; e-mail generalsecretary@wesleyhistoricalsociety.org.uk; internet www.wesleyhistoricalsociety.org.uk; f. 1893; promotes study of history and literature of Methodism; annual lecture, supporting programme; residential conf. every 3 years; access to network of regional historical socs; library at Westminster Institute of Education, Oxford Univ.; 600 mems; Pres. Prof. EDWARD ROYLE; Gen. Sec. Dr JOHN A. HARGREAVES; publ. *Proceedings* (3 a year).

LANGUAGE AND LITERATURE

Alliance Française: 1 Dorset Sq., London, NW1 6PU; tel. (20) 7723-6439; e-mail info@alliancefrancaise.org.uk; internet www.alliancefrancaise.org.uk; offices in Bath, Belfast, Bristol, Cambridge, Exeter, Glasgow, Jersey, Loughborough, Manchester, Milton Keynes, Oxford, Totnes, York; Dir CHRYSTEL HUG.

Alliance of Literary Societies: 59 Bryony Rd, Birmingham, B29 4BY; tel. (121) 475-1805; e-mail l.j.curry@bham.ac.uk; internet www.allianceofliterarysocieties.org.uk; f. 1973; provides a voice for literary and authors' socs in defence of sites and legacies of literary importance; 125 mem. socs; Pres. JENNY UGLOW; Chair. LINDA CURRY; publ. *ALSo* (1 a year).

Association for Language Learning: Univ. of Leicester, University Rd, Leicester, LE1 7RH; tel. (116) 229-7600; e-mail info@all-languages.org.uk; internet www.all-languages.org.uk; f. 1990; offers help, in-service training and support to language teachers; professional devt activities; 4,500 mems; Dir LINDA PARKER; publs *Deutsch: Lehren und Lernen* (2 a year), *Francophonie* (2 a year), *Language Learning Journal* (3 a year), *Languages Today* (3 a year), *Language World* (4 a year), *Rusistika* (1 a year), *Tuttitalia* (1 a year), *Vida Hispánica* (2 a year).

Association of British Science Writers: 76 Glebe Lane, Barming, ME16 9BD; e-mail info@absw.org.uk; internet www.absw.org.uk; f. 1947; works to improve the standard of science journalism in the UK; study trips, briefings, workshops, lunches and social events; 600 mems; Pres. MARTIN INCE (acting); Sec. JULIA DURBIN; publ. *The Science Reporter* (online, 4 a year).

British Association for Applied Linguistics: c/o Dovetail Management Consultancy, POB 6688, London, SE15 3WB; tel. (20) 7639-0090; e-mail admin@baal.org.uk; internet www.baal.org.uk; f. 1967; promotes study of language and applied linguistics; 750 individual mems, 30 mem. publishers and univ. depts; Chair. GREG MYERS; Sec. DAWN KNIGHT; publ. *Applied Linguistics* (4 a year).

British Association of Academic Phoneticians: Dept of English Language and Applied Linguistics, Univ. of Reading, Whiteknights, Reading, RG6 6AA; tel. (118) 378-6089; internet www.baap.ac.uk; f. 1984; encourages teaching phonetics in higher education, and application of phonetic knowledge in speech and language therapy, speech technology and forensic science; 150 mems; Pres. Dr FRANCIS NOLAN; Hon. Sec. Dr JANE E. SETTER; Archivist Dr MICHAEL ASHBY.

Brontë Society: The Brontë Parsonage Museum, Church St, Haworth, BD22 8DR; tel. (1535) 642323; e-mail bronte@bronte.org.uk; internet www.bronte.org.uk; f. 1893, inc.

1902; collects Brontë manuscripts and artefacts, administers Brontë Parsonage Museum; 3,000 mems; Exec. Dir Prof. ANN SUMNER; Chair. SALLY MCDONALD; publ. *Brontë Studies* (3 a year).

Charles Lamb Society: BM Elia, London, WC1N 3XX; internet www.charleslambsociety.com; f. 1935; studies the life, works and times of Charles and Mary Lamb; publishes essays and lectures of interest to Elians; colln of Eliana at Guildhall Library, London; 300 mems; Pres. DUNCAN WU; Chair. and Treas. NICK POWELL; publ. *The Charles Lamb Bulletin* (2 a year).

Chartered Institute of Linguists: 4th Fl., Dunstan House, 14A St Cross St, London, EC1N 8XA; tel. (20) 7940-3100; e-mail info@iol.org.uk; internet www.iol.org.uk; f. 1910; language assessment and awarding organization; offers Ofqual (Office of Qualification and Examination Regulation) accredited qualifications; 6,000 mems; library of 6,000 vols; Pres. Dr NICHOLAS BOWEN; Exec. Dir ALAN PEACOCK; publ. *The Linguist* (6 a year).

Classical Association: Senate House, Malet St, London, WC1E 7HU; tel. (1923) 239300; e-mail office@classicalassociation.org; internet www.classicalassociation.org; f. 1903; promotes education and research in languages, literature and civilization of ancient Greece and Rome; 3,500 mems; Pres. MARTHA KEARNEY; Chair. Prof. R. K. GIBSON; publs *CA News* (2 a year), *Classical Quarterly* (2 a year), *Classical Review* (2 a year), *Greece and Rome* (2 a year).

Dickens Fellowship: Dickens House, 48 Doughty St, London, WC1N 2LX; tel. (20) 7405-2127; e-mail postbox@dickensfellowship.org; internet www.dickensfellowship.org; f. 1902; promotes the knowledge and appreciation of Charles Dickens' works; assists in the preservation and purchase of buildings and objects associated with Dickens or mentioned in his works; museum; 7,000 mems; Pres. Prof. JENNY HARTLEY; Hon. Sec.-Gen. LEE AULT; Hon. Gen. Sec PAUL GRAHAM; publs *Mr Dick's Kite* (3 a year), *The Dickensian* (3 a year).

Early English Text Society: Lady Margaret Hall, Oxford, OX2 6QA; internet www.eets.org.uk; f. 1864; publishes Old and Middle English literary texts; 900 mems; Hon. Dir Prof. VINCENT GILLESPIE; Exec. Sec. Prof. DANIEL WAKELIN.

English Association: Univ. of Leicester, Leicester, LE1 7RH; tel. (116) 229-7622; e-mail engassoc@le.ac.uk; internet www.le.ac.uk/engassoc; f. 1906; promotes knowledge and appreciation of the English language and its literature through confs, lectures and publs; 1,000 mems; Pres. and Chair. ADRIAN BARLOW; Treas. Prof. GORDON CAMPBELL; publs *English* (4 a year), *English 4–11* (3 a year), *Essays and Studies*, *The Use of English* (3 a year), *The Year's Work in Critical and Cultural Theory*, *The Year's Work in English Studies*.

English Centre of International PEN: Free Word Centre, 60 Farringdon Rd, London, EC1R 3GA; tel. (20) 7324-2535; e-mail enquiries@englishpen.org; internet www.englishpen.org; f. 1921; 990 mems; Dir JO GLANVILLE.

English Speaking Board: 9 Hattersley Court, Burscough Rd, Ormskirk, L39 2AY; tel. (1695) 573439; e-mail admin@esbuk.org; internet www.esbuk.org; f. 1953; promotes and encourages all aspects of spoken English; individual and corporate mems in 34 countries; arranges courses and examinations in spoken English at all levels; 450 mems; Hon. Pres. JOCELYN BELL; Chair. QUENTIN OLIVER (acting); publ. *Speaking English* (2 a year).

Francis Bacon Society Inc.: c/o G. N. Salway, Flat 1, Lee House, 75A Effra Rd, London, SW19 8PS; tel. (20) 8542-4689; internet www.baconsocietyinc.org; f. 1886; registered charity; studies the works and life of Francis Bacon; library of 1,300 vols and pamphlets; Pres. PETER A. WELSFORD; Sec. GERALD N. SALWAY; publ. *Baconiana*.

Goethe-Institut: 50 Princes Gate, Exhibition Rd, London, SW7 2PH; tel. (20) 7596-4000; e-mail info@london.goethe.org; internet www.goethe.de/london; offers courses and exams in German language; promotes German culture; offers cultural exchange with Germany;; attached centres in Glasgow and Manchester; library of 17,000 vols; Dir ANGELA KAYA.

Institute of Translation and Interpreting: Suite 165, Milton Keynes Business Centre, Foxhunter Dr., Linford Wood, Milton Keynes, MK14 6GD; tel. (1908) 325250; e-mail info@iti.org.uk; internet www.iti.org.uk; f. 1986; promotes high standards in translation and interpreting; provides information on these services to govt, industry; support translators and interpreters in their own professional devt; 3,000 mems; Chair. IWAN DAVIES.

Instituto Cervantes: 102 Eaton Sq., London, SW1W 9AN; tel. (20) 7235-0353; e-mail cenlon@cervantes.es; internet londres.cervantes.es; f. 1991; offers courses and exams in Spanish language; promotes Spanish culture; offers cultural exchange with Spain and Spanish-speaking Latin and Central America; attached centre in Manchester; library of 20,000 vols, 33,000 documents; Dir JULIO CRESPO MACLENNAN.

Joseph Conrad Society: c/o POSK, 238–246 King St, London, W6 0RF; e-mail theconradian@aol.com; internet www.josephconradsociety.org; f. 1973; provides a forum and resource for scholars of Conrad's work; 200 mems; library of 800 vols; Hon. Sec. Dr HUGH EPSTEIN; publ. *The Conradian* (2 a year).

Kipling Society: 31, Brookside, Billericay, CM11 1DT; tel. (20) 7286-(77)1432 6532; e-mail john.lambert1@btinternet.com; internet www.kipling.org.uk; f. 1927; interested in the prose and verse, and life and times, of Rudyard Kipling; organizes 5 meetings a year and a luncheon with guest speakers; awards the Kipling Essay Prize; 500 mems; Pres. Lt. Col. R.C. AYERS; Hon. Sec. JOHN LAMBERT; publ. *The Kipling Journal* (4 a year).

Linguistics Association of Great Britain: c/o Dr Andrew Hippisley, School of Electronics and Physical Sciences, University of Surrey, Guildford, GU2 7XH; e-mail lagb.office@gmail.com; internet www.lagb.org.uk; f. 1959; 600 mems; Pres. Prof. APRIL MCMAHON; Hon. Sec. Dr AD NEELEMAN; publ. *Journal of Linguistics* (2 a year).

Llenyddiaeth Cymru/Literature Wales: Fourth Floor, Cambrian Bldgs, Mount Stuart Sq., Cardiff, CF10 5FL; tel. (29) 2047-2266; e-mail post@literaturewales.org; internet www.literaturewales.org; f. 2011; promotes interests of writers and literatures of Wales; 950 mems (300 in Welsh-language section, 650 in English-language section); Chief Exec. LLEUCU SIENCYN; Chair Dr DAMIAN WALFORD-DAVIES; publ. *Taliesin* (3 a year, in Welsh).

Malone Society: c/o Dr Conor Wyer, Institute of English Studies, Univ. of London, Senate House, Malet St, London, WC1E 7HU; tel. (20) 7862-8679; e-mail sonia.massai@kcl.ac.uk; internet www.malonesociety.com; f. 1906; produces copies of early plays; advances education in English drama; grants fellowships and bursaries; 670

mems; Chair. LEAH SCRAGG; Exec. Sec. Prof. KATHARINE CRAIK.

Philological Society: School of Oriental and African Studies, Univ. of London, Thornhaugh St, Russell Sq., London, WC1H 0XG; e-mail secretary@philsoc.org.uk; internet www.philsoc.org.uk; f. 1842, inc. 1879; investigates and promotes study and knowledge of the structure, affinities and history of languages; 832 mems; Pres. Prof. W. AYRES-BENNETT; Sec Prof. P. RUSSELL; publ. *Transactions* (3 a year).

Poetry Society: 22 Betterton St, London, WC2H 9BX; tel. (20) 7240-9880; e-mail info@poetrysociety.org.uk; internet www.poetrysociety.org.uk; f. 1909; promotes study, appreciation and enjoyment of poetry; organizes poetry reading, educational activities; awards the Foyle Young Poets of Year prize; 4,000 mems; Dir JUDITH PALMER; publs *Poetry News* (4 a year), *Poetry Review* (4 a year).

Royal Society of Literature of the United Kingdom: Somerset House, Strand, London, WC2R 1LA; tel. (20) 7845-4678; e-mail info@rslit.org; internet www.rslit.org; f. 1820; lectures and literary discussions; awards 3 prizes annually; master classes with the Booker Prize Foundation; 900 mems; Chair. ANNE CHISHOLM; Dir MAGGIE FERGUSSON; publ. *The RSL Review* (2 a year).

Society for the Promotion of Hellenic Studies: Senate House, Malet St, London, WC1E 7HU; tel. (20) 7862-8730; e-mail office@hellenicsociety.org.uk; internet www.hellenicsociety.org.uk; f. 1879; engages in promotion of hellenic studies; advances the study of Greek language, literature, history, art and archaeology in the Ancient, Byzantine and Modern periods; 1,400 mems; library: see under entry for Joint Library of the Hellenic and Roman Societies; Pres. Prof. A. W. GOMME; Hon. Sec. Dr MARGARET MOUNTFORD; publs *Journal of Hellenic Studies* (1 a year), *Archaeological Reports* (1 a year).

Society for the Promotion of Roman Studies: Senate House, Malet St, London, WC1E 7HU; tel. (20) 7862-8727; e-mail office@romansociety.org; internet www.romansociety.org; f. 1910; promotes the study of Rome and the Roman Empire; 2,000 mems; library: see under Libraries and Archives; Pres. Prof. DOMINIC RATHBONE; Hon. Sec. F. JANE FISHER-HUNT; Hon. Treas. Dr PHILIP KAY; publs *Britannia* (1 a year), *Journal of Roman Studies* (1 a year).

Society for the Study of Medieval Languages and Literature: c/o Dr Corinne Saunders, Department of English Studies, University of Durham, Hallgarth House, 77 Hallgarth St, Durham, DH1 3AY; e-mail ssmll@history.ox.ac.uk; internet www.mod-langs.ox.ac.uk/ssmll; f. 1932; disseminates research through its journal and monographs; organizes confs; annual essay prize; Pres. Dr ANTHONY LAPPIN; Hon. Sec. Dr SIMON HOROBIN; publ. *Medium Ævum* (2 a year).

Society of Authors: 84 Drayton Gardens, London, SW10 9SB; tel. (20) 7373-6642; e-mail info@societyofauthors.org; internet www.societyofauthors.org; f. 1884; promotes and protects the rights of authors; 9,000 mems; Chief Exec. NICOLA SOLOMON; publ. *The Author* (4 a year).

H. G. Wells Society: c/o Dr. Emma V. Miller, Durham Univ., Room A 69, Elvet Riverside, New Elvet, Durham, DH1 3JT; internet hgwellsusa.50megs.com; f. 1960; promotes interest in the life, work and thought of H. G. Wells; organizes annual conf. (September); 200 mems; library of 300 vols (H. G. Wells Colln, Library, London

Metropolitan Univ.–N London campus); Treas. PAUL ALLEN; publ. *The Wellsian* (1 a year).

MEDICINE

Academy of Medical Sciences: 41 Portland Pl., London, W1B 1QH; tel. (20) 3176-2150; e-mail info@acmedsci.ac.uk; internet www.acmedsci.ac.uk; f. 1998; promotes medical science and its translation; influences policy to improve health and wealth; promotes research and provides information; 1,017 mems; Pres. Prof. Sir JOHN TOOKE; Registrar Prof. MOIRA WHYTE.

Anatomical Society: Dept of Anatomy and Human Sciences, King's College (Guy's Campus), Room HB5.9N, Hodgkin Bldg, London, SE1 1UL; tel. (20) 7848-8234; e-mail anatsoc@portland-services.com; internet www.anatsoc.org.uk; f. 1887; promotes, develops and advances anatomical and related sciences; research into the anatomical and related sciences; publishes research relevant to anatomical sciences; promotes and advances education in the anatomical sciences; 400 mems; Pres. Prof. T. CLIVE LEE; Exec. Admin. MARY-ANNE PIGGOTT; publs *Aging Cell* (4 a year), *Journal of Anatomy* (12 a year).

The Worshipful Society of Apothecaries of London: Apothecaries' Hall, Black Friars Lane, London, EC4V 6EJ; tel. (20) 7236-1189; e-mail examoffice@apothecaries.org; internet www.apothecaries.org; f. 1617 by King James I; offers education in medical sciences; grants a registrable medical qualification; archives; 1,600 mems; Master Prof. P. J. H. TOOLEY; Registrar JENNIFER MACLEAN.

Association for the Study of Medical Education: 12 Queen St, Edinburgh, EH2 1JE; tel. (131) 225-9111; e-mail info@asme.org.uk; internet www.asme.org.uk; f. 1957; 1,200 individual mems, 85 corporate mems; CEO NICKY PENDER; publs *Medical Education* (12 a year), *The Clinical Teacher* (2 a year).

Association of Anaesthetists of Great Britain and Ireland: 21 Portland Pl., London, W1B 1PY; tel. (20) 7631-1650; e-mail info@aagbi.org; internet www.aagbi .org; f. 1932; promotes devt and study of anaesthetics and their admin. and maintains the high standard of this br. of medicine; 10,000 mems; Pres. Dr WILLIAM HARROP-GRIFFITHS; Exec. Dir KARIN PAPPENHEIM; publs *Anaesthesia* (12 a year), *Anaesthesia News* (12 a year).

Association of British Neurologists: Ormand House, 4th Fl., 27 Boswell St, London, WC1N 3JZ; tel. (20) 7405-4060; e-mail info@theabn.org; internet www.abn .org.uk; f. 1932; aims to improve the health and well-being of people with neurological disorders by advancing the knowledge and practice of neurology in the British Isles; 1,500 mems; Exec. Dir JOANNE LAWRENCE.

Association of Surgeons of Great Britain and Ireland: c/o The Royal College of Surgeons, 35–43 Lincoln's Inn Fields, London, WC2A 3PE; tel. (20) 7973-0300; e-mail admin@asgbi.org.uk; internet www.asgbi.org .uk; f. 1920; advances the science and art of surgery; Chief Exec. Prof. NICHOLAS P. GAIR; publ. *Journal of the ASGBI.*

British Association for Sexual Health and HIV: Chester House, 68 Chestergate, Macclesfield, SK11 6DY; tel. (1625) 664523; e-mail admin@bashh.org; f. 1922 as Medical Society for the Study of Venereal Diseases; studies sexually transmitted and allied diseases; 900 mems; Pres. Dr JANET WILSON;

Gen. Sec. Dr ELIZABETH CARLIN; publ. *Sexually Transmitted Infections* (6 a year).

British Association of Plastic, Reconstructive and Aesthetic Surgeons: c/o The Royal College of Surgeons, 35–43 Lincoln's Inn Fields, London, WC2A 3PE; tel. (20) 7831-5161; e-mail secretariat@bapras .org.uk; internet www.bapras.org.uk; f. 1946; protects and preserves public health by the promotion and devt of plastic surgery; Pres. G. PERKS; Hon. Sec. A. PANDYA; publ. *Journal of Plastic, Reconstructive and Aesthetic Surgery (JPRAS).*

British Dental Association: 64 Wimpole St, London, W1G 8YS; tel. (20) 7935-0875; e-mail enquiries@bda.org; internet www.bda .org; f. 1880; acts as trade union for dental profession; promotes policies on dental practice and dental care; 20,000 mems, 3,500 student mems; library of 10,000 vols; Pres. BARRY MCGONIGLE; publs *BDA News* (12 a year), *British Dental Journal* (24 a year).

British Dietetic Association: 5th Fl., Charles House, 148–149 Great Charles St Queensway, Birmingham, B3 3HT; tel. (121) 200-8080; e-mail info@bda.uk.com; internet www.bda.uk.com; f. 1936; regulates relations between dietitians and their employer through the BDA Trade Union; 5,000 mems; Chair. SIÁN O'SHEA; Pres. MARY TURNER; publ. *Journal of Human Nutrition and Dietetics* (6 a year).

British Geriatrics Society: Marjory Warren House, 31 St John's Sq., London, EC1M 4DN; tel. (20) 7608-1369; e-mail president@ bgs.org.uk; internet www.bgs.org.uk; f. 1947; improves standards of medical care for elderly patients and encourages research into the problems of old age; 2,750 mems; Pres. PAUL KNIGHT; CEO COLIN NEE; publ. *Age and Ageing.*

British Institute of Radiology: 48-50 St John St, London, EC1M 4DG; tel. (20) 3668-2220; e-mail admin@bir.org.uk; internet www.bir.org.uk; f. 1897; promotes study and practice of radiology, radiobiology and the medical applications of nuclear science; current and historic radiological library; 1,700 mems; Chief Exec. JACQUELINE FOWLER; publs *The British Journal of Radiology* (12 a year), *Imaging* (4 a year).

British Medical Association: BMA House, Tavistock Sq., London, WC1H 9JP; tel. (20) 7387-4499; e-mail info.web@bma.org.uk; internet www.bma.org.uk; f. 1832; scientific and educational body, guides doctors throughout all stages of their career; 137,000 mems; library: see under Libraries and Archives; Pres. Sir SABARATNAM ARULKUMARAN; Chair. Dr IAN WILSON; publs *BMA News* (48 a year), *British Medical Journal* (48 a year).

British Nutrition Foundation: Imperial House, Sixth Floor, 15–19 Kingsway, London, WC2B 6UN; tel. (20) 7557-7930; e-mail postbox@nutrition.org.uk; internet www .nutrition.org.uk; f. 1967; Hon. Pres. Prof. ALAN SHENKIN; Dir-Gen. Prof. JUDITH BUTTRISS; publ. *Nutrition Bulletin* (4 a year).

British Orthodontic Society: c/o Dr Stephen Rudge, Hon. Sec., British Orthodontic Soc., 12 Bridewell Pl., London, EC4V 6AP; tel. (20) 7353-8680; e-mail hon.sec@bos.org .uk; internet www.bos.org.uk; f. 1994; encourages research and education in orthodontics; Chair. Dr JOHN D. MUIR; Hon. Sec. Dr STEPHEN RUDGE; publ. *Journal of Orthodontics* (4 a year).

British Orthopaedic Association: 35–43 Lincoln's Inn Fields, London, WC2A 3PE; tel. (20) 7405-6507; e-mail secretary@boa.ac.uk; internet www.boa.ac.uk; f. 1918; advances science and art of orthopaedic surgery; 3,486

mems; Pres. IAN WINSON; Hon. Sec. GORDON MATTHEWS; publ. *Journal of Bone and Joint Surgery.*

British Pharmacological Society: 16 Angel Gate, City Rd, London, EC1V 2PT; tel. (20) 7239-0171; e-mail info@bps.ac.uk; internet www.bps.ac.uk; f. 1931; 3,000 mems; Pres. Prof. HUMPHREY RANG; publs *British Journal of Clinical Pharmacology* (12 a year), *British Journal of Pharmacology* (24 a year).

British Psychoanalytical Society: Byron House, 112A Shirland Rd, Maida Vale, London, W9 2BT; tel. (20) 7563-5000; e-mail admin@iopa.org.uk; internet www .psychoanalysis.org.uk; f. 1913 as The London Psychoanalytical Society, current name adopted 1919; training of psychoanalysts, devt of the theory and practice of psychoanalysis, advancement of psychoanalysis as a science; maintains clinical and scientific standards of psychoanalysis; 400 mems; library of 22,000 vols, incl. 1,600 monographs, 300 journals; Pres. Dr NICHOLAS TEMPLE; publ. *The International Journal of Psycho-Analysis* (6 a year).

British Society for Research on Ageing: c/o Dr Matthew Hardman, Faculty of Life Sciences, AV Hill Bldg, Univ. of Manchester, Manchester, M13 9PT; internet www.bsra .org.uk; f. 1945; holds an annual scientific meeting; Chair. Prof. ANNE MCARDLE; Sec. Dr MATTHEW HARDMAN; publs *e-Lifespan* (12 a year, online), *Lifespan* (2 a year), *Mechanisms of Ageing and Development.*

British Society for Rheumatology: Bride House, 18–20 Bride Lane, London, EC4Y 8EE; tel. (20) 7842-0900; e-mail bsr@ rheumatology.org.uk; internet www .rheumatology.org.uk; f. 1984; promotes treatment of people with arthritis and musculo-skeletal conditions and supports those delivering it; 1,500 mems; CEO LAURA GUEST; Pres. MARION BROWN; publs *Musculoskeletal Care, Rheumatology.*

British Society of Gastroenterology: 3 St Andrews Pl., Regent's Park, London, NW1 4LB; tel. (20) 7935-3150; e-mail enquiries@ bsg.org.uk; internet www.bsg.org.uk; f. 1937; conducts training programmes, research workshops and scientific and clinical confs; 3,400 mems; Pres. Dr IAN FORGACS; Sec. Dr CATHRYN EDWARDS; Sec. JAYNE EADEN; publs *Frontline Gastroenterology* (6 a year), *Gut* (12 a year).

Chartered Society of Physiotherapy: 14 Bedford Row, London, WC1R 4ED; tel. (20) 7306-6666; e-mail enquiries@csp.org.uk; internet www.csp.org.uk; f. 1894 as Society of Trained Masseuses, became Incorporated Society of Trained Masseuses 1900, granted Royal Charter 1920, merged with Institute of Massage and Remedial Gymnastics, current name adopted 1944; professional, educational and trade union body for chartered physiotherapists, support workers and physiotherapy students in the UK; 51,000 mems; Chair. SUE REES; publs *Physiotherapy Frontline* (24 a year), *Physiotherapy Journal* (4 a year).

College of Optometrists: 42 Craven St, London, WC2N 5NG; tel. (20) 7839-6000; e-mail optometry@college-optometrists.org; internet www.college-optometrists.org; f. 1980; improves and conserves human vision; provides pre-registration training and assessment; incl. a library and museum; 13,357 mems incl. over 9,000 practising UK mems and fellows; library of 7,000 vols, incl. optical books, pamphlets and audiovisual titles, journals, British Standards, govt publs, college publs, gen. reference materials, historical collns; Chair. Dr CINDY TROMANS; publs *Ophthalmic and Physiological Optics*

(6 a year, online), *Optometry in Practice* (4 a year, print).

Diabetes UK: 10 Parkway, London, NW1 7AA; tel. (345) 123-2399; e-mail info@ diabetes.org.uk; internet www.diabetes.org .uk; f. 1934; promotes greater public understanding about diabetes and supports research; 190,000 mems; Chief Exec. BARBARA YOUNG; publs *Balance for Beginners* (1 a year), *Balance Magazine* (6 a year), *Diabetic Medicine* (10 a year), *Diabetes Update* (4 a year).

Harveian Society of London: Lettsom House, 11 Chandos St, London, W1G 9EB; tel. (20) 7580-1043; e-mail harveiansoclondon@btconnect.com; internet www.harveiansocietyoflondon.btck.co.uk; f. 1831; promotes the advancement of medical science; meets weekly; 210 mems; Pres. Prof. DAVID THOMAS; Hon. Sec. Prof. CHARLES POLKEY.

Institute of Biomedical Science: 12 Coldbath Sq., London, EC1R 5HL; tel. (20) 7713-0214; e-mail mail@ibms.org; internet www .ibms.org; f. 1912; promotes biomedical science and its practitioners within health care; award qualifications; establishes and maintains professional standards; 19,000 mems; Pres. NICK KIRK; publs *British Journal of Biomedical Science* (4 a year), *The Biomedical Scientist* (12 a year).

Medical Society of London: Lettsom House, 11 Chandos St, London, W1G 9EB; tel. (20) 7580-1043; e-mail medicalsoclondon@btconnect.com; internet www.medsoclondon.org; f. 1773; organises lectures and social activities; 410 mems; library of 4,500 vols; Pres. Dr ROY PALMER; publ. *Transactions* (1 a year).

MIND: Granta House, 15–19 Broadway, Stratford, London, E15 4BQ; tel. (20) 8519-2122; e-mail contact@mind.org.uk; internet www.mind.org.uk; f. 1946; works to create a better life for people with experience of mental distress; produces information and publs; offers services incl. advocacy, counselling, crisis helplines, drop-in centres, employment and training schemes, supported housing; 1,600 mems, 200 local asscns, 7 regional offices; Chief Exec. PAUL FARMER; publ. *Mind Membership News* (4 a year).

Northern Ireland Association for Mental Health: Central Office, 80 University St, Belfast, BT7 1HE; tel. (28) 9032-8474; internet www.niamh.co.uk; f. 1959 as Beacon House; provides counselling, training and consultancy for employers on mental health in the workplace; influences policy and public opinion; Chief Exec. PETER MCBRIDE.

Nutrition Society: 10 Cambridge Court, 210 Shepherds Bush Rd, London, W6 7NJ; tel. (20) 7602-0228; e-mail office@ nutritionsociety.org; internet www .nutritionsociety.org; f. 1941; over 2,200 mems; Pres. CATHERINE GEISSLER; Chief Exec. FREDERICK WENTWORTH-BOWYER; publ *British Journal of Nutrition* (12 a year), *Journal of Nutritional Science*, *Nutrition Research Reviews* (2 a year), *Proceedings* (6 a year), *Public Health Nutrition* (8 a year).

Pathological Society: 2 Carlton House Terrace, London, SW1Y 5AF; tel. (20) 7976-1260; e-mail admin@pathsoc.org; internet www.pathsoc.org; f. 1906; enhances research and education in pathology; awards grants; 1,500 mems; Pres. Prof. IAN O ELLIS; Gen. Sec. Dr RICHARD BYERS; Treas. Dr N. ROONEY; publs *Journal of Pathology*, *Diagnostic Histopathology*.

Disability Rights UK: 12 City Forum, 250 City Rd, London, EC1V 8AF; tel. (20) 7250-3222; e-mail enquiries@disabilityrightsuk .org; internet www.disabilityrightsuk.org; f. 1977 as Royal Association for Disability and Rehabilitation; current name adopted 2012; a coordinating organization concerned with the needs and rights of disabled people in the UK; led by disabled people; Chief Exec. LIZ SAYCE; publ. *Disability and Welfare Rights Updates* (24 a year).

Royal College of Anaesthetists: Churchill House, 35 Red Lion Sq., London, WC1R 4SG; tel. (20) 7092-1500; e-mail info@rcoa.ac.uk; internet www.rcoa.ac.uk; f. 1948; responsible for the science of anaesthesia throughout the UK; ensures quality of patient care through the maintenance of standards in anaesthesia, critical care and pain medicine; 14,000 fellows, mems and trainees; Pres. Dr J. P. VAN BESOUW; publ. *British Journal of Anaesthesia* (12 a year).

Royal College of General Practitioners: 30 Euston Sq., London, NW1 2FB; tel. (20) 3188-7400; internet www.rcgp.org.uk; f. 1952; 21,000 mems; Chair. Dr MAUREEN BAKER; Hon. Sec. Prof. NIGEL MATHERS; publ. *British Journal of General Practice* (12 a year).

Royal College of Nursing of the United Kingdom: 20 Cavendish Sq., London, W1G 0RN; tel. (20) 7409-3333; internet www.rcn .org.uk; f. 1916; 410,000 mems; library of 60,000 vols, 3,500 journals, newsletters and magazines, 1,000 theses; Pres. ANDREA SPYROPOULOS; publ. *Nursing Standard* (48 a year).

Royal College of Obstetricians and Gynaecologists: 27 Sussex Pl., Regent's Park, London, NW1 4RG; tel. (20) 7772-6200; internet www.rcog.org.uk; f. 1929; 10,705 mems; library of 15,000 vols; Pres. Dr DAVID RICHMOND; publs *British Journal of Obstetrics and Gynaecology* (12 a year), *The Obstetrician and Gynaecologist* (4 a year).

Royal College of Ophthalmologists: 17 Cornwall Terrace, London, NW1 4QW; tel. (20) 7935-0702; e-mail contact@rcophth.ac .uk; internet www.rcophth.ac.uk; f. 1988; provides training in ophthalmology; 3,200 mems; Pres. HARMINDER DUA; Chief Exec. KATHY EVANS; publ. *Eye* (6 a year).

Royal College of Paediatrics and Child Health: 5–11 Theobalds Rd, London, WC1X 8SH; tel. (20) 7092-6000; e-mail enquiries@ rcpch.ac.uk; internet www.rcpch.ac.uk; f. 1928; 7,800 mems; Pres. HILARY CASS; Registrar IAN MACONOCHIE; publ. *Archives of Disease in Childhood* (12 a year).

Royal College of Pathologists: 2 Carlton House Terrace, London, SW1Y 5AF; tel. (20) 7451-6700; e-mail info@rcpath.org; internet www.rcpath.org; f. 1962; 8,474 fellows and mems; library of 2,100 vols (spec. colln); Pres. Dr ARCHIE PRENTICE; Chief Exec. DANIEL ROSS.

Royal College of Physicians: 11 St Andrews Pl., Regent's Park, London, NW1 4LE; tel. (20) 3075-1539; e-mail enquiries@ rcplondon.ac.uk; internet www.rcplondon.ac .uk; f. 1518; aims to promote the values of the medical profession, improve standards of clinical practice; sets and monitors the standards of medical training; communicates with govt, the public and the profession and provides leadership on health and health care issues; 22,000 mems (13,000 fellows, 9,000 collegiate mems); library: see under Libraries and Archives; Pres. Sir RICHARD THOMPSON; Chief Exec. PATRICIA WRIGHT; publ. *Clinical Medicine* (6 a year).

Royal College of Physicians and Surgeons of Glasgow: 232–242 St Vincent St, Glasgow, G2 5RJ; tel. (141) 221-6072; internet www.rcpsg.ac.uk; f. 1599; medical licensing corporation; provides training to its mems; 10,000 mems; library: see under Libraries and Archives; Pres. Dr FRANCIS G. DUNN; Hon. Sec. Prof. HAZEL SCOTT.

Royal College of Physicians of Edinburgh: 9 Queen St, Edinburgh, EH2 1JQ; tel. (131) 225-7324; e-mail president@rcpe.ac .uk; internet www.rcpe.ac.uk; f. 1681; helps qualified doctors pursue careers in specialist (internal) medicine; library: see under Libraries and Archives; Pres. Dr N. G. DEWHURST; CEO ELAINE TAIT; publ. *Journal* (4 a year).

Royal College of Psychiatrists: 21 Prescot St, London, E1 8BB; tel. (20) 7235-2351; e-mail reception@rcpsych.ac.uk; internet www.rcpsych.ac.uk; f. 1971 by Charter, previously Royal Medico-Psychological Asscn; sets standards and promotes excellence in psychiatry and mental healthcare; 16,000 fellows and mems; Pres. Prof. SUE BAILEY; Registrar Dr LAURENCE MYNORS-WALLIS; Chief Exec. V. CAMERON; publs *Advances in Psychiatric Treatment* (6 a year), *British Journal of Psychiatry* (12 a year), *The Psychiatrist* (12 a year).

Royal College of Radiologists: 63 Lincoln's Inn Fields, London, WC2A 3JW; tel. (20) 7405-1282; e-mail enquiries@rcr.ac.uk; internet www.rcr.ac.uk; f. 1939; advances practice of radiology and oncology; 6,600 mems; Pres. Dr GILES MASKELL; publs *Clinical Oncology* (8 a year), *Clinical Radiology* (12 a year).

Royal College of Surgeons of Edinburgh: Nicolson St, Edinburgh, EH8 9DW; tel. (131) 527-1600; e-mail mail@rcsed.ac.uk; internet www.rcsed.ac.uk; f. 1505; advances surgical and dental practice; postgraduate education and assessment in surgery; c. 20,000 mems; Pres. IAN RITCHIE; publs *Surgeon News* (4 a year), *The Surgeon* (6 a year).

Royal College of Surgeons of England: 35–43 Lincoln's Inn Fields, London, WC2A 3PE; tel. (20) 7405-3474; e-mail education@ rcseng.ac.uk; internet www.rcseng.ac.uk; f. 1800; supervises training of surgeons in approved posts; provides educational and practical workshops for surgeons and other medical professionals; promotes surgical research; acts as an advisory body to the Dept of Health and other health authorities, trusts, hospitals; attached information centre for surgeons in the library and museums; 20,000 fellows and mems; library of 100,000 vols; Pres. NORMAN WILLIAMS; publ. *Annals of the Royal College of Surgeons of England* (8 a year).

Royal Medical Society: Students' Centre, 5/5 Bristo Sq., Edinburgh, EH8 9AL; tel. (131) 650-2672; e-mail enquiries@ royalmedical.co.uk; internet www .royalmedical.co.uk; f. 1737; 2,000 mems; library of 2,000 vols; Pres. RUHITH ARIYAPALA; publ. *Res Medica* (2 a year).

Royal Pharmaceutical Society: 1 Lambeth High St, London, SE1 7JN; tel. (20) 7572- 2737; e-mail support@rpharms.com; internet www.rpharms.com; f. 1841; professional body for pharmacists in England, Scotland and Wales; works with stakeholders across the profession to develop the role of pharmacy; c. 30,000 mems; library of 80,000 vols, pamphlets and MSS, 300 journals, colln of pharmacopoeias and formularies; Pres. MARTIN ASTBURY; CEO HELEN GORDON; publs *Annual Register of Pharmaceutical Chem-*

ists, *British National Formulary* (jtly with the British Medical Asscn), *Journal of Pharmacy and Pharmacology* (12 a year), *Martindale: The Extra Pharmacopoeia, Medicines and Ethics, Pharmaceutical Sciences* (12 a year), *The Clinical Pharmacist* (11 a year), *The International Journal of Pharmacy Practice* (4 a year), *The Pharmaceutical Journal* (52 a year).

Royal Society for Public Health: John Snow House, 59 Mansell St, London, E1 8AN; tel. (20) 7265-7300; e-mail info@rsph .org.uk; internet www.rsph.org.uk; f. 2008 by merger of Royal Soc. for the Promotion of Health and the Royal Institute of Public Health; advises on policy devt, provides education and training services, encourages scientific research on human health and wellbeing; examining body for food hygiene; holds confs. and lectures; 5,700 mems; Pres. LORD HUNT OF KING'S HEATH; Chief Exec. SHIRLEY CRAMER; publs *Perspectives in Public Health* (6 a year), *Public Health* (12 a year).

Royal Society of Medicine: 1 Wimpole St, London, W1G 0AE; tel. (20) 7290-2900; e-mail membership@rsm.ac.uk; internet www.rsm.ac.uk; f. 1805, first Royal Charter 1834; undertakes over 400 meetings a year covering 58 sections of medicine and surgery; provides accredited courses for continuing professional development; 23,000 mems; library: see under Libraries and Archives; Pres. Sir MICHAEL RAWLINS; Chief Exec. IAN BALMER; publs *Aids and Hepatitis Digest* (6 a year), *Annals of Clinical Biochemistry* (6 a year, online), *Clinical Governance Bulletin* (6 a year, also online), *Clinical Risk* (6 a year, online), *Effective Health Care* (6 a year, also online), *Handbook of Practice Management* (4 a year, online), *Health Information on the Internet* (6 a year, online), *Health Services Management Research* (4 a year, also online), *International Journal of STD and AIDS* (12 a year, also online), *Journal of Health Services Research and Policy* (4 a year, online), *Journal of Integrated Care Pathways* (3 a year), *Journal of Laryngology and Otology* (12 a year, also online), *Journal of Medical Biography* (4 a year), *Journal of Medical Screening* (4 a year, also online), *Journal of Telemedicine and Telecare* (6 a year, online), *Journal of the British Menopause Society* (4 a year, also online), *Journal of the Royal Society of Medicine* (12 a year, also online), *Laboratory Animals* (4 a year, online), *Phlebology* (4 a year, also online), *Tropical Doctor* (4 a year).

Royal Society of Tropical Medicine and Hygiene: Northumberland House, 303–306 High Holborn, London, WC1V 7JZ; tel. (20) 7405-2628; e-mail info@rstmh.org; internet www.rstmh.org; f. 1907; 2,000 mems; Pres. Prof. SIMON HAY; publs *International Health* (4 a year), *Transactions* (12 a year).

Society for Endocrinology: 22 Apex Court, Woodlands, Bradley Stoke, Bristol, BS32 4JT; tel. (1454) 642200; e-mail info@ endocrinology.org; internet www .endocrinology.org; f. 1946; 2,000 mems; Pres. A. B. GROSSMAN; publs *Endocrine-Related Cancer* (4 a year, online), *Journal of Endocrinology* (12 a year), *Journal of Molecular Endocrinology* (6 a year, print; 12 a year, online), *The Endocrinologist* (4 a year).

Society of British Neurological Surgeons: 35–43 Lincoln's Inn Fields, London, WC2A 3PE; tel. (20) 7869-6892; e-mail admin@sbns.org.uk; internet www.sbns.org .uk; f. 1926; promotes safe and effective Neurosurgical treatment through the Soc.'s involvement in the education and the examination of neurosurgeons; 640 mems; Pres. Prof. RICHARD NELSON; Sr Administrator

SUZANNE MURRAY; publ. *Proceedings* (in *British Journal of Neurosurgery*).

Society of Occupational Medicine: Hamilton House, Mabledon Pl., London, WC1H 9BB; tel. (20) 7554-8628; e-mail admin@som.org.uk; internet www.som.org .uk; f. 1935; stimulates interest and research in Occupational Medicine; works with the govt, the healthcare community, health charities and other bodies to promote a healthier workforce; 1,800 mems; Pres. A. M. LECKIE; Hon. Sec. Dr E. D'SOUZA; publ. *Occupational Medicine* (8 a year).

St John's Dermatological Society: St John's Institute of Dermatology, St Thomas' Hospital, Lambeth Palace Rd, London, SE1 7EH; tel. (20) 7188-9352; internet www .st-johns-society.co.uk; meeting at St John's Hospital for Diseases of the Skin; f. 1911 to promote the knowledge and study of dermatology by presentation and discussion of rare and interesting cases; 250 Fellows; Pres. Dr ANDREW PEMBROKE; Hon. Sec. Dr NUALA O'DONOGHUE; publ. *Clinical and Experimental Dermatology* (1 a year).

Stroke Association: 240 City Rd, London, EC1V 2PR; tel. (20) 7566-0300; e-mail info@ stroke.org.uk; internet www.stroke.org.uk; f. 1899, fmrly The Chest, Heart and Stroke Asscn; provides stroke information for stroke patients, their families and carers through community services, welfare grants and health education; Chair. Sir DAVID VARNEY; Chief Exec. JON BARRICK; publ. *Stroke News* (3 a year).

Tavistock Institute of Medical Psychology: 70 Warren St, London, W1T 5PB; tel. (20) 7380-1975; e-mail timp@tccr.org.uk; internet www.tccr.org.uk; f. 1929; promotes the study and practice of psychotherapy and provides grants for related small research projects; administers the Tavistock Centre for Couple Relationships; trains counsellors; CEO SUSANNA ABSE; publ. *In Brief* (1 a year).

NATURAL SCIENCES

General

Association for Science Education: College Lane, Hatfield, AL10 9AA; tel. (1707) 283000; e-mail info@ase.org.uk; internet www.ase.org.uk; f. 1901; organizes meetings and workshops locally and nationally; aims to improve science teaching and to provide a medium of expression for science teachers; 21,000 mems; CEO JOHN OVERSBY; publs *Education in Science* (5 a year), *Primary Science Review* (5 a year), *School Science Review* (4 a year), *Science Teacher Education* (3 a year).

British Science Association: Wellcome Wolfson Bldg, 165 Queen's Gate, London, SW7 5HD; tel. (870) 770-7101; e-mail info@ britishscienceassociation.org; internet www .britishscienceassociation.org; f. 1831; promotes and advances public understanding and awareness of science and technology; annual British Science Festival, National Science and Engineering Week, regional and local events, and an extensive programme for young people; 5,670 mems; Chief Exec. IMRAN KHAN; publ. *People & Science* (4 a year).

British Society for the History of Science: POB 3401, Norwich, NR7 7JF; tel. (1603) 516236; e-mail office@bshs.org.uk; internet www.bshs.org.uk; f. 1947; promotes and advances the study of the history and philosophy of science, technology, medicine and their changing relationship with society; organizes meetings and confs; 750 mems; Pres. HASOK CHANG; publ. *British Journal for the History of Science* (4 a year).

Cambridge Philosophical Society: Central Science Library, Arts School, Bene't St, Cambridge, CB2 3PY; tel. (1223) 334743; e-mail philosoc@hermes.cam.ac.uk; internet www.cambridgephilosophicalsociety.org; f. 1819; promotes scientific enquiry and facilitates the communication of facts connected with the advancement of science; Studentship Fund; 1,900 mems; Pres. Prof. C. L.-H. HUANG; publs *Biological Reviews* (4 a year), *Mathematical Proceedings* (6 a year).

Council for Environmental Education: c/o SEEd, 9–13 Kean St, London, WC2B 4AY; tel. (118) 950-2550; e-mail info@se-ed.org.uk; internet www.cee.org.uk; f. 1968; umbrella org. for national and associated orgs working in environmental and sustainable development education; increases the effectiveness of the environmental education movement by developing and influencing policy and supporting and encouraging good practice; library: reference library and resource centre; 84 mems; Dir LIBBY GRUNDY; publs *CEEmail* (3 a year), *CEEview* (4 a year), *Earthlines* (3 a year).

Field Studies Council: Preston Montford, Montford Bridge, Shrewsbury, SY4 1HW; tel. (1743) 852100; e-mail enquiries@ field-studies-council.org; internet www .field-studies-council.org; f. 1943; operates 17 residential and day centres throughout the UK, offering a range of courses for schools and colleges; leisure learning and professional devt courses are offered in the UK and overseas; provides outreach education, training and consultancy; publishes a number of titles to support its work, incl. identification guides; 4,000 mems; Pres. Prof. IAN MERCER; Chair. Prof. TIMOTHY P. BURT.

Foundation for Science and Technology: 10 Carlton House Terrace, London, SW1Y 5AH; tel. (20) 7321-2220; e-mail office@foundation.org.uk; internet www .foundation.org.uk; f. 1977; debates science, engineering, technology and medical science policy; Chair. JAMES SMITH; Chief Exec. Dr DAVID CLARKE; publ. *FST Journal* (4 a year).

Institution of Environmental Sciences: 2nd Fl., 34 Grosvenor Gardens, London, SW1W 0DH; tel. (20) 7730-5516; e-mail enquiries@ies-uk.org.uk; internet www .ies-uk.org.uk; f. 1971; promotes interdisciplinary studies of the environment; provides professional advice on environmental sciences; 1,003 individual mems; CEO ADAM DONNAN; Chair. Dr HEATHER BARRETT-MOLD; publ. *The Environmental Scientist* (3 a year).

Kindrogan Field Studies Centre: Kindrogan Field Centre, Enochdhu, Blairgowrie, PH10 7PG; tel. (1250) 870150; e-mail enquiries.kd@field-studies-council.org; internet www.field-studies-council.org/centres/ kindrogan.aspx; f. 1945; provides residential courses and a venue for fieldwork in biology and geography; centre for biodiversity and outdoor learning; recreational areas for residents; 400 mems; Chair. MARTYN JAMIESON.

London Natural History Society: c/o The Secretary, 381B Whitton Ave, Greenford, UB6 0JU; tel. (20) 8426-6621; e-mail davidhowdon@virgin.net; internet www.lnhs .org.uk; f. 1858; shares knowledge on wild plants, mammals, birds, invertebrates and fungi; organizes field meetings, talks, training days, recording of species and habitats; reading circles; 1,000 individual mems, 25 corporate mems; library of 3,500 vols, 5,000 periodicals; library at the Angela Marmont Centre for UK Biodiversity at the Natural History Museum, London; Pres. Prof. TED TUDDENHAM; Sec. DAVID HOWDON; publs *London Bird Report* (1 a year), *The London Naturalist* (1 a year).

Royal Institution of Great Britain: 21 Albemarle St, London, W1S 4BS; tel. (20) 7409-2992; e-mail ri@ri.ac.uk; internet www.rigb.org; f. 1799; promotes science by lectures, demonstrations and discussions; Davy Faraday Research Laboratory; Faraday Museum; 3,200 mems; library: library: see Libraries and Archives; museum: see Museums and Art Galleries; Pres. HRH THE DUKE OF KENT; Chair. Sir RICHARD SYKES.

United Kingdom Science Park Association: Chesterford Research Park, Little Chesterford, Saffron Walden, CB10 1XL; tel. (1799) 532050; e-mail info@ukspa.org.uk; internet www.ukspa.org.uk; f. 1984; authority on planning and devt of science parks; mems: 65 science parks; Chair. DAVID HARDMAN; Chief Exec. PAUL WRIGHT; publ. *Innovation Into Success* (4 a year).

Wildlife Trusts: The Kiln, Waterside, Mather Rd, Newark, NG24 1WT; tel. (1636) 677711; e-mail enquiry@wildlifetrusts.org; internet www.wildlifetrusts.org; f. 1912 as Royal Society for Nature Conservation; inc. by Royal Charter 1916 and 1976; promotes the conservation of nature for study and research; educates the public in the understanding and appreciation of nature; 11,000 events a year; acts as the nat. office for 46 wildlife trusts, urban wildlife groups and Wildlife Watch (junior br.); 800,000 mems; Pres. SIMON KING; publ. *Natural World* (3 a year).

Biological Sciences

Association for the Study of Animal Behaviour: Harold Mitchell Bldg, Univ. of St Andrews, St Andrews, G12 8QQ; e-mail dms14@st-andrews.ac.uk; internet asab.nottingham.ac.uk; f. 1936; 2,000 mems; Pres. Prof. TIM BIRKHEAD; Sec. Dr DAVID SHUKER; publ. *Animal Behaviour* (12 a year).

Association of Applied Biologists: Warwick Enterprise Park, Wellesbourne, Warwick, CV35 9EF; tel. (2476) 575195; internet www.aab.org.uk; f. 1904; promotes study and advancement of all brs of biology, with spec. reference to their applied aspects; 800 mems; Pres. PETER SHEWRY; Gen. Sec. Dr ELIZABETH STOCKDALE; publ. *Annals of Applied Biology* (6 a year).

Biochemical Society: Charles Darwin House, 12 Roger St, London, WC1N 2JU; tel. (20) 7685-2400; e-mail genadmin@biochemistry.org; internet www.biochemistry.org; f. 1911; 5,000 mems; Chief Exec. KATE BAILLIE; publs *Biochemical Journal* (24 a year), *Biochemical Society Transactions* (6 a year), *Biology of the Cell* (12 a year), *Biotechnology and Applied Biochemistry* (6 a year), *Clinical Science* (12 a year), *Essays in Biochemistry* (2 a year), *Symposia* (1 a year), *The Biochemist* (6 a year).

Botanical Society of Scotland: c/o Royal Botanic Garden Edinburgh, 20A Inverleith Row, Edinburgh, EH3 5LR; tel. (131) 552-7171; internet www.botsocscot.org.uk; f. 1836 as Botanical Soc. of Edinburgh; incorporates the Cryptogamic Soc. of Scotland; 300 mems and fellows; Pres. Prof. JOHN GRACE; Hon. Gen. Sec. Dr BARBRA HARVIE; publ. *Plant Ecology and Diversity* (2 a year).

Botanical Society of Britain and Ireland: c/o Dept of Botany, Natural History Museum, Cromwell Rd, London, SW7 5BD; tel. (20) 7942-5002; e-mail coordinator@bsbi.org.uk; internet www.bsbi.org.uk; f. 1836 as the Botanical Society of London; studies British native flowering plants and ferns; exhibitions, confs, field meetings; 2,800 mems; Pres. IAN DENHOLM; publs *BSBI News* (3 a year), *Watsonia* (2 a year).

British Biophysical Society: c/o Dr Tharin Blumenschein, School of Chemistry, Univ. of East Anglia, Norwich Research Park, Norwich NR4 7TJ; tel. (1603) 592963; e-mail t.blumenschein@uea.ac.uk; internet www.britishbiophysics.org.uk; f. 1960; promotes studies in Biophysics and Biophysical Chemistry; works with the Biophysical Chemistry group of the Royal Chemical Society, and the Biological Physics group of the Institute of Physics; 500 mems; Chair. ANTHONY WATTS; Sec. Dr THARIN BLUMENSCHEIN.

British Ecological Society: Charles Darwin House, 12 Roger St, London, WC1N 2JU; tel. (20) 7685-2500; e-mail info@britishecologicalsociety.org; internet www.britishecologicalsociety.org; f. 1913; studies the impact of depleting natural resources on ecological systems; publ. of scientific literature, incl. five internationally renowned journals; funding of numerous grant schemes, education work and policy work; 4,000 mems; Exec. Dir Dr HAZEL J. NORMAN; publs *Symposium* (1 a year), *Journal of Ecology* (6 a year), *Journal of Animal Ecology* (6 a year), *Journal of Applied Ecology* (6 a year), *Functional Ecology* (6 a year).

British Mycological Society: City View House, Union St, Ardwick, Manchester, M12 4JD; tel. (161) 277-7638; e-mail admin@britmycolsoc.info; internet www.britmycolsoc.org.uk; f. 1896; devoted to the study of fungi; promotes mycology through scientific meetings, publs and education; 1,206 mems and 644 assocs; Pres. Dr GEOFF ROBSON; Treas. Dr GEOFFREY M. GADD; publs *Field Mycology* (4 a year), *Fungal Biology* (12 a year), *Fungal Biology Reviews* (4 a year), *Fungal Ecology* (4 a year).

British Ornithologists' Union: POB 417, Peterborough, PE7 3FX; tel. (1865) 8281842; e-mail bou@bou.org.uk; internet www.bou.org.uk; f. 1858; 1,800 ordinary mems, plus hon. mems and corresp. mems; Pres. Dr J. GILL; Hon. Sec. Dr K. SMITH; publ. *Ibis* (4 a year).

British Society for Plant Pathology: Charles Darwin House, 12 Roger St, London, WC1N 2JU; e-mail secretary@bspp.org.uk; internet www.bspp.org.uk; f. 1981; 650 mems; Pres. Prof. LESLEY TORRANCE; Sec. Dr ROGER WILLIAMS; publs *BSPP News* (4 a year), *Molecular Plant Pathology* (9 a year), *New Disease Reports* (4 a year), *Plant Pathology* (6 a year).

British Trust for Ornithology: The Nunnery, Thetford, IP24 2PU; tel. (1842) 750050; e-mail info@bto.org; internet www.bto.org; f. 1933; promotes and encourages wider understanding, appreciation and conservation of birds; projects incl. Nat. Bird Ringing Scheme, Nest Records Scheme, Wetland Bird Survey, Breeding Bird Survey, Garden Bird Watch, Bird Atlas; offers advisory services; 13,000 mems; Dir ANDY CLEMENTS; publs *Bird Study* (4 a year), *Bird Table* (4 a year), *BTO News* (6 a year), *Ringing and Migration* (2 a year).

Fauna & Flora International: Fourth Floor, Jupiter House, Station Rd, Cambridge, CB1 2JD; tel. (1223) 571000; e-mail info@fauna-flora.org; internet www.fauna-flora.org; f. 1903; protects threatened species and ecosystems from extinction worldwide; chooses solutions that are sustainable; improves the livelihoods of local people; 140 projects in 40 countries; 3,000 mems; CEO MARK ROSE; publ. *Oryx* (4 a year).

Freshwater Biological Association: The Ferry Landing, Far Sawrey, Ambleside, LA22 0LP; tel. (15394) 42468; e-mail info@fba.org.uk; internet www.fba.org.uk; f. 1929; promotes study and application of freshwater biology and management of water resources; ferry landing on shores of Windermere, Cumbria; River Laboratory, East Stoke, Wareham, Dorset sited on River Frome; 1,650 mems; library of 150,000 vols, 10,000 vols. of scientific periodicals; Pres. Sir J. BEDDINGTON; publs *FBA News* (3 a year), *FBA Scientific Publications* (irregular), *Freshwater Forum* (irregular), *Freshwater Reviews* (2 a year, online), *Inland Waters* (4 a year, online).

Genetics Society: c/o Portland Customer Services Charles Darwin House 12 Roger St, London, WC1N 2JU; tel. (20) 7685-2444; e-mail theteam@genetics.org.uk; internet www.genetics.org.uk; f. 1919; all aspects of genetics, pure and applied; 2,000 mems; Pres. Prof. JONATHAN HODGKIN; Hon. Sec. Dr JOHN ARMOUR; publs *Genes and Development* (24 a year), *Genetics Society News* (12 a year), *Heredity* (12 a year).

Linnean Society of London: Burlington House, Piccadilly, London, W1J 0BF; tel. (20) 7434-4479; e-mail info@linnean.org; internet www.linnean.org; f. 1788; maintains Carl Linnaeus's plants and animals and other collns and personal library; holds scientific meetings; 2,100 fellows, incl. 50 foreign mems and 20 hon. fellows; library: see Libraries and Archives; Pres. Prof. DIANNE EDWARDS; publs *Biological Journal* (12 a year), *Botanical Journal* (12 a year), *Pulse* (4 a year), *Symposium*, *Synopses of the British Fauna* (irregular), *Zoological Journal* (12 a year).

Malacological Society of London: c/o Dr V. Flari, Central Science Laboratory, Sand Hutton, York, YO4 1LZ; tel. (1904) 462349; e-mail vasiliki@flari.fsnet.co.uk; internet www.malacsoc.org.uk; f. 1893; promotes study of mollusca; awards for research and travel to students; 300 mems; library: Radley Library deposited at University College London; Pres. TONY WALKER; publ. *Journal of Molluscan Studies* (4 a year).

Marine Biological Association of the United Kingdom: The Laboratory, Citadel Hill, Plymouth, PL1 2PB; tel. (1752) 633207; e-mail sec@mba.ac.uk; internet www.mba.ac.uk; f. 1884; promotes scientific research into all aspects of life in the sea; receives grants from univs, research charities and other public bodies; incl. Nat. Marine Biological Library; 1,400 mems; library of 60,000 vols; Pres. Sir GEOFFREY HOLLAND; Sec. and Dir Prof. COLIN BROWNLEE; publ. *Journal* (8 a year).

Physiological Society: Hodgkin Huxley House, 30 Farringdon Lane, London, EC1R 3AW; tel. (20) 7269-5710; e-mail admin@physoc.org; internet www.physoc.org; f. 1876; promotes the advancement of physiology and facilitates communication between physiologists at home and abroad; 3,000 mems; Pres. JONATHAN ASHMORE; publs *Experimental Physiology* (12 a year online, 6 a year in print), *The Journal of Physiology* (26 a year), *The Physiological Society Magazine* (4 a year).

Ray Society: c/o Dr Tim Ferrero, Department of Zoology, The Natural History Museum, Cromwell Rd, London, SW7 5BD; tel. (7753) 764095; internet www.raysociety.org.uk; f. 1844; publishes works primarily concerned with the natural history of the British Isles and NW Europe; advised by a ccl of eminent British naturalists and scientists; 270 mems; Pres. E. PLATTS; Hon. Sec. Dr T. J. FERRERO.

Royal Entomological Society: The Mansion House, Chiswell Green Lane, St Albans, AL2 3NS; tel. (1727) 899387; e-mail info@royensoc.co.uk; internet www.royensoc.co.uk; f. 1833 as the Entomological Society of London; 2,025 fellows; library of 11,000 vols, 750 periodicals, 30,000 reprints; Pres. Prof. JEREMY THOMAS; Registrar W. H. F. BLAKE-

MORE; publs *Agricultural and Forest Entomology* (4 a year), *Antenna* (4 a year), *Ecological Entomology* (4 a year), *Insect Molecular Biology* (4 a year), *Medical and Veterinary Entomology* (4 a year), *Physiological Entomology* (4 a year), *Systematic Entomology* (4 a year).

Royal Society for the Protection of Birds: The Lodge, Potton Rd, Sandy, SG19 2DL; tel. (1767) 680551; internet www.rspb.org.uk; f. 1889, inc. 1904; protects wild birds and their natural habitat; owns and manages 200 nature reserves; 195,000 mems; library of 9,000 vols; Pres. MIRANDA KRESTOVNIKOFF; Chair. Prof. STEVE ORMEROD; publs *Bird Life* (6 a year), *Birds* (4 a year).

Royal Zoological Society of Scotland: Edinburgh Zoo, 134 Corstorphine Rd, Edinburgh, EH12 6TS; tel. (131) 334-9171; e-mail info@rzss.org.uk; internet www.rzss.org.uk; f. 1909, inc. by Royal Charter 1913; promotes conservation of animal species and wild places by captive breeding, environmental education and scientific research; 23,000 mems; Pres. JOHN SPENCE; Chief Exec. CHRIS WEST; publ. *Lifelinks* (4 a year).

Scottish Association for Marine Science: Scottish Marine Institute, Dunstaffnage Marine Laboratory, Oban, PA37 1QA; tel. (1631) 559215; e-mail info@sams.ac.uk; internet www.sams.ac.uk; f. 1884; involved with science in society initiatives, organizes scientific meetings, hosts confs and administers a marine science bursary scheme; 300 mems; Pres. Prof. Sir JOHN ARBUTHNOT.

Selborne Society Ltd: 36, Ferrymead Gardens, Greenford, UB6 9NF; tel. (78) 7859-4290; e-mail contact@selbornesociety.org.uk; internet www.perivalewood.k-hosting.co.uk; f. 1885; observes and records wildlife in part of W London and manages and conserves Perivale Wood Local Nature Reserve as the Gilbert White Memorial; 1,024 mems; Hon. Sec. ANDREW PEDLEY.

Society for General Microbiology: Charles Darwin House, 12 Roger St, London, WC1N 2JU; tel. (20) 7685-2400; e-mail info@sgm.ac.uk; internet www.sgm.ac.uk; f. 1945; promotes advancement of microbiology; organizes int. scientific conf.; 5,300 individual mems, 550 schools; Chief Exec. SIMON FESTING; publs *International Journal of Systematic and Evolutionary Microbiology* (12 a year), *Journal of General Virology* (12 a year), *Journal of Medical Microbiology* (12 a year), *Microbiology* (12 a year), *Microbiology Today* (4 a year).

Society of Biology: Charles Darwin House, 12 Roger St, London, WC1N 2JU; tel. (20) 7685-2550; e-mail education@societyofbiology.org; internet www.societyofbiology.org; f. 2009 by merger of the Biosciences Federation and the Institute of Biology; advises the govt and influences policies; works towards education and professional devt; 80,000 mems; Chief Exec. Dr MARK DOWNS; publs *Journal of Biological Education*, *The Biologist* (6 a year).

Systematics Association: c/o Dept of Plant Sciences, Oxford Univ., South Parks Rd, Oxford, OX1 3RB; tel. (1865) 275059; internet www.systass.org; f. 1937; studies systematics in relation to biology and evolution; organizes int. conf.; training courses; 500 mems; Pres. Dr ROBERT SCOTLAND; Sec. Dr PETER WILKIE.

Zoological Society of London: Regent's Park, London, NW1 4RY; tel. (844) 225-1826; internet www.zsl.org; f. 1826; promotes worldwide conservation of animals and their habitats; consists of: ZSL London Zoo and ZSL Whipsnade Zoo; conservation programmes in 50 countries; 40,000 mems; library of 180,000 vols, 1,300 periodicals;

Pres. Prof. Sir PATRICK BATESON; Sec. Prof. GEOFF BOXSHALL; publs *Animal Conservation* (6 a year), *Conservation Science and Practice Book Series* (2 a year), *International Zoo Yearbook* (1 a year), *Journal of Zoology* (12 a year).

Mathematical Sciences

British Society for the History of Mathematics: c/o Andrew Thurburn & Co, 38 Tamworth Rd, Croydon, CR0 1XU; internet www.bshm.org; f. 1971; promotes historical studies of mathematics; organizes confs, workshops, visits; 500 mems; Pres. Prof. ROBIN WILSON; publ. *Bulletin* (3 a year).

Institute of Mathematics and its Applications: Catherine Richards House, 16 Nelson St, Southend-on-Sea, SS1 1EF; tel. (1702) 354020; e-mail post@ima.org.uk; internet www.ima.org.uk; f. 1964, inc. by Royal Charter 1990; enhances mathematical culture in UK; promotes education in mathematics and its applications in science, engineering, economics; 5,000 mems; Pres. Prof. Dame CELIA HOYLES; publs *IMA Journal of Applied Mathematics* (6 a year), *IMA Journal of Management Mathematics* (4 a year), *IMA Journal of Mathematical Control and Information* (4 a year), *IMA Journal of Numerical Analysis* (4 a year), *IMA Teaching Mathematics and its Applications* (4 a year), *Information and Inference: a Journal of the IMA*, *Mathematical Medicine and Biology* (4 a year).

London Mathematical Society: De Morgan House, 57–58 Russell Sq., London, WC1B 4HS; tel. (20) 7637-3686; e-mail lms@lms.ac.uk; internet www.lms.ac.uk; f. 1865; promotes and extends mathematical knowledge; publishes journals and books, provides grants and organizes meetings and lectures; 2,300 mems; Exec. Sec. FIONA NIXON; publs *Journal* (6 a year), *Nonlinearity* (6 a year), *Proceedings* (6 a year).

Physical Sciences

Association of Public Analysts: Burlington House, Piccadilly, London, W1J 0BA; tel. (1224) 491648; e-mail nmichie@aberdeencity.gov.uk; internet www.the-apa.co.uk; f. 1953; supports analysts engaged in the public protection enforcement service, which tests foodstuffs, fertilizers and other areas of consumer protection; 120 mems and assoc. mems; Pres. LIZ MORAN; publ. *Journal of the Association of Public Analysts* (online).

British Astronomical Association: Burlington House, Piccadilly, London, W1J 0DU; tel. (20) 7734-4145; e-mail office@britastro.org; internet www.britastro.org; f. 1890; encourages observational astronomy; provides astronomical information and observational material; recognizes contributions to astronomy through awards; 3,000 mems; Pres. HAZEL McGEE; publs *Handbook* (1 a year), *Journal* (6 a year).

British Cryogenics Council: 7 Leverton Gdns, Wantage, OX12 9NY; e-mail admin@bcryo.org.uk; internet www.bcryo.org.uk; f. 1967; fosters and encourages devt and application of cryogenics in Britain by means of contacts, education and research; quarterly meetings; 100 mem. instns; Chair. Prof. HARRY JONES; Treas. JOHN VANDORE; publ. *Low Temperature News* (4 a year).

British Horological Institute: Upton Hall, Upton, Newark, NG23 5TE; tel. (1636) 813795; e-mail research@bhi.co.uk; internet www.bhi.co.uk; f. 1858; 3,000 mems; Chair. RAY WALFORD; publ. *The Horological Journal* (12 a year).

British Interplanetary Society: 27/29 S Lambeth Rd, London, SW8 1SZ; tel. (20) 7735-3160; e-mail mail@bis-space.com;

internet www.bis-space.com; f. 1933; promotes study and research in space and astronautics, meetings, symposia, publs, visits and exhibitions; library; 3,300 mems (1,800 fellows, 1,500 mems); Pres. ROBERT PARKINSON; Exec. Sec. SUSZANN PARRY; publs *Journal of the British Interplanetary Society* (*JBIS*) (12 a year), *Space Chronicle* (2 a year), *Spaceflight* (12 a year).

Challenger Society for Marine Science: c/o Nat. Oceanography Centre, Waterfront Campus, European Way, Southampton, SO14 3ZH; tel. (23) 8059-5106; e-mail jxj@noc.soton.ac.uk; internet www.challenger-society.org.uk; f. 1903; promotes study of oceanography and marine sciences; contributes to public debate and govt policy; 500 mems; Pres. Prof. HILARY KENNEDY; publ. *Ocean Challenge* (2 a year).

Geological Society of London: Burlington House, Piccadilly, London, W1J 0BG; tel. (20) 7434-9944; e-mail enquiries@geolsoc.org.uk; internet www.geolsoc.org.uk; f. 1807; investigates the mineral structure of the Earth; 10,000 mems; library: see under Libraries and Archives; Pres. DAVID SHILSTON; publs *Geochemistry, Exploration, Environment, Analysis* (4 a year), *Journal* (6 a year), *Petroleum Geoscience* (4 a year), *Quarterly Journal of Engineering Geology and Hydrogeology*.

Geologists' Association: Burlington House, Piccadilly, London, W1J 0DU; tel. (20) 7434-9298; internet www.geologistsassociation.org.uk; f. 1858; fosters the science of geology and encourages research; 2,000 mems; Pres. RORY MORTIMER; Exec. Sec. SARAH STAFFORD; publs *GA Magazine* (4 a year), *Proceedings* (4 a year).

Institute of Acoustics: 3rd Fl., St Peter's House, 45–49 Victoria St, St Albans, AL1 3WZ; tel. (1727) 848195; e-mail ioa@ioa.org.uk; internet www.ioa.org.uk; f. 1974; promotes ideas in aerodynamics, architectural acoustics, building acoustics, electroacoustics, engineering dynamics, noise and vibration, hearing, speech, underwater acoustics, and their environmental aspects; 3,000 mems; Pres. BRIDGET SHIELD; publ. *Acoustics Bulletin* (6 a year).

Institute of Physics: 76 Portland Place, London, W1B 1NT; tel. (20) 7470-4800; e-mail physics@iop.org; internet www.iop.org; f. 1918, chartered 1970; professional body for physicists in the UK and Ireland; supports research through grants; 34,500 mems; Chief Exec. PAUL HARDAKER; publs *Chinese Physics* (12 a year), *Chinese Physics Letters* (12 a year), *Combustion Theory and Modelling* (4 a year), *European Journal of Physics* (6 a year), *Inverse Problems* (6 a year), *Journal of Cosmology and Astroparticle Physics* (online), *Journal of High Energy Physics* (online), *Journal of Micromechanics and Microengineering* (12 a year), *Journal of Physics* (series A 50 a year, B 24 a year, CM 50 a year, D 24 a year and G 12 a year), *Journal of Radiological Protection* (4 a year), *Journal of Turbulence* (online), *Measurement Science and Technology* (12 a year), *Metrologia* (6 a year), *Modelling and Simulation in Materials Science and Engineering* (8 a year), *Nanotechnology* (12 a year), *New Journal of Physics* (online, www.njp.org), *Nonlinearity* (6 a year), *Nuclear Fusion* (12 a year), *Physics Education* (6 a year), *Physics in Medicine and Biology* (24 a year), *Physiological Measurement* (6 a year), *Plasma Physics and Controlled Fusion* (12 a year), *Plasma Sources Science and Technology* (4 a year), *Reports on Progress in Physics* (12 a year), *Semiconductor Science and Technology* (12 a year), *Smart Materials and Struc-*

tures (6 a year), *Superconductor Science and Technology* (12 a year).

Mineralogical Society of Great Britain and Ireland: 12 Baylis Mews, Amyand Park Rd, Twickenham, TW1 3HQ; tel. (20) 8891-6600; e-mail info@minersoc.org; internet www.minersoc.org; f. 1876; scientific publishing and promotion of the mineral sciences through scientific meetings and special interest groups; 1,000 mems; Pres. Prof. BEN HARTE; Gen. Sec. Dr MARK HODSON; Exec. Sec. Dr ADRIAN LLOYD-LAWRENCE; publs *Clay Minerals* (4 a year), *Mineralogical Magazine* (6 a year).

Palaeontographical Society: c/o Dept of Palaeontology, Natural History Museum, Cromwell Rd, London, SW7 5BD; tel. (20) 7942-5011; internet www.palaeosoc.org; f. 1847; illustration and description of British fossils; 181 individual mems, 174 mem. orgs; Pres. Dr PAUL M. BARRETT; Sec. Dr S. K. DONOVAN; publ. *Monograph of the Palaeontographical Society* (1 a year).

Quekett Microscopical Club: c/o Natural History Museum, Cromwell Rd, London, SW7 5BD; tel. (20) 7942-5213; e-mail president@quekett.org; internet www .quekett.org; f. 1865; encourages study of every br. of microscopical science; 500 mems; library of 1,000 vols; Pres. CAREL SARTORY; publ. *Quekett Journal of Microscopy* (2 a year).

Royal Astronomical Society: Burlington House, Piccadilly, London, W1J 0BQ; tel. (20) 7734-4582; e-mail info@ras.org.uk; internet www.ras.org.uk; f. 1820, granted Royal Charter in 1831; promotes study of astronomy, solar-system science and geophysics; 3,500 mems; library: see Libraries and Archives; Pres. Prof. DAVID J. SOUTHWOOD; Exec. Sec. PAMELA MORTIMER; publs *Astronomy and Geophysics* (6 a year), *Geophysical Journal International* (12 a year).

Royal Meteorological Society: 104 Oxford Rd, Reading, RG1 7LL; tel. (118) 956-8500; e-mail info@rmets.org; internet www.rmets .org; f. 1850 as The British Meteorological Society; offers vocational qualifications; 3,000 mems; Pres. Prof. JOANNA HAIGH; Chief Exec. LIZ BENTLEY; publs *Atmospheric Science Letters* (online), *International Journal of Climatology* (15 a year), *Meteorological Applications* (4 a year), *Quarterly Journal*, *Weather* (12 a year), *Weather Front* (12 a year), *WIREs Climate Change* (online).

Royal Microscopical Society: 37–38 St Clements St, Oxford, OX4 1AJ; tel. (1865) 254760; e-mail info@rms.org.uk; internet www.rms.org.uk; f. 1839, granted Royal Charter 1866; promotes microscopical science and its application in academics and industries; 1,333 mems; Pres. Prof. PETER NELLIST; publs *infocus* (4 a year), *Journal of Microscopy* (12 a year).

Royal Society of Chemistry: Burlington House, Piccadilly, London, W1J 0BA; tel. (20) 7437-8656; e-mail sales@rsc.org; internet www.rsc.org; f. 1980 from merger of the Chemical Soc. (f. 1841) and the Royal Inst. of Chemistry (f. 1877); professional body for chemical scientists; 49,000 mems; library: see under Libraries and Archives; Pres. Prof. LESLEY YELLOWLEES; Chief Exec. Dr ROBERT PARKER; publs *The Analyst* (12 a year), *Analytical Abstracts* (12 a year), *Catalysts and Catalysed Reactions* (12 a year), *Chemical Biology* (12 a year), *Chemical Communications* (52 a year), *Chemical Science* (12 a year), *Chemical Society Reviews* (12 a year), *Chemical Technology* (12 a year), *Chemistry World* (12 a year), *Chromatography Abstracts* (12 a year), *CrystEngComm* (electronic only, 12 a year), *Dalton Transactions* (52 a year), *Education in Chemistry* (6 a

year), *Faraday Discussions* (3 a year), *Green Chemistry* (12 a year), *Journal of Analytical Atomic Spectroscopy* (12 a year), *Journal of Environmental Monitoring* (12 a year), *Journal of Materials Chemistry* (52 a year), *Lab on a Chip* (12 a year), *Laboratory Hazards Bulletin* (12 a year), *Mass Spectrometry Bulletin* (12 a year), *Methods in Organic Synthesis* (12 a year), *Molecular BioSystems* (12 a year), *Natural Product Reports* (6 a year), *Natural Product Updates* (12 a year), *New Journal of Chemistry* (12 a year), *Organic and Biomolecular Chemistry* (26 a year), *PCCP–Physical Chemistry Chemical Physics, Photochemical and Photobiological Sciences* (12 a year), *Soft Matter* (12 a year); publ. *Chemistry World* (12 a year).

SCI (Society of Chemical Industry): 14/15 Belgrave Sq., London, SW1X 8PS; tel. (20) 7598-1500; e-mail secretariat@soci.org; internet www.soci.org; f. 1881; provides opportunity for sharing information between sectors such as biotechnology, environmental science, food and agriculture, pharmaceuticals and safety; 6,000 mems; Pres. PAUL BOOTH; Exec. Dir Dr JULIET CORBETT; publs *Chemistry & Industry* (24 a year), *Journal of Chemical Technology and Biotechnology* (12 a year), *Journal of the Science of Food and Agriculture* (15 a year), *Pest Management Science* (12 a year), *Polymer International* (12 a year).

Yorkshire Geological Society: c/o Patrick Boylan, 2A, Compass Rd, Leicester, LE5 2HF; internet www.yorksgeolsoc.org.uk; f. 1837; works in fields of geology and the wider earth sciences of N England; coordinates the annual Yorkshire Geology Month each May; 600 mems; library of 5,000 vols; Pres. Prof. PATRICK BOYLAN; Gen. Sec. PAUL HILDRETH; publ. *Proceedings of the Yorkshire Geological Society* (2 a year).

PHILOSOPHY AND PSYCHOLOGY

Aristotelian Society: Room 281, Stewart House, Russell Sq., London, WC1B 5DN; tel. (20) 7862-8685; e-mail mail@aristoteliansociety.org.uk; internet www .aristoteliansociety.org.uk; f. 1880; involved in systematic study of philosophy; meets fortnightly in London, throughout the academic year, to hear and discuss philosophical papers; 700 individual mems, 1,357 mem. libraries; Hon. Dir LUCY O'BRIEN; publs *Proceedings* (1 a year), *Supplementary Volume* (1 a year).

British Psychological Society: St Andrews House, 48 Princess Rd E, Leicester, LE1 7DR; tel. (116) 254-9568; e-mail enquiries@bps.org.uk; internet www.bps.org .uk; f. 1901; 40,000 mems; Pres. Dr GERRY MULHERN; Hon. Gen. Sec. Prof. PAM MARAS; publs *British Journal of Clinical Psychology* (4 a year), *British Journal of Developmental Psychology* (4 a year), *British Journal of Educational Psychology* (4 a year), *British Journal of Health Psychology* (4 a year), *British Journal of Mathematical & Statistical Psychology* (4 a year), *British Journal of Psychology* (4 a year), *British Journal of Social Psychology* (4 a year), *Journal of Occupational & Organisational Psychology* (4 a year), *Legal and Criminological Psychology* (4 a year), *Psychology and Psychotherapy: Theory, Research and Practice* (4 a year), *Selection & Development Review* (4 a year), *The Psychologist* (12 a year).

British Society of Aesthetics: POB 271, Cheadle, SK8 9BU; e-mail admin@british-aesthetics.org; internet www .british-aesthetics.org; f. 1960; promotes study, research and discussion of the fine arts; provides grants for research in aesthetics; essay prize; Pres. RICHARD WOLLHEIM;

Sec. KATHLEEN STOCK; publ. *British Journal of Aesthetics* (4 a year).

Experimental Psychology Society: Dept of Experimental Psychology, Univ. of Bristol, 12A Priory Rd, Bristol, BS8 1TU; e-mail eps-enquiries@nottingham.ac.uk; internet www.eps.ac.uk; f. 1946; furthers scientific enquiry in the field of psychology and cognate subjects; holds meetings and disseminates educational material; 756 mems; Pres. Prof. K. E. PATTERSON; Hon. Sec. Dr H. J. CASSADAY; publ. *Quarterly Journal of Experimental Psychology* (4 a year).

Leeds Philosophical and Literary Society Ltd: c/o Leeds City Museum, Cookridge St, Leeds, LS2 8BH; internet www .leedsphilandlit.org.uk; f. 1819; promotes advancement of science, literature and the arts; organizes public lectures and visits; 135 mems; Pres. J. M. HILL.

Manchester Literary and Philosophical Society: Mabel Tylecote Bldg, Cavendish St, Manchester, M15 6BG; tel. (161) 247-6774; e-mail admin@manlitphil.ac.uk; internet www.manlitphil.ac.uk; f. 1781; promotes advancement of education and encourages public interest in, and appreciation of, any form of literature, science, the arts and public affairs; 500 mems; library of 4,000 vols; Administrator ALLAN JEFFERIS; Administrator MARGARET GALLAGHER; Hon. Sec. PETER BARNES; Hon. Sec. DEREK CALDWELL; publ. *Manchester Memoirs* (1 a year).

Mind Association: c/o Dr Miranda Fricker, Dept of Philosophy, Univ. of Sheffield, 45 Victoria St, Sheffield, S3 7QB; tel. (20) 7631-6383; internet www.mindassociation.org; f. 1900; supports philosophical research; organizes annual confs jtly with the Aristotelian Soc.; 300 mems; Dir Prof. MIRANDA FRICKER; publ. *MIND* (4 a year).

Philosophical Society of England: 6 Craghall Dean Rd, Newcastle, NE3 1QR; tel. (191) 284-1223; internet www.philsoc.co .uk; f. 1913; organizes lectures, confs and workshops; sponsors local philosophical groups; 150 mems; Pres. Prof. BRENDA ALMOND; Chair. MICHAEL BAVIDGE; publ. *The Philosopher* (2 a year).

Royal Institute of Philosophy: 14 Gordon Sq., London, WC1H 0AR; tel. (20) 7387-4130; e-mail think@royalinstitutephilosophy.org; internet www.royalinstitutephilosophy.org; f. 1925; 700 mems; Pres. LORD SUTHERLAND OF HOUNDWOOD; Chair. Prof. JOHN HALDANE; publs *Conference Proceedings* (1 a year), *Philosophy* (4 a year), *Think* (4 a year).

Royal Philosophical Society of Glasgow: D12, 160 Bothwell St, Glasgow, G2 7EL; tel. (141) 564-3841; e-mail info@royalphil.org; internet www.royalphil.org; f. 1802; aids study and advancement of arts and sciences; organizes lectures and promotes philosophical debate; 950 mems; Pres. Dr JEFFREY JAY; Hon. Sec. Dr FELICITY GRAINGER.

Victoria Institute/Philosophical Society of Great Britain/Faith and Thought: 3 Dukes Pl., 19 Watford Rd, Croxley Green, Rickmansworth, WD3 3DP; tel. (1702) 472-710; e-mail apkerry@aol.com; internet www .faithandthought.org.uk; f. 1865; Pres. Sir COLIN J. HUMPHREYS; publs *Faith & Thought* (2 a year), *Science and Christian Belief* (2 a year).

William Morris Society: Kelmscott House, 26 Upper Mall, Hammersmith, London, W6 9TA; tel. (20) 8741-3735; e-mail info@williammorrissociety.org.uk; internet www .williammorrissociety.org.uk; f. 1955; encourages wider appreciation and understanding of the life, work and influence of William Morris and his circle; 1,400 mems; library of

2,000 vols; Sec. PENNY LYNDON; publ. *Journal* (2 a year).

RELIGION, SOCIOLOGY AND ANTHROPOLOGY

African Studies Association of the United Kingdom: 36 Gordon Sq., London, WC1H 0PD; tel. (20) 3073-8335; e-mail secretary@asauk.net; internet www.asauk .net; f. 1963; advances academic studies relating to Africa; holds inter-disciplinary confs and symposia; offers fellowships and workshops; 1,000 mems; Hon. Pres. Prof. STEPHANIE NEWELL; Hon. Sec. Dr NICI NELSON.

British Association for South Asian Studies: c/o Royal Asiatic Society, 14 Stephenson Way (Second Fl.), London, NW1 2HD; tel. (20) 7388-5490; e-mail basas@basas .org.uk; internet www.basas.org.uk; f. 1972 as the Soc. for S Asian Studies; merged with British Asscn for S Asian Studies 2007; supports research in humanities and social sciences of S Asia; 600 mems; Chair. Prof. IAN TALBOT; Sec. Dr PHILIPPA WILLIAMS; publs *Contemporary South Asia* (1 a year), *South Asian Studies* (1 a year).

British Association for the Study of Religions: e-mail b.schmidt@tsd.ac.uk c/o Dr Bettina Schmidt, School of Theology, Religious Studies and Islamic Studies, Univ. of Wales, Trinity Saint David, Lampeter, SA48 7ED; tel. (131) 650-8942; internet basr.open.ac.uk; f. 1954 as British Association for the History of Religions; affiliated to Int. Association for the History of Religions; organizes annual conf.; 250 mems; Pres. and Chair Dr GRAHAM HARVEY; Hon. Sec. Dr BETTINA SCHMIDT.

British Society for Middle Eastern Studies: Institute for Middle Eastern and Islamic Studies, Univ. of Durham, Al-Qasimi Bldg, Elvet Hill Rd, Durham, DH1 3TU; tel. (191) 334-5179; e-mail a.l.haysey@durham.ac.uk; internet www.brismes.ac.uk; f. 1973; promotes study of the Middle Eastern region from the end of classical antiquity and the rise of Islam; organizes discussion and debates; 550 mems; Pres. FRANCES GUY; Exec. Dir Prof. JAMES DICKINS; publ. *British Journal of Middle Eastern Studies* (4 a year).

British Sociological Association: Bailey Suite, Palatine House, Belmont Business Park, Belmont, Durham, DH1 1TW; tel. (191) 383-0839; e-mail enquiries@britsoc.org .uk; internet www.britsoc.co.uk; f. 1951; promotes interest in sociology; holds confs, seminars and workshops; 2,500 mems; Chief Exec. JUDITH MUDD; publs *Cultural Sociology* (3 a year), *Network* (3 a year), *Sociology* (6 a year), *Work Employment and Society* (6 a year).

Ecclesiological Society: EcclSoc, 38 Rosebery Ave, New Malden, KT3 4JS; tel. (20) 8942-2111; e-mail info@ecclsoc.org; internet www.ecclsoc.org; f. 1879 as St Paul's Ecclesiological Soc.; promotes arts, architecture or liturgy of the Christian Church; lectures, confs, visits, publs; 950 mems; Chair. TREVOR COOPER; publ. *Ecclesiology Today* (2 a year).

Folklore Society: c/o Warburg Inst., Woburn Sq., London, WC1H 0AB; tel. (20) 7862-8564; e-mail thefolkloresociety@gmail .com; internet www.folklore-society.com; f. 1878; c. 1,000 mems and subscribers; library of 11,000 vols; Pres. ROBERT MCDOWALL; Hon. Sec. Prof. JAMES H. GRAYSON; Librarian Dr CAROLINE OATES; publs *FLS News* (3 a year), *Folklore* (3 a year).

Galton Institute: 19 Northfields Prospect, Northfields, London, SW18 1PE; tel. (20) 8874-7257; e-mail betty.nixon@talk21.com; internet www.galtoninstitute.org.uk; f.

1907; advances understanding of human genetics and population problems; promotes research and understanding in the biosocial sciences; 400 mems; Pres. Prof. Sir WALTER BODMER; Sec. PATRICK JAMES.

Henry Bradshaw Society: Music Collections, The British Library, 96 Euston Rd, London, NW1 2DB; e-mail nicolas.bell@bl.uk; internet www.henrybradshawsociety.org; f. 1890; publishes facsimiles and editions of rare texts relating to the liturgy of the medieval Christian church; 134 institutional mems, 152 individual mems; Pres. THE RIGHT REVEREND ABBOT DOM CUTHBERT JOHNSON; Chair. Prof. SUSAN RANKIN.

Institute of Race Relations: 2–6 Leeke St, King's Cross Rd, London, WC1X 9HS; tel. (20) 7837-0041; e-mail info@irr.org.uk; internet www.irr.org.uk; f. 1958; promotes scientific study and publs on race and racism; Chair. COLIN PRESCOD; publ. *Race & Class* (4 a year).

Maghreb Studies Association: c/o The Maghreb Bookshop, 45 Burton St, London, WC1H 9AL; tel. (20) 7388-1840; e-mail maghreb@maghreb-studies-association.co .uk; internet www .maghreb-studies-association.co.uk; f. 1981; promotes research and the exchange of ideas in anthropology, economics, environmental studies, history, linguistics, literature, political science, sociology, and the Islamic culture of the Maghreb and Mediterranean region; 155 mems; Chair. Prof. HÉDI BOURAOUI; Vice-Chair. Prof. ALLAN CHRISTELOW; Exec. Sec. MOHAMED BEN-MADANI; publ. *Maghreb Review* (4 a year).

Modern Church: 32 Gratton Rd, Cheltenham, GL50 2BU; tel. (845) 345-1909; e-mail office@modernchurch.org.uk; internet www .modernchurch.org.uk; f. 1898; promotes liberal theology; 650 mems; Chair. JAN VAN DER LELY; Gen. Sec. GUY ELSMORE; publ. *Modern Believing* (4 a year).

National Society for Promoting Religious Education: Church House, Great Smith St, Westminster, London, SW1P 3AZ; tel. (20) 7898-1000; e-mail webmaster@ churchofengland.org; internet www .churchofengland.org/education/national-society; f. 1811; attached to Church of England; promotes religious education in accordance with the principles of the Church of England; Chief Education Officer and Gen. Sec. JAN AINSWORTH.

Royal African Society: 36 Gordon Sq., London, WC1H 0PD; tel. (20) 3073-8335; e-mail ras@soas.ac.uk; internet www .royalafricansociety.org; f. 1901; promotes Africa in business, politics, culture and academia; 1,000 mems; Dir RICHARD DOWDEN; publ. *African Affairs* (4 a year).

Royal Anthropological Institute of Great Britain and Ireland: 50 Fitzroy St, London, W1T 5BT; tel. (20) 7387-0455; e-mail admin@therai.org.uk; internet www.therai .org.uk; f. 1843; dedicated to the furtherance of anthropology; lectures and film festivals; manages various trust and scholarship funds; awards medals and prizes; raises funds for research; 2,000 mems; library: borrowing rights to 120,000 vols; Pres. Prof. CLIVE GAMBLE; Hon. Sec. Dr ERIC HIRSCH; publs *Anthropology Today* (6 a year), *Journal of the Royal Anthropological Institute* (incorporating *Man*, 5 a year).

Royal Asiatic Society of Great Britain and Ireland: 14 Stephenson Way, London, NW1 2HD; tel. (20) 7388-4539; e-mail info@ royalasiaticsociety.org; internet www .royalasiaticsociety.org; f. 1823; studies the history, religions, instns, customs, languages, literature and art of Asia; brs in various Asian cities; 800 mems; library: see

under Libraries and Archives; Dir Dr ALISON OHTA; publ. *Journal* (4 a year).

Royal Commonwealth Society: Award House, 7-11 St Matthew St, London, SW1P 2JT; tel. (20) 7766-9200; e-mail info@thercs .org; internet www.thercs.org; f. 1868; improves lives and prospects of Commonwealth citizens worldwide; 10,000 mems worldwide; Dir MICHAEL LAKE.

Royal Society for Asian Affairs: 25 Eccleston Pl., London, SW1W-9NF; tel. (20) 7235-5122; e-mail info@rsaa.org.uk; internet www.rsaa.org.uk; f. 1901; promotes knowledge and understanding of Asia and countries from the Middle East to Japan; hosts lectures and encourages debate on topics like literature, arts, exploration, environment, history and current affairs; holds social functions; 1,080 mems; library of 5,000 vols; Pres. Lord DAVIES OF ABERSOCH; Hon. Treas. NEVILLE GREEN; publ. *Asian Affairs* (3 a year).

Swedenborg Society: 20–21 Bloomsbury Way, London, WC1A 2TH; tel. (20) 7405-7986; e-mail info@swedenborg.org.uk; internet www.swedenborg.org.uk; f. 1810; translates and publishes writings of Emanuel Swedenborg, Swedish scientist, philosopher and theologian; organizes events: lectures, conferences, exhibitions, performances and film screenings; library of 15,000 vols; works of Swedenborg in Latin and translated in modern languages; colln of collateral literature (mainly 19th century); periodicals since 1790; 850 mems; Sec. RICHARD LINES; Librarian ALEX MURRAY; publ. *Journal of the Swedenborg Society* (1 a year).

Young Foundation: 18 Victoria Park Sq., London, E2 9PF; tel. (20) 8980-6263; e-mail reception@youngfoundation.org; internet www.youngfoundation.org; f. 2005; works to create a more equal and just society; social research on poverty, deprivation and comparative social policy; housing, urban planning and community; social innovation and investment; health, well-being and ageing; education; Chief Exec. AMANDA MERCER.

TECHNOLOGY

British Computer Society: First Fl., Block D, N Star House, N Star Ave, Swindon, SN1 1FA; tel. (1793) 417417; e-mail bcshq@hq.bcs .org.uk; internet www.bcs.org.uk; f. 1957; industry body for IT professionals; sets standards for education and training through the BCS Professional Examination and through the inspection and accreditation of university courses and company training schemes; awards the Chartered IT Professional (CITP) qualification; licensed by the Engineering Council and the Science Council to appoint chartered and incorporated engineers and chartered scientists; 70,000 mems; library: joint library with Instn of Electrical Engineers; Pres. DAVID MORRISS; Registrar MANDY BRYAR; publs *The Computer Journal* (6 a year), *IT Now* (4 a year), *IEE Proceedings —Software* (6 a year, in conjunction with IEE), *Interacting with Computers Journal* (4 a year), *Formal Aspects of Computing Journal* (6 a year).

British Society of Rheology: c/o Prof. Simon Cox, Institute of Mathematics and Physics, Aberystwyth Univ., Aberystwyth SY23 3BZ; tel. (1970) 622764; e-mail secretary@bsr.org.uk; internet www.bsr.org .uk; f. 1940; promotes rheology, the science of the deformation and flow of matter; library at Aberystwyth Univ.; holds conf. and seminars; 400 mems; Pres. Prof. RHODRI P. WILLIAMS; Sec. Prof. SIMON COX.

BSI Group (British Standards Institution): 389 Chiswick High Rd, London, W4

4AL; tel. (20) 8996-9000; e-mail cservices@ bsi-global.com; internet www.bsigroup.com/ en-gb; f. 1901 as Engineering Standards Committee; inc. 1918 as British Engineering Standards Association, f. 1929 under Royal Charter and Supplemental Charter in 1931, when scope was extended; ind. certification of management systems and products; product-testing services; operates BSI British Standards; helps businesses improve performance, reduce risk and achieve sustainable growth; 15,000 subscribing mems; CEO HOWARD KERR; publs *British Standards*, *BSI Catalogue* (1 a year), *Business Standards* (4 a year), *Standards Update* (12 a year).

Chartered Institute of Building: 1 Arlington Sq., Downshire Way, Bracknell, RG12 1WA; tel. (1344) 630700; e-mail reception@ ciob.org.uk; internet www.ciob.org.uk; f. 1834, inc. by Royal Charter 1980; promotes the science and practice of building and construction; accredits university degrees, educational courses and training; 46,000 mems; library of 40,000 vols, 400 British Standards, 150 journals; Pres. PETER JACOBS; Chief Exec. CHRIS BLYTHE; publs *Construction Innovation and Development* (4 a year), *Construction Manager* (10 a year), *Icon* (4 a year).

Chartered Institute of Logistics and Transport: Earlstrees Court, Earlstrees Rd, Corby, NN17 4AX; tel. (1536) 740-100; e-mail enquiry@ciltuk.org.uk; internet www .ciltuk.org.uk; f. 1919, inc. by Royal Charter 1926; promotes study and research of transport; brs in Argentina, Australia, Bangladesh, Canada, Cyprus, Ghana, Greece, Hong Kong, India, Ireland, Kenya, Malawi, Malaysia, Malta, Mauritius, Nepal, New Zealand, Nigeria, Pakistan, Singapore, S Africa, Spain, Sri Lanka, Thailand, Uganda, United Arab Emirates, USA, West Indies, Zambia, Zimbabwe and elsewhere; 32,000 mems; Chief Exec. STEVE AGG.

Chartered Institute of Patent Attorneys: 95 Chancery Lane, London, WC2A 1DT; tel. (20) 7405-9450; e-mail mail@cipa.org.uk; internet www.cipa.org.uk; f. 1882, chartered 1891, current name adopted 2006; professional and examining body for patent attorneys in UK; 3,500 mems; Pres. ROGER BURT; Chief Exec. LEE DAVIES; publs *CIPA* (12 a year), *Register of Patent Attorneys* (1 a year).

Chartered Institution of Building Services Engineers: 222 Balham High Rd, London, SW12 9BS; tel. (20) 8675-5211; e-mail membership@cibse.org; internet www .cibse.org; supports science, art and practice of building services engineering; associated with the built environment and industrial processes and the advancement of education and research in building services engineering; 20,000 mems; Pres. GEORGE ADAMS; Chief Exec. and Sec. STEPHEN MATTHEWS; publs *Building Services Engineering Research and Technology* (4 a year), *Building Services Journal* (12 a year), *Lighting Research and Technology* (4 a year).

Chartered Institution of Water and Environmental Management: 106-109 Saffron Hill, London, EC1N 8QS; tel. (20) 7831-3110; e-mail reception@ciwem.org; internet www.ciwem.org; f. 1895; advances the science and practice of water and environmental management for public benefit; promotes education, training, study and research in those areas; 10,000 mems; Pres. MIKE SUMMERGILL; Chief Exec. Dr SIMON FESTING; publs *Journal of Flood Risk Management (JFRM)* (4 a year), *The Environment Magazine* (12 a year), *Water and Environment Magazine* (4 a year).

Chartered Management Institute: 2 Savoy Court, Strand, London, WC2R 0EZ;

Management House, Cottingham Rd, Corby, NN17 1TT; tel. (1536) 204222; e-mail enquiries@managers.org.uk; internet www .managers.org.uk; f. 1947 as British Institute of Management, renamed 1992; granted Royal Charter 2002; encourages and supports the lifelong devt of managers; influences policy-makers and opinion-formers on management issues; awards Chartered Manager qualification; 100,000 individual mems, 600 company mems; library: 80,000 items, 200 periodicals; Chair. PETER AYLIFFE; CEO ANN FRANCKE; publ. *Professional Manager* (6 a year).

Chartered Society of Designers: 1 Cedar Court, Royal Oak Yard, Bermondsey St, London, SE1 3GA; tel. (20) 7357-8088; e-mail info@csd.org.uk; internet www.csd .org.uk; f. 1930, incorporated by Royal Charter 1976; promotes sound principles of design; professional body for designers practising in product design, fashion and textiles design, interiors and graphics, design management, education and professional development; 4,000 mems; Pres. DAVID CALLCOTT; publ. *CSD Magazine* (4 a year).

Design Council: Angel Bldg, 407 St John St, London, EC1V 4AB; tel. (20) 7420-5200; e-mail info@designcouncil.org.uk; internet www.designcouncil.org.uk; f. 1944; Chief Exec. JOHN MATHERS.

Energy Institute: 61 New Cavendish St, London, W1G 7AR; tel. (20) 7467-7100; e-mail info@energyinst.org; internet www .energyinst.org; f. 2003 by merger of the Institute of Petroleum (f. 1913) and Institute of Energy (f. 1927); promotes safe and efficient supply and use of energy; research into oil, gas and other primary fuels and renewable sources of energy; power generation, transmission and distribution, sustainable devt; 12,000 individual mems and 400 group mems; library of 17,000 vols, 200 periodicals; Chief Exec. LOUISE KINGHAM; Library and Information Service Man. CATHERINE COSGROVE; publs *Energy World* (11 a year), *Journal of the Energy Institute* (4 a year), *Petroleum Review* (12 a year).

Engineering Council UK: 246 High Holborn, London, WC1V 7EX; tel. (20) 3206-0500; e-mail info@engc.org.uk; internet www .engc.org.uk; f. 1981 by Royal Charter; represents interests of UK engineers; advances education and training of engineers and technologists; sets up and maintains relevant professional, educational and training standards; Chair. NIGEL GUILD.

Environmental Protection UK: c/o Land and Environmental Services, Glasgow City Council, 231 George St, Glasgow, G1 1RX; tel. (1273) 878770; internet www .environmental-protection.org.uk; f. 1899 as Coal Smoke Abatement Soc., merged with the Smoke Abatement League of Great Britain 1929, fmrly Nat. Soc. for Clean Air and Environmental Protection; current name adopted 2007; conducts discussions on air pollution, contaminated land and noise control, environmental protection; provides critical analysis of UK government and European Union policy proposals; 1,500 mems, incl. learned socs, local authorities, industrial concerns, etc.; Pres. JOHN MURLIS; publ. *NSCA Briefing* (12 a year).

Faculty of Royal Designers for Industry: RSA, 8 John Adam St, London, WC2N 6EZ; tel. (20) 7930-5115; e-mail general@rsa.org .uk; internet www.thersa.org; f. 1936; furthers the devt of design and in particular its application to industrial purposes; offers fellowships; no. of holders of RDI limited to 200 (135 at present plus 54 Hon.); Chief Exec. MATTHEW TAYLOR.

Gemmological Association Great Britain: 21 Ely Pl., London, EC1N 6TD; tel. (20) 7404-3334; e-mail information@gem-a.com; internet www.gem-a.com; f. 1908; promotes study of gemmology and the science of gems; est. provider of gem and jewellery education; 3,000 mems; Pres. H. LEVY; CEO JAMES H. RILEY; publs *Gem and Jewellery* (9 a year), *GemTalk*, *The Journal of Gemmology* (4 a year).

Institute of Corrosion: The Newton Bldg, St George's Ave, Northampton, NN2 6JB; tel. (1604) 893883; e-mail admin@icorr.org; internet www.icorr.org; f. 1959 as the British Association of Corrosion Engineers (BACE); current name adopted 1975; promotes research to fight corrosion in all areas of industry; 1,600 mems; Pres. TREVOUR OSBORNE; Hon. Sec. Dr JANE LOMAS; publs *Corrosion Management* (6 a year), *Corrosion Science* (12 a year).

Institute of Ergonomics and Human Factors: Elms Court, Elms Grove, Loughborough, LE11 1RG; tel. (1509) 234904; e-mail iehf@ergonomics.org.uk; internet www.ergonomics.org.uk; f. 1949; professional organization for ergonomists and human factors practitioners; fosters evolution of ergonomics; 1,400 mems; Pres. Dr RICHARD GRAVELING; Chief Exec. DAVID O'NEILL; publ. *The Ergonomist* (12 a year).

Institute of Food Science and Technology: 5 Cambridge Court, 210 Shepherd's Bush Rd, London, W6 7NJ; tel. (20) 7603-6316; e-mail info@ifst.org; internet www.ifst .org; f. 1964; promotes the knowledge, devt and application of science and technology of food, and the provision of a professional body for food scientists and technologists; 2,000 mems; Pres. MARGARET PATTERSON; Chief Exec. JON POOLE; publs *Food Science and Technology* (4 a year, print and online, www.fstjournal.org), *International Journal of Food Science and Technology* (12 a year, print and online).

Institute of Management Services: Brooke House, 24 Dam St, Lichfield, WS13 6AA; tel. (1543) 266909; e-mail admin@ ims-stowe.fsnet.co.uk; internet www .ims-productivity.com; f. 1941; promotes practices for improving productivity and quality; 1,800 mems; Chair. Dr ANDREW MUIR; publ. *Management Services Journal* (4 a year).

Institute of Marine Engineering, Science and Technology (IMarEST): Aldgate House, 33 Aldgate High St, London, EC3N 1EN; tel. (20) 7382-2600; e-mail info@imarest .org; internet www.imarest.org; f. 1889 as Institute of Marine Engineers, current name adopted 2002; represents those involved in marine engineering, science and technology; 15,000 mems; Pres. A. I. CHRYSOSTOMOU; publs *Journal of Offshore Technology* (6 a year), *Marine Engineers' Review* (10 a year), *The Marine Scientist* (4 a year), *Maritime Electronics* (6 a year).

Institute of Materials, Minerals and Mining: 1 Carlton House Terrace, London, SW1Y 5DB; tel. (20) 7451-7300; e-mail admin@iom3.org; internet www.iom3.org; f. 2002, merger of Institute of Materials and Institution of Mining and Metallurgy; advances the science and practice of engineering; administers scholarships and fellowships; 22,000 mems; library of 65,000 vols, 1,000 periodicals; Pres. Prof. J. G. P. BINNER; publs *Advances in Applied Ceramics* (8 a year), *Energy Materials* (4 a year), *Historical Metallurgy* (2 a year), *Interdisciplinary Science Reviews* (4 a year), *International Heat Treatment and Surface Engineering* (4 a year), *International Materials Reviews* (8 a year), *International Wood Products Journal*

(4 a year), *Ironmaking and Steelmaking* (10 a year), *Materials Science and Technology* (15 a year), *Plastics, Rubber and Composites* (10 a year), *Powder Metallurgy* (5 a year), *Science and Technology of Welding and Joining* (8 a year), *Steel World* (2 a year), *Surface Engineering* (12 a year), *The Packaging Professional* (6 a year), *Tribology* (4 a year).

Institute of Measurement and Control: 87 Gower St, London, WC1E 6AF; tel. (20) 7387-4949; e-mail ceo@instmc.org.uk; internet www.instmc.org.uk; f. 1944, inc. by Royal Charter 1975; promotes the professional excellence of engineers and technologists; 4,100 mems; Chief Exec. Peter Martindale; publs *Measurement and Control* (10 a year, incl. *Inst MC Interface*, of which 2 a year), *Transactions* (5 a year), *Instrument Engineer's Yearbook*.

Institute of Physics and Engineering in Medicine: Fairmount House, 230 Tadcaster Rd, York, YO24 1ES; tel. (1904) 610821; e-mail office@ipem.ac.uk; internet www.ipem.ac.uk; f. 1995; promotes advancement of physics and engineering applied to medicine and biology and advances public education in the field; ensures better healthcare; 4,000 mems; Pres. Prof. Stephen Keevil; Hon. Sec. Dr Joanna Barraclough; publs *Medical Engineering and Physics* (10 a year), *Physics in Medicine and Biology* (26 a year), *Physiological Measurement* (12 a year).

Institute of Quarrying: McPherson House, 8a Regan Way, Chetwynd Business Park, Chilwell, Nottingham, NG9 6RZ; tel. (115) 972-9995; e-mail mail@quarrying.org; internet www.quarrying.org; f. 1917; provides education and training to improve science and practice of quarrying; forum for technical discussion; 5,000 home and overseas mems; Pres. Colin Jenkins; Chair. Miles Watkins; publ. *Quarry Management* (12 a year).

Institute of Refrigeration: Kelvin House, 76 Mill Lane, Carshalton, SM5 2JR; tel. (20) 8647-7033; e-mail ior@ior.org.uk; internet www.ior.org.uk; f. 1899 as the Cold Storage and Ice Asscn; promotes advancement of refrigeration and air conditioning in all its applications; 2,600 mems; Pres. Dr Andy Pearson; Sec. M. Rodway.

Institute of Science and Technology: Kingfisher House, 90 Rockingham St, Sheffield, S1 4EB; tel. (114) 2763197; e-mail office@istonline.org.uk; internet www.istonline.org.uk; f. 1954 from the Science Technologists' Assoc. (f. 1948); current name adopted 2008; professional and qualifying body for specialist, technical and managerial staff; provides training for vocational qualifications and continuing professional devt; provides awards and prizes; 1,000 mems; Pres. (vacant); Chair. Terry Croft; publ. *Science Technology Journal* (2 a year).

Institute of Scientific and Technical Communicators: Airport House, Purley Way, Croydon, CR0 0XZ; tel. (20) 8253-4506; e-mail istc@istc.org.uk; internet www.istc.org.uk; f. 1972; encourages professional devt and standards, research resources and networking opportunities for its members and industry affiliates; 1,500 mems; Pres. Paul Ballard; Exec. Administrator Elaine Cole; publ. *Communicator* (4 a year).

Institution of Chemical Engineers: 165–189 Railway Terrace, Rugby, CV21 3HQ; tel. (1788) 578214; e-mail customerservices@icheme.org; internet www.icheme.org; f. 1922 inc. by Royal Charter; promotes the science and practice of chemical engineering, qualifying body for chemical engineers; 25,000 mems; Chief Exec. Dr David Brown; publs *Chemical Engineering Research and Design* (12 a year), *Food and Bioproducts Processing*

(4 a year), *Process Safety and Environmental Protection* (6 a year), *The Chemical Engineer* (12 a year).

Institution of Civil Engineers: 1 Great George St, Westminster, London, SW1P 3AA; tel. (20) 7222-7722; e-mail secretariat@ice.org.uk; internet www.ice.org.uk; f. 1818 inc. by Royal Charter 1828; promotes civil engineering; talks to nat. and local govt and to the media; provides civil engineering qualification; 80,000 corporate and non-corporate mems; library of 100,000 vols; Pres. Geoff French; Dir-Gen. Nick Baveystock; publs *New Civil Engineer* (48 a year), *New Civil Engineer International* (12 a year).

Institution of Electronics: 12 Bentfield Close, Higher Bebington, CH63 8NB; tel. (151) 608-4236; e-mail info@institutionofelectronics.ac.uk; internet www.institutionofelectronics.ac.uk; f. 1930, inc. 1935; furthers the science of electronics and other scientific subjects; holds lectures, discussions, publication of papers and correspondence with public bodies and individuals; over 2,500 mems; Chair. Alan Hollinshead-Jones; Membership Officer Tim Hatch; publs *Electron* (4 a year, online), *Proceedings* (4 a year, online).

Institution of Engineering and Technology: Michael Faraday House, Six Hills Way, Stevenage, SG1 2AY; tel. (1438) 313311; e-mail postmaster@theiet.org; internet www.theiet.org; f. 1871, inc. by Royal Charter 1921; promotes advancement of science, engineering and technology; facilitates exchange of information and ideas on those subjects; 150,000 mems; library: see under Libraries and Archives; Pres. Sir Robin Saxby; Chief Exec. and Sec. Nigel Fine; publs *Communications Engineer* (6 a year), *Computing and Control Engineering* (6 a year), *Electronics Education* (3 a year), *Electronics Systems and Software* (6 a year), *Engineering Management* (6 a year), *Engineering & Technology* (12 a year), *Flipside* (6 a year), *Information Professional* (6 a year), *Manufacturing Engineer* (6 a year), *Power Engineer* (6 a year), *Proceedings* (6 a year), *Systems Biology* (4 a year).

Institution of Engineering Designers: Courtleigh, Westbury Leigh, Westbury, BA13 3TA; tel. (1373) 822801; e-mail staff@ied.org.uk; internet www.ied.org.uk; f. 1945; a nominated body of the Engineering Council; advances education in engineering and product design; 5,300 mems; Sec. and Chief Exec. Libby Brodhurst; publ. *Engineering Designer* (6 a year).

Institution of Engineers and Shipbuilders in Scotland: Clydeport, 16 Robertson St, Glasgow, G2 8DS; tel. (141) 248-3721; e-mail secretary@iesis.org; internet www.iesis.org; f. 1857; 600 mems; Pres. Prof. Iain MacLeod; publ. *Transactions* (1 a year).

Institution of Fire Engineers: 64–66 Cygnet Court, Timothy's Bridge Rd, Stratford-upon-Avon, CV37 9NW; tel. (1789) 261463; e-mail info@ife.org.uk; internet www.ife.org.uk; f. 1918, inc.1924; awards internationally recognized membership grades and fire-related qualifications; 11,000 home and overseas mems; Chair. Grant Lupton; publ. *Fire Prevention and Fire Engineers Journal* (online, 12 a year).

Institution of Gas Engineers and Managers: IGEM House, 28 High St, Kegworth, DE74 2DA; tel. (844) 678182; e-mail general@igem.org.uk; internet www.igem.org.uk; f. 1863; Royal Charter 1929; promotes research and discussion for better production, distribution or utilization of gas and its by-products; 5,000 mems; library of 10,000 vols; Chief Exec. Sarb Bajwa; publ. *Gi* (10 a year).

Institution of Highways and Transportation: 119 Britannia Walk, London, N1 7JE; tel. (20) 7336-1555; e-mail info@ciht.org.uk; internet www.iht.org; f. 1930 as the Institution of Highway Engineers, current name adopted 1987; concerned with the design, construction, maintenance and operation of sustainable transport systems and infrastructure; serves as a representative body for the profession; offers Chartered and Incorporated Engineer qualifications; 12,000 mems; Chief Exec. Sue Percy; publ. *Transportation Professional* (10 a year).

Institution of Lighting Professionals: Regent House, Regent Place, Rugby, CV21 2PN; tel. (1788) 576492; e-mail info@theilp.org.uk; internet www.theilp.org.uk; f. 1924; promotes, encourages and improves the science and art of efficient lighting in all fields; facilitates exchange of information and ideas on this subject; provides training and professional devt; 1,900 mems; Pres. Mark Johnson; Chief Exec. Richard Frost; publ. *Lighting Journal* (6 a year).

Institution of Mechanical Engineers: 1 Birdcage Walk, London, SW1H 9JJ; tel. (20) 7222-7899; e-mail enquiries@imeche.org; internet www.imeche.org; f. 1847, inc. by Royal Charter 1930; principal organisation for professional mechanical engineers in the UK, and qualifying body for chartered and incorporated mechanical engineers; promotes research in the fields of energy, environment, transport, manufacturing, and education of engineers; 100,000 mems; library of 60,000 books and various other documents; Pres. Patrick Kniveton; publs *Automotive Engineer* (10 a year), *Environmental Engineering* (4 a year), *Institution of Diesel and Gas Turbine Engineers* (6 a year), *Professional Engineering* (22 a year).

The Nuclear Institute: CK International House, 1–6 Yarmouth Pl., London, W1J 7BU; tel. (20) 3475-4701; e-mail admin@nuclearinst.com; internet www.nuclearinst.com; f. 2009 by merger of the British Nuclear Energy Society and the Institution of Nuclear Engineers; 1,700 mems; Pres. Tim Chittenden; publ. *Nuclear Future* (6 a year).

Institution of Structural Engineers: 11 Upper Belgrave St, London, SW1X 8BH; tel. (20) 7235-4535; e-mail mail@istructe.org; internet www.istructe.org; f. 1908 as the Concrete Inst., current name adopted 1922; inc. by Royal Charter 1934; library of 15,000 vols; 27,000 mems; Pres. Nick Russell; publ. *The Structural Engineer* (6 a year).

Newcomen Society for the Study of the History of Engineering and Technology: Science Museum, Exhibition Rd, S Kensington, London, SW7 2DD; tel. (20) 7371-4445; e-mail office@newcomen.com; internet www.newcomen.com; f. 1920; visits to sites of engineering interest; 1,000 mems and subscribers; Pres. Geoff Wallis; publs *Links* (4 a year), *Transactions of the Newcomen Society/The International Journal for the History of Engineering and Technology* (2 a year).

Oil and Colour Chemists' Association: The Oval, 14 West Walk, Leicester, LE1 7NA; tel. (116) 257-5488; e-mail admin@occa.org.uk; internet www.occa.org.uk; f. 1918; promotes technology of the paint, oil, printing ink and allied industries; 2,400 mems; Pres. Keith Dobell; Hon. Sec. Brenda Peters; publs *Surface Coatings International Part A* (10 a year), *Surface Coatings International Part B* (4 a year).

Radio Society of Great Britain: 3 Abbey Court, Fraser Rd, Priory Business Park, Bedford, MK44 3WH; tel. (1234) 832700; e-mail ar.dept@rsgb.org.uk; internet www.rsgb.org; f. 1913; promotes radio-communication by amateurs; 30,000 mems; Pres. Dr

BOB WHELAN; publ. *Radio Communication* (12 a year).

Remote Sensing and Photogrammetry Society: c/o School of Geography, Univ. of Nottingham, Nottingham, NG7 2RD; tel. (115) 951-5435; e-mail office@rspsoc.org.uk; internet www.rspsoc.org.uk; f. 2001; 1,000 mems; library of 2,000 vols; Chair. COLM JORDAN; publs *International Journal of Remote Sensing* (24 a year), *The Photogrammetric Record* (4 a year).

Royal Academy of Engineering: 3 Carlton House Terrace, London, SW1Y 5DG; tel. (20) 7766-0600; internet www.raeng.org.uk; f. 1976; conducts engineering and educational studies, sponsors links between industry and higher education; 1,390 mems (1,266 fellows, 90 foreign mems, 34 hon. fellows); Pres. Sir JOHN PARKER; Chief Exec. PHILIP GREENISH; publ. *Ingenia* (4 a year).

Royal Aeronautical Society: 4 Hamilton Place, London, W1J 7BQ; tel. (20) 7670-4300; e-mail raes@aerosociety.com; internet www.aerosociety.com; f. 1866; advances aeronautical art, science and engineering; 18,500 mems; library of 27,000 books, 1,300 periodicals (of which 300 current), 20,000 technical reports, 100,000 photographs; Pres. JENNY BODY; publs *Aerospace International* (12 a year), *Aerospace Professional* (12 a year), *The Aeronautical Journal* (12 a year).

Royal Institution of Naval Architects: 8–9 Northumberland St, London, WC2N 5DA; tel. (20) 7235-4622; e-mail hq@rina.org.uk; internet www.rina.org.uk; f. 1860; advances naval architecture and marine technology; involves in design, construction, maintenance and operation of all marine vessels and structures; 9,500 mems; Pres. PETER FRENCH; Chief Exec. TREVOR BLAKELEY; publs *Transactions Part A: International Journal of Maritime Engineering* (4 a year), *Transactions Part B: International Journal of Small Craft Technology* (2 a year), *The Naval Architect* (10 a year), *Ship and Boat International* (6 a year), *Ship Repair and Conversion Technology* (4 a year), *Significant Ships* (1 a year), *Significant Small Ships* (1 a year), *Warship Technology* (5 a year), *Offshore Marine Technology* (4 a year).

SCI/Steel Construction Institute: Silwood Park, Ascot, SL5 7QN; tel. (1344) 636525; e-mail reception@steel-sci.com; internet www.steel-sci.com; f. 1986; develops and promotes the proper and effective use of steel as a construction material; provides technical expertise; 850 mems; library of 11,000 vols; Dir Dr G. H. COUCHMAN; publ. *New Steel Construction* (10 a year).

Society for Underwater Technology: 1 Fetter Lane, London, EC4A 1BR; tel. (20) 3440-5535; e-mail info@sut.org; internet www.sut.org.uk; f. 1966; promotes understanding of the underwater environment and proper economic and sociological usage of resources; 1,000 individual and 110 corporate mems; Exec. Sec. Dr R. L. ALLWOOD; publ. *Underwater Technology* (4 a year).

Society of Consulting Marine Engineers and Ship Surveyors: 202 Lambeth Rd, London, SE1 7JW; tel. (20) 7261-0869; e-mail sec@scmshq.org; internet www.scmshq.org; f. 1920; Sec. P. R. OWEN.

Society of Dyers and Colourists: Perkin House, POB 244, 82 Grattan Rd, Bradford, BD1 2JB; tel. (1274) 725138; e-mail info@sdc.org.uk; internet www.sdc.org.uk; f. 1884; promotes advancement of the science and technology of colour and coloration; awards chartered qualifications; colour experience; 2,500 mems; Pres. Dr SANJIV KAMAT; Chief Exec. Dr GRAHAM CLAYTON; publs *Colour Index*, *Coloration Technology* (6 a year), *The Colourist* (4 a year).

Society of Glass Technology: 9 Churchill Way, Chapeltown, Sheffield, S35 2PY; tel. (114) 263-4455; e-mail info@sgt.org; internet www.sgt.org; f. 1916; promotes the assocn of persons interested in glass technology; publishes books, journals and conf. proceedings; organizes int. and local confs on glass; Student Project Prize; 400 mems; library of 10,000 vols; located at Univ. of Sheffield Applied Science Library; Hon. Sec. JOHN HENDERSON; publs *Glass Technology: European Journal of Glass Science and Technology Part A* (6 a year), *Physics and Chemistry of Glasses: European Journal of Glass Science and Technology Part B* (6 a year).

Society of Operations Engineers: 22 Greencoat Pl., London, SW1P 1PR; tel. (20) 7630-1111; e-mail soe@soe.org.uk; internet www.soe.org.uk; f. 2000; formed by merger of Institute of Road Transport Engineers (IRTE) and Instn of Plant Engineers (IPlantE); represents mems of road transport, plant engineering and engineer surveying industries; 15,000 mems; Pres. GERRY FLEMING; publs *Plant Engineer* (6 a year), *Transport Engineer* (12 a year).

South Wales Institute of Engineers Educational Trust: Suite 2, Bay Chambers, W Bute St, Cardiff, CF10 5BB; tel. (1792) 879409; e-mail sandra.chapman@swieet2007.org.uk; internet www.swieet2007.org; f. 1857; develops an interest in engineering among the young; Chair. PHILIP E. HOURAHINE.

Textile Institute: see under International Organizations (Engineering and Technology).

TWI: Granta Park, Great Abington, Cambridge, CB21 6AL; tel. (1223) 899000; e-mail twi@twi.co.uk; internet www.twi.co.uk; f. 1946; undertakes gen. and contract research; advances welding technology in all aspects; provides consultancy and laboratory services; improves professional status and qualification of mems; specialized information services on materials-joining technology; training courses in welding engineering, welding inspection, practical welding, non-destructive testing, structural integrity, microjoining; 10,500 mems (3,500 research, 7,000 professional); library of 10,000 vols; Chief Exec. Dr CHRISTOPH WIESNER; publ. *Connect* (6 a year).

Research Institutes

GENERAL

Asia Research Centre: 10th Fl., Tower Two, Houghton St, London, WC2A 2AE; tel. (20) 7955-7388; e-mail arc@lse.ac.uk; internet www.lse.ac.uk/asiaresearchcentre; f. 1997; attached to London School of Economics and Political Science, Univ. of London; conducts and supports research on issues concerning Asia; organizes public lectures on topical issues of Asian countries; Dir Prof. ATHAR HUSSAIN.

Automotive Safety Centre: Edgbaston, Birmingham, B15 2TT; f. 1963; attached to Univ. of Birmingham; studies vehicle crashes; identifies injury causation and develops solutions for injury mitigation; Head Prof. AHAMEDALI HASSAN.

Cambridge Institute for Sustainability Leadership (CISL): 1 Trumpington St, Cambridge, CB2 1QA; tel. (1223) 768850; e-mail info@cisl.cam.ac.uk; internet www.cisl.cam.ac.uk; f. 1988; attached to Univ. of Cambridge; builds strategic leadership capacity to tackle critical global challenges; Dir POLLY COURTICE.

Centre for Alcohol and Drug Studies: Paisley Campus, Paisley, PA1 2BE; tel. (141) 848-3788; attached to Univ. of the West of Scotland; Dir K. BARRIE.

Centre for Business Research: The Judge Business School Bldg, Trumpington St, Cambridge, CB2 1AG; tel. (1223) 765320; e-mail enquiries@cbr.cam.ac.uk; internet www.cbr.cam.ac.uk; f. 1994; attached to Univ. of Cambridge; conducts interdisciplinary research on enterprise, innovation and governance in contemporary market economies; Dir Prof. SIMON DEAKIN.

Centre for Early Modern Studies: Dept of History, College of Humanities, Amory Bldg, Rennes Dr., Exeter, EX4 4RJ; tel. (1392) 264297; e-mail histoff@ex.ac.uk; internet humanities.exeter.ac.uk/history/research/centres/earlymodern; f. 2007; attached to Univ. of Exeter; areas of research incl. religious culture, social and economic relations, political and intellectual thought, gender and sexuality, space, landscape and national identities, history of the book, theatre and performance for the period between 1500 and 1800; Dir Prof. PHILIP SCHWYZER; Asst Dir Prof. JANE WHITTLE.

Centre for Enterprise and Regional Development: College Rd, Bangor, LL57 2DG; attached to Bangor Univ.; Dir Prof. DYLAN JONES-EVANS.

Centre for Gymnastics Research: Loughborough, LE11 3TU; e-mail m.r.yeadon@lboro.ac.uk; internet www.lboro.ac.uk/microsites/ssehs/biomechanics/gymnastics; f. 2004; attached to Loughborough Univ.; Dir Prof. FRED YEADON.

Centre for Innovation and Service Research: Univ. of Exeter Business School, Streatham Court, Rennes Dr., Exeter, EX4 4PU; tel. (1392) 722557; internet business-school.exeter.ac.uk/research/areas/centres/isr; attached to Univ. of Exeter; Dir Prof. ANDI SMART.

Centre for International Studies: Houghton St, London, WC2A 2AE; internet www.lse.ac.uk/internationalrelations/centresandunits/cis; f. 1967; attached to London School of Economics and Political Science, Univ. of London; promotes research in all aspects of int. studies; Centre Dir Dr KIRSTEN AINLEY.

Centre for Leadership Studies: Univ. of Exeter Business School, Streatham Court, Streatham Campus, Exeter, EX4 4ST; tel. (1392) 723463; e-mail m.l.bishop@exeter.ac.uk; internet business-school.exeter.ac.uk/research/areas/centres/cls; f. 1997; attached to Univ. of Exeter; research area ranges from applied evaluation of leadership devt processes to the philosophical underpinnings of modern leadership; Dir Prof. JONATHAN GOSLING.

Centre for Olympic Studies & Research: School of Sport, Exercise and Health Sciences, Loughborough Univ., Loughborough, LE11 3TU; e-mail cosar@lboro.ac.uk; internet www.lboro.ac.uk/microsites/ssehs/olympic-studies; f. 2004; attached to Loughborough Univ.; promotes, facilitates and conducts academic research on Olympism, Olympic games, Olympic movement and Olympic sports; Dir Prof. IAN HENRY; Deputy Dir Dr MAHFOUD AMARA.

Centre for the Study of Human Rights: Houghton St, London, WC2A 2AE; tel. (20) 7955-6428; e-mail z.gillard@lse.ac.uk; internet www.lse.ac.uk/humanrights; f. 1998; attached to London School of Economics and Political Science, Univ. of London; trans-disciplinary centre for human rights; Dir Prof. CHRISTINE CHINKIN (acting); Man. ZOE GILLARD.

Centre for War, State and Society: Dept of History, College of Humanities, Armory Bldg, Rennes Dr., Exeter, EX4 4RJ; tel. (1392) 264297; e-mail histoff@ex.ac.uk; internet humanities.exeter.ac.uk/history/research/centres/warstateandsociety; f. 2005; attached to Univ. of Exeter; researches on effects of armed conflict on states, societies, cultures; explores themes of warfare and societal transformation; insurgencies and counter-insurgencies; war and occupation; conflict resolution, peace-building and human rights; Dir Prof. MARTIN THOMAS.

Centre of Postcolonial Studies: Stirling, FK9 4LA; tel. (1786) 467495; internet www.stir.ac.uk/arts-humanities/research/centres/centre-of-postcolonial-studies; f. 1985; attached to Univ. of Stirling; postgraduate and undergraduate work relating to Commonwealth countries, particularly African history, African and Caribbean culture, writing and religion, Australian writing and painting, literature of India and New Zealand, and post-colonial critical theory; Dir Prof. DAVID RICHARDS.

Communications Research Centre: Dept of Social Sciences, Loughborough Univ., Loughborough, LE11 3TU; tel. (1509) 223368; e-mail ssenquiries@lboro.ac.uk; internet www.lboro.ac.uk/departments/socialsciences/research/centres/crc; attached to Loughborough Univ.; communication studies, culture and media, discourse and social interaction; Dir LIESBAT VAN ZOONEN.

Crucible Centre for Human Rights Research: tel. (20) 8392-5026; e-mail michele.lamb@roehampton.ac.uk; internet www.roehampton.ac.uk/crucible; attached to Roehampton Univ.; conducts research, teaching and training in the field of human rights, social justice and int. relations; Dir Dr MICHELE LAMB.

David Livingstone Centre for Sustainability: Graham Hills Bldg, 50 Richmond St, Glasgow, G1 1XQ; tel. (141) 548-4078; e-mail dlcs@strath.ac.uk; internet www.strath.ac.uk/dlcs; f. 2007 by merger of Graduate School of Environmental Studies (f. 1991) and David Livingstone Institute of International Development Studies (f. 1973); attached to Univ. of Strathclyde; research activities incl. Scotland chikhwawa health initiative, climate change risk and uncertainty, environmental forensics, emerging pollution and health risks, remediation of contaminated land, sustainable infrastructure; Dir Dr CHARLES KNAPP.

Early Childhood Research Centre: Dept of Education, Froebel College, Univ. of Roehampton, London, SW15 5PJ; tel. (20) 8392-3276; e-mail mathias.urban@roehampton.ac.uk; internet www.roehampton.ac.uk/research-centres/early-childhood-research-centre; attached to Univ. of Roehampton; interdisciplinary research in early childhood history and policy, measures of quality in early years provision, professional devt; Dir Prof. MATHIAS URBAN.

European Construction Institute: John Pickford Bldg, Loughborough Univ., Loughborough, LE11 3TU; tel. (1509) 222620; e-mail eci@lboro.ac.uk; internet www.eci-online.org; f. 1990; attached to Loughborough Univ.; focuses on delivering construction excellence; regional centres in the UK, Italy and Benelux; Pres. MICHEL VIRLOGEUX; Chair. JOHN OLIVER.

European Institute: Houghton St, London, WC2A 2AE; e-mail europeaninstitute@lse.ac.uk; tel. (20) 7955-6839; internet www.lse.ac.uk/europeaninstitute; f. 1991; attached to London School of Economics and Political Science; research focused on 4 interdisciplinary themes: governance and democracy in the European Union, European society, political economy in Europe, Europe beyond the EU; Head Prof. MAURICE FRASER.

European Research Institute: Edgbaston, Birmingham, B15 2TT; tel. (121) 414-6346; e-mail p.a.carr@bham.ac.uk; internet www.eri.bham.ac.uk; f. 2001; attached to Univ. of Birmingham; research in the fields of culture and society, economics, European politics, history, law; Head Prof. MARK WEBBER.

Institute for Creative Enterprises: Coventry Univ. Enterprises, Puma Way, Coventry, CV1 2NE; tel. (24) 7615-8300; e-mail receptionice@cad.coventry.ac.uk; internet www.coventry.ac.uk/business/institute-for-creative-enterprise; attached to Coventry Univ.; applied research activities for arts practice, communication and cultural studies, media, performing arts; postgraduate courses in performance, media, digital art; Project Man. Dr PETE McLUSKIE.

Institute for Retail Studies: Stirling, FK9 4LA; tel. (1786) 467386; e-mail irst1@stir.ac.uk; internet www.stir.ac.uk/management/research/irs; attached to Univ. of Stirling; Dir Prof. PAUL FREATHY; Deputy Dir Prof. LEIGH SPARKS.

Institute of Rehabilitation: 215 Anlaby Rd, Kingston upon Hull, HU3 2PG; tel. (1482) 675602; e-mail l.g.walker@hull.ac.uk; internet www.lgwalker.com/institute.html; f. 1997; attached to Univ. of Hull; research groups on cancer rehabilitation, elderly rehabilitation, and pain and therapies; Dir Prof. LESLIE G. WALKER (acting); Deputy Dir Dr DONALD M. SHARP.

Institute of Youth Sport: School of Sport, Exercise and Health Sciences, Loughborough Univ., Ashby Rd, Loughborough, LE11 3TU; e-mail c.e.taylor@lboro.ac.uk; internet www.lboro.ac.uk/microsites/ssehs/youth-sport; f. 1998; attached to Loughborough Univ.; promotes research on the welfare, education, performance and devt of young people participating in sports and physical education; Dir Dr MARY NEVILL; Sec. CATHIE TAYLOR.

Managerial Economics and Strategy Group: Houghton St, London, WC2A 2AE; tel. (20) 7955-7920; internet www.lse.ac.uk/management/research/academic-groups/managerial-economics-and-strategy; f. 1990; attached to London School of Economics and Political Science, Univ. of London; research areas incl. corporate governance, corporate restructuring, network economics, game theoretic approaches to strategy, executive compensation, organizational structure, negotiation, and system dynamics; Head Prof. LUIS GARICANO.

Loughborough Design School: Loughborough Univ., Loughborough, LE11 3TU; tel. (1509) 226900; e-mail dsoffice@lboro.ac.uk; internet www.lboro.ac.uk/departments/lds; f. 2010 by merger of Dept of Design and Technology, Dept of Human Sciences (Ergonomics) and the Ergonomics and Safety Research Institute (ESRI); attached to Loughborough Univ.; research, training and enterprise; Dean Prof. TRACY BHAMRA (acting).

LSE Gender Institute: Houghton St, London, WC2A 2AE; tel. (20) 7955-7602; internet www.lse.ac.uk/genderinstitute; f. 1993; attached to London School of Economics and Political Science, Univ. of London; addresses major intellectual challenges posed by contemporary changes in gender relations; Dir Prof. DIANE PERRONS; publs European Journal of Women's Studies (4 a year), European Urban and Regional Studies (4 a year), Feminist Review (online), Population Studies (3 a year).

Paisley Enterprise Research Centre: Paisley, PA1 2BE; internet www.uws.ac.uk/schools/business-school/research/paisley-enterprise-research-centre; f. 1995; attached to Univ. of the West of Scotland; Dir Prof. DAVID DEAKINS.

Peter Harrison Centre for Disability Sport: School of Sport, Exercise and Health Sciences, Loughborough Univ., Epinal Way, Loughborough, LE11 3TU; tel. (1509) 226387; e-mail phc@lboro.ac.uk; internet www.lboro.ac.uk/research/phc; f. 2005; attached to Loughborough Univ.; promotes knowledge in disability sport through applied research; 3 main research strands: sport science, performance health and psychosocial health and well-being; Dir Prof. VICKY TOLFREY; publs Health and Well-being, Sport Culture and Science, Sport Science.

Professional and Management Development Centre: Sir Richard Morris Bldg, Loughborough Univ., Loughborough, LE11 3TU; tel. (1509) 223140; e-mail pmdc@lboro.ac.uk; internet www.lboro.ac.uk/departments/sbe/pmdc; attached to Loughborough Univ.; Dir J. WHITTAKER.

Research Centre Wales/Canolfan Ymchwil Cymru: Univ. of Wales, Bangor, LL57 2DG; tel. (1248) 382220; e-mail cyc@bangor.ac.uk; internet www.cyc.bangor.ac.uk; f. 1985; attached to Bangor Univ.; research directly related to the needs of the region and its communities; Dir Prof. C. R. BAKER.

Social Science Research Unit: 18 Woburn Sq., London, WC1H 0NR; tel. (20) 7612-6397; e-mail ssru@ioe.ac.uk; internet www.ioe.ac.uk/research/54489.html; f. 1990; attached to Institute of Education, Univ. of London; promotes rigorous, ethical and participative social research to support education, health and welfare; Dir Prof. DAVID GOUGH; Deputy Dir SANDY OLIVER.

Stirling Centre for Scottish Studies: Stirling, FK9 4LA; tel. (1786) 467495; e-mail english@stir.ac.uk; internet www.stir.ac.uk/arts-humanities/research/centres/stirling-centre-for-scottish-studies; f. 1998; attached to Univ. of Stirling; promotes research, publ. and postgraduate recruitment in Scottish Studies, literature, art, music, history, media, philosophy, politics, social issues and cultural theory; Dir Dr SCOTT HAMES.

Stirling Media Research Institute: Stirling, FK9 4LA; tel. (1786) 467520; e-mail stirling.media@stir.ac.uk; internet www.stir.ac.uk/arts-humanities/research/centres/stirlingmediaresearchinstitute; attached to Univ. of Stirling; Dir Prof. NEIL BLAIN; publ. International Journal of Media and Cultural Politics.

AGRICULTURE, FISHERIES AND VETERINARY SCIENCE

Agri-Food and Biosciences Institute: AFBI HQ, Newforge Lane, Belfast, BT9 5PX; tel. (28) 9025-5636; e-mail info@afbini.gov.uk; internet www.afbini.gov.uk; f. 2006 by merger of Dept of Agriculture and Rural Devt (DARD) Science Service and the Agricultural Research Institute of Northern Ireland (ARINI); conducts high technology research and devt, statutory, analytical and diagnostic testing functions; offers scientific capabilities in areas of agriculture, animal health, food, environment and biosciences; Chair. SEÁN HOGAN; CEO Prof. SEAMUS KENNEDY.

Animal Health and Veterinary Laboratories Agency: Woodham Lane, Addlestone, KT15 3NB; tel. (1932) 341111; e-mail corp.weybridge@ahvla.gsi.gov.uk; internet www.defra.gov.uk/ahvla; f. 2011 by merger of 2 agencies: Animal Health and the Veterinary Laboratories Agency; exec. agency of the Dept for Environment, Food and Rural Affairs; safeguards animal health and welfare as well as public health; protects the economy and enhances food security through research, surveillance and inspection; CEO CHRIS HADKISS.

Animal Health and Welfare: Dept of Agriculture and Rural Development, Dundonald House, Upper Newtownards Rd, Belfast, BT4 3SB; tel. (28) 9052-4999; e-mail dardhelpline@dardni.gov.uk; internet www .dardni.gov.uk/index/animal-health-and-welfare; attached to Dept of Agriculture and Rural Devt; animal and animal product imports and by-products, diseases, control and prevention, animal welfare, artificial reproduction, export certification; library of 11,000 vols.

Animal Health Trust: Lanwades Park, Kentford, Newmarket, CB8 7UU; tel. (1638) 751000; e-mail info@aht.org.uk; internet www.aht.org.uk; f. 1942; aims to advance veterinary science and provide specialist clinical services for all companion animals; Pres. HRH THE PRINCESS ROYAL; CEO Dr MARK VAUDIN.

Biotechnology and Biological Sciences Research Council: Polaris House, North Star Ave, Swindon, SN2 1UH; tel. (1793) 413200; e-mail press.office@bbsrc.ac.uk; internet www.bbsrc.ac.uk; f. 1994; promotes economic growth, wealth and job creation; improves quality of life in the UK and beyond; Chair. Prof. TOM BLUNDELL; Chief Exec. Prof. JACKIE HUNTER..

Institutes and Units:

Babraham Institute: Babraham Research Campus, Cambridge, CB22 3AT; tel. (1223) 496000; e-mail babraham .contact@babraham.ac.uk; internet www .babraham.ac.uk; f. 1948; advances understanding of function in animal cells and systems, with emphasis on cell signalling, recognition mechanisms and mammalism devt; Dir Prof. MIACHAEL WAKELAM (acting).

Institute of Food Research: Norwich Research Park, Colney Lane, Norwich, NR4 7UA; tel. (1603) 255000; e-mail ifr .communications@ifr.ac.uk; internet www .ifr.ac.uk; f. 1986; harnesses food for health and prevents food-related diseases; Dir Prof. DAVID BOXER; publ. *Science+Innovation*.

Institute of Biological, Environmental and Rural Sciences—IBERS—Aberystwyth University: Edward Llwyd Building, Pengalis Campus, Aberystwyth, SY23 3DA; tel. (1970) 621986; e-mail ibers@aber .ac.uk; internet www.aber.ac.uk/en/ibers; f. 2008; conducts basic, strategic and applied research from genes and molecules to organisms and the environment; Dir Prof. WAYNE POWELL.

John Innes Centre: Norwich Research Park, Norwich, NR4 7UH; tel. (1603) 450000; e-mail jic.communications@jic.ac .uk; internet www.jic.ac.uk; f. 1994; carries out fundamental and strategic research; uses a wide range of disciplines in the biological and chemical sciences, incl. microbiology, cell biology, biochemistry, chemistry, genetics, molecular biology, computational and mathematical biology; Dir Prof. DALE SANDERS.

Pirbright Institute: Pirbright Laboratory, Ash Rd, Pirbright, GU24 0NF; tel. (1635) 578411; e-mail enquiries@pirbright .ac.uk; internet www.pirbright.ac.uk; f. 1986; conducts research on virus diseases of farm animals and viruses that spread from animals to humans; Dir Prof. JOHN FAZAKERLEY.

Roslin Institute (Edinburgh): Univ. of Edinburgh, Easter Bush Roslin, EH25 9PS; tel. (131) 6519100; e-mail info@roslin .ed.ac.uk; internet www.roslin.ed.ac.uk; f. 1993; basic and strategic research on farm animals; Dir Prof. DAVID HUME.

Rothamsted Research: Rothamsted, Harpenden, AL5 2JQ; tel. (1582) 763133; e-mail foi.rothamsted@rothamsted.ac.uk; internet www.rothamsted.ac.uk; f. 1843; basic, strategic and applied research on soils and crop plants; Dir Prof. MAURICE MOLONEY.

Sustainable Bioenergy Centre: e-mail info.bsbec@bbsrc.ac.uk; internet www .bbsrc.ac.uk/research/biotechnology-bioenergy/bsbec; f. 2009; 6 dedicated programmes in bioenergy research; centres have offices at universities incl. Cambridge, Dundee, Nottingham and York.

Centre for Applied Marine Sciences: Marine Science Laboratories, Menai Bridge Anglesey, Bangor, LL59 5AB; tel. (1248) 382888; e-mail enquiries@cams.bangor.ac .uk; internet www.cams.bangor.ac.uk; f. 1977; attached to Bangor Univ.; divs of analytical chemistry, applied marine biology, applied oceanography, coastal zone management, marine geosciences and survey and instrumentation; Dir LEWIS LE LAY; Deputy Dir JONATHAN KING.

Centre for Environment, Fisheries and Aquaculture Science (CEFAS): Pakefield Rd, Lowestoft, NR33 0HT; tel. (1502) 562244; e-mail lowlibrary@cefas.co.uk; internet www .cefas.defra.gov.uk; exec. agency of the Dept for the Environment, Food and Rural Affairs; provides contract research, consultancy and training services in environmental impact assessment, environmental research and monitoring, aquaculture health and hygiene, and fisheries science and management; extensive research library; br at Weymouth; Chief Exec. MIKE WALDOCK.

Centre for Rural Policy Research: College of Social Sciences and Int. Studies, Room 339/340, Armory Bldg, Rennes Dr., Exeter, EX4 4RJ; tel. (1392) 722438; e-mail crprmail@exeter.ac.uk; internet socialsciences.exeter.ac.uk/research/centres/ crpr; f. 1960 as Agricultural Economics Unit, renamed as Centre for Rural Research, current name adopted 2007; attached to Univ. of Exeter; researches into aspects of rural economy and society with focus on agricultural, environmental and bioenergy policies; environmental resource management; agro-food regulation; sustainable communities; social and economic devt of agriculture; impacts of climate change on farming and land use; Co-Dir Prof. MICHAEL WINTER; Co-Dir Dr MATT LOBLEY.

Food and Environment Research Agency (FERA): Sand Hutton, York, YO41 1LZ; tel. (1904) 462000; e-mail info@fera.gsi .gov.uk; internet www.fera.defra.gov.uk; f. 2009; exec. agency of the Dept for Environment, Food and Rural Affairs; research and advice in the fields of: plant health; the authenticity, chemical and microbiological safety and nutritional value of the food supply; pesticide safety (incl. the monitoring of residues in food); veterinary drug residues; proficiency testing schemes; the control of pests and diseases of growing and stored crops; the impact of food production on the environment and the consumer; alternative crops and biotechnology; animal health and welfare; and conservation and wildlife management; response and recovery from unforeseen and emergency situations; Chief Exec. ADRIAN BELTON.

Forest Research: Alice Holt Lodge, Farnham, GU10 4LH; tel. (1420) 22255; e-mail research.info@forestry.gsi.gov.uk; internet www.forestry.gov.uk/forestresearch; f. 1997; attached to Forestry Commission; informs and supports forestry's contribution to UK governmental policies; provides the evidence base for UK forestry practices and supports innovation; provides a range of products and services to support the land management and environmental technologies sectors; 2 research stations cover the following research domains: ecosystems, social forestry, biosecurity, sustainable forestry and climate change; library of 20,000 vols, 60 current journals; CEO Dr JAMES PENDLEBURY.

Research Station:

Northern Research Station: Roslin, EH25 9SY; tel. (131) 445-2176; e-mail nrs@forestry.gsi.gov.uk.

Garden Organic: Ryton Organic Gardens, Coventry, CV8 3LG; tel. (24) 7630-3517; e-mail enquiry@gardenorganic.org.uk; internet www.gardenorganic.org.uk; f. 1954, current name adopted 2005; conducts research in organic agriculture, with focus on commercial organic horticulture in temperate regions and subsistence agriculture in developing countries; maintains vegetable seed colln; sets standards for organic amenity horticulture; services to the public incl. membership of the asscn and access to organic display gardens; Dir for Research Dr MARGI LENNARTSSON.

Hull International Fisheries Institute: Cottingham Rd, Hull, HU6 7RX; internet www2.hull.ac.uk/science/biological_sciences/ research/hifi.aspx; f. 1989; attached to Univ. of Hull; research, education, training and consultancy in fisheries, conservation and aquatic-resource management; Dir Prof. Dr IAN G. COWX.

National Institute of Agricultural Botany: Huntingdon Rd, Cambridge, CB3 0LE; tel. (1223) 342200; e-mail info@niab.com; internet www.niab.com; f. 1919; applied, basic and translational research in crops and agronomy, genetics and breeding, varieties and seeds; Chair. JEREMY LEWIS; CEO Dr TINA BARSBY.

Oxford Forestry Institute: University of Oxford, Department of Plant Sciences, South Parks Rd, Oxford, OX1 3RB; tel. (1865) 275000; e-mail ofi@plants.ox.ac.uk; internet www.plants.ox.ac.uk/ofi; f. 1924 as Imperial, later Commonwealth Forestry Inst.; attached to Dept of Plant Sciences, Univ. of Oxford; library of 200,000 vols, in conjunction with CAB International; Dir Prof. J. BURLEY.

Science and Advice for Scottish Agriculture (SASA): Roddinglaw Rd, Edinburgh, EH12 9FJ; tel. (131) 244-8890; e-mail info@ sasa.gsi.gov.uk; internet www.sasa.gov.uk; f. 1992 as the Scottish Agricultural Science Agency, current name adopted 2008; attached to Scottish Govt Agriculture, Food and Rural Communities Directorate; carries out scientific exec. work, associated research and consultation on: seed testing, testing of candidate cultivators of crop plants for Nat. Listing and Plant Breeders' Rights, certification of seed and planting stock, production of disease-tested clonal stocks of potatoes, statutory aspects of pest and disease control, pesticide usage assessment, pesticide residues, ecology of mammals and birds of actual or potential pest status; Head of SASA (vacant)..

Research Institute:

James Hutton Institute: Invergowrie, Dundee, DD2 5DA; tel. (844) 928-5428; e-mail info@hutton.ac.uk; internet www

.hutton.ac.uk; f. 2011 by merger of Macaulay Land Use Research Institute and SCRI; researches on plants and their interactions with the environment, particularly in managed ecosystems; addresses the public goods of sustainability and high-quality and healthy food, particularly crops of potatoes, barley and soft fruit; Chief Exec. Prof. IAIN GORDON.

Woburn Experimental Station (Lawes Agricultural Trust): Husborne Crawley, Bedford; f. 1876; runs as outstation of Rothamsted Experimental Station; Dir L. FOWDEN.

ARCHITECTURE AND TOWN PLANNING

Built Environment Research Institute: Room 04F14, School of the Built Environment, Univ. of Ulster, Jordanstown campus, Shore Rd, Newtownabbey, BT37 0QB; tel. (28) 9036-6566; e-mail ws.mcgreal@ulster.ac.uk; internet www.beri.ulster.ac.uk; f. 1994; attached research centres: Centre for Sustainable Technologies (CST), Centre for Research on Property and Planning (RPP), Fire Safety Engineering Research and Technology Centre (FireSERT), Hydrogen Safety Engineering and Research (HySAFER); conducts research that enhances the quality of the built environment and addresses the changing needs of society in a more sustainable manner; Dir Prof. STANLEY MCGREAL; Sec. SADIE MAGEE.

Cities Programme: Houghton St, London, WC2A 2AE; tel. (20) 7955-6828; e-mail cities@lse.ac.uk; internet www.lse.ac.uk/lsecities/citiesprogramme; f. 1996; attached to London School of Economics and Political Science, Univ. of London; undertakes design-based teaching and research on social, technical and economic aspects of cities and urban systems; Dir RICKY BURDETT.

Housing Policy and Practice Unit: School of Applied Social Science, Colin Bell Bldg, Univ. of Stirling, Stirling, FK9 4LA; tel. (1786) 467719; e-mail hppu1@stir.ac.uk; internet www.dass.stir.ac.uk; attached to Univ. of Stirling; teaching and research in sociology, social policy, social work, housing, services to people with dementia and addictions; Dir Prof. ISOBEL ANDERSON.

LSE Housing and Communities: Houghton St, London, WC2A 2AE; tel. (20) 7955-6330; e-mail lsehousingandcommunities@lse.ac.uk; internet sticerd.lse.ac.uk/lsehousing; f. 1989; attached to London School of Economics and Political Science, Univ. of London; multi-disciplinary research centre; focuses on the exploration of different dimensions of social disadvantage; examines the impact of public policy on individuals, communities and areas; Dir Prof. ANNE POWER.

Parallelism, Algorithms and Architectures Research Centre: Dept of Computer Science, Loughborough Univ., Loughborough, LE11 3TU; tel. (1509) 222692; e-mail h.e.bez@lboro.ac.uk; internet parc.lboro.ac.uk; attached to Loughborough Univ.; research areas incl. coding and signal processing, concurrency, fundamental theoretical research, future architectures of parallel computers, parallel algorithms, vision and visualization; Co-Dir Dr HELMUT BEZ; Co-Dir Dr ONDREJ SYKORA.

Prince's Foundation for Building Community: 19–22 Charlotte Rd, London, EC2A 3SG; tel. (20) 7613-8500; e-mail enquiry@princes-foundation.org; internet www.princes-foundation.org; f. 1992; research into all areas of sustainable traditional architecture, urbanism, regeneration and building crafts; public lectures, seminars and exhibitions; educational courses and consultancy; library of 10,200 vols; Chair. Sir MICHAEL HINTZE; Librarian CARLA MARCHESAN.

ECONOMICS, LAW AND POLITICS

Bracton Centre for Legal History Research: Law School, Amory Bldg, Rennes Dr., Exeter, EX4 4RJ; internet socialsciences.exeter.ac.uk/law/research/groups/legalhistory; f. 2009; attached to Univ. of Exeter; Dir Prof. CHANTAL STEBBINGS; Dir Prof. ANTHONY MUSSON.

Centre for Comparative Criminology and Criminal Justice: School of Social Sciences, Bangor Univ., Bangor, LL57 2DG; tel. (1248) 382007; e-mail j.wardhaugh@bangor.ac.uk; f. 1991; attached to Bangor Univ.; promotes research, postgraduate teaching and consultancy on matters relating to crime and deviance, law, order and social control; Dir Dr JULIA WARDHAUGH.

Centre for Economic Performance: Houghton St, London, WC2A 2AE; tel. (20) 7955-7673; e-mail cep.info@lse.ac.uk; internet cep.lse.ac.uk; f. 1990; attached to London School of Economics and Political Science, Univ. of London; studies determinants of economic performance; also globalization, technology and instns and their impact on productivity, inequality, employment, stability, wellbeing; Dir Prof. JOHN VAN REENEN.

Centre for Elections, Media and Participation (CEMaP): Univ. of Exeter, Queen's Dr., Exeter, EX4 4QJ; tel. (1392) 723183; internet centres.exeter.ac.uk/cemap; f. 2008; attached to Univ. of Exeter; research on campaigns, elections, political parties from both a British and comparative perspective; Dir NICOLE BOLLEYER.

Centre for European Governance: Dept of Politics, Univ. of Exeter, Armory Bldg, Rennes Dr., Exeter, EX4 4RJ; tel. (1392) 661000; e-mail c.radaelli@exeter.ac.uk; internet centres.exeter.ac.uk/ceg; f. 1979 as Centre for European Studies; merged with the Centre for Regulatory Governance; attached to Univ. of Exeter; provides training and conducts research in EU politics, regulatory governance, public opinion, constitutional politics, political economy of European integration; Dir Prof. CLAUDIO RADAELLI; publ. *European Journal of Political Research.*

Centre for European Legal Studies: School of Law, Univ. of Exeter, Armory Bldg, Rennes Dr., Exeter, EX4 4RJ; tel. (1392) 263365; e-mail lawlib@exeter.ac.uk; internet socialsciences.exeter.ac.uk/law/research/groups/cels; f. 1972; attached to Univ. of Exeter; conducts research on EU and comparative law; evaluates its effects in the UK and other mem. states; Dir Prof. JAMES DEVENNEY.

Centre for Professional Legal Studies: Graham Hills Bldg, 50 George St, Glasgow, G1 1BA; tel. (141) 548-3738; internet www.strath.ac.uk/humanities/lawschool/centreforprofessionallegalstudies; attached to Univ. of Strathclyde; access to justice and legal aid, the legal profession, professional ethics and the judiciary; Dir Prof. ALAN PATERSON.

Centre for Research into Economics and Finance in Southern Africa: Room G409, 20 Kingsway, London School of Economics and Political Science, Houghton St, London, WC2A 2AE; e-mail crefsa@lse.ac.uk; internet www.lse.ac.uk/researchandexpertise/units/crefsa; f. 1990; attached to London School of Economics and Political Science, Univ. of London; undertakes research into management of int. finance, foreign-exchange policy and domestic financial policy in S Africa, and macroeconomic and financial issues in S African region; Dir Dr JONATHAN LEAPE.

Centre for the Study of Public Policy: McCance Bldg, 16 Richmond St, Glasgow, G1 1XQ; e-mail cspp@strath.ac.uk; internet www.cspp.strath.ac.uk; f. 1976; attached to Univ. of Strathclyde; research areas incl. the growth of govt, social welfare, elections and democratization and social capital and health; Dir Prof. RICHARD ROSE; Sec. OHNA ROBERTSON.

Department of International Development: 6–8th Fl., Connaught House, Houghton St, London, WC2A 2AE; tel. (20) 7955-7425; internet www.lse.ac.uk/internationaldevelopment; f. 1990 as Development Studies Institute; attached to London School of Economics and Political Science, Univ. of London; promotes interdisciplinary post-graduate teaching and research on processes of social, political and economic devt and change; Head Prof. TIM ALLEN.

Economic Research Council: 5 Albany Courtyard, Piccadilly, London, W1J 0HF; tel. (20) 7340-6016; e-mail info@ercouncil.org; internet www.ercouncil.org; f. 1943; non-profit-making research and educational org. in the field of economics and monetary practice; Pres. The Rt Hon. Lord LAMONT OF LERWICK; Chair. DAMON DE LASZLO; Hon. Sec. JIM BOURLET; publ. *Britain and Overseas* (4 a year).

Economic Research Institute of Northern Ireland: Pearl Assurance House, 1–3 Donegall Sq. East, Belfast, BT1 5HB; tel. (28) 9023-2180; e-mail contact@erini.ac.uk; internet www.erini.ac.uk; f. 2003, merger of Northern Ireland Economic Research Centre (NIERC) and the Northern Ireland Economic Council (NIEC) 2004; ind. economic research and analyses; public policy making; research consultancy; Dir VICTOR HEWITT; Head of Research Dr MICHAEL ANYADIKE-DANES; publs *ERINI Research Reports*, *ERINI Working Papers* (print and online, irregular), *NIEC Publications* (print and online, irregular), *NIERC Northern Ireland Studies* (print and online, irregular), *NIERC Reports* (print and online, irregular).

European Policies Research Centre: School of Government and Public Policy, Univ. of Strathclyde, 40 George St, Glasgow, G1 1QE; tel. (141) 548-3672; e-mail eprc@strath.ac.uk; internet www.eprc.strath.ac.uk; f. 1983; attached to Univ. of Strathclyde; research on regional problems and policies in Europe and on the evaluation of structural funds programmes and projects within the EU; Dir Prof. JOHN BACHTLER; Dir FIONA WISHLADE.

Exeter Centre for Ethno-Political Studies (EXCEPS): Institute of Arab and Islamic Studies, Stocker Rd, Univ. of Exeter, Exeter, EX4 4ND; tel. (1392) 269250; e-mail z.jennings@exeter.ac.uk; internet centres.exeter.ac.uk/exceps; f. 2007; attached to Univ. of Exeter; conducts interdisciplinary research covering culture, memory and conflict, dynamics and management of ethnic conflict, unrecognised states, migrations and diasporas, language, literature and culture, security and terrorism; Dir Prof. GARETH STANSFIELD; Deputy Dir Prof ILAN PAPPE; Deputy Dir Dr JONATHAN GITHENS-MAZER.

Financial Markets Group Research Centre: Lionel Robbins Bldg, 4th Fl., Houghton St, London, WC2A 2AE; tel. (20) 7955-7002; e-mail fmg@lse.ac.uk; internet www.lse.ac.uk/fmg; f. 1987; attached to London School of Economics and Political Science, Univ. of London; conducts research into financial markets; Dir Prof. CHRISTOPHER POLK.

Fraser of Allander Institute: Sir William Duncan Bldg, 130 Rottenrow, Glasgow, G4 0GE; tel. (141) 548-3958; e-mail fraser@strath.ac.uk; internet www.strath.ac.uk/fraser; f. 1975; attached to Univ. of Strathclyde; carries out research on regional issues generally and the Scottish economy in particular, incl. forecasting and the analysis of short-term and medium-term movements in Scottish economic activity; Dir KIM SWALES; Deputy Dir RICHARD BELLINGHAM; publ. *Fraser of Allander Economic Commentary* (3 a year).

Greater London Group: Houghton St, London, WC2A 2AE; tel. (20) 7955-6522; f. 1958; attached to London School of Economics and Political Science, Univ. of London; studies the devt, economy and social aspects of urban areas in Britain and overseas; Dir TONY TRAVERS.

Institute for European Finance: Bangor Business School, Bangor Univ., Bangor, LL57 2DG; tel. (1248) 382277; e-mail ief@bangor.ac.uk; internet www.bangor.ac.uk/business/research_and_inst/ief; f. 1973; attached to Bangor Univ.; provides specialist consultancy and project reports to banks, financial services firms, trade asscns, govts, int. orgs and public sector orgs; Dir Prof. KLAUS SCHAECK.

Institute for Social & Economic Research: Wivenhoe Park, Colchester, CO4 3SQ; tel. (1206) 872957; e-mail iser@essex.ac.uk; internet www.iser.essex.ac.uk; attached to Univ. of Essex; conducts research in social science disciplines, incl. economics, sociology, demography, geography and statistics; Dir HEATHER LAURIE.

Institute of Development Studies: Library Rd, Brighton, BN1 9RE; tel. (1273) 606261; e-mail ids@ids.ac.uk; internet www.ids.ac.uk; f. 1966; attached to Univ. of Sussex; nat. centre concerned with Third World devt and relationships between rich and poor countries; offers teaching and supervision for univ. graduate degrees; official depository for UN publs; library of 200,000 vols; Dir Prof. LAWRENCE BEZANSON.

Institute of European Law: Birmingham Law School, Univ. of Birmingham, Edgbaston, Birmingham, B15 2TT; tel. (121) 414-6282; e-mail iel@contacts.bham.ac.uk; internet www.birmingham.ac.uk/research/activity/iel; f. 1989; attached to Univ. of Birmingham; provides interdisciplinary centre for research on European law; Dir Dr MARTIN TRYBUS; Deputy Dir Dr LUCA RUBINI.

Institute of European Public Law: Cottingham Rd, Hull, HU6 7RX; tel. (1482) 465742; internet www2.hull.ac.uk/fass/law/research/iepl.aspx; f. 1992; attached to Univ. of Hull; promotes research and post-graduate teaching in European public law; Dir Prof. PATRICK BIRKINSHAW; Deputy Dir Dr MIKE VARNEY; publ. *European Public Law Journal*.

Institute of Judicial Administration: Birmingham Law School, Univ. of Birmingham, Edgbaston, Birmingham, B15 2TT; tel. (121) 414-3637; e-mail law@bham.ac.uk; internet www.birmingham.ac.uk/research/activity/ija; f. 1968; attached to Univ. of Birmingham; initiates, coordinates and develops teaching and research in all aspects of the admin. of justice in England and Wales; Dir Dr MARIANNE WADE.

International Institute for Strategic Studies: Arundel House, 13–15 Arundel St, Temple Pl., London, WC2R 3DX; tel. (20) 7379-7676; e-mail iiss@iiss.org; internet www.iiss.org; f. 1958; promotes the adoption of sound policies to further global peace and security; Chair. FRANÇOIS HEISBOURG; Dir-Gen. and Chief Exec. Dr JOHN CHIPMAN; publs *Strategic Survey* (1 a year), *Survival* (4 a year).

Jill Dando Institute of Security and Crime Science: 35 Tavistock Sq., London, WC1H 9EZ; tel. (20) 3108-3206; e-mail jdi@ucl.ac.uk; internet www.ucl.ac.uk/jdi; f. 2001; attached to Univ. College London; promotes multi-disciplinary research in crime and security; conferences, events, training and short courses; Dir Prof. RICHARD WORTLEY.

LSE London: Room PS300, Portsmouth St, Houghton St, London, WC2A 2AE; tel. (20) 7955-6522; e-mail lselondon@lse.ac.uk; internet www.lse.ac.uk/geographyandenvironment/research/london; f. 1998; attached to London School of Economics and Political Science, Univ. of London; studies economic and social issues of London region, as well as problems and potential of other urban and metropolitan regions; Dir TONY TRAVERS.

Mannheim Centre of Criminology: Houghton St, London, WC2A 2AE; internet www.lse.ac.uk/socialpolicy/researchcentresandgroups/mannheim/home.aspx; f. 1990; attached to London School of Economics and Political Science, Univ. of London; coordinates research in criminology and criminal justice; Co-Dir Prof. JENNIFER BROWN.

Midlands Centre for Criminology and Criminal Justice: Brockington Bldg, Loughborough Univ., Loughborough, LE11 3TU; tel. (1509) 228369; e-mail g.farrell@lboro.ac.uk; attached to Loughborough Univ.; research areas incl. environmental criminology, crime analysis and crime prevention, criminal justice system, drug policy, policing; Dir Prof. GRAHAM FARRELL.

National Institute of Economic and Social Research: 2 Dean Trench St, Smith Sq., London, SW1P 3HE; tel. (20) 7222-7665; e-mail enquiries@niesr.ac.uk; internet www.niesr.ac.uk; f. 1938; carries out research to improve understanding of the economic and social forces that affect people's lives, and the ways in which policy can bring about change; library of 10,000 vols, 300 periodicals; Pres. Prof. CHARLES BEAN (acting); Dir JONATHAN PORTES; publ. *National Institute Economic Review* (4 a year).

Overseas Development Institute: 203 Blackfriars Rd, London, SE1 8NJ; tel. (20) 7922-0300; e-mail odi@odi.org.uk; internet www.odi.org.uk; f. 1960; inspires and informs policy and practice to reduce poverty and improve livelihoods; library of 20,000 vols; Chair. JAMES CAMERON; Exec. Dir KEVIN WATKINS; publs *Development Policy Review* (4 a year), *Disasters: The Journal of Disaster Studies and Management* (4 a year).

Policy Studies Institute: 50 Hanson St, London, W1W 6UP; tel. (20) 7911-7500; e-mail admin@policystudiesinstitute.org.uk; internet www.psi.org.uk; f. 1978; attached to Univ. of Westminster; undertakes and publishes research studies relevant to social, economic, industrial and environmental policy; Dir MALCOLM RIGG.

Royal United Services Institute for Defence and Security Studies: Whitehall, London, SW1A 2ET; tel. (20) 7747-2600; e-mail director@rusi.org; internet www.rusi.org; f. 1831; engages in defence and security research; library: see under Libraries and Archives; Dir-Gen. Prof. MICHAEL CLARKE; publs *Defence Systems* (3 a year), *Journal* (6 a year).

Scottish Economic Policy Network: Stirling, FK9 4LA; tel. (1786) 473171; attached to Univ. of Stirling; Dir Prof. D. BELL.

Suntory and Toyota International Centres for Economics and Related Disciplines: Houghton St, London, WC2A 2AE; tel. (20) 7955-6699; e-mail sticerd@lse.ac.uk; internet www.sticerd.lse.ac.uk; f. 1978; attached to London School of Economics and Political Science, Univ. of London; promotes research into applied economics and related fields; incl. Centre for Analysis of Social Exclusion; Dir Prof. ORIANA BANDIERA; Deputy Dir Prof. JOHN HILLS.

Transitional Justice Institute: Jordanstown Campus, Shore Rd, Newtownabbey, BT37 0QB; tel. (2890) 366202 Magee Campus, Northland Rd, Londonderry, BT48 7JL; tel. (2871) 375146; e-mail transitionaljustice@ulster.ac.uk; internet www.transitionaljustice.ulster.ac.uk; f. 2003; attached to Univ. of Ulster; promotes theoretical and practical understanding of 'transitional justice'; raises awareness of gender and other issues in the realization of peace and justice; Dir Prof. BILL ROLSTON; Assoc. Dir Prof. FIONNUALA NÍ AOLÁIN.

EDUCATION

Centre for Applied Research in Educational Technologies (CARET): Cambridge University Library, Digital Services, Cambridge CB3 9DR; tel. (1223) 765040; e-mail john@caret.cam.ac.uk; internet www.caret.cam.ac.uk; attached to Univ. of Cambridge; Dir JOHN NORMAN.

Centre for Educational Research and Development: Univ. of Lincoln, Brayford Pool, Lincoln, LN6 7TS; tel. (1522) 837017; e-mail jhubbard@lincoln.ac.uk; internet www.lincoln.ac.uk/cerd; attached to Univ. of Lincoln; Head Dr ANDREA ABBAS (acting).

Centre for Educational Studies: 3rd Fl., Wilberforce Bldg, Univ. of Hull, Cottingham Rd, Hull, HU6 7RX; tel. (1482) 465974; e-mail facultyofeducation@hull.ac.uk; internet www2.hull.ac.uk/ifl/ces.aspx; attached to Faculty of Education, Univ. of Hull; conducts research on education and technology, professionals and practice, policy: theory and practice; Co-Dir JAYNE KNOTT (acting); Co-Dir EILEEN WAKE.

Centre for International Education and Research: School of Education, Univ. of Birmingham, Edgbaston, Birmingham, B15 2TT; tel. (121) 414-4809; e-mail m.schweisfurth@bham.ac.uk; internet www.birmingham.ac.uk/research/activity/education/cier; attached to Univ. of Birmingham; promotes role of education in economic, social, political devt; Dir Dr MICHELE SCHWEISFURTH.

Centre for Learning Development: Cottingham Rd, Hull, HU6 7RX; e-mail cld@hull.ac.uk; attached to Univ. of Hull; Head Prof. G. CHAMBERS (acting).

Centre for Mediterranean Studies: Dept of Classics and Ancient History, Univ. of Exeter, Queen's Dr., Exeter, EX4 4RJ; tel. (1392) 264203; e-mail l.g.mitchell@ex.ac.uk; internet centres.exeter.ac.uk/cms; f. 1992; attached to Univ. of Exeter; promotes interdisciplinary teaching and research into history, culture and people of Mediterranean; Dir Dr LYNETTE MITCHELL.

Centre for Research in the Arts, Social Sciences and Humanities: Alison Richard Bldg, 7 W Rd, Cambridge, CB3 9DT; tel. (1223) 766886; e-mail enquiries@crassh.cam.ac.uk; internet www.crassh.cam.ac.uk; attached to Univ. of Cambridge; Dir Prof. SIMON GOLDHILL (King's College).

Centre for Russian and East European Studies: Muirhead Tower, Sixth Fl., Univ. of Birmingham, Edgbaston, Birmingham, B15 2TT; tel. (121) 414-6346; e-mail d.l.averre@bham.ac.uk; internet www.birmingham.ac.uk/schools/government-society/departments/

russian-east-european-studies; f. 1963; attached to Univ. of Birmingham; research programmes incl. studies of Russian, Ukrainian and Central European politics, society and culture, post-socialist economic transformation, history of Russia and the Soviet Union, security studies; library of 90,000 vols; Dir Dr TIM HAUGHTON.

Centre for the Economics of Education: London School of Economics and Political Science, Houghton St, London, WC2A 2AE; tel. (20) 7955-7673; e-mail cee@lse.ac.uk; internet cee.lse.ac.uk; f. 2000; attached to London School of Economics and Political Science, Univ. of London; Dir Prof. STEPHEN MACHIN.

Centre of Advanced International Studies: c/o Politics Dept, Univ. of Exeter, Amory Bldg, Rennes Dr., Exeter, EX4 4RJ; tel. (1392) 723164; e-mail politics@exeter.ac.uk; internet socialsciences.exeter.ac.uk/politics/research/centres/cais; f. 2000; attached to Univ. of Exeter; researches into aspects of global social relations across political, economic, cultural realms; Dir Prof. DOUG STOKES; Deputy Dir Dr ALEX PRICHARD.

Centre of African Studies: Alison Richard Bldg, 7 W Rd, Cambridge, CB3 9DT; tel. (1223) 334396; e-mail centre@african.cam.ac.uk; internet www.african.cam.ac.uk; f. 1965; attached to Univ. of Cambridge; Dir Dr HARRI ENGLUND; Librarian MARILYN GLANFIELD.

Centre of Latin American Studies: Alison Richard Bldg, 7 W Rd, Cambridge, CB3 9DT; tel. (1223) 335390; e-mail jac46@cam.ac.uk; internet www.latin-american.cam.ac.uk; f. 1966; attached to Univ. of Cambridge; promotes research and teaching on Latin America; library of 12,500 vols; Dir Dr CHARLES A. JONES.

Centre of South Asian Studies: Alison Richard Bldg, 7 West Rd, Cambridge, CB3 9DT; tel. (1223) 338-094; e-mail admin@s-asian.cam.ac.uk; internet www.s-asian.cam.ac.uk; f. 1964; attached to Univ. of Cambridge; promotes within the Univ. the study of India, Pakistan, Sri Lanka, Bangladesh, the Himalayan kingdoms and Burma; library of 40,000 vols; Dir Prof. C. A. BAYLY.

Education Research Group: Houghton St, London, WC2A 2AE; f. 1990; attached to London School of Economics and Political Science, Univ. of London; carries out research into current educational topics incl. choice of schools, schools' admissions, nat. curriculum, funding of education, and European and int. issues; Dir Dr ANNE WEST.

Institute for Advanced Studies in the Humanities: Hope Park Sq., Edinburgh, EH8 9NP; tel. (131) 650-4671; e-mail iash@ed.ac.uk; internet www.iash.ed.ac.uk; f. 1969; attached to Univ. of Edinburgh; Dir Prof. JO SHAW (acting); Sec. DONALD FERGUSON.

Institute for Cultural Research: POB 2227, London, NW2 3BW; tel. (20) 8452-0960; e-mail admin@i-c-r.org.uk; internet i-c-r.org.uk; f. 1965; library of 59 monographs; Chair. of Ccl CLARE MAXWELL-HUDSON; Hon. Sec. PATTI SCHNEIDER; Hon. Treas. RAMSAY WOOD.

Institute of Continuing Education: Madingley Hall, Madingley, Cambridge, CB23 8AQ; tel. (1223) 746262; e-mail registration@ice.cam.ac.uk; internet www.ice.cam.ac.uk; f. 1873; attached to Univ. of Cambridge; offers Masters programmes; Dir Dr REBECCA J. LINGWOOD.

Library and Information Statistics Unit/LISU: Loughborough Univ., Loughborough, LE11 3TU; tel. (1509) 635680; e-mail lisu@lboro.ac.uk; internet www.lboro.ac.uk/

microsites/infosci/lisu; f. 1987; attached to Loughborough Univ.; research and information centre for library and information services; collects, analyzes, interprets, publishes statistical information for and about the library domain in the UK; Dir CLAIRE CREASER.

National Foundation for Educational Research: The Mere, Upton Park, Slough, SL1 2DQ; tel. (1753) 574123; e-mail enquiries@nfer.ac.uk; internet www.nfer.ac.uk; f. 1946; provides ind. research, assessment and information services for education, training and children's services; improves the practice and understanding of those who work with and for learners; library of 20,000 vols, 300 journals; Pres. Sir JAMES ROSE; Chair. RICHARD BUNKER; CEO CAROLE WILLIS; publ. *Educational Research* (2 a year).

SCRE Centre: St Andrew's Bldg, 11 Eldon St, Glasgow, G3 6NH; tel. (141) 330-3490; e-mail scre.info@scre.ac.uk; internet www.scre.ac.uk; f. 1928 as Scottish Council for Research in Education; attached to Univ. of Glasgow; conducts educational research; Dir Prof. PAUL BRNA.

Society for Research into Higher Education: 73 Collier St, London, N1 9BE; tel. (20) 7427-2350; e-mail srheoffice@srhe.ac.uk; internet www.srhe.ac.uk; f. 1964; Pres. Prof. Sir ROBERT BURGESS; Dir HELEN PERKINS; publs *Higher Education Quarterly*, *Research into Higher Education Abstracts* (3 a year), *Studies in Higher Education* (8 a year).

FINE AND PERFORMING ARTS

Applied Music Research Centre: attached to Roehampton Univ.; conducts research on music and its relationship with psychology, education, special educational needs, medicine and neuropsychology; Dir Prof. ADAM OCKELFORD.

Centre for Advanced Welsh Music Studies: School of Music, Bangor Univ., College Rd, Bangor, LL57 2DG; tel. (1248) 382181; e-mail s.harper@bangor.ac.uk; internet www.bangor.ac.uk/music/cawms; f. 1994; attached to Bangor Univ.; promotes scholarly debate and writing in English and Welsh; Dir Dr SALLY HARPER; publ. *Welsh Music History Journal* (every 2 years).

Centre for Dance Research: Roehampton Univ., Roehampton Lane, London SW15 5PH; tel. (20) 8392-4482; e-mail theresa.buckland@roehampton.ac.uk; attached to Roehampton Univ.; research projects in historical, analytical, anthropological, cultural studies and professional choreography; hosts seminars and international confs; Dir Prof. THERESA BUCKLAND.

Centre for Educational Research in Equalities, Policy and Pedagogy: internet http://www.roehampton.ac.uk/research-centres/centre-for-educational-research-in-equalities-policy-and-pedagogy; attached to Roehampton Univ.; Dir Prof. GILL CROZIER.

Centre for Research in Film and Audiovisual Cultures: Queen's Bldg, Roehampton Univ., Roehampton Lane, London, SW15 5PH; tel. (20) 8392-5043; internet www.roehampton.ac.uk/research-centres/centre-for-research-in-film-and-audiovisual-cultures; attached to Roehampton Univ.; critical, historical, analytical and practical research relating to film and other audiovisual media; supports research on cinema, television, video cassettes/DVD, interactive platforms and online media; Co-Dir Dr MICHAEL WITT; Dir Prof. HEATHER NUNN.

Research Institute for Art and Design: Room 82E02, School of Art and Design, Univ.

of Ulster, Belfast Campus, Belfast, BT15 1ED; tel. (2890) 366521; e-mail adbe@ulster.ac.uk; internet www.riad.ulster.ac.uk; f. 2004; attached to Univ. of Ulster; conducts research on art and conflict, art and context, creative ecologies, design for living, future and virtual worlds, space and place; Dir Prof KAREN FLEMING.

Sainsbury Institute for the Study of Japanese Arts and Culture: 64 The Close, Norwich, NR1 4DH; tel. (1603) 597507; e-mail sisjac@sainsbury-institute.org; internet www.sainsbury-institute.org; f. 1999; affiliated to Univ. of East Anglia, The British Museum, School of Oriental and African Studies and Univ. of London; promotes world class research in the study of Japanese arts and cultures; Research Dir NICOLE COOLIDGE ROUSMANIERE; Exec. Dir MAMI MIZUTORI.

HISTORY, GEOGRAPHY AND ARCHAEOLOGY

Business History Unit: London School of Economics and Political Science, Houghton St, London, WC2A 2AE; tel. (20) 7955-7073; e-mail t.r.gourvish@lse.ac.uk; internet www.lse.ac.uk/economichistory/bhu; f. 1978, jtly with Imperial College London; attached to London School of Economics and Political Science, Univ. of London; promotes research into business history, incl. technological aspects; Dir Dr TERENCE R. GOURVISH.

Centre for City and Regional Studies: Dept of Geography, Univ. of Hull, Cottingham Rd, Hull, HU6 7RX; tel. (1482) 465330; internet www.hull.ac.uk/ccrs; attached to University of Hull; conducts research on nat., regional and local policy for economic devt and environmental protection; Dir Prof. DAVID GIBBS; Dir Prof. GRAHAM HAUGHTON.

Centre for Medieval Studies: College of Humanities, Amory Bldg, Rennes Dr., Exeter, EX4 4RJ; tel. (1392) 264364; e-mail j.g.clark@exeter.ac.uk; internet humanities.exeter.ac.uk/history/research/centres/medieval; attached to Univ. of Exeter; Dir Prof. JAMES CLARK.

Centre for Research in History and Theory: Dept of Humanities, Univ. of Roehampton, Roehampton Lane, London, SW15 5PH; tel. (20) 8392-3345; e-mail c.hamilton@roehampton.ac.uk; internet www.roehampton.ac.uk/research-centres/centre-for-research-in-history-and-theory; f. 2006; attached to Roehampton Univ.; research in art history, classical civilisation, dance, and drama, history, philosophy, theology and religious studies; Dir Dr CARRIE HAMILTON.

Centre for Research in Polish History: Stirling, FK9 4LA; tel. (1786) 467580; e-mail historyandpolitics@stir.ac.uk; f. 2000; attached to Univ. of Stirling; Dir Dr PETER D. STACHURA.

Centre for Research in Renaissance Studies: Univ. of Roehampton, London, SW15 5PU; tel. (20) 8392-3334; e-mail s.greenhalgh@roehampton.ac.uk; internet www.roehampton.ac.uk/research-centres/research-group-in-renaissance-studies; attached to Roehampton Univ.; research in classics, drama, English, history and art history, particularly in the fields of Italian Renaissance history; 17th-century politics; Shakespearean after lives in literature, theatre, and the media; gender and performance; early modern court and domestic cultures; textual editing; and Renaissance visual cultures and mythographies; Dir SUSANNE GREENHALGH.

Centre for South-Western Historical Studies: c/o Devon and Exeter Institution, 7 The Close, Exeter, EX1 1EZ; tel. (1392)

263292; e-mail r.burt@exeter.ac.uk; internet people.exeter.ac.uk/rburt/swhs; f. 1985; attached to Univ. of Exeter; promotes historical research into all aspects of counties of Cornwall, Devon, Dorset, Somerset; Dir Prof. ROGER BURT.

German Historical Institute London: 17 Bloomsbury Sq., London, WC1A 2NJ; tel. (20) 7309-2050; e-mail ghil@ghil.ac.uk; internet www.ghil.ac.uk; f. 1976; promotes research on the comparative history of Germany and Britain, the British Empire and Commonwealth and Anglo-German relations; library of 75,000 vols, 200 periodicals; Dir Prof. Dr ANDREAS GESTRICH; Librarian MICHAEL SCHAICH.

Institute of Contemporary British History: King's Bldg, King's College London, Strand, London, WC2R 2LS; tel. (20) 7848-7045; e-mail icbh@kcl.ac.uk; internet www.kcl.ac.uk/innovation/groups/ich; f. 1986, fmrly Centre for Contemporary British History, current name adopted 2010; archive of oral source material derived from Witness Seminars; Dir Prof. ROBERT BLACKBURN; Deputy Dir Dr VIRGINIA PRESTON; publs *Contemporary British History* (4 a year), *Modern History Review* (4 a year), *Twentieth Century British History* (4 a year).

Royal Archaeological Institute: c/o Society of Antiquaries of London, Burlington House, Piccadilly, London, W1J 0BE; e-mail admin@royalarchinst.org; internet www.royalarchinst.org; f. 1844; awards grants for archaeological research and excavations; undergraduate and masters dissertations; Pres. Prof. DAVID A. HINTON; Hon. Sec. Dr GILL HEY; Hon. Treas. Dr ANDREW WILLIAMS; publ. *Archaeological Journal* (1 a year).

Scott Polar Research Institute: Univ. of Cambridge, Lensfield Rd, Cambridge, CB2 1ER; tel. (1223) 336540; e-mail enquiries@spri.cam.ac.uk; internet www.spri.cam.ac.uk; f. 1920; attached to Univ. of Cambridge; research and information centre on the polar regions (glaciology, geophysics, oceanography, remote sensing, history, anthropology, socio-economics); library of 250,000 vols, 700 periodicals; archives; photographic library; Dir Prof. JULIAN A. DOWDESWELL; Librarian HEATHER LANE; publs *Polar and Glaciological Abstracts* (3 a year), *Polar Record* (4 a year).

Wetland Archaeology and Environments Research Centre: Dept of Geography, Environment & Earth Sciences, Univ. of Hull, Cottingham Rd, Hull, HU6 7RX; tel. (1482) 465325; e-mail waerc@hull.ac.uk; internet www2.hull.ac.uk/science/waerc.aspx; f. 2000; attached to Univ. of Hull; research into preservation of wetlands and excavation of past landscapes; Dir Dr MALCOLM LILLIE.

LANGUAGE AND LITERATURE

Arts and Humanities Research Council: Polaris House, N Star Ave, Swindon, SN2 1FL; tel. (1793) 416000; e-mail enquiries@ahrc.ac.uk; internet www.ahrc.ac.uk; f. 2005; Chair. Prof. Sir ALAN WILSON; Chief Exec. Prof. RICK RYLANCE.

Centre for Advanced Research in English: Dept of English, Arts Bldg, Edgbaston, Birmingham, B15 2TT; internet www.birmingham.ac.uk/facilities/care; attached to Univ. of Birmingham; Dir Dr SUGANTHI JOHN; Admin. MICHELLE DEVEREUX.

Centre for South West Writing: Univ. of Exeter, Queen's Dr., Exeter, EX4 4QJ; tel. (1392) 264343; internet centres.exeter.ac.uk/southwestwriting; attached to Univ. of Exeter; promotes appreciation of the region's creative writers; Dir ANDY BROWN.

Centre for the Standardisation of Terminology: Bangor, LL57 2DG; f. 1996; attached to Bangor Univ.; develops standardized dictionaries and glossaries of contemporary technical terms in Welsh; Dir Dr LLION JONES.

CILT, the National Centre for Languages: CfBT Education Trust, 60 Queens Rd, Reading, RG1 4BS; tel. (118) 902-1000; e-mail info@cilt.org.uk; internet www.cilt.org.uk; f. 1966 merged with CfBT Education Trust 2011; Chief Exec. KATE BOARD.

Dictionary Research Centre: Edgbaston, Birmingham, B15 2TT; tel. (121) 414-3364; e-mail english@bham.ac.uk; internet www.birmingham.ac.uk/schools/edacs/departments/english/research/projects/drc.aspx; f. 2001; attached to Univ. of Birmingham; research activities incl. work on Johnson's A Dictionary of the English Language, sourcing of Johnson's citations; corpus-based lexicography; bilingual and multilingual lexicography; lexicographical description of collocation; language of definitions; perceptions of dictionaries; metaphor and dictionaries; Dir Dr ROSAMUND MOON.

English Language and Applied Linguistics Postgraduate Centre: J. G. Smith Bldg, Univ. of Birmingham, Edgbaston, Birmingham, B15 2TT; tel. (121) 414-5695; e-mail elalpg@contacts.bham.ac.uk; internet www.birmingham.ac.uk/pg-english; attached to Univ. of Birmingham; Dir Dr JEANNETTE LITTLEMORE.

Foreign Language Centre: College of Humanities, 2nd Fl., Queen's Bldg, Queen's Dr., Exeter, EX4 4QH; tel. (1392) 724306; e-mail languages@exeter.ac.uk; internet humanities.exeter.ac.uk/flc; attached to Univ. of Exeter; languages offered: Arabic, British Sign Language (BSL), Catalan, French, German, Greek, Italian, Japanese, Korean, Latin, Mandarin Chinese, Portuguese, Russian, Spanish and Turkish; Dir JONATHAN LIPPMAN.

Hispanic Research Centre: tel (20) 8392-5027; internet www.roehampton.ac.uk/research-centres/hispanic-research-centre; attached to Roehampton Univ.; Dir Dr ELVIRA ANTÓN-CARRILLO.

Institute for Advanced Research in Arts and Social Sciences: 91 Oakfield Rd, Selly Park, Birmingham, B29 7HL; attached to Univ. of Birmingham; Hon. Dir Prof. E. W. IVES.

Institute of Cornish Studies: Penryn Campus, Treliever Rd, Penryn, TR10 9FE; tel. (1326) 371-8888; e-mail cornishstudies@exeter.ac.uk; internet humanities.exeter.ac.uk/history/research/centres/ics; f. 1971; attached to Univ. of Exeter; promotes knowledge of historical and contemporary Cornwall; Dir Prof. PHILIP J. PAYTON; Asst Dir Dr GARRY TREGIDGA; publ. *Cornish Studies* (1 a year).

Leopardi Centre: Ashley Bldg, Dept of Italian Studies, Univ. of Birmingham, Edgbaston, Birmingham, B15 2TT; tel. (121) 414-5996; e-mail franco.dintino@umiroma1.it; internet www.birmingham.ac.uk/research/activity/leopardi; f. 1998; attached to Univ. of Birmingham; promotes study and knowledge of Leopardi and his European context at postdoctoral, postgraduate, undergraduate level; facilitates research on Leopardi and on related topics, incl. the European reception of Leopardi's work; acts as a UK focus for research into the cultures of 18th- and 19th-century Italy; organizes research seminars and colloquia with specialists in 18th- and 19th-century studies and related fields from Italy, the UK and other countries; maintains and enhances colln of publs relating to Leopardi in the European languages; collects

relevant bibliographical material; Dir Dr FRANCO D'INTINO.

Modern Humanities Research Association: 1 Carlton House Terrace, London, SW1Y 5AF; e-mail mail@mhra.org.uk; internet www.mhra.org.uk; f. 1918; encourages and promotes advanced study and research in the field of modern humanities; Hon. Sec. Dr BARBARA BURNS; publs *Austrian Studies* (1 a year), *Modern Language Review* (4 a year), *Portuguese Studies* (2 a year), *The Slavonic and East European Review* (4 a year), *Yearbook of English Studies* (1 a year).

National Centre for Research in Children's Literature: Dept of English and Creative Writing, Roehampton Univ., Roehampton Lane, London, SW15 5PH; tel. (20) 8392-3346; e-mail k.reynolds@roehampton.ac.uk; internet www.roehampton.ac.uk/research-centres/national-centre-for-research-in-children-s-literature; f. 1993; attached to Roehampton Univ.; postgraduate MA and PhD programmes, confs and staff publs; Dir Dr LISA SAINSBURY.

R. S. Thomas Study Centre: English Dept, Bangor Univ., Bangor, LL57 2DG; tel. (1248) 382113; internet rsthomas.bangor.ac.uk; f. 2000; attached to Bangor Univ.; archive contains all of R. S. Thomas's published works, together with a comprehensive colln of reviews, critical books and articles, interviews and audiovisual material; Dir Dr JASON WALFORD DAVIES; Dir Prof. TONY BROWN.

Shakespeare Institute: Mason Croft, Stratford upon Avon, CV37 6HP; tel. (121) 414-9500; e-mail shakespeare@bham.ac.uk; internet www.birmingham.ac.uk/schools/edacs/departments/shakespeare; attached to Univ. of Birmingham; conducts research on Renaissance drama, the afterlife of Shakespeare in performance, culture of Renaissance England and the impact of Shakespeare on modern culture; library of 60,000 vols; Dir Prof. MICHAEL DOBSON; Librarian KARIN BROWN.

MEDICINE

Arthritis Research UK: Copeman House, St Mary's Gate, Chesterfield, S41 7TD; tel. (300) 790-0400; e-mail enquiries@arthritisresearchuk.org; internet www.arthritisresearchuk.org; f. 1936 as the Arthritis and Rheumatism Ccl; raises funds to promote medical research into causes, treatment and cure of arthritis and related musculoskeletal conditions; educates medical professionals and provides information to patients and the general public; Chief Exec. Dr LIAM O'TOOLE.

Asthma UK: Summit House, 70 Wilson St, London, EC2A 2DB; tel. (20) 7786-4900; e-mail info@asthma.org.uk; internet www.asthma.org.uk; f. 1927; ind. UK charity; funds research into asthma and provides advice and information; works with asthma patients, health professionals and researchers; influences health care policies; 7,000 mems; Chair. Prof. ROB WILSON; Chief Exec. KAY BOYCOTT; publ. *Asthma Magazine* (4 a year).

BHF National Centre for Physical Activity and Health: School of Sport, Exercise and Health Sciences, Loughborough Univ., Epinal Way, Loughborough, LE11 3TU; tel. (1509) 226421; e-mail bhfnc@lboro.ac.uk; internet www.bhfactive.org.uk; f. 2000; attached to Loughborough Univ.; Dir ELAINE MCNISH.

Bone and Joint Research Unit, William Harvey Research Institute: John Vane Bldg, Charterhouse Sq., London, EC1M 6BQ; tel. (20) 7882-2471; e-mail y.chernajovsky@

qmul.ac.uk; internet www.whri.qmul.ac.uk/research/boneandjoint.html; f. 1978; attached to Queen Mary's School of Medicine and Dentistry, Univ. of London; research into causes of arthritic diseases and lupus erythematosus with emphasis on the devt of new targeted therapies by protein design, antibody engineering, gene delivery and stem cell engineering; Centre Lead Prof. YUTI CHERNAJOVSKY.

Bristol Institute of Clinical Neurosciences: Dept of Neurology, Frenchay Hospital, Bristol, BS16 1LE; tel. (117) 340-6632; internet www.bristol.ac.uk/neuroscience/clinical/icns; f. 1999; Dir Prof. NEIL J. SCOLDING.

Cancer Research UK: Angel Bldg, 407 St John St, London, EC1V 4AD; tel. (20) 7242-0200; internet www.cancerresearchuk.org; f. 2002, by merger of Imperial Cancer Research Fund (f. 1902) and Cancer Research Campaign (f. 1923); library of 4,000 vols, 300 periodicals; Chair. and CEO HARPAL KUMAR; Exec. Dir Prof. IAIN FOULKES.

Cancer Research UK Beatson Institute: Garscube Estate, Switchback Rd, Bearsden, Glasgow, G61 1BD; tel. (141) 330-3953; e-mail beatson@gla.ac.uk; internet www.beatson.gla.ac.uk; f. 1890; library of 1,000 textbooks, 83 journals; Dir Prof. KAREN H. VOUSDEN.

Cancer Research UK Manchester Institute: Univ. of Manchester, Wilmslow Rd, Withington, Manchester, M20 4BX; tel. (161) 446-3156; e-mail enquiries@cruk.manchester .ac.uk; internet www.cruk.manchester.ac.uk; f. 1932 as Paterson Institute for Cancer Research; present name 2006; attached to Univ. of Manchester; conducts basic and clinical cancer research; Dir RICHARD MARAIS.

Centre for Child and Family Research: Dept of Social Sciences, Brockington Bldg, Loughborough Univ., Loughborough, LE11 3TU; tel. (1509) 228758; e-mail ccfr@lboro.ac .uk; internet www.lboro.ac.uk/research/ccfr; f. 2002; attached to Loughborough Univ.; Dir Prof. HARRIET WARD; Asst Dir LISA HOLMES.

Centre for Health and Rehabilitation Technologies: Room 01B102, School of Health Sciences, Jordanstown Campus, Univ. of Ulster, Shore Rd, Newtownabbey, BT37 0QB; tel. (28) 9036-6851; e-mail science@ulster.ac.uk; internet www.science .ulster.ac.uk/inhr/chart; attached to Univ. of Ulster; research in physiotherapy, speech and language therapy, occupational therapy, radiography, podiatry and clinical physiology; Head Prof SUZANNE MC DONOUGH.

Centre for Medical History: College of Humanities, Univ. of Exeter, Amory Bldg, Rennes Dr., Exeter, EX4 4RJ; tel. (1392) 723289; e-mail cfmhmail@exeter.ac.uk; internet humanities.exeter.ac.uk/history/research/centres/medicalhistory; f. 1997; attached to Univ. of Exeter; Dir Prof. JONATHAN BARRY; Co-Dir Prof. JOSEPH MELLING.

Centre for Social Policy Research and Development: College Rd, Bangor, LL57 2DG; f. 1986; attached to Bangor Univ.; scientific research primarily in areas of human devt, health studies and social care provision; Dir VANESSA BURHOLT.

Children's Health and Exercise Research Centre (CHERC): Univ. of Exeter, St Luke's Campus, Exeter, EX1 2LU; tel. (1392) 724890; e-mail sshs-school-office@ exeter.ac.uk; internet sshs.exeter.ac.uk/research/centres/cherc; f. 1987; attached to Univ. of Exeter; research in paediatric exercise science; paediatric clinical trials; child and adolescent nutrition; sport and the youth athlete; Dir Prof. CRAIG WILLIAMS.

Dementia Services Development Centre: Univ. of Stirling, Iris Murdoch Bldg, Stirling, FK9 4LA; tel. (1786) 467740; internet dementia.stir.ac.uk; attached to Univ. of Stirling; library of 12,000 vols; Dir Prof. JUNE ANDREWS; Deputy Dir JEMMA GALBRAITH.

Essex Biomedical Sciences Institute: School of Biological Sciences, Univ. of Essex, Wivenhoe Park, Colchester, CO4 3SQ; tel. (1206) 872918; e-mail bwilk@essex.ac.uk; internet www.essex.ac.uk/bs/ebsi; attached to Univ. of Essex; promotes clinically-relevant, biomedical and health-related translational research; Dir Prof. ELENA KLENOVA; Assoc. Dir Dr TONY ELSTON.

Exeter MR Research Centre: Univ. of Exeter, St Lukes Campus, Magdalen Rd, Exeter, EX1 2LU; tel. (1392) 262982; internet centres.exeter.ac.uk/pmrrc; f. 2002; collaboration of the Univ. of Exeter, the Peninsula Medical School and the Univ. of Plymouth; jtly run by the Schools of Physics, Sports Science and Psychology at Exeter, the Institute of Neuroscience at Plymouth and the Peninsula Medical School; research projects incl. MRI, EEG, MEG, eyetracker; Dir Dr JUDITH MEAKIN.

Health Protection Agency: Manor Farm Rd, Porton Down, Salisbury, SP4 0JG; tel. (1980) 612100; e-mail business@hpa.org.uk; internet www.hpa.org.uk; f. 2003; attached to Public Health England, Dept of Health; protects the UK population against biological, chemical and radiological health threats.

History of Medicine Unit: 90 Vincent Dr., Edgbaston, Birmingham, B15 2SP; tel. (121) 415-8122; e-mail j.reinarz@bham.ac.uk; internet www.birmingham.ac.uk/research/activity/mds/centres/histmed; f. 2000; attached to Univ. of Birmingham; supports and promotes teaching and research in the history of medicine; Dir Dr JONATHAN REINARZ.

Institute for Ageing and Health: Newcastle Univ., Campus for Ageing and Vitality, Newcastle upon Tyne, NE4 5PL; tel. (191) 208-1100; internet www.ncl.ac.uk/iah; f. 1994; Dir Prof. DAVID BURN.

Institute of Cancer Research: see under Univ. of London.

Institute of Medical and Social Care Research: Bangor Univ., Bangor, LL57 2DG; tel. (1248) 388771; e-mail imscar@ bangor.ac.uk; internet www.bangor.ac.uk/imscar; f. 1997; attached to Bangor Univ.; Head Prof. BOB WOODS (acting); Man. NEIL HAROLD.

Institute of Neurology: Queen Sq., London, WC1N 3BG; tel. (20) 3456-7890; internet www.ucl.ac.uk/ion; f. 1950; attached to Univ. College London; 8 research depts: neurodegenerative disease; molecular neuroscience, clinical and experimental epilepsy; motor neuroscience and movement disorders; imaging neuroscience; brain repair and rehabilitation, neuroinflammation and clinical neurosciences; library of 16,000 vols; Dir Prof. MICHAEL G. HANNA; Sec. ROBERT WALKER.

Institute of Nursing and Health Research: Room G242, School of Nursing, Univ. of Ulster, Coleraine Campus Cromore Rd, Coleraine, BT52 1SA; tel. (28) 7012-4094; internet www.science.ulster.ac.uk/inhr; attached to Univ. of Ulster; activities related to intellectual and developmental disabilities, managing chronic illness, maternal foetal and infant research, health and rehabilitation technologies; Dir Prof BRENDAN MCCORMACK; Sec. JULIE CUMMINS.

Liverpool School of Tropical Medicine: Pembroke Pl., Liverpool, L3 5QA; tel. (151) 705-3100; e-mail lstminfo@liv.ac.uk; internet www.lstmliverpool.ac.uk; f. 1898; attached to Univ. of Liverpool; trains medical and para-medical personnel in all aspects of individual or community medicine in the tropics; conducts original research into tropical diseases and their control; library of 50,000 vols and periodicals, incl. Ronald Ross collection; Chair. JAMES ROSS; Dir Prof. JANET HEMINGWAY; publs *Paediatrics and International Child Health, Pathogens and Global Health*.

LSE Health and Social Care: Cowdray House, London School of Economics and Political Science, Houghton St, London, WC2A 2AE; tel. (20) 7955-6840; e-mail lse_health@lse.ac.uk; internet www.lse.ac .uk/lsehealthandsocialcare; f. 2000; attached to London School of Economics and Political Science, Univ. of London; research on health policy and health economics, social care policy and mental health economics, and social care practice; Chair. Prof. ALISTAIR MCGUIRE; Dir Prof. ELIAS MOSSIALOS.

Medical Research Council (MRC): 14th Fl., One Kemble St, London, WC2B 4AN; tel. (20) 7395-2345; e-mail corporate@headoffice .mrc.ac.uk; internet www.mrc.ac.uk; f. 1913; promotes research for improvement of human health; undertakes research in molecular science and public health in a network of 64 research establishments complementing the research resources of univs and hospitals; supports research training by means of fellowships, studentships and grants to scientists; CEO Sir JOHN SAVILL; Chief Operating Officer BRUCE MINTY..

Attached Research Establishments:

Centre for Brain Ageing and Vitality: Institute for Ageing and Health, Univ. of Newcastle Upon Tyne, Campus for Ageing and Vitality, Newcastle Upon Tyne, NE4 5PL; tel. (191) 248-1200; e-mail cbav@ncl .ac.uk; internet www.ncl.ac.uk/cbav; Dir Prof. DOUG TURNBULL.

Centre for Cognitive Ageing and Cognitive Epidemiology: Dept of Psychology, Univ. of Edinburgh, 7 George Sq., Edinburgh, EH8 9JZ; tel. (131) 650-8275; e-mail ccace@ed.ac.uk; internet www.ccace .ed.ac.uk; Dir Prof. IAN J. DEARY.

Crucible Centre: Univ. College London, Gower St, London, WC1E 6BT; tel. (20) 7679-1597; e-mail r.thoreau@ucl.ac.uk; internet www.ucl.ac.uk/crucible; research on all aspects of ageing process from philosophy, biology, economics, clinical practice to design of the built environment; Dir Prof. NICK TYLER.

Gray Institute for Radiation Oncology & Biology: Univ. of Oxford, Old Road Campus Research Bldg, Roosevelt Dr., Oxford, OX3 7DQ; tel. (1865) 617330; e-mail enquiries@oncology.ox.ac.uk; internet www.rob.ox.ac.uk; Dir Prof. GILLIES MCKENNA.

MRC Anatomical Neuropharmacology Unit: Mansfield Rd, Oxford, OX1 3TH; tel. (1865) 271865; e-mail mary.gilgunn-jones@ pharm.ox.ac.uk; internet www.mrc.ox.ac .uk; f. 1984; Dir Prof. PETER SOMOGYI.

MRC Asthma UK Centre in Allergic Mechanisms of Asthma: King's College London, School of Medicine, 5th Floor, Thomas Guy House, Guy's Hospital, London, SE1 9RT; tel. (20) 7188-1943 Imperial College London, S Kensington Campus, Sir Alexander Fleming Bldg, London, SW7 2AZ; tel. (20) 7594-3159; internet www .asthma-allergy.ac.uk; Dir at KCL Prof. TAK LEE; Dir at ICL Prof. SEB SEB JOHNSTON.

MRC Biomedical Nuclear Magnetic Resonance Centre: Nat. Institute for Medical Research, The Ridgeway, Mill Hill, London, NW7 1AA; tel. (20) 8816-2427; e-mail tom.frenkiel@nimr.mrc.ac.uk; internet www.nmrcentre.mrc.ac.uk; f. 1980; Head Dr TOM FRENKIEL.

MRC Biostatistics Unit: Institute of Public Health, Univ. Forvie Site, Robinson Way, Cambridge, CB2 0SR; tel. (1223) 330397; internet www.mrc-bsu.cam.ac.uk; f. 1970; Dir SYLVIA RICHARDSON.

MRC Cancer Unit: Univ. of Cambridge, Hutchison/MRC Research Centre, Hills Rd, POB 197, Cambridge Biomedical Campus, Cambridge, CB2 0XZ; tel. (1223) 763240; e-mail contact@mrc-cu.cam.ac.uk; internet www.mrc-cu.cam.ac.uk; f. 2001, current name adopted 2013; Dir Prof. ASHOK VENKITARAMAN.

MRC/Cancer Research UK/BHF Clinical Trial Service Unit & Epidemiological Studies Unit (CTSU): Richard Doll Bldg, Old Rd Campus, Roosevelt Dr., Oxford, OX3 7LF; tel. (1865) 743743; e-mail enquiries@ctsu.ox.ac.uk; internet www.ctsu.ox.ac.uk; Co-Dir Prof. RORY COLLINS; Co-Dir Prof. RICHARD PETO.

MRC Centre for Behavioural and Clinical Neuroscience Institute (BCNI): Dept of Experimental Psychology, Univ. of Cambridge, Downing Site, Cambridge, CB2 3EB; tel. (1223) 333558; internet www.psychol.cam.ac.uk/bcni; Dir Prof. TREVOR ROBBINS.

MRC Centre for Developmental and Biomedical Genetics: Firth Court, Univ. of Sheffield, Western Bank, Sheffield, S10 2TN; tel. (114) 222-2710; e-mail cdbg@sheffield.ac.uk; internet cdbg.shef.ac.uk; f. 1997 as Centre for Developmental Genetics, present status 2004; Dir Prof. MARYSIA PLACZEK (acting).

MRC Centre for Developmental Neurobiology: King's College London, New Hunt's House, 4th Fl., Guy's Hospital Campus, London, SE1 1UL; tel. (20) 7848-8148; e-mail lauren.ryan@kcl.ac.uk; internet www.kcl.ac.uk/biohealth/research/divisions/devneuro; Dir Prof. ANDREW LUMSDEN.

MRC Centre for Drug Safety Science: Dept of Pharmacology and Therapeutics, Univ. of Liverpool, Sherrington Bldg, Ashton St, Liverpool, L69 3GE; tel. (151) 794-5852; e-mail neil.french@liverpool.ac.uk; internet www.liv.ac.uk/drug-safety; Dir Prof. KEVIN PARK.

MRC Centre for Genomics and Global Health: Roosevelt Dr., Oxford, OX3 7BN; tel. (1865) 287500; internet www.cggh.ox.ac.uk; Dir Prof. DOMINIC KWIATKOWSKI.

MRC Centre for Neuromuscular Diseases: POB 102, Nat. Hospital for Neurology and Neurosurgery, Queen Sq., London, WC1 3BG; tel. (20) 3448-8013; e-mail cnmd.contact@ucl.ac.uk; internet www.cnmd.ac.uk; Dir Prof. MIKE HANNA.

MRC Centre for Neuropsychiatric Genetics and Genomics: Cardiff Univ. School of Medicine, Hadyn Ellis Bldg, Maindy Rd, Cathays, Cardiff, CF24 4XQ; tel. (29) 2068-7065; e-mail psychmedadmin@cf.ac.uk; internet www.cardiff.ac.uk/cngg; Dir Prof. MICHAEL OWEN.

MRC Centre for Reproductive Health: Queen's Medical Research Institute, 47 Little France Crescent, Edinburgh, EH16 4TJ; tel. (131) 242-2694; internet www.crh.ed.ac.uk; Dir Prof. JEFFREY POLLARD.

MRC Centre for Virus Research: Garscube Campus, Univ. of Glasgow, Glasgow, G61 1QH; tel. (141) 330-6262; e-mail s.lyden@mrcvu.gla.ac.uk; internet www.cvr.ac.uk; f. 2010; carries out multidisciplinary research on viruses and viral diseases of humans and animals; Dir Prof. MASSIMO PALMARINI (acting).

MRC Centre for Outbreak Analysis and Modelling: Dept of Infectious Disease Epidemiology, Imperial College London, Medical School Bldg, Norfolk Pl., London, W2 1PG; tel. (20) 7594-3296; internet www1.imperial.ac.uk; Dir Prof. NEIL FERGUSON.

MRC Centre for Regenerative Medicine: Scottish Centre for Regenerative Medicine Bldg, Univ. of Edinburgh, Five Little France Dr., Edinburgh, EH16 4UU; tel. (131) 651-9500; internet www.crm.ed.ac.uk; Dir Prof. CHARLES FFRENCH-CONSTANT.

MRC Centre for Transplantation: King's College London, 5th Fl., Tower Wing, Guy's Hospital, Great Maze Pond, London, SE1 9RT; tel. (20) 7188-5669; e-mail mrccentre@kcl.ac.uk; internet transplantation.kcl.ac.uk; Dir Prof. STEVE SACKS.

MRC Clinical Sciences Centre: Faculty of Medicine, Imperial College London, Hammersmith Hospital Campus, Du Cane Rd, London, W12 0NN; tel. (20) 3313-1000; internet www.csc.mrc.ac.uk; f. 1994; Dir Prof. AMANDA FISHER.

MRC Clinical Trials Units: Aviation House, 125 Kingsway, London, WC2B 6NH; tel. (20) 7670-4700; e-mail enquiries@ctu.mrc.ac.uk; internet www.ctu.mrc.ac.uk; f. 1998; Dir Prof. MAHESH PARMAR.

MRC Cognition and Brain Sciences Unit: 15 Chaucer Rd, Cambridge, CB2 7EF; tel. (1223) 355294; e-mail info@mrc-cbu.cam.ac.uk; internet www.mrc-cbu.cam.ac.uk; f. 1944; investigates fundamental human mental processes such as attention, emotion, memory and knowledge, speech and language; conducts behavioural experiments to probe the functional properties of psychological systems and build computer models of their operation; carries out neuropsychological and neuroimaging (PET, MRI, MEG, EEG) studies of the underlying neural mechanisms in the brain and explores the clinical implications of the research for patient therapy and rehabilitation; Dir Prof. SUSAN GATHERCOLE.

MRC Epidemiology Unit: Institute of Metabolic Science, POB 285, Cambridge Biomedical Campus, Cambridge, CB2 0QQ; tel. (1223) 330315; internet www.mrc-epid.cam.ac.uk; f. 2003; Dir Prof. NICK WAREHAM.

MRC Functional Genomics Unit: Dept of Physiology, Anatomy and Genetics, Univ. of Oxford, S Parks Rd, Oxford, OX1 3PT; tel. (1865) 282690; e-mail mrc.fgu@dpag.ox.ac.uk; internet www.mrcfgu.ox.ac.uk; f. 1999; Dir Prof. KAY E. DAVIES.

MRC Human Genetics Unit: Univ. of Edinburgh, Western Gen. Hospital, Crewe Rd, Edinburgh, EH4 2XU; tel. (131) 332-2471; e-mail enquiries@hgu.mrc.ac.uk; internet www.hgu.mrc.ac.uk; f. 1967; Dir Prof. NICHOLAS HASTIE.

MRC Human Immunology Unit: Weatherall Institute of Molecular Medicine, Univ. of Oxford, John Radcliffe Hospital, Headington, Oxford, OX3 9DS; tel. (1865) 222443; internet www.imm.ox.ac.uk/mrc-human-immunology-unit; Dir Prof. VINCENZO CERUNDOLO.

MRC Human Nutrition Research: Elsie Widdowson Laboratory, 120 Fulbourn Rd, Cambridge, CB1 9NL; tel. (1223) 426356; e-mail reception.office@mrc-hnr.cam.ac.uk; internet www.mrc-hnr.cam.ac.uk; f. 1998; Dir Dr ANN PRENTICE.

MRC Institute of Hearing Research: Univ. of Nottingham, Univ. Park, Nottingham, NG7 2RD; tel. (115) 922-3431; e-mail enquiries@ihr.mrc.ac.uk; internet www.ihr.mrc.ac.uk; f. 1977; Dir Prof. ALAN PALMER.

MRC Integrative Epidemiology Unit: Senate House, Tyndall Ave, Bristol, BS8 1TH; tel. (117) 928-9000; e-mail mrc-ieu@bristol.ac.uk; internet www.bristol.ac.uk/integrative-epidemiology; Dir Prof. GEORGE DAVEY SMITH.

MRC International Nutrition Group: London School of Hygiene & Tropical Medicine, Keppel St, London, WC1E 7HT; tel. (20) 7958-8140; internet www.ing.mrc.ac.uk; Dir Prof. ANDREW PRENTICE.

MRC Laboratories, The Gambia: POB 273, Banjul, Gambia; tel. 4495442; e-mail information@mrc.gm; internet www.mrc.gm; f. 1947; researches into improvement of health care for developing countries; areas of speciality include virology, malaria, bacterial diseases and genetics; Dir Prof. UMBERTO D'ALESSANDRO.

MRC Laboratory for Molecular Cell Biology: Univ. College London, Gower St, London, WC1E 6BT; tel. (20) 7679-7806; internet www.ucl.ac.uk/lmcb; Dir Prof. MARK MARSH.

MRC Laboratory of Molecular Biology (LMB): Francis Crick Ave, Cambridge Biomedical Campus, Cambridge, CB2 0QH; tel. (1223) 267000; e-mail enquiries@mrc-lmb.cam.ac.uk; internet www2.mrc-lmb.cam.ac.uk; f. 1947, moved to present site 1962; Dir HUGH PELHAM.

MRC Lifecourse Epidemiology Unit: Southampton Gen. Hospital, Southampton, SO16 6YD; tel. (23) 8077-7624; e-mail postmaster@mrc.soton.ac.uk; internet www.mrc.soton.ac.uk; f. 2010; Dir Dr CYRUS COOPER.

MRC Metabolic Diseases Unit: Univ. of Cambridge Metabolic Research Laboratories, Level 4, Institute of Metabolic Science, POB 289, Addenbrooke's Hospital, Cambridge, CB2 0QQ; tel. (1223) 336792; internet www.mrc-cord.org; f. 2007; Dir Prof. STEVE O'RAHILLY.

MRC Mitochondrial Biology Unit: Wellcome Trust/MRC Bldg, Hills Rd, Cambridge, CB2 0XY; tel. (1223) 252700; internet www.mrc-mbu.cam.ac.uk; Dir MASSIMO ZEVIANI.

MRC Molecular Haematology Unit: Weatherall Institute of Molecular Medicine, John Radcliffe Hospital, Headington, Oxford, OX3 9DS; tel. (1865) 222359; f. 1980; Dir Prof. DOUG HIGGS.

MRC Prion Unit: Queen Sq. House, Queen Sq., London, WC1N 3BG; tel. (20) 7837-4888; e-mail michelle.gorham@uclh.nhs.uk; internet www.prion.ucl.ac.uk; f. 1998; Dir Prof. JOHN COLLINGE.

MRC Protein Phosphorylation and Ubiquitylation Unit: Sir James Black Centre, College of Life Sciences, Univ. of Dundee, Dow St, Dundee, DD1 5EH; tel. (1382) 384238; internet www.ppu.mrc.ac.uk; f. 1990; Dir Prof. DARIO ALESSI.

MRC Social and Public Health Sciences Unit: 4 Lilybank Gardens, Glasgow, G12 8RZ; tel. (141) 357-3949; e-mail enquiries@sphsu.mrc.ac.uk; internet www.sphsu.mrc.ac.uk; f. 1998; Dir Prof. LAURENCE MOORE.

MRC Social, Genetic and Developmental Psychiatry Centre: Institute of Psychiatry-PO80, De Crespigny Park, London, SE5 8AF; tel. (20) 7848-0873; internet www.kcl.ac.uk/iop/depts/mrc; f. 1994; Dir Prof. FRANCESCA HAPPÉ.

MRC Technology: Lynton House, 7-12 Tavistock Sq., London, WC1H 9LT; tel. (20) 7391-2700; e-mail info@tech.mrc.ac.uk; internet www.mrctechnology.org; CEO Dr DAVID TAPOLCZAY.

MRC Toxicology Unit: Hodgkin Bldg, POB 138, Lancaster Rd, Leicester, LE1 9HN; tel. (116) 252-5544; internet www.tox.mrc.ac.uk; f. 1947; Dir Prof. ANNE WILLIS (acting).

MRC Unit for Lifelong Health and Ageing: 33 Bedford Pl., London, WC1B 5JU; tel. (20) 7670-5700; internet www.nshd.mrc.ac.uk; f. 2008; incl. MRC Nat. Survey of Health and Devt; Dir Prof. DI KUH.

MRC/UCL Centre for Medical Molecular Virology: Univ. College London, Cruciform Bldg, Gower St, London, WC1E 6BT; tel. (20) 3018-2116; e-mail lauren.collins@ucl.ac.uk; internet www.ucl.ac.uk/infection-immunity/mrc_ucl-centre; Dir Prof. MARY COLLINS.

MRC/University of Birmingham Centre for Immune Regulation: Dept of Immunology, Univ. of Birmingham, Edgbaston, Birmingham, B15 2TT; tel. (121) 414-4068; internet www.mrcbcir.bham.ac.uk; Dir Prof. ERIC J. JENKINSON.

MRC/University of Edinburgh Centre for Inflammation Research: Queen's Medical Research Institute, 47 Little France Crescent, Edinburgh, EH16 4TJ; tel. (131) 242-9195; e-mail paula.saikko@ed.ac.uk; internet www.cir.med.ed.ac.uk; f. 1999; Dir Prof. JOHN IREDALE.

MRC/University of Sussex Centre in Genome Damage and Stability: Science Park Rd, Univ. of Sussex, Falmer, Brighton, BN1 9RQ; tel. (1273) 678123; e-mail gdsc@sussex.ac.uk; internet www.sussex.ac.uk/gdsc; Dir Prof. ANTHONY CARR.

MRC/UVRI Uganda Research Unit on AIDS: Uganda Virus Research Institute, POB 49, Entebbe, Uganda; tel. (417) 704000; e-mail mrc@mrcuganda.org; internet www.mrcuganda.org; f. 1989; Dir Dr PONTIANO KALEEBU.

MRC National Institute for Medical Research: The Ridgeway, Mill Hill, London, NW7 1AA; tel. (20) 8959-3666; e-mail enquiries@nimr.mrc.ac.uk; internet www.nimr.mrc.ac.uk; f. 1914; Dir Prof. JIM SMITH; publ. *Mill Hill Essays* (1 a year).

Scottish Collaboration for Public Health Research and Policy: MRC Human Genetics Unit, W. Gen. Hospital, Crewe Rd, Edinburgh, EH4 2XU; tel. (131) 332-2471; internet www.scphrp.ac.uk; f. 2008; Dir Prof. JOHN FRANK.

Miles Dyslexia Centre: Bangor Univ., Bangor, LL57 2DG; tel. (1248) 382203; e-mail dyslex-admin@bangor.ac.uk; internet www.dyslexia.bangor.ac.uk; f. 1977; attached to Bangor Univ.; student support teaching service and training workplace assessment; Dir Dr MARKETA CARAVOLAS.

MRC Toxicology Unit: Hodgkin Bldg, POB 138, Lancaster Rd, Leicester, LE1 9HN; tel. (116) 252-5544; internet tox.mrc.ac.uk; f. 1947; examines effects of chemicals, radiation and external biological agents on cellular exposure; Dir Prof. ANNE WILLIS.

National Centre for Prosthetics and Orthotics: Curran Bldg, 131 St James' Rd,

Glasgow, G4 0LS; tel. (141) 548-3433; e-mail contact-ncpo@strath.ac.uk; attached to Univ. of Strathclyde; Dir Prof. JACQUELINE HUGHES.

School of Health and Human Sciences: Wivenhoe Park, Colchester, CO4 3SQ; tel. (1206) 873765; e-mail hhs@essex.ac.uk; internet www.essex.ac.uk/hhs; attached to Univ. of Essex; applied teaching, training and research in health incl. nursing, occupational therapy, oral health, physiotherapy and speech and language therapy; Head of School VIKKI-JO SCOTT; Dir for Research Dr EWEN SPEED.

Strangeways Research Laboratory: Worts' Causeway, Cambridge, CB1 8RN; tel. (1223) 740145; internet www.phpc.cam.ac.uk/about-the-dphc/history/strangeways-research-laboratory; f. 1905, current name adopted 1928; attached to Univ. of Cambridge; research into cell biology, developmental biology, cancer; primary research into cancer genetics, epidemiology, cardiovascular disease and diabetes; Co-Dir Prof. JOHN DANESH.

Strathclyde Institute of Pharmacy and Biomedical Sciences: 161 Cathedral St, Glasgow, G4 0RE; tel. (141) 548-2125; e-mail hodsipbs@strath.ac.uk; internet www.strath.ac.uk/sipbs; attached to Univ. of Strathclyde; Head Prof. PHILIP WINN.

The Gurdon Institute: Henry Wellcome Building of Cancer and Developmental Biology, Univ. of Cambridge, Tennis Court Rd, Cambridge, CB2 1QN; tel. (1223) 334088; e-mail info@gurdon.cam.ac.uk; internet www.gurdon.cam.ac.uk; f. 1989 as Wellcome Trust and Cancer Research UK Institute, current name adopted 2004; attached to Univ. of Cambridge; promotes research in developmental biology and cancer biology; Dir Prof. DANIEL ST JOHNSTON; Deputy Dir TONY KOUZARIDES.

Thomas Coram Research Unit: Institute of Education, 27–28 Woburn Sq., London, WC1H 0AA; tel. (20) 7612-6957; e-mail tcru@ioe.ac.uk; internet www.ioe.ac.uk/research/54490.html; f. 1973; attached to Institute of Education, Univ. of London; conducts research with a focus on children and young people in families, and in health, education, care and social service settings; Unit Dir Prof. MARGARET O'BRIEN.

Trafford Centre for Medical Research: University of Sussex, Falmer, Brighton, BN1 9RH; attached to Univ. of Sussex; Dir Prof. A. L. MOORE (acting).

NATURAL SCIENCES

General

Engineering and Physical Sciences Research Council: Polaris House, North Star Ave, Swindon, SN2 1ET; tel. (1793) 444100; e-mail infoline@epsrc.ac.uk; internet www.epsrc.ac.uk; f. 1994; Chair. Dr PAUL GOLBY; CEO Prof. PHILIP NELSON; publs *Connect*, *Pioneer* (4 a year).

Natural Environment Research Council (NERC): Polaris House, North Star Ave, Swindon, SN2 1EU; tel. (1793) 411500; e-mail requests@nerc.ac.uk; internet www.nerc.ac.uk; f. 1965; funds and manages research, training and knowledge exchange in the environmental sciences, conducts research on human health, genetic make-up of life on Earth etc.; Chair. Sir ANTHONY CLEAVER; Chief Exec. Prof. DUNCAN WINGHAM; publ. *Planet Earth* (4 a year).

Research Centres:

British Antarctic Survey: High Cross, Madingley Rd, Cambridge, CB3 0ET; tel. (1223) 221400; e-mail information@bas.ac.uk; internet www.antarctica.ac.uk; f. 1945 as Falkland Islands Dependencies Survey;

current name adopted 1962; operates 4 research stations, 2 Royal Research Ships and 5 aircraft in and around Antarctica; undertakes a programme of science in the Antarctic and related regions and aims to address key global and regional issues; undertakes jt research projects and over 120 nat. and int. collaborations; library of 8,500 vols, 330 periodicals; Dir Prof. JANE FRANCIS.

British Geological Survey: Kingsley Dunham Centre, Nicker Hill, Keyworth, Nottingham, NG12 5GG; tel. (115) 936-3100; e-mail enquiries@bgs.ac.uk; internet www.bgs.ac.uk; f. 1835; survey and monitoring, modelling and research, data and knowledge; Exec. Dir Prof. JOHN LUDDEN; publ. *Earthwise* (2 a year).

Centre for Ecology & Hydrology: Maclean Bldg, Benson Lane, Crowmarsh Gifford, Wallingford, OX10 8BB; tel. (1491) 838800; e-mail enquiries@ceh.ac.uk; internet www.ceh.ac.uk; delivers ind. research, survey, training and knowledge transfer in the environmental sciences to advance knowledge of planet Earth as a complex, interacting system; Dir Prof. MARK J. BAILEY..

Constituent Institutes:

CEH Bangor: Environment Centre Wales, Deinol Rd, Bangor, LL57 2UW; tel. (1248) 374500; e-mail enquiries@ceh.ac.uk; internet www.ceh.ac.uk/sites/bangor.html; Head Prof. BRIDGET EMMETT.

CEH Edinburgh: Bush Estate, Penicuik, EH26 0QB; tel. (131) 445-4343; e-mail enquiries@ceh.ac.uk; internet www.ceh.ac.uk; Head Dr ALISTAIR DAWSON.

CEH Lancaster: Lancaster Environment Centre, Library Ave, Bailrigg, Lancaster, LA1 4AP; tel. (1524) 595800; e-mail lancaster@ceh.ac.uk; internet www.ceh.ac.uk/sites/lancaster.html; Head of Site Prof. RICHARD SHORE.

CEH Wallingford: Maclean Bldg, Benson Lane, Crowmarsh Gifford, Wallingford, OX10 8BB; tel. (1491) 838800; e-mail jsw@ceh.ac.uk; internet www.nwl.ac.uk; Dir Prof. JIM WALLACE.

Proudman Oceanographic Laboratory: 6 Brownlow St, Liverpool, L3 5DA; tel. (151) 795-4800; e-mail polenquiries@pol.ac.uk; internet www.pol.ac.uk; Dir Dr ANDREW WILLMOTT.

National Centre for Atmospheric Science: School of Earth and Environment, Univ. of Leeds, Leeds, LS2 9JT; tel. (113) 343-6408; e-mail admin@ncas.ac.uk; internet www.ncas.ac.uk; conducts research on the science of climate change, atmospheric condition, weather etc.; Dir Prof. STEPHEN MOBBS.

National Centre for Earth Observation: Dept of Meteorology, Univ. of Reading, Earley Gate Bldg 58, Reading, RG6 6BB; tel. (118) 378-6728; internet www.nceo.ac.uk; Dir Prof. PETER JAN VAN LEEUWEN; publ. *Blue Marble* (2 a year).

National Oceanography Centre: Univ. of Southampton Waterfront Campus, European Way, Southampton, SO14 3ZH; tel. (23) 8059-6666; internet www.noc.ac.uk; f. 2010 by merger of Proudman Oceanographic Laboratory, Liverpool and National Oceanography Centre, Southampton; undertakes integrated ocean research and technology development from the coast to the deep ocean; Dir Prof. ED HILL.

Biological Sciences

Biocomposites Centre: Bangor Univ., Deiniol Rd, Bangor, LL57 2UW; tel. (1248) 370588; e-mail bc@bangor.ac.uk; internet www.bc.bangor.ac.uk; f. 1989; attached to Bangor Univ.; undertakes collaborative research projects to develop sustainable bio-based technologies that will minimize the impact of materials on the environment; Dir Dr ROBERT ELIAS.

Biomedical Sciences Research Institute: School of Biomedical Sciences, Univ. of Ulster, Cromore Rd, Coleraine, BT52 1SA; tel. (28) 7012-4163; e-mail c.adams@ulster.ac.uk; internet biomed.science.ulster.ac.uk/bmsri; f. 2004; attached to Univ. of Ulster; studies of biological mechanisms associated with degenerative diseases like cancer, diabetes, heart disease, osteoporosis and visual deterioration; Dir Prof. TONY BJOURSON; Sec. CAROLINE ADAMS.

Biosciences Graduate Research School: School of Biosciences, Univ. of Birmingham, Edgbaston, Birmingham, B15 2TT; tel. (121) 414-5891; e-mail biosciences-phd@bham.ac.uk; internet www.birmingham.ac.uk/schools/biosciences/courses/postgraduate/phd.aspx; attached to Univ. of Birmingham; Dir Dr NEIL HOTCHIN.

Cambridge University Botanic Garden: 1 Brookside, Bateman St, Cambridge, CB2 1JE; tel. (1223) 336265; e-mail enquiries@botanic.cam.ac.uk; internet www.botanic.cam.ac.uk; f. 1846; teaching and research in botany and horticulture; library of 9,000 vols; Dir Prof. BEVERLEY GLOVER; publs *Friends' News* (1 a year), *Seed List* (1 a year).

Chelsea Physic Garden: 66 Royal Hospital Rd, Chelsea, London, SW3 4HS; tel. (20) 7352-5646; e-mail enquiries@chelseaphysicgarden.co.uk; internet www.chelseaphysicgarden.co.uk; f. 1673; botanic garden and centre for research and education on plants, conservation of rare plants; specializes in medicinal plants, tropical corridor glasshouse, cool fernery, listed pond rockery, beehives; adult learning programme of lectures and short courses; library: restricted-access library of 300 vols, incl. Soc. of Apothecaries Dale bequest; Curator CHRISTOPHER BAILES; publ. *Index Seminum* (1 a year).

Egenis, the Centre for the Study of Life Sciences: Univ. of Exeter, Byrne House, St German's Rd, Exeter, EX4 4PJ; tel. (1392) 725140; e-mail egenis@exeter.ac.uk; internet www.exeter.ac.uk/egenis; f. 2002 as part of the ESRC Genomics Network; attached to Univ. of Exeter; conducts research on social science, biology, philosophy and history; Dir Prof. JOHN DUPRÉ; publ. *History and Philosophy of the Life Sciences*.

Institute of Zoology: Zoological Society of London, Regent's Park, London, NW1 4RY; tel. (20) 7449-6610; e-mail enquiries@ioz.ac.uk; internet www.zsl.org/science; f. 1977; conducts research on behavioural and population ecology; biodiversity and macroecology; evolution and molecular ecology; people, wildlife and ecosystems; wildlife epidemiology; Dir Prof. TIM BLACKBURN (acting); publ. *Journal of Zoology* (1 a year).

Interdisciplinary Research Centre in Biomedical Materials: Queen Mary, Univ. of London, Mile End Rd, London, E1 4NS; tel. (20) 7882-5151; f. 1991; attached to Queen Mary, University of London; funded by EPSRC as nat. centre; innovation of analogue biomaterials for tissue and joint replacement; second-generation implants and prostheses for medical and dental applications; offers PhD, MD and MS degrees.

International Bee Research Association (IBRA): Unit 6 Centre Court, Main Avenue, Treforest, CF37 5YR; tel. (29) 2037-2409; e-mail mail@ibra.org.uk; internet www.ibra.org.uk; f. 1949; Pres. Prof. OCTAAF VAN LAERE (Belgium); Chair. HANS KJAERSGAARD; Sec. DAVID SMITH; publs *Bee World* (4 a year),

Journal of Apicultural Research (4 a year, online), *Journal of ApiProduct and ApiMedical Science* (4 a year, online).

National Institute for Biological Standards and Control: Blanche Lane, S Mimms, Potters Bar, EN6 3QG; tel. (1707) 641000; e-mail enquiries@nibsc.org; internet www.nibsc.org; f. 1976; controls and standardizes biological substances used in human medicines; library of 5,000 vols, 200 periodicals; Dir Dr STEPHEN INGLIS; publ. *Biological Reference Materials*.

Royal Botanic Garden, Edinburgh: 20A Inverleith Row, Edinburgh, EH3 5LR; tel. (131) 552-7171; e-mail info@rbge.org.uk; internet www.rbge.org.uk; f. 1670; int. centre for the study of plant biodiversity and conservation; courses leading to HND in horticulture with plantsmanship; MSc course in biodiversity and plant taxonomy; Inverleith House Gallery with art exhibitions inspired by nature; regional gardens at Bentmore, Dawyck and Logan; herbarium of 2,000,000 specimens; library: see under Libraries and Archives; Chair. Sir MUIR RUSSELL; Regius Keeper Prof. STEPHEN BLACKMORE; publs *Botanics Magazine* (4 a year), *Edinburgh Journal of Botany* (3 a year).

Royal Botanic Gardens, Kew: Richmond upon Thames, TW9 3AB; tel. (20) 8332-5000; e-mail info@kew.org; internet www.kew.org; f. 1759; taxonomic botany, horticulture, conservation, economic botany, biochemistry, genetics, mycology, propagation and seed storage; also gardens and facilities at Wakehust Place, W Sussex; library: see under Libraries and Archives; Dir Prof. RICHARD DEVERELL; Dir of Science KATHY WILLIS; publs *Curtis's Botanical Magazine* (4 a year), *Kew Bulletin* (4 a year), *Kew Record of Taxonomic Literature* (4 a year).

University of Bristol Botanic Garden: Hollybush Lane, Stoke Bishop, Bristol, BS9 1JB; The Holmes, Stoke Park Rd, Stoke Bishop, Bristol, BS9 1JG; tel. (117) 331-4906; e-mail botanic-gardens@bristol.ac.uk; internet www.bristol.ac.uk/botanic-garden; f. 1882; advances public education and promotes teaching and research into botany and its related subjects; Dir Prof. SIMON HISCOCK; Curator NICHOLAS WRAY; publ. *Annual Seed List*.

University of Oxford Botanic Garden: Rose Lane, Oxford, OX1 4AZ; tel. (1865) 286690; internet www.botanic-garden.ox.ac.uk; f. 1621; 6,000 plant species in glasshouses, walled garden, water garden, rock garden and seasonal borders; educational lectures and tours; Harcourt Arboretum south of Oxford; library of 1,000 vols on horticulture; Dir TIMOTHY WALKER.

Wildfowl & Wetlands Trust: Slimbridge, GL2 7BT; tel. (1453) 891900; e-mail enquiries@wwt.org.uk; internet www.wwt.org.uk; f. 1946; safeguards and improves wetlands for wildlife and people; comparative colln of living wildfowl at Slimbridge; centres at Arundel, Caerlaverock, Co. Down, London, Burscough, Llanelli, Tyne and Wear, Wisbech; Chair. Sir GEORGE RUSSELL; Chief Exec. MARTIN SPRAY; publs *Waterlife* (4 a year), *Wildfowl* (1 a year).

Mathematical Sciences

Hull Institute for Mathematical Science and Applications: Cottingham Rd, Hull, HU6 7RX; attached to Univ. of Hull; Dir Prof. V. VLADIMIROV.

Isaac Newton Institute for Mathematical Sciences: 20 Clarkson Rd, Cambridge, CB3 0EH; tel. (1223) 335999; e-mail info@newton.ac.uk; internet www.newton.ac.uk; f. 1992; attached to Univ. of Cambridge; library

of 6,000 vols; access by appointment only; Dir Prof. JOHN TOLAND.

Mathematics Education Centre: Schofield Bldg, Loughborough Univ., Loughborough, LE11 3TU; tel. (1509) 228250; e-mail mec@lboro.ac.uk; internet www.lboro.ac.uk/departments/mec; f. 2002; attached to Loughborough Univ.; research in different fields of mathematics; curriculum devt projects; organizes courses and seminars; Dir Dr CAROL ROBINSON.

National Computing Centre: Norduck House, Moat Lane, Aston Abbotts, HP22 4NF; tel. (870) 908-8767; e-mail info@ncc.co.uk; internet www.ncc.co.uk; f. 1966; promotes the effective use of IT; represents mems views at nat. and int. level; provides consultancy and training services, software packages and other products; cooperates with other bodies to foster standards and best practices; Exec. Chair. MICHAEL GOUGH; Man. Dir STEFAN FOSTER; publ. *IT Adviser* (4 a year).

SIMBIOS Centre: Level 5, Kydd Bldg, Univ. of Abertay Dundee, Bell St, Dundee, DD1 1HG; tel. (1382) 308533; e-mail simbios@abertay.ac.uk; internet simbios.abertay.ac.uk; attached to Univ. of Abertay Dundee; conducts multi-disciplinary research on ecological, biological and environmental problems; Co-Dir Prof. WILFRED OTTEN; Co-Dir Prof. JIM BOWN.

XFi Centre for Finance and Investment: Univ. of Exeter Business School, Streatham Court, Rennes Dr., Exeter, EX4 4ST; tel. (1392) 726504; internet business-school.exeter.ac.uk/research/areas/centres/xfi; f. 2001; attached to Univ. of Exeter; financial market research; Dir Prof. RICHARD HARRIS.

Physical Sciences

Astronomy Unit: School of Physics and Astronomy, Queen Mary, Univ. of London, Mile End Rd, London, E1 4NS; tel. (20) 7882-3460; internet astro.qmul.ac.uk; attached to Queen Mary, Univ. of London; nat. centre conducting research in astronomy and astrophysics; Dir RICHARD NELSON.

Biocatalysis Centre: Henry Wellcome Bldg for Biocatalysis, Stocker Rd, Exeter, EX4 4QD; tel. (1392) 263489; internet www.exeter.ac.uk/biocatalysis; f. 2003; attached to Univ. of Exeter; researches into aspects of biocatalysis incl. relationships between protein structure and function, protein engineering, molecular graphics, protein crystallography; Head Dr CLIVE BUTLER.

Armagh Observatory: College Hill, Armagh, BT61 9DG; tel. (28) 3752-2928; e-mail info@arm.ac.uk; internet star.arm.ac.uk; f. 1789; study of astronomy, climate, stellar astrophysics and the solar system; library of 15,000 vols; Dir Prof. MARK E. BAILEY; Admin. EMMA-JANE KENNEDY.

Astrophysics Group, Cavendish Laboratory: JJ Thomson Ave, Cambridge, CB3 0HE; tel. (1223) 337294; e-mail k.scrivener@mrao.cam.ac.uk; internet www.mrao.cam.ac.uk; f. 1945; attached to Univ. of Cambridge; conducts research on optical interferometry, cosmic microwave background (CMB) radiation, galaxy evolution, star formation and exoplanets; Head Prof. PAUL ALEXANDER.

Centre for Advanced Research in International Agricultural Development: Alun Roberts Bldg, Bangor Univ., Deniol Rd, Bangor, LL57 2UW; tel. (1248) 382346; e-mail cariad@bangor.ac.uk; internet cariad.bangor.ac.uk; f. 1983 as Centre for Arid Zone Studies, current name adopted 2010; attached to Bangor Univ.; promotion of agricultural and forestry devt and the provision of technological and scientific innovation to improve natural resource devt and management; Dir Dr IAN ROBINSON.

Centre for Electromagnetic Materials Research (CEMR): Harrison Bldg, N Park Rd, Exeter, EX4 4QF; tel. (1392) 263628 Physics Bldg, Stocker Rd, Exeter, EX4 4QL; tel. (1392) 264151; e-mail cemr@exeter.ac.uk; internet centres.exeter.ac.uk/cemr; attached to Univ. of Exeter; research areas include diffractive optics, photonic control of light-matter interactions, thin-film magnetics, magnetic, optical, probe data storage, micro-wave photonics and plasmonics, phase-change materials, photonics in biology, ter-ahertz photonics and plasmonics, liquid crystals; Head Prof. ROY SAMBLES.

Centre for Energy and Environment: Unit M1, The Innovation Centre (Phase 1), Univ. of Exeter, Rennes Dr., Exeter, EX4 4RN; tel. (1392) 724144; internet emps .exeter.ac.uk/research/energy-environment/ cee; f. 1975; attached to Univ. of Exeter; conducts applied research into sustainable bldgs, energy policy and impact of climate change on the built environment; Dir ANTHONY NORTON.

Centre for Environmental History and Policy: Stirling, FK9 4LA; tel. (1786) 467-861; internet www.stir.ac.uk/cehp; f. 1999; attached to Univ. of Stirling; research on disciplinary backgrounds, incl. history, politics, environmental science, law; Dir Dr PAUL ADDERLEY.

Centre for Environmental Studies: Loughborough Univ., Loughborough, LE11 3TU; tel. (1509) 222558; internet www.lboro .ac.uk/research/cens; f. 2000; attached to Loughborough Univ.; provides multi-disciplinary approach to education and research in environmental studies; Coordinator Dr LOIS E. CHILD.

Centre of Environmental and Waste Management: Univ. of the West of Scotland, Paisley, PA1 2BE; tel. (141) 848-3249; e-mail cewm@uws.ac.uk; internet www.uws.ac.uk/ schools/school-of-science/departments/cen-tre-for-environmental-and-waste-manage-ment; f. 1991; attached to Univ. of the West of Scotland; consultancy, courses and training on health and safety, environment and waste management; Dir Dr JENNIFER McQUAID-COOK.

Centre for Hazard & Risk Management: Loughborough Univ., Loughborough, LE11 3TU; tel. (1509) 222155; e-mail sbe.ohs@lboro .ac.uk; attached to Loughborough Univ.; applied research in environmental pollution control, human factors and safety culture, organizational health and safety management, risk and continuing professional devt.

Centre for Maritime Historical Studies: College of Humanities, Amory Bldg, Rennes Dr., Exeter, EX4 4RJ; tel. (1392) 724456; e-mail history@exeter.ac.uk; internet humanities.exeter.ac.uk/history/research/ centres/maritime; f. 1991; attached to Univ. of Exeter; promotes research on economic, social, political, naval, environmental aspects of British and European maritime history; Dir Dr MARIA FUSARO.

Centre for Philosophy of Natural and Social Science: Lakatos Bldg, London School of Economics and Political Science, 7 Portugal St, London, WC2A 2AE; tel. (20) 7955-7573; e-mail philcent@lse.ac.uk; internet www.lse.ac.uk/cpnss; f. 1990; attached to London School of Economics and Political Science, Univ. of London; Dir ROMAN FRIGG.

Centre for Renewable Energy Systems Technology: Holywell Park, School of Electronic and Electrical Engineering, Loughborough Univ., Loughborough, LE11 3TU; tel.

(1509) 635340; internet www.lboro.ac.uk/ departments/eese/research/centres/crest; f. 1993; attached to Loughborough Univ.; Dir Prof. PHIL EAMES.

Centre for Research in Ecology: Dept of Life Sciences, Whitelands College, Roehampton Univ., Holybourne Ave, London, SW15 4JD; tel. (20) 8392-3456; internet www .roehampton.ac.uk/research-centres/centre-for-research-in-ecology; attached to Roehampton Univ.; specializes in study of fresh-water ecology, terrestrial ecology and whole-animal behavioural-physiology; Dir Prof. ANNE ROBERTSON.

Centre for Sustainable Design: Univ. for the Creative Arts, Farnham Campus, Farnham, GU9 7DS; tel. (1252) 892772; internet www.cfsd.org.uk; f. 1995; attached to Univ. for the Creative Arts; Dir MARTIN CHARTER; publ. *Journal of Sustainable Product Design* (4 a year).

Centre for Water Systems (CWS): College of Engineering, Mathematics and Physical Sciences, Univ. of Exeter, N Park Rd, Exeter, EX4 4QF; tel. (1392) 263637; e-mail cws@ exeter.ac.uk; internet emps.exeter.ac.uk/ engineering/research/cws; f. 1994; attached to Univ. of Exeter; researches into water systems engineering focusing mainly on water supply and distribution systems, waste water and urban drainage systems, integrated modelling, risk and uncertainty, whole-life costing, water efficiency, catch-ment-based management, spatial water management; Co-Dir Prof. DAVID BUTLER; Co-Dir Prof. DRAGAN SAVIC.

Environmental Sciences Research Institute: Room G157, School of Environmental Sciences, Univ. of Ulster, Cromore Rd, Coleraine, BT52 1SA; tel. (28) 7012-4242; internet www.science.ulster.ac.uk/esri; attached to Univ. of Ulster; research on natural hazards and climate change, and human and physical influences in ecological, freshwater, coastal and maritime systems; Dir Prof. SANDY STEACY; Sec. LINDA ALLEN.

Hull Environment Research Institute (HERI): Cottingham Rd, Hull, HU6 7RX; internet www2.hull.ac.uk/science/heri.aspx; f. 2004; attached to Univ. of Hull; Dir Prof. L. FROSTICK.

Institute of Astronomy: Univ. of Cambridge, Madingley Rd, Cambridge, CB3 0HA; tel. (1223) 337548; e-mail ioa@ast.cam .ac.uk; internet www.ast.cam.ac.uk; f. 1972 by merger of Observatory (f. 1823), Solar Physics Observatory (f. 1912) and Institute of Theoretical Astronomy (f. 1967); Univ. of Cambridge; teaching and research in the fields of theoretical and observational astronomy; library of 35,800 vols; Dir ANDREW C. FABIAN.

Institute of Estuarine and Coastal Studies: Univ. of Hull, Cottingham Rd, Hull, HU6 7RX; tel. (1482) 464120; e-mail iecs@hull.ac .uk; internet www.hull.ac.uk/iecs; f. 1982; attached to Univ. of Hull; research on benthic ecology, fish and epifaunal ecology, marine ornithology, estuarine and terrestrial ornithology, marine mammals; biotope mapping and habitat assessment; vegetation surveys; Dir Dr MIKE ELLIOTT; Deputy Dir NICK CUTTS.

Jodrell Bank Observatory: Univ. of Manchester, Macclesfield, SK11 9DL; tel. (1477) 571321; e-mail simon.garrington@ manchester.ac.uk; internet www.jb.man.ac .uk; f. 1945; attached to Univ. of Manchester; the observatory uses 7 large steerable radio telescopes, incl. the Lovell 250-ft diameter radio telescope; research on galactic and extra-galactic astrophysical continuum and spectral line radio emissions and cosmic microwave background; observations of radio

emission from quasars, pulsars and stars; multi-telescope interferometry and very long base-line interferometry; Dir Prof. SIMON GARRINGTON.

Met Office: Fitzroy Rd, Exeter, EX1 3PB; tel. (1392) 885680; e-mail enquiries@ metoffice.gov.uk; internet www.metoffice.gov .uk; f. 1854; provides a nat. meteorological service and implements the objectives of the World Meteorological Org. (see Int. Org.); provides forecasting and consultative services; library: see under Libraries and Archives; Chair. GREG CLARKE; Chief Exec. JOHN HIRST..

Attached Research Centre:

Met Office Hadley Centre: Fitzroy Rd, Exeter, EX1 3PB; tel. (870) 900-0100; e-mail enquiries@metoffice.gov.uk; internet www.metoffice.gov.uk/ climate-change/resources/hadleycentre; f. 1990; monitors, understands and predicts global and regional climate variability and change; provides advocacy services to govt on climate change issues; Head Prof. STEPHEN BELCHER; publ. *COP Climate Change* (1 a year).

Oxford Institute for Energy Studies: 57 Woodstock Rd, Oxford, OX2 6FA; tel. (1865) 311377; e-mail information@oxfordenergy .org; internet www.oxfordenergy.org; f. 1982; attached to Univ. of Oxford; conducts research on the economics of petroleum, gas, coal, nuclear power, solar and renewable energy; politics and sociology of energy; int. relations of oil-producing and oil-consuming nations; economic devt of oil-producing countries and the energy problems of other; developing countries; economics and politics of the environment in its relationship with energy; library of 13,000 vols; Pres. CHRISTOPHER ALLSOP; Dir BASSAM FATTOUH.

Science and Technology Facilities Council: Polaris House, N Star Ave, Swindon, SN2 1SZ; tel. (1793) 442000; e-mail enquiries@stfc.ac.uk; internet www.stfc.ac .uk; f. 2007 by merger of the Particle Physics and Astronomy Research Centre (PPARC) and the Council for the Central Laboratory of the Research Councils (CCLRC); operates large-scale research facilities and provides strategic advice to British Govt on their devt; coordinates and promotes research, innovation and skills devt in distinct fields; Chair. Prof. MICHAEL STERLING; CEO Prof. JOHN WOMERSLEY..

Attached Centre:

UK Astronomy Technology Centre: Royal Observatory, Blackford Hill, Edinburgh, EH9 3HJ; tel. (131) 668-8100; e-mail library@roe.ac.uk; internet www .stfc.ac.uk/ukatc; f. 1998; conducts research on dust and planets around nearby stars, galaxy formation and evolution, nearby young stellar populations; library of 75,000 vols; Dir GILLIAN WRIGHT.

Scottish Institute for Wood Technology: Bell St, Dundee, DD1 1HG; attached to Univ. of Abertay Dundee; Sr Research Dir Prof. JOHN W. PALFREYMAN.

Strathclyde Fermentation Centre: Univ. of Strathclyde, SIPBS, Hamnett Wing, 161 Cathedral St, Glasgow, G4 0RE; e-mail b .mcneil@strath.ac.uk; f. 1986; attached to Univ. of Strathclyde; bioprocessing; monitoring and control; animal and microbial cell culture; Dir Prof. B. McNEIL.

Tyndall Centre for Climate Change Research: Zuckerman Institute for Connective Environmental Research, School of Environmental Sciences, Univ. of East Anglia, Norwich, NR4 7TJ; tel. (1603) 593-900; e-mail tyndall@uea.ac.uk; internet www

.tyndall.ac.uk; attached to Univ. of East Anglia; Dir Prof. CORINNE LE QUÉRÉ.

UK Atomic Energy Authority: Culham Science Centre, Abingdon, OX14 3DB; tel. (1235) 528822; e-mail foienquiries@uk-atomic-energy.org.uk; internet www.gov.uk/government/organisations/uk-atomic-energy-authority; f. 1954; carries out fusion research in the UK; manages JET fusion project on behalf of the EU; Chair. Prof. ROGER CASHMORE; CEO Prof. STEVEN COWLEY.

University of London Observatory: 553 Watford Way, Mill Hill Park, London, NW7 2QS; tel. (20) 3108-1613; e-mail amira.valbaker@ucl.ac.uk; internet www.ulo.ucl.ac.uk; f. 1929; attached to Dept of Physics and Astronomy, Univ. College London; teaching and research in astronomy; specialized astronomical library; Dir Prof. IAN D. HOWARTH.

PHILOSOPHY AND PSYCHOLOGY

Anna Freud Centre: 12 Maresfield Gdns, London, NW3 5SU; tel. (20) 7794-2313; e-mail www@annafreud.org; internet www.annafreud.org; f. 1947 by Anna Freud, daughter of Sigmund Freud, 1952–1982 as the Hampstead Child Therapy Course and Clinic, current name adopted 1982; psychotherapeutic treatment of children and young people with emotional difficulties and family support; academic courses and training for professionals; research into child devt and psychotherapeutic techniques; library of 3,500 vols; Chair. of Directorial Team Prof. LINDA MAYES; Chief Exec. Prof. PETER FONAGY.

Centre for Experimental Consumer Psychology: College Rd, Bangor, LL57 2DG; tel. (1248) 382211; e-mail psychology@bangor.ac.uk; f. 2000; attached to Bangor Univ.; undergraduate and postgraduate courses; research and consulting services; Dir Dr JAMES INTRILIGATOR.

Clinical and Health Psychology Research Centre: Dept of Psychology, Whitelands College, Roehampton Univ., Holybourne Ave, London, SW15 4JD; tel. (20) 8392-3744; e-mail l.gibson@roehampton.ac.uk; internet www.roehampton.ac.uk/research-centres/clinical-and-health-psychology-research-centre; attached to Roehampton Univ.; promotes research on interaction of behavioural, biological environmental and sociocultural factors in the aetiology, maintenance and prevention of health problems, and in health promotion; Dir Dr LEIGH GIBSON.

Psychology Research Institute: Room G213, School of Psychology, Coleraine Campus, Cromore Rd, Coleraine, BT52 1SA; tel. (28) 7012-4418; e-mail f.harkin@ulster.ac.uk; internet www.science.ulster.ac.uk/psyri; attached to Univ. of Ulster; conducts internationally recognized research within 4 research groups: psychological epidemiology and mental health; peace, conflict and equality; behavioural neuroscience; health and wellbeing; Dir Prof. MAURICE STRINGER; Sec. FIONA HARKIN.

RELIGION, SOCIOLOGY AND ANTHROPOLOGY

Centre for Analysis of Social Exclusion: London School of Economics and Political Science, Houghton St, London, WC2A 2AE; tel. (20) 7955-6679; e-mail case@lse.ac.uk; internet sticerd.lse.ac.uk/case; f. 1997; attached to London School of Economics and Political Science, Univ. of London; conducts research on poverty, exclusion and equalities; children, families and education; health and social care; housing, neighbourhoods and environment; wealth and social mobility; employment and income; tax, benefits and pensions; regions and area inequalities; methodology, concepts and measures; Dir Prof. JOHN HILLS; Deputy Dir Dr TANIA BURCHARDT.

Centre for Biblical Studies: Univ. of Exeter, Amory Bldg, Exeter, EX4 4RJ; tel. (1392) 724288; internet humanities.exeter.ac.uk/theology/research/centres/biblicalstudies; f. 2008; attached to Dept of Theology and Religion, Univ. of Exeter; provides a forum for research in biblical studies; organizes seminars, hosts academic visitors and public lectures; Dir Prof. DAVID HORRELL.

Centre for Crime and Justice Studies: 2 Langley Lane, London, SW8 1GB; tel. (20) 7840-6110; e-mail info@crimeandjustice.org.uk; internet www.crimeandjustice.org.uk; f. 1931, current name adopted 1999; advances public understanding of crime, criminal justice and social harm; Chair. of Ccl ELIZABETH HILL; Dir RICHARD GARSIDE; Deputy Dir WILL McMAHON; publs *British Journal of Criminology* (4 a year), *Criminal Justice Matters* (4 a year).

Centre for Research in Evolutionary and Environmental Anthropology: Dept of Life Sciences, Whitelands College, Roehampton Univ., Holybourne Ave, London, SW15 4JD; tel. (20) 8392-3528; e-mail s.semple@roehampton.ac.uk; internet www.roehampton.ac.uk/research-centres/centre-for-research-in-evolutionary-and-environmental-anthropology; f. 2002; attached to Roehampton Univ.; research on fields in primatology, incl. socioecology, life history strategies, communication, welfare, reproductive endocrinology, comparative morphology and crop-raiding behaviour; Dir STUART SEMPLE.

Centre for Research in Social Policy: Loughborough, LE11 3TU; tel. (1509) 222222; e-mail crsp@lboro.ac.uk; internet www.lboro.ac.uk/research/crsp; f. 1983; attached to Loughborough Univ.; conducts applied social research and policy analysis on issues related to poverty, living standards and income adequacy; Dir DONALD HIRSCH.

Centre for the Advanced Study of Religion in Wales: Bangor, LL57 2DG; tel. (1248) 382079; e-mail theology@bangor.ac.uk; f. 1998; attached to Bangor Univ.; Dir Prof. D. DENSIL MORGAN; Dir Dr ROBERT POPE.

Centre for the Study of Migration: Mile End Rd, London, E1 4NS; e-mail b.schwarz@qmul.ac.uk; internet www.qmul.ac.uk/migration; f. 1995; attached to Queen Mary, Univ. of London; Dir Prof. BILL SCHWARZ; publ. *Crossings: Journal of Migration & Culture* (2 a year).

Centre for the Study of the Christian Church: Dept of Theology, Univ. of Exeter, Exeter, EX4 4QH; tel. (1392) 264242; e-mail theology@exeter.ac.uk; internet centres.exeter.ac.uk/cscc; attached to Univ. of Exeter; Dir Rev. Dr PAUL AVIS; publ. *International Journal for the Study of the Christian Church* (2 a year).

Economic and Social Research Council: Polaris House, North Star Ave, Swindon, SN2 1UJ; tel. (1793) 413000; e-mail comms@esrc.ac.uk; internet www.esrc.ac.uk; f. 1965; research and training agency; provides research on issues of importance to business, public sector and govt; Chair. Dr ALAN GILLESPIE; Chief Exec. Prof. PAUL BOYLE; publs *Britain in 2014* (1 a year), *Society Now* (3 a year).

European Muslim Research Centre: Amory Bldg, Rennes Dr., Exeter, EX4 4RJ; tel. (1392) 723367; e-mail emrc@exeter.ac.uk; internet centres.exeter.ac.uk/emrc; attached to Univ. of Exeter; researches on roles that Muslim communities play in European soc.; Co-Dir Dr JONATHAN GITHENS-MAZER; Co-Dir Dr ROBERT LAMBERT.

Exeter Centre for the Study of Esotericism (EXESESO): Univ. of Exeter, Queen's Dr., Exeter, EX4 4QJ; tel. (1392) 723252; internet centres.exeter.ac.uk/exeseso; f. 2005; attached to Univ. of Exeter; researches into historical and comparative aspects of esoteric traditions from Hellenistic period in late antiquity through Renaissance and early modern period to present; offers Masters programme and doctorate in Western Esotericism; library: 1m. vols of books and journals; Dir (vacant).

Exeter Turkish Studies: Amory Bldg, Rennes Dr., Exeter, EX4 4RJ; tel. (1392) 264195; e-mail exts@exeter.ac.uk; internet centres.exeter.ac.uk/exts; f. 2009; attached to Univ. of Exeter; researches Turkish history and culture; Dir STEPHEN MITCHELL; Co-Dir GERALD MacLEAN.

Family Assessment and Support Unit: Cottingham Rd, Hull, HU6 7RX; tel. (1482) 464304; internet www2.hull.ac.uk/fass/familyassessmentandsupport.aspx; f. 1996; attached to Univ. of Hull; Man. JANE McLOCKLAN.

Institute of Applied Social Studies: Muirhead Tower, Birmingham, B15 2TT; tel. (121) 414-2676; internet www.birmingham.ac.uk/schools/social-policy/departments/applied-social-studies; attached to Univ. of Birmingham; research in social policy and social work; Head DAVID STEPHENSON.

Institute of Arab and Islamic Studies: Univ. of Exeter, Stocker Rd, Exeter, EX4 4ND; tel. (1392) 724029; e-mail iais-info@exeter.ac.uk; internet socialsciences.exeter.ac.uk/iais; attached to Univ. of Exeter; Dir Prof. GARETH STANSFIELD.

Institute of Ismaili Studies: 210 Euston Rd, London, NW1 2DA; tel. (20) 7756-2700; e-mail info@iis.ac.uk; internet www.iis.ac.uk; f. 1977; research into Islam, with emphasis on Shi'ism and Ismaili tariqah; library of 30,000 vols, MSS and audiovisual items; Co-Dir Dr FARHAD DAFTARY.

London Middle East Institute: SOAS, Univ. of London, MBI Al Jaber Bldg, 21 Russell Sq., London, WC1B 5EA; tel. (20) 7898-4330; e-mail lmei@soas.ac.uk; internet www.soas.ac.uk/lmei; attached to School of Oriental and African Studies (SOAS), Univ. of London; provides teaching, training, research, publ., consultancy, outreach and other services related to the Middle East; Chair. Prof. PAUL WEBLEY; Dir Dr HASSAN HAKIMIAN; publ. *The Middle East in London* (5 a year).

Department of Methodology: Columbia House, London School of Economics, Houghton St, London, WC2A 2AE; tel. (20) 7955-6156; internet www.lse.ac.uk/methodology; f. 1991, jtly with external research bodies; attached to London School of Economics and Political Science, Univ. of London; researches methodological aspects of social surveys; Dir Prof. GEORGE GASKELL.

Muslim Institute: 109 Fulham Palace Rd, London, W6 8JA; tel. (20) 8563-1995; e-mail info@musliminstitute.com; internet www.musliminstitute.org; f. 2010; research in early history of Islam, Islamic economics, philosophy of science, international relations, global Islamic movement; teaching (short courses) in political thought, philosophy of science, Arabic language, journalism; monthly meetings of academics, writers and activists dealing with issues such as reform within Islam, Islamic identity and citizenship and the future of Islam in Europe; Co-Dir MERRYL WYN DAVIES; Co-Dir HASSAN

MAHAMDALLIE; publ. *Critical Muslim* (4 a year).

Network for Religion in Public Life: Dept of Theology, Univ. of Exeter, Exeter, EX4 4RJ; tel. (1392) 264241; e-mail e.d.reed@exeter.ac.uk; internet humanities.exeter.ac.uk/theology/research/centres/nrpl; f. 2007; attached to Univ. of Exeter; promotes understanding and cooperation between academics and religious communities; Dir Dr ESTHER D. REED.

Oxford Centre for Buddhist Studies: Linton Rd, Oxford, OX2 6UD; tel. (1865) 274098; e-mail info@ocbs.org; internet www.ocbs.org; f. 2004; attached to Univ. of Oxford; promotes the academic study of Buddhist texts, societies, theories and practices; holds confs and lecture series, and sponsors guest lectures; Academic Dir Prof. RICHARD GOMBRICH; publ. *Journal of the Oxford Centre for Buddhist Studies* (2 a year).

Oxford Centre for Hebrew and Jewish Studies: Yarnton Manor, Yarnton, Kidlington, Oxford, OX5 1PY; tel. (1865) 377946; e-mail enquiries@ochjs.ac.uk; internet www.ochjs.ac.uk; f. 1972; attached to Univ. of Oxford; promotes Jewish history, religion and culture, and Jewish interactions with other cultures; library: see under Libraries and Archives; Pres. Prof. MARTIN GOODMAN (acting); publ. *Journal of Jewish Studies* (2 a year).

Oxford Centre for Hindu Studies: 13–15 Magdalen St, Oxford, OX1 3AE; tel. (1865) 304300; e-mail info@ochs.org.uk; internet www.ochs.org.uk; f. 1997; attached to Univ. of Oxford; study of Hindu culture, soc., philosophies, religions and languages in all parts of the world and of all periods; preserves India's cultural heritage and promotes understanding of it through education, publishing and research; library of 20,000 vols; Dir SHAUNAKA RISHI DAS; Librarian REMBERT LUTJEHARMS; publ. *Journal of Hindu Studies* (2 a year).

Oxford Centre for Islamic Studies: George St, Oxford, OX1 2AR; tel. (1865) 278730; e-mail islamic.studies@oxcis.ac.uk; internet www.oxcis.ac.uk; f. 1985; attached to Univ. of Oxford; Dir Dr FARHAN AHMAD NIZAMI (Magdalen College); publ. *The Journal of Islamic Studies* (3 a year).

Population Investigation Committee: Room POR.2.01, London School of Economics, Houghton St, London, WC2A 2AE; tel. (20) 7955-7666; e-mail pic@lse.ac.uk; internet www.lse.ac.uk/socialpolicy/researchcentresandgroups/pic; f. 1936; attached to London School of Economics and Political Science, Univ. of London; promotes and undertakes research into population questions; promotes study of demography in both its quantitative and qualitative aspects; Chair. Prof. JOHN CLELAND; Gen. Sec. ANNE SHEPHERD; publ. *Population Studies: A Journal of Demography* (3 a year, print and online, www.popstudies.net).

School of Theology and Ministry Studies: Brayford Pool, Lincoln, LN6 7TS; attached to Univ. of Lincoln; Head Rev. Dr MARK HOCKNULL.

Social Work Research Centre: Stirling, FK9 4LA; tel. (1786) 473171; attached to Univ. of Stirling; Dir Prof. G. McIVOR.

Tavistock Institute: 30 Tabernacle St, London, EC2 A4UE; tel. (20) 7417-0407; e-mail hello@tavinstitute.org; internet www.tavinstitute.org; f. 1947; study of human relations in conditions of well-being, conflict or breakdown in the family, the work group, the community and the larger organization; CEO Dr ELIAT ARAM; publs *Evaluation* (4 a year), *Human Relations* (12 a year).

Welsh National Centre for Religious Education: College of Education and Lifelong Learning, Bangor Univ., Bangor, LL57 2DG; tel. (1248) 383594; e-mail ems023@bangor.ac.uk; internet wncre.bangor.ac.uk; f. 1979; attached to Bangor Univ.; promotes the devt of religious education in schools, colleges and churches of all types throughout Wales; Chair. VAUGHAN SALISBURY; Dir Prof. LESLIE J. FRANCIS.

TECHNOLOGY

Advanced Virtual Reality Research Centre: Holywell Park, Loughborough Univ., Loughborough, LE11 3TU; tel. (1509) 635678; internet www.lboro.ac.uk/research/avrrc; f. 1995; attached to Loughborough Univ.; research and devt in advanced modelling, simulation and visualization techniques; Dir Prof. ROY KALAWSKY.

Animation Research Centre: Falkner Rd, Farnham, GU9 7DS; f. 2000; attached to Univ. for the Creative Arts; encourages interdisciplinary relationships between animation, visual and film theories, architecture and the fine arts; Dir Dr SUZANNE BUCHAN.

Building Research Establishment (BRE): Bucknalls Lane, Garston, Watford, WD25 9XX; tel. (1923) 664000; e-mail enquiries@bre.co.uk; internet www.bre.co.uk; f. 1921 as Building Research Station, current name adopted 1972; research and consultancy covering building, construction, energy efficiency and the prevention and control of fire; certification of building products, accreditation of product installers and energy assessors; environmental assessment of bldgs; Chief Exec. Dr PETER BONFIELD.

Centre for Automotive Management: Loughborough, LE11 3TU; tel. (7805) 201823; internet www.lboro.ac.uk/departments/sbe/executive-education/areas/automotive-management; f. 1997; attached to Loughborough Univ.; provides training in automotive dealership; Dir Prof. JIM SAKER.

Centre for Engineering and Design Education: Keith Green Bldg, Loughborough Univ., Loughborough, LE11 3TU; tel. (1509) 227191; e-mail cede@lboro.ac.uk; internet cede.lboro.ac.uk; f. 1997, current name adopted 2011; attached to Loughborough Univ.; provides engineering and design education activities; Head MELANIE KING.

Centre for Innovative and Collaborative Construction Engineering: Loughborough Univ., Loughborough, LE11 3TU; tel. (1509) 228549; e-mail cice@lboro.ac.uk; internet www.lboro.ac.uk/research/cice; f. 1999; attached to Loughborough Univ.; Dir Prof. STEPHEN ISON; Deputy Dir Prof. JACQUELINE GLASS.

Centre for Internet Computing: Cottingham Rd, Hull, HU6 7RX; attached to Univ. of Hull; Head Dr CRAIG GASKELL.

Centre for Mobile Communications Research: School of Electronic, Electrical and Systems Engineering, Loughborough Univ., Loughborough, LE11 3TU; tel. (1509) 227006; internet www.lboro.ac.uk/research/cmcr; f. 1998; attached to Loughborough Univ.; research in the design of antennas and associated components for mobility applications; encourages cross fertilization between physical, firm and soft aspects of communications technology; Dir Dr ROB EDWARDS.

Centre for MR Investigations: Hull Royal Infirmary, Anlaby Rd, Hull, HU3 2JZ; tel. (1482) 674078; internet www.hull.ac.uk/mri; f. 1992; attached to Univ. of Hull; breast research programme, brain research programme, radiotherapy planning and bone marrow imaging; Scientific Dir Prof. LINDSAY W. TURNBULL.

Centre for Particle Characterization and Analysis: Paisley, PA1 2BE; tel. (141) 848-3241; e-mail cpca@uws.ac.uk; f. 1994; attached to Univ. of the West of Scotland; Man. Dr ANDREW HURSTHOUSE.

CIRIA: Griffin Court, 15 Long Lane, London, EC1A 9PN; tel. (20) 7549-3300; e-mail enquiries@ciria.org; internet www.ciria.org; f. 1960; improves the quality, efficiency, cost-effectiveness and safety in both the provision and operation of the modern built environment; Chief Exec. BILL HEALY; publ. *Evolution* (2 a year).

Computer Science Research Institute: Room L113, School of Computing and Information Engineering, Univ. of Ulster, Coleraine Campus, Cromore Rd, Coleraine, BT52 1SA; tel. (28) 7012-4648; internet www.compeng.ulster.ac.uk/csri.php; f. 2004; attached to Univ. of Ulster; research in artificial intelligence and applications, information and communication engineering, intelligent systems and smart environments; attached research centres: Electronics Production and Innovation (EPI) Centre, Intelligent Systems Research Centre, Wireless Technology Research Centre; Dir Prof. BRYAN W. SCOTNEY.

Computer Security Research Centre: Tower One, Houghton St, London, WC2A 2AE; tel. (20) 7955-6398; f. 1991; attached to London School of Economics and Political Science, Univ. of London; studies computer security issues from organizational, management, social and technical perspectives; Dir Dr JAMES BACKHOUSE.

Defence Science and Technology Laboratory (DSTL): Porton Down, Salisbury, SP4 0JQ; tel. (1980) 613121; e-mail centralenquiries@dstl.gov.uk; internet www.dstl.gov.uk; f. 2001; attached to Min. of Defence; library: MOD Scientific Reports Colln of 750,000 items from WWII to the present; Chair. Sir RICHARD MOTTRAM; Chief Exec. JONATHAN LYLE.

Engineering Innovation Institute: Cottingham Rd, Hull, HU6 7RX; tel. (1482) 466470; e-mail eii@hull.ac.uk; attached to Univ. of Hull; coordinates contract research and devt business; Dir GAVIN CUTLER.

Hasselblad Centre for High Resolution Digital Imaging: Fort Pitt, Rochester, ME1 1DZ; attached to Univ. for the Creative Arts; Contact Prof. ORI GERSHT.

Health Design and Technology Institute: Coventry Univ. Technology Park, Puma Way, Coventry, CV1 2TT; tel. (24) 7615-8000; e-mail hdti.info@coventry.ac.uk; internet www.coventry.ac.uk/research/research-directory/allied-health/health-design-technology-institute; attached to Coventry Univ.; research in areas such as bldg and vehicle adaptations, walking aids and wheelchairs, consumer health products and healthcare technology for the elderly and people with disabilities; Dir SIMON FIELDEN.

Industrial Control Centre: Dept of Electronic and Electrical Engineering, Univ. of Strathclyde, Royal College Bldg, 204 George St, Glasgow, G1 1XW; tel. (141) 548-2378; internet www.icc.strath.ac.uk; attached to Univ. of Strathclyde; promotes research in mathematical modelling, numerical simulation and dynamic control of complex systems; Dir Prof. WILLIAM E. LEITHEAD; Sec. SHEILA CAMPBELL.

Institute for Energy and Environment: Royal College Bldg, 204 George St, Glasgow, G1 1XW; tel. (141) 548-2268; e-mail instee@eee.strath.ac.uk; internet www.strath.ac.uk/

eee/research/iee; attached to Univ. of Strathclyde; Dir Prof. JIM McDONALD.

Institute of Bioelectronic and Molecular Microsystems: Dean St, Bangor, LL57 1UT; tel. (1248) 382-010; e-mail info@ibmm-microtech.co.uk; internet www.bangor.ac.uk/eng/business/ibmm.php; f. 1983; attached to Bangor Univ.; Dir Prof. D. M. TAYLOR.

Intelligent Systems Research Group: Bell St, Dundee, DD1 1HG; attached to Univ. of Abertay Dundee; Dir Prof. DAVID A. BRADLEY.

Interdisciplinary Research Centre in Materials Processing: Univ. of Birmingham, Edgbaston, Birmingham, B15 2TT; tel. (121) 414-3446; internet www.birmingham.ac.uk/research/activity/irc-materials-processing; f. 1989, current name adopted 2001; attached to Univ. of Birmingham; research on metals and ceramics, covering processing, property and microstructural studies; Head Dr STUART BLACKBURN.

International Centre for Computer Games and Virtual Entertainment: Bell St, Dundee, DD1 1HG; f. 2001; attached to Univ. of Abertay Dundee; academic research and devt centre for computer games and digital entertainment industry; Head Prof. LOUIS NATANSON.

National Physical Laboratory: Hampton Rd, Teddington, TW11 0LW; tel. (20) 8977-3222; e-mail enquiry@npl.co.uk; internet www.npl.co.uk; f. 1900; establishes measurement standards; undertakes research into improved techniques, engineering materials and IT; Managing Dir Dr BRIAN BOWSHER.

Natural Resources Institute: Univ. of Greenwich, Central Ave, Chatham Maritime, ME4 4TB; tel. (1634) 880088; e-mail nri@greenwich.ac.uk; internet www.nri.org; f. 1987; attached to Univ. of Greenwich; undertakes research, consultancy and training to support global food security, sustainable devt and poverty reduction in developing countries; library of 300,000 vols and information service; Dir Dr ANDREW WESTBY; publ. *NRI Annual Review*.

Pera Technology: Nottingham Rd, Melton Mowbray, LE13 0PB; tel. (1664) 501501; e-mail enquiries@peratechnology.com; internet www.peratechnology.com; f. 1946; a multi-disciplinary technology centre specializing in all aspects of manufacture, incl. materials, quality training, methods, computer applications, human resources and manufacturing integration; Exec. Chair. JOHN HILL; CEO PAUL TRANTER.

QinetiQ: Cody Technology Park, Ively Rd, Farnborough, GU14 0LX; tel. (1252) 392000; internet www.qinetiq.com; f. 2001 as govt-owned UK PLC following reorganization of the fmr Defence Evaluation and Research Agency (DERA); researches and develops services and technologies in: defence, maritime, aviation, security, energy and power, automative, finance, health, highways and traffic, public sector, rail, space, telecoms, media and electronics; CEO LEO QUINN.

Scottish Microelectronics Centre: School of Engineering, Univ. of Edinburgh, Kings Bldgs, Edinburgh, EH9 3JF; tel. (131) 650-5620; internet www.see.ed.ac.uk/~ajw/facilities.html; attached to Univ. of Edinburgh; research and devt in semiconductor sector; delivers services in 4 areas: incubation, analytical, processing and assembly; Dir Prof. ANTHONY J. WALTON.

Scottish Universities Environmental Research Centre: Rankine Ave, Scottish Enterprise Technology Park, E Kilbride, Glasgow, G75 0QF; tel. (1355) 223332; e-mail director@suerc.gla.ac.uk; internet www.gla.ac.uk/research/az/suerc; f. 1963; provides research and teaching facilities in radioactive and stable isotopes in the environment, ultratrace analysis, radiation mapping, nuclear waste disposal, thermoluminescence dating and dosimetry, food irradiation, radiochemistry, environmental studies, geochronology, isotope geology, stable isotope geochemistry, carbon dating and cosmogenic isotope analysis, including accelerator mass spectrometry; Dir Prof. ROB ELLAM.

Smith Institute for Industrial Mathematics and System Engineering: Surrey Technology Centre, Surrey Research Park, Guildford, GU2 7YG; tel. (1483) 579108; e-mail office@smithinst.co.uk; internet www.smithinst.co.uk; f. 1997; jt industry/academic institute for research in industrial mathematics and system engineering; training in energy, telecommunications and insurance sectors; Chair. Dr BRUCE SMITH; Dir Dr ROBERT LEESE.

Sports Technology Institute: Loughborough Park, Loughborough Univ., Loughborough, LE11 3TU; tel. (1509) 564819; internet sti.lboro.ac.uk; attached to Loughborough Univ.; Dir Dr ANDY HARLAND.

SPRU—Science and Technology Policy Research: Jubilee Bldg, Univ. of Sussex, Falmer, Brighton, BN1 9SL; tel. (1273) 686758; e-mail spru@sussex.ac.uk; internet www.sussex.ac.uk/spru; f. 1966; attached to Univ. of Sussex; analysis of science, technology and innovation; research in the field of social sciences; Dir Prof. JOHAN SCHOT.

Systems Engineering Innovation Centre: Sir Denis Rooke Bldg, Holywell Park, Loughborough Univ., Loughborough, LE11 3TU; tel. (1509) 635678; e-mail seic@lboro.ac.uk; internet www.lboro.ac.uk/departments/eese/research/centres/seic; f. 2002; attached to Loughborough Univ.; Technical Head Dr ROY KALAWSKY.

Thin Film Centre: High St, Paisley, PA1 2BE; tel. (141) 848-3610; e-mail thinfilmcentre@uws.ac.uk; internet www.uws.ac.uk/schools/school-of-engineering/research/thin-film-research-centre; f. 2000; attached to Univ. of the West of Scotland; devt of deposition processes for thin films; design and fabrication of thin film products; characterization of thin films; Dir Prof. FRANK PLACIDO.

TRL Ltd: Crowthorne House, Nine Mile Ride, Wokingham, RG40 3GA; tel. (1344) 773131; e-mail enquiries@trl.co.uk; internet www.trl.co.uk; f. 1933; specializes in road materials and construction, structures, road safety and traffic, vehicle safety, environment, security, travel behaviours and attitudes, software; library of 200,000 vols, 250 current journals; Chief Exec. ROB WALLIS; publ. *TRL Journal of Research* (3 or 4 a year).

Tun Abdul Razak Research Centre: Brickendonbury, Hertford, SG13 8NL; tel. (1992) 584966; e-mail general@tarrc.co.uk; internet www.tarrc.co.uk; f. 1938; research focused towards the advancement of the Malaysian rubber industry through compounding and processing, materials and product devt, engineering design, evaluation and testing and production technology; library of 3,000 books and 200 periodicals, information retrieval system containing 100,000 items; CEO Dr KAMARUDIN AB-MALEK; Dir for Research STUART COOK.

Urban Water Technology Centre: Level 5, Kydd Bldg, Bell St, Dundee, DD1 1HG; tel. (1382) 308170; e-mail uwtc@abertay.ac.uk; internet www.uwtc.tay.ac.uk; f. 1993; attached to Univ. of Abertay Dundee; research on anaerobic digestion, wastewater and waste treatment, sustainable urban drainage systems, biofuels and sustainability assessment, modelling and visualization; Co-Dir Prof. DAVID BLACKWOOD; Co-Dir Dr JOE AKUNNA.

Water, Engineering and Development Centre: John Pickford Bldg, Loughborough Univ., Loughborough, LE11 3TU; tel. (1509) 222885; e-mail wedc@lboro.ac.uk; internet wedc.lboro.ac.uk; f. 1971; attached to Loughborough Univ.; develops knowledge and capacity in water and sanitation for sustainable devt and emergency relief; Dir ANDREW COTTON.

WRc PLC: Frankland Rd, Blagrove, Swindon, SN5 8YF; tel. (1793) 865000; e-mail solutions@wrcplc.co.uk; internet www.wrcplc.co.uk; f. 1927; provides consultancy in the water, waste and environment sectors; Man. Dir TONY GRIFFITHS; Man. Dir MARK SMITH.

Libraries and Archives

Aberdeen

Aberdeen City Library and Information Services: Central Library, Rosemount Viaduct, Aberdeen, AB25 1GW; tel. (1224) 652500; e-mail centrallibrary@aberdeencity.gov.uk; internet www.aberdeencity.gov.uk/libraries; f. 1884; 20 brs; Central Library—Adult Lending Library, Children's Library, Media Centre, Internet access, Aberdeen College Learning Centre, Information Service, Local Studies, Community Contacts Directory; Careers Information, Scottish Parliament information, Nat. Library of Scotland Partner, Europe Direct Centre Enquiry and Research service, Migrant Communities Information Point, Enquire online nat. reference service; 500,000 vols; spec. collns incl. Scottish genealogy, local photographs, North Sea oil, British patent abstracts, 10,000 standard specifications, trademarks, business information; Library and Information Services Man. FIONA CLARK.

Robert Gordon University Library: Riverside E, Garthdee Rd, Aberdeen, AB10 7GJ; tel. (1224) 263450; e-mail library@rgu.ac.uk; internet www.rgu.ac.uk/library; f. 1992; 218,750 vols, incl. books and bound journals; Dir for Library Services MICHELLE ANDERSON.

University of Aberdeen: Library, Special Collections and Museums: Bedford Rd, Aberdeen, AB24 3AA; tel. (1224) 273330; e-mail library@abdn.ac.uk; internet www.abdn.ac.uk/library; f. 1495; consists of The Sir Duncan Rice Library and Special Collections Centre, Taylor Library and European Documentation Centre on the Old Aberdeen campus and the Medical Library on the Foresterhill Campus; 1,300,000 vols, 200,000 rare printed books, incl. 4,000 16th century items; McBean Jacobite colln, O'Dell railway colln, Aberdeen Bestiary colln, Biesenthal Hebrew colln, Taylor psalmody colln, G. W. Wilson photographic colln, Oral History Archive and other spec. collns; Univ. Librarian and Dir LAURENCE BEBBINGTON (acting).

Aberystwyth

Aberystwyth University, Hugh Owen Library: Penglais Campus, Aberystwyth, SY23 3DZ; tel. (1970) 622400; e-mail library@aber.ac.uk; internet www.aber.ac.uk; f. 1872; 730,000 vols, 3,647 periodicals; spec. collns in Hugh Owen Library incl. Celtic Colln (25,000 vols), Gregynog Press books and private press books since beginning of 20th century, George Powell Colln (19th century English and French literature, fine art and music), James Camden Hotten

Colln, Rudler Colln of geological pamphlets, Duff Colln of pamphlets (Classics), League of Nations and UN Documents, microforms incl. Early American Imprints 1639–1800, David De Lloyd Papers (Welsh folksongs), Lily Newton Papers (water pollution), Thomas Webster letters (19th century geologist); British Soc. of Rheology Library; spec. collns in Thomas Parry Library (incl. Welsh Institute of Rural Studies Library) incl. Horton Colln (early children's books), Appleton Colln (Victorian colour printing and binding), Whittingham colln; Dir for Information Services TIM DAVIES.

Ceredigion Library: Queen's Sq., Aberystwyth, SY23 2EB; tel. (1970) 633703; e-mail llyfrgell.library@ceredigion.gov.uk; f. 1996; attached to Ceredigion County Ccl; 7 brs, 6 mobile libraries; 290,000 vols; County Libraries Officer WILLIAM H. HOWELLS.

National Library of Wales: Aberystwyth, SY23 3BU; tel. (1970) 632800; e-mail enquiry@llgc.org.uk; internet www.llgc.org.uk; f. 1907; legal deposit library; 5m. printed books, 30,000 MSS, 800,000 photographs, 3.5m. deeds and documents and 200,000 maps, prints and drawings; Sir John Williams' Colln, Welsh and Celtic collns, diaries and correspondence of David Lloyd George; Librarian ALED GRUFFYDD JONES; publ. *The National Library of Wales Journal* (irregular, online).

Aldershot

Prince Consort's Library: Knollys Rd, Aldershot, GU11 1PS; tel. (1252) 349381; e-mail pcl@alibs.detsa.co.uk; f. 1860; public access by written appointment only; open to the public for Heritage Open Days; military history library; 80,000 vols; Head of Library Services TIM WARD.

Armagh

Armagh Public Library: 43 Abbey St, Armagh, BT61 7DY; tel. (28) 3752-3142; e-mail admin@armaghpubliclibrary.co.uk; internet armaghpubliclibrary.arm.ac.uk; f. 1771, by Archbishop Richard Robinson, museum status 2001; 17th- and 18th-century books on theology, philosophy, classic and modern literature, travels, history, medicine and law; library colln incl. subjects on art, history, religion, Ireland, Armagh City and County, Jonathan Swift, St Patrick, Church of Ireland, Rokeby Colln (prints), Beresford Colln (Irish artefacts), drawings of William Conor; 45,000 vols; Keeper Very Rev. GREGORY DUNSTAN.

Southern Education and Library Board: 3 Charlemont Pl., The Mall, Armagh, BT61 9AX; tel. (28) 3751-2200; e-mail selb.hq@selb.org; internet www.selb.org; f. 1973; 23 brs, 6 mobile libraries; serves the district ccl areas of Armagh, Banbridge, Cookstown, Craigavon, Dungannon and S Tyrone, Newry and Mourne; 1,450,000 vols; Chief Exec. GAVIN BOYD.

Ashton under Lyne

Tameside Metropolitan Borough Council Libraries: Old St, Ashton under Lyne, OL6 7SG; tel. (161) 342-2031; e-mail information.direct@tameside.gov.uk; internet www.tameside.gov.uk/libraries; f. 1974; 288,078 vols, 150 periodicals; spec. collns: local studies and archives, sound recordings, video cassettes, computer software; Head of Library Services MANDY KINDER.

Aylesbury

Buckinghamshire County Libraries: Gallery Suite, Walton St, Aylesbury, HP20 1UU; tel. (845) 230-3232; e-mail library@buckscc.gov.uk; internet www.buckscc.gov

.uk/libraries; f. 1918; 33 brs; 927,000 vols; Library Systems Man. HAZEL EDWARDS.

Ballymena

North Eastern Education and Library Board: County Hall, 182 Galgorm Rd, Ballymena, BT42 1HN; tel. (28) 2566-3333; e-mail foi@neelb.org.uk; internet www.neelb.org.uk; f. 1973; 28 brs, 8 mobile libraries; 2m. vols; Chief Exec. SHANE McCURDY.

Bangor

Library and Archives Service, Bangor University: College Rd, Bangor, LL57 2DG; tel. (1248) 382981; e-mail library@bangor.ac.uk; internet www.bangor.ac.uk/library; f. 1884; Bangor Cathedral Library; local Estate archives; 6 brs; 500,000 vols; Univ. Librarian SUE HODGES.

Barry

Vale of Glamorgan Libraries: Provincial House, Kendrick Rd, Barry, CF62 8BF; tel. (1446) 709381; e-mail barrylibrary@valeofglamorgan.gov.uk; internet www.valeofglamorgan.gov.uk/libraries; 9 brs; 200,000 vols, 6,000 audio books, 7,000 CDs, 9,000 DVDs; Prin. Librarian CHRISTOPHER EDWARDS.

Bath

University of Bath Library: Bath, BA2 7AY; tel. (1225) 385000; e-mail library@bath.ac.uk; internet www.bath.ac.uk/library; 500,000 vols; spec. collns: All England Women's Hockey Association (AEWHA) Colln, A. K. Chesterton Colln, Joseph Black Colln, Royal Bath and West of England Society Colln; Sir Isaac Pitman's private library colln; Univ. Librarian KATE ROBINSON.

Bedford

Bedford Borough Libraries: Bedford Borough Council, Borough Hall, Cauldwell St, Bedford, MK42 9AP; tel. (1234) 267422; e-mail bedfordshirelibraries@bedford.gov.uk; internet www.bedford.gov.uk/leisure_and_culture/libraries.aspx; 8 brs, mobile library; Man. ANDY BAKER.

Belfast

Belfast Education and Library Board: 40 Academy St, Belfast, BT1 2NQ; tel. (28) 9056-4000; e-mail info.belb@belb.co.uk; internet www.belb.org.uk; f. 1973; Central Library, 20 community libraries and 2 mobile libraries; Central Lending Library 57,000 vols; Central Reserve colln 100,000 vols; Humanities and Gen. Reference Library 120,000 vols; Irish Library 40,000 books, pamphlets and MSS on all aspects of Ireland, Ulster and Belfast; Fine Arts and Literature 74,000 vols; Music Library 12,000 vols, 24,000 scores, 24,000 records and cassettes; Business, Science and Technology Library 68,000 vols; other spec. collns: bibliographies, govt and agency publs, patents, rare books, microfilms; Chief Librarian KATHERINE McCLOSKEY.

Linen Hall Library: 17 Donegall Sq., N, Belfast, BT1 5GB; tel. (28) 9032-1707; e-mail info@linenhall.com; internet www.linenhall.com; f. 1788 as Belfast Reading Soc., still known as Belfast Library and Soc. for Promoting Knowledge for legal purposes; 350,000 vols; spec. colln: 70,000 Irish colln incl. early Ulster printing and colln of political ephemera relating to civil conflict since 1968; 5,000 17th-century pamphlets, 18th- and 19th-century travel, biography; Pres. G. PRIESTLEY; Vice-Pres. A. DAVIES; Hon. Sec. H. CAMPBELL; Hon. Treas. C. HUNTER; Deputy Dir PATRICIA SAUNDERS; Librarian JOHN

KILLEN; Deputy Librarian MONICA McERLANE.

Public Record Office of Northern Ireland: 2 Titanic Blvd, Belfast, BT3 9HQ; tel. (28) 9053-4800; e-mail proni@dcalni.gov.uk; internet www.proni.gov.uk; f. 1924; attached to Dept of Culture, Arts and Leisure for Northern Ireland; retains official and private records relating mainly to the history of Northern Ireland (c. 1600); Dir MAGGIE SMITH; Head of Public Services STEPHEN SCARTH.

Queen's University Library: Information Services, Queen's Univ., Belfast, BT7 1LS; tel. (28) 9097-6322; e-mail library@qub.ac.uk; internet www.qub.ac.uk/lib; f. 1849; 1.2m. vols, periodicals, pamphlets, MSS, theses and microforms; spec. collns: Hibernica Colln (incl. R. M. Henry Colln, O'Rahilly Colln), Antrim Presbytery Library, MacDouall Colln (Philology), Hamilton Harty Music Colln, Thomas Percy Library; Asst Dir for Library Services ELIZABETH TRAYNOR; Head of Spec. Collns & Archives DEIRDRE WILDY.

South Eastern Education and Library Board: Grahambridge Rd, Dundonald, Belfast, BT16 2HS; tel. (28) 9056-6200; e-mail info@seelb.org.uk; internet www.seelb.org.uk; f. 1973; 24 brs, 5 mobile libraries; 652,000 vols, 6,000 maps, 18,000 microforms, 22,000 CDs, 3,000 video recordings, 2,000 DVDs; Chief Exec. and Accounting Officer STANTON G. SLOAN.

Birmingham

Aston University Library & Information Services: Aston Triangle, Birmingham, B4 7ET; tel. (121) 204-4525; e-mail library@aston.ac.uk; internet www.aston.ac.uk/library; f. 1895; 139,593 vols, 32 print journal titles, 85,664 ebooks, 67,249 ejournal titles; Dir Dr NICK SMITH.

Library of Birmingham: Centenary Sq., Broad St, Birmingham, B1 2ND; tel. (121) 242-4242; e-mail enquiries@libraryofbirmingham.com; internet www.libraryofbirmingham.com; f. 2013; 39 community libraries; mobile library; archives, photography, rare books; incl. gallery space, studio theatre, recording studio, BFI Mediathèque providing access to the Nat. Film Archive; spec. collns: Shakespeare Library, Warwickshire Photographic Survey, Anstey College Archive, Parker Colln, Wingate Bett Colln, Railway Colln, Benjamin Stone Photographic Colln, Modern Photographic Colln, Birmingham Portrait Colln incl. cartes de visite and cabinet cards; collns of postcards from the USA, song sheets, music scores for silent films, Samuel Johnson, Milton, Cervantes, Baskerville and war poetry collns, early printed books, fine bindings and private press books, and Shakespeare Library—f. 1864, 45,000 vols in 90 languages); Dir BRIAN GAMBLES.

Orchard Learning Resources Centre: Hamilton Dr., Weoley Park Rd, Selly Oak, Birmingham, B29 6QW; tel. (121) 415-8454; e-mail olrc@bham.ac.uk; internet www.birmingham.ac.uk/libraries; f. 1997; attached to Univ. of Birmingham; anthropology and world area studies, communications, devt economics, Islamic, Christian theology and missiology, social studies, world religions, education, child and youth studies; 225,000 vols; spec. collns: Baykov Colln (100,000 vols), European Documentation Colln (10,000 vols), German Documentation Colln (3,000 vols), Arabic Colln, Oriental Colln; Resource Centre Man. DOROTHY VUONG.

University of Birmingham Libraries: Edgbaston, Birmingham, B15 2TT; tel. (121) 414-5828; e-mail library@bham.ac.uk;

internet www.birmingham.ac.uk/libraries; f. 1880 as Mason Science College Library; 2,671,174 vols, 50,000 print and electronic periodicals, 275,000 ebooks, 3m. MSS, 120,000 pre-1850 vols; spec. collns: archives of Joseph, Austen and Neville Chamberlain, Anthony Eden, W. H. Dawson, Francis Brett Young, Harriet Martineau, Bishop E. W. Barnes, Sir Oliver Lodge, Church Missionary Society Archives (pre-1950), YMCA archives; St Mary's, Warwick and Bengeworth parish libraries, Wigan Library from Bewdley, Worcs, Baskerville colln; Birmingham and Midland Institute pamphlet colln; Dir DIANE JOB.

Blackburn
Blackburn with Darwen Libraries: Central Library, Town Hall St, Blackburn, BB2 1AG; tel. (1254) 661221; e-mail library@blackburn.gov.uk; internet www.blackburn.gov.uk/libraries; f. 1998; unitary authority with 5 public libraries and mobile services; Head of Library and Information Services KATH SUTTON; Sr Librarian CATHERINE SNELLING.

Blackpool
Blackpool Library Service: Queen St, Blackpool, FY1 1PX; tel. (1253) 478080; e-mail central.library@blackpool.gov.uk; internet www.blackpool.gov.uk/libraries; 8 br libraries; 152,284 vols, 43 periodicals; Head of Libraries ANNE ELLIS.

Bournemouth
Bournemouth Libraries: 22 The Triangle, Bournemouth, BH2 5RQ; tel. (1202) 454848; e-mail bournemouth@bournemouthlibraries.org.uk; internet www.bournemouth.gov.uk/libraries; 277,404 vols, 41,237 audiovisual items, 13,276 sheet music, 16,720 microforms, 2,339 maps, 532 newspapers and periodicals; Area Services and Arts Man. CAROLYN DATE.

Bracknell
Bracknell Forest Borough Libraries: Bracknell Library, Town Sq., Bracknell, RG12 1BH; tel. (1344) 423149; e-mail bracknell.library@bracknell-forest.gov.uk; internet www.bracknell-forest.gov.uk/libraries; f. 1998; 9 brs; Head of Libraries and Information RUTH BURGESS.

Bradford
Bradford Libraries & Information Services: Centenary Sq., Bradford, BD1 1SD; tel. (1274) 430094; e-mail public.libraries@bradford.gov.uk; internet www.bradford.gov.uk/libraries; f. 1887; 32 libraries and 3 mobile libraries, provides general collns; Central Library specializes in local history, business information, Asian languages and audio and video services; Head of Service JOHN TRIFFITT.

University of Bradford Library: Bradford, BD7 1DP; tel. (1274) 233301; e-mail library@bradford.ac.uk; internet www.bradford.ac.uk/library; f. 1966; J. B. Priestley Library; Management Library; 580,000 vols; Commonwealth Colln, spec. J. B. Priestley Colln; Head of Library Services GRACE HUDSON.

Bridgend
Bridgend Library and Information Service: Angel St, Bridgend, CF31 4WB; tel. (1656) 754800; e-mail blis@bridgend.gov.uk; internet www.bridgend.gov.uk/libraries; 10 brs, mobile library; Prin. Officer Libraries RICHARD BELLINGER.

Bridgwater
Somerset County Council Library Service: Mount St, Bridgwater, TA6 3ES; tel. (1823) 340317; e-mail enquiry@somerset.gov.uk; internet www.somerset.gov.uk/libraries; f. 1919; 34 brs, 6 mobile libraries; 933,217 vols and sound recordings; Libraries Service Man. SUE CROWLEY; Information and Skills Devt Man. MAGGIE HARRIS.

Brighton
Brighton and Hove City Libraries: Jubilee Library, Jubilee St, Brighton, BN1 1GE; tel. (1273) 290800; e-mail libraries@brighton-hove.gov.uk; internet www.brighton-hove-rpml.org.uk/libraries; holdings incl. 45,000 rare and historical books at Jubilee Library; 13 brs; Head of Libraries SALLY McMAHON.

University of Sussex Library: Falmer, Brighton, BN1 9QL; tel. (1273) 678163; e-mail library@sussex.ac.uk; internet www.sussex.ac.uk/library; f. 1961; Mass Observation Archive; 750,000 vols; Librarian KITTY INGLIS.

Bristol
Bristol City Council Libraries: Central Library, College Green, Bristol, BS1 5TL; tel. (117) 903-7200; e-mail bristol.library.service@bristol.gov.uk; internet www.bristol.gov.uk/libraries; f. 1613; 27 brs; reference library; learning centre; 876,332 vols; Head of Libraries KATE MURRAY.

University of Bristol Library: Tyndall Ave, Bristol, BS8 1TJ; tel. (117) 928-8000; e-mail library-enquiries@bris.ac.uk; internet www.bris.ac.uk/library; f. 1876; 1.5m. vols and pamphlets; spec. collns incl. the English novel to 1850, the Sir Allen Lane Penguin colln, business histories, early geology, medicine, mathematics, chemistry and physics, Pinney Papers (17th–19th century), Brunel workbooks and papers, British philosophers, landscape gardening, courtesy books, Gen. Election addresses (part of the Nat. Liberal Club Library), Wiglesworth Ornithological Library, EDC, Addington Symonds Papers, Papers of the Somerset Miners' Asscn; Dir for Library Services Dr JESSICA GARDNER.

Caernarfon
Gwynedd Libraries: Caernarfon Library, Pavilion Hill, Caernarfon, LL55 1AS; tel. (1286) 679463; e-mail library@gwynedd.gov.uk; internet www.gwynedd.gov.uk; f. 1996; 17 brs; 320,089 vols; Prin. Librarian HYWEL JAMES.

Caerphilly
Caerphilly Library Service: The Twyn, Caerphilly, CF83 1JL; tel. (29) 2085-3911; e-mail libcaer@caerphilly.gov.uk; internet www.caerphilly.gov.uk/libraries; 18 brs, mobile library; Sr Man. GARETH EVANS.

Cambridge
Bible Society's Library: Cambridge Univ. Library, West Rd, Cambridge, CB3 9DR; tel. (1223) 333075; e-mail bslib@lib.cam.ac.uk; internet www.lib.cam.ac.uk/deptserv/biblesociety; f. 1804, fmrly British and Foreign Bible Society's Library; large colln of printed Bibles, over 39,000 vols of scripture in more than 2,500 languages, 500 MSS; archives of the Bible Society from 1804; Librarian P. M. MEADOWS.

Cambridge University Library: West Rd, Cambridge, CB3 9DR; tel. (1223) 333000; e-mail library@lib.cam.ac.uk; internet www.lib.cam.ac.uk; f. 1400; legal deposit library; 7,115,065 printed books and serial vols, numerous spec. collns, 157,186 MSS, large collns of papers and correspondence, 1,151,087 maps, 1,800,324 microforms; the collns have been accumulating since the beginning of the 15th century; Librarian ANNE JARVIS..

College Libraries:

Christ's College Library: Cambridge, CB2 3BU; tel. (1223) 334905; e-mail library@christs.cam.ac.uk; internet www.christs.cam.ac.uk/library; f. 1448, refounded 1505; 100,000 vols, incunabula, periodicals; spec. collns: works of John Milton, incl. items published before 1700, Charles Lesingham Smith colln of early mathematical and scientific books, William Robertson Smith Oriental Library, Sir Stephen Gaselee colln of Coptic studies, A. H. Wratislaw colln of Slavonic language and literature, W. H. D. Rouse colln of Indian studies and 16th-century English books, D. Dickson colln of C.P. Snow, David Stanbury Darwin colln; College Librarian AMELIE ROPER; Fellow Librarian Dr JAMES WADE.

Churchill College Library: Cambridge, CB3 0DS; tel. (1223) 336138; e-mail librarian@chu.cam.ac.uk; internet www.chu.cam.ac.uk; f. 1960; 58,000 vols; spec. collns incl. political, military and scientific archives mainly since late 19th century, C. P. Snow colln, Powys colln, Winston Churchill's books on Napoleon; Librarian MARY KENDALL.

Clare College Library: Memorial Court, Clare College, Cambridge, CB3 9AJ; tel. (1223) 333202; e-mail library@clare.cam.ac.uk; internet www.clare.cam.ac.uk/libraries; f. 1326; 38,000 vols; comprises Fellows' Library (8,000 vols); Forbes Mellon Library (30,000 vols); spec. collns: Cecil Sharp MSS, papers of Duncan Forbes, Geoffrey Elton, Mike Majerus, Philip Ford; Fellows' Librarian Dr FIONA EDMONDS; Forbes Mellon Librarian ANNE C. HUGHES.

Corpus Christi College: Parker Library: Trumpington St, Cambridge, CB2 1RH; tel. (1223) 338025; e-mail parker-library@corpus.cam.ac.uk; internet www.corpus.cam.ac.uk; f. 1352; spec. collns: Parker bequest of MSS and early printed books, Lewis colln of coins, gems and other antiquities (at present on loan to the Fitzwilliam Museum); Stokes colln on Jewish history; readers by appointment; 20,000 vols, 600 MSS; Fellow Librarian Dr C. DE HAMEL.

Downing College: The Maitland Robinson Library: Regent St, Cambridge, CB2 1DQ; tel. (1223) 334829; internet www.dow.cam.ac.uk; f. 1800, Maitland Robinson Library opened 1993; 50,000 vols; spec. collns of Bowtell MSS relating to the city and univ. of Cambridge; 500 vols of naval history and navigation and large colln of law, Civil War and Interregnum newspapers; College Librarian KAREN LUBARR.

Emmanuel College Library: St Andrew's St, Cambridge, CB2 3AP; tel. (1223) 334233; e-mail library@emma.cam.ac.uk; internet www.emma.cam.ac.uk/library; f. 1584; 72,000 vols, rare book collns, incl. the Graham Watson Colln and library of William Sancroft, Archbishop of Canterbury; 400 MSS; Librarian Dr H. C. CARRON.

Fitzwilliam College Library: Cambridge, CB3 0DG; tel. (1223) 332042; e-mail library@fitz.cam.ac.uk; internet www.fitz.cam.ac.uk/library; f. 1963; 44,000 vols; Librarian CHRISTINE ROBERTS LEWIS.

Girton College Library: Huntingdon Rd, Cambridge, CB3 0JG; tel. (1223) 338970; e-mail library@girton.cam.ac.uk; internet www.girton.cam.ac.uk/library; f. 1869; spec. collns: Blackburn Colln of women's rights materials, Newall Colln of Scandinavian material, Frere Colln of Hebrew MSS, Crews Colln of Judeo-Spanish material, Somerville Colln of science and mathematics, Bibas Colln of 18th-century French works; College Archive covers the history of higher education for women via the College's institutional records and personal papers collns; 95,000 vols; Librarian and Curator FRANCES GANDY.

Gonville and Caius College Library: Cambridge, CB2 1TA; tel. (1223) 332419; e-mail library@cai.cam.ac.uk; internet www.cai.cam.ac.uk; f. 1348; 85,000 vols, 900 incunabula, 1,000 MSS related to medieval law and science; Librarian MARK STATHAM; Fellow Librarian Prof. D. S. H. ABULAFIA.

Jesus College Old Library: Jesus College, Cambridge, CB5 8BL; tel. (1223) 339405; e-mail old-library@jesus.cam.ac.uk; f. 1500; spec. collns: Civil War tracts, military science, library of the Malthus family, large theological colln; 8,600 vols, 39 incunabula, 80 medieval MSS from north-country monasteries, 17 Oriental MSS; Keeper of the Old Library Prof. S. C. HEATH.

King's College Library: Cambridge, CB2 1ST; tel. (1223) 331232; e-mail library@kings.cam.ac.uk; internet www.kings.cam.ac.uk/library; f. 1441; spec. collns: MSS of Sir Isaac Newton (available on microfilm in the Univ. Library), 20th-century MSS, notably major collns of Rupert Brooke, E. M. Forster, T. S. Eliot, J. M. Keynes, Joan Robinson; incl. the Rowe Music Library; f. 1928; 25,000 vols; 125,000 vols; Librarian P. M. JONES.

Magdalene College Old Library: Cambridge, CB3 0AG; tel. (1223) 332125; e-mail library@magd.cam.ac.uk; MSS of works by Thomas Hardy, Rudyard Kipling, T. S. Eliot, I. A. Richards and 38 medieval MSS, incl. a 13th-century Apocalypse; papers of Ferrar family of Little Gidding; incunabula, foreign-printed books of 16th, 17th and 18th centuries, early theological works; Diaries of A. C. Benson, W. R. Inge and letters of George Mallory; 17,000 vols; Keeper Dr JANE HUGHES.

Newnham College Library: Cambridge, CB3 9DF; tel. (1223) 335740; e-mail librarian@newn.cam.ac.uk; internet www.library.newn.cam.ac.uk; f. 1871; 9 medieval MSS, incunabula, early edns of poets, dramatists and chroniclers of 16th and 17th centuries; Skilliter Centre for Ottoman Studies holds 4,500 vols relating to Ottoman history; 90,000 vols; Librarian DEBORAH HODDER.

Pembroke College Library: Cambridge, CB2 1RF; tel. (1223) 338121; e-mail library@pem.cam.ac.uk; f. 1347; spec. collns: papers of Gray, William Mason, R. Storrs; 65,000 vols, 317 medieval MSS; Librarian PATRICIA ASKE.

Pepys Library (Magdalene College): Cambridge, CB3 0AG; tel. (1223) 332125; e-mail pepyslibrary@magd.cam.ac.uk; f. 1724 in its present location; Pepys's own colln (MSS, books, music, maps, prints and drawings), not added to since his death in 1703; Pepys's own catalogue; spec. collns: Pepys MSS (incl. Diary), medieval MSS, naval and historical MSS (mostly English, 16th- and 17th-century), colln of calligraphy, prints of London and Westminster, incunabula, broadside ballads, plays; 3,000 vols in original bookcases; Pepys Librarian Dr JANE HUGHES.

Peterhouse (Perne) Library: Cambridge, CB2 1RD; tel. (1223) 338251; e-mail perne@pet.cam.ac.uk; internet www.pet.cam.ac.uk; f. 1594; 5,000 vols, 80 incunabula, 280 medieval MSS, 16th- and 17th-century musical MSS (on permanent deposit in Univ. Library); spec. collns incl. first edns of classics in science, 16th-century theological books; Librarian S. H. MANDELBROTE.

Queens' College Old Library: Cambridge, CB3 9ET; tel. (1223) 335549; e-mail librarian@queens.cam.ac.uk; internet www.queens.cam.ac.uk; f. 1448; colln incl. medieval MSS and incunabula, 28,000 vols; catalogue by Thomas Hartwell Horne (1827); Milner colln of works on history of Reformation and 18th-century science and mathematics; Thomas Smith colln of Renaissance humanist writings; College Librarian Dr T. EGGINGTON.

St Catharine's College Library: Cambridge, CB2 1RL; tel. (1223) 338343; e-mail librarian@caths.cam.ac.uk; internet www.caths.cam.ac.uk/library; f. 1473; 69,000 vols (44,000 vols in undergraduate library; 25,000 vols in spec. collns: 17th-century political and religious tracts, 184 vols of 18th-century medical works (Addenbrooke colln), medieval Romance literature, Spanish books and MSS of 16th and 17th centuries (Chaytor colln); MSS; 30 incunabula; Librarian COLIN HIGGINS.

St John's College Library: Cambridge, CB2 1TP; tel. (1223) 338662; e-mail library@joh.cam.ac.uk; internet www.joh.cam.ac.uk/library; f. 1511; MSS; spec. collns: 15th-century books, Matthew Prior bequest, Sir Soulden Lawrence law colln, Thomas Baker's colln of printed books and MSS, Samuel Butler colln, Smith colln of Rabelais literature, Wordsworthiana, papers of Sir Cecil Beaton, mathematical works of historical interest from libraries of Adams, Todhunter and Pendlebury, Udny Yule colln of Thomas à Kempis edns, Hugh Gatty colln, Sparrow bequest of Samuel Parr books, papers of Sir Fred Hoyle; Librarian Dr MARK NICHOLLS.

Selwyn College Library: Grange Rd, Cambridge, CB3 9DQ; tel. (1223) 335880; e-mail lib@sel.cam.ac.uk; internet www.sel.cam.ac.uk/library; f. 1892; 40,000 vols, MSS, incunabula; spec. collns incl. diaries and papers of George Augustus Selwyn (1809–78) Primate of New Zealand and later Bishop of Lichfield, large colln of theological works incl. 19th-century sermons, 19th-century missionary colln with particular emphasis on Melanesia and New Zealand, and 3,000 19th-century English ecclesiastical pamphlets; Librarian SARAH STAMFORD.

Sidney Sussex College Library: Cambridge, CB2 3HU; tel. (1223) 338852; e-mail librarian@sid.cam.ac.uk; internet www.sid.cam.ac.uk/life/lib; f. 16th century; 38,000 vols, 70 periodicals; Muniment Room: 7,300 vols, 119 MSS, incunabula; spec. collns incl. 18th- and 19th-century mathematical books; Taylor Mathematical Library (separately administered); Librarian ALAN STEVENS.

Trinity College Library: Cambridge, CB2 1TQ; tel. (1223) 338488; e-mail college.library@trin.cam.ac.uk; internet www.trin.cam.ac.uk; f. 1546; 300,000 vols; spec. collns incl. medieval Western and Oriental MSS; literary MSS of Milton, Tennyson, Housman, Capell colln of Shakespeareana; Rothschild library of 18th-century English literature; Isaac Newton's library; papers of economists, philosophers, politicians since 19th century; Librarian Prof. D. MCKITTERICK.

Trinity Hall Library: Cambridge, CB2 1TJ; tel. (1223) 332546; e-mail library@trinhall.cam.ac.uk; internet www.trinhall.cam.ac.uk/about/library; f. 1350; 25,000 vols, 31 MSS; spec. collns incl. early canon law, Larman Bequest of books and MSS relating to Reformation and Tudor periods, particularly heraldry, ecclesiastical history and theology; Dir of Library Services DOMINIQUE RUHLMANN.

Special Libraries:

Balfour and Newton Libraries: Univ. of Cambridge, Dept of Zoology, Downing St, Cambridge, CB2 3EJ; tel. (1223) 336648; e-mail library@zoo.cam.ac.uk; internet www.zoo.cam.ac.uk/department/library; Balfour Library f. 1883, Newton Library f. 1907; 155,000 vols, incl. over 19,600 books, 22,600 periodicals and over 110,000 reprints; Librarian JANE ACRED (acting).

Churchill Archives Centre: Churchill College, Cambridge, CB3 0DS; tel. (1223) 336087; e-mail archives@chu.cam.ac.uk; internet www.chu.cam.ac.uk/archives; f. 1973; houses papers of Sir Winston Churchill, Lady Thatcher and many other senior political figures; Dir ALLEN PACKWOOD.

Marshall Library of Economics: Austin Robinson Bldg, Sidgwick Ave, Cambridge, CB3 9DB; tel. (1223) 335217; e-mail marshlib@econ.cam.ac.uk; internet www.marshall.econ.cam.ac.uk; f. 1925; 70,000 vols, incl. books, working papers, pamphlets and dissertations, 30,000 journals; spec. collns: archival materials of the economists Keynes, Marshall, Pigou; Librarian CLEMENS GRESSER.

Squire Law Library: 10 West Rd, Cambridge, CB3 9DZ; tel. (1223) 330077; internet www.squire.law.cam.ac.uk; f. 1904; 130,000 vols; spec. collns incl. Roman law, legal history, comparative law, conflict of laws, int. law, environmental law, intellectual property, political biographies; research library; Librarian DAVID WILLS.

Cambridgeshire Libraries, Archives and Information: 7 Lion Yard, Cambridge, CB2 3QD; tel. (345) 045-5225; e-mail your.library@cambridgeshire.gov.uk; internet www.cambridgeshire.gov.uk/library; f. 1974; 32 brs, 4 mobile libraries; 1,155,000 vols; Library Man. IAN DOUGLAS; Head of Libraries, Archives and Information CHRISTINE MAY.

East Asian History of Science Library: 8 Sylvester Rd, Cambridge, CB3 9AF; tel. (1223) 311545; e-mail administration@nri.org.uk; internet www.nri.org.uk/library.html; f. 1976; attached to Needham Research Institute; collns assembled since 1937 by Dr Joseph Needham and Dr Lu Gwei-Djen from sources in China and the West; 30,000 vols, 800 serial titles, 20,000 items of off-prints, MSS in Asian and European languages, also archival and iconographic material (notes, photographs, maps, microfilms, etc.); spec. colln on the history of science, technology and medicine in E Asia; open to research scholars by appointment; Dir Prof. MEI JIANJUN; Librarian JOHN P. C. MOFFETT.

Tyndale House Library: 36 Selwyn Gardens, Cambridge, CB3 9BA; tel. (1223) 566604; e-mail librarian@tyndale.cam.ac.uk; internet www.tyndale.cam.ac.uk; f. 1944; residential centre for biblical research; 49,000 vols; Librarian SIMON SYKES.

Canterbury

Canterbury Cathedral Archives and Library: The Precincts, Canterbury, CT1 2EH; tel. (1227) 865330 (Archives); tel. (1227) 865287 (Library); e-mail archives@canterbury-cathedral.org; internet www.canterbury-cathedral.org/conservation/library; f. c. 597; documents since 8th century; MSS of Christ Church Cathedral Priory and the Dean and Chapter of Canterbury; archives of the Diocese of Canterbury; archives of Canterbury City and District Parish; records for parishes in the Archdeaconry of Canterbury (eastern Kent); 52,000 printed books: early printed books, Bibles, prayer books, Catholic and anti-Catholic writings, natural science, travel, theology, history, 17th–19th century pamphlets, material on the slave trade, music; 2 parish libraries (Elham and Preston-next-Wingham); Cannon Librarian CHRISTOPHER IRVINE; Sr Library Asst KAREN BRAYSHAW; Archivist CRESSIDA WILLIAMS.

Templeman Library: Canterbury, CT2 7NU; tel. (1227) 824777; e-mail library-enquiry@kent.ac.uk; internet www.kent.ac.uk/library/templeman; f. 1964; attached to Univ. of Kent; 800,000 vols; spec. collns incl. Cartoon Centre (80,000 original political cartoons), Victorian and Edwardian Popular Theatre (Pettingell, Melville and Reading-Rayner MSS and printed plays, mainly 19th century), Maddison colln (history of science), C. P. Davies Wind and Watermill colln, the papers of Lord Weatherill; Dir of Information Services and Librarian JOHN SOTILLO.

Cardiff

Amgueddfa Cymru—National Museum Wales Library: Cathays Park, Cardiff, CF10 3NP; tel. (29) 2057-3202; e-mail library@museumwales.ac.uk; internet www.museumwales.ac.uk/library; 220,000 vols, books and periodicals relevant to the museum collns; spec. collns: Tomlin (conchology), Willoughby Gardner (early natural history), Vaynor (James) Colln (early works on astronomy); also houses libraries of Cardiff Naturalists' Soc. and Cambrian Archaeological Asscn; Librarian JOHN R. KENYON.

Cardiff Libraries: Central Library, The Hayes, Cardiff, CF10 1FL; tel. (29) 2038-2116; e-mail centrallibrary@cardiff.gov.uk; internet www.cardiff.gov.uk/libraries; f. 1862, present bldg 2009; main library incl. lending and reference books; music and sound recordings library; children's library; local studies library incl. maps, prints and MSS; 20 brs; 547,269 vols incl. 10,000 Welsh language and 10,000 community language items, 10,000 CDs and DVDs, large colln of Welsh history; Central Library Man. NIC RICHARDS; Operational Man. of Libraries ELSPETH MORRIS.

Cardiff University Libraries: Information Services Directorate, 40–41 Park Pl., Cardiff, CF10 3BB; tel. (29) 2087-4818; e-mail library@cardiff.ac.uk; internet www.cardiff.ac.uk/insrv/libraries; f. 1883; consists of 17 libraries: Aberconway (business, economics and transport), Archie Cochrane (medicine), architecture, arts and social studies, biomedical sciences, Brian Cooke Dental, Bute, Cancer Research Wales, law, legal practice, music, nursing and health care studies, school of nursing and midwifery studies, science, Senghennydd (mathematics and lifelong learning), Sir Herbert Duthie (medicine), Trevithick (engineering and science); research collns: Ann Griffiths colln, architecture rare books colln, arts and social studies special colln, Cochrane archive, Cudlipp colln, David Bainton archive, European Documentation Centre, First Edition arch-

ive, Historical Book colln (Healthcare), Osman archive (Photojournalism), Salisbury colln (Welsh History), UCAC (Undeb Cenedlaethol Athrawon Cymru) archive; Dir of Libraries and Univ. Librarian JANET PETERS.

Carlisle

Cumbria Libraries: Carlisle Library Globe Lane, Carlisle, CA3 8NX; tel. (1228) 227290; e-mail libraries@cumbria.gov.uk; internet www.cumbria.gov.uk/libraries.

Carmarthen

Carmarthenshire County Libraries: Public Library, St Peter's St, Carmarthen, SA31 1LN; tel. (1267) 224824; e-mail library@carmarthenshire.gov.uk; internet libraries.carmarthenshire.gov.uk; 17 brs, 5 mobile libraries; 660,000 vols; spec. collns: coal mine plans, Theodore Nichol Colln, the library of the Carmarthenshire Antiquarian Soc.; Library Services Man. MARK JEWELL; Library Services Man. MYRDDIN MORGAN; Library Services Man. WIL PHILLIPS.

Chatham

Medway Libraries: Chatham Library, Community Hub Chatham, Gun Wharf, Dock Rd, Chatham, ME4 4TX; tel. (1634) 337799; e-mail chatham.library@medway.gov.uk; internet www.medway.gov.uk/libraries; f. 1998; 16 brs, 2 mobile libraries; Medway Archives and Local Studies Centre; Head of Libraries SIMON SWIFT.

Chelmsford

Anglia Ruskin University Library: Queen's Bldg, Bishop Hall Lane, Chelmsford, CM1 1SQ; tel. (1245) 686705; internet www.libweb.anglia.ac.uk; 293,150 vols, 906 current journal titles, 81,790 ebooks, 20,043 ejournals, 206 databases; Librarian JOLENE CUSHION.

Essex County Council Libraries: County Hall, Market Rd, Chelmsford, CM1 1LH; tel. (1245) 430430; e-mail answers.people@essex.gov.uk; internet www.essex.gov.uk/libraries; 74 brs, 11 mobile libraries; Dir for Libraries and Culture MARTIN PALMER.

Chepstow

Monmouthshire Libraries & Information Service: Chepstow Library, Manor Way, Chepstow, NP16 5HZ; tel. (1291) 635730; e-mail informationcentre@monmouthshire.gov.uk; internet libraries.monmouthshire.gov.uk; 5 brs, mobile library; 150,000 vols; Prin. Librarian ANN JONES.

Chester

Cheshire Libraries: Cheshire County Council, Libraries and Culture, Room 286, County Hall, Chester, CH1 1SF; tel. (1244) 606034; e-mail webmaster@cheshire.gov.uk; internet www.cheshire.gov.uk/library/home.htm; f. 1922; 1,500,000 vols; 35 full-time, 6 part-time, 3 dual use brs, 6 mobile libraries and 1 research library; HQ spec. collns; Education Library Service; County Libraries Officer I. DUNN.

Chichester

West Sussex County Council Libraries: Chichester Library, Tower St, Chichester, PO19 1QJ; tel. (1243) 777351; e-mail chichester.library@westsussex.gov.uk; internet www.westsussex.gov.uk/libraries; f. 1925; 36 brs, 2 mobile libraries; 1,117,000 vols; Libraries Service Man. LESLEY SIM.

Colchester

University of Essex, The Albert Sloman Library: Wivenhoe Park, Colchester, CO4

3UA; tel. (1206) 873192; e-mail libline@essex.ac.uk; internet libwww.essex.ac.uk; f. 1964; 1.8m. vols and microforms, 14,370 current periodicals; spec. collns: Latin America, fmr USSR, Social Democratic Party (SDP) archives, SDP papers of Lord Rodgers of Quarrybank, Tawney Soc. archives, Nat. Viewers' and Listeners' Asscn archives, Boundary Comm. for England archives (1992–93 public enquiries), papers and publs of the Cttee on Standards in Public Life (Nolan Cttee), Sigmund Freud and related collns (papers and publs), papers of Lord Alport, Sir Vincent Evans colln, Paul Sieghart memorial archive, SCOPE-ENUWAR archive, papers of Lord Brimelow, Gaudier-Brzeska colln, Royal Statistical Soc. (historical) colln, Essex Soc. for Archaeology and History Library, John Hassall colln, Lord Hill of Wivenhoe papers, Lord Thomson of Monifieth papers, T. E. Lawrence letters, Samuel Harsnett Library (Archbishop of York, 1629–31), Ellis East European Elections colln, Windscale Inquiry (1977) papers, archives of the Talking Newspaper Asscn of the UK, Margery Allingham/Philip Youngman Carter colln, Bernie Hamilton (Human Rights) archive, Georg Groddeck archive, papers of Sir Frederick Warner, Papers of Enid Balint (Psychoanalyst), Papers of Lord Brimelow (Under-Sec. of State, Foreign Office, 1969–73), Charter 88 Archives (1990–97), Colohester Medical Society Library (f. 1774), Levine/Sky Television Internet Video Archive, B. B. Zeitlyn Memorial Library (Psychology and Psychoanalysis); Librarian ROBERT BUTLER.

Coventry

Coventry Libraries and Information Services: Central Library, Smithford Way, Coventry, CV1 1FY; tel. (24) 7683-2314; e-mail central.library@coventry.gov.uk; internet www.coventry.gov.uk/libraries; f. 1868; 17 community libraries, mobile library; 480,000 vols; spec. collns on trade unions and industrial relations; Head of Libraries and Information Services CARMEL REED; Central Library Man. CAROL ROBINSON (acting).

University of Warwick Library: Gibbet Hill Rd, Coventry, CV4 7AL; tel. (24) 7652-2026; e-mail library@warwick.ac.uk; internet library.warwick.ac.uk; f. 1963; 1.2m. printed vols, 13 km of archives; spec. collns: British and foreign statistical serials (trade, finance, production), current and retrospective, pre-1948 collns of Howard League for Penal Reform, Modern Records Centre (labour history, employers' records, industrial relations, political org. archives), Modern German Literature, Ethnicity and Migration collns (combined collns of the Centre for Research in Ethnic Relations and the Institute of Race Relations), Official Pubs (incl. Stationery Office, other UK and European official publs); European documentation centre; Librarian ROBIN GREEN.

Darlington

Darlington Libraries: Central Library, Crown St, Darlington, DL1 1ND; tel. (1325) 462034; e-mail crown.street.library@darlington.gov.uk; internet www2.darlington.gov.uk; f. 1885; Libraries Man. LYNNE LITCHFIELD; Local Studies and Reference Librarian KATHERINE WILLIAMSON.

Derby

Derby City Libraries: Central Library, The Wardwick, Derby, DE1 1HS; tel. (1332) 641702; e-mail central.library@derby.gov.uk; internet www.derby.gov.uk/libraries; f. 1997; Head of Libraries DAVID POTTON.

Dorchester

Dorset County Libraries: South Walks House, Charles St, Dorchester, DT1 1EE; tel. (1305) 224440; e-mail dorchesterlibrary@ dorsetcc.gov.uk; internet www.dorsetforyou .com/libraries; f. 1920, reorganized 1997; 25 brs; 5 mobile libraries; 625,000 vols; spec. collns: Dorset colln, Powys colln, Thomas Hardy colln; Head of Community Services P. LEIVERS.

Dundee

Dundee Libraries: Central Library, The Wellgate, Dundee, DD1 1DB; tel. (1382) 431500; e-mail central.library@ leisureandculturedundee.com; internet www .leisureandculturedundee.com/library; f. 1869; 13 brs, mobile library; spec. collns: local history and genealogy, music, Wighton Colln of Nat. Music (620 vols), British Standards; Head of Library and Information Services JUDY DOBBIE.

University of Dundee Library and Learning Centre: Dundee, DD1 4HN; tel. (1382) 384087; e-mail llc@dundee.ac.uk; internet www.dundee.ac.uk/library; f. 1881; 684,352 vols, 4,804 periodicals; spec. colls: 10,000 theological books and MSS of Episcopal Diocese of Brechin, Allan Ramsay Colln, Joan Auld Memorial Colln, Leng Colln of Scottish Philosophy, Nicoll Colln, Thoms Mineralogy Colln, William Lyon Mackenzie Canadiana Colln; Dir RICHARD PARSONS.

Durham

Durham County Libraries: County Hall, Durham, DH1 5UL; tel. (191) 383-3595; e-mail durhamclayportlibrary@durham.gov .uk; internet www.durham.gov.uk/libraries; f. 1923; 39 brs, mobile library, bookbus for the elderly; 876,000 vols; Dir PATRICK CONWAY.

Durham University Library: Stockton Rd, Durham, DH1 3LY; tel. (191) 334-3042; e-mail main.library@durham.ac.uk; internet www.dur.ac.uk/library; f. 1833; 1.5m. vols on 4 sites, incl. Middle East Documentation Unit; dept of Archives and Spec. Collns houses 70,000 books printed before 1850 incl. 300 incunables, 100 medieval MSS, 30,000 maps and prints, 100,000 photographs, 3,400 m of archives and artefacts; printed book spec. collns incl. those formed by Bishop Cosin, M. J. Routh, Bishop Maltby, Dr Winterbottom and the Sharp Library from Bamburgh Castle; modern literary MSS (C. C. Abbott, Basil Bunting, William Plomer Collns), Earl Grey Papers, Malcolm MacDonald Papers, Durham Cathedral Archives, Durham diocesan and probate records, Howard of Naworth Papers and other collns of local family and estate records, Sudan Archive; Librarian JON PURCELL.

Ebbw Vale

Blaenau Gwent Libraries: 21 Bethcar St, Ebbw Vale, NP23 6HS; tel. (1495) 303069; e-mail libraries@blaenau-gwent.gov.uk; internet www.blaenau-gwent.gov.uk/leisure/ 273.asp; 6 brs, 2 mobile libraries; 120,000 vols; Prin. Librarian SUE WHITE.

Edinburgh

Edinburgh City Libraries and Information Services: Central Library, George IV Bridge, Edinburgh, EH1 1EG; tel. (131) 242-8000; e-mail eclis@edinburgh.gov.uk; internet www.edinburgh.gov.uk/libraries; f. 1890; 1,365,000 items; 25 community libraries, 4 mobile libraries; Central Reference (incl. business information, British Standards, electronic information; 346,229 items); spec. collns: Edinburgh Room (contains information on life in Edinburgh and on Scott, Stevenson, Ballantyne; press cuttings; illustrations; playbills; 120,000 items), Scottish (especially genealogy, history and Scottish Parliament information; 97,000 items), Music and Audio (CDs, scores, Scottish music; 148,000 items), Fine Art (includes costume, fashion and photography; slides, Japanese prints, video cassettes, artists' books, press cuttings on Scottish art, architecture, design and photography; 90,000 items); City Librarian BILL WALLACE.

Edinburgh University Library, Museums and Galleries: George Sq., Edinburgh, EH8 9LJ; tel. (131) 650-3384; e-mail library@ed.ac.uk; internet www.lib.ed.ac.uk; f. 1580; 3,462,947 printed items, 279,814 microforms, 111,832 maps in sheets, 7,700 m of MSS and archives, 33,808 theses, 6,826 audiovisual items, 4,417 electronic and 4,430 print current periodicals; Drummond (of Hawthornden) Collection; Laing Charters and MSS; Halliwell-Phillipps Collection; MSS on Scottish history and the Scottish literary renaissance; Arthur Koestler MSS and part library; Corson Sir Walter Scott Collection; New Zealand Studies Collection; MSS and printed books on early 20th-century English literature; Scottish Enlightenment; history of science and medicine; African, E Asian, Islamic and Middle Eastern studies; includes the Main Library, Law and Europa Library, Moray House Library (Education), New College Library (Divinity), Science Libraries and Royal (Dick) School of Veterinary Studies Libraries, Royal Infirmary Library, Reid Concert Hall Museum of Instruments (John Donaldson Collection), St Cecilia's Hall Museum of instruments (Raymond Russell Collection of Early Keyboard Instruments) and the Talbot Rice Gallery; Dir for Library Services SHEILA E. CANNELL.

Heriot-Watt University Library: Riccarton, Edinburgh, EH14 4AS; tel. (131) 451-3570; e-mail libhelp@hw.ac.uk; internet www .hw.ac.uk/library; f. 1821; 164,800 vols, 20,000 print and e-journals; Librarian G. A. McDONALD (acting).

National Archives of Scotland: HM General Register House, Edinburgh, EH1 3YY; tel. (131) 535-1314; e-mail enquiries@nas.gov .uk; internet www.nas.gov.uk; f. 1993 as an Executive Agency; local and church records; records of Scottish govt and law since 12th century; contains private and business collns; Keeper of the Records of Scotland GEORGE P. MacKENZIE.

National Library of Scotland: George IV Bridge, Edinburgh, EH1 1EW; tel. (131) 623-3700; e-mail enquiries@nls.uk; internet www .nls.uk; f. 1680 as the Advocates' Library; legal deposit library; contains 13m. vols and pamphlets and a large colln of MSS; Library's Inter-Library Services (33 Salisbury Pl., Edinburgh, EH9 1SL) maintain a stock (120,000 vols) of scarce books to supplement the reserves of Scottish public libraries, act as the headquarters for Scottish inter-library co-operation, and house Scottish Union Catalogue; Chair. of the Trustees Prof. MICHAEL ANDERSON; Nat. Librarian MARTYN WADE; publ. *Discover NLS* (4 a year).

Attached Library:

National Library of Scotland Map Library: 159 Causewayside, Edinburgh, EH9 1PH; tel. (131) 623-3970; e-mail maps@nls.uk; internet maps.nls.uk; f. 1958; modern topographic and thematic map coverage of most parts of the world; particular interest in early/modern maps with Scottish association; Sr Map Curator CHRIS FLEET.

National Museums Scotland Library: Chambers St, Edinburgh, EH1 1JF; tel. (131) 247-4137; e-mail library@nms.ac.uk; internet www.nms.ac.uk; f. 1854; 320,000 vols, esp. European decorative arts, N European archaeology and Scottish history; MS collns incl. Society of Antiquaries of Scotland, Harvie Brown (natural sciences), William Spiers Bruce (Antarctic exploration), Sir William Jardine (natural sciences); Head of Information Services EVELYN SIMPSON.

Royal Botanic Garden Library: 20A Inverleith Row, Edinburgh, EH3 5LR; tel. (131) 248-2853; e-mail library@rbge.org.uk; internet www.rbge.org.uk; f. 1670; nat. reference colln for specialist botanical and horticultural resources; 100,000 vols, incl. pre-Linnean literature on botany, horticulture, agriculture and medicine; 70,000 monographs, 100,000 pamphlets and separates; 4,000 (1,500 current) periodicals; colln of botanical drawings and prints; Head of Library Services LORNA MITCHELL; publs *Catalogue of Plants* (irregular), *Edinburgh Journal of Botany* (3 a year), *Sibbaldia: an occasional series of horticultural notes* (irregular).

Royal College of Physicians of Edinburgh Library: 9 Queen St, Edinburgh, EH2 1JQ; tel. (131) 225-7324; e-mail library@ rcpe.ac.uk; internet www.rcpe.ac.uk; f. 1681; 50,000 books, 1,000 vols of MSS; open to all bona fide enquirers; particularly rich in the early sources of medical knowledge; colln of periodicals; Librarian I. A. MILNE.

Royal College of Surgeons of Edinburgh Library and Archive: Nicolson St, Edinburgh, EH8 9DW; tel. (131) 527-1630; e-mail library@rcsed.ac.uk; internet www.library .rcsed.ac.uk; f. 1505; historical and contemporary medical and surgical stock; images library; college archive since 1505; private library for Fellows and members (access to researchers by appointment); 50,000 vols, 170 periodicals; CEO ALISON ROONEY; publs *Surgeons' News*, *The Surgeon*.

Signet Library: Parliament Sq., Edinburgh, EH1 1RF; tel. (131) 220-3249; e-mail library@wssociety.co.uk; internet www .signetlibrary.co.uk; f. 1594, but there were Writers to HM's Signet as early as 1460; library of a private soc.; Scots law and Scottish history and genealogy; 60,000 vols; Librarian JAMES HAMILTON; publ. *Signet Magazine* (2 a year).

Eton

Eton College Library: Eton College, Windsor, SL4 6DB; tel. (1753) 671221; e-mail collections@etoncollege.org.uk; internet www .etoncollege.com/collegelibrary.aspx; f. 1440; 150,000 vols, incl. 200 medieval MSS, 200 incunabula; important collns of edns of classical writers and related material (16th–18th centuries), early science, Elizabethan, Jacobean and Restoration drama, large colln of Civil War and early 18th century English pamphlets, 16th century Italian books; bindings, English and Continental, since 12th century; Topham colln of drawings and engravings (2,500 items); Etoniana colln (5,000 printed books, drawings, prints, scrapbooks, MSS); School Books colln; Parikian colln of Armenian printed books 1500–1900; Kessler colln of books on China and Russia; English literature since 19th century, incl. Elizabeth Barrett Browning, Anne Thackeray Ritchie, Thomas Hardy, Edward Gordon Craig, Moelwyn Merchant collns; mezzotint colln (1,000 items); Librarian SARAH WARREN-MACMILLAN; Archivist ELEANOR CRACKNELL.

Exeter

Devon Libraries: Great Moor House, Bittern Rd, Sowton, Exeter, EX2 7NL; tel. (1392) 384315; e-mail devlibs@devon.gov.uk; internet www.devon.gov.uk/libraries; f. 1924; 50 brs, 7 mobile libraries; 1,169,987 vols; Head of Libraries CIARA EASTELL.

Exeter Cathedral Library and Archives: c/o Cathedral Office, 1 The Cloisters, Exeter, EX1 1HS; tel. (1392) 421423; e-mail library@ exeter-cathedral.org.uk; internet www .exeter-cathedral.org.uk/visiting/cathedrallibrary.ashx; f. 11th century when Bishop Leofric gave 66 MSS to the Cathedral Church; 20,000 vols; MSS incl. Exeter Book of Old English Poetry and Exon Domesday Book; spec. collns incl. Cathedral MSS and archives, early printed books in medicine and science, Cook Colln (16th–19th century works, early linguistics), printed tracts (mainly English Civil War period), Harington Colln (16th–19th century theology, ecclesiastical history, history); archive of 50,000 items; Cathedral Librarian PETER W. THOMAS; Cathedral Archivist ELLIE JONES.

National Meteorological Library and Archive: Met Office, Fitzroy Rd, Exeter, EX1 3PB; tel. (1392) 884841; e-mail metlib@ metoffice.gov.uk; internet www.metoffice.gov .uk/learning/library; f. 1870; incl. comprehensive records of data published by British and foreign instns; early weather diaries; official weather records and charts; ships' weather log books; separate record stores for Scotland (Edinburgh) and N Ireland (Belfast); 300,000 vols and 5,000 images.

University of Exeter Library: Stocker Rd, Exeter, EX4 4PT; tel. (1392) 723867; e-mail library@exeter.ac.uk; internet as.exeter.ac .uk/library; f. 1937; 1.2m. vols; administers Library of Devon and Exeter Instn (36,000 vols); Head of Library and Culture Services (vacant).

Falkirk

Falkirk Community Trust Libraries: Falkirk Library, Hope St, Falkirk, FK1 5AU; tel. (1324) 506800; e-mail libraries@ falkirkcommunitytrust.org; internet www .falkirkcommunitytrust.org/libraries; local history colln; 8 brs, mobile library; Culture and Libraries Man. LESLEY O'HARE (acting).

Flitwick

Central Bedfordshire Libraries: Coniston Rd, Flitwick, MK45 1QJ; tel. (300) 300-8305; e-mail customers@centralbedfordshire.gov .uk; internet www.centralbedfordshire.gov .uk/leisure/libraries; 15 brs.

Glasgow

Glasgow Caledonian University Library: The Saltire Centre, Glasgow Caledonian University, Cowcaddens Rd, Glasgow, G4 0BA; tel. (141) 273-1000; e-mail library@gcu.ac.uk; internet www.gcu.ac.uk/ library; f. 1993; 275,000 vols; 39,000 ebooks and access to 35,000 journals online; Dir of Library Services ROBERT RUTHVEN; Sr Librarian and Resource Man. MARIAN MILLER.

Glasgow Libraries: 20 Trongate, Glasgow, G1 5ES; tel. (141) 287-4350; e-mail info@ glasgowlife.org.uk; internet www.glasgowlife .org.uk; 32 district libraries; spec. collns of foreign literature and local history; 2,145,000 vols; Head of Libraries and Community Facilities KAREN CUNNINGHAM..

Attached Library:

Mitchell Library: North St, Glasgow, G3 7DN; tel. (141) 287-2999; e-mail archives@ csglasgow.org; internet www .mitchelllibrary.org; f. 1874; 1,235,000 vols; special collns: on Glasgow (20,000 vols), music (43,000 vols), Robert Burns (5,000 vols), Scottish poetry (12,000 vols) and Patent Depository Library; business users' service; receives a copy of every publication issued by HMSO, and is also a Depository Library for the unrestricted publications of the UN, UNESCO and FAO; Librarian F. MACPHERSON.

Royal College of Physicians and Surgeons of Glasgow Library: 234 St Vincent St, Glasgow, G2 5RJ; tel. (141) 227-3234; e-mail library@rcpsg.ac.uk; internet www .rcpsg.ac.uk; f. 1698; houses works on all aspects of medicine and surgery incl. early examples of medical texts from the 16th and 17th centuries; Glasgow Colln, books relating to the history of Glasgow and the West of Scotland; archives since 1602; 35,000 vols; Library and Heritage Man. CAROL PARRY.

University of Glasgow Library: Hillhead St, Glasgow, G12 8QE; tel. (141) 330-6704; e-mail library@lib.gla.ac.uk; internet www .lib.gla.ac.uk; f. 15th century; 1.3m. books, 7,308 m of MSS, archives; 15,000 serial titles; incorporates Trinity College Glasgow Library (Church of Scotland); Hunterian Books and MSS, Euing Collns of the Bible and music, Farmer Music Colln, Laver, MacColl and Wright Papers on fine art, Hamilton Colln of philosophy, Ferguson Colln of the history of chemistry, Stirling Maxwell Colln of Emblem books, J. M. Whistler archive, David Murray regional history colln, Scottish Theatre Archive, Edwin Morgan Papers, Trotsky Colln; Univ. Librarian HELEN DURNDELL.

University of Strathclyde: The Andersonian Library: 101 St James' Rd, Glasgow, G4 0NS; tel. (141) 548-4444; e-mail library@ strath.ac.uk; internet www.strath.ac.uk/ library; f. 1796; spec. collns incl. Anderson colln (founder's library), Young colln (alchemy and early chemistry), Laing colln (mathematics vols from the 18th and 19th centuries), Robertson colln (Scottish history and topography); 887,646 vols and 548330 e-books; Univ. Librarian and Asst Dir for Information Services Directorate DILYS YOUNG; Head of Information Management ELAINE BLAXTER.

Gloucester

Gloucestershire Libraries and Information HQ: Shire Hall, Westgate St, Gloucester, GL1 2TG; tel. (845) 230-5420; e-mail libraryhelpline@gloucestershire.gov.uk; internet www.gloucestershire.gov.uk/ libraries; spec. collns incl. Gloucestershire Colln; Head for Library Services SUE LAURENCE.

Grays

Thurrock Libraries: Grays Central Library, Thameside Complex, Orsett Rd, Grays, RM17 5DX; tel. (1375) 413976; e-mail grays.library@thurrock.gov.uk; internet www.thurrock.gov.uk/libraries; 9 brs, mobile library; Head of Libraries ANN HALLIDAY.

Guildford

Surrey Libraries: Enquiries Direct, c/o Guildford Library, 77 North St, Guildford, GU1 4AL; tel. (1483) 543599; e-mail libraries@surreycc.gov.uk; internet www .surreycc.gov.uk/libraries; offers public library service to Surrey; 52 brs and an enquiries dept; 1,913,000 vols, 78,400 audiovisual items; Head of Libraries and Culture PETER MILTON.

University of Surrey Library: George Edwards Bldg, Guildford, GU2 7XH; tel. (1483) 689235; e-mail library-enquiries@ surrey.ac.uk; internet www.surrey.ac.uk/ library; f. 1894; 625,000 vols, 7,900 periodicals; spec. collns incl. Nat. Resource Centre for Dance, E. H. Shepard archive; Head of Learning and Research Services VIVIEN SIEBER.

Hatfield

Hertfordshire Libraries: New Barnfield, Travellers Lane, Hatfield, AL10 8XG; tel. (1438) 737333; e-mail hertsdirect@hertscc .gov.uk; internet www.hertsdirect.org/ libraries; f. 1925; 47 brs, 7 mobile libraries; 1,373,048 vols, other media 119,852 items; spec. collns: performing arts, local history, business information, official publs; Head of Libraries ANDREW BIGNELL.

Haverfordwest

Pembrokeshire Libraries: Former Youth Club, Off Dew St, Haverfordwest, SA61 1ST; tel. (1437) 775244; e-mail haverfordwestlibrary@pembrokeshire.gov .uk; internet www.pembrokeshire.gov.uk/ libraries; reference library, incl. the Pembrokeshire Colln; local studies colln; 12 br. lending libraries; Prin. Librarian for Devt ANITA THOMAS.

Hawarden

Gladstone's Library: Church Lane, Hawarden, CH5 3DF; tel. (1244) 532350; e-mail library@gladlib.org; internet www .gladstoneslibrary.org; f. 1894 by William Ewart Gladstone (1809–98); theology, philosophy, history (esp. 19th century), classics, English literature, Gladstonian studies; accommodation for 40 residents; 250,000 vols, 57 current journal titles; spec. collns: Gladstone Foundation Colln, Bishop Moorman Franciscan Colln, Francis Colln, Richard L. Hills History of Technology Colln, West Colln; Warden Rev. PETER FRANCIS; Dir for Collns and Research LOUISA YATES.

Hereford

Herefordshire Council Libraries: Broad St, Hereford, HR4 9AU; tel. (1432) 383600; e-mail herefordlibrary@herefordshire.gov .uk; internet www.herefordshire.gov.uk/ libraries; f. 1998; 10 libraries, volunteer-run service; 186,294 vols, 11,104 media items; Libraries Man. JON CHEDGZOY.

Huddersfield

Kirklees Libraries and Information Centres: Civic Centre 1, High St, Huddersfield, HD1 2NF; tel. (1484) 221000; e-mail customer.enquiries@kirklees.gov.uk; internet www.kirklees.gov.uk/libraries; f. 1974; 1,250,000 vols; Head of Library and Information Services CAROL STUMP; Asst Dir for Customer and Exchequer Services JANE BRADY.

University of Huddersfield Library: Queensgate, Huddersfield, HD1 3DH; tel. (1484) 473830; e-mail lc@hud.ac.uk; internet www.hud.ac.uk/library; f. 1841; 374,000 vols, 62,000 ebooks, 24,500 journal titles; Dir for Library Services SUE WHITE.

Ipswich

Suffolk Libraries IPS Ltd.: Ipswich County Library, Northgate St, Ipswich, IP1 3DE; tel. (1473) 263810; e-mail help@ suffolklibraries.co.uk; internet www .suffolklibraries.co.uk; f. 2012; 44 libraries, 3 mobile libraries; 1.2m. vols; Gen. Man. ALISON WHEELER.

Keele

University of Keele Library: Keele, ST5 5BG; tel. (1782) 733535; e-mail library.hq@ keele.ac.uk; internet www.keele.ac.uk/ library; f. 1949; 620,000 vols; Librarian PAUL REYNOLDS.

Keyworth

British Geological Survey Library: British Geological Survey, Keyworth, NG12 5GG; tel. (115) 936-3205; e-mail libuser@bgs.ac.uk; internet www.bgs.ac.uk; f. 1837; regional office library at Edinburgh; information office in London; open access repository; 500,000 vols, 400 current periodicals, 200,000 maps and atlases, 20,000 archives, nat. collns of

100,000 photographs largely illustrating British scenery and geology; Library Service Man. ANNE DIXON.

Kingston upon Hull

Kingston upon Hull City Libraries: Central Library, Albion St, Hull, HU1 3TF; tel. (1482) 300300; e-mail lending.library@hullcc.gov.uk; internet www.hullcc.gov.uk/libraries; f. 1903; reference and information service; Asst Head of Libraries and Information Service MICHELLE ALFORD.

University of Hull, Library and Learning Innovation: Cottingham Rd, Hull, HU6 7RX; tel. (1482) 466581; e-mail libhelp@hull.ac.uk; internet www.hull.ac.uk/lib; f. 1929; 1,000,000 vols; spec. collns: SE Asia, India, British Labour history; Dir for Library and Learning Innovation and Univ. Librarian Dr RICHARD HESELTINE.

Kirkcaldy

Fife Council Libraries and Archives: 16 East Fergus Pl., Kirkcaldy, KY1 1XT; tel. (1592) 583204; e-mail fife.libraries@onfife.com; internet www.onfife.com/fife-libraries; 51 community libraries, 3 mobile libraries, 1 housebound service; 628,000 vols; Chief Exec. HEATHER STUART.

Lampeter

Lampeter Campus Learning Resource Centre: Lampeter, SA48 7ED; tel. (1570) 424798; e-mail lampeterlrc@tsd.ac.uk; internet www.tsd.ac.uk/en/lrc; attached to Univ. of Wales Trinity Saint David; 275,000 vols, incl. Tract colln of 11,000 items; Head of Library and Learning Resources ALISON HARDING; publ. *Trivium*.

Lancaster

Lancaster University Library: Bailrigg, Lancaster, LA1 4YH; tel. (1524) 592516; e-mail librba@lancaster.ac.uk; internet libweb.lancs.ac.uk; f. 1963; 936,000 vols, pamphlets and other items, 3,000 current serials; spec. collns: business history, Quaker, Redlich (music), Socialist, European Documentation Centre; Librarian CLARE POWNE..

Branch Library:

Ruskin Library and Research Centre: Lancaster Univ., Bailrigg, Lancaster, LA1 4YH; tel. (1524) 593587; e-mail ruskin.library@lancaster.ac.uk; internet www.lancaster.ac.uk/depts/ruskinlib; Whitehouse colln of documents relating to the writer and thinker John Ruskin (1819–1900), incl. 1,700 works of art by Ruskin and his circle, Ruskin's diaries, 8,000 letters, 200 MSS, 3,500 books and 1,000 original photographs; Dir and Curator Prof. STEPHEN WILDMAN; Sec. JEN SHEPHERD; publ. *Ruskin Review and Bulletin* (2 a year).

Leeds

Leeds Library and Information Services: Central Library, Calverley St, Leeds, LS1 3AB; tel. (113) 247-6016; e-mail enquiry.express@leeds.gov.uk; internet www.leeds.gov.uk/libraries; f. 1884; 37 brs and 7 mobile libraries; central library incl. specialist central depts: business and patents, local and family history, art and music, and the information centre housing spec. collns (Porton colln of Judaica, Gott bequest of early gardening books, Leeds pottery drawing books and pattern books and the Gascoigne colln of militaria); Chief Officer, Libraries, Arts and Heritage CATHERINE BLANSHARD.

Leeds University Library: Leeds, LS2 9JT; tel. (113) 343-5663; e-mail library@leeds.ac.uk; internet library.leeds.ac.uk; f. 1874; includes fmr Ripon Cathedral Library

containing early MSS, Service Books, Books of Hours, MSS since the 13th century, printed books from 15th–18th century; Liddle Colln of First World War archive materials; 2.8m. vols, pamphlets and microforms, incl. the Brotherton Colln of 50,000 vols, pamphlets, MSS, deeds and letters, 500,000 ebooks, 37,000 print and online journals; Univ. Librarian and Keeper of the Brotherton Colln STELLA BUTLER.

Leicester

De Montfort University Library and Learning Services: Kimberlin Library, The Gateway, Leicester, LE1 9BH; tel. (116) 257-7042; e-mail justask@dmu.ac.uk; internet www.library.dmu.ac.uk; spec. collns: Kodak Colln, Nat. Youth Colln, Fashion and Textiles colln incorporating the library of Hosiery and Allied Trades Research Asscn (HATRA); Dir for Library and Learning Services JO WEBB.

Leicester City Libraries: Central Library, Bishop St, Town Hall Sq., Leicester, LE1 6AA; tel. (116) 454-3540; e-mail libraries@leicester.gov.uk; internet www.leicester.gov.uk/libraries; Head of Libraries and Information Services ADRIAN WILLS.

Leicestershire Library Services: County Hall, Glenfield, Leicester, LE3 8TD; tel. (116) 232-3232; e-mail libraries@leics.gov.uk; internet www.leics.gov.uk/libraries; f. 1974; 7 brs, mobile library; Head of Library Services NIGEL THOMAS.

University of Leicester Library: POB 248, University Rd, Leicester, LE1 9QD; tel. (116) 252-2043; e-mail library@leicester.ac.uk; internet www.le.ac.uk/library; f. 1921; 1m. vols; spec. collns: local history of England and Wales, papers of Joe Orton and of Sue Townsend; Univ. Librarian CAROLINE TAYLOR.

Lewes

East Sussex Library and Information Service: County Hall, St Anne's Crescent, Lewes, BN7 1UE; tel. (1273) 481870; e-mail libraries@eastsussex.gov.uk; internet www.eastsussex.gov.uk/libraries; 28 brs; 750,000 vols; Asst Dir for Libraries and Culture Dr IRENE CAMPBELL.

Lichfield

Dean Savage Library: 19A The Close, Lichfield, WS13 7LD; tel. (1543) 306175; e-mail library@lichfield-cathedral.org; internet www.lichfield-cathedral.org/visiting-lichfield-cathedral/dean-savage-library.html; f. 1924; attached to Lichfield Cathedral; books on theology and ecclesiastical history; library is currently closed; 3,000 vols; Man. CLARE TOWNSEND.

Lincoln

Discover Stamford—Heritage at your library: Stamford Library, High St, Lincoln, PE9 2BB; tel. (1522) 782010; e-mail stamford.library@lincolnshire.gov.uk; internet www.lincolnshire.gov.uk/stamfordlibrary; f. 2012; attached to Lincoln Heritage Services; stories of the town through objects, pictures, interactive trails.

Lincolnshire County Council Communities Directorate—Libraries: County Offices, Newland, Lincoln, LN1 1YL; tel. (1522) 552222; e-mail library.support@lincolnshire.gov.uk; internet www.lincolnshire.gov.uk; f. 1974 from 7 fmr Lincolnshire library authorities; 46 brs, 11 mobile libraries; 1,528,773 vols; spec. collns: music, drama, Lincolnshire material, Alfred Lord Tennyson; Head of Libraries JONATHAN PLATT.

Liverpool

Liverpool Libraries and Archives: Central Library, William Brown St, Liverpool, L3 8EW; tel. (151) 233-3069; e-mail recoffice.central.library@liverpool.gov.uk; internet liverpool.gov.uk/libraries; f. 1852; reference services, services to business, record office, family history service; EU depository library; 1m. vols, incl. Hornby Library: 15,000 rare books, fine bindings, MSS, prints and a patents library; Head of Libraries JOYCE LITTLE.

University of Liverpool Library: POB 123, Liverpool, L69 3DA; tel. (151) 794-2679; e-mail ask@liv.ac.uk.libanswers.com; internet www.liv.ac.uk/library; f. 1881; over 1.9m. vols; spec. collns incl. 254 incunabula, T. G. Rylands colln (early cartography, Lancashire and Cheshire history), William Blake colln, Scott Macfie colln (gypsy studies), William Noble colln (Kelmscott and other private presses), Knowsley colln (17th- to 19th-century English pamphlets), Peers colln (Spanish Civil War), Fraser colln (c. 900 books and pamphlets on tobacco; material on positivism and secularism), Robert Graves colln, Merseyside poets; modern MSS incl. the Rathbones papers, Blanco White, Brunner and Glasier papers, Science Fiction Foundation colln, Olaf Stapledon colln; Education Library with colln of children's books; Univ. Librarian PHIL SYKES.

Llandrindod Wells

Powys Library Service: Cefnllys Lane, Llandrindod Wells, LD1 5LD; tel. (1597) 826860; e-mail library@powys.gov.uk; internet library.powys.gov.uk; f. 1974; 17 brs, 4 mobile libraries; spec. local history collns; 300,000 vols; Prin. Librarian KAY THOMAS.

Llandudno

Conwy Libraries: Library Bldg, Mostyn St, Llandudno, LL30 2RP; tel. (1492) 576139; e-mail library@conwy.gov.uk; internet www.conwy.gov.uk/libraries; f. 1996; 12 brs, mobile library, home library service; 200,000 vols; spec. collns: local history, Welsh language and literature; Section Head for Culture and Information ANN LLOYD WILLIAMS.

Llangefni

Isle of Anglesey County Libraries: Llangefni Library, Lôn y Felin, Llangefni, LL77 7RT; tel. (1248) 752095; e-mail libraries@anglesey.gov.uk; internet www.anglesey.gov.uk/libraries; Head of Services JOHN REES THOMAS.

London

Aslib-IMI Information and Library Service: Temple Chambers, 3–7 Temple Ave, London, EC4Y 0HP; tel. (20) 7583-8900; e-mail aslib@aslib.co.uk; internet www.aslib.com/info; 16,000 vols on information management, incl. documentation, information science, special libraries and related subjects, 370 current periodicals of the world and about 25,000 references to articles, reports, etc., on library and information science; publs *Aslib Book Guide* (12 a year), *Aslib Guide to Copyright* (3 a year), *Aslib Proceedings* (10 a year), *Current Awareness Abstracts* (10 a year), *Forthcoming International Scientific and Technical Conferences* (4 a year), *Journal of Documentation* (5 a year), *Managing Information* (10 a year), *Online and CD Notes* (10 a year), *Program: Electronic Library and Information Systems* (4 a year), *Records Management Journal* (3 a year).

Barking and Dagenham Libraries: Barking Library, 2 Town Sq., Barking, IG11 7NB;

tel. (20) 8724-8725; e-mail 3000direct@lbbd
.gov.uk; internet www.lbbd.gov.uk/libraries;
f. 1888; public library service in the London
Borough of Barking and Dagenham; 10 brs
throughout the borough, mem. of the LLC
(London Libraries Consortium); 600,000 vols;
Group Man. Libraries ZOINUL ABIDIN.

Barnet Libraries: Bldg 4, North London
Business Park, Oakleigh Rd South, London,
N11 1NP; tel. (20) 8359-2000; e-mail first
.contact@barnet.gov.uk; internet www
.barnet.gov.uk/libraries; f. 1965; 66,000 vols;
spec. colln of sociology; Libraries Man.
HANNAH RICHENS.

Bexley Libraries: Foots Cray Offices, Maidstone Rd, Sidcup, London, DA14 5HS; tel.
(20) 8303-7777; e-mail libraries@bexley.gov
.uk; internet www.bexley.gov.uk/libraries;
12 brs; 3 mobile libraries, reference library;
Local Studies and Archive Centre; 600,000
vols; Library Services Man. JUDITH MITLIN.

Brent Libraries: Brent Civic Centre,
Engineers Way, Wembley, London, HA9
0FJ; tel. (20) 8937-3144; e-mail libraries@
brent.gov.uk; internet www.brent.gov.uk/
libraries; f. 1965; 6 brs, mobile library,
housebound service, Grange Museum of
Local History; 580,000 vols; Head of Libraries KAREN TYERMAN.

British Architectural Library: RIBA, 66
Portland Pl., London, W1B 1AD; tel. (20)
7307-3882; e-mail info@riba.org; internet
www.architecture.com/librarydrawingsand-
photographs/home.aspx#.uwmm9wksy0c; f.
1834; attached to Royal Institute of British
Architects; 150,000 vols, 2,000 periodicals
titles, 1,400 dead runs, 1m. drawings, 1.5m.
archive items, 1.5m. photographs, 300,000
negatives, 700 m of MSS; spec. collns: Early
Imprints Colln (4,000 books published from
1478–1840), Charles Handley-Read Colln
(500 vols), Modern Movement Colln (600
vols); Dir WENDY FISH.

BFI National Archive: 21 Stephen St,
London, W1T 1LN; tel. (20) 7255-1444;
e-mail pressoffice@bfi.org.uk; internet www
.bfi.org.uk; f. 1935 as a div. of the British
Film Institute; 60,000 fiction films, 120,000
non-fiction titles and 750,000 television programmes; 600 spec. collns, 30,000 unpublished scripts, 1m. still images, 15,000
posters, 3,000 production and costume
designs; J. Paul Getty Jr Conservation
Centre (in Berkhamsted); BFI Reuben
Library; 51,000 vols, 7,000 journal titles,
4,000 audio cassettes, 4m. newspaper cuttings; Head Curator ROBIN BAKER; Head of
Collns and Information GABRIELE POPP.

**British Geological Survey, London
Information Office:** Natural History
Museum Earth Galleries, Cromwell Rd,
London, SW7 5BD; tel. (20) 7589-4090;
e-mail bgslondon@bgs.ac.uk; internet www
.bgs.ac.uk; f. 1986; information and advisory
service; public reference colln of British
Geological Survey; publs incl. geological
maps, memoirs, reports, research reports
and information illustrating the geology of
the British Isles; online access to British
Geological Survey databases; some overseas
maps and textbooks; Man. CLARE M. TOM-
BLESON.

British Library: St Pancras, 96 Euston Rd,
London, NW1 2DB; tel. (843) 208-1144;
e-mail press-and-pr@bl.uk; internet www.bl
.uk; f. 1973; legal deposit library; 150m.
items in most known languages, incorporating books, newspapers, periodicals, MSS,
maps, prints and drawings, music scores,
patents and the Nat. Sound Archive; document supply service at Boston Spa,
Wetherby, West Yorks., LS23 7BQ; Chair.
Baroness BLACKSTONE; Chief Exec. ROLY

KEATING; publ. *British Library Journal*
(online only).

**British Library of Political and Eco-
nomic Science:** London School of Economics, 10 Portugal St, London, WC2A 2HD; tel.
(20) 7955-7229; e-mail library.enquiries@lse
.ac.uk; internet www.lse.ac.uk/library; f.
1896 as The British Library of Political
Science, current name adopted 1925; colln
incl. economics, political science, law (esp.
int. law), sociology, history, geography; 4m.
bibliographic items comprising journals, govt
publs, other serial publs and 1.2m. monographs; Dir for Library Services ELIZABETH
CHAPMAN; Deputy Dir for Library Services
NICOLA WRIGHT.

British Medical Association Library:
BMA House, Tavistock Sq., London, WC1H
9JP; tel. (20) 7383-6625; e-mail bma-library@
bma.org.uk; internet www.bma.org.uk/
library; f. 1887; provides expert medical
information services to members and staff;
specializes in current clinical practice, medical ethics and education; 30,000 vols, 2,000
periodicals, 3,500 films and video cassettes;
Librarian JACKY BERRY.

Bromley Libraries: Central Library, High
St, Bromley, BR1 1EX; tel. (20) 8461-7155;
e-mail informationservices@bromley.gov.uk;
internet www.bromley.gov.uk/libraries; f.
1894; 15 brs, mobile library; 51,945
audiovisual items, 676 multimedia items,
98,878 microtext items; spec. collns: Crystal
Palace, Walter de la Mare, H. G. Wells; Head
of Libraries JUDITH MITLIN.

Camden Libraries: 7th Fl., Town Hall
Extension, Argyle St, London, WC1H 8EQ;
tel. (20) 7974-4444; internet www.camden
.gov.uk/libraries; 759,500 vols; Head of
Libraries DAVID JONES.

Canning House Library: Maughan
Library, Chancery Lane, London, WC2A
1LR; tel. (20) 7848-2424; e-mail enquiries@
canninghouse.org; internet www
.canninghouse.org; f. 1947; attached to Hispanic and Luso-Brazilian Council; 70,000
vols; collns from Spanish- and Portuguese-
speaking countries on social sciences and
humanities; Library and Information Services Man. ALAN BIGGINS.

**City of Westminster Libraries and Arch-
ives:** Dept of Environment and Leisure,
Westminster City Hall, Victoria St, London,
SW1E 6QP; tel. (20) 7641-1300; internet
www.westminster.gov.uk/libraries; 11 community libraries, total stock: 1,196,903 books
and other materials; Dir DAVID RUSE; Head of
Library Operations IONA CAIRNS..

Notable Constituent Libraries:

City of Westminster Archives Centre:
10 St Ann's St, London, SW1P 2DE; tel.
(20) 7641-5180; e-mail archives@
westminster.gov.uk; internet www
.westminster.gov.uk/services/libraries/
archives; collns document the socio-economic, cultural, admin. and community
history; houses the archives of Jaeger,
Liberty and Gillows; 200,000 vols, pamphlets, directories, newspapers, journals,
maps and plans, prints, drawings and
photographs, local govt records, electoral
registers, census returns, parish registers
and business archives; Archives Man.
ADRIAN AUTTON.

Westminster Music Library: 160 Buckingham Palace Rd, London, SW1W 9UD;
tel. (20) 7641-6200; e-mail musiclibrary@
westminster.gov.uk; internet www
.westminster.gov.uk/services/libraries/spe-
cial/music; f. 1946; 62,400 items on music
(not recordings); Music Services
Coordinator RUTH WALTERS.

Westminster Reference Library: 35 St
Martin's St, London, WC2H 7HP; tel. (20)
7641-1300; e-mail referencelibrarywc2@
westminster.gov.uk; internet www
.westminster.gov.uk/libraries/findalibrary/
westref.cfm; 432,000 vols; key collns incl.
law and British official publs (Hansard,
LexisNexis); performing arts (theatre, film,
television, radio, dance); art and design
(MLA designated colln of nat. importance);
business information (market research
reports, directories and online services);
Gen. Reference Librarian EVELEEN ROO-
NEY.

College of Arms: 130 Queen Victoria St,
London, EC4V 4BT; tel. (20) 7248-2762;
e-mail enquiries@college-of-arms.gov.uk;
internet www.college-of-arms.gov.uk; f.
1484; genealogical, heraldic, antiquarian
collns; Arundel MSS, deeds and charters;
30,000 vols; Archivist LYNSEY DARBY; Librarian PETER O'DONOGHUE.

Croydon Libraries: Central Library,
Katharine St, Croydon, CR9 1ET; tel. (20)
8726-6900; e-mail croydon.centrallibrary@
laing.com; internet www.croydon.gov.uk/
leisure/libraries; f. 1888; 695,000 vols, 23,592
audio items; Libraries Officer A. BATT.

**Department for Children, Schools and
Family Library:** Sanctuary Bldgs, Great
Smith St, London, SW1P 3BT; tel. (20) 7925-
5040; f. 1854; 210,000 vols; Chief Librarian
GILL BAKER.

Department of Health Library: tel. (11)
3254-5080; e-mail knowledgecentre-qh@dh
.gsi.gov.uk; internet www.dh.gov.uk; f. 1834;
200,000 vols and pamphlets, 650 print periodicals and various databases and electronic
journals on public health, health-services
policy and management, medicine, hospitals
and social care; Head of Knowledge Management and IT Skills Devt KAREN LEWIS; Sr
Librarian NATALIE GUDGEON; publs *DH-Data*
(online), *DH-Data Thesaurus* (print), *HMIC*
(online and CD-ROM).

Associated Library:

**Department of Health Knowledge
Centre:** Room 1W28, Quarry House,
Quarry Hill, Leeds, LS2 7UE; tel. (113)
254-5080; e-mail knowledgecentre-qh@dh
.gsi.gov.uk; archive of Dept of Health (incl.
predecessors) publs; producer of DH data;
Sr Librarian NATALIE GUDGEON.

Dr Williams's Library: 14 Gordon Sq.,
London, WC1H 0AR; tel. (20) 7387-3727;
e-mail enquiries@dwlib.co.uk; internet www
.dwlib.co.uk; f. 1729; lending and reference
library of theological, philosophical and historical works, relating in particular to religious non-conformity and esp. to
Congregational, English Presbyterian and
Unitarian traditions; 300,000 vols; Dir Dr
DAVID L. WYKES; publ. *Lectures of Friends of
Dr Williams's Library* (1 a year).

Attached Library:

Congregational Library: 14 Gordon Sq.,
London, WC1H 0AR; tel. (20) 7387-3727;
e-mail enquiries@dwlib.co.uk; internet
conglib.co.uk; f. 1831; 70,000 vols, mainly
relating to Church history, the history and
activities of the Nonconformists, theology,
religious liberty and hymnology.

Ealing Libraries: Perceval House, 14–16
Uxbridge Rd, Ealing, London, W5 2HL; tel.
(208) 825-7261; e-mail ealing.libraryuser@
laing.com; internet www.ealing.gov.uk/
libraries; f. 1965; 650,000 vols; Library Man.
for Devt and Stock KATE GODDARD.

Enfield Libraries: Enfield Town Library,
66 Church St, Enfield, EN2 6AX; tel. (20)
8379-8393; e-mail enfield.town.library@
enfield.gov.uk; internet www.enfield.gov.uk/
library; f. 1965; 17 brs, mobile library;

620,000 vols; spec. collns: linguistics, local history; Head of Library Services JULIE GIBSON.

Geological Society of London, Library and Information Services: Burlington House, Piccadilly, London, W1J 0BG; tel. (20) 7432-0999; e-mail library@geolsoc.org .uk; internet www.geolsoc.org.uk/library; f. 1807; earth science library; lending restricted to the UK via British Library Document Supply Centre; reference access by appointment; 300,000 vols, 600 current journal titles, 40,000 maps; Library and Information Services Man. FABIENNE MICHAUD.

Gray's Inn Library & Archives: 5 South Sq., Gray's Inn, London, WC1R 5ET; tel. (20) 7458 7822; e-mail library.information@ graysinn.org.uk; internet www.graysinn.org .uk/index.php/library; f. c. 1488; Legal Reference Library for mems of Gray's Inn, others admitted on application; 60,000 vols; spec. collns: 12th- to 14th-century MSS, pre-1800 books incl. Francis Bacon colln; Librarian T. L. THOM; Archivist ANDREW MUSSELL.

Greenwich Libraries: Plumstead Library, 232 Plumstead High St, London, SE18 1JL; tel. (20) 8317-4466; e-mail libraries@ greenwich.gov.uk; internet www .royalgreenwich.gov.uk/libraries; f. 1905; 750,800 vols, 85,213 sound recordings; Borough Librarian and Head of Community Services JULIA NEWTON.

Guardian News and Media Archive: Kings Pl., 90 York Way, London, N1 9GU; tel. (20) 3353-3304; e-mail archives@ theguardian.com; internet www.theguardian .com/gnm-archive; f. 2002 as the Newsroom; archives of orgs and people associated with the Guardian and Observer newspapers; photographic libraries; microfilm, bound hard-copy and digital back-issues; permanent display details history of the two newspapers; Archivist MARIAM YAMIN.

Guildhall Library, City of London: Aldermanbury, London, EC2V 7HH; tel. (20) 7332-1868; e-mail guildhall.library@cityoflondon .gov.uk; internet www.cityoflondon.gov.uk/ guildhalllibrary; f. 1425; MSS records of the city livery cos, stock exchange and Lloyd's of London; public reference library, particularly rich in books on all aspects of London history, business history, maritime history, food and wine, clock making; Dir of Libraries and Guildhall Art Gallery DAVID PEARSON; Prin. Librarian Dr PETER ROSS; Head of Library SARA PINK..

Branch Library:

City Business Library, City of London: Guildhall, Aldermanbury, London, EC2V 7HH; tel. (20) 7332-1812; e-mail cbl@ cityoflondon.gov.uk; internet www .cityoflondon.gov.uk/cbl; f. 1970; contains co-financial data, country information (incl. global markets) and market research information; Head SARA PINK.

Hackney Libraries: Hackney Central Library, 1 Reading Lane, London, E8 1GQ; tel. (20) 8356-4358; e-mail info@hackney.gov .uk; internet www.hackney.gov.uk/ cl-libraries; f. 1965; 8 brs; Hackney Archives housed in attached Dalston C. L. R. James Library; 250,000 vols, 57,000 CDs and DVDs; spec. collns: mechanic trades, woodwork and furniture, local history, John Dawson Colln; Head of Libraries EDWARD ROGERS.

Hammersmith & Fulham Libraries: Hammersmith Library, 181 King St, Hammersmith, London, W6 9JT; tel. (20) 8753-3820; e-mail libraries@lbhf.gov.uk; internet www.lbhf.gov.uk; f. 1888; 234,000 vols; spec. collns: law, politics, Christianity,

HMSO publs since 1970, video and audio cassettes, DVDs, CDs; Man. ANN COOPER.

Haringey Libraries: Central Library, 187-197A High Rd, Wood Green, London, N22 6XD; tel. (20) 8489-2781; e-mail library .service@haringey.gov.uk; internet www .haringey.gov.uk/data/libraries; 1m. vols; Head of Libraries DIANA EDMONDS.

Harrow Libraries: POB 4, Civic Centre, Station Rd, Harrow, London, HA1 2UU; tel. (20) 8424-1055; e-mail civiccentre.library@ harrow.gov.uk; internet www.harrow.gov .uk/libraries; f. 1965; 11 brs; 412,000 vols, 38,000 audiovisual items; spec. collns: architecture and building; Library Services Man. TIM BRYAN.

Havering Libraries: Central Library, St Edward's Way, Romford, RM1 3AR; tel. (1708) 432389; e-mail central.library@ havering.gov.uk; internet www.havering.gov .uk/libraries; f. 1964; 10 brs; 500,000 vols; Library Services Man. ANN RENNIE.

Hillingdon Libraries: Central Library, 14 High St, Uxbridge, UB8 1HD; tel. (1895) 250600; e-mail librarycontact@hillingdon.gov .uk; internet www.hillingdon.gov.uk/ libraries; f. 1965; 843,105 vols; Dir (vacant).

Home Office Information Services Centre: Lower Ground, Seacole Bldg, 2 Marsham St, London, SW1P 4DF; tel. (20) 7035-6699; e-mail informationservicescentre@homeoffice.gsi .gov.uk; internet www.homeoffice.gov.uk; 42,000 vols, 100,000 microforms, 2,000 periodicals; Library and Information Services JACKIE KING; Customer Liaison Man. JANET COCKAYNE.

Hounslow Library Network: Hounslow Community Services, CentreSpace, Treaty Centre, High St, Hounslow, TW3 1ES; tel. (845) 456-2800; e-mail hounslow-info@laing .com; internet www.hounslow.info; Dir of Culture and Heritage (vacant).

House of Commons Library: London, SW1A 0AA; tel. (20) 7219-4272; e-mail hcinfo@parliament.uk; internet www .parliament.uk/mps-lords-and-offices/offices/ commons/commonslibrary; f. 1818; research div. issues internal reference sheets and background papers on subjects of current interest to mems; library private to MPs; Information Office handles enquiries on Parliament from the gen. public; over 260,000 vols, Parliamentary Papers; reference library files contain more than 700 periodicals, 1,500 ejournals, 100 newspapers; Dir-Gen. of Information Services and Librarian JOHN PULLINGER; Head of Library Resources KATHARINE MARKE; publ. *POST Notes*.

House of Lords Library: London, SW1A 0PW; tel. (20) 7219-5242; e-mail hllibrary@ parliament.uk; f. 1826; 120,000 vols, legal and parliamentary history, gen. literature and reference; Dir of Information Services and Librarian Dr ELIZABETH HALLAM SMITH.

Imperial College of London Libraries: S Kensington, London, SW7 2AZ; tel. (20) 7594-8810; e-mail library@imperial.ac.uk; internet www.imperial.ac.uk/library; central library on S Kensington campus; 5 Faculty of Medicine libraries at Charing Cross, Chelsea and Westminster, Royal Brompton, St Mary's and Hammersmith campuses; also Michael Way Library at Silwood Park; 580,000 vols, 25,000 ejournal titles, 1,000 print titles; Dir of Library Services CHRIS BANKS.

Inner Temple Library: Inner Temple, London, EC4Y 7DA; tel. (20) 7797-8217; e-mail library@innertemple.org.uk; internet www.innertemplelibrary.org.uk; f. 1500; 80,000 vols, mostly legal and historical;

spec. colln of 10,000 MSS, incl. Petyt MSS; Librarian MARGARET CLAY.

Institute of Advanced Legal Studies Library: Univ. of London, 17 Russell Sq., London, WC1B 5DR; tel. (20) 7862-5790; e-mail ials@sas.ac.uk; internet www.ials.sas .ac.uk; f. 1947; serves academic researchers nationally and internationally; 300,000 vols, 3,073 current serials; comprehensive colln of legal literature (except for Oriental laws and literature of East European law in East European languages), with spec. emphasis on the legal systems of the UK, the Commonwealth, the USA, Western Europe and Latin America; comparative law; int. law; incl. the Foreign and Commonwealth Office Commonwealth Law Library; the Records of Legal Education Archives; Librarian and Dir of Institute Prof. JULES WINTERTON.

Institute of Historical Research Library: Univ. of London, Senate House, London, WC1E 7HU; tel. (20) 7862-8760; e-mail ihr.library@sas.ac.uk; internet www .history.ac.uk/library; f. 1921; colln of printed historical sources covering W Europe and its colonial history, from end of Roman period; 171,000 vols; Collns and Periodicals Librarian METTE LUND NEWLYN.

Institution of Engineering and Technology Library and Archives: Savoy Pl., London, WC2R 0BL; tel. (20) 7344-5461; e-mail libdesk@theiet.org; internet www .theiet.org/library; f. 1871; 75,000 books, 200,000 bound vols of periodicals, 850 current periodicals, 20,000 reports and pamphlets; spec. collns of historical electrical works; Sir Francis Ronalds Colln (6,000 vols and pamphlets), Sylvanus P. Thompson Library (4,500 vols and 8,000 pamphlets), Faraday MSS, and library, notebooks and MSS of Oliver Heaviside; holds library of British Computer Society; produces INSPEC database and provides specialized information services; Man. of Library and Archives Services JOHN W. COUPLAND; publs *Engineering and Technology* (12 a year), *IET Proceedings* (6 a year), *IET Research Journals*.

Islington Library and Heritage Services: Central Library, 2 Fieldway Crescent, London, N5 1PF; tel. (20) 7527-6900; e-mail centralref.library@islington.gov.uk; internet www.islington.gov.uk/libraries; f. 1905; 10 libraries incl. Central Reference Library, Lewis Carroll Children's Library, Islington Local History Centre, Islington museum and 2 adult learning centres: First Steps Learning Centre and Islington Computer Skills Centre; 544,357 vols; Head of Library and Heritage Service ROSEMARY DOYLE; Information and Learning Man. JOHN SMITH.

Joint Library of the Hellenic and Roman Societies: Senate House, Malet St, London, WC1E 7HU; tel. (20) 7862-8709; e-mail colin.annis@sas.ac.uk; internet icls .sas.ac.uk/library/home.htm; f. 1879, since 1953 run in asscn with Univ. of London's Institute of Classical Studies Library; art, classical archaeology, history, language, literature, philosophy and religion; 130,000 vols, 19,500 periodicals, 650 current periodicals; classified colln of 6,800 coloured slides, 200 CD-ROMs; Librarian COLIN ANNIS.

Kensington and Chelsea Libraries: Central Library, Phillimore Walk, London, W8 7RX; tel. (20) 7361-3010; e-mail libraries@ rbkc.gov.uk; internet www.rbkc.gov.uk/ leisureandlibraries.aspx; f. 1888; 620,000 vols; spec. collns: genealogy and heraldry, biography, languages, folklore, costume and local history; Head of Libraries JANE BATTYE.

King's College London Library: Maughan Library, Chancery Lane, London, WC2A 1LR; tel. (20) 7848-2424; e-mail libraryservices@kcl.ac.uk; internet www.kcl

.ac.uk/library; f. 1829; sites incl. Chancery Lane (humanities, law, science), Denmark Hill Campus (medicine, dentistry), Guy's Campus (medicine, dentistry, biomedical sciences), St Thomas's Campus (medicine) and Waterloo Campus (life sciences, nursing and midwifery, education, management); 1,200,000 vols; spec. collns: Foyle Library (170,000 printed works, maps, slides, sound recordings and MSS; Dir of Library Services ROBERT HALL.

Kingston Council Libraries: Fairfield Rd, Kingston upon Thames, KT1 2PS; tel. (20) 8547-5006; e-mail kingston.library@rbk .kingston.gov.uk; internet www.kingston.gov .uk/libraries; f. 1882; 230,000 vols; Strategic Man. for Library and Heritage Service GRACE MCELWEE.

Lambeth Libraries and Archives: Brixton Library, Brixton Oval, London, SW2 1JQ; tel. (20) 7926-1056; e-mail libraries@lambeth.gov .uk; internet www.lambeth.gov.uk/libraries; f. 1888; 9 brs; mobile library and home visit library service; archives and local history service; over 600,000 vols; Head of Service SANDRA GOODWIN.

Lambeth Palace Library: Lambeth Palace Rd, London, SE1 7JU; tel. (20) 7898-1400; e-mail archives@churchofengland.org; internet www.lambethpalacelibrary.org; f. 1610; 200,000 printed items (esp. Church history) and 4,500 vols of 9th–20th century MSS; Sion College Library MSS and early printed books; archives; Librarian and Archivist GILES MANDELBROTE.

Law Society Library: 113 Chancery Lane, London, WC2A 1PL; tel. (20) 7320-5946; e-mail library@lawsociety.org.uk; internet www.lawsociety.org.uk/library; f. 1825; private library for solicitors who are mems of the Law Soc. of England and Wales; 55,000 vols, 3,500 current legal practitioner textbooks, 1,100 journal titles, 60 legal journals; Head Librarian MICHAEL MAHER.

Lewisham Library Service: Town Hall, Catford, London, SE6 4RU; tel. (20) 8314-6399; e-mail libraries@lewisham.gov.uk; internet www.lewisham.gov.uk/ leisureandculture/libraries; f. 1890; 700,000 vols; 12 brs, Central Reference Library, Local History Centre, Open Learning Centre; Head of Library and Information Services JOHN HUGHES; publs *Looking Back at Lewisham*, local history publs.

Library of Anti-Slavery International: Thomas Clarkson House, The Stableyard, Broomgrove Rd, London, SW9 9TL; tel. (20) 7501-8920; e-mail library@antislavery.org; internet www.antislavery.org/english/ resources/library.aspx; f. 1839; literature, photographs and video cassettes on historical and contemporary slavery and human rights issues (modern issues incl. bonded labour, child labour, descent-based slavery, forced labour, indigenous peoples and trafficking; historical issues incl. the Transatlantic Slave Trade and colonialism); 3,000 vols, 250 images; Librarian (vacant).

Library of the Religious Society of Friends in Britain: Friends House, Euston Rd, London, NW1 2BJ; tel. (20) 7663-1135; e-mail library@quaker.org.uk; internet www .quaker.org.uk/library; f. 1673; collects and preserves Quakers' historic and continuing recorded heritage; increases access to information about the Society of Friends; encourages study in Quaker and related activities, incl. peace, prison reform, humanitarian assistance and the anti-slavery movement; 80,000 vols of books and pamphlets, 3,000 vols of periodicals, 4,000 MSS, 40,000 prints and photographs; Head of Library and Archives DAVID BLAKE.

Lilian Storey Memorial Library, Theosophical Society in England: 50 Gloucester Pl., London, W1U 8EA; tel. (20) 7563-9816; e-mail books@theosoc.org.uk; internet www.theosoc.org.uk; f. 1875; 15,000 vols; publ. *Esoterica*.

Lincoln's Inn Library: Holborn, London, WC2A 3TN; tel. (20) 7242-4371; e-mail library@lincolnsinn.org.uk; internet www .lincolnsinn.org.uk; f. 1475; 170,000 vols on law and 2,000 vols of MSS, incl. the Hale Colln; Librarian G. F. HOLBORN.

Linnean Society Library: Burlington House, Piccadilly, London, W1J 0BF; tel. (20) 7434-4479; e-mail library@linnean.org; internet www.linnean.org; f. 1788; books on natural history, incl. Linnaeus's own library; collns of MSS, engravings and portraits; 95,000 vols; Librarian LYNDA BROOKS; Deputy Librarian ELAINE CHARWAT.

London Library: 14 St James's Sq., London, SW1Y 4LG; tel. (20) 7930-7705; e-mail membership@londonlibrary.co.uk; internet www.londonlibrary.co.uk; f. 1841; open to subscribing mems; an educational charity; 1m. vols mainly in the arts, humanities and social sciences; Librarian INEZ T. P. A. LYNN.

London Oratory Library: The Oratory, Brompton Rd, S Kensington, London, SW7 2RP; tel. (20) 7808-0900; e-mail bromptonoratory@aol.com; internet www .bromptonoratory.com; f. 1854; contains 40,000 vols and 3,000 pamphlets on theology and Church history; separate library (4,000 vols) of David Lewis, Tractarian convert; Librarian and Archivist Fr LIBRARIAN.

Library & Archives Service, London School of Hygiene and Tropical Medicine: Keppel St, London, WC1E 7HT; tel. (20) 7927-2276; e-mail library@lshtm.ac.uk; internet www.lshtm.ac.uk/library; f. 1899; archive collns incl. the papers of Sir Ronald Ross and many other eminent public health and tropical medicine professionals; Head of Library and Archives Service CAROLINE LLOYD.

Marx Memorial Library: Marx House, 37A Clerkenwell Green, London, EC1R 0DU; tel. (20) 7253-1485; e-mail info@marxlibrary.org .uk; internet www.marxlibrary.org.uk; f. 1933; 150,000 vols; pamphlets, files of Labour, Socialist and Communist periodicals; spec. collns: Peace Movement, Spanish Civil War, USA, and the Hunger Marches; James Klugmann colln of Chartist and early British working-class history; lectures and discussion confs; Dir of Archives and Librarian (vacant).

Merton Libraries and Heritage Service: Wimbledon Library, 35 Wimbledon Hill Rd, Wimbledon, SW19 7NB; tel. (20) 8545-3770; e-mail library.enquiries@merton.gov.uk; internet www.merton.gov.uk/council/ departments/ch/librariesandheritagedept .htm; f. 1887; 500,000 vols; spec. collns: William Morris, Nelson; Head of Library and Heritage Services INGRID LACKAJIS.

Middle Temple Library (The Honourable Society of the Middle Temple): Ashley Bldg, Middle Temple Lane, London, EC4Y 9BT; tel. (20) 7427-4830; e-mail library@middletemple.org.uk; internet www .middletemplelibrary.org.uk; f. 1641; private library for members of the Hon. Soc. of the Middle Temple; non-members admitted at the discretion of the librarian; 125,000 vols of works on British, American, Public Int. and European Communities law, ecclesiastical law, capital punishment; spec. collns: 80 incunabula, misc. tracts, mainly 17th-century, 83 vols from John Donne's library; Librarian V. HAYWARD.

Ministry of Defence, Information Services: Ministry of Defence Main Bldg, Whitehall, London, SW1A 2HB; tel. (20) 7218-4445; e-mail cio-svcslibrary-office@mod .uk; covers defence policy, defence forces, military, naval and aviation strategy and technology, int. relations, politics, management and computer science; 50,000 vols, 300 periodicals; Chief Librarian PATRICK RYAN.

National Archives: Ruskin Ave, Kew, Richmond upon Thames, TW9 4DU; tel. (20) 8876-3444; e-mail enquiry@nationalarchives .gov.uk; internet www.nationalarchives.gov .uk; f. 2003 following merger of the Public Record Office (f. 1838) and the Historical Manuscripts Comm. (f. 1869); nat. archives for England and Wales and for the United Kingdom; holds the records of central govt and the central courts of law since 11th century; central UK advisory body on archives and MSS relating to British history; Chief Exec. CLEM BROHIER (acting); publ. *Magna* (3 a year).

National Art Library: Victoria and Albert Museum, Cromwell Rd, London, SW7 2RL; e-mail nal.enquiries@vam.ac.uk; internet www.vam.ac.uk/nal; f. 1837; attached to Victoria and Albert (V&A) Museum; reference library for the int. documentation of art and design; 1m. vols on art and allied subjects; spec. collns: Dyce (1869) and Forster (1876) literary libraries, Clements Colln of armorial book-bindings, Piot Colln of festival literature, and many others; Keeper of the Word and Image Dept JULIUS BRYANT..

Attached Archive:

> **Archive of Art and Design:** 23 Blythe Rd, Olympia, London, W14 0QX; tel. (20) 7603-1514, ext. 209; e-mail archive@vam .ac.uk; internet www.vam.ac.uk/resources/ archives/aad; f. 1978; colln of principally 20th-century archives of designers, design asscns and cos involved in the design process; Keeper of the Word and Image Dept JULIUS BRYANT.

Natural History Museum, Library and Archives: Cromwell Rd, London, SW7 5BD; tel. (20) 7942-5460; e-mail library@nhm.ac .uk; internet www.nhm.ac.uk; f. 1881; print and e-resources covering botany, entomology, museum techniques, palaeontology, mineralogy, parasitology, physical anthropology, zoology and ornithology; 1m. vols; spec. collns: Carl Linnaeus, Sir Joseph Banks, Alfred Russel Wallace; 1,800 MSS, 400,000 original works of art; Head of Library JANE SMITH; publs *Journal of Systematic Palaeontology* (4 a year), *Systematics and Biodiversity* (4 a year).

Newham Public Libraries: Stratford Library, 3 The Grove, Stratford, London, E15 1EL; tel. (20) 8430-2000; e-mail customer.services@newham.gov.uk; internet www.newham.gov.uk/libraries; f. 1965; 10 brs; 500,530 vols, 57,243 reference stock, 14,031 audio items.

Queen Mary, University of London, Library: Mile End Rd, London, E1 4NS; tel. (20) 7882-7379; e-mail library-acquisitions@qmul.ac.uk; internet www.library.qmul.ac.uk; f. 1887; European Documentation Centre; 600,000 vols on the arts, engineering, medicine, law, sciences and social studies; Dir of Library Services EMMA BULL..

Medical Libraries:

> **St Bartholomew's and the Royal London, Queen Mary's School of Medicine and Dentistry, Libraries:** Turner St, London, E1 2AD; tel. (20) 7882-7112; internet www.library.qmul.ac.uk; incl. Whitechapel, W Smithfield, London Chest

Hospital, Wolfson Institute of Preventive Medicine.

Richmond upon Thames Libraries: Richmond Library, Little Green, Richmond, TW9 1QL; Information and Reference Library, Old Town Hall, Whittaker Ave, Richmond, TW9 1TP; tel. (20) 8734-3308; e-mail information@ richmond.gov.uk; internet www.richmond .gov.uk/libraries; f. 1880; 14 libraries; incl. Borough Local Studies Colln; Head of Libraries and Culture IAN DODDS.

Royal Academy of Arts Library: Burlington House, Piccadilly, London, W1J 0BD; tel. (20) 7300-5737; e-mail library@royalacademy .org.uk; internet www.royalacademy.org.uk/ collectionsandlibrary; f. 1768; 60,000 vols on the fine arts and standard reference books; original drawings, MSS, prints and photographs; Librarian ADAM WATERTON.

Royal Academy of Music Library: Marylebone Rd, London, NW1 5HT; tel. (20) 7873-7323; e-mail library@ram.ac.uk; internet www.ram.ac.uk/library; f. 1822; 150,000 vols, 5,500 sets of orchestral parts, sound recordings; spec. collns incl. MSS and early editions, Sir Henry Wood Library, Angelina Goetz Library, David Munrow Library, Sullivan Archive, Robert Spencer Colln, Foyle Menuhin Archive; Librarian KATHRYN ADAMSON.

Royal Asiatic Society Library: 14 Stephenson Way, London, NW1 2HD; tel. (20) 7388-4539; e-mail library@ royalasiaticsociety.org; internet www .royalasiaticsociety.org; f. 1823; holds lectures, organizes study days, publishes 2–3 books a year; 80,000 vols; collns incl. 1,500 Asian MSS, 2,000 paintings and drawings, 5,000 photographs; spec. collns: Tod colln of Indian MSS and paintings, Hodgson colln of Buddhist Sanskrit MSS, Ram Raz colln of architectural drawings, Raffles and Maxwell colls of Malay MSS, Howell colln of early photographs of China and Japan; Dir Dr ALISON OHTA; Librarian KATHY LAZENBATT; publ. *Journal* (4 a year).

Royal Astronomical Society Library and Archives: Burlington House, Piccadilly, London, W1J 0BQ; tel. (20) 7734-4582; e-mail info@ras.org.uk; internet www.ras .org.uk/library; f. 1820; 11,000 vols, incl. 4,000 items published before 1851, 3,000 journals, 300 current periodicals in astronomy and geophysics; spec. colln: Herschel Archive; Librarian S. PROSSER.

Royal Botanic Gardens, Kew, Library, Art & Archives: Kew, Richmond upon Thames, TW9 3AE; tel. (20) 8332-5414; e-mail library@kew.org; internet www.kew .org; f. 1852; botany (esp. taxonomic, floristic and economic aspects), history of gardening, botanical art, conservation, biochemistry, anatomy, genetics, molecular systematics, propagation and seed science and storage; 300,000 vols, 170,000 monographs, 5,000 periodicals, 150,000 pamphlets, 200,000 botanical illustrations, 4,600 collns within archives consisting of 250,000 letters and MSS and registered files; Head of Library, Art and Archives CHRISTOPHER MILLS.

Royal College of Art Library: Kensington Gore, London, SW7 2EU; tel. (20) 7590-4224; e-mail library@rca.ac.uk; internet www.rca .ac.uk; f. 1953; 70,000 vols on the visual arts, history and philosophy of design; history and criticism of the arts; Colour Reference Library: comprehensive colln of books and articles on all aspects of colour; Head of Information and Learning Services PETER HASSELL; Library Man. DARLENE MAXWELL.

Royal College of Music Library: Prince Consort Rd, S Kensington, London, SW7 2BS; tel. (20) 7591-4325; e-mail library@rcm .ac.uk; internet www.rcm.ac.uk/library; f.

1883; admission for reference only; 400,000 vols, incl. MSS and early printed music; Librarian PETER LINNITT.

Royal College of Physicians' Library Archive and Museum Services: 11 St Andrews Pl., Regent's Park, London, NW1 4LE; tel. (20) 3075-1539; e-mail enquiries@ rcplondon.ac.uk; internet www.rcplondon.ac .uk/resources/library; f. 1518; services incl. enquiry service, exhibitions, research facilities, tours; services for fellows and mems incl. loans, expert search and information retrieval; medical education resource centre; 60,000 vols (mostly related to history of medicine, but some on current medical issues), 100 incunabula, 200 linear m of MSS, 30,000 portrait photographs and other pictorial items; spec. collns: 130 books printed before 1501, 4,500 tracts from 17th–19th century, Dorchester colln (3,000 vols), Evan Bedford colln, John Dee colln; Man. JULIE BECKWITH; publs *Munk's Roll* (online, munksroll.rcplondon.ac.uk), *The Royal College of Physicians and its Collections*.

Royal College of Surgeons of England Library: 35–43 Lincoln's Inn Fields, London, WC2A 3PE; tel. (20) 7869-6555; e-mail library@rcseng.ac.uk; internet www.rcseng .ac.uk/library; f. 1800; 100,000 vols of monographs and periodicals, 30,640 pamphlets; Dir THALIA KNIGHT; publs *Annals of The Royal College of Surgeons of England*, FDJ.

Royal College of Veterinary Surgeons Knowledge Library: Belgravia House, 62–64 Horseferry Rd, London, SW1P 2AF; tel. (20) 7202-0752; e-mail library@ rcvsknowledge.org; internet www.rcvslibrary .org.uk; f. 1844; 30,000 vols; Librarian CLARE BOULTON.

Royal Geographical Society (with the Institute of British Geographers) Library: Kensington Gore, London, SW7 2AR; tel. (20) 7591-3044; e-mail enquiries@ rgs.org; internet www.rgs.org; f. 1830; 250,000 books and bound periodicals; 500 current periodicals; map room contains 1m. maps and charts, 3,000 atlases, large selection of gazetteers and expedition reports; picture library of 500,000 images; archives; Prin. Librarian E. M. RAE; Map Curator D. MCNEILL; publs *Area*, *Geographical Journal*, *Transactions*.

Royal Institute of International Affairs Library: Chatham House, 10 St James's Sq., London, SW1Y 4LE; tel. (20) 7957-5723; e-mail library@chathamhouse.org; internet www.chathamhouse.org/library; f. 1920; Chatham House archives; private research library; 75,000 vols, 200 current periodicals, 1,500 journals; Library and Information Services Man. DAVID BATES; publs *International Affairs* (6 a year), *The World Today* (6 a year).

Royal Institution of Great Britain Archives: 21 Albemarle St, London, W1S 4BS; tel. (20) 7409-2992; e-mail archivist@ri.ac.uk; internet www.rigb.org; f. 1799; 25,000 vols on all brs of science, early scientific books and journals especially of 18th and 19th centuries, spec. collns: admin. papers of the Royal Instn and collected papers of associated individuals incl. Michael Faraday, Humphry Davy and William and Lawrence Bragg; Head of Collns and Heritage Prof. FRANK JAMES.

Royal Society Centre for History of Science: 6–9 Carlton House Terrace, London, SW1Y 5AG; tel. (20) 7451-2606; e-mail library@royalsociety.org; internet royalsociety.org/library; f. 1660; 150,000 vols; colln on history of science and scientists, science policy, science education, science and the public; Library Man. RUPERT BAKER; Head of Library and Information Services

KEITH MOORE; publ. *Notes and Records: the Royal Society Journal of the History of Science* (4 a year).

Royal Society of Chemistry Library and Information Centre: Burlington House, Piccadilly, London, W1J 0BA; tel. (20) 7440-3373; e-mail library@rsc.org; internet www .rsc.org; f. 1841; 100,000 vols; Library Operations Specialist KATE BENNETT.

Royal Society of Medicine Library: 1 Wimpole St, London, W1G 0AE; tel. (20) 7290-2940; e-mail library@rsm.ac.uk; internet www.rsm.ac.uk/library; f. 1805; 600,000 vols, 1,200 current periodicals, 10,000 back titles; lending restricted to mems; back-up library to British Library; worldwide mail order photocopy service; historical colln since 1474; medical portrait colln; Dir of Library Services WAYNE SIME; Librarian NICOLA WOOD.

Royal United Services Institute Library of Military History: 61 Whitehall, London, SW1A 2ET; tel. (20) 7930-5854; e-mail library@rusi.org; internet www.rusi.org/ about/library; f. 1831; maintains 3 in-house research depts covering int. security studies, military science and nat. security and resilience; organizes lectures, seminars and confs; 20,000 vols on military history incl. British regimental and unit histories; c. 4,000 biographies, memoirs and personal experiences (published works, the library does not keep MSS or similar documents); books lent to RUSI mems and to other libraries, mems of the public should apply to the librarian for reference access; Librarian TONY PILMER; publs *RUSI Defence Systems* (3 a year), *RUSI Journal* (6 a year), *RUSI Newsbriefs* (6 a year), *Whitehall Papers* (2 a year), *Whitehall Reports* (irregular).

St Bride Library: Bride Lane, Fleet St, London, EC4Y 8EE; tel. (20) 7353-4660; e-mail nigel@sbf.org.uk; internet www .stbride.org; f. 1891, opened 1895; early technical literature, drawings, MSS, prospectuses, patents, printing, papermaking, bookbinding, illustration, graphic design, materials for printing and type founding; organizes exhibitions and lectures; 3 annual confs; printing workshop educational programme; 50,000 books and pamphlets, 3,500 periodical titles; Librarian NIGEL ROCHE; publs *Printing History News* (4 a year), *Ultrabold* (2 a year).

St Paul's Cathedral Library: London, EC4M 8AE; tel. (20) 7246-8342; e-mail library@stpaulscathedral.org.uk; internet www.stpauls.co.uk; f. 1707; 13,500 vols and 11,500 pamphlets; early printed books of theology and Greek and Latin classics, 20 medieval MSS; Librarian JO WISDOM.

School of Oriental and African Studies Library: Univ. of London, Thornhaugh St, Russell Square, London, WC1H 0XG; tel. (20) 7898-4160; e-mail libenquiry@soas.ac.uk; internet www.soas.ac.uk; f. 1916; back-up library to the British Library for loans; 859,000 vols and pamphlets, 4,500 periodicals, 2,700 MSS and archive collections dealing with Asian and African languages, literature, philosophy, religions, history, law, cultural anthropology, art and archaeology, social sciences; Librarian ANNE POULSON.

Science Museum Library: Imperial College Rd, S Kensington, London, SW7 5NH; tel. (20) 7942-4242; e-mail smlinfo@ sciencemuseum.ac.uk; internet www .sciencemuseum.org.uk/library; f. 1883; printed and archive collns; provides access to academics, students, authors, general public and schools; access to Swindon collns by appointment; 500,000 vols; collns housed in London incl. history, biography and social context of all brs of science, technology and medicine, also 400 current journal titles; collns housed in Swindon incl. contemporary science technology and medicine books and journals, published in 15th–20th centuries, reports, directories, trade literature; also at Swindon the Archives colln containing original MSS, letters, company records, drawings, etc., on scientific, technical and medical subjects; Head of Library and Archives NICHOLAS WYATT.

Senate House Library, University of London: Senate House, Malet St, London, WC1E 7HU; tel. (20) 7862-8500; e-mail shl .enquiries@london.ac.uk; internet www .senatehouselibrary.ac.uk; f. 1838; research library principally in the arts, humanities and social sciences, incl. special collns, e.g. Goldsmiths' Library of Economic Literature, Harry Price Colln, Sterling Library, Durning-Lawrence Library, Eliot-Phelips Colln, Bromhead Library, Carlton Shorthand Colln, Porteus Library, Malcolm Morley Theatre Colln and the Libraries of the Canadian and Australian High Commissions; 2m. vols; Dir of Research Library Services MARY NIXON (acting).

Sir John Soane's House and Museum Library: 13 Lincoln's Inn Fields, London, WC2A 3BP; tel. (20) 7440-4251; e-mail library@soane.org.uk; internet www.soane .org; f. 1837; contains Sir John Soane's colln of 8,000 vols on art, antiquities, architecture, classical and gen. literature, architectural drawings, personal and business archive; Librarian Dr STEPHANIE COANE.

Society of Antiquaries Library & Collections: Burlington House, Piccadilly, London, W1J 0BE; tel. (20) 7479-7084; e-mail library@sal.org.uk; internet www.sal.org.uk; f. 1707; 100,000 vols, 650 current periodicals on British and foreign archaeology and history, heraldry, genealogy, etc.; brass rubbings, drawings, early printed books, MSS, paintings, prints, museum objects, seal casts; Head of Library and Collns HEATHER ROWLAND; publ. *Antiquaries Journal* (1 a year).

Southwark Culture, Libraries, Learning and Leisure: 160 Tooley St, London, SE1 2QH; tel. (20) 7525-2000; e-mail southwark .libraries@southwark.gov.uk; internet www .southwark.gov.uk/libraries; 600,000 vols; 12 brs; 1 museum; Head of Culture, Libraries, Learning and Leisure ADRIAN WHITTLE.

Supreme Court Library: Royal Courts of Justice, Ministry of Justice, Strand, London, WC2A 2LL; tel. (20) 7947-6587; internet www.justice.gov.uk; f. 1970; 300,000 vols; spec. collns: Court of Appeal (Civil Div.) Transcripts 1950–; old edns of legal textbooks (in Supreme Court Library—Bar—f. 1883); Librarian J. ROBERTSON.

Sutton Library Service: Central Library, St Nicholas Way, Sutton, Surrey, SM1 1EA; tel. (20) 8770-4740; e-mail sutton.library@ sutton.gov.uk; internet www.sutton.gov.uk; f. 1936; 9 libraries; 316,100 vols, 26,759 audio items, 9,067 visual items; spec. colln: genealogy and heraldry; Exec. Head of Leisure and Libraries COLIN BEECH.

Tower Hamlets Idea Stores: John Onslow House, 1 Ewart Pl., London, E3 5EQ; tel. (20) 7364-4332; e-mail ideastore@towerhamlets .gov.uk; internet www.ideastore.co.uk; f. 1965; local history library; colln of books, CDs and DVDs in Bengali, Chinese, Somali, Urdu and Vietnamese; 627,564 vols; Head of Idea Store JUDITH ST JOHN.

Treasury and Cabinet Office Library: Parliament St, London, SW1P 3AG; tel. (20) 7270-5290; 120,000 vols, 1,500 periodicals; covers economics, finance and public administration; Librarian JEAN CLAYTON.

UCL Ear Institute and Action on Hearing Loss Libraries: 330–336 Gray's Inn Rd, London, WC1X 8EE; tel. (20) 3456-5145; e-mail rnidlib@ucl.ac.uk; internet www.ucl .ac.uk/library/rnidlib.shtml; f. 1911; 18,000 books and 200 current journals on all aspects of deafness, audiology and other communication disorders; Librarian ALEX STAGG.

UCL Library Services: Gower St, London, WC1E 6BT; tel. (20) 7679-7793; e-mail library@ucl.ac.uk; internet www.ucl.ac.uk/ library; f. 1828; libraries incl.: main arts and humanities library, science library, Bartlett Library, Cruciform Library, UCL Institute of Archaeology Library, UCL Ear Institute and RNID libraries at the Royal Nat. Throat, Nose and Ear Hospital, UCL Eastman Dental Institute Library, UCL Institute of Child Health Library, UCL Institute of Neurology, Queen Square Library, UCL Institute of Ophthalmology Library, Institute of Orthopaedics Library, UCL Language and Speech Science Library, Royal Free Medical Library, UCL School of Pharmacy Library, UCL School of Slavonic and East European Studies Library and Information Services, Whittington Library and Information Services; spec. collns: medieval period to present day; 2m. vols, c. 30,000 journals printed and electronic format; Dir PAUL AYRIS.

University of Greenwich, Information and Library Services: Old Royal Naval College, Greenwich, London, SE10 9LS; tel. (20) 8331-9660; internet www.gre.ac.uk/lib; Information Services Man. VIRGINIA MALONE.

University of West London Library: Villiers House, Haven Green, Ealing, London, W5 2NU; tel. (20) 8231-2246; e-mail lib .enq@uwl.ac.uk; internet library.uwl.ac.uk; f. 1992; 2 libraries, main campus library temporarily relocated and the other in the Health Bldg in Brentford; 180,000 vols; Univ. Librarian TIM WALES.

Upper Norwood Joint Library: 39–41 Westow Hill, London, SE19 1TJ; tel. (20) 8670-2551; e-mail info@uppernorwoodlibrary .org; internet www.uppernorwoodlibrary.org; f. 1900; 60,000 vols; collns on the Crystal Palace and its historical background, the Gerald Massey colln, the J. B. Wilson colln; Chief Librarian BRADLEY MILLINGTON.

Vaughan Williams Memorial Library: English Folk Dance and Song Soc., Cecil Sharp House, 2 Regents Park Rd, London, NW1 7AY; tel. (20) 7485-2206; e-mail library@efdss.org; internet www.vwml.org; f. 1930; maintained by English Folk Dance and Song Soc. (q.v.); England's main source of information on traditional song, dance, customs and folk culture; 20,000 vols, MS collns, microfilms, press cuttings, broadsides, 10,000 audiovisual items, 15,000 photographic images; open to public for reference; Library Dir MALCOLM TAYLOR; publs *English Dance and Song (EDS)* (4 a year), *Folk Music Journal* (1 a year).

Victoria and Albert Museum, Library of the: see National Art Library.

Vision Redbridge Leisure and Libraries: Central Library, Clements Rd, Ilford, IG1 1EA; tel. (20) 8708-2420; e-mail central .library@visionrcl.org.uk; internet www2 .redbridge.gov.uk/cms/leisure_and_libraries .aspx; f. 1965; 633,104 vols; Information Heritage Librarian IAN DOWLING (acting).

Waltham Forest Public Libraries: Walthamstow Library, High St, Walthamstow, London, E17 7JN; tel. (20) 8496-5134; e-mail wf.libs@walthamforest.gov.uk; internet www.walthamforest.gov.uk; f. 1893; 448,427 vols; spec. collns: cookery, domestic economy, fiction authors; Librarian CAROLINE RAE.

Wandsworth Public Libraries: Town Hall, Room 223, Wandsworth High St, London, SW18 2PU; tel. (20) 8871-6369; e-mail libraries@wandsworth.gov.uk; internet www.wandsworth.gov.uk/libraries; f. 1883; 11 brs; reference library, 2 music libraries, local history library, home delivery library service; spec. collns: architecture, town planning, European history, geography and travel, occult sciences, local history, early children's books, G. A. Henty; 721,101 vols; Head of Library and Heritage Service ANDREW GREEN.

Warburg Institute Library: Woburn Sq., London, WC1H 0AB; tel. (20) 7862-8949; e-mail warburg.library@sas.ac.uk; internet warburg.sas.ac.uk/library; f. 1922; cultural and intellectual history of Europe from Classical Antiquity to modern times, incl. history of art, literature, science, religion, humanism; houses libraries of the Royal and British Numismatic Socs; 350,000 vols, 1,100 current serials, 450,000 photographs; Librarian Prof. JILL KRAYE; publ. *Journal of the Warburg and Courtauld Institutes* (1 a year).

Wellcome Library: 183 Euston Rd, London, NW1 2BE; tel. (20) 7611-8722; e-mail library@wellcome.ac.uk; internet wellcomelibrary.org; f. 1913, opened to the public in 1949; records medicine and its role in society; includes popular science, biomedical ethics and the public understanding of science; 700,000 vols, ephemera, 55,000 pamphlets, 2,700 periodical titles, 9,000 Western MSS, 12,000 Oriental MSS in 43 languages, 200,000 prints, drawings, photographs, paintings, 700 collns of medical archives, 2,500 films, 700 incunabula; Head of Library Dr SIMON CHAPLIN.

Westminster Abbey Library and Muniment Room: E Cloister, London, SW1P 3PA; tel. (20) 7654-4830; e-mail library@ westminster-abbey.org; internet www .westminster-abbey.org/library-research; f. 1623; 20,000 vols since the 16th century, predominantly theological but also general literature and music; Abbey records and other documents since the 11th century; Librarian and Head of Abbey Collns Dr TONY TROWLES; Keeper of Muniments MATTHEW PAYNE.

The Wiener Library: 29 Russell Sq., London, WC1B 5DP; tel. (20) 7636-7247; e-mail info@wienerlibrary.co.uk; internet www .wienerlibrary.co.uk; f. in Amsterdam in 1933, moved to London 1939; 65,000 vols incl. books and pamphlets; 3,000 periodicals; 2,000 catalogued documents on the Holocaust, anti-Semitism, the Third Reich, Fascism, Neo-Fascism, contemporary German-Jewish history and exile studies; Dir BEN BARKOW; Archivist HOWARD FALKSOHN.

Women's Library: 25 Old Castle St, London, E1 7NT; tel. (20) 7955-7229; e-mail library.enquiries@lse.ac.uk; internet www .lse.ac.uk/library; f. 1926 as London Society for Women's Service Library, present status 1977; attached to London School of Economics; documents changing role of women in society; women's history and women's contemporary lives in the UK; suffrage collns; organizes exhibitions; 60,000 vols, 3,500 periodicals, 5,000 museum objects, 300 web archives, 500 personal and organizational archives; Collns Man. TERESA DOHERTY.

Zoological Society of London Library: Regent's Park, London, NW1 4RY; tel. (20) 7449-6293; e-mail library@zsl.org; internet www.zsl.org; f. 1826; library; archives of Zoological Soc. of London; information about zoos, animals and their conservation; 200,000 vols, 5,000 journal titles, incl. 1,300 current journals; Librarian ANN SYLPH; Archivist MICHAEL PALMER; publs *Animal Conser-*

vation, International Zoo Yearbook, Journal of Zoology.

Loughborough

Loughborough University—Pilkington Library: Loughborough, LE11 3TU; tel. (1509) 222360; e-mail library@lboro.ac.uk; internet www.lboro.ac.uk; f. 1909; incl. the Univ. Archives; 550,000 vols, 4,000 periodicals; Univ. Librarian RUTH JENKINS.

Luton

Luton Cultural Services Trust: Luton Libraries, St George's Sq., Luton, LU1 2NG; tel. (1582) 547440; e-mail libraryinfo@lutonculture.com; internet www.lutonlibraries.co.uk; Luton Libraries is now part of Luton Cultural Services Trust; Dir of Libraries NARINDER BHOURLAY.

Maidenhead

Royal Borough of Windsor and Maidenhead Libraries: Maidenhead Library, St Ives Rd, Maidenhead, SL6 1QU; tel. (1628) 796969; e-mail maidenhead.library@rbwm.gov.uk; Head of Library, Arts and Heritage MARK TAYLOR.

Maidstone

Kent Libraries, Registration and Archives: Kent History and Library Centre, James Whatman Way, Maidstone, ME14 1LQ; tel. (1622) 696438; e-mail libraries.informationservices@kent.gov.uk; internet www.kent.gov.uk/libraries; f. 1921; 70,000 vols; Head of Libraries and Archives CATH ANLEY.

Manchester

Chetham's Library: Long Millgate, Manchester, M3 1SB; tel. (161) 834-7961; e-mail librarian@chethams.org.uk; internet www.chethams.org.uk; f. 1653 as a free public reference library; local history records; 100,000 vols, incl. 60,000 vols published before 1851; spec. collns: 40 medieval MSS, Belle Vue Zoo and Gardens archive, numerous ephemera of bookplates, postcards, chapbooks, broadsides, ballads, theatre programmes, posters, trade cards and bill heads; Librarian Dr MICHAEL POWELL.

University of Manchester Library: Oxford Rd, Manchester, M13 9PP; tel. (161) 275-3751; internet www.library.manchester.ac.uk; f. 2004 by merger of the John Rylands University Library of Manchester (f. 1972 by merger of John Rylands Library—f. 1900—with Manchester University Library—f. 1851) and the Library of UMIST (f. 1824); 4.5m. printed books, 1m. MSS or archival items, 800,000 titles on microform, 9,000 current serials, 500,000 ebooks, 41,000 ejournals; numerous spec. collns, Althorp Library of 2nd Earl Spencer and manuscript portion of Bibliotheca Lindesiana, containing 220,000 books printed before 1801, incl. 4,500 incunabula and 1,500 aldines; Univ. Librarian and Dir of John Rylands Library JAN WILKINSON.

Manchester Libraries: Central Library, St Peter's Sq., Manchester, M2 5PD; tel. (161) 234-1900; e-mail libraries@manchester.gov.uk; internet www.manchester.gov.uk/libraries; f. 1852; regional local studies and archives centre, lending and reference libraries, business and information library, Henry Watson Music Library, exhibition spaces, computer facilities and performance space; 24 community libraries; prison library service; 2,430,000 vols, 54,000 audiovisual items; spec. collns incl. the Newman Flower, Henry Watson and Gaskell; Head of Libraries and Archives NEIL MACINNES.

Manchester Metropolitan University Library: Sir Kenneth Green Library, All Saints, Manchester Metropolitan University, Manchester, M15 6BH; tel. (161) 247-6104; internet www.library.mmu.ac.uk; f. 1970; 867,000 vols; Librarian GILL BARRY.

Matlock

Derbyshire Libraries and Heritage Division: Matlock Library, Steep Turnpike, Matlock, DE4 3DP; tel. (1629) 533190; e-mail derbyshire.libraries@derbyshire.gov.uk; internet www.derbyshire.gov.uk/libraries; f. 1923; 46 brs; 1m. vols; Strategic Dir of Health and Communities DAVID LOWE.

Merthyr Tydfil

Merthyr Tydfil Libraries: Central Library, High St, Merthyr Tydfil, CF47 8AF; tel. (1685) 353480; e-mail library.services@merthyr.gov.uk; internet www.libraries.merthyr.gov.uk; f. 1935; 163,210 vols; local history colln; Prin. Librarian JANE SELLWOOD.

Middlesbrough

Middlesbrough Libraries: Central Library, Centre Sq., Middlesbrough, TS1 2AY; tel. (1642) 729001; e-mail reference_library@middlesbrough.gov.uk; internet www.middlesbrough.gov.uk/libraries; 11 brs; 400,000 vols; Library Services Man. JEN BRITTAIN (acting).

Teesside University Library & Information Services: Library & Information Services, Borough Rd, Middlesbrough, TS1 3BA; tel. (1642) 342100; e-mail libraryhelp@tees.ac.uk; internet lis.tees.ac.uk; 290,000 vols; Dir LIZ JOLLY.

Milton Keynes

Milton Keynes Council Libraries: Milton Keynes Central Library, 555 Silbury Blvd, Saxon Gate East, Central Milton Keynes, MK9 3HL; tel. (1908) 254050; e-mail central.library@milton-keynes.gov.uk; internet www.milton-keynes.gov.uk/libraries; f. 1981; Reference and Information Librarian AGGIE O'HARA.

Open University Library Services: Walton Hall, Milton Keynes, MK7 6AA; tel. (1908) 659001; e-mail lib-help@open.ac.uk; internet www.open.ac.uk/library; f. 1969; 206,000 books, 450 current periodicals, 50,000 ejournal titles; Dir for Library Services NICKY WHITSED.

Mold

Flintshire Library and Information Service: County Hall, Mold, CH7 6NW; tel. (1352) 704400; e-mail libraries@flintshire.gov.uk; internet www.flintshire.gov.uk/libraries; f. 1996; 13 libraries, mobile library, library for the housebound; spec. collns: Arthurian literature, local studies; Head of Culture and Leisure LAWRENCE RAWSTHORNE.

Morpeth

Northumberland County Library: Gas House Lane, Morpeth, NE61 1TA; tel. (1670) 500390; e-mail mylibrary@northumberland.gov.uk; internet www.northumberland.gov.uk/default.aspx?page=749; f. 1924; 34 brs, 4 mobile libraries; 635,000 vols; spec. collns: local history, vocal scores, cinema, drama, Northern Poetry Library; Service Man. for Libraries JUDITH WALKER.

Newbury

West Berkshire Libraries: Newbury Central Library, The Wharf, Newbury, RG14 5AU; tel. (1635) 519900; e-mail newburylibrary@westberks.gov.uk; internet www.westberks.gov.uk/libraries; f. 1998; 9 brs and 2 mobile libraries; Library Services Man. MIKE BROOK; Information & Local Studies Librarian PAUL GAHAN.

Newcastle upon Tyne

Newcastle Libraries and Information Service: City Library, Charles Avison Bldg, 33 New Bridge St West, Newcastle upon Tyne, NE1 8AX; tel. (191) 277-4100; e-mail information@newcastle.gov.uk; internet www.newcastle.gov.uk/libraries; f. 1880; extensive local and family history resources; Thomas Bewick Colln (first edns, engravings, original woodblocks, Bewick's worktable and toolbox), Thomlinson Library (4,351 vols from the 16th, 17th and 18th centuries, mainly theological); City Library and 17 brs; 600,000 vols, 50,000 audiovisual items; Service Man. ANDREW SCROGHAM.

Newcastle University The Robinson Library: Newcastle upon Tyne, NE1 7RU; tel. (191) 222-7662; e-mail lib-readerservices@ncl.ac.uk; internet www.ncl.ac.uk/library; f. 1871 as Library of Durham College of Physical Science; 1.2m. vols, 10,000 periodicals (electronic and print); spec. collns incl. Pybus (medical history), Robert White, Gertrude Bell, Runciman Papers, Trevelyan Papers, Catherine Cookson, Wallis, Butler, Booktrust (children's literature); Librarian WAYNE CONNOLLY.

Newport (Gwent)

Newport City Libraries: Central Library, John Frost Sq., Newport, NP20 1PA; tel. (1633) 656656; e-mail central.library@newport.gov.uk; internet www.newport.gov.uk/libraries; 12 brs; Community Learning and Libraries Man. GILL JOHN.

Newport (Isle of Wight)

Isle of Wight Council Library Services: 5 Mariners Way, Somerton Industrial Estate, Cowes, PO31 8PD; tel. (1983) 203880; e-mail libraries@iow.gov.uk; internet www.iwight.com/thelibrary; f. 1904; 6 brs; Head of Libraries and Information Services ROB JONES.

Newtownabbey

University of Ulster Library: Shore Rd, Newtownabbey, BT37 0QB; tel. (28) 9036-6399; internet library.ulster.ac.uk; f. 1985; campus libraries at Belfast, Coleraine, Jordanstown and Londonderry; 698,349 vols (all campuses); Univ. Librarian JANET PEDEN (acting)..

Campus Libraries:

Belfast Campus Library, University of Ulster: York St, Belfast, BT15 1ED; tel. (28) 9536-7268; e-mail illbfast@ulster.ac.uk; internet library.ulster.ac.uk/info/belfast.php; 56,561 vols, mostly arts-related: painting, history of art and architecture, sculpture, design, fashion, film and photography, museum studies, Irish language; Man. MARION KHORSHIDIAN.

Coleraine Campus Library: Cromore Rd, Coleraine, BT52 1SA; tel. (28) 7012-4345; e-mail illcol@ulster.ac.uk; internet library.ulster.ac.uk/info/coleraine.php; 218,795 vols; spec. collns: First and Second World Wars, Henry Davis Gift of incunabula, Henry Morris Colln of Irish material, Stelfox natural history colln; Man. STEPHANIE McLAUGHLIN.

Jordanstown Campus Library: Shore Rd, Newtownabbey, BT37 0QB; tel. (28) 9036-6399; e-mail illjord@ulster.ac.uk; internet library.ulster.ac.uk/info/jordanstown.php; 204,704 vols; spec. collns: American and women's studies, UK, USA and Irish radical newspapers and periodicals on microfilm; Man. LAURA MILLS.

Magee Campus Library: Northland Rd, Londonderry, BT48 7JL; tel. (28) 7167-5264; e-mail illmagee@ulster.ac.uk; internet library.ulster.ac.uk/info/magee .php; 102,067 vols; American studies, dance, drama, history, informatics, law and social work, modern languages, music; Irish Colln of 5,400 books and 800 pamphlets, rare books colln; Derry & Raphoe Diocesan Library; Man. CIARAN CREGAN.

Northallerton

North Yorkshire Libraries and Archives: County Library Headquarters, 21 Grammar School Lane, Northallerton, DL6 1DF; tel. (1609) 533800; e-mail libraries@ northyorks.gov.uk; internet www.northyorks .gov.uk/libraries; 42 brs, mobile library service; 1,059,000 vols; Head of Libraries and Community Services JULIE BLAISDALE.

Northampton

Northamptonshire Library Service: Northamptonshire Central Library, Abington St, Northampton, NN1 2BA; tel. (1604) 237955; e-mail centlib@northamptonshire .gov.uk; internet www.northamptonshire.gov .uk/libraries; f. 1927; 36 brs, 6 mobile libraries; 1,224,000 vols, 107,000 sound recordings and video cassettes; spec. collns: Beeby Thompson Colln, H. E. Bates Colln, Henry Dryden Colln, Mary Pendered Colln, Philip Doddridge Colln; Library Man. CARL DORNEY.

Norwich

Norfolk Library and Information Service: Norfolk and Norwich Millennium Library, The Forum, Millennium Plain, Norwich, NR2 1AW; tel. (1603) 774774; e-mail libraries@norfolk.gov.uk; internet www.norfolk.gov.uk/libraries; f. 1925, reorganized 1974; 47 libraries incl. Norfolk and Norwich Millennium Library, 14 mobile libraries, services to hospitals, prisons, residential settings, school library service, home library service; 1,153,295 vols; Head of Libraries and Information JENNIFER HOLLAND.

Norwich Cathedral Library: 12 The Close, Norwich, NR1 4DH; tel. (1603) 218443; e-mail library@cathedral.org.uk; internet www.cathedral.org.uk/learning; medieval monastic (Benedictine) foundation; privately managed by Norwich Cathedral; 20,000 vols modern theology loan colln; 8,000 vols historic colln, some incunabula and MSS; houses 450 vols of the Swaffham Parochial Church Library and other parish books; spec. collns: Brian Runnett Music Library, Norwich Diocesan Asscn of Ringers Colln; Canon Librarian Dr P. DOLL; Librarian GUDRUN WARREN.

University of East Anglia Library Services: Norwich Research Park, Norwich, NR4 7TJ; tel. (1603) 592993; e-mail lib .helpdesk@uea.ac.uk; internet www.uea.ac .uk/is/lib; f. 1962; 725,000 vols, 7,000 journal titles, 10,000 CDs; spec. collns: illustrated books (600 vols), Broke colln (150 vols on 18th- and 19th-century military science), Abbott colln (1,500 vols), Ketton-Cremer colln (1,000 vols), Kimber colln (500 vols), Oriental art books (1,350 vols); Library Dir NICK LEWIS.

Nottingham

Nottingham City Libraries and Information Service: Central Library, Angel Row, Nottingham, NG1 6HP; tel. (115) 915-2828; e-mail enquiryline@nottinghamcity.gov.uk; internet www.nottinghamcity.gov.uk/ libraries; f. 1868; 480,000 vols, 33,000 sound recordings; spec. collns incl. local history, D. H. Lawrence, Byron and Robin Hood; Sr Devt Librarian PHIL SELLARS.

University of Nottingham Libraries: King's Meadow Campus, Lenton Lane, Nottingham, NG7 2NR; tel. (115) 846-8555; e-mail is-admin-team@nottingham.ac.uk; internet www.nottingham.ac.uk/library; f. 1881; 1.3m. vols and pamphlets, 23,000 current periodicals; MSS and archives (Portland, Newcastle, Middleton, Manvers) 3m. items; spec. collns incl. D. H. Lawrence, early children's books, French Revolution, meteorology, ornithology; incl. Hallward Library (arts, social sciences and law), George Green Library of Science and Engineering, James Cameron Gifford Library of Agricultural and Food Sciences (Sutton Bonington), Greenfield Medical Library, Music Library, Business Library and Djanogly Learning Resources Centre (education and computer science); Dir CAROLINE WILLIAMS.

Oakham

Rutland Library Service: Oakham Library, Catmos St, Oakham, LE15 6HW; tel. (1572) 722918; e-mail libraries@rutland .gov.uk; internet www.rutland.gov.uk/ libraries; f. 1997; 55,327 vols; Head of Culture and Leisure ROBERT CLAYTON; Library and Heritage Man. EMILY BARWELL.

Omagh

Western Education & Library Board: 1 Hospital Rd, Omagh, BT79 0AW; tel. (28) 8241-1411; e-mail info@welbni.org; internet www.welbni.org; provides library services in the council areas of Omagh, Fermanagh, Londonderry, Strabane and Limavady; Chief Exec. BARRY MULHOLLAND.

Oxford

Bodleian Library: Broad St, Oxford, OX1 3BG; tel. (1865) 277000; e-mail communications@bodleian.ox.ac.uk; internet www.bodleian.ox.ac.uk/bodley; f. 1602; legal deposit library; the principal library of Oxford Univ.; incl. the Old Library, the Radcliffe Camera, Weston Library and the following dependent libraries: Radcliffe Science Library, Social Science Library, Bodleian Law Library, Indian Institute Library, Bodleian Library for Commonwealth and African Studies (at Rhodes House), Vere Harmsworth Library (for the history of the United States), Bodleian Japanese Library, Philosophy Library, Oriental Institute Library and Institute for Chinese Studies Library; 11m. vols; Librarian RICHARD OVENDEN; publ. *The Bodleian Library Record* (2 a year).

Oxfordshire Libraries Headquarters: Customer Services Unit, Library Support Services, Holton, Oxford, OX33 1QQ; tel. (1865) 810240; e-mail librarycustomerservicesunit@oxfordshire .gov.uk; internet www.oxfordshire.gov.uk/ libraries; 43 static libraries, 5 mobile libraries; 930,000 vols, 40,000 scores, 18,000 sound recordings, 38,000 DVDs; Library Service Man. JILLIAN SOUTHWELL.

Sackler Library: St John St, Oxford, OX1 2LG; tel. (1865) 288190; e-mail sac-enquiries@bodleian.ox.ac.uk; internet www.saclib.ox.ac.uk; f. 2001, fmrly Ashmolean Library (since 1683); 270,000 vols; archaeology, ancient history, ancient Near Eastern studies, Byzantine studies, numismatics, classical languages and literature, Western art and architecture; special collns incl. Grenfell and Hunt Papyrological Library, Griffith Egyptological Library, Haverfield and Richmond Archives and original documentation of principal archaeological expeditions and explorations and classification of artefacts; Librarian-in-Charge Dr G. PIDDOCK.

Taylor Institution Library: Oxford Univ. Library Services, St Giles', Oxford, OX1 3NA; tel. (1865) 278158; e-mail tay-enquiries@ bodleian.ox.ac.uk; internet www.bodleian.ox .ac.uk/taylor; f. 1847; 600,000 vols; medieval and modern continental European (and related) languages and literature (esp. French, German, Italian, Spanish, Portuguese, incl. the languages and literature of Latin America, the literature of Canada, and North and sub-Saharan Africa); Dutch, Yiddish, Celtic, Afrikaans, Romanian; linguistics and philology; spec. collns incl.: Voltaire and the French Enlightenment; Dante and Futurist holdings; the G. B. Guarini colln; Golden Age literature; literature of the former German Democratic Republic; Luther *Flugschriften* and the Fiedler colln; letters and papers of Modern European writers; and the Strachan colln of *livres d'artistes*; Slavonic, East European and Modern Greek languages and literature housed separately; Operations Man. FRANK EGERTON.

University of Oxford Libraries:.

Constituent Libraries:

Balliol College Library: Oxford, OX1 3BJ; tel. (1865) 277709; e-mail library@ balliol.ox.ac.uk; internet www.balliol.ox.ac .uk/library; f. 1263; 90,000 vols, 468 MSS; Librarian NAOMI TILEY.

Brasenose College Library: Oxford, OX1 4AJ; tel. (1865) 277827; e-mail library@bnc.ox.ac.uk; internet www.bnc.ox .ac.uk; f. 1509; 60,000 vols; Fellow Librarian Dr E. H. BISPHAM; College Librarian LIZ KAY.

Christ Church Library: Oxford, OX1 1DP; tel. (1865) 276169; e-mail library@ chch.ox.ac.uk; internet www.chch.ox.ac .uk; f. 1546; 130,000 vols.

Codrington Library (All Souls College): Oxford, OX1 4AL; tel. (1865) 279318; e-mail codrington.library@ all-souls.ox.ac.uk; internet www.all-souls .ox.ac.uk; f. 1710; 178,000 vols; spec. collns: medieval and modern history, military history, strategic studies and law; Librarian Prof. I. MACLEAN.

Corpus Christi College Library: Oxford, OX1 4JF; tel. (1865) 276744; e-mail library.staff@ccc.ox.ac.uk; internet www.ccc.ox.ac.uk/library-and-archives; f. 1517; 80,000 vols, MSS; spec. collns: incunabula, early English printed books, 17th- and 18th-century Italian books, English, French and German books on 19th-century philosophy; Fellow Librarian Dr. H. MOORE; Librarian JOANNA SNELLING.

Exeter College Library: Oxford, OX1 3DP; tel. (1865) 279657; e-mail library@ exeter.ox.ac.uk; f. 1314; library open for lending to members of Exeter College only; 40,000 vols on open shelves, 35,000 vols in spec. collns; College Librarian JOANNA BOWRING.

Green Templeton College Library: Oxford, OX2 6HG; tel. (1865) 274770; e-mail library@green.ox.ac.uk; internet library.green.ox.ac.uk; f. 1979; 10,000 vols; Librarian GILL EDWARDS.

Hertford College Library: Oxford, OX1 3BW; tel. (1865) 279409; e-mail library@ hertford.ox.ac.uk; internet www.hertford .ox.ac.uk; 50,000 vols; 17th-century colln from Magdalen Hall (forerunner of Hertford College); Fellow Librarian Dr O. NOBLE WOOD; Librarian KIRSTY TAYLOR.

Jesus College Library: Oxford, OX1 3DW; tel. (1865) 279704; e-mail librarian@jesus.ox.ac.uk; internet www .jesus.ox.ac.uk/library; f. 1571; 65,000 vols, incl. periodicals; Celtic colln; Fellows' Library (f. 1571): 12,000 early printed books, 150 MSS; spec. collns: library of Lord Herbert of Cherbury, material relating to T. E. Lawrence (of Arabia); Meyricke Library (f. 1865); Fellow Librarian Dr J. MAGORRIAN; College Librarian OWEN MCKNIGHT; Archivist CHRIS JEENS.

Keble College Library: Oxford, OX1 3PG; tel. (1865) 272797; e-mail library@ keble.ox.ac.uk; internet www.keble.ox.ac .uk; f. 1876; 40,000 vols in working library; spec. collns: medieval MSS, incunabula and early printed books, Brooke colln, Millard colln, Hatchett-Jackson colln, Port-Royal, John Keble's own library, part of Henry Liddon's library, 19th-century archive material; Librarian M. M. SZURKO.

Lincoln College Library: Oxford, OX1 3DR; tel. (1865) 279831; e-mail library@ lincoln.ox.ac.uk; internet www.lincoln.ox .ac.uk/library; f. 1427; 40,000 vols; Librarian F. M. PIDDOCK.

Magdalen College Library: Oxford, OX1 4AU; tel. (1865) 276045; e-mail library@ magd.ox.ac.uk; internet www.magd.ox.ac .uk/college_life/libraries_and_archives .shtml; f. 1458; 120,000 vols; spec. collns: 16th- to 18th-century books, late medieval English history, late medieval MS books, early printed botanical books and medical books; Fellow Librarian Dr CHRISTINE Y. FERDINAND.

Merton College Library: Oxford, OX1 4JD; tel. (1865) 276380; e-mail library@ merton.ox.ac.uk; internet www.merton.ox .ac.uk/library-and-archives; f. 1264; 70,000 vols; Librarian Dr JULIA WALWORTH.

New College Library: Holywell St, Oxford, OX1 3BN; tel. (1865) 279580; e-mail naomi.vanloo@new.ox.ac.uk; internet www.new.ox.ac.uk/ library-and-archives; f. 1379; 100,000 vols; spec. collns: medieval MSS, incunabula, early archives, modern papers of Milner Colln (deposited in Bodleian Library); Librarian NAOMI VAN LOO; publ. *New College Notes*.

Nuffield College Library: Oxford, OX1 1NF; tel. (1865) 278550; e-mail librarian@ nuffield.ox.ac.uk; internet www.nuffield.ox .ac.uk/library; f. 1937; postgraduate research library in the social sciences covering politics, int. relations, sociology and economics; spec. collns: modern political MSS, labour history, trade unions, political parties, William Cobbett, Daniel Defoe, William Morris, Lord Nuffield; 200,000 vols; Librarian ELIZABETH MARTIN.

Oriel College Library: Oxford, OX1 4EW; tel. (1865) 276558; e-mail library@ oriel.ox.ac.uk; f. 1326; 100,000 vols; spec. colln of personages who attended Oriel College; Librarian MARJORY SZURKO.

Pembroke College, McGowin Library: Oxford, OX1 1DW; tel. (1865) 276409; e-mail library@pmb.ox.ac.uk; internet www.pmb.ox.ac.uk; f. 1624; 40,000 vols; Chandler colln of Aristotelia; Librarian LUCIE WALKER.

Queen's College Library: High St, Oxford, OX1 4AW; tel. (1865) 279130; e-mail library@queens.ox.ac.uk; internet www.queens.ox.ac.uk/library; f. 1341; 150,000 vols; Librarian A. J. SAVILLE.

St Edmund Hall Library: Queen's Lane, Oxford, OX1 4AR; tel. (1865) 279062; e-mail book.loans@seh.ox.ac.uk; internet www.seh.ox.ac.uk/about-college/library; f. 1970; 45,000 vols; spec. collns: Emden (naval and military history), Aularian (Hall members' publs), John Oldham, Thomas Hearne; Librarian BLANCA MARTIN.

St John's College Library: Oxford, OX1 3JP; tel. (1865) 277300; e-mail library@sjc .ox.ac.uk; internet www.sjc.ox.ac.uk/385/ library-and-archives; f. 1598; 80,000 vols; spec. collns incl. 400 MSS (200 Medieval); 20,000 early printed books; archives of papers of Robert Graves, A.E. Housman and Spike Milligan; Librarian STEWART TILEY.

Trinity College Library: Oxford, OX1 3BH; tel. (1865) 279863; e-mail alison .felstead@trinity.ox.ac.uk; internet www .trinity.ox.ac.uk/college/library; Librarian ALISON FELSTEAD.

University College Library: Oxford, OX1 4BH; tel. (1865) 276621; e-mail library@univ.ox.ac.uk; internet www.univ .ox.ac.uk/content/libraries-and-archives; f. 1249; 60,000 vols, 200 MSS; spec. collns: Attlee Papers and Robert Ross Memorial Colln, are deposited in the Bodleian Library (see above); collns housed on site incl. the Browne Colln and the Alport Colln; Librarian ELIZABETH ADAMS.

Wadham College Library: Oxford, OX1 3PN; tel. (1865) 277914; e-mail library@ wadh.ox.ac.uk; internet www.wadham.ox .ac.uk/about-wadham/library; f. 1610; 55,000 vols; spec. collns: 16th-century theology, 17th-century science; Persian history and literature; Fellow Librarian Prof. R. W. FIDDIAN; Librarian TIM KIRTLEY.

Worcester College Library: Oxford, OX1 2HB; tel. (1865) 278354; internet www.worc.ox.ac.uk/library; f. 1714; 75,000 vols; spec. collns: Clarke Papers (Civil War and Commonwealth documents), architectural books and drawings (Inigo Jones, Hawksmoor), English poetry and drama from 1550–1750, Pottinger colln of 19th-century pamphlets, 17th- and 18th-century print colln; Librarian Dr JOANNA PARKER.

Paisley

Paisley Campus Library, University of West of Scotland: Paisley Campus, Paisley, PA1 2BE; tel. (141) 848-3758; e-mail library@ uws.ac.uk; internet www.uws.ac.uk/library; holds the spec. collns of Univ. of West of Scotland, incl. aeronautical history, Ayrshire Sound Archive, Burgh Records, Colour Chemistry Archive, Community Relations Council (CRC) West of Scotland Archive, Hugh MacDiarmid Colln, Hugh McMahon European Parliament papers, Janey Buchan Parliamentary papers, Konrad Hopkins Collns, local history, maps of Scottish Railways Archive 1839–1924, Penguin Specials Series, Scottish Poetry Library, Scottish Schools Essay Competition Archive; 12,114 online journals; Campus Librarian PHILOMENA MILLAR.

Renfrewshire Libraries: Central Library, 68 High St, Paisley, PA1 2BB; tel. (141) 840-3003; e-mail libraries.els@renfrewshire.gov .uk; internet www.renfrewshire.gov.uk/ libraries; 13 libraries, incl. Paisley Central Reference Library; toy library; 2 mobile libraries; 321,500 vols, 29,000 audiovisual items; Libraries Man. JENIFER MCFARLANE (acting).

Peterborough

Peterborough Cathedral Archives & Library: c/o Cathedral Office, Minster Precincts, Peterborough, PE1 1XS; tel. (1733) 355315; e-mail library@ peterborough-cathedral.org.uk; internet www.peterborough-cathedral.org.uk/the-cathedral-archives-library.html; f. c. 1672; open to only researchers by appointment; 4,500 vols, 60 incunabula (books and MSS printed before 1800 are now deposited in the Cambridge University Library, except those

of local concern); Librarian Canon JACK HIGHAM.

Peterborough Libraries and Archives: Peterborough Central Library, Broadway, Peterborough, PE1 1RX; tel. (1733) 864280; e-mail libraryenquiries@ vivacity-peterborough.com; internet www .peterborough.gov.uk/libraries; f. 1892; 10 brs, 2 mobile libraries; Library Service Man. HEATHER WALTON.

Plymouth

Plymouth Library and Information Services: Central Library, Drake Circus, Plymouth, PL4 8AL; tel. (1752) 305900; e-mail library@plymouth.gov.uk; internet www .plymouth.gov.uk/libraries; 16 brs; City Librarian ALASDAIR MACNAUGHTAN.

Pontypool

Torfaen Libraries: Pontypool Library, Hanbury Rd, Pontypool, NP4 6JL; tel. (1495) 766160; e-mail pontypool.library@ torfaen.gov.uk; internet www.torfaen.gov.uk/ libraries; 3 brs, 1 mobile service; 110,000 vols; Information Man. CHRISTINE GEORGE.

Poole

Borough of Poole Libraries: Poole Central Library, Dolphin Centre, Poole, BH15 1QE; tel. (1202) 262424; e-mail libraries@poole.gov .uk; internet www.boroughofpoole.com/ libraries; 10 brs, mobile library; 152,195 vols; Head of Service KEVIN MCERLANE.

Port Talbot

Neath Port Talbot Libraries: Reginald St, Velindre, Port Talbot, SA13 1YY; tel. (1639) 899829; e-mail npt.libhq@neath-porttalbot .gov.uk; internet www.npt.gov.uk/libraries; f. 1996; 17 brs, 2 mobile libraries; 391,000 vols; Co-Librarian WAYNE JOHN.

Porth

Rhondda Cynon Taff Library Service: Penygraig Library, Penygraig, CF40 1LA; tel. (1443) 431309; e-mail penygraig.library@ rhondda-cynon-taff.gov.uk; internet www .rctcbc.gov.uk/libraries; f. 1996; 27 brs, 4 mobile libraries; 550,000 vols; Head of Libraries ROS WILLIAMS.

Portsmouth

Portsmouth City Council library Services: Central Library, Guildhall Sq., Portsmouth, PO1 2DX; tel. (23) 9281-9311; e-mail libraries@portsmouthcc.gov.uk; internet www.portsmouth.gov.uk/learning/libraries .html; f. 1976; 9 brs, 3 mobile libraries; spec. collns: Charles Dickens and Arthur Conan Doyle; Library and Archive Services Man. LINDY ELLIOTT (acting).

University of Portsmouth Library: Cambridge Rd, Portsmouth, P01 2ST; tel. (23) 9284-3228; e-mail elibrary@port.ac.uk; internet www.port.ac.uk/library; print colln incl. books, journals, dissertations and theses, map library, rare book colln, Parliamentary Papers, Univ. Archives; European Documentation Centre; 600,000 vols; Univ. Librarian ROISIN GWYER.

Preston

Lancashire Libraries: East Cliff, POB 162, Preston, PR1 3EA; tel. (1772) 534008; e-mail library@lancashire.gov.uk; internet www .lancashire.gov.uk/libraries; f. 1924; 74 brs, 8 mobile libraries; 3,018,000 vols; Head of Library Service TRACEY WYKE.

Reading

Reading Libraries: Central Library, Abbey Sq., Reading, RG1 3BQ; tel. (118) 901-5950; e-mail info@readinglibraries.org.uk; internet www.reading.gov.uk/libraries; f. 1883; 7 brs, mobile library; Local Studies Library; 280,000 vols; Dir for Environment, Culture and Sport AMAR DAVE (acting).

University of Reading Library: Whiteknights, POB 233, Reading, RG6 6AE; tel. (118) 378-8770; e-mail library@reading.ac.uk; internet www.reading.ac.uk/library; f. 1892; 1.1m. catalogued items, 29,000 current periodical subscriptions, 28,000 eperiodicals; Univ. Museums and Spec. Collns Service gives access to MLA Designated Collns of British Publishers' Archives and material by and about Samuel Beckett; also Overstone Library, Stenton Library on English history, Cole Library on early zoology, Finzi collns of music and English poetry, Turner Colln of French Revolution pamphlets, Stendhal Colln, agricultural history, children's books, papers of Lord and Lady Astor; Univ. Librarian JULIA MUNRO.

Runcorn

Halton Libraries: Halton Lea, Runcorn, WA7 2PF; tel. (151) 511-7744; e-mail haltonlea.library@halton.gov.uk; internet kohalibrary.halton.gov.uk; f. 1998; 4 brs, mobile library; Librarian SALLY SHAW.

Ruthin

Denbighshire Libraries and Archives: The Old Gaol, 46 Clwyd St, Ruthin, LL15 1HP; tel. (1824) 708250; e-mail library.services@denbighshire.gov.uk; internet www.denbighshire.gov.uk; 8 libraries, mobile library, home library service; 219,260 vols; spec. collns: Welsh music, local history; Head of Libraries R. ARWYN JONES.

St Andrews

University of St Andrews Library: North St, St Andrews, KY16 9TR; tel. (1334) 462283; e-mail library@st-andrews.ac.uk; internet www.st-andrews.ac.uk/library; f. 1612; 1m. vols, MSS, maps and numerous spec. collns, incl. Donaldson (classics and education), J. D. Forbes (science), Von Hügel (theology and philosophy), 200,000 early and rare printed vols, MSS holdings and photographic colln, 33,900 ejournals; Univ. Librarian and Dir for Library Services JOHN MACCOLL.

Salford

University of Salford Library: Clifford Whitworth Library, The Crescent, Salford, M5 4WT; tel. (161) 295-5535; e-mail library@salford.ac.uk; internet www.salford.ac.uk/library; f. 1896; 600,000 vols, 400,000 ebooks, 35,000 ejournals, 600,000 misc. items; spec. collns: Bartington Hall Papers, Duke of Bridgewater Archive, Robert Dockray Colln, Stanley Houghton Colln; Univ. Photographic Colln; Univ. Librarian JULIE BERRY.

Salisbury

Salisbury Cathedral Library and Archives: The Cathedral, Wyndham House, 65 The Close, Salisbury, SP1 2EN; e-mail library@salcath.co.uk; internet www.salisburycathedral.org.uk/learning/library-and-archives; f. 11th century; contains printed books and medieval MSS; open only to bona fide research students by appointment; Canon Chancellor Rev. EDWARD PROBERT; Librarian SUZANNE EWARD.

Sheffield

Sheffield Hallam University Library: Student and Learning Centre, City Campus, Howard St, Sheffield, S1 1WB; tel. (114) 225-3333; e-mail learning.centre@shu.ac.uk; internet library.shu.ac.uk; 520,000 vols, 38,700 ebooks, 50,590 ejournal titles, 42,300 audiovisual items; Dir NUALA DEVLIN.

Sheffield Libraries and Archives: Central Library, Surrey St, Sheffield, S1 1XZ; tel. (114) 273-4712; e-mail libraries@sheffield.gov.uk; internet www.sheffield.gov.uk/libraries; f. 1856; 29 community libraries, mobile library; 915,000 vols (excluding MSS); local spec. collns incl. 19th-century periodicals, botanical illustrations, climbing library, patents, standards and the World Metal Index; central library (incl. private press books, books printed in England 1765–79); business, science and technology standards, local studies, circulation services (incl. Whitworth Colln of organ books, Climbing colln, Alan Rowse colln), Sheffield Archives (incl. Strafford papers, Edmund Burke papers, Edward Carpenter papers, Fairbank map colln); Head of Libraries, Archives and Information Services ANDREW MILROY (acting).

University of Sheffield Library: Western Bank, Sheffield, S10 2TN; tel. (114) 222-7200; e-mail library@sheffield.ac.uk; internet www.shef.ac.uk/library; f. 1905; 1.4m. vols; spec. collns: Sir Charles Firth's colln of 17th-century tracts and 19th-century broadside ballads, Samuel Hartlib Papers, papers of Sir Hans Krebs (FRS and Nobel Laureate), Nat. Fairground Archive, Sir Thomas Beecham Music Library; Dir for Library Services and Univ. Librarian MARTIN LEWIS.

Shrewsbury

Shropshire Libraries: Shirehall, Abbey Foregate, Shrewsbury, SY2 6ND; tel. (1743) 255000; e-mail libraries@shropshire.gov.uk; internet www.shropshire.gov.uk/library.nsf; f. 1925; 22 brs, 4 mobile libraries; 510,000 vols, audiovisual collns; Library Service Man. MICHAEL LEWIS.

Slough

Slough Libraries: Slough Library, 85 High St, Slough, SL1 1EA; tel. (1753) 535166; e-mail libraries@slough.gov.uk; internet www.slough.gov.uk/libraries; 3 brs, mobile library; Head of Libraries and Information YVONNE COPE.

Southampton

Southampton City Libraries: Central Library, Civic Centre, Southampton, SO14 7LW; tel. (23) 8083-3007; e-mail library@southampton.gov.uk; internet www.southampton.gov.uk/libraries; 11 brs, mobile library; Libraries Man. DAVID BALDWIN; Central Librarian MARTIN PAVEY.

University of Southampton Library: Highfield, Southampton, SO17 1BJ; tel. (23) 8059-2180; e-mail libenqs@soton.ac.uk; internet www.library.soton.ac.uk; f. 1862 as Hartley Instn; Health Services Library, Nat. Oceanographic Library, Winchester School of Art Library, Ford Colln of Parliamentary Papers (since 1801), Wellington Papers, Broadlands Archives (Palmerston, Shaftesbury, Mountbatten), Cope colln of Hampshire material, Perkins Agricultural Library, Parkes Library (relationship between Jewish and non-Jewish worlds), archive collns relating to Anglo-Jewry, Hampshire Field Club Library; 2,400,000 vols, 22,000 current periodicals; Librarian JANE SAVIDGE; Deputy Librarian RICHARD WAKE.

Southend on Sea

Southend-on-Sea Libraries: Southend Library, Victoria Ave, Southend-on-Sea, SS2 6EX; tel. (1702) 215011; e-mail library@southend.gov.uk; internet www.southend.gov.uk/libraries; 7 brs, mobile library; Libraries Services Man. SIMON MAY.

Stafford

Staffordshire Library and Information Services: Shire Hall, Market St, Stafford, ST16 2LQ; tel. (1785) 278585; internet www.staffordshire.gov.uk; f. 1916; 44 brs, 13 mobile libraries; 1,067,000 vols, 38,000 CDs, 17,000 DVDs; Commr for Culture and Leisure JANENE COX; Libraries Man. CATHERINE MANN.

Stirling

Stirling Council Library Services: Borrowmeadow Rd, Springkerse Industrial Estate, Stirling, FK7 7TN; tel. (1786) 237535; e-mail libraryheadquarters@stirling.gov.uk; internet www.stirling.gov.uk/libraries; 16 brs, 2 mobile libraries; 330,000 vols; Libraries and Archives Service Man. ROBERT AIRD.

University of Stirling Library: Stirling, FK9 4LA; tel. (1786) 467235; e-mail library@stir.ac.uk; internet www.stir.ac.uk/is; f. 1967; 350,000 vols, 4,000 periodicals, 50,000 ebooks, 45,000 eperiodicals; spec. collns: works by Sir Walter Scott and contemporaries, John Grierson archive, Lindsay Anderson archive, Musicians' Union archive, Howietoun Fish Farm archive, Norman McLaren archive, Victorian illustrated books, labour history colln; Dir of Information Services (vacant).

Stockport

RNIB National Library Service: Far Cromwell Rd, Bredbury, Stockport, SK6 2SG; tel. (303) 123-9999; e-mail library@rnib.org.uk; internet www.rnib.org.uk/livingwithsightloss/reading/services/rnibnationallibrary/pages/national_library_service.aspx; f. 1882, present status 2008 by merger of the Nat. Library for the Blind and the Royal Nat. Institute of Blind People; attached to Royal Nat. Institute of Blind People; 4m. vols (incl. music, in Braille, giant print and audio—incl. talking books); Head of Nat. Library Service HELEN BRAZIER; publs *New Books* (4 a year), *Read On* (2 a year).

Stoke on Trent

Staffordshire University Library: College Rd, Stoke-on-Trent, ST4 2DE; tel. (1782) 295770; e-mail libraryhelpdesk@staffs.ac.uk; internet www.staffs.ac.uk/library; 300,000 vols; spec. collns: Arts Archive, Badminton Colln, Ceramic History Colln, Dorothy Thompson Colln, Eysenck Colln, Iris Strange Colln, Local Studies Colln, Mining Colln, Stoke-on-Trent (S) Constituency Labour Party Archive, Victoria Theatre Colln; Library and Learning Services Man. ALISON POPE.

Stoke-on-Trent Libraries and Archives: City Central Library, Bethesda St, Hanley, Stoke-on-Trent, ST1 3RS; tel. (1782) 238455; e-mail central.library@stoke.gov.uk; internet www.stoke.gov.uk/libraries; attached City Archives located in City Central Library; 352,000 vols; Solon ceramics colln; Strategic Man. JANET THURSFIELD; City Archivist CHRIS LATIMER.

Stratford upon Avon

Shakespeare Centre Library and Archive, Shakespeare Birthplace Trust: Henley St, Stratford upon Avon, CV37 6QW; tel. (1789) 204016; e-mail scla@shakespeare.org.uk; internet www.shakespeare.org.uk; f. 1864; Shakespeare Birthplace Trust the Shakespeare collns: all aspects of Shakespeare's life, work and times; the local collns: history of Stratford-upon-Avon and surrounding area) and the Royal Shakespeare Company Archive (incl. its admin. and production archives, prompt books, photographs, programmes, press clippings, playbills and ephemera); 55,000 vols; Head of Collns and Interpretation DELIA GARRATT; Collns Man. PAUL TAYLOR.

Swansea

City and County of Swansea Library and Information Service: Central Library, Civic Centre, Oystermouth Rd, Swansea, SA1 3SN; tel. (1792) 636464; e-mail libraryline@swansea.gov.uk; internet www .swansea.gov.uk/libraries; 986,546 vols; spec. collns: Dylan Thomas, Welsh and local history; Head of Libraries STEVE HARDMAN; Library Man. KERRY PILLAI.

Swansea University Libraries: Singleton Park, Swansea, SA2 8PP; tel. (1792) 295697; e-mail library@swan.ac.uk; internet www .swan.ac.uk/iss/libraries; f. 1920; 800,000 vols; Dir for Information Services and Systems KEVIN DANIEL.

Swindon

Swindon Borough Libraries: Central Library, Regent Circus, Swindon, SN1 1QG; tel. (1793) 463238; e-mail central.library@ swindon.gov.uk; internet www.swindon.gov .uk/libraries; f. 1943; Librarian ROGER TRAYHURN; Libraries Services Man. ALLYSON JORDAN.

Telford

Telford & Wrekin Libraries: Telford Town Centre Library, St Quentin Gate, Telford, TF3 4JG; tel. (1952) 292151; e-mail libraryenquiries@telford.gov.uk; internet www.telford.gov.uk/libraries; 9 brs, mobile library; Libraries and Heritage Services Man. PAT DAVIS.

Torquay

Torbay Libraries: Torquay Library, Lymington Rd, Torquay, TQ1 3DT; tel. (1803) 208300; e-mail torquaylibrary@ torbay.gov.uk; internet www.torbay.gov.uk/ libraries; f. 1907; 4 brs, mobile library; local studies colln; 191,000 vols; Exec. Head of Residents and Visitors Services SUE CHERITON.

Trowbridge

Wiltshire Libraries and Heritage and Arts: County Hall, Bythesea Rd, Trowbridge, BA14 8JN; tel. (1225) 716700; e-mail customerservices@wiltshire.gov.uk; internet www.wiltshire.gov.uk/libraries; f. 1919; 30 brs, 4 mobile libraries; 869,000 vols, audio and video cassettes, CDs; spec. collns: Wiltshire, agriculture, life of Christ, anthropology and sociology of the family; public and private archives for Wiltshire and the Diocese of Salisbury; Assistant Dir for Libraries and Heritage PAULINE PALMER.

Truro

Cornwall Libraries: Unit 17, Threemilestone Industrial Estate, Threemilestone, Truro, TR4 9LD; tel. (1872) 324676; e-mail libraries@cornwall.gov.uk; internet www .cornwall.gov.uk/library; f. 1925; 37 brs, 6 mobile libraries; 835,000 vols; Asst Head of Shared Services ANNE MCSEVENEY.

Warrington

LiveWire Libraries: Warrington Library, Museum St, Warrington, WA1 1JB; tel. (1925) 442889; e-mail library@ livewirewarrington.org; internet www .livewirewarrington.co.uk/library; f. 1848; 11 brs; Head of Culture, Libraries and Heritage MARTIN GAW.

Warwick

Warwickshire Library and Information Service: Resources Group, Shire Hall, Warwick, CV34 4RR; tel. (1926) 412657; e-mail libraryenquiryteam@warwickshire.gov.uk; internet www.warwickshire.gov.uk/libraries; f. 1920; 33 libraries, mobile library; 1,105,000 vols; spec. collns: Warwickshire Colln, George Eliot Colln; Head of Libraries and Culture SIMON ROBSON.

West Bretton

National Arts Education Archive: Lawrence Batley Centre, Bretton Hall, West Bretton, WF4 4LG; tel. (1924) 830690; e-mail info@ysp.co.uk; internet www.ysp.co .uk/page/national-arts-education-archive/es; f. 1985; attached to Yorkshire Sculpture Park; establish an illustrated 'trace' of work in art and design education from 1880 to date; colln of works of art illustrating the devt of the Child Art and Basic Design movements in art education; colln incl. books, original papers, letters, slides, films, video and audio cassettes; Admin. LEONARD BARTLE.

Winchester

Hampshire Libraries and Information Service: Moorside Place, Moorside Rd, Winchester, SO23 7FZ; tel. (1962) 225391; e-mail library@hants.gov.uk; internet www3 .hants.gov.uk/library; f. 1974; 53 brs; 4 mobile libraries; 2,840,000 vols; spec. collns: Aviation Colln (5,000 vols), Military Colln (18,000 vols), Naval Colln, Railway Colln (11,000 vols), Jane Austen Colln; Head of Library Operations ALEC KENNEDY.

Worcester

Worcestershire Libraries and Learning: Worcestershire County Council, County Hall, Spetchley Rd, Worcester, WR5 2NP; tel. (1905) 822722; e-mail librarieshq@ worcestershire.gov.uk; internet www .worcestershire.gov.uk/libraries; f. 1998; 24 brs, 3 mobile libraries; Head of Libraries and Learning KATHY KIRK.

Wrexham

Wrexham Library & Information Service: 16 Lord St, Wrexham, LL11 1LG; tel. (1978) 297442; e-mail library@wrexham.gov .uk; internet www.wrexham.gov.uk/libraries; 12 brs, mobile library, library for the housebound; spec. collns: business information centre, Europe Direct, BFI Mediatheque; 220,500 vols; Libraries Officer DYLAN HUGHES.

York

City of York Libraries and Archives: York Explore Library, Library Sq., York, YO1 7DS; tel. (1904) 552828; e-mail exploreyork@york.gov.uk; internet www .york.gov.uk/libraries; f. 1893; 16 brs, mobile library; Head of Libraries and Heritage FIONA WILLIAMS.

University of York Library: Heslington, York, YO10 5DD; tel. (1904) 323873; e-mail lib-enquiry@york.ac.uk; internet www.york .ac.uk/library; f. 1963; 1m. vols, 3,500 audiovisual items; spec. collns: 16th- 20th-century medical books (2,500 vols), Yorkshire history (1,500 items), 18th- and 19th-century engravings; Dir STEPHEN TOWN.

York Minster Library: The Old Palace, Dean's Park, York, YO1 7JQ; tel. (8449) 390021; e-mail library@yorkminster.org; internet www.yorkminster.org/ treasures-and-collections/historic-collections/ library; f. 7th–8th century; 125,000 vols, 115 incunabula, 101 medieval MSS, 200 music MSS; spec. collns incl. Civil War Tracts and Yorkshire local history; Librarian SARAH GRIFFIN; Archivist PETER YOUNG.

Museums and Art Galleries

Aberdeen

Aberdeen Art Gallery and Museums: Schoolhill, Aberdeen, AB10 1FQ; tel. (1224) 523700; e-mail info@aagm.co.uk; internet www.aagm.co.uk; collns incl. fine art; applied art; maritime history; science, technology and industry; archaeology; coins, banknotes, medals and tokens; Art Gallery and Museums Man. CHRISTINE REW; Lead Curator ALISON FRASER..

Selected Museums and Galleries:

Aberdeen Art Gallery: Schoolhill, Aberdeen, AB10 1FQ; tel. (1224) 523700; e-mail info@aagm.co.uk; internet www.aagm.co .uk/venues/aberdeenartgallery; f. 1885; fine and decorative arts; major collns of British art since the 18th century; Museum Supervisor BRIAN JOHNSTONE.

Aberdeen Maritime Museum: Shiprow, Aberdeen, AB11 5BY; tel. (1224) 337700; e-mail info@aagm.co.uk; internet www .aagm.co.uk/venues/aberdeenmaritimemuseum; f. 1984; displays covering all aspects of Aberdeen and the NE of Scotland's maritime heritage; Museum Supervisor MIKE HEPBURN.

Alloway

Robert Burns Birthplace Museum: Murdoch's Lone, Alloway, Ayr, KA7 4PQ; tel. (1292) 443700; e-mail burns@nts.org.uk; internet www.burnsmuseum.org.uk; f. 1881; collns incl. 5,500 MSS, books, personal artefacts and artworks relating to Robert Burns and his legacy; Curator JOHN MANSON.

Anstruther

Scottish Fisheries Museum: St Ayles, Harbourhead, Anstruther, KY10 3AB; tel. (1333) 310628; e-mail enquiries@ scotfishmuseum.org; internet www .scotfishmuseum.org; f. 1969; visual historical record of every aspect of the Scottish fishing industry from prehistoric times to the present; touring boat; library of 1,500 vols; Dir SIMON HAYHOW; Curator LINDA FITZPATRICK.

Bangor

Gwynedd Museum and Art Gallery/ Amgueddfa ac Oriel Gwynedd: Ffordd Gwynedd, Bangor, LL57 1DT; tel. (1248) 353368; e-mail gwyneddmuseum@gwynedd .gov.uk; internet www.gwynedd.gov.uk/ gwy_doc.asp?doc=13261&langua-ge=1&p=1&c=1; f. 1884; artefacts relating to social history of N Wales, incl. archaeology, furniture, costume and Welsh textiles, domestic items; exhibitions incl. painting, photography and sculpture by local and int. artists; Curator ESTHER ELIN ROBERTS.

Barnard Castle

Bowes Museum: Barnard Castle, DL12 8NP; tel. (1833) 690606; e-mail info@ thebowesmuseum.org.uk; internet www .thebowesmuseum.org.uk; f. 1892; collns formed 1862–75 by John and Joséphine Bowes, mainly of all forms of European fine and decorative art, incl. works by Canaletto, El Greco, Courbet and Turner; ceramics, furniture and textiles; Dir ADRIAN JENKINS.

Bath

American Museum in Britain: Claverton Manor, Bath, BA2 7BD; tel. (1225) 460503; e-mail enquiries@americanmuseum.org; internet www.americanmuseum.org; f. 1961; illustrates the devt of American decorative arts from the 17th to the 19th century; textile colln; printed maps from the

15th and 16th centuries; library of 11,000 vols; Dir Dr RICHARD WENDORF; Curator LAURA BERESFORD; publ. *America in Britain* (1 a year).

Holburne Museum: Great Pulteney St, Bath, BA2 4DB; tel. (1225) 388569; e-mail enquiries@holburne.org; internet www .holburne.org; f. 1893; paintings, silver, sculpture, porcelain and furniture in an 18th-century bldg; library of 3,000 vols; Dir Dr ALEXANDER STURGIS.

Beamish

Beamish Museum: Beamish, DH9 0RG; tel. (191) 370-4000; e-mail museum@beamish.org .uk; internet www.beamish.org.uk; f. 1970; includes a colliery village, railway station, a working farm and The Town of around 1913; Pockerley Manor and horse yard illustrate yeoman farming lifestyle in early 19th century; working replica of George Stephenson's *Locomotion No. 1* railway engine, and *Steam Elephant* of 1815; library of 20,000 vols, 10,000 trade catalogues; photographic archive containing 250,000 photographs; oral history colln with 800 audio cassette recordings; Dir RICHARD EVANS.

Beaulieu

National Motor Museum: Beaulieu, Brockenhurst, SO42 7ZN; tel. (1590) 614650; e-mail nmmt@beaulieu.co.uk; internet www .nationalmotormuseum.org.uk; f. 1972; houses designated collns of 250 vehicles, 42,000 objects, 1m. photographic images, 100 linear m of motoring archives; CEO RUSSELL BOWMAN.

Belfast

National Museums Northern Ireland: Cultra, Holywood, BT18 0EU; tel. (845) 608-0000; e-mail info@nmni.com; internet www .nmni.com; holds over 1m. objects across the collns of the Ulster Museum, Ulster Folk & Transport Museum, Ulster American Folk Park and Armagh County Museum; Dir and Chief Exec. TIM COOKE..

Constituent Museums:

Armagh County Museum: The Mall East, Armagh, BT61 9BE; tel. (28) 3752-3070; e-mail acm.info@nmni.com; internet www.nmni.com; f. 1935; collns in archaeology, art, domestic life, history, natural world, transport, textiles and costumes, social life and traditions; Curator Dr GREER RAMSEY.

Ulster American Folk Museum: 2 Mellon Rd, Castletown, Omagh, BT78 5QU; tel. (28) 8224-3292; f. 1976; open-air museum illustrating history of emigration from Ulster to the USA during the 18th and 19th centuries; reconstructions of bldgs and activities; full-size reconstruction of 19th-century sailing ship; Curator Dr PHILIP MOUNT.

Ulster Folk and Transport Museum: Cultra, Holywood, BT18 0EU; tel. (28) 9042-8428; f. 1964; nat. museum comprising open-air museum with authentic bldgs illustrating Ulster folk life, both rural and urban; separate transport museum; library of 18,000 vols; Chair. M. ELLIOTT; Divisional Head JONATHAN BELL; publ. *Ulster Folklife* (1 a year).

Ulster Museum: Botanic Gardens, Belfast, BT9 5AB; tel. (28) 9044-0000; f. 1833; fine and applied arts, archaeology, ethnography, history, botany, geology, zoology; Chief Exec. TIM COOKE.

Birmingham

Birmingham Museums and Art Gallery: Chamberlain Sq., Birmingham, B3 3DH; tel. (121) 303-1966; e-mail bmag.enquiries@ birminghammuseums.org.uk; internet www .bmag.org.uk; f. 1885; depts of fine and applied art; Staffordshire hoard, archaeology, ethnography and local history (collections from Ancient Egypt, Ur, Nineveh, Jericho, Nimrud, Vinca, Jerusalem, Petra, Vounos, Mexico and Peru, Prehistoric, Roman and British Medieval antiquities, British 20th century); pacific ethnography colln; British coin colln; restricted access to comprehensive collections of minerals, gemstones and molluscs, British birds, lepidoptera and coleoptera; Midlands flora; prints; br. museums incl. Aston Hall, Blakesley Hall, Weoley Castle, Sarehole Mill, Soho House, Museum of the Jewellery Quarter; picture library; Dir Dr ELLEN McADAM; Deputy Dir SIMON CANE.

Thinktank, Birmingham Science Museum: Millennium Point, Curzon St, Birmingham, B4 7XG; tel. (121) 202-2222; e-mail findout@thinktank.ac; internet www .thinktank.ac; f. 2001; consists of 10 galleries of interactive exhibits on science, technology, medicine, natural and local history; digital planetarium; Chief Exec. NICK WINTERBOTHAM.

Bishop's Stortford

Bishop's Stortford Museum: South Rd, Bishop's Stortford, CM23 3JG; tel. (1279) 651746; e-mail museum@ rhodesbishopsstortford.org.uk; internet www .rhodesbishopsstortford.org.uk; f. 1938 as the Rhodes Memorial Museum, current name adopted 2005; exhibits relating to the life and times of colonialist Cecil Rhodes (1853–1902); African art and culture; also incorporates local history museum; Curator Dr SARAH TURNER.

Blackburn

Blackburn Museum and Art Gallery: Museum St, Blackburn, BB1 7AJ; tel. (1254) 667130; e-mail museum@blackburn .gov.uk; f. 1874; collns of Japanese prints, the Hart colln of books, coins and medieval MSS.

Bradford

National Media Museum: Bradford, BD1 1NQ; tel. (844) 856-3797; e-mail talk@ nationalmediamuseum.org.uk; internet www .nationalmediamuseum.org.uk; f. 1983 as Nat. Museum of Photography, Film and Television, current name adopted 2006; collns incl. photography, cinematography, television, new media; the Museum houses an IMAX projection system, with cinema screen and a Cinerama cinema; Head JO QUINTON-TULLOCH.

Brighton

Booth Museum of Natural History: 194 Dyke Rd, Brighton, BN1 5AA; tel. (3000) 290900; e-mail visitor.services@ brighton-hove.gov.uk; internet www .brighton-hove-rpml.org.uk/museums/boothmuseum; f. 1874; colln of 525,000 insects, 50,000 minerals and rocks, 30,000 plants and 5,000 microscopic slides; library of 15,000 vols; Keeper of Natural Sciences JOHN COOPER; Curator of Natural Sciences LEE ISMAIL.

Brighton Museum and Art Gallery: Royal Pavilion Gardens, Brighton, BN1 1EE; tel. (3000) 290900; e-mail visitor.services@ brighton-hove.gov.uk; internet www .brighton-hove-rpml.org.uk/museums/brightonmuseum; f. 1873; colln of paintings since the 15th century, drawings and prints; English pottery and porcelain, incl. the Willett Collection; decorative art and furniture of Art Nouveau and Art Deco periods; fashion gallery; ethnography; local history; Assistant Dir of Heritage PAULINE SCOTT-GARRETT.

Royal Pavilion: 4–5 Pavilion Bldgs, Brighton, BN1 1EE; tel. (3000) 290900; e-mail visitor.services@brighton-hove .gov.uk; internet www.brighton-hove-rpml .org.uk/royalpavilion; f. 1851; regency seaside palace of King George IV with Mughal-style exterior and Chinese-style interiors; audio guides in Cantonese, English, French, German, Italian, Mandarin, Spanish; Head of Museums and Royal Pavilion JANITA BAGSHAWE.

Bristol

Bristol Museum and Art Gallery: Queen's Rd, Bristol, BS8 1RL; tel. (117) 922-3571; e-mail general.museum@bristol.gov.uk; internet www.bristol.gov.uk/page/ leisure-and-culture/bristol-museum-and-art-gallery; galleries incl. Old Masters, French School, British colln, Modern Art and Bristol School; decorative arts colln incl. Eastern Art, ceramics, silverware and glassware; minerals, fossils and natural history collns; archaeological colln; also 16th-century Red Lodge (Park Row), Georgian House (Gt George St), Blaise Castle House Museum (Henbury), Bristol Industrial Museum (Princes Wharf); Kingsweston Roman Villa; Dir KATE BRINDLEY.

Burnley

Towneley Hall Art Gallery and Museums: Towneley Hall, Towneley Park, Burnley, BB11 3RQ; tel. (1282) 477130; e-mail towneleyhall@burnley.gov.uk; internet www.burnley.gov.uk/residents/ towneley-hall; f. 1902; collns incl. natural history, Egyptology, local history, textiles, decorative art and furniture; art colln focuses on 19th-century British artists; Curator MIKE TAREND.

Cambridge

Fitzwilliam Museum: Trumpington St, Cambridge, CB2 1RB; tel. (1223) 332900; e-mail fitzmuseum-enquiries@lists.cam.ac .uk; internet www.fitzmuseum.cam.ac.uk; f. 1816; attached to Univ. of Cambridge; art collns of the Univ. of Cambridge; paintings, drawings, prints, sculpture; rare coins and medals; ceramics, glass, textiles, arms and armour, and other applied arts; Greek, Roman, Cypriot, western Asiatic and Egyptian antiquities; library of 250,000 vols and medieval, literary and music MSS, autograph letters, early printed books, illuminated medieval books of hours, printed music, books on history of art; Dir TIM KNOX.

Museum of Archaeology and Anthropology: Downing St, Cambridge, CB2 3DZ; tel. (1223) 333516; e-mail admin@maa.cam.ac .uk; internet maa.cam.ac.uk; f. 1884; attached to Univ. of Cambridge; archaeological collns, anthropological collns, photographic collns, modern and contemporary art and archival material; Dir and Curator Prof. NICHOLAS J. THOMAS.

University Museum of Zoology: Downing St, Cambridge, CB2 3EJ; tel. (1223) 336650; e-mail umzc@zoo.cam.ac.uk; internet www .museum.zoo.cam.ac.uk; f. 1815; attached to Univ. of Cambridge; collns of recent and fossil zoological species; Dir Prof. PAUL BRAKEFIELD.

Cardiff

Amgueddfa Cymru/National Museum Wales: Cathays Park, Cardiff, CF10 3NP; tel. (29) 2057-3951; internet www .museumwales.ac.uk; f. 1907; Pres. ELISABETH ELIAS; Dir-Gen. DAVID ANDERSON..

Associated Museums:

Big Pit National Coal Museum: Blaenafon, NP4 9XP; tel. (29) 2057-3650; internet www.museumwales.ac.uk/bigpit;

f. 1980; working coal mine and exhibits relating to Welsh mining history; Man. PETER WALKER.

National Museum Cardiff: Cathays Park, Cardiff, CF10 3NP; tel. (29) 2039-7951; internet www.museumwales.ac.uk/cardiff; f. 1927; houses Welsh nat. archaeology, art, geology and natural history collns as well as major touring and temporary exhibitions; library: 2m. vols; Dir MICHAEL TOOBY.

National Roman Legion Museum: High St, Caerleon, NP18 1AE; tel. (29) 2057-3550; internet www.museumwales.ac.uk/roman; f. 1850; fmr Roman fortress, comprising ruins and relevant exhibits; open by appointment; Man. DAI PRICE.

National Slate Museum: Llanberis, LL55 4TY; tel. (29) 2057-3700; internet www.museumwales.ac.uk/slate; f. 1972; machinery, relics and bldgs relating to the Wales slate industry; Keeper DAFYDD ROBERTS.

National Waterfront Museum: Oystermouth Rd, Maritime Quarter, Swansea, SA1 3RD; tel. (29) 2057-3600; e-mail waterfront@museumwales.ac.uk; internet www.museumwales.ac.uk/swansea; 15 themed display areas on the effect of the Industrial Revolution on Welsh life.

National Wool Museum: Dre-fach Felindre, SA44 5UP; tel. (29) 2057-3070; e-mail gwlan@amgueddfacymru.ac.uk; internet www.museumwales.ac.uk/wool; f. 1976; displays of bldgs and artefacts relating to the Welsh woollen industry, incl. working historic textile machinery and textile gallery; Man. ANN WHITTALL.

St Fagans National History Museum: St Fagans, Cardiff, CF5 6XB; tel. (29) 2057-3500; internet www.museumwales .ac.uk/stfagans; f. 1948; museum of Welsh social history, with over 40 original bldgs re-erected on site; Dir BETHAN LEWIS.

Carmarthen

Carmarthenshire County Museum: Abergwili, Carmarthen, SA31 2JG; tel. (1267) 228696; e-mail museums@carmarthenshire.gov.uk; internet www .carmarthenshire.gov.uk/english/education/museums/carmarthenshirecountymuseum; f. 1978; local authority museum; geology, archaeology, social history, folk life, furniture, ceramics, art, costume; County Museums Man. ANN DORSETT.

Chawton

Jane Austen's House Museum: Chawton, Alton, GU34 1SD; tel. (1420) 83262; e-mail enquiries@jahmusm.org.uk; internet www .jane-austens-house-museum.org.uk; f. 1949; portraits, documents, furniture and objects relating to Jane Austen and her family; Chair. ISABEL HUGHES; Curator MARY GUYATT.

Cirencester

Corinium Museum: Park St, Cirencester, GL7 2BX; tel. (1285) 655611; e-mail coriniummuseum@slm-ltd.co.uk; internet www.coriniummuseum.org; important colln of Roman material; mosaic pavements, sculpture, military and civil tombstones, household domestic utensils, personal ornaments, and Samian and coarse pottery; Curator AMANDA HART.

Devizes

Wiltshire Heritage Museum: 41 Long St, Devizes, SN10 1NS; tel. (1380) 727369; e-mail wanhs@wiltshireheritage.org.uk; internet www.wiltshiremuseum.org.uk; f. 1853; collects and preserves history of the

county; archaeological and historical collns from Wiltshire, incl. Stonehenge, with emphasis on Bronze Age period; Wiltshire art colln; archives relating to Wiltshire; library of 8,000 vols; Dir DAVID DAWSON; Curator LISA BROWN; publ. *Wiltshire Archaeological and Natural History Magazine* (1 a year).

Doncaster

Doncaster Museum and Art Gallery: Chequer Rd, Doncaster, DN1 2AE; tel. (1302) 734293; e-mail museum@doncaster .gov.uk; internet www.doncaster.gov.uk/sections/leisureandculture/museumsandgalleries/doncastermuseumandartgallery; f. 1909; regional natural history, geology, archaeology and local history collns; permanent art colln, paintings, ceramics and glass; Regimental colln of the King's Own Yorkshire Light Infantry; Man. C. DALTON; Asst Man. J. ADAMS.

Dorchester

Dorset County Museum: High West St, Dorchester, DT1 1XA; tel. (1305) 262735; e-mail enquiries@dorsetcountymuseum.org; internet www.dorsetcountymuseum.org; f. 1845; natural history, palaeontology, archaeology, fine arts, geology, literature (incl. Thomas Hardy), and the local history of Dorset; lectures, confs and seminars in the first half of the year; library of 30,000 vols; Pres. Capt. MICHAEL FULFORD-DOBSON; Dir of the Museum and Sec. to the Society Dr JON MURDEN.

Dumfries

Dumfries Museums: The Observatory, Rotchell Rd, Dumfries, DG2 7SW; tel. (1387) 253374; e-mail dumfriesmuseum@dumgal.gov.uk; internet www .dumfriesmuseum.com; f. 1836 as an observatory and camera obscura; building erected as a windmill c. 1790; exhibits Roman relics, Stone and Bronze Age artefacts, natural and local history from Dumfries and Galloway; incorporates Dumfries Museum, Thornhill Museum, Langholm Museum and Myrseth Museum collns; MSS concerning Carlyle and Barrie; camera obscura; period rooms at Old Bridge House (1660) nearby; Robert Burns Centre in Dumfries Town Mill (1781): exhibitions on Burns and his life in SW Scotland; Burns House: period house occupied by Burns 1793–96 and where he died: exhibits incl. MSS, first editions, personal belongings; Sanquhar Museum in Adam-designed Town House (1735) covers local history and geology; Museum Officer SIOBHAN RATCHFORD.

Dundee

McManus: Dundee's Art Gallery & Museum: Albert Sq., Meadowside, Dundee, DD1 1DA; tel. (1382) 307200; e-mail themcmanus@leisureandculturedundee.com; internet www.themcmanus-dundee.gov.uk; f. 1873; operates 4 heritage sites open to the public: The McManus: Dundee's Art Gallery & Museum (Victorian Scottish paintings, contemporary art and photography, decorative arts, local history displays from time of earliest settlers to modern era, costume gallery, natural history); Broughty Castle Museum (history of Broughty Ferry, natural history of the seashore, paintings from the Orchar Colln), Mills Observatory (10-inch Victorian telescope, modern 12-inch reflecting telescope with 'go to' technology, displays on the solar system and space exploration, displays of historic equipment and information of local importance; planetarium), McManus Collns Unit (city's history, archaeology and natural history collns); Cultural Services Man. BILLY GARTLEY.

Durham

Oriental Museum: Elvet Hill, off South Rd, Durham, DH1 3TH; tel. (191) 334-5694; e-mail oriental.museum@durham.ac.uk; internet www.dur.ac.uk/oriental.museum; f. 1960; attached to Durham Univ.; Duke of Northumberland's colln of Egyptian antiquities; MacDonald colln of Chinese ceramics; Charles Hardinge colln of Chinese jades; Henry de Laszlo colln of Chinese art and other examples of oriental art and archaeology covering Ancient Egypt and the Near East, the Indian subcontinent, Japan and SE Asia; Curator Dr CRAIG P. BARCLAY.

Killhope, the North of England Lead Mining Museum: Near Cowshill, Upper Weardale, DL13 1AR; tel. (1388) 537505; e-mail info@killhope.org.uk; internet www .killhope.org.uk; f. 1984 as Killhope Lead Mining Centre; current name adopted 2000; fully restored 19th-century lead mine; Dir MIKE BOASE.

Edinburgh

Edinburgh Museums and Galleries: City Art Centre, 2 Market St, Edinburgh, EH1 1DE; tel. (131) 529-2427; e-mail museumsandgalleries@edinburgh.gov.uk; internet www.edinburghmuseums.org.uk; comprises 13 museums and galleries: City Art Centre, Museum of Childhood, Museum of Edinburgh, People's Story Museum, Writer's Museum, Lauriston Castle, Queensferry Museum, Museum Collection Centre, Travelling Gallery, Brass Rubbing Centre, Scott Monument, Nelson Monument, Old City (Playfair) Observatory; Museums Man. FRANK LITTLE.

National Galleries of Scotland: The Mound, Edinburgh, EH2 2EL; tel. (131) 624-6200; e-mail enquiries@nationalgalleries.org; internet www .nationalgalleries.org; f. 1859; collns of Western art ranging from the Middle Ages to the present day; Dir-Gen. Sir JOHN LEIGHTON..

Constituent Galleries:

Scottish National Gallery: The Mound, Edinburgh, EH2 2EL; tel. (131) 624-6200; e-mail nginfo@nationalgalleries.org; internet www.nationalgalleries.org/visit/about-the-scottish-national-gallery; f. 1859; nat. collection of fine art from the early Renaissance to the late 19th century; Dir MICHAEL CLARKE.

Scottish National Gallery of Modern Art: 75 Belford Rd, Edinburgh, EH4 3DR; tel. (131) 624-6200; e-mail gmainfo@nationalgalleries.org; internet www .nationalgalleries.org/visit/about-the-scottish-national-gallery-of-modern-art; f. 1960; displays Scottish and European paintings, drawings, prints and sculptures since beginning of 20th century; int. postwar works; library of 50,000 vols; Dir Dr SIMON GROOM.

Scottish National Portrait Gallery: 1 Queen St, Edinburgh, EH2 1JD; tel. (131) 624-6200; e-mail pginfo@nationalgalleries .org; f. 1889; portraits of Scottish historical interest; an extensive reference section of engravings and photographs of portraits; the nat. photography colln; Dir CHRISTOPHER BAKER.

National Museums Scotland: Chambers St, Edinburgh, EH1 1JF; tel. (131) 225-7534; e-mail info@nms.ac.uk; internet www.nms.ac .uk; f. 1985; Dir Dr GORDON RINTOUL..

Constituent Museums:

Museum of Flight: East Fortune Airfield, East Lothian, EH39 5LF; tel. (131) 247-4238; e-mail info@nms.ac.uk; internet www.nms.ac.uk/flight; colln of aircraft, rockets and aeroengines displayed in the hangars of a former RAF wartime station; houses a decommissioned Concorde aircraft; archives, propellers, incl. reference library; Curator ALISTAIR DODDS.

National Museum of Costume: New Abbey, DG2 8HQ; tel. (131) 247-4030; e-mail info@nms.ac.uk; internet www.nms .ac.uk/costume; f. 1977; 19th-century country house; changing exhibitions of costume from the 1870s to the 1950s; Man. MARGARET ROBERTS.

National Museum of Rural Life: Philipshill Rd, Wester Kittochside, East Kilbride, G76 9HR; tel. (131) 247-4369; e-mail info@nms.ac.uk; internet www.nms.ac.uk/ our_museums/museum_of_rural_life.aspx; f. 2001, fmrly Museum of Scottish Country Life; includes Georgian farmhouse and a 1950s working farm; Gen. Man. DUNCAN DORNAN.

National Museum of Scotland: Chambers St, Edinburgh, EH1 1JF; tel. (131) 225-7534; e-mail info@nms.ac.uk; internet www.nms.ac.uk/scotland; f. 1998; history and geology of Scotland; Dir Dr GORDON RINTOUL.

National War Museum: Edinburgh Castle, Edinburgh, EH1 2NG; tel. (131) 247-4413; e-mail info@nms.ac.uk; internet www.nms.ac.uk/war; f. 1930; collns of the Scottish experience of war and military service since 1700; Curator ALLAN CARSWELL.

Royal Museum: Chambers St, Edinburgh, EH1 1JF; tel. (131) 247-4422; e-mail info@nms.ac.uk; internet www.nms .ac.uk/royal; f. 1854; int. collns of decorative arts, archaeology, ethnography, natural history, geology, science and technology; Dir Dr GORDON RINTOUL.

Gateshead

BALTIC Centre for Contemporary Art: Gateshead Quays, S Shore Rd, Gateshead, NE8 3BA; tel. (191) 478-1810; e-mail info@ balticmill.com; internet www.balticmill.com; f. 2002; Dir GODFREY WORSDALE; Deputy Dir AGNES WILKIE.

Glasgow

Glasgow Museums: 200 Woodhead Rd, Nitshill, Glasgow, G53 7NN; tel. (141) 276-9300; e-mail museums@glasgowlife.org.uk; internet www.glasgowlife.org.uk/museums; colln displayed in 10 venues across the city of Glasgow; incl. Glasgow Museums Resource Centre; Museum Man. GARETH JAMES..

Constituent Museums:

Burrell Collection: Pollok Country Park, 2060 Pollokshaws Rd, Glasgow, G43 1AT; tel. (141) 287-2550; e-mail museums@ glasgowlife.org.uk; internet www .glasgowlife.org.uk/museums/burrell-collection; f. 1983; antiquities from Iraq, Egypt, Greece and Italy; Oriental art, incl. Chinese ceramics, bronzes and jades, Japanese prints, Near Eastern carpets, rugs, ceramics and metal work; European decorative arts of 14th–18th centuries incl. tapestries, stained glass, sculpture, furniture, glass, silver and ceramics; fine art, especially French 19th-century works by Degas, Boudin, Monet and Daumier; Sr Curator, Ancient Civilizations SIMON ECCLES.

Gallery of Modern Art (GOMA): Royal Exchange Sq., Glasgow, G1 3AH; tel. (141) 287-3050; e-mail museums@glasgowlife .org.uk; internet www.glasgowlife.org.uk/ museums/goma; f. 1996; exhibits work by local, nat. and int. artists; aims to address contemporary social issues through major biennial projects; museum bldg combines old and new architecture and incorporates

a number of artists' commissions; Man. VICTORIA HOLLOWS.

Glasgow Museums Resource Centre (GMRC): 200 Woodhead Rd, Nitshill, Glasgow, G53 7NN; tel. (141) 276-9300; e-mail museums@glasgowlife.org.uk; internet www.glasgowlife.org.uk/ museums/gmrc; f. 2003; publicly accessible store of 200,000 items held by Glasgow's museum service; home of the Open Museum; formal and informal learning programmes; research facilities; Man. GARETH JAMES.

Kelvingrove Art Gallery and Museum: Argyle St, Glasgow, G3 8AG; tel. (141) 276-9599; e-mail museums@glasgowlife.org.uk; internet www.glasgowlife.org.uk/ museums/kelvingrove; f. 1901; collns incl. Dutch Old Masters and French Impressionist paintings, Scottish colourists, arms and armour, Charles Rennie Mackintosh and the Glasgow Style, natural history, technology, costume; discovery and study centres.

People's Palace and Winter Gardens: Glasgow Green, Glasgow, G40 1AT; tel. (141) 276-0795; e-mail museums@ csglasgow.org; internet www.glasgowlife .org.uk/museums/peoples-palace; f. 1898; local and social history museum; story of the city of Glasgow and its inhabitants since 1750; the Winter Gardens houses exotic palms and plants; Curator FIONA HAYES.

Pollok House: Pollok Country Park, 2060 Pollokshaws Rd, Glasgow, G43 1AT; tel. (844) 493-2202; e-mail pollokhouse@nts .org.uk; internet www.nts.org.uk; 18th-century Palladian house with Victorian additions, furnished c. 1750–1820 and with Stirling Maxwell colln of Spanish and European paintings; managed by the Nat. Trust of Scotland on behalf of Glasgow Museums; Property Man. IAN McGREEVY (acting); Admin. Asst ALISON SIMMS.

Provand's Lordship: 3 Castle St, Glasgow, G4 0RB; tel. (141) 276-1625; e-mail museums@glasgowlife.org.uk; internet www.glasgowlife.org.uk/museums/pro-vands-lordship; built 1471, the oldest house in Glasgow, with period room displays; home to the St Nicholas Garden, a herb garden containing 15th-century medicinal plants, the Tontine Faces (colln of carved stone faces originally carved for the new Town Hall 1740); Man. SANDRA EWIRI.

Riverside Museum: 100 Pointhouse Pl., Glasgow, G3 8RS; tel. (141) 287-2720; e-mail museums@glasgowlife.org.uk; internet www.glasgowlife.org.uk/ museums/riverside/pages/default.aspx; f. 1964; displays incl. Glasgow trams and buses, Scottish-built cars, commercial vehicles, cycles and motorcycles, railway locomotives, fire engines, horse-drawn vehicles, ship models; toy cars, prams, the oldest surviving pedal cycle in the world and a reproduction of a typical Glasgow street of 1938; Man. LAWRENCE FITZGERALD.

St Mungo Museum of Religious Life and Art: 2 Castle St, Glasgow, G4 0RH; tel. (141) 276-1625; e-mail museums@ glasgowlife.org.uk; internet www .glasgowlife.org.uk/museums/st-mungos/ pages/default.aspx; f. 1993; art objects associated with religious faiths; displays on religion in art, world faiths, religion in Scottish history; permanent Zen garden; Man. SANDRA EWIRI.

Scotland Street School Museum: 225 Scotland St, Glasgow, G5 8QB; tel. (141) 287-0513; e-mail museums@glasgowlife .org.uk; internet www.glasgowmuseums

.com/scotland-street; f. 1906; designed by Charles Rennie Mackintosh between 1903 and 1906; history of Scotland Street Public School, and devts in education in Scotland; reconstructed classrooms from the Victorian period, World War II, the 1950s and 1960s; colln of old school photographs; Curator for Decorative Arts ALISON BROWN; Curator for Social History ISOBEL McDONALD.

Hunterian Museum: Univ. of Glasgow, University Ave, Glasgow, G12 8QQ; tel. (141) 330-4221; e-mail hunterian-enquiries@ glasgow.ac.uk; internet www.gla.ac.uk/ hunterian; f. 1807; attached to Univ. of Glasgow; based around the collns of the Surgeon Extraordinary to Queen Charlotte, William Hunter (1718–83); geological, prehistoric, Roman, ethnographical and coin collns, scientific instruments; zoological, anatomical and pathological collns in univ. depts of zoology, anatomy and pathology; books and MSS in univ. library; Dir Prof. DAVID GAIMSTER..

Attached Gallery:

Hunterian Art Gallery: Univ. of Glasgow, 82 Hillhead St, Glasgow, G12 8QQ; tel. (141) 330-4221; e-mail hunterian-enquiries@glasgow.ac.uk; internet www.gla.ac.uk/museum; f. 1980; collns of C. R. Mackintosh and J. M. Whistler; works by Chardin, Stubbs and Reynolds; Scottish painting since 18th century; old master and modern prints; Dir DAVID GAIMSTER.

Gloucester

Gloucester City Museum and Art Gallery: Brunswick Rd, Gloucester, GL1 1HP; tel. (1452) 396131; e-mail museums@ gloucester.gov.uk; internet www.gloucester .gov.uk/museums; f. 1859; natural history, archaeology (before AD 1500), fine and applied art; temporary art, science, archaeology, natural sciences and textile exhibitions; Museum Man. ANGELA SMITH.

Gloucester Folk Museum: 99–103 Westgate St, Gloucester, GL1 2PG; tel. (1452) 396868; e-mail museum@gloucester.gov.uk; internet venues.gloucester.gov.uk/freetime/ museums/folkmuseum.aspx; f. 1935; local history, crafts, trades and industries of City and County of Gloucester since 1500; housed in Tudor and Jacobean timber-framed bldgs with new extensions; regular spec. exhibitions, activities and events; social history reference colln (access by appointment); Curator SARAH ORTON.

Grasmere

Dove Cottage and the Wordsworth Museum: Dove Cottage, Grasmere, Ambleside, LA22 9SH; tel. (1539) 435544; e-mail enquiries@wordsworth.org.uk; internet www .wordsworth.org.uk; f. 1890; fmr home of William and Dorothy Wordsworth and, later, of Thomas de Quincey; contains original furniture and personal effects, and a museum containing MSS, books, paintings, diaries, letters, poetry books, as well as personal items, clothing, pictures, sculptures, objects relating to the poet, and to Grasmere life of the period; library of 20,000 vols relating to the Romantic period, The Jerwood Centre; Dir MICHAEL McGREGOR; Curator JEFF COWTON.

Grays

Thurrock Museum: 2nd Fl., Thameside Complex, Orsett Rd, Grays, RM17 5DX; tel. (1375) 413965; e-mail thurrock.museum@ thurrock.gov.uk; internet www.thurrock.gov .uk/thurrock-museum; f. 1956; 1,500 objects; archaeology and history of Thurrock with accent on the growth of technology in a

Thameside landscape; Museum and Heritage Officer JONATHAN CATTON.

Haverfordwest

Pembrokeshire Museum Service: Scolton Manor, Bethlehem, Haverfordwest, SA62 5QL; tel. (1437) 731328; e-mail scolton.enq@pembrokeshire.gov.uk; internet www.pembrokeshire.gov.uk; f. 1967; Museums Officer NICOLA CALDWELL..

Attached Museums:

Penrhos Cottage: Pembrokeshire Museum Service, The County Library, Dew St, Haverfordwest, SA61 1SU; Llanycefn, Clunderwen; tel. (1437) 779500; e-mail adam@writegood.co.uk; f. 1971; traditional thatched Welsh cottage with original furniture; open by appointment only; Museums Officer NICK SUFFOLK.

Scolton Manor Museum: Bethlehem, Haverfordwest; tel. (1437) 731328; e-mail scolton.enq@pembroke-shire.gov.uk; internet www.pembrokeshirevirtualmuseum.co.uk; f. 1972; regional history of Pembrokeshire; includes period rooms in early Victorian manor, World War II exhibition, railway exhibits, geology, river fishing, coal mining, servant life, costume; history of the domestic iron; County Museums Officer MARK THOMAS.

High Wycombe

National Trust, Hughenden Manor: Hughenden Manor, High Wycombe, HP14 4LA; tel. (1494) 755565; e-mail hughenden@nationaltrust.org.uk; internet www.nationaltrust.org.uk/hughenden; f. 1947; Disraeli's country estate; contains Disraeli's books, furniture, paintings and personal effects; property of the National Trust (*q.v.*); library of 4,000 vols; Gen Man. JIM FOY; Regional Curator LUCY PORTEN.

Huddersfield

Tolson Memorial Museum: Ravensknowle Park, Wakefield Rd, Huddersfield, HD5 8DJ; tel. (1484) 223830; e-mail tolson.museum@kirklees.gov.uk; f. 1922; illustrates natural and human history of the district; prehistory, folk-life, devt of woollen industry; colln of costume and textiles, decorative and applied art, music, weapons and war, coins and medals, personalities, science and technology, vehicles.

Ironbridge

Ironbridge Gorge Museums: Coach Rd, Coalbrookdale, TF8 7DQ; tel. (1952) 884391; e-mail information@ironbridge.org.uk; internet www.ironbridge.org.uk; f. 1968; explains and interprets the industrial and social history of the East Shropshire Coalfield; 6-mile site on the River Severn comprising: Coalbrookdale Museum of Iron and Darby Furnace, Ironbridge with the Museum of the Gorge, the world's first Iron Bridge (built 1779), Blists Hill Victorian Town, Coalport China Museum, Jackfield Tile Museum, Ironbridge Institute at Coalbrookdale, Rosehill and Dale House (restored home of the Darby family), Tar Tunnel (200-year-old source of natural bitumen), Broseley Pipeworks, 'Enginuity' (engineering and technological exhibits); designated a World Heritage Site by UNESCO; library of 50,000 vols; Chief Exec. STEVE MILLER.

Kendal

Kendal Museum: Station Rd, Kendal, LA9 6BT; tel. (1539) 815597; e-mail info@kendalmuseum.org.uk; internet www.kendalmuseum.org.uk; f. 1796; Westmorland Gallery of local history and archaeology, World Wildlife gallery, natural history gallery of geology, flora and fauna of the district; Curator CAROL DAVIES.

Museum of Lakeland Life & Industry: Abbot Hall, Kendal, LA9 5AL; tel. (1539) 722464; e-mail info@lakelandmuseum.org.uk; internet www.lakelandmuseum.org.uk; f. 1962 (gallery), 1971 (museum); gallery provides changing exhibitions of local and int. interest; houses permanent collns of 18th-century furniture, paintings, modern paintings, sculpture and drawings; museum features the working and social life of the area; Chief Exec. GORDON WATSON; Dir EDWARD KING.

Kirkcaldy

Kirkcaldy Museum and Art Gallery: War Memorial Gardens, Kirkcaldy, KY1 1YG; tel. (1592) 583213; e-mail kirkcaldy.museum@fife.gov.uk; internet www.fifedirect.org.uk/museums; f. 1925; local history, archaeology, earth and natural sciences, industrial history, decorative arts, costume, ceramics; Scottish paintings since 19th century; Service Devt Man., Heritage and Art DALLAS MECHAN.

Leeds

Leeds Museums and Galleries: Carlisle Road, Hunslet, Leeds, LS10 1LB; tel. (113) 378-2100; e-mail museumsandgalleries@leeds.gov.uk; internet www.leeds.gov.uk/museumsandgalleries; f. 1820; Head of Collns CAMILLA NICHOL; publ. *Museums and Galleries Review* (1 a year).

Selected Museums and Galleries:

Abbey House Museum: Abbey Walk, Kirkstall, Leeds, LS5 3EH; tel. (113) 230-5492; e-mail abbey.house@leeds.gov.uk; internet www.leeds.gov.uk/abbeyhouse; f. 1927; gatehouse of Kirkstall Abbey, recreation of Victorian Leeds; Curator SAMANTHA FLAVIN.

Armley Mills (Leeds Industrial Museum): Canal Rd, Armley, Leeds, LS12 2QF; tel. (113) 263-7861; e-mail armley.mills@leeds.gov.uk; internet www.leeds.gov.uk/armleymills; f. 1969; textiles, printing, cinematography, history of engine and locomotive manufacturing in Leeds; manager's and mill-workers' houses; Keeper NINA BAPTISTE.

Leeds Art Gallery: The Headrow, Leeds, LS1 3AA; tel. (113) 247-8256; e-mail city.art.gallery@leeds.gov.uk; internet www.leeds.gov.uk/artgallery; f. 1888; 19th-century English and European paintings; early English watercolours, incl. Kitson and Lupton collns; modern paintings and sculpture; library: Print Room and Art Library; linked with Henry Moore Institute Archive and Library supporting the study of sculpture; Curator, Contemporary Art NIGEL WALSH.

Lotherton Hall: Lotherton Lane, Aberford, Leeds, LS25 3EB; tel. (113) 378-2959; e-mail museumsandgalleries@leeds.gov.uk; internet www.leeds.gov.uk/lothertonhall; f. 1969; country house dating from the 19th and 20th centuries; Gascoigne Colln of furniture, silver, ceramics, costume and paintings from the 17th to 19th centuries; modern crafts; oriental gallery; Curator ADAM WHITE.

Temple Newsam House: Temple Newsam Rd, off Selby Rd, Leeds LS15 0AE; tel. (113) 336-7461; e-mail temple.newsam.house@leeds.gov.uk; internet www.leeds.gov.uk/templenewsamhouse; f. 1923; Tudor-Stuart house, birthplace of Lord Darnley; contains extensive collns of old master and Ingram family paintings and the decorative arts; Curator POLLY PUTNAM.

Royal Armouries Museum: Armouries Dr., Leeds, LS10 1LT; tel. (113) 220-1999; e-mail enquiries@armouries.org.uk; internet www.royalarmouries.org; f. 1996; nat. colln of arms and armour and artillery; Master of the Armouries Dr EDWARD IMPEY; publ. *Arms and Armour: Journal of the Royal Armouries*.

Leicester

Leicestershire Museums: Leicestershire County Council, Leicester Rd, Glenfield, Leicester, LE3 8TB; tel. (116) 305-6642; e-mail museums@leics.gov.uk; internet www.leics.gov.uk/museums; f. 1849; local museums incl. Charnwood Museum, Donington-le-Heath Manor House, Harborough Museum, Melton Carnegie Museum, Snibston Discovery Park and the Record Office at Wigston Magna; Leicester 'Open Museum' comprises exhibits for hire within the county; museums concentrate on archaeology, natural life, cultural life, working life, Leicestershire history and education; Head Y. C. COURTNEY.

National Space Centre: Exploration Dr., Leicester, LE4 5NS; e-mail info@spacecentre.co.uk; internet www.spacecentre.co.uk; f. 2001; displays about space and space exploration; incl. space science research unit; Chief Exec. CHAS BISHOP.

Lincoln

Lincolnshire Heritage Services: Cultural Services Branch, Lincolnshire County Council Offices, Newland, Lincoln, LN1 1YQ; tel. (1522) 552222; e-mail customer_services@lincolnshire.gov.uk; internet www.lincolnshire.gov.uk; f. 1974; operates 7 museums (see below) and several other sites, incl. Lincoln Castle, Judge's Lodgings, Battle of Britain Memorial Flight Visitor Centre, Lincolnshire Archives, and windmills in Alford, Burgh le Marsh, Heckington and Lincoln; Head of Heritage and Regeneration HEATHER CUMMINS..

Attached Museums:

The Collection: Art and Archaeology in Lincolnshire: Danes Terrace, Lincoln, LN2 1LP; tel. (1522) 550990; e-mail thecollection@lincolnshire.gov.uk; internet www.thecollectionmuseum.com; f. 1906 as City and County Museum, present status 2005; comprises exhibits from the fmr City and County Museum (artefacts since medieval era, incl. collns of coins, medals, arms and natural science) and the Usher Gallery (fine, decorative and contemporary arts); Collns Officer DAWN HEYWOOD; Collns Officer ANTONY LEE.

Gainsborough Old Hall: Parnell St, Gainsborough, DN21 2NB; tel. (1427) 612669; e-mail gainsborougholdhall@lincolnshire.gov.uk; internet www.lincolnshire.gov.uk/gainsborougholdhall; f. 1974; 15th-century timber-framed manor house with great hall, medieval kitchen; guided tours; events and exhibits; heritage education programme; Site Coordinator VICTORIA MASON.

Grantham Museum: St Peter's Hill, Grantham, NG31 6PY; tel. (1476) 568783; e-mail info@granthammuseum.org.uk; internet www.granthammuseum.org.uk; f. 1923; local prehistoric artefacts, Roman and Saxon archaeology, Grantham local history, trades and industries, display of Victorian dolls, and a colln devoted to notable figures born locally, incl. Sir Isaac Newton and Margaret Thatcher; District Man. NICOLA ROGERS.

Museum of Lincolnshire Life: Burton Rd, Lincoln, LN1 3LY; tel. (1522) 528448; e-mail lincolnshire_museum@lincolnshire.gov.uk; f. 1969; displays illustrating the social, agricultural and industrial history of Lincolnshire over the 17th–20th centuries; also contains Lincolnshire Regiment Museum; manages the Ellis Windmill; Dist. Man. N. ROGERS.

Usher Gallery: Lindum Rd, Lincoln, LN2 1NN; tel. (1522) 527980; e-mail usher.gallery@lincolnshire.gov.uk; internet www.thecollection.lincoln.museum; attached to The Collection (county archaeological collns; see above); houses the Usher colln of watches, miniatures and decorative art, and a colln of fine art, sculpture and coins, incl. works by De Wint, Lowry, Turner and contemporary artists Grayson Perry and Terry Frost; Area Service Man. JEREMY WEBSTER.

Liverpool

National Museums Liverpool: 127 Dale St, Liverpool,; tel. (151) 207-0001; internet www.liverpoolmuseums.org.uk; f. 1986 as Nat. Museums and Galleries on Merseyside, current name adopted 2003; groups the 7 museums of Liverpool, incl. the Museum of Liverpool; Dir DAVID FLEMING..

Constituent Museums and Galleries:

Conservation Centre: Midland Railway Bldg, 1 Peter St, Liverpool, L1 6BL; tel. (151) 478-41812; e-mail val.ward@liverpoolmuseums.org.uk; internet www.liverpoolmuseums.org.uk; f. 1996; illustrates the arts and science of the conservation of museum exhibits; depts of ceramics, conservation science, frames, metals, organics, paintings, paper, sculpture, shipkeeping, taxidermy and textiles; Head of Conservation SALLY ANN YATES.

Lady Lever Art Gallery: Port Sunlight Village, Wirral, CH62 5EQ; tel. (151) 478-4136; internet www.liverpoolmuseums.org.uk/ladylever; f. 1922; colln of British Pre-Raphaelite 18th- and 19th-century paintings, 18th-century furniture; colln of Wedgewood and Chinese porcelain.

Merseyside Maritime Museum: Albert Dock, Liverpool, L3 4AQ; tel. (151) 478-4499; internet www.liverpoolmuseums.org.uk/maritime; f. 1980; set in Liverpool's docklands; displays and exhibits on the region's maritime past; gallery of maritime paintings; library: reference library of maritime material, incl. archives and records.

Seized! Border and Customs Uncovered: Merseyside Maritime Museum, Albert Dock, Liverpool, L3 4AQ; tel. (151) 478-4499; internet www.liverpoolmuseums.org.uk/maritime; f. 1994 fmrly HM Customs and Excise National Museum; exhibits relating to smuggling and revenue colln since 1700; holds nat. colln of Dept of Customs and Excise and UK Border Agency; displays of equipment, prints, paintings and photographs; Press Assist. ALISON CORNMELL.

Sudley House: Mossley Hill Rd, Liverpool; tel. (151) 724-3245; internet www.liverpoolmuseums.org.uk; f. 1986; fmr home of 19th-century shipowner; 18th- and 19th-century art incl. works by Gainsborough, Landseer and artists of the Pre-Raphaelite movement; Dir of Art Galleries REYAHN KING.

Walker Art Gallery: William Brown St, Liverpool L3 8EL; tel. (151) 478-4199; internet www.liverpoolmuseums.org.uk/walker; collns of European art since 1300; sculpture gallery; Keeper JULIAN TREUHERZ.

World Museum Liverpool: William Brown St, Liverpool, L3 8EN; tel. (151) 478-4399; internet www.liverpoolmuseums.org.uk/wml; f. 1851, rebuilt 1964–69, current name adopted 2005; spec. collns incl. the Mayer-Fejérvàry Gothic ivories, the Bryan Fausset group of Anglo-Saxon antiquities, the Lord Derby and Tristram ornithological collns; bug house, aquarium, ethnology, time and space gallery, planetarium, Clore natural history centre, Weston discovery centre; Dir Dr STEVE JUDD.

London

Bank of England Museum: Bartholomew Lane, London, EC2R 8AH; tel. (20) 7601-5545; e-mail museum@bankofengland.co.uk; internet www.bankofengland.co.uk/education/pages/museum/visiting/default.aspx; f. 1694; illustrates the history of the bank and its current work; collns incl. banknotes and coins, books and documents, furniture, pictures and photographs, statues and other artefacts; Curator JOHN KEYWORTH.

British Museum: Great Russell St, London, WC1B 3DG; tel. (20) 7323-8299; e-mail information@britishmuseum.org; internet www.britishmuseum.org; f. 1753 opened 1759, present bldgs begun 1823, completed 1852; 8m. objects; collns and exhibitions of prehistoric, Egyptian, Assyrian, medieval, oriental and other archaeological collns, ethnography, prints, drawings, ceramics, coins, medals and banknotes; Dir NEIL MACGREGOR; Keeper (Africa, Oceania and the Americas Dept) LISSANT BOLTON; Keeper (Ancient Egypt and Sudan Dept) NEAL SPENCER; Keeper (Asia Dept) JAN STUART; Keeper (Coins and Medals Dept) PHILIP ATTWOOD; Keeper (Conservation and Scientific Research Dept) DAVID SAUNDERS; Greece and Rome Dept J. LESLEY FITTON; Keeper (Middle East Dept) JONATHAN N. TUBB; Keeper (Prehistory and Europe Dept) ROGER BLAND; Keeper (Prints and Drawings Dept) HUGO CHAPMAN.

British Postal Museum & Archive: Freeling House, Phoenix Place, London, WC1X 0DL; tel. (20) 7239-2570; e-mail info@postalheritage.org.uk; internet www.postalheritage.org.uk; f. 2004; colln of stamps, essays, drawings and official documents dating back to Rowland Hill's proposals for Uniform Penny Postage in 1837–39; Post Office colln of stamps of the world and of British stamps since the early 20th century, philatelic archives (1855–1965) of Thomas De La Rue and Co., security printers, on microfilm; postboxes and other postal exhibits; Dir Dr ADRIAN STEEL; Deputy Dir TIM ELLISON.

Carlyle's House: 24 Cheyne Row, Chelsea, London, SW3 5HL; tel. (20) 7352-7087; e-mail carlyleshouse@nationaltrust.org.uk; contains books, paintings, furniture and personal relics of Thomas Carlyle.

Courtauld Gallery: Somerset House, Strand, London, WC2R 0RN; tel. (20) 7848-2526; e-mail galleryinfo@courtauld.ac.uk; internet www.courtauld.ac.uk/gallery; f. 1932; Old Master, Impressionist and Post-Impressionist paintings, prints and drawings, (incl. works by Botticelli, Cézanne, Goya, Manet, Michelangelo, Rembrandt, Renoir, Rubens, Tiepolo, Turner and Van Gogh); sculpture and applied arts; Head Dr ERNST VEGELIN.

Cuming Museum (Borough of Southwark): 151 Walworth Rd, London, SE17 1RY; tel. (20) 7525-2332; e-mail cuming.museum@southwark.gov.uk; internet www.southwark.gov.uk/cumingmuseum; f. 1906; worldwide collns of the Cuming family; local history of Southwark from Roman times to the present; display galleries currently closed.

Design Museum: Shad Thames, London, SE1 2YD; tel. (20) 7403-6933; e-mail info@designmuseum.org; internet www.designmuseum.org; f. 1989; ind. museum set up by the Conran Foundation, promotes awareness of the importance of design in education, industry, commerce and culture; colln of mass-produced design; Chair. LUQMAN ARNOLD; Dir DEYAN SUDJIC.

Dulwich Picture Gallery: Gallery Rd, London, SE21 7AD; tel. (20) 8693-5254; e-mail enquiries@dulwichpicturegallery.org.uk; internet www.dulwichpicturegallery.org.uk; f. 1811; houses colln of European old masters, incl. Rembrandt, Rubens, Cuyp, Van Dyck, Teniers, Poussin, Claude, Watteau, Raphael, Tiepolo, Gainsborough, Murillo, etc.; Dir IAN DEJARDIN.

Estorick Collection of Modern Italian Art: 39A Canonbury Sq., London, N1 2AN; tel. (20) 7704-9522; e-mail info@estorickcollection.com; internet www.estorickcollection.com; f. 1998; 20th-century Italian art, especially Futurist; library of 2,000 vols, periodicals and catalogues; Dir ROBERTA CREMONCINI.

Fashion and Textile Museum: 83 Bermondsey St, London, SE1 3XF; tel. (20) 7407-8664; e-mail info@ftmlondon.org; internet www.ftmlondon.org; f. 2003; colln relates to the design and production of fashion, textiles and jewellery; Head of Museum CELIA JOICEY; Curator DENNIS NOTHDRUFT.

Foundling Museum: 40 Brunswick Sq., London, WC1N 1AZ; tel. (20) 7841-3600; e-mail enquiries@foundlingmuseum.org.uk; internet www.foundlingmuseum.org.uk; f. 2004; 2 principal collns: the Foundling hospital colln and the Gerald Coke Handel colln; paintings, sculpture, prints, MSS, furniture, clocks and historical documents; Dir CARO HOWELL.

Freud Museum: 20 Maresfield Gdns, London, NW3 5SX; tel. (20) 7435-2002; e-mail info@freud.org.uk; internet www.freud.org.uk; f. 1986; fmr London home of Sigmund Freud and his daughter Anna; incl. Sigmund Freud's colln of antiquities, including 1,500 Egyptian, Greek, Roman and Oriental antiquities; his psychoanalytical couch, library and furniture; also a psychoanalysis research centre; library of 1,600 vols from Sigmund Freud's colln; Dir DAWN KEMP (acting).

Geffrye Museum: 136 Kingsland Rd, London, E2 8EA; tel. (20) 7739-9893; e-mail info@geffrye-museum.org.uk; internet www.geffrye-museum.org.uk; f. 1914; English furniture, textiles, domestic objects and paintings arranged in a series of period rooms from 1600–2000; herb and period gardens; library and archive; Dir DAVID DEWING.

Hampton Court Palace: Surrey, KT8 9AU; tel. (844) 482-7777; e-mail hamptoncourt@hrp.org.uk; internet www.hrp.org.uk/hamptoncourtpalace; home of Henry VIII, contains colln of paintings and tapestries, incl. Andrea Mantegna's 9 great tempera paintings of 'The Triumphs of Julius Caesar'; Palace Dir PAUL GRAY; Superintendent of the Royal Colln C. STEVENS.

Hayward Gallery: South Bank Centre, Belvedere Rd, London, SE1 8XZ; tel. (20) 7921-08138; e-mail hginfo@hayward.org.uk; internet www.southbankcentre.co.uk/venues/hayward-gallery; f. 1968; contemporary perspectives on art past and present, focusing on individual artists, historical themes and artistic movements, other cultures, and contemporary art; administers national touring exhibitions and the Arts Council Collection (7,500 items); Dir CAROLINE FELTON (acting).

Horniman Museum and Gardens: 100 London Rd, Forest Hill, London, SE23 3PQ; tel. (20) 8699-1872; e-mail enquiry@ horniman.ac.uk; internet www.horniman.ac .uk; f. 1901; 3 major collns: ethnography, natural history and musical instruments (incl. archive documents); aquarium; 16 acres of gardens; education activities with schools, community groups and gen. public; specialist research library; library of 30,000 vols, mainly on African history, entomology, botany, ethnography, natural history, musical instruments; Chief Exec. JANET VITMAYER; Keeper (Anthropology) ROBERT STORRIE; Keeper (Musical Instruments) MARGARET BIRLEY; Keeper (Natural History) JOANNE HATTON.

Hunterian Museum: Royal College of Surgeons, 35–43 Lincoln's Inn Fields, London, WC2A 3PE; tel. (20) 7869-6560; e-mail museums@rcseng.ac.uk; internet www .rcseng.ac.uk/museums/hunterian/; f. 1813; colln of anatomist and surgeon John Hunter (1728–93); collns of comparative anatomy and pathology specimens, skeletons, skulls and teeth, teaching models, historical surgical and dental instruments, paintings, drawings and sculpture; temporary exhibitions; Dir of Museums and Archives Dr SAMUEL ALBERTI; Curator SARAH PEARSON; Head of Conservation Unit MARTYN COOKE.

Imperial War Museums: Lambeth Rd, London, SE1 6HZ; tel. (20) 7416-5000; e-mail mail@iwm.org.uk; internet www.iwm .org.uk; f. 1917; collns cover all aspects of 20th and 21st century conflict involving Britain, the Commonwealth and other former empire countries; library of 270,000 items, incl. pamphlets, periodicals, maps and drawings; Chair. of the Board of Trustees Sir FRANCIS RICHARDS; Dir-Gen. DIANE LEES..

Branches:

Churchill War Rooms: Clive Steps, King Charles St, London, SW1A 2AQ; tel. (20) 7930-6961; e-mail cwr@iwm.org.uk; internet www.iwm.org.uk/visits/ churchill-war-rooms; Churchill's underground headquarters; explores the life of Winston Churchill (1874–1965); Dir PHIL REED.

HMS Belfast: The Queen's Walk, London, SE1 2JH; tel. (20) 7940-6300; e-mail hmsbelfast@iwm.org.uk; internet www .iwm.org.uk/visits/hms-belfast; Second World War cruiser moored in the Pool of London; Dir E. J. WENZEL.

Imperial War Museum Duxford: Duxford, Cambridgeshire, CB22 4QR; tel. (1223) 835000; e-mail duxford@iwm.org .uk; internet www.iwm.org.uk/duxford; f. 1977; airfield that featured in the Battle of Britain (1940), housing historic colln of aircraft, military vehicles, tanks and artillery; incl. American Air Museum (aam.iwm.org.uk); interactive exhibitions; Dir RICHARD ASHTON.

IWM North: The Quays, Trafford Wharf Rd, Manchester, M17 1TZ; tel. (161) 836-4000; e-mail iwmnorth@iwm.org.uk; internet www.iwm.org.uk; f. 2002; war and its effect on the 20th and 21st centuries, through exhibits, audiovisual shows and interactive exhibits and changing programme of events; Dir GRAHAM BOXER.

Iveagh Bequest: Kenwood, Hampstead Lane, London, NW3 7JR; tel. (20) 8348-1286; left to the nation by Edward Cecil Guinness, first Earl of Iveagh, in 1927; includes paintings of British, Dutch, Flemish and French schools, housed in an 18th-century mansion (Kenwood House) designed by Robert Adam, containing an ornate library; exhibitions on aspects of 18th-century art;

Dir of E. H. London Region RICHARD FREELAND.

London Transport Museum: Covent Garden Piazza, London, WC2E 7BB; tel. (20) 7379-6344; e-mail enquiry@ltmuseum.co.uk; internet www.ltmuseum.co.uk; f. 1961, present name 2002; offers people an understanding of the capital's past devt of transport and engages in the debate about its future; collns incl. vehicles, rolling stock, posters and original artworks, signs, uniforms, photographs, ephemera, maps and engineering drawings; library of 14,000 vols incl. books, journals and spec. collns; Chief Exec. and Dir SAM MULLINS.

Museum of London: 150 London Wall, London, EC2Y 5HN; tel. (20) 7001-9844; e-mail info@museumoflondon.org.uk; internet www.museumoflondon.org.uk; f. 1976 by merger of Guildhall Museum (f. 1826) and London Museum (f. 1912); social history of London from prehistory to 20th century; exhibits incl. the Lord Mayor's coach, 18th-century prison cell, Victorian shop fronts; Dir SHARON AMENT..

Constituent Museums:

Museum of London Docklands: No 1 Warehouse, West India Quay, London, E14 4AL; tel. (20) 7001-9844; e-mail info .docklands@museumoflondon.org.uk; internet www.museumoflondon.org.uk/ docklands; exhibits on activities and industries in London's docklands, incl. conservation, employment and social history; Dir DAVID SPENCE.

National Army Museum: Royal Hospital Rd, Chelsea, London, SW3 4HT; tel. (20) 7730-0717; e-mail info@nam.ac.uk; internet www.nam.ac.uk; f. 1960; displays depicting the history of the British Army since 1066 until the present day, the Indian Army until Independence in 1947, and colonial land forces; reference collns of 43,000 books, 30,000 pamphlets, 300 mof archives, 50,000 prints, drawings and watercolours, 5,000,000 photographs; 80,000 uniforms, 250,000 badges; 20,000 medals and weapons; personal equipment and a sound and film archive; Dir-Gen. JANICE MURRAY; Dir MIKE O'CONNOR.

National Gallery: Trafalgar Sq., London, WC2N 5DN; tel. (20) 7747-2885; e-mail information@ng-london.org.uk; internet www.nationalgallery.org.uk; f. 1824; contains examples of all the principal schools of Western European painting from 1250 to 1900; a selection of British painters from Hogarth to Turner; picture library; Chair. MARK GETTY; Dir Dr NICHOLAS PENNY.

National Maritime Museum: Romney Rd, Greenwich, London, SE10 9NF; tel. (20) 8858-4422; internet www.rmg.co.uk/ national-maritime-museum; f. 1934; colln incl. portraits and sea pieces, models, ship's plans, instruments, maps and charts, weapons, medals; Queen's House: 17th-century royal apartments of Queen Henrietta Maria; also the Royal Observatory Greenwich, where the displays illustrate themes concerned with astronomy, time and navigation, the meridian line, and a planetarium; library of 20,000 vols on maritime history and MSS; photo library of 330,000 images and negatives; Dir KEVIN FEWSTER; Deputy Dir MARGARETTE LINCOLN; publ. *Journal for Maritime Research.*

National Portrait Gallery: St Martin's Pl., London, WC2H 0HE; tel. (20) 7306-0055; internet www.npg.org.uk; f. 1856; portraits of eminent people in British history; library of 40,000 vols; Dir SANDY NAIRNE.

Natural History Museum: Cromwell Rd, London, SW7 5BD; tel. (20) 7942-5000;

internet www.nhm.ac.uk; f. 1881, current name adopted 1992; originates from the Natural History Depts of the British Museum, and a br. comprising the Natural History Museum at Tring, Herts.; incorporates the Geological Museum; library: see under Libraries and Archives; Chair. of the Board of Trustees (vacant); Dir Dr MICHAEL DIXON; Keeper of Botany PHILIP STEPHEN RAINBOW; Keeper of Entomology ANDREW POLASZEK; Keeper of Palaeontology Prof. NORMAN MACLEOD; Keeper of Zoology Prof. PHILIP STEPHEN RAINBOW; publ. *Evolve* (4 a year).

Polish Institute and Sikorski Museum: 20 Princes Gate, London, SW7 1PT; tel. (20) 7589-9249; internet www.pism.co.uk; f. 1945; archives, museum, research centre and publishing house; incl the Sikorski Colln (personal belongings, memorabilia, wartime diary, etc. of Gen. Wladyslaw Sikorski, 1881–1943), militaria (over 10,000 items), maps, paintings and engravings, sculptures, porcelain, miniatures, coins and medals.

Royal Academy of Arts: Burlington House, Piccadilly, London, W1J 0BD; tel. (20) 7300-8000; internet www.royalacademy.org.uk; f. 1768; colln incl. paintings, sculptures, drawings, prints, architectural designs, historic books, archives, historic photographs and plaster casts; contains 935 paintings, 350 sculptures, 700 plaster casts, 25,000 prints and drawings and 5,000 historic photographs; Pres. Sir CHRISTOPHER LE BRUN; Keeper EILEEN COOPER.

Royal Air Force Museum: Grahame Park Way, London, NW9 5LL; tel. (20) 8205-2266; e-mail london@rafmuseum.org; internet www.rafmuseum.org; f. 1972; exhibits 100 full-size British and foreign aircraft from 1909 to the present, material recording the history of the Royal Air Force and the devt of aviation; br. at Cosford (West Midlands); library of 100,000 vols, and archives and photographic colln; Dir-Gen. PETER DYE.

Royal Armouries: HM Tower of London, London, EC3N 4AB; tel. (20) 3166-6660; e-mail enquiries@armouries.org.uk; internet www.royalarmouries.org; nat. museum of arms and armour and museum of the Tower of London, originating from the working arsenal at the Tower and the colln of royal armour begun by Henry VIII; first open to the public c. 1660; the nat. and royal collns cover the devt of arms and armour since c. AD 1000; Royal Small Arms Factory; library: Leeds-based reference library of 40,000 vols and 167,000 prints, transparencies and slides; also libraries at the Tower of London and Fort Nelson; Master of the Armouries Dr EDWARD IMPEY; Chair. WES PAUL; publ. *Arms and Armour* (2 a year).

Museum of Instruments: Prince Consort Rd, S Kensington, London, SW7 2BS; tel. (20) 7591-4842; e-mail museum@rcm.ac.uk; internet www.cph.rcm.ac.uk/genmuseum .htm; f. 1970; attached to Royal College of Music; colln of 800 instruments and accessories since 1480, incl. Donaldson, Tagore, Hipkins, Ridley, Hartley, Fleming, Walton and Steele-Perkins collns; Curator JENNY NEX.

Faraday Museum: 21 Albemarle St, London, W1S 4BS; tel. (20) 7409-2992; e-mail archivist@ri.ac.uk; internet www.rigb.org/ visit-us/faraday-museum; f. 1799; attached to Royal Institution; original apparatus made and used by Faraday and other key scientists such as Humphry Davy, John Tyndall and William and Lawrence Bragg; incl. Faraday's magnetic laboratory; library of 30,000 vols (works on physics and chemistry since the 1700s); Head of Collns and Heritage Prof FRANK JAMES.

Saatchi Gallery: Duke of York's HQ, King's Rd, London, SW3 4RY; e-mail admin@saatchigallery.com; internet www.saatchigallery.com; f. 1985; colln of mostly modern art from contemporary British artists (incl. Damien Hirst, Tracey Emin, Sarah Lucas, Jenny Saville, Chapman brothers), modern art from China; Dir REBECCA WILSON.

Science Museum: Exhibition Rd, S Kensington, London, SW7 2DD; tel. (20) 7942-4000; e-mail info@sciencemuseum.ac.uk; internet www.sciencemuseum.org.uk; f. 1857; collns: science, medicine, information and communications technologies, engineering technologies; library: see under Libraries and Archives; Dir Prof. IAN BLATCHFORD.

Sir John Soane's Museum: 13 Lincoln's Inn Fields, London, WC2A 3BP; tel. (20) 7405-2107; e-mail admin@soane.org.uk; internet www.soane.org; f. 1837; colln incl. paintings by Hogarth, the Egyptian Sarcophagus of Seti I, Italian bronzes, paintings, antique sculpture, 18th-century English sculpture, models, 30,000 architectural drawings; library: see under Libraries and Archives; Dir ABRAHAM THOMAS; Deputy Dir HELEN DOREY.

South London Gallery: 65–67 Peckham Rd, London, SE5 8UH; tel. (20) 7703-6120; e-mail mail@southlondongallery.org; internet www.southlondongallery.org; f. 1891; regular exhibitions of innovative contemporary art supported by a full programme of education events and workshops; Dir MARGOT HELLER; Deputy Dir HIRAANI HIMONA.

Tate: Millbank, London, SW1P 4RG; tel. (20) 7887-8888; e-mail information@tate.org.uk; internet www.tate.org.uk; f. 1897; Dir Sir NICHOLAS SEROTA..

Constituent Museums:

Tate Britain: Millbank, London, SW1P 4RG; tel. (20) 7887-8888; e-mail information@tate.org.uk; internet www.tate.org.uk; f. 1897 by Sir Henry Tate; nat. gallery of British art since 1500, incl. works by Hogarth, Blake, Constable and the Pre-Raphaelites, with the Turner Collection housed in the Clore Gallery; Dir Dr PENELOPE CURTIS..

Research Centre:

Tate Library and Archive: Hyman Kreitman Reading Rooms, Tate Britain, Millbank, London, SW1P 4RG; tel. (20) 7887-8838; e-mail reading.rooms@tate.org.uk; internet www.tate.org.uk/research/reading-rooms; f. 2002; covers British art from 1500 and int. art from 1900 exhibition catalogues, monographs, artists' books, ephemera; Archive colln (700 individual archives) covers British art from 1900, incl. unpublished material on British artists, art world figures and orgs; Tate Public Records colln; library of 250,000 vols; Head of Library and Archive and Colln Access JANE BRAMWELL.

Tate Liverpool: Albert Dock, Liverpool, L3 4BB; tel. (151) 702-7400; e-mail visiting.liverpool@tate.org.uk; internet www.tate.org.uk/liverpool; f. 1988; home of the Nat. Colln of Modern Art in the North; 4 floors displaying work selected from the Tate Colln and spec. exhibitions of artwork loaned from around the world; modern and contemporary art since 1900, incl. painting and sculpture, photography, video installations; tours and lectures; Exec. Dir ANDREA NIXON.

Tate Modern: Bankside, London, SE1 9TG; tel. (20) 7887-8888; e-mail visiting.modern@tate.org.uk; internet www.tate.org.uk; f. 2000; int. modern art since 1900; Dir CHRIS DERCON.

Tate St Ives: Porthmeor Beach, St Ives, TR26 1TG; tel. (1736) 796226; e-mail tatestives@tate.org.uk; internet www.tate.org.uk; f. 1993; modern painting, sculpture and ceramics by artists associated with St Ives, as well as int. figures; incl. Barbara Hepworth Museum and Sculpture Garden; Exec. Dir MARK OSTERFIELD.

Victoria and Albert (V&A) Museum: S Kensington, Cromwell Rd, London, SW7 2RL; tel. (20) 7942-2000; e-mail vanda@vam.ac.uk; internet www.vam.ac.uk; f. 1852; all forms of art and design, with collns of ceramics, furniture, fashion, glass, jewellery, metalwork, sculpture, textiles and paintings; Dir MARTIN ROTH; Keeper (Asian Dept) ANNA JACKSON; Keeper (Furniture, Textiles and Fashion Dept) CHRISTOPHER WILK; Keeper (Sculpture, Metalwork, Ceramics and Glass Dept) PAUL WILLIAMSON; Keeper (Word and Image Dept) JULIUS BRYANT..

Constituent Museum:

V&A Department of Theatre and Performance—National Museum for the Performing Arts: Reading Room, Blythe House, 23 Blythe Rd, London, W14 0QX; tel. (20) 7942-2697; e-mail tmenquiries@vam.ac.uk; internet www.vam.ac.uk/page/t/theatre-and-performance; f. 1974, opened to the public 1987; nat. record of stage performance; history, craft and practice of the performing arts in Britain; library of 100,000 vols (incorporating British Theatre Asscn colln and library of the Soc. for Theatre Research); spec. archive collns incl. D'Oyly Carte Co., English Stage Co., English Shakespeare Co., Arts Council of Great Britain, Diaghilev's Ballets Russes and Edward Gordon Craig; spec. photographic archives incl. Houston Rogers, Gordon Anthony and Anthony Crickmay; Nat. Video Archive of Performance; Dir GEOFFREY MARSH.

V&A Museum of Childhood: Cambridge Heath Rd, London, E2 9PA; tel. (20) 8983-5200; e-mail mocbookings@vam.ac.uk; internet www.museumofchildhood.org.uk; f. 1872 as Bethnal Green Museum, current name adopted 1974; collns of childhood objects, toys, dolls, dolls' houses, games, puzzles; Dir RHIAN HARRIS.

Wallace Collection: Hertford House, Manchester Sq., London, W1U 3BN; tel. (20) 7563-9500; e-mail enquiries@wallacecollection.org; internet www.wallacecollection.org; f. 1900; collns of 18th-century French pictures, furniture, Sèvres porcelain and sculpture; 17th-century paintings, armoury and objets d'art, bequeathed to the nation in 1897 by Lady Wallace; library of 20,000 vols; Dir Dr CHRISTOPH VOGTHERR.

White Cube: 144–152 Bermondsey St, London, SE1 3TQ; tel. (20) 7930-5373; e-mail enquiries@whitecube.com; internet www.whitecube.com; f. 2011; modern British art; Man. Dir JAY JOPLING.

Whitechapel Gallery: 77–82 Whitechapel High St, London, E1 7QX; tel. (20) 7522-7888; e-mail info@whitechapelgallery.org; internet www.whitechapelgallery.org; f. 1901, reopened 2009; temporary exhibitions, principally of modern or contemporary art; no permanent colln; charitable trust supported by the Arts Council, local authorities, charitable bodies and the business community; Chair. ROBERT TAYLOR; Dir IWONA BLAZWICK.

Manchester

Manchester City Galleries: Mosley St, Manchester, M2 3JL; tel. (161) 235-8888; internet www.manchestergalleries.org; f. 1823; dept of Manchester City Ccl, operates 4 galleries in and around Manchester..

Constituent Galleries:

Gallery of Costume: Platt Hall, Rusholme, Manchester, M14 5LL; tel. (161) 245-7245; e-mail m.lambert@manchester.gov.uk; internet www.manchestergalleries.org/our-other-venues/platt-hall-gallery-of-costume; f. 1947; 18th-century fmr textile merchant's house; 20,000 items of clothing and fashion accessories from 17th century to the present; library of 20,000 vols, 25000 portrait photographs, fashion journals, tailoring and etiquette books, shop catalogues, paper patterns; Sr Curator Dr MILES LAMBERT.

Manchester Art Gallery: Mosley St, Manchester, M2 3JL; tel. (161) 235-8888; e-mail galleryeducation@notes.manchester.gov.uk; internet www.manchestergalleries.org; f. 2002 following reorganization of the fmr Manchester City Art Gallery; 25,000 items; fine art colln includes 2,000 oil paintings, 3,000 watercolours and drawings, 250 sculptures, 90 miniatures, 1,000 prints, notable works by the Pre-Raphaelites: Rossetti, Millais, Hunt, Burne-Jones; colln of decorative arts ranges from ancient Greek pottery to contemporary furniture; contemporary local art and design, incl. works by Lowry; gallery of craft and design.

Manchester Museum: Univ. of Manchester, Oxford Rd, Manchester, M13 9PL; tel. (161) 275-2648; e-mail museum@manchester.ac.uk; internet www.museum.manchester.ac.uk; f. 1888; attached to Univ. of Manchester; colln of 4.5m objects in subject areas of ancient Egypt, archaeology, archery, earth sciences, human remains, vivarium, living cultures, money, plants, zoology and birds and insects; Dir Dr NICHOLAS MERRIMAN.

Museum of Science and Industry: Liverpool Rd, Castlefield, Manchester, M3 4FP; tel. (161) 832-2244; internet www.mosi.org.uk; f. 1983; housed in the world's oldest passenger railway station; explores the history, science and industry of Manchester, with displays focusing on textiles, communications, utilities, steam power and the railways, cameras, aircraft; Dir JEAN M. FRANCZYK (acting).

National Football Museum: Urbis Bldg, Cathedral Gardens, Manchester, M4 3BG; tel. (161) 605-8200; e-mail info@nationalfootballmuseum.com; internet www.nationalfootballmuseum.com; f. 2001; colln of 140,000 items, incl. FIFA colln; Dir KEVIN MOORE; Deputy Dir DAVID PEARSON.

Newcastle upon Tyne

Tyne and Wear Archives & Museums: Discovery Museum, Blandford Sq., Newcastle upon Tyne, NE1 4JA; tel. (191) 232-6789; internet www.twmuseums.org.uk; f. 1974; Dir IAIN WATSON..

Selected Museums and Galleries:

Arbeia Roman Fort & Museum: Baring St, South Shields, NE33 2BB; tel. (191) 456-1369; e-mail info@arbeiaromanfort.org.uk; internet www.twmuseums.org.uk/arbeia; f. 1953; Roman coins, military equipment, pottery, jewellery; excavations and reconstructions; Curator ALEX CROOM.

Discovery Museum: Blandford Sq., Newcastle upon Tyne, NE1 4JA; tel. (191) 232-6789; e-mail info@discoverymuseum.org.uk; internet www.twmuseums.org.uk/discovery; f. 1934; displays of fashion, military history, social history and maritime history, and ship *Turbinia*; Museum Man. HAZEL EDWARDS.

Great North Museum: Hancock: Barras Bridge, Newcastle upon Tyne, NE2 4PT; tel. (191) 208-6765; e-mail info@

greatnorthmuseum.org.uk; internet www .twmuseums.org.uk/great-north-museum .html; f. 2009, incorporates collns from the Hancock Museum (f. 1829), Newcastle Univ.'s Museum of Antiquities (f. 1813), the Shefton Museum (f. 1956) and the Hatton Gallery; reserve natural science and archaeology collns comprising 500,000 items; large-scale, interactive model of Hadrian's Wall, displays of the animal and plant kingdoms, objects from ancient Greece, mummies from ancient Egypt, planetarium.

Laing Art Gallery: New Bridge St, Newcastle upon Tyne, NE1 8AG; tel. (191) 232-7734; e-mail info@laingartgallery.org.uk; internet www.twmuseums.org.uk/ laing-art-gallery.html; f. 1904; British oil paintings and watercolours since 1700 (incl. works by Reynolds, Gainsborough, Turner, Landseer, Burne-Jones, Holman Hunt, Spencer); silver, ceramics and glass (incl. display of enamelled glass by William Beilby); Curator JULIE MILNE.

Segedunum Roman Fort, Baths and Museum: Buddle St, Wallsend, NE28 6HR; tel. (191) 236-9347; e-mail info@ segedunumromanfort.org.uk; internet www.twmuseums.org.uk/segedunum; f. 2000; Roman colln incl. defensive missiles from the fort; Industry Gallery has artefacts associated with coalmining and shipbuilding, incl. model of the ship *Carpathia*; Curator GEOFF WOODWARD.

Shipley Art Gallery: Prince Consort Rd, Gateshead, NE8 4JB; tel. (191) 477-1495; e-mail info@shipleyartgallery.org.uk; internet www.twmuseums.org.uk/ shipley-art-gallery; f. 1917; contemporary craft; design; decorative arts; British and European paintings; Curator AMY BARKER.

South Shields Museum and Art Gallery: 4 Ocean Rd, South Shields, NE33 2JA; tel. (191) 456-8740; e-mail info@ southshieldsmuseum.org.uk; internet www.twmuseums.org.uk/south-shields; local history in relation to S Tyneside; Catherine Cookson gallery; local art and crafts; Curator ALISDAIR WILSON.

Stephenson Railway Museum: Middle Engine Lane, North Shields, NE29 8DX; tel. (191) 200-7146; e-mail info@ stephensonrailwaymuseum.org.uk; internet www.twmuseums.org.uk/stephenson; colln of steam, diesel and electric locomotives, incl. the early locomotive *Billy*; social history relating to railways; Curator JOHN CLAYSON.

Newport (Gwent)

Newport Museum and Art Gallery: John Frost Sq., Newport, NP20 1PA; tel. (1633) 656656; e-mail museum@newport.gov.uk; internet www.newport.gov.uk/heritage/ index.cfm/museum; f. 1888; collns of Roman material from Caerleon and Caerwent; oils, early English watercolours and prints, and other paintings (incl. by Lowry); teapot displays; ceramics; natural and local history collns; Museums Officer (Collns) BRUCE CAMPBELL; Museums and Heritage Officer MIKE LEWIS.

Norwich

Norfolk Museums and Archaeology Service: The Shirehall, Market Ave, Norwich, NR1 3JQ; tel. (1603) 493625; e-mail museums@norfolk.gov.uk; internet www .museums.norfolk.gov.uk; Head of Museums VANESSA TREVELYAN..

Selected Museums:

Ancient House Museum: 21–23 White Hart St, Thetford, IP24 1AA; tel. (1842) 752599; e-mail ancienthouse@norfolk.gov

.uk; 15th-century timber-framed bldg; local history; Curator OLIVER BONE.

Bridewell Museum: NMAS, Shirehall, Market Ave, Norwich, NR1 3JQ; tel. (1603) 493625; e-mail museums@norfolk .gov.uk; local industries and crafts in medieval house; Curator of Community History HANNAH HENDERSON.

Cromer Museum: East Cottages, Tucker St, Cromer, NR27 9HB; tel. (1263) 513543; e-mail cromer.museum@norfolk.gov.uk; internet www.museums.norfolk.gov.uk; f. 1978; local history, archaeology, geology, natural history; Curator ALISTAIR MURPHY; Area Museum Officer JAMIE EVERITT.

Elizabethan House Museum: Elizabethan House, 4 S Quay, Great Yarmouth, NR30 2QH; tel. (1493) 855746; e-mail yarmouth.museums@norfolk.gov.uk; domestic life, toys, porcelain, glassware.

Gressenhall Farm and Workhouse: Gressenhall, Dereham, NR20 4DR; tel. (1362) 869263; e-mail gressenhall .museum@norfolk.gov.uk; historic workhouse; social and rural history displays and collections; farm with rare breeds of animal.

Lynn Museum: Market St, King's Lynn, PE30 1NL; tel. (1553) 775001; e-mail lynn .museum@norfolk.gov.uk; social history, natural history, archaeology and geology of West Norfolk.

Norwich Castle Museum and Art Gallery: NMAS, Shirehall, Market Ave, Norwich, NR1 3JQ; tel. (1603) 493625; e-mail museums@norfolk.gov.uk; internet www .museums.norfolk.gov.uk; f. 1894; Norman keep; fine art, ceramics, social history, natural history, archaeology.

Royal Norfolk Regimental Museum: NMAS, Shirehall, Market Ave, Norwich, NR1 3JQ; tel. (1603) 493625; e-mail museums@norfolk.gov.uk; social history of the county regiment since 1685.

Time and Tide Museum of Great Yarmouth Life: Blackfriars Rd, Great Yarmouth, BR30 3BX; tel. (1493) 743930; various aspects of East Anglian maritime history.

Tolhouse Museum: Tolhouse St, Great Yarmouth; tel. (1493) 858900; e-mail yarmouth.museums@norfolk.gov.uk; internet www.museums.norfolk.gov.uk; history of crime and punishment in Great Yarmouth.

Sainsbury Centre for Visual Arts: Univ. of East Anglia, Norwich, NR4 7TJ; tel. (1603) 593199; e-mail scva@uea.ac.uk; internet www.scva.ac.uk; f. 1978; modern European art, sculpture and design of other cultures and periods; library of 13,000 vols (mainly non-Western art and anthropology); Dir Prof. PAUL GREENHALGH.

Nottingham

Nottingham Castle Museum: Lenton Rd, Nottingham, NG1 6EL; tel. (115) 876-1400; e-mail nottingham.castle@nottinghamcity .gov.uk; internet www.nottinghamcity.gov .uk/article/22175/nottingham-castle; f. 1878; archaeology and ethnography, fine and applied arts, military, social and local history; Dir MICHAEL WILLIAMS.

Nottingham Natural History Museum/ Wollaton Hall and Park: Wollaton Hall, Nottingham, NG8 2AE; tel. (115) 915-3900; internet www.nottinghamcity.gov.uk/article/ 22178/wollaton-hall-and-park; f. 1867; collns of botanical, zoological and geological material; extensive British and foreign herbaria, Crowfoot colln of exotic butterflies, Pearson colln of European butterflies, Fowler colln of British Coleoptera, Hollier colln of Wenlock

Limestone fossils, Carrington series of Mountain Limestone fossils; library of 3,500 vols; Sr Keeper G. WALLEY.

Overton

National Coal Mining Museum for England: Caphouse Colliery, New Rd, Overton, Wakefield, WF4 4RH; tel. (1924) 848806; e-mail info@ncm.org.uk; internet www.ncm .org.uk; f. 1988; mine workings and mine exhibits; library of 20,000 vols; Museum Dir Dr MARGARET FAULL; Librarian ANISHA CHRISTISON.

Oxford

Ashmolean Museum: Beaumont St, Oxford, OX1 2PH; tel. (1865) 278002; e-mail director@ashmus.ox.ac.uk; internet www .ashmolean.org; f. 1683; attached to Univ. of Oxford; contains the art and archaeological collns of the Univ. of Oxford; British, European, Mediterranean, Egyptian and Near Eastern archaeology; Italian, Dutch, Flemish, French and English oil paintings; Old Master and modern drawings, watercolours and prints; miniatures; European ceramics; sculpture and bronzes; English silver; objects of applied art; Hope colln of engraved portraits; coins and medals of all countries and periods; Chinese and Japanese porcelain, paintings and lacquer; Chinese bronzes, Tibetan art; Indian sculpture and painting; Islamic pottery and metalwork; Dir Dr CHRISTOPHER BROWN.

Modern Art Oxford: 30 Pembroke St, Oxford, OX1 1BP; tel. (1865) 722733; e-mail info@modernartoxford.org.uk; internet www .modernartoxford.org.uk; f. 1965; exhibits contemporary and modern art, sculpture, design, photography, architecture, film and video; Dir PAUL HOBSON.

Pitt Rivers Museum: S Parks Rd, Oxford, OX1 3PP; tel. (1865) 270927; e-mail prm@ prm.ox.ac.uk; internet www.prm.ox.ac.uk; f. 1884; attached to Univ. of Oxford; ethnographic, archaeological and related photographic and manuscript collns; Dir Dr MICHAEL O'HANLON.

Plymouth

Plymouth City Museum and Art Gallery: Drake Circus, Plymouth, PL4 8AJ; tel. (1752) 304774; e-mail museum@plymouth.gov.uk; internet www.plymouth.gov.uk/ museumpcmag.htm; f. 1897; illustrates the arts and sciences of the West Country; comprises the Cottonian Colln of early printed and illuminated books, Old Master engravings and drawings, portraits by Sir Joshua Reynolds; gen. collns of Fine Art (since 16th century) and of Decorative Arts incl. Plymouth silver and William Cookworthy's Plymouth and Bristol porcelain; natural history, ethnography, archaeology and local history; the Merchant's House (f. 1977), 33 St Andrew's St (16th–17th centuries); the Elizabethan House (f. 1929), 32 New St (16th century) and Smeaton's Tower lighthouse, The Hoe; Curator NICOLA MOYLE.

Portsmouth

Portsmouth City Museum and Records Office: Museum Rd, Portsmouth, PO1 2LJ; tel. (23) 9282-6722; e-mail mvs@ portsmouthcc.gov.uk; internet www .portsmouthmuseums.co.uk; f. 1972; local history, fine and decorative art; re-creation of domestic interiors from various periods; Arthur Conan Doyle Colln; Fine and Decorative Art Gallery; Records Office contains official records of the City of Portsmouth since 14th century; Museums and Records Services Man. Dr JANE MEE..

Branch Museums:

Charles Dickens Birthplace: 393 Old Commercial Rd, Portsmouth, PO1 4QL; tel. (23) 9283-4744; e-mail mvs@portsmouthcc .gov.uk; internet www .portsmouthmuseums.co.uk; f. 1904; built 1805; birthplace of Charles Dickens in 1812; small terraced house restored, decorated and furnished in the Regency style; Museums and Records Services Man. Dr JANE MEE.

D-Day Museum and Overlord Embroidery: Clarence Esplanade, Southsea, PO5 3NT; tel. (23) 9283-4744; e-mail mvs@ portsmouthcc.gov.uk; internet www .ddaymuseum.co.uk; f. 1984; houses the 'Overlord Embroidery', commemorating the D-Day Landings; displays of original archive material, vehicles, uniforms and artefacts; Museums and Records Services Man. Dr JANE MEE.

Southsea Castle: Clarence Esplanade, Southsea, PO5 3PA; tel. (23) 9283-4744; e-mail mvs@portsmouthcc.gov.uk; internet www.portsmouthmuseums.co.uk; f. 1967; built 1544 by Henry VIII to protect Portsmouth harbour; 'Life in the Castle' experience; history of the defences of Portsmouth; displays on the Tudors, the English Civil War, 18th century and the Victorian period; audiovisual show and underground passages; Museums and Records Services Man. Dr JANE MEE.

Preston

Harris Museum and Art Gallery: Market Sq., Preston, PR1 2PP; tel. (1772) 258248; e-mail harris.museum@preston.gov.uk; internet www.harrismuseum.org.uk; f. 1893; fine art, costumes and textiles, ceramics and glass, contemporary art, digital media, archaeology, local history; Head of Arts and Heritage Services ALEXANDRA WALKER.

Reading

Museum of English Rural Life: Univ. of Reading, Redlands Rd, Reading, RG1 5EX; tel. (118) 378-8660; e-mail merl@reading.ac .uk; internet www.reading.ac.uk/merl; f. 1951; nat. colln of objects, photographs, archives, records and publs relating to English rural and agricultural history; library of 70,000 vols incl. large sections on agricultural sciences and technology and pre-1950 agricultural devt overseas; Dir KATE ARNOLD-FORSTER.

Reading Museum: Blagrave St, Reading, RG1 1QH; tel. (118) 937-3400; e-mail curator@readingmuseum.org.uk; internet www.readingmuseum.org.uk; f. 1883; collns cover art, archaeology, local history, world history and natural history; over 400,000 objects of local, regional and nat. importance incl. archaeological finds from the Roman site at Silchester, British artworks from between the wars, Romanesque carvings from Reading Abbey and the Huntley and Palmers Colln relating to the famous Reading biscuit company; Museum Man. MATTHEW WILLIAMS.

Salisbury

Salisbury and South Wiltshire Museum: The King's House, 65 The Close, Salisbury, SP1 2EN; tel. (1722) 332151; e-mail museum@salisburymuseum.org.uk; internet www.salisburymuseum.org.uk; f. 1860; archaeology, local history, ceramics, costume, Pitt Rivers colln, topographical pictures, numismatics; temporary exhibitions; Dir ADRIAN GREEN.

Selborne

Gilbert White's House and Garden and the Oates Collection: The Wakes, High St, Selborne, GU34 3JH; tel. (1420) 511275; e-mail info@gilbertwhiteshouse.org.uk; internet www.gilbertwhiteshouse.org.uk; f. 1954; private collns funded by the Oates Memorial Trust; furnished period rooms, original MSS about the natural history of Selborne; 18th-century plants grown in the garden; exploration in Africa by Frank Oates and in Antarctica by Capt. Lawrence Oates; Oates Memorial Library; Gen. Man. MIRIAM TONG.

Sheffield

Kelham Island Museum: Alma St, Sheffield, S3 8RY; tel. (114) 272-2106; e-mail ask@simt.co.uk; internet www.simt.co.uk/kelham-island-museum/about; f. 1982; objects, pictures and archives relating to Sheffield's industrial heritage; Exec. Dir JOHN HAMSHERE.

Weston Park Museum: Western Bank, Sheffield, S10 2TP; tel. (114) 278-2600; e-mail info@museums-sheffield.org.uk; internet www.museums-sheffield.org.uk/museums/weston-park; f. 1875 as Sheffield City Museum and Mappin Art Gallery; collns of Sheffield cutlery, old Sheffield plate, British and European cutlery, coins and medals, ceramics, local archaeology, natural sciences, local geology; Victorian paintings, old masters; Dir NICK DODD.

Singleton

Weald and Downland Open Air Museum: Singleton, Chichester, PO18 0EU; tel. (1243) 811363; e-mail office@wealddown.co.uk; internet www.wealddown.co.uk; f. 1967; working exhibits incl. a watermill and treadwheel; working farm with animals; continuing education courses for adults in bldg conservation, traditional bldg methods and traditional rural trades and crafts; Dir RICHARD PAILTHORPE; Head of Learning DIANA ROWSELL.

Skegness

The Village Church Farm: Church Rd South, Skegness, PE25 2HF; tel. (1754) 766658; e-mail info@churchfarmvillage.org .uk; internet www.churchfarmvillage.org .uk; f. 1976; a complex of 18th- and 19th-century farmhouse and agricultural bldgs with displays of agricultural equipment typical of the area; Dir TREVOR MONAHAN.

Southampton

Southampton City Art Gallery: Civic Centre, Commercial Rd, Southampton, SO14 7LP; tel. (23) 8083-3007; e-mail art .gallery@southampton.gov.uk; internet www .southampton.gov.uk/art; f. 1939; collns incl. Old Masters, French 19th- and 20th-century Schools, British painting since the 18th century, with emphasis on the Camden Town School; large colln of British contemporary painting and sculpture; library of 1,500 vols; Curator of Art TIM CRAVEN.

Southport

Atkinson Art Gallery: Lord St, Southport, PR8 1DH; tel. (151) 934-2024; e-mail info@ theatkinson.co.uk; internet www .theatkinson.co.uk; f. 1878; British oils and watercolours since the 18th century; contemporary sculpture, paintings and prints; Man. (Museum and Gallery) STEPHEN WHITTLE.

Stoke on Trent

Stoke on Trent Museums: Bethesda St, Hanley, Stoke on Trent, ST1 3DW; tel. (1782) 232323; e-mail museums@stoke.gov.uk; internet www.stokemuseums.org.uk; Head of Museums IAN LAWLEY..

Constituent Museums:

Gladstone Pottery Museum: Uttoxeter Rd, Longton, Stoke on Trent, ST3 1PQ; tel. (1782) 237777; e-mail gladstone@stoke.gov .uk; internet www.stokemuseums.org.uk/visit/gpm; f. 1974; complete Victorian pottery factory; workshops demonstrating traditional skills; Visitor Services KERRY WALTERS, ALISON PORTER.

Potteries Museum and Art Gallery: Bethesda St, City Centre, Stoke on Trent, ST1 3DW; tel. (1782) 232323; e-mail museums@stoke.gov.uk; internet www .stokemuseums.org.uk/visit/pmag/; Staffordshire pottery and porcelain, art, natural history, archaeology, local history; Strategic Man. KEITH BLOOR.

Wakefield

Wakefield Metropolitan District Council Access and Culture—Libraries and Museums: Wakefield Art Gallery, Wentworth Terrace, Wakefield, WF1 3QW; tel. (1924) 305796; e-mail cmacdonald@wakefield .gov.uk; internet www.wakefield.gov.uk/culture; f. 1934; museums and sites incl. Wakefield Art Gallery, Wakefield Museum, Pontefract Museum, Castleford Museum Room, Pontefract Castle, Sandal Castle, Clarke Hall Educational Museum; Head of Libraries and Museums COLIN MACDONALD.

Weybridge

Brooklands Museum: Brooklands Rd, Weybridge, KT13 0QN; tel. (1932) 857381; e-mail info@brooklandsmuseum.com; internet www.brooklandsmuseum.com; f. 1991; cars, motorcycles, aircraft, historic Brooklands racetrack; Dir ALLAN WINN.

Widnes

Catalyst—Science Discovery Centre and Museum: Mersey Rd, Widnes, WA8 0DF; tel. (151) 420-1121; e-mail info@catalyst.org.uk; internet www.catalyst.org.uk; f. 1987; informs the public about the role of chemistry in society past and present, incl. its relationship to the environment; enthuses school pupils about science through workshops, science demonstrations and interactive galleries; colln of relevant artefacts; Marketing Officer MERYL JAMESON.

Wolverhampton

Wolverhampton Art Gallery and Museums: Lichfield St, Wolverhampton, WV1 1DU; tel. (1902) 552055; e-mail artgallery@wolverhampton.gov.uk; internet www.wolverhamptonart.org.uk/about-wolverhampton-art-gallery/; f. 1884; collns of fine art since the 18th century and temporary exhibitions; br. museums: Bantock House (period house, enamels, japanned ware); Bilston Craft Gallery (contemporary craft and temporary exhibitions); Head of Arts and Museums CORINNE MILLER.

York

Jorvik Viking Centre: Coppergate, York, YO1 9WT; tel. (1904) 615505; e-mail jorvik@ yorkat.co.uk; internet jorvik-viking-centre.co .uk; f. 1984; reconstruction of part of the Viking city of Jorvik, based on archaeological evidence; artefacts from the York Archaeological Trust's excavation on display in the Gallery; Dir of Attractions SARAH MALTBY.

National Railway Museum: Leeman Rd, York, YO26 4XJ; tel. (844) 815139; e-mail nrm@nrm.org.uk; internet www.nrm.org.uk; f. 1975; part of the Science Museum (q.v.); collns incl. 1m. objects from over 300 years of railway history, incl. locomotives, carriages, wagons, models, signalling equipment, photos and paintings; library of 20,000 vols, 800 journals; Dir PAUL KIRKMAN.

York Castle Museum: Eye of York, York, YO1 9RY; tel. (1904) 687687; e-mail castle .museum@ymt.org.uk; internet www .yorkcastlemuseum.org.uk; f. 1938; England's first major folk museum; Kirk colln illustrates English life since the 17th century, including reconstructed shops and streets; also costumes, arms and armour, craft workshops, 1960s exhibition and the 18th-century Castle Prison; Museums Man. DAVID ARMSTRONG.

York Art Gallery: Exhibition Sq., York, YO1 7EW; tel. (1904) 687687; e-mail art .gallery@ymt.org.uk; internet www .yorkartgallery.org.uk; f. 1879; paintings of the Italian, Dutch, Flemish, German, French, Spanish and British schools; William Etty colln; large colln of 20th-century studio ceramics; library of 7,000 vols; Gallery Man. LORNA SERGEANT.

Yorkshire Museum: Museum Gardens, York, YO1 7FR; tel. (1904) 687687; e-mail yorkshire.museum@ymt.org.uk; internet www.yorkshiremuseum.org.uk; f. 1822; archaeology (Roman, Anglo-Saxon, Viking and medieval life); natural history and geology; Museums Man. HELEN YOUNG.

Universities in England

ANGLIA RUSKIN UNIVERSITY

Chelmsford Campus: Bishop Hall Lane, Chelmsford, CM1 1SQ
Cambridge Campus: East Rd, Cambridge, CB1 1PT

Telephone: (1245) 683757
E-mail: advertising@anglia.ac.uk
Internet: www.anglia.ac.uk

Founded 1858, present status 1992, current name adopted 2005
Academic year: September to July

Chancellor: Lord ASHCROFT
Vice-Chancellor: Prof. MICHAEL THORNE
Deputy Vice-Chancellor: Prof. ALAN SIBBALD
Deputy Vice-Chancellor: Prof. HELEN VALENTINE
Deputy Vice-Chancellor: Prof. LESLEY DOBREE
Librarian: NICKY KERSHAW

Library of 152,885 vols, 73,000 ebooks, 16,920 electronic and print journals
Number of teachers: 710
Number of students: 31,000

DEANS

Faculty of Arts, Law and Social Science: DERRIK FERNEY
Faculty of Health, Social Care and Education: Prof. DAVID HUMBER
Faculty of Science and Technology: Prof. EAMON STRAIN
Lord Ashcroft International Business School: Dr TREVOR BOLTON

ASTON UNIVERSITY

Aston Triangle, Birmingham, B4 7ET
Telephone: (121) 204-3000
E-mail: prospectus@aston.ac.uk
Internet: www.aston.ac.uk

Founded 1895, present status 1966
Academic year: October to June

Chancellor: Sir MICHAEL BETT
Pro-Chancellor: Dr PAUL GOLBY
Vice-Chancellor: Prof. JULIA KING
Sr Pro-Vice-Chancellor: Prof. HELEN HIGSON
Pro-Vice-Chancellor for Business Partnerships and Knowledge Transfer: Dr PHIL EXTANCE

Pro-Vice-Chancellor for Learning and Teaching Innovation: Prof. ALISON HALSTEAD
Pro-Vice-Chancellor for Research: Prof. MARTIN GRIFFIN
Univ. Sec.: ADELE MACKINLAY
Dir of Library and Information Services: Dr NICK SMITH
Library: see under Libraries and Archives
Number of teachers: 340
Number of students: 6,620 (5,700 full-time, 920 part-time)

DEANS

Aston Business School: Prof. MIKE WEST
School of Engineering and Applied Science: Prof. ROBERT BERRY
School of Languages and Social Science: Prof. PAM MOORES
School of Life and Health Sciences: Prof. HELEN GRIFFITHS

PROFESSORS

ANDERSON, S., Clinical Neuroscience
BAILEY, C., Pharmacology
BARKER, P., Chemical Engineering
BENNET, D., Technology Management and Head of International Liaison, Aston Business School
BENNION, I., Opto-Electronics
BHATTACHARYYA, G., Sociology
BLOW, K., Photonic Systems
BOOTH, R., Occupational Health and Safety
BRETT, P., Medical Engineering
BRIDGWATER, T., Engineering and Applied Science
BRIGNALL, S., Finance Accounting and Law, Aston Business School
BROOKES, J., Life and Health Sciences
BROWN, M., Pharmacy
CHELLEY-STEELEY, P., Finance Accounting and Law, Aston Business School
COLEMAN, M., Toxicology, Medicinal Chemistry
COULTHARD, M., Forensic Linguistics
FLOOD, J., Electronic Engineering
FURLONG, P., Clinical Neuroimaging
GAFFNEY, J., Languages and Social Sciences
GEOFFREY, G., Chemical Engineering
GEORGESON, M., Vision Sciences
GIBSON, J., Ophthalmology
GILMARTIN, B., Optometry
GREEN, S., Languages and Social Sciences
GRIFFIN, M., Biochemistry
HARDING, G., Life and Health Sciences
HART, M., Small Business and Entrepreneurship
HOMER, J., Chemistry
HORNUNG, A., Chemical Engineering
JARZABKOWSKI, P., Strategic Management, Aston Business School
JOSEPH, N., Finance Accounting and Law, Aston Business School
LOWE, A., Finance Accounting and Law, Aston Business School
LOWE, D., Informatics
MARRIOTT, J., Pharmacy Practice
NABNEY, T., Computer Science
PEARCE, G., Finance Accounting and Law, Aston Business School
PENNY, J., Engineering Systems and Management
POOLE, J., Commercial Law
PORTER, K., Chemical Engineering
REERSHEMIUS, G., German Linguistics
ROBERTS, B., Auditory Perception
ROGERS, M., Economics and Strategy, Aston Business School
ROPER, S., Business Innovation, Aston Business School
SAAD, D., Information Maths
SAUNDERS, J., Marketing, Aston Business School
SCHWALBE, C., Medicinal Chemistry
SCOTT, G., Chemical Engineering
SERI, S., Clinical Neurophysiology

SHAW, D., Operations and Information Management, Aston Business School
SILLINCE, J., Operations and Information Management, Aston Business School
STEELEY, J., Finance Accounting and Law, Aston Business School
STEVENS, A., European Studies
SULLIVAN, D., Surface Science
TANSLEY, G., Mechanical Engineering
THANASSOULIS, E., Operations and Information Management, Aston Business School
TIGHE, J., Polymer Chemistry
TISDALE, M., Cancer Biochemistry
TURITSYN, S., Electronic Engineering
ZHANG, L., Electronic Engineering

BATH SPA UNIVERSITY

Newton Park Campus: Newton St Loe, Bath, BA2 9BN

Telephone: (1225) 875875

Sion Hill Campus: Lansdown, Bath, BA1 5SF

Telephone: (1225) 875875
E-mail: enquiries@bathspa.ac.uk
Internet: www.bathspa.ac.uk

Founded 1853, granted taught degree-awarding powers 1992; present name and status 2005
Academic year: September to June

Vice-Chancellor: Prof. CHRISTINA SLADE
Deputy Vice-Chancellor: Dr ALUN THOMAS
Deputy Vice-Chancellor: Prof. NEIL SAMMELLS
Deputy Vice-Chancellor: JON BRADY
Registrar: CHRISTOPHER ELLICOTT
Head of Library and Information Services: Prof. ALISON BAUD
Number of teachers: 600
Number of students: 8,500

DEANS

Art and Design: Prof. MIKE TOOBY
Education: Dr CHRISTINE EDEN
Humanities and Cultural Industries: Dr STEVE MAY
Music and Performing Arts: JOE BENNETT
Science, Enterprise and Environment: Prof. ROB MEARS

BIRMINGHAM CITY UNIVERSITY

Perry Barr, Birmingham, B42 2SU

Telephone: (121) 331-5000
E-mail: choices@bcu.ac.uk
Internet: www.bcu.ac.uk

Founded 1971, as Birmingham Polytechnic, gained university status in 1992 and was renamed Univ. of Central England in Birmingham, present name 2007
Academic year: October to July

Chancellor: Lord Mayor of Birmingham, Cllr MICHAEL NANGLE
Vice-Chancellor: Prof. DAVID TIDMARSH
Pro-Vice-Chancellor: SALLY WESTNEY
Pro-Vice-Chancellor: Prof. MARY CARSWELL
Pro-Vice-Chancellor for Corporate Devt: Prof. DAVID MAGUIRE
Univ. Sec.: CHRISTINE ABBOTT

Library of 950,000 vols, 9,000 journals
Number of teachers: 700
Number of students: 25,000

DEANS

Birmingham City Business School: Prof. CHRISTOPHER PRINCE
Birmingham Institute of Art and Design: Prof. CHRIS O'NEIL
Faculty of Education, Law and Social Sciences: Prof. R. WOODS
Faculty of Health: Prof. IAN BLAIR
Faculty of Performance, Media and English: Prof. JOHN ROUSE

Faculty of Technology, Engineering and Environment: Prof. MELVYN LEES

BISHOP GROSSETESTE UNIVERSITY

Lincoln, LN1 3DY

Telephone: (1522) 527347
E-mail: reception@bishopg.ac.uk
Internet: www.bishopg.ac.uk

Founded 1862 present status 2012
State control

Undergraduate, postgraduate and work-based programmes in education, arts and humanities and cultural industries

Chancellor: Dame JUDITH MAYHEW JONAS
Vice-Chancellor: Rev. Prof. PETER S. NEIL
Head of Library Services: EMMA SANSBY

BOURNEMOUTH UNIVERSITY

Fern Barrow, Poole, BH12 5BB

Telephone: (1202) 524111
E-mail: enquiries@bournemouth.ac.uk
Internet: www.bournemouth.ac.uk

Founded 1976, as Dorset Institute of Higher Education, became Bournemouth Polytechnic 1990, present name and status 1992

Academic year: September to July

Chancellor: Lord NICHOLAS PHILLIPS
Vice-Chancellor: Prof. JOHN VINNEY
Deputy Vice-Chancellor: Prof. TIM MCINTYRE-BHATTY
Pro-Vice-Chancellor: Prof. MATTHEW BENNETT
Chief Operating Officer: JIM ANDREWS
Exec. Dir for Finance and Performance: ANDY RIGGS
Librarian: JILL BEARD
Library of 271,000 vols
Number of teachers: 626
Number of students: 14,851 incl. full-time and part-time

DEANS

Business School: Prof. ROGER PALMER
Media School: STEPHEN JUKES
School of Applied Sciences: Prof. B. GAIL THOMAS
School of Design, Engineering and Computing: Prof. JIM ROACH
School of Health and Social Care: Prof. B. GAIL THOMAS
School of Tourism: Dr KEITH WILKES

BRUNEL UNIVERSITY

Kingston Lane, Uxbridge, UB8 3PH

Telephone: (1895) 274000
E-mail: admissions@brunel.ac.uk
Internet: www.brunel.ac.uk

Founded 1966 as Brunel College of Technology, College of Advanced Technology 1962, Univ. Charter 1966, inc. W London Institute into the Univ. in 1995
State control
Language of instruction: English
Academic year: September to June

Chancellor: Sir RICHARD SYKES
Pro-Chancellor: NAZIR AFZAL
Vice-Chancellor and Prin.: Prof. JULIA BUCKINGHAM
Vice-Prin.: Prof. MANSOOR SARHADI
Vice-Prin. for Education and International: Prof. ANDREW J. GEORGE
Pro-Vice-Chancellor for Quality Affairs: Dr MARIANN RAND-WEAVER
Pro-Vice-Chancellor for Research: Prof. GEOFF RODGERS
Pro-Vice-Chancellor for Strategy, Devt and External Relations: Prof. DANY NOBUS
Library of 458,000 vols, 17,000 journals
Number of teachers: 1,057

Number of students: 15,201

PROFESSORS

AL-RAWESHIDY, H., Electronic and Computer Engineering
ANDERSON, N., Business and Management
ANGELIDES, M., Electronic and Computer Engineering
ATHREYE, S., Business and Management
BAHAI, H., Mechanical Engineering
BALACHANDRAN, W., Electronic and Computer Engineering
BALMER, J. M. T., Business and Management
BALTZOPOULOS, V., Sport
BANTEKAS, I., Law
BARNETT, J., Information Systems
BARRELL, R., Economics and Finance
BAURLEY, S., Design
BEASLEY, J. M. T., Mathematical Sciences
BENNETT, J. M. T., Economics and Finance
BERESFORD, P., Social Care
BHATTACHARYA, A., Wolfson Centre
BIRRINGER, J., Drama
BOURLAKIS, M., Business and Management
BOYD, I., Experimental Techniques Centre
BRACKENRIDGE, C., Sport
BRADFORD, S., Health Sciences and Social Care
BRAGANZA, A., Business and Management
BRETT, P., Brunel Institute of Bioengineering
BROADHURST, S., Drama
BRODY, D., Mathematical Sciences
BUCKINGHAM, S., Social Care
BULL, J., Civil Engineering
BULPETT, R., Experimental Techniques Centre
BUNCE, D., Psychology
BUXTON, M., Health Economics Research Group
CAMPOS, N., Economics and Finance
CAPEL, S., School of Sport and Education
CAPORALE, G., Economics and Finance
CHENG, K., Mechanical Engineering
CHIGARA, B., Law
COSMAS, J., Electronic and Computer Engineering
DESOUZA, L., Health Sciences and Social Care
DICKSON, K., Business and Management
ESAT, I., Mechanical Engineering
EVANS, R., Biological Sciences
FISHER, D., Brunel Institute of Bioengineering
FISHER, J., Social Sciences
FOX-RUSHBY, G., Music
FOX-RUSHBY, J., Health Economics Research Group
GAN, T., Electronic and Computer Engineering
GERZINA, G., English Studies
GHOSH, S., Economics and Finance
GIACOMIN, J., Design
GILHOOLY, M., Health Studies and Community Health
GONZALEZ-ALONSO, J., Sport
GOODWIN, R., Psychology
HACKNEY, R., Business and Management
HANNEY, S., Health Economics Research Group
HARRISON, D., Design
HARWIN, J., Social Care
HIERONS, R., Information Systems
HOBSON, P., Electronic and Computer Engineering
HUGHES, M., Politics and History
IRANI, Z., Brunel Business School
IRVING, M., Electronic and Computer Engineering
JAFFEY, P., Law
JARVIS, R., Business and Management
JOBLING, S., Environmental Studies
KARANASOS, M., Economics and Finance
KARAYIANNIS, T., Mechanical Engineering
KATHIRGAMANATHAN, P., Wolfson Centre
KHAN, A., Electronic and Computer Engineering
KING, G., Media

KNOWLES, J., English Studies
KOLOKOTRONI, M., Electronic and Computer Engineering
KORTENKAMP, A., Environmental Studies
KOSHY, V., Education
KRAHMANN, E., Politics and History
KRZYWINSKA, T., Media
KULJIS, J., Information Systems
LEROY, S., Environmental Studies
LIU, G., Economics and Finance
LIU, X., Information Systems
LOUVIERIS, P., Information Systems
LYCETT, M., Information Systems
MACREDIE, R., Information Systems
MADGE, N., Social Care
MCCONNELL, A., Sport
MEGARITIS, A., Mechanical Engineering
MELEWAR, T. C., Business and Management
MIKHAILOV, S., Mathematical Sciences
MORGAN, K., Politics and History
MOSCONE, F., Business and Management
MYERS, L., Psychology
NEOCLEOUS, M., Politics and History
NEWBOLD, R., Cancer, Genetics and Pharmaceuticals
NIBLOCK, S., Media
NOBUS, D., School of Social Sciences
OLOWOFOYEKU, A., Brunel Law School
OZBILGIN, M., Business Management
PETLEY, J., Media
PIPER, C., Law
RAMANI, S., Business and Management
RAWLINS, A., Mathematical Sciences
RAY, A. K., Wolfson Centre
REHMAN, J., Law
RIVERS, I., Education
RODGERS, G., PVC Research
ROJEK, C., Sociology
SADKA, A., Electronic and Computer Engineering
SALA, A., Biological Sciences
SAUNDERS, N., Biological Sciences
SCAMANS, G., BCAST
SEALE, C., Sociology
SELF, W., English Studies
SERMON, P. A., Wolfson Centre
SHARIF, A., Business and Management
SHEPPERD, M., Information Systems
SILVER, J., Wolfson Centre
SIMPSON, R., Business and Management
SKINNER, F., Economics and Finance
SONG, J., Mechanical Engineering
SPURLIN, W., English Studies
STELARC, X., Performance Arts
STOLARSKI, T., Mechanical Engineering
STONHAM, T., Electronic and Computer Engineering
SUMPTER, J., Institute for the Environment
SUTHERLAND, I., Brunel Institute of Bioengineering
TARVERDI, K., Wolfson Centre
TASSOU, S., School of Engineering and Design
TEW, P., English Studies
VASEGHI, S., Electronic and Computer Engineering
VICTOR, C. R., Health Studies and Community Health
WAINWRIGHT, S. P., Sociology
WANG, H., Electronic and Computer Engineering
WANG, Z., Information Systems
WATKIN, W., English Studies
WATTS, M., Education
WAYNE, M., Media
WHITEMAN, J., Mathematical Sciences
WIEGOLD, P., Music
WILLIAMS, A. M., Sport
WILLIAMS, C., Sociology
WROBEL, L., Mechanical Engineering
WYDELL, T., Psychology
YOUNG, T., Information Systems
ZEPHANIAH, B., English Studies
ZHAO, H., Mechanical Engineering

BUCKINGHAMSHIRE NEW UNIVERSITY

Queen Alexandra Rd, High Wycombe, HP11 2JZ

Telephone: (1494) 522141
E-mail: advice@bucks.ac.uk
Internet: bucks.ac.uk

Founded 1893; present name and status 2007

Vice-Chancellor and CEO: Prof. RUTH FARWELL
Deputy Vice-Chancellor: Prof. DEREK GODFREY
Pro-Vice-Chancellor: Prof. CHRIS KEMP
Pro-Vice-Chancellor: Dr ALISON CHAMBERS
Pro-Vice-Chancellor: Prof. TREVOR NICHOLLS
Dir for Business Planning: STEPHEN DEWHURST
Number of students: 9,017

DEANS

Faculty of Design, Media and Management: Prof. CHRIS KEMP
Faculty of Society and Health: Dr ALISON CHAMBERS
School of Advanced and Continuing Practice: LAUREN GRIFFITHS (Head)
School of Applied Management and Law: Dr LORRAINE WATKINS-MATHYS (Head)
School of Applied Production and New Media: FRAZER MACKENZIE (Head)

CANTERBURY CHRIST CHURCH UNIVERSITY

N Holmes Rd, Canterbury, CT1 1QU

Telephone: (1227) 767700
E-mail: admissions@canterbury.ac.uk
Internet: www.canterbury.ac.uk

Founded 1962 as a Church of England Teacher Training College; Univ. College 1995; present name and status 2005
State control
Academic year: September to June

Chancellor: Dr JUSTIN WELBY
Vice-Chancellor: Prof. RAMA THIRUNAMACHANDRAN (acting)
Pro-Chancellor: Prof. PETER HERMITAGE
Deputy Pro-Chancellor: STEPHEN CLARK
Sr Pro-Vice-Chancellor: Prof. JANET DRUKER
Pro-Vice-Chancellor for Research and Knowledge Exchange: Prof. TONY LAVENDER
Pro-Vice-Chancellor for Academics: Prof. SUE PIOTROWSKI
Pro-Vice-Chancellor for Learning and Quality: Dr KEITH GWILYM
Pro-Vice-Chancellor for Students: Prof. MARGARET ANDREWS
Strategic Dir: DAVID LEAH
Number of teachers: 1,330
Number of students: 19,100

Publication: *Inspire*

DEANS

Faculty of Arts and Humanities: Prof. RODERICK WATKINS
Faculty of Education: Dr JOHN MOSS
Faculty of Health and Social Care: Prof. DEBRA TEASDALE (acting)
Faculty of Social and Applied Sciences: Dr JANET HADDOCK-FRASER (acting)

CITY UNIVERSITY LONDON

Northampton Sq., London, EC1V 0HB

Telephone: (20) 7040-5060
E-mail: registry@city.ac.uk
Internet: www.city.ac.uk

Founded 1894 as Northampton Institute, Northampton College of Advanced Technology 1957, Univ. Charter 1966
Academic year: September to July

Chancellor: THE LORD MAYOR OF LONDON
Vice-Chancellor: Prof. PAUL CURRAN

Deputy Vice-Chancellor: Prof. DAVID BOLTON
Deputy Vice-Chancellor for Devt and Int.: Prof. DINOS ARCOUMANIS
Pro-Vice-Chancellor for Research and Enterprise: Prof. JOHN FOTHERGILL
Pro-Vice-Chancellor for Strategy and Planning: Prof. RICHARD VERRALL
Univ. Sec.: FRANK TOOP
Head of Library Services: MAIRE LANIGAN
Library of 350,000 vols
Number of teachers: 1,840
Number of students: 21,730

Publication: *City*

DEANS

Cass Business School: Prof. STEVE HABERMAN
City Law School: Prof. CARL STYCHIN
Conjoint School of Informatics and School of Engineering and Mathematics: Prof. ROGER CROUCH
School of Arts and Social Sciences: Prof. ANDREW JONES
School of Health Sciences: Prof. STANTON NEWMAN

PROFESSORS

AMIR, E., Finance
ATKIN, C., Mechanical and Aeronautical Engineering
AYERS, S., Early Years
AYOUB, A., Civil Engineering
AYTON, P., Psychology
BACON, N., Management
BADEN FULLER, C., Management
BALABANIS, G., Management
BANERJEE, R., Mechanical and Aeronautical Engineering
BANERJEE, S., Management
BARBUR, J., Optometry and Visual Science
BATCHELOR, R., Finance
BAWDEN, D., Computer Science
BEBER, A., Finance
BEN GAD, M., Economics
BHALLA, A., Management
BISHOP, P., Software Reliability
BLAKE, D., Finance
BLOOMFIELD, R., Software Reliability
BOOTH, P., Actuarial Science and Insurance
BOSWELL, L., Civil Engineering
BOUCHER, J., Psychology
BOWLER, D., Psychology
BRANDT, M., Finance
BROCK, G., Journalism
BROMLEY, M., Journalism
BROOKE, H., Journalism
BROOM, M., Mathematical Science
BRYAR, R., Early Years
CARAHER, M., Food Policy
CARLTON, J., Mechanical and Aeronautical Engineering
CERNY, A., Finance
CHALABY, J., Sociology
CHIAT, S., Language and Communication Science
CHOO, A., Law
CHRYSTAL, K., Finance
CHUANG, J., Mathematical Science
CLARE, A., Finance
COLLINS, R., Journalism
CONWAY, M., Psychology
COTTRELL, S., Creative Practice and Enterprise
CRABB, D., Optometry and Visual Science
CROUCH, R., Engineering and Mathematical Sciences and Informatics
CUTHBERTSON, K., Finance
DE RUYTER, J., Management
D'MELLO, C., Civil Engineering
DOUGLAS, R., Optometry and Visual Science
DYKES, J., Computer Science
EDGAR, D., Optometry and Visual Science
ELFORD, J., Health Services Research and Management
EMPSON, L., Management
FILATOTCHEV, I., Management

FLEMING, P., Management
FRANCIS, J., Health Services Research and Management
FRANKS, S., Journalism
FRING, A., Mathematical Science
FUERTES, A., Finance
GABER, I., Journalism
GAVAISES, E., Mechanical and Aeronautical Engineering
GIETZMANN, M., Finance
GLASS, C., Actuarial Science and Insurance
GOND, J., Management
GRAMMENOS, C., Finance
GRATTAN, K., Electrical and Electronic Engineering
GREENSLADE, R., Journalism
HALIKIAS, G., Electrical and Electronic Engineering
HAMPTON, J., Psychology
HARDY, S., Adult Years
HARROW, J., Management
HATGIOANNIDES, Y., Finance
HENNIG, T., Management
HOLTHAM, C., Management
HOWE, M., Psychology
HULL, C., Optometry and Visual Science
IORI, G., Economics
IOSIFIDIS, P., Sociology
JAFAREY, S., Economics
JAIN, N., Economics
JOFRE BONET, M., Economics
JONES, A., School of Arts and Social Sciences
JONES, K., Computer Science
KAISHEV, V., Actuarial Science and Insurance
KAPPOS, A., Civil Engineering
KARCANIAS, N., Electrical and Electronic Engineering
KESSAR, R., Mathematical Science
KEY, J., Finance
KHAN, S., Electrical and Electronic Engineering
KOVACEVIC, A., Mechanical and Aeronautical Engineering
KYRIACOU, P., Electrical and Electronic Engineering
LAMPEL, J., Management
LANG, T., Food Policy
LANZOLLA, G., Management
LASFER, M., Finance
LAWRENSON, J., Optometry and Visual Science
LEIGH, D., Journalism
LI, F., Management
LIATSIS, P., Electrical and Electronic Engineering
LINCKELMANN, M., Mathematical Science
LITTLEWOOD, B., Software Reliability
LOGAN, J., Management
MA, Q., Civil Engineering
MACFARLANE, A., Early Years
MAIDEN, N., Human Computer Interaction Design
MANOEL DE MENEZES, W., Management
MARSH, I., Finance
MARSHALL, J., Language and Communication Science
MATHON, J., Mathematical Science
MAYHEW, J., Actuarial Science and Insurance
MCCOURT, C., Early Years
MELVILLE, W., Management
MEYER, J., Adult Years
MILLER, B., Creative Practice and Enterprise
MITCHELL, V., Management
MOELLER, S., Finance
MONTES ROJAS, G., Economics
MORGAN, G., Language and Communication Science
MORGAN, M., Optometry and Visual Science
NEWBY, M., Electrical and Electronic Engineering
NEWMAN, S., School of Health Sciences
NICOLAOU, N., Management
NIELSEN, J., Actuarial Science and Insurance
NOMIKOS, N., Finance
NOURI, J., Mechanical and Aeronautical Engineering

OSWICK, C., Management
OWEN, J., Journalism
PALAN, R., International Politics
PALMER, P., Management
PARMAR, I., International Politics
PARSONS, C., Actuarial Science and Insurance
PAYNE, R., Finance
PEARLMAN, J., Economics
PEDERSEN, T., Management
PHAROAH, C., Management
PHYLAKTIS, E., Finance
PILBEAM, K., Economics
POPE, P., Finance
PRING, T., Language and Communication Science
PULLEN, K., Mechanical and Aeronautical Engineering
PURVIS, S., Journalism
QUINSEE, S., Learning Development Centre
RAHMAN, B., Electrical and Electronic Engineering
RAVASI, D., Management
RICKAYZEN, B., Actuarial Science and Insurance
ROWLEY, C., Management
ROY, P., Language and Communication Science
SARNO, L., Finance
SAYMA, A., Mechanical and Aeronautical Engineering
SCHIFFERES, S., Journalism
SHANE SCOTT, S., Management
SILVESTER, J., Psychology
SIMPSON, A., Adult Years
SIMS, D., Management
SIU TAK, K., Actuarial Science and Insurance
SMITH, I., Mechanical and Aeronautical Engineering
SODHI, M., Management
SOLOMON, J., Optometry and Visual Science
SOUITARIS, V., Management
SPANOUDAKIS, G., Computer Science
SPICER, A., Management
STALLEBRASS, S., Civil Engineering
STANTON, S., Creative Practice and Enterprise
STOSIC, N., Mechanical and Aeronautical Engineering
STRIGINI, L., Software Reliability
STUPPLES, D., Electrical and Electronic Engineering
STYCHIN, C., Law
SUN, T., Electrical and Electronic Engineering
SZYMANSKI, S., Finance
TAMVAKIS, M., Finance
TAYLOR, R., Civil Engineering
THOMAS, P., Electrical and Electronic Engineering
THOMAS, S., Finance
TUMBER, H., Journalism
URGA, G., Finance
WEBSTER, F., Sociology
WILLIG, C., Psychology
WOLSTENHOLME, L., Actuarial Science and Insurance
WOOD, J., Computer Science
WOOTTON, L., Mechanical and Aeronautical Engineering
ZAUNER, K., Economics
ZISMAN, A., Computer Science

COVENTRY UNIVERSITY

Priory St, Coventry, CV1 5FB
Telephone: (24) 7688-7688
E-mail: info.rao@coventry.ac.uk
Internet: www.coventry.ac.uk

Founded 1970, by merger of Coventry College of Art, Lanchester College of Technology and Rugby College of Engineering Technology, present name and status 1992
Academic year: September to June

Chancellor: Sir JOHN EGAN
Vice-Chancellor: Prof. MADELAINE ATKINS
Deputy Chancellor for Business Devt: JOHN LATHAM
Deputy Vice-Chancellor for Academics: Prof. IAN MARSHALL
Deputy Vice-Chancellor for Planning and Resources: DAVID SOUTTER
Pro-Vice-Chancellor for Continuous Improvement: DONNA KENDALL
Pro-Vice-Chancellor for Int. Experience and Mobility Service: Dr DAVID PILSBURY
Pro-Vice-Chancellor for Student Empowerment: IAN DUNN
Registrar and Sec.: KATE QUANTRELL
Librarian: P. NOON
Library of 400,000 vols
Number of teachers: 600
Number of students: 18,000
Publications: *Biological Agriculture and Horticulture* (4 a year), *Coventry University Law Journal* (2 a year), *The Holocene, International Journal of Media and Cultural Politics, Ultrasonics – Sonochemistry*

DEANS

Faculty of Business, Environment and Society: Prof. DAVID NOON
Faculty of Engineering and Computing: Prof. PAUL IVEY
Faculty of Health and Life Sciences: Dr LINDA MERRIMAN
School of Art and Design: Prof. JILL JOURNEAUX
School of Lifelong Learning Staff: SUE RIVERS (acting)

PROFESSORS

Faculty of Business, Environment and Society:
BAKER, B., African Security
BARRETT, H., Development Geography
BEIDER, H., Community Cohesion
BRODERICK, A., Marketing/Advertising
CANTLE, E.
CHADWICK, S., Sport Management and Marketing
DONNELLY, T., Automotive Business
FARNELL, R., Neighbourhood Regeneration
FORBES, N., International History
HARRIS, P., Plant Design
HUNTER, A., Asian Studies
MCINTOSH, M., Human Security
MITCHELL, B., Criminal Law and Criminal Justice
NESI, H., English Language
NOON, D., Economic Regeneration
RENWICK, N., Global Security
RIGBY, A., Peace Studies
SKINNER, D., Human Resource Management
WORRALL, L., Strategic Analysis

Faculty of Engineering and Computing:
BENJAMIN, S., Fluid Dynamics
BLUNDELL, M., Vehicle Dynamics and Impact
BURNHAM, K., Industrial Control Systems
CHAO, K., Computing
CLAISSE, P., Construction Materials
HOLDO, A., Energy and Environment
IVEY, P.
JAMES, A., Data Systems Architecture
LAWSON, D., Mathematics and Education
LEHANEY, B., Statistics and Operational Research Subject Group
MOLOKOV, S., Applied Mathematics
NAGUIB, R., Biomedical Computing
POPPLEWELL, K., Engineering Manufacture and Management
WHITE, P., Thermofluid Dynamics

Faculty of Health and Life Sciences:
BARLOW, J., Health Psychology
HARRISON, K., Physiotherapy and Dietetics
MASON, T., Chemistry
SAVIN-BADEN, M., Higher Education Research
TOFT, B., Patient Safety
WALLACE, L., Psychology and Health
WOOLLARD, M., Pre-Hospital and Emergency Care

School of Art and Design:
DUTTON, S., Creative Practice
HALL, G., Media and Performing Arts
JOURNEAUX, J., Fine Art Education
RICHARDS, C., Information Design
WHATLEY, S., Dance
WOODCOCK, A., Educational Ergonomics and Design

CRANFIELD UNIVERSITY

Cranfield Campus: College Rd, Cranfield, MK43 0AL

Telephone: (1234) 750111

Shrivenham Campus: CDT, Shrivenham, Swindon, SN6 8LA

Telephone: (1793) 785810
E-mail: info@cranfield.ac.uk
Internet: www.cranfield.ac.uk

Founded 1946
Academic year: October to September
Chancellor: Baroness BARBARA YOUNG OF OLD SCONE
Vice-Chancellor: Prof. Sir PETER GREGSON
Deputy Vice-Chancellor: Prof. CLIFFORD FRIEND
Pro-Vice-Chancellor: Prof. LYNETTE RYALS
Sec. and Registrar: Prof. WILLIAM STEPHENS
Univ. Librarian: SIMON BEVAN
Library of 440,915 vols, 9,708 journals (electronic and print)
Number of students: 2,300, 20,000 short-course delegates per annum

PROFESSORS

AKHAVAN, J., Explosive Chemistry
ASPINALL, R., Translational Medicine
ASSADIAN, F., Automotive Engineering
BAINES, P., Political Marketing
BARR, H., Clinical
BOURLAKIS, M., Logistics and Supply Chain Management
BOURNE, M., Business Performance
BOWMAN, C., Strategic Management
BRAITHWAITE, G., Transport and Safety Engineering
BRENNAN, F., Energy and Power Engineering
BURKE, A., Entrepreuneurship
CARR, K., Centre for Human System
CARTMELL, E., Water Technology
CULLEN, D., Bioanalytical Technology
DENYER, D., Organizational Change
DICKMANN, M., International Human Resources Management
DOREY, R., Nanomaterials
DRIKAKIS, D., Engineering Sciences
FITZ-GERALD, A., Security Sector Management
FOOTE, P., Composites
GARRY, K., Aerodynamics
GELMAN, L., Vibro-Acoustic Monitoring
GOFFIN, K., Innovation & New Product Development
GRAYSON, D., Corporate Social Responsibility
GU, S., Bio Energy Technology
GUENOV, M., Aerospace Engineering
HAMEED, A., Defence Engineering
HARRIS, J., Environmental Technology
HIGSON, S., Bio- and Electroanalysis
HORSFALL, I., Armour Systems
HORWITZ, F., International Human Resource Management
IRVING, P., Damage Tolerance
JEFFERSON, B., Water Engineering
JEFFREY, P., Water Management
JENKINS, M., Business Strategy
JENNIONS, I., Integrated Vehicle Health Management
JOLLY, M., Sustainable Manufacturing
JUDD, S., Membrane Technology

KELLIHER, C., Work and Organization
KIRK, G., Soil Systems
KNOWLES, K., Aeromechanical Systems
LADKIN, D., Leadership and Ethics
LUK, P., Electrical Engineering
MAGAN, N., Applied Mycology
MALKIN, P., Electrical Power Engineering
MANOVIC, V., Carbon Systems Engineering
MATTHEWS, R., Defence Economics
MBA, D., Rotating Machines Technology
MURRAY, S., Engineering and Applied Science for Defence and Security
NEAL, D., Strategic Change for Defence
NICHOLLS, J., Coatings Technology
OAKEY, J., Energy Technology
ORMONDROYD, R., Communication Networks
PATEL, M., Mechanical Engineering
PILIDIS, P., Power and Propulsion
POLLARD, S., Environmental Science and Technology
POSHAKWALE, S., International Finance
REINMOELLER, P., Strategic Management
RICHARDSON, M., Electronic Warfare
RICKSON, J., Soil Erosion and Conservation
RITZ, K., Soil Biology
ROGERS, K., Materials in Medical Science
ROY, R., Manufacturing and Materials
RYALS, L., Strategic Sales and Account Management
SAVILL, M., Computational Aerodydnamics
SHORE, P., Ultra-Precision Engineering
SMITH, H., Aircraft Design
STARR, A., Maintenance Systems
SZWEJCZEWSKI, M., Operations Strategy
TATAM, R., Engineering Photonics
TERRY, L., Soil and AgriFoods
THOMPSON, C., Engineering Computing
TIBBETT, M., Soil Ecology
TIWARI, A., Manufacturing Informatics
TOMIYAMA, T., Life Cycle Engineering
TOTHILL, S., Biosensors in Health
TSOURDOS, A., Control Engineering
TURNBULL JAMES, K., Executive Learning
VIGNJEVIC, R., Astronautics and Advanced Structures
VINNICOMBE, S., Women and Leadership
WEATHERHEAD, K., Water Resources and Climate Adaptation
WEBB, P., Aeronautical System Design
WEEKS, J., Environmental Risk Analysis
WILDING, R., Supply Chain Strategy
WILLIAMS, S., Welding Science and Technology
WILSON, H., Strategic Marketing
YEUNG, H., Flow Process Assurance
ZBIKOWSKI, R., Control Engineering
ZHAO, H., Corporate Finance

DE MONTFORT UNIVERSITY

The Gateway, Leicester, LE1 9BH

Telephone: (116) 255-1551
E-mail: enquiry@dmu.ac.uk
Internet: www.dmu.ac.uk

Founded 1969, as Leicester Polytechnic, later became Leicester Polytechnic; present name and status 1992

Chancellor: Lord WAHEED ALLI
Pro-Chancellor: DAVID STEVENS
Vice-Chancellor: Prof. DOMINIC SHELLARD
Pro-Vice-Chancellor for Research: (vacant)
Pro-Vice-Chancellor for Teaching, Learning and Student Experience: Prof. HEIDI MACPHERSON
Acad. Registrar: EUGENE CRITCHLOW
Univ. Librarian: K. ARNOLD

Library of 479,135 vols, 16,490 periodicals
Number of teachers: 3,240
Number of students: 20,500

DEANS

Faculty of Art and Design: Dr GERARD MORAN
Faculty of Business and Law: Prof. DAVID WILSON

Faculty of Health and Life Sciences: Prof. BARRY MITCHELL
Faculty of Humanities: Prof. TIM O'SULLIVAN
Faculty of Technology: Prof. ADRIAN HOPGOOD

EDGE HILL UNIVERSITY

St Helens Rd, Ormskirk, L39 4QP

Telephone: (1695) 575171
Internet: www.edgehill.ac.uk

Founded 1885, present status 2008

Chancellor: Prof. TANYA BYRON
Pro-Chancellor: CHRIS TRINICK
Vice-Chancellor: Dr JOHN CATER
Deputy Vice-Chancellor: Prof. STEVE IGOE
Pro-Vice-Chancellor for Education: ROBERT SMEDLEY
Pro-Vice-Chancellor for Health and Social Care: (vacant)
Univ. Sec. and Clerk to Governors: SETH CROFTS
Academic Registrar: (vacant)
Dean of Learning Services: LESLEY MUNRO
Number of teachers: 4,000
Number of students: 24,000

DEANS

Faculty of Arts and Sciences: GEORGE TALBOT
Faculty of Education: ROBERT SMEDLEY
Faculty of Health: SETH CROFTS

KINGSTON UNIVERSITY

River House, 53–57 High St, Kingston upon Thames, KT1 1LQ

Telephone: (20) 8417-9000
E-mail: admissions-info@kingston.ac.uk
Internet: www.kingston.ac.uk

Founded 1899, as Kingston Technical Institute, present name and status 1992
Academic year: September to July

Chancellor: BONNIE GREER
Vice-Chancellor: Prof. JULIUS WEINBERG
Deputy Vice-Chancellor: Dr DAVID MACKINTOSH
Pro-Vice-Chancellor: Prof. MARTYN JONES
Pro-Vice-Chancellor for Corporate Affairs and Univ. Sec.: NEIL LATHAM
Pro-Vice-Chancellor for Education: Prof. LESLEY-JANE EALES-REYNOLDS
Pro-Vice-Chancellor for Research and Enterprise: Prof. PENNY SPARKE
Acad. Registrar: MARIE SHEEHAN
Head of Library Services: GRAHAM BULPITT

Library of 450,000 vols
Number of teachers: 950
Number of students: 23,100

Publication: Kingston review

DEANS

Faculty of Art, Design and Architecture: Prof. STEVEN SPIER
Faculty of Arts and Social Sciences: Prof. MARTIN McQUILLAN
Faculty of Business and Law: Prof. JEAN-NOEL EZINGRARD
Faculty of Health and Social Care Education: Prof. FIONA ROSS
Faculty of Science, Engineering and Computing: Prof. EDITH SIM

LEEDS METROPOLITAN UNIVERSITY

City Campus, Leeds, LS1 3HE

Telephone: (113) 812-0000
E-mail: helpzone@leedsmet.ac.uk
Internet: www.leedsmet.ac.uk

Founded 1970 as Leeds Polytechnic; present name and status 1992

Chancellor: BRENDAN FOSTER
Vice-Chancellor: Prof. SUSAN PRICE

Pro-Vice-Chancellor and Provost: SALLY BROWN
Deputy Vice-Chancellor for Research and Enterprise: Prof. ANDREW SLADE
Deputy Vice-Chancellor for Strategic Devt: Dr PAUL SMITH
Deputy Vice-Chancellor for Student Experience: Prof. SALLY GLEN
Sec. and Registrar: STEVE DENTON
Dir of Libraries and Learning Innovation: JO NORRY

Library of 330,000 vols, 22,000 periodicals
Number of teachers: 3,000
Number of students: 30,000

DEANS

Faculty of Arts, Environment and Technology: Prof. CHRISTOPHER BAILEY
Faculty of Business and Law: BARBARA COLLEDGE
Faculty of Health and Social Sciences: Prof. IEUAN ELLIS
Carnegie Faculty of Sports and Education: GARETH DAVIES

LEEDS TRINITY UNIVERSITY

Brownberrie Lane, Leeds, LS18 5HD

Telephone: (1132) 837100
E-mail: enquiries@leedstrinity.ac.uk
Internet: www.leedstrinity.ac.uk

Founded 1980 by merger of Leeds Trinity and All Saints College, present status 2012

Depts of business, management and marketing, children, young people and families, English, history, journalism, media, film and culture, primary education, psychology, secondary education, sport, health and nutrition, theology and religious studies, Victorian studies

Chancellor: GABBY LOGAN
Vice-Chancellor: Prof. MARGARET HOUSE
Deputy Vice-Chancellor: MARK SHIELDS

Library of 400,000 vols of ebooks, 25,000 ejournals
Number of students: 3,000

LIVERPOOL HOPE UNIVERSITY

Hope Park, Liverpool, L16 9JD

Telephone: (151) 291-3000
E-mail: enquiry@hope.ac.uk
Internet: www.hope.ac.uk

Founded 1844; present name 1995, present status 2005
Academic year: September to July

Chancellor: Baroness CAROLINE COX
Vice-Chancellor and Rector: Prof. GERALD PILLAY
Pro-Vice-Chancellor for Academic Devt: Prof. KENNETH NEWPORT
Pro-Vice-Chancellor for Resource Management and Planning: Dr IAN VANDEWALLE
Univ. Sec.: GRAHAM DONELAN
Number of students: 7,500

DEANS

Arts and Humanities: Prof. NICK REES
Education: Prof. BART McGETTRICK
Sciences and Social Sciences: Dr JOHN BRINKMAN

LIVERPOOL JOHN MOORES UNIVERSITY

Roscoe Court, 4 Rodney St, Liverpool, L1 2TZ

Telephone: (151) 231-5090
E-mail: communications@ljmu.ac.uk
Internet: www.livjm.ac.uk

Founded 1825, as Liverpool Mechanics' School of Arts, present name and status 1992
Academic year: September to May

Chancellor: Dr BRIAN MAY
Vice-Chancellor and Chief Exec.: Prof.
MICHAEL BROWN
Pro-Vice-Chancellor for Admin. and Univ.
Sec.: ALISON WILD
Pro-Vice-Chancellor for Acad. and Enhancement: Prof. DIANA BURTON
Pro-Vice-Chancellor for Student Experience:
STEVE KENNY
Pro-Vice-Chancellor for Infrastructure:
ALLAN BICKERSTAFFE
Dir of Learning and Information Services:
MAXINE MELLING

Number of teachers: 2,800
Number of students: 24,000

DEANS

Faculty of Business and Law: Prof. ROGER
WEBSTER
Faculty of Education, Community and Leisure: KATE JOHNSTON
Faculty of Health and Applied Social Sciences: Prof. GODFREY MAZHINDU
Faculty of Media, Arts and Social Science:
Prof. ROGER WEBSTER
Faculty of Science: Prof. PETER WHEELER
Faculty of Technology and Environment:
Prof. DIANE MEEHAN

LONDON METROPOLITAN UNIVERSITY

London City Campus: 133 Whitechapel High
St, London, E1 7QA
North London Campus: 166–220 Holloway
Rd, London, N7 8DB
Telephone: (20) 7423-0000
E-mail: admissions@londonmet.ac.uk
Internet: www.londonmet.ac.uk
Founded 2002, by merger of Univ. of North
London and London Guildhall Univ.

Pres.: Sir RODERICK CASTLE FLOUD
Vice-Chancellor and Chief Exec.: Prof. MAL-
COLM GILLIES
Deputy Vice-Chancellor for Acad. Affairs:
BOB AYLETT
Deputy Vice-Chancellor for Planning and
Resources: MAX WEAVER
Deputy Vice-Chancellor for Research and
Devt: Prof. PAUL LISTER
Acad. Registrar: JILL GRINSTEAD
Number of students: 33,000

Publication: *The Metropolitan* (1 a year)

LONDON SOUTH BANK UNIVERSITY

103 Borough Rd, London, SE1 0AA
Telephone: (20) 7928-8989
E-mail: lsbuinfo@lsbu.ac.uk
Internet: www.lsbu.ac.uk
Founded 1970 as South Bank Polytechnic,
present name and status 1992
State control
Academic year: September to July

Chancellor: RICHARD FARLEIGH
Vice-Chancellor: Prof. DAVID PHOENIX
Pro-Vice-Chancellor for Academic Affairs:
Prof. PHIL CARDEW
Pro-Vice-Chancellor for External Affairs: BEV
JULLIEN
Univ. Sec.: JAMES STEVENSON
Registrar: R. PHILLIPS
Librarian: J. AKEROYD
Library of 280,000 vols
Number of teachers: 652
Number of students: 25,441

DEANS

Faculty of Arts and Human Sciences: Prof.
MIKE MOLAN
Faculty of Business: MIKE MOLAN (acting)
Faculty of Engineering, Science and Built
Environment: Prof. RAO BHAMIDIMARRI

Faculty of Health and Social Care: Prof.
JUDITH ELLIS

LOUGHBOROUGH UNIVERSITY

Loughborough, LE11 3TU
Telephone: (1509) 263171
E-mail: k.j.raine@lboro.ac.uk
Internet: www.lboro.ac.uk
Founded 1966, as univ.; fmrly Loughborough
College of Advanced Technology, univ.
charter 1966
Academic year: September to June

Chancellor: Sir NIGEL RUDD
Vice-Chancellor and Pres.: Prof. ROBERT
ALLISON
Deputy Vice-Chancellor and Provost: Prof.
CHRIS LINTON
Pro-Vice-Chancellor for Enterprise: Prof.
STEVE ROTHBERG
Pro-Vice-Chancellor for Research: Prof. MYRA
NIMMO
Pro-Vice-Chancellor for Teaching: Prof.
MORAG BELL
Dir for Finance: ANDY STEPHENS
Librarian: JEFF BROWN (acting)
Library of 500,000 vols, 19,000 e-journals
Number of teachers: 773
Number of students: 16,237

DEANS

Aeronautical, Automotive, Chemical and
Materials Engineering: Prof. JON BINNER
Loughborough Design School: Prof. TRACY
BHAMRA
School of Business and Economics: Prof.
ANGUS LAING
School of Civil and Building Engineering:
Prof. TONY THORPE
School of Electronic, Electrical and Systems
Engineering: Prof. DAVID PARISH
School of Mechanical and Manufacturing
Engineering: Prof. ROB PARKIN
School of Science: Dr PAUL CHUNG
School of Social, Political and Geographical
Sciences: Prof. JONATHAN POTTER
School of Sport, Exercise and Health Sci-
ences: Prof. MARK LEWIS
School of the Arts, English and Drama: Prof.
TERRY KAVANAGH

PROFESSORS

ACKERS, P., Industrial Relations and Labour
History
ALEXANDROV, A., Theoretical Physics
ALLEN, D., European and International Pol-
itics
ANDERSON, J., Physical Geography
ANDREWS, J., Risk and Reliability Analysis
ANTAKI, C., Language and Psychology
ANUMBA, C., Construction Engineering and
Informatics
ARNOLD, J., Organizational Behaviour
AUSTIN, S., Structural Engineering
BABITSKY, V., Dynamics
BACKHOUSE, C., Product Innovation
BAGILHOLE, B., Social Policy and Equal
Opportunities
BAIRNER, A., Sport and Social Theory
BELL, M., Cultural Geography
BIDDLE, S., Exercise and Sport Psychology
BILLIG, M., Social Sciences
BOUCHLAGHEM, D., Architectural Engineering
BOWMAN, R., Organic Chemistry
BRISTOW, A., Transport Studies
BUCK, T., International Business
BURNS, N., Manufacturing Systems
CADOGAN, J., Marketing
CAINE, M., Sports Technology and Innovation
CALLOW, G., Industrial Professor
CAMERON, N., Human Biology
CARRILLO, P., Strategic Management in Con-
struction
CASE, K., Computer-aided Engineering

CHAMBERS, J., Communications and Signal
Processing
CHUNG, P., Computer Science
COHEN, L., Organization Studies
CONWAY, P., Manufacturing Processes
COUPLAND, J., Applied Optics
CRAMER, D., Psychological Health
CREASER, C., Analytical Chemistry
DAINTY, A. R. J., Construction Sociology
DAMODARAN, L., Participative Design and
Change Management
DANIELS, K., Organizational Psychology
DAVIDSON, I., Accounting and Finance
DICKENS, J., Engineering Education
DICKENS, P., Manufacturing Technology
DIXON, N., Geotechnical Engineering
DOBSON, P., Competition Economics
DOHERTY, N., Information Management
EBBATSON, R., English Studies
EDWARDS, D., Psychology
EVANS, J., Sociology of Education and Phys-
ical Education
FARRELL, G., Criminology
FAULKNER, R., Physical Metallurgy
FEATHER, J., Library and Information Studies
FITZGERALD, L., Management Accounting
FLETCHER, S., Physical Chemistry
FORBES, W., Accounting and Finance
GANE, M., Sociology
GARNER, C., Applied Thermodynamics
GERSTNER, E., Marketing and Retail
GIBB, A., Construction Engineering Manage-
ment
GILBERT, M., Polymer Technology
GLEESON, M., Exercise Biochemistry
GOLDING, P., Sociology
GOODALL, R., Control Systems Engineering
GREEN, C., Banking and Finance
GRIFFITHS, J., Applied Mathematics
GRIMSHAW, R. H. J., Mathematical Sciences
GROVES, M., Mathematics
HAGUE, R., Innovative Manufacturing
HALL, M., Banking and Financial Regulation
HALLIWELL, N., Optical Engineering
HANKINSON, G., Safety Engineering
HANTRAI, L., European Social Policy
HARGRAVE, G., Optical Diagnostics
HASLAM, R., Health and Safety Ergonomics
HAVENITH, G., Environmental Physiology and
Ergonomics
HENRY, I., Leisure Policy and Management
HENSHAW, M., Systems Engineering
HEWITT, C., Pharmaceutical Engineering
HOBBY, E., 17th-century Studies
HOCKING, B., International Relations
HOGERVORST, E., Psychology
HOLDICH, R., Chemical Engineering
HORNE, J., Psychophysiology
HOULIHAN, B., Sport Policy
HOWCROFT, B., Retail Banking
HUBBARD, P., Urban Social Geography
HUNTLEY, J., Applied Mechanics
ISON, S., Transport Policy
JONES, R., Organic and Biological Chemistry
JONES, R., Sports Technology
KALAWSKY, R., Human-Computer Integration
KAVANAGH, T., Design
KHOMSKII, D., Novel Material
KING, M., Management Sciences
KONG, M., Bioelectrics Engineering
KORCZYNSKI, M., Sociology of Work
KRYLOV, V., Acoustics and Vibration
KUSMARTSEV, F., Condensed Matter Theory
LINTON, C., Applied Mathematics
LISTER, R., Social Policy
LIU, J., Operations Management
LLEWELLYN, D., Money and Banking
LOUCOPOULOS, P., Information Systems
LOUGHLAN, J., Aerospace Structures
LOVEDAY, D., Building Physics
MCCAFFER, R., Construction Management
MCGUIGAN, J., Cultural Analysis
MCGUIRK, J., Aerodynamics
MCIVER, P., Applied Mathematics
MCKEE, V., Inorganic Chemistry
MCKNIGHT, C., Information Studies

MAGUIRE, J., Sociology of Sport
MATTHEWS, G., Information Management
MAUGHAN, R., Sport and Exercise Nutrition
MILLS, T., Applied Statistics and Econometrics
MORGAN, K., Gerontology
MORRIS, A., Information Science
MORTIMER, R., Physical Chemistry
NEISHTADT, A., Applied Mathematics
NIMMO, M., Exercise Physiology
OPPENHEIM, C., Information Science
OVERTON, W., Literature
PAGE, P., Organic Chemistry
PARISH, D., Communication Networks
PARKIN, R., Mechatronics
PARRY-JONES, R., Industrial Professor
PARSONS, K., Environmental Ergonomics
PENTECOST, E., Economics
PORTER, M., Design Ergonomics
POTTER, J., Discourse Analysis
POYAGO-THEOTOKY, J., Microeconomics
PRICE, A., Project Management
RADLEY, A., Social Psychology
RAHNEJAT, H., Dynamics
RAMAN, K., Marketing
RAOOF, M., Structural Engineering
RASTOGI, S., Polymer Technology
REID, I., Physical Geography
RENDELL, H., Physical Geography
RIELLY, C., Chemical Engineering
ROTHBERG, S., Vibration Engineering
SEAL, W., Accounting
SHAW, M., English
SHIONO, K., Environmental Hydrodynamics
SILBERSCHMIDT, V., Mechanics of Materials
SINGH, S., Autonomous Systems
SKELTON, T., Critical Geographies
SLATER, D., Human Geography
SMITH, D., Sociology
SMITH, I., Electrical Power Engineering
SMITH, M., European Politics
SMITH, R., Analytical Chemistry
SMITH, R., Mathematical Engineering
STAROV, V., Chemical Engineering
STOBART, R. K., Automotive Engineering
STURGES, P., Library Studies
SUMMERS, R., Information Science
TAYLOR, P., Geography
THOMAS, P., Analytical Chemistry
THOMSON, R., Materials Engineering
THORPE, A., Construction Information Technology
THRING, R., Fuel Cell Engineering
TIPPETT, M., Accounting and Finance
TIWARI, A., Renewable Energy Systems
VARDAXOGLOU, Y., Wireless Communications
VESELOV, A., Mathematics
WAKEMAN, R., Chemical Engineering
WARD, H., Child and Family Research
WARWICK, P., Environmental Radiochemistry
WELLS, P., Animation
WESTON, R., Flexible Automation
WEYMAN-JONES, T., Industrial Economics
WHEATLEY, A., Water Technology
WILKINSON, S., Feminism and Health Studies
WILLIAMS, C., Sports Science
WILLIAMS, D., Healthcare Engineering
WILSON, J., Operational Research
WOLFREYS, J., Modern Literature and Culture
WOOD, N., Literature
WOODHEAD, M., Systems Engineering
WOODWARD, B., Underwater Acoustics
WRIGHT, J., Building Optimization
YANG, S., Networks and Control
YEADON, F., Computer Simulation in Sport
ZHAO, H., Mathematics
ZIEBECK, K., Physics

MANCHESTER METROPOLITAN UNIVERSITY

All Saints Bldg, Manchester, M15 6BH
Telephone: (161) 247-2000
E-mail: enquiries@mmu.ac.uk

Internet: www.mmu.ac.uk
Founded 1970, as Manchester Polytechnic, present name and status 1992
Academic year: September to July
Chancellor: Dame JANET SMITH
Pro-Chancellor: ALAN BENZIE
Vice-Chancellor: Prof. JOHN BROOKS
Deputy Vice-Chancellor for Strategic Planning: Prof. GERRY KELLEHER
Deputy Vice-Chancellor for Student Experience: Prof. KEVIN BONNETT
Registrar: GWYN ARNOLD
Librarian: Prof. C. HARRIS
Library: see under Libraries and Archives
Number of teachers: 5,820
Number of students: 34,970
Publication: *Success*

DEANS

Business School: Prof. RUTH ASHFORD
Faculty of Art and Design: Prof. DAVID CROW
Faculty of Health, Psychology and Social Care: Prof. V. K. RAMPROGUS
Faculty of Humanities, Law and Social Science: Prof. J. BEER
Faculty of Science and Engineering: Prof. M. NEAL
Hollings Faculty: Prof. RICHARD MURRAY
Institute of Education: ANDY JONES
MMU Cheshire: DENNIS DUNN

MIDDLESEX UNIVERSITY

The Burroughs, London, NW4 4BT
Telephone: (20) 8411-5555
E-mail: intadmissions@mdx.ac.uk
Internet: www.mdx.ac.uk
Founded 1973, as Middlesex Polytechnic, present name and status 1992; comprises fmr Enfield and Hendon Colleges of Technology, Hornsey College of Art, New College of Speech and Drama, Trent Park College of Education, College of All Saints and North London College of Health Studies
Academic year: September to July
Chancellor: Lord SHEPPARD OF DIDGEMERE
Vice-Chancellor: Prof. MICHAEL DRISCOLL
Deputy Vice-Chancellor: STEVE KNIGHT
Deputy Vice-Chancellor: KATIE BELL
Deputy Vice-Chancellor for Academics: Prof. MARGARET HOUSE
Deputy Vice-Chancellor for Int. Affairs: Dr TERRY BUTLAND
Deputy Vice-Chancellor for Finance and External Relations: MELVYN KEEN
Deputy Vice-Chancellor for Research and Enterprise: Prof. WAQAR AHMAD
Library of 540,000 vols, 130,000 vols of periodicals
Number of teachers: 850
Number of students: 35,000

DEANS

School of Arts and Education: Prof. EDWARD J. ESCHE
School of Engineering and Information Sciences: Prof. MARTIN LOOMES
School of Health and Social Sciences: Prof. JAN WILLIAMS
Middlesex University Business School: ANNA KYPRIANOU

NEWCASTLE UNIVERSITY

Exec. Office, King's Gate, Newcastle upon Tyne, NE1 7RU
Telephone: (191) 208-6000
E-mail: postmaster@ncl.ac.uk
Internet: www.ncl.ac.uk
Founded 1834, present status 1963
Academic year: September to June
Chancellor: Prof. Sir LIAM DONALDSON

Chair. of Ccl and Pro-Chancellor: MARK I'ANSON
Vice-Chancellor: Prof. CHRIS BRINK
Deputy Vice-Chancellor: Prof. ELLA RITCHIE
Dean for Int. Business Devt and Student Recruitment: Prof. GERARD CORSANE
Pro-Vice-Chancellor for Learning and Teaching: Prof. SUZANNE CHOLERTON
Pro-Vice-Chancellor for Planning and Resources: Prof. TONY STEVENSON
Pro-Vice-Chancellor for Research and Innovation: Prof. NICK WRIGHT
Registrar: Dr JOHN HOGAN
Librarian: WAYNE CONNOLLY
Library of 1,000,000 vols, 500,000 ebooks, 10,500 periodicals
Number of teachers: 2,430
Number of students: 22,874

PRO-VICE-CHANCELLORS

Faculty of Humanities and Social Sciences: Prof. CHARLES HARVEY
Faculty of Medical Sciences: Prof. CHRIS DAY
Faculty of Science, Agriculture and Engineering: Prof. STEVE HOMANS

NORTHUMBRIA UNIVERSITY

Ellison Pl., Newcastle upon Tyne NE1 8ST
Telephone: (191) 232-6002
E-mail: er.pressoffice@northumbria.ac.uk
Internet: www.northumbria.ac.uk
Founded 1969, as Newcastle upon Tyne Polytechnic, present name and status 1992
Academic year: September to July
Chancellor: Lord STEVENS OF KIRKWHELPINGTON
Chair and Pro-Chancellor: Sir LESLIE ELTON
Vice-Chancellor and Chief Exec.: Prof. ANDREW WATHEY
Deputy Vice-Chancellor and Finance Dir: DAVID CHESSER
Deputy Vice-Chancellor for Learning and Teaching: Prof. PAUL CRONEY
Deputy Vice-Chancellor for Region, Engagement and Partnerships: LUCY WINSKELL
Deputy Vice-Chancellor for Research and Innovation: Prof. PETER GOLDING
Deputy Vice-Chancellor for Strategic Planning: Prof. IAN POSTLETHWAITE
Academic Registrar: PAUL KELLY
Univ. Sec.: PHILIP BOOTH (acting)
Library of 550,000 vols with 2,500 titles available as ebooks
Number of teachers: 920 (full-time)
Number of students: 34,020 (23,186 full-time and sandwich, 10,834 part-time)

DEANS

School of Arts and Social Sciences: Prof. LYNN DOBBS
School of Built and Natural Environment: STEPHEN HODGSON (acting)
School of Computing, Engineering and Information Science: Prof. ALISTAIR SAMBELL
School of Design: Prof. STEVEN KYFFIN
School of Health, Community and Education Studies: Prof. KATH McCOURT (acting)
School of Life Sciences: Prof. PAM BRIGGS
Newcastle Business School: Prof. SHARON MAVIN (acting)
Northumbria Law School: Prof. PHILIP PLOWDEN

NOTTINGHAM TRENT UNIVERSITY

Burton St, Nottingham, NG1 4BU
Telephone: (115) 941-8418
E-mail: cor.web@ntu.ac.uk
Internet: www.ntu.ac.uk
Founded 1843, as Nottingham Government School of Design, present name and status 1992
Academic year: September to July

Chancellor: Sir MICHAEL PARKINSON
Vice-Chancellor: Prof. NEIL T. GORMAN
Sr Pro-Vice-Chancellor: Prof. PETER JONES
Pro-Vice-Chancellor: Prof YVONNE BARNETT
Pro-Vice-Chancellor: Prof. NIGEL HASTINGS
Pro-Vice-Chancellor: ANN PRIEST
Registrar: D. W. SAMSON
Head of Libraries and Learning Resources: MARK TOOLE

Library of 467,299 vols, 2,550 periodicals, 7,150 electronic journals, 261 databases
Number of teachers: 927 (767 full-time, 160 part-time)
Number of students: 24,000

Publications: *Collapsing Soil Communique* (2 a year), *Comparative American Studies* (4 a year), *Gearing and Transmissions Journal* (2 a year), *Interventions Journal* (3 a year), *John Clare Society Journal* (1 a year), *Journal of Construction Procurement* (2 a year), *Journal for Critical Realism* (3 a year), *Journal of Strategic Change* (8 a year), *Loess Letter* (2 a year), *Mercian Geologist* (1 a year), *Nottingham Law Journal* (2 a year), *Studies in Travel Writing* (2 a year)

DEANS

School of Animal, Rural and Environmental Sciences: Dr EUNICE SIMMONS
School of Architecture, Design and Built Environment: PETER WESTLAND
School of Art and Design: Prof. JUDITH MOTTRAM
School of Arts and Humanities: Prof. MURRAY PRATT
School of Education: Dr GILL SCOTT
School of Science and Technology: Prof. ROGER ECCLESTON
School of Social Sciences: CHRIS POLE
Nottingham Business School: Prof. BABACK YAZDANI
Nottingham Law School: ANDREA NOLLENT

OPEN UNIVERSITY

Walton Hall, Milton Keynes, MK7 6AA
POB 197, Milton Keynes, MK7 6BJ

Telephone: (1908) 274066
E-mail: general-enquiries@open.ac.uk
Internet: www.open.ac.uk

Founded 1969
Academic year: variable; teaching takes place over up to 9 months, depending on courses

Chancellor: Lord PUTTNAM
Pro-Chancellor: Baron HASKINS OF SHIDBY
Treas.: RICHARD DEL BRIDGE
Vice-Chancellor: MARTIN BEAN
Pro-Vice-Chancellor for Academic Affairs: Prof. MUSA MIHSEIN
Pro-Vice-Chancellor for Learning, Teaching and Quality: Prof DENISE KIRKPATRICK
Pro-Vice-Chancellor for Research and Staff: Prof. BRIGID HEYWOOD
Pro-Vice-Chancellor for Strategy and External Affairs: Prof. DAVID VINCENT
Pro-Vice-Chancellor for Students, Quality and Standards: Prof. ALAN COCHRANE
Univ. Sec.: FRASER WOODBURN
Finance Dir: HILES HEDGET
Dir for Students: WILLIAM SWANN
Dir for Library Services: NICKY WHITSED

Number of teachers: 8,200 (7,000 tutors and 1,200 full-time)
Number of students: 250,000

Publications: *Open Business School Brochure*, *PGCE Brochure*, *Research Degree Prospectus*, *Studying with the Open University*, *Taught Master's Degree Prospectuses*

DEANS

Faculty of Arts: Prof DAVID ROWLAND

Faculty of Education and Language Studies: Dr SHARON DING
Faculty of Health and Social Care: JEREMY ROCHE
Faculty of Mathematics, Computing and Technology: Prof. ANNE DE ROECK
Faculty of Science: Prof PHILIP POTTS
Faculty of Social Sciences: Prof SIMON BROMLEY
Open University Business School: Prof. JAMES FLECK

DIRECTORS OF UNITS

Institute of Educational Technology: Prof. JOSIE TAYLOR
Knowledge Media Institute: Dr PETER SCOTT

REGIONAL DIRECTORS

East Midlands Region: G. LAMMIE
East of England Region: HELEN WILDMAN
Ireland: Dr R. HAMILTON
London Region: ROSEMARY MAYES
North Region: DAVID KNIGHT
North West Region: LYNDA BRADY
Scotland: PETER SYME
South East Region: LIZ GRAY
South Region: CELIA COHEN
South West Region: LINDA BRIGHTMAN
Wales: ROB HUMPHREYS
West Midlands Region: Dr MICHAEL ROOKES
Yorkshire Region: NICK BERRY

PROFESSORS

ALDGATE, P. J., Social Care
ALLEN, J. R., Social Science
APPLEBY, C., Business Development
ATKINSON, D., Learning Disability
BASSINDALE, A., Organometallic Chemistry
BENNETT, T., Sociology
BENTON, T. J., Art History
BERRY, F., Inorganic Chemistry
BISSELL, C. C., Telematics
BLOWERS, A. T., Social Sciences
BORNAT, J., Oral History
BRAITHWAITE, N., Engineering Physics
BRANNAN, D. A., Pure Mathematics
BROWN, S., Philosophy
BURROWS, D. J., Music
BURTON, K. W., Isotope Geochemistry
BUSH, P.
CANDLIN, C. N., Applied Linguistics
CHAMBERS, E.
CHATAWAY, J. C., Development Manager
CLARKE, J., Social Policy
COCHRANE, A., Public Policy
COCKELL, C. S., Geomicrobiology
COLEMAN, J. A., Languages
COLLINS, R. E., Media Studies
COOK, G., Education
CRITCHLEY, F., Statistics
CROSS, N. G., Design Studies (Technology)
DANIEL, E. M., Information Management
DAVIES, C., Health Care
DE ROECK, A. N., Computing
DOBSON, A. N. H., Politics
DU GAY, P. L. J., Sociology
EARL, C., Engineering Product Design
EDWARDS, L., Structural Integrity
EISENSTADT, M., Artificial Intelligence
ELLIOTT, D., Technology Policy
EMSLEY, C., Arts
ENGLANDER, R., History
FORRESTER-PATON, R., Social Enterprise
GARTHWAITE, P. H., Statistics
GELLATLY, A. R. H., Cognitive Psychology
GLATTER, R. G., Education
GOODMAN, D. C., History of Science and Technology
GOWER, J. C., Statistics
GRANNELL, M. J., Pure Mathematics
GRANT, J., Education in Medicine
GRAY, J. J., History of Mathematics
GRIGGS, T. S., Pure Mathematics
HALL, P. A. V., Computing
HALLIDAY, T. R., Evolutionary Biology

HAMMERSLEY, M., Educational and Social Research
HARDWICK, L. P., Classical Studies
HARRIS, N. B. W., Tectonics
HARRISON, C. T., Art History
HERBERT, T., Music
HIMMELWEIT, S. F., Economics
HOLLWAY, W., Psychology
INCE, D. C., Computing
ISON, R. L., Systems
JOHNSON, J., Complexity, Science and Design
JONES, B. W., Astronomy
JONES, M. C., Statistics
KAYE, G. R., Information Management
KING, C., Art History
LAING, A. W., Marketing
LAURENCE, E. A., History
LENTIN, A., History
LEWIS, V., Education
McCORMICK, R., Learning Schools Programme
McDONNELL, J. A., Planetary Space Science
MACKINTOSH, M., Economics
MALE, D., Immunology
MASON, J. H., Mathematics Education
MASON, N., Physics
MASON, R., Educational Technology
MASSEY, D. B., Geography
MERCER, N., Education
MONK, J. S., Digital Systems
MOON, R. E., Education
MUNCIE, J. P., Criminology
NAUGHTON, J., Public Understanding of Technology
NEWMAN, J. E., Social Policy
NUSEIBEH, B., Computing
O'DAY, R., History
OWENS, W. R., Art
PETERS, G., Systems Strategy
PHOENIX, A. A., Psychology
PILLINGER, C. T., Planetary Sciences
PLUMBRIDGE, W. J., Materials
POND-JANZEN, C. M., Biological Sciences
QUINTAS, P. R., Knowledge Management
RICHARDS, D., Applied Mathematics
RICHARDSON, J. T. E., Student Learning and Assessment
ROSE, S. P. R., Biology
ROY, R., Design and Environment
RUTTERFORD, J., Financial Management
SALAMAN, G., Organization Studies
SAWARD, M., Politics
SCANLON, E., Educational Technology
SEGAL-HORN, S., International Strategy
SELF, S., Volcanology
SHUKER, D. E. G., Organic Chemistry
SILVERTOWN, J. W., Ecology
SLAPPER, G., Law
SLATER, J. B.
SPICER, R. A., Earth Sciences
STEWART, D.
STEWART, M. G., Neuroscience
STOREY, J., Human Resource Management
SWITHENBY, S. J., Physics
THOMPSON, G. F., Political Economy
THORPE, M. S., Educational Technology
WALDER, D. J., Literature
WATSON, S., Sociology
WETHERELL, M., Business
WHATMORE, S. J., Geography
WIELD, D. V., Innovation and Development
WILKINSON, M., Applied Mathematics
WILSON, R. C. L., Earth Sciences
WOLFFE, J. R., Religious History
ZARNECKI, J., Space Sciences

OXFORD BROOKES UNIVERSITY

Gipsy Lane, Headington, Oxford, OX3 0BP

Telephone: (1865) 484848
E-mail: query@brookes.ac.uk
Internet: www.brookes.ac.uk

Founded 1865, as Oxford School of Art, became Oxford Polytechnic 1970, university status 1992

State control
Academic year: September to July
Chancellor: SHAMI CHAKRABARTI
Pro-Chancellor: DANBY BLOCH
Vice-Chancellor: Prof. JANET BEER
Pro-Vice-Chancellor for Research: Prof DIANA WOODHOUSE
Pro-Vice-Chancellor for Student Experience: Prof. JOHN RAFTERY
Registrar: PAUL LARGE (acting)
Library of 500,000 vols
Number of teachers: 750
Number of students: 18,170
Publication: *Observe*

DEANS

Faculty of Business: Prof. CHRIS COOPER
Faculty of Health and Life Sciences: JUNE GIRVIN
Faculty of Humanities and Social Sciences: DEREK ELSOM
Faculty of Technology, Design and Environment: MARS STREET

PLYMOUTH UNIVERSITY

Drake Circus, Plymouth, PL4 8AA
Telephone: (1752) 600600
E-mail: publicrelations@plymouth.ac.uk
Internet: www.plymouth.ac.uk
Founded 1970 as Plymouth Polytechnic, name changed to Polytechnic South West in 1989, present name and status 1992
Academic year: September to June
Vice-Chancellor and Chief Exec.: Prof. WENDY PURCELL
Deputy Vice-Chancellor: Prof. DAVID COSLETT
Deputy Vice-Chancellor: Prof. RAYMOND PLAYFORD
Pro-Vice-Chancellor for Health: Prof. RICHARD STEPHENSON
Pro-Vice-Chancellor for Regional Enterprise: Prof. JULIAN BEER
Pro-Vice-Chancellor for Research: Prof. JOHN SCOTT
Pro-Vice-Chancellor for Teaching and Learning: Prof. PAULINE KNEALE
Dean for Students: Dr MAUREEN POWERS
Dir for External Relations: JANE CHAFER
Dir for Human Resources: VIKKI MATTHEWS
Dir for Research and Innovation: Prof. JIM GRIFFITHS
Library of 450,000 vols, 14,000 journal titles
Number of teachers: 2,942
Number of students: 32,933
Publication: *Research Report*

DEANS

Academic Partnerships: Prof. SIMON PAYNE
Faculty of Arts: Prof. DAFYDD MOORE
Faculty of Business: Prof. NIKOLAOS TZOKAS
Faculty of Health and Human Sciences: Prof. RICHARD STEPHENSON
Faculty of Science and Technology: Prof. SIMON HANDLEY (acting)
Plymouth University International College: Prof. PETER MCDONNELL (Prin.)
Plymouth University Peninsula Schools of Medicine and Dentistry: Prof. ROBERT SNEYD

ROEHAMPTON UNIVERSITY

Erasmus House, Roehampton Lane, London, SW15 5PU
Telephone: (20) 8392-3232
E-mail: enquiries@roehampton.ac.uk
Internet: www.roehampton.ac.uk
Founded 1841, present status 2004
Chancellor: JOHN SIMPSON
Pro-Chancellor: WILLIAM MACINTYRE
Pro-Vice-Chancellor: ANDREW MASHETER
Vice-Chancellor: Prof. PAUL O'PREY

Deputy Vice-Chancellor and Provost: Prof. JANE BROADBENT
Pro-Vice-Chancellor: CHRIS COBB
Pro-Vice-Chancellor: ANDY MASHETER
Dir for Finance: REGGIE BLENNERHASSETT
Univ. Sec. and Registrar: ROBIN GELLER
Prin. of Digby Stuart College: PAUL HODGES
Prin. of Froebel College: SIMON DORMAN
Prin. of Southlands College: YVONNE GUERRIER
Prin. of Whitelands College: Rev. Prof. GEOFFREY WALKER

DEANS

School of Arts: LYNDIE BRIMSTONE
School of Business and Social Sciences: Prof. YVONNE GUERRIER
School of Education: Dr JEANNE KEAY
School of Human and Life Sciences: MICHAEL BARHAM
Business School: Prof. ELAINE HARRIS (Dir)

PROFESSORS

School of Arts:
  FISHER, A., Art History
  JORDAN, S., Dance
  READ, A., Drama and Theatre Studies
School of Business and Social Sciences:
  BALES, K., Sociology
  EADE, J., Sociology and Anthropology
  FENNELL, G., Sociology and Social Policy
  GLOVER, J., Employment Studies
  GUERRIER, Y., Organizational Studies
School of Education:
  BREHONY, K. J., Early Childhood Studies
  HARGREAVES, D., Child Development
  MAHONY, P., Education
  MASON, R., Art Education
  WATTS, M., Education
School of English and Modern Languages:
  COATES, J., English Languages and Linguistics
  DOBSON, M., English Literature
  HARTLEY, J., English Literature
  HEADLAM-WELLS, R., English Literature
  LEADER, Z., English Literature
  PRIESTMAN, M., English Literature
School of Humanities and Cultural Studies:
  DEAN, T., Medieval History
  EDWARDS, P., History
  GIBSON, A., Philosophy
  TOSH, J., History
School of Initial Teacher Education:
  BEST, R., Education
School of Human and Life Sciences:
  MACLARNON, A., Evolutionary Anthropology
School of Psychology and Therapeutic Studies:
  BEAUMONT, G., Neuropsychology
  ESSAU, C., Developmental Psychopathology
  REID, M., Nutritional Psychology
  VOGELE, C., Clinical and Health Psychology

SHEFFIELD HALLAM UNIVERSITY

City Campus, Howard St, Sheffield, S1 1WB
Telephone: (114) 225-5555
E-mail: admissions@shu.ac.uk
Internet: www.shu.ac.uk
Founded 1969, as Sheffield Polytechnic, later Sheffield City Polytechnic; present name and status 1992
Academic year: September to June
Chancellor: Lord WINSTON
Vice-Chancellor: Prof. PHILIP JONES
Deputy Vice-Chancellor: CLIFF ALLAN
Pro-Vice-Chancellor for Research: MIKE SMITH
Dir of Human Resources: PHILL DIXON

Sec. and Registrar: LIZ WINDERS
Academic Registrar: GWYN ARNOLD
Library of 540,000 vols
Number of teachers: 960
Number of students: 28,280 (20,994 undergraduate, 7,286 postgraduate)

DEANS

Faculty of Arts, Computing Engineering and Sciences: Prof. ALISTAIR SAMBELL
Faculty of Devt and Society: SYLVIA JOHNSON
Faculty of Health and Wellbeing: Prof. RHIANNON BILLINGLSEY
Sheffield Business School: CHRISTINE BOOTH

SOUTHAMPTON SOLENT UNIVERSITY

East Park Terrace, Southampton, SO14 0YN
Telephone: (23) 8031-9000
E-mail: ask@solent.ac.uk
Internet: www.solent.ac.uk
Founded 1855, as a school of art; present name and status 2005
Chancellor: Admiral Lord WEST OF SPITHEAD
Vice-Chancellor: Prof. VAN GORE
Deputy Vice-Chancellor: Dr RICHARD BLACKWELL
Deputy Vice-Chancellor: Prof. JANE LONGMORE
Deputy Vice-Chancellor: Dr MIKE WILKINSON
Number of students: 16,000
Publications: *Headway*, *Issue*

DEANS

Faculty of Business, Sport and Enterprise: Prof. JENNY ANDERSON
Faculty of Media, Arts and Society: Prof. ROD PILLING
Faculty of Technology: Prof. JOHN REES
Warsash Maritime Academy: JOHN MILLICAN

STAFFORDSHIRE UNIVERSITY

College Rd, Stoke on Trent, ST4 2DE
Telephone: (1782) 294000
E-mail: international@staffs.ac.uk
Internet: www.staffs.ac.uk
Founded 1970 as North Staffordshire Polytechnic, became Staffordshire Polytechnic 1988; present name and status 1992
Academic year: September to July
Chancellor: Sir Lord BILL MORRIS
Vice-Chancellor and Chief Exec.: Prof. MICHAEL GUNN
Deputy Vice-Chancellor and Deputy Chief Exec.: PAUL RICHARDS
Univ. Sec.: KEN SPROSTON
Academic Registrar: FRANCESCA FRANCIS
Librarian: LIZ HART
Library of 300,000 vols, 2,000 periodicals
Number of teachers: 590
Number of students: 16,580 (10,994 full-time undergraduate, 1,973 postgraduate, 3,613 part-time)
Publications: *Horizon* (journal for former students; 3 a year), *Research Report* (1 a year), *Shine On* (1 a year)

DEANS

Business School: Prof. SUSAN FOREMAN
Faculty of Arts, Media and Design: Dr ASTRID HERHOFFER
Faculty of Computing, Engineering and Technology: Prof. MIKE GOODWIN
Faculty of Health: HILARY JONES
Faculty of Sciences: Prof. DAVID WHITE (acting)
Law School: ROSEMARY EVANS

TEESSIDE UNIVERSITY

Borough Rd, Middlesbrough, TS1 3BA
Telephone: (1642) 218121
E-mail: enquiries@tees.ac.uk
Internet: www.tees.ac.uk

Founded 1929 as Constantine College of Technology, became Teesside Polytechnic 1970, present name and status 1992
Academic year: September to June
Chancellor: Lord SAWYER OF DARLINGTON
Vice-Chancellor and Chief Exec.: Prof. GRAHAM HENDERSON
Deputy Vice-Chancellor for Academics: Prof. EILEEN MARTIN
Deputy Vice-Chancellor for Partnerships: Prof. CAROLINE MACDONALD
Deputy Vice-Chancellor for Research and Business Engagement: Prof. CLIFF HARDCASTLE
Pro Vice-Chancellor for Quality: LIZ HOLEY
Deputy Chief Executive (Chief Operating Officer): MALCOLM PAGE
Dir of Library and Information Services: LIZ JOLLY

Library of 369,641 vols
Number of teachers: 800
Number of students: 22,000

DEANS

Graduate Research School: Prof. ZULFI ALI
School of Arts and Media: Prof. GERDA ROPER
School of Computing: Dr SIMON STOBART
School of Health and Social Care: Prof. PAUL KEANE
School of Science and Engineering: Prof. SIMON HODGSON
School of Social Sciences and Law: Dr MARK SIMPSON
Teesside Univ. Business School: ALASTAIR THOMSON

THAMES VALLEY UNIVERSITY

St Mary's Rd, Ealing, London, W5 5RF
Telephone: (20) 8579-5000
E-mail: learning.advice@tvu.ac.uk
Internet: www.tvu.ac.ukWellington St, Slough, SL1 1YG
Telephone: (1753) 534585

Founded 1860, as Lady Byron School, present name and status 1992
Academic year: September to July
Chancellor: Lord BILIMORIA
Vice-Chancellor: Prof. PETER JOHN
Pro-Vice-Chancellor for Academic Affairs and Student Services: Prof. KATH MITCHELL
Deputy Vice-Chancellor for Enterprise and External Services: Dr IAN TUNBRIDGE
Univ. Sec. and Clerk to the Board: MAUREEN SKINNER
Head of Registry Services: (vacant)

Library of 270,000 vols, 1,300 print journals
Number of teachers: 638 (388 full-time, 250 part-time)
Number of students: 25,741 (9,004 full-time and sandwich, 16,737 part-time and distance learning)

DEANS

Faculty of Arts: ROSY CREHAN
Faculty of Health and Human Sciences: ANDREW MACCALLUM
Faculty of Professional Studies: Prof. DAVID JONES

UNIVERSITY FOR THE CREATIVE ARTS

Canterbury Campus: New Dover Rd, Canterbury, CT1 3AN
Telephone: (1227) 817302
E-mail: admissionscanterbury@ucreative.ac.uk
Epsom Campus: Ashley Rd, Epsom, KT18 5BE
Telephone: (1372) 728811
E-mail: admissionsepsom@ucreative.ac.uk
Farnham Campus: Falkner Rd, Farnham, GU9 7DS
Telephone: (1252) 722441
E-mail: admissionsfarnham@ucreative.ac.uk
Maidstone Campus: Oakwood Park, Maidstone, ME16 8AG
Telephone: (1622) 620000
E-mail: admissionsmaidstone@ucreative.ac.uk
Rochester Campus: Fort Pitt, Rochester, ME1 1DZ
Telephone: (1634) 888702
E-mail: admissionsrochester@ucreative.ac.uk
Internet: www.ucreative.ac.uk

Founded 2005, as Univ. College for Creative Arts by merger of Kent Inst. of Art and Design (f. 1987) and Surrey Inst. of Art and Design, University College (f. 1995); present name 2008
Academic year: September to May
Vice-Chancellor: Prof. ELAINE THOMAS
Deputy Vice-Chancellor: Prof. MARK HUNT
Pro-Vice-Chancellor for Corporate Resources: ALAN COOKE
Pro-Vice-Chancellor for Further Education and Widening Participation: Prof. DIANNE TAYLOR GEARING
Pro-Vice-Chancellor for Learning and Teaching: Prof. PAUL COYLE
Pro-Vice-Chancellor for Research and Devt: Dr SEYMOUR ROWORTH-STOKES
Sec.: MARION WILKS
Number of students: 6,500

UNIVERSITY OF BATH

Claverton Down, Bath, BA2 7AY
Telephone: (1225) 388388
E-mail: registry@bath.ac.uk
Internet: www.bath.ac.uk

Founded 1856, designated College of Advanced Technology 1960, independent instn with direct-grant status 1962, Univ. Charter 1966
Academic year: September to June
Chancellor: Lord TUGENDHAT OF WIDDINGTON
Vice-Chancellor: Prof. GLYNIS BREAKWELL
Deputy Vice-Chancellor: Prof. KEVIN EDGE
Pro-Vice-Chancellor for Internationalization: Prof. COLIN GRANT
Pro-Vice-Chancellor for Learning and Teaching: Prof. BERNIE MORLEY
Pro-Vice-Chancellor for Research: Prof. JANE MILLAR
Univ. Sec.: MARK HUMPHRISS
Univ. Librarian: KATE ROBINSON

Library: see under Libraries and Archives
Number of teachers: 880
Number of students: 15,140

DEANS

Faculty of Engineering and Design: Prof. GARY HAWLEY
Faculty of Humanities and Social Sciences: Prof. ROGER EATWELL
Faculty of Science: Prof. DAVID BIRD
School of Management: Prof. RICHARD ELLIOTT

PROFESSORS

ACHARYA, K., Biology and Biochemistry
ADAMS, M., Management
AGGARWAL, R., Electronic and Electrical Engineering
ALMOND, D., Mechanical Engineering
ARNOULD, E., Management
BAYLISS, B., Management
BENDING, S., Physics
BEVERLAND, M., Management
BIRD, D., Physics
BIRKS, T., Physics
BOWEN, C., Mechanical Engineering
BREAKWELL, G.
BRINER, R., Management
BRITTON, N., Mathematical Sciences
BROWN, D., Biology and Biochemistry
BROWN, A., Management
BUDD, C., Mathematical Sciences
BULL, A., Politics, Languages and International Studies
BURSTALL, F., Mathematical Sciences
BURTON, G., Mathematical Sciences
BUTLER, I., Social and Policy Sciences
CALDERBANK, D., Mathematical Sciences
CHAUDHURI, J., Chemical Engineering
CLEGG, P., Architecture and Civil Engineering
COLEMAN, P., Physics
COLEY, D., Architecture and Civil Engineering
COOKE, L., Social and Policy Sciences
COPESTAKE, J., Social and Policy Sciences
CRITTENDEN, B., Chemical Engineering
CULLEY, S., Mechanical Engineering
CULLIS, J., Economics
DANSON, M., Biology and Biochemistry
DAVENPORT, J., Computer Science
DAVIDSON, M., Chemistry
DIMOV, D., Management
DOOLEY, A., Mathematical Sciences
EARNEST, C., Health
EATWELL, R., Politics, Languages and International Studies
ECCLESTON, C., Health
EDGE, K.
ELLIOTT, R., Management
FARAWAY, J., Mathematical Sciences
FEIL, E., Biology and Biochemistry
FINUS, M., Economics
FROST, C., Chemistry
GABRIEL, Y., Management
GALAKTIONOV, V., Mathematical Sciences
GILL, H., Mechanical Engineering
GILLESPIE, D., Politics, Languages and International Studies
GILMORE, A., Health
GOODBODY, A., Politics, Languages and International Studies
GOODWIN, P., Management
GOUGH, S., Education
GRAHAM, I., Mathematical Sciences
GRANT, C.
GRAVES, A., Management
GREGG, P., Social and Policy Sciences
GRIFFIN, C., Psychology
GURSUL, I., Mechanical Engineering
GUY, R., Pharmacy and Pharmacology
HAMMOND, G., Mechanical Engineering
HARLAND, C., Management
HARRIS, R., Architecture and Civil Engineering
HART, V., Architecture and Civil Engineering
HAWLEY, J., Mechanical Engineering
HILL, M., Chemistry
HOLMAN, G., Biology and Biochemistry
HOPE HAILEY, V., Management
HUDSON, J., Economics
HUISMAN, J., Management
HURST, L., Biology and Biochemistry
HUSBANDS, S., Pharmacy and Pharmacology
HYDE-PRICE, A., Politics, Languages and International Studies
IBELL, T., Architecture and Civil Engineering
IOANNIDIS, C., Economics
ISLAM, M., Chemistry
JAMES, T., Chemistry
JAMES, C., Education
JENNISON, C., Mathematical Sciences
JOHNSON, P., Computer Science
JONES, P., Economics
JUDGE, K., Health

KELSH, R., Biology and Biochemistry
KEOGH, P., Mechanical Engineering
KING, A., Mathematical Sciences
KNIGHT, J., Physics
KOLACZKOWSKI, S., Chemical Engineering
KYPRIANOU, A., Mathematical Sciences
LAUDER, H., Education
LEAK, D., Biology and Biochemistry
LEES, C., Politics, Languages and International Studies
LEWIS, M., Management
LEWIS, A., Psychology
LI, F., Electronic and Electrical Engineering
LINDSAY, M., Pharmacy and Pharmacology
LOCK, G., Mechanical Engineering
LOGEMANN, H., Mathematical Sciences
MARKEN, F., Chemistry
MAROPOULOS, P., Mechanical Engineering
MAROUKIS, A., Social and Policy Sciences
MARTIN, C., Economics
MAYER, M., Management
MCCUSKER, G., Computer Science
MILES, A., Mechanical Engineering
MILEWSKI, P., Mathematical Sciences
MILLAR, J.
MILLER, D., Social and Policy Sciences
MILLINGTON, A., Management
MITCHELL, C., Electronic and Electrical Engineering
MITCHELL, N., Electronic and Electrical Engineering
MOLLOY, K., Chemistry
MORLEY, B.
MORTERS, P., Mathematical Sciences
MRSNY, R., Pharmacy and Pharmacology
MULLINEUX, G., Mechanical Engineering
NANDEIBAM, S., Economics
NEWMAN, S., Mechanical Engineering
PARKER, S., Chemistry
PAVELIN, S., Management
PAYNE, S., Computer Science
PENROSE, M., Mathematical Sciences
PETER, L., Chemistry
PLUMMER, A., Mechanical Engineering
POTTER, B., Pharmacy and Pharmacology
PRICE, G., Chemistry
PRICE, R., Pharmacy and Pharmacology
RAITHBY, P., Chemistry
RICHENS, P., Architecture and Civil Engineering
RIDGE, T., Social and Policy Sciences
ROOM, G., Social and Policy Sciences
RYAN, E., Mathematical Sciences
SALKOVSKIS, P., Psychology
SALMON, P., Physics
SANKARAN, G., Mathematical Sciences
SCHEICHL, R., Mathematical Sciences
SCOTT, R., Biology and Biochemistry
SESSIONS, J., Economics
SHANKAR, A., Management
SIVALOGANATHAN, J., Mathematical Sciences
SKRYABIN, D., Physics
SPENCE, A., Mathematical Sciences
SQUIRE, B., Management
STABLES, A., Education
STANTON FRASER, D., Psychology
SWART, J., Management
SZEKELY, T., Biology and Biochemistry
TAYLOR, J., Electronic and Electrical Engineering
THOMPSON, E., Management
THREADGILL, M., Pharmacy and Pharmacology
TONKS, I., Management
TOSH, D., Biology and Biochemistry
TYRRELL, R., Pharmacy and Pharmacology
VERPLANKEN, B., Psychology
VINCE, R., Management
VOROBJOV, N., Computer Science
WALKER, P., Architecture and Civil Engineering
WALKER, A., Physics
WALTER, J., Social and Policy Sciences
WANG, W., Electronic and Electrical Engineering
WARD, S., Pharmacy and Pharmacology

WEISS, M., Pharmacy and Pharmacology
WELHAM, M., Pharmacy and Pharmacology
WELLER, M., Chemistry
WHITTLESEY, M., Chemistry
WHITTY, G., Management
WILDING, N., Physics
WILLIAMS, J., Chemistry
WILLIAMS, I., Chemistry
WILLIS, P., Computer Science
WILSON, C., Chemistry
WONNACOTT, S., Biology and Biochemistry
WOOD, W., Biology and Biochemistry
WOOD, S., Mathematical Sciences
WRIGHT, A., Architecture and Civil Engineering
WYVILL, B., Computer Science
ZALEWSKA, A., Management

UNIVERSITY OF BEDFORDSHIRE

Park Sq., Luton, LU1 3JU

Telephone: (1582) 489286

E-mail: admission@beds.ac.uk

Internet: www.beds.ac.uk

Founded 2006, by merger of Univ. of Luton (f. 1993) and De Montfort Univ.'s Bedford campus

Academic year: September to September

Chancellor: JOHN BERCOW

Vice-Chancellor and Chief Exec.: Prof. LES EBDON

Deputy Vice-Chancellor for Acad. Affairs: Prof. MARY MALCOLM

Deputy Vice-Chancellor for Resources: DONALD HARLEY

Registrar: ALICE HYNES

Librarian: TIM STONE

Library of 250,000 vols

Number of teachers: 1,200

Number of students: 21,000

DEANS

Bedfordshire Business School: Prof. PAUL BURNS

Faculty of Creative Arts, Technologies and Science: Prof. JAMES CRABBE

Faculty of Education, Sport and Tourism: Prof. MARILYN LEASK

Faculty of Health and Social Sciences: Prof. MICHAEL PRESTON-SHOOT

UNIVERSITY OF BIRMINGHAM

Edgbaston, Birmingham, B15 2TT

Telephone: (121) 414-3344

Internet: www.bham.ac.uk

Founded 1900

Academic year: September to June

Chancellor: Sir DOMINIC CADBURY

Vice-Chancellor and Prin.: Prof. DAVID EASTWOOD

Provost and Vice-Prin.: Prof. MICHAEL SHEPPARD

Pro-Vice-Chancellor for Estates and Infrastructure: Prof. JOHN HEATH

Pro-Vice-Chancellor for Research and Knowledge Transfer: (vacant)

Pro-Vice-Chancellor for Teaching, Learning and Quality: Prof. ADRIAN RANDALL

Registrar and Sec.: LEE SANDERS

Librarian: M. SHOEBRIDGE (acting)

Library: see under Libraries and Archives

Number of teachers: 2,290

Number of students: 26,070

Publications: *Court Reporter* (1 a year), *Medlines* (2 a year), *The Birmingham Magazine* (1 a year)

PROFESSORS

ABELL, S., Functional Materials
ADAMS, D. H., Hepatology
AHMED, A., Reproductive Physiology
AL-RUBEAI, M., Biotechnology
ALCOCK, P., Social Policy and Administration

ALEXANDER, D., Accounting
ALLEMANN, R., Chemical Biology
AMANN, R., Soviet Politics
ARNULL, A. M., European Law
BACKHOUSE, R. E., History and Philosophy of Economics
BACON, P. A., Rheumatology
BALDWIN, J., Judicial Administration
BALE, J. S., Environmental Biology
BANFIELD, S. D., Music
BARBER, K., African Popular Culture
BARKER, A., Classics
BARNDEN, J., Artificial Intelligence
BARNETT, A. H., Diabetic Medicine
BATLEY, R. A., Development Administration
BEEVERS, D. G., Medicine
BELL, T., Metallurgy
BESRA, G., Biosciences
BIDDLESTONE, A. J., Chemical Engineering
BIRKETT, J., French Studies
BLACKBURN, S., Solids Processing
BLAKE, J. R., Applied Mathematics
BOOTH, D. A., Psychology
BOOTH, I. W., Paediatric Gastroenterology and Nutrition
BOWEN, P., Mechanical Metallurgy
BOWERY, N. G., Pharmacology
BRADBURY, A., Vascular Surgery
BREUILLY, J. J., Modern History
BROOKS, N. P., Medieval History
BROWN, N. L., Molecular Genetics and Microbiology
BROWNE, K., Forensic and Family Psychology
BRYAN, S., Health Economics
BUCKLEY, C., Rheumatology
BURKE, F., Primary Dental Care
BUSBY, S. J. W., Biochemistry
BUTLER, M. G., Modern German Literature
BUTLER, P. J., Comparative Physiology
CAESAR, M. P., Italian
CALLOW, J. A., Botany
CAMPBELL, J., Casting Technology
CARROLL, D., Applied Psychology
CHAPPLE, I., Periodontology
CHENG, K. K., Public Health and Epidemiology
CHILD, J., Commerce (International Management and Organization)
CHIPMAN, J., Cell Toxicology
CLARK, L. A., Structural Engineering
CLARKE, M., Public Policy
CLIFFORD, C. M., Nursing
COCHRANE, R., Psychology
COLE, J. A., Microbial Physiology and Biochemistry
COOPER, J. M., Russian Economic Studies
COOTE, J. H., Physiology
COULTHARD, R. M., English Language and Linguistics
COX, A. W., Business Strategy and Procurement
CROFT, S. J., International Relations
CROSSLEY, E. C. D., 19th-Century French Studies
CRUIKSHANK, G. S., Neurosurgery
CRUISE, A. M., Astrophysics and Space Research
CURTIS, R., Combinatorial Algebra
DADSON, T. J., Hispanic Studies
DANIELS, H. R. J., Special Education and Educational Psychology
DANIELS, P. W., Geography
DAVIES, G., Engineering
DAVIES, L., English
DAVIES, M. L., International Education
DAVIS, A., Social Work
DAWE, D. J., Structural Mechanics
DE CHERNATONY, L., Brand Marketing
DEAN, T. A., Manufacturing Engineering
DEB, S., Neuropsychiatry and Intellectual Disability
DELECLUSE, H.-J., Molecular Pathology
DENT, N. J. H., Philosophy
DICKENSON, D., Global Ethics
DOE, W., Medicine
DOLING, J. F., Housing Studies

DOWDEN, K., Classics
DUDA, J., Sports Psychology
DUTTA, J., Economics
EDWARDS, A., Education
EDWARDS, P. P., Inorganic Chemistry
ELLIS, E. D., Public Law
ELLIS, S., English Literature
ENONCHONG, N., Law
EVANS, H., Metallurgy and Materials
FADDY, M., Statistics
FELDMAN, D. J., Jurisprudence
FENDER, J., Macroeconomics
FORGAN, E. M., Condensed Matter Physics
FRAME, J. W., Oral Surgery
FRANKLIN, F., Plant Molecular Biology
FRANKLYN, J. A., Medicine
FREEMANTLE, N., Clinical Epidemiology and
  Biostatistics
FRYER, P. J., Chemical Engineering
GALLIMORE, P. H., Cancer Studies
GARVEY, J., Particle Physics
GORDON, J., Cellular Immunology
GRAY, R., Medical Statistics
GREAVES, C., Solid-State Chemistry
GUNN, J. M. F., Theoretical Physics
HALDON, J. F., Byzantine Studies
HALL, P. S., Communications Engineering
HAM, C. J., Health Policy and Management
HARBER, C., International Education
HARRIS, I. R., Materials Science
HARRIS, J., Law
HARRIS, K. D. M., Structural Chemistry
HARRISON, R. M., Environmental Health
HAWKEY, P., Immunology
HAY, C., Political Analysis
HEATH, J. K., Biochemistry
HENDERSON, W., Continuing Education
HICKS, C., Health Care Psychology
HOBBS, F. D. R., Primary Care and General
  Practice
HUGHES, A., 20th-Century French Literature
HUMPHREYS, G. W., Cognitive Psychology
HUNTER, J. R., Ancient History and Archae-
  ology
HUTTON, P., Anaesthetics and Intensive Care
JACKSON, J. B., Bioenergetics
JEFFERIES, R., Molecular Immunology
JEFFERY, C., German Politics
JEFFERYS, J. G. R., Basic Neuroscience
JENKINSON, E. J., Experimental Immunology
JENNINGS, J., Political Theory
JOHNSON, P., Oncology and Translational
  Research
JONES, D. A., Sport and Exercise Sciences
JONES, E. L., Pathology
JONES, I. P., Physical Metallurgy
JONES, P. M., French History
JONES, R. H., Public Sector Accounting
JUNG, A., Computer Science
KAPLAN, J., Drama and Theatre Arts
KEARSEY, M., Biometrical Genetics
KEIGHLEY, M. R. B., Surgery
KELSEY, D., Economic Theory
KENDALL, K., Chemical Engineering
KENDALL, M., Clinical Pharmacology
KERALI, R., Highway Engineering and Man-
  agement
KILBY, M., Maternal and Foetal Medicine
KINSON, J. B., High Energy Physics
KLAPPER, J., Foreign Language Pedagogy
KNIGHT, D., Water Engineering
KNOTT, J. F., Metallurgy and Materials
KNOWLES, P. J., Theoretical Chemistry
KWIATKOWSKA, M., Computer Science
LAIRD, W. R. E., Prosthetic Dentistry
LANCASTER, M., Communications Engineer-
  ing
LAWRANCE, A. J., Statistics
LE SUEUR, A., Jurisprudence
LEATHER, P., Urban and Regional Studies
LERNER, I., Theoretical Physics
LEWIS, A., Special Education and Educational
  Psychology
LILFORD, R., Public Health and Epidemiology
LLOYD-BOSTOCK, S., Law and Psychology
LOGAN, A., Molecular Neuroscience

LOTE, C., Experimental Nephrology
LUCAS, W., American Studies
LUESLEY, D. M., Gynaecology
LYDDIATT, A., Process Biotechnology
MACARTHUR, C., Maternal and Child Epi-
  demiology
MACASKIE, L., Applied Microbiology
McCASKIE, T., Asante History
MACKAY, R., Hydrogeology
MACLENNAN, I. C. M., Immunology
MADELIN, K. B., Civil Engineering
MAHER, E., Medical Genetics
MALLIN, C., Business Finance
MARQUIS, P. M., Biomaterials
MARSH, D., Political Science and Inter-
  national Studies
MARSHALL, J. M., Cardiovascular Science
MARTIN, G. R., Avian Sensory Science
McLEOD, D. H., Church History
MENON, A., European Studies
MICHELL, R. H., Biochemistry
MILLER, C. J., English Law
MINNIKIN, D., Microbial Chemistry
MOAYYEDI, P., Primary Care and General
  Practice
MORRISON, K., Neurology
MORTON, D. B., Biomedical Science and
  Biomedical Ethics
MOSS, P. A. H., Haematology
MULLINEUX, A. W., Global Finance
MURIE, A., Urban and Regional Studies
MURINDE, V., Developmental Finance
MURRAY, P. I., Ophthalmology
NASH, G., Cardiovascular Rheology
NEAL-STURGESS, C. E., Automotive Engineer-
  ing
NELSON, J. M., Nuclear Physics
NIELSEN, J., Theology
NIENOW, A. W., Biochemical Engineering
NOONAN, H., Philosophy
NORTON, J. P., Control Engineering
OLIVER, C., Clinical Psychology
ORFORD, J. F., Clinical and Community
  Psychology
PALIWODA, S., Marketing
PALLEN, M., Infection
PALMER, R. E., Experimental Physics
PARKER, D., Textual Criticism and Palaeo-
  graphy
PARLE, J., Primary Care
PARRATT, J., Third-World Theologies
PATERSON, W. E., German Studies
PECK, E., Health Services Management
PENN, C., Molecular Microbiology
PERRIE, M., Russian History
PERRY, J. G., Civil Engineering
PETTS, G., Physical Geography
PETTS, J., Environmental Risk Management
PIDDOCK, L., Microbiology
PILKINGTON, H., Sociology and Russian Area
  Studies
PONMAN, T., Astrophysics
PRESTON, P., Political Sociology
PREWETT, P., Microsystems Manufacture
RAFTERY, J. P., Health Economics
RAINE, J., Management in Criminal Justice
RAKODI, C., Public Policy
RANDALL, A. J., English Social History
RANSON, P. R. S., Education
REDDY, U., Computer Science
REDMOND, J., European Studies
RICHARDS, S., Public Management
RICKINSON, A. B., Cancer Studies
RIDDOCH, M., Cognitive Neuropsychology
ROBINSON, G., Pure Mathematics
ROGERS, C., Geotechnical Engineering
RUSSELL, M., Electronic and Electrical Engin-
  eering
SALMON, M., Experimental Rheumatology
SAMUELS, J. M., Business Finance
SAVAGE, C., Nephrology
SCASE, W., Medieval English Literature
SCHOFIELD, A., Theoretical Physics
SCOTT, I. R., Law
SEN, S., Development Economics
SEVILLE, J. P. K., Chemical Engineering

SHARPLES, M., Educational Technology
SHEPPARD, M. C., Medicine
SHUTE, S., Criminal Law and Criminal Just-
  ice
SIEBERT, W. S., Labour Economics
SIMNETT, G. M., High-Energy Astrophysics
SINCLAIR, P. J. N., Economics
SKELCHER, C., Local Government Studies
SLOMAN, A., Artificial Intelligence and Cog-
  nitive Science
SMALL, I. C., English Literature
SMITH, A., Oral Biology
SMITH, M., Experimental Neurology
SORAHAN, T., Occupational Epidemiology
SOUTHWOOD, T., Paediatric Rheumatology
SPEIRS, R. C., German
SPENCER, K. M., Local Policy
SPURGEON, P. C., Health Services Manage-
  ment
STEVENS, A., Public Health
STEWART, P. M., Medicine
STRAIN, A., Biochemistry
SUGDEN, R., Commerce
SUGIRTHARAJAH, R., Biblical Hermeneutics
SWANSON, R., Medieval Ecclesiastical History
TANN, J., Commerce
TAYLOR, A., Economics
TAYLOR, A. M. R., Cancer Genetics
TAYLOR, E. W., Animal Physiology
TAYLOR, M., World Faiths Development Dia-
  logue
TELLAM, J., Hydrogeology
TEMPLE, J. G., Surgery
TEUBERT, W., English
THEOBALD, M. F., Accounting
THOMAS, C. M., Molecular Genetics
THOMAS, C. R., Biochemical Engineering
THOMAS, H. R., Economics of Education
TIMMS, C. R., Music
TOOLAN, M., Applied English Linguistics
TRAYER, I. P., Biochemistry
TURNBULL, P., Marketing
TURNER, B. M., Experimental Genetics
TZIOVAS, D. P., Modern Greek Studies
USTORF, W., Mission
VERDI, R., Fine Art and Art History
VINZENT, M., Theology
WAKELAM, M. J. O., Molecular Pharmacology
WALMSLEY, A., Dentistry
WALSH, M., English Literature
WALTON, D., Mechanical Engineering
WEBBER, J., Theology
WEST, S., Art History
WESTBROOK, G. K., Geophysics
WESTBURY, D. R., Physiology
WHARTON, C., Biochemistry
WHEATLEY, K., Medical Statistics
WHENHAM, E., Music History
WHITEHAND, J. W. R., Urban Geography
WHITTLE, M. J., Foetal Medicine
WICKHAM, C. J., Early Medieval History
WILSON, J. S., Pure Mathematics
WILSON, R., Group Theory
WING, A. M., Human Movement
WINTERBOTTOM, J., Chemical Reaction Engin-
  eering
WOOD, D. M., French Literature
WOODMAN, G., Comparative Law
WRIGHTSON, P., Physiotherapy
YAO, X., Computer Science
YOUNG, F. M., Theology
YOUNG, L. S., Cancer Biology

UNIVERSITY OF BOLTON

Deane Rd, Bolton, BL3 5AB
Telephone: (1204) 900600
E-mail: enquiries@bolton.ac.uk
Internet: www.bolton.ac.uk

Founded 1824, present status 2005
State control
Language of instruction: English
Academic year: September to July

Chancellor: Rt Hon. Lord Justice ERNEST
NIGEL RYDER

Vice-Chancellor: Dr GEORGE HOLMES
Pro-Vice-Chancellor: Prof. ROB CAMPBELL
Library Man.: TREVOR HODGSON
Library of 180,000 vols, 18,000 books, 8,000 ebooks, 400 print journals, 15,000 ejournals
Number of teachers: 320
Number of students: 9,240 (7,446 undergraduate, 1,794 postgraduate)
Publication: *The Bolt* (4 a year)

DEANS

Faculty of Advanced Engineering and Sciences: ANDY GRAHAM
Faculty of Arts and Media Technologies: SAM JOHNSON
Faculty of Well Being and Social Sciences: Prof. CAROLE TRUMAN

UNIVERSITY OF BRADFORD

Richmond Rd, Bradford, BD7 1DP
Telephone: (1274) 232323
E-mail: enquiries@bradford.ac.uk
Internet: www.bradford.ac.uk
Founded 1882, as Bradford Technical College, Royal Charter 1966
Academic year: September to May (2 semesters)
Chancellor: IMRAN KHAN
Vice-Chancellor and Prin.: Prof. MARK CLEAREY
Pro-Chancellor and Chair.: PAUL JAGGER
Treas. and Pro-Chancellor: ROLAND CLARK
Pro-Chancellor: DIANA CHAMBERS
Sec.: MARY-ROSE MILLIN
Deputy Vice-Chancellor: S. KERSHAW
Deputy Vice-Chancellor for Academic Affairs: Prof. GEOFF LAYER
Dir of Learning Resources Unit: Dr S. J. HOUGHTON
Librarian: J. J. HORTON
Library: see under Libraries and Archives
Number of teachers: 540
Number of students: 8,430
Publications: *News and Views*, *Vice-Chancellor's Research Report* (1 a year)

DEANS

Engineering, Design and Technology: Prof. A. S. WOOD
Health Studies: Prof. G. BRADSHAW
School of Computing, Informatics and Media: Dr I. J. PALMER
School of Life Sciences: Prof. D. COATES
School of Lifelong Education and Devt: N. MIRZA
School of Management: Prof. A. FRANCIS
School of Social and Int. Studies: Prof. J. CUSWORTH

PROFESSORS

ALDERSON, G., Medical Microbiology
ANDERSON, D., Biomedical Sciences
ASHLEY, R. M., Urban Water
ASHMORE, M. R., Environmental Science
BAILES, P. J., Process Engineering
BALMER, J. M. T., Corporate Identity
BARRY, B. W., Pharmaceutical Technology
BENKREIRA, H., Coating and Polymer Processing
BIBBY, M. C., Cancer Research
CHALMERS, M. G., International Politics
CHOUDHRY, T., Finance
CHRYSTYN, H., Clinical Pharmacy
CLARK, B. J., Pharmaceutical Technology
COATES, P. D., Polymer Engineering
COSTALL, B., Neuropharmacology
COWLING, P. I., Computing
CUSWORTH, J. W., International Development Management
DANDO, M. R., International Security
DAY, A. J., Quality Engineering

DOUBLE, J. A., Experimental Cancer Chemotherapy
DOWNS, M. G., Dementia Studies
DUNCAN, S. S., Comparative Social Policy
EARNSHAW, R. A., Electronic Imaging
EDWARDS, H. G. M., Molecular Spectroscopy
EXCELL, P. S., Applied Electromagnetics
FELL, A. F., Pharmaceutical Chemistry
FILOTOTCHEV, I. R., Strategic Management
FRANCIS, F. A. S., Management
GALLAGHER, T. G. P., Ethnic Conflict and Peace
GARDINER, J. G., Electronic Engineering
GARDNER, M. L. G., Physiological Biochemistry
GRAVES-MORRIS, P. R., Numerical Analysis
GREEN, J. N., Romance Linguistics
HOGARTH-SCOTT, S., Marketing and Entrepreneurship
HOPE, C. A., Service Quality
HUSBAND, C. H., Social Analysis
JAMES, A. L., Social Sciences
JAMES, P. W., Environmental Sciences
JENKINS, T. C., Drugs Design
JIANG, J., Electronic Imaging and Media Communications
JOBBER, D., Marketing
KOUVATSOS, D. D., Computer Systems Modelling
LAYER, G. M., Lifelong Learning
LUCAS, J., Learning and Teaching
McCOLM, I. J., Ceramic Materials
MELLORS, C., Political Science
MIRZA, H. R., International Business
MUHLEMANN, A. P., Operations Management
NAYLOR, R. J, Pharmacology
NEWELL, R. J., Nursing Research
O'HEAR, A., Philosophy
OSTELL, A. E., Organizational Health and Behaviour
PEARCE, J. V., Latin American Politics
PIKE, R. H., Finance and Accounting
POLLARD, A. M., Archaeological Sciences
PRICE, D. H. R., Operational Research
RADAELLI, C. M., Public Policy
RAMSBOTHAM, O. P., Peace Studies
RANDALL, V. A., Biomedical Sciences
ROGERS, P. F., Peace Studies
SCHALLREUTER, K. U., Clinical and Experimental Dermatology
SEAWARD, M. R. D., Environmental Biology
SHEPHERD, S. J., Cryptography and Computer Communications Security
SHERIFF, R. E., Mobile Communications
SMALL, N. A., Community and Primary Care
TAYLOR, W. A., Business Information Systems
TOROPOV, V. V., Computational Mechanics
VOURDAS, A., Computing
WALLS, J. R., Chemical Engineering
WEISS, J. A., Development Economics
WHALLEY, R., Mechanical Engineering
WHITAKER, D. J., Optometry
WILLIAMS, A. C., Contemporary German Studies
WINN, B., Optometry
WOOD, J. M., Medical Biochemistry
WOODHOUSE, T., Conflict Resolution
WOODWARD, M. E., Telecommunications
YORK, P., Physical Pharmaceutics
ZAIRI, M., Best Practice Management

UNIVERSITY OF BRIGHTON

Mithras House, Lewes Rd, Brighton, BN2 4AT
Telephone: (1273) 600900
E-mail: enquiries@brighton.ac.uk
Internet: www.brighton.ac.uk
Founded 1970 as Brighton Polytechnic, present name and status 1992
Academic year: September to June
Vice-Chancellor: Prof. JULIAN CRAMPTON
Deputy Vice-Chancellor: STUART LAING

Pro-Vice-Chancellor for Business and Marketing: COLIN MONK
Pro-Vice-Chancellor for Research: Prof. BRUCE BROWN
Registrar and Sec.: CAROL BURNS
Dir of Finance: SUE McHUGH
Dir of Information Services: MARK TOOLE
Library of 550,000 vols
Number of teachers: 1,122 (f.t.e.)
Number of students: 23,000

DEANS

Brighton and Sussex Medical School: Prof. JON COHEN
Faculty of Arts: Prof. BRUCE BROWN
Faculty of Education and Sport: PAUL GRIFFITHS
Faculty of Health and Social Science: Prof. DAVID TAYLOR
Faculty of Management and Information Sciences: Prof. DAVID ARNOLD
Faculty of Science and Engineering: Prof. ANDREW LLOYD

UNIVERSITY OF BRISTOL

Senate House, Tyndall Ave, Bristol, BS8 1TH
Telephone: (117) 928-9000
Internet: www.bristol.ac.uk
Founded 1909, previously established as Univ. College, Bristol, 1876
Academic year: October to July
Chancellor: Baroness HALE OF RICHMOND
Vice-Chancellor: Prof. ERIC THOMAS
Deputy Vice-Chancellor: Prof. DAVID CLARKE
Pro-Vice-Chancellor for Education and Students: Prof. AVRIL WATERMAN-PEARSON
Pro-Vice-Chancellor for Enterprise: Prof. GUY ORPEN
Registrar: DEREK PRETTY
Library: see under Libraries and Archives
Number of teachers: 2,130
Number of students: 18,620
Publications: *re:search*, *Subtext*

DEANS

Faculty of Arts: Prof. CHARLES MARTINDALE
Faculty of Engineering: Prof. NICK LIEVEN
Faculty of Medical and Veterinary Sciences: Prof. CLIVE ORCHARD
Faculty of Medicine and Dentistry: Prof. PETER MATHIESON
Faculty of Science: Prof. JON KEATING
Faculty of Social Sciences and Law: Prof. JUDITH SQUIRES

PROFESSORS

(Some professors serve in more than one faculty)
Faculty of Arts (Senate House, Tyndall Ave, Bristol, BS8 1TH; tel. (117) 928-8897; internet www.bris.ac.uk/depts/artspgc/facart.htm):

BANFIELD, S. D., Music
BANN, S., History of Art
BENNETT, A. J., English
BIRD, A. J., Philosophy
BROOKSHAW, D. R., Luso-Brazilian Studies
BRYCE, J. H., Italian
BUXTON, R. G. A., Greek Language and Literature
CLARK, E. G., Ancient History
CORNWELL, N. J., Russian and Comparative Literature
DOYLE, W., History
FOWLER, R. L. H., Greek
FREEMAN, M. J., French Language and Literature
HARRISON, R. J., European Prehistory
HOOK, D., Hispanic Studies
HOPKINS, D. W., English Literature
HUTTON, R. E., History
KENNEDY, D. F., Latin Literature and Theory of Criticism

KERSHAW, B. R., Drama
KOSENINA, A., German
LOWE, R., Contemporary History
MARTINDALE, C. A., Latin
OFFORD, D. C., Russian Intellectual History
PARKIN, J., French Literary Studies
PARRY, M. M., Italian Linguistics
POOLE, G. R., Composition
PUNTER, D. G., English
SAMPSON, R. B. K., Romance Philology
STREET, S. C. J., Film
UNWIN, T. A., French
VINCENT, J. R., History
WEBB, E. T., English
WHITE, M. E., Theatre
WILLIAMS, P. M., Indian and Tibetan Philosophy

Faculty of Engineering (Queen's Building, University Walk, Bristol, BS8 1TR; tel. (117) 928-9760; internet www.fen.bris.ac.uk):

ADAMS, R. D., Applied Mechanics
BEACH, M. A., Radio Systems Engineering
BLOCKLEY, D. I., Civil Engineering
BOWES, S. R., Electrical and Electronic Engineering
BULL, D. R., Digital Systems Processing
CANAGARAJAH, C. N., Multimedia Signal Processing
CHALMERS, A. G., Computer Graphics
CHAMPNEYS, A. R., Applied Non-linear Mathematics
CLUCKIE, I. D., Worldwide Water Management
DAGLESS, E. L., Microelectronics
FLACH, P. A., Artificial Intelligence
FRISWELL, M. I., Aerospace Engineering
HOGAN, S. J., Mathematics
JOSZA, R. O., Computer Science
KRAUSKOPF, B., Applied Non-linear Mathematics
LIEVEN, N. A. J., Aerospace Dynamics
MAY, M. D., Computer Science
MCGEEHAN, J. P., Communications Engineering
MELLOR, P. H., Electrical Engineering
MUIR WOOD, D., Civil Engineering
NIX, A. R., Wireless Communication Systems
PRADHAN, D. K., Computer Science
QUARINI, G. L., Process Engineering
RAILTON, C. J., Electrical and Electronic Engineering
RARITY, J. G., Optical Communications Systems
SMART, N. P., Cryptology
SMITH, D. J., Mechanical Engineering
STOTEN, D. P., Dynamics and Control
TAYLOR, C. A., Earthquake Engineering
WISNOM, M. R., Aerospace Structures

Faculty of Medical and Veterinary Sciences (University Walk, Bristol, BS8 1TD; tel. (117) 331-7484; internet www.bristol.ac.uk/fmvs/):

BANTING, R. L., Molecular Cell Biology
BASHIR, Z. I., Cellular Neuroscience
BENNETT, P. M., Bacterial Genetics
BRADY, R. L., Biochemistry
BROWN, M. W., Anatomy and Cognitive Neuroscience
CLARKE, A. R., Biochemistry
COLLINGRIDGE, G., Neuroscience in Anatomy
CULLEN, P. J., Biochemistry
DAY, M. J., Veterinary Pathology
DENTON, R. M., Biochemistry
DUFFUS, W. P. H., Veterinary Medicine
GRUFFYDD-JONES, T. J., Feline Medicine
HALESTRAP, A. P., Biochemistry
HALFORD, S. E., Biochemistry
HALL, E. J., Companion Animal Studies
HALL, L., Molecular Genetics
HASSAN, A. B., Adult Oncology
HEADLEY, P. M., Physiology
HENDERSON, G., Pharmacology
HENLEY, J. M., Molecular Neuroscience

HEYDERMAN, R. S., Infectious Diseases and International Health
HOLT, P. E., Veterinary Surgery
HUMPHREY, T. J., Veterinary Zoonotic Bacteriology
KUWABARA, P. E., Genomics
LAWSON, S. N., Physiology
LISNEY, S. J. W., Physiology
MACGOWAN, A. P., Clinical Microbiology and Antimicrobial Therapeutics
MARRION, N. V., Neuroscience
MARTIN, P. B., Cell Biology
MOLNAR, E., Anatomy
MULLER, R. L., Neuroscience
NICOL, C. J., Animal Welfare
ORCHARD, C. H., Physiology
PARASKEVA, M. M., Experimental Oncology
PATON, J. F. R., Physiology
PIGNATELLI, M., Histopathology
RIVETT, A. J., Biochemistry
ROBERTS, P. J., Neurochemical Pharmacology
RUTTER, G. A., Biochemistry and Cell Biology
SIDDELL, S. G., Virology
STOKES, C. R., Mucosal Immunology
TAVARE, J. M., Biochemistry
VAZQUEZ-BOLAND, J. A., Veterinary Molecular Biology
VIRJI, M., Molecular Microbiology
WATERMAN-PATERSON, A. E., Veterinary Anaesthesia
WILLIAMS, N. A., Immunology
WOOD, J. D., Food Animal Science
WRAITH, D. C., Pathological Sciences

Faculty of Medicine and Dentistry (Senate House, Tyndall Ave, Bristol, BS8 1TH; tel. (117) 928-9951; internet www.medici.bris.ac.uk/medf/):

ADDY, M., Periodontology
ALDERSON, D., Gastrointestinal Surgery
ANGELINI, G., Cardiac Surgery
ARMITAGE, W. J., Opthalmology
BINGLEY, P. J., Diabetes
CAMPBELL, A. V., Ethics in Medicine
COLLINGRIDGE, G., Neuroscience in Anatomy
COWPE, J. G., Oral Surgery
DAVEY SMITH, G., Clinical Epidemiology
DICK, A. D., Ophthalmology
DONOVAN, J. L., Social Medicine
EBRAHIM, S. B. J., Epidemiology of Ageing
EMOND, A. M., Community Child Health
EVESON, J. W., Head and Neck Pathology
FINN, A. H. R., Paediatrics
FLEMING, P. J., Infant Health and Developmental Psychology
FRANKEL, S. J., Epidemiology and Public Health Medicine
GALE, E. A. M., Diabetic Medicine
GOLDING, M. J., Paediatric and Perinatal Epidemiology
GUNNELL, D. J., Epidemiology
HANKS, G. W. C., Palliative Medicine
HARRISON, G. L., Mental Health
HOLLANDER, A. P., Rheumatology and Tissue Engineering
HOLLY, J. M., Clinical Sciences
JAGGER, D. C., Restorative Dentistry
JENKINSON, H. F., Oral Microbiology
KARSCH, K. R., Cardiology
KIRWAN, J. R., Rheumatic Diseases
LEARMONTH, I. D., Orthopaedic Surgery
LEWIS, G. H., Psychiatric Epidemiology
LIGHTMAN, S. L., Medicine
LOPEZ BERNAL, A., Human Reproductive Biology
LOVE, S., Neuropathology
MATHIESON, P. W., Renal Medicine
MURPHY, D., Experimental Medicine
NEWBY, A. C., Vascular Cell Biology
NUTT, D. J., Psychopharmacology
PETERS, T. J., Primary Health Care Services Research
PIGNATELLI, M. M., Histopathology

PRIME, S. S., Experimental Pathology
REES, M. R., Clinical Radiology
SALISBURY, C. J., Primary Health Care
SANDY, J. R., Orthodontics
SCOLDING, N. J., Clinical Neurosciences
SHARP, D. J., Primary Health Care
SOOTHILL, P. W., Maternal and Foetal Medicine
STEVENS, M. C. G., Paediatric Oncology
THORESEN, M., Neonatal Neuroscience
UNEY, J. B., Molecular Neuroscience
WHITELAW, A. G. L., Neonatal Medicine
WILCOCK, G. K., Care of the Elderly
WILLIAMS, G., Medicine and Dentistry
WOLF, A. R., Anaesthesia
WYNICK, D., Molecular Medicine

Faculty of Science (Senate House, Tyndall Ave, Bristol, BS8 1TH; tel. (117) 928-9957; internet www.bris.ac.uk/depts/science/sciweb.htm):

AGGARWAL, V. K., Synthetic Organic Chemistry
ALAM, M. A., Physics
ALLAN, N. L., Physical Chemistry
ALLEN, G. C., Materials Science
ANDERSON, M. G., Geography
ANNETT, J. F., Physics
ASHFOLD, M. N. R., Physical Chemistry
BALINT-KURTI, G. G., Theoretical Chemistry
BAMBER, J. L., Geography
BATES, P. D., Hydrology
BENTON, M. J., Vertebrate Palaeontology
Sir BERRY, MICHAEL, Physics
BIRKINSHAW, M., Cosmology and Astrophysics
BLUNDY, J. D., Petrology
BRERETON, R. G., Chemometrics
CHERNS, D., Physics
CLOKE, P. J., Geography
CONNELLY, N. G., Inorganic Chemistry
CONREY, J. B., Number Theory
COSGROVE, T., Physical Chemistry
CUTHILL, I. C., Behavioural Ecology
DAVIS, A. P., Supramolecular Chemistry
EASTOE, J. G., Chemistry
EDWARDS, K. J., Cereal Functional Genomics
EGGERS, J. G., Applied Mathematics
EVANS, D. V., Applied Mathematics
EVANS, R., Physics
EVERSHED, R. P., Chemistry
FOSTER, B., Physics
FRANKS, N. R., Animal Behaviour and Ecology
FREEMAN, N. H., Cognitive Development
GALLAGHER, T. C., Organic Chemistry
GIBSON, W. C., Protozoology
GOLDSTEIN, H., Statistics
GREEN, B. J., Pure Mathematics
GREEN, P. J., Statistics
HANNAY, J. H., Theoretical Physics
HARRIS, S., Environmental Sciences
HAWKESWORTH, C. J., Earth Sciences
HAYDEN, S. M., Physics
HAYES, P. K., Biology
HEATH, G. P., Physics
HELFRICH, G. R., Seismology
HENSHAW, D. L., Physics
HOOD, B. M., Development Psychology
HOUSTON, A. I., Theoretical Biology
JONES, G., Biological Sciences
JONES, K., Human Quantitative Geography
KEATING, J. P., Mathematical Physics
KEMPSON, H. E., Personal Finance and Social Policy Research
KENDALL, J.-M., Earth Sciences
LARNER, W. J., Human Geography and Sociology
LINDEN, N., Theoretical Physics
LISKEVICH, V., Mathematics
LLOYD-JONES, G. C., Chemistry
MANN, S., Chemistry
MCNAMARA, J. M., Mathematics and Biology

MANNERS, I., Inorganic Materials and Chemistry
MILES, M. J., Physics
NASON, G. P., Statistics
OBERAUER, K., Psychology
ORPEN, A. G., Structural Chemistry
ORR-EWING, A. J., Chemistry
PEREGRINE, D. H., Applied Mathematics
POPESCU, S., Physics
PRENTICE, I. C., Earth System Science
PRINGLE, P. G., Inorganic Chemistry
RAGNARSDOTTIR, K. V., Environmental Geochemistry
RICHARDSON, R. M., Physics
RICKARD, J. C., Mathematics
ROBERT, D., Bionanoscience
ROBERTS, A., Zoology
ROGERS, P. J., Biological Psychology
SCHOFIELD, A. H., Pure Mathematics
SHERMAN, D. M., Geochemistry
SIEGERT, M. J., Physical Geography
SIMPSON, T. J., Organic Chemistry
SMART, P. L., Geography
SPARKS, R. S. J., Geology
STEEDS, J. W., Physics
STOBART, A. K., Plant Biochemistry
TICKELL, A. T., Human Geography
TINSLEY, R. C., Zoology
TRANTER, M., Geography
TROSCIANKO, T. S., Psychology
VALDES, P. J., Physical Geography
VAN DEN BERG, M., Pure Mathematics
VINCENT, B., Physical Chemistry
VINEY, M. E., Biological Sciences
WALL, R. L., Zoology
WALSBY, A. E., Botany
WELCH, P. D., Mathematics
WIGGINS, S. R., Applied Mathematics
WILLIS, C. L., Organic Chemistry
WOOD, B. J., Earth Sciences
WORRALL, D. M., Physics

Faculty of Social Sciences and Law (Senate House, Tyndall Ave, Bristol, BS8 1TH; tel. (117) 928-7797; internet www.bris.ac.uk/depts/socsci):

ASHTON, D. J., Accountancy and Finance
ATTFIELD, C. L. F., Econometrics
BAILEY-HARRIS, R. J., Law
BRADLEY, H. K., Sociology
BREWER, A. A., History of Economics
BURGESS, S. M., Economics
CARVER, T. F., Political Theory
COWAN, D. S., Law and Policy
CROSSLEY, M. W., Comparative and International Education
DEEM, R., Education
DOYAL, L., Health and Social Care
DUGDALE, D., Management Accounting
FARMER, E. R. G., Child and Family Studies
FENTON, C. S., Sociology
FORREST, R. S., Urban Studies
FORSTER, A. W., Politics and International Relations
FOX, K. R., Exercise and Health Sciences
FRIEDMAN, A. L., Management and Economics
GORDON, D., Social Justice
GREGG, P. A., Economics
GROUT, P. A., Political Economy
HESTER, M., Gender, Violence and International Policy
HILL, J. D., Law
HUGHES, R. M., Education
JOHNSON, M. L., Health and Social Policy
KERRIDGE, J. R., Law
KYLE, J. G., Deaf Studies
LEVITAS, R., Sociology
LITTLE, R., International Politics
MCFARLANE, A. E., Education
MCLENNAN, G., Sociology
MCMEEL, G. P., Law
MODOOD, T., Sociology, Politics and Public Policy
MOK, K. J., East Asian Studies
OSBORN, M. J., Education

PARK, I.-U., Industrial Organization
PARTINGTON, T. M., Law
PRIDHAM, G. F. M., European Politics
PROPPER, C., Economics
PROSSER, J. A. W., Public Law
QUINTON, D. L., Psychosocial Development
REA-DICKINS, P. M., Applied Linguistics in Education
ROBERTSON, S. L., Education (Sociology)
ROSE, F. D., Commercial Law
SKULTANS SHELLEY, V., Social Anthropology
STANTON, K. M., Law
SUFRIN, B. E., Law
SUTHERLAND, R. J., Education
TEMPLE, J. R. W., Economics
WARD, L. M., Disability and Social Policy
WEBSTER, A., Educational Psychology

UNIVERSITY OF BUCKINGHAM

Hunter St, Buckingham, MK18 1EG
Telephone: (1280) 814080
E-mail: info@buckingham.ac.uk
Internet: www.buckingham.ac.uk
Founded 1976, Royal Charter 1983
Private control
Academic year: January to December (4 10-week terms)

Chancellor: Lord TANLAW
Chair. of Ccl: CHLOE WOODHEAD
Vice-Chancellor: Dr TERENCE KEALEY
Deputy Vice-Chancellor: Prof. ANDREW MILES
Registrar: Prof. LEN EVANS
Librarian: LOUISE HAMMOND
Number of teachers: 160 (91 full-time, 89 part-time)
Number of students: 1,000
Publication: *Denning Law Journal* (1 a year)

DEANS

School of Business: Dr JANE TAPSELL
School of Humanities: Prof. MARTIN RICKETTS
School of Law: Prof. SUSAN EDWARDS
School of Medicine: Prof. KAROL SIKORA (Dean-Elect)
School of Sciences: Prof. MIKE CAWTHORNE

PROFESSORS

ADAMS, C. J., Information Systems
ADAMSON, J., Modern History
ALCOCK, A., Corporate Law
ALDERMAN, G., Politics and Contemporary History
ARCH, J., Metabolic Research
CAWTHORNE, M. A., Metabolic Research
CLARKE, J. C., History
DURAND, A., European Law
EDWARDS, S., Law
FOSTER, N., European Law
GLEES, A., Security/Intelligence Studies
JASSIM, S., Mathematics
O'HEAR, A., Philosophy and Education
O'KEEFE, D., Education
RICKETTS, M., Economic Organization
RIDLEY, J., History
SMITHERS, A., Education
WOOD, G., Economics
WOODHEAD, C., Education

UNIVERSITY OF CAMBRIDGE

Cambridge, CB2 1TN
Telephone: (1223) 337733 (Central Switchboard); (1223) 332200 (Central Administration/Secretariat)
E-mail: registry@admin.cam.ac.uk
Internet: www.cam.ac.uk
Founded 13th century
Academic year: October to June

Chancellor: Lord SAINSBURY OF TURVILLE
Vice-Chancellor: Prof. Sir LESZEK BORYSIEWICZ
Sr Pro-Vice-Chancellor for Planning and Resources: Prof. STEVE YOUNG

Pro-Vice-Chancellor for Education: Prof. JOHN RALLISON
Pro-Vice-Chancellor for Institutional Affairs: Prof. JEREMY SANDERS
Pro-Vice-Chancellor for Int. Strategy: Dr JENNIFER BARNES
Pro-Vice-Chancellor for Research: Prof. LYNN GLADDEN
High Steward: Lord WATSON OF RICHMOND
Registrary: Dr JONATHAN NICHOLLS
Librarian: ANNE JARVIS

Number of teachers: 1,600
Number of students: 18,190 (11,943 undergraduate, 6,24 postgraduate)

PROFESSORS

Faculty of Architecture and History of Art (1–5 Scroope Terrace, Trumpington St, Cambridge, CB2 1PX; tel. (1223) 332950; e-mail enquiries@aha.cam.ac.uk; internet www.aha.cam.ac.uk):

BINSKI, P., History of Medieval Art (Gonville and Caius College)
ECHENIQUE, M. H., Land Use and Transport Studies (Churchill College)
JOANNIDES, P. E., Art History
MASSING, J. M., History of Art (King's College)
PENZ, F., Architecture and the Moving Image (Darwin College)
SHORT, A., Architecture (Clare Hall)
STEEMERS, K., Sustainable Design (Wolfson College)

Faculty of Asian and Middle Eastern Studies (Sidgwick Ave, Cambridge, CB3 9DA; tel. (1223) 335106; e-mail enquiries@ames.cam.ac.uk; internet www.ames.cam.ac.uk):

DE LANGE, N., Hebrew and Jewish Studies (Wolfson College)
KHAN, G., Hebrew
KORNICKI, P., Japanese/East Asian Studies (Robinson College)
MELVILLE, C., Persian History (Pembroke College)
MONTGOMERY, J. E., Classical Arabic (Trinity Hall)
POSTGATE, N., Assyriology (Trinity College)
RAY, J. D., Egyptology (Selwyn College)
STERCKX, R., Chinese History, Science and Civilization (Clare College)
SULEIMAN, Y., Modern Arabic Studies (King's College)
VAN DE VEN, H., Modern Chinese History

Faculty of Biology (School of the Biological Sciences, 17 Mill Lane, Cambridge, CB2 1RX; tel. (1223) 766894; e-mail mb422@admin.cam.ac.uk; internet www.bio.cam.ac.uk):

AFFARA, N. A., Cellular Molecular Pathology (Hughes Hall)
AKAM, M., Zoology (Darwin College)
AMOS, W., Evolutionary Genetics
BALMFORD, A., Conservation Science (Clare College)
BARLOW, H. B., Physiology, Development and Neuroscience (Trinity College)
BARON-COHEN, S., Developmental Psychopathology (Trinity College)
Sir BAULCOMBE, D. C., Plant Sciences
Sir BLUNDELL, TOM L., Biochemistry (Sidney Sussex College)
BRAKEFIELD, P. M., Zoology (Trinity College)
BRAND, A., Molecular Biology (Jesus College)
BRAY, S., Developmental Biology
BRINDLE, K., Biochemistry (Fitzwilliam College)
BROWN, G., Cellular Biochemistry
BURTON, G., Physiology of Reproduction
BUSSEY, T., Behavioural Neuroscience (Pembroke College)
CARPENTER, R., Oculomotor Physiology (Gonville and Caius College)

CARRINGTON, M., Molecular Biology (St John's College)

CLACK, J. A., Vertebrate Palaeontology

CLAYTON, N. S., Comparative Cognition (Clare College)

CLUTTON-BROCK, T. H., Ecology and Evolutionary Biology (Magdalen College)

COLLEDGE, W., Reproductive Physiology

COLLINS, V. P., Histopathology

COOKE, A., Immunobiology (King's College)

COOPER, D., Pharmacology (Wellcome Trust Sanger Institute)

CRAWFORD, A. C., Neurophysiology (Trinity College)

DAVIES, N. B., Behavioural Ecology (Pembroke College)

DICKINSON, A., Comparative Psychology (Hughes Hall)

DU, M.-Q., Pathology

DUNNE, D., Parasitology (King's College)

DUPREE, P., Biochemistry (Magdalene College)

EDWARDSON, J. M., Pharmacology (Christ's College)

EVAN, G. I., Biochemistry (Christ's College)

EVERITT, B. J., Behavioural Neuroscience (Downing College)

FARNDALE, R. W., Biochemistry

FERGUSON-SMITH, A., Genetics (Downing College)

FIELD, M. C., Cell Biology and Parasitology (St Edmund's College)

FITZSIMONS, J. T., Physiology, Development and Neuroscience (Gonville and Caius College)

FOWDEN, A. L., Perinatal Physiology (Girton College)

FRANKLIN, R., Neuroscience (Pembroke College)

GAY, N. J. A., Biochemistry (Christ's College)

GILLIGAN, C. A., Mathematical Biology (King's College)

GIUSSANI, D. A., Developmental Cardiovascular Physiology and Medicine (Caius College)

GLOVER, B., Plant Systematics and Evolution (Queens' College)

GLOVER, D. M., Genetics (Fitzwilliam College)

GOLOMBOK, S., Family Research (Newnham College)

GOODFELLOW, I., Virology

GOSWAMI, U., Cognitive Developmental Neuroscience (St John's College)

GRAY, J. C., Plant Molecular Biology (Robinson College)

GRIFFITHS, H., Plant Ecology (Clare College)

HARDIE, R. C., Cellular Neuroscience

HARRIS, W. A., Physiology, Development and Neuroscience (Clare College)

HEENEY, J. L., Comparative Pathology

HERRTAGE, M., Small Animal Medicine (St Edmund's College)

HINES, M., Pyschology (Churchill College)

HOLT, C., Developmental Neuroscience (Gonville and Caius College)

HOWE, C., Plant and Microbial Biochemistry (Corpus Christi College)

HUANG, C. H., Cell Physiology (Murray Edwards College)

HUGHES, C., Microbiology (Trinity College)

HUGHES, C., Experimental Psychology (Newnham College)

IRVINE, R. F., Molecular Pharmacology (Corpus Christi College)

JACKSON, R. J., Biochemistry (Pembroke College)

JACKSON, S., Biology

JOHNSON, R. S., Molecular Physiology and Pathology

JOHNSTONE, R., Evolution and Behaviour

KAUFMAN, J., Comparative Immunogenetics (Hughes Hall)

KEYNES, R. J., Physiology, Development and Neuroscience (Trinity College)

KILNER, R. M., Evolutionary Biology (Sidney Sussex College)

KORONAKIS, V., Molecular Biology (Wolfson College)

KOURTZI, Z., Experimental Psychology

KOUZARIDES, T., Virology (Gurdon Institute)

LAMB, M., Psychology (Sidney Sussex College)

LAUE, E. D., Structural Biology (St John's College)

LAUGHLIN, S. B., Neurobiology (Churchill College)

LEADLAY, P. F., Biochemistry (Clare College)

LEYSER, H. M. O., Plant Development (Sainsbury Laboratory)

LILLEY, K., Cellular Dynamics (Jesus College)

LUISI, B., Structural and Molecular Cell Biology

LUMMIS, S., Biochemistry (King's College)

MCCAFFERTY, J., Biochemistry

MCNAUGHTON, P. A., Pharmacology (Christ's College)

MARTINEZ ARIAS, A., Genetics

MASKELL, D., Farm Animal Health, Food Science and Food Safety (Wolfson College)

MINSON, A. C., Virology (Wolfson College)

MISKA, E., Molecular Genetics (Pembroke College)

MOFFETT, A., Reproductive Immunology (King's College)

MOLLON, J. D., Visual Neuroscience (Gonville and Caius College)

MOORE, B. C. J., Auditory Perception (Wolfson College)

MORTON, J., Physiology, Development and Neuroscience (Newnham College)

OLIVER, S., Systems Biology and Biochemistry (Wolfson College)

PARKER, J. S., Plant Cytogenetics (St Catharine's College)

PATTERSON, R. D., Physiology, Development and Neuroscience

PAULSEN, O., Physiology (St John's College)

PERHAM, R. N., Structural Biochemistry (St John's College)

ROBBINS, T. W., Cognitive Neuroscience (Downing College)

ROBERTS, A. C., Behavioural Neuroscience (Girton College)

RUDD, C. E, Molecular Immunology

RUSSELL, S., Genetics

RUST, J., Psychology (Darwin College)

ST JOHNSTON, R. D., Developmental Genetics (Peterhouse)

SALMOND, G. P. C., Molecular and Microbiology (Wolfson College)

SCHULTZ, W., Neuroscience (Churchill College)

SKAER, H., Developmental Biology (Jesus College)

SMITH, A. G., Plant Biochemistry (Corpus Christi College)

SMITH, A. G., Biochemistry (Wellcome Trust Centre for Stem Cell Research)

SMITH, C., Biochemistry

SMITH, D., Infectious Disease Informatics

SMITH, G. L., Pathology (Emmanuel College)

STANLEY, M. A., Epithelial Biology (Christ's College)

SURANI, M. A. H., Physiology of Reproduction (King's College)

SUTHERLAND, W. J., Conservation Biology (Clare College)

TAYLOR, C. W., Cellular Pharmacology (Downing College)

Dame THOMAS, J. O., Macromolecular Biochemistry (St Catherine's College)

TROWSDALE, J., Immunology

TYLER, L. K., Cognitive Neuroscience (Clare College)

WATSON, C. J., Cell and Cancer Biology

WATT, F. M., Molecular Genetics

WILLIAMS, A., Veterinary Diagnostic Pathology (Wolfson College)

WOOD, J., Equine and Farm Animal Science (Wolfson College)

WUTZ, A., Biochemistry

ZERNICKA-GOETZ, M., Developmental Biology

Faculty of Classics (Sidgwick Site, Sidgwick Ave, Cambridge, CB3 9DA; tel. (1223) 335151; internet www.classics.cam.ac.uk):

BEARD, M., Classics (Newnham College)

CARTLEDGE, P. A., Greek Culture (Clare College)

GOLDHILL, S., Greek Literature and Culture (King's College)

HOLTON, D. W., Modern Greek (St John's College)

HORROCKS, G. C., Comparative Philology (St John's College)

HUNTER, R. L., Greek (Trinity College)

MILLETT, M. J., Classical Archaeology (Fitzwilliam College)

OAKLEY, S. P., Latin (Emmanuel College)

OSBORNE, R., Ancient History (King's College)

SEDLEY, D. N., Ancient Philosophy (Christ's College)

Faculty of Divinity (West Rd, Cambridge, CB3 9BS; tel. (1223) 763002; e-mail faculty-office@divinity.cam.ac.uk; internet www.divinity.cam.ac.uk):

COAKLEY, S., Divinity (Murray Edwards College)

DE LANGE, N. R. M., Hebrew and Jewish Studies (Wolfson College)

DUFFY, E., History of Christianity (Magdalene College)

FORD, D. F., Divinity (Selwyn College)

FOWDEN, G., Abrahamic Faiths (Peterhouse)

LIEU, J., Divinity (Robinson College)

SOSKICE, J., Philosophical Theology (Jesus College)

Faculty of Earth Sciences and Geography (Downing Place, Cambridge, CB2 3EN; tel. (1223) 766571; e-mail secretary@esg.cam.ac.uk; internet www.esg.cam.ac.uk):

ADAMS, B., Conservation and Development (Downing College)

AMIN, A., Geography (Christ's College)

BAYLISS-SMITH, T., Pacific Geography (St John's College)

BICKLE, M. J., Tectonics, Basin and Crustal Development and Sedimentology (Queens' College)

CARPENTER, M. A., Mineralogy and Mineral Physics (Magdalene College)

CONWAY MORRIS, S., Evolutionary Palaeoecology (St John's College)

DOWDESWELL, J. A., Physical Geography (Jesus College)

ELDERFIELD, H., Environmental Change and Marine Geochemistry (St Catharine's College)

GIBBARD, P., Quaternary Palaeoenvironments (Darwin College)

GRAF, H.-F., Environmental Systems Analysis (Darwin College)

HAINING, R. P., Human Geography (Fitzwilliam College)

HODELL, D. A., Climate Change and Earth-Ocean-Atmosphere Systems (Clare College)

HOLNESS, M., Petrology (Trinity College)

JACKSON, J., Active Tectonics (Queens' College)

LEADER-WILLIAMS, N., Conservation Leadership (Dir (Churchill College)

MCKENZIE, D. P., Geophysics, Geodynamics and Tectonics (King's College)

MARTIN, R. L., Economic Geography (St Catharine's College)

OPPENHEIMER, C., Volcanology (St Catharine's College)

OWENS, S., Environment and Policy (Newnham College)

PRIESTLEY, K., Geophysics, Geodynamics and Tectonics (Queens' College)

RADCLIFFE, S., Latin American Geography (Christ's College)

REDFERN, S., Mineral Sciences (Jesus College)

RICHARDS, K. S., Geography (Emmanuel College)

SALJE, E. K. H., Mineralogy and Petrology (Clare Hall)

WHITE, N., Geophysics, Geodynamics and Tectonics

WHITE, R. S., Geophysics, Geodynamics and Tectonics (St Edmund's College)

WOLFF, E., Climate Change and Earth-Ocean-Atmosphere Systems

WOODS, A. W., Geophysics, Geodynamics and Tectonics (St John's College)

Faculty of Economics (Austin Robinson Bldg, Sidgwick Ave, Cambridge, CB3 9DD; tel. (1223) 335200; e-mail faculty@econ.cam.ac.uk; internet www.econ.cam.ac.uk):

CHATTERJI, M., Economics (Sidney Sussex College)

CORSETTI, G., Macroeconomics (Clare College)

EVANS, R., Microeconomics

GOYAL, S., Economics (Christ's College)

HARRIS, C. J., Economics (King's College)

HARVEY, A. C., Econometrics (Corpus Christi College)

LINTON, O., Political Economy (Trinity College)

LOW, H., Economics (Trinity College)

MUNSHI, K., Economics

OGILVIE, S., Economic History

SABOURIAN, H., Economics and Game Theory (King's College)

SMITH, R. J., Econometric Theory and Economic Statistics (Gonville and Caius College)

TEULINGS, C., Economics

Faculty of Education (184 Hills Rd, Cambridge, CB2 8PQ; tel. (1223) 767600; e-mail reception@educ.cam.ac.uk; internet www.educ.cam.ac.uk):

ARNOT, M., Sociology of Education (Jesus College)

GRAY, J. M., Education (Homerton College)

GRONN, P., Education (Hughes Hall)

HOWE, C., Education (Lucy Cavendish College)

MERCER, N., Education (Hughes Hall)

NIKOLAJEVA, M., Education (Homerton College)

REAY, D., Education

RUTHVEN, K., Education (Hughes Hall)

STYLES, M., Children's Literature and Education (Homerton College)

VERMUNT, J., Education (Wolfson College)

VIGNOLES, A. F., Education (Wolfson College)

Faculty of English (9 West Rd, Cambridge, CB3 9DP; tel. (1223) 335070; e-mail english-faculty@lists.cam.ac.uk; internet www.english.cam.ac.uk):

BEADLE, R., English (St John's College)

COLLINI, S. A., English

CONNOR, S., English (Peterhouse)

COOPER, H., English (Magdalene College)

DE BOLLA, P., English (King's College)

GLEN, H. J., English (Murray Edwards College)

HAWKINS, J., Research Centre for English and Applied Linguistics

HEATH, S., English (Jesus College)

JACOBUS, M. L., English (Churchill College)

JARVIS, S., English (Robinson College)

KERRIGAN, J. F., English (St John's College)

LEIGHTON, A., English (Trinity College)

PAGE, C., English (Sidney Sussex College)

POOLE, A., English (Trinity College)

RAVEN, J., English (Magdalene College)

TROTTER, D., English (Gonville and Caius College)

WARD, G., English (Homerton College)

WINDEATT, B. A., English (Emmanuel College)

Faculty of History (West Rd, Cambridge, CB3 9EF; tel. (1223) 335340; e-mail gen.enq@hist.cam.ac.uk; internet www.hist.cam.ac.uk):

ABULAFIA, D. S. H., Mediterranean History (Gonville and Caius College)

ANDREW, C. M., Modern and Contemporary History (Corpus Christi College)

BADGER, A. J., American History since 1930 (Clare College)

BASHFORD, A., Modern History

Sir BAYLY, CHRISTOPHER, Modern Indian History and the History of the Expansion of Europe (St Catharine's College)

BIAGINI, E., Modern and Contemporary History (Sidney Sussex College)

BLIGHT, D. W., American History (Sidney Sussex College)

CARPENTER, M. C., Medieval English History

CARTLEDGE, P., Ancient and Medieval History (Clare College)

CLARK, C., Modern Europe (St Catharine's College)

DAUNTON, M. J., Economic History (Trinity Hall)

DUFFY, E., Religious History (Magdalene College)

EVANS, R. J., Modern European History (Wolfson College)

GAMBLE, A., Political Thought and Intellectual History (Queens' College)

HASLAM, J., History of International Relations (Corpus Christi College)

HATCHER, M. J., Economic and Social History (Corpus Christi College)

HILTON, B., British History (Trinity College)

KEYNES, S., Anglo-Saxon History (Trinity College)

LIEVEN, D., Russian History (Trinity College)

MANDLER, P., Modern Cultural History (Gonville and Caius College)

MAXWELL, D., Ecclesiastical History (Emmanuel College)

McKITTERICK, R. D., Medieval History (Sidney Sussex College)

MORRILL, J. S., British and Irish History (Selwyn College)

O'BRIEN, M., American Intellectual History (Jesus College)

OSBORNE, R., Ancient History (King's College)

PARRY, J. P., Modern British History (Pembroke College)

REYNOLDS, D., International History (Christ's College)

ROBERTSON, J., History of Political Thought (Clare College)

ROTHSCHILD, E., History and Economics (Magdalene College)

RUBLACK, U., Early Modern European History (St John's College)

RUNCIMAN, D., Political Thought and Intellectual History (Trinity Hall)

SIMMS, B. P., History of International Relations (Peterhouse)

STEDMAN-JONES, G., Political Science (King's College)

SZRETER, S., History and Public Policy (St John's College)

TOMBS, R., Modern French and European History (St John's College)

VAN DE VEN, H., World History (St Catharine's College)

VAUGHAN, M., Commonwealth History (King's College)

WALSHAM, A., Modern History (Trinity College)

WHALEY, J., German History and Thought (Gonville and Caius College)

Faculty of Human, Social, and Political Science (Free School Lane, Cambridge, CB2 3RQ; tel. (1223) 334520; e-mail enquiries@hsps.cam.ac.uk; internet www.hsps.cam.ac.uk; merger of Faculty of Archaeology and Anthropology and Faculty of Politics, Psychology, Sociology and International Studies 2011):

ALEXANDER, J. C., American History and Institutions

BAERT, P., Social Theory (Selwyn College)

BARKER, G., Archaeology (St John's College)

CASTELLS, M., Sociology (St John's College)

CHAKRABARTI, D., South Asian Archaeology (McDonald Institute for Archaeological Research)

FOLEY, R. A., Human Evolution (King's College)

FRANKLIN, S., Sociology (Christ's College)

FRENCH, C. A. I., Geoarchaeology

GAMBLE, A. M., Politics (Queens' College)

HALPER, S., American Studies (Magdalene College)

HAMILTON, L., Political Theory (Clare Hall)

HASLAM, J. G., History of International Relations (Corpus Christi College)

Sir HILL, CHRISTOPHER J., International Relations (Sidney Sussex College)

HUMPHREY, C., Collaborative Anthropology (King's College)

JOFFE, G., International Studies (Robinson College)

JONES, M. K., Archaeological Science

KEIGER, J., International History

KING, L. P., Sociology (Emmanuel College)

LOUGHLIN, J., European Politics (St Edmund's College)

MASCIE-TAYLOR, C. G. N., Biological Anthropology (Churchill College)

Sir MELLARS, P. A., Prehistory and Human Evolution (Corpus Christi College)

MILLETT, M. J., Classical Archaeology (Fitzwilliam College)

MOORE, H. L., Social Anthropology (Jesus College)

POSTGATE, N., Assyriology (Trinity College)

RAY, J., Egyptology (Selwyn College)

Lord RENFREW OF KAIMSTHORN, Archaeology (McDonald Institute for Archaeological Research)

ROBBINS, J., Social Anthropology

RUNCIMAN, D., Politics (Trinity Hall)

SCOTT, J. L., Empirical Sociology (Queens' College)

SIMMS, B. P., History of International Relations (Peterhouse)

THOMPSON, J. B., Sociology (Jesus College)

WELLER, M., International Law and International Constitutional Studies (Hughes Hall)

Faculty of Law (10 West Rd, Cambridge, CB3 9DZ; tel. (1223) 330033; e-mail enquiries@law.cam.ac.uk; internet www.law.cam.ac.uk):

ALLAN, T. R. S., Jurisprudence and Public Law (Pembroke College)

ANDREWS, N. H., Civil Justice and Private Law (Clare College)

ARMSTRONG, K., European Law (Sidney Sussex College)

BARNARD, C., European Union Law (Trinity College)

BELL, J. S., Law (Pembroke College)

BENTLY, L. A. F., Intellectual Property (Emmanuel College)

Sir BOTTOMS, ANTHONY E., Criminology (Fitzwilliam College)

CHEFFINS, B. R., Corporate Law (Trinity Hall)

CRAWFORD, J. R., International Law (Jesus College)

DEAKIN, S. F., Law (Peterhouse)

EISNER, M. P., Comparative and Developmental Criminology (Violence Research Centre, Institute of Criminology)

FARRINGTON, D. P., Psychological Criminology (Darwin College)

FELDMAN, D., English Law (Downing College)

FENTIMAN, R., Private International Law (Queens' College)

FERRAN, E. V., Company and Securities Law (St Catharine's College)

FORSYTH, C. F., Public Law and Private International Law (Robinson College)

GELSTHORPE, L. R. R., Criminology and Criminal Justice (Pembroke College)

GRAY, C. D., International Law (St John's College)

HOOLEY, R. J. A., Law (Fitzwilliam College)

IBBETSON, D. J., Civil Law (Corpus Christi College)

KRAMER, M. H., Legal and Political Philosophy (Churchill College)

LIEBLING, A., Criminology and Criminal Justice (Trinity Hall)

LÖSEL, F., Criminology (Dir of Research—Institute of Criminology)

McHUGH, P. G., Law and Legal History (Sidney Sussex College)

SHERMAN, L. W., Criminology (Darwin College/Dir of Institute of Criminology)

SIMESTER, A. P., Law (Wolfson College)

SPENCER, J. R., Law (Selwyn College)

VIRGO, G. J., English Private Law (Downing College)

WELLER, M., International Law and International Constitutional Studies (Hughes Hall)

WIKSTROM, P. O., Ecological and Developmental Criminology (Girton College)

WORTHINGTON, S., Laws of England (Trinity College)

YATES, A. D., Law (Robinson College)

VINUALES, J. E., Law and Environmental Policy

Faculty of Mathematics (Centre for Mathematical Sciences, Wilberforce Rd, Cambridge, CB3 0WA; tel. (1223) 765000; e-mail reception@maths.cam.ac.uk; internet www.maths.cam.ac.uk):

ALLANACH, B., Applied Mathematics and Theoretical Physics

BARROW, J. D., Applied Mathematics (Clare Hall)

BEARDON, A. F., Complex Analysis (St Catharine's Hall)

BERLOFF, N. G., Applied Mathematics (Jesus College)

COATES, J. H., Pure Mathematics (Emmanuel College)

DAFERMOS, M. C., Mathematical Physics

DAVIS, A.-C., Mathematical and Theoretical Physics (King's College)

DAWID, A. P., Statistics (Darwin College)

DOREY, N., Theoretical Physics

FOKAS, A. S., Nonlinear Mathematical Science (Clare College)

GIBBONS, G. W., Theoretical Physics (Clare College)

GIBSON, A., Pure Mathematics and Mathematical Statistics (Trinity College)

GOLDSTEIN, R. E., Complex Physical Systems (Churchill College)

GOWERS, W. T., Mathematics (Trinity College)

GREEN, M. B., Mathematics (Clare Hall)

GRIMMETT, G. R., Mathematical Statistics (Churchill College)

GROJNOWSKI, I., Mathematics

GROSS, M., Algebraic and Differential Geometry

HAWKING, S. W., Gravitational Physics (Gonville and Caius College)

HAYNES, P. H., Applied Mathematics (Queens' College)

HINCH, E. J., Fluid Mechanics (Trinity College)

HORGAN, R. R., Theoretical and Mathematical Physics (Sidney Sussex College)

HYLAND, J. M. E., Mathematical Logic (King's College)

ISERLES, A., Numerical Analysis of Differential Equations (King's College)

JOHNSTONE, P. T., Foundations of Mathematics (St John's College)

JOZSA, R., Quantum Physics (King's College)

KELLY, F. P., Mathematics of Systems (Christ's College)

KÖRNER, T. W., Fourier Analysis (Trinity Hall)

LEADER, I. B., Pure Mathematics (Trinity College)

LINDEN, P. F., Fluid Mechanics (Downing College)

LISTER, J. R., Fluid Dynamics (Trinity College)

MANTON, N. S., Mathematical Physics (St John's College)

MARKOVIC, V., Pure Mathematics

MARKOWICH, P. A., Applied Mathematics (Clare Hall)

MOUHOT, C., Mathematical Sciences (King's College)

NORRIS, J. R., Stochastic Analysis (Churchill College)

OGILVIE, G. I., Mathematical Astrophysics (Clare College)

PAPALOIZOU, J. C. B., Mathematical Physics

PATERNAIN, G. P., Mathematics (Trinity College)

PEAKE, N., Applied Mathematics (Emmanuel College)

PERRY, M. J., Theoretical Physics (Trinity College)

PROCTOR, M. R. E., Astrophysical Fluid Dynamics (Trinity College)

QUEVEDO, F., Theoretical Physics (Gonville and Caius College)

RALLISON, J. M., Fluid Dynamics (Trinity College)

REALL, H. S., Theoretical Physics (Trinity College)

ROGERS, L. C. G., Statistical Science (St John's College)

SAMWORTH, R. J., Statistics (St John's College)

SAXL, J., Algebra (Gonville and Caius College)

SCHOLL, A. J., Number Theory and Algebra

SHELLARD, E. P. S., Cosmology (Trinity College)

SMITH, I., Geometry (Gonville and Caius College)

SPIEGELHALTER, D. J., Public Understanding of Risk (Churchill College)

TAVARÉ, S., Oncology and Applied Mathematics (Christ's College)

THOMASON, A. G., Combinatorial Mathematics (Clare College)

TONG, D., Theoretical Physics (Trinity College)

TOTARO, B. J., Astronomy and Geometry

TOWNSEND, P. K., Theoretical Physics (Queens' College)

WADHAMS, P., Ocean Physics (Clare Hall)

WEBER, R. R., Mathematics for Operational Research (Queens' College)

WILSON, P. M. H., Algebraic Geometry (Trinity College)

WORSTER, M. G., Mathematics for Natural Sciences (Trinity College)

Faculty of Modern and Medieval Languages (Sidgwick Ave, Cambridge, CB3 9DA; tel. (1223) 335000; e-mail mml-faculty-office@lists.cam.ac.uk; internet www.mml.cam.ac.uk):

BENNETT, W., French Philology and Linguistics (Murray Edwards College)

BOLDY, S., Latin American Literature (Emmanuel College)

BOYLE, N., German (Magdalene College)

BURGWINKLE, B., Medieval French and Occitan Literature (King's College)

EPPS, B., Spanish (King's College)

ETKIND, A., Russian Literature and Cultural History (King's College)

FINCH, A., French (Churchill College)

FRANKLIN, S. C., Slavonic Studies (Clare College)

GORDON, R., Modern Italian Culture (Gonville and Caius College)

HOLTON, D. W., Modern Greek (Selwyn College)

HUOT, S., Medieval French Literature (Pembroke College)

JASZCZOLT, K. M., Linguistics and Philosophy of Language (Newnham College)

KIRKPATRICK, R., Italian and English (Robinson College)

LEDGEWAY, A., Italian/Romance Philology (Downing College)

LISBOA, M. M., Portuguese Literature and Culture (St John's College)

MIDGLEY, D., German Literature and Intellectual History (St John's College)

MORIARTY, M., French (Peterhouse)

NOLAN, F. J., Phonetics

ROBERTS, I. G., Linguistics (Downing College)

SINCLAIR, A., Modern Spanish Literature and Intellectual History (Clare College)

WEBBER, A. J., Modern German and Comparative Culture (Churchill College)

WHALEY, J., German History and Thought (Gonville and Caius College)

WILSON, E., French Literature and the Visual Arts (Corpus Christi College)

YOUNG, C., Modern and Medieval German Studies (Pembroke College)

Faculty of Music (11 West Rd, Cambridge, CB3 9DP; tel. (1223) 763481; e-mail scr25@cam.ac.uk; internet www.mus.cam.ac.uk):

COOK, N. J., Music (Darwin College)

CROSS, I., Music and Science (Wolfson College)

FENLON, I. A., Historical Musicology (King's College)

RANKIN, S. K., Medieval Music (Emmanuel College)

RINK, J. S., Musical Performance Studies (St John's College)

Faculty of Philosophy (Sidgwick Ave, Cambridge, CB3 9DA; tel. (1223) 335090; e-mail phil-admin@lists.cam.ac.uk; internet www.phil.cam.ac.uk):

CRANE, T., Philosophy (Peterhouse)

GEUSS, R., Philosophy

HOLTON, R., Philosophy (Peterhouse)

LANGTON, R., Philosophy (Newnham College)

MARENBON, J., Medieval Philosophy (Trinity College)

OLIVER, A., Philosophy (Gonville and Caius College)

POTTER, M., Logic (Fitzwilliam College)

PRICE, H., Philosophy (Trinity College)

Faculty of Physics and Chemistry (Institute of Astronomy, Madingley Rd, Cambridge, CB3 0HA; tel. (1223) 766644; e-mail vbennett@ast.cam.ac.uk; internet www.ast.cam.ac.uk/physchemfaculty):

ABELL, C., Biological Chemistry (Christ's College)

ALAVI, A., Chemistry (Trinity College)

ALEXANDER, P., Astrophysics (Jesus College)

ALTHORPE, S., Theoretical Chemistry (St Catharine's College)

ARTACHO, E., Theoretical Mineral Physics (Clare Hall)

BALASUBRAMANIAN, S., Medicinal Chemistry (Trinity College)

BAUMBERG, J. J., Nanophotonics (Jesus College)

BEST, S. M., Materials Science (St John's College)

BHADESHIA, H. K. D. H., Metallurgy (Darwin College)

BLAMIRE, M. D., Device Materials (Hughes Hall)

BURSTEIN, G. T., Materials Chemistry and Corrosion (Selwyn College)

CAMERON, R. E., Materials Science (Lucy Cavendish College)

CHEETHAM, A. K., Materials Science (Downing College)

CHIN, J. W., Chemistry and Chemical Biology (Trinity College)

CLARKE, C. J., Institute of Astronomy (Clare College)

CLARKE, J., Molecular Biophysics (Trinity Hall)

CLEGG, W. J., Materials Science and Metallurgy (Selwyn College)

CLYNE, T. W., Mechanics of Materials (Downing College)

COLE, J., Structure and Dynamics

COOPER, J. R. C., Quantum Matter (Darwin College)

COOPER, N. R., Theoretical Physics (Pembroke College)

COWBURN, R. P., Physics (Dir of Research, Cavendish Laboratory)

DAVIES, P. B., Laser Spectroscopy (Corpus Christi College)

DOBSON, C. M., Chemistry (St John's College)

DONALD, A. M., Experimental Physics (Robinson College)

DRISCOLL, J. L., Materials Science (Trinity College)

EFSTATHIOU, G. P., Astrophysics (King's College)

ELLIOTT, S. R., Chemistry (Trinity College)

EVANS, W., Astrophysics (King's College)

FABIAN, A. C., Astronomy and Astrophysics (Darwin College)

FRAY, D. J., Materials Chemistry

FRENKEL, D., Chemistry (Trinity College)

Sir FRIEND, RICHARD, Physics (St John's College)

GAUNT, M., Chemistry

GIBSON, V., High-Energy Physics (Trinity College)

GILMORE, G. F., Experimental Philosophy (King's College)

GLEN, R. C., Chemistry (Clare College)

GLOWACKI, B. A., Energy and Materials Science

GREENHAM, N. C., Optoelectronics (Clare College)

GREER, A. L., Materials Science (Sidney Sussex College)

GREY, C. P., Materials Chemistry (Pembroke College)

GULL, S., Physics (St John's College)

HAEHNELT, M., Cosmology and Astrophysics

HANIFF, C. A., Astrophysics (Downing College)

HEWETT, P. C., Institute of Astronomy

HILLS, R. E., Radio Astronomy (St Edmund's College)

HOBSON, M., Astrophysics (Trinity Hall College)

Sir HUMPHREYS, COLIN J., Materials Science (Selwyn College)

JONES, R., Photochemistry (Queens' College)

JONES, W., Materials Chemistry (Sidney Sussex College)

KENNICUTT, R. C., Astronomy and Experimental Philosophy (Churchill College)

Sir KING, DAVID, Physical Chemistry (Downing College)

KLENERMAN, D., Chemistry (Christ's College)

KLINOWSKI, J., Chemical Physics (Peterhouse)

KÖHL, M., Atomic, Mesoscopic and Optical Physics

LAMBERT, R. M., Physical Chemistry (King's College)

LASENBY, A. N., Astrophysics and Cosmology (Queens' College)

LEY, S. V., Organic Chemistry (Trinity College)

LONZARICH, G. G., Theoretical Physics (Trinity College)

MACKAY, C. D., Institute of Astronomy

MACKAY, D., Natural Philosophy

McMAHON, R. G., Institute of Astronomy

MAIOLINO, R., Astrophysics (Cavendish Laboratory)

MATHUR, N. D., Materials Physics (Churchill College)

MIDGLEY, P. A., Materials Science

NEEDS, R., Theoretical Physics (Robinson College)

PARKER, A., High-Energy Physics (Peterhouse)

PATERSON, I., Chemistry (Jesus College)

PAYNE, M. C., Theory of Condensed Matter (Pembroke College)

PETTINI, M., Observational Astronomy (Institute of Astronomy)

PHILLIPS, R. T., Physics (Clare College)

PYLE, J. A., Atmospheric Chemistry (St Catharine's College)

RITCHIE, D. A., Experimental Physics (Robinson College)

SANDERS, J. K. M., Inorganic Chemistry (Selwyn College)

SCOTT, J., Quantum Matter

SIMONS, B. D., Theoretical Physics (St John's College)

SIRRINGHAUS, H., Electron Device Physics (Churchill College)

SMITH, C. G., Semiconductor Physics (Clare Hall)

SPRIK, M., Chemistry (Clare College)

SPRING, D., Chemistry (Trinity College)

STEINER, U., Physics of Materials (St Edmund's College)

TERENTJEV, E. M., Polymer Physics (Queens' College)

THOMSON, M., Experimental Particle Physics (Emmanuel College)

VENDRUSCOLO, M., Biophysics

WALES, D., Chemistry (Downing College)

WARD, D. R., Particle Physics (Queens' College)

WARNER, M., Theoretical Physics (Corpus Christi College)

WEBBER, B. R., Theoretical High Energy Physics (Emmanuel College)

WINDLE, A. H., Materials Science (Trinity College)

WITHINGTON, S., Analytical Physics (Downing College)

WRIGHT, D., Inorganic Chemistry (Gonville and Caius College)

School of Clinical Medicine (Addenbrooke's Hospital, Box 111, Hills Rd, Cambridge, CB2 0SP; tel. (1223) 336700; e-mail school-enquiries@medschl.cam.ac.uk; internet www.medschl.cam.ac.uk):

ALLAIN, J.-P., Transfusion Medicine (Corpus Christi College)

BALASUBRAMANIAN, S., Oncology

BARKER, R., Clinical Neuroscience (Corpus Christi College)

BARON, J.-C., Stroke Medicine

BARON-COHEN, S., Developmental Psychopathology (Trinity College)

BENNETT, M. R., Cardiovascular Sciences

BLACKWELL, J. M., Genetics and Health

BRADLEY, J. A., Surgery (Wolfson College)

BRAYNE, C. E. G., Public Health (Darwin College)

BRINDLE, K., Oncology (Fitzwilliam College)

BROWN, M. J., Clinical Pharmacology (Gonville and Caius College)

BULLMORE, E. T., Psychiatry

BURNET, N. G., Radiation Oncology

CALDAS, C., Cancer Medicine

CARRELL, R. W., Haematology (Trinity College)

CHARNOCK-JONES, D. S., Reproductive Biology

CHATTERJEE, V. K. K., Endocrinology (Churchill College)

CHILVERS, E. R., Respiratory Medicine (St Edmund's College)

CLAYTON, D., Biostatistics

COMPSTON, D. A. S., Neurology (Jesus College)

COX, T. M., Medicine (Sidney Sussex College)

DANESH, J., Epidemiology and Medicine

DUNGER, D. B., Paediatrics

EASTON, D., Genetic Epidemiology

EISEN, T., Medical Oncology (Gonville and Caius College)

FAWCETT, J. W., Medicine (King's College)

FEARON, D. T., Immunology (Trinity College)

FITZGERALD, R., Oncology (Trinity College)

FLETCHER, P., Health Neuroscience (Clare College)

FRANKLIN, R., Stem Cell Medicine (Pembroke College)

GASTON, J. S. H., Rheumatology (St Edmund's College)

GILBERT, F. J., Radiology

GILLARD, J. H., Neuroradiology (Christ's College)

GOODYER, I. M., Child and Adolescent Psychiatry (Wolfson College)

GOTTGENS, B., Molecular Haematology

GREEN, A. R., Haematology

GRIBBLE, F., Clinical Biochemistry

GRIFFIN, S., General Practice (Primary Care Unit)

GRIFFITHS, G., Immunology and Cell Biology (King's College)

GRIFFITHS, J., Molecular Imaging

HOLLAND, A. J., Learning Disability

HUGHES, I. A., Paediatrics (Clare Hall)

HUNTINGTON, J., Haematology

HUPPERT, F., Psychology (Darwin College)

JODRELL, D., Cancer Therapeutics

JONES, P. B., Psychiatry (Wolfson College)

KARET, F. E., Nephrology

KASER, A., Gastroenterology

KHAW, K.-T., Clinical Gerontology (Gonville and Caius College)

KINMONTH, A. L., General Practice (St John's College)

LEHNER, P. J., Medicine

LEVER, A. M. L., Infectious Diseases (Peterhouse)

LOMAS, D. A., Respiratory Medicine (Trinity College)

LOMAS, D. J., Radiology (Emmanuel College)

LUZIO, J. P., Clinical Biochemistry (St Edmund's College)

MAHER, E., Medical Genetics

MANT, J., Primary Care Research

MARTEAU, J., Behaviour and Health Research (Christ's College)

MENON, D. K., Anaesthesia (Queens' College)

MORRELL, N. W., Cardiopulmonary Medicine (St Catharine's College)

MURPHY, G., Oncology (Wolfson College)

NEAL, D. E., Surgical Oncology (Clare Hall)

O'BRIEN, J. T., Old Age Psychiatry
Sir O'RAHILLY, S., Clinical Biochemistry and Medicine (Churchill College)
OUWEHAND, W. H., Experimental Haematology
OWEN, D., Clinical Biochemistry
PEACOCK, S., Clinical Microbiology
PEDERSEN, R., Regenerative Medicine (Churchill College)
PICKARD, J. D., Neurosurgery (St Catharine's College)
Sir PONDER, B. A. J., Clinical Oncology (Jesus College)
READ, R. J., Haematology
ROBINSON, M., Clinical Biochemistry
ROLAND, M., Health Services Research
RON, D., Cellular Pathophysiology and Clinical Biochemistry (Churchill College)
RUBINSZTEIN, D., Molecular Neurogenetics
RUDD, C., Pathology
RUSHTON, N., Orthopaedic Research (Magdalene College)
SADAF FAROOQI, I., Metabolism and Medicine
SAHAKIAN, B. J., Clinical Neuropsychology (Clare Hall)
ST GEORGE-HYSLOP, P., Clinical Neurosciences
SIDDLE, K., Molecular Endocrinology (Churchill College)
SINCLAIR, J. H., Molecular Virology (Wolfson College)
SMITH, G. C. S., Obstetrics and Gynaecology
SMITH, K., Medicine (Pembroke College)
SUTTON, S. R., Behavioural Science
TAVARÉ, S., Cancer Research/Bioinformatics (Christ's College)
THOMPSON, S., Biostatistics (Wolfson College)
TODD, J. A., Medical Genetics (Gonville and Caius College)
TROWSDALE, J., Pathology (Trinity Hall)
VENTIKARAMAN, A. R., Cancer Research (New Hall)
VIDAL-PUIG, A., Molecular Nutrition and Metabolism
WAREHAM, N., Epidemiology (Wolfson College)
WARREN, A. J., Haematology
WATSON, C., Transplantation
WICKER, L., Medical Genetics (Wolfson College)
WILKINSON, I., Therapeutics (Trinity Hall)
WOODS, G., Medical Genetics

Department of Chemical Engineering and Biotechnology (New Museums Site, Pembroke St, Cambridge, CB2 3RA; tel. (1223) 334777; e-mail webmaster@ceb.cam.ac.uk; internet www.ceb.cam.ac.uk):

BAHN, S., Neuropsychiatric Research (Lucy Cavendish College)
CHASE, H., Biochemical Engineering (Magdalene College)
DENNIS, J., Chemical Reaction Engineering (Selwyn College)
GLADDEN, L. F., Chemical Engineering (Trinity College)
HALL, E. A. H., Analytical Biotechnology (Queens' College)
KAMINSKI, C., Chemical Physics (Robinson College)
KRAFT, M., Chemical Engineering (Churchill College)
LAPKIN, A., Sustainable Reaction Engineering (Wolfson College)
LOWE, C., Biotechnology (Trinity College)
SLATER, N. K. H., Chemical Engineering (Fitzwilliam College)
TUNNACLIFFE, A., Molecular Biotechnology (Pembroke College)

Department of Engineering (Trumpington St, Cambridge, CB2 1PZ; tel. (1223) 332600; e-mail reception@eng.cam.ac.uk; internet www.eng.cam.ac.uk):

AMARATUNGA, G. A. J., Electrical Engineering (Churchill College)
BABINSKY, H., Aerodynamics (Magdalene College)
BOLTON, M. D., Soil Mechanics (Churchill College)
BRITTER, R. E., Engineering (Pembroke College)
BYRNE, W. J., Information Engineering (Clare College)
CANT, R. S., Engineering (Selwyn College)
CARDWELL, D. A., Superconducting Engineering (Fitzwilliam College)
CEBON, D., Mechanical Engineering (Queens' College)
CHU, D. P., Electrical Engineering (Selwyn College)
CIPOLLA, R., Information Engineering (Jesus College)
CLARKSON, P. J., Engineering Design
COLES, H. J., Electrical Engineering (St Catharine's College)
COLLINGS, N., Engineering (Robinson College)
DAVIDSON, P., Fluid Mechanics (Churchill College)
DAWES, W. N., Aeronautical Engineering (Churchill College)
DESHPANDE, V. S., Materials Engineering (Pembroke College)
Dame DOWLING, ANN, Mechanical Engineering (Sidney Sussex College)
EVANS, S., Industrial Sustainability
FERRARI, A. C., Nanotechnology (Pembroke College)
FITZGERALD, W. J., Applied Statistics and Signal Processing (Christ's College)
FLECK, N. A., Mechanics of Materials (Pembroke College)
GHAHRAMANI, Z., Information Engineering (St John's College)
GLOVER, K., Information Engineering (Sidney Sussex College)
GODSILL, S. J., Statistical Signal Processing (Corpus Christi College)
Sir GREGORY, MICHAEL J., Manufacturing Engineering (Churchill College)
GUTHRIE, P. M., Engineering (St Edmund's College)
HARVEY, J. K., Engineering
HOCHGREB, S., Experimental Combustion
HODSON, H. P., Aerothermal Engineering (Girton College)
HOPPER, A., Communications (Corpus Christi College)
HUNT, G. R., Fluid Mechanics
HUTCHINGS, I. M., Manufacturing Engineering (St John's College)
KELLY, M. J., Electrical Engineering (Trinity Hall)
KINGSBURY, N. G., Signal Processing (Trinity College)
LANGLEY, R. S., Mechanical Engineering (Fitzwilliam College)
LIDDELL, W. I., Engineering
McFARLANE, D., Industrial Informational Engineering
MACIEJOWSKI, J. M., Control Engineering (Pembroke College)
MACKAY, D. J. C., Engineering
MADABHUSHI, G. S. P., Engineering
MAIR, R. J., Geotechnical Engineering (Jesus College)
MASTORAKOS, E., Energy Technologies (Fitzwilliam College)
MATSUDA, K., Engineering
MIGLIORATO, P., Electrical Engineering (Trinity College)
MILES, J. C., Transitional Energy Strategies (Emmanuel College)
MILLER, R. J., Aerothermal Technology (Gonville and Caius College)

MILNE, W. I., Electrical Engineering (Churchill College)
NATHAN, A., Electrical Engineering
O'NEILL, W., Laser Engineering (Downing College)
PENTY, R. V., Photonics (Sidney Sussex College)
PRAGER, R. V., Medical Imaging (Queens' College)
PURNELL, A. J., Engineering (Trinity Hall)
ROBERTSON, J., Electrical Engineering (Churchill College)
SCHOLTES, S., Health Management
SEPULCHRE, R., Engineering (Sidney Sussex College)
SMITH, M. C., Control Engineering (Gonville and Caius College)
SOGA, K., Civil Engineering (Churchill College)
SWAMINATHAN, N., Engineering
TUCKER, P. G., Engineering
UDREA, F., Electrical Engineering (Girton College)
WELLAND, M. E., Nanotechnology (St John's College)
WHITE, I. H., Electrical Engineering (Jesus College)
WILKINSON, T. D., Photonic Engineering (Jesus College)
WILLIAMS, J. A., Engineering Tribology
WOLPERT, D., Engineering (Trinity College)
WOODHOUSE, J., Engineering (Clare College)
WOODLAND, P., Information Engineering (Peterhouse)
XU, L., Turbomachinery (Downing College)
YOUNG, J. B., Applied Thermodynamics (King's College)
YOUNG, S. J., Information Engineering (Emmanuel College)

Department of History and Philosophy of Science (Free School Lane, Cambridge, CB2 3RH; tel. (1223) 334500; e-mail hps-admin@lists.cam.ac.uk; internet www.hps.cam.ac.uk):

CHANG, H., History and Philosophy of Science (Clare Hall)
FORRESTER, J. P., History and Philosophy of Psychoanalysis and Human Sciences (King's College)
LEWENS, T., History and Philosophy of Physical Science (Clare College)
SCHAFFER, S., History and Philosophy of Physical Science (Darwin College)
SECORD, J. A., History and Philosophy of Science (Christ's College)
TAUB, L., History and Philosophy of Science (Newnham College)

Department of Land Economy (16–21 Silver St, Cambridge, CB3 9EP; tel. (1223) 337147; e-mail landecon-ugadmissions@lists.cam.ac.uk; internet www.landecon.cam.ac.uk):

ALLMENDINGER, P., Land Economy (Clare College)
ARESTIS, P., Land Economy (Wolfson College)
HODGE, I., Rural Economy (Hughes Hall)
LIZIERI, C., Real Estate Finance (Pembroke College)
McCOMBIE, J., Regional and Applied Economics (Downing College)
McHUGH, P. G., Law (Sidney Sussex College)
NEEDHAM, B., Land Economy
TYLER, P., Land Economy (St Catharine's College)
VIÑUALES, J. E., Law and Environmental Policy
WEBSTER, C., Land Economy
WHITEHEAD, C., Housing Economics

Department of Veterinary Medicine (Madingley Rd, Cambridge, CB3 0ES; tel. (1223) 337694; e-mail enquiries@vet.cam.ac.uk; internet www.vet.cam.ac.uk):

BRYANT, C., Innate Immunity (Queens' College)

FRANKLIN, R., Neuroscience (Pembroke College)

HEENEY, J. L., Comparative Pathology (Darwin College)

HERRTAGE, M. E., Small Animal Medicine (St Edmund's College)

WILLIAMS, A., Veterinary Diagnostic Pathology (Wolfson College)

WOOD, J., Equine and Farm Animal Science (Wolfson College)

Judge Business School (Trumpington St, Cambridge, CB2 1AG; tel. (1223) 339700; e-mail enquiries@jbs.cam.ac.uk; internet www.jbs.cam.ac.uk; f. 1990 as Judge Institute of Management Studies, current name adopted 2005):

BARRETT, M., Information Systems and Innovation Studies (Hughes Hall)

Dame DAWSON, S., Management (Sidney Sussex College)

DISSANAIKE, G., Corporate Governance (Trinity College)

HUGHES, A., Enterprise Studies (Sidney Sussex College)

KAVADIAS, S., Enterprise Studies in Innovation and Growth

LAMBRECHT, B., Finance

LOCH, C. H., Management Studies

MEEKS, G., Financial Accounting

NOLAN, P. H., Chinese Management (Jesus College)

PRABHU, J., Indian Business and Enterprise (Clare College)

RALPH, D., Operations Research (Churchill College)

RAU, R., Finance

RUNDE, J., Economics and Organization (Girton College)

SCHOLTES, S., Health Management

TRACEY, P., Innovation and Organization

Computer Laboratory (William Gates Bldg, 15 J. J. Thomson Ave, Cambridge, CB3 0FD; tel. (1223) 763500; e-mail departmental-secretary@cl.cam.ac.uk; internet www.cl.cam.ac.uk):

ANDERSON, R. J., Security Engineering

BACON, J. M., Distributed Systems (Jesus College)

BRISCOE, E. J., Computational Linguistics (Girton College)

COPESTAKE, A., Computational Linguistics (Wolfson College)

CROWCROFT, J. A., Communications Systems (Wolfson College)

DAUGMAN, J. G., Computer Vision and Pattern Recognition

DAWAR, A., Logic and Algorithms (Robinson College)

DODGSON, N., Graphics and Imaging (Emmanuel College)

FIORE, M., Mathematical Foundations of Computer Science (Christ's College)

GORDON, M. J. C., Computer Assisted Reasoning (King's College)

HOPPER, A., Computer Technology (Corpus Christi College)

LESLIE, I. M., Computer Science (Christ's College)

MYCROFT, A., Computing (Robinson College)

PAULSON, L. C., Computational Logic (Clare College)

PITTS, A. M., Theoretical Computer Science (Darwin College)

ROBINSON, P., Computer Technology (Gonville and Caius College)

SEWELL, P., Computer Science (Wolfson College)

WINSKEL, G., Computer Science (Emmanuel College)

WOMEN'S COLLEGES

Lucy Cavendish College: Lady Margaret Rd, Cambridge, CB3 0BU; tel. (1223) 332190; e-mail lcc-admin@lists.cam.ac.uk; internet www.lucy-cav.cam.ac.uk; f. 1965; library of 27,000 vols; Pres. Prof. JANET TODD.

Murray Edwards College: New Hall, Univ. of Cambridge, Cambridge, CB3 0DF; tel. (1223) 762100; e-mail enquiries@murrayedwards.cam.ac.uk; internet www.murrayedwards.cam.ac.uk; f. 1954 as New Hall; present name 2008; Pres. Dame BARBARA STOCKING (acting).

Newnham College: Sidgwick Ave, Cambridge, CB3 9DF; tel. (1223) 335700; e-mail enquiries@newn.cam.ac.uk; internet www.newn.cam.ac.uk; f. 1871; library of 90,000 vols; Prin. Prof. Dame CAROL M. BLACK.

MIXED COLLEGES

Christ's College: St Andrew's St, Cambridge, CB2 3BU; tel. (1223) 334900; e-mail library@christs.cam.ac.uk; internet www.christs.cam.ac.uk; f. 1505 for men; women admitted 1978; library of 100,000 vols; Master Prof. FRANK KELLY.

Churchill College: Storey's Way, Cambridge, CB3 0DS; tel. (1223) 336000; e-mail register@chu.cam.ac.uk; internet www.chu.cam.ac.uk; f. 1960 for men; women admitted 1972; Master Prof. Sir DAVID WALLACE.

Clare College: Trinity Lane, Cambridge, CB2 1TL; tel. (1223) 333200; e-mail bursar@clare.cam.ac.uk; internet www.clare.cam.ac.uk; f. 1326 for men; women admitted 1972; Master Prof. A. J. BADGER.

Corpus Christi College: Trumpington St, Cambridge, CB2 1RH; tel. (1223) 338000; e-mail admissions@corpus.cam.ac.uk; internet www.corpus.cam.ac.uk; f. 1352 for men; women admitted 1983; Master STUART LAING.

Downing College: Regent St, Cambridge, CB2 1DQ; tel. (1223) 334800; e-mail college-office@dow.cam.ac.uk; internet www.dow.cam.ac.uk; f. 1800 for men; women admitted 1978; Master Prof. GEOFFREY GRIMMETT.

Emmanuel College: St Andrew's St, Cambridge, CB2 3AP; tel. (1223) 334200; e-mail co@emma.cam.ac.uk; internet www.emma.cam.ac.uk; f. 1584 for men; women admitted 1978; library of 60,000 vols; Master Dame FIONA REYNOLDS.

Fitzwilliam College: Storey's Way, Cambridge, CB3 0DG; tel. (1223) 332000; e-mail admissions@fitz.cam.ac.uk; internet www.fitz.cam.ac.uk; f. 1966 for men, women admitted 1978; library of 40,000 vols; Master NICOLA PADFIELD.

Girton College: Huntingdon Rd, Cambridge, CB3 0JG; tel. (1223) 338999; e-mail admissions@girton.cam.ac.uk; internet www.girton.cam.ac.uk; f. 1869 for women, men admitted 1977; library of 95,000 vols; Mistress Prof. SUSAN J. SMITH.

Gonville and Caius College: Trinity St, Cambridge, CB2 1TA; tel. (1223) 332400; internet www.cai.cam.ac.uk; f. 1348 for men; women admitted 1978; Master Prof. Sir ALAN FERSHT.

Homerton College: Hills Rd, Cambridge, CB2 8PH; tel. (1223) 747111; e-mail porters@homerton.cam.ac.uk; internet www.homerton.cam.ac.uk; f. 1824 as a Training College (Approved Society 1976); men readmitted 1978; Prin. Prof. GEOFFREY WARD.

Hughes Hall: Mortimer Rd, Cambridge, CB1 2EW; tel. (1223) 334898; e-mail enquiries@hughes.cam.ac.uk; internet www.hughes.cam.ac.uk; f. 1885 as the Cambridge Training College for Women (Approved Foundation 1968); Pres. SARAH SQUIRE.

Jesus College: Jesus Lane, Cambridge, CB5 8BL; tel. (1223) 339339; internet www.jesus.cam.ac.uk; f. 1496 for men; women admitted 1978; Master Prof. IAN WHITE.

King's College: King's Parade, Cambridge, CB2 1ST; tel. (1223) 331100; e-mail info@kings.cam.ac.uk; internet www.kings.cam.ac.uk; f. 1441 for men; women admitted 1972; library of 130,000 vols; Provost Prof. MICHAEL PROCTOR.

Magdalene College: Magdalene St, Cambridge, CB3 0AG; tel. (1223) 332100; e-mail enquiries@magd.cam.ac.uk; internet www.magd.cam.ac.uk; f. 1428 for men; women admitted 1987; Master Dr ROWAN WILLIAMS.

Pembroke College: Trumpington St, Cambridge, CB2 1RF; tel. (1223) 338100; e-mail enquiries@pem.cam.ac.uk; internet www.pem.cam.ac.uk; f. 1347 for men; women admitted 1983; library of 37,000 vols; Master Sir RICHARD DEARLOVE.

Peterhouse: Trumpington St, Cambridge, CB2 1RD; tel. (1223) 338200; e-mail info@pet.cam.ac.uk; internet www.pet.cam.ac.uk; f. 1284, women admitted 1984; Master Prof. ADRIAN DIXON.

Queens' College: Silver St, Cambridge, CB3 9ET; tel. (1223) 335511; e-mail enquiries@queens.cam.ac.uk; internet www.queens.cam.ac.uk; f. 1448 for men; women admitted 1979; Pres. Prof. Lord EATWELL.

Robinson College: Grange Rd, Cambridge, CB3 9AN; tel. (1223) 339100; e-mail apply@robinson.cam.ac.uk; internet www.robinson.cam.ac.uk; f. 1979; Warden Prof. A. DAVID YATES.

St Catharine's College: Trumpington St, Cambridge, CB2 1RL; tel. (1223) 338300; e-mail info@caths.cam.ac.uk; internet www.caths.cam.ac.uk; f. 1473 for men; women admitted 1978; library of 60,000 vols; Master Prof. Dame JEAN THOMAS.

St Edmund's College: Mount Pleasant, Cambridge, CB3 0BN; tel. (1223) 336250; e-mail reception@st-edmunds.cam.ac.uk; internet www.st-edmunds.cam.ac.uk; f. 1896 for men; (Approved Foundation 1975); women admitted 1978; Master Prof. J. PAUL LUZIO; Dean Fr ALBAN McCOY.

St John's College: St John's St, Cambridge, CB2 1TP; tel. (1223) 338600; e-mail reception@joh.cam.ac.uk; internet www.joh.cam.ac.uk; f. 1511 for men; women admitted 1981; Master Prof. CHRISTOPHER M. DOBSON.

Selwyn College: Grange Rd, Cambridge, CB3 9DQ; tel. (1223) 335846; e-mail admissions@sel.cam.ac.uk; internet www.sel.cam.ac.uk; f. 1882 for men; women admitted 1976; Master ROGER MOSEY.

Sidney Sussex College: Sidney St, Cambridge, CB2 3HU; tel. (1223) 338800; e-mail enquiries@sid.cam.ac.uk; internet www.sid.cam.ac.uk; f. 1596 for men; women admitted 1976; Master Prof. RICHARD PENTY.

Trinity College: Trinity St, Cambridge, CB2 1TQ; tel. (1223) 338400; e-mail college.office@trin.cam.ac.uk; internet www.trin.cam.ac.uk; f. 1546 for men; women admitted 1977; library of 300,000 vols; Master Sir GREGORY WINTER.

Trinity Hall: Trinity Lane, Cambridge, CB2 1TJ; tel. (1223) 332500; e-mail info@trinhall.cam.ac.uk; internet www.trinhall.cam.ac.uk; f. 1350 for men; women admitted 1977; Master Prof. MARTIN DAUNTON.

MIXED COLLEGES FOR GRADUATE STUDENTS

Clare Hall: Herschel Rd, Cambridge, CB3 9AL; tel. (1223) 332360; e-mail college.secretary@clarehall.cam.ac.uk; internet www.clarehall.cam.ac.uk; f. 1966 (Approved Foundation); Pres. Prof. DAVID IBBETSON.

Darwin College: Silver St, Cambridge, CB3 9EU; tel. (1223) 335660; e-mail deanery@darwin.cam.ac.uk; internet www.dar.cam.ac.uk; f. 1964; Master Prof. MARY FOWLER; Dean Dr LEO HOWE.

Wolfson College: Barton Rd, Cambridge, CB3 9BB; tel. (1223) 335900; e-mail registrar@wolfson.cam.ac.uk; internet www.wolfson.cam.ac.uk; f. 1965; Pres. Prof. Sir RICHARD EVANS

UNIVERSITY OF CENTRAL LANCASHIRE

Preston, PR1 2HE

Telephone: (1772) 201201
E-mail: cenquiries@uclan.ac.uk
Internet: www.uclan.ac.uk

Founded 1828, as Instn for the Diffusion of Knowledge, present name and status 1992
Academic year: September to July

Chancellor: Sir RICHARD EVANS
Vice-Chancellor: Prof. GERRY KELLEHER
Deputy Vice-Chancellor for Academic Affairs: GRAHAM BALDWIN
Pro-Vice-Chancellor for Int. Affairs: ANGELA MURPHY
Pro-Vice-Chancellor for Research: (vacant)
Pro-Vice-Chancellor for Student Experience: ROD DUBROW-MARSHALL
Librarian: KEVIN ELLARD

Number of teachers: 1,000
Number of students: 35,000

DEANS

Grenfell-Baines School of Architecture, Construction and Environment: Prof. AKIN AKINTOYE
Lancashire Business School: DHARMA KOVVURI
Lancashire Law School: LYNNE LIVESEY
School of Art, Design And Performance: GLENDA BRINDLE
School of Computing, Engineering and Physical Sciences: ROBERT WALLACE
School of Education and Social Sciences: Prof. KEITH FAULKS
School of Forensic and Investigative Sciences: Dr ALLISON JONES
School of Health: NIGEL HARRISON
School of Journalism and Digital Communication: Dr ANDREW IRELAND
School of Language, Literature and International Studies: ISABEL DONNELLY
School of Medicine and Dentistry: Prof. StJOHN CREAN
School of Pharmacy and Biomedical Sciences: Prof. TONY D'EMANUELE
School of Psychology: Prof. LINDEN BALL
School of Social Work: Prof. AIDAN WORSLEY
School of Sport, Tourism and The Outdoors: Dr JOHN MINTEN

UNIVERSITY OF CHESTER

Parkgate Rd, Chester, CH1 4BJ

Telephone: (1244) 511000
E-mail: enquiries@chester.ac.uk
Internet: www.chester.ac.uk

Founded 1839, present status 2005

Vice-Chancellor and Prin.: Prof. TIMOTHY WHEELER
Sr Pro-Vice-Chancellor for Resources and Quality: Dr MALCOLM RHODES
Pro-Vice-Chancellor: Prof. PETER HARROP
Pro-Vice-Chancellor for Acad.: Prof. MIKE THOMAS
Pro-Vice-Chancellor for Acad. Sec.: ADRIAN LEE
Pro-Vice-Chancellor for Student Experience and Corporate Performance: Dr CHRIS HASLAM

Univ. Sec.: DAVID STEVENS
Number of teachers: 413
Number of students: 14,000

DEANS

Applied Sciences: Prof. SARAH ANDREW
Arts and Media: BRENDAN O'SULLIVAN
Business, Enterprise and Lifelong Learning: Prof. PHIL HARRIS
Education and Children's Services: ANNA SUTTON
Health and Social Care: Prof. MICHAEL THOMAS
Humanities: Prof. ROB WARNER
Social Sciences: DAVID BALSAMO

UNIVERSITY OF CHICHESTER

Bishop Otter Campus, College Lane, Chichester, PO19 6PE

Telephone: (1243) 816000
E-mail: help@chi.ac.uk
Internet: www.chi.ac.uk

Founded 1839; became Univ. College Chichester 1999, present name and status 2005
Language of instruction: English
Academic year: September to July

Vice-Chancellor: Prof. CLIVE BEHAGG
Deputy Vice-Chancellor: IAN CHILD
Deputy Vice-Chancellor for Academic Affairs: Dr SARAH GILROY

Library of 202,712 vols and 2,000 periodical titles
Number of teachers: 450
Number of students: 6,000

Publication: *Showcase*

DEANS

Arts, Business and Humanities: MARK MASON (Deputy Dean)
Education, Social Sciences and Sport: GILL BUTLER (Deputy Dean)

UNIVERSITY OF DERBY

Kedleston Rd, Derby, DE22 1GB

Telephone: (1332) 590500
E-mail: askadmissions@derby.ac.uk
Internet: www.derby.ac.uk

Founded 1851, present name and status 1998, merged with Leek College 2012
Academic year: September to June

Chancellor: Duke Of Devonshire PEREGRINE CAVENDISH
Vice-Chancellor and Chief Exec.: Prof. JOHN COYNE
Deputy Vice-Chancellor: Prof. MARGARET BARNES
Deputy Vice-Chancellor: Prof. ROD DUBROW MARSHALL
Deputy Vice-Chancellor: Prof. PHILIP PLOWDEN
Dean for Learning Enhancement and Innovation: Dr RUTH AYRES
Librarian: PATRICIA JOHNSON

Library of 332,148 vols
Number of teachers: 671
Number of students: 22,300

DEANS

Faculty of Arts, Design and Technology: Prof. HUW DAVIES
Faculty of Business, Computing and Law: Prof. KEITH HORTON
Faculty of Education, Health and Sciences: Prof. GUY DALY
University of Derby College, Buxton: Prof. PETER DEWHURST

UNIVERSITY OF DURHAM

University Office, Old Elvet, Durham, DH1 3HP

Telephone: (191) 334-2000
E-mail: pro.directory@durham.ac.uk
Internet: www.dur.ac.uk

Founded 1832
Academic year: October to June (3 terms)

Chancellor: Sir THOMAS ALLAN
Vice-Chancellor and Warden: Prof. CHRISTOPHER HIGGINS
Deputy Warden: Prof. JOHN ASHWORTH
Pro-Vice-Chancellor for Education: Prof. ANTHONY FORSTER
Pro-Vice-Chancellor for Research: Prof. TOM McLEISH
Pro-Vice-Chancellor for the Faculty of Arts and Humanities: Prof. SETH KUNIN
Pro-Vice-Chancellor for the Faculty of Science: Prof. ANDREW DEEKS
Pro-Vice-Chancellor for the Faculty of Social Sciences and Health: Prof. ROBIN CONINGHAM
Pro-Vice-Chancellor: Prof. RAY HUDSON
Registrar and Sec.: CAROLYN FOWLER
Treas.: PAULINA LUBACZ
Librarian: JON PURCELL

Library: see Libraries and Archives
Number of teachers: 1,450
Number of students: 15,770

PROFESSORS

Faculty of Arts and Humanities:

ARCHER, R. L. A., Spanish
BAGULEY, D., French
BARCLAY, J. M. G., Divinity
BARNES, G. L., Japanese
BROOKS, C. W., History
BROWN, D. W., Divinity
CLARK, T. J. A., English Studies
COOPER, D. E., Philosophy
COWLING, D. J., French
DAVIES, D. J., Study of Religion
DIBBLE, J. C., Music
HALL, E. M., Greek Cultural History
HARRIS, E., Classics and Ancient History
HARRIS, H. J., History
HAYWARD, C. T. R., Hebrew
LOUTH, A., Patristic and Byzantine Studies
LOWE, E. J., Philosophy
MANNING, P. D., Music
MICHIE, R. C., History
O'MEARA, P., Russian
O'NEILL, M. S. C., English Studies
PADDISON, M. H., Music
PRESTWICH, M. C., History
REGAN, S., English Studies
RHODES, P. J., Ancient History
ROLLASON, D. W., History
ROWE, C. J., Greek
SANDERS, A. L., English Studies
SAUL, N. D. B., German
STUCKENBRUCK, L. T., Biblical Studies
TAYLOR, J. H. M., French
WAUGH, P., English Studies
WILLIAMSON, P. A., History

Faculty of Science:

ABRAM, R. A., Physics
ABRASHKIN, V. A., Mathematics
ADAMS, C. S., Physics
APPLETON, E., Engineering
BADYAL, J. P., Chemistry
BENNETT, K. H., Engineering
BOWER, R. G., Physics
BROERSMA, H. J., Computer Science
BRYCE, M. R., Chemistry
CAMPBELL, A. C., Psychology
CHAMBERLAIN, J. M., Applied Physics
CROUCH, R., Engineering
DAVIDSON, J. P., Earth Sciences
DOREY, P. E., Mathematics
EDWARDS, R., Biological and Biomedical Sciences

FARBER, M. S., Pure Mathematics
FINDLAY, J. M., Psychology
FLOWER, D. R., Physics
FOULGER, G. R., Earth Sciences
FRENK, C. S., Fundamental Physics
GATHERCOLE, S. E., Psychology
GLOVER, E. W. N., Physics
GOLDSTEIN, M., Statistics
GOULTY, N. R., Earth Sciences
HATTON, P. D., Physics
HE, L., Engineering
HEYWOOD, C. A., Psychology
HOLDSWORTH, R. E., Earth Sciences
HOWARD, J. A. K., Chemistry
HUNTLEY, B., Biological and Biomedical Sciences
HUSSEY, P. J., Plant Molecular Cell Biology
HUTCHISON, C. J, Animal Cell Biology
HUTSON, J. M., Chemistry
LINDSAY, S. W., Biological and Biomedical Sciences
LINDSEY, K., Plant Molecular Biology
MANSFIELD, P., Mathematics
MARDER, T. B., Chemistry
MAROPOULOS, P., Engineering
MENSHIKOV, M. V., Statistics
MILNER, A. D., Cognitive Neuroscience
MONKMAN, A. P., Physics
MUNRO, M., Computer Science
NIU, Y., Earth Sciences
PARKER, D., Chemistry
PENNINGTON, M. R., Mathematical Sciences and Physics
PETTY, M. C., Engineering
PURVIS, A., Engineering
QUINLAN, R. A., Biomedical Sciences
SALOUS, S., Engineering
SEARLE, R. C., Geophysics
SHANKS, T., Physics
SHARPLES, R. M., Physics
SLABAS, A. R., Plant Sciences
STEWART, I. A., Computer Science
STIRLING, W. J., Mathematical Sciences and Physics
STRAUGHAN, B., Numerical Analysis
TANNER, B. K., Physics
TAVNER, P., Engineering
THOMPSON, R. N., Geology
TUCKER, M. E., Geological Sciences
UNSWORTH, A., Engineering
WALMSLEY, A. R., Infectious Diseases
WARD, M. J., Physics
WARD, R. S., Mathematics
ZAKRZEWSKI, W. J., Mathematics

Faculty of Social Sciences and Health:
ABHYANKAR, A., Finance
ALLEN, T., Law
ALLISON, R. J., Geography
AMIN, A., Geography
ANTONIOU, A., Business School
BAILEY, D., Applied Social Sciences
BAILIFF, I. K., Archaeology
BARR, D. G., Business School
BASU, P., Economics
BILSBOROUGH, A., Anthropology
BLACKMAN, T. J., Applied Social Sciences
BOHLANDER, M., Law
BOYNE, R. D., Sociology and Social Policy
BURT, T. P., Geography
BYRAM, M. S., Education
BYRNE, D. S., Applied Social Sciences
CAMPBELL, D., Cultural and Political Geography
CAMPBELL, I. D., Law
CARRITHERS, M. B., Anthropology
CLARK, T., Organizational Behaviour
COCKERILL, T. A. J., Business Management and Economics
COOPER, B., Education
DARNELL, A. C., Business School
DEGELING, P., Clinical Management Development
DIXON, R., Managerial Accounting
EHTESHAMI, A., Middle Eastern and Islamic Studies

ELLIOTT, J., Education
EVANS, H. M., Humanities in Medicine
FENWICK, H. M., Law
FERGUSON, R. I., Physical Geography
GLOVER, G. R., Public Mental Health
GOTT, R., Education
GRAHAM, S., Geography
GREAVES, R.-M., European Law
HAMILTON, J. D., Academic Director of Phase 1 Medicine
HOBBS, R. F., Law
HOLMES, P. R., Business School
HUDSON, R., Geography
HUNGIN, A. P. S., Health
HUNTER, D. J., Health Policy and Management
JOHNSON, P. S., Business School
KOUKRAKOS, P., Law
LAFFIN, M., Public Policy and Management
LANE, S., Geography
LAYTON, R. H., Anthropology
LEIGH, I. D., Law
LINSTEAD, S., Organizational Analysis
LONG, A. J., Geography
MASON, J., Health
McGLYNN, C. M. S., Law
McKENDRICK, D. G., Strategy
MEYER, J. H. F., Education
MOORE, G., Business School
NEWTON, L. D., Education
PAINTER, J. M., Geography
PALMER-COOPER, J. A., Education
PARKER, S. C., Entrepreneurship
PAUDYAL, K., Business School
POLOS, L., Business School
PRICE, A. J., Archaeology
READ, D., Business School
REDMAN, T., Business School
RIDGWAY, J. E., Education
RIGG, J. D., Geography
ROBERTS, C. A., Archaeology
SCOTT, S. J., Applied Social Sciences
SHENNAN, I., Geography
SHONE, R., Business School
SILLITOE, P., Anthropology
SMITH, R. D., Education
SMITH, S. J., Human Geography
SULLIVAN, G. R., Law
TOWNSEND, A. R., Regional Regeneration and Development Studies
TYMMS, P. B., Education
van WITTELOOSTUIJN, A., Strategy
WARBRICK, C. J., Law
WATSON, R., Financial Management
WILLIAMS, R. J., Politics
WILSON, R. J. A., Middle Eastern and Islamic Studies
WRIGHT, G., Management

COLLEGES

College of St Hild and St Bede: Durham, DH1 1SZ; tel. (191) 334-8300; internet www .dur.ac.uk/hild-bede; f. 1975, by merger of College of the Venerable Bede (for men) and St Hild's College (for women); Prin. Prof. CHRIS HUTCHISON; Vice-Prin. LAURA WILSON.

Collingwood College: South Rd, Durham, DH1 3LT; tel. (191) 334-5000; e-mail collingwood.collegeoffice@durham.ac.uk; internet www.dur.ac.uk/collingwood; f. 1972; 1,100 students; Prin. Prof. EDWARD CORRIGAN.

Grey College: South Rd, Durham, DH1 3LG; tel. (191) 334-5900; e-mail grey .college@durham.ac.uk; internet www.dur.ac .uk/grey.college; f. 1959; Master Prof. J. M. CHAMBERLAIN.

Hatfield College: N Bailey, Durham, DH1 3RQ; tel. (191) 334-2633; e-mail hatfield .reception@durham.ac.uk; internet www.dur .ac.uk/hatfield.college; f. 1846; Master Prof. TIM BURT (acting).

John Snow College: Stockton-on-Tees, TS17 6BH; tel. (191) 334-0046; e-mail snow .college@durham.ac.uk; internet www.dur.ac

.uk/johnsnow.college; f. 2001; Prin. Prof. CAROLYN SUMMERBELL.

Josephine Butler College: South Rd, Durham, DH1 3DF; tel. (191) 334-7260; e-mail jbcollege.secretary@durham.ac.uk; internet www.dur.ac.uk/butler.college; f. 2001; 800 students; Prin. ADRIAN SIMPSON.

Queen's Campus, Stockton: Thornaby, Stockton-on-Tees, TS17 6BH; tel. (191) 334-0022; internet www.dur.ac.uk/queens-campus; f. 1992 as Univ. College Stockton; awards jt qualifications of Univs of Durham and Teesside; Dean Prof. JO PHOENIX.

St Aidan's College: Windmill Hill, Durham, DH1 3LJ; tel. (191) 334-5769; e-mail aidans .reception@durham.ac.uk; internet www.dur .ac.uk/st-aidans.college; f. 1895, known as St Aidan's Society until 1961; Prin. J. S. ASHWORTH.

St Chad's College: 18 N Bailey, Durham, DH1 3RH; tel. (191) 334-3358; e-mail chads@ dur.ac.uk; internet www.dur.ac.uk/stchads; f. 1904; 500 students; Prin. Rev. Canon Dr J. P. M. CASSIDY.

St Cuthbert's Society: 12 S Bailey, Durham, DH1 3EE; tel. (191) 334-3400; e-mail st-cuthberts.society@durham.ac.uk; internet www.dur.ac.uk/st-cuthberts.society; f. 1888, known as non-Collegiate until 1947; Prin. Prof. GRAHAM TOWL.

St John's College with Cranmer Hall: 3 S Bailey, Durham, DH1 3RJ; tel. (191) 334-3894; e-mail enquiries@cranmerhall.co; internet www.dur.ac.uk/cranmerhall; f. 1909; Prin. Rev. Dr DAVID WILKINSON.

St Mary's College: Elvet Hill Rd, Durham, DH1 3LR; tel. (191) 334-5719; e-mail reception.stmarys@durham.ac.uk; internet www.dur.ac.uk/st-marys.college; f. 1899; Prin. Prof. SIMON HACKETT.

Stephenson College: Stockton-on-Tees, TS17 6JZ; tel. (191) 334-0560; e-mail stephenson@durham.ac.uk; internet www .dur.ac.uk/stephenson; f. 2001; Prin. Prof. A. C. DARNELL.

Trevelyan College: Elvet Hill Rd, Durham, DH1 3LN; tel. (191) 334-7000; e-mail admissions.trevelyan@durham.ac.uk; internet www.dur.ac.uk/trevelyan.college; f. 1966; 600 students; Prin. Prof. H MARTYN EVANS.

University College: Durham Castle, Palace Green, Durham, DH1 3RW; tel. (191) 334-4099; e-mail pro.directory@durham.ac.uk; internet www.dur.ac.uk/university.college; f. 1832; Master Prof. M. E. TUCKER.

Ushaw College: Durham, DH7 9RH; tel. (191) 373-8517; e-mail courses@ushaw.ac.uk; internet www.ushaw.ac.uk; f. 1808; Rector Rev. T. P. DRAINEY.

Ustinov College: Howlands Farm, Durham, DH1 3DE; tel. (191) 334-7241; e-mail ustinov .college@durham.ac.uk; internet www.dur.ac .uk/ustinov.college; f. 1965; Prin. Dr PENELOPE WILSON (acting).

Van Mildert College: Mill Hill Lane, Durham, DH1 3LH; tel. (191) 334-7100; e-mail vm.reception@durham.ac.uk; f. 1963; academic year October to June; 1,000 students; Prin. Prof. DAVID HARPER

UNIVERSITY OF EAST ANGLIA

Norwich, NR4 7TJ
Telephone: (1603) 456161
Internet: www.uea.ac.uk
Founded 1963
Academic year: September to June
Chancellor: Sir BRANDON GOUGH
Vice-Chancellor: Prof. EDWARD ACTON

Pro-Vice-Chancellor for Academics: Prof. TOM WARD
Pro-Vice-Chancellor for Research, Enterprise and Engagement: Prof. TREVOR DAVIES
Registrar and Sec.: BRIAN SUMMERS
Librarian: JEAN C. STEWARD
Library of 800,000 items (700,000 books, CDs and DVDs, 100,000 print periodicals)
Number of teachers: 1,000
Number of students: 14,320
Publications: *Pretext* (2 a year), *Reactions* (1 a year), *Scandinavica* (2 a year)

DEANS

Faculty of Arts and Humanities: Prof. DAVID PETERS CORBETT
Faculty of Health: Prof. IAN HARVEY
Faculty of Science: Prof. DAVID RICHARDSON
Faculty of Social Sciences: Prof. NEIL WARD

PROFESSORS

School of American Studies (tel. (1603) 592220; e-mail wwweas@uea.ac.uk; internet www.uea.ac.uk/eas):

BIGSBY, C. W. E.
CROCKATT, R.
HOMBERGER, E.

School of Biological Sciences (tel. (1603) 593503; e-mail diana.cook@uea.ac.uk; internet www.uea.ac.uk/bio):

DAWSON, A., Biology
DUNCAN, G., Biology
EDWARDS, D. R., Cancer Studies
HEWITT, G. M., Biology
JOHNSTON, A. W. B., Biology
REYNOLDS, J., Biology
RICHARDSON, D. J.
SUTHERLAND, W. J., Biology
WATKINSON, A. R., Ecology

School of Chemical Sciences and Pharmacy (tel. (1603) 593145; e-mail k.e.bezants@uea.ac.uk; internet www.uea.ac.uk/cap):

ANDREWS, D. L., Chemistry
BELTON, P., Chemistry
BOCHMANN, M., Chemistry
COOK, M. J., Chemistry
CRAIG, D., Pharmacy
FIELD, R., Chemistry
MOORE, G. R., Chemistry
ROBINSON, B. H., Chemistry
RUSSELL, D., Chemistry
THOMSON, A. J., Chemistry

School of Computing Sciences (tel. (1603) 592847; e-mail www-admin@uea.ac.uk; internet www.cmp.vea.uea.ac.uk):

BANGHAM, J. A., Electronic Systems Engineering
GLAUERT, J., Computing Science
FINLAYSON, G., Information Systems
FORREST, A. R., Computing Science
RAYWARD-SMITH, V. J., Computing Science
SLEEP, M. R., Computing Science

School of Developmental Studies (tel. (1603) 592807; e-mail dev.general@uea.ac.uk; internet www.uea.ac.uk/dev):

ELLIS, F. T., Development Studies
JENKINS, R., Development Studies
SEDDON, D., Development Studies
STOCKING, M. A., Development Studies

School of Economics (tel. (1603) 592070; e-mail m.watling@uea.ac.uk; internet www.uea.ac.uk/eco):

CUBITT, R., Economics
DAVIES, S. W., Economics
HARGREAVES HEAP, S. P., Economics
LAWSON, S., International Relations
LOOMES, G., Economics
LYONS, B. R., Economics
SUGDEN, R., Economics

School of Education and Lifelong Learning (tel. (1603) 591451; e-mail edv.reception@uea.ac.uk; internet www.uea.ac.uk/edu):

BRIDGES, D., Education
ELLIOTT, J., Education
NORRIS, N. F. J., Education
SCHOSTAK, J. F., Education
TICKLE, L., Education
WALKER, R., Education

School of Environmental Sciences (tel. (1603) 592542; e-mail env@uea.ac.uk; internet www.uea.ac.uk/env):

BATEMEN, I., Environmental Sciences
BENTHAM, C. G., Environmental Sciences
BRIMBLECOMBE, P., Environmental Sciences
HEY, R. D., Environmental Sciences
HULME, M., Environmental Sciences
JICKELLS, T. D., Environmental Sciences
LEEDER, M. R., Environmental Sciences
LISS, P. S., Environmental Sciences
O'RIORDAN, T., Environmental Sciences
PENKETT, S. A., Environmental Sciences
PIDGEON, N. F., Environmental Sciences
PLANE, J. M. C., Environmental Sciences
SCHELLNHUBER, J., Environmental Sciences
TURNER, R. K., Environmental Studies
VINCENT, C. E., Environmental Sciences
WATKINSON, A. R., Ecology
WIGLEY, T. M. C., Environmental Sciences

School of Film and Television Studies (tel. (1603) 593820; e-mail k.durnford@uea.ac.uk; internet www.uea.ac.uk/eas):

BARR, C. J. A., Film Studies
HIGSON, A., Film Studies
JANCOVICH, M., Film Studies
TASKER, Y., Contemporary Popular Culture

School of History (tel. (1603) 593521; e-mail h.ashdown@uea.ac.uk; internet www.uea.ac.uk/his):

CHARMLEY, J. D., Modern British History
DAVIS, J. C., English History
HARPER-BILL, C., English History
HOWE, A. C., Modern History
RAWCLIFFE, C., English History
SANDERSON, M., Modern Social History
VINCENT, N., English and European History

School of Language, Linguistics and Translation Studies (tel. (1603) 592750; e-mail pg.llt@uea.ac.uk; internet www.uea.ac.uk/llt):

CHILTON, P., Linguistics

School of Law (tel. (1603) 593042; e-mail pglaw@uea.ac.uk; internet www.uea.ac.uk/law):

HVIID, M., Competition and Contract Law
MULLIS, A., International Commercial Law
PATTENDEN, R. D., Law
PRIME, T., Law
SMITH, I. T., Employment Law
WINSHIP, P., Law

School of Literature and Creative Writing (tel. (1603) 593820; e-mail k.durnford@uea.ac.uk; internet www.uea.ac.uk/eas):

DUNCKER, P., Creative Writing
HOLMES, R., Literature
ROBERTS, M., Creative Writing
ROBINSON, M., Scandinavian Studies
SAGE, V., Literature
SALES, R., English Literature
SCOTT, C., European Literature (French)
YARROW, R., Drama

School of Management (tel. (1603) 593029; e-mail pg.mgt@uea.ac.uk; internet www.mgt.uea.ac.uk):

DREW, S., Management
FLETCHER, K. P., Management
TZOKAS, N., Customer Relationship Management
WADDAMS, C., Management

School of Mathematics (tel. (1603) 592597; e-mail ann.barnes@uea.ac.uk; internet www.mth.uea.ac.uk):

EVEREST, G. R., Mathematics
JOHNSON, J. A., Mathematics
VANDER-BROECK, J. M., Applied Mathematics
WARD, T., Pure Mathematics
ZALESSKII, A., Pure Mathematics

School of Medicine (tel. (1603) 593061; e-mail e.newport@uea.ac.uk; internet www.med.uea.ac.uk):

BACHMANN, M., Healthcare Interfaces
BARRETT, A., Clinical Oncology
HARVEY, I., Epidemiology and Public Health
HOWE, A. C., Clinical Professor
HUNTER, P. R., Clinical Professor
MACGREGOR, A., Public Health
MUGFORD, M., Health Economics
REYNOLDS, S., Medicine

School of Music (tel. (1603) 592452; e-mail n.swan@uea.ac.uk; internet www.uea.ac.uk/mus):

CHADD, D., Music

School of Nursing and Midwifery (tel. (1603) 421422; e-mail nam.admissions@uea.ac.uk; internet www.uea.ac.uk/nam):

SALTER, B., Health Services Research

School of Philosophy (tel. (1603) 593717; e-mail m.watling@uea.ac.uk; internet www.uea.ac.uk/phi):

O'HAGAN, T., Philosophy

School of Political, Social and International Studies (tel. (1603) 593717; e-mail m.watling@uea.ac.uk; internet www.uea.ac.uk/psi):

GOODWIN, B., Politics
LAWSON, S., International Relations
STREET, J. R., Politics

School of Social Work and Psychosocial Sciences (tel. (1603) 592068; e-mail pgswk@uea.ac.uk; internet www.uea.ac.uk/swk):

HOWE, D. K., Social Work
THOBURN, J., Social Work

School of World Art Studies and Museology (tel. (1603) 592817; e-mail pgwam1@uea.ac.uk; internet www.uea.ac.uk/art):

HODGES, R. A., Visual Arts
JORDANOVA, L., Visual Arts
ONIANS, J. B., Visual Arts

UNIVERSITY OF EAST LONDON

University Way, Docklands, London, E16 2RD

Telephone: (20) 8223-3000
E-mail: study@uel.ac.uk
Internet: www.uel.ac.uk

Founded 1970, as North East London Polytechnic, later became Polytechnic of East London, present name and status 1992
Academic year: September to July

Chancellor: Lord RIX
Vice-Chancellor: Prof. PATRICK MCGHEE
Deputy Vice-Chancellor: Prof. JOHN JOUGHIN
Pro-Vice-Chancellor: NIRMAL BORKHATARIA
Pro-Vice-Chancellor for Int. Affairs: JOHN SHAW
Pro-Vice-Chancellor for Learning, Teaching and Student Experience: GRAHAM CURTIS
Pro-Vice-Chancellor for Strategic Planning and External Devt: SELENA BOLINGBROKE
Univ. Sec. and Registrar: JILL GRINSTEAD
Librarian: ANDREW MCDONALD

Library of 248,000 vols, 1,400 current periodicals; 150,000 books and journals in Stratford Library colln
Number of teachers: 530 (485 full-time, 45 part-time)
Number of students: 23,000

DEANS

Cass School of Education: ANN SLATER
Royal Docks Business School: Prof. LEN SHACKLETON
School of Architecture and the Visual Arts: PETE COBB (acting)
School of Computing, Information Technology and Engineering: Prof. MOHAMMAD DASTBAZ
School of Health and Bioscience: Prof. NEVILLE PUNCHARD
School of Humanities and Social Sciences: STEVEN P. TREVILLION
School of Law: FIONA FAIRWEATHER
School of Psychology: Prof. MARK DAVIES

UNIVERSITY OF ESSEX

Wivenhoe Park, Colchester, CO4 3SQ

Telephone: (1206) 873333*East 15 (Loughton) Campus*, Hatfields, Rectory Lane, Loughton, IG10 3RY

Telephone: (20) 8508-5983*Southend Campus*, Elmer Approach, Southend-on-Sea, SS1 1LW

Telephone: (1702) 328200
E-mail: enquiries@essex.ac.uk
Internet: www.essex.ac.uk

Founded 1964
Academic year: October to July
Chancellor: Lord PHILLIPS OF SUDBURY
Vice-Chancellor: Prof. COLIN RIORDAN
Pro-Vice-Chancellor for Academic and Regional Devt: Prof. NIGEL SOUTH
Pro-Vice Chancellor for Academic Standards: Prof. JANE WRIGHT
Pro-Vice Chancellor for Learning and Teaching: Prof. ANDY DOWNTOWN
Pro-Vice-Chancellor for Research and Enterprise: Prof. DAVID SANDERS
Deputy Vice-Chancellor and Pro-Vice-Chancellor for Sustainability and Resources: Prof. JULES PRETTY
Dean, Univ. of Essex Southend: Prof. STUART MANSON
Dean, Academic Partnerships: Dr AULAY MACKENZIE
Registrar and Sec.: Dr TONY RICH
Librarian: ROBERT BUTLER
Library: see under Libraries and Archives
Number of teachers: 610
Number of students: 10,280

DEANS

Faculty of Health: Prof. JOHN CLIBBENS
Faculty of Humanities and Comparative Studies: Dr LEON BURNETT
Faculty of Law and Management: PETER LUTHER
Faculty of Science and Engineering: Dr DAVID PEVALIN
School of Social Sciences: Dr MIKE JONES
Graduate School: Prof. PAM COX

PROFESSORS

ADAMS, M., Computer Science and Electronic Engineering
ADES, D., Art History and Theory
BAKER, N., Biological Sciences
BALKAN, A., Computer Science and Electronic Engineering
BARRY, C., Psychology
BENEKE, R., Biological Sciences
BENTON, E., Sociology
BLACKBURN, R., Sociology
BOOTH, A., Economics
BORSLEY, R., Language and Linguistics
BOYLE, C., Law
BUSFIELD, N., Sociology
CALLAGHAN, V., Computer Science and Electronic Engineering
CHAMBERS, M., Economics
CLAHSEN, H., Language and Linguistics

CLIBBENS, J., Faculty of Science and Engineering
COAKLEY, J., Essex Business School
COLBECK, I., Biological Sciences
COLES, M., Economics
COOPER, C., Biological Sciences
COX, N., Art History and Theory
DEWS, P., Philosophy
DORUSSEN, H., Government
DOWNTON, A., Computer Science and Electronic Engineering
ELSON, D., Sociology
ERMISCH, J., Institute for Social and Economic Research
FERNANDEZ, N., Biological Sciences
FIGLIO, K., Centre for Psychoanalytic Studies
FOX, E., Psychology
FRANCESCONI, M., Economics
FRASER, V., Art History and Theory
GALEOTTI, A., Economics
GEIDER, R., Biological Sciences
GHANBARI, M., Computer Science and Electronic Engineering
GHIGLINO, C., Economics
GILBERT, G., Law
GILLIES, J., Literature, Film and Theatre Studies
GLEDITSCH, K., Government
GLUCKSMANN, M., Sociology
GOBERT, J., Law
GRAY, R., Literature, Film and Theatre Studies
GREEN, G., Health and Human Sciences
HADFIELD, B., Law
HAGRAS, H., Computer Science and Electronic Engineering
HAMILTON, C., Law
HAMPSON, F., Law
HANLEY, J., Psychology
HAN-PILE, B., Philosophy
HARVEY, M., Sociology
HATTON, T., Economics
HAWKINS, R., Language and Linguistics
HAWKSFORD, M., Computer Science and Electronic Engineering
HENNING, I., Computer Science and Electronic Engineering
HENSON, M., Computer Science and Electronic Engineering
HIGGINS, P., Mathematical Sciences
HIGGS, E., History
HINSHELWOOD, R., Centre for Psychoanalytic Studies
HOPFL, H., Essex Business School
HU, H., Computer Science and Electronic Engineering
HULME, P., Literature, Film and Theatre Studies
HUNT, P., Law
IVERSEN, M., Art History and Theory
JENKINS, S., Institute for Social and Economic Research
KING, A., Government
LANDMAN, T., Government
LANDMAN, T., Institute for Democracy and Conflict Resolution
LEADER, S., Law
LUBBOCK, J., Art History and Theory
LUCAS, S., Computer Science and Electronic Engineering
LYNN, P., Institute for Social and Economic Research
MANSON, S., Essex Business School
MARKOSE-CHERIAN, S., Economics
MARTIN, W., Philosophy
MCDONALD-MAIER, K., Computer Science and Electronic Engineering
MEDDIS, R., Psychology
MILLARD, F., Government
MIRSHEKAR-SYAHKAL, D., Computer Science and Electronic Engineering
MITRA, J., Essex Business School (Southend)
MORAWSKA, E., Sociology
MORRIS, L., Sociology
MUGASHA, A., Law
MULLINEAUX, P., Biological Sciences

NANKERVIS, J., Essex Business School
NEDWELL, D., Biological Sciences
NORTON, J., Biological Sciences
ORBELL, S., Psychology
PACKER, F., Human Rights Centre
PAPADOPOULOS, R., Centre for Psychoanalytic Studies
PATRICK, P., Language and Linguistics
PEERS, S., Law
PLUMPER, T., Government
POLI, R., Computer Science and Electronic Engineering
PRETTY, J., Biological Sciences
PUDNEY, S., Institute for Social and Economic Research
RADFORD, A., Language and Linguistics
RAINES, C., Biological Sciences
RANDALL, M., Government
RAVEN, J., History
REYNOLDS, C., Biological Sciences
ROBERSON, D., Psychology
RODLEY, N., Law
ROPER, M., Sociology
RUBIN, L., East 15 Acting School, Loughton Campus
RUSSO, R., Psychology
SACKER, A., Institute for Social and Economic Research
SADLER, L., Language and Linguistics
SAMUELS, A., Centre for Psychoanalytic Studies
SANDERS, D., Government
SANTOS SILVA, J., Economics
SCHURER, K., UK Data Archive
SHERER, M., Essex Business School
SIKKA, P., Essex Business School
SIMEONIDOU, D., Computer Science and Electronic Engineering
SMITH, E., Economics
SMITH, S., History
SOUTH, N., Sociology
SPENCER, A., Language and Linguistics
SQUINTANI, F., Economics
STANWAY, G., Biological Sciences
STONE, P., Law
STONES, R., Sociology
SUNKIN, M., Law
SUTHERLAND, H., Institute for Social and Economic Research
TEMPLE, C., Psychology
TSANG, E., Computer Science and Electronic Engineering
TURNER, R., Computer Science and Electronic Engineering
UNDERWOOD, G., Biological Sciences
UPTON, G., Mathematical Sciences
VEGA-REDONDO, F., Economics
VERGO, P., Art History and Theory
WALKER, S., Computer Science and Electronic Engineering
WALTER, J., History
WARD, H., Government
WARD, G., Psychology
WARNER, M., Literature, Film and Theatre Studies
WHITELEY, P., Government
WILKINS, A., Psychology
WILSON, M., Biological Sciences
WRIGHT, J., Law
ZHANG, Q., Computer Science and Electronic Engineering

UNIVERSITY OF EXETER

Northcote House Exeter, EX4 4QJ
Telephone: (1392) 661000
E-mail: ug-ad@exeter.ac.uk
Internet: www.exeter.ac.uk
Founded 1922, as University College, present status 1955
Academic year: October to July
Chancellor: Baroness FLOELLA BENJAMIN
Vice-Chancellor and Chief Exec.: Prof. STEVE SMITH

Deputy Vice-Chancellor for Education: Prof. JANICE KAY

Deputy Vice-Chancellor for External Affairs: Prof. MARK OVERTON

Deputy Vice-Chancellor for Research and Knowledge Transfer: Prof. NICHOLAS J. TALBOT

Sr Deputy Vice-Chancellor: Prof. NEIL ARMSTRONG

Chief Operating Officer: Dr CLAIRE BAINES

Asst Dir for Library Research and Support: Dr JESSICA GARDNER

Library: see under Libraries and Archives

Number of teachers: 1,800

Number of students: 18,500 (17,400 fulltime, 1,100 part-time)

Publications: *Bracton Law Journal* (1 a year), *Cornish Studies* (1 a year), *FACT: Focus on Alternative and Complementary Therapies* (4 a year), *New Arabian Studies* (1 a year), *Studies in Theatre Production* (2 a year)

DEANS

Business School: Prof. ROBIN MASON

College of Engineering, Mathematics and Physical Sciences: Prof. KEN EVANS

College of Humanities: Prof. NICK KAYE

College of Life and Environmental Sciences: Prof. MARK GOODWIN

College of Social Sciences and International Studies: Prof. ROBERT VAN DE NOORT

University of Exeter Medical School: Prof. STEVE THORNTON

UNIVERSITY OF GLOUCESTERSHIRE

The Park, Cheltenham, GL50 2RH

Telephone: (1242) 714666

E-mail: admissions@glos.ac.uk

Internet: www.glos.ac.uk

Founded 1990 as Cheltenham and Gloucester College of Further Education through merger of existing colleges, present name and status 2001

State control

Chancellor: Lord CAREY OF CLIFTON

Vice-Chancellor and Chief Exec.: STEPHEN MARSTON

Deputy Vice-Chancellor: RICHARD O'DOCHERTY

Academic Registrar and Clerk to the Council: JULIE THACKRAY

Head of Library Services: LESLEY CARSTONS

Number of teachers: 390

Number of students: 9,410

Publications: *Business School Research Journal* (4 a year), *Contexts* (2 a year), *Journal of Learning and Teaching* (2 a year), *Landscape Issues* (2 a year)

DEANS

Media, Arts and Technology: Dr BEN CALVERT

Natural and Social Sciences: MIKE COGGER

UNIVERSITY OF GREENWICH

Old Royal Naval College, Park Row, London, SE10 9LS

Telephone: (20) 8331-8590

E-mail: courseinfo@greenwich.ac.uk

Internet: www.greenwich.ac.uk

Founded 1890, later became Thames Polytechnic; present name and status 1992

Academic year: September to July

Chancellor: Lord HART OF CHILTON

Vice-Chancellor: Baroness TESSA BLACKSTONE

Deputy Vice-Chancellor for Academic Devt: Prof. SIMON JARVIS

Deputy Vice-Chancellor for Resources: Prof. NEIL GARROD

Deputy Vice-Chancellor for Research and Enterprise: Prof. TOM BARNES

Registrar and Sec.: LINDA CORDING

Librarian: D. HEATHCOTE

Library of 610,000 vols

Number of teachers: 710

Number of students: 24,840

Publications: *Applied Mathematical Modelling* (12 a year), *Computational Fluid Dynamics News* (4 a year)

DEANS

Business School: Prof. BARRY CURNOW

Greenwich Maritime Institute: Prof. CHRIS BELLAMY (Dir)

Medway School of Pharmacy: Prof. IAIN CUMMING

Natural Resources Institute: Prof. ANDREW WESTBY (Dir)

School of Architecture and Construction: Prof. NEIL SPILLER

School of Computing and Mathematical Sciences: Dr LIZ BACON

School of Education: CHRIS PHILPOTT

School of Engineering: Prof. NDY EKERE

School of Health and Social Care: LIZ MEERABEAU

School of Humanities and Social Sciences: Prof. JOANNE FINKELSTEIN

School of Science: Prof. MARTIN SNOWDEN

Urban Renaissance Institute: LOUISE THOMAS (Dir)

UNIVERSITY OF HERTFORDSHIRE

College Lane, Hatfield, AL10 9AB

Telephone: (1707) 284800

E-mail: admissions@herts.ac.uk

Internet: www.herts.ac.uk

Founded 1952, as Hatfield Technical College, became Hatfield Polytechnic in 1969; present name and status 1992

Academic year: October to June

Main campus in Hatfield and Law campus in St Albans

Chancellor: Lord MACLAURIN OF KNEBWORTH

Vice-Chancellor: Prof. QUINTIN MCKELLAR

Deputy Vice-Chancellor: Prof. GRAHAM GALBRAITH

Pro-Vice-Chancellor for Enterprise: JULIE NEWLAN

Pro-Vice-Chancellor for Int. Affairs: Prof. BARRY HUNT

Pro-Vice-Chancellor for Regional Affairs: Dr STEPHEN BOFFEY

Pro-Vice-Chancellor for Research: Prof. JOHN SENIOR

Pro-Vice-Chancellor for Student Experience: Dr ANDREW CLUTTERBUCK

Sec. and Registrar: PHILIP E. WATERS

Librarian: D. MARTIN

Library of 600,000 vols

Number of teachers: 2,700

Number of students: 24,500

DEANS

Business School: JULIE NEWLAN

Faculty of Engineering and Information Sciences: Prof. JOHN SENIOR

Faculty of Health and Human Sciences: Prof. BARRY HUNT

Faculty of Humanities, Law and Education: Dr ANDREW CLUTTERBUCK

Faculty of Interdisciplinary Studies: Dr STEPHEN BOFFEY

UNIVERSITY OF HUDDERSFIELD

Queensgate, Huddersfield, HD1 3DH

Telephone: (1484) 422288

E-mail: admissions@hud.ac.uk

Internet: www.hud.ac.uk

Founded 1841, formerly Huddersfield College of Technology, became Polytechnic of

Huddersfield 1970, present name and status 1992

Academic year: September to June

Chancellor: Prof. Sir PATRICK STEWART

Vice-Chancellor: Prof. BOB CRYAN

Deputy Vice-Chancellor: Prof. PETER SLEE

Pro-Vice-Chancellor for Teaching and Learning: Prof. TIM THORNTON

Pro-Vice-Chancellor for Research and Enterprise: Prof. ANDREW BALL

Univ. Sec.: TONY MEARS

Acad. Registrar: KATHY SHERLOCK

Library of 416,000 vols

Number of teachers: 1,900

Number of students: 23,000

DEANS

Business School: Prof. CHRIS COWTON

School of Applied Sciences: Prof. BOB CYWINSKI

School of Art, Design and Architecture: EMMA HUNT

School of Computing and Engineering: Prof. STEVE DONNELLY

School of Education and Professional Devt: Prof. CHRISTINE JARVIS

School of Human and Health Sciences: SUE BERNHAUSER

School of Music, Humanities and Media: Prof. MIKE RUSS

UNIVERSITY OF HULL

Cottingham Rd, Hull, HU6 7RX

Telephone: (1482) 346311

E-mail: international@hull.ac.uk

Internet: www.hull.ac.uk

Founded 1928, as Univ. College of Hull, Univ. Charter 1954

Academic year: September to June

Chancellor: Baroness BOTTOMLEY

Vice-Chancellor: Prof. CALIE PISTORIUS

Deputy Vice-Chancellor and Pro-Vice Chancellor for Acad. Affairs: Prof. J. W. BRUCE

Pro-Vice-Chancellor for Engagement: Prof. JOHN LEACH

Pro-Vice-Chancellor for Learning and Teaching: Prof. GLENN BURGESS

Pro-Vice-Chancellor for Research and Enterprise: Prof. BARRY WINN

Quality Dir, Univ. Registrar and Sec.: FRANCES OWEN

Librarian and Academic Services Dir: Dr R. G. HESELTINE

Library: see under Libraries and Archives

Number of teachers: 1,030

Number of students: 20,000

DEANS

Business School: Prof. M. JACKSON

Faculty of Arts and Social Sciences: Prof. VALERIE SANDERS (acting)

Faculty of Education: DINA LEWIS

Faculty of Health and Social Care: CHRISTINE ENGLISH

Faculty of Science: DEREK P. WILLS

Hull York Medical School: Prof. TREVOR SHELDON

Postgraduate Medical Institute: Prof. NICHOLAS D. STAFFORD

PROFESSORS

ALEKSEEVSKY, D., Mathematics

ATTENBOROUGH, K., Engineering

BENNETT, J., Hull York Medical School

BINKS, B., Chemistry

BIRKINSHAW, P. J., Law

BOSCH, P., Mathematics

BOTTERY, M., Educational Studies

BROOKES, G. R., Computer Science

BURGESS, M., Politics

BURGESS, P., History

CAMPION, P. D., Public Health and Primary Care Medicine

CARVALHO, G., Biological Science
CHESTERS, G., IfL Office
CLELAND, J., Cardiology
COLQUHOUN, D., Educational Studies
CRAIG, G., Comparative and Applied Social Sciences
CROUCH, D., History
CUMMINGS, A., Engineering Design and Manufacture
CUTLAND, N. J., Pure Mathematics
DAVIES, K., International Leadership Centre
DYER, P. E., Physics
ELTIS, D., Economic Studies
FLETCHER, P. D., Chemistry
FROSTICK, L. E., Geography and Earth Resources
GIBBS, D. C., Geography and Earth Resources
GILBERT, P., Philosophy
GILLESPIE, W., Hull York Medical School
GOODBY, J. W., Chemistry
GRABBE, L. L., Theology
GREEN, R., Economics
GRIFFIN, G., Gender Studies
HARDISTY, J. H., Geography and Earth Resources
HARRIS, R. J., Politics
HASWELL, S., Chemistry
HAUGHTON, G., Geography
HAYWOOD, S., Engineering
HOPPEN, T., History
JACKSON, M., Business School
JESSHOPE, C., Computer Science
JOHNSTON, R., Psychology
KILLICK, S. R., Obstetrics and Gynaecology
KING, V. T., Politics
KITCHEN, P., Business School
LA TORRE, M., Law
LEIGHTON, A., English
LIND, M. J., Oncology
LLOYD, H. A., History
LOVEJOY, P., History
McCOLLUM, P. T., Surgery
McNAUGHTON, L., Sport Science
MAUNDERS, K. T., Accounting, Business and Finance
MONSON, J. R. T., Surgery
MORICE, A. H., Respiratory Medicine
MORTIMER, A., Psychiatry
Lord NORTON OF LOUTH, Politics
OKELY, J. M., Comparative and Applied Social Sciences
O'SULLIVAN, N. K., Politics
PATTON, R. J., Electronic Engineering
PHILLIPS, R., Computer Science
RATLEDGE, C., Biological Science
RICHARDSON, P. D., Economic Studies
RIGBY, B., English
SANDERS, V., English Literature
SCHLUDERMANN, B., Dutch Studies
SHNIRELMAN, A., Mathematics
SMITH, P. M., French
STAFFORD, N., Otolaryngology and Head and Neck Surgery
SWIFT, K. G., Engineering Design and Manufacture
TOWNSHEND, A., Chemistry
TURNBULL, L. W., Magnetic Resonance Investigation
TURNER, G., Biological Science
TURNER, M. E., Economic Studies
VLADIMIROV, V., Mathematics
WALKER, L., Rehabilitation
WATSON, R., Care of the Older Person
WILLIAMS, D., French

UNIVERSITY OF KEELE

Keele, ST5 5BG
Telephone: (1782) 732000
E-mail: international@mac.keele.ac.uk
Internet: www.keele.ac.uk

Founded 1949, as Univ. College of North Staffordshire, present name and status 1962

State control
Academic year: August to July

Chancellor: JONATHAN PORRITT
Vice-Chancellor: Prof. NICHOLAS FOSKETT
Deputy Vice-Chancellor: RAMA THIRUNAMA-CHANDRAN
Pro-Vice-Chancellor for Community and Partnerships: KEVIN MATTINSON
Pro-Vice-Chancellor for Education and Student Experience: Prof. MARILYN ANDREWS
Pro-Vice-Chancellor for Research: Prof. MARK ORMEROD
Librarian: PAUL REYNOLDS
Library: see under Libraries and Archives
Number of teachers: 604
Number of students: 8,371 (f.t.e.)
Publications: *British Journal for the History of Philosophy*, *Sociological Review*

DEANS

Faculty of Health: Prof. ANDY GARNER
Faculty of Humanities and Social Sciences: Prof. DAVID SHEPHERD
Faculty of Natural Sciences: Prof. PATRICK BAILEY

PROFESSORS

ADAM, C., Forensic Science
ADDAMS, H., Economics and Management
AHALL, L., International Relations
AMIGONI, D., Victorian Literature
ANDERSON, B., History
ANDREW, J., Literature and Culture
ANDREWS, M., Professional Education in Health
ARIES, A., Health and Rehabilitation
ARMSTRONG, C., Nursing
ASHBY, S., Nursing
ASHWORTH, J., Anaesthesia and Pain Medicine
ATHERTON, I., History
AUDZEYEVA, A., Management
BAIASU, S., Philosophy
BAILEY, C., American Politics
BAILEY, P., Natural Sciences
BALLINGER, A., Criminology
BANKART, J., Biostatistics
BARTLAM, B., Mixed Methods
BEDFORD, D., Mathematics
BEDSON, J., General Practice
BEECH, R., Health Services
BELL, I., American Literature
BENTLEY, N., English
BERKSON, R., Bioscience
BERNARD, M., Social Gerontology
BERRY, D., Psychology
BISHOP, A., Physiotherapy
BLACK, P., Pharmacy
BLADEN-HOVELL, R., Economics
BOADO-PENAS, M., Economics and Management
BOYLAN, J., Public Policy and Professional Practice
BRADNEY, A., Law
BRAMMER, A., Law
BRANNAN, M., Economics and Management
BREEN, D., Public Policy and Professional Practice
BRERETON, P., Software Engineering
BRIGHT, R., History
BRUCE, S., English
BRUNT, M., Oncology
BUCHER, C., Health and Rehabilitation
BUCKNALL, M., Statistics
CAGE, A., Environmental Science and Physical Geography
CAO, X., Economics and Management
CARRIGAN, A., English
CARTER, E., Politics
CASSIDY, N., Applied Geophysics
CATNEY, P., Politics
CHADWICK, E., Biomedical Engineering
CHANNON, A., Computing and Mathematics
CHAPMAN, C., Applied Mathematics
CHAPMAN, S., Prescribing Studies

CHARI, D., Physiological Medicine
CHEN, R., Clinical Pharmacy and Pharmacology
CHESTERTON, L., Health and Rehabilitation
CHEW-GRAHAM, C., General Practice
CLARK, S., Basin Analysis and Sedimentology
COLLIN, J., Nursing
CORCORAN, M., Criminology
COWLING, M., Radiology
COWNIE, F., Law
CROFT, P., Epidemiology
CROOK, M., French History
CROPPER, S., Management
CURTIS, A., Organic and Medicinal Chemistry
CUSHING, A., Medieval History
D'ORO, G., Philosophy
DANAHER, J., Law
DARTON, R., Physical Chemistry
DAVIES, S., Nephrology
DAVITTI, D., Law, Ethics and Society
DAWSON, P., Economics and Management
DAY, C., Computing and Mathematics
DENT, G., Pharmacology
DIECKMANN, C., Modern European History
DIXSON, B., Criminology
DOBSON, A., Politics
DOBSON, J., Biophysics and Biomedical Engineering
DOHERTY, B., Politics
DOOR, V., Public Policy and Professional Practice
DOUGLAS, J., Nursing
DOYLE, T., Politics and International Relations
DREZOV, K., Politics
DRIJFHOUT, F., Analytical Chemistry
DUNN, K., Epidemiology
DZIEDZIC, K., Musculoskeletal Therapies
EDELSTYN, N., Psychology
EDWARDS, M., Organic Chemistry
EGAN, S., Geology
EGGER, C., Chemistry and Forensic Science
EGGLESTON, P., Molecular Entomology
EKRUM, A., Economics and Management
EL HAJ, A., Cell Engineering
EMMERICH, F., Law, Ethics and Society
ESSEX, J., Public Policy and Professional Practice
ESTACIO, E., Psychology
EVANS, A., Astrophysics
EVANS, M., Neuroscience
EXLEY, C., Bioinorganic Chemistry
FARRELL, W., Human Genomics
FEATHERSTONE, M., Sociology
FINDLOW, S., Social Policy
FINNEY, A., Nursing
FISCHMAN, S. R., Musical Composition
FLETCHER, P., Mathematics
FLETCHER, R., Law
FLOOD, Y., Nursing
FORSYTH, N., Stem Cell Biology
FORSYTH, T., Biophysics
FOSTER, C., Psychology
FOSTER, N., Musculoskeletal Health
FRANCIS, A., Law
FRENCH, S., Economics and Management
FRICKER, R., Biomedical Sciences
FRYER, A., Clinical Biochemistry
FU, Y., Applied Mathematics
FURNESS, D., Neuroscience
GARNER, A., Health Sciences
GARRO, D., Music
GATES, M., Medicine and Neuroscience
GEORGE, S., Environmental Sustainability and Green Technology
GERTISSER, R., Mineralogy and Petrology
GIBBS, M., Nursing
GIFFORD, L., Pharmacy Education
GIRLING, E., Criminology
GLAZEWSKI, S., Neuroscience
GODFREY, B., Criminology
GOKAY, B., International Relations
GOOL, P., Physiotherapy
GOULDING, C., Economics and Management
GRANGE, J., Psychology
GRAY, R., Modern History

GREEN, J., Nursing
GREENHOUGH, T., Structural Biology
GRIFFITHS, C., Criminology
HALEY, M., Property Law
HALL, A., Ultrasonography
HAMILTON, G., Chemical Ecology
HAMILTON, L., Economics and Management
HAN, J., Pharmaceutics
HARDIE-BICK, J., Sociology
HARPER, A., Bioscience
HARRIS, O., American Studies
HART, S., Bioscience
HAWKINS, C., Clinical Neurology
HAXTON, K., Chemistry
HAY, E., Community Rheumatology
HAYCOCK, P., Environmental Engineering
HEAD, E., Sociology
HEALY, J., Computing and Mathematics
HECKL, M., Applied Mathematics
HEGARTY, J., Psychology
HELLIER, C., Astrophysics
HERBERT, J., Politics and International Relations
HIDER, S., Rheumatology
HILL, C., Nursing
HILL, J., Arthritis
HIRSCHI, R., Physics and Astrophysics
HOLDSWORTH, C., Social Geography
HOLOHAN, S., Sociology
HOOLE, D., Fish Diseases
HOPE, S., Biochemistry
HORROCKS, P., Molecular Biology
HORTON, J., Political Philosophy
HOSKINS, C., Pharmaceutics
HOWLETT, J., Public Policy and Professional Practice
HUCKFIELD, L., Physiotherapy
HUGHES, A., Early Modern History
HUGHES, N., Economics and Management
HUGHES, R., Primary Care Health Sciences
HUNT, K., British History
HUNTER, S., Parasitology
HURD, H., Parasitology
HUSSAIN, M., Economics
JACKSON, P., Medieval History
JACKSON, R., Chemistry
JACOB, M., Law
JEFFRIES, R., Astrophysics
JINKS, C., Primary Care Health Sciences
JOHNSON, B., English
JOHNSON, D., Nursing
JONES, G., Organic Chemistry
JONES, M., Medical Statistics
JONES, P., Statistics
JONES, R., Chemistry and Medicinal Chemistry
JONES, R., Social Work
JORDAN, K., Biostatistics
KADAM, U., General Practice
KAPLUNOV, J., Mathematics
KAUDERS, A., History
KAZMI, S., Economics and Management
KEAMAN, T., Criminology
KELEMEN, M., Management Studies
KELLY, B., Musicology
KELLY, C., Bioscience
KELSALL, G., Cultural and Media Studies
KENT, A., Psychology
KEREN-PEZ, T., Law
KERFOOT, D., Economics and Management
KING, C., Earth Science Education
KIRK, W., Ecology and Entomology
KITCHENHAM, B., Quantitative Software Engineering
KNIGHT, P., Geography
KONSTANTINOU, K., Spinal Physiotherapy
KOSKINA, A., Economics and Management
KRISHNADAS, J., Law
KUIPER, J., Biomechanics
KUIPER, N., Biomedical Sciences
KYRIACOU, T., Computing and Mathematics
LADRECH, R., Politics
LAM, K., Computing and Mathematics
LAMONT, A., Psychology
LAU, L., Geography
LEACH, R., Sociology

LEECE, D., Economics and Management
LEGRENZI, G., Economics and Management
LEIGHTON, G., Psychology
LENNEY, W., Child Health
LEWIS, M., Biostatistics
LI, W., Analytical Biochemistry
LILLIE, K., Nursing
LIPPENS, R., Criminology
LIST, P., Psychological Research
LLOYD, L., International Relations
LUSTIG, T., American Studies
LUTHER, K., Politics
MAARABOUNI, M. M., Human Biology
MACGREGOR, S., Politics
MAGUINNESS, N., Social Work
MAHENDRASINGAM, A., Physics
MAIN, C., Psychology (Pain Management)
MALLEN, C., General Practice
MANGAN, A., Economics and Management
MARTENS, L., Sociology
MASLIN-PROTHERO, S., Nursing
MATHER, K., Economics and Management
MATTEY, D., Rheumatology
MAXTED, P., Physics
MAZZOCCHI-JONES, D., Neuroscience
McBETH, J., Chronic Pain in Older People
McCRACKEN, M., English Literature
McGARVEY, D., Physical Chemistry
McKAY, D., Social Geography and Environmental Politics
McLAUGHLIN, D., Astrophysics
McMURTY, L., Law
MERRICK, C., Biology
MILLER, C., Economics and Management
MILLS, E., Pharmacy
MITCHELL, L., Economics and Management
MONTENARI, M., Palaeontology and Statigraphy
MOOKHERJEE, M., Political Philosophy
MORGAN, C., English
MORGAN, P., History
MORRIS, G., Biochemistry
MOSS, G., Pharmaceutics
MUNRO, L., English
MURRAY, M., Psychology
MYERS, H., Occupational Therapy
NAIRE, S., Computing and Mathematics
NARDINI, E., Astrophysics
NELIGWA, T., Computing and Mathematics
O'BRIEN, M., Chemistry and Medicinal Chemistry
O'BRIEN, S., Obstetrics and Gynaecology
O'DRISCOLL, B., Igneous and Metamorphic Petrology
OAKES, H., Economics and Management
OBOKATA, T., Law, Ethics and Society
OLIVEIRA, J., Astrophysics
OLIVER, I., Environmental Science
ONG BIE, N., Health Services Research
ORMEROD, M., Inorganic Materials Chemistry
OSBOURNE, A., Computing and Mathematics
OULTRAM, T., Economics and Management
PACKHAM, J., Rheumatology
PANDYAN, A., Rehabilitation Technology for Health
PARISH, J., Sociology
PARKER, J., Politics
PARR, H., Politics
PARROTT, L., Social Work
PARSONS, E., Economics and Management
PASKINS, Z., Rheumatology
PATON, C., Public Policy
PEACOCK, J., American Studies
PEARSON, R., Organic and Medicinal Chemistry
PEAT, G., Clinical Epidemiology
PEREZ-MORENO, C., Cultural and Media Studies
PHILLIPSON, C., Applied Social Studies and Social Gerontology
POOLE, E., Media Communications and Culture
POOLER, A., Nursing
POOLEY, R., English
PREATER, J., Operational Research

PRINGLE, J., Engineering and Environmental Geosciences
PROST, M., Law
PROTHEROE, J., General Practice
PUGH, R., Social Work
QUINNEY, D., Computer Assisted Learning in Mathematics
RAAB, R., Economics
RADU, A., Chemistry
RAFTPOULOU, C., Economics and Management
RAY, M., Public Policy and Professional Practice
READ, S., Nursing
REEVES, J., Astrophysics
REYLAND, N., Music
RICHARDSON, A., Pharmacology
RICHARDSON, J., Primary Care Health Science
RIGBY, C., Economics and Management
RIMINGTON, L., Health and Rehabilitation
ROACH, P., Biomedical/Cell Engineering
ROBINSON, Z., Environmental Science and Sustainability
ROBSON, M., Psychology
ROCHE, J., Law
RODDY, E., Primary Care Health Sciences
ROFFE, C., Stroke Medicine
ROGERSON, G., Applied Mathematics
ROSENFELD, D., Sociology
ROTENBERG, K., Psychology
ROTH, C., Nursing
ROWLEY, M., Psychology
RUGG, G., Computing and Mathematics
RUSHTON, C., Nursing
RUTHERFORD, A., Psychology
RUTTEN, F., Physical Chemistry
RYAN, B., International Relations
SANDY, L., American Studies
SARGEANT, K., Nursing
SCARBOROUGH, H., Economics and Management
SCHAEFER, A., American Studies
SCRIVNER, D., International Relations
SEAGER, N., English
SEMENOV, S., Imaging
SHAIN, F., Public Policy and Professional Practice
SHAPELY, M., General Practice
SHARMA, S., Colonial/Post-Colonial History
SHARPE, A., Law
SHEARD, J., English
SHEARS, J., English
SHEIKH, N., International Relations
SHEPHERD, D., Humanities and Social Sciences
SHERMAN, S., Psychology
SHRIRA, V., Applied Mathematics
SHRIVE, A., Life Science
SIKDAR, S., Economics and Management
SIM, J., Health Care Research
SIMPSON, P., Geography, Geology and Environment
SKIDMORE, M., Biochemistry
SMALLEY, B., Physics and Astrophysics
SMITH, D., Chemical Physics
SOUSOUNIS, P., Economics and Management
SOWDEN, G., Physiotherapy
SPANEL, P., Trace Gas Analysis
SPASOV, M., Music
STANNARD, R., Public Policy and Professional Practice
STEPHENS, R., Psychology
STEVENSON, K., Physiotherapy
STIFF, C., Psychology
STIMPSON, I., Geophysics
STRANGE, R., Clinical Biochemistry
STRETCH, J., English
STYLES, P., Applied and Environmental Geophysics
STYNES, S., Physiotherapy
SULE-SUSO, J., Oncology
SURMAN, E., Economics and Management
SWIFT, D., Public Policy and Professional Practice
SYMONS, E., Economics and Management
SZKORNIK, K., Physical Geography

TARTAGLIA, J., Philosophy
TAYLOR, S., Ecology
TELLING, N., Biomagnetics
THOMAS, E., Biostatistics
THOMAS, P., Botanical and Environmental Science
THOMPSON, D., Forensic Science
THOMSON, M., Law, Culture and Society
THORNLEY, C., Economics and Management
TOMKINS, A., History
TREBILCOCK, J., Criminology
TRINGHAM, N., History
TRIPET, F., Molecular Biology
TRUEMAN, M., Psychology
TWEATS, R., Public Policy and Professional Practice
UDUMAN, S., Music
UL CHONNACHTAIGH, S., Law
ULLAH, S., Environmental Science
VAN DER WINDT, D., Primary Care Epidemiology
VAN LOON, J., Physics and Astrophysics
VARBIRO, G., Biochemistry
VARNEY, E., Law
VAUGHAN, M., Humanities
VOGLER, J., International Relations
WALLER, R., Physical Geography
WASHINGTON, K., Nursing
WASIK, M., Criminal Justice
WASS, V., Medical Education
WATERFIELD, J., Health and Rehabilitation
WATKINS, C., Health and Rehabilitation
WEARDEN, A., Psychology
WEISSMEYER, C., Economics and Management
WELLS, H., Criminology
WERBNER, P., Social Anthropology
WESTON, S., Criminology
WILKINSON, S., Bioethics
WILLIAMS, A., Music
WILLIAMS, G., Biochemistry
WILLIAMS, G., Structural Geology
WOOD, I., Nursing
WORRALL, A., Criminology
WRIGLEY, A., Law
YANG, Y., Biomaterials
YARDLEY, S., Medical Education
ZHOLOBENKO, V., Chemistry and Forensic Science
ZHOU, H., Economics and Management
ZIELENIEC, A., Sociology

UNIVERSITY OF KENT

The Registry, Canterbury, CT2 7NZ
Telephone: (1227) 764000
E-mail: information@kent.ac.uk
Internet: www.kent.ac.uk

Founded 1965
State control
Academic year: September to June

Chancellor: Sir ROBERT WORCESTER
Vice-Chancellor: Prof. JULIA GOODFELLOW
Sr Deputy Vice-Chancellor: DAVID NIGHTINGALE
Deputy Vice-Chancellor: Prof. KEITH MANDER
Deputy Vice-Chancellor: DENISE EVERITT
Pro Vice-Chancellor: Prof. JOHN BALDOCK
Pro Vice-Chancellor: Prof. ALEX HUGHES
Sec. of Council: KAREN GOFFIN
Head of Library Services: CAROLE PICKAVER

Library: 1.3m. vols
Number of teachers: 630
Number of students: 17,000

DEANS

Faculty of Humanities: Prof. KARL LEYDECKER
Faculty of Sciences: Prof. MARK BURCHELL
Faculty of Social Sciences: Prof. JOHN WIGHTMAN

PROFESSORS

Faculty of Humanities (Marlowe Bldg, Univ. of Kent, Canterbury, CT2 7NR; tel. (1227) 764000):

ALLAIN, P., Theatre and Performance
ANDERSON, G., Classics
ANDREWS, M. Y., Victorian and Visual Studies
AYERS, D., Modernism and Critical Theory (English)
BEECH, A., Fine Art
CARRETTE, J., Religion and Culture
CONNELLY, M., Modern British History
COWIE, E., Film Studies
DITCHFIELD, G., 18th-Century History
FINCHAM, K., Early Modern History
FONTANA-GIUSTI, G., Regional Regeneration
GILL, R., Theology
GOLDSTEIN, L., Philosophy
GURNAH, A., English and Postcolonial Literatures
HOWIE, T., Contemporary Music
KLEIN, B., English Literature
LANDRY, D., English and American Literature
LEYDECKER, K., German and Comparative Literature
LYNCH, G., Modern Theology
MONTEFIORE, J., English and American Literature
NIKOLOPOULOU, M., Sustainable Architecture
PAVIS, P., Drama and Theatre Studies
READ, P. F., French
SCHMIDT, U., Modern History
SMITH, C. W., History of Science
SMITH, M., Film Studies
WELCH, D. A., Modern European History
WELLER, S., Comparative Literature
WILLIAMSON, J., Reasoning, Inference and Scientific Method

Faculty of Sciences (School of Mathematics, Statistics and Actuarial Science, Univ. of Kent Canterbury, CT2 7NR; tel. (1227) 764000):

BOWMAN, H., Cognition and Logic (Computing)
BROWN, D., Structural Biology
BROWN, M., Actuarial Science
BROWN, P., Medieval English Literature
BROWN, P. J., Medical Statistics
BURCHELL, M., Space Sciences
CARPENTER, I., Human Ageing
CHADWICK, A. V., Physical Chemistry
CHADWICK, D., Informations Systems Security
CLARKSON, P., Mathematics
COLCHESTER, A. C. F., Clinical Neuroscience and Medical Image Computing
FAIRHURST, M. C., Computer Vision
FARRELL, P., Digital Communications
FINCHER, S., Computing Education
FLEISCHMAN, P., Mathematics
GEEVES, M. A., Physical Biochemistry
GRIFFIN, D., Genetics
GRIFFITHS, R., Biological Conservation
GULLICK, W., Cancer Biology
HONE, A., Mathematics
HOWARD, P., Ethnobotany
JACKSON, D. A., Applied Optics
JEFFRIES, P., Mycology
JONES, R., Computer Systems
KOLLING, M., Computer Science
KRSKA, J., Clinical and Professional Practice (Pharmacy)
MANDER, K., Computer Science
MANSFIELD, E., Mathematics
MATHIE, A., Pharmacology
MICHAELIS, M., Cell Biology
MORGAN, B. J. T., Applied Statistics
NEWPORT, R., Materials Physics
PODOLEANU, A., Biomedical Optics
RIDOUT, M., Applied Statistics

SMALES, M., Mammalian Cell Biotechnology
SMITH, M., Astrophysics
SPURGEON, S., Control Engineering
STRANGE, P., Actuarial Science
SWEETING, P., Actuarial Science
THOMPSON, S., Logic and Computation
TUITE, M., Molecular Biology
USHKARYOV, Y., Biological Sciences
WALKER, S., Statistics
WANG, J., Telecommunications
WANG, F., Future Computing
WARREN, M. J., Biochemistry
WAYMAN, J., Biometric Information Technology
WELCH, P. H., Parallel Computing
WENT, M., Forensic Science and Chemistry
YAN, Y., Electronic Instrumentation
ZHANG, J., Statistics

Faculty of Social Sciences (Marlowe Bldg, University of Kent, Canterbury, CT2 7NR; tel. (1227) 764000):

ABRAMS, W. D. J., Social Psychology
BALDOCK, J., Social Policy
BEECHAM, J., Health and Social Care Economics
BURGESS, M., Federal Studies
CALNAN, M., Sociology of Health Studies
CARRUTH, A., Economics
CHADHA, J., Economics
CONAGHAN, J., Law
COOPER, D., Law
COULTON, S., Health Services Research
CRISP, R., Psychology
DAVIDOVA, S., European Agricultural Policy
ELLEN, R. F., Anthropology and Human Ecology
EVANS, M. S., Women's Studies
FISCHER, M., Anthropological Sciences
FITZPATRICK, J., Law
FRASER, R., Economics
FUNNELL, W., Accounting and Finance
FUREDI, F., Sociology
GRIEF, N., Law
HALE, C., Criminology
HARROP, S., Wildlife Management Law
HEADY, C., Economics
HERMAN, D., Law
HOUSTON, D., Psychology
HOWARTH, W., Environmental Law
HUBBARD, P., Urban Studies
HUNTER, R., Law
IRELAND, P., Law
JOHNSTON, R., Cognitive Psychology
KERR, N., Psychology
KROLZIG, H., Economics
LEON-LEDESMA, M., Economics
LUI, S. W., Management Science and Computational Mathematics
MACMILLAN, D., Conservation and Applied Resource Economics
MANSELL, W., Law
MAR, M., Management Science
MIALL, A., International Relations
MOHR, A., Strategy (Business)
MURPHY, G., Applied Psychology of Learning Disability
NETTEN, A., Social Welfare
PHILLIPS, P., Strategic Management
RAMSAY, I., Law
RAY, L., Sociology
ROOTES, C., Environmental Politics and Political Sociology
RUBIN, G., Law
RUTLAND, A., Developmental Psychology
SAKWA, R., Russian and European Politics
SALHI, S., Management Science
SAMUEL, G., Law
SAYERS, J., Psychoanalytic Psychology
SAYERS, S., Philosophy
SCHEPEL, H., Law
SHAUGHNESSY, R., Theatre
SHELDON, S., Law
SHILLING, C., Sociology

STEPHENSON, G., Social Psychology
STEVENS, A., Criminal Justice
TAYLOR-GOOBY, P., Social Policy
THIRLWALL, A. P., Applied Economics
TUNARU, R., Quantitative Finance
TWIGG, J., Social Policy and Sociology
UGLOW, S., Criminal Justice
VICKERMAN, R. W., Regional and Transport Economics
VICKERSTAFF, S., Social Policy, Sociology, Social Research
WHITMAN, R., Politics and International Relations
WILLIAMS, T., Law
YOUNG, J., Sociology

UNIVERSITY OF LANCASTER

Univ. House, Lancaster, LA1 4YW
Telephone: (1524) 65201
E-mail: ugadmissions@lancaster.ac.uk
Internet: www.lancs.ac.uk

Founded 1964
Academic year: October to July

Chancellor: Sir CHRISTIAN BONINGTON
Pro-Chancellor: BRYAN GRAY
Vice-Chancellor: Prof. PAUL WELLINGS
Deputy Vice-Chancellor: Prof. ROBERT MCKINLAY
Pro-Vice-Chancellor for Colleges and Student Experience: Prof. AMANDA CHETWYND
Pro-Vice-Chancellor for Research: Prof. TREVOR J. MCMILLAN
Univ. Sec.: FIONA AIKEN
Librarian: CLARE POWNE

Library: see under Libraries and Archives
Number of teachers: 800
Number of students: 16,500

DEANS

Faculty of Arts and Social Sciences: Prof. TONY MCENERY
Faculty of Science and Technology: Prof. MARY SMYTH
School of Health and Medicine: Prof. TONY GATRELL
Management School: Prof. SUE COX

PROFESSORS

ACKROYD, S. C., Organizational Behaviour
ALDERSON, J. C., Linguistics and English Language Education
ALLSOP, D., Neuroscience
ARAUJO, L., Industrial Marketing
ARCHARD, D., Philosophy
ASTON, E., Theatre Studies
BARDGETT, R. D., Ecology
BARTON, D., Language and Literacy
BEVEN, K. J., Environmental Science
BINLEY, A., Hydrogeophysics
BLACKLER, F. H. M., Behaviour in Organizations
BLAIR, G. S., Distributed Systems
BLINKHORN, R. M., History
BLOOMFIELD, B., Organizational Behaviour
BRADLEY, S., Economics
BRAY, R. W., Music
BREMNER, J. G., Developmental Psychology
BURGOYNE, J. G., Management Learning
BYGATE, M., Linguistics
CARTER, R. G., Electronic Engineering
CHADWICK, R., Philosophy
CHAPMAN, G. P., Geography
CHETWYND, A. G., Mathematics and Statistics
CLARK, D., Medical Sociology
CLARKE, I., Marketing
COLLINSON, D., Management Learning
COULSON, G., Distributed Systems
COX, S. J., Safety and Risk Management
CROUCHLEY, R., Applied Statistics
DAVIES, N.A. J., Computing
DAVIES, W. J., Environmental Physiology
DAVISON, W., Environmental Chemistry
DENVER, D. T., Politics
DIGGLE, P. J., Mathematics and Statistics

DILLON, G. M., Politics
DIX, A., Computing
DUFFIELD, M., Politics
EASTERBY-SMITH, M. P. V., Management Learning
EASTON, G., Marketing
EMERSON, E., Clinical Psychology
EVANS, E. J., Social History
FAIRCLOUGH, N. L., Linguistics
FALKO, V., Condensed Matter Theory
FIDDLER, A., German and Austrian Studies
FILDES, R. A., Management Science
FINDLAY, A., Renaissance Drama
FORDE, B., Plant Biotechnology
FOX, S., Social and Management Learning
FRANCIS, B. J., Social Statistics
FRANKLIN, S., Sociology
GATRELL, A. C., Health
GELLERSEN, H.-W., Computing
GRAHAM, H., Social Policy
HAMILTON, M. E., Adult Learning and Literacy
HANLEY, K. A., English Literature
HARMAN, P. M., History of Science
HATTON, C. R., Psychology, Health and Social Care
HEELAS, P. L. F., Religion and Modernity
HENDERSON, R., Biostatistics
HETHERINGTON, A. M., Plant Cell Physiology
HEWITT, C. N., Atmospheric Chemistry
HONARY, B., Communications Engineering
HONARY, F., Space Plasma and Radio Science
HOPKINS, J. B., Psychology
HUGHES, J. A., Sociological Analysis
HUTCHISON, D., Computing
INTRONA, L., Organization, Technology and Ethics
IVANIC, R., Linguistics and Education
JESSOP, R. D., Sociology
JOHNES, G., Economics
JOHNSON, K., Linguistics and Language Education
JONES, K. C., Environmental Chemistry and Ecotoxicology
KATAMBA, F. X., Linguistics
KIRBY, M. W., Economic History
KRIER, A., Semiconductor Physics
KUHN, A. F., Film Studies
LAMBERT, C. J., Theoretical Condensed Matter Physics
LAMBRECHT, B. M., Accounting and Finance
LAW, J., Sociology
LEA, P. J., Biological Sciences
LEWIS, C. N., Family and Developmental Psychology
LYTH, D., Astro-Particle Physics
MACDONALD, R., Environmental Science
MAHER, B., Geography
MAY-CHAHAL, C., Applied Social Science
MCCLINTOCK, P. V. E., Physics
MCENERY, A. M., English Language and Linguistics
MCMILLAN, T. J., Cancer Biology
MCNEILL, M., Women's Studies and Cultural Studies
MORRIS, P. E., Psychology
MULLETT, M. A. A., Cultural and Religious History
NIEDUSZYNSKI, I. A., Connective Tissue Biochemistry
O'HANLAN, J. F., Finance
O'NEILL, J. F., Philosophy
ORMEROD, T., Cognitive Psychology
OTLEY, D. T., Accounting and Finance
PAYNE, J. P., German Studies
PEARCE, L., Literary Theory and Women's Writing
PEASNELL, K. V., Accounting and Finance
PENN, R. D., Economic Sociology and Statistics
PERCY, K. A., Adult Continuing Education
PICCIOTTO, S., Law
PICKETT, G. R., Low-Temperature Physics
PIDD, M., Management Science
PINKERTON, H., Physical Volcanology
POOLEY, C. G., Geography

POPAY, J., Social and Public Health
POPE, P. F., Accounting and Finance
POWER, S. C., Mathematics
RATOFF, P. N., Experimental Particle Physics
READER, I. J., Religious Studies
REYNOLDS, P. M., Management Learning
RICHARDS, J. M., Cultural History
RICHARDSON, A. M. D., Microsystems Engineering
ROBERTS, G., Mathematics
RODWELL, J. S., Plant Ecology
ROGERS, C. G., Educational Research
ROSE, M., Entrepreneurship
ROTHSCHILD, R., Economics
ROWE, P., Law
SAUNDERS, M. S., Evaluation in Education and Work
SAYER, R. A., Sociology
SEGAL, R., Theories of Religion
SEWARD, D. W., Engineering Design
SHAPIRO, D. Z., Sociology
SHORT, M. H., Linguistics
SIEWIERSKA, A. M., Linguistics
SMITH, D. B., Criminology
SMITH, L., Educational Research
SMYTH, M. M., Experimental Psychology
SOMMERVILLE, I. F., Computing
SOOTHILL, K. L., Social Research
STACEY, J., Women's Studies and Cultural Studies
STRINGER, K. J., Medieval British History
SUCHMAN, L., Sociology
SUGARMAN, D., Law
TAWN, J. A., Statistics
TAYLOR, J., Economics
TAYLOR, S. J., Finance
THORPE, D. H., Applied Social Science
TIHANOV, G., Comparative Literature
TROWLER, P., Higher Education
TUCKER, R. W., Mathematical Physics
TURVEY, G. J., Engineering Mechanics
URRY, J. R., Sociology
WEBER, C. L., Politics
WHITELEY, N. S., Visual Arts
WHITTAKER, J. B., Biological Sciences
WHITTON, D. W., French Theatre
WHYTE, I. D., Historical Geography
WIGMORE, J. K., Condensed Matter Physics
WILSON, L., Environmental Science
WILSON, R. F., Renaissance Studies
WISE, S., Social Justice
WYNNE, B. E., Science Studies
XYDEAS, C. S., Communications Engineering
YADAV, P. K., Accounting and Finance

UNIVERSITY OF LEEDS

Leeds, LS2 9JT

Telephone: (113) 243-1751
E-mail: enquiry@leeds.ac.uk
Internet: www.leeds.ac.uk

Founded 1874 as Yorkshire College of Science, Univ. Charter 1904
Academic year: September to June

Chancellor: Lord BRAGG
Pro-Chancellor: LINDA POLLARD
Vice-Chancellor: Prof. MICHAEL ARTHUR
Deputy Vice-Chancellor: Prof. JOHN FISHER
Pro-Vice-Chancellor for Int. Partnerships: Prof. RICHARD WILLIAMS
Pro-Vice-Chancellor for Research and Innovation: Prof. ANDREW THOMPSON
Pro-Vice-Chancellor for Staff: Prof. STEPHEN SCOTT
Pro-Vice-Chancellor for Student Education: Prof. VIVIEN JONES
Sec: ROGER GAIR
Librarian and Keeper of Brotherton Colln: MARGARET COUTTS

Library: see under Libraries and Archives
Number of students: 32,500

DEANS

Faculty of Arts: Prof. FRANK FINLAY

Faculty of Biological Sciences: Prof. STEVE HOMANS

Faculty of Business: Prof. PETER MOIZER

Faculty of Education, Social Sciences and Law: Prof. JEREMY HIGHAM (acting)

Faculty of Engineering: Prof. PETER JIMACK

Faculty of Environment: Prof. JANE FRANCIS

Faculty of Mathematics and Physical Sciences: Prof. MICHAEL WILSON

Faculty of Medicine and Health: Prof. PETER McWILLIAM

Faculty of Performance, Visual Arts and Communications: Prof. DAVID COOPER

PROFESSORS

Faculty of Arts:

AGIUS, D. A., Arabic and Islamic Material Culture

ATACK, M. K., French

BLACK, R. D., Renaissance History

BROCK, R. W., Renaissance History

BUTLER, M. H., Renaissance Drama

CANTOR, G. N., History of Science

CHARTRES, J. A., Social and Economic History

CHILDS, J. C. R., Military History

DIXON, S. M., Modern History

ELLIOTT, J. K., New Testament Textual Criticism

FAIRER, D., 18th-Century English Literature

FINLAY, F. J., German

FRENCH, S. R. D., Philosophy of Science

GARNER, P., Spanish

GIDLEY, CM., American Literature

GOOCH, J., International History

HAMMOND, P., 17th-Century English Literature

HARTLEY, T., Translation Studies

HEATH, M. F., Greek Language and Literature

HILL, J., Visiting Professor

HOLMES, D., French

HUGGAN, G., Commonwealth and Postcolonial Literatures

JOHNSON, S., Linguistics

JONES, V., 18th-Century Gender and Culture

KILLICK, R., Quebec Studies and 19th-Century French Studies

KING, V. T., South-East Asian Studies

KNIGHT, R. A., Language Centre

KNOTT, K., Religious Studies

KOCIENSKI, P., Chemistry

LARRISSY, E., English Literature

LEVENE, D. S., Latin Language and Literature

LINDLEY, D., Renaissance Literature

LOOSELY, D. L., Contemporary French Culture

LOUD, G. A., Medieval Italian History

MALTBY, R., Latin Philology

McFADYEN, A. I., Theology and Religious Studies

MORRIS, R. H., Medieval Studies

NAGIB, L., Centenary Professor of World History

NELSON, M. T., Philosophy

NETTON, I. R., Arabic Studies

PLATTEN, D. P., French

POIDEVIN, R. LE, Metaphysics

RICHARDSON, B. F., Italian

SILVERMAN, M., Modern French Studies

SIMONS, P. M., Philosophy

SPIERS, E. M., Strategic Studies

SUTTON, J. F., Russian

TABERNER, S. J., German

TOLLIDAY, S. W., Economic History

WAWN, A., Anglo-Icelandic Studies

WILLIAMS, M. B., East Asian Studies

WILSON, K. M., International Politics

WOOD, I. N., Early Medieval History

Faculty of Biological Sciences:

ALEXANDER, R. M., Biology

ALTRINGHAM, J. D., Biomechanics

ATKINSON, H. J., Nematology

BALDWIN, S. A., Biochemistry

BAUMBERG, S., Bacterial Genetics

BEECH, D. J., Cellular and Molecular Physiology

BENTON, T. G., Population Ecology

BOOTH, A. G., Online Learning

BROWN, S. B., Biochemistry

BUCKLEY, N. J., Neuroscience

CARDING, S., Molecular Immunology

CHOPRA, I., Microbiology

FINDLAY, J. B. C., Biochemistry

FORBES, J. M., Agricultural Sciences

GILMARTIN, P. M., Plant Molecular Genetics

HANDYSIDE, A., Developmental Biology

HENDERSON, P. J. F., Biochemistry and Molecular Biology

HOLDEN, A. V., Computational Biology

HOLLAND, K. T., Microbiology

HOMANS, S. W., Structural Biology

HOOPER, N. M., Biochemistry

HUGHES, I. E., Pharmacology Education

INGHAM, E., Medical Immunology

ISAAC, R. E., Comparative Biochemistry

KILLINGTON, R. A., Virology Education

KRAUSE, J., Behavioural Ecology

McPHERSON, M. J., Biochemistry and Molecular Biology

MEYER, P., Plant Genetics

ORCHARD, C. H., Physiology

PHILLIPS, S. E. V., Biophysics

RADFORD, S. E., Structural Molecular Biology

RAYNER, J. M. V., Zoology

ROBERTSON, B., Neurobiology

ROWLANDS, D. J., Molecular Virology

SHORROCKS, B., Population Biology

SMITH, J. E., Parasitology

STOCKLEY, P. G., Biological Chemistry

TRINICK, J. A., Animal Cell Biology

TURNER, A. J., Biochemistry

WARD, S. A., Sport and Exercises

WILCOX, M. H., Medical Microbiology

WITHINGTON, D. J., Auditory Neuroscience

WOOD, E. J., Biochemistry

WRAY, D. A., Pharmacology

YATES, M. S., Biomedical Sciences

Faculty of Earth and Environment:

ALEXANDER, R. M., Biology

BAILEY, A. J., Population Geography

BELL, M., Traffic and Environmental Pollution

BEST, J. L., Process Sedimentology

BONSALL, P. W., Transport Planning

CARSTEN, O., Transport Safety

CLARKE, G. P., Business Geography

CLARKE, M. C., Geographic Modelling

FAIRHEAD, J. D., Applied Geophysics

FORBES, R. D., Business Geography

FRANCIS, J. E., Paleoclimatology

GUBBINS, D., Geophysics

HAISEMAN, G. A., Geophysics

KNEALE, P. E., Applied Hydrology

KNIPE, R. J., Structural Geology

KROM, M. D., Marine and Environmental Geochemistry

LLOYD, J. J., Centenary Professor of Earth Science Systems

McDONALD, A. T., Environmental Management

MACKIE, P. J., Transport Studies

MAY, A. D., Transport Engineering

MOBBS, S. D., Atmospheric Dynamics

NASH, C. A., Transport Economics

RAISWELL, R. W., Sedimentary Geochemistry

REES, P. H., Population Geography

SMITH, M. H., Atmospheric Physics

SMITH, N. J., Project and Transport Infrastructure Management (joint post with Faculty of Engineering)

STILLWELL, J. C. H., Migration and Regional Development

TZEDAKIS, P. C., Quarternary Earth System History

VALENTINE, G., Human Geography

WATLING, D., Centenary Professor of Transport Analysis

WILSON, B. M., Igneous Petrogenesis

YARDLEY, B. W. D., Metamorphic Geochemistry

Faculty of Education, Social Sciences and Law:

ACKERS, H. L., European Law

BAGGULEY, P., Sociology and Social Policy

BARNES, C., Disability Studies

BATES, I., Education and Work

BAYNHAM, M. J., TESOL

BELL, D. S., French Government and Politics

BLUTH, C., International Studies

CAMERON, L. J., Applied Linguistics

CHASE, M. S., Continuing Education

CRAWFORD, T. A., Criminology and Criminal Justice

DEACON, A. J., Social Policy

DONNELLY, J. F., Science Education

HALSON, D. R., Law

HODKINSON, P. M., Lifelong Learning

KEAY, A., Corporate and Commercial Law

KERR, A., Sociology

LEACH, J., Science Education

LODGE, J., European Studies

McCARGO, D., Politics and International Studies

McMULLEN, J., Labour Law

ORMEROD, D., Law

OSLER, A. H., Education

PEARSON, R., Development Studies

RADICE, H. K., International Political Economy

ROSENEIL, S., Sociology and Gender Studies

SCOTT, P., Science Education

SHORROCKS-TAYLOR, D., Assessment and Evaluation in Education

SUBEDI, S. P., International Law

SUGDEN, D. A., Special Needs in Education

THEAKSTON, K., British Government

VINCENT-JONES, P., Law

WALKER, C. P., Criminal Justice

WALL, D. S., Legal History

WILLIAMS, F., Social Policy

ZUKAS, M., Adult Education

Faculty of Engineering:

ANDREWS, G. E., Combustion Engineering

BARTON, D. C., Solid Mechanics

BELL, A. J., Electronic Materials

BERZINS, M., Scientific Computation

BIGGS, S. R., Particle Science and Technology

BONSALL, P. W., Transport Planning

BOYLE, R. D., Computing

BRADLEY, D., Mechanical Engineering

BRODLIE, K. W., Visualization

CHILDS, T. H. C., Manufacturing Engineering

COHN, A. G., Automated Reasoning

DAVIES, A. G., Electronic and Photonic Engineering

DE PENNINGTON, A., Computer-aided Engineering

DEW, P. M., Computer Science

DOWSON, D., Mechanical Engineering

DYER, M. E., Theoretical Computer Science

EDMONDS, D. V., Metallurgy

FAIRWEATHER, R. M., Thermofluids and Combustion

FISHER, J., Mechanical Engineering

GASKELL, P. H., Fluid Mechanics

GHADIRI, M., Chemical Engineering

HARRISON, P. H., Quantum Electronics

HOGG, D. C., Artificial Intelligence

HOWES, M. J., Electronic Engineering

HOYLE, B. S., Vision and Image Systems

HUNTER, I. C., Microwave Signal Processing

JHA, A., Applied Materials Science

JIMACK, P., Scientific Computing

JIN, Z. M., Computational Biomechanics/Bioengineering
LINFIELD, E., Terahertz Electronics
MARA, D. D., Civil Engineering
MARKARIAN, G., Communication Systems
MCINTOSH, A. C., Thermodynamics and Combustion Theory
MILES, R. E., Semiconductor Electronics
NEVILLE, A., Engineering Tribology
PAGE, C. L., Civil Engineering Materials
POLLARD, R. D., High-Frequency Measurements
POURKASHANIAN, M., High-Temperature Combustion Processes
PRIEST, M., Engineering Tribology
RAND, B., Ceramics
RHODES, J. D., Electronic and Electrical Engineering
ROBERTS, K. J., Chemical Engineering
ROBERTSON, I. D., Centenary Professor of Microwave and Millimetre Wave Circuits
SHEPPARD, C. G. W., Applied Thermodynamics and Combustion Science
SMITH, N. J., Project and Transport Infrastructure Management (joint position with Transport Studies)
VIRK, G. S., Robotics and Control
WILLIAMS, P. T., Environmental Engineering
WILLIAMS, R. A., Mineral and Process Engineering
XU, J., Computing

Faculty of Mathematics and Physical Sciences:

BATCHELDER, D. N., Physics
BEDDARD, G., Chemical Physics
BLOOR, M. I. G., Applied Mathematics
BODEN, N., Physical Chemistry
BRINDLEY, J., Applied Mathematics
COOPER, S. B., Pure Mathematics
CRAWLEY-BOEVEY, W. W., Pure Mathematics
CYWINSKI, R., Experimental Physics
DALES, H. G., Pure Mathematics
DICKINSON, E., Food Colloids
DYSON, J. E., Astronomy
EVANS, S. D., Molecular and Nanoscale Physics
FALLE, S. A. E. G., Astrophysical Fluid Dynamics
FORDY, A. P., Nonlinear Mathematics
GREIG, D., Physics
GRIFFITHS, J. F., Functional Dye Chemistry
GRIGG, R. E., Organic Chemistry
GUTHRIE, J. T., Polymer and Surface Coatings, Science and Technology
HAMLEY, I. W., Polymer Materials
HARTQUIST, T. W., Astrophysics
HEARD, D. E., Atmospheric Chemistry
HICKEY, B., Physics
HILLAS, A. M., Physics
HUGHES, D. W., Applied Mathematics
INGHAM, D. B., Applied Mathematics
JOHNSON, A. P., Computational Chemistry
KENNEDY, J. D., Inorganic Chemistry
KENT, J. T., Statistics
KOCIEŃSKI, P. J., Organic Chemistry
LANCE, E. C., Pure Mathematics
LAWRIE, I. D., Theoretical Physics
LEWIS, D. M., Colour Chemistry
LUO, M. R., Colour and Imaging Science
MACPHERSON, H. D., Pure Mathematics
MARDIA, K. V., Applied Statistics
MCLEISH, T. C. B., Polymer Physics
MERKIN, J. H., Applied Mathematics
MIKHAILOV, A. V., Mathematical Physics
MORGAN, G. J., Theoretical Physics
MORGAN, M. R., Food Biochemistry
NIJHOFF, F. W., Mathematical Physics
PARTINGTON, J. R., Pure Mathematics
PILLING, M. J., Physical Chemistry
POVEY, M. J. W., Food Physics
RATHJEN, M., Pure Mathematics
READ, C. J., Pure Mathematics

ROBINSON, D. S., Food Science
ROBSON, J. C., Pure Mathematics
SAVAGE, M. D., Thin Liquid Films and Coatings
SCOTT, S. K., Mathematical Chemistry
SLEEMAN, B. D., Applied Mathematics
TAYLOR, C. C., Statistics
TRUSS, J. K., Pure Mathematics
VEDRAL, V., Centenary Professor of Quantum Information Science
VERETENNIKOV, A. Y., Statistics
WAINER, S. S., Pure Mathematics
WARD, I. M., Physics
WATSON, A. A., Physics
WEDZICHA, B. L., Food Science
WHITAKER, B. J., Chemical Physics
WILSON, M. J., Applied Mathematics
WOOD, J. C., Pure Mathematics

Faculty of Medicine and Health:

ADAMS, C., Adult Psychiatry and Mental Health Services Research
ALIMO-METCALFE, B. M., Leadership Studies
BALL, S. G., Cardiology
BARKHAM, M., Clinical and Counselling Psychology
BIRD, H. A., Pharmacological Rheumatology
BISHOP, T., Genetic Epidemiology
BLUNDELL, J. E., Psychobiology
BONIFER, C., Experimental Haematology
BONTHRON, D. T., Molecular Medicine
BOYLSTON, A. W., Pathology
BRUNTON, P. A., Restorative Dentistry
CADE, J., Nutritional Epidemiology and Public Health
CHEATER, F., Public Health Nursing
CLEREHUGH, M. A., Periodontology
CLOSS, J., Nursing Research
COTTRELL, D. J., Child and Adolescent Psychiatry
CUCKLE, H. S., Reproductive Epidemiology
DICKSON, R. A., Orthopaedic Surgery
DRIFE, J. O., Obstetrics and Gynaecology
DUGGAL, M. S., Child Dental Health
EMERY, P., Rheumatology
FORMAN, D., Cancer Epidemiology
GIANNOUDIS, P. P., Orthopaedic Surgery
GRANT, P. J., Molecular Vascular Medicine
GREEN, A., International Health Planning
GUILLOU, P. J., Surgery
HALE, C., Clinical Nursing
HALL, A. S., Clinical Cardiology
HANBY, A. M., Breast Pathology
HAWARD, R., Cancer Studies
HAY, A., Environmental Toxicology
HEWISON, J., Healthcare Psychology
HEYWOOD, P. L., Primary Care
HILLHOUSE, E., Dean of the School of Medicine and Health
HOPKINS, P. M., Anaesthesia
HOUSE, A. O., Liaison Psychiatry
HOWDLE, P. D., Clinical Education
HULL, M. A., Molecular Gastroenterology
HUME, W. J., Oral Pathology
INGLEHEARN, C., Molecular Ophthalmology
KAPLAN, R. S., Clinical Cancer Studies
KEEN, J., Health Politics and Information Management
KELLETT, M., Restorative Dentistry
KIRKHAM, J., Oral Biology
KNOWLES, M., Experimental Cancer Research
LEVENE, M. I., Paediatrics and Child Health
LONG, A., Health Systems Research
MACLENNAN, K., Tumour Pathology
MARKHAM, A. F., Medicine
MARSH, P. D., Oral Microbiology
MCDERMOTT, M., Experimental Rheumatology
MCGONAGLE, D., Investigative Rheumatology
MCMAHON, M. J., Surgery

MCWILLIAM, P. N., Cardiovascular Physiology
MORLEY, S. J., Clinical Psychology
MURDOCH-EATON, D., Medical Education
PEERS, C. S., Cellular Physiology
QUIRKE, P., Pathology
RAYNOR, D. K., Pharmacy Practice, Medicine and its Users
ROBERTS, T. E., Medical Education
ROBINSON, C., Oral Biology
RODGERS, R. J., Behavioural Pharmacology
SANDLE, G. I., Clinical Science
SELBY, P. J., Cancer Medicine
SEYMOUR, M., Gastro-intestinal Medicine
TENNANT, A., Rehabilitation Studies
TWELVES, C. J., Clinical Pharmacology and Oncology
WALKER, J. J., Obstetrics and Gynaecology
WILD, C., Molecular Epidemiology
WILLIAMS, S. A., Oral Health Services Research
WISTOW, G., Health and Social Care
WOOD, D. J, Dental Materials
WOOD, E. J., Biochemistry

Faculty of Performance, Visual Arts and Communications:

BARBER, G. D., Performance Studies (Music)
BOON, R., Performance Studies
BROWN, C., Applied Musicology
BROWN, R. C. M., International Communications
BURKINSHAW, S. M., Textile Chemistry
CASSIDY, T., Design
COOPER, D. G., Music
DANIELS, S. M., Performance and Cultural Industries
GREEN, V., Fine Art, Film and Media
HANN, M. A., Design Theory
HAY, K. G., Contemporary Art Practice
HILL, D., Fine Art
LAWRENCE, C. A., Textile Engineering
MCQUILLAN, M., Fine Art, History of Art and Cultural Studies
MORRISON, D. E., Communications Research
ORTON, L. F., Art History and Theory
PALMER, R., Fine Art
POLLOCK, G. F. S., Social and Critical Histories of Art
RASTALL, G. R., Historical Musicology
TAYLOR, P. M., International Communications
WALLIS, M., Performance and Culture
WESTLAND, S., Colour Science and Technology

Leeds University Business School:

BUCKLEY, P. J., International Business
CLEGG, L. J., European Integration and International Business Management
COLLINS, M., Financial History
GERRARD, W. J., Sport Management and Finance
HAYES, J., Management Studies
HILLIER, D., Financial Markets
HODGKINSON, G. P., Organizational Behaviour and Strategic Management
KATSIKEAS, C. S., Marketing and International Management
KEASEY, K., Financial Services
LOCK, A. R., Marketing and Business Administration
MACKIE, P. J., Transport Studies
MAULE, A. J., Human Decisions
MCNULTY, T. H., Management and Governance
MICHELL, P. C. N., Marketing and Communications
MOIZER, P., Accounting
NASH, C. A., Transport Economics
NOLAN, P. J., Industrial Relations
OAKLAND, J. S., Business Excellence and Quality Management
PEARMAN, A. D., Management Decision Analysis

PÉROTIN, V., Economics
SAWYER, M. C., Economics
SCHENK-HOPPÉ, K. R., Renaissance History
SHIN, Y., Applied Econometrics
STUART, M., Human Resources Management and Employment Relations
THORPE, R., Management Development
WILSON, N., Credit Management

UNIVERSITY OF LEICESTER

University Rd, Leicester, LE1 7RH
Telephone: (116) 252-2522
Internet: www.le.ac.uk
Founded 1918 as Univ. College, Charter 1950, Univ. Charter 1957
Academic year: September to June
Visitor: HER MAJESTY THE QUEEN
Chancellor: (vacant)
Pro-Chancellor: (vacant)
Pro-Chancellor: P. BATEMAN
Vice-Chancellor: Prof. Sir R. G. BURGESS
Sr Pro-Vice-Chancellor: Prof. M. P. THOMPSON
Pro-Vice-Chancellor: C. FYFE
Pro Vice-Chancellor: Prof. K. SCHÜRER
Registrar and Sec.: D. E. HALL
Head of Library Services: L. JONES

Library: see under Libraries and Archives
Number of teachers: 750 full-time
Number of students: 23,000

Publications: *Graduates' Review* (1 a year), *Insider*, *LE1* (2 a year)

PRO-VICE-CHANCELLORS AND HEADS OF COLLEGE

College of Arts, Humanities and Law: Prof. D. TALLACK
College of Medicine, Biological Sciences and Psychology: Prof. D. WYNFORD-THOMAS
College of Science and Engineering: Prof. M. BARSTOW
College of Social Sciences: Prof. E. MURPHY

PROFESSORS

College of Arts, Humanities and Law (tel. (116) 252-2679; e-mail kxb@le.ac.uk; internet www2.le.ac.uk/colleges/artshumlaw):

FOXHALL, L., Ancient History
HOUSLEY, N. J., History
MATTINGLY, D. J., Roman Archaeology
SHIPLEY, D. G. J., Ancient History
STANNARD, M. J., Modern English Literature
WOOD, S., Modern Languages

College of Medicine, Biological Sciences and Psychology (tel. (116) 252-2969; e-mail med-admis@le.ac.uk; internet www.le.ac.uk/medicine):

ABRAMS, K. R., Epidemiology and Public Health
ANDREW, P. W., Microbial Pathogenesis
BAKER, R. H., Quality in Health Care
BRUGHA, T. S., Psychiatry
BURTON, P. R., Genetic Epidemiology
COLMAN, A. M., Psychology
DAVIES, M., Diabetes Medicine
DYER, M. J. S., Pathology
EPERON, I. C., Biochemistry
FIELD, D. J., Neonatal Medicine
FORSYTHE, I. D., Neuroscience
GOTTLOB, I., Ophthalmology
HESLOP-HARRISON, J. S., Plant Cell Biology, Molecular Cytogenetics
HOLLIN, C. R., Criminological Psychology
Sir JEFFREYS, A., Genetics
JONES, D. R., Medical Statistics
KETLEY, J. M., Genetics
KYRIACOU, C. P., Behavioural Genetics
LONDON, N. J. M., Surgery
MELLON, J. K., Urology
NG, L. L., Medicine and Therapeutics
NICHOLSON, K. G., Infectious Diseases
NICHOLSON, M. L., Transplant Surgery
O'CALLAGHAN, C. L. P., Paediatrics

PANERAI, R. B., Physiological Measurement
PETERSEN, S. A., Medical Education
ROBERTS G. C. K., Biochemistry
ROWBOTHAM, D. J., Anaesthesia and Pain Management
RUTTY, G. N., Forensic Pathology
SAMANI, N. J., Cardiovascular Medicine
STEWARD, W. P., Oncology
THOMPSON, J. R., Ophthalmology
TWELL, D., Plant Biology
VOSTANIS, P., Child and Adolescent Psychiatry
WARDLAW, A. J., Respiratory Medicine
WILLIAMS, B., Medicine
WOODS, K. L., Therapeutics

College of Science and Engineering (tel. (116) 252-5012; e-mail science@le.ac.uk; internet www.le.ac.uk/science):

BINNS, C., Physics and Astronomy
BRADSHAW, M. J., Human Geography
COWLEY, S. W. H., Solar-Planetary Physics
CULLIS, P. M., Organic Chemistry
FISHER, P. F., Geographical Information
FOTHERGILL, J. C., Engineering
FRASER, G. W., Detector Physics
HILLMAN, A. R., Physical Chemistry
HOPE, E. G., Inorganic Chemistry
KING, A. R., Astrophysics
LESTER, M., Physics and Astronomy
LOVELL, M. A., Petrophysics
NORRIS, C., Surface Physics
PAN, J., Mechanics and Materials
PARRISH, R. R., Isotope Geology
RAMAN, R., Computer Science
ROBINSON, T. R., Space Plasma Physics
SAUNDERS, A. D., Geochemistry
THOMAS, R. M., Mathematics and Computer Science
WARWICK, R. S., X-Ray Astronomy

College of Social Sciences (tel. (116) 252-2842; e-mail socsci@le.ac.uk; internet www.le.ac.uk/socsci):

BURRELL, G., Organization Theory
CHAREMZA, W., Economics
DEMETRIADES, P. O., Financial Economics
FRASER, C. D., Economics
JACKSON, P. M., Economics; Public Sector Economics
SNELL, K. D. M., English Local History

School of Law (tel. (116) 252-2363; e-mail law@le.ac.uk; internet www.le.ac.uk/law):

CLARKSON, C. M. V., Law
GRAHAM, C., Law
SHAW, M. N., International Law
SZYSZCZAK, E. M., Competition and Labour Law
WHITE, R. C. A., Law

UNIVERSITY OF LINCOLN

Brayford Pool, Lincoln, LN6 7TS
Telephone: (1522) 882000
E-mail: enquiries@lincoln.ac.uk
Internet: www.lincoln.ac.uk
Founded 1861 as School of Art and Design; as Humberside College of Higher Education 1978; Humberside Polytechnic 1990; University of Humberside 1992; University of Lincolnshire and Humberside 1996; incorporated Lincoln School of Art and Lincolnshire School of Agriculture 2001; present name and status 2001
Vice-Chancellor: Prof. MARY STUART
Sr Deputy Vice-Chancellor for Research, Innovation and Enterprise: Prof. ANDREW ATHERTON
Deputy Vice-Chancellor for Devt: Dr FRANCES MANNSAKER
Deputy Vice-Chancellor for Teaching Quality and Student Experience: Prof. SCOTT DAVIDSON
Registrar: EDMUND FITZPATRICK

Dir of Learning Support: MICHELLE ANDERSON

Library of 240,000 vols, 1,000 periodicals
Number of teachers: 570
Number of students: 10,680

Publications: *Institute of Communication Ethics* (4 a year), *Lincoln Magazine*

DEANS

Faculty of Agriculture, Food and Animal Sciences: VAL BRAYBROOKS
Faculty of Art, Architecture and Design: Prof. NORMAN CHERRY
Faculty of Business and Law: Prof. DAVID HEAD
Faculty of Health, Life and Social Science: Prof. SARA OWEN
Faculty of Media, Humanities and Technology: Prof. DAVID SLEIGHT

UNIVERSITY OF LIVERPOOL

Liverpool, L69 3BX
Telephone: (151) 794-2000
Internet: www.liv.ac.uk
Founded 1882, as Univ. College, Royal Charter 1903

Chancellor: Prof. Sir DAVID KING
Pro-Chancellor: Prof. JAMES KEATON
Vice-Chancellor: Prof. Sir HOWARD NEWBY
Deputy Vice-Chancellor: Prof. JON SAUNDERS
Exec. Pro-Vice-Chancellor: Prof. ANDREW DERRINGTON
Exec. Pro-Vice-Chancellor: Prof. STEPHEN HOLLOWAY
Exec. Pro-Vice-Chancellor: Prof. IAN GREER
Pro-Vice-Chancellor for Int. Affairs: Prof. MICHAEL HOEY
Pro-Vice-Chancellor for Student Experience: Prof. KELVIN EVEREST
Registrar: M. D. CARR
Librarian: PHILIP SYKES

Library: see under Libraries and Archives
Number of teachers: 1,400
Number of students: 18,000

Publications: *Bulletin of Hispanic Studies* (4 a year), *Third World Planning Review* (4 a year), *Town Planning Review* (4 a year)

PROFESSORS

Faculty of Arts:

BATE, A. J., English Literature
BELCHEM, J. C., History
CLARK, S. R. L., Philosophy
DAVIES, J. K., Ancient History and Classical Archaeology
ELLIOTT, M., Irish Studies
EVEREST, K. D., Modern English
FISHER, J. R., Latin-American History
FORSDICK, C., French
GASKIN, R. M., Philosophy
GOWLETT, J. A. J., Archaeology, Classics and Oriental Studies
HIGGINS, J., Latin American Literature
HOEY, M. P., English Language
LEE, W. R., Economic and Social History
MEE, C., Archaeology, Classics and Oriental Studies
MILLARD, A. R., Hebrew and Ancient Semitic Languages
MILLS, A. D., English Language and Literature
SAUL, N. D. B., German
SEED, D., English
SEVERIN, D. S., Spanish
SHAW, J., Archaeology, Classics and Oriental Studies
SLATER, E. A., Archaeology
STAFFORD, P. A., History
TALBOT, M. O., Music
WRIGHT, R. H. P., Hispanic Studies

Faculty of Engineering:

BACON, D. J., Materials Science and Engineering
BUNGEY, J. H., Civil Engineering
BURROWS, R., Environmental Hydraulics
CANTWELL, W. J., Engineering
CHALKER, P. R., Engineering
ECCLESTON, W., Electronic Engineering
ESCUDIER, M. P., Mechanical Engineering
FANG, M. T. C., Applied Electromagnetism
GOODHEW, P. J., Materials Engineering
HALL, S., Electrical Engineering and Electronics
HON, K. K. B., Manufacturing Systems
JONES, G. R., Electrical Engineering and Electronics
JONES, N., Mechanical Engineering
LUCAS, J., Electrical Engineering and Electronics
MOTTERSHEAD, J. E., Applied Mechanics
NANDI, A. K., Electrical Engineering and Electronics
OWEN, I., Mechanical Engineering
PADFIELD, G. D., Engineering
POND, R. C., Materials Science and Engineering
TATLOCK, G. J., Engineering
WATKINS, K. G., Engineering
WU, Q. H., Electrical Engineering

Faculty of Medicine:

ASHFORD, R. W., Parasite and Vector Biology
BACK, D. J., Pharmacology and Therapeutics
BURGOYNE, R. D., Physiology
CALVERLEY, P. M. A., Rehabilitation Medicine
CAPEWELL, S. J., Public Health
CARTY, H. M. L., Paediatric Radiology
CAWLEY, J. C., Haematology
CHADWICK, D. W., Neurology
COOKE, R. W. I., Paediatric Medicine
DIMALINE, R., Physiology
DOCKRAY, G. J., Physiology
DOWRICK, C. F., Primary Care
EMBERY, G., Clinical Dental Sciences
FIELD, J. K., Molecular Oncology
FOSTER, C. S., Pathology
FRASER, W. D., Clinical Chemistry
FROSTICK, S. P., Orthopaedics
GALLAGHER, J. A., Human Anatomy and Cell Biology
GARNER, P. A., Tropical Medicine
GOSDEN, C. M., Medical Genetics
GOWERS, S. G., Adolescent Psychiatry
GRIERSON, I., Experimental Ophthalmology
GRIFFITHS, R. D., Medicine
HART, C. A., Medical Microbiology
HART, G., Medicine
HILL, J., Child and Development Psychiatry
HOMMEL, M., Tropical Medicine
HUNTER, J. M., Anaesthesia
JACKSON, M. J., Cellular Pathophysiology
JOHNSON, P. M., Immunology
KROEGER, A., International Community Health
LEUWER, M., Anaesthesia
LLOYD, D. A., Paediatric Surgery
MOLYNEUX, M. E., Tropical Medicine
MORRISS, R. K., Psychiatry
NEILSON, J. P., Obstetrics and Gynaecology
NEOPTOLEMOS, J. P., Surgery
NURMIKKO, T. J., Neurology
PARK, B. K., Pharmacology and Therapeutics
PETERSEN, O. H., Physiology
PINE, C. M., Clinical Dental Sciences
PIRMOHAMED, M., Pharmacology and Therapeutics
QUINN, J. P., Human Anatomy and Cell Biology
RHODES, J. M., Medicine
ROBERTS, J. N., Magnetic Resonance
SALMON, P., Clinical Psychology
SCOTT, J., Oral Diseases
SHENKIN, A., Clinical Chemistry
SMYTH, R. L., Child Health
STEWART, J. P., Medical Microbiology
TEPIKIN, A. V., Physiology
THEAKSTON, R. D. G., Tropical Medicine
TOWNSON, H., Medical Entomology
TRAYHURN, P., Medicine
TREES, A. J., Tropical Medicine
VARRO, A., Physiology
WALLEY, T. J., Clinical Pharmacology
WARD, S., Tropical Medicine
WARENIUS, H. M., Research Oncology
WARNKE, P. C., Neurology
WATSON, A. J. M., Medicine
WATTS, A., Restorative Dentistry
WEINDLING, A. M., Child Health
WHITEHEAD, M. M., Public Health
WILKINSON, D. G., Liaison Psychiatry
WILLIAMS, D. F., Clinical Engineering
WILLIAMS, G., Medicine
WILSON, K. C. M., Psychiatry of Old Age
WINSTANLEY, P. A., Pharmacology and Therapeutics
WRAY, S. C., Physiology

Faculty of Science:

ALLPORT, P., Physics
APPLEBY, P. G., Mathematical Sciences
BEGON, M. E., Biological Sciences
BHANSALI, R. J., Mathematical Sciences
BOWCOCK, T. J. V., Physics
BRUCE, J. W., Pure Mathematics
CANTER, D. V., Psychology
COOPER, S. J., Psychology
COSSINS, A. R., Biological Sciences
CRAMPTON, J. M., Molecular Biology
DAINTON, J. B., Physics
DEROUANE, E. G. J., Chemistry, Innovative Catalysis
DONALD, I., Psychology
DUNBAR, R. I. M., Psychology
EDWARDS, C., Biological Sciences
EDWARDS, S. W., Biological Sciences
ELLIOTT, T. J., Geology
FISHER, M. D., Computer Science
FLINT, S. S., Earth Sciences
GIBLIN, P., Mathematical Sciences
GORYUNOV, W., Mathematical Sciences
HEATON, B. T., Inorganic Chemistry
HETHERINGTON, M. M., Psychology
HOLLOWAY, S., Chemical Physics
IRVING, A. C., Mathematical Sciences
JONES, A. C., Chemistry
KEMP, S. J., Biological Sciences
KUSZNIR, N. J., Geophysics
MARRS, R. H., Applied Plant Biology
MAYES, A. R., Psychology
McCARTHY, A. J., Biological Sciences
McLENNAN, A. G., Biological Sciences
MICHAEL, C., Theoretical Physics
MORTON, H. R., Mathematical Sciences
MOSS, B., Botany
MOVCHAN, A., Mathematical Sciences
MUELLER, M. M., Psychology
NIKULIN, W., Mathematical Sciences
NORTON, T. A., Marine Biology
PARKER, G. A., Zoology
RAVAL, R., Chemistry
REES, H. H., Biological Sciences
REES, S. M., Mathematical Sciences
RITCHIE, D. A., Genetics
ROBERTS, S. M., Organic Chemistry
ROSSEINSKY, M. J., Chemistry
RUDLAND, P. S., Biochemistry
SAUNDERS, J. R., Genetics and Microbiology
SCHIFFRIN, D. J., Physical Chemistry
SHAW, J., Earth Sciences
STIRLING, W. G., Experimental Physics
TOMSETT, A. B., Biological Sciences
VAN DEN BERG, C. M. G., Earth Sciences
VAN DER HOEK, W., Computer Science
VEDRINE, J., Chemistry
WEIGHTMAN, P., Physics
WOOLDRIDGE, M. J., Computer Science

Faculty of Social and Environmental Studies:

ARORA, A., Law
BARON, J. S., Management
BATEY, P. W. J., Town and Regional Planning
CORNER, J., Politics and Communication Studies
DEARING, J. A., Geography
DELANTY, G., Sociology
DRUMMOND, H., Decision Sciences
DUNSTER, D., Architecture
ELLIOTT, D., Management
GIBBS, B. M., Acoustics
GILLESPIE, R., Politics
GOULD, W. T. S., Geography
HADRI, K., Economics and Accounting
HARVEY, A. M., Geography
HILL, J. J., Management
HOJMAN, D. E., Economics and Accounting
JONES, C., Social Policy and Social Work
JONES, M. A., Law
KAVANAGH, D. A., Politics and Communication Studies
KEHOE, D. F., Management
LYON, C. M., Common Law
MACLEOD, J. K., Law
McCABE, B. P. M., Economics
McGOLDRICK, D., Law
MUNCK, R. P., Sociology
NEUWAHL, N. A. E. M., European Law
OLDHAM, D. J., Building Engineering
PEPPER, S. M., Architecture and Building Engineering
ROBERTS, K., Sociology
RUSSELL, T., Centre for Research into Primary Science and Technology
SADLER, D., Geography
SAPSFORD, D. R., Economics and Accounting
SMITH, D., Management
SMITHERS, A. G., Education
TAYLOR, P. J., Economics and Accounting
WARBURTON, J., Law
WONG, Y. L. C., Civic Design
WOODS, R. I., Geography

Faculty of Veterinary Science:

BENNETT, M., Veterinary Pathology
BEYNON, R. J., Veterinary Pre-Clinical Science
CARTER, S. D., Veterinary Science
DOBSON, H., Veterinary Reproduction
EDWARDS, G. B., Equine Studies
GASKELL, C. J., Small Animal Studies
GASKELL, R. M., Veterinary Pathology
HURST, J. L., Animal Science
INNES, J. F., Veterinary Clinical Science and Animal Husbandry
MORGAN, K. L., Epidemiology
SHIRAZI-BEECHEY, S. P., Veterinary Pre-Clinical Science

UNIVERSITY OF LONDON

Senate House, Malet St, London, WC1E 7HU

Telephone: (20) 7862-8000
E-mail: enquiries@london.ac.uk
Internet: www.london.ac.uk

Founded 1836, as examining body, became also a teaching body in 1898

Chancellor: HRH THE PRINCESS ROYAL
Vice-Chancellor: Prof. Sir ADRIAN SMITH
Deputy Vice-Chancellor: Prof PAUL WEBLEY
Dir of Admin.: CATHERINE SWARBRICK
Academic Registrar: GILLIAN ROBERTS

Library: see under Libraries and Archives
Number of teachers: 7,880
Number of students: 170,000 (incl. students of distance learning)..

COLLEGES OF THE UNIVERSITY

Birkbeck, University of London

Malet St, London, WC1E 7HX

Telephone: (20) 7631-6000

Internet: www.bbk.ac.uk

Founded 1823, Charter of Incorporation 1926

State control

Academic year: September to July

Master: Prof. DAVID S. LATCHMAN
Vice-Master: Prof. PHILIP DEWE
Dean of College: Dr KATE MACKENZIE DAVEY
Sec.: KEITH HARRISON
Registrar (vacant)
Dir for Library and Media Services: ROBERT ATKINSON

Library of 364,102 vols
Number of teachers: 927
Number of students: 18,000

DEANS

School of Arts: Prof. HILARY FRASER
School of Business, Economics and Informatics: Prof. PHILIP POWELL
School of Law: Prof. PATRICIA TUITT
School of Science: Prof. NICHOLAS KEEP
School of Social Sciences, History and Philosophy: Prof. MIRIAM ZUKAS

PROFESSORS

School of Arts:

BALE, A., Medieval Studies
CHRISTIE, I., Film and Media History
COOMBES, A., Material and Visual Culture
FINLAY, A., Medieval English and Icelandic Studies
FRASER, H., 19th-Century Studies
JONES, R., Creative Writing
LESLIE, E., Political Aesthetics
LUCKHURST, R., Modern and Contemporary Literature
MULVEY, L., Film Studies
NEAD, L., History of Art
ROSEN, M., Children's Literature
ROWE, W., Poetics
SEGAL, N., French and German Studies
SWAIN, R., Theatre Practice
WATTS, C., Literature and Poetics
WISEMAN, S., 17th-Century Literature

School of Business, Economics and Informatics:

ANDERSEN, B., Economics and Management Innovation
ARCHIBUGI, D., Innovation, Governance and Public Policy
BRUMMELHUIS, R., Mathematical Finance
CALDWELL, R., Organizational Change
CHRISTODOULIDES, G., Management
DEWE, P., Organizational Psychology
DRIFFILL, J., Economics
FENNER, T., Computer Science
GARRATT, A., Economics
GEMAN, H., Mathematical Finance
HART, S., Mathematics
IBEH, K., Marketing and International Business
KAPUR, S., Financial Economics
KELLY, J., Industrial Relations
LAWTON-SMITH, H., Entrepreneurship
LEVENE, M., Computer Science
MAGOULAS, S., Computer Science
MAYBANK, G., Computer Science
NIELSEN, K., Institutional Economics
POULOVASSILIS, A., Computer Science
POWELL, P., Management
PSARADSKIS, Z., Econometrics
SIBERT, A., Economics
SMITH, R., Applied Economics
SNOWER, D., Economics
SOLA, M., Economics
TINSLEY, P., Economics
TISSINGTON, P., Industrial Psychology
TRENBERTH, L., Management
WRIGHT, S., Economics

XIAMING, L., International Business
ZAKHARYASCHEV, M., Computer Science
ZOEGA, G., Economics

School of Law:

BOWRING, B., Law
DOUZINAS, C., Law
EVERSON, M., Law
FITZPATRICK, P., Law
GEAREY, A., Law
HANAFIN, P., Law
HOUGH, M., Criminal Policy
MACMILLAN, F., Law
MCAUSLAN, P., Law
MORAN, L., Law
MULCAHY, L., Law and Society
SALECL, R., Psychoanalysis and Law
TUITT, P., Law
WEAIT, M., Law and Policy

School of Science:

BARNES, J., Psychology
BARNES, P., Applied Crystallography
BELSKY, J., Psychology
BRISTOW, C., Sedimentology
CARTER, A., Earth Sciences
COOPER, R., Cognitive Science
CRAWFORD, I., Planetary Science and Astrobiology
CSIBRA, G., Psychology
DERAKHSHAN, N., Psychology
DOWNES, H., Geochemistry
EIMER, M., Psychology
HAHN, U., Psychology
JOHNSON, M., Psychology
KARMILOFF-SMITH, A., Psychology
KEEP, N., Biomolecular Science
MARESCHAL, D., Psychology
MCDONALD, N., Structural Biology
MELHUISH, E., Human Development
MOSS, D., Biomolecular Structure
MULLER, H., Cognitive Psychology
OAKSFORD, M., Psychology
ORLOVA, E., Macromolecular Systems
RICHARDS, A., Psychology
ROBERTS, G., Earthquake Geology
SAIBIL, H., Structural Biology
SERENO, M., Psychology
SLINGSBY, C., Structural Biology
SMITH, J., Psychology
THOMAS, M., Psychology
USHER, M., Psychology
WAKSMAN, G., Structural Molecular Biology
WALLACE, B., Crystallography

School of Social Sciences, History and Philosophy:

ARNOLD, J., Medieval History
BOURKE, J., History
CALLENDER, C., Higher Education Policy
COOLE, D., Political and Social History
DEWAELE, J., Applied Linguistics and Multilingualism
EDGINGTON, D., Philosophy
EDWARDS, C., Ancient History and Culture
FELDMAN, D., History
FIGES, O., History
FROSH, S., Psychology
GARDNER-CHLOROS, P., Sociolinguistics and Language Contact
GEMES, K., Philosophy
GUTTENPLAN, S., Philosophy
HARDING, V., London History
HENDERSON, J., Italian Renaissance History
HORNSBY, J., Philosophy
HUMFRESS, C., History
INNES, M., History
JACKSON, S., Lifelong Learning and Gender Studies
JAMES, S., Philosophy
KAUFMANN, A., Psychology
KARMILOFF-SMITH, E., Politics
LI, W., Linguistics
LILLEHAMMER, H., Philosophy
LINNEBO, O., Philosophy

LORCH, M., Neurolinguistics
LOVENDUSKI, J., Politics
MABBETT, D., Public Policy
PICK, D., History
PRICE, A., Philosophy
RIALL, L., History
ROSENEIL, S., Sociology and Social Theory
RUMFITT, I., Philosophy
SEGAL, L., Psychology and Gender Studies
SENGOOPTA, C., History
SHIMAZU, N., History
SINGH, R., Politics
SWANN, J., Early Modern History
TRENTMAN, F., History
WACHSMANN, N., Modern European History
WHITE, J., History
ZHU, H., Applied Linguistics and Communication
ZUKAS, M., Applied Linguistics and Communication

Courtauld Institute of Art

Somerset House, Strand, London, WC2R 0RN

Telephone: (20) 7848-2777

E-mail: ugadmissions@courtauld.ac.uk

Internet: www.courtauld.ac.uk

Founded 1932, became an ind. college of the Univ. of London 2002

Academic year: September to July

Dir: Dr DEBORAH SWALLOW
Dean and Deputy Dir: Prof. DAVID SOLKIN
Sec. and Registrar: MICHAEL ARTHUR
Academic Registrar: Dr GARETH MORGAN

Number of teachers: 30
Number of students: 380 (328 full-time, 52 part-time)

Publication: *Journal of the Warburg and Courtauld Institutes* (1 a year)

PROFESSORS

CORMACK, R., History of Art
CROSSLEY, P., History of Art
CUNO, J., History of Art
GREEN, C., History of Art
HOUSE, J., History of Art
LOWDEN, J., History of Art
RIBEIRO, A., History of Dress
RUBIN, P., History of Art
SOLKIN, D., History of Art

Goldsmiths, University of London

New Cross, London, SE14 6NW

Telephone: (20) 7919-7171

E-mail: communications@gold.ac.uk

Internet: www.gold.ac.uk

Founded 1891

Academic year: September to June

Warden: PATRICK LOUGHREY
Deputy Warden for Academic Devt: Prof. JANE POWELL
Pro-Warden for Interdisciplinary Devt: Prof. ROGER BURROWS
Pro-Warden for Research and Enterprise: Prof. MARK D'INVERNO
Pro-Warden of Students and Learning Devt: MICHAEL YOUNG
Registrar and Sec.: LIZ BROMLEY

Library of 300,000 vols
Number of teachers: 410 and 318 visiting tutors and 169 assoc. tutors
Number of students: 10,150

Publications: *African Affairs, African Identities, Death and Dying, Economy and Society* (4 a year), *Goldsmiths Journal of Education* (2 a year), *History Workshop Journal* (4 a year), *Journal of Buddhist Ethics, Scriblerian* (2 a year), *Social Identities, Street Signs* (2 a year), *Third Text*

PROFESSORS

AHMED, S., Media and Communications

ANIM-ADDO, J., English and Comparative Literature
ARCHER, M., Art
ATKINSON, D., Educational Studies
BALDICK, C., English and Comparative Literature
BELL, V., Sociology
BERRY, C., Media and Communications
BHATTACHARYA, J., Psychology
BISHOP, M., Computing
BOLDRINI, L., English and Comparative Literature
BOWERS, J., Design
BURROWS, R., Sociology
CAMPBELL, J., Social, Therapeutic and Community Studies
CASSIDY, R., Anthropology
COHEN, J., English and Comparative Literature
CUBITT, S., Media and Communications
CURRAN, J. P. P., Media and Communications
DAVIDOFF, J., Psychology
DAVIS, A., Media and Communications
DAY, S., Anthropology
D'INVERNO, M., Computing
DOWNIE, A., English and Comparative Literature
DRYDEN, W., Social, Therapeutic and Community Studies
DUTTMAN, A., Visual Cultures
DUTTON, M., Politics
FRENCH, C., Psychology
FURSE, A., Theatre and Performance
GEORGE, R., Educational Studies
GODDARD, V., Anthropology
GORDON, R., Theatre and Performance
GREGORY, E., Educational Studies
HEATON, P., Psychology
IVASHKIN, A., Music
KEMBER, S., Media and Communications
KNOWLES, C., Sociology
LATHAM, W., Computing
LEYMARIE, F. F., Computing
LOMAX, Y., Art
LONDON, J., Theatre and Performance
MARTIN, J., Politics
MCDONALD, R., English and Comparative Literature
MCROBBIE, A., Media and Communications
MICHAEL, M., Sociology
MOORE-GILBERT, B., English and Comparative Literature
MORLEY, D., Media and Communications
MORRISON, B., English and Comparative Literature
NASH, K., Sociology
NEGUS, K., Music
NEWMAN, M., Art
NUGENT, S., Anthropology
OKAGBUE, O., Theatre and Performance
PAECHTER, C., Educational Studies
PICKERING, A., Psychology
PLAMPER, J., History
PLATT, L., Professional and Community Education
PRING, L., Psychology
PROPHET, J. A., Computing
RENTON, A., Art
ROGOFF, I., Visual Cultures
RUTLAND, A., Psychology
SETH, S., Politics
SHEVTSOVA, M., Drama
SIMONE, A. M., Sociology
TARLO, E., Anthropology
VALENTINE, T., Psychology
WEIZMAN, E., Visual Cultures

Heythrop College

Univ. of London, Kensington Sq., London, W8 5HN

Telephone: (20) 7795-6600
E-mail: enquiries@heythrop.ac.uk
Internet: www.heythrop.ac.uk

Founded 1614, became part of Univ. of London 1970

Academic year: September to June

Specialist courses in theology and philosophy; receives grant from Higher Education Funding Council for England (HEFCE)

Prin.: Rev. Dr JOHN MCDADE
Academic Registrar: ANNABEL CLARKSON
Asst Registrar: ANTONY CHARLES

Library of 180,000 vols
Number of teachers: 40
Number of students: 920

Publications: *Heythrop Journal* (4 a year), *Heythrop Studies in Contemporary Philosophy, Religion and Theology* (2 a year)

Imperial College London

South Kensington Campus, London, SW7 2AZ

Telephone: (20) 7589-5111
E-mail: info@imperial.ac.uk
Internet: www.imperial.ac.uk

Founded 1907 by fed. of Royal College of Science, Royal School of Mines, and City and Guilds College, (1988) St Mary's Hospital Medical School, (1995) Nat. Heart and Lung Institute, (1997) Charing Cross and Westminster Medical School and Royal Postgraduate Medical School, and (2000) Wye College

Academic year: October to June

Rector: Sir KEITH O'NIONS
Deputy Rector: Prof. STEPHEN RICHARDSON
Pro-Rector for Education and Academic Services: Prof. JULIA BUCKINGHAM
Pro-Rector for Enterprise: EDWARD ASTLE
Pro-Rector for Int. Affairs: Prof. SIMON BUCKLE
Pro-Rector for Research: Prof. DONAL BRADLEY
College Sec.: Dr RODNEY EASTWOOD
Academic Registrar: NIGEL WHEATLEY
Dir of Library Services: DEBORAH SHORLEY

Number of teachers: 1,240
Number of students: 13,960

PRINCIPALS

Business School: Prof. DAVID BEGG
Faculty of Engineering: Prof. JEFF MAGEE
Faculty of Medicine: Prof. ANTHONY NEWMAN TAYLOR
Faculty of Natural Sciences: MAGGIE DALLMAN
Graduate School: Prof. ANDREW GEORGE (Dir)

PROFESSORS

ADCOCK, I. M., Respiratory Cell and Molecular Biology
ALBANESE, C., Mathematical Finance
ALBERTI, J. G. M. M., Metabolic Medicine
ALIABADI, F. M. H., Aerostructures
ALLDAY, M. J., Virology
ALLEN-MERSH, T. G., Gastrointestinal Surgery
ALTON, E. W. F. W., Gene Therapy
AMIS, A. A., Orthopaedic Biomechanics
ANAND, P., Clinical Neurology
ANDERSON, R. M., Infectious Disease Epidemology
APSIMON, H. M., Air Pollution Studies
ARMSTRONG, A., Organic Chemistry
ARST, H. N., Microbial Genetics
ATKINSON, A., Materials Chemistry
ATKINSON, C., Applied Mathematics
BALDING, D. J., Statistical Genetics
BALOGH, A., Space Physics
BANGHAM, C., Immunology
BARBER, J., Biochemistry
BARLOW, J. G., Technology and Innovation Management
BARNES, P. J., Thoracic Medicine
BARNES, T. R. E., Clinical Psychiatry
BARNHAM, K. W. J., Physics
BARRETT, A. G. M., Organic Chemistry
BARRETT, J. W., Numerical Analysis

BEDDINGTON, J. R., Applied Population Biology
BEGG, D. K. H., Economics
BELL, A. R., Plasma Physics
BELL, J. N. B., Environmental Pollution
BELL, M. G. H., Transport Operations
BELVISI, M., Respiratory Pharmacology
BENNETT, P. R., Obstetrics and Gynaecology
BLACKMOND, D. G., Catalysis
BLANE, D., Medical Sociology
BLOMLEY, M. J., Radiology
BLOOM, S. R., Metabolic Medicine
BLUNT, M. J., Petroleum Engineering
BOOBIS, A. R., Biochemical Pharmacology
BOSANQUET, N. F. G., Health Policy
BOTTO, M., Rheumatology
BRADLEY, D. D. C., Experimental Solid-State Physics
BRANDON, N. P., Sustainable Development in Energy
BRENNAN, F. M., Immunopathology
BRIDSON, M. R., Pure Mathematics
BRIGGS, D. J., Public Health
BRINSON, C. E. J., German Studies
BRISCOE, B. J., Interface Engineering
BRONSTEIN, A. M., Clinical Neurology
BROOKS, D. J., Neurology
BROSENS, J. J., Reproductive Sciences
BUCHANAN, D. L., Mining Geology
BUCK, K. W., Plant and Fungal Virology
BUCK, M., Molecular Microbiology
BUCKINGHAM, J. C., Pharmacology
BUENFELD, N. R., Concrete Structures
BULPITT, C. J., Geriatric Medicine
BUSH, A., Paediatric Respirology
BUTLER, D., Water Engineering
CALLAN, M. F. C., Immunology and Rheumatology
CARGILL, P. J., Physics
CASH, J. R., Numerical Analysis
CASS, A. E. G., Chemical Biology
CAWLEY, P., Mechanical Engineering
CHADWICK, D., Applied Catalysis
CHATURVEDI, N., General Practice
CHEN, Y., Mathematical Physics
CHEUNG, P., Digital Systems
CHRISTOFIDES, N., Operational Research
CHUNG, K. F., Respiratory Medicine
CLARK, K. L., Computational Logic
COLLINS, P., Clinical Cardiology
CONNERADE, J.-P., Atomic and Molecular Physics
CONSTANTINIDES, A. G., Signal Processing
CONWAY, G. R., International Development
COOK, H. T., Renal Pathology
COOKSON, W. O. C., Respiratory Genetics
COOMBES, R. C. D. S., Medical Oncology
COUCHMAN, J. R., Cell Biology
COUTELLE, C. C., Gene Therapy
COWBURN, R. P., Nanotechnology
COWIE, M. R., Cardiology
COWLEY, S. R., Plasma Physics
CRAIG, D. D. C., Organic Synthesis
CRASTER, R. V., Applied Mathematics
CRAWLEY, M. J., Community Ecology
CRISANTI, A., Molecular Parasitology
CROWDER, M. J., Stochastic Modelling
CUMPSTY, N. A., Mechanical Engineering
CUTHBERTSON, K., Finance
DAINTY, J. C., Applied Optics
DALLMAN, M. J., Immunology
DAMZEN, M. J., Experimental Laser Physics
DARLINGTON, J., Programming Methodology
DARZI, A., Minimal Access Surgery
DAVIS, M. H. A., Mathematics
DE BELLEROCHE, J. S., Neurochemistry
DE MELLO, A. J., Chemical Nanosciences
DELL, A., Carbohydrate Biochemistry
DERWENT, R. G., Atmospheric Chemistry
DJAMGOZ, M. B. A., Neurobiology
DOKAL, I. S., Haematology
DONALDSON, S. K., Pure Mathematics
DONNELLY, C., Statistical Epidemiology
DORNAN, P. J., Experimental Particle Physics
DOUGHERTY, M. K., Space Physics
DREW, J. E., Astrophysics

DRIVER, C., Economics
DUGWELL, D. R., Chemical Engineering
DURHAM, S. R., Allergy and Clinical Immunology
DURUCAN, S., Mining and Environmental Engineering
EDALAT, A., Computer Science and Mathematics
EDGERTON, D. E. H., History of Science, Technology and Medicine
EDWARDS, A. D., Neonatology
ELGIN, J. N., Applied Mathematics
ELLAWAY, P. H., Physiology
ELLIOTT, P., Epidemiology and Public Health Medicine
EVANS, A. W., Risk Management
EVANS, J., Tropical Forestry
EWINS, D. J., Vibration Engineering
FARRELL, P. J., Tumour Virology
FELDMAN, M., Cellular Immunology
FENNER, R. T., Engineering Computation
FENWICK, A., Tropical Parasitology
FERENCZI, M. J., Physiological Sciences
FERGUSON, N. M., Mathematical Biology
FIRMIN, D., Biomedical Imaging
FIRTH, J. A., Anatomy
FISK, D. J., Engineering for Sustainable Development
FISK, N. M., Obstetrics and Gynaecology
FOSTER, R. G., Molecular Neurology
FOULKES, W. M. C., Physics
FOXWELL, B. M., Immune Cell Signalling
FRANKEL, G., Molecular Pathenogenesis
FRANKS, N. P., Biophysics
FRANKS, S., Reproductive Endocrinology
FRASER, R. W., Agricultural Economics
FREEMONT, P. S., Structural Biology
FRENCH, P. M. W., Physics
FRIEDLAND, J. S., Infectious Diseases and Microbiology
FROGUEL, P., Genomic Medicine
GABRA, H., Medical Oncology
GABRIEL, J., Organizational Theory
GANN, D. M., Technology and Innovation Management, Built Environment
GARNETT, G., Microparasite Epidemiology
GARRALDA HUALDE, M. E., Child and Adolescent Psychiatry
GAUNTLETT, J. P., Theoretical Physics
GELENBE, S. E., Computer and Communication Networks
GEORGE, A., Molecular Immunology
GHATEI, M., Peptide Endocrinology
GHOSH, S., Gastroenterology
GIBBON, J. D., Applied Mathematics
GIBSON, S. E., Chemistry
GIBSON, V. C., Organic Chemistry
GILKS, C. F., International Health
GILLON, R., Medical Ethics
GLAISTER, S., Transport and Infrastructure
GLOVER, V. A., Perinatal Psychobiology
GODFRAY, H. C. J., Evolutionary Biology
GOGOLIN, A. O., Mathematical Physics
GORDON, M. Y. A., Experimental Haematology
GOSMAN, A. D., Computational Fluid Dynamics
GOTCH, F. M., Immunology
GRAEBER, M., Neuroscience
GRAHAM, J. M. R., Unsteady Aerodynamics
GRAHAM, N. J. D., Environmental Engineering
GRASBY, P. M., Psychiatry
GREENHALGH, R. M., Surgery
GRIFFITHS, D. S., Human Resource Management
GRIGORYAN, A., Pure Mathematics
GRIMES, R. W., Materials Science
GRIMM, S. W., Toxicology
GRINGARTEN, A., Petroleum Engineering
GRUZELIER, J. G., Psychology
GUO, Y., Computing Science
HABIB, N. A., Hepto-biliary Surgery
HAIGH, J. D., Atmospheric Physics
HAJNAL, J. V., Imaging Science
HALL, G., Physics

HALL, P., Applied Mathematics
HALL, S. G. F., Economics
HALLIWELL, J. J., Theoretical Physics
HAND, D. J., Statistics
HANKINS, M. W., Visual Neuroscience
HARDIE, R. J., Insect Physiology
HARDING, S., Cardiac Pharmacology
HARRIES, J. E., Earth Observation
HARRISON, N., Chemistry
HARRISON, P. G., Computing Science
HASKARD, D. O., Cardiovascular Medicine
HASSELL, M. P., Insect Ecology
HENCH, L. L., Ceramic Materials
HENRY, J. A., Accident and Emergency Medicine
HIGGINS, C. F., Clinical Sciences
HIGGINS, J. S., Polymer Science
HILL, B., Policy Analysis
HILLIER, R., Compressible Flow
HINDS, E. A., Quantum Optics
HODKINSON, I., Logic and Computation
HODSON, M. E., Respiratory Medicine
HOLDEN, D. W., Molecular Microbiology
HOLM, D. D., Applied Mathematics
HOLMES, A. B., Organic and Polymer Chemistry
HOPKINS, C. R., Biochemistry
HUDSON, J. A., Rock Mechanics
HUGHES, A. D., Clinical Pharmacology
HUGHES, S. F. R., Orthopaedic Surgery
HUHTANIEMI, I. T., Reproductive Biology
HULL, C., Theoretical Physics
IMREGUN, M., Computational Engineering Dynamics
ISHAM, C. J., Theoretical Physics
IVANOV, A. A., Pure Mathematics
IWATA, C. J., Biochemistry
JACKSON, G., Chemical Physics
JAMES, G. D., Pure Mathematics
JARDINE, R. J., Geomechanics
JARVELIN, M., Lifecourse Epidemiology
JEGER, M., Agroecology
JENSEN, H. J., Mathematics
JOHNSON, H. D., Petroleum Geology
JOHNSTON, D. G., Clinical Endocrinology
JOHNSTON, S. L., Respiratory Medicine
JONES, T. S., Physical Chemistry
JONES, W. G., High-Energy Physics
JONES, W. P., Combustion
KANDIYOTI, R., Chemical Engineering
KELSALL, G. H., Electrochemical Engineering
KENNARD, C., Clinical Neurology
KILNER, J. A., Materials Science
KING, P. R., Petroleum Engineering
KINLOCH, A. J., Adhesion
KITNEY, R. I., Biomedical Systems Engineering
KLUG, D., Chemical Biophysics
KLUMPES, P. J. M., Accounting
KNIGHT, P. L., Quantum Optics
KORNYSHEV, A. A., Chemical Physics
KRAMER, J., Distributed Computing
KRUSHELNICK, K. M., Plasma Physics
KYDD, J., Agricultural Economics and Business Management
LALANI, E. M. A., Molecular and Cell Pathology
LANE, D. A., Molecular Haematology
LAWRENCE, C., Fluid Mechanics
LAYCOCK, J. F., Endocrine Physiology
LEATHERBARROW, R., Chemical Biology
LESCHZINER, R., Computational Aerodynamics
LESTER, J. N., Water Technology
LEUNG, K. K., Internet Technology
LEVER, M. J., Physiological Mechanics
LEVIN, M., Paediatrics
LIEBECK, M. W., Pure Mathematics
LIMEBEER, D. J. N., Control Engineering
LINDSTEDT, R. P., Thermofluids
LIVINGSTON, A. G., Chemical Engineering
LLOYD SMITH, D., Structural Mechanics
LOMAX, M. A., Animal Sciences
LONG, K. R., Experimental Particle Physics
LUCKHAM, P. F., Particle Technology
LUK, W. W.-C., Computer Engineering

MACCHIETTO, S., Process Systems Engineering
MACCULLOCH, R. J., Economics
MACDERMOT, J., Clinical Pharmacology
MACKINNON, A., Theoretical Solid-State Physics
MADEN, A., Psychiatry
MAGEE, A. I., Membrane Biology
MAGEE, J. N., Computing Science
Sir MAINI, R. N., Rheumatology
MAJEED, F. A., Primary Healthcare and General Practice
MAMDANI, E. H., Telecommunications Strategy and Services
MANSFIELD, J., Biology
MARANGOS, J. J., Laser Physics
MAROS, I., Computational Methods of Operations Research
MARSTON, S. B., Cardiovascular Biochemistry
MATHIAS, C. J., Neurovascular Medicine
MATTHEWS, S. J., Chemical and Structural Biology
MAXWELL, P. H., Nephrology
MAZE, M., Anaesthetics
McCLURE, M. O., Retrovirology
MEADE, N., Quantitative Finance
MEIKLE, W. P. S., Astrophysics
MILLER, A., Organic Chemistry and Structural Biology
MITCHELL, J., Pharmacology in Critical Care
MOORE, G. E., Molecular Genetics
MUGGLETON, S. H., Bioinformatics
MUMFORD, J., Natural Resource Management
MUNTONI, F., Paediatric Neurology
NAGASE, H., Rheumatology
NETHERCOT, D. A., Civil Engineering
NEW, G. H. C., Non-linear Optics
NICHOLSON, J. K., Biological Chemistry
NORTHOVER, J. M. A., Intestinal Surgery
OPENSHAW, P. J. M., Experimental Medicine
OWENS, I., Evolutionary Ecology
PANTELIDES, C. C., Chemical Engineering
PARKER, K. H., Physiological Fluid
PARKER, M. G., Obstetrics and Gynaecology
PARRY, A. O., Statistical Physics
PARRY, G., Applied Physics
PARRY, S., Radiochemistry
PARTRIDGE, M. R., Respiratory Medicine
PASVOL, G., Infection and Tropical Medicine
PAVLOVIC, M., Structural Engineering and Mechanics
PENDRY, J. B., Theoretical Solid-State Physics
PENNELL, D. J., Cardiology
PEPPER, J., Cardiothoracic Surgery
PERRAUDIN, W. R. M., Finance
PETERS, N. S., Cardiac Electrophysiology
PHILLIPS, C. C., Experimental Solid-State Physics
PHILLIPS, D., Physical Chemistry
PISTIKOPOULOS, E. N., Chemical Engineering
PLANT, J. A., Applied Geochemistry
PLAYFORD, R., Gastroenterology
PLENIO, M. B., Quantum Physics
POLAK, J. M., Endocrine Pathology
POTTS, D. M., Analytical Soil Mechanics
POULTER, N. R., Preventative Cardiovascular Medicine
PRABHU, J. C., Marketing
PUSEY, C. D., Renal Medicine
QUIRKE, N., Physical Chemistry
RAWLINGS, R. D., Materials Science
REED, M. J., Steroid Biochemistry
REGAN, L., Obstetrics and Gynaecology
REYNOLDS, R., Cellular Neurobiology
RICHARDS, B., Computing Science
RICHARDSON, S., Public Health
RICHARDSON, S. M., Chemical Engineering
RITTER, M. A., Immunology
RIVERS, R. J., Theoretical Physics
ROBB, M. A., Chemistry
ROBERTS, I., Paediatrics Haematology
ROSE, M. L., Transport Immunology
ROWAN-ROBINSON, G. M., Astrophysics
RUDD, C. E., Haematology
RUSSELL, N. J., Biology

RUSTEM, B., Computational Methods in Operations
RZEPA, H. S., Computational Fluid Dynamics
SAKLATVALA, J., Experimental Pathology
SANDERSON, D. J., Geology
SCHROTER, R. C., Biological Mechanics
SCHWARTZ, S. J., Space Physics
SCOTT, J., Medicine
SCREATON, G. R., Medicine
SEABRA, M. C., Molecular Genetics
SECKL, M., Molecular Cancer Medicine
SEDDON, J. M., Physical Chemistry
SEFTON, J. A., Economics
SELKIRK, M. E., Biochemical Parasitology
SENSKY, J., Applied Mathematics
SERGOT, M. J., Computational Logic
SEVER, P. S., Clinical Pharmacology and Therapeutics
SEVERS, N. J., Cell Biology
SHAH, N., Process Systems Engineering
SHAUNAK, S., Infectious Diseases
SHAW, R. J., Thoracic Medicine
SHERIDAN, D. J., Clinical Cardiology
SINDEN, R. E., Parasite Cell Biology
SKOROBOGATOV, A. N., Pure Mathematics
SLOMAN, M. S., Distributed Systems Management
SMITH, G. L., Experimental Pathology
SMITH, R. A., Mechanical Engineering
SMITH, R. W., Physics
SOBEY, R. J., Fluid Mechanics
SOUTHWOOD, D. J., Physics
SPIKES, H. A., Lubrication
SPRATT, B. G., Molecular Microbiology
SQUIRE, J. M., Structural Biophysics
STAMP, G. W. M., Histopathology
STARK, J., Applied Mathematics
STEER, P. J., Obstetrics and Gynaecology
STELLE, K. S., Physics
STERNBERG, M. J. E., Structural Bioinformatics
STUCKEY, D. C., Biochemical Engineering
SUGDEN, P. H., Cellular Biochemistry
SUMMERFIELD, J. A., Experimental Medicine
SUMNER, T. J., Experimental Astrophysics
SUTTON, A. P., Nanotechnology
SWAN, C., Hydrodynamics
SYMS, R. R., Microsystems
SZYMANSKI, S. A., Economics
TAYLOR, A., Neurophysiology
TAYLOR, A. M. K. P., Thermofluids
TAYLOR, J. R., Ultrafast Physics and Technology
TAYLOR, K. M., Cardiac Surgery
TEMPLER, R., Biophysical Chemistry
THIRTLE, C. G., Agricultural Economics
THOMAS, H. C., Medicine
THOMPSON, R. C., Experimental Physics
TOUMAZOU, C., Analogue Circuit Design
TRUSLER, J. P. M., Thermophysics
TSEYTLIN, A., Theoretical Physics
TYRER, P. J., Community Psychiatry
UNDERWOOD, S. R., Cardiac Imaging
VAN HEEL, M., Structural Biology
VASSILICOS, C., Fluid Mechanics
VAZ DE MELO, J., Molecular Haematology
VENABLES, P. J., Viral Immunorheumatology
VINEIS, P., Environmental Epidemiology
VINTER, R. B., Control Theory
VIRDEE, T. S., Physics
VVEDENSKY, D., Theoretical Solid-State Physics
WAAGE, J. K., Applied Ecology
WALDEN, A. T., Statistics
WANG, Y., Reservoir Geophysics
WARK, D. L., High Energy Physics
WARNER, M. R., Geophysics
WARWICK, A. C., History of Science
WAXMAN, J., Medical Oncology
WEBER, J. N., Genito-urinary Medicine and Communicable Diseases
WEBSDALE, D. M., Physics
WEBSTER, J. P. G., Agricultural Business Management
WHEATER, H. S., Hydrology
WILKINS, M. R., Clinical Pharmacology

WILLIAMS, A. J., Membrane Biophysics
WILLIAMS, T. J., Applied Pharmacology
WINSTON, R. M., Fertility Studies
WISE, C. M., Civil Engineering Design
WISE, R. J. S., Neurology
WOOD, D. A., Clinical Epidemiology
WOODS, J. D., Oceanography
WRIGHT, D. J., Pest Management
YANG, G. Z., Medical Image Computing
YOUNG, D. B., Medical Microbiology
ZEGARLINSKI, B., Pure Mathematics

Institute of Education

20 Bedford Way, London, WC1H 0AL

Telephone: (20) 7612-6000
E-mail: info@ioe.ac.uk
Internet: www.ioe.ac.uk

Founded 1902 as London Day Training College, transferred to control of Univ. of London in 1932, became School of Univ. in 1987

Academic year: September to June

Dir: Prof. CHRIS HUSBANDS
Sec.: BRYN MORRIS
Academic Registrar: Dr LORETO LOUGHRAN
Librarian: ANNE PETERS

Library of 270,000 vols, 1,160 periodicals
Number of teachers: 180
Number of students: 4,420 (1,370 full-time, 3,050 part-time)

Publication: *London Review of Education* (3 a year)

PROFESSORS

AGGLETON, P., Education
ALDERSON, P., Childhood Studies
ALDRICH, R., History of Education
BALL, S., Sociology of Education
BARNETT, R., Higher Education
BARTON, L., Inclusive Education
BLATCHFORD, P., Education and Psychology
BRANNEN, J., Sociology of the Family
BRIGHOUSE, H., Philosophy of Education
BUCKINGHAM, D., Education
BYNNER, J., Education
CAMERON, D., Languages
DAVID, N., Educational Technology
DOCKRELL, J., Psychology and Special Needs
DOLTON, P., Education
ELBOURNE, D., Evidence-informed Policy and Practice
EVANS, K., Education (Lifelong Learning)
GILLBORN, D., Education
GOLDSTEIN, H., Statistical Methods
GORDON, P., History of Education
GREEN, A., Education
GUNDARA, J., Education
HALPIN, D., Education
HIRST, P., Education
HOYLES, C. M., Mathematics Education
JOSHI, H., Education
KENT, A., Geography Education
KRESS, G., English
LAWTON, D., Education
LEONARD, D., Sociology of Education and Gender
LEVACIC, R., Economics and Finance of Education
LITTLE, A., Education with spec. reference to Developing Countries
LUNT, I., Educational Psychology
MACGILCHRIST, B., Education
MAYALL, B., Childhood Studies
MOSS, P., Early Childhood Provision
NOSS, R., Mathematics Education
OAKLEY, A. R., Sociology and Social Policy
POWER, S., Education
REISS, M., Science Education
ST JAMES ROBERTS, I., Child Development
SAMMONS, P., Education
SHATTOCK, M., Higher Education Management
SIRAJ-BLATCHFORD, I., Early Childhood Education

WELCH, G., Music Education
WHITE, J., Philosophy of Education
WHITTY, G. J., Sociology of Education
WOLF, A., Education

King's College London

Strand, London, WC2R 2LS

Telephone: (20) 7836-5454

Denmark Hill Campus: 10 Cutcombe Rd, London, SE5 9RJ
Guy's Campus: New Hunts House, London, SE1 1UL

Telephone: (20) 7848-6004

St Thomas' Campus: Westminster Bridge Rd, London, SE1 7EH

Telephone: (20) 7188-7188

Waterloo Campus: James Clerk Maxwell Bldg, 57 Waterloo Rd, London, SE1 8WA
E-mail: ceu@kcl.ac.uk
Internet: www.kcl.ac.uk

Founded 1829 by merger of Queen Elizabeth College and Chelsea College 1985, the Institute of Psychiatry 1997, and United Medical and Dental Schools of Guy's and St Thomas' Hospitals 1998

Academic year: September to June

Prin. and Pres.: Prof. RICK TRAINOR (acting)
Vice-Prin. for Arts and Sciences: Prof. KEITH HOGGART
Vice-Prin. for Education: Prof. EEVA LEINO-NEN
Vice-Prin. for Health: Prof. ROBERT LECHLER
Vice-Prin. for Research and Innovation: CHRIS MOTTERSHEAD
Vice-Prin. for Strategy and Devt: Prof. Sir LAWRENCE FREEDMAN
Head of Admin. and College Sec.: IAN CREAGH
Chief Information Officer and College Librarian: KAREN STANTON

Library: see under Libraries and Archives
Number of teachers: 1,530
Number of students: 23,000 (incl. School of Medicine and Dentistry)

Publications: *Dispatches* (3 a year), *King's College Law Journal* (2 a year)

PROFESSORS

Guy's, King's and St Thomas' School of Biomedical Sciences (1st Fl., Henrietta Raphael House, London, SE1 1UL; tel. (20) 7848-6400; e-mail biomed.admin@kcl.ac.uk):

BERRY, M., Anatomy
BRAIN, S. D., Pharmacology
BUCKLAND-WRIGHT, J. C., Radiological Anatomy
CICLITIRA, P. J., Gastroenterology
FILE, S. E., Psychopharmacology
FRASER, L. R., Reproductive Biology
GOULD, H. G., Biophysics
HALLIWELL, B., Biochemistry
HEARSE, D. J., Cardiovascular Biochemistry
HOLDER, N. H., Anatomy
HOWELL, S. L., Physiology
JENNER, P. G., Pharmacology
JONES, G. E., Cell Biology
LITTLETON, J. M., Pharmacology
LUMSDEN, A. G. S., Developmental Neurobiology
MADEN, M., Developmental Biology
MANN, G. E., Vascular Physiology
MARSHALL, J., Ophthalmology
McMAHON, S. B., Physiology
McNAUGHTON, P. A., Physiology
NAFTALIN, R. J., Physiology
NEAL, M. J., Pharmacology
PAGE, C. P., Pharmacology
PATIENT, R. K., Molecular Genetics
PEARSON, J. D., Physiology
PRICE, R. G., Biochemistry
QUINN, P. J., Biochemistry
RICE-EVANS, C., Biochemistry
RITTER, J. M., Clinical Pharmacology

RUTTER, M., Psychopathology
SIMMONS, R., Biophysics
STANDRING, S. M., Applied Neurobiology
THURSTON, C. F., Microbiology
TIMBRELL, J. A., Biochemical Toxicology
WEBSTER, K., Anatomy
WILLIAMS, W. P., Environmental Science

Guy's, King's and St Thomas' School of Dentistry (Guy's Tower, Guy's Hospital, London, SE1 9RT; tel. (20) 7188-7188):

BEIGHTON, D., Oral Microbiology
CHALLACOMBE, S. J., Oral Medicine
ELEY, B. M., Periodontology
GELBIER, S., Dental Public Health
GIBBONS, D. E., Oral Health Services Research
JOHNSON, N., Dental Sciences
KIDD, E. A., Cariology
LANGDON, J., Oral and Maxillofacial Surgery
LINDEN, R., Craniofacial Biology
MCGURK, M., Oral and Maxillofacial Surgery
MEIKLE, M. C., Orthodontics
MEREDITH SMITH, M., Evolutionary Dentoskeletal Biology
PALMER, R. M., Implant Dentistry and Periodontology
PITT-FORD, T. R., Endodontology
SHARPE, P. T., Craniofacial Biology
SMITH, B. G. N., Conservative Dental Surgery
SMITH, N. J. D., Dentistry
WADE, W. G., Oral Microbiology
WATSON, R., Prosthetic Dentistry

School of Education (Franklin-Wilkins Bldg (WBW), Waterloo Rd, London, SE1 9NN; tel. (20) 7848-3183):

BROWN, M. L., Education
COX, M. J., Information Technology in Education
DUSCHL, R., Science Education
JOHNSON, D. C., Education
STREET, B. U., Language in Education
WILLIAM, D. A. P. R., Educational Assessment

School of Health and Life Sciences (Franklin-Williams Bldg, 150 Stamford St, London, SE1 9NN; e-mail health-life@kcl.ac.uk):

CAMMACK, R., Health and Life Sciences
COWAN, D. A., Pharmaceutical Toxicology
COWLEY, S. A., Community Practice Development
EBRINGER, A. M. A., Immunology
FRANK, L. S., Children's Nursing Research
GEISSLER, C. A., Nutrition
HALL, D. O., Health and Life Sciences
HIDER, R. C., Pharmacy
MARRIOTT, C., Pharmacy
REDFERN, S. J., Nursing Studies
ROSS MURPHY, S. B., Life Sciences
SANDERS, T. A., Nutrition
STAINES, N. A., Immunology
TINKER, A. M., Gerontology
WHILE, A. E., Nursing Studies
WILSON-BARNETT, J., Nursing Studies

School of Humanities (Strand, London, WC2R 2LS; tel. (20) 7848-2374; e-mail humanities@kcl.ac.uk):

ADLER, J. D., German
BANNER, M. C., Moral and Social Theology
BEATON, R. M., Modern Greek
BIRTWISTLE, H., Musical Composition
BOND, B. J., War Studies
BRIDGE, C., Australian Studies
BUSH, C., American Literature
BUTT, J. W., Modern Hispanic Studies
CHABAL, P. E., Lusophone-African Studies
CLARKE, M., Defence Studies
CLARKE, P. B., History and Sociology of Religion
DANDEKER, C., Military Sociology
DEATHRIDGE, J. W., King Edward Chair of Music

DOCKRILL, M. L., Diplomatic History
DREYFUS, L., Music
FREEDMAN, L. D., War Studies
GANZ, D., Palaeography
GARNETT, J., Defence Studies
GAUNT, S. B., French Language and Literature
GILLIES, D. A., Philosophy of Science and Mathematics
GRIFFITHS, R. M., French Studies
HAMNETT, C., Human Geography
HEATH, M. J., French Literature
HELM, P., Theology and Religious Studies
HERRIN, J. E., Late Antique and Byzantine Studies
HOGGART, K., Geography
HOOK, D., Spanish Medieval Studies
IFE, B. W., Spanish and Spanish-American Studies
JORDANOVA, L., Modern History
KARSH, E., Mediterranean Studies
KNIBB, M. A., Old Testament Studies
LAPPIN, S., Linguistics
LIEU, J., New Testament Studies
MCCABE, M. M. A., Ancient Philosophy
MACEDO, H. M., Portuguese and Brazilian Studies
MACHOVER, M., Philosophy
MAYER, R. G. M., Classics
NELSON, J. L., Medieval History
NEWITT, M. D. D., History
NEWSON, L. A., Geography
NOKES, D. L., English Literature
ORMOND, L., Victorian Studies
OVERY, R. J., Modern History
PAPINEAU, D. C., Philosophy
PORTER, A. N., History
PROUDFOOT, G. R., English
ROBERTS, J. A., English Language and Medieval Literature
ROSEVEARE, H. G., History
RUSSELL, C. S. R., History
SABIN, P. A. G., Strategic Studies
SAINSBURY, R. M., Philosophy
SAVILE, A. B., Philosophy
SCHIESARO, A., Latin Language and Literature
SILK, M. S., Latin Language and Literature
SORABJI, R. R. K., Philosophy
STOKES, J., English Literature
THORNES, J. B., Geography
WAYWELL, G. B., Classics
WHITE, J. J., German

School of Law (Strand, London, WC2R 2LS; tel. (20) 7836-5454; e-mail gen.genlaw@kcl.ac.uk):

BLACKBURN, R., Law
EECKHOUT, P. O. V., Law
EWING, K. D., Law
GEARTY, C. A., Human Rights Law
GLOVER, J. C. B., Ethics (Dir)
GUEST, A. G., Law
HAYTON, D. J., Law
LOMNICKA, E. Z., Law
MARTIN, J. E., Law
MORSE, C. G., Law
MULLERSON, R., International Law
NORRIE, A. W., Criminal Law and Criminal Justice
PHILLIPS, J. C., Law
WHISH, R., Law

Guy's, King's and St Thomas' School of Medicine (1st Fl., Hodgkin Bldg, London, SE1 9RT; tel. (20) 7848-6971):

ADAM, A., Interventional Radiology
ADAMS, A. P., Anaesthetics
AMIEL, S., Diabetic Medicine
BANATVALA, J. E., Clinical Virology
BATES, G. P., Neurogenetics
BENJAMIN, I., Surgery
BOURAS, N., Psychiatry of Learning Difficulties
BRAUDE, P. R., Obstetrics and Gynaecology
BURNAND, K. G., Vascular Surgery
BURNEY, P. G. J., Public Health Medicine

COLLINS, W. P., Obstetrics and Gynaecology
CRAIG, T. K., Community Psychiatry
DAVID, A., Cognitive Neuropsychiatry
DAVIS, H. M., Child Health Psychology
DOHERTY, P., Cell Biology
EADY, R. A., Experimental Dermatopathology
EASTERBROOK, P. J., Medicine
EYKYN, S. J., Clinical Microbiology
FABRE, J., Clinical Sciences
FARZANEH, F., Molecular Medicine
FENTIMAN, I. S., Surgical Oncology
FOGELMAN, I., Nuclear Medicine
FORSLING, M. L., Neuroendocrinology
FRENCH, G. L., Medical Microbiology
GARETY, P. A., Clinical Psychology
GIANNELLI, F. B., Molecular Genetics
GLEESON, M. J., Otolaryngology
GREAVES, M. W., Dermatology
GREENOUGH, A., Clinical Respiratory Physiology
HART, I. R., Cancer Research
HAWK, J. L. M., Dermatological Photobiology
HAWKES, D. J., Computational Imaging
HAY, R. J., Cutaneous Medicine
HAYCOCK, G. B., Paediatrics
HAYDAY, A. C., Immunobiology
HEATLEY, F. W., Orthopaedic Surgery
HENDRY, B., Renal Medicine
HIGGINSON, I., Palliative Care
HIGGS, R., General Practice
HUGHES, R. A. C., Neurology
JACKSON, S., Clinical Gerontology
JONES, R. H., General Practice
KALRA, L., Stroke Medicine
KEMENY, D. M., Immunology
KOPELMAN, M. D., Neuropsychiatry
LEE, T. H., Allergy and Respiratory Medicine
LEHNER, T., Basic and Applied Immunology
LOWY, C., Endocrinology
LUCAS, S. B., Clinical Histopathology
MACDONALD, A. J. D., Old-Age Psychiatry
MAISEY, M. N., Radiological Sciences
MARTEAU, T. M., Health Psychology
MATHEW, C. G. P., Molecular Genetics
MCGREGOR, A., Medicine
MILLS, K. R., Clinical Neurophysiology
MILNER, A. D., Neonatology
MUFTI, G., Haematological Oncology
NICOLAIDES, K., Obstetrics and Gynaecology
PANAYI, G. S., Rheumatology
PEARSON, T. C., Haematology
PETERS, T. J., Clinical Biochemistry
POLKEY, C., Neurosurgery of Epilepsy
POSTON, L., Foetal Health
RAMIREZ, A. J., Liaison Psychiatry
RICHARDS, M. A., Palliative Medicine
ROBERTS, V. C., Clinical Prof.
ROBINSON, R. O., Paediatric Neurology
ROSS, E., Community Paediatrics
RUBENS, R. D., Clinical Oncology
SACKS, S. H., Nephrology
SAVIDGE, G. F., Coagulation Medicine
SCOTT, D. L., Clinical Rheumatology
SELLER, M. J., Developmental Genetics
SHEPHERD, G. W., Mental Health Rehabilitation
SIMONOFF, E. A., Child and Adolescent Psychiatry
SOLOMON, E., Human Genetics
SONKSEN, P. H., Endocrinology
SWAMINATHAN, R., Clinical Biochemistry
SWIFT, C., Health Care of the Elderly
TYNAN, M. J., Paediatric Cardiology
VIBERTI, G., Diabetes and Metabolic Medicine
WATSON, J. P., Psychiatry
WEINMAN, J. A., Psychology Applied to Medicine
WESSELEY, S., Liaison Psychiatry
WILLIAMS, D. G., Medicine

Florence Nightingale School of Nursing and Midwifery (James Clerk Maxwell Bldg, 57 Waterloo Rd, London, SE1 8WA; tel. (20) 7848-4698; e-mail nightingale@kcl.ac.uk; internet www.kcl.ac.uk/nursing):

COWLEY, S.
FRANCK, L.
HUMPHREY, C.
NORMAN, I.
RICHARDSON, A.
SANDALL, J.
WHILE, A.

School of Physical Sciences and Engineering (Strand, London, WC2R 2LS; tel. (20) 7848-2267; e-mail pse.schooloffice@kcl.ac.uk):

AGHVAMI, A. H., Telecommunications Engineering
BUSHNELL, C. J., Mathematics
CLARKSON, T. G., Electrical Engineering
COLLINS, A. T., Physics
DAVIES, A. C., Electrical Engineering
DAVIES, E. B., Mathematics
DAVIES, G., Physics
GABBAY, D. M., Logic
GAUNT, D. S., Physics
GIBSON, S. E., Chemistry
GOSPEL, H. F., Management
HALL, T. J., Optoelectronics
HEATH, C. C., Work and Orgs
HIBBERT, F., Chemistry
HOLWILL, M. E. J., Biological Physics
HOWE, P. S., Applied Mathematics
HUGHES, M. N., Chemistry
LAUGHLIN, R., Physical and Engineering Sciences
PIKE, E. R., Physical and Engineering Sciences
PRESSLEY, A. N., Mathematics
ROBB, M. A., Chemistry
ROBINSON, D. C., Mathematics
ROGERS, A. J., Electrical Engineering
SAFAROV, Y., Mathematics
SANDLER, M. B., Signal Processing
SARKAR, S., Theoretical Physics
SAUNDERS, P. T., Mathematics
STREATER, R. F., Mathematics
SWANSON, J. G., Electrical Engineering
TURNER, C. W., Electrical Engineering
UFF, J., Engineering Law
WEST, P. C., Mathematics
WINDER, R., Computer Science
YIANNESKIS, M., Fluid Mechanics

Institute of Psychiatry (De Crespigny Park, London, SE5 8AF; tel. (20) 7836-5454; e-mail spjgams@iop.kcl.ac.uk; internet www.iop.kcl.ac.uk):

ANDERTON, B. H., Neuroscience
BANERJEE, S. S., Mental Health and Ageing
BARKER, G. J., Magnetic Resonance Physics
BOLTON, D., Philosophy and Psychopathology
CHALDER, T., Psychological Medicine
CRAIG, T. K. J., Psychological Medicine
GOODMAN, R., Child and Adolescent Psychiatry
HEMSLEY, D. R., Psychology
HOTOPF, M., General Hospital Psychiatry
HUXLEY, P. J., Social Work
JONES, E., History of Medicine and Psychiatry
KNAPP, M. R. J., Health Economics
MACDONALD, A. J. D., Psychological Medicine
McGUFFIN, P., Social, Genetic and Developmental Psychiatry
MORRIS, R. G., Neuropsychology
SALKOVSKIS, P. M., Psychology
STOLERMAN, I., Behavioural Pharmacology
STRANG, J., Addiction Research
WESSELY, S., Epidemiological and Liaison Psychiatry

ATTACHED CENTRE

Centre for Defence Studies: King's College London, Strand, London, WC2R 2LS; tel. (20) 7848-2892; e-mail jessica.marcos@kcl.ac.uk; internet www.kcl.ac.uk/sspp/departments/warstudies/research/groups/cds/index.aspx; f. 1990; Dir for CDS Prof. JOHN GEARSON

London Business School

Regent's Park, London, NW1 4SA
Telephone: (20) 7000-7000
E-mail: webenquiries@london.edu
Internet: www.london.edu
Founded 1965
Academic year: August to July
Dean: Sir ANDREW LIKIERMAN
Deputy Dean for Faculty: Prof. STEPHEN SCHAEFER
Deputy Dean for Programmes: Prof. ANDREW SCOTT

Number of teachers: 160
Number of students: 1,700 (postgraduate); over 8,000 exec. education participants

PROFESSORS

BIRKINSHAW, J., Strategic and International Management
BUNN, D. W., Decision Sciences
CORNELLI, F., Finance
DEGRAEVE, Z., Decision Sciences
DIMSON, E., Finance
FRANKS, J. R., Finance
GOFFEE, R. E., Organizational Behaviour
GRATTON, L., Organizational Behaviour
HENNESSY, C., Finance
LIKIERMAN, A., Accounting (Dean)
MARKIDES, C., Strategic and International Management
NAIK, N., Finance
NICHOLSON, N., Organizational Behaviour
PETERSON, R., Organizational Behaviour
PILLUTLA, M., Organizational Behaviour
PORTES, R., Economics
RAMDAS, K., Management Science and Operations
REY, H., Economics
SCOTT, A., Economics
SHIVAKUMAR, L., Accounting
TALMOR, E., Accounting
WARREN, K., Management Science and Operations
WEBER, B., Management Science and Operations

ATTACHED RESEARCH INSTITUTES

Aditya Birla India Centre: e-mail indiacentre@london.edu; Co-Dir NIRMALYA KUMAR; Co-Dir PHANISH PURANAM.

Centre for Corporate Governance: e-mail vfarnell@london.edu; Academic Dir JULIAN FRANKS.

Coller Institute of Private Equity: e-mail peinstitute@london.edu; Founder and Chair. Prof. ELI TALMOR.

Foundation and Endowment Asset Management: e-mail sacharya@london.edu; Academic Dir ELROY DIMSON.

Hedge Fund Centre: e-mail hedgefunds@london.edu; Dir NARAYAN NAIK.

Management Lab: e-mail jbirkinshaw@london.edu; Co-Founder and Research Dir JULIAN BIRKINSHAW

London School of Economics and Political Science

Houghton St, London, WC2A 2AE
Telephone: (20) 7405-7686
E-mail: stu.rec@lse.ac.uk
Internet: www.lse.ac.uk
Founded 1895
Academic year: October to July

Dir: Prof. CRAIG CALHOUN
Pro-Dir for Planning and Resources: Prof. GEORGE GASKELL
Pro-Dir for Teaching and Learning: Prof. JANET HARTLEY
Pro-Dir: Prof. S CORBRIDGE
Sec. and Dir of Admin.: ADRIAN HALL
Library: see under Libraries and Archives
Number of teachers: 580 (full-time)
Number of students: 9,500 (8,700 full-time, 800 part-time)

Publications: *BioSocieties* (4 a year), *British Journal of Industrial Relations* (4 a year), *Economica* (4 a year journal of economics, economic history and statistics), *Journal of Global History* (3 a year), *Journal of Transport Economics and Policy* (3 a year), *Population Studies* (3 a year), *The British Journal of Sociology* (4 a year), *The International Bibliography of the Social Sciences* (4 vols, 1 a year)

PROFESSORS

ALPERN, S. R., Mathematics
ANDERSON, R. W., Accounting and Finance
ANGELL, I. O., Information Systems
BALDWIN, R., Law
BALFOUR, S., Government
BARKER, E. V., Sociology
BARKER, R. S., Government
BARR, N. A., European Institute
BEAN, C. R., Economics/Centre for Economic Performance
BESLEY, T. J., Economics
BHATTACHARYA, S., Accounting and Finance
BIGGS, N. L., Mathematics
BLOCH, M. E. F., Anthropology
BRIGHTWELL, G. R., Mathematics
BROMWICH, M., Accounting and Finance
BROWN, C. J., International Relations
BUZAN, B. G., International Relations
CARTWRIGHT, N. L. D., Philosophy
CHANT, S. H., Geography and Environment
CHARVET, J. C. R., Government
CHESHIRE, P. C., Geography and Environment
CHINKIN, C. M., Law
CIBORRA, C., Information Systems
COHEN, S., Sociology
COLEMAN, J., Government
COLLEY, L. J., European Institute
COLLINS, H. G., Law
CONNOR, G., Accounting and Finance
CORBRIDGE, S. E., Geography and Environment
COWELL, F. A., Economics
COX, M., International Relations
CRAFTS, N. F. R., Economic History/Centre for Economic Performance
DAVIES, P. L., Law
DESAI, LORD, Economics
DOWDING, K. M., Government
DOWNES, D. M., Social Policy
DUNLEAVY, P., Government
DYSON, T. P., Population Studies
EPSTEIN, S. R., Economic History
FEATHERSTONE, K., European Institute
FELLI, L., Economics
FREEMAN, R. B., Centre for Economic Performance
FULLER, C. J., Anthropology
GALLIERS, R., Information Systems
GASKELL, G. D., Social Psychology
GEARTY, C. A., Sociology
GORDON, I. R., Geography and Environment
GRAY, J. N., Government
GREENWOOD, C. J., Law
HALLIDAY, F., International Relations
HARDMAN MOORE, J., Economics
HARRISS, J. C., Development Studies Institute
HARTLEY, T. C., Law
HELD, D., Government
HEMMER, T., Accounting and Finance
HIDALGO, F. J., Economics

HILL, C. J., International Relations
HILLS, J. R., Suntory and Toyota International Centres for Economics and Related Disciplines
HOBCRAFT, J. N., Population Studies, Social Policy
HOWSON, C., Philosophy
HUMPHREY, N. K., Centre for Philosophy of Natural and Social Science
HUMPHREY, P. C., Social Psychology
HUTTER, B. M., Centre for Analysis of Risk and Regulation
HYMAN, R., Industrial Relations
JACKMAN, R. A., Economics
JOHNSON, P. A., Economic History
JONES, D. K. C., Geography and Environment
JONES, G. W., Government
KALDOR, M. H., Centre for the Study of Global Governance
KELLY, J. E., Industrial Relations
KIERNAN, K. E., Social Policy
KIYOTAKI, N., Economics
KNAPP, M. R. J., Social Policy
KNOX, M. B., International History
LACEY, N. M., Law
LAYARD, P. R. G., Economics/Centre for Economic Performance
LE GRAND, J., Social Policy
LIEVEN, D. C. B., Government
LIGHT, M. M., International Relations
LINTON, O., Economics
LIVINGSTONE, S. M., Social Psychology
LOUGHLIN, M., Law
MACVE, R. H., Accounting and Finance
MANNING, A. P., Economics
MANSELL, R. E., Sociology
MARSDEN, D. W., Industrial Relations
McGUIRE, A. J., Social Policy
METCALF, D. H., Industrial Relations/Centre for Economic Performance
MILLER, P. B., Accounting and Finance
MOORE, H. L., Anthropology
MORGAN, M. S., Economic History
MOUZELIS, N. P., Sociology
MURPHY, M. J., Population Studies
MURPHY, T., Law
NEWBURN, W. H. T., Social Policy
NICKELL, S. J., Economics
NORBERG, R., Statistics
O'LEARY, B., Government
PAGE, E. C., Government
PARRY, J. P., Anthropology
PHILIP, G. D. E., Government
PHILLIPS, A. M., Gender Institute
PIACHAUD, D. F. J., Social Policy
PICCIONE, M., Economics
PISCHKE, J. S., Economics
PISSARIDES, C. A., Economics
POWER, A. E., Social Policy
POWER, M. K., Accounting and Finance
PRESTON, P., International History
QUAH, D., Economics
RAWLINGS, R., Law
REES, J. A., Geography and Environment
REINER, R., Law
REYNIERS, D. J., Interdisciplinary Institute of Management
ROBERTS, S. A., Law
ROBINSON, P. M., Economics
ROCK, P. E., Sociology
RODRIGUEZ-SALGADO, M., International History
ROSE, N. S., Sociology
ROSENHEAD, J. V., Operational Research
RYDIN, Y. J., Geography and Environment
SAITH, A., Development Studies Institute
SASSEN, S., Geography and Environment
SENNETT, R., Sociology
SHIN, H. S., Accounting and Finance
SMITH, A. D. S., Government
STERN, N. H., Economics
STEVENSON, D., International History
SUTTON, J., Economics
TAYLOR, P. G., International Relations
TEUBNER, G., Law
TIMMERMANN, A. G., Accounting and Finance

TONG, H., Statistics
VENABLES, A. J., Economics
WADE, R., Development Studies Institute
WALLACE, W., International Relations
WEBB, D. C., Accounting and Finance
WHITEHEAD, C. M. E., Economics
WILLIAMS, H. P., Operational Research
WORRALL, J., Philosophy
YAHUDA, M. B., International Relations
YAO, Q., Statistics

London School of Hygiene & Tropical Medicine

Keppel St, London, WC1E 7HT
Telephone: (20) 7636-8636
E-mail: registry@lshtm.ac.uk
Internet: www.lshtm.ac.uk
Founded 1899
Academic year: September to September
Dir: PETER PIOT
Sec. and Registrar: RICHARD BENSON
Library: see under Libraries and Archives
Number of teachers: 432 (incl. research staff)
Number of students: 1,800
Publications: *Health Policy and Planning,*
Journal of Tropical Medicine and Hygiene

DEANS

Faculty of Epidemiology and Population Health: JOHN EDMUNDS
Faculty of Infectious and Tropical Diseases: SIMON CROFT
Faculty of Public Health and Policy: RICHARD SMITH

PROFESSORS

ACKERS, J., Postgraduate Education in Public Health
BERRIDGE, V., History
BLACK, N. A., Health Services Research
CAIRNCROSS, A. M., Environmental Health
CAIRNS, J., Health Economics
CLELAND, J., Medical Demography
COLEMAN, M. P., Epidemiology and Vital Statistics
COUSENS, S. N., Epidemiology and Medical Statistics
CROFT, S. L., Parasitology
CURTIS, C., Medical Entomology
DOCKRELL, H., Immunology
DOWIE, J., Health Impact Analysis
ELBOURNE, D., Health Care Evaluation
FINE, P. E. M., Communicable Disease Epidemiology
FLETCHER, A., Epidemiology and Ageing
FOSTER, A., International Eye Health
GREENWOOD, B. M., Communicable Diseases
GRUNDY, E., Demographic Gerontology
HALL, A. J., Infectious Disease Epidemiology
HAYES, R. J., Epidemiology and International Health
HILL, A. A., Community Nutrition
KAYE, P. M., Cellular Immunology
KELLY, J. M., Molecular Biology
KENWARD, M. G., Biostatistics
KIRKWOOD, B. R., Epidemiology and International Health
LEON, D., Epidemiology
MABEY, D., Communicable Diseases
McADAM, K. P. W., Clinical Tropical Medicine
McKEE, C. M., European Public Health
MILES, M. A., Medical Protozoology
MILLS, A. J., Health Economics and Policy
MULHOLLAND, K., Infectious Disease Epidemiology
NOAH, N. D., Public Health
PETO, J., Cancer Epidemiology
POCOCK, S. J., Medical Statistics
PRENTICE, A., International Nutrition
RILEY, E. M., Infectious Disease Immunology
ROBERTS, I., Epidemiology and Public Health
RODRIGUES, L., Infectious Disease Epidemiology

ROY, P., Virology
SMITH, P. G., Tropical Epidemiology
TAYLOR, M. G., Medical Helminthology
UAUY, R., Public Health Nutrition
WALT, G., International Health Policy
WELLINGS, K., Sexual and Reproductive Health
WHITWORTH, J. A., International Public Health
WREN, B. W., Microbial Pathogenesis

Queen Mary, University of London

Mile End Rd, London, E1 4NS
Telephone: (20) 7882-5315
E-mail: international-office@qmul.ac.uk
Internet: www.qmul.ac.uk
Founded 1989 as Queen Mary and Westfield College, following merger of Queen Mary College (f. 1934) and Westfield College (f. 1882); current name adopted 2000
Academic year: September to June
Prin.: Prof. SIMON GASKELL
Sr Vice-Prin.: Prof. PHILIP OGDEN
Vice-Prin. for External Relations: Prof. RAY PLAYFORD
Vice-Prin. for Humanities and Social Sciences: Prof. MORAG SHIACH
Vice-Prin. for Research and Int. Affairs: Prof. EVELYN WELCH
Vice-Prin. for Science and Engineering: Prof. JEREMY KILBURN (acting)
Vice-Prin. for Teaching and Learning: Prof. SUSAN DILLY
Vice-Prin. and Warden, Barts and the London School of Medicine and Dentistry: Prof. RICHARD TREMBATH
Chief Admin. Officer: DEAN CURTIS
Sec. to Ccl and Academic Registrar: WENDY APPLEBY
Dir of Library Services: E. J. BULL
Library: see under Libraries and Archives
Number of teachers: 1,000
Number of students: 16,500

PROFESSORS
Faculty of Arts:
ADAMOWICZ, E., French
ADGER, D. J., Linguistics
BOFFEY, J., English
CHESHIRE, J. L., Linguistics
DADSON, T. J., Hispanic Studies
DELGADO, M. M., Drama and Theatre Arts
DEYERMOND, A. D., Spanish
EDWARDS, M. J., Classics
ELLIS, M., English Literary History
EVANS, P. W., Film Studies
GOERNER, R., German
GUSSENHOVEN, C., Linguistics
HAMILTON, P. W. A., English
HENNESSY, P. J., Contemporary History
HOBSON JEANNERET, M. E., French Language and Literature
JACKSON, J., History
JANOWITZ, A., English
JARDINE, L. A., English and Drama
MILLER, J. L., History
MORIARTY, M. M., French Literature and Thought
OLSCHNER, L. M., German
PARSONS, D. W., Public Policy
PENNY, R. J., Romance Philology
RAMSDEN, J. A., Modern History
RANAWAKE, S. A., German
RAYFIELD, D., Russian
REES, G. C., English
ROSE, J., English
RUBIN, M., History
SASSOON, D., History
SHIACH, M., Cultural History
Faculty of Engineering and Mathematical Sciences:
ALIABADI, M. H., Engineering
ANDREWS, E. H., Materials
ARROWSMITH, D. K., Mathematics

ASHBY, D., Mathematics
BADER, D. L., Engineering
BAILEY, R. A., Statistics
BULLET, S. R., Mathematics
CAMERON, P. J., Mathematics
CARR, B. J., Mathematics and Astronomy
CLARRICOATS, P., Electrical Engineering
CROOKES, R., Combustion Engineering
CUTHBERT, L. G., Electronic Engineering
DAVIES, K. L., Materials
DONKIN, S., Pure Mathematics
DRIKAKIS, D., Engineering
EDIRISINGHE, M., Materials
EVANS, J., Materials
GASTER, M., Experimental Aerodynamics
GOLDSHEID, I., Probability Theory
GUO, Z. X., Materials
HODGES, W. A., Mathematics
HOGG, P., Materials
LAUGHTON, M. A., Electrical and Electronic Engineering
LAWN, C. J., Thermo-fluids Engineering
LEEDHAM-GREEN, C. R., Pure Mathematics
LESCHZINER, M. A., Engineering
LINDSAY, P., Electrical Engineering
MacCALLUM, M. A. H., Applied Mathematics
MURRAY, C. D., Mathematics and Astronomy
O'HEARN, P., Computer Science
OLVER, A. D., Electrical and Electronic Engineering
PAKER, Y., Parallel Computing
PAPALOIZOU, J. C. B., Mathematics and Astronomy
PARINI, C., Antenna Engineering
ROBINSON, E., Computer Science
ROSE, J. W., Mechanical Engineering
ROXBURGH, I. W., Mathematics and Astronomy
SCHWARTZ, S. J., Space Plasma Physics
STARK, J. P. W., Aeronautical Engineering
TANNER, K., Materials
WEHRFRITZ, B. A. F., Pure Mathematics
WILLIAMS, I. P., Mathematics and Astronomy

Faculty of Law and Social Sciences:

ADAMS, J., Property Law
ATKINSON, B. W., Geography
BAILLIE, R. T., Economics
BLAKENEY, M., Intellectual Property Law
COTTERRELL, R. B. M., Legal Theory
CURTIS, S., Geography
FITZPATRICK, P., Law
FLETCHER, I. F., Commercial Law
GHIGLINO, C., Economics
HASKEL, J., Economics
LAHORE, J. C., Intellectual Property Law
LEE, R., Geography
MALGOSIA, F.
McCONVILLE, S. D. M., Criminal Justice
NORTON, J. J., Banking Law
O'DONOVAN, K., Law
OGDEN, P. E., Geography
REED, C., Electronic Commerce Law
RICHARDSON, G. M., Public Law
SMITH, D. M., Geography
SORGER, G., Economics
SPENCE, N. A., Human Geography
THOMAS, G., Equity and Property Law
TZAVALIS, E., Economics
VAN BUEREN, G., International Human Rights Law
YELLAND, J. L., Law

Faculty of Natural Sciences:

ADE, P. A. R., Experimental Astrophysics
AYLETT, B. J., Chemistry
BONNETT, R., Research Chemistry
BRADLEY, D. C., Chemistry
BUGG, D. V., Nuclear Physics
CARTER, A. A., Particle Physics
CHARAP, J. M., Theoretical Physics
CLEGG, P. E., Astrophysics
COVNEY, P. V., Physical Chemistry
DUCKETT, J. G., Botany

DUNSTAN, D. J., Experimental Physics
EDGINGTON, J. A., Physics
EMERSON, J., Physics
GRIFFITHS, D. V., Organic Chemistry
HILDREW, A. G., Ecology
KALMUS, P., Physics
LICHTENSTEIN, C. P., Molecular Biology
MARTIN, D., Physics
PERCIVAL, I. C., Physics
PYE, J. D., Biological Sciences
RANDALL, E. W., Research Chemistry
SEWELL, G., Physics
SULLIVAN, A., Inorganic Chemistry
THOMPSON, G., Physics
THORPE, A., Biology
UTLEY, J. H. P., Organic Chemistry
VLCEK, A., Inorganic Chemistry
WARREN, M. J., Biological Sciences
WHITE, G. J., Physics and Astronomy
WILSON, E. G., Physics

Barts and the London School of Medicine and Dentistry (Turner St, London, E1 2AD; tel. (20) 7377-7611; e-mail medicaladmissions@qmul.ac.uk; internet www.mds.qmul.ac.uk):

ANSEAU, M. R., Institute of Dentistry
ARMSTRONG, P., Haematology, Oncology and Imaging
ARMSTRONG-JAMES, M. A., Biomedical Sciences
ASHBY, D., Wolfson Institute of Preventive Medicine
BENJAMIN, N., Pharmacology
BERRY, C. L., Molecular Pathology, Infection and Immunity
BESSER, G. M., Metabolism
BRADLEY, P. F., Institute of Dentistry
BRITTON, K. E., Haematology, Oncology and Imaging
BROCKLEHURST, K., Biomedical Sciences
BURRIN, J., Metabolism
CARTER, Y. H., Community Sciences
CHARD, T., Haematology, Oncology and Imaging
CLARK, A. J. L., Metabolism
COHEN, R. D., Metabolism
COID, J. W., Community Sciences
COSTELOE, K., Metabolism
CURTIS, M., Oral Microbiology
DAVIES, R. J., Molecular Pathology, Infection and Immunity
DOYAL, L., Metabolism
ELLIOTT, J. C., Institute of Dentistry
FELDMAN, R. A., Surgery, Clinical Neuroscience and Intensive Care
FLOWER, R. J., Pharmacology
GALTON, D., Metabolism
GOODE, A. W., Surgery, Clinical Neuroscience and Intensive Care
GOWLAND, G., Pharmacology
GROSSMAN, A., Metabolism
GRUDZINSKAS, J. G., Community Sciences
HAJ, M., Metabolism
HAJEK, P., Clinical Psychology
HARDIE, J. M., Institute of Dentistry
HEATH, M., Institute of Dentistry
HILLIER, S. M., Community Sciences
HITMAN, G. A., Metabolism
HUGHES, F., Periodontology
ILES, R. A., Metabolism
JACOBS, I., Gynaecological Oncology
JEFFRIES, R. A., Molecular Pathology, Infection and Immunity
KOPELMAN, P. G., Metabolism
KUMAR, P., Clinical Medical Education
LEIGH, I. M., Haematology, Oncology and Imaging
LESLIE, R. D. G., Metabolism
LILLEYMAN, J. S., Metabolism
LISTER, T. A., Haematology, Oncology and Imaging
LOWE, D. G., Molecular Pathology, Infection and Immunity
LUMLEY, J. S., Surgery, Clinical Neurosurgery and Intensive Care
MacDONALD, T. T., Metabolism

MARTIN, J. E., Molecular Pathology, Infection and Immunity
MILLER, G., Epidemiology
MILLER, N. E., Metabolism
MONSON, J., Clinical Endocrinology
NEWLAND, A. C., Haematology, Oncology and Imaging
OLIVER, R. T. D., Haematology, Oncology and Imaging
OXFORD, J., Molecular Pathology, Infection and Immunity
PERRETT, D., Metabolism
PHILLIPS, I. R., Biomedical Sciences
PINCHING, A. J., Molecular Pathology, Infection and Immunity
PRICE, C. P., Metabolism
PRIEBE, S., Community Sciences
PRIESTLEY, J. V., Biomedical Sciences
REES, L. H., Metabolism
REZNEK, R., Haematology, Oncology and Imaging
SANDERSON, I. R., Metabolism
SAVAGE, M., Metabolism
STRUNIN, L., Surgery, Clinical Neuroscience and Intensive Care
SUGDEN, M. C., Biomedical Sciences
SWAIN, C., Gastrointestinal Endoscopy
SWASH, M., Surgery, Clinical Neuroscience and Intensive Care
TABAQCHALI, S., Molecular Pathology, Infection and Immunity
THIEMERMANN, C., Pharmacology
TOMLINSON, D. R., Biomedical Sciences
TROTT, K. R., Haematology, Oncology and Imaging
VINSON, G. P., Biomedical Sciences
WALD, N. J., Wolfson Institute of Preventive Medicine
WHITTLE, B. J., Pharmacology
WILLIAMS, D. M., Institute of Dentistry
WILLIAMS, N. S., Surgery, Clinical Neuroscience and Intensive Care
WILLOUGHBY, D. A., Pharmacology
WINGATE, D. L., Metabolism

Royal Academy of Music

Marylebone Rd, London, NW1 5HT

Telephone: (20) 7873-7373
E-mail: go@ram.ac.uk
Internet: www.ram.ac.uk

Founded 1822, inc. by Royal Charter 1830
State control

Pres.: HRH THE DUCHESS OF GLOUCESTER
Prin.: Prof. JONATHAN FREEMAN-ATTWOOD
Deputy Prin.: MARK RACZ
Deputy Prin. for Programmes and Research: TIMOTHY JONES
Academic Registrar: PHILIP WHITE

Library of 125,000 vols, incl. colln of early sheet music and MSS
Number of teachers: 155
Number of students: 700

Publication: *RAM Magazine* (2 a year)

Royal Holloway, University of London

Egham Hill, Egham, TW20 0EX

Telephone: (1784) 434455
E-mail: admissions@rhul.ac.uk
Internet: www.rhul.ac.uk

Founded 1886 as Royal Holloway College, present status 1985

Prin.: Prof. PAUL LAYZELL
Deputy Prin.: Prof. ROB KEMP
Dir of Library Services: JOHN TUCK
Library of 600,000 vols, 17,000 ejournals
Number of teachers: 1,525
Number of students: 8,500

DEANS

Faculty of Arts: Prof. KATIE NORMINGTON
Faculty of History and Social Sciences: Prof. ROSEMARY DEEM
Faculty of Science: Prof. PHILIP BEESLEY

PROFESSORS

Faculty of Arts:

ALSTON, R., Classics
ARMSTRONG, T. D., English Literature
BOEHMER, E. D., English
BOWIE, A., German
BRADBY, D. H., Drama and Theatre Studies
BRATTON, J. S., Theatre and Cultural History
BRUZZI, S., Film Studies
CARROLL, J. F. M., Philosophy and German
CAVE, R. A., Drama and Theatre Studies
CHARLTON, D. P., Music
COOK, N. J., Music
DZELAINIS, M. M., Early Modern Literature and Thought
ELLIS, J. C. P., Media Arts
EVERSON, J. E., Italian Literature
GARNETT, A., Media Arts
GIBSON, A. W., Modern Literature and Theory
GOULD, W. L., English Literature
GUNDLE, S., Italian
HAMPSON, R. G., Modern Literature
HILL, W. J., Media Arts
HUGHES, E. J., Modern French Literature
HUGHES, J., German and Comparative Literature
KAHANE, A., Classics
LEE SIX, A. E., Hispanic Studies
LONGERICH, P., German History
MERCK, A. J., Media Arts
MOTION, A., Creative Writing
O'BRIEN, J. P., French Renaissance Literature
PIKE, L., Music
POWELL, J. G. F., Classics
RINK, J., Music
ROBERTSON, E., French
RYAN, K. J. P., English Language and Literature
SAMSON, J., Music
SCHAFER, E. J., Drama
TOSI, A., Italian Studies
VILAIN, R. L., German and Comparative Literature
VILASECA, D., Spanish
WATHEY, A., Music History
WHITE, I. A., German
WILES, D., Theatre
WILLIAMS, J., French Literature and Film

Faculty of History and Social Sciences:

ANSARI, K. H., Islam and Culture
BARN, R., Health and Social Care
BARRON, C. M., History of London
BROADBENT, P. J., Management
CESARANI, D., History
CHAMPION, J. A. I., Early Modern Ideas
CLAEYS, G. R., History of Political Thought
CORFIELD, P. J., History
CROFT, J. P., Early Modern History
DENNEY, D., Applied Social Studies
DREWRY, G., Public Administration
EDWARDS, J. R., Social Policy
FAULKNER, D. O., Management
FERLIE, E. B., Management
FRANK, J. L., Economics
GRAHAM, H. E., History
HACKLEY, C. E., Marketing
HEYES, A., Economics
LEE, R. M., Social Research Methods
MCSWEENEY, L. B., Management
MANDLER, M., Economics
MATTEN, D., Management
MCCONVILLE, S. D. M., Criminal Justice
NEWELL, S. M., Management
NORMAN, H., Economics
PILBEAM, P., Modern European History
ROBINSON, F. C. R., History of South-East Asia
ROSENBERG, D., Information and Communication Management
SAUL, N. E., Medieval History
SELZER, A., Economics
SMITH, C. D., Organization Studies

SPAGAT, M., Economics
STONE, D., Modern History

Faculty of Science:

ANDREWS, B. D., Abnormal Psychology
BLACKBURN, S., Mathematics
BLAIR, G. A., Physics
BOLWELL, G. P., Plant Biochemistry
BOWYER, J. R., Plant Biochemistry
BRADLEY, C., Health Psychology
BRAMLEY, P. M., Biochemistry
BRYSBAERT, M. M. C., Psychology
CASTIELLO, U., Psychology
CATCHPOLE, C. K., Animal Behaviour
CHERVONENKIS, A. Y., Computer Science
COHEN, D. A., Computer Science
COLLINSON, M. E., Plant Palaeobiology
COWAN, B. P., Physics
CRANG, P. A., Geography
DAVIES, E. R., Machine Vision
DICKSON, J. G., Molecular Cell Biology
DRIVER, F. F., Human Geography
DUDEN, R., Biological Sciences
EBINGER, C. J., Tectonics
EYSENCK, M. W., Psychology
FOWLER, C. M. R., Geography
FUNNELL, E., Neuropsychology
GAMBLE, C. S., Geography
GAMMERMAN, A., Computer Science
GREEN, M. G., Particle Physics
GUTIN, Z., Computer Science
HALL, R., Geology
HARMAN, G., Mathematics
HARRIS, M., Psychology
IMRIE, R. F., Human Geography
JANSEN, V., Mathematical Biology
KEMP, R. A., Physical Geography
LEA, M. J., Physics
LOEWENTHAL, C., Psychology
LOWE, J. J., Geography
LUO, Z., Computer Science
MACLEOD, A. K., Psychology
MCCLAY, K. R., Structural Geology
MENZIES, M. A., Geochemistry
MITCHELL, C. J., Information Security
MOORE, A. M., Crystallography
MURPHY, S. P., Mathematics
MURTAGH, F., Computer Science
NISBET, E. G., Geology
O'MAHONY, P. F., Applied Mathematics
PATERSON, K. G., Mathematics
PETRASHOV, V. T., Physics
ROSE, J., Geography
SAUNDERS, J., Low-Temperature Physics
SCHACK, R., Mathematics
SCOTT, A. C., Applied Palaeobotany
SIMON, D., Development Geography
SMITH, A. T., Psychology
SOLOVYEV, W., Computer Science
STRONG, J. A., Experimental Physics
THIRLWALL, M. F., Isotope Geochemistry
UNWIN, P. T., Geography
VAPNIK, V., Computer Science
VOVK, V. G., Computer Science
WILD, P. R., Mathematics
ZANKER, J. M., Neuroscience

Royal Veterinary College

Royal College St, London, NW1 0TU
Telephone: (20) 7468-5000
E-mail: registry@rvc.ac.uk
Internet: www.rvc.ac.uk
Founded 1791
Academic year: September to July
Prin.: Prof. STUART REID
Asst Prin. and Sec.: ELAINE ACASTER
Librarian: SIMON JACKSON
Number of teachers: 110
Number of students: 1,060

PROFESSORS

BROWNLIE, J., Veterinary Pathology
CHANTLER, P. D., Veterinary Molecular and Cellular Biology
CHURCH, D. B., Small Animal Studies

ELLIOTT, J., Pharmacology
GOODSHIP, A. E., Orthopaedic Sciences
GREGORY, N. G., Animal Welfare Physiology
HOWARD, C. R., Veterinary Microbiology and Parasitology
JACOBS, D. E., Veterinary Parasitology
JOHNSTON, A. M., Veterinary Public Health
LANYON, L., Veterinary Anatomy
LEES, P., Veterinary Pharmacology
LLOYD, D. H., Veterinary Dermatology
MAY, S. A., Equine Medicine and Surgery
MCGOWAN, M., Farm-Animal Medicine and Surgery
PFEIFFER, D. U., Veterinary Epidemiology
SCARAMUZZI, R. J., Veterinary Physiology
SKERRY, T. M., Developmental Biology
SMITH, R., Equine Orthopaedics
STICKLAND, N. C., Veterinary Anatomy
STOKER, N. G., Molecular Bacteriology
WATHES, D. C., Veterinary Reproduction
WATSON, P. F., Reproductive Biology
WILLIAMS, A. E., Veterinary Pathology

St George's Hospital Medical School

Cranmer Terrace, London, SW17 0RE
Telephone: (20) 8672-9944
E-mail: webmaster@stgeorges.nhs.uk
Internet: www.sghms.ac.uk
Founded 1751
Academic year: September to August
Prin.: Prof. PETER KOPELMAN
Deputy Prin.: Prof. SEAN HILTON
Academic Registrar and Sec.: SOPHIE BOWEN
Library of 150,000 vols
Number of teachers: 400
Number of students: 6,070

PROFESSORS

ANDERSON, H. R., Epidemiology and Public Health
AUSTEN, B. M., Protein Science
BELL, B. A., Neurosurgery
BENNETT, D. C., Anatomy
BENNETT, E. D., Anaesthesia
BLAND, J. M., Medical Statistics
BOLTON, T. B., Pharmacology
BROWN, N., Anatomy and Developmental Biology
BURNS, T. P., Community Psychiatry
CAMM, A. J., Clinical Cardiology
CAMPBELL, S., Obstetrics and Gynaecology
CAPPUCCIO, F., General Practice and Primary Care
CARTER, N. D., Developmental Biochemistry
CHALMERS, R. A., Paediatric Metabolism
CHAMBERS, T. J., Tissue Pathology
CLEMENS, M. J., Biochemistry
COATES, A. R. M., Medical Microbiology
COLLIER, J. G., Clinical Pharmacology
COOK, D., Epidemiology
DALGLEISH, A. G., Oncology
DUFF, M. J. B., Physiological Medicine
EASTMAN, N. L. G., Psychiatry
FISHER, L. M., Biochemistry
GHODSE, A. H., Psychiatry of Addictive Behaviour
GILLBERG, C., Psychiatry
GORDON-SMITH, E. C., Haematology
GRIFFIN, G. E., Infectious Diseases and Medicine
GRIFFITHS, J. R., Medical Biochemistry
HALL, G. M., Anaesthesia
HAY, F. C., Immunology
HERMON-TAYLOR, J., Surgery
HILTON, S. R., General Practice and Primary Care
HOLLINS, S. C., Psychiatry of Learning Disability
HORTON, R., Clinical Pharmacology
HOWLIN, P. A., Clinical Psychology
JOHNSTONE, A. P., Molecular Immunology
JONES, I., Sociology of Health and Illness
JONES, P. W., Medicine
KASKI, J. C., Cardiological Sciences

KRISHNA, S., Infectious Diseases
LACEY, J. H., Psychiatry
LARGE, W. A., Pharmacology
LEVICK, J. R., Physiology
MacGREGOR, G. A., Cardiovascular Medicine
MALIK, M., Cardiology
MARKUS, H., Clinical Neuroscience
McKENNA, W. J., Cardiac Medicine
McLAREN, S., Nursing
MORTIMER, P. S., Physiological Medicine
OLIVEIRA, D. B. G., Renal Medicine
PATTON, M., Medical Genetics
ROSS, F., Nursing Primary Care
SEYMOUR, C. A., Clinical Biochemistry and Metabolism
STRACHAN, D. P., Public Health
VICTOR, C. R., Public Health Sciences
WALLER, G., Psychiatry
WALTERS, D. V., Child Health
WEST, R. J., Psychology
WHINCUP, P. H., Public Health Sciences
WHIPP, B. J., Physiology
XU, Q., Cardiological Sciences

School of Oriental and African Studies

Thornhaugh St, Russell Sq., London, WC1H 0XG

Telephone: (20) 7637-2388
E-mail: study@soas.ac.uk
Internet: www.soas.ac.uk
Founded 1916
Academic year: September to June
Dir and Prin.: Prof. PAUL WEBLEY
Pro-Dir for Learning and Teaching: Prof. NIRMALA RAO
Pro-Dir for Research and Enterprise: Prof. GRAHAM FURNISS
Registrar and Sec.: DONALD BEATON
Library: see under Libraries and Archives
Number of teachers: 200
Number of students: 4,700

Publications: *Journal of African Law, The China Quarterly*

DEANS

Faculty of Arts and Humanities: Prof. GURHARPAL SINGH
Faculty of Languages and Cultures: Prof. ANNE PAUWELS
Faculty of Law and Social Sciences: Prof. STEPHEN CHAN

PROFESSORS

ABDEL-HALEEM, M. A. S., Islamic Studies
ACHCAR, G., Development Studies and International Relations
AL-ALI, N., Gender Studies
ASH, R., Economics (Taiwan)
AUSTIN, P., Linguistics
ASHIAGBOR, D., Law
BADERIN, M., Law
BANDA, F., Law
BARRETT, T. H., East Asian History
BEHRENS-ABOUSEIF, D., Islamic Art and Archaeology
BOOTH, A., Economics (Asia)
BRAMALL, C., Economics (Asia Pacific)
BROWN, I., Economic History (South East Asia)
CLARENCE-SMITH, W., Economic History (Asia and Africa)
CONTADINI, A., History of Art and Archaeology
CRAMER, C., Development Studies
CRAVEN, M., Law
CULLET, P., Law
DORWARD, A., Development Economics
DRIVER, C., Financial Economics
DWYER, R., South Asia (Indian Cultures and Cinema)
FARDON, R., Anthropology (West Africa)
FATTOUH, B., Finance and Management (Middle East)
FINE, B., Economics

FORTNA, B., History of the Middle East
FUEHRER, B., Sinology
FURNISS, G., African Languages, Literature and Popular Culture
GEORGE, A., Babylonian
GERSTLE, A., Japanese and Korean Studies
GOODHAND, J., Development Studies
HARRIS, L., Economics
HARRIGAN, J., Economics
HEWITT, G., Caucasian Languages
HEZSER, C., Jewish Studies
HINTZE, A., Study of Religions
HOBART, M., Critical Media and Cultural Studies (South East Asia)
HOCKX, M., Chinese
HOWARD, K., Music
HOWE, C., Chinese Business and Management
HUTT, M., Nepali and Himalayan Studies
HUXLEY, A., Law
NIKOLAEVA, I., Linguistics
ISMAIL, S., Comparative and International Politics (Middle East)
JAGGAR, P., Language and Cultures (Africa)
KABEER, N., Development Studies
KARSHENAS, M., Economics (Middle East)
KENNEDY, D., Law
KENNEDY, H., Arabic
KHAN, M., Economics
KRATZ, U., Indonesian and Malay
LAPAVITSAS, C., Economics (Japan)
LAU, M., Law
NISSANKE, M., Economics
OUGHTON, C., Managerial Economics
PALMER, M., Law
PAUWELS, A., Sociolinguistics
PEEL, J., Anthropology and Sociology (Africa)
PERRY-KESSARIS, A., Economic Law
PICTON, J., African Art
POTTIER, J., Anthropology (Africa)
RATHBONE, R., Modern African History
REID, R., History of Africa
ROBB, P., History of India
SAAD-FILHO, A., Political Economics
SACHDEV, I., Linguistics
SAEZ, L., Politics and International Studies
SCARAMOZZINO, P., Economics
SHINDLER, C., Near and Middle East
SCREECH, T., History of Art (Japan)
SCOBBIE, I., Law, Peace Building, Human Rights
SHANKAR, B., Development, Environment and Policy
SIMS-WILLIAMS, N., Iranian and Central Asian Studies
SREBERNY, A., Global Media and Communications
SRIRAM, C., Law
SUN, L., Business and Management (China)
TOPOROWSKI, J., Economics and Finance
TRIPP, C., Politics (Middle East)
WEEKS, J., Development Economics
WELCHMAN, L., Law
WEST, H., Anthropology
WIDDESS, R., Music
WRIGHT, O., Musicology of the Middle East

University College London

Gower St, London, WC1E 6BT

Telephone: (20) 7679-2000
E-mail: international@ucl.ac.uk
Internet: www.ucl.ac.uk
Founded 1826, merged with Royal Free Hospital School of Medicine 1998
Pres. and Provost: Prof. MALCOLM GRANT
Vice-Provost for Academic and Int. Affairs: Prof. MICHAEL WORTON
Vice-Provost for Enterprise: Prof. STEPHEN CADDICK
Vice-Provost for Health: Prof. Sir JOHN TOOKE
Vice-Provost for Operations: REX KNIGHT
Vice-Provost for Research: Prof. G. DAVID PRICE
Registrar: CHRISTOPHER HALLAS

Library: see under Libraries and Archives
Number of teachers: 4,080
Number of students: 21,130
Publications: *The World of UCL, UCL Universe*

DEANS

Faculty of Arts and Humanities: Prof. HENRY WOUDHUYSEN
Faculty of Biomedical Sciences: Prof. IAN JACOBS
Faculty of the Built Environment: Prof. ALAN PENN
Faculty of Engineering Sciences: Prof. ANTHONY C. W. FINKELSTEIN
Faculty of Laws: Prof. Dame HAZEL GENN
Faculty of Life Sciences: Prof. MARY K. L. COLLINS
Faculty of Mathematical and Physical Sciences: Prof. RICHARD CATLOW
Faculty of Social and Historical Sciences: Prof. STEPHEN R. SMITH

PROFESSORS

ADLER, M. W., Sexually Transmitted Diseases
AEPPLI, G., Physics
AGHION, P., Economics of Public Policy
AIELLO, L. C., Biological Anthropology
AIKEN, J., Fine Art
AKBAR, A. N., Immunology
ANDERSON, J. E., Organic Chemistry
ANDERSON, J. M., Mathematics
ANDERSON, P. N., Experimental Neuroscience
ANDERSON, R. H., Paediatric Cardiac Morphology
ANDREWS, D. J., Engineering Design
ARRIDGE, S. R., Image Processing
ASHMORE, J. F., Biophysics
ASHTON, R. D., English Language and Literature
ATKINSON, J., Psychology
ATTANASIO, O. P., Economics
ATTWELL, D. I., Physiology
AYAZI SHAMLOU, P., Biochemical Engineering
AYNSLEY-GREEN, A., Child Health
BABIKER, A. G., Medical Statistics and Epidemiology
BALL, K. M., Mathematics
BANISTER, D. J., Transport Planning
BARENDT, E. M., Law of Media of Communication and Expression
BARKER, J. A., Hydrogeology
BARLOW, M. J., Astrophysics
BARNES, M. P., Scandinavian Studies
BARTLETT, R. P., Russian History
BARTLEY, M., Medical Sociology
BATE, S. P., Health Services Management
BATTARBEE, R. W., Environmental Change
BATTY, J. M., Spatial Analysis and Planning
BAYVEL, P., Optical Communications and Networks
BEBBINGTON, P. E., Social and Community Psychiatry
BEGENT, R. H. J., Oncology
BERGER, M. A., Mathematics
BETTERIDGE, D. J., Endocrinology and Metabolism
BEVAN, S. J., Pharmacology
BEVERLEY, P. C. L., Tumour Immunology
BHATTACHARYA, S. S., Experimental Ophthalmology
BINDMAN, D., History of Art
BIRD, A. C., Clinical Ophthalmology
BISHOP, S. R., Non-linear Dynamics
BLUNDELL, R., Economics
BLUNN, G. W., Biomedical Engineering
BOGLE, I. D. L., Chemical Engineering
BOLSOVER, S. R., Cell Physiology
BORDEN, I. M., Architecture and Urban Culture
BORGERS, T., Economics
BOSHOFF, C. H., Cancer Medicine
BOSTOCK, H., Neurophysiology

BOULOS, P. B., Surgery
BOWLING, A., Health Services Research
BOWMAKER, J., Visual Research
BOWN, S. G., Laser Medicine and Surgery
BOYD, I. W., Electronic Materials
BRAMWELL, S. T., Physical Chemistry
BREWIN, C. R., Clinical Psychology
BRIDGE, M. G., Commercial Law
BROCKES, J. P., Cell Biology
BRODY, M. B., Linguistics
BROWN, D. A., Pharmacology
BROWN, M. M., Stroke Medicine
BROWN, R. A., Tissue Engineering
BROWN, S. N., Mathematics
BROWNE, E. J., History of Medicine
BRUCKDORFER, K. R., Biochemistry
BRYSON, W. N., History and Theory of Art
BURGESS, J. A., Geography
BURK, K. M., Modern and Contemporary History
BURNHAM, P. C., Social Anthropology
BURNSTOCK, G., Anatomy
BURROUGHS, A. K., Hepatology
BUTLER, W. E., Comparative Law
BUTTERWORTH, B. L., Cognitive Neuropsychology
BUXTON, B. F., Information Processing
BYNUM, W. F., History of Medicine
CALLARD, R., Immunology
CAMPBELL, J. A., Computer Science
CAMPBELL, R., Communication Disorders
CARLIN, W. J., Economics
CATLOW, C. R. A., Chemistry
CHAIN, B. M., Immunology
CHARLES, I. G., Molecular Biology
CHESHER, A. D., Economics
CLARK, J. B., Neurochemistry
CLARK, R. J. H., Chemistry
CLARKE, P. E. L., Physics
CLAYTON, P. T., Paediatric Metabolic Disease and Hepatology
CLOUT, H. D., Geography
COCKCROFT, S., Cell Physiology
COLHOUN, H. M., Clinical Epidemiology
COLLINGE, J., Neurodegenerative Disease
COLLINS, M. K. L., Immunology
COLQUHOUN, D., Pharmacology
CONWAY, S. R., History
COOK, P. F. C., Architecture
COOTER, R. J.
COPP, A. J., Developmental Neurobiology
COVENEY, P. V., Physical Chemistry
CRAGGS, M. D., Applied Neurophysiology
CRAIG, G., Paediatric Genetics
CRANE, T. M., Philosophy
CRAWFORD, M. H., Ancient History
CROLL, J. G. A., Civil and Environmental Engineering
CROSS, P. A., Geomatic Engineering
CULHANE, J. L., Physics
CULL-CANDY, S. G., Pharmacology
CURRAN, H. V., Psychopharmacology
CUZNER, M. L., Neurochemistry
D'AVRAY, D. L., History
DACRE, J. E., Medical Education
DANPURE, C. J., Molecular Cell Biology
DARBYSHIRE, J. H., Epidemiology
DAVIDSON, B. R., Surgery
DAVIES, S. W., Experimental Neuropathology
DAVIES, W. E., History
DAWID, A. P., Statistics
DAYAN, P., Computational Neuroscience
DEAN, M. C., Anatomy
DEEMING, A. J., Chemistry
DELETANT, D. J., Romanian Studies
DELHANTY, J. D. A., Human Genetics
DELPY, D. T., Medical Photonics
DENNIS, I. H., English Law
DEZATEUX, C. A., Paediatric Epidemiology
DHILLON, A. P., Histopathology
DICKENSON, A. H., Neuropharmacology
DIMITRIOU, H., Planning Studies
DOLAN, R., Neuropsychiatry
DOLPHIN, A., Pharmacology
DOWD, P. M., Dermatology

DOWMAN, I. J., Photogrammetry and Remote Sensing
DUCHEN, M. R., Physiology
DUNCAN, J. S., Clinical Neurology
DUNNILL, P., Biochemical Engineering
DUSHEIKO, G. M., Medicine
DWORKIN, R. M., Jurisprudence
EDWARDS, J. C. W., Connective-tissue Medicine
EDWARDS, Y. H., Human Genetics
EKINS, R. P., Biophysics
ELL, P. J., Nuclear Medicine
ELTON, L., Higher Education
EMERY, V. C., Virology
EVANS, A. W., Transport Safety
EVANS, M. C. W., Plant Chemistry
FEARN, T., Applied Statistics
FERGUSSON-PELL, M., Neuromuscular Restoration and Rehabilitation
FINE, L. G., Medicine
FINKELSTEIN, A. C. W., Software Systems Engineering
FINNEY, J. L., Physics
FISH, D. R., Clinical Neurophysiology and Epilepsy
FISHER, A. J., Physics
FISHER, E. M. C., Neurogenetics
FITZGERALD, M., Developmental Neurobiology
FITZKE, F. W., Visual Optics
FLETCHER, I. F., International Commercial Law
FONAGY, P., Psychoanalysis
FOOT, M. M., Library and Archive Studies
FOREMAN, J. C., Immunopharmacology
FORGACS, D. A., Italian
FORGE, A., Auditory Cell Biology
FORTY, J. A., History of Architecture
FOURNIER, C. L., Architecture and Urban Planning
FOWLER, C. J., Uro-neurology
FRACKOWIAK, R. S. J., Cognitive Neurology
FRANCK, L. S., Children's Nursing Research Studies
FREEMAN, M. D. A., English Law
FRENCH, D. W., History
FRISTON, K. J., Imaging Neuroscience
FRITH, C. D., Neuropsychology
FRITH, U., Cognitive Development
FRY, C. H., Cellular Physiology
FULBROOK, M. J. A., German History
FULLER, J. H., Clinical Epidemiology
FURNHAM, A. F., Psychology
GABELLA, G., Histology and Cytology
GAGE, S. A., Innovative Technology in Architecture
GALLIVAN, S., Mathematics
GARB, T., History of Art
GARDINER, R. M., Paediatrics
GARDNER-MEDWIN, A. R., Physiology
GARTHWAITE, J., Experimental Neuroscience
GELLER, M. J., Jewish Studies
GENN, H. G., Socio-Legal Studies
GILBERT, A. G., Geography
GILLAN, M. J., Physics
GILLESPIE, S. H., Medical Microbiology
GOADSBY, P. J., Clinical Neurology
GODOVAC-ZIMMERMANN, J., Protein Biochemistry
GOLDSPINK, G., Anatomy
GOLDSTEIN, D. B., Evolutionary and Population Genetics
GOLDSTONE, A. H., Haematology
GOODSHIP, A. E., Orthopaedic Sciences
GOODWIN, P. B., Transport Policy
GOSWAMI, U., Cognitive Developmental Psychology
GRAFFY, J. J., Russian Literature and Cinema
GRANTHAM-MCGREGOR, S. M., Child Health and Nutrition
GRASS, A. J., Fluid Mechanics
GREEN, C. J., Surgery
GREENHALGH, P. M., Primary Care Development
GREENWOOD, J., Biomedical Research
GREGORY, J., Water Chemistry

GRIFFITHS, H. D., Electronics
GRIFFITHS, P. D., Virology
GUERRINI, R., Paediatric Neurology
GUEST, J. E., Planetary Science
GUEST, S. F. D., Legal Philosophy
GURLING, H. M., Molecular Psychiatry
HALE, K. J., Chemistry
HALL, A., Molecular Biology
HALL, C., Modern British Social and Cultural History
HALL, C. M., Paediatric Radiology
HALL, P. G., Planning Studies
HAMILTON-MILLER, J. M. T., Medical Microbiology
HAMMOND, P., Dental and Medical Informatics
HANN, I., Paediatric Haematology and Oncology
HANSON, J. M., House Form and Culture
HARRIS, J. M., Linguistics
HARRIS, R., Geography
HARRISON, C. M., Geography
HARRISON, M. J. G., Clinical Neurology
HART, S. M., Hispanic Studies
HARTLEY, J. A., Cancer Studies
HARVEY, N. J. W., Judgement and Decision Research
HASSAN, F. A., Archaeology
HATCH, D. J., Paediatric Anaesthesia
HAUSSER, M. A., Neuroscience
HAWKINS, P. N., Medicine
HAWLEY, C., Architectural Studies
HAWORTH, S. G., Developmental Cardiology
HAZELL, R. J. D., Government and the Constitution
HEBDEN, J. C., Biomedical Optics
HERMANS, T. J., Dutch and Comparative Literature
HERTZMAN, C., Paediatric Radiology
HEYDECKER, B. G., Transport Studies
HEYES, C. M., Psychology
HILLIARD, A. J., Fine Art Media
HILLIER, W. R. G., Architectural and Urban Morphology
HILLSON, S. W., Bioarchaeology
HITCHINGS, R. A., Glaucoma and Allied Studies
HOARE, M., Biochemical Engineering
HOBKIRK, J. A., Dental Prosthetics
HOBSON, R. P., Developmental Psychopathology
HOCKEY, S. M., Library and Information Studies
HODGSON, H., Medicine
HOMEWOOD, K. M., Human Ecology
HOPPIT, J., British History
HORNBLOWER, N. S. R., Classics and Ancient History
HORNE, F. P., English Language and Literature
HORTON, M. A., Bone Biology and Mineral Metabolism
HOSKING, G. A., Russian History
HOWARTH, I. D., Astronomy
HOWELL, P., Experimental Psychology
HUDSON, R. A., Linguistics
HUGHES, H. A. J., Russian History
HUMBERSTON, J. W., Physics
HUMPHRIES, S. E., Cardiovascular Genetics
HUNT, D. M., Molecular Genetics
HUNT, J. C. R., Climate Modelling
HUNT, N. P., Orthodontics
HUNT, S. P., Molecular Neurobiology
HYAMS, J. S., Cell Biology
ICHIMURA, H., Economics
INGRAM, D., Health Informatics
ISENBERG, D. A., Rheumatology
ISHAM, V. S., Probability and Statistics
JANOSSY, G., Immunology
JARVIS, M. J., Health Psychology
JAUNIAUX, E. R. M., Obstetrics and Fetal Medicine
JAYNE, J. E., Mathematics
JEHIEL, P., Economics
JESSEN, K. R., Developmental Neurobiology

JOHNSON, A. M., Primary Care and Population Sciences
JOHNSON, E. R., Mathematics
JOHNSON, F. E. A., Mathematics
JOHNSTON, A., Psychology
JONES, A. G., Chemical Engineering
JONES, D. T., Bioinformatics
JONES, J. S., Human Genetics
JONES, T. W., Physics
JORDAN, D., Physiology
JOWELL, J. L., Public Law
KAPLAN, B. J., Dutch History
KARLIN, D. R., English
KATONA, C. L. E., Psychiatry of the Elderly
KATZ, D. R., Immunopathology
KEMP, D. T., Auditory Biophysics
KHAW, P. T., Glaucoma Studies and Wound Healing
KING, M., Primary Care Psychiatry
KINNON, C., Molecular Immunology
KIRBY, D. G., Modern History
KIRSTEIN, P. T., Computer Systems
KLIER, J. D., Modern Jewish History
KOERNER, J. L., History of Art
KOLANKIEWICZ, J. M., Sociology
KUHRT, A. T. L., Ancient Near Eastern History
KULLMANN, D. M., Neurology
LARMAN, D. G., Mathematics
LAST, D. M., Anthropology
LATCHMAN, D. S., Human Genetics
LAURENT, G. J., Pulmonary Biochemistry
LAWRENCE, C. J., History of Medicine
LAYCOCK, G. K., Crime Science
LEES, A. J., Clinical Neurology
LEES, W. R., Medical Imaging
LEMON, R. N., Neurophysiology
LEONARD, J. V., Paediatric Metabolic Disease
LEWIS, A. D. E., Comparative Legal History
LIEBERMAN, A. R., Anatomy
LIGHTMAN, S. L., Clinical Ophthalmology
LIM, L., Neurochemistry
LINCH, D. C., Clinical Haematology
LINDON, J. M. A., Italian Studies
LITTLEWOOD, R., Anthropological Psychiatry
LLOYD, M. H., General Practice
LONDEI, M., Autoimmunity
LONGLEY, P. A., Geographic Information
LUMLEY, R., Italian Cultural History
LUND, V. J., Rhinology
LUTHERT, P. J., Pathology
LUXON, L. M., Audiological Medicine
LYDYARD, P. M., Immunology
MACHIN, S. J., Economics
MACHIN, S. J., Haematology
MACKETT, R. L., Transport Studies
MACLEAN, A. B., Obstetrics and Gynaecology
MACRORY, R. B., Environmental Law
MAJEED, F. A., Primary Care and Public Health
MALLET, J., Biological Diversity
MALONE-LEE, J. G., Geriatric Medicine
MARGETTS, H. Z., Political Science
MARKESINIS, B., Common Law and Civil Law
MARMOT, M. G., Epidemiology and Public Health
MARTIN, B. R. C., Physics
MARTIN, J. F., Cardiovascular Medicine
MARTIN, M. G. F., Philosophy
MARTIN, P., Tissue Repair
MASON, K. O., Astronomy
MASTERS, J. R. W., Experimental Pathology
MATHEWS, T. P., French
MATHIAS, C. J., Neurovascular Medicine
MCARTHUR, J. M., Geochemistry
MCCARTHY, M., Public Health
MCDOWELL, L. M., Economic Geography
MCEWEN, K. A., Physics
MCGUIRE, W. J., Geological Hazards
MCLEAN, P., Fine Art
MCMANUS, I. C., Psychology and Medical Education
MCMILLAN, P. F., Solid State Chemistry
MCMILLIN, A. B., Russian Literature
MCMULLEN, P., Mathematics
MEGHIR, C. H. D., Economics

MEREDITH, P. G., Rock Physics
MIDWINTER, J. E., Electrical Engineering
MILLA, P. J., Paediatric Gastroenterology
MILLER, A. I., History and Philosophy of Science
MILLER, D. H., Clinical Neurology
MILLER, D. J., Physics
MILLER, D. M. S., Anthropology
MIRSKY, R., Developmental Neurobiology
MOBBS, P. G., Physiology
MONCADA, S., Experimental Biology and Therapeutics
MONK, M., Molecular Embryology
MOORE, A. T., Ophthalmology
MORRIS, P. W. G., Construction and Project Management
MOSS, S. E., Biomedical Research
MOSS, S. J., Molecular Pharmacology and Cell Biology
MOTHERWELL, W. B., Chemistry
MULLER, J.-P. A. L., Image Understanding and Remote Sensing
MUNDY, A. R., Urology
MUNTON, R. J. C., Geography
MYTHEN, M. G., Paediatric Anaesthesia
NAZARETH, I. D., Primary Care and Population Science
NEILD, G. H., Nephrology
NEVILLE, B., Paediatric Neurology
NEWELL, M. L., Paediatric Epidemiology
NEWELL, W. R., Physics
NEWMAN, A. F., Economics
NEWMAN, S. P., Health Psychology
NORTH, J. A., History
NUGENT, J. H. A., Plant Biochemistry
NUTT, B. B., Facility and Environment Management
NUTTON, V., History of Medicine
O'DALY, G. J. P., Latin
O'HARE, M. J., Cell Biology
O'HIGGINS, P., Anatomy
O'KEEFE, J., Cognitive Neuroscience
O'KEEFFE, D., European Law
O'NEILL, M. E., Mathematics
O'REILLY, J. J., Telecommunications
ODA, H., Japanese Law
OLIVER, A. D. H., Constitutional Law
OLSEN, I., Cell Biology and Tissue Engineering
ONO, S. J., Ocular Immunology
ORDIDGE, R. J., Medical Physics
ORENGO, C. A., Bioinformatics
ORESZCZYN, T., Energy and Environment
ORTON, C. R., Quantitative Archaeology
OWEN, J. S., Molecular Medicine
PALMER, N. E., Law of Art and Cultural Property
PARKIN, I. P., Chemistry
PARMAR, M. K. B., Medical Statistics and Epidemiology
PARNAVELAS, J. G., Neuroanatomy
PARTRIDGE, L., Biometry
PATTISON, J. R., Medical Microbiology
PEARCE, D. W., Economics
PEARCE, F. L., Biological Chemistry
PECKHAM, C., Paediatric Epidemiology
PEPYS, M., Medicine
PERKINS, R. M., Norse Studies
PERKINS, S. J., Structural Biochemistry
PETTET, B. G., Company and Capital Markets Law
PHILLIPS, A., Epidemiology and Biostatistics
PICKERING, K. T., Sedimentology and Stratigraphy
PIERRO, A., Paediatric Surgery
PIPER, P. W., Molecular Microbiology
PITT, C. W., Electrical Engineering
PLATT, J. P., Geology
PLOTKIN, H. C., Psychobiology
POLLOCK, A. M., Health Services Policy
POMIANKOWSKI, A., Genetics
PORTER, J. B., Haematology
PORTER, S. R., Oral Medicine
POULTER, L. W., Immunology
POUNDER, R. E., Medicine
POVEY, M. S., Human Somatic Cell Genetics

POWER, C., Epidemiology and Public Health
POWIS, S. H., Renal Medicine
PRASHER, D. K., Audiology
PREECE, M., Child Health and Growth
PREISS, D., Pure Mathematics
PRICE, C. A., Archaeological Conservation
PRICE, G. D., Mineral Physics
PRICE, S. D., Chemical Physics
PRICE, S. L., Chemistry
PROWSE, P., Theatre Design
PYNSENT, R. B., Czech and Slovak Literature
QUINN, N. P., Clinical Neurology
RADEMACHER, T. W., Molecular Medicine
RAWSON, P. F., Geology
REHREN, T. H. H., Archaeological Materials and Technologies
REVELL, P. A., Histopathology
RICH, P. R., Bioenergetics
RICHARDS, C. D., Experimental Physiology
RICHARDS, P., Anthropology
RICHARDSON, W. D., Biology
ROBERTS, B. P., Chemistry
ROBERTS, G. J., Children's Dentistry
ROBERTSON, M. M., Neuropsychiatry
RODECK, C. H., Obstetrics and Gynaecology
ROEMER, C. E., Papyrology
RON, M. A., Neuropsychiatry
ROOK, G. A. W., Medical Microbiology
ROSEN, F. R., History of Political Thought
ROSEN, S., Speech and Hearing Sciences
ROTHWELL, J. C., Human Neurophysiology
ROWLAND, S. C. W., Higher Education
ROWLANDS, M. J. J., Material Culture
RUBIN, G. S., Visual Function and Rehabilitation
RUSSELL, M. A., Addiction
RYAN, J. M., Post-Conflict Recovery
SAGGERSON, E. D., Biochemistry
SALT, J., Geography
SALT, T. E., Visual Science
SALVERDA, R., Dutch Language and Literature
SAMMONDS, P. R., Geophysics
SANDER, J. W. A., Epilepsy
SANDS, P. J., Law
SAUNDERS, M. I., Oncology
SCAMBLER, G. N., Medical Sociology
SCAMBLER, P. J., Molecular Medicine
SCARAVILLI, F., Neuropathology
SCHAPIRA, A. H. V., Neurology
SCHOFIELD, T. P., History of Legal and Political Thought
SCULLY, C. M., Special Needs Dentistry
SEEDS, A. J., Opto-electronics
SEGAL, A. W., Medicine
SENN, S. J., Pharmaceutical and Health Statistics
SEYMOUR, R. M., Mathematics
SHALLICE, T., Psychology
SHANKS, D. R., Experimental Psychology
SHARPLES, R. W., Classics
SHEIHAM, A., Dental Public Health
SHENNAN, S. J., Theoretical Archaeology
SHEPHARD, E. A., Molecular Biology
SHEPHERD, P. R., Cellular Signalling
SHERR, L., Clinical and Health Psychology
SHORVON, S. D., Clinical Neurology
SILLITO, A. M., Visual Science
SIMONS, S. J. R., Chemical Engineering
SINDET-PEDERSEN, S., Oral Implantology
SINGER, A., Gynaecological Research
SINGER, M., Intensive Care Medicine
SLATER, M., Virtual Environments
SMART, T. G., Pharmacology
SMITH, A., Detector Physics
SMITH, A. H., Political Economy
SMITH, F. T., Mathematics
SMITH, N. V., Linguistics
SMITH, S. R., Economics
SNOWDON, P. F.
SOMMER, V., Evolutionary Anthropology
SOUTHGATE, L. J., Primary Care and Education
SPEIGHT, P. M., Oral Pathology
SPELLER, R. D., Medical Physics
SPIRO, S. G., Respiratory Medicine

SPOOR, C. F., Evolutionary Anatomy
SPYER, K. M., Physiology
STANFORD, J. L., Medical Microbiology
STEADMAN, J. P., Urban and Built Form Studies
STEPHENS, J. A., Physiology
STEPTOE, A. P. A., Psychology
STOCKMAN, A., Investigative Eye Research
STOCKS, J., Respiratory Medicine
STONEHAM, A. M., Physics
STOREY, P. J., Physics
STROBEL, S., Paediatrics and Clinical Immunology
SURTEES, R. A. H., Paediatric Neurology
SUTHERLAND, J. A., Modern English Literature
SUTTON, S. R., Social and Health Psychology
SWALES, M. W., German
SWALLOW, D. M., Biology
SWANN, P. F., Molecular Oncology
SWANSON, T. M., Law and Economics
TAIT, W. J., Egyptology
TAYLOR, B., Community Child Health
TAYLOR, I., Surgery
TEDDER, R. S., Medical Virology
TENNYSON, J., Physics
THIMBLEBY, H. W., Human Interaction with Systems
THOMAS, D. G. T., Neurological Surgery
THOMAS, K. D., Human Palaeoecology
THOMPSON, A. J., Clinical Neurology and Neurorehabilitation
THOMPSON, E. J., Neurochemistry
THORNTON, J. M., Biomolecular Structure
THRASHER, A. J., Paediatric Immunology
TILLEY, C. Y., Anthropology and Archaeology
TITCHENER-HOOKER, N. J., Biochemical Engineering
TOBIAS, J. S., Cancer Medicine
TODD, C. J., Network Science
TODD-POKROPEK, A. E., Medical Physics
TOFTS, P. S., Medical Physics
TOMKINS, A. M., International Child Health
TONETTI, M., Periodontology
TOOK, J. F., Dante Studies
TRELEAVEN, P. C., Computer Science
TRIMBLE, M. R., Behavioural Neurology
TURNER, M. W., Molecular Immunology
TURNER, R., Anthropology
TWINING, W. L., Jurisprudence
TYLER, N. A., Communities and Transport
UCKO, P. J., Comparative Archaeology
UNWIN, R., Nephrology and Physiology
VALLANCE, P., Clinical Pharmacology
VAN DER LELY, H. K. J., Developmental Language Disorders and Cognitive Neuroscience
VAN GRIETHUYSEN, W. J., Naval Architecture
VAN REENEN, J. M., Economics
VARGHA-KHADEM, F., Developmental Cognitive Neuroscience
VERGANI, D., Immunopathology
WAKELY, P. I., Urban Development
WALTON, S. J., Norwegian
WARDLE, F. J., Clinical Psychology
WARNER, A. E., Developmental Biology
WASHBROOK, J., Computer Science
WATERFIELD, M. D., Biochemistry
WEIS, R. J., English
WEISS, R. A., Viral Oncology
WELLER, I. V. D., Sexually Transmitted Diseases
WELLS, J. C., Phonetics
WESTON, H. D., History of Art
WHITEHOUSE, R. D., Archaeology
WIGZELL, F. C. M., Russian Literature and Culture
WILBUR, S. R., Distributed Systems
WILKIN, C., Physics
WILLIAMS, G. H., Histopathology
WILLIAMS, R. S., Hepatology
WILLIS, A. J., Astronomy
WILSON, D. S. M., Linguistics
WILSON, E. J., Latin American Literature
WILSON, M., Microbiology
WILSON, S. W., Developmental Genetics

WINCHESTER, B. G., Biochemistry
WINGHAM, D. J., Climate Physics
WINSLET, M. C., Surgery
WINTER, R. M., Clinical Genetics
WOLEDGE, R. C., Experimental Physiology
WOLFF, J., Philosophy
WOLPERT, D. M., Motor Neuroscience
WOLPERT, L., Biology as applied to Medicine
WOO, P. M. M., Paediatric Rheumatology
WOOD, N. W., Clinical Neurogenetics
WOOD, P. A., Geography
WOOLF, A. S., Nephrology
WORTON, M. J., French Language and Literature
WOTTON, R. S., Biology
WOUDHUYSEN, H. R., English Language and Literature
WRIGHT, A., Otorhinolaryngology
WU, G., Computational Fluid Dynamics
WYATT, J. S., Neonatal Paediatrics
YANG, Z., Statistical Genetics
YATES, J. G., Chemical Engineering
YELLON, D. M., Cellular Cardiology
YIP, M. J., Linguistics
YOUSRY, T. A., Neuroradiology
YUDKIN, J. S., Medicine
ZEKI, S., Neurobiology
ZUMLA, A., Infectious Diseases and International Health

SCHOOLS OF THE COLLEGE

UCL School of Pharmacy: 29–39 Brunswick Sq., London, WC1N 1AX; tel. (20) 7753-5800; e-mail sop.director@ucl.ac.uk; internet www.ucl.ac.uk/pharmacy; f. 1842, merged with Univ. College London 2012; engages in education, research and policy devt; focuses on 4 key areas—drug discovery, formulation sciences, medicines use and health, and neuroscience; develops new areas of significance such as behavioural medicine, gene therapy, nanomedicines and paediatric pharmacy; 1,300 students; Dir Prof. DUNCAN CRAIG; Head of Registry JOHN PECK.

UCL School of Slavonic and East European Studies: Univ. of London, London, WC1E 7HU; tel. (20) 7636-8000; f. 1915, merged with Univ. College London 1999; library of 400,000 vols; 60 teachers; 500 students (460 full-time, 40 part-time); Dir Dr ROBIN P. AIZLEWOOD; Academic Registrar CAROL PEARCE; publ. *The Slavonic and East European Review* (4 a year).

UNIVERSITY INSTITUTES

University of London Institute in Paris

9–11 rue de Constantine, 75340 Paris Cedex 07, France

Telephone: (1) 44-11-73-73
E-mail: french@ulip.lon.ac.uk
Internet: www.ulip.lon.ac.uk

Founded 1894 as 'Guilde Franco-Anglaise', attached to Univ. of Paris 1927, now a central institute of Univ. of London, partner of Queen Mary and Royal Holloway, Univ. of London

Languages of instruction: French, English
Academic year: September to July

Dean: Prof. ANDREW HUSSEY
Project Man.: ANNA GRAY
Office Man.: COLLETTE BROWN
Librarian: ERICA BURNHAM

Library of 10,000 vols, 25 journals and electronic subscriptions
Number of teachers: 13
Number of students: 160 f.t.e.

Publication: *Francosphères*

PROFESSOR

HUSSEY, A., French Studies

University Marine Biological Station Millport

Millport, Isle of Cumbrae, Scotland, KA28 0EG

Telephone: (1475) 530581
E-mail: tracy.price@millport.gla.ac.uk
Internet: www.gla.ac.uk/marinestation

Founded 1970 in asscn with Univ. of Glasgow
Teaches and researches in marine biology
Library of 5,000 vols

Dir: Prof. JIM ATKINSON (acting)
Deputy Dir: FIONA HANNAH
Sec.: TRACY E. PRICE

PROFESSORS

ATKINSON, R. J. A., Marine Biology
MOORE, P. G., Marine Biology.

CONSTITUENT INSTITUTES OF THE SCHOOL OF ADVANCED STUDY

Dean of the School of Advanced Study: Prof. ROGER KAIN

Institute of Advanced Legal Studies

17 Russell Sq., London, WC1B 5DR

Telephone: (20) 7862-5800
E-mail: ials@sas.ac.uk
Internet: www.ials.sas.ac.uk
Academic year: October to December
Founded 1947

Man.: Dr CONOR WYER
Dir: JULES WINTERTON
Library: see under Libraries and Archives
Publication: *Amicus Curiae*

PROFESSORS

DAINTITH, T. C., Constitutional and Admin. Law, Economic Law
RIDER, B. A. K., Company Law, Commercial Criminal Law
SHERR, A. H., Legal Education, Legal Profession, Legal Services
XANTHAKI, H., Law and Legislative Studies

Institute of Classical Studies

Senate House, Malet St, London, WC1E 7HU

Telephone: (20) 7862-8700
E-mail: admin.icls@sas.ac.uk
Internet: www.icls.sas.ac.uk
Founded 1953

Library of basic research books complemented by library of Hellenic and Roman Socs (jt library of 100,000 vols); seminars and lectures for students

Dir: Prof. JOHN NORTH
Sec.: Dr OLGA KRZYSZKOWSKA

Institute of Commonwealth Studies

Second Fl., S Block, Senate House, Malet St, London, WC1E 7HU

Telephone: (20) 7262-8844
E-mail: ics@sas.ac.uk
Internet: commonwealth.sas.ac.uk
Founded 1949
Academic year: September to June

Dir: Prof. PHILIP MURPHY
Admin. Man.: ALISON STEWART
Information Resources Man.: DAVID CLOVER

Library of 190,000 vols, 9,000 periodical and serial publs, 230 archival collns
Number of teachers: 5 (full-time)
Number of students: 80

Publication: *Journal of Imperial and Commonwealth History* (4 a year)

PROFESSORS

HOLLAND, R., Imperial and Commonwealth History
MANOR, J., Emeka Anyaoku Prof. of Commonwealth Studies

MURPHY, P., British and Commonwealth History

ATTACHED INSTITUTE

Commonwealth Policy Studies Unit (CPSU): internet www.cpsu.org.uk; Head Dr VICTORIA TE VELDE; Asst Dir Dr LEO ZEILIG

Institute of English Studies

School of Advanced Study, Senate House, Malet St, London, WC1E 7HU

Telephone: (20) 7862-8675
E-mail: ies@sas.ac.uk
Internet: ies.sas.ac.uk

Founded 1991 as Centre for English Studies; present name 1999
State control
Academic year: September to June

Dir: Prof. WARWICK GOULD
Number of teachers: 35
Number of students: 28

Institute of Germanic and Romance Studies

Senate House, Malet St, London, WC1E 7HU

Telephone: (20) 7862-8677
E-mail: igrs@sas.ac.uk Germanic Studies Library: 29 Russell Sq., London, WC1B 5DP

Telephone: (20) 7862-8967
E-mail: igslib@sas.ac.uk
Internet: igrs.sas.ac.uk

Founded 2004, by merger of Institute of Germanic Studies (f. 1950) and Institute of Romance Studies (f. 1989)
Academic year: October to June

Dir: Prof. NAOMI SEGAL
Admin. Sec.: ROSEMARY LAMBETH
Librarian: WILLIAM ABBEY; 1,320 mems
Library of 100,000 vols
Number of teachers: 6
Number of students: 25

Publications: *Journal of Romance Studies* (3 a year), *London German Studies* (irregular)

Institute of Historical Research

Senate House, Malet St., London, WC1E 7HU

Telephone: (20) 7862-8740
E-mail: ihr@sas.ac.uk
Internet: www.history.ac.uk

Founded 1921
Language of instruction: English
Academic year: October to September

Dir: Prof. MILES TAYLOR
Institute Administrator: ELAINE WALTERS
Librarian: KATE WILCOX

Library: see under Libraries and Archives
Number of teachers: 8
Number of students: 57

Publications: *Historical Research* (4 a year), *Past and Future, Teachers of History* (1 a year), *Theses in Progress and Theses Completed* (1 a year)

PROFESSORS

ROBERTS, R., Contemporary British History
TAYLOR, M., Modern History
THANE, P., Contemporary British History

Institute of Musical Research

Senate House, Malet St, London, WC1E 7HU

Telephone: (20) 7664-4865
E-mail: music@sas.ac.uk
Internet: music.sas.ac.uk

Founded 2005, began operating 2006

Funded by Higher Education Funding Ccl for England (HEFCE); fosters collaborative research; hosts visiting scholars; organizes confs and other events; provides research training support for postgraduate students

Dir: Dr PAUL ARCHBOLD
Administrator: VALERIE JAMES

Institute of Philosophy

Senate House, Malet St, London, WC1E 7HU

Telephone: (20) 7862-8683
E-mail: philosophy@sas.ac.uk
Internet: www.philosophy.sas.ac.uk

Founded 2005

Promotes and disseminates research in philosophy

Dir: Prof. BARRY C. SMITH
Administrator: Dr SHAHRAR ALI

Institute for the Study of the Americas

Senate House, Malet St, London, WC1H 7HU

Telephone: (20) 7862-8870
E-mail: americas@sas.ac.uk
Internet: www.americas.sas.ac.uk

Founded 2004 by merger of Institute of Latin American Studies (f. 1964) and Institute of United States Studies (f. 1965)
Academic year: October to July

Dir: Prof. MAXINE MOLYNEUX
Admin. Man.: PAUL SULLIVAN
Librarian: CHRISTINE ANDERSON
Number of teachers: 9
Number of students: 80

Publication: *Journal of Latin American Studies* (4 a year)

PROFESSORS

MIDDLEBROOK, K., Politics
MOLYNEUX, M., Sociology
MORGAN, I., United States Studies

Warburg Institute

Woburn Sq., London, WC1H 0AB

Telephone: (20) 7862-8949
E-mail: warburg@sas.ac.uk
Internet: www.warburg.sas.ac.uk

Founded 1921
Academic year: October to September

Dir: Prof. P. W. D. MACK
Librarian: Dr RAPHAELE MOUREN

Library: see under Libraries and Archives
Number of teachers: 8
Number of students: 40

Publications: *Journal of the Warburg and Courtauld Institutes* (1 a year), *Warburg Institute Colloquia* (20 a year), *Warburg Studies and Texts* (irregular)

PROFESSORS

BURNETT, C. S. F., History of Islamic Influences in Europe
KRAYE, J. A., History of Renaissance Philosophy
MACK, P. W. D., History of the Classical Tradition.

ASSOCIATE INSTITUTION

The following institution has recognized teachers of the University of London on its staff and offers courses leading to degrees of the University.

Institute of Cancer Research: 123 Old Brompton Rd, London, SW7 3RP; tel. (20) 7352-8133; internet www.icr.ac.uk; f. 1909; library of 25,000 vols; Chief Exec. Prof. ALAN ASHWORTH; Sec. CATHY SCIVIER; Academic Dean Prof. ALAN HORWICH

UNIVERSITY OF MANCHESTER

Oxford Rd, Manchester, M13 9PL

Telephone: (161) 306-6000
E-mail: ug-admissions@manchester.ac.uk
Internet: www.manchester.ac.uk

Founded 2004 following merger of Univ. of Manchester (f. 1851) and UMIST (f. 1824)
Academic year: September to June

Chancellor: TOM BLOXHAM
Pres. and Vice-Chancellor: Prof. Dame NANCY J. ROTHWELL
Deputy Pres. and Deputy Vice-Chancellor: Prof. ROD COOMBS
Pro-Chancellor: NORMAN ASKEW (Chair. of the Board of Governors)
Pro-Chancellor: Sir JOHN KERR
Registrar and Sec.: ALBERT MCMENEMY
Vice-Pres.: Prof. COLIN BAILEY
Vice-Pres.: Prof. KEITH BROWN
Vice-Pres.: Prof. MARTIN HUMPHRIES
Vice-Pres.: Prof. ALAN NORTH
Vice-Pres. for Research and Innovation: Prof. LUKE GEORGHIOU
Vice-Pres. for Teaching and Learning: Prof. COLIN STIRLING
Univ. Librarian: JAN WILKINSON

Library: see under Libraries and Archives
Number of teachers: 3,970
Number of students: 37,020

DEANS

Faculty of Engineering and Physical Sciences: Prof. COLIN BAILEY
Faculty of Humanities: Prof. KEITH BROWN
Faculty of Life Sciences: Prof. MARTIN HUMPHRIES
Faculty of Medical and Human Sciences: Prof. ALAN NORTH

PROFESSORS

Faculty of Engineering and Physical Sciences

School of Chemical Engineering and Analytical Science:

ALDER, J. F.
CILLIERS, J.
DAVEY, R.
DEWHURST, R.
DYAKOWSKI, T.
FIELDEN, P.
GODDARD, N.
GRIFFITHS, R.
HEGGS, P.
MANN, R.
MAVITUNA, F.
MCCARTHY, J.
PERSAUD, K.
ROBERTS, S.
SHARRATT, P.
SMITH, R.
SNOOK, R.
TIDDY, G.
VICKERMAN, J.
WEBB, C.

School of Chemistry:

ANDERSON, N. W.
BAILEY, P. D.
CLARKE, J. H. R.
CLAYDEN, J. P.
CONNOR, J. N. L.
GASKELL, S. J.
HELLIWELL, J. R.
HILLIER, I. H.
KELL, D. B.
LIVENS, F. R.
MORRIS, G. A.
MUNN, R. W.
O'BRIEN, P.
STOODLEY, R. J.
SUTHERLAND, J.
TAIT, P. J. T.
THOMAS, E. J.
TURNER, M.
VICKERMAN, J. C.
WAUGH, K. C.
WINPENNY, R.
WOODPENNY, L. V.

School of Computer Science:

ACZEL, P.
BARRINGER, H.

BARTON, S.
BREE, D.
FURBER, S.
GOBLE, C.
GURD, J.
HORROCKS, I.
HUBBOLD, R.
KAHN, H.
MIDDLETON, B.
PATON, N.
RECTOR, A.
TAYLOR, C.
VORONKOV, A.
WARBOYS, B.
WATSON, I.

School of Earth, Atmospheric and Environmental Sciences:

CHOULARTON, T. W., Atmospheric Physics
CURTIS, C., Geochemistry
GAWTHORPE, R., Sedimentation and Tectonics
HENDERSON, M., Petrology
JONAS, P. R., Atmospheric Physics
PATTRICK, R., Earth Sciences
RUTTER, E., Earth Sciences
SELDEN, P., Earth Sciences
TURNER, G., Earth Sciences
VAUGHAN, D., Mineralogy
VAUGHAN, G., Atmospheric Sciences
ZUSSMAN, Z., Earth Sciences

School of Electrical and Electronic Engineering:

ALLINSON, N. M.
BROWN, A. K.
DAVIS, L. E.
GOTT, G. F.
HICKS, P. J.
JENKINS, N.
KIRSCHEN, D.
McCANN, H.
MISSOUS, M.
MUNRO, N.
PEAKER, A. R.
REZAZADEH, A.
STRBAC, G.
WANG, H.
WILLIAMSON, S.
YORK, T. A.

School of Materials:

DERBY, B., Materials Science
FREER, R., Materials Science
HUMPHREYS, F. J., Materials Science
LORIMER, G., Materials Science
LOVELL, P., Polymer Science
O'BRIEN, P., Inorganic Materials, Chemistry
ROBERTS, J., Textiles and Paper
SALE, F., Chemical Metallurgy and Materials Science
SHERRY, A., Corrosion and Protection
STANFORD, J., Polymer Materials Science
STOTT, H., Corrosion and Protection
THOMPSON, G., Corrosion and Protection
WITHERS, P., Materials Science
YOUNG, R., Polymer Science and Technology

School of Mathematics:

ABRAHAMS, I. D., Applied Mathematics
ACZEL, P. H., Mathematical Logic and Computing Science
BOROVIK, A., Pure Mathematics
BROOMHEAD, D., Applied Mathematics
BRYANT, R., Pure Mathematics
DODSON, K., Geometry
DOLD, J., Applied Mathematics
DONEY, R. A., Probability Theory
DUCK, P. W., Applied Mathematics
GLENDINNING, P., Applied Mathematics
HIGHAM, N. J., Applied Mathematics
PARIS, J. B., Pure Mathematics
PLYMEN, R. J., Pure Mathematics
PREMET, A. A., Algebra
PREST, M., Pure Mathematics
RAY, N., Pure Mathematics

ROWLEY, P., Mathematics
RUBAN, A., Computational Fluid Dynamics
SILVESTER, D., Applied Mathematics
SUBBA RAO, T., Statistics
TAYLOR, M. J., Pure Mathematics
WOOD, R. M. W., Algebra

School of Mechanical, Aerospace and Civil Engineering:

AL-HASSANI, S. T. S., Mechanical Engineering
BAILEY, C., Structural Engineering
BALL, A. D., Maintenance Engineering
COOPER, J. E., Engineering
DAVIES, M., Structural Engineering
HAYHURST, D. R., Design, Manufacture and Materials
HINDUJA, S., Mechanical Engineering
JACKSON, J. D., Mechanical and Nuclear Engineering
LAUNDER, B. E., Mechanical Engineering
LAURENCE, D., Computational Fluid Dynamics
LEUNG, A., Engineering
LEVERMORE, G., Built Environment
LI, L., Laser Engineering
MARSDEN, B., Nuclear Graphite Technology
REID, S. R., Mechanical Engineering
SANDOZ, D. J., Control Engineering
SMITH, I., Geotechnics
STANSBY, P., Hydrodynamics
THOMPSON, G., Mechanical Engineering
TURAN, A., Mechanical Engineering
VARLOW, B. R., Industrial Liaison
WINCH, G., Construction Project Management
WOOD, N., Aerospace Engineering
WRIGHT, J. R., Mechanical Engineering

School of Physics and Astronomy:

BARLOW, S. J., Particle Physics
BISHOP, R. F., Theoretical Physics
BRAY, A. J., Theoretical Physics
DIAMOND, P. D., Astronomy and Astrophysics
DURELL, J. L., Nuclear Physics
FLAVELL, W. R., Photon Physics
FORSHAW, J. R., Particle Physics
GEIM, A. K., Condensed Matter Physics
GLEESON, H. F., Nonlinear and Liquid Crystal Physics
KING, G. C., Photon Physics
KING, T. A., Photon Physics
LAFFERTY, G. D., Particle Physics
LU, J., Biological Physics
LYNE, A. G., Astronomy and Astrophysics
MARSHALL, R., Particle Physics
MILLAR, T. J., Astronomy and Astrophysics
MOORE, M. A., Theoretical Physics
MULLIN, T., Nonlinear and Liquid Crystal Physics
WALET, N. R., Theoretical Physics
WILKINSON, P. N., Astronomy and Astrophysics
WYATT, T. R., Particle Physics
ZIJLSTRA, A. A., Astronomy and Astrophysics

Faculty of Humanities

School of Arts, Histories and Culture:

ADAMSON, S., Linguistics and Literary History
ALEXANDER, P., Post-Biblical Jewish Studies
BERGIN, J., Modern History
BROOKE, G. J., Biblical Studies
CASKEN, J., Music
CAUSEY, A., Modern Art History
COOPER, B., Music
CORNELL, T., Ancient History
CROWLEY, T., Modern English Literature
DENISON, D., English Linguistics
EAGLETON, T., Cultural Theory
FALLOWS, D., Music
FANNING, D., Music
FOURACRE, P., History

GARDNER, V., Theatre Studies
GATRELL, P., Modern History
GRAHAM, E. L., Social and Pastoral Theology
GRANGE, P., Music
HAMMOND, G., English Literature
HOGG, R. M., English Language and Medieval English Literature
JACKSON, B. S., Modern Jewish Studies
JANTZEN, G. M., Philosophy of Religion
JONES, A., History of Art
JOYCE, P., Modern History
LANGSLOW, D., Classics
LING, R., Archaeology
MILLWARD, R., Economic History
PARKIN, T., Ancient History
PEARSON, J., English Literature
PITTOCK, M., Scottish and Romantic Literature
SCRAGG, D., Anglo-Saxon Studies
SHARROCK, A., Classics
SUMMERFIELD, P., Modern History
THOMAS, J., Archaeology
WARD, B., American Studies
WARD, G., Contextual Theology
WOOLFORD, J., 19th-Century Literature and Culture

School of Education:

AINSCOW, M., Education
BAMFORD, J., Audiology and Deaf Education
CONTI-RAMSDEN, G., Specific Language Impairment
DAVIES, A., Education
DYSON, A., Education
FARRELL, P., Educational Psychology
THOMPSON, L., Language and Literacy Studies
WEST, M., Educational Leadership
WILLIAMS, J. S., Mathematics Education

School of Environment and Development:

AGNEW, C., Geography
ALLOTT, T., Geography
BEBBINGTON, A., Management in International Development
BRADFORD, M., Geography
CASTREE, N., Geography
COOK, P., Economics and Development Policy
DOUGLAS, I., Geography
HANDLEY, J., Land Restoration and Management
HEBBERT, M., Town Planning
HENDERSON, J., International Economic Sociology
HULME, D., Development Studies
KIRKPATRICK, C., Development Economics
MacDOUGALL, G., Architecture and Advanced Technology
ROBSON, B., Geography
STONEHOUSE, R., Architecture
THOMAS, R., Geography
WILLIAMS, G., Urban Planning and Development
WOOD, C., Environmental Planning

School of Informatics:

BLENKHORN, P., Interactive Systems Design
KEANE, J., Data and Decision Engineering
LOUCOPOULOS, P., Information Systems
MACAULAY, L., System Design
RAMSAY, A., Data and Decision Engineering
SUTCLIFFE, A., Interactive Systems Design
WASTELL, D., Information Systems
WOOD, J., Information Systems
WOOD-HARPER, A., Information Systems

School of Languages, Linguistics and Cultures:

ALEXANDER, P. S., Middle Eastern Studies
BERGER, S., Modern German and Comparative European History
DURRELL, M., German
GÜNSBERG, M., Italian

LAWRANCE, J., Spanish
PARKER, S., German
PERRIAM, C., Hispanic Studies
SMITH, G. R., Middle Eastern Studies
TOLZ, V., Russian

School of Law:

BRAZIER, M., Law
BRAZIER, R., Law
DOBASH, R., Law
DUXBURY, N., Law
GIBBONS, T., Law
HARRIS, J., Law
HARRIS, N., Law
HÄYRY, M., Law
JACONELLI, J., Law
McCORMACK, G., Law
McGEE, A., Law
MILLMAN, D., Law
OGUS, A., Law
QURESHI, A., Law
SANDERS, A., Law
SHAW, J., Law
TSUJII, J., Text Mining

Manchester Business School:

BARRAR, P., Operations Management
BOWE, M., International Finance
BRUCE, M., Design Management and
    Retailing
CHITTENDEN, F., Small Business Finance
CONYON, M., Corporate Governance
COOMBS, R., Technology Management
DAVIDSON, M., Managerial Psychology
DAVIES, G., Corporate Reputation
EASINGWOOD, C., Marketing
EDWARDS, P., Accountancy
FRENCH, S., Information and Decision Sci-
    ences
GARRETT, I., Accounting and Finance
GEORGHIOU, L., Technology and Entrepre-
    neurship Management and Policy
GHAURI, P., International Business
GREEN, K., Technology and Entrepreneur-
    ship Management and Policy
HASSARD, J., Organizational Analysis
HIGGINS, J., Health Policy
HOWELLS, J., Innovation and Competition
HUMPHREY, C., Accounting
JACKSON, P., Corporate Communications
KANG, J., Marketing
LEWIS, B., Marketing
LITTLER, D., Strategic Management
MARCHINGTON, M., Human Resource Man-
    agement
McGOLDRICK, P., Retailing
MILES, I., Technology and Entrepreneur-
    ship Management and Policy
NAUDÉ, P., Marketing
NEWMAN, M., Management Accounting and
    Information Systems
OAKEY, R., Business Development
OGDEN, S., Accounting and Finance
O'LEARY, T., Accounting
PAXSON, D., Finance
POON, S.-H., Finance
RICKARDS, T., Creativity and Organiza-
    tional Change
ROBSON, K., Accounting
RUBERY, J., Comparative Employment Sys-
    tems
SANGHAVI, N., Retail Marketing and Strat-
    egy
SCAPENS, R., Management Accounting and
    Information Systems
SPARROW, P., International Human
    Resource Management
STAPLETON, R., Finance
STARK, A., Accounting
STEPHEN, F., Regulation
STRONG, N., Finance
TURLEY, S., Accounting
WADDINGTON, J., Human Resource Man-
    agement
WALKER, M., Finance and Accounting
WALSH, V., Innovation Management

WALSHE, K., Health Policy and Manage-
    ment
WILLIAMS, K., Accounting and Political
    Economy
YANG, J.-B., Decision Sciences and Oper-
    ations Management

School of Social Sciences:

AGÉNOR, P.-R., Economics
BLACKBURN, K., Economics
CALLAHAN, W., International Politics
COLMAN, D., Economics
EVSTIGNEEV, I., Economics
GLEDHILL, J., Social Anthropology
HARVEY, P., Social Anthropology
HENLEY, P., Social Anthropology
MADDEN, P., Economics
MASON, J., Sociology
METCALFE, S., Economics
NIXSON, F., Economics
OSBORN, D., Economics
SMART, C., Sociology
WADE, P., Social Anthropology
WERBNER, R., Social Anthropology
YOUNG, T., Economics

Faculty of Life Sciences:

ABADI, R.
ATTWOOD, T.
BALMENT, R.
BARNES, G.
BRASS, A.
BROWN, T. A.
BULLEID, N.
CASE, M.
CHARMAN, W.
CRONLY-DILLON, J.
CROSSMAN, A.
DAVID, R.
DIXON, M.
DUNNE, M.
EDDY, A.
EFRON, N.
FERGUSON, M.
FOSTER, D.
GARROD, D.
GRANT, M.
GRENCIS, R.
HARDINGHAM, T.
HIGH, S.
HUMPHRIES, M.
HUTCHINSON, I.
HYDE, J. E.
ITZHAKI, R.
KADLER, K.
KAUPPINEN, R.
KIELTY, C.
KULIKOWSKI, J.
LIAN, L. Y.
LOUDON, A.
McCARTHY, J. E. G.
MOORE, A.
NORTH, R. A.
OLIVER, S.
PICKSTONE, J.
POLLER, L.
ROBERTS, I.
ROTHWELL, N.
SHARROCKS, A.
SIBLEY, C.
STERN, P.
STIRLING, C.
STREULI, C.
TERENGHI, G.
TOMLINSON, D.
TRINCI, A.
TURNER, S.
VERKHRATSKY, A.
WESTON, A.
WHETTON, A. D.
WHITE, A.
WORBOYS, M.

Faculty of Medical and Human Sciences
School of Dentistry:

BLINKHORN, A. S., Oral Health
DIXON, M. J., Dental Genetics

FERGUSON, M. W. J., Basic Dental Sciences
O'BRIEN, K. D., Orthodontics
SHAW, W. C., Orthodontics and Dentofacial
    Development
SLOAN, P., Experimental Oral Pathology
THORNHILL, M. H., Medicine in Dentistry
WILSON, N. H. F., Restorative Dentistry

School of Medicine:

ADAMS, J. E., Diagnostic Radiology
AGIUS, R., Occupational and Environmen-
    tal Medicine
BIRCH, J. M., Cancer Research Campaign,
    Paediatric and Familial Cancer
    Research Group
BOULTON, A. J. M., Medicine
BURNIE, J. P., Medical Microbiology
CASE, R. M., Physiology
CHERRY, N. M., Occupational and Environ-
    mental Medicine
CROSSMAN, A. R., Anatomy
DAVID, T. J., Child Health and Paediatrics
DAVIS, J. R. E., Medicine
DUNN, G., Biomedical Statistics
DURRINGTON, P. N., Medicine
EDEN, O. B., Paediatric Oncology
EISNER, D., Cardiac Physiology
FREEMONT, A. J., Tissue Pathology
GALASKO, C. S. B., Orthopaedic Surgery
GALLAGHER, S. T., Oncology
GARROD, D. R., Developmental Biology
GORDON, D., Medicine
GRANT, M. E., Medical Biochemistry
GREEN, R., Physiology
GRENCIS, R. K., Immunology
GRIFFITHS, C. E. M., Dermatology
HAWKINS, R. E., Medical Oncology
HEAGERTY, A., Medicine
HELLER, R., Public Health
HERHOLZ, K., Clinical Neurosciences
HICKMAN, J., Molecular Pharmacology
HORAN, M. A., Geriatric Medicine (South)
HOWELL, A., Medical Oncology
HUTCHINSON, I. V., Immunology
IRVING, M. H., Surgery
JACKSON, A., Neuroradiology
KIERNAN, C. C., Behavioural Studies in
    Mental Handicap
KIRKWOOD, T. B. L., Biological Gerontology
KITCHENER, H. C., Gynaecological Oncology
LOWENSTEIN, P. R., Molecular Medicine and
    Gene Therapy
MALLICK, N. P., Renal Medicine
MAWER, E. B., Bone and Mineral Metabol-
    ism
MAYES, A., Cognitive Neuroscience
McALLISTER, I., Medicine
McCLURE, J., Pathology
McCOLLUM, C. N., Surgery
McCORD, J. F., Restorative Care of the
    Elderly
McLEOD, D., Ophthalmology
MÜLLER, R., Pharmaceutics, Biopharma-
    ceutics and Biotechnology
O'BRIEN, K. D., Orthodontics
OLLIER, W. E. R., Immunogenetics
POLLARD, B. J., Anaesthesia
PRICE, P., Radiation Oncology
READ, A. P., Human Genetics
RECTOR, A. L., Medical Informatics
ROLAND, M. O., General Practice
SCARFFE, J. H., Oncology
SEYMOUR, L., Gene Therapy
SIBBALD, B. S., Health Services Research
SIBLEY, C. P., Child Health and Physiology
SILMAN, A. J., Rheumatic Diseases Epi-
    demiology
STANLEY, J. K., Hand Surgery
TALLIS, R. C., Geriatric Medicine (Salford)
TAYLOR, C. J., Medical Biophysics
THATCHER, N., Oncology
THOMPSON, D. G., Gastroenterology
VADGAMA, P., Clinical Biochemistry
WHITE, A., Endocrine Sciences
WHITEHOUSE, C. R., Teaching Medicine in
    the Community

WILKIN, D., Health Services Research
WOODMAN, C. B. J., Cancer Epidemiology and Public Health
YATES, D. W., Accident and Emergency Surgery

School of Nursing, Midwifery and Social Work:

CARLISLE, E., Education in Nursing and Midwifery
LUKER, K., Nursing and Midwifery
THOMSON, A., Midwifery
TODD, C., Primary Care and Community Health
WATERMAN, H., Nursing and Midwifery

School of Pharmacy and Pharmaceutical Sciences:

ATTWOOD, D.
CANTRILL, J.
CLARKE, D.
COLLETT, J.
DIVE, C.
DOUGLAS, K.
GIFFORD, L.
GILBERT, P.
HOUSTON, J. B.
NOYCE, P.
ROWLAND, M.
STRATFORD, I.

School of Psychological Sciences:

BAMFORD, J.
BARROWCLOUGH, C.
BEATTIE, G.
BENTALL, R.
CONTI-RAMSEN, G.
DAVIS, A.
LAMBON-RALPH, M.
LIEVEN, E.
MEUDELL, P.
PARKER, D.
TARRIER, N.
WEARDEN, J. H.

UNIVERSITY OF NORTHAMPTON

Park Campus, Boughton Green Rd, Northampton, NN2 7AL
Ave Campus, St George's Ave, Northampton, NN2 6JD

Telephone: (1604) 735500
E-mail: study@northampton.ac.uk
Internet: www.northampton.ac.uk

Founded 1975 by merger of College of Education, College of Technology and College of Art, present name and status 2005
Academic year: September to July

Chancellor: Baroness FALKNER OF MARGRAVINE
Vice-Chancellor: ANN TATE
Vice-Chancellor: Prof. NICK PETFORD
Pro-Vice-Chancellor for Acad.: Prof. PETER BUSH
Pro-Vice-Chancellor for Research and Devt: Dr FRANK BURDETT
Pro-Vice-Chancellor for Strategic Planning and Resources: JOHN HOSKINSON

Library of 375,000 vols, 15,000 journals
Number of teachers: 470
Number of students: 10,000

DEANS

School of Education: Prof. ANN SHELTON MAYES
School of Health: Dr SUE ALLEN
School of Science and Technology: Prof. KAMAL BECHKOUM
School of Social Sciences: CHRIS MOORE
School of the Arts: PAUL MIDDLETON
Northampton Business School: Dr IAN BROOKS

UNIVERSITY OF NOTTINGHAM

University Park, Nottingham, NG7 2RD
Telephone: (115) 951-5151
Internet: www.nottingham.ac.uk
Founded 1881, Univ. Charter 1948
Academic year: September to August
Chancellor: Prof. YANG FUJIA
Vice-Chancellor: Prof. Sir DAVID GREENAWAY
Pro-Vice-Chancellor for Environment, Infrastructure and Information Services: Prof. ALAN DODSON
Pro-Vice-Chancellor for Human Resources, Access and Community Relations: Prof. KAREN COX
Pro-Vice-Chancellor for Internationalization: Prof. CHRISTINE ENNEW
Pro-Vice-Chancellor for Knowledge Transfer, Business Engagement, Devt and Alumni Relations Office: Prof. CHRIS RUDD
Pro-Vice-Chancellor for Research and Graduate School: Prof. BOB WEBB
Pro-Vice-Chancellor for Teaching and Learning: Prof. SAUL TENDLER
Registrar: Dr PAUL GREATRIX

Library: see under Libraries and Archives
Number of teachers: 2,700
Number of students: 32,040

Publications: *Exchange Magazine*, *Gazette*, *Global Review*

DEANS

Faculty of Arts: Prof. ALAN FORD
Faculty of Engineering: Prof. HAI-SUI YU
Faculty of Medicine and Health Sciences: Prof. IAN HALL
Faculty of Science: Prof. EDMUND BURKE
Faculty of Social Sciences: Prof. SARAH O'HARA
Graduate School: Prof. CLAIRE O'MALLEY

PROFESSORS

AITKENHEAD, A., Anaesthesia and Intensive Care
ALDRICH, R. J., Politics
ARCHER, D. B., Microbiology
ARMOUR, E. A. G., Mathematical Physics
ARROWSMITH, S. L., Law
ASHER, G. M., Electrical and Electronic Engineering
ASHWORTH, J., American and Canadian Studies
AZZOPARDI, B. J., Chemical, Environmental and Mining Engineering
BACKHOUSE, R. C., Computer Science and Information Technology
BAILEY, S. H., Law
BALL, F. G., Statistics
BARNARD, C. J., Animal Behaviour and Ecology
BATES, C., Physics and Astronomy
BATH, P., Stroke Medicine
BECKER, A. A., Mechanical Engineering
BECKETT, J. V., History
BEHNKE, J. M., Infections and Immunity
BELAVKIN, V., Mathematical Physics
BENFORD, S. D., Computer Science and Information Technology
BENNETT, M. J., Plant Science
BENNETT, T., Biomedical Sciences
BENSON, T. M., Electrical and Electronic Engineering
BERRY, R. H., Accounting and Finance
BETON, P. H., Physics and Astronomy
BINKS, M. R., Institute for Enterprise and Innovation
BIRCH, D. J., Law
BLACK, C. R., Plant Science
BLEANEY, M. F., Economics
BOWLEY, R. M., Physics and Astronomy
BOWTELL, R. W., Physics and Astronomy
BRADLEY, J. E., Infections and Immunity
BRADSHAW, C. M., Psychiatry
BRAILSFORD, D. F., Computer Science and Information Technology

BRIGGS, D., Pharmaceutical Sciences
BRINCAT, M. P., Nurture Unit
BRITTON, J., Respiratory Medicine
BROOK, J. D., Genetics
BROUGHTON-PIPKIN, F., Obstetrics and Gynaecology
BROWN, A. D., Business School
BROWN, S. F., Civil Engineering
BRUCE, A. C., Economics and Insurance
BURKE, E. K., Computer Science and Information Technology
BURKHARDT, H., Education
BUTTERY, P. J., Nutritional Biochemistry
BYCROFT, B. W., Pharmaceutical Sciences
CALLEN, A. E., Art History
CAMPBELL, K. H., Animal Physiology
CARDWELL, R. A., Hispanic and Latin American Studies
CARTER, R. A., English Studies
CASEY, P. M., Theology
CHALLIS, R. E., Electrical and Electronic Engineering
CHESTERS, M. A., Physical Chemistry
CHOI, K.-S., Fluid Mechanics
CHOONARA, I., Human Devt
CHRISTOPOULOS, C., Electrical and Electronic Engineering
CLARK, J. S., Organic Chemistry
CLARKE, B., Genetics
CLARKE, D. D., Psychology
COLES, P., Physics and Astronomy
COLLIS, J., Atmospheric Environment
CONNERTON, I., Food Sciences
COOKE, M., Music
COX, K., Nursing
COX, T. R., Institute of Work, Health and Orgs
CREMONA, J. E., Mathematical Sciences
CURRIE, G., Business School
CURRIE, G., Philosophy
DANCHEV, A., Int. Relations
DANIELS, S., Geography
DAVIES, M. C., Pharmaceutical Sciences
DAVIS, S. S., Pharmaceutical Sciences
DAVIS, T., Orthopaedic and Accident Surgery
DAY, C., Education
DENBY, B., Chemical, Environmental and Mining Engineering
DERRINGTON, A. M., Psychology
DEVLIN, J., Marketing
DIACON, S. R., Business School
DINGWALL, R. W. J., Institute for the Study of Genetics, Biorisks and Society
DISNEY, R. F., Economics
DODSON, A. H., Civil Engineering
DONNELLY, R., Vascular Medicine
DOWD, K., Centre for Risk Insurance Studies
DRYDEN, I. L., Statistics
DUNCAN, A. S., Economics
EAVES, L., Physics and Astronomy
ELLIMAN, D. G., Computer Science and Information Technology
ENNEW, C. T., Business School
EVETTS, J. A., Sociology and Social Policy
FALVEY, R. E., Economics
FAWCETT, A. P., Architecture
FAWCETT, J. J., Law
FENN, P. T., Business School
FESENKO, I., Pure Mathematics
FINCH, R., Microbiology and Infectious Diseases
FLINT, A. P. F., Animal Physiology
FORBES, I., Politics
FORD, G. A., Theology
FORD, P. H., Computer Science and Information Technology
FOXON, C. T. B., Physics and Astronomy
FRANCIS, R. A., French
FRASER, D., Midwifery
GARDINER, S. M., Biomedical Sciences
GARNER, C. D., Inorganic Chemistry
GARVEY, S. D., Mechanical Engineering
GEARY, R. J., History
GILL, P. M. W., Physical Chemistry
GILLIES, P. A., Public Health Sciences

GINDY, N. N. Z., Manufacturing Engineering and Operations Management
GLASS, R. E., Genetics
GOW, I. T., Business School
GRAVELLS, N. P., Law
GREENAWAY, D., Economics
GREENHAFF, P. L., Biomedical Sciences
GRIERSON, D., Plant Science
GRIFFITHS, A., Institute of Work, Health and Orgs
HALL, I., Therapeutics
HAMMOND, B. S., English Studies
HARDING, S. E., Food Sciences
HARGREAVES, A., Education
HARRIS, D. J., Law
HARRISON, C., Economics
HASLAM, R., Institute of Work, Health and Orgs
HEFFERNAN, M. J., Geography
HENDERSON, J., Archaeology
HEPTINSTALL, S., Cardiovascular Medicine
HERVEY, T. K., Law
HEWITT, N., French
HEYWOOD, P. M., Politics
HILL, S. J., Biomedical Sciences
HOLLIS, C., Psychiatry
HOPKINSON, B., Vascular Surgery
HOWDLE, S. M., Inorganic Chemistry
HYDE, T. H., Mechanical Engineering
IRVING, W., Microbiology and Infectious Diseases
JACKSON, S., Psychology
JAKEMAN, E., Electrical and Electronic Engineering
JAKEMAN, E., Theoretical Mechanics
JAMES, R., Microbiology and Infectious Diseases
JAMES, V. C., Nursing
JENSEN, O. E., Theoretical Mechanics
JESCH, J., English Studies
JOHNSON, C. M., French
JOHNSON, I. R., Human Devt
JONES, R. G., Physical Chemistry
JORDAN, T. R., Psychology
KENDALL, D. A., Biomedical Sciences
KENNER, J., European Law
KING, J. R., Theoretical Mechanics
KING, R. H., American and Canadian Studies
KNIGHT, D. M., French
LANGLEY-EVANS, S., Human Nutrition
LARKINS, E., Electrical and Electronic Engineering
LAYBOURN-PARRY, J., Life and Environmental Sciences
LEDGEWAY, T., Vision Research
LEICESTER, M., Continuing Education
LEYBOURNE, S. J., Economics
LEYSHON, A., Geography
LINCOLN, N. B., Psychology
LLOYD, R. G., Genetics
MCCARTNEY, D. G., Materials Engineering and Materials Design
MCCORQUODALE, R. G., Law
MCCOUSTRA, M., Chemical Physics
MACDONALD, I. A., Biomedical Sciences
MCGUIRK, B. J., Hispanic and Latin American Studies
MCRAE, J., English Studies
MADELEY, R., Community Health Sciences
MAHAJAN, R., Anaesthesia and Intensive Care
MANNING, N. P., Sociology and Social Policy
MARLOW, N., Human Devt
MARSDEN, C. A., Biomedical Sciences
MATHER, P. M., Geography
MAYER, R. J., Biomedical Sciences
MAYHEW, T. M., Biomedical Sciences
MELLER, H. E., History
MEPHAM, B., Biosciences
MERRIFIELD, M. R., Physics and Astronomy
MESSENT, P. B., American and Canadian Studies
MILES, N. J., Chemical, Environmental and Mining Engineering
MILLINGTON, M. I., Hispanic and Latin American Studies

MILNE, L. M., Russian and Slavonic Studies
MILNER, C. R., Economics
MITCHELL, J. R., Food Sciences
MITCHELL, P., Psychology
MITHEN, R. F., Agricultural Sciences
MONTEITH, S., American Studies
MOON, J., Int. Centre for Corporate Social Responsibility
MOORE, T., Engineering Surveying and Space Geodesy
MORGAN, W. J., Continuing Education
MORRIS, P. G., Physics and Astronomy
MORSE, G. K., Law
MURPHY, R. J. L., Education
MURPHY, S., Biomedical Sciences
NEWBOLD, P., Economics
NEWMAN, J. A., American and Canadian Studies
O'BRIEN, C., Manufacturing Engineering and Operations Management
O'CONNELL-DAVIDSON, J., Sociology and Social Policy
O'SHEA, P. S., Biomedical Sciences
OC, T., Built Environment
PARKER, S., Continuing Education
PASHBY, I. R., Manufacturing Engineering and Operations Management
PATIENT, R. K., Genetics
PATTENDEN, G., Chemistry
PEBERDY, J. F., Institute for Enterprise and Innovation
PERKINS, A., Human Devt
PIERSON, C., Politics
POLIAKOFF, M., Inorganic Chemistry
POWER, H., Mechanical Engineering
PRINGLE, M., General Practice
PRITCHARD, D. I., Pharmaceutical Sciences
RAY, D., Biomedical Sciences
REES, W., Int. Security
REEVE, D. E., Civil Engineering
RIFFAT, S. B., Built Environment
RILEY, D. S., Theoretical Mechanics
ROBERTS, J. A., Plant Science
RODDEN, T. A., Computer Science and Information Technology
ROSSLYN, W., Russian and Slavonic Studies
ROWLANDS, B. J., Gastrointestinal Surgery
RUDD, C., Mechanical Engineering
RUSSELL, N., Haematology
SABLITZKY, F., Genetics
SARRE, P. J., Physical Chemistry
SCHOLEFIELD, J., Surgery
SCHRODER, M., Inorganic Chemistry
SEABROOK, M. F., Agricultural Sciences
SEDDON, A. B., Materials Engineering and Materials Design
SHAKESHEFF, K., Pharmaceutical Sciences
SHARP, P. M., Genetics
SHAW, P. E., Biomedical Sciences
SHAW, R., Obstetrics and Gynaecology
SHAYLER, P. J., Mechanical Engineering
SIMESTER, A. P., Law
SIMPKINS, N. S., Organic Chemistry
SINCLAIR, M. T., Business School
SNAPE, C. E., Chemical, Environmental and Mining Engineering
SOCKET, E., Bacterial Genetics
SOMEKH, M. G., Electrical and Electronic Engineering
SOMMERSTEIN, A. H., Classics
SPIESS, M. K., Pure Mathematics
STARKEY, K. P., Business School
STARMER, C. V., Economics
STEPHENSON, T., Child Health
STEVENS, M. F. G., Pharmaceutical Sciences
STILL, J. M., French
TALLACK, D. G., American and Canadian Studies
TATTERSFIELD, A., Respiratory Medicine
TAYLOR, A. J., Food Sciences
TENDLER, S. J. B., Pharmaceutical Sciences
THORNE, C. R., Geography
THORNTON, J., Obstetrics and Gynaecology
TOMS, J. S., Business School
TUCK, B., Electrical and Electronic Engineering

TUCKER, G. A., Nutritional Biochemistry
TURVILLE-PETRE, T. F. S., English Studies
TYNAN, A. C., Business School
UNDERWOOD, G., Psychology
VAN ZYL SMIT, D., Law
WAITES, W. M., Food Sciences
WALKER, R. L., Sociology and Social Policy
WALLACE, W. A., Orthopaedic and Accident Surgery
WARD, C., Rehabilitation and Ageing
WEBB, R., Agricultural Sciences
WESTHEAD, P., Business School
WHITE, N. D., Law
WHYNES, D. K., Economics
WILCOX, R. G., Cardiovascular Medicine
WILKINSON, R., Epidemiology and Public Health Sciences
WILLIAMS, H., Medical and Surgical Sciences
WILLIAMS, P., Institute of Infections and Immunity
WILLIAMS, P., Pharmaceutical Sciences
WILSON, J., Business School
WILSON, J. R., Manufacturing Engineering and Operations Management
WILSON, R. J. A., Archaeology
WINGFIELD, J., Pharmaceutical Sciences
WOOD, A. T., Statistics
WOOD, D. J., Psychology
WOOD, J. V., Materials Engineering and Materials Design
WOODS, R. A. M., German
WORTHEN, J., English Studies
WRIGHT, D. M., Business School
WRIGHT, N., Environmental Fluid Mechanics
WRIGLEY, C. J., History
YOUNG, J. W., History
YOUNG, L., Molecular Embryology
YU, H., Civil Engineering

UNIVERSITY OF OXFORD

Univ. Offices, Wellington Sq., Oxford, OX1 2JD

Telephone: (1865) 270000
E-mail: information.office@admin.ox.ac.uk
Internet: www.ox.ac.uk

Founded 12th century
Academic year: October to June

Chancellor: Rt Hon. the Lord PATTEN OF BARNES
High Steward: Rt Hon. the Lord MANCE
Vice-Chancellor: Prof. ANDREW HAMILTON
Pro-Vice-Chancellor for Devt and External Affairs: Prof. NICK RAWLINS
Pro-Vice-Chancellor for Education: Prof.e SALLY MAPSTONE
Pro-Vice-Chancellor for Personnel and Equality: Dr STEPHEN GOSS
Pro-Vice-Chancellor for Planning and Resources: Prof. WILLIAM JAMES
Pro-Vice-Chancellor for Research, Academic Services and Univ. Collns: Prof. IAN WALMSLEY
Registrar: Prof. EWAN MCKENDRICK
Deputy Registrar: MICHAEL SIBLY
Bodley's Librarian: RICHARD OVENDEN
Chief Information Officer: Prof. ANNE TREFETHEN

Library: the Bodleian Libraries comprise some 40 libraries, excl. college libraries, and holds over 11m. printed items and 50,000 ejournals
Number of teachers: 1,050 f.t.e.
Number of students: 22,180 (incl. 20,094 full-time and 2,086 part-time)

PROFESSORS

Note: Faculties, Schools, Depts, etc. are grouped by Div. (each Div. has a full-time head and an elected board who are responsible for day-to-day operations incl. finance and planning) as follows: *Humanities Div.*(- Rothermere American Institute, Faculty of Classics, Faculty of English Language and Literature, Ertegun Graduate Scholarship

Programme in the Humanities, Faculty of Linguistics, Philology and Phonetics, Faculty of Medieval and Modern European Languages, Faculty of History, Faculty of Music, Faculty of Oriental Studies, Faculty of Philosophy, Ruskin School of Art, Faculty of Theology and Religion, Voltaire Foundation, TORCH: The Oxford Research Centre in the Humanities); *Mathematical, Physical and Life Sciences Div.*(Begbroke Science Park, Dept of Chemistry, Dept of Computer Science, Dept of Earth Sciences, Dept of Engineering Science, Dept of Materials, Mathematical Institute, Dept of Physics, Dept of Plant Sciences, Dept of Statistics, Dept of Zoology, Oxford e-Research Centre); *Medical Sciences Div.*(Dept of Biochemistry, Nuffield Dept of Clinical Medicine, Nuffield Dept of Clinical Neurosciences (incorporating the Division of Clinical Neurology, the Nuffield Laboratory of Ophthalmology, the Nuffield Division of Anaesthetics and the Oxford Centre for Functional Magnetic Resonance Imaging of the Brain), Dept of Experimental Psychology, Radcliffe Dept of Medicine (incorporating the Div. of Cardiovascular Medicine, the Nuffield Div. of Clinical Laboratory Sciences, the Oxford Centre for Diabetes, Endocrinology and Metabolism, the Investigative Medicine Div. and the MRC Weatherall Institute of Molecular Medicine), Nuffield Dept of Obstetrics and Gynaecology, Dept of Oncology, Nuffield Dept of Orthopaedics, Rheumatology and Musculoskeletal Sciences, Dept of Paediatrics, Sir William Dunn School of Pathology, Dept of Pharmacology, Dept of Physiology, Anatomy and Genetics, Nuffield Dept of Population Health, Nuffield Dept of Primary Care Health Sciences, Dept of Psychiatry, Nuffield Dept of Surgical Sciences.); *Social Sciences Div.*(School of Anthropology and Museum Ethnography, School of Archaeology, Blavatnik School of Government, Saïd Business School (Faculty of Management), Dept of Economics, Dept of Education, School of Geography and the Environment, School of Interdisciplinary Area Studies, Oxford Dept of International Development (Queen Elizabeth House), Oxford Internet Institute, Faculty of Law, Oxford Martin School, Oxford-Man Institute of Quantitative Finance, Dept of Politics and International Relations, Dept of Social Policy and Intervention, Dept of Sociology). *Dept for Continuing Education* is not part of a Div.

Rothermere American Institute (1A South Parks Rd, Oxford, OX1 3UB; tel. (1865) 282710; e-mail enquiries@rai.ox.ac.uk; internet www.rai.ox.ac.uk):

Dir N. Bowles (Corpus Christi College)

School of Anthropology and Museum Ethnography (51–53 Banbury Rd, Oxford, OX2 6PE; tel. (1865) 274624; e-mail information@anthro.ox.ac.uk; internet www.anthro.ox.ac.uk):

ANDERSON, B., Migration and Citizenship
BANKS, M. J., Visual Anthropology (Wolfson College)
GELLNER, D. N., Social Anthropology (All Souls College)
Hsu, E., Anthropology (Green Templeton College)
KEITH, M., Migration, Policy and Society (Merton College)
RAYNER, S., Science and Civilization (Keble College)
ULIJASZEK, S. J., Human Ecology (St Cross College)
WHITEHOUSE, H., Social Anthropology (Magdalen College)
ZEITLYN, D., Social Anthropology (Wolfson College)

School of Archaeology (36 Beaumont St, Oxford, OX1 2PG; tel. (1865) 278240; e-mail administrator@arch.ox.ac.uk; internet www.arch.ox.ac.uk; comprises the Institute of Archaeology (located on Beaumont St) and the Research Laboratory for Archaeology and the History of Art (located in the Dyson Perrins Bldg on South Parks Rd)):

BARTON, R. N. E., Palaeolithic Archaeology (Hertford College)
GOSDEN, C. H., European Archaeology (Keble College)
HAMEROW, H. F., Archaeology (St Cross College)
LEE-THORP, J., Scientific Archaeology (St Cross College)
MITCHELL, P. J., African Prehistory (St Hugh's College)
PETRAGLIA, M., Human Evolution and Prehistory (Linacre College)
POLLARD, A. M., Archaeological Science (Linacre College)
RAMSEY, C. B., Archaeological Science (Merton College)
Dame RAWSON, J., Chinese Art and Archaeology (Merton College)
ROBINSON, M. A., Environmental Archaeology (St John's College)

Department of Biochemistry (South Parks Rd, Oxford, OX1 3QU; tel. (1865) 613200; e-mail admin@bioch.ox.ac.uk; internet www.bioch.ox.ac.uk):

ARMITAGE, J. P., Biochemistry (Merton College)
BARR, F., Mechanistic Cell Biology (Trinity College)
BERKS, B., Biochemistry (Wadham College)
BROCKDORFF, N., Biochemistry
DAVIS, I., Cell Biology (Jesus College)
FERGUSON, S. J., Biochemistry (St Edmund Hall)
GARMAN, E. F., Molecular Biophysics (Brasenose College)
HANDFORD, P. A., Biochemistry (St Catherine's College)
HODGKIN, J. A., Genetics (Keble College)
KLEANTHOUS, (K) C., Microbial Biochemistry (Linacre College)
MAHADEVAN, L. C., Biochemistry (Trinity College)
MELLOR, E. J. C., Biochemistry (The Queen's College)
NASMYTH, K., Biochemistry (Trinity College)
NOVÁK, B., Integrative Systems Biology (Merton College)
REDFISH, C., Molecular Biophysics (Wolfson College)
SANSOM, M. S. P., Molecular Biophysics (Corpus Christi College)
WATTS, A., Biochemistry (St Hugh's College)
WHITBY, M. C., Molecular Genetics
ZITZMANN, N., Glycobiology (Merton College)

Department of Chemistry (Chemistry Research Laboratory, 12 Mansfield Rd, Oxford, OX1 3TA; tel. (1865) 285000; internet www.chem.ox.ac.uk):

AARTS, D. G. A. L., Chemistry (Christ Church)
ALDRIDGE, S., Main Group Chemistry (The Queen's College)
ANDERSON, H. L., Chemistry (Keble College)
ARMSTRONG, F. A., Chemistry (St John's College)
BATTLE, P. D., Chemistry (St Catherine's College)
BAYLEY, J. H. P., Chemical Biology (Hertford College)
BEER, P. D., Chemistry (Wadham College)
BROUARD, M., Chemistry (Jesus College)
BROWN, T., Nucleic Acid Chemistry

CLARY, D. C., Chemistry (Magdalen College)
COMPTON, R. G., Chemistry (St John's College)
DAVIES, S. G., Chemistry (Magdalen College)
DAVIS, B. G., Chemistry (Pembroke College)
DIXON, D. J., Chemistry (Wadham College)
DONOHOE, T. J., Chemistry (Magdalen College)
EDWARDS, P. P., Inorganic Chemistry (St Catherine's College)
FAULKNER, S., Chemistry (Keble College)
FLEET, G. W. J., Chemistry (St John's College)
FOORD, J. S., Chemistry (St Catherine's College)
GOUVERNEUR, V., Chemistry (Merton College)
HAMILTON, A. D., Organic Chemistry (Harris Manchester College and Kellogg College)
HODGSON, D. M., Chemistry (Oriel College)
HORE, P. J., Physical Chemistry (Corpus Christi College)
LOGAN, D. E., Theoretical Chemistry (University College)
MANOLOPOULOS, D. E., Theoretical Chemistry (St Edmund Hall)
McGRADY, J., Computational Inorganic Chemistry (New College)
MOLONEY, M. G., Chemistry (St Peter's College)
MOUNTFORD, P., Organometallic Chemistry and Catalysis (St Edmund Hall)
O'HARE, D. M., Chemistry (Balliol College)
Dame ROBINSON, CAROL V., Chemistry (Exeter College)
SCHOFIELD, C. J., Chemistry (Hertford College)
SOFTLEY, T. P., Chemical Physics (Merton College)
TSANG, S. C. E., Chemistry (University College)
WELLER, A. S., Chemistry (Magdalen College)
WILLIS, M. C., Chemistry (Lincoln College)

Faculty of Classics (Ioannou Centre for Classical and Byzantine Studies, 66 St Giles', Oxford, OX1 3UL; tel. (1865) 288372; e-mail enquiries@classics.ox.ac.uk; internet www.classics.ox.ac.uk):

HARRISON, S. J., Literature (Corpus Christi College)
HORNBLOWER, S., Classics and Ancient History (All Souls College)
HOWGEGO, C. J., Greek and Roman Numismatics (Wolfson College)
HUTCHINSON, G. O., Greek and Latin Languages and Literature (Exeter College)
LEIGH, M. G. L., Classical Languages and Literature (St Anne's College)
LEMOS, I. S., Classical Archaeology (Merton College)
PARKER, R. C. T., Ancient History (New College)
PELLING, C. B. R., Greek—Regius (Christ Church)
PURCELL, N., Ancient History (Brasenose College)
REINHARDT, T., Latin Language and Literature (Corpus Christi College)
SMITH, R. R. R., Classical Archaeology and Art (Lincoln College)
THOMAS, R., Ancient Greek History (Balliol College)
WILLI, A., Comparative Philology (Worcester College)
WILSON, A. I., Archaeology of the Roman Empire (All Souls College)

Nuffield Department of Clinical Medicine (John Radcliffe Hospital, Headington, Oxford, OX3 9DU; tel. (1865) 221325; e-mail enquiries@ndm.ox.ac.uk; internet www.ndm.ox.ac.uk):

BACHMANN, M., Immunology
CORNALL, R. J., Immunology (Corpus Christi College)
CROOK, D. W. M., Microbiology
DAY, N. P. J., Tropical Medicine
DONDORP, A., Tropical Medicine
DONG, T., Immunology
FLINT, J., Molecular Psychiatry (Merton College)
GILBERT, S. C., Vaccinology
GODING, C. R., Oncology
GRÜNEWALD, K., Structural Cell Biology
HANKE, T., Vaccine Immunology
HARPER, S., Gerontology (Nuffield College)
HIEN, T., Tropical Medicine
HILL, A. V. S., Human Genetics (Magdalen College)
JONES, E. Y., Protein Crystallography (Jesus College)
KLENERMAN, P., Immunology (Brasenose College)
KNAPP, S., Structural Biology
KWIATKOWSKI, D., Genomics and Global Health (St John's College)
LU, X., Cancer Medicine (Magdalen College)
MARSH, K., Tropical Medicine (St Cross College)
MCMICHAEL, A. J., Molecular Medicine (Corpus Christi College)
MCSHANE, H., Vaccinology (Harris Manchester College)
MCVEAN, G., Statistical Genetics (Linacre College)
MOTT, R. F., Bioinformatics and Statistical Genetics
NOSTEN, F. H., Tropical Medicine
O'CALLAGHAN, C. A., Medicine (The Queen's College)
PAVORD, I. D., Respiratory Medicine (St Edmund Hall)
PHILLIPS, R. E., Clinical Medicine (Pembroke College)
POWRIE, F. M., Gastroenterology (Green Templeton College)
PRICE, R., Tropical Medicine (All Souls College)
PUGH, C. W., Renal Medicine (Kellogg College)
RATCLIFFE, S. P., Clinical Medicine (Magdalen College)
ROWLAND-JONES, S. L., Immunology (Christ Church)
SIMMONS, C. P., Infectious Diseases
SNOW, R. W., Tropical Public Health
STUART, D., Biochemistry (Hertford College)
TOMLINSON, I., Molecular and Population Genetics (The Queen's College)
WHITE, N. J., Tropical Medicine (St John's College)
WILLIAMS, T. N., Tropical Medicine

Nuffield Department of Clinical Neurosciences (Level 6, West Wing, John Radcliffe Hospital, Headley Way, Headington, Oxford, OX3 9DU; tel. (1865) 231511; e-mail enquiries@ndcn.ox.ac.uk; internet www.ndcn.ox.ac.uk; incorporates the Div. of Clinical Neurology, the Nuffield Laboratory of Ophthalmology, the Nuffield Div. of Anaesthetics and the Oxford Centre for Functional Magnetic Resonance Imaging of the Brain):

BEESON, D. M. W., Neuroscience (St Cross College)
BEHRENS, T., Computational Neuroscience
BROWN, P., Experimental Neurology (Brasenose College)
FOSTER, R. G., Circadian Neuroscience (Brasenose College)
FUGGER, L., Clinical Neuroimmunology (Oriel College)
HANKINS, M. W., Visual Neuroscience

HUSAIN, M., Neurology and Cognitive Neuroscience (New College)
JEZZARD, P., Neuroimaging (University College)
JOHANSEN-BERG, H., Cognitive Neuroscience (St Edmund Hall)
KENNARD, C., Clinical Neurology (Brasenose College)
MACLAREN, R., Ophthalmology (Merton College)
ROTHWELL, P. M., Clinical Neurology (St Edmund Hall)
SMITH, S. M., Biomedical Engineering
TALBOT, K., Motor Neuron Biology
TRACEY, I. M. C., Anaesthetic Science (Pembroke College)

Department of Computer Science (Wolfson Bldg, Parks Rd, Oxford, OX1 3QD; tel. (1865) 273838; e-mail enquiries@cs.ox.ac.uk; internet www.cs.ox.ac.uk):

ABRAMSKY, S., Computing (Wolfson College)
BENEDIKT, M., Computing Science (University College)
BURRAGE, K., Computational and Systems Biology (New College)
BYRNE, H., Computational Biology (Keble College)
CARDELLI, L. A., Royal Society Research Professor
COECKE, B., Quantum Foundations, Logics and Structures (Wolfson College)
CREESE, S., Cybersecurity (Worcester College)
DAVIES, J. W. M., Software Engineering (Kellogg College)
DE FREITAS, J. F. G., Computer Science (Linacre College)
DE MOOR, O., Computer Science (Magdalen College)
GAVAGHAN, D. J., Computational Biology (New College)
GIBBONS, J., Computing (Kellogg College)
GOLDBERG, L. A., Computer Science (St Edmund Hall)
GOLDBERG, P., Computer Science
GOTTLOB, G., Informatics (St John's College)
HORROCKS, I. R., Computing Science (Oriel College)
JEAVONS, P. G., Computer Science (St Anne's College)
KROENING, D., Computer Science (Magdalen College)
KWIATKOWSKA, M. Z., Computing Systems (Trinity College)
LOWE, G., Computer Science (St Catherine's College)
LUKASIEWICZ, T., Computer Science
MELHAM, T. F., Computer Science (Balliol College)
ONG, C. H. L., Computer Science (Merton College)
OUAKNINE, J., Computer Science (St John's College)
PULMAN, S. G., Computational Linguistics (Somerville College)
ROSCOE, A. W., Computing Science (University College)
WOOLDRIDGE, M., Computer Science (Hertford College)
WORRELL, J., Computer Science (Green Templeton College)

Department for Continuing Education (Rewley House, 1 Wellington Sq., Oxford, OX1 2JA; tel. (1865) 270360; e-mail enquiries@conted.ox.ac.uk; internet www.conted.ox.ac.uk):

DU SAUTOY, M. P. F., Public Understanding of Science (New College)
HAWKINS, A., Modern British History (Keble College)
MICHIE, J., Innovation and Knowledge Exchange (Kellogg College)

Ruskin School of Fine Art (74 High St, Oxford, OX1 4BG; tel. (1865) 276940; e-mail info@ruskin-sch.ox.ac.uk; internet www.ruskin-sch.ox.ac.uk):

CATLING, B. D., Fine Art (Linacre College)
CHEVSKA, M., Fine Art (Brasenose College)

Department of Earth Sciences (South Parks Rd, Oxford, OX1 3AN; tel. (1865) 272000; e-mail enquiries@earth.ox.ac.uk; internet www.earth.ox.ac.uk):

BALLANTINE, C., Geochemistry (St Hugh's College)
CARTWRIGHT, J., Earth Sciences (St Peter's College)
ENGLAND, P. C., Geology (University College)
FRASER, D. G., Earth Sciences (Worcester College)
HALLIDAY, A. N., Geochemistry (St Hugh's College)
HENDERSON, G. M., Earth Sciences (University College)
KHATIWALA, S., Earth Sciences (Linacre College)
PARSONS, B. E., Geodesy and Geophysics (St Cross College)
PYLE, D. M., Earth Sciences (St Anne's College)
RICKABY, R. E. M., Biogeochemistry (Wolfson College)
SEARLE, M. P., Earth Sciences (Worcester College)
WATTS, A. B., Marine Geology and Geophysics (Wolfson College)
WOOD, B., Earth Sciences (Wolfson College)

Department of Economics (Manor Rd Bldg, Manor Rd, Oxford, OX1 3UQ; tel. (1865) 271089; e-mail reception@economics.ox.ac.uk; internet www.economics.ox.ac.uk):

ANAND, S., Quantitative Economic Analysis (St Catherine's College)
ARMSTRONG, M., Economics (All Souls College)
BROWNING, M. J., Economics (Nuffield College)
CRAWFORD, V. P., Political Economy (All Souls College)
JAVORCIK, B. S., Economics (All Souls College)
KEANE, M., Economics (Nuffield College)
KELLER, R. G., Microeconomic Theory (Nuffield College)
KLEMPERER, P. D., Economics (Nuffield College)
MUKERJI, S., Economics (University College)
NEARY, J. P., Economics (Merton College)
QUAH, J. K.-H., Economic Theory (St Hugh's College)
ROBERTS, K. S. W., Economics (Nuffield College)
STEVENS, M. J., Economics (Lincoln College)
VAN DER PLOEG, R., Economics (New College)
VENABLES, A. J., Economics (New College)
VINES, D. A., Economics (Balliol College)
YOUNG, H. P., Economics (Nuffield College)

Department of Education (15 Norham Gardens, Oxford, OX2 6PY; tel. (1865) 274024; e-mail general.enquiries@education.ox.ac.uk; internet www.education.ox.ac.uk):

BAIRD, J.-A., Educational Assessment (St Anne's College)
DANIELS, H., Education (Green Templeton College)
EDWARDS, A., Educational Studies (St Hilda's College)
KEEP, E., Education, Training and Skills
MAYHEW, K., Education and Economic Performance (Pembroke College)
MELHUISH, E. C., Human Development

MENTER, I., Teacher Education (Kellogg College)

NUNES, T., Educational Studies (Harris Manchester College)

OZGA, J., Sociology of Education (Green Templeton College)

SAMMONS, P., Education (Jesus College)

SEBBA, J., Fostering and Education (Green Templeton College)

STAMBACH, A., Educational Studies (St Edmund Hall)

STRAND, S., Education (St Cross College)

Department of Engineering Science (17 Parks Rd, Oxford, OX1 3PJ; tel. (1865) 273000; e-mail enquiries@eng.ox.ac.uk; internet www.eng.ox.ac.uk):

BLAKEBOROUGH, A., Engineering Science (Worcester College)

CLEVELAND, R., Engineering Science (Magdalene College)

COCKS, A. C. F., Materials Engineering (St Anne's College)

COUSSIOS, C. C., Biomedical Engineering (Magdalen College)

CUI, Z. F., Chemical Engineering (Hertford College)

DANIEL, R. W., Engineering Science (Brasenose College)

DARTON, R. C., Engineering Science (Keble College)

DUNCAN, S. R., Engineering Science (St Hugh's College)

ELSTON, S. J., Engineering Science (St John's College)

FIELD, R., Engineering Science (Balliol College)

FOX, J. P., Engineering Science

HE, L., Computational Aerothermal Engineering (Lady Margaret Hall)

HILLS, D. A., Engineering Science (Lincoln College)

HOULSBY, G. T., Civil Engineering (Brasenose College)

IRELAND, P. T., Turbomachinery (St Catherine's College)

KIM, J. M., Electrical Engineering (St Hugh's College)

KORSUNSKY, A. M., Engineering Science (Trinity College)

LIMEBEER, D. J. N., Control Engineering (New College)

MURRAY, D. W., Engineering Science (St Anne's College)

NEWMAN, P., Information Engineering (Keble College)

NOBLE, J. A., Biomedical Engineering (St Hilda's College)

NOWELL, D., Engineering Science (Christ Church)

O'BRIEN, D., Engineering Science (Balliol College)

PETRINIC, N., Engineering Science

REED, R., Engineering Science (St Anne's College)

ROBERTS, S. J., Engineering Science (Somerville College)

ROY, R., Mechanical Engineering (Harris Manchester College)

SHAMONINA, K., Electrical Engineering (Wadham College)

STONE, C. R., Engineering Science (Somerville College)

TARASSENKO, L., Electrical Engineering (St John's College)

TAYLOR, P. H., Engineering Science (Keble College)

THOMPSON, I. P., Engineering Science (St Edmund Hall)

TORR, P. H. S., Engineering Science (St Catherine's College)

WILLIAMS, M. S., Engineering Science (New College)

WILSON, T., Engineering Science (Hertford College)

ZISSERMAN, A. P., Computer Vision Engineering (Brasenose College)

Faculty of English Language and Literature (St Cross Bldg, Manor Rd, Oxford, OX1 3UL; tel. (1865) 271055; e-mail english.office@ell .ox.ac.uk; internet www.english.ox.ac.uk):

ACHINSTEIN, S., Renaissance Literature (St Edmund Hall)

BALLASTER, R. M., 18th-Century Studies (Mansfield College)

BOEHMER, E. D., World Literature in English (Wolfson College)

BRADSHAW, D., English Literature (Worcester College)

BREWER, C. D., English Language and Literature (Hertford College)

CAMERON, D. J., Language and Communication (Worcester College)

GILLESPIE, V. A., English Language and Literature (Lady Margaret Hall)

HERMIONE, D. L., 20th- and 21st-century English Literature (Wolfson College)

HILL, G. W., Poetry (Keble College)

HOROBIN, S., English Language and Literature (Magdalen College)

Dame LEE, HERMIONE, 20th- and 21st-century English Literature (Wolfson College)

MAGUIRE, L. E., English Language and Literature (Magdalen College)

MAPSTONE, S., Older Scottish Literature (St Hilda's College)

MARCUS, L., English Literature (New College)

McCABE, R. A., English Language and Literature (Merton College)

McCULLOUGH, P., English (Lincoln College)

McDONALD, P. D., English and Related Literature (St Hugh's College)

MUGGLESTONE, L. C., History of English (Pembroke College)

NEWLYN, L. A., English Language and Literature (St Edmund Hall)

ORCHARD, A. P. M., Anglo-Saxon (Pembroke College)

PALFREY, S., English Literature (Brasenose College)

ROMAINE, S., English Language (Merton College)

SHUTTLEWORTH, S., English Language and Literature (St Anne's College)

SMALL, H., English Literature (Pembroke College)

STAFFORD, F. J., English Language and Literature (Somerville College)

STERN, T., Early Modern Drama (University College)

SUTHERLAND, K., Bibliography and Textual Criticism (St Anne's College)

WAKELIN, D., Medieval English Palaeography (St Hilda's College)

WOMERSLEY, D. J., English Literature (St Catherine's College)

Oxford e-Research Centre (7 Keble Rd, Oxford, OX1 3QG; tel. (1865) 610600; e-mail info@oerc.ox.ac.uk; internet www.oerc.ox.ac .uk):

CHEN, M., Scientific Visualization (Pembroke College)

DE ROURE, D., e-Research (Wolfson College)

Department of Experimental Psychology (Tinbergen Bldg, 9 South Parks Rd, Oxford, OX1 3UD; tel. (1865) 271444; e-mail general@psy.ox.ac.uk; internet www.psy.ox .ac.uk):

BANNERMAN, D., Behavioural Neuroscience

BISHOP, D. V. M., Developmental Neuropsychology (St John's College)

CLARK, D. M., Psychology (Magdalen College)

DUNBAR, R., Evolutionary Psychology (Magdalen College)

EHLERS, A., Experimental Psychopathology (Wolfson College)

FLINT, J., Neuroscience (Merton College)

FOX, E., Cognitive and Affective Psychology (Magdalen College)

HEWSTONE, M. R. C., Social Psychology (New College)

HEYES, C. M., Psychology (All Souls College)

HUMPHREYS, G., Psychology (Wolfson College)

HUSAIN, M., Neurology and Cognitive Neuroscience (New College)

MARTIN, R. M. A., Abnormal Psychology (St Edmund Hall)

NATION, K., Experimental Psychology (St John's College)

NOBRÉ, A. C. DE O., Cognitive Neuroscience (New College)

PLUNKETT, K. R., Cognitive Neuroscience (St Hugh's College)

RAWLINS, J. N. P., Psychology (Wolfson College)

RUSHWORTH, M. F. S., Cognitive Neuroscience

SPENCE, C. J., Experimental Psychology (Somerville College)

VINCENT, C. A., Psychology

School of Geography and the Environment (Dyson Perrins Bldg, South Parks Rd, Oxford, OX1 3QY; tel. (1865) 285070; e-mail enquiries@geog.ox.ac.uk; internet www.geog .ox.ac.uk):

ALLEN, M. R., Geosystem Science (Linacre College)

BANISTER, D., Transport Studies (St Anne's College)

CLARK, G. L., Geography (St Peter's College)

DORLING, D., Geography (St Peter's College)

HALL, J., Climate and Environmental Risks (Linacre College)

JEFFREY, C., Development Geography (St John's College)

McDOWELL, L. M., Human Geography (St John's College)

MALHI, Y. S., Ecosystem Science (Oriel College)

PALLOT, J., Human Geography of Russia (Christ Church)

THOMAS, D. S. G., Geography (Hertford College)

VILES, H. A., Biogeomorphology and Heritage Conservation (Worcester College)

WASHINGTON, R., Climate Science (Keble College)

WHATMORE, S. J., Environment and Public Policy (Linacre College)

WHITTAKER, R. J., Biogeography (St Edmund Hall)

Blavatnik School of Government (10 Merton St, Oxford OX1 4JJ; tel. (1865) 614343; e-mail enquiries@bsg.ox.ac.uk; internet www.bsg.ox.ac.uk):

COLLIER, SIR P., Economics and Public Policy (St Antony's College)

TOFT, M. D., Government and Public Policy (University College)

WOODS, N., Global Economic Governance (University College)

YIP, W., Health Policy and Economics (Green Templeton College)

Faculty of History (Old Boys' School, George St, Oxford, OX1 2RL; tel. (1865) 615000; e-mail board.admin@history.ox.ac.uk; internet www.history.ox.ac.uk):

BELICH, J., Imperial and Commonwealth History (Balliol College)

BETTS, P., Modern European History (St Antony's College)

BLAIR, W. J., Medieval History and Archaeology (The Queen's College)

BROCKLISS, L. W. B., Early Modern French History (Magdalen College)

BROERS, M., Western European History (Lady Margaret Hall)

CLAVIN, P. M., International History (Jesus College)

CLUNAS, C., History of Art (Trinity College)

CORSI, P., History of Science (Linacre College)

FOSTER, R. F., Irish History (Hertford College)

GILDEA, R. N., Modern History (Worcester College)

HAMALAINEN, P., American History (St Catherine's College)

HAMEROW, H. F., Archaeology (St Cross College)

HARRIS, R., Modern History (New College)

HARRISON, M., History of Medicine (Green Templeton College)

HAWKINS, A. B., History (Kellogg College)

HEALEY, D., Modern Russian History (St Antony's College)

HOTSON, H. B., Early Modern Intellectual History (St Anne's College)

HUMPHRIES, K. J., Economic History (All Souls College)

MITTER, R. S. R., History and Politics of Modern China (St Cross College)

O'ROURKE, K. H., Economic History (All Souls College)

ROPER, L. A., Modern History—Regius (Oriel College)

SHARPE, R., Diplomatic (Wadham College)

SMITH, S. A., History (All Souls College)

STARGARDT, N., Modern European History (Magdalen College)

STRACHAN, SIR H., History of War (All Souls College)

WICKHAM, C. J., Medieval History (All Souls College)

School of Interdisciplinary Area Studies (12 Bevington Rd, Oxford, OX2 6LH; tel. (1865) 284996; e-mail enquiries@area.ox.ac.uk; internet www.area-studies.ox.ac.uk):

BEINART, W., Race Relations (St Antony's College)

GOODMAN, R. J., Modern Japanese Studies (St Antony's College)

KARIYA, T., Sociology of Japanese Society (St Antony's College)

NEARY, I. J., Politics of Japan (St Antony's College)

PAYNE, L. A., Sociology—Latin American Societies (St Antony's College)

PENSLAR, D. J., Israel Studies (St Anne's College)

Oxford Department of International Development (Queen Elizabeth House, 3 Mansfield Rd, Oxford, OX1 3TB; tel. (1865) 281800; e-mail qeh@qeh.ox.ac.uk; internet www.qeh.ox.ac.uk):

ADAM, C., Development Economics (St Cross College)

ALEXANDER, J., Commonwealth Studies (Linacre College)

CHATTY, D., Anthropology and Forced Migration (St Cross College)

DERCON, S., Development Economics (Wolfson College)

FU, X., Technology and International Development (Green Templeton College)

GOLLIN, D., Development Economics (St Antony's College)

PLATTEAU, J.-P., Development Economics

Oxford Internet Institute (1 St Giles, Oxford, OX1 3JS; tel. (1865) 287210; e-mail enquiries@oii.ox.ac.uk; internet www.oii.ox.ac.uk):

FLORIDI, L., Philosophy and Ethics of Information (St Cross College)

MARGETTS, H., Society and the Internet (Mansfield College)

MAYER-SCHÖNBERGER, V., Internet Governance and Regulation (Keble College)

SCHROEDER, R., e-Science

Faculty of Law (St Cross Bldg, St Cross Rd, Oxford, OX1 3UL; tel. (1865) 271491; e-mail lawfac@law.ox.ac.uk; internet www.law.ox.ac.uk):

ARMOUR, J. H., Law and Finance (Oriel College)

ASHWORTH, A. J., English Law (All Souls College)

BRIGGS, A., Private International Law (St Edmund Hall)

BRIGHT, S. L., Land Law (New College)

BURROWS, A., Law of England (All Souls College)

CARTWRIGHT, J., Law of Contract (Christ Church)

COLLINS, H., English Law (All Souls College)

CRAIG, P. P., English Law (St John's College)

DAVIES, A., Law and Public Policy (Brasenose College)

DICKINSON, A., Law (St Catherine's College)

DINWOODIE, G. B., Intellectual Property and Information Technology Law (St Peter's College)

DOUGLAS-SCOTT, S., European and Human Rights Law (Lady Margaret Hall)

ENCHELMAIER, S., European and Comparative Law (Lincoln College)

ENDICOTT, T. A. O., Legal Philosophy (Balliol College)

ENRIQUES, L., Corporate Law (Jesus College)

EZRACHI, A., Competition Law (Pembroke College)

FREDMAN, S., Laws of the British Commonwealth and the United States (Pembroke College)

FREEDMAN, J. A., Taxation Law (Worcester College)

GALLIGAN, D. J., Socio-legal Studies (Wolfson College)

GARDNER, J. B., Jurisprudence (University College)

GARDNER, S., Law (Lincoln College)

GETZLER, J., Law and Legal History (St Hugh's College)

GOODWIN-GILL, G. S., International Refugee Law (All Souls College)

GREEN, L., Philosophy of Law (Balliol College)

GULLIFER, L., Commercial Law (Harris-Manchester College)

HERRING, J., Law (Exeter College)

HOYLE, C., Criminology (Green Templeton College)

LOADER, I., Criminology (All Souls College)

PAYNE, J., Corporate Finance Law (Merton College)

PEEL, E., Law (Keble College)

REDGWELL, C., Public International Law (All Souls College)

RINGE, W.-G., International Commercial Law

ROBERTS, J. V., Criminology (Worcester College)

SAROOSHI, D., Public International Law (The Queen's College)

STEVENS, R., English Private Law (Lady Margaret Hall)

VOGENAUER, S., Comparative Law (Brasenose College)

WEATHERILL, S. R., European Law (Somerville College)

WHITTAKER, S. J., European Comparative Law (St John's College)

ZEDNER, L. H., Criminal Justice (Corpus Christi College)

ZUCKERMAN, A. A. S., Civil Procedure (University College)

Faculty of Linguistics, Philology and Phonetics (Centre for Linguistics and Philology, Clarendon Press Institute, Walton St, Oxford, OX1 2HG; tel. (1865) 280400; e-mail enquiries@ling-phil.ox.ac.uk; internet www.ling-phil.ox.ac.uk):

COLEMAN, J. S., Phonetics (Wolfson College)

DALRYMPLE, M. E., Syntax (Linacre College)

LAHIRI, A., Linguistics (Somerville College)

MAIDEN, M., Romance Languages (Trinity College)

WILLI, A., Comparative Philology (Worcester College)

Faculty of Management (Saïd Business School) (Saïd Business School, Park End St, Oxford, OX1 1HP; tel. (1865) 288800; e-mail reception@sbs.ox.ac.uk; internet www.sbs.ox.ac.uk):

BARKER, R., Accounting (Christ Church)

DEVEREUX, M., Business Taxation (Oriel College)

DOPSON, S., Organizational Behaviour (Green Templeton College)

FELIN, T., Strategic Management

FLYVBJERG, B., Major Programme Management (St Anne's College)

HELLMAN, T., Entrepreneurship and Innovation

HOLWEG, M., Operations Management

JENKINSON, T. J., Finance (Keble College)

JIN, L., Emerging Markets

MAYER, C. P., Management Studies (St Edmund Hall)

MORRIS, T. J., Management Studies (Green Templeton College)

MORRISON, A. D., Law and Finance (Merton College)

NICHOLLS, A., Social Entrepreneurship (Harris Manchester College)

NOE, T. H., Management Studies (Balliol College)

PETTIGREW, A. M., Strategy and Organization (Brasenose College)

POWELL, T. C., Strategy (St Hugh's College)

RAMADORAI, T., Financial Economics (St Catherine's College)

SAKO, M., Management Studies (Green Templeton College)

SCOTT, L., Entrepreneurship and Innovation (Green Templeton College)

SUZUKI, T., Accounting (Hertford College)

TAYLOR, J. W., Decision Science (St Cross College)

TUFANO, P., Finance (Balliol College)

UPTON, D. M., Operations Management (Christ Church)

WESTBROOK, R. K., Operations Management (St Hugh's College)

WHITTINGTON, R. C., Strategic Management (New College)

WOOLGAR, S. W., Marketing (Green Templeton College)

Oxford Martin School (34 Broad St, Oxford OX1 3BD; tel. (1865) 287430; internet www.oxfordmartin.ox.ac.uk):

ABRAMSKY, S., Computing (Wolfson College)

ALLEN, M., Geosystem Science (Linacre College)

ARMOUR, J., Law and Finance (Oriel College)

ARREGUÍN-TOFT, I., Public Policy (Pembroke College)

SIR ATKINSON, TONY, Economics (Nuffield College)

BANISTER, D., Transport Studies (St Anne's College)

SIR BEDDINGTON, JOHN, Natural Resources Management

BOSTROM, N., Philosophy (St Cross College)

BRIGGS, A., Nanomaterials (St Anne's College)

CANEY, S., Political Theory (Magdalen College)

CASTLES, S., Sociology

COECKE, B., Quantum Foundations, Logics and Structures (Wolfson College)

COLLIER, S. P., Economics (St Antony's College)

CORNISH, P., Strategic Studies

CREESE, S., Cybersecurity

DARTON, R., Engineering Science (Keble College)

DE ROURE, D., e-Research

DEUTSCH, D. E., Physics

DOLAN, L., Botany (Magdalen College)

DUTTON, W. H., Internet Studies (Balliol College)

FARMER, J. D., Mathematics

FERREIRA, P. G., Astrophysics (Oriel College)

FLINT, J., Molecular Psychiatry (Merton College)

FOOT, C., Physics (St Peter's College)

FREDMAN, S., Laws of the British Commonwealth and the United States (Pembroke College)

GERCKE, M., Cybercrime

GILBERT, S., Vaccinology

GODFRAY, H. C. J., Zoology (Jesus College)

GODING, C., Oncology

GOLDIN, I., Globalization and Development (Balliol College)

GOLDSMITH, M., Cybersecurity

GOLLIN, D., Development Economics (St Antony's College)

GORIELY, A., Mathematical Modelling (St Catherine's College)

GOSSELIN, D., Strategy and Marketing

GOTTLOB, G., Informatics (St John's College)

GROVENOR, C., Materials (St Anne's College)

GUPTA, S., Theoretical Epidemiology

HALL, J., Climate and Environmental Risks

HARPER, S., Gerontology (Nuffield College)

HENDERSON, G. M., Earth Sciences

Sir HENDRY, DAVID F., Economics (Nuffield College)

HEPBURN, C., Environmental Economics (New College)

HILL, A., Human Genetics (Magdalen College)

HOULSBY, G. T., Civil Engineering (Brasenose College)

JAMES, W., Virology (Brasenose College)

JONES, J., Atomic and Laser Physics (Brasenose College)

KEITH, M., Sociology and Migration Studies (Merton College)

KLENERMAN, P., Immunology

KWIATKOWSKA, M., Computing Systems (Trinity College)

LANGDALE, J., Plant Development (The Queen's College)

LEA, S., Microbiology (Wadham College)

MCLEAN, A., Mathematical Biology (All Souls College)

MACMAHON, S., Medicine

MCSHANE, H., Vaccinology

MAIDEN, M., Molecular Epidemiology (Hertford College)

MALHI, Y., Ecosystems Science (Oriel College)

MARROW, J., Energy Materials

MARSHAL, D., Physical Oceanography

MIESENBÖCK, G., Physiology (Magdalen College)

MUELLBAUER, J., Economics (Nuffield College)

MÜLLER, V. C., Philosophy

NORTON, R., Public Health

PALMER, T., Climate Physics (Jesus College)

PHILLIPS, R. E., Clinical Medicine (Pembroke College)

POLLARD, A., Paediatric Infection and Immunity (St Cross College)

PYBUS, O., Evolution and Infectious Disease (New College)

RAYNER, S., Science and Civilization (Keble College)

REDGWELL, C., Public International Law (All Souls College)

REINERT, G., Statistics (Keble College)

ROSCOE, B., Computing Science (University College)

SASSE, M. A., Human-centred Technology

SATTENTAU, Q., Immunology (Magdalen College)

SAUNDERS, S., Philosophy of Physics (Merton College)

SAVULESCU, J., Practical Ethics (St Cross College)

STEANE, A., Physics (Exeter College)

TANG, C., Cellular Pathology (Exeter College)

TAYLOR, R., Condensed Matter Physics (The Queen's College)

THOMAS, J., Ecology (New College)

TURBERFIELD, A., Physics (Magdalen College)

ULIJASZEK, S., Human Ecology (St Cross College)

UPTON, D., Operations Management

VEDRAL, V., Quantum Information Science (Wolfson College)

VENABLES, A., Economics (New College)

VINES, D., Economics (Balliol College)

WADDELL, S., Neurobiology

WALMSLEY, I. A., Experimental Physics (St Hugh's College)

WELSH, J., International Relations (Somerville College)

WEST, G., Theoretical Physics

WILLIS, K., Biodiversity (Merton College)

YOUNG, H. P., Economics (Nuffield College)

Department of Materials (16 Parks Rd, Oxford, OX1 3PH; tel. (1865) 273700; e-mail enquiries@materials.ox.ac.uk; internet www .materials.ox.ac.uk):

BRIGGS, G. A. D., Nanomaterials (St Anne's College)

BRUCE, P. G., Materials (St Edmund Hall)

CASTELL, M. R., Materials (Linacre College)

GRANT, P. S., Materials (St Catherine's College)

GROBERT, N., Nanomaterials (Corpus Christi)

GROVENOR, C. R. M., Materials (St Anne's College)

KIRKLAND, A. I., Materials (Linacre College)

MARROW, T. J., Energy Materials (Mansfield College)

NELLIST, P. D., Materials (Corpus Christi)

REED, R. C., Materials and Solid Mechanics (St Anne's College)

ROBERTS, S. G., Materials (St Edmund Hall)

TODD, R. I., Materials (St Catherine's College)

WILKINSON, A. J., Materials (St Cross College)

WILSHAW, P. R., Materials (St Anne's College)

Mathematical Institute (Andrew Wiles Bldg, Radcliffe Observatory Quarter, Woodstock Rd, Oxford, OX2 6GG; tel. (1865) 273525; e-mail enquiries@maths.ox.ac.uk; internet www.maths.ox.ac.uk):

ALDAY, L. F., Mathematical Physics (Hertford College)

Sir BALL, JOHN M., Natural Philosophy (The Queen's College)

BATTY, C. J. K., Analysis (St John's College)

BRIDSON, M. R., Pure Mathematics (Magdalen College)

BYRNE, H., Computational Biology (Keble College)

CANDELAS, P., Mathematics (Wadham College)

CHAPMAN, S. J., Mathematics and its Applications (Mansfield College)

CHEN, G.-Q. G., Analysis of Partial Differential Equations (Keble College)

DANCER, A., Mathematics (Jesus College)

DRUTU, B. C., Mathematics (Exeter College)

DU SAUTOY, M. P. F., Public Understanding of Science (New College)

EKERT, A., Quantum Information (Merton College)

ETHERIDGE, A. M., Probability (Magdalen College)

FARMER, J. D., Mathematics

FLYNN, E. V., Mathematics (New College)

GILES, M. B., Scientific Computing (St Hugh's College)

GORIELY, A., Mathematical Modelling (St Catherine's College)

GOULD, N. M., Numerical Optimization (Exeter College)

GREEN, B. J., Pure Mathematics (Magdalen College)

GRINDROD, P., Mathematics

HAMBLY, B., Mathematics (St Anne's College)

HEATH-BROWN, D. R., Pure Mathematics (Worcester College)

HENKE, A. E., Mathematics (Pembroke College)

HITCHIN, N. J., Geometry (New College)

HOWISON, S. D., Applied Mathematics (Christ Church)

JOYCE, D. D., Mathematics (Lincoln College)

KEEVASH, P., Mathematics (Mansfield College)

KIM, M., Number Theory (Merton College)

KIRWAN, F. C., Mathematics (Balliol College)

KRAMKOV, D., Mathematical Finance

KRISTENSEN, J., Mathematics (Magdalen College)

LACKENBY, M., Mathematics (St Catherine's College)

LYONS, T. J., Mathematics (St Anne's College)

MAINI, P. K., Mathematical Biology (Brasenose College)

MASON, L. J., Mathematics (St Peter's College)

PLEASE, C., Applied Mathematics (Mansfield College)

RIORDAN, O., Discrete Mathematics (St Edmund Hall)

SCOTT, A. D., Mathematics (Merton College)

SEREGIN, G. A., Pure Mathematics (St Hilda's College)

SHKOLLER, S., Mathematics (Trinity College)

SPARKS, J., Mathematical Physics (Oriel College)

SÜLI, E., Numerical Analysis (Worcester College)

TANNER, J., Mathematics of Information (Exeter College)

TILLMANN, U. L., Mathematics (Merton College)

TOD, K. P., Mathematical Physics (St John's College)

TREFETHEN, L. N., Numerical Analysis (Balliol College)

WETTLAUFER, J., Applicable Mathematics (Jesus College)

WILES, Sir A., Royal Society Research Professor (Merton College)

ZHOU, X., Mathematical Finance (St Hugh's College)

ZILBER, B., Mathematical Logic (Merton College)

Radcliffe Department of Medicine (Level 6, West Wing, John Radcliffe Hospital, Headington, Oxford OX3 9DU; e-mail enquiries@ rdm.ox.ac.uk; internet www.rdm.ox.ac.uk; f. 2012 by merger of the Dept of Cardiovascular Medicine; the Oxford Centre for Diabetes,

Endocrinology and Metabolism; the majority of research groups from the MRC Weatherall Institute of Molecular Medicine; the Nuffield Department of Clinical Laboratory Sciences; the Oxford Acute Vascular Imaging Centre; and the academic groups in Geratology and Stroke):

AHMED, A. A., Gynaecological Oncology (St Hugh's College)
BANHAM, A. H., Haemato-oncology
BANNING, A., Interventional Cardiology
BEESON, D., Neuroscience (St Cross College)
Sir BELL, JOHN I., Medicine—Regius (Christ Church)
BHATTACHARYA, S., Cardiovascular Medicine (Green Templeton College)
BOULTWOOD, J., Molecular Haematology (Wolfson College)
BUCHAN, A., Stroke Medicine (Corpus Christi College)
CASADEI, B., Cardiovascular Medicine
CERUNDOLO, V., Immunology (Merton College)
CHANNON, K. M., Cardiovascular Medicine (Lady Margaret Hall)
CHOUDHURY, R. P., Cardiovascular Medicine (Balliol College)
DAVIS, S. J., Molecular Immunology (Corpus Christi)
DONG, T., Immunology
FARRALL, M., Cardiovascular Genetics (Keble College)
FERGUSON, D. J. P., Ultrastructural Morphology
FERRY, B. L., Immunology (Green Templeton College)
FUGGER, L., Clinical Neuroimmunology (Oriel College)
GATTER, K. C., Pathology (St John's College)
GIBBONS, R., Clinical Genetics (Green Templeton College)
GOUGH, S. C. L., Diabetic Medicine (Harris Manchester College)
GROSSMAN, A. B., Endocrinology (Green Templeton College)
HARRIS, A. L., Medical Oncology (St Hugh's Coollege)
HIGGS, D. R., Haematology (Brasenose College)
HOLLÄNDER, G., Paediatrics (Jesus College)
HOLMAN, R. R., Diabetic Medicine
JACKSON, D. G., Human Immunology (Harris Manchester College)
JOHNSON, P., Paediatric Surgery (St Edmund Hall)
KARPE, F., Metabolic Medicine (Pembroke College)
KERR, D., Cancer Medicine
LEESON, P., Cardiovascular Science (Wolfson College)
MCCARTHY, M., Diabetic Medicine (Green Templeton College)
MURPHY, M., Blood Transfusion Medicine
NERLOV, C., Stem Cell Biology
NEUBAUER, S., Cardiovascular Medicine (Christ Church)
NEWBOLD, C. I., Tropical Medicine (Green Templeton College)
OGG, G., Dermatology (Christ Church)
PATIENT, R., Developmental Haemopoiesis (Weatherall Institute of Molecular Medicine)
PEZZELLA, F., Tumour Pathology (New College)
RABBITTS, T. H., Molecular Biology
ROBERTS, D. J., Haematology (Trinity College)
RORSMAN, P., Diabetic Medicine (Harris Manchester College)
THAKKER, R. V., Medicine (Somerville College)
TOMLINSON, J. W., Medicine (Somerville College)

TOWNSEND, A. R., Molecular Immunology (New College)
VYAS, P., Haematology (St Anne's College)
WASS, J. A. H., Endocrinology (Green TempletonCollege)
WATKINS, H. C., Cardiovascular Medicine (Exeter College)
WATT, S. M., Haematology
WILKIE, A. O. M., Pathology

Faculty of Medieval and Modern European Languages (41 & 47 Wellington Sq., Oxford, OX1 2JF; tel. (1865) 270570; e-mail reception@mod-langs.ox.ac.uk; internet www .mod-langs.ox.ac.uk):

BONSAVER, G., Italian Cultural History (Pembroke College)
COOPER, R. A., French (Brasenose College)
CRONK, N. E., French Literature (St Edmund Hall)
FIDDIAN, R. W., Spanish (Wadham College)
HOWELLS, C. M., French (Wadham College)
JEFFERSON, A. M., French Literature (New College)
KAHN, A. S., Russian Literature (St Edmund Hall)
KELLY, C. H. M., Russian (New College)
KOHL, K. M., German Literature (Jesus College)
LAUXTERMANN, M. D., Byzantine and Modern Greek Language and Literature (Exeter College)
LEEDER, K. J., Modern German Literature (New College)
MCGUINNESS, P. R. A., French and Comparative Literature (St Anne's College)
MCLAUGHLIN, M. L., Italian Studies (Magdalen College)
MAIDEN, M. D., Romance Languages (Trinity College)
MALLINSON, G. J., Early Modern French Literature (Trinity College)
PARISH, R. J., French (St Catherine's College)
PEARSON, R. A. G., French (Queen's College)
ROBERTSON, R. N. N., German Language and Literature (The Queen's College)
ROTHWELL, P., Portuguese Studies (St Peter's College)
SHERINGHAM, M. H. T., French Literature (All Souls College)
VIALA, A., French Literature (Lady Margaret Hall)
VOLFING, A. M., Medieval German Studies (Oriel College)
WILLIAMSON, E. H., Spanish Studies (Exeter College)
ZORIN, A. L., Russian (New College)

Faculty of Music (St Aldate's, Oxford, OX1 1DB; tel. (1865) 276125; e-mail office@music .ox.ac.uk; internet www.music.ox.ac.uk):

BORN, G., Music and Anthropology (Mansfield College)
CLARKE, E. F., Music (Wadham College)
CROSS, J. G. E., Musicology (Christ Church)
DREYFUS, L., Music (Magdalen College)
LEACH, E. E., Music (St Hugh's College)
SAXTON, R. L. A., Composition (Worcester College)
WOLLENBERG, S., Music (Lady Margaret Hall)

Nuffield Department of Obstetrics and Gynaecology (Level 3, Women's Centre, John Radcliffe Hospital, Oxford, OX3 9DU; tel. (1865) 221004; e-mail enquiries@obs-gyn .ox.ac.uk; internet www.obs-gyn.ox.ac.uk):

AHMED, A. A., Gynaecological Oncology (St Hugh's College)
KENNEDY, S., Reproductive Medicine (Green Templeton College)
POULTON, J., Mitochondrial Genetics (Lady Margaret Hall)

SARGENT, I. L., Reproductive Science (Mansfield College)
VILLAR, J., Perinatal Medicine

Department of Oncology (Old Road Campus Research Bldg, Roosevelt Drive, Oxford, OX3 7DQ; tel. (1865) 617330; e-mail enquiries@ oncology.ox.ac.uk; internet www.oncology.ox .ac.uk; merged with Dept of Clinical Pharmacology):

Sir BRADY, M., Oncological Imaging (Keble College)
BROWN, T., Nucleic Acid Chemistry
HARRIS, A. L., Medical Oncology (St Hugh's College)
LA THANGUE, N. B., Cancer Biology (Linacre College)
MCKENNA, W. G., Radiation Oncology and Biology (Wolfson College)
MAUGHAN, T., Clinical Oncology (Linacre College)
MIDDLETON, M., Experimental Cancer Medicine
MUSCHEL, R., Molecular Pathology (St Hilda's College)
SEYMOUR, L. W., Genetic Therapy (Wolfson College)
VALLIS, K. A., Experimental Radiotherapeutics
VOJNOVIC, B., Biophysics

Faculty of Oriental Studies (Oriental Institute, Pusey Lane, Oxford, OX1 2LE; tel. (1865) 278200; e-mail orient@orinst.ox.ac .uk; internet www.orinst.ox.ac.uk):

BRAY, J., Arabic (St John's College)
FRAENKL, C., Study of the Abrahamic Religions (Lady Margaret Hall)
FRELLESVIG, B., Japanese Linguistics (Hertford College)
GOODMAN, M. D., Jewish Studies (Wolfson College)
HARRISON, H., Modern Chinese Studies (St Cross College)
HERZIG, E., Persian Studies (Wadham College)
HOYLAND, R., Islamic History (Wolfson College)
JOHNS, J., Art and Archaeology of the Islamic Mediterranean (Wolfson College)
MINKOWSKI, C. Z., Sanskrit (Balliol College)
O'HANLON, P., Indian History and Culture (St Cross College)
PARKINSON, R. B., Egyptology (The Queen's College)
RAMADAN, T., Contemporary Islamic Studies (St Antony's College)
SANDERSON, A. G. J. S., Eastern Religions and Ethics (All Souls College)
SMITH, M. J., Egyptology (University College)
TER HAAR, B. J., Chinese (University College)
VAN LINT, T. M., Armenian Studies (Pembroke College)
WATSON, O. J., Islamic Art and Architecture (Wolfson College)
ZACCHETTI, S., Buddhist Studies (Balliol College)

Nuffield Department of Orthopaedics, Rheumatology and Musculoskeletal Sciences (Nuffield Orthopaedic Centre, Windmill Rd, Headington, Oxford, OX3 7HE; tel. (1865) 227374; internet www.ndorms.ox.ac.uk):

ARDEN, N. K., Rheumatic Diseases (Lady Margaret Hall)
ATHANASOU, N. A., Osteoarticular Pathology (Wadham College)
BEARD, D., Musculoskeletal Sciences (Kellogg College)
BOWNESS, P., Experimental Rheumatology
CARR, A. J., Orthopaedic Surgery (Worcester College)
COOPER, C., Musculoskeletol Epidemiology (St Peter's College)
FAIRBANK, J. C. T., Spinal Surgery

Sir FELDMANN, MARC, Immunology

LAMB, S. E., Trauma Rehabilitation (Wadham College)

LUQMANI, R., Rheumatology (Green Templeton College)

MONACO, C., Cardiovascular Inflammation

MURRAY, D., Orthopaedic Surgery

NAGASE, H., Matrix Biology

NANCHAHAL, J., Hand, Plastic and Reconstructive Surgery

OPPERMANN, U. C. T., Muskuloskeletol Sciences (St Catherine's College)

PRICE, A., Orthopaedic Surgery (Worcester College)

SAKLATVALA, J., Cell Signalling

TAYLOR, P., Musculoskeletal Sciences (St Peter's College)

UDALOVA, I., Molecular Immunology

VENABLES, P., Viral Immunorheumatology

VINCENT, T., Musculoskeletal Biology

WILLETT, K. M., Orthopaedic Trauma Surgery (Wolfson College)

WORDSWORTH, B. P., Rheumatology (Green Templeton College)

Department of Paediatrics (Level 2, Children's Hospital (John Radcliffe), Headington, Oxford, OX3 9DU; tel. (1865) 234240; e-mail enquiries@paediatrics.ox.ac.uk; internet www.paediatrics.ox.ac.uk):

GOULDER, P. J. R., Immunology (Brasenose College)

HOLLÄNDER, G. A. P., Paediatrics (Jesus College)

POLLARD, A. J., Paediatric Infection and Immunity (St Cross College)

ROBERTS, I. A. G., Paediatric Haematology

WILKINSON, A. W., Paediatrics (All Souls College)

Sir William Dunn School of Pathology (South Parks Rd, Oxford, OX1 3RE; tel. (1865) 275500; e-mail enquiries@path.ox.ac.uk; internet www.path.ox.ac.uk):

BARCLAY, A. N., Chemical Pathology (Lincoln College)

COBBOLD, S. P., Cellular Immunology (Christ Church)

FODOR, E., Virology (Exeter College)

FREEMAN, M., Pathology (Lincoln College)

GREAVES, D., Inflammation Biology (Hertford College)

HASSAN, A. B., Medical Oncology (Lincoln College)

JAMES, W. S., Virology (Brasenose College)

LEA, S., Microbiology (Wadham College)

NORBURY, C., Molecular Pathology (The Queen's College)

PROUDFOOT, N. J., Molecular Biology (Brasenose College)

RAFF, J. W., Cancer Cell Biology (Lincoln College)

SATTENTAU, Q. J., Immunology (Magdalen College)

TANG, C., Cellular Pathology (Exeter College)

VAUX, D., Cell Biology (Lincoln College)

Department of Pharmacology (Mansfield Rd, Oxford, OX1 3QT; tel. (1865) 271850; e-mail info@pharm.ox.ac.uk; internet www.pharm.ox.ac.uk):

EMPTAGE, N., Neuropharmacology (Lincoln College)

GALIONE, A. G., Pharmacology (Lady Margaret Hall)

GARLAND, C. J., Vascular Pharmacology (Magdalen College)

PLATT, F. M., Biochemistry and Pharmacology (Merton College)

SHARP, T., Neuropharmacology (Corpus Christi College)

SITSAPESAN, R., Pharmacology (Hertford College)

TERRAR, D. A., Cardiac Electrophysiology (Worcester College)

Faculty of Philosophy (Radcliffe Humanities, Radcliffe Observatory Quarter, Woodstock Rd, Oxford, OX2 6GG; tel. (1865) 276926; e-mail enquiries@philosophy.ox.ac.uk; internet www.philosophy.ox.ac.uk):

ARNTZENIUS, F., Philosophy (University College)

BOBZIEN, S., Philosophy (All Souls College)

BOSTROM, N. R. L., Applied Ethics (St Cross College)

BROWN, H. R., Physics (Wolfson College)

COOPE, U. C., Ancient Philosophy (Corpus Christi College)

CRISP, R. S., Moral Philosophy (St Anne's College)

DAVIES, M. K., Mental Philosophy (Corpus Christi College)

FABRE, C. M. Y., Political Philosophy (All Souls College)

HALBACH, V., Philosophy (New College)

HAWTHORNE, J., Metaphysical Philosophy (Magdalen College)

HILLS, A., Moral Philosophy (St John's College)

HYMAN, J., Aesthetics (The Queen's College)

IRWIN, T. H., Ancient Philosophy (Keble College)

MILLICAN, P., Early Modern Philosophy (Hertford College)

MOORE, A. W., Philosophy (St Hugh's College)

MULHALL, S. J., Philosophy (New College)

RODRIGUEZ-PEREYRA, G., Metaphysics (Oriel College)

SAUNDERS, S. W., Philosophy of Physics (Linacre College)

SAVULESCU, J., Practical Ethics (St Cross College)

SHIELDS, C. J., Classical Philosophy (Lady Margaret Hall)

TRIFOGLI, C., Medieval Philosophy (All Souls College)

WILLIAMSON, T., Logic (New College)

Department of Physics (Clarendon Laboratory, Parks Rd, Oxford, OX1 3PU; tel. (1865) 272200; e-mail enquiries@physics.ox.ac.uk; internet www.physics.ox.ac.uk):

ALLEN, M., Geosystem Science (Linacre College)

BALBUS, S. A., Astronomy (New College)

BARTOLINI, R., Accelerator Physics

BILLER, S. D., Particle Physics (Mansfield College)

BINNEY, J. J., Physics (Merton College)

BLUNDELL, K. M., Astrophysics (St John's College)

BLUNDELL, S. J., Physics (Mansfield College)

BOOTHROYD, A. T., Physics (Oriel College)

BURROWS, P. N., Physics (Jesus College)

CAVALLERI, A., Physics (Merton College)

CHALKER, J. T., Physics (St Hugh's College)

COOPER, S., Experimental Physics (St Catherine's College)

COOPER-SARKAR, A. M., Particle Physics (St Hilda's College)

DALTON, G., Astrophysics (St Cross College)

DAVIES, R. L., Astrophysics (Christ Church)

ESSLER, F. H. L., Physics (Worcester College)

EWART, P., Physics (Worcester College)

FENDER, R., Physics (Brasenose College)

FERREIRA, P. G., Astrophysics (Oriel College)

FOOT, C. J., Physics (St Peter's College)

FOSTER, B., Experimental Physics (Balliol College)

GOLESTANIAN, R., Theoretical Condensed Matter Physics (St Cross College)

GRAY, L., Atmospheric Physics (St Cross College)

GREGG, J. F., Physics (Magdalen College)

GREGORI, G., Physics (Lady Margaret Hall)

HARNEW, N., Physics (St Anne's College)

HERZ, L., Physics (Brasenose College)

HOOK, I. M., Astrophysics (Christ Church)

HOOKER, S. M., Atomic and Laser Physics (Merton College)

IRWIN, P. G. J., Planetary Physics (St Anne's College)

JAKSCH, D., Physics (Keble College)

JONES, J. A., Physics (Brasenose College)

JONES, M. E., Experimental Cosmology

KAPANIDIS, A., Biological Physics (St Cross College)

KRAUS, H. A. P., Physics (Corpus Christi College)

LUKAS, A., Theoretical Physics (Balliol College)

MARCH-RUSSELL, J., Theoretical Physics (New College)

MARSHALL, D. P., Physical Oceanography (St Hugh's College)

MILLER, L., Astrophysics (St Catherine's College)

NICHOLAS, R. J., Physics (University College)

PALMER, T. N., Royal Society Research Professor in Climate Physics (Jesus College)

PODSIADLOWSKI, P., Physics (St Edmund Hall)

RADAELLI, P., Experimental Philosophy (Wadham College)

READ, P. L., Physics (Trinity College)

ROCHE, P. F., Physics (Hertford College)

RYAN, J. F., Physics (Christ Church)

SARKAR, S., Physics (Linacre College)

SERYI, A., Accelerator Physics (Wolfson College)

SHIPSEY, I., Experimental Physics (St Catherine's College)

SIMON, S. H., Theoretical Condensed Matter Physics (Somerville College)

SNAITH, H. J., Physics

STEANE, A. M., Physics (Exeter College)

TAYLOR, R., Condensed Matter Physics (The Queen's College)

THATTE, N., Astrophysics (Keble College)

TURBERFIELD, A. J., Physics (Magdalen College)

VEDRAL, V., Quantum Information Science (Wolfson College)

WALMSLEY, I. A., Experimental Physics (St Hugh's College)

WARK, J. S., Physics (Trinity College)

WEBER, A., Physics (University College)

WILKINSON, G., Physics (Christ Church)

YASSIN, G., Astrophysics (The Queen's College)

YEOMANS, J. M., Physics (St Hilda's College)

ZANDERIGHI, G., Physics (Wadham College)

Department of Physiology, Anatomy and Genetics (Le Gros Clark Bldg, South Parks Rd, Oxford, OX1 3QX; tel. (1865) 272169; e-mail enquiries@dpag.ox.ac.uk; internet www.dpag.ox.ac.uk):

ASHCROFT, F. M., Physiology (Trinity College)

CLARKE, K., Physiological Biochemistry (Merton College)

Dame DAVIES, K. E., Anatomy (Hertford College)

KING, A. J., Neurophysiology (Lincoln College)

MIESENBÖCK, G., Physiology (Magdalen College)

MOLNAR, Z., Developmental Neurobiology (St John's College)

PAREKH, A. K., Physiology (Lady Margaret Hall)

PARKER, A. J., Physiology (St John's College)

PATERSON, D. J., Cardiovascular Physiology (Merton College)

PONTING, C. P., Genomics

RILEY, P. R., Development and Reproduction (Jesus College)

ROBBINS, P. A., Physiology (The Queen's College)

SCHNUPP, J., Neuroscience (St Peter's College)

VAUGHAN-JONES, R. D., Cellular Physiology (Exeter College)

WADDELL, S., Neurobiology

WOOD, M., Neuroscience (Somerville College)

ZACCOLO, M., Cell Biology (Balliol College)

Department of Plant Sciences (South Parks Rd, Oxford, OX1 3RB; tel. (1865) 275000; e-mail reception@plants.ox.ac.uk; internet www.plants.ox.ac.uk):

DOLAN, L., Botany (Magdalen College)

HARBERD, N. P., Plant Sciences (St John's College)

HECTOR, A., Ecology (Linacre College)

JARVIS, R. P., Plant Cell Biology (Wolfson College)

LANGDALE, J. A., Plant Development Genetics (The Queen's College)

MACKAY, J., Forest Sciences (Linacre College)

POOLE, P., Plant Microbiology

RATCLIFFE, R. G., Plant Sciences (New College)

SMITH, J. A. C., Plant Sciences (Magdalen College)

Department of Politics and International Relations (Manor Rd Bldg, Manor Rd, Oxford, OX1 3UQ; tel. (1865) 278700; e-mail enquiries@politics.ox.ac.uk; internet www .politics.ox.ac.uk):

ANSELL, B., Democratic Institutions (Nuffield College)

BERMEO, N., Comparative Politics (Nuffield College)

CANEY, S., Political Theory (Magdalen College)

CAPLAN, R. D., International Relations (Linacre College)

CAPOCCIA, G., Comparative Politics (Corpus Christi College)

CEADEL, M. E., Politics (New College)

DE VRIES, C., European Politics (Lincoln College)

DEIGHTON, A. F., European International Politics (Wolfson College)

EVANS, G., Sociology of Politics (Nuffield College)

HURRELL, A. J., International Relations (Balliol College)

JOHNSON, D., International Relations (St Antony's College)

KHONG, Y. F., International Relations (Nuffield College)

KING, D. S., American Government (Nuffield College)

MACFARLANE, S. N., International Relations (St Anne's College)

MCNAY, L., Theory of Politics (Somerville College)

MATTLI, W., International Political Economy (St John's College)

NEARY, I. J., Politics of Japan (St Antony's College)

NICOLAIDIS, K. A., International Relations (St Antony's College)

RUEDA, F. D., Quantitative Political Science (Nuffield College)

SNIDAL, D. J., International Relations (Nuffield College)

STEARS, M., Political Theory (University College)

WALDRON, J. J., Social and Political Theory (All Souls College)

WELSH, J. M., International Relations (Somerville College)

WHITEFIELD, S. D., Comparative Russian and East European Politics and Society (Pembroke College)

ZIELONKA, J., European Politics (St Antony's College)

Nuffield Department of Population Health (Richard Doll Bldg, Old Rd Campus, Roosevelt Dr, Headington, Oxford, OX3 7LF; tel. (1865) 289600; internet www.dph.ox.ac.uk; est. as amalgamation of Dept of Public Health, Cancer Epidemiology Unit, and Clinical Trial Service Unit and Epidemiological Studies Unit):

ARMITAGE, J., Clinical Trials and Epidemiology

BAIGENT, C., Epidemiology (Green Templeton College)

BERAL, V., Epidemiology (Green Templeton College)

CHEN, Z., Epidemiology

Sir COLLINS, RORY, Public Health (St Cross College)

DARBY, S. C., Medical Statistics

FITZPATRICK, R., Public Health and Primary Care (Nuffield College)

GOLDACRE, M. J., Public Health (Magdalen College)

GRAY, A., Health Economics

GRAY, R., Medical Statistics

JENKINSON, C. P., Health Services Research (Harris Manchester College)

JHA, V., Nephrology

KEY, T., Epidemiology

KURINCZUK, J. J., Perinatal Epidemiology

MACMAHON, S., Medicine

NORTON, R., Global Health

PARKER, M. J., Bioethics (St Cross College)

Sir PETO, RICHARD, Medical Statistics and Epidemiology (Green Templeton College)

SHEPHERD, S., Health Services Research (Kellogg College)

WOODWARD, M., Statistics and Epidemiology (Green Templeton College)

Nuffield Department of Primary Care Health Sciences (New Radcliffe House, 2nd Floor, Walton St, Oxford, OX2 6NW; tel. (1865) 289300; internet www.phc.ox.ac.uk):

AVEYARD, P., Behavioural Medicine (Wolfson College)

FARMER, A. J., General Practice (Exeter College)

GLASZIOU, P. P., Evidence-based Medicine (Kellogg College)

HENEGHAN, C., Evidence-based Medicine (Kellogg College)

HOBBS, R., Primary Care Health Sciences (Harris Manchester College)

JEBB, S., Diet and Population Health

MCMANUS, R., Primary Care Health Sciences (Green Templeton College)

ZIEBLAND, S., Medical Sociology (Green Templeton College)

Department of Psychiatry (Warneford Hospital, Oxford, OX3 7JX; tel. (1865) 223635; e-mail information@psych.ox.ac.uk; internet www.psych.ox.ac.uk):

COOPER, Z., Clinical Psychology

COWEN, P. J., Psychopharmacology

EBMEIER, K. P., Old Age Psychiatry (Linacre College)

FAIRBURN, C. J. A. G., Psychiatry (Merton College)

FLINT, J., Molecular Psychiatry (Merton College)

FREEMAN, D., Clinical Psychology (University College)

GEDDES, J., Epidemiological Psychiatry

GOODWIN, G. M., Psychiatry (Merton College)

HARMER, C., Cognitive Neuroscience (Corpus Christi College)

HARRISON, P. J., Psychiatry (Wolfson College)

HAWTON, K. E., Psychiatry (Green Templeton College)

HOLMES, E., Clinical Psychology

LOVESTONE, S., Translational Neuroscience

NEWTON, C. R. J. C., Psychiatry (St John's College)

SHARPE, M., Psychological Medicine (St Cross College)

STEIN, A. L., Child and Adult Psychiatry (Linacre College)

Oxford-Man Institute of Quantitative Finance (Eagle House, Walton Well Rd, Oxford OX2 6ED; tel. (1865) 616600; e-mail adminteam@oxford-man.ox.ac.uk; internet www.oxford-man.ox.ac.uk):

DOUCET, A., Statistics (Hertford College)

GILES, M., Scientific Computing (St Hugh's College)

GOTTLOB, G., Computing Science (St John's College)

HAMBLY, B., Mathematics (St Anne's College)

HOLMES, C., Biostatistics (Lincoln College)

HOWISON, S., Mathematics (Christ Church)

LYONS, T., Mathematics (St Anne's College)

RAMADORAI, T., Financial Economics

ROBERTS, S., Engineering Science

ZHOU, X., Mathematical Finance (St Hugh's College)

Begbroke Science Park (Begbroke Hill, Woodstock Rd, Begbroke OX5 1PF; tel. (1865) 283700; e-mail enquiries@begbroke .ox.ac.uk; internet www.begbroke.ox.ac.uk):

GRANT, P. S., Materials (St Catherine's College)

Department of Social Policy and Intervention (Barnett House, 32 Wellington Sq., Oxford, OX1 2ER; tel. (1865) 270325; e-mail info@spi .ox.ac.uk; internet www.spi.ox.ac.uk):

COLEMAN, D. A., Demography (St John's College)

DALY, M., Sociology and Social Policy (Green Templeton College)

GARDNER, F. E. M., Child and Family Psychology (Wolfson College)

MONTGOMERY, P., Psycho-social Intervention (Green Templeton College)

NOBLE, M. W. J., Social Policy (Green Templeton College)

SEELEIB-KAISER, M., Comparative Social Policy (St Cross College)

WALKER, R. L., Social Policy (Green Templeton College)

Department of Sociology (Manor Road Bldg, Manor Rd, Oxford, OX1 3UQ; tel. (1865) 281740; e-mail enquiries@sociology.oxford.ac .uk; internet www.sociology.ox.ac.uk):

BILLARI, F., Sociology and Demography (Nuffield College)

DE GRAAF, N. D., Sociology (Nuffield College)

ERMISCH, J., Family Demography (Nuffield College)

GERSHUNY, J., Economic Sociology (St Hugh's College)

JONSSON, J. O., Sociology (Nuffield College)

KARIYA, T., Sociology of Japanese Society (St Antony's College)

MILLS, M., Sociology (Nuffield College)

PAYNE, L. A., Sociology—Latin American Societies (St Antony's College)

SULLIVAN, O., Sociology of Gender (St Hugh's College)

VARESE, F., Criminology (Linacre College)

Department of Statistics (1 South Parks Rd, Oxford, OX1 3TG; tel. (1865) 272860; e-mail info@stats.ox.ac.uk; internet www.stats.ox .ac.uk):

DEANE, C., Structural Bioinformatics (Kellogg College)

DONNELLY, P. J., Statistical Science (St Anne's College)

DOUCET, A., Statistics (Jesus College)

ETHERIDGE, A. M., Mathematics (Magdalen College)

HEIN, J. J., Bioinformatics (University College)

HOLMES, C., Biostatistics (Lincoln College)

MCDIARMID, C. J. H., Combinatorics (Corpus Christi College)

MCVEAN, G. A. T., Statistical Genetics (Linacre College)

REINERT, G., Statistics (Keble College)

RIPLEY, B. D., Applied Statistics (St Peter's College)

SILVERMAN, B. W., Statistics (Green Templeton College)

TEH, Y. W., Statistical Machine Learning (University College)

Nuffield Department of Surgical Sciences (Business Administration Unit, Room 6607, Level 6, John Radcliffe Hospital, Headington, Oxford, OX3 9DU; tel. (1865) 220302; e-mail enquiries@nds.ox.ac.uk; internet www.nds.ox.ac.uk):

AUSTYN, J. M., Immunobiology (Wolfson College)

AZIZ, T. Z., Neurosurgery

BYRNE, J. V., Neuroradiology

FRIEND, P. J., Transplantation (Green Templeton College)

HAMDY, F. C., Surgery (Balliol College)

JOHNSON, P. R. V., Paediatric Surgery (St Edmund Hall)

PLOEG, R., Transplant Biology

TAGGART, D. P., Cardiovascular Surgery

WOOD, K. J., Immunology (Green Templeton College)

Faculty of Theology and Religion (34 St Giles, Oxford, OX1 3LD; tel. (1865) 270790; e-mail general.administrator@theology.ox.ac.uk; internet www.theology.ox.ac.uk):

BIGGAR, N. J., Moral and Pastoral Theology—Regius (Christ Church)

BOCKMUEHL, M., Biblical and Early Christian Studies (Keble College)

FIDDES, P. S., Systematic Theology (Regent's Park College)

FOOT, S. R. I., Ecclesiastical History—Regius (Christ Church)

LEFTOW, B., Philosophy of the Christian Religion (Oriel College)

MACCULLOCH, D. N. J., History of the Church (St Cross College)

MCGRATH, A., Science and Religion (Harris Manchester College)

WARD, G., Divinity—Regius (Christ Church)

Department of Zoology (The Tinbergen Bldg, South Parks Rd, Oxford, OX1 3PS; tel. (1865) 271234; internet www.zoo.ox.ac.uk):

COULSON, T., Zoology (Jesus College)

DAWKINS, M., Animal Behaviour (Somerville College)

FOSTER, K., Evolutionary Biology (Magdalen College)

GODFRAY, H. C. J., Zoology—Entomology (Jesus College)

GRAFEN, A., Theoretical Biology (St John's College)

GUILFORD, T. C., Animal Behaviour (Merton College)

GUPTA, S., Theoretical Epidemiology (Linacre College)

HAY, S. I., Epidemiology (St John's College)

HOLLAND, P. W. H., Zoology (Merton College)

KACELNIK, A., Behavioural Ecology (Pembroke College)

MACDONALD, D. W., Wildlife Conservation (Lady Margaret Hall)

MAIDEN, M. C. J., Molecular Epidemiology (Hertford College)

Lord MAY, Zoology (Merton College)

MCLEAN, A. R., Mathematical Biology (St Catherine's College)

NUTTALL, P., Arbovirology (Wolfson College)

PYBUS, O., Evolution and Infectious Disease (New College)

ROGERS, D. J., Ecology (Green Templeton College)

SHELDON, B. C., Field Ornithology (Wolfson College)

THOMAS, J. A., Ecology (New College)

WEST, S. A., Evolutionary Biology (Magdalen College)

WILLIS, K. J., Biodiversity (Merton College)

DIRECTORS AND HEADS OF UNIVERSITY INSTITUTIONS AND DEPARTMENTS

Institute of Archaeology (36 Beaumont St, Oxford, OX1 2PG; tel. (1865) 278240; e-mail administrator@arch.ox.ac.uk; internet www.archinst.ox.ac.uk):

Dir Prof. C. GOSDEN, European Archaeology (Keble College)

Institute for Chinese Studies (Clarendon Institute Bldg, Walton St, Oxford, OX1 2HG; tel. (1865) 280387; e-mail enquiries@chinese.ox.ac.uk; internet www.orinst.ox.ac.uk/ea/chinese):

Administrator R. GOSI

Institute of European and Comparative Law (St Cross Bldg, St Cross Rd, Oxford, OX1 3UL; tel. (1865) 281610; e-mail enquiries@iecl.ox.ac.uk; internet www.iecl.ox.ac.uk):

Dir Prof. S. VOGENAUER, Comparative Law (Brasenose College)

Institute of Social and Cultural Anthropology (51–53 Banbury Rd, Oxford, OX2 6PE; tel. (1865) 274624; e-mail information@anthro.ox.ac.uk; internet www.isca.ox.ac.uk):

Dir Prof. S. ULIJASZEK, Human Ecology (St Cross College)

Centre for Criminology (3rd Floor, Manor Road Bldg, Manor Rd, Oxford, OX1 3UQ; tel. (1865) 274444; e-mail cfc@crim.ox.ac.uk; internet www.crim.ox.ac.uk):

Dir Prof. C. HOYLE, Criminology (Green Templeton College)

Centre for Linguistics and Philology (Walton St, Oxford, OX1 2HG; tel. (1865) 280400; e-mail enquiries@ling-phil.ox.ac.uk; internet www.ling-phil.ox.ac.uk):

Curator Prof. A. LAHIRI, Linguistics (Somerville College)

Centre for Socio-Legal Studies (Manor Road Bldg, Manor Rd, Oxford, OX1 3UQ; tel. (1865) 284220; e-mail admin@csls.ox.ac.uk; internet www.csls.ox.ac.uk):

Dir Dr F. PIRIE, Socio-Legal Studies (St Cross College)

Environmental Change Institute (Oxford University Centre for the Environment, South Parks Rd, Oxford, OX1 3QY; tel. (1865) 275885; e-mail enquiries@eci.ox.ac.uk; internet www.eci.ox.ac.uk):

Dir Prof. J. HALL, Climate and Environmental Risks (Linacre College)

Nissan Institute of Japanese Studies (27 Winchester Rd, Oxford, OX2 6NA; tel. (1865) 274570; e-mail secretary@nissan.ox.ac.uk; internet www.nissan.ox.ac.uk):

Dir Prof. I. J. NEARY, Politics of Japan (St Antony's College)

Oriental Institute (Pusey Lane, Oxford, OX1 2LE; tel. (1865) 278200; e-mail orient@orinst.ox.ac.uk; internet www.orinst.ox.ac.uk):

Chair. of Bd of Oriental Studies Prof. B. FRELLESVIG, Japanese Linguistics (Hertford College)

Oxford Learning Institute (Littlegate House, 16/17 St Ebbe's St, Oxford, OX1 1PT; tel. (1865) 286808; e-mail services@learning.ox.ac.uk; internet www.learning.ox.ac.uk):

Dir Dr S. GOSS, Teaching and Learning in Higher Education (Wadham College)

Oxford University Language Centre (12 Woodstock Rd, Oxford, OX2 6HT; tel. (1865) 283360; e-mail admin@lang.ox.ac.uk; internet www.lang.ox.ac.uk):

Dir R. N. VANDERPLANK (Kellogg College)

Latin American Centre (St Antony's College, Oxford, OX2 6JF; tel. (1865) 274486; e-mail enquiries@lac.ox.ac.uk; internet www.lac.ox.ac.uk):

Dir Prof. L. A. PAYNE, Sociology (St Antony's College)

Philosophy Centre (Radcliffe Humanities, Radcliffe Observatory Quarter, Woodstock Rd, Oxford, OX2 6GG; tel. (1865) 276926; e-mail enquiries@philosophy.ox.ac.uk; internet www.philosophy.ox.ac.uk):

Chair. of the Faculty Bd Prof. C. SHIELDS, Classical Philosophy (Lady Margaret Hall)

Department of the History of Art and Centre for Visual Studies (Suite 9, Littlegate House, St Ebbe's, Oxford, OX1 1PT; tel. (1865) 286830; e-mail admin@hoa.ox.ac.uk; internet www.hoa.ox.ac.uk):

Head A. C. CLUNAS, History of Art (Trinity College)

Ruskin School of Art (74 High St, Oxford, OX1 4BG; tel. (1865) 276940; e-mail info@ruskin-sch.ox.ac.uk; internet www.ruskin-sch.ox.ac.uk):

Head J. GAIGER, Fine Art (St Edmund Hall)

Life Sciences Interface Doctoral Training Centre (Rex Richards Bldg, South Parks Rd, Oxford, OX1 3QU; tel. (1865) 610660; e-mail dtcenquiries@dtc.ox.ac.uk; internet www.lsi.ox.ac.uk):

Dir D. J. GAVAGHAN, Computational Biology (New College)

Inorganic Chemistry Laboratory (South Parks Rd, Oxford, OX1 3QR; tel. (1865) 272600; internet www.chem.ox.ac.uk/icl):

Head Prof. P. MOUNTFORD, Inorganic Chemistry (St Edmund Hall)

Organic Chemistry Laboratory (Chemistry Research Laboratory, 12 Mansfield Rd, Oxford, OX1 3TA; tel. (1865) 285000; internet www.chem.ox.ac.uk/oc):

Head Prof. C. J. SCHOFIELD, Organic Chemistry (Hertford College)

Phonetics Laboratory (41 Wellington Sq., Oxford, OX1 2JF; tel. (1865) 270444; e-mail enquiries@phon.ox.ac.uk; internet www.phon.ox.ac.uk):

Dir Prof. J. S. COLEMAN, Phonetics (Wolfson College)

Physical and Theoretical Chemistry Laboratory (South Parks Rd, Oxford, OX1 3QZ; tel. (1865) 275400; internet ptcl.chem.ox.ac.uk):

Head Prof. M. BROUARD, Chemistry (Jesus College)

Research Laboratory for Archaeology and the History of Art (Dyson Perrins Bldg, South Parks Rd, Oxford, OX1 3QY; tel. (1865) 285222; internet www.rlaha.ox.ac.uk):

Head A. M. POLLARD, Archaeological Science (Linacre College)

Smith School of Enterprise and the Environment (South Parks Rd, Oxford, OX1 3QY; tel. (1865) 614963; e-mail enquiries@smithschool.ox.zc.uk; internet www.smithschool.ox.ac.uk):

Dir Prof. G. CLARK, Geography (St Edmund Hall)

Oxford University Archives (Bodleian Library, Broad St, Oxford, OX1 3BG; tel. (1865) 277145; e-mail enquiries@oua.ox.ac.uk; internet www.oua.ox.ac.uk):

Keeper S. BAILEY (Linacre College)

Ashmolean Museum of Art and Archaeology (Beaumont St, Oxford, OX1 2PH; tel. (1865) 278002; internet www.ashmolean.org):

Dir Dr A. STURGIS (Worcester College)

Museum of the History of Science (Old Ashmolean Bldg, Broad St, Oxford, OX1 3AZ; tel. (1865) 277280; e-mail museum@mhs.ox.ac.uk; internet www.mhs.ox.ac.uk):

Dir Dr S. ACKERMANN (Linacre College)

Pitt Rivers Museum (South Parks Rd, Oxford, OX1 3PP; tel. (1865) 270927; e-mail prm@prm.ox.ac.uk; internet www.prm.ox.ac.uk):

Dir Dr M. O'HANLON (Linacre College)

Oxford University Museum of Natural History (Parks Rd, Oxford, OX1 3PW; tel. (1865) 272950; e-mail info@oum.ox.ac.uk; internet www.oum.ox.ac.uk):

Dir Prof. P. SMITH (Kellogg College)

Bodleian Library (Broad St, Oxford, OX1 3BG; tel. (1865) 277000; e-mail enquiries@bodley.ox.ac.uk; internet www.bodleian.ox.ac.uk):

Bodley's Librarian R. (Balliol College)

Botanic Garden and Harcourt Arboretum (Rose Lane, Oxford, OX1 4AZ; tel. (1865) 286690; internet www.botanic-garden.ox.ac.uk):

Dir: (vacant)

National Perinatal Epidemiology Unit (Old Rd Campus, Headington, Oxford, OX3 7LF; tel. (1865) 289700; e-mail general@npeu.ox.ac.uk; internet www.npeu.ox.ac.uk):

Dir Prof. J. KURINCZUK, Perinatal Epidemiology

Transport Studies Unit (Oxford University Centre for the Environment, South Parks Rd, Oxford, OX1 3QY; tel. (1865) 285066; e-mail enquiries@tsu.ox.ac.uk; internet www.tsu.ox.ac.uk):

Dir Prof. D. BANISTER, Transport Studies (St Anne's College)

Wellcome Unit for the History of Medicine (45–47 Banbury Rd, Oxford, OX2 6PE; tel. (1865) 274600; e-mail wuhmo@wuhmo.ox.ac.uk; internet www.wuhmo.ox.ac.uk):

Dir Prof. M. HARRISON, History of Medicine (Green Templeton College)

COLLEGES

All Souls College: High St, Oxford, OX1 4AL; tel. (1865) 279379; internet www.all-souls.ox.ac.uk; f. 1438; for Fellows only; Warden Prof. Sir JOHN VICKERS.

Balliol College: Broad St, Oxford, OX1 3BJ; tel. (1865) 277777; e-mail academic.registrar@balliol.ox.ac.uk; internet www.balliol.ox.ac.uk; f. 1263; Master Prof. Sir DRUMMOND BONE; publ. *Floreat Domus* (1 a year).

Brasenose College: Radcliffe Sq., Oxford, OX1 4AJ; tel. (1865) 277830; e-mail college.office@bnc.ox.ac.uk; internet www.bnc.ox.ac.uk; f. 1509; Prin. Prof. ALAN K. BOWMAN.

Christ Church: St Aldates, Oxford, OX1 1DP; tel. (1865) 276150; e-mail enquiries@chch.ox.ac.uk; internet www.chch.ox.ac.uk; f. 1546; Dean The Very Rev. Dr CHRISTOPHER A. LEWIS.

Corpus Christi College: Merton St, Oxford, OX1 4JF; tel. (1865) 276700; e-mail college.office@ccc.ox.ac.uk; internet www.ccc.ox.ac.uk; f. 1517; Pres. Prof. RICHARD CARWARDINE.

Exeter College: Turl St, Oxford, OX1 3DP; tel. (1865) 279600; e-mail academic.administrator@exeter.ox.ac.uk; internet www.exeter.ox.ac.uk; f. 1314; Rector FRANCES CAIRNCROSS.

Green Templeton College: 43 Woodstock Rd, Oxford, OX2 6HG; tel. (1865) 274770; internet www.gtc.ox.ac.uk; f. 2008; Prin. Prof. Sir DAVID WATSON.

Harris Manchester College: Mansfield Rd, Oxford, OX1 3TD; tel. (1865) 271006; e-mail enquiries@hmc.ox.ac.uk; internet www.hmc.ox.ac.uk; f. 1786 for mature students; Prin. The Rev. Dr RALPH WALLER.

Hertford College: Catte St, Oxford, OX1 3BW; tel. (1865) 279400; internet www.hertford.ox.ac.uk; f. 1740; Prin. WILL HUTTON.

Jesus College: Turl St, Oxford, OX1 3DW; tel. (1865) 279700; e-mail lodge@jesus.ox.ac.uk; internet www.jesus.ox.ac.uk; f. 1571; Prin. Lord KREBS.

Keble College: Parks Rd, Oxford, OX1 3PG; tel. (1865) 272727; e-mail enquiries@keble.ox.ac.uk; internet www.keble.ox.ac.uk; f. 1870; Warden Sir JONATHAN PHILLIPS.

Kellogg College: Banbury Rd, Oxford, OX2 6PN; tel. (1865) 612000; e-mail college.office@kellogg.ox.ac.uk; internet www.kellogg.ox.ac.uk; f. 1990 for adult, part-time and professional devt students; Pres. Prof. Dr JONATHAN MICHIE.

Lady Margaret Hall: Norham Gardens, Oxford, OX2 6QA; tel. (1865) 274300; e-mail enquiries@lmh.ox.ac.uk; internet www.lmh.ox.ac.uk; f. 1878; Prin. Dr FRANCES LANNON.

Linacre College: St Cross Rd, Oxford, OX1 3JA; tel. (1865) 271650; e-mail college.secretary@linacre.ox.ac.uk; internet www.linacre.ox.ac.uk; f. 1962, as Linacre House for graduates; Prin. Dr NICK BROWN.

Lincoln College: Turl St, Oxford, OX1 3DR; tel. (1865) 279800; e-mail info@lincoln.ac.uk; internet www.linc.ox.ac.uk; f. 1427; Rector Prof. HENRY WOUDHUYSEN.

Magdalen College: High St, Oxford, OX1 4AU; tel. (1865) 276000; internet www.magd.ox.ac.uk; f. 1458; Pres. Prof. DAVID CLARY.

Mansfield College: Mansfield Rd, Oxford, OX1 3TF; tel. (1865) 270999; e-mail admissions@ox.ac.uk; internet www.mansfield.ox.ac.uk; f. 1886; Prin. Baroness HELENA KENNEDY.

Merton College: Merton St, Oxford, OX1 4JD; tel. (1865) 276310; internet www.merton.ox.ac.uk; f. 1264; Warden Prof. Sir MARTIN TAYLOR.

New College: Holywell St, Oxford, OX1 3BN; tel. (1865) 279500; internet www.new.ox.ac.uk; f. 1379; Warden Sir CURTIS PRICE.

Nuffield College: New Rd, Oxford, OX1 1NF; tel. (1865) 278500; e-mail lodge@nuffield.ox.ac.uk; internet www.nuff.ox.ac.uk; f. 1958; Warden ANDREW DILNOT.

Oriel College: Oriel Sq., Oxford, OX1 4EW; tel. (1865) 276555; e-mail lodge@oriel.ox.ac.uk; internet www.oriel.ox.ac.uk; f. 1326; Provost MOIRA WALLACE.

Pembroke College: St Aldate's, Oxford, OX1 1DW; tel. (1865) 276444; internet www.pmb.ox.ac.uk; f. 1624; Master Dame LYNNE J. BRINDLEY.

Queen's College, The: High St, Oxford, OX1 4AW; tel. (1865) 279120; internet www.queens.ox.ac.uk; f. 1341; Provost Prof. PAUL A. MADDEN.

St Anne's College: 56 Woodstock Rd, Oxford, OX2 6HS; tel. (1865) 274800; e-mail enquiries@st-annes.ox.ac.uk; internet www.st-annes.ox.ac.uk; f. 1878 as Society of Oxford Home Students; Prin. TIM GARDAM.

St Antony's College: 62 Woodstock Rd, Oxford, OX2 6JF; tel. (1865) 284700; e-mail info@sant.ox.ac.uk; internet www.sant.ox.ac.uk; f. 1953; Warden Prof. MARGARET MACMILLAN.

St Catherine's College: Manor Rd, Oxford, OX1 3UJ; tel. (1865) 271700; e-mail college.office@stcatz.ox.ac.uk; internet www.stcatz.ox.ac.uk; f. 1868, reconstituted as a full college 1963; Master Prof. ROGER W. AINSWORTH.

St Cross College: 61 St Giles, Oxford, OX1 3LZ; tel. (1865) 278490; internet www.stx.ox.ac.uk; f. 1965 for graduate students and fellows; Master Sir MARK JONES.

St Edmund Hall: Queen's Lane, Oxford, OX1 4AR; tel. (1865) 279000; e-mail college.secretary@seh.ox.ac.uk; internet www.seh.ox.ac.uk; f. c. 1278; Prin. Prof. KEITH GULL.

St Hilda's College: Cowley Pl., Oxford, OX4 1DY; tel. (1865) 276884; e-mail enquiries@st-hildas.ox.ac.uk; internet www.st-hildas.ox.ac.uk; f. 1893; Prin. SHEILA FORBES.

St Hugh's College: St Margaret's Rd, Oxford, OX2 6LE; tel. (1865) 274900; e-mail academic.administrator@st-hughs.ox.ac.uk; internet www.st-hughs.ox.ac.uk; f. 1886; Prin. Dame ELISH F. ANGIOLINI.

St John's College: St Giles', Oxford, OX1 3JP; tel. (1865) 277300; e-mail college.office@sjc.ox.ac.uk; internet www.sjc.ox.ac.uk; f. 1555; Pres. Prof. MAGGIE SNOWLING.

St Peter's College: New Inn Hall St, Oxford, OX1 2DL; tel. (1865) 278900; internet www.spc.ox.ac.uk; f. 1929 as St Peter's Hall; Master MARK DAMAZER (acting); Dean Dr ROGER ALLEN.

Somerville College: Woodstock Rd, Oxford, OX2 6HD; tel. (1865) 270600; e-mail enquiries@some.ox.ac.uk; internet www.some.ox.ac.uk; f. 1879; Prin. Dr ALICE PROCHASKA.

Trinity College: Broad St, Oxford, OX1 3BH; tel. (1865) 279900; internet www.trinity.ox.ac.uk; f. 1555; Pres. Sir IVOR ROBERTS.

University College: High St, Oxford, OX1 4BH; tel. (1865) 276602; e-mail lodge@univ.ox.ac.uk; internet www.univ.ox.ac.uk; f. 1249; Master Sir IVOR CREWE.

Wadham College: Parks Rd, Oxford, OX1 3PN; tel. (1865) 277900; e-mail lodge@wadh.ox.ac.uk; internet www.wadham.ox.ac.uk; f. 1610; Warden Lord KEN MACDONALD.

Wolfson College: Linton Rd, Oxford, OX2 6UD; tel. (1865) 274100; internet www.wolfson.ox.ac.uk; f. 1965 for graduates; Pres. Prof. Dame HERMIONE LEE (acting).

Worcester College: Walton St, Oxford, OX1 2HB; tel. (1865) 278300; internet www.worc.ox.ac.uk; f. 1714; Provost Prof. JONATHAN BATE.

PERMANENT PRIVATE HALLS

Blackfriars Hall: 64 St Giles', Oxford, OX1 3LY; tel. (1865) 278400; e-mail secretary@bfriars.ox.ac.uk; internet www.bfriars.ox.ac.uk; f. 1221; Regent Very Revd Dr SIMON GAINE.

Campion Hall: Brewer St, Oxford, OX1 1QS; tel. (1865) 286100; e-mail enquiries@campion.ox.ac.uk; internet www.campion.ox.ac.uk; f. 1896; Master Rev. Dr JAMES HANVEY.

Regent's Park College: Pusey St, Oxford, OX1 2LB; tel. (1865) 288120; e-mail enquiries@regents.ox.ac.uk; internet www.rpc.ox.ac.uk; f. 1752; Prin. Rev. Dr ROBERT ELLIS.

St Benet's Hall: 38 St Giles', Oxford, OX1 3LN; tel. (1865) 280556; e-mail enquiries@stb.ox.ac.uk; internet www.st-benets.ox.ac.uk; f. 1897; Domestic Bursar MARIA BYRNE.

St Stephen's House: 16 Marston St, Oxford, OX4 1JX; tel. (1865) 613500; e-mail enquiries@ssho.ox.ac.uk; internet www.ssho

.ox.ac.uk; f. 1876; Prin. Rev. Canon Dr ROBIN WARD.

Wycliffe Hall: 52–54 Banbury Rd, Oxford, OX2 6PW; tel. (1865) 274200; e-mail enquiries@wycliffe.ox.ac.uk; internet www .wycliffe.ox.ac.uk; f. 1877; Prin. Rev. Dr MICHAEL LLOYD.

UNIVERSITY OF PORTSMOUTH

University House, Winston Churchill Ave, Portsmouth, PO1 2UP

Telephone: (23) 9284-8484
E-mail: info.centre@port.ac.uk
Internet: www.port.ac.uk

Founded 1869, as Portsmouth School of Science and Art, became Portsmouth Polytechnic in 1969; present name and status 1992

Academic year: September to June

Chancellor: Lord PALUMBO
Vice-Chancellor: Prof. JOHN CRAVEN
Deputy Vice-Chancellor: REBECCA BUNTING
Pro-Vice-Chancellor: Dr DAVID ARRELL
Pro-Vice-Chancellor: Prof. JOHN TURNER
Acad. Registrar: A. REES
Univ. Librarian: ROISIN GWYER

Library of 600,000 vols
Number of teachers: 1,200
Number of students: 19,000

DEANS

Faculty of Creative and Cultural Industries: Dr SIMON CLARIDGE
Faculty of Humanities and Social Sciences: DAVE RUSSELL
Faculty of Science: Prof. PAUL HAYES
Faculty of Technology: Prof. DJAMEL AIT-BOUDAOUD
Portsmouth Business School: ANN RIDLEY

UNIVERSITY OF READING

Whiteknights, POB 217, Reading, RG6 6AH
Telephone: (118) 987-5123
E-mail: communications@reading.ac.uk
Internet: www.reading.ac.uk

Founded 1892, as Univ. Extension College, univ. status 1926

Academic year: October to July

Chancellor: Sir JOHN MADEJSKI
Vice-Chancellor: Prof. GORDON MARSHALL
Deputy Vice-Chancellor: Prof. TONY DOWNES
Pro-Vice-Chancellor for Int. and External Engagement: Prof. STEVEN MITHEN
Pro-Vice-Chancellor for Research and Innovation: Prof. CHRISTINE WILLIAMS
Pro-Vice-Chancellor for Teaching and Learning: Prof. ROB ROBSON
Dir of Student Services: JENNIFER GHANDHI
Treas.: Dr PETER WARRY
Librarian: JULIA MUNRO

Library: see Libraries and Archives
Number of teachers: 2,000
Number of students: 17,500

Publication: *Research Review* (2 a year)

DEANS

Faculty of Arts and Humanities: Prof. SUE WALKER
Henley Business School: Prof. CHRIS BONES
Faculty of Life Sciences: Prof. RICHARD ELLIS
Faculty of Science: Prof. GAVIN BROOKS
Faculty of Social Sciences: Prof. DIANNE BERRY

PROFESSORS

(Some professors serve in more than one faculty)

Faculty of Arts and Humanities (Whiteknights, POB 218, Reading, RG6 6AA; tel. (118) 931-8063):

ARNOLD, B. C. B., History

BARANSKI, Z., Italian Studies
BARBER, M. C., History
BIDDISS, M. D., History
BROWN, C. C., English and American Literary Studies
BUCKLEY, S., Arts and Communication Design
BULL, J., Arts and Communication Design
BULLEN, J. B., English and American Literary Studies
COOK, G. W. D., Linguistics and Applied Language Studies
COOPER, P. J., Psychology
COTTINGHAM, J. G., Humanities
CURRY, A. E., History
DANCY, J. P., Humanities
DUNSBY, J. M., Arts and Communication Design
ELIOT, S. J., Arts and Communication Design; English and American Literary Studies
EVANS, A. W., Environmental Economics
GARMAN, M. A. G., Linguistics and Applied Language Studies
GILCHRIST, R., Archaeology
HOOKER, B., Humanities
HOULBROOKE, R. A., History
HOWELLS, C. A., English and American Literary Studies
JAMES, E. F., History
LUNA, P., Arts and Communication Design
NOBLE, P. S., Modern Languages
PARRINDER, J. P., English and American Literary Studies
PILLING, J., English and American Literary Studies
POTTS, A., Humanities
ROACH, P. J., Linguistic and Applied Language Studies
ROBEY, D. J. B., Modern Languages
RUTHERFORD, I. C., Humanities
SANDFORD, J. E., Modern Languages
SEGAL, N., Modern Languages
STRAWSON, G. J., Humanities
TUCKER, G. H., Modern Languages
WALLACE-HADRILL, A. F., Humanities
WARBURTON, I. P., Linguistic Science
WILKINS, D. A., Linguistics and Applied Language Studies
WOODWARD, P. R., Politics

Faculty of Economic and Social Sciences (Whiteknights, POB 218, Reading, RG6 6AA; tel. (118) 931-8183; e-mail fasug@ reading.ac.uk):

BELLAMY, R., Politics and Sociology
BREHENY, M. J., Business
BUCKLEY, R. A., Law
BUSH, A. W., Education
CANTWELL, J. A., Business
CASSON, M. C., Business
CROLL, P., Education
CROSBY, F. N., Business
DAVIES, J. C. H., Politics and Sociology
DOWNES, T. A., Law
EDWARDS, V. K., Education
EVANS, A. W., Business
FIDLER, F. B., Education
FRANZONI, R., Politics and Sociology
GHANDI, P. R., Law
GILBERT, J. K., Education
GRAY, C. S., Politics and Sociology
JONES, G. G., Business
KEENE, J., Health and Social Care
LIZIERI, C. M., Business
MALVERN, D. D., Education
MURDOCH, J. R., Law
NOBES, C. W., Business
PATTERSON, K. D., Business
PEMBERTON, J., Business
POPE, M. L., Education
RICHARDS, B. J., Education
SCOTT-QUINN, B., Business
SOUTHWORTH, G. W., Education
STYCHIN, C., Law
UTTON, M. A., Business

WADDINGTON, P. A. J., Politics and Sociology
WARD, C. W., Business
WOODWARD, P. R., Politics and Sociology

Faculty of Life Sciences (Whiteknights, POB 200, Reading, RG6 6AF; tel. (118) 931-8342; e-mail sciug@reading.ac.uk):

BARNETT, J. R., Plant Sciences
BEEVER, D. E., Agriculture, Policy and Development
BISBY, F. A., Plant Sciences
BROWN, V. K., Agriculture, Policy and Development
CALIGARI, P. D. S., Plant Sciences
COLLINS, M. D., Food Biosciences
CRABBE, M. J. C., Animal and Microbial Sciences
DUNWELL, J. M., Plant Sciences
ELLIS, R. H., Agriculture, Policy and Development
FRANCE, J., Agriculture, Policy and Development
GARFORTH, C. J., Agriculture, Policy and Development
GIBSON, G. R., Food Biosciences
HADLEY, P., Plant Sciences
HOLLAND, P. W. H., Animal and Microbial Sciences
JOHN, P., Plant Sciences
JONES, I. M., Animal and Microbial Sciences
KNIGHT, P. G., Animal and Microbial Sciences
LEDWARD, D. A., Food Biosciences
LOWRY, P. J., Animal and Microbial Sciences
MOTTRAM, D. V., Food Biosciences
OWEN, E., Agriculture, Policy and Development
PAGEL, M., Animal and Microbial Sciences
PAYNE, C. C., Plant Sciences
PYLE, D. L., Food Biosciences
ROBSON, R. L., Animal and Microbial Sciences
SCHOFIELD, J. D., Food Biosciences
SIBLY, R. M., Animal and Microbial Sciences
STRANGE, P., Animal and Microbial Sciences
SWINBANK, A., Agriculture, Policy and Development
TRAILL, B., Agriculture, Policy and Development
WHITEHEAD, J. R., Applied Statistics
WILLIAMS, C. M., Food Biosciences

Faculty of Science (Whiteknights, POB 200, Reading, RG6 6AF; tel. (118) 931-8342; e-mail sciug@reading.ac.uk):

ALLOWAY, B. J., Human and Environmental Sciences
ANDREWS, B., Computer Science, Cybernetics and Electronic Engineering
ASTILL, G. G., Human and Environmental Sciences
ATKINS, A. G., Construction Management and Engineering
BAKER, K. D., Computer Science, Cybernetics and Electronic Engineering
BASSETT, D. C., Mathematics, Meteorology and Physics
BERRY, D. C., Psychology
BON, R., Construction Management and Engineering
BOWKER, M., Chemistry
BRADLEY, R. J., Human and Environmental Sciences
BROWNING, K. A., Mathematics, Meteorology and Physics
CARDIN, D. J., Chemistry
CHAPLIN, C. R., Construction Management and Engineering
CHAPMAN, R. W., Human and Environmental Sciences
CLEMENTS-CROOME, T. D. J., Construction Management and Engineering

CODLING, K., Mathematics, Meteorology and Physics
COLEMAN, M. L., Human and Environmental Sciences
COLQUHOUN, H. M., Chemistry
COOPER, P. J., Psychology
DREW, M. G. B., Chemistry
FISHER, G. N., Construction Management and Engineering
FLANAGAN, R., Construction Management and Engineering
FULFORD, M. G., Human and Environmental Sciences
GILBERT, A., Chemistry
GILCHRIST, R., Human and Environmental Sciences
GREGORY, P. J., Human and Environmental Sciences
GURNEY, R., Mathematics, Meteorology and Physics
HAINES, K., Mathematics, Meteorology and Physics
HARRISON, R., Computer Science, Cybernetics and Electronic Engineering
HARWOOD, L. M., Chemistry
HILTON, A. J. W., Mathematics, Meteorology and Physics
HOSKINS, B. J., Mathematics, Meteorology and Physics
JERONIMIDIS, G., Construction Management and Engineering
MCKENNA, F. P., Psychology
MEGSON, G. M., Computer Science, Cybernetics and Electronic Engineering
MITCHELL, G. R., Mathematics, Meteorology and Physics
MITHEN, S. J., Human and Environmental Sciences
MURRAY, L., Psychology
NEEDHAM, D. J., Mathematics, Meteorology and Physics
NICHOLS, N. K., Mathematics, Meteorology and Physics
O'NEILL, A., Mathematics, Meteorology and Physics
PORTER, D., Mathematics, Meteorology and Physics
RICE, D. A., Chemistry
SELLWOOD, B. W., Human Sciences
SHARKEY, P. M., Computer Science, Cybernetics and Electronic Engineering
SHINE, K. P., Mathematics, Meteorology and Physics
SLINGO, G. M., Mathematics, Meteorology and Physics
SMITH, P. T., Psychology
THORPE, A. J., Mathematics, Meteorology and Physics
VALDES, P. J., Mathematics, Meteorology and Physics
WADGE, G. M., Mathematics, Meteorology and Physics
WALSH, R., Chemistry
WANN, J. P., Psychology
WARBURTON, D. M., Psychology
WARWICK, K., Computer Science, Cybernetics and Electronic Engineering
WHITEHEAD, P. G., Human and Environmental Sciences
WRIGHT, A. C., Mathematics, Meteorology and Physics
WRIGHT, J. D. M., Mathematics, Meteorology and Physics

Rural History Centre (Whiteknights, POB 229, Reading, RG6 6AG; tel. (118) 931-8342; e-mail rhc@reading.ac.uk):

HOYLE, R. W.

UNIVERSITY OF SALFORD

Salford, Greater Manchester, M5 4WT
Telephone: (161) 295-5000
E-mail: office-exrel@salford.ac.uk
Internet: www.salford.ac.uk

Founded 1896, as the Royal Technical Institute, later Royal College of Advanced Technology, Univ. Charter granted 1967
Academic year: October to July
Chancellor: Dr IRENE KHAN
Vice-Chancellor: Prof. MARTIN HALL
Dean for Students: SAM GROGAN
Deputy Vice-Chancellor and Registrar and Sec.: Dr ADRIAN GRAVES
Pro-Vice-Chancellor for Academics: Prof. HUW MORRIS
Pro-Vice-Chancellor for Int. Affairs: Prof. CYNTHIA PINE
Pro-Vice-Chancellor for Research and Innovation: Prof. GHASSAN AOUAD
Pro-Vice-Chancellor for Strategic Partnerships: KEITH BARNES
Dir of Academic Information Services and Librarian: TONY LEWIS
Number of teachers: 800
Number of students: 18,000

DEANS

Arts and Social Sciences: Prof. HUW MORRIS
Health and Social Care: Prof. CYNTHIA PINE
Science and Technology: Prof. GHASSAN AOUAD

PROFESSORS

ALEXANDER, K., Construction and Property Management
ALSHAWI, M., Surveying
AOUAD, G., Surveying
ARMOUR, D. G., Physics
ARNELL, R. D., Aeronautical, Mechanical and Manufacturing Engineering
AVIS, N., Information Technology Institute
AYLETT, R., Information Systems Institute
BAKER, R. D., Accounting, Economics and Management Service
BARIC, L. F., Information Technology Institute
BARRETT, P. S., Surveying
BETTS, M. P., Surveying
BLAKEMORE, D. L., Modern Languages
BOARDMAN, A. D., Physics
BOOTH, J. G., Physics
BOTHAM, D., Management
BOWKER, P., Rehabilitation
BRANDON, P. S., Surveying
BROWN, G. R., Surveying
BRYANT, C. G. A., Sociology
BULL, M. J., Politics and Contemporary History
CALDWELL, D., Electronic and Electrical Engineering
CARTER, G., Physics
CHADWICK, D. W., Information System Institute
CHRISTER, A. H., Computer and Mathematics Science
COLLIER, C. G., Civil and Environmental Engineering
COLLIGON, J. S., Electronic and Electrical Engineering
COLLINS, D. N., Geography
COLQUHOUN, H. M., Chemistry and Applied Chemistry
COOK, R., Media and Performance
COOPER, G., Information Technology
COOPER, I., Centre for Regional Development and Sustainability
COOPER, R., Art and Design Technology
CRAIG, P. S., Biological Sciences
CROSSLEY, T. R., Aeronautical, Mechanical and Manufacturing Engineering
DANGERFIELD, B. C., Accounting, Economics and Management Science
DANSON, F. M., Environment and Life Sciences
DAVIES-COOPER, R., Art and Design Technology
DONNELLY, S. E., Physics
EASSON, A. W., English
EDGELL, S. R., Sociology

EDWARDS, J., Rehabilitation
EKERE, N. N., Aeronautical, Mechanical and Manufacturing Engineering
FERNANDO, T. P., Information Systems Institute
FLYNN, R., Sociology
GARSIDE, P. L., European Studies Research Institute
GERBER, R., Physics
GLEAVE, M. B., Geography
GOLDSMITH, M. J. F., Politics and Contemporary History
GRAY, J. O., Electronic and Electrical Engineering
GRUNDY, P. J., Physics
HARDING, A., Regional Development and Urban Politics
HARRIS, G. T., Modern Languages
HICKEY, L. D., Modern Languages
HILL, R., Computer and Mathematical Sciences
HORNER, A., English
HUGHES, R., Chemistry and Applied Chemistry
KAY, S., Health and Social Care
KEIGER, J. F. V., Modern Languages
KOBBACY, K. A. H., Accounting, Economics and Management Science
LAM, Y. W., Acoustics and Electronic Engineering
LARMOUTH, J., Information Technology Institute
LAWSON, R., Biological Sciences
LEONARD, J., Sciences
LINGE, N., Electronic and Electrical Engineering
LONG, A. F., Health Care Practice
LONGHURST, B. J., English, Sociology, Politics and Contemporary History
LORD, D., Physics
MARVIN, S., Centre for Regional Development and Sustainability
MASON, R. S., Business Studies
MAY, T., Sociology
MELBOURNE, C., Civil and Environmental Engineering
MORGAN, C. G., Biological Sciences
NAGY, F. L. N., Information Technology
NEAL, F., European Studies
PEMBLE, M. E., Chemistry and Applied Chemistry
POPAY, J., Public Health Research and Resource Centre
POWELL, J. A., Information Technology
PROCTER, G., Chemistry and Applied Chemistry
RAYNES, N., Health and Social Care
REZGUI, Y., Information Systems Institute
RICHARDS, J., Science
ROSS, D. K., Physics
SAMPSON, A. A., Economics
SANGER, D. J., Aeronautical, Mechanical and Manufacturing Engineering
SARSHAR, M., Construction and Property Management
SCOTT, D. B., Music
SHARDLOW, S. M., Social Work
SIMMONS, C., Accounting, Economics and Management Science
STEELE, A., Environment and Life Sciences
STOREY, D. M., Biological Sciences
TAYLOR, I. R., Sociology
TOLZ, V., English, Sociology, Politics and Contemporary History
TOMLINSON, P., Languages
TONGE, J., English, Sociology, Politics and Contemporary History
TOWELL, R. J., Modern Languages
VADERA, S., Sciences
WALKDEN, F., Computer and Mathematics Science
WEBSTER, P. J., Civil and Environmental Engineering
WHITEHEAD, C., Physics
WHITELEY, S., Media, Music and Performance
WHITELOCK, J., Management

WOOD, J. R. G., Computer and Mathematical Sciences, Information and Educational and Materials Development
WOOD, L., Business and Informatics
WOOD-HARPER, A. T., Computer and Mathematics Science
WRIGHT, F., Surveying
WYN JONES, E., Chemistry and Applied Chemistry

UNIVERSITY OF SHEFFIELD

Firth Court, Western Bank, Sheffield, S10 2TN
Telephone: (114) 222-2000
E-mail: externalrelations@sheffield.ac.uk
Internet: www.sheffield.ac.uk
Founded 1879 as Univ. College, Royal Charter 1905
Academic year: September to June
Chancellor: Lord DAINTON
Pro-Chancellor: K. E. RIDDLE
Pro-Chancellor: P. FIRTH
Pro-Chancellor: ANTHONY PAUL PEDDER
Vice-Chancellor: Prof. KEITH BURNETT
Pro-Vice-Chancellor for Int. Affairs: Prof. REBECCA HUGHES
Pro-Vice-Chancellor for Learning and Teaching: Prof. PAUL WHITE
Pro-Vice-Chancellor for Research and Innovation: Prof. RICHARD JONES
Pro-Vice-Chancellor for the Faculty of Arts and Humanities: Prof. MICHAEL BRADDICK (acting)
Pro-Vice-Chancellor for the Faculty of Engineering: Prof. MICHAEL HOUNSLOW
Pro-Vice-Chancellor for the Faculty of Medicine, Dentistry and Health: Prof. ANTHONY WEETMAN
Pro-Vice-Chancellor for the Faculty of Science: Prof. ANTHONY RYAN
Pro-Vice-Chancellor for the Faculty of Social Sciences: Prof. ANTHONY PAYNE
Registrar and Sec.: P. HARVEY
Librarian: MARTIN LEWIS
Library: see under Libraries and Archives
Number of teachers: 1,500
Number of students: 24,920

PROFESSORS

(Some staff serve in more than one faculty)
Faculty of Architectural Studies:
BLUNDELL JONES, P. M., Architecture
CAMPBELL, H., Town and Regional Planning
CROOK, A. D. H., Town and Regional Planning
HENNEBERRY, J., Town and Regional Planning
KANG, J., Architecture
LAWSON, B. R., Architecture
PLANK, R. J., Architecture
SWANWICK, C. A., Landscape
TILL, J., Architecture
TREGENZA, P. R., Architecture
Faculty of Arts:
AINSWORTH, P. F., French
Canon ALEXANDER, L. C. A., Biblical Studies
BARRETT, J. C., Archaeology
BELL, D. A., Philosophy
BENNET, J., Archaeology
BRADDICK, M. J., History
BRANIGAN, K., Archaeology
BROOKSBANK JONES, A., Hispanic Studies
CLARKE, E. F., Music
CLINES, D. J. A., Biblical Studies
COLLIS, J. R., Archaeology and Prehistory
COOK, R. J., History
CROSS, M. F., French
DENNELL, R. W., Archaeology
DIVERS, J., Philosophy
DUFFIELD, N. G., English Language and Linguistics

ENGLAND, J. P., Hispanic Studies
EXUM, J. C., Biblical Studies
GREENGRASS, M., History
HAFFENDEN, J., English Literature
HATTAWAY, M., English Literature
HILL, P. H. A. W., Music
HOOKWAY, C. J., Philosophy
HOPKINS, R., Philosophy
JONES, G. E. M., Archaeology
Sir KERSHAW, I., Modern History
KING, E. J., History
LEATHERBARROW, W. J., Russian and Slavonic Studies
LINN, A. R., English Language and Linguistics
MCMAHON, A. M. S., English Language and Linguistics
OWENS, D. J., Philosophy
PERRAUDIN, M. F., Germanic Studies
PHIMISTER, I. P., International History
ROBERTS, N. J., English Literature
RUSSELL, R., Russian and Slavonic Studies
SAUL, J. M., Philosophy
SHELLARD, D. M., English Literature
SHEPHERD, D. G., Russian and Slavonic Studies
SHOEMAKER, R. B., History
SHUTTLEWORTH, S. A., English Literature
SIMEONE, N. A., Music
STAUB, M. H., History
STERN, R. A., Philosophy
STOCK, J. P. J., Music
SWANSON, P., Hispanic Studies
WALKER, D. H., French
WHITELAM, K. W., Biblical Studies
ZVELEBIL, M., Archaeology

Faculty of Engineering:
ALLEN, R. W. K., Chemical and Process Engineering
ALLERTON, D. J., Automatic Control and Systems Engineering
ALLINSON, N. M., Electronic and Electrical Engineering
ANDERSON, W. F., Civil and Structural Engineering
ASHLEY, R. M., Civil and Structural Engineering
ASKES, H., Civil and Structural Engineering
BANKS, S. P., Automatic Control and Systems Engineering
BANWART, S. A., Civil and Structural Engineering
BEYNON, J. H., Metallurgy
BILLINGS, S. A., Control Engineering
BOLLER, C., Mechanical Engineering
BROWN, M. W., Mechanical Engineering
BURGESS, I. W., Civil and Structural Engineering
CHAMBERS, B., Electronic and Electrical Engineering
CULLIS, A. G., Electronic and Electrical Engineering
DALEY, S., Automatic Control and Systems Engineering
DAVID, J. P. R., Electronic and Electrical Engineering
DAVIES, H. A., Engineering Materials
FLEMING, P. J., Automatic Control and Systems Engineering
GIBBS, M. R. J., Engineering Materials
HARDING, J., Engineering Materials
HOUNSLOW, M. J., Chemical and Process Engineering
HOUSTON, P. A., Electronic and Electrical Engineering
HOWARD, I. C., Mechanical Engineering
HOWE, D., Electrical Engineering
JAMES, P. F., Engineering Materials
JOHNSON, C. M., Electronic and Electrical Engineering
JONES, F. R., Engineering Materials
JONES, H., Engineering Materials
LEE, W. E., Engineering Materials
LERNER, D. N., Civil Engineering

MACNEIL, S., Tissue Engineering
MATTHEWS, A., Engineering Materials
OWENS, D. H., Automatic Control and Systems Engineering
PAVIC, A., Civil and Structural Engineering
PILAKOUTAS, K., Civil and Structural Engineering
QIN, N., Mechanical Engineering
RAINFORTH, W. M., Engineering Materials
REES, G. J., Electronic and Electrical Engineering
RIDGWAY, K., Mechanical Engineering
SAUL, A. J., Civil and Structural Engineering
SHARIFI, V. N., Chemical and Process Engineering
SHORT, R. D., Engineering Materials
SOUTIS, C., Aerospace Engineering
SWITHENBANK, J., Chemical and Process Engineering
TOMLINSON, G. R., Engineering Dynamics
UNGAR, G., Engineering Materials
WALDRON, P., Civil and Structural Engineering
WEST, A. R., Engineering Materials
WILSON, C. W., Mechanical Engineering
WORDEN, K., Mechanical Engineering
WRIGHT, P. C., Chemical and Process Engineering
WRIGHT, P. V., Engineering Materials
YATES, J. R., Mechanical Engineering
ZHU, Z. Q., Electronic and Electrical Engineering

Faculty of Law ():
ADAMS, J. N., Intellectual Property
BEYLEVELD, D., Law
BIRDS, J. R., Commercial Law
BRADGATE, J. R., Commercial Law
BRADNEY, T. A., Law
DIGNAN, J., Criminology and Restorative Justice
DITTON, J., Criminology
HARDEN, I., Law
HOLDAWAY, S. D., Sociology
KINDERLERER, J., Biotechnical Law
LEWIS, N. D., Constitutional Law, Sociology of Law
LUXTON, P., Property Law
MERRILLS, J. E. G., International Law
SHAPLAND, J. M., Criminal Justice

Faculty of Medicine (Beech Hill Rd, Sheffield, S10 2RX):
AHMEDZAI, S., Palliative Medicine
AKEHURST, R. L., Health Economics
BARBER, D. C., Medical Imaging and Medical Physics
BAX, N. D. S., Medical Education
BISHOP, N. J., Paediatric Bone Disease
BOISSONADE, F. M., Oral and Maxillofacial Surgery
BRAZIER, J. E., Health Economics
BROOK, A. H., Oral Health and Development
BROOK, I. M., Oral and Maxillofacial Surgery
BROOKER, C. G. D., Mental Health
BROWN, B. H., Medical Physics
BROWN, B. L., Cell Signalling and Endocrinology
BROWN, N. J., Surgical Sciences
CAMPBELL, M. J., Medical Statistics
CANNINGS, C., Mathematics and Informatics
COLEMAN, R., Medical Oncology
CROSSMAN, D. C., Cardiology
CROUCHER, P. I., Bone Biology
DOLAN, P. H. R., Health Economics
DOWER, S. K., Molecular Immunology
DUFF, G. W., Molecular Medicine
EASTELL, R., Bone Metabolism
EL-NAHAS, A. M., Nephrology
ENDERBY, P. M., Community Rehabilitation
FORREST, A. R. W., Clinical Chemistry

GERRISH, K., Nursing Practice Development
GRANT, G. W. B., Cognitive Disability
GRIFFITHS, P. D., Academic Radiology
Sir HALL, D. M. B., Community Paediatrics
HAMDY, F., Urology
HANCOCK, B. W., Clinical Oncology
HATTON, P. V., Adult Dental Care
HELLEWELL, P. G., Vascular Biology
HENDERSON, I. W., Functional Genomics
HUTCHINSON, A., Public Health Medicine
INCE, P., Neuropathology
KERSHAW, B., Nursing and Midwifery
KIRKHAM, M. J., Midwifery
LEDGER, W. L., Obstetrics and Gynaecology
LENNON, M. A., Oral Health and Development
LEWIS, C. E., Molecular and Cellular Pathology
MacNEIL, S., Tissue Engineering
MATHERS, N., General Practice
MEUTH, M., Cellular Genetics
MILROY, C. M., Forensic Pathology
MOORE, H. D. M., Reproductive Biology
NICHOLL, J. P., Medical Care Research Centre
NICOLSON, P., Health Psychology
NOLAN, M. R., Gerontological Nursing
PALEY, M. N. J., Magnetic Resonance Physics
PARKER, S. G., Health Care for Elderly People
PARRY, G. D., Applied Psychological Therapies
PAYNE, S., Palliative Care Nursing
PEAKE, I. R., Molecular Medicine
PERKINS, M. R., Human Communications Science
PHILP, I., Health Care for Elderly People
POCKLEY, A. G., Immunobiology
POWERS, H. J., Nutritional Biochemistry
QWARNSTRÖM, E. E., Cell Biology
READ, R. C., Infectious Diseases
READ, S. M., Acute and Critical Care Nursing
REED, M. W. R., Surgical Oncology
REILLY, C. S., Anaesthesia
RENNIE, I. G., Ophthalmology
ROBINSON, P. G., Oral Health and Development
ROBINSON, P. P., Oral and Maxillofacial Surgery
ROLF, C. G., Sports Medicine
ROSS, R. J. M., Endocrinology
SAYERS, J. R., Functional Genomics
SHAW, P. J., Neurology
SPEIGHT, P. M., Oral Pathology
STACKHOUSE, R. J., Human Communication Science
TANNER, M. S., Paediatrics
TANTAM, D. J. H., Psychotherapy
TAYLOR, C. J., Paediatric Gastroenterology
THOMPSON, D. R., Acute and Critical Care
TUCKER, G. T., Molecular Pharmacology and Pharmacogenetics
UNDERWOOD, J. C. E., Pathology
van NOORT, R., Adult Dental Care
WALSH, T. F., Adult Dental Care
WARNES, A. M., Social Gerontology
WEETMAN, A. P., Medicine
WELLS, M., Gynaecological Pathology
WELLS, W. B., Human Communication Science
WHYTE, M. K. B., Respiratory Medicine
WOLL, P. J., Medical Oncology
WOODRUFF, P. W. R., Academic Clinical Psychiatry

Faculty of Pure Science:
ANDERSON, C. W., Mathematics and Statistics
ANDREWS, P. W., Biomedical Science
ARMS, S. P., Chemistry
ARMSTRONG, H. W., Geography
ARTYMIUK, P. J., Molecular Biology and Biotechnology

ATKIN, R. J., Applied Mathematics
BAILEY, G. J., Applied Mathematics
BEERLING, D. J., Palaeoclimatology
BIGG, G. R., Geography
BIGGINS, J. D., Probability and Statistics
BINGHAM, N. H., Probability and Statistics
BIRKHEAD, T. R., Zoology
BLACKSTOCK, W., Molecular Biology and Biotechnology
BULLOUGH, P. A., Molecular Biology and Biotechnology
BURKE, T. A., Molecular Ecology
BUTLIN, R. K., Evolutionary Biology
CALLAGHAN, T. V., Arctic Ecology
CALOW, P., Zoology
CARSWELL, D. A., Geology
CHATWIN, P. C., Applied and Computational Mathematics
CIRAVEGNA, F., Computer Science
COOKE, M. P., Computer Science
DEAN, P., Psychology
DERRICK, J., Computer Science
DORLING, D. F. L., Geography
EBDON, J. R., Chemistry
EISER, C., Psychology
EISER, J. R., Psychology
FLEMING, A. J., Plant Sciences
FOSTER, S. J., Molecular Biology and Biotechnology
FRISBY, J. P., Psychology
GAIZAUSKAS, R., Computer Science
GASTON, K. J., Biodiversity and Conservation
GEHRING, G. A., Solid-State Physics
GREEN, J., Molecular Biology and Biotechnology
GREEN, P. D., Computer Science
GREENLEES, J. P. C., Probability and Statistics
GREGSON, N., Geography
GRUNDY, D., Biomedical Science
HARDY, G., Clinical Psychology
HEATHWAITE, A. L., Geography
HIGGINS, J. A., Molecular Biology and Biotechnology
HOCKEY, G. R. J., Psychology
HOLCOMBE, W. M. L., Computer Science
HOLLEY, M. J., Biomedical Science
HORTON, P., Molecular Biology and Biotechnology
HUGHES, D. W., Physics and Astronomy
HUNTER, C. A., Chemistry
HUNTER, C. N., Molecular Biology and Biotechnology
INGHAM, P. W., Biomedical Science
JACKSON, P. A., Human Geography
JACKSON, R. F. W., Synthetic Chemistry
JONES, R. A. L., Physics
JORDAN, D. A., Pure Mathematics
KELLY, D. J., Molecular Biology and Biotechnology
LEE, J. A., Environmental Biology
LEEGOOD, R. C., Plant Biochemistry
LEGGETT, G. J., Nanoscale Analytical Science
MALTBY, L., Environmental Biology
MANN, B. E., Chemistry
MAYHEW, J. E. W., Psychology
McLEOD, C. W. M., Chemistry
MOERDIJK, I., Pure Mathematics
MOORE, H. D. M., Reproductive Biology
MOORE, R., Computer Science
NICOLSON, R. I., Psychology
NIRANJAN, M., Computer Science
O'HAGAN, A., Probability and Statistics
OUTHWAITE, C. W., Mathematics and Statistics
PARSONS, L. M., Psychology
PATTIE, C. J., Geography
PICKUP, B. T., Chemistry
PIPER, B., Molecular Biology and Biotechnology
PLACZEK, M., Biomedical Science
POOLE, R. K., Molecular Biology and Biotechnology
PRESS, M. C., Physiological Ecology

QUEGAN, S., Applied and Computational Mathematics
QUICK, W. P., Plant Physiology
RATNIEKS, F. L. W., Apiculture
READ, D. J., Plant Sciences
REDGRAVE, P., Psychology
REES, M., Plant Ecology
RICE, D. W., Molecular Biology and Biotechnology
ROSZKOWSKI, L., Physics and Astronomy
RUDERMAN, M. S., Applied Mathematics
RYAN, A. J., Chemistry
SCHOLES, J. D., Plant and Microbial Science
SHARKEY, N. E., Computer Science
SHARP, R. Y., Pure Mathematics
SHEERAN, P., Psychology
SIEGAL, M., Psychology
SKOLNICK, M. S., Experimental Condensed Matter
SLADE, P., Clinical Psychology
SMALLWOOD, R., Computer Science
SMYTHE, C., Biomedical Science
SMYTHE, E., Biomedical Science
SNAITH, V. P., Pure Mathematics
SPENCER, C. P., Psychology
SPOONER, N. J. C., Physics
STRICKLAND, N. P., Pure Mathematics
SURPRENANT, A., Biomedical Science
TADHUNTER, C. N., Physics and Astronomy
THOMPSON, M.J., Applied Mathematics
TURNER, G., Genetics
TURPIN, G., Clinical Psychology
VALENTINE, G., Geography
von FÁY-SIEBENBÜRGEN, R., Applied Mathematics
WALL, T. D., Psychology
WALKER, M., Computer Science
WALTHO, J. P., Molecular Biology and Biotechnology
WARD, M. D., Chemistry
WHITE, P. E., Geography
WILKS, Y., Computer Science
WILLIAMSON, M. P., Molecular Biology and Biotechnology
WOODWARD, F. I., Plant Ecology
WYATT, L. R., Applied Mathematics
ZINOBER, A. S. I., Applied Mathematics

Faculty of Social Sciences:
ADCOCK, C. J., Financial Econometrics
ARMSTRONG, D., Education
BEAULIEU, M., Management
BOOTH, T. A., Social Policy
BROOKES, R. G., Education
CARR, W., Education
CASSELL, C. M., Management
CHAPPELL, D., Mathematical Economics
CLEGG, C. W., Work Psychology
COLE, P., Journalism
CORRALL, S., Librarianship and Information Management
FORD, N. J., Information Studies
FRANKLIN, R., Media Communications
GAMBLE, A. M., Politics
GEDDES, A. P., Politics
GRAYSON, J. H., East Asian Studies
GRUGEL, J. B., Politics
GUNTER, B., Journalism
HANNON, P. W., Education
HEALD, D. E. A, Management
HOCKEY, J. L., Sociological Studies
HOOK, G. D., Japanese Studies
HOOPER, B. J., East Asian Studies
JAMES, A., Sociological Studies
JENKINS, R., Sociology
KENNEDY-PIPE, C., International Relations, Politics
MacDONALD, S., Management
MALTBY, J. A., Management
MARSH, P., Child and Family Welfare
McCONNELL, D., Education
MOSLEY, P., Economics
NIXON, J. D., Education
NORRIS, C. A., Sociology
PARRY, G., Education

PAYNE, A. J., Politics
REDMAN, T. A., Management
SMITH, M. J., Politics
STANDISH, P., Education
TAYLOR, A. J., Politics
TAYLOR, P. D., Leisure Management
TYLECOTE, A. B., Economics and Management of Technological Change
USHERWOOD, R. C., Information Studies
VINCENT, A. W., Politics
WALKER, A. C., Social Policy
WEBB, S. C., Institute of Lifelong Learning
WELLINGTON, J. J., Education
WHITTAKER, S. J., Information Studies
WILLETT, P., Information Studies
WOOD, S. J., Work Psychology
WRIGHT, T., East Asian Studies

ATTACHED SCHOOLS

School of Health and Related Research: e-mail scharr.reception@sheffield.ac.uk; Dean Prof. R. L. AKEHURST.

School of Management: e-mail mgt .reception@sheffield.ac.uk; Dir Prof. M. BEAULIEU

UNIVERSITY OF SOUTHAMPTON

University Rd, Southampton, SO17 1BJ

Telephone: (23) 8059-5000
E-mail: admissns@soton.ac.uk
Internet: www.soton.ac.uk

Founded 1952; opened as the Hartley Institution 1862; incorporated as the Hartley Univ. College 1902
Academic year: October to July
Vice-Chancellor: Prof. DON NUTBEAM
Provost and Deputy Vice-Chancellor: Prof. ADAM WHEELER
Pro-Vice-Chancellor: Prof. PHILIP NELSON
Pro-Vice-Chancellor: MARK SPEARING
Pro-Vice-Chancellor for Education: Prof. DEBRA HUMPHRIS
Chief Operating Officer: MALCOLM ACE
Registrar: TESSA HARRISON
Head Student Information and Records: GILLIAM HOLF
Librarian: Dr MARK BROWN
Library: see under Libraries and Archives
Number of teachers: 2,280
Number of students: 22,830 (20,867 full-time and 1,963 part-time)

DEANS

Faculty of Business and Law: Prof. JEREMY HOWELLS
Faculty of Engineering and the Environment: Prof. WILLIAM POWRIE
Faculty of Health Sciences: Prof. JESSICA CORNER
Faculty of Humanities: Prof. ANNE CURRY
Faculty of Medicine: Prof. IAIN CAMERON
Faculty of Natural and Environmental Sciences: Prof. STEPHEN HAWKINS
Faculty of Physical and Applied Sciences: Prof. Dame WENDY HALL
Faculty of Social and Human Sciences: Prof. JUDITH PETTS

UNIVERSITY OF SUNDERLAND

Edinburgh Bldg, City Campus, Chester Rd Sunderland, SR1 3SD

Telephone: (191) 515-2000
E-mail: student-helpline@sunderland.ac.uk
Internet: www.sunderland.ac.uk

Founded 1969 as Sunderland Polytechnic; present name and status 1992
Academic year: September to June
Chancellor: STEVE CRAM
Vice-Chancellor and Chief Exec.: Prof. PETER FIDLER
Deputy Vice-Chancellor for Resources: SHIRLEY ATKINSON

Deputy Vice-Chancellor (Academic): Prof. PETER STRIKE
Deputy Vice-Chancellor (Academic): Prof. JULIE MENNELL
Sec. and Clerk to the Board: J. D. PACEY
Dir of Information Services: Prof. ANDREW MACDONALD
Library of 280,000 vols
Number of teachers: 1,300
Number of students: 18,950

DEANS

Faculty of Applied Sciences: Prof. JOHN MACINTYRE
Faculty of Arts, Design and Media: GRAEME THOMPSON
Faculty of Business and Law: VIVIAN KINNAIRD
Faculty of Education and Society: Prof. G. SHIELD

PROFESSORS

ALABASTER, T., Environmental Informatics
ARTHUR, W. W., Population Biology
BAINBRIDGE, E., Fine Art
BRAYNE, H., Law
CHILTON, P., Politics and Peace Studies
COCKTON, G., Computer Software Engineering
COX, C. S., Control Engineering
CRISELL, A. P., Broadcasting Studies
CROZIER, G., Education
DARBY, J., Humanities
EDWARDS, H. M., Computer Software Engineering
ELLIOTT, J., Education
ELLIS, P., Performance Arts
FLETCHER, E. J., Applied Computing
GROUNDWATER, P. W., Organic Chemistry
HANMER, J., Humanities
HARVEY, B. P., Humanities
HEPBURN, A., Modern Irish History
HESTER, M., Social Studies
HARRISON, R., Renewable Energy
ITZIN, C., Health and Community Studies
LEES, G., Neurophysiology and Neuropharmacology
LILLEY, T. H., Physical Chemistry
MACINTYRE, J., Computer Software Engineering
MALIN, N. A., Health Services Research
MOSCARDINI, A. O., Mathematical Modelling
O'BRIEN, M., Librarian, Communication and Media Studies
OVER, D. E., Philosophical Logic
PALOVA, Z., Design and Creative Arts
PETROVA, S., Glass
PODCZECK, G. F., Pharmaceutics
PRENTICE, R. C., Tourism
PRINGLE, K., Comparative Social Policy
REED, M. A., Criminal and Private International Law
RICHARDS, D. S., International Business and Cross-Cultural Management
SIM, S. D., Critical Theory
SINGH, G., Pharmacy
STOREY, J. C., Librarian, Communication and Media Studies
TAIT, J. I., Computer Software Engineering
THOMPSON, B., Design and Creative Arts
THORNHAM, S., Librarian, Communication and Media Studies
TINDLE, J., Computer Software Engineering
VAN LEEUWEN, C. C., Psychology
VAN ZON, H., Social Studies
WALDRON, P., Modern European History
WERMTER, S., Information Systems
WILSON, P. H., Early Modern History

UNIVERSITY OF SURREY

Guildford, GU2 5XH
Telephone: (1483) 300800
Internet: www.surrey.ac.uk

Founded 1891 as Battersea Polytechnic Institute, designated a College of Advanced Technology 1956, University Charter 1966
Academic year: October to June
Chancellor: HRH THE DUKE OF KENT
Vice-Chancellor and Chief Exec.: Prof. CHRISTOPHER M. SNOWDEN
Sr Deputy Vice-Chancellor: Prof. NIGEL SEATON
Deputy Vice-Chancellor for Academic Devt: Prof. GILLIAN NICHOLLS
Deputy Vice-Chancellor for Research and Innovation: Prof. STEPHEN WILLIAMSON
Pro-Vice-Chancellor for Int. Relations: Prof. COLIN GRANT
Univ. Registrar: CAROLINE JOHNSON (acting)
Dir of Corporate Services: GREG MELLY
Dir of Finance: DAVID SHARKEY
Dir of Information Services and University Librarian: T. J. A. CRAWSHAW
Number of teachers: 1,000 (incl. 350 part-time assoc. lecturers)
Number of students: 15,190
Publication: *Surrey Matters*

DEANS

Faculty of Arts and Human Sciences: Prof. PHILLIP POWRIE
Faculty of Engineering and Physical Sciences: Prof. MICHAEL KEARNEY
Faculty of Health and Medical Sciences: Prof. JOHN HAY
Faculty of Management and Law: Prof. DAVID ALLEN

PROFESSORS

School of Arts:
  ANDERMAN, G. M., Translation Studies
  BARTA, P., Russian and Cultural Studies
  CORBETT, G. G., Linguistics and Russian Language
  EADE, J.
  FLOCKTON, C. H., European Economic Studies
  FLOOD, C. G., European Studies
  FORBES, S.
  GRANT, C. B., Communication Studies
  HOLFORD, J. A. K.
  HUTCHINGS, S. C., Russian
  JARVIS, P., Continuing Education
  JUDGE, A., French
  LANSDALE, J. H., Dance Studies
  LUTZEIER, P. R., German
  McNAIR, S., Education
  MIDDLEHURST, R. M., Higher Education
  MOORE, A., Music
  UPEX, R. V., Law

School of Biomedical and Life Sciences:
  ADAMS, M. R., Food Microbiology
  BUSHELL, M. E., Microbial Physiology
  CLIFFORD, M. N., Food Safety
  DALE, J. W., Molecular Microbiology
  DANIL DE NAMOR, A., Chemistry
  FERNS, G. A. A., Metabolic and Molecular Medicine
  GIBSON, G. G., Molecular Toxicology
  GOLDFARB, P. S. G., Molecular Biology
  HAY, J. N., Materials Chemistry
  HEYES, D. M., Chemistry
  HINDMARCH, I., Human Psychopharmacology
  HOURANI, S. M. O., Pharmacology
  HOWELL, N. K., Food Science
  KITCHEN, I., Neuropharmacology
  LYNCH, J. M., Life Sciences
  McFADDEN, J., Molecular Genetics
  MILLWARD, D. J., Nutrition
  ROBERTSON, W. R.
  SERMON, P., Physical Chemistry
  SKENE, D. J., Neuroendocrinology
  SLADE, R. C. T., Inorganic Chemistry
  SMITH, C., Functional Genomics

School of Electronics and Physical Sciences:
  ADAMS, A. R.

AHMAD, KH., Artificial Intelligence
ALLAM, J., Ultra-fast Optoelectronics
BRIDGES, T. J., Mathematics
CLOUGH, A. S.
COWERN, N. E. B., Nanoscale Materials Processing
EVANS, B. G., Information Systems
GELLETLY, W.
HESS, O., Computational Quantum Electronics
HOMEWOOD, K. P., Semiconductor Optoelectronics
ILLINGWORTH, J., Machine Vision
KEARNEY, M. J., Electronic Device Engineering
KITTLER, J. V., Machine Intelligence
KONDOZ, A. M., Multimedia Communication Systems
KRAUSE, P. J., Software Engineering
MCDONALD, P. J.
MELBOURNE, I., Mathematics
PAVLOU, G., Communication and Information Systems
PETROU, M., Image Analysis
REED, G. T., Optoelectronics
ROBERTS, R. M., Mathematics
ROGERS, A. J.
SANDSTEDE, B., Mathematical Sciences
SCHNEIDER, S. A., Computing
SEALY, B. J., Solid State Devices and Ion Beam Technology
SILVA, S. R. P., Solid State Electronics
SPYROU, N. M.
Sir SWEETING, MARTIN, Satellite Engineering
TAFAZOLLI, R., Mobile Communications
THOMPSON, I. J.
TOSTEVIN, J. A.
WALKER, P. M.
WEBB, R. P., Ion Beam Physics
WEISS, B. L., Microelectronics

School of Engineering:

AZAPAGIC, A., Sustainable Engineering
CHEW, J. W., Mechanical Engineering
CHRYSSANTHOPOULOS, M. K., Structural Systems
CLIFT, R., Environmental Technology
CROCOMBE, A. D., Structural Mechanics
GILLAN, M. A., Aerospace Engineering
GORINGE, M. J., Materials
HOLLAWAY, L. C., Composite Structures
JACKSON, T., Sustainable Development
JEFFERIS, S., Civil Engineering
KOKOSSIS, A. C., Process Systems Engineering Optimization
LAWSON, M., Construction Systems
LLOYD, B. J., Environmental Health Engineering
NOOSHIN, H., Space Structures
PARKE, C. A. R., Structural Engineering
PARKER, G. A., Mechanical Engineering
ROBINS, A. G., Environmental Fluid Mechanics
SMITH, P. A., Composite Materials
THORPE, R., Multiphase Engineering
TOY, N., Fluid Mechanics
TSAKIROPOULOS, P., Metallurgy
TÜZÜN, U., Process Engineering
WATTS, J. F., Materials Science

School of Human Sciences:

ARBER, S. L., Sociology
BAG, P., Economics
BARRETT, M. D., Psychology
BIRD, G. R., Economics
BROWN, J. M., Forensic Psychology
BULMER, M. I. A., Sociology
CRAWFORD, I., Economics
DAVIES, I. R. L., Psychology
EMLER, N., Social Psychology
FIELDING, N. G., Sociology
GILBERT, G. N., Sociology
GROEGER, J. A., Cognitive Psychology
HAMPSON, S. E., Psychology and Health
HUNT, L. C., Economics
LEVINE, P., Economics

OGDEN, J., Health Psychology
RICKMAN, N. J., Economics
SHEPHERD, R., Psychology
STERR, A., Cognitive Neuroscience and Neuropsychology
TARLING, R., Sociology
UZZELL, D. L., Environmental Psychology
ZIJLSTRA, F., Occupational and Organizational Psychology

School of Management:

AIREY, D. W., Tourism Management
ARCHER, G. S. H., Financial Management
BUTLER, R. W., Tourism
DESOMBRE, T., Health Care Management
GILBERT, D., Marketing
HALES, C., Organizational Behaviour
JONES, P. L. M., Productions and Operations Management
KIRBY, D., Entrepreneurship
LIU, X., International Business
LOCKWOOD, A. J., Hospitality Management
LOWE, M., Retail Management
O'KEEFE, R. M., Information Management
PHILLIPS, P. A., Hotel Management
RILEY, M. J., Organizational Behaviour
SADLER-SMITH, E., Management Development and Organizational Behaviour

European Institute of Health and Medical Sciences:

BRYAN, K., Clinical Practice
BUCKLE, P., Health Ergonomics
HUNT, G.
POPE, R., Nurse Education
ROBBINS, I., Mental Health Practice
SMITH, P. A., Nurse Education
STUBBS, D. A., Ergonomics

Postgraduate Medical School:

FARMER, R. D. T., Epidemiology
THOMAS, H., Oncology

UNIVERSITY OF SUSSEX

Sussex House, Brighton, BN1 9RH
Telephone: (1273) 606755
E-mail: information@sussex.ac.uk
Internet: www.sussex.ac.uk
Founded 1961
Academic year: October to June
Chancellor: SANJEEV BHASKAR
Vice-Chancellor: Prof. MICHAEL FARTHING
Deputy Vice-Chancellor and Pro-Vice-Chancellor for Research: Prof. BOB ALLISON
Pro-Vice-Chancellor for Int. Affairs: Prof. CHRIS MARLIN
Pro-Vice-Chancellor for Teaching and Learning: Prof. CLARE MACKIE
Registrar and Sec.: JOHN DUFFY
Librarian: KITTY INGLIS
Library: see under Libraries and Archives
Number of teachers: 550
Number of students: 11,480

PROFESSORS

ABBS, P. F., Creative Writing
ABRAHAM, J. W., Sociology
ABRAHAM, S. C. S., Psychology
ARMES, S. P., Chemistry
BACON, J. P., Neuroscience
BAILIN, D., Theoretical Physics
BEEBEE, J. J. C., Molecular Ecology
BENJAMIN, P. R., Neuroscience
BILLINGHAM, N. C., Chemistry
BLISS, J. F., Education
BODEN, M. A., Philosophy and Psychology
BUXTON, H., Visual Intelligence
CAWSON, A., Digital Media
CHATWIN, C. R., Manufacturing Systems
CHERRY, D., History of Art
CLARK, A. J., Philosophy
CLARK, T. D., Physical Electronics
CLOKE, F. G. N., Chemistry
CLUNAS, A. C., History of Art
COATES, R. A., Linguistics

COLCLOUGH, C. L., Development Studies
COLLETT, T. S., Neurobiology
COPELAND, E. J., Theoretical Physics
DARWIN, C. J., Experimental Psychology
DAVEY, G. C. L., Psychology
DEARLOVE, J. N., Politics
DOMBEY, N. D., Theoretical Physics
DU BOULAY, J. B. H., Artificial Intelligence
DUNFORD, M. F., Economic Geography
DYHOUSE, C. A., History
ERAUT, M. R., Education
FAIRHEAD, J., Social Anthropology
FALLOWFIELD, L. J., Psycho-Oncology
FENDER, S. A., American Studies
FIELDING, A. J., Human Geography
FLOWERS, T. J., Plant Physiology
GANN, D. M., Science and Technology Policy Research
GARDINER, J. M., Psychology
GARNHAM, A., Experimental Psychology
GAZDAR, G. J. M., Computational Linguistics
GOLDIE, C. M., Statistics
GOUGH, M. P., Space Science
GRAY, F. G., Continuing Education
GRIFFITH-JONES, S., Development Studies
GRILLO, R. D., Social Anthropology
GRIMSDALE, R. L., Electronic Engineering
HANSON, J. R., Chemistry
HART, V. M., American Studies
HENNESSY, M., Computer Science
HINDS, E. A., Experimental Physics
HIRSCHFELD, J. W. P., Mathematics
HOBDAY, M. G., Science and Technology Policy Research
HOLMWOOD, J. M., Sociology
HOWKINS, A. J., Social History
HUMPHREY, C. J., Development Studies
HUTCHINGS, M. J., Ecology
JAYAWANT, B. V., Electrical and Systems Engineering
KAPLINSKY, R. M., Development Studies
KEDWARD, H. R., History
KING, R. L., Geography
Sir KROTO, H. W., Chemistry
LAND, M. F., Neurobiology
LEACH, M. A., Development Studies
LEHMANN, A. R., Molecular Genetics
LEWIN, K. M., Education
LIDDLE, A. R., Astrophysics
LISTER, P. F., Electronics
LLEWELLYN, N. G., History of Art
MANOR, J. G., Development Studies
MARTIN, B. R., Science and Technology Policy Research
MATHER, G. W., Experimental Psychology
MCCAFFERY, A. J., Chemistry
MELLOR, D. A., History of Art
MILNER-GULLAND, R. R., Russian
MITTER, P., History of Art
MOORE, A. L., Biochemistry
MOORE, M. P., Development Studies
MURPHY, R. J., German, Comparative Literature and Film
NICHOLLS, P. A., English and American Literature
NIXON, J. F., Chemistry
O'SHEA, M. R., Neuroscience
OAKHILL, J. V., Experimental Psychology
OSMOND-SMITH, D., Music
OUTHWAITE, R. W., Sociology
PAIN, V. M., Biochemistry
PARSONS, P. J., Organic Chemistry
PAVITT, K. L. R., Science and Technology Policy Studies
PENDLEBURY, J. M., Experimental Physics
PERRY-ROBINSON, J. P., Science and Technology Policy Research
PLATT, J. A., Sociology
POWNER, E. T., Electronic Engineering
PRASSIDES, K., Chemistry
RAJAK, H. H., Law
RICHARDS, R. L., Chemistry
RÖHL, J. C. G., History
ROLLO, J. M. C., European Economic Integration
ROPER, T. J., Biology

Ross, M. G., European Law
Royle, N. W. O., English
Russell, I. J., Neurobiology
Ryan, C. J., Italian
Sampson, G. R., Natural Language Computing
Schmitz, H., Development Studies
Shaw, M., International Relations and Politics
Short, B. M., Geography
Sinfield, A. J., English
Skeldon, R., Geography
Smith, L. J., English
Smith, P. B., Social Psychology
Smith, P. H., Media Studies
Sobolev, A. V., Mathematics
Stace, A. J., Chemistry
Steinmueller, W. E., Science and Technology Policy Research
Stephens, D. N., Experimental Psychology
Stobart, R. K., Automotive Engineering
Sumner, M. T., Economics
Tapper, E. R., Politics
Taylor, I. J., Social Care and Social Work
Temkin, J., Law
Tidd, J., Science and Technology Policy Research
Timms, E. F., German Studies
Torrance, H., Education
Townsend, P. D., Experimental Physics
Troscianko, T., Psychology
Turner, A. B., Mechanical Engineering
van Der Pijl, K., International Relations
van Gelderen, M. A. J., Intellectual History
Vance, R. N. C., English
Vincent, R., Medical Science
von Tunzelmann, G., Economics of Science and Technology
Wagstaff, R. A. S., Economics
Wallis, M., Biochemistry
Wark, D. L., Physics
Watts, C. T., English
Webb, P. D., Politics
Wilkinson, R. G., Trafford Centre for Graduate Medical Education and Research
Winters, L. A., Economics
Worden, A. B., Early Modern History
Young, D. W., Chemistry
Zhang, K., Pure Mathematics

UNIVERSITY OF THE ARTS LONDON

272 High Holborn, London, WC1V 7EY
Telephone: (20) 7514-6000
E-mail: info@arts.ac.uk
Internet: www.arts.ac.uk

Founded 2004

Rector: Sir Nigel Carrington
Deputy Rector of Academic Devt and Quality: Elizabeth Rouse
Deputy Rector of Planning and Operations: William Bridge
Dir for Information Services: Pat Christie
Library of 400,000 vols, 3,500 magazines and periodicals, 10,000 video cassettes and other media, 130 databases, 170 electronic resources and 12,000 ejournals
Number of teachers: 1,230
Number of students: 22,050 ..

COLLEGES OF THE UNIVERSITY

Camberwell College of Arts

Peckham Rd, London, SE5 8UF
Telephone: (20) 7514-6302
E-mail: info@camberwell.arts.ac.uk
Internet: www.camberwell.arts.ac.uk

Founded 1898

Main subject areas: ceramics, design products, conservation, drawing, graphic design, illustration, painting, photography, sculpture; another campus at Wilson Rd
Head: Chris Wainwright

Dean: Natalie Brett
Number of teachers: 150
Number of students: 1,750

Central Saint Martins College of Art and Design

Southampton Row, London, WC1B 4AP
Telephone: (20) 7514-7022
E-mail: info@csm.arts.ac.uk
Internet: www.csm.arts.ac.uk

Founded 1989 by merger of Central School of Arts and Crafts (f. 1896) and St Martin's School of Art (f. 1854), incorporated Drama Centre London (f. 1962) 1999 and London Studio Centre 2003

Incl. Drama Centre London and the Cochrane Theatre; three schools: school of art, school of graphic and industrial design, school of fashion and textiles
Head: Jane Rapley
Library of 80,000 vols
Number of students: 4,880

Chelsea College of Art and Design

Millbank, London, SW1P 4JU
Telephone: (20) 7541-7751
E-mail: enquiries@chelsea.arts.ac.uk
Internet: www.chelsea.arts.ac.uk

Founded 1895

Main subject areas: fine art, communication design, interior and spatial design, textile design, history and theory of visual and multimedia cultures
Dean: Prof. David Gracia
Head: Prof. Chris Wainwright
Number of teachers: 80
Number of students: 1,750

London College of Communication

Elephant and Castle, London, SE1 6SB
Telephone: (20) 7514-6500
E-mail: info@lcc.arts.ac.uk
Internet: www.lcc.arts.ac.uk

Founded 1894, fmrly London College of Printing, present name 2004

Main subject areas: animation, graphic design, graphic communication, journalism, media, photography
Head: Prof. Sandra Kemp
Number of students: 5,430

London College of Fashion

20 John Princes St, London, W1G 0BJ
Telephone: (20) 7514-7400
E-mail: enquiries@fashion.arts.ac.uk
Internet: www.fashion.arts.ac.uk

Founded 1906, as Shoreditch Technical Institute Girls School

Head of College: Frances Corner
Number of students: 5,110
Publication: *Pigeons and Peacocks*

Wimbledon College of Art

Merton Hall Rd, London, SW19 3QA
Telephone: (20) 7514-9641
E-mail: info@wimbledon.arts.ac.uk
Internet: www.wimbledon.arts.ac.uk

Founded 1890, as an Art Class in the Rutlish School for Boys, present name and status 2006

Schools of specialist art and design
Head: Chris Wainwright
Dean: Prof. George Blacklock
Library of 28,000 vols
Number of teachers: 50
Number of students: 1,120

UNIVERSITY OF THE WEST OF ENGLAND (UWE)

Frenchay Campus, Coldharbour Lane, Bristol, BS16 1QY
Telephone: (117) 965-6261
E-mail: admissions@uwe.ac.uk
Internet: www.uwe.ac.uk

Founded 1969 as Bristol Polytechnic, present name and status 1992
Language of instruction: English
Academic year: September to June

Chancellor: Sir Ian Carruthers
Vice-Chancellor: Prof. Steven West
Deputy Vice-Chancellor for Academic Affairs: Prof. Paul Gough
Deputy Vice-Chancellor for Resources, Planning and Infrastructure: John Rushforth
Academic Registrar: Andrea Cheshire
Librarian: Cathy Rex

Library of 561,219 vols, 516,105 books and e-books, 45,114 journals
Number of teachers: 1,190
Number of students: 27,500 (21,170 full-time and 6,332 part-time)

DEANS

Faculty of Arts, Creative Industries and Education: Alex Gilkison
Faculty of Business and Law: Dr Jane Harrington (acting)
Faculty of Environment and Technology: Prof. Paul Olomolaiye
Faculty of Health and Life Sciences: Prof. Helen Langton

UNIVERSITY OF WARWICK

Coventry, CV4 7AL
Telephone: (24) 7652-3523
Internet: www.warwick.ac.uk

Founded 1965
Academic year: September to July

Chancellor: Sir Richard Lambert
Vice-Chancellor: Prof. Nigel Thrift
Provost: Prof. Stuart Croft
Pro-Vice-Chancellor for Academic Planning and Resources: Prof. Lawrence Young
Pro-Vice-Chancellor for Postgraduate and Transnational Education: Prof. Jan Palmowski
Pro-Vice-Chancellor for Science, Engineering and Medicine: Prof. Tim Jones
Pro-Vice-Chancellor for Teaching and Learning: Prof. Christina Hughes
Registrar: Ken Sloan
Librarian: Robin Green
Library: 1m. vols
Number of teachers: 930
Number of students: 23,420

DEANS

School of Engineering: Prof. Nigel Stocks
Warwick Business School: Prof. Mark Taylor
Warwick Medical School: Prof. Peter Winstanley

PROFESSORS

Faculty of Arts (internet www2.warwick.ac.uk/fac/arts):

Bassnett, S. E., Centre for Translation and Comparative Cultural Studies
Bate, J., English and Comparative Literary Studies
Beacham, R. C., Theatre Studies
Bell, M., English
Bennett, O., Theatre Studies
Berg, M. L., History
Brunsdon, C. M., Film and Television Studies
Burns, R. A., German Studies
Caesar, A., Italian
Capp, B. S., History

CLARK, C. F., History
DABYDEEN, D., Caribbean Studies
DAVIS, C. J., French Studies
DAVIS, J., Theatre Studies
DOCHERTY, T., English and Comparative Literary Studies
DYER, R. W., Film and Television Studies
GARDNER, J., History of Art
HEUMAN, G. J., Caribbean Studies, History
HILL, L. J., French Studies
HINDLE, S., History
HINTON, J. S., History
HUGHES, D. W., English
JONES, C. D. H., History
KING, J. P., History
LAZARUS, N., English
MACK, P. W. D., English
McFARLANE, A. J., History
MULRYNE, J. R., English
NYE, D., History
O'BRIEN, K., English and Comparative Literary Studies
PATERSON, L. M., French Studies
READ, C. J., History
ROSENTHAL, M. J., History of Art
RUTTER, C. C., English and Comparative Literary Studies
SHARPE, K., English
STEEDMAN, C. K., Social History
SWAIN, S. C. R., Classics
TREGLOWN, J. D., English
VINCENDEAU, G. O. R., Film and Television Studies
WHITBY, L. M., Classics

Faculty of Medicine, Warwick Medical School (internet www2.warwick.ac.uk/fac/med):

CARTER, Y., Dean, Warwick Medical School
DALE, J., Division of Health in the Community
FULFORD, K. W. N., Philosophy and Mental Health
GRIFFIN, D., Orthopaedics and Trauma
HUNDT, G. A., School of Health and Social Studies
KUMAR, S., Medicine, Diabetes and Metabolism
LAMB, S., Physiotherapy and Rehabilitation
LEHNERT, H., Medicine
PEILE, E., Medical Education
SINGER, D., Clinical Pharmacology
SPANSWICK, D., Molecular Neurosciences
STANFIELD, P. R., Dept of Biological Sciences
STEWART-BROWN, S., Public Health
THORNTON, S., Biological Sciences
THOROGOOD, M., Epidemiology
WEICH, S., Psychiatry

Faculty of Science (internet www2.warwick.ac.uk/fac/sci; some members also serve in the Faculty of Medicine):

ANDERSON, D., Civil and Mechanical Engineering
BALL, R. C., Theoretical Physics
BARKLEY, D., Mathematics
BHATTACHARYYA, S. K., Manufacturing Systems
BRIGHT, S.
BROWN, G. D. A., Psychology
BRYANSTON-CROSS, P. J., Civil and Mechanical Engineering
BUGG, T. D. H., Biological Chemistry
BURNS, I.
CAMPBELL-KELLY, M., Computer Science
CARPENTER, P. W., Mechanical Engineering
CHAPMAN, S. C., Physics
CHATER, N., Psychology
CHETWYND, D. G., Civil and Mechanical Engineering
COOPER, M. J., Physics
COPAS, J. B., Statistics
CRITOPH, R. E., Civil and Mechanical Engineering
DALE, N., Biological Sciences
DALTON, H., Biological Sciences

DAVEY, J., Biological Sciences
DERRICK, P. J., Chemistry
DIMMOCK, N. J., Biological Sciences
DOWSETT, M. G., Physics
DOWSON, C. G., Biological Sciences
DUPREE, R., Physics
EASTON, A. J., Biological Sciences
ELWORTHY, K. D., Mathematics
FIRTH, D., Statistics
FLOWER, J. O., Engineering
FREEDMAN, R. B., Biological Sciences
FRIESECKE, G., Mathematics
FULFORD, K. W. M., Philosophy and Mental Health
FULOP, V., Biological Sciences
GARDNER, J. W., Electronic Engineering
GODFREY, K. R., Electrical and Electronic Engineering
GREEN, R. J., Electronic Communication Systems
HADDLETON, D. M., Chemistry
HARRISON, P. F., Physics
HOLT, D. F., Mathematics
HUANG, T., Civil and Mechanical Engineering
HUTCHINS, D. A., Electrical and Electronic Engineering
HUTTON, J. L., Statistics
JONES, G. V., Psychology
JONES, J. D. S., Mathematics
KEMP, T. J., Chemistry
KENDALL, W. S., Statistics
KERR, R., Mathematics
KERR, R. M., Civil and Mechanical Engineering
LAMBERTS, K., Psychology
LAWRENCE, A. J., Statistics
LEWIS, M. H., Physics
LORD, J. M., Biological Sciences
MacKAY, R., Mathematics
MANN, N. H., Biological Sciences
MARSH, T., Physics
MAYOR, E. A., Psychology
McCONVILLE, C. F., Physics
McCRAE, M. A., Biological Sciences
MEDLEY, G. F. H., Biological Sciences
MILLAR, A. J., Biological Sciences
MILLS, P.
MOND, D. M. Q., Mathematics
MOORE, P., Chemistry
MURRELL, J. C., Biological Sciences
NUDD, G. R., Computer Science
PARKER, E. H. C., Semiconductor Physics
PATERSON, M. S., Computer Science
PAUL, D. McK., Physics
PELED, D., Computer Science
POLLICOTT, M., Mathematics
RAND, D. A., Mathematics
RAWNSLEY, J. H., Mathematics
REID, M. A., Mathematics
ROBERTS, L. M., Biological Sciences
ROBINSON, C., Biological Sciences
RODGER, P. M.
ROURKE, C. P., Mathematics
SCOTT, D., Chemistry
SERIES, C. M., Mathematics
SHIPMAN, M., Chemistry
SMITH, J. Q., Statistics
SMITH, M. E., Physics
STANFIELD, P. R., Biological Sciences
STAUNTON, J. B., Physics
STEEL, M. F., Statistics
STEWART, I. N., Mathematics
STRIEN, S. VAN, Mathematics
STUART, A., Mathematics
TAYLOR, P. R., Chemistry
THOMAS, B.
THORNTON, S., Obstetrics and Gynaecology
UNWIN, P. R., Chemistry
WALTERS, P., Mathematics
WELLINGTON, E. M. H., Biological Sciences
WHALL, T. E., Physics
WHIPPS, J.
WILLS, M., Chemistry
WILSON, A. J., Medical Physics
WILSON, R. G., Computer Science

WILSON, T. M. A., Biological Sciences
WOODLAND, H. R., Biological Sciences
WOODRUFF, D. P., Physics

Faculty of Social Studies (internet www2.warwick.ac.uk/fac/soc; some members also serve in the Faculty of Medicine):

ALI, S. S., Law
ANSELL-PEARSON, K., Philosophy
ANWAR, M., Ethnic Relations
ARCHER, M. S, Sociology
ARULAMPALAM, S. W., Economics
AUBREY, C., Institute of Education
BAXI, U., Law
BEALE, H. G., Law
BECKFORD, J. A., Sociology
BENINGTON, J., Business Studies
BLACKORBY, A. B., Economics
BRESLIN, S., Politics and International Studies
BREWER, B., Philosophy
BRIDGES, L. T., Law
BROADBERRY, S. N., Economics
BRYER, R. A., Accounting and Finance
BURNELL, P. J., Politics and International Studies
BURNHAM, P., Politics and International Studies
BURRIDGE, R. H. M., Law
CAMPBELL, R. J., Institute of Education
CARNALL, C., Business Studies
CAVE, M., Centre for Management under Regulation
CHARLES, N., Sociology
CLARKE, S. R. C., Sociology
CLUBB, C., Accounting and Finance
COHEN, R., Sociology
COWLING, K. G., Industrial Economics
CROUCH, C., Governance and Public Management
CURRIE, W., Information Systems
DALE, J., Primary Care
DAVIES, R., Business Studies
DEVEREUX, M. P., Economics and Business Studies
DICKENS, L. J., Business Studies
DUTTA, B., Economics
DYSON, R. G., Business Studies
EDWARDS, P. K., Business Studies
EILAN, N. H., Philosophy
ELIAS, D. P. B., Employment Research
ELLIOTT, R., Business Studies
FAUNDEZ, J., Law
FINE, R. D., Sociology
FULFORD, K. W. M., Philosophy and Mental Health
FULLER, S., Sociology
GEMMILL, G., Accounting and Finance
GHOSAL, S., Economics
GLEESON, D., Institute of Education
GRANT, W. P., Politics and International Studies
HARRIS, A., Institute of Education
HARRIS, J., Health and Social Studies
HARRISON, R. M., Economics
HARTLEY, J., Local Government Centre
HIGGOTT, R. A., Politics and International Studies
HODGES, S. D., Financial Management
HOSKIN, K. W., Business Studies
HOULGATE, S., Philosophy
HUDDLESTON, P. J., Institute of Education
HURLEY, S., Politics and International Studies
IRELAND, N. J., Economics
JACKSON, R. M. D., Institute of Education
JOHNSTON, R., Business Studies
JOLY, D., Centre for Research in Ethnic Relations
LAYTON-HENRY, Z. A., Politics and International Studies
LEGGE, K., Business Studies
LEWANDO-HUNDT, G., Social Sciences and Health
LINDLEY, R. M., Employment Research
LINDSAY, G. A., Special Educational Needs

LOCKWOOD, B., Economics
LOVELL, T. A., Women and Gender
LUNTLEY, M., Philosophy
MARGINSON, P., Industrial Relations
MASSON, J. M., Law
MAWSON, J., Local Government Centre
MCCONVILLE, M. J., Law
MCELDOWNEY, J. F., Law
MCGEE, J., Marketing and Strategic Management
MILLER, M. H., Economics
MITCHELL, C., Centre for Management under Regulation
MORGAN, G., Industrial Relations
MULLENDER, A., Social Work
NAYLOR, R. A., Economics
NEAL, A., Law
NEUBERGER, A., Accounting and Finance
OSWALD, A. J., Economics
PALIWALA, A., Law
PERRONI, C., Economics
PHIZACKLEA, A. M., Sociology
PIERCY, N., Marketing and Strategic Management
POGANY, S. I., Law
RAI, S. M., Politics and International Studies
RANKIN, N., Economics
RATCLIFFE, P. B., Sociology
REEVE, A. W., Politics and International Studies
SALMON, M., Accounting and Finance
SARNO, L., Business Studies
SCARBOROUGH, H., Business Studies
SCHOLTE, J. A., Politics and International Studies
SKIDELSKY, R., Political Economy
SLACK, N. D. C., Manufacturing and Strategy Policy
SLADE, M., Economics
SMITH, H., Politics and International Studies
SMITH, R. J., Economics
SPENCER, N. J., Community Paediatrics
STEWART, M. B., Economics
STONEMAN, P., Business Studies
STOREY, D. J., Business Studies
STURDY, A., Industrial Relations and Organizational Behaviour
SWAN, J. A., Organizational Behaviour
SZCZEPURA, A., Business Studies
TALL, D. O., Institute of Education
TAYLOR, M. P., Economics
TERRY, M. A., Business Studies
THOMAS, H., Business Studies
TRIGG, R. H., Philosophy
TSOUKOS, H., Industrial Relations and Organizational Behaviour
WAGNER, P., Sociology
WALKER, I., Economics
WARHURST, A., Corporate Citizenship Unit
WATERSON, M. J., Economics
WENSLEY, J. R. C., Marketing and Strategic Management
WHALLEY, J., Development Economics
WHITE, B., Politics and International Studies
WHITESIDE, N., Sociology
WILLCOCKS, L., Information Management and e-Business
WILSON, D. C., Strategic Management
WOODERS, M., Economics
WRAY, D., Institute of Education

UNIVERSITY OF WESTMINSTER

309 Regent St, London W1B 2UW
Telephone: (20) 7911-5000
E-mail: course-enquiries@westminster.ac.uk
Internet: www.westminster.ac.uk
Founded 1838 as Polytechnic Institution; became Royal Polytechnic Institution 1839 and Polytechnic of Central London 1970; present name and status 1992
Academic year: September to August

Vice-Chancellor and Rector: Prof. GEOFFREY PETTS
Deputy Vice-Chancellor and Pro-Vice-Chancellor: Prof. RIKKI MORGAN-TAMOSUNAS
Registrar and Sec.: CAROLE MAINSTONE
Dir for Finance: MICHAEL WEBB
Dir for Information Services: SUZANNE ENRIGHT
Library of 420,000 vols
Number of teachers: 1,204
Number of students: 23,000

DEANS

Faculty of Architecture and Built Environment: Prof. DAVID DERNIE
Faculty of Media, Arts and Design: KERSTIN MEY
Faculty of Science and Technology: Prof. JANE LEWIS
Faculty of Social Sciences and Humanities: Prof. ROLAND DANNREUTHER
Westminster Business School: Prof. BARBARA ALLAN

UNIVERSITY OF WINCHESTER

Sparkford Rd, Winchester, SO22 4NR
Telephone: (1962) 841515
E-mail: course.enquiries@winchester.ac.uk
Internet: www.winchester.ac.uk
Founded 1840, present name and status 2005
Chancellor: MARY FAGAN
Vice-Chancellor: Prof. JOY CARTER
Univ. Librarian: DAVID FARLEY
Deputy Vice-Chancellor: TOMMY GEDDES
Pro-Vice-Chancellor: Prof. ELIZABETH STUART
Pro-Vice-Chancellor: NEIL MARRIOTT
Dir for Finance and Strategy: SIMON COWHIG
Library of 250,000 vols
Number of teachers: 650 (f.t.e.)
Number of students: 5,900

DEANS

Faculty of Arts: Prof. ANTHONY DEAN
Faculty of Business, Law and Sport: Prof. NEIL MARRIOTT
Faculty of Education, Health and Social Care: Prof. JOYCE GOODMAN
Faculty of Humanities and Social Sciences: Prof. KRISTYAN SPELMAN MILLER

UNIVERSITY OF WOLVERHAMPTON

Molineux St, Wolverhampton, WV1 1SB
Telephone: (1902) 321000
E-mail: enquiries@wlv.ac.uk
Internet: www.wlv.ac.uk
Founded 1969 as Wolverhampton Polytechnic; present name and status 1992
Constituent Colleges: City of Wolverhampton College, Dudley College, Rodbaston College, Sandwell College, South Birmingham College, Telford College of Arts and Technology, Walsall College of Arts and Technology
Chancellor: Lord PAUL OF MARYLEBONE
Vice-Chancellor: Prof. CAROLINE GIPPS
Deputy Vice-Chancellor: Prof. GEOFF HAMPTON
Deputy Vice-Chancellor and Dir of Finance: GARRY SPROSTON
Pro-Vice-Chancellor for Academic Affairs: Prof. SALLY GLEN
Pro-Vice-Chancellor and Dir for Corporate Services: HELEN LLOYD WILDMAN
Pro-Vice-Chancellor for Student Affairs: JANE NELSON
Pro-Vice-Chancellor for Research and Enterprise: Prof. IAN OAKES
Registrar: PAUL TRAVILL
Dir for Learning and Information Services: FIONA PARSONS
Dean for Students: JON ELSMORE
Univ. Sec.: A. W. (TONY) LEE

Library of 363,471 vols
Number of teachers: 980
Number of students: 23,080

DEANS

Applied Sciences: Prof. JOHN DARLING
Art and Design: Dr BRYONY CONWAY
Education: Prof. KIT FIELD
Health and Wellbeing: Prof. LINDA LANG
Institute for Learning Enhancement: Dr GLYNIS COUSIN
Law, Social Sciences and Communications: Dr JUDITH BURNETT
Sport, Performing Arts and Leisure: JOHN PYMM
Technology: Prof. ROBERT MORETON
University of Wolverhampton Business School: Prof. KIT FIELD (acting)

UNIVERSITY OF WORCESTER

Henwick Grove, Worcester, WR2 6AJ
Telephone: (1905) 855000
E-mail: admissions@worc.ac.uk
Internet: www.worc.ac.uk
Founded 1946 as Emergency Teacher Training College, present name and status 2005
Academic year: September to May
Chancellor: HRH PRINCE RICHARD, THE DUKE OF GLOUCESTER
Vice-Chancellor and Chief Exec.: Prof. DAVID GREEN
Deputy Vice-Chancellor: Prof. ROSALIND FOSKETT
Pro-Vice-Chancellor for Resources: Dr MARTIN DOUGHTY
Registrar and Univ. Sec.: JOHN RYAN
Library of 130,000 vols, 400 print periodicals, 12,000 e-periodicals
Number of teachers: 700
Number of students: 10,100

UNIVERSITY OF YORK

Heslington, York, YO10 5DD
Telephone: (1904) 320000
E-mail: admissions@york.ac.uk
Internet: www.york.ac.uk
Founded 1963
Academic year: October to June (3 terms)
Chancellor: GREG DYKE
Vice-Chancellor: Prof. KOEN LAMBERTS
Deputy Vice-Chancellor and Pro-Vice-Chancellor for Students: Prof. JANE GRENVILLE
Pro-Vice-Chancellor for Business and Community: Prof. COLIN MELLORS
Pro-Vice-Chancellor for Research: Prof. DEBORAH SMITH
Pro-Vice-Chancellor for Teaching, Learning and Information: Prof. JOHN ROBINSON
Registrar and Sec.: Dr DAVID DUNCAN
Dir for Corporate Planning: DAVID MUCKERSIE
Dir for External Relations: JOAN CONCANNON
Dir for Finance: GRAHAM GILBERT
Dir for Human Resources: PAT LOFTHOUSE
Dir for Information and Univ. Librarian: STEPHEN TOWN
Library: see under Libraries and Archives
Number of teachers: 770
Number of students: 13,000
Publication: *University of York Magazine* (6 a year)

PROFESSORS

ABADIR, K., Economics, Mathematics
AFSHAR, H., Politics
ANDREWS, R., Educational Studies
ARTHURS, A. M., Mathematics
ATTRIDGE, D., English
BABIKER, M., Physics
BALDWIN, T. R., Philosophy
BARRELL, J. C., English
BEHRINGER, W., History

BERTHOUD, J. A., English
BESSEL, R., History
BILLER, P., History
BOWLBY, R., English
BOWLES, D. J., Biology
BRADSHAW, J. R., Social Policy
BRAUNSTEIN, S., Quantum Computing
BURNS, A., Computer Science
BURR, A., Electronics
CALLINICOS, A., Politics
CAMPBELL, C., Sociology
CARR-HILL, R., Health Economics
CARVER, M. O., Archaeology
CLARK, J. H., Chemistry
CORRIGAN, E., Mathematics
CRESSER, M., Environment
CULYER, A. J., Economics
DE FRAJA, G., Economics
DITCH, J. S., Social Policy and Social Work
DIVALL, C., Railway Studies
DIXON, H. D., Economics
DODSON, E., Chemistry
DODSON, G. G., Chemistry
DODSON, M., Mathematics
DOLLIMORE, J., English
DRUMMOND, M. F., Health Economics
EL-GOMATI, M. M., Electronics
ELLIS, A. W., Psychology
FITTER, A. H., Biology
FORD, J. R., Housing Policy
FORREST, A. I., History
FOUNTAIN, J., Mathematics
GILBERT, B. C., Chemistry
GODBY, R., Physics
GODFREY, C., Centre for Health Economics, Health Services
GODFREY, L. G., Social and Economic Statistics
GRAHAM, I., Biology
GRAVELLE, H. S. E., Economics
GUEST, H., English
HALL, G., Psychology
HARRISON, M. D., Computer Science
HARTLEY, K., Economics
HEY, J. D., Social and Economic Statistics
HITCH, G., Psychology
HOLMAN, J., Chemistry
HOWARD, D., Electronics
HOWELL, D., Politics
HUBBARD, R., Chemistry
HULME, C., Psychology
HUTTON, J. P., Economics and Econometrics
INESON, P., Biology
JACKSON, S. F., Women's Studies
JONES, A., Economics
KEMP, P., Social Policy Research Unit
KITZINGER, C., Sociology
KLEIJNEN, J. E., Centre for Reviews and Dissemination
LAMARQUE, P., Philosophy
LAMBERT, P., Economics
LE FANU, N., Music
LEESE, H. J., Biology
LEWIN, R. J., Health Studies
LINDSAY SMITH, J., Chemistry
LOCAL, J. K., Linguistics
MACPHAIL, E., Psychology
MAITLAND, N. J., Biology
MARKS, R., History of Art
MARSH, R., Music
MARVIN, A. C., Electronics
MATTHEW, J. A. D., Physics
MAYNARD, A. K., Health Studies
MAYNARD, M. A., Social Policy and Social Work
MAYSTON, D. J., Public Sector Economics
McDERMID, J. A., Computer Science
McDOUGALL, C., Criminal Justice
McQUEEN-MASON, S., Biology
MENDUS, S., Politics
MILLAR, R., Educational Studies
MILNER, A. J., Biology
MINNIS, A. J., Medieval Literature
MONK, A., Psychology
MULKAY, M., Sociology
MULLER-DETHLEFS, K., Chemistry

O'CONNOR, T., Archaeology
O'GRADY, K., Physics
ORMROD, M., History
PARRY, G., English
PERRINGS, C., Environment
PERT, G. J., Computational Physics
PERUTZ, R. N., Chemistry
PHILLIPS, P., Economics
POSNETT, J., York Health Economics Consortium
PRUTTON, M., Physics
QURESHI, H., Social Policy and Social Work
RAFFAELLI, D., Environment
RAINEY, L. S., English
RIDDY, F J., English
ROBARDS, A. W., Biology
ROBINSON, J., Electronics
ROYLE, E., History
RUNCIMAN, C., Computer Science
RUSSELL, I. T., Health Sciences
SANDERS, D., Biology
SHARPE, J. A., History
SHAW, I., Social Work
SHELDON, T., Health Sciences
SIMMONS, P. J., Economics
SINCLAIR, I. A. C., Social Work
SLOPER, P., Social Policy Research Unit
SMITH, D. M., Borthwick Institute
SMITH, P. C., Economics
SNOWLING, M. S., Psychology
SOUTHGATE, J., Biology
SPARROW, J., Biology
STEIN, M., Social Work
SUDBERY, A., Mathematics
TAYLOR, R. J. K., Chemistry
THOMPSON, D. R., Health Studies
TYRRELL, A. M., Electronics
VULLIAMY, G., Educational Studies
WALTON, P., Chemistry
WALVIN, J., History
WAND, I. C., Computer Science
WARD, N. A.-M. F., English
WARNER, A. R., Language
WATT, I. S., Health Studies
WEBSTER, A., Sociology
WELLINGS, A. J., Computer Science
WICKENS, M. R., Economics
WILKINSON, A. J., Chemistry
WILLIAMS, A. H., Economics
WILSON, K., Chemistry
WILSON, R. A., Biology
WOOLHOUSE, R., Philosophy
YEARLEY, S., Sociology
YOUNG, A. W., Psychology
YOUNG, J. P. W., Biology

YORK ST JOHN UNIVERSITY

Lord Mayor's Walk, York, YO31 7EX
Telephone: (1904) 624624
Internet: w3.yorksj.ac.uk

Founded 1841, as York Diocesan Training School, present name and status 2006
Chancellor: Archbishop of York, Dr JOHN SENTAMU
Vice-Chancellor: Prof. DAVID FLEMING
Deputy Vice-Chancellor: Prof. DAVID MAUGHAN BROWN
Registrar: ALISON KENNELL
Number of teachers: 235
Number of students: 6,500
Publication: *The White Rose* (1 a year)

DEANS

Faculty of Arts: Dr FIONA THOMPSON
Faculty of Education and Theology: Prof. JULIAN STERN
Faculty of Health and Life Sciences: Prof. PAMELA DAWSON
York St John Business School: JACKIE MATHERS

University Colleges in England

University Colleges have taught degree awarding powers only and do not carry out research.

Arts University College at Bournemouth: Wallisdown, Poole, BH12 5HH; tel. (1202) 363-233; e-mail general@aucb.ac.uk; internet www.aucb.ac.uk; f. 1885; specialist instn; diploma, undergraduate, postgraduate degree courses in art, design and creative media; library: 45,000 vols, 40,000 ebooks, 300 specialist journals; 3,000 students.

BPP University College: Aldine House, Aldine Place, 142–144 Uxbridge Rd, London, W12 8AW; tel. (20) 7633-4410; e-mail admissions@bpp.com; internet www.bppuc.com; f. 1992; consists of business school and law school; undergraduate, postgraduate and professional programmes; campuses in Birmingham, Bristol, Leeds, Manchester and in 3 centres in London; acquired by Apollo Global, Inc.; library: 6,200 vols; 64 teachers; 600 full-time postgraduate students; Prin. CARL LYGO.

College of Law: Braboeuf Manor, Portsmouth Rd, St Catherines, Guildford, GU3 1HA; tel. (1483) 216-000; internet www.college-of-law.co.uk; f. 1967, degree awarding powers 2006; postgraduate courses; brs in Birmingham, Bristol, Chester, London, Manchester and York; Chief Exec. Prof. NIGEL SAVAGE; Chair. DAVID YATES; Deputy Chair. JONATHAN HAW; Deputy Chair. GUY BERINGER.

Greenwich School of Management: Meridian House, Royal Hill, Greenwich, London SE10 8RD; tel. (20) 8516-7800; e-mail admissions@greenwich-college.ac.uk; internet www.greenwich-college.ac.uk; f. 1973 incorporates the Greenwich School of Law; provides univ. MBA, MSc, EMBA, BSc, LLB, BBA PhD, DBA, CIPS, undergraduate, postgraduate, doctoral programmes and professional courses; Prin. Dr WILLIAM HUNT.

Henley Business School: Whiteknights, Reading, RG6 6UD; tel. (118) 378-5044; e-mail helpdesk@henley.com; internet www.henley.reading.ac.uk; f. 1945; attached to Univ. of Reading; has campus in Greenland; courses in accountancy, business, management, finance, real estate, planning, informatics and coaching; 7,000 students; Dean Prof. JOHN BOARD; Deputy Dean Prof. GINNY GIBSON.

ifs School of Finance: 36 Monument St, London, EC3R 8LJ; tel. (20) 7444-7111; e-mail customerservices@ifslearning.ac.uk; internet www.ifslearning.ac.uk; f. 1879 as Institute of Bankers, present name 2006, acquisition of taught degree-awarding powers 2010; courses in banking and financial management; Chair. BRUCE CARNEGIE-BROWN; Prin. GAVIN SHREEVE; Treas. ROY RANSLEY.

Newman University College: Genners Lane, Bartley Green, Birmingham, B32 3NT; tel. (121) 476-1181; e-mail admissions@newman.ac.uk; internet www.newman.ac.uk; f. 1968; offers foundation degrees, BA (Hons), professional graduate certificate of education, teacher training courses; postgraduate research students awarded by Univ. of Leicester; library: 90,000 books, 500 periodicals; Prin. and CEO Prof. PETER LUTZEIER; Vice-Prin. KATHRYN SOUTHWORTH; Registrar and Univ. College Sec. HEATHER SOMERFIELD.

Norwich University College of the Arts: 3–7 Redwell St, Norwich, NR2 4SN; tel. (1603) 610561; e-mail info@nuca.ac.uk;

internet www.nuca.ac.uk; f. 1845, as Norwich School of Design, present name and status 2008; library: 30,000 vols, 2,500 DVDs, 100 journals; 1,500 students; Prin. Prof. JOHN LAST.

Royal Agricultural College: Stroud Rd, Cirencester, GL7 6JS; tel. (1285) 652-531; e-mail admissions@rac.ac.uk; internet www.rac.ac.uk; f. 1842, royal charter granted in 1845; education, research and consultancy; undergraduate and postgraduate courses in agricultural, land, business management, food, equine, property industries; library: 40,000 vols, 1,000 journal subscriptions, 50,000 ebooks; 49 full-time teachers; 25 visiting professors; 650 full-time students; Prin. Prof. CHRIS GASKELL.

St Mary's University College: Strawberry Hill, Twickenham, London TW1 4SX; tel. (20) 8240-4000; internet www.smuc.ac.uk; f. 1850, present status 2006; library: 11,500 vols, 13,500 journals; 100 teachers; Prin. FRANCIS CAMPBELL; Vice-Prin. Prof. MICHAEL HAYES; Vice-Prin. DAVID LEEN.

University College Birmingham: Summer Row, Birmingham, B3 1JB; tel. (121) 604-1000; internet www.ucb.ac.uk; f. 1918, present name and status 2007; library: 75,000 vols, 1,000 journals; 7,500 students; Prin. Prof. RAY LINFORTH.

University College Falmouth: Woodlane, Falmouth, TR11 4RH; tel. (1326) 211077; e-mail admissions@falmouth.ac.uk; internet www.falmouth.ac.uk; f. 1902, merged with Dartington College of Arts in 2008; college of arts; campuses at Woodlane in Falmouth and Tremough in Penryn; library: 100,000 vols; 80 teachers; 1,700 students; Rector and CEO Prof. ANNE CARLISLE.

University College Plymouth St Mark and St John: Derriford Rd, Plymouth, PL6 8BH; tel. (1752) 636700; e-mail info@ucpmarjon.ac.uk; internet www.marjon.ac.uk; f. 1926, by merger of St John's College and St Mark's College, present name and status 2007; library: 120,000 vols; 3,500 students; Prin. Prof. MARGARET NOBLE; Vice-Prin. for Academic Dr GEOFF STOAKES; Vice-Prin. for Resources KAREN COOK.

Colleges in England

These institutions are not able to award their own degrees, but offer courses leading to a degree from a recognized body.

GENERAL

Accrington and Rossendale College: Broad Oak Rd, Accrington, BB5 2AW; tel. (1254) 389933; e-mail info@accross.ac.uk; internet www.accross.ac.uk; 3 campuses; degree courses in health, sports, technology validated by Buckinghamshire New Univ. and Univ. of Bolton; Prin. SUE TAYLOR.

Alpha Meridian College: Meridian House, Greenwich High Rd, Greenwich, London, SE10 8TL; tel. (20) 8853-5697; e-mail info@alphameridian.co.uk; internet www.alphameridian.co.uk; f. 1994; private ind. educational instn; business management, information technology, management of information systems, travel tourism and hospitality management.

Aylesbury College: Oxford Rd, Aylesbury, HP21 8PD; tel. (1296) 588588; e-mail enquiries@aylesbury.ac.uk; internet www.aylesbury.ac.uk; f. 1962 as Aylesbury College of Further Education, current name adopted 1993; vocational courses incl. hospitality and catering, construction, care, hair and beauty and sport; 5,500 (4,500 part-

time, 1,000 full-time); Prin. and Chief Exec. KAREN MITCHELL.

Bishop Burton College: York Rd, Bishop Burton, Beverley, HU17 8QG; tel. (1964) 553000; e-mail enquiries@bishopburton.ac.uk; internet www.bishopburton.ac.uk; f. 1954; land-based college; degrees validated by Univ. of Hull, Leeds Metropolitan Univ.; library: 46,000 items; 370 journal and magazine subscriptions; Prin JEANETTE DAWSON.

Blackpool and The Fylde College: Ashfield Rd, Bispham, Blackpool, FY2 0HB; tel. (1253) 352352; e-mail info@blackpool.ac.uk; internet www.blackpool.ac.uk; attached to Lancaster Univ.; offers undergraduate, professional and vocational courses; 30,000 students; Prin. and Chief Exec. BEV ROBINSON.

Bradford College: Great Horton Rd, Bradford, BD7 1AY; tel. (1274) 433333; e-mail information@bradfordcollege.ac.uk; internet www.bradfordcollege.ac.uk; f. 1832; provides undergraduate, postgraduate and professional courses; consists of law school, business school and school of teaching, health and care; Prin. KATHRYN OLDALE.

Bromley College of Further and Higher Education: Rookery Lane, Bromley, BR2 8HE; tel. (20) 8295-7000; e-mail info@bromley.ac.uk; internet www.bromley.ac.uk; Bachelors degrees and HNDs in vocational subjects; validated by Univ. of Greenwich; 600 teachers; 10,000 students; Prin. SAM PARRETT.

Chesterfield College: Infirmary Rd, Chesterfield, S41 7NG; tel. (1246) 500500; e-mail advice@chesterfield.ac.uk; internet www.chesterfield.ac.uk; f. 1841; HNDs and undergraduate degrees; library: 340,000 books, journals, magazines and DVDs; 8,000 students (incl. part-time); Prin. TREVOR CLAY.

City College Brighton and Hove: Pelham St, Brighton, BN1 4FA; tel. (1273) 667788; e-mail info@ccb.ac.uk; internet www.ccb.ac.uk; 3 campuses; Bachelors courses validated by Univ. of Brighton; library: 40,000 vols, 3,000 ebooks, 300 current periodicals, 3,000 video cassettes, 2,000 DVDs; 10,000 students; Prin. LYNN THACKWAY.

City College Norwich: Ipswich Rd, Norwich, NR2 2LJ; tel. (1603) 773311; e-mail information@ccn.ac.uk; internet www.ccn.ac.uk; HNDs, undergraduate and postgraduate degrees, English language qualification; validated by Univ. of East Anglia; library: 80,000 books, 700 periodicals; Prin. CORRIENNE PEASGOOD.

City of London College: 71 Whitechapel High St, London, E1 7PL; tel. (20) 7247-2177; e-mail info@clc-london.ac.uk; internet www.clc-london.ac.uk; f. 1979; Bachelors and Masters degrees validated by Univ. of London, Univ. of Wales; library: 2,500 vols; Man. Dir Dr S. YOUSUF; Prin. DAVID J. NIXON.

Colchester Institute: Colchester Campus, Sheepen Rd, Colchester, CO3 3LL; tel. (1206) 712000; e-mail info@colchester.ac.uk; internet www.colchester.ac.uk; 3 campuses; higher nat. certificate, diploma, undergraduate and postgraduate courses validated by Univ. of Essex; Prin. and Chief Exec. ALISON ANDREAS (acting).

College of West Anglia: King's Lynn Campus, Tennyson Ave, King's Lynn, PE30 2QW; tel. (1553) 761144; e-mail enquiries@col-westanglia.ac.uk; internet www.cwa.ac.uk; f. 1894 as King's Lynn Technical School, current name adopted 1998; 4 campuses; offers degrees and HNDs; courses validated by Anglia Ruskin Univ.; Prin. DAVID POMFRET.

Cornwall College: Cornwall College Camborne, Trevenson Rd, Pool, Redruth, TR15 3RD; tel. (1209) 611611; e-mail enquiries@cornwall.ac.uk; internet www.cornwall.ac.uk; f. 1929; 7 campuses; Bachelors and Masters courses validated by Plymouth Univ.; Prin. and CEO AMARJIT BASI.

Craven College: Aireville Campus, Gargrave Rd, Skipton, BD23 1US; tel. (1756) 791411; e-mail enquiries@craven-college.ac.uk; internet www.craven-college.ac.uk; BA (Hons) in fine art validated by the Open Univ.; Prin. ROBERT BELLFIELD.

Croydon College: College Rd, Croydon, CR9 1DX; tel. (20) 8686-5700; e-mail info@croydon.ac.uk; internet www.croydon.ac.uk; Bachelors degrees validated by Univ. of Sussex; 8,000 students; Prin. and Chief Exec. FRANCES WADSWORTH; Dean for Univ. Centre JASON PEMBERTON-BILLING.

Doncaster College: High Melton, Doncaster, DN5 7SZ; tel. (1302) 553553; e-mail he@don.ac.uk; internet www.don.ac.uk; 2 campuses, undergraduate and postgraduate degrees validated by the Univ. of Hull; 1,100 teachers; 20,000 students; Prin. and Chief Exec. GEORGE TROW; publs *UCD Journal of Research and Scholarship*, *USpeak*.

East Riding College: Beverley Campus, Gallows Lane, Beverley, HU17 7DT; e-mail info@eastridingcollege.ac.uk; internet www.eastridingcollege.ac.uk; 3 campuses; diploma courses, Bachelors degree courses; Prin. and Chief Exec. DEREK BRANTON; publ. *Student Life*.

EThames Graduate School: 412–416 Eastern Ave, Ilford, IG2 6NQ; tel. (20) 8518-5190; e-mail admissions@etgs.org.uk; internet etgs.org.uk; schools of business and finance, computing, English, health and social care, hospitality and tourism; degrees awarded by Univ. of Sunderland; Prin. SUSAN J. HINDLEY.

Exeter College: Hele Rd, Exeter, EX4 4JS; tel. (1392) 400500; e-mail info@exe-coll.ac.uk; internet www.exe-coll.ac.uk; f. 1970; Bachelors degrees, postgraduate certificate in education, English language courses; validated by Plymouth Univ., Univ. of Exeter, Univ. of St Mark and St John Plymouth, Kingston Univ.; Prin. RICHARD ATKINS.

Furness College: Channelside, Barrow-in-Furness, LA14 2PJ; tel. (1229) 825017; e-mail info@furness.ac.uk; internet www.furness.ac.uk; undergraduate and postgraduate degrees validated by Univ. of Central Lancashire, Univ. of Cumbria and Lancaster Univ.; Prin. ANNE ATTWOOD.

Gateshead College: Baltic Campus, Quarryfield Rd, Gateshead, NE8 3BE; tel. (191) 490-0300; e-mail info@gateshead.ac.uk; internet www.gateshead.ac.uk; Bachelors degree courses validated by Northumbria Univ., Univ. of Sunderland, Univ. of Teesside; Prin. JUDITH DOYLE.

Grimsby Institute: Nuns Cnr, Grimsby, DN34 5BQ; tel. (1472) 311222; e-mail infocent@grimsby.ac.uk; internet www.grimsby.ac.uk; undergraduate, postgraduate degree programmes; courses validated by Leeds Metropolitan Univ. and Univ. of Hull; Prin. and Chief Exec. SUE MIDDLEHURST; publ. *Journal of Research & Scholarly Output*.

Guildford College: Stoke Rd, Guildford, GU1 1EZ; tel. (1483) 448500; e-mail info@guildford.ac.uk; internet www.guildford.ac.uk; f. 1939; 3 campuses; undergraduate and other college courses validated by London South Bank Univ., Surrey Univ., Univ. of Greenwich; library: 50,000 vols, magazines, video cassettes and DVDs; Prin. and CEO MIKE POTTER.

Harlow College: Velizy Ave, Harlow, CM20 3EZ; tel. (1279) 868000; e-mail reception@harlow-college.ac.uk; internet www.harlow-college.ac.uk; Bachelors degrees validated by Anglia Ruskin Univ.; Prin. KAREN SPENCER.

Havering College of Further and Higher Education: Ardleigh Green Rd Campus, Ardleigh Green Rd, Hornchurch, RM11 2LL; tel. (1708) 455011; e-mail information@havering-college.ac.uk; internet www.havering-college.ac.uk; undergraduate degrees and postgraduate programmes in vocational and academic subjects; validated by the Open University; Prin. and Chief Exec. MARIA THOMPSON.

Kaplan Holborn College: 179–191 Borough High St, London, SE7 8LN; tel. (20) 3740-7889; e-mail international@kaplan.co .uk; internet www.holborncollege.ac.uk; f. 1969 as Holborn College, current name adopted 2005; undergraduate, postgraduate law and business degrees validated by Anglia Ruskin Univ., Univ. of the West of England, Univ. of Wales; library: 10,000 vols; Head of College JENNY BIRCH; Dean TIM HARRIS.

Holy Cross College: Manchester Rd, Bury, BL9 9BB; tel. (161) 762-4500; e-mail information@holycross.ac.uk; internet www .holycross.ac.uk; Bachelors degrees validated by Liverpool Hope Univ. and Edge Hill Univ.; library: 20,000 vols; Prin. DAVID FROST.

Hull College: Queen's Gardens, Chesters Bldg, Hull, HU1 3DG; tel. (1482) 329943; e-mail info@hull-college.ac.uk; internet www .hull-college.ac.uk; BA (Hons) degrees; Chief Exec. GARY WARKE; Prin. GRAHAM TOWSE; publ. *The Review.*

Manchester College: Ashton Old Rd, Openshaw, Manchester, M11 2WH; tel. (161) 909-6655; e-mail enquiries@ themanchestercollege.ac.uk; internet www .themanchestercollege.ac.uk; f. 2008 by merger of Manchester College of Arts and Technology and City College Manchester; fulltime and part-time HNDs and Bachelors degree courses validated by Univ. of Salford; Chief Exec. JOHN THORNHILL; Deputy CEO and Prin. JACK CARNEY.

Middlesbrough College: Dock St, Middlesbrough, TS2 1AD; tel. (1642) 333700; e-mail courseinfo@mbro.ac.uk; internet www.mbro .ac.uk; f. 2002 by merger of Middlesbrough College and Teesside Tertiary College; courses leading to higher national diplomas/ certificates, BA (Hons), BSc (Hons), univ. certificates, professional qualifications; degrees awarded by Teesside Univ.; library: 30,000 vols; 10,000 students; Prin. ZOE LEWIS.

New College Durham: Framwellgate Moor Campus, Durham, DH1 5ES; tel. (191) 375-4000; e-mail help@newdur.ac.uk; internet www.newcollegedurham.ac.uk; f. 1977 by merger of Neville's Cross College and Durham Technical College; higher nat. diplomas/ certificates, degrees and professional qualifications; validated by Teesside Univ.; library: 60,000 vols, 3,000 ebooks, 200 journals; Prin. and Chief Exec. JOHN WIDDOWSON.

New College Nottingham: The Adams Bldg, Stoney St, Nottingham, NG1 1NG; tel. (115) 910-0100; e-mail enquiries@ncn.ac .uk; internet www.ncn.ac.uk; 6 centres; undergraduate courses validated by Nottingham Trent Univ.; Prin. and Chief Exec. DAWN WHITEMORE.

Newham College: East Ham Campus, High St South, London, E6 6ER; tel. (20) 8257-4000; e-mail on-line.enquiries@newham.ac .uk; internet www.newham.ac.uk; f. 1985 by merger of East Ham and West Ham technical colleges; 2 main campuses; courses offered in business, management, combined studies, counselling, professional devt; Prin. and Chief Exec. MARTIN TOLHURST.

North Lindsey College: Kingsway, Scunthorpe, DN17 1AJ; tel. (1724) 281111; e-mail info@northlindsey.ac.uk; internet www.northlindsey.ac.uk; partner college of Univ. of Lincoln; Bachelors degrees validated by Bishop Grosseteste Univ. and Univ. of Lincoln; Prin. ANNE TYRRELL.

South Cheshire College: Dane Bank Ave, Crewe, CW2 8AB; tel. (1270) 654654; e-mail info@scc.ac.uk; internet www.scc.ac.uk; graduate diploma in counselling validated by Manchester Metropolitan Univ.; Prin. and Chief Exec. JASBIR DHESI.

South Essex College: Nethermayne, Basildon, SS16 5NN; tel. (1268) 820130; e-mail learning@southessex.ac.uk; internet www .southessex.ac.uk; f. 2010, by merger of Thurrock and Basildon College and South East Essex College; degrees validated by Univ. of Essex, Univ. of East London, Anglia Ruskin Univ.; campuses in Basildon and Thurrock; Prin. and Chief Exec. ANGELA O'DONOGHUE.

South Thames College: Wandsworth High St, London, SW18 2PP; tel. (20) 8918-7777; e-mail info@south-thames.ac.uk; internet www.south-thames.ac.uk; f. 1895 as Wandsworth Technical Institute; degrees validated by Kingston Univ., London South Bank Univ., Univ. of Cumbria, Christ Church Canterbury Univ.; 21,000 students; Prin. SUE RIMMER.

St Patrick's International College: 15–19 Great Chapel St, London, W1F 8FN; tel. (20) 7287-6664; e-mail info@st-patricks.ac.uk; internet www.st-patricks.ac.uk; f. 1803 as St. Patrick's School, present name and status 1998; Bachelors degree in law awarded by Univ. of London; Prin. and Chief Exec. GIRISH CHANDRA.

St Helens College: Water St, St Helens, WA10 1PP; tel. (1744) 733766; e-mail enquire@sthelens.ac.uk; internet www .sthelens.ac.uk; degree courses validated by Univ. of Central Lancashire, Edge Hill Univ., Liverpool John Moores Univ., Sheffield Hallam Univ., York St John Univ.; library: 50,000 vols; Prin. Dr JETTE BURFORD.

St Mary's College: Shear Brow, Blackburn, BB1 8DX; tel. (1254) 580464; e-mail reception@stmarysblackburn.ac.uk; internet www.stmarysblackburn.ac.uk; honours degree validated by Liverpool Hope Univ.; Prin. F. DIXON.

South Gloucestershire and Stroud College: Stratford Rd, Stroud, GL5 4AH; tel. (1453) 763424; e-mail info@sgscol.ac.uk; internet www.sgscol.ac.uk; f. 2012 by merger of Stroud College and Filton College; Bachelors and Masters courses validated by Univ. of Gloucestershire; library: 14,000 vols; 15,500 students; Prin. and Chief Exec. KEVIN HAMBLIN.

Swindon College: North Star Ave, Swindon, SN2 1DY; tel. (1793) 491591; internet www.swindon-college.ac.uk; degrees validated by Oxford Brookes Univ. and Univ. of Bath; library: 32,000 vols; 9,500 students; Prin. ANDREW MILLER; Deputy Prin. for Finance and Resources NICK LETCHET; Vice-Prin. for Curriculum and Quality JOHN EVANS.

Tresham College of Further and Higher Education: Oakley Rd, Corby, NN17 1NE; tel. (845) 658-8990; e-mail info@tresham.ac .uk; internet www.tresham.ac.uk; f. 1978 by merger of 2 technical colleges in Kettering and Corby, present name and status 1992 by merger of Wellingborough College and Tresham College; degree courses validated by Univ. of Northampton and Univ. of Bedfordshire; courses in engineering, business and management, sport, computing, art and

design, accounting; 10,000 students; Chair. E. R. BAINES; Prin. and Chief Exec. MARK SILVERMAN.

Tyne Metropolitan College: Battle Hill Dr., Wallsend, NE28 9NL; tel. (191) 229-5000; e-mail enquiries@tynemet.ac.uk; internet www.tynemet.ac.uk; campuses in Benton and N Shields; higher education courses in education and teaching, therapeutic counselling; Prin. and CEO JON VINCENT; Deputy Prin. for Finance and Corporate Devt ANN-MARIE CROZIER; Deputy Prin. for Curriculum and Business Devt AUDREY KINGHAM.

University Campus Suffolk: Neptune Quay, Ipswich, IP4 1QJ; tel. (1473) 338000; e-mail info@ucs.ac.uk; internet www.ucs.ac .uk; f. 2007; centres in Bury St Edmunds, Great Yarmouth, Lowestoft and Otley; degrees jtly validated by Univ. of East Anglia and Univ. of Essex; Provost and CEO Prof. MIKE SAKS; Head of Learning Resources STEVE PHILIPS.

Uxbridge College: Park Rd, Uxbridge, UB8 1NQ; tel. (1895) 853333; e-mail enquiries@ uxbridgecollege.ac.uk; internet www .uxbridge.ac.uk; f. 1965; courses validated by Thames Valley Univ. and Univ. of Greenwich; Prin. LARAINE SMITH.

Wakefield College: Margaret St, Wakefield, WF1 2DH; tel. (1924) 789789; e-mail admissions@wakefield.ac.uk; internet www .wakefield.ac.uk; f. 1868; Bachelors degrees validated by Leeds Metropolitan Univ., Teesside Univ., Univ. of Huddersfield; 10,000 students; Prin. SAM WRIGHT.

West London College: Parliament House, 35 North Row, Mayfair, London, W1K 6DB; tel. (20) 7491-1841; e-mail courses@ westlondoncollege.com; internet www .westlondoncollege.com; Bachelors degree validated by Heriot-Watt Univ.; Prin. PAUL SMITH; Librarian AIDHA BABIRYE.

Wiltshire College: Cocklebury Rd, Chippenham, SN15 3QD; tel. (1249) 464644; e-mail info@wiltshire.ac.uk; internet www .wiltshire.ac.uk; f. 2000, merger with Salisbury College 2008; 4 campuses; Bachelors degrees validated by Bournemouth Univ., Univ. of Bath; library: 20,000 vols, incl. books, magazines, DVDs; 10,000 students; Prin. DIANE DALE.

Yeovil College: Univ. Centre, 91 Preston Rd, Yeovil, BA20 2DN; tel. (1935) 845454; e-mail ucy@yeovil.ac.uk; internet www.yeovil .ac.uk; f. 1974; Bachelors degrees validated by Bournemouth Univ., Univ. of Gloucestershire, Univ. of the West of England; all higher education courses taught at Univ. Centre; Prin. JOHN EVANS.

AGRICULTURE

Askham Bryan College: Askham Bryan, York, YO23 3FR; tel. (1904) 772277; e-mail enquiries@askham-bryan.ac.uk; internet www.askham-bryan.ac.uk; f. 1948 as Yorkshire Institute of Agriculture; Bachelors degree validated by Harper Adams Univ.; Prin. and Chief Exec. LIZ PHILIP.

Brooksby Melton College: Melton Campus, Melton Mowbray, LE13 0HJ; tel. (1664) 855444; e-mail info@brooksbymelton.ac.uk; internet www.brooksbymelton.ac.uk; 4 campuses; ind. college specializing in animal care and agriculture, also performing arts college; Bachelors degrees validated by Univ. of Bolton; Prin. CHRIS BALL.

Hadlow College: Hadlow Campus, Hadlow, Tonbridge, TN11 0AL; tel. (1732) 850551; e-mail enquiries@hadlow.ac.uk; internet www.hadlow.ac.uk; f. 1969 by merging Sittingbourne Farm Institute and Swanley

Horticultural Institute; Bachelors degrees validated by Univ. of Greenwich; library: 20,000 vols; Prin. and Chief Exec. PAUL HANNAN.

Moulton College: West St, Moulton, NN3 7RR; tel. (1604) 491131; e-mail enquiries@ moulton.ac.uk; internet www.moulton.ac.uk; Bachelors and Masters degrees validated by Univ. of Northampton; Prin. STEPHEN M. DAVIES.

Reaseheath College: Nantwich, CW5 6DF; tel. (1270) 625131; e-mail enquiries@ reaseheath.ac.uk; internet www.reaseheath .ac.uk; f. 1921 as Cheshire School of Agriculture, present name and status 1967; Bachelors degrees validated by Harper Adams Univ. and Univ. of Chester; Prin. MEREDYDD DAVID.

Writtle College: Chelmsford, CM1 3RR; tel. (1245) 424200; e-mail info@writtle.ac.uk; internet www.writtle.ac.uk; f. 1893; Bachelors and Masters degrees validated by Univ. of Essex; library: 40,000 vols, 300 periodical titles; Prin. and CEO Dr STEVE WAITE; Library Head RACHEL HEWINGS.

ART AND DESIGN

Christie's Education: 153 Great Titchfield St, London, W1W 5BD; tel. (20) 7665-4350; e-mail london@christies.edu; internet www .christies.edu; degrees validated by Univ. of Glasgow; Academic Dir Dr M. A. MICHAEL.

City and Guilds of London Art School: 124 Kennington Park Rd, London, SE11 4DJ; tel. (20) 7735-2306; e-mail info@ cityandguildsartschool.ac.uk; internet www .cityandguildsartschool.ac.uk; f. 1879; BA (Hons) degree courses in painting, sculpture, fine arts; library: 5,500 vols, 750 films and cinema titles, 1,400 slides, 30 journal subscriptions; Prin. TONY CARTER.

Cleveland College of Art & Design: Green Lane, Linthorpe, Middlesbrough, TS5 7RJ; tel. (1642) 288000; internet www.ccad.ac.uk; partnership with Univ. of Teeside; library: 25,000 books, 100 magazines and journals, 1,600 DVDs and video cassettes; Prin. MARTIN RABY.

Courtauld Institute of Art: part of University of London (see entry).

Hereford College of Arts: Folly Lane, Hereford, HR1 1LT; tel. (1432) 273359; e-mail enquiries@hca.ac.uk; internet www .hca.ac.uk; f. 1851; Bachelors degrees and Masters degrees validated by Univ. of Wales and Univ. of Wales Trinity Saint David respectively; library: 24,000 books, 80 specialist journals; Prin. and Chief Exec. RICHARD HEATLY.

Inchbald School of Design: 7 Eaton Gate, London, SW1W 9BA; tel. (20) 7730-5508; e-mail interiors@inchbald.co.uk; internet www.inchbald.co.uk; f. 1960; 2 campuses; ind. school of design offering Masters degree validated by Univ. of Wales; Prin. JACQUELINE DUNCAN.

Leeds College of Art: Blenheim Walk, Leeds, LS2 9AQ; tel. (113) 202-8000; e-mail info@leeds-art.ac.uk; internet www.leeds-art .ac.uk; f. 1846 as Leeds School of Art; Bachelors and Masters degrees validated by Open Univ.; library: 45,000 vols, 156 journals; Prin. SIMONE WONNACOTT.

Northumbria Design: Northumbria Univ., City Campus East, Newcastle upon Tyne, NE1 8ST; tel. (191) 227-4913; e-mail de .admissions@northumbria.ac.uk; internet www.northumbria.ac.uk/sd/academic/scd; attached to Northumbria Univ.; Bachelors,

Masters and doctoral degree courses in design, fashion management, interior design; 120 teachers; 1,600 students; Dean STEVEN KYFFIN.

Norwich School of Art and Design: Francis House, 3–7 Redwell St, Norwich, NR2 4SN; tel. (1603) 610-561; e-mail info@ nuca.ac.uk; internet www.nuca.ac.uk; f. 1846 became Norwich University College of the Arts in 2008; undergraduate, postgraduate and doctoral courses in arts, design and media disciplines; library: 30,000 vols, 80,000 photographs, 2,500 DVDs, 100 journals; 1,500 students; Prin. JOHN LAST.

Plymouth College of Art: Tavistock Pl., Plymouth, PL4 8AT; tel. (1752) 203434; e-mail enquiries@plymouthart.ac.uk; internet www.plymouthart.ac.uk; f. 1856 as Plymouth School of Art; Bachelors and Masters degrees validated by Open Univ.; library: 20,000 vols, subscriptions to 130 journals, magazines and newspapers; Prin. Prof. ANDREW BREWERTON.

Prince's School of Traditional Arts: 19–22 Charlotte Rd, London, EC2A 3SG; tel. (20) 7613-8500; e-mail enquiry@psta.org.uk; internet www.psta.org.uk; f. 2004; research and postgraduate degrees in traditional arts validated by Univ. of Wales; Chair. Sir DAVID GREEN; Dir Dr KHALED AZZAM.

Ravensbourne College of Design and Communication: Ravensbourne, 6 Penrose Way, London, SE10 0EW; tel. (20) 3040-3500; e-mail info@rave.ac.uk; internet www .ravensbourne.ac.uk; f. 1962; Dir and CEO Prof. ROBIN BAKER.

Royal Academy Schools: Burlington House, Piccadilly, London, W1J 0BD; tel. (20) 7300-5857; e-mail schools@ royalacademy.org.uk; internet www .royalacademy.org.uk/raschools; f. 1768; offers three-year, full-time postgraduate fine arts course; Head of Schools ELIZA BONHAM CARTER.

Royal College of Art: Kensington Gore, London, SW7 2EU; tel. (20) 7590-4444; e-mail info@rca.ac.uk; internet www.rca.ac .uk; f. 1837, awarded Charter 1967 empowering it to grant its own degrees; postgraduate instn receiving direct grant from Higher Education Funding Ccl for Architectural Asscn; schools of architecture, communication, design, fine art, humanities, material; library: 70,000 vols, 120 periodical subscriptions; Visitor HRH The DUKE OF EDINBURGH; Provost Sir JAMES DYSON; Rector and Vice-Provost Dr PAUL THOMPSON; Registrar CORINNE SMITH.

School of Architecture, Architectural Association: 36 Bedford Sq., London, WC1B 3ES; tel. (20) 7887-4000; e-mail info@aaschool.ac.uk; internet www.aaschool .ac.uk; f. 1847; 1-year foundation course; 5-year course leading to AA Dipl.; postgraduate courses and research in architecture, building conservation, conservation (landscape and gardens), emergent technologies and design, environment and energy, histories and theories of architecture, housing and urbanism, landscape urbanism; campus at Hooke Park; library: 46,000 vols, 10,000 student drawings, paintings, 500,000 images, incl. lantern slides, transparencies, negatives and prints, DVD colln of lectures, confs, symposia held at Architectural Asscn; Dir BRETT STEELE; publ. AA Files (2 a year).

Slade School of Fine Art: Univ. College London, Gower St, London, WC1E 6BT; tel. (20) 7679-2313; e-mail slade.enquiries@ucl.ac .uk; internet www.ucl.ac.uk/slade; f. 1871; attached to Univ. College London; Bachelors, Masters and doctoral degrees in fine art; 42 teachers; Dir and Slade Prof. Prof. SUSAN

COLLINS; publ. Rubric (4 a year, print and online).

Somerset College: Wellington Rd, Taunton, TA1 5AX; tel. (1823) 366366; e-mail enquiries@somerset.ac.uk; internet www .somerset.ac.uk; f. 1856 as School of Art and Science; Bachelors degrees validated by the Open Univ. and Univ. of Plymouth; Prin. and Chief Exec. RACHEL DAVIES.

Sotheby's Institute of Art: 30 Bedford Sq., Bloomsbury, London, WC1B 3EE; tel. (20) 7462-3232; e-mail admissions@ sothebysinstitute.com; internet www .sothebysinstitute.com; campuses in New York, Los Angeles and Singapore; Masters degrees in art business, contemporary art, contemporary design, east Asian art, fine and decorative art, photography; degrees validated by Univ. of Manchester; library: 15,000 vols, 50 current journal titles; Dir Dr JOS HACKFORTH-JONES; Academic Dir Dr MEGAN ALDRICH.

BUSINESS AND COMMERCE

Ashridge Business School: Berkhamsted, HP4 1NS; tel. (1442) 843491; e-mail contact@ ashridge.org.uk; internet www.ashridge.org .uk; f. 1959 as Ashridge Management College, present status 2008; MBA, MSc, doctorate, diploma and executive devt programmes; 90 full-time teachers; 6,000 students; library: 8,000 vols, spec. colln incl. Ashridge learning guides; CEO KAI PETERS; Library and Information Services Man. LORRAINE OLIVER; publs 360°, The Ashridge Journal (2 a year), Converse (1 a year).

Chartered Management Institute: see under Learned Societies.

College of Estate Management: Whiteknights, Reading, RG6 6AW; tel. (118) 921-4696; e-mail enquiries@cem.ac.uk; internet www.cem.ac.uk; f. 1919, Royal Charter 1922; Bachelors and Masters degrees in real estate and construction; Prin. and CEO ASHLEY WHEATON.

European Business School London: Regent's College, Inner Circle, Regent's Park, London, NW1 4NS; tel. (20) 7487-7505; e-mail ebsl@regents.ac.uk; internet www.ebslondon.ac.uk; f. 1979 in UK, centres also in Germany, France, Italy, Japan, Russia, Spain and USA; BA (Hons) degree in European Business Administration, and other degrees with business and language mix; summer courses; library: 25,500 vols; 750 full-time students; Dir Prof. MICHAEL SCRIVEN.

European College of Business and Management: 69–71 Great Eastern St, London, EC2A 3HU; tel. (20) 7749-5930; e-mail study@eurocollege.org.uk; internet www .ecbm-london.de; f. 1988 as British-German School for Vocational Training, current name adopted 2000; Bachelors and Masters courses in business and management; centre in Germany; Dir RICHARD BILLS; Treas. PHIL SAMPSON.

European School of Economics: 8/9 Grosvenor Pl., London, SW1X 7SH; tel. (20) 7245-6148; e-mail info@eselondon.ac.uk; internet www.eselondon.ac.uk; private college of higher education in int. business; Bachelors, Masters, MBA, and certificate programmes; validated by Univ. of Buckingham; Pres. ELIO D'ANNA.

Henley Business School: Greenlands Campus, Henley-on-Thames, RG9 3AU; tel. (1491) 571454; e-mail pressoffice@reading.ac .uk; internet www.henley.reading.ac.uk; f.

1945; attached to Univ. of Reading; Bachelors, Masters and doctoral degrees; campuses at Whiteknights, Reading; library: 18,000 vols; 150 teachers; 5,000 students; Dean Prof. JOHN BOARD; publ. *Journal of General Management* (4 a year).

Kensington College of Business: Wesley House, 4 Wild Court, London, WC2B 4AU; tel. (20) 7404-6330; e-mail kcb@kensingtoncoll.ac.uk; internet www.kensingtoncoll.ac.uk; f. 1982; Bachelors and Masters degrees validated by Glyndŵr Univ., Univ. of London and Univ. of Wales; Prin. IAN PIRIE.

LCA Business School: 19 Charter House St, London, EC1N 6RA; tel. (20) 7400-6789; e-mail enquiry@lca.anglia.ac.uk; internet www.londoncollege.org; f. 2000 as London College of Accountancy; attached to Anglia Ruskin Univ.; Chair. RAVI GILL; Prin. DAVID SEXTON.

London School of Commerce: Chaucer House, White Hart Yard, London, SE1 1NX; tel. (20) 7357-0077; e-mail info@lsclondon.co.uk; internet www.lsclondon.co.uk; Bachelors and MBA courses; assoc. college of Cardiff Metropolitan Univ.; Dean Prof. GEOFFREY LANCASTER.

Manchester Business School: Booth St West, Manchester, M15 6PB; tel. (161) 820-8343; e-mail ug-admissions@manchester.ac.uk; internet www.mbs.ac.uk; f. 2004 by merger of Institute of Innovation Research, Victoria Univ. of Manchester's School of Accounting and Finance, UMIST's Manchester School of Management and Manchester Business School; attached to Univ. of Manchester; courses in accounting and finance, business systems, marketing, int. business and strategy and management; 200 teachers; 2,000 students; Head of School Prof. FIONA DEVINE.

Oxford Business College: 65 George St, Oxford, OX1 2BQ; tel. (1865) 791908; e-mail admissions@oxfordbusinesscollege.co.uk; internet www.oxfordbusinesscollege.net; f. 1985; Prin. DAVID FOGG.

Regent's Business School London: Inner Circle, Regent's Park, London, NW1 4NS; tel. (20) 7487-7505; e-mail rbsl@regents.ac.uk; internet www.rbslondon.ac.uk; f. 1997; foundation courses, undergraduate and postgraduate degrees in business, finance and management; 60 teachers; 430 students; Academic Dir Dr RICHARD GREGSON.

Resource Development International: 1A Brandon Lane, Coventry, CV3 3RD; tel. (24) 7651-5700; e-mail info@rdi.co.uk; internet www.rdi.co.uk; f. 1990; MBA degrees validated by Anglia Ruskin Univ., Univ. of Bradford, Univ. of Sunderland; CEO Dr PHILIP HALLAM.

MEDICINE, THERAPY, COUNSELLING AND HEALTHCARE

Anglo-European College of Chiropractic: 13–15 Parkwood Rd, Bournemouth, BH5 2DF; tel. (1202) 436200; e-mail aecc@aecc.ac.uk; internet www.aecc.ac.uk; f. 1965; Bachelors degrees validated by Bournemouth Univ.; library: 10,000 vols, 100 current periodicals; Prin. Prof. HAYMO THIEL.

College of Integrated Chinese Medicine: 19 Castle St, Reading, RG1 7SB; tel. (118) 950-8880; e-mail admin@cicm.org.uk; internet www.acupuncturecollege.org.uk; f. 1993; BSc (Hons) Acupuncture validated by Kingston Univ.; 40 teachers; Prin. and Co-Founder ANGELA HICKS; Prin. and Co-Founder JOHN HICKS; Dean PETER MOLE; publ. *Jing Shen*.

College of Medical and Dental Sciences: Edgbaston, Birmingham, B15 2TT; tel. (121) 414-3858; e-mail mdsenquiries@contacts.bham.ac.uk; internet www.medicine.bham.ac.uk; f. 2008; attached to Univ. of Birmingham; Bachelors, Masters and doctoral degrees in dentistry, medicine, nursing, pharmacy, physiotherapy, public health; schools of cancer sciences, clinical and experimental medicine, dentistry, health and population sciences, and immunity and infection; Head Prof. LAWRENCE YOUNG.

College of Osteopaths: 13 Furzehill Rd, Borehamwood, WD6 2DG; tel. (20) 8905-1937; e-mail admin@collegeofosteopaths.ac.uk; internet www.collegeofosteopaths.ac.uk; f. 1948; Bachelors and Masters in osteopathy in collaboration with Middlesex Univ.; Prin. PAT HAMILTON.

Conductive College: Cannon Hill House, Russell Rd, Moseley, Birmingham, B13 8RD; tel. (121) 442-5556; e-mail mmccann@conductive-education.org.uk; internet www.conductivecollege.org.uk; f. 1997, current name adopted 2011; attached to National Institute of Conductive Education; BA (Hons) Conductive Education from Univ. of Wolverhampton.

European School of Osteopathy: Boxley House, The Street, Boxley, Maidstone, ME14 3DZ; tel. (1622) 671558; e-mail info@eso.ac.uk; internet www.eso.ac.uk; f. 1965; integrated Masters degree in osteopathy validated by Univ. of Greenwich; library: 7,500 vols; Prin. ADRIAN BARNES.

Hull York Medical School: John Hughlings Jackson Bldg, University of York, Heslington York, YO10 5DD; Cottingham Rd, Hull, HU6 7RX; tel. (1482) 463074; e-mail admissions@hyms.ac.uk; internet www.hyms.ac.uk; f. 2003; partnership between Univ. of Hull and Univ. of York; medical school with undergraduate, postgraduate courses; library: 2m. vols, 20,000 journal titles; Dean Prof. TREVOR SHELDON; publ. *Pioneer*.

International College of Oriental Medicine: Van Buren House, Green Hedges Ave, East Grinstead, RH19 1DZ; tel. (1342) 313106; e-mail info@orientalmed.ac.uk; internet www.orientalmed.ac.uk; f. 1972; BSc (Hons) in acupuncture validated by Univ. of Greenwich; Prin. SAM PATEL.

McTimoney College of Chiropractic: McTimoney House, 1 Kimber Rd, Abingdon, OX14 1BZ; tel. (1235) 468575; e-mail courseoffice@mctimoney-college.ac.uk; internet www.mctimoney-college.ac.uk; f. 1982; Bachelors and Masters degrees in chiropractic validated by BPP Univ.; Prin. Prof. CHRISTINA CUNLIFFE.

Metanoia Institute: 13 Gunnersbury Ave, Ealing, London, W5 3XD; tel. (20) 8579-2505; e-mail info@metanoia.ac.uk; internet www.metanoia.ac.uk; Bachelors and Masters degrees validated by Middlesex Univ.; CEO Prof. SHEILA OWEN-JONES.

National Institute of Medical Herbalists: Clover House, James Court, South St, Exeter, EX1 1EE; tel. (1392) 426022; e-mail info@nimh.org.uk; internet www.nimh.org.uk; f. 1864 as Nat. Asscn of Medical Herbalists; BSc in herbal medicine; publ. *Journal of Herbal Medicine* (4 a year).

School of Psychotherapy and Counselling Psychology: Regent's Park, London, NW1 4NS; tel. (20) 7487-7505; e-mail spc@regents.ac.uk; internet www.spc.ac.uk; f. 1990; attached to Regent's College; validation by Univ. of Wales; Head Dr JOHN NUTTALL (acting).

Sherwood Psychotherapy Training Institute: Thiskney House, 2 St James Terrace, Nottingham, NG1 6FW; tel. (115) 844-7904; e-mail enquiries@spti.net; internet www.spti.net; f. 1987; BSc and MSc degrees in counselling and psychotherapy; Dir ROSEMARY LANGFORD-BELLABY.

MUSIC, DANCE AND DRAMA

Academy of Contemporary Music: Rodboro Bldgs, Bridge St, Guildford, GU1 4SB; tel. (1483) 500800; e-mail enquiries@acm.ac.uk; internet www.acm.ac.uk; music industry education; degree courses in music; other courses in music production; Founding Dir PHIL BROOKES.

Academy of Live and Recorded Arts: Studio 24, Royal Victoria Patriotic Bldg, John Archer Way, London, SW18 3SX; tel. (20) 8870-6475; e-mail info@alra.co.uk; internet www.alra.co.uk; f. 1979; courses accredited by Nat. Council for Drama Training; centre in Wigan; Chair. HARRY COWD; Co-Dir CLIVE DUNCAN; Co-Dir ADRIAN HALL.

Arts Educational Schools London: Cone Ripman House, 14 Bath Rd, Chiswick, London, W4 1LY; tel. (20) 8987-6666; internet www.artsed.co.uk; f. 1939 as the Cone Ripman School; Bachelors and Masters degrees validated by City Univ. London; Prin. JANE HARRISON.

Bird College: The Centre, 27 Station Rd, Sidcup, DA15 7E; tel. (20) 8300-6004; internet www.birdcollege.co.uk; f. 1946; performing arts college; offers degrees, foundation courses and diplomas validated by Univ. of Greenwich, Trinity College London; Prin. and Chief Exec. SHIRLEY COEN; publ. *Action Network Magazine*.

Birmingham School of Acting: Millennium Point, Curzon St, Birmingham, B4 7XG; tel. (121) 331-7220; e-mail info@bsa.bcu.ac.uk; internet www.bcu.ac.uk/pme/school-of-acting; f. 1936; attached to Faculty of Performance, Media and English at Birmingham City Univ.; specialist instn offering full-time higher education courses at undergraduate and postgraduate level; Dir STEPHEN SIMMS.

Brighton Institute of Modern Music: 38–42 Brunswick St West, Hove, BN3 1EL; tel. (1273) 626666; e-mail info@bimm.co.uk; internet www.bimm.co.uk; 4 centres in Brighton and Bristol, 10 core courses in various areas; degree, diploma and certificate; validated by Univ. of Sussex; Prin. VASEEMA HAMILTON.

Conservatoire for Dance and Drama: Tavistock House, Tavistock Sq., London, WC1H 9JJ; tel. (20) 7387-5101; e-mail info@cdd.ac.uk; internet www.cdd.ac.uk; f. 2001; comprises 8 schools listed below; not directly involved in training students but acts as an admin. unit for the 8 schools; library: 51,000 vols, 78 titles of print and electronic periodicals, 1,200 CDs, 2,750 DVDs, large colln of photographs; 271 teachers (58 full-time, 213 part-time), 1,120 students (960 undergraduate, 160 graduate); Prin. EDWARD KEMP; Prin. Prof. VERONICA LEWIS; Exec. Dir JULIE CROFTS; Academic Registrar Dr SIMON PARKER..

Attached Schools:

Bristol Old Vic Theatre School: 2 Downside Rd, Clifton, Bristol, BS8 2XF; tel. (117) 973-3535; e-mail enquiries@oldvic.ac.uk; internet www.oldvic.ac.uk; f. 1946; Bachelors and Masters degrees validated by Univ. of the West of England; Prin. PAUL RUMMER.

Central School of Ballet: 10 Herbal Hill, Clerkenwell Rd, London, EC1R 5EG; tel.

(20) 7837-6332; e-mail info@csbschool.co.uk; internet www.centralschoolofballet.co.uk; f. 1982; Bachelors in professional dance and performance and Masters in choreography; library of 1,500 vols, 1,000 periodicals, 50 CDs, 350 DVDs; 21 teachers (10 full-time, 11 part-time); 112 students (110 undergraduate, 2 graduate); Dir SARA MATTHEWS; Deputy Dir WILLIAM GLASSMAN.

Circus Space: Coronet St, London, N1 6HD; tel. (20) 7613-4141; e-mail info@circusspace.co.uk; internet www.circusspace.co.uk; BA (Honours) in Circus Arts validated by the Univ. of Kent; library of 816 bound vols, 11 titles of periodicals, 123 CDs, 130 DVDs, several photographs; Charlie Holland Book Colln; 46 teachers; 58 students; Registrar TONY CULLEN; Head of Studies JOANNA McPHERSON; Administrator JODIE DIAZ.

London Academy of Music and Dramatic Art: 155 Talgarth Rd, London, W14 9DA; tel. (20) 8834-0500; e-mail enquiries@lamda.org.uk; internet www.lamda.org.uk; f. 1861; professional theatrical training, acting and stage management; 22 teachers; 259 students; Prin. JOANNA READ.

London Contemporary Dance School: The Place, 17 Duke's Rd, London, WC1H 9PY; tel. (20) 7121-1020; e-mail info@theplace.org.uk; internet www.lcds.ac.uk; f. 1966; BA (Hons), postgraduate diploma, MA in contemporary dance; undergraduate course validated by Univ. of Kent; 24 teachers; Dir Prof. VERONICA LEWIS.

Northern School of Contemporary Dance: 98 Chapeltown Rd, Leeds, LS7 4BH; tel. (113) 219-3000; e-mail info@nscd.ac.uk; internet www.nscd.ac.uk; f. 1986; Bachelors in performing arts: contemporary dance and choreography; library of 12,148 vols; 20 teachers; 212 students; Prin. JANET SMITH; Librarian SAMANTHA KING.

Rambert School of Ballet and Contemporary Dance: Clifton Lodge, St Margaret's Dr., Twickenham, TW1 1QN; tel. (20) 8892-9960; e-mail info@rambertschool.org.uk; internet www.rambertschool.org.uk; f. 1920; Bachelors in ballet and contemporary dance and Masters in advanced dance performance with specialization in ritual and related somatic studies; library of 2,135 vols, 324 audiovisual items (63 video cassettes, 76 CDs, 185 DVDs); 14 teachers (6 full-time, 8 part-time); 110 students (106 undergraduate, 4 graduate); Prin. and Artistic Dir Dr ROSS McKIM.

Royal Academy of Dramatic Art (RADA): 62–64 Gower St, London, WC1E 6ED; tel. (20) 7636-7076; e-mail enquiries@rada.ac.uk; internet www.rada.ac.uk; f. 1904; vocational training for actors, stage managers, directors, designers and technical stage craft specialists; library of 30,000 vols, incl. 10,000 plays, 1,000 video cassettes, 500 DVDs; Dir EDWARD KEMP.

Guildford School of Acting: Stag Hill Campus, Guildford, GU2 7XH; tel. (1483) 684040; e-mail gsaenquiries@gsa.surrey.ac.uk; internet www.gsauk.org; f. 1935 as Grant-Bellairs School of Dance and Drama, current name adopted 1964; Bachelors and Masters degrees; subsidiary company of Univ. of Surrey; Head TERRIE FENDER.

Guildhall School of Music and Drama: Silk St, Barbican, London, EC2Y 8DT; tel. (20) 7628-2571; e-mail info@gsmd.ac.uk; internet www.gsmd.ac.uk; f. 1880; BMus degree, Masters degrees in composition, music, leadership, performance; 300 teachers; 900 students; Prin. Prof. BARRY IFE.

Italia Conti Academy of Theatre Arts: Italia Conti House, 23 Goswell Rd, London, EC1M 7AJ; tel. (20) 7608-0044; e-mail admin@italiaconti.com; internet www.italiaconti.com; f. 1911; Bachelors degree in acting validated by Univ. of East London; Prin. A. M. SHEWARD.

Leeds College of Music: 3 Quarry Hill, Leeds, LS2 7PD; tel. (113) 222-3400; e-mail enquiries@lcm.ac.uk; internet www.lcm.ac.uk; f. 1965 as Leeds Music Centre; higher and further education courses in jazz, classical and popular music, music production; Prin. PHILIP MEADEN.

Liverpool Institute for the Performing Arts: Mount St, Liverpool, L1 9HF; tel. (151) 330-3000; e-mail reception@lipa.ac.uk; internet www.lipa.ac.uk; f. 1996; Bachelors degrees validated by Liverpool John Moores Univ.; Prin. and CEO MARK FEATHERSTONE-WITTY.

London Studio Centre: 5 Nether St, Tally Ho cnr, North Finchley, London, N1 9AB; tel. (20) 7837-7741; e-mail info@londonstudiocentre.org; internet www.londonstudiocentre.org; f. 1978; Bachelors degree in theatre dance validated by Middlesex Univ.; Dir and CEO NIC ESPINOSA; Librarian FIONA COMPTON.

Mountview Academy of Theatre Arts: Clarendon Rd, London, N22 6XF; tel. (20) 8881-2201; e-mail enquiries@mountview.org.uk; internet www.mountview.org.uk; Bachelors and Masters degrees in acting, direction, production; Prin. STEPHEN JAMESON.

Rose Bruford College of Theatre and Performance: Lamorbey Park, Burnt Oak Lane, Sidcup, DA15 9DF; tel. (20) 8308-2600; e-mail enquiries@bruford.ac.uk; internet www.bruford.ac.uk; f. 1951; MPhil and PhD research degrees validated by Univ. of London; Hons degree in professional acting and theatre practice validated by Univ. of Manchester; Prin. and CEO Prof. MICHAEL EARLEY.

Royal Academy of Dance: 36 Battersea Sq., London, SW11 3RA; tel. (20) 7326-8000; e-mail info@rad.org.uk; internet www.rad.org.uk; f. 1920; Bachelors and Masters degrees in dance validated by Univ. of Surrey; centres in Wales and Scotland; Chief Exec. LUKE RITTNER; publs *Dance Gazette*, *UK & Ireland diary* (3 a year).

Royal Academy of Music: see University of London.

Royal Central School of Speech & Drama: Eton Ave, London, NW3 3HY; tel. (20) 7722-8183; e-mail enquiries@cssd.ac.uk; internet www.cssd.ac.uk; f. 1906; attached to Univ. of London; undergraduate, postgraduate, PhD and research courses in art, design and the performing arts, in education and in therapy; 55 teachers; Prin. Prof. GAVIN HENDERSON.

Royal College of Music: Prince Consort Rd, S Kensington, London, SW7 2BS; tel. (20) 7591-4300; e-mail info@rcm.ac.uk; internet www.rcm.ac.uk; f. 1882; BMus (Hons) degree, BSc in Physics with musical performance; Masters and Doctorate in music; library: see under Libraries and Archives; Dir Prof. COLIN LAWSON; publ. *Upbeat* (3 a year).

Royal Northern College of Music: 124 Oxford Rd, Manchester, M13 9RD; tel. (161) 907-5200; e-mail info@rncm.ac.uk; internet www.rncm.ac.uk; f. 1973; BMus (Hons) in association with Univ. of Manchester; the Graduate School in Music; library: contains extensive colln of MSS, reference works, gramophone records, cassettes, CDs, video cassettes, periodicals, and important archive material incl. an historical instrument colln;

450 teachers; 700 students; Prin. Prof. LINDA MERRICK.

Trinity Laban Conservatoire of Music and Dance: King Charles Court, Old Royal Naval College, London, SE10 9JF; tel. (20) 8305-4444; e-mail info@tcm.ac.uk; internet www.trinitylaban.ac.uk; f. 2005 by merger of Trinity College of Music and Laban; Bachelors and Masters degrees in music and dance; Prin. Prof. ANTHONY BOWNE; Dir of Dance MIRELLA BARTRIP; Dir of Music CLAIRE MERA-NELSON; publ. *Dance Theatre Journal* (4 a year).

SCIENCE AND TECHNOLOGY

British Institute of Technology and E-Commerce: 252–262 Romford Rd, London, E7 9HZ; tel. (20) 8552-3071; e-mail info@bite.ac.uk; internet bite.ac.uk; f. 2000; Bachelors, Masters, MBAs and other professional qualifications; degrees validated by Univ. of Wales; CEO Prof. MUHAMMAD FARMER; Prin. Dr JAMES MacASKILL; publ. *e-Britain*.

Camborne School of Mines: Penryn Campus, Penryn, TR10 9FE; tel. (1326) 371800; e-mail cornwall@exeter.ac.uk; internet emps.exeter.ac.uk/csm; f. 1888; attached to College of Engineering, Mathematics and Physical Sciences, Univ. of Exeter; undergraduate, postgraduate and research degree programmes in geology, mining, minerals processing and renewable energy; library: 30,000 vols; Head Prof. HYLKE J. GLASS.

CECOS London College: 59 Compton Rd, Islington, London, N1 2YT; tel. (20) 7359-3316; e-mail info@cecos.co.uk; internet www.cecos.co.uk; f. 1998; courses in information technology, business admin., computer sciences; Dir Dr KEITH SHARP.

Farnborough College of Technology: Farnborough Campus, Boundary Rd, Farnborough, GU14 6SB; tel. (1252) 405555; e-mail info@farn-ct.ac.uk; internet www.farn-ct.ac.uk; f. 1957; 2 campuses, degrees validated by Univ. of Surrey; Prin. CHRISTINE SLAYMAKER.

National Computing Centre Education: Wilmslow Rd, Manchester, M20 2EZ; tel. (161) 438-6200; e-mail customer.service@nccedu.com; internet www.nccedu.com; f. 1966; courses in business studies, business admin., computing and information systems; degrees validated by Univ. of Wales, Univ. of Greenwich and Univ. of Hertfordshire; centres in Asia (incl. Hong Kong), Africa, Middle East; Man. Dir Prof. FELIX STRAVENS.

National Film and Television School: Beaconsfield Studios, Station Rd, Beaconsfield, HP9 1LG; tel. (1494) 671234; e-mail info@nfts.co.uk; internet www.nftsfilm-tv.ac.uk; f. 1971 as Nat. Film School; MA degrees in film and television production validated by Royal College of Art; Dir NIK POWELL.

SAE Institute: 297 Kingsland Rd, London, E8 4DD; tel. (20) 7923-9159; e-mail london@sae.edu; internet london.sae.edu; f. 1985; Bachelors degrees validated by Middlesex Univ.; campuses in Oxford, Liverpool, Glasgow; Man. LUCA BARASSI; publ. *SAE Magazine*.

THEOLOGY AND RELIGIOUS STUDIES

All Nations Christian College: Easneye, Ware, SG12 8LX; tel. (1920) 443500; internet www.allnations.ac.uk; f. 1971 by merger of 3 missionary colleges; Bachelors and Masters degrees validated by the Open Univ.; library: 50,000 books, papers, maps and audiovisual items; Exec. Dir MIKE WALL.

Cambridge Theological Federation: Wesley House, Jesus Lane, Cambridge, CB5

8BQ; tel. (1223) 741055; e-mail general-enquiries@theofed.cam.ac.uk; internet www.theofed.cam.ac.uk; f. 1972; Bachelors and Masters degrees validated by Anglia Ruskin Univ. and Cambridge Univ.; Registrar ROWENA SMALL; Librarian Dr CAROL REEKIE.

Centre for Youth Ministry: Trinity Business Centre, Stonehill Green, Swindon, SN5 7DG; tel. (1793) 418336; e-mail enquiries@ centreforyouthministry.ac.uk; internet www .centreforyouthministry.ac.uk; Bachelors degrees validated by Staffordshire Univ., Univ. of Gloucestershire; centres in Wales and Ireland; CEO NICK SHEPHERD.

Cliff College: Calver, Hope Valley, S32 3XG; tel. (1246) 584200; e-mail reception@ cliffcollege.ac.uk; internet www.cliffcollege .ac.uk; Bachelors and Masters degrees accredited by Univ. of Manchester; library: 30,000 vols; Prin. Rev. Dr CHRIS BLAKE; publ. *Cliff Today* (3 a year).

College of the Resurrection: Stocks Bank Rd, Mirfield, WF14 0BW; tel. (1924) 490441; e-mail hscott@mirfield.org.uk; internet college.mirfield.org.uk; undergraduate, postgraduate and research degrees validated by Univ. of Sheffield; library: 13,000 vols; Prin. Fr PETER ALLAN.

Islamic College: The Islamic College, 133 High Rd, Willesden, London, NW10 2SW; tel. (20) 8451-9993; e-mail info@islamic-college .ac.uk; internet www.islamic-college.ac.uk; f. 1998; Bachelors and Masters degrees validated by Middlesex Univ.; Prin. MOHAMMAD JAFAR ELMI; publ. *Journal of Shi'a Islamic Studies* (4 a year).

Leo Baeck College: The Sternberg Centre, 80 East End Rd, London, N3 2SY; tel. (20) 8349-5600; internet www.lbc.ac.uk; f. 1956 as Jewish Theological College; Bachelors and Masters degrees in Jewish education validated by Univ. of Winchester; library: 60,000 vols; Prin. DEBORAH KAHN-HARRIS; Librarian Dr ANNETTE M. BOECKLER; publ. *European Judaism*.

Markfield Institute of Higher Education: Ratby Lane, Markfield, LE67 9SY; tel. (1530) 244922; e-mail info@mihe.org.uk; internet mihe.org.uk; f. 2000; associate college of Univ. of Gloucestershire; library: 30,000 vols, 420 serials with 85 current journals; Dir Dr ZAHID PARVEZ.

Maryvale Institute: Maryvale House, Old Oscott Hill, Birmingham, B44 9AG; tel. (121) 360-8118; internet www.maryvale.ac.uk; f. 1980; int. Catholic distance-learning college for theology and religious education at undergraduate and postgraduate levels; courses validated by Open University; library: 15,000 vols; Dir Fr EDWARD CLARE (acting).

Oxford Centre for Mission Studies: Woodstock Rd, Oxford, OX2 6HR; tel. (1865) 556071; e-mail ocms@ocms.ac.uk; internet www.ocms.ac.uk; library: 16,000 vols; Exec. Dir Dr WONSUK MA; publ. *Transformation*.

Queen's Foundation: Somerset Rd, Edgbaston, Birmingham, B15 2QH; tel. (121) 454-1527; e-mail enquire@queens.ac.uk; internet www.queens.ac.uk; f. 1828; graduate, postgraduate and research degrees validated by Univ. of Birmingham; library: 50,000 vols, 80 journals; Prin. Rev. Dr DAVID HEWLETT.

Redcliffe College: Wotton House, Horton Rd, Gloucester, GL1 3PT; tel. (1452) 308097; internet www.redcliffe.org; f. 1892; Bachelors and Masters degrees validated by Univ. of Gloucestershire; Prin. ROB HAY; publ. *Encounters Mission Journal* (4 a year, online, www.redcliffe.org/SpecialistCentres/ EncountersMissionJournal).

Regents Theological College: West Malvern Rd, West Malvern, WR14 4AY; e-mail info@regents-tc.ac.uk; internet www .regents-tc.ac.uk; Bachelors and Masters degrees validated by Univ. of Chester; library: 36,000 vols, 160 journal titles; Prin. NIGEL TWEEN.

Spurgeon's College: 189 South Norwood Hill, London, SE25 6DJ; tel. (20) 8653-0850; e-mail enquiries@spurgeons.ac.uk; internet www.spurgeons.ac.uk; f. 1856; Bachelors and Masters degrees in theology and Christian though validated by Univ. of Manchester; library: 60,000 vols; spec. colln: C. H. Spurgeon Archive; Chair. SARAH KING; Prin. ROGER STANDING; Librarian JUDY POWLES.

St John's College: Chilwell Lane, Bramcote, Nottingham, NG9 3DS; tel. (115) 925-1114; e-mail enquiries@stjohns-nottm.ac.uk; internet www.stjohns-nottm.ac.uk; undergraduate and postgraduate courses in theology for ministry and theology validated by Univ. of Chester and Univ. of Durham; Prin. Rev. Dr DAVID HIBORN; Librarian Dr AMANDA HODGSON.

Wesley Study Centre: 3 South Bailey, Durham, DH1 3RJ; tel. (191) 334-3850; e-mail p.a.bissell@durham.ac.uk; internet www.dur.ac.uk/wsc.online; attached to Univ. of Durham; graduate and postgraduate theology and ministry courses validated by Univ. of Durham; Dir Rev. Dr CALVIN SAMUEL.

YMCA George Williams College: 199 Freemasons Rd, Canning Town, London, E16 3PY; tel. (20) 7540-4900; e-mail registry@ymca.ac.uk; internet www.ymca.ac .uk; f. 1970; Bachelors degrees in youth and community work validated by Canterbury Christ Church Univ.; library: 25,000 vols; Prin. and Chief Exec. MAXINE GREEN; Librarian SAMANTHA MAKWANA.

Universities in Northern Ireland

QUEEN'S UNIVERSITY BELFAST

University Rd, Belfast, BT7 1NN
Telephone: (28) 9024-5133
E-mail: vc.office@qub.ac.uk
Internet: www.qub.ac.uk

Founded 1845, as Queen's College, original Univ. Charter 1908, present Charter 1982
State control
Language of instruction: English
Academic year: September to September

Chancellor: KAMALESH SHARMA
Pro-Chancellor: Sir DAVID FELL
Pro-Chancellor: ROTHA JOHNSTON
Pres. and Vice-Chancellor: Prof. PETER GREGSON
Pro-Vice-Chancellor for Academic Planning and External Relations: Prof. TONY GALLAGHER
Pro-Vice-Chancellor for Education and Students: Prof. ELLEN DOUGLAS-COWIE
Pro-Vice-Chancellor for Research and Postgraduates: Prof. JAMES MCELNAY
Registrar: JAMES O'KANE
Library Systems Man.: ELIZABETH TRAYNOR
Library: see under Libraries and Archives
Number of teachers: 1,600 full-time
Number of students: 17,500 (full-time and part-time); 10,000 part-time students enrolled at Institute of Lifelong Learning

DEANS

Faculty of Arts, Humanities and Social Sciences: Prof. SHANE O'NEILL

Faculty of Engineering and Physical Sciences: Prof. TOM MILLAR
Faculty of Medicine, Health and Life Sciences: Prof. SEAN GORMAN

PROFESSORS

Faculty of Arts, Humanities and Social Sciences (73 University Rd, Belfast, BT7 1NN; tel. (28) 9097-5347; e-mail deansofficeahss@ qub.ac.uk; internet www.qub.ac.uk/fhum):

ALCORN, M., Music and Sonic Arts
ANDREW, M., English
BALES, R., Languages, Literatures and (Performing) Arts
BELL, D., Languages, Literatures and (Performing) Arts
BEW, P., Politics, International Studies and Philosophy
BOWLER, P., History and Anthropology
BURNETT, M., English
CAMPBELL, J., History and Anthropology
CARAHER, B., English
CAREY, M., Management and Economics
CARSON, C., English
CLOUGH, P., Education
CONNOLLY, P., Education
CONNOLLY, S., History and Anthropology
CULLEN, B., Politics, International Studies and Philosophy
DALY, M., Sociology, Social Policy and Social Work
DAVIES, S., Languages, Literatures and (Performing) Arts
DAWSON, N., Law
DEMIRAG, S., Management and Economics
DICKSON, B., Law
DONNAN, H., History and Anthropology
DOUGLAS COWIE, E., Arts, Humanities and Social Sciences
ELWOOD, J., Education
ENGLISH, R., Politics, International Studies and Philosophy
EVANS, J., Politics, International Studies and Philosophy
FORKER, J., Management and Economics
GALLAGHER, A., Education
GARDNER, J., Arts, Humanities and Social Sciences
GEOGHEGAN, V., Politics, International Studies and Philosophy
GORMAN, J., Politics, International Studies and Philosophy
GRAY, P., History and Anthropology
GREEN, I., History and Anthropology
GUELKE, A., Politics, International Studies and Philosophy
HARVEY, C., Law
HAYTON, D., History and Anthropology
HELLAWELL, P., Music and Sonic Arts
HILLYARD, P., Sociology, Social Policy and Social Work
HYNDMAN, N., Management and Economics
JACKSON, J., Law
JEFFCUTT, P., Management and Economics
JEFFERY, K., History and Anthropology
JOHNSTON, D., Languages, Literatures and (Performing) Arts
KENNEDY, L., History and Anthropology
LEITH, P., Law
MACDONALD, C., Politics, International Studies and Philosophy
MAGENNIS, H., English
MANN, M., Sociology, Social Policy and Social Work
McEVOY, J., Politics, International Studies and Philosophy
McEVOY, K., Law
McKILLOP, D., Management and Economics
McLAUGHLIN, E., Sociology, Social Policy and Social Work
MILTON, K., History and Anthropology
MOORE, M., Management and Economics
MORISON, J., Law
MULLETT, M., History and Anthropology

O'Dowd, L., Sociology, Social Policy and Social Work
O'Dowd, M., History and Anthropology
O'Hearn, D., Sociology, Social Policy and Social Work
O'Neill, S., Politics, International Studies and Philosophy
Philip, G., Management and Economics
Pinkerton, J., Sociology, Social Policy and Social Work
Prior, L., Sociology, Social Policy and Social Work
Scraton, P., Law
Sheehan, E., English
Simpson, P., English
Smaczny, J., Music and Sonic Arts
Teague, P., Management and Economics
Thompson, J., English
Turner, J., Management and Economics
Turner, S., Law
Walker, B., Politics, International Studies and Philosophy
Walker, G., Politics, International Studies and Philosophy
Wheeler, S., Law
Whitehead, D., History and Anthropology
Whitehouse, H., History and Anthropology
Wiener, A., Politics, International Studies and Philosophy
Wilford, R., Politics, International Studies and Philosophy
Williams, F., Arts, Humanities and Social Sciences
Woodfield, I., Music and Sonic Arts

Faculty of Engineering and Physical Sciences (NI Technology Centre, Cloreen Park, Belfast, BT9 5HN; tel. (28) 9097-5443; e-mail deaneps@qub.ac.uk; internet www.qub.ac.uk/feng):

Allen, S. J., Chemical Engineering
Armitage, D. H., Pure Mathematics
Armstrong, C. G., Mechanical and Manufacturing Engineering
Armstrong, G. A., Electrical and Electronic Engineering
Atkinson, R., Physics and Astronomy
Basheer, P. A. M., Civil Engineering
Bell, D. A., Computer Science
Bell, K. L., Applied Mathematics and Theoretical Physics
Blair, G. P., Mechanical and Aerospace Engineering
Boyd, D. R., Chemistry
Burch, R., Chemistry
Campbell, B., Geography
Cleland, D. J., Civil Engineering
Clint, M., Computer Science
Cowan, C. F. N., Electrical and Electronic Engineering
Cowie, R., Psychology
Crawford, R., Mechanical and Aerospace Engineering
Crookes, D., Computer Engineering
Crossley, P., Electrical and Electronic Engineering
Crothers, D. S. F., Applied Mathematics and Theoretical Physics
de Silva, A. P., Chemistry
Douglas, R., Mechanical and Manufacturing Engineering
Dufton, P. L., Physics and Astronomy
Fee, A. J., Mechanical and Manufacturing Engineering
Finnis, M. W., Physics and Astronomy
Fleck, R., Mechanical and Manufacturing Engineering
Fusco, V. F., Electrical and Electronic Engineering
Gamble, H. S., Electrical and Electronic Engineering
Graham, W. G., Physics and Astronomy
Hall, V., Archaeology and Palaeoecology
Hardacre, C., Chemistry

Harkin-Jones, E. M. A., Mechanical and Manufacturing Engineering
Hepper, P., Psychology
Hibbert, A., Applied Mathematics and Theoretical Physics
Howe, J., Environmental Planning
Hu, P., Chemistry
Irwin, G. W., Electrical and Electronic Engineering
Kalin, R. M., Civil Engineering
Keenan, F. P., Applied Mathematics and Theoretical Physics
Latimer, C. J., Physics and Astronomy
Lewis, C. L. S., Physics and Astronomy
Livingstone, D. N., Mechanical and Aerospace Engineering
Magee, T. R. A., Chemical Engineering
Mallory, J., Archaeology and Palaeoecology
Mann, J., Chemistry
Marshall, A. J., Electrical and Electronic Engineering
McCanny, J. V., Electrical and Electronic Engineering
McCormac, G., Archaeology and Palaeoecology
McEldowney, J. M., Environmental Planning
McGarvey, J. J., Chemistry
McGuinness, C., Psychology
Orford, J. D., Geography
Orr, J. F., Mechanical and Manufacturing Engineering
Perrott, R. H., Computer Science
Raghunathan, S. R., Aeronautical Engineering
Scott, N. S., Computer Science
Seddon, K. R., Chemistry
Sheehy, N., Psychology
Smith, B., Geography
Smyth, A., Environmental Planning
Taylor, K. T. A., Applied Mathematics and Theoretical Physics
Walmsley, D. G., Physics and Astronomy
Walters, H. R. J., Applied Mathematics and Theoretical Physics
Whalley, W. B., Geography
Whitaker, M. A. B., Physics and Astronomy
Wickstead, A. W., Pure Mathematics
Williams, I., Physics and Astronomy
Woods, R., Electrical and Electronic Engineering
Woolley, T. A., Architecture

Faculty of Medicine, Health and Life Sciences (Whitla Medical Bldg, 97 Lisburn Rd, Belfast, BT9 7BL; tel. (28) 9097-5177; e-mail dean-mhls@qub.ac.uk; internet www.qub.ac.uk/fmhs):

Ames, J., Biological and Food Sciences
Campbell, F., Biomedical Sciences
Chakravarthy, U., Biomedical Sciences
Cosby, S., Biomedical Sciences
Davies, R., Biological and Food Sciences
Dring, M., Biological and Food Sciences
Elborn, J., Medicine and Dentistry
Elwood, R., Biological and Food Sciences
Ennis, M., Medicine and Dentistry
Evans, A., Medicine and Dentistry
Fee, J., Medicine and Dentistry
Freeman, R., Medicine and Dentistry
Gorman, S., Pharmacy
Hall, P., Medicine and Dentistry
Hamilton, P., Biomedical Sciences
Harkin, D., Biomedical Sciences
Hay, R., Medicine and Dentistry
Hirst, D., Pharmacy
Hughes, A., Medicine and Dentistry
Hughes, C., Pharmacy
Hutchinson, G., Biological and Food Sciences
Johnston, G., Medicine and Dentistry
Johnston, J., Biomedical Sciences
Johnston, P., Biomedical Sciences
Jones, D., Pharmacy

Kee, F., Medicine and Dentistry
Lamey, P., Medicine and Dentistry
Lappin, T., Biomedical Sciences
Larkin, M., Biological and Food Sciences
Lewis, S., Medicine and Dentistry
Linden, G., Medicine and Dentistry
Lynch, E., Medicine and Dentistry
Maggs, C., Biological and Food Sciences
Maule, A., Biological and Food Sciences
Maxwell, A., Medicine and Dentistry
McClure, N., Medicine and Dentistry
McDermott, B., Medicine and Dentistry
McElnay, J., Medicine, Health and Life Sciences
McVeigh, G., Biomedical Sciences
Mirakhur, R., Medicine and Dentistry
Montgomery, W., Biological and Food Sciences
Orr, J., Nursing and Midwifery
Porter, S., Nursing and Midwifery
Reilly, P., Medicine and Dentistry
Reynolds, G., Medicine and Dentistry
Rima, B., Biomedical Sciences
Savage, J., Medicine and Dentistry
Shaw, C., Pharmacy
Shields, M., Medicine and Dentistry
Stitt, A., Biomedical Sciences
Stout, R., Medicine and Dentistry
Trimble, E., Medicine and Dentistry
Vandenbroeck, K., Pharmacy
Walker, B., Pharmacy
Woolfson, D., Pharmacy
Young, I., Medicine and Dentistry

UNIVERSITY OF ULSTER

Coleraine Campus, Cromore Rd, Coleraine, BT52 1SA
Jordanstown Campus, Shore Rd, Newtownabbey, BT37 0QB
Belfast Campus, York St, Belfast, BT15 1ED
Magee Campus, Northland Rd, Londonderry, BT48 7JL

Telephone: (28) 7012-3456
E-mail: online@ulster.ac.uk
Internet: www.ulster.ac.uk

Founded 1984 by Royal Charter following merger of New Univ. of Ulster and Ulster Polytechnic
State control
Academic year: September to May

Chancellor: Dr James Nesbitt
Pro-Chancellor: Prof. Rosemary Peter-Gallagher
Pro-Chancellor: Dr Jeremy Harbinson
Pro-Chancellor: Gerry Mallon
Vice-Chancellor: Prof. Richard Barnett
Pro-Vice-Chancellor for Communication and Provost of Coleraine and Magee Campuses: Prof. Deirdre Heenan
Pro-Vice-Chancellor for Devt and Provost of Jordanstown and Belfast Campuses: Prof. Alastair Adair
Pro-Vice-Chancellor for Educational Partnerships and Int. Affairs: Prof. Anne Moran
Pro-Vice-Chancellor for Research and Innovation: Prof. Hugh McKenna
Pro-Vice-Chancellor for Teaching and Learning: Prof. Denise McAlister

Number of teachers: 1,047
Number of students: 26,642 (18,744 full-time, 7,898 part-time)

DEANS

Faculty of Arts: Prof. Jan Jedrzejewski
Faculty of Art, Design and the Built Environment: Prof. Ian Montgomery
Faculty of Computing and Engineering: Prof. Richard Millar
Faculty of Life and Health Sciences: Prof. Carol Curran
Faculty of Social Sciences: Prof. Paul Carmichael
Ulster Business School: Prof. Marie McHugh

PROFESSORS

Faculty of Arts (Univ. of Ulster Coleraine Campus, Cromore Rd, Coleraine, BT52 1SA; tel. (28) 7032-4517; e-mail arts@ulster.ac.uk; internet www.arts.ulster.ac.uk):

BORSJE, H., Medieval Irish Culture and Religion
BRADFORD, R., Literary History and Theory
CROOKE, E., Museum and Heritage Studies
EAGLETON, T., Critical Theory
EDGE, S., Photography and Cultural Studies
EKINS, R. J. M., Media Studies
FOSTER, J. W., Modern Irish Literature
GARGETT, G., French Culture and Ideas
GILLESPIE, J., French Language and Literature
IRVINE, B., Music
KENNEDY, L., Modern Economic and Social History of Ulster
KENNEDY-ANDREWS, E., English
KOCKEL, U., Irish and European Ethnology
LILEY, A., Creative Industries
LYONS, F., Arts and Humanities
MAC MATHUNA, S., Irish and Celtic Studies
MACRAILD, D., British and Irish History
MCKEVITT, P., Digital Multimedia
MESSENGER DAVIES, M., Media Studies
MOORE, G., Creative Technologies
O'CORRAIN, A., Irish and Celtic Studies
THATCHER, I., History

Faculty of Art, Design and the Built Environment (Univ. of Ulster, Belfast Campus, York St, Belfast, BT15 1ED; tel. (28) 9036-6310; e-mail jai.montgomery@ulster.ac.uk; internet www.adbe.ulster.ac.uk):

ALI, F., Structural Engineering
BERRY, J., Urban Planning and Property Development
CURL, J., Architecture
DASS, B., Design
DELICHATSIOS, M., Fire Safety and Engineering
DOHERTY, W., Video Art
FLEMING, K., Textile Art
GRAY, P., Housing
HEANEY, S., Construction
HEWITT, N., Energy/Sustainable Technologies
HINE, J., Translink Chair Transport
LERM HAYES, C., Iconology
LEVENDIS, Y. A., Fire Safety Science
LLOYD, G., Urban Planning
MAGUIRE, J., Animation
MCGREAL, W., Property Research
MOLKOV, V., Fire Safety Science
NADJAI, A., Fire Structural Engineering
NOVOZHILOV, V., Fire Dynamics
PARR, M., Photography
SEAWRIGHT, P., Photography
VAN DER KRABBEN, E., Real Estate
WALKER, P., Architecture
WALLINGER, M., Fine Art
WRIGHT, T., Visual Arts
YOHANIS, Y., Building Services Engineering

Faculty of Computing and Engineering (Univ. of Ulster, Jordanstown Campus, Shore Rd, Newtownabbey, BT37 0QB; tel. (28) 9036-6855; e-mail engineering@ulster.ac.uk; internet www.compeng.ulster.ac.uk):

AGRAWAL, S. K., Robotics
BLACK, N., Medical Informatics
BUSTARD, D., Computing Science
BYRNE, J., Photocatalysis
CLARKE, R., Mechanical Engineering
DAVIS, J., Biomedical Sensors
ESCALONA, O., Cardiovascular Research
FARAHMAND, K., Mathematics
HANNA, J. R. P., Computing & Mathematics
KELSO, S., Computational Neuroscience
MAGUIRE, L., Computational Intelligence
MAGUIRE, P., Plasmas and Nanofabrication

MCCLEAN, S., Mathematics
MCDAID, L. J., Computational Neuroscience
MCGINNITY, T., Systems Engineering
MCLAUGHLIN, J., Functional Materials
MEENAN, B., Biomedical Materials
MILLAR, R., Computer Science
MORROW, P. J., Computer Vision
MULVENNA, M., Computer Science
NUGENT, C., Biomedical Engineering
PAPAKONSTANTINOU, P., Advanced Materials
PARR, G., Telecommunications
PRASAD, G., Intelligent Systems
SCOTNEY, B., Informatics
TURNER, C., Engineering
WALLACE, J., Innovation
WANG, H., Computer Science

Faculty of Life and Health Sciences (Univ. of Ulster, Coleraine Campus, Cromore Rd, Coleraine, BT52 1SA; tel. (28) 7032-4491; e-mail science@ulster.ac.uk; internet www.science.ulster.ac.uk):

ADAMSON, G., Psychology
ANDERSON, R., Vision Science
BANAT, I., Microbial Biotechnology
BARR, O., Nursing
BJOURSON, A., Biomedical Sciences Research
BRADBURY, I., Statistical Science
BRADLEY, J., Physiotherapy
BRENNAN, D., Physical Education and Sport
BUNTING, B., Psychology
CALLAN, J., Pharmacy
CLARK, P. U., Quaternary Science
CLAUSS, M., Biomedical Sciences
COATES, V., Nursing Research
COOPER, J., Coastal Studies
CUNNINGHAM, G., Child and Family Therapy
CURRAN, C., Life and Health Sciences
DAVIDSON, G., Exercise Biochemistry and Physiology
DOLK, H., Epidemiology and Health Services Research
DOOLEY, J., Microbiology
DOWNES, C., Cancer Biology
DUBITZKY, W., Bioinformatics
ELKLIT, A., Psychology
FITZSIMONS, D., Nursing
FLATT, P., Biological and Biomedical Sciences
GAULT, V., Experimental Medicine
GIBNEY, M. J., Biomedical Sciences
GILES, M., Psychology
GOEKE-MOREY, M. C., Psychology
HANNIGAN, B., Immunology
HARRIS, R., Physical Activity and Health Research
HASSAN, D., Sport Policy and Management
HOWARD, V., Bioimaging
JACKSON, D., Coastal Geomorphology
JORDAN, P., Catchment Science
KEENAN, M., Behaviour Analysis
KERNOHAN, W., Health Research
LESLIE, J., Psychology
LIDDELL, C., Psychology
LIVINGSTONE, M., Nutrition
MARCHANT, R., Microbial Biotechnology
MATTOUSSI, H., Pharmaceutical Nanotechnology
MCCANCE, T., Nursing Research and Development
MCCARRON, P., Pharmaceutics
MCCAUGHAN, E., Cancer Care
MCCLENAGHAN, N., Innovation and Enterprise
MCCLOSKEY, J., Geophysics
MCCORMACK, J., Nursing Research
MCDONOUGH, S., Health and Rehabilitation
MCHALE, A., Medical Biotechnology
MCKEOWN, S. R., Cancer Biology
MCKILLOP, A., Biomedical Sciences

MCMULLAN, G., Microbiology
MCNULTY, H., Nutritional Science
MERRILEES, C. E., Psychology
MOORE, C., Personalised Medicine
MOORE, A., Environmental Sciences
MOSER, D., Cardiovascular Nursing
MURPHY, M., Sports and Exercise
O'HARTE, F., Endocrinology and Metabolism
O'NEILL, S., Mental Health Sciences
PARAHOO, K., Nursing and Health Research
RIPPEY, B., Environmental Science
SAKMANN, B., Biomedical Sciences
SAUNDERS, K. J., Optometry and Vision Science
SHEVLIN, M., Psychology
SINCLAIR, M., Midwifery Research
SMYTH, W. F., Pharmacy
SOTO, A., Cancer Development
STEACY, S., Earthquake Physics
STRAIN, S., Human Nutrition
STRINGER, M., Psychology
WALLACE, E., Sports Biomechanics
WALSH, C., Genetics
WARD, M., Nutrition and Dietetics
WILSON, R., Psychology

Faculty of Social Sciences (Univ. of Ulster, Jordanstown Campus, Shore Rd, Newtownabbey, BT37 0QB; tel. (28) 9036-6157; e-mail socsci@ulster.ac.uk; internet www.socsci.ulster.ac.uk):

AUGHEY, A., Politics
AUSTIN, R., Education
BIRRELL, W., Social Administration and Social Policy
CARMICHAEL, P., Policy/Government
CLARKE, L., Education
COLLINS, C., Transitional Justice
ERRIDGE, A., Public Policy and Management
HAMBER, B., International Conflict Research
HARGIE, O., Communication
HENRY, A., Linguistics
KNOX, C., Comparative Public Policy
LEAVEY, G., Mental Health and Wellbeing
LUNDY, P., Sociology
MCCOLGAN, M., Sociology and Applied Social Studies
MCWILLIAMS, M., Women's Studies
NI AOLAIN, F., Law
O'CONNELL, R., Human Rights and Constitutional Law
O'CONNOR, J., Social Policy
OFFER, J., Social Theory and Policy
ROBINSON, G., Social Research
SMITH, A., Education
TAYLOR, B., Social Work
TEITEL, R., Transitional Justice
TRENCH, A., Politics
WILLS, S., Law
WILSON, J., Communication

Ulster Business School (Univ. of Ulster, Coleraine Campus, Cromore Rd, Coleraine, BT52 1SA; tel. (28) 9036-8126; e-mail business@ulster.ac.uk; internet www.business.ulster.ac.uk):

ARMSTRONG, G. A., Accounting, Finance & Economics
BALLANTINE, J., Accounting
BEAMISH, P., Management
BOYD, S., Tourism
BROWN, S., Marketing Research
CAREY, M., Management
COTTE, J., Management
DURKIN, M., Marketing
FANG, Y., Management
FARLEY, H., Management and Leadership
GIBSON, N., Economic Policy
GILMORE, A., Services Marketing
HUMPHREYS, P., Operations Management
KIRK, R., Accounting and Finance
MCADAM, R., Innovation Management

MCGOWAN, P., Entrepreneurship and Business Development
MCHUGH, M., Organizational Behaviour
MCIVOR, R., Operations Management
OSMANI, S. R., Developmental Economics
QUINN, B., Retail Marketing
RAMSEY, E., Business Innovation
TRIDIMAS, Political Economy
WARD, A., Accounting
WIENGARTEN, F., Management
WU, W., Management
YEUNG, A., Management

Colleges in Northern Ireland

These institutions are not able to award their own degrees, but offer courses leading to a degree from a recognized body.

Belfast Bible College: Glenburn Rd S, Dunmurry, Belfast, BT17 9JP; tel. (28) 9030-1551; e-mail info@belfastbiblecollege.com; internet www.belfastbiblecollege.com; f. 1943, as Belfast Bible School and Missionary Training Home; attached to Queen's Univ. Belfast; offers certificate, diploma, undergraduate and postgraduate courses in conjunction with Queen's Univ. Belfast and Univ. of Cumbria; library: 16,000 vols, 87 journals and specialist texts in biblical studies, mission, youth ministry, historical theology and theological education; 200 students; Prin. IAN DICKSON (acting); publ. *The Link* (2 a year).

Belfast Metropolitan College: Millfield Campus, 125–153 Millfield, Belfast, BT1 1HS; tel. (28) 9026-5000; e-mail studentportal@belfastmet.ac.uk; internet www.belfastmet.ac.uk; f. 1991, from College of Technology (f. 1901), College of Business Studies and Rupert Stanley College 2007; acad. depts of business and management, community education and training, computing and admin. studies, continuing education, creative and health studies, general education, hospitality, leisure and tourism, technology; 1,000 teachers; 37,000 students; Prin. and Chief Exec. THÉRÈSE MCGIVERN.

College of Agriculture, Food and Rural Enterprise: Greenmount Campus, 45 Tirgracy Rd, Antrim, BT41 4PS; tel. (28) 9442-6666; e-mail enquiries@cafre.ac.uk; internet www.cafre.ac.uk; higher national certificate, diploma and degree courses; campuses in Antrim, Enniskillen, Loughry; Prin. STEVEN BLACK.

Irish Baptist College: 19 Hillsborough Rd, Moira, BT67 0HG; tel. (28) 9261-9267; e-mail info@irishbaptistcollege.co.uk; internet www.irishbaptistcollege.co.uk; f. 2003; undergraduate, postgraduate and part-time courses; accrediting universities Queen's Univ. Belfast and Univ. of Chester; 50 students; Prin. EDWIN EWART; Registrar VALERIE HAMILTON; publ. *ABC Insight* (12 a year).

Northern Regional College: Newtownabbey Campus, 400 Shore Road, Newtownabbey, BT37 9RS; tel. (28) 9085-5000; internet www.nrc.ac.uk; campuses in Ballymena, Ballymoney, Coleraine, Larne, Magherafelt and Newtownabbey; library: 35,000 vols, 3,000 ebooks, 70 journal titles; Chair. GERRY GILPIN; Prin. and Chief Exec. TREVOR NEILANDS; publ. *Babble*.

North West Regional College: Londonderry Campus, Strand Rd, Londonderry, BT48 7AL; tel. (28) 7127-6000; internet www.nwrc.ac.uk; f. 2007 formed by by merger of Limavady College and North West Institute; 3 campuses: Derry-Londonderry,

Limavady, Stabane, and 8 academic schools; 24,000 students; Prin. and Chief Exec. S MURPHY; Library Man. JONATHAN MOOR; publ. @nwrc (print and online, www.nwrc.ac.uk/our_college/news_events/@nwrc).

Saint Mary's University College: 191 Falls Rd, Belfast, BT12 6FE; tel. (28) 9032-7678; internet www.stmarys-belfast.ac.uk; f. 1900, as St Mary's Training College, current name adopted 1985; attached to Queen's Univ. Belfast; offers Bachelors degrees in education and liberal arts, PGCE (Irish Medium Education), and Masters in education; library: 90,000 vols, 320 ebooks, 4,500 print and online journals; Chair. Rev. NOEL TREANOR; Vice-Chair. Rev. DONAL MCKEOWN; Prin. Prof. PETER B. FINN; Librarian ELAINE MULHOLLAND.

South Eastern Regional College: Lisburn Campus, 39 Castle St, Lisburn, BT27 4SU; tel. (28) 9267-7225; e-mail info@serc.ac.uk; internet www.serc.ac.uk; f. 1914; main campuses in Bangor, Downpatrick, Lisburn, Newtownards, Newcastle and Ballynahinch; HND courses; 1,185 teachers; 32,000 students; Chair. ROBSON DAVISON; Prin. and Chief Exec. KEN WEBB.

Southern Regional College: East/West Buildings, Patrick St, Newry, BT35 8DN; tel. (28845) 3026-1071; e-mail info@src.ac.uk; internet www.src.ac.uk; 6 campuses; foundation degrees, HNDs and full degrees; 1,100 teachers; 45,000 students; Chief Exec. BRIAN DORAN; publ. *SRCzine*.

South West College: Enniskillen Campus, Fairview, 1 Dublin Rd, Enniskillen, BT74 6AE; tel. (845) 603-1881; e-mail enquiries@swc.ac.uk; internet www.swc.ac.uk; campuses in Cookstown, Dungannon, Enniskillen and Omagh; 500 teachers; 14,000 students; Dir MALACHY MCALEER (acting).

Stranmillis University College: Stranmillis Rd, Belfast, BT9 5DY; tel. (28) 9038-1271; e-mail info@stran.ac.uk; internet www.stran.ac.uk; f. 1922; attached to Queen's Univ. Belfast; offers teacher education courses at BEd, PGCE and MEd level; BA (Early Childhood Studies), BSc (Health and Leisure Studies), part-time MA (Arts in the Community), part-time MA (Early Childhood Studies) and one year, full-time PGCE course for Early Years specialists; library: 70,000 vols; Chair. S. COSTELLO; Vice-Chair. S. E. D. BELL; Prin. and Chief Exec. Dr ANNE HEASLETT.

Union Theological College: 108 Botanic Ave, Belfast, BT7 1JT; tel. (28) 9020-5080; e-mail admin@union.ac.uk; internet www.union.ac.uk; f. 1853 as Assembly's College; current name adopted 1978; attached to Institute of Theology, Queen's University Belfast; offers Bachelors, Masters and Doctoral level courses; library: 70,000 vols, 20,000 pamphlets, 70 journals and periodicals on theology; 17,000 students; Prin. STAFFORD CARSON; Librarian DAVID KERRY.

Universities in Scotland

EDINBURGH NAPIER UNIVERSITY

Sighthill Campus, Edinburgh, EH11 4BN
Telephone: (131) 455-3555
E-mail: info@napier.ac.uk
Internet: www.napier.ac.uk

Founded 1964 as Napier Technical College, present name and status 2014
Academic year: September to May
Chancellor: TIM WATERSTONE
Prin. and Vice-Chancellor: Prof. ANDREA NOLAN
Vice-Prin.: Dr ALISTAIR SAMBELL

Vice-Prin.: Prof. JOHN DUFFIELD
Univ. Sec.: Dr GERRY WEBBER
Dir of Learning Information Services: CHRIS PINDER

Library of 210,000 vols
Number of teachers: 1,644
Number of students: 17,264

DEANS

Business School: Prof. GEORGE STONEHOUSE
Faculty of Engineering, Computing and Creative Industries: Dr SANDRA CAIRNCROSS
Faculty of Health, Life and Social Sciences: IAIN MCINTOSH

GLASGOW CALEDONIAN UNIVERSITY

Cowcaddens Rd, Glasgow, G4 0BA
Telephone: (141) 331-3000
E-mail: helpline@gcal.ac.uk
Internet: www.caledonian.ac.uk

Founded 1971 as Glasgow Polytechnic; merged with The Queen's College; present name and status 1993
State control
Academic year: September to June
Chancellor: Prof. Dr MUHAMMAD YUNUS
Prin. and Vice-Chancellor: Prof. PAMELA GILLIES
Vice-Prin. and Pro-Vice-Chancellor for External Relations: Prof. KAREN STANTON
Vice-Prin. and Pro-Vice-Chancellor for Learning and Teaching: Prof. MIKE MANNION
Pro-Vice-Chancellor for Strategy: Prof. MIKE SMITH
Vice-Prin. and Exec. Dir of Finance: DAVID BEEBY
Vice-Prin. and Univ. Sec.: JAN HULME
Chief Information Officer: JEFF MURRAY (acting)
Number of students: 17,000

DEANS

Caledonian Business School: Prof. ŽELJKO ŠEVIĆ
School of Built and Natural Environment: Prof. PETER KENNEDY
School of Engineering and Computing: Prof. MALCOLM ALLAN (acting)
School of Health: Prof. FRANK CROSSAN
School of Law and Social Sciences: Prof. BILL HUGHES (acting)
School of Life Sciences: Prof. KEVAN M. A. GARTLAND

HERIOT-WATT UNIVERSITY

Edinburgh Campus: Edinburgh, EH14 4AS
Scottish Borders Campus: Netherdale, Galashiels, TD1 3HF

Telephone: (131) 449-5111 (Edinburgh); (1896) 753351 (Scottish Borders)
E-mail: enquiries@hw.ac.uk
Internet: www.hw.ac.uk

Founded 1821 as Edinburgh School of Arts; became Heriot-Watt College 1885; present name and status 1966
Academic year: September to August
Chancellor: Baroness SUSAN GREENFIELD
Prin. and Vice-Chancellor: Prof. STEVE CHAPMAN
Vice-Prin.: Prof. JULIAN D. C. JONES
Sr. Deputy Prin.: Prof. ANDY C. WALKER
Deputy Prin. for Learning and Teaching: Prof. ROBERT J. M. CRAIK
Deputy Prin. for Research and Knowledge Transfer: Prof. ALAN MILLER
Sec.: ANN MARIE DALTON
Librarian: GILL A. MCDONALD (acting)

Number of teachers: 450
Number of students: 23,000

HEADS OF SCHOOLS

Edinburgh Business School: Prof. KEITH G. LUMSDEN (Dir)

Institute of Petroleum Engineering: Prof. S. STEWART

School of Built Environment: Prof. GARRY PENDER

School of Engineering and Physical Sciences: (vacant)

School of Life Sciences: Prof. D. HOPKINS

School of Management and Languages: Prof. G. HOGG

School of Mathematical and Computer Sciences: Prof. PHILIP DE WILDE

School of Textiles and Design: Prof. ALISON J. HARLEY (acting)

PROFESSORS

School of the Built Environment (tel. (131) 451-4644; e-mail a.j.ormston@hw.ac.uk):

ASPINALL, P., Building Engineering and Surveying

BANFILL, P., Construction Materials

BRAMLEY, G., Urban Studies

CAO, Z., Civil Engineering

CHRISP, T., Civil Engineering

CRAIK, R., Acoustics, Deputy Principal (Teaching and Learning)

DHILLON, B., Building Engineering and Surveying

HULL, A., Spatial Planning

JENKINS, P., Architecture and Human Settlements

JONES, C., Estate Management

JOWITT, P., Sustainable Technology

KAKA, A., Construction Economics and Management and William Watson Chair, Dubai Campus

MAY, I., Civil Engineering

McCARTER, W., Civil Engineering Materials

OGUNLANA, S., Construction Project Management

PAWSON, H., Housing Policy

PENDER, G., Civil Engineering

PRIOR, A., Planning and Housing

ROAF, S., Architectural Engineering

ROBERSTON, B., School of the Built Environment

SWAFFIELD, J., Building Services Engineering

WANG, Y., Urban Studies

School of Engineering and Physical Sciences (tel. (131) 451-3082; e-mail l.bruce@hw.ac.uk):

ADAMS, D., Chemistry

BAKER, H., Physics

BULLER, G., Physics

CLOSE, A., Electrical Engineering

DESMULLIEZ, M., Electrical Engineering

GALBRAITH, I., Physics

GREENAWAY, A., Physics

GREENHALGH, D., Physics

GUTOWSKI, M., Chemistry

HALL, D., Physics

HAND, D., Physics

HARVEY, A., Electrical Engineering

JOHN, P., Chemistry

JONSON, M., Physics

JONES, J., Physics

KAR, A., Physics

KEANE, M., Chemical Engineering

LANE, D., Electrical Engineering

MACGREGOR, S., Chemistry

MARKX, G., Chemical Engineering

McCOUSTRA, M., Chemical Physics

McKENDRICK, K., Chemistry

MOORE, A., Mechanical Engineering

NI, X., Chemical Engineering

OCONE, R., Chemical Engineering

PETILLOT, Y., Electrical Engineering

POWELL, A., Chemistry

REAY, D., Electrical Engineering

REID, D., Physics

REUBEN, R., Mechanical Engineering

RICHARDS, B., Mechanical Engineering

RITCHIE, J., Mechanical Engineering

TAGHIZADEH, M., Physics

WALKER, A., Physics

WALLACE, A., Electrical and Electronic Engineering

WELCH, A., Chemistry

WHERRETT, B., Theoretical Physics

WILSON, J., Physics

School of Life Sciences (tel. (131) 451-3456; e-mail j.e.j.lodder@hw.ac.uk):

GREEN, P., Psychology

HUGHES, P., Brewing and Distilling

MAIR, J., Marine Biology

NORTH, A., Psychology

QUAIN, D., Brewing

SCHWEIZER, H., Biological Sciences

WILKINSON, M., Marine Biology

School of Management and Languages (tel. (131) 451-8143; e-mail enquiries@sml.hw.ac.uk):

BOSER, U., Languages and Intercultural Studies

COBHAM, D., Economics

CRAIG, V., Employment Law

FERNIE, J., Retail Marketing

HARE, P., Economics

JAMASB, T., Economics

MARSTON, C., Accountancy

MASON, I., Languages

McKINNON, A., Logistics

MELITZ, J., Economics

PEREZ, I., Languages

ROSLENDER, R., Accounting

SAWKINS, J., Economics

SCHAFFER, M., Economics

SHARWOOD SMITH, M., Languages

TOWERS, N., Business Management

TURNER, G., Translation, Languages

School of Mathematical and Computer Sciences (tel. (131) 451-3420; e-mail enquiries@macs.hw.ac.uk):

AYLETT, R., Computer Science

CAIRNS, A., Actuarial Mathematics and Statistics

CARR, J., Mathematics

CHANTLER, M., Computer Science

CORNE, D., Computer Science

DE WILDE, P., Computer Science

DUNCAN, D., Mathematics

EILBECK, J., Mathematics

FOSS, S., Actuarial Mathematics and Statistics

GIBSON, G., Statistics

HOWIE, J., Mathematics

JOHNSTON, D., Mathematics

KAMAREDDINE, F., Computer Science

KONSTANTOPOULOS, P., Actuarial Mathematics

KUKSIN, S., Mathematics

LACEY, A., Mathematics

LORD, G., Mathematics

MACDONALD, A., Actuarial Mathematics

McNEIL, A., Actuarial Mathematics

MICHAELSON, G., Computer Science

RYNNE, B., Mathematics

SHERRATT, J., Mathematics

SZABO, R., Mathematics

TAYLOR, N., Computer Science

TRINDER, P., Computer Science

WATERS, H., Actuarial Mathematics and Statistics

WILKIE, A., Actuarial Mathematics and Statistics

WILLIAMS, M., Computer Science

Institute of Petroleum Engineering (tel. (131) 451-3567; e-mail jane.wells@pet.hw.ac.uk):

CHRISTIE, M., Reservoir Engineering

CORBETT, P., Geoengineering

COUPLES, G., Petroleum Engineering

DAVIES, D., Petroleum Engineering

FORD, J., Petroleum Engineering

MACBETH, C., Reservoir Geophysics; Time-lapse and Multi Components

SIDE, J., Civil Engineering

SMART, B., Petroleum Engineering

SORBIE, K., Petroleum Engineering

STEWART, S., Petroleum Engineering

STOW, D., Petroleum Engineering

TODD, A., Petroleum Engineering

TOHIDI KALORAZI, B., Petroleum Engineering

School of Textiles and Design (tel. (1896) 753351; e-mail l.a.lindsay@hw.ac.uk):

CHRISTIE, R., Colour Chemistry

HARLEY, A., Textiles and Design

SHENK, P., Textile Design

STYLIOS, G., Textiles

WARDMAN, R., Textiles

Edinburgh Business School (tel. (131) 451-3090; e-mail enquiries@ebs.hw.ac.uk):

KAY, N., Economics

LOTHIAN, N., Accounting

LUMSDEN, K., Economics

O'FARRELL, P., Consultant

POOLEY, R., Computer Science

SCOTT, A., Economics

SIMMONS, J., Mechanical Engineering

QUEEN MARGARET UNIVERSITY

Musselburgh, Edinburgh, EH21 6UU

Telephone: (131) 474-0000

Internet: www.qmu.ac.uk

Founded 1875, present name and status 2007

Chancellor: Sir TOM FARMER

Prin. and Vice-Chancellor: Prof. PETRA WEND

Vice-Prin. for Resources and Devt and Univ. Sec.: ROSALYN MARSHALL

Vice-Prin. for Academics: Prof. ALAN GILLORAN

Dir for Campus Services: STEVE SCOTT

Dir for Finance: MALCOLM CUTT

Dir for Human Resources: DEE DENHOLM

Dir for Registry and Secretariat: IRENE HYND

Library of 67,423 vols and 112,251 e-titles, 142 printed journals, 19,744 ejournals

Number of teachers: 460

Number of students: 6,330

DEANS

School of Arts and Social Sciences: Dr CHRISTINE BOVIS-CNOSSEN

School of Health Sciences: Dr FIONA COUTTS

ROBERT GORDON UNIVERSITY

Schoolhill, Aberdeen, AB10 1FR

Telephone: (1224) 262000

E-mail: international@rgu.ac.uk

Internet: www.rgu.ac.uk

Founded 1750, present name and status 1992

Academic year: September to July

Chancellor: Sir IAN WOOD

Prin. and Vice-Chancellor: Prof. FERDINAND VON PRONDZYNSKI

Sec.: Dr ADRIAN GRAVES

Acad. Registrar: HILARY DOUGLAS

Chief Librarian: ELAINE DUNPHY

Library of 250,946 vols, 1,901 periodicals, 4,939 online journals

Number of teachers: 700 (full-time)

Number of students: 15,000

DEANS

Aberdeen Business School: Prof. RITA MARCELLA

Faculty of Design and Technology: Prof. JOHN WATSON

Faculty of Health and Social Care: Prof. VALERIE MAEHLE

HEADS OF SCHOOLS

Aberdeen Business School (Garthdee Rd, Aberdeen, AB10 7QE; tel. (1224) 263550; e-mail j.dey@rgu.ac.uk):

Accounting and Finance: ELIZABETH GAMMIE

Business and Management: MORAG HAMILTON

Information and Media: IAN M. JOHNSON

Public Administration and Law: VERONICA STRACHAN

Faculty of Design and Technology (Scott Sutherland School, Garthdee Rd, Aberdeen, AB10 7QB; tel. (1224) 263750; e-mail c.black@rgu.ac.uk):

School of Computing: Prof. SUSAN CRAW
School of Engineering: Prof. JOHN WATSON
Gray's School of Art: Prof. MIKE PRESS
Scott Sutherland School: Prof. ROBERT W. POLLOCK

Faculty of Health and Social Care (Garthdee Rd, Aberdeen, AB10 7QG; tel. (1224) 263050; e-mail s.barnett@rgu.ac.uk):

Applied Social Studies: Prof. JOYCE LISHMAN

Health Sciences: ELIZABETH HANCOCK
Life Sciences: Prof. MAUREEN MELVIN
Nursing and Midwifery: JENNIE PARRY
Pharmacy: Prof. TERENCE M. HEALEY

ROYAL CONSERVATOIRE OF SCOTLAND

100 Renfrew St, Glasgow, G2 3DB

Telephone: (141) 332-4101
E-mail: principal@rcs.ac.uk
Internet: www.rcs.ac.uk

Founded 1847 as The Glasgow Athenaeum, became The Scottish Nat. Acad. of Music 1928, The Royal Scottish Acad. of Music 1944, present status 1993, present name 2011

Academic year: September to June

Patron: HRH Prince CHARLES
Pres.: Sir CAMERON MACKINTOSH
Chair.: Lord JEFFREY SHARKEY
Prin.: Prof. JOHN WALLACE
Vice-Prin.: Prof. MAGGIE KINLOCH

Library of 80,120 music vols, 13,750 books, 7,570 sound recordings
Number of students: 836

DEANS

School of Drama and Dance: HUGH HODGART
School of Music: HAVILLAND WILLSHIRE

UHI MILLENNIUM INSTITUTE

12B Ness Walk, Inverness, IV3 5SQ

Telephone: (1463) 279-000
E-mail: info@uhi.ac.uk
Internet: www.uhi.ac.uk

Founded 1993, present status 2008
Private control

Rector: GARRY COUTTS
Prin. and Vice-Chancellor: Prof. CLIVE MULHOLLAND
Vice-Prin. for Research and Enterprise: Dr JEFF HOWARTH
Vice-Prin. for Acad.: Dr CRICHTON LANG
Sec.: FIONA LARG
Librarian: GILLIAN ANDERSON
Number of students: 8,156

DEANS

Faculty of Arts, Humanities and Business: Dr NEIL SIMCO
Faculty of Science, Health and Education: IAN LESLIE

UNIVERSITY OF ABERDEEN

King's College, Aberdeen AB24 3FX

Telephone: (1224) 272000
E-mail: pubrel@abdn.ac.uk
Internet: www.abdn.ac.uk

Founded 1495

Chancellor: Lord WILSON OF TILLYORN
Prin. and Vice-Chancellor: Prof. IAN DIAMOND
Rector: STEPHEN ROBERTSON
Sec.: STEVE CANNON
Sr Vice-Prin.: Prof. STEPHEN LOGAN
Vice-Prin. for Culture and Communities: Prof. CHRIS GANE
Vice-Prin. for Curriculum Reform: Prof. BRYAN MACGREGOR
Vice-Prin. for Learning and Teaching: Prof. PETER MCGEORGE
Vice-Prin. for Research and Commercialization: Prof. DOMINIC HOULIHAN
Acad. Registrar: Dr GILLIAN MACKINTOSH
Librarian: CHRIS BANKS

Library: see under Libraries and Archives
Number of teachers: 1,400
Number of students: 16,000

Publications: *Aberdeen University Review, Gaudeamus* (1 a year)

PROFESSORS

College of Arts and Social Sciences (Univ. of Aberdeen, King's College, Aberdeen, AB24 3FX; tel. (1224) 272084; e-mail adf076@abdn.ac.uk):

ADAMS, C. D., Land Economy
ARTER, D., Politics and International Relations
BEAUMONT, P. R., Law
BEBBINGTON, K. J., Accountancy
BLAIKIE, J. A. D., Sociology and Anthropology
BRIDGES, R. C., History and Economic History
BRITTON, C. M., French
BRUCE, C., Sociology
BRYDEN, J. M., Geography
BUCKLAND, R., Accountancy
BURGESS, G. J., German
CAMERON, J. R., Philosophy
CAREY-MILLER, D. L., Law
CHAPMAN, K., Geography
CLARK, B., Geography
DAWSON, P. M., Management Studies
DEVINE, T. M., Research Institute of Irish and Scottish Studies
DUFF, P. R., Law
DUKES, P., History and Economic History
DUNKLEY, J., French
EDWARDS, K. J., Geography
ELLIOTT, R. F., Economics
EVANS-JONES, R., Law
FERGUSSON, D. A. S., Divinity with Religious Studies
FORTE, A. D. M., Law
FRASER, P., Accountancy
GANE, C. H. W., Law
GRAHAM, L. G., Philosophy
HARRIS, D. R., Hispanic Studies
HARRISON, R. T., Management Studies
HEALD, D. A., Accountancy
HENDERSHOTT, P. H., Land Economy
HENDRY, L. B., Centre for Educational Research
HEWITT, D. S., English
HOESLI, M. E. R., Accountancy
HOTSON, H., Early Modern History
INGOLD, T., Sociology and Anthropology
JOHNSTONE, W., Divinity with Religious Studies
JORDAN, A. G., Politics and International Relations
KEATING, M. J., Politics and International Relations
KEMP, A. G., Economics
KIDD, M., Economics
LEBOUTTE, R. F. M. P., History
LEE, C. H., Economics
LYALL, F., Law
MACDONALD, I. R., Hispanic Studies
MACGREGOR, B. D., Land Economy
MACINNES, A. I., History
MANNINGS, D., History of Art
MATHER, A. S., Geography

MATTHEWS, E. H., Philosophy
MCKEE, L., Management Studies
MEEK, D. E., Celtic
MILLER, D., Law
MURRAY, I., English
O'BOYLE, C. J. M., Celtic
OHLMEYER, J., History
PAYNE, P. L., History and Economic History
PORTER, J. W., English (Elphinstone Institute)
ROBERTS, C., Accountancy
ROBERTSON, R., Sociology
ROWAN-ROBINSON, J. R., Law
SALMON, T. C., Politics and International Relations
SAUNDERS, A. M., French
SEWEL, J. B., Politics and International Relations
SHEEHAN, M. J., Politics and International Relations
SHUCKSMITH, D. M., Land Economy
SOULSBY, C., Geography
SWANSON, P., Hispanic Studies
THEODOSSIOU, I., Economics
THOMANECK, J. K. A., German
TORRANCE, I. R., Divinity with Religious Studies
URWIN, D. W., Politics and International Relations
VAN DER MERWE, C. G., Law
WALKER, N. C., Law
WALKER, S., Geography
WATSON, F. B., Divinity with Religious Studies
WATSON, G. J. B., English

College of Life Sciences and Medicine (Univ. of Aberdeen, Polworth Bldg, Foresterhill, Aberdeen, AB25 2ZD; tel. (1224) 552504; internet w3.abdn.ac.uk/medicine):

ALEXANDER, D. A., Mental Health
ASHFORD, M. L. J., Biomedical Sciences
BOOTH, I. R., Microbiology
BROWN, A. J. P., Molecular and Cell Biology
CASSIDY, J., Medicine and Therapeutics (Oncology)
CATTO, G. R. D., Medicine and Therapeutics
DOCHERTY, K., Molecular and Cell Biology (Biochemistry)
EL-OMAR, E. M., Medicine and Therapeutics
FORRESTER, J. V., Ophthalmology
FOTHERGILL, J. E., Molecular and Cell Biology (Biochemistry)
GILBERT, F. J., Radiology
GODDEN, D. J., Highlands and Islands Health Research Institute
GOLDEN, M. H. N., Medicine and Therapeutics
GOODAY, G. W., Molecular and Cell Biology
GOW, N. A. R., Molecular and Cell Biology
GRANT, A. M., Public Health
GREAVES, M., Medicine and Therapeutics (Haematology)
HAITES, N. E., Medicine and Therapeutics, and Molecular and Cell Biology
HAMILTON, W. A., Medical Microbiology
HANNAFORD, P., Primary Care
HARRIS, W. J., Molecular and Cell Biology (Genetics)
HAWKSWORTH, G. M., Biomedical Sciences, and Medicine and Therapeutics
HELMS, P. J. B., Child Health
HUHTANIEMI, I. T., Obstetrics and Gynaecology
HUKINS, D. W. L., Biomedical Physics and Bioengineering
HUTCHISON, J. D., Surgery (Orthopaedics)
KIDD, C., Biomedical Sciences (Physiology)
LITTLE, J., Medicine and Therapeutics (Epidemiology)
LOGAN, S. D., Biomedical Sciences (Neuroscience)

MACLEOD, A. M., Medicine and Therapeutics

MAUGHAN, R. J., Environmental and Occupational Medicine

MCCAIG, C. D., Biomedical Sciences

NEEDHAM, G., Medical Faculty

NORMAN, J. N., General Practice and Primary Care

ODDS, F. C., Molecular and Cell Biology

PENNINGTON, T. H., Medical Microbiology

PERTWEE, R. G., Biomedical Sciences

POPE, M. H., Medicine and Therapeutics

PRICE, D. B., General Practice and Primary Care

PROSSER, J. I., Molecular and Cell Biology

RALSTON, S. H., Medicine and Therapeutics

REES, A. J., Medicine and Therapeutics

REID, D. M., Medicine and Therapeutics

RITCHIE, L. D., General Practice and Primary Care

RUSSELL, E. M., Public Health

SEATON, A., Environmental and Occupational Medicine

SEYMOUR, D. G., Medicine and Therapeutics, and General Practice and Primary Care

SHARP, P. F., Biomedical Physics and Bioengineering

SHAW, D. J., Molecular and Cell Biology

SMITH, W. C. S., Public Health

TEMPLETON, A. A., Obstetrics and Gynaecology

VAN DER MOLEN, T., General Practice and Primary Care

WALKER, F., Pathology

WEBSTER, N. R., Medicine and Therapeutics (Anaesthesia and Intensive Care)

WHALLEY, L. J., Mental Health

WISCHIK, C. M., Mental Health

College of Physical Sciences (Univ. of Aberdeen, King's College, Aberdeen, AB24 3FX; tel. (1224) 272081; e-mail adf073@abdn.ac.uk):

ALEXANDER, I. J., Plant and Soil Sciences

ARCHBOLD, R. J., Mathematical Sciences

BAKER, M. J., Engineering

BOYLE, P. R., Zoology

CHANDLER, H. W., Engineering

CRAWFORD, J. E., Psychology

DELLA SALA, S. F., Psychology

DEREGOWSKI, J. B., Psychology

DUFFY, J. A., Chemistry

ENGLISH, P. R., Agriculture

FLIN, R., Psychology

FORRESTER, A. R., Chemistry

FREESTON, M. W., Computing Science

GLASSER, F. P., Chemistry

GORMAN, D. G., Engineering

GRAY, P. M. D., Computing Science

HALL, G. S., Mathematical Sciences

HOULIHAN, D. F. J., Zoology

HOWE, R. F., Chemistry

HUBBUCK, J. R., Mathematical Sciences

HUNTER, J., Computing Science

HURST, A., Geology and Petroleum Geology

INGRAM, M. D., Chemistry

JOLLIFFE, I. T., Mathematical Sciences

KILLHAM, K. S., Plant and Soil Sciences

LOGIE, R. H., Psychology

LOMAX, M. A., Agriculture

MACDONALD, D. I. M., Geology and Petroleum Geology

MEHARG, A. A., Plant and Soil Sciences

MILLER, H. G., Agriculture and Forestry

MITCHELL, C. P., Agriculture and Forestry

MORDUE, W., Zoology

NAYLOR, R. E. L., Agriculture

PENMAN, J., Engineering

PLAYER, M. A., Engineering

PRIEDE, I. G., Zoology

RACEY, P. A., Zoology

ROBINSON, D., Plant and Soil Sciences

RODGER, A. A., Engineering

SECOMBES, C. J., Zoology

SLEEMAN, D. H., Computing Science

SPEAKMAN, J. R., Zoology

SPRACKLEN, C. T., Engineering

THOMSON, K. J., Agriculture

VAS, P., Engineering

WIERCIGROCH, M., Engineering

WILLETTS, B. B., Engineering

UNIVERSITY OF ABERTAY DUNDEE

Bell St, Dundee, DD1 1HG

Telephone: (1382) 308000

E-mail: sro@abertay.ac.uk

Internet: www.abertay.ac.uk

Founded 1888 as Dundee Technical Institute, present name and status 1994

Academic year: October to June

Chancellor: Lord DOUGLAS CULLEN

Vice-Chancellor and Prin.: Prof. Dr NIGEL SEATON

Vice-Prin. and Deputy Vice-Chancellor: Prof. NICHOLAS TERRY

Pro-Vice-Chancellor for Acad. Devt: Prof. STEVE OLIVIER

Pro-Vice-Chancellor for Recruitment and Student Experience: Prof. ROSITSA BATESON

Head of Information Services: MICHAEL TURPIE

Library of 120,000 vols, 400 journals

Number of teachers: 380 (230 full-time, 150 part-time)

Number of students: 5,080

HEADS OF SCHOOL

Dundee Business School: Prof. HEATHER TARBERT

School of Computing and Engineering Systems: Dr COLIN MILLER

School of Contemporary Sciences: Prof. JOHN W. PALFREYMAN

School of Social and Health Sciences: RAY LLOYD

UNIVERSITY OF DUNDEE

Dundee, DD1 4HN

Telephone: (1382) 383000

E-mail: university@dundee.ac.uk

Internet: www.dundee.ac.uk

Founded 1881 as Univ. College, Dundee, Royal Charter 1967

Academic year: September to August

Chancellor: Lord NAREN PATEL

Rector: BRIAN COX

Prin. and Vice-Chancellor: Prof. C. PETER DOWNES

Vice-Prin.: Prof. DOREEN CANTRELL (acting)

Vice-Prin.: Prof. J. CALDERHEAD

Vice-Prin.: Prof. CHRISTOPHER WHATLEY

Vice-Prin.: Prof. Dr IRENE LEIGH

Deputy Prin.: Prof. GEORGINA FOLLETT

Sec.: Dr J. MCGEORGE

Librarian: Dr RICHARD PARSONS

Library: see under Libraries and Archives

Number of teachers: 3,000

Number of students: 17,000

DEANS

College of Art, Science and Engineering: Prof. STEPHEN DECENT

College of Arts and Social Sciences: Prof. CHRISTOPHER WHATLEY

College of Life Sciences: Prof. M. A. J. FERGUSON

College of Medicine, Dentistry and Nursing: Prof. IRENE LEIGH

PROFESSORS

College of Arts and Social Sciences (Tower Bldng, Dundee, DD1 4HN; tel. (1382) 384935; e-mail cassoffice@dundee.ac.uk; internet www.dundee.ac.uk/cass):

ANDREWS-SPEED, C., Energy Policy

BELCHER, C., Law

BENNETT, R., Developmental Biology

BONELL, M., Catchment Science

BROWN, C., Religious and Cultural History

CAMERON, P., International Energy Law and Policy

CHALKLEY, M. J., Economics

CHATTERJI, M., Applied Economics

CHURCHILL, R., Law

COLLISON, D., Accounting and Society

DAY, A., English Literature

DEWHURST, J. H. L., Economic, Social and Regional Statistics

DOBSON, A. P., Politics

FERGUSON, Scots Law

FINDLAY, A. M., Geography

FISCHER, M., Psychology

FYFE, N., Human Geography

GUNN, K., Creative Writing

HARRIS, R., Social Care

HASLAM, J., Business Finance

HOBER, K., International Law

HUDSON, B., Education

KELLY, T., Social Work

KITSON, P., English Literature

MCELEAVY, P., Law

MCKEAN, C., Scottish Architectural History

MCLEAN, J., Law

MOLANA, H., Economics

MONTAGNA, ., Economic Studies

POWER, D., Business Finance

RAITT, F., Law

REID, C., Environmental Law

RODRIGUES, S., Science Education

SPRAY, C., Water Science

TOMLINSON, J., Bonar Modern History

WERRITTY, A., Physical Geography

WILLIAMS, J., European Philosophy

WILLSON, P., History

WOUTERS, P., International Water Law and Policy

College of Art, Science and Engineering (Queen Mother Bldg, Dundee, DD1 4HN; tel. (1382) 386610; e-mail case@dundee.ac.uk; internet www.dundee.ac.uk/case/index.htm):

ABEL, E. W., Biomedical Engineering

ARNOTT, J. L., Communication Systems

CHAPLAIN, M. A., Mathematical Biology

COLVIN, C. M., Fine Art Photography

DAVIES, P. A., Fluid Dynamics

DONG, P., Coastal Engineering

FISHER, G. R.,

GILLESPIE, Sculpture

HANSON, V. L., Inclusive Technologies

INNS, T. G., Design

JENG, D., Civil Engineering

JOHNSON, N. M., Numerical Analysis/Computational Mathematics

LIN, P., Numerical Analysis/Computational Mathematics

MACDONALD, M J S., History Of Scottish Art

MARTIN, T., Animal Conservation

MCKENNA, S. J., Computer Vision

MELZER, A., Foundation Director Of Imsat

MUIR WOOD, D., Geotechnical Engineering

PARTRIDGE, S., Media Art

PRESS, M., Design Policy

REED, C. A., Art And Policy

RENWICK, G. T., Assistive Systems And Healthcare Computing

RICKETTS, I. W.

ROSE, M. J., Physical Electronics

SHEMILT, T. E., Fine Art Printmaking

TRUCCO, E., Inclusive Technologies

Faculty of Education, Social Work and Community Education (Gardyne Rd, Dundee, DD5 1NY; tel. (1382) 464000; e-mail edusocwk@dundee.ac.uk; internet www.dundee.ac.uk/facedusoc):

BALDWIN, N., Child Care and Protection

DANIEL, D. M., Child Care and Protection

HARTLEY, J. D., Educational Theory and Policy

TOPPING, K. J., Educational and Social Research

Faculty of Engineering and Physical Sciences (Carnegie Bldg, Dundee, DD1 4HN; tel. (1382) 344190; e-mail engineering@dundee .ac.uk; internet www.dundee.ac.uk/ facengphys):

ABEL, E. W., Biomedical Engineering
ARNOTT, J. L., Communications Systems
CHAPLAIN, M. A., Mathematical Biology
DAVIES, M. C. R., Civil Engineering
DAVIES, P. A., Fluid Dynamics
DHIR, R. K., Concrete Technology
FITZGERALD, A. G., Physics
FLETCHER, R., Mathematics
GOODMAN, T. N. T., Applied Analysis
HORNER, R. M. W., Engineering Management
NEWELL, A. F., Electronics and Microcomputer Systems
PANFILOV, A., Mathematical Biology
RICKETTS, I. W., Assistive Systems and Healthcare Computing
VARDY, A. E., Civil Engineering
WATSON, G. A., Numerical Analysis

Faculty of Law (Scrymgeour Bldg, Dundee, DD1 4HN; tel. (1382) 344185; e-mail lawandaccy@dundee.ac.uk; internet www .dundee.ac.uk/faclawacc):

BELCHER, C. A., Law
BISSETT-JOHNSON, A., Private Law
CAMERON, P. D., International Energy Law and Policy
FERGUSON, P. R., Scots Law
GRINYER, J. R., Accountancy
HELLIER, C. V., Accountancy and Business Finance
NIXON, W. A. J., Accountancy
PAGE, A. C., Public Law
PALMER, K. F., Mineral Policy
POUNDER, D. J., Forensic Medicine
POWER, D. M., Business Finance
REID, C. T., Environmental Law
STEVENS, P., Petroleum Policy and Economics
WALDE, T. W., International Economic, Energy and Natural Resources Law

College of Life Sciences (MSI/WTB/JBC Complex, Dow St, Dundee, DD1 4HN; tel. (1382) 385136; e-mail d.a.hill@dundee.ac.uk; internet www.lifesci.dundee.ac.uk):

BARTON, G. J., Bioinformatics
BIRCH, P. R. J., Plant Pathology
BLACK, S. M., Anatomy and Forensic Anthropology
BLOW, J. J., Chromosome Maintenance
BROWN, J. W. S., Molecular Plant Sciences
CODD, G. A., Microbiology
FAIRLAMB, A. H., Wellcome Trust Building
FLAVELL, A. J., Plant Genomics
GADD, G. M., Microbiology
GILBERT, I. H., Medicinal Chemistry
HALPIN, C., Plant Biology And Biotechnology
HARDIE, D. G., Cellular Signalling
HAY, R. T., Molecular Biology
HOPKINS, A. L., Medicinal Informatics
HUNDAL, H. S., Molecular Physiology
HUNTER, W. N., Structural Biology
LAMOND, A. I., Biochemistry
LILLEY, D. M. J., Molecular Biology
NATHKE, I. S., Epithelial Biology
OWEN-HUGHES, T. A., Chromatin Structure And Dynamics
PALMER, T., Molecular Microbiology
SARGENT, F., Bacterial Physiology
SCHAAP, P., Developmental Signalling
SOAMES, M., Anatomy
STARK, M. J. R., Yeast Molecular Biology
SWEDLOW, J. R., Quantitative Cell Biology
VAN AALTEN, D. M. F., Biological Chemistry
WATTS, C., Immunobiology
WEIJER, C. J., Developmental Physiology
WILLIAMS, J. A., Developmental Biology
WYATT, P. G., Drug Discovery

College of Medicine, Dentistry and Nursing (Ninewells Hospital and Medical School, Dundee, DD1 9SY; tel. (1382) 232763; e-mail cmdn-office@dundee.ac.uk; internet www.dundee.ac.uk/cmdn):

ABBOUD, R. J., Education in Biomechanics
ANDERSON, A. S., Food Choice
ASHFORD, M. L. J., Neuroscience
BALFOUR, D. J. K., Behavioural Pharmacology
BARBOUR, R., Health and Social Care
BARRATT, C., Reproductive Medicine
BEARN, D., Orthodontics
BELCH, J. J. F., Vascular Medicine
CADDEN, S. W., Oral Biology
CLARKE, P. R., Cancer Cell Biology
CLARKSON, J. E., Clinical Effectiveness
COLHOUN, H., Public Health
CROMBIE, I. K., Public Health
DAVEY, P. G., Pharmacoeconomics
DONNAN, P. T., Epidemiology and Biostatistics
ENTWISTLE, V. A., Values in Health Care
EVANS, A., Breast Imaging
FLEMING, S., Cellular and Molecular Pathology
FREEMAN, R. E., Dental Public Health Research
GUTHRIE, B., Primary Care Medicine
HALES, T. G., Anaesthesia
HAYES, J. D., Molecular Carcinogenesis
HIOM, K., Biomedical Research Institute
HOUSTON, S., Imaging
HUME, R., Developmental Medicine
JOVANOVIC, A., Experimental Medicine
KEARNEY, N., Nursing And Midwifery
LAMBERT, J. J., Neuropharmacology
LANG, C. C., Cardiology
LIPWORTH, B. J., Allergy and Respiratory Medicine
MACDONALD, T. M., Clinical Pharmacology and Pharmacoepidemiology
MACFARLAINE, G. T., Bacteriology
MCLEAN, W. H. I., Human Genetics
MCMURDO, M. E. T., Ageing and Health
MIRES, G. J., Perinatal Health and Education
MORRIS, A. D., Diabetic Medicine
MOSSEY, P. A., Craniofacial Development and Dentofacial Orthopaedics
MUNRO, A. J., Radiation Oncology
OGDEN, G. R., Oral and Maxillofacial Surgery
PALMER, C. N. A., Pharmacogenomics
PARKIN, I. G., Applied Clinical Anatomy
PETERS, J. A., Pharmacology
PITTS, N. B., Dental Health
RANKIN, E. M., Cancer Medicine
REES, C., Education Research
RICKETTS, D. N. J., Cariology and Conservative Dentistry
SCHWEIGER, S., Molecular Medicine
STEELE, J. D., Neuro-Imaging
STEELE, R. J., Surgery
STONEBRIDGE, P. A., Vascular Surgery
STRUTHERS, A. D., Cardiovascular Medicine and Therapeutics
SULLIVAN, F. M., General Practice and Primary Care
TAYLOR, J. S., Family Health
THOMPSON, A. M., Surgical Oncology
WOLF, C. R., Molecular Pharmacology
WRIGHT, E. G., Experimental Haematology
WYATT, J., Health Informatics

Faculty of Duncan of Jordanstone College (Perth Rd, Dundee, DD1 4HT; tel. (1382) 345213; internet www.dundee.ac.uk/ facdjcad):

COLVIN, C., Fine Art Photography
FISHER, G. R., Sculpture
FOLLETT, G. L. P., Design
INNS, T. G., Design
PARTRIDGE, S., Media Art
ROBB, A., Fine Art
UNWIN, S. D. A., Architecture

UNIVERSITY OF EDINBURGH

Old College, South Bridge, Edinburgh EH8 9YL

Telephone: (131) 650-1000
E-mail: communications.office@ed.ac.uk
Internet: www.ed.ac.uk
Founded 1583
Academic year: September to June
Chancellor: HRH THE PRINCESS ROYAL
Prin.: Prof. Sir TIMOTHY O'SHEA
Rector: PETER MCCOLL
Sec.: Dr KIM WALDRON
Hon. Vice-Prin.: Prof. CHRIS BREWARD
Vice-Prin. for Academic Enhancement: Prof. DAI HOUNSELL
Vice-Prin. for Devt: YOUNG DAWKINS
Vice-Prin. for Equality and Diversity: Prof. LORRAINE WATERHOUSE
Vice-Prin. for High Performance Computing: Prof. RICHARD KENWAY
Vice-Prin. for Int. Affairs: Prof. STEVE HILLIER
Vice-Prin. for Knowledge Management and Chief Information Officer: Prof. JEFF HAYWOOD
Vice-Prin. for Planning, Resources and Research Policy: Prof. APRIL MCMAHON
Vice-Prin. for Research, Training and Community Relations: Prof. MARY BOWNES
Dir of Registry: RIO WATT
Dir of Finance: JON GORRINGE
Dir of Int. Office: ALAN MACKAY
CEO of Edinburgh Research and Innovation: DEREK WADDELL
Librarian: Prof. JEFF HAYWOOD
Library: see under Libraries and Archives
Number of teachers: 2,730
Number of students: 27,000
Publications: EDIT Magazine (2 a year), Scottish Affairs (4 a year), Scottish Studies (1 a year), The University of Edinburgh Journal (2 a year)

HEADS OF COLLEGES

Edinburgh College of Art: Prof. IAN HOWARD (Prin.)
College of Humanities and Social Science: Prof. DOROTHY MIELL
College of Medicine and Veterinary Medicine: Prof. Sir JOHN SAVILL
College of Science and Engineering: Prof. NIGEL BROWN

PROFESSORS

College of Humanities and Social Science (Administration Office, 55–56 George Sq., Edinburgh, EH8 9JU; tel. (131) 650-4646; internet www.hss.ed.ac.uk):

ABHYONKAR, A., Financial Markets
ADLER, M. E., Socio-Legal Studies
ALTHAUS-REID, M., Contextual Theology
ANDERSON, R. D., Modern History
ANGOLD, M. J., Byzantine History
ANSELL, J. I., Risk Management
ARCHIBALD, T. W., Business Modelling
BAILEY, P., Modern Chinese History
BANKOWSKI, Z., Legal Theory
BANNER, M. C., Ethics and Public Policy in Life Sciences
BARKER, A. W., Austrian Studies
BARNARD, A. J., Anthropology of Southern Africa
BARRINGER, J. M., Greek Art and Archaeology
BARSTAD, H. M., Hebrew and Old Testament Studies
BLOOR, D., Sociology of Science
BLOXHAM, D., Modern History
BOYLE, A. E., Public International Law
BRAY, F., Social Anthropology
BRODIE, D., Employment Law
BROWN, S. J., Ecclesiastical History
BRUCE, V., Psychology
CAIRNS, D. L., Classics

CAIRNS, J. W., Legal History
CAMPBELL, I., Scottish and Victorian Literature
CARR, C. H., Corporate Strategy
CARR, D., Philosophy of Education
CARSTEN, J. F., Social and Cultural Anthropology
CASTLES, F. G., Social and Public Policy
CLARK, A., Logic and Metaphysics
CLARK, C., Social Work Ethics
CLASON, J., Comparative Social Policy
COGLIANO, F. D., American History
COLEBROOK, C. M., Literary Theory
COLVIN, S., German
COWLING, E. G., 20th-Century European Art
COX, J. L., Religious Studies
COYNE, A. R., Architectural Computing
CREE, V. E., Social Work Studies
CROOK, J. N., Business Economics
CURRIE, C., Child and Adolescent Health
DAVIDSON, R., Social History
DAWSON, J., Reformation History
DAYAN, P., French
DEARY, I. J., Differential Psychology
DELLA SALA, S., Human Cognitive Neuroscience
DEVINE, T. M., Scottish History and Palaeography
DUFFY, J. H., French
ERSKINE, A., Ancient History
FABRE, C., Political Theory
FERGUSSON, D., Divinity
FERREIRA, F., Language and Cognition
FRANSMAN, M., Economics
FROTH, S., Music
GENTZ, N., Chinese
GIEGERICH, H. J., English Linguistics
GILLIES, W., Celtic Languages, Literature, History and Antiquities
GILMORE, W. C., Int. Criminal Law
GOODE, A., Social Anthropology in Practice
GREASLEY, D. G., Economic History
GREEN, J., Medieval History
GRETTON, G. L., Law
GRIFFITHS, A., Anthropology of Law
GRIFFITHS, M., Classroom Learning
HARDING, D. W., Archaeology
HARDMAN MOORE, J. H., Political Economy
HAYWARD, T., Environmental Political Theory
HAYWOOD, J., Education and Technology
HENDERSON, J., Visual Cognition and Cognitive Neuroscience
HENLEY, J. S., Int. Management
HEYCOCK, C., Syntax
HIGGINS, P., Outdoor and Environmental Education
HILLENBRAND, C., Islamic History
HILLENBRAND, R., Islamic Art
HIMSWORTH, C. M. G., Admin. Law
HOPKINS, E. H. K., Economics
HOUNSELL, D., Higher Education
HURFORD, J. R., General Linguistics
HURTADO, L. W., New Testament Language, Literature and Theology
JACKSON, A., History
JAMIESON, L. H. A., Sociology of Families and Relationships
JEFFERY, C., Politics
JEFFERY, P. M., Sociology
JEFFERY, R., Sociology of South Asia
JEFFREYS-JONES, R., American History
JOSEPH, J. E., Applied Linguistics
KREBER, C., Teaching and Learning in Higher Education
LADD, D. R., Linguistics
LAPSLEY, I. McL., Accountancy
LAURIE, G. T., Medical Jurisprudence
LIM, T. M., Hebrew Bible and Second Temple Judaism
LINGARD, R., Education
LOGIE, R. H., Human Cognitive Neuroscience
MacDONALD, A. J., Architectural Studies
MacINNES, J., Sociology

MacKENZIE, D. A., Sociology
MacQUEEN, H. L., Private Law
MAHER, G., Criminal Law
MAIN, B. G. M., Business Economics
MANNING, S., English Literature
MARDER, R., Midwifery
MARSHALL, D. W., Marketing and Consumer Behaviour
McCRONE, D., Sociology
McDOUGALL, B. S., Chinese
McMAHON, A., English Language
McMILLAN, J. F., History
MEEK, D. E., Scottish and Gaelic Studies
MELIA, K. M., Nursing Studies
MEYERHOFF, M., Sociolinguistics
MITCHELL, F., Management Accounting
MOLINA, A. H., Technology Strategy
MUNN, P., Curriculum Research
MUNRO, C. R., Constitutional Law
MYERS, A., Organology
NELSON, P., Music and Technology
NICHOLSON, C. E., 18th-Century and Modern Literature
NORTHCOTT, M. S., Ethics
NUGENT, P., Comparative African History
NUTLEY, S., Public Management
O'DONOVAN, O., Christian Ethics and Practical Theology
OLIVER, N., Management
OSBORNE, N., Music
OSBORNE, S., Int. Public Management
OZGA, J., Educational Research
PATERSON, L., Educational Policy
PEDRESCHI, R., Architectural Technology
PELTENBURG, E. J., Archaeology
PETERSON, J., Int. Politics
PICKERING, M., Psychology of Language and Communication
POLLOCK, A., Health Policy
POWER, M. J., Clinical Psychology
PRITCHARD, D., Philosophy
PULLUM, G., General Linguistics
RAAB, C. D., Govt
RAFFE, D., Sociology of Education
RALSTON, I., Prehistoric European Archaeology
REID, K. G. C., Property Law
RIDDELL, S., Inclusion and Diversity
RIDGE, M. R., Moral Philosophy
ROBBINS, J. M. W., Hispanic Studies
RODGER, R., Economic and Social History
ROSA, P., Entrepreneurship and Family Business
SAKOVICS, J., Economic Theory
SANDERS, R., Sport Science
SCALTSAS, T., Ancient Philosophy
SCHOFIELD, J., Healthcare Management
SCOTT, A. G., European Union Studies
SHAW, J., European Institutions
SNELL, A. J., Economics and Econometrics
SORACE, A., Developmental Linguistics
SPARKS, R., Criminology
SPENCER, J., Anthropology of South Asia
STANLEY, E., Sociology
STEPHENSON, A. J. R., Modern German History
STEVENSON, R., 20th-Century Literature
TAFFER, R., Finance and Investment
TETT, L., Community Education and Lifelong Learning
THOMAS, J. P., Economics
THOMSON, R., Fine Art
USHER, J., Italian
WASOFF, F., Family Policies
WATERHOUSE, L. A. M., Social Work
WEBB, J., Sociology of Organizations
WHYTE, I. B., Architectural History
WHYTE, W. J., Social Work
WILLIAMS, R., Social Research on Technology
WISHART, J. G., Developmental Disabilities in Childhood
YEARLEY, S., Sociology of Scientific Knowledge

College of Medicine and Veterinary Medicine (The Queen's Medical Research Institute, 47 Little France Crescent, Edinburgh, EH16 4TJ; tel. (131) 242-9300; e-mail mvm@ed.ac.uk; internet www.mvm.ed.ac.uk):

AMOS, A., Health Promotion
AMYES, S. G. B., Microbial Chemotherapy
ANDERSON, R., Clinical Reproductive Science
ARGYLE, D., Veterinary Clinical Studies
BACKETH-MILLBURN, K. C., Sociology of Families and Health
BALL, K., Biochemistry and Cell Signalling
BARD, J., Bio-informatics and Devt
BATEMAN, D. N., Clinical Toxicology
BELL, J. E., Neuropathology
BEST, J. J. K., Medical Radiology
BHOPAL, R., Public Health
BLACKWOOD, D., Psychiatric Genetics
BOYD, K. M., Medical Ethics
BROPHY, P. J., Veterinary Anatomy and Cell Biology
CALDER, A. A., Obstetrics and Gynaecology
CAMPBELL, H., Genetic Epidemiology and Public Health
CLUTTON, E., Veterinary Anaesthesiology
CORCORAN, B. M., Veterinary Cardiopulmonary Medicine
CRAWFORD, D. H., Bacteriology
CRITCHLEY, H., Reproductive Medicine
CUMMING, A. D., Medical Education
CUNNINGHAM-BURLEY, S. J., Medical and Family Sociology
DAVIES, J., Experimental Anatomy
DENNIS, M. S., Stroke Medicine
DEWHURST, D., Student Learning (e-Learning)
DIXON, P. M., Equine Surgery
DONALDSON, K., Respiratory Toxicology
DOUGLAS, N. J., Respiratory and Sleep Medicine
DROUSFIELD, I., Leukocyte and Lung Cell Biology
DUNLOP, M. G., Coloproctology
EBMEIER, K. P., Psychiatry
ELSE, R. W., Diagnostic Veterinary Pathology
FALLON, M. T., Palliative Medicine
FAZAKERLEY, J., Virology
FEARON, K. C. H., Surgical Oncology
FFRENCH-CONSTANT, C., Multiple Sclerosis
FLEETWOOD-WALKER, S. M., Sensory Neuroscience
FORBES, S. J., Transplantation and Regenerative Medicine
FOWKES, F. G. R., Epidemiology
FOX, K. A. A., Cardiology
GALLY, D. L., Microbial Genetics
GARDEN, O. J., Clinical Surgery
GHAZAL, P., Molecular Genetics and Biomedicine
GOVAN, J. R. W., Microbial Pathogenecity
GRANT, S. G. N., Molecular Neuroscience
GREENING, A. P., Pulmonary Disease
GREGORY, C. D., Inflammatory Cell Biology
GUNN-MOORE, D., Feline Medicine
HARKISS, G. D., Veterinary Immunopathology
HARMAR, A. J., Molecular Pharmacology
HARRISON, D. J., Pathology
HASLETT, C., Respiratory Medicine
HAYES, P. C., Hepatology
HECK, M., Cell Biology and Genetics
HILLIER, S. G., Reproductive Endocrinology
HOOPER, M. L., Molecular Pathology
HOPKINS, J., Veterinary Immunology
HOWIE, S. E. M., Immunopathology
HUPP, E., Cancer Research
IBBETSON, R. J., Dental Primary Care
IREDALE, J., Medicine
IRONSIDE, J. W., Clinical Neuropathology
JARMAN, A. P., Developmental Cell Biology
JODRELL, D., Cancer Therapeutics
JOHNSTONE, E. C., Psychiatry
KAUFMAN, M. H., Anatomy

LAMB, J. R., Veterinary Clinical Immunology
LAWRIE, S. M., Psychiatric Imaging
LENG, G., Experimental Physiology
LINCOLN, Q. A., Biological Tuning
LUDWIG, M., Neurophysiology
MACNEE, W., Respiratory and Environmental Medicine
MACPHERSON, S. G., Postgraduate Medical Education
MARSHALL, I., Magnetic Resonance Physics
MASON, J. I., Clinical Biochemistry
MCCULLOCH, J., Neuropharmacology
MCDICKEN, W. N., Medical Physics and Medical Engineering
MCGORUM, B. C., Equine Medicine
MCINTOSH, N., Child Life and Health
MCQUEEN, D. S., Sensory Pharmacology
MCKEEVER, D., Veterinary Clinical Science
MELTON, D. W., Somatic Cell Genetics
MIMS, R. A., Paediatric Neurology
MORRIS, R. G. M., Neuroscience
MURRAY, G. D., Medical Statistics
MURRAY, S. A., Primary Palliative Care
NASH, A. A., Veterinary Pathology
NEWBY, D., Cardiology
OWENS, D. G. C., Clinical Psychiatry
PETTIGREW, G. W., Bioenergetics
PORTEOUS, D. J., Human Molecular Genetics and Medicine
POWER, I., Anaesthetics, Critical Care and Pain
POXTON, I. R., Microbial Infection and Immunity
PRESCOTT, R. J., Health Technology Assessment
PRICE, D. J., Developmental Neurobiology
RALSTON, S. H., Rheumatology
REES, J. L., Dermatology
RHIND, S. M., Veterinary Medical Education
ROCHESTER, R. R., Cellular Neuroscience
ROSS, J. A., Liver Cell Biology
ROSSI, A., Respiratory and Inflammation Pharmacology
RUSSELL, J. A., Neuroendocrinology
SALLER, D. M., Osteoarticular Pathology
SANDERCOCK, P., Medical Neurology
SATSANGI, J., Gastroenterology
SAVILL, J. S., Experimental Medicine
SECKL, J. R., Molecular Medicine
SETHI, T. J., Respiratory and Lung Cancer Biology
SHARPE, M., Psychological Medicine and Symptoms Research
SHEIKH, A., Primary Care Research and Devt
SHIPSTON, M. J., Physiology
SIMMONDS, P., Virology
SIMPSON, A. H. R. W., Orthopaedic Surgery
SIMPSON, J. W., Canine Medecine
SMYTH, J. F., Medical Oncology
TAYLOR, D. W., Tropical Animal Health
THODAY, K. L., Veterinary Dermatology
TURNER, A. N., Nephrology
TURNER, M., Cellular Therapy
VAN HEYNINGEN, S., Learning and Teaching
WALKER, B. R., Endocrinology
WARDLAW, J. M., Applied Neuroimaging
WARLOW, C. P., Medical Neurology
WATSON, E. D., Veterinary Reproduction
WEBB, D. J., Clinical Pharmacology
WELBURN, S., Medical and Veterinary Molecular Epidemiology
WELLER, D., General Practice
WHITTLE, I. R., Surgical Neurology
WILL, R. G., Clinical Neurology
WILMUT, I., Reproductive Science
WOOLHOUSE, M. E. J., Veterinary Public Health and Quantitative Epidemiology

College of Science and Engineering (Weir Bldg, King's Bldgs, West Mains Rd, Edinburgh, EH9 3JY; tel. (131) 650-5759; e-mail sciengmail@ed.ac.uk; internet www.scieng .ed.ac.uk):

ACKLAND, G. J., Computer Simulation
AITKEN, A., Protein Biochemistry
AITKEN, C. G. G., Forensic Statistics
ALLEN, J. E., Immunology
ALLSHIRE, R., Chromosome Biology
ANDERTON, X., Therapeutic Immunology
ARSLAN, T., Integrated Electronic Systems
ATKINSON, M. P., e-Science
ATTFIELD, J. P., Materials Science at Extreme Conditions
BALL, R. D., Mathematical Physics
BARLOW, P. N., Structural Biology
BARTHOLEMIE, R. J., Renewable Energy
BARTON, N. H., Evolutionary Genetics
BAXTER, R. L., Chemical Biology
BEGGS, J. D., Molecular Biology
BIALEK, J. W., Electrical Engineering
BIRD, A. P., Genetics
BISHOP, C. M., Computer Science
BLAXTER, M. L., Evolutionary Genomics
BONDI, E., Social Geography
BOULTON, G. S., Geology
BOWNES, M., Developmental Biology
BRADEN, H. W., Integrable Systems
BRADLEY, N., Chemical Biology
BRAND, P. W. J. L., Astrophysics
BRANDONI, S., Chemical Engineering
BRANFORD, D., Photonuclear Physics
BRUCE, A. D., Statistical Physics
BRYDON, I. G., Renewable Energy
BULFIELD, G., Animal Genetics
BUNDY, A. R., Automated Reasoning
BUNEMAN, P., Database Systems
CAMPBELL, D. M., Musical Acoustics
CARBERY, A., Mathematics
CATES, M., Natural Philosophy
CHAPMAN, S. K., Biological Inorganic Chemistry
CHEUNG, R., Nanoelectronics
CLARKE, P., e-Science
COOPER, J. M., Micro- and Nanosystems
CRAIN, J., Applied Physics
CROWLEY, T., Earth Systems Science
DAVIE, A. M., Mathematical Analysis
DAVIES, M., Signal Processing
DAVIS, I., Cell Biology
DONOVAN, R. J., Chemistry
DUGMORE, A. J., Geosciences
DUNLOP, J. S., Extragalactic Astronomy
EASSON, W. J., Fluid Mechanics
FAN, W., Web Data Management
FARMER, J. G., Environmental Geochemistry
FIGUEROA-O'FARRILL, J., Geometric Physics
FINNEGAN, D. J., Molecular Genetics
FISHER, R. B., Computer Vision
FITTON, J. G., Igneous Petrology
FORDE, M. C., Civil Engineering Construction
FOURMAN, M. P., Computer Systems
FRY, S. C., Plant Biochemistry
GILLESPIE, T. A., Mathematical Analysis
GONDZIS, J., Optimization
GORDON, I., Mathematics
GORYANIN, I., Systems Biology
GRACE, J., Environmental Biology
GRAHAM, C. M., Experimental Geochemistry
GRANT, P. M., Electronic Signal Processing
GRAY, D., Immunology
GYÖNGY, I. J., Probability
HALL, C., Materials
HALLIDAY, I., Physics
HARLEY, S. L., Lower Crustal Processes
HARRISON, A., Solid-State Chemistry
HARTE, B., Metaphorism
HASZELDINE, S., Sedimentary Geology
HEAVENS, A. F., Theoretical Astrophysics
HEGGIE, D. C., Mathematical Astronomy
HILLSTON, J., Quantitative Modelling
HUDSON, A. D., Developmental Genetics
HUXLEY, A., Physics, Quantum Ordering at Extreme Positions
ILLIUS, A. W., Animal Ecology
JACK, M. A., Electronic Systems
JACOBS, J. M., Cultural Geography

JERRUM, M. R., Algorithms and Complexity
KEIGHTLEY, P. D., Evolutionary Genetics
KENNEDY, A. D., Computational Science
KENWAY, R. D., Mathematical Physics
KLEIN, E., Cognitive Systems
KROON, D., Geology
LAWRENCE, A., Astronomy
LEACH, D. R. F., Molecular Genetics
LEIGH, D. A., Organic Chemistry
LEIGH BROWN, A. J., Evolutionary Genetics
LEIM-KUHLER, B., Applied Mathematics
LENAGAN, T. H., Non-commutative Algebra
LIBKIN, L., Foundations of Data Management
LOAKE, G. J., Molecular Plant Sciences
LU, Y., Structural Mechanics
MADDON, P., Physical Chemistry
MAIN, I. G., Seismology and Rock Physics
MAIZELS, R. M., Zoology
MATTHEWS, K., Parasite Biology
MCKINNON, K. I. M., Operational Research
MCLAUGHLIN, S., Electronic Communications Systems
MCMAHON, M., High Pressure Physics
MCNABB, H., Heterocyclic Chemistry
MEDVINSKY, A., Haematopoietic Stem Cell Biology
METCALFE, S. E., Environmental Change
MILLER, A. J., Systems Biology
MONCRIEFF, J., Micrometeorology
MOORE, J. D., Artificial Intelligence
MULGREW, B., Signals and Systems
MULHEIM, F., Particle Physics
MURRAY, A. F., Neural Electronics
NEE, S., Social Evolution
NELMES, R. J., Physical Crystallography
O'BOYLE, M., Computer Science
OBERLANDER, J., Epistemics
OOI, J., Particulate Solid Mechanics
OPARKA, K. J., Plant Science
PARKER, D. F., Applied Mathematics
PARSONS, S., Crystallography
PEACOCK, J. A., Cosmology
PEMBERTON, J. M., Molecular Ecology
PLAYFER, S. M., Experimental Particle Physics
PLOTKIN, G. D., Computation Theory
PONTON, J. W., Chemical and Process Systems Engineering
POON, W. C. K., Condensed Matter Physics
PUSEY, P. N., Physics
RANICKI, A. A., Algebraic Surgery
RANKIN, D. W. H., Structural Chemistry
READ, A. F., Natural History
REID, G. A., Molecular Microbiology
RENALS, S., Speech Technology
RESBOL, N. D., Fungal Cell Biology
ROBERTSON, A. H. F., Geology
ROTTER, J. M., Civil Engineering
ROUNSEVELL, M., Rural Economy and Environmental Sustainability
SANNELLA, D. T., Computer Science
SAWYER, L., Biomolecular Structure
SCHÄFER, A., Environmental Engineering
SEATON, N. A., Interfacial Engineering
SHEIKHDESLAMI, R., Chemical Process Engineering
SHOTTER, A. C., Experimental Physics
SIEGERT, M. J., Geoscience
SINGER, M., Geometry
SMOKTURNOWICZ, A., Algebra
STAEHELI, L., Geography
STEEDMAN, M., Cognitive Science
STENNING, K., Human Communications
STIRLING, C., Computation Theory
SUGDEN, D. E., Geography
SUMMERFIELD, M. A., Geomorphology
TASKER, P. A., Industrial Chemistry
TATE, A., Knowledge-based Systems
TELEMAN, C., Mathematics
TETT, S. F. B., Earth Systems Dynamics
THOMPSON, R., Environmental Geophysics
TOPHAM, N. P., Computer Systems
TORERO, J. L., Fire Safety Engineering
TREW, A. S., Computational Science
TUDHOPE, A. W., Climate Science

TYER, S. M. D., Systems Biology
UNDERHILL, J. R., Seismic Stratigraphy
UNDERWOOD, I., Electronic Displays
USAMI, A. S., Structural Engineering and Computational Mechanics
VOLBERG, A., Mathematical Sciences
WALDER, P., Theoretical Computer Science
WALKINSHAW, M. D., Structural Biochemistry
WALLACE, A. R., Renewable Energy Systems
WALTON, A. J., Microelectronic Manufacturing
WEBBER, B., Intelligent Systems
WEST, S. A., Evolutionary Ecology
WHALER, K. A., Geophysics
WHITTEMORE, C. T., Agriculture and Rural Economy
WILLIAMS, C. K. I., Machine Learning
WILLIAMS, W., Mineral Physics
WILLSHAW, D., Computational Neurobiology
WITHERS, C. W. J., Geography
WOODS, P. J., Nuclear Physics
WRIGHT, J., Mathematical Analysis
YELLOWLEES, L. J., Inorganic Electrochemistry
ZIOLKOWSKI, A. M., Petroleum Geoscience

CONSTITUENT COLLEGE

New College/School of Divinity: Mound Pl., Edinburgh, EH1 2LX; tel. (131) 650-8959; e-mail divinity@ed.ac.uk; internet www.ed.ac.uk/schools-departments/divinity; f. 1846 as an ind. college, merged with Faculty of Divinity of Univ. of Edinburgh 1935; Head Prof. PAUL FOSTER

UNIVERSITY OF GLASGOW

Glasgow, G12 8QQ

Telephone: (141) 330-2000
E-mail: media@gla.ac.uk
Internet: www.gla.ac.uk

Founded 1451, reconstituted 1577
Academic year: October to June

Chancellor: Prof. Sir KENNETH CALMAN
Prin. and Vice-Chancellor: Prof. ANTON MUSCATELLI
Pro-Vice-Prin.: Prof. JOHN COGGINS
Sr Vice-Prin. and Deputy Vice-Chancellor: ANDREA NOLAN
Vice-Prin. for Learning and Teaching: Prof. FRANK COTON
Vice-Prin. for Life Sciences and Medicine: Prof. JOHN COGGINS
Vice-Prin. for Research and Enterprise: Prof. STEVE P. BEAUMONT
Vice-Prin. for Strategy and Resources: Prof. NEAL JUSTER
Clerk of Senate: Prof. GRAHAM CAIE
Rector: CHARLES KENNEDY
Sec. of Court: DAVID NEWALL
Librarian: HELEN DURNDELL

Library: see under Libraries and Archives
Number of teachers: 2,600
Number of students: 21,950

Publications: *Avenue* (2 a year), *News Review* (2 a year)

HEADS OF COLLEGES AND SCHOOLS

Arts Lab: Prof. JOHN CAUGHIE (Dir)
Business School: Prof. FARHAD NOORBAKHSH
College of Arts: Prof. MURRAY PITTOCK
College of Medical, Veterinary and Life Sciences: Prof. ANNA DOMINICZAK
College of Science and Engineering: Prof. JOHN CHAPMAN
College of Social Sciences: Prof. ANNE ANDERSON
School of Chemistry: Prof. STEPHEN CLARK
School of Computing Science: Prof. JOSEPH S. SVENTEK

School of Critical Studies: Prof. NIGEL J. LEASK
School of Culture and Creative Arts: Prof. NICHOLAS J. PEARCE
School of Education: Prof. ROBERT A. DAVIS
School of Engineering: Prof. JOHN H. MARSH
School of Geographical and Earth Sciences: Prof. TREVOR HOEY
School of Humanities/Sgoil nan Daonnachdan: Prof. SIMON J. BALL
School of Interdisciplinary Studies: Prof. DAVID CLARK (Dir)
School of Law: Prof. ROSA GREAVES
School of Life Sciences: Dr ROBERT AITKEN
School of Mathematics and Statistics: Prof. NICHOLAS A. HILL
School of Medicine: Prof. DAVID H. BARLOW
School of Modern Languages and Cultures: Prof. JOHN MACKLIN
School of Physics and Astronomy: Prof. ANDREW R. LONG
School of Psychology: Prof. ANTHONY M. BURTON
School of Social and Political Sciences: Prof. MICHAEL J. FRENCH
School of Veterinary Medicine: Prof. STUART W. REID

PROFESSORS

Faculty of Arts (6 University Gardens, Glasgow, G12 8QQ; tel. (141) 330-6319; e-mail dean@arts.gla.ac.uk; internet www.arts.gla.ac.uk):

ABRAMS, L. C., Gender History
ADAMS, A. R., Emblem Studies
BISHOP, P. C., German
BLACK, C. F., Italian History
BROADIE, A., Logic and Rhetoric
BUTT, J. A., Music (Gardiner Chair)
CAIE, G. D., English Language
CARTER, A. B., Moral Philosophy
CASTILLO, S., American Literature (John Nichol Chair)
CAUGHIE, J. M., Film and Television Studies
CLANCY, T. O., Celtic
COHN, S. K., Medieval History
COWAN, E. J., Scottish History
CRONIN, R., English Literature
GERAGHTY, C., Film and TV Studies
GEYER-KORDESCH, J. M., European Natural History and Medicine
GIFFORD, D. G., Scottish Literature
GONZALEZ, M. A., Latin American Studies
GRANT, R. A., Cultural and Political Thought
GREEN, R. P., Humanity
HAIR, G. B., Music
HANSON, W. S., Roman Archaeology
HAZLETT, W. I., Ecclesiastical History
HOPKINS, D., Art History
JASPER, D., Literature and Theology
KAY, C. J., English Language
KIDD, C., Modern History (Chair)
KIRK, J., Scottish History
KNAPP, A. B., Mediterranean Archaeology
KNOWLES, D. R., Political Philosophy
LEASK, N., English Language and Literature (Regius Chair)
LEONARD, T. A., Creative Writing
MACKENZIE, A. L., Spanish (Ivy McClelland Research Chair)
MACMAHON, M. K. C., Phonetics
MALEY, W. T., Renaissance Studies
MARSHALL, W. J., Modern French Studies
MAWDSLEY, E., International History
MCDONALD, J. B., Drama (James Arnott Chair)
MCLEOD, M. D., African Studies
MOIGNARD, E. A., Classical Art and Archaeology
MORRIS, C. D., Archaeology
MOSS, M. S., Archival Studies
NEWLANDS, G. M., Divinity

NEWMAN, S. P., American Studies (Sir Denis Brogan Chair)
O'MAOLALAIGH, R., Celtic
O'DOCHARTAIGH, C. N. O., Celtic
PEACOCK, N. A., French (Marshall Chair)
READER, K. A., Modern French Studies
RIACH, A. S., Scottish Literature
ROBERTSON, P. B., Mackintosh Studies
ROSS, S., Humanities Informatics and Digital Curation
RYCROFT, M. E., Music
SCHMIDT-LEUKEL, P. H., World Religions for Peace
SMITH, J. J., English Philology
STALLEY, R. F., Ancient Philosophy
STEPHENSON, R. H., German Language and Literature; Modern Languages (William Jacks Chair)
TAYLOR, R. C., Social Policy and Social Work
THORP, N. R., History of Art
TODD, J., English Literature (Francis Hutcheson Chair)
WARD, M. G., German Language and Literature
YARRINGTON, A. W., Fine Art (Richmond Chair)

Faculty of Biomedical and Life Sciences (Room 237, West Medical Bldg, Glasgow, G12 8QQ; tel. (141) 339-8855; e-mail ilbs-acstaff@bio.gla.ac.uk; internet www.gla.ac.uk/ibls/faculty/html):

BIRKBECK, T. H., Marine Microbiology
BLATT, M. R., Botany (Regius Chair)
CAMPBELL, A. M., Biochemical Immunology
CLEMENTS, J. B., Virology
COGDELL, R. J., Botany (Hooker Chair)
COGGINS, J. R., Molecular Enzymology
COOMBS, G. H., Biochemical Parasitology
CROZIER, A., Plant Biochemistry and Human Nutrition
CUSHLEY, W., Molecular Immunology
DAVIES, R. W., Biotechnology (Robertson Chair)
DOW, J. A. T., Molecular and Integrative Physiology
ELLIOTT, R. M., Molecular Virology
EVANS, D. J., Virology
FERRELL, W. R., Clinical Physiology
FURNESS, R. W., Seabird and Fishing Interactions
GILLESPIE, D. A. F., Molecular and Cell Biology
GOULD, G. W., Membrane Biology
HAGAN, P., Parasitology
HOUSLAY, M. D., Biochemistry (Gardiner Chair)
HOUSTON, D. C., Zoology
HUNTINGFORD, F. A., Functional Ecology
JENKINS, G. I., Plant Cell and Molecular Biology
KENNEDY, M. W., Infection Biology
KOLCH, W., Molecular and Cellular Biology
LA THANGUE, N. B., Biochemistry (Cathcart Chair)
LINDSAY, J. G., Medical Biochemistry
MACLEAN, M. R., Pulmonary Pharmacology
MARTIN, W., Cardiovascular Pharmacology
MAXWELL, D. J., Neuroanatomy
MCGRATH, J. C., Physiology (Regius Chair)
METCALFE, N. B., Behavioural Ecology
MILLIGAN, G., Molecular Pharmacology
MILNER-WHITE, E. J., Structural Bioinformatics
MITCHELL, T. J., Microbiology
MONAGHAN, P., Animal Ecology
MONCKTON, D. G., Human Genetics
MORRIS, B. J., Molecular Neurobiology
MUTRIE, N., Physical Activity and Health Science
NIMMO, H. G., Plant Biochemistry
PAGE, R. D., Taxonomy
PAYNE, A. P., Anatomy
PHILLIPS, R. S., Parasitology
PRICE, N. C., Protein Science

RUXTON, G. D., Theoretical Ecology
SMITH, G. L., Cardiovascular Physiology
STARK, W. M., Molecular Genetics
STONE, T. W., Pharmacology
TAYLOR, A. C., Physiological Ecology
TODD, A. J., Neuroscience
TURNER, C. M. R., Parasitology
WHITE, R. J., Gene Transcription

Faculty of Education (St Andrew's Bldg, Glasgow, G12 8QQ; tel. (141) 330-3700; e-mail faculty@educ.gla.ac.uk; internet www.gla.ac.uk/faculties/education):

BARON, S., Urban Education
BARR, J. L., Adult and Continuing Education
CONROY, J. C., Religious and Philosophical Education
MCGETTRICK, B. J., Educational Studies
MCGONIGAL, J., English in Education
MENTER, I. J., Teacher Education
PETERS, M. A., Education
PREECE, J., Adult and Lifelong Education
WHITEHEAD, R. R., Theoretical Physics
WILKINSON, J. E., Education

Faculty of Engineering (James Watt South Bldg, Glasgow, G12 8QQ; tel. (141) 330-3733; internet www.eng.gla.ac.uk):

ACHA, E., Electrical Power Systems
AITCHISON, J. S., Photonics
ARNOLD, J. M., Applied Electromagnetics
ASENOV, A. M., Device Modelling
BARKER, J. R., Electronics
BARLTROP, N. D. P., Naval Architecture and Ocean Engineering (John Elder Chair)
BICANIC, N. J. D., Civil Engineering (Regius Chair)
CARTMELL, M. P., Mechanical Engineering
COOPER, J. M., Bioelectronics and Bioengineering
COTON, F. N., Low Speed Aerodynamics
COWLING, M. J., Marine Technology
CUMMING, D., Microelectronics
DAS, P. K., Marine Structures
DAVIES, J. H., Physical Electronics
DE LA RUE, R. M., Optoelectronics
ERVINE, D. A., Water Engineering
GALBRAITH, R. A. M., Engineering (Shoda Chair)
HANCOCK, J. W., Mechanical Engineering
HUNT, K. J., Mechanical Engineering (Wylie Chair)
HUTCHINGS, D., Optical and Quantum Electronics
IRONSIDE, C. N., Quantum Electronics
MARSH, J. H., Optoelectronic Systems
MCINNES, C. R., Space Systems Engineering
MILLER, T. J. E., Electrical Engineering
MURRAY-SMITH, D. J., Engineering Systems and Control
O'REILLY, J., Control Engineering
SEWELL, J. I., Electronic Systems
STANLEY, C. R., Semiconductor Materials
THAYNE, I., Ultrafast Systems
VASSALOS, D., Naval Architecture
WEAVER, J. M. R., Applied Nanofabrication
WHEELER, S. J., Civil Engineering (Cormack Chair)
WILKINSON, C. D. W., Electrical Engineering (James Watt Chair)

Faculty of Information and Mathematical Sciences (Room 311, Boyd Orr Bldg, Glasgow, G12 8QQ; tel. (141) 330-4269; e-mail gs@fims.gla.ac.uk; internet www.gla.ac.uk/faculties/ims):

ANDERSON, A. H., Psychology
ATKINSON, M. P., Computing Science
BOWMAN, A. W., Statistics
BREWSTER, S. A., Human Computer Interaction
BROWN, K. A., Mathematics
BURTON, A. M., Psychology
CALDER, M., Formal Methods

COHEN, S. D., Number Theory
FEARN, D. R., Applied Mathematics
FORD, I., Biostatistics
GARROD, S. C., Cognitive Psychology
GILBERT, D. R., Biomedical Informatics
HILL, N. A., Mathematics (Simson Chair)
JOHNSON, C. W., Computing Science
JONES, B. T., Psychology
KROPHOLLER, P. H., Mathematics
O'DONNELL, P.
OGDEN, R. W., Mathematics (George Sinclair Chair)
PRIDE, S. J., Mathematics
SANFORD, A. J., Psychology
SCHWEINBERGER, S. R., Psychology
SCHYNS, P. G., Visual Cognition
SCOTT, E. M., Environmental Statistics
SENN, K. S. J., Statistics
SMITH, P. F., Mathematics
SVENTEK, J., Communications Systems
TITTERINGTON, D. M., Statistics
VAN RIJSBERGEN, K. J., Computing Science
WATT, D. A., Computing Science
WEBB, J. R. L., Mathematics
WELLAND, R. C., Software Engineering

Faculty of Law and Financial Studies (5–9 Stair Bldg, The Square, Univ. of Glasgow, Glasgow, G12 8QQ; tel. (141) 330-6075; e-mail faculty@law.gla.ac.uk; internet www.gla.ac.uk/faculties/law):

BEATTIE, V. A., Accounting
BURROWS, N., European Law
CRERAR, L. D., Banking Law
DANBOLT, J., Finance
DAVIDSON, F. P., Law, Commercial Law (Alexander Stone Chair)
EMMANUEL, C. R., Accountancy
FARMER, L. A., Law
GRAY, R. H., Accounting
HOLLAND, J. B., Accountancy
KINNON, D. H., Accounting (Johnstone Smith Chair)
MCLEAN, S. A., Law and Ethics in Medicine (International Bar Assoc Chair)
MCPHAIL, K., Social and Ethical Accounting
MULLEN, T. J., Law
MURDOCH, J. L., Public Law
OPONG, K. K., Finance and Accounting
ORUCU, E., Comparative Law
REES, W., Accountancy
RENNIE, R., Conveyancing
SHACKLETON, J. K., Accounting History
THOMSON, J. M., Law (Regius Chair)
TOMKINS, A., Public Law (John Millar Chair)
WOOLFSON, C. A., Labour Studies

Faculty of Medicine (Wolfson Medical Bldg, University Ave, Univ. of Glasgow, Glasgow, G12 8QQ; tel. (141) 330-5921; e-mail postmaster@student.gla.ac.uk; internet www.gla.ac.uk/faculties/medicine):

AYOUB, A. F., Oral Surgery
BAGG, J., Clinical Microbiology
BAKER, A. H., Molecular Medicine
BARLOW, D. H., Reproductive Medicine
BROWN, R., Cancer Therapeutics
CASSIDY, J., Oncology
COBBE, S. M., Medical Cardiology (Walton Chair)
CONNELL, J. M. C., Endocrinology
CONNOR, J. M., Medical Genetics (Burton Chair)
COOKE, T. G., Surgery (St Mungo Chair)
COOPER, S. A., Learning Disabilities
DOMINICZAK, A. F., Cardiovascular Medicine
ELLIOTT, A. T., Clinical Physics
ESPIE, C. A., Clinical Psychology
EVANS, J. J., Applied Neuropsychology
EVANS, T. J., Molecular Microbiology
FRANKLIN, I. M., Transfusion Medicine
GARSIDE, P., Immunobiology
GEMMELL, C. G., Bacterial Infection and Epidemiology

GEORGE, W. D., Surgery (Regius Chair)
GRAHAM, G. J., Molecular and Structural Immunology
GREER, I. A., Obstetrics and Gynaecology (Muirhead Chair)
GUSTERSON, B. A., Pathology
HANLON, P. W., Public Health
HARNETT, M. M., Immune Signalling
HILLAN, E. M., Midwifery
HILLIS, W. S., Cardiovascular and Exercise Medicine
HOLE, D. J., Epidemiology and Biostatistics
HOLYOAKE, T., Experimental Haematology
JUDGE, K. F., Health Promotion Policy (HEBS Chair)
KEITH, W. N., Molecular Oncology
KENNEDY, P. G. E., Neurology (Burton Chair)
KENNY, G. N. C., Anaesthesia
LANGHORNE, P., Stroke Care
LEAN, M. E. J., Human Nutrition (Rank Chair)
LEES, K. R., Cerebrovascular Medicine
LIEW, F. Y., Immunology (Gardiner Chair)
LOWE, G. D. O., Vascular Medicine
LUMSDEN, M. A., Medical Education and Gynaecology
LYALL, F., Maternal and Fetal Health
MACDONALD, D. G., Oral Pathology
MACFARLANE, P. W., Electrocardiology
MACRAE, I. M., Neuroscience
MCCOLL, K. E. L., Gastroenterology
MCINNES, G. T., Clinical Pharmacology
MCINNES, I. B., Experimental Medicine
MCKILLOP, J. H., Medicine (Muirhead Chair)
MCMILLAN, T., Clinical Neuropsychology
MCMURRAY, J. I. V., Medical Cardiology
MILLAR, K., Behavioural Science
MORRISON, J. M., General Practice
MOWAT, A. M., Mucosal Immunology
MURRAY, T. S., General Practice
O'DWYER, P. J., Gastrointestinal Surgery
OLIVER, J. S., Forensic Toxicology
RAMPLING, R. P., Neuro-oncology
REID, J. L., Materia Medica, Medicine and Therapeutics (Regius Chair)
REID, M., Professor of Women's Health
SATTAR, N. A., Metabolic Medicine
SHEPHERD, J., Pathological Biochemistry
SMITH, L. N., Nursing Studies
STONE, D. H., Paediatric Epidemiology
STOTT, D. J., Geriatric Medicine (David Cargill Chair)
STURROCK, R. D., Rheumatology (McLeod/Arthritis and Rheumatism Council Chair)
THOMSON, N. C., Respiratory Medicine
WATT, G. C. M., General Practice (Norrie-Miller Chair)
WEAVER, L. T., Child Health (Samson Gemmell Chair)
WELBURY, R. R., Paediatric Dentistry
WELSH, J., Palliative Medicine (Dr Olav Kerr Chair)
WHEATLEY, D. J., Cardiac Surgery
WILLISON, H. J., Neurology
WRAY, D., Oral Medicine

Faculty of Physical Sciences (Room 234, Kelvin Bldg, Univ. of Glasgow, Glasgow, G12 8QQ; tel. (141) 330-4374; e-mail physci@gla.ac.uk; internet www.facps.gla.ac.uk):

BARRON, L. D., Physical Chemistry (Gardiner Chair)
BISHOP, P. M., Geography
BRIGGS, J. A., Geography
BROWN, J. C., Astrophysics, Astronomy (Regius Chair)
BROWN, R. W., Earth Sciences
CHAPMAN, J. N., Physics
COOPER, A., Biophysical Chemistry
CRAVEN, A. J., Physics
DAVIES, C. T., Physics
DOYLE, A. T., Physics

FALLICK, A. E., Isotope Geosciences
FROGGATT, C. D., Physics
GILMORE, C. J., Crystallography
HOEY, T., Numerical Geoscience
HOUGH, J., Physics
ISAACS, N. W., Protein Crystallography (Joseph Black Chair)
JACKSON, S. D., Catalysis Science
KOCOVSKY, P., Chemistry (Ramsay Chair)
LEAKE, R. E., Endocrine Oncology
LONG, A. R., Physics
PADDISON, R., Geography
PADGETT, M. J., Physics
PHILO, C., Geography
ROBERTSON, N. A., Experimental Physics
ROBINS, D. J., Bio-organic Chemistry
ROSNER, G., Natural Philosophy (Cargill Chair)
RUSSELL, M. J., Applied Geology (Dixon Chair)
SAXON, D. H., Physics (Kelvin Chair)
STRAIN, K. A., Physics
WILSON, C., Chemistry (Regius Chair)
WINFIELD, J. M., Inorganic Chemistry

Faculty of Social Sciences (Adam Smith Bldg, 40 Bute Gardens, Glasgow, G12 8RT; tel. (141) 330-0347; e-mail enquiries@socsci.gla.ac.uk; internet www.gla.ac.uk/faculties/socialsciences):

ADAMS, C. D., Ian Mactaggart Chair of Property and Urban Studies
BEAUMONT, P. B., Employee Relations
BERRY, C. J., Political Theory
BURMAN, M., Criminology
CORRIN, C. A., Feminist Politics
CROWTHER, M. A., Social History
FERGUSON, H., Sociology
FRENCH, M. J., Economic History
FRISBY, D. P., Sociology
FURLONG, A., Sociology
GIRVIN, B., Comparative Politics
GOODLAD, R., Housing and Urban Studies
GORDON, E. J., Gender and Social History
HARRIS, R., Cairncross Professor of Applied Economics
HILL, M., Study of the Child (St Kentigern Chair)
KEARNS, A. J., Urban Studies
LAING, A. W., Business and Management
MACBETH, D. K., Supply Chain Management
MACDONALD, R., Bonar-Macfie Chair of Economics
MACLENNAN, D., Urban Studies, Economics and Finance (Mactaggart Chair of Urban Studies)
MALLEY, J., Economics
MCGREGOR, A. M., Housing and Urban Studies
MCKEGANEY, N. P., Drug Misuse Research
MILLER, W. L., Politics (Edward Caird Chair)
MOUTINHO, L. A., Marketing
MUSCATELLI, A., Economics (Daniel Jack Chair)
NOORBAKHSH, F., Development Economics
ORME, J. E., Social Work
PARR, J. B., Regional and Urban Economics
PATON, R. A., Management
PETCH, A. J., Nuffield Trust Professor of Community Care
PETERSON, J. C., European Politics (Jean Monnet Chair)
PHILO, G., Communications and Social Change
SCHENK, C., International Economic History
STOKES, R. G., International Industrial History
TUROK, I. N., Urban Economic Development
VIRDEE, S., Sociology
WATSON, N., Disability Studies
WEAVER, R., Entrepreneurship

WHITE, J. D., Russian and East European History
WHITE, S. L., Government
WILSON, F. M., Organizational Behaviour

Faculty of Veterinary Medicine (464 Bearsden Rd, Glasgow, G61 1QH; tel. (141) 330-5700; internet www.gla.ac.uk/faculties/vet):

BARRY, J. D., Molecular Parasitology
BENNETT, D., Small Animal Clinical Studies
CAMERON, E. R., Molecular and Cellular Oncology
CAMPO, M. S., Viral Oncology
CARMICHAEL, S., Veterinary Clinical Studies
DEVANEY, E., Parasite Immunobiology
ECKERSALL, P. D., Veterinary Biochemistry
FITZPATRICK, J. L., Farm Animal Medicine
GRIFFITHS, I., Comparative Neurology
HOLMES, P. H., Veterinary Physiology
JARRETT, R. F., Molecular Pathology
LOVE, S., Equine Clinical Studies
MOTTRAM, J. C., Molecular and Cellular Parasitology
NASH, A. S., Small Animal Medicine
NEIL, J. C., Virology and Molecular Oncology
NOLAN, A., Veterinary Pharmacology
ONIONS, D. E., Veterinary Pathology
O'SHAUGHNESSY, P. J., Reproductive Biology
PALMARINI, M., Molecular Pathogenesis
PARKINS, J. J., Animal Health
REID, J., Veterinary Anaesthesia
REID, S. W. J., Veterinary Informatics and Epidemiology
ROBERTS, M., Molecular Bacteriology
STEAR, M. J., Veterinary Medicine
SULLIVAN, M., Veterinary Surgery and Diagnostic Imaging
TAIT, A., Veterinary Parasitology
TAYLOR, D. J., Veterinary Bacteriology and Public Health

Hunterian Museum and Art Gallery: (see Museums and Art Galleries)

UNIVERSITY OF ST ANDREWS

St Andrews KY16 9AJ
Telephone: (1334) 476161
Internet: www.st-and.ac.uk
Founded 1413
Chancellor: Sir MENZIES CAMPBELL
Prin. and Vice-Chancellor: Prof. Dr LOUISE RICHARDSON
Deputy Prin. and Vice-Prin. for Research: Prof. CHRISTOPHER HAWKESWORTH
Vice-Prin. for External Relations: STEPHEN MAGEE
Vice-Prin. for Governance and Planning: Prof. RONALD PIPER
Vice-Prin. for Learning and Teaching: Prof. PAT WILLMER
Rector: KEVIN DUNION
Master of the United College: Prof. NEVILLE V. RICHARDSON
Proctor: Prof. PETER CLARK
Quaestor and Factor: DEREK WATSON
Dir of Library Services: JEREMY UPTON (acting)
Library: see under Libraries and Archives
Number of teachers: 935
Number of students: 7,730

DEANS

Faculty of Arts: Prof. ROY DILLEY
Faculty of Divinity: Prof. IVOR DAVIDSON
Faculty of Medicine: Prof. HUGH MACDOUGALL
Faculty of Science: Prof. ALYSON TOBIN

PROFESSORS

Faculty of Arts:
BARTLETT, R. J., Medieval History

BEATH, J. A., Economics and Finance
BEBBINGTON, J., Management
BENTLEY, M. J., Modern History
BROADIE, S., Moral Philosophy
BROWN, K. M., Scottish History
CARRADICE, I. A., Art History
CHAMBERS, H. E., German
CRAWFORD, R., English
DAVIES, H. T. O., Management
DE GROOT, G. J., Modern History
DENNIS, N., Spanish
DUNN, D. E., English
FERGUSON, R., French
FITZROY, F. R., Economics and Finance
GIVEN-WILSON, C. J., Medieval History
GOW, P., Philosophical and Anthropological Studies
GRATWICK, A., Classical Philology
GRAY, R. H., Management
HALDANE, J. J., Moral Philosophy
HALLIWELL, F. S., Greek
HARRIES, J. D., Ancient History
HINNEBUSCH, R., International Relations
HOUSTON, R. A., Modern History
HUDSON, J., History
HUGHES-HALLETT, A., Economics and Finance
HUMFREY, P., Art History
LITTLER, C., Management Centre for Business Education
MAGDALINO, P., Medieval History
MCKIERNAN, P., Management
MCKINLAY, A., Management
NOLAN, C., Economics and Finance
PETTEGREE, A. D. M., Modern History
POLLMANN, K., Classics
PRIEST, G., Philosophy
RAPPORT, N. J., Social Anthropology
REID, G. C., Economics and Finance
RENGGER, N. J., International Relations
RHODES, N., English
ROE, N. H., English
SCOTT, H. M., Modern History
SELLERS, S. C., English
SKORUPSKI, J., Moral Philosophy
SMITH, C. J., Classics
SUTHERLAND, A. J., Economics and Finance
WALKER, W. B., International Relations
WOOLF, G. D., Classics
WRIGHT, C. J. G., Logic and Metaphysics

Faculty of Divinity:
ESLER, P. F., Divinity
HART, T. A., Divinity
PIPER, R. A., Divinity
TORRANCE, A. J., Divinity

Faculty of Medicine:
HERRINGTON, S., Medicine
HUMPHRIS, G., Medicine
MACDOUGALL, R. H., Medicine
RICHES, A., Medicine

Faculty of Science:
BALLANTYNE, C. K., Geography and Geosciences
BOYD, I., Biology
BOYLE, P. J., Geography and Geosciences
BROWN, V., Psychology
BRUCE, P. G., Chemistry
BUCKLAND, S. T., Mathematics and Statistics
BYRNE, R. W., Psychology
CAIRNS, R. A., Applied Mathematics
CAMERON, A. C., Physics and Astronomy
COLE-HAMILTON, D. J., Chemistry
DEARLE, A., Computer Science
DHOLAKIA, K., Physics and Astronomy
DRITSCHEL, D. G., Mathematics
DUNN, M. H., Photonics
FALCONER, K. J., Mathematics and Statistics
FLOWERDEW, R., Geography and Geosciences
HARWOOD, J., Biology
HOOD, A. W., Mathematics
HORNE, K. D., Physics and Astronomy

IRVINE, J. T. S., Chemistry
JOHNSTON, I. A., Comparative Physiology
KRAUSS, T. F., Physics and Astronomy
LEE, S., Physics and Astronomy
LEONHARDT, U., Physics and Astronomy
MACKENZIE, A., Physics and Astronomy
MACLEOD, M., Psychology
MAGURRAN, A. E., Biology
MEAGHER, T. R., Biology
MORRIS, R., Chemistry
NAISMITH, J. H., Chemistry
O'HAGAN, D., Chemistry
PATERSON, D. M., Biology
PERRETT, D. I., Psychology
PRIEST, E. R., Theoretical Solar Physics
RANDALL, R. E., Biology
REICHER, S., Psychology
RICHARDSON, N. V., Chemistry
RITCHIE, M. G., Biology
ROBERTS, B., Mathematics
SAMUEL, I., Physics and Astronomy
SIBBETT, W., Natural Philosophy
SILLAR, K. T., Biology
TAYLOR, G. L., Biology
TODD, C. D., Biology
WALTON, J. C., Chemistry
WHITEN, D. A., Psychology
WILLMER, P. G., Biology
WINN, P., Psychology
WOOLLINS, J. D., Chemistry

UNIVERSITY OF STIRLING

Stirling, FK9 4LA

Telephone: (1786) 473171

Internet: www.stir.ac.uk

Founded 1967

State control

Academic year: September to May (two semesters)

Chancellor: Dr JAMES NAUGHTIE
Prin. and Vice-Chancellor: Prof. GERRY MCCORMAC
Sr Deputy Prin.: Prof. STEVE BURT
Deputy Prin. for Education and Students: Prof. JOHN GARDNER
Deputy Prin. for Research: Prof. EDMUND BURKE
Univ. Sec. and Chief Operating Officer: EILEEN SCHOFIELD
Chair. of the Univ. Court: ALAN SIMPSON
Library: see Libraries and Archives
Number of teachers: 1,400
Number of students: 12,300

Publication: *Stirling Minds*

UNIVERSITY OF STRATHCLYDE

16 Richmond St, Glasgow, G1 1XQ

Telephone: (141) 552-4400

E-mail: rkes@strath.ac.uk

Internet: www.strath.ac.uk

Founded 1796 as Anderson's Institution, present status 1964

Academic year: September to June

Chancellor: Lord SMITH OF KELVIN
Prin. and Vice-Chancellor: Prof. SIR JIM MCDONALD
Vice-Prin.: Prof. KENNETH MILLER
Assoc. Deputy Prin.: Prof. COLIN GRANT
Assoc. Deputy Prin.: Prof. DAVID LITTLEJOHN
Assoc. Deputy Prin.: Prof. TIM BEDFORD
Assoc. Deputy Prin.: Prof. VAL BELTON
Chief Operating Officer: HUGH HALL
Chief Financial Officer: DAVID COYLE

Library of 887,646 vols
Number of teachers: 1,415
Number of students: 23,665 (14768 undergraduate, 8897 postgraduate)

DEANS

Faculty of Engineering: Prof. SCOTT MACGREGOR

Faculty of Humanities and Social Sciences: Prof. TONY MCGREW
Faculty of Science: Prof. IAIN HUNTER
Strathclyde Business School: Prof. SUSAN HART

PROFESSORS

ACKERMANN, F., Management Science
ALEXANDER, J., Immunology
ANDERSON, J., Bioscience
ANDONOVIC, I., Electronic and Electrical Engineering
ASHCROFT, B. K., Economics
BACHTLER, J., European Policy
BALENDRA, R., Design, Manufacture and Engineering Management
BANKS, W. M., Advanced Materials
BATES, T., Law
BAUM, T. G., Hospitality Management
BEDFORD, T., Management Science
BELTON, V., Management Science
BINGHAM, R., Physics
BIRCH, D. J. S., Photophysics
BITITCI, U., Design, Manufacture and Engineering Management
BLACKIE, J. W. G., Scots Law
BOYLE, J. T., Mechanics of Materials
BRIDGES, A., Architecture
BRYCE, T. G. K, Education
CARTER, S., Marketing
CHAKRABARTI, M., Social Work
CLARKE, J. A., Energy Systems
COMMON, M., Environmental Studies
CONNOLLY, P., Bioengineering
CONNOR, R., Computer and Information Sciences
COOPER, C., Accounting and Finance
CORCORAN, M., Architecture
CROSS, R. B., Economics
CULSHAW, B., Optoelectronics
CURTICE, J., Government
DAVIES, J. B., Psychology
DUNLOP, J., Communications Engineering
DURRANI, T., Signal Processing
DUXBURY, G., Chemical Physics
EDEN, C., Graduate School of Business
ELPHINSTONE, M., Writing
FABB, N., English
FARRELL, J., Modern Languages
FERGUSON, A. I., Photonics
FINN, G., Educational Studies
FIRTH, W. J., Experimental Physics
FOOT, H. C., Psychology
GETTINBY, G. C., Statistics
GIBB, F., Computer and Information Sciences
GORMAN, D., Mechanical Engineering
GRANT, C. D., Chemical Engineering
GRANT, M., Bioengineering
GRAY, T. G. F., Fracture Mechanics
GRIMBLE, M. J., Industrial Systems
GURNEY, W. S. C., Mathematical Ecology
HALLING, P. J., Biocatalyst Science
HARNETT, W., Immunology
HART, S., Marketing
HARVEY, A. L., Pharmacology
HIGHAM, D., Mathematics
HILLIER, D., Accounting and Finance
HOGWOOD, B. W., Politics
HUNTER, I., Molecular Microbiology
HUTTON, N., Law
HUXHAM, C., Management Science
JACKSON, M., Environmental Health
JAROSZYNSKI, D., Physics
JOHNSON, G., Strategic Management
JOHNSON, M., Electronic and Electrical Engineering
JUDGE, D., Politics
KAY, N. M., Business Economics
KENDRICK, A., Childcare Initiative
KERR, W., Pure and Applied Chemistry
LEITHEAD, W., Electronic and Electrical Engineering
LITTLEJOHN, D., Analytical Chemistry
LO, K. L., Power Engineering
LOVE, J., Economics
MACDONALD, J., Power Engineering

MACFARLANE, C. J., Subsea Engineering
MACGREGOR, S., Electronic and Electrical Engineering
MAO, X., Statistics
MAVER, T. W., Computer-aided Design
MCBRIDE, A., Mathematics
MCGETTRICK, A. D., Computer and Information Sciences
MCGREGOR, P., Economics
MCKEE, S., Mathematics
MILLER, K., Employment Law
MULVEY, R. E., Inorganic Chemistry
MURDOCH, A., Mathematics
MURPHY, J., Preparative Chemistry
NICOL, A., Bioengineering
NICOLSON, D., Law
NORRIE, K., Law
O'DONNELL, K., Physics
OPPO, G.-L., Physics
OSIPOV, M., Mathematics
PACIONE, M., Geography
PADGETT, S., Government
PATERSON, A. A., Law
PETHRICK, R. A., Physical Chemistry
PHELPS, A., Plasma Physics
PLEVIN, R., Physiology and Pharmacology
PYNE, N., Physiology and Pharmacology
RENSHAW, E., Statistics and Modelling Science
RHODES, J., Mechanics of Materials
ROBERTSON, C., Statistics
ROBSON, P., Law
RODGER, B., Law
SHAW, S. A., Marketing
SHERRINGTON, D. C., Polymer Chemistry
SLOAN, D. McP., Numerical Analysis
SMITH, W. E., Inorganic Chemistry
STACK, M., Mechanical Engineering
STEVENS, H., Pharmaceutical Sciences
STIMSON, W. H., Immunology
SUCKLING, C. J., Chemistry
SUMMERS, H. P., Theoretical Atomic Physics
THOMPSON, P., Human Resource Management
THOMSON, J., Psychology
UTTAMCHANDANI, D., Electronic and Electrical Engineering
VASSALOS, D., Naval Architecture and Marine Engineering
WALLS, L., Management Science
WILLIAMS, H., Management Science
WILSON, C. G., Pharmacy
WILSON, S., Mathematics
WRIGHT, G., Business Administration
WRIGHT, H. D., Structural Engineering
WRIGHT, R., Business
YUILL, D., European Policies

UNIVERSITY OF THE WEST OF SCOTLAND

Paisley, PA1 2BE

Telephone: (141) 848-3000

E-mail: uni-direct@paisley.ac.uk

Internet: www.paisley.ac.uk

Founded 1897 as Paisley College of Technology, present name and status 2007

Academic year: October to June

Chancellor: Sir ROBERT SMITH
Prin. and Vice-Chancellor: Prof. SEAMUS MCDAID (acting)
Vice-Prin.: PAUL MARTIN
Deputy Prin. and Vice-Prin. for Strategy: GILL TROUP (acting)
Vice-Prin. for Research and Commercialization: Prof. RODDY WILLIAMSON
Vice-Prin. for Teaching and Learning: Prof. MALCOLM FOLEY
Sec.: KENNETH ALEXANDER
Librarian: STUART JAMES

Number of teachers: 2,000
Number of students: 20,000

DEANS

School of Education: IAN SMITH

School of Engineering and Science: Prof. ROGER MCLEAN

School of Health, Nursing and Midwifery: Prof. JACK RAE

School of Information Communication Technologies: Dr CHRIS HALSALL

School of Media: ALEX GILKISON

School of Social Sciences: Dr TONY CLARKE

Paisley Business School: ALAN GODFREY

Colleges in Scotland

These institutions are not able to award their own degrees, but offer courses leading to a degree from a recognized body.

Al-Maktoum Institute for Arabic and Islamic Studies: 124 Blackness Rd, Dundee, DD1 5PE; tel. (1382) 908070; e-mail info@almcollege.org.uk; internet www .almcollege.org.uk; offers Masters programmes accredited by Scottish Qualifications Authority (SQA) and PhDs; library: 19,000 vols; Prin. Dr HOSSEIN GODAZGAR.

City of Glasgow College: 60 North Hanover St, Glasgow, G1 2BP; tel. (1412) 566-6222; e-mail enquiries@cityofglasgowcollege .ac.uk; internet www.cityofglasgowcollege.ac .uk; f. 1956 as Stow College of Hairdressing; current name adopted 2010; courses in accounting, advertising, art and design, business studies, computing, distribution, hairdressing and beauty therapy, librarianship, marketing, office studies, sports therapy; 1,200 teachers; 32,500 students; Prin. PAUL G. K. LITTLE.

Edinburgh College of Art: Lauriston Place, Edinburgh, EH3 9DF; tel. (131) 651-5800; e-mail eca@ed.ac.uk; internet www.eca .ac.uk; f. 1907; attached to The University of Edinburgh; art, design, architecture and landscape architecture programmes at undergraduate, postgraduate and doctoral levels; library: 85,000 vols, 350 periodicals; 300 teachers; 3,000 students; Prin. Prof. CHRIS BREWARD.

Free Church of Scotland College: The Mound, Edinburgh, EH1 2LS; tel. (131) 226-5286; e-mail secretary@freescotcoll.ac.uk; internet www.freescotcoll.ac.uk; f. 1843; undergraduate, postgraduate and part-time courses in biblical studies, Christian theology and related disciplines; 8 teachers; Prin. IVER M. MARTIN.

Glasgow School of Art: 167 Renfrew St, Glasgow, G3 6RQ; tel. (141) 353-4500; e-mail info@gsa.ac.uk; internet www.gsa.ac.uk; f. 1845; offers undergraduate, postgraduate and doctoral degrees; library: 80,000 vols, 59,000 slides, 250 periodicals of art, design, craft and architecture; 400 teachers; 1,900 students; Dir Prof. TOM INNS; publ. *FLOW Magazine*.

International Christian College: 110 St James Rd, Glasgow, G4 0PS; tel. (1415) 524040; e-mail college@icc.ac.uk; internet www.icc.ac.uk; f. 1998 by merger of Glasgow Bible College and Northumbria Bible College; undergraduate, postgraduate and certificate courses in Christian studies and theology; library: 45,000 vols, 180 periodical titles, 40 CD-ROMs; 20 teachers; Prin. Rev. RICHARD TIPLADY.

International Correspondence Schools Ltd: Breckenridge House, 274 Sauchiehall St, Glasgow, G2 3EH; tel. (141) 302-5487; e-mail courseadvisors@icslearn.co.uk; internet www.icslearn.co.uk; f. 1890; distance learning courses; 36,000 students; Man. Dir SALLY PULVERTAFT.

Scotland's Rural College (SRUC): SRUC Riverside Campus, University Ave, Ayr, KA8 0SX; tel. (1292) 886200; e-mail recruitment@ sruc.ac.uk; internet www.sac.ac.uk/learning; f. 1900; partners are Barony, Elmwood and Oatridge Colleges and Scottish Agricultural Colleges (SAC); campuses in Aberdeen, Ayr, Barony, Edinburgh, Elmwood and Oatridge; undergraduate, postgraduate courses in agriculture and land-based studies; library: 50,000 vols, 670 current journal titles; 250 teachers; 1,200 students; Chief Exec. JANET SWADLING (acting).

Scottish Baptist College: K202, Univ. of the West of Scotland, High St, Paisley, PA1 2BE; tel. (141) 848-3988; e-mail scottishbaptistcollege@uws.ac.uk; internet www.scottishbaptistcollege.org; f. 1894 as Baptist Theological College of Scotland; attached to Univ. of West of Scotland; Bachelors courses in Christian theology; Prin. Rev. Dr STUART BLYTHE.

Scottish Institute of Human Relations: Park Business Centre, 5 La Belle Place, Glasgow, G3 7LH; tel. (141) 332-0011; e-mail info@sihr.org.uk; internet www.sihr .org.uk; f. 1971; postgraduate programmes and services for psychoanalytic, psychodynamic and systemic thinking; validated by Univ. of Strathclyde; Exec. Dir AMANDA CORNISH.

Universities in Wales

ABERYSTWYTH UNIVERSITY

Visualisation Centre, Penglais Campus, Aberystwyth, SY23 3BF

Telephone: (1970) 623111

E-mail: dym@aber.ac.uk

Internet: www.aber.ac.uk

Founded 1872, present status 2007

Languages of instruction: English, Welsh

Academic year: September to June

Pres.: Sir EMYR JONES PARRY

Vice-Pres.: ELIZABETH FRANCE

Vice-Pres.: Dr GLYN ROWLANDS

Vice-Pres.: GWERFYL PIERCE JONES

Vice-Chancellor: Prof. APRIL MCMAHON

Pro-Vice-Chancellor: Prof. JOHN GRATTAN

Pro-Vice-Chancellor: REBECCA DAVIES

Pro-Vice-Chancellor: Dr RHODRI LLWYD MORGAN

University Sec.: GERAINT PUGH

Library: see under Libraries and Archives

Number of teachers: 900

Number of students: 11,700

Publication: *Prom* (1 a year)

DEANS

Faculty of Arts: Prof. TIM S. WOODS

Faculty of Postgraduate Studies: Prof. COLIN J. MCINNES

Faculty of Science: Prof. NEIL GLASSER

Faculty of Social Sciences: Prof. LEN V. SCOTT

PROFESSORS

ALEXANDER, M. S., International Politics

BARNES, D. P., Computer Science

BARRY, P. T., English and Creative Writing

BEUMERS, B., Theatre, Film and Television

BOOTH, K., International Politics

BORSAY, P. N., History

BOYLE, R. D., Institute of Biological, Environmental and Rural Sciences

BRIDLE, C., Sport and Exercise Science

BROPHY, P. M., Institute of Biological, Environmental and Rural Sciences

BULLEN, K. S., Psychology

CHRISTIE, M., Management and Business

CLARK, I., International Politics

CLARKE, A. H., Law and Criminology

COX, N. S., Law and Criminology

COX, S. J., Mathematics

CRAIG, H. C., International Politics

DONNISON, I. S., Institute of Biological, Environmental and Rural Sciences

DOONAN, J. H., Institute of Biological, Environmental and Rural Sciences

DRAPER, J., Institute of Biological, Environmental and Rural Sciences

DULLER, G. A. T., Earth Sciences

EDKINS, J. A., International Politics

ELLIS, D., Information Studies

ELLIS, T. H., Institute of Biological, Environmental and Rural Sciences

ERSKINE, T. A., International Politics

EVANS, D. A., Physics

FOLEY, M., International Politics

FUGE, R., Geography and Earth Sciences

GLASSER, N. E., Geography

GOUGH, J. E., Mathematics

GOUGH, R. A., Theatre, Film and Television

GRANDE, M., Physics

GREAVES, G. N., Physics

HAMBREY, M. J., Earth Sciences

HANNAH, M. G., Geography

HARDING, C. S. P., Law and Criminology

HARESIGN, W., Institute of Biological, Environmental and Rural Sciences

HARVEY, J., Art

HAYCOCK, M. E., Cymraeg and Welsh

HENLEY, A. G., Management and Business

HILLS, M. J., Theatre, Film and Television

HOFFMANN, K. F., Institute of Biological, Environmental and Rural Sciences

HUBBARD, B. P., Geography

HUTTON, S. C., English and Creative Writing

JACKSON, R. H., Management and Business

JONES, A. G., Cymraeg and Welsh

JONES, J. A., Geography and Earth Sciences

JONES, M. R., Geography

JONES, R. A., Geography

JONES, R. N., Institute of Biological, Environmental and Rural Sciences

KAY, D., Earth Sciences

KEAR, A. C., Theatre, Film and Television

KOPPEL, G., Theatre, Film and Television

KURKI, M. H., International Politics

LAMB, H., Geography

LEE, M. H., Computer Science

LINKLATER, A., International Politics

LUCAS, R. M., Geography and Earth Sciences

MACKLIN, M. G., Geography

MALTMAN, A. J., Geography and Earth Sciences

MARGGRAF TURLEY, R. J., English and Creative Writing

McGUIRE, S. M., Management and Business

McINNES, C. J., International Politics

MEYRICK, R. K., Art

MIDMORE, P. R., Management and Business

MISHURIS, G., Mathematics

MORUS, I. R., History

NEWBOLD, C. J., Institute of Biological, Environmental and Rural Sciences

O'MALLEY, T. P., Theatre, Film and Television

PASHA, M. K., International Politics

PEARCE, N. J. G., Geography and Earth Sciences

PEARSON, M. J., Theatre, Film and Television

PERDIKIS, N., Management and Business

PIOTROWICZ, R. W., Law and Criminology

POWELL, W., Institute of Biological, Environmental and Rural Sciences

PRESCOTT, S. H., English and Creative Writing

PRICE, C. J., Computer Science

RABEY, D. I., Theatre, Film and Television

ROGOSIN, S., Mathematics

ROMS, H. P., Theatre, Film and Television

ROWLAND, D., Law and Criminology

SCHOFIELD, P. R., History

SCOLLAN, N. D., Institute of Biological, Environmental and Rural Sciences

SCOTT, L. V., International Politics

SHAW, P. W., Institute of Biological, Environmental and Rural Sciences

SHEN, Q., Computer Science

SIMS-WILLIAMS, P. P., Cymraeg and Welsh

SLEPYAN, L., Mathematics and Physics
SUGANAMI, H., International Politics
THOMAS, B. A., Lifelong Learning
THOMAS, C. J., Institute of Biological, Environmental and Rural Sciences
THOMAS, D. A., Management and Business
THOMPSON, M. J., Management and Business
TROTTER, D. A., European Languages
VINCENTELLI, M. M., Art
WALFORD DAVIES, D., English and Creative Writing
WEILER, B. K. U., History
WHITEHEAD, M. J., Geography
WILLIAMS, J. R., Law and Criminology
WOODS, M. J., Geography and Earth Sciences
WOODS, T. S., English and Creative Writing
ZWIGGELAAR, R., Computer Science

BANGOR UNIVERSITY

Bangor LL57 2DG
Telephone: (1248) 351151
E-mail: admissions@bangor.ac.uk
Internet: www.bangor.ac.uk
Founded 1884
Academic year: September to June
Pres.: Rt Hon. Lord ELIS-THOMAS OF NANT CONWY
Vice-Chancellor: Prof. JOHN HUGHES
Deputy Vice-Chancellor: Prof. DAVID SHEPHERD
Pro-Vice-Chancellor for Students: Prof. CAROL TULLY
Pro-Vice-Chancellor for Teaching and Learning: Prof. OLIVER TURNBULL
Pro-Vice-Chancellor for Welsh Medium and Civic Engagement: Prof. WYN THOMAS
Academic Registrar: Dr DAVID ROBERTS (acting)
Library: see under Libraries and Archives
Number of teachers: 690
Number of students: 11,440

DEANS

College of Arts and Humanities: Dr A. EDWARDS
College of Business, Law, Education and Social Sciences: Prof. PHIL MOLYNEUX
College of Health and Behavioural Sciences: Prof. N. CALLOW
College of Natural Sciences: Prof. COLIN JAGO
College of Physical and Applied Sciences: Prof. PAUL SPENCER

PROFESSORS

College of Arts and Humanities:
BROWN, A. D., English
BUSHELL, A., Modern Languages
CLAYDON, A., History and Welsh History
CORNS, T. N., English
DEUCHAR, M., Linguistics and English Language
EDWARDS, N., History and Welsh History
EVANS, V., Linguistics and English Language
GREGSON, I., English
HARPER, J., Musicology
HISCOCK, A., English
HUNTER, J., Welsh
KARL, R., History and Welsh History
LEWIS, A.P., Music
LYNCH, P., Welsh
MENNEN, I., Linguistics and English Language
PRYCE, A. H., History and Welsh History
SULLIVAN, C., English
TULLY, C., Modern Languages
WILCOX, H., English
WILIAMS, G., Welsh
College of Business, Law, Education and Social Sciences:
ALDER, J., Law
ALTUNBAŞ, Y., Banking and Finance

BATIZ-LAZO, B., Business History and Bank Management
CAHILL, D., Law
CARBO-VALVERDE, S., Economics and Finance
CHAKRAVARTY, S. P., Economics
DAVIES, H., Social Theory
EBRAHIM, M. S., Islamic Banking and Finance
FENG, A., Education
GODDARD, J., Financial Economics
GWILYM, O., Finance
HODGKINSON, L., Accounting and Finance
LINTON, S., International Law
MOLYNEUX, P., Banking and Finance
NIKOLOPOULOS, K., Decision Sciences
POOLE, R., Social Psychiatry
ROBINSON, C., Social Policy Research
SAMBROOK, S., Human Resource Development
SCHAECK, K., Empirical Banking
THORNTON, J., Global Finance
SHIU, E., Marketing
WILLIAMS, J., Banking and Finance
College of Health and Behavioural Sciences:
CLARE, L., Clinical Psychology and Neuropsychology
COX, W. M., Psychology of Addictive Behaviours
DOWNING, P., Cognitive Neuroscience
GATHERCOLE, V. M., Psychology
HARDY, L., Sport, Health and Exercise Sciences
HASTINGS, R. P., Psychology
HORNE, P., Psychology
HUTCHINGS, J. M., Psychology
LEEK, C., Psychology
LEMMY, A., Exercise Physiology
LOWE, C. F., Psychology
MILLS, D., Psychology
NOYES, J., Nursing
RAFAL, R. D., Psychology of Neuroscience and Neuropsychology
REES, M. R., Vascular Studies
RYCROFT-MALONE, J., Nursing
STUART, N. S. A., Cancer Studies
THIERRY, G., Cognitive Neuroscience
TURNBULL, O., Psychology
WALSH, N., Exercise Physiology
WARD, R., Psychology
WOODMAN, T., Sport Psychology
WOODS, R. T., Clinical Psychology of the Elderly
College of Natural Sciences:
BOWERS, D., Ocean Science
CARVALHO, G. R., Biological Sciences
CHADWICK, D. R., Sustainable Land-Use Systems
DAVIES, A. G., Physical Oceanography
DELUCA, T., Environmental Sciences
FREEMAN, C., Biological Sciences
GOLYSHIN, P. N., Environmental Genomics
HEALEY, J. R., Forest Sciences
HUGHES, R. N., Biological Sciences
JAGO, C., Ocean Sciences
JOHNSON, D. P., Biological Sciences
JONES, D. L., Soil and Environmental Science
KAISER, M. J., Ocean Sciences
PULLIN, A. S., Evidence-based Conservation
RICHARDSON, C., Ocean Sciences
SCOURSE, J. D., Ocean Sciences
SIMPSON, J. H., Ocean Sciences
THOMAS, D. N., Ocean Sciences
THORPE, R. S., Biological Sciences
TOMOS, A. D., Biological Sciences
WEBSTER, S., Biological Sciences
College of Physical and Applied Sciences:
BAIRD, M. S., Chemistry
HANCOCK, C., Electronic Engineering
HOPE, S., Computer Science
JOHN, N. W., Computing
KUNCHEVA, L. I., Computer Science

PAIZS, B., Chemistry
PEREPICHKA, I. F., Chemistry
SHORE, K. A., Electronic Engineering
SPENCER, P. S., Electronic Engineering
TANG, J., Electronic Engineering
TAYLOR, D. M., Electronic Engineering

CARDIFF UNIVERSITY

Cardiff, CF10 3XQ
Telephone: (29) 2087-4000
E-mail: prospectus@cardiff.ac.uk
Internet: www.cardiff.ac.uk
Founded 2004 by merger of Cardiff University (f. 1883) and University of Wales College of Medicine (f. 1931)
Academic year: September to June
Pres.: Prof. Sir MARTIN EVANS
Vice-Chancellor: Dr DAVID GRANT
Deputy Vice-Chancellor: Prof. ELIZABETH TREASURE
Pro-Vice-Chancellor for Education and Students: Prof. JONATHAN OSMOND
Pro-Vice-Chancellor for Engagement and Int.: Prof. HYWEL THOMAS
Pro-Vice-Chancellor for Estates: Prof. TIM WESS
Pro-Vice-Chancellor for Research: Prof. GRAHAM HUTCHINGS
Pro-Vice-Chancellor for Staff and Diversity: Prof. TERRY THREADGOLD
Dean of Strategic Futures and Interdisciplinary Studies: Prof. PETER HALLIGAN
Library: see under Libraries and Archives
Number of teachers: 2,920
Number of students: 28,000

HEADS OF SCHOOLS

College of Humanities and Sciences:
Architecture: Prof. PHIL JONES
Business School: Prof. GEORGE BOYNE
Chemistry: Prof. PETER KNOWLES
City and Regional Planning: Prof. CHRISTOPHER WEBSTER
Computer Science: Dr. ROGER WHITAKER
Earth and Ocean Sciences: Prof. JOHN PARKES
Engineering: Prof. HYWEL THOMAS
English, Communication and Philosophy: Prof. MARTIN KAYMAN
European Studies: Prof. DAVID BOUCHER
History, Archaeology and Religion: Prof. PETER COSS
Journalism, Media and Cultural Studies: Prof. JUSTIN LEWIS
Law School: Prof. NIGEL LOWE
Lifelong Learning: Dr RICHARD EVANS
Mathematics: Prof. A RUSSELL DAVIES
Music: Prof. DAVID WYN JONES
Physics and Astronomy: Prof. WALTER GEAR
Social Sciences: Prof. MALCOLM WILLIAMS
Welsh: Prof. SIONED DAVIES
Wales College of Medicine, Biology, Life and Health Sciences:
Biosciences: Prof. OLE PETERSEN
Dentistry: Prof. ELIZABETH TREASURE
Healthcare Studies: Prof. PATRICIA PRICE
Medicine: Prof. PAUL MORGAN
Nursing and Midwifery Studies: Prof. SHEILA HUNT
Optometry and Vision Sciences: Prof. TIM WESS
Pharmacy: Prof. GARY BAXTER
Postgraduate Medical and Dental Education: Prof. DEREK GALLEN
Psychology: Prof. DYLAN JONES

PROFESSORS

College of Humanities and Sciences
Architecture:
WESTON, R.

Business School:

BLYTON, P. R.
BOYNE, G. A.
CHANDLER, R. A.
CLARKE, R.
COLLIE, D. R.
COPELAND, L.
DAVIES, A. J.
DELBRIDGE, R. I.
EDWARDS, J. R.
EZZAMEL, M. A.
FOREMAN-PECK, J.
FOSH, P.
FOXALL, G. R.
HARRIS, L. C.
HEERY, E. J.
HINES, P. A.
HUGHES HALLET, A.
JONES, D. T.
JONES, M. J.
KNOTT, J. H.
MAKEPEACE, G. H.
MARTIN, S. J.
MATTHEWS, K. G. P.
MCNABB, R.
MELLETT, H. J.
MINFORD, A. P. L.
MORRIS, J. L.
NAIRN, M. M.
OGBONNA, E.
PEATTIE, K. J.
PEEL, M. J.
PENDLEBURY, M. W.
POOLE, M. J. F.
REED, M. I.
RHYS, D. G.
SILVER, M. S.
TOWILL, D. R.
TURNBULL, P. J.
WALKER, S. P.
WHITFIELD, K. L.
XU, X.

Chemistry:

ATTARD, G. A.
BOWKER, M.
CAVELL, K. J.
EDWARDS, P. G.
HARRIS, K. D. M.
HEWLINS, M. J. E.
JONES, C.
KNIGHT, D. W.
KNOWLES, P. J.
MCKEOWN, N. B.
ROBERTS, M. W.
WELLS, P. B.
WILLIAMS, D. R.
WIRTH, T.

City and Regional Planning:

ALDEN, J. D.
CLAPHAM, D. F.
COOKE, P. N.
GUY, C. M.
HOOPER, A. J.
LOVERING, J.
MORGAN, K. J.
MURDOCH, J. L.
PUNTER, J. V.
WEBSTER, C. J.
WILLIAMS, H. C. W. L.

Computer Science:

AVIS, N. J.
BATCHELOR, B. G.
BROWN, B. M.
GRAY, W. A.
JONES, A. J.
JONES, C. B.
MARTIN, R. R.
WALKER, D. W.

Earth and Ocean Sciences:

BOWEN, D. Q.
CARTWRIGHT, J. A.
EDWARDS, D.
HARRIS, C.

LISLE, R. J.
O'HARA, M. J.
PARKES, R. J.
PEARCE, J. A.
PEARSON, P. N.
RICKARD, D. T.
SCHULTZ, A.
WRIGHT, V. P.
ZAHN, R.

Engineering:

BARR, B. I. G.
BARROW, D. A.
BORODICH, F. M.
CHAMBERS, J. A.
EVANS, H. P.
DIMOV, S. S.
FALCONER, R. A.
HUGHES, T. G.
KARIHALOO, B. L.
LEVER, K. V.
MILES, J. C.
MORGAN, D. V.
MOSES, A. J.
PHAM, D. T.
POOLEY, F. D.
ROWE, D. M.
SNIDLE, R. W.
SYRED, N.
TASKER, P. J.
WATTON, J.
WILLIAMS, F. W.

English, Communication and Philosophy:

ATTFIELD, R.
BELSEY, C.
COUPLAND, N. J. R.
KAYMAN, M. A.
KNIGHT, S. T.
NORRIS, C. C.
SARANGI, S. K.
SKILTON, D. J.
VAN LEEUWEN, T.
WEEDON, C. M.

European Studies:

BERENDSE, G.-J.
BOUCHER, D.
BRYDEN, K. M.
COLE, A. M.
DYSON, K. H. F.
HADDOCK, B. A.
HANLEY, D. L.
JACKSON, D. A.
LOUGHLIN, J. P.

History and Archaeology:

BENTON, G.
COSS, P. R.
EDBURY, P. W.
FREESTONE, I. C.
FISHER, N. R. E.
HINES, J.
HUDSON, P.
PRINGLE, R. D.
WHITTLE, A. W. R.

Journalism, Media and Cultural Studies:

HARGREAVES, I. R.
KITZINGER, J.
LEWIS, J. W.
MILLER, B. T. A.
TAIT, R.

Law School:

CAMPBELL, I. D.
CHURCHILL, R. R.
DOE, C. N.
DOUGLAS, G. F.
FENNELL, P. W. H.
HARPWOOD, V.
HOLM, S.
LEE, R. G.
LEWIS, R. K.
LOWE, N. V.
MIERS, D. R.
MORGAN, D. M.
MURCH, M.
NELKEN, D.

SMITH, K. J. M.
THOMAS, P. A.
WELLS, C. K.
WYLIE, J. C. W.

Mathematics:

BOURENKOV, K.
EVANS, D. E.
EVANS, W. D.
HOOLEY, C.
HUXLEY, M. N.
PHILLIPS, T. N.
WICKRAMASINGHE, N. C.
ZHIGLJAVSKY, A. A.

Music:

THOMAS, A. T.
TYRELL, J.
WALSH, S.

Physics and Astronomy:

ADE, P. A. R.
BLOOD, P.
DISNEY, M. J.
GEAR, W. K.
GRIFFIN, M. J.
GRISHCHUK, L.
INGLESFIELD, J. E.
IVANOV, A. L.
SATHYAPRAKASH, B. S.
WHITWORTH, A. P.

Religious and Theological Studies:

SAMUEL, G. B.
TREVETT, C.

Social Sciences:

ADAM, B. E.
ATKINSON, P.
BROWN, P.
COLLINS, H. M.
CROZIER, W. R.
DAVIES, W. B.
DRAKEFORD, M.
EPSTEIN, D. A.
FAIRBROTHER, P.
FEVRE, R. W.
FITZ, J.
GLASNER, P. E.
LAWN, M.
LEVI, M.
MAGUIRE, E. M. W.
MOORE, L. A. R.
NICHOLS, W. A. T.
POWER, S. A. R.
PRIOR, L. F.
REES, G. M.
REES, T. L.
WALKERDINE, V.
WALTERS, D.
WILLIAMS, G. H.

Welsh:

JONES, R. O.
THOMAS, P. W.
WILLIAMS, C. H.

Wales College of Medicine, Biology, Life and Health Sciences

Biosciences:

ARCHER, C. W.
BENJAMIN, M.
BODDY, L.
BOWEN, I. D.
BRUFORD, M. W.
BUCHMAN, V.
CATERSON, B.
CLARKE, A. R.
COAKLEY, W. T.
CRUNELLI, V.
DALE, T. C.
DAVIES, A. M.
DUANCE, V. C.
DUNNETT, S. B.
ECCLES, R.
EHRMANN, M.
FOX, K. D.
FRY, J. C.
HARWOOD, A. J.

HARWOOD, J. L.
JACOB, T. J. C.
JOHN, R. A.
KAY, J.
MOXHAM, B. J.
ORMEROD, S. J.

Dentistry:

DUMMER, P. M. H., Adult Dental Health
GLANTZ, P.-O. J., Adult Dental Health
JONES, M. L., Dental Health and Development
LEWIS, M. A. O., Oral Medicine
MACKENZIE, I. C., Adult Dental Health
RICHMOND, S., Dental Health and Development
SHEPHERD, J. R., Oral Surgery and Pathology
TREASURE, E. T., Dental Public Health
WHITTAKER, D. K., Basic Dental Science
WILTON, J. M. A., Adult Dental Health

Healthcare Studies:

PALASTANGA, N.

Medicine:

BURNETT, A. K., Haematology
CAMPBELL, A. K., Medical Biochemistry
CLARKE, A. J., Medical Genetics
COOPER, D. N., Human Molecular Genetics
DAVIES, D. P., Child Health
DUERDEN, B. I., Medical Microbiology
EVANS, W. H., Medical Biochemistry
FELCE, D., Mental Handicap Research
FIANDER, A., Obstetrics and Gynaecology
FINLAY, A. Y., Dermatology
FINLAY, I. G., Palliative Care
FRENNEAUX, N. P., Cardiology
GRIFFITH, T. M., Medical Imaging
HARDING, K. G., Rehabilitation Medicine
HARMER, M., Anaesthetics and Intensive Care Medicine
HARPER, P. S., Medical Genetics
HOUSTON, H. L. A., General Practice
KRAWCZAK, M., Mathematical Genetics
LAI, F. A., Cell Signalling
LEWIS, M. J., Cardiovascular Pharmacology
MANSEL, R. E., Surgery
MASON, M., Clinical Oncology
MORGAN, B. P., Medical Biochemistry
O'DONOVAN, M. C., Psychological Medicine
OWEN, M. J., Neuropsychiatric Genetics
OWENS, D. R., Diabetes
PALMER, S. R., Epidemiology, Statistics and Public Health
PILL, R., General Practice
ROUTLEDGE, P., Clinical Pharmacology
ROWE, M., Cell Biology
SAMPSON, J. R., Medical Genetics
SCANLON, M. F., Endocrinology
SHALE, D. J., Respiratory and Communicable Diseases
SIBERT, J. R., Community Child Health
SMITH, P. J., Cancer Biology
STEPHENS, S. D. G., Audiology
THAPAR, A., Child and Adolescent Psychiatry
WHEELER, M. H., Surgery
WILES, C. M., Neurology
WILKINSON, C., General Practice
WILLIAMS, B. D., Rheumatology
WILLIAMS, G. T., Pathology
WILLIAMS, J. D., Nephrology
WOODCOCK, J. P., Bioengineering
WOODHOUSE, K. W., Geriatric Medicine
WORWOOD, M., Haematology
WYNFORD-THOMAS, D., Pathology

Nursing and Midwifery Studies:

BURNARD, P., Nursing and Midwifery Education
LYNE, P. A., Nursing Research
TUCKER, A., Nursing and Midwifery

Optometry and Vision Sciences:

MEEK, K. M. A.
ROVAMO, J. M.

WESS, T. J.
WILD, J.

Pharmacy:

AKHTAR, S.
BROADLEY, K. J.
DUNCAN, R.
LUSCOMBE, D. K.
McGUIGAN, C.
MRSNY, R. J.
NICHOLSON, R. I.
RUSSELL, A. D.
WALKER, R. D.

Psychology:

AGGLETON, J. P.
ELLIS, H. D.
HALLIGAN, P.
HAY, D. F.
HONEY, R. C.
MANSTEAD, A. S. R.
OAKSFORD, M. R.
PAYNE, S. J.
PEARCE, J. M.
PIDGEON, N.
SMITH, A. P.
SNOWDEN, R. J.
SPEARS, R.
WRIGHT, P.

SWANSEA UNIVERSITY

Singleton Park, Swansea, SA2 8PP

Telephone: (1792) 205678

Internet: www.swan.ac.uk

Founded 1920

Academic year: September to June

Vice-Chancellor: Prof. RICHARD B. DAVIES
Pro-Vice-Chancellor for Acad. Devt: Prof. NOEL THOMPSON
Pro-Vice-Chancellor for Internationalization: Prof. IWAN DAVIES
Pro-Vice-Chancellor for Science and Engineering: Prof. IAN CLUCKIE
Pro-Vice-Chancellor for Student Experience and Acad. Quality Enhancement: Prof. ALAN SPEIGHT

Library: see Libraries and Archives
Number of teachers: 800
Number of students: 12,500

HEADS OF DEPARTMENTS

College of Arts and Humanities: Prof. JOHN SPURR
College of Engineering: Prof. JAVIER BONET
College of Human and Health Sciences: Prof. MELANIE JASPER
College of Medicine: Prof. GARETH MORGAN
College of Science: Prof. STEVE WILKS
Department of Adult Continuing Education: Prof. COLIN TROTMAN
School of Business and Economics: Prof. STEVEN COOK (acting)
School of Law: Prof. NOEL THOMPSON (acting)

UNIVERSITY OF GLAMORGAN

Pontypridd, CF37 1DL

Telephone: (1443) 480480

E-mail: enquiries@glam.ac.uk

Internet: www.glam.ac.uk

Founded 1913 as South Wales and Monmouthshire School of Mines, present name and status 1992

Academic year: September to July

Chancellor: Rt Hon Lord MORRIS OF ABERAVON
Vice-Chancellor: Prof. JULIE LYDON
Deputy Vice-Chancellor for Academic and Business Devt: HELEN MARSHALL
Deputy Vice-Chancellor for Research and Student Experience: Prof. CLIVE MULLHOLLAND
Deputy Vice-Chancellor for Strategic Resources: Dr HUW WILLIAMS

Academic Registrar: WILLIAM CALLAWAY
Library of 245,000 vols, 1,600 current periodicals
Number of teachers: 610
Number of students: 23,990

DEANS

Cardiff School of Creative and Cultural Industries: Prof. PETER ROBERTSON
Faculty of Advanced Technology: VASSILIS KONSTANTINOU
Faculty of Business and Society: Dr MONICA GIBSON-SWEET
Faculty of Health, Sport and Science: Prof. DONNA MEAD

UNIVERSITY OF WALES

University Registry, King Edward VII Ave, Cathays Park, Cardiff, CF10 3NS

Telephone: (29) 2037-6999

E-mail: uniwales@wales.ac.uk

Internet: www.wales.ac.uk

Founded 1893

Languages of instruction: English, Welsh

Chancellor: HRH Prince CHARLES, PRINCE OF WALES
Pro-Chancellor: The Most Revd Dr BARRY MORGAN, ARCHBISHOP OF WALES
Vice-Chancellor and Chief Exec.: Prof. MARC CLEMENT
Pro-Vice-Chancellor: Prof. NIGEL PALASTANGA
Sec.-Gen.: Dr LYNN E. WILLIAMS
Number of students: 80,000

Publication: *Campus*..

INSTITUTIONS AWARDING UNIVERSITY OF WALES DEGREES

Glyndŵr University

Mold Rd, Wrexham, LL11 2AW

Telephone: (1978) 290666

Internet: www.glyndwr.ac.uk

Founded 1887, present name and status 2008

Languages of instruction: English, Welsh

Academic year: September to June

Vice-Chancellor and Chief Exec.: Prof. MICHAEL SCOTT
Pro-Vice-Chancellor for Academic Affairs: Prof. GRAEME WILKINSON
Pro-Vice-Chancellor for Operations: Dr ALLAN HOWELLS

Library of 120,000 vols, DVDs, 6,000 e-journals
Number of students: 6,000

Swansea Metropolitan University

Mount Pleasant, Swansea, SA1 6ED

Telephone: (1792) 481000

E-mail: enquiry@smu.ac.uk

Internet: www.smu.ac.uk

Founded 1976 by merger of Swansea College of Art (f. 1853), Swansea College of Education (f. 1872) and Swansea Technical College (f. 1897), present name and status 2008

Languages of instruction: English, Welsh

Vice-Chancellor: Prof. DAVID WARNER
Chair.: Dr GERALD LEWIS

Library of 200,000 vols
Number of teachers: 320
Number of students: 7,000

University of Wales, Newport

Caerleon Campus, Lodge Rd, Caerleon, Newport, NP18 3QT

Telephone: (1633) 432432

E-mail: uic@newport.ac.uk

Internet: www.newport.ac.uk

Founded 1841, present name and status 1996

Vice-Chancellor: Dr PETER NOYES

EHRENBERG, M., Molecular Biology with Kinetics
EKELÖF, T., Experimental Elementary Particle Physics
EKMAN, J., Population Biology
ELLEGREN, H., Evolutionary Biology
ENGMAN, L., Organic Chemistry
ENGSTRÖM, P., Physiological Botany
ERICSSON, T., Materials Physics
ERIKSSON, O., Condensed Matter Physics
FÄLDT, G. L., Theoretical Physics
FROELICH, P., Quantum Chemistry
GEE, D. G., Orogenic Dynamics
GELIUS, U., Physics
GESTBLOM, B., Physics
GOSCINSKI, O., Quantum Chemistry
GRANQVIST, C.-G., Solid-State Physics
GUNNINGBERG, P., Computer Communication
GUSTAFSSON, B., Numerical Analysis
GUSTAFSSON, B., Theoretical Astrophysics
GUSTAFSSON, L., Animal Ecology
GUT, A., Mathematical Statistics
HAGERSTEN, E., Computer Architecture
HAJDU, J., Biochemistry
HÅKANSSON, L., Sedimentology
HÅKANSSON, P., Ion Physics
HALLDIN, S., Hydrology
HALLGREN, A., Experimental Physics
HEJHAL, D. A., Mathematics
HELLMAN, L., Molecular and Comparative Immunology
HERMANSSON, K. G., Inorganic Chemistry
HILBORN, J., Polymer Chemistry
HÖGLUND, J., Population Biology
HOGMARK, S., Materials Science
HÖISTAD, B., Nuclear Physics
HOLMER, L., Historical Geology and Palaeontology
HUGHES, D., Evolutionary Biology
INGELMANN, G., High-Energy Physics
ISRAELSSON, S. O., Meteorology
JACOBSON, S., Materials Science
JANSON, S., Mathematics
JANSSON, U., Inorganic Chemistry
JOHANSSON, B., Condensed Matter Theory
JOHANSSON, S., Materials Science
JOHANSSON, T., Nuclear Physics
JONES, A., Structural Molecular Biology
JONSSON, B., Computer Systems
JUHL-JÖRICKE, B., Mathematics
KAISER, S. G., Mathematics
KÄLLNE, J., Neutron Physics
KARLSSON, L., Experimental Physics
KIRSEBOM, L., Evolutionary Biology
KISELMAN, C. O., Mathematics
KOLSTRUP, E., Physical Geography
LÅNGSTROM, B., Radiopharmaceutical Organic Chemistry
LANSHAMMER, H., Systems and Control
LEIJON, M., Electricity
LIBERMAN, M., Theoretical Statistical Physics
LILJAS, L., Evolutionary Biology
LINDBLAD, P., Evolutionary Biology
LINDER, C., Physical Didactics
LINDGREN, J. B. R., Inorganic Chemistry
LÖTSTEDT, P., Numerical Analysis
LUNDAHL, P., Biochemistry
LUNDBERG, A., Evolutionary Biology
LUNDBERG, B., Solid Mechanics
LUNELL, S. G., Applied Quantum Chemistry
MANNERVIK, B., Biochemistry
MARKIDES, K., Analytical Chemistry
MÅRTENSSON, N., Physics of Metals and Metal Surfaces
MATTSSON, O. L., Organic Chemistry
McGREEVY, R. L., Neutron Research
MILBRINK, G., Animal Ecology
MOLLER, F., Computing Science
NIEMI, A., Theoretical Physics
NIKLASSON, G., Materials Science and Solar Energy
NILSSON, A., Chemical Physics
NILSSON, A., Systematic Botany

NORDBLAD, P., Solid-State Physics
NORDGREN, J., Soft X-ray Physics
NYHOLM, L., Analytical Chemistry
OHLSSON, R., Developmental Zoology
OLSSON, E., Experimental Physics
PAMILO, P., Conservation Biology
PAROSH, A., Computer Systems
PAVLENKO, V. P., Astronomy
PEDERSEN, L. B., Solid Earth Physics
PEEL, J. S., Historical Geology and Palaeontology
PETTERSSON, K. I., Evolutionary Biology
PILSTRÖM, L. H., Immunology
PISKOUNOV, N., Astronomy
POSSNERT, G., Accelerator Mass Spectrometry
RIBBING, C.-G., Solid-State Physics
RICKMAN, H., Astronomy
ROBERTS, R., Solid Earth Physics
RODHE, A., Hydrology
RONQUIST, F., Systematic Zoology
ROOS, A., Solid-State Physics
RYDIN, H., Plant Ecology
SAXENA, S., Theoretical Geochemistry
SCHWEITZ, J.-A., Materials Science
SIEGBAHN, H., Atomic and Molecular Physics
SJÖBERG, S., Organic Chemistry
SKÖLD, K., Neutron Research
SMEDMAN, A.-S., Meteorology
SÖDERHÄLL, K. T., Physiological Mycology
SÖDERSTRÖM, T., Automatic Control
STERNAD, M., Signals and Systems
STOICA, P., Systems Modelling
STOLTENBERG-HANSEN, V., Logic of Mathematics
STRÖMQUIST, L., Applied Environmental Impact Analysis
SUNDQVIST, B. U. R., Ion Physics
SVEDLINDH, P., Solid-State Physics
SVENSSON, B. W., Animal Ecology
SVENSSON, S., Physics
TALBOT, C. J., Geodynamics and Tectonics
TAPIA-OLIVARES, O., Physical Chemistry
TÄRNLUND, S. A., Computer Science
TEGELSTRÖM, H., Conservation Biology and Genetics
TEGENFELT, J. S., Inorganic Chemistry
THOMAS, J. O., Solid-State Electro-chemistry
THOTTAPPILLIL, R., Electricity
THULIN, M., Systematic Botany
THUNE, M., Scientific Computing
TIBELL, L. B., Systematic Botany
TINTAREV, K., Mathematics
TOTTMAR, O., Comparative Physiology
TRANVIK, L., Limnology
VIRO, O., Mathematics
VIRTANEN, A., Molecular Cell Biology
WAGNER, G., Microbiology
WAHLBERG, C., Astronomy
WANG, Y., Computer Systems
WÄPPLING, R., Physics
ZILITINKEVICH, S., Meteorology

Faculty of Social Sciences:

AGELL, J., Economics
ANDERSSON, R. K. G., Housing and Urban Research
BÄCK, L., Urban Geography
BÄCKMAN, L., Cognitive Psychology
BLOMQUIST, S., Local Public Economics
BOHLIN, G., Developmental Psychology
BORGEGÅRD, L.-E., Urban Geography
BÖRJESSON, E. A., Psychology
BROADY, D., Education
BURNS, T., Sociology
CARLSNAES, W., Political Science
CHRISTOFFERSSON, A. L., Statistics
DIMBERG, U., Psychology
EDIN, P.-A., Labour Market Relations
EKEHAMMAR, B., Psychology
ENGWALL, L., Business Studies
EYERMAN, R., Sociology
FOGELKLOU, A., East European Studies

FORSGREN, M. O., International Business Studies
FREDRIKSON, M., Clinical Psychology
GERNER, K., East European Studies
GOTTFRIES, N., Economics
GUSTAFSSON, C., Education
HADENIUS, A., Political Science
HAGEKULL, B., Developmental Psychology
HÅKANSSON, K. G., Sociology
HALLEN, L., Business Studies
HAMFELT, A., Computer Science
HAMMARSTRÖM, G., Sociology
HANSSON, A., Computer Science
HEDLUND, S., East European Studies
HEDMAN, L., Media and Communication
HERMANSSON, B. J., Political Science
HOLMLUND, B., Economics
HOPPE, G., Economic Geography
ISACSON, M., Economic History
KEMENY, P. J., Urban Sociology
KLEVMARKEN, A., Econometrics
LEWIN, L., Political Science
LINDBLAD, S., Education
LINDH, T., Economics
LUNDGREN, E., Sociology
LUNDGREN, U. P., Education
MAGNUSSON, L., Economic History
MALMBERG, A., Economic Geography
MELIN, L. G., Clinical Psychology
ÖBERG, S., Social and Economic Geography
OHLSSON, H., Economics
PETERSSOHN, E., Business Administration
RIIS, U., Education
RISCH, T., Computer Science
SAHLIN-ANDERSSON, K., Business Studies
SÖDER, M., Sociology
SÖDERSTEN, J., Economics
SOMMESTAD, L., Economic History
TORNSTAM, L., Sociology
TURNER, B., Housing Economics
VEDUNG, E., Housing Policy
von HOFSTEN, C., Perceptional Psychology
WALLENSTEEN, P. N., Peace and Conflict
WIGREN, R., Economics
WITTROCK, B., Advanced Study in the Social Sciences

Faculty of Theology:

BÄCKSTRÖM, A., Sociology of Religion
BEXELL, O., Ecclesiology
BRÅKENHIELM, C.-R., Studies of Faiths and Ideologies
BRODD, S.-E., Studies of Churches and Religious Denominations
de MARINIES, VALERIE, Psychology of Religion
FRANZÉN, R., Church History
GRENHOLM, C.-H., Ethics
HERRMANN, E., Philosophy of Religions
HULTGÅRD, A., History of Religions
NORIN, S., Old Testament Exegesis
PETTERSSON, T., Sociology of Religion
SCHALK, P., History of Religions
SYREENI, K., New Testament Exegesis
WIKSTRÖM, O., Psychology of Religion

University Colleges

Ersta Sköndal Högskola (Ersta Sköndal University College): Stigbergsgatan 30, POB 11189, SE-100 61 Stockholm; tel. (8) 555-050-00; e-mail info@esh.se; internet www.esh.se; f. 1998; depts of diaconal studies, church music and theology, health care sciences, social sciences and St Lukas Educational Institute; 1,400 students; Vice-Chancellor JAN-HÅKAN HANSSON; Sec. ANN-MARGRET BERGMAN; Chief Librarian ANN-KRISTIN FORSBERG.

Högskolan Dalarna (Dalarna University College): SE-791 88 Falun; tel. (23) 77-80-00; e-mail ioffice@du.se; internet www.du.se; f. 1977; schools of health and social sciences, humanities and media studies, technology and business studies; 800 teachers; 18,000 students; Vice-Chancellor Prof. MARITA HILLIGES; Library Dir MARGARETA MALMGREN.

Högskolan i Borås (University College of Borås): SE-501 90 Borås; Allégatan 1, Borås; tel. (33) 435-40-00; e-mail registrator@hb.se; internet www.hb.se; f. 1977; schools of business and informatics, education and behavioural sciences, engineering, health sciences, library and information science, textiles; library: see under Libraries and Archives; 650 teachers; 13,820 students; Rector Prof. BJÖRN BRORSTRÖM; Pro-Rector MARTIN HELLSTRÖM; Head of Library SVANTE KRISTENSSON.

Högskolan i Gävle (Gävle University College): SE-801 76 Gävle; Kungsbackavägen 47, Gävle; tel. (26) 64-85-00; e-mail registrator@hig.se; internet www.hig.se; f. 1977; faculties of education and business, engineering and sustainable development, health and occupational studies; library: 90,000 vols, 550 periodicals; 700 teachers; 14,500 students; Vice-Chancellor Prof. Dr MAJ-BRITT JOHANSSON; Pro-Vice-Chancellor and Head of the Education and Research Office Dr SVANTE BRUNÅKER; Chief Admin. Officer ELISABETH DAUNELIUS; Head of Library MAIVOR HALLÉN.

Högskolan i Halmstad (Halmstad University): POB 823, SE-301 18 Halmstad; Kristian IV:s väg 3, Halmstad; tel. (35) 16-71-00; e-mail registrator@hh.se; internet www.hh .se; f. 1973; schools of business and engineering, humanities, information science, computer and electrical engineering, social and health sciences, teacher education; library: 130,000 vols, 50,000 ebooks, 10,000 ejournals, 500 printed journals; 260 teachers; 10,100 students; Vice-Chancellor Dr MIKAEL ALEXANDERSSON; Pro-Vice-Chancellor Dr CARINA IHLSTRÖM ERIKSSON; Univ. Director and Registrar INGER M. JOHANSSON.

Högskolan i Jönköping (Jönköping University): POB 1026, SE-551 11 Jönköping; Gjuterigatan 5, SE-553 18 Jönköping; tel. (36) 10-10-00; e-mail info@hj.se; internet www.hj.se; f. 1977; schools of business, education and communication, engineering, health sciences; library: see under Libraries and Archives; 500 teachers; 8,600 students; Rector Dr ANITA HANSBO.

Högskolan i Skövde (University of Skövde): POB 408, SE-541 28 Skövde; Högskolevägen, Skövde; tel. (500) 44-80-00; e-mail registrator@his.se; internet www.his.se; f. 1977, present status 1983; schools of humanities and informatics, life sciences, technology and society; library: see under Libraries and Archives; 320 teachers; 4,500 full-time students; Rector and Vice-Chancellor Prof. Dr SIGBRITT KARLSSON; Pro-Rector LARS NIKLASSON; Vice-Rector for Education ANITA KJELLSTRÖM; Vice-Rector for Internationalization AFROUZ BEHOUDI; Dir JOHAN ALMER.

Högskolan Kristianstad (Kristianstad University): SE-291 88 Kristianstad; Elmetorpsvägen 15, SE-291 88 Kristianstad; tel. (44) 20-30-00; e-mail info@hkr.se; internet www.hkr.se; f. 1977; depts of behavioural sciences, business studies, humanities and social sciences, health sciences and mathematics and science; school of engineering; 2 campuses: Campus Kristianstad and Campus Hässleholm; library: see under Libraries and Archives; 500 teachers; 14,000 students; Rector SANIMIR RESIC.

Högskolan på Gotland (Gotland University): Cramérgatan 3, SE-621 67 Visby; tel. (498) 29-99-00; e-mail info@hgo.se; internet www.hgo.se; f. 1998; primarily business administration and international management and coastal zone management, secondary subjects incl. archaeology, osteology,

information technology and business administration, international business relations, technology, art and new media, building restoration, Russian, history, human geography, ethnology, ecology, art history and cross-cultural communication; 110 teachers; 2,500 students; Rector Dr ERIKA SANDSTRÖM; Pro-Rector OLLE JANSSON.

Högskolan Väst (University West): SE-461 86 Trollhättan; Gustava Melins gata 2, Trollhättan; tel. (520) 22-30-00; e-mail registrator@hv.se; internet www.hv.se; f. 1990 as Högskolan Trollhättan/Uddevalla, present name 2006; depts of economics and IT, engineering science, nursing, health and culture, social and behavioural studies; 500 teachers; 11,000 students; Rector and Vice-Chancellor Prof. KERSTIN NORÉN; Pro-Rector JAN THELIANDER; Vice-Rector for Innovation Prof. STEFAN CHRISTIERNIN; Dir MARITA JOHANSON (acting).

Mälardalens Högskola (Mälardalen University): POB 883, SE-721 23 Västerås; tel. (21) 10-13-00; e-mail info@mdh.se; internet www.mdh.se; f. 1977; schools of business, society and engineering, education, culture and communication, health, care and social welfare, innovation, design and engineering; library: see under Libraries and Archives; 460 teachers; 12,000 students; Vice-Chancellor KARIN RÖDING; Pro-Vice-Chancellor Prof. PAUL PETTERSSON; Deputy-Vice-Chancellor KARIN AXELSSON; Univ. Dir MARIE ERIKSSON.

Malmö Högskola (Malmö University): SE-205 06 Malmö; tel. (40) 665-70-00; e-mail intsek@mah.se; internet www.mah.se; f. 1998; faculties of health and society, culture and society, education and society, odontology, technology and society; 1,440 teachers; 25,000 students (full-time and part-time); Vice-Chancellor Prof. STEFAN BENGTSSON; Deputy Vice-Chancellor CECILIA CHRISTERSSON; Pro-Vice-Chancellor EVA ENGQUIST; Pro-Vice-Chancellor Prof. HANS LINDQUIST.

Södertörns Högskola (Sodertorn University): SE-141 89 Huddinge; Alfred Nobels allé 7, SE-141 52 Huddinge; tel. (8) 608-40-00; e-mail international@sh.se; internet www.sh .se; f. 1996; schools of culture and education, historical and contemporary studies, natural sciences, technology and environmental studies, social sciences; library: 119,313 vols; 450 teachers; 13,500 students; Vice-Chancellor Prof. MOIRA VON WRIGHT; Pro-Vice-Chancellor Dr NILS EKEDAHL; Pro-Vice-Chancellor Dr REBECKA LETTEVALL; Chief Administrative Officer BJÖRN SANDAHL (acting); Library Dir KARIN GRÖNVALL.

Sophiahemmet Högskola (Sophiahemmet University): POB 5605, SE-114 86 Stockholm; Lindstedtsvägen 8, Solhemmet, Stockholm; tel. (8) 406-20-00; e-mail info@ sophiahemmethogskola.se; internet www .sophiahemmethogskola.se; f. 1884 as Drottningens Sjuksköterskeskola (Queen's School of Nursing); Bachelors and Masters degree courses in nursing science; library: 20,000 vols, 100 periodicals; 1,300 students; Rector JAN ÅKE LINDGREN; Library Dir WAHLFRIDSSON EVA UNEMO.

Other Institutes of University Standing

Blekinge Tekniska Högskola (Blekinge Institute of Technology): SE-371 79 Karlskrona; Campus Gräsvik (Valhallavägen 1), Karlskrona; tel. (455) 38-50-00; e-mail info@ bth.se; internet www.bth.se; f. 1989, present name adopted 2000; schools of computing, engineering, health science, management,

planning and media design; 140 teachers; 8,800 students; Vice-Chancellor ANDERS HEDERSTIERNA; Pro-Vice-Chancellor HENRIC JOHNSON; Head of Admin. HENRICK GYLLBERG.

Chalmers Tekniska Högskola (Chalmers University of Technology): SE-412 96 Gothenburg; tel. (31) 772-10-00; e-mail info@adm.chalmers.se; internet www .chalmers.se; f. 1829; depts of applied information technology, applied mechanics, applied physics, architecture, chemical and biological engineering, civil and environmental engineering, computer science and engineering, Earth and space sciences, energy and environment, fundamental physics, materials and manufacturing technology, mathematical sciences, microtechnology and nanoscience, product and production devt, shipping and marine technology, signals and systems, technology management and economics; maintains 44 attached centres; library: see under Libraries and Archives; 1,600 teachers; 11,000 students; Pres. and CEO Prof. Dr KARIN MARKIDES; First Vice-Pres. Prof. MATS VIBERG; Dean. JOHAN CARLSTEN; Vice-Pres. for Advancement LARS BORJESSON; Vice-Pres. for Research and Research Education Prof. ALF-ERIK ALMSTEDT; Vice-Pres. for Strategy and Sustainable Devt Prof. JOHN HOLMBERG; Vice-Pres. for Undergraduate and Master Programmes Prof. Dr MARIA KNUTSON WEDEL; Libraries Dir L. NELLDE.

Gymnastik- och Idrottshögskolan (Swedish School of Sport and Health Sciences): POB 5626, SE-114 86 Stockholm; Lidingövägen 1, SE-114 33 Stockholm; tel. (8) 120-537-00; e-mail registrator@gih.se; internet www .gih.se; f. 1813, fmrly Stockholm Univ. College of Physical Education and Sports, present name 2005; programmes incl. physical education teaching, sports science and coaching, sports science and health science; library: 60,000 vols, 6,000 periodicals; 60 teachers; 650 students; Rector Prof. KARIN HENRIKSSON-LARSEN; Pro-Rector Dr KARIN REDELIUS; Vice-Rector Dr HANS ROSDAHL; Vice-Rector TAGE STERNER; Registrar and Sec. AMANDA WEBRINK; Head of Library LOTTA HAGLUND.

Handelshögskolan i Stockholm (Stockholm School of Economics): POB 6501, SE-113 83 Stockholm; Sveavägen 65, Stockholm; tel. (8) 736-90-00; e-mail info@hhs.se; internet www.hhs.se; f. 1909; depts of accounting, economics, finance, law, languages and economic statistics, management and organization, marketing and strategy; library: see under Libraries and Archives; 170 teachers; 2,000 students; Pres. ROLF WOLFF; Sr Exec. Vice-Pres. for Administration LARS ÅGREN; Vice-Pres. for Internationalization LARS STRANNEGÅRD; Dir for Academic Affairs LENA HILDEHY; Dir for Student Services CHRISTINA ZANDER; Library Dir MARIE-LOUISE FENDIN.

Högskolan för Design och Konsthantverk (School of Design and Crafts): POB 131, SE-405 30 Gothenburg; Kristinelundsgatan 6–8, SE-405 30 Gothenburg; tel. (31) 786-00-00; e-mail info@hdk.gu.se; internet www.hdk .gu.se; f. 1848, merger of School of Craft and Design, Dals Långed 2012; attached to Gothenburg Univ.; product design, interior and graphic design, ceramic art, textile art, jewellery design, film scenography; library: 20,000 vols; 40 teachers; 250 students; Head BITTE NYGREN; Deputy Head JEFF KALLER; Head of Admin. JEANETTE JOHANSSON; Librarian KARIN SUNDÉN.

Högskolan för Scen och Musik (Academy of Music and Drama): POB 210, SE-405 30 Gothenburg; Fågelsången 1, Gothenburg; tel.

1974; repository for official, non-governmental records, private papers relating to Bermuda from 1615 to present; Dir BEVERLEY MORFITT (acting).

Bermuda National Library: Bermuda Youth Library, 74 Church St, Hamilton HM 12; Par-la-Ville, 13 Queen St, Hamilton HM 11; tel. 295-2905; e-mail bdanatlib@gov.bm; internet www.bnl.bm; f. 1839, present bldg (Adult Library) 1916; attached to Min. of Education; spec. colln of Bermudiana materials; extensive talking book and large print collns; 117,655 vols (incl. 12,700 vols at the Youth Library); Head Librarian C. JOANNE BRANGMAN; Librarian for Adult Services JULIE BEAN; Librarian for Youth Services MARLA SMITH; Librarian for Colln Management PATRICE CARVELL; publ. *Bermuda National Bibliography* (4 a year; print and online).

Museums and Art Galleries
Flatts
Bermuda Aquarium, Museum & Zoo: POB FL 145, Flatts FL BX; 40 North Shore Rd, Flatts FL 04; tel. 293-2727; e-mail info.bzs@gov.bm; internet www.bamz.org; f. 1926; live zoological colln; aquarium with large reef tank; local natural history and other exhibits; library of 3,000 vols; Prin. Curator Dr IAN WALKER; publ. *Wild Tales* (4 a year).

Hamilton
Bermuda National Gallery: Suite 191, 48 Par-la-Ville Rd, Hamilton HM 11; City Hall Arts Centre, Church St, Hamilton; tel. 295-9428; e-mail director@bng.bm; internet www.bng.bm; f. 1992; attached to Bermuda Fine Art Trust; nat. art colln; spec. colln of historic European paintings; educational and social events; Chair., Bermuda Fine Art Trust GARY L. PHILLIPS; Dir LISA HOWIE; Curator SOPHIE CRESSALL.

Bermuda National Trust Museum at the Globe Hotel: POB HM 61, Hamilton HM AX; 32 York St, St George's; tel. 297-1423; e-mail palmetto@bnt.bm; internet www.bnt.bm; f. 1970, housed at the Globe Hotel (built c. 1700); attached to Bermuda Nat. Trust; displays depict Bermuda's role in the American Civil War; colln of antique furniture; Dir AMANDA OUTERBRIDGE.

Masterworks Museum of Bermuda Art: POB HM 1929, Hamilton HM HX; The Botanical Gardens 183, South Rd, Paget DV 04; tel. 236-2950; e-mail mworks@logic.bm; internet www.bermudamasterworks.com; f. 2008; not-for-profit org.; art storage facilities; classroom, main gallery and a smaller gallery dedicated to local artists; Founder and Creative Dir TOM BUTTERFIELD; Chair. MICHAEL HAMER; Treas. JUDITH HOWE-TUCKER.

Tucker House Museum: POB HM 61, Hamilton HM AX; 5 Water St, St George's; tel. 297-0545; e-mail palmetto@bnt.bm; internet www.bnt.bm; f. 1970, bldg 1750; attached to Bermuda Nat. Trust; 18th-century house with colln of Tucker family silver, china, crystal, English mahogany and Bermuda cedar furniture; Dir AMANDA OUTERBRIDGE.

Verdmont Museum: POB HM 61, Hamilton HM AX; 6 Verdmont Lane, off Collector's Hill, Smith's Parish; tel. 236-7639; e-mail palmetto@bnt.bm; internet www.bnt.bm; f. built 1710, sold to the Bermuda Nat. Trust 1951; attached to Bermuda Nat. Trust; 18th-century house with period furniture; early Georgian architecture; Exec. Dir JENNIFER GRAY.

Sandys
Bermuda Arts Centre at Dockyard: POB MA 66, Mangrove Bay MA BX; tel. 234-2809; e-mail artcentre@ibl.bm; internet www.artbermuda.bm; f. 1984; not-for-profit org.; forum for local artists; art workshops; display and sale of local artwork.

Bermuda Maritime Museum: POB MA 133, Sandys, MA BX; tel. 234-1333; e-mail info@bmm.bm; internet www.bmm.bm; f. 1975; area incl. fortress of Bermuda Dockyard and exhibits represent Bermuda maritime history; Exec. Dir Dr EDWARD C. HARRIS; Curator ELENA STRONG; publs *Bermuda Journal of Archaeology and Maritime History* (1 a year), *MARITimes* (members' magazine).

College
Bermuda College: POB PG 297, Paget PG BX; Stonington Ave, South Rd, Paget PG 04; tel. 236-9000; e-mail info@college.bm; internet www.college.bm; f. 1974, by merger of Bermuda Technical Institute (est. 1956), Bermuda Hotel and Catering College (est. 1965) and Academic Sixth Form Centre (est. 1967); divs of applied science and technology, business and hospitality, liberal arts, professional and career education; 52 teachers; 1,366 students; library: 30,000 vols; Pres. Dr DURANDA GREENE; Head Librarian JAMES AGEE.

CAYMAN ISLANDS

The Higher Education System
The Government administers the University College Cayman Islands (founded in 1985; present status and name adopted in 1987 and 2004, respectively) and the Cayman Islands Law School (founded in 1982, and affiliated to the United Kingdom's University of Liverpool). The Cayman Islands are also home to the International College of the Cayman Islands (founded in 1970), which offers Associate, Bachelors and Masters degrees; St Matthew's University (founded in 1997), which operates a medical school and a veterinary medicine school; and the Institute for Theological and Leadership Development (founded in 1989; now a constituent institute of the International University of the Caribbean, founded in 2005 by the United Church in Jamaica and the Cayman Islands), which offers Certificate, Diploma, Bachelors and Masters programmes in a limited number of theological fields. Distance-learning programmes are available from the University of the West Indies, in conjunction with the University College Cayman Islands. In 2008/09 a total of 912 students were enrolled in tertiary level education.

Regulatory and Representative Bodies
GOVERNMENT
Ministry of Education, Employment and Gender Affairs: Govt Admin. Bldg, POB 108, George Town, Grand Cayman, KY1-9000; Govt Admin. Bldg, Fifth Floor, 133 Elgin Ave, George Town, Grand Cayman; tel. 244-2417; e-mail education@gov.ky; internet www.education.gov.ky; Minister TARA RIVERS.

Ministry of Health, Sports, Youth & Culture: Govt Admin. Bldg, Third Floor, George Town, Grand Cayman, KY1-9000; tel. 244-2318; internet www.ministryofhealth.gov.ky; Minister Hon. OSBOURNE BODDEN.

ACCREDITATION
Accreditation Commission on Colleges of Medicine (ACCM): see under Ireland.

Learned Societies
GENERAL
Cayman National Cultural Foundation: F. J. Harquail Cultural Centre, Harquail Dr. 17, POB 30201, Grand Cayman, KY1-1201; tel. 949-5477; e-mail admincncf@candw.ky; internet www.artscayman.org; f. 1984; facilitates and preserves cultural and artistic expression, particularly preservation and exploration of Caymanian performing, visual and literary arts; Chair. MARTYN C. W. BOULD.

National Trust for the Cayman Islands: POB 31116, Grand Cayman, KY1-1205; S Church St 558, Grand Cayman; tel. 749-1121; e-mail info@nationaltrust.org.ky; internet www.nationaltrust.org.ky; f. 1990; preserves natural environments and places of historic significance; Pres. CARLA REID; Sec. LOIS BLUMENTHAL; publ. *The Preserver* (4 a year).

FINE AND PERFORMING ARTS

Visual Arts Society of the Cayman Islands: POB 31060, Grand Cayman, KY1-1205; tel. 327-0751; e-mail topureart@candw.ky; internet www.visualartcayman.com; f. 1978; art appreciation, enhancement and learning; 75 mems; Chair. IVAN BURGES; Sec. SHIRLEY SCOTT.

Research Institutes
NATURAL SCIENCES
Biological Sciences

Central Caribbean Marine Institute (CCMI): POB 37, Little Cayman KY3-2501; tel. 948-1094; e-mail info@reefresearch.org; internet www.reefresearch.org; f. 1998; sustains marine biodiversity through research, education, outreach and conservation programmes; Little Cayman research centre; Pres. Dr CARRIE MANFRINO; Sec. CHRISTOPHER HUMPHRIES; publ. *Green Guides*.

Queen Elizabeth II Botanic Park: POB 203, Grand Cayman, KY1-1701; tel. 947-3558; e-mail ma@botanic-park.ky; internet www.botanic-park.ky; f. 1994; preserves natural environments; incl. floral garden, heritage garden, lake and wetland area, nursery, woodland trail; Gen. Man. JOHN LAWRUS.

Libraries and Archives
George Town

Cayman Islands National Archive: POB 10160, KY1-1002; Archive Lane 37, George Town, Grand Cayman; tel. 949-9809; e-mail cina@gov.ky; internet www.cina.gov.ky; f. 2007; archive and records preservation, records policy unit and reprographics unit; Dir J. KIMLON LAWRENCE.

Cayman Islands Public Library Service: POB 1172, Grand Cayman, KY1-1102; Edward St 68, George Town, Grand Cayman; tel. 949-5159; e-mail foi.lib@gov.ky; internet www.cipl.gov.ky; f. 1920; 5 br. libraries and learning centre; local history reference colln; 64,025 vols; Dir K. C. WILLIAMS-COCKFIELD (acting).

Museums and Art Galleries
Cayman Brac

Cayman Brac Museum: POB 240, Cayman Brac, KY2-2101; tel. 948-2222; e-mail naturecayman@gov.ky; internet www.naturecayman.com; flora and fauna of the island; conserves natural environments; items of Cayman Brackers seafaring days.

George Town

Cayman Islands National Museum: POB 2189, George Town, KY1-1105; tel. 949-8368; internet www.museum.ky; f. 1990; preservation, research and dissemination of Caymanian heritage; over 8,000 items, incl. natural history specimens and rare documents; Dir MARGARET (PEGGY) LESHIKAR-DENTON.

National Gallery of the Cayman Islands: POB 10197, Esterley Tibbetts Highway, Grand Cayman, KY1-1002; tel. 945-8111; e-mail administration@nationalgallery.org.ky; internet www.nationalgallery.org.ky; f. 1996; promotes and encourages appreciation and practice of visual arts; reference library with books and DVDs on history of art, design, and arts education and production; Chair. HENRY HARFORD; Dir NATALIE URQUHART; publ. *The Viewer* (4 a year).

Universities
ST MATTHEW'S UNIVERSITY

POB 32330, Grand Cayman, KY1-1209
Telephone: 945-3199
E-mail: admissions@stmatthews.edu
Internet: www.stmatthews.edu

Founded 1997
Language of instruction: English
Academic year: September to August (3 semesters)
Chancellor: JOHN MARVIN
Library of 3,000 vols, 200 periodicals
Number of teachers: 280 (incl. 40 full-time)
Number of students: 1,000

DEANS

Faculty of Basic Sciences: Dr SENTHIL KUMAR
Faculty of Clinical Sciences: Dr JOHN RANDALL
Faculty of Veterinary Medicine: Dr KAREN ROSENTHAL

UNIVERSITY COLLEGE CAYMAN ISLANDS

Olympic Way 168, POB 702, George Town, Grand Cayman, KY1-1107
Telephone: 623-8224
E-mail: suggestions@ucci.edu.ky
Internet: www.ucci.edu.ky
Founded 1985, present status 1987, present name 2004
State control
Academic year: September to July
Pres.: ROY BODDEN
Registrar: JOHN FREDERICK
Librarian: LUCILLE KONG
Library of 18,000 vols, 50 journals
Publication: *The Pipeline*

Colleges

Cayman Islands Law School: POB 1568, Grand Cayman, KY1-1110; Old CIBC Bldg, 2nd–3rd Fl., George Town, Grand Cayman; tel. 945-0077; e-mail lovisa.vernon@gov.ky; internet www.lawschool.gov.ky; f. 1982; degree accredited by Univ. of Liverpool (UK); Dir MITCHELL DAVIES; Asst Dir D. BARKER.

International College of the Cayman Islands: Hirst Rd 595, POB 136, Grand Cayman, KY1-1501; tel. 947-1100; e-mail info@myicci.com; internet www.icci.edu.ky; f. 1970; undergraduate and postgraduate courses in science and business admin.; Dean SCOTT CUMMINGS.

GIBRALTAR

The Higher Education System

There are no higher education institutions offering degree programmes in Gibraltar. Students wishing to pursue higher education generally apply to institutions located in the United Kingdom; the Government of Gibraltar operates a scholarship and grant system, which allocates funding for students studying in the United Kingdom. The Gibraltar College of Further Education, which is administered by the Government, offers professional programmes of study leading to British vocational awards such as Business and Technology Education Council (BTEC), Royal Society of Arts (RSA) and City & Guilds qualifications. In 2010 there were approximately 400 full-time students enrolled at the College.

Regulatory Bodies

GOVERNMENT

Ministry of Education, Financial Services, Gaming, Telecommunications and Justice: 23 Queensway; tel. 20077486; e-mail info.edu@gibraltar.gov.gi; Minister Hon. GILBERT LICUDI.

Ministry of Sports, Culture, Heritage and Youth: 310 Main St; tel. 20047592; e-mail culture.info@culture.gov.gi; Minister STEVEN E. LINARES.

Learned Society

NATURAL SCIENCES

Biological Sciences

Gibraltar Ornithological & Natural History Society: Field Centre, Jews' Gate, Upper Rock Nature Reserve, POB 843; tel. 20072639; e-mail info@gonhs.org; internet www.gonhs.org; f. 1976; attached to Strait of Gibraltar Bird Observatory; research and conservation of nature in Gibraltar; environmental and biological education; 450 mems;

Gen. Sec. CHARLES PEREZ; publs *Alectoris* (1 a year), *Gibraltar Bird Report* (1 a year), *Gibraltar Nature News* (2 a year), *Iberis* (scientific journal).

Libraries and Archives

Gibraltar

Gibraltar Archives: 6 Convent Pl.; tel. 20079461; e-mail archives@gibraltar.gov.gi; internet www.gibraltar.gov.gi/gibraltar-archives; f. 1969; attached to Min. of Sports, Culture, Heritage and Youth; colln and preservation of public and historical records from 18th to 20th century; research services; liaises with schools and other instns; Archivist T. J. FINLAYSON.

Gibraltar Garrison Library: Governor's Parade; tel. 20077418; e-mail gibgarlib@gibconnect.net; internet gibraltargarrisonlibrary.info; f. 1793; culture and travel; lithographs and art prints; local history colln; colln of books published in 18th and 19th centuries; 45,000 books, incl. rare vols; Trust Sec. FRED TIBBO.

John Mackintosh Hall Library: 308 Main St, POB 939; tel. 20075669; e-mail gfjmh@gibraltar.gi; f. 1964; attached to European Documentation Centre; 3 exhibition galleries, theatre, reference library, information office and conf. rooms; 33,000 vols; Dir Dr GERALDINE FINLAYSON.

Museum

Gibraltar

Gibraltar Museum: 18/20 Bomb House Lane, POB 939; tel. 20074289; e-mail enquiries@museum.gib.gi; internet www.gib.gi/museum; f. 1930; colln of local natural history, archaeology and palaeontology (especially Palaeolithic, Neolithic and Phoenician) and military history; displays incl. Evelegh colln (colln of miniature ordnance 1779–83), artefacts from Gibraltar's Islamic past (711–1464), medieval baths built in 1333; Dir, Heritage Div. Dr CLIVE FINLAYSON; Dir, Institute for Gibraltarian Studies GERALDINE FINLAYSON; Deputy Dir DARREN FA; publ. *Gibraltar Heritage Magazine* (2 a year).

GUERNSEY

The Higher Education System

There are no universities on Guernsey, and consequently students wishing to pursue degree-level education must do so overseas, many choosing to apply to institutions in the United Kingdom. Students enrolled in British universities receive state financial support towards maintenance and tuition fees, calculated on an assessment of parental income. Recent proposals to introduce student loans for those from middle- and upper-income households, as part of austerity measures intended to address an increasingly large public deficit, met with staunch opposition. As a number of UK universities have begun to charge Guernsey students overseas tuition fees, the Government has decided to cap its participation to funding at the home tuition rates; from 2014 any difference is to be paid by the student. Vocational programmes of study are available at the Guernsey College of Further Education (founded in 1969 as the Technical Training Centre; present name adopted in 1971). In 2010/11 more than 3,000 students were enrolled at the College, of whom around 400 were enrolled on a full-time basis. The GTA University Centre (founded in 1996), which is affiliated to the United Kingdom's University of Bournemouth, provides a range of professional and postgraduate programmes, and, from 2012, a Bachelors (Honours) degree programme in business studies was introduced. Additionally, professional training courses, primarily aimed at those in the finance and support industries, are provided by a number of private companies.

Regulatory Bodies
GOVERNMENT

Culture and Leisure Department: Information Centre, N Esplanade, St Peter Port, GY1 2LQ; tel. (1481) 713888; e-mail enquiries@cultureleisure.gov.gg; internet www.gov.gg/cultureleisure; Min. MIKE G. O'HARA.

Education Department: POB 32, Grange Rd, St Peter Port, GY1 3AU; tel. (1481) 733000; e-mail office@education.gov.gg; internet www.education.gg; Min. ROBERT SILLARS.

Learned Societies
GENERAL

Alderney Society: The Alderney Society Museum, High St, St Anne, GY9 3TG; tel. (1481) 823222; e-mail info@alderneysociety .org; internet www.alderneysociety.org; f. 1966; promotes awareness and encourages historical, environmental, scientific activities relating to the Island of Alderney; 600 mems; Pres. LOUIS JEAN; publ. *Bulletin* (1 a year).

La Société Guernesiaise: Candie Gardens, St Peter Port, GY1 1UG; tel. (1481) 725093; e-mail societe@cwgsy.net; internet www .societe.org.gg; f. 1882; activities incl. archaeology, astronomy, botany, entomology, family history, geology, historic buildings, history and philology, marine biology, nature conservation, ornithology; also manages island's

nature reserves; 2,000 mems; Pres. RODNEY COLLENETTE; Sec. KATE LEE; publs *Communiqué* (3 a year), *Transactions* (1 a year).

HISTORY, GEOGRAPHY AND ARCHAEOLOGY

Alderney Maritime Trust: POB 1, St Anne, GY9 3AA; tel. (1481) 822249; e-mail hugo@alderneywreck.com; internet www .alderneywreck.com; f. 1996 by the States of Alderney; preserves, protects and manages the historic Elizabethan shipwreck off the coast of Alderney and its contents; artefacts from the wreck are either stored or on display at the Alderney Soc. Museum; Chair. STUART TROUGHT; Excavation Dir MENSUN BOUND; Treas. DICKIN DREW.

Libraries and Archives
St Peter Port

Guille Allès Library: Market St, St Peter Port, GY1 1HB; tel. (1481) 720392; e-mail ga@library.gg; internet www.library.gg; f. 1882; admin. by the Guille Allès Trust to provide free library services for the community; Chief Librarian MAGGIE FALLA; Deputy Chief Librarian LAURA MILLIGAN.

Priaulx Library: Candie Rd, St Peter Port, GY1 1UG; tel. (1481) 721998; e-mail info@ priaulxlibrary.co.uk; internet www .priaulxlibrary.co.uk; f. 1889; based on personal colln of Osmond de Beauvoir Priaulx; also incl. archives of local newspapers on

microfilm, civil and ecclesiastical records, family history files and military colln; rare vols and incunabula; local studies in French and English; 30,000 vols; Chief Librarian AMANDA BENNETT; Deputy Chief Librarian SUE LAKER.

Museums and Art Galleries
St Anne

Alderney Society Museum: The Museum, High St, St Anne, GY9 3TG; tel. (1481) 823222; e-mail info@alderneymuseum.org; internet www.alderneysociety.org/museum .html; f. 1966, registered in 1993; attached to The Alderney Society; colln of 12,000 items incl. artefacts, documents, photographs; Admin. DON OAKDEN.

St Peter Port

Guernsey Museums & Galleries: Candie Gardens, St Peter Port, GY1 1UG; tel. (1481) 726518; internet www.museums.gov.gg; f. 1907, present status 2004; attached to Culture and Leisure Dept; history of Guernsey and its people; art gallery displays pictures of Guernsey by Guernsey painters; associated maritime and military museums at Fort Grey and Castle Cornet; Guernsey Telephone Museum; Dir Dr JASON MONAGHAN; Sr Curator ALAN HOWELL.

ISLE OF MAN

The Higher Education System

The Isle of Man College (founded in 1947 as the School of Technology, Arts and Crafts) is the principal institution of higher education on the Isle of Man. In 2012 it merged with the Isle of Man International Business School (founded in 1999) to become the Isle of Man College of Further and Higher Education. Bachelors degree courses are offered in partnership with the University of Chester and Liverpool John Moores University, with degrees being awarded by the UK institutions. Distance-learning degree and other programmes are available through the Open University. In 2009/10 some 1,429 students were enrolled within higher education on the island. The Department of Education and Children provides financial support for those students enrolled within higher education institutions either on the Isle of Man or within the United

Kingdom; at 2011 the Department paid such students' tuition fees in their entirety. Approximately 1,100 undergraduate and 120 postgraduate Isle of Man students enrolled within universities in the United Kingdom are supported by the Department each year, while around a further 250 are supported at the Isle of Man College of Further and Higher Education. Means-tested maintenance grants are also available, subject to household income. Higher education programmes for employees in the Department of Health are provided by the Government and include the three-year Bachelor of Science (Honours) in Nursing, awarded by the University of Chester. Four new nursing degree programmes, including Bachelor of Science (Honours) and Master of Science degrees in specialist community public health nursing, were introduced by the Department at the beginning of the 2011/12 academic year.

Regulatory Body
GOVERNMENT

Department of Education and Children: Hamilton House, Peel Rd, Douglas, IM1 5EZ; tel. (1624) 685820; e-mail admin@doe.gov.im; internet www.gov.im/education; Minister TIM CROOKALL.

Learned Societies
HISTORY, GEOGRAPHY AND ARCHAEOLOGY

Isle of Man Family History Society: Derby Lodge, Derby Rd, Peel, IM5 1HH; tel. (1624) 843105; e-mail iomfhs@manx.net; internet www.iomfhs.im; f. 1979; local genealogy and family history; attached

library; Chair. ERNEST CLEATOR; Sec. PAT NICHOLSON; Treas. DAVID CHRISTIAN; publ. *Fraueyn as Banglaneyn* (Roots and Branches, 4 a year).

Isle of Man Natural History and Antiquarian Society: Ballacrye Stream Cottage, Ballaugh, IM7 5EB; tel. (1624) 897306; internet www.manxantiquarians .com; f. 1879; archaeology, geography, geology, history, literature and natural history; organizes excursions in summer and lectures in winter; 500 mems; Pres. KATE CHAPMAN; Hon. Sec. CLARE BRYAN; Hon. Treas. IAN WRENCH; Hon. Librarian PETER BOND; publ. *Proceedings* (every 2 years).

Research Institutes

HISTORY, GEOGRAPHY AND ARCHAEOLOGY

Centre for Manx Studies: Stable Bldg, Univ. Centre, Old Castletown Rd, Douglas, IM2 1QB; tel. (1624) 695777; e-mail cms@liv.ac.uk; internet www.liv.ac.uk/manxstudies; f. 1992; attached to Archaeology, Classics and Egyptology, School of Histories, Languages and Cultures, Univ. of Liverpool; research in history, archaeology, culture and environment of the Isle of Man; Dir Prof. HAROLD MYTUM; Admin. GILL WILSON; publ. *Studeyrys Manninagh* (Journal of Manx Studies, online, dbweb.liv.ac.uk/manxstudies/sm/smdefault.htm).

Libraries and Archives

Castletown

Castletown Library: Civic Centre, Farrants Way, Castletown, IM9 1NR; tel. (1624) 829355; e-mail library@castletown.org; internet www.castletown.gov.im; 15,000 vols, audio and video cassettes, CDs, DVDs; Librarian PAULINE CRINGLE.

Douglas

Henry Bloom Noble Library: 10 Victoria St, Douglas, IM1 2LH; tel. (1624) 696461; e-mail library@douglas.gov.im; internet library.douglas.gov.im; f. 1886, present location 2003; dedicated colln on Manx that comprises maps, photographs, postcards, newspaper clippings, DVDs and cassettes; Librarian JAN MACARTNEY.

Manx National Heritage—National Library and Archives Service: Douglas, IM1 3LY; tel. (1624) 648040; e-mail library@mnh.gov.im; internet www.manxnationalheritage.im/what-we-do/our-collections/library-archives; f. 1923; nat. library and archives of the Isle of Man; covers all aspects of Manx heritage and acts as a place of deposit for public and diocesan records; Library and Archive Services Officer PAUL WEATHERALL.

Tynwald Library: Legislative Bldgs, Finch Rd, Douglas, IM1 3PW; tel. (1624) 685520; e-mail library@tynwald.org.im; internet www.tynwald.org.im; f. 1975; 5,000 vols, documents issued by the Isle of Man legislature (Tynwald) and govt; spec. collns: Manx Statutes from 1417 and secondary legislation from the 18th century to date, Blackhall Statutes, English Statutes; Head of Chamber and Information Service J. CORKISH.

Onchan

Onchan Library: Willow House, Main Rd, Onchan, IM3 1AJ; tel. (1624) 621228; e-mail onchan.library@onchan.org.im; internet www.library.onchan.org.im; f. 1944, present location 1989; Librarian PAM HAND.

Peel

Ward Library: 38 Castle St, Peel, IM5 1AL; tel. (1624) 843533; internet www.peelonline.net/ward; f. 1897; 15,000 vols; large colln of audio books and print books for the visually impaired; spec. colln of Manx reference books; Librarian CAROL HORTON.

Port Erin

George Herdman Library: Bridson St, Port Erin, IM9 6AL; tel. (1624) 832365; internet www.porterin.gov.im; 20,000 vols, spec. colln on art and crafts, travel, war and history.

Ramsey

Ramsey Town Library: Town Hall, Parliament Sq., Ramsey, IM8 1RT; tel. (1624) 810100; internet ramsey.gov.im; public library; colln of govt publs, audio books, DVDs and video cassettes; Librarian and Archivist P. BOULTON.

Museums and Art Galleries

Ballasalla

Manx Aviation and Military Museum: Ronaldsway Airport, Ballasalla, IM9 2AT; tel. (1624) 829294; e-mail airmuseum@manx.net; internet www.maps.org.im/museum; f. 2000; exhibits, models, wartime stories and facts, photographs and recovered aircraft crash parts; section devoted to civil aviation; archive of Manx military history open to researchers by appointment; Chair. JOHN HUXLEY; Dir IVOR RAMSDEN.

Castletown

Nautical Museum: Bridge St, Castletown, IM9 1AX; tel. (1624) 648000; internet www.manxnationalheritage.im/attractions/nautical-museum; f. 1951; attached to Manx Nat. Heritage (Eiraght Ashoonagh Vannin); located in the house of Capt. George Quayle and exhibits his 18th-century armed yacht the 'Peggy'; considered of maritime importance on the Nat. Historic Ships Register.

Cregneash

Cregneash Village: A31 Sound Rd, Cregneash, IM9 5PX; internet www.manxnationalheritage.im; f. 1938; attached to Manx Nat. Heritage (Eiraght Ashoonagh Vannin); provides a living, working illustration of life in a typical 19th- and early 20th-century Manx upland crofting community; organizes spec. events, incl. Hop tu Naa celebrations in October.

Douglas

Manx Museum: Kingswood Grove, Douglas, IM1 3LY; tel. (1624) 648000; e-mail enquiries@mnh.gov.im; internet www.manxnationalheritage.im/attractions/manx-museum; f. 1922; attached to Manx Nat. Heritage (Eiraght Ashoonagh Vannin); Manx history and archaeology; art and map galleries; Chair. ANTHONY JOHN BRADLEY PASS.

Jurby

Jurby Transport Museum: Hangar 230, Jurby, IM7 3BD; e-mail jtminfo@manx.net; internet jtmiom.im; wide range of exhibits, incl. buses, trams, lorries, steam cars and a traction engine; also a replica Spitfire, an airborne lifeboat and parts of an Airship (G-MAAC).

Peele

Leece Museum: Old Courthouse, E Quay, Peel, IM5 1AR; tel. (1624) 845366; e-mail leecemuseum@manx.net; internet www.peelonline.net/leece; f. 1984, present location 2000; exhibits objects, photographs and documents specifically relating to Peel; spec. archive of documents and photographs useful for researchers of family history; Chair. of Commrs RAY HARMER.

Port Erin

Port Erin Railway Museum: Station Rd, Port Erin; tel. (1624) 836855; internet www.visitisleofman.com/placestovisit/museums/railway.xml; charts the history of steam-powered railway from its inception in 1873 to the present, incl. the now defunct lines connecting Peel, Ramsey and Foxdale; exhibits steam engines and carriages; large display of photographs, posters and memorabilia.

Ramsey

Grove Museum of Victorian Life: A9 Andreas Rd, Ramsey, IM8 3UA; tel. (1624) 648000; e-mail enquiries@mnh.gov.im; internet www.manxnationalheritage.im/attractions/grove-museum-of-victorian-life; attached to Manx Nat. Heritage (Eiraght Ashoonagh Vannin); originally a summer retreat of the Gibbs family of Liverpool; exhibits Victorian furniture, fashion and fineries; early farm equipment, incl. a horse-drawn threshing mill.

College

Isle of Man College of Further & Higher Education/Colleish Ellan Vannin son Ynsagh Sodjey as Syrjey: Homefield Rd, Douglas, IM2 6RB; tel. (1624) 648200; e-mail mail@iomcollege.ac.im; internet www.iomcollege.ac.im; f. 1947 as School of Technology, Arts and Crafts, present name 2012 following merger with Isle of Man Int. Business School; publicly funded instn; assoc. college of the Univ. of Chester, affiliated to Liverpool John Moores Univ., offers jt degree courses in addition to gen. further education studies; main college campus offers degree courses in art, design and media, computer studies, construction, education, engineering, health and social care, heritage and Manx studies, languages, teacher training; Univ. Campus (fmrly Isle of Man Int. Business School) located at The Nunnery in Douglas provides business degree courses, MBA programmes and management training; library: 30,000 vols, CDs, DVDs, video cassettes, maps, atlases, prospecti and the Manx Colln; Prin. Prof. RONALD BARR; Sr Librarian CAROLE GRAHAM.

JERSEY

The Higher Education System

There are no universities on Jersey, and most students wishing to pursue degree-level education do so at universities in the United Kingdom; for such students, tuition fees are generally higher than for United Kingdom residents but not as high as for foreign students. There is no student loan system in place; however, limited means-tested student grants and bursaries are available. Highlands College (founded in 1881; present name and status adopted 1972),

which is administered by the Department of Education, Sport and Culture, offers a limited number of degree courses at its University Centre, which was opened in 2009: Foundation degree programmes, which are offered in a number of professional fields, require two years' study, while the Bachelor of Science (Honours) degree, which is currently only available in the field of social sciences, is a three-year course. The College also provides a range of vocational training and adult education programmes.

Regulatory Body

GOVERNMENT

Department for Education, Sport and Culture: POB 142, Highlands Campus, St Helier, JE4 8QJ; tel. (1534) 445504; e-mail esc@gov.je; internet www.gov.je/esc; Minister for Education, Sport and Culture PATRICK RYAN.

Learned Societies

GENERAL

Société Jersiaise: 7 Pier Rd, St Helier, JE2 4XW; tel. (1534) 758314; e-mail societe@societe-jersiaise.org; internet www.societe-jersiaise.org; f. 1873; promotes the study of the history, archaeology, natural history, language and other fields relative to Jersey; library: Lord Coutanche Library contains books, newspapers, maps, prints, parish records and other material concerning the Channel Islands, Normandy, Brittany and southern England; 75,000 images in photographic archive; Pres. ROWLAND ANTHONY; Exec. Dir PAULINE SYVRET; publ. *Library and Photographic Archive* (online).

AGRICULTURE, FISHERIES AND VETERINARY SCIENCE

Royal Jersey Agricultural & Horticultural Society: Royal Jersey Showground, La Route de la Trinité, Trinity, JE3 5JP; tel. (1534) 866555; e-mail society@royaljersey.co.uk; internet www.royaljersey.co.uk; f. 1833; agricultural dept: provides a range of services to support the modern dairy industry; responsible for the management of the Jersey breed in the island; horticulture dept: promotes horticulture through talks, shows, garden competitions and general advice; Royal Jersey Showground: holds indoor and outdoor events; conference and exhibition facilities.

ECONOMICS, LAW AND POLITICS

Law Society of Jersey: POB 493, St Helier, JE4 5SZ; tel. (1534) 613920; e-mail ceolawsoc@gmail.com; internet www.jerseylawsociety.je; governing body of lawyers practising as advocates and solicitors of the Royal Court of Jersey; operates a free complaints procedure; Pres. C. M. B. THACKER; Sec. S. E. FITZ; Hon. Treas. M. H. RICHARDSON; Hon. Librarian C. G. PARSLOW.

HISTORY, GEOGRAPHY AND ARCHAEOLOGY

Channel Islands Family History Society: POB 507, St Helier, JE4 5TN; e-mail cifhs@localdial.com; internet www.jerseyfamilyhistory.org; f. 1978; research colln held at Jersey Archive; Pres. JOHN NOEL; Sec. PAT NEALE; Treas. HARRY BAUDAINS; publ. *Journal* (4 a year).

Jersey Heritage: The Weighbridge, St Helier, JE2 3NF; tel. (1534) 633300; e-mail info@jerseyheritagetrust.org; internet www.jerseyheritagetrust.org; f. 1981; ind. org. funded by States of Jersey; promotes and preserves Jersey's heritage; main collns of archaeology, art, archives and social history; Chair. C. JONES; Vice-Chair. P. LE BROCQ; Dir JONATHAN CARTER.

Research Institute

MEDICINE

Cancer Research UK Jersey: Woodlands Court, La Route des Cotils, Grouville, JE3 9AP; tel. (1534) 500420; internet www.cancerresearchukjersey.org; f. 1953 as Jersey Committee; fund-raising and research into the causes of cancer, means of treating cancer more effectively and ways of reducing the incidence of cancer; Chair. ROBERT CHRISTENSEN; Treas. CAROL RAFFERTY.

Libraries and Archives

St Helier

Jersey Archive: Clarence Rd, St Helier, JE2 4JY; tel. (1534) 833135; e-mail archives@jerseyheritage.org; internet www.jerseyheritage.org/research-centre/jersey-archive; f. 1993; attached to Jersey Heritage; preserves records of the States of Jersey, State cttees and depts, Royal Court, Lt-Governor, parishes, churches, businesses, societies and individuals; Head of Archives and Collns LINDA ROMERIL.

Jersey Library: Halkett Pl., St Helier, JE2 4WH; tel. (1534) 448700; e-mail je.library@gov.je; internet www.gov.je/library; gen. lending colln, local and British newspapers and periodicals since the 18th century; Chief Librarian PAT DAVIS.

Museums and Art Galleries

Grouville

La Hougue Bie Museum: La Route de la Hougue Bie, Grouville, JE2 7UA; internet www.jerseyheritage.org; attached to Jersey Heritage; passage graves; life and history of Jersey's neolithic community.

St Helier

Jersey Museum and Art Gallery: The Weighbridge, St Helier, JE2 3NG; tel. (1534) 633300; e-mail info@jerseyheritage.org; internet www.jerseyheritage.org; attached to Jersey Heritage; history of neolithic to modern - day Jersey; spec. items on display incl. Bronze Age gold torque and Millais' portrait of Lillie Langtry; works of Claude Cahun; Victorian merchant town house with traditional gas lamps and period furniture.

Maritime Museum: New North Quay, St Helier, JE2 3ND; tel. (1534) 633372; e-mail info@jerseyheritagetrust.org; internet www.jerseyheritage.org; f. 1997; attached to Jersey Heritage; seafaring and navigation; displays selected objects from maritime collector and Jersey resident Tony Titterington's collns incl. a torpedo, propeller and shaft, a restored 88-mm deck gun and sonar from a German armed trawler; ship bells, bronze cannon from HMS *Determinée*, a British man-of-war wrecked off Noirmont in 1803.

Occupation Tapestry Gallery: New N Quay, St Helier, JE2 3ND; tel. (1534) 633372; e-mail info@jerseyheritage.org; internet www.jerseyheritage.org; attached to Jersey Heritage; displays 12 panels of tapestry depicting life in Jersey during the Second World War.

St Lawrence

Hamptonne Country Life Museum: La Rue de la Patente, St Lawrence, JE3 1HS; tel. (1534) 633300; e-mail info@jerseyheritage.org; internet www.jerseyheritage.org; attached to Jersey Heritage; farm bldgs and meadows; cluster of restored farmhouses and outbuildings displaying 17th-century rural life in Jersey.

Jersey War Tunnels: Les Charrières Malorey, St Lawrence, JE3 1FU; tel. (1534) 860808; e-mail info@jerseywartunnels.com; internet www.jerseywartunnels.com; tunnel complex fmrly known as Höhlgangsanlage 8 (Ho8); hosts a series of galleries detailing the occupation of Jersey during the Second World War.

College

Highlands College: POB 1000, St Saviour, JE4 9QA; tel. (1534) 608608; e-mail hcwebsite@highlands.ac.uk; internet www .highlands.ac.uk; f. 1881 as naval training college, present name and status 1972; attached to Dept for Education, Sport and Culture; vocational and leisure courses; adult education service; partnership with Plymouth and London South Bank Univs; attached Univ. Centre for undergraduate and graduate study; 6,000 students; Prin. and Chief Exec. Prof. EDWARD SALLIS; Deputy Prin. Dr GARY JONES; Vice-Prin. PETER WADE (acting).

UNITED STATES OF AMERICA

The Higher Education System

Institutions of higher education predate the USA's independence from the United Kingdom in 1776, the oldest being Harvard University, which was founded in 1636. Over 500 universities and colleges were founded during the 19th century, particularly following the Morrill Land-Grants Acts of 1862 and 1890, which gave over federal lands to the States for the purpose of establishing and funding educational institutions; the so-called 'A&M' (agricultural and mechanical) universities are among the most prominent of these institutions. There is no federal system of higher education, which is primarily provided by state governments and private institutions. However, the federal Department of Education is responsible for promoting education at all levels, dispensing federal aid and enforcing civil rights statutes. The Bill of Rights of the US Constitution guarantees academic freedom at all levels. Higher education is offered by universities and two-year, four-year and community colleges. In 2009 there were 4,409 degree-granting universities and colleges. In 2010 student enrolment figures stood at 20,427,709 for full- and part-time students enrolled in both private and public institutions at tertiary level.

Admission to higher education is often on the basis of the High School Graduation Diploma and results in Scholastic Aptitude Tests (SATs), with institutions also applying their own criteria. Two-year Associate degrees are offered by both four-year institutions and two-year junior, technical and community colleges (junior colleges are usually privately run institutions and community colleges are funded by State or local governments). Students who have been awarded Associate degrees may transfer into four-year universities and colleges to complete full degrees. The Bachelors is the main undergraduate degree and typically lasts four years, consisting of two years of general education and then two years of study in a 'major' subject. However, Bachelors degrees in specialist or technical fields last five years. Most degrees are awarded on a 'credit-semester' basis, under which the student is required to accumulate a specified number of credits each semester in order to graduate. The minimum number of credits required for the award of the Bachelors degree is 120.

Postgraduate education in US institutions is referred to as 'graduate school' because degrees at this level are administered by university graduate schools. Admission to graduate school requires the Bachelors and an application supported by transcripts, statements of purpose and letters of recommendation. Applicants will also be required to achieve good scores in at least one of several standardized tests, depending on the subject area. Among these tests are Graduate Record Examinations, Miller Analogies Test, Graduate Management Admissions Test, Law School Admissions Test and the Medical College Admission Test. Masters degrees last between one and three years and are available on a taught or research basis, the difference being that taught degrees prepare students for professional entry and research degrees prepare students for further postgraduate studies. The PhD is the most common doctoral-level degree, and lasts between five to 10 years following the award of the Bachelors, depending on the subject and on whether the student has first undertaken a Masters or professional postgraduate degree; programmes in the humanities and professional fields generally take longer to complete than those in the physical sciences and engineering. The PhD consists of a period of intensive study leading to examinations before the student undertakes research for a doctoral dissertation, which is presented and defended before a panel.

There is no established federal framework of post-secondary technical and vocational qualifications. Occupational training takes place in the workplace, and educational certificates, diplomas and degrees consist of both classroom-based learning and practical experience.

Accreditation of universities and colleges is administered by the six main regional accrediting bodies, which are recognized by the Department of Education and are members of the Council for Higher Education Accreditation. They are: Middle States Association of Colleges and Schools (MSA), Northwest Commission on Colleges and Universities (NWCCU), North Central Association of Colleges and Schools (NCA), New England Association of Schools and Colleges, Inc./Commission on Institutions of Higher Education (NEASC–CIHE), Southern Association of Colleges and Schools/Commission on Colleges (SACS–CC) and Western Association of Schools and Colleges/Accrediting Commission for Senior Colleges and Universities (WASC–Sr). There are also professional bodies and single-subject agencies that accredit specialist schools and individual programmes.

In 2009 President Barack Obama enacted legislation to make college more affordable by making working families eligible for a tax credit to help offset the cost of tuition and by expanding the Perkins Loan Programme. In March 2010 Obama enacted the Student Aid and Fiscal Responsibility Act, which provided for the investment of more than US $36,000m. into the Pell Grants programme over a 10-year period, and raised the maximum Pell Grant amount for the 2010/11 academic year to $5,500. Owing to a shortfall in funding, Congress voted in mid-2011 to reduce the average amount of aid available to students via the Pell Grant for 2011/12, although the maximum payment was to remain unchanged at $5,500. Obama also had plans to reform the nation's student loan system by decreasing the role of private lenders and placing the responsibility on the federal Government.

Regulatory and Representative Bodies

GOVERNMENT

Department of Education: 400 Maryland Ave, SW, Washington, DC 20202; tel. (202) 401-2000; internet www.ed.gov; Sec. of Education ARNE DUNCAN.

ACCREDITATION

ABET: 111 Market Pl., Suite 1050, Baltimore, MD 21202-4012; tel. (410) 347-7700; e-mail comms@abet.org; internet www.abet.org; f. 1932 as Engineers Council for Professional Devt, present location 1996, present name 2005; advances quality education in applied science, computing, engineering and technology; manages operations and resources; consults and assists in devt and advancement of education in a financially self-sustaining manner; accredits over 3,100 programmes at more than 660 colleges and univs in 23 countries; 31 mem. socs; Exec. Dir Dr MICHAEL K. J. MILLIGAN; Pres. LARRY A. KAYE; Sec. JEFFREY J. SIIROLA.

Accreditation Council for Business Schools and Programs: 11520 West 119th St, Overland Park, KS 66213; tel. (913) 339-9356; e-mail info@acbsp.org; internet www.acbsp.org; f. 1988; promotes continuous improvement and recognizes excellence in accreditation of business education programmes around the world; Exec. Dir DOUGLAS VIEHLAND.

Accrediting Commission of Career Schools and Colleges (ACCSC): 2101 Wilson Blvd, Suite 302, Arlington, VA 22201; tel. (703) 247-4212; internet www.accsc.org; f. 1965 as Accrediting Comm. of the Nat. Asscn of Trade and Technical Schools, present name and status 2009; serves as reliable authority on educational quality; promotes enhanced opportunities for students by establishing, sustaining and enforcing standards and practices contributing to devt of highly trained and competitive workforce through quality career-oriented education; 800 mems; Exec. Dir and CEO Dr MICHALE S. MCCOMIS.

Accrediting Council for Independent Colleges and Schools (ACICS): 750 First St, NE, Suite 980, Washington, DC 20002-4223; tel. (202) 336-6780; e-mail info@acics .org; internet www.acics.org; f. 1912; not-for-profit org.; advances educational excellence at ind., non-public career schools, colleges and orgs in the USA and other countries; accredits more than 900 instns throughout the USA; Exec. Dir and CEO Dr ALBERT C. GRAY.

American Association of Colleges of Nursing: 1 Dupont Circle, NW, Suite 530, Washington, DC 20036; tel. (202) 463-6930; internet www.aacn.nche.edu; f. 1969; autonomous accrediting agency; works to establish quality standards for nursing education; 690 mems; Exec. Dir JENNIFER BUTLIN.

American Bar Association: see under Learned Societies.

Association for Biblical Higher Education: 5850 T. G. Lee Blvd, Suite 130, Orlando, FL 32822; tel. (407) 207-0808; internet www.abhe.org; f. 1947 as Accrediting Asscn of Bible Institutes and Bible Colleges, present name 2004; nat., faith-based accrediting agency; specializes in biblical ministry formation and professional leadership education; Pres. Dr RALPH E. ENLOW, JR.

Association of Theological Schools—Commission on Accrediting: 10 Summit Park Dr., Pittsburgh, PA 15275-1110; tel. (412) 788-6505; e-mail communications@ats .edu; internet www.ats.edu; f. 1918 as Conf. of Theological Schools, present status 2005; accredits theological schools in USA and Canada offering post-baccalaureate professional and academic degree programmes in theological disciplines; 264 mems (230 USA, 34 Canada); Pres. J. DORCAS GORDON; Sec. PATRICIA SCHOELLES; Exec. Dir DANIEL O. ALESHIRE; publ. *Theological Education* (2 a year).

Council for Higher Education Accreditation: One Dupont Circle, NW, Suite 510, Washington, DC 20036-1135; tel. (202) 955-6126; e-mail chea@chea.org; internet www .chea.org; f. 1966; nat. advocate and institutional voice for self-regulation of academic quality through accreditation; recognizes 60 institutional and programmatic accrediting orgs; 3,000 mems (degree-granting colleges and univs); Pres. Dr JUDITH S. EATON.

Council for Interior Design Accreditation (CIDA): 206 Grandville Ave, Suite 350, Grand Rapids, MI 49503-4014; tel. (616) 458-0400; e-mail info@accredit-id.org; internet accredit-id.org; f. 1970 as Foundation for Interior Design Education Research, present name 2006; establishes and periodically updates standards for interior design education; evaluates and accredits interior design programmes of colleges and univs; facilitates outreach and collaboration with stakeholders in interior design community; Exec. Dir HOLLY MATTSON; Dir of Accreditation MEGAN SCANLAN.

Distance Education and Training Council (DETC): 1601 18th St, NW, Suite 2, Washington, DC 20009; tel. (202) 234-5100; internet www.detc.org; f. 1926 as Nat. Home Study Council, present status 1955, present name 1994; defines, maintains and promotes educational excellence in distance education instns; focuses on quality assurance, protection of rights of students and institutional self-improvement through voluntary accreditation via peer evaluation; 100 mems; Chair. TIMOTHY MOTT; Exec. Dir MICHAEL P. LAMBERT.

ENIC/NARIC United States of America: 5209 Sangamore Rd, Bethesda, MD 20816; tel. (301) 320-3842; internet www.enic-naric .net.

Middle States Commission on Higher Education: 3624 Market St, Second Fl., W, Philadelphia, PA 19104-2680; tel. (267) 284-5000; e-mail info@msche.org; internet www .msche.org; f. 1919; attached to Middle States Asscn of Colleges and Schools; voluntary, non-governmental, membership asscn that defines, maintains and promotes educational excellence across instns with diverse missions, student populations and resources; accredits degree-granting instns incl. colleges, military academics, religious seminaries and univs in Middle States region, which incl. DE, DC, FL, MD, NJ, NY, PA, Puerto Rico, the US Virgin Islands and several locations internationally; Pres. Dr ELIZABETH H. SIBOLSKI.

National Association of Schools of Art and Design (NASAD): 11250 Roger Bacon Dr., Suite 21, Reston, VA 20190-5248; tel. (703) 437-0700; e-mail info@arts-accredit.org; internet nasad.arts-accredit.org; f. 1944; produces statistical research, provides professional devt for leaders of art and design schools and engages in policy analysis; 309 mems; Exec. Dir SAMUEL HOPE.

National Association of Schools of Music: 11250 Roger Bacon Dr., Suite 21, Reston, VA 20190-5248; tel. (703) 437-0700; e-mail info@arts-accredit.org; internet nasm .arts-accredit.org; f. 1924; aims at better understanding among instns of higher education engaged in work in music; establishes a more uniform method of granting credit; develops and maintains basic, threshold standards for the granting of degrees and other credentials; provides specialized accreditation to free-standing instns and units within multipurpose instns offering curricula in music; 647 mems; Exec. Dir KAREN P. MOYNAHAN.

National Association of Schools of Public Affairs and Administration (NASPAA): 1029 Vermont Ave, NW, Suite 1100, Washington, DC 20005-3517; tel. (202) 628-8965; e-mail naspaa@naspaa.org; internet www.naspaa.org; f. 1970; promotes excellence in public service education; 280 mems; Exec. Dir LAUREL McFARLAND.

National Council for Accreditation of Teacher Education (NCATE): 2010 Massachusetts Ave, NW, Suite 500, Washington, DC 20036; tel. (202) 466-7496; e-mail ncate@ ncate.org; internet www.ncate.org; f. 1954; works to make a difference in the quality of teaching, teachers, school specialists and administrators; Chair. DENNIS VAN ROEKEL.

New England Association of Schools and Colleges: Commission on Institutions of Higher Education (NEASC—CIHE): New England Asscn of Schools and Colleges, 209 Burlington Rd, Suite 201, Bedford, MA 01730-1433; tel. (781) 271-0022; e-mail cihe@neasc.org; internet cihe.neasc .org; f. 1885; regional accreditation agency for over 234 colleges and univs in 6 New England states: CT, ME, MA, NH, RI and VT; 2 instns in Greece, 3 in Switzerland and 1 in Bulgaria, Bermuda and Lebanon, respectively, are also affiliated with CIHE; 242 mems; Pres. and Dir of Comm. Dr BARBARA E. BRITTINGHAM.

Higher Learning Commission: 230 S LaSalle St, Suite 7-500, Chicago, IL 60604-1411; tel. (312) 263-0456; e-mail info@ hlcommission.org; internet www.ncahlc.org; f. 1895; attached to North Central Asscn of Colleges and Schools; ind. corpn that accredits degree-granting post-secondary educational instns in N Central region: AR, AZ, CO, IA, IL, IN, KS, MI, MN, MO, ND, NE, OH, OK, NM, SD, WI, WV and WY; Pres. Dr SYLVIA MANNING.

Northwest Commission on Colleges and Universities: 8060 165th Ave, NE, Suite 100, Redmond, WA 98052; tel. (425) 558-4224; internet www.nwccu.org; f. 1917, fmrly Commission on Colleges and Univs, present status 1952; ind., non-profit membership org.; recognized as regional authority on educational quality and institutional effectiveness of higher education instns in 7-state NW region of AK, ID, MT, NV, OR, UT and WA; establishes accreditation criteria and evaluation procedures by which the region's 162 instns are reviewed; Pres. Dr SANDRA E. ELMAN.

Southern Association of Colleges and Schools: Commission on Colleges: 1866 Southern Lane, Decatur, GA 30033; tel. (404) 679-4500; e-mail questions@sacscoc.org; internet www.sacscoc.org; f. 1895; recognized regional accrediting body in 11 US Southern states (AL, FL, GA, KY, LA, MS, NC, SC, TN, TX and VA) and in Latin America for those instns of higher education that award Assoc., Bachelors, Masters or doctoral degrees; Pres. of Comm. Dr BELLE S. WHEELAN.

Teachers Standards and Practices Commission: 250 Div. St, NE, Salem, OR 97301-1012; tel. (503) 378-3586; e-mail contact .tspc@state.or.us; internet www.oregon.gov/ tspc; establishes, upholds and enforces professional standards of excellence, and communicates those standards to the public and educators for benefit of Oregon's students; Exec. Dir VICTORIA CHAMBERLAIN.

Western Association of Schools and Colleges: Accrediting Commission for Senior Colleges and Universities: 985 Atlantic Ave, Suite 100, Alameda, CA 94501; tel. (510) 748-9001; e-mail wascsr@ wascsenior.org; internet www.wascsenior .org; f. 1962; promotes welfare, interests and devt of education in the W region; accredits 161 instns in CA, HI and the Pacific Basin; Chair. LINDA JOHNSRUD; Pres. and Exec. Dir RALPH A. WOLFF.

FUNDING

Alfred P. Sloan Foundation: 630 Fifth Ave, Suite 2550, New York, NY 10111; tel. (212) 649-1649; e-mail officeofthepresident@ sloan.org; internet www.sloan.org; f. 1934; makes grants for research and broad-based education related to science and technology, standard of living and economic performance, and education and careers in science and technology; Chair. STEPHEN L. BROWN; Pres. PAUL L. JOSKOW.

Bureau of Educational and Cultural Affairs (ECA): US Dept of State, SA-5, 2200 C St, NW, Washington, DC 20522-0500; tel. (202) 632-6445; e-mail educationusa@state.gov; internet exchanges .state.gov; f. 1959; attached to US Dept of State; advances US foreign policy objectives through educational and cultural programmes that enhance mutual understanding between the USA and other nations; reflects diversity of the USA and global soc., its programmes, funding and other activities encouraging involvement of American and int. participants incl. women, racial and ethnic minorities and people with disabilities; Prin. Deputy Asst Sec. of State for Educational and Cultural Affairs J. ADAM ERELI.

Foundation Center: 79 Fifth Ave, 16th St, New York, NY 10003-3076; tel. (212) 620-4230; e-mail communications@ foundationcenter.org; internet foundationcenter.org; f. 1956; offices in Washington, DC, San Francisco, CA, Cleveland, OH, and Atlanta, GA; makes available information about philanthropic foundations; maintains colln of foundation reports; library of 2,500 vols, 3,250 pamphlets and articles, 500 foundation reports, computer files of foundation grants, aperture card system containing foundation IRS returns; Chair. M. CHRISTINE DEVITA; Pres. BRADFORD K. SMITH; publs *Foundation Directory* (online and 1 a year), *Foundation Grants to Individuals* (every 2 years), *Grant Guides in 30 Subjects* (1 a year), *Guide to Funding for International and Foreign Programs*, *National Directory of Corporate Giving* (1 a year).

Institute of Museum and Library Services: 1800 M St NW, Ninth Fl., Washington, DC 20036-5802; tel. (202) 653-4657; internet www.imls.gov; f. 1996; inspires libraries and museums to advance innovation, learning and cultural and civic engagement through research, policy devt and grants; Dir SUSAN HILDRETH.

National Science Foundation: 4201 Wilson Blvd, Arlington, VA 22230; tel. (703) 292-5111; e-mail oies@nsf.gov; internet www.nsf.gov; f. 1950; funds research and education in fields of science and engineering; accounts for 20 per cent of fed. support to academic instns for basic research by US colleges and univs; supports nat. research centres, user facilities, certain oceanographic vessels, Antarctic research stations and cooperative research between univs and industry; Dir Dr SUBRA SURESH.

Rockefeller Foundation: 420 Fifth Ave, New York, NY 10018; tel. (212) 869-8500; internet www.rockfound.org; f. 1913; makes grants in the fields of agriculture, health, population sciences, global environment, African initiatives; organized under Int. Programme to Support Science-Based Devt; arts and humanities; equal opportunity; school reform; offices in San Francisco, CA, Italy, Kenya and Thailand; Man. Dir CLAUDIA JUECH; Pres. JUDITH RODIN.

US Department of Energy—Office of Science: US Dept of Energy, 1000 Independence Ave, SW, Washington, DC 20585; tel. (202) 586-5430; e-mail the.secretary@hq.doe.gov; internet science.energy.gov; f. 1977 as Office of Energy Research, present name 1998; funds researchers in univs and dept of energy nat. laboratories; devt of individual research programmes of outstanding scientists early in their careers; funds advanced scientific computing research, biological and environmental research, basic energy sciences, fusion energy sciences, high-energy physics and nuclear physics; Dir Dr WILLIAM F. BRINKMAN; Sec. Dr STEVEN CHU.

Woodrow Wilson International Center for Scholars: 1 Woodrow Wilson Plaza, 1300 Pennsylvania Ave, NW, Washington, DC 20004-3027; tel. (202) 691-4000; e-mail wwics@wilsoncenter.org; internet www.wilsoncenter.org; f. 1968; non-partisan instn supported by public and private funds; fosters research, study, discussion and collaboration among a full spectrum of individuals concerned with policy and scholarship in nat. and world affairs; library of 20,000 vols, 250 periodicals; Chair. JOSEPH B. GILDENHORN; Pres., CEO and Dir JANE HARMAN; publ. *Wilson Quarterly*.

NATIONAL BODIES

American Association of Collegiate Registrars and Admissions Officers (AACRAO): One Dupont Circle, NW, Suite 520, Washington, DC 20036; tel. (202) 293-9161; e-mail oies@aacrao.org; internet www.aacrao.org; f. 1910; provides professional devt, guidelines and voluntary standards to be used by higher education officials regarding the best practices in records management, admissions, enrolment management,

admin. information technology and student services; 10,000 mems in 40 countries; Pres. NORA MCLAUGHLIN; Exec. Dir (vacant); publ. *College & University* (4 a year).

American Association of State Colleges and Universities (AASCU): 1307 New York Ave, NW, Fifth Fl., Washington, DC 20005-4701; tel. (202) 293-7070; internet www.aascu.org; f. 1961; improves higher education within its mem. instns through cooperative planning, studies, research on common educational problems and devt of a more unified programme of action; 420 mems; Chair. MICKEY BURNIM; Pres. Dr MURIEL A. HOWARD; publ. *Public Purpose*.

American Association of University Professors: 1133 19th St, NW, Suite 200, Washington, DC 20036-3655; tel. (202) 737-5900; e-mail aaup@aaup.org; internet www.aaup.org; f. 1915; advances academic freedom and shared governance; defines fundamental professional values and standards for higher education; ensures higher education's contribution to common good; 47,000 mems; Pres. CARY NELSON; Sec. and Treas. HOWARD BUNSIS; publs *AAUP Journal of Academic Freedom* (online), *Academe: Magazine of the AAUP* (6 a year).

American Council on Education: One Dupont Circle, NW, Washington, DC 20036-1193; tel. (202) 939-9300; e-mail comments@ace.nche.edu; internet www.acenet.edu; f. 1918; represents press and chancellors of US accredited, degree-granting instns: community colleges and four-year instns, private and public univs and non-profit and for-profit colleges; advocates on behalf of key higher education issues; ensures higher education has diverse, skilled and ample leadership; 1,859 mems; Chair. EDUARDO J. PADRÓN; Pres. MOLLY CORBETT BROAD; publ. *The Presidency* (3 a year).

American Federation of Teachers (AFT): AFL-CIO, 555 New Jersey Ave, NW, Washington, DC 20001; tel. (202) 879-4400; internet www.aft.org; f. 1916; represents economic, social and professional interests of classroom teachers; 1.5m. mems; Pres. RANDI WEINGARTEN; Sec. and Treas. ANTONIA CORTESE; publs *AFT On Campus*, *American Academic* (irregular), *American Educator* (4 a year), *American Teacher* (6 a year), *Healthwire* (6 a year), *PSRP Reporter*, *Public Employee Advocate* (6 a year).

Association for Career and Technical Education (ACTE): 1410 King St, Alexandria, VA 22314; tel. (703) 683-3111; e-mail acte@acteonline.org; internet www.acteonline.org; f. 1926; assures growth in local, state and fed. funding for career and technical programmes by communicating and working with legislators and govt leaders; increases public awareness and appreciation for career and technical programmes; 27,000 mems; Pres. JAMES W. COMER; Exec. Dir JAN BRAY; publ. *Techniques* (8 a year).

Association for Institutional Research (AIR): 1435 E Piedmont Dr., Suite 211, Tallahassee, FL 32308; tel. (850) 385-4155; e-mail air@airweb.org; internet www.airweb.org; f. 1965; supports its mems in facilitating quality, data-informed decisions for enhancement of higher education; 4,000 mems and 160 int. mems; Exec. Dir Dr RANDY SWING; Pres. JENNIFER A. BROWN; Sec. ELIZABETH C. STANLEY; publs *AIR Professional File* (online), *IR Applications* (online), *Research in Higher Education*.

Association of American Colleges and Universities (AAC&U): 1818 R St, NW, Washington, DC 20009; tel. (202) 387-3760; e-mail pub_desk@aacu.org; internet www.aacu.org; f. 1915 as Asscn of American Colleges; current named adopted 1995; pro-

motes liberal education at national and local levels; helps individual colleges and universities focus on quality of student learning in a changing environment; 1,300 mems; Pres. Dr CAROL GEARY SCHNEIDER; Chair. MILDRED GARCÍA; publs *Diversity Digest* (3 a year), *Liberal Education* (4 a year), *Peer Review* (4 a year), *AAC&U News* (10 a year).

Association of American Universities: 1200 New York Ave, NW, Suite 550, Washington, DC 20005; tel. (202) 408-7500; internet www.aau.edu; f. 1900; 62 mems (60 American, 2 Canadian); Chair. SCOTT S. COWEN; Pres. HUNTER R. RAWLINGS, III; publ. *AAU Community Services Directory* (1 a year).

Association of Community College Trustees: 1233 20th St, NW, Suite 301, Washington, DC 20036; tel. (202) 775-4667; e-mail acctinfo@acct.org; internet www.acct.org; promotes effective board governance through advocacy and education; governs community, technical and junior colleges in the USA and beyond; 1,200 mems; Chair. ROBERTO URANGA; Pres. and CEO J. NOAH BROWN; Sec. and Treas. LEROY W. MITCHELL; publ. *Trustee Quarterly* (4 a year).

Association of Governing Boards of Universities and Colleges: 1133 20th St, NW, Suite 300, Washington, DC 20036; tel. (202) 296-8400; e-mail info@agb.org; internet www.agb.org; f. 1921; strengthens and protects the country's unique form of institutional governance through its research, services and advocacy; 1,250 mems; Chair. JIM GER-INGER; Pres. RICHARD D. LEGON; Sec. DAVID MILES; publ. *Trusteeship* (6 a year).

Association of Public and Land-Grant Universities: 1307 New York Ave, NW, Suite 400, Washington, DC 20005-4722; tel. (202) 478-6040; internet www.aplu.org; f. 1887 as American Association of Agricultural Colleges and Experiment Stations, merger of American Asscn of Land-Grant Colleges and Univs with Nat. Asscn of State Univs 1963, present name 2009; research and advocacy org. of public research univs, land-grant instns and state univ. systems with mem. campuses in 50 states, US territories and District of Columbia; 217 mem. instns, incl. 74 US land-grant instns; Chair. GENE D. BLOCK; Pres. M. PETER MCPHERSON.

Center for Quality Assurance in International Education: 2001 Mayfair McLean Court, Falls Church, VA 22043; tel. (703) 534-6384; e-mail cqaie@cqaie.org; internet www.cqaie.org; f. 1991; facilitates comparative study of nat. quality and competency assurance mechanisms to improve efforts within countries and promote mobility among nat. systems; assists countries in devt or enhancement of quality assurance systems for higher education; promotes globalization of professions; monitors issues of quality in transnational movement of higher education; offices in Washington, DC, Hanoi, Viet Nam, Abu Dhabi, United Arab Emirates; Chair. CAROL BOBBY; Pres. Dr BETHANY S. JONES.

College Board: 45 Columbus Ave, New York, NY 10023-6917; tel. (212) 713-8000; e-mail apexams@info.collegeboard.com; internet www.collegeboard.com; f. 1900 as College Entrance Examination Board; not-for-profit membership asscn; connects students to college success and opportunity; offices in New York, Washington, DC, Albany, NY, Reston, VA, Bala Cynwyd, PA, Chicago, IL, Waltham, MA, Duluth, GA, Tallahassee, FL, Austin, TX, San Jose, CA, Sacramento, CA and San Juan, PR; 5,900 mem. schools, colleges, univs and other educational orgs; Pres. GASTON CAPERTON.

Council on International Educational Exchange: 300 Fore St, Portland, ME 04101; tel. (207) 553-4000; e-mail contact@ciee.org; internet ciee.org; f. 1947 as Council on Student Travel, present name 1967; non-profit, non-governmental int. exchange org.; creates and administers programmes that allow high school and univ. students and educators to study and teach abroad; office Boston, MA; Chair. ROBERT E. FALLON; Pres. and CEO Dr JAMES P. PELLOW; Sec. KENTON KEITH.

Education Commission of the States: 700 Broadway, Suite 810, Denver, CO 80203-3442; tel. (303) 299-3600; e-mail ecs@ecs.org; internet www.ecs.org; f. 1967; helps states develop effective policy and practice for public education by providing data, research, analysis and leadership; 49 mem. states; Chair. JOHN HICKENLOOPER; Pres. ROGER SAMPSON; publ. *The Progress of Education Reform* (6 a year).

Institute of International Education: 809 United Nations Pl., New York, NY 10017; tel. (212) 883-8200; e-mail development@iie.org; internet www.iie.org; f. 1919; ind. non-profit org.; promotes closer educational relations between the people of the USA and other countries; strengthens and link instns of higher learning globally; rescues threatened scholars and advances academic freedom; builds leadership skills and enhances capacity of individuals and orgs to address local and global challenges; 18 offices in the USA, Europe, Middle East and N Africa, Sub-Saharan Africa, South and Central Asia and East Asia and the Pacific; 1,100 mems; Chair. THOMAS S. JOHNSON; Pres. and CEO Dr ALLAN E. GOODMAN; publ. *Open Doors*.

NAFSA: Association of International Educators: 1307 New York Ave, NW, Eighth Fl., Washington, DC 20005-4701; tel. (202) 737-3699; e-mail inbox@nafsa.org; internet www.nafsa.org; f. 1948 as Nat. Asscn of Foreign Student Advisers, present name 1990; promotes int. education and provides professional devt opportunities; sets and upholds standards of good practice, and provides training opportunities; 10,000 mems; Pres. and Chair. of Board Dr MEREDITH M. MCQUAID; Sec. Dr CHARLES A. S. BANKART; publ. *International Educator* (6 a year), *Journal of Studies in International Education* (5 a year), *Policy Brief* (electronic, irregular).

National Academy of Education: 500 Fifth St, NW, Washington, DC 20001; tel. (202) 334-2341; e-mail info@naeducation.org; internet www.naeducation.org; f. 1965; promotes the highest quality educational research and its use in policy formulation and practice; 165 mems, 46 foreign assocs; Exec. Dir GREGORY WHITE; Pres. Dr SUSAN FUHRMAN; Sec. and Treas. SUSAN MOORE JOHNSON.

National Association for Equal Opportunity in Higher Education: 209 Third St, SE, Washington, DC 20003; tel. (202) 552-3300; internet www.nafeo.org; f. 1969; not-for-profit org. of Historically Black Colleges and Univs (HBCU) and Predominantly Black Institutions (PBI); advocates policies, programmes and practices designed to preserve and enhance HBCUs and PBIs; builds capacity of HBCUs; Pres. and CEO LEZLI BASKERVILLE.

National Association of State Boards of Education: 2121 Crystal Dr., Suite 350, Arlington, VA 22202; tel. (703) 684-4000; e-mail boards@nasbe.org; internet www.nasbe.org; f. 1958; works to strengthen state leadership in educational policy-making, promote excellence in education of all students, advocate equality of access to educational opportunity and assure continued citizen support for public education; Exec. Dir JIM KOHLMOOS; Pres. GAYLE MANCHIN; Sec. and Treas. ROB HOVIS; publs *Headline Review* (52 a year), *State Education Standard*.

National Association of State Directors of Career Technical Education Consortium: 8484 Georgia Ave, Suite 320, Silver Spring, MD 20910; tel. (301) 588-9630; internet www.careertech.org; f. 1920; provides leadership for career technical education's role in education, workforce preparation and economic devt; 200 mems; Exec. Dir KIMBERLY A. GREEN; Pres. Dr PATRICK AINSWORTH; Sec. and Treas. MARK WILLIAMS.

National Association of State Directors of Teacher Education and Certification: 1629 K St, NW, Suite 300, Washington, DC 20006; tel. (202) 204-2208; e-mail philrogers@nasdtec.com; internet www.nasdtec.org; f. 1928; represents professional standards boards and comms and state depts of education in all 50 states, DC, the Dept of Defense Education Activity, the US Territories, AB, BC and ON that are responsible for the preparation, licensure, and discipline of educational personnel; promotes high standards for educators, teacher mobility across state lines, comprehensive personnel screening and a database on teacher discipline; Pres. BRIAN DEVINE; Exec. Dir Dr PHILIP ROGERS; publs *NASDTEC KnowledgeBase* (irregular, online), *The Communicator* (4 a year, online).

National Education Association: 1201 16th St, NW, Washington, DC 20036-3290; tel. (202) 833-4000; internet www.nea.org; f. 1857; advocates for education professionals; focuses on improving quality of teaching, increasing student achievements and making schools safer; 3.2m. mems; Exec. Dir JOHN C. STOCKS; Pres. DENNIS VAN ROEKEL; Sec. and Treas. REBECCA S. PRINGLE; publs *Almanac* (1 a year), *NEA Today* (4 a year), *This Active Life* (6 a year), *Thought & Action* (1 a year), *Tomorrow's Teachers* (1 a year).

State Higher Education Executive Officers: 3035 Center Green Dr., Suite 100, Boulder, CO 80301-2205; tel. (303) 541-1600; e-mail sheeo@sheeo.org; internet www.sheeo.org; f. 1954; works to develop and sustain excellent systems of higher education; emphasizes importance of state planning and coordination for higher education by promoting effective strategic planning and statewide coordination and governance; speaks as nat. org. in public and private forums, promoting interests of states in effectively planning and financing higher education; Chair. GEORGE PERNSTEINER; Pres. Dr PAUL E. LINGENFELTER.

United States Network for Education Information: US Dept of Education, 400 Maryland Ave, SW, Room 6W108, Washington, DC 20202; tel. (202) 401-0430; internet www.ed.gov/about/offices/list/ous/international/usnei/edlite-index.html; f. 1996; information centre under Lisbon Convention on the Recognition of Qualifications Concerning Higher Education in the European Region, 1 of 6 UNESCO regional recognition conventions; provides guide to American and foreign systems of education to facilitate int. educational mobility; Man. Dr E. STEPHEN HUNT.

Learned Societies

GENERAL

American Academy of Arts and Letters: 633 W 155th St, New York, NY 10032-1799; tel. (212) 368-5900; e-mail academy@artsandletters.org; internet www.artsandletters.org; f. 1904, merger with Nat. Institute of Arts and Letters (f. 1898) 1976; fosters and sustains interest in literature, music and fine arts; identifies and encourages individual artists by administering awards and prizes, exhibiting art and MSS, funding stage readings and performances of new works and purchasing works of art to be donated to museums; 250 mems; library of 25,000 vols; Pres. HENRY N. COBB; Exec. Dir VIRGINIA DAJANI; Sec. BILLIE TSIEN; publ. *Proceedings* (1 a year).

American Academy of Arts & Sciences: 136 Irving St, Cambridge, MA 02138; tel. (617) 576-5000; e-mail aaas@amacad.org; internet www.amacad.org; f. 1780; ind. policy research centre; focuses on science and technology policy, global security, social policy, the humanities and culture, and education; 4,600 mems (4,000 American fellows, 600 foreign hon. mems); Chair. LOUIS W. CABOT; Pres. LESLIE C. BERLOWITZ; Sec. JERROLD MEINWALD; Treas. JOHN S. REED; publs *Bulletin* (4 a year), *Daedalus* (4 a year), *Occasional Papers*.

American Council of Learned Societies: 633 Third Ave, 8th Fl., New York, NY 10017-6795; tel. (212) 697-1505; e-mail grants@acls.org; internet www.acls.org; f. 1919; private non-profit fed.; supports humanities research through fellowships and grants; represents humanities scholars and promotes the scholarly humanities in the USA and internationally; provides a forum for learned societies to discuss and suggest improvements in scholarship, education and communication; 71 mems; Chair. JAMES J. O'DONNELL; Pres. PAULINE YU; publ. *ACLS Occasional Papers*.

American Philosophical Society: 104 S Fifth St, Philadelphia, PA 19106-3387; tel. (215) 440-3400; internet www.amphilsoc.org; f. 1743; promotes useful knowledge in sciences and humanities through excellence in scholarly research, professional meetings, publs, library resources and community outreach; mems from various fields: mathematical and physical sciences, biological sciences, social sciences, humanities, and the professions, arts and affairs; conducts symposia, lectures and presents awards (incl. the Magellanic Premium, the oldest American scientific award); offers grants for research; museum and exhibition programme; 1,004 mems (834 US citizens, 170 foreign); library of 350,000 vols, 11m. MSS, 250,000 images; Pres. BARUCH S. BLOMBERG; Exec. Officer MARY PATTERSON MCPHERSON; publs *Biographical Memoirs of Members of the American Philosophical Society*, *Proceedings* (4 a year), *Transactions* (1 a year), *Year Book*.

Asia Foundation: POB 193223, San Francisco, CA 94119-3223 (Main Office); 465 California St, Ninth Fl., San Francisco, CA 94104; tel. (415) 982-4640; e-mail info@asiafound.org; internet www.asiafoundation.org; f. 1954; offices in Washington, DC, and 18 Asian and Pacific island countries; assists Asian economic and social devt through private American support to Asian instns, orgs and individuals working towards constructive social change, stable political devt and equitable economic growth within their socs; provides grants; Books for Asia Program distributes books and journals to libraries and instns in Asia; library of 3,370 vols on current Asian and world affairs; Pres. DAVID D. ARNOLD; publ. *Occasional Papers*.

Connecticut Academy of Arts and Sciences: POB 208211, New Haven, CT 06520-8211; tel. (203) 432-3113; e-mail caas@yale.edu; internet www.yale.edu/caas; f. 1799; disseminates scholarly information through lectures and extensive publs; library merged with Yale Univ. Library; 400 mems; Pres. ERNEST I. KOHORN; Sec. MARGOT L. KOHORN; Treas. JANETTE MURDOCK; publs *A Manual of the Writings in Middle English* (irregular), *Memoirs* (irregular), *Transactions* (irregular).

English-Speaking Union of the United States: 144 E 39th St, New York, NY 10016; tel. (212) 818-1200; e-mail info@esuus.org; internet www.esuus.org; f. 1920; non-profit org.; promotes communication and understanding among people of all nationalities through the medium of the English language; initiates and implements innovative educational programmes; 10,000 mems; library of 6,000 vols; Chair. PATRICIA S. SCHROEDER; Pres. and Exec. Dir ALICE BOYNE; Sec. MATILDE JONES; Treas. HOLLISTER STURGES; publ. *E-SU Today*.

Hispanic Society of America: 613 W 155th St, New York, NY 10032; tel. (212) 926-2234; e-mail info@hispanicsociety.org; internet www.hispanicsociety.org; f. 1904; 400 mems; professional research staff; reference library and museum; library of 25,000 vols and periodicals, 15,000 rare books; Dir MITCHELL A. CODDING.

National Academies: 500 Fifth St, NW, Washington, DC 20001; tel. (202) 334-2000; e-mail worldwidewebfeedback@nas.edu; internet national-academies.org; f. 1863; est. by Congressional charter; linked group of instns, coordinating their advice to Fed. Govt; publs *ILAR Journal* (4 a year), *The National Academies In Focus*.

Individual Institutions:

Institute of Medicine: 500 Fifth St, NW, Washington, DC 20001; tel. (202) 334-2352; e-mail iomwww@nas.edu; internet www.iom.edu; f. 1970; 1,700 mems; Pres. HARVEY V. FINEBERG; Exec. Officer JUDITH A. STALERNO; publs *Informing the Future, IOM News* (4 a year).

National Academy of Engineering: 500 Fifth St, NW, Washington, DC 20001; tel. (202) 334-3200; internet www.nae.edu; f. 1964; promotes technological welfare of the nation by marshalling expertise and insights of eminent mems of engineering profession; 2,000 mems; Pres. CHARLES M. VEST; Home Sec. THOMAS F. BUDINGER; Foreign Sec. VENKATESH (VENKY) NARAYA-NAMURTI; Exec. Officer LANCE A. DAVIS; publ. *The Bridge* (4 a year).

National Academy of Sciences: 500 Fifth St, NW, Washington, DC 20001; tel. (202) 334-2000; internet www.nas.edu; f. 1863; sections: anthropology, applied mathematical sciences, applied microbial sciences, applied physical sciences, computer and information sciences, astronomy, biochemistry, biophysics and computational biology, chemistry, cellular and developmental biology, cellular and molecular neuroscience, economic sciences, engineering sciences, evolutionary, biology, environmental, sciences and ecology, genetics, geology, geophysics, haematology and oncology, human environmental sciences, immunology, psychology, mathematics, medical genetics, microbial biology, nutritional and plant, soil and microbial sciences, physics, physiology and metabolism, physiology and pharmacology, plant biology, social and political sciences and systems neuroscience; 2,200 mems and 400 assocs; Pres. RALPH J. CICERONE; Home Sec. SUSAN WESSLER; Foreign Sec. MICHAEL T. CLEGG; publs *Issues in Science and Technology, Proceedings of the National Academy of Sciences* (52 a year).

National Research Council: 500 Fifth St, NW, Washington, DC 20001; e-mail worldwidewebfeedback@nas.edu; internet www.national-academies.org/nrc; f. 1916; improves govt decision making and public policy; increases public understanding; promotes acquisition and dissemination of knowledge in matters involving science, engineering, technology and health; Chair., National Research Council RALPH J. CICERONE; Vice-Chair. CHARLES M. VEST.

National Foundation on the Arts and the Humanities: 1100 Pennsylvania Ave, NW, Washington, DC 20506; f. 1965; an ind. agency in the Exec. Br. of Govt; develops and promotes a broadly conceived nat. policy of support for the humanities and the arts in the United States..

Constituent Institutions:

Federal Council on the Arts and the Humanities: c/o Nat. Endowment for the Arts, 1100 Pennsylvania Ave, NW, Washington, DC 20506-0001; f. 1965; coordinates activities of the two Endowments with related fed. agencies and carries out fed. indemnity programme; mems incl. Chairmen of two Endowments; Secs of Depts of Education, Interior, State, Commerce, Transportation, Housing and Urban Devt and Labor; Commissioners of Fine Arts Comm., Admin. on Aging, and Public Bldgs Service; Administrators of Veterans' Admin. and Gen. Services Admin.; Dirs of Nat. Science Foundation, and Institute of Museum and Library Services; Librarian of Congress; Archivist of the US; Chair. of Nat. Museum Services Board; mems who do not vote on indemnity incl. Dir, Nat. Gallery of Art; Sec. of Senate; Sec., Smithsonian Institution; Mem., House of Representatives.

National Council on the Arts: c/o Nat. Endowment for the Arts, 1100 Pennsylvania Ave, NW, Washington, DC 20506-0001; tel. (202) 682-5433; internet www.arts.endow.gov/about/nca/about_nca.html; f. 1964; advises Chair. of Nat. Endowment for the Arts on policies, programmes and procedures and reviews applications for financial assistance; Chair. of Council is Chair. of the Arts Endowment; 20 mems (14 private citizens appointed by Pres. for a 6-year term, 6 *ex-officio* from Congress).

National Council on the Humanities: Washington, DC 20506; f. 1965; advises the Chair. of the Nat. Endowment for the Humanities on policies, programmes and procedures and reviews applications for financial assistance; 26 private citizen mems appointed by the Pres. for 6-year terms (approx. one-third of the appointments expire every 2 years); Chair. of Council is Chair. of the Humanities Endowment.

National Endowment for the Arts: 1100 Pennsylvania Ave, NW, Washington, DC 20506; tel. (202) 682-5400; e-mail webmgr@arts.gov; internet arts.endow.gov; f. 1965; establishes and carries out a programme of grants-in-aid to non-profit groups, individuals of exceptional talent and state art agencies, which promote progress in the arts; Chair. ROCCO LANDESMAN (acting); publ. *NEA Arts Magazine* (4 a year).

National Endowment for the Humanities: 1100 Pennsylvania Ave, NW, Washington, DC 20506-0001; e-mail webmgr@arts.endow.gov; tel. (202) 606-8400; internet www.neh.gov; f. 1965; carries out a programme supporting projects of research, education and public activity in the humanities; Chair. JIM LEACH; publ. *Humanities* (6 a year).

New York Academy of Sciences: 7 World Trade Center, 250 Greenwich St, 40th Fl., New York, NY 10007-2157; tel. (212) 298-8600; e-mail nyas@nyas.org; internet www.nyas.org; f. 1817; sections of anthropology, atmospheric sciences and geology, biochemical pharmacology, chemical biology, computional biology and bioinformatics, emerging infectious diseases, environmental sciences, genome integrity, genomic medicine, history and philosophy of science, imaging, microbiology, nanobiotechnology, neurogenerative diseases, neuroimmunology, psychology, RNAi, science education, systems biology, vision research, women investigators' network, women in science; 24,000 mems; Pres and CEO ELLIS RUBINSTEIN; Chair. NANCY ZIMPHER; Treas. ROBERT CATELL; Sec. LARRY SMITH; publs *eBriefings* (online), *The Annals of the New York Academy of Sciences* (irregular), *The New York Academy of Sciences Magazine* (3 a year).

North American Spanish Language Academy/Academia Norteamericana de la Lengua Española: POB 349, New York, NY 10116; tel. (718) 761-0556; e-mail info@anle.us; internet www.anle.us; f. 1973; mem. of Asociación de Academias de la Lengua Española; corresp. of Real Academia, Spain; 36 tenured mems, and 150 corresponding mems; Dir D. GERARDO PIÑA-ROSALES; Sec. D. JORGE I. COVARRUBIAS; Treas. D. EMILIO BERNAL LABRADA; publs *Boletín de la Academia Norteamericana* (every 2 years), *Glosas* (4 a year).

Smithsonian Institution: POB 37012, SI Bldg, Rm 153, MRC 010, Washington, DC 20013-7012; 1000 Jefferson Dr., Washington, DC 20560-033; tel. (202) 633-1000; e-mail info@si.edu; internet www.si.edu; f. 1846; a museum, education and research complex for the 'increase and diffusion of knowledge' by bequest of English scientist James Smithson; 137m. artefacts, works of art and specimens; 17 mems of the Board of Regents, incl. the Chief Justice of the USA and the Vice-Pres. of the USA, 3 mems of the Senate and of the House of Representatives, and 9 citizen mems; library: 1.8m. vols; Sec. G. WAYNE CLOUGH; Chancellor THE CHIEF JUSTICE OF THE UNITED STATES; Deputy Sec. SHEILA BURKE; publs *American Art Journal, Archives of American Art Journal, Smithsonian Contributions to Anthropology, Smithsonian Contributions to Astrophysics, Smithsonian Contributions to Botany, Smithsonian Contributions to the Earth Sciences, Smithsonian Contributions to the Marine Sciences, Smithsonian Contributions to Paleobiology, Smithsonian Contributions to Zoology, Smithsonian Studies in Air and Space, Smithsonian Studies in History and Technology*.

Constituent libraries and archives; (unless indicated otherwise, each institution listed below has a separate entry in the USA chapter):

Air and Space Museum Archives: see entry for National Air and Space Museum.

American History Museum Archives Center: see entry for National Museum of American History.

Archives of American Art.

Archives of American Gardens: see entry for Smithsonian Horticulture Services Division.

Eliot Elisofon Photographic Archives: see entry for National Museum of African Art, Smithsonian Institution.

Juley Photographic Archive: see entry for Smithsonian American Art Museum and its Renwick Gallery.

National Anthropological Archives and Human Studies Film Archives: see entry for National Museum of Natural History.

Ralph Rinzler Folklife Archives and Collections: see entry for Center for Folklife and Cultural Heritage.

Smithsonian Institution Archives.

Smithsonian Institution Libraries: 22-branch library system: for details of individual libraries, see under entries for Smithsonian instns. For general details of the system, see main Smithsonian libraries entry.

Constituent museums and art galleries; (unless indicated otherwise, each institution listed below has a separate entry in the USA chapter):

Anacostia Museum and Center for African American History and Culture.

Arts and Industries Building.

Cooper-Hewitt, National Design Museums.

Freer Gallery of Art and Arthur M. Sackler Gallery.

Hirshhorn Museum and Sculpture Garden.

National Air and Space Museums.

National Museum of African Art.

National Museum of American History, Behring Center.

National Museum of the American Indian.

National Museum of Natural History.

National Portrait Gallery.

National Postal Museum.

National Zoological Park.

Smithsonian American Art Museum and the Renwick Gallery.

Smithsonian Institution Building—the Castle: see main Smithsonian entry for address and contact details.

Constituent science centres; (unless indicated otherwise, each institution listed below has a separate entry in the USA chapter):

Astrophysical Observatory (SAO): see entry for Harvard-Smithsonian Center for Astrophysics.

Carrie-Bow Marine Field Station—Caribbean Coral Reef Ecosystems (CCRE): see entry in Belize chapter.

Center for Earth and Planetary Studies.

Conservation and Research Center: see entry for Smithsonian National Zoological Park.

Environmental Research Center (SERC).

Marine Science: network of Smithsonian instns—see entries for Environmental Research Center (SERC), Marine Station at Fort Pierce, CCRE, Tropical Research Institute, National Museum of Natural History, and National Zoological Park.

Migratory Bird Center: see entry for Smithsonian National Zoological Park.

Natural History Museum Research and Collections: see entry for National Museum of Natural History.

Tropical Research Institute (STRI): see entry in Panama chapter.

Conservation research units; (unless indicated otherwise, each institution listed below has a separate entry in the USA chapter):

African Art Museum Conservation Research Department: see entry for National Museum of African Art.

Center for Materials Research and Education.

Freer and Sackler Galleries Department of Conservation and Scientific Research: see entries for Freer Gallery of Art and Arthur M. Sackler Gallery.

Cultural and scholarly programmes; (unless indicated otherwise, each institution listed below has a separate entry in the USA chapter):

Asian Pacific American Program: f. 1997 to provide leadership and support for all Asian Pacific America (APA) activities at the Smithsonian; Dir FRANKLIN ODO.

Center for Education and Museum Studies.

Center for Folklife and Cultural Heritage.

Jerome and Dorothy Lemelson Center for the Study of Invention and Innovation.

Latino Initiatives: see entry for Smithsonian Center for Latino Initiatives.

National Science Resources Center.

AGRICULTURE, FISHERIES AND VETERINARY SCIENCE

Agricultural History Society: Dept of History, Mississippi State Univ., POB H, Mississippi State, MS 39762; tel. (662) 268-2247; internet www.aghistorysociety.org; f. 1919; inc. 1924 as a non-profit org.; encourages interest in, promotes study of and facilitates research and publ. on history of agriculture; 1,400 mems; Pres. BRIAN CANNON; Exec. Sec. JAMES C. GIESEN; Treas. ALAN I. MARCUS; publ. *Agricultural History* (4 a year).

American Dairy Science Association: 2441 Village Green Place, Champaign, IL 61822; tel. (217) 356-5146; e-mail adsa@adsa .org; internet www.adsa.org; f. 1906 as Nat. Asscn of Dairy Instructors and Investigators, present name 1916; int. org. of educators, scientists and industry representatives committed to advancing dairy industry; serves as an open forum where a full range of views on critical scientific questions may be addressed; publishes original research, reviews and timely information; 4,500 mems; Pres. ROBERT F. ROBERTS; Exec. Dir PETER STUDNEY; Treas. ALOIS G. KERTZ; publ. *Journal of Dairy Science* (12 a year).

American Forests: POB 2000, Washington, DC 20013; 734 15th St NW, Suite 800, Washington, DC 20005; tel. (202) 737-1944; e-mail info@americanforests.org; internet www.americanforests.org; f. 1875 as American Forestry Association, current name adopted 1990; protects and restores forests, distributes information and educates public on forest protection issues, advocates sound forest policy; 35,000 mems; Chair. ANN NICHOLS; CEO SCOTT STEEN; publ. *American Forests* (4 a year).

American Society for Horticultural Science: 1018 Duke St, Alexandria, VA 22314-2851; tel. (703) 836-4606; internet www.ashs .org; f. 1903; promotes and encourages scientific research and education in all brs of horticulture; 5,000 mems; Chair. FRED T. DAVIES; Pres. DEWAYNE INGRAM; Treas. CURT R. ROM; Exec. Dir MICHAEL W. NEFF; publs *HortScience* (12 a year), *HortTechnology* (6 a year), *Journal* (6 a year).

American Society of Agricultural and Biological Engineers: 2950 Niles Rd, St Joseph, MI 49085; tel. (269) 429-0300; e-mail hq@asabe.org; internet www.asabe.org; f. 1907; develops efficient and environmentally sensitive methods of producing food, fibre, timber and renewable energy sources; 9,000 mems; Pres. SONIA M. MAASSEL JACOBSEN; Treas. STEPHEN W. SEARCY; Exec. Dir DARRIN J. DROLLINGER; publs *Applied Engineering in Agriculture* (6 a year), *Biological Engineering Transactions* (4 a year), *Journal of Agricultural Safety and Health* (4 a year), *Resource Magazine: Engineering & Technology for a Sustainable World* (6 a year), *Transactions of the ASABE* (6 a year).

American Society of Agronomy: 5585 Guilford Rd, Madison, WI 53711-5801; tel. (608) 273-8080; e-mail headquarters@ sciencesocieties.org; internet www.agronomy .org; f. 1907; conserves and wisely uses natural resources to produce food, feed and fibre crops while maintaining and improving the environment; 12,600 mems; Pres. NEWELL KITCHEN; Exec. Vice-Pres. Dr ELLEN BERGFELD; CEO ELLEN G. M. BERGFELD; publs *Agronomy Journal* (6 a year), *Crop Science* (6 a year), *Journal of Environmental Quality* (6 a year), *Journal of Natural Resources and Life Sciences Education* (1 a year), *Journal of Plant Registrations* (3 a year), *Soil Science Society of America* (6 a year), *Soil Survey Horizons* (4 a year), *The Plant Genome*, *Vadose Zone* (4 a year).

American Society of Animal Science: 2441 Village Green Pl., Champaign, IL 61822; tel. (217) 356-9050; e-mail asas@ asschq.org; internet www.asas.org; f. 1908; promotes devt of sciences beneficial to animal production; 6,500 mems; Pres. Dr MARGARET E. BENSON; Exec. Dir Dr MEGHAN WULSTER-RADCLIFFE; publ. *Journal of Animal Science* (12 a year).

American Veterinary Medical Association: 1931 N Meacham Rd, Suite 100, Schaumburg, IL 60173-4360; tel. (800) 248-2862; e-mail avmainfo@avma.org; internet www.avma.org; f. 1863; helps to improve animal and human health and advances veterinary medical profession; 81,500 mems; Pres. Dr RENÉ A. CARLSON; Treas. BARBARA SCHMIDT; Exec. Vice-Pres. Dr W. RON DeHAVEN; library of 5,000 vols, 400 periodicals; publs *American Journal of Veterinary Research* (12 a year), *Journal of the AVMA* (26 a year).

Association for International Agricultural and Extension Education: c/o Mark Erbaugh, 113 Ag. Admin. Bldg., 2120 Fyffe Rd, Columbus, OH 43210; tel. (353) 392-0502; internet www.aiaee.org; f. 1984; a professional network of agricultural educators; improves and strengthens developing countries through agricultural education programmes and institutions; 200 mems; Pres. JAMES LINDNER; Sec. T. GRADY ROBERTS; Treas. J. MARK ERBAUGH; publ. *Journal of International Agricultural and Extension Education* (4 a year).

Council for Agricultural Science and Technology: 4420 W Lincoln Way, Ames, IA 50014-3447; tel. (515) 292-2125; e-mail cast@cast-science.org; internet www .cast-science.org; f. 1972; non-profit consortium of scientific socs, orgs, cos, scientists and citizens interested in public policy and science of food and agriculture; compiles scientific information for Congress, the public, journalists and educators; 3,000 mems; Pres. NATHANIEL TABLANTE; Exec. Vice-Pres. and CEO Dr JOHN M. BONNER; Treas. TURNER SUTTON; publs *CAST Commentaries* (4 a year), *Issue Paper*, scientific publs.

Poultry Science Association Inc.: 1800 S Oak St, Suite 100, Champaign, IL 61820; tel. (217) 356-5285; e-mail psa@assochq.org; internet www.poultryscience.org; f. 1908; application and dissemination of knowledge, stimulates discovery, facilitates exchange of information on various segments of the poultry industry; 1,400 mems; Pres. Dr MICHAEL O. SMITH; Sec. and Treas. R. MICHAEL HULET; Exec. Dir Dr STEPHEN E. KOENIG; publs *Journal of Applied Poultry Research* (4 a year), *Poultry Science* (12 a year).

Society of American Foresters: 5400 Grosvenor Lane, Bethesda, MD 20814-2198; tel. (301) 897-8720; e-mail safweb@safnet .org; internet www.safnet.org; f. 1900; provides access to information and networking opportunities to prepare mems for challenges and changes that face natural resource professionals; 18,000 mems; Pres. MICHAEL B. LESTER; Exec. Vice-Pres. and CEO MICHAEL T. GOERGEN, JR; publs *Forest Science* (6 a year), *Journal of Forestry* (8 a year), *Northern Journal of Applied Forestry* (4 a year), *Southern Journal of Applied Forestry* (4 a year), *The E-Forester*, *The Forestry Source* (12 a year), *Western Journal of Applied Forestry* (4 a year).

Soil Science Society of America: 5585 Guilford Rd, Madison, WI 53711-5801; tel. (608) 273-8080; e-mail headquarters@soils .org; internet www.soils.org; f. 1936; provides information about soils in relation to crop production, environmental quality, ecosystem sustainability, bioremediation, waste management, recycling and wise land use; works closely with American Soc. of Agronomy and Crop Science Soc. of America; 6,000 mems; Pres. CHARLES RICE; CEO Dr ELLEN BERGFELD; publs *Journal of Environmental Quality* (6 a year), *Soil Science Society of America Journal* (6 a year), *Soil Survey Horizons* (irregular), *Vadose Zone Journal* (4 a year, online).

ARCHITECTURE AND TOWN PLANNING

American Institute of Architects: 1735 New York Ave, NW, Washington, DC 20006-5292; tel. (202) 626-7300; e-mail infocentral@ aia.org; internet www.aia.org; f. 1857; sponsors continuing education experiences to help architects maintain their licensure; sets industry standard in contract documents used in design and construction industry; provides web-based resources for emerging architecture professionals; conducts market research and provides analysis of economic factors that affect business of architecture; serves as an advocate of architecture profession; promotes design excellence and outstanding professional achievement through an awards programme; 74,000 mems; library of 30,400 vols; Pres. MICKEY JACOB; publs *Forward*, *Practice Management Digest*, *The Academy Journal* (1 a year).

American Planning Association: 122 N Michigan Ave, Suite 1600, Chicago, IL 60601; tel. (312) 431-9100; e-mail joinapa@planning .org; internet www.planning.org; f. 1978 following merger of American Institute of Planners and the American Society of Planning Officials; non-profit research, educational and professional org. for city planners and others involved in land use and community devt; incl. American Institute of Certified Planners (AICP); 40,000 mems; Pres. MITCHELL J. SILVER; Dir ANNA BREINICH; publs *Journal of the American Planning Association* (4 a year), *Planning & Environmental Law* (12 a year), *Planning Magazine* (12 a year), *Practicing Planner* (4 a year, online), *The Commissioner* (4 a year), *The New Planner* (4 a year, online), *Zoning Practice* (12 a year).

National Trust for Historic Preservation: 1785 Massachusetts Ave, NW, Washington, DC 20036-2117; tel. (202) 588-6000; e-mail info@nthp.org; internet www .preservationnation.org; f. 1949; encourages preservation of bldgs, sites and objects significant in American history and culture; 200,000 mems; library: (at Architecture School, Univ. of Maryland, College Park) of 14,000 vols, 400 periodicals; Pres. and CEO STEPHANIE MEEKS; Exec. Vice-Pres. and Chief Preservation Officer DAVID J. BROWN; publs *Forum*, *Preservation* (6 a year), *Preservation Law Reporter*.

Society of Architectural Historians: 1365 N Astor St, Chicago, IL 60610-2144; tel. (312) 573-1365; e-mail info@sah.org; internet www .sah.org; f. 1940; preserves and promotes the study of important structures, landscapes and bldgs; mems incl. architects, architectural historians, preservationists, professionals and students; 3,500 mems; Pres. Prof. DIANNE HARRIS; Sec. Prof. GAIL FENSKE; Treas. HENRY KUEHN; publ. *Journal of the Society of Architectural Historians* (4 a year).

BIBLIOGRAPHY, LIBRARY SCIENCE AND MUSEOLOGY

American Association of Law Libraries: 105 W Adams St, Suite 3300, Chicago, IL 60603-6225; tel. (312) 939-4764; e-mail support@aall.org; internet www.aallnet.org; f. 1906; promotes and enhances value of law libraries to legal and public communities; fosters profession of law librarianship; provides leadership in the field of legal information; 5,000 mems; Pres. DARCY KIRK; Sec. DEBORAH RUSIN; Treas. SUSAN LEWIS; Exec. Dir KATE HAGAN; publs *AALL Spectrum* (9 a year), *Index to Foreign Legal Periodicals* (4 a year), *Law Library Journal* (4 a year).

American Association of Museums: 1575 Eye St, NW, Suite 400, Washington, DC 20005; tel. (202) 289-1818; e-mail infocenter@ aam-us.org; internet www.aam-us.org; f. 1906; strengthens museums through leadership, advocacy, collaboration and service; programmes incl. accreditation, museum assessment, technical information service, continuing education, govt Affairs, int. programmes and AAM/ICOM; 21,000 mems (incl. 18,000 individuals and 3,000 institutions); Pres. FORD BELL; Chair. DOUGLAS G. MYERS; publs *Museum* (6 a year), *The Official Museum Directory* (1 a year).

American Library Association: 50 E Huron, Chicago, IL 60611; tel. (312) 944-6780; e-mail ala@ala.org; internet www.ala .org; f. 1876; promotes effective library and information services and public access to information; offers professional services and publs to mems and non-mems; 62,000 mems; library of 12,000 vols; Pres. COURTNEY JONES; Treas. MARIO GONZALEZ; Exec. Dir KEITH MICHAEL FIELS; Librarian KAREN MULLER; publs *American Libraries* (6 a year), *Booklist* (22 a year), *CHOICE: Current Reviews for Academic Libraries* (12 a year).

American Society for Information Science and Technology (ASIS&T): 1320 Fenwick Lane, Suite 510, Silver Spring, MD 20910; tel. (301) 495-0900; e-mail asis@asis .org; internet www.asis.org; f. 1937 as American Documentation Institute, present name 2000; concerned with devt of advanced methodologies and techniques; acts as a bridge between research and devt and requirements of diverse types of information systems; 4,000 mems; Pres. DIANE SONNENWALD; Treas. VICKI GREGORY; Exec. Dir RICHARD HILL; publs *Annual Proceedings* (1 a year), *Bulletin of the American Society for Information Science and Technology* (6 a year), *Journal of the American Society for Information Science and Technology (JASIST)* (12 a year).

American Theological Library Association: 300 S Wacker Dr., Suite 2100, Chicago, IL 60606-6701; tel. (312) 454-5100; e-mail atla@atla.com; internet www.atla .com; f. 1946; professional asscn; fosters study of theology and religion by enhancing devt of theological and religious studies libraries and librarianship; 1,000 mems; library of 30,000 monologue titles preserved on microfiche and microfilm, 2,000 microfilm serial titles; Pres. JOHN B. WEAVER; Sec. CARRIE M. HACKNEY; Exec. Dir BRENDA BAILEY-HAINER; publs *Summary of Proceedings* (1 a year), *Theology Cataloging Bulletin* (4 a year).

Art Libraries Society of North America (ARLIS/NA): c/o Technical Enterprises, Inc., 7044 S 13th St, Oak Creek, WI 53154, Canada; tel. (414) 768-8000; e-mail arlisna@ igs.net; internet www.arlisna.org; f. 1972; sponsors confs and workshops; distributes publs; grants awards for art book publ. and student essays on visual librarianship; affiliated with ARLIS (UK), ARLIS (Australia—New Zealand), ARLIS (Norge), ARLIS (Norden), American Library Asscn, Visual Resources Asscn and College Art Asscn; 1,000 mems; Pres. JON EVANS; Sec. ALAN MICHELSON; Treas. TOM RIEDEL; publs *Art Documentation* (2 a year), *ARLIS/NA Update* (6 a year), *Handbook and List of Members* (1 a year), *Occasional Papers* (irregular), *Topical Papers* (irregular).

Association for Library and Information Science Education: 65 E Wacker Pl., Suite 1900, Chicago, IL 60601-7246; tel. (312) 795-0996; e-mail contact@alise.org; internet www .alise.org; f. 1915 as The Asscn of American Library Schools, current name adopted 1983; non-proft org.; promotes excellence in research, teaching, and service; provides understanding of values and ethos of library and information science; 500 individual mems, 60 institutional mems; Pres. Prof. CLARA CHU; Sec. and Treas. STEVEN MAC-CALL; Exec. Dir KATHLEEN COMBS; publs *Journal of Education for Library and Information Science* (4 a year), *Library and Information Science Education Statistical Report* (1 a year).

Association of Academic Health Sciences Libraries: 2150 N 107th St, Suite 205, Seattle, WA 98133; tel. (206) 367-8704; e-mail aahsl@sbims.com; internet www.aahsl .org; f. 1978; supports academic health sciences libraries and dirs in advancing patient care, research, education and community service missions of academic health centres through visionary exec. leadership and expertise in health information, scholarly communication and knowledge management; 149 mems; Pres. PATRICIA THIBODEAU; Exec. Dir LOUISE MILLER; Sec. and Treas. JETT MCCANN; publ. *Annual Statistics of Medical School Libraries in the United States and Canada* (1 a year).

Association of Art Museum Directors: 120 E 56th St, Suite 520, New York, NY 10022; tel. (212) 754-8084; internet www .aamd.org; f. 1916; forum for sharing news and ideas among art museum directors, establishes and maintains the highest standards of professional practice, encourages communication among art museum directors; 224 mems (208 American, 16 int.); Pres. KIMBERLY RORSCHACH; Exec. Dir CHRISTINE ANAGNOS.

Association of Research Libraries: 21 Dupont Circle, NW, Suite 800, Washington, DC 20036; tel. (202) 296-2296; e-mail arlhq@ arl.org; internet www.arl.org; f. 1932;

advances goals of its mem research libraries; provides leadership in public and information policy to scholarly and higher education communities; fosters exchange of ideas and expertise; facilitates emergence of new roles for research libraries; shapes future environment that leverages its interests with those of allied orgs; 126 institutional mems; Pres. WINSTON TABB; Exec. Dir CHARLES B. LOWRY; publs *ARL Annual Salary Survey* (1 a year), *ARL Statistics* (1 a year), *Research Library Issues: A Bimonthly Report from ARL, CNI, and SPARC* (6 a year, online), *SPEC Kits* (6 a year).

Association of Vision Science Librarians: c/o D. J. Matthews, M. B. Ketchum Memorial Library, S California College of Optometry, Fullerton, CA 92831; tel. (714) 449-7438; internet www.avsl.org; f. 1968; fosters collective and individual acquisition and dissemination of visual science information; improves services to those seeking such information; develops libraries' standards; 100 individual mems and 75 institutions; Chair. D. J. MATTHEWS; Chair.-Elect and Sec. NANCY HENDERSON; Treas. ELAINE WELLS; publs *Opening Day Book List* (every 2 years), *Standards for Vision Science Libraries*, *Vision Union List of Serials* (every 3 years).

Bibliographical Society of America: POB 1537, Lenox Hill Station, New York, NY 10021; tel. (212) 452-2710; e-mail bsa@bibsocamer.org; internet www.bibsocamer.org; f. 1904, inc. 1927; dedicated to the study of books and MSS as physical objects; promotes bibliographical research and issues bibliographical publs; 1,000 mems; Pres. JOHN NEAL HOOVER; Sec. CAROLINE DURO-SELLE-MELISH; Treas. G. SCOTT CLEMONS; Exec. Sec. MICHÈLE E. RANDALL; publ. *Papers of the Bibliographical Society of America* (4 a year).

Bibliographical Society of the University of Virginia: POB 400152, Alderman Library, Charlottesville, VA 22904-4152; tel. (434) 924-7013; e-mail ar3g@virginia.edu; internet www.bsuva.org; f. 1947; promotes study of books, MSS, printing and the graphic arts, bibliography and textual criticism; 450 mems; Pres. G. THOMAS TANSELLE; Sec. and Treas. ANNE G. RIBBLE; publ. *Studies in Bibliography* (1 a year).

California Library Association: 2471 Flores St, San Mateo, CA 94403; tel. (650) 376-0886; e-mail info@cla-net.org; internet www.cla-net.org; f. 1895 as Library Asscn of Central California, present name 1906; non-profit charitable org.; 2,400 mems; Pres. WAYNE DISHER; Treas. JACKIE GRIFFIN; Exec. Dir CAROL SIMMONS; publ. *California Libraries* (12 a year).

California School Library Association: 6444 E Spring St 237, Long Beach, CA 90815-1553; tel. (888) 655-8480; e-mail info@csla.net; internet www.csla.net; f. 1977; advocates, educates and collaborates, ensuring that all California students and educators are effective users of ideas and information; Pres. JANE LOFTON; Sec. NINA JACKSON; Treas. KATHIE MAIER; publ. *CSLA Journal* (2 a year).

Catholic Library Association: 205 W Monroe St, Suite 314, Chicago, IL 60606-5061; tel. (312) 739-1776; e-mail cla2@cathla.org; internet www.cathla.org; f. 1921, present status 1931; initiates, fosters and encourages activities and library programmes that promote literature and libraries, not only of a Catholic nature but also of an ecumenical spirit; 1,000 mems; Pres. MALACHY R McCARTHY; Exec. Dir JEAN R. BOSTLEY; publs *Catholic Library World* (4 a year), *Catholic Periodical and Literature Index* (4 a year).

Council on Library and Information Resources: 1752 N St, NW, Suite 800, Washington, DC 20036; tel. (202) 939-4750; internet www.clir.org; f. 1997 by merger of Council on Library Resources (f. 1956) with Comm. on Preservation and Access (f. 1986); fosters new approaches to management of digital and nondigital information resources so that they will be available in the future; expands leadership capacity in the information professions; analyzes changes in information landscape and helps practitioners prepare for them; Pres. CHARLES HENRY; Chair. STEPHEN NICHOLS; publs *CLIR Issues* (6 a year), *Reports* (ireegular).

Medical Library Association: 65 E Wacker Pl., Suite 1900, Chicago, IL 60601-7246; tel. (312) 419-9094; e-mail info@mlahq.org; internet www.mlanet.org; f. 1898; non-profit educational org.; provides information for delivery of healthcare, education of health professionals, conduct of research and public's understanding of health; 4,700 mems (incl. 3,600 individuals and 1,100 instns); Pres. GERALD (JERRY) PERRY; Sec. CYNTHIA L. HENDERSON; Treas. MARIANNE COMEGYS; Exec. Dir CARLA J. FUNK; publ. *Journal of the Medical Library Association* (4 a year).

Minnesota State Library Services: 1500 Highway 36W, Roseville, MN 55113-4266; tel. (651) 582-8791; e-mail mde.lst@state.mn.us; internet education.state.mn.us/mde/stusuc/lib/statelibserv; f. 1899; attached to Minnesota Dept of Education; resource and information centre serving state and local govt, libraries and library support groups; administers state library programmes and federal LSTA grant programme; State Librarian and Dir NANCY WALTON (acting); publ. *Minnesota Libraries*.

Music Library Association: 8551 Research Way, Suite 180, Middleton, WI 53562; tel. (608) 836-5825; e-mail mla@areditions.com; internet www.musiclibraryassoc.org; f. 1931; professional forum for librarians, archivists and those who support the world's musical heritage; 2,900 mems; Pres. JERRY L. McBRIDE; publs *Index and Bibliography Series* (irregular), *Music Cataloging Bulletin* (12 a year), *Notes: Quarterly Journal of the Music Library Association* (4 a year), *Technical Reports—Information for Music Media Specialists* (irregular).

Society of American Archivists: 17 N State St, Suite 1425, Chicago, IL 60602-4061; tel. (312) 606-0722; e-mail servicecenter@archivists.org; internet www2.archivists.org; f. 1936; a professional asscn for archivists and institutions interested in the preservation and use of archives, MSS and current records; 5,500 individual and institutional mems; Exec. Dir NANCY PERKIN BEAUMONT; publ. *The American Archivist* (2 a year).

Special Libraries Association: 331 S Patrick St, Alexandria, VA 22314-3501; tel. (703) 647-4900; e-mail sla@sla.org; internet www.sla.org; f. 1909; activities: professional devt, résumé referral service, employment clearing-house and career advisory service, chapters and div. services, book publishing, govt relations, public relations; Information Resources Center provides telephone reference service; research; 9,000 mems; library of 3,000 vols; Pres. CINDY ROMAINE; Treas. DAN TREFETHEN; Dir MARILYN BROMLEY; CEO JANICE R. LACHANCE; publ. *Information Outlook* (12 a year, online).

Theatre Library Association: c/o New York Public Library for the Performing Arts, 40 Lincoln Center Plaza, New York, NY 10023; e-mail info@tla-online.org; internet www.tla-online.org; f. 1937; supports librarians and archivists affiliated with theatre, dance, performance studies, popular entertainment, motion picture and broadcasting collns; promotes professional best practices in acquisition, org., access and preservation of performing arts resources in libraries, archives, museums, private collns and the digital environment; 327 mems; Pres. NANCY FRIEDLAND; Vice-Pres. ANGELA WEAVER; Exec. Sec. REBECCA LORD; Treas. COLLEEN REILLY; publs *BROADSIDE* (Newsletter, 3 a year), *Performing Arts Resources* (irregular).

ECONOMICS, LAW AND POLITICS

Academy of Political Science: 475 Riverside Dr., Suite 1274, New York, NY 10115-1274; tel. (212) 870-2500; e-mail aps@psqonline.org; internet www.psqonline.org; f. 1880; promotes objective, scholarly analyses of political, social, and economic issues; 8,000 mems; Chair. PETER J. GOULANDRIS; Pres. DEMETRIOS JAMES CARALEY; publ. *Political Science Quarterly* (4 a year).

American Academy of Political and Social Science: Annenberg Public Policy Center, 202 S 36th St, Philadelphia, PA 19104-3806; tel. (215) 746-6500; internet www.aapss.org; f. 1889; brings together public officials and scholars from across disciplines to tackle issues ranging from racial inequality and intractable poverty to threat of nuclear terrorism; conducts confs and symposia; 5,000 mems; Chair. HEIDI HARTMANN; Pres. DOUGLAS S. MASSEY; Exec. Dir Dr PHYLLIS KANISS; publ. *The Annals of the American Academy of Political and Social Science* (6 a year).

American Accounting Association: 5717 Bessie Dr., Sarasota, FL 34233-2399; tel. (941) 921-7747; e-mail info@aaahq.org; internet aaahq.org; f. 1916 as American Asscn of Univ. Instructors in Accounting, present name 1936; professional soc. for educators, practitioners and students of accounting; promotes worldwide excellence in accounting education, research and practice; 9,000 mems; Pres. KAREN PINCUS; Exec. Dir TRACEY SUTHERLAND; publs *Accounting Horizons* (4 a year), *Issues in Accounting Education* (4 a year), *The Accounting Review* (6 a year).

American Arbitration Association: 1633 Broadway, 10th Fl., New York, NY 10019; tel. (212) 716-5800; e-mail websitemail@adr.org; internet www.adr.org; f. 1926; non-profit org. that offers broad range of dispute resolution services to business executives, attorneys, individual employees, trade asscns, unions, management, consumers, families, communities and all levels of govt; conducts seminars, confs, etc.; 5,400 mems, over 50,000 arbitrators on nat. panel; library of 23,500 vols, 244 periodical titles; Pres. WILLIAM K. SLATE, II; publs *AAA Yearbook*, *Arbitration in the Schools*, *Arbitration Journal*, *Arbitration Times*, *Dispute Resolution Journal*, *Forum New York*, *Labor Arbitration in Government*, *Lawyers' Arbitration Letter* (4 a year), *New York No-Fault Arbitration Reports* (12 a year), *Summary of Labor Arbitration Awards*, *The Claims Forum*.

American Bar Association: 321 N Clark St, Chicago, IL 60654; tel. (312) 988-5000; internet www.americanbar.org; f. 1878; provides law school accreditation, continuing legal education, information about the law, programmes to assist lawyers and judges in their work and initiatives to improve legal system for public; 400,000 mems; library of 50,000 vols; Pres. W. T. (BILL) ROBINSON, III; publs *ABAJournal* (12 a year), *ABA Journal of Labor & Employment Law* (3 a year), *Antitrust Law Journal* (3 a year), *Criminal Justice* (4 a year), *Family Law Quarterly* (4 a year), *Franchise Law Journal* (4 a year), *GPSolo* (8 a year), *Human Rights* (4 a year), *Judges' Journal* (4 a year), *Litigation* (4 a year), *Natural Resources & Environment* (4 a year), *Probate & Property* (6 a year), *Reports* (1 a year), *Student Lawyer* (12 ayear), *The International Lawyer* (4 a year), *The Professional Lawyer* (4 a year), *The Urban Lawyer* (4 a year).

American Economic Association: 2014 Broadway, Suite 305, Nashville, TN 37203-2418; tel. (615) 322-2595; e-mail aeainfo@vanderbilt.edu; internet www.aeaweb.org; f. 1885; encourages economic discussion, research and publs on economic subjects; c. 18,000 mems; Pres. ORLEY ASHENFELTER; Sec. and Treas. JOHN J. SIEGFRIED; publs *American Economic Review, American Economic Journal: Applied Economics, American Economic Journal: Economic Policy, American Economic Journal: Macroeconomics, American Economic Journal: Microeconomics, Journal of Economic Literature* (4 a year), *Journal of Economic Perspectives* (4 a year).

American Finance Association: Univ. of Utah, David Eccles School of Business, 1655 E Campus Center Dr., Salt Lake City, UT 84112; tel. (801) 581-4434; internet www.afajof.org; f. 1940; makes available knowledge on current devts in the field of finance; 11,000 mems; Pres. LUIGI ZINGALES; Exec. Sec. and Treas. JAMES SCHALLHEIM; publ. *Journal of Finance* (6 a year).

American Judicature Society: The Opperman Center at Drake Univ., 2700 University Ave, Des Moines, IA 50311; tel. (515) 271-2281; internet www.ajs.org; f. 1913; ind., non-partisan, membership org.; promotes effective admin. of justice; 6,000 mems; Pres. PETER D. WEBSTER; Chair. MARTIN H. BELSKY; Sec. Hon. JON B. COMSTOCK; Treas. THOMAS C. LEIGHTON; publ. *Judicature* (6 a year).

American Law Institute: 4025 Chestnut St, Philadelphia, PA 19104; tel. (215) 243-1600; internet www.ali.org; e-mail ali@ali.org; f. 1923; promotes clarification and simplification of the law; research work; 4,000 mems, 3,000 elected; library of 5,000 vols; Pres. ROBERTA COOPER RAMO; Dir LANCE LIEBMAN; publs *Model and Uniform Codifications, Restatements of the Law.*

American Law Institute-American Bar Association: Continuing Professional Education, 4025 Chestnut St, Philadelphia, PA 19104; tel. (215) 243-1600; e-mail custserv@ali-aba.org; internet www.ali-aba.org; f. 1947; post-admission legal education; organizes, develops and carries out a nat. programme of continuing education of the bar; library of 5,000 vols; Pres. MAURY B. POSCOVER; Exec. Dir JULENE FRANKI; publs *ALI-ABA Estate Planning Course Materials Journal* (6 a year), *The Practical Lawyer* (4 a year), *The Practical Real Estate Lawyer* (6 a year), *The Practical Tax Lawyer* (4 a year).

American Peace Society: 1319 18th St, NW, Washington, DC 20036-1802; f. 1828; Pres. Dr EVRON M. KIRKPATRICK; Sec. L. EUGENE HEDBERG; publ. *World Affairs* (4 a year).

American Political Science Association: 1527 New Hampshire Ave, NW, Washington, DC 20036-2106; tel. (202) 483-2512; e-mail apsa@apsanet.org; internet www.apsanet.org; f. 1903; promotes scholarly research and communication, domestically and internationally; 15,000 mems; Pres. G. BINGHAM POWELL; Sec. LISA L. MARTIN; Treas. JONATHAN BENJAMIN-ALVARADO; Exec. Dir MICHAEL A. BRINTNALL; publs *American Political Science Review* (4 a year), *Perspectives on Politics* (4 a year), *PS: Political Science & Politics* (4 a year).

American Society for Public Administration: 1301 Pennsylvania Ave, NW, Suite 700, Washington, DC 20004; tel. (202) 393-7878; e-mail info@aspanet.org; internet www.aspanet.org; f. 1939; advances the art, science, teaching and practice of public and non-profit admin.; promotes value of joining and elevating public service profession; builds bridges among all who pursue public purposes nationally and internationally; provides networking and professional devt opportunities to those committed to public service values; achieves innovative solutions to the challenges of governance; nat. and regional confs, management institutes; 80 local chapters; 11,000 mems; Exec. Dir ANTOINETTE SAMUEL; publs *Public Administration Review* (6 a year), *Public Integrity.*

American Society of International Law: 2223 Massachusetts Ave, NW, Washington, DC 20008; tel. (202) 939-6000; e-mail services@asil.org; internet www.asil.org; f. 1906, inc. 1950; fosters study of int. law and promotes establishment and maintenance of int. relations on the basis of law and justice; 4,000 mems; library of 22,000 vols; Pres.-Elect DONALD FRANCIS DONOVAN; Sec. JAMES NAFIZGER; Treas. NANCY L. PERKINS; Exec. Dir ELIZABETH ANDERSEN; publs *Academic Bulletin* (3 a year), *American Journal of International Law* (4 a year), *Cultural Heritage and the Arts Review* (2 a year), *Proceedings of the Annual Meeting* (1 a year), *IL.post, International Law In Brief* (24 a year), *International Legal Materials* (6 a year), *Law of the Sea Reports* (online).

American Statistical Association: 732 N Washington St, Alexandria, VA 22314-1943; tel. (703) 684-1221; e-mail asainfo@amstat.org; internet www.amstat.org; f. 1839; promotes inclusion of statistics in policy-making and funding of statistics research; sponsors educational programmes and meetings to enrich statistical knowledge; acknowledges and recognizes mems who have made outstanding contributions to statistics or the asscn by sponsoring awards, honours, scholarships and fellowships; 18,000 mems; Pres. NANCY L. GELLER; Sec. and Exec. Dir RONALD L. WASSERSTEIN; publs *CHANCE* (4 a year), *Journal of Agricultural, Biological and Environmental Statistics* (4 a year), *Journal of Business & Economic Statistics* (4 a year), *Journal of Computational and Graphical Statistics* (4 a year), *Journal of Educational and Behavioral Statistics* (4 a year), *Journal of Statistical Software, Journal of Statistics Education, Journal of the American Statistical Association* (4 a year), *Significance, Statistical Analysis and Data Mining, Statistics in Biopharmaceutical Research, Statistics Survey, Technometrics* (4 a year), *The American Statistician* (4 a year).

Association of American Law Schools: 1201 Connecticut Ave, NW, Suite 800, Washington, DC 20036-2717; tel. (202) 296-8851; e-mail aals@aals.org; internet www.aals.org; f. 1900; promotes improvement of legal profession through legal education; 172 institutional mems; Exec. Dir and CEO SUSAN WESTERBERG PRAGER; Pres. MICHAEL A. OLIVAS; publs *Clinical Law Review* (2 a year), *Directory of Law Teachers* (1 a year), *Journal of Legal Education* (4 a year), *Placement Bulletin* (4 a year), *Proceedings* (1 a year).

Atlantic Council of the United States: 1101 15th St, NW, 11th Fl., Washington, DC 20005; tel. (202) 463-7226; e-mail info@acus.org; internet www.acus.org; f. 1961; non-partisan instn that promotes transatlantic cooperation and int. security; 130 board mems, 200 councillors, 400 acad. assocs; Chair. CHUCK HAGEL; Pres. and CEO FREDERICK KEMPE; Sec. WALTER B. SLOCOMBE; publs *Bulletin* (irregular), *Occasional Papers* (irregular), *Policy Papers* (irregular).

Carnegie Endowment for International Peace: 1779 Massachusetts Ave, NW, Washington, DC 20036-2103; tel. (202) 483-7600; e-mail info@carnegieendowment.org; internet www.carnegieendowment.org; f. 1910; private, non-profit and non-partisan org. dedicated to advancing cooperation between nations and promoting active int. engagement by the USA; offices also in Moscow, Beijing, Beirut and Brussels; 130 mems; library of 8,000 vols; Pres. JESSICA T. MATHEWS; Chair. RICHARD GIORDANO; publs *Foreign Policy* (6 a year), *International Economic Bulletin* (52 a year), *Pro et Contra* (4 a year), *Sada* (online).

Century Foundation: 41 E 70th St, New York, NY 10021; tel. (212) 535-4441; e-mail info@tcf.org; internet www.tcf.org; f. 1919; non-partisan foundation for public policy research on major economic, political and soc. insts and issues; Chair. ALAN BRINKLEY; Pres. JANICE NITTOLI; Treas. LEWIS B. KADEN; Sec. ALICIA H. MUNNELL.

Council for European Studies at Colombia University: 420 W 118th St, MC 3307 Int. Affairs Bldg, Room 1209, New York, NY 10027; tel. (212) 854-4172; e-mail ces@columbia.edu; internet www.ces.columbia.edu; f. 1970; attached to Columbia Univ.; European studies programmes at over 80 univs in the USA, Canada and Europe; encourages greater scholarly interest in Europe; emphasizes commonality of problems that face nations of Europe and N America; sponsors research, information services, graduate student training; holds biennial conf. in Chicago; 800 mem. orgs; Chair. JOHN BOWEN; Dir SIOVAHN A. WALKER; publ. *Perspectives on Europe* (2 a year).

Council of State Governments: 2760 Research Park Dr., POB 11910, Lexington, KY 40578-1910; tel. (859) 244-8000; e-mail membership@csg.org; internet www.csg.org; f. 1933; offices in Washington, DC, New York, Atlanta, GA, Chicago, IL, and San Francisco, CA; a non-partisan org. est. by the USA for service to the USA; region-based forum that fosters exchange of insights and ideas to help state officials shape public policy; Chair. BOB GODFREY; Pres. BRIAN SCHWEITZER; Exec. Dir DAVID ADKINS; publs *Book of the States* (2 a year), *CSG State Directories* (1 a year), *Spectrum* (4 a year), *State Government News* (12 a year), *Suggested State Legislation* (12 a year).

Council on Foreign Relations, Inc.: The Harold Pratt House, 58 E 68th St, New York, NY 10065; tel. (212) 434-9400; e-mail communications@cfr.org; internet www.cfr.org; f. 1921; ind., non-partisan membership org.; promotes understanding of foreign policy and America's role in the world; 4,500 mems; library: Foreign Relations library of 18,000 vols, 300 periodicals, clippings files; Co-Chair. CARLA A. HILLS; Co-Chair. ROBERT E. RUBIN; Pres. RICHARD N. HAASS; publ. *Foreign Affairs* (6 a year).

Counterpart International: 2345 Crystal Dr., Suite 301, Arlington, VA 22202; tel. (703) 236-1200; e-mail communications@counterpart.org; internet www.counterpart.org; f. 1965 as Foundation for the South Pacific (FSP), present name 1992; empowers people and communities to implement innovative and enduring solutions to social, economic and environmental challenges; attached offices in New York and Los Angeles, CA; operates programmes in Armenia, Azerbaijan, Belarus, Bosnia and Herzegovina, Bulgaria, Fiji, Georgia, Guatemala, India, Iraq, Kazakhstan, Kiribati, Kyrgyzstan, Moldova, Papua New Guinea, Russia,

Samoa, Senegal, Solomon Islands, Tajikistan, Tonga, Turkmenistan, Tuvalu, Ukraine, Uzbekistan, Vanuatu and Viet Nam; Chair. JEFFREY T. LARICHE; Pres. and CEO JOAN C. PARKER.

Economic History Association: Dept of Economics, 500 El Camino Real, Santa Clara Univ., Santa Clara, CA 95053-0385; tel. (408) 554-4348; internet www.eh.net/eha; f. 1940; promotes teaching, research and publ. in all fields of economic history; 1,200 individual mems and 2,210 library mems; Pres. JEREMY ATACK; Exec. Dir ALEXANDER J. FIELD; publ. *Journal of Economic History* (4 a year).

Federal Bar Association: 1220 N Fillmore St, Suite 444, Arlington, VA 22201; tel. (571) 481-9100; e-mail fba@fedbar.org; internet www.fedbar.org; f. 1920; works to promote admin. of justice and independence of judiciary; provides scholarships and opportunities for judges and lawyers to professionally and socially interact; 15,000 mems, 99 Chapters, 20 sections in fields of federal law; Exec. Dir JACK D. LOCKRIDGE; Pres. FERN C. BOMCHILL; Treas. Hon. GUSTAVO GELPI; publ. *The Federal Lawyer* (10 a year).

Foreign Policy Association: 470 Park Ave S, New York, NY 10016; tel. (212) 481-8100; e-mail info@fpa.org; internet www.fpa.org; f. 1918; non-profit org.; promotes citizen education in world affairs; assists orgs, communities and educational instns; develops programmes for citizen understanding and constructive participation in world affairs; advances public understanding of foreign policy problems through nat. programmes and publs of a non-partisan character based upon the principles of freedom, justice and democracy; Chair. GONZALO DE LAS HERAS; Pres. and CEO NOEL V. LATEEF; publs *Great Decisions* (2 a year), *Headline Series* (4 a year).

History of Economics Society: c/o Tim Leonard, Dept of Economics, Princeton Univ., Fisher Hall, Princeton, NJ 08544; internet historyofeconomics.org; f. 1974; non-profit corpn; promotes interest and inquiry into the history of economics and related parts of intellectual history; 300 mems; Pres. PHILLIP MIROWSKI; Sec. THOMAS LEONARD; Treas. NEIL B. NIMAN; publs *ERN History of Economics Journal*, *Journal of the History of Economic Thought* (4 a year).

Institute for Mediterranean Affairs, Inc.: Nat. Press Bldg, Suite 984, 14th and F Sts, NW, Washington, DC 120045; tel. (202) 662-7655; e-mail medquarterly@aol.com; internet www.mediterraneanquarterly.com; est. under charter of the Univ. of the State of New York to evolve a better understanding of the historical background and contemporary political and socio-economic problems of the nations and regions that border on the Mediterranean Sea; to analyse the various tensions in the Eastern Mediterranean and to investigate the basic problems of the area; special attention is given to the Israeli–Arab conflict; 250 Academic Advisory mems; Man. Dir J. YAMPOLSKY; publ. *Mediterranean Quarterly: A Journal of Global Issues* (4 a year).

Institute for Operations Research and the Management Sciences: 5521 Research Park Dr., Catonsville, MD 21228; tel. (443) 757-3500; e-mail informs@informs.org; internet www.informs.org; f. 1995 by merger of Operations Research Soc. of America (f. 1952) and Institute for Management Sciences (f. 1953); serves scientific and professional needs of operations research educators, investigators, scientists, students, managers and consultants; nat. and int. confs for academics and professionals; 11,000 mems; Pres. Prof. STEPHEN ROBINSON; Sec. Prof.

BRIAN DENTON; Treas. Prof. NICHOLAS G. HALL; Exec. Dir MELISSA MOORE; publs *Decision Analysis* (4 a year), *Information Systems Research* (4 a year), *INFORMS Journal on Computing* (4 a year), *INFORMS Transactions on Education* (3 a year), *Interfaces* (6 a year), *Management Science* (12 a year), *Manufacturing & Service Operations Management* (4 a year), *Marketing Science* (6 a year), *Mathematics of Operations Research* (4 a year), *Operations Research* (6 a year), *Organization Science* (6 a year), *Transportation Science* (4 a year).

Society of Actuaries: 475 N Martingale Rd, Suite 600, Schaumburg, IL 60173-2226; tel. (847) 706-3500; e-mail feedback@soa.org; internet www.soa.org; f. 1949; educational, research and professional membership soc. for actuaries in life and health insurance and pension planning; spec. collns, reports and transactions from US, Canadian and int. actuarial orgs; 22,000 mems; library of 3,900 vols; Pres. TONYA MANNING; Exec. Dir GREG HEIDRICH; publs *The Actuary Magazine* (6 a year), *The North American Actuarial Journal* (4 a year).

World Peace Foundation: 169 Holland St, Somerville, MA 02144; tel. (617) 627-2255; e-mail worldpeace1910@gmail.com; internet www.worldpeacefoundation.org; f. 1910; an operating foundation that does not give outside grants; policy-orientated studies in world affairs; research concerning causes of state failure; Exec. Dir ALEX DE WAAL; Chair. PHILIP S. KHOURY; Pres. ROBERT I. ROTBERG; Treas. THOMAS M. O'REILLY; publ. sponsors *International Organization* (4 a year).

EDUCATION

Carnegie Corporation of New York: 437 Madison Ave, New York, NY 10022; tel. (212) 371-3200; internet www.carnegie.org; f. 1911 to promote advancement and diffusion of knowledge and understanding in the USA, and, with subsequent amendment of the charter, to some British overseas Commonwealth countries; makes grants to promote international peace and to advance education and knowledge; 17 mems; Pres. VARTAN GREGORIAN; Chair. JANET L. ROBINSON; publs *Carnegie Reporter* (2 a year), *Carnegie Results* (4 a year).

International Montessori Society: 9525 Georgia Ave, Suite 200, Silver Spring, MD 20910; tel. (301) 589-1127; internet www.imsmontessori.org; f. 1979; supports effective application of Montessori scientific educational principles; provides teacher education through correspondence; organizes workshops, mail-order book sales, audio CD and study guide; library; 400 mems; Dir LEE HAVIS.

Philosophy of Education Society: c/o Cris Mayo, PES Exec. Dir, Education Policy, Organization and Leadership, 1310 S Sixth St, Univ. of Illinois at Urbana Champaign, Champaign, IL 61820; tel. (217) 333-3673; internet philosophyofeducation.org; f. 1941; promotes fundamental philosophic treatment of problems of education; promotes clarification of agreements and differences among several philosophies of education through opportunities for discussion afforded by annual meetings; advances and improves teaching in philosophy of education both in schools for education of teachers and in other educational instns; cultivates fruitful relationships between workers in general philosophy of education and workers in philosophy of education and between scholars in philosophy of education and those in other areas of education; encourages promising students in the field of philosophy of education; 550 mems; Pres. GERT BIESTA; Exec. Dir CRIS

MAYO; publs *Contemporary Pragmatism*, *Education and Culture* (2 a year), *Educational Philosophy and Theory*, *Educational Theory* (4 a year), *Journal of Educational Controversy*, *Journal of Philosophy of Education*, *Studies in Philosophy and Education*, *Yearbook* (1 a year).

FINE AND PERFORMING ARTS

American Federation of Arts: 305 E 47th St, 10th Fl., New York, NY 10017; tel. (212) 988-7700; e-mail pubinfo@afaweb.org; internet www.afaweb.org; f. 1909; works to strengthen ability of museums to enrich public's experience and understanding of art; organizes nat. and int. travelling art exhibitions and develops educational programmes in cooperation with museum community; Chair. TOM L. FREUDENHEIM; Pres. JASON N. R. HERRICK; Sec. RICHARD S. LANE; Treas. SCOTT A. DAHNKE; Dir GEORGE G. KIN; publ. *Memo to Members* (4 a year).

American Musicological Society: 6010 College Station, Brunswick, ME 04011-8451; tel. (207) 798-4243; e-mail ams@ams-net.org; internet www.ams-net.org; f. 1934; research in the various fields of music as a br. of learning and scholarship; 3,300 individual mems, 1,200 institutional mems; Pres. CHRISTOPHER REYNOLDS; Sec. PAMELA F. STARR; Treas. JAMES LADEWIG; Exec. Dir ROBERT JUDD; publs *Abstracts of Papers read at the Annual Meeting* (1 a year), *Journal of the American Musicological Society* (3 a year).

Americans for the Arts: 1 E 53rd St, Second Fl., New York, NY 10022; tel. (212) 223-2787; internet www.artsusa.org; f. 1960; provides extensive arts-industry research and professional devt opportunities for community arts leaders via specialized programmes and services; 150,000 organizational and individual mems; library of 5,000 vols; Pres. and CEO ROBERT L. LYNCH; Chair. C. KENDRIC FERGESON; Sec. MICHAEL SPRING; Treas. JULIE MURACO.

American Society for Aesthetics: POB 915, Pooler, GA 31322-0915; tel. (912) 748-9524; e-mail secretary-treasurer@aesthetics-online.org; internet www.aesthetics-online.org; f. 1942; research and publ. in aesthetics, criticism and theory of the arts; sponsors confs; 1,000 mems; Pres. Prof. DOMINIC MCIVER LOPES; Sec. and Treas. Dr DABNEY TOWNSEND; publs *ASAGE* (ASA Graduate ejournal), *Journal of Aesthetics and Art Criticism* (4 a year).

American Society for Theatre Research: POB 1798, Boulder, CO 80306-1798; tel. (303) 530-1838; e-mail info@astr.org; internet www.astr.org; f. 1956; serves needs of theatre and performance studies historians and fosters knowledge of theatre in the USA and overseas; 706 mems; Pres. Prof. RHONDA BLAIR; Sec. Prof. MARLA CARLSON; Treas. TOBIN NELLHAUS; publ. *Theatre Survey* (2 a year).

American Society of Composers, Authors and Publishers (ASCAP): 1 Lincoln Plaza, New York, NY 10023; tel. (212) 621-6000; e-mail info@ascap.com; internet www.ascap.com; f. 1914; a non-profit asscn of composers, songwriters, lyricists, and music publishers of every kind of music; issues licences for public performance of mems' copyright works; 420,000 mems; Pres. PAUL WILLIAMS; Treas. JAMES M. KENDRICK; publs *ASCAP Biographical Dictionary*, *ASCAP Playback* (4 a year).

College Art Association: 50 Broadway, 21st Fl., New York, NY 10004; tel. (212) 691-1051; e-mail nyoffice@collegeart.org; internet www.collegeart.org; f. 1911; advances scholarship and excellence in the teaching and practice of art and art history; 12,000 individual mems, 2,000 institutional mems; Pres. BARBARA NESIN; Sec. DEWITT GODFREY; Treas. JOHN HYLAND, JR; Exec. Dir LINDA DOWNS; publs *Art Bulletin* (4 a year), *Art Journal* (4 a year), *caa.reviews.*

Printing Industries of America: 200 Deer Run Rd, Sewickley, PA 15143-2600; tel. (412) 741-6860; e-mail printing@printing.org; internet www.printing.org; f. 1887, merged with GATF 1999; non-profit scientific research and technical education org. serving int. graphic communications community; conducts technical workshops, in-plant assessments, seminars worldwide on various aspects of graphic communications; 14,000 mems in 60 countries; library: over 6,000 vols and periodicals; Chair. MICHAEL R. KEENE; Pres. and CEO MICHAEL MAKIN; Treas. HAL SLAGER; publs *Learning Modules, Second Sight* (technical reports), *The Magazine* (6 a year).

National Academy: Five E 89th St, New York, NY 10128; tel. (212) 996-1908; e-mail info@nationalacademy.org; internet www .nationalacademy.org; f. 1825; membership exclusively of artists; sections: painting, sculpture, watercolour, graphic arts, architecture; attached art museum, art library and art school; 450 mems; Chair. DAVID KAPP; Pres. BRUCE FOWLE; Sec. DAWN HAND-LER HARBART; Treas. STEPHEN VOGEL; Dir CARMINE BRANAGAN; publ. *Bulletin* (2 a year).

National Sculpture Society: 75 Varick St, 11th Fl., New York, NY 10013; tel. (212) 764-5645; e-mail news@nationalsculpture.org; internet www.nationalsculpture.org; f. 1893, inc. 1896; disseminates knowledge of American sculpture; promotes excellence in sculpture inspired by the natural world; 3,000 mems (incl. 300 elected mems); library of 400 vols; Pres. MICHEL LANGLAIS; Sec. GREG WYATT; Exec. Dir GWEN PIER; publ. *Sculpture Review* (4 a year).

Society for Ethnomusicology: Morrison Hall 005, 1165 E Third St, Bloomington, IN 47405-3700; tel. (812) 855-6672; e-mail sem@ indiana.edu; internet www.ethnomusicology .org; f. 1955; dedicated to the study of all forms of music; examines music as central to human experience throughout space and time; 1,800 mems; Exec. Dir STEVE STUEMP-FLE; Pres. BEVERLEY DIAMOND; Sec. ZOE SHERINIAN; Treas. GREGORY BARZ; publ. *Ethnomusicology* (3 a year).

HISTORY, GEOGRAPHY AND ARCHAEOLOGY

American Antiquarian Society: 185 Salisbury St, Worcester, MA 01609-1634; tel. (508) 755-5221; e-mail library@ americanantiquarian.org; internet www .americanantiquarian.org; f. 1812; focuses on American history before 1877; sponsors research, education, publs, lectures and concerts; library of 680,000 vols, 2m. MSS collns, 2m. newspaper issues, 200,300 items of graphic art; 950 mems; Chair. SIDNEY LAPI-DUS; Pres. ELLEN S. DUNLAP.

American Association for State and Local History: 1717 Church St, Nashville, TN 37203-2991; tel. (615) 320-3203; e-mail membership@aaslh.org; internet www.aaslh .org; f. 1904 as Conf. of State and Local Historical Socs, present name and status 1940; exchanges information on local and regional history and historical socs; dissemination of knowledge through scholarly and popular publs of professional material and interpretative articles; 5,900 mems; Chair. D. STEPHEN ELLIOTT; Pres. and CEO TERRY DAVIS; publs *History News* (4 a year, professional news), *History News Dispatch* (12 a year).

American Catholic Historical Association: Dealy Hall, Room 637, 441 E Fordham Rd, Bronx, NY 10458; tel. (718) 817-3830; e-mail acha@fordham.edu; internet www .achahistory.org; f. 1919; promotes interest in the history of the Catholic Church broadly considered; research work; 660 mems; Pres. Prof. MAGGIE MCGUINNESS; Exec. Sec. and Treas. Rev. Dr R. BENTLEY ANDERSON S.J.; publ. *The Catholic Historical Review* (4 a year).

American Historical Association: 400 A St, SE, Washington, DC 20003-3889; tel. (202) 544-2422; e-mail aha@historians.org; internet www.historians.org; f. 1884; promotes historical studies; collects and preserves historical documents and artefacts; disseminates historical research; 16,000 mems; Pres. Prof. JAN GOLDSTEIN; Exec. Dir JAMES R. GROSSMAN; Controller RANDY NOR-ELL; publs *American Historical Review* (5 a year), *Perspectives* (9 a year), *Program of the Annual Meeting* (1 a year).

American Irish Historical Society: 991 Fifth Ave, New York, NY 10028; tel. (212) 288-2263; e-mail aihs@aihs.org; internet aihs .org; f. 1897; offers use of library and archives to researchers, writers and scholars; research into the history of the Irish in America; 800 mems; library of 10,000 vols; Dir WILLIAM COBERT; Chair. DONALD R. KEOUGH; Librarian Rev. JOSEPH A. O'HARE; publ. *The Recorder* (2 a year).

American Jewish Historical Society: 15 W 16th St, New York, NY 10011; tel. (212) 294-6160; e-mail publicservices@cjh.org; internet www.ajhs.org; f. 1892; nat. ethnic historical org.; collects and publishes material bearing upon the history of Jews in America; promotes the study of American-Jewish history; contains many rare and valuable MSS from the 16th century; American-Jewish periodicals from the 18th century; 3,200 mems; library of 50,000 vols and 2m. MSS; Pres. PAUL B. WARHIT; Sec. JOSHUA H. LANDES; Treas. STEVEN D. OPPENHEIM; Exec. Dir JONATHAN KARP; publ. *American Jewish History* (4 a year).

American Numismatic Society: 75 Varick St, 11th Fl., New York, NY 10013; tel. (212) 571-4470; e-mail membership@numismatics .org; internet www.numismatics.org; f. 1858; non-profit org.; dedicated to the study of coins, currency, medals and tokens; 2,000 mems; library of 100,000 vols (incl. periodicals, MSS, photographs, pamphlets, auction catalogues and microforms); Chair. KENNETH L. EDLOW; Pres. ROGER S. SIBONI; Sec. and Exec. Dir UTE WARTENBERG KAGAN; publs *American Journal of Numismatics* (1 a year), *Ancient Coins in the North American Collections* (irregular), *ANS Magazine* (4 a year), *Numismatic Literature* (1 a year), *Numismatic Notes and Monographs* (irregular), *Numismatic Studies* (irregular), *Proceedings of the Coinage of the Americas Conference* (irregular), *Sylloge Nummorum Graecorum* (irregular), *The Collection of the American Numismatic Society* (irregular).

American Society for Eighteenth-Century Studies: POB 7867, Wake Forest Univ., Winston-Salem, NC 27109; tel. (336) 727-4694; e-mail asecs@wfu.edu; internet asecs.press.jhu.edu; f. 1969, inc. 1970; ind. soc.; works through publs and meetings to foster interest and encourage interdisciplinary investigation in achievements of the 18th century in America and Europe; 2,500 mems, 50 instns and 1,077 libraries; Pres. Prof. LAURA BROWN; Treas. WILLIAM EDMISTON; Exec. Dir BYRON R. WELLS; publs *Eighteenth-Century Studies* (4 a year), *Studies in Eighteenth-Century Culture* (1 a year).

American Society of Church History: POB 2793, Santa Rosa, CA 95405-2793; tel. (707) 538-6005; e-mail asch@churchhistory .org; internet www.churchhistory.org; f. 1888, reorganized 1906; scholarly study of history of Christianity and its relationship to surrounding cultures in all periods, locations and contexts; encourages study of Christian church and faith, its figures and movements, in institutional and non-institutional settings; 1,500 mems; Pres. Prof. THOMAS NOBLE; Exec. Sec. Dr KEITH FRANCIS; publ. *Church History: Studies in Christianity and Culture* (4 a year).

Archaeological Institute of America: Boston Univ., 656 Beacon St, Sixth Fl., Boston, MA 02215-2006; tel. (617) 353-9361; e-mail aia@aia.bu.edu; internet www .archaeological.org; f. 1879; non-profit org.; promotes vivid and informed public interest in cultures and civilizations of the past; supports archaeological research, fosters sound professional practice of archaeology; advocates preservation of world's archaeological heritage; represents the discipline in the wider world; 200,000 mems; CEO PETER HERDRICH; Exec. Dir BONNIE R. CLENDENNING; Pres. ELIZABETH BARTMAN; Treas. BRIAN J. HEIDTKE; publs *American Journal of Archaeology* (4 a year), *Archaeological Field Work Opportunities Bulletin, Archaeology* (6 a year, illustrated).

Arizona Archaeological and Historical Society: Arizona State Museum, POB 210026, Univ. of Arizona, Tucson, AZ 85721-0026; internet www.az-arch-and-hist .org; f. 1916; attached to Arizona State Museum; non-profit, educational org.; encourages scholarly pursuits in history and anthropology of the SW USA and N Mexico; encourages preservation of archaeological and historical sites; publishes results of archaeological, historical and ethnographic investigations; organizes lectures, field trips and other activities; 1,150 mems; Pres. SCOTT O'MACK; Sec. JUDITH BILLINGS; Treas. GEORGE HARDING; publ. *Kiva* (4 a year).

Association of American Geographers: 1710 16th St, NW, Washington, DC 20009-3198; tel. (202) 234-1450; e-mail gaia@aag .org; internet www.aag.org; f. 1904; non-profit scientific and educational soc.; conducts educational and research projects that advance geographic understanding, geographic literacy and geographic learning; 10,700 mems; Exec. Dir DOUGLAS RICHARD-SON; Pres. ERIC S. SHEPPARD; Sec. JENNY ZORN; Treas. AMY GLASMEIER; publs *Annals of the Association of American Geographers* (4 a year), *The Professional Geographer* (4 a year).

Brooklyn Historical Society: 128 Pierrepont St, Brooklyn, NY 11201; tel. (718) 222-4111; e-mail membership@brooklynhistory .org; internet www.brooklynhistory.org; f. 1863 as Long Island Historical Soc.; preserves and encourages study of Brooklyn's 400-year history; 1,250 mems; library of 155,000 bound vols, 100,000 graphic images, 600 m of MSS, 2,000 maps and atlases; Chair. JAMES ROSSMAN; Pres. DEBORAH SCHWARTZ.

California Historical Society: 678 Mission St, San Francisco, CA 94105; tel. (415) 357-1848; e-mail info@calhist.org; internet www.californiahistoricalsociety.org; f. 1871; holds primary and secondary materials on social, cultural, economic and political devt of California; 4,500 mems; library of 55,000 vols, rare MSS, pamphlets and maps, 500,000 historic photographs; Exec. Dir ANTHEA HARTIG; Pres. THOMAS R. OWENS;

Sec. LARRY GOTLIEB; Treas. JOHN BROWN; publ. *California History* (4 a year).

Dallas Historical Society: POB 150038, Dallas, TX 75315-0038; The Hall of State at Fair Park, 3939 Grand Ave., Dallas, TX 75210; tel. (214) 421-4500; internet www .dallashistory.org; f. 1922; encourages historical enquiry; collects, preserves and exhibits historical materials; custodian of the Hall of State (see under Museums and Galleries), which it operates as a museum and archive of Texas and Dallas history; 2,000 mems; library of 10,000 vols, 3m. archival items, 10,000 museum artefacts and 30,000 photographs; Exec. Dir JACK BUNNING; publ. *Legacies* (2 a year, published jtly with other orgs).

Historical Society of Pennsylvania: 1300 Locust St, Philadelphia, PA 19107; tel. (215) 732-6200; e-mail hsppr@hsp.org; internet www.hsp.org; f. 1824; historical and genealogical collns; 2,300 mems; library of 600,000 vols and pamphlets, 20m. MSS, 300,000 graphics; Pres. and CEO KIM SAJET; Chair. BRUCE K. FENTON; publs *Pennsylvania Legacies* (2 a year), *The Pennsylvania Magazine of History and Biography* (4 a year).

Kansas Historical Society: 6425 SW Sixth Ave, Topeka, KS 66615-1099; tel. (913) 272-8681; e-mail reference@kshs.org; internet www.kshs.org; f. 1875; preserves and shares Kansas history by collecting, preserving, and interpreting materials and information pertaining to state govt and history for enhancing govt accountability, providing economic devt assistance and educating people of Kansas; state archives, newspapers and census, archaeology; manuscript, photograph and maps dept, museum, folk arts dept, education dept; library of 440,459 vols, 11,128 cu ft MSS, 79,629 microfilm reels, 511,856 photographs and audiovisual items, 59,487 cu ft state records, 42,646 cu ft State Archives materials, 32,279 maps and architectural drawings; Exec. Dir JENNIE A. CHINN; Pres. PAUL M. BUCHANAN; Sec. DEBORAH BARKER; Treas. JAMES MAAG; publs *Kansas History: A Journal of the Central Plains* (4 a year), *Reflections*.

Maryland Historical Society: 201 W Monument St, Baltimore, MD 21201-4647; tel. (410) 685-3750; internet www.mdhs.org; f. 1844; preserves remnants of Maryland's past; museum, library, press, and educational programmes; see Museums and Art Galleries; 5,000 mems; library: 7m. vols, incl. documents on Maryland's history; Pres. BURT KUMMEROW; Dir ROBERT R. NEALL; Sec. JAMES W. CONSTABLE; Treas. CECIL E. FLAMER; publ. *Maryland Magazine of Genealogy* (2 a year).

Massachusetts Historical Society: 1154 Boylston St, Boston, MA 02215-3695; tel. (617) 536-1608; internet www.masshist.org; f. 1791; collects, preserves, makes accessible and communicates MSS that promote study of Massachusetts and the nation; ind. research library and MSS repository; holds documents and artefacts vital to study of American history; library: see under Libraries and Archives; Pres. DENNIS A. FIORI; Chair. CHARLES C. AMES; publ. *The Massachusetts Historical Review* (1 a year).

Medieval Academy of America: 104 Mount Auburn St, 5th Fl., Cambridge, MA 02138; tel. (617) 491-1622; e-mail info@ themedievalacademy.org; internet www .medievalacademy.org; f. 1925; promotes research, publ. and instruction in medieval archaeology, art, history, languages, literature, life, philosophy, records, science and all other aspects of medieval civilization; 4,100 mems; Pres. MARYANNE KOWALESKI; Treas. EUGENE W. LYMAN; Exec. Dir EILEEN GARDINER; Exec. Dir RONALD G. MUSTO; publ.

Speculum: A Journal of Medieval Studies (4 a year).

Minnesota Historical Society: 345 W Kellogg Blvd, St Paul, MN 55102-1906; tel. (651) 259-3000; e-mail reference@mnhs.org; internet www.mnhs.org; f. 1849; history museum; state historic preservation office; state archives; colln of artefacts; archaeology; newspaper and audiovisual library; 78,000 cu ft of MSS; 26 historic sites and museums; 8,000 mems; library of 500,000 vols; Pres. WILLIAM R. STOERI; Dir and Sec. D. STEPHEN ELLIOTT; Treas. MISSY STAPLES THOMPSON; publ. *Minnesota History* (4 a year).

National Geographic Society: 1145 17th St, NW, Washington, DC 20036-4688; tel. (202) 857-7000; e-mail askngs@ nationalgeographic.com; internet www .nationalgeographic.com; f. 1888; non-profit scientific and educational instn; promotes environmental and historical conservation; 4m. mems; library: see under Libraries and Archives; Pres. and CEO GARY KNELL; publs *National Geographic* (12 a year), *National Geographic Little Kids* (6 a year), *National Geographic Kids* (10 a year), *National Geographic Traveler* (8 a year).

New York Historical Society: 170 Central Park W, New York, NY 10024-5194; tel. (212) 873-3400; e-mail info@nyhistory.org; internet www.nyhistory.org; f. 1804; museum of 17th–19th-century American art, antiques and history, incl. portraits, landscapes and genre paintings; 3,300 mems; library of 350,000 vols, 10,000 newspaper titles, 10,000 published maps and atlases, 15,000 pieces of sheet music; Pres. and CEO Dr LOUISE MIRRER; Chair. ROGER HERTOG.

Omohundro Institute of Early American History and Culture: POB 8781, Williamsburg, VA 23187-8781; 400 Landrum Dr., Williamsburg, VA 23185; tel. (757) 221-1114; e-mail ieahc1@wm.edu; internet oieahc.wm.edu; f. 1943 as Institute of Early American History and Culture, current name adopted 1996; annually awards post-doctoral fellowships, sponsors confs and publishes books; sponsored jtly by the College of William and Mary and the Colonial Williamsburg Foundation; 800 assoc. mems; library of 7,000 vols, 880 periodicals, 2,000 microfilms; Dir Prof. RONALD HOFFMAN; Chair. ROBERT C. RITCHIE; publ. *William and Mary Quarterly* (4 a year).

Oregon Historical Society: 1200 SW Park Ave, Portland, OR 97205-2483; tel. (503) 222-1741; e-mail orhist@ohs.org; internet www .ohs.org; f. 1898; educates and informs through collecting, preserving and interpreting Oregon's past; 85,000 museum artefacts from Neolithic period to discovery, settlement of Oregon Country, Pacific NW; 6,500 mems; library of 30,000 vols, 25,000 maps, 8.5m. ft of film and video cassettes, 16,000 rolls of microfilm, and 12,000 linear ft of documents, 2.5m. photographic archives; Exec. Dir KERRY TYMCHUK; Pres. Dr JERRY HUDSON; Sec. Dr LESLEY HALLICK; Treas. PAT RITZ; publ. *Oregon Historical Quarterly* (4 a year).

Organization of American Historians: 112 N Bryan Ave, Bloomington, IN 47408-4141; tel. (812) 855-7311; e-mail help@oah .org; internet www.oah.org; f. 1907; promotes historical study of American history; 9,300 indiv. mems, 2,400 institutional mems; Pres. ALICE KESSLER-HARRIS; Exec. Dir KATHERINE M. FINLEY; publs *Journal of American History* (4 a year), *OAH Magazine of History*.

Pilgrim Society: 75 Court St, Plymouth, MA 02360; tel. (508) 746-1620; e-mail director@pilgrimhallmuseum.org; internet www.pilgrimhallmuseum.org; f. 1820; main-

tains pilgrim Hall Museum, the oldest public museum in N America; collns of pilgrim decorative arts, furnishings, prehistoric Native American collns; 600 mems; library of 12,000 vols and rare MSS collns dealing with the Plymouth Colony; Dir ANN BERRY.

Presbyterian Historical Society: 425 Lombard St, Philadelphia, PA 19147-1516; tel. (215) 627-1852; e-mail refdesk@history .pcusa.org; internet www.history.pcusa.org; f. 1852; nat. archives of the Presbyterian Church (USA); serves church's nat. agencies, mid-councils and local congregations as well as scholars and gen. public; 700 mems; library of 250,000 vols (incl. monographs, serials and rare books), 30,000 cu ft archive material; Exec. Dir FREDERICK J. HEUSER, JR; Chair. PAUL G. WATERMULDER; publ. *The Journal of Presbyterian History* (2 a year).

Renaissance Society of America: The Graduate School and Univ. Center, The City Univ. of New York, 365 Fifth Ave, Room 5400, New York, NY 10016; tel. (212) 817-2130; e-mail rsa@rsa.org; internet www .rsa.org; f. 1954; interdisciplinary study of the period 1300–1650 in USA; 2,400 individual mems, 1,100 library mems; Pres. ELIZABETH CROPPER; Exec. Dir ANN E. MOYER; publ. *Renaissance Quarterly* (4 a year).

Rhode Island Historical Society: 110 Benevolent St, Providence, RI 02906; tel. (401) 331-8575; e-mail execdirector@rihs.org; internet www.rihs.org; f. 1822; collects, preserves and shares Rhode Island's history; 1,700 mems; library of 100,000 vols, 400,000 photographs and maps, 5,000 MSS; Pres. BARRY G. HITTNER; Sec. LAURIE WHITE; Treas. JAMES P. LORING; Exec. Dir Dr C. MORGAN GREFE; publ. *Rhode Island History* (2 a year).

Society of American Historians: Columbia Univ., 603 Fayerweather, MC 2538, New York, NY 10027; tel. (212) 854-6495; e-mail amhistsociety@columbia.edu; internet www .sah.columbia.edu; f. 1939; promotes historical studies and interests; awards prizes; 250 authors, 14 publishers; Pres. PAULINE MAIER; Exec. Sec. ANDIE TUCHER.

Vermont Historical Society: 60 Washington St, Barre, VT 05641-4209; tel. (802) 479-8500; e-mail vhs-info@state.vt.us; internet www.vermonthistory.org; f. 1838; objects: educational work in Vermont and American history; colln of books, documents and MSS relating to Vermont; publ. of historical magazines and books; maintenance of Vermont History Museum in Montpelier and Vermont History Center in Barre; Leahy Library Genealogy Research Center; 2,800 mems; library of 40,000 vols, early Vermont imprints; Pres. LAURA WARREN; Exec. Dir MARK HUDSON; publs *History Connections* (4 a year), *Vermont History* (2 a year).

Western Reserve Historical Society: 10825 E Blvd, Cleveland, OH 44106; tel. (216) 721-5722; e-mail info@wrhs.org; internet www.wrhs.org; f. 1867; preserves and presents history of people of NE Ohio; maintains a historical museum, family and regional history library, auto-aviation museum, two historical sites; 6,400 mems; library of 235,000 vols, 25,000 vols of newspapers, 30,500 rolls of microfilm, 1m. prints and photos, 6m. MSS; Pres. and CEO GAINOR B. DAVIS; Chair. DONALD J. DAILEY; Sec. GREGORY M. JELINEK; Treas. MARK W. BICHÉ.

Wisconsin Historical Society: 816 State St, Madison, WI 53706-1417; tel. (608) 264-6400; internet www.wisconsinhistory.org; f. 1846; 7,200 mems; library of 1,085,000 vols (incl. pamphlets and govt documents), 1,888,000 microforms, 39,000 cu ft MSS, 49,000 cu ft public records, 25,000 maps and atlases, 1m. pictures and negatives, 14,000 cinema and television films from major Hollywood studios, 2m. motion picture and theatre promotional graphics; Dir GEORGE VOGT; Pres. ELLEN D. LANGILL; Sec. ELLSWORTH H. BROWN; Treas. SID BREMER; publs *Columns* (6 a year), *Wisconsin Magazine of History* (4 a year), *Wisconsin Public Documents* (6 a year).

LANGUAGE AND LITERATURE

Alliance Française: 618 SW 8th St, Miami, FL 33130; tel. (305) 859-8760; e-mail dgo@alliance-us.org; internet www.alliance-us.org; offers courses and examinations in French language and culture and promotes cultural exchange with France; attached teaching offices in Albuquerque (NM), Atlanta (GA), Austin (TX), Berkeley (CA), Beverly Hills (CA), Bloomfield Hills (MI), Bonita Springs (FL), Boston (MA), Buffalo (NY), Chicago (IL), Cincinnati (OH), Denver (CO), Doylestown (PA), Earlysville (VA), Evanston (IL), Fort Lauderdale (FL), Fresno, (CA), Greenwich (CT), Hartford (CT), Hawaii (HI), Houston (TX), Jackson (MS), Jacksonville (FL), Kansas City (MO), Louisville (KY), Lynchburg (VA), Madison (WI), Miami (FL), Milwaukee (WI), Minneapolis-St Paul (MI), Missoula (MT), Napa (CA), Naperville (TN), New Haven (CT), New Orleans (LA), New York (NY), Newport Beach (CA), Norfolk (VA), Orlando (FL), Pasadena (CA), Philadelphia (PA), Phoenix (AZ), Pittsburg (PA), Portland (OR), Providence (RI), Sacramento (CA), Saint-Louis (MO), Salt Lake City (UT), San Antonio (TX), San Diego (CA), San Francsico (CA), San Rafael (CA), Santa Clara Valley (CA), Santa Cruz County (CA), Sarasota (FL), Saratoga (CA), Seattle (WA), Toledo (OH), Tulsa (OK), Washington, DC, White Plains (NY), Wilmington (DE), Woodbury (CT); Dir of Operations, USA PIERRE HUDELOT; Chair. MARGARET GANONG.

American Center of PEN: 588 Broadway, Suite 303, New York, NY 10012; tel. (212) 334-1660; e-mail pen@pen.org; internet www.pen.org; f. 1922; promotes friendship and intellectual cooperation among writers, exchange of ideas and freedom of expression; confs, workshops, emergency fund for writers, translation prize; administers PEN/Nabokov Award and other literary awards; programme for inmate-writers in American prisons; 3,400 mems; library of 1,000 vols; Exec. Dir STEVEN L. ISENBERG; Pres. Prof. KWAME ANTHONY APPIAH; Sec. ROXANA ROBINSON; Treas. MARIA CAMPBELL; publs *Grants and Awards Available to American Writers* (every 2 years), *PEN America* (2 a year).

American Classical League: Miami Univ., 422 Wells Mill Dr., Oxford, OH 45056; tel. (513) 529-7741; e-mail info@aclclassics.org; internet www.aclclassics.org; f. 1919; promotes study of classical languages in the USA and Canada; 3,400 mems; Pres. PETER HOWARD; Sec. CATHERINE STURGILL; Treas. DEB HEATON; publ. *The Classical Outlook* (4 a year).

American Comparative Literature Association: Univ. of South Carolina, Dept of Languages, Literatures and Cultures, 1620 College St, Room 813A, Columbia, SC 29208; tel. (803) 777-3021; e-mail info@acla.org; internet www.acla.org; f. 1960; promotes study of intercultural relations that cross nat. boundaries, multi-cultural relations within a particular soc. and interactions between literature and other forms of human activity, incl. arts, sciences, philosophy and cultural artefacts of all kinds; 2,000 mems; Pres. LOIS PARKINSON ZAMORA; Sec. and Treas. ALEXANDER BEECROFT; publ. *Comparative Literature* (4 a year).

American Dialect Society: c/o Allan Metcalf, Dept of English, MacMurray College, Jacksonville, IL 62650; tel. (217) 479-7014; e-mail americandialect@mac.edu; internet www.americandialect.org; f. 1889; study of English language in N America, together with other languages or dialects of other languages influencing it or being influenced by it; sponsor of *Dictionary of American Regional English*; 350 mems; Pres. LUANNE VONNE SCHNEIDEMESSER; Exec. Sec. ALLAN METCALF; publ. *American Speech* (4 a year, with annual supplement).

American Philological Association: Univ. of Pennsylvania, 220S, 40th St, Suite 201E, Philadelphia, PA 19104-3512; tel. (215) 898-4975; e-mail apaclassics@sas.upenn.edu; internet www.apaclassics.org; f. 1869; study of classical languages, literatures and history; 3,200 mems; Pres. KATHRYN GUTZWILLER; Exec. Dir ADAM D. BLISTEIN; publs *Amphora* (1 a year), *Transactions of the American Philological Association (TAPA)* (2 a year).

British Council: c/o British Embassy, 3100 Massachusetts Ave, NW, Washington, DC 20008-3600; e-mail info-us@britishcouncil.org; internet www.britishcouncil.org/usa; offers courses and examinations in English language and British culture, and promotes cultural exchange with the UK; Dir SHARON MEMIS.

Goethe-Institut: 72 Spring St, 11th Fl., New York, NY 10012; tel. (212) 439-8700; e-mail info@newyork.goethe.org; internet www.goethe.de/newyork; offers courses and examinations in German language and culture, and promotes cultural exchange with Germany; attached centres in Boston (MA), Chicago (IL), Los Angeles (CA), San Francisco (CA) and Washington, DC; library of 12,000 vols; Exec. Dir Dr CHRISTOPH BARTMANN.

Instituto Cervantes: 211 E 49th St, New York, NY 10017; tel. (212) 308-7720; e-mail cenny@cervantes.es; internet nyork.cervantes.es; offers courses and examinations in Spanish language and culture, and promotes cultural exchange with Spain and Spanish-speaking Latin and Central America; attached centres in Albuquerque (NM) and Chicago (IL); library of 85,000 vols (incl. books, magazines, DVDs, CDs and electronic resources); Exec. Dir ANTONIO MUÑOZ MOLINA.

Linguistic Society of America: 1325 18th St, NW, Suite 211, Washington, DC 20036-6501; tel. (202) 835-1714; e-mail lsa@lsadc.org; internet www.lsadc.org; f. 1924; linguistic institute; annual meeting; web-based resources; cttees; fellowships; awards; 5,000 mems (incl individual and instns); Pres. KEREN RICE; Sec. and Treas. PAUL CHAPIN; Exec. Dir ALYSON W. REED; publs *eLanguage*, *Language* (4 a year).

Modern Language Association: 26 Broadway, Third Fl., New York, NY 10004-1789; tel. (646) 576-5000; e-mail info@mla.org; internet www.mla.org; f. 1883; provides opportunities for its mems to share their scholarly findings and teaching experiences with colleagues and to discuss trends in the acad.; 30,000 mems; Pres. RUSSELL BERMAN; Exec. Dir Prof. ROSEMARY G. FEAL; publs *ADE Bulletin* (online), *ADFL Bulletin* (3 a year), *MLA International Bibliography of Books and Articles on the Modern Languages and Literatures* (1 a year), *PMLA* (4 a year), *Profession* (1 a year).

National Communication Association: 1765 N St, NW, Washington, DC 20036; tel. (202) 464-4622; e-mail inbox@natcom.org; internet www.natcom.org; f. 1914; promotes widespread appreciation of the importance of communication in public and private life, application of competent communication to improve quality of human life and relationships and use of knowledge about communication to solve human problems; 7,500 mems; Pres. Dr LYNN H. TURNER; Exec. Dir Dr NANCY KIDD; publs *Communication and Critical/Cultural Studies* (4 a year), *Communication Education* (4 a year), *Communication Monographs* (4 a year), *Communication Teacher* (4 a year), *Critical Studies in Media Communication* (5 a year), *Journal of Applied Communication Research* (4 a year), *Journal of International and Intercultural Communication* (4 a year), *Quarterly Journal of Speech* (4 a year), *Review of Communication* (4 a year, online), *Text and Performance Quarterly* (4 a year).

Poetry Society of America: 15 Gramercy Park, New York, NY 10003; tel. (212) 254-9628; internet www.poetrysociety.org; f. 1910; service org. for poets and readers of poetry; sponsors readings, lectures, workshops and annual prize-giving; 2,000 mems; library of 8,000 vols of American poetry; Exec. Dir ALICE QUINN; Pres. RUTH KAPLAN; Sec. GEORGE MINKOFF; Treas. ELLEN RACHLIN; publ. *Journal* (2 a year).

Society of Biblical Literature: POB 133158, Atlanta, GA 30333; The Luce Center, 825 Houston Mill Rd, Atlanta, GA 30329; tel. (404) 727-3100; e-mail sblexec@sbl-site.org; internet www.sbl-site.org; f. 1880; study of biblical and related literature, language, history, religions; 8,500 mems; Chair. BRUCE C. BIRCH; Pres. CAROL NEWSOM; Sec. CHRISTINE M. THOMAS; Treas. and Exec. Dir JOHN F. KUTSKO; publs *International Voices in Biblical Studies*, *Journal of Biblical Literature* (4 a year), *TC: A Journal of Biblical Textual Criticism*.

MEDICINE

Aerospace Medical Association: 320 S Henry St, Alexandria, VA 22314-3579; tel. (703) 739-2240; e-mail inquiries@asma.org; internet www.asma.org; f. 1929; advancement of aerospace medicine, life sciences, bio-astronautics and environmental medicine; annual awards; 3,500 mems; Exec. Dir JEFFREY C. SVENTEK; Pres. Dr FANANCY L. ANZALONE; Sec. Dr ESTRELLA FORSTER; Treas. Dr HERNANDO ORTEGA; publ. *Aviation, Space and Environmental Medicine* (12 a year).

American Academy of Allergy, Asthma & Immunology: 555 E Wells St, Suite 1100, Milwaukee, WI 53202-3823; tel. (414) 272-6071; e-mail info@aaaai.org; internet www.aaaai.org; f. 1943 as American Acad. of Allergy, merger of Soc. for the Study of Asthma and Allied Conditions (on the East Coast) with American Asscn for the Study of Allergy (on the West Coast); for the advancement of the knowledge and practice of allergy, asthma and immunology for optimal patient care; 6,500 mems; Pres. Dr DENNIS K. LEDFORD; Sec. and Treas. Dr LINDA COX; publs *AAAAI Impact* (4 a year), *The Journal of Allergy and Clinical Immunology* (12 a year).

American Academy of Family Physicians: POB 11210, Shawnee Mission, KS 66207-1210; 11400 Tomahawk Creek Parkway, Leawood, KS 66211-2680; tel. (913) 906-6000; e-mail contactcenter@aafp.org; internet www.aafp.org; f. 1947 as American Acad. of General Practice, present name 1971; promotes and maintains high standards in the gen./family practice of medicine; 100,300 mems; Pres. Dr GLEN R. STREAM; Chair. ROLAND A. GOERTZ; publs *American Family Physician* (24 a year), *Annals of Family Medicine* (6 a year), *Family Practice Management* (10 a year).

American Academy of Ophthalmology: 655 Beach St, POB 7424, San Francisco, CA

94120-7424; 655 Beach St, San Franciso, CA 94109; tel. (415) 561-8500; e-mail aaoe@aao.org; internet www.aao.org; f. 1896, inc. 1979; advances lifelong learning and professional interests of ophthalmologists to ensure that public can obtain best possible eye care; 20,777 mems; Chair. ALBERT CASTILLO; Dir TIM D. COUCH; publs *EyeNet*, *Ophthalmology*.

American Academy of Otolaryngology—Head and Neck Surgery: 1650 Diagonal Rd, Alexandria, VA 22314-2857; tel. (703) 836-4444; e-mail info@entnet.org; internet www.entnet.org; f. 1896; representing specialists who treat ear, nose, throat and related structures of head and neck; offers more than 500 continuing medical educational courses at annual meetings and through correspondence courses throughout the USA and abroad; 12,000 US and non-US fellows, scientific and assoc. mems; Pres. Dr RODNEY P. LUSK; Sec. and Treas. Dr JOHN W. HOUSE; Exec. Vice-Pres. and CEO Dr DAVID R. NIELSEN; publs *The Bulletin* (12 a year), *Otolaryngology—Head and Neck Surgery* (12 a year, peer-reviewed scientific journal).

American Academy of Pediatrics: 141 NW Point Blvd, Elk Grove Village, IL 60007-1098; tel. (847) 434-4000; e-mail kidsdocs@aap.org; internet www.aap.org; f. 1930; works for physical, mental and social health, and well-being for all infants, children, adolescents and young adults; 60,000 mems; Pres. Dr ROBERT W. BLOCK; Exec. Dir Dr ERROL R. ALDEN; publs *AAP Grand Rounds* (12 a year, online), *Neoreviews* (12 a year, online), *Pediatrics* (12 a year, online), *Pediatrics in Review* (12 a year, online), *PREP Audio* (audio journal).

American Academy of Periodontology: 737 N Michigan Ave, Suite 800, Chicago, IL 60611-6660; tel. (312) 787-5518; internet www.perio.org; f. 1914 as American Acad. of Oral Prophylaxis and Periodontology, present name 1919; advances periodontal and gen. health of public and promotes excellence in the practice of periodontics; 8,000 mems; Pres. PAMELA K. MCCLAIN; Sec. and Treas. JOAN OTOMO-CORGE; Exec. Dir GERALD M. BOWERS; publs *Annals of Periodontology* (1 a year), *Clinical Advances in Periodontics* (4 a year, online), *Journal of Periodontology* (12 a year).

American Association of Anatomists: 9650 Rockville Pike, Bethesda, MA 20814-3998; tel. (301) 634-7910; e-mail exec@anatomy.org; internet www.anatomy.org; f. 1888; serves as professional home for an int. community of biomedical researchers and educators focusing on anatomical form and function; researches and conducts professional devt activities; 2,753 mems; Exec. Dir ANDREA PENDLETON; Pres. Dr JEFFREY LAITMAN; Sec. and Treas. Dr RICHARD L. DRAKE; publs *AAA Proceedings* (1 a year), *Anatomical Record* (12 a year), *Anatomical Sciences Education* (6 a year), *Developmental Dynamics* (12 a year).

American Association of Immunologists: 9650 Rockville Pike, Bethesda, MD 20814; tel. (301) 634-7178; e-mail infoaai@aai.org; internet www.aai.org; f. 1913; ind. body for exchange of information and advancement of knowledge in immunology and related fields; 7,400 mems; Chair. Dr BETTY DIAMOND; Exec. Dir Dr M. MICHELE HOGAN; Pres. Dr LESLIE J. BERG; Sec. and Treas. Dr MITCHELL KRONENBERG; publ. *Journal of Immunology* (24 a year).

American Cancer Society: 250 Williams St NW, Atlanta, GA 30303; tel. (866) 228-4327; internet www.cancer.org; f. 1913 as American Soc. for the Control of Cancer, present name 1945; voluntary health agency; strives to eliminate cancer as a major health problem by preventing cancer, saving lives and diminishing suffering from cancer, through research, education, advocacy and service; library of 16,000 vols; Chair. STEPHEN L. SWANSON; Pres. Dr EDWARD E. PARTRIDGE; Sec. LILA R. JOHNSON; Treas. DANIEL P. HEIST; publs *Ca-A* (6 a year, cancer journal for clinicians), *Cancer* (24 a year), *Cancer Cytopathology* (6 a year).

American College of Obstetricians and Gynecologists: POB 96920, Washington, DC 20090-6920; tel. (202) 638-5577; e-mail registrar@acog.org; internet www.acog.org; f. 1951; advocates for quality health care for women; maintains highest standards of clinical practice and continuing education for its mems; promotes patient education and stimulates patient understanding of and involvement in medical care; increases awareness among its mems and public of changing issues facing women's health care; 55,000 mems; Exec. Dir Dr RALPH HALE; publ. *Obstetrics and Gynecology* (12 a year).

American College of Physicians: 190 N Independence Mall W, Philadelphia, PA 19106-1572; tel. (215) 351-2400; internet www.acponline.org; f. 1915, merger with American Soc. of Internal Medicine (f. 1956) 1998; enhances quality and effectiveness of health care by fostering excellence and professionalism in practice of medicine; 132,000 mems; Pres. Dr VIRGINIA L. HOOD; Chair., Board of Regents Dr YUL D. EJNES; Treas. Dr DENNIS SCHABERG; publs *ACP Hospitalist* (52 a year), *Annals of Internal Medicine* (26 a year).

American College of Rheumatology: 2200 Lake Blvd NE, Atlanta, GA 30319; tel. (404) 633-3777; e-mail acr@rheumatology.org; internet www.rheumatology.org; education, research, advocacy and practice support; 4,000 mems; Pres. Dr DAVID BORENSTEIN; Sec. Dr JOSEPH FLOOD; Treas. Dr AUDREY UKNIS; publs *Arthritis & Rheumatism* (12 a year), *Arthritis Care & Research* (12 a year), *Hotline*.

American College of Surgeons: 633 N St Clair St, Chicago, IL 60611-3211; tel. (312) 202-5000; e-mail postmaster@facs.org; internet www.facs.org; f. 1913; monitors and analyses socioeconomic, legislative and regulatory issues affecting field of surgery; works to improve the care of injured and critically ill patients; provides gen. information to public about surgeons and surgical care; improves quality of care for surgical patient by setting high standards for surgical education and practice; 77,000 mems, incl. 4,000 fellows in other countries; Exec. Dir DAVID B. HOYT; Pres. PATRICIA J. NUMANN; Sec. COURTNEY M. TOWNSEND, JR; Treas. ANDREW L. WARSHAW; publ. *Journal of the American College of Surgeons* (12 a year).

American Dental Association: 211 E Chicago Ave, Chicago, IL 60611-2678; tel. (312) 440-2500; e-mail membership@ada.org; internet www.ada.org; f. 1859; nat. dental soc.; provides oral health-related information for dentists and their patients; 156,000 mems; library of 50,000 vols; Exec. Dir Dr JAMES BRAMSON; publs *American Dental Directory* (1 a year), *The Journal of the American Dental Association* (12 a year, online).

American Dietetic Association: 120 S Riverside Plaza, Chicago, IL 60606-6995; tel. (312) 899-0040; e-mail membrshp@eatright.org; internet www.eatright.org; f. 1917; advances science of dietetics; promotes education in these and allied fields; strives to improve nutrition of human beings; 70,000 mems; library of 1,000 vols; CEO PATRICIA M. BABJAK; Pres. SYLVIA A. ESCOTT-STUMP; Treas. MARY K. RUSSELL; publ. *Journal* (12 a year, online).

American Geriatrics Society: 40 Fulton St, 18th Fl., New York, NY 10038; tel. (212) 308-1414; e-mail info.amger@americangeriatrics.org; internet www.americangeriatrics.org; f. 1942; works towards the improvement of the health, independence and quality of life of all older people; provides leadership to health care professionals, policy makers and public by implementing and advocating for programmes in patient care, research, professional and public education and public policy; 6,000 mems; Chair. Dr JAMES T. PACALA; Pres. Dr CATHY ALESSI; Sec. Dr STEVEN COUNSELL; Treas. Dr ELLEN FLAHERTY; publs *Annals of Long-term Care* (12 a year), *Clinical Geriatrics* (12 a year), *Journal of the American Geriatrics Society* (12 a year), *The American Journal of Geriatric Pharmacotherapy*.

American Gynecological and Obstetrical Society: 230 W Monroe, Suite 710, Chicago, IL 60606; tel. (312) 676-3920; e-mail agos@agosonline.org; internet www.agosonline.org; f. 1982 by merger of American Gynecological Soc. with American Asscn of Obstetricians and Gynecologists; advances health of women by providing dedicated leadership and promoting excellence in research, education and medical practice; 200 fellows, 92 life fellows, 43 hon. fellows; Exec. Dir JENNA CUMMINS; Pres. Dr MARY E. D'ALTON; Sec. Dr LARRY J. COPELAND; Treas. DONALD R. COUSTAN.

American Heart Association: Nat. Center, 7272 Greenville Ave, Dallas, TX 75231; tel. (214) 570-5978; e-mail sessionsadmin@heart.org; internet www.americanheart.org; f. 1924; dedicated to the reduction of disability and death from cardiovascular diseases and stroke; supports cardiovascular research and brings its benefits to the public through professional education and community service programmes; coordinates efforts of all medical and lay groups in combating cardiovascular diseases; informs public of progress in cardiovascular field; 27,000 mems; CEO NANCY BROWN; Pres. GORDON F. TOMASELLI; Chair. BILL ROACH; publs *Arteriosclerosis, Thrombosis, and Vascular Biology* (12 a year), *Circulation* (52 a year), *Circulation: Arrhythmia and Electrophysiology* (6 a year), *Circulation: Cardiovascular Genetics* (6 a year), *Circulation: Cardiovascular Imaging* (6 a year), *Circulation: Cardiovascular Interventions* (6 a year), *Circulation: Cardiovascular Quality and Outcomes* (6 a year), *Circulation: Heart Failure* (6 a year), *Circulation Research* (24 a year), *Hypertension* (12 a year), *Stroke* (12 a year).

American Hospital Association: 155 N Wacker Dr., Chicago, IL 60606; tel. (312) 422-3000; internet www.aha.org; f. 1898; leads, represents and serves hospitals, health systems and other related orgs that are accountable to the community and committed to health improvement; advances health of individuals and communities; 40,000 individual mems, 5,000 institutional mems; library of 63,000 vols; Chair. JOHN W. BLUFORD, III; Pres. and CEO RICHARD UMBDENSTOCK; Senior Vice-Pres. LISA ALLEN; publs *H&HN Daily*, *Health Facilities Management*, *Hospitals & Health Networks* (12 a year), *Trustee* (12 a year).

American Institute of the History of Pharmacy: 777 Highland Ave, Madison, WI 53705-2222; tel. (608) 262-5378; e-mail aihp@aihp.org; internet www.pharmacy.wisc.edu/aihp; f. 1941; attached to School of Pharmacy, Univ. of Wisconsin-Madison; documents and preserves pharmaceutical heritage; 1,000 mems; Exec. Dir Dr GREGORY J. HIGBY; publ. *Pharmacy in History* (4 a year).

American Laryngological, Rhinological and Otological Society, Inc (Triological Society): 13930 Gold Circle, Suite 103, Omaha, NE 68144; tel. (402) 346-5500; e-mail info@triological.org; internet www.triological.org; f. 1895; disseminates scientific information by presenting latest basic science and clinical information at scientific meetings and through publs; promotes research into the causes of and treatments for otolaryngic diseases; 1,200 mems; Pres. Dr ROBERT H. OSSOFF; Exec. Sec. Dr PATRICK E. BROOKHOUSER; Treas. Dr MYLES L. PENSAK; publ. *The Laryngoscope* (12 a year).

American Lung Association (ALA): 1301 Pennsylvania Ave, NW, Suite 800, Washington, DC 20004; tel. (202) 785-3355; e-mail info@lung.org; internet www.lungusa.org; f. 1904; 115 affiliated asscns nationally; works to improve lung health and prevent lung disease; 11,000 mems; Chair. Dr ALBERT A. RIZZO; Pres. and CEO CHARLES DEAN. CONNOR; Sec. and Treas. CHRISTINE L. BRYANT.

American Medical Association: 515 N State St, Chicago, IL 60654; tel. (800) 621-8335; e-mail mediarelations@jama-archives.org; internet www.ama-assn.org; f. 1847; promotes art and science of medicine and betterment of public health; 296,000 mems; CEO and Exec. Vice-Pres. Dr JAMES L. MADARA; publs *American Medical News* (online, www.amednews.com), *Disaster Medicine and Public Health Preparedness* (4 a year), *JAMA* (48 a year), *JAMA Dermatology* (12 a year), *JAMA Facial Plastic Surgery* (6 a year), *JAMA Internal Medicine* (24 a year), *JAMA Neurology* (12 a year), *JAMA Ophthalmology* (12 a year), *JAMA Otolaryngology—Head & Neck Surgery* (12 a year), *JAMA Pediatrics* (12 a year), *JAMA Psychiatry* (12 a year), *JAMA Surgery* (12 a year).

American Medical Technologists: 10700 W Higgins Rd, Suite 150, Rosemont, IL 60018; tel. (847) 823-5169; e-mail mail@americanmedtech.org; internet www.americanmedtech.org/default.aspx; f. 1939; nationally and internationally recognized certification agency and membership soc. for allied health professionals; 29,000 mems; Exec. Dir CHRISTOPHER A. DAMON; Pres. ROXANN CLIFTON; Sec. SUSANNA HANCOCK; Treas. EVERETT BLOODWORTH; publs *AMT Events* (4 a year), *Journal of Continuing Education Topics & Issues* (3 a year).

American Neurological Association: 5841 Cedar Lake Rd, Suite 204, Minneapolis, MN 55416; tel. (952) 545-6284; e-mail ana@llmsi.com; internet www.aneuroa.org; f. 1875; trains and educates neurologists and other physicians in neurologic sciences; expands understanding of diseases of nervous system and ability to treat them; 1,000 mems; Exec. Dir LINDA SCHER; Pres. Dr EVA L. FELDMAN; Treas. STEVEN P. RINGEL; publ. *Annals of Neurology* (1 a year).

American Occupational Therapy Association, Inc: 4720 Montgomery Lane, POB 31220, Bethesda, MD 20824-1220; tel. (301) 652-2682; e-mail ajotsis@aota.org; internet www.aota.org; f. 1917; assures quality of occupational therapy services; improves consumer access to health care services; promotes professional devt of mems; 42,000 mems; library of 4,000 vols; Pres. Dr FLORENCE CLARK; Sec. PAUL A. FONTANA; publs *American Journal of Occupational Therapy* (7 a year, incl. 1 online supplement), *OT Practice* (22 a year).

American Optometric Association, Inc: 243 N Lindbergh Blvd, St Louis, MO 63141; tel. (314) 991-4100; internet www.aoa.org; f. 1898; promotes art and science of optometry; improves vision care and health of public;

sets professional standards, helping its mems conduct patient care efficiently and effectively; lobbies with govt and other orgs; provides research and education leadership; 36,000 mems; Pres. Dr DORI M. CARLSON; Sec. and Treas. Dr DAVID A. COCKRELL; publ. *Optometry* (12 a year).

American Pediatric Society/Society for Pediatric Research: 3400 Research Forest Dr., Suite B7, The Woodlands, TX 77381; tel. (281) 419-0052; e-mail info@aps-spr.org; internet www.aps-spr.org; f. 1888; 855 active mems; Exec. Dir DEBBIE ANAGNOSTELIS; Pres. Dr F. BRUDER. STAPLETON; Sec. and Treas. Dr JUDY L. ASCHNER; publ. *Pediatric Research* (12 a year).

American Physical Therapy Association: 1111 N Fairfax St, Alexandria, VA 22314-1488; tel. (703) 684-2782; e-mail memberservices@apta.org; internet www.apta.org; f. 1921 as American Women's Physical Therapeutic Asscn, inc. 1930; develops art and science of physical therapy; represents and promotes the profession; 77,000 mems; library of 3,000 colln focus: physical rehabilitation, available to researchers by appointment only; CEO JOHN D. BARNES; Pres. Dr R. SCOTT WARD; Sec. LAURITA M. HACK; Treas. ELMER PLATZ; publs *Perspective Magazine* (3 a year), *Physical Therapy* (12 a year), *PT in Motion Magazine* (11 a year).

American Physiological Society: 9650 Rockville Pike, Bethesda, MD 20814-3991; tel. (301) 634-7164; e-mail info@the-aps.org; internet www.the-aps.org; f. 1887; non-profit org.; fosters education, scientific research and dissemination of information in the physiological sciences; 10,500 mems; Pres. Dr JOE P. GRANGER; Exec. Dir Dr MARTIN FRANK; publs *Advances in Physiology Education* (4 a year, online), *American Journal of Physiology—Consolidated* (24 a year), *American Journal of Physiology—Cell Physiology* (12 a year, online), *American Journal of Physiology—Endocrinology and Metabolism* (12 a year, online), *American Journal of Physiology—Gastrointestinal and Liver Physiology* (12 a year, online), *American Journal of Physiology—Heart and Circulatory Physiology* (12 a year, online), *American Journal of Physiology—Lung Cellular and Molecular Physiology* (12 a year, online), *American Journal of Physiology—Regulatory, Integrative and Comparative Physiology* (12 a year, online), *American Journal of Physiology—Renal Physiology* (12 a year, online), *APS Journal Legacy Content* (online), *Comprehensive Physiology* (4 a year), *Journal of Applied Physiology* (12 a year, online), *Journal of Neurophysiology* (12 a year, online), *Physiological Genomics* (24 a year, online), *Physiological Reviews* (4 a year), *Physiology* (6 a year, online), *The Physiologist* (6 a year, online).

American Psychiatric Association: 1000 Wilson Blvd, Suite 1825, Arlington, VA 22209-3901; tel. (703) 907-7300; e-mail apa@psych.org; internet www.psych.org; f. 1844; ensures humane care and effective treatment for all persons with mental disorders, incl. intellectual developmental disorders and substance use disorders; 36,000 mems; library of 10,000 vols; Pres. JOHN OLDHAM; publs *Academic Psychiatry* (6 a year), *FOCUS: The Journal of Lifelong Learning in Psychiatry* (4 a year), *The American Journal of Psychiatry* (12 a year), *The Journal of Neuropsychiatry and Clinical Neurosciences* (4 a year), *Psychiatric Services* (12 a year).

American Public Health Association: 800 I St, NW, Washington, DC 20001-3710; tel. (202) 777-2742; e-mail comments@apha

.org; internet www.apha.org; f. 1872; interests incl. environment, personal health services, social factors, manpower and training in public health, global and int. health; 50,000 mems; Exec. Dir Dr J. ALAN BAKER; Pres. Dr MELVIN D. SHIPP; Treas. Dr RICHARD J. COHEN; publ. *American Journal of Public Health* (12 a year).

American Society for Clinical Laboratory Science: 2025 M St, NW, Suite 800, Washington, DC 20036; tel. (202) 367-1174; e-mail ascls@ascls.org; internet www.ascls.org; f. 1933 as American Soc. of Clinical Laboratory Technicians, inc. 1936, present name 1993; local, state and regional socs; activities incl. education, education and research funding, professional affairs and membership services; 13,000 mems; Pres. CATHY OTTO; Sec. and Treas. GILMA RONCANCIO-WEEMER; publ. *Clinical Laboratory Science* (4 a year).

American Society for Clinical Pathology: 33 W Monroe St, Suite 1600, Chicago, IL 60603; tel. (312) 541-4999; e-mail info@ascp.org; internet www.ascp.org; f. 1922; non-profit medical soc. for promotion of pathology and laboratory medicine; 100,000 mems; library of 25,500 vols; Pres. Dr C. BRUCE ALEXANDER; Sec. Dr WILLIAM G. FINN, JR; Treas. Dr KENNETH EMANCIPATOR; publs *American Journal of Clinical Pathology* (12 a year), *LABMEDICINE* (12 a year).

American Society for Investigative Pathology: 9650 Rockville Pike, Suite E133, Bethesda, MD 20814-3993; tel. (301) 634-7130; e-mail asip@asip.org; internet www.asip.org; f. 1976; investigates mechanisms of disease; advocates for practice of investigative pathology and fosters professional career devt and education of its mems; 2,500 mems; Pres. Dr MARTHA FURIE; Sec. and Treas. Dr WILLIAM B. COLEMAN; Exec. Officer Dr MARK E. SOBEL; publs *American Journal of Pathology* (12 a year), *The Journal of Molecular Diagnostics* (6 a year).

American Society for Microbiology: 1752 N St, NW, Washington, DC 20036-2904; tel. (202) 737-3600; e-mail service@asmusa.org; internet www.asm.org; f. 1899, present name 1961; supports programmes of education, training and public information; publishes journals and books; convenes meetings, workshops and colloquia; promotes contributions and promise of microbiological sciences; recognizes achievement and distinction among its practitioners; 39,000 mems; Exec. Dir MICHAEL I. GOLDBERG; Pres. DAVID C. HOOPER; Sec. JOSEPH M. CAMPOS; publs *Antimicrobial Agents and Chemotherapy* (12 a year), *Applied and Environmental Microbiology* (24 a year), *Clinical and Diagnostic Laboratory Immunology* (12 a year), *Clinical and Vaccine Immunology (CVI)* (12 a year), *Clinical Microbiology Reviews* (4 a year), *Eukaryotic Cell* (12 a year), *Infection and Immunity* (12 a year), *Journal of Bacteriology* (24 a year), *Journal of Clinical Microbiology* (12 a year), *Journal of Microbiology & Biology Education* (2 a year), *Journal of Virology* (24 a year), *Microbiology and Molecular Biology Reviews* (4 a year), *Molecular and Cellular Biology* (24 a year).

American Society for Nutritional Sciences: 9650 Rockville Pike, Bethesda, MD 20814; tel. (301) 634-7050; e-mail mem@nutrition.org; internet www.nutrition.org; f. 1928; develops and extends knowledge of nutrition and facilitates personal contact between investigators in nutrition and related fields of interest; 3,100 mems; Exec. Officer Dr JOHN E. COURTNEY; Pres. Dr SHARON DONOVAN; Sec. Dr MARIAN L. NEUHOUSER; Treas. Dr CHERYL ROCK; publs *Advances in Nutrition* (6 a year), *The Ameri-*

can Journal of Clinical Nutrition (12 a year), *The Journal of Nutrition* (12 a year).

American Society for Pharmacology and Experimental Therapeutics: 9650 Rockville Pike, Bethesda, MD 20814-3995; tel. (301) 634-7060; e-mail info@aspet.org; internet www.aspet.org; f. 1908; basic and clinical pharmacological research in academia, industry and govt; helps develop new medicines and therapeutic agents to fight existing and emerging diseases; 4,800 mems; Pres. Dr LYNN WECKER; Sec. and Treas. Dr MARY E. VORE; Exec. Officer Dr CHRISTINE K. CARRICO; publs *Drug Metabolism and Disposition* (12 a year), *Journal of Pharmacology and Experimental Therapeutics* (12 a year), *Molecular Pharmacology* (12 a year), *Pharmacological Reviews* (4 a year).

American Society of Clinical Hypnosis: 140 N Bloomingdale Rd, Bloomingdale, IL 60108-1017; tel. (630) 980-4740; e-mail info@asch.net; internet www.asch.net; f. 1957; ind. org. of professional people in medicine, dentistry, and psychology who share scientific and clinical interests in hypnosis; provides educational programmes to further understanding and acceptance of hypnosis as important tool of ethical clinical medicine and scientific research; 2,400 mems; Pres. Dr ELGAN L. BAKER; Exec. Dir for Governance and Policy MICHAEL WHITE; Sec. Dr ASSEN ALLADIN; publ. *The American Journal of Clinical Hypnosis* (4 a year).

American Society of Tropical Medicine and Hygiene: 111 Deer Lake Rd, Suite 100, Deerfield, IL 60015; tel. (847) 480-9592; e-mail info@astmh.org; internet www.astmh.org; f. 1951 by merger of American Soc. of Tropical Medicine (f. 1903) with Nat. Malaria Soc. (f. 1940); promotes global health through prevention and control of infectious and other diseases that disproportionately afflict global poor; 3,000 mems; Exec. Dir BRIAN MADDOX; Pres. Dr PETER J. HOTEZ; Sec. and Treas. Dr JOSH D. BERMAN; publ. *American Journal of Tropical Medicine and Hygiene* (12 a year).

American Speech-Language-Hearing Association: 2200 Research Blvd, Rockville, MD 20850-3289; tel. (301) 296-5700; e-mail actioncenter@asha.org; internet www.asha.org; f. 1925, fmrly American Acad. of Speech Correction, present name 1978; advocates on behalf of persons with communication and related disorders; advances communication science; promotes effective human communication; 145,000 mems; Pres. PAUL R. RAO; Exec. Dir ARLENE A. PIETRANTON; publs *American Journal of Audiology* (2 a year, online), *American Journal of Speech-Language Pathology* (4 a year, online), *Journal of Speech, Language, and Hearing Research* (4 a year, online), *Language Speech and Hearing Services in Schools* (4 a year, online).

American Surgical Association: 900 Cummings Center, Suite 221-U, Beverly, MA 01915; tel. (978) 927-8330; e-mail asa@prri.com; internet www.americansurgical.info; f. 1880; org. for surgical science and scholarship; provides a nat. forum for presenting developing state of gen. and subspeciality surgery; 1,000 mems; Pres. Dr TIMOTHY J EBERLEIN; Sec. Dr E. CHRISTOPHER ELLISON; Treas. Dr RUSSELL G. POSTIER; publ. *Annals of Surgery* (12 a year).

American Urological Association: 1000 Corporate Blvd, Linthicum, MD 21090; tel. (410) 689-3700; e-mail aua@auanet.org; internet www.auanet.org; f. 1902; helps in advancement of urologic patient care through education, research and in the formulation of health care policy; 17,000 mems; Pres. Dr SUSHIL S. LACY; Sec. Dr GOPAL H. BADLANI; Treas. RICHARD A. MEMO; publs

Health Policy Brief (12 a year), *The Journal of Urology* (12 a year).

ARRS: American Roentgen Ray Society: 44211 Slatestone Court, Leesburg, VA 20176-5109; tel. (703) 729-3353; e-mail info@arrs.org; internet www.arrs.org; f. 1900; int. org. of physicians and scientists working in radiology and related fields; 20,000 mems; Exec. Dir SUSAN BROWN CAPPITELLI; Pres. MELISSA ROSADO DE CHRISTENSON; Sec. and Treas. BERNARD KING; publs *AJR: American Journal of Roentgenology* (12 a year), *InPractice* (4 a year).

Association of American Medical Colleges: 2450 N St, NW, Washington, DC 20037-1126; tel. (202) 828-0400; e-mail amcas@aamc.org; internet www.aamc.org; f. 1876; works for betterment of medical care by supporting education, research and patient care activities; 136 US and 17 Canadian medical schools; more than 400 teaching hospitals and 93 academic and professional socs; 313,000 mems (incl. faculty mems, medical students and resident physicians); Pres. and CEO Dr DARRELL G. KIRCH; Chair. Dr MARK R. LARET; publs *AAMC Curriculum Directory* (1 a year), *AAMC Directory of Medical Education* (1 a year), *Academic Medicine* (12 a year), *Medical School Admission Requirements* (1 a year).

Association of American Physicians: 45685 Harmony Lane, Belleville, MI 48111; tel. (734) 699-1217; e-mail admin@aap-online.org; internet www.aap-online.org; f. 1885; pursues medical knowledge; makes advancement through experimentation and discovery of basic and clinical science and their application to clinical medicine; 1,750 mems; Exec. Dir LORI ENNIS; Pres. DAVID BRENNER; Sec. RICHARD LIFTON; Treas. TIMOTHY LEY.

Center for the Study of Aging and Human Development: POB 3003, Duke Univ. Medical Center, Room 3502 Busse Bldg, Blue Zone, Duke S, Durham, NC 27710; tel. (919) 660-7500; internet www.geri.duke.edu; f. 1955; attached to Duke Univ.; research incl. studies of age-related functional decline and dysmobility, genomic, proteonic and metabolomic biomarkers of ageing, exercise, osteoporosis, Alzheimer's disease, cancer and ageing, viral diseases of ageing, depression in later life, caregiver stress and religion/spirituality and health; Dir Dr HARVEY JAY COHEN.

College of Physicians of Philadelphia: 19 S 22nd St, Philadelphia, PA 19103-3097; tel. (215) 563-3737; e-mail info@collphyphil.org; internet www.collphyphil.org; f. 1787; increases understanding between health professions and gen. public; incl. Historical Medical Library, Mutter Museum (pathology and anatomy) and Francis C. Wood Institute for the History of Medicine; 1,500 fellows; library of 340,000 vols; CEO MARK HOCHBERG; Pres. Dr BENNETT LORBER; Sec. Dr ROGER J. PORTER; Treas. Dr MARJORIE A. BOWMAN; College Librarian ANNEMARIE BROGAN.

Commonwealth Fund: 1 E 75th St, New York, NY 10021; tel. (212) 606-3800; e-mail info@cmwf.org; internet www.commonwealthfund.org; f. 1918; helps Americans live healthy and productive lives; helps young people realize their potential through mentoring and educational enhancement programmes; improves health care services; promotes healthier life styles and betters health care of minorities; awards Harkness Fellowships to study social issues in the USA; Chair. of Board JAMES R. TALLON; Pres. Dr KAREN DAVIS.

Gerontological Society of America: 1220 L St, NW, Suite 901, Washington, DC 20005; tel. (202) 842-1275; e-mail geron@geron.org;

internet www.geron.org; f. 1945; multidisciplinary sciences org., incl. an educational unit, AGHE (Asscn for Gerontology in Higher Education) and a policy institute, NAAS (Nat. Acad. on an Aging Soc.); 5,400 mems; Exec. Dir JAMES APPLEBY; Pres. TERRY T. FULMER; publs *Gerontology & Geriatrics Education* (4 a year), *Journals of Gerontology* (Series A: Biological Sciences and Medical Sciences; Series B: Psychological Sciences and Social Sciences), *Public Policy and Aging Report* (4 a year), *The Gerontologist* (6 a year).

Industrial Health Foundation, Inc: 34 Penn Circle W, Pittsburgh, PA 15206-3612; tel. (412) 363-6600; f. 1935; a non-profit org. for advancement of healthy working conditions in industry; 120 mem cos and asscns; library of 2,000 vols; publs *Industrial Hygiene Digest* (12 a year), spec. technical bulletins.

John A. Hartford Foundation: 55 E 59th St, 16th Fl., New York, NY 10022-1713; tel. (212) 832-7788; e-mail mail@jhartfound.org; internet www.jhartfound.org; f. 1929; ageing and health programme; health care training, research and service innovations that ensures well-being and vitality of older adults; Chair. of the Board NORMAN H. VOLK; Pres. KATHRYN D. WRISTON; Sec. WILLIAM T. COMFORT; Exec. Dir and Treas. CORINNE H. RIEDER.

Medical Society of the State of New York: 865 Merrick Ave, Westbury, New York, NY 11590; tel. (516) 488-6100; e-mail mssny@mssny.org; internet www.mssny.org; f. 1807; non-profit org.; advocates health-related rights, responsibilities and issues; 30,000 mems; library of 45,000 vols; Pres. Dr PAUL A. HAMLIN; Sec. MALCOLM D. REID; Treas. ANDREW Y. KLEINMAN; Exec. Dir WILLIAM R. ABRAMS; publ. *Medical Directory of New York State* (every 2 years).

Mental Health America: 2000 N Beauregard St, 6th Fl., Alexandria, VA 22311; tel. (703) 684-7722; e-mail info@mentalhealthamerica.net; internet www.mentalhealthamerica.net; f. 1909 as Nat. Mental Health Asscn; 320 affiliates nationally; educates public about ways to preserve and strengthen its mental health; fights for access to effective care and an end to discrimination against people with mental and addictive disorders; fosters innovation in research, practice, services and policy; provides support to individuals and families living with mental health and substance use problems; Pres. and CEO DAVID L. SHERN; Chair. PENDER McELROY; Sec. and Treas. JEANNE ROHNER.

National Association for Biomedical Research: 818 Connecticut Ave, Suite 900, Washington, DC 20006; tel. (202) 857-0540; e-mail info@nabr.org; internet www.nabr.org; f. 1979; advocates sound public policy that recognizes vital role of humane animal use in biomedical research, higher education and product safety testing; stands for scientific community on legislative, regulatory and legal matters affecting laboratory animal research; 300 institutional mems; Pres. FRANKIE L. TRULL; publs *NABR Alert* (26 a year), *NABR Update* (26 a year), *State Laws*.

New York Academy of Medicine: 1216 Fifth Ave, 103rd St, New York, NY 10029; tel. (212) 822-7200; internet www.nyam.org; f. 1847; ind. org. that addresses health challenges facing world's urban population through interdisciplinary approaches to policy leadership, innovative research, evaluation, education and community engagement; 2,000 mems; library: see under Libraries and Archives; Pres. Dr JO IVEY BOUFFORD; Treas. THESEA HAVELL.

Radiological Society of North America: 820 Jorie Blvd, Oak Brook, IL 60523-2251; tel. (630) 571-2670; e-mail membership@rsna.org; internet www.rsna.org; f. 1915; continuing medical education in radiology; 48,000 mems; Chair. Dr SARAH S. DONALDSON; Pres. Dr BURTON P. DRAYER; Sec. and Treas. GEORGE S. BISSET, III; publs *Index to Imaging Literature* (online index of 38 journals), *RadioGraphics* (6 a year), *Radiology* (12 a year), *Radiology Legacy Collection*.

Society of Medical Jurisprudence: POB 20678, New York, NY 10021-0073; f. 1883; investigation, study and advancement of science of medical jurisprudence, and attainment of a higher standard of medical testimony; mems incl. physicians, lawyers, chemists, forensic odontologists, health professionals and teachers in approved law or medical schools; 250 mems; publ. *Proceedings* (9 a year).

NATURAL SCIENCES
General

Academy of Natural Sciences of Drexel University: 1900 Benjamin Franklin Parkway, Philadelphia, PA 19103-1195; tel. (215) 299-1000; e-mail presentsoffice@ansp.org; internet www.ansp.org; f. 1812 as Acad. of Natural Sciences of Philadelphia; natural history museum; research into systematics and evolutionary biology, ecology, limnology and geology, and environmental monitoring; 24m. specimen collns of plants, animals and fossils of worldwide scope; teaching at all levels; innovative exhibits, publs and educational programmes; 200,000 mems; library: see under Libraries and Archives; Pres. and CEO GEORGE W. GEPHART, JR (acting); Chair. CYNTHIA HECKSCHER; Sec. JUDITH E. SOLTZ; Treas. DAVID P. LAZAR, SR; publs *Notulae Naturae*, *Proceedings of the Academy of Natural Sciences*, *Special Publications*.

American Association for the Advancement of Science: 1200 New York Ave, NW, Washington, DC 20005; tel. (202) 326-6400; e-mail media@aaas.org; internet www.aaas.org; f. 1848; int. non-profit org.; aims to advance science and serve soc. through initiatives in science policy; int. programmes; science education; 128,000 mems, 262 affiliates; Chair. Dr ALICE S. HUANG; Pres. Dr NINA V. FEDOROFF; CEO Dr ALAN I. LESHNER; publs *Science* (52 a year), *Science Signaling* (52 a year), *Science Translational Medicine* (52 a year).

American Society of Limnology and Oceanography: 5400 Bosque Blvd, Suite 680, Waco, TX 76710-4446; tel. (979) 845-5706; e-mail secretary@aslo.org; internet aslo.org; f. 1936 as Limnological Soc. of America, present name 1948; creates, integrates and communicates knowledge across the full spectrum of aquatic sciences, advances public awareness and education about aquatic resources and research; promotes scientific stewardship of aquatic resources; 3,800 mems; Pres. DEBORAH BRONK; Sec. LISA CAMPBELL; Treas. PATRICIA MATRAI; publs *Limnology and Oceanography* (6 a year), *Limnology and Oceanography Bulletin* (4 a year), *Limnology and Oceanography: Fluids and Environments* (online), *Limnology and Oceanography: Methods* (1 a year).

Buffalo Society of Natural Sciences: c/o Buffalo Museum of Science, 1020 Humboldt Parkway, Buffalo, NY 14211; tel. (716) 896-5200; internet www.sciencebuff.org; f. 1861; administers the Buffalo Museum of Science

and Tifft Nature Preserve; samples of natural life in the USA; cultures from other eras to the present; Whem Ankh: The Cycle of Life in Ancient Egypt; Dinosaurs and Company; research into anthropology, botany, entomology, geology, mycology, ornithology, palaeontology, vertebrate zoology, with collns in these fields; 11,000 mems; library of 40,000 vols; Chair. RANDALL E. BURKARD; Sec. LAURIE DANN; publ. *Bulletin* (irregular).

California Academy of Sciences: 55 Music Concourse Dr., Golden Gate Park, San Francisco, CA 94118; tel. (415) 379-8000; internet www.calacademy.org; f. 1853; promotes advancement of natural sciences through public education and research; inc. under the laws of the State of California 1871; 20,000 mems, incl. 300 fellows; Pres. Dr JOHN HAFERNIK; Exec. Dir Dr GREGORY C. FARRINGTON; publs *California Wild*, *Memoirs*, *Occasional Papers*, *Pacific Discovery* (4 a year), *Proceedings of the California Academy of Sciences*.

Chicago Academy of Sciences: c/o Peggy Notebaert Nature Museum2430 N Cannon Dr., Chicago, IL 60614; tel. (773) 755-5100; e-mail membership@naturemuseum.org; internet www.chias.org; f. 1857; research colln of plants, animals, fossils and minerals; also maintains Peggy Notebaert Nature Museum, with interactive displays treating the relationship between people and nature; 2,200 mems; library of 3,000 vols, 2,000 periodicals; Chair. STEPHEN R. FERRARA; Sec. JIM MURRAY; publs *Bulletin*, *Natural History Miscellanea*.

Cranbrook Institute of Science: POB 801, 39221 N Woodward Ave, Bloomfield Hills, MI 48303-0801; tel. (248) 645-3200; internet science.cranbrook.edu; f. 1904; non-profit org. with exhibits and educational programmes in astronomy, mineralogy, geology, botany, zoology, ecology, anthropology, mathematics and physics; 4,000 mems; library of 18,000 vols; Dir Dr MICHAEL D. STAFFORD; Chair. LLOYD E. REUSS; Sec. CAROL A. WALTERS; Treas. FREDERICK M. ADAMS, JR; publ. *Homes for Wildlife*.

Franklin Institute: 222 N 20th St, Philadelphia, PA 19103; tel. (215) 448-1200; e-mail membership@fi.edu; internet www2.fi.edu; f. 1824 as The Franklin Institute of the State of Pennsylvania for the Promotion of the Mechanic Arts; non-profit science centre dedicated to public science education and to advancing knowledge in the physical sciences; its cttee on science and arts awards several medals, incl. Franklin Medal, for contributions to science and technology; also administers Bower Awards for science and business; incorporates Franklin Institute Science Museum (*q.v.*), Fels Planetarium, The Tuttleman Omniverse Theater and Musser Choices Forum, and houses Benjamin Franklin Nat. Memorial; observatory open to public; Pres. and CEO Dr DENNIS M. WINT; publ. *Journal*.

History of Science Society: 440 Geddes Hall, Univ. of Notre Dame, Notre Dame, IN 46556; tel. (574) 631-1194; e-mail info@hssonline.org; internet www.hssonline.org; f. 1924; understands science, technology, medicine and their interactions with soc. in historical context; 3,500 mems; Exec. Dir ROBERT JAY MALONE; Pres. Prof. LYNN K. NYHART; Sec. MARSHA RICHMOND; Treas. ADAM APT; publs *Isis* (4 a year), *Isis Current Bibliography* (1 a year), *Osiris* (1 a year).

Mellon Institute: see Carnegie Mellon University under Universities and Colleges—Pennsylvania.

National Science Teachers Association: 1840 Wilson Blvd, Arlington, VA 22201-3000; tel. (703) 243-7100; e-mail pubinfo@nsta.org; internet www.nsta.org; f. 1944; advances science teaching and science education at elementary, secondary and college levels; 60,000 mems; Pres. Dr PATRICIA SIMMONS; Exec. Dir and Sec. Dr FRANCIS Q. EBERLE; Treas. LEROY LEE; publs *Journal of College Science Teaching*, *Science & Children* (4 a year), *Science Scope* (4 a year), *The Science Teacher*.

Ohio Academy of Science: 1500 W Third Ave, Suite 223, Columbus, OH 43212-2817; tel. (614) 488-2228; e-mail oas@iwaynet.net; internet www.ohiosci.org; f. 1891; fosters curiosity, discovery, understanding, dissemination and practice of education, science, mathematics, engineering, technology or their applications; 2,000 mems; CEO LYNN E. ELFNER; Pres. and Chair. HORTON H. HOBBS, III; Sec. DON R. GRUBBS; Treas. MICHAEL S. HERSCHLER; publs *Legislative Bulletin*, *The Ohio Journal of Science* (4 a year).

Sigma Xi, the Scientific Research Society: POB 13975, 3106 E NC Highway 54, Research Triangle Park, NC 27709; tel. (919) 549-4691; e-mail memberinfo@sigmaxi.org; internet www.sigmaxi.org; f. 1886; encourages scientific research; publishes new scientific discoveries; 65,000 mems; Pres. MICHAEL CROSBY; Exec. Dir Dr JEROME F. BAKER; publ. *American Scientist* (6 a year).

Southern California Academy of Sciences: 900 Exposition Blvd, Los Angeles, CA 90007; tel. (909) 607-2836; internet scas.jsd.claremont.edu; f. 1891, inc. 1907; promotes fellowship among scientists and those interested in science; contributes to scientific literature through publ. of pertinent MSS; encourages and promotes scholarship among young scientists; provides information to mems, public and public agencies on such matters as may be of joint interest to the sciences and to soc.; 400 mems; Pres. JON ROBERTS; Sec. EDITH REED; Treas. Dr DANIEL GUTHRIE; publ. *Bulletin of the Southern California Academy of Science* (3 a year).

World Future Society: 7910 Woodmont Ave, Suite 450, Bethesda, MD 20814; tel. (301) 656-8274; e-mail info@wfs.org; internet www.wfs.org; f. 1966; private, non-profit org. promoting free discussion and study of alternative futures esp. on technological and social themes; 30,000 mems; Pres. TIMOTHY C. MACK; Sec. KENNETH W. HARRIS; Treas. KENNETH W. HUNTER; publs *Future Survey* (12 a year), *Outlook* (1 a year), *The Futurist* (10 a year), *World Future Review* (4 a year).

Biological Sciences

American Genetic Association: 2030 SE Marine Science Dr., Newport, OR 97365; tel. (541) 867-0334; e-mail agajoh@oregonstate.edu; internet www.theaga.org; f. 1903, fmrly American Breeders Asscn, current name adopted 1914; publishes journals of plant and animal genetics; organizes and supports annual symposium and workshops; 300 mems; Pres. Dr KATIE PEICHEL; Sec. Dr OLIVER RYDER; publ. *Journal of Heredity* (6 a year).

American Institute of Biological Sciences: 1900 Campus Commons Dr., Suite 200, Reston, VA 20191; tel. (703) 674-2500; e-mail admin@aibs.org; internet www.aibs.org; f. 1947; advances biological research and education; 250,000 mems; Pres. JAMES P.

COLLINS; Sec. JUDITH SKOG; Treas. LOUIS GROSS; Exec. Dir Dr RICHARD O'GRADY; publ. *BioScience* (11 a year).

American Malacological Society: Dept of Zoology, Univ. of Rhode Island, Kingston, RI 02881; internet www.malacological.org; f. 1931, fmrly American Malacological Union; study of phylum mollusca–systematics, ecology, functional morphology, evolution; medical, neotological and palaeontological aspects; 750 mems; Pres. GARY ROSENBERG; Sec. AMANDA LAWLESS; Treas. DAWN DITTMAN; publ. *American Malacological Bulletin* (2 a year).

American Ornithologists Union: 5400 Bosque Blvd, Suite 680, Waco, TX 76710; e-mail aou@aou.org; internet www.aou.org; f. 1883; scientific study of birds; 3,000 mems; Exec. Dir MELINDA PRUETT-JONES; Pres. SUSAN HAIG; Sec. SARA R. MORRIS; publs *AOU Check-List of North American Birds* (irregular), *Birds of North America*, *The Auk* (4 a year).

American Phytopathological Society: 3340 Pilot Knob Rd, St Paul, MN 55121; tel. (651) 454-7250; e-mail aps@scisoc.org; internet www.apsnet.org; f. 1908; provides credible and beneficial information related to plant health; advocates and participates in exchange of knowledge with public, policy makers and larger scientific community; promotes and provides opportunities for scientific communication, career preparation and professional devt for its mems; plant health management; plant management network; 5,000 mems; Pres. CAROL A. ISHIMARU; publs *Molecular Plant-Microbe Interactions* (12 a year), *Phytopathology* (12 a year), *Plant Disease* (12 a year), *Plant Health Progress*.

American Society for Photobiology: POB 1897, Lawrence, KS 66044; tel. (785) 843-1235; e-mail phot@allenpress.com; internet www.photobiology.org; f. 1972; promotes research into photobiology, integration of different photobiology disciplines, dissemination of photobiology knowledge; provides information on photobiological aspects of nat. and int. issues; 600 mems; Pres. ELIZABETH GAILLARD; Sec. DON FORBES; Treas. JOHN STREICHER; publ. *Photochemistry and Photobiology* (6 a year).

American Society of Human Genetics: 9650 Rockville Pike, Bethesda, MD 20814-3998; tel. (301) 634-7000; e-mail society@ashg.org; internet www.ashg.org; f. 1948; serves research scientists, health professionals and public by providing forums; 8,000 mems; Pres. MARY-CLAIRE KING; Sec. Dr BRENDAN LEE; Treas. DANIEL L. VAN DYKE; Exec. Dir ELAINE STRASS; publ. *American Journal of Human Genetics* (12 a year).

American Society of Ichthyologists and Herpetologists: c/o Maureen A. Donnelly, Florida Int. Univ., Dept of Biological Sciences, 11200 SW 8th St, Miami, FL 33199; tel. (305) 348-1235; e-mail asih@fiu.edu; internet www.asih.org; f. 1913; scientific study of fishes, amphibians and reptiles; publs, confs and symposia; 2,400 mems; Pres. MICHAEL E. DOUGLAS; Sec. MAUREEN A. DONNELLY; Treas. MARGARET A. NEIGHBORS; publ. *Copeia* (4 a year).

American Society of Mammalogists: 810 E 10th St, POB 1897, Lawrence, KS 66044-8897; tel. (785) 843-1235; e-mail asm@allenpress.com; internet www.mammalsociety.org; f. 1919, inc. 1920; promotes interest in mammalogy by holding meetings, issuing serial or other publs and aiding research; 4,500 mems; Pres. MICHAEL A. MARES; Sec. and Treas. RONALD A. VAN DEN BUSSCHE; publs *Journal of Mammalogy* (4 a year), *Mammalian Species* (irregular).

American Society of Naturalists: 4328 Storer Hall, Univ. of California, Davis, CA 95616-8755; tel. (530) 752-1114; internet www.asnamnat.org; f. 1883; study of ecology, evolution and behaviour; 1,835 mems; Pres. Dr ROBERT E. RICKLEFS; Sec. Dr DANIEL I. BOLNICK; Treas. KATHLEEN DONOHUE; publ. *The American Naturalist* (12 a year).

American Society of Parasitologists: c/o Dennis J. Minchella, Dept of Biological Sciences, Purdue Univ., West Lafayette, IN 47907-2054; tel. (765) 494-8188; internet amsocparasit.org; f. 1924; contributes to devt of parasitology as a discipline, and also to primary research in systematics, medicine, molecular biology, immunology, physiology, ecology, biochemistry and behaviour; 1,000 mems; Sec. and Treas. Dr DENNIS J. MINCHELLA; publ. *The Journal of Parasitology* (6 a year).

Biophysical Society: 11400 Rockville Pike, Suite 800, Rockville, MD 20852; tel. (240) 290-5600; e-mail society@biophysics.org; internet www.biophysics.org; f. 1957; dissemination of knowledge in biophysics through meetings, publs and cttee outreach activities; 9,000 mems; Pres. RICHARD ALDRICH; Sec. LUKAS TAMM; Treas. LINDA KENNEY; Exec. Dir ROSALBA KAMPMAN; publ. *Biophysical Journal* (24 a year).

Botanical Society of America: POB 299, St Louis, MO 63166-0299; tel. (314) 577-9566; e-mail bsa-manager@botany.org; internet www.botany.org; f. 1893, fmrly Botanical Club of the American Asscn; studies of plants and allied organisms, and functions as an umbrella org. covering all specialities; 3,000 mems; Pres. STEPHEN G. WELLER; Sec. PAMELA DIGGLE; Treas. AMY LITT; Exec. Dir BILL DAHL; publs *American Journal of Botany* (12 a year), *Botany for the Next Millennium*, *Plant Science Bulletin* (4 a year).

Ecological Society of America: 1900 M St, NW, Suite 700, Washington, DC 20036; tel. (202) 833-8773; e-mail esahq@esa.org; internet www.esa.org; f. 1915; promotes ecological science by improving communication among ecologists; raises public's level of awareness of importance of ecological science; increases resources available for conduct of ecological science; ensures appropriate use of ecological science in environmental decision making by enhancing communication between the ecological community and policy-makers; 10,000 mems; Exec. Dir KATHERINE S. McCARTER; Pres. STEWARD A. PICKETT; Sec. CHARLES D. CANHAM; publs *Bulletin* (4 a year), *Ecological Applications* (8 a year), *Ecological Monographs* (4 a year), *Ecology* (12 a year), *Ecosphere* (12 a year, online), *Frontiers in Ecology and the Environment* (10 a year).

Entomological Society of America: 10001 Derekwood Lane, Suite 100, Lanham, MD 20706-4876; tel. (301) 731-4535; e-mail esa@entsoc.org; internet www.entsoc.org; f. 1889; professional and scientific needs of entomologists and people in related disciplines; 6,000 mems; Pres. Dr ERNEST S. DELFOSSE; Exec. Dir DAVID GAMMEL; publs *American Entomologist* (4 a year), *Annals of the Entomological Society of America* (6 a year), *Anthropod Management Tests* (1 a year), *Environmental Entomology* (6 a year), *Journal of Economic Entomology* (6 a year), *Journal of Integrated Pest Management* (4 a year, online), *Journal of Medical Entomology* (6 a year).

Environmental Mutagen Society: 1821 Michael Faraday Dr., Suite 300, Reston, VA 20190; tel. (703) 438-8220; e-mail emshq@ems-us.org; internet www.ems-us.org; f. 1969; scientific research into causes and consequences of damage to genome and epigenome; promotes basic and applied studies of mutagenesis; informs and supports nat. and int. efforts to ensure a healthy, sustainable environment; 600 mems; Exec. Dir TONIA MASSON; Pres. CATHERINE B. KLEIN; Sec. SUZANNE M. MORRIS; Treas. BARBARA S. SHANE; publ. *Environmental and Molecular Mutagenesis* (8 a year).

Federation of American Societies for Experimental Biology: 9650 Rockville Pike, Bethesda, MD 20814; tel. (301) 634-7000; e-mail info@faseb.org; internet www.faseb.org; f. 1912; promotes progress and education in biological and biomedical sciences; policy devt related to biomedical science and engineering for legislators, fed. agencies and media; 100,000 mems and 24 scientific socs.; library of 2,500 vols; Pres. Dr JOSEPH C. LaMANNA; Sec. and Exec. Dir Dr GUY FOGLEMAN; Treas. Dr FRED D. FINKELMAN; publ. *The FASEB Journal* (12 a year).

Genetics Society of America: 9650 Rockville Pike, Bethesda, MD 20814-3998; tel. (301) 634-7300; e-mail society@genetics-gsa.org; internet www.genetics-gsa.org; f. 1931 by merger of Joint Genetics Sections of American Soc. of Zoologists and Botanical Soc. of America; works towards a unified science of genetics and to maximize its intellectual and practical impact; 5,000 mems; Exec. Dir Dr ADAM P. FAGEN; Pres. Dr VICKI CHANDLER; publs *GENETICS* (12 a year, online, www.genetics.org), *G3: Genes | Genomes | Genetics* (online, www.g3journal.org).

Mycological Society of America: c/o Dr Jessie A. Glaeser, USFS Northern Research Station, 1 Gifford Pinchot Dr., Madison, WI 53726; tel. (608) 231-9215; e-mail msasec1@yahoo.com; internet msafungi.org; f. 1937; study of fungi of all kinds incl. mushrooms, moulds, truffles, yeasts, lichens, plant pathogens and medically important fungi; 1,300 mems; Pres. Dr DAVID S. HIBBETT; Sec. Dr JESSIE A. GLAESER; Treas. Dr MARC CUBETA; publ. *Mycologia* (6 a year, online).

National Audubon Society: 225 Varick St, 7th Fl., New York, NY 10014; tel. (212) 979-3000; e-mail join@audubon.org; internet www.audubon.org; f. 1905; works to conserve and restore natural ecosystems; focuses on birds, other wildlife, and their habitats for the benefit of humanity and the earth's biodiversity; 518 local chapters; 550,000 mems; Pres. and CEO DAVID YARNOLD; publs *Audubon* (6 a year), *Audubon Field Notes* (4 a year).

National Wildlife Federation: 11100 Wildlife Center Dr., Reston, VA 20190-5362; tel. (703) 438-6000; internet www.nwf.org; f. 1936; conservation org.; protects and restores wildlife habitat, confronts global warming and connects with nature; 47 state affiliates; 4 m. mems; Pres. and CEO LARRY J. SCHWEIGER; Chair. STEPHEN K. ALLINGER; publs *Conservation Directory*, *International Wildlife Magazine*, *National Wildlife Magazine* (6 a year), *Ranger Rick* (10 a year), *Wild Animal Baby* (10 a year), *Your Big Backyard* (10 a year).

Nature Conservancy: Suite 100, 4245 N Fairfax Dr., Arlington, VA 22203-1606; tel. (703) 841-5300; e-mail member@tnc.org; internet nature.org; f. 1951; int. non-profit org. committed to preserving biological diversity by protecting lands and waters; 1m. mems; Pres. and CEO MARK R. TERCEK; Sec. FRANK E. LOY; Treas. MUNEER A. SATTER; publ. *Nature Conservancy* (6 a year).

Society for Developmental Biology: 9650 Rockville Pike, Bethesda, MD 20814-3998; tel. (301) 634-7815; e-mail sdb@sdbonline.org; internet www.sdbonline.org; f. 1939;

furthers study of devt in all organisms and at all levels; represents and promotes communication among students of devt; promotes field of developmental biology; 2,100 mems; Pres. MIKE LEVINE; Sec. MARY C. MULLINS; Treas. SALLY MOODY; publ. *Developmental Biology* (26 a year).

Society for Economic Botany: POB 299, St Louis, MO 63166-0299; tel. (314) 882-3038; e-mail seb@econbot.org; internet www .econbot.org; f. 1959; encourages scientific research, education and related activities on past, present and future uses of plants; relationship between plants and people, and to make results of such research available to scientific community; 1,000 mems; Pres. RAINER BUSSMANN; Sec. HEATHER MCMILLEN; Treas. SY SOHMER; publ. *Economic Botany* (4 a year).

Society for Experimental Biology and Medicine: 334 Maple Ave, W 134, Vienna, VA 22180-5612; tel. (201) 962-3519; e-mail ed@sebm.org; internet www.sebm.org; f. 1903; promotes investigation in biomedical sciences; 1,500 mems, 1,300 subscribers; Pres. Dr MICHAEL J. FRIEDLANDER; Exec. Dir FELICE O'GRADY; publ. *Experimental Biology and Medicine* (12 a year).

Society of Vertebrate Paleontology: 9650 Rockville Pike, Bethesda, MD 20814; tel. (301) 634-7814; e-mail svp@vertpaleo.org; internet www.vertpaleo.org; f. 1940; advances science of vertebrate paleontology; field occurrence, colln and study of fossil vertebrates; conservation and preservation of fossil sites; 2,300 mems; Exec. Dir JENNIFER HOLLAND; Pres. CATHERINE A FORSTER; Sec. GLENN STORRS; publs *Bibliography of Fossil Vertebrates* (online), *Journal of Vertebrate Paleontology* (6 a year), *SVP Memoir Series* (1 a year).

Wildlife Conservation Society: 2300 S Blvd, Bronx, NY 10460; tel. (718) 220-5100; e-mail membership@wcs.org; internet www .wcs.org; f. 1895; saves wildlife and wild places worldwide through science, global conservation, education and management of world's largest system of urban wildlife parks; operates the Bronx Zoo, New York Aquarium, Central Park Zoo, Queens Zoo, Prospect Park Zoo, and c. 500 conservation field projects in over 60 nations; education programmes developed at the Bronx Zoo are in 50 states and 16 countries from K-12 grade with professional devt components; 100,000 mems; library of 6,000 vols; Chair. WARD W. WOODS; Pres. and CEO Dr STEVEN E. SANDERSON; Sec. ANDREW H. TISCH; Treas. BRIAN J. HEIDTKE; publ. *Wildlife Conservation* (6 a year).

Wildlife Management Institute: 1440 Upper Bermudian Rd, Gardners, PA 17324; tel. (717) 677-4480; internet www .wildlifemanagementinstitute.org; f. 1911; scientific and educational org. dedicated to conservation, enhancement and professional management of N America's wildlife and other natural resources; Pres. STEVEN A. WILLIAMS; publs *North American Wildlife and Natural Resources Conference Transactions* (1 a year), *Outdoor News Bulletin* (12 a year).

Wildlife Society: 5410 Grosvenor Lane, Suite 200, Bethesda, MD 20814-2144; tel. (301) 897-9770; e-mail tws@wildlife.org; internet joomla.wildlife.org; f. 1937; develops and promotes sound stewardship of wildlife resources and of environments upon which wildlife and humans depend; undertakes active role in preventing human-induced environmental degradation; increases awareness and appreciation of wildlife values; seeks highest standards in all activities of wildlife profession; 9,100 mems; Exec. Dir

and CEO MICHAEL HUTCHINS; publs *Journal of Wildlife Management* (8 a year), *The Wildlife Professional*, *The Wildlifer*, *Wildlife Monographs* (irregular), *Wildlife Society Bulletin* (4 a year).

Mathematical Sciences

American Mathematical Society: 201 Charles St, Providence, RI 02904-2294; tel. (401) 455-4000; e-mail ams@ams.org; internet www.ams.org; f. 1888; sponsors meetings, symposia, seminars and institutes; provides employment services in the mathematical sciences; 30,000 mems; Exec. Dir Dr DONALD MCCLURE; Pres. Prof. DAVID VOGAN; Sec. Prof. CARLA SAVAGE; Treas. JANE M. HAWKINS; publs *Abstracts of Papers Presented to the American Mathematical Society* (4 a year), *Bulletin of the American Mathematical Society* (4 a year), *Conformal Geometry and Dynamics* (electronic only), *Current Mathematical Publications* (17–18 a year), *Employment Information in the Mathematical Sciences* (5 a year), *Journal of the American Mathematical Society* (4 a year), *Mathematical Reviews* (12 a year), *Mathematics of Computation* (4 a year), *Memoirs of the American Mathematical Society* (6 a year), *Notices of the American Mathematical Society* (11 a year), *Proceedings of the American Mathematical Society* (12 a year), *Representation Theory* (electronic only), *St Petersburg Mathematical Journal* (6 a year), *Sugaku Expositions* (2 a year), *Theory of Probability and Mathematical Statistics* (2 a year), *Transactions of the American Mathematical Society* (12 a year), *Transactions of the Moscow Mathematical Society* (1 a year).

Dozenal Society of America: 5106 Hampton Ave Suite 205, St Louis, MO 63109-3115; tel. (631) 351-7456; e-mail contact@dozenal .org; internet www.dozenal.org; f. 1944 as the Duodecimal Soc. of America; educational corpn organized to conduct research and educate public in the use of base 12 in calculations, mathematics, weights and measures, and other brs of pure and applied science; 144 mems; library of 120 vols; Chair. Prof. JAY SCHIFFMAN; Pres. MICHAEL DE VLIEGER; publ. *Duodecimal Bulletin* (2 a year).

Mathematical Association of America: 1529 18th St, NW, Washington, DC 20036-1358; tel. (202) 387-5200; e-mail maahq@maa .org; internet www.maa.org; f. 1915; non-profit, ind. org.; advances mathematical sciences, esp. at collegiate level; 21,000 mems; Exec. Dir MICHAEL PEARSON; Pres. ROBERT DEVANEY; Sec. BARBARA T. FAIRES; Treas. JIM DANIEL; publs *Mathematics Magazine* (5 a year), *Math Horizons* (4 a year), *The American Mathematical Monthly* (10 a year), *The College Mathematics Journal* (5 a year).

Society for Industrial and Applied Mathematics Society: 3600 Market St., 6th Fl., Philadelphia, PA 19104-2688; tel. (215) 382-9800; e-mail service@siam.org; internet www.siam.org; f. 1951; promotes a better understanding of how mathematics may be used in the solution of complex problems in industry; 13,000 individual mems, 500 institutional mems; Pres. LLOYD TREFETHEN; Sec. L. PAMELA COOK; Treas. SAMUEL GUBINS; publs *SIAM review* (4 a year), 12 specialist journals, mainly 4 a year.

Physical Sciences

Acoustical Society of America: 2 Huntington Quadrangle, Suite 1NO1, Melville, NY 11747-4502; tel. (516) 576-2360; e-mail asa@aip.org; internet asa.aip.org; f. 1929; dedicated to increasing and diffusing knowledge of acoustics and its practical applications; 7,500 mems; Pres. MARDI C. HASTINGS; Exec. Dir CHARLES E. SCHMID; publs *Acous-

tics Today*, *Journal of the Acoustical Society of America* (12 a year), *Proceedings of Meetings on Acoustics* (online).

American Association of Petroleum Geologists: POB 979, Tulsa, OK 74101-0979; 1444 S Boulder, Tulsa, OK 74119; tel. (918) 584-2555; e-mail bulletin@aapg.org; internet www.aapg.org; f. 1917; int. geological, professional geoscience org.; 31,995 mems; Exec. Dir DAVID CURTISS; Pres. LEE KRYSTINIK; Sec. RICHARD BALL; publs *AAPG Explorer* (12 a year), *Environmental Geosciences* (4 a year).

American Astronomical Society: 2000 Florida Ave, NW, Suite 400, Washington, DC 20009-1231; tel. (202) 328-2010; e-mail aas@aas.org; internet www.aas.org; f. 1899, inc. 1928; promotes interest in astronomy; disseminates and archives results of astronomical research; facilitates and strengthens interactions among mems through professional meetings; supports mem. divs representing specialized research and astronomical interests; represents goals of mems to the nation and the world; trains, mentors and supports next generation of astronomers; promotes increased participation of historically under-represented groups in astronomy; assists mems to develop skills in fields of education and public outreach; 7,000 mems; Exec. Officer Dr KEVIN MARVEL; Pres. DEBRA M. ELMEGREEN; publs *Astronomy Education Review* (online), *Bulletin of the American Astronomical Society*, *The Astronomical Journal* (12 a year), *The Astrophysical Journal* (36 a year).

American Chemical Society: 1155 16th St, NW, Washington, DC 20036; tel. (202) 872-4600; e-mail help@acs.org; internet www .chemistry.org; f. 1876; publishes numerous scientific journals and databases, convenes major research confs and provides educational, science policy and career programmes in chemistry; 163,000 mems; Pres. NANCY B. JACKSON; Exec. Dir and CEO Dr MADELEINE JACOBS; publs *Accounts of Chemical Research*, *Advances in Chemistry*, *Analytical Chemistry*, *Biochemistry*, *Bioconjugate Chemistry*, *Biomacromolecules*, *Biotechnology Progress*, *Chemical Research in Toxicology*, *Chemical Reviews*, *Chemistry of Materials*, *Crystal Growth & Design*, *Energy & Fuels*, *Environmental Science & Technology*, *Industrial & Engineering Chemistry Research*, *Inorganic Chemistry*, *Journal of the American Chemical Society* (52 a year), *Journal of Agricultural and Food Chemistry*, *Journal of Chemical & Engineering Data*, *Journal of Chemical Education*, *Journal of Chemical Information and Modeling* (12 a year), *Journal of Chemical Theory and Computation*, *Journal of Medicinal Chemistry*, *Journal of Natural Products*, *Journal of Proteome Research*, *Langmuir*, *Macromolecules*, *Molecular Pharmaceutics*, *Nano Letters*, *Organic Letters*, *Organic Process Research & Development*, *Organometallics*, *The Journal of Organic Chemistry*, *The Journal of Physical Chemistry A*, *The Journal of Physical Chemistry B*, *The Journal of Physical Chemistry Letters*.

American Crystallographic Association, Inc.: POB 96, Ellicott Station, Buffalo, NY 14205-0096; tel. (716) 898-8690; e-mail aca@ hwi.buffalo.edu; internet www .amercrystalassn.org; f. 1949 by merger of American Soc. for X-Ray and Electron Diffraction with Crystallographic Soc. of America; promotes interactions among scientists who study structure of matter at atomic (or near atomic) resolution; 2,200 mems; Pres. THOMAS KOETZLE; Sec. CARRIE WILMOT; CEO WILLIAM L. DUAX; publs *Program and Abstracts* (1 a year), *Transactions* (1 a year).

American Geophysical Union: 2000 Florida Ave, NW, Washington, DC 20009-1277; tel. (202) 462-6900; e-mail service@agu.org; internet www.agu.org; f. 1919; publishes journals and books; sponsors scientific meetings and a variety of other educational and scientific activities; 60,000 mems; Pres. MIKE MCPHADEN; Exec. Dir and CEO CHRISTINE W. MCENTEE, JR; publs *Earth Interactions* (electronic journal), *Geochemistry, Geophysics, Geosystems* (online), *Geophysical Research Letters* (26 a year), *Global Biogeochemical Cycles* (4 a year), *Journal of Advances in Modeling Earth Systems* (irregular), *Journal of Geophysical Research* (7 sections, 12 a year), *Nonlinear Processes in Geophysics* (4 a year), *Paleoceanography* (6 a year), *Radio Science* (6 a year), *Reviews of Geophysics* (4 a year), *Space Weather* (4 a year), *Tectonics* (6 a year), *Water Resources Research* (12 a year).

American Geosciences Institute: 4220 King St, Alexandria, VA 22302-1502; tel. (703) 379-2480; e-mail agi@agiweb.org; internet www.agiweb.org; f. 1948; provides information services; promotes geoscience education; strives to increase public understanding of the vital role the geosciences play in society's use of resources, resilience to natural hazards and interaction with environment; 49 mem. socs; Exec. Dir P. PATRICK LEAHY; Pres. Dr WAYNE D. PENNINGTON; Sec. Dr BERRY H. TEW, JR; Treas. MICHAEL D. LAWLESS; publ. *EARTH* (12 a year).

American Institute of Chemists: 315 Chestnut St, Philadelphia, PA 19106-2702; tel. (215) 873-8224; e-mail info@theaic.org; internet www.theaic.org; f. 1923; professional aspects of chemical practice, incl. nat. certification programme, involvement in governmental activities, awards, and sponsorship, through the AIC Foundation; honours top college chemistry seniors; 6,000 mems; Exec. Dir SHARON DOBSON; Pres. Dr DAVID M. MANUTA; Sec. Dr E. GERRY MEYER; Treas. Dr J. STEPHEN DUERR; publ. *The Chemist* (online).

American Institute of Physics: One Physics Ellipse, College Park, MD 20740-3843; tel. (301) 209-3100; e-mail aipinfo@aip.org; internet www.aip.org; f. 1931; advances science of physics; tracks employment and education trends; Fosters connections between science and industry; promotes science in public realm; 550 student chapters; Niels Bohr Library; 95,000 mems, 18 affiliated socs, 94 corporate assocs; Chair. LOUIS J. LANZEROTTI; Exec. Dir and CEO H. FREDERICK DYLLA; publ. 46 publs, incl. *Physics Today*, journals, bulletins, translated Russian and Chinese journals, and secondary information services.

American Meteorological Society: 45 Beacon St, Boston, MA 02108-3693; tel. (617) 227-2425; e-mail amsinfo@ametsoc .org; internet www.ametsoc.org; f. 1919, inc. 1920; promotes devt and dissemination of information and education on atmospheric and related oceanic and hydrologic sciences; 14,000 mems; Exec. Dir KEITH L. SEITTER; Pres. JON MALAY; Sec. and Treas. RICHARD D. ROSEN; publs *Bulletin of the American Meteorological Society* (12 a year), *Earth Interactions*, *Journal of Applied Meteorology and Climatology* (12 a year), *Journal of Atmospheric and Oceanic Technology* (12 a year), *Journal of Climate* (24 a year), *Journal of Hydrometeorology* (12 a year), *Journal of Physical Oceanography* (12 a year), *Journal of the Atmospheric Sciences* (12 a year), *Monthly Weather Review* (12 a year), *Weather and Forecasting* (6 a year), *Weather, Climate, and Society* (4 a year).

American Microscopical Society: c/o Dr John Zardus, The Citadel, 171 Moultrie St, Dept of Biology, Washington College, Chestertown, Charleston, SC 29407; tel. (843) 953-7511; internet www.amicros.org; f. 1878; publishes reports of research into invertebrate biology; conducts annual meetings on research using microscopy; organizes workshops on techniques of microscopy and biology of organisms studied by microscopy; 695 mems; Pres. Dr KATHRYN A. COATES; Sec. Dr JOHN ZARDUS; Treas. Dr DAVID BRUCE CONN; publ. *Invertebrate Biology* (4 a year).

American Nuclear Society: 555 N Kensington Ave, La Grange Park, IL 60526; tel. (708) 352-6611; e-mail nucleus@ans.org; internet www.ans.org; f. 1954; 17 professional divs: fusion energy, education and training, environmental sciences, isotopes and radiation, materials science and technology, mathematics and computation, nuclear criticality safety, fuel cycle and waste management, human factors, nuclear reactor safety, radiation protection and shielding, power and operations, reactor physics, robotics and remote systems technology, thermal hydraulics, biology and medicine, decommissioning, decontamination and reutilization, accelerator applications; 52 local sections, 8 overseas local sections (Japan, S Korea, Latin America, Austria, Switzerland, Italy, France, Taiwan); 51 student brs; 11,000 mems; Pres. ERIC P. LOEWEN; Exec. Dir ROGER W. TILBROOK; publs *Fusion Science and Technology* (8 a year), *Nuclear Science and Engineering* (9 a year), *Nuclear Technology* (12 a year), nuclear standards.

American Pharmacists Association: 2215 Constitution Ave,NW, Washington, DC 20037; tel. (202) 628-4410; e-mail infocenter@aphanet.org; internet www .pharmacist.com; f. 1852 as American Pharmaceutical Asscn; provides a forum for discussion, consensus building and policy setting for the profession of pharmacy; 60,000 mems; library of 6,000 vols; Exec. Vice-Pres. and CEO THOMAS E. MENIGHAN; Pres. MARIALICE S. BENNETT; publs *APhA Drug Infoline* (12 a year), *Journal of Pharmaceutical Sciences* (12 a year), *Journal of the American Pharmacists Association* (6 a year), *Student Pharmacist* (6 a year), *Pharmacy Today* (12 a year).

American Physical Society: 1 Physics Ellipse, College Park, MD 20740-3844; tel. (301) 209-3243; e-mail exoffice@aps.org; internet www.aps.org; f. 1899; advances and diffuses knowledge of physics through research journals, scientific meetings, and education, outreach, advocacy and int. activities; 50,000 mems; Pres. MICHAEL S. TURNER; Exec. Officer Dr KATE P. KIRBY; publs *Physical Review A-E*, *Physical Review* (in 6 series), *Physical Review Letters* (52 a year), *Physical Review Special Topics–Accelerators and Beams* (12 a year), *Physical Review Special Topics–Physics Education Research*, *Physics* (online), *Reviews of Modern Physics* (4 a year).

American Society for Biochemistry and Molecular Biology: 11200 Rockville Pike, Suite 302, Rockville, MD 20852-3110; tel. (240) 283-6600; e-mail asbmb@asbmb.org; internet www.asbmb.org; f. 1906 as American Soc. of Biological Chemists; advances science of biochemistry and molecular biology through publ. of scientific and educational journals; 12,000 mems; Exec. Dir BARBARA A. GORDON; Pres. SUZANNE R. PFEFFER; Sec. MARK A. LEMMON; Treas. MERLE S. OLSON; publs *Journal of Biological Chemistry* (52 a year), *Journal of Lipid Research* (12 a year), *Molecular and Cellular Proteomics* (12 a year).

Electrochemical Society: 65 S Main St, Bldg D, Pennington, NJ 08534-2839; tel. (609) 737-1902; e-mail ecs@electrochem.org; internet www.electrochem.org; f. 1902; advances theory and practice of electrochemistry, solid-state science, and allied subjects; encourages research and dissemination of knowledge in these fields; assures availability of adequate training and education of fundamental and applied scientists and engineers in these fields; 8,000 individual mems, 100 corporate mems; Exec. Dir ROQUE J. CALVO; Pres. ESTHER TAKEUCHI; Sec. JOHNA LEDDY; Treas. CHRISTINA BOCK; publs *ECS Transactions* (online), *Electrochemical and Solid-State Letters* (12 a year, print and online), *Interface* (4 a year, print and online), *Journal of the Electrochemical Society* (12 a year, print and online).

Geochemical Society: Dept of Earth and Planetary Sciences, Washington Univ., 1 Brookings Dr., CB 1169, St Louis, MO 63130-4899; tel. (314) 935-4131; e-mail gsoffice@geochemsoc.org; internet www .geochemsoc.org; f. 1955; encourages application of chemistry to solve geological and cosmological problems; 1,800 mems; Pres. SAMUEL MUKASA; Sec. EDWIN SCHAUBLE; Treas. SAM SAVIN; publs *Elements* (6 a year), *Geochemistry, Geophysics, Geosystems* (online), *Geochimica et Cosmochimica Acta* (24 a year).

Geological Society of America: POB 9140, Boulder, CO 80301-9140; 3300 Penrose Place, Boulder, CO 80301-1806; tel. (303) 357-1000; e-mail gsaservice@geosociety.org; internet www.geosociety.org; f. 1888; provides access to elements that are essential to the growth of earth scientists at all levels of expertise and from all sectors: academic, govt, business and industry; 24,000 mems; Pres. JOHN W. GEISSMAN; Exec. Dir and Sec. JOHN W. HESS; Treas. JONATHAN G. PRICE; publs *Environmental & Engineering Geoscience* (4 a year, online), *Geology* (12 a year), *Geosphere* (6 a year, online), *GSA Bulletin* (6 a year), *Lithosphere* (6 a year), *Memoirs* (1–2 a year).

Microscopy Society of America: 12100 Sunset Hills Rd, Suite 130, Reston, VA 20190; tel. (703) 234-4115; e-mail associationmanagement@microscopy.org; internet www.microscopy.org; f. 1942; annual meeting, presenting technical papers and exhibits; increases and diffuses knowledge of microscopy and related instruments and results obtained through their use; 2,300 mems; Pres. JANET WOODWARD; Sec. IAN ANDERSON; Treas. JOAN HUDSON; Man. Dir PETER DOHERTY; publs *Microscopy & Microanalysis* (6 a year), *Microscopy Today* (6 a year).

Mineralogical Society of America: 3635 Concorde Pkwy Suite 500, Chantilly, 20151-1110; tel. (703) 652-9950; e-mail business@ minsocam.org; internet www.minsocam.org; f. 1919; encourages fundamental research about natural materials; supports teaching of mineralogical concepts and procedures; encourages preservation of mineral collns, displays, mineral localities, type minerals and scientific data; 2,700 mems; Exec. Dir Dr J. ALEX SPEER; Pres. Dr MICHAEL F. HOCHELLA, JR; Sec. ANDREA M. KOZIOL; Treas. DARRELL J. HENRY; publs *Elements* (6 a year), *Reviews in Mineralogy and Geochemistry* (3–6 a year), *The American Mineralogist* (8 a year).

Oak Ridge Associated Universities: POB 117, MC100-44, Oak Ridge, TN 37831-0117; tel. (865) 576-3146; e-mail communications@ orau.org; internet www.orau.org; f. 1946; promotes collaborative partnerships with univs, fed. laboratories and industry; manages the Oak Ridge Institute for Science and Education for the US Dept of Energy (DOE); carries out research and devt, training and education, technical assistance activities for DOE and other fed. and private orgs; concentrates on the following major areas: science/engineering education, worldwide emergency response and training, workforce health and safety research and training, technical training systems and environmental monitoring; manages educational programmes for undergraduate, graduate and postdoctoral students and academic staff; develops training processes that encompass design, delivery and evaluation of training networks; performs radiological site investigations and verification surveys; manages Univ. Radioactive Ion Beam (UNIRIB) user facility; maintains medical, training and energy/environment library; 101 mem univs; Pres. and CEO ANDY PAGE.

OSA—The Optical Society: 2010 Massachusetts Ave, NW, Washington, DC 20036; tel. (202) 223-8130; e-mail info@osa.org; internet www.osa.org; f. 1916, present name 2008; devoted to the advancement of optics and the service of all who are interested in any aspect of that science; 16,000 mems; Pres. Prof. CHRISTOPHER DAINTY; CEO ELIZABETH ROGAN; publs *Advances in Optics & Photonics* (4 a year), *Applied Optics* (36 a year), *Biomedical Optics Express* (12 a year), *Journal of the Optical Society of America A* (12 a year), *Journal of the Optical Society of America B* (12 a year), *Optics Express* (26 a year), *Optics Letters* (24 a year), *Optical Materials Express* (12 a year).

Palaeontological Society: POB 9044, Boulder, CO 80301; tel. (855) 357-1032; e-mail paleosoc@geosociety.org; internet www.paleosoc.org; f. 1908; publishes and disseminates palaeontological research; 550 institutional subscribers; 1,500 mems; Pres. SANDRA CARLSON; Sec. MARK A. WILSON; Treas. PETER HARRIES; publs *Journal of Paleontology* (6 a year), *Memoirs of the Paleontological Society* (irregular), *Paleobiology* (4 a year), *Palaeontologica Electronica*, *Paleontological Society Papers* (irregular), *Short Course Notes* (1 a year).

Seismological Society of America: 201 El Cerrito Plaza Professional Bldg, El Cerrito, CA 94530-4003; tel. (510) 525-5474; e-mail info@seismosoc.org; internet www.seismosoc.org; f. 1906; seismology, earthquake engineering, earthquake geology; 1,900 mems; Exec. Dir SUSAN B. NEWMAN; Pres. CHRISTA VON HILLEBRANDT-ANDRADE; Sec. KEITH KNUDSEN; Treas. MITCH WITHERS; publs *Bulletin of the Seismological Society of America* (6 a year), *Seismological Research Letters* (6 a year).

SEPM Society for Sedimentary Geology: 4111 S Darlington, Suite 100, Tulsa, OK 74135-6373; tel. (918) 610-3361; internet www.sepm.org; f. 1926; disseminates scientific information on sedimentology, stratigraphy, paleontology, environmental sciences, marine geology, hydrogeology and many additional related specialities; 5,000 mems; Pres. CHRIS R. FIELDING; Sec. and Treas. DIANE KAMOLA; Exec. Dir Dr HOWARD HARPER; publs *Journal of Sedimentary Research* (6 a year), *PALAIOS* (6 a year), *The Sedimentary Record* (4 a year).

Society of Economic Geologists: 7811 Shaffer Parkway, Littleton, CO 80127-3732; tel. (720) 981-7882; e-mail seg@segweb.org; internet www.segweb.org; f. 1919; advances science of geology through scientific investigation of mineral deposits and mineral resources; 5,000 mems; Pres. M. STEPHENS ENDERS; Exec. Dir BRIAN G. HOAL; publ. *Economic Geology* (8 a year).

PHILOSOPHY AND PSYCHOLOGY

American Philosophical Association: Univ. of Delaware, 31 Amstel Ave, Newark, DE 19716-4797; tel. (302) 831-1112; e-mail apaonline@udel.edu; internet www.apaonline.org; f. 1900; promotes exchange of ideas among philosophers; encourages creative and scholarly activity in philosophy and facilitates professional work of teachers of philosophy; 10,000 mems; Chair. MICHAEL BRATMAN; Exec. Dir AMY FERRER; publ. *Proceedings and Addresses* (5 a year).

American Psychological Association: 750 First St, NE, Washington, DC 20002-4242; tel. (202) 336-5500; e-mail public.affairs@apa.org; internet www.apa.org; f. 1892; advances psychology as a science, a profession, and as a means of promoting health, education and human welfare; 154,000 mems; library of 2,500 vols; Pres. Dr DONALD BERSOFF; Exec. Vice-Pres. and CEO Dr NORMAN B. ANDERSON; publs *American Psychologist, Journal of Experimental Psychology: General* (4 a year), *Neuropsychology* (24 a year), and 65 others.

Metaphysical Society of America: c/o Brian Martine, Dept of Philosophy, Univ. of Alabama, Huntsville, AL 35899; tel. (205) 895-6555; internet web02.gonzaga.edu/faculty/henning/metaphysical_society/index.htm; f. 1950; studies of metaphysical problems without regard to sectarian divisions; 700 mems; Pres. EDWARD HALPER; Sec. and Treas. BRIAN MARTINE.

Philosophy of Science Association: Dept of Philosophy, Bloomsburg Univ., Bloomsburg, PA 17815; tel. (570) 389-4174; internet www.philsci.org; f. 1934; promotes research, teaching and free discussion of issues in philosophy of science from diverse standpoints; 1,000 mems; Pres. JAMES WOODWARD; Exec. Sec. and Treas. GARY HARDCASTLE; publ. *Philosophy of Science* (4 a year).

Psychometric Society: c/o Terry Ackerman, 320 SOEB, 1300 Spring Garden St, Univ. of North Carolina at Greensboro, Greensboro, NC 27402; tel. (336) 334-3439; e-mail taackerm@uncg.edu; internet www.psychometricsociety.org; f. 1935; advancement of quantitative measurement practices in psychology, education and social sciences; 800 mems; Pres. MARK WILSON; Sec. TERRY ACKERMAN; Treas. LUZ BAY; publ. *Psychometrika* (4 a year).

RELIGION, SOCIOLOGY AND ANTHROPOLOGY

African Studies Association: Rutgers Univ., Livingston Campus, 54 Joyce Kilmer Ave, Piscataway, NJ 08854-8045; tel. (848) 445-8173; e-mail asapub@rci.rutgers.edu; internet www.africanstudies.org; f. 1957; encourages research and collects and disseminates information on Africa; 1,700 mems; Pres. AILI TRIPP; Exec. Dir KAREN JENKINS; publs *African Studies Review* (3 a year), *History in Africa: A Journal of Method* (1 a year).

American Academy of Religion: 825 Houston Mill Rd, NE, Suite 300, Atlanta, GA 30329-4205; tel. (404) 727-3049; e-mail adminasst@aarweb.org; internet www.aarweb.org; f. 1909; professional asscn of teachers and research scholars in the field of religion and religious studies; 10,000 mems; Exec. Dir JOHN R. FITZMIER; Pres. KWOK PUI LAN; Sec. MICHEL DESJARDINS; Treas. DONNA BOWMAN; publ. *Journal of the American Academy of Religion (JAAR)* (4 a year).

American Anthropological Association: 2200 Wilson Blvd, Suite 600, Arlington, VA 22201-3357; tel. (703) 528-1902; e-mail members@aaanet.org; internet www.aaanet.org; f. 1902; fosters and supports devt of spec. anthropological socs organized on regional or functional basis; publishes and promotes publ. of anthropological monographs and journals; encourages anthropological research; maintains effective liaison with related sciences and their orgs; 11,000 mems; Pres. VIRGINIA R. DOMINGUEZ; Sec. DEB MARTIN; Exec. Dir BILL DAVIS; publs *American Anthropologist* (4 a year), *American Ethnologist* (4 a year), *Annals of Anthropological Practice* (2 a year), *Anthropology and Education Quarterly* (4 a year), *Anthropology and Humanism* (2 a year), *Anthropology of Consciousness* (2 a year), *Anthropology of Work Review* (2 a year), *Archeological Papers of the AAA* (1 a year), *City and Society* (3 a year), *Cultural Anthropology* (4 a year), *Culture, Agriculture, Food and Environment* (2 a year), *Ethos* (4 a year), *General Anthropology* (2 a year), *Journal of Latin American and Caribbean Anthropology* (2 a year), *Journal of Linguistic Anthropology* (2 a year), *Medical Anthropology Quarterly* (4 a year), *Museum Anthropology* (2 a year), *North American Dialogue* (2 a year), *PoLAR: Political and Legal Anthropology Review* (2 a year), *Transforming Anthropology* (2 a year), *Visual Anthropology Review* (2 a year).

American Counseling Association: 5999 Stevenson Ave, Alexandria, VA 22304; tel. (703) 823-9800; e-mail membership@counseling.org; internet www.counseling.org; f. 1952; counselling, guidance and student personnel services; divs: American College Counseling Asscn, Asscn for Counselor Education and Supervision, Nat. Career Devt Asscn, Counseling Asscn for Humanistic Education and Devet, American School Counselor Asscn, American Rehabilitation Counseling Asscn, Asscn for Assessment in Counseling, Nati. Employment Counseling Asscn, Asscn for Multicultural Counseling and Devt, Asscn for Spiritual, Ethical and Religious Values in Counseling, Int. Asscn of Addictions and Offender Counselors, American Mental Health Counselors Asscn, Asscn for Counselors and Educators in Govt, Asscn for Adult Devt and Aging, Asscn for Gay, Lesbian and Bisexual Issues in Counseling, Int. Asscn of Marriage and Family Counselors; Asscn for Creativity in Counseling; Asscn for Specialists in Group Work; Counselors for Social Justice; 50,427 mems; Pres. Dr DON W. LOCKE; Exec. Dir RICHARD YEP; publs *Counseling Outcome Research and Evaluation, Journal for Social Action in Counseling and Psychology, Journal for Specialists in Group Work, Journal of Creativity in Mental Health, Journal of LGBT Issues in Counseling, Journal of Mental Health Counseling, Measurement and Evaluation in Counseling and Development, Professional School Counseling, Rehabilitation Counseling Bulletin, The Family Journal.*

American Folklore Society: Mershon Center, Ohio State Univ., 1501 Neil Ave, Columbus, OH 43201-2602; tel. (614) 292-4715; e-mail americanfolkloresociety@gmail.com; internet www.afsnet.org; f. 1888; asscn of people who study and communicate knowledge about folklore throughout the world; 2,200 mems; Pres. DIANE GOLDSTEIN; Exec. Dir TIMOTHY LLOYD; publ. *Journal of American Folklore* (4 a year).

American Oriental Society: Hatcher Graduate Library, Univ. of Michigan, Ann Arbor, MI 48109-1190; internet www.umich.edu/~aos; f. 1842; encourages basic research in the languages and literatures of Asia incl. archaeology, biography, epigraphy, linguistics, literary criticism, paleography, philology, textual criticism, and the history of the intellectual and imaginative aspects of Oriental civilizations, esp. of art and folklore, philosophy and religion; 1,350 mems; library of 22,000 vols; Pres. ROBERT JOE. CUTTER; Sec. and Treas. JONATHAN RODGERS; publ. *Journal of American Oriental Society* (4 a year).

American Society for Ethnohistory: Dept of Anthropology, McGraw Hall, Cornell Univ., Ithaca, NY 14853; tel. (607) 277-0109; internet www.ethnohistory.org; f. 1954 as Ohio Valley Historic Indian Conf., present 1966; scholarly org. that studies histories of cultures and socs in all areas of the world; 1,200 mems; Pres. KEVIN TERRACIANO; Sec. LARRY NESPER; Treas. CHARLOTTE GRADIE; publ. *Ethnohistory* (4 a year).

American Sociological Association: 1430 K St, NW, Suite 600, Washington, DC 20005; tel. (202) 383-9005; e-mail executive.office@ asanet.org; internet www.asanet.org; f. 1905; non-profit asscn; articulates policy and implements programmes likely to have broadest possible effect on sociology now and in future; 14,000 mems; Pres. ERIK OLIN WRIGHT; Sec. CATHERINE BERHEIDE; Exec. Officer SALLY T. HILLSMAN; publs *American Sociological Review* (6 a year), *City and Community* (4 a year), *Contemporary Sociology* (6 a year), *Contexts* (4 a year), *Journal of Health and Social Behavior* (4 a year), *Social Psychology Quarterly*, *Sociological Methodology* (1 a year), *Sociological Theory* (4 a year), *Sociology of Education* (4 a year), *Teaching Sociology* (4 a year).

Association for Asian Studies, Inc.: 825 Victors Way, Suite 310, Ann Arbor, MI 48108; tel. (734) 665-2490; e-mail postmaster@aasianst.org; internet www .aasianst.org; f. 1941; scholarly, non-political, non-profit professional asscn open to all persons interested in Asia; 8,000 mems; Pres. GAIL HERSHATTER; Exec. Dir MICHAEL PASCHAL; publs *Bibliography of Asian Studies Online* (4 a year, electronic database), *Education about Asia* (3 a year), *Journal of Asian Studies* (4 a year).

Association for the Study of African American Life and History: Howard Center, 2225 Georgia Ave, NW, Suite 331, Washington, DC 20059; tel. (202) 238-5910; e-mail info@asalh.net; internet www.asalh .org; f. 1915; promotes research, preservation, interpretation and dissemination of information about Black life, history and culture to global community; 2,200 mems; Pres. Dr JAMES STEWART; Sec. ZENDE CLARK; Treas. TROY THORNTON; Exec. Dir SYLVIA Y. CYRUS; publs *Black History Bulletin* (2 a year), *Fire!!! The Multimedia Journal of Black Studies*, *Journal of African American History* (4 a year), *The Woodson Review* (1 a year).

National Institute of Social Sciences: 161 E 91st St, New York, NY 10128-2018; tel. (212) 831-0560; f. 1899; 850 mems; Pres. J. SINCLAIR ARMSTRONG; Sec. BRUCE E. BALDING.

Pacific Sociological Association: Dept of Sociology, San Diego State Univ., 5500 Campanile Dr., San Diego, CA 92182-4423; tel. (619) 594-5522; e-mail pacificsoc@csus.edu; internet www.pacificsoc.org; f. 1929 as Pacific Southwest Sociological Soc.; advances scholarly research into all social processes and areas of social life; promotes high-quality teaching of sociological knowledge; mentors next generation of sociologists; 1,200 mems; Exec. Dir DEAN S. DORN; publ. *Sociological Perspectives* (4 a year).

Population Association of America: 8630 Fenton St, Suite 722, Silver Spring, MD 20910-3812; tel. (301) 565-6710; e-mail membersvc@popassoc.org; internet www .populationassociation.org; f. 1930, fmrly American Nat. Cttee of the Int. Union for the Scientific Study of Population (f. 1927);

non-profit, scientific, professional org. that promotes research into population issues; 3,000 mems; Exec. Dir STEPHANIE DUDLEY; Pres. DAVID A. LAM; Sec. and Treas. ANN E. BIDDLECOM; publ. *Demography* (4 a year).

Population Council: 1 Dag Hammarskjold Plaza, Ninth Fl., New York, NY 10017; tel. (212) 339-0500; e-mail pubinfo@popcouncil .org; internet www.popcouncil.org; f. 1952; seeking to improve the well-being and reproductive health of current and future generations around the world and to help achieve a humane, equitable and sustainable balance between people and resources; conducts research worldwide to improve policies, programmes and products in 3 areas (HIV/AIDS; poverty, gender and youth; reproductive health); conducts fundamental biomedical research into reproduction; develops contraceptives and other products for improvement of reproductive health; conducts studies to improve the quality and outreach of services related to family planning, HIV/AIDS and reproductive health; carries out research into reproductive health and behaviour, family structure and function, causes and consequences of population growth; works to strengthen professional resources in developing countries through collaborative research, awards, fellowships and training; Pres. Dr PETER J. DONALDSON; Chief Financial Officer and Treas. SCOTT NEWMAN; Gen. Counsel and Sec. PATRICIA C. VAUGHAN; publs *Population and Development Review* (4 a year), *Studies in Family Planning* (4 a year).

Religious Research Association: 618 SW 2nd Ave, Galva, IL 61434-1912; tel. (309) 932-2727; e-mail william_swatos@baylor .edu; internet rra.hartsem.edu; f. 1951 as Religious Research Fellowship; promotes religious research; cooperates with other socs interested in study of religion; meets annually in conjunction with the Soc. for the Scientific Study of Religion; 325 mems; Pres. Dr JOY CHARLTON; Sec. Dr JAMES C. CAVENDISH; Treas. DAVID A. ROOZEN; publ. *Review of Religious Research* (4 a year).

Russell Sage Foundation: 112 E 64th St, New York, NY 10065; tel. (212) 750-6000; e-mail info@rsage.org; internet www .russellsage.org; f. 1907; promotes improvement of social and living conditions in the USA; supports projects on the future of work, immigration and the social psychology of cultural contact; library of 2,000 vols; Chair. ROBERT E. DENHAM; Pres. ERIC WANNER; Sec. PATRICIA WOODFORD; Treas. SHELLEY E. TAYLOR.

Society for Applied Anthropology: POB 2436, Oklahoma City, OK 73101-2436; tel. (405) 843-5113; e-mail info@sfaa.net; internet www.sfaa.net; f. 1941; application of the social and behavioural sciences to contemporary problems; 3,000 mems; Exec. Dir Dr JUDE THOMAS MAY; Pres. MERRILL EISENBERG; Sec. SUSAN CHARNLEY; Treas. SHARON D. MORRISON; publs *Human Organization* (4 a year), *Practicing Anthropology* (4 a year).

Society for the Scientific Study of Religion: c/o Dr Arthur E. Farnsley, II, Indiana Univ.—Purdue Univ. Indianapolis: Center for the Study of Religion and American Culture, Cavanaugh Hall 417, 425 Univ. Blvd, Indianapolis, IN 46202-5140; tel. (317) 278-6491; e-mail sssr@iupui.edu; internet www.sssrweb.org; f. 1949; dedicated to research and scholarly publs relating to religious phenomena; examining consequences of religious beliefs on individual and social behaviour, effect of religious orgs on other instns and problems of continuity and change within religious groups; c. 1,500 mems; Pres. JAMES BECKFORD; Sec. KORIE

EDWARDS; Treas. JAMES CAVENDISH; Exec. Officer ARTHUR FARNSLEY; publ. *Journal for the Scientific Study of Religion* (4 a year).

Society for the Study of Evolution: c/o Judy Stone, Dept of Biology, Colby College, Waterville, ME 04901; tel. (207) 859-5736; internet www.evolutionsociety.org; f. 1946; promotes study of organic evolution and integration of various fields of science concerned with evolution; 3,000 mems; Pres. Prof. JERRY COYNE; publ. *Evolution* (12 a year).

TECHNOLOGY

American Ceramic Society: POB 6136, Westerville, OH 43086-6136; 600 N Cleveland Ave., Suite 210, Westerville, Ohio 43082; tel. (866) 721-3322; e-mail customerservice@ceramics.org; internet www.ceramics.org; f. 1898; advances study, understanding and use of ceramics and related materials; 9,500 mems; library of 11,000 vols; Pres. GEORGE G. WICKS; Exec. Dir CHARLIE SPAHR; publs *Bulletin* (12 a year), *Ceramic Engineering and Science Proceedings* (5 a year), *Ceramic Source* (1 a year), *International Journal of Applied Ceramic Technology* (6 a year), *International Journal of Applied Glass Science* (4 a year), *Journal of the American Ceramic Society* (12 a year).

American Council of Engineering Companies: 1015 15th St, NW, 8 Fl., Washington, DC 20005-2605; tel. (202) 347-7474; e-mail acec@acec.org; internet www.acec .org; f. 1909, fmrly as American Institute of Consulting Engineers; represents engineering industries of USA; 5,800 mems; Chair. TERRY F. NEIMEYER; Pres. and CEO DAVID A. RAYMOND; publs *American Consulting Engineer*, *Directory*, *Engineering Inc.*

American Institute of Aeronautics and Astronautics: 1801 Alexander Bell Dr., Suite 500, Reston, VA 20191-4344; tel. (703) 264-7500; e-mail custserv@aiaa.org; internet www.aiaa.org; f. 1963 by merger of American Rocket Soc. (f. 1930) with Institute of Aerospace Science (f. 1932); enables global movement of people and goods; leads global acquisition and dissemination of information and data; advances nat. security interests; provides source of scientific progress and inspiration by pushing the boundaries of exploration and innovation; 31,000 mems; Pres. Dr BRIAN DAILEY; Exec. Dir ROBERT DICKMAN; publs *AIAA Journal* (12 a year), *AIAA Student Journal* (4 a year, online), *Journal of Aerospace Computing, Information and Communication* (12 a year, online only), *Journal of Aircraft* (24 a year), *Journal of Guidance, Control and Dynamics* (24 a year), *Journal of Propulsion and Power* (24 a year), *Journal of Spacecraft and Rockets* (24 a year), *Journal of Thermophysics and Heat Transfer* (4 a year).

American Institute of Chemical Engineers: 3 Park Ave, New York, NY 10016-5991; tel. (203) 702-7660; e-mail xpress@aiche.org; internet www.aiche.org; f. 1908; org. for chemical engineering professionals; provides access to information on recognized and promising chemical engineering processes and methods; 40,000 mems; Exec. Dir JUNE WISPELWEY; Pres. MARIA K. BURKA; Sec. KIMBERLY L. OGDEN; Treas. ANDRE R. DA COSTA; publs *AIChE Journal* (12 a year), *Biotechnology Progress* (6 a year), *Chemical Engineering Faculty Directory* (1 a year), *Chemical Engineering Progress* (12 a year), *Environmental Progress & Sustainable Energy* (4 a year), *Process Safety Progress* (4 a year).

American Institute of Mining, Metallurgical and Petroleum Engineers: 12999 E

Adam Aircraft Circle, Englewood, CO 80112; tel. (303) 325-5185; e-mail aime@aimehq.org; internet www.aimehq.org; f. 1871; 4 mem socs; 130,000 mems; library of 550 vols; Pres. Dr BRAJENDRA MISHRA; Exec. Dir L. MICHELE LAWRIE-MUNRO.

American Iron and Steel Institute: 1140 Connecticut Ave, NW, Suite 705, Washington, DC 20036; tel. (202) 452-7100; internet www.steel.org; f. 1855, fmrly American Iron Asscn, present status 1908, present location 1974; advocates for public policies that support a competitive environment for domestic manufacturing; provides high-quality, value-added products to a wide array of customers; leads the world in innovation and technology in production of steel; produces steel in safe and environmentally friendly manner; increases market for N American steel in both traditional and innovative applications; 31 corporate mems; Chair. JOHN SURMA; Pres. and CEO THOMAS J. GIBSON.

American National Standards Institute: 25 W 43rd St, Fourth Fl., New York, NY 10036; tel. (212) 642-4900; e-mail membership@ansi.org; internet www.ansi.org; f. 1918; coordinates devt of voluntary nat. standards; approves American Nat. Standards, and represents US interests in the ISO and the IEC; 125,000 mem companies; Chair. Dr ARTHUR E. COTE; Pres. and CEO S. JOE BHATIA; publs *Standards Action* (52 a year), *The ANSI Reporter* (4 a year).

American Society for Engineering Education: 1818 N St, NW, Suite 600, Washington, DC 20036-2479; tel. (202) 331-3500; e-mail aseeexec@asee.org; internet www.asee.org; f. 1893; promotes improvement of higher and continuing education for engineers and engineering technologists, incl. teaching, counselling, research, ethics, etc.; 12,000 individual mems, 500 institutional mems; Exec. Dir and Sec. NORMAN FORTENBERRY; Pres. DON P. GIDDENS; publs *Advances in Engineering Education* (1 a year), *Chemical Engineering Education Journal* (4 a year), *Computers in Education Journal* (4 a year), *Engineering Design Graphics Journal* (1 a year, online), *Journal of Engineering Education* (4 a year), *Journal of Engineering Technology* (2 a year), *Prism* (12 a year), *Profiles of Engineering and Engineering Technology Colleges* (1 a year), *The Engineering Economist* (4 a year).

American Society for Photogrammetry and Remote Sensing: 5410 Grosvenor Lane, Suite 210, Bethesda, MD 20814-2160; tel. (301) 493-0290; e-mail asprs@asprs.org; internet www.asprs.org; f. 1934; aerial photography, photogrammetry, photo-interpretation, remote sensing, geographic information systems (GIS), surveying, mapping, cartography; 6,000 mems; Pres. GARY R. FLORENCE; Exec. Dir and Sec. JAMES R. PLASKER; Treas. Dr DONALD T. LAUER; publ. *Photogrammetric Engineering and Remote Sensing* (12 a year, in print and online).

American Society of Civil Engineers: 1801 Alexander Bell Dr., Reston, VA 20191-4400; tel. (703) 295-6300; internet www.asce.org; f. 1852; works for advancement of technology to enhance quality, knowledge, competitiveness, sustainability and environmental stewardship; 140,000 mems; Pres. ANDREW W. HERRMANN; Exec. Dir and Sec. PATRICK J. NATALE; Treas. MICHAEL H. WENNING; publs *ASCE* (12 a year), *Journal of Aerospace Engineering* (4 a year), *Journal of Architectural Engineering* (4 a year), *Journal of Energy Engineering* (3 a year), *International Journal of Geomechanics* (4 a year), and 28 online journals, *Publications Information* (6 a year).

American Society of Heating, Refrigerating and Air-Conditioning Engineers: 1791 Tullie Circle, NE, Atlanta, GA 30329; tel. (404) 636-8400; e-mail ashrae@ashrae.org; internet www.ashrae.org; f. 1894 by merger of American Soc. of Heating and Ventilating Engineers with American Soc. of Refrigerating Engineers; advances arts and sciences of heating, ventilation, air conditioning and refrigeration to serve humanity and promote a sustainable world through research, standards writing, publishing and continuing education; 51,000 mems; Pres. RONALD JARNAGIN; Exec. Vice-Pres. JEFF H. LITTLETON; Treas. WILLIAM BAHNFLETH; publs *ASHRAE Journal* (12 a year), *ASHRAE Handbook* (1 a year), *ASHRAE Transactions* (2 a year), *High Performing Buildings* (4 a year), *HVAC&R Research* (6 a year).

American Society of Mechanical Engineers: 3 Park Ave, New York, NY 10016-5990; tel. (973) 882-1170; e-mail infocentral@asme.org; internet www.asme.org; f. 1880; enables collaboration, knowledge sharing and skill devt across all engineering disciplines; 120,000 mems; Exec. Dir THOMAS G. LOUGHLIN; Pres. VICTORIA ROCKWELL; Sec. and Treas. WILBUR J. MARNER; publs *Applied Mechanics Reviews* (12 a year), *Journal of Nanotechnology in Engineering and Medicine* (4 a year), *Mechanical Engineering* (12 a year), *Transactions* (divided into 17 periodicals, each published 4 times a year): *Biomechanical Engineering, Dynamic Systems, Engineering for Industry, Electronic Packaging, Energy Resources Technology, Engineering for Gas Turbines and Power, Engineering Materials and Technology, Fluids Engineering, Heat Transfer Mechanisms, Journal of Applied Mechanics, Manufacturing Review Measurement and Control, Pressure Vessel Technology, Solar Energy Engineering, Tribology, Transmissions and Automationin Design, Turbomachinery, Vibration and Acoustics.*

American Society of Naval Engineers: 1452 Duke St, Alexandria, VA 22314-3458; tel. (703) 836-6727; e-mail asnehq@navalengineers.org; internet www.navalengineers.org; f. 1888; conceives, designs, develops, tests, constructs, outfits, operates and maintains complex naval and maritime ships, submarines and aircraft and their associated systems and subsystems; 5,000 mems; Pres. RONALD K. KISS; Exec. Dir, Sec. and Treas. Capt. (Retd) DENNIS K. KRUSE; publ. *Naval Engineers Journal* (4 a year).

American Welding Society: 550 NW Le Jeune Rd, Miami, FL 33126; tel. (305) 443-9353; e-mail education@aws.org; internet www.aws.org; f. 1919, present location 1971; welding education seminars and confs, qualification and certification, annual int. exposition; 66,000 mems; Pres. JOHN L. MENDOZA; Exec. Dir R. W. SHOCK; publs *Inspection Trends* (4 a year), *Welding Journal* (12 a year), *Welding Handbook* (every 3 years).

ASM International: 9639 Kinsman Rd, Materials Park, OH 44073-0002; tel. (440) 338-5151; e-mail memberservicecenter@asminternational.org; internet www.asminternational.org; f. 1913 as The Steel Treaters Club; technical soc. concerned with advanced materials technology; 36,000 mems; Pres. Prof. Dr CHRISTOPHER BERNDT; Man. Dir STANLEY C. THEOBALD; Treas. ROBERT FULTON; publs *Advanced Materials and Processes* (12 a year), *Alloy Digest* (12 a year), *Electronic Device Failure Analysis, International Materials Reviews* (6 a year, with Institute of Materials), *Journal of Failure Analysis and Prevention, Journal of Materials Engineering and Performance* (6 a year), *Journal of Phase Equilibria and Diffusion* (6 a year), *Journal of Thermal Spray Technology* (4 a year), *Metallography, Microstructure, and Analysis, Metallurgical Transactions A and B (6 a year) (with TMS–AIME)* (12 a year).

Association for Iron and Steel Technology: 186 Thorn Hill Rd, Warrendale, PA 15086-7528; tel. (724) 814-3000; e-mail memberservices@aist.org; internet www.aistech.org; attached to American Institute of Mining Metallurgical and Petroleum Engineers; holds int. confs, expositions and technical presentations concerning steel-related technologies; 11,268 mems; Exec. Dir RONALD E. ASHBURN; publ. *Iron and Steel Maker* (12 a year).

Association of Consulting Chemists and Chemical Engineers: POB 902, Murray Hill, NJ 07974-0902; tel. (908) 464-3182; e-mail accce@chemconsult.org; internet www.chemconsult.org; f. 1928; non-profit membership corpn; consultants serving chemical and related industries with expertise based on a wide variety of technical and business knowledge; 160 mems; Pres. Dr JOSEPH V. PORCELLI; Exec. Dir Dr JOHN BONACCI; publ. *Consulting Services Directory*.

ASTM International: 100 Barr Harbor Dr., POB C700, W Conshohocken, PA 19428-2959; tel. (610) 832-9500; e-mail service@astm.org; internet www.astm.org; f. 1898 as American Section of the Int. Asscn for Testing and Materials, fmrly American Soc. for Testing and Materials, present name 2001; non-profit org. providing a global forum for the devt and publ. of voluntary consensus standards for materials, products, systems and services; 30,000 mems; Chair. CATHERINE H. PILARZ; Pres. JAMES A. THOMAS; publs *Cement, Concrete and Aggregates, Geotechnical Testing Journal, Journal of ASTM International, Journal of Composites, Technology and Research, Journal of Forensic Sciences, Journal of Testing and Evaluation.*

Edison Electric Institute: 701 Pennsylvania Ave, NW, Washington, DC 20004-2696; tel. (202) 508-5000; e-mail news@eei.org; internet www.eei.org; f. 1933; provides public policy leadership, critical industry data, market opportunities, strategic business intelligence, one-of-a-kind confs and forums; 390 mems; Chair. THOMAS F. FARRELL, II; Exec. Dir RICHARD S. TEMPCHIN; Pres. THOMAS R. KUHN; Corporate Sec. EDWARD H. COMER; Treas. JOHN S. SCHLENKER; publ. *Electric Perspectives* (6 a year).

Illuminating Engineering Society: 120 Wall St, 17th Fl., New York, NY 10005-4001; tel. (212) 248-5000; e-mail ies@ies.org; internet www.ies.org; f. 1906; dedicated to promoting the art and science of quality lighting to its mems, allied professional orgs and public; 8,000 mems; Pres. DENIS LAVOIE; publs *LEUKOS* (4 a year, online, 1 a year, printed compilation), *LD+A* (12 a year).

Industrial Designers Society of America: 45195 Business Court, Suite 250, Dulles, VA 20166-6717; tel. (703) 707-6000; e-mail idsa@idsa.org; internet www.idsa.org; f. 1965; advances profession of industrial design through education, information, community and advocacy; organizes confs; 3,300 mems; Chair. GEORGE MCCAIN; Sec. and Treas. PETER BRESSLER; CEO CLIVE ROUX; Exec. Dir BOB SCHWARTZ; publ. *Innovation* (4 a year).

Institute of Electrical and Electronics Engineers: 3 Park Ave, 17th Fl., New York, NY 10016-5997; tel. (212) 419-7900; e-mail society-info@ieee.org; internet www.ieee.org; f. 1884; serves professionals involved in all aspects of electrical, electronic and computing fields and related areas of science and technology that underlie modern civilization;

395,000 mems; Pres. and CEO Dr MOSHE KAM; Sec. Prof. ROGER D. POLLARD; Treas. HAROLD L. FLESCHER; Exec. Dir Dr E. JAMES PRENDERGAST; publs *IEEE Journal of Selected Topics in Quantum Electronics* (1 a year), *IEEE Potentials* (12 a year), *Journal of Selected Topics in Signal Processing (J-STSP)*, *Proceedings* (12 a year), *Society and Council Transactions*.

Institute of Food Technologists: 525 W Van Buren, Suite 1000, Chicago, IL 60607; tel. (312) 782-8424; e-mail info@ift.org; internet www.ift.org; f. 1939; advocates for food science and acts as catalyst for change around the world; educates media and policy makers and works with govts to shape regulations; 26,000 mems; Pres. ROGER CLEMENS; publs *Comprehensive Reviews in Food Science and Food Safety* (6 a year), *Food Technology* (12 a year), *Journal of Food Science* (12 a year, online), *Journal of Food Science Education* (4 a year).

Institute of Industrial Engineers: 3577 Parkway Lane, Suite 200, Norcross, GA 30092; tel. (770) 449-0460; e-mail executiveoffices@iienet.org; internet www .iienet.org; f. 1948 as American Institute of Industrial Engineers, present name 1981; provides leadership for application, education, training, research and development of industrial engineering; 30,000 mems; Pres. G. DON TAYLOR; Sec. JESSICA O. MATSON; Treas. DOUGLAS R. RABENECK; CEO and Exec. Dir DON H. GREENE; publs *IIE Transactions* (12 a year), *IIE Transactions on Healthcare Systems Engineering* (4 a year), *IIE Transactions on Occupational Ergonomics and Human Factors* (4 a year), *Industrial Engineer* (12 a year), *Industrial Management* (6 a year), *Journal of Enterprise Transformation* (4 a year), *The Engineering Economist* (4 a year).

International Communication Association: 1500 21st St, NW, Washington, DC 20036; tel. (202) 955-1444; e-mail icahdq@icahdq.org; internet www.icahdq.org; f. 1950 as Nat. Soc. for the Study of Communication; brings together academics and professionals concerned with research and application of human communication theory; officially associated with the UN as a non-governmental asscn (NGO); 4,300 mems; Pres. LARRY GROSS; Exec. Dir MICHAEL L. HALEY; publs *Communication, Culture, & Critique*, *Communication Theory* (4 a year), *Human Communication Research* (4 a year), *Journal of Communication* (4 a year), *Journal of Computer-Mediated Communication*, *The Communication Yearbook* (1 a year).

International Society of Automation (ISA): POB 12277, 67 Alexander Dr., Research Triangle Park, NC 27709; tel. (919) 549-8411; e-mail info@isa.org; internet www.isa.org; f. 1945 as Instrument Soc. of America; develops standards; certifies industry professionals; provides education and training; publishes books and technical articles; hosts confs and exhibitions for automation professionals; 30,000 mems; CEO ROB RENNER; Exec. Dir PATRICK GOUHIN; Pres. KIM MILLER DUNN; publs *InTech* (12 a year), *ISA Directory of Automation* (1 a year), *ISA Transactions* (4 a year).

Markle Foundation: 10 Rockefeller Pl., 16th Fl., New York, NY 10020-1903; tel. (212) 713-7600; e-mail info@markle.org; internet www.markle.org; f. 1927; seeks to improve mass media and realize the potential of communications technology; addresses critical public needs, particularly in the areas of health and nat. security; collaborates with innovators and thought leaders from the public and private sectors whose expertise lies in the areas of information technology,

privacy, civil liberties; 25 mems; Chair. LEWIS B. KADEN; Pres. ZOË BAIRD BUDINGER; Man. Dir and Chief Financial Officer KAREN D. BYERS.

Minerals, Metals and Materials Society: 184 Thorn Hill Rd, Warrendale, PA 15086-7514; tel. (724) 776-9000; e-mail tmsgeneral@tms.org; internet www.tms.org; attached to American Institute of Mining, Metallurgical and Petroleum Engineers; professional org. dealing with minerals processing and primary metals production; basic research and advanced applications of different materials; 10,000 mems; Pres. GARRY W. WARREN; Sec. and Exec. Dir Dr WARREN HUNT, JR; publs *Journal of Electronic Materials* (12 a year), *Journal of Metals* (12 a year), *Metallurgical and Materials Transactions A* (12 a year), *Metallurgical and Materials Transactions B* (12 a year).

National Society of Professional Engineers: 1420 King St, Alexandria, VA 22314-2794; tel. (703) 684-2800; e-mail memserv@nspe.org; internet www.nspe.org; f. 1934; professional aspects of engineering; administers licensure and licensure preparation; operates a Board of Ethical Review; 45,000 mems; Pres. CHRISTOPHER M. STONE; Exec. Dir and Sec. LAWRENCE A. JACOBSON; Treas. LEANNE H. PANDURE; publ. *Engineering Times* (12 a year).

Society for Mining, Metallurgy and Exploration: 12999 E. Adam Aircraft Circle, Englewood, CO 80112; tel. (303) 948-4200; e-mail sme@smenet.org; internet www .smenet.org; attached to American Institute of Mining, Metallurgical and Petroleum Engineers; int. soc. of professionals in minerals industry; 8 divs: coal and energy, environmental, industrial minerals and aggregates, mineral and metallurgical processing, mining and exploration, Underground Construction Asscn (UCA), Int. Marine Minerals Soc. (IMMS) and woman's auxiliary to the AIME (WAAIME); 14,000 mems; Pres. JOHN N. MURPHY; Exec. Dir DAVID L. KANAGY; publs *Minerals & Metallurgical Processing* (4 a year), *Mining Engineering* (12 a year), *Transactions* (1 a year), *Tunneling and Underground Construction (T&UC)* (4 a year).

Society for the History of Technology: c/o Dept of Science, Technology & Soc., Univ. of Virginia, POB 400744, Charlottesville, VA 22904-4744; tel. (434) 987-6230; e-mail shot@virginia.edu; internet www .historyoftechnology.org; f. 1958; concerned with history of technological devices and processes, relations of technology with science, politics, social change, the arts and humanities, and economics; affiliated to the American Asscn for the Advancement of Science, the American Council of Learned Socs; 1,500 mems; Pres. RON KLINE; Sec. BERNIE CARLSON; Treas. HUGH GORMAN; publ. *Technology and Culture* (4 a year).

Society of Automotive Engineers: 400 Commonwealth Dr., Warrendale, PA 15096-0001; tel. (724) 776-4841; e-mail magazines@sae.org; internet www.sae.org; f. 1905; global body of scientists, engineers, and practitioners that advances self-propelled vehicle and system knowledge in a neutral forum for the benefit of soc.; 128,000 mems; Pres. RICHARD E. KLEINE; Sec. Dr DAVID L. SCHUTT; Treas. CAROL STORY; publs *Aerospace Engineering* (12 a year), *Automotive Engineering International* (12 a year), *Off-Highway Engineering* (6 a year), *SAE Handbook* (1 a year), *SAE Transactions* (1 a year), *SAE Update* (12 a year), *Vehicle Electrification*.

Society of Manufacturing Engineers: POB 930, Dearborn, MI 48121-0930; 1 SME Dr., Dearborn, MI 48128; tel. (313) 425-3000;

e-mail communications@sme.org; internet www.sme.org; f. 1932 as Soc. of Tool Engineers, present name 1969; advances scientific knowledge in the field of manufacturing and applies its resources to research, writing, publishing and disseminating information; 25,000 mems; library of 7,000 vols; Pres. LAROUX GILLESPIE; Sec. and Treas. MICHAEL F. MOLNAR; Exec. Dir and Gen. Man. MARK C. TOMLINSON; publs *Composites in Manufacturing* (4 a year), *Electronics Manufacturing Engineering* (4 a year), *Finishing Line* (4 a year), *Forming and Fabricating* (12 a year), *Integrated Design and Manufacturing* (12 a year), *Journal of Manufacturing Processes* (4 a year), *Journal of Manufacturing Systems* (4 a year), *Machining Technology* (4 a year), *Plastics Insights* (4 a year), *Rapid Prototyping* (4 a year), *Robotics Today* (4 a year), *Transactions*, *Vision* (4 a year).

Society of Naval Architects & Marine Engineers: 601 Pavonia Ave, Suite 400, Jersey City, NJ 07306; tel. (201) 798-4800; internet www.sname.org; f. 1893; encourages exchange and recording of information; sponsors applied research; offers career guidance; supports education; enhances professional status and integrity of its membership; 10,000 mems; Pres. EDWARD N. COMSTOCK; Exec. Dir ERIK W. SEITHER; publs *Journal of Ship Production and Design* (4 a year), *Journal of Ship Research* (4 a year), *Marine Technology* (4 a year).

Society of Petroleum Engineers: 222 Palisades Creek Dr., Richardson, TX 75080-2040; tel. (972) 952-9393; e-mail service@spe .org; internet www.spe.org; f. 1957, inc. 1985; collects, disseminates and exchanges technical knowledge concerning exploration, devt and production of oil and gas resources and related technologies; 97,191 mems; Pres. GANESH C. THAKUR; Exec. Dir MARK A. RUBIN; publs *Journal of Canadian Petroleum Technology* (12 a year), *Oil and Gas Facilities* (6 a year), *SPE Drilling & Completion* (4 a year, online), *SPE Economics & Management* (4 a year, online), *SPE Journal* (4 a year), *SPE Production & Operations* (4 a year), *SPE Projects, Facilities & Construction* (4 a year), *SPE Reservoir Evaluation & Engineering* (6 a year).

Society of Rheology: c/o A. Jeffrey Giacomin, Rheology Research Center, Univ. of Wisconsin, Madison, WI 53706; tel. (608) 262-7473; internet www.rheology.org; f. 1929; study of those properties of materials which determine their response to mechanical force; 1,700 mems; Pres. A. JEFFREY GIACOMIN; Sec. ALBERT CO; publs *Journal of Rheology* (6 a year), *Rheology Bulletin* (2 a year).

Research Institutes

GENERAL

Albert Schweitzer Institute: 275 Mount Carmel Ave, Hamden, CT 06518; tel. (203) 582-3144; e-mail schweitzer@quinnipiac.edu; internet www.quinnipiac.edu/institutes-and-centers/albert-schweitzer-institute; f. 1984 as Albert Schweitzer Memorial Foundation, present name 2002; attached to Quinnipiac Univ.; focuses on health, humanitarian and peace efforts; supports health care devt in under-served areas; Exec. Dir DAVID T. IVES.

Getty Research Institute: Suite 1100, 1200 Getty Center Dr., Los Angeles, CA 90049-1688; tel. (310) 440-7335; e-mail reference@getty.edu; internet www.getty .edu/research; f. 1983; operating programme of the J. Paul Getty Trust; furthers knowledge and advances understanding of the visual arts through its expertise, its active collecting programme, public programmes, institutional collaborations, exhibitions, publs, digital services and residential scholars programme; library: 1m. vols, incl. reference rare materials, serials and auction catalogues; Dir Prof. THOMAS W. GAEHTGENS; Deputy Dir ANDREW PERCHUK; Assoc. Dir GAIL FEIGENBAUM; publ. *Getty Research Journal.*

Institute for the Arts and Humanities: Ihlseng Cottage, University Park, PA 16802; tel. (814) 865-0495; e-mail arts-humanities@ psu.edu; internet www.research.psu.edu/iah; f. 1966; attached to Pennsylvania State Univ.; areas of research incl: philosophy, music, history, dance, comparative literature, landscape architecture; Dir Dr MICHAEL BÉRUBÉ.

National Humanities Center: POB 12256, 7 Alexander Dr., Research Triangle Park, NC 27709-2256; tel. (919) 549-0661; e-mail gharpham@nationalhumanitiescenter.org; internet nationalhumanitiescenter.org; f. 1977; encourages scholarship in the humanities and enhances the usefulness and influence of the humanities in the USA; awards fellowships (40 a year) to pursue advanced post-doctoral research and writing at the centre; organizes seminars, lectures, confs; library: reference works, bibliographical aids, microfilm catalogue comprises 4 small collns; Chair. ALAN BRINKLEY; Pres. and Dir GEOFFREY GALT HARPHAN; Sec. JOHN F. ADAMS; Treas. MERRIL M. HALPERN.

RAND Corporation: 1776 Main St, POB 2138, Santa Monica, CA 90407-2138; tel. (310) 393-0411; internet www.rand.org; f. 1948; non-profit instn receiving funds from federal, state and local govt, foundations and the private sector; brs in Arlington, VA, Boston, MA, Jackson, MA, Pittsburgh, PA, New Orleans, LA, Cambridge (UK), Brussels (Belgium), and Doha (Qatar); research on matters affecting public interest; education, civil and criminal justice, health sciences, int. affairs, labour and population, science and technology, national security, information processing systems; 950 research professionals; Pres. and CEO MICHAEL D. RICH; publ. *Rand Review* (3 a year).

Research Institute for Telecommunications Marketing (RITM): College of Business Admin., Ballentine Hall, Univ. of Rhode Island, Seven Lippitt Rd, Kingston, RI 02881-0802; tel. (401) 874-5065; e-mail ritim@etal.uri.edu; internet ritim.cba.uri .edu; f. 1989; attached to College of Business Admin., Univ. of Rhode Island; focuses on marketing, behavioural, organizational and strategic aspects of telecommunications and information technology industries; Dir Dr RUBY ROY DHOLAKIA; Assoc. Dir Dr NIK DHOLAKIA.

Sierra Nevada Research Institute (SNRI): 5200 N Lake Rd, Merced, CA 95343; tel. (209) 228-4400; e-mail snri@ ucmerced.edu; internet snri.ucmerced.edu; attached to Univ. of California, Merced; conducts basic and applied research into natural resources, physical and biological diversity; promotes social well being in the San Joaquin Valley and Sierra Nevada regions of California; operates 2 facilities in the Great Valley and Sierra Nevada region: Environmental Analytical Laboratory and Yosemite Field Station at Wawona; Dir Dr ROGER BALES; Exec. Dir DAVID HOSLEY.

AGRICULTURE, FISHERIES AND VETERINARY SCIENCE

Forest Products Society: 2801 Marshall Court, Madison, WI 53705-2295; tel. (608) 231-1361; internet www.forestprod.org; f. 1947; technology transfer concerning all areas of the forest products industry; Pres. PAUL MERRICK; Pres.-Elect PATRICE TARDIF; Vice-Pres. TIMOTHY M. YOUNG; Exec. Vice-Pres. STEFAN BERGMANN; publs *Forest Products Journal* (10 a year), *International Journal of Forest Engineering* (2 a year), *Journal of Forest Products Business Research* (online), *Wood Design Focus* (4 a year).

Louisiana State University Agricultural Center: POB 25203, Baton Rouge, LA 70894; 101 Efferson Hall, Baton Rouge, LA 70803; tel. (225) 578-4161; e-mail web@ agcenter.lsu.edu; internet www.lsuagcenter .com; attached to Louisiana State Univ. System; focus areas incl. alternative fuels, crop adaptability, coastal restoration, functional foods, childhood obesity, sustainable housing and rural initiatives; Chancellor WILLIAM B. RICHARDSON; Vice-Chancellor and Dir for Louisiana Agricultural Experiment Station JOHN RUSSIN; Vice-Chancellor and Dir for Louisiana Cooperative Extension Service PAUL COREIL; publ. *Louisiana Agriculture* (4 a year).

Ohio Agricultural Research and Development Center: 209 Research Services, 1680 Madison Ave, Wooster, OH 44691-4096; tel. (330) 263-3701; e-mail oardc@osu .edu; internet www.oardc.ohio-state.edu; f. 1882 as Ohio Agricultural Experiment Station (OAES), current name adopted 1965; attached to College of Food, Agricultural, and Environmental Sciences, Ohio State Univ.; research into better food and fibre production, environmental and water quality issues for both rural and urban population; emphasis on new, improved and safer products for use in the agricultural endeavours of both the state of Ohio and the world community; Dir STEVEN A. SLACK; Librarian CONSTANCE J. BRITTON.

Rhode Island Agricultural Experiment Station: Woodward Hall, 9 E Alumni Ave, Kingston, RI 02881-0804; tel. (401) 874-5493; internet riaes.cels.uri.edu; f. 1888; attached to Univ. of Rhode Island; conducts research dedicated to addressing challenges in agriculture, food production and processing, nutrition, natural resource policy and natural resource management, and renewable energy and climate change; Dir Dr RICHARD C. RHODES, III.

BIBLIOGRAPHY, LIBRARY SCIENCE AND MUSEOLOGY

Getty Conservation Institute: 1200 Getty Center Dr., Suite 700, Los Angeles, CA 90049-1684; tel. (310) 440-7325; e-mail gciweb@getty.edu; internet www.getty.edu/ conservation; f. 1985; programme of the J. Paul Getty Trust; works for the preservation of the world's cultural heritage; library of 60,000 vols; Dir TIMOTHY P. WHALEN; Assoc. Dir for Admin. KATHLEEN GAINES; Assoc. Dir for Programmes JEANNE MARIE TEUTONICO; publs *Art and Archaeology Technical Abstracts* (online, aata.getty.edu/nps), *GCI e-Bulletin* (6 a year).

National Federation of Advanced Information Services (NFAIS): 1518 Walnut St, Suite 1004, Philadelphia, PA 19102-3403; tel. (215) 893-1561; e-mail nfais@nfais.org; internet www.nfais.org; f. 1958, present location 1965; a global non-profit org.; aims to serve the world's information community through education, research, and publ.; Pres. KEITH MacGREGOR; Exec. Dir BONNIE LAWLOR; Pres.-Elect BARBARA DOBBS MACKENZIE; Sec. MARK GAUTHIER; Treas. SUZANNE BEDELL.

Smithsonian Center for Education and Museum Studies (SCEMS): POB 37012, MRC 508, Washington, DC 20003-7012; Capital Gallery, 600 Maryland Ave, Suite 1005, Washington, DC 20024; tel. (202) 633-5330; e-mail learning@si.edu; internet www .museumstudies.si.edu; f. 1971 as Office of Museum Programs, renamed as Center for Museum Studies in 1995, current name adopted 1999 after merger with Smithsonian Office of Education; assists the museum community in acquiring and strengthening its understanding and practices of museology, increases the Smithsonian Institution's influence as a nat. educational org.; library: merged library of collns from the Museum Reference Center and Central Reference and Loan Services br. libraries; part of the Smithsonian Institution libraries system of 20 libraries; Exec. Dir STEPHANIE NORBY; publs *Air & Space Magazine* (6 a year), *Smithsonian in Your Classroom.*

Smithsonian Museum Conservation Institute: Museum Support Center, 4210 Silver Hill Rd, Suitland, MD 20746; tel. (301) 238-1240; e-mail mciweb@si.edu; internet www.si.edu/mci; f. 1963 as Conservation Research Laboratory; research into the fields of conservation and the scientific study of colln materials; conducts technical research studies and interpretation of anthropological, artistic, biological and historical objects; Dir Dr ROBERT J. KOESTLER; Deputy Dir PAULA T. DEPRIEST.

ECONOMICS, LAW AND POLITICS

Brookings: 1775 Massachusetts Ave, NW, Washington, DC 20036; tel. (202) 797-6000; e-mail communications@brookings.edu; internet www.brook.edu; f. 1916; research, education, and publishing into the fields of economics, govt and foreign policy; library of 75,000 vols, 700 periodical titles; not open to public; Pres. STROBE TALBOTT; Chair. JOHN L. THORNTON; Man. Dir WILLIAM ANTHOLIS; publs *Brookings Papers on Economic Activity* (2 a year), *Brookings Papers on Education Policy, Brookings Trade Forum* (1 a year), *Brookings—Wharton Papers on Financial Services, Brookings—Wharton Papers on Urban Affairs* (1 a year), *Economia* (2 a year).

Center for Strategic & International Studies (CSIS): 1800 K St, NW, Washington, DC 20006; tel. (202) 887-0200; internet www.csis.org; f. 1962; research into new challenges to nat. and int. peace and security; helps to develop new methods of governance for the global age through programmes in technology and public policy, energy, and int. trade and finance; Chair. SAM NUNN; Pres. and CEO JOHN J. HAMRE; publ. *The Washington Quarterly.*

Center for the Study of Democratic Institutions: 10951 West Pico Blvd, Suite 300, Los Angeles, CA 90064; tel. (310) 474-0011; e-mail nfo@npq.org; internet www .digitalnpq.org; f. 1959, fmrly Robert Maynard Hutchins Center for the Study of Democratic Institutions; Exec. Dir (vacant); publ. *New Perspectives Quarterly.*

East-West Center: 1601 East-West Rd, Honolulu, HI 96848-1601; tel. (808) 944-7111; e-mail ewcinfo@eastwestcenter.org; internet www.eastwestcenter.org; f. 1960; a public, non-profit educational instn with an int. board of governors; research fellows, graduate students, and professionals in govt, academia and business each year work with the Center's int. staff in cooperative study, training, and research; they examine major issues related to int. relations, population, resources, economic devt and the environment in Asia, the Pacific and the USA; library of 50,000 vols, unpublished documents, periodicals and electronic resources; Pres. Dr CHARLES E. MORRISON; Chair. PUONGPUN SANANIKONE; Treas. RICKY KUBOTA; publs *Asia Pacific Issues Paper* (irregular), *Observer* (4 a year).

Institute for the Study of International Aspects of Competition: Dept of Economics, Univ. of Rhode Islands, 806 Chafee Hall, 10 Chafee Rd, Kingston, RI 02881-0808; tel. (401) 874-9195; internet www.uri.edu/research/isiac; attached to Dept of Economics, Univ. of Rhode Island; areas of research incl. industrial org. and int. economics; Exec. Dir Dr JOHN P. BURKETT; Research Dir Dr MENG-JIEU CHEN.

Institute of International Business: J. Mack Robinson College of Business, Georgia State Univ., 14th Fl., Suite 1437, 35 Broad St, Atlanta, GA 30303; tel. (404) 413-7275; e-mail iib@gsu.edu; internet robinson.gsu.edu/iib; attached to J. Mack Robinson College of Business, Georgia State Univ.; focuses on cross-border activities and studies political, cultural and commercial environment within which cross-border trade and investment activities take place; Dir Dr DANIEL BELLO.

International Center for Economic Growth: University of the Pacific, 3601 Pacific Ave, Stockton, CA 95211; tel. (209) 946-3265; f. 1985; attached to School of Int. Studies, Univ. of the Pacific; promotes economic growth and human devt in developing and post-socialist countries, by strengthening the capacity of local research institutes to provide project leadership; operates in conjunction with 370 mem. institutes globally; sponsors confs and seminars; CEO ROBERT HODAM.

International Marketing Institute: c/o Carroll School of Management, Boston College, Fulton Hall 510, 140 Commonwealth Ave, Chestnut Hill, MA 02467; tel. (617) 552-8420; f. 1960; supported by Carroll School of Management, Boston College; int. executive devt and management training programmes in management education, with marketing as the primary focus; Exec. Dir JOSEPH B. GANNON.

Marketing Science Institute: 1000 Massachusetts Ave, Cambridge, MA 02138-5396; tel. (617) 491-2060; e-mail msi@msi.org; internet www.msi.org; f. 1961; non-profit marketing consortium that stimulates, supports and reports research in order to advance marketing knowledge and practice; sponsors and publishes academic research on all areas of marketing; 71 mem. companies. Chair. GORDON A. WYNER; Chief Operating Officer MARNI ZEA CLIPPINGER; Exec. Dir JOHN A. DEIGHTON; publs *Fast Forward Series*, *MSI Reports* (4 a year).

National Bureau of Economic Research: 1050 Massachusetts Ave, Cambridge, MA 02138; tel. (617) 868-3900; e-mail info@nber.org; internet www.nber.org; f. 1920; fundamental qualitative analysis of the US economy; 50 dirs; br. in NY; Chair. JOHN CLARKESON; Pres. and CEO JAMES POTERBA; Treas. ROBERT MEDNICK; publs *Bulletin on Aging and Health*, *Digest* (12 a year), *NBER Reporter* (4 a year).

Nelson A. Rockefeller Center at Dartmouth College: 6082 Rockefeller Hall, Hanover, NH 03755; tel. (603) 646-3874; e-mail rockefeller.center@dartmouth.edu; internet rockefeller.dartmouth.edu; f. 1983; supports research into policy-related topics; Dir ANDREW A. SAMWICK; Deputy Dir SADHANA HALL; publ. *Direct Line* (4 a year).

Scripps Gerontology Center: Scripps Gerontology Center, 396 Upham Hall, Oxford, OH 45056; tel. (513) 529-2914; e-mail scripps@muohio.edu; internet www.scripps.muohio.edu; f. 1922 as Scripps Foundation for Research in Population Problems; present status 1972; attached to Miami Univ.; research incl. health, disability, and longevity; long-term care policy, systems, and services; workforce issues and older workers; income security; racial and ethnic diversity and ageing; translational health; quality improvement; supports undergraduate and graduate gerontology education at the univ.; promotes public awareness of ageing issues; specializes in evaluation research and provides applied research to legislators, public administrators, planners, service providers, gerontology students, academicians, other researchers and gen. public; library of 4,000 vols; Dir Dr SUZANNE R. KUNKEL.

EDUCATION

American Educational Research Association: 1430 K St, NW, Suite 1200, Washington, DC 20005; tel. (202) 238-3200; e-mail pubs@aera.net; internet www.aera.net; f. 1916; improves educational process by encouraging scholarly inquiry related to education and evaluation and by promoting the dissemination and practical application of research results; Pres. ARNETHA F. BALL; Pres.-Elect WILLIAM G. TIERNEY; Exec. Dir Dr FELICE J. LEVINE; publs *American Educational Research Journal*, *Educational Evaluation and Policy Analysis*, *Educational Researcher* (9 a year), *Journal of Educational and Behavioral Statistics*, *Review of Educational Research*, *Review of Research in Education* (1 a year).

Center for the Study of Higher Education: 400 Rackley Bldg, University Park, PA 16802; tel. (814) 865-6346; e-mail cshe@psu.edu; internet www.ed.psu.edu/cshe; f. 1969; attached to College of Education, Pennsylvania State Univ.; conducts theory-based research to improve higher education practice and policy; provides data and analysis to institutional, state, and fed. policymakers; supports graduate training for students in higher education programmes; Dir Dr ROBERT M. HENDRICKSON.

Cohn-Haddow Center for Judaic Studies: Wayne State Univ., 2311 Faculty Admin. Bldg, 656 W Kirby, Detroit, MI 48202; tel. (313) 577-2679; e-mail cohnhaddowcenter@wayne.edu; internet www.judaicstudies.wayne.edu; f. 1988; attached to Wayne State Univ.; serves as a resource to the Univ. and to the larger community in Jewish studies and related areas; conducts biannual int. confs, symposia and lectures; Dir Prof. HOWARD N. LUPOVITCH; Chair. CHARLES SOBERMAN.

Institute of Education Sciences (IES): 555 New Jersey Ave, NW, Washington, DC 20208; tel. (202) 219-1385; internet ies.ed.gov; f. 2002; fmrly the Office of Educational Research and Improvement (f. 1980), present name and status 2002; attached to US Dept of Education; funds research studies on ways to improve academic achievement, conducts large-scale evaluations of federal education programmes and reports a wide array of statistics on the condition of education, disseminates information through 10 regional education laboratories and 10 nat. research and devt centres; Dir JOHN Q. EASTON; publ. *National Assessment of Educational Progress*.

National Science Resources Center: 901 D St, SW, Suite 704B, Washington, DC 20024; tel. (202) 633-2966; internet www.nsrconline.org; f. 1985; operated by the Smithsonian Instn, National Academy of Sciences, National Academy of Engineering and Institute of Medicine to improve the teaching of science in schools; builds awareness of science education, provides new services and products to support science teaching, provides K-12 instructional materials; Dir THOMAS A. EMRICK (acting).

FINE AND PERFORMING ARTS

Institute of Contemporary Art: Porteous Bldg, 522 Congress St, Portland, ME 04101; tel. (207) 699-5040; e-mail ica@meca.edu; internet www.meca.edu/meca-life/campus-resources/ica; f. 1997; attached to Maine College of Art; research and devt of exhibitions; Dir DANIEL FULLER.

HISTORY, GEOGRAPHY AND ARCHAEOLOGY

Center for Reformation Research: Concordia Seminary, 801 Seminary Pl., St Louis, MO 63105; tel. (314) 505-7134; internet www.csl.edu/library/the-center-for-reformation-resources-collection; f. 1957 as Foundation for Reformation Research, present name 1974; attached to Concordia Seminary; microfilm library of original MSS and printed materials of the 15th and 16th centuries; reference library; library of 3,000 vols; Dir Prof. ROBERT ROSIN.

Leo Baeck Institute: Center for Jewish History, 15 W 16th St, New York, NY 10011; tel. (212) 744-6400; e-mail lbaeck@lbi.cjh.org; internet www.lbi.org; f. 1955; research and documentation on German Jewish history; exhibitions and lectures; library of 80,000 vols in German, English and Hebrew, archives of family papers, community histories, business and public records, 2,000 personal memoirs, 35,000 photographs, 10,000 archival records (access to archive and library materials is available only through reading room of the Center for Jewish History); art colln; Pres. BERNARD BLUM; Vice-Pres. MICHAEL A. BAMBERGER; Exec. Dir CAROL KAHN STRAUSS; Head Librarian RENATE EVERS; Treas. LAWRENCE RAMER; publs *Jüdischer Almanach des LBI* (in German), *LBI News*, *Leo Baeck Yearbook*, *Overview*, *Stammbaum*.

Mississippi Office of Geology: POB 2279, Jackson, MS 39225; 700 N State St, Jackson, MS 39202; tel. (601) 961-5500; internet deq.state.ms.us/mdeq.nsf/page/geology_home; f. 1850; researches the geological and mineral resources of the state, regulates the reclamation of mined land; Dir MICHAEL B. E. BOGRAD; publ. maps, charts, soil surveys, bulletins.

Paleontological Research Institution: 1259 Trumansburg Rd, Ithaca, NY 14850; tel. (607) 273-6623; e-mail info@museumoftheearth.org; internet www.museumoftheearth.org; f. 1932; focuses on fossil and modern molluscs from the SE USA, Caribbean, and Latin America; also works on abundant Devonian marine invertebrates and Pleistocene mastodons of New York State and general fields of evolutionary palaeobiology and macroevolution; colln of 3m. specimens; library of 50,000 vols; Dir Dr WARREN D. ALLMON; Assoc. Dir for Science Dr PAULA M. MIKKELSEN; publs *American Paleontologist* (4 a year), *Bulletins of American Paleontology* (2 a year), *Palaeontographica Americana* (irregular).

School for Advanced Research: POB 2188, Santa Fe, NM 87504-2188; 660 Garcia St, Santa Fe, NM 87505; tel. (505) 954-7200; e-mail info@sarsf.org; internet www.sarweb.org; f. 1907 as School of American Archaeology; centre for advanced studies in anthropology and the humanities; grants to 6 resident scholars, incl. 1 native American, annually; native artist fellows; advanced seminars in anthropology; anthropological publs; extensive collns in SW American

Indian art; library of 8,600 books and MSS; Pres. and CEO JAMES F. BROOKS; Chair. STEVE BOHLIN; Sec. DIANE STANLEY VENNEMA; Treas. JASON BRADY; publ. *Annual Review: Creativity and Research at SAR.*

LANGUAGE AND LITERATURE

Harry Ransom Center, The University of Texas at Austin: POB 7219, Austin, TX 78713-7219; 300 W 21st St, Austin, TX 78712; tel. (512) 471-8944; internet www .hrc.utexas.edu; f. 1957 as Humanities Research Center at The Univ. of Texas at Austin, present location 1972, current name adopted 1983; specializes in American, British and French literature and art since 19th century; library of 800,000 vols, 40m. MSS, 5m. photographs; Dir THOMAS F. STALEY.

H. H. Meeter Center for Calvin Studies: Hekman Library, 1855 Knollcrest Circle, SE, Grand Rapids, MI 49546; tel. (616) 526-7081; e-mail meeter@calvin.edu; internet www .calvin.edu/meeter; f. 1981; attached to Calvin College; specializes in John Calvin, Calvinism, the Reformation and early modern studies; library of 700,000 vols; Dir Dr KARIN MAAG; Curator PAUL FIELDS; publ. *John Calvin Bibliography.*

MEDICINE

American Association for Cancer Research: c/o Dr Margaret Foti, 615 Chestnut St, 17th Fl., Philadelphia, PA 19106-4404; tel. (215) 440-9300; e-mail aacr@aacr .org; internet www.aacr.org; f. 1907; facilitates communication and dissemination of knowledge among scientists and others dedicated to cancer research; Pres. Dr CHARLES L. SAWYERS; Pres.-Elect Dr CARLOS L. ARTEAGA; CEO Dr MARGARET FOTI; Treas. Dr WILLIAM N. HAIT; publs *Cancer Epidemiology, Biomarkers & Prevention* (12 a year), *Cancer Discovery* (12 a year), *Cancer Prevention Research* (12 a year), *Cancer Research* (24 a year), *Clinical Cancer Research* (12 a year), *Molecular Cancer Research* (12 a year), *Molecular Cancer Therapeutics* (12 a year).

American Federation for Medical Research: 500 Cummings Center, Suite 4550, Beverly, MA 01915; tel. (978) 927-8330; e-mail afmr@prri.com; internet www .afmr.org; f. 1940 as American Federation for Clinical Research, current name adopted 1996; asscn of scientists engaged in all areas of biomedical investigation-patient-oriented and basic research; fosters research into the medical sciences; provides leadership in articulating and publicizing the aims and goals of scientific research; disseminates the knowledge generated by medical research; Pres. Dr SHARMA S. PRABHAKAR; Sec. and Treas. Dr ROBERT J. FREISHTAT; publ. *Journal of Investigative Medicine* (24 a year).

American Pediatric Society/Society for Pediatric Research: 3400 Research Forest Dr., Suite B-7, The Woodlands, TX 77381; tel. (281) 419-0052; e-mail info@aps-spr.org; internet www.aps-spr.org; f. 1929; Exec. Dir DEBBIE ANAGNOSTELIS; Pres. Dr F. BRUDER STAPLETON; Vice-Pres. Dr BARBARA J. STOLL; Sec and Treas. Dr JUDY L. ASCHNER.

Association for Research in Nervous and Mental Disease: Weill Medical College of Cornell Univ., Dept of Psychiatry, 1300 York Ave, POB 171, Room F-1231, New York, NY 10065; tel. (212) 746-3770; e-mail daw2026@med.cornell.edu; internet www .arnmd.org; f. 1920; brings together scientists from the fields of psychiatry, neurology and neuroscience to advance the scientific knowledge and understanding of neuropsychiatry at all levels; promotes dissemination of information about nature of scientific discovery and results and implications of latest neuropsychiatric research; provide annual conf. that presents ground-breaking research in a topical area encouraging the participation and attendance of physicians and trainees in these fields; Chair. JACK D. BARCHAS; Exec. Dir ANNLOUISE GOODERMUTH; Sec. and Treas. FRANCIS LEE; publ. *Clinical Neuroscience Research* (6 a year).

Association for Research in Vision and Ophthalmology: 1801 Rockville Pike, Suite 400, Rockville, MD 20852; tel. (240) 221-2900; e-mail arvo@arvo.org; internet www .arvo.org; f. 1928 as Asscn for Research in Ophthalmology in Washington, DC, current name adopted 1970, present location 2001; encourages and assists research, training, publication and dissemination of knowledge in vision and ophthalmology; Pres. Dr JEFFREY. H. BOATRIGHT; Pres.-Elect Dr PENG T. KHAW; Exec. Dir Dr JOANNE G. ANGLE; Vice-Pres. Dr PAUL MITCHELL; Vice-Pres. Dr ROBERT FRANCIS MILLER; publs *Investigative Ophthalmology and Visual Science* (online, www.iovs.org), *Journal of Vision* (irregular, online, www.journalofvision.org).

Barbara Ann Karmanos Cancer Institute: 4100 John R., Detroit, MI 48201; e-mail info@karmanos.org; internet www.karmanos .org; f. 1943 as Detroit Institute for Cancer Research, present name 1995; attached to Wayne State Univ., School of Medicine; focuses on prevention, early detection, treatment and eradication of cancer; conducts basic, behavioural, clinical, epidemiological and translational research; Pres. and CEO Dr GEROLD BEPLER; publ. *Karmanos Hope* (4 a year).

Bioengineering Center: 818 W Hancock, Detroit, MI 48201; tel. (313) 577-0252; internet www.bioengineeringcenter.org; f. 1939; attached to Biomedical Engineering Dept, College of Engineering, Wayne State Univ.; conducts research in areas of impact trauma, low back pain and orthopaedic biomechanics; Dir Prof. Dr KING H. YANG.

California Pacific Medical Center Research Institute: POB 7999, San Francisco, CA 94120; tel. (415) 600-1600; internet www.cpmc.org/professionals/research; f. 1993 by merger of Medical Research Institute of San Francisco with California Pacific Medical Center; non-profit research div. of medical centre conducting patient-orientated research in arthritis, HIV/AIDS, cancer, incl. leukemia and monoclonal antibodies, heart disease, immunology and infectious diseases, artificial heart research, organ transplantation and preservation, neurology, maternal foetal medicine, child health and human devt; CEO WARREN S. BROWNER; Scientific Dir Dr MICHAEL C. ROWBOTHAM; publ. *Currents* (1 a year).

Center for Molecular Medicine and Genetics: 3127 Scott Hall, 540 E Canfield, Detroit, MI 48201; tel. (313) 577-5323; e-mail newgradapp@wayne.edu; internet cmmg.biosci.wayne.edu; f. 1986; attached to School of Medicine, Wayne State Univ.; focuses on molecular biology, molecular medicine, and genetics to increase understanding, diagnosis, treatment and prevention of human disease; library of 3,000 vols; Dir Prof. Dr LAWRENCE I. GROSSMAN.

Center to Advance Palliative-Care Excellence: 4201 St Antoine, Suite 5C-UHC, Detroit, MI 48201; tel. (313) 577-5751; internet capewayne.med.wayne.edu; attached to School of Medicine, Wayne State Univ.; interdisciplinary community of scholars, educators, researchers and clinicians dedicated to improving lives of people suffering from terminal illness; Dir Dr ROBERT J. ZALENSKI.

Developmental Disabilities Institute: Wayne State Univ., 4809 Woodward Ave, Suite 268, Dettroit, MI 48202; tel. (313) 577-2654; e-mail ddi@wayne.edu; internet ddi .wayne.edu; attached to Wayne State Univ.; works towards devt of inclusive communities, enhancement of quality of life of people with disabilities; enriches the field of disability research and service; Dir Dr BARBARA LEROY.

Eppley Institute for Research in Cancer and Allied Diseases: 985950 Nebraska Medical Center, Omaha, NE 68198-5950; tel. (402) 559-4090; e-mail info@eppleyits .com; internet www.unmc.edu/eppley; f. 1960; attached to Univ. of Nebraska Medical Center; understands causes of cancer; researches to improve methods for diagnosis of cancer and treatment and prevention of cancer and similar disorders; offers undergraduate, graduate and postdoctoral students; Dir Dr KENNETH H. COWAN.

Fox Chase Cancer Center: 333 Cottman Ave, Philadelphia, PA 19111-2497; tel. (215) 728-7784; internet www.fccc.edu/research; f. 1904 as American Oncologic Hospital; researches on new technologies and cancer treatment, incl. fundamental mechanisms of biomolecular reactions and treatment; library of 23,000 vols, incl. 5,000 books and 450 scientific journals; Chair. DAVID G. MARSHALL; Pres. and CEO Dr MICHAEL V. SEIDEN; Chief Scientific Officer JONATHAN CHERNOFF.

Gallaudet Research Institute: Dawes House, 800 Florida Ave, NE, Washington, DC 20002-3695; tel. (202) 651-5575; internet www.gallaudet.edu/gallaudet_research_institute; attached to Gallaudet Univ.; conducts studies of language and learning processes in American Sign Language and English among deaf people from diverse cultural and educational backgrounds; Dir CAROL J. ERTING; publ. *Deaf Studies Digital Journal.*

Gerontology Institute: POB 3984, Atlanta, GA 30302-3984; tel. (404) 413-5210; e-mail gerontology@gsu.edu; internet www.gsu.edu/ gerontology; attached to College of Arts and Sciences, Georgia State Univ.; develops and coordinates research, instruction and service in gerontology; research areas incl. long-term care of older persons with disabilities and ethnicity and ageing; Dir Prof. ELISABETH O. BURGESS.

Huntington Medical Research Institutes: 734 Fairmount Ave, Pasadena, CA 91105-3104; tel. (626) 397-5805; internet www.hmri.org; f. 1952; oncology, cell biology, differentiated cell culture, cancer genetics, prostate cancer, immunotherapy, biomedical magnetic resonance spectroscopy, cardiology, devt of neural prosthetic devices; Pres. Dr WILLIAM OPEL.

Institute of Gerontology: Wayne State Uinv., 87 E Ferry St, 226 Knapp Bldg, Detroit, MI 48202; tel. (313) 664-2600; e-mail ioginfo@wayne.edu; internet www.iog .wayne.edu; attached to Wayne State Univ.; research into social and behavioural sciences, cognitive neuroscience and issues related to ageing and urban health; offers pre-doctoral, graduate certificate and continuing education programmes in gerontology; Dir Dr PETER LICHTENBERG; Deputy Dir Dr CATHY LYSACK.

Institute of Public Health: Georgia State Univ., POB 3995, Atlanta, GA 30302-3995; Urban Life Bldg, 140 Decatur St, Suite 848, Atlanta, GA 30303; tel. (404) 413-1130; e-mail publichealth@gsu.edu; internet publichealth.gsu.edu; f. 2004; attached to Georgia State Univ.; focuses on finding solutions to pressing urban health issues; offers PhD in public health and Masters in public health with spec. emphasis on prevention sciences, health promotion and behaviour or health policy and management; Dir Prof. Dr MICHAEL ERIKSON.

Jackson Laboratory: 600 Main St, Bar Harbor, ME 04609-1500; tel. (207) 288-6000; e-mail pubinfo@jax.org; internet www.jax .org; f. 1929; research in molecular genetics, cell biology, biochemistry, immunology and physiological genetics; library of 4,000 vols, 5,000 ejournals, 80 print journals, 5,000 photographs; Assoc. Dir and Chair. of Research Dr ROBERT BRAUN; publs *Inside the Jackson Laboratory* (4 a year), *Search*, *Scientific Report* (1 a year), *Training for Research* (1 a year).

Lovelace Respiratory Research Institute: 2425 Ridgecrest Dr., SE, Albuquerque, NM 87108-5127; tel. (505) 348-9400; e-mail info@lrri.org; internet www.lrri.org; f. 1947; research into prevention, treatment, and cure of respiratory diseases; areas of research incl. asthma, emphysema, lung cancer, inhalation toxicology, aerosol science, inhalation drug delivery, bronchitis, allergies, science service contracting, pulmonary fibrosis, pulmonary hypertension, infectious disease, radiation studies, chemical exposure research and clinical trials; library of 10,000 vols, 25,000 bound journals, 116 current journals; Pres. and CEO ROBERT RUBIN; publs *Advances*, *Breathe*.

Mayo Clinic: 200 First St SW, Rochester, MN 55905; tel. (507) 284-2511; internet www .mayoresearch.mayo.edu/mayo/research/ departments-mcr.cfm; f. 1919; clinical medicine, medical research, graduate and undergraduate education; also located at Scottsdale, AZ, and Jacksonville, FL; library of 275,000 vols and 3,500 periodicals; Chair. MARILYN CARLSON NELSON; Pres. and CEO JOHN H. NOSEWORTHY; Dir for Research Dr ROBERT A. RIZZA; publs *Discovery's Edge* (2 a year, online), *Forefront* (1 a year), *Mayo Clinic Magazine* (2 a year), *Mayo Clinic Proceedings* (12 a year), *Sharing Mayo Clinic* (4 a year).

Memorial Sloan-Kettering Cancer Center: 1275 York Ave, New York, NY 10065; tel. (212) 639-2000; e-mail publicaffairs@ mskcc.org; internet www.mskcc.org; f. 1884 as New York Cancer Hospital, present location 1939, present status and name 1960; research into physical and biological sciences contributing to devt of new and better therapies for treatment of cancer; postdoctoral research training in laboratory investigations with scientific staff; graduate instruction with Cornell Univ.; Chair. DOUGLAS A. WARNER, III; Pres. and CEO Dr CRAIG B. THOMSON; Sec. NORMAN C. SELBY; Treas. CLIFTON S. ROBBINS.

Menninger: 2801 Gessner Dr., Houston, TX 77280-9045; tel. (713) 333-3320; e-mail developmentoffice@menninger.edu; internet www.menningerclinic.com; f. 1925, present location 2003; attached to Baylor College of Medicine and Methodist Hospital; non-profit mental health centre for inpatient and outpatient treatment of mental illness through preventive psychiatry, clinical treatment, research and professional education; library of 50,000 vols; Pres. and CEO IAN AITKEN; publs *Bulletin of the Menninger Clinic* (4 a year), *Menninger Perspective* (4 a year).

Munroe-Meyer Institute: 985450 Nebraska Medical Center, Omaha, NE 68198-5450; tel. (402) 559-6430; e-mail munroemeyer@unmc.edu; internet www .unmc.edu/mmi; f. 1968; attached to Univ. of Nebraska Medical Center; conducts basic investigations in developmental neurosciences like genetics of autism and other neurodevelopmental disorders to applied

studies of treatments for disorders of movement, severe behaviour, feeding, communication, sleep, paediatric pain and learning; Dir Dr J. MICHAEL LEIBOWITZ.

National Institutes of Health: 9000 Rockville Pike, Bethesda, MD 20892; tel. (301) 496-4000; e-mail nihinfo@od.nih.gov; internet www.nih.gov; f. 1887; attached to US Dept of Health and Human Services; biomedical research, research training, and biomedical communications; Nat. Library of Medicine: see under Libraries and Archives; Dir Dr FRANCIS S. COLLINS.

Constituent Institutes:

Eunice Kennedy Shriver National Institute of Child Health and Human Development: Bldg 31, Room 2A32, MSC 2425, 31 Center Dr., Bethesda, MD 20892-2425; tel. (301) 496-5133; e-mail nichdinformationresourcecenter@mail.nih .gov; internet www.nichd.nih.gov; f. 1962; supports, fosters and coordinates research and training in areas of maternal health, child health and human devt, focusing on the continuing process of growth and devt, biological and behavioural; also supports research into the population sciences, incl. contraceptive devt and evaluation, reproductive health, behavioural and demographic research, and medical rehabilitation; Dir Dr ALLAN GUTTMACHER.

National Cancer Institute: National Cancer Institute Public Inquiries Office, Cancer Information Service, 9609 Medical Center Dr., Bethesda, MD 20892-9760; tel. (301) 435-3848; e-mail cancergovstaff@ mail.nih.gov; internet www.cancer.gov; f. 1937; principal fed. govt agency for cancer research; supports research into the causes, prevention, early detection and treatment of cancer, and into supportive care; cooperates with state and local health agencies and voluntary bodies; Dir Dr HAROLD E. VARMUS.

National Eye Institute: Information Office, 31 Center Dr., MSC 2510, Bethesda, MD 20892-2510; tel. (301) 496-5248; e-mail 2020@nei.nih.gov; internet www.nei.nih .gov; f. 1968; conducts and supports research, training, health information dissemination, and other programmes relating to blinding eye diseases, visual disorders, mechanisms of visual function, preservation of sight; special health problems and requirements of the blind; research performed in Institute's own laboratories and through contracts; supports training and directs Nat. Eye Health Education Program; Dir Dr PAUL A. SIEVING; publ. *Eye on NEI* (12 a year, online).

National Heart, Lung and Blood Institute: POB 30105, Bethesda, MD 20824-0105; Bldg 31, Room 5A52, 31 Center Dr., MSC 2486, Bethesda, MD 20892; tel. (301) 592-8573; e-mail nhlbiinfo@nhlbi.nih.gov; internet www.nhlbi.nih.gov; f. 1948 as Nat. Heart Institute, redesignated 1969 and 1976; performs and supports research into diseases of the heart, blood vessels, lungs (exclusive of pulmonary malignancies) and blood; Dir Dr SUSAN B. SHURIN (acting).

National Human Genome Research Institute (NHGRI): Bldg 31, Room 4B09, 31 Center Dr., MSC 2152, 9000 Rockville Pike Bethesda, MD 20892-2152; tel. (301) 402-0911; internet www.genome .gov; f. 1989 as National Center for Human Genome Research; directs and supports work on the sequencing of the human genome; funds research into the genome's structure, function and role in health and disease; supports studies on the ethical,

legal and social implications (ELSI) of genome research; Dir Dr ERIC D. GREEN.

National Institute for Biomedical Imaging and Bioengineering (NIBIB): Clinical Center Office of Communications, 10 Cloister Court, Bldg 61, Room 100, Bethesda, MD 20892; tel. (301) 496-2563; e-mail ni@nibib.nih.gov; internet www .nibib.nih.gov; f. 2000; accelerates pace of discovery and speeds devt of biomedical technologies that prevent illnesses or treat them when they strike; Dir Dr RODERIC I. PETTIGREW.

National Institute of Allergy and Infectious Diseases: 6610 Rockledge Dr., MSC 6612, Bethesda, MD 20892-6612; tel. (301) 496-5717; e-mail ocpostoffice@niaid.nih.gov; internet www .niaid.nih.gov; f. 1887, current name adopted 1955; supports basic and translational research to prevent, diagnose and treat infectious diseases such as HIV/AIDS and other sexually transmitted infections, influenza, tuberculosis, malaria and illness from potential agents of bioterrorism; supports research into transplantation and immune-related illnesses, incl. autoimmune disorders, asthma and allergies; Dir Dr ANTHONY S. FAUCI.

National Institute of Arthritis and Musculoskeletal and Skin Diseases: Bldg 31, Room 4C02, 31 Center Dr., MSC 2350, Bethesda, MD 20892-2350; tel. (301) 496-8190; e-mail niamsinfo@mail.nih.gov; internet www.niams.nih.gov; f. 1986; research into the causes, treatment and prevention of arthritis and musculoskeletal and skin diseases; training of basic and clinical scientists to carry out this research; dissemination of information on progress in research; Dir Dr STEPHEN I. KATZ; Deputy Dir ROBERT H. CARTER; publs *NIAMS Update* (12 a year), *Multicultural Outreach News* (4 a year).

National Institute of Dental and Craniofacial Research: Nat. Institutes of Health, 31 Center Dr., MSC 2290, Bethesda, MD 20892-2190; tel. (866) 232-4528; e-mail nidcrinfo@mail.nih.gov; internet www.nidcr.nih.gov; f. 1948; conducts and supports research and training with the aim of preventing, diagnosing and treating dental, oral and craniofacial diseases and conditions; Dir Dr MARTHA J. SOMERMAN.

National Institute of Diabetes and Digestive and Kidney Diseases: Office of Communications and Public Liaison, Bldg 31, Rm 9A06 31 Center Dr., MSC 2560, Bethesda, MD 20892-2560; tel. (301) 496-3583; e-mail niddk_inquiries@nih.gov; internet www.niddk.nih.gov; f. 1950 as Nat. Institute of Arthritis and Metabolic Diseases, present name 1986; conducts and supports research into diabetes, endocrinology, metabolic diseases, digestive diseases, nutrition, kidney and urologic diseases and haematology; information and education activities; Dir Dr GRIFFIN P. RODGERS.

National Institute of Environmental Health Sciences: POB 12233, MD K3-16 Research Triangle Park, NC 27709-2233; tel. (919) 541-3345; internet www.niehs .nih.gov; f. 1969; conducts, fosters and coordinates research into the biological effects of chemical, physical and biological substances present in or introduced into the environment; Dir Dr LINDA S. BIRNBAUM; publ. *Environmental Health Perspectives* (12 a year).

National Institute of General Medical Sciences: 45 Center Dr., MSC 6200, Bethesda, MD 20892-6200; tel. (301) 496-

7301; e-mail info@nigms.nih.gov; internet www.nigms.nih.gov; f. 1962; supports a programme of research and training in the basic medical sciences; Dir Dr JON LORSCH; publ. *Findings* (1 a year).

National Institute of Mental Health (NIMH): Science Writing, Press, and Dissemination Br., 6001 Exec. Blvd, Room 8184, MSC 9663, Bethesda, MD 20892-9663; tel. (301) 443-4513; e-mail nimhinfo@nih.gov; internet www.nimh.nih.gov; f. 1946; improves mental health through biomedical research into the mind, brain and behaviour; Dir Dr THOMAS R. INSEL.

National Institute of Neurological Disorders and Stroke: POB 5801, Bethesda, MD 20284; tel. (301) 496-5751; e-mail braininfo@ninds.nih.gov; internet www.ninds.nih.gov; f. 1950; conducts, supports, fosters and coordinates research into the causes, prevention, diagnosis and treatment of disorders of the brain and nervous system; Dir Dr STORY C. LANDIS.

National Institute of Nursing Research: c/o Nat. Institutes of Health, 31 Center Dr., Room 5B10, Bethesda, MD 20892-2178; tel. (301) 496-0207; internet www.ninr.nih.gov; f. 1985, present status 1993; supports and conducts scientific research and research training to strengthen nursing practice and health care for prevention and amelioration of disease and disability; Dir Dr PATRICIA A. GRADY.

National Institute on Aging: Bldg 31, Room 5C27, 31 Center Dr., MSC 2292, Bethesda, MD 20892; tel. (301) 496-1752; e-mail nianews3@mail.nih.gov; internet www.nia.nih.gov; f. 1974; conducts and supports biomedical, social and behavioural research and training related to the ageing process and diseases, and other special problems and needs of the aged; Dir Dr RICHARD J. HODES.

National Institute on Alcohol Abuse and Alcoholism (NIAAA): 5635 Fishers Lane, MSC 9304, Bethesda, MD 20892-9304; tel. (301) 443-3860; e-mail niaaaweb-r@exchange.nih.gov; internet www.niaaa.nih.gov; f. 1970; conducts and supports research into a wide range of scientific areas, incl. genetics, neuroscience, epidemiology, health risks and benefits of alcohol consumption, prevention and treatment; Dir Dr GEORGE KOOB; publs *Alcohol Alert* (4 a year), *Alcohol Research & Health* (4 a year).

National Institute on Deafness and Other Communication Disorders: 31 Center Dr., MSC 2320, Bethesda, MD 20892-2320; tel. (301) 496-7243; e-mail nidcdinfo@nidcd.nih.gov; internet www.nidcd.nih.gov; f. 1988; supports and conducts research into the normal processes and diseases of human communication, incl. hearing, balance, smell, taste, voice, speech and language; fosters training and disseminates science-based health information; Dir Dr JAMES F. BATTEY, JR.

National Institute on Drug Abuse (NIDA): 6001 Executive Blvd, Room 5213, Bethesda, MD 20892-9561; tel. (301) 443-1124; e-mail information@nida.nih.gov; internet www.nida.nih.gov; f. 1974; provides strategic support and conducts research on improving prevention and treatment on drug abuse and addiction; Dir Dr NORA D. VOLKOW.

National Institute on Minority Health and Health Disparities: 6707 Democracy Blvd, Suite 800, Bethesda, MD 20892-5465; tel. (301) 402-1366; e-mail ncmhdinfo@od.nih.gov; internet www.ncmhd.nih.gov; f. 1993; promotes, assists

and supports research capacity building activities in the minority and medically under-served communities; Dir Dr JOHN RUFFIN.

Naval Aerospace Medical Institute: 340 Hulse Rd, Pensacola, FL 32508-104; tel. (850) 452-2933; e-mail nomi-info@med.navy.mil; internet www.med.navy.mil/sites/navmedmpte/nomi/nami; f. 1939; provides expert aeromedical consultation; develops services and application of aeromedical standards; trains aeromedical personnel for operational assignments; library of 20,000 vols; Officer in Charge Capt. CHARLES A. CICCONE.

Schepens Eye Research Institute—Massachusetts Eye and Ear Foundation: 20 Staniford St, Boston, MA 02114; tel. (617) 912-0100; e-mail development@schepens.harvard.edu; internet www.theschepens.org; f. 1950 as Retina Foundation, present name and status 2011; basic and clinical research into causes, prevention and treatment of eye diseases, devt of diagnostic and therapeutic devices, instruments and techniques for ophthalmology, study of the processes of vision; library of 200 vols, 100 journals; Chair. KENNETT F. BURNES; Pres. JOHN FERNANDEZ; publ. *Sundial*.

Texas Biomedical Research Institute: POB 760549, San Antonio, TX 78425-0549; 7620 NW Loop 410, San Antonio, TX 78227-5301; tel. (210) 258-9400; internet www.sfbr.org; f. 1941, fmrly Southwest Foundation for Research and Education; basic research in biomedical sciences; designated in 1999 one of the regional primate research centres (Southwest Regional Primate Research Center); library of 50,000 journal vols; 6,700 books; Chair. JOHN R. HURD; Pres. KENNETH P. TREVETT; Chief Scientific Officer Dr JOHN L. VANDEBERG; publ. *Progress in Biomedical Research* (irregular).

Wistar Institute of Anatomy and Biology: 3601 Spruce St, Philadelphia, PA 19104; tel. (215) 898-3700; internet www.wistar.org; f. 1892, present status 1972; ind. research centre, cellular and subcellular research into human diseases; library of 10,000 vols; Pres. and CEO Dr RUSSEL E. KAUFMAN; publ. *Focus* (2 a year).

Worcester Foundation for Biomedical Research: 222 Maple Ave, Shrewsbury, MA 01545; tel. (508) 842-8921; f. 1944, present name 1995, present status 1997; attached to Univ. of Massachusetts Medical School; supports biomedical research at the Univ. of Massachusetts Medical School, ind. biomedical research centre; emphasis on cell biology, molecular biology, neurobiology and developmental-reproductive biology; conducts joint PhD programme with Clark Univ., Worcester Polytechnic Inst. and Univ. of Massachusetts Medical School; library of 25,000 vols; spec. collns: cellular/molecular biology, developmental biology, neurobiology, endocrine/reproductive biology; Chair. MORTON H. SIGEL; Sec. WARNER S. FLETCHER; publs *Research Reporter* (4 a year), *Scientific Report*.

NATURAL SCIENCES

General

Bioanthropology Research Institute: 275 Mount Carmel Ave, Hamden, CT 06518-1908; tel. (203) 582-8200; internet www.quinnipiac.edu/x1978.xml; f. 1998; attached to School of Health Sciences, Quinnipiac Univ.; research areas incl. biology, archaeology, anthropology and palaeopathology through diagnostic imaging, video endoscopy and laboratory analysis; Co-Exec. Dir RONALD BECKETT; Co-Exec. Dir Prof. GERALD CONLOGUE.

Carnegie Institution for Science: 1530 P St, NW, Washington, DC 20005; tel. (202) 387-6400; internet www.carnegiescience.edu; f. 1902; research and education in astronomy, developmental biology, Earth and planetary sciences, global ecology and plant biology; Chair. Board of Trustees MICHAEL GELLERT; Pres. Dr RICHARD A. MESERVE; publs *Carnegie Science* (3 a year), *Yearbook*

Attached Departments:

Department of Embryology: 3520 San Martin Dr., Baltimore, MD 21218; tel. (410) 246-3001; internet www.ciwemb.edu; f. 1913; cellular, developmental and genetic biology; Dir ALLAN C. SPRADLING.

Department of Global Ecology: 260 Panama St, Stanford, CA 94305; tel. (650) 462-1047; e-mail cfield@ciw.edu; internet dge.stanford.edu; f. 2002; located in Stanford Univ.; conducts basic research into the interactions among the earth's ecosystems, land, atmosphere and oceans; Dir CHRISTOPHER B. FIELD; publ. *Science Literature*.

Department of Plant Biology: 260 Panama St, Stanford, CA 94305; tel. (650) 325-1521; internet dpb.carnegiescience.edu; f. 1903 as Desert Laboratory; basic problems of how plants function and grow; Dir WOLF B. FROMMER.

Department of Terrestrial Magnetism: 5241 Broad Branch Rd, NW, Washington, DC 20015-1305; tel. (202) 478-8820; internet www.dtm.ciw.edu; f. 1904; maps the geomagnetic field of the Earth; discovers planets outside the solar system; determines age and structure of universe; studies causes of earthquakes and volcanoes; Dir SEAN C. SOLOMON.

Geophysical Laboratory: 5251 Broad Branch Rd, NW, Washington, DC 20015; tel. (202) 478-8900; internet www.gl.ciw.edu; f. 1905, current location 1990; understands processes that control composition and structure of the Earth; also researches biology of the Earth, chemistry and physics; Dir GEORGE D. CODY.

Observatories of the Carnegie Institution: 813 Santa Barbara St, Pasadena, CA 91101; tel. (626) 577-1122; e-mail questions@obs.carnegiescience.edu; internet www.obs.carnegiescience.edu; f. 1904 as Mount Wilson Solar Observatory; basic research into astronomy; studies early universe, Milky Way, galaxies; Dir WENDY FREEDMAN.

Institute for Advanced Study: Einstein Dr., Princeton, NJ 08540; tel. (609) 734-8000; e-mail contactus@ias.edu; internet www.ias.edu; f. 1930; encourages and supports fundamental research into the sciences and humanities; Dir ROBBERT DIJKGRAAF.

MRI Global: 425 Volker Blvd, Kansas City, MO 64110-2241; tel. (816) 753-7600; internet www.mriglobal.org; f. 1944 as Midwest Research Institute, present name 2011; non-profit org.; conducts programmes in life sciences, agriculture and food safety, energy and environment, engineering and infrastructure, and nat. security and defence; Pres. and CEO Dr MICHAEL F. HELMSTETTER; Exec. Vice-Pres. Dr DAN E. ARVIZU; Vice-Pres. and Chief Information Officer LYLA PERRODIN; Sr Vice-Pres. and Chief Financial Officer R. THOMAS FLEENER; Sr Vice-Pres. and Dir for Technical Operations Dr THOMAS M. SACK.

Southern Research: 2000 Ninth Ave. S, POB 55305, Birmingham, AL 35205-5305; tel. (205) 581-2000; internet www.southernresearch.org; f. 1941; attached to Univ. of Alabama, Birmingham; contract scientific research in the areas of advanced engineering, environmental protection, drug discovery and preclinical drug devt; library of 40,000 vols; Pres. and CEO Dr JOHN A. SECRIST, III; Chair. Dr CAROL GARRISON; Sec. Dr SHIRLEY SALLOWAY KAHN; Treas. RICHARD MARGISON.

World Resources Institute: 10 G St NE, Suite 800, Washington, DC 20002; tel. (202) 729-7600; e-mail pveit@wri.org; internet www.wri.org; f. 1982; provides information about global resources and environmental conditions, analysis of emerging issues, and devt of creative yet workable policy responses; seeks to deepen public understanding by publishing a variety of reports and papers, undertaking briefings, seminars and confs, and offering material for use in the press and on air; br. in Beijing, China; library of 10,000 vols, 200 journals; Pres. and Exec Vice-Pres. and Man. Dir MANISH BAPNA.

Biological Sciences

Boyce Thompson Institute for Plant Research: 533 Tower Rd, Ithaca, NY 14853-1801; tel. (607) 254-1234; e-mail bmr6@cornell.edu; internet bti.cornell.edu; f. 1924; non-profit ind. affiliate of Cornell Univ.; research into plants and human health, incl. air and water pollution, biochemistry, entomology, molecular biology, plant pathology, plant physiology; library of 4,700 vols; Chair. EZRA CORNELL; CEO and Pres. Dr DAVID B. STERN; Vice-Pres. for Research Dr ERIC RICHARDS; Sec. DONNA L. CLAES; Treas. SOPHIA DARLING; publ. *Transcript* (4 a year).

Center for Bioethics & Human Dignity: 2065 Half Day Rd, Deerfield, IL 60015; tel. (847) 317-8180; e-mail info@cbhd.org; internet www.cbhd.org; f. 1994, present status 2007; attached to Trinity Int. Univ.; Exec. Dir Dr PAIGE C. CUNNINGHAM; Man. Dir Dr MICHAEL J. SLEASMAN; Dir for Devt JOEL DILLON.

Coastal Institute: Narragansett Bay Campus, Rm 124, Univ. of Rhode Island, Narragansett, RI 02882; tel. (401) 874-6513; e-mail ci@edc.uri.edu; internet www.ci.uri.edu; attached to Univ. of Rhode Island; advances knowledge and develops solutions to environmental problems in coastal ecosystem; Dir JUDITH SWIFT.

Cold Spring Harbor Laboratory: 1 Bungtown Rd, Cold Spring Harbor, NY 11724; tel. (516) 367-8800; e-mail pubaff@cshl.edu; internet www.cshl.org; f. 1890, present status 1962, current name adopted 1970; non-profit instn; research into bioinformatics and genomics, cancer biology, molecular neuroscience, plant genetics, professional education, structural biology and DNA literacy; library of 30,000 vols, special collns on history of science and genetics; Chair. JAMIE C. NICHOLLS; Pres Dr BRUCE W. STILLMAN; Chief Operating Officer W. DILLAWAY AYRES, JR; Sec. EDWARD TRAVAGLIANTI; Treas. LEO A. GUTHART; publs *Cold Spring Harbor Perspectives in Biology* (12 a year, online, www.cshperspectives.cshlp.org), *Cold Spring Harbor Protocols* (12 a year), *Genes & Development* (6 a year), *Genome Research* (12 a year), *Learning & Memory* (6 a year), *RNA* (12 a year, online, www.rnajournal.cshlp.org).

Desert Research Institute: 2215 Raggio Parkway, Reno, NV 89512; tel. (775) 673-7300; internet www.dri.edu; f. 1959, present status 1969; attached to Nevada System of Higher Education; conducts research in air, land and life and water quality across Nevada, the USA and on every continent; campuses in Reno and Las Vegas; Pres. Dr STEPHEN G. WELLS; Exec. Vice-Pres. for Research Dr TERRENCE SURLES; Sr Vice-Pres. for Finance and Admin. and Chief

Operations Officer ELLEN OPPENHEIM; Vice-Pres. for Devt RUSSEL KOST; Library Dir MELANIE SCOTT.

Institute of Arctic Studies: 6048 Haldeman Center, Dartmouth College, Hanover, NH 03755; tel. (603) 646-2023; e-mail dickey.center@dartmouth.edu; internet www.dartmouth.edu/~arctic; f. 1989; attached to The John Sloan Dickey Center for Int. Understanding, Dartmouth College; focuses on environmental, cultural and political dimensions of the N and effect of climate change; Dir ROSS VIRGINIA.

Institute for Energy & the Environment: New Mexico State Univ., POB 3000, Las Cruces, NM 88003-8001; tel. (575) 646-2038; e-mail iee@nmsu.edu; internet iee.nmsu.edu; attached to New Mexico State Univ.; centres on devt, transfer, promotion and commercialization of renewable energy technologies through advancing education, training, outreach and research on areas related to the environment, energy, water and food safety; meets increased global energy and energy-related needs; fosters advanced electric power delivery, public policy, alternative resources, materials sciences, and environmental surety; Dir Prof. ABBAS GHASSEMI.

Institute of Environmental Health Science: Eugene Applebaum College of Pharmacy and Health Sciences, Wayne State Univ., 259 Mack Ave, Rm 5137, Detroit, MI 48201; tel. (313) 577-0100; e-mail iehs_info@wayne.edu; internet www.iehs.wayne.edu; attached to Eugene Applebaum College of Pharmacy and Health Sciences, Wayne State Univ.; engages in basic mechanistic studies using animal and cellular models and human investigations to determine the complex role of environmental exposure in disease devt; Dir Dr MELISSA RUNGE-MORRIS.

Lincoln Park Zoological Gardens: 2001 N Clark St, Chicago, IL 60614; tel. (312) 742-2000; e-mail guestservices@lpzoo.org; internet www.lpzoo.org; f. 1868; specimens of mammals, birds, reptiles, and amphibians; farm; specialities: great apes, primates, perching birds, snakes, big cats; spec. programmes: Farm in the Zoo, Travelling Zoo and Endangered Species educational programmes; scientific studies incl. nutrition, behaviour, reproductive biology, physiology, African, Asian and S American field work; research centres: Alexander Center for Applied Population Biology, Davee Center for Epidemiology and Endocrinology and Lester E. Fisher Center for the Study and Conservation of Apes; library of 2,000 vols; Chair. JOHN ALEXANDER; Pres. and CEO KEVIN J. BELL; publ. *Lincoln Park Zoo Magazine* (3 a year).

MBL: 7 MBL St, Woods Hole, MA 02543; tel. (508) 289-7423; e-mail comm@mbl.edu; internet www.mbl.edu; f. 1888 as Marine Biological Laboratory; research and teaching instn; offers courses and seminars on ecology, behaviour, developmental biology, microbiology, neurobiology, parasitology, cell and molecular biology and biological techniques, global infectious diseases; library of 150,000 vols, 3,000 periodicals; Chair. JOHN W. ROWE; Dir and CEO GARY G. BORISY; publs *Catalyst* (2 a year), *MBL Guide to Research and Education* (1 a year), *The Biological Bulletin* (6 a year).

Missouri Botanical Garden: 4344 Shaw Blvd., St Louis, MO 63110; tel. (314) 577-5100; e-mail tourism@mobot.org; internet www.mobot.org; f. 1859; botanical research, exploration, education and display, with emphases on monographic and floristic studies in N America, tropical Latin America and Africa; archives and non-book materials; herbarium colln (5.8m. vascular plants and

300,000 bryophytes); library of 160,300 vols, 2,000 current periodicals, 3,000 reference works, 40,000 microfiche, 500 images (incl. glass plate negatives, hand-tinted prints, stereographs, postcards and MSS); spec. collns: Art (7,000 items), Ewan (11,000 vols), Linnaean (900 vols), Niederlander (600 vols), Sturtevant Pre-Linnaean (1,000 vols), Steere (3, 000, vols incl. titles on bryology and pamphlets); also incl. rare book colln (3,000 vols), folio colln (1,000 vols), maps and atlas colln (7,000 items); Chair. ARNOLD W. DONALD; Pres. Dr PETER WYSE JACKSON; publs *Annals of the Missouri Botanical Garden* (4 a year), *Bulletin* (7 a year), *Novon* (4 a year).

Moss Landing Marine Laboratories: 8272 Moss Landing Rd, Moss Landing, CA 95039; tel. (831) 771-4400; e-mail frontdesk@mlml.calstate.edu; internet www.mlml.calstate.edu; f. 1966; research, undergraduate and postgraduate education in the marine sciences; library of 10,000 vols; Dir Dr JAMES T. HARVEY.

Mote Marine Laboratory: 1600 Ken Thompson Parkway, Sarasota, FL 34236; tel. (941) 388-4441; e-mail info@mote.org; internet www.mote.org; f. 1955; ind., non-profit marine research org.; research includes environmental assessment, estuarine and coastal ecology, marine chemistry, toxicology, biology, aquaculture, biomedical research, and behaviour of fishes and marine mammals; aquarium and environmental education programmes; library: Arthur Vining Davis Library and Archives, 26,000 vols, 16,000 books and reports, 508 journal titles, 4,500 reprints; Chair. EUGENE BECKSTEIN; Pres. and CEO Dr MICHAEL CROSBY; publs *Collected Papers* (every 3 years), *Mote Magazine* (1 a year).

New England Aquarium: Central Wharf, Boston, MA 02110-3399; tel. (617) 973-5200; e-mail comments@neaq.org; internet www.neaq.org; f. 1969; public aquarium, conservation and research programmes, incl. bycatch and aquaculture, climate change and the oceans, endangered species and habitats and sustainable fisheries; library of 3,000 vols; Pres. and CEO BUD RIS; Exec. Vice-Pres., Chief Operating Officer and Treas. WALTER J. FLAHERTY; Sr Vice-Pres. Dr GREGORY STONE; publ. *Blue* (4 a year).

New Mexico Water Resources Research Institute: New Mexico State Univ., MSC 3167, POB 30001, Las Cruces, NM 88003-8001; Stucky Hall, 3170 S Espina St, Las Cruces, NM 88003-8001; tel. (575) 646-4337; e-mail nmwrri@wrri.nmsu.edu; internet wrri.nmsu.edu; f. 1963; attached to New Mexico State Univ.; develops and disseminates knowledge that will assist the state and nation in solving water problems; funds research conducted by faculty and students from univs across the state to address water problems critical to NM and SW; mem. of Nat. Institutes for Water Resources and Powell Consortium; Dir SAM FERNALD; publ. *Journal of Transboundary Water Resources*.

New York Botanical Garden: 2900 S Blvd, Bronx, NY 10458-5126; tel. (718) 817-8700; internet www.nybg.org; f. 1891; conducts basic research in plant biology and studies all species of plants and fungi; William and Lynda Steere Herbarium houses 7.3m. specimens; library: over 1m. items, incl. 196,000 vols; CEO GREGORY LONG; Chair. MAUREEN CHILTON; Sec. and Treas. THOMAS J. HUBBARD; publs *Botanical Review* (4 a year), *Brittonia* (4 a year), *Economic Botany* (4 a year).

Pennington Biomedical Research Center: 6400 Perkins Rd, Baton Rouge, LA 70808-4124; tel. (225) 763-2500; internet www.pbrc.edu; f. 1988; attached to Louisiana State Univ.; houses 53 laboratories; research areas incl. epidemiology and prevention, physical activity and health, cancer, diabetes, obesity, neurodegeneration, genomics and molecular genetics, stem cell and devt biology, neurobiology and nutrient sensing and signalling; Exec. Dir Dr STEVEN B. HEYMSFIELD.

Rhode Island Sea Grant: 220 S Ferry Rd, Narragansett, RI 02882; tel. (401) 874-6800; internet seagrant.gso.uri.edu; attached to Graduate School of Oceanography, Univ. of Rhode Island; supports research, extension, legal, and education programmes that address issues in the thematic areas of sustainable coastal devt, healthy coastal ecosystems, and safe and sustainable seafood; Dir Prof. BARRY A. COSTA-PIERCE; publ. *41°N*.

Salk Institute for Biological Studies: POB 85800, San Diego, CA 92186-5800; 10010 N Torrey Pines Rd, La Jolla, CA 92037; tel. (858) 453-4100; e-mail communications@salk.edu; internet www .salk.edu; f. 1960; advanced biological research into HIV/AIDS, cell biology, chemistry and proteomics, computational and theoretical biology, metabolic research, molecular biology and genetics; neurosciences, plant biology, regulatory biology and stem cell biology; 9 research centres; library of 15,000 vols; Chair. IRWIN MARK JACOBS; Pres. Dr WILLIAM R. BRODY; Exec. Vice-Pres. Dr MARSHA A. CHANDLER; publs *From the Bench, InsideSalk, Stories of Discovery*.

Smithsonian Environmental Research Center (SERC): POB 28, 647 Contees Wharf Rd, Edgewater, MD 21037-0028; tel. (443) 482-2200; internet www.serc.si.edu; f. 1965 as Chesapeake Center for Field Biology, present name 1985; attached to Smithsonian Institution; multi-disciplinary instn dedicated to increasing knowledge of the biological and physical processes that sustain life on earth; scientific programmes: animal–plant interactions, bio-geochemistry, chemical ecology, ecological modelling, estuarine zoology, forest ecology, invasion studies, micro–zooplankton, phyto-plankton, plant ecophysiology, plant ecology, plant physiology, solar radiation, terrestrial animal ecology; part of the Smithsonian Marine Science Network; library: br. library of the Smithsonian Instn Libraries system: 12,500 books and bound journals, 120 current journals, colln of *Chesapeakiana*; Dir TUCK HINES; Librarian ANGELA N. HAGGINS.

Smithsonian Gardens: POB 37012, Capital Gallery, Suite 3300, MRC 506, Washington, DC 20013-7012; tel. (202) 633-2220; e-mail gardens@si.edu; internet gardens.si .edu; f. 1972; research and educational programmes; manages grounds of the Smithsonian Instn museums and creates horticultural exhibitions; Smithsonian Orchid colln (10,000 plants); library: Archives of American Gardens: 80,000 photographic images, records of historic and contemporary American gardens; special collns: Garden Club of America (40,000 images), J. Horace McFarland (glass lantern slides and photographs), Thomas Warren Sears (glass negatives).

Smithsonian Marine Station at Fort Pierce: 701 Seaway Dr., Fort Pierce, FL 34949; tel. (772) 462-6220; internet www.sms .si.edu; f. 1969 as Fort Pierce Bureau, current name adopted 1998; attached to Nat. Museum of Natural History, Smithsonian Instn; research into marine biodiversity and ecosystems of FL; Head Scientist Dr VALERIE PAUL.

Smithsonian National Zoological Park: National Zoo Information, DEVS, POB 37012, MRC 5516, Washington, DC 20013-7012; 3001 Connecticut Ave, NW, Washington, DC 20008; tel. (202) 633-4888; e-mail nationalzoo@nzp.si.edu; internet nationalzoo .si.edu; f. 1889; attached to Smithsonian Instn; scientific research into behaviour, biodiversity monitoring, conservation ecology and nutrition, population management, reproductive biology and veterinary medicine; animal colln of 2,800 specimens from 435 species; Chair. JOHN W. MARRIOTT, III; Dir DENNIS W. KELLY; publ. *Smithsonian Zoogoer* (6 a year)

Attached Research Institutes:

Smithsonian Conservation Biology Institute: 1500 Remount Rd, Front Royal, Front Royal, VA 22630; tel. (202) 633-3055; internet nationalzoo.si.edu/scbi; f. 2010 fmrly Conservation and Research Center; veterinary and reproductive research; 6 centers of excellence: Center for Animal Care Sciences, Center for Conservation Ecology, Center for Conservation and Evolutionary Genetics, Center for Species Survival, Migratory Bird Center, Center for Conservation Education and Sustainability.

Stone Laboratory: 1314 Kinnear Rd, Area 100, Columbus, OH 43212-1156; tel. (614) 292-8949; e-mail stonelab@osu.edu; internet www.stonelab.osu.edu; f. 1895; attached to Ohio State Univ.; freshwater biological field station; addresses problems facing the Great Lakes; Dir Dr JEFFERY M. REUTTER.

University of Maryland Center for Environmental Science: POB 775, Cambridge, MD 21613; tel. (410) 228-9250; e-mail info@umces.edu; internet www.ca.umces .edu; research, education, service instn; focuses on science of coastal environments and their watersheds; incl. 4 laboratories; Pres. Prof. Dr DONALD F. BOESCH.

Physical Sciences

Argonne National Laboratory: 9700 S Cass Ave, Argonne, IL 60439; tel. (630) 252-2000; e-mail media@anl.gov; internet www .anl.gov; f. 1942 as Metallurgical Laboratory, present name 1946; attached to Univ. of Chicago; U.S. Dept of Energy's nat. laboratory for science and engineering research; primary focus on basic research in the physical, life and environmental sciences, and on technology-directed research in fission, fossil and fusion energy as well as conservation and renewable energy; library of 65,000 books, 550,000 technical reports, 4,000 journals and numerous standards, media, maps, translations and patents; Chair. R. J. ZIMMER; CEO D. H. LEVY; Dir Dr ERIC ISAACS; publ. *Argonne Now* (2 a year).

Association of Universities for Research in Astronomy (AURA): 1212 New York Ave NW, Suite 450, Washington, DC 20005; tel. (202) 483-2101; e-mail dnarcisso@ aura-astronomy.org; internet www .aura-astronomy.org; f. 1957; consortium of univs; operates the Space Telescope Science Institute, Baltimore, MD, and the Nat. Optical Astronomy Observatories, Tucson, AZ, which consist of the Kitt Peak Nat. Observatory, AZ, the Nat. Solar Observatory, AZ and NM, and Cerro Tololo Inter-American Observatory, Chile; manages the Int. Gemini Project, Tucson, AZ; library of 30,000 vols; Chair. Dr DAN CLEMENS; Pres. WILLIAM S. SMITH; Exec. Vice-Pres. HEIDI B. HAMMEL; Vice-Pres. for Admin. DEBORAH NARCISSO.

Byrd Polar Research Center at the Ohio State University: Scott Hall, Room 108, 1090 Carmack Rd, Ohio State Un., Columbus, OH 43210-1002; tel. (614) 292-6531; internet bprc.osu.edu; f. 1960; research focuses on the role of cold regions in the Earth's overall climate system, and encompasses geological sciences, geochemistry, glaciology, paleoclimatology, meteorology, remote sensing, ocean dynamics and the history of polar exploration; library of 12,000 vols, 1,000 maps, also holds papers and memorabilia of Richard E. Byrd, Sir Hubert Wilkins and other polar explorers; Dir Dr ELLEN MOSLEY-THOMPSON; publs *Report* (irregular), *Technical Report* (irregular).

Case Western Reserve University Astronomy: 10900 Euclid Ave, Cleveland, OH 44106-7164; tel. (216) 368-3728; e-mail dept@astronomy.case.edu; internet astronomy.case.edu; f. 1881; attached to Dept of Astronomy; astronomical research and education in galaxy formation and evolution, stellar chemical abundances, and telescope instrumentation and design; uses a 9½" telescope on the Cleveland campus; owns and operates Burrell Schmidt Telescope; library of 3,000 vols, 4,000 bound periodicals, 480 linear ft of observatory publs; Dept Chair Dr CHRIS MIHOS.

Center for Earth and Planetary Studies (CEPS): Smithsonian Institution, POB 37012, Nat. Air and Space Museum, MRC 315, Washington, DC 20013-7012; tel. (202) 633-2470; e-mail info@si.edu; internet www .nasm.si.edu/ceps; f. 1974; attached to Smithsonian Nat. Air and Space Museum; research into planetary and terrestrial geology and geophysics; application of remote sensing data from Earth-orbiting satellites and space missions; designated Regional Planetary Image Facility (RPIF); colln of Space Shuttle photographs; responsible for museum galleries 'Exploring the Planets' and 'Looking at Earth'; Chair. Dr JOHN GRANT; Programme Man. PRISCILLA STRAIN.

Fermilab: POB 500, Batavia, IL 60510-5011; Wilson and Kirk Rds, Batavia, IL 60510-5011; tel. (630) 840-3000; e-mail fermilab@fnal.gov; internet www.fnal.gov; f. 1967 as Nat. Accelerator Laboratory, present name 1974; attached to US Dept of Energy; research into high-energy physics; library of 15,000 vols, 250 periodicals; Dir PIERMARIA J. ODDONE; Deputy Dir YOUNG-KEE KIM; publs *International Science Grid This Week* (54 a year, online, www.isgtw.org), *Symmetry* (12 a year).

Harvard–Smithsonian Center for Astrophysics (CfA): 60 Garden St, Cambridge, MA 02138; tel. (617) 495-7463; internet sao-www.harvard.edu; f. 1973 by merger of Harvard College Observatory (f. 1839) with Smithsonian Astrophysical Observatory (f. 1890); scientific divs: atomic and molecular physics, high-energy astrophysics, optical and infrared astronomy, radio and geoastronomy, solar, stellar and planetary sciences, theoretical astrophysics, science education; library: John G. Wolbach Library and Information Resource Center (combines libraries of the SAO and HCO) of 75,000 vols, 40,000 astronomic photographic plates; Dir CHARLES ALCOCK; Deputy Dir ROGER BRISSENDEN.

Lamont-Doherty Earth Observatory: POB 1000, 61 Route 9W, Palisades, NY 10964-1000; tel. (845) 359-2900; e-mail director@ldeo.columbia.edu; internet www .ldeo.columbia.edu; f. 1949 as Lamont Geological Observatory, current name adopted 1993; attached to Earth Institute, Columbia Univ.; research into atmospheric processes, climate, ecology and ecosystems, earth and ocean sciences, polar science, solid earth dynamics and surface and environmental processes; library of 30,000 vols, 500 journals; Dir Prof. SEAN C. SOLOMON; publs *List of Scientific Publications, Year Book*.

Lick Observatory: POB 85, Mount Hamilton, CA 95140; tel. (831) 459-5933; e-mail giftshop@ucolick.org; internet mthamilton .ucolick.org; f. 1888; attached to Univ. of California Observatories; optical and near-infrared astronomy and astrophysics; library of 2,000 vols, 150,000 plates, 450 linear ft archival material; Dir SANDRA FABER; Deputy Dir JOHN WAREHAM.

Liquid Crystal Institute: POB 5190, 1425 Univ. Esplanade, Kent, OH 44242-0001; tel. (330) 672-2654; internet www.lcinet.kent .edu; f. 1965 as Glenn H. Brown Liquid Crystal Institute; attached to Kent State Univ.; addresses entire range of multidisciplinary topics associated with the science and technology of liquid crystals and related self-organized materials and devices; Dir and CEO Dr HIROSHI YOKOYAMA.

Lowell Observatory: 1400 W Mars Hill Rd, Flagstaff, AZ 86001; tel. (928) 774-3358; e-mail info@lowell.edu; internet www.lowell .edu; f. 1894; non-profit research instn; conducts research on a range of solar system and astrophysical topics using ground-based, airborne and space-based telescopes; library: astronomical research library of 12,000 vols; Dir JEFFREY HALL; Librarian LAUREN AMUNDSON; publ. *The Lowell Observer*.

Lunar and Planetary Institute: 3600 Bay Area Blvd, Houston, TX 77058; tel. (281) 486-2100; e-mail info@lpi.usra.edu; internet www .lpi.usra.edu; f. 1968 as Lunar Science Institute; attached to Univs Space Research Asscn (USRA); provides support services to NASA and planetary science community; centre for lunar and planetary science; conducts research into formation, evolution and current state of the Moon, planets, comets, asteroids, planetary satellites, cosmic dust and solar system; library of 60,000 vols (incl. books, documents, maps and globes, video cassettes), 100 periodicals, also photographic and cartographic data from planetary spacecraft missions; Dir Dr STEPHEN MACKWELL.

Maria Mitchell Association: 4 Vestal St, Nantucket, MA 02554; tel. (508) 228-9198; e-mail info@mmo.org; internet www.mmo .org; f. 1902; astronomical research, research training, public lectures and viewings; manages Hinchman House Natural Science Museum, Loines Observatory, Maria Mitchell Observatory, Mitchell House (birthplace of Maria Mitchell), Science Library, Aquarium; library of 8,000 vols of rare and out-of-print natural science, astronomy, and Nantucket books; Exec. Dir Dr JANET E. SCHULTE; Dir of Natural Sciences and Education and Programmes ANDREW MCKENNA-FOSTER; Dir of Astronomy Dr VLADIMIR STRELNITSKI.

Materials Research Institute: N-317 Millennium Science Complex, Pollock Rd, University Park, PA 16802-7003; tel. (814) 863-8407; e-mail mri-info@research.psu.edu; internet www.mri.psu.edu; f. 1992; attached to Pennsylvania State Univ.; vertically integrates discovery of new substances with scientific understanding and engineering devt of their properties, and in parallel, links them with the materials integration and systems performance required to solve problems; materials for research incl. biomedical materials and devices, electronic materials and devices, materials, processes and tools, nanomaterials, nanostructures and nanofabrication and polymeric systems; Dir Prof. CARLO PANTANO; publ. *Focus On Materials*.

Mount Graham International Observatory (MGIO): 1480 W Swift Trail, Safford, AZ 85546; tel. (928) 428-2739; e-mail mgiomail@as.arizona.edu; internet mgpc3.as .arizona.edu; attached to Steward Observatory, Dept of Astronomy, Univ. of Arizona; operates and maintains facilities in the Pinaleño Mountains in SE Arizona; Dir BUDDY E. POWELL.

Constituent Centres:

Arizona Radio Observatory (ARO): Univ. of Arizona, 933 N Cherry Ave, Tucson, AZ 85721; tel. (520) 621-5290; e-mail opersmt@as.arizona.edu; internet aro.as.arizona.edu; operates the Heinrich Hertz Submillimeter Telescope (HHSMT); Dir Dr LUCY ZIURYS.

Large Binocular Telescope Observatory (LBTO): Univ. of Arizona, 933 N Cherry Ave, Room 552, Tucson, AZ 85721-0065; tel. (520) 626-5231; internet www .lbto.org; f. 1988, operational 2007; the world's most powerful optical telescope; consists of two 8.4-m mirrors on a common mount; a collaboration between the Italian astronomical community (represented by the Istituto Nazionale di Astrofisica—*q.v.*—the Univ. of Arizona, Arizona State Univ., Northern Arizona Univ., the LBT Beteiligungsgesellschaft in Germany, the Ohio State Univ., Research Corpn in Tucson and the Univ. of Notre Dame; Dir RICHARD F. GREEN.

Vatican Observatory Research Group (VORG): Steward Observatory, Univ. of Arizona, Tucson, AZ 85721; tel. (520) 621-3225; e-mail mgiomail@as.arizona.edu; internet vaticanobservatory.org; f. 1981; attached to Vatican Observatory, Vatican City; operates the 1.8-m Alice P. Lennon Telescope with its Thomas J. Bannan Astrophysics Facility, known together as the Vatican Advanced Technology Telescope (VATT), on Mount Graham, Arizona; Vice-Dir for the Vatican Observatory for VORG Dr CHRISTOPHER J. CORBALLY.

NASA Goddard Institute for Space Studies: 2880 Broadway, New York, NY 10025; tel. (212) 678-5500; internet www.giss.nasa .gov; f. 1961; attached to Earth Sciences Div., Goddard Space Flight Center; global climate, biogeochemical cycles, cloud studies, planetary atmospheres, global habitability; library of 15,000 vols; Dir Dr JAMES HANSEN.

National Center for Atmospheric Research (NCAR): POB 3000, Boulder, CO 80307-3000; 3090 Center Green Dr., Boulder, CO 80301; tel. (303) 497-2525; internet www.ncar.ucar.edu; f. 1960; sponsored by Nat. Science Foundation; operated by the Univ. Corpn for Atmospheric Research (UCAR); research in weather prediction, causes of climatic trends, solar processes and influences of the sun on weather and climate, convective storms and global air quality; library of 100,000 items, 900 current journals; Dir Dr ROGER WAKIMOTO; Deputy Dir Dr MAURA HAGAN; publs *Highlights* (every 2 years), *NCAR Scientific Report*, *UCAR* (4 a year).

National Radio Astronomy Observatory: 520 Edgemont Rd, Charlottesville, VA 22903-2475; tel. (434) 296-0211; e-mail nthisdel@ nrao.edu; internet www.nrao.edu; f. 1956; funded by the Nat. Science Foundation, operated under cooperative agreement by Assoc. Univs, Inc.; research into radio astronomy, radio astronomy electronics, design of radio telescopes; observing radio telescopes, incl. a 27-element array of 82-ft radio telescopes in New Mexico (Very Large Array); a 10-element array of 82-ft radio telescopes located in 7 states and the US Virgin Islands (Very Long Baseline Array) dedicated to very long baseline interferometry; and a 100-m fully steerable telescope in West Virginia (Robert C. Byrd Green Bank Telescope); library of 27,000 vols; Dir TONY BEASLEY; Deputy Dir PHIL JEWELL.

National Solar Observatory: NSO Sacramento Peak, 3010 Coronal Loop, Sunspot, NM 88349; tel. (575) 434-7000; internet www .nso.edu; f. 1952; operated by AURA (*q.v.*); national centre for solar research; offers telescope use to astronomical community; conducts solar research; 50 staff, incl. 11 astrophysicists; library of 8,000 vols; Dir STEPHEN L. KEIL.

Physical Science Laboratory: POB 30002, Las Cruces, NM 88003-8002; Anderson Hall, cnr of Stewart and Espina, Las Cruces, NM 88003; tel. (575) 646-9200; e-mail director@ psl.nmsu.edu; internet www.psl.nmsu.edu; f. 1946; attached to New Mexico State Univ.; areas of research incl: sub-orbital platforms, unmanned aircraft research and devt and airspace integration, information modeling for predictive decision making, specialized intelligence community support, advanced NASA scientific exploration and experimentation, homeland security sensing and detection technologies, and advanced weapons and countermeasures devt and testing; Dir Dr JAY JORDAN.

Radiation Research Society: POB 7050, Lawrence, KS 66044-8897; 810 E 10th St, Lawrence, KS 66044-8897; e-mail info@ radres.org; internet www.radres.org; f. 1952; facilitates inter-disciplinary cooperative research between biology, chemistry, medicine and physics in the study of the properties and effects of radiation; promotes dissemination of knowledge in these and related fields through publications, meetings and educational symposia; Pres. Dr JACQUELINE P. WILLIAMS; Pres.-Elect Dr TOM K. HEI; Exec. Dir KATHY VOTAW; Sec. and Treas. Dr ELEANOR A. BLAKELY; publ. *Radiation Research* (12 a year).

Scripps Institution of Oceanography: 8622 Kennel Way, La Jolla, CA 92093-0210; tel. (858) 534-3624; e-mail scrippsnews@ucsd .edu; internet www.scripps.ucsd.edu; f. 1903, present status 1912; attached to Univ. of California, San Diego; ocean and earth science research; education and public service; main depts: associated Univ. of California institutes: institute of geophysics and planetary physics, California space institute, centre for atmospheric sciences, centre for coastal studies, centre for marine biotechnology and biomedicine, climate research, geosciences research, marine biology research, marine physical laboratory, marine research, marine life research group, physical oceanography, Scripps graduate dept; spec. facilities incl. hydraulics laboratory; operates 4 research vessels and 1 platform; public aquarium (Birch Aquarium) and museum; geological and biological collns; library of 227,000 vols, 700 print periodicals, more than 100,000 vols digitized; Dir Dr MARGARET LEINEN; publs *explorations now* (irregular), *Scripps Wide*.

Sproul Observatory: Computer Science Dept, Swarthmore College, 500 College Ave, Swarthmore, PA 19081-1397; tel. (610) 328-8272; e-mail info@cs.swarthmore.edu; internet www.cs.swarthmore.edu/program/ history/sproul.html; f. 1906; attached to Swarthmore College; hosts occasional physics and astronomy observing sessions; 61-cm reflector and echelle spectrometer; astrometry and stellar spectroscopy; library of 9,000 vols.

United States Naval Observatory: 3450 Massachusetts Ave, NW, Washington, DC 20392-5420; tel. (202) 762-1467; e-mail usno_pao@navy.mil; internet www.usno .navy.mil/usno; f. 1830 as Depot of Charts and Instruments, present location 1893; provides astronomical data and products; serves as official source of time for the US Dept of

Defense and standard of time for the USA; substation at Flagstaff, AZ; library of 75,000 vols; Superintendent Capt. R. SCOTT STEADLEY; Scientific Dir Dr KENNETH JOHNSTON; publs *Air Almanac, Astronomical Almanac, Astronomical Papers, Astronomical Phenomena, Multi-year Interactive Computer Almanac, Nautical Almanac, NavObs Circulars, Time Service Bulletins*, star catalogues.

Vanderbilt Dyer Observatory: 1000 Oman Dr., Brentwood, TN 37027; tel. (615) 373-4897; e-mail lynn.d.mcdonald@ vanderbilt.edu; internet www.dyer .vanderbilt.edu; f. 1953; attached to Vanderbilt Univ.; specializes in research on local structure of the Milky Way, photo-electric photometry of eclipsing binaries and variable stars, pre-planetary discs around young stars; equipped with combination 60-cm reflecting and Baker-Schmidt telescope, 40-cm computer-controlled automatic telescope, 30-cm and 40-cm Cassegrain reflecting telescopes and 15-cm refracting telescope; library of 12,000 vols; Dir ROCKY ALVEY; publ. *IAPPP Communications* (4 a year).

Woods Hole Oceanographic Institution: 266 Woods Hole Rd, Woods Hole, MA 02543-1050; tel. (508) 289-2252; e-mail information@whoi.edu; internet www.whoi .edu; f. 1930; research into physical, chemical and biological oceanography, marine geology and marine geophysics, ocean acoustics, ocean engineering and marine policy; 4 ocean institutes: Coastal Oceans Institute, Deep Ocean Exploration Institute, Ocean and Climate Change Institute, and Ocean Life Institute; conducts jt PhD programme with Massachusetts Institute of Technology, postdoctoral fellowship programme and summer student fellowship programme; library of 150,000 vols, 5,000 periodicals, jt library with Marine Biological Laboratory; Pres. and Dir SUSAN K. AVERY; Dir of Research Dr LAURENCE P. MADIN; publs *Oceanus* (3 a year), *Woods Hole Currents* (irregular).

Yale Southern Observatory, Inc: Dept of Astronomy, Yale Univ., POB 208101, New Haven, CT 06520-8101; J. W. Gibbs Laboratory, Second Fl., 260 Whitney Ave, Yale Univ., New Haven, CT 06511; tel. (203) 432-3000; internet www.astro.yale.edu/ astrom/yso.html; f. 1962 as Yale-Columbia Southern Observatory, Inc., present status and name 1975; attached to Dept of Astronomy, Yale Univ.; non-profit corpn; provides framework for Yale faculty mems to perform astronomical research into the Southern Hemisphere; holds Double Astrograph telescope consisting of 2 lenses, each 20 inches in diameter: one designed for blue light and the other for visual light; publs *Bright Star Catalogue* (and supplement), *General Catalogue of Trigonometric Stellar Parallaxes, Transactions*.

Yerkes Observatory: 373 W Geneva St, Williams Bay, WI 53191; tel. (262) 245-5555; internet astro.uchicago.edu/yerkes; f. 1897; attached to Dept of Astronomy and Astrophysics, Univ. of Chicago; provides laboratory space and access to telescopes for research and instruction; library of 25,000 books and journals; Dir Dr KYLE M. CUDWORTH.

PHILOSOPHY AND PSYCHOLOGY

American Society for Psychical Research: 5 W 73rd St, New York, NY 10023; tel. (212) 799-5050; e-mail aspr@aspr .com; internet www.aspr.com; f. 1885; study of paranormal phenomena such as telepathy, clairvoyance, precognition and psychokinesis; library of 10,000 vols, 3,000 periodicals, rare MSS and photos; Exec. Dir PATRICE KEANE; publ. *ASPR Journal* (4 a year).

RELIGION, SOCIOLOGY AND ANTHROPOLOGY

Africana Studies and Research Center: 310 Triphammer Rd, Ithaca, NY 14850; tel. (607) 255-4625; e-mail africana@cornell.edu; internet www.asrc.cornell.edu; attached to Cornell Univ.; studies African people, global migrations and reconstruction of African peoples, as well as patterns of linkages to the African continent; library of 17,000 vols; Dir ELIZABETH ADKINS-REGAN.

American Institutes for Research: 1000 Thomas Jefferson St, NW, Washington, DC 20007; tel. (202) 403-5000; e-mail inquiry@ air.org; internet www.air.org; f. 1946; ind., non-profit org. conducting research, devt, analysis and evaluation studies in the behavioural and social sciences and quality of education, health care, and workplace for clients in govt and the private sector; brs in San Mateo and Sacramento, CA, Atlanta, GA, Honolulu, HI, Chicago, IL, Baltimore, Frederick and Silver Spring, MD, Boston Area, MA, New York, NY, Chapel Hill, NC, Columbus, OH, Portland, OR; int. offices in Egypt, Ethiopia, Georgia, Haiti, Honduras, Kenya, Liberia, Malawi, Nicaragua, Pakistan, South Africa and Zambia; Chair. PATRICIA B. GURIN; Pres. and CEO DAVID MYERS.

American Research Center in Egypt (ARCE): 8700 Crownhill Blvd, Suite 507, San Antonio, TX 78209-1130; tel. (210) 821-7000; e-mail info@arce.org; internet www .arce.org Cairo Office: 2 Midan Simón Bolívar, Garden City, Cairo, 11461, Egypt; tel. (2) 2794-8239; e-mail cairo@arce.org; f. 1948; ind., non-profit-making; promotes research into Egypt and the Middle East in the fields of archaeology, art, architecture, history, culture, social sciences; library: (in Cairo) of 25,000 vols, 300 journal titles; Pres. Dr SAMEH ISKANDER; Vice-Pres. CAROL REDMOUNT; Treas. JANET IRWINE; Asst Dir for US Operations RACHEL MAULDIN; Cairo Dir GERRY DEE SCOTT, III; publs *Bulletin of the American Research Center in Egypt* (2 a year), *Journal of the American Research Center in Egypt (JARCE)* (1 a year).

American Schools of Oriental Research: Boston Univ., 656 Beacon St, 5th Fl., Boston, MA 02215-2010; tel. (617) 353-6570; e-mail asor@bu.edu; internet www.asor.org; f. 1900; promotes research into the cultures of the Near E and supports activities of ind. archaeological instns abroad: Albright Institute of Archaeological Research (Jerusalem, Israel), American Center of Oriental Research (Amman, Jordan), and Cyprus American Archaeological Research Institute (Nicosia, Cyprus); Pres. SUSAN ACKERMAN; Exec. Dir Dr ANDREW G. VAUGHN; publs *Journal of Cuneiform Studies* (1 a year), *Near Eastern Archaeology* (4 a year).

Arctic Studies Center: POB 37012, Dept of Anthropology, MRC 112, Washington, DC 20013-7012; tel. (202) 633-1887; e-mail arctics@si.edu; internet www.mnh.si.edu/ arctic; f. 1988; attached to Dept of Anthropology of the Smithsonian Instn's Nat. Museum of Natural History; research into peoples, history, archaeology and social change in the circumpolar regions; Dir WILLIAM W. FITZHUGH.

Regional Office:

Alaska Office: 625C St, Anchorage, AK 99501; tel. (907) 929-9207; e-mail crowella@si.edu; publs *Contributions to Circumpolar Anthropology, Field Reports* (1 a year).

Calvin Center for Christian Scholarship: 3201 Burton St, SE, Grand Rapids, MI 49546; 2041 Raybrook, Suite 201G Grand Rapids, MI 49546; tel. (616) 526-7162; e-mail

info@calvin.edu; internet www.calvin.edu/ admin/cccs; f. 1976; attached to Calvin College; coordinates and provides leadership for the project of advancing and improving intentional Christian scholarship at Calvin College; Dir Prof. Dr SUSAN M. FELCH.

Center for Advanced Study in the Behavioral Sciences: 75 Alta Rd, Stanford, CA 94305-8170; tel. (650) 736-0100; e-mail casbs-info@stanford.edu; internet www.casbs .org; f. 1954; attached to Stanford Univ.; basic understanding of the social, psychological, historical, biological and cultural foundations of behaviour and soc.; library of 1,700 vols, colln of Ralph W. Tyler; Dir STEPHEN M. KOSSLYN; publ. *Reports*.

Center for Social Research: Calvin College, Raybrook Bldg 2041, Suite 103, 3201 Burton, SE, Grand Rapids, MI 49546; tel. (616) 526-7799; e-mail csr@calvin.edu; internet www.calvin.edu/admin/csr; f. 1970; attached to Dept of Sociology, Calvin College; scholarly research into social science; organizes grant-funded research projects; Dir Dr NEIL CARLSON.

Center for the Study of Citizenship: 656 W Kirby, Faculty Admin. Bldg, Detroit, MI 48202; tel. (313) 577-2593; internet www.clas .wayne.edu/citizenship; attached to College of Liberal Arts and Sciences, Wayne State Univ.; promotes interdisciplinary research and exchange about citizenship within a global community of scholars, students, political community and business leaders and gen. public; Dir Dr MARC W. KRUMAN.

Center for Urban Studies: 5700 Cass, 2207 A/AB, Detroit, MI 48202; tel. (313) 577-2208; e-mail cusinfo@wayne.edu; internet www.cus.wayne.edu; f. 1967; attached to Wayne State Univ.; conducts research and provides support to scholars, community organizations, businesses, municipalities, foundations, non-profits and others throughout SE Michigan; involved in education and policy analysis, geographic information systems and mapping, data colln, sampling, grants and data analysis; Dir Dr LYKE THOMPSON; Man. Dir CHARO HULLEZA.

Justice System Training & Research Institute: School of Justice Studies, 1 Old Ferry Rd, Bristol, RI 02809-2921; tel. (401) 254-3731; internet www.rwu.edu/academics/ schools/sjs/jstri; attached to School of Justice Studies, Roger Williams Univ.; trains public safety personnel; provides information for criminal justice community; acts as applied research resource; Dir Dr ROBERT MCKENNA.

Labor Studies Center—Labor@Wayne: 656 W Kirby St, 3178 Faculty Admin. Bldg, Detroit, MI 48201; tel. 313) 577-2191; e-mail ac6644@wayne.edu; internet www.clas .wayne.edu/lsc; attached to College of Liberal Arts and Sciences, Wayne State Univ.; labour education centre; strengthens capacity of organized labour to represent needs and interests of workers; conducts research and teaching on labour and workplace issues; Dir GAYLE HAMILTON.

Lewis Center for Church Leadership: 4500 Massachusetts Ave, NW, Washington, DC 20016; tel. (202) 885-8757; e-mail lewiscenter@wesleyseminary.edu; internet www.churchleadership.com; f. 2003; attached to Wesley Theological Seminary; seeks holistic understanding of leadership that brings together theology and management, scholarship and practice, research and application; Chair. C. RANDALL NUCKOLLS; Dir Dr LOVETT H. WEEMS, JR.

Middle American Research Institute: Tulane Univ., Dinwiddie Hall, 3rd Fl., 6823 St, Charles Ave, New Orleans, LA 70118-5698; tel. (504) 865-5110; e-mail mari@tulane

.edu; internet www.tulane.edu/~mari; f. 1924 as Dept of Middle American Research; attached to Tulane Univ.; research, education and publs related to Mexico and Central America; supports archaeological excavation and research into humanities and social sciences; small museum gallery; anthropological collns; engages in exhibitions, workshops, and symposia; Dir MARCELLO A. CANUTO; publ. *Bulletin* (2 a year).

Middle East Institute: 1761 N St, NW, Washington, DC 20036-2882; tel. (202) 785-1141; e-mail information@mei.edu; internet www.mideasti.org; f. 1946; a non-profit, non-advocating resource centre; promotes American understanding of the Middle East, N Africa, the Caucasus and Central Asia; coordinates cultural presentations; library of 25,000 vols; Chair. ANTHONY ZINNI; Pres. WENDY J. CHAMBERLIN; Vice-Pres. KATE SEELYE; publs *Middle East Journal* (4 a year), *Encounters* (online), *Policy Briefs* (online), *Policy Insights* (online), *Viewpoints* (online).

Oak Institute for the Study of International Human Rights: Colby College, 5319 Mayflower Hill, Waterville, Maine 04901; tel. (207) 859-5319; e-mail oakhr@colby.edu; internet www.colby.edu/oak; f. 1998; attached to Colby College; sponsors Oak Human Rights Fellow to teach and conduct research while residing at the College; organizes lectures and other events; Dir WALTER HATCH.

Population Research Institute: 601 Oswald Tower, University Park, PA 16802-6211; tel. (814) 865-0486; e-mail info@pop.psu.edu; internet www.pop.psu.edu; f. 1972; attached to Pennsylvania State Univ.; encourages, organizes and supports innovative research and training in population sciences; Dir Dr JENNIFER VAN HOOK.

Reformed Church Center: New Brunswick Campus, 17 Seminary Pl., New Brunswick, NJ 08901; tel. (732) 247-5241; e-mail helpdesk@nbts.edu; internet www.nbts.edu/newsite/rcc.cfm; attached to New Brunswick Theological Seminary; offers programmes and research opportunities to scholars interested in reformed tradition; 2 scholarships for research students: Albert A. Smith Fellowship and Alvin J. Poppen and John R. Young; Dir Rev. BARBARA FILLETTE.

Smithsonian Center for Folklife and Cultural Heritage: POB 37012, MRC 520, Washington, DC 20013-7012; Capital Gallery Bldg, 600 Maryland Ave, SW, Suite 2001, MRC 520, Washington, DC 20024; tel. (202) 633-6440; e-mail folklife-info@si.edu; internet www.folklife.si.edu; promotes the understanding and continuity of contemporary grassroots cultures in the USA and abroad; runs Smithsonian Folklife Festival, Smithsonian Folkways recordings, exhibitions, documentary films, symposia; library: Ralph Rinzler Folklife Archives and Collns: 17,300 commercial discs, 4,000 acetate discs, 45,000 audiotapes, 2,000 CDs, 1m. stills, 2,500 video casettes, 500,000 ft of motion picture film; Moses and Frances Asch colln, consisting of recordings and material relating to Folkways Records; records and archives of the centre; Dir DANIEL SHEEY; publ. *Folkways Magazine*.

Smithsonian Latino Center: Capital Gallery, 600 Maryland Ave, SW, Suite 7042, MRC 512, Washington, DC 20024; tel. (202) 633-1240; internet latino.si.edu; f. 1997; coordinates all Smithsonian-related Latino exhibitions, initiatives, research and educational programmes; library: archive of papers of Latino and Latin American artists; Chair. PATRICIA Q. STONESIFER; Exec. Dir EDUARDO DIAZ (acting).

Social Science Research Council (SSRC): 1 Pierrepont Plaza, 15th Fl., 300 Cadmon Plaza W, Brooklyn, NY 11021; tel. (212) 377-2700; e-mail info@ssrc.org; internet www.ssrc.org; f. 1923; ind., non-profit int. org.; plans for critical areas of social research; improves research training through training institutes and fellowship programmes; supports individual research through postdoctoral grants; sponsors interdisciplinary and int. research confs; Chair. MICHAEL KENNEDY; Pres. CRAIG CALHOUN; publ. *Items* (4 a year).

Wenner-Gren Foundation: 470 Park Ave S, 8th Fl., New York, NY 10016; tel. (212) 683-5000; e-mail inquiries@wennergren.org; internet www.wennergren.org; f. 1941 as the Viking Fund; supports research into all brs of anthropology and closely related disciplines concerned with human origins, devt and variation; grants to aid individual research, incl. dissertation research, fellowships and post-PhD research grants; Conf. Grants Program; Historical Archives Program; Professional Devt Int. Fellowships and Int. Collaborative Research Grants; Chair. SETH MASTERS; Vice-Chair. Dr JOHN IMMERWAHR; Pres. Dr LESLIE C. AIELLO; Treas. WILLIAM COBB; publ. *Current Anthropology* (5 a year).

TECHNOLOGY

Applied Research Laboratory (ARL): POB 30, State College, PA 16804; N Atherton St, State College, PA 16801; tel. (814) 865-6343; internet www.arl.psu.edu; f. 1945; attached to Pennsylvania State Univ.; champions transfer of advanced technologies and manufacturing processes, in partnership with industry and Navy research devt centres, to acquisition programmes and fleet operations, as well as to other govt agencies and private sector; performs basic and applied research, exploratory and advanced devt and manufacturing technology in support of the Navy technology base; Dir Dr EDWARD G. LISZKA.

Battelle Memorial Institute: 505 King Ave, Columbus, OH 43201-2696; tel. (614) 424-6424; e-mail solutions@battelle.org; internet www.battelle.org; f. 1929; serves industry and govt in the generation, application and commercialization of technology; supports research and devt activities of clients in 30 countries; major areas of activity are community and education, energy, health and life sciences, nat. security and defense, and laboratory management; research operations in the USA and Europe; 130 offices worldwide; library: more than 150,000 vols; Pres. and CEO CARL E. KOHRT; Library Man. KEMBERLY LANG.

Board on Infrastructure and the Constructed Environment: The National Academies, 500, Fifth St, NW, Washington, DC 20001; tel. (202) 334-3505; e-mail bice@nas.edu; internet www.nas.edu/bice; f. 1946 as Bldg Research Advisory Board unit of Div. on Engineering and Physical Sciences of the Nat. Research Council (NRC); advises exec. and legislative brs of govt and private sector on technology, science and public policy; develops strategic plans and oversees cttee activities involving studies, briefings, workshops, symposia, information dissemination activities; Chair. DAVID NASH; Dir DENNIS CHAMOT (acting).

Brookhaven National Laboratory: POB 5000, Upton, Long Island, NY 11973-5000; tel. (631) 344-8000; internet www.bnl.gov; f. 1947; operated by Brookhaven Science Assocs, under contract with the US Dept of Energy; basic and applied research by staff and visiting scientists in the fields of applied sciences, biology, chemistry, energy, environment, mathematics, medicine, particle accelerators, and physics, incl. the design, devt, acquisition and operation of large-scale facilities; training of scientists and engineers; dissemination of scientific and technical knowledge; library of 82,000 vols; Dir SAMUEL ARONSON; publs *Brookhaven Bulletin* (56 a year), *Discover Brookhaven*.

Center for Innovative Materials Research (CIMR): College of Engineering, Lawrence Technological Univ., 21000 W Ten Mile Rd, Southfield, MI 48075-1058; tel. (248) 204-2556; internet www.ltu.edu/cimr; attached to College of Engineering, Lawrence Technological Univ.; f. 2005; researches and tests carbon fibre composite materials for defence applications; Dir Dr NABIL F. GRACE.

Combustion Institute: 5001 Baum Blvd, Suite 635, Pittsburgh, PA 15213-1851; tel. (412) 687-1366; e-mail office@combustioninstitute.org; internet www.combustioninstitute.org; f. 1954; non-profit educational scientific soc.; promotes and disseminates research in combustion science; offices in 34 countries; Pres. Prof. KATHARINA KOHSE-HOEINGHAUS; Vice-Pres.and Pres.-Elect Prof. JAMES DRISCOLL; Sec. Prof. REGINALD MITCHELL; publs *Combustion and Flame* (12 a year), *Combustion Science and Technology* (12 a year), *Combustion Theory and Modelling* (6 a year), *The Proceedings of the Combustion Institute* (every 2 years).

HERTY Advanced Materials Development Center: 110 Brampton Rd, Savannah, GA 31408; tel. (912) 963-2600; e-mail info@herty.com; internet www.herty.com; f. 1938; non-profit contractual research and devt of wood, non-wood and synthetic fibres; Chair. EUGENE CARTLEDGE; Pres. and CEO Dr WILLIAM G. BRUNDAGE.

Industrial Research Institute: 2200 Clarendon Blvd, Suite 1102, Arlington, VA 22201-3331; tel. (703) 647-2580; internet www.iriweb.org; f. 1938; offers services to research and devt, and innovation to professionals in the US and China; Chair. ROBERT J. KUMPF; Pres. EDWARD BERNSTEIN; publ. *Research-Technology Management* (6 a year).

Institute for Security, Technology, and Society: Dartmouth College, 6211 Sudikoff Laboratory, Hanover, NH 03755; tel. (603) 646-0700; e-mail info@ists.dartmouth.edu; internet www.ists.dartmouth.edu; f. 2000; attached to Dartmouth College; engages in interdisciplinary research, education and outreach programmes that focus on information technology (IT) and its role in soc.; nurtures leaders and scholars, educates students and the community, and collaborates with its partners to develop and deploy IT, and to better understand how IT relates to socio-economic forces, cultural values and political influences; Dir DENISE ANTHONY.

Institute of Textile Technology: North Carolina State Univ., College of Textiles, 2401 Research Dr., POB 8301, Raleigh, NC 27695-8301; tel. (919) 513-7704; internet www.itt.edu; f. 1944; research, graduate education and open funding of applied textile research; Pres. and CEO Dr W. GILBERT O'NEAL; Dir for Research Dr HENRY BOYTER.

Lemelson Center for the Study of Invention and Innovation: Nat. Museum of American History, Smithsonian Instn, Room 1210, MRC 604, Smithsonian, POB 37012, Washington, DC 20013-7012; tel. (202) 633-3450; e-mail lemcen@si.edu; internet invention.smithsonian.org; f. 1995; attached to Smithsonian Nat. Museum of American History; documents, interprets and disseminates information about invention and innovation; encourages inventive creativity in young people; Dir ARTHUR MOLELLA; Deputy Dir JEFFREY BRODIE.

National Aeronautics and Space Administration (NASA): Suite 5κ 39, Washington, DC 20546-0001; tel. (202) 358-0001; e-mail public-inquiries@hq.nasa.gov; internet www.nasa.gov; f. 1958, fmrly Nat. Advisory Cttee for Aeronautics (f. 1915); conducts space and scientific research through 3 prin. org., aeronautics, human explorations and operations and science; Administrator CHARLES F. BOLDER, JR.

Main Research Centres:

Ames Research Center: c/o NASA HQ, Suite 5κ 39, Washington, DC 20546-000; NASA, Moffett Field, CA 94035; tel. (650) 604-5000; internet www.nasa.gov/centers/ames; f. 1939; supercomputing, networking and intelligent systems, aerospace and thermal protection systems, astrobiology, biotechnology, fundamental space biology, human factors and nanotechnology; Dir Dr SIMON P. WORDEN; Deputy Dir LEWIS S. G. BRAXTON, III.

Dryden Flight Research Center: POB 273, Edwards, CA 93523-0273; tel. (661) 276-3311; e-mail drydenpao@nasa.gov; internet www.nasa.gov/centers/dryden; f. 1946; research into aeronautics and space technology; Dir DAVID D. MCBRIDE.

George C. Marshall Space Flight Center: Nat. Aeronautics and Space Admin., Huntsville, AL 35812; tel. (256) 544-1382; e-mail marshallpublicinquiries@msfc.nasa.gov; internet www.nasa.gov/centers/marshall; f. 1960; develops and operates space systems the USA needs to journey into low Earth orbit and beyond; Dir ROBERT M. LIGHTFOOT, JR.

Glenn Research Center: NASA, 21000 Brookpark Rd, Cleveland, OH 44135; tel. (216) 433-4000; internet www.nasa.gov/centers/glenn; f. 1941 as Aircraft Engine Research Laboratory, present name 1999; researches, designs, develops and tests innovative technology for aeronautics and spaceflight; Dir RAMON LUGO, III.

Goddard Space Flight Center: NASA, Public Inquiries, Mail Code 130, Greenbelt, MD 20771; tel. (301) 286-2000; internet www1.nasa.gov/centers/goddard; f. 1959; builds spacecraft, instruments and new technology to study Earth, sun, solar system and the universe; library of 57,000 vols, 35,000 periodicals; Dir ROB STRAIN.

Jet Propulsion Laboratory: 4800 Oak Grove Dr., Pasadena, CA 91109; tel. (818) 354-4321; internet www.nasa.gov/centers/jpl; centre for robotic exploration of the solar system; operated by California Institute of Technology; Dir Dr CHARLES ELACHI.

John F. Kennedy Space Center: NASA, FL 32899; tel. (321) 867-5000; e-mail ksc-public-inquiries@mail.nasa.gov; internet www1.nasa.gov/centers/kennedy; f. 1962 as Launch Operations Center, current name adopted 1963; previously Launch Operations Center; space vehicle launch facility; library of 32,000 vols, 106,000 documents and reports, 589 periodicals; Dir ROBERT D. CABANA.

Langley Research Center: NASA, Hampton, VA 23681-2199; tel. (757) 864-3293; internet www1.nasa.gov/centers/langley; f. 1917, current name adopted 1958; research areas incl. aeronautics, atmospheric sciences and exploration; Dir LESA B. ROSE; publ. *Researcher News* (online).

Lyndon B. Johnson Space Center: 2101 NASA Parkway, Houston, TX 77058; tel. (281) 483-0123; internet www.nasa.gov/centers/johnson/home/index.html; f. 1961; responsible for the design, devt and testing of manned spacecraft and associated systems, for the selection and training of astronauts and for the operation of manned space flights; operates White Sands Test Facility at Las Cruces, NM; library: Johnson Space Center Technical library of 49,000 vols, 550,000 technical reports, 600 periodicals; Dir MIKE COATS.

Stennis Space Center: Office of Public Affairs, MS, 39529; tel. (228) 688-2211; e-mail public-inquiries@ssc.nasa.gov; internet www.nasa.gov/centers/stennis; f. 1961 as Mississippi Test Operations, present name 1988; Dir PATRICK SCHEUERMANN.

National Institute of Standards and Technology: 100 Bureau Dr., Stop 1070, Gaithersburg, MD 20899-1070; tel. (301) 975-6478; e-mail inquiries@nist.gov; internet www.nist.gov; f. 1901; attached to US Dept of Commerce; works with industry to develop and apply technology, measurements and standards; laboratory research focused on infrastructural technologies; operates research org JILA in CO with the Univ. of Colorado, Institute for Bioscience and Biotechnology Research (IBBR) (fmrly CARB), Rockville, MD, with Univ. of Maryland Biotechnology Institute, Joint Quantum Institute (JQI), MD with Univ. of Maryland and Hollings Marine Laboratory, Charleston, SC with 5 other univ. partners; Dir Dr PATRICK D. GALLAGHER; publs *Building Science*, *Journal of Research*, *National Standard Reference Database*.

National Renewable Energy Laboratory: 15013 Denver W Parkway, Golden, CO 80401; tel. (303) 275-3000; internet www.nrel.gov; f. 1977 as the Solar Energy Research Institute; a national centre; develops long-range high-risk renewable energy technologies and practices, advances related science and engineering, and transfers knowledge and innovations; library: consists of the NREL Library and the Wind Technical Library.; Dir Dr DAN ARVIZU; publ. *Continuum Magazine* (4 a year).

New Mexico Bureau of Geology and Mineral Resources: New Mexico Institute of Mining and Technology, 801 Leroy Pl., Socorro, NM 87801-4796; tel. (575) 835-5420; internet www.geoinfo.nmt.edu; f. 1927 as New Mexico Bureau of Mines and Mineral Resources, current name adopted 2001; attached to New Mexico Institute of Mining and Technology; conducts research and interacts with State and Fed. agencies; serves as the geological survey for State of New Mexico; provides information to scientists, decision makers, and the New Mexico population on the state's geologic infrastructure, mineral and energy resources and geohydrology; provides timely information on potential geologic hazards, incl. earthquakes, volcanic events, soils- and subsidence-related problems, and flooding; provides public education and outreach through college teaching; offices in Albuquerque and Carlsbad; incl. Geologic Information Center and a mineralogical museum; library of 5,000 vols, 5,000 maps, 2,000 photographs, 1,200 theses and dissertations; Dir L. GREER PRICE; Librarian Dr MAUREEN WILKS; publs *Lite Geology* (4 a year), *New Mexico Geology* (4 a year).

New Mexico Space Grant Consortium: POB 3001, MSC SG, Las Cruces, NM 88003; tel. (505) 646-6414; e-mail nmsgc@nmsu.edu; internet spacegrant.nmsu.edu; f. 1989; attached to New Mexico State Univ.; mem. of Nat. Space Grant College and fellowship programme of NASA; encourages interdisciplinary training, research and public service programmes on aerospace; encourages cooperative programmes among univs, aerospace industry and fed., state and local govts; establishes and maintains a nat. network of univs with interests and capabilities in aeronautics, space and related fields; recruits and trains US citizens in aerospace science and technology; Dir Dr PAT HYNES.

Southwest Research Institute: POB 28510, 6220 Culebra Rd, San Antonio, TX 78228-0510; 9503 W Commerce, San Antonio, TX 78227-1301; tel. (210) 522-2122; e-mail bd@swri.org; internet www.swri.edu; f. 1947; ind. non-profit org. conducting research and devt in the engineering and physical sciences for govt, business and industry around the world; library of 50,000 vols; Pres. J. DAN BATES; publ. *Technology Today* (3 a year).

Southwest Technology Development Institute: POB 3001, MSC 3SOLAR, Las Cruces, NM 88003-8001; tel. (575) 646-6105; e-mail tdi@nmsu.edu; internet www.nmsu.edu/~tdi; f. 1977 as New Mexico Solar Energy Institute; attached to College of Engineering, New Mexico State Univ.; focuses on the devt, transfer, promotion and commercialization of renewable energy technologies; areas incl: solar and wind energy systems, geothermal research, energy systems simulation, resource assessment and environmental analysis.; Dir ANDREW L. ROSENTHAL.

SRI International: 333 Ravenswood Ave, Menlo Park, CA 94025-3453; tel. (650) 859-2000; e-mail info@sp.sri.com; internet www.sri.com; f. 1946 as Stanford Research Institute, present status 1970, present name 1977; non-profit-making; centres for diversified research for industry and govt in pure and applied science and engineering; br. in Washington, DC, and other locations; overseas offices in Tokyo, Japan, Hong Kong, China, Greenland, Sharjah and UAE; Chair. VERN E. CLARK; Pres. and CEO CURTIS R. CARLSON.

TRI Princeton: 601 Prospect Ave, POB 625, Princeton, NJ 08542; tel. (609) 430-4820; e-mail info@triprinceton.org; internet www.triprinceton.com; f. 1930; fundamental and applied research and continuing education in the physical and engineering sciences relating to fibrous materials, films, polymers, human hair, and porous and nanoporous materials; library of 5,000 vols; Chair. ROBERT J. BIANCHINI; Pres. Dr MICHAEL A. DRZEWINSKI; Sec. and Treas. ELEANOR LEHMAN.

Libraries and Archives
Alabama

Alabama Department of Archives and History: POB 300100, Montgomery, AL 36130; 624 Washington Ave, Montgomery, AL 36130; tel. (334) 242-4435; e-mail reference@archives.alabama.gov; internet www.archives.alabama.gov; f. 1901; records and artefacts of historical value; Dir ED BRIDGES.

Autauga-Prattville Public Library: 254 Doster St, Prattville, AL 36067-3900; tel. (334) 365-3396; internet www.appl.info; Alabama Room: spec. colln of local history and genealogy materials; Dir JAN EARNEST; Chair. WILLIS BRADFORD.

B. B. Comer Memorial Library: 314 N Broadway Ave, Sylacauga, AL 35150-2528; tel. (256) 249-0961; e-mail bbclibrary@sylacauga.net; internet www.sylacauga.net/library; f. 1936 as Sylacauga Public Library; Dir SHIRLEY SPEARS.

Bessemer Public Library: 400 19th St N, Bessemer, AL 35020-4819; tel. (205) 428-

7882; e-mail bessemerlibrary@gmail.com; internet www.bessemerlibrary.org; f. 1907 as Bessemer Carnegie Library, present name 1967; research database incl. encyclopaedias, biographies, genealogy, literature, social sciences, health, science, magazines and newspapers; Dir DONNA SCHREMSER; Pres. DORIS LEWIS.

Birmingham Public Library: 2100 Park Pl., Birmingham, AL 35203; tel. (205) 226-3600; e-mail bpldirector@bham.lib.al.us; internet www.bplonline.org; f. 1886; spec. collns: Agee Cartographical Colln (incl. Joseph H. Woodward Colln), Catherine Collins Colln of Dance, Scruggs Philately Colln, Tutwiler Colln of Southern History and Literature, govt documents, archives, MSS, musical recordings, film and video; DIALOG Online Computer Reference Service, Books by Mail Service; 19 brs; 900,000 vols, 1m. pieces of microfilm, 30,000,000 archival documents, 400,000 photographs; Dir RENEE BLALOCK.

Boaz Public Library: 404 Thomas Ave, Boaz, AL 35957; tel. (256) 593-3000; e-mail library@cityofboaz.org; internet www .boazpubliclibrary.org; f. 1973; newspapers on microfilm from 1893 to 1983; colln on ancestry of Abraham Lincoln; 60,000 vols; Librarian LYNN BURGESS.

Cheaha Regional Library: 935 Colleman St, Heflin, AL 36264-1313; tel. (256) 463-7125; e-mail info@cheaharegionallibrary.org; internet www.cheaharegionallibrary.org; f. 1976, fmrly Public Library of Anniston, present location 1989; multi-county library system; incl. 8 mem. libraries across 5 counties; 1 bookmobile; Dir EVI JONES.

Cullman County Public Library System: 200 Clark St NE, Cullman, AL 35055; tel. (256) 734-1068; internet www.ccpls.com; f. 1890; photographic collns of Beyer-Karter, Herfurth and Johnson documenting history of Cullman County until the 1970s; artefacts incl. archaeological relics from Battle of Hog Mountain (1863); genealogical and historical periodicals; brs. incl. Cullman (HQ), Garden City, Guy Hunt Library-Holly Pond, Hanceville and Tom Bevill Library-Colony; 150,000 vols (incl. print and electronic); Dir MAX HAND; Chair. RON HOGUE.

Daphne Public Library: POB 1225, 2607 US Highway 98, Daphne, AL 36526-1225; tel. (251) 621-2818; e-mail daphlib3@bellsouth .net; internet www.daphneal.com/residents/ library; f. 1969; spec. colln incl. state and local folk life, digitized photographs and articles; 68,000 vols; Dir TONJA YOUNG.

Demopolis Public Library: 211 E Washington St, Demopolis, AL 36732; tel. (334) 289-1595; e-mail demopolis.public .library@demopolisal.com; internet www .demopolislibrary.info; f. 1922; 25,000 vols; spec. colln on history of Alabama, Marengo County and Demopolis; Luther Franklin Bragg, Jr, colln: genealogical and local history records focusing on Alabama and other areas of Marengo County; Dir MORGAN GRIMES; Chair. BETTY McCANTS.

Enterprise Public Library: 101 E Grubbs St, Enterprise, AL 36330-2531; tel. (334) 347-2636; e-mail epl@sanman.net; internet www .enterpriselibrary.org; f. 1923; colln of audio cassettes and CDs for the visually impaired and physically disabled; 53,000 vols; Dir DENISE UNRUH-KITCH; Chair. BRUCE KEEL; Sec. CATHERINE ROTH; Treas. MARY PENNY.

Fairhope Public Library: 501 Fairhope Ave, Fairhope, AL 36532; tel. (251) 928-7483; e-mail director@fairhopelibrary.org; internet www.fairhopelibrary.org; f. 1900; Dir TAMARA DEAN; Chair. MARTIN LANAUX.

Florence-Lauderdale Public Library: 350 N Wood Ave, Florence, AL 35630-4709; tel. (256) 764-6564; e-mail events@flpl.org; internet www.flpl.org; f. 1885 as The Ladies' Library, present location 2002; colln of records on local Lauderdale; Colbert (original part of Franklin) and Franklin co histories incl. Lauderdale County Probate Court record books on microfilm from 1820 to 1927 and local newspapers since 1824; colln of records on several New England, Southern and Mid-Western states; 100,000 vols; Exec. Dir NANCY SANFORD; Chair. PATRICIA BULLS BUTLER.

Gardendale Martha Moore Public Library: 995 Mount Olive Rd, Gardendale, AL 35071-4654; tel. (205) 631-6639; internet gardendale.lib.al.us; f. 1959; database incl. magazine and newspaper index; a health reference centre; 55,200 vols; Dir CONNIE SMITH.

Shelby County Public Library System: Harrison Library—System HQs, 50 Lester St, Columbiana, AL 35051; tel. (205) 669-3910; e-mail info@shelbycounty-al.org; internet www.shelbycounty-al.org; f. 1940; 14 libraries: Harrison Regional Library (HQ), 11 mem. libraries, 2 brs and 1 mem.-br. library; Dir BARBARA ROBERTS.

Hoover Public Library: 200 Municipal Dr., Hoover, AL 35216-5510; tel. (205) 444-7800; internet www.hooverlibrary.org; f. 1983; colln: literature, directories, encyclopedias, magazines and newspapers; 240,578 vols; Dir LINDA R. ANDREWS.

Horseshoe Bend Regional Library: 20 NW St, Dadeville, AL 36853-1355; tel. (256) 825-9232; e-mail horseshoebend@bellsouth .net; internet www.horseshoebendlibrary .org; 8 public libraries in Coosa, Elmore, Lee and Tallapoosa counties; Dir SUSIE ANDERSON.

Luverne Public Library: 148 E Third St, Luverne, AL 36049; tel. (334) 335-5326; e-mail library@luverne.org; internet library .luverne.org; local history colln; Dir KATHRYN TOMLIN.

Montgomery City-County Public Library: 2885-B E South Blvd, Montgomery, AL 36116-2513; tel. (334) 240-4842; internet www.mccpl.lib.al.us; f. 1899, present status 1974; 11 brs; comprehensive colln of books and data; 600,000 vols; Dir JAUNITA OWES.

State Law Library: 300 Dexter Ave, Montgomery, AL 36104; tel. 334 229-0578; e-mail reference@alalinc.net; internet www.alalinc .net/library; f. 1828; US govt depository; colln incl. reported decisions of the state and fed. appellate courts in the USA; statutes of all 50 states and the District of Columbia; 200,000 vols; Dir and State Law Librarian TIMOTHY A. LEWIS.

Tuscaloosa Public Library: 1801 Jack Warner Parkway, Tuscaloosa, AL 35401-1099; tel. (205) 345-5820; e-mail info@ tuscaloosa-library.org; internet www .tuscaloosa-library.org; f. 1879; genealogy and local history colln with microforms; Brown br. and Weaver Bolden br.; 2 bookmobiles; Exec. Dir MARY ELIZABETH HARPER; Chair. SHERIE GILES; Sec. Dr SAMORY PRUITT; Treas. J. BRAD SPRINGER.

University of Alabama Library: POB 870266, Tuscaloosa, AL 35487-0266; tel. (205) 348-6047; internet www.lib.ua.edu; f. 1831; regional depository for fed. documents; departmental libraries for business, education, engineering, sciences; spec. collns on Alabama and Southern history and literature; 2m. vols, 1m. govt documents, 3.5m. microform units and 2.75m. maps; Dean of Libraries LOUIS A. PITSCHMANN.

Washington County Public Library: POB 1057, Chatom, AL 36518; 14102 St Stephens Ave, Chatom, AL 36518; tel. (251) 847-2097; internet www.wcpls.org; f. 1956; main library in Chatom and br. in McIntosh; Dir JESSICA M. ROSS; Chair. ASHLI PAGE.

Alaska

Alaska Resources Library and Information Services: Library Bldg, Suite 111, 3211 Providence Dr., Anchorage, AK 99508; tel. (907) 272-7547; e-mail reference@arlis.org; internet www.arlis.org; provides access to natural and cultural resources information; 10,117 vols.

Alaska State Library: POB 110571, 333 Willoughby Ave, Eighth Fl, Juneau, AK 99811-0571; tel. (907) 465-2920; e-mail asl@ alaska.gov; internet library.alaska.gov; f. 1900 as Alaska Historical Library and Museum, current name adopted 1966; 154,533 vols: information services 72,857 vols, historical collns 78,643 vols, incl. 849 MSS and 515 photographic collns; 3,033 vols in Anchorage office; information service; br. in Anchorage, Alaska with talking book centre; incl. service to Alaska govt and the gen. public; historical collns; library devt; Dir LINDA THIBOADEAU.

Delta Community Library: 2291 Deborah St, Delta Junction, AK 99737-0229; tel. (907) 895-4102; internet www.ci.delta-junction.ak .us; f. 1960.

Elmer E. Rasmuson and BioSciences Libraries: POB 756800, 310 Tanana Loop, Fairbanks, AK 99775-6800; tel. (907) 474-7481; e-mail fyref@uaf.edu; internet www .library.uaf.edu; f. 1922; attached to Univ. of Alaska Fairbanks (UAF); 1.75m. vols; Dean of Libraries Dr BELLA KARR GERLICH.

Haines Borough Public Library: POB 1089, 111 Third Ave, Haines, AK 99827; tel. (907) 766-2545; e-mail director@ haineslibrary.org; internet www .haineslibrary.org; f. 1958; Dir PATRICIA BROWN.

Homer Public Library: 500 Hazel Ave, Homer, AK 99603; tel. (907) 235-3180; e-mail library@ci.homer.ak.us; internet www .cityofhomer-ak.gov/library; f. 1940; 45,000 vols; Library Dir ANN DIXON.

Joyce K. Carver Soldotna Public Library: 235 N Binkley St, Soldotna, AK 99669; tel. (907) 262-4227; e-mail kmcleod@ci .soldotna.ak.us; internet www.ci.soldotna.ak .us/library.html; Librarian TERRI BURDICK.

Juneau Public Libraries: 292 Marine Way, Juneau, AK 99801; tel. (907) 586-5249; internet www.juneau.org/library; 3 brs; 124,000 vols; Library Dir BARBARA BERG.

Kegoayah Kozga Library: POB 1168, 223 Front St, Nome, AK 99762; tel. (907) 443-6628; e-mail library@nomealaska.org; internet www.nomealaska.org; Library Dir MARGUERITE LA RIVIERE.

Keith B. Mather Library: Geophysical Institute, Int. Arctic Research Center, 930 Koyukuk Dr., POB 757355, Fairbanks, AK 99775-7355; tel. (907) 474-7503; e-mail gilibrary@gi.alaska.edu; internet www2.gi .alaska.edu/services/library; f. 1946; attached to Geophysical Institute, Univ. of Alaska, Fairbanks; colln incl. atmospheric sciences, glaciology, global change, ice, snow, permafrost, remote sensing, seismology, space physics and volcanology; US Patent and Trademark depository library; Librarian FLORA GRABOWSKA.

Ketchikan Campus Library: Ziegler Bldg, 2600 Seventh Ave, Ketchikan, AK 99901; tel. (907) 228-4567; e-mail libket@uas.alaska .edu; internet www.ketch.alaska.edu/

library; attached to Univ. of Alaska, SE; Librarian KATHLEEN WIECHELMAN.

Ketchikan Public Library: 629 Dock St, Ketchikan, AK 99901; tel. (907) 225-3331; e-mail library@firstcitylibraries.org; internet www.firstcitylibraries.org; f. 1901, present bldg 1969.

Petersburg Public Library: POB 549, 12 Nordic Dr., Petersburg, AK 99833; tel. (907) 772-3349; e-mail library@ci.petersburg.ak .us; internet www.psglib.org; f. 1932, present bldg 1960; City Librarian TARA ALCOCK.

Seward Community Library: POB 2389, 238 Fifth Ave, Seward, AK 99664; tel. (907) 224-4082; e-mail tmorrow@cityofseward.net; internet www.cityofseward.net/library; Library Dir PATRICIA LINVILLE.

Tuzzy Consortium Library: POB 2130, Barrow, AK 99723; tel. (907) 852-4050; e-mail tuzzy@tuzzy.org; internet www.tuzzy .org; Tuzzy Consortium Library is a mem. of OCLC (Online Computer Library Center); Library Dir DAVID ONGLEY.

Valdez Consortium Library: POB 609, Valdez, AK 99686; tel. (907) 835-4632; e-mail vnvl@uaa.alaska.edu; internet www .ci.valdez.ak.us/library; combined public and college library; Head Librarian MOLLIE GOOD.

Wasilla Meta-Rose Public Library: 391 N Main St, Wasilla, AK 99654; tel. (907) 376-5913; e-mail library@ci.wasilla.ak.us; internet www.cityofwasilla.com; f. 1917; Librarian K. J. MARTIN-ALBRIGHT.

Z. J. Loussac Public Library: 3600 Denali St, Anchorage, AK 99503; tel. (907) 343-2975; internet www.muni.org/departments/library; 4 brs; Dir NANCY TILESTON.

Arizona

Apache County Library District: POB 2760, 30 S Second W, St Johns, AZ 85936; tel. (928) 337-4923; internet www .apachecountylibraries.com; operates 7 public libraries located in Alpine, Concho, Greer, Round Valley, Sanders, St Johns, and Vernon communities; Dir JUDITH PEPPLE.

Arizona Historical Society Library and Archives: 949 E Second St, Tucson, AZ 85719; tel. (520) 628-5774; e-mail ahsref@ azhs.gov; internet www .arizonahistoricalsociety.org/library_an d_archives; 4 regional repositories in Flagstaff, Tempe, Tucson and Yuma; MSS, maps, personal papers, photographs, films, oral histories, books on history of Arizona, W and N Mexico; non-circulating libraries; colln of 500,000 prints, slides and original negatives showcases visual record of Arizona since 1870s; Exec. Dir ANNE I. WOOSLEY.

Arizona State Library, Archives and Public Records: 1700 W Washington, Suite 200, Phoenix, AZ 85007; tel. (602) 926-4035; e-mail services@azlibrary.gov; internet www .azlibrary.gov; f. 1864; attached to Sec. of State; historical MSS, govt records, books and photographs of Arizona and its peoples, genealogy, fed. and state documents; library extension assistance to public libraries, archives of historical records, library for the blind and physically handicapped, museums, public records; Carnegie Center; 1.2m. vols; State Librarian JOAN CLARK.

Arizona State University Libraries: POB 871006, Arizona State Univ., Tempe, AZ 85287; 113 Hayden Library, Tempe, AZ 85287-1006; tel. (480) 965-6164; e-mail askalib@asu.edu; internet lib.asu.edu; Univ. Archives; 8 brs on 4 campuses: Downtown Phoenix Campus, Polytechnic Campus, Tempe Campus, West Campus; repository of govt and fed. documents; Labriola Nat. American Indian Data Center; 2.5m. vols,

200,000 maps; spec. colln: 45,000 books, 2,000 linear ft of MSS and photographs, sound and video recordings; Univ. Librarian SHERRIE SCHMIDT.

Flagstaff City-Coconino County Public Library: Main Library, 300 W Aspen Ave, Flagstaff, AZ 86001; tel. (928) 779-7673; internet www.flagstaffpubliclibrary.org; f. 1884, present status 1927; incl. East Flagstaff Community Library; 4 brs; 4 affiliated public libraries; bookmobile services; Dir HEIDI HOLLAND.

Glendale Public Library: 5959 W Brown St, Glendale, AZ 85302; tel. (623) 939-0532; internet www.glendaleaz.com/library; f. 1890; 1 main library and 2 brs; Dir SUE KOMERNICKY; Library Man. KATHLEEN HAMEL.

Maricopa County Library District: 2700 N Central Ave, Suite 700, Phoenix, AZ 85004; tel. (602) 652-3000; internet www.mcldaz .org; 17 brs; 7 affiliated libraries; Dir CINDY KOLACZYNSKI.

Parker Public Library: 1001 Navajo Ave, Parker, AZ 85344; tel. (928) 669-2622; internet www.parkerpubliclibraryaz.org; f. 1956; Library Man. RUTHIE DAVIS.

Phoenix Public Library: 1221 N Central Ave, Phoenix, AZ 85004; tel. (602) 262-4636; internet www.phoenixpubliclibrary.org; f. 1898; 16 brs; Arizona and SW materials; art gallery and exhibitions; audiovisual material; 1.7m. vols; Chair. ABRAHAM JAMES; City Librarian RITA HAMILTON.

Pima County Public Library: 101 N Stone Ave, Tucson, AZ 85701; tel. (520) 791-4010; internet www.library.pima.gov; f. 1883 as Carnegie Free Library, present name and status 2006; HQ and colln at Joel D. Valdez Main Library; local, state and fed. govt documents; holds records from Postal History Foundation Library and Tucson Museum of Art Research Library; 25 brs and bookmobile service; affiliate library: Oro Valley Public Library; Dir NANCY LEDEBOER; Pres. OBDÚLIA GONZÁLEZ.

Prescott Valley Public Library: 7401 E Civic Circle, Prescott Valley, AZ 86314; tel. (928) 759-3040; internet www.pvlib.net; part of Yavapai Library Network; 65,000 vols; Dir STUART MATTSON; Pres. DONNA MORGAN; Sec. KARYL COLOZZE.

Sedona Public Library: 3250 White Bear Rd, Sedona, AZ 86336; tel. (928) 282-7714; internet www.sedonalibrary.org; f. 1958, present location 1994; mem. of Yavapai County Library Network; village service centre at Oak Creek; Dir VIRGINIA VOLKMAN; Pres. ANNE URUBURU; Sec. SANDRA IMMERSO; Treas. ROGER SHLONSKY.

Superior Court Law Library: East Court Bldg, 101 W Jefferson St, Phoenix, AZ 85003; tel. (602) 506-3461; e-mail services@scll .maricopa.gov; internet www.superiorcourt .maricopa.gov/lawlibrary; f. 1913; provides legal research assistance in Maricopa co; colln incl. Arizona's legal materials, court admin. documents, fed. legal materials, foreign and int. legal treaties and monographs, books on legal topics, session laws and state and local bar asscn journals; 150,000 vols; Dir MARCUS REINKENSMEYER; publ. *The Court Informer* (6 a year).

University of Arizona Library: Main Library A349, POB 210055, Tucson, AZ 85721-0055; 1510 E University Blvd, Tucson, AZ 85721-0055; tel. (520) 621-2101; internet www.library.arizona.edu; f. 1891; spec. collns: history of science, SW Americana and borderlands history, fine and theatre arts, British and American literature, rare books, MSS collns, photographs and other materials; 5,266,051 vols, 645,463 ebooks,

54,464 ejournals; Dean for Univ. Libraries CARLA STOFFLE.

Arkansas

Arkansas History Commission Library: One Capitol Mall, Little Rock, AR 72201; tel. (501) 682-6900; e-mail state.archives@ arkansas.gov; internet www.ark-ives.com; f. 1905; attached to Arkansas Dept of Parks and Tourism; official state archives; copy and edit official records and other historical material; encourages historical work and research; 2 brs: NE Arkansas Regional Archives (NEARA) and Southwest Arkansas Regional Archives (SARA); Dir Dr WENDY RICHTER; Librarian SHEILA BEVILL.

Arkansas State Library: Suite 100, 900 W Capitol, Little Rock, AR 72201; tel. (501) 682-2053; internet www.library.arkansas.gov; f. 1979; genealogy; state and fed. records; US patent and trademark depository; State Librarian CAROLYN ASHCRAFT.

Arkansas Supreme Court Library: Justice Bldg, 625 Marshall St, Suite 1500, Little Rock, AR 72201; tel. (501) 682-2147; internet courts.arkansas.gov/library; f. 1851, present bldg 1958; serves justices and staff of Arkansas Supreme Court, judges and staff of Arkansas Court of Appeals and judicial agencies; state and fed. depository library; maintains 13 satellite libraries; 100,000 vols; Dir AVA M. HICKS; Librarian JACQUELINE S. WRIGHT.

Boone County Library: 221 W Stephenson, Harrison, AR 72601; tel. (870) 741-5913; internet www.boonecountylibrary.org; 84,000 vols; Dir and Librarian LAVOYCE EWING.

Columbia County Library: POB 668, 2057 N Jackson St, Magnolia, AR 71754; tel. (870) 234-1991; e-mail library@cocolib.org; internet www2.youseemore.com/columbia; f. 1929 as Magnolia City Library, present name 1942; incl. Lafayette Co Library, Stamps Public Library and Taylor Public Library; Dir LAURA CLEVELAND.

Conway County Library: 101 W Church St, Morrilton, AR 72110; tel. (501) 354-5204; internet www2.youseemore.com/conwaycl; f. 1916; 35,000 vols; Chair. JANNA VIRDEN; Dir JAY CARTER.

Crawford County Library: 1409 Main St, Van Buren, AR 72956; tel. (479) 471-3226; e-mail ccls@crawfordcountylib.org; internet www2.youseemore.com/crawfordcl; f. 1999; brs at Alma, Cedarville, Mountainburg and Mulberry; Van Buren Public Library (HQ); 143,351 vols; Dir EVA WHITE.

Craighead County Jonesboro Public Library: 315 W Oak Ave, Jonesboro, AR 72401-3594; tel. (870) 935-5133; e-mail reference@libraryinjonesboro.org; internet www.libraryinjonesboro.org; f. 1917; 7 brs; 145,000 vols, 13,776 books on cassettes, DVDs, video cassettes and CDs; Chair. MICHAEL JOHNSON.

Donald W. Reynolds Library: 300 Library Hill, Mountain Home, AR 72653; tel. (870) 580-0987; internet www.baxtercountylibrary .org; f. 2010; attached to Baxter County Library; br. at Gassville; 75,000 vols; Chair. JOHN AHRENS; Dir GWEN KHAYAT.

Fayetteville Public Library: 401 W Mountain St, Fayetteville, AR 72701; tel. (479) 856-7000; e-mail questions@faylib.org; internet www.faylib.org; f. 1916, 245,000 vols (incl. books, CDs, DVDs, video cassettes, audio cassettes, ebooks and parenting kits); Exec. Dir DAVID JOHNSON; Pres. SUZANNE CLARK; Sec. KIM AGEE; Treas. MAYLON RICE.

Fort Smith Public Library: 3201 Rogers Ave, Fort Smith, AR 72903; tel. (479) 783-0229; e-mail reference@fortsmithlibrary.org;

internet www.fortsmithlibrary.org; f. 1891; 3 brs; genealogy dept in main library; Pres. TRACY LONG; Sec. BRIAN DELUNG; Treas. ROBERT KELLY.

Marion County Library: 308 Old Main, Yellville, AR 72687; tel. (870) 449-6015; e-mail librarian@marcolib.org; internet marcolib.org; f. 1944; Dir ANITA PAULSON.

Springdale Public Library: 405 S Pleasant St, Springdale, AR 72764; tel. (479) 750-8180; e-mail askus@springdalelibrary.org; internet www.springdalelibrary.org; f. 1927; newspaper on microfilm since May 1887; cemetery indexes for Washington and Benton counties; mem. of Washington County Library System; Dir MARCIA RANSOM; Pres. TODD WOOD.

University of Arkansas Libraries: 365 N McIlroy Ave, Fayetteville, AR 72701-4002; tel. (479) 575-4104; e-mail refer@uark.edu; internet ibinfo.uark.edu; David W. Mullins Library (main research facility), Robert A. and Vivian Young Law Library, Fine Arts Library, Chemistry and Biochemistry Library, Physics Library, Performing Arts and Media Library; spec. collns: local politics, Civil War, women's records, maps; 1.9m. vols, 5.5m. microforms, 100,000 pictures and photographs; Dean of Libraries CAROLYN HENDERSON ALLEN.

William F. Laman Public Library System: 2801 Orange St, North Little Rock, AR 72114; tel. (501) 758-1720; e-mail library .information@lamanlibrary.org; internet www.lamanlibrary.org; f. 1947; 1 br; 175,000 vols, 8,000 CDs and audiobooks, 3,000 DVDs; Dir JEFFREY L. BASKIN; Chair. RON OLIVER.

William J. Clinton Presidential Library and Museum: 1200 President Clinton Ave, Little Rock, AR 72201; tel. (501) 374-4242; e-mail clinton.library@nara.gov; internet www.clintonlibrary.gov; f. 2004; 10,000 vols (incl. Head of State gifts and non-Head of State gifts), 78m. pages of official records, 20m. email records, 2m. photographs, 5,900 audio cassettes and 12,500 video cassettes; Dir TERRI GARNER.

California

Alameda County Law Library: 125 12th St, Oakland, CA 94607-4912; tel. (510) 208-4800; internet www.acgov.org/law; f. 1891; provides free access to the judiciary, state and county officials, members of the bar and residents of the county; colln incl. legal research materials; 196,941 vols, 105,000 vols in hard copy and 91,941 vols in microform; publ. *Recent Acquisitions List* (12 a year); Law Library Dir MARK E. ESTES.

Belvedere-Tiburon Library: 1501 Tiburon Blvd Tiburon, CA 94920; tel. (415) 789-2665; e-mail refdesk@bel-tib-lib.org; internet www .thelibrary.info; f. 1997; 53,904 vols, 47,654 adult colln, 69,279 electronic media, 14,918 multimedia, 2,867 reference colln, 319 periodicals; Library Dir DEBORAH MAZZOLINI.

California State Library: POB 942837, Sacramento, CA 94237-0001; tel. (916) 654-0266; e-mail cslinfo@library.ca.gov; internet www.library.ca.gov; f. 1850; library service to state govt; preservation of CA materials; govt document depository; law library; books for the blind, and physically handicapped service; administrator of the state and fed. aid to public libraries; 696,000 vols, 3,011,835 govt publs; State Librarian STACEY A. ALDRICH; publs *California Library Directory* (1 a year), *California Library Laws* (1 a year), *California Library Statistics* (1 a year), *California State Publications* (2 a year).

County of Los Angeles Public Library: A C Bilbrew Library, 150 E El Segundo Blvd, Los Angeles, CA 90061; tel. (310) 538-3350; e-mail lacountylibrary@gmail.com; internet www.colapublib.org; f. 1912; 84 regional and community libraries; 1 institutional library; 4 bookmobiles; 5,488,446 vols, 789,237 titles, 6,742 periodicals, 59,352 govt publs, 298,033 audio materials, 600,095 video cassettes, 2,118 CDs; County Librarian MARGARET DONNELLAN TODD.

Dr Martin Luther King, Jr, Library: 150 E San Fernando St, San Jose, CA 95112; tel. (408) 808-2000; internet www.sjlibrary.org; f. 1997; also known as King Library; spec. colln: materials related to Dr Martin Luther King, Jr, and the Civil Rights movement; 1.5m. vols.

Hoover Institution on War, Revolution and Peace: 434 Galvez Mall, Stanford, CA 94305-6010; tel. (650) 723-1754; internet www.hoover.org; f. 1919; attached to Stanford Univ.; centre of documentation and research on int. and domestic political, social and economic change since beginning of the 20th century; 60m. documents, 100,000 political posters; 4,772 archival units on the causes and consequences of war and revolutionary movements, and on efforts to achieve peace; with emphasis on int. rivalries and global cooperation; research programme on political, economic and social problems in the USA; ind., within the framework of Stanford Univ.; Dir RICHARD SOUSA; publs *China Leadership Monitor* (4 a year), *Education Next* (4 a year), *Hoover's Digest* (4 a year), *Policy Review* (6 a year).

Huntington Library, Art Collections and Botanical Gardens: 1151 Oxford Rd, San Marino, CA 91108; tel. (626) 405-2100; e-mail publicinformation@huntington.org; internet www.huntington.org; f. 1919; collns incl. 375,000 rare books, 6m. MSS, working reference library of 500,000 vols and 600,000 photographs; available to scholars and others engaged in research work on application to the Registrar; collns concentrate on British and American history, literature and art; particular strengths incl. English medieval and Renaissance, British drama, American colonial, American Civil War, American frontier, MSS since 19th century, early science; separate reference libraries located in the Botanical Div., the latter incl. 300,000 photographs, paintings and 6,000 British drawings; public programmes, lectures, exhibitions; See also Museums and Art Galleries; 6m. vols, incl. books, MSS and photographs; Pres. STEVEN KOBLIK; Avery Dir of the Library DAVID S. ZEIDBERG; publ. *Huntington Frontiers* (2 a year).

Kern County Library: 701 Truxtun Ave, Bakersfield, CA. 93301; tel. (661) 868-0700; internet www.kerncountylibrary.org; 25 brs, 1 main library, 2 bookmobiles; 1,097,438 vols (incl. 16,172 govt documents, 14,358 microforms, 191 periodicals subscriptions, and 65,003 audiovisual items; Dir of Libraries SHERRY GOMEZ.

LA Law Library (Los Angeles County Law Library): 301 W First St, Los Angeles, CA 90012-3100; tel. (213) 785-2529; e-mail reference@lalawlibrary.org; internet www .lalawlibrary.org; f. 1891 as Los Angeles County Law Library; br collns in courthouses in Long Beach and Torrance; programmes for mems of the California State Bar MCLE; public training classes; public library partnerships: Compton, Lancaster; Pasadena, Van Nuys; 1m. vols (incl. print, media, microfilm and microfiche); collns of USA and int. legal materials; self-help colln for self-represented litigants; Exec. Dir SANDRA J. LEVIN; Sr Dir JAYE STEINBRICK.

Los Angeles Public Library: 630 W Fifth St, Los Angeles, CA 90071; tel. (213) 228-7272; e-mail asklapl@hotmail.com; internet www.lapl.org; f. 1872; 70 brs; California, children's literature, cookery, genealogy, North American Indians, modern languages, orchestral scores, US patents, standards and specifications, English language, theatre, congressional documents and hearings, business and finance, corporate annual reports, video cassettes, DVDs, CDs, audiobooks, telephone and trade directories; 6m. vols; Dir Central Library GIOVANNA MANNINO (acting); Dir Br. Libraries CHERYL COLLINS (acting); City Librarian MARTÍN GÓMEZ.

Nixon Presidential Library and Museum: 18001 Yorba Linda Blvd, Yorba Linda, CA 92886; tel. (714) 983-9120; e-mail nixon@nara.gov; internet www.nixonlibrary .gov; f. 2007; 4,000 of 'off air' video recordings; nearly 4,469 audio recordings; 30,000 gifts from foreign heads of states, American citizens, and others; 500,000 photographs; 700 hours of film; 46m. pages of documents; 3,700 hours of recorded presidential conversations; Dir TIMOTHY NAFTALI.

Oakland Public Library: 125 14th St, Oakland, CA 94612; tel. (510) 238-3134; e-mail tdowns@oaklandlibrary.org; internet www.oaklandlibrary.org; f. 1878 as Oakland Free Library; 15 brs; 1 main library; 1 bookmobile; Dir of Library Services CARMEN L. MARTINEZ.

OC Public Libraries: Aliso Viejo Library, One Journey, Aliso Viejo, CA 92656; tel. (949) 360-1730; e-mail libraryadmin@occr.ocgov .com; internet www.ocpl.org; 33 brs; County Librarian HELEN FRIED.

Pasadena Public Library: 285 E Walnut St, Pasadena, CA 91101; tel. (626) 744-4066; internet www.ci.pasadena.ca.us; 1 main library; 9 brs; 775,469 vols,; Dir JAN SANDER.

Placer County Library: 350 Nevada St, Auburn, CA 95603; tel. (530) 886-4550; e-mail library@placerlibrary.org; internet www.placer.ca.gov; 11 brs; 1 bookmobile; Dir of Library Services MARY GEORGE.

Plumas County Library: 445 Jackson St, Quincy, CA 95971; tel. (530) 283-6310; internet www.countyofplumas.com; f. 1905; 1 main library, 3 brs; County Librarian DORA MITCHELL.

Ronald Reagan Presidential Library: 40 Presidential Dr., Simi Valley, CA 93065; tel. (805) 577-4000; e-mail reagan.library@nara .gov; internet www.reagan.utexas.edu; f. 1991; repository of presidential records for Pres. Reagan's admin; 50m. pages of presidential documents, 1.6m. photographs, 500,000 ft of motion picture film.

Roseville Public Library: Downtown Library, 225 Taylor St, Roseville, CA 95678; tel. (916) 774-5221; e-mail library@roseville .ca.us; internet www.roseville.ca.us/library; f. 1912; 3 brs; contains a large history colln, and other research materials such as books, magazines and online databases; 190,360 vols; City Librarian NATASHA CASTEEL.

Sacramento Public Library: 828 I St, Sacramento, CA 95814; tel. (916) 264-2700; e-mail contact@saclibrary.org; internet www .saclibrary.org; f. 1879; spec. collns: Sacramento current and historical information, California colln, business colln, printing history, Sacramento area authors, art and music colln; central library, 26 brs; 2m. vols; Chair. SANDY SHEEDY; Dir RIVKAH K. SASS.

San Diego County Public Law Library: 1168 Union St, San Diego, CA 92101-3904; tel. (619) 531-3900; e-mail refdesk@sdcpll .org; internet www.sdcpll.org; f. 1891; colln of California and US legal materials, such as statutes and codes, administrative regulations, case law; secondary legal resources, incl. federal, microform, reference, archival, electronic and self-help collections; main library under construction; 250,000 vols; Pres. JULIA C. KELETY; Dir JOHN ADKINS.

San Diego Public Library: 820 E St, San Diego, CA 92101-6416; tel. (619) 236-5800; e-mail librarydirector@sandiego.gov; internet www.sandiego.gov/public-library; f. 1882; 1 central library and 35 brs; adult literacy programme office (READ/San Diego); 4.2m. books, incl. ebooks, 3,888 periodicals, 1.6m. govt. documents, 291,000 books in 25 languages other than English; Dir DEBORAH BARROW.

San Francisco Law Library: 401 Van Ness Ave, Room 400, San Francisco, CA 94102; tel. (415) 554-6821; e-mail sflawlibrary@sfgov .org; internet www.sflawlibrary.org; f. 1870; colln of materials relevant to legal research with an emphasis on California law; 3 brs; open to public; 246,000 vols (main library), 30,367 vols (br. libraries); Dir MARCIA R. BELL; Pres. KURT W. MELCHIOR; Treas. KATHLEEN V. FISHER.

San Francisco Public Library: 100 Larkin St, San Francisco, CA 94102-4733; tel. (415) 557-4400; e-mail citylibrarian@sfpl.org; internet www.sfpl.org; 7,051,190 vols; City Librarian LUIS HERRERA.

Santa Cruz County Law Library: 701 Ocean St, Room 070, Santa Cruz, CA 95060; tel. (831) 420-2205; e-mail scclawlib@yahoo .com; internet www.lawlibrary.org; f. 1896; 16,000 vols; Pres. JOHN GALLAGHER.

St Helena Public Library: 1492 Library Lane, St. Helena, CA 94574; tel. 963-5244; e-mail director@shpl.org; internet www.shpl .org; f. 1875, present bldg 1979; 96,000 vols; Library Dir JENNIFER BAKER.

Stanford University Libraries: Stanford, CA 94305; tel. (650) 725-1064; e-mail infocenter@stanford.edu; internet www .library.stanford.edu; f. 1885; 19 libraries incl. the Green Library, Hoover Institution on War, Revolution and Peace, and 45 departmental and school libraries, of which the major ones are: Lane Medical Library, Robert Crown Law Library, Cubberley Education Library, Branner Earth Sciences Library, J. Hugh Jackson Business Library, Linear Accelerator Center Library, Falconer Biology Library, Hopkins Marine Station Library, Mathematical and Computer Sciences Library, Swain Chemistry Library, Art and Architecture, Music, Archive of Recorded Sound, Physics, Engineering; 9m. vols, 6m. vols of microform, 75,000 serials, 1.5m. ebooks, 1.5m. audiovisual materials; spec. collns: transportation, music, British and American Literature, history of science, book arts and history of the book, children's literature, Judaica and Hebraica; Univ. Librarian MICHAEL A. KELLER.

University of Southern California Libraries: 3550 Trousdale Parkway, DML 335, Los Angeles, CA 90089-0183; tel. (213) 740-2543; e-mail library@usc.edu; internet www.usc.edu/isd/libraries; f. 1880; spec. collns: Cervantes, Lewis Carroll, Max Reinhardt; American literature; cinema and television, European philosophy; German exile literature; gerontology; international relations; Korean studies, Latin American studies, natural history, Southern California history, Univ. Archives; 4,180,515 vols, 109,352 serial titles, 3,192,549 visual materials, 161,720 maps and cartographic materials, 6,472,630 microfilm units, 37,032 audio recordings, 37,980 film and video recordings, 49,251 linear ft MSS and archives, 399,112 ebooks, 76,399 ejournals, 255,935 digital archive items; Dean for Libraries CATHERINE QUINLAN.

Colorado

Arapahoe Library District: 12855 E Adam Aircraft Circle, Englewood, CO 80112; tel. (303) 542-7279; internet arapahoelibraries .org; f. 1966; serves Byers and Deer Trail, cities of Bow Mar, Centennial, Cherry Hills Village, Columbine, Glendale, Greenwood Village and Sheridan, and unincorporated areas of Arapahoe co; 8 br. libraries and 1 bookmobile; Man. ELOISE MAY.

Auraria Library: 1100 Lawrence St, Denver, CO 80204; tel. (303) 556-2740; internet library.auraria.edu; archives and spec. colln; serves downtown Denver campus of Univ. of Colorado Denver, Auraria Higher Education Center, Metropolitan State Univ. of Denver and Community College of Denver; Dir MARY M. SOMERVILLE.

Berthoud Community Library District: POB 1259, 236 Welch Ave, Berthoud, CO 80513-2259; tel. (970) 532-2757; e-mail director.bpl@gmail.com; internet berthoud .colibraries.org; f. 1931; Dir SARA WRIGHT; Pres. KATHRYN CHURCHILL; Sec. LAURI WEAVER; Treas. PEG OBENHAUS.

Cardinal Stafford Library: 1300 S Steele St, Denver, CO 80210; tel. (303) 715-3146; e-mail infosjv@archden.org; internet www .sjvdenver.edu/library; f. 1910; attached to St John Vianney Theological Seminary; colln on Catholic theology, church history, biblical studies, liturgy, canon law, religious art, philosophy and literature; spec. collns: over 500 rare books dating back to early 16th century and periodicals dating back to the 1800s; 150,000 vols, 300 print periodicals; E. M. Womack Colln: 10,000 vols; Dir STEPHEN SWEENEY.

Clear Creek County District Library: POB 666, Georgetown, CO 80444; 614 Taos St, Georgetown, CO 80444; tel. (303) 569-2403; e-mail director@clearcreeklibrary.org; internet www2.youseemore.com/ clearcreeklibrary; incl. John Tomay Memorial Library and Idaho Springs Public Library; Dir SUE LATHROP; Pres. MARIANNE LORITZ; Sec. SUSAN SERPA; Treas. VICTORIA COLLE.

Colorado State Archives: 1313 Sherman, Room 1B20 Denver, CO 80203; tel. (303) 866-2358; internet www.colorado.gov/dpa/doit/ archives; f. 1953; attached to Colorado Dept of Personnel and Admin.; preserves Colorado's legal and historical records and promotes their use by public; 1m. archival entries; State Archivist TERRY KETELSEN.

Colorado State Library: 201 E Colfax Ave, Room 309, Denver, CO 80203; tel. (303) 866-6900; internet www.cde.state.co.us/cdelib; f. 1959; attached to Colorado Dept of Education; access to information produced by state govt; free recorded Braille and large-print library materials; Asst Commr EUGENE HAINER.

Colorado State University Libraries: Morgan Library, Colorado State Univ., 501 University Ave, 1019 Campus Delivery, Fort Collins, CO 80523-1019; tel. (970) 491-1841; internet lib.colostate.edu; f. 1880; br. library in Veterinary Medical Center; fed. depository; 2,073,333 vols, 31,372 current serials (incl. magazines, journals and periodicals), 1.6 km of archival materials, 24,106 ejournals; Dean for Libraries PATRICK BURNS.

Colorado Supreme Court Library: 101 W Colfax Ave, Suite A, Denver, CO 80202; tel. (303) 837-3720; e-mail library@judicial.state .co.us; internet cscl.colibraries.org; colln for research of judiciary and mems of the bar; open to public; colln on primary law from fed. and state govts, treatise colln and other practice-oriented materials incl. form books, Colorado Continuing Legal Education mater-

ials and practice manuals; 80,000 vols, 12,000 titles.

Denver Public Library: 10 W 14th Ave, Pkwy, Denver, CO 80204; tel. (720) 865-1111; internet www.denverlibrary.org; f. 1889 as a wing of Denver High School, new building opened in 1995; 2,236,686 items; 24 brs; specializes in W US history, conservation of natural resources, energy and the environment, genealogy, fine printing, folk music, US 10th Mountain Div. soldiers; holds events and classes; Pres. KEVIN O'CONNOR; City Librarian SHIRLEY AMORE.

DOC Boulder Laboratories Library: 325 Broadway MC-5, Boulder, CO 80305; tel. (303) 497-3271; e-mail boulderlabs.main .library@noaa.gov; internet library.bldrdoc .gov; f. 1954; attached to US Dept of Commerce; 45,000 vols, 350 current journals, 38,000 bound journal vols, 1,000 ejournals; Dir JOAN SEGAL (acting).

Douglas County Libraries: 100 S Wilcox St, Castle Rock, CO 80104; tel. (303) 791-7323; internet douglascountylibraries.org; f. 1929; libraries in Highlands Ranch, Lone Tree, Louviers, Parker, Castle Rock, Littleton; 713,448 vols; Dir JAMIE LaRUE; Pres. AMY HUNT; Sec. DAVID STARCK; Treas. BOB McLAUGHLIN.

Garfield County Libraries: POB 832, Rifle, CO 81650; 207 E Ave, Rifle, CO 81650; tel. (970) 625-4270; internet www .garfieldlibraries.org; f. 1938; 6 brs; Ancestry Library Edn with 4 billion records in census data, vital records, directories and photos from N America, Europe and Australia; 182,655 vols; Exec. Dir AMELIA SHELLEY; Pres. NELLA BARKER.

Grand County Library District: POB 1050, Granby, CO 80446; 225 E Jasper Ave, Granby, CO 80446; tel. (970) 887-9411; e-mail adminoffice@gcld.org; internet www .gcld.org; f. 1995; provides sources and advisory to create new libraries; 5 brs; Exec. Dir MARY ANNE HANSON-WILCOX; Pres. JOHN KACIK; Sec. DEDE FAY; Treas. KIM JENSEN.

HealthONE Denver Medical Library: 1719 E 19th Ave, Denver, CO 80218; tel. (303) 839-6670; e-mail info@denvermedlib .org; internet www.denvermedlib.org; f. 1893 as Colorado Medical Library Asscn; open only to mems; Man. SHARON MARTIN.

Mesa County Libraries: 443 N Sixth St, Grand Junction, CO 81501; tel. (970) 243-4442; internet www.mcpld.org; 7 brs; Dir EVE TALLMAN; Pres. LINDA DAVIDSON; Sec. LAURIE TASHIRO.

Pikes Peak Library District: POB 1579, Colorado Springs, CO 80901; tel. (719) 531-6333; internet library.ppld.org; f. 1903; incl. Community Breast Cancer Resource Center; bookmobile services; 13 brs; Exec. Dir PAULA J. MILLER.

University of Colorado at Boulder Libraries: 184 UCB, 1720 Pleasant St, Boulder, CO 80309-0184; tel. (303) 492-8705; e-mail reflib@colorado.edu; internet ucblibraries.colorado.edu; f. 1877 as Teller Library; 5 brs; spec. collns: mountaineering, photobooks, peace and justice, western Americana; 3,928,431 vols, 6,993,960 microforms, 963,779 govt documents, 38,518 linear ft MSS and archives, 69,010 audio cassettes, 16,697 films and video cassettes; Dean of Libraries JAMES F. WILLIAMS.

Connecticut

Acton Public Library: 60 Old Boston Post Rd, Old Saybrook, CT 06475; tel. (860) 395-3184; e-mail actonpubliclibrary@gmail.com; f. 1854; offers information in all areas incl. municipal, medical and career field; 75,000 vols; Dir MICHELE VAN EPPS.

Ansonia Library: 53 S Cliff St, Ansonia, CT 06401; tel. (203) 734-6275; e-mail ansonialibrary@biblio.org; internet www .ansonialibrary.org; f. 1892; Dir JOYCE CEC- CARELLI; Chair. MARGARET SULLIVAN; Treas. VIOLET O'DONNELL.

Avon Free Public Library: 281 Country Club Rd, Avon, CT 06001; tel. (860) 673-9712; e-mail avonref@avonctlibrary.info; internet www.avonctlibrary.info; f. 1798; Marian Hunter History Room incl. photographs, postcards, scrapbooks, maps, deeds and other pieces of memorabilia; 100,403 vols; Dir VIRGINIA VOCELLI; Pres. MARY LaBELLE SUTER; Sec. RUTH TIMME; Treas. THOMAS IEZZI.

Bakerville Library: 6 Maple Hollow Rd, New Hartford, CT 06057; tel. (860) 482-8806; internet www.bakervillelibrary.org; f. 1949; colln of audio books, popular fiction and reference material; 14,000 vols; Librarian JULIE LaSATA; Chair. DIANNE LITCHFIELD.

Bethlehem Public Library: 32 Main St S, Bethlehem, CT 06751; tel. (203) 266-7792; internet www.ci.bethlehem.ct.us/library .htm; f. 1857, present name and status 1900; 23,000 vols; Dir ANNE SMALL.

Bill Memorial Library: 240 Monument St, Groton, CT 06340; tel. (860) 445-0392; e-mail info@billmemorial.org; internet www .billmemorial.org; f. 1888; genealogy or local history room for research; colln incl. best-sellers, current non-fiction, classics and large print books; 21,000 vols.

Bridgeport Library: 925 Broad St, Bridge-port, CT 06604; tel. (203) 576-7777; internet www.bportlibrary.org; f. 1881; brs: Bur-roughs and Saden, Black Rock, Newfield, North and Old Mill Green; City Librarian SCOTT HUGHES; Pres. JIM O'DONNELL; Sec. and Treas. TOM ERRICHETTI.

Cheshire Public Library: 104 Main St, Cheshire, CT 06410-2406; tel. (203) 272-2245; e-mail cheshire@cheshirelibrary.org; internet www.cheshirelib.org; f. 1892; local history and genealogy, large print books and audio books for visually impaired; Dir RAMONA BURKEY; Chair. CAROL DiPIETRO.

Connecticut State Library: 231 Capitol Ave, Hartford, CT 06106; tel. (860) 757-6500; e-mail isref@cslib.org; internet www.cslib .org; f. 1854, present bldg 1910; Connecticut newspapers, genealogy, history, law, legisla-tive reference, public policy, Connecticut and US govt publs; 2.5m. vols; Chair. MOLLIE KELLER; State Librarian KENDALL F. WIGGIN.

Cora J. Belden and Library: 33 Church St, Rocky Hill, CT 06067; tel. (860) 258-7623; internet www.rockyhilllibrary.info/index .htm; f. 1794, present name and status 1950; Dir MARY HOGAN; Chair. CATHY PUGLISI CARONE; Sec. W. MURRAY LICHTNER.

Cragin Memorial Library: 8 Linwood Ave, Route 16, Colchester, CT 06415; tel. (860) 537-5752; e-mail library@colchesterct.gov; internet www.colchesterct.gov; f. 1905; 63,000 vols; Dir KATE BYROADE.

East Hartford Public Library System: 840 Main St, East Hartford, CT 06108; tel. (860) 289-6429; internet www.ehtfdlib.info; brs: Raymond Library and Wickham Library; 200,000 vols, 10,000 CDs, audio and video cassettes, and DVDs; Dir PAT JONES.

East Lyme Public Library: 39 Society Rd, Niantic, CT 06357-1100; tel. (860) 739-6926; e-mail elpl@ely.lioninc.org; internet www.ely .lioninc.org; f. 1888 as Niantic Library and Reading Room Asscn, present location 1990; 147,000 vols.

Granby Public Library: 15 N Granby Rd, Granby, CT 06035; tel. (860) 844-5275; internet www.granby-ct.gov/ public_documents/granbyct_library/index; f.

1982; 2 brs: Granby Public Library and Frederick H. Cossitt Library; reference colln incl. 1,500 items; 63,000 vols; Dir for Library Services JOAN M. FOX.

Greenwich Library: 101 W Putnam Ave, Greenwich, CT 06830-5387; tel. (203) 622-7900; internet www.greenwichlibrary.org; f. 1805; brs: Byram Shubert, Cos Cob and Perrot Memorial Library; Dir CAROL MAHO-NEY; Pres. JENNIFER BALDOCK; Sec. MARY JACOBSON; Treas. SUZANNE PEISCH.

Hamden Public Library: 2901 Dixwell Ave, Hamden, CT 06518; tel. (203) 287-2680; e-mail info@hamdenlibrary.org; internet www.hamdenlibrary.org; f. 1950; brs: Miller Memorial Central Library, Whit-neyville Branch Library and Brundage Com-munity Branch Library; colln incl. 21,101 video cassettes and audio cassettes, spec. colln of books, MSS and photographs on the history of Hamden; 191,264 vols (incl. books, paperbacks and magazines); Dir BOB GUAL-TIERI.

Harwinton Public Library: 80 Bentley Dr., Harwinton, CT 06791; tel. (860) 485-9113; e-mail staff@harwintonpl.org; internet www2.youseemore.com/harwinton; 35,297 vols, 43 periodicals, 4,370 audio recordings and 1,942 video cassettes; Dir STASIA MOTU-ZICK.

Hotchkiss Library of Sharon: POB 277, Sharon, CT 06069; 10 Upper Main St, Sharon, CT 06069; tel. (860) 364-5041; internet www.hotchkisslibrary.org; f. 1893; historical colln of books and archives dating back to the Revolutionary War; 14,000 vols; Dir LOUISE MANTEUFFEL.

Levi E. Coe Library: 414 Main St, POB 458, Middlefield, CT 06455; tel. (860) 349-3857; e-mail staff@leviecoe.com; internet www.leviecoe.com; f. 1893; 10,000 works of fiction; colln incl. educational, cultural and recreational resources; 25,000 vols; Dir LOREN WEBBER.

Russell Library: 123 Broad St, Middletown, CT 06457; tel. (860) 347-2528; e-mail infodept@russell.lioninc.org; internet www .russelllibrary.org; f. 1875; local history colln; microfilm archives incl. Mellili church records and discontinued Middletown news-papers; Dir ARTHUR MEYERS; Pres. RICHARD B. KAMINS; Sec. ANDREW E. BECKER; Treas. MARVIN FARBMAN.

Russell Library: 123 Broad St, Middletown, CT 06457; tel. (860) 347-2528; e-mail infodept@russell.lioninc.org; internet www .russelllibrary.org; f. 1875; local history colln; microfilm archives incl. Mellili church records and discontinued Middletown news-papers; Dir ARTHUR MEYERS; Pres. RICHARD B. KAMINS; Sec. ANDREW E. BECKER; Treas. MARVIN FARBMAN.

Henry Carter Hull Library: 10 Killing-worth Turnpike, Clinton, CT 06413; tel. (860) 669-2342; internet www.hchlibrary.org; f. 1910; Lincoln colln: 250 books on Civil War and Abraham Lincoln; rare books and pamphlets about history of Connecticut; 85,000 vols; Dir MARIBETH BREEN; Pres. RICH SANTANELLI.

University of Connecticut Library: 369 Fairfield Way, Storrs, CT 06269-2005; tel. (860) 486-2518; e-mail elibrary@uconn.edu; internet www.lib.uconn.edu; f. 1881; largest public research colln in the state, incl. Arch-ives and Special Collns, Homer Babbidge Library, Music and Dramatic Arts Library, Pharmacy Library; 5 regional libraries; 3.5m. vols, 98,500 current print and electronic periodicals, 25,000 electronic journals, 2.8m. microforms, 35,500 reference sources, 180,000 maps and a large repository of

electronic information resources; Vice-Prov-ost for Univ. Libraries MARTHA BEDARD.

Yale University Library: POB 208240, 130 Wall St, New Haven, CT 06520-8240; 130 Wall St, New Haven, CT 06511; tel. (203) 432-1810; e-mail smlref@yale.edu; internet www.library.yale.edu; f. 1701; each of the 12 undergraduate colleges has its own library; 13m.vols; Univ. Librarian SUSAN GIBBONS.

Delaware

Corbit-Calloway Memorial Library: POB 128, 115 High St, Odessa, DE 19730; tel. (302) 378-8838; internet corbitlibrary.org; f. 1847; colln incl. books, pamphlets, magazines and newspapers, photographs and postcards, posters and prints; 9,000 vols (Delmarva Colln); Pres. MARGARET RYAN; Treas. VIRGINIA BRICCOTTO; Sec. JANET BUTLER.

Delaware Division of Libraries: 121 Duke of York St, Dover, DE 19901; tel. (302) 739-4748; internet www.state.lib.de.us; f. 1901; attached to Delaware Dept of State; spec. collns: US govt documents, talking books; Dir Dr ANNE E. C. NORMAN; Deputy Dir BETH-ANN RYAN; Sr Librarian MARIE CUNNINGHAM; Sr Librarian STEVE NEWTON.

Delaware Public Archives: 121 Duke of York St, Dover, DE 19901; tel. (302) 744-5000; e-mail aarchives@state.de.us; internet www.archives.delaware.gov; f. 1905, present location 2000; attached to Dept of State; 95,000 cu ft of govt records and historical documents, incl. records of the exec., legisla-tive and judicial brs of Delaware's state govt and holdings of county and municipal records since late 17th century (incl. 800,000 histor-ical photographs); 500 rolls of microfilm holdings; MSS; reference library; Dir STE-PHEN M. MARZ.

Dover Public Library: 45 S State St, Dover, DE 19901; tel. (302) 736-5025; internet www.cityofdover.com/home-library; Library Dir MARGERY CYR.

Jewish Historical Society of Delaware Archives: 505 N Market St, Wilmington, DE 19801; tel. (302) 655-6232; e-mail jhsdel@ yahoo.com; internet www.jhsdelaware.org; f. 1974; audiovisual materials, artefacts, docu-ments, memorabilia newspapers, oral histor-ies, private papers and photographs that record and document the organizational, cultural, religious, educational, business and family activities of the Jewish Commu-nity in Delaware; 350 linear ft of archival space; records from the Jewish Community Center of Wilmington, Jewish Federation of Delaware, Adas Kodesch Shel Emeth Con-gregation, Congregation Beth Shalom, Con-gregation Beth Emeth, and other Delaware synagogues and Vaad Hakashruth; Holo-caust-related materials.

John Eugene Derrickson Memorial Library: Delaware Technical and Commu-nity College, Wilmington Campus, W Bldg, First Floor, 333 Shipley St, Wilmington, DE 19801; tel. (302) 573-5422; internet www .library.dtcc.edu/wilmlib; attached to Dela-ware Technical and Community College; 2 sections: main library and audiovisual library and education centre; 50,000 vols (incl. colln of Stanton Campus), 500 period-icals; Librarian KARENE CHESTER.

Lewes Historical Society Library: 110 Shipcarpenter St, Lewes, DE 19958; tel. (302) 645-7670; e-mail research@ historiclewes.org; internet www .historiclewes.org/research/library.html; his-tory of Delaware, Delmarva history, natural and maritime history, some gen. American history works, family bibles, genealogy, spec. collns, 19th century medical texts, 19th- and early 20th-century school texts, and texts dealing with aspects of the Soc.'s museum collns; comprises libraries of John Farrace, Alice Watts and Joseph Enos; 4,000 vols; Pres. FRAN RICHMANN; Sec. H. EDWARD MAULL, JR; Treas. SUSAN McELLIGOTT-McKAY.

Stanton Campus Library: Room D 201, Delaware Technical and Community College, Stanton Campus, 400 Stanton-Christiana Rd, Newark, DE 19713; tel. (302) 453-3716; internet www.library.dtcc.edu/stantlib; attached to Delaware Technical and Community College; colln supports the technologies taught at the campus; 29,000 vols, 1,500 audiovisual items, 270 periodical titles; Librarian JANET CHIN.

Stephen J. Betze Library: Seashore Hwy, POB 630, Georgetown, DE 19947; tel. (302) 856-9033; internet www.library.dtcc.edu/owenslib; attached to Delaware Technical and Community College, Owens Campus; fiction and paperback colln; spec. collns incl. Quarto (oversized books), historical Delaware resource materials and pamphlets; also holds fed. govt documents; Dir Dr SHIRIN JAMASB.

Terry Campus Library: 100, Campus Dr., Dover, DE 19904; tel. (302) 857-1060; internet www.dtcc.edu/terry/library; attached to Delaware Technical and Community College; serves students in Terry campus' educational programmes, Delaware Tech credit courses, Univ. of Delaware assoc. in arts courses, and corporate and community programmes and training programmes; Head Librarian Dr MARGARET PROUSE.

University of Delaware Library: 181 S College Ave, Newark, DE 19717-5267; tel. (302) 831-2965; internet www.lib.udel.edu; incl. Hugh M. Morris Library and 3 br. libraries in Newark (agriculture library, chemistry library and physics library) and 1 br. library in Lewes (Marine Studies Library); Mark Samuels Lasner Colln: British literature and art from 1850 to 1900, with an emphasis on the Pre-Raphaelites and writers and illustrators of the 1890s; 7,500 first and other edns (incl. signed and asscn copies), MSS, letters, works on paper and ephemera; 2.8m. vols, 330,000 ebooks, 32,000 ejournals, 3.4m. microforms, 510,000 DVDs and maps, 8,800 linear ft of MSS and archives, 26,000 film and video programmes; Vice-Provost and May Morris Univ. Librarian SUSAN BRYNTESON.

William C. Jason Library: 1200 N DuPont Highway, Dover, DE 19901-2277; tel. (302) 857-6191; internet www.desu.edu/library; attached to Delaware State Univ.; African-American Colln; Claude E. Phillips Herbarium Library; 800 vols of local, state and regional research materials; 1,000 titles of history of the univ.; yearbooks and books written by Delaware State Univ. profs and alumni; 475,033 vols; Dean of Univ. Libraries Dr R. BATSON.

District of Columbia

Archives of American Art: Smithsonian Instn, POB 37012, Victor Bldg, Suite 2200, MRC, 937, Washington, DC 20013-7012; 750 Ninth St, NW, Victor Bldg, Suite 2200, Washington, DC 20001; tel. (202) 633-7940; internet www.aaa.si.edu; f. 1954; attached to Smithsonian Instn; research centre; collects, preserves and provides access to primary sources that document history of visual arts in America; colln incl. letters, diaries and scrapbooks of artists, dealers, and collectors; MSS of critics and scholars; business and financial records of museums, galleries, schools and asscns; photographs of art, world figures and events; sketches and sketchbooks; rare printed material; film, audio and video recordings; 16m. items; Dir LIZA KIRWIN (acting); publ. *Journal* (2 a year).

Commerce Departmental Library: 1401 Constitution Ave, NW, Washington, DC 20230; tel. (202) 482-1154; e-mail lawlibrary@doc.gov; internet www.library.doc.gov; f. 1913; attached to US Dept of Commerce; colln incl. legislative histories, Congressional hearings, reports, prints and documents, Code of Fed. Regulations, Fed. Register, treaties and journals; current legal material that supports the work of the Office of the Gen. Counsel; 50,000 vols, 2,000 vols microform; Dir JANE SESSA.

Department of the Treasury Library: Main Treasury Bldg, 1500 Pennsylvania Ave, NW, Washington, DC 20220; tel. (202) 622-2000; e-mail ofe@treasury.gov; internet www.treasury.gov; f. c.1817; spec. collns: taxation, public finance, int. economic affairs, Treasury history; 74,000 vols, 495,000 microfiches and 7,800 reels of microfilm.

Department of Veterans Affairs, Headquarters Library: 810 Vermont Ave, NW, Washington, DC 20420; tel. (202) 461-5669; internet www.va.gov; planning, policy, devt, training, centralized support services for the VA Library Network (VALNET); comprises 176 library services at 172 VA facilities; combined library holdings 1,398,000 vols, 145,000 audiovisual items, 75,655 journal subscriptions; Chief of VALNET GINNY DuPONT; Chief of Library CARYL KAZEN.

District of Columbia Public Library: 901 G St, NW, Washington, DC 20001; tel. (202) 727-0321; e-mail boardoflibrarytrustees@dc.gov; internet www.dclibrary.org; f. 1896; Martin Luther King, Jr, Memorial Library (central library); 25 brs; Library for the Blind and the Physically Handicapped; spec. collns: Washingtoniana, Washington Star Colln, Black Studies, Musical Scores; 2,672,488 vols; Chief Librarian GINNIE COOPER; Pres. JOHN W. HILL, JR.

Dumbarton Oaks Research Library and Collection: 1703 32nd St, NW, Washington, DC 20007; tel. (202) 339-6401; e-mail dumbartonoaks@doaks.org; internet www.doaks.org; f. 1940; attached to Harvard Univ.; collns of early Christian and Byzantine art and of Pre-Columbian art of Mexico; Central and S America; research programmes in Byzantine and Pre-Columbian studies, and studies in landscape architecture; incl. museum with collns of Byzantine and Pre-Columbian art and European masterpieces; 200,000 vols, 10,000 vols of rare book colln and 500,000 images; Dir of Library SHEILA KLOS; publs *Colloquium Papers*, *Conference Proceedings* (irregular), *Dumbarton Oaks Papers* (1 a year), *Dumbarton Oaks Texts* (irregular), *Studies in Pre-Columbian Art and Archaeology* (irregular).

EPA National Library Network: POB 3404T, 1200 Pennsylvania Ave, NW, Washington, DC 20460; tel. (202) 566-0556; e-mail epalibrarynetwork@epa.gov; internet www.epa.gov/natlibra; attached to US Environmental Protection Agency; provides access to information about environment and related scientific, technical, management and policy information.

Folger Shakespeare Library: 201 E Capitol St, SE, Washington, DC 20003; tel. (202) 544-4600; e-mail reference@folger.edu; internet www.folger.edu; f. 1932; fellowships; Folger Institute; public and educational programmes; theatre; lectures; poetry readings; concerts; exhibitions; 350,000 vols, 60,000 MSS; 250,000 playbills; 200 oil paintings, 50,000 drawings, watercolours, prints and photographs; collns incl. original edns and reprints of Shakespeare; English Renaissance books 1475–1700; 16th- and 17th-century Continental European books incl.

German Reformation, festival books and Italian drama; 17th- and 18th-century Strozzi MSS; Dryden colln; 16th-, 17th- and 18th-century English plays; 60,000 MSS since 16th century relating to early modern Britain, and the history of theatre and Shakespearean scholarship; 50,000 literary and theatrical prints and engravings; Chair. LOUIS R. COHEN; Dir Dr MICHAEL WITMORE; Librarian DANIEL DE SIMONE; publs *Folger Magazine* (3 a year), *Shakespeare Quarterly* (4 a year).

George Washington University Libraries: Estelle and Melvin Gelman Library, 2130H St, NW, Washington, DC 20052; tel. (202) 994-6558; internet www.gelman.gwu.edu; Gelman Library System consists of Melvin Gelman Library at the Foggy Bottom campus, Eckles Library at the Mount Vernon Campus (both in Washington, DC) and Virginia Science and Technology Campus Library in Ashburn, Virginia; 2m. vols; 60,000 vols in Eckles Library; Univ. Librarian JACK A. SIGGINS.

Georgetown University Library: 37th and O St, NW, Washington, DC 20057-1174; tel. (202) 687-7425; e-mail reference@georgetown.edu; internet www.library.georgetown.edu; f. 1796; incl. Joseph Mark Lauinger Memorial Library, Blommer Science Library, Woodstock Theological Center Library, Bioethics Research Library, Dahlgren Memorial Library, Riggs Memorial Library, Edward Bennett Williams Law Library, John Wolff Int. and Comparative Law Library and Maternal and Child Health Library; library in Qatar, Doha; 2.4m. vols, 400,000 ebooks, 1.3m. microforms, 100,000 rare books, 700 MSS colln, 300,000 photographs and slides, 10,000 films, audio cassettes, video cassettes and phonograph recordings; Univ. Librarian ARTEMIS KIRK.

House of Representatives Library: c/o Office of the Clerk, US Capitol, Room H154, Washington, DC 20515-6601; tel. (202) 225-7000; e-mail info.clerkweb@mail.house.gov; internet library.clerk.house.gov; f. 1792; div. of the Legislative Resource Center; spec. bound collns of all House of Representatives publs since c. 1800; 125,000 vols; Librarian RAE ELLEN BEST.

Howard University Library System: 500 Howard Pl., NW, Washington, DC 20059; tel. (202) 806-7252; internet www.howard.edu/library; consists of a central library group (comprised of the Founders Library/Undergraduate Library and 4 br. libraries in professional schools—Architecture, Business, Divinity, and Social Work); Moorland-Spingarn Research Center; Louis Stokes Health Sciences Library; Law Library; Ralph J. Bunche Int. Affairs Center Library and Afro-American Studies Resource Center; 2.5m. vols, 16,600 current journal subscriptions, 4.2m. microforms, 18,000 MSS and thousands of audiovisual items; Dir Dr ARTHUREE R. WRIGHT.

Library of Congress: 101 Independence Ave, SE, Washington, DC 20540; tel. (202) 707-5000; internet www.loc.gov; f. 1800; provides services to other libraries; incl. the devt of scientific schemes of classification (Library of Congress and Dewey Decimal); a centralized acquisition and cataloguing programme; a 755-vol. *National Union Catalog: Pre-1956 Imprints*; an inter-library loan system; registers creative work for copyright; 144m. items (incl. 33m. books and other print material in 460 languages, 63m. MSS); Librarian of Congress JAMES H. BILLINGTON.

Moorland-Spingarn Research Center: 500 Howard Place, NW, Washington, DC 20059; tel. (202) 806-7240; internet www

.howard.edu/msrc; f. 1914; attached to Howard Univ.; documents the history and culture of people of African descent in the Americas, Africa and Europe; rare works dating from the 16th century; 200,000 vols, 650 MSS and archival collns, 700 oral histories, 150,000 photographs and other images and 3,000 pieces of sheet music; Dir Dr HOWARD DODSON.

National Geographic Society Library and Archives: 1145 17th St, NW, Washington, DC 20036-4688; tel. (202) 857-7783; e-mail library@ngs.org; internet www.ngslis.org; f. 1903; reference reading room open to the public since 1920 for research by appointment; 30,000 vols; spec. collns: polar, natural history, exploration and discovery, soc. publs; publs *National Geographic Explorer*, *National Geographic Kids*, *National Geographic Magazine*, *National Geographic Traveler*.

National Library of Education: 400 Maryland Ave, SW, Washington, DC 20202; tel. (202) 205-5015; e-mail askalibrarian@ed.gov; internet ies.ed.gov/ncee/projects/nat_ed_library.asp; f. 1870 as Bureau of Education library, current name adopted 1994; attached to US Dept of Education; fed. govt's primary resource centre for education information providing collns and information services to public, education community and other govt agencies on current and historical programmes, activities and publs of the US Dept of Education; fed. education policy and education research and statistics; complete ERIC (Education Resources Information Center) microfiche colln, archives of official print and electronic documents published by Dept of Education and histories and documentation of education legislation passed by the Congress; depositary library; 70,000 vols, 800 periodicals; Dir PAMELA TRIPP-MELBY (acting).

Navy Department Library: 805 Kidder Breese St, SE, Washington, DC 20374-5060; tel. (202) 433-4132; e-mail navylibrary@navy.mil; internet www.history.navy.mil/library/index.htm; f. 1800; attached to US Dept of Navy; periodicals and govt documents on naval, military and nautical history; incl. foreign navies; colln of historical literature on the US Navy; serves as fed. depository; 201,000 vols; Dir GLENN E. HELM.

Pentagon Library: Washington HQ Services, 1155 Defense Pentagon, Washington, DC 20301-1155; tel. (703) 695-1997; internet www.whs.mil/library; f. 1944; 100 databases that helps to access to full text articles, abstracts, financial data, govt documents and reports; ejournal management system; newsletters, magazines and newspapers; 4,000 digital versions of print books; 100,000 vols, 1,800 periodicals and 1m. documents; Acquisitions Librarian RICHARD C. MAY.

Ralph J. Bunche Library of the Department of State: US Dept of State, Room 3239, 2201 C St, NW, Washington, DC 20520-3239; tel. (202) 647-1099; e-mail library@state.gov; internet www.state.gov/m/a/ls; f. 1789, current name adopted 1997; materials relate primarily to economic, ngsitical and social conditions in foreign areas; treaties and agreements; int. relations and diplomatic history; 400,000 vols; Chief Librarian HUGH HOWARD.

Smithsonian Institution Archives: POB 37012, MRC 507, Washington, DC 20013-7012; Capital Gallery Bldg, Suite 3000, 600 Maryland Ave, SW, Washington, DC 20024-2520; tel. (202) 633-5870; e-mail osiaref@osia.si.edu; internet www.si.edu/archives; f. 1970; repository for the official records of the Instn since its foundation in 1846, and

official repository for numerous other orgs; personal papers of noted Smithsonian staff, artists, researchers and museum founders; 35,000 cu ft of materials; 17,273 finding aids, digitized images, documents and publs; Dir ANNE VAN CAMP.

Smithsonian Libraries: Office of the Dir, POB 37012, MRC 154, Washington, DC 20013-7012; Nat. Museum of Natural History Bldg, Room 29, Washington, DC 20560; tel. (202) 633-2240; e-mail libmail@si.edu; internet library.si.edu; f. 1846; exhibition gallery and annual colln-based curated exhibition; displays in Nat. Museum of American History, Nat. Air and Space Museum and Nat. Museum of Natural History; active exhibition loan programme; 20 brs; 1,969,547 vols (incl. spec. colln of 40,000 rare books), 2,109 linear ft of MSS, 190,207 microfilms, 5,534 journal subscriptions and 2,667 ejournals; Dir Dr NANCY E. GWINN.

United States Senate Library: Russell Senate Office Bldg, Washington, DC 20510; tel. (202) 224-7106; f. 1871; research and reference for the use of the Senate and its cttees; services incl. legislative and gen. reference, automated information retrieval, Micrographics Center and photoduplication facilities; 250,000 vols, incl. spec. colln of legislative proceedings and documents from 1774; Senate Librarian LEONA I. FAUST; Head of Reference and Information Services ZOE DAVIS.

US Department of Justice Library System: Main Library, Robert F. Kennedy Justice Bldg, 950 Pennsylvania Ave, NW, Washington, DC 20530-0001; tel. (202) 514-3775; e-mail askdoj@usdoj.gov; internet www.justice.gov/jmd/ls; f. 1831; open to the public by appointment only; research facility with legal and non-legal holdings; service is provided mainly to the offices, boards and divs of the Dept of Justice; 11 br. libraries support the litigating divs and maintain specialized collns; 300,000 vols, 1m. items of microfiche and microfilm; Library Dir BLANE K. DESSY.

US Department of the Interior Library: 1849c St, NW, MS 1151, Washington, DC 20240; tel. (202) 208-5815; e-mail library@nbc.gov; internet library.doi.gov; f. 1850; consists of 8 libraries; 1m. vols, incl. 15,000 serials and 2,500 periodicals; Dir GEORGE FRANCHOIS; publ. *Bibliographies*.

Wirtz Labor Library: US Dept of Labor, 200 Constitution Ave, NW, Room N-2445, Washington, DC 20210; tel. (202) 693-6600; e-mail library@dol.gov; internet www.dol.gov/oasam/library; f. 1917; attached to US Dept of Labor; access to both public and employees of the US Dept of Labor; colln incl. history of labour, labour unions and the growth and devt of the labour; consolidation of the libraries of the fmr Children's Bureau and the Bureau of Labor Statistics; spec. colln: James Taylor Colln, Trade Union Periodicals, Folio Colln and Portrait Colln; incl. Labor Law Library; 140,000 vols, 5,000 electronic and print periodical titles, 3,000 journals; Library Dir JAMES IGOE.

Florida

Boynton Beach City Library: 208 S Seacrest Blvd, Boynton Beach, FL 33435; tel. (561) 742-6395; e-mail reference@boyntonlibrary.org; internet www.boyntonlibrary.org; spec. colln of books dealing with Florida history; 100,000 vols; Dir CRAIG CLARK.

Brockway Library: 10021 N E Second Ave, Miami Shores, FL 33138; tel. (305) 758-8107; internet www.brockwaylibrary.org; f. 1949; colln of books, magazines, newspapers, audio-books and large print books; 64,147 vols (incl. 1,892 large print books, 1,871

audio books and books on CD, 3,563 recreational and educational video cassettes and DVDs, 115 current magazines and newspapers); Chair. CHERYL GOWING; Dir ELIZABETH ESPER.

Broward County Division of Libraries: 100 South Andrews Ave, Fort Lauderdale, FL 33301; tel. (954) 357-7444; internet www.broward.org/library; f. 1974; consists of a flagship main library, the African-American Research Library and Cultural Center, the Alvin-Sherman Library, Research, and Information Technology Center at Nova Southeastern Univ., 5 regional libraries, 37 br. libraries and 2 reading centres; spec. collns: black heritage, Spanish language, Floridiana; main library is a depository for govt documents; 3m.vols; Dir ROBERT E. CANNON.

Clearwater Public Library System: 100 N Osceola Ave, Clearwater, FL 33755-4083; tel. (727) 562-4970; internet www.myclearwater.com/cpl; f. 1916; brs: Beach Library, Countryside Library, East Library and North Greenwood Library; 600,000 vols; Chair. JAN REGULSKI; Dir BARBARA PICKELL.

Delray Beach Public Library: 100 W Atlantic Ave, Delray Beach, FL 33444; tel. (561) 266-0194; e-mail info.delraylibrary@gmail.com; internet www.delraylibrary.org; f. 1913; book and media colln incl. audio and large print books, foreign language materials and video cassettes; 250,000 vols; Dir ALAN KORNBLAU.

Eustis Memorial Library: 120 N Center St, Eustis, FL 32726; tel. (352) 357-5686; e-mail contactus@eustismemoriallibrary.org; internet www.eustismemoriallibrary.org; f. 2002; 117,000 vols, current and back issues of 200 periodicals and newspapers, 5,600 video cassettes and 2,400 audio cassettes.

Flagler County Public Library System: 2500 Palm Coast Parkway. NW, Palm Coast, FL 32137; tel. (386) 446-6763; internet www.flaglercounty.org; f. 1987; 2 brs: main and Bunnell; depository of genealogical information; books for visually impaired; Dir HOLLY ALBANESE.

Florida State University Libraries: 116 Honors Way, Tallahassee, FL 32306-2047; tel. (850) 644-5211; internet www.lib.fsu.edu; f. 1851; incl. 8 libraries: Strozier Library, Dirac Science Library, Claude Pepper Library, College of Music Allen Music Library, School of Library and Information Studies Goldstein Library, College of Law Research Center, College of Medicine Maguire Medical Library, FAMU/FSU Engineering Reading Room/Library; 3m. vols (incl. 549,000 ebooks, 78,000 periodicals); Dean of Univ. Libraries JULIA ZIMMERMAN.

George A. Smathers Libraries: Univ. of Florida, POB 117000, Gainesville, FL 32611-7000; tel. (352) 273-2505; internet www.uflib.ufl.edu; f. 1853 as East Florida Seminary; current name adopted 1991; attached to Univ. of Florida; spec. collns: children's literature in English before 1900, contemporary American and British poetry, contemporary American creative writing, Floridiana, history of printing and book arts, Judaica, Latin Americana, New England literature before 1900, performing arts, United States Borderlands (Florida), Irish literature; 5m. vols; Dean of Univ. Libraries JUDITH RUSSELL.

Jacksonville Public Library: 303 N Laura St, Jacksonville, FL 32202; tel. (904) 630-2665; internet www.jaxpubliclibrary.org; f. 1878; 20 brs and the Main Library downtown; spec. collns: African-American Colln, Delius Colln, Digital Library Colln, Florida Colln, Genealogy Colln, Govt Documents Colln, Holocaust Colln, Lewis Ansbacher

Map Colln; 3,023,307 vols; Chair. JIM SELZER; Dir BARBARA A. B. GUBBIN.

Lake Worth Public Library: 15 N M St, Lake Worth, FL 33460; tel. (561) 533-7354; e-mail lwreference@lakeworth.org; internet www.lakeworth.govoffice.com; f. 1912; Library Services Man. VICKIE JOSLIN.

LeRoy Collins Leon County Public Library System: 200 W Park Ave, Tallahassee, FL 32301; tel. (850) 606-2665; internet www.leoncountylibrary.org; f. 1955; brs: Dr B. L. Perry, Eastside Br. Library, Fort Braden Br. Library, Jr Br. Library, Lake Jackson Br. Library, NE Br. Library, Woodville Branch Library; Dir CAY HOHMEISTER.

Lynn Haven Library: 901 Ohio Ave, Lynn Haven, FL 32444; tel. (850) 265-2781; internet www2.youseemore.com/lynnhaven; f. 1911, present name and status in 1990; 25,000 vols.

Maitland Public Library: 501 S Maitland Ave, Maitland, FL 32751; tel. (407) 647-7700; e-mail board@maitlandpubliclibrary.org; internet www.maitlandpubliclibrary.org; f. 1896; 85,000 vols; Chair. SARAH CHAPMAN; Pres. WILLIAM WHITACRE; Sec. JOANNE MULINARE; Treas. BEN AYCRIGG.

Miami-Dade Public Library System: 101 West Flagler St, Miami, FL 33130-1523; tel. (305) 375-2665; internet www.mdpls.org; f. 1971; main library, 49 brs, 4 mobile libraries; 3,878,771 vols; spec. collns incl. Florida history, Spanish books, urban affairs, genealogy; Dir RAYMOND SANTIAGO.

Orlando Public Library: 101 E Central Blvd, Orlando, FL 32801; tel. (407) 835-7323; e-mail comments@ocls.info; internet www.ocls.lib.fl.us; f. 1920; acts as HQ and resource centre for the Orange Co Library System; 1.5m. vols; Dir and CEO MARY ANNE HODEL; Pres. RICHARD MALADECKI.

Osceola Library System: 211 E Dakin Ave, Kissimmee, FL 34741; tel. (407) 742-8888; e-mail thelibrary@osceolalibrary.org; internet www.osceolalibrary.org; f. 1989; brs: Hart Memorial Central Library, Poinciana Br. Library, Veterans Memorial Library-St Cloud, Buenaventura Lakes Br. Library, West Osceola Br. Library and Kenansville Br. Library; colln incl. resources related to Florida and Federal laws; 70,000 vols; Chair. JEFFEREY (SCOTT) MOUSSEAU.

Palm Beach County Library System: 3650 Summit Bold, West Palm Beach, FL 33406; tel. (561) 233-2600; internet www.pbclibrary.org; f. 1967; main library, 15 brs and a bookmobile; 1.7m. vols; Dir JOHN J. CALLAHAN, III.

Palm Harbor Library: 2330 Nebraska Ave, Palm Harbor, FL 34683; tel. (727) 784-3332; internet www.palmharborlibrary.org; f. 1978; 126,916 vols; Dir GENE P. COPPOLA.

Sanibel Public Library: 770 Dunlop Rd, Sanibel, FL 33957; tel. (239) 472-2483; internet www.sanlib.org; f. 1994; local history colln; 60,000 vols, 10,000 audiovisual items; Dir MARGARET MOHUNDRO.

Seminole County Public Library: 215 N Oxford Rd, Casselberry, FL 32707; tel. (407) 665-1500; internet www.seminolecountyfl.gov; f. 1978; 5 brs: East Br. Library, Northwest Br. Library, Jean Rhein Central Br. Library, North Br. Library and West Br. Library; 500,000 vols; Library Services Man. CHRISTINE PATTEN.

St. Lucie County Library System: 180 SW Prima Vista Blvd, Port St Lucie, FL 34983; tel. (772) 462-1615; internet www.stlucieco.gov; f. 1903, present status 1954; attached to Dept of Housing and Community Services; 6 brs: Fort Pierce, Lakewood Park, Morning-Side, Port St Lucie, St Lucie W and Z. N. Hurston; Library Man. SUSAN JACOB.

State Library of Florida: R. A. Gray Bldg, 500 S Bronough St, Tallahassee, FL 32399-0250; tel. (850) 245-6600; e-mail state.fl.us; internet dlis.dos.state.fl.us/library; attached to Florida Dept of State, Div. of Library and Information Services; provides information resources to Florida Legislature and all state agencies; coordinates and helps to fund activities of public libraries; framework for library initiatives in the state; archival and records management services of published and unpublished documentary history of the state; 312,000 vols; 350,000 microforms; 60,000 books, MSS, maps, memorabilia and periodicals; 140,000 state documents; 150,000 federal publs since 1789; Dir JUDITH RING.

Wilderness Coast Public Libraries: 1180 W Washington St, Monticello, FL 32344; tel. (850) 997-7400; e-mail cturner@wildernesscoast.org; internet www.wild.lib.fl.us; f. 1992; admin. office for cooperative multi-county library system for Wakulla, Jefferson and Franklin counties; 100,000 vols; Chair. CORA RUSS; Sec. MARILYN LEWIS; Central Administrator CHERYL TURNER.

Georgia

Atlanta-Fulton Public Library System: 1 Margaret Mitchell Sq., Atlanta, GA 30303; tel. (404) 730-1700; internet www.afplweb.com; e-mail librarycomments@fultoncountyga.gov; f. 1902 as the Carnegie Library of Atlanta, current named adopted 2004; 34 brs, offers classes, workshops, seminars for all levels; instructional learning centre, bookmobiles, meeting rooms; 2.5m. vols, incl. books, periodicals, CDs and DVDs; Dir ANNE T. HAIMES.

Bartow County Library System: 429 W Main St, Cartersville, GA 30120; tel. (770) 382-4203; e-mail info@bartowlibrary.org; internet www.bartowlibraryonline.org; f. 1980; brs: Cartersville Public Library, Emmie Nelson Public Library and Adairsville Public Library; 137,521 vols; Dir CARMEN SIMS; Chair. KEN MILLER; Sec. JO TAYLOR; Treas. BRYAN CANTY.

Chattahoochee Valley Libraries: 3000 Macon Rd, Columbus, GA 31906; tel. (706) 243-2669; e-mail contact@cvrls.net; internet www.thecolumbuslibrary.org; serves counties of Muscogee, Chattahoochee, Marion and Stewart; research materials on local history, biographical and historical resources, newspapers and maps; 7 brs; Dir CLAUDYA MULLER; Chair. ABBIE DILLARD.

Chestatee Regional Library System: 342 Allen St, Dawsonville, GA 30534; tel. (706) 344-3690; internet www.chestateelibrary.org; f. 1953; 2 brs: Dawson Co Library and Lumpkin Co Library; history of Lumpkin and Dawson Counties; 115,124 vols; Dir CLAUDIA GIBSON; Chair. SUSANNE NEIL.

Clayton County Library System: 865 Battle Creek Rd, Jonesboro, GA 30236; tel. (770) 473-3850; internet www.claytonpl.org; f. 1941; 6 brs; 475,740 vols, 8,730 audio cassettes and CDs, 4,766 video cassettes and DVDs, 539 journals; Dir CAROL STEWART.

Cobb County Public Library System: Central Library, 266 Roswell St, Marietta, GA 30060; tel. (770) 528-2320; e-mail contactus@cobbcat.org; internet www.cobbcat.org; f. 1959; 17 br. libraries of Marietta and Cobb Co; Chair. CHARLES D. SWITZER; Sec. CHERRIE COLEMAN-GRAFFREAD.

Conyers-Rockdale Library System: Nancy Guinn Memorial Library, 864 Green St, Conyers, GA 30012; tel. (770) 388-5041; internet www.conyersrockdalelibrary.org; f. 1920; 100,000 books, audio books, video cassettes, CDs and other materials in Nancy Guinn Memorial Library; Chair. MIKE KESSLER; Treas. JEANNE TALLEY.

DeKalb County Public Library: 215 Sycamore St, Decatur, GA 30030; tel. (404) 370-8450; internet www.dekalb.public.lib.ga.us; f. 1925 fmrly Decatur Library; 1 central library and 21 brs; spec. colln incl. items related to Georgia history and genealogy; early local, state and area newspapers on microfilm; 808,682 vols, 46,612 audio cassettes and CDs, 46,633 video cassettes and DVDs; Dir ALISON WEISSINGER; Chair. DEBORAH TORBUSH.

East Central Georgia Regional Library: Augusta Library, 823 Telfair St, Augusta, GA 30901; tel. (706) 821-2600; internet www.ecgrl.public.lib.ga.us; 15 libraries in 5 counties; Talking Book Center; 500,000 vols; Dir TERESA COLE.

Forsyth County Public Library: 585 Dahlonega Rd, Cumming, GA 30040; tel. (770) 781-9840; internet www.forsythpl.org; f. 1938; 3 brs: Cumming, Hampton Park and Sharon Forks; 300,000 vols; Dir JON McDANIEL.

Hall County Library System: 127 Main St NW, Gainesville, GA 30501; tel. (770) 532-3311; e-mail info@hallcountylibrary.org; internet www.hallcountylibrary.org; f. 1937; 5 brs: Gainesville (HQ), Blackshear Place, Murrayville, Spout Springs, North Hall; Dir ADRIAN MIXSON; Chair. KILLIAN EDWARDS.

Henry County Library System: McDonough Public Library, 1001 Florence McGarity Blvd, McDonough, GA 30252; tel. (770) 954-2806; e-mail md-reference@mail.henry.public.lib.ga.us; internet www.henry.public.lib.ga.us; f. 1959; brs: McDonough, Fairview, Locust Grove, Fortson and Cochran; 737,338 vols; Dir CAROLYN T. FULLER.

Jimmy Carter Library & Museum: 441 Freedom Parkway, Atlanta, GA 30307-1498; tel. (404) 865-7100; internet www.jimmycarterlibrary.gov; f. 1980; attached to Nat. Archives and Records Admin.; 50,000 photographs and hundreds of hours film, audio and video cassettes; 27m. pages of Jimmy Carter's White House material, papers of admin. associates, incl. documents, memoranda and correspondence; Dir JAY HAKES.

Live Oak Public Libraries: 2002 Bull St, Savannah, GA 31401; tel. (912) 652-3600; internet www.liveoakpl.org; f. 1903 as Savannah Public Library, present name 2002; 18 brs serving Chatham, Effingham and Liberty counties; 1 bookmobile; Dir CHRISTIAN KRUSE; Chair. Dr ALLEN BERGER.

Middle Georgia Regional Library System: Washington Memorial Library, 1180 Washington Ave, Macon, GA 31201-1790; tel. (478) 744-0800; internet www.co.bibb.ga.us/library; f. 1836, present name 1939; serving Bibb, Crawford, Jones, Macon, Twiggs and Wilkinson counties; Genealogical and Historical Room colln incl. 32,000 vols and 24,000 microforms; MSS and archival records of historical significance for Middle Georgia; Dir THOMAS JONES.

Mountain Regional Library System: 698 Miller St, POB 159, Young Harris, GA 30582; tel. (706) 379-3732; e-mail mountain@mountainregionallibrary.org; internet www.mountainregionallibrary.org; f. 1946, present name and status 1957; attached to Univ. System of Georgia; incl. HQ library and 3 brs: Towns Co Public Library, Union Co Public Library and Fannin Co Public Library; 105,948 vols; Dir DONNA W. HOWELL.

Newton County Library System: Covington Br. Library, 7116 Floyd St, Covington,

GA 30014; tel. (770) 787-3231; e-mail library@newtonlibrary.org; internet www .newtonlibrary.org; f. 1916, present name and status 1998; local history and genealogy colln; garden colln; Dir LACE KEATON.

Pine Mountain Regional Library System: POB 709, Manchester GA 31816; 218 Perry St, Manchester, GA 31816; tel. (706) 846-2186; e-mail libraryh@pinemtnlibrary .org; internet www.pinemtnlibrary.org; f. 1938, present name 1958; 7 brs in Meriwether, Upson, Talbot and Taylor Counties; Dir CHARLES B. GEE.

Roddenbery Memorial Library: 320 N Broad St, Cairo, GA 39828; tel. (229) 377-3632; e-mail rml@rmlibrary.org; internet www.rmlibrary.org; f. 1939 as Cairo Public Library, present location 1964; The Cairo Messenger, newspaper, on microfilm and print since 1904; Dir PAM GRIGG.

Statesboro Regional Public Libraries: 124 S Main St, Statesboro, GA 30458-5246; tel. (912) 764-1341; internet www.strl.info; brs: Claxton, Metter, Richmond Hill, Pembroke, Swainsboro and Statesboro; 182,000 vols; Dir SHARON C. ROWE.

Twin Lakes Library System: Mary Vinson Memorial Library, 151 S Jefferson St SE, Milledgeville, GA 31061-3419; tel. (478) 452-0677; internet twinlakeslibrarysystem.org; f. 1938; genealogy and local history colln; large print books; Dir BARRY REESE; Chair. DOROTHY BROWN.

Hawaii

Bishop Museum's Library and Archives: 1525 Bernice St, Honolulu, HI 96817; tel. (808) 848-4148; e-mail archives@ bishopmuseum.org; internet www .bishopmuseum.org/research/library; 50,000 vols, 1,000 periodicals, historical photographs, films, works of art, audio recordings and MSS.

Edwin H. Mookini Library: Univ. of Hawai'i at Hilo, 200 W Kawili St, Hilo, HI 96720; tel. (808) 932-7286; e-mail mookini@ hawaii.edu; internet guides.library.uhh .hawaii.edu; f. 1981; attached to Univ. of Hawaii at Hilo; 232,120 vols, 3,000 journals, 78 current serial titles, 86,560 microforms, 10,026 audiovisual items, 108,780 ebooks, 38,569 online periodical titles, 145 databases; spec. Hawaiian colln of 40,000 items incl. maps, historic periodicals and microfilm; depository colln of federal and state govts; Univ. Librarian HELEN M. ROGERS.

Hamilton and Sinclair Libraries: 2550 McCarthy Mall, Honolulu, HI 96822; tel. (808) 956-7214; e-mail emailref@hawaii.edu; internet library.manoa.hawaii.edu; f. 1920; attached to Univ. of Hawaii at Manoa; 3.4m. vols, 15,000 MSS and archives, 50,000 serial and journal titles, 73,000 audiovisual items, 95,000 maps and aerial photographs; Univ. Librarian PAULA MOCHIDA.

Hawaiian Historical Society Library: 560 Kawaiahao St, Honolulu, HI 96813; tel. (808) 537-6271; internet www .hawaiianhistory.org/lib/libmain.html; Hawaiian history resources; language books; newspapers published in Hawai'i; 19th- and early 20th-century maps of Honolulu, the Hawaiian Islands, and the Pacific Ocean; 300 broadsides published in Hawai'i from 1829 to the early 1900s; 12,000 vols, 35 linear ft of MSS, 10,000 photographs; Admin. Dir and Librarian BARBARA DUNN.

Hawaii Legislative Reference Bureau: Hawaii State Capitol, Room 005, Honolulu, HI 96813; tel. (808) 587-0690; e-mail lrb@ capitol.hawaii.gov; internet lrbhawaii.org; f. 1943 as a dept of Univ. of Hawaii, present status 1996; provides services to legislators, legislative cttee, and some mems of the

public; legislative studies and exec. agency reports from Hawaii and across the country; Hawaii statutes, journals, court cases and county codes; statutes from 12 other states; fed. statutes and US Supreme Court cases; Dir CHARLOTTE CARTER-YAMAUCHI (acting).

Hawaii State Law Library System: Supreme Court Law Library, Ali'iolani Hale, Room 115, 417 S King St, Honolulu, HI 96813; tel. (808) 539-4964; e-mail lawlibrary@courts.hawaii.gov; internet www .state.hi.us/jud/library; f. 1966; legal reference library; contains materials on laws for all federal and state jurisdictions, and practice materials for all major areas of law; 5 brs: Supreme Court Law Library in Oahu, Second Circuit Court Law Library in Maui, Third Circuit Court Law Libraries in Hilo and Kona, and a Fifth Circuit Court Law Library in Kauai; collns incl. print, microfilm, microfiche, audio, video and CD-ROM formats; a depository for materials published by the State Justice Institute.

Honolulu Community College Library: 874 Dillingham Blvd, Honolulu, HI 96817; tel. (808) 845-9199; e-mail library@hcc .hawaii.edu; internet www2.honolulu.hawaii .edu/library; Head Librarian IRENE MESINA.

Leeward Community College Library: 96-045 Ala Ike, Pearl City, HI 96782; tel. (808) 455-0210; e-mail lccref@hawaii.edu; internet www.leeward.hawaii.edu/lib; Head Librarian CHRIS MATZ.

Municipal Reference Center: 558 S King St, Honolulu, HI 96813; tel. (808) 768-3765; e-mail csdaccess@honolulu.gov; internet www1.honolulu.gov/csd/mrc; f. 1929; artefacts, permanent records, publs of depts and agencies of the City and County of Honolulu.

Sullivan Family Library: Chaminade Univ. of Honolulu, 3140 Waialae Ave, Honolulu, HI 96816; tel. (808) 735-4725; e-mail library@chaminade.edu; internet www .chaminade.edu/library; f. 1957, present name 2008; attached to Chaminade Univ. of Honolulu; 70,000 vols, 239 journals subscriptions, 40,000 ebooks, 19,000 ejournal subscriptions, 1,500 DVDs and CDs; Librarian PUANANI AKAKA.

University of Hawaii Maui College Library: 310 W Ka'ahumanu Ave, Kahului, HI 96732; tel. (808) 984-3233; e-mail mcclib@ hawaii.edu; internet maui.hawaii.edu/ library; 155,291 vols, 274 print periodicals, 5,429 video cassettes, DVDs and audio CDs; Public Services Librarian ELLEN PETERSON.

William S. Richardson School of Law Library: Univ. of Hawaii at Mānoa, 2525 Dole St, Honolulu, HI 96822-2328; tel. (808) 956-7583; e-mail lawcirc@hawaii.edu; internet www.law.hawaii.edu/library; f. 1983; attached to Univ. of Hawaii at Mānoa; Dir VICTORIA SZYMCZAK.

Idaho

Ada Community Library: 10664 W Victory Rd, Boise, ID 83709; tel. (208) 362-0181; e-mail mdewalt@adalib.org; internet www .adalib.org; f. 1989; 4 brs; 160,000 vols (incl. 1,000 journals); Dir MARY DEWALT.

Boise Public Library: 715 S Capitol Blvd, Boise, ID 83702; tel. (208) 384-4076; e-mail askalibrarian@cityofboise.org; internet www .boisepubliclibrary.org; f. 1895; 3 brs; Dir KEVIN BOOE.

Coeur d'Alene Public Library: 702 E Front Ave, Coeur d'Alene, ID 83814; tel. (208) 769-2315; e-mail info@cdalibrary.org; internet www.cdalibrary.org; f. 1905; 500,000 vols; Library Dir BETTE AMMON.

Eagle Public Library: 100 N Stierman Way, Eagle, ID 83616; tel. (208) 939-6814; internet www.eaglepubliclibrary.org; f. 1963;

S Idaho's regional library consortium; 98,000 vols; Library Dir JANICE CAMPBELL.

Idaho Falls Public Library: 457 W Broadway, Idaho Falls, ID 83402; tel. (208) 612-8460; e-mail director@ifpl.org; internet www .ifpl.org; f. 1884; microfilm copies of the Post Register and its predecessors dating back to 1880; 180 magazines and 26 newspaper subscription; Chair. HAL PETERSON.

Idaho State Law Library: 322 E Front St, Suite 560, Boise, ID 83702; tel. (208) 364-4555; e-mail lawlibrary@idcourts.net; internet www.isll.idaho.gov; f. 1869; primarily a research library; holds state and fed. law, as well as legal periodicals, digests, citators, encyclopaedias and treatises of law; 192,000 vols.

Marshall Public Library: 113 S Garfield Ave, Pocatello, ID 83204; tel. (208) 232-1263; e-mail admin@marshallpl.org; internet www .marshallpl.org; f. 1907; 160,000 vols; Dir ERIC SUESS.

Mountain Home Public Library: 790 N 10th E, Mountain Home, ID 83647; tel. (208) 587-4716; internet mountainhome.lili.org; f. 1903; Dir LUISE HOUSE.

Nampa Public Library: 101-11th Ave S, Nampa, ID 83651; tel. (208) 468-5803; internet www.nampalibrary.org; f. 1900; Library Dir MARK ROSE.

Oneida County Library: 31 N 100, POB 185, Malad, ID 83252; tel. (208) 766-2229; e-mail oclib@atcnet.net; internet www .maladidaho.org/library; f. 1977; 26,000 vols; Dir KAY CALDWELL.

Illinois

Abraham Lincoln Presidential Library and Museum: *Library*: 112 N 6th St, Springfield, IL; *Museum*: 212 N 6th St, Springfield, IL; tel. (217) 558-8844; internet www.alplm.org; f. 2002; fmr Illinois State Historical Library (f. 1889) of 12m. items; spec. colln: Henry Horner Lincoln Colln of 46,000 items incl. 1,500 signed MSS, 10,000 books and pamphlets, 1,000 posters, 1,000 prints and photographs, Gettysburg Address, Second Inaugural Address, Anti-Slavery Statement; Exec. Dir RICK BEARD.

Chicago Public Library: 400 S State St, Chicago, IL 60605-1203; tel. (312) 747-4300; e-mail info@chipublic.org; internet www .chipublib.org; f. 1873; 5,691,321 vols; Commr BRIAN BANNON; Board Pres. LINDA JOHNSON RICE; Sec. CRISTINA BENITEZ.

Cook County Law Library: 50 W Washington St, 29th Fl., Chicago, IL 60602; tel. (312) 603-5423; internet lawlibrary .cookcountyil.gov; f. 1966; provides services at main library and 5 brs; collns of law books, statutes, case law and digests for all 50 states and numerous Illinois practice manuals, treatises, int. law; print and electronic formats; 350,000 vols; Dir and Exec. Law Librarian MONTELL DAVENPORT.

Illinois Institute of Technology Libraries: 35 W 33rd St, Chicago, IL 60616; tel. (312) 567-3616; e-mail library@iit.edu; internet www.iit.edu/libraries; 6 br. libraries at different campuses; 1.8m. vols (incl. 30,000 print and online journals, magazines and newspapers); Dean of Libraries KRISTIN STANDAERT.

Illinois State Archives: Margaret Cross Norton Bldg, Capitol Complex, Springfield, IL 62756; tel. (217) 782-4682; internet www .cyberdriveillinois.com/departments/archives/archives.html; f. 1921; depository of public records of Illinois state and local govt agencies of permanent admin., legal and historical research values documents; admin. of Illinois Regional Archives Depositories (IRAD); 53,000 cu ft of state governmental records; State Archivist JESSE WHITE; Dir DAVID A. JOENS.

Illinois State Library: Gwendolyn Brooks Bldg, 300 S Second St, Springfield, IL 62701-1796; tel. (217) 785-5600; e-mail islinformationonline@ilsos.net; internet www.cyberdriveillinois.com/departments/library/home.html; f. 1839; permanent colln of 33 works of visual art by contemporary Illinois artists; 5m. items and documents; State Librarian JESSE WHITE; Dir ANNE CRAIG; publ. *Illinois Literacy* (4 a year).

Illinois Supreme Court Library: Supreme Court Bldg, 200 E Capitol Ave, Springfield, IL 62701; tel. (217) 782-2424; internet www .state.il.us/court/supremecourt/library.asp; f. 1842, present location 1908; serves state, fed. and local govts, the bar and gen. public; 100,000 vols, 350 legal periodicals; Librarian BRENDA LARISON.

John Crerar Library of the University of Chicago: 5730 S Ellis Ave, Chicago, IL 60637; tel. (773) 702-7715; e-mail crerar-reference@lib.uchicago.edu; internet www.lib.uchicago.edu/e/crerar; f. 1984 by merger of John Crerar Library (f. 1892) and Univ. of Chicago; organizes Kathleen A. Zar symposium and science exhibits and lectures; 1.4m. vols on biological, medical, physical sciences, general science and the philosophy and history of science, medicine, technology; Dir BARBARA KERN; Dir ANDREA TWISS-BROOKS.

Newberry Library: 60 West Walton St, Chicago, IL 60610-7324; tel. (312) 255-3666; e-mail research@newberry.org; internet www.newberry.org; f. 1887; ind. research libray; maintains research and academic programmes in its Center for Renaissance Studies, Family and Community History Center, McNickle Center for American Indian and Indigenous Studies, Scholl Center for American Culture, and Smith Center for the History of Cartography; spec. collns on the American Indians, history of printing and book arts, music, American and English history and literature, exploration and early cartography, Portugal, the Renaissance in England and Europe, European history from the Renaissance to 1815, the Philippine Islands, colonial Latin America, American dances; 1.5m. vols in the humanities, 5m. MSS pages; Pres. and Librarian DAVID SPADAFORA; Chair. VICTORIA J. HERGET; Sec. PAUL J. MILLER; Treas. DAVID E. MCNEEL.

Northwestern University Libraries: 1970 Campus Dr., Evanston, IL 60208-2300; tel. (847) 491-7658; e-mail library@ northwestern.edu; internet www.library .northwestern.edu; f. 1856; Northwestern Univ. Library (humanities and social sciences, with spec. collns on Africa: comprehensive historically on sub-Sahara, francophone West Africa and South Africa; extensive holdings in Art Nouveau, dada, surrealism, futurism and expressionism, Samuel Johnson, siege and commune of Paris 1870–71, women's liberation movement; libraries for music and transportation); brs for science-eng., geology and mathematics; professional libraries (dentistry, law, medicine) and the Schaffner Library in Chicago; 4,930,613 vols, 4,603,214 microforms, 18,069 linear ft of archives and MSS, 208,757 maps, 601,153 graphic images, 66,977 audio files, 33,882 film and video cassettes, 98,844 journals; Dean of Libraries SARAH M. PRITCHARD.

Rockford Public Library: 215 N Wyman St, Rockford, IL 61101; tel. (815) 965-7606; internet www.rockfordpubliclibrary.org; f. 1872; 5 brs; Andrew M. Potter Colln: 300 vols of 19th-century memoirs, regimental histories, histories of campaigns and materials dealing with accounts of Civil War;

Rockford area music colln; 494,261 vols, 5,615 audiobook CDs, 4,996 video cassettes, 39,734 DVDs, 22,799 CDs, 1,274 CD-ROMs; Exec. Dir FRANK NOVAK; Pres. PAUL A. LOGLI; Sec. and Treas. EDWARD J. GEESER.

Ryerson & Burnham Libraries: 111 S Michigan Ave, Chicago, IL 60603-6404; tel. (312) 443-7279; e-mail reference@artic.edu; internet www.artic.edu/research; f. 1957 by merger of Ryerson Library with Burnham Library of Architecture; attached to Art Institute of Chicago; incl. archives; 450,000 vols, 1,200 current serial subscriptions; art and architecture research colln; architecture of the 18th to 20th centuries and 19th-century painting, prints, drawings, and decorative arts; spec. colln incl. Percier and Fontaine Colln of 17th–19th century architectural books, Mary Reynolds Colln on Dada and Surrealism, George R. Collns Archive of Catalan Art and Architecture and Mrs. James Ward Thorne Colln of illustrated books; Exec. Dir JACK BROWN.

University of Chicago Library: 1100 E 57th St, Chicago, IL 60637-1502; tel. (773) 702-8740; e-mail info@lib.uchicago.edu; internet www.lib.uchicago.edu; f. 1892; comprises Regenstein (humanities, business and social sciences), Crerar (science, medicine, technology), Harper (college), D'Angelo Law (nat. and int. law), Joe and Rika Mansueto, Eckhart (mathematics, statistics and computer science) and Social Services Admin. (social welfare and social work); Spec. Collns Research Center, incl. rare books, MSS, the Chicago Jazz Archive, Univ. Archives; E Asia, S Asia, Middle E, Slavic and E European area studies; 11,397,412 vols (incl. print and eholdings); Dir and Univ. Librarian JUDITH NADLER.

University of Illinois (Urbana-Champaign) Library: 1408 W Gregory Dr., Urbana, IL 61801; tel. (217) 333-2290; e-mail writeus@library.illinois.edu; internet www.library.illinois.edu; f. 1867; 40 departmental libraries; spec. collns in classical literature and history, English literature, incl. Milton and Shakespeare, Western US history, Lincolniana, Italian history, music, architecture, science and technology; 12m. vols, 9m. microforms, 90,000 periodicals and journals, 148,000 audio-recordings, over 930,000 audiovisual materials, over 280,000 ebooks, 12,000 films, 650,000 maps; Dean of Libraries and Univ. Librarian JOHN P. WILKIN.

Indiana

Alexandrian Public Library: 115 W Fifth St, Mount Vernon, IN 47620; tel. (812) 838-3286; e-mail alexpl@evansville.net; internet www.apl.lib.in.us; f. 1895; serves city of Mount Vernon and communities of Black, Marrs, Robinson, Lynn and Point townships; 92,383 vols, 4,554 video cassettes, 5,848 audio materials; Dir MARISSA PRIDDIS.

Allen County Public Library: 900 Library Pl., Fort Wayne, IN 46802; tel. (260) 421-1252; e-mail ask@acpl.info; internet www .acpl.lib.in.us; f. 1895 as Fort Wayne Public Library; Fred J. Reynolds Historical Genealogy Colln; 13 brs; 3.7m. vols; Pres. JOHN GERNI; Vice-Pres. GENE G. HOEMIG; Dir JEFFREY R. KRULL.

Delphi Public Library: 222 E Main St, Delphi, IN 46923; tel. (765) 564-2929; e-mail dplibrar@carrollnet.org; internet www .carrollnet.org/dpl; f. 1904; NW Carroll Br. Library at Yeoman; 61,063 vols, 5,777 video cassettes and DVDs, 3,456 audiobooks and CDs, 209 magazines and newspapers; Dir KELLY CURRIE; Pres. ANGIE MURRAY; Sec. KATHY ZINK; Treas. ROBERTA BLUE.

Fulton County Public Library: POB 307, 514 State Road 25, Fulton, IN 46931; tel. (574) 857-3895; e-mail fulton@fulco.lib.in.us; internet www.fulco.lib.in.us; 3 brs; local genealogy colln; Dir BECKY WILLIAMS; Pres. GEORGE HAPNER; Sec. ROSA METZGER; Treas. BOB UHRICH.

Hancock County Public Library: 900 W McKenzie Rd, Greenfield, IN 46140-1741; tel. (317) 462-5141; e-mail reference@hcplibrary .org; internet www.hcplibrary.org; f. 1878; colln in local history of Indiana and genealogy; br. in New Palestine; Dir and CEO DIANNE OSBORNE; Pres. PEGGY PRITZKE; Sec. JANE PFAFF; Treas. DEBBI BARNHART.

Harrison County Public Library: 105 N Capitol Ave, Corydon, IN 47112; tel. (812) 738-4110; e-mail hcpl@hcpl.lib.in.us; internet www.hcpl.lib.in.us; f. 1914 as Corydon Public Library, present name 1998; 3 brs; Frederick Porter Griffin Center for Local History and Genealogy; Dir VI ECKART.

Indiana State Archives: 6440 E 30th St, Indianapolis, IN 46219; tel. (317) 591-5222; e-mail arc@icpr.in.gov; internet www.in.gov/ icpr/2358.htm; records of the executive, legislative, and judicial brs of govt since 1790s; military records incl. holdings from the War of 1812, Black Hawk War, Mexican War, Civil War, Spanish-American War and veterans' enrollments from 1886, 1890 and 1894; 100,000 aerial photographs incl. colln from the Dept of Natural Resources and State Fair Comm; 25,000 cu ft of records; Dir and State Archivist JIM CORRIDAN.

Indiana State Library: 315 W Ohio St, Indianapolis, IN 46202; tel. (317) 232-3675; e-mail ldo@library.in.gov; internet www .library.in.gov; f. 1825; provides library service to state govt, advice and counsel to the libraries and librarians of the state, reference service and materials for local school, public, spec., and academic libraries; genealogy and spec. research collns; Indiana history colln; service to the blind and physically handicapped; library for Indiana Acad. of Science; 70,000 vols incl. histories, biographies, directories, magazines and newsletters, atlases, state documents, and works of fiction by Indiana authors, 50,000 pamphlets, 3m. MSS, 40,000 genealogy colln; State Librarian ROBERTA L. BROOKER; publs *Focus on Indiana Libraries* (12 a year), *Indiana Libraries* (4 a year).

Indiana Supreme Court Law Library: State House 316, 200 W Washington St, Indianapolis, IN 46204; tel. (317) 232-2557; internet www.in.gov/judiciary/supreme; f. 1867; primary law library for state agencies, Office of Gov., the legislature, mems of private bar and gen. public; repository for publs produced under grants from State Justice Institute; 70,000 vols; Head Librarian TERRI LEA ROSS.

Indiana University Bloomington Libraries: 1320 E 10th St, Bloomington, IN 47405; tel. (812) 855-1673; e-mail libtechs@indiana .edu; internet www.libraries.iub.edu; f. 1829; 9,516,606 vols, 40,557 linear ft MSS, 252,763 music scores, 350,058 slides, 301,850 maps and charts, 311,751 audio recordings, 116,604 serial titles (print and electronic) serials, 3,106,419 graphic materials (incl. photos), 1.1m. govt publs; Dean of Libraries BRENDA JOHNSON.

Indianapolis-Marion County Public Library: POB 211, Indianapolis, IN 46206-0211; One Library Sq., 40 E St, Clair St, Indianapolis, IN 46204; tel. (317) 275-4100; internet www.imcpl.org; f. 1873; 22 brs; 3 bookmobiles; 2.1m. vols; CEO JACKIE NYTES.

Lawrenceburg Public Library District: 150 Mary St, Lawrenceburg, IN 47025; tel. (812) 537-2775; e-mail lawplib@lpld.lib.in.us;

internet www.lpld.lib.in.us; N Dearborn Br. Library at West Harrison; Dir SALLY STEGNER; Pres. PATRICIA RITZMANN; Sec. MARITA CIZEK.

Purdue University Libraries: 504 W State St, West Lafayette, IN 47907-2058; tel. (765) 494-2900; e-mail libinfo@purdue.edu; internet www.lib.purdue.edu; f. 1869; divs of Archives and Special Collns (ASC), Health and Life Sciences (HLS), Humanities, Social Sciences, Education, and Business (HSSEB) and Physical Sciences, Engineering and Technology (PSET); 14 brs; 2,586,297 vols, 3,074,243 microform units, 483,072 govt documents, 59,268 serials; Dean of Libraries Prof. Dr JAMES L. MULLINS.

University of Notre Dame Hesburgh Libraries: 221 Hesburgh Library, Notre Dame, IN 46556; tel. (574) 631-6258; internet www.library.nd.edu; f. 1873; 4m. vols, 77,500 current journals, 175,000 vols of rare books; spec. collns: Ambrosiana, American Catholic Studies, O'Neill Irish Music, Joyce Sports Research, medieval education, Descartes, Jacques Maritain, Dante, orchids, historical botany, Irish maps and sea charts, Irish Rebellion of 1798, Irish postage stamps; Univ. Librarian DIANE PARR WALKER.

Iowa

Carnegie-Stout Public Library: 360 W 11th St, Dubuque, IA 52001; tel. (563) 589-4225; internet www.dubuque.lib.ia.us; f. 1902, present bldg 1981; spec. colln: obituary file dating from the late 1850s and a newspaper index to the Telegraph Herald and other local newspapers; Grant Wood art colln; works by Lasansky, Thieme, Charlet, de Vlaminck and Crane; 180,000 vols, 500 periodical and newspaper subscriptions; databases and digital colln; Dir SUSAN HENRICKS; Pres. of Board of Trustees PAULA CONNORS.

Cedar Falls Public Library: 524 Main St, Cedar Falls, IA 50613; tel. (319) 273-8643; e-mail cedarfallslibrary@gmail.com; internet www.cedar-falls.lib.ia.us; f. 1878; 140,195 vols; Dir SHERYL MCGOVERN; Pres. LYNN BLAIR-BROEKER; Sec. ELAINE PFALZGRAF.

Des Moines Public Library: 1000 Grand, Des Moines, IA 50309; tel. (515) 283-4152; e-mail trustees@dmpl.org; internet www.pldminfo.org; f. 1866 as Des Moines Library Asscn; selective fed. depository library for govt documents; colln on history of Iowa, esp. city of Des Moines; Shoah Visual History Colln: testimonies by Holocaust survivors and witnesses; 1 Central Library and 5 brs; Dir GREG HEID; Pres. KEVIN W. TECHAU.

Fayette Community Library: POB 107, 104 W State St, Fayette, IA 52142; tel. (563) 425-3344; e-mail director@fayettelibrary.lib.ia.us; internet www.fayettelibrary.lib.ia.us; f. 1934; Dir LINDA K. ADAMS.

Herbert Hoover Presidential Library—Museum: 210 Parkside Dr., West Branch, IA 52358; tel. (319) 643-5301; e-mail hoover.library@nara.gov; internet hoover.archives.gov; f. 1962; administered by the Nat. Archives and Records Admin.; official and personal papers of 31st Pres. of USA; 300 MSS collns; 20,000 vols, 8,247,000 MSS, 39,500 photographs, 420 hours sound recordings and 153,000 ft of film, 2,770 rolls of microfilm, 443 oral history transcripts covering history since beginning of the 20th century, economics and political science; Dir Dr THOMAS SCHWARTZ; publ. *Historical Materials in the Herbert Hoover Presidential Library.*

Iowa City Public Library: 123 S Linn St, Iowa City, IA 52240; tel. (319) 356-5200; internet www.icpl.org; f. 1896; 230,597 vols (incl. 182,993 books and ebooks, 40,824 nonprint materials, 6,340 print and e-reference,

440 periodicals and newspapers); Dir SUSAN CRAIG; Pres. THOMAS S. MARTIN; Sec. MEREDITH RICH-CHAPPELL.

Iowa State University Library: cnr of Osborn Dr. and Morrill Rd, Ames, IA 50011-2140; tel. (515) 294-3642; e-mail spclref@iastate.edu; internet www.lib.iastate.edu; f. 1868; fed. depository; also comprises Archives of American Agriculture, Archives of American Veterinary Medicine, American Archives of the Factual Film, Women in Science and Eng. Archives, Univ. Archives; 2,626,074 vols, 3,527,542 microform units, 936,687 photographs and slides, 18,051 audio materials, 18,409 linear ft of MSS and archives, 85,655 ejournals, 33,769 films and video cassettes, 99,209 aerial photographs and maps; Dean OLIVIA M. A. MADISON.

Mason City Public Library: 225 Second St SE, Mason City, IA 50401; tel. (641) 421-3670; e-mail admin@masoncity.lib.ia.us; internet www.mcpl.org; f. 1940; Lee P. Loomis Archive: historical documents and photos, city directories, artefacts and Autograph Colln; colln of genealogical materials; Dir MARY MARKWALTER; Pres. DAVE GROOTERS.

Ossian Public Library: POB 120, 123 Main St, Ossian, IA 52161; tel. (563) 532-9461; e-mail director@ossian.lib.ia.us; internet www.ossian.lib.ia.us; f. 1956; Dir JUDE ZWEIBOHMER; Pres. KAY ELSBERND; Sec. ERICA DAVIS.

Scott County Library System: 200 N Sixth Ave, Eldridge, IA 52748; tel. (563) 285-4794; internet www.scottcountylibrary.org; 5 brs; bookmobile services; Dir PAUL SEELAU; Pres. LINDA TUBBS; Sec. JENI CRISWELL.

Sioux City Public Library: 529 Pierce St, Sioux City, IA 51101; tel. (712) 255-2933; internet www.siouxcitylibrary.org; 1 main library and 2 brs; 220,000 vols; Dir BETSY THOMPSON.

State Historical Society of Iowa State Archives & Records Program: 600 E Locust, Des Moines, IW 50319-0290; tel. (515) 281-5111; internet www.iowahistory.org/archives; br. in Iowa City; colln of genealogical material, records of functions and responsibilities of Office of Gov. and Lt Gov., military records of Iowa regiments fought in the Mexican War, Civil War and Spanish-American War, newspaper, MSS, audiovisual and map collns; spec. colln of photographs incl. old specimens of daguerreotype to digital; State Archivist JEROME THOMPSON; publ. *Iowa Heritage Illustrated* (4 a year); publ. *The Annals of Iowa* (4 a year).

State Library of Iowa: Miller Bldg, 1112 E Grand Ave, Des Moines, IA 50319; tel. (515) 281-4105; internet www.statelibraryofiowa.org; f. 1838 as territorial library, present name and status 1846; attached to Iowa Dept of Education; focuses on improving library services and delivers specialized information services to state govt and public; law library; State Librarian MARY WEGNER.

University of Iowa Libraries: 100 Main Library (LIB), Iowa City, IA 52242-1420; tel. (319) 335-5299; e-mail lib-ref@uiowa.edu; internet www.lib.uiowa.edu; f. 1847; 11 departmental libraries; depository for fed., State of Iowa, UN, and EU information; rare books since 15th century; Map Colln; Iowa Women's Archives; 5m. vols, 200,000 rare books, 800 MSS; Univ. Librarian NANCY L. BAKER.

Urbandale Public Library: 3520 86th St, Urbandale, IW 50322; tel. (515) 278-3945; e-mail reference@urbandale.org; internet www.urbandalelibrary.org; f. 1961; Dir JULIE

WELLS; Pres. JULIE KROLL; Sec. THOMAS P. GRAVES.

Waterloo Public Library: 415 Commercial St, Waterloo, IA 50701; tel. (319) 291-4480; e-mail infowiz.wpl@gmail.com; internet www.waterloo.lib.ia.us; f. 1896; 172,580 vols; Dir SHERYL MCGOVERN.

Kansas

Arkansas City Public Library: 120 E Fifth Ave, Arkansas City, KS 67005; tel. (620) 442-1280; e-mail arkcitypl@acpl.org; internet www.arkcity.org; f. 1892; 46,900 vols (incl. books, audio cassettes, audio CDs, video cassettes, DVDs, music CDs, microfilm and magazines); Dir DALENE MCDONALD.

Bonner Springs City Library: 201 N Nettleton Ave, Bonner Springs, KS 66012; tel. (913) 441-2665; internet www.bonnerlibrary.org; f. 1964; 50,000 vols; Dir KIMBERLY BEETS; Pres. VICKY WHEELER; Sec. JANE RINK; Treas. TED STOLFUS.

Dwight D. Eisenhower Presidential Library and Museum: POB 339, 200 SE Fourth St, Abilene, KS 67410; tel. (785) 263-6700; e-mail eisenhower.library@nara.gov; internet www.eisenhower.archives.gov; f. 1962; documents related to fmr Pres. Eisenhower, and MSS of important persons in Eisenhower's admin. and military career; museum with 70,000 artefacts; 28,500 vols, 26m. MSS pages, 33,120 pages oral history transcripts, 335,000 still photographs, 768,000 ft of motion picture film; Dir KARL WEISSENBACH; publ. *Overview* (4 a year).

Hays Public Library: 1205 Main St, Hays, KS 67601; tel. (785) 625-9014; internet www.hayspublib.org; f. 1895 as Saturday Afternoon Club; mem. of Central Kansas Library System; Chair. AVRY ST PETER; Dir ERIC NORRIS; Sec. KERRI SUNLEY; Treas. JENIFER RIAT.

Johnson County Kansas Law Library: 100 N Kansas Ave, First Fl., Olathe, KS 66061; tel. (913) 715-4154; e-mail lawlib@jocogov.org; internet lawlibrary.jocogov.org; collns incl. statutes and case law, fed. statutes and case law, case law of other states, Missouri statutes and case law, practice handbooks covering Kansas and Missouri law in many areas, legal encyclopedias, treatises, recent legal periodicals.

Kansas Supreme Court Law Library: Kansas Judicial Center, 301 SW 10th Ave, First Fl., Topeka, KS 66612-1507; tel. (785) 296-3257; e-mail lawlibrary@kscourts.org; internet www.kscourts.org/kansas-courts/law-library; colln incl. statutory and case law for all 50 states, treatises on various legal subjects, fed. documents, briefs of Kansas appellate level cases and court-related materials; fed. depository; 185,000 vols, 600 periodical titles; Dir (vacant).

K-State Libraries: 137 Hale Library, 1100 Mid-Campus Dr., Manhattan, KS 66506; tel. (785) 532-3014; e-mail library@k-state.edu; internet www.lib.k-state.edu; f. 1863; attached to Kansas State Univ.; research collns incl. cookery, the consumer movement, military history, biosecurity and food safety, grain science and milling, prairie studies, and children's literature; 5 brs (veterinary medical, engineering, maths and physics, architecture and technology and aviation); Consumer Movement Archives; 2.6m. vols; Dean of Libraries LORI A. GOETSCH; publs *KSU Library Cassette Series on Library Technology* (irregular), *Library Bibliography Series* (irregular).

Leavenworth Public Library: 417 Spruce St, Leavenworth, KS 66048; tel. (913) 682-5666; internet www.leavenworthpubliclibrary.org; f. 1860, fmrly Leavenworth Mercantile Library, present location 1987; Dir KIM BAKER; Pres. PAULINE GRAEBER; Sec. JUSTIN STEWART; Treas. JENNIFER BRENNEMAN TOBEY.

Macksville City Library: 333 N Main St, Macksville, KS; tel. (620) 348-3555; e-mail macksvillecitylibrary@hotmail.com; internet macksville.mykansaslibrary.org; f. 1935; mem. of S Central Kansas Library System; Dir JODY SUITER; Pres. JON ZWINK; Sec. AUDREY AUSTIN; Treas. KAREN SPENCER.

Manhattan Public Library: 629 Poyntz Ave, Manhattan, KS 66502; tel. (785) 776-4741; e-mail refstaff@manhattan.lib.ks.us; internet www.manhattan.lib.ks.us; f. 1856; resource centre for N Central Kansas Libraries System; Dir LINDA KNUPP; Pres. TODD SIMON.

Marysville Public Library: 1009 Broadway, Marysville, KS 66508; tel. (785) 562-2491; e-mail maryslb@bluevalley.net; internet marysville.mykansaslibrary.org; f. 1935; 36,000 vols; Dir JAMIE KELLEY; Pres. AMY HEIMAN; Sec. STACY WULLSCHLEGER; Treas. DANA PIESCHL.

Rossville Community Library: POB 618, Rossville, KS 66533; 407 N Main, Rossville, KS 66533; tel. (785) 584-6454; e-mail director@rossvillelibrary.org; internet www .rossvillelibrary.org; f. 1950; 11,614 vols; Dir ADRIENNE OLEJNIK; Pres. ANDREW FOSTER; Sec. SEAN BIRD; Treas. ALICIA VANATTA.

Salina Public Library: 301 W Elm St, Salina, KS 67401; tel. (785) 825-4624; e-mail ask4info@salpub.org; internet www .salinapubliclibrary.org; f. 1868; Dir JOE MCKENZIE; Pres. SANDIE JOHNSON; Sec. and Treas. BRIAN SCHMIDT.

State Library of Kansas: Capitol Bldg, Room 169-W, 300 SW 10th Ave, Topeka, KS 66612-1593; tel. (785) 296-3296; e-mail infodesk@library.ks.gov; internet www.kslib .info; f. 1855; provides information services for state and local govts, for local libraries and their users; collects and shares resources and govt information; educates librarians and trustees; advocates for open and equitable access, intellectual freedom and excellence in library services and support; depository for fed. documents since 1900; newspaper clippings dating back to 1913; 40,000 state govt documents dating back to 1856; State Librarian JO BUDLER.

Topeka and Shawnee County Public Library: 1515 SW 10th Ave, Topeka, KS 66604-1374; tel. (785) 580-4400; internet www.tscpl.org; f. 1870 as Ladies Library Asscn, present name and status 1992; incl. Alice C. Sabatini Gallery; bookmobile services; genealogy and local history colln; spec. colln of handmade artist's books and book objects, miniature books, fore-edge books, pop-up books, first edns; Moses Colln of scholarly fine arts books; 500,000 vols; CEO GINA MILLSAP; Chair. DAN GUENTHER; Sec. MELISSA MASONER; Treas. ROBERT HARDER.

KU Libraries University of Kansas: Suite 502, 1425 Jayhawk Blvd, Lawrence, KS 66045-7544; tel. (785) 864-8983; internet www.lib.ku.edu; f. 1866; 3.8m. vols, 322,000 maps, 3,370,000 microforms, 3m. graphics (mostly photographs), 30,000 sound recordings, 691,000 govt documents, 15,000 linear ft MSS, spec. colln: 250,000 vols printed since the mid-15th century and 500,000 MSS from Antiquity to present; Dean of Libraries LORRAINE J. HARICOMBE.

Kentucky

Allen County Public Library: 106 W Public Sq., Scottsville, KY 42164; tel. (270) 237-3861; internet www2.youseemore.com/ allen; f. 1954; 35,000 vols; Dir SHELIA STOVALL.

Boyd County Public Library: 1740 Central Ave, Ashland, KY 41101; tel. (606) 329-0518; e-mail reference@thebookplace.org; internet www.thebookplace.org; f. 1981; spec. colln incl. Arnold Hanners Tri-State photograph colln, Boyd Co historical records colln, Hilton colln and KY vital records (1911–95); microfilm colln incl. KY Federal Census and regional census materials; genealogy and local history; 2 brs; 150,000 vols (incl. books, large print, movies, audio books, downloadable movies, downloadable audio books, iPods, and newspaper and magazine colln); Dir DEBBIE COSPER.

Clark County Public Library: 370 S Burns Ave, Winchester, KY 40391-1876; tel. (859) 744-5661; e-mail clarkbooks@gmail .com; internet www.clarkpublib.org; 1 bookmobile; Dir JULIE MARUSKIN; Pres. EDDIE WILLIAMS; Sec. CINDY DARLING CODELL; Treas. BRENDA ROYSE.

Daviess County Public Library: 2020 Frederica St, Owensboro, KY 42301; tel. (270) 684-0211; e-mail daviess@dcplibrary .org; internet www.dcplibrary.org; f. 1913 as Carnegie Free Public Library, present location 2007, current name adopted 1995; 190,000 vols, 46,325 vols digital material, 12,257 movies in DVD and Blu-ray format, 247 video games, 235 magazines, 35 newspapers; Pres. POLLY REYNOLDS; Dir JAMES BLANTON.

Grant County Public Library: 201 Barnes Rd, Williamstown, KY 41097; tel. (859) 824-2080; e-mail grantcountypubliclibrary@fuse .net; internet www.grantlib.org; f. 1954; local history colln; 21,000 vols, 1,900 movies on DVD and VHS, 600 audio books on CD or audio cassettes, 950 music CDs, 100 newspaper and magazine subscriptions; Dir SUSAN NIMERSHEIM; Public Services Librarian WYNITA WORLEY.

Graves County Public Library: 601 N 17th St, Mayfield, KY 42066; tel. (270) 247-2911; e-mail dianegcpl@bellsouth.net; internet www.gcpl.org; f. 1940; 50,000 vols; Dir DIANE BENNETT; Pres. MARTHA BABB; Sec. KATHY O'NAN; Treas. PETE GALLOWAY.

Grayson County Public Library: 130 E Market St, Leitchfield, KY 42754; tel. (270) 259-5455; e-mail jones@ graysoncountylibrary.org; internet www2 .youseemore.com/grayson; co and state histories, family records, News-Gazette on microfilm since 1940s; 40,000 vols, 60 periodicals, 1,000 video cassettes and 400 audio books; Dir LISA JONES.

Henderson County Public Library: 101 S Main St, Henderson, KY 42420; tel. (270) 826-3712; internet www.hcpl.org; f. 1904; large print books, genealogy and local history photo colln; 112,000 vols (incl. books, newspapers, magazines, audiovisual materials, microfilms); Pres. KEN CHRISTOPHER; Sec. LINDA A. MIODUSZEWSKI; Treas. STEPHEN W. MARTIN.

Jessamine County Public Library: 600 S Main St, Nicholasville, KY 40356-1839; tel. (859) 885-3523; e-mail jcplcirculation@ jesspublib.org; internet www.jesspublib.org; f. 1975 as Withers Memorial Public Library, present name and status 2001; Dir Dr RON CRITCHFIELD; Pres. BILLIE GOODWILL; Sec. TERRY MORGAN; Treas. ROB AMBURGEY.

Kenton County Public Library: 2171 Chamber Center Dr., Fort Mitchell, KY 41017; tel. (859) 341-3200; internet www .kenton.lib.ky.us; f. 1901; brs: Mary Ann Mongan Library Covington, Erlanger Br., William E. Durr Br.; 584,938 vols; Dir DAVE SCHROEDER.

Kentucky Department for Libraries and Archives: POB 537 Frankfort, KY 40602-

0537; 300 Coffee Tree Rd, Frankfort, KY 40601; tel. (502) 564-8300; internet www .kdla.ky.gov; 18,600 vols, 3,189 audiovisual items, 5,797 audio books, 33,502 govt documents, 149,133 ebooks, 18,771 journals; State Librarian and Commr WAYNE ONKST.

Laurel County Public Library: 120 College Park Dr., London, KY 40741; tel. (606) 864-5759; internet www.laurellibrary.org; f. 1916; 120,000 vols and 10,000 audiovisual colln; Dist. Dir LORI ACTON.

Lexington Public Library: 140 E Main St, Lexington, KY 40507; tel. (859) 231-5500; internet www.lexpublib.org; f. 1795; brs: Beaumont, Eagle Creek, Northside, Tates Creek and Village; 623,186 vols; Exec. Dir ANN HAMMOND; Dir of Library Services SUSIE LAWRENCE.

Logan County Public Library: 201 W Sixth St, Russellville, KY 42276; tel. (270) 726-6129; internet www.loganlibrary.org; 3 brs: Central Library, Adairville br. and Auburn br; Dir LINDA KOMPANIK; Pres. OBIE VAN CLEAVE; Sec. NORARGENTINA LACAYO; Treas. MARTHA DAVENPORT.

Louisville Free Public Library: 301 York St, Louisville, KY 40203; tel. (502) 574-1611; internet www.lfpl.org; f. 1908; attached to Louisville/Jefferson County Metro Govt; 36,000 phono-discs, 70,000 programmes on electronic tape, operates 2 FM radio stations for music and educational programmes; 18 brs, 1 bookmobile; spec. Kentucky History Colln; houses a 'Louisville Art Gallery'; Talking Book Library for the blind and physically handicapped; 1,172,236 vols; Chair. TAD THOMAS; Dir CRAIG BUTHOD; publ. *Library News*.

Mt Sterling—Montgomery County Library: 241 W Locust St, Mt Sterling, KY 40353; tel. (859) 498-2404; e-mail askmtsterlinglibrary@yahoo.com; internet www.youseemore.com/mtsterling; f. 1878; Dir MELISSA SMATHERS-BARNES; Chair. JOHN WENZ; Sec. KIM TONNING.

Nelson County Public Library: 201 Cathedral Manor, Bardstown, KY 40004; tel. (502) 348-3714; e-mail ncpl@nelsoncopublib.org; internet www.nelsoncopublib.org; f. 1946; present name and status 1968; 2 brs: Bloomfield Br. and New Haven Br.; 1 bookmobile; Dir SHARON SHANKS; Pres. VAL DOWNS; Sec. BARBARA HEADDY.

Nicholas County Public Library: 223 N Broadway, Carlisle, KY 40311; tel. (859) 289-5595; internet www.nicholascountylibrary .com; f. 1947, present location 1967; 1 bookmobile; 26,000 vols; Dir BECKY REID.

Rowan County Public Library: 175 Beacon Hill Dr., Morehead, KY 40351; tel. (606) 784-7137; e-mail email@rowancountylibrary .org; internet www.youseemore.com/rowan; 140 vols (incl. newspapers and magazine subscriptions); Dir HELEN WILLIAMS; Pres. HELEN NORTHCUTT; Sec. KAY FREELAND; Treas. RYAN NEFF.

Spencer County Library: 168 Taylorsville Rd, Taylorsville, KY 40071; tel. (502) 477-8137; e-mail scpl@insightbb.com; internet members.iglou.com/scpl; f. 1979; spec. colln incl. genealogy items; Dir DEBRA LAWSON.

University of Kentucky Libraries: Lexington, KY 40506-0456; tel. (859) 218-2048; e-mail refdesk@uky.edu; internet libraries .uky.edu; f. 1909; 12 br. and collegiate libraries; regional depository for govt publs and a depository for EU and Canadian publs, British parliamentary papers, Kentucky govt publs, and technical reports from US fed. agencies; King Library Press; univ. and audiovisual archives; Digital Library Service creates digital content for the Kentucky Digital Library, incl. electronic texts, digitized photographs, images and archival finding aids; 4,107,758 vols; incl. 656,644 ebooks, 415 commercial databases, 26,780 linear ft of MSS and archives; large colln of Kentuckiana, spec. collns of 19th century British literature, French and Spanish drama from 1600 to 1900, modern political manuscript collns, broadsides, ballads and chapbooks, Cortot colln of music theory, typography, history of books, Appalachian Regional Commission archives, oral history colln; Dean of Libraries TERRY BIRDWHISTELL; Sr Assoc. Dean MARY BETH THOMSON.

Woodford County Library: 115 N Main St, Versailles, KY 40383; tel. (859) 873-5191; internet woodfordcountylibrary.org; 2 brs: Main Br. and Midway Br. (opened 2009); 1 bookmobile; 70,000 vols; Dir KAREN KASACAVAGE; Pres. CHARLANN WOMBLES; Sec. TIM MIDDLETON; Treas. Dr MICHAEL R. NICHOLS.

Louisiana

Allen Parish Libraries: 320 S Sixth St, Oberlin, LA 70655; tel. (337) 639-4315; e-mail jsmith2@state.lib.la.us; internet www .allen.lib.la.us; f. 1957; Oberlin (HQ) and brs at Oakdale and Kinder; Dir GERALDINE HARRIS.

Ascension Parish Library: 708 S Irma Blvd, Gonzales, LA 70737; tel. (225) 647-8924; internet www.myapl.org; f. 1960; Donaldsonville (HQ); brs: Dutchtown, Gonzales and Galvez; 324,151 vols; Dir ANGELLE DESHAUTELLES.

Beauregard Parish Public Library: 205 S Washington Ave, DeRidder, LA 70634; tel. (337) 463-6217; e-mail admin@beau.org; internet www.beau.lib.la.us/lib; f. 1947; brs: East Beauregard, Fields, Merryville, South Beauregard and Singer; local history colln has information on people, places and events; adult new readers colln incl. reading materials for literacy activities; 61,498 vols.

Bienville Parish Library: 2768 Maple St, Arcadia, LA 71001; tel. (318) 263-7410; internet www.bienvillelibrary.org; f. 1964; Arcadia (HQ); brs: Ringgold, Saline and Castor; Dir PEGGY WALLS.

East Baton Rouge Parish Library: 7711 Goodwood Blvd, Baton Rouge, LA 70806; tel. (225) 231-3700; e-mail eref@ebrpl.com; internet www.ebrpl.com; f. 1939; brs: main library and 12 brs; 2 bookmobiles; 2m. vols; Dir DAVID FARRAR; Dir KIZZY A. PAYTON; Treas. LAURENCE LAMBERT.

Iberia Parish Library System: 445 E Main St, New Iberia, LA 70560; tel. (337) 364-7024; e-mail newiberialib@yahoo.com; internet www.iberia.lib.la.us; f. 1947; spec. colln: I.A. and Carroll Martin Photo Colln and the Bunk Johnson Colln; 7 brs; 210,000 vols; Dir KATHLEEN MILES.

Jefferson Davis Parish Library: 4747 W Napoleon Ave, Metairie, LA 70001; tel. (504) 838-1100; internet www.jefferson-davis.lib.la .us; f. 1949; Jennings HQ; 4 brs and 1 bookmobile; Dir LON DICKERSON; Pres. JANICE ESTHAY; Treas. LEAVON LADNER.

Lafayette Public Library System: 301 W Congress St, Lafayette, LA 70501; tel. (337) 261-5775; internet www .lafayettepubliclibrary.org; f. 1897; brs: Broussard, Butler Memorial, Chenier, Duson, Jefferson St, Milton, N Regional, Scott, S Regional and Youngsville; main library closed for renovation; Dir SONA J. DOMBOURIAN; Pres. ANDREW DUHON.

LaSalle Parish Library: 3108 N First St, Jena, LA 71342; tel. (318) 992-5675; internet www.lasalle.lib.la.us; f. 1963; main library and Olla br.; spec. colln incl. genealogy colln and microfilm; Dir ANDREA BOOK (acting); Pres. SAMMY FRANKLIN.

Law Library of Louisiana: 400 Royal St, Second Fl., New Orleans, LA 70130-2104; tel. (504) 310-2400; e-mail library@lasc.org; internet www.lasc.org/law_library/library_information.asp; f. 1855; colln incl. complete chronology of both statutes and court reports for all states and fed. govt; 230,000 vols.

Livingston Parish Library: POB 397, Livingston, LA 70754; 13986 Florida Blvd, Livingston, LA 70754; tel. (225) 686-2489; internet www.mylpl.info; f. 1946; Livingston (HQ); brs: Albany-Springfield, Denham Springs-Walker, S and Watson; Dir GIOVANNI TAIROV; Asst Dir JENNIFER SENECA.

Louisiana State University Libraries: Baton Rouge, LA 70803; tel. (225) 578-5652; internet www.lib.lsu.edu; f. 1860; UN, fed. and state depositories; spec. collns incl. E. A. McIlhenny Natural History Colln, Louisiana Colln, sugar technology, Southern history, agriculture, plant pathology, petroleum, bibliography colln, aquaculture, incl. crawfish, wetlands research and marine biology; archives on Lower Mississippi Valley; 3m. vols, 5,375,405 microforms and 12m. MSS, databases, ebooks and ejournals; Dean JENNIFER CARGILL; publ. *Library Lectures*.

New Orleans Public Library: 219 Loyola Ave, New Orleans, LA 70112; tel. (504) 596-2570; internet nutrias.org; f. 1843; 12 brs; spec. collns: city archives colln, civil and criminal courts colln, carnivals, maps, photographs, rare books, early sheet music, early jazz recordings and MSS; incl. African American Resource Center and Business and Science Div.; 1,043,471 vols; Chair. LEE C. REID; Head of Main Public Services LINDA MARSHALL HILL.

Ouachita Parish Public Library: 1800 Stubbs Ave, Monroe, LA 71201; tel. (318) 327-1490; internet www.ouachita.lib.la.us; f. 1884; main library and brs: Anna Meyer, Carver Br., Louise Williams, Ollie Burns, Ouachita Valley, Cptl J R Searcy, Sterlington Memorial, W Monroe and W Ouachita; Dir ROBIN TOMS; Pres. DARRIS WAREN.

Rapides Parish Library: 430 St James St, Alexandria, LA 71301; tel. (318) 445-6436; internet www.rpl.org; f. 1942; brs: Westside Regional Library, Boyce, Gunter, Hineston, J. W. McDonald Memorial, Johnson, King, Martin and Robertson; main library and 1 bookmobile; Dir STEVE ROGGE; Pres. SUSIE C. SMITH.

Sabine Parish Library: 705 Main St, Many, LA 71449; tel. (318) 256-4150; internet www.sabine.lib.la.us; f. 1933; Sabine Parish (HQ); brs: Toledo, Converse, Pleasant Hill and Zwolle; Dir REBECCA MORRIS; Pres. LORENE JONES.

South St Landry Community Library: 235 Marie St, Sunset, LA 70584; tel. (337) 662-3442; internet www .southstlandrylibrary.com; f. 1989, present name and status 1991; 34,000 vols; Dir BARBARA A. MALBRUE; Chair. ARMAND BRINKHAUS; Sec. ANDY DAKIN.

St. Tammany Parish Library: 310 W 21st Ave, Covington, LA 70433; tel. (985) 871-1219; e-mail covington@stpl.us; internet www.sttammany.lib.la.us; f. 1946; spec. colln incl. selected documents issued by state governmental agencies; census on microfilm; family histories and a local newspaper archive in geneology colln; Dir DONALD WESTMORELAND; Pres. Dr ARGIRO MORGAN; Sec. and Treas. MARY RENEAU.

State Library of Louisiana: POB 131, Baton Rouge, LA 70821-0131; 701 N Fourth St, Baton Rouge, LA 70802-5345; tel. (225) 342-4923; e-mail admin@state.lib.la.us; internet www.state.lib.la.us; f. 1920, fmrly

Louisiana Library Comm.; colln supplements Louisiana public libraries and meets research needs of state govt employees; 11m. vols; State Librarian REBECCA HAMILTON; publ. *Hotlines* (4 a year).

Terrebonne Parish Library System: 151 Library Dr., Houma, LA 70360; tel. (985) 876-5861; internet www.mytpl.org; f. 1927; main br.; brs: Bourg, Chauvin, Dularge, E Houma, Gibson, Grand Caillou, Montegut and N Terrebonne; Dir MARY COSPER LEBOEUF.

Tulane University Libraries: 7001 Freret St, New Orleans, LA 70118; tel. (504) 865-5605; e-mail libref@tulane.edu; internet library.tulane.edu; f. 1834; incl. 16 libraries; 3.6m. vols, incl. law, medicine and 6 other collns; spec. collns on New Orleans, Louisiana and S USA history; Latin America, architecture and jazz; Dean of the Library LANCE QUERY.

Union Parish Library: 202 W Jackson St, Farmerville, LA 71241; tel. (318) 368-9226; internet www.youseemore.com/unionparish; f. 1955; 62,000 vols; Dir STEPHANIE ANTLEY HERRMANN; publ. *Beacon Bulletin* (12 a year).

Vermilion Parish Library: POB 640, Abbeville, LA 70510; 405 E St Victor St, Abbeville, LA 70510; tel. (337) 893-2674; e-mail abbeville@vermilion.lib.la.us; internet www.vermilion.lib.la.us; f. 1942; brs: Abbeville, Delcambre, Erath, Gueydan, Kaplan and Maurice; Dir CHARLOTTE TROSCLAIR; Pres. RICKY LUQUETTE.

Maine

Auburn Public Library: 49 Spring St, Auburn, ME 04210; tel. (207) 333-6640; e-mail email@auburnpubliclibrary.org; internet www.auburn.lib.me.us; f. 1890; Dir LYNN LOCKWOOD; Pres. RICHARD L. TRAFTON.

Bangor Public Library: 145 Harlow St, Bangor, ME 04401; tel. (207) 947-8336; e-mail bplill@bpl.lib.me.us; internet www .bpl.lib.me.us; f. 1830; spec. colln incl. co histories, local history resources and State and Fed. Census state resources like Maine Register Town Histories; Dir BARBARA McDADE; Pres. NORMAN MINSKY.

Boothbay Harbor Memorial Library: 4 Oak St, Boothbay Harbor, ME 04538; tel. 207-633-3112; e-mail bbhlibrary@bmpl.lib .me.us; internet www.bmpl.lib.me.us; f. 1924; 22,000 vols; Exec. Dir BETTY HUGHES; Pres. TOM CHURCHILL; Sec. JANE GARDNER; Treas. JOYCE ARMENDARIS.

Cary Library: 107 Main St, Houlton, ME 04730; tel. (207) 532-1302; e-mail library@cary.lib.me.us; internet www.cary.lib.me.us; f. 1904; 55,000 vols, incl. 800 large print titles, 1,400 audio CDs, 1,700 video cassettes and DVDs and 90 periodicals; spec. colln incl. historical genealogical information from Houlton, Maine and its surrounding communities in the S Aroostook Co area; Dir LINDA FAUCHER.

Curtis Memorial Library: 23 Pleasant St, Brunswick, ME 04011; tel. (207) 725-5242; e-mail director@curtislibrary.com; internet www.curtislibrary.com; f. 1883; 146,625 vols; Dir ELISABETH DOUCETT; Pres. CHRISTOPHER GOODWIN; Sec. and Treas. LESTER HODGDON.

Falmouth Memorial Library: 5 Lunt Rd, Falmouth, ME 04105; tel. (207) 781-2351; internet www.falmouth.lib.me.us; f. 1944; 47,392 vols, 2,560 video cassettes and DVDs, 1,871 music CDs, 1,806 audio books and 107 periodicals; Dir LYNDA L. SUDLOW; Pres. JULIE RABINOWITZ.

Farmington Public Library: 117 Academy St, Farmington, ME 04938; tel. (207) 778-4312; internet www.farmington.lib.me.us; f. 1890; colln of Maine authors; local and town history; genealogy reference library; 30,000 vols; Librarian MELANIE COOMBS.

Gardiner Public Library: 152 Water St, Gardiner, ME 04345-2195; tel. (207) 582-3312; internet www.gpl.lib.me.us; f. 1796; Community Archives Room incl. colln on genealogy, state, county and local histories; Dir ANNE ESTRADA DAVIS.

Lithgow Public Library: 45 Winthrop St, Augusta, ME 04330; tel. (207) 626-2415; internet www.lithgow.lib.me.us; f. 1894; 65,000 vols; Dir ELIZABETH POHL.

Maine State Archives: 84 State House Station, Augusta, ME 04333; 230 State St, Augusta, ME 04333; tel. (207) 287-5790; internet www.state.me.us/sos/arc; attached to Dept of the Sec. of State; colln incl. bills introduced in Legislature; Governor's Exec. Council reports; deeds to and from Maine; maps; fed. census records up to 1930; co court records dating back to 1639; 95m. pages of official State records; State Archivist DAVE CHEEVER.

Maine State Library: 64 State House Station, Augusta, ME 04333-0064; 230 State St, Augusta, ME 04333-0064; tel. (207) 287-5600; e-mail reference.desk@maine.gov; internet www.maine.gov/msl; f. 1836; 350,615 vols, 703 periodicals, 848 audio cassettes, 650 video cassettes, 250,888 govt docs; State Librarian LINDA H. LORD.

Mark & Emily Turner Memorial Library: 39 Second St, Presque Isle, ME 04769; tel. (207) 764-2571; internet www.presqueislelibrary.org; f. 1874; colln incl. genealogy resources and historical texts and memorabilia of Presque Isle and surrounding area; Dir SONJA PLUMMER-MORGAN; Chair. KEVIN SIPE; Sec. PAUL HAMLIN; Treas. ELAINE SIPE.

McArthur Public Library: 270 Main St, Biddeford, ME; tel. (207) 284-4181; e-mail reference@mcarthur.lib.me.us; internet www.mcarthurpubliclibrary.org; f. 1902; colln of antique photographs of the city and surrounding areas; 65,000 vols, 170 magazine subscriptions, 1,500 music cassettes or CDs, 2,000 video cassettes or DVDs, 1,500 audiobooks; Dir JEFF CABRAL.

Portland Public Library: 5 Monument Sq., Portland, ME 04101; tel. (207) 871-1700; e-mail reference@portland.lib.me.us; internet www.portlandlibrary.com; f. 1867; 1 main library; 3 brs: Burbank, Peaks Island and Riverton; Exec. Dir STEPHEN J. PODGAJNY; Pres. NATHAN H. SMITH.

Rumford Public Library: 56 Rumford Ave, Rumford, ME 04276; tel. (207) 364-3661; internet www.rumford.lib.me.us; f. 1903; Dir LUKE SORENSEN; Chair. CAROLYN KENNARD.

Scarborough Public Library: 48 Gorham Rd, Scarborough, ME 04074; tel. (207) 883-4723; e-mail askspl@scarborough.lib.me.us; internet www.library.scarborough.me.us; f. 1899; 62,703 vols, 5,503 video cassettes, 4,334 audio books colln; Dir NANCY E. CROWELL.

South Berwick Public Library: 37 Portland St, S Berwick, ME 03908; tel. (207) 384-3308; e-mail sbpl@south-berwick.lib.me.us; internet www.south-berwick.lib.me.us; f. 1971; colln incl. S Berwick History Colln, Sarah Orne Jewett Colln and large print books.

Thomaston Public Library: 60 Main St, Thomaston, ME 04861; tel. (207) 354-2453; e-mail tpl@thomaston.lib.me.us; internet www.thomaston.lib.me.us; f. 1898; 26,000 vols (incl. 23,800 books, 2,080 movies); Dir BRIAN SYLVESTER; Chair. JANET BOSWORTH; Sec. SHEILAGH GUYER; Treas. WILLIAM DASHIELL.

Wells Public Library: POB 699, Wells, ME 04090; 1434 Post Rd, Wells, ME 04090; tel. (207) 646-8181; e-mail libstaff@wellstown.org; internet www.wells.lib.me.us; f. 1978; colln of large print books for visually impaired; Dir CINDY SCHILLING; Chair. AMY ANDERSON.

William Fogg Public Library: POB 359, 116 Old Rd, Eliot, ME 03903; tel. (207) 439-9437; e-mail front-desk@william-fogg.lib.me.us; internet www.william-fogg.lib.me.us; f. 1907; Fogg antiquarian book colln; American regional history, which incl. state histories, westward expansion, Revolutionary, Civil War, and Indian War materials; Dir and Head of Adult Services SUSAN SINNOTT.

Windham Public Library: 217 Windham Center Rd, Windham, ME 04062; tel. (207) 892-1908; internet www.windham.lib.me.us; f. 1971; spec. colln on genealogy and books that deal with the state of Maine; 42,000 vols, 3,300 movies, 1,500 audio recordings, 850 music recordings, 80 periodicals and newspapers; Chair. ROBERT A. ROSBOROUGH.

Maryland

Allegany County Library System: 31 Washington St, Cumberland, MD 21502; tel. (301) 777-1200; e-mail washingtonstlibrary@allconet.org; internet www.home.alleganycountylibrary.info; f. 1960; incl. 6 libraries and 1 bookmobile; spec. colln incl. Maryland Room colln of print materials of interest for local history and genealogy, incl. histories of Maryland and Allegany Co and nearby cities, towns, churches and businesses; Dir JOHN TAUBE.

Baltimore County Circuit Court Law Library: County Courts Bldg, 401 Bosley Ave, Towson, MD 21204; tel. (410) 887-3086; internet www.baltimorecountymd.gov/agencies/circuit/library; provides legal information and information services to judges, attorneys, paralegals, govt officials and citizens representing themselves in legal matters who reside or practice in Baltimore Co, Maryland; colln incl. laws and cases of all 50 states and the Fed. govt; spec. emphasis on Maryland law and subject specific treatises; collns incl. Co codes, Court of Appeals briefs on microfiche, all currently available MICPELs, over 50 law reviews and extensive tax and labour collns; Dir STEPHANIE LEVASSEUR.

Caroline County Public Library: 100 Market St, Denton, MD 21629; tel. (410) 479-1343; e-mail info@carolib.org; internet www.carolib.org; f. 1961; 3 brs; colln incl. Maryland history geographic and economic studies; works by local authors; Caroline Co information; Spanish language colln; Central Library Man. ANN REINECKE.

Enoch Pratt Free Library: 400 Cathedral St, Baltimore, MD 21201-4484; tel. (410) 396-5430; e-mail slrc@prattlibrary.org; internet www.pratt.lib.md.us; f. 1882; spec. collns: H. L. Mencken colln, Maryland history colln; 2,290,042 vols, 91,000 maps, 5,000 films, 19,094 video cassettes, 38,450 slides, 486 filmstrips, 34,802 recordings; CEO CARLA D. HAYDEN; publ. *Menckeniana* (4 a year).

Johns Hopkins University Libraries: Baltimore, MD 21218; tel. (410) 516-8335; e-mail asklib@jhu.edu; internet webapps.jhu.edu/jhuniverse/libraries; f. 1876; incl. the Milton S. Eisenhower Library, 1 of the Sheridan libraries and the main research library of the univ.; spec. collns in medicine, int. affairs, music and earth and space science; 2,961,160 vols; Dean of Univ. Libraries WINSTON TABB.

Maryland State Archives: Dr Edward C. Papenfuse State Archives Bldg, 350 Rowe Blvd, Annapolis, MD 21401; tel. (410) 260-6400; e-mail archives@mdsa.net; internet www.msa.md.gov; f. 1935, fmrly Hall of Records, present name 1984; central depository for government records; holdings date from Maryland's founding in 1634, and incl. colonial and state exec., legislative, and judicial records; co probate, land and court records; church records; business records; state publs and reports; spec. collns of private papers, maps, photographs and newspapers; State Archivist Dr EDWARD C. PAPENFUSE.

Maryland State Law Library: Robert C. Murphy Courts of Appeal Bldg, 361 Rowe Blvd, Annapolis, MD 21401; tel. (410) 260-1430; e-mail lawlibrary@mdcourts.gov; internet www.lawlib.state.md.us; f. 1826 as State Library, present location 1972, present name 1978; legal and govt information resources; spec. colln: Anglo-American legal collns; Maryland legislative task force and comm. reports; Maryland govt pubs in the State and Code of Fed. Regulations; Dir STEVEN P. ANDERSON.

National Agricultural Library: Abraham Lincoln Bldg, 10301 Baltimore Ave, Beltsville, MD 20705-2351; tel. (301) 504-5755; e-mail agref@ars.usda.gov; internet www.nal.usda.gov; f. 1862; attached to US Dept of Agriculture; agriculture and related sciences; spec. collns: Layne R. Beaty Papers (farm radio and television broadcasting); foreign and domestic nursery seed trade catalogues; flock, herd and stud books; audiovisual colln on food and nutrition; apiculture; Forest Service and USDA Photo colln on optical laser discs; M. Truman Fossum Colln (floriculture); James M. Gwin Colln (poultry); Charles E. North Colln (milk sanitation); Pomology Colln (original pomological art); Charles Valentine Riley Colln (entomology); plant exploration photograph colln; food and nutrition micro-computer software; MAPP colln of family life education materials; computer database (AGRICOLA) of 3m. records for books and journal articles in agriculture; information centres on agricultural trade and marketing, alternative farming systems, animal welfare, aquaculture, biotechnology, food and nutrition, plant genome, rural information, technology transfer, water quality and youth devt; 3.5m. vols; Dir Dr SIMON Y. LIU; publs *Agriculture Libraries Information Notes* (12 a year), *Quick Bibliography* (irregular).

National Archives and Records Administration: 8601 Adelphi Rd, College Park, MD 20740-6001; tel. (301) 837-2000; internet www.archives.gov; f. 1934; ensures, for citizens and federal officials, ready access to essential evidence that documents the rights of American citizens, the actions of federal officials, and the nat. experience; establishes policies and procedures for managing US Govt records and assists federal agencies in documenting their activities, administering record management programmes, scheduling records, and retiring non-current records; obtains, arranges, describes, preserves and provides access to the essential documentation of the 3 brs of govt, manages the presidential libraries system, and publishes the laws, regulations, and presidential and other public documents; assists the Information Security Oversight Office, which manages federal classification and declassification policies, and the Nat. Historical Publs and Records Comm., which makes grants nationwide to help non-profit orgs identify, preserve, and provide access to materials that document American history; consists of 33 facilities nationwide, incl. 18 regional records services facilities and 10 presidential Libraries; on permanent display in the Exhibition Hall are the Declaration of Independence, the Constitution of the United

States, and the Bill of Rights; 9,000m. pages of textual records; 7.2m. maps, charts and architectural drawings; over 20m. still photographs; billions of machine-readable data sets; over 365,000 reels of film and 110,000 video cassettes; Archivist of the United States DAVID S. FERRIERO; publ. *Prologue* (4 a year).

National Institute of Standards and Technology Research Library: 100 Bureau Dr., Stop 2500, Gaithersburg, MD 20899-2500; tel. (301) 975-3052; e-mail library@nist.gov; internet www.nist.gov; f. 1912; spec. collns: science, engineering and technology; archives colln incl. catalogued documents, artefacts, photographs, films, video cassettes, oral histories, biographical files, subject files and other material; not open to the public; 300,000 vols, 1,000 journals; Dir Dr PATRICK D. GALLAGHER; Chief Information Officer DELWIN BROCKETT; publ. *Journal of Research of the National Institute of Standards and Technology*.

National Institutes of Health Library: Bldg 10, Room 1L25, 10 Center Dr., MSC 1150, Bethesda, MD 20892-1150; tel. (301) 496-5612; internet nihlibrary.nih.gov; f. 1903; biomedical research library: biology, medicine, health sciences, chemistry, physiology, physics; 70,000 books, 160,000 periodicals, 9,000 journal subscriptions, 2,898 microforms; Library Dir SUZANNE GREFSHEIM; Librarian JEAN WEISS.

National Oceanic and Atmospheric Administration Central Library: 1315 EW Highway, SSMC3, Second Fl., Silver Spring, MD 20910; tel. (301) 713-2600; e-mail library.reference@noaa.gov; internet www.lib.noaa.gov; f. 1807; attached to US Dept of Commerce; 35 libraries and information centres; networks with 30 NOAA libraries; disciplines incl. aeronomy, cartography, coastal studies, ecosystems, geodesy, marine ecology, marine resources, mathematics, oceanography, ocean engineering, nautical charting statistics and weather and atmospheric sciences; 1m. vols; Dir NEAL KASKE.

Nimitz Library: 589 McNair Rd, Annapolis, MD 21402-5029; tel. (410) 293-2420; internet www.usna.edu/library; f. 1973; attached to United States Naval Acad. (USNA); open for midshipmen and faculty; services also provided to USNA military and civilian staff and their family members and personnel attached to the other activities of the Annapolis Area Naval Complex; local retired faculty members and retired military personnel; 30,000 vols, 40,000 photographs and 400 MSS colln; Dir JAMES RETTIG.

Prince George's County Memorial Library System: 6532 Adelphi Rd, Hyattsville, MD 20782; tel. (301) 699-3500; internet www.pgcmls.info; 18 Community Libraries; Co Correctional Center Library; 1,906,457 vols (incl. 1,613,086 books, 76,630 serials, 120,328 audio recordings, 89,425 video cassettes, 246,662 journals); Dir KATHLEEN TEAZE; Pres. MARK POLK.

Ruth Enlow Library of Garrett County: 6 N Second St, Oakland, MD 21550; tel. (301) 334-3996; internet www.relib.net; f. 1915 as Oakland Free Public Library, present bldg 1950; print, non-print and e-resources; 1 main library (Oakland) and 4 brs in Accident, Friendsville, Grantsville and Kitzmiller; Dir CATHY ASHBY; Pres. SHERRY GEORG; Treas. KATHY HELBIG.

Somerset County Library System: 11767 Beechwood St, Princess Anne, MD 21853; tel. (410) 651-0852; internet www.some.lib.md.us; f. 1967, present location 1988; Princess Anne Public Library; Corbin Memorial Library in Crisfield; Elwell School library in Smith Island; Dir JENNIFER RANCK.

University of Maryland Libraries: College Park, MD 20742-7011; tel. (301) 405-0800; e-mail govdocs@umd.edu; internet www.lib.umd.edu; f. 1856; 8 campus libraries: McKeldin Library, Hornbake Library, Art Library, Architecture Library, Eng. and Physical Sciences Library, Michelle Smith Performing Arts Library, Shady Grove Library and Media Center, White Memorial (Chemistry) Library; 3,930,013 vols, 68,514 current serial titles; Dean PATRICIA A. STEELE.

US Census Bureau Library: 4600 Silver Hill Rd, Suitland, MD 20746; tel. (301) 763-2511; e-mail library@census.gov; internet www.census.gov/prod/www/library; f. 1952; attached to US Dept of Commerce; collects, preserves and provides access to information resources produced by the Census Bureau; 250,000 vols, spec. int. colln 115,000 vols; Dir ROBERT M. GROVES.

US National Library of Medicine: 8600 Rockville Pike, Bethesda, MD 20894; tel. (301) 594-5983; e-mail custserv@nlm.nih.gov; internet www.nlm.nih.gov; f. 1836; houses old and rare medical works; materials, information and research services in all areas of biomedicine and healthcare; 13m. vols; Dir Dr DONALD A. B. LINDBERG; publ. *Index Medicus* (12 a year).

Wicomico Public Library: 122 S Div. St, Salisbury, MD 21801; tel. (410) 749-3612; e-mail askus@wicomico.org; internet www.wicomicolibrary.org; f. 1869; main library, centre br., Bivalve Station and Pittsville br.; 1 bookmobile; Dir TOM HEHMAN; Chair. VALERIE MURPHY; Sec. SUSAN BOUNDS; Treas. WINNIE STOKES.

Massachusetts

Abbot Library: 235 Pleasant St, Marblehead, MA 01945; tel. (781) 631-1481; e-mail mar@noblenet.org; internet www.abbotlibrary.org; f. 1878; Dir PATRICIA J. ROGERS.

Amherst Center for Russian Culture: POB 2268, Amherst College, Amherst, MA 01002-5000; tel. (413) 542-8204; internet www.amherst.edu; f. 1991; attached to Amherst College; rare Russian books, MSS, newspapers and periodicals; 15,000 vols; Dir Prof. STANLEY J. RABINOWITZ.

Amherst Libraries: 43 Amity St, Amherst, MA 01002; tel. (413) 259-3090; e-mail info@joneslibrary.org; internet www.joneslibrary.org; Jones Library (HQ); brs: Munson Memorial Library and N Amherst Library; 210,845 vols and 25,516 audio and video materials; spec. colln: local and regional history, genealogy and Amherst authors; Dir SHARON SHARRY.

Athol Public Library: 568 Main St, Athol, MA 01331; tel. (978) 249-9515; e-mail info@athollibrary.org; internet www.athollibrary.org; f. 1878; 50,000 vols (incl. books, magazines, periodicals, books on tape, video cassettes, CDs); Dir DEBRA BLANCHARD; Chair. MARGARET YOUNG.

Bedford Free Public Library: 7 Mudge Way, Bedford, MA 01730; tel. (781) 275-9440; e-mail bedford@minlib.net; internet www.bedfordlibrary.net; f. 1876; spec. colln incl. MSS, pamphlets and audiovisual materials focusing on Bedford history and culture; Nickerson Colln on learning and developmental disabilities; Chinese Language Colln: books in Chinese, Chinese music CDs, Chinese-language periodicals, and Chinese movies and TV series on DVD and VCD; Andrew Zuckerman Memorial Colln: global poverty, Southeast Asia (languages, music, books, histories, travel, memoirs, etc.), Eastern religions, Native American beliefs, sustainable agriculture, volunteering and social

action, ecology and environment, medicinal plants and herbs, wildlife conservation; 119,287 vols; Dir RICHARD CALLAGHAN.

Belmont Public Library: 336 Concord Ave, POB 125, Belmont, MA 02478; tel. (617) 489-2000; e-mail belmont@minlib.net; internet www.belmont.lib.ma.us; f. 1868; Claflin Room: colln incl. 2 murals of old Belmont, original art, town reports, books by Belmont authors, materials relating to the town and historical artefacts; Dir MAUREEN CONNERS.

Boston Athenaeum: $10\frac{1}{2}$ Beacon St, Boston, MA 02108-3777; tel. (617) 227-0270; e-mail reference@bostonathenaeum.org; internet www.bostonathenaeum.org; f. 1807, present location 1849; ind. research library; 1.5m. vols, 600,000 books; history, biography, English and American literature, fine and decorative arts; spec. collns incl. confederate states imprints, books from libraries of George Washington, Gen. Henry Knox and the Adams Family, the King's Chapel Colln (1698), Gypsy literature, private press publs, 19th-century tracts, early US govt documents, maps, charts and atlases, and the Charles E. Mason print colln; Bartlett Hayes poster colln; 19th-century photographs; Dir and Librarian PAULA MATTHEWS; Pres. DEBORAH H. BORNHEIMER; Sec. ALEXANDER ALTSCHULLER; Treas. GILBERT M. RODDY, JR.

Boston Public Library: 700 Boylston St, Boston, MA 02116; tel. (617) 536-5400; e-mail ask@bpl.org; internet www.bpl.org; f. 1848, present location 1895; oldest free municipal library supported by public taxation in the world; 25 brs; 22m. vols; Chair. JEFFREY B. RUDMAN; Pres. AMY E. RYAN.

Boston University Libraries: 771 Commonwealth Ave, Boston, MA 02215; tel. (617) 353-2700; e-mail ask@bu.edu; internet www.bu.edu/library; f. 1839; 5 major libraries: Mugar Memorial Library (6 brs humanities and social sciences), Howard Gotlieb Archival Research Center (rare books and MSS), Pappas Law Library (fed. and state primary legal materials; major serials, treatises and other secondary materials; legal documents and reports and int. law materials), Medical Library, School of Theology Library (theology, Bible, church history, min., and historic Judaism); 2.4m. vols, 45,264 serials titles, 77,000 media titles and 28,000 periodicals; Univ. Librarian ROBERT HUDSON.

Burlington Public Library: 22 Sears St, Burlington, MA 01803; tel. (781) 270-1738; internet www.burlingtonpubliclibrary.org; f. 1857; 91,681 vols; Dir LORI HODGSON.

Cambridge Public Library: 449 Broadway, Cambridge, 02138; tel. (617) 349-4041; internet www.cambridgema.gov/cpl.aspx; f. 1849; 6 brs: Boudreau, Central Square, Collins, O'Connell, O'Neill and Valente; Dir SUSAN FLANNERY.

Chelmsford Public Library: 25 Boston Rd, Chelmsford, MA 01824; tel. (978) 256-5521; e-mail askus@mvlc.org; internet www.chelmsfordlibrary.org; f. 1894; main library and Anna C. MacKay Br. Library; 140,000 vols (incl. books, periodicals, audio books, CDs, DVDs, video cassettes and newspapers); Dir BECKY HERRMANN.

Francis A. Countway Library of Medicine: 10 Shattuck St, Boston, MA 02115; tel. (617) 432-4888; internet countway.harvard.edu; f. 1965; serves the Harvard Medical School, Harvard School of Public Health, Harvard School of Dental Medicine, Boston Medical Library and Massachusetts Medical Soc; promotes advancement of education, research, scholarship and professional practice in medicine, biological sciences, public health and dentistry; 630,000 vols, 3,500 journals, 10,000 non-current biomedical journals, medical history collection; Dir Dr ISAAC

KOHANE; Dir of Center for the History of Medicine SCOTT PODOLSKY.

East Longmeadow Public Library: 60 Center Sq., East Longmeadow, MA 01028; tel. (413) 525-5400; e-mail steale@cwmars .org; internet www.eastlongmeadow.org/ library; f. 2004; colln in Local History Room incl. books, documents, photographs and maps related to the town's history; 80,606 vols; Chair. ARTHUR MCGUIRE; Sec. AMIE SINGH; Dir SUSAN M. PETERSON.

Edgartown Public Library: 58 N Water St, POB 5249, Edgartown, MA 02539; tel. (508) 627-4221; e-mail director@ edgartownlibrary.org; internet www .edgartownlibrary.org; f. 1903; 40,725 vols (incl. 30,083 books, 1,787 audio CDs, 4,954 video DVD and VHS, 411 microfilms, 215 journals); Chair. PAT ROSE; Dir FELICIA CHENEY; Sec. HERBERT FOSTER.

Falmouth Public Library: 300 Main St, Falmouth, MA 02540; tel. (508) 457-2555; e-mail info@falmouthpubliclibrary.org; internet www.falmouthpubliclibrary.org; f. 1876; brs: E Falmouth Br. and N Falmouth Br.; spec. colln on genealogy, local history (from 1876 to the present day) and rep. colln of work of Katharine Lee Bates; Chair. OTIS PORTER, JR; Dir LESLIE A. MORRISSEY; Sec. SYLVIA SZULKIN.

Hamilton-Wenham Public Library: 14 Union St, S Hamilton, MA 01982; tel. (978) 468-5577; internet www.hwlibrary.org; f. 2001 by merger of Wenham Town Library (f. 1885) with Hamilton Public Library (f. 1891); 105,993 vols, 464 print periodicals, newspapers and other print serials, 7,748 audio materials and 8,472 video materials; Dir JAN DEMPSEY.

Harvard University Library: Office of the Dir, Wadsworth House-1341, Massachusetts Ave, Cambridge, MA 02138; tel. (617) 495-3650; e-mail administration@hulmail .harvard.edu; internet hul.harvard.edu; f. 1638; oldest library in the USA; central collns are housed in Widener, Houghton, Pusey, Lamont, Hilles, Cabot Science, Harvard-Yenching, Littauer, Loeb Music, Tozzer, Fine Arts and Geological Sciences Libraries; important collns in nearly every field of learning and 4,000 vols printed before 1501; 17m. vols; Exec. Dir HELEN SHENTON; Univ. Librarian ROBERT DARNTON; publ. *Harvard Library Bulletin*.

Jacob Edwards Library: 236 Main St, Southbridge, MA 01550; tel. (508) 764-5426; e-mail refjel@cwmars.org; internet www .jacobedwardslibrary.org; f. 1870; colln about local history; books, photographs, maps, directories and memorabilia; local newspaper colln on microfilm; digital colln: agricultural and industrial history of Central and Western Massachusetts; Holmes Ammidown Colln: 18th-century library that belonged to a prominent early citizen of Southbridge; 73,493 vols; Chair. JOAN MENARD; Dir MARGARET MORRISSEY; Treas. PAULA DACOLES.

John F. Kennedy Presidential Library and Museum: Columbia Point, Boston, MA 02125; tel. (617) 514-1541; e-mail kennedy .library@nara.gov; internet www.jfklibrary .org; f. 1963; colln of textual documents, audiovisual items and museum artefacts of John F. Kennedy, Robert F. Kennedy, Joseph P. Kennedy and Rose Kennedy; 600 other colln incl. Kennedy family mems, authors, politicians and individuals; Ernest Hemingway Colln: MSS materials; 48m. items; Dir THOMAS J. PUTNAM; Museum Curator STACEY BREDHOFF.

Marlborough Public Library: 35 W Main St, Marlborough, MA 01752; tel. (508) 624-6900; e-mail mcardello@marlborough-ma .gov; internet www.marlborough-ma.gov/ gen/marlboroughma_publibrary/index; f. 1871; 115,819 vols; Dir SALVATORE GENOVESE.

Massachusetts Historical Society Library: 1154 Boylston St, Boston, MA 02215-3695; tel. (617) 536-1608; e-mail library@masshist.org; internet www .masshist.org/library; f. 1791; MSS: letters, diaries, and other personal papers of individuals and families who lived in Massachusetts; many famous documents such as Paul Revere's own account of his famous ride, MSS copies of the Declaration of Independence by both Thomas Jefferson and John Adams; 250,000 vols, 3,600 MSS collns; Chair. WILLIAM C. CLENDANIEL; Librarian PETER DRUMMEY; Librarian STEPHEN T. RILEY; Sec. JOHN F. MOFFITT; Treas. WILLIAM R. COTTER; publs *Proceedings* (1 a year), *The Massachusetts Historical Review* (1 a year).

Massachusetts Institute of Technology Libraries: 14S–216, 77 Massachusetts Ave, Cambridge, MA 02139-4307; tel. (617) 253-5655; e-mail diroff-lib@mit.edu; internet libraries.mit.edu; f. 1861; 5 major subject libraries: architecture and planning, engineering, humanities, science, management and social science, as well as 5 specialized libraries and the Institute archives; 3m. vols and pamphlets, 17,000 current journals, 55,000 databases and electronic journals; Dir of Libraries ANN J. WOLPERT.

Salisbury Public Library: 17 Elm St, Salisbury, MA 01952; tel. (978) 465-5071; e-mail librarian@salisburyma.gov; internet www.salisburylibrary.org; f. 1885; provides access to holdings at more than 40 local libraries as well as libraries outside the region; Dir TERRY KYRIOS; Asst Librarian JOAN BOMBA.

Sargent Memorial Library: 427 Massachusetts Ave, Boxborough, MA 01719; tel. (978) 263-4680; internet www.boxlib.org; f. 1891, present location 2005; 35,000 vols (incl. books, periodicals, VHS video cassettes, DVDs, music and books on audio cassettes and CDs); Dir MAUREEN STRAPKO.

Springfield City Library: 220 State St, Springfield, MA 01103; tel. (413) 263-6828; e-mail askalibrarian@springfieldlibrary.org; internet www.springfieldlibrary.org; f. 1857, present bldg 1912; has 6 brs; 668,856 vols, 32,490 audio recordings, 20,804 video cassettes, 3,933 CD-ROMs, 296 periodicals; Dir EMILY BADER.

State Library of Massachusetts: 24 Beacon St, State House, Room 341, Boston, MA 02133; tel. (617) 727-2590; e-mail library .director@state.ma.us; internet www.mass .gov/lib; f. 1826; govt and public affairs library serving research and research needs of the exec. and legislative brs of Massachusetts state govt; depository for printed documents of the same and for selected fed. documents; collns esp. strong in public law, public affairs, state and local history; 822,083 vols; State Librarian ELVERNOY JOHNSON; publ. *Commonwealth of Massachusetts Publications Received by the State Library* (4 a year).

Waltham Public Library: 735 Main St, Waltham, MA 02451; tel. (781) 314-3425; e-mail waltham@minlib.net; internet www .waltham.lib.ma.us; f. 1865; spec. colln of materials relating to the Waltham Watch Factory and other watch cos; 155,000 vols, 400 magazines or newspapers, 22,000 CDs and 18,000 video cassettes and DVDs; Dir KATE TRANQUADA.

Westfield Athenaeum Library: 6 Elm St, Westfield, MA 01085; tel. (413) 568-7833; e-mail cpennington@westath.org; internet www.westath.org; f. 1830; 500 linear ft of maps, drawings, papers, MSS, stereoscopes, Mayoral papers, diaries, business ledgers and emphera giving insight into life in Westfield; Dir CHRISTOPHER LINDQUIST.

Worcester Public Library: 3 Salem Sq., Worcester, MA 01608; tel. (508) 799-1655; internet www.worcpublib.org; f. 1859; 3 sites: main library at Salem Sq., Frances Perkins Library at Greendale and Great Brook Valley Br. Library; largest selective depository of fed. documents in central Massachusetts; 634,000 vols, 14,500 audio cassettes, 15,500 video cassettes and 120,700 microforms; Head Librarian CHRISTOPHER J. KORENOWSKY; Pres. KEVIN DOWD; Sec. JYOTI DATTA; Treas. DONNA J. MCGRATH.

Michigan

Adams-Pratt Oakland County Law Library: 1200 N Telegraph Rd, Bldg 14E, Pontiac, MI, 48341-0481; tel. (248) 858-0012; e-mail lawlib@oakgov.com; internet www .oakgov.com/lawlib; f. 1904, present name 1976; colln incl. Michigan and fed. statutes, digests, reports, Shepard's citators, treatises, law reviews, statutes and case law for all states; Chair. ROBERT GAYLOR; Sec. ROBERT TERA.

Alcona County Library: POB 348, 312 W Main, Harrisville, MI 48740; tel. (989) 724-6796; internet library.alcona.lib.mi.us; brs in Harrisville (HQ), Lincoln, Caledonia and Mikado; Dir CAROL LUCK; Chair. PAM KERSTEN.

Ann Arbor District Library System: 343 S Fifth Ave, Ann Arbor, MI 48104; tel. (734) 327-4200; internet www.aadl.org; Downtown library and 4 brs: Malletts Creek, Traverwood, West and Pittsfield; 581,250 vols (incl. books, DVDs, CDs, magazines, CD-Roms, audio books, art prints, pamphlets and maps, language materials); Dir JOSIE PARKER; Pres. MARGARET LEARY; Sec. JAN BARNEY NEWMAN; Treas. BARBARA MURPHY.

Bay County Library System: 500 Center Ave, Bay City, MI 48708; tel. (989) 894-2837; internet www.baycountylibrary.org; f. 1974; 3 br. libraries, 1 main library and a bookmobile; 360,000 vols; incl. business resource centre and core reference colln; local history and genealogy colln; Dir TOM BIRCH; Chair. ROBERT LA CHANCE; Sec. and Treas. FRANK QUINN.

Brighton District Library: 100 Library Dr., Brighton, MI 48116; tel. (810) 229-6571; internet brightonlibrary.info; serves Brighton, Genoa and Green Oak Townships; Dir Dr NANCY B. JOHNSON; Pres. JEANNETTE HILL; Sec. SALLY MCKEE; Treas. JANE PETRIE.

Chelsea District Library: 221 S Main St, Chelsea, MI 48118; tel. (734) 475-8732; internet www.chelsea.lib.mi.us; f. 1931, present name and status 2006; serves City of Chelsea, Dexter, Lima, Lyndon and Sylvan townships; 66,142 vols (incl. 54,757 print and 11,088 media materials); Dir WILLIAM H. HARMER; Pres. GARY ZENZ; Sec. DAWN CAPLIS; Treas. MARY BUDZINSKI.

Chippewa River District Library System: 301 S University, Mount Pleasant, MI 48858; tel. (989) 773-3242; internet www2 .youseemore.com/chippewa; f. 1998; brs incl. Veterans Memorial Library in Mount Pleasant and Faith Johnston Memorial Library in Rosebush; Dir LISE MITCHELL.

Detroit Public Library: 5201 Woodward Ave, Detroit, MI 48202; tel. (313) 481-1300; e-mail dir@detroitpubliclibrary.org; internet www.detroitpubliclibrary.org; f. 1865, present location 1921; main library and 21 brs and a bookmobile service; spec. collns: Burton Historical Colln (Michigan, Great Lakes and Old NW Territory), Labor History Colln, Hackley Colln, Nat. Automotive History Colln; 7.1m. vols; Exec. Dir JO ANNE MONDOWNEY.

Gerald R. Ford Presidential Library & Museum: 1000 Beal Ave, Ann Arbor, MI 48109; tel. (734) 205-0555; e-mail ford .library@nara.gov; internet www .fordlibrarymuseum.gov; f. 1981; archival materials on US domestic issues, foreign relations, and political affairs during the Cold War era; fed. records; papers of Betty Ford; pre- and post-presidential papers of Gerald Ford; presidential papers of Gerald Ford and his White House staff; 25m. pages of memos, letters, meeting notes, reports and historical documents, 450,000 photographs, 787,000 ft motion picture film; Dir ELAINE DIDIER.

Jackson District Library: 244 W Michigan Ave, Jackson, MI 49201; tel. (517) 788-4087; internet www.myjdl.com; f. 1901; 13 brs; 417,200 vols, 25,000 audio CDs, 16,000 video cassettes and DVDs, 700 magazines and newspapers; Dir ISHWAR LAXMINARAYAN; Pres. DARRELL J. DURHAM; Sec. and Treas. THEORDORE R. KOLMAN.

Library of Michigan: 702 W Kalamazoo St, Lansing, MI 48915; tel. (517) 373-1300; e-mail librarian@michigan.gov; internet www.michigan.gov/libraryofmichigan; f. 1828; attached to Michigan Dept of Education; operates main and law library; specializes in MI history, current information, public policy issues, state and fed. govt document depositories; 2.7m. vols; State Librarian NANCY R. ROBERTSON; publs *Directory of Michigan Libraries* (online), *District Library Law* (online), *Michigan Public Library Statistics* (online), *Michigan Public Libraries: Data Digest* (1 a year, online).

Michigan State University Libraries: Main Library, 100 Library, East Lansing, MI 48824-1048; tel. (517) 353-8700; internet www.lib.msu.edu; f. 1855; br. libraries within main bldg incl. Africana, Digital and Multimedia Center, Fine Arts, Govt Documents, Map Library, Spec. Collns (incl. Chicano and Boricua), Turfgrass Information Center, Vincent Voice Library; br. libraries outside main bldg incl. William C. Gast Business Library (incl. Human Resources and Labor Relations Library), Dubai Library, Engineering Library, Gull Lake Library, Law College Library, Mathematics Library, Veterinary Medical Center Library; Africana Colln, Cesar E. Chavez Colln; 4.5m. vols, 2,600 books, 4,000 current periodicals, 10,000 multimedia items, 3m. govt documents, 119,000 reels of microfilm, 1.1m. microfiche and microcards, 200,000 sheet maps, 4,000 atlases, gazetteers and other reference aids; Dir CLIFFORD H. HAKA.

MLibrary University of Michigan: 818 Hatcher S, Ann Arbor, MI 48109-1190; tel. (734) 764-9356; internet lib.umich.edu; f. 1817; 6 sub-libraries; online video gallery, academic publishing services; 11,073,632 vols, incl. 8.5m. print collections, online journals, digital images and rare books; spec. collns in ancient papyri, early economics, early military science, Elsevier imprints, English and American drama, French historical pamphlets; Univ. Librarian PAUL N. COURANT.

Monroe County Library System: Mary K. Daume Library Service Center, 840 S Roessler St, Monroe, MI 48161; tel. (734) 241-5770; internet monroe.lib.mi.us; f. 1934; 16 brs; genealogy colln; depository for fed., state, local and nuclear documents; George Armstrong Custer Colln; Dir NANCY BELLAIRE; Chair. MARYANNE BOURQUE; Sec. ELIZABETH TAYLOR.

Northville District Library: 212 W Cady St, Northville, MI 48167-1560; tel. (248) 349-3020; internet www.northville.lib.mi.us; f. 1889, present name and status 1996; Dir

JULIE HERRIN; Chair. JOSEPH CORRIVEAU; Sec. MIKE DEFRANCESCO; Treas. JEAN HANSEN.

Salem-South Lyon District Library: 9800 Pontiac Trail, South Lyon, MI 48178; tel. (248) 437-6431; internet www.south-lyon.lib .mi.us; f. 1939; 65,546 vols, 1,525 magazines, 6,306 DVDs, 3,422 music CDs, 2,419 audiobooks; Dir DOREEN HANNON; Pres. KEN KNEISEL; Sec. ROBIN WHITE FANNING; Treas. W. DAVID MCNEILL.

Wayne State University Libraries: 5150 Anthony Wayne Dr., Detroit, MI 48202; tel. (313) 577-4023; e-mail acquisitions@wayne .edu; internet www.lib.wayne.edu; Shiffman Medical Library, Arthur Neef Law Library; spec. colln: Arthur L. Johnson African-American History Colln, Curriculum Guide Colln, Florence Nightingale Colln, Jeheskel (Hezy) Shoshani Library Endowed Colln, Trybom Memorial Colln, Juvenile Colln, Leonard Simons Colln of Rare Michigan History, Kasle Colln, Merrill-Palmer Institute Colln, Mildred Jeffrey Colln of Peace and Conflict Resolution, Millicent A. Wills Colln of Urban Ethnic Materials, Purdy/Kresge Microform Colln, Ramsey Colln of Literature for Young People, William Alfred Boyce Storytelling Colln; 3,665,805 vols, 360,223 ebooks, 3,899,273 microforms, 56,346 maps and other cartographic materials, 50,109 audio recordings, 30,604 films and video recordings; Dean of Library Services Dr SANDRA G. YEE.

Minnesota

Duluth Public Library: 520 W Superior St, Duluth, MN 55802; tel. (218) 730-4200; e-mail webmail@duluth.lib.mn.us; internet www.duluth.lib.mn.us; 2 brs; 620,101 vols, incl. 414,007 books and bound serials; Pres. DANIEL D'ALLAIRD; Library Man. CARLA POWERS.

East Central Regional Library: 244 S Birch St, Cambridge, MN 55008; tel. (763) 689-7390; e-mail ecregion@ecrl.lib.mn.us; internet ecrl.lib.mn.us; 14 brs; bookmobile services; 396,800 vols; Dir BARBARA MISSELT; Pres. WAYNE ZAUDTKE; Sec. JAMES RAISANEN; Treas. CHARLOTTE KRAMERSMEIER.

Gilbert Public Library: POB 758, 17 N Broadway, Gilbert, MN 55741; tel. (218) 748-2230; e-mail illgil@arrowhead.lib.mn.us; internet www.gilbert.lib.mn.us; mem. of Arrowhead Library System; Chair. ROCCO LEONI; Dir NICK PRIEVE; Sec. JUDY THORSON.

Great River Regional Library: 1300 W Saint Germain St, St Cloud, MN 56301; tel. (320) 650-2500; internet www.griver.org; f. 1969; 32 brs; 955,483 vols; Dir KIRSTY SMITH; Pres. GERALD RUDA; Sec. LOUISE KUESTER; Treas. SPENCER BUERKLE.

Hennepin County Library: 12601 Ridgedale Dr., Minnetonka, MN 55305-1909; tel. (612) 543-8500; internet www.hclib.org; f. 1922, merged with Minneapolis Public Library (f. 1885) 2008; 41 brs; 5m. vols, CDs, DVDs, electronic resources; Dir LOIS LANGER THOMPSON.

James Jerome Hill Reference Library: 80 W Fourth St, Saint Paul, MN 55102; tel. (651) 265-5500; e-mail info@jjhill.org; internet www.jjhill.org; f. 1921; applied business and commerce; 240,000 vols (incl. business books, magazines, industry reports); Chair. GREG HEINEMANN; Dir of Library Services NIKKI MARCHAND.

Lake Agassiz Regional Library: POB 900, Moorhead, MN 56561-0900; 118 Fifth St S, Moorhead, MN 56560-2756; tel. (218) 233-3757; internet larl.org; f. 1961; 13 brs; 300,000 vols; Regional Library Dir KATHY FREDETTE.

Marshall-Lyon County Public Library: 201 C St, Marshall, MN 56258; tel. (507) 537-7003; e-mail library@marshalllyonlibrary .org; internet www.marshalllyonlibrary.org; 2 brs; Dir HOLLY MARTIN HUFFMAN; Pres. PAM SUKALSKI; Treas. MARK GOODENOW.

Minnesota Historical Society Library: 345 Kellogg Blvd, W, Saint Paul, MN 55102-1906; tel. (651) 259-3300; e-mail reference@mnhs.org; internet www.mnhs .org/library; f. 1849; N American history particularly relating to Minnesota and the Upper Midwest (esp. travel accounts, fur trade, Scandinavian and other immigration, labour, political and church history, railway records, local history and genealogy); 500,000 vols, 95m. MSS pages, 4,000 govt documents, 950,000 artefacts of archeology, 6,000 paintings, prints and drawings; Dir for Library and Collns JENNIFER JONES.

Minnesota State Archives: c/o Minnesota Historical Soc., 345 W Kellogg Blvd, St. Paul, MN 55102-1906; tel. (651) 259-3260; internet www.mnhs.org/preserve/records; f. 1913; attached to Minnesota Historical Soc.; identifies, collects and preserves historically valuable records of 4,000 units of state and local govt; colln from exec. br. of state, legislative and judicial brs and local govt; local history colln; State Archivist SHAWN ROUNDS.

Minnesota State Law Library: Room G25, Minnesota Judicial Center, 25 Rev Dr Martin Luther King, Jr, Blvd, St Paul, MN 55155; tel. (651) 296-2775; e-mail askalibrarian@ courts.state.mn.us; internet www.lawlibrary .state.mn.us; f. 1849; Marvin R. Anderson Spec. Collns Room: trials of American and British, France, Germany and fmr Soviet Union and series British notable trials; 400,000 vols; State Law Librarian JUDY REHAK (acting).

Minnesota State University Library: POB 8419, Mankato, MN 56002-8419; tel. (507) 389-5952; internet lib.mnsu.edu; depository for state documents, nat. govt documents, US geological survey maps; univ. archives and Southern Minnesota Historical Center; Marilyn J. Lass Center for Minnesota Studies; 1.2m. vols, 55,000 periodicals (incl. print and electronic); Dean of Library Services JOAN ROCA.

Rochester Public Library: 101 Second St, SE, Rochester, MN 55904; tel. (507) 328-2310; internet www.rochesterpubliclibrary .org; f. 1865; 437,815 vols; Dir AUDREY S. BETCHER; Pres. DIANE MOENCH; Sec. JANICE M. ENGBERG.

Saint Paul Public Library: 90 W Fourth St, Saint Paul, MN 55102; tel. (651) 266-7000; e-mail spplweb@ci.stpaul.mn.us; internet www.sppl.org; f. 1856; central library, 12 brs and a bookmobile; fed. depository; 1,131,578 vols; Dir KIT HADLEY.

Two Harbors Public Library: 320 Waterfront Dr., Two Harbors, MN 55616; tel. (218) 834-3148; e-mail thpl@arrowhead.lib.mn.us; internet www.two-harbors.lib.mn.us; f. 1896, fmrly Carnegie Library; Archive Room holds scrapbooks, history and local newspapers dating back to the late 1890s; mem. of Arrowhead Library System; 30,000 vols; Pres. TONY LOCKHART; Sec. PATRICIA TOFTE.

University of Minnesota Libraries: 499 Wilson Library, 309 19th Ave S, Minneapolis, MN 55455; tel. (612) 626-2227; e-mail enge@ umn.edu; internet www.lib.umn.edu; f. 1851; gen. and 14 departmental libraries; spec. collns: law, immigration history, social welfare history, data processing, medicine, children's literature, horticulture, literary MSS; 7,111,311 vols, 109,681 serial subscriptions; Univ. Librarian Prof. WENDY PRADT LOUGEE; publ. *continuum* (1 a year).

Washington County Law Library: Washington County Courthouse, 14949 62nd St N, Room 1005, Stillwater, MN 55082; tel. (651) 430-6330; e-mail lawlibrary@co.washington.mn.us; internet www.co.washington.mn.us/lawlibrary; f. 1956; primary sources of Minnesota state law, fed. law, Wisconsin statutes annotated, Wisconsin rules of court, Wisconsin practice materials, Treatises, CLEs, form books, practice manuals, jury instructions and periodicals; organizes legal advice clinics; Law Librarian PAULINE AFUSO; Law Librarian PATRICIA DOLAN.

Mississippi

Bolivar County Library System: 104 S Leflore Ave, Cleveland, MS 38732; tel. (662) 843-2774; internet www.bolivar.lib.ms.us; f. 1958; brs: Robinson-Carpenter Memorial Library (HQ), Dr Robert T. Hollingsworth Public Library, Mound Bayou Public Library, Thelma Rayner Memorial Library, Rosedale Public Library, Gunnison Public Library, Benoit Public Library and Field Memorial Library; Dir LYNN F. SHURDEN.

Central Mississippi Regional Library System: POB 1749, Brandon, MS 39043; 100 Tamberline St, Brandon, MS 39042; tel. (601) 825-0100; e-mail custsvc@cmrls.lib.ms.us; internet www.cmrls.lib.ms.us; 20 br. libraries in Rankin, Scott, Simpson and Smith counties; Dir KAILEEN THIELING.

Dixie Regional Library System: 111 N Main St, Pontotoc, MS 38863; tel. (662) 489-3960; e-mail jmcneece@dixie.lib.ms.us; internet www.dixie.lib.ms.us; library services in Pontotoc, Calhoun and Chickasaw counties; Dir JUDY MCNEECE.

Hancock County Library System: 312 Highway 90, Bay St Louis, MS 39520; tel. (228) 467-5282; e-mail info@hancocklibraries .info; internet www.hancock.lib.ms.us; f. 1934, present status 1965; brs: Bay St Louis-Hancock County Library, Kiln Public Library, Pearlington Public Library and Waveland Public Library; Chair. DOLLY LUNNDBERG; Exec. Dir PATTY FURR.

Jackson/Hinds County Library System: 300 N State St, Jackson, MS 39201; tel. (601) 968-5811; e-mail reference@jhlibrary.com; internet www.jhlibrary.com; f. 1986; 14 brs and a main library; Margaret Walker Alexander Library incl. spec. colln of African-American history; 639,253 vols (incl. books, video cassettes, audio cassettes, CDs and multimedia kits); Exec. Dir CAROLYN McCALLUM; Chair. LOUIS WRIGHT; Sec. ROSALYN SYLVESTER; Treas. MARIA L. BROWN.

Laurel-Jones County Library System, Inc.: 530 Commerce St, Laurel, MS 39440-3998; tel. (601) 428-4313; internet www .laurel.lib.ms.us; f. 1919 as Laurel Library Asscn, present location 1979; Laurel Jones Co Library (HQ) and Ellisville Public Library br.; Dir MARY LOUISE BRELAND.

Madison County Library System: 102 Priestly St, Canton, MS 39046; tel. (601) 859-3202; e-mail feedback@mcls.ms; internet www.mcls.ms; brs: Canton, Camden, Flora, Madison and Ridgeland; Dir SANDRA SANDERS.

Meridian Lauderdale County Public Library: 2517 Seventh St, Meridian, MS 39301; tel. (601) 693-6771; e-mail library@ meridian.lib.ms.us; internet www.meridian .lib.ms.us; f. 1913; 192 magazine subscriptions and 31 local, state and nat. newspapers; microfilm edns of periodicals, incl. the *Meridian Star* dating 1898; Chair. J. D. WATSON.

Noxubee County Public Library: 103 E King St, Macon, MS 39341; tel. (662) 726-5461; internet www.noxubee.lib.ms.us; f. 1984; brs: Macon, Brooksville and Shuqua-

lak; Harold Gibson Brown Research Colln; Dir SHAMEKA CONNER.

Pearl River County Library System: 900 Goodyear Blvd, Picayune, MS 39466; tel. (601) 798-5081; internet www.pearlriver.lib .ms.us; f. 1974; Margaret Reed Crosby Memorial Library and Cultural Center (HQ) and Poplarville Public Library; Dir LINDA TUFARO.

Starkville-Oktibbeha County Library System: 326 Univ. Dr, Starkville, MS 39759; tel. (662) 323-2766; internet www .starkville.lib.ms.us; brs: Maben and Sturgis; Dir VIRGINIA HOLTCAMP.

Warren County-Vicksburg Public Library: 700 Veto St, Vicksburg, MS 39180; tel. (601) 636-6411; internet www .warren.lib.ms.us; f. 1916, present status 1986; incl. genealogy items, newspapers and local history materials; Dir DEB MITCHELL.

Washington County Library System: 341 Main St, Greenville, MS 38701; tel. (662) 335-2331; e-mail wash-ref@washington.lib .ms.us; internet www.washington.lib.ms.us; f. 1967; brs: Greenville (HQ), Arcola, Avon, Glen Allan, Hollandale, Metcalfe and Leland; Dir K. CLANTON; Chair. JAMES SCOTT; Sec. MARGIE JOHNSON.

Waynesboro-Wayne County Library System: 1103A Mississippi Dr., Waynesboro, MS 39367-2415; tel. (866) 735-2268; e-mail wlib@wwcls.lib.ms.us; internet www.wwcls .lib.ms.us; f. 1934; genealogy colln incl. books, periodicals and family histories; 3,508 video/DVD colln, 880 audio titles; Dir PATSY C. BREWER; Pres. BECKY RHINEHART.

Missouri

Adair County Public Library: One Library Lane, Kirksville, MO 63501; tel. (660) 665-6038; e-mail acpl@adairco.org; internet www2.youseemore.com/adaircpl; f. 1986; Dir GLENDA HUNT; Pres. RON BRAND; Sec. SANDRA FLEAK; Treas. MARK LAUGHLIN.

Barry-Lawrence Regional Library: 213 Sixth St, Monett, MO 65708; tel. (417) 235-6646; e-mail monett@blrlibrary.org; internet www2.youseemore.com/blrl; 10 br. libraries in Barry and Lawrence counties; HQ at Monett Br. Library; Dir GINA MILBURN; Pres. ANN HALL; Sec. and Treas. FELICITY NESBITT.

Boonslick Regional Library: 219 W Third St, Sedalia, MO 65301; tel. (660) 827-7111; internet brl.lib.mo.us; brs in Benton, Cooper and Pettis counties; bookmobile services; Dir LINDA ALLCORN.

Daniel Boone Regional Library: POB 1267, 100 W Broadway, Columbia, MO 65205-1267; tel. (573) 443-3161; internet www.dbrl.org; f. 1959; Columbia Public Library (HQ); incl. Callaway County Public Library and Southern Boone County Public Library; bookmobile services; 549,502 vols; Dir MELISSA CARR; Pres. SUSAN DALY; Sec. JESSICA ROBINSON.

Dunklin County Library: 209 N Main, Kennett, MO 63857; tel. (573) 888-3561; internet dunklin-co.lib.mo.us; 8 brs; genealogy colln; 140,000 vols; Dir JONELL MINTON; Pres. Dr LEWIS E. AUKES; Sec. LEON GODLEY; Treas. BILL BRIGANCE.

Harry S. Truman Library and Museum: 500 W US Highway 24, Independence, MO 64050-1798; tel. (816) 268-8200; e-mail truman.library@nara.gov; internet www .trumanlibrary.org; f. 1957; administered by the Nat. Archives and Records Admin.; 30,000 objects in museum related to Truman and his family; 15m. pages of MSS, 6.5m. White House files, 112,000 photographs, 1,000 hours of audio disc and tape recordings, 400 motion pictures, 75 hours of video

cassette recordings, 30,000 books, 10,000 serials, 1,400 microfilm copies of printed materials; Dir Dr MICHAEL J. DEVINE.

Jefferson County Library: 5678 State Rd PP, High Ridge, MO 63049; tel. (636) 677-8689; e-mail info@jeffersoncountylibrary.org; internet www.jeffersoncountylibrary.org; f. 1983; 3 brs; Dir PAM KLIPSCH; Pres. RETTA TUGGLE; Sec. BILL BUOL; Treas. SHARON REINERI.

Kansas City Public Library: 14 W 10th St, Kansas City, MO 64105; tel. (816) 701-3400; internet www.kclibrary.org; f. 1873 as Public School Library of Kansas City; a central library and 9 brs; spec. historical collns incl. the Missouri Valley Colln (local history), Ramos Colln (African American history) and Western expansion materials; 2,326,922 vols; Exec. Dir R. CROSBY KEMPER, III; Deputy Exec. Dir CHEPTOO KOSITANY-BUCKNER.

Linda Hall Library: 5109 Cherry St, Kansas City, MO 64110-2498; tel. (816) 363-4600; e-mail reference@lindahall.org; internet www.lindahall.org; f. 1946; ind., non-profit, public access, science, engineering and technology library, specializing in periodicals and scientific and technical research materials; document supplier; fee-based literature search services; 1m. vols, 12,330 current periodicals, 47,425 total serial titles, 528,000 monographs, 1,550,000 govt-contracted technical reports, incl. 70,000 maps, 170,000 standards and specifications, History of Science Colln (10,000 vols), US patent and trademark colln; Pres. LISA BROWAR.

Livingston County Library: 450 Locust St, Chillicothe, MO 64601; tel. (660) 646-0547; e-mail librarian@ livingstoncountylibrary.org; internet www .livingstoncountylibrary.org; f. 1920; 50,000 vols; Dir ROBIN WESTPHAL; Pres. MARION HARTER; Sec. MARGARET VANCE; Treas. LINDY CHAPMAN.

Missouri State Archives: POB 1747, 600 West Main St, Jefferson City, MO 65102; tel. (573) 751-3280; e-mail archref@sos.mo.gov; internet www.sos.mo.gov/archives; f. 1965; official repository for state records of permanent and historical value; holdings date from 1770 and incl. exec., legislative and judicial records, records of state depts and agencies, land records, military records, state publ, photographic collns, co and municipal records on microfilm and MSS and reference collns; 336m. pages of paper, 400,000 photographs, 9,000 maps, 61,000 reels of microfilm, 560 cu ft of published state documents and 1,000 audiovisual items; State Archivist JOHN DOUGAN.

Missouri State Library: POB 387, 600 W Main St, Jefferson City, MO 65101; tel. (573) 751-0586; e-mail mostlib@sos.mo.gov; internet www.sos.mo.gov/library; f. 1945; provides service in support of exec. and legislative brs of Missouri state govt; 80,000 vols, 495 periodicals, Wolfner Library of 360,000 vols and 70 periodicals; spec. colln: Missouri state documents; State Librarian MARGARET M. CONROY; publ. *Show Me Express* (52 a year).

MU Libraries University of Missouri: 104 Ellis Library, Columbia, MO 65201-5149; tel. (573) 882-4701; e-mail ellisref@ missouri.edu; internet library.missouri.edu; f. 1839; 7 brs; 3,152,151 vols, 53,394 periodicals, 7,518,745 microform units, 1,688,651 govt documents, 12,609 MSS and archives, 26,656 audio cassettes, 5,782 film and video materials; spec. collns: Western historical MSS and Missouriana; Dir JAMES COGSWELL.

Riverside Regional Library: POB 389, 1997 E Jackson Blvd, Jackson, MO 63755; tel. (573) 243-8141; e-mail librarylady98@

gmail.com; internet www .riversideregionallibrary.org; 5 brs; Dir NANCY HOWLAND.

St Charles City-County Library District: POB 529, 77 Boone Hills Dr., St Peters, MO 63376; tel. (636) 441-2300; internet www .youranswerplace.org; f. 1973 by merger of Kathryn Linnemann Library of St Charles with St Charles Co Library Dist.; 3 regional brs incl. larger collns and subject specialists; 4 gen. purpose brs; 2 Library Express; 3 mini brs in remote areas; spec. colln of local history and genealogy, business and public management, consumer health and govt documents; 1,079,783 vols (incl. 839,234 books, 64,070 DVDs, 64,112 CDs, 44,966 magazines, 4,907 govt documents, 26,522 edocuments, 9,356 ebooks); Dir JIM BROWN; Pres. MYRA CROOK; Sec. MARY REESE; Treas. JOHN THOELKE.

St Louis County Library: 1640 S Lindbergh Blvd, St Louis, MO 63131-3598; tel. (314) 994-3300; e-mail reference@slcl.org; internet www.slcl.org; f. 1946; 20 brs and 7 bookmobiles; 2,044,682 vols; Dir KRISTEN SORTH; Pres. LYNN BECKWITH, JR; Pres. Dr CHINGLING TAI; Sec. and Treas. ELENA KENYON; publ. *PastPorts* (12 a year, online).

St Louis Public Library: 1301 Olive St, St Louis, MO 63103-2389; tel. (314) 241-2288; e-mail webref@slpl.org; internet www.slpl .org; f. 1865 as Public School Library Soc. of St Louis; 15 brs; Fed. Documents Depository since 1866; spec. collns incl. the Julia Davis Colln (African American history and culture), genealogical sources since 1902, Steedman Colln (architecture); 4,702,299 vols; Exec. Dir WALLER McGUIRE; Pres. JACQUE LAND; publ. *Missouri Union List of Serial Publications.*

Saint Louis University Library: 3650 Lindell Blvd, St Louis, MO 63108; tel. (314) 977-3087; e-mail piusref@slu.edu; internet libraries.slu.edu; f. 1818; Omer Poos Law Library, Pius XII Memorial Library, Medical Center Library; Knights of Columbus Vatican Film Library (microfilm colln of medieval and renaissance MSS studies), univ. archives; spec. colln: MSS (Walter J. Ong colln, Tristan da Cunha colln), rare books (16th–19th century theology, church history, patristics, Jesuitica); 1,849,584 vols, 105,559 maps; Asst Vice-Pres. for Univ. Libraries Dr GAIL M. STAINES; publ. *Manuscripta* (2 a year).

Springfield-Greene County Library District: POB 760, 4653 S Campbell Ave, Springfield, MO 65801-0760; tel. (417) 883-5366; e-mail humanresources@thelibrary .org; internet thelibrary.org; f. 1971 by merger of Greene Co Library (f. 1945) with Springfield Public Library (f. 1905); 10 br. libraries; bookmobile services; 550,000 vols; Exec. Dir REGINA GREER COOPER; Pres. DAVID RICHARDSON; Sec. JAMES JEFFRIES; Treas. KIM KOLLMEYER.

Montana

Belgrade Community Library: 106 N Broadway, Belgrade, MT 59714; tel. (406)388-4346; internet www .belgradelibrary.org; f. 1932; 35,000 vols; Dir GALE BACON.

Bozeman Public Library: 626 E Main St, Bozeman, MT 59715; tel. (406) 582-2400; internet www.bozemanlibrary.org; 133,055 vols; Dir SUSAN GREGORY.

Kohrs Memorial Library: 501 Missouri Ave, Deer Lodge, MT 59722-1152; tel. (406) 846-2622; e-mail wkkohrs@mtlib.org; internet kohrslibrary.org; Library Dir KATHY MORA.

Lewis & Clark Library: 120 S Last Chance Gulch, Helena, MT 59601; tel. (406) 447-1690; internet www.lewisandclarklibrary

.org; f. 1868; 3 brs; 115,000 vols; Dir JUDY HART.

Missoula Public Library: 301 E Main, Missoula, MT 59802; tel. (406) 721-2665; e-mail mslaplib@missoula.lib.mt.us; internet missoulalibrary.com; f. 1894; 5 brs and 1 bookmobile; also provides Web on Wheels Bus services; Dir HONORE BRAY.

Montana State Library: POB 201800, 1515 E Sixth Ave, Helena MT 59620-1800; tel. (406) 444-3115; e-mail msl@mt.gov; internet msl.mt.gov; State Librarian JENNIE STAPP.

Parmly Billings Library: 510 N Broadway, Billings, MT 59101; tel. (406) 657-8258; e-mail circdesk@ci.billings.mt.us; internet ci .billings.mt.us; f. 1901; Library Dir BILL COCHRAN.

Nebraska

Kilgore Memorial Library: 520 Nebraska Ave, York, NE 68467-3035; tel. (402) 363-2620; internet yorklib.org; f. 1885, present name and status 1986; 75,000 vols; Dir STAN SCHULZ; Pres. LEONARD HOSKINS.

Lincoln City Libraries: 136 S, 14th St, Third Fl., Lincoln, NE 68508-1899; tel. (402) 441-8500; e-mail library@lincolnlibraries .org; internet www.lincolnlibraries.org; 7 brs and 1 bookmobile; 903,992 vols; Dir PAT LEACH; Pres. MAJA HARRIS.

Link Library: Concordia Univ., 800 N Columbia Ave, Seward, NE 68434; tel. (402) 643-7254; e-mail library@cune.edu; internet www.cune.edu/library; f. 1960; attached to Concordia Univ.; 150,000 vols; Dir PHILIP HENDRICKSON.

Morton-James Public Library: 923 First Corso, Nebraska City, NE 68410; tel. (402) 873-5609; e-mail mlibrary@neb.rr.com; internet www.morton-jamespubliclibrary .com; f. 1896; 64,760 vols; Pres. BONNIE GOODMAN; Dir BARBARA HEGR.

Nebraska State Historical Society Library and Archives: POB 82554, 1500 R St, Lincoln, NE 68501; tel. (402) 471-4751; e-mail nshs.libarch@nebraska.gov; internet www.nebraskahistory.org/lib-arch; incl. Dept of Public Instruction Reports, govt and prison records, State Newspaper Project; newspapers dating back to 1854; archival collns incl. state and local govt records, incl. those of most Nebraska governors; photographs incl. sod house images taken by Solomon D. Butcher; private MSS collns incl. famous Nebraskans (Willa Cather, John Falter); 80,000 vols, 3,000 maps and atlases, 2,500 MSS, 500,000 photographs; Assoc. Dir ANDREA FALING.

Nebraska State Library: POB 98931, 325 State Capitol, 1445 K St, Lincoln, NE 68509; tel. (402) 471-3189; e-mail nsc.lawlibrary@nebraska.gov; internet supremecourt.ne.gov/1082/ state-library; f. 1871; reference and research library for law books; serves Nebraska Supreme Court, Nebraska Legislature, Nebraska Court of Appeals, attorneys within the State of Nebraska and general public; 130,000 vols.

Newman Grove Public Library: POB 430, 615 Hale Ave, Newman Grove, NE 68758; tel. (402) 447-2331; e-mail ngpl@megavision.com; internet www.megavision.net/ngpl; f. 1923; 14,000 vols; Dir ARDIS VON SEGGERN; Pres. BRUCE BACKHAUS; Sec. MARY ROBERG.

North Platte Public Library: 120 W Fourth St, N Platte, NE 69101; tel. (308) 535-8036; e-mail library@ci.north-platte.ne .us; internet www.ci.north-platte.ne.us/ library; Dir CECELIA LAWRENCE.

Omaha Public Library: 215 S. 15th St, Omaha, NE 68102; tel. (402) 444-4833; internet www.omahapubliclibrary.org; 11

brs; HQ in W. Dale Clark Main Library; Dir GARY WASDIN; Pres. STUART CHITTENDEN; Sec. MARY A. HOLLAND.

University of Nebraska Libraries: POB 884100, 318 Love Library, Univ. of Nebraska-Lincoln, Lincoln, NE 68588-4100; tel. (402) 472-2526; internet libraries.unl .edu; 6 brs; spec. colln of MSS, univ. records and rare book collns; 3.5m. vols, 39,000 serial subscriptions; Dean of Libraries Prof. Dr JOAN R. GIESECKE.

Wayne Public Library: 410 Pearl St, Wayne, NE 68787; tel. (402) 375-3135; internet www.cityofwayne.org; f. 1902, present status 1910; Dir LAURAN LOFGREN; Pres. JOEL ANKENY; Sec. MOLLIE SPIEKER.

Nevada

Boulder City Library: 701 Adams Blvd, Boulder City, NV 89005; tel. (702) 293-1281; internet bclibrary.org; Chair. AMY CARVALHO; Dir LYNN SCHOFIELD-DAHL.

Elizabeth Sturm Library: Truckee Meadows Community College, 7000 Dandini Blvd, SIER LIB, Reno, NV 89512-3999; tel. (775) 674-7600; internet www.tmcc.edu/ library; f. 1971, present name 1988; attached to Truckee Meadows Community College; 20,000 vols; Library Dir MICHELLE NOEL.

Elko-Lander-Eureka County Library System: 720 Court St, Elko, NV 89801; tel. (775) 738-3066; internet www .elkocountylibrary.org; 11 brs; Library Dir JEANETTE HAMMONS.

Great Basin College Library: McMullen Hall, 1500 College Parkway, Elko, NV 89801; tel. (775) 753-2222; internet www.gbcnv.edu/ library; depository for govt documents; Library Dir DAVID ELLEFSEN.

Las Vegas-Clark County Library District: 7060 W Windmill Lane, Las Vegas, NV 89113; tel. (702) 734-7323; e-mail administration@lvccld.org; internet www .lvccld.org; 25 brs; 2.7m. vols; Exec. Dir JEANNE GOODRICH.

Pahrump Community Library: 701 E St, Pahrump, NV 89048; tel. (775) 727-5930; e-mail director@pahrumplibrary.com; internet www.pahrumplibrary.com; f. 1978 as Doris, Shirky Community Library.

Washoe County Law Library: Second Judicial District Court, 75 Court St, Room 101, Reno, NV 89501; tel. (775) 328-3250; internet www.co.washoe.nv.us; partial selective depository for US govt documents.

Washoe County Library: 301 S Center St, Reno, NV 89501; tel. (775) 327-8341; e-mail libraryboard@washoecounty.us; internet www.washoecountylibrary.us; f. 1904; Dir ARNOLD MAURINS.

New Hampshire

Amherst Town Library: 14 Main St, Amherst, NH 03031; tel. (603) 673-2288; e-mail library@amherst.lib.nh.us; internet www.amherst.lib.nh.us; f. 1892; Archives Room colln incl. historical items on Amherst and New Hampshire; 70,000 vols; Dir AMY LAPOINTE; Chair. DONALD HOLDEN; Sec. HELEN ROWE; Treas. RICHARD MARTINI.

Bedford Public Library: Three Meetinghouse Rd, Bedford, NH 03110; tel. (603) 472-2300; internet www.bedford.lib.nh.us; Dir MARY ANN SENATRO; Chair. EDWARD MORAN; Treas. ANTHONY FREDERICK.

Derry Public Library: 64 E Broadway, Derry, NH 03038; tel. (603) 432-6140; e-mail derrylib@derrypl.org; internet www.derry.lib .nh.us; f. 1905; Dir CHERYL LYNCH; Chair. ELIZABETH IVES; Sec. JOAN CRIMLISK; Treas. JACK ROBILLARD.

Dover Public Library: 73 Locust St, Dover, NH 03820-3753; tel. (603) 516-6050; e-mail libraryquestions@dover.nh.gov; internet www.dover.lib.nh.us; f. 1883; historical photographs colln of Dover; Dir CATHLEEN BEAUDOIN.

Durham Public Library: Seven Mill Rd Unit H, Durham, NH 03824; tel. (603) 868-6699; e-mail durhampl@gmail.com; internet www.durhampubliclibrary.org; f. 1900; Dir THOMAS MADDEN; Chair. DOUGLAS BENCKS; Sec. SIBYLLE CARLSON; Treas. ROBIN BALDUCCI.

Hollis Social Library: POB 659, Hollis, NH 03049-0659; Two Monument Sq., Hollis, NH 03049-0659; tel. (603) 465-7721; e-mail helpdesk@hollislibrary.org; internet www .hollislibrary.org; f. 1799; colln. incl. reference section on genealogy; maps and history of Hollis and New Hampshire; Dir LUCINDA MAZZA; Chair. ROBERT BARTIS; Sec. JONE LaBOMBARD; Treas. STEPHANIE STACK.

Hooksett Public Library: 31 Mount St Marys Way, Hooksett, NH 03106; tel. (603) 485-6092; e-mail hplbooks@hooksettlibrary .org; internet www.hooksett.lib.nh.us; Dir HEATHER SHUMWAY; Chair. MARY FARWELL; Sec. TAMMY HOOKER; Treas. BARBARA DAVIS.

Howe Library: 13 S St, Hanover, NH 03755; tel. (603) 643-4120; e-mail reference@thehowe.org; internet www .thehowe.org; f. 1900; 73,000 vols; Dir MARY WHITE.

Keene Public Library: 60 Winter St, Keene, NH 03431; tel. (603) 352-0157; internet www.keenepubliclibrary.org; f. 1801; colln incl. large print books and New Hampshire town histories; Keene Sentinel microfilm since 1799; full text of the New York Times from 1851 to present (online); 130,000 vols; Dir NANCY VINCENT; Pres. DON WILMETH; Sec. JOE DuMOND; Treas. HOPE THERRIEN.

Kelley Library: 234 Main St, Salem, NH 03079; tel. (603) 898-7064; e-mail kelleylb@ kelleylibrary.org; internet www.kelleylibrary .org; f. 1894; colln incl. local histories, town reports, and local and state govt documents; 112,391 vols, 297 magazines and newspapers, 4,105 music CDs and other electronic media, 2,838 audio books, 7,038 video cassettes and DVDs; Dir ALISON BAKER; Chair. MARTHA BREEN; Treas. KATE NORTON.

Lane Memorial Library: Two Academy Ave, Hampton, NH 03842; tel. (603) 926-3368; e-mail library@hampton.lib.nh.us; internet www.hampton.lib.nh.us; f. 1881; local history colln; Dir AMANDA REYNOLDS COOPER; Chair. LINDA SADLOCK; Sec. ROBERT LAMOTHE; Treas. MARY LOU HERAN.

Manchester City Library: 405 Pine St, Manchester, NH 03104; tel. (603) 624-6550; e-mail library@manchesternh.gov; internet www.manchester.lib.nh.us; f. 1854; Manchester City Library (HQ) and West Community Br. Library; 350,000 vols; Dir DENISE VAN ZANTEN; Chair. MARSHA BEECY; Sec. PATRICIA CORNELL; Treas. JEFF HICKOK.

Merrimack Public Library: 470 Daniel Webster Highway, Merrimack, NH 03054; tel. (603) 424-5021; e-mail mmkpl@ merrimack.lib.nh.us; internet www .merrimack.lib.nh.us; f. 1892; colln incl. rare New Hampshire books, town histories and local archives; 85,326 vols; Dir JANET ANGUS.

New Hampshire Law Library: Supreme Court Bldg, One Charles Doe Dr., Concord, NH 03301; tel. (603) 271-3777; e-mail lawlibrary@courts.state.nh.us; internet www .courts.state.nh.us/lawlibrary/index.htm; f. 1816, present name and status 1994; depository for US govt documents; legal information and related services to judicial, legislative and exec. brs of govt; 94,000 vols; Dir MARY S. SEARLES.

New Hampshire State Library: 20 Park St, Concord, NH 03301-6314; tel. (603) 271-2392; internet www.nh.gov/nhsl; f. 1717, present building 1895; spec. collns of historical children's books, New Hampshire govt, town records and history; 600,000 vols; State Librarian MICHAEL C. YORK.

Pelham Public Library: 24 Village Green, Pelham, NH 03076-3172; tel. (603) 635-7581; e-mail librarydirector@pelhamweb.com; internet pelhampubliclibrary.org; f. 1893; 30,000 vols; Dir ROBERT (BOB) RICE, JR; Chair. FRANCIS (FRAN) GARBOSKI; Sec. DIANE CHUBB; Treas. SUSAN SNIDE.

Portsmouth Public Library: 175 Parrott Ave, Portsmouth, NH 03801; tel. (603) 427-1540; e-mail info@lib.cityofportsmouth.com; internet www.cityofportsmouth.com/library; f. 1881; Dir MARY ANN LIST; Chair. JODY RECORD; Sec. GRACE LESSNER; Treas. JOHN O'LEARY.

Richards Free Library: 58 N Main St, Newport, NH 03773; tel. (603) 863-3430; e-mail rfl@newport.lib.nh.us; internet www .newport.lib.nh.us; f. 1888; 40,000 vols; Dir ANDREA THORPE.

Rye Public Library: 581 Washington Rd, Rye, NH 03870; tel. (603) 964-8401; e-mail contact@ryepubliclibrary.org; internet www .ryepubliclibrary.org; f. 1911; Dir ANDREW RICHMOND; Chair. KAREN W. OLIVER; Sec. BILL McDADE; Treas. GARRY LAYMAN.

Seabrook Library: 25 Liberty Lane, Seabrook, NH 03874; tel. (603) 474-2044; e-mail ocean@sealib.org; internet www.sealib.org; 47,000 vols; Dir ANN ROBINSON.

Wadleigh Memorial Library: 49 Nashua St, Milford, NH 03055; tel. (603) 673-2408; e-mail wadleigh@wadleighlibrary.org; internet www.wadleighlibrary.org; 70,000 vols and 200 magazines and newspapers, 2,000 CDs, 3,000 video cassettes and DVDs; Dir MICHELLE SAMPSON; Chair. MARY BURDETT.

New Jersey

Atlantic City Free Public Library: One N Tennessee Ave, Atlantic City, NJ 08401; tel. (609) 345-2269; e-mail reflib@acfpl.org; internet www.acfpl.org; f. 1901; magazines, newspapers, journals, audio books, ebooks on health, education, business, languages and immigration and naturalization; Alfred M. Heston Colln; 135,000 vols, 7,615 DVDs, 7,519 CDs and 28,357 books; Dir MAUREEN SHERR FRANK; Pres. WILLIAM K. CHEATHAM.

Atlantic County Library System: 40 Farragut Ave, Mays Landing, NJ 08330; tel. (609) 625-2776; e-mail contactus@aclsys.org; internet www.atlanticlibrary.org; 10 brs, 1 community reading centre and 1 bookmobile; 507,671 vols; Dir KAREN L. GEORGE; Chief Librarian GAIR HELFRICH.

Belleville Public Library and Information Center: 221 Washington Ave, Belleville, NJ 07109-3189; tel. (973) 450-3434; internet www.bellepl.org; spec. collns incl. Spanish language materials, business, New Jersey history, Italian-American History and local history; Dir JOAN TAUB; Sec. FLORENCE PENTOL; Treas. LOUIS J. MESSANO, JR.

Bergen County Cooperative Library System: 810 Main St, Hackensack, NJ 07601; tel. (201) 489-1904; e-mail bccls@ bccls.org; internet www.bccls.org; f. 1979; 74 public libraries in Bergen, Essex, Hudson and Passaic Counties; 5,481,163 vols; Exec. Dir ROBERT WHITE; Dir ARLENE SAHRAIE.

Berkeley Heights Public Library: 290 Plainfield Ave, Berkeley Heights, NJ 07922; tel. (908) 464-9333; e-mail reference@bhplnj .org; internet www.bhplnj.org; f. 1946; collns incl. encyclopedias, foreign language learn-

ing databases, literature and audio books; Dir STEPHANIE BAKOS; Pres. HOPE DANZIS; Sec. LESLIE KALTENBACH; Treas. SHEILA BUTHE.

Bernadsville Public Library: One Anderson Hill Rd, Bernardsville, NJ 07924; tel. (908) 766-0118; e-mail librarian@ bernardsvillelibrary.org; internet www .bernardsvillelibrary.org; f. 1840; books on local history; ebooks; audio books; Exec. Dir KAREN BRODSKY; Pres. DONALD BURSET; Sec. TERRY THOMPSON; Treas. JOHN La DUC.

Butler Public Library: One Ace Rd, Butler, NJ 07405; tel. (973) 838-3262; internet www.butlerlibrary.org; f. 1928; colln incl. databases of newspaper and magazine articles; business; health and well-being and reference directories; Dir ROCHELLE LEVIN; Treas. MARIE PRA.

Camden County Library System: Vogelson Br., 203 Laurel Rd, Voorhees, NJ 08043; tel. (856) 772-1636; internet www.camden.lib .nj.us; f. 1921; 7 brs; Dir LINDA DEVLIN.

Cherry Hill Public Library: 1100 Kings Highway N, Cherry Hill, NJ 08034-1911; tel. (856) 667-0300; e-mail info@chplnj.org; internet www.chplnj.org; incl. research section; Dir MANUEL PAREDES.

Free Public Library & Cultural Center of Bayonne: 697 Ave C, cnr of 31st St, Bayonne, NJ 07002; tel. (201) 858-6970; e-mail library@bayonnelibrary.org; internet www.bayonnelibrary.org; f. 1890 as Bayonne Public Library, present bldg 1904, current name adopted 1989; art and music colln; audio books; reference section incl. traditional and ebooks, newspapers, journals, maps, military history and oral history of Bayonne veterans; archives of Bayonne Public Library; Dir SNEH BAINS; Pres. CARMINE BORZELLI; Sec. BERNARD P. JABLONSKI; Treas. MARY-ANN D. ROWLAND.

Mercer County Library System: Lawrence HQ Br., 2751 Brunswick Pike, Lawrenceville, NJ 08648; tel. (609) 882-9246; e-mail director@mcl.org; internet webserver .mcl.org; 9 brs. incl Lawrence HQ br; Dir ELLEN BROWN.

New Jersey State Library: POB 520, Trenton, NJ 08625-0520; 185 W State St, Trenton, NJ 08625-0520; tel. (609) 278-2640; e-mail refdesk@njstatelib.org; internet www .njstatelib.org; f. 1796; affiliate of Thomas Edison State College; databases, online journals and ebooks; 2m. vols and documents, 800 current periodicals, 750,000 items on microfiche and microfilm; State Librarian NORMA E. BLAKE.

Newark Public Library: POB 630, 5 Washington St, Newark, NJ 07101-0630; tel. (973) 733-7779; e-mail reference@npl .org; internet www.npl.org; f. 1888; collns: art, sheet music, science, technology, business histories, American and British literature, US patent specifications and drawings since 1790, US govt documents regional depository, NJ documents, NJ history, fine printing, Black studies, Newark Evening News Morgue; 8 brs; 1,685,365 vols; Library Dir WILMA J. GREY; Prin. Librarian JANE SEIDEN.

Ocean City Free Public Library: 1735 Simpson Ave, Suite 4, Ocean City, NJ 08226-3071; tel. (609) 399-2434; internet home .oceancitylibrary.org; Dir CHRIS MALONEY.

Princeton Library: 65 Witherspoon St, Princeton, NJ 08542; tel. (609) 924-9529; e-mail comments@princetonlibrary.org; internet www.princeton.lib.nj.us; f. 1910; African-American history; genealogy; health and medicine; history and social sciences; languages; spec. colln public art; Dir LESLIE BURGER; Pres. KATHERINE McGAVERN.

Princeton University Library: One Washington Rd, Princeton, NJ 08544; tel. (609) 258-1470; e-mail libhr@princeton.edu; internet libweb.princeton.edu; f. 1746; spec. collns incl. 450 medieval and Renaissance codices, 10,000 Islamic MSS, cuneiform tablets, stone seals and papyri, pre-Columbian indigenous materials (especially Mayan), George Cruikshank and Aubrey Beardsley, American theatre (incl. papers of Max Gordon and Otto Kahn), archives of American publishers, especially Charles Scribner's Sons, the Morris L. Parrish Colln of Victorian Novelists, early American family papers, especially Edward Livingston and Blair-Lee, public policy papers since early 20th century, especially John Foster Dulles, Adlai Stevenson and the American Civil Liberties Union, 'Boom' period Latin American writers (incl. Mario Vargas Llosa); 6.9m. vols, 6m. microforms, 35,000 linear ft of MSS; Univ. Librarian KARIN A. TRAINER; publ. *Princeton University Library Chronicle*.

Ramsey Free Public Library: 30 Wyckoff Ave, Ramsey, NJ 07446; tel. (201) 327-1445; e-mail ramscirc@bccls.org; internet www.ramseylibrary.org; f. 1907; open borrowing library with M.A.I.N., PALS, LMxAC and SWELL BCCLS' patrons; Dir WENDY B. BLOOM; Pres. EMILY J. RENNIE; Sec. MARIE O'NEILL; Treas. FRANK HURLEY.

Rutgers University Libraries: 169 College Ave, CAC, New Brunswick, NJ 08901-1163; tel. (732) 932-7505; internet www.libraries.rutgers.edu; f. 1766; 26 libraries on Rutgers campuses in Camden, Newark and New Brunswick; spec. collns in medicine, physics, chemistry, mathematics, microbiology, art, alcohol studies, labour and management relations, urban research, law and music; 3m. vols; Univ. Librarian MARIANNE GAUNT.

Sussex County Library System: 125 Morris Turnpike, Newton, NJ 07860; tel. (973) 948-3660; internet www.sussexcountylibrary.org; f. 1942 as bookmobile; main library in Frankford and 5 brs in Newton, Sussex, Franklin, Hopatcong and Vernon; fed. depository; Dir STAN POLLAKOFF; Chief Librarian ELLEN CALLANAN.

University Libraries: George F. Smith Library of the Health Sciences, 30 12th Ave, POB 1709, Newark, NJ 07101-1709; tel. (973) 972-4580; e-mail libcwis@umdnj.edu; internet libraries.umdnj.edu; attached to Univ. of Medicine and Dentistry of New Jersey; George F. Smith Library of the Health Sciences, Newark campus; Robert Wood Johnson Library of the Health Sciences, NB/Piscataway Campus; Health Sciences Library at Stratford; Reuben L. Sharp Health Science Library, Camden Campus; Coriell Library, study annex campus; 92,802 vols, 703 ebooks, 173,951 journals, 158 print journal subscriptions, 4,610 ejournal subscriptions and 84 database subscriptions; Univ. Librarian JUDY COHN.

Warren and Reba Lummis Library: 981 Ye Greate St, POB 16, Greenwich, NJ 08323; tel. (856) 455-8580; e-mail cchistsoc@verizon.net; internet www.cchistsoc.org/lummis; attached to Cumberland Co Historical Soc.; holdings incl. genealogical and historical files, directories, maps, newspapers, deeds and indentures and microfilms on the USA and New Jersey census; 815 vols; Dir WARREN Q. ADAMS; Librarian CONSTANCE C. SCHUCHARD.

New Mexico

Albuquerque/Bernalillo County Library System: 501 Copper Ave, NW, Albuquerque, NM 87102; tel. (505) 768-5170; e-mail library@cabq.gov; internet www.abclibrary.org; 17 brs; Dir DEAN P. SMITH.

Capitan Public Library: POB 1169, 101 E Second St, Capitan, NM 88316; tel. (575) 354-3035; e-mail capitanlibrary@gmail.com; internet www.capitanlibrary.org; f. 1996; Dir PAT GARRETT; Pres. GEORGE HINCH; Sec. ANN CURTIS; Treas. SADIE MANN.

Clovis-Carver Public Library: 701 N Main St, Clovis, NM; tel. (575) 769-7840; e-mail library@cityofclovis.org; internet www.library.cityofclovis.org; f. 1949, current location 1991; 117,688 vols, 2,038 audio cassettes, 2,591 DVDs.

El Rito Library: POB 5, 182 Placitas Rd, El Rito, NM 87530; tel. (575) 581-4608; e-mail elritopubliclibrary@yahoo.com; internet www.elritolibrary.org; f. 1986; spec. collns: arts, crafts and culture; Spanish language (books, video cassettes, audio books); gardening and nature; 11,245 vols, 1,723 DVDs and video cassettes, 711 audio books and audio cassettes; Dir CHRISTINE TRUJILLO; Librarian RITA LARROW; Librarian TOM FORTSON.

Española Public Library: Richard Lucero Center, 313 N Paseo de Oñate, Española, NM 87532; tel. (505) 747-6087; internet www2.youseemore.com/espanola; f. 1925; depository for New Mexico State documents; 41,000 vols; Dir TEDDIE RIEHL.

Los Alamos County Library System: 133 Longview Dr., Los Alamos, NM 87544; tel. (505) 662-8253; e-mail libweb@lacnm.us; internet www.losalamosnm.us/library; incl. Rock Br. Library and Mesa Public Library; 182,050 vols, 152,692 books and magazines, 8,126 sound recordings, 130 framed art prints, 9,810 video recordings, 4,025 ebooks and 1,879 audio books; Chair. LINDA ANDERMAN; Library Man. BERNADINE GOLDMAN (acting).

Los Alamos National Laboratory Research Library: POB 1663, MS-P362, Los Alamos, NM 87545-1362; tel. (505) 667-5809; e-mail library@lanl.gov; internet library.lanl.gov; offers literature searching, training and outreach services; 150,000 vols, 100,000 print titles of books, 50,000 ebooks, 10,000 journals, 8,500 ejournals, 150,000 bound journals, 1.5m. print and microfiche reports, 790 video and audio cassettes; Dir MIRIAM BLAKE; publs *1663–Los Alamos Science and Technology Magazine*, *National Security Science*.

New Mexico Archives and Historical Services Division: New Mexico Library, Archives and Records Center Bldg, 1205 Camino Carlos Rey, Santa Fe, NM 87507; tel. (505) 476-7948; e-mail archives@state.nm.us; internet www.nmcpr.state.nm.us/archives/archives_hm.htm; attached to Nat. Archives and Records Admin.; colln of govt records since 1621, co records from 1850 to 1912, non-govt MSS, film and video colln, genealogy materials (Catholic church records, census, published family histories), private papers: letters, diaries, wills, maps and photographs related to New Mexico or SW; Dir MELISSA SALAZAR.

New Mexico State Library: 1209 Camino Carlos Rey, Santa Fe, NM 87507-5166; tel. (505) 476-9702; e-mail reference@state.nm.us; internet www.nmstatelibrary.org; f. 1929; attached to Dept of Cultural Affairs (State Govt); 110 brs statewide; 3 bookmobiles; provides state agencies with library resources and services, and serves as a primary reference source for libraries in the state; spec. collns: Southwest Resources (books, journals and newspapers on the history of the southwestern area of the USA), New Mexico Documents (publs of the various depts, agencies, commissions comprising the state govt), Fed. Documents (selective depository focus on New Mexico federal agency publs); 2m. vols; State Librarian DEVON SKEELE; publ. *Directory of New Mexico Libraries*.

Santa Fe Public Library: 145 Washington St, Santa Fe, NM 87501; tel. (505) 955-6789; e-mail library@santafenm.gov; internet www.santafelibrary.org; f. 1896; 2 brs; 230,166 vols, 10,795 video cassettes and DVDs, 6,505 audiobooks on cassettes and CDs, 4,787 music CDs, 388,003 other items; Pres. JENNIFER JARAMILLO.

University of New Mexico Libraries: MSC05 3020, One Univ. of New Mexico, Albuquerque, NM 87131-0001; tel. (505) 277-9100; internet elibrary.unm.edu; f. 1892; brs: Centennial Science and Engineering library, Parish Memorial Library for Business and Economics, Fine Arts and Design Library and Zimmerman Library; regional depository for fed. documents since 1968; spec. collns: Center for Southwest Research and Spec. Collns, Chicano/Hispano/Latino Research Program, Div. of Iberian and Latin American Resources and Services, Indigenous Nations Library Program; 3m. vols, 60,000 journal subscriptions, 663,000 govt documents, 348,149 ebooks, 14,728 linear ft MSS and archives, 235,000 maps and cartographic images, 3.8m. microform units, 37,000 audio materials, 9,300 film and video materials; Dean of Univ. Libraries MARTHA BEDARD.

New York

American Museum of Natural History Research Library: Central Park W, 79th St, New York, NY 10024-5192; tel. (212) 769-5400; e-mail libref@amnh.org; internet library.amnh.org; f. 1869; subject areas incl. anthropology, astronomy, exploration and travel, geology, history of science, museology, palaeontology, zoology; incl. astronomy colln transferred from Hayden Planetarium; 487,000 vols, 21,000 periodicals, 1m. photographs, 3,000 films, 13,000 rare vols; Dir TOM BAIONE; publs *Anthropological Papers of the American Museum of Natural History*, *Memoirs of the American Museum of Natural History*, *Novitates* (irregular).

Association of the Bar of the City of New York Library: 42 W 44th St, New York, NY 10036; tel. (212) 382-6666; e-mail library@nycbar.org; internet www.nycbar.org/index.php/library/overview-hours; f. 1870; colln of current and early edn treatises; current and superseded statutes for Fed. and all state jurisdictions; case reporters; law reviews and int. law material; colln of US and New York State appellate court briefs and records on appeal; 600,000 vols; Dir RICHARD TUSKE.

Brooklyn Public Library: 10 Grand Army Plaza, Brooklyn, NY 11238; tel. (718) 230-2100; internet www.brooklynpubliclibrary.org; f. 1892; 58 brs; spec. collns incl. Brooklyn history; business library; 7,189,998 items; Pres. and CEO LINDA E. JOHNSON; Chair. ANTHONY W. CROWELL; Sec. ANTONIA YUILLE WILLIAMS; Treas. PETER ASCHKENASY.

Buffalo and Erie County Public Library System: 1 Lafayette Sq., Buffalo, NY 14203; tel. (716) 858-8900; internet www.buffalolib.org; f. 1886; 37 brs (incl. 8 city br. libraries); 3,639,922 vols; Dir MARY JEAN JAKUBOWSKI.

Center for Inquiry Libraries: POB 741, Amherst, NY 14226-0741; 3965 Rensch Rd, Amherst, NY 14228; tel. (716) 636-4869; internet www.cfilibraries.org; incl.: John and Mary Frantz Skeptics' Library, James Hervey Johnson Freethought and Humanist Library, Jo Ann Boydston Library of American Philosophical Naturalism, Humanist Institute colln (incl. the Joseph Blau colln), Arnold B. Levy colln of Literary, Artistic and Scientific Hoaxes in Honor of Steve Allen,

Hal Verb Little Blue Book colln, Rare Book Room, Prometheus Repository; incl. microforms, microfiche, reference colln; Dir TIMOTHY BINGA.

Center for Jewish History: 15 W 16th St, New York, NY 10011; tel. (212) 294-8301; e-mail inquiries@cjh.org; internet www.cjh .org; f. 2000; 5 partner orgs: American Jewish Historical Soc. American Seephardi Fed., Leo Baeck Institute, Yeshiva Univ. Museum, YIVO Institute for Jewish Research; artwork, textiles and ritual objects, music, films and photographs covering 600 years of Jewish history; 500,000 vols, 100m. archival documents; Co-Chair. JOSEPH S. STEINBERG; Co-Chair. WILLIAM A. ACKMAN; Dir for Archive and Library Services LAURA E. LEONE; Sec. THEODORE N. MIRVIS; Treas. SIDNEY LAPIDUS.

Chancellor Robert R. Livingston Masonic Library: 71 W 23rd St, 14th Fl., New York, NY 10010-4171; tel. (212) 337-6620; e-mail info@nymasoniclibrary.org; internet www.nymasoniclibrary.org; f. 1850 as Masonic Library of the Grand Lodge, present state 1983, present location 1986; books on Masonic history, origins, philosophy, symbolism, current events, esoterica and occultism; Masonic periodicals from all over the USA and the world since 1700s; collns of Masonic memorabilia, ritual artefacts, jewellery, aprons and other textile artefacts, artwork, engravings, paintings and collns by Past Grand Masters of New York; 60,000 vols; Dir THOMAS M. SAVINI; Pres. BRUCE RENNER; Sec. RICHARD C. MILLS.

Clinton Essex Franklin Library System: 33 Oak St, Plattsburgh, NY 12901-2810; tel. (518) 563-5190; e-mail info2@cefls.org; internet www.cefls.org; f. 1954; 30 public libraries, 1 bookmobile and 3 reading centres; Dir EWA JANKOWSKA; Pres. CHRIS DE GRANDPRÉ; Sec. LISA MINNICH; Treas. Dr NANCY CHURCH.

Columbia University Libraries: 535 W 114th St, New York, NY 10027; tel. (212) 854-7309; e-mail lio@columbia.edu; internet www .library.columbia.edu; f. 1754; 22 libraries at Columbia Univ. and its affiliated instns; collns in architecture, business, humanities, history, law, medicine, engineering, sciences and social sciences; 10.4m. vols; 144,787 current serial subscriptions; 6,379,196 microforms; 26m. MSS and 979,096 rare books; 156,717 video cassettes, DVDs, CDs, sound recordings; 174,032 govt documents; Vice-Pres. for Information Services and Univ. Librarian JAMES G. NEAL.

Cornell University Library: 201 Olin Library, Ithaca, NY 14853; tel. (607) 255-3393; e-mail libadmin@cornell.edu; internet www.library.cornell.edu; f. 1868; collns in SE Asia studies, industrial relations, viticulture, Old Norse and Icelandic materials, agriculture, astronomy, chemistry, classics, French history and literature, human devt, mathematics, medieval studies, microbiology, N European language and literature, physics, and W European social sciences; 8m. vols, 8.5m. microforms, 71,000 cu ft of MSS; Univ. Librarian ANNE R. KENNEY.

Department of Records and Information Services: Surrogate's Court Bldg, 31 Chambers St, New York, NY 10007; tel. (212) 788-8602; internet www.nyc.gov/html/records; f. 1977; comprises Municipal Archives of the City of New York, City Hall Library and Municipal Records Management Div; 250,000 vols, 160,000 items in records div., 1m. photographs; Deputy Commr EILEEN M. FLANNELLY.

Finger Lakes Library System: 119 E Green St, Ithaca, NY 14850; tel. (607) 273-4074; internet www.flls.org; f. 1958; 33 mem.

libraries; central library Tompkins Co Public Library; serves the public libraries in Cayuga, Cortland, Seneca, Tioga, and Tompkins counties; Exec. Dir KIMBERLY A. IRACI, Pres. CHRISTINE GRIFFIN; Sec. GRACE MILLER; Treas. DEBORA KELSEY.

Franklin D. Roosevelt Presidential Library and Museum: 4079 Albany Post Rd, Hyde Park, NY 12538; tel. (845) 486-1142; e-mail roosevelt.library@nara.gov; internet www.fdrlibrary.marist.edu; f. 1941; attached to Nat. Archives and Records Admin.; MSS, photographs, printed and museum materials concerning life and times of Franklin and Eleanor Roosevelt, incl. 4,700 lin. ft of Roosevelt's and his contemporaries papers; museum with 34,000 items; 72,000 vols, 17m. MSS pages, 130,000 photographs; Dir LYNN A. BASSANESE.

Frick Art Reference Library: 10 E 71st St, New York, NY 10021; tel. (212) 547-0641; e-mail library@frick.org; internet www.frick .org/library; f. 1920; repository for archives and spec. collns documenting the history of art and collecting in America; public and private collns date back to the 18th century; research databases and ejournals related to the study of art and art history; 285,000 vols, 80,000 auction catalogues and more than 1m. photographs; Dir ANNE L. POULET; Chair. MARGOT BOGERT; Sec. JOHN P. BIRKELUND; Treas. FRANKLIN W. HOBBS.

Hispanic Society of America Library: 613 W 155 St, New York, NY 10032; Audubon Terrace, Broadway, 155 and 156 Sts, New York, NY; tel. (212) 926-2234; e-mail library@hispanicsociety.org; internet www.hispanicsociety.org/hispanic/library .htm; f. 1904; art, history and literature of Spain, Portugal and Hispanic America; 300,000 MSS; 15,000 books printed before 1701, incl. 250 incunabula; 250,000 later books; Curator of Modern Books EDWIN X. ROLON; Curator of MSS and Rare Books JOHN O'NEILL.

Jewish Theological Seminary Library: 3080 Broadway, New York, NY 10027; tel. (212) 678-8844; e-mail library@jtsa.edu; internet www.jtsa.edu/library.xml; f. 1893; Louis Ginzberg Microfilm library (foreign collns of Hebrew MSS); incunabula; Bible, Rabbinics, Jewish history, liturgy, theology, early Yiddish, Hebrew literature, history of science and medicine; Haggadahs; Megillot (Esther scrolls); Ketuboth (marriage contracts); prints and photographs; musical scores; microfilms; video cassettes; sound recordings; e-resources; 400,000 vols, 11,000 MSS, 35,000 leaves of Cairo Genizah, Archives; Librarian DAVID KRAEMER; publ. *Quntres* (1 a year, online).

Library of Agudas Chassidei Chabad—Ohel Yosef Yitzchak—Lubavitch (Central Chabad Lubavitch Library and Archive Center): 770 E Parkway, Brooklyn, NY 11213; tel. (718) 493-1537; e-mail library@chabad .org; internet www.chabadlibrary.org; f. 1941; Judaic library; several thousand MSS on Chabad Chasidic philosophy; archive of correspondence and writings relating to Chabad philosophy and movement; incl. Chabad research centre; 250,000 vols (incl. 200,000 in Hebrew and Yiddish, and 50,000 in other languages); Lubavitch Colln, Colln of Rabbi Yosef Yitzchak and Colln of Lubavitcher Rebbe Menachem M. Schneerson; colln of photographs of Chasidim and Chabad activities sent to Rabbi Yosef Yitzchak and his successor Rabbi Menachem M. Schneerson.

Medical Research Library of Brooklyn: 450 Clarkson Ave, POB 14, Brooklyn, NY 11203; tel. (718) 270-7410; internet library .downstate.edu; f. 1962 as the jt library of the

Acad. of Medicine of Brooklyn, Inc. (f. 1845) and the State Univ. of New York Downstate Medical Center (f. 1860); provides service to College of Medicine, College of Nursing, College of Health-Related Professions, School of Graduate Studies, School of Public Health, Univ. Hospital and Graduate Medical Education of SUNY Downstate Medical Center; 67,078 vols, 388,320 printed journals, 4000 ejournals and 356 ebooks; Dir for Libraries Dr RICHARD M. WINANT.

Middletown Thrall Library: 11–19 Depot St, Middletown, NY 10940; tel. (845) 341-5454; e-mail thrall7@warwick.net; internet www.thrall.org; f. 1901; literature, law, encyclopedias, science and technology, local history, language and health; incl. govt information centre; 321,042 vols; Dir MATTHEW PFISTERER; Pres. CARL S. BERKOWITZ; Sec. LOIS RUCKERT; Treas. BARBARA KAY.

Monroe County Library System: Central Library of Rochester and Monroe Co, 115 S Ave, Rochester, NY 14604-1896; tel. (585) 428-7300; internet www.libraryweb.org/ central; f. 1912; fed. of 20 ind. public libraries in Monroe Co; 1,344,621 vols; Dir PATRICIA UTTARO; publ. *Rochester History* (2 a year).

Morgan Library & Museum: 225 Madison Ave, New York, NY 10016; tel. (212) 685-0008; e-mail readingroom@themorgan.org; internet www.themorgan.org; f. 1924; public museum and research library; collns formed by Pierpont Morgan and his son; regular public lectures and exhibitions; incl. Medieval and Renaissance MSS from the 5th to the 16th century; colln of 10,000 drawings by artists since the 15th century; colln of Rembrandt prints; Paris Review Archives; Pierre Matisse Gallery Archives; major monuments in the history of printing and typography, from Gutenberg and Caxton to modern times; comprehensive group of fine bindings; literary and historical MSS, incl. Dickens, Ruskin, the Brontës, Austen, Thoreau and Steinbeck; Carter Burden Colln of American Literature; colln of autograph scores, incl. works by Beethoven, Mahler, Mozart and Stravinsky; extensive Gilbert and Sullivan archive; photography; Dir WILLIAM M. GRISWOLD.

New York Academy of Medicine Library: 1216 Fifth Ave, New York, NY 10029; tel. (212) 822-7200; e-mail library@nyam.org; internet www.nyam.org/library; f. 1847; spec. collns incl. medical Americana, history of medicine, medical biography, rare medical books and incunabula; Coller Rare Book Room; 550,000 vols, 182,910 catalogued pamphlets, 275,788 catalogued illustrations and portraits, 2,700 serials; Pres. Dr JO IVEY BOUFFORD; publ. *Grey Literature Report* (6 a year).

New York Law Institute Library: 120 Broadway, Suite 932, New York, NY 10271-0043; tel. (212) 732-8720; e-mail library@nyli .org; internet www.nyli.org; f. 1828; law library for practising attorneys; spec. collns and edns incl. George Washington's copy of the Code de Louis XIII: the Plantation Laws of Virginia, autographed by Richard Henry Lee; 300,000 vols, 1,450 reels of microfilm, 16,300 microfiches; Exec. Dir RALPH MONACO.

New York Public Library: Stephen A. Schwarzman Bldg, Fifth Ave and 42nd St, New York, NY 10018; tel. (917) 275-6975; e-mail nyplweb@nypl.org; internet www.nypl .org; f. 1895 by merger of Astor, Tilden and Lenox Libraries; scholarly research collns; incl. Gutenberg Bible and Jefferson's MSS copy of the Declaration of Independence, Berg colln of English and American literature, Arents colln of books on tobacco and books in parts and Spencer colln of illustrated books; focuses on humanities and social sciences; performing arts; black history and culture; business and industry; network of neighbourhood libraries throughout Bronx, Manhattan and Staten Island; 90 local brs and 4 research centres; 65m. vols; Pres. and CEO Dr ANTHONY W. MARX; publs *Bookmark* (3 a year), *NOW* (3 a year), *Roar! UpRoar* (4 a year).

New York State Archives: New York State Education Dept, Cultural Education Center, Albany, NY 12230; tel. (518) 474-6926; e-mail dhs@mail.nysed.gov; internet www.archives .nysed.gov; f. 1971; archives and records of New York since 17th century; 200m. documents; Pres. ROBERT E. BULLOCK; Chief of Archival Services MARIA HOLDEN; publ. *New York Archives* (4 a year).

New York State Library: Cultural Education Center, 222 Madison Ave, Albany, NY 12230; tel. (518) 474-5355; e-mail circ@mail .nysed.gov; internet www.nysl.nysed.gov; f. 1818; attached to Office of Cultural Education, New York State Education Dept; serves Research Library, Talking Book and Braille Library and Div. of Library Devt; American and New York State history, law, medicine, education, technology and genealogy; MSS and spec. collns; US govt depository; digital collns incl. 18th- and 19th-century historical materials from the Revolutionary War, the Civil War, Native American materials, New York State laws and natural history; 20m. items; spec. colln of 19m. items in Talking Book and Braille Library; State Librarian BERNARD A. MARGOLIS.

New York University Libraries: The Elmer Holmes Bobst Library, New York Univ., 70 Washington Square S, New York, NY 10012; tel. (212) 998-2500; e-mail libweb@nyu.edu; internet www.nyu.edu/ library; f. 1835; 9 brs; Bobst Library has 3 specialized research centres (digital projects, arts, labour history); Courant Institute of Mathematical Sciences focuses on research-level material in mathematics, computer science and related fields; Stephen Chan Library of Fine Arts houses collns in art history and archaeology; Jack Brause Real Estate Library; Frederick L. Ehrman Medical Library; the Dental Center's Waldman Memorial Library, Jack Brause Library; Institute for the Study of the Ancient World and the Law Library; 5.1m. vols; Dean of Div. of Libraries CAROL MANDEL.

Queens Library: 89–11 Merrick Blvd, Jamaica, NY 11432; tel. (718) 990-0700; e-mail foundation@queenslibrary.org; internet queenslibrary.org; f. 1858, inc. 1907; books on literature and languages, social sciences, business, science and technology; spec. collns incl. Carter G. Woodson and Augusta Baker collns of African-American materials; 61 community libraries; 9.7m. vols, 1.25m. books, 2,100 periodical subscriptions in print, 90,000 govt documents, 20,000 video cassettes, DVDs and CDs, 517 16mm film titles, 42,000 music scores, 500 libretti, 23,000 music CDs, 3,500 music cassettes, 700 CD-ROMs, 500 titles of language study materials on cassettes and CDs and 2,000 phonorecords; Pres. and CEO THOMAS W. GALANTE; publs *Enrich Your Life* (6 a year), *The Guide* (12 a year).

Stephen B. Luce Library: Maritime College, SUNY, Six Pennyfield Ave, Fort Schuyler, Throgs Neck, NY 10465; tel. (718) 409-7231; e-mail library@sunymaritime.edu; internet www.sunymaritime.edu/ stephenblucelibrary; attached to Maritime College, SUNY; marine engineering, naval architecture, marine transportation, oceanography, transportation economics and management and meteorology; 80,000 vols, 374

magazines and journals subscriptions, 7,000 microfilms; Dir CONSTANTIA CONSTANTINOU.

Syracuse University Library: E. S. Bird Library, 222 Waverly Ave, Syracuse, NY 13244-5040; tel. (315) 443-2093; e-mail libref@syr.edu; internet libwww.syr.edu; f. 1870; divs incl. Science and Technology Library, Spec. Collns Research Center and Belfer Audio Archive; 2,992,795 vols, 22,000 ejournals, 1.9m. ebooks, 270,000 maps, 5,000 atlases, and 80,000 historical air photographs, 300,000 print and electronic fed., state and int. documents, 200,000 rare books and printed materials, 340,000 sound recordings of music, 300 sets of architectural drawings; Dean and Univ. Librarian SUZANNE E. THORIN (acting).

Burke Library at Union Theological Seminary: 3041 Broadway, New York, NY 10027; tel. (212) 851-5606; e-mail burke@ libraries.cul.columbia.edu; internet www .library.columbia.edu/indiv/burke; f. 1836; attached to Columbia Univ. Libraries; colln incl. theological disciplines; periodicals, pamphlets, reports, MSS, microforms, digital resources and archival material; 700,000 vols; spec. colln: Americana colln, Christian Science colln, Gillett colln of American History and Theology, MSS colln, McAlpin colln of British History and Theology, Missionary Research colln, Reformation Tracts colln, Thompson colln and Van Ess colln; Library Dir BETH BIDLACK.

United Nations Dag Hammarskjöld Library: 405 E 42nd St, Library Bldg, New York, NY 10017; tel. (212) 963-7412; e-mail unreference@un.org; internet www.un.org/ depts/dhl; f. 1949, present name 1961; colln of UN documents; specialized agencies and the League of Nations; activities and history of the UN; int. affairs since 1918; 600,000 vols, 10,000 serials, 6.5m. documents, 80,000 maps, 9,800 periodical titles; spec. colln of 8,600 vols of League documents and 6,500 related books and pamphlets; Head Librarian IAIN WATTS; publ. *Indices to Proceedings of the General Assembly, Security Council, Economic and Social Council and Trusteeship Council.*

United States Military Academy Library: Jefferson Hall, 758 Cullum Rd, West Point, NY 10996-1711; tel. (845) 938-8301; e-mail 8lib@usma.edu; internet www .library.usma.edu; f. 1802; military-historical records (since 1802), academic, govt documents, rare books; 50,000 vols, 1,500 linear ft MSS; Librarian and Assoc. Dean CHRISTOPHER BARTH.

University at Buffalo Libraries: 433 Capen Hall, Buffalo, NY 14260-1625; tel. (716) 645-2965; e-mail library@buffalo.edu; internet library.buffalo.edu/libraries; Architecture and Planning Library, Health Sciences Library, Law Library, Libraries Annex, Lockwood Memorial Library, Music Library and Oscar A. Silverman Library; spec. colln comprises poetry, rare books and univ. archives; digital colln consists of 3-D objects, photographs, slides, video and audio; 3.6m. vols, 350 research databases and more than 10,000 ejournals; Vice-Provost for Univ. Libraries H. AUSTIN BOOTH.

University of Rochester Libraries: River Campus Libraries, 755 Library Rd, POB 270055, Rochester, NY 14627-0055; tel. (585) 275-4471; internet www.rochester.edu/ libraries; f. 1850; River Campus Libraries; Sibley Music Library; Miner Library; Allen Library; 3.5m. vols.

Vassar College Libraries: POB 20, 124 Raymond Ave, Poughkeepsie, NY 12604-0020; tel. (845) 437-5760; e-mail libfacil@ vassar.edu; internet library.vassar.edu; f. 1865; incl. art library, music library, visual

resources library; spec. colln incl. Virginia B. Smith Memorial MSS colln; 1m. vols, 50,000 serial titles, 612,000 microforms; Dir SABRINA PAPE.

Waterford Public Library: 117 Third St, Waterford, NY 12188; tel. (518) 237-0891; e-mail watpublibrary@gmail.com; internet www.waterfordlibrary.net; full-text magazine and newspaper articles; current health and business information; 24,500 vols, 1,000 DVDs, 400 music CDs, 1,000 books on audio cassettes and CDs; Dir TIMOTHY McDONOUGH; Pres. MICHAEL MARCHESE; Sec. ANNE-MARIE MORRISSEY; Treas. JOANNE McLEOD.

Westchester Library System: 540 White Plains Rd, Suite 200, Tarrytown, NY 10591; tel. (914) 674-3600; internet www .westchesterlibraries.org; f. 1958; collaborates with 38 libraries in Westchester Co; spec. colln incl. fed. govt documents, Helen Whitman Colln of Herbs, Horticulture and Gdns, John C. Jutkowitz Memorial Theatre Arts Colln, New York Govt Documents and Mills Law Colln; Exec. Dir TERRY L. KIRCHNER; Pres. PATRICIA N. DOHRENWEND; Sec. NASEEM JAMALI; Treas. DAVE DONELSON.

Yonkers Public Library: Riverfront Library, 1 Larkin Center, Yonkers, NY 10701; tel. (914) 337-1500; internet www.ypl .org; f. 1893; 3 brs: Riverfront, Grinton I. Will and Crestwood; business, technical and govt information sources in printed and e-formats; fine arts dept in Grinton I. Will br. houses visual and performing arts, sound recordings and musical scores; Dir STEPHEN E. FORCE; Pres. WILLIAM E. SHEERIN.

North Carolina

Alamance County Public Libraries: 342 S Spring St, Burlington, NC 27215; tel. (336) 229-3588; e-mail reference.staff@ alamancelibraries.org; internet www .alamancelibraries.org; May Memorial Library (HQ); brs: Graham Public Library, Mebane Public Library, N Park Library and S Annex Library; 250,000 vols; Dir M. J. WILKERSON.

Burke County Public Library: 204 S King St, Morganton, NC 28655; tel. (828) 437-5638; e-mail admin@bcpls.org; internet www .bcpls.org; f. 1923; brs: Valdese Public Library, Morganton Public Library and C. B. Hildebrand Public Library; Chair. BAKHTIAR ALAM; Sec. ANNA WILSON.

Charlotte Mecklenburg Library: 310 N Tryon St, Charlotte, NC 28202; tel. (704) 416-0100; internet www.plcmc.org; f. 1903, fmr name Public Library of Charlotte and Mecklenburg County, present name 2009; colln of foreign-language publs, local history and genealogy; 23 br. libraries; 1.5m. vols; Dir of Libraries CHARLES M. BROWN; Man. JONITA EDMONDS.

Chatham County Public Libraries: 197 NC Highway 87N, Pittsboro, NC 27312; tel. (919) 545-8084; e-mail mail@ chathamlibraries.org; internet www .chathamnc.org; Chatham Community Library (HQ); brs: Goldston Library and Wren Memorial Library; 90,000 vols; Dir LINDA CLARKE.

Cumberland County Public Library & Information Center: 300 Maiden Lane, Fayetteville, NC 28301-5000; tel. (910) 483-7727; e-mail library@cumberland.lib.nc.us; internet www.cumberland.lib.nc.us; f. 1932, present name 1945; brs: HQ, Cliffdale Regional, E Regional, N Regional, W Regional, Bordeaux, Hope Mills, Spring Lake, Law Library; 5,000,000 vols (incl. 33,000 foreign language books); Dir JODY RISACHER; Chair. OLE SORENSEN.

Duke University Library: POB 90193, Durham, NC 27708-0193; tel. (919) 660-

5800; e-mail asklib@duke.edu; internet library.duke.edu; f. 1838; British history and literature of 17th–19th centuries; gen. European history since 1870; French Revolution; church history of Reformation; E Asia; advertising history; American and Latin American history; S Americana; women's history; history of economic thought; labour history; French, English, Italian, German Baroque and American literature; int. law; 6 br. libraries and 4 professional school libraries: Law (Ford Library), medicine, business and divinity; 6,172,205 vols, 51,827 linear ft of MSS and archives; Univ. Librarian and Vice-Provost for Library Affairs Dr DEBORAH JAKUBS; publ. *Duke University Libraries* (3 a year).

Forsyth County Public Library: 660 W Fifth St, Winston-Salem, NC 27101; tel. (336) 703-2665; internet www.forsyth.cc/library; Central Library (HQ); brs: Carver School Rd, Clemmons, Kernersville, Kernersville, Malloy/Jordan E Winston, Reynolda Manor, Rural Hall, Southside and Walkertown; fed. depository; Dir SYLVIA SPRINKLE-HAMLIN; Chair. DONNA L. STALEY.

Gaston-Lincoln Regional Library: 1555 E Garrison Blvd, Gastonia, NC 28054-5156; tel. (704) 868-2164; e-mail celler@co.gaston.nc.us; internet www.glrl.lib.nc.us; Dir CINDY W. MOOSE; Chair. RALPH S. ROBINSON, JR.

Haywood County Public Library: 678 S Haywood St, Waynesville, NC 28786; tel. (828) 452-5169; internet www.haywoodlibrary.org; f. 1891 as Waynesville Library; attached to Haywood County Govt; Waynesville (HQ); brs: Canton, Maggie Valley and Fines Creek; 158,000 vols, 11,500 audio cassettes, 9,000 video cassettes, 545 journals; Dir SHARON WOODROW; Chair. BETTE SPRECHER; Sec. JOAN ROUTH.

Henderson County Public Library: 301 N Washington St, Hendersonville, NC 28739; tel. (828) 697-4725; internet www.henderson.lib.nc.us; f. 1914; brs: HQ, Fletcher, Edneyville, Etowah, Green River and Mills River; Chair. MORTON LAZARUS; Sec. STAN SHELLEY.

Hickory Public Library: 375 Third St NE, Hickory, NC 28601; tel. (828) 304-0500; internet www.ci.hickory.nc.us/library; f. 1893; Patrick Beaver Memorial Library (HQ) and Ridgeview Br.; genealogy colln incl. Catawba and surrounding counties; 115,396 vols, 272 video cassettes, 6,946 audio recordings, 377 periodicals; Dir LOUISE HUMPHREY.

McDowell County Public Library: 90 W Court St, Marion, NC 28752; tel. (828) 652-3858; e-mail mcdowellcountypubliclibrary@yahoo.com; internet www.mcdowellpubliclibrary.org; f. 1920; McDowell Co Public Library (HQ); brs: Marion Davis Memorial Br. and McDowell Co Law Library; Dir ELIZABETH HOUSE.

Rockingham County Public Library: 527 Boone Rd, Eden, NC 27288; tel. (336) 627-1106; e-mail reference@rcpl.org; internet www.rcpl.org; brs: Eden, Madison, Mayodan, Reidsville and Stoneville; colln of genealogy and local history materials; Dir MICHAEL P. ROCHE; Chair. MICHAEL ROSE.

Rowan Public Library: 201 W Fisher St, Salisbury, NC 28144; tel. (704) 216-8228; e-mail info@rowancountync.gov; internet www.rowancountync.gov/government/departments/publiclibrary/tabid/145/default.aspx; f. 1911; Salisbury (HQ); brs: S Rowan Regional and East Br., Rockwell; Dir JEFF HALL.

Town of Chapel Hill Public Library: University Mall, 201 S. Estes Dr., Chapel Hill, NC 27514; tel. (919) 968-2780; e-mail library@townofchapelhill.org; internet www.chapelhillpubliclibrary.org; f. 1958; Dir KATHLEEN THOMPSON; Chair. MARTHA DIEFENDORF; Sec. PAUL JONES.

Transylvania County Library: 212 S Gaston St, Brevard, NC 28712; tel. (828) 884-3151; internet library.transylvaniacounty.org; f. 1912, present location 2006; Rowell Bosse North Carolina Room incl. colln of reference book titles, unpublished family histories, co heritage vols and church histories; Dir ANNA YOUNT; Chair. MICHAEL H. SHELLEY.

University of North Carolina Library: Chapel Hill, NC 27514-8890; tel. (919) 962-1301; e-mail reference@unc.edu; internet www.lib.unc.edu; f. 1795; spec. collns on North Carolina, South Americana, the history of the book, incunabula, 16th-century books, incl. large colln of Estienne imprints, *crónicas* of the discovery and conquest of the New World, also Johnson, Boswell, Dickens, Shaw and selected contemporary authors, Napoleon and the French Revolution, World War I and World War II materials, early Americana, Confederate imprints, Spanish, Catalan and Portuguese drama, John Murray and Smith, Elder and Co imprints, Afro-American materials, fed. and state documents, Latin America, Mazarinades, music and historical MSS; 10 departmental libraries in scientific and other fields; Institute of Govt Library; separate libraries in Law, Health Sciences, Population and a Data Library; 6,526,824 vols; Univ. Librarian and Assoc. Provost for Univ. Libraries SARAH C. MICHALAK.

Wake County Public Libraries: 4020 Carya Dr., Raleigh, NC 27610; tel. (919) 250-1200; internet www.wakegov.com/libraries; f. 1901; 6 regional libraries and 14 community libraries; genealogy and local history library; 1 bookmobile; Dir MICHAEL J. WASILICK.

North Dakota

Adams County Library: Hettinger, ND 58639; tel. (701) 567-2741; internet adamscountylibrary.org; f. 1913; Dir PAT ANDERSON.

Cavalier County Library: 600 Fifth Ave, Langdon, ND 58249; tel. (701) 256-5353; internet ccl.utma.com; f. 1897, present name and status 1986, present bldg 1988; 27,500 vols, 1,000 video cassettes and DVDs; Librarian SHANNON NUELLE.

Dickinson Area Public Library: 139 Third St, West Dickinson, ND, 58601; tel. (701) 456-7700; e-mail dickinson.library@sendit.nodak.edu; internet www.dickinsonlibrary.com; f. 1908; 90,000 vols; Dir RENEE PAASCH.

Grand Forks Public Library: 2110 Library Circle, Grand Forks, ND 58201; tel. (701) 772-8116; e-mail gfplreference@hotmail.com; internet www.gflibrary.com; f. 1892, present bldg 1972; 314,310 vols (incl. 25,108 audio items, 21,054 DVDs and video cassettes), 341 journals, 6,000 ebooks; Dir WENDY WENDT; Chair. BRIAN SCHILL.

Lake Region Public Library: 423 Seventh St, NE, Devils Lake, ND 58301-2529; tel. (701) 662-2220; e-mail lakeregion.pl@sendit.nodak.edu; internet www.dvlnd.com/departments/library.html; f. 2003 established in Carnegie library in 1910; spec. colln: Scandinavian Section, George Johnson Genealogical Section and microfilm; 42,582 vols; Dir JAMES CHATTIN; Pres. NANCY LUNDON.

North Dakota State Library: 604 E Blvd Ave, Bismarck, ND 58505-0800; tel. (701) 328-4622; e-mail statelib@nd.gov; internet www.library.nd.gov; f. 1907 as Public Library Comm., present name 1979; State Librarian HULEN E. BIVINS.

North Dakota State University Libraries: POB 6050, NDSU Dept 2080, Fargo, ND 58108-6050; tel. (701) 231-8753; e-mail ndsu-library-librarians@listserv.nodak.edu; internet library.ndsu.edu; f. 1891; incl. Main Library, Architecture Library, Barry Library (Business), Chemistry Library, Health Sciences Library, Institute for Regional Studies and Univ. Archives, Germans for Russia Heritage Colln; 922,470 vols, 10,829 periodicals, 530,000 govt documents; Dean of Libraries MICHELE M. REID.

State Historical Society of North Dakota State Archives: 612 E Blvd Ave, Bismarck, ND 58505; tel. (701) 328-2091; e-mail archives@nd.gov; internet history.nd.gov; f. 1905; historic records of state and local govt in ND; genealogical resources; State Archivist ANN B. JENKS.

University of North Dakota Libraries: 3051 University Ave, Grand Forks, ND 58202-9000; tel. (701) 777-2189; internet www.library.und.edu; f. 1883; incl. Chester Fritz Library (US Patent and Trademark and govt publs depository), Energy and Environmental Research Center Library, F. D. Holland Geology Library, Gordon Erickson Music Library, Harley E. French Library of the Health Sciences and Thormodsgard Law Library; 2m. vols, access to 40,000 ejournals; Dir for Libraries WILBUR STOLT.

West Fargo Public Library: 109 Third St E, West Fargo, ND 58078; tel. (701) 433-5460; internet www.westfargolibrary.org; 58,409 vols; Dir SANDRA HANNAHS; Pres. LEIGHAN AKER-MONSON.

Ohio

Akron Law Library: 209 S High St, Fourth Fl., Akron, OH 44308-1675; tel. (330) 643-2804; internet akronlawlib.summitoh.net; f. 1888; colln on legal issues and Ohio-specific colln; 81,500 vols; Dir ALAN CANFORA.

Akron-Summit County Public Library: 60 S High St, Akron, OH 44326; tel. (330) 643-9000; internet ascpl.lib.oh.us; f. 1874; also has 2 bookmobiles; a mobile service van; 17 brs in Summit County; 2m. vols (incl. books, CDs, DVDs); Dir DAVID JENNINGS; Deputy Dir PAM HICKSON-STEVENSON.

Butler County Law Library: 10 Journal Sq., Suite 200, Hamilton, OH 45011; tel. (513) 887-3455; internet www.bclawlib.org; f. 1889; provides materials used for regular legal research: legal education materials from the Ohio State Bar Asscn and selected law reviews, legal periodicals and newspapers, incl. bar publs; colln of fed. practice and procedure materials, form books and legal encyclopedic works in print and electronic format; state codes, administrative codes and state court opinions; legal encyclopedia and legal dictionary; legal forms set; pleading and practice forms set; American Law Institute Restatements; uniform laws annotated; Dir JOE HODNICKI.

Case Western Reserve University Libraries: 11055 Euclid Ave, Cleveland, OH 44106-7151; tel. (216) 368-3506; internet www.case.edu/dir/libraries.html; f. 1826; Kelvin Smith Library is the main Univ. Library; other libraries are Astronomy Library, Cleveland Health Sciences Library, Allen Memorial Medical Library, Health Center Library, Kulas Music Library, Law School Library and Technology Resources, Lillian F. and Milford J. Harris Library; spec. collns: early American children's books, German literature and philology, history of medicine, history of printing, history of science and technology, environmental sciences, natural history, public housing and urban devt; Kelvin Smith Library: 1.7m. vols (incl. books, journals, microfilm, scripts, electronic content, media, theses and dissertations—electronic and in print, digital collns); Astronomy Library: 3,000 books, 4,000 bound periodical vols, 480 linear ft of observatory publs; Cleveland Health Sciences Library: 380,000 vols and 1,700 journals; Kulas Music Library: 42,000 items, incl. music scores, books on music, sound recordings, microforms and music periodicals; Kulas Music Library: 42,000 items, incl. music scores, books on music, sound recordings, microforms, music periodicals; Law School Library and Technology Resources: 410,000 books of fed. and state law, law reviews, current law services, an extensive British and Commonwealth colln, and spec. collns in taxation, labour law, foreign investments, int. law, environmental law; Lillian F. and Milford J. Harris Library: 40,000 books and pamphlets, 325 journals, 700 media items; Univ. Librarian ARNOLD HIRSHON; Deputy Dir TIMOTHY ROBSON.

Clermont County Law Library Association: Clermont County Court House, 270 E Main St, Batavia, OH 45103; tel. (513) 732-7109; e-mail cclaw@cclla.org; internet www.cclla.org; f. 1937; Dir CAROL SUHRE; Chair. GARY OSTENDARP.

Cleveland Law Library: 1 W Lakeside Ave, Fourth Fl., Cleveland, OH 44113-1023; tel. (216) 861-5070; e-mail lawlib@clelaw.lib.oh.us; internet clelaw.lib.oh.us; f. 1869 as Cleveland Law Library Assocn; Dir and Librarian KATHLEEN M. SASALA; Pres. JOSEPH N. GROSS.

Cleveland Public Library: 325 Superior Ave, NE, Cleveland, OH 44114-1271; tel. (216) 623-2800; e-mail info@cpl.org; internet www.cpl.org; f. 1869; 28 brs; services to hospitals, the homebound, the physically handicapped and the blind; telephone reference service; fee-based research service; 3,723,666 vols, 45,000 edns classical music and jazz in Naxos Music Library, 900 linear ft archives; spec. colln: Schweinfurth Colln (rare architectural publs), Chess and Checkers Collns, Folklore, Gypsies and Orientalia, Miniature Books, Tobacco Colln; Dir FELTON THOMAS, Jr; Deputy Dir CINDY LOMBARDO (acting); Pres. THOMAS D. CORRIGAN; Sec. ALAN SEIFULLAH.

Columbus Metropolitan Library: 96 S Grant Ave, Columbus, OH 43215; tel. (614) 645-2275; internet www.columbuslibrary.org; f. 1873; 20 brs; also jtly operates Northwest Library in cooperation with Worthington Libraries; 3m. vols; Exec. Dir PATRICK A. LOSINSKI; Chief Operating Officer CHRIS TAYLOR; Treas. DEWITT HARRELL.

Dayton Metro Library: 215 E Third St, Dayton, OH 45402; tel. (937) 463-2665; internet www.daytonmetrolibrary.org; f. 1847; 20 brs; bookmobile service; service to homebound, elderly and blind; circulating colln of 16-mm films, records and cassettes; 1,509,623 vols; Exec. Dir TIM KAMBITSCH.

Hamilton County Law Library: 1000 Main St, Room 601, Hamilton County Courthouse, Cincinnati, OH 45202; tel. (513) 946-5300; e-mail reference@cms.hamilton-co.org; internet www.hamilton-co.org/cinlawlib; f. 1834, present name and status 2010; 150,000 vols; Dir and Law Librarian MARY JENKINS; Chair. JAMES T. O'REILLY.

Lake County Law Library: Lake County Courthouse, 47 N Park Pl., Painesville, OH 44077; tel. (440) 350-2638; e-mail lawlibrary@lakecountyohio.org; internet www.lakecountyohio.org/lawlibrary; 3 brs in Municipal Courts of Mentor, Painesville and Willoughby; materials related to fed., state, tax, family, probate, real estate and labour

law; Dir and Law Librarian SANDRA E. MURPHY; Chair. KENNETH R. GAUNTNER, JR.

Lorain County Law Library: Lorain County Admin. Bldg, First Fl., 226 Middle Ave, Elyria, OH; tel. (440) 329-5567; internet lorainlawlib.org/information.htm; 22,000 vols, 35,000 microfiche, 500 audio cassettes, 200 video cassettes and 70 CD-ROMs; Dir MARY KOVACS; Chair. JAMES TAYLOR.

Mahoning Law Library Association: Fourth Fl., Courthouse, 120 Market St, Youngstown, OH 44503-1752; tel. (330) 740-2295; e-mail mlladir@mahoninglawlibrary.org; internet www.mahoninglawlibrary.org; f. 1906; local court rules and ordinances, case law, treatises, legal periodicals, legal reference material, fed. and state statutes; 32,000 vols; Librarian ANNA PACZELT; Pres. ALAN R. KRETZER; Sec. and Treas. CHRISTOPHER J. SCHIAVONE.

Mansfield/Richland County Public Library: 43 W Third St, Mansfield, OH 44902; tel. (419) 521-3100; internet www.mrcpl.org; f. 1887; 8 brs; Dir JOSEPH C. PALMER; Pres. VIN BLACK; Sec. JACK WELSH.

Medina County District Library: 210 S Broadway, Medina, OH 44256; tel. (330) 725-0588; internet www.medina.lib.oh.us; f. 1877, present name and status 1982; 1 main library and 5 brs; bookmobile services; Dir CAROLE KOWELL; Pres. ADRIENNE APPLEBY-BURES; Sec. PATRICIA BOYLE.

Montgomery County Law Library: 505 Montgomery County Courts Bldg, 41 N Perry St, POB 972, Dayton, OH 45422; tel. (937) 225-4496; internet www.mcohio.org/government/law_library; f. 1868, fmrly Dayton Law Library Assocn, present name and status 2010; Law Librarian JOANNE R. BEAL.

Ohio Historical Society Archives and Library: Ohio History Center, 800E, 17th Ave, Columbus, OH 43211; tel. (614) 297-2510; e-mail reference@ohiohistory.org; internet www.ohiohistory.org/resource/archlib; colln of documents related to operation of state and local govts; incl. State Archives; 82,500 vols, 10,700 cu ft MSS, 13,500 cu ft local govt records, 15,000 maps, 85,000 rolls microfilm, 12,000 sheets microfiche, 4,500 newspapers, 1m. photographs, 20,000 cu ft State Archives; State Archivist FRED PREVITS.

Ohio State University Libraries: 1858 Neil Ave Mall, Columbus, OH 43210-1286; tel. (614) 292-6785; e-mail library@osu.edu; internet www.lib.ohio-state.edu; f. 1873; Main (Thompson) Library and 26 deptl and affiliated libraries; 6,161,657 vols, 108,051 monographs, 6,147,566 microforms, 90,965 serials incl. periodicals, 16,328 govt documents, 36,829 linear ft MSS and archives, 87,485 audio and video materials; spec. collns incl. American fiction, theatre, cartoons and cartooning, medieval Slavic MSS on microfilm; Dir of Libraries CAROL PITTS DIEDRICHS.

Public Library of Cincinnati and Hamilton County: 800 Vine St, Cincinnati, OH 45202-2009; tel. (513) 369-6900; internet www.cincinnatilibrary.org; f. 1853; US Documents Depository; 41 brs; regional library for the blind and physically handicapped; spec. collns incl. local history, genealogy, theology, art, music, theatre, US patents and trademarks, Inland Rivers Library, Bibles, English-language dictionaries, Cincinnatiana, first edns of English and American authors, Edgar Rice Burroughs Colln, Theodore Langstroth Colln, Lafcadio Hearn Colln, Loeb Colln; 4,887,372 books, 150,000 maps; Exec. Dir KIMBER L. FENDER; Pres. WILLIAM J. MORAN; Sec. ROSS A. WRIGHT.

Rutherford B. Hayes Presidential Center Library: Spiegel Grove, Fremont, OH

43420-2796; tel. (419) 332-2081; e-mail hayeslib@rbhayes.org; internet www.rbhayes.org/hayes/library; f. 1916, present name 1981; 12,000 vol of personal library and archival material from Pres. Hayes's military and political career (1877–81); colln areas incl. Rutherford B. Hayes and the Hayes family, Gilded Age, local history and local govt, The Great Lakes and the Erie Islands and spec. collns; 70,000 vols; Head Librarian BECKY HILL.

Stark County Law Library: 110 Central Plaza, S Suite 401, Canton, OH 44702; tel. (330) 451-7380; e-mail inform@starklawlibrary.org; internet www.starklawlibrary.org; f. 1889; colln of revised code, gen. code, admin. code, reported and unreported cases, form books, legislative history materials, law journals, atty gen. opinions, local court rules for co courts, local municipal and township ordinances; 62,000 vols; Dir ANN CAPOZZI.

State Library of Ohio: 274 East First Ave, Columbus, OH 43201; tel. (614) 644-7061; internet winslo.state.oh.us; f. 1817; 1.4m. vols; a spec. library for state govt, incl. periodicals, documents, pamphlets, services and microforms; spec. colln of management, genealogy, local history, education and health; State Librarian JO BUDLER.

Toledo-Lucas County Public Library: 325 Michigan St, Toledo, OH 43604; tel. (419) 259-5200; internet www.toledolibrary.org; f. 1970; 18 brs; 1 outreach service; 1.9m. vols; Dir CLYDE S. SCOLES.

University of Cincinnati Libraries: POB 210033, Cincinnati, OH 45221-0033; tel. (513) 556-1424; internet www.libraries.uc.edu; f. 1819; incl. Walter C. Langsam Library, Archives and Rare Books Library, Donald C. Harrison Health Sciences Library and 8 college and dept libraries; 4,267,945 vols; spec. colln: Archives and Rare Books Library (German-Americana Colln), Artists' Books, CCM Library Spec. Collns, Cohen Colln, Elliston Poetry Room, Emile Male Colln, Geology Guidebook Colln, Historic K-12 Textbook Colln, Oesper Collns in the History of Chemistry, Henry R. Winkler Center for the History of the Health Professions Colln; Dean and Univ. Librarian XUE-MAO WANG.

Warren-Trumbull County Public Library: 444 Mahoning Ave NW, Warren, Ohio 44483; tel. (330) 399-8807; internet www.wtcpl.lib.oh.us; f. 1890; 5 brs and a bookmobile; Dir JAMES A. WILKINS; Pres. LILLIE JOHNSON; Sec. JAMES MCFARLAND.

Oklahoma

Anadarko Community Library: 215 West Broadway, Anadarko, OK 73005; tel. (405) 247-7351; internet www.anadarkopl.okpls.org; f. 1903, present name and status 1990; Dir CHRISTINA OWEN.

Bartlesville Public Library: 600 S Johnstone, Bartlesville, OK 74003; tel. (918) 338-4161; e-mail bpl@bartlesville.lib.ok.us; internet www.bartlesville.lib.ok.us; f. 1898; Dir JOAN SINGLETON.

Chickasaw Regional (Public) Library System: 601 Railway Express, Ardmore, OK 73401; tel. (580) 223-3164; e-mail reference@crlsok.org; internet www.crlsok.org; brs in Atoka, Davis, Healdton, Tishomingo, Marietta, Sulphur and Wilson; provides free public library service to S-Central Oklahoma; Dir LYNN MCINTOSH.

Duncan Public Library: 2211 N Highway 81, Duncan, OK 73533; tel. (580) 255-0636; internet www2.youseemore.com/duncan; f. 1921; Dir JAN COLE; Pres. RICK RODGERS; Sec. CAROL EUBANKS (acting).

Jay C. Byers Memorial Library: 215 E Wichita Ave, Cleveland, OK 74020; tel. (918) 358-2676; e-mail info@jcbyers.lib.ok.us; internet www.jcbyerslibrary.okpls.org; f. 1936, present name 2002; Chair. L. RUSTIN FERGUSON; Dir MICHELLE MILLER; Sec. JAN STEPHENS.

Mabel C. Fry Public Library: 1200 Lakeshore Dr., Yukon, OK 73099; tel. (405) 354-8232; internet www.cityofyukonok.gov/city-departments/mabel-c-fry-public-library/; f. 1905, present location 1997; Chair. DONELDA WHEATLEY; Sec. JOYCE ROMAN; Head Librarian SARA SCHIEMAN.

Margaret Carder Library: 201 W Lincoln, Mangum, OK 73554; tel. (580) 782-3185; e-mail mangumlibrary@gmail.com; internet www.mangumpubliclibrary.com; f. 1922 as Mangum Public Library, present name 1995; 14,000 vols; Librarian MARTHA YOUNG; Pres. PAULA BANISTER; Sec. BRENDA SCOTT.

Miami Public Library: 200 N Main St, Miami, OK 74354-5918; tel. (918) 541-2292; internet www.miami.lib.ok.us; Dir MARCIA JOHNSON; Head Librarian GAY FAIRCHILD; Chair. RON GILBERT; Sec. MICHELLE BASHORE.

Oklahoma Department of Libraries: 200 NE 18th St, Oklahoma City, OK 73105-3298; tel. (405) 521-2502; internet www.odl.state.ok.us; f. 1967; state archives, state and federal govt depository; incl. Jan Eric Cartwright Memorial Library, State Records Center, Allen Wright Memorial Library; Dir SUSAN C. MCVEY; Chair. HANNIBAL JOHNSON.

Oklahoma State University Libraries: 216 Library, Oklahoma State Univ., Stillwater, OK 74078-1071; tel. (405) 744-9775; e-mail okstatelibrary@hotmail.com; internet www.library.okstate.edu; f. 1953; 3 brs: Mary L. Williams Curriculum Materials Library, John Rex Cunningham Architecture Library and Veterinary Medicine Library; N Boomer Annex; 3,468,428 vols, 198,512 govt documents, 70,030 print and e-serials, 4,567,900 microforms, 321,418 maps, 799,332 ebooks; Dean of Libraries SHEILA GRANT JOHNSON.

Okmulgee Public Library: 218 S Okmulgee, Okmulgee, OK 74447; tel. (918) 756-1448; e-mail library@okmcity.net; internet www.okmulgeelibrary.org; bookmobile and inter-library services; genealogical colln; Dir KRISTIN CUNNINGHAM.

Ponca City Library: POB 1450, Ponca City, OK 74602; 516 E Grand, Ponca City, OK 74601; tel. (580) 767-0339; e-mail library@poncacityok.gov; internet www.poncacitylibrary.com; f. 1904; Matzene Art Colln of artwork from Oriental and Western art; Richard Gordon Matzene colln incl. oils, charcoals, and water colours and three-dimensional bronze and pottery pieces; 80,000 vols; Dir HOLLY LABOSSIERE.

Public Library of Enid and Garfield County: 120 W Maine, Enid, OK 73701; tel. (580) 234-6313; e-mail publiclibrary@enid.org; internet www.enid.org/index.aspx?page=62; f. 1959 by merger of Enid Public Library with Garfield County Library; Dir MICHELLE R. MEARS.

Stillwater Public Library: 1107 S Duck, Stillwater, OK 74074; tel. (405) 372-3633; e-mail askalibrarian@stillwater.org; internet library.stillwater.org; f. 1922; spec. collns: multi-language, graphic novels, genealogy, and local govt and historical documents; 90,000 vols; Chair. SUSAN SIMMONS; Dir LYNDA REYNOLDS.

Tulsa City-County Library: 400 Civic Center, Tulsa, OK 74103; tel. (918) 549-7323; internet www.tulsalibrary.org; 25 br. libraries; incl. Ruth G. Hardman Adult Literacy Services; 1,740,123 vols, 68,224 maps,

185,273 microforms, 524,669 govt documents; CEO GARY SHAFFER.

University of Oklahoma Libraries: 401 W Brooks St, Norman, OK 73019; tel. (405) 325-4142; e-mail librarian@ou.edu; internet libraries.ou.edu; f. 1892; depository for fed. govt documents since 1893; 5 brs; 5m. vols, 63,000 serials subscriptions, 17,000 linear ft of MSS and archives, 1.6m. photographs, 1.5m. maps, 70 incunabula; spec. collns: Western history, John and Mary Nichols Rare Books and Spec. Collns, Bass Business History Colln, History of Science Collns; Dean for Univ. Libraries RICHARD E. LUCE.

Oregon

Cedar Mill Community Library: 12505 NW Cornell Rd, Suite 13, Portland, OR 97229; tel. (503) 644-0043; e-mail askcarmill@wccls.org; internet library.cedarmill.org; f. 1974; 2 brs, 284,000 vols.

Chetco Community Public Library: 405 Alder St, Brookings, OR 97415; tel. (541) 469-7738; internet www.chetcolibrary.org; f. 1927; 70,000 vols (incl. books, DVDs, video cassettes, audiobooks, magazines and pamphlets); Chair. VIOLET LOVEJOY.

Eugene Public Library: 100 W 10th Ave, Eugene, OR 97401; tel. (541) 682-5450; e-mail libraryaskus@ci.eugene.or.us; internet www.eugene-or.gov; 400,000 vols (incl. CDs, DVDs, audio books, large print books, magazines and newspapers).

Jefferson County Library: 241 SE Seventh St, Madras, OR 97741; tel. (541) 475-3351; e-mail library@jcld.org; internet www.jcld.org; f. 1916; Library Dir DERESE HALL.

Multnomah County Library: 801 SW 10th Ave, Portland, OR 97205; tel. (503) 988-5402; internet www.multcolib.org; f. 1864; 19 brs; 2m. vols; Dir VAILEY OEHLKE.

Oregon State Library: 250 Winter St, NE, Salem, OR 97301-3950; tel. (503) 378-4243; e-mail library.help@state.or.us; internet www.oregon.gov/osl; f. 1905; develops local library services; provides service to state agencies and print-disabled persons; spec. collns: OR and OR authors; 1,140,680 vols; Librarian MARGIE HARRISON.

Springfield Public Library: 225 Fifth St, Springfield, OR 97477-4636; tel. (541) 726-3766; e-mail library@ci.springfield.or.us; internet www.ci.springfield.or.us/library; f. 1908; Dir ROB EVERETT.

University of Oregon Libraries: 1299 Univ. of Oregon, Eugene, OR 97403-1299; tel. (541) 346-3053; internet libweb.uoregon.edu; f. 1876; 3.1m. vols, 481,414 govt documents, 783,154 maps, 4.2m. microfilm units; 420,557 computer files; Dean of Libraries DEBORAH A. CARVER; Head of Licensing, Grants and Collns Analysis Assoc. Prof. DAVID C. FOWLER.

Wilsonville Public Library: 8200 SW Wilsonville Rd, Wilsonville, OR 97070; tel. (503) 682-2744; e-mail reference@wilsonvillelibrary.org; internet www.wilsonville.lib.or.us; access to over 1.5m. items from the Library Information Network of Clackamas County; 120,000 vols; Library Dir PATRICK DUKE.

Pennsylvania

Adams County Library System: 140 Baltimore St, Gettysburg, PA 17325; tel. (717) 334-5716; internet www.adamslibrary.org; incl. 6 libraries and 1 bookmobile; main br. Gettysburg.

American Philosophical Society Library: 105 S Fifth St, Philadelphia, PA 19106-3386; tel. (215) 440-3400; internet www.amphilsoc.org; f. 1743; nat. centre for research in the history of the sciences, medi-

cine and technology; MSS collns range from 18th-century natural history, American Indian linguistics and culture, to nuclear physics, computer devt and medical science; 350,000 vols, 11m. MSS, 250,000 images; spec. collns on Benjamin Franklin, Thomas Paine, history of science, genetics, quantum physics, Darwinism; Librarian MARTIN LEVITT; publ. *Bulletin* (2 a year).

Athenaeum of Philadelphia: 219 S Sixth St, Philadelphia, PA 19106; tel. (215) 925-2688; internet www.philaathenaeum.org; f. 1814; colln incl. history and antiquities of America and useful arts; resources incl. for the period of 1800–1945; Exec. Dir Dr SANDRA L. TATMAN.

Beaver County Library System: 109 Pleasant Dr., Suite 101, Aliquippa, PA 15001; tel. (724) 378-6227; e-mail foundationcenter@beaverlibraries.org; internet www.beaverlibraries.org; f. 1971; 11 public libraries and 1 bookmobile.

Carnegie Library of Pittsburgh: 4400 Forbes Ave, Pittsburgh, PA 15213-4080; tel. (412) 622-3114; e-mail info@carnegielibrary.org; internet www.carnegielibrary.org; f. 1895; 19 local brs; incl. main library and library for the blind and physically handicapped; 5,267,012 vols; Pres. and Dir MARY FRANCES COOPER.

Chester County Library System: 450 Exton Sq. Parkway, Exton, PA 19341; tel. (610) 280-2600; internet www.ccls.org; f. 1965; Dist. Center Library and 17 mem. libraries; Exec. Dir JOSEPH L. SHERWOOD; Pres. RICHARD HANKIN; Sec. BUCK JONES; Treas. JO ANN WEINBERGER.

Dauphin County Library System: 101 Walnut St, Harrisburg, PA 17101; tel. (717) 234-4961; e-mail exec-dir@dcls.org; internet www.dcls.org; incl. 8 libraries; 351,234 vols; Exec. Dir RICH BOWRA; Pres. BRUCE SENFT; Sec. CHRISTINE MUMMERT; Treas. Dr THOMAS CAREY.

David Library of the American Revolution: POB 748, Washington Crossing, PA 18977; 1201 River Rd, Washington Crossing, PA 18977; tel. (215) 493-6776; e-mail librarian@dlar.org; internet www.dlar.org; f. 1959, present bldg 1974; specialized research library for the study of American history c. 1750–1800; spec. colln incl. materials on women, families, African Americans and Native Americans, the French and Indian War and early nat. periods; 40,000 vols, 10,000 reels of microfilm; Chief Operating Officer MEG MCSWEENEY; Librarian KATHERINE A. LUDWIG; Treas. BARBARA B. FAHERTY.

Delaware County Library System: 340 N Middletown Rd, Fair Acres Bldg 19, Media, PA 19063; tel. (610) 891-8622; e-mail support@delcolibraries.org; internet www.delcolibraries.org; 26 libraries; 1.2m. vols; Exec. Dir DAVID BELANGER; Pres. L. JAMES BIDDLE; Sec. DAVID GALLO; Treas. VICTORIA GERSTENFELD.

Donald F. and Mildred Topp Othmer Library of Chemical History: 315 Chestnut St, Philadelphia, PA 19106; tel. (215) 873-8205; e-mail reference@chemheritage.org; internet www.chemheritage.org/research/library-research/index.aspx; f. 1988; attached to Chemical Heritage Foundation; rare books, oral histories, photographs about history of chemistry and related sciences and industries; spec. colln incl. alchemy, engineering, environmental topics, gen. science, industries, medicine, mining and chemical manufacturers, pathology, pharmacy and material medica, pharmacology, physics, physiology, technology, toxicology; Dir ELSA ATSON.

Ewell Sale Stewart Library and Archives of the Academy of Natural Sciences: 1900 Benjamin Franklin Parkway, Philadelphia, PA 19103-1195; tel. (215) 299-1040; e-mail library@ansp.org; internet www.ansp.org/library; f. 1812; attached to Drexel Univ.; works published in the 1500s to current serials and monographs from all over the world; expedition literature, incl. works of scientists such as Lewis and Clark and published journals of amateur naturalists; illustrated works in natural sciences, from the pre-Linnaean classics of Gesner, Aldrovandi and Catesby (published before 1750) to the great bird books of Gould, Audubon, Elliot and Wilson, and the flora of Redouté, Sowerby and the Bauers, to the modern masters of wildlife art, F. L. Jaques, L. A. Fuertes and Terence Shortt; 200,000 vols, 2,500 current periodicals, 250,000 MSS, 1m. archival items; Pres. and CEO GEORGE W. GEPHART, JR; Sec. JUDITH E. SOLTZ; Treas. DAVID P. LAZAR, SR.

Free Library of Philadelphia: Central Library, 1901 Vine St, Philadelphia, PA 19103-1189; tel. (215) 686-5322; internet www.library.phila.gov; f. 1891; 54 brs citywide, incl. 3 larger regional libraries and Library for the Blind and Physically Handicapped; spec. collns incl.: Fleisher orchestral music; Carson history of common law; Widener incunabula; Drinker Choral Library; Lewis Illuminated MSS, European and Oriental; History of the Automobile; Elkins Americana, Dickens, Goldsmith, Gimbel Poe; Lewis cuneiform tablets; theatre colln; map colln (over 130,000 single-sheet maps and atlases); 6m. items; Pres. and Dir SIOBHAN A. REARDON; Sec. DARWIN BEAUVAIS; Treas. MELISSA GRIMM.

Jenkins Law Library: 833 Chestnut St, Suite 1220, Philadelphia, PA 19107-4429; tel. (215) 574-7900; e-mail circulation@jenkinslaw.org; internet www.jenkinslaw.org; f. 1802 as Law Library Company of the City of Philadelphia; legal and non-legal resources, incl. fed. and state cases, statutes, regulations, court records and briefs and treatises; rare and out-of-print materials; 600,000 vols; Pres. ALEXANDER KERR; Exec. Dir and Sec. REGINA L. SMITH; Treas. HAROLD CRAMER.

Joseph P. Horner Memorial Library: German Soc. of Pennsylvania, 611 Spring Garden St, Philadelphia, PA 19123; tel. (215) 627-2332; e-mail librarian@germansociety.org; internet www.germansociety.org/library; f. 1783; attached to German Soc. of Pennsylvania; books in German language; books published after 1917; German-American Archive (10,000 books and pamphlets, 75 linear ft of MSS collns); 60,000 vols; Librarian CHRISSY BELLIZZI.

Library Company of Philadelphia: 1314 Locust St, Philadelphia, PA 19107; tel. (215) 546-3181; e-mail cking@librarycompany.org; internet www.librarycompany.org; f. 1731; American history and culture from the 17th through the 19th centuries; colln incl. rare books, MSS, broadsides, ephemera, prints, photographs and works of art; spec. colln incl. Afro-Americana; German-Americana; history of printing and publishing; American Judaica; printmaking, mapmaking, and photography in Philadelphia; libraries of James Logan and Benjamin Franklin; 500,000 vols; Dir Dr JOHN C. VAN HORNE; Librarian JAMES N. GREEN.

Pennsylvania Horticultural Society's McLean Library: 100 N 20th St, Philadelphia, PA 19103-1495; tel. (215) 988-8772; e-mail mcleanlibrary@pennhort.org; internet www.pennsylvaniahorticulturalsociety.org/garden/libraryhome.html; books and DVDs on gardening and plant care, botany, urban greening; rare gardening books; vintage seed catalogue colln and archives of the Soc. incl. Philadelphia Flower Show archives; 15,000 vols; Pres. DREW BECHER; publ. *Green Scene* (6 a year).

Pennsylvania State University Libraries: 510 Paterno Library, University Park, PA 16802-1812; tel. (814) 865-6368; e-mail s2w@psulias.psu.edu; internet www.libraries.psu.edu; f. 1859; 36 libraries at 24 locations throughout the Commonwealth of Pennsylvania; 5,441,121 vols, 430,694 maps, 3,553,455 microforms, 127,834 film and video materials, 47,000 online full-text journals and 125,000 ebooks; Dean of Libraries BARBARA I. DEWEY.

State Library of Pennsylvania: PA Dept of Education, Office of Commonwealth Libraries, Bureau of State Library, 607 S Dr., Harrisburg, PA 17120-0600; tel. (717) 783-5950; e-mail alubrecht@pa.gov; f. 1745; attached to PA Dept of Education; colln incl. American history, education, political science, sociology, library science, law and genealogy, PA history; PA newspapers, maps; spec. colln: original PA Assembly colln; 1.6m. vols; Dir ALICE LUBRECHT.

Union County Library System: 255 Reitz Blvd, Lewisburg, PA 17837; tel. (570) 523-1172; internet www.unioncountylibrarysystem.com; f. 1998; Public Library for Union Co, Lewisburg; Herr Memorial Library, Mifflinburg; West End Library, Laurelton; Pres. SUSAN JORDAN; Sec. and Treas. KAREN SHIPTON.

University of Pennsylvania Library: 3420 Walnut St, Philadelphia, PA 19104-6206; tel. (215) 898-7555; e-mail library@pobox.upenn.edu; internet www.library.upenn.edu; f. 1750; central library and 14 dept and affiliated libraries; incl. books on archaeology, anthropology, Leibniz, Descartes, history of philosophy and science, Lithuanian history and literature, history of chemistry, criminology, French Revolution, Judaica, modern Jewish history, modern Hebrew literature, Aristotelianism, Occam, medieval history, medieval Church history, Inquisition, Middle East and Islamic studies, Italian Renaissance literature, Spanish literature of the Golden Age, Shakespeareana (Furness Library), Restoration drama, 18th- and early 19th-century English fiction, American drama, fiction, and poetry; 6,096,588 vols; Vice-Provost and Dir of Libraries H. CARTON ROGERS.

University of Pittsburgh Libraries: Pittsburgh, PA 15260; tel. (412) 648-7747; internet www.pitt.edu/libraries.html; f. 1873; 22 separate libraries on or near main campus and 4 regional campus libraries in Bradford, Greensburg, Johnstown and Titusville; academic research library; 6.1m. vols, 5.4m. microforms, over 87,000 current serials, 5,500 ejournals, 200,000 ebooks; Dir RUSH MILLER.

US Army War College Library: 122 Forbes Ave, Carlisle, PA 17013-5220; tel. (717) 245-3660; e-mail usawc.libraryr@us.army.mil; internet www.carlisle.army.mil/library; military strategy and operations, int. relations, foreign policy, regional studies, management and economics; 171,800 vols, 450 ejournals, 500 print journal subscriptions.

Rhode Island

Brown University Library: Providence, RI 02912; tel. (401) 863-2165; e-mail libweb@brown.edu; internet dl.lib.brown.edu/libweb; f. 1764; incl. John D. Rockefeller, Jr, Library (research library for humanities, social sciences, fine arts), Sciences Library, Owing Music Library, John Hay Library (spec. collns, rare books, MSS archives), Art Slide Library; 6.8m. vols; Univ. Librarian HARRIETTE HEMMASI.

George Hail Free Library: 530 Main St, Warren, RI 02885; tel. (401) 245-7686; e-mail epatricrn@yahoo.com; internet www.georgehail.org; f. 1871; Pres. JOHN MILLARD; Dir PATRICIA REDFEARN.

Jamestown Philomenian Library: 26 N Rd, Jamestown, RI 02835; tel. (401) 423-7280; e-mail library@jamestownri.com; internet www.jamestownri.com/library; f. 1874; Pres. HEIDI KELLER MOON; Sec. CRAIG WATSON; Treas. DELIA KLINGBEIL; Dir DONNA FOGARTY.

John Carter Brown Library: Brown Univ., POB 1894, Providence, RI 02912; Brown Univ., 94 George St Providence, RI 02906; tel. (401) 863-2725; e-mail jcbl_information@brown.edu; internet www.jcbl.org; f. 1846, current location 1901; independently funded and administered centre for advanced research in history and the humanities at Brown Univ.; contains primary historical sources pertaining to the colonial period of the Americas 1492–1825; offers fellowships, sponsors lectures and confs; regularly mounts exhibitions and publishes catalogues, bibliographies, and other works that interpret its holdings; 50,000 rare books, 16,000 reference books; Dir Dr NEIL SAFIER.

North Kingstown Free Library: 100 Boone St, North Kingstown, RI 02852; tel. (401) 294-3306; internet www.nklibrary.org; f. 1898; 136,592 vols; Chair. RICK MOORE; Dir CYNDI DESROCHERS.

North Scituate Public Library: 606 W Greenville Rd, N Scituate, RI 02857; tel. (401) 647-5133; e-mail reference@scituatelibrary.org; internet scituatelibrary.org; f. 1906; Pres. JEFFREY AMYLON; Sec. TARA ANDERSON; Treas. PATIA BERTRAM; Dir LESLIE B. MCDONOUGH.

Providence Public Library: 150 Empire St, Providence, RI 02903; tel. (401) 455-8000; e-mail pplref@provlib.org; internet www.provlib.org; f. 1875; colln represents 4,000 years of human history and culture; Genealogy Coll: city directories, house directories, family biographies, Arnold's Vital Records and regimental histories of the Civil War; Rhode Island Colln: 10,000 books, 7,000 photographs of people, places and bldgs (print and online), historic and current maps pertaining to Rhode Island cities and towns, clippings, pamphlets, selected documents from the State of Rhode Island and the City of Providence; 40,000 vols (incl. books, MSS, pamphlets, ephemera, newspapers, maps, broadsides, art and artefacts), 15,000 scores and song books; Chair. WILLIAM S. SIMMONS; Sec. JULIUS KOLAWOLE; Treas. ELLEN K. HAYES; Dir DALE THOMPSON.

Providence Public Library: 150 Empire St, Providence, RI 02903; tel. (401) 455-8000; e-mail pplref@provlib.org; internet www.provlib.org; f. 1876; 1m. vols (incl. 40,000 books, MSS, pamphlets, ephemera, newspapers, maps, broadsides, art and artefacts representing over 4,000 years of human history and culture); Chair. WILLIAM S. SIMMONS; Dir M. DALE THOMPSON; publ. *Occasional Nuggets* (4 a year).

Tiverton Public Library: 238 Highland Rd, Tiverton, RI 02878; tel. (401) 625-6796; internet www.tivertonlibrary.org; brs: Essex Public Library and Union Br. Library; Chair. BARBARA DONNELLY; Dir ANN GREALISH-RUST.

South Carolina

Anderson County Library System: 300 N McDuffie St, POB 4047, Anderson, SC 29621; tel. (864) 260-4500; e-mail administration@

andersonlibrary.org; internet www .andersonlibrary.org; f. 1840; brs: Belton, Honea Path, Iva, Pendleton, Piedmont, Piedmont, Westside and Williamston; 1 main library and a bookmobile; 300,000 vols; an expanded video and audio book colln; music CD colln: 4,000 titles in classical, jazz, rock, blues, country, R&B, gospel, and bluegrass music, as well as Broadway shows and movie themes; Dir FAITH LINE.

Berkeley County Library System: 1003 Highway 52, Moncks cnr, SC 29461; tel. (843) 719-4223; e-mail bcls@berkeley.lib.sc.us; internet www.bcls.sc.gov; f. 1934; brs: Daniel Island, Sangaree, Goose Creek, Hanahan and St Stephen; Moncks Corner (HQ); Dir DONNA OSBORNE.

Charleston County Public Library: 68 Calhoun St, Charleston, SC 29401; tel. (843) 805-6930; internet www.ccpl.org; f. 1930; 16 brs; 1 bookmobile; Jerry and Anita Zucker Holocaust Colln: books and CDs on Nazi persecution and destruction of European Jewry and other minorities; Shoah Visual History Colln; Exec. Dir DOUGLAS HENDERSON; Chair. JANET SEGAL; Sec. MAYA HOLLINSHEAD; Treas. STEVEN E. CLEM.

Darlington County Library System: 204 N Main St, Darlington, SC 29532; tel. (843) 398-4940; internet www.darlington-lib.org; f. 1968; Darlington (HQ), Hartsville, Lamar and Society Hill; Chair. JENELLE DAVIS; Sec. and Treas. ANNE BALDWIN; Dir NANCY RAY.

Florence County Library System: 509 S Dargan St, Florence, SC 29506; tel. (843) 662-8424; e-mail reference@florencelibrary .org; internet www.florencelibrary.org; f. 1903; 1 main library (Florence), 5 brs (Johnsonville, Lake City, Olanta, Pamplico and Timmonsville), 1 bookmobile; Chair. CHARLES HOWLE; Sec. and Treas. ANGELA LORENZ.

Greenville County Library System: 25 Heritage Green Pl., Greenville, SC 29601; tel. (864) 242-5000; e-mail maincirc@ greenvillelibrary.org; internet www .greenvillelibrary.org; f. 1921; 11 brs and 1 bookmobile; colln of materials that assist researchers interested in historical and genealogical research; 737,547 vols, 170,532 audio and visual items; Chair. DOUGLAS A. CHURDAR; Sec. SUSAN BARRY; Treas. S. ALLAN HILL; Exec. Dir BEVERLY JAMES.

Horry County Memorial Library: 1008 Fifth Ave, Conway, SC 29526; tel. (843) 248-1544; internet www.horry.lib.sc.us; f. 1949; brs: Conway (HQ), Aynor, Bucksport, Green Sea/Floyds, Little River, Loris, North Myrtle Beach, Socastee and Surfside Beach; bookmobile; Dir CLIFTON BOYER.

Marion County Library: 101 E Court St, Marion, SC 29571; tel. (843) 423-8300; e-mail marionlibr@spiritcom.net; internet www .marioncountylibrary.org; f. 1898; brs: Marion (HQ), Mullins and Nichols; 1 bookmobile; 86,534 vols; Chair. H. PAUL DOVE, JR; Sec. ESTHER W. ROGERS; Treas. VIOLA D. EDWARDS.

Oconee County Public Library: 501 W S Broad St, Walhalla, SC 29691-2105; tel. (864) 638-4133; internet www.youseemore.com/ oconee; f. 1948; brs: Walhalla (HQ), Salem, Seneca and Westminster; 1 mobile library; S Carolina history and local genealogy colln; family histories, historical maps, cemetery listings and indexes, biographies of noted South Carolinians and local newspapers on microfilm; Dir SUE BALDWIN.

Orangeburg County Library: 510 Louis St, Orangeburg, SC 29115; tel. (803) 531-4636; e-mail oclnotify@orangeburgcounty .org; internet www.orangeburgcounty.org/ ocl; f. 1936; incl. libraries in Orangeburg,

North, Holly Hill, Elloree, Santee and Springfield; Dir ROBERTA R. BIBBINS.

Richland County Public Library: 1431 Assembly St, Columbia, SC 29201; tel. (803) 799-9084; internet www.richland.lib.sc.us; f. 1896; incl. Main Library and 10 brs; 1.1m. books; 900 magazine titles in print; 15,000 online magazine titles; 150 newspaper titles; 90,000 video cassettes, DVDs and CDs; 80 electronic databases; Exec. Dir MELANIE HUGGINS.

South Carolina State Library: POB 11469, Columbia, SC 29211; tel. (803) 734-8026; e-mail reference@statelibrary.sc.gov; internet www.statelibrary.sc.gov; f. 1929, present name and status 1969; fed. depository library since 1970; colln of pubns on governance, management and admin., applied technology, history and social sciences; 303,681 vols, 264,144 federal documents, 94,564 state documents and 651,842 microforms, 2,088 periodicals, 4,553 audiovisual; Dir DAVID GOBLE; Chair. DAN B. MACKEY.

York County Library: 138 E Black St, Rock Hill, SC 29730; tel. (803) 981-5858; internet www.yclibrary.org; f. 1966; brs: Rock Hill (HQ), Clover, Fort Mill, Lake Wylie and York; books, periodicals, audio books, DVDs and video cassettes; book mobile: 3,000 vols; Dir COLLEEN KAPHENGST.

South Dakota

Brookings Public Library: 515 Third St, Brookings, SD 57006; tel. (605) 692-9407; internet www.brookingslibrary.org; f. 1911; Dir ELVITA LANDAU.

Deadwood Public Library: 435 Williams St, Deadwood, SD 57732-2821; tel. (605) 578-2821; e-mail dwd@sdln.net; internet dwdlib .sdln.net; f. 1876; Dir JEANETTE CHANEY-MOODIE; Librarian CAROL HAUCK.

Grant County Public Library: 207 E Park Ave, Milbank, SD 57252; tel. (605) 432-6543; e-mail gclibrary21@hotmail.com; internet grantcountylibrary.com; f. 1979; 1 main library and 4 brs; Dir ROBIN SCHRUPP; Pres. MARJORIE BOHN.

Rapid City Public Libraries: 610 Quincy St, Rapid City, SD 57701-3630; tel. (605) 394-6139; internet www.rcgov.org/library; f. 1879; 2 brs; Dir GRETA CHAPMAN.

South Dakota State Archives: 900 Governors Dr., Pierre, SD 57501; tel. (605) 773-3804; e-mail archref@state.sd.us; internet history.sd.gov/archives; f. 1975; attached to SD State Historical Soc.; collects, appraises, accessions, describes, organizes, preserves, determines significance, and makes available MSS collns, SD state, county, and town govt records, photographs, maps and other archival materials that have permanent historical and research value; 12,000 cu ft of records documenting SD's history and heritage; State Archivist CHELLE SOMSEN; Govt Archivist VIRGINIA HANSON; Govt Archivist SARA CASPER.

South Dakota State Library: MacKay Bldg, 800 Governors Dr., Pierre, SD 57501; tel. (605) 773-3131; e-mail library@state.sd .us; internet library.sd.gov; state govt publ. depository; 3,403,015 vols; State Librarian DAN SIEBERSMA; Pres. JUDY TRZYNKA.

South Dakota State University Library: POB 2115, Brookings, SD 57007; Briggs Library, SDSU, 1300 N Campus Dr., Brookings, SD 57007; tel. (605) 688-5107; internet www.sdstate.edu/library; incl. archives and spec. colln of MSS and archival materials, books, serials, audiovisual materials, artefacts and photographs related to S Dakota history and life; Chief Univ. Librarian Prof. Dr KRISTI TORNQUIST.

University of South Dakota Libraries: 414 E Clark St, Vermillion, SD 57069; tel. (605) 677-5373; e-mail library@usd.edu; internet www.usd.edu/library; incl. archives and spec. colln; pre-1900 US govt publs and resources; genealogy colln; spec. collns: Chilson Colln (materials related to local histories, S Dakota history and Native American cultures), Mahoney Music Colln (violin and violin family instruments), Richardson Colln (MSS collns focusing on S Dakota's cultural, political and economic history), USD Photograph Colln; 488,000 vols; Dean of Univ. Libraries Dr ANNE COOPER MOORE.

Watertown Regional Library: POB 250, Watertown, SD 57201-0250; 160 Sixth St, NE, Watertown, SD 57201-0250; tel. (605) 882-6220; e-mail adminwat@sdln.net; internet watweb.sdln.net; f. 1899; Pres. JUDY TRZYNKA.

Yankton Community Library: 515 Walnut St, Yankton, SD 57078; tel. (605) 668-5275; e-mail ycllibrary@sdln.net; internet www.cityofyankton.org/yankton/library; f. 1868, present location 1974; 70,000 vols, 150 magazine and newspaper subscriptions; Dir KATHY JACOBS; Pres. ALICIA CORNEMANN.

Tennessee

C. E. Weldon Public Library: 100 Main St., Martin, TN 38237; tel. (731) 587-3148; e-mail cew@ceweldonlibrary.org; internet www.ceweldonlibrary.org; f. 1925 as Woman's Club Library, present name and status 1984; colln incl. genealogical files, large print books, video cassettes, CDs, DVDs, audio books and microfilms; 40,000 vols; Dir ROBERTA PEACOCK.

Clarksville Montgomery County Public Library: 350 Pageant Lane, Suite 501, Clarksville, TN 37040; tel. (931) 648-8826; e-mail librarydirector@clarksville.org; internet cmc-websvr.clarksville.org; f. 1894, present name and status 1959; colln incl. genealogy, periodicals, audio books; Dir MARTHA HENDRICKS.

Jean and Alexander Heard Library: 419 21st Ave S, Nashville, TN 37203-2427; tel. (615) 322-7100; internet www.library .vanderbilt.edu; f. 1873; attached to Vanderbilt Univ.; housed in central, science and engineering, biomedical, divinity, education, law, management and music libraries; 3.5m. vols, 3.1m. microform, 1.2m. digital colln, 266,061 govt publs and 55,260 periodicals; Dean of Libraries CONNIE VINITA DOWELL.

Johnson City Public Library: 100 W Millard St, Johnson City, TN 37604; tel. (423) 434-4450; e-mail info@jcpl.net; internet www.jcpl.net; f. 1895; 125,000 vols; Pres. POLLY PETERSON; Sec. MICHAEL CLARK; Dir BOB SWANAY.

Knox County Public Library: 500 W Church Ave, Knoxville, TN 37902; tel. (865) 215-8750; e-mail reference@knoxlib.org; internet knoxrooms.sirsi.net; f. 1873; 20 facilities; local history and genealogy colln; 1m. books, periodicals, CDs, films and audio books; Dir MYRETTA BLACK.

Lawrence County Public Library: 519 E Gaines St, Lawrenceburg, TN 38464; tel. (931)-762-4627; e-mail librarian@co .lawrence.tn.us; internet www .lawcopubliclibrary.com; f. 1941; colln incl. items on genealogy; Dir TERESA NEWTON.

Memphis Public Library & Information Center: 3030 Poplar Ave, Memphis, TN 38111-3527; tel. (901) 415-2749; internet www.memphislibrary.org; f. 1893; 18 brs; CATV and colour videotaping studio; information and referral service (LINC-Library Information Center); 4.5m. vols; Dir KEENON McCLOY; publ. *Kaleidoscope* (12 a year).

Nashville Public Library: 615 Church St, Nashville, TN 37219; tel. (615) 862-5800; internet www.library.nashville.org; f. 1903; 21 brs; audiobooks on audio cassettes and CDs; govt documents colln; spec. colln: historic colln of non-book materials, from newspaper photographs and recordings made by civil rights-era leaders, to an 1857 map of Nashville drawn by bookseller William A. Eichbaum and a hand-blocked poster promoting Helen Hayes' appearance at the Ryman Auditorium in the 1930s; Wilson Limited Editions Colln: 800 books dating from 1929 to the present; Chair. MARGARET ANN ROBINSON; Dir DONNA NICELY.

Tennessee State Library and Archives: 403 Seventh Ave N, Nashville, TN 37243-1102; tel. (615) 741-2764; e-mail reference .tsla@tn.gov; internet www.tennessee.gov/ tsla; colln incl. county records and MSS, bibliographies; photographs depicting Tennessee; records dating back to 1763; 50,000 vols, 70 magazines; State Librarian and Archivist CHARLES A. SHERRILL.

University of Tennessee, Knoxville Libraries: 607 John C. Hodges Library, 1015 Volunteer Blvd, Knoxville, TN 37996-1000; tel. (865) 974-6600; e-mail eref@utk .edu; internet www.lib.utk.edu; f. 1794; spec. collns incl. Tennesseana, North American Indians; 3.5m. vols; Dean STEVE SMITH.

Watauga Regional Library: 2700 S Roan St, Suite 435, Johnson City, TN 37601; tel. (423) 926-2951; e-mail nrenfro@wrlibrary .org; internet www.wrlibrary.org; consortium of libraries in Carter, Greene, Johnson, Sullivan, Unicoi and Washington counties; not open to the public; Dir NANCY RENFRO.

Texas

Amarillo Public Library: 413 E Fourth, Amarillo, TX 79101; tel. (806) 378-3054; e-mail reference@amarillolibrary.org; internet www.amarillolibrary.org; Downtown (central library); brs: SW, E, N and NW; 800,000 vols (incl. books, magazines and media materials).

Austin Public Library: POB 2287, Austin, TX 78768-2287; tel. (512) 974-7400; internet www.ci.austin.tx.us/library; f. 1926; 20 brs; system maintains a comprehensive colln of books, magazines, newspapers, recordings, audio cassettes and video cassettes; Austin History Center contains materials on history of Austin and Travis County; 4,316,785 vols; Dir BRENDA BRANCH.

Bastrop Public Library: 1100 Church St, Bastrop, TX 78602; tel. (512) 321-5441; e-mail genealogy@bastroplibrary.org; internet www.bastroplibrary.org; f. 1852, closed 1927, reopened 1971; 48,500 vols; Pres. MARY JO JENKINS; Dir MICKEY DUVALL.

Bedford Public Library: 2424 Forest Ridge Dr., Bedford, TX 76021; tel. (817) 952-2330; internet lib.bedford.tx.us; f. 1964; 100,000 vols; Man. MARIA REDBURN.

Brazoria County Library System: 451 N Velasco, Suite 250, Angleton, TX 77515; tel. (979) 864-1505; e-mail bcls@bcls.lib.tx.us; internet www.bcls.lib.tx.us; 12 libraries; Pres. MATINA BONNEN; Sec. STEWART COFFMAN; Library Dir DAVID THRASH.

Brownsville Public Library System: 2600 Central Blvd, Brownsville, TX 78521; tel. (956) 548-1055; e-mail ask@brownsville .lib.tx.us; internet www2.youseemore.com/ brownsville; f. 1906; brs: Central and Southmost; 200,000 vols.

Central Texas Library System, Inc.: 1005 W 41st St, Suite 100, Austin, TX 78756; tel. (512) 583-0704; e-mail pat.tuohy@ctls.net; internet www.ctls.net; f. 1969; 79 mem. libraries; Chair. PEGGY GIBSON; Sec. LYLE

THORMANN; Treas. EILEEN ALTMILLER; Exec. Dir PATRICIA TUOHY.

Dallas Public Library: 1515 Young St, Dallas, TX 75201-5415; tel. (214) 670-1760; e-mail askalibrarian@dallaslibrary.org; internet www.dallaslibrary.org; f. 1901, present bldg 1954; 6,143,644 vols; Dir CORRINE HILL.

Fort Bend County Libraries: 1001 Golfview, Richmond, TX 77469; tel. (281) 342-4455; e-mail genref@fortbend.lib.tx.us; internet www.fortbend.lib.tx.us; f. 1948; 9 brs; George Memorial Library (HQ); microfilm newspaper colln incl. Herald Coaster (since 1920s); foreign language colln; Dir CLARA RUSSELL.

Fort Worth Public Library: 500 W Third St, Fort Worth, TX 76102-7305; tel. (817) 392-7705; e-mail librarywebmail@ fortworthlibrary.org; internet www .fortworthlibrary.org; f. 1901; 15 brs; spec. collns: genealogy, local history, sheet music, postcards, bookplates; US and Texas govt depository; 2,066,000 vols; Dir Dr GLENIECE A. ROBINSON.

George H. W. Bush Presidential Library and Museum: 1000 George Bush Dr. W, College Station, TX 77845; tel. (979) 691-4000; e-mail library.bush@nara.gov; internet bushlibrary.tamu.edu; f. 1997; museum of 100,000 items related to the life and career of Pres. George H. W. Bush (1989–93) incl. 3,000 gifts received; museum classroom; art and essay contests; 44m. documents, 2m. photographs, 10,000 video cassettes, sound recordings; Dir Dr WARREN L. FINCH, JR.

Harris County Public Library: 8080 El Rio St, Houston, TX 77054; tel. (713) 749-9000; internet www.hcpl.net; 26 brs; 2,312,482 vols, incl. traditional printed books, magazines, newspapers, video cassettes, CDs and DVDs; Dir RHODA GOLDBERG; Man. for Br. Services BRUCE FARRAR.

Houston Area Library System: 500 McKinney St, Suite 400, Houston, TX 77002-5000; tel. (832) 393-1397; internet www.hals.lib.tx.us; mem. libraries across 28 counties in SE Texas; Library Chief and Coordinator ELIZABETH SWAN.

Houston Public Library: 500 McKinney St, Houston, TX 77002; tel. (832) 393-1300; e-mail website@hpl.lib.tx.us; internet www .houstonlibrary.org; f. 1854 as Houston Lyceum, present status 1904; 35 brs; spec. collns: Bibles, Civil War, Salvation Army posters, early Houston photographs, early printing and illuminated MSS, juvenile literature, petroleum, sheet music, Texana, US and Texas depository; specializes in genealogy, art, architecture, business, management; jazz, Afro-American and Hispanic archives; 3.6m. items; Dir of Libraries RHEA BROWN LAWSON.

Jacksonville Public Library: 502 S Jackson St, Jacksonville, TX 75766; tel. (903) 586-7664; internet www.jacksonvillelibrary.com; f. 1913; colln on geneaology; 65,000 vols; Dir BARBARA CROSSMAN.

Lyndon Baines Johnson Library & Museum: 2313 Red River St, Austin, TX 78705; tel. (512) 721-0200; e-mail johnson .library@nara.gov; internet www.lbjlibrary .org; f. 1971; administered by Nat. Archives and Records Admin.; audiovisual colln documenting Lyndon B. Johnson's life, career and presidency; spec. colln incl. vols on American politics and history; 45m. pages of historical documents; Dir MARK K. UPDEGROVE.

Midland County Public Library: 301 W Missouri, Midland, TX 79701; tel. (432) 688-4320; e-mail circulation@co.midland.tx.us; internet www.co.midland.tx.us/lib; f. 1928;

Downtown Library, Centennial Library (HQ) and Law Library; Dir JOHN TRISCHITTI.

Port Arthur Public Library: 4615 Ninth Ave, Port Arthur, TX 77642-5818; tel. (409) 985-2238; internet www.pap.lib.tx.us; spec. colln of historic photographs on Port Arthur history; 140,000 vols (incl. 15,000 books on genealogy), 3,500 DVDs and VHS, 2,000 CDs; Dir JOSE MARTINEZ.

Quitman Public Library: POB 1677, Quitman, TX 75783-1677; 202 E Goode St, Quitman, TX 75783; tel. (903) 763-4191; e-mail quitmanlibrarian@gmail.com; internet www .quitmanlibrary.org; genealogy colln; 30,000 vols; Dir DELENE H. ALLEN.

Seguin-Guadalupe County Public Library: 707 E College St, Seguin, TX 78155; tel. (830) 401-2422; e-mail library@ seguintexas.gov; internet www.seguin.lib.tx .us; local history and genealogy research materials; historic photographs and microfilmed copies of local newspapers dating back to 1847; 60,000 vols; Chair. MICHELLE JOHNSON; Dir JACKI GROSS.

Sevier County Public Library System: 408 High St, Sevierville, TX 37862; tel. (865) 453-3532; e-mail dvess@sevierlibrary.org; internet www.sevierlibrary.org; f. 1968; brs: King Family, Kodak and Seymour; Chair. DAVID SARTEN; Treas. JUDY GODFREY; Dir ROBIN COGDILL.

University of Texas Libraries: University of Texas at Austin, POB P, Austin, TX 78713-8916; tel. (512) 495-4350; e-mail lib-hr@lib .utexas.edu; internet www.lib.utexas.edu; f. 1883; 8m. vols, also Arlington: 893,155 vols, El Paso: 746,308 vols, Permian Basin: 215,945 vols, San Antonio: 367,583 vols, Health Science Center, Houston: 54,000 vols, Health Science Center, Dallas: 224,732 vols, Health Science Center, Dallas: 224,732 vols, Health Science Center, San Antonio: 173,143 vols, Medical Br., Galveston: 291,326; Vice-Provost and Dir Dr FRED HEATH.

Weatherford Public Library: 1014 Charles St, Weatherford, TX 76086; tel. (817) 598-4150; e-mail libinfo@ci .weatherford.tx.us; internet www.wpltx.com; spec. genealogy colln on Weatherford, Parker co and Texas; fed. census for Texas from 1850 to 1930; microfilm of local newspapers since 1901; 90,000 vols; Dir DALE FLEEGER.

William T. Cozby Public Library: 177 N Heartz Rd, Coppell, TX 75019; tel. (972) 304-3655; e-mail library@coppelltx.gov; internet www.coppelltx.gov/library; f. 1974; 93,000 vols, 170 periodicals and newspapers; Dir VICTORIA CHIAVETTA.

Utah

Brigham City Carnegie Library: 26 E Forest St, Brigham City, UT 84302; tel. (435) 723-5850; e-mail brighamlibrary@gmail.com; internet bcpl.lib.ut.us; f. 1898; Dir SUE HILL.

City Library: 210 E 400S, Salt Lake City, UT 84111; tel. (801) 524-8200; internet www .slcpl.lib.ut.us; f. 1851; 5 brs; 1m. vols; Dir LINDA HAMILTON (acting).

Family History Library of the Church of Jesus Christ of Latter-day Saints: 35 N West Temple St, Salt Lake City, UT 84150-3400; tel. (866) 406-1830; e-mail fhl@ ldschurch.org; internet www.familysearch .org; f. 1894; 356,000 bound vols, 2.4m. reels of microfilm, 727,000 microfiches, 4,500 periodicals and 3,725 e-resources; Dir DON ANDERSON.

Giovale Library: 1840 S 1300E, Salt Lake City, UT 84105; tel. (801) 832-2250; internet www.westminstercollege.edu/library; attached to Westminster College; Dir DIANE VANDERPOL.

J. Willard Marriott Library: 295 S 1500E, Salt Lake City, UT 84112-0860; tel. (801) 581-8558; internet www.lib.utah.edu; f. 1850, present name 1969; attached to Univ. of Utah; spec. collns: archives, Middle East, MSS, rare books, W Americana, oral history; US state and UN documents depository; 3,159,576 vols, 86,266 serials; Dean and Univ. Librarian (vacant) JOYCE L. OGBURN.

Orem Public Library: 58 N State St, Orem, UT 84057; tel. (801) 229-7050; internet lib .orem.org; 285,000 vols, 13,000 video cassettes, 20,000 DVDs, 31,000 CDs.

Park City Library: 1255 Park Ave, Park City, UT 84060; tel. (435) 615-5600; internet www.parkcitylibrary.org; f. 1888, present location 1993; 71,164 vols; Library Dir LINDA TILLSON.

President Millard Fillmore Library: 25 S 100W, Fillmore, UT 84631; tel. (435) 743-5314; e-mail info@fillmorelibrary.org; internet www.fillmorelibrary.org; f. 1925; Dir STEPHANIE ALEMAN.

Utah State Library Division: 250 N, 1950W, Suite A, Salt Lake City, UT 84116-7901; tel. (801) 715-6777; internet library .utah.gov; f. 1957; Library Dir DONNA JONES MORRIS.

Vermont

Bennington Free Library: 101 Silver St, Bennington, VT 05201; tel. (802) 442-9051; e-mail reference@bfli.org; internet www .benningtonfreelibrary.org; f. 1865; colln on history of Bennington and Vermont; 57,000 vols (incl. books, periodicals and research materials); Dir LYNNE FONTENEAU McCANN.

John G. McCullough Free Library: 2 Main St, POB 339, North Bennington, VT 05257; tel. (802) 447-7121; e-mail mclibrary@ comcast.net; internet www.mccullough.lib.vt .us; f. 1921; colln incl. periodicals and newspapers, biography and reference books, CDs (music and audio books), books on audio cassettes, DVDs and video cassettes, large print books; 20,000 vols; Chair. PRESTON McADOO; Sec. VIRGINIA SANDY; Treas. RACHEL SCHUMACHER; Dir SUSANNE WARREN.

Kellogg-Hubbard Library: 135 Main St, Montpelier, VT 05602; tel. (802) 223-3338; e-mail info@kellogghubbard.org; internet www.kellogghubbard.org; f. 1885; remnants of Ancient Greece and Renaissance Italy; Pres. JOHN PAGE; Sec. JESSICA TURNER; Treas. TANYA MOREHOUSE; Dir ROBIN SALES.

Pierson Library: 5376 Shelburne Rd, Shelburne, VT 05482; tel. (802) 985-5124; e-mail pierson@vals.state.vt.us; internet www .piersonlibrary.org; f. 1888, present name 1922, present bldg 2001; 32,000 vols and 104 periodicals; Chair. MELISSA FLETCHER; Treas. MARLEEN MOORE; Dir KIP ROBERSON.

St. Albans Free Library: 11 Maiden Lane, Saint Albans, VT 05478; tel. (802) 524-1507; e-mail stalbans@vals.state.vt.us; internet www.stalbans.lib.vt.us; f. 1855 as Vermont Central Railroad Library Asscn, present bldg 1902; colln incl. Vermont town histories; US Census on microfilm (1810–1910) and information for family researchers; Chair. D. JOE DAVISON; Sec. DONNA HOWARD; Treas. LINDA LANG.

Stowe Free Library: 90 Pond St, Stowe, VT 05672; tel. (802) 253-6145; internet www .stowelibrary.org; f. 1866; 34,000 vols, 3,700 film titles, 1,400 audio books on CDs, 200 music CDs, 100 magazine, journal and newspaper subscriptions; Dir CINDY WEBER; Sec. ELIZABETH WECHSLER.

University of Vermont Libraries: 538 Main St, Burlington, VT 05405-0036; tel. (802) 656-2023; e-mail bhref@uvm.edu; internet library.uvm.edu; Bailey/Howe

Library houses spec. collns of Vermont materials, rare books, govt documents and maps, and univ. archives; Dana Medical Library; Library Research Annex; 1,523,977 vols, 1,123,993 govt documents, 2,037,527 microforms, 220,637 graphic materials; Dean of Libraries and Information Services MARA SAULE.

Howard and Alba Leahy Library: 60 Washington St, Barre, VT 05641-4209; tel. (802) 479-8500; e-mail vhs-info@state.vt.us; internet www.vermonthistory.org; f. 2002 as Vermont Historical Society Library, present name 2007; collns of books and pamphlets dating from 1770; large genealogical colln; Librarian PAUL CARNAHAN; publ. *Vermont History* (1 a year).

Vermont State Archives and Records Administration Vermont Office of the Secretary of State: 1078 Route 2, Middlesex, Montpelier, VT 05633-7701; tel. (802) 828-3700; e-mail archives@sec.state.vt.us; internet vermont-archives.org; f. 2008 by merger of Vermont State Archives and Div. of Public Records, Dept of Bldgs and Gen. Services; Sec. of State JAMES C. CONDOS; State Archivist GREGORY SANFORD; publ. *Records and Information Management Update* (4 a year).

Westford Public Library: 1717 Vermont Route 128, POB 86, Westford, VT 05494; tel. (802) 878-5639; e-mail westford_pl@vals .state.vt.us; internet www.westford.lib.vt.us; f. 1895, present bldg 1974; colln on Westford, Chittenden co and Vermont history; large print books and magazines; Chair. LINELL VILASECA; Sec. PETER JONES; Treas. ANDREA LETORNEY; Librarian VICTORIA TIBBITS.

Virginia

Alexandria Library: 5005 Duke St, Alexandria, VA 22304-2903; tel. (703) 746-1702; internet www.alexandria.lib.va.us; f. 1794; 4 brs; spec. colln incl. historical materials related to Alexandria and Northern Virginia; historical photographs; govt documents on Civil War; microfilm of local newspapers; rare book colln of Alexandria Library Company and journals on history, genealogy and historic preservation; 300,000 vols, 3,000 audiovisual materials (Charles E. Beatley, Jr, Central Library); 110,000 vols (Kate Waller Barrett Br.); 18,000 books and audiovisual materials (Ellen Coolidge Burke Br.); 75,000 books and audio-visual materials (James M. Duncan Br.); Chair. DOROTHY KOOPMAN; Sec. GWENDOLYN DAY-FULLER; Treas. ANNE PAUL; Dir for Libraries ROSE T. DAWSON.

Fairfax County Public Library: 12000 Government Center Parkway, Suite 324, Fairfax, VA 22035-0012; tel. (703) 324-3100; e-mail wwwlib@fairfaxcounty.gov; internet www.co.fairfax.va.us/library; f. 1939; 21 brs; also CD-ROMs, microfilm, audio and video cassettes, periodicals, recorded and talking books, CATV hook-up; 3m. vols; Dir EDWIN S. CLAY, III.

Fauquier County Public Library: Old Town Warrenton, 11 Winchester St, Warrenton, VA 20186; tel. (540) 422-8500; internet www.fauquiercounty.gov/government/ departments/library; f. 1969; brs: Warrenton, Bealeton, John Marshall and New Baltimore; 210,625 vols; Chair. BARBARA SEVERIN; Sec. and Treas. JACK WHITING.

Hampton Public Library: 4207 Victoria Blvd, Hampton, VA 23669; tel. (757) 727-1154; internet www.hamptonpubliclibrary .org; f. 1926; colln on Virginia and Hampton history; local newspapers on microfilm; current City of Hampton documents; brs: Main, Northampton, Phoebus, Willow Oaks and

George Wythe Law; 1 bookmobile; 316,828 vols; Dir ROBERT CARPENTER.

Jefferson-Madison Regional Library: 201 E Market St, Charlottesville, VA 22902; tel. (434) 979-7151; e-mail reference@jmrl .org; internet www.jmrl.org; f. 1972; 9 brs and 1 bookmobile; 500,000 vols; spec. colln incl. Roland E. Beauford, Sr African-American colln by or about African-Americans; periodicals, photographs, MSS and maps on community history; newspapers and magazines on microfilm; Pres. TIMOTHY F. JOST TOLSON; Dir JOHN HALLIDAY.

Jones Memorial Library: 2311 Memorial Ave, Lynchburg, VA 24501; tel. (434) 846-0501; e-mail refdesk@jmlibrary.org; internet www.jmlibrary.org; f. 1908; specializes in genealogy and local history; Lynchburg newspapers on microfilms; co histories and court records, family histories and genealogies; 300 MSS.

Library of Virginia: 800 E Broad St, Richmond, VA 23219-8000; tel. (804) 692-3500; internet www.lva.virginia.gov; f. 1823, present location 1997; Virginia, Southern US history, Civil War, genealogy; NewsBank's America's Newspapers which offers current and archived edns of more than 600 local, regional, and nat. newspapers; archive colln of 55,000 cu ft; 700,000 vols, 834 current periodicals; Librarian SANDRA GIOIA TREADWAY; publ. *Virginia Cavalcade.*

Mariners' Museum Library: 100 Museum Dr., Newport News, VA 23606-3759; tel. (757) 591-7782; e-mail library@ marinersmuseum.org; internet www .mariner.org/library; f. 1933; library of materials related to human interaction with the world's waterways; spec. collns: Edwin Levick Colln of photographs of passenger ships, yachts, and America's Cup Races; A. Aubrey Bodine Colln of images of life on Chesapeake Bay; Chris-Craft Colln documenting the construction of boats by one of America's most important pleasure boat builders; 1,750,000 vols (incl. books, magazines, rare books, MSS, maps and charts, vessel plans, newspaper articles, photographs, Chris-Craft archives, and The Mariners' Museum's archives); Dir SUSAN BERG.

Norfolk Public Library: 1155 Pineridge Rd, Norfolk, VA 23502; tel. (757) 664-7328; e-mail npl.comments@norfolk.gov; internet www.npl.lib.va.us; f. 1904; ltd Fed. Govt Depository; brs: Norfolk Main, Sargeant Memorial Room, Barron F. Black, Blyden, Horace C. Downing, Janaf, Jordan-Newby, Lafayette, Larchmont, Little Creek, Park Place, Mary D. Pretlow Anchor and Van Wyck; bookmobile; colln incl. classic and popular items since late 19th century; Dir NORMAN L. MAAS.

Patent and Trademark Office Scientific and Technical Information Center: Remsen Bldg, Lobby Level, Room 1D58, 400 Dulany St, Alexandria, VA; tel. (571) 272-2520; e-mail usptoinfo@uspto.gov; internet www.uspto.gov; f. 1836; foreign patent documents in electronic, print, and micro formats since 1617 from 73 countries; 200,000 vols; Dir of the US Patent and Trademark Office DAVID KAPPOS; Commr for Patents ROBERT L. STOLL; Commr for Trademarks DEBORAH COHN.

Richmond Public Library: 101 E Franklin St, Richmond, VA 23219; tel. (804) 646-4256; internet www.richmondpubliclibrary.org; f. 1924; 1 main library and 8 brs; 810,066 vols; Chair. CLARE OSDENE SCHAPIRO; Dir HARRIET HENDERSON COALTER.

University of Virginia Library: POB 400113, Charlottesville, VA 22904-4113; tel. (804) 924-3021; e-mail library@virginia.edu; internet www.lib.virginia.edu; f. 1819; 5.1m.

vols, 53,015 journals, 150,362 maps, 447,020 slides and photographs, 87,642 video and audio recordings, 70,000 CDs, 16m. MSS and archives; spec. collns incl. American history and literature, incl. McGregor Library of American History and the Barrett Library of American Literature, Massey-Faulkner colln, Streeter colln on Southeastern railways, optics, evolution, Thomas Jefferson, Scott Sporting Colln, Victorian fiction, Greek and Latin literature, music, int. law, history of printing, Gothic novels, Matthew Arnold, Jorge Luis Borges colln, Gordon colln of French books, Tibetan colln, Paul Mellon colln of Americana and Virginiana; Librarian KARIN WITTENBORG.

US Geological Survey Libraries Program: 12201 Sunrise Valley Dr., MS 950, Reston, VA 20192; tel. (703) 648-4301; e-mail library@usgs.gov; internet library.usgs.gov; f. 1879; incl. 5 brs at Denver, CO, Flagstaff, AZ, Lafayette, LA, Menlo Park, CA and Reston, VA; part of Core Science Systems within USGS; 1.7m. vols, 700,000 maps, 370,000 microforms, 270,000 pamphlets, 260,000 black and white photographs, 60,000 colour transparencies, 15,000 field record notebooks, 250 video cassettes.

Virginia Beach Public Library: 4100 Virginia Beach Blvd, Virginia Beach, VA 23452; tel. (757) 385-4321; e-mail library@vbgov.com; internet www.vbgov.com; 10 brs; a bookmobile; colln of old newspapers and magazines; 875,169 vols, 11,000 books; Dir MARCY SIMS.

Washington County Public Library System: 205 Oak Hill St, Abingdon, VA 24210; tel. (276) 676-6222; e-mail charlotte@wcpl .net; internet www.wcpl.net; f. 1954; Abingdon (HQ); brs: Damascus, Glade Spring, Hayters Gap and Mendota; local history and genealogy colln; 30,000 ebooks; Chair. KENNY SHUMAN; Dir CHARLOTTE LEWIS PARSONS.

Williamsburg Regional Library: 7770 Croaker Rd, Williamsburg, VA 23188; tel. (757) 259-4050; internet www.wrl.org; f. 1909, present location 1973; brs: Williamsburg Library and James City County Library; serves Williamsburg, James City Co and York Co; colln on periodicals and news content from New York Times since 1995; mobile library services; 345,000 vols; Chair. MICHAEL J. FOX; Dir JOHN A. MOORMAN.

Washington

Enumclaw Public Library: 1700 First St, Enumclaw, WA 98022; tel. (360) 825-2938; e-mail library@ci.enumclaw.wa.us; internet www.enumclaw.lib.wa.us; f. 1923; photography colln; colln documents social, industrial, commercial and agricultural heritage in Enumclaw and surrounding region; 50,000 vols; Chair. FRED FLEISCHMANN.

Everett Public Library: 2702 Hoyt Ave, Everett, WA 98201; tel. (425) 257-8022; e-mail libref@ci.everett.wa.us; internet www .epls.org; f. 1894 as Everett Woman's Book Club; 2 brs; 236,359 vols, 805 magazine and newspaper titles, 3,972 vols govt documents, 11,694 DVDs, 5,712 video cassettes; Dir EILEEN SIMMONS.

Fort Vancouver Regional Library District: 1007 E Mill Plain Blvd, Vancouver, WA 98663; tel. (360) 695-1561; e-mail contact@fvrl.org; internet www.fvrl.org; f. 1950; 13 libraries, 3 bookmobiles and a Vancouver operations centre; 721,000 books, magazines, video cassettes, DVDs, and audio book CDs, cassettes; Exec. Dir PATTY DUITMAN.

Longview Public Library: 1600 Louisiana St, Longview, WA 98632; tel. (360) 442-5300;

internet www.longviewlibrary.org; f. 1922; Dir CHRIS SKAUGSET.

North Olympic Library System (NOLS): 2210 S Peabody St, Port Angeles, WA 98362; tel. (360) 417-8525; e-mail director@nols.org; internet www.nols.org; 4 brs; 260,000 vols; Dir PAULA BARNES.

Pierce County Library System: Processing and Administrative Center, 3005 112th St, E, Tacoma, WA 98446; tel. (253) 548-3300; e-mail director@piercecountylibrary .org; internet www.piercecountylibrary.org; f. 1946; 18 brs and 3 bookmobiles; 1.3m. books, CDs, DVDs and audiobooks; Exec. Dir NEEL PARIKH.

Puyallup Public Library: 324 S Meridian, Puyallup, WA 98371; tel. (253) 841-5454; e-mail puylib@ci.puyallup.wa.us; internet www.cityofpuyallup.org; f. 1877; Library Dir MARY JO TORGESON.

Roslyn Public Library: 109 S First St, POB 451, Roslyn, WA 98941; tel. (509) 649-3420; e-mail rpl@inlandnet.com; internet www.roslynlibrary.org; f. 1898; 10,000 vols, 5,000 ebooks and e-audiobooks; Librarian ERIN KRAKE.

Seattle Public Library: 1000 Fourth Ave, Seattle, WA 98104-1109; tel. (206) 386-4636; e-mail city.librarian@spl.org; internet www .spl.org; f. 1891; spec. collns: Aeronautics, Pacific NW Americana; 23 brs; 2m. vols, 20,000 int. and nat. newspapers and magazines; Pres. MARIE MCCAFFREY; City Librarian MARCELLUS TURNER.

Tacoma Public Library: 1102 Tacoma Ave S, Tacoma, WA 98402; tel. (253) 292-2001; internet www.tacomapubliclibrary.org; 1 main library; 7 brs; Library Dir SUSAN ODENCRANTZ.

University of Washington Libraries: POB 352900, Seattle, WA 98195-2900; tel. (206) 543-0242; e-mail libquest@u .washington.edu; internet www.lib .washington.edu; f. 1862; incl. Law Library (separately administered; Librarian PENNY HAZELTON), Health Sciences Library, Odegaard Undergraduate Library, East Asia Library, Spec. Collns Div. and 9 br. libraries; 7,203,156 vols, 63,221 current serials, 8,006,590 microforms; Dir and Dean, Univ. of Washington Libraries LIZABETH A. WILSON.

Washington State Library: POB 42460, Olympia, WA 98504-2460; tel. (360) 704-5200; e-mail askalibrarian@sos.wa.gov; internet www.sos.wa.gov/library; f. 1853; spec. collns: Washington authors, Pacific NW, Washington state documents, Washington state newspapers, transportation, labour and industries, utilities; 167,094 vols, 1,241,563 fed. and state documents, 198,142 microfiche, 49,183 microfilms, 8,914 films, 456,320 audio and video cassettes; State Librarian Dr RAND SIMMONS (acting).

West Virginia

Cabell County Public Library: 455 Ninth St Plaza, Huntington, WV 25701; tel. (304) 528-5700; e-mail cabelllibrary@cabell.lib.wv .us; internet cabell.lib.wv.us; f. 1897, present bldg 1980; 7 brs and 1 main library; also serves libraries located in Logan, Mason, Mingo, Putnam and Wayne counties; Dir JUDY K. RULE; Pres. ROBERT JACKSON.

Greenbrier County Public Library: 152 Robert W McCormick Dr., Lewisburg, WV 24901; tel. (304) 647-7568; e-mail greenbrier .library@mail.mln.lib.wv.us; internet greenbrier.lib.wv.us; f. 1941; genealogical material; local history room with colln of books related to local history.

Hampshire County Public Library: 153 W Main St, Romney, WV 26757; tel. (304) 822-3185; internet www

.hampshirecopubliclib.com; f. 1935; Dir AMANDA SNYDER; Head Librarian NORMA CZERNICKI; Pres. JOHN ZEILOR; Sec. KATHEE ROGERS; Treas. STEVE MORELAND.

Jackson County Public Library: 208 N Church St, Ripley, WV 25271; tel. (304) 372-5343; internet jackson.park.lib.wv.us; f. 1949; HQ in Ripley and br. in Ravenswood; 50,000 vols; Pres. TERESA EVANS.

Kanawha County Public Library: 123 Capitol St, Charleston, WV 25301; tel. (304) 343-4646; internet www.kanawhalibrary .org; f. 1908 as Charleston Public Library, present name 1934; 1 main library, 9 brs and 1 mobile library; affiliation with Nitro Public Library and shares resources with libraries in Kanawha Co Schools system; 600,000 vols; Dir ALAN ENGELBERT; Pres. MICHAEL ALBERT.

Marion County Public Library: 321 Monroe St, Fairmont, WV 26554; tel. (304) 366-1210; internet www .marioncountypubliclibrary.org; f. 1892, present name and status 1939; HQ in Fairmont; 2 brs; bookmobile services; Dir ERIKA REED.

Monroe County Public Library: 103 South St, Union, WV 24983; tel. (304) 772-3038; internet monroe.lib.wv.us; f. 1947; 30,000 vols; Dir DORIS MCCURDY; Pres. ELIZABETH MCLAY IRONS; Sec. CATHY ABERNATHY; Treas. JANE PEIRICK.

Ohio County Public Library: 52 16th St, Wheeling, WV 26003; tel. (304) 232-0244; e-mail ocplweb@weirton.lib.wv.us; internet www.ohiocountylibrary.org; f. 1882; Chair. JIMMIE MCCAMIC; Sec. and Treas. GREG MARQUART.

Parkersburg and Wood County Public Library: 3100 Emerson Ave, Parkersburg, WV 26104-2414; tel. (304) 420-4587; internet parkersburg.lib.wv.us; 3 brs; Dir BRIAN E. RAITZ.

Pocahontas County Free Libraries: 500 Eigth St, Marlinton, WV 24954; tel. (304) 799-6000; e-mail info@pocahontaslibrary.org; internet www.pocahontaslibrary.org; br. libraries in Green Bank, Marlinton, Hillsboro, Durbin and Slatyfork; spec. collns: Pearl S. Buck E Pluribus Unum Colln, West Virginia/Appalachian Colln, Railroad and Logging Colln; Heritage Colln; Pres. SUE ANN HEATHERLY; Sec. DENISE MCNEEL; Treas. ELIZABETH LITTLE.

Putnam County Libraries: 4219 State Route 34, Hurricane, WV 25526; tel. (304) 757-7308; internet putnam.lib.wv.us; f. 1961; 4 brs and 1 main library; Pres. SAM SENTELLE.

Raleigh County Public Library: 221 N Kanawha St, Beckley, WV 25801; tel. (304) 255-0511; e-mail referen@raleigh.lib.wv.us; internet rcpl.lib.wv.us; 1 main library, 3 brs and bookmobile services; edns of Beckley Register Herald dating back to 1907; select edns of Charleston Gazette and New York Times on microfilm; Pres. CAROLYN LUCAS; Dir AMY LILLY.

Roane County Library: 110 Parking Plaza, Spencer, WV 25276; tel. (304) 927-1130; internet roanecountylibrary.org; f. 1951; 2 brs; Dir MARY FURY.

State Law Library: State Capitol Bldg, Room E-404, 1900 Kanawha Blvd, E, Charleston, WV 25305; tel. (304) 558-2607; internet www.state.wv.us/wvsca/library/ menu.htm; attached to Supreme Court of Appeals West Virginia; 28 circuit court libraries; congressionally designated depository for US govt documents; State Law Librarian KAYE L. MAERZ.

Taylor County Public Library: 200 Beech St, Grafton, WV 26354; tel. (304) 265-6121; e-mail taylib@clark.lib.wv.us; internet taylor .clark.lib.wv.us; f. 1981; 20,000 vols; Pres.

PAUL ELDER; Sec. NANCY ELLEN JUDY; Treas. JULIE GREGORY.

West Virginia State Archives: c/o Archives and History Library, The Culture Center, 1900 Kanawha Blvd, E, Charleston, WV 25305-0300; tel. (304) 558-0230; internet www.wvculture.org/history/wvsamenu.html; f. 1905 as Bureau of Archives and History; attached to West Virginia Div. of Culture and History; genealogical colln related to West Virginia counties; colln of maps, MSS, periodicals, photographs, newspapers, state publs, state govt records, yearbooks, co court records on microfilm units; State Historian and Archivist JOSEPH N. GEIGER, JR.

West Virginia University Libraries: POB 6069, Morgantown, WV 26506-6069; 1549 University Ave, Morgantown, WV 26506-6069; tel. (304) 293-4040; e-mail ask_a_librarian@mail.wvu.edu; internet www.libraries.wvu.edu; f. 1867; incl. Downtown Campus Library, Evansdale Library, Health Sciences Library, Law Library, WVU Charleston Health Sciences Library; spec. collns: W Virginia historical art, Appalachian, Myers, rare books; 1.6m. vols, 2.3m. microforms, 24,000 ejournals; Dean JON E. CAWTHORNE.

Wisconsin

American Geographical Society Library: Univ. of Wisconsin-Milwaukee, POB 399, Milwaukee, WI 53201; UWM Libraries, Third Fl., E Wing, 2311 E Hartford Ave, Milwaukee, WI 53211; tel. (414) 229-6282; e-mail agsl@uwm.edu; internet www.uwm.edu/libraries/agsl; f. 1851, present status 1978; attached to Univ. of Wisconsin-Milwaukee Libraries; specialized academic research library with emphasis on discovery and exploration, history of cartography, history of geographical thought, historical geography and geographical themes with a significant historical component; 2 research fellowship programmes available to support visiting scholars; sponsors various lecture series; home of the Map Soc. of Wisconsin; 222,000 vols, 512,000 maps, 10,700 atlases, 114 globes, 33,676 pamphlets, 450,000 photographs and slides, 2,450 CD-ROMs, 800 gigabytes of data storage; Curator MARCY BIDNEY.

Antigo Public Library: 617 Clermont St, Antigo, WI 54409; tel. (715) 623-3724; internet www.antigopl.org; 3 brs; Dir CYNTHIA TAYLOR; Pres. NANCY BUGNI; Treas. SHARON KIND.

Dwight Foster Public Library: 209 Merchants Ave, Fort Atkinson, WI 53538; tel. (920) 563-7790; e-mail connect@fortlibrary.org; internet www.fortlibrary.org; f. 1892; 90,000 vols; Dir KELLY M. TERKEURST; Pres. ANN ENGELMAN; Sec. RITA GRAY.

Edgerton Public Library: 101 Albion St, Edgerton, WI 53534; tel. (608) 884-4511; internet als.lib.wi.us/epl; f. 1907; mem. of Arrowhead Library System; 32,000 vols (incl. books, magazines, video recordings, audio recordings and historical materials); Dir SHERRY MACHONES; Pres. Dr WALT FRANCIS; Sec. KATHY KLEIN; Treas. Dr MARK IRGENS.

Frank L. Weyenberg Library of Mequon—Thiensville: 11345 N Cedarburg Rd, Mequon, WI 53092; tel. (262) 242-2593; e-mail admin@flwlib.org; internet www.flwlib.org; f. 1953, present location 1971; 130,000 vols; Dir LINDA A. BENDIX; Pres. DAVID J. HASE; Sec. MIMI ROSING; Treas. DREW WALLACH.

Greendale Public Library: 5647 Broad St, Greendale, WI 53129; tel. (414) 423-2136; e-mail grnd.ref@mcfls.org; internet www.greendalepubliclibrary.org; f. 1972; mem. of Milwaukee County Federated Library Sys-

tem; 75,908 vols; Dir GARY WARREN NIEBUHR; Pres. STEPHANIE MARES.

Kenosha Public Library: POB 1414, 812 56th St, Kenosha, WI 53141-1414; tel. (262) 564-6100; internet www.mykpl.info; f. 1872, present name 1978; resource library for Kenosha County Library System; 4 brs; bookmobile services; 403,476 vols; Dir DOUGLAS BAKER; Pres. DIANE KASTELIC; Treas. GORDON WYLLIE.

Lake Geneva Public Library: 918 W Main St, Lake Geneva, WI 53147; tel. (262) 249-5299; e-mail lakegene@lakegeneva.lib.wi.us; internet www.lakegeneva.lib.wi.us; f. 1898; Dir ANDREA W. PETERSON; Pres. DUANNE LAFRENZ; Sec. DIANE JONES.

Madison Public Library: 201 W Mifflin St, Madison, WI 53703; tel. (608) 266-6300; e-mail libraryadministration@cityofmadison.com; internet www.madisonpubliclibrary.org; f. 1875 as Madison Free Library, present name 1958; spec. collns: Art of the Picture Book Colln, Audiobooks Colln, Comics and Anime Colln, Education, Employment and Housing Colln, Film and Film History Colln; mem. of S Central Library System; 9 brs; Dir BARBARA DIMICK; Pres. TRIPP WIDDER, III; Sec. and Treas. LAWRENCE PALM.

Menominee Tribal/County Library: POB 1090, W2760 Chief Little Wave Rd, Keshena, WI 54135; tel. (715) 799-5212; internet www.nfls.lib.wi.us/kes; mem. of Nicolet Federated Library System; 9,000 vols; Chair. MABEL BROWN; Dir MICHAEL WILBER.

Milwaukee Public Library: 814 W. Wisconsin Ave, Milwaukee, WI 53233; tel. (414) 286-3000; internet www.mpl.org; f. 1878; 2.7m. vols and magazines, newspapers, records, cassettes, CDs, video cassettes and 1.5m. govt documents; spec. collns incl. African-American colln, business journals and company annual reports, historic photos, historical sheet music, historic recipes, colln of local newspapers and magazines, land ownership books, 40 books on local artists, genealogy; depository for US Fed. Documents, US Geological Survey, US Defense Mapping Agency maps and US Patent Office; 13 br. libraries, Wisconsin Regional Library for the Blind and Physically Handicapped headquarters, 1 mobile library, 2 library vans, computer classes; 3,170,711 vols; Pres. ALDERMAN ASHANTI HAMILTON; Dir PAULA A. KIELY.

Park Falls Public Library: 121 N Fourth Ave, Park Falls, WI 54552; tel. (715) 762-3121; e-mail pfpl@ifls.lib.wi.us; internet www.parkfallslibrary.org; 46,000 vols; Dir GARY OLSON; Pres. DOROTHY HARRIS; Sec. LUCY ROSS.

Pewaukee Public Library: 210 Main St, Pewaukee, WI 53072; tel. (262) 691-5670; e-mail pwlib@pewaukee.lib.wi.us; internet www.pewaukeelibrary.org; jt library of the City and village of Pewaukee; incl. Harken Observatory; Dir JENNIE J. STOLTZ; Pres. DALE NOLL; Sec. LISA JANSEN; Treas. LAURA MUCHOWSKI.

University of Wisconsin-Madison Library: 728 State St, Madison, WI 53706; tel. (608) 262-3193; e-mail userview-l@library.wisc.edu; internet www.library.wisc.edu; f. 1848; 59 campus libraries; Chester H. Thordarson Colln incl. rare books, MSS and archives, printed ephemera, pictorial materials, English and American literature, history of science, history of the book, European collns, and philosophy and theology; 7.3m. vols, 55,000 serial titles, 6.2m. microforms, 160 linear ft of MSS, 7m. govt documents, maps, musical scores, 20,000 ejournals; Dir-Gen. for Library System VAN GEMERT ED.

Waukesha Public Library: 321 Wisconsin Ave, Waukesha, WI 53186; tel. (262) 524-3680; e-mail refemail@waukesha.lib.wi.us; internet www.waukesha.lib.wi.us; 326,459 vols; Dir JANE AMEEL; Pres. PAUL KASPROWICZ; Sec. JEFF FOWLE.

Waupaca Area Public Library: 107 S Main St, Waupaca, WI 54981; tel. (715) 258-4414; e-mail wau@mail.owls.lib.wi.us; internet www.waupacalibrary.org; mem. of Outagamie Waupaca Library System; 75,230 vols, 12,867 ebooks, 6,476 audio materials, 8,127 video materials; Dir PEG BURINGTON; Pres. MARY TRICE; Sec. and Treas. CONNIE ANDRASCHKO.

Winchester Public Library: 2117 Lake St, Winchester, WI 54557-9104; tel. (715) 686-2926; internet winchester.wislib.org; f. 1985; mem. of Northern Waters Library Service; Dir CELA MCGINNIS; Pres. BILL HORNER; Sec. JUDY HABERMAN; Treas. FELICIA GORMAN.

Wisconsin State Law Library: POB 7881, Madison, WI 53707; 120 Martin Luther King, Jr, Blvd, Madison, WI 53703; tel. (608) 267-9696; e-mail wsll.ref@wicourts.gov; internet wilawlibrary.gov; f. 1836 as Wisconsin State Library, present name and status 1876; colln of primary law for all fed. and state jurisdictions and practice materials for all major areas of law; spec. collns incl. Appendices and Briefs for the Wisconsin Supreme Court and Court of Appeals and the Judicial Council colln; 140,000 vols; State Law Librarian JULIE TESSMER.

Wyoming

Albany County Public Library: 310 S Eighth St, Laramie, WY 82070-3969; tel. (307) 721-2580; e-mail info@albanycountylibrary.org; internet www.albanycountylibrary.org; Rock River Br. Library and Centennial Valley Br. Library; Chair. ANTONIO BENDEZU; Sec. and Treas. REBECCA ROBERTS; Co Librarian SUSAN SIMPSON.

Big Horn County Library: POB 231, Basin, WY 82410-0231; 430 W C St, Basin, WY 82410-0231; tel. (307) 568-2388; e-mail director@bhclibrary.org; internet www.bhclibrary.org; 5 brs; Dir DONNA CAPELLEN; Librarian VICKI WALLACE.

Campbell County Public Library System: 2101 S 4J Rd, Gillette, WY 82718-5205; tel. (307) 687-0009; internet ccpls.org; incl. Wright Br. Library; Exec. Dir PATTY MYERS; Chair. KEVIN ANDERS; Treas. MATT SORENSON.

Carbon County Library System: 215 W Buffalo St, Rawlins, WY 82301; tel. (307) 328-2618; internet carbonlibraries.org; f. 1925; 8 brs; 119,806 vols (incl. 104,588 print vols, 95 magazines, 11,005 audio cassettes, 7,025 video cassettes, 94 e-databases); Dir KRISTIN E. HERR; Chair. LARRY MOORE; Sec. JULIE EVANS; Treas. PATTI HAYS.

Converse County Library: 300 Walnut St, Douglas, WY 82633; tel. (307) 358-3644; e-mail glenrockbranchlibrary@conversecountylibrary.org; internet www.conversecountylibrary.org; f. 1905 as Douglas library, present bldg 1968; br. at Glenrock; 60,828 vols; Dir KAREN HOPKINS; Pres. SCOTT BARBER; Sec. and Treas. JEREMY MATTER.

Crook County Public Library System: POB 910, 414 Main St, Sundance, WY 82729-0910; tel. (307) 283-1006; e-mail crookcountylib@rangeweb.net; internet www-wsl.state.wy.us/crook; incl. Moorcroft Br. Library and Hulett Br. Library; main br. at Sundance; Dir JILL MACKEY; Chair. DEE MCGIRR; Sec. JOANN BOHMONT; Treas. SHARON MILLAY.

Johnson County Library System: 171 N Adams Ave, Buffalo, WY 82834; tel. (307) 684-5546; internet www.jclwyo.org; 1 main library and 2 brs; Dir CYNTHIA TWING; Chair. KATHY URRUTY; Sec. JENNIFER LOMPE; Treas. HELEN JONES.

Laramie County Library: 2200 Pioneer Ave, Cheyenne, WY 82001; tel. (307) 634-3561; internet www.lclsonline.org; f. 1886; 2 brs; bookmobile services; genealogy colln; 337,000 vols; Co Librarian LUCIE OSBORN; Chair. BARB COOK; Sec. BETH HOWARD; Treas. JEFF WHITE.

Lincoln County Library System: 519 Emerald St, Kemmerer, WY 83101; tel. (307) 877-6961; internet www.linclib.org; 5 brs; Dir BRENDA MCGINNIS; Chair. ROSALIE TRATNIK; Treas. SUSAN PARK.

Natrona County Public Library: 307 E Second St, Casper, WY 82601; tel. (307) 237-4935; e-mail reference@ natronacountylibrary.org; internet www .natronacountylibrary.org; f. 1902, present name and status 1909; 2 brs and 1 bookmobile; 200,166 vols; Dir BILL NELSON; Pres. RANDY BUFFINGTON; Sec. BOB HOPKINS; Treas. SHAWN HOUCK.

Platte County Public Library System: 904 Ninth St, Wheatland, WY 82201; tel. (307) 322-2689; e-mail pcpl@ plattecountylibrary.org; internet will.state .wy.us/platte; 1 main library and 3 brs; Dir JULIE HENION; Pres. PATSY PARKIN; Sec. JANE WILLIS; Treas. JEANNIE MITCHELL.

Sheridan County Public Library System: 335 W Alger St, Sheridan, WY 82801; tel. (307) 674-8585; e-mail diverson@will .state.wy.us; internet www .sheridanwyolibrary.org; 4 brs; 152,147 vols (incl. 134,231 print vols, 4,661 audio cassettes, 9,445 video cassettes, 3,810 magazines, 78 e-databases); Dir CAMERON DUFF; Chair. CHASE MCFADDEN; Sec. TONY WENDTLAND; Treas. LINDA THOMPSON.

University of Wyoming Libraries: Dept 3334, 1000 E University Ave, Laramie, WY 82071; tel. (307) 766-3279; e-mail ncyrus@ uwyo.edu; internet www-lib.uwyo.edu; br. libraries incl. American Heritage Center, Coe Library, Geology-Brinkerhoff Geology Library, Law Library, Learning Resource Center, Rocky Mountain Herbarium, Univ. of Wyoming-National Park Service Research Centre, Library Annex; 1,552,501 vols, 838,395 ebooks, 13,878 periodicals and serials, 75,150 ejournals, 1,912,170 microforms, 170,313 maps, 1,498,819 govt documents; Dean for Libraries MAGGIE FARRELL.

Wyoming State Archives: Barrett Bldg, 2301 Central Ave, Cheyenne, WY 82002; tel. (307) 777-7826; e-mail wyarchive@state.wy .us; internet wyoarchives.state.wy.us; f. 1895; sponsors and participates in workshops and confs related to Wyoming history and preservation and management of records; Archives and Historical Research Supervisor CURTIS GREUBEL.

Wyoming State Law Library: Supreme Court Bldg, 2301 Capitol Ave, Cheyenne, WY 82002; tel. (307) 777-7509; e-mail library@ courts.state.wy.us; internet www.courts .state.wy.us/lawlibrary; colln of reported cases of American courts, fed. and state laws and statutes, fed. admin. regulations and decisions, US and Wyoming attorney-general opinions, legal treatises, legal periodicals and newspapers, selected US govt publs; Dir KATHY CARLSON.

Wyoming State Library: 2800 Central Ave, Cheyenne, WY 82002; tel. (307) 777-6333; internet will.state.wy.us; State Librarian LESLEY BOUGHTON; publ. *Wyoming Library Roundup* (4 a year).

Museums and Art Galleries

Alabama

Alabama Museum of Natural History: POB 870340, Tuscaloosa, AL 35487-0340; tel. (205) 348-7550; e-mail museum.programs@ ua.edu; internet amnh.ua.edu; f. 1910; displays of geology, zoology, mineralogy, paleontology, ethnology, history, and photography, incl. the Hodges meteorite, the only meteorite known to have struck a human being; courses, field trips, gift shop; Dir Dr RANDY MECREDY; publ. *Museum Chronicle* (irregular); publ. *Nature South*.

Aliceville Museum: 104 Broad St, Aliceville, AL 35442; tel. (205) 373-2363; e-mail museum@nctv.com; internet www .cityofaliceville.com; f. 1995; camp artefacts of Camp Aliceville (Second World War German prisoner of war camp dating from 1942 to 1945); colln incl. wooden objects, weapons, photographs, uniforms, books, sculptures and other artefacts made by German prisoners of war; Exec. Dir JOHN GILLUM.

Birmingham Civil Rights Institute: 520 16th St N, Birmingham, AL 35203; tel. (205) 328-9696; e-mail bcri@bcri.org; internet www .bcri.org; f. 1992; colln on American Civil Rights Movement, struggle of African-American citizens in Birmingham to be part of city's govt and business community; Pres. and CEO Dr LAWRENCE J. PIJEAUX, JR; Chair. ROBERT HOLMES, JR; Sec. PEGGIE F. MYLES; Treas. WALTER HOWLETT, JR.

Birmingham Museum of Art: 2000 Rev. Abraham Woods, Jr, Blvd, Birmingham, AL 35203-2278; tel. (205) 254-2565; internet www.artsbma.org; f. 1951; 24,000 paintings, sculptures, prints and drawings dating from ancient to modern times; holdings of Asian, European, American, African and native American art; library of 35,000 vols; Chair. RALPH COOK; Dir DANNETTA K. THORNTON OWENS; Dir GAIL ANDREWS; Chief Curator JEANNINE A. O'GRODY.

Gadsden Museum of Art: 515 Broad St, Gadsden, AL 35901; tel. (256) 546-7365; internet www.gadsdenmuseum.com; f. 1963; colln of paintings, sculptures, artefacts and items of historical significance depicting local history of Gadsden and Etowah Co; Dir STEVE TEMPLE.

History Museum of Mobile: 111 S Royal St, POB 2068, Mobile, AL 36602; tel. (251) 208-7569; e-mail museum@cityofmobile.org; internet www.historymuseumofmobile.com; f. 1831; 80,000 artefacts incl. furniture and antique silver depicting local history; library of 5,000 vols; Dir Dr DAVID ALSOBROOK.

Huntsville Museum of Art: 300 Church St, Huntsville, AL 35801; tel. (256) 535-4350; internet www.hsvmuseum.org; f. 1970; 3,000 objects of 19th- and 20th-century American art focusing on SE; 200 prints in S photography; 400 paintings, drawings and sculptures in Sellars colln of art dating from 1850 to 1940; Chair. SARAH GESSLER; Sec. RICHARD CRUNKLETON; Treas. PATSY HAWS; Exec. Dir CHRISTOPHER MADKOUR.

Jule Collins Smith Museum of Fine Art: Auburn Univ., 901 S College St, Auburn, AL 36849; tel. (334) 844-1484; e-mail jcsm@ auburn.edu; internet jcsm.auburn.edu; f. 1948; attached to Auburn Univ.; Louise Hauss and David Brent Miller Audubon colln comprises 100 prints of Audubon; late 19th- and 20th-century European modernism work by Pierre-Auguste Renoir, Henri Matisse, Pablo Picasso, Joan Miró, Salvador Dalí and Marc Chagall; Dir MARILYN LAUFER.

Karl C. Harrison Museum of George Washington: 50 Lester St, Columbiana, AL 35051; tel. (205) 669-8767; e-mail info@ washingtonmuseum.com; internet www .washingtonmuseum.com; f. 1982; 1,000 artworks and artefacts dating from colonial period to 1865; original 1787 Samuel Vaughn sketch of Mount Vernon grounds and writing instruments and tools from George Washington's survey case; Curator BONNIE ATCHISON.

Montgomery Museum of Fine Arts: POB 230819, Montgomery, AL 36123-0819; One Museum Dr., Montgomery, AL 36117; tel. (334) 240-4333; e-mail museuminfo@mmfa .org; internet www.mmfa.org; f. 1930; 4,000 objects dating from Colonial period portraiture to 20th century: American art, old master prints, S, regional and decorative arts; library of 5,000 vols, 17 periodicals; Dir MARK M. JOHNSON; Sr Curator MARGARET LYNNE AUSFELD.

National African American Archives & Museum: 564 Dr Martin Luther King, Jr, Ave, Mobile, AL 36603; tel. (251) 433-8511; e-mail dnaaamus@aol.com; internet nationalafricanamericanarchives.org; f. 1932 as Davis Avenue Br. of the Mobile Public Library; colln on African-American history; colln incl. portraits, biographies, African carvings, family histories and other memorabilia; Pres. and Exec. Dir DELORES S. DEES.

Southern Museum of Flight: 4343 73rd St N, Birmingham, AL 35206-3642; tel. (205) 833-8226; e-mail southernmuseumofflight@ yahoo.com; internet www .southernmuseumofflight.org; colln incl. 75 aircrafts, engines, artefacts, photographs and paintings; Alabama Aviation Hall of Fame: 65 biographical plaques presenting Alabama aviation history through collective biography; Dir JAMES T. GRIFFIN.

United States Army Aviation Museum: POB 620610-0610, Fort Rucker, AL 36362; tel. (334) 598-2508; internet www .armyaviationmuseum.org; f. 1956; colln incl. 170 military aircrafts and helicopters; 3,000 items in historical property colln; library: 1,600 technical and field manuals, 95,000 photographs; Dir ROBERT S. MAXHAM; Curator ROBERT D. MITCHELL.

Alaska

Alaska Museum of Science and Nature: 201 N Bragaw, Anchorage, AK 99508; tel. (907) 274-2400; e-mail education@ alaskamuseum.org; internet www .alaskamuseum.org; f. 1994; holds 10,000 objects of Alaskan anthropological, biological, geological, historical, artistic and educational significance; Exec. Dir KATCH BACHELLER; Education Dir KERRI JACKSON; Museum Man. JUDY LIND; Collns Man. SAM WINER.

Alaska Native Heritage Center Museum: 8800 Heritage Center Dr., Anchorage, AK 99504; tel. (907) 330-8000; internet www .alaskanative.net; f. 1989; workshops, demonstrations and guided tours of indoor exhibits and outdoor village sites showcasing native traditions and customs; Board Chair. GAIL R. SCHUBERT; Pres. and CEO ANNETTE EVANS SMITH.

Alaska State Museum: 395 Whittier St, Juneau, AK 99801-1718; tel. (907) 465-2901; e-mail bob.banghart@alaska.gov; internet www.museums.state.ak.us; f. 1900, opened to the public 1920; 27,000 objects; Alaskan history, Alaska's native people, Russian America, art, natural history and ethnographic materials; state-wide assistance to museums in Alaska; Alaska State Chief Curator BOB BANGHART; Dir for Libraries, Archives and Museums LINDA THIBODEAU.

Attached Museum:

Sheldon Jackson Museum: 104 College Dr., Sitka, AK 99835; tel. (907) 747-8981; internet www.museums.state.ak.us; f. 1888; 6,000 objects; Alaska Native artefacts; Chief Curator NADIA JACKINSKY-HORRELL (acting).

Alutiiq Museum Archaeological Repository: 215 Mission Rd Suite 101, Kodiak, AK 99615-7326; tel. (907) 486-7004; internet www.alutiiqmuseum.org; f. 1995; holds 250,000 items related to culture and history of the Alutiiq people, incl. archaeological materials, photographs, ethnographic objects, archival items, film and audio recordings, and natural history specimens; library of 1,700 vols, 1,400 journals, articles, catalogues, conf. papers, maps, newsletters, speeches, pamphlets, presentations, recordings, technical reports, transcripts and unpublished MSS (both original and copied); Exec. Dir Dr SVEN D. HAAKANSON.

Anchorage Museum: Rasmuson Center, 625 C St Anchorage, AK 99501; tel. (907) 929-9201; e-mail museum@anchoragemuseum.org; internet www.anchoragemuseum.org; f. 1968; collects, preserves, exhibits and interprets art, history, anthropology and science of Arkansas and its relationship to the Circumpolar N; 17,500 objects and an additional education colln of 2,000 artefacts; 350,000 historical photographs; Dir and CEO JAMES PEPPER HENRY; Chair. GLORIA O'NEILL; Chair. KAREN COMPTON; Treas. SUSAN KNOWLES.

Baranov Museum: Kodiak Historical Soc., 101 Marine Way, Kodiak, AK 99615; tel. (907) 486-5920; e-mail baranov@ak.net; internet www.baranovmuseum.org; f. 1954 incorporated by the Kodiak Historical Society; located within Kodiak's 200-year-old Nat. Historic Landmark bldg known as the Russian American Magazin or the Erskine House; colln of 2,000 objects dating from several thousand years ago to the present; comprehensive colln of 18th- and 19th-century Alutiiq and Aleut (Alaska Native) material culture that incl. items from daily life as well as ceremonial objects; Exec. Dir TIFFANY K. BRUNSON; Curator of Collns ANJULI GRANTHAM; Pres. NANCY KEMP; Sec. THERESA MILLER; Treas. PAT SZABO.

Clausen Museum: POB 708, Petersburg, AK 99833; 203 Fram St, Petersburg, AK 99833; tel. (907) 772-3598; e-mail clausenmuseum@aptalaska.net; internet www.clausenmuseum.net; f. 1968; colln of 5,000 artefacts (fishing industry related items), 45,000 photographs and negatives; 200 archival colln; Dir SUE McCALLUM; Pres. BEV SIERCKS; Sec. SUZANNE PETERSON.

Fairbanks Community Museum: 410 Cushman St, Fairbanks, AK 99701; tel. (907) 457-3669; internet www.fairbankshistorymuseum.com; f. 1996; exhibits of the history and culture of the Fairbanks area; Exec. Dir BOB ELEY.

Hammer Museum: POB 702, 108 Main St, Haines, AK 99827; tel. (907) 766-2374; internet www.hammermuseum.org; f. 2002; 1,500 hammers ranging from ancient times to the present.

Iñupiat Heritage Center: POB 749, Barrow, AK 99723; 5421 N Star St, Barrow, AK 99723; tel. (907) 852-4594; internet www.co.north-slope.ak.us/departments/planning/ihc.php; Iñupiaq culture, history and language through exhibits, classes, performances and educational activities; Facility Dir BEVERLY HUGO; Museum and Cultural Affairs Coordinator QAIYAAN HARCHAREK (acting).

Museum of the Aleutians: POB 648, Unalaska, AK, 99685; 314 Salmon Way, Unalaska, AK, 99685; tel. (907) 581-5150; e-mail museum@akwisp.com; internet www.aleutians.org; f. 1999; unique artefacts, quotes and historic photographs depicting the purchase of Alaska Territory by the USA in 1867; artefacts from World War period; Chair. SHARON SVARNY-LIVINGSTON; Exec. Dir ZOYA JOHNSON; Sec. and Treas. DONNA DETWEILER.

Palmer Museum of History & Art: 723 S Valley Way, Palmer, AK 99645; tel. (907) 746-7668; internet www.palmermuseum.org; colln incl. items that depict the history of the Palmer region, such as the region's art history, exploration, settlement, agriculture, and trade, cultural and social devt; Exec. Dir MELISSA JENSKI.

Pratt Museum: 3779 Bartlett St, Homer, AK 99603; tel. (907) 235-8635; e-mail info@prattmuseum.org; internet www.prattmuseum.org; f. 1968; natural history museum with 24,000 objects; focuses on art, natural history, native cultures, homesteading, fishing, marine ecology and the Exxon Valdez oil spill, Alaskan wildlife dioramas and the saltwater aquaria; library of 1,500 vols; Museum Dir Dr DIANE CONVERSE.

Sheldon Museum & Cultural Center: 11 Main St, POB 269, Haines, AK 99827; tel. (907) 766-2366; e-mail director@sheldonmuseum.net; internet www.sheldonmuseum.org; a cultural and historical centre for the Chilkat Valley; photographs since 1880; Dir HELEN ALTEN; Pres. JIM HEATON.

Sitka Historical Society and Museum: 330 Harbor Dr., Sitka, AK 99835; tel. (907) 747-6455; e-mail sitka.history@yahoo.com; internet www.sitkahistory.org; f. 1967; exhibits, photographs, artefacts and archives related to Sitka's Tlingit, Russian and American history; particularly, period surrounding and following Alaska's 1867 transfer from Russia; Dir BOB MEDINGER.

Tongass Historical Museum: 629 Dock St, Ketchikan, AK 99901; tel. (907) 225-5600; collects, preserves and interprets history, art and culture of Ketchikan and SE Alaska; Dir MICHAEL NAAB.

Totem Heritage Center: 629 Dock St Ketchikan, AK 99901; 601 Deermount St Ketchikan AK 99901; tel. (907) 225-5900; f. 1976; preserves endangered 19th-century totem poles retrieved from uninhabited Tlingit and Haida village sites near Ketchikan; also preserves the traditional arts and crafts of Tlingit, Haida and Tsimshian cultures; Dir MICHAEL NAAB.

University of Alaska Museum of the North: POB 756960, 907 Yukon Dr., Fairbanks, AK 99775; tel. (907) 474-7505; e-mail museum@uaf.edu; internet www.uaf.edu/museum; f. 1926; 1.4m. artefacts and specimens incl. archaeology, birds, documentary film, earth sciences, ethnology/history, fine arts, fishes/marine invertebrates, insects, mammals and plants; Museum Dir Dr CAROL DIEBEL.

Valdez Museum & Historical Archive: POB 8, Valdez, AK 99686; tel. (907) 835-2764; e-mail info@valdezmuseum.org; internet www.valdezmuseum.org; f. 1901; textiles, photographs and documents that trace the community's history since its founding; Mary Whalen Colln; Owen Meals Colln; All-America City Colln; Pipeline Contruction Colln; Marine Colln; library of 2,000 vols; 35,000 photographs, MSS, documents; 510 maps; 5,500 edns of newspapers; Exec. Dir PATRICIA RELAY; Pres. DANNY SPARRELL; Sec. CAROL HARRIS; Treas. SPIKE GILSON.

Arizona

Arizona-Sonora Desert Museum: 2021 N Kinney Rd, Tucson, AZ 85743; tel. (520) 883-1380; e-mail info@desertmuseum.org; internet www.desertmuseum.org; f. 1952; zoo, natural history museum and botanical garden; exhibits 300 animal species and 1,200 kinds of plants; 14,095 catalogued specimens of gem, mineral and fossils; vertebrate palaeontology colln; art institute; library of 6,000 vols and 83 periodical subscriptions; Dir CRAIG S. IVANYI.

Arizona State Museum: POB 210026, Univ. of Arizona, Tucson, AZ 85721-0026; 1013 E University Blvd, Tucson, AZ 85721-0026; tel. (520) 621-6302; e-mail dfl@email.arizona.edu; internet www.statemuseum.arizona.edu; f. 1893; attached to Univ. of Arizona; collns of American Indian basketry; 25,000 woven pieces of rare baskets, sandals, cradle boards, mats, cordage and preserved fibres; collns of 300,000 catalogued archaeological artefacts, 40,000 ethnographic artefacts, 500,000 photographic negatives and original prints; research colln incl. Mogollon and Hohokam cultures; Navajo textile collns; collns of Casas Grandes pottery; 500 Mexican folk masks from Cordry colln; 4,000 comparative vertebrate skeletons; library of 70,000 vols, incl. rare titles, 1,500 periodicals, 6,000 maps, 1,500 linear ft of paper documents, 800 original sound recordings; Dir Dr PATRICK LYONS.

Arizona State University Art Museum: 10th St and Mill Ave, POB 872911, Tempe, AZ 85287-2911; tel. (480) 965-2787; internet asuartmuseum.asu.edu; f. 1950; attached to ASU Herberger Institute of Design and the Arts, Arizona State Univ.; 12,000 artefacts; contemporary art of new media and innovative methods of presentation; American ceramics; historic and contemporary prints; American and European paintings; SW art of Latino artists; historic American and modernist and contemporary Latin American works; Dir GORDON KNOX.

Heard Museum: 2301 N Central Ave, Phoenix, AZ 85004; tel. (602) 252-8848; e-mail contact@heard.org; internet www.heard.org; f. 1929; art from ancestral artefacts to contemporary paintings and jewellery; colln of American Indian fine art, paintings, drawings, prints, photography and sculpture; resource colln on 25,000 American Indian artists, 300,000 historic and contemporary photographs; Scott L. Libby, Jr, Amphitheater; library: 300 linear ft of MSS, personal collns and cultural materials, incl. 150 linear ft of institutional records; Dir JAMES PEPPER HENRY.

International Wildlife Museum: 4800 W Gates Pass Rd, Tucson, AZ 85745; tel. (520) 629-0100; internet www.thewildlifemuseum.org; f. 1988; exhibits natural history; 400 species of insects, mammals and birds; dioramas depicting wild animals in their natural settings, video cassettes, interactive computers, and hands-on exhibits; promotes wildlife appreciation and conservation; wildlife theatre; Dir RICHARD WHITE.

Jewish History Museum: POB 889, Tucson, AZ 85702; 564 S Stone Ave, Tucson, AZ 85701; tel. (520) 670-9073; e-mail jhmtucson@gmail.com; internet www.jewishhistorymuseum.org; f. 1910; collects, preserves and teaches history, culture and traditions of Jewish people, from SW Pioneers to Jews of contemporary times; Pres. BARRY A. FRIEDMAN; Exec. Dir EILEEN WARSHAW.

Museum of Northern Arizona: 3101 N Ft. Valley Rd, Flagstaff, AZ 86001; tel. (928) 774-5213; e-mail info@mna.mus.az.us; internet www.musnaz.org; f. 1928; collects, studies, interprets and preserves Colorado Plateau's natural and cultural heritage; 600,000 artefacts of anthropology, biology, geology and fine arts; fed. and tribal research collns; library of 50,000 vols, 25,000 separates, 300 MSS and 250,000 photographic images; Dir Dr ROBERT G. BREUNIG; Chair. DAVID CONNELL; Sec. MARGARET TAYLOR; Treas. BRAD RYAN; publ. *Plateau: Land and People of the Colorado Plateau* (2 a year).

Northern Arizona University Art Museum: POB 6021, Flagstaff, AZ 86011-6021; tel. (928) 523-3471; e-mail art.museum@nau.edu; internet www4.nau.edu/art_museum; attached to College of Art and Letters, Norther Arizona Univ.; 448 framed pieces of lithographs, paintings and etchings; 300 pieces of ceramic, sculpture and textiles; colln dates from early 1700s to the present; Dir Dr GEORGE V. SPEER.

Phippen Museum: 4701 Highway 89N, Prescott, AZ 86301; tel. (928) 778-1385; e-mail phippen@phippenartmuseum.org; internet www.phippenartmuseum.org; f. 1984; colln of paintings, etchings, drawings, bronze sculptures, photography, American Indian artefacts and jewellery from late 19th century to early 21st century; library of 580 vols and 60 video cassettes; Exec. Dir KIM VILLALPANDO; Chair. DICK CORNWELL; Treas. MAUREEN SHAFFER.

Phoenix Art Museum: McDowell Rd and Central Ave, 1625 N Central Ave, Phoenix, AZ 85004-1685; tel. (602) 257-1880; e-mail info@phxart.org; internet www.phxart.org; f. 1959; 18,000 works of American, Asian, European, Latin American, W American, modern and contemporary art and fashion design; organizes festivals, live performances, ind. art films and educational programmes; library of 40,000 vols.

Pima Air & Space Museum: 6000 E Valencia Rd, Tucson, AZ 85756; tel. (520) 574-0462; internet www.pimaair.org; f. 1976; 300 aircraft and spacecraft from all over the world; 125,000 artefacts; Exec. Dir YVONNE MORRIS.

Pueblo Grande Museum: 4619 E Washington St, Phoenix, AZ 85034; tel. (602) 495-0901; e-mail pueblo.grande.museum.pks@phoenix.gov; internet phoenix.gov/recreation/arts/museums/pueblo; f. 1929; attached to City of Phoenix Parks and Recreation Dept; archaeological site museum; repository for professionally excavated archaeological project collns from Phoenix metropolitan area; collects historic and contemporary Native American art objects, esp. from cultures with long-standing ties to the Salt River Valley, such as the Akimel O'odham (Pima) and Piipash (Maricopa); cultural materials from site of Pueblo Grande and Greater SW; Dir ROGER LIDMAN.

Smoki Museum: 147 N Arizona Ave, POB 10224, Prescott, AZ 86304-0224; tel. (928) 445-1230; e-mail director@smokimuseum.org; internet www.smokimuseum.org; American Indian art and culture; Man. Dir CINDY GRESSER; Pres. JIM CHRISTOPHER; Sec. LINDA YOUNG; Treas. KENT ROBINSON.

Tucson Museum of Art and Historic Block: 140 N Main Ave, Tucson, AZ 85701; tel. (520) 624-2333; e-mail info@tucsonmuseumofart.org; internet www.tucsonmuseumofart.org; f. 1924 as Tucson Fine Arts Asscn, present name and status 1975; art of Latin America, art of the American W, modern and contemporary art and Asian art, MSS and rare books; J. Knox Corbett House, La Casa Cordova, Edward Nye Fish House, Romero House and Stevens/Duffield House; library of 13,000 vols; Pres. ANNE LYMAN; CEO ROBERT E. KNIGHT; Sec. JEAN S. COOPER; Treas. HARRY GEORGE.

University of Arizona Museum of Art: POB 210002, Tucson, AZ 85721-0002; tel. (520) 621-7567; e-mail vca@email.arizona.edu; internet artmuseum.arizona.edu; 6,000 paintings, sculptures, prints and drawings with emphasis on European and American fine art from 14th century to present; Exec. Dir CHARLES A. GUERIN.

West Valley Art Museum: POB 6377, Peoria, AZ 85385; tel. (623) 972-0635; e-mail info@wvam.org; internet www.wvam.org; 1,651 items from 75 countries and 1,000 pieces of ethnic dress and textiles; 300 fine art prints; 19th-century historic Japanese woodcut prints; ethnographic artefacts incl. Chinese snuff bottles, calligraphy tools, ethnographic sculptures, Japanese fans, chopsticks and scrolls; Pres. Dr G. WILLIAM BENZ; Sec. and Treas. W. MCMILLIN.

Arkansas

Arkansas Air Museum: 4290 S School Ave, Fayetteville, AR 72701-8008; tel. (479) 521-4947; internet www.arkairmuseum.org; f. 1986; colln of classic aircraft in flight service condition from the 1920s and 1930s; modern planes from the post-Second World War era; static displays of key military aircraft from the Viet Nam era; still-flying aircraft on loan from private owners.

Arkansas Arts Center: POB 2137, Little Rock, AR 72203-2137; 501 E Ninth St, Little Rock, AR 72202; tel. (501) 372-4000; e-mail info@arkarts.com; internet www.arkarts.com; f. 1960; colln of sheets by Cézanne, Van Gogh, Jackson Pollock, Georgia O'Keeffe, Alison Saar, Rembrandt and Rubens; 135 drawings and watercolours by Paul Signac, 100 Post-Minimalist drawings, Arthur Dove's Sketchbook 'E' and 80 works by Will Barnet; paintings by Diego Rivera, Odilon Redon and Francesco Bassano; sculpture by Henry Moore, Louise Nevelson and Roy Lichtenstein; prints by Rembrandt, Whistler and Dürer; contemporary objects in craft media, incl. teapots by contemporary artists, contemporary baskets, turned wood objects, studio glass, ceramics, metalwork and jewellery; library of 5,000 vols (incl. dictionaries, indexes, monographs, catalogues raisonnés and exhibition catalogues); Exec. Dir TODD HERMAN.

Arkansas Inland Maritime Museum: 120 Riverfront Park Dr., N Little Rock, AR 72114; tel. (501) 371-8320; e-mail events@aimm.museum; internet www.aimm.museum; f. 2005; exhibition of historic naval vessels with emphasis on the era of Second World War through the present; artefacts incl. plaques, scrapbooks, brochures, patrol reports and photographs; incl. theatre; outdoor exhibits, incl. the Snook Memorial; library of 2,500 vols.

Arkansas State University Museum: POB 490, State Univ., Jonesboro, AR 72467; tel. (870) 972-2074; e-mail museum@astate.edu; internet www.astate.edu/a/museum; f. 1985; 70,000 objects of natural history, archaeology and history of state; archives and photographic colln; library of 7,000 vols; Dir Dr MARTI L. ALLEN.

Arts & Science Center: 701 Main St, Pine Bluff, AR 71601; tel. (870) 536-3375; e-mail info@artssciencecenter.org; internet www.artssciencecenter.org; f. 1968; 1,000 artworks incl. paintings, sculptures, photography, drawings and prints by African-American artists, Arkansas artists and artists of S region of USA; organizes art exhibitions, performing arts, education and science exhibits; Exec. Dir LENORE SHOULTS; Chair. ADAM ROBINSON; Sec. LEIGH PHILIPPI; Treas. CAROL F. JONES.

Crystal Bridges Museum of American Art: 600 Museum Way, Bentonville, AR 72712; tel. (479) 418-5700; e-mail info@crystalbridges.org; internet www.crystalbridges.org; f. 2011; American art works since colonial era incl. iconic images Rosie the Riveter by Norman Rockwell, Asher B. Durand's Kindred Spirits and Maxfield Parrish's The Lantern Bearers; library of 50,000 vols; Chair. ALICE WALTON; Pres. DON BACIGALUPI.

Fort Smith Regional Art Museum: POB 1257, Fort Smith, AR 72902; 701 Rogers Ave, Fort Smith, AR 72901; tel. (479) 784-2787; e-mail info@fsram.org; internet www.fsram.org; f. 1948; paintings, sculpture, lithographs, drawings, photographs and mixed media by int., regional and local artists; travelling exhibitions and works by regional artists; Exec. Dir LEE ORTEGA; Pres. MARTA JONES; Sec. SUZZANNE SALSBURY; Treas. SHAREN REEDER.

Historic Arkansas Museum: 200 E Third St, Little Rock, AR 72201; tel. (501) 324-9351; e-mail info@historicarkansas.org; internet www.historicarkansas.org; f. 1973; 5 pre-Civil War houses; collns of art and paintings, furniture, guns, hunting horns, jewellery, knives, photographs, pottery, pottery of Caddo, quilts and silver; Dir BILL WORTHEN.

Museum of Discovery: Suite 150, 500 President Clinton Ave, Little Rock, AR 72201; tel. (501) 396-7050; e-mail info@museumofdiscovery.org; internet museumofdiscovery.org; f. 1927 as Museum of Natural History and Antiquities, current name adopted 1998; operates mobile science museum; sponsors educational programmes; exhibits at partner museums and educational venues; exhibition related to media and science; colln of dinosaur fossils; Exec. Dir NAN SELZ.

Old State House Museum: 300 W Markham St, Little Rock, AR 72201; tel. (501) 324-9685; e-mail info@oldstatehouse.org; internet www.oldstatehouse.com; f. 1947; state police colln of Arkansas criminal justice history and memorabilia; colln of Arkansas's First Ladies' Gowns; quilts made by mems of Arkansas's black community since 1880; Dir BILL GATEWOOD.

Shiloh Museum of Ozark History: 118 W Johnson Ave, Springdale, AR 72764; tel. (479) 750-8165; e-mail shiloh@springdalear.gov; internet www.shilohmuseum.org; f. 1965; Guy Howard Colln of Native American prehistoric and historic artefacts; Lockwood and Annabel Searcy Colln; Mooney-Barker Drugstore Colln; Morris Family Colln of First World War items; Jeanne Hoffer-Tucker Colln of paintings; Ada Lee Shook Colln; Lucy Cartmell Leming Colln; Robert G. Winn Colln; McGarrah-Reed Colln; 500,000 photographs; Dir ALLYN LORD; Pres. MYRON ENG; Sec. CAROLYN BAYLEY; Treas. Dr MARSHA JONES.

California

Asian Art Museum: Chong-Moon Lee Center for Asian Art and Culture, 200 Larkin St, San Francisco, CA 94102; tel. (415) 581-3500; e-mail pr@asianart.org; internet www.asianart.org; f. 1969, present name 1994; museum and centre of research on outstanding collns of Chinese, Japanese, Korean, Indian, SE Asian, Himalayan and Islamic art; colln of 17,000 artworks spanning 6,000 years of history; library of 40,000 vols; Chair. ANTHONY SUN; Sec. JANE CHANG TOM; Treas. TIMOTHY F. KAHN.

Autry: 4700 Western Heritage Way, Los Angeles, CA 90027-1462; tel. (323) 495-4349; e-mail rroom@theautry.org; internet www.theautry.org; f. 2003, by merger of

Autry Museum of Western Heritage with Southwest Museum of the American Indian and Women of the West Museum; colln of 500,000 pieces of art and artefacts; 2 research libraries: Braun Research Library and Autry Library; library of 21,000 vols (incl. books, MSS, diaries and visual materials in the Rosenstock Colln of Western Americana) and 1,200 scripts; Pres. and CEO W. RICHARD WEST, JR; publ. *Convergence* (irregular).

California African American Museum: 600 State Dr., Exposition Park, Los Angeles, CA 90037; tel. (213) 744-7432; internet www .caamuseum.org; f. 1981; historic and contemporary colln of art, books, photographs and written materials about African Americans in California and the USA; library of 20,000 vols, incl. books, periodicals and records; Exec. Dir CHARMAINE JEFFERSON.

California Palace of the Legion of Honor: Lincoln Park, 34th Ave and Clement St, San Francisco, CA 94121; tel. (415) 750-3600; e-mail contact@famsf.org; internet legionofhonor.famsf.org; f. 1924; attached to Fine Arts Museums of San Francisco; European decorative arts and paintings; ancient art; sculpture by Auguste Rodin; Achenbach Foundation for Graphic Arts has largest colln of prints and drawings in the Western USA (see also de Young Museum); Dir JOHN E. BUCHANAN, JR; Pres. DIANE B. WILSEY; publ. *Fine Arts Magazine* (3 or 4 a year).

Chinese American Museum: 125 Paseo de la Plaza, Suite 300, Los Angeles, CA 90012; 425 N Los Angeles St, Los Angeles, CA 90012; tel. (213) 485-8567; e-mail pr@camla .org; internet www.camla.org; f. 2003, fmrly Museum of Chinese American History; arts, documents, images, and artefacts depicting history of Chinese immigrants in the US that began in mid-19th century; Exec. Dir PAULINE WONG; Pres. ALFRED H. SOO-HOO; Sec. JOE L. QUAN; Treas. DOROTHY HALL TAMASHIRO; Curator STEVE Y. WONG.

Craft and Folk Art Museum: 5814 Wilshire Blvd, Los Angeles, CA 90036; tel. (323) 937-4230; e-mail info@cafam.org; internet www.cafam.org; f. 1965 as The Egg and The Eye, present name and status 1973; displays folk art and contemporary craft; Chair. WALLY MARKS, III; Exec. Dir SUZANNE ISKEN.

Drum Barracks Civil War Museum: 1052 Banning Blvd, Wilmington, CA 90744; tel. (310) 548-7509; e-mail susan.ogle@lacity.org; internet www.drumbarracks.org; f. 1987; preservation of memorabilia concerning the Civil War and California's contribution towards it; library of 259 vols; Dir SUSAN OGLE; publs *American Heritage* (irregular), *Civil War Illustrated* (irregular).

de Young Museum: 50 Hagiwara Tea Garden Dr., Golden Gate Park, San Francisco, CA 94118; tel. (415) 750-3600; e-mail contact@famsf.org; internet www .deyoungmuseum.org; f. 1894 as Fine Arts Bldg, reopened 2005; attached to Fine Arts Museums of San Francisco; collns of American art since 17th century; art of the native Americas, Africa and the Pacific (see also California Palace of the Legion of Honor); Dir JOHN E. BUCHANAN, JR; Pres. DIANE B. WILSEY; publ. *Fine Arts Magazine* (4 a year).

FIDM Museum & Galleries: 919 S Grand Ave, Suite 250, Los Angeles, CA 90015; tel. (213) 623-5821; e-mail info@fidmmuseum .org; internet www.fidmmuseum.org; f. 1978; colln of 15,000 objects covering more than 200 years of fashion history: 1800 to the present; film costumes, haute couture and ready-to-wear, jewellery and fragrance, non-Western dress, textiles; Dir BARBARA BUNDY; Curator KEVIN JONES.

Fort MacArthur Museum—Battery Osgood-Farley Historic Site: 3601 S Gaffey St, San Pedro, CA 90731; tel. (310) 548-2631; e-mail director@ftmac.org; internet www.ftmac.org; f. 1985; preserves and interprets history of Fort MacArthur; US Army post that guarded the Los Angeles harbour from 1914 to 1974; Museum Dir and Curator STEPHEN NELSON.

Fowler Museum at UCLA: POB 951549, Los Angeles, CA 90095-1549; 308 Charles E Young Dr. N, Los Angeles, CA 90095; tel. (310) 825-4361; e-mail fowlerws@arts.ucla .edu; internet www.fowler.ucla.edu; f. 1963, present name 2006; colln of 150,000 art and ethnographic and 600,000 archaeological objects representing ancient, traditional and contemporary cultures of Africa, Native and Latin America, and Asia and the Pacific; Dir and Exhibition Curator MARLA C. BERNS.

Getty Villa: 17985 Pacific Coast Highway, Pacific Palisades, CA 90272; tel. (310) 440-7300; e-mail visitorservices@getty.edu; internet www.getty.edu/museum/home .html; f. 1953, reopened in 2006 after major renovations; educational centre and museum dedicated to the study of the arts and cultures of ancient Greece, Rome and Etruria, incl. re-creation of a Roman seaside villa, the Villa dei Papiri, which was destroyed by the eruption of Vesuvius in AD 79; houses permanent colln of 44,000 Greek, Roman and Etruscan antiquities, 1,200 of which are on public display; a library and other facilities for scholars supports research and study programmes; Dir (vacant).

Grammy Museum: 800 W Olympic Blvd, Suite A245, Los Angeles, CA 90015; tel. (213)765-6800; e-mail grammyinfo@ grammymuseum.org; internet www .grammymuseum.org; f. 2008; keeps records of and explores all forms of music and musical legends in Grammy history; Exec. Dir BOB SANTELLI; Asst Curator TORY MILLIMAKI.

Griffith Observatory: 2800 E Observatory Rd, Los Angeles, CA 90027; tel. (213) 473-0800; internet www.griffithobservatory.org; f. 1935; 3 main divs: the Observatory, with Zeiss twin 12-inch and 9-inch refracting telescopes and 3 solar telescopes; more than 100 exhibits; the Samuel Oschin Planetarium, with its Zeiss star projector and laser video all-dome animation; Dir Dr E. C. KRUPP; publ. *The Griffith Observer* (12 a year).

Hammer Museum: 10899 Wilshire Blvd, Los Angeles, CA 90024; tel. (310) 443-7000; e-mail info@hammer.ucla.edu; internet www .hammer.ucla.edu; f. 1990; contemporary and historical work in all media of visual arts; paintings, garden sculptures and video cassettes; Chair. and Pres. JOHN V. TUNNEY; Dir ANN PHILBIN; Treas. STEVEN A. OLSEN.

Hollywood Heritage Museum: POB 2586, Hollywood, CA 90078; Lasky-DeMille Barn, 2100 N Highland Ave, Hollywood, CA; tel. (323) 874-4005; e-mail museum@ hollywoodheritage.org; internet www .hollywoodheritage.org; f. 1985; located within the restored Lasky-DeMille Barn; photographs from the silent movie days of motion picture production, movie props, historic documents and other movie related memorabilia; Pres. RICHARD ADKINS; Sec. ALAN SIMON; Treas. RANDY HABERKAMP.

Hollywood Museum: 1660 N Highland Ave, Hollywood Blvd, Hollywood, CA 90028; tel. (323) 464-7776; internet www .thehollywoodmuseum.com; colln of props, photographs, costumes and other memorabilia belonging to Hollywood history; Pres. DONELLE DADIGAN.

Huntington Library, Art Collections and Botanical Gardens: 1151 Oxford Rd, San Marino, CA 91108; tel. (626) 405-2100; e-mail publicinformation@huntington.org; internet www.huntington.org; f. 1919; British and French paintings from 18th to 19th centuries (incl. full-length portraits by Reynolds, Gainsborough and Lawrence); 18th-century French sculpture, furniture and porcelain; European decorative arts from 16th to 18th centuries; American painting, furniture and decorative arts from 1730 to 1930; botanical gardens of 120 acres with 15,000 plant species; see under Libraries and Archives; library of 500,000 rare books, 500,000 ref. books, 6m. MSS, prints, 600,000 photographs and maps; Chair. STEWART R. SMITH; Pres. STEVEN S. KOBLIK; Dir Art Collns JOHN MURDOCH; publ. *Huntington Frontiers* (2 a year).

J. Paul Getty Museum: 1200 Getty Center Dr., Los Angeles, CA 90049-1687; tel. (310) 440-7330; e-mail gettymuseum@getty.edu; internet www.getty.edu; f. 1954; Greek, Roman and Etruscan antiquities, European paintings; drawings, MSS, decorative arts; European and American photographs, modern and contemporary European and American outdoor sculpture; conservation work and symposia; Dir DAVID BOMFORD (acting).

Japanese American National Museum: 369 E First St, Los Angeles, CA 90012; tel. (213) 625-0414; e-mail hr@janm.org; internet www.janm.org; f. 1985; colln of Japanese American objects, images and documents that provide insight into the ancestry of Japanese-American people in the USA; Co-Exec. Dir NANCY ARAKI; Co-Exec. Dir MIYOKO OSHIMA.

Korean American Museum: 3727 W Sixth St, Suite 400, Los Angeles, CA 90020; tel. (213) 388-4229; e-mail info@kamuseum.org; internet www.kamuseum.org; f. 1991; works towards the interpretation and preservation of the Korean American community and its history; Chair. KI SUH PARK; Programme Coordinator Dr CHANGMII BAE; publs *The Korea Central Daily (Joong-ang-ilbo)*, *The Korea Times (Han-kook-ilbo)*.

Korean Cultural Centre Los Angeles: 5505 Wilshire Blvd, Los Angeles, CA 90036; tel. (323) 936-7141; internet www.kccla.org; colln of historical and contemporary Korean artefacts and a variety of replicas of historical pieces from Korea's dynastic kingdoms such as Three Kingdoms Period and Joseon Dynasty (1329–1910); library of 26,000 vols; Dir JAEWON KIM.

LACMA–Los Angeles County Museum of Art: 5905 Wilshire Blvd, Los Angeles, CA 90036; tel. (323) 857-6000; e-mail publicinfo@ lacma.org; internet www.lacma.org; f. 1910, fmrly Los Angeles Museum of History, Science and Art, present name and status 1961; 100,000 objects dating from ancient times to the present; colln incl. Asian, Japanese, Latin American, Islamic, pre-Columbian art and modern art; CEO and Dir MICHAEL GOVAN.

Los Angeles Municipal Art Gallery (LAMAG): 4800 Hollywood Blvd, Los Angeles, CA 90027; tel. (323) 644-6269; e-mail info@lamag.org; internet www.lamag .org; f. 1954; attached to City of Los Angeles Dept of Cultural Affairs; colln focusing on the artists and art of S California; colln incl. painting, sculpture, photography, architecture, design, video, sound, electronic, performance and installation works; Curator and Dir SCOTT CANTY.

Los Angeles Museum of the Holocaust: 100 S The Grove Dr., Los Angeles, CA 90036; tel. (323) 651-3704; e-mail info@lamoth.org; internet www.lamoth.org; f. 1961; created by

Holocaust survivors; colln of memorabilia: relics and other primary source materials from the Holocaust period (1933–45); Exec. Dir SAMARA HUTMAN; Dir of Archive, Library and Historical Curatorship Dr VLADIMIR MELAMED.

Los Angeles Police Historical Society: 6045 York Blvd, Los Angeles, CA 90042; tel. (323) 344-9445; e-mail e@laphs.org; internet www.laphs.org; colln of memorabilia concerning the Los Angeles Police Dept history; Exec. Dir GLYNN MARTIN; Chair. TERRY HARA; Sec. TRACEY SCHUSTER; Treas. DAVE BROOKS.

Martial Arts History Museum: 2319 W Magnolia Blvd, Burbank, CA 91506; tel. (818) 478-1722; e-mail info@mamuseum .com; internet www.martialartsmuseum .com; f. 1999; Pres. MICHAEL MATSUDA.

Museum of Neon Art: POB 631, Glendale, CA 91209; tel. (213) 489-9918; e-mail info@ neonmona.org; internet www.neonmona.org; f. 1981; preserves, collects and interprets neon art; Exec. Dir KIM KOGA.

Museum of Tolerance: Simon Wiesenthal Plaza 9786, W Pico Blvd, Los Angeles, CA 90035; tel. (310) 553-8403; e-mail info@ museumoftolerance.com; internet www .museumoftolerance.com; f. 1993; attached to Simon Wiesenthal Center Museum; works towards educating people concerning prejudice, the Holocaust, civil rights, and to prevent hatred and genocide.

Natural History Museum of Los Angeles County: 900 Exposition Blvd, Los Angeles, CA 90007; tel. (213) 763-3466; e-mail info@ nhm.org; internet www.nhm.org; f. 1910; Western USA and American History, New World ethnology and archaeology, palaeontology, geology, mineralogy, botany, ichthyology, mammalogy, entomology, herpetology, invertebrate zoology, ornithology; active research centre in areas of living and fossil invertebrates, vertebrates, mineralogy, anthropology (Native American, pre-Columbian and Pacific) and history (California and Southwestern); incl. Page Museum at La Brea Tar Pits and William S. Hart Museum; library of 100,000 vols; Pres. Dr JANE G. PISANO; Dir JAMES L. POWELL; publs *Contributions in Science* (irregular), *Naturalist*, *Science Series* (irregular), *Terra* (6 a year).

San Diego Museum of Art: POB 122107, San Diego, CA 92112-2107; 1450 El Prado, Balboa Park, San Diego, CA; tel. (619) 232-7931; e-mail information@sdmart.org; internet www.sdmart.org; f. 1925; Renaissance and Baroque paintings of Spanish, Italian, Dutch, Flemish and French schools; major works by El Greco, Zurbarán, Goya, Crivelli, Tiepolo, Guardi, Rubens, Rembrandt, Ruysdael, Hals, Matisse, Braque; early and contemporary American artists; Asiatic arts and sculpture, graphics and decorative arts from many countries; Latin American art; lectures, concerts and classes; library of 30,000 vols, 15,000 bound vols of art periodicals and 18,000 auction sale catalogues; Exec. Dir ROXANA VELASQUEZ; Pres. TOM GILDRED; Sec. CHARLES HELLERICH; Treas. KEN WILLIAMS.

San Diego Natural History Museum: POB 121390, San Diego, CA 92112-1390; 1788 El Prado, San Diego, CA 92101; tel. (619) 232-3821; e-mail collections@sdnhm .org; internet www.sdnhm.org; f. 1917; depts of botany, herpetology, birds and mammals, entomology, palaeontology and marine invertebrates; Laurence Klauber Herpetology Colln; library of 56,000 vols (incl. standard and obscure references, journals, rare books and maps); Chair. VIRGINIA CROCKETT; Pres. Dr MICHAEL W. HAGER; Sec. WALT DAVIS; Treas. JEFF WITT; Library Dir MARGARET

DYKENS; publs *Proceedings* (irregular), *Transactions* (irregular).

San Francisco Museum of Modern Art: 151 Third St, San Francisco, CA 94103; tel. (415) 357-4000; e-mail collections@sfmoma .org; internet www.sfmoma.org; f. 1935; 27,000 artworks, photographs and design objects; contemporary art; permanent colln: early Modernism, Analytical Cubism, Abstract Expressionism and other major schools since the beginning of the 20th century; also German Expressionism, Modernist Mexican painting, figurative art of the San Francisco Bay area; important photography dept with colln of images since the 1840s; dept of architecture and design focusing on works by architects and designers of the Pacific region; dept of media arts incl. multimedia, videotape, film and other works created in moving-image or image-reproduction media; library of 60,000 vols, incl. 1,890 periodicals, 45,000 artists files, 1,100 vols of Sydney Tillim colln, 700 CDs from Skowhegan Lecture Archive; Chair. CHARLES R. SCHWAB; Dir NEAL BENEZRA; Sec. and Treas. DENNIS J. WONG.

University of California, Berkeley Art Museum & Pacific Film Archive: 2625 Durant Ave, Berkeley, CA 94720-2250; tel. (510) 642-0808; e-mail bampfa@berkeley.edu; internet www.bampfa.berkeley.edu; f. 1970; 10 exhibition galleries, sculpture garden; permanent colln of Asian and Western art; Hans Hofmann colln; 16,000 objects and 14,000 films and video cassettes; serves the univ. and San Francisco Bay Area community with exhibitions, study collns, etc.; organizes and receives travelling exhibitions from major museums internationally; screens 550–600 films annually; library of 8,000 vols; 150 journal titles; 7,500 posters; 35,000 stills; 1,500 audio cassettes; 95,000 documentation files containing film reviews, press kits, and articles on filmmakers, performers, nat. cinemas, genres and other topics; Chair. BARCLAY SIMPSON; Dir LAWRENCE RINDER; Chief Curator and Dir of Programmes and Colln LUCINDA BARNES.

Colorado

Clyfford Still Museum: 1250 Bannock St, Denver, CO 80204; tel. (720) 354-4880; e-mail info@clyffordstillmuseum.org; internet www .clyffordstillmuseum.org; f. 2004; 2,400 works of Clyfford; artist's archives of letters, sketchbooks, MSS, photograph albums and personal effects; 825 paintings and 1,575 works on paper; Dir DEAN SOBEL.

Colorado Springs Fine Arts Center: 30 W Dale St, Colorado Springs, CO 80903; tel. (719) 634-5581; e-mail info@csfineartscenter .org; internet www.csfineartscenter.org; f. 1936; permanent colln of masterworks by American artists Richard Diebenkorn, Georgia O'Keeffe, Walt Kuhn, John Singer Sargent and artists associated with the Broadmoor Art Acad.; collns of Hispanic and American Indian art; 9 permanent colln galleries, 2 travelling exhibition galleries and Tactile Gallery; Chair. MARTHA MARZOLF; Pres. and CEO SAM GAPPMAYER; Sec. DAN O'REAR; Treas. KIMBERLEY SHERWOOD; publ. *ArtsFocus*.

Colorado Springs Pioneers Museum: 215 S Tejon St, Colorado Springs, CO 80903; tel. (719) 385-5990; e-mail cosmuseum@ springsgov.com; internet www.springsgov .com; f. 1903; 60,000 objects incl. nationally significant collns of quilts, Van Briggle art pottery and regional art colln; native American colln of items rep. of the Ute, Cheyenne and Arapaho cultures; reconstruction of author Helen Hunt Jackson's house; collns related to founding of the City, area's mining and agricultural history, its early promin-

ence as a health resort and its recent significance as centre for military training and operations; incl. Starsmore Centre for Local History, archives and research library; Dir MATT MAYBERRY.

CU Art Museum: Univ. of Colorado at Boulder, 318 UCB, Boulder, CO 80309; 1085 18th St., Boulder, CO 80309; tel. (303) 492-8300; internet cuartmuseum.colorado .edu; f. 1939; attached to Univ. of Colorado at Boulder; 6,000 works of art; colln of ancient Greek ceramics, Pop Art paintings, Old Master works on paper, SW American and S American santos, SE Asian and Iranian pottery, African sculpture, 18th-century British engraving, 19th-century photography, Japanese ukiyo-e, American prints of 1930s and 1940s, minimalist works on paper and contemporary sculpture, prints, photographs and paintings; Dir LISA TAMIRIS BECKER; Chair. WALTER DIETRICH; Sec. KELLY FEENEY.

Denver Art Museum: 100 W 14th Ave Parkway, Denver, CO 80204-2788; tel. (720) 865-5000; e-mail info@denverartmuseum .org; internet www.denverartmuseum.org; f. 1893 as Artists' Club of Denver, current location 1971, extension opened 2006; exhibitions and art education programmes for children and adults; permanent collns incl. architecture, design and graphics, Asian; modern and contemporary; native art (incl. American Indian, African and Oceanic artworks); New World (incl. pre-Columbian and Spanish Colonial); painting and sculpture (incl. American and European); photography; Western American art; textile art; temporary exhibitions; Dir Dr CHRISTOPH HEINRICH; Chief Curator NANCY BLOMBERG; publs *On & Off the Wall* (6 a year), *Western Passages* (1 a year).

Denver Museum of Nature and Science: 2001 Colorado Blvd, Denver, CO 80205-5978; tel. (303) 370-6000; e-mail feedback@dmns .org; internet www.dmns.org; f. 1900; depts of anthropology and archaeology, archives, photographic archives, earth sciences, zoology, conservation, exhibitions, youth programmes, adult programmes; Gates Planetarium, Hall of Life, IMAX theatre, auditorium; permanent exhibition: Egyptian mummies, expedition health, gems and minerals, N American Indian cultural artefacts, wildlife exhibits, space odyssey, prehistoric dinosaurs skeletons and fossils; library of 53,000 vols, incl. 2,000 children's books, 2,500 rare books and 9,000 vols of scientific periodicals, 700,000 photographs; Chair. JAMES H. CROCKER; Chief Curator Dr KIRK R. JOHNSON; Pres. and CEO GEORGE W. SPARKS; publ. *Denver Museum of Nature & Science Annals*.

Kirkland Museum of Fine & Decorative Art: 1311 Pearl St, Denver, CO 80203; tel. (303) 832-8576; e-mail info@ kirklandmuseum.org; internet www .kirklandmuseum.org; f. 1910; 3,300 works of 20th-century decorative arts on view of arts and crafts, art nouveau, Glasgow style, Wiener Werkstätte, De Stijl, Bauhaus, art deco, modern and pop art; retrospective of painter Vance Kirkland; incl. historic studio of Vance Kirkland; Dir and Curator HUGH A. GRANT.

Koshare Indian Museum: POB 580, La Junta, CO 81050; 115 W 18th St, La Junta, CO 81050; tel. (719) 384-4411; e-mail kiva_clerk@ojc.edu; internet www .kosharehistory.org; f. 1949; Joseph Imhof colln (Imhof works of art by Taos founders, artists from Taos and Sante Fe, and Native American artists); sculptures and paintings by Ernesto Zepeda; Andy Anderson woodcarving and caricature carving figures; letter colln of Daniel Kills Alive; colln of guns and

W items dating from Civil War; colln of pottery, kachinas, basketry, beadwork, tools, dolls, quill work, jewellery and handicraft artwork; Dir and Curator JEREMY MANYIK.

Leanin' Tree Museum and Sculpture Garden of Western Art: 6055 Longbow Dr., Boulder, CO 80301; e-mail mediadirector@leanintree.com; internet www.leanintreemuseum.com; f. 1949; fine art paintings and bronzes of W America created after 1930, incl. cowboys, Indians, wildlife and landscapes; 250 paintings and 150 bronze sculptures by 100 artists; Chair. ED TRUMBLE.

Littleton Museum: 6028 S Gallup St, Littleton, CO 80120; tel. (303) 795-3950; e-mail mutn@littletongov.org; internet www.littletongov.org/museum; 40,000 historically significant artefacts; Dir TIM NIMZ.

Longmont Museum & Cultural Center: 400 Quail Rd, Longmont, CO 80501; tel. (303) 651-8374; internet www.ci.longmont.co.us/museum; f. 1936, present status 1970; exhibits history and culture of Longmont and the St Vrain River Valley; colln incl. Lyons, Colorado, artist Kathy Bradford's sandblasted glass wall Hidden Paths, Unseen Trails; 3 pieces of public art; incl. archives; Dir WESLEY JESSUP.

Museo de las Americas: 861 Santa Fe Dr., Denver, CO 80204; tel. (303) 571-4401; e-mail info@museo.org; internet www.museo.org; f. 1991; 4,000 artefacts on ancient art of the Americas and Latin America; Exec. Dir MARUCA SALAZAR; Pres. GEORGE S. MARTINEZ; Treas. MARIA MONTOYA.

Museum of Western Colorado: POB 20000, Grand Junction, CO 81502-5020; tel. (970) 242-0971; e-mail info@westcomuseum.org; internet www.museumofwesternco.com; incl. Museum of the West, Dinosaur Journey Museum, Cross Orchards Historic Site, Loyd Files Research Library and Whitman Educational Centre; Exec. Dir MIKE PERRY; Pres. DALE TOOKER; Sec. RICK ADLEMAN; Treas. WILLIAM VOSS.

University Art Museum: 1778 Campus Delivery, Fort Collins, CO 80523-1778; tel. (970) 491-1989; internet www.artmuseum.colostate.edu; attached to Colorado State Univ.; 3,000 artworks incl. prints, photographs, paintings, sculpture, textiles and ceramics; modern and contemporary works on paper, incl. Soviet era photography and 250 prints by 19th-century lithographer and social critic, Honoré-Victorin Daumier; 200 19th-century and early 20th-century Japanese prints and African objects and textiles; Dir LINNY FRICKMAN.

University of Colorado Museum of Natural History: Henderson Bldg, 15th and Broadway, Boulder, CO 80309; tel. (303) 492-6892; e-mail cumuseum@colorado.edu; internet cumuseum.colorado.edu; f. 1909; colln of 4m. objects in anthropology, botany, entomology, paleontology and zoology; Dir PATRICK KOCIOLEK.

Connecticut

Bruce Museum: 1 Museum Dr., Greenwich, CT 06830-7157; tel. (203) 869-6786; e-mail info@brucemuseum.org; internet brucemuseum.org; f. 1908; 15,000 objects of fine and decorative art, natural history and anthropology; local repository for archaeological sites and artefacts in Greenwich and Fairfield co; Exec. Dir and CEO PETER C. SUTTON; Co-Chair. NATHANIEL B. DAY; Co-Chair. TAMARA HOLLIDAY; Sec. MARTHA R. ZOUBEK; Treas. LAURENCE B. SIMON.

Connecticut State Museum of Natural History and Archaeology Center: 2019 Hillside Rd, Unit 1023, Storrs, CT 06269-1023; tel. (860) 486-4460; e-mail csmnhinfo@uconn.edu; internet www.cac.uconn.edu; attached to College of Liberal Arts and Sciences, Univ. of Connecticut; 500,000 archaeological and ethnographic items primarily of Native North and South American origin, incl. 19th-century Plains Indian shirts and Palaeolithic stone tools dating from over 250,000 years ago; repository for artefacts from more than 400 archaeological sites from Connecticut, representing every town within the State; State Archaeologist Dr NICHOLAS BELLANTONI; Dir LEANNE KENNEDY HARTY.

Connecticut Trolley Museum: POB 360, East Windsor, CT 06088; 58 North Rd, East Windsor, CT 06088; tel. (860) 627-6540; e-mail office@ceraweb.org; internet www.ct-trolley.org; f. 1940; 70 pieces of rail equipment since 1869; colln incl. elevated railway cars, locomotives (diesel and electric) and passenger and freight railroad cars; Chair. FRED STOINEY; Pres. GALEN SEMPREBON; Treas. STEPHEN TAYLOR.

Custom House Maritime Museum: 150 Bank St, New London, CT 06320; tel. (860) 447-2501; e-mail nlmaritimedirector@gmail.com; internet www.nlmaritimesociety.org; f. 1983; colln promotes and interprets maritime life and history of port of New London and surrounding regions; library of 2,000 vols; Pres. and Chair. GEORGE SPRECACE; Sec. GWENDOLYN BOSCO; Treas. JOHN DESJARDINS; Dir SUSAN TAMULEVICH.

Danbury Railway Museum: POB 90, 120 White St, Danbury, CT 06813-0090; tel. (203) 778-8337; internet www.danbury.org/drm; f. 1994; 70 pieces of historic railroad equipment and artefacts; colln incl. Boston and Maine 1455 steam engine; Pres. WADE ROESE; Sec. STEVE GOULD; Treas. PATTY OSMER.

Discovery Museum and Planetarium: 4450 Park Ave, Bridgeport, CT 06604; tel. (203) 372-3521; e-mail info@discoverymuseum.org; internet www.discoverymuseum.org; f. 1958 as The Museum of Art Science and Industry; incl. Henry B. duPont Planetarium, Challenger Learning Center, interactive science galleries and educational programmes; Chair. JOSEPH D'AVANZO; Dir for Finance and Admin. LAUREL ANDERSON.

Fairfield Museum and History Center: 370 Beach Rd, Fairfield, CT 06824; tel. (203) 259-1598; e-mail info@fairfieldhs.org; internet www.fairfieldhistory.org; f. 2007; colln on 375 years of Fairfield history; early 19th-century store items, genealogy records and resources, arms and weapons from mid-18th century to First World War and civil defence items from Second World War and Cold War era; repository for town records incl. real estate tax records dating back to 1890; Exec. Dir MICHAEL A. JEHLE; Pres. WILLIAM J. VOGEL; Sec. MISSY PALMISANO; Treas. STEVE WAGENBACH.

Florence Griswold Museum: 96 Lyme St, Old Lyme, CT 06371; tel. (860) 434-5542; internet www.flogris.org; f. 1936; paintings and sculptures by artists in Connecticut dating from late Colonial period to early 20th century; library of 1,000 vols; Dir JEFF ANDERSEN; Curator AMY KURTZ LANSING.

Hill-Stead Museum: 35 Mountain Rd, Farmington, CT 06032; tel. (860) 677-4787; internet www.hillstead.org; f. 1947; 1,800 photographs, 55 paintings, 13 sculptures, 170 works on paper, 860 pieces of ceramic, glass and silver, 620 items of textile, 330 pieces of furniture and 25,800 archival documents; French Impressionist paintings; library of 3,300 vols; Dir DEBRA K. PASQUALE; Pres. M. TIMOTHY CORBETT; Sec. and Treas. JAMES W. FANELLI.

Keeler Tavern Museum & Garden House: POB 204, 132 Main St, Ridgefield, CT 06877; tel. (203) 438-5485; e-mail info@keelertavernmuseum.org; internet keelertavernmuseum.org; f. 1966; paintings, prints, samplers and sculpture from early 19th century to mid-20th century; original engraving of Battle of Ridgefield published 1780; hand-carved decorative urns in gardens recreated in Italy from original blueprints; Pres. CHERYL CROWL; Sec. MARY KALETTA; Treas. GEORGE STUECK.

Lyman Allyn Art Museum: 625 Williams St, New London, CT 06320; tel. (860) 443-2545; e-mail info@lymanallyn.org; internet www.lymanallyn.org; f. 1932; 10,000 paintings, drawings, prints, sculptures, furniture and decorative arts focusing on American art dating from 16th to 20th century; Registrar and Asst Curator JANE LeGROW.

Mark Twain House & Museum: 351 Farmington Ave, Hartford, CT 06105; tel. (860) 247-0998; e-mail info@marktwainhouse.org; internet www.marktwainhouse.org; f. 2003; home of author Samuel L. Clemens (also known as Mark Twain) and his family from 1874 to 1891; 16,000 artefacts incl. period decorative and fine arts pieces and 12-vols set of Twain's works in Russian; library of 6,000 vols, 5,280 photographs; Pres. GREGORY BOYKO; Sec. RICHARD F. AHLES; Treas. GREGORY SERVODIDIO; Exec. Dir JEFFREY L. NICHOLS.

New Britain Museum of American Art: 56 Lexington St, New Britain, CT 06052-1412; tel. (860) 229-0257; e-mail nbmaa@nbmaa.org; internet www.nbmaa.org; f. 1953 as New Britain Institute, present name and status 1957; 10,236 works of American art incl. 1,133 oils and acrylics, 2,710 drawings, 1,518 graphics, 202 sculptures, 216 photographs and 1,782 illustrations; colonial and federal portraits, impressionist colln and mural series; Chair. KATHRYN COX; Sec. LINDA TOMASSO; Treas. HENRY R. MARTIN; Dir DOUGLAS HYLAND.

Railroad Museum of New England: POB 400, Thomaston, CT 06787-0400; tel. (860) 283-7245; internet www.rmne.org; f. 1968; focus on historically significant examples of railroad equipment of New England; colln incl. steam and diesel locomotives, passenger cars and freight cars spanning several eras.

Wadsworth Atheneum Museum of Art: 600 Main St, Hartford, CT 06103; tel. (860) 278-2670; e-mail info@wadsworthatheneum.org; internet www.wadsworthatheneum.org; f. 1842; early American furniture, Hudson River School landscapes, Renaissance and Baroque paintings, African-American art; Meissen and Sèvres porcelain; costume and textiles; 19th-century French and Impressionist paintings; modernist and surrealist masterpieces; MATRIX Gallery for Contemporary Art; colln of 50,000 works of art spanning 5,000 years; library: Auerbach library of 40,000 vols; Dir and CEO SUSAN TALBOT; Chief Curator LINDA ROTH; Pres. SUSAN A. ROTTNER; Sec. HY J. SCHWARTZ; Treas. HENRY R. MARTIN.

Yale Peabody Museum of Natural History: Yale Univ., POB 208118, New Haven, CT 06520-8118; Yale Univ., 170–210 Whitney Ave, New Haven, CT 06511; tel. (203) 432-3752; e-mail peabody.director@yale.edu; internet www.peabody.yale.edu; f. 1866; attached to Yale Univ.; extensive collns in the fields of anthropology, meteorites, botany, palaeobotany, invertebrate palaeontology, mineralogy, vertebrate palaeontology, invertebrate zoology and vertebrate zoology, historic scientific instruments, each with its own curator; also Yale Peabody Museum Field Station; Dir DEREK E. G. BRIGGS; publs *Bulletin*, *Discovery*, *Postilla*.

Yale University Art Gallery: POB 208271, New Haven, CT 06520-8271; tel. (203) 432-0600; e-mail artgalleryinfo@yale.edu; internet artgallery.yale.edu; f. 1750; colln of 185,000 works of African art, American paintings and sculpture dating from colonial America to mid-20th century; European art: paintings and sculpture from early Renaissance Tuscany to 19th-century France; coins, medals and paper money since 7th century BC; modern and contemporary art; Asian art; Ancient art; Dir JOCK REYNOLDS.

Delaware

Biggs Museum of American Art: POB 711, Dover, DE 19903; 406 Federal St, Dover, DE 19901; tel. (302) 674-2111; e-mail admin@biggsmuseum.org; internet biggsmuseum .org; f. 1993; representational American paintings colln on the Delmarva Peninsula with highlights by the Peale family, Albert Bierstadt, Gilbert Stuart and Childe Hassam; sculptures by Hiram Powers and images by Brandywine School illustrator, Frank E. Schoonover; colln of regional silver; Dir LINDA A. K. DANKO; Curator RYAN GROVER.

Delaware Agricultural Museum & Village: 866 N DuPont Highway, Dover, DE 19901; tel. (302) 734-1618; e-mail damv@verizon.net; internet www .agriculturalmuseum.org; f. 1980; non-profit org.; depicts technological growth and change in Delaware and Delmarva agricultural history; displays 10,000 artefacts: from butter churns to threshers, from an 18th-century log house to the first broiler chicken house; library of 442 vols, incl. 1,458 images, also houses archival material, oral histories and artefacts pertaining to Delaware agriculture; Pres. CHESTER DICKERSON, JR; Treas. ROBIN TALLEY; Sec. FRANCES WEST.

Delaware Art Museum: 2301 Kentmere Parkway, Wilmington, DE 19806; tel. (302) 571-9590; e-mail info@delart.org; internet www.delart.org; f. 1938 as Delaware Art Center, present name and status 1972; colln of American art since 19th century; pre-Raphaelite collns of Samuel Bancroft, Jr; paintings of Howard Pyle; artworks by John Sloan; library of 30,000 vols (incl. exhibition catalogues, monographs, periodicals, reference works and vertical files relating to individual artists); Exec. Dir DANIELLE RICE; Chief Curator MARGARETTA S. FREDERICK; Librarian RACHAEL DiELEUTERIO.

Delaware History Museum: 504 Market St, Wilmington, DE 19801; tel. (302) 656-0637; e-mail hsd@hsd.org; internet www.hsd .org/dhm.htm; attached to Delaware Historical Soc.; 3 galleries of changing interactive exhibits on Delaware history; displays rare items of everyday life, costumes, children's toys, regional decorative arts and paintings; library: 2m. MSS, 12,000 references, maps, prints and photographs, 700 rare book titles, 110 rare pamphlets and periodicals, 83 almanacs and 300 Delaware imprints; CEO SCOTT W. LOEHR; publ. *Delaware History* (2 a year).

Delaware Museum of Natural History: 4840 Kennett Pike, POB 3937, Wilmington, DE 19807-0937; tel. (302) 658-9111; internet www.delmnh.org; f. 1972; 117,000 bird specimens and 220,000 lots of molluscs (shells); library of 10,000 vols (incl. works on molluscs, recent monographs, reprints and journals); Exec. Dir HALSEY SPRUANCE; publ. *Nemouria: Occasional Papers of the Delaware Museum of Natural History*.

Delaware State Police Museum: 1425 N DuPont Highway, POB 430, Dover, DE 19903-0430; tel. (302) 739-7700; internet www.delawaretrooper.com/museum; f. 1998; showcases history of Delaware State Police; displays vehicles used by Delaware police and their uniform since the time of its inception; Pres. ROBERT M. GOUGE; Treas. PAUL R. KANE; Curator JOHN ALSTADT.

DiscoverSea Shipwreck Museum: 708 Coastal Highway, Fenwick Island, DE 19944; tel. (302) 539-9366; e-mail dsmuseum@aol.com; internet www .discoversea.com; f. 1995; preserves Delmarva's maritime heritage; displays 10,000 artefacts: both regional and worldwide shipwreck and recovered artefacts; Dir DALE W. CLIFTON, JR.

Hagley Museum and Library: POB 3630, Wilmington, DE 19807-0630; 298 Buck Rd E, Wilmington, DE 19807-0630; tel. (302) 658-2400; e-mail info@hagley.org; internet www .hagley.org; f. 1972; non-profit org.; collects, preserves and interprets the unfolding history of American enterprise; incl. restored mills, workers' community and ancestral home and gardens of the du Pont family; library of 280,000 vols, 34,000 linear ft in the MSS and Archives Dept, 2m. visual items; Exec. Dir GEOFF HALFPENNY; Dir Museum Services JOAN HOGE-NORTH; Curator of Collns and Exhibits DEBRA HUGHES.

Historic Odessa Foundation: POB 697, Odessa, DE 19730; tel. (302) 378-4119; e-mail info@historicodessa.org; internet www .historicodessa.org; f. 2005; 18th- and early 19th-century bldgs, incl. Corbit-Sharp House (c. 1774); Wilson-Warner House (c. 1769), Collins-Sharp House (c. 1700), Brick Hotel (c. 1822) and Odessa Bank (c. 1853); 4,000 objects spannig an interpretive period in regional decorative arts from 1760 to 1850; colln of regional paintings, prints, textiles, silver, pewter and other metals; Exec. Dir DEBORAH BUCKSON; Pres. ELIZABETH A SHARP; Treas. WILLIAM GOTWALS.

Milford Museum: 121 S Walnut St, Milford, DE 19963; tel. (302) 424-1080; internet www .milforddemuseum.org; f. 1983; displays local historic events since 1700s; historic doll colln; Victorian silverware colln; early Milford baseball; Exec. Dir CLAUDIA FURNISH LEISTER; Pres. DAVID KENTON; Sec. JOAN LOFLAND; Treas. DONALD ABRUTYN.

Milton Historical Society: POB 112, Milton, DE 19968; tel. (302) 684-1010; e-mail info@historicmilton.org; internet www .historicmilton.org; collects, preserves, and interprets stories, artefacts and documents related to Milton and the Broadkill Hundred for study and education; exhibits show Milton's heyday as a shipbuilding centre and offers a snapshot of Milton from the Civil War through the 1960s; Exec. Dir MELINDA LINDERER HUFF; Pres. DENNIS HUGHES; Treas. DAVID CAREY; Sec. BONNIE HUDSON.

Museum of Business History and Technology: 100 Philadelphia Pike, Wilmington, DE 19809; tel. (302) 798-2100; internet www.mbht.com; f. 2001; 2,000 artefacts showcasing evolution of business technology; collns incl. machines of American manufactures between 1873 and 1940, such as automatic typewriters, calculating machines, copying machines, dictating machines, paging and calling systems, postage machines and word-processing machines; James Watt's 1795 copier and Thomas Decolmar's 1820 calculator.

New Castle Historical Society: 2 E Fourth St, New Castle, DE 19720; tel. (302) 322-2794; e-mail nchistorical@aol.com; internet www.newcastlehistory.org; f. 1934; 3 museums: Amstel House, Dutch House and Old Library Museum; collns of New Castle Library Company; also holds books, ceramics, documents, furniture, MSS, metals, photographs, textiles and works-on-paper preserving 300 years of local and nat. history; Exec. Dir MICHAEL CONNOLLY.

Seaford Museum: 203 High St, Seaford, DE 19973; tel. (302) 628-9828; e-mail info@seafordhistoricalsociety.com; internet www .seafordhistoricalsociety.com/index .cfm?ref=89265; f. 2003; attached to Seaford Historical Soc.; holds artefacts on early agriculture, shipbuilding, canning, chicken industry and railroads.

University Museums: Univ. of Delaware, 208 Mechanical Hall, Newark, DE 19716; tel. (302) 831-8037; e-mail universitymuseums@udel.edu; internet www.udel.edu/museums; f. 1979 as Univ. Gallery; attached to Univ. of Delaware; 20th- and 21st-century American art (Brandywine School); African-American art, photography, minerals; displays 10,000 objects; 3 museums: Mechanical Hall, Mineralogical Museum and Old College Gallery; Dir Dr JANIS A. TOMLINSON; Curator of African-American Art Dr JULIE MCGEE; Curator of the Mineralogical Museum Dr SHARON FITZGERALD; Collns Man. JANET BROSKE.

Winterthur Museum, Garden & Library: 5105 Kennett Pike, Wilmington, DE 19735; tel. (302) 888-4600; e-mail tourinfo@winterthur.org; internet www.winterthur .org; f. 1951; 90,000 American antiquities from 1630 to 1860 (colln incl. ceramics, glass, furniture, metalwork, paintings and prints, and textiles and needlework); MA programme in early American culture and MS programme in art conservation, both in conjunction with Univ. of Delaware; colln of over; library of 100,000 vols, 500,000 MSS, 20,000 rare American and European imprints, 110,000 photographs; Exec. Dir DAVE ROSELLE; publ. *Winterthur Portfolio* (4 a year).

Zwaanendael Museum: 102 Kings Highway, Lewes, DE 19958; tel. (302) 645-1148; internet history.delaware.gov/museums/zm/zm_main.shtml; f. 1931; showcases history of Sussex County, Lewes area maritime, military and social history; 11,000 years of Lewes culture through 5 thematic sections; artefacts, maps, sketches, lithographs and photographs of period bldgs.

District of Columbia

Anacostia Community Museum: 1901 Fort Pl., SE, Washington, DC 20020; tel. (202) 633-4820; e-mail acminfo@si.edu; internet www.anacostia.si.edu; f. 1967; attached to Smithsonian Instn; artefacts, photographs, archival documents, media and art objects that document family and community locally, regionally, nationally and internationally; Griffith Family Colln; Lillian Evans-Tibbs Colln; Lorenzo Dow Turner Colln; library of 3,500 vols, 100 periodicals; Dir CAMILLE GIRAUD AKEJU; Chair. JAMES LARRY FRAZIER.

Arthur M. Sackler Gallery: Smithsonian Instn, 1050 Independence Ave, SW, POB 37012, MRC 707, Washington, DC 20013-7012; tel. (202) 633-1000; e-mail publicaffairsasia@si.edu; internet www.asia .si.edu; f. 1987; attached to Smithsonian Instn; colln incl. ancient Chinese jades and bronzes in the world and contemporary art from Asia as well as int. loan exhibitions; interlinked with Freer Gallery whose colln incl. 19th-century American art; jt Sackler and Freer scientific and research dept; library of 80,000 vols; Dir JULIAN RABY; publs *Ars Orientalis* (1 a year), *Occasional Papers Series* (irregular).

Art Museum of the Americas: Org. of American States, 1889 F St, NW, Washington, DC 20006; 201 18th St, NW, Washington, DC 20006; tel. (202) 458-6016; e-mail artmus@oas.org; internet www.museum.oas.org; f. 1976; attached to Org. of American States; 2,000 objects incl. painting, sculpture, installations, prints, drawings and photographs of America; contemporary Latin American and Caribbean art; works incl. early 20th-century American paintings and art; Dir LYDIA BENDERSKY.

Arts and Industries Building: 900 Jefferson Dr., SW, Washington, DC; tel. (202) 633-1000; e-mail info@si.edu; internet www.si.edu/museums/arts-and-industries-building; f. 1881; attached to Smithsonian Instn; exhibitions of Smithsonian Instn and other museums; art, history, natural history, history of technology, portraiture, air and space history, African-American and Native American history.

Corcoran Gallery of Art: Corcoran College of Art and Design, 500 17th St, NW, Washington, DC 20006-4840; tel. (202) 639-1700; e-mail provostoffice@corcoran.org; internet www.corcoran.org; f. 1869; 16,000 items from 19th and 20th centuries; American and European painting, sculpture and photography, incl. works by Cuyp, Degas, Delacroix, Hopper, Elsworth Kelly, Monet, Picasso, Man Ray, Renoir, Rodin, Sargent, Warhol, Whistler; also houses the Corcoran College of Art and Design; Dir and Pres. KRISTIN GUITER; Man. of Curatorial Affairs LISA STRONG; Chair. HARRY F. HOPPER, III; Sec. SARAH E. CHAPOTON; Treas. FREDERICK W. KNOPS, III.

DAR Museum: c/o Nat. Soc. Daughters of the American Revolution, 1776D St, NW, Washington, DC 20006-5303; tel. (202) 628-1776; e-mail historian@dar.org; internet www.dar.org/museum; f. 1890; attached to Nat. Soc. Daughters of the American Revolution; comprises 31 period rooms and 2 galleries; 30,000 decorative and fine arts objects spanning the 18th and 19th centuries, incl. furniture, glass, ceramics, textiles and silver; spec. colln: folk art and Americana, artefacts of the abolitionist movement; library of 180,000 vols; Dir DIANE DUNKLEY; publ. *American Spirit*.

Fondo Del Sol Visual Arts Center: 2112R St, NW, Washington, DC 2008; tel. (202) 483-2777; e-mail info@fondodelsol.org; internet www.fondodelsol.org; f. 1973; colln of 800 paintings, prints and drawings; 500 photographic images; pre-Columbian, Santero and 20th-century Latino and Carribean art; film and video archive of over 200 works; Chair., Dir and Chief Curator MARC ZUVER; Treas. BRUCE TOONE.

Hillwood Estate, Museum & Gardens: 4155 Linnean Ave, NW, Washington, DC 20008; tel. (202) 686-8500; internet www.hillwoodmuseum.org; 16,000 works of art; colln of imperial Russian and 18th-century French decorative arts; library of 30,000 vols; Exec. Dir KATE MARKERT; Chief Curator LIANA PAREDES; Pres. ELLEN M. CHARLES; Sec. MICHAEL CANTACUZÈNE; Treas. RILEY K. TEMPLE.

Hirshhorn Museum and Sculpture Garden: Smithsonian Instn, POB 37012, MRC Code 350, Washington, DC 20013-7012; Independence Ave, Seventh St, SW, Washington, DC 20560; tel. (202) 633-4674; e-mail hmsginquiries@si.edu; internet hirshhorn.si.edu; f. 1960; attached to Smithsonian Instn; modern and contemporary int. art; sculpture of major artists of the 20th and 21st centuries; library of 62,000 vols, 50 serials, 980 non-colln photograph files, 13,000 slides from 900 contemporary artists; Chair. J. TOMILSON HILL; Sec. DANIEL SALLICK; Treas. PAUL C. SCHORR, III.

International Spy Museum: 800 F St, NW, Washington, DC 20004; tel. (202) 393-7798;

e-mail other@spymuseum.org; internet www.spymuseum.org; f. 2002; history and contemporary role of espionage from a global perspective; colln of int. espionage artefacts; Exec. Dir PETER EARNEST; Chair. MILTON MALTZ.

Kreeger Museum: 2401 Foxhall Rd, NW, Washington, DC 20007; tel. (202) 337-3050; e-mail visitorservices@kreegermuseum.org; internet www.kreegermuseum.org; f. 1959; colln incl. works since 1850s; paintings of Pablo Picasso's life and career and that by 20th-century European artists as well as traditional African and Asian art; Dir JUDY A. GREENBERG.

National Air and Space Museum: Independence Ave, Sixth St, SW, Washington, DC 20560; tel. (202) 633-1000; e-mail info@si.edu; internet www.nasm.si.edu; f. 1946 as Nat. Air Museum; attached to Smithsonian Instn; records the nat. devt of aeronautics and astronautics; collects, preserves and displays aeronautical and astronautical equipment of historical interest and significance: 38,200 aviation artefacts, 14,900 space related artefacts and 4,400 works of art; provides educational material for the historical study of aeronautics and astronautics; colln contains original full-size aircraft, spacecraft, recovered space exploration vehicles, engines, instruments, flight clothing, accessories of technical, historical, and biographical interest, photographs, scale models and extensive reference data; Paul E. Garber Preservation, Restoration and Storage Facility and Steven F. Udvar-Hazy Center; incl. Center for Earth and Planetary Studies (*q.v.*); library of 40,000 vols, archives: 14,000 cu ft of materials, 2m. photographs, 20,000 motion picture and video items, 16,000 reels of microfilm, 2m. technical drawings; Dir Gen. JOHN R. DAILEY.

National Building Museum: 401 F St, NW, Washington, DC 20001; tel. (202) 272-2448; e-mail editor@nbm.org; internet www.nbm.org; f. 1985; 75,000 photographic images; 68,000 architectural prints and drawings; 100 linear ft of documents and 4,500 objects; material samples, architectural fragments and 2,200 architectural toys; spec. collns: S. H. Kress and Co Colln, Wurts Brothers Photography Colln and NW Terra Cotta Colln; Exec. Dir CHASE W. RYND; Vice-Pres. for Exhibitions and Collns CATHY CRANE FRANKEL.

National Gallery of Art: 2000B South Club Dr., Landover, MD 20785; Nat. Mall, Third and Ninth St, NW, Constitution Ave, Washington, DC 20565; tel. (202) 737-4215; e-mail pressinfo@nga.gov; internet www.nga.gov; f. 1937; European and American paintings, sculpture and graphic arts since 12th century; photographic archives; slide colln; library of 365,000 vols, 2,321 periodicals; Pres. VICTORIA P. SANT; Dir EARL A. POWELL, III; publ. *Studies in the History of Art*.

National Museum of African Art: POB 37012, MRC 708, Washington, DC 20013-7012; 950 Independence Ave, SW, Washington, DC 20560; tel. (202) 633-4600; e-mail nmafaweb@nmafa.si.edu; internet africa.si.edu; f. 1964; attached to Smithsonian Instn; 8,000 items from Africa, incl. traditional and contemporary art; library of 25,000 vols, the Eliot Elisofon Photographic Archives: 300,000 photographic prints and transparencies, 120,000 ft of motion picture film and video cassettes; Dir Dr JOHNNETTA B. COLE; Chair. STUART BOHART.

National Museum of American History: Kenneth E. Behring Center, Dept of Education for Interpretation and Visitor Experience, POB 37012, MRC 603, Washington, DC 20013-7012; The Nat. Mall, 14th St and

Constitution Ave, NW, Washington, DC 20560; tel. (202) 633-1000; e-mail info@si.edu; internet americanhistory.si.edu; f. 1964 as the Nat. Museum of History and Technology, present name 1980; attached to Smithsonian Instn; 3m. artefacts incl. gowns and locomotives; Archives Center with 1,200 documents, photographs and other works; lectures and concerts; Dir MARC PACHTER; Curator, Archives Center VANESSA BROUSSARD SIMMONS.

Attached Research Institute:

Jerome and Dorothy Lemelson Center for the Study of Invention and Innovation: see separate entry.

National Museum of American Jewish Military History: 1811R St, NW, Washington, DC 20009; tel. (202) 265-6280; e-mail nmajmh@nmajmh.org; internet www.nmajmh.org; f. 1958; 5,000 artefacts, incl. objects from every American military conflict, with spec. emphasis on Second World War; incl. archival colln of American Jewish military history since the Civil War; Dir HERB ROSENBLEETH; Pres. NORMAN ROSENSHEIN; publ. *Hall of Heroes*.

National Museum of Natural History: POB 37012, Smithsonian Instn, Washington, DC 20013-7012; tel. (202) 357-2661; e-mail naturalexperience@si.edu; internet www.mnh.si.edu; f. 1910; attached to Smithsonian Instn; 126m. natural science specimens and cultural artefacts; items incl. fossilized pollen, bones of Tyrannosaurus rex, algal samples, slab of a giant sequoia tree, tiny crustaceans, giant squid, DNA samples of whale skulls, ancient spear points, Chinese shoes, Hope Diamond and Moon rocks; 30m. insects; 7m. fish in liquid-filled jars; 2m. cultural artefacts; 400,000 photographs housed in the Nat. Anthropological Archives; 20,000 works of native art, 1,200 aluminium discs by J. P. Harrington; human studies film archives: 8m. ft of film and video; Chair. KATHRYN S. FULLER; Dir Dr CRISTIÁN SAMPER (acting); publ. *Smithsonian Contributions* (separate series for Anthropology, Botany, Earth Sciences, Palaeobiology, Zoology and Marine Sciences)

Attached Research Institutes:

Arctic Research Centre: see separate entry.

Carrie-Bow Marine Field Station—Caribbean Coral Reef Ecosystems (CCRE): see separate entry in Belize chapter.

Marine Station at Fort Pierce: see separate entry.

National Museum of the US Navy: Washington Navy Yard, 805 Kidder Breese St, SE, Washington, DC 20374-5060; tel. (202) 433-4882; e-mail navymuseum@navy.mil; internet www.history.navy.mil/branches/org8-1.htm; f. 1961; attached to Naval History and Heritage Command; naval artefacts, models, documents and fine art depicting the history of the US Navy from the American Revolution to the present conflicts; interactive exhibits of Navy's wartime heroes and battles as well as peacetime contributions in exploration, diplomacy, navigation and humanitarian service; Dir Rear Admiral JAY A. DELOACH.

National Museum of Women in the Arts: 1250 New York Ave, NW, Washington, DC 20005-3970; tel. (202) 783-5000; internet www.nmwa.org; f. 1981; more than 3,000 works of art by women since 16th century; Renaissance paintings of Elisabetta Sirani, modern photographs by Barbara Morgan and Louise Nevelson's contemporary sculptures; archives on women artists: colln of research files of personal and biographic information of 18,000 women artists; library of 18,500 vols; Dir SUSAN FISHER STERLING; Chief Curator JORDANA POMEROY; Chair. WILHELMINA COLE HOLLADAY; Sec. CHARLOTTE CLAY BUXTON; Treas. SHEILA SHAFFER; publ. *Women in the Arts* (4 a year).

National Portrait Gallery: POB 37012, Victor Bldg, Suite 8300, MRC 973, Washington, DC 20013-7012; Eighth and F St, NW, Washington, DC 20001; tel. (202) 633-1000; e-mail npgnews@si.edu; internet npg.si.edu; f. 1962; attached to Smithsonian Instn; portraits of persons who have made significant contributions to the history, devt or culture of the people of the USA; Dir KIM SAJET; publ. *PROFILE* (4 a year).

National Postal Museum: POB 37012, MRC 570, Washington, DC 20013-7012; 2 Massachussetts Ave, NE, Washington, DC 20002; tel. (202) 633-5555; internet www .postalmuseum.si.edu; f. 1886 as Nat. Philatelic Colln, present name and location 1993; attached to Smithsonian Instn; Nat. Philatelic Colln of 6m. items; incl. delivery vehicles, mailboxes and mailbags, uniforms and equipment and other items of postal history; library of 13,000 vols; Dir ALLEN R. KANE; Chief Curator of Philately CHERYL GANZ.

Phillips Collection: 1600 21st St, NW, Washington, DC 20009; tel. (202) 387-2151; e-mail director@phillipscollection.org; internet www.phillipscollection.org; f. 1918; 3,000 works by American and European artists; Center for the Study of Modern Art; library of 9,500 vols; Dir DOROTHY KOSINSKI; Chair. GEORGE VRADENBURG; Sec. BRIAN D. DAILEY; Treas. THOMAS D. RUTHERFOORD, JR.; Chief Curator ELIZA RATHBONE.

Sewall-Belmont House & Museum: 144 Constitution Ave, NE, Washington, DC 20002-5608; tel. (202) 546-1210; e-mail info@sewallbelmont.org; internet www .sewallbelmont.org; colln incl. 800 suffrage banners, archives, capes, sashes and ribbons used by the National Woman's Party for parades; artefacts of the suffrage movement and the campaign for Equal Rights Amendment; books, scrapbooks, political cartoons, textiles, photographs, organizational records, fine arts and decorative arts; library of 10,000 vols (incl. early women's magazines and suffrage journals written by and about women since 1880); Exec. Dir PAGE HARRINGTON; Pres. DIANNE CHASEN LIPSEY; Sec. SALLY PATTERSON; Treas. ALICIA DALY.

Smithsonian American Art Museum and the Renwick Gallery: POB 37012, MRC 970, Washington, DC 20013-7012; 750 Ninth St, NW, Washington, DC 20001; tel. (202) 633-7970; e-mail americanartinfo@si.edu; internet americanart.si.edu; f. 1829; largest colln of American art in the world; 41,000 artworks since 18th century; incl. Lunder Conservation Center (permanent displays of the museum's preservation work) and provides information on conservation science and techniques; other centres incl. Luce Foundation Center for American Art (art storage and study centre): 3,300 objects on display, incl. a discussion of each artwork, artist biographies, audio interviews, videoclips and still images; specialized art research databases of 500,000 records, incl. Inventory of American Paintings and Sculpture; pre-1877 Art Exhibition Catalogue Index and findings from the Save Outdoor Sculpture programme; photographic archives: 250,000 photographs, negatives and slides; Peter A. Juley and Son colln (127,000 images documenting the work of 11,000 American artists from the 1890s to 1975); and the Walter Rosenblum colln (7,500 black-and-white photographs docu-

menting the New York art scene from 1945 to 1970); Graphic Arts Study Center (28,000 works on paper, including prints, drawings, watercolours and photographs) and the Joseph Cornell Study Center; Renwick Gallery of craft work; now part of the Donald W. Reynolds Center; library of 180,000 vols; Dir ELIZABETH BROUN; publ. *American Art* (3 a year).

Textile Museum: 2320 S St, NW, Washington, DC 20008-4088; tel. (202) 667-0441; e-mail info@textilemuseum.org; internet www.textilemuseum.org; f. 1925; 9,000 objects spanning 5,000 years dating from 3,000 BC to the present; colln incl. 15th-century Mamluk rugs from Egypt, Spanish carpets and classical Indian carpet fragments; also incl. pre-Columbian Peruvian textiles; library of 20,000 vols; Dir MARY-CLAIRE RAMSEY; Pres. BRUCE P. BAGANZ; publ. *Members' Magazine* (4 a year).

United States Holocaust Memorial Museum: 100 Raoul Wallenberg Pl., SW, Washington, DC 20024-2126; tel. (202) 488-0400; e-mail curator@ushmm.org; internet www.ushmm.org; f. 1993; collects and preserves historical record of the Holocaust; colln incl. original documents, photographs and artefacts related to Holocaust; 10,000 art and artefacts; 12,500 oral history testimonies and access to 52,000 oral histories from the USC Shoah Foundation Institute; 2 theatres; interactive computer learning centre; classrooms and a memorial space; library of 92,025 vols; Dir SARA J. BLOOMFIELD.

United States National Arboretum: 3501 New York Ave, NE, Washington, DC 20002-1958; tel. (202) 245-2726; internet www.usna .usda.gov; f. 1927; attached to Beltsville Agricultural Research Center, Agricultural Research Service, US Dept of Agriculture; aquatic plants; Asian collns; Fern Valley Native Plant collns; Flowering Tree colln; Flowering Tree Walk; Friendship gdn; Gotelli Dwarf and Slow-Growing Conifer colln; Introduction gdn; Nat. Bonsai and Penjing Museum; Nat. Capitol Columns; Nat. Grove of State Trees; Nat. Herb Gdn; library of 11,000 vols, 100 journals; Dir Dr COLIEN HEFFERAN.

Florida

Appleton Museum of Art: College of Central Florida, 4333 E Silver Springs Blvd, Ocala, FL 34470-5001; tel. (352) 291-4455; e-mail ormej@cf.edu; internet www .appletonmuseum.org; f. 1982, present status 2004; attached to College of Central Florida; 16,000 objects of European, American, Asian, African, Contemporary and pre-Columbian art and artefacts from 17th to 19th century; library of 2,000 vols; Dir Dr JOHN Z. LOFGREN; Chief Curator RUTH GRIM.

Bass Museum of Art: 2100 Collins Ave, Miami Beach, FL 33139; tel. (305) 673-7530; e-mail info@bassmuseum.org; internet www .bassmuseum.org; f. 1963; 3,000 art works incl. European paintings and sculptures since 15th century; textiles, tapestries and artefacts dating from 7th to 20th century; 20th- and 21st-century N American, Latin American, Asian and Caribbean art, photographs, prints and drawings; Exec. Dir and Chief Curator SILVIA KARMAN CUBIÑA; Pres. GEORGE LINDEMANN; Sec. LIDA RODRIGUEZ-TASEFF; Treas. ALAN RANDOLPH.

Boca Raton Museum of Art: 501 Plaza Real, Mizner Park, Boca Raton, FL 33432; tel. (561) 392-2500; e-mail info@bocamuseum .org; internet www.bocamuseum.org; f. 1962, current name adopted 1985; colln incl. European paintings and sculptures dating from 1775 to 1945; modern and contemporary artworks since 1960s; 300 objects of African

arts and artefacts; 800 European and American prints and drawings from 19th century; Dir STEVEN MAKLANSKY; Pres. PAUL W. CARMAN; Sec. ANDREA KLINE; Treas. JOSEPH BORROW.

Cornell Fine Arts Museum: 1000 Holt Ave, Winter Park, FL 32789-4499; tel. (407) 646-2526; internet www.rollins.edu/cfam; f. 1941 as Morse Gallery of Art, present name 1978; attached to Rollins College; 5,000 objects from antiquity to contemporary, Middle E artefacts, religious iconography and fine paintings; works of Albert Bierstadt, Alex Katz, John Frederick Kensett, Henri Matisse, Thomas Moran and Pablo Picasso; public talks, film screenings and educational programmes; Dir Dr ENA HELLER (acting); Curator JONATHAN F. WALZ.

Cummer Museum of Art & Gardens: 829 Riverside Ave, Jacksonville, FL 32204; tel. (904) 356-6857; internet www.cummer.org; f. 1958; 5,000 art works spanning 2100BC through 21st century; Dir HOPE McMATH; Chief Curator HOLLY KERIS.

Dalí Museum: One Dali Blvd, St Petersburg, FL 33701; tel. (727) 823-3767; e-mail info@thedali.org; internet thedali.org; f. 1982; colln of 1,300 graphics, sculptures and photographs; oil paintings dating from 1917 to 1970; Dir HANK HINE.

Florida State University Museum of Fine Arts: 530 W Call St, Room 250, Tallahassee, FL 32306-1140; tel. (850) 644-6836; e-mail mofa@fsu.edu; internet www .mofa.fsu.edu; f. 1950; 5,000 objects from pre-Columbian pottery to contemporary art; Dir ALLYS PALLADINO-CRAIG; publ. *Athanor* (1 a year).

Harn Museum of Art: POB 112700, Gainesville, FL 32611-2700; SW 34th St and Hull Rd, Gainesville, FL 32611-2700; tel. (352) 392-9826; e-mail info@harn.ufl.edu; internet www.harn.ufl.edu; f. 1990; attached to Univ. of Florida; 8,000 objects from Mesoamerica, Central America and Central Andes; 2,000 objects from Neolithic period to contemporary art; modern colln incl. 1,000 artworks dating from 19th to 20th century; Dir Dr REBECCA M. NAGY.

John and Mable Ringling Museum of Art: 5401 Bay Shore Rd, Sarasota, FL 34243; tel. (941) 359-5700; e-mail info@ringling.org; internet www.ringling.org; f. 1927; attached to Florida State Univ.; comprises Museum of Art (European, American and Non-Western art), 2 Circus Museums incl. the Tibbals Learning Center, home of the world's largest miniature circus, Cà d'Zan Mansion (former Ringling winter residence), Historic Asolo Theater (18th-century Venetian theatre from Asolo, Italy), 66-acre waterfront estate; 14,000 objects of European, American and Asian art; Koger Colln of Chinese ceramic; library of 80,000 vols and exhibition catalogues, 100 periodicals; Chair. PATRICK J. HENNIGAN; Sec. MICHÉLE D. REDWINE; Treas. MICHAEL E. URETTE; Exec. Dir Dr JOHN WETENHALL.

Lowe Art Museum: 1301 Stanford Dr., Coral Gables, FL 33124-6310; tel. (305) 284-3535; internet lowemuseum.org; f. 1952; attached to Univ. of Miami; world art colln of over 18,500 objects; Dir BRIAN DURSUM.

Mennello Museum of American Art: 900 E Princeton St, Orlando, FL 32803; tel. (407) 246-4278; internet www.mennellomuseum .com; colln of paintings by Earl Cunningham (1893–1977) and other American Artists; Exec. Dir FRANK HOLT.

Miami Art Museum: 101 W Flagler St, Miami, FL 33130; tel. (305) 375-3000; e-mail curatorial@miamiartmuseum.org; internet www.miamiartmuseum.org; f. 1996, fmrly

Center for the Fine Arts; 800 artworks with focus on int. art of 20th and 21st centuries; Chair. AARON PODHURST; Pres. GAIL S. MEYERS; Sec. M. THÉRÈSE VENTO; Treas. JEFF KRINSKY.

Museum of Art—Fort Lauderdale: 1 E Las Olas Blvd, Andrews Ave, Fort Lauderdale, FL 33301; tel. (954) 525-5500; e-mail info@moafl.org; internet www.moafl.org; f. 1958 as Fort Lauderdale Art Center, current name adopted 1963; attached to Nova Southeastern Univ.; 6,000 artworks reflecting cultures of S Florida and Caribbean; Chair. DAVID HORVITZ; Sec. STANLEY GOODMAN; Exec. Dir IRVIN LIPPMAN; Curator JORGE HILKER SANTIS.

Museum of Arts & Sciences: 352 S Nova Rd, Daytona Beach, FL 32114; tel. (386) 255-0285; e-mail groupinfo@moas.org; internet www.moas.org; f. 1955; 30,000 objects of Cuban and Florida art, American fine and decorative arts, European fine and decorative arts, pre-Columbian and African artefacts, Pleistocene fossils, Florida history and regional natural history; Anderson C. Bouchelle Center for Decorative Arts: Russian enamels, French gilt bronze, and American Brilliant Period Glass; Abraham and Dorothy Frischer Sculpture Garden; planetarium; Pres. BARBARA COLEMAN; Sec. MELINDA DAWSON; Treas. MICHAEL SLICK; Exec. Dir DEBORAH B. ALLEN; Chief Curator CYNTHIA DUVAL; publ. *Arts & Sciences* (4 a year).

Museum of Contemporary Art: Joan Lehman Bldg, 770 NE 125th St, N Miami, FL 33161; tel. (305) 893-6211; e-mail info@mocanomi.org; internet mocanomi.org; f. 1996, fmrly Center of Contemporary Art (f. 1981); 600 works of contemporary art; Pres. RAY ELLEN YARKIN; Chair. MICHAEL COLLINS; Sec. FRANCINE BIRBRAGHER-ROZENCWAIG; Treas. CARLOS J. ARRIZURIETA; Exec. Dir and Chief Curator BONNIE CLEARWATER.

Museum of Fine Arts: 255 Beach Dr., NE, St Petersburg, FL 33701-3498; tel. (727) 896-2667; internet www.fine-arts.org; f. 1965; colln of 14,000 objects since antiquity (spanning 4,500 years); European Art Colln: 17th to 19th century; American Art Colln: 18th and 19th centuries; Greek and Roman Antiquities and Pre-Columbian and Asian art; Dir Dr KENT LYDECKER; Chief Curator Dr JENNIFER HARDIN; publ. *MOSAIC* (4 a year).

Museum of Florida History: 500 S Bronough, Tallahassee, FL 32399; tel. (850) 245-6400; internet www.museumoffloridahistory.com; f. 1977; attached to Florida Dept of State; 45,300 artefacts on Florida history dating from prehistoric era to mid-19th century; military artefacts since 1830s; Florida's Second World War Living Memorial; Chair. BILL HERRLE; Dir JEANA BRUNSON; Curator CLINT FOUNTAIN.

Norton Museum of Art: 1451 S Olive Ave, West Palm Beach, FL 33401; tel. (561) 832-5196; e-mail museum@norton.org; internet www.norton.org; f. 1941; 7,000 works of 19th- to 20th-century American art; jades produced for emperor of China in mid-1700s; European art comprises paintings, sculpture, prints and drawings dating from 1450 to 1950; 2,200 photographs since 19th century; Chair. KEMP C. STICKNEY; Dir and CEO HOPE ALSWANG; Chief Curator ROGER WARD.

Patricia & Phillip Frost Art Museum: Florida Int. Univ., University Park, 10975 SW 17th St, Miami, FL 33199; tel. (305) 348-2890; e-mail artinfo@fiu.edu; internet thefrost.fiu.edu; f. 1977, fmrly The Art Museum at FIU, current name adopted 2003; attached to Florida Int. Univ.; represents American printmaking from the 1960s and 1970s; 2,300 objects incl. sculptures,

photographs and paintings of 20th century, Japanese Netsukes and ancient bronzes from Asian and African cultures; pre-Columbian objects dating from AD 200–500; Dir Dr CAROL DAMIAN; publ. *Frost on View* (2 a year).

Pensacola Museum of Art: 407 S Jefferson St, Pensacola, FL 32502; tel. (850) 432-6247; e-mail info@pensacolamuseumofart.org; internet www.pensacolamuseumofart.org; f. 1954 as Pensacola Art Asscn, current name adopted 1982; colln incl. 20th- and 21st-century artworks representing modern and contemporary styles and periods, incl. Cubism, Realism, Pop art, Non-objective art, Folk art and Illustration; decorative arts colln of European and American glass and African tribal art; Exec. Dir SONYA DAVIS.

Polk Museum of Art: 800 E Palmetto St, Lakeland, FL 33801; tel. (863) 688-7743; e-mail info@polkmuseumofart.org; internet polkmuseumofart.org; f. 1966 as Imperial Youth Museum, current name adopted 1983; colln on modern and contemporary art, Asian art, European and American decorative arts and pre-Columbian art; artistic works ranging from 2,500-year-old vessels made by the Chavin culture (now Peru) to contemporary artworks; Curator of Art ADAM JUSTICE.

Tampa Museum of Art: 120 W Gasparilla Plaza, Tampa, FL 33602; tel. (813) 274-8130; internet www.tampamuseum.org; f. 1979; colln of material culture of Mediterranean region from Bronze Age to Roman Imperial period; 2,149 photographs incl. 19th-century photographs related to Greece and Rome and photography created after 1970; Chair. PETER M. HEPNER; Sec. EDWARD M. WALLER; Treas. JOHN T. WATTS; Exec. Dir TODD D. SMITH.

University of South Florida Contemporary Art Museum: 3821 Holly Dr., Tampa, Fl 33620-7360; tel. (813) 974-4133; e-mail caminfo@arts.usf.edu; internet ira.usf.edu; f. 1968; attached to Institute for Research in Art, Univ. of S Florida; 5,000 artworks incl. contemporary photography and African art; graphics and sculptures by int. artists; Dir MARGARET A. MILLER; Curator JANE SIMON.

Wolfsonian—Florida International University: 1001 Washington Ave, Second Fl., Miami Beach, FL 33139; tel. (305) 531-1001; e-mail info@thewolf.fiu.edu; internet www.wolfsonian.org; f. 1986, present status 1997; 150,000 artefacts, rare books, ephemeral items, and archives of N American and European origin dating from 1885 to 1945; library of 45,000 vols; Dir CATHY LEFF; Curator SARAH SCHLEUNING.

Georgia

Albany Museum of Art: 311 Meadowlark Dr., Albany, GA 31707; tel. (229) 439-8400; e-mail info@albanymuseum.com; internet www.albanymuseum.com; f. 1964, present name and status 1983; colln incl. 2,100 works of art comprising 19th- and 20th-century American and European paintings, sculptures, prints, photographs and traditional African art in SE; Pres. BANKS MARGESON; Treas. TODD HOCKMAN; Sec. NEALY STAPLETON; Exec. Dir KAREN KEMP.

Atlanta History Center: 130 W Paces Ferry Rd, NW, Atlanta, GA 30305-1366; tel. (404) 814-4000; internet www.atlantahistorycenter.com; f. 1926, present name and status 1990; Decorative Arts and Material Culture Colln: 7,000 artefacts from 19th and 20th century, incl. furniture, fine art and glass work; Textiles and Social History Colln: 10,000 objects of clothing, accessories and household textiles; Civil War and Military Colln: 12,000 historical

artefacts; Centennial Olympic Games Colln; Urban History Colln; houses Atlanta History Museum, Centennial Olympic Games Museum, Swan House, Smith Family Farm, 6 historic gardens and Kenan Research Center; Pres. and CEO SAL CILELLA; Chair. BILL SHEARER; Sec. BRAND MORGAN; Treas. LAURA MILES.

Augusta Museum of History: 560 Reynolds St, Augusta, GA 30907; tel. (706) 722-8454; e-mail amh@augustamuseum.org; internet www.augustamuseum.org; f. 1937; colln incl. objects on 12,000 years of local history; 1900 farm wagon and 1917 steam locomotive; Exec. Dir NANCY J. GLASER; Pres. PERRY M. SMITH; Treas. JEFFERSON B. A. KNOX, SR.

Booth Western Art Museum: POB 3070, Cartersville, GA 30120; 501 Museum Dr., Cartersville, GA 30120; tel. (770) 387-1300; e-mail director@boothmuseum.org; internet www.boothmuseum.org; f. 2003; colln incl. Western art, Civil War art, Presidential letters and portraits.

Columbus Museum: 1251 Wynnton Rd, Colombus, GA 31906; tel. (706) 748-2562; e-mail information@columbusmuseum.com; internet www.columbusmuseum.com; f. 1953; drawings, paintings, sculptures and decorative arts spanning over 300 years; 18th- and 19th-century American art colln; library of 4,000 vols; Dir CHARLES T. BUTLER.

Fernbank Museum of Natural History: 767 Clifton Rd NE, Atlanta, GA 30307; tel. (404) 929-6300; internet www.fernbankmuseum.org; f. 1989; documentation of prehistoric human activity on island dating back 5,000 years; Dorothy Methvin McClatchey colln: objects from Central and SE Asia, N America, Africa and Europe; Chair. DOROTHY SMITH HINES; Pres. and CEO SUSAN E. NUEGENT; Sec. KRISTINE PETERSON RUDOLPH; Treas. RONALD B. BOBO.

Georgia Museum of Art: 90 Carlton St, Univ. of Georgia, Athens, GA 30602-6719; tel. (706) 542.4662; internet www.georgiamuseum.org; f. 1945; attached to Univ. of Georgia; 8,000 object colln incl. 19th- and 20th-century American paintings, S decorative arts and Asian art; American, European and Asian works on paper; Samuel H. Kress Study colln of Italian Renaissance paintings; library of 5,000 vols; Dir WILLIAM U. EILAND; Chief Curator PAUL MANOGUERRA.

Hammonds House Museum: 503 Peeples St, SW, Atlanta, GA 30310; tel. (404) 612-0500; internet www.hammondshouse.org; f. 1988; Haitian paintings and 350 artworks by African American artists from mid-19th century; Pres. IMARA CANADY; Exec. Dir MYRNA ANDERSON-FULLER; Sec. DENIECE ACOSTA GRIFFIN; Treas. ISAAC WASHINGTON.

High Museum of Art: 1280 Peachtree St, NE, Atlanta, GA 30309; tel. (404) 733-4400; internet www.high.org; colln incl. 12,000 art works comprising anthology of 19th- and 20th-century American art; European paintings, decorative art, African American art and modern and contemporary art; Chair. LOUISE SAMS.

Michael C. Carlos Museum: 571 S Kilgo Circle, Atlanta, GA 30322; tel. (404) 727-4282; e-mail mburell@emory.edu; internet www.carlos.emory.edu; f. 1876; attached to Emory Univ.; colln of ancient art and artefacts; colln of works on paper since Renaissance; colln of art objects from ancient Egypt, Nubia, Near East, Greece, Rome, Africa and Asia; Dir BONNIE SPEED.

Morris Museum of Art: 1 10th St, Augusta, GA 30901-0100; tel. (706) 724-7501; internet themorris.org; f. 1985; 5,000 paintings, works on paper, photographs and sculptures since the late 18th century; Civil War painting from 1861 to 1865; colln on late 20th century and contemporary art; library of 13,000 vols; Dir and Curator KEVIN GROGAN.

Museum of Aviation: POB 2469, Warner Robins, GA 31099; tel. (478) 926-6870; internet www.museumofaviation.org; f. 1984; colln incl. 6,000 historical artefacts, 100 aircrafts, missiles and cockpits dating from replica of early 1896 glider to modern-era aircraft such as B-1B bomber, SR-71 Blackbird, U-2 Dragon Lady and F-15 Eagle; Dir Col (Retd) KENNETH R. EMERY, II; Curator MIKE ROWLAND.

Museum of Contemporary Art of Georgia: 75 Bennett St, Suite A2, Atlanta, GA 30309; tel. (404) 367-8700; e-mail info@mocaga.org; internet www.mocaga.org; f. 2000; colln incl. 750 works of contemporary art by 200 Georgia artists since mid-1940s in various media (from painting to digital works) and styles (from folk to minimalism); Pres., CEO and Dir ANNETTE CONE-SKELTON.

National Infantry Museum & Soldier Center: 1775 Legacy Way, Colombos, GA 31903; tel. (706) 685-5800; internet www.nationalinfantrymuseum.com; 70,000 artefacts depicting 236 years of American history; Exec. Dir Lt Gen. CARMEN CAVEZZA.

Robert C. Williams Paper Museum: POB 0620, Institute of Paper Science and Technology, Georgia Tech, 500 10th St, NW, Atlanta, GA 30332-0620; tel. (404) 894-7840; internet www.ipst.gatech.edu/amp; f. 1939, present name and status 1954; 10,000 watermarks, papers, tools, machines and MSS; library of 2,000 vols; Dir TERI WILLIAMS.

Roosevelt's Little White House: 401 Little White House Rd, Warm Springs, GA 31830; tel. (706) 655-5870; internet www.fdr-littlewhitehouse.org; f. 1932; under direction of Georgia Dept of Natural Resources; remains as it was when Pres. Franklin Delano Roosevelt died here in 1945; exhibits and film of Roosevelt in Georgia; Franklin Delano Roosevelt Memorial Museum opened in April 2004 with expanded and updated exhibits and films; Superintendent (vacant); Volunteer Coordinator LYNN BARFIELD.

Telfair Museums: 121 Barnard St, Savannah, GA 31401; tel. (912) 790-8800; e-mail info@telfair.org; internet telfair.org; f. 1883; colln incl. 4,500 objects from America, Europe and Asia dating from 18th to 20th centuries; colln of visual art by Lebanese writer Kahlil Gibran; Chair. ALICE JEPSON; Dir LISA GROVE.

William Breman Jewish Heritage & Holocaust Museum: 1440 Spring St NW, Atlanta, GA 30309; tel. (678) 222-3700; internet www.thebreman.org; f. 1984; colln on history of the Holocaust and Jewish life in Georgia; Exec. Dir JANE D. LEAVEY; Pres. JOYCE SHLESINGER; Pres. SPRING ASHER; Sec. MARGIE STERN; Treas. MICHAEL WOOCHER.

Hawai'i

Bailey House Museum: 2375-A Main St, Wailuku, HI 96793; tel. (808) 244-3326; e-mail baileyhousemuseum@clearwire.net; internet www.mauimuseum.org; f. 1957; attached to Maui Historical Soc.; colln of Hawai'ian artefacts, paintings and furnishings from 19th century; Exec. Dir NICOLE McMULLEN; Pres. LUISE BRAUN; Sec. MELISSA KIRKENDALL; Treas. GEORGE ANDRADE.

Bishop Museum: 1525 Bernice St, Honolulu, HI 96817; tel. (808) 847-3511; e-mail library@bishopmuseum.org; internet www.bishopmuseum.org; f. 1889; 25m. works of art, plant and animal specimens; cultural artefacts representing Native Hawaiian, Pacific Island and Hawai'i immigrant life;

23m. specimens of plant and animal life; library of 115,000 vols and 1m. historic photographs, films, works of art, audio recordings and MSS; Pres. and CEO BLAIR D. COLLIS; publ. *Ka'Elele* (12 a year)

Attached Institute:

Amy B. H. Greenwell Ethnobotanical Garden: POB 1053, Captain Cook, HI 96704; tel. (808) 323-3318; e-mail agg@bishopmuseum.org; internet www.bishopmuseum.org/greenwell; f. 1974; 200 species of endemic, indigenous and Polynesian introduced plants; insect house; archaeological site; Man. PETER VAN DYKE.

Hawai'i State Art Museum: 1 Capitol Dist. Bldg, 250 S. Hotel St, Second Fl., Honolulu, HI 96813; tel. (808) 586-0300; internet sfca.hawaii.gov/hisam; f. 1965; attached to Hawaii State Foundation on Culture and the Arts; collns reflect culture, arts and history of Hawai'i; Museum Educator SUSAN HOGAN.

Honolulu Academy of Arts: 900 S Beretania St, Honolulu, HI 96814-1495; tel. (808) 532-8700; e-mail info@honoluluacademy.org; internet www.honoluluacademy.org; f. 1927; 60,000 works spanning 5,000 years (incl. 20,000 works of Asian art, 10,000 Japanese ukiyo-e woodblock prints, 15,000 works on paper); American and European painting and decorative arts, 19th- and 20th-century art, Asian textiles, and traditional works from Africa, Oceania, and the Americas; museum and art school; educational programmes for adults and young people; Doris Duke Theatre with frequent films, lectures, concerts and performances; outdoor gardens; arts festivals; guided tours/gallery talks; art classes and educational programmes for children and adults; spec. exhibitions; Robert Allerton Art Research Library; library of 45,000 vols; Dir STEPHAN JOST; Chair. LYNNE JOHNSON; publ. *Calendar News* (bulletin for members, 6 a year).

Hui No'eau Visual Arts Center: 2841 Baldwin Ave, Makawao, HI 96768; tel. (808) 572-6560; e-mail info@huinoeau.com; internet www.huinoeau.com; f. 1934, present status 1976; works of art and sculptures; Exec. Dir CAROLINE KILLHOUR; Pres. SHANNON HOEKSTRA; Sec. ROBIN FERRIER; Treas. SARAH BREDHOFF.

Isaacs Art Center Museum and Gallery: 65–1692 Kohala Mountain Rd, Kamuela, HI 96743; 65–1268 Kawaihae Rd, Kamuela, HI 96743; tel. (808) 885-5884; e-mail isaacsartcenter@hpa.edu; internet www.isaacsartcenter.hpa.edu; f. 2002; attached to Hawai'i Preparatory Acad.; works of art, paintings, books, furniture, jewellery and photographs; Dir GAYLORD DILLINGHAM.

John Young Museum of Art: Outreach College, Univ. of Hawai'i at Mānoa, Krauss Hall, 2500 Dole St, Honolulu, HI 96822; tel. (808) 956-3634; internet www.outreach.hawaii.edu/jymuseum; f. 1999; attached to Univ. of Hawai'i at Mānoa Outreach College; objects incl. Neolithic pottery jars that date as far back as 3000–2000 BC, Han Dynasty tomb figures (206 BC–220 CE), early Ming Dynasty (14th century); several pieces from the Korean Three Kingdoms (5th–6th centuries) and early Goryeo (10th–11th centuries); Curator L. B. NERIO.

Kaua'i Museum: 4428 Rice St, Lihu'e, HI 96766; tel. (808) 245-6931; e-mail director@kauaimuseum.org; internet www.kauaimuseum.org; f. 1954; colln incl. exhibit on early sugar plantation life, Missionary era furniture, pottery, photographs, books, artwork, quilts, saddles, and Second World War memorabilia; Dir JANE KAMAHAOKALANI GRAY; Collns Curator CHRIS FAYE; Pres.

HOLBROOK GOODALE; Sec. STEVE C. TODD; Treas. KEITH HOLDEMAN.

Koa Art Gallery: 4303 Diamond Head Rd, Honolulu, HI 96816; tel. (808) 734-9374; e-mail koaglry@hawaii.edu; internet koagallery.kcc.hawaii.edu; f. 1980; Dir and Curator DAVID BEHLKE.

Shangri La: 4055 Papu Circle, Honolulu, HI 96816; tel. (808) 734-1941; internet www.shangrilahawaii.org; f. 1935; attached to the Doris Duke Foundation for Islamic Art; 3,500 items of Islamic art and craft: architectural features, furniture, ceramics, textiles and paintings; library of 1,500 vols; Exec. Dir DEBORAH POPE; Curator Dr KEELAN OVERTON.

Idaho

Basque Museum and Cultural Center: 611 Grove St, Boise, ID 83702; tel. (208) 343-2671; e-mail info@basquemuseum.com; internet www.basquemuseum.com; f. 1985; Juanita Uberuaga Hormachea Colln.

Boise Art Museum: 670 Julia Davis Dr., Boise, ID 83702; tel. (208) 345-8330; internet www.boiseartmuseum.org; f. 1937 as the Boise Gallery of Art, current name adopted 1988; private, non-profit; permanent colln of 2,300 works of 20th-century American art with emphasis on artists of the Pacific Northwest, American Realism and ceramics; art classes, education programmes; Pres. NICOLE SNYDER; Exec. Dir MELANIE FALES.

Clearwater Historical Museum: POB 1454, 315 College Ave, Orofino, ID 83544-1454; tel. (208) 476-5033; e-mail info@clearwatermuseum.org; internet www.clearwatermuseum.org; f. 1976; 4,500 historical photographs, Nez Perce Indian history and artefacts; old mining history and logging pictures; Orofino newspapers since 1899; Chinese artefacts.

Discovery Center of Idaho: 131 Myrtle St, Boise, ID 83702; tel. (208) 343-9895; e-mail dcifilter@gmail.com; internet www.scidaho.org; photograph exhibits, artefacts and other material concerning devt and progress of engineering, mathematics, technology and science; Exec. Dir JANINE BOIRE; Pres. BRUCE SCHREPPLE; Sec. HILARY SOLTMAN; Treas. STEVE SIMPSON.

Idaho Black History Museum: 508 Julia Davis Dr., Boise, ID 83702-7694; tel. (208) 433-0017; e-mail info@ibhm.org; internet www.ibhm.org; f. 1995; exhibits; educational and community outreach programmes incl. lectures, films, workshops, literacy programmes and musical performances.

Idaho Museum of Natural History: 921 S Eight Ave, Stop 8096, Pocatello, ID 83209; tel. (208) 282-3168; internet imnh.isu.edu; f. 1934 as Historical Museum at the Southern Br. of the Univ. of Idaho, current name adopted 1977; attached to Idaho State Univ.; collns of Anthropology, Earth Sciences, and Life Sciences; 500,000 specimens that document the natural history of Idaho and the Intermountain W; Dir and Research Curator Dr HERBERT MASCHNER.

Idaho State Historical Museum: 610 N Julia Davis Dr., Boise, ID 83702; tel. (208) 334-2120; internet history.idaho.gov/idaho-state-historical-museum; f. 1893; attached to Idaho State Historical Soc.; 250,000 artefacts incl. arms, agricultural items, clothing and textile artefacts, tools and transportation artefacts depicting the history of Idaho.

Museum of Idaho: 200 N E Ave, Idaho Falls, ID 83402; tel. (208) 522-1400; internet www.museumofidaho.org; f. 1982; Eagle Rock USA exhibit: representative of the architecture and furnishings of the time; Race for Atomic Power Exhibit.

Museum of North Idaho: POB 812, Coeur d'Alene, ID 83816-0812; tel. (208) 664-3448; e-mail dd@museumni.org; internet www .museumni.org; f. 1973; 35,000 images and archive material relating to the history of the Coeur d'Alene region; 3-D artefacts; Dir DOROTHY DAHLGREN.

Nez Perce National Historical Park: 39063 US Highway 95, Spalding, ID 83540-9715; tel. (208) 843-7020; e-mail nepe_visitor_information@nps.gov; internet www.nps.gov/nepe; attached to Nat. Park Service, US Dept of the Interior; Nez Perce (Nimiipuu) history and culture; 38 sites marking important events related to war of 1877; incl. White Bird Battlefield, Big Hole National Battlefield and Bear Paw Battlefield.

Priest Lake Museum: POB 44, Coolin, ID 83821-0044; 38 Priest Lake Museum Rd, Priest Lake, ID 83856; tel. (208) 443-2676; e-mail priestlakemuseum@gmail.com; internet plmuseum.org; f. 1979; photos and artefacts depicting history of the Priest Lake region, incl. the natural and cultural characteristics.

Wallace District Mining Museum: POB 469, 509 Bank St, Wallace, ID 83873; tel. (208) 556-1592; e-mail info@ wallaceminingmuseum.org; internet wallaceminingmuseum.org; mining history with artefacts and exhibits depicting the hardships, toil and home life of the period.

Illinois

Adler Planetarium: 1300 S Lake Shore Dr., Chicago, IL 60605-2403; tel. (312) 922-7827; internet www.adlerplanetarium.org; f. 1930; collns incl. astronomical artefacts, world's oldest known window sundial (dated 1529) and telescope made by William Herschel; 2,000 items of Scientific Instrument Colln incl. models from 12th to 20th century, celestial globes and gores; interactive virtual environments; sky shows, classes in astronomy, navigation and telescope making; public observation sessions, demonstrations, lectures, films; library of 5,000 vols, 3,000 vols of rare book colln; Chair. JOHN W. ESTEY; Pres. Dr PAUL H. KNAPPENBERGER, Jr; Sec. IRENE SIRAGUSA PHELPS; Treas. THOMAS A. NARDI.

Art Institute of Chicago: 111 S Michigan Ave, Chicago, IL 60603-6404; tel. (312) 443-3600; internet www.artic.edu; f. 1879, present location 1893; American painting and sculpture; European painting since 13th century, medieval and Renaissance art; prints and drawings; sculpture; Asian arts (covering 5,000 years); African and Amerindian art; textiles; decorative arts; photography; architecture; Thorne Miniature Rooms (European interiors from late 13th century to 1930s and American furnishings from 17th century to 1930s); School of Art; Ryerson Library (f. 1901); Burnham Library of Architecture (f. 1912); Kraft Education Centre; library of 400,000 vols, 100,000 auction catalogues, 1,200 serial subscriptions and 340,000 slides on art and architecture; Chair. THOMAS J. PRITZKER; Dir JAMES CUNO; Pres. DOUGLAS DRUICK; Treas. FREDERICK H. WADDELL; publ. *Member Magazine* (6 a year).

Art Museum: 116 Altgeld Hall, Northern Illinois Univ., DeKalb, IL 60115; tel. (815) 753-1936; internet www.niu.edu/artmuseum; f. 1960 present name and status 1990; attached to College of Visual and Performing Arts, Northern Illinois Univ.; incl. 1,000 art objects of 20th-century works of art on paper (prints, drawings and photographs) and contemporary paintings and sculpture; organizes art exhibitions with written educational material, gallery talks, artist lectures, panel discussions and symposia; Dir JO BURKE.

Cedarhurst Center for the Arts: 2600 Richview Rd, POB 923, Mt Vernon, IL 62864; tel. (618) 242-1236; e-mail vonda@ cedarhurst.org; internet www.cedarhurst .org; f. 1973 as Mitchell Museum; 400 artworks and decorative objects incl. works by Thomas Eakins, Robert Henri, William Glackens, George Luks, John Sloan, Arthur B. Davies and Maurice Prendergast, mems of The Eight, Childe Hassam and J. Alden Weir, mems of The Ten and Mary Cassatt and John Singer Sargent; 60 large-scale sculptures by Dennis Oppenheim, Alexander Liberman, Fletcher Benton and Chakaia Booker; Exec. Dir SHARON BRADHAM.

Field Museum: 1400 S Lake Shore Dr., Chicago, IL 60605-2496; tel. (312) 922-9410; e-mail media@fieldmuseum.org; internet www.fieldmuseum.org; f. 1893 as Columbian Museum of Chicago, present location 1921; depts of anthropology, botany, geology, zoology (birds, fishes, insects, invertebrates, mammals, reptiles and amphibians); more than 20m. specimens; large colln of books on China, incl. several thousand in Chinese; Ornithological Section incl. many rare and illustrated vols; library of 275,000 vols, 300,000 photographs; Chair. JOHN A. CANNING, Jr; Pres. and CEO JOHN W. MCCARTER, Jr; publs *Fieldiana* (peer-reviewed publs in anthropology, botany, geology and zoology; in two series: Fieldiana Anthropology and Fieldiana Life and Earth Sciences), *In The Field*.

Freeport Art Museum: 121 N Harlem Ave, Freeport, IL 61032; tel. (815) 235-9755; e-mail info@freeportartmuseum.org; internet www.freeportartscenter.org; f. 1975; 4,000 artefacts, incl. antiquities, ethnographic objects from SE Asia, and Papua New Guinea, Pre-Columbian and Native American artefacts, 15th- to 19th-century European paintings, prints and sculpture, textiles from around the world and contemporary American prints, paintings and sculpture; Dir JENNIFER KIRKER PRIEST; Pres. VANESSA HUGHES; Sec. HEATHER MCPHERSON; Treas. GERALD POLLEY.

Illinois State Museum: 502 South Spring St, Springfield, IL 62706-5000; tel. (217) 782-7386; e-mail internet@museum.state.il.us; internet www.museum.state.il.us; f. 1877; natural history and anthropology (recreations of American Indian villages and natural habitats); 'At Home in the Heartland' exhibition of decorative arts in Illinois since 1750; historic and contemporary works by Illinois artists are exhibited in the fine and applied arts galleries; research laboratories and a Technology Learning Center; colln incl. 8m. archaeological specimens and ethnographic objects, 14,000 aesthetic and historical objects in fine and decorative arts colln, 111,000 botanical specimens, 200,000 specimens in geology collns, 140,000 specimens in zoology colln; library of 15,000 vols of monographs, 800 serials; Dir BONNIE W. STYLES; publs *Events and Activities* (4 a year), *Impressions* (4 a year), *The Living Museum* (4 a year)

Attached Museums and Galleries:

Dickson Mounds Museum: 10956 N Dickson Mounds Rd, Lewistown, IL 61542; tel. (309) 547-3721; internet www .museum.state.il.us/ismsites/dickson; on-site archaeological museum covering 12,000 years of Illinois history; Nat. Historic Site; Dir Dr MICHAEL WIANT.

Illinois State Museum Lockport Gallery: 201 West 10th St, Lockport, IL 60441; tel. (815) 838-7400; e-mail jzimmer@museum.state.il.us; internet www.museum.state.il.us/ismsites/lockport; f. 1987; exhibitions of art by past and contemporary Illinois artists and artisans; Dir JIM ZIMMER; Curator JENNIFER JASKOWIAK.

ISM Chicago Gallery: James R. Thompson Center, 100 W Randolph, Suite 2-100, Chicago, IL 60601-3219; tel. (312) 814-5322; e-mail jstevens@museum.state.il.us; internet www.museum.state.il.us/ismsites/ chicago/exhibitions.html; f. 1985; exhibitions of art by contemporary and historical Illinois artists; Dir of Art KENT SMITH.

Southern Illinois Art and Artisans Center: 14967 Gun Creek Trail, Whittington, IL 62897-1000; tel. (618) 629-2220; internet www.museum.state.il.us/ismsites/ so-il; houses Southern Illinois Art Gallery: fine art, decorative art, and ethnographic collns of the Illinois State Museum to southern Illinois; Dir MARYLOU GALLOWAY.

John G. Shedd Aquarium: 1200 S Lake Shore Dr., Chicago, IL 60605; tel. (312) 939-2438; e-mail contactus@sheddaquarium.org; internet www.sheddaquarium.org; f. 1930; exhibits both freshwater and saltwater species; oceanarium recreates a Pacific Northwest Coast environment and a Falkland Islands habitat; 90,000-gallon Coral Reef exhibit; Wild Reef re-creates a coral reef in the Philippines and offers a diverse shark habitat and garden eels; Pres. and CEO TED A. BEATTIE.

Lakeview Museum of Arts & Sciences: 1125 W Lake Ave, Peoria, IL 61614-5985; tel. (309) 686-7000; e-mail development@ lakeview-museum.org; internet www .lakeview-museum.org; f. 1954; 16,000 works and items of fine arts (paintings, sculptures, works on paper), decorative arts (furniture, ceramics, metal, glass, textiles), folk art (paintings, sculptures, graphics, decorative arts), ethnographic arts (Native American, African, Oceanic, Asian) and natural sciences (mineralogy, geology, entomology, conchology); planetarium, Illinois Folk Art Gallery, Discovery Center; Pres. and CEO JIM RICHERSON.

Mary and Leigh Block Museum of Art: 40 Arts Circle Dr., Evanston, IL 60208-2410; tel. (847) 491-4000; e-mail block-museum@ northwestern.edu; internet www .blockmuseum.northwestern.edu; f. 1980; attached to Northwestern Univ.; 4,000 works of art; historical and contemporary prints; Griffin architectural drawings and photographs; bronze sculptures; organizes lectures, symposia and workshops with artists and scholars; screens classic and contemporary films; Chair. CHRISTINE O. ROBB; Dir DAVID ALAN ROBERTSON.

Museum of Contemporary Art Chicago: 220 E Chicago Ave, Chicago, IL 60611; tel. (312) 280-2660; e-mail jwolski@mcachicago .org; internet mcachicago.org; f. 1967; colln of visual art from 1945 to present with focus on surrealism, minimalism, conceptual photography and work by Chicago-based artists; 2,500 objects (painting, sculpture, and photography, installation and video); library of 15,000 vols; Dir MADELEINE GRYNSZTEJN; Chair. MARY ITTELSON; Sec. STEFAN EDLIS; Treas. MICHAEL CANMANN.

Museum of Contemporary Photography: c/o Columbia College Chicago, 600 S Michigan, Chicago, IL 60605; tel. (312) 663-5554; e-mail mocp@colum.edu; internet www.mocp .org; f. 1984, fmrly Chicago Center for Contemporary Photography (f. 1976); attached to Columbia College Chicago; 9,000 photographs and photographically related objects produced since 1936; Dir NATASHA EGAN; Curator and Assoc. Dir KAREN IRVINE.

Museum of Science and Industry: 57th St and Lake Shore Dr., Chicago, IL 60637; tel. (773) 684-1414; e-mail contact@msichicago .org; internet www.msichicago.org; f. 1933; 35000 artefacts, incl. metals, power, physics, chemistry, electronics, transportation, petroleum, food, space eng., communications and medical sciences; over 2,000 exhibit units incl. re-creation of a coal mine, German submarine, walk-through model of human heart, Colleen Moore's Fairy Castle, 'Yesterday's Main Street', actual Apollo 8 spacecraft, Henry Crown Space Center, 'Omnimax' theatre, and exhibits on space exploration and energy research; archival images of exhibits from past and photographs relating to *U-505 Submarine*, Pioneer Zephyr train, Chicago World's Fairs; Chair. DAVID B. SPEER; Pres. and CEO DAVID R. MOSENA; Sec. EILEEN M. CABRERA; Treas. DAVID J. VITALE.

National Veterans Art Museum: 4041 N Milwaukee Ave, Chicago, IL 60641; tel. (312) 326-0270; e-mail info@nvam.org; internet www.nvam.org; f. 1981, present status 1996, current name adopted 2010; 2,000 works of art, incl. paintings, photography, sculpture, poetry and music by 255 artists; Exec. Dir LEVI MOORE; Chair. LIONEL RABB; Sec. KEN NIELSEN; Treas. CAROL SHERMAN.

Oriental Institute Museum: 1155 E 58th St, Chicago, IL 60637; tel. (773) 702-9514; e-mail oi-museum@uchicago.edu; internet oi .uchicago.edu/museum; f. 1919; attached to Univ. of Chicago; holds 202,000 registered objects from Egypt, Iran, Iraq, Israel, Jordan, Palestinian Autonomous Territories, Sudan, Syria and Turkey; research arm supports archaeological excavations in Egypt, Iran, Sudan, Syria and Turkey; has dictionary projects in Demotic Egyptian, Sumerian, Akkadian and Hittite; divs of collections: Museum Registration, Tablet Colln, Archives, Conservation, and Research Library; temporary exhibitions; library of 60,000 vols; Dir GIL STEIN; Chief Curator JACK GREEN; publ. *Journal of Near Eastern Studies* (2 a year).

Rockford Art Museum: 711 N Main St, Rockford, IL 61103; tel. (815) 968-2787; internet www.rockfordartmuseum.org; f. 1888 as Rockford Sketch Club, present name 1913; 1,600 works of modern and contemporary American art; American masters from 1830 to 1940; photography, contemporary glass and outsider art; Exec. Dir LINDA DENNIS; Pres. JANE SMITH; Sec. SUSAN CARLIN; Treas. MIKE ABRAHAMS.

Smart Museum of Art: Univ. of Chicago, 5550 S Greenwood Ave, Chicago, IL 60637; tel. (773) 702-0200; e-mail smart-museum@ uchicago.edu; internet smartmuseum .uchicago.edu; f. 1974; attached to Univ. of Chicago; central repository for Univ.'s fine arts colln spanning 5,000 years of artistic creation; Asian art, European art, contemporary art, modern art and design; Dir ANTHONY HIRSCHEL; Deputy Dir and Chief Curator. STEPHANIE SMITH; Sr Curator RICHARD A. BORN.

Tarble Arts Center: Eastern Illinois Univ., 600 Lincoln Ave, Charleston IL 61920-3099; tel. (217) 581-2787; e-mail tarble@eiu.edu; internet www.eiu.edu/tarble; f. 1982; attached to College of Arts and Humanities, Eastern Illinois Univ.; 20th-century Illinois folk arts with archive of audio and video cassettes; photographs and interviews of musicians, artists and crafts persons; prints, drawings and watercolours by contemporary Midwestern artists; American Scene or Regionalists prints and watercolours c. 1930s and 1940s; contemporary art in other media and art from other cultures and historical periods in various media; organizes education and outreach programmes, lectures and demonstrations by artists, chamber music concerts and other performing arts; Dir MICHAEL WATTS.

Terra Foundation for American Art: 980 N Michigan Ave, Suite 1315, Chicago, IL 60611; tel. (312) 664-3939; e-mail contact@ terraamericanart.org; internet www .terraamericanart.org; f. 1978; colln of American art from 1740 to 1945; 725 paintings, prints, drawings, photographs and sculptures; resource centre in Paris; library of 9,000 vols; Chair. GERHARD CASPER; Pres. and CEO ELIZABETH GLASSMAN.

Ukrainian Institute of Modern Art: 2320 W Chicago Ave, Chicago, IL 60622; tel. (773) 227-5522; internet www.uima-chicago.org; f. 1971; collns of Ukrainian and Ukrainian-American abstract and minimalist works from the 1950s, 1960s and 1970s; Pres. PAUL NADZIKEWYCH; Sec. KALYNA POMIRKO; Treas. LUBOMYR KLYMKOWYCH; Curator STANISLAV GREZDO.

University Museum: 1000 Faner Dr., POB 4508, Southern Illinois Univ., Carbondale, IL 62901; 2469 Faner Hall, Southern Illinois Univ., Carbondale, IL 62901; tel. (618) 453-5388; e-mail museum@siu.edu; internet www .museum.siu.edu; f. 1874; attached to Southern Illinois Univ. Carbondale; encyclopedic museum; 2,500 objects in fine and decorative arts; paintings, prints and drawings, sculpture, photography; ethnic arts collns of 20th-century regional, nat. and int. artists; science colln with 26,000 geological specimens; humanities colln of 22,000 artefacts reflecting history, world cultures and archaeological past; organizes workshops and art festivals; Dir Dr DONA R. BACHMAN.

Indiana

Art Museum of Greater Lafayette: 102 S Tenth St, Lafayette, IN 47905; tel. (765) 742-1128; internet artlafayette.org; f. 1909, present name 2000; 900 works of 19th- and 20th-century American art, with focus on Indiana artists; spec. colln of work of Laura Ann Fry; Exec. Dir KENDALL SMITH II; Pres. ELIZABETH LOCKREY; Curator MICHAEL ATWELL.

Brauer Museum of Art: Center for the Arts, Valparaiso Univ., 1709 Chapel Dr., Valparaiso, IN 46383-6493; tel. (219) 464-5365; internet www.valpo.edu/artmuseum; attached to Valparaiso Univ.; 19th-, 20th- and 21st-century American art (works of Frederic Edwin Church, Asher B. Durand, Childe Hassam, Georgia O'Keeffe, and Ed Paschke); world religious art and Midwestern regional art (incl. paintings, sculpture, drawings, prints and photographs); spec. colln of works by Junius R. Sloan; Dir and Curator GREGG HERTZLIEB.

Conner Prairie: 13400 Allisonville Rd, Fishers, IN 46038; tel. (317) 776-6006; e-mail info@connerprairie.org; internet www.connerprairie.org; f. 1934; 5 themed historic areas—1863 Civil War Journey: Raid on Indiana, Prairietown, Animal Encounters Barn, Loom House at Conner Homestead, Lenape Indian Camp incl. Indian trading post about Lenape or Delaware Indians, 1859 Balloon Voyage in tethered helium-filled balloon; Chair. J. CHRISTOPHER COOKE; Pres. and CEO ELLEN M. ROSENTHAL; Sec. Dr MARY E. BUSCH; Treas. DAVID T. FRONEK.

David Owsley Museum of Art: 2021 W Riverside Ave, Ball State Univ., Muncie, IN 47306; tel. (765) 285-5242; e-mail artmuseum@bsu.edu; internet cms.bsu.edu/ web/museumofart.aspx; f. 1892 as Art Students' League, present bldg 1935, current name adopted 2011; 11,000 artworks of ancient, medieval, Renaissance, 17th century, 18th century, 19th century, modern, Asian, Africa, Oceania, the Americas; European and American decorative arts and furniture and works on paper, incl. drawings, prints and photographs; Dir CARL SCHAFER.

Eiteljorg Museum of American Indians and Western Art: White River State Park, 500 W Washington St, Indianapolis, IN 46204; tel. (317) 636-9378; e-mail president@eiteljorg.com; internet www .eiteljorg.org; f. 1989; showcases Western and Native American art; contemporary works of art incl. paintings, photography, prints, drawings and sculpture and installations, incl. artists T. C. Cannon, N. C. Wyeth, Andy Warhol, Georgia O'Keeffe, Allan Houser, Frederic Remington, Charles Russell and Kay WalkingStick; library of 5,000 vols; Pres. and CEO JOHN VANAUSDALL; Chair. BETSY HARVEY; Chief Curatorial Officer JAMES NOTTAGE.

Evansville Museum of Arts, History & Science: 411 SE Riverside Dr., Evansville, IN 47713; tel. (812) 425-2406; e-mail info@ emuseum.org; internet www.emuseum.org; f. 1906, present name and status 1938; collns in areas of art, history, anthropology and science; paintings and graphic works from 16th century to the present; anthropology colln on North and South American native life since 13,000 BC; Science Center, Koch Planetarium; Exec. Dir JOHN STREETMAN; Pres. STEVE KROHN; Sec. ELAINE McCARTHY; Treas. SARA ABU-HUSSEIN; publ. *COPIA*.

Fort Wayne Museum of Art: 311 E Main St, Fort Wayne, IN 46802; tel. (260) 422-6467; e-mail mail@fwmoa.org; internet www .fwmoa.org; f. 1921, present status 1977; 1,400 American paintings, sculpture, drawings, prints and photographs; colln incl. paintings by Janet Fish, William Forsyth, George Inness, Thomas Moran and Larry Rivers; sculpture by Mark di Suvero and George Rickey; colln of 56 Indiana Amish quilts; Exec. Dir CHARLES A. SHEPARD, III; Pres. BEN EISBART; Sec. JUDY PURSLEY; Treas. CINDY GOODMAN.

Indianapolis Museum of Art: 4000 Michigan Rd, Indianapolis, IN 46208-3326; tel. (317) 923-1331; e-mail ima@imamuseum.org; internet www.imamuseum.org; f. 1883 as Art Asscn of Indianapolis, present name 1969; collns of African art, American painting and sculpture up to 1945; ancient art of the Americas (incl. Mesoamerican cultures, Olmec and civilizations of the Gulf Coast of Mexico, the Colima, and the Maya); ancient art of Mediterranean (displays objects from Italy, Cyprus, Iran, Greece, and Egypt); 400 artworks showing 4,000 years of Asian art from China, Japan, Korea, India, Tibet, and West and SE Asia; contemporary works of art; S Pacific art from Melanesia, Polynesia, Micronesia and Indonesia; textile and fashion arts in Irish embroidery, prints, drawings and photographs of famous artists; incl. Virginia B. Fairbanks Art and Nature Park and Oldfields–Lilly House and Gardens; library of 2,000 vols, 1,000 linear ft museum records, MSS, personal papers, ephemera, scrapbooks, photographs, video cassettes; Dir and CEO MAXWELL L. ANDERSON; Chair. STEPHEN RUSSELL; Sec. THOMAS HIATT; Treas. DANIEL CANTOR.

Indiana State Museum: 650 W Washington St, Indianapolis, IN 46204; tel. (317) 232-1637; e-mail museumcommunication@ indianamuseum.org; internet www .indianamuseum.org; f. 1862, present location 2002; 542,000 cultural and natural history items ranging from prehistoric fossils to current popular culture items; also holds

25,000 items from Lincoln Financial Foundation Colln; Pres. and CEO THOMAS A. KING.

Indiana University Art Museum: 1133 E Seventh St, Bloomington, IN 47405-7509; tel. (812) 855-5445; e-mail iuam@indiana.edu; internet www.iub.edu/~iuam; f. 1941; 40,000 objects incl. ancient gold jewellery, African masks and paintings by Monet and Picasso; Dir ADELHEID GEALT.

Purdue University Galleries: 552 W Wood St, West Lafayette, IN 47907-2002; tel. (765) 494-3061; e-mail galleries@purdue.edu; internet www.purdue.edu/galleries; artwork of regional, nat. and int. artists; organizes visual art exhibitions and lectures; serves as cultural resource for the Greater Lafayette; Stewart Center Gallery, Robert L. Ringel Gallery, Patti and Rusty Rueff Galleries; Dir CRAIG MARTIN; Asst Dir MICHAL HATHAWAY.

Richmond Art Museum: 350 Hub Etchison Parkway, Richmond, IN 47375-0816; tel. (765) 966-0256; internet www .richmondartmuseum.org; f. 1898; colln of American Impressionists, Taos School, Hoosier Group, Richmond School and regional artists; local ceramic artists incl. works by potters of Arts and Craft Movement, Overbeck Sisters and Bethel Pike potters; organizes workshops and art classes; Exec. Dir SHAUN DINGWERTH.

Snite Museum of Art: POB 368, Moose Krause Circle, Univ. of Notre Dame, Notre Dame, IN 46556-0368; tel. (574) 631-5466; e-mail sniteart@nd.edu; internet sniteartmuseum.nd.edu; attached to Univ. of Notre Dame; 24,000 works of art; Jack and Alfrieda Feddersen colln of Rembrandt etchings; the Noah L. and Muriel Butkin colln of 19th-century French art; John D. Reilly colln of Old Master and 19th-century drawings; Janos Scholz colln of 19th-century European photographs and the Mr and Mrs Russell G. Ashbaugh, Jr, colln of Mestrovic sculpture and drawings; Olmec and Preclassic Mesoamerican art; 20th-century art, N Native American art, decorative and design arts and 2 kinetic sculptures by George Rickey; Dir CHARLES R. LOVING; publs *Events* (2 a year), *Notre Dame magazine* (4 a year).

Swope Art Museum: 25 S Seventh St, Terre Haute, IN 47807; tel. (812) 238-1676; e-mail info@swope.org; internet www.swope.org; f. 1942; 2,000 works of American art incl. 19th- and 20th-century paintings, sculptures and works on paper; paintings from 'American Regionalist' group incl. works by Thomas Hart Benton, Charles Burchfield, Edward Hopper, Reginald Marsh and Grant Wood; art from latter half of 20th century incl. works of Alexander Calder, Moses and Raphael Soyer, Robert Motherwell, Eva Hesse, Robert Rauschenberg and Leonard Baskin; screenprints from Robert Indiana (Decade Portfolio) and Andy Warhol (Marilyn); artworks by women artists; Exec. Dir MARIANNE RICHTER; Pres. RICHARD SHAGLEY; Sec. KATHY BRENTLINGER; Treas. TOM FRANCIS.

University Art Gallery: Dept of Art, FA108, Indiana State Univ., Terre Haute, IN 47809; tel. (812) 237-3720; internet www .indstate.edu/artgallery; f. 1985 as Turman Gallery; attached to Indiana State Univ.; collects, preserves and exhibits modern and contemporary art; organizes exhibitions, workshops, gallery talks and lectures; promotes understanding and appreciation for visual arts; encourages visual artwork scholarship; Dir MELISSA VANDENBERG; Univ. Curator BARBARA RACKER.

Iowa

Blanden Art Museum: 920 Third Ave S, Fort Dodge, IA 50501; tel. (515) 573-2316; internet www.blanden.org; visual artworks related to World Wars; Pres. KENNETH ADAMS; Dir MARGARET SKOVE.

Cedar Rapids Museum of Art: 410 Third Ave SE, Cedar Rapids, IA 52401; tel. (319) 366-7503; e-mail info@crma.org; internet www.crma.org; f. 1905; 7,000 artworks since Roman antiquity; colln incl. works of art by Grant Wood, Roman portrait busts and temporary exhibitions; Exec. Dir SEAN ULMER; Pres. TIM HILL; Sec. PHIL LASANSKY; Treas. BRIAN COLLER; publs *Art in Roman Life: Villa To Grave, Clary Illian: A Potter's Potter*.

Des Moines Art Center: 4700 Grand Ave, Des Moines, IA 50312-2099; tel. (515) 277-4405; internet www.desmoinesartcenter.org; f. 1948; Irma and Julian Brody colln, John C. Huseby Print colln, Louise Noun Colln of Art by Women, Paul and Anastasia Polydoran colln and Nathan Emory Coffin colln; Pres. WOODWARD G. BRENTON; Vice-Pres. and Treas. JAMES HUBBELL, III; Sec. PATRICIA MCFARLAND; Dir JEFF FLEMING; Sr Curator GILBERT VICARIO.

Dubuque Museum of Art: 701 Locust St, Dubuque, IA 52001; tel. (563) 557-1851; e-mail info@dbqart.com; internet www .dbqart.com; f. 1874; 20th-century American art emphasizing on American Regionalism; 2,100 works of art, incl. works by Iowa Regionalist Grant Wood, Edward S. Curtis, N American Indian photogravures and texts, nat. artists incl. John Steuart Curry, Adrian Dornbush and Mauricio Lasansky, local artists incl. Francesco Licciardi, Louise Halliburton, Joseph Walter and Dorothy Rossiter and 900 etchings by artist and author Arthur Geisert; also organizes art classes and workshops; Exec. Dir MARK WAHLERT.

Figge Art Museum: 225 W Second St, Davenport, IA 52801; tel. (563) 326-7804; internet figgeart.org; f. 1925 as Davenport Municipal Art Gallery, present name and location 2003; 3,500 paintings, sculptures and works on paper since 16th century; American colln of works from Colonial period to 1945, incl. 19th-century landscape traditions of the Hudson River School artists Asher B. Durand, John Kensett and Albert Bierstadt; Midwest Regionalist colln focuses on works of Grant Wood, Thomas Hart Benton, John Steuart Curry and Mid W artists who defined style in 1930s and 1940s; Mexican Colonial colln on growth of painting in New Spain in 17th and 18th centuries; Haitian colln on artistic tradition in Haiti since 1940s; Pres. ANDREW J. BUTLER; Sec. TARA BARNEY; Treas. KEN KOUPAL.

Iowa Museum Association: 1116 Washington St, Cedar Falls, IA 50613; tel. (319) 239-2236; e-mail imasweet@cfu.net; internet www.iowamuseums.org; f. 1976; provides training and devt to Iowa museum professionals and volunteers; provides education, communication, networking opportunities and advocacy for Iowa's museums; art centres and museums, botanical gardens, children's museums, historic sites, historical socs, living history sites, nature centres, natural history museums, planetariums, science and technology centres and zoos; Pres. LINDA WILLEKE; Exec. Dir CYNTHIA SWEET; Sec. SHALLA WILSON; Treas. ELAINE RALEIGH.

Iowa State University Museums: 290 Scheman Bldg, Ames, IA 50011-1110; tel. (515) 294-3342; e-mail dwitter@iastate.edu; internet www.museums.iastate.edu; f. 1961; incl. Anderson Sculpture Garden, Art on Campus Colln, Brunnier Art Museum, Christian Petersen Art Museum and Farm House Museum; 30,000 objects of art ranging from ancient to modern art; Dir and Chief Curator LYNETTE POHLMAN.

MacNider Art Museum: 303 Second St SE, Mason City, IA 50401; tel. (641) 421-3666; e-mail macnider@macniderart.org; internet www.macniderart.org; f. 1966; paintings, prints, drawings, photographs, sculptures, ceramics and puppets on American art; Dir EDITH BLANCHARD.

National Mississippi River Museum & Aquarium: 350 E Third St, Port of Dubuque, IA 52001; tel. (563) 557-9545; e-mail info@ rivermuseum.com; internet www .rivermuseum.com; attached to Dubuque Co Historical Soc.; archives of 20,000 items for river research incl. lithographs, glass plate negatives, boat blueprints, original contract and correspondence documents; artefact colln of small boats of 19th and 20th century; 1,200 steamboat artefacts; natural history specimens, Native American artefacts, minerals, fossils and early Dubuque history dating to 1870; fine art colln of furnishings about life in Dubuque in mid-19th century incl. china, parlour furniture and paintings; colln of large vessels; National Rivers Hall of Fame honouring people related to America's rivers and river industries; William Woodward Discovery Center and Fred W. Woodward Riverboat Museum; library of 4,000 vols; Exec. Dir JERRY ENZLER; Curator CRISTIN WATERBURY.

Sioux City Art Center: 225 Nebraska St, Sioux City, IA 51101-1712; tel. (712) 279-6272; internet www.siouxcityartcenter.org; f. 1938; 1,000 works from Midwest, nat. and int. artists; organizes art classes; Chair. DOUG PALMER; Dir AL HARRIS-FERNANDEZ.

University of Iowa Museum of Art: 1375 Highway 1W, 1840 Studio Arts Bldg, Iowa City, IA 52242; tel. (319) 335-1727; e-mail uima@uiowa.edu; internet uima.uiowa.edu; f. 1969; European and American art; colln of traditional African arts; European and American prints; drawings and photographs: 1900–70; artefacts of ancient Americas and native America; ceramics and metal work; Iowa gallery (digital art collns); temporary exhibitions; Provost WALLACE LOH; Exec. Dir SEAN O'HARROW; Sec. BETTY BREAZEALE; Chief Curator KATHLEEN EDWARDS; publ. *UIMA Magazine*.

University of Iowa Museum of Natural History: 10 Macbride Hall, Iowa City, IA 52242; tel. (319) 335-0480; e-mail mus-nat-hist@uiowa.edu; internet www .uiowa.edu/~nathist; f. 1858; spec. collns incl. geology, ecology and native cultures; giant Ice Age sloth; N American birds; Mammal Hall incl. a skeleton of an Atlantic Right Whale; Dir JOHN LOGSDON; Curator TRINA ROBERTS.

Waterloo Center for the Arts: 225 Commercial St, Waterloo, IA 50701-1313; tel. (319) 291-4490; e-mail museum@waterloo-ia .org; internet www.waterloocenterforthearts .org; f. 1962; Mid W regionalist art (incl. works by Grant Wood and Thomas Hart Benton), Haitian/Caribbean folk art, American decorative arts, int. folk art, murals and mosaics spread across city of Waterloo; organizes lectures, symposia, films and performances; Dir CAMMIE SCULLY; Curator KENT SHANKLE.

Kansas

Birger Sandzén Memorial Gallery: 401 N First St, POB 348, Lindsborg, KS 67456-0348; tel. (785) 227-2220; e-mail fineart@ sandzen.org; internet www.sandzen.org; f. 1957; colln of Birger Sandzén's paintings, prints, drawings and watercolours; colln of works of Henry Varnum Poor, Doel Reed, Carl Milles, Marsden Hartley, B. J. O. Nordfelt, John Bashor, Lester Raymer, Raymond Jonson and John Stuart Curry; colln of prints from European to American regionalist printmakers and Asia; organizes temporary exhibitions, gallery talks, chamber music concerts and docent tours; incl. archives.

Coutts Memorial Museum of Art: 110 N Main, El Dorado, KS 67042-0001; tel. (316) 321-1212; e-mail coutts@coutts.kscoxmail .com; internet www.skyways.org/museums/ coutts; f. 1970; colln of 1,000 objects of art, incl. paintings, sculptures, prints and drawings from Russia, China, France, Holland, England and S America; contemporary work of Prairie Printmakers incl. Seward, Foltz, Capps, Hotvedt, N. B. Hall, A. W. Hall, Thomas Hart Benton, Birger Sandzen, Americo, Eva Makk and son A. B. and Kansas artists Robert Carver, Charles Sanderson, Frederic James, J. R. Hamil, Charles Rogers and James Fallier; Dir ROD SEEL; Pres. CONNIE WALTON; Sec. JEREMY SUNDGREN; Treas. TED FARMER.

Kansas African American Museum: 601 N Water, Wichita, KS 67203; tel. (316) 262-7651; e-mail info@tkaamuseum.net; internet www.tkaamuseum.org; f. 1917 as Calvary Baptist Church, present name and status 1997; permanent colln of African artefacts, incl. tribal masks, headdresses and statues, photographs from Kansas native Gordon Parks, artwork from Dr Samella Lewis, Elizabeth Catlett and Jacob Lawrence and jazz and blues photographs from area performers; temporary exhibitions related to stories of the African American experience in Kansas; Exec. Dir PRISCA BARNES; Pres. GWYNNE BIRZER; Sec. TEKETA HARDING.

Kansas Aviation Museum: 3350 S George Washington Blvd, Wichita, KS 67210; tel. (316) 683-9242; e-mail ksaviation@ kansasaviationmuseum.org; internet kansasaviationmuseum.org; f. 1991; 40 historically significant aircrafts; engines from earliest aircraft power plants to jet turbines; incl. Kansas Aviation Hall of Fame honouring people related to aviation by state, nat. or worldwide; library of 10,000 vols, 250,000 photographs, negatives and slides of rare aircraft, 15,000 journals, periodicals and printed matter; Exec. Dir LON SMITH; Pres. TIM BONNELL, SR; Sec. CHERYL KASTNER; Treas. JAMES WIEBE.

Kansas Museum of History: 6425 SW Sixth Ave, Topeka, KS 66615-1099; tel. (785) 272-8681; e-mail reference@kshs.org; internet www.kshs.org/portal_museum; f. 1875; colln of African American, American Indian artefacts, archaeology, ceramic, furniture, clothing, photographs, quilts, toys and railroads related to history of Kansas; Dir BOB KECKEISEN; Curator LAUREL FRITZSCH; Curator BLAIR TARR.

Marianna Kistler Beach Museum of Art: Kansas State Univ., 14th and Anderson, 701 Beach Lane, Manhattan, KS 66506; tel. (785) 532-7718; e-mail beachart@ksu.edu; internet beach.k-state.edu; f. 1996; attached to Kansas State Univ.; 7,000 objects of art; colln of historical through contemporary art in all media; also promotes research and teaching mission of Kansas State Univ.; Dir LINDA DUKE; Chair. JACKIE HARTMAN; Sec. KATHY BORCK; Sr Curator BILL NORTH.

Mulvane Art Museum: 1700 SW Jewell Ave, Washburn Univ., Topeka, KS 66621; tel. (785) 670-1124; e-mail mulvane.info@ washburn.edu; internet www.washburn.edu/ main/mulvane; f. 1922, present name 1981; attached to Washburn Univ.; colln of 4,000 pieces of fine art from around the world incl. paintings, prints, drawings, sculptures, photographs and decorative art with focus on artists from Kansas and the MidWest and American art of 20th century; Dir CINDI

MORRISON; Pres. MARK BORANYAK; Treas. CHRIS SCHULTZ.

Natural History Museum, University of Kansas: 1345 Jayhawk Blvd, Lawrence, KS 66045-7593; tel. (785) 864-4450; e-mail naturalhistory@ku.edu; internet naturalhistory.ku.edu; f. 1903; attached to Univ. of Kansas Biodiversity Institute; covers 50,000 sq ft; exhibits and dioramas of the animals and plants of N America; 8m. specimens of plants and animals, from prehistoric to living species and from every continent and ocean, 1.2m. archeological artefacts; collns: botany, entomology, herpetology, ichthyology, ichthyology tissue, invertebrate palaeontology, invertebrate zoology, mammalogy, ornithology, palaeobotany, vertebrate palaeontology; Dir LEONARD KRISHTALKA; Curator MARY ADAIR.

Nerman Museum of Contemporary Art: c/o Johnson Co Community College, 12345 College Blvd, Overland Park, KS 66210; tel. (913) 469-3000; e-mail foundation.dept@jccc .edu; internet www.nermanmuseum.org; f. 2007; attached to Johnson Co Community College; colln of outdoor sculpture and paintings, ceramics, photography and works on paper; Dir BRUCE HARTMAN; Chair. JON STEWART; Sec. MELODY RAYL; Treas. LYNN MITCHELSON.

Prairie Museum of Art and History: 1905 S Franklin, Colby, KS 67701; tel. (785) 460-4590; e-mail prairiem@st-tel.net; internet www.prairiemuseum.org; colln of 40,000 artefacts, incl. 28,000 works of art from Kuska Colln of glass, furniture, ceramics, toys, dolls, stamps, clocks, coins, silver and jewellery; incl. sod house, one-room school, country church and 1930s farmstead; Dir SUE TAYLOR.

Spencer Museum of Art, University of Kansas: 1301 Mississippi St, Lawrence, KS 66045-7500; tel. (785) 864-4710; e-mail spencerart@ku.edu; internet www .spencerart.ku.edu; f. 1928; 7 galleries; 37,000 artworks and artefacts in all media; incl. European and American art from ancient to contemporary; significant holdings of E Asian art; recently reopened 20/21 Gallery of modern and contemporary objects; spec. collns incl. medieval art; European and American paintings, sculpture and prints; photography; Japanese Edo-period painting and prints; 20th-century Chinese painting; Kansas Univ.'s ethnographic colln: incl. 10,000 Native American, African, Latin American and Australian works; runs public programmes, programmes for school children, Kansas Univ. students; objects not on view in the galleries are available by appointment; works on paper are accessible for viewing in the Print Room every Friday; organizes exhibitions of local, regional, national and int. interest; also houses Kress Foundation Dept of Art History and the Murphy Library of Art and Architecture; library of 165,000 vols in Murphy Library of Art and Architecture; 17,700 images in Digital Library Colln; Dir SARALYN REECE HARDY; publs *Register* (1 a year), *The Franklin D. Murphy Lecture* (1 a year).

Ulrich Museum of Art: Wichita State Univ., 1845 Fairmount St, Wichita, KS 67260-0046; tel. (316) 978-3664; e-mail ulrich@wichita.edu; internet ulrich.wichita .edu; f. 1974; attached to Wichita State Univ.; colln of 6,300 works of 20th and 21st centuries; colln of works by Robert Henri, Milton Avery, Joan Miro, Alexander Calder, Robert Motherwell, Jacob Lawrence, Joan Mitchell, Claus Oldenburg, Luis Jiménez, Jr, Zhang Huan, Andy Goldsworthy and Jules de Balincourt; photography colln by Berenice Abbott, Margaret Bourke-White, Edward

Weston, Gordon Parks, W. Eugene Smith, Diane Arbus and Nikki Lee; outdoor sculpture colln; Chair. KELLY CALLEN; Dir Dr PATRICIA MCDONNELL.

Wichita Art Museum: 1400 W Museum Blvd, Wichita, KS 67203-3296; tel. (316) 268-4921; e-mail info@wichitaartmuseum.org; internet wichitaartmuseum.org; f. 1935; permanent colln of 7,000 works of American art, spanning 3 centuries of painting, sculpture, glasses, works on paper and decorative arts, incl. Mary Cassatt, Winslow Homer, Horace Pippin, Edward Hopper and Charles M. Russell; library of 10,000 vols and 2,000 artist files; Dir CHARLES K. STEINER; Chief Curator STEPHEN GLEISSNER.

Kentucky

African American Heritage Center, Inc: POB 353, Franklin, KY 42135-0353; tel. (270) 598-9986; e-mail africanamericanh@ bellsouth.net; internet www.aahconline.org; f. 1994; academic research of African American achievements; highlights early account of foodways, burial customs, traditions, religion, education, social life, vital statistics, genealogy and employment.

Art Museum at the University of Kentucky: 405 Rose St, Lexington, KY 40506-0241; tel. (859) 257-5716; e-mail artmuseum@email.uky.edu; internet www .uky.edu/artmuseum; 4,500 objects of American and European paintings, drawings, photographs, prints and sculptures; art of Africa and Asia; Dir KATHY WALSH-PIPER; Curator JANIE WELKER.

Behringer—Crawford Museum: 1600 Montague Rd, Devou Park, Covington, KY 41011; tel. (859) 491-4003; e-mail info@ bcmuseum.org; internet www.bcmuseum .org; f. 1950 as William Behringer Memorial Museum, present name 1980; regional cultural history, minerals, fossils, and American Indian artefacts, transportation objects, art collns of Harlan Hubbard, Dr Wolfgang Ritschel and Mary Bruce Sharon; Exec. Dir LAURIE RISCH; Pres. JOHN BOH; Treas. MARK NEIKIRK.

Frazier History Museum: 829 W Main St, Louisville, KY 40202; tel. (502) 753-5663; e-mail info@fraziermuseum.org; internet www.fraziermuseum.org; f. 2004 as Frazier Historical Arms Museum; 5,000 artefacts spanning over 1,000 years of American and international artefacts and British Royal Armouries; Chair. OWSLEY BROWN FRAZIER; Sec. A. BETH REID; Exec. Dir Dr MADELEINE BURNSIDE.

Headley-Whitney Museum: 4435 Old Frankfort Pike, Lexington, KY 40510; tel. (859) 255-6653; e-mail hwm@ headley-whitney.org; internet www .headley-whitney.org; f. 1968; George Headley's colln of jewellery, bibelots and mounted semi-precious stones; library of 1,500 vols; Exec. Dir (vacant).

Kentucky Historical Society: 100 W Broadway, Frankfort, KY 40601; tel. (502) 564-1792; e-mail refdesk@ky.gov; internet history.ky.gov; f. 1836; more than 12,000 artefacts; incl. a 'Historymobile' and 'Museums to go'; library of 90,000 vols, 16,000 reels of microfilm, 200,000 historic photographs, 1,900 cu ft of MSS and 2,000 maps; Exec. Dir KENT WHITWORTH.

Museums:

Kentucky Military History Museum: 125 E Main St, Frankfort, KY 40601; the Old State Arsenal, a 2-storey brick Gothic-Revival 'castle' standing on a cliff overlooking the Kentucky River and the downtown area, built in 1850, houses the weapons and equipment of the Kentucky Militia, State Guard, and other volunteer military orgs, from the Revolution to the Gulf War; collns of firearms, edged weapons, artillery, uniforms, flags, photographs, personal items.

Old State Capitol: 300 W Broadway, Frankfort, KY 40601; f. 1830; nat. historical landmark introduced Greek-Revival architecture to the USA west of the Appalachian Mountains; bldg served as capitol of the Commonwealth of Kentucky from 1830 to 1910; site of the assassination of William Goebel, the only Governor in US history to die in office as a result of assassination; re-creation of State Law Library.

Thomas D. Clark Center for Kentucky History: 100 W Broadway, Frankfort, KY 40601; prehistoric times to the present: First Kentuckians (10,000 BC to AD 1750), The Kentucky Frontier (1750–1800), The Antebellum Age (1800–60), War and Aftermath (1860–75), Continuity and Change (1875–1900), The New Century (1900–30), Depression and War (1930–50), and Many Sides of Kentucky (since 1950); Pure Kentucky highlights the lives and contributions of famous Kentuckians through artefacts.

Kentucky Museum: Western Kentucky Univ., 1444 Kentucky St, Bowling Green, KY 42101; tel. (270) 745-2592; e-mail kymus@wku.edu; internet www.wku.edu/library/museum; f. 1939; attached to Western Kentucky Univ.; archaeology colln: 70,000 items incl. axes, mortars and scrapers; art colln: 1,000 art works; clothing and textiles colln: 7,000 items of 19th- and 20th-century textiles; Julius Rather colln: 10,000 items of political memorabilia; glassware and ceramics colln: 1,300 items; Man. DEBORAH COLE.

Lincoln Museum: 66 Lincoln Sq., Hodgenville, KY 42748; tel. (270) 358-3163; e-mail abe@lincolnmuseum-ky.org; internet lincolnmuseum-ky.org; f. 1991; exhibits depicting life of Abraham Lincoln; paintings, drawings and other artworks related to Lincoln era.

Locust Grove: 561 Blankenbaker Lane, Louisville, KY 40207; tel. (502) 897-9845; e-mail lghh@locustgrove.org; internet www.locustgrove.org; f. 1964; nat. historic landmark; colln incl. late 18th- and early 19th-century furniture, ceramics, metals, prints, paintings, textiles, books, firearms, tools and domestic objects; Exec. Dir CAROL ELY.

Portland Museum: 2308 Portland Ave, Louisville, KY 40212; tel. (502) 776-7678; e-mail pmuse@iglou.com; internet www.goportland.org; f. 1978; colln on history and material culture of Portland incl. photographs, documents, artefacts, costumes, paintings, drawings, oral histories and vernacular objects; Pres. DENISE MELCHER GOODALE; Sec. BRYAN WARREN; Treas. MIKE LALLY; Exec. Dir NATHALIE TAFT ANDREWS.

Speed Art Museum: 2035 S Third St, Louisville, KY 40208; tel. (502) 634-2700; e-mail info@speedmuseum.org; internet www.speedmuseum.org; f. 1925 as J. B. Speed Memorial Museum; colln incl. Ancient, African, American, Contemporary, European and native American art; Dir and CEO Dr CHARLES L. VENABLE; Chief Curator RUTH CLOUDMAN.

Louisiana

Alexandria Museum of Art: POB 1028, Alexandria, LA 71309-1028; 933 Second St, Alexandria, LA 71309-1028; tel. (318) 443-3458; internet www.themuseum.org; f. 1977; colln of contemporary Louisiana art and N Louisiana folk art; Chair. JOE LIPSEY; Exec. Dir CATHERINE M. PEARS; Curator SARA FUHRER.

DeQuincy Railroad Museum: 400 Lake Charles Ave, DeQuincy, LA 70633; tel. (337) 786-2823; e-mail dqgary@aol.com; internet www.dequincyrailroadmuseum.com; f. 1974; colln of railroad memorabilia incl. restored 1913 steam locomotive, 1947 passenger coach and 2 vintage cabooses; Pres. GARY W. COOPER; Sec. JOLENE CONSTANCE; Treas. EVALIN HESTER.

Historic New Orleans Collection: 533 Royal St, New Orleans, LA 70130; tel. (504) 523-4662; e-mail wrc@hnoc.org; internet www.hnoc.org; f. 1966; museum, research centre and publisher for study and preservation of history and culture of New Orleans and Gulf S region; library of 35,000 vols, 350,000 photographs, prints and drawings; Exec. Dir PRISCILLA LAWRENCE.

Louisiana Military Hall of Fame & Museum: POB 61930, Lafayette, LA 70596; 911 Revis Sirmon Loop, Abbeville, LA 70510; tel. (337) 898-9645; internet walshwebworks.net/lamilitary; f. 1991; colln incl. memorabilia, facts of First World War, Second World War, Korean conflict, Viet Nam War, Gulf War and Iraq War; Pres. Gen. BOB LEBLANC; Sec. N. R. BUBBA BROUSSARD, JR; Treas. JOEY LEROUGE.

Louisiana State Museum: POB 2448, New Orleans, LA 70176; tel. (504) 568-6968; internet www.crt.state.la.us/museum; f. 1906; decorative arts colln on Louisiana-related artefacts from 1790 to 1890; costumes and textiles colln since late 18th century; early Louisiana portraiture dating from 1780s to 1890s; 2,000 paintings and 14,000 works of art on paper; museum incl. Cabildo, Presbytere, 1850 House, old US mint, Madame John's Legacy, Patterson, Baton Rouge and E. D. White historic site in Thibodaux; Chair. ROSEMARY EWING; Sec. DARRYL GISSEL; Treas. RALPH LUPIN; Dir ROBERT WHEAT.

Louisiana State University Museum of Art: Shaw Center for the Arts, 100 Lafayette St, Baton Rouge, LA 70801; tel. (225) 389-7200; internet www.lsumoa.com; f. 2005; 5,000 artwork colln incl. American and British portraiture and decorative arts, pre-Civil War silver, American arts and crafts, Chinese jade, modern and contemporary paintings, sculptures and photography; Exec. Dir THOMAS A. LIVESAY; Curator NATALIE MAULT.

Meadows Museum of Art: 2911 Centenary Blvd, Shreveport, LA 71104; tel. (318) 869-5169; internet www.centenary.edu/meadows; f. 1967; attached to Centenary College of Louisiana; Indochina Colln of Jean Despujols: 1,500 objects incl. artworks by George Grosz, Emilio Amero, Mary Cassatt and Alfred Maurer; Dir DIANE DUFILHO.

New Orleans Museum of Art: POB 19123, New Orleans, LA 70179; 1 Collins Diboll Circle, City Park, New Orleans, LA 70124; tel. (504) 658-4100; e-mail education@noma.org; internet www.noma.org; f. 1911; paintings, sculpture, prints, drawings, photographs and decorative arts; spec. collns incl. history of glass; 150-year colln of photographs; Japanese paintings of the Edo Period; Chinese pottery and stone sculpture; 17th to 20th-century French paintings; Italian and Spanish paintings from Renaissance and Baroque periods; 16th- to 18th-century Low Countries paintings; tribal arts of sub-Saharan Africa; 18th- and 19th-century French porcelain; 20th-century American art and pottery; Spanish colonial Latin American paintings and sculpture; English and Continental portrait miniatures; P. C. Fabergé jewelled objects; 18th- to 20th-century American and English silver; arts of pre-Columbian Mexico, and of Central America and S America; N American Indian arts;

Sculpture Garden containing 50 works by Henry Moore, Fernando Botero, Elisabeth Frink, Barbara Hepworth and others; library of 20,000 vols, 70 periodicals; Dir SUSAN M. TAYLOR; publ. *Arts Quarterly.*

R. W. Norton Art Gallery: 4747 Creswell Ave, Shreveport, LA 71106-1899; tel. (318) 865-4201; e-mail gallery@rwnaf.org; internet www.rwnaf.org; f. 1966; colln of 4,000 art work incl. 400 paintings by 100 artists dating from Renaissance old masters to modernist iconoclasts and contemporary neo-realists; 6 tapestries dating from 16th century; colln of American and European paintings, sculptures and decorative arts spanning over 4 centuries; library of 10,000 vols.

West Baton Rouge Museum: 845 N Jefferson Ave, Port Allen, LA 70767; tel. (225) 336-2422; e-mail contact_us@wbrmuseum.org; internet www.westbatonrougemuseum.com; colln of photos, documents and arts on history and culture of West Baton Rouge Parish since late 18th century; Aillet House (c. 1830); Allendale Plantation Cabin (c. 1850); Reed Shotgun House (c. 1938); Dir JULIA ROSE.

Maine

Abbe Museum: POB 286, Bar Harbor, ME 04609; 26 Mount Desert St, Bar Harbor, ME 04609; tel. (207) 288-3519; e-mail info@abbemuseum.org; internet www.abbemuseum.org; f. 1926; colln of 50,000 objects on 10,000 years of native American culture and history; repository for cultural resource management archaeology colln in Maine; CEO CINNAMON CATLIN-LEGUTKO; Pres. Dr SANDRA K. WILCOX; Sec. Dr WILLIAM HAVILAND; Treas. JEFF DALRYMPLE.

Bowdoin College Museum of Art: 9400 College Station, Brunswick, ME 04011-8494; tel. (207) 725-3275; e-mail artmuseum@bowdoin.edu; internet www.bowdoin.edu/art-museum; f. 1894; colln incl. 20,000 objects of decorative arts, paintings, sculptures and works on paper; Co-Dir ANNE COLLINS GOODYEAR; Co-Dir FRANK GOODYEAR; Curator JOACHIM HOMANN.

Brick Store Museum: 117 Main St, Kennebunk, ME 04043; tel. (207) 985-4802; e-mail info@brickstoremuseum.org; internet www.brickstoremuseum.org; f. 1936; colln on history of the Kennebunks; colln of 70,000 items incl. artefacts and papers on maritime heritage of Kennebunks and paintings by Thomas Badger, John Brewster, Jr, Abbott Fuller Graves; Exec. Dir CHRISTOPHER FARR; Pres. STEPHEN P. SPOFFORD; Sec. KATHY GRAHAM; Treas. DAVID N. MORAVICK.

Colby College Museum of Art: 5600 Mayflower Hill Dr., Waterville, ME 04901-8840; tel. (207) 859-5600; e-mail museum@colby.edu; internet www.colby.edu/museum; f. 1959; 6,000 works of 18th- to 21st-century American art; Dir and Chief Curator SHARON CORWIN.

Davistown Museum: POB 144, Hulls Cove, ME 04644; tel. (207) 288-5126; e-mail curator@davistownmuseum.org; internet www.davistownmuseum.org; f. 1999; incl. regional history, tools (18th- and 19th-century hand tools) and art museum; Curator H. G. SKIP BRACK.

Farnsworth Art Museum: 16 Museum St, Rockland, ME 04841; tel. (207) 596-6457; e-mail writeus@farnsworthmuseum.org; internet www.farnsworthmuseum.org; f. 1948 as William A. Farnsworth Library and Art Museum; colln of 10,000 art works related to Maine; works by sculptor Louise Nevelso; Wyeth Center; library of 10,000 vols; Exec. Dir CHRISTOPHER BROWNAWELL; Pres. RICHARD ARONEAU; Sec. MARY BALDWIN COLLINS; Treas. JOHN W. ROSENBLUM.

Hudson Museum: Univ. of Maine, Collins Center for Arts, Orono, ME 04469-5746; tel. (207) 581-1901; e-mail hudsonmuseum@umit.maine.edu; internet www.umaine.edu/hudsonmuseum; f. 1986; attached to Univ. of Maine; 8,000 ethnographic and archaeological objects, incl. 2,828 pre-Columbian ceramics, lithics and gold work dating from 2000BC to Spanish conquest; Dir GRETCHEN F. FAULKNER.

Maine Archives and Museums: POB 46, Cumberland Center, ME 04021; tel. (207) 400-6965; e-mail info@mainemuseums.org; internet www.mainemuseums.org; directory of 201 museums in Maine; Pres. JAY ADAMS; Dir LEIGH HALLETT; Curator CANDACE KANES; Sec. PATRICIA BURDICK; Treas. PATRICIA HENNER.

Maine Maritime Museum: 243 Washington St, Bath, ME 04530; tel. (207) 443-1316; e-mail curator@maritimeme.org; internet www.mainemaritimemuseum.org; f. 1962 as Marine Research Soc. of Bath, present name 1975; 20,000 objects incl. shipbuilding tools, 550 ship models, 475 maritime paintings, more than 140 historic Maine watercraft of nat. significance, ceramics, engines, furniture, fishing and boat gear, jewellery, textiles and navigational equipment; library of 17,000 vols, 53,000 periodicals, 130,000 historical photographs, 42,000 sheets of ship plans, 2,000 linear ft MSS, 1,000 maps and charts, 482 video cassettes; Chair. WILLIAM A. ROGERS, JR; Sec. JACKSON PARKER; Treas. JEFFREY W. PETERS; Exec. Dir AMY LENT.

Maine State Museum: 83 State House Station, Augusta, ME 04333-0083; 230 State St, Augusta, ME 04330; tel. 207-287-2301; e-mail maine.museum@maine.gov; internet mainestatemuseum.org; f. 1965; colln of 500,000 artefacts on prehistory, history and natural science of Maine; 24,000 historic images; geological colln dates from 1830s; Dir JOSEPH R. PHILLIPS.

Matthews Museum of Maine Heritage: POB 582, Union, ME 04862; tel. (207) 542-2379; e-mail matthewsmuseum@gmail.com; internet www.matthewsmuseum.org; agricultural museum with colln of 10,000 exhibits incl. agricultural tools and equipment, carriages and musical instruments; Sec. MARTHA HOOPER.

Museum of African Culture: 13 Brown St, Portland, ME 04101; tel. (207) 871-7188; e-mail africart@museumafricanculture.org; internet www.museumafricanculture.org; f. 1998; colln of 1,500 objects incl. carved wooden masks, textiles, ceramic, bone, ivory and composite objects; 1,000 years old bronzes figures; 2,000 years old ivory flutes and clay vessels; Exec. Dir OSCAR O. MOKEME; Sec. LORRAINE KARDASH.

Ogunquit Museum of American Art: POB 815, Ogunquit, ME 03907; tel. (207) 646-4909; internet www.ogunquitmuseum.org; f. 1953; colln of 1,600 art works incl. paintings, sculptures, photography and graphics on American Art; Pres. TIMOTHY B. ELLIS; Sec. CAROLE J. AARON; Treas. MARK CONNOLLY; Exec. Dir RONALD L. CRUSAN.

Peary-MacMillan Arctic Museum & Arctic Studies Center: Bowdoin College, 9500 College Station, Brunswick, ME 04011-8495; tel. (207) 725-3416; e-mail ahawkes@bowdoin.edu; internet www.bowdoin.edu/arctic-museum; f. 1985; attached to Bowdoin College; colln incl. material donated by Donald B. MacMillan collected during his career as arctic explorer and researcher; colln incl. 20,000 images from E N American Arctic (1908–54); Dir SUSAN A. KAPLAN; Curator GENEVIEVE LeMOINE.

Portland Museum of Art: Seven Congress Sq., Portland, ME 04101; tel. (207) 775-6148; e-mail info@portlandmuseum.org; internet www.portlandmuseum.org; f. 1882; 17,000 fine and decorative arts since 18th century housed in 3 bldgs of architectural note: Charles Shipman Payson Bldg, L. D. M. Sweat Memorial Galleries, McLellan House; Maine artists such as Winslow Homer, Marsden Hartley, Rockwell Kent, Louise Nevelson; European collns incl. works by Cassatt, Degas, Magritte, Monet, Munch, Picasso, Rodin; Dir MARK BESSIRE; Chief Curator KAREN SHERRY; Curator JESSICA MAY.

Saco Museum: 371 Main St, Saco, ME 04072; tel. (207) 283-3861; e-mail museum@sacomuseum.org; internet www.sacomuseum.org; f. 1866 as York Institute, present name 2000; colln of 10,000 fine, decorative and historic artefacts incl. documented local furniture, clocks, decorative arts such as silver, ceramics, textiles and costumes; Dir TARA VOSE RAISELIS.

Maryland

Allegany Museum: 3 Pershing St, Cumberland, MD 21502; tel. (301) 777-7200; e-mail info@alleganymuseum.org; internet www.alleganymuseum.org; f. 1999 as Allegany County Museum, current name 2008, current location 2010; colln of over 50,000 items; spec. colln incl. King James Bible, artefacts of Kelly-Springfield Tire Co, glassware, models showcasing Maryland's transportation history, canon boat models and photo display of Cumberland; Pres. GARY BARTIK; Sec. JERRY ROBINETTE; Treas. MIKE FETCHERO.

Annapolis Maritime Museum: POB 3088, Annapolis, MD 21403; 723 Second St, Annapolis, MD 21403; tel. (410) 295-0104; e-mail office@amaritime.org; internet www.amaritime.org; preserves and commemorates maritime heritage of Annapolis and neighbouring waters of Chesapeake Bay; Dir JEFF HOLLAND.

B & O Railroad Museum: 901 W Pratt St, Baltimore, MD 21223; tel. (410) 752-2490; e-mail info@borail.org; internet www.borail.org; f. 1953; attached to Smithsonian Instn; collects, preserves and interprets artefacts (incl. locomotives and rolling stock, historic bldgs and small objects) related to early American railroading focusing on continuum of railroad technology history since 1830, particularly the Baltimore and Ohio, Chesapeake and Ohio, W Maryland, and other mid-Atlantic railroads; also located at Ellicott City; Exec. Dir COURTNEY B. WILSON; Chief Curator DAVID SHACKELFORD; Chair. FRANCIS X. SMYTH; Sec. ROBERT F. SCHOLZ; Treas. GREGORY A. FARNO.

Baltimore Museum of Art: 10 Art Museum Dr., Baltimore, MD 21218-3898; tel. (443) 573-1700; internet www.artbma.org; f. 1914; total colln of 90,000 items; Cone Colln of post-impressionist and modern art (incl. 500 works by Matisse, and examples by Picasso, Cézanne and Van Gogh); West Wing for Contemporary Art housing 16 galleries of art since 1960s; Old Master and 19th-century European paintings and sculpture; prints, drawings and photographs since 15th century; American paintings, sculpture and decorative arts from the 17th to the 19th century; Maryland period rooms; African, Asian, Native American, and Oceanic art; 3-acre sculpture garden; library of 71,000 vols; Chair. STILES TUTTLE COLWILL; Dir and Sec. DOREEN BOLGER; Treas. FREDERICK SINGLEY KOONTZ; publ. *BMA Today* (4 a year).

Baltimore Museum of Industry: 1415 Key Highway, Baltimore, MD 21230; tel. (410) 727-4808; e-mail info@thebmi.org; internet www.thebmi.org; colln of 100,000 objects; spec. colln incl. historic 1850s shipyard bell, early wooden gas pipe, rare 1820s Acorn printing press, 1922 Linotype machine, antique sewing machines and the entire colln from the Mount Vernon Museum of Incandescent Lighting; 250,000 photographs and negatives; Schneidereith Print Colln; incl. Maryland Center for Career and Technology Education Studies and Downtown Sailing Center; Exec. Dir ROLAND H. WOODWARD; Chair. STUART FITZGIBBON; Sec. C. WILLIAM SCHNEIDEREITH, JR; Treas. CHERYL GRAVEEN.

Banneker-Douglass Museum: 84 Franklin St, Annapolis, MD 21401; tel. (410) 216-6180; e-mail bdmprograms@goci.state.md.us; internet www.bdmuseum.com; f. 1984; state's official repository of African American material culture; African permanent exhibit incl. American history in Maryland since 1633; incl. Sylvia Gaither Garrison Library; Pres. Dr JONI JONES; Curator of Collns TABITHA PRYOR.

Evergreen Museum & Library: Johns Hopkins Univ., 4545 N Charles St, Baltimore, MD 21210; tel. (410) 516-0341; e-mail evergreenmuseum@jhu.edu; internet www.museums.jhu.edu/evergreen.php; attached to John Hopkins Univ.; 500,000 objects incl. architecture, paintings, decorative arts, rare books, philanthropy, Baltimore's railroad history; Garret family holdings; European paintings by Edgar Degas, Amedeo Modigliani and Ignacio Zuloaga; library of 30,000 vols; Dir and Curator JAMES ARCHER ABBOTT.

F. Brooke Whiting House & Museum: 632 Washington St, Cumberland, MD 21502; tel. (301) 777-7782; e-mail info@thewhitinghouse.org; internet www.thewhitinghouse.org; f. 1998; colln of art from Brooke Whiting's travels around the world: Asian Works of Art and American, British and European decorative arts; arts from USA, UK, Netherlands, France, Spain, Portugal, Italy, Greece, Egypt, Lebanon, Iran, India, China, Thailand, Viet Nam, Korea, Japan, Russia and Mexico; library of 1,500 vols, incl. photographic materials and ephemera from his travels.

Glenn L. Martin Maryland Aviation Museum: POB 5024, Baltimore, MD 21220; 701 Wilson Point Rd, Hangar Five, Suite 531, Baltimore, MD 21220; tel. (410) 682-6122; e-mail other@marylandaviationmuseum.org; internet www.marylandaviationmuseum.org; f. 1990; preserves and documents aviation and space history in Maryland; contributions of Glenn L. Martin and his Co; 13 historic aircraft; thousands of original motion picture films, plans, documents, research models, aircraft tools, and components; 200,000 aviation and Co's photographs; Exec. Dir ROBERT BYRNES.

Homewood Museum: The Johns Hopkins Univ., 3400 N Charles St, Baltimore, MD 21218; tel. (410) 516-5589; e-mail homewoodmuseum@jhu.edu; internet www.museums.jhu.edu/homewood.php; attached to Johns Hopkins Univ.; colln incl. architecture (palladian and fed.), silver, Baltimore furniture, American history; Carroll family's fine and decorative arts objects; English ceramics, silver and furniture and items of Chinese and French manufacture; Dir and Curator CATHERINE ROGERS ARTHUR.

Jefferson Patterson Park and Museum, State Museum of Archaeology: 10515 Mackall Rd, St Leonard, MD 20685; tel. (410) 586-8501; e-mail jppm@mdp.state.md.us; internet www.jefpat.org; f. 1983; Maryland Archaeological Conservation Laboratory (MAC Lab): over 8m. artefacts; library of 12,000 vols; Exec. Dir MARK THOMPSON.

Johns Hopkins Archaeological Museum: 150 Gilman Hall, 3400 N Charles St, Baltimore, MD 21218; tel. (410) 516-0383; e-mail archmuseum@jhu.edu; internet www .archaeologicalmuseum.jhu.edu; f. 1882; attached to Johns Hopkins Univ.; 700 archaeological objects from ancient Greece, Rome, Egypt, the Near E and ancient Americas; Dir Dr BETSY M. BRYAN; Curator SANCHITA BALACHANDRAN.

Maryland Historical Society Museum and Library: 201 W Monument St, Baltimore, MD 21201-4674; tel. (410) 685-3750; e-mail reference@mdhs.org; internet www .mdhs.org; f. 1844; exhibits Francis Scott Key's original MSS of The Star-Spangled Banner and the war of 1812; 350,000 objects, incl. paintings and miniatures, pieces of furniture, sculpture, drawings, silver, ceramics, jewellery, textiles, examples of porcelain and pottery, works on paper, misc. household, office and agricultural equipment, toys, dolls, games, silver holloware and flatware, maritime objects; MSS room incl. Calvert Papers, papers of Benjamin Henry Latrobe, over 1,300 letters and documents of the Lords Baltimore and their families, genealogical colln and several hundreds of prints and drawings; maritime colln emphasizing crafts of Chesapeake Bay; library: 7m. vols; Pres. BURT KUMMEROW; Chief Curator ALEXANDRA DEUTSCH; publ. *Maryland Historical Magazine* (4 a year).

Maryland Science Center: 601 Light St, Baltimore, MD 21230; tel. (410) 685-2370; e-mail observatory@marylandsciencecenter .org; internet www.mdsci.org; f. 1797 as Maryland Acad. of Sciences; exhibits incl. travelling, earth science, life science, physical science and space science; Davis Planetarium and IMAX theatre; educational instn focusing on science, technology, engineering and mathematics; Pres. and CEO VAN R. REINER; Sec. PHYLLIS S. CLEMENTS; Treas. RICHARD M. HESSE.

National Cryptologic Museum: 9800 Savage Rd No 6272, Fort Meade, MD 20755; tel. (301) 688-5849; e-mail crypto_museum@nsa .gov; internet www.nsa.gov/about/ cryptologic_heritage/museum; f. 1993; attached to Nat. Security Agency; colln of artefacts preserving the history of the cryptologic profession; school programmes; library: collns of commercial codebooks, declassified documents, released VENONA documents, NSA's Special Research Histories (SRH), oral histories; Dir of Nat. Security Agency Gen. KEITH B. ALEXANDER.

Reginald F. Lewis Museum of Maryland African American History & Culture: 830 E Pratt St, Baltimore, MD 21202; tel. (443) 263-1800; e-mail emailus@maamc.org; internet www.africanamericanculture.org; attached to Smithsonina Instn; colln incl. art, artefacts, textiles, material culture, photographs, rare books and other items; African American military experience, early American jazz recordings and Maryland community history; Exec. Dir Dr A. SKIPP SANDERS; Chair. Dr LESLIE KING-HAMMOND; Sec. KATHLEEN PONTONE; Treas. CARLA HAYDEN.

Richardson Maritime Museum: POB 1198, 401 High St, Cambridge, MD 21613; tel. (410) 221-1871; e-mail info@ richardsonmuseum.org; internet www .richardsonmuseum.org; more than 50 Chesapeake Bay wooden boat models; boatbuilding tools; watermen's equipment and gear; spec. colln incl. skipjack Nathan of Dorchester, the last skipjack built in the 20th century and life and work of James B; Chair. VICTOR H. MACSORLEY; Curator MELVIN HICKMAN.

Thrasher Carriage Museum: 19 Depot St, Frostburg, MD 21532; tel. (301) 689-3380;

e-mail info@thethrashercarriagemuseum .com; internet www .thethrashercarriagemuseum.com; f. 1975; collns of horse-drawn vehicles, pleasure vehicles, funeral wagons, sleighs, carts; vehicles representing every walk of life; spec. collns: Extension Front Brougham, Queen Body Phaeton and Governess Cart.

United States Naval Academy Museum: Preble Hall, 118 Maryland Ave, Annapolis, MD; tel. (410) 293-2108; internet www.usna .edu/museum; f. 1845 as Naval School Lyceum, present location 1939; colln incl. ship models, paintings, prints, flags, uniforms, swords, firearms, medals, sculptures, MSS, rare books, photographs, ship instruments and gear and personal memorabilia; spec. colln incl. 6,000 prints of Beverley R. Robinson, United States Navy Trophy Flag and Malcolm Storer Naval Medals colln; Dir Dr J. SCOTT HARMON; Sr Curator JAMES CHEEVERS.

Walters Art Museum: 600 N Charles St, Baltimore, MD 21201; tel. (410) 547-9000; e-mail info@thewalters.org; internet www .thewalters.org; f. 1931; 35,000 objects: collns range from predynastic Egypt to 20th-century Europe; Chinese, Japanese and Indian art; ancient Egyptian, Greek and Roman art; Byzantine art; Romanesque, early Gothic art; later Gothic art; Renaissance sculpture and decorative arts; MSS illumination; incunabula, arms and armour; old master paintings, 19th-century paintings, decorative arts; spec. colln incl. ancient Egyptian mummy masks and medieval armour and 19th-century French Impressionism; library of 120,000 vols; Chair. ANDREA B. LAPORTE; Dir and Sec. GARY VIKAN; Treas. FRANK K. TURNER, JR; Sr Curator WILLIAM R. JOHNSTON; publs *Journal* (1 a year), *The Walters Magazine* (4 a year).

Washington County Museum of Fine Arts: POB 423, 401 Museum Dr., Hagerstown, MD 21741; tel. (301) 739-5727; e-mail info@wcmfa.org; internet www.wcmfa.org; f. 1929; 6,000 objects from Old Masters to 20th-century paintings, sculpture and decorative arts; conducts research on all works of art in its colln; art library.

Massachusetts

Adams National Historical Park: 135 Adams St, Quincy, MA 02169-1749; tel. (617) 773-1177; e-mail adam_visitor_center@nps.gov; internet www .nps.gov/adam; f. 1946; attached to Nat. Park Service; donated to the USA in December 1946 by the Adams Memorial Soc.; designated a nat. historic site under the admin. of the Nat. Park Service of the Dept of the Interior; built in 1731 by Major Leonard Vassall of Boston; bought by John Adams in 1787; at the end of his term, he lived in the house until his death in 1826; the house then passed to his son, John Quincy Adams, in the middle of his term as sixth Pres.; the Adams family continued to live there until 1927; the house, contents, and garden are as the Adams family left them; the separate stone library, standing in the garden, was built in 1870 by Charles Francis Adams—comprises most of the libraries of John Quincy Adams and Charles Francis Adams, and some of the libraries of John Adams, Henry and Brooks Adams; library of 12,000 vols; Dir JONATHAN B. JARVIS; Superintendent MARIANNE PEAK.

Addison Gallery of American Art: Phillips Acad., 180 Main St, Andover, MA 01810-4161; tel. (978) 749-4015; e-mail addison@ andover.edu; internet www.andover.edu/ museums/addison; f. 1931; 17,000 objects in media-painting, sculpture, photography, drawings, prints and decorative arts since

18th century; Dir BRIAN T. ALLEN; Curator ALLISON N. KEMMERER.

Art Complex Museum: 189 Alden St, POB 2814, Duxbury, MA 02331; tel. (781) 934-6634; e-mail director@artcomplex.org; internet www.artcomplex.org; f. 1971; 8,000 objects on American paintings, prints, Shaker furniture and Asian art; library of 6,000 vols; Dir CHARLES WEYERHAEUSER; Librarian CHERYL O'NEILL.

Beneski Museum of Natural History: POB 5000, Amherst College, Amherst, MA 01002-5000; 11 Barrett Hill Rd, Amherst College, Amherst, MA 01002-5000; tel. (413) 542-2165; internet www.amherst.edu/ museums/naturalhistory; f. 1821, present name and status 2011; attached to Amherst College; natural history colln of 200,000 objects; archaeology colln incl. 15,000 items made by Americans from New England and New York; rep. sample of 18 original meteorites; Dir PETER CROWLEY.

Berkshire Museum: 39 S St, Route 7, Pittsfield, MA 01201; tel. (413) 443-7171; internet www.berkshiremuseum.org; f. 1903; 19th- and 20th-century sculptures by American and European artists; artefacts of ancient history and natural science incl. fossil colln and 143-lb meteorite; neoclassical marble sculptures dating from 19th century; Exec. Dir VAN W. SHIELDS.

Cahoon Museum of American Art: POB 1853, 4676 Falmouth Rd, Cotuit, MA 02635; tel. (508) 428-7581; internet www .cahoonmuseum.org; f. 1984; colln incl. folk paintings of Cahoon and 19th- and 20th-century contemporary American art; Dir RICHARD WATERHOUSE.

Concord Museum: POB 146, 200 Lexington Rd, Concord, MA 01742-0146; tel. (978) 369-9763; e-mail cm1@concordmuseum.org; internet www.concordmuseum.org; f. 1886; history and decorative arts museum with 16 period rooms and galleries, with artefacts from Concord area; museum rooms chronicle life in Concord from Native American habitation to present; spec. collns incl. relics from the battle at N Bridge, the largest colln of Thoreau artefacts from his stay at Walden Pond, and the contents of Emerson's study; over 35,000 objects; Exec. Dir PEGGY BURKE.

Danforth Art: 123 Union Ave, Framingham, MA 01702-8291; tel. (508) 620-0050; e-mail info@danforthart.org; internet www .danforthart.org; f. 1975; 3,500 works of art with focus on American art since 18th century; spec. colln incl. 19th- and 20th-century American art by artists incl. Gilbert Stuart, Faith Ringgold and Albert Bierstadt; exhibitions and education programmes; Exec. Dir KATHERINE FRENCH.

Davis Museum and Cultural Center: Wellesley College, 106 Central St, Wellesley, MA 02481-8203; tel. (781) 283-2051; internet www.davismuseum.wellesley.edu; f. 1889; attached to Wellesley College; colln incl. paintings, sculptures, works on paper, photographs and decorative objects since antiquity; Dir LISA FISCHMAN.

DeCordova Sculpture Park and Museum: 51 Sandy Pond Rd, Lincoln, MA 01773-2600; tel. (781) 259-8355; e-mail info@ decordova.org; internet www.decordova.org; f. 1950 as deCordova Museum and Sculpture Park, present name 2009; 3,400 works of modern and contemporary art in photography, prints, painting, drawing and sculpture; Pres. FAITH PARKER; Treas. ANNE COLUMBIA; Exec. Dir DENNIS KOIS; Curator DINA DEITSCH.

Emily Dickinson Museum: 280 Main St, Amherst, MA 01002; tel. (413) 542-8161; e-mail info@emilydickinsonmuseum.org;

internet www.emilydickinsonmuseum.org; f. 2003; attached to Amherst College; colln of 8,000 objects incl. furniture, artwork and personal items of Emily Dickinson; Exec. Dir JANE WALD; Chair. JOHN ARMSTRONG; Sec. JAMES C. FRASER.

Fitchburg Art Museum: 25 Merriam Parkway, Fitchburg, MA 01420; tel. (978) 345-4207; e-mail info@fitchburgartmuseum.org; internet www.fitchburgartmuseum.org; f. 1925; American and European paintings, prints, drawings, ceramics and decorative arts; Greek, Roman, Asian and pre-Columbian antiquities; 14 galleries; Dir NICK CAPASSO.

Harvard Art Museums: 32 Quincy St, Cambridge, MA 02138; tel. (617) 495-9400; internet www.harvardartmuseums.org; f. 1891; incl. Arthur M. Sackler Museum (ancient, Asian, Islamic and later Indian art), Busch-Reisinger Museum (art from German-speaking countries), Fogg Museum (Western art from the Middle Ages to the present), Center for the Technical Study of Modern Art, Harvard Art Museum Archives, Straus Center for Conservation, the US HQ for the Archaeological Exploration of Sardis; library of 3,000 vols of conservation-related books in the Straus Center, 3,000 linear ft of historical records and artists papers in the archives (since 1895); Dir THOMAS W. LENTZ; Deputy Dir MAUREEN DONOVAN; Chief Curator DEBORAH MARTIN KAO; publ. *Index* (3 a year).

Higgins Armory Museum: 100 Barber Ave, Worcester, MA 01606-2444; tel. (508) 853-6015; e-mail higgins@higgins.org; internet www.higgins.org; f. 1931 as John Woodman Higgins Armory; 4,500 artefacts on arms and armours from medieval and Renaissance Europe, Feudal Japan and ancient Greece and Rome; European colln incl. 3,000 armours and components, 1,000 weapons and accessories, 500 swords and daggers and 100 firearms; 1,000 African, Islamic, Indian and Japanese arms; Exec. Dir SUZANNE MAAS.

Isabella Stewart Gardner Museum: 280 The Fenway, Boston, MA 02115; tel. (617) 566-1401; e-mail information@isgm.org; internet www.gardnermuseum.org; f. 1903; 2,500 objects incl. paintings, sculptures, textiles, drawings, silver, ceramics, illuminated MSS, rare books, photographs and letters from ancient Rome, medieval Europe, Renaissance Italy, Asia, Islamic world and 19th-century France and America; Dir ANNE HAWLEY.

Mead Art Museum: POB 5000, Amherst College, Amherst, MA 01002-5000; tel. (413) 542-2335; e-mail mead@amherst.edu; internet www.amherst.edu/museums/mead; f. 1949; attached to Amherst College; colln incl. 16,000 works of art from America, Europe, Mexico, Asia, Africa and Russia; Dir and Chief Curator Dr ELIZABETH E. BARKER.

Milton Art Museum: 900 Randolph St, Canton, MA 02021; tel. (781) 821-2222; e-mail miltonmuseum@hotmail.com; internet miltonartmuseum.org; f. 1986; colln incl. fine art, limited prints, sculpture, photography and Asian art; Remington and Russell cast bronzes; American and European etchings and lithographs from 18th to 20th century; 17th-century oil painting by Dutch painter Cornelius Bisschop; Chair. and Interim Treas. ELLYN MOLLER; Sec. DAVID EHRMANN.

Museum of Fine Arts, Boston: 465 Huntington Ave, Boston, MA 02115; tel. (617) 267-9300; e-mail customerservice@mfa.org; internet www.mfa.org; f. 1876; 450,000 objects; rare and important works incl. masters of American painting, Impressionist art, Asian scrolls and Egyptian mummies; art classes, educational programmes, tours for blind; library of 320,000 items; spec. collns the William Morris Hunt Memorial Library, the W. Van Alan Clark, Jr, Library, and nine curatorial department libraries; Dir MALCOLM ROGERS.

Museum of Science: 1 Science Park, Boston, MA 02114; tel. (617) 723-2500; e-mail information@mos.org; internet www.mos.org; f. 1830 as Boston Soc. of Natural History; exhibits on astronomy, natural history, physical science, technology, medicine, etc.; educational programmes with more than 550 interactive exhibits; houses the Charles Hayden Planetarium, the Mugar Omni Theater and the Lyman Library; library of 40,000 vols and journals; Chair. HOWARD MESSING; Pres. and Dir IOANNIS N. MIAOULIS; publ. *Magazine* (2 a year).

Norman Rockwell Museum: Nine Route 183, Stockbridge, MA 01262; tel. (413) 298-4100; internet www.nrm.org; f. 1969; museum houses American painter and illustrator Norman Rockwell's 574 original paintings and drawings; more than 100,000 items, incl. working photographs, letters, personal calendars, fan mail and business documents; Chair. THOMAS L. PULLING.

Peabody Essex Museum: East India Sq., 161 Essex St, Salem, MA 01970-3738; tel. (978) 745-9500; internet www.pem.org; f. 1799; 1m. works; maritime art and history, Asian, Oceanic, Indian, African and Native American art; American art and architecture; incl. Phillips Library; library of 400,000 vols, a mile in linear ft of MSS, colln of ephemera, broadsides, pamphlets, and periodicals; Exec. Dir and CEO DAN L. MONROE; Pres. ROBERT N. SHAPIRO; Sec. CARLA B. HERWITZ; Treas. C. RICHARD CARLSON; publs *American Neptune* (4 a year), *Quarterly Review of Archaeology*.

Peabody Museum of Archaeology and Ethnology: Harvard Univ., 11 Divinity Ave, Cambridge, MA 02138; tel. (617) 496-1027; e-mail peapub@fas.harvard.edu; internet www.peabody.harvard.edu; f. 1866; works in cooperation with the Dept of Anthropology of Harvard; collns of ethnology, archaeology and physical anthropology; Maya archaeology colln, Old World archaeology colln, Pacific Islands ethnology colln; material representing the native tribes of Africa, South America, and the Plains and NW Coast Indians of N America; archaeology of SW USA, incl. the Pueblo Indian area; Tozzer Library of anthropology; library of 250,000 vols and pamphlets; Dir Prof. DAVID PILBEAM; publs *RES: Anthropology and Aesthetics*, *Symbols* (1 a year).

Scottish Rite Masonic Museum & Library: 33 Marrett Rd, Lexington, MA 02421; tel. (781) 861-6559; internet www.nationalheritagemuseum.org; f. 1975; colln on history of American Freemasonry and fraternalism; colln incl. decorative arts, documents, photographs and fine art on American history; library of 60,000 vols; Exec. Dir RICHARD V. TRAVIS.

Smith College Museum of Art: Elm St at Bedford Terrace, Northampton, MA 01063; tel. (413) 585-2760; e-mail artmuseum@smith.edu; internet www.smith.edu/artmuseum; f. 1879, present bldg 2003; collns incl. examples from most periods and cultures with spec. emphasis on European and American paintings, sculpture, drawings, prints and photographs since 17th century; Cunningham Center houses over 1,600 drawings, 5,700 photographs and over 8,000 prints by artists from Dürer to contemporary print makers; Dir and Chief Curator JESSICA NICOLL; Assoc. Dir DAVID DEMPSEY.

Spellman Museum of Stamps & Postal History: 235 Wellesley St, Regis College, Weston, MA 02493; tel. (781) 768-8367; e-mail info@spellman.org; internet www.spellman.org; f. 1960 as Cardinal Spellman Philatelic Museum; 2m. items incl. those from Pres. Dwight David Eisenhower, violinist Jascha Heifetz and Gen. Matthew Ridgway; library of 4,800 vols; Pres. and Chair. NANCY CLARK; Sec. Sr ANN MARIE GRADY; Treas. LYNNE LINNEHAN.

Sterling and Francine Clark Art Institute: 225 S St, Williamstown, MA 01267; tel. (413) 458-2303; internet www.clarkart.edu; f. 1950; colln of European and American painting, sculpture, works on paper and decorative art dating from Renaissance to early 20th century; 19th-century European and American paintings; Dir MICHAEL CONFORTI.

USS Constitution Museum: POB 291812, Boston, MA 02129-0215; Charlestown Navy Yard, Bldg 22, Charlestown, MA 02129; tel. (617) 426-1812; e-mail museumadmin@ussconstitutionmuseum.org; internet www.ussconstitutionmuseum.org; f. 1972; colln related to duty naval vessel USS Constitution; art and artefact colln incl. swords, pistols and muskets from 18th and 19th century; 7,500 items in MSS colln; library of 2,000 vols; Chair. JAMES C. STOKES; Sec. PAUL F. McDONOUGH, JR; Treas. WILLIAM WHITE.

Williams College Museum of Art: 15 Lawrence Hall Dr., Suite 2, Williamstown, MA 01267-3248; tel. (413) 597-2429; internet wcma.williams.edu; f. 1926; attached to Williams College; 13,000 objects incl. Assyrian reliefs to contemporary photography; colln of American art since late 18th century; Dir KATY KLINE.

Worcester Art Museum: 55 Salisbury St, Worcester, MA 01609; tel. (508) 799-4406; e-mail information@worcesterart.org; internet www.worcesterart.org; f. 1898; 40,000-piece colln of paintings, sculptures, decorative arts, photographs, prints, drawings and new media illustrating the evolution of art from early Egyptian civilization to modern times; esp. notable are ancient Egyptian, Greek, Roman, Asian and medieval sculpture; mosaics from Antioch; a French Romanesque Chapter House; Italian and other European schools of painting since 13th century; American collns since 17th century; pre-Columbian art; Japanese and Western prints; offers a year-round studio art and art appreciation programme; library of 45,000 vols; Dir MATTHIAS WASCHEK.

Michigan

Cranbrook Art Museum: 39221 Woodward Ave, POB 801, Bloomfield Hills, MI 48303-0801; e-mail artmuseum@cranbrook.edu; internet www.cranbrookart.edu/museum; f. 1930; attached to Cranbrook Academy of Art; 6,000 works of art, architecture and design from the Arts and Crafts Movement to the present; colln incl. sculpture, paintings, models and drawings, ceramics, glass, furniture, textiles and metalwork, decorative, applied and fine arts; Dir GREGORY WITTKOPP.

Dennos Museum Center: 1701 E Front St, Traverse City, MI 49686; tel. (231) 995-1055; e-mail dmc@nmc.edu; internet www.dennosmuseum.org; f. 1991; 2,000 works of art incl. Inuit prints, painting, sculpture and photography and sculptures; contemporary works by Michigan artists, 19th- and 20th-century American and European graphic art, 18th- and 19th-century Japanese prints, and 20th-century Great Lakes Indian and Canadian Indian art; incl. 3 exhibit galleries, sculpture court, Discovery Gallery, Inuit

Art Gallery and Milliken auditorium; Exec. Dir EUGENE JENNEMAN.

Detroit Institute of Arts: 5200 Woodward Ave, Detroit, MI 48202; tel. (313) 833-7900; e-mail operator@dia.org; internet www.dia .org; f. 1885 as Detroit Museum of Art, present name and location 1927; comprehensive fine arts colln from prehistoric to contemporary times; colln of American, Dutch, Flemish, French, Italian and German Expressionist painting; Ancient, African, Oceanic and New World cultures; Asian, Native American and Islamic art since the beginning of the 20th century; graphic arts; American and European decorative arts since the beginning of the 20th century; theatre arts colln; 100 galleries, art reference library and state-of-the-art conservation services laboratory; library of 190,000 vols; Dir, Pres. and CEO GRAHAM W. J. BEAL; Chief Curator KENNETH J. MYERS; publs *Bulletin of the Detroit Institute of Arts* (1 a year), *Your DIA* (12 a year).

Ella Sharp Museum of Art and History: 3225 Fourth St, Jackson, MI 49203; tel. (517) 787-2320; e-mail info@ellasharp.org; internet www.ellasharp.org; f. 1965; Andrews Gallery of Wildlife Art, Jackson History Gallery and 3 galleries of temporary exhibitions; outdoor sculpture colln; historic sites of Ella Sharp's 19th-century Hillside Farmhouse, Dibble One-Room Schoolhouse, Eli Stilson's Log House and Merriman-Sharp Tower Barn.

Flint Institute of Arts: 1120 E Kearsley St, Flint, MI 48503; tel. (810) 234-1695; internet www.flintarts.org/museum/museum.html; f. 1928 as Enos and Sarah DeWaters Art Center; 8,000 American, European, Native American, African, and Asian art incl. paintings, sculptures, prints, drawings, and decorative arts; colln incl. 15th- to 18th-century English, French and Italian decorative arts, panel by Peter Paul Rubens, 17th-century French tapestries, 18th- and 19th-century paperweights and European glass, American and French Impressionist and Post-Impressionist paintings, Hudson River School paintings, Regional and Great Lakes paintings, Modernist and Abstract Expressionist and Photorealist paintings; Dir JOHN HENRY; Pres. SAMUEL M. HARRIS; Sec. MARILYN KOPP; Treas. DIANE LINDHOLM; publ. *fia magazine*.

Grand Rapids Art Museum: 101 Monroe Center, Grand Rapids, MI 49503; tel. (616) 831-1000; internet www.artmuseumgr.org; f. 1910, present name 1963; 19th- and 20th-century art, design and modern craft, prints, drawings and photographs; library of 8,000 vols; Dir and CEO DANA FRIIS-HANSEN; Pres. SCOTT WIERDA; Sec. and Treas. TONY S. LAWRENCE.

Grand Rapids Public Museum: 272 Pearl St NW, Grand Rapids, MI 49504; tel. (616) 929-1700; e-mail info@grmuseum.org; internet www.grmuseum.org; f. 1854; Roger B. Chaffee planetarium; museum sites: Voigt House, Community Archives, Calkins Law Office, Veen Observatory, Norton Mounds, 54 Jefferson and Van Andel Museum Center; colln of 250,000 artefacts and specimens incl. ethnographic cultural materials, historically significant fine art, bldgs and architectural fragments, archeological materials, fossils, rocks and minerals, clothing and textiles, decorative arts; archival colln of paper records, publs, photographs, artwork, letters and diaries; Pres. and CEO DALE ROBERTSON; Chair. DAN GAYDOU; Sec. and Treas. RICH NOREEN.

Holland Museum: 31 W 10th St, Holland, MI 49423; tel. (616) 796-3321; e-mail hollandmuseum@hollandmuseum.org; internet www.hollandmuseum.org; f. 1897, cur-

rent name and status 1992; colln of works of art of Netherlands, Indonesia, local history, Hispanic and SE Asian, Native American, Cappon House, 1867 Settlers House; Archives incl. 1,585 linear ft of material; temporary exhibitions; Exec. Dir CHRISTOPHER SHIRES; Chair. GEOFFREY REYNOLDS; Sec. ANNE STEWART.

Kalamazoo Institute of Arts: 314 S Park St, Kalamazoo, MI 49007; tel. (269) 349-7775; e-mail museum@kiarts.org; internet www .kiarts.org; f. 1924; American paintings, sculpture and ceramics, American and European works on paper since 16th century, photography, oceanic objects, Pre-Columbian gold and ceramics, African art and E Asian art; library of 11,000 vols, 350 DVDs and video cassettes, 40 art-related periodicals; Exec. Dir JAMES BRIDENSTINE; Pres. COURTENAY VANDERMOLEN; Sec. LINDA DUNN; Treas. BRIAN HUDSON.

Kelsey Museum of Archaeology: 434 S State St, Ann Arbor, MI 48109-1390; tel. (734) 764-9304; e-mail kelseymuse@umich .edu; internet www.lsa.umich.edu/kelsey; f. 1928, present name and status 1953; attached to Univ. of Michigan; colln of 100,000 Greek, Near E and Roman artefacts (painted Egyptian mummy coffin, magical amulets from the ancient Near E, array of glass vessels, Greek pottery, Roman sculptures, and large-scale watercolour representation of Villa of the Mysteries murals from ancient Pompeii); excavation records and archive of 25,000 archaeological and fine arts photographs; library of 20,000 vols; Dir SHARON HERBERT.

Michigan State University Museum: W Circle Dr., East Lansing, MI 48824; tel. (517) 355-2370; e-mail pr@museum.msu.edu; internet www.museum.msu.edu; f. 1857; colln of 1m. archaeological items, 25,000 ethnographic artefacts, 63,000 historical and cultural artefacts, 300 quilts and 5,000 files on Michigan quilts and quilters, cultural and folk art, 38,500 natural science specimens, 100,000 historical 3-D objects, archive of documents and photographs; temporary exhibitions; Dir GARY MORGAN.

Muskegon Museum of Art: 296 W Webster Ave, Muskegon, MI 49440; tel. (231) 720-2570; internet www.muskegonartmuseum .org; f. 1912, present name 1980; Exec. Dir JUDITH HAYNER; Chair. LARRY HINES; Treas. TRIP JOHNSON; Sec. STACIE BEHLER; Sr Curator E. JANE CONNELL.

Saginaw Art Museum: 1126 N Michigan Ave, Saginaw, MI 48602-4763; tel. (989) 754-2491; e-mail staff@saginawartmuseum.org; internet www.saginawartmuseum.org; f. 1948, present name 1967; colln of 2,500 art and artefacts spanning 4,500 years of art history; American and European artworks incl. decorative arts, drawings, MSS, paintings, prints, sculpture and textiles from 15th to 20th centuries; Asian art colln of decorative art, paintings, sculpture, textiles and woodcuts from China, India, Japan and Korea; modern and contemporary art holdings incl. prints, drawings and photographs by Robert Estes, Jasper Johns, and Claes Oldenburg and regional artists; library of 1,200 vols (incl. books, catalogues and periodicals); Exec. Dir STACEY GANNON.

The Henry Ford: 20900 Oakwood Blvd, Dearborn, MI 48124-5029; tel. (313) 982-6001; internet www.thehenryford.org; f. 1929; indoor and outdoor living museum of US history from European settlement to the present; public life, agriculture and industry, leisure and entertainment, transportation, communication and IT, decorative arts, historic structures; incl. Henry Ford Museum, Greenfield Village, Ford Rouge Factory Tour,

IMAX Theatre and Benson Ford Research Center; library of 43,500 vols, 1,500 periodicals, 30,000 trade literature items, 25,000 linear ft of archival material incl. records of the Ford Motor Co, 2m. photographic images and 50,000 graphic items; Chair. S. EVAN WEINER; Pres. and Sec. PATRICIA E. MOORADIAN.

University of Michigan Museum of Art: 525 S State St, Ann Arbor, MI 48109-1354; tel. (734) 764-0395; e-mail umma-press@ umich.edu; internet www.umma.umich.edu; f. 1856; colln of 18,000 art works of African, American, Asian, European, Middle E, modern and contemporary, prints, drawings and photographs; 18 galleries; Dir JOSEPH ROSA; Chair. ROBERT BOHLEN; publ. *UMMA magazine* (6 a year).

Minnesota

American Museum of Asmat Art at the University of St. Thomas: c/o Dept of Art History, Univ. of St Thomas, 2115 Summit Ave, St Paul, MN 55105; tel. (651) 962-5512; internet www.stthomas.edu/arthistory/ asmat; Chair. GERALD D. BRENNAN; Dir Dr JULIE RISSER.

Minneapolis Institute of Arts: 2400 Third Ave S, Minneapolis, MN 55404; tel. (612) 870-3131; internet www.artsmia.org; f. 1883 as Minneapolis Soc. of Fine Arts; 7 divs of colln: arts of Africa and Americas; contemporary art; decorative arts, textiles and sculpture; Asian art; paintings; photography and new media; prints and drawings; textiles; library of 60,000 vols mainly on history of art; Dir and Pres. KAYWIN FELDMAN.

Minnesota Lakes Maritime Museum: POB 1216, 205 Third Ave W, Alexandria, MN 56308; tel. (320) 759-1114; e-mail boat@ mnlakesmaritime.org; internet www .mnlakesmaritime.org; Pete and Mado Pederson Gallery: local resort hotel industry history on Lake Minnetonka; Mahan-Zimmerman Gallery: 3 historic launches—The Dungeness, Frieda and Stella and colln of toy boats; Mammel Foundation Exhibit Hall: classic wood boats; M. M. "Bud" Peterson Gallery: restored Larson boats from Mikkelson Colln in Willmar; Summer Porch-Minnesouri Club Exhibit; Fishing Gallery: antique tackle, fish mounts, guide stories and fishing memorabilia; New North Hall-History of Chris-Craft: chronological display of Chris-Craft co history and boat builder and racer Gar Wood Exhibit; Dir BRUCE OLSON.

Minnesota Museum of American Art: Historic Hamm Bldg, 408 St Peter St, Suite 419, St Paul, MN 55102; tel. (651) 797-4057; e-mail info@mmaa.org; internet www.mmaa .org; 3,800 works of art incl. American art since 19th century, with spec. emphasis on paintings of School of the Eight, mid-century studio craft, modern drawings and artists from Minnesota and region; Exec. Dir Dr KRISTIN MAKHOLM; Chair. A. DAVID KELLY; Sec. ANN M. HEIDER; Treas. MATTHEW BELLIN.

Rourke Art Museum: 521 Main Ave, Moorhead, MN 56560; tel. (218) 236-8861; e-mail museum@rourkeart.org; internet www.wix .com/therourke/rourke; f. 1975 as Plains Art Museum, present status 1996; 3,000 contemporary paintings, prints, drawings, sculptures, photographs, African, Native American, Pre-Columbian and Hispanic works of art; Rourke Gallery.

Science Museum of Minnesota: 120 W Kellogg Blvd, St Paul, MN 55102; tel. (651) 221-9444; e-mail info@smm.org; internet www.smm.org; f. 1907; collns and research in anthropology, biology, palaeontology, ethnology, zoology, archaeology, geology and geography; outdoor research centre; a 300-seat omnitheatre; nature centre and public science education centre; Pres. ERIC J. JOLLY; Chair. JOHN M. STANOCH; Sec. RUSS NELSON; Treas. RICHARD O. LUND.

Thunder Bay National Marine Sanctuary: 500 W Fletcher, Alpena, MI 49707; tel. (989) 356-8805; e-mail thunderbay@noaa .gov; internet thunderbay.noaa.gov; f. 2000; attached to Nat. Oceanic and Atmospheric Admin. and State of Michigan; protects nationally significant collns of shipwrecks and related maritime heritage resources; historic and archaeological features incl. stations, lighthouses, historic boats and ships, commercial fishing camps, docks and working ports; conducts, supports, promotes, and coordinates geological and archaeological research into prehistoric sites; Chair. STEVE KROLL.

Tweed Museum of Art: Univ. of Minnesota Duluth, 1201 Ordean Court, Duluth, MN 55812-2496; tel. (218) 726-7823; e-mail tweed@d.umn.edu; internet www.d.umn.edu/ tma; f. 1958; attached to Univ. of Minnesota Duluth; 8,000 art objects on major themes: Stories in Art, People and Places (artworks from USA, Italy, Holland, Japan, W Africa and Cuba), Art and Environment and the Language of Art (paintings, sculptures, prints and photographs); 374 images of the Royal Canadian Mounted Police Force; Dir KEN BLOOM.

Walker Art Center: 1750 Hennepin, Minneapolis, MN 55403; tel. (612) 375-7600; e-mail info@walkerart.org; internet www .walkerart.org; f. 1927; modern paintings, drawings, prints, sculpture, photography; extensive music, dance, film and video, theatre and education programmes; incl. Minneapolis Sculpture Garden; 800 holdings in Ruben Bentson Film and Video Study Colln; library of 35,000 vols; Dir OLGA VISO.

Weisman Art Museum: 333 E River Rd, Minneapolis, MN 55455; tel. (612) 625-9494; e-mail wamdir@umn.edu; internet weisman .umn.edu; f. 1934, present bldg 1993; attached to Univ. of Minnesota; colln of 1,700 works of art incl. 20th-century American artists, incl. Georgia O'Keeffe and Marsden Hartley, ceramics, Korean furniture and contemporary art; Dir LYNDEL KING; Curator DIANE MULLIN.

Mississippi

DeSoto County Museum: 111 E Commerce St, Hernando, MS 38632; tel. (662) 429-8852; e-mail info@desotomuseum.org; internet www.desotomuseum.org; artefacts and exhibits featuring history and devt of DeSoto Co since 1541; Dir BRIAN HICKS.

Dunn-Seiler Geology Museum: Mississippi State Univ., Dept of Geosciences, 108 Hilbun Hall, POB 5448, Mississippi, MS 39762-5448; tel. (662) 325-3915; internet www.geosciences.msstate.edu/museum.htm; f. 1946 as Franklin Seiler Museum, present name 1962; attached to Dept of Geosciences, Mississippi State Univ.; colln incl. mineral, rock, meteorites and fossils; Dir RENEE CLARY; Curator AMY MOE HOFFMAN.

Jacqueline House African American Museum: 1325 Main St, Vicksburg, MS 39183; tel. (601) 636-0941; internet www .stmaryvicksburg.org/jh; f. 1995; 20,000 items incl. photographs, books and MSS on history and culture of people of African descent in Vicksburg-Warren Co; Curator TILLMAN WHITLEY.

Lauren Rogers Museum of Art: POB 1108, Laurel, Laurel, MS 39441-1108; 565 N Fifth Ave, Laurel, MS 39440; tel. (601) 649-6374; e-mail info@lrma.org; internet lrma.org; f. 1923; colln incl. 19th- and 20th-century European and American art, Native American baskets, British Georgian silver and

Japanese woodblock prints; library of 10,000 vols; Dir GEORGE BASSI; Curator JILL CHANCEY.

Meridian Museum of Art: 628 25th Ave, Meridian, MS 39301-4917; tel. 601-693-1501; e-mail meridianmuseum@bellsouth.net; internet www.meridianmuseum.org; focus on collecting and displaying work of renowned regional and Mississippi artists; Exec. Dir KATE CHERRY.

Mississippi Armed Forces Museum: Bldg 850, Camp Shelby, MS 39407; tel. (601) 558-2757; internet www.armedforcesmuseum.us; military history museum; exhibits of War of 1812, Mexican War, American Civil War, Spanish-American War, First and Second World War, Korean War, Viet Nam Conflict; Dir CHAD DANIELS.

Mississippi Museum of Art: 380 S Lamar St, Jackson, MS 39201; tel. (601) 960-1515; internet www.msmuseumart.org; f. 1911, fmrly Mississippi Art Asscn, present name and status 1979; permanent colln of 3,800 pieces with an emphasis on mid-19th and 20th-century American art; incl. paintings, sculptures, prints, drawings and photographs by Albert Bierstadt, Arthur B. Davies, Robert Henri, George Inness, Georgia O'Keeffe, Thomas Sully, J. A. M. Whistler; photographs and works on paper incl. works by Thomas Hart Benton, Alexander Calder, William Eggleston, Walker Evans, Andy Warhol, Eudora Welty; Annie Laurie Swaim Hearin Memorial Exhibition Series hosts world-class exhibitions every 2 years; Chair. ROY D. CAMPBELL; Dir BETSY BRADLEY; Sec. MAYO FLYNT; Treas. DAVID FOWLER.

Mississippi Museum of Natural Science: 2148 Riverside Dr., Jackson, MS 39202-1353; tel. (601)576-6000; e-mail rebeccag@mmns .state.ms.us; internet www.msnaturalscience .org; f. 1932; an aquarium system with over 200 living species of native fish, reptiles, amphibians and aquatic invertebrates; 1,700-sq. ft greenhouse called 'The Swamp' with another 20,000-gallon aquarium, provides a home for alligators, turtles, fish and a lush native plant garden; 200-seat auditorium, library, biological archives; 870,000 specimens; Chair. BRYAN JONES; Exec. Dir Dr SAM POLLES; Museum Dir LIBBY HARTFIELD.

University of Mississippi Museum: POB 1848, Oxford, MS 38677; tel. (662) 915-7073; internet museum.olemiss.edu; f. 1939 as Mary Buie Museum, present status 1974; colln incl. S folk art, Greek and Roman antiquities and American fine art; 500 19th-century scientific instruments; 200 artworks by Theora Hamblett; Dir WILLIAM PITTMAN ANDREWS.

Walter Anderson Museum of Art: 510 Washington Ave, Ocean Springs, MS 39564-4632; tel. (228) 872-3164; e-mail wama@ walterandersonmuseum.org; internet www .walterandersonmuseum.org; f. 1991; watercolours, drawings, oils, block prints, ceramics and carvings by the 3 Anderson brothers; Exec. Dir LINDA STUART-LAND; Pres. MORRIS SHOEMAKER; Sec. LORI CARTER; Treas. Dr LARRY SHOEMAKER.

Missouri

Albrecht-Kemper Museum of Art: 2818 Frederick Ave, St Joseph, MO 64506; tel. (816) 233-7003; e-mail frontdesk@ albrecht-kemper.org; internet albrecht-kemper.org; f. 1913, present name and status 1991; collns of 18th-, 19th- and 20th-century American art in the Mid W region, incl. colonial portraits, American landscape paintings and American Impressionism; Dir TERRY OLDHAM.

Daum Museum of Contemporary Art: 3201 W 16th St, Sedalia, MO 65301; tel. (660) 530-5888; e-mail info@daummuseum .org; internet www.daummuseum.org; f. 2002; attached to State Fair Community College in Sedalia; 1,000 objects of modern and contemporary works of art and design, incl. abstract paintings, drawings, prints, works in clay and sculpture created since mid-20th century; Dir THOMAS PICHÉ, JR.

International Photography Hall of Fame and Museum: 3415 Olive St, St Louis, MO 63103; tel. (314) 535-1999; e-mail info@iphf.org; internet www.iphf.org; f. 1965; photographic equipment colln; photographic images colln; Pres. ROBERT WAGNER; Sec. DAVID HANLON; Exec. Dir JOHN WM. NAGEL.

Kansas City Museum: 3218 Gladstone Blvd, Kansas City, MO 64123-1199; tel. (816) 483-8300; internet kansascitymuseum .org; f. 1940; incl. Corinthian Hall, Beaux Arts limestone residence, Carriage House, StoryTarium in the fmr Conservatory; administered by Kansas City Museum Asscn; features films, lectures and other history-related programming on Kansas City's local and regional history; Dir CHRISTOPHER LEITCH.

Kemper Museum of Contemporary Art: 4420 Warwick Blvd, Kansas City, MO 64111; tel. (816) 753-5784; e-mail visitorservices@ kemperart.org; internet www.kemperart.org; f. 1994; colln of 1,000 works, incl. painting, sculpture, installations, prints and works on paper, photography and time-based media; works by Louise Bourgeois, Christian Boltanski, Manuel Neri, Jasper Johns, Helen Frankenthaler, Frank Stella, Joan Mitchell, Jackson Pollock, Robert Rauschenberg, Hung Liu, Robert Motherwell, Deborah Butterfield, Fairfield Porter, Wayne Thiebaud, Grace Hartigan, William Wegman, Red Grooms, Georgia O'Keeffe, Christopher Brown, Willem de Kooning, and Robert Mapplethorpe; 3 museum locations; Chair. CROSBY KEMPER; Dir and CEO RACHAEL BLACKBURN COZAD.

Mildred Lane Kemper Art Museum: c/o Washington Univ., 1 Brookings Dr., POB 1214, St Louis, MO 63130; tel. (314) 935-5490; e-mail kemperartmuseum@wustl.edu; internet wustl.edu/community/visitors/tour/ danforth/kemper-art-museum.html; f. 1881 as St Louis School and Museum of Fine Arts, present name 2006; attached to Washington Univ.; 19th-, 20th- and 21st-century European and American paintings, sculptures, prints, installations and photographs; colln also incl. some Egyptian and Greek antiquities and more than 100 Old Master prints; Dir and Chief Curator Dr SABINE ECKMANN.

Museum of Art and Archaeology: 1 Pickard Hall, Columbia, MO 65211-1420; tel. (573) 882-3591; e-mail museumuser@ missouri.edu; internet maa.missouri.edu; f. 1957 as Study Collns for Art History and Archaeology, current name adopted 1961; attached to Univ. of Missouri; colln of art works and artefacts of Greek, Roman and Near Eastern, ancient Egypt and Byzantium, European and American art since 15th century, incl. Samuel H. Kress Study Colln of European paintings, Asian, African, Ancient Americas and Oceanic cultures; incl. archives; Dir ALEX BARKER; publ. *MVSE* (1 a year).

National World War I Museum at Liberty Memorial: 100 W 26th St, Kansas City, MO 64108; tel. (816) 784-1918; e-mail info@ theworldwar.org; internet www.theworldwar .org; f. 1921 as Liberty Memorial, present status 2004; colln of 55,000 items in museum, library and archives; exhibits weapons, tanks, soldiers' uniforms, series of trenches, chronology walls giving data about the war; incl. memory hall; promotes research on First World War; 60,000 archival documents; library of 6,000 vols; Pres. and CEO BRIAN ALEXANDER; Chair. JAMES H. BERNARD, JR; Sec. JEANNETTE NICHOLS.

Nelson-Atkins Museum of Art: 4525 Oak St, Kansas City, MO 64111; tel. (816) 751-1278; e-mail press@nelson-atkins.org; internet www.nelson-atkins.org; f. 1933; depts of Asian art, prints, photography, modern and contemporary art, American art, American Indian art, European art, decorative arts, ancient art, African art, Chinese art, Japanese art, S and SE Asian art, Kansas City Sculpture Park (incl. monumental bronzes by Henry Moore); works by Thomas Hart Benton; library of 180,000 vols, 650 current periodicals; Dir and CEO JULIÁN ZUGAZAGOITIA.

Saint Louis Art Museum: 1 Fine Arts Dr., Forest Park, St Louis, MO 63110-1380; tel. (314) 721-0072; e-mail publicrelations@slam.org; internet www.slam.org; f. 1879; publicly owned colln of about 35,000 art objects; important collns of Oceanic art, pre-Columbian and American art, ancient Chinese bronzes, and European and American art of the late 19th and 20th centuries, with particular strength in 20th-century German painting, Asian art, decorative arts and design, contemporary and modern art, Islamic art, African art, photographs, prints and drawings; temporary exhibitions; library of 100,000 vols, 425 periodicals; Chair. BARBARA W. ROBERTS; Dir BRENT R. BENJAMIN; Sec. CHERI J. FROMM; Treas. JOAN O'NEILL; publ. *Magazine*.

Springfield Art Museum: 1111 E Brookside Dr., Springfield, MO 65807; tel. (417) 837-5700; e-mail artmuseum@springfieldmo.gov; internet www.springfieldmo.gov/art; f. 1928, present status 1958; colln of 8,895 art objects incl. 19th-, 20th- and 21st-century American paintings, watercolour sculpture and prints; Dir JERRY A. BERGER; Pres. JOAN MENCHETTI; Sec. NANCY DAILEY.

State Historical Society of Missouri: 1020 Lowry St, Columbia, MO 65201; tel. (573) 882-7083; e-mail shsofmo@umsystem.edu; internet shs.umsystem.edu/art; colln of paintings, engravings and lithographs by George Caleb Bingham and Thomas Hart Benton; editorial cartoon colln incl. drawings by Daniel Fitzpatrick, S. J. Ray, Bill Mauldin, Don Hesse and Tom Engelhardt; library of 460,000 vols, 500,000 MSS, 800 reels of microfilmed MSS, 150,000 state archival records and 2,900 maps; Exec. Dir, Sec. and Librarian GARY KREMER; Curator JOAN STACK; Pres. STEPHEN N. LIMBAUGH, JR; Treas. SABRINA MCDONNELL.

Montana

Blaine County Museum: 501 Indiana St, Chinook, MT 59523; tel. (406) 357-2590; e-mail blmuseum@mtintouch.net; internet www.blainecountymuseum.com; artefacts, photographs and documents depicting history of Blaine county; Exec. Dir JUDE SHEPPARD.

C. M. Russell Museum: 400 13th St N, Great Fall, MT 59401; tel. (406) 727-8787; internet cmrussell.org; artwork concerning the culture of the W during the late 1800s and early 1900s, incl. many works by Russell; Exec. Dir DARRELL BEAUCHAMP; Chief Curator SARAH BURT; Chair. JOE MASTERSON.

Holter Museum of Art: 12E, Lawrence, Helena, MT 59601; tel. (406) 442-6400; internet www.holtermuseum.org; f. 1987; visual arts exhibition programme that incl. all media; Exec. Dir KAREN BOHLINGER; Co-

Pres. TERESA OLCOTT COHEA; Co-Pres. KATHERINE ORR; Sec. SIDNEY ARMSTRONG; Treas. DAVE HUNTER.

Huntley Project Museum of Irrigated Agriculture: POB 353, 770 Railroad Highway, Huntley, MT 59037; tel. (406) 348-2533; e-mail curator@huntleyprojectmuseum.org; internet www.huntleyprojectmuseum.org; history of the homesteading era; records and photographs of the Huntley Project Communities; Curator and Dir MELISSA KOCH; Pres. JAMES KNAPP; Sec. MARY KNAPP; Treas. MARVIN HAMMERSMARK.

Montana Cowboy Hall of Fame: 218 Third Ave, So - Suite C, Wolf Point, MT 59201; tel. (406) 653-3800; internet www.montanacowboyfame.com; f. 1991; collns concerning W culture and heritage; Exec. Dir CHRISTY STENSLAND; Pres. DUWAYNE WILSON; Sec. KATHY MCLANE; Treas. MICHAEL NEUTGENS.

Montana Historical Society Museum: POB 201201, 225 N Roberts, Helena, MT 59620-1201; tel. (406) 444-2694; e-mail mhslibrary@mt.gov; internet mhs.mt.gov/museum; f. 1865; 50,000 fine art, historical, archaeological and ethnological artefacts that pertain to Montana and its adjoining geographic region; Native American Colln of 6,000 objects; incl. original Governor's Mansion and Moss Mansion historic house; Pres. STEVE LOZAR; Dir BRUCE WHITTENBERG; State Historic Preservation Officer Dr MARK BAUMLER; Sr Curator JENNIFER BOTTOMLY-O'LOONEY; publ. *Montana The Magazine of Western History* (4 a year).

Museum of the Rockies: 600 W Kagy Blvd, Bozeman, MT 59717; tel. (406) 994-2251; e-mail museum@montana.edu; internet museumoftherockies.org; f. 1957 as McGill Museum, present name 1965; attached to Montana State Univ.; cultural and natural history; palaeontology colln; on-site 19th-century farm; incl. planetarium, dinosaur complex and tyrannosaurus rex; fed. repository for fossils; Dean and Exec. Dir SHELDON MCKAMEY; Pres. PAT DOWNEY.

Paris Gibson Square Museum of Art: 1400 First Ave N, Great Falls, MT 59401,; tel. (406) 727-8255; e-mail info@the-square.org; internet www.the-square.org; f. 1977; 611 pieces, incl. NW regional contemporary art, American Indian contemporary art and American self-taught art; Exec. Dir KATHY LEAR; Curator of Art COREY GROSS; Pres. REBECCA BOGDEN-RICHARDS; Sec. JULIE EASTON; Treas. MICHELLE KLUNDT.

Rocky Mountain Museum of Military History: c/o Tate Jones, POB 7263, Missoula, MT 59807; tel. (406) 549-5346; e-mail info@fortmissoula.org; internet www.fortmissoula.org; f. 1936; commemoration and study of the US armed services: from the Frontier Period to the war on terrorism; Exec. Dir TATE JONES; Pres. GARY R. LANCASTER; Treas. BO FOSTER.

Ursuline Centre: 2300 Central Ave, Great Falls, MT 59401; tel. (406) 452-8585; e-mail ursuline@in-tch.com; internet www.ursulinecentre.com; f. 1912; unique Native American artefacts, 1900s antique furnishings, musical instruments and other artefacts; colln of over 100 years of history of the Ursuline Sisters, their lives and how they helped shape the history of Montana; Dir HARRY THOLEN.

World Museum of Mining: POB 33, 155 Museum Way, Butte, MT 59703; tel. 406-723-7211; e-mail info@miningmuseum.org; internet www.miningmuseum.org; f. 1963; 7,000 catalogued photos; company day books, maps, diaries, engineering diagrams, journals, log books and payroll records; Exec. Dir

TINA DAVIS; Pres. BOB MCCARTHY; Sec. COURTNEY MCKEE; Treas. LINDA ROSIN.

Yellowstone Art Museum: 401 N 27th St, Billings, MT 59101; tel. (406) 256-6804; e-mail artinfo@artmuseum.org; internet yellowstone.artmuseum.org; f. 1964 as Yellowstone Arts Center, present name 1998; contemporary and historic art; Montana Colln of 1,925 regional artefacts; Virginia Snook Colln incl. illustrations from Will James, paintings and drawings from Joseph Henry Sharp, Charles M. Russell; Exec. Dir and Acting Curator ROBYN G. PETERSON; Pres. LINDA SHELHAMER; Sec. GLADYS PHELPS; Treas. SUSAN SULLIVAN.

Nebraska

Bone Creek Museum of Agrarian Art: 575 E St, David City, NE 68632; tel. (402) 367-4488; internet www.bonecreek.org; f. 2007; colln of artworks of Agrarian Artists Winslow Homer, Harvey Dunn, John Steuart Curry, Thomas Hart Benton, Robert Gwathmey, Birger Sandzen, Augustus Dunbier, Peter Helck, Robert Wesley Amick, Gary Ernest Smith, Robert Bateman, Mark L. Moseman, Charles Banks Wilson, Jane Scott, Raymond Knaub, Jim Hamil, Hal Holoun, Robert Sudlow and John Roush; organizes artist talks and workshops; Pres. ANNA NOLAN; Vice-Pres. and Chief Curator MARK L. MOSEMAN; Sec. ALLEN COVAULT; Treas. MICHAEL MORAVEC.

Great Plains Art Museum: c/o Univ. of Nebraska-Lincoln, 1155 Q St, Hewit Place, POB 880250, Lincoln, NE 68588-0250; tel. (402) 472-6220; e-mail gpac@unl.edu; internet www.unl.edu/plains/gallery/gallery.shtml; f. 1981; attached to Center for Great Plain Studies, Univ. of Nebraska-Lincoln; colln of bronze sculptures, paintings and drawings, other works on paper, photographs; artwork by Albert Bierstadt, William de la Montagne Cary, Robert F. Gilder, William Henry Jackson, Frederic Remington, Charles M. Russell and Olaf Wieghorst; 20th Native American paintings from Patricia J. and Stanley H. Broder; Richard Lane colln of Western fiction and history; Regina Colln of Canadian Plains literature, Lyman Byxbe, Ray Ellis, John Falter, Michael Forsberg, Charles Guildner, Veryl Goodnight, Cliff Hollestelle, Laurie Houseman-Whitehawk, Keith Jacobshagen, Ted Long, Herb Mignery, Andrew Peters, Martha and Del Pettigrew, Jackson Pollock, Norman Rockwell, and Grant Wood; library of 7,500 vols; Museum Administrator and Curator AMBER MOHR.

Hastings Museum of Natural and Cultural History: POB 1286, Hastings, NE 68902; 1330 N Burlington Ave, Hastings, NE 68900; tel. (402) 461-4629; e-mail museum@hastingsmuseum.org; internet www.hastingsmuseum.org; f. 1927; incl. J. M. McDonald Planetarium, Groundwater Discovery Adventure and theatre; colln of species of animals set in their natural habitats incl. whooping cranes; colln tells history of the early inhabitants of the Nebraska; Dir REBECCA MATTICKS.

Joslyn Art Museum: 2200 Dodge St, Omaha, NE 68102-1292; tel. (402) 342-3300; internet www.joslyn.org; f. 1931; colln of ancient, European, American Indian, art of the American W, Latin American, Asian, modern and contemporary works of art; Peter Kiewit Foundation Sculpture Garden; Exec. Dir and CEO Dr JACK F. BECKER; Chair. JOHN P. NELSON; Sec. BRYAN E. SLONE; Treas. KIRK L. KELLNER; Chief Curator TOBY JUROVICS.

Lester F. Larsen Tractor Museum: POB 830833, Lincoln, NE 68583; tel. (402) 472-8389; e-mail tractormuseum2@unl.edu;

internet tractormuseum.unl.edu; f. 1998; attached to Univ. of Nebraska-Lincoln; collects, preserves, researches and interprets the traditions and technologies of agriculture; Curator Prof. LOUIS I. LEVITICUS.

Museum of Nebraska Art: 2401 Central Ave, Kearney, NE 68847; tel. (308) 865-8559; e-mail mona@unk.edu; internet monet.unk .edu/mona; f. 1976 as Nebraska Art Colln, present name and status 1986; 5,000 works by George Catlin, early Nebraskans Robert Henri and J. Laurie Wallace, modern era artists Grant Reynard and John Falter, Nebraska wildlife artwork by John James Audubon; Cliff Hillegass Sculpture Garden; Dir AUDREY S. KAUDERS; Pres. SUE TALLMAN; Sec. DEANNA BOSSELMAN; Treas. TAMI HELLMAN; Curator TELIZA V. RODRIGUEZ.

Nebraska State Historical Society: POB 82554, Lincoln, NE 68501-2554; 1500 R St, Lincoln, NE 68501; tel. (402) 471-4754; e-mail nshs.museum@nebraska.gov; internet www.nebraskahistory.org/museum; f. 1878; state-wide network of historical sites and museums, incl. Chimney Rock Nat. Historic Site, Fort Robinson Museums, Gerald R. Ford Conservation Center, John G. Neihardt State Historic Site, K St Govt Records Facility, Nebraska History Museum, Neligh Mill State Historic Site, Senator George W. Norris State Historic Site, Thomas P. Kennard House Nebraska Statehood Memorial, Willa Cather State Historic Site; documentation of bldg first transcontinental railroad through Union Pacific Railroad colln; 300,000 photographs, incl. colln of sod house photographs taken by Solomon D. Butcher; library of 80,000 vols, 12,000 film and video reels, 35,000 reels of microfilm with state newspapers since 1854; Dir and CEO MICHAEL J. SMITH; Sr Curator LAURA MOONEY; publs *Nebraska History News* (4 a year), *Nebraska History* (4 a year).

Sheldon Museum of Art: POB 880300, Lincoln, NE 68588-0300; 12 and R Sts, Lincoln, NE 68588-0300; tel. (402) 472-2461; internet www.sheldonartmuseum.org; f. 1888; houses collns of Sheldon Art Asscn (f. 1888) and Univ. of Nebraska (f. 1929); 12,000 works of art in all media, incl. 19th-century landscape and still life, American impressionism, early modernism, geometric abstraction, abstract expressionism, pop, minimalism and contemporary art; 30 sculptures by Gaston Lachaise, Jacques Lipchitz, Claes Oldenburg and Coosje van Bruggen, David Smith, William Tucker, Bryan Hunt, Mark di Suvero, Michael Heizer and Richard Serra; library of 10,000 vols; Dir CHRISTIN J. MAMIYA.

Strategic Air & Space Museum: 28210 W Park Highway, Ashland, NE 68003; tel. (402) 944-3100; e-mail llessmann@ strategicairandspace.com; internet www .sasmuseum.com; f. 1959; exhibits photographs, letters and personal mementos left at Viet Nam Memorial Wall in Washington, DC; artefacts incl. flight suits, flown shuttle tyre and cameras used by Gemini astronaut, Wally Schirra; Linebacker II display outlines men and machines of the US Seventh Air Force and US Navy Task Force 77 that took part in bombing missions on Haiphong and Hanoi, N Viet Nam on December 1972; commemorates the Martin Bomber Plant; Doolittle's Tokyo Raiders; equipments of the 9th Air Force; Exec. Dir SCOTT TARRY; Chair. W. DAVID SCOTT; Sec. NICK BAXTER.

Stuhr Museum of the Prairie Pioneer: 3133 W Highway 34, Grand Island, NE 68801; tel. (308) 385-5316; e-mail info@ stuhrmuseum.org; internet www .stuhrmuseum.org; f. 1961; colln of historical objects and information relating to life in

Nebraska's prairie communities from the 1840s to 1920; 150,000 historical artefacts, incl. 60 historic bldgs and railroad equipment; archives and research library; Exec. Dir JOE BLACK; Pres. DENSEL RASMUSSEN; Exec. Sec. SHARON MANKIN; Treas. MARK HOCK.

University of Nebraska State Museum: 307 Morrill Hall, Univ. of Nebraska-Lincoln, Lincoln, NE 68588-0338; tel. (402) 472-2642; e-mail afox1@unl.edu; internet www .museum.unl.edu; incl. Mueller Planetarium; educational programming; collns and research in following: anthropology, botany, entomology, invertebrate palaeontology, parasitology, vertebrate palaeontology, zoology; Dir PRISCILLA C. GREW.

Affiliated Museums:

Ashfall Fossil Beds State Historical Park: 86930 517th Ave, Royal, NE 68773; tel. (402) 893-2000; e-mail ashfall2@unl .edu; internet www.ashfall.unl.edu; f. 1991; fossil site of int. significance left intact for public viewing; Superintendent RICK OTTO; Museum Specialist SANDY MOSEL.

Trailside Museum of Natural History: Fort Robinson State Park, Crawford, NE 69339; tel. (308) 665-2929; internet trailside.unl.edu; f. 1961; geological and natural history; publ. *The Mammoth* (4 a year).

Nevada

Fleischmann Planetarium & Science Center: POB 272, 1650 N Virginia St, Univ. of Nevada, Reno, Reno, NV 89557; tel. (775) 784-4812; internet planetarium.unr .nevada.edu; f. 1964 as Fleischmann Atmospherium-Planetarium; attached to Univ. of Nevada, Reno; public star shows and large-format films; Spitz SciDome digital projector; Dir and Assoc. Vice-Provost for Extended Studies Dr DEE HENDERSON.

Hispanic Museum of Nevada: 3680 S Maryland Parkway, Suite 140, Las Vegas, NV 89169; tel. (702) 773-2203; e-mail hispanicmuseumnv@hotmail.com; internet www.hispanicmuseumnv.com; f. 1991; education and resources of the diverse Hispanic cultures and traditions to enhance intercultural understanding among community mems; Founder and Exec. Dir LYNNETTE SAWYER; Sec. and Treas. FELICIA ALAVA.

International Scouting Museum: Suite 2, Krolak Center, 2915 W Charleston Blvd, Las Vegas, NV 89102; tel. (702) 878-7268; internet www.worldscoutingmuseum.org; f. 1996; colln of Scouting memorabilia; Exec. Dir R. LYNN HORNE; Pres. GWEN KROGEN; Treas. JACQUES BEHAR; Sec. DEBORAH MARTZ.

Marjorie Barrick Museum: Univ. of Nevada, Las Vegas, POB 4009 4505 S Maryland Parkway, Las Vegas, NV 89154-4009; tel. (702) 895-3381; e-mail barrick.museum@ unlv.edu; internet barrickmuseum.unlv.edu; f. 1969, current name adopted 1989; attached to Univ. of Nevada, Las Vegas; cultural objects concerning the American SW, Mesoamerica and their environs; Pre-Columbian Colln: objects from nearly every culture of Pre-Columbian Latin America as well as Mexican dance masks and retablos; Guatemalan, Bolivian and Navajo textiles; Paiute and Hopi basketry; Navajo jewellery; Programme Dir AURORE GIGUET; Sec. TORI KLEIN.

National Atomic Testing Museum: 755 E Flamingo Rd, Las Vegas, NV 89119; tel. (702) 794-5151; e-mail atm@atomictestingmuseum .org; internet www.atomictestingmuseum .org; Exec. Dir ALLAN PALMER; Curator KAREN GREEN.

Nevada Museum of Art: 160 W Liberty St, Reno, NV 89501; tel. (775) 329-3333; e-mail art@nevadaart.org; internet www.nevadaart .org; f. 1931 as Nevada Art Gallery, current name adopted 1988; altered landscape incl. 600 pieces of contemporary landscape photography; contemporary colln focuses on W coast and Nevada-based artists; Sierra Nevada/Great Basin colln surveys artists' impressions of the landscape over 150 years; historical colln incl. paintings and sculptures; work-ethic themed E. L. Wiegand Colln; Curator of Exhibitions and Collns ANN M. WOLFE; Exec. Dir and CEO DAVID B. WALKER; Chair. JOHN WORTHINGTON; Sec. JENNIFER L. PATTERSON; Treas. RON ZIDECK.

Nevada State Museum and Historical Society: 309 S Valley View Blvd, Las Vegas, NV 89107; tel. (702) 486-5205; biological sciences, earth sciences, regional history; Dir DAVID MILLMAN.

Walker African American Museum: 705 W Van Buren, Las Vegas, NV 89106; tel. (702) 399-8016; e-mail walkeraamuseum1@ yahoo.com; internet www .churchesinlasvegas.com/walkermuseum; books, magazines, dolls, stamps, postcards, trade cards, figurines, statues, sports and political items, newspapers and clippings, signs, church histories, biographies, prints, posters, painting, etc. about the history of people of African descent belonging to Nevada.

W. M. Keck Earth Science and Mineral Engineering Museum: Mackay School of Earth Sciences and Engineering, Univ. of Nevada, Reno, 1664 N Virginia St, Reno, NV 89557; tel. (775) 784-4528; internet www .mines.unr.edu/museum; f. 1908, present name 1988; colln of fossils, minerals, ores and photographs related to mining; emphasis on early NV mining history; Mackay Silver Colln; Dir RUSS FIELDS.

New Hampshire

American Independence Museum: 1 Governors Lane, Exeter, NH 03833; tel. (603) 772-2622; e-mail info@independencemuseum .org; internet www.independencemuseum .org; f. 1991; focus on study, research, education and interpretation of American Revolution; colln incl. 2 rare drafts of the US Constitution, American furnishings, ceramics, silver, textiles and military ephemera; museum comprises 18th-century Ladd-Gilman House and Folsom Tavern; Exec. Dir GAIL NESSELL COLGLAZIER; Curator WENDY BERGERON.

Currier Museum of Art: 150 Ash St, Manchester, NH 03104-4393; tel. (603) 669-6144; e-mail visitor@currier.org; internet www.currier.org; f. 1929; 12,000 American and European works of art featuring decorative arts, photographs and sculptures; permanent colln incl. works by Picasso, Matisse, Monet, O'Keeffe, Calder and Wyeth; owns Frank Lloyd Wright's 1950 Zimmerman House; year-round exhibitions, tours and classical music performances; library of 15,000 vols; Dir and CEO SUSAN STRICKLER; Pres. DAVID A. JENSEN.

Exeter Historical Society: POB 924, 47 Front St, Exeter, NH 03833; tel. (603) 778-2335; e-mail info@exeterhistory.org; internet www.exeterhistory.org; f. 1931; colln on local history; Native American artefacts and 1740 English Common Press; Chair. LIONEL INGRAM; Curator BARBARA RIMKUNAS.

Hood Museum of Art: Dartmouth College, Hanover, NH 03755; tel. (603) 646-2808; e-mail hood.museum@dartmouth.edu; internet hoodmuseum.dartmouth.edu; f. 1985; attached to Dartmouth College; 65,000 works of art and artefacts of different cultures and historical periods; Dir MICHAEL TAYLOR.

Laconia Historical & Museum Society: POB 1126, Laconia, NH 03247; 695 Main St, Laconia, NH 03246; tel. (603) 527-1278; e-mail lhmslpl@metrocast.net; internet www.laconiahistorical.org; f. 1998 by merger of Laconia Historical Soc. (f. 1951) with Laconia Museum Soc. (f. 1994); Jewett colln: 10,000 objects incl. photographs, MSS, etc. spanning 200 years; Pres. ERNEST BOLDUC; Exec. Dir BRENDA M. POLIDORO; Curator LINDSAY BURKE.

Mariposa Museum & World Culture Center: 26 Main St, Peterborough, NH 03458; tel. (603) 924-4555; e-mail admin@mariposamuseum.org; internet www.mariposamuseum.org; f. 2001; colln of folk-art, textiles, costumes, art, puppets and instruments from 6 continents; Chair. S. MARTIN; Exec. Dir (vacant).

Millyard Museum: 200 Bedford St, Manchester, NH 03101; tel. (603) 622-7531; e-mail history@manchesterhistoric.org; internet www.manchesterhistoric.org/mill.htm; f. 1896; attached to Manchester Historic Asscn; colln incl. 600,000 documents and artefacts on local history.

Museum of Art: Univ. of New Hampshire, Paul Creative Arts Center, 30 Academic Way, Durham, NH 03824-3538; tel. (603) 862-3712; e-mail museum.of.art@unh.edu; internet www.unh.edu/moa; f. 1960; attached to Univ. of New Hampshire; 1,600 historical and modern works by American, European and other artists; colln of 19th- and 20th-century prints and drawings; 200 Japanese wood block prints; Dir KRISTINA L. DUROCHER.

University of New Hampshire Museum: Room 103, Dimond Library, 18 Library Way, Durham, NH 03824; tel. (603) 862-1081; internet www.izaak.unh.edu/museum; f. 1966; colln incl. over 1,000 univ. memorabilia and historic artefacts since 1940s; Curator DALE VALENA.

Woodman Institute Museum: POB 1916, Dover, NH 03821; 182 Central Ave, Dover, NH 03820-4058; tel. (603) 742-1038; e-mail contact@woodmaninstitutemuseum.org; internet woodmaninstitutemuseum.org; f. 1916; 4 historic bldgs: colonial garrison house (1675), Hale House (1813), Keefe House (1825) and Woodman House (1818); colln incl. 800 items of area history, 1,300 specimens of minerals, Civil War artefacts and memorabilia.

Wright Museum of WWII History: POB 1212, 77 Center St, Wolfeboro, NH 03894; tel. (603) 569-1212; e-mail info@wrightmuseum.org; internet www.wrightmuseum.org; f. 1983; artefacts of Second World War incl. vintage military vehicles and Army Air Corps mission map; Exec. Dir NORMAN STEVENS.

New Jersey

African Art Museum: 23 Bliss Ave, Tenafly, NJ 07670; tel. (201) 894-8611; e-mail museum@smafathers.org; internet smafathers.org/museum; f. 1980; attached to Soc. of African Missions; sub-Saharan sculpture and painting, costumes, textiles and decorative arts, religion and folklore; Dir BOB KOENIG.

Atlantic City Art Center: POB 1061, Atlantic City, NJ 08401; New Jersey Ave and Boardwalk, Atlantic City, NJ 08401; tel. (609) 347-5837; e-mail acartcenter@aol.com; internet www.acartcenter.org; f. 1908; features artwork by contemporary artists and artisans at nat., regional and local level; Exe. Dir KALEEM SHABAZZ.

Belskie Museum of Art & Science: 280 High St, Closter, NJ 07624; tel. (20l) 768-0286; e-mail contact@belskiemuseum.com; internet www.belskiemuseum.com; f. 1993; preserves, houses and exhibits works of Abram Belskie, a sculptor and medical illustrator.

Camp Olden Civil War Round Table & Museum, Inc.: POB 10565, Hamilton, NJ 08690; 2202 Kuser Rd, Hamilton, NJ; e-mail president@campolden.org; internet www.campolden.org; f. 1992; exhibits incl. uniforms, weapons, equipment and material relating to the experience of the common soldier in the Civil War; Pres. BRUCE SIRAK; Curator BRUCE SMITH.

Franklin Mineral Museum: 32 Evans St, Franklin, NJ 07416; tel. (973) 827-3481; e-mail fmm1954@earthlink.net; internet www.franklinmineralmuseum.com; f. 1964; archaeological, geological, historical, mineralogical themes; 4,000 mineral specimens on display; a life-sized mine replica.

Hiram Blauvelt Art Museum: 705 Kinderkamack Rd, Oradell, NJ 07649; tel. (201) 261-0012; e-mail info@blauveltartmuseum.com; internet www.blauveltartmuseum.com; f. 1957 as a natural history museum; works by contemporary wildlife artists; Dir MARIJANE SINGER.

Hunterdon Art Museum: Seven Lower Center St, Clinton, NJ 08809-1303; tel. (908) 735-8415; internet www.hunterdonartmuseum.org; f. 1952; contemporary art and design, incl. works on paper since 1930s; spec. colln: Anne Steele Marsh Colln; Dir of Exhibitions JONATHAN GREENE.

Macculloch Hall Historical Museum: 45 Macculloch Ave, Morristown, NJ 07960; tel. (973) 538-2404; e-mail info@macullochhall.org; internet www.macullochhall.org; f. 1949; Thomas Nast's original works in the USA; 50 specimens of French, German, English and Chinese export porcelain dating from 750 to 1850; presidential colln incl. silver, porcelain, letters, images, documents, and a Thanksgiving proclamation; Exec. Dir CARRIE FELLOWS; Curator RYAN HYMAN; Pres. JO ANN BURK; Sec. EUNICE LYNCH; Treas. SHARON CROSS.

Monmouth County Historical Association Museum & Library: 70 Court St, Freehold, NJ 07728; tel. (732) 462-1466; internet www.monmouthhistory.org; f. 1898; 30,000 objects, incl. 1,550 paintings, drawings, watercolours, prints and miniatures of American art from the mid-18th to the mid-20th centuries; 900 pieces of furniture, incl. 72 wainscot chair made by Scottish immigrant Robert Rhea; artefacts and objects related to the Battle of Monmouth; items related to Monmouth Co steamboat industry; kitchen and household equipment since early 18th century; over 300 pieces of folk art, incl. local retail signs and carving; 3,500 pieces of historic clothing and textiles colln; Dir Dr LEE ELLEN GRIFFITH; Curator BERNADETTE ROGOFF; Pres. CLAIRE KNOPF; Sec. NANCY STEWART; Treas. GEORGE J. DITTMAR, III.

Montclair Art Museum: Three S Mountain Ave, Montclair, NJ 07042-1747; tel. (973) 746-5555; internet www.montclairartmuseum.org; f. 1914; 12,000 works; 18th- and 19th-century American art; traditional and contemporary American Indian art and artefacts showcasing the cultural achievements in weaving, pottery, wood carving, jewellery, and textiles of indigenous Americans from 7 major regions—NW Coast, California, SW, Plains, Woodlands, SE and the Arctic; Yard School of Art; library of 44,000 vols; Dir LORA S. URBANELLI; Chief Curator GAIL STAVITSKY; Pres. NEWTON B. SCHOTT, JR; Sec. LYNN GLASSER; Treas. IRA A. WAGNER.

Montclair State University Art Gallery: Montclair State Univ., Normal Ave, Montclair, NJ 07043; tel. (973) 655-3382; e-mail artgalleries@mail.montclair.edu; internet www.montclair.edu/arts/galleries; 16th- to 19th-century European paintings; incl. George Segal Gallery: colln of modern and contemporary art; Cosla Colln and MFA Gallery; Wingert Colln of traditional African and Oceanic masks and sculptures; Dir M. TERESA LAPID RODRIGUEZ.

Morris Museum: Six Normandy Heights Rd, Morristown, NJ 07960; tel. (973) 971-3700; e-mail info@morrismuseum.org; internet www.morrismuseum.org; colln of 48,700 objects, incl. costumes and textiles, fine art, decorative art, dolls and toys, natural science, geology and palaeontology and anthropology; Exec. Dir LINDA S. MOORE; Curator DAVID NALVEN (acting); Chair. PAUL J. LAUD; Sec. RICHARD A. WATSON; Treas. JOHN S. HEMMENDINGER.

Museum of Early Trades & Crafts: 9 Main St, Madison, NJ 07940; tel. (973) 377-2982; e-mail info@metc.org; internet www.metc.org; f. 1970; preserves and interprets the tools used before the rise of industrialization in the USA; 8,800 artefacts related to 21 different trades; research library; Exec. Dir VIVIAN C. R. JAMES; Chair. ALLEN BLACK; Sec. ASTRI BAILLIE; Treas. IRENE MARONEY.

New Jersey Maritime Museum: 528 Dock Rd, Beach Haven, NJ 08008; tel. (609) 492-0202; e-mail curator@njmaritimemuseum.org; internet www.museumofnjmh.com; US life saving service exhibit; rare post-card colln of New Jersey towns, USLSS stations, lighthouses and other maritime-related fields; shipwreck artefacts recovered from various wreck sites off the New Jersey coast; china plates, platters, pitchers and other artefacts recovered from the 1827 wreck of the Aurora off Sandy Hook; Pres. DEBORAH WHITCRAFT; Sec. BEVERLY TROMM; Treas. ROBERT CUNNINGHAM.

New Jersey State Museum: POB 530, New Jersey Dept of State, 205 W State St, Trenton, NJ 08625; tel. (609) 292-6464; e-mail feedback@sos.state.nj.us; internet www.state.nj.us/state/museum; f. 1895; archaeology and ethnology colln of 2m. prehistoric and historic specimens from nearly 100 years of excavation and over 2,000 ethnographic objects; fine art colln incl. paintings, prints, drawings, sculpture and photographs since 1965; cultural history colln of 13,000 artefacts showcasing New Jersey's cultural, economic, military, political and social history; natural history colln; Planetarium; Exec. Dir ANTHONY GARDNER; Pres. STEVEN M. RICHMAN.

Newark Museum: 49 Washington St, Newark, NJ 07102; tel. (973) 596-6550; e-mail director@newarkmuseum.org; internet www.newarkmuseum.org; f. 1909; 80 galleries of collns incl. American, Asian, African and Classical; Natural Science Galleries feature 83,000 specimens; Alice and Leonard Dreyfuss Planetarium; library: 2,500 linear ft of paper records, 26,000 documentary photographs and 200 published articles; Dir and CEO STEVEN KERN; Sr Curator ULYSSES GRANT DIETZ; Chair. ARLENE LIEBERMAN.

Paul Robeson Galleries: Rutgers Univ., 350 Dr Martin Luther King Jr Blvd, Newark, NJ 07102; tel. (973) 353-1610; e-mail galleryr@andromeda.rutgers.edu; internet andromeda.rutgers.edu/artgallery; attached to Rutgers Univ.; dedicated to Paul Robeson; artistic and cultural centre of Rutgers Univ.; holds educational and public programmes; arts and visual cultural exhibitions; Dir and Curator ANONDA BELL.

Trenton City Museum: Ellarslie Mansion in Cadwalader Park, Trenton, NJ; tel. (609) 989-3632; e-mail collections@ellarslie.org; internet www.ellarslie.org; f. 1978; colln of fine and decorative arts, cultural history and industrial artefacts; 19th- and 20th-centuries colln of tableware, sanitary ware and art ware.

Zimmerli Art Museum at Rutgers University: 71 Hamilton St, New Brunswick, NJ 08901-1248; tel. (848) 932-7237; e-mail press@zimmerli.rutgers.edu; internet www.zimmerlimuseum.rutgers.edu; f. 1966; attached to Rutgers, The State Univ. of New Jersey; 60,000 works of art, from ancient to contemporary: 19th-century French art, Russian art from icons to the avant-garde; Soviet nonconformist art from the Dodge Colln; American art incl. prints and original illustrations for children's books; art inspired by Japan; library of 4,000 vols; Dir MARTI MAYO.

New Mexico

Albuquerque Museum of Art and History: 2000 Mountain Rd NW, Albuquerque, NM 87104; tel. (505) 243-7255; e-mail albuquerquemuseum@cabq.gov; internet albuquerquemuseum.org; f. 1967; colln of 7,000 works of art incl. Native American jewellery and ceramics, Hispanic religious and domestic folk arts, documentary sketches and paintings from Territorial-era exploration, late 19th- and early 20th-century Taos and Santa Fe artists Ernest Blumenschein, John Sloan and Georgia O'Keeffe, contemporary reflections on land, landscape and regional cultures; outdoor Sculpture Garden; photoarchives; Casa San Ysidro: The Gutiérrez/Minge House; Dir CATHY L. WRIGHT; Chair. CHRISTINE S. GLIDDEN; Sec. and Treas. JACOBO DE LA SERNA; publ. *abqmuseum* (4 a year).

Anderson Museum of Contemporary Art: 409 E College Blvd, Roswell, NM 88201; tel. (575) 623-5600; e-mail email@roswellamoca.org; internet www.roswellamoca.org; f. 1994; 300 works of art; fibreglass sculptures; paintings; ceramic sculpture and golf bag sharks; new media pieces; colln of photographs.

Georgia O'Keeffe Museum: 217 Johnson St, Santa Fe, NM 87501; tel. (505) 946-1000; internet www.okeeffemuseum.org; f. 1997; colln of 2,989 works incl. 1,149 O'Keeffe paintings, drawings and sculptures dating from 1901 to 1984 and 1,840 by other artists; Research Center; Dir ROBERT A. KRET; Chair. ANNE W. MARION; Pres. SAUL COHEN; Sec. BARRY G. KING, JR; publ. *O'Keeffe* (3 a year).

Harwood Museum of Art: 238 Ledoux St, Taos, NM 87571; tel. (575) 758-9826; e-mail info@harwoodmuseum.org; internet harwoodmuseum.org; f. 1916; 3,000 works of art and photographic archive of 17,000 images since 19th century; colln incl. Hispanic works, prints, drawings and photographs, works by Taos Soc. of Artists, contemporary art, Taos moderns; Dir SUSAN LONGHENRY; Chair. LINDA WARNING; Sec. MARCIA WINTER; Treas. WYNN GOERING.

Indian Pueblo Cultural Center: 2401 12th St NW, Albuquerque, NM 87104; tel. (505) 724-3564; internet indianpueblo.org; f. 1976; 2,000 colln of contemporary and historic forms of pottery; colln of jewellery, textiles, baskets, photographs, prints, paintings and murals to archaeological objects from each of the 19 Pueblos and other tribes of the greater SW; incl. archives and library and Institute for Pueblo Indian Studies; Museum Dir MARTH BECKTELL.

Maxwell Museum of Anthropology: 1 Univ. of New Mexico, Albuquerque, NM 87131; tel. (505) 277-4405; e-mail maxwell@unm.edu; internet www.maxwellmuseum.unm.edu; f. 1932 as Museum of Anthropology of the Univ. of New Mexico, present name 1972; attached to Univ. of New Mexico; anthropological collns from North, South and Central America, Africa, Asia, Australia and the Pacific Islands; assoc. research institutes: Office of Contract Archaeology, Alfonso Ortiz Center for Intercultural Studies and Maxwell Center for Anthropological Research; Dir E. JAMES DIXON.

Millicent Rogers Museum: POB 1210, Taos, NM 87571; 1504 Millicent Rogers Rd, Taos, NM 87571; tel. (575) 758-2462; e-mail mrm@millicentrogers.org; internet www.millicentrogers.org; f. 1956; colln of Native American, Hispanic arts, pottery, contemporary arts and designs from all cultures in Northern New Mexico, 1,000 pieces of Native American jewellery; Exec. Dir PAUL FIGUEROA; Pres. PHILIP PERALTA-RAMOS; Sec. YALE I. JONES; Treas. DOUG CLARK.

Museum of Contemporary Native Arts: 108 Cathedral Pl., Santa Fe, NM 87501; tel. (505) 983-8900; internet www.iaia.edu/museum; f. 1972; attached to Institute of American Indian Arts; colln of 7,500 artworks incl. paintings, works on paper, sculpture, ceramics, jewellery, photography, contemporary apparel, textiles, cultural arts, new media and installations; Dir PATSY PHILLIPS; Chief Curator RYAN RICE.

Museum of New Mexico: POB 2087, Santa Fé, NM 87504-2087; internet www.museumofnewmexico.org; f. 1909; state agency, under Bd of Regents appointed by Governor, divs in anthropology, history, fine arts, int. folk art, Indian arts and culture, state monuments located in separate bldgs; library of 50,000 vols; Dir THOMAS A. LIVESAY; publ. *El Palacio* (4 a year).

Constituent Museums:

Museum of Indian Arts and Culture: 710 Camino Lejo, Santa Fe, NM 87505; tel. (505) 476-1250; e-mail miac.info@state.nm.us; internet www.indianartsandculture.org; f. 1987; Native art and material culture; incl. Laboratory of Anthropology; archives with institutional and ethnographic records incl. 8,000 historic and contemporary images, MSS archives documenting early Laboratory of Anthropology staff projects, papers and correspondence relating to history of anthropology in the SW; Dir SHELBY TISDALE.

Museum of International Folk Art: 706 Camino Lejo, Santa Fe, NM 87505; tel. (505) 476-1200; e-mail internationalfolkart@gmail.com; internet www.internationalfolkart.org; f. 1953; 135,000 artefacts in 4 divs: Bartlett, Girard, Hispanic Heritage and Neutrogena; Dir MARSHA C. BOL.

New Mexico Museum of Art: 107 W Palace Ave, Santa Fe, NM 87501; tel. (505) 476-5072; internet www.mfasantafe.org; f. 1917 as Art Gallery for the Museum of New Mexico; 23,000 objects, focusing on the areas of photography and works on paper; paintings, sculpture and furniture since the beginning of the 20th century; Dir MARY KERSHAW.

New Mexico State Monuments: 725 Camino Lejo, Santa Fe, NM 87504; tel. (505) 476-1150; internet www.nmmonuments.org; f. 1931; incl. Coronado State Monument (where Francisco Vásquez de Coronado—with 300 soldiers and 800 Indian allies from New Spain—entered the valley while looking for the fabled Seven Cities of Gold; Fort Seldon State Monument (est. in 1865 in an effort to bring peace to the south central region of present day New Mexico); Jemez State Monument (incl. stone ruins of a 500-year-old Indian village and the San José de los Jemez church dating to 1610); Lincoln State Monument (incl. 7 structures and outbuildings from 1870 and 1880s); El Camino Real International Heritage Center (commemorates El Camino Real de Tierra Adentro, the historic trade route and its impact on New Mexico); Bosque Redondo Memorial at Fort Sumner State Monument (inc. story of how the US Army forcibly moved the Navajo and Mescalero Apache people from their traditional homelands to the land surrounding this lonely outpost); Dir RUDY ACOSTA.

Palace of the Governors: 105 W Palace Ave, Santa Fe, NM 87501; tel. (505) 476-5100; internet www.palaceofthegovernors.org; constructed in the early 17th century as Spain's seat of govt in what is today the American South-West; chronicles the history of Santa Fe, as well as New Mexico and the wider region; photo archives of 800,000 items incl. historic photographic prints, cased photographs, glass plate negatives, film negatives, stereographs, photo postcards, panoramas, colour transparencies and lantern slides; Fray Angélico Chávez History Library; Dir FRANCES LEVINE.

Museum of Spanish Colonial Art: 750 Camino Lejo, Santa Fe, NM 87505; tel. (505) 982-2226; e-mail museum@spanishcolonial.org; internet www.spanishcolonial.org; f. 1925; attached to Spanish Colonial Arts Soc.; art of the Hispanic SW; colln of 3,700 works of art, incl. historically significant and contemporary works; Pueblo Revival-style bldg; Sr. Curator ROBIN FARWELL GAVIN.

New Mexico Museum of Natural History and Science: 1801 Mountain Rd NW, Albuquerque, NM 87104; tel. (505) 841-2800; internet www.nmnaturalhistory.org; exhibits dinosaurs cast in bronze, Tyrannosaurus rex, space exhibition, beginnings of life on Earth; Bioscience Colln of plants, mammals, birds, reptiles and amphibians, insects and molluscs; fossil and mineralogical collns; planetarium and Sandia Mountain Natural History Center; Dir CHARLIE WALTER.

New Mexico State University Museum: Kent Hall, MSC 3564, POB 30001, Las Cruces, NM 88003-88001; tel. (575) 646-5161; e-mail museum@nmsu.edu; internet www.nmsu.edu/museum; f. 1959; 170,000 archaeological items; 5,000 ethnographic items; 10,000 historical items; Dir Dr MONTE MCCROSSIN; Curator Dr JENNIFER ROBLES.

Roswell Museum and Art Center: 100 W 11th St, Roswell, NM 88201; tel. (575) 624-6744; internet www.roswellmuseum.org; f. 1935; fine art and historical materials that chronicle specific areas of cultural change in the SW, incl. 71 watercolour sketches from the 1880s, modernist works from Santa Fe and Taos art colonies, public colln of regionalists, contemporary fine arts, int. print colln since 16th century, hand-crafted furniture and decorative objects; planetarium; library of 8,000 vols; Dir LAURIE J. RUFE; Pres. ROBERT PHILLIPS; Sec. and Treas. ELINOR MULKEY.

Silver City Museum: 312 W Broadway, Silver City, NM 88061; tel. (575) 538-5921; e-mail info@silvercitymuseum.org; internet www.silvercitymuseum.org; f. 1967; colln of 20,000 objects; archival material incl. 5,000 household and personal objects dating from late 19th to early 20th century; artefacts rep. of Anglo and Hispanic settlers incl. clothing and accessories, furnishings and firearms; Native American artefacts of pieces of pottery and lithic material from the Mimbres, Mogollon and Casas Grandes peoples and ancient cultures; mining exhibits incl. the Tyrone Room; 50 ranching artefacts; H. B. Ailman House 1881 Mansard/Italianate structure; 17,000 photographs; Dir TRACY SPIKES; Pres. SANDRA HICKS; Sec. LUCY WHITMARSH.

Taos Art Museum: 227 Paseo del Pueblo Norte, POB 1848, Taos, NM 87571; tel. (575) 758-2690; e-mail museum@taosartmuseum .org; internet www.taosartmuseum.org; f. 1994; colln of approx. 300 paintings, drawings and prints by Taos founders; art of early 20th-century Taos; colln of paintings by the masters of the Taos Soc. of Artists; Exec. Dir ERION SIMPSON.

University of New Mexico Art Museum: 1 Univ. of New Mexico, Albuquerque, NM 87131-0001; tel. (505) 277-4001; e-mail artmuse@unm.edu; internet unmartmuseum .unm.edu; colln of 30,000 objects incl. photographs, prints and old master paintings; Dir E. LUANNE McKINNON.

Wheelwright Museum of the American Indian: POB 5153, 704 Camino Lejo, Santa Fe, NM 87502; tel. (505) 982-4636; e-mail info@wheelwright.org; internet www .wheelwright.org; f. 1937; access by appointment; houses collns of artefacts, archives, sound recordings and photographs, documenting Native American (esp. Navajo) culture, both historic and contemporary; contemporary and traditional American Indian art; Dir JONATHAN BATKIN; Curator CHERI FALKENSTIEN-DOYLE.

New York

Albright-Knox Art Gallery: 1285 Elmwood Ave, Buffalo, NY 14222-1096; tel. (716) 882-8700; e-mail info@albrightknox.org; internet www.albrightknox.org; f. 1862 as Buffalo Fine Arts Acad., current name adopted 1962; colln of paintings since the 18th century; post-war American and European art; abstract expressionism; pop art and art from the 1970s; library of 45,000 vols; Dir LOUIS GRACHOS; Chief Curator Dr DOUGLAS DREISHPOON.

American Folk Art Museum: 2 Lincoln Sq., Columbus Ave, 66th St, New York, NY 10023-6214; tel. (212) 595-9533; internet www.folkartmuseum.org; f. 1961 as Museum of Early American Folk Arts, present name 2001; holdings of 18th- and 19th-century artworks and objects from New England and the Mid-Atlantic states; works of folk art symbolizing utility, community, individuality and symbolism; Contemporary Center; Henry Darger Study Center for multidisciplinary research; library of 10,000 vols; Dir LINDA DUNNE (acting); Chair. LAURA PARSONS.

American Museum of Natural History: Central Park W, 79th St, New York, NY 10024-5192; tel. (212) 769-5100; internet www.amnh.org; f. 1869; divs of anthropology, invertebrate zoology, paleontology, physical sciences, vertebrate zoology; Center for Biodiversity and Conservation; Sackler Institute for Comparative Genomics; SW Research Station; Hayden Planetarium; library: see Libraries and Archives; Chair. LEWIS W. BERNARD; Pres. ELLEN V. FUTTER; Sec. SIBYL R. GOLDEN; Treas. CHARLES H. MOTT; publs *American Museum Novitates, Anthropological Papers of the American Museum of Natural History, Bulletin of the American Museum of Natural History.*

Asia Society Museum: 725 Park Ave, 70th St, New York, NY 10021; tel. (212) 288-6400; e-mail info@asiasociety.org; internet asiasociety.org/arts/asia-society-museum; f. 1956; exhibitions of both traditional and contemporary Asian and Asian American art; objects from cultures across Asia that date from the 11th century to the 19th century; spec. colln: Rockefeller colln of Asian art in the USA; Dir MELISSA CHIU.

Binghamton University Art Museum: POB 6000, Binghamton, NY 13902-6000; Fine Arts Bldg, Rooms 179 and 213, 4400 Vestal Parkway E, Binghamton, NY 13902; tel. (607) 777-2000; e-mail info@binghamton .edu; internet www2.binghamton.edu/ art-museum; Italian Baroque painting, Asian art, African art prints and decorative arts, sculpture, prints, photographs, drawings, glass, ceramic, metalwork, MSS pages and textiles from Egypt, Greece, Asia, Africa, Europe, N America and pre-Columbian cultures; 3,000 objects from all major periods of art history and most parts of the world; Assistant Dir JACKIE HOGAN.

Bronx Museum: 1040 Grand Concourse, Bronx, NY 10456-3999; tel. (718) 681-6000; e-mail info@bronxmuseum.org; internet www.bronxmuseum.org; f. 1971; 20th- and 21st-century works by artists of African, Asian and Latin American ancestry; Exec. Dir HOLLY BLOCK; Chair. R. DOUGLASS RICE; Sec. ALESSANDRA DiGIUSTO.

Brooklyn Botanic Garden: 1000 Washington Ave, Brooklyn, NY 11225; tel. (718) 623-7200; e-mail feedback@bbg.org; internet www.bbg.org; f. 1910; living colln of 12,000 species and varieties; herbarium with 250,000 specimens; education programmes; plant information service; library of 30,000 vols, 150 current serials; Chair. FREDERICK BLAND; Sec. ELIZABETH GILE; Treas. SUZANNE T. MARQUARD; Curator KERRY BARRINGER; publ. *Urban Habitats* (online, www.urbanhabitats.org).

Brooklyn Museum: 200 E Parkway, Brooklyn, NY 11238-6052; tel. (718) 638-5000; e-mail information@brooklynmuseum.org; internet www.brooklynmuseum.org; f. 1823; Native American art; Peruvian textiles; pre-Columbian gold; Costa Rican sculpture; collns from Africa, Melanesia and Polynesia; collns from China, Korea, SE Asia, Japan, India and Persia; Colonial S American art; American period rooms; sculpture garden; American and European paintings; prints and drawings; ancient art of the Near East, Egypt, Greece and Rome; American and European costumes; American glass, pewter and silver; contemporary paintings and sculpture; Elizabeth A. Sackler Center for Feminist Art, art reference library and Egyptological library; library of 170,000 vols, 11,710 glass lantern slides; Dir ARNOLD L. LEHMAN; Chief Curator KEVIN STAYTON; Dir ARNOLD L. LEHMAN; Chair. JOHN S. TAMAGNI; Sec. CONSTANCE L. CHRISTENSEN; Treas. RICHARD M. CASHIN.

Buffalo Museum of Science: 1020 Humboldt Parkway, Buffalo, NY 14211; tel. (716) 896-5200; internet www.sciencebuff.org; f. 1929; attached to Buffalo Soc. of Natural Sciences; exhibition halls feature insects, dinosaurs and other fossils, birds, wild flowers and fungi, vertebrates, minerals, flora and fauna of the Niagara Frontier, life in ancient Egypt, solar system and space exploration, geology; solar and lunar observatory; loan collns, lectures, day and evening classes, etc.; operates Tifft Nature Preserve, S Buffalo; library of 45,000 vols, 400 journals; Pres. and CEO MARK MORTENSON; Curator of Collns KATHRYN LEACOCK; Chair. RANDALL E. BURKARD; Sec. ROBERT GENCO; Treas. CHRISTOPHER HOGAN; publ. *Bulletin of the Buffalo Society of Natural Sciences.*

Cooper-Hewitt, National Design Museum: 2 E 91st St, New York, NY 10128; tel. (212) 849-8400; e-mail redesignch@si.edu; internet www .cooperhewitt.org; f. 1897, present status 1967; attached to Smithsonian Instn; 250,000 items, incl. collns of original drawings and designs for architecture and the decorative arts; prints since 15th century; textiles, lace, woodwork and furniture, ceramics, glass, etc.; drawings and paintings by F. E. Church, W. Homer and other 19th-century American artists; library of 70,000 vols, incl. 8,000 rare books; 1,000 items: books, journals, guides, ephemera; 13,000 drawings and 4,300 black and white photographs; Dir BILL MOGGRIDGE; Pres. BETH COMSTOCK (acting); Sec. JUDY FRANCIS ZANKEL; Treas. ERIC A. GREEN; Curatorial Dir CARA McCARTY.

Dia Beacon Riggio Galleries: Three Beekman St, Beacon, NY 12508; tel. (845) 440-0100; e-mail info@diaart.org; internet www .diaart.org/sites/main/beacon; f. 2003; attached to Dia Art Foundation; art since 1960s; Dir PHILIPPE VERGNE; Curator YASMIL RAYMOND.

El Museo del Barrio: 1230 Fifth Ave, 104th St, New York, NY 10029; tel. (212) 831-7272; e-mail info@elmuseo.org; internet www .elmuseo.org; f. 1969; 6,500 objects spanning more than 800 years of Latin American, Caribbean and Latino art, incl. pre-Columbian Taíno artefacts, traditional arts, 20th-century drawings, paintings, sculptures and installations, as well as prints, photography, documentary films, and video; Exec. Dir MARGARITA AGUILAR; Dir of Curatorial Programmes DEBORAH CULLEN; Chair. TONY BECHARA; Sec. MICHAEL J. GARCÍA; Treas. MARY McCAFFREY.

Everson Museum of Art: 401 Harrison St, Syracuse, NY 13202; tel. (315) 474-6064; e-mail everson@everson.org; internet www .everson.org; f. 1897 as Syracuse Museum of Fine Arts, present location 1968; 11,000 objects, incl. American paintings, with 700 artworks spanning 2 centuries; 2,000 pieces of American Art pottery colln; 600 works on paper of 19th- and 20th-century art movements; 100 decorative objects; Exec. Dir STEVEN KERN; Pres. PATRICK PEDRO; Sec. EUGENIA BRIEVA; Treas. RICHARD DRISCOLL.

Frick Collection: 1 E 70th St, New York, NY 10021; tel. (212) 288-0700; e-mail info@ frick.org; internet www.frick.org; f. 1920; European paintings from 13th to 19th centuries; French 18th-century sculpture, furniture and porcelains; Italian Renaissance bronzes and furniture; Limoges enamels of the Renaissance; Oriental porcelains; works of art mostly assembled by industrialist Henry Clay Frick; library: see under Libraries and Archives; Dir IAN WARDROPPER.

Grey Art Gallery: New York Univ., 100 Washington Sq. E, New York, NY 10003; tel. (212) 998-6780; e-mail greyartgallery@nyu .edu; internet www.nyu.edu/greyart; f. 1927 as A. E. Gallatin's Museum of Living Art, current name adopted 1975; attached to New York Univ.; collects, preserves, studies, documents, interprets and exhibits evidence of human culture; 6,000 objects of late-19th-and 20th-century works, ranging from Pablo Picasso's Bust of Sylvette to Joseph Cornell box and Chocolat Menier, from 1952; American paintings since 1940s.

Solomon R. Guggenheim Museum: 1071 Fifth Ave at 89th St, New York, NY 10128-0173; tel. (212) 423-3500; e-mail visitorinfo@ guggenheim.org; internet www.guggenheim .org; f. 1939 as Museum of Non-Objective Painting with approx. 600 artworks from Solomon Guggenheim's private collection; 7 large collns: Thanhauser colln, Panza colln, Karl Neiderdorf Estate, Katherine S. Dreier Bequest, Hilla Rebay Colln, Robert Mapplethorpe Foundation Gift, Bohen Foundation Gift; Brancusi sculptures, Kandinsky paintings, works by Klee, Braque, Chagall, Delaunay, Dubuffet, Léger, Marc, Mondrian and Picasso; Sackler Center for Arts Education; library of 20,000 vols on modern and contemporary art, architecture, and photography; global Guggenheim exhibition catalogues and rare books; Dir RICHARD ARMSTRONG; Chief Curator NANCY SPECTOR.

Harbor Defense Museum: 230 Sheridan Loop, Fort Hamilton Military Community, Brookyln, NY 11252-5701; tel. (718) 630-4349; internet www.harbordefensemuseum .com; f. 1825; US Army weapons, uniforms, small arms, cannons and accoutrements since 18th century; military art and historical items from Fort Hamilton; Dir PAUL MORANDO.

Hispanic Society of America Museum and Library: 613 W 155th St, New York, NY 10032; Audubon Terrace, Broadway, between 155th and 156th Sts, New York, NY 10032; tel. (212) 926-2234; e-mail info@ hispanicsociety.org; internet www .hispanicsociety.org; f. 1904; concentrates on culture of the Iberian Peninsula and Latin America: paintings, prints and drawings (since 14th century), sculpture (since 13th century), archaeology, decorative arts (ceramics, textiles, metalwork, furniture); library of 250,000 vols, 200,000 MSS, 15,000 vols printed before 1701; Dir Dr MITCHELL A. CODDING; Curator of Paintings and Drawings MARCUS BURKE; Curator of Iconography PATRICK LENAGHAN.

Jacques Marchais Museum of Tibetan Art: 338 Lighthouse Ave, Staten Island, NY 10306; tel. (718) 987-3500; internet www .tibetanmuseum.org; f. 1948; colln of Jacques Marchais during the early 1920s to the late 1940s, incl. sculptures, thangka or scroll paintings, ritual artefacts, musical instruments, furniture and historic photographs of Tibet; Exec. Dir MEG VENTRUDO; Pres. BEVERLY GARCIA-ANDERSO; Sec. RUTH SPRUTE; Treas. GEORGE SIEGHARDT.

Jewish Museum: 1109 Fifth Ave, 92nd St, New York, NY 10128; tel. (212) 423-3200; e-mail info@thejm.org; internet www .thejewishmuseum.org; f. 1904; explores scope and diversity of 4,000 years of Jewish art and culture through 27,000 objects; Dir CLAUDIA GOULD.

Metropolitan Museum of Art: 1000 Fifth Ave, New York, NY 10028-0198; tel. (212) 535-7710; e-mail communications@ metmuseum.org; internet www.metmuseum .org; f. 1866; art of Africa, Oceania and the Americas; American paintings and sculpture; American decorative arts; ancient Near Eastern art; Asian art; drawings and prints; European paintings; European sculpture and decorative arts; Greek and Roman art; Islamic art; Robert Lehman Colln; medieval art; musical instruments; photographs; 20th-century art; 2m. works of art and 6,500 objects; library of 240,000 vols, 1,400 periodicals; photograph and slide library; Chair. DANIEL BRODSKY; Pres. EMILY K. RAFFERTY; Dir and CEO THOMAS P. CAMPBELL; publs *Metropolitan Museum of Art Bulletin, Metropolitan Museum Journal, Now at the Met.*

Museum of Chinese in America: 215 Centre St, New York, NY 10013; tel. (212) 619-4785; e-mail info@mocanyc.org; internet www.mocanyc.org; f. 1980, present location 2009; collns incl. 60,000 letters and documents, business and organizational records, oral histories, clothing and textiles, photographs and precious artefacts of Chinese American history; colln and research centre in Mulberry St; Dir JESSICA CHAO; Curator and Dir of Exhibitions HERB HOI CHUN TAM; Sec. PATRICIA P. TANG.

Museum of Jewish Heritage: Edmond J. Safra Plaza, 36 Battery Pl., New York, NY 10280; tel. (646) 437-4202; e-mail info@ mjhnyc.org; internet www.mjhnyc.org; f. 1997; 25,000 items on modern Jewish history and Holocaust; incl. 4,000 audio and video testimonies by Holocaust survivors, liberators, rescuers, Jews who served in the Allied Armies during Second World War; Dir Dr DAVID G. MARWELL; Sr Curator ESTHER BRUMBERG; Chair. ROBERT M. MORGENTHAU.

Museum of Modern Art: 11 W 53rd St, New York, NY 10019-5497; tel. (212) 708-9400; internet www.moma.org; f. 1929; paintings, drawings, prints, sculptures, industrial and graphic design, photographs, architecture and design since 1880s; large colln of American, British, French, German and Russian films, 1,200 of which are available to educational organizations; colln of modern and contemporary photography in the world; daily film showings; organizes exhibitions worldwide in all the visual arts; library of 300,000 vols, incl. 300 periodicals and 40,000 vertical files; Dir GLENN D. LOWRY; Chair. JERRY I. SPEYER; Sec. PATTY LIPSHUTZ; Treas. RICHARD E. SALOMON.

Museum of the City of New York: 1220 Fifth Ave, 103rd St, New York, NY 10029; tel. (212) 534-1672; e-mail info@mcny.org; internet www.mcny.org; f. 1923; colln of 1.4m. paintings, sculptures, prints, photographs, costumes, toys reflecting historical and modern New York city; Pres. and Dir SUSAN HENSHAW JONES; Chair. JAMES G. DINAN; Sec. JAMES P. DRUCKMAN; Treas. JANE B. O'CONNELL.

National Museum of the American Indian: George Gustav Heye Center, Alexander Hamilton US Custom House, One Bowling Green, New York, NY 10004; tel. (212) 514-3700; e-mail nmai-ny@si.edu; internet www.nmai.si.edu; f. 1989; attached to Smithsonian Instn; colln of the material culture of the native people of the W Hemisphere; 800,000 items from the colln of George Gustav Heye; film and audiovisual collns; paper archives; photography archive of more than 300,000 images; also located in Washington, DC; library of 40,000 vols, 90,000 photographs and negatives, 1,500 linear ft of records; Dir KEVIN GROVER.

Neue Galerie: Museum for German and Austrian Art, 1048 Fifth Ave, New York, NY 10028; tel. (212) 628-6200; e-mail museum@ neuegalerie.org; internet www.neuegalerie .org; f. 2001; early 20th-century German and Austrian art and design; Dir RENÉE PRICE; Pres. RONALD S. LAUDER.

Noble Maritime Collection: 1000 Richmond Terrace, Bldg D, Staten Island, NY 10301; tel. (718) 447-6490; internet www .noblemaritime.org; f. 1987; preserves and interprets art and writings of marine artist, John A. Noble; House Boat Studio, Ship Model Gallery with colln from Sailors' Snug Harbor; sailing vessels, steamships and collns from the 18th, 19th and 20th centuries; Exec. Dir ERIN M. URBAN; Chair. JAMES J. DEVINE; Sec. KEVIN J. MAHONEY; Treas. JOHN J. PINTO.

Paley Center for Media: 25 W 52nd St, New York, NY 10019; tel. (212) 621-6800; e-mail groupvisitsny@paleycenter.org; internet www.paleycenter.org; f. 1975 as The Museum of Broadcasting, present name 2007; 150,000 television and radio programmes and advertisements reflecting the history of television and radio; incl. a screening room to browse and watch programmes; br. in Los Angeles, CA; Pres. and CEO PAT MITCHELL.

Rochester Museum & Science Center: 657 E Ave, Rochester, NY 14607-2177; tel.

(585) 271-4320; internet www.rmsc.org; f. 1912; collns of 1.2m. objects: incl. 164,000 history objects, 20,960 ethnology objects, 800,000 archaeology objects; RMSC's Natural Sciences colln incl. 26,000 specimens; Strasenburgh Planetarium; Cumming Nature Center: environmental education facility in Naples, NY; library of 25,000 vols, 1,400 serial titles, 60,000 archived documents, 40,000 photographs; Pres. KATE BENNETT.

Rubin Museum of Art: 150 W 17th St, New York, NY 10011; tel. (212) 620 5000; e-mail info@rmanyc.org; internet www.rmanyc.org; f. 1999; museum of Himalayan art; 2,000 works of art incl. paintings, sculptures and textile of the Himalayan region incl. Nepal, Tibet and Bhutan as well as the inter-related traditions of India, Mongolia and China spanning a period from the 2nd to the 20th century; education centre; Exec. Dir PATRICK SEARS; Dir for Exhibitions, Collns and Research JAN VAN ALPHEN.

Whitney Museum of American Art: 945 Madison Ave, 75th St, New York, NY 10021; tel. (212) 570-3600; e-mail info@whitney.org; internet www.whitney.org; f. 1930; 19,000 paintings, sculptures, drawings, prints, photographs, films, video cassettes and new media by more than 2,900 artists; library of 50,000 vols, 500 current periodicals; Dir ADAM D. WEINBERG; Chief Curator and Deputy Dir DONNA DE SALVO; Pres. NEIL G. BLUHM; Sec. JOANNE LEONHARDT CASSULLO; Treas. HENRY CORNELL.

Yager Museum of Art & Culture: POB 4020, Oneonta, NY 13820; tel. (607) 431-4480; e-mail museum@hartwick.edu; internet www.hartwick.edu/academics/ museum; f. 1929, present location 1967; attached to Hartwick College; 17,000 objects of fine arts, Upper Susquehanna Indian artefacts, SW pottery, baskets and rugs; Museum Coordinator DONNA ANDERSON.

Yeshiva University Museum: 15 W 16th St, New York, NY 10011; tel. (212) 294-8330; e-mail info@yum.cjh.org; internet www .yumuseum.org; f. 1973; colln of more than 8,000 artefacts, incl. fine and folk art, ethnographic and archaeological artefacts, clothing and textiles, Jewish ceremonial objects, documents, books and MSS; colln represents 2,000 years of Jews living throughout the world; spec. colln incl. archaeological artefacts dating from the Bronze Age to the late antique period; Torah scroll and Tefillin of the Baal Shem Tov, founder of the Hassidic movement; Dir JACOB WISSE.

North Carolina

Ackland Art Museum: Univ. of North Carolina at Chapel Hill, POB 3400, Chapel Hill, NH 27599-3400; tel. (919) 966-5736; e-mail ackland@email.unc.edu; internet www.ackland.org; f. 1958; attached to Univ. of North Carolina; 16,000 works of art; art glass colln dating from 1880s to 1950s; African art colln incl. ancient Nok terracotta sculpture; European paintings from Renaissance to 20th century; paintings and sculptures from modernist period; Dir EMILY KASS; Chief Curator PETER NISBET.

Asheville Art Museum: POB 1717, 2 S Pack Sq., Asheville, NC 28802-1717; tel. (828) 253-3227; e-mail mailbox@ashevilleart .org; internet www.ashevilleart.org; f. 1948; 3,000 objects and 4,000 architectural drawings; 20th- and 21st-century American art; Exec. Dir PAMELA L. MYERS; Curator FRANK THOMSON.

Aurora Fossil Museum: POB 352, 400 Main St, Aurora, NC 27806-0352; tel. (252) 322-4238; e-mail aurfosmus@yahoo.com; internet www.aurorafossilmuseum.com; f.

1976; colln incl. Pleistocene Age mastodon tusk and rare fossil cetacean skeleton; archaeology colln incl. stone tools, jewellery and cooking implements of native Americans from E North Carolina.

Bechtler Museum of Modern Art: 420 S Tryon St, Charlotte, NC 28202; tel. (704) 353-9200; e-mail info@bechtler.org; internet www.bechtler.org; f. 2010; colln comprises mid-century modern art by artists incl. Alberto Giacometti, Joan Miro, Jean Tinguely and Barbara Hepworth; Pres. and CEO JOHN BOYER; Chair. CYNDEE PATTERSON; Sec. ROBERT S. LILIEN; Treas. LYNN GOOD.

Cape Fear Museum of History and Science: 814 Market St, Wilmington, NC 28401; tel. (910) 798-4350; internet www.capefearmuseum.com; f. 1898; 50,000 objects (photographs, household items, industrial tools, etc.) on history, science and cultures of lower Cape Fear; Dir RUTH HAAS; Curator BARBARA ROWE.

Carolinas Aviation Museum: 4672 First Flight Dr., Charlotte, NC 28208; tel. (704) 997-3770; e-mail info@carolinasaviation.org; internet www.carolinasaviation.org; f. 1991; colln incl. aircraft, helicopters, equipment, artefacts and printed material spanning years of aviation history; Exec. Dir WALLY COPPINGER; Education and Exhibits Dir KATIE MCCLAMROCK.

Chatham Historical Museum: POB 93, Pittsboro, NC 27312; e-mail history@chathamhistory.org; internet www.chathamhistory.org; f. 1990; local history museum; colln incl. early settlement and formation of Chatham Co, colonial warrant signed by William Hooper who signed Declaration of Independence, 1880 census of agriculture and early maps; Pres. BARBARA PUGH; Sec. WINNCIE JANE HINNANT; Treas. DAN PERRY; Curator JANE PYLE.

Colburn Earth Science Museum: 2 S Pack Sq., Asheville, NC 28801-3521; tel. (828) 254-7162; e-mail colburngroupon@gmail.com; internet www.colburnmuseum.org; f. 1960 as Burnham S. Colburn Memorial Museum, present name 2002; 4,500 specimens incl. examples of 350 minerals in North Carolina; 500 fossil specimens; 1,000 cut gemstones from around the world; Dir VICKY BALLARD; Pres. JOSEPH NUNAN.

Cowan Museum of History and Science: POB 950, 411 S Main St, Kenansville, NC 28349; tel. (910) 296-2149; e-mail curator@cowanmuseum.org; internet www.cowanmuseum.org; f. 1981; artefacts incl. early audio equipment, farm equipment, geological specimens, household utensils, woodworking tools, dating from 18th and 19th century that highlight early rural North Carolina and Duplin Co; historical park; Curator and Dir ROBIN GROTKE.

Fine Art Museum: 199 Centennial Dr., Cullowhee, NC 28723; tel. (828) 227-3591; e-mail museum@wcu.edu; internet www.wcu.edu/museum; f. 2005; attached to Western Carolina Univ.; 1,200 pieces of contemporary fine art since 1945 and craft media by regional, nat. and int. artists; Dir DENISE DRURY.

Gaston County Museum: POB 429, Dallas, NC 28034; 131 W Main St, Dallas, NC; tel. (704) 922-7681; e-mail museum@co.gaston.nc.us; internet www.gastoncountymuseum.org; f. 1975; 5,000 objects, 20,000 documents and 400,000 photos on Gaston Co dating from the 1500s to 21st century; Dir JEFF PRUETT; Chair. BRENT MESSER; Sec. JOHN BROOKS; Treas. VAN NOBLETT; Curator STEPHANIE ELLIOTT.

Greensboro Historical Museum: 130 Summit Ave, Greensboro, NC 27401; tel.

(336) 373-2043; internet www.greensborohistory.org; f. 1924; 25,000 items incl. militaria, costumes, textiles and decorative arts; MSS, photographs, printed materials and artwork since 1700; 11,000 American artefacts from 1979 excavations; Dir LINDA EVANS (acting).

Gregg Museum of Art & Design: POB 7306, Raleigh, NC 27695-7306; tel. (919) 515-3503; e-mail gregg@ncsu.edu; internet www.ncsu.edu/gregg; f. 1992, current name and status 1998; attached to North Carolina State Univ.; 26,000 objects incl. textiles, ceramics, photography, glass and sculpture; Native American art and artefacts; Pres. BERNARD HYMAN; Dir ROGER MANLEY.

Mint Museum: 2730 Randolph Rd, Charlotte, NC 28207; tel. (704) 337-2000; internet www.mintmuseum.org; f. 1936; contemporary art colln incl. paintings, drawings, sculptures and photography; American art colln incl. fed. portraiture, 19th-century landscape paintings and early 20th-century realism; 12,500 objects of decorative arts holdings from England and continental Europe, American art pottery and Asian porcelain; 1 br; library of 15,000 vols; Chair. RICHARD T. WILLIAMS.

Morehead Planetarium and Science Center: CB 3480, UNC-CH, Chapel Hill, NC 27599; tel. (919) 962-1236; e-mail mhplanet@unc.edu; internet www.moreheadplanetarium.org; f. 1947; educational programmes for adults and children; daily planetarium shows; digital video theatre; Star Theatre; exhibitions; Dir TODD BOYETTE; Dir for Finance and Admin. SUSAN DURHAM; publ. *Sundial.*

Nasher Museum of Art at Duke University: 2001 Campus Dr., Durham, NC 27705; tel. (919) 684-5135; e-mail nasherinfo@duke.edu; internet nasher.duke.edu; f. 1969 as Duke Univ. Museum of Art, present name 2005; colln incl. 10,000 works of medieval art, art of Americas, antiquities, Russian art, modern and int. contemporary art, traditional African art and Asian art; Dir KIMERLY RORSCHACH.

North Carolina Museum of Art: 4630 Mail Services Centre, Raleigh, NC 27607-6494; 2110 Blue Ridge Rd, Raleigh, NC 27607-6494; tel. (919) 839-6262; internet ncartmuseum.org; f. 1924; colln incl. European paintings from Renaissance to 19th century, African, ancient American, pre-Columbian and Oceanic art, and Jewish ceremonial objects; library of 40,000 vols; Dir LAWRENCE J. WHEELER; Chief Curator LINDA JOHNSON DOUGHERTY; publ. *Preview* (4 a year).

North Carolina Museum of History: Five E Edenton St, Raleigh, NC 27601-1011; tel. (919) 807-7900; internet ncmuseumofhistory.org; f. 1898, present name 1965; 150,000 artefacts representing 6 centuries of North Carolina history; Dir KENNETH B. HOWARD; Curator ROANN BISHOP; Curator JEANNE MARIE WARZESKI.

North Carolina Museum of Natural Sciences: 11 W Jones St, Raleigh, NC 27601-1029; tel. (919) 733-7450; internet www.naturalsciences.org; f. 1879 as North Carolina State Museum; colln of 3m. specimens focusing on zoology, geology and paleontology of North Carolina and SE USA; Dir Dr BETSY M. BENNETT.

Reynolda House Museum of American Art: POB 7287, Winston-Salem, NC 27109-7287; 2250 Reynolda Rd, Winston-Salem, NC 27106; tel. (336) 758-5150; e-mail reynolda@reynoldahouse.org; internet www.reynoldahouse.org; f. 1967; American art colln of painting and sculpture from 3 centuries, since colonial times; architectural

drawings, documents, oral histories and photographs; 700 articles of clothing, representing 2 generations of the Reynolds Family from 1890 to 1965; library of 3,650 vols; Exec. Dir ALLISON C. PERKINS.

Weatherspoon Art Museum: POB 26170, UNC Greensboro, Greensboro, NC 27402-6170; tel. (336) 334-5770; e-mail weatherspoon@uncg.edu; internet weatherspoon.uncg.edu; f. 1941; attached to Univ. of North Carolina; 6,000 works incl. modern and contemporary American art; American art since 1900; Lenoir C. Wright colln of Japanese wood block prints; Dir NANCY DOLL.

North Dakota

Bonanzaville: 1351 W Main Ave, POB 719, West Fargo, ND 58078; tel. (701) 282-2822; internet www.bonanzaville.com; f. 1955; attached to Cass Co Historical Soc.; 400,000 artefacts in 43 historical bldgs; Eugene Dahl Car Museum, Eagles Air Museum, Horse Drawn Vehicle Bldg, Law Enforcement Museum, Medical Display, Melroe Tractor Bldg, Moum Agricultural Bldg and Telephone Museum; Exec. Dir TROY WHITE; Pres. ROBERT CLARKE; Treas. PAUL MEYERS; Curator ANDREW NIELSEN.

Dakota Dinosaur Museum: 200 E Museum Dr., Dickinson, ND 58601; tel. (701) 225-3466; e-mail info@dakotadino.com; internet www.dakotadino.com; f. 1987; geological and palaeontological specimens of dinosaurs; skeletal casts, replicas of real bones; dinosaur sculptures; Dir and Curator ALICE LEAGUE; Dir and Curator LARRY LEAGUE.

Dickinson Museum Center: 188 Museum Dr. E, Dickinson, ND 58601; tel. (701) 456-6225; e-mail info@dickinsonmuseumcenter.org; internet www.dickinsonmuseumcenter.org; Joachim Regional Museum: art and history exhibits of regional significance; Museum Dir DANIELLE STUCKLE.

Fargo Air Museum: 1609 19th Ave N, Fargo, ND 58102; tel. (701) 293-8043; internet www.fargoairmuseum.org; aircraft colln; Chair. REX A. HAMMARBACK; Sec. TIMOTHY MCPHERSON; Treas. ROBERT THIBIDEAU.

North Dakota Museum of Art: 261 Centennial Dr., Grand Forks, ND 58202; tel. (701) 777-4195; e-mail ndmoa@ndmoa.com; internet www.ndmoa.com; f. 1975 as Univ. of N Dakota Art Galleries, present name and status 1981; contemporary, int. art in all media starting with the early 1970s; colln contemporary Native American art; Dir LAUREL REUTER.

Pembina State Museum: Off Interstate 29, 805 Highway 59; POB 456, Pembina, ND 58271; tel. (701) 825-6840; e-mail histsoc@nd.gov; internet www.history.nd.gov; f. 1996; attached to State Historical Soc. of North Dakota; 2 exhibition galleries; observation tower with a view of the Red River Valley; pre-glacial fossils; bone and stone tools; frontier military forts; current trends in industry, agriculture, and recreation in NE of North Dakota; temporary exhibitions; natural history, history, archaeology and ethnology; interpretive programming; Dir MERL PAAVERUD.

Pioneer Trails Regional Museum: 12 First Ave NE, POB 78, Bowman, ND 58623; tel. (701) 523-3600; e-mail ptrm@ptrm.org; internet www.ptrm.org; colln and research on anthropology, archaeology, astronomy, botany, genealogy, local history and palaeontology.

Plains Art Museum: 704 First Ave N, Fargo, ND 58102; tel. (701) 232-3821; e-mail museum@plainsart.org; internet plainsart

.org; f. 1965 as Red River Art Center, present name 1975; 3,000 works incl. nat. and regional contemporary art, traditional American Indian art and traditional folk art; Hannaher's, Inc. Print Studio, Dawson Studio and Goldberg Resource Library; Dir and CEO COLLEEN SHEEHY; Chair. ARLETTE PRESTON; Sec. KATE HAUGAN; Treas. JIM HAMBRICK.

Prairie Village Museum: 102 HWY 2 SE, POB 232, Rugby, ND 58368-2444; tel. (701) 776-6414; e-mail prairievillagemuseum@gmail.com; internet www.prairievillagemuseum.com; f. 1964; colln incl. bldgs, artefacts, household items, clothing, buggies, automobiles and farm machinery dating from late 1880s to the present, focussing on turn of the century; Exec. Dir CATHY JELSING.

Ohio

Akron Art Museum: 1 S High, Akron, OH 44308; tel. (330) 376-9185; e-mail mail@akronartmuseum.org; internet www.akronartmuseum.org; f. 1922 as Akron Art Institute, present name 1980; 5,000 art works produced since 1850; public colln of glass by artist Paul Stankard; library of 11,000 vols, 38 journals, 5,200 artist biographical files; Dir and CEO Dr MITCHELL KAHAN.

Allen Memorial Art Museum: c/o Oberlin College, 87 N Main St, Oberlin, OH 44074; tel. (440) 775-8665; internet www.oberlin.edu/amam; f. 1917; attached to Oberlin College; colln of 14,000 artworks incl. European and American paintings and sculpture since 15th century; Asian paintings, scrolls, sculpture and decorative art, incl. ukiyo-e prints, African, Pre-Columbian and ancient art and photographs; Dir Dr STEPHANIE WILES.

Butler Institute of American Art: The Beecher Center, 524 Wick Ave, Youngstown, OH 44502; tel. (330) 743-1107; e-mail info@butlerart.com; internet www.butlerart.com; f. 1919; 20,000 individual works spanning 4 centuries; Marine colln; impressionist works; early 20th-century works; contemporary works; brs in Salem and Howland Township; Dir and Chief Curator Dr LOUIS A. ZONA.

Canton Museum of Art: 1001 Market Ave N, Canton, OH 44702; tel. (330) 453-7666; internet www.cantonart.org; f. 1935 as Little Civic Art Gallery, current name adopted 1995; colln of American watercolours from 19th and 20th centuries and contemporary ceramics; Exec. Dir M. J. ALBACETE; Pres. ADAM LUNTZ; Sec. TRAVIS MAXWELL; Treas. RON VAN HORN.

Cincinnati Art Museum: 953 Eden Park Dr., Cincinnati, OH 45202; tel. (513) 639-2995; e-mail information@cincyart.org; internet www.cincinnatiartmuseum.org; f. 1881; colln incl. ancient art of Egypt, Greece, Rome and Near and Far Eastern art, art of Africa and the Americas, costume and textiles, prints, drawings, photographs, paintings, sculpture, decorative art, and contemporary art; colln of ancient Nabataean art, Herbert Greer French colln of old master prints and colln of European and American portrait miniatures; temporary exhibitions; library of 52,000 vols, 250,000 pamphlets and clippings; Chair. LARRY A. SHEAKLEY; Chief Curator Dr JAMES CRUMP; Dir AARON BETSKY (acting); Pres. GEORGE H. VINCENT; publ. *CANVAS* (6 a year).

Cleveland Museum of Art: 11150 E Blvd, Cleveland, OH 44106; tel. (216) 421-7340; e-mail info@clevelandart.org; internet www.clevelandart.org; f. 1913; archives; collns incl. African art, American painting and sculpture, ancient Egyptian, near East, Greek and Roman art, art of the Americas, decorative arts and design, drawings, Chinese art, contemporary art, European painting and sculpture from 1500 to 1800, modern European painting and sculpture, Indian and SE Asian art, Japanese and Korean art, medieval art, photographs, prints, textiles and Islamic art; temporary exhibitions; library of 450,000 vols; Chair. R. STEVEN KESTNER; Dir, Pres. and CEO Dr DAVID FRANKLIN; Sec. SARAH S. CUTLER; Treas. JANET G. ASHE; publ. *Cleveland Studies in the History of Art* (1 a year).

Cleveland Museum of Natural History: One Wade Oval Dr., University Circle, Cleveland, OH 44106-1767; tel. (216) 231-4600; internet www.cmnh.org; f. 1920; research and colln in fields of archaeology, botany, cultural anthropology, invertebrate paleontology, invertebrate zoology, mineralogy, ornithology, physical anthropology, vertebrate paleontology, vertebrate zoology; 5m. artefacts and specimens incl. the Hamann-Todd Osteological Colln; protects 4,500 acres of rare natural habitats throughout Northeast Ohio; Shafran Planetarium; Mueller Observatory (incl. $10^{1}/_{2}$-inch Warner and Swasey telescope built in 1899); Wade Gallery (colln of 1,500 gems and minerals); library: Harold T. Clark Library of 60,000 vols (incl. 40,000 periodicals and 20,000 books), 1,000 Rare Book Colln; Exec. Dir and CEO Dr EVALYN GATES; Pres. A. CHACE ANDERSON; Sec. GORDON D. KINDER; Treas. JONATHON L. GRIMM; publs *Explorer* (4 a year), *Kirtlandia* (scientific papers), *Tracks* (6 a year).

Columbus Museum of Art: 480 E Broad St, Columbus, OH 43215; tel. (614) 221-6801; e-mail info@cmaohio.org; internet www.columbusmuseum.org; colln of late 19th- and early 20th-century American and European modern art; regional collns of woodcarvings; paintings and lithographs; photographs; Philip and Suzanne Schiller Colln of American Social Commentary Art 1930–70; Exec. Dir NANNETTE V. MACIEJUNES; Pres. JAY VORYS; Sec. LOANN W. CRANE; Treas. MICHAEL A. PETRECCA.

Dayton Art Institute: 456 Belmonte Park N, Dayton, OH 45405; tel. (937) 223-4278; e-mail info@daytonart.org; internet www.daytonartinstitute.org; f. 1919; collns of 26,000 objects spanning 5,000 years of art history, incl. ancient, European, Oceanic, Asian, Pre-Columbian and American fine and decorative art; outdoor sculptures; Chair. BEAR MONITA; Dir and CEO MICHAEL R. ROEDIGER.

Kennedy Museum of Art: Lin Hall, Ohio Univ., Athens, OH 45701; tel. (740) 593-1304; e-mail kennedymuseum@ohio.edu; internet www.ohio.edu/museum; attached to Ohio Univ.; colln of 8,000 objects incl. SW Native American arts and crafts, 700 Navajo weavings, 1,200 jewellery items and silverware, post-1945 print colln, 20th-century American Art and works on paper; 300 objects of African art incl. textiles, sculpture, jewellery, clothing and ceremonial items; Dir EDWARD E. PAULEY; Curator PETRA KRALICKOVA; publ. *KMA Magazine* (2 a year).

Kent State University Museum: 515 Hilltop Dr., POB 5190, Rockwell Hall, Kent, OH 44242-0001; E Main St and S Lincoln St, Kent, OH 44242-0001; tel. (330) 672-3450; e-mail museum@kent.edu; internet www.kent.edu/museum; f. 1985; colln of 20,000 objects incl. American glass, clothing and textiles, furniture, paintings and decorative arts; Dir JEAN DRUESEDOW; Curator Asst Prof. SARA HUME.

Massillon Museum: 121 Lincoln Way E, Massillon, OH 44646; tel. (330) 833-4061; internet www.massillonmuseum.org; f. 1933 as Baldwin Museum, present name 1938; 100,000 objects incl. paintings and prints, ceramics, glass, photographs, textiles, costumes, military artefacts, city records, agricultural equipment, Native American objects, quilts, books, musical instruments, medical equipment, furniture, toys, household equipment and circus memorabilia; 60,000 photographs; 18,000 archival and reference documents; 700 geological specimens and fossils; Exec. Dir and Curator ALEXANDRA NICHOLIS; Chair. JUDY PAQUELET; Treas. and Sec. MAUDE SLAGLE.

Miami University Art Museum: 801 S Patterson Ave, Oxford, OH 45056; tel. (513) 529-2232; e-mail artmuseum@muohio.edu; internet arts.muohio.edu/art-museum; f. 1978; 16,000 artworks incl. prints, paintings and sculptures; incl. Outdoor Sculpture Park; William Holmes McGuffey Museum (open by appointment); Charles M. Messer Leica Camera Colln; Dir Dr ROBERT S. WICKS.

National Museum of the US Air Force: 1100 Spaatz St, Wright-Patterson Air Force Base, OH 45433-7102; tel. (937) 255-3286; e-mail nationalmuseum.usaf@wpafb.af.mil; internet www.nationalmuseum.af.mil; f. 1923; displays of historical events, individuals and materials incl. 360 aircraft and missiles; preservation of milestones in aerospace technology; study of aviation and aerospace history; Research Center available by appointment only; 12 field museums; 7 heritage centres; Dir JOHN L. HUDSON; Sr Curator TERRY AITKEN.

Ohio River Museum: 601 Front St, Marietta, OH 45750; tel. (740) 373-3750; e-mail cmmoriv@ohiohistory.org; internet ohsweb.ohiohistory.org/places/se09; attached to Ohio Historical Soc.; colln depicting origins and natural history of the Ohio River and history of steamboat on the Ohio River system; colln of boat building, mussels and tool and equipment from steamboat era; Site Man. F. BARMANN.

Southern Ohio Museum: 825 Gallia St, Portsmouth, OH 45662; tel. (740) 354-5629; e-mail info@somacc.com; internet www.somacc.com; f. 1979; Anna Louise Stanton Doll Colln of 18th, 19th and early 20th century in bisque, china, papier-mâché and tin; Art of the Ancients Colln: 10,000 objects between 1,500 to 8,000 years old; Carl Ackerman Colln: 10,000 historic local photographs; library of 1,000 vols; Exec. Dir MARK CHEPP; Artistic Dir CHARLOTTE GORDON.

Springfield Museum of Art: 107 Cliff Park Rd, Springfield, OH 45501; tel. (937) 325-4673; internet www.springfieldart.museum; f. 1946 as Springfield Art Asscn, present name 1989; works of Berenice Abbott, George Bellows, Robert Brackman, Alfred T. Bricher, Thomas Doughty, Emil S. Carlsen, Ethel Cook, Stuart Davis and Charles Demuth; Dir ANN FORTESCUE; Curator CHARLOTTE GORDON.

Taft Museum of Art: 316 Pike St, Cincinnati, OH 45202; tel. (513) 241-0343; e-mail taftmuseum@taftmuseum.org; internet www.taftmuseum.org; f. 1820, present name and status 1932; European and American master paintings; Chinese ceramics and works of art; European decorative arts; 17th- to 19th-century watches; pieces of early 19th-century American furniture and European and American sculptures; Dir and CEO DEBORAH EMONT SCOTT; Chief Curator LYNNE AMBROSINI.

Toledo Museum of Art: POB 1013, Toledo, OH 43697; 2445 Monroe St, Toledo, OH 43620; tel. (419) 255-8000; internet www.toledomuseum.org; f. 1901; 30,000 works of art: American and European painting, history of art in glass, ancient Greek, Roman and Egyptian works, Asian and African art, medieval art, sculpture, decorative arts, graphic arts, and modern and contemporary art; sculpture garden and glass pavilion; Dir and CEO Brian P. Kennedy; Chair. Elizabeth Brady; Vice-Chair. and Sec. John S. Szuch; Vice-Chair. and Treas. George L. Chapman; Chief Curator Carolyn Putney.

Zanesville Museum of Art: 620 Military Rd, Zanesville, OH 43701; tel. (740) 452-0741; internet www.zanesvilleart.org; colln of Ohio glass and pottery, decorative arts ancient to Tiffany and works by Cezanne, Grandma Moses, Lautrec, Matisse, Picasso, Rembrandt, Rubens; Asian, Indian, African, Pre-Columbian collns; Madame Alexander Doll Colln; Dir Susan Talbot-Stanaway.

Oklahoma

Cherokee Strip Museum: 2617 W Fir Ave, Perry, OK 73077-7903; tel. (580) 336-2405; e-mail csmuseum@okhistory.org; internet www.cherokee-strip-museum.org; f. 1968; attached to Oklahoma Historical Soc.; artefacts, photographs and documents tracing history of the Cherokee Outlet and its people; original furnishings and memorabilia of Henry S. Johnston and fmr gov., Henry Bellmon; beadwork artefacts of Otoe-Missouria Indians; music room; tamac pottery; guns and lawmen; early 1900s kitchen; Historical Facility Man. Peggy Haxton.

Cherokee Strip Regional Heritage Center: 507 S Fourth St, Enid, OK 73701; tel. (580) 237-1907; e-mail csrhcinfo@okhistory.org; internet www.csrhc.org; f. 1960, present location 1975, present name and status 2005; attached to Oklahoma Historical Soc.; living history area, Humphrey Heritage Village, which is colln of 4 historically significant blgs incl. 1893 US Land Office; Dir Andi Holland; Curator Dave Kennedy; Chair. Lew O. Ward; Sec. Daron Rudy; Treas. Dr. David Russell.

Fred Jones Jr Museum of Art: 555 Elm Ave, Norman, OK 73019-3003; tel. (405) 325-4938; e-mail museuminfo@ou.edu; internet www.ou.edu/fjjma.html; f. 1936, current name adopted 1992; attached to Univ. of Oklahoma; 16,000 objects incl. Eugene B. Adkins Colln and James T. Bialac Native American Art Colln, French Impressionism, 20th-century American painting and sculpture, traditional and contemporary Native American art, art of the Southwest, ceramics, photography, contemporary art, Asian art and graphics from 16th century to the present; Museum Dir Emily Neff.

Mabee-Gerrer Museum of Art: 1900 W MacArthur Dr., Shawnee, OK 74804; tel. (405) 878-5300; e-mail info@mgmoa.org; internet www.mgmoa.org; f. 1919; Egyptian, Greek and Roman objects; art from the Middle Ages and Renaissance through early 20th century and Native American, African, Oceanic and E cultural artefacts; Dir and Chief Curator Dane Pollei; Chair. Paul Hammond; Treas. Chris Rick.

Museum of the Western Prairie: 1100 Memorial Dr., Altus, OK 73521; tel. (580) 482-1044; e-mail muswestpr@okhistory.org; internet www.okhistory.org/outreach/museums/westernprairie.html; attached to Oklahoma Historical Soc.; showcases natural history to industrial history of SW Oklahoma; Dir Jennie Buchanan.

National Cowboy & Western Heritage Museum: 1700 NE 63rd St, Oklahoma City, OK 73111; tel. (405) 478-2250; e-mail info@nationalcowboymuseum.org; internet www.nationalcowboymuseum.org; f. 1955; classic and contemporary Western art; colln of American cowboy, rodeos, Native American culture, Victorian firearms, frontier military

and Western performers; sponsors educational programmes and scholarly research; Donald C. & Elizabeth M. Dickinson Research Center; Pres. Robert A. Funk.

Oklahoma City Museum of Art: 415 Couch Dr., Oklahoma City, OK 73102; tel. (405) 236-3100; e-mail info@okcmoa.com; internet www.okcmoa.com; f. 1989 by merger of Oklahoma Art Center with Oklahoma Museum of Art; paintings, prints, photographs and sculptures of American, European, post-war and contemporary art from 1945 to present; drawings and prints from 16th century to the present; art glass; library of 5,000 vols; Chair. Elby J. Beal; Pres. and CEO Glen Gentele; Sec. John R. Bozalis; Treas. Peter B. Delaney; publ. *CONNECT* (3 a year).

Oklahoma History Center: 800 Nazih Zuhdi Dr., Oklahoma City, OK 73105; tel. (405) 522-5248; e-mail okhc@okhistory.org; internet www.okhistorycenter.org; f. 2005; attached to Oklahoma Historical Society, affiliate of the Smithsonian Institute; five galleries with approx. 200 hands-on audio, video and computer activities, 50 topics and 2,000 artefacts on Oklahoma's past; outdoor oilfield exhibits, Red River Journey walking tour, research centre; Dir Dan Provo.

Oklahoma Territorial Museum: 402 E Oklahoma, Guthrie, OK 73044; tel. (405) 282-1889; e-mail guthriecomplex@okhistory.org; internet www.okhistory.org/outreach/museums/territorialmuseum.html; attached to Oklahoma Historical Soc.; artefacts, photographs and paintings showcasing history of Oklahoma's Territorial period; Carnegie Library; Dir Nathan V. Turner.

Philbrook Museum of Art: POB 52510, Tulsa, OK 74152-0510; 2727 S Rockford Rd, Tulsa, OK 74114-4104; tel. (918) 749-7941; e-mail curator@philbrook.org; internet www.philbrook.org; African art; American and European paintings and sculptures; Asian art; Italian Renaissance; Modern and Contemporary art; Native American art; outdoor sculpture; works on paper; library of 25,000 vols, 90 periodicals; Chief Curator Catherine Whitney.

Pioneer Heritage Townsite Center: 201 N Ninth St, Frederick, OK 73542; tel. (580) 335-5844; e-mail pioneer@okhistory.org; internet www.okhistory.org/outreach/museums/pioneertownsite.html; f. 1977; attached to Oklahoma Historical Soc.; house structures, barn and churches of 1920s; Tillman County Historical Museum exhibits life in SW Oklahoma community during territorial period, World Wars and Depression era; implement shed exhibits tractors, harrows, plows, grain separators and other pieces of early farm machinery from late 1800s to 1950s.

Pioneer Woman Museum: 701 Monument Rd, Ponca City, OK 74604-3910; tel. (580) 765-6108; e-mail piown@okhistory.org; internet www.okhistory.org/outreach/museums/pioneerwoman.html; f. 1958; attached to Oklahoma Historical Soc.; preserves legacy of women from all races, creeds and nationalities who have contributed to devt of Oklahoma; Pioneer Woman Statue; Dir Jean Winchester.

Price Tower Arts Center: 510 Dewey Ave, Bartlesville, OK 74003; tel. (918) 336-4949; e-mail dwoodall@pricetower.org; internet pricetower.org; 3,000 works of art; Exec. Dir Timothy L. Boruff; publ. *The View.*

Route 66 Museum: 2229 W Gary Blvd, Clinton, OK 73601; tel. (580) 323-7866; e-mail rt66mus@okhistory.org; internet www.route66.org; f. 1968 as Museum of the Western Trails, present status 1991, present name 1995; attached to Oklahoma Historical

Soc.; vehicles and artefacts exhibiting history and culture of each decade concerning road construction, transportation, lodging, restaurants, garages, curio shops; Dir Pat Smith.

Sam Noble Museum: 2401 Chautauqua Ave, Norman, OK 73072-7029; tel. (405) 325-4712; internet www.snomnh.ou.edu; f. 1899; attached to Univ. of Oklahoma; 7m. objects and specimens in 12 collns: archaeology, ethnology, herpetology, ichthyology, invertebrates, invertebrate paleontology, mammalogy, ornithology, Native American languages, paleobotany and micropaleontology, Okla colln of genomic resources and vertebrate paleontology; Dir Dr Michael A. Mares.

Science Museum Oklahoma: 2100 NE 52nd St, Oklahoma City, OK 73111-7107; tel. (405) 602-6664; e-mail communications@sciencemuseumok.org; internet www.sciencemuseumok.org; f. 1962 as Oklahoma Science and Arts Foundation, present name 2004; planetarium and Dome Theatre; Chair. James W. Farris; Pres. Donald R. Otto; Sec. Kym Koch Thompson.

Sherwin Miller Museum of Jewish Art: 2021 E 71st St, Tulsa, OK 74136; tel. (918) 492-1818; e-mail director@jewishmuseum.net; internet jewishmuseum.net; f. 1965, present name 2000; colln of 10,000 artefacts showing 5,000 year history of the Jewish people from pre-Canaanite era through settling of the Jewish community in Tulsa and the American SW; Julius and Gertrude Livingston Oklahoma Jewish Archives, Tulsa Jewish Genealogical Soc. and Markovitz Jewish Genealogy Study and Research Center; Exec. Dir Arthur Feldman; Curator Dr Karen York.

Spiro Mounds Archaeological Center: 18154 First St, Spiro, OK 74959; tel. (918) 962-2062; e-mail spiro@okhistory.org; internet www.okhistory.org/outreach/museums/spiromounds.html; f. 1978; attached to Oklahoma Historical Soc.; 150-acre site encompassing 12 southern mounds containing evidence of an Indian culture that occupied the site from AD 850 to 1450; organizes solstice and equinox alignment tours; Dir Dennis Peterson.

Thomas Gilcrease Museum: 1400 N Gilcrease Museum Rd, Tulsa, OK 74127-2100; tel. (918) 596-2700; internet www.gilcrease.org; f. 1949; attached to Univ. of Tulsa; anthropological colln of 250,000 specimens, covering prehistoric and historic archaeology and ethnographic materials from Native American, Hispanic and Anglo-American cultural traditions; 10,000 paintings, drawings, prints and sculptures from colonial times to the present; library of 100,000 vols of rare books, MSS and archival material; Exec. Dir Dr Duane H. King; Chair. Hans C. Helmerich; Sec. Joan B. Atkinson.

Oregon

3D Center of Art & Photography: 1928 NW Lovejoy, Portland, OR 97209; tel. (503) 227-6667; internet www.3dcenter.us; f. 1994; history of 3-D: antique stereocards to View-Master, contemporary 3-D photography, lenticulars, anaglyphs and computer generated 3-D art; Dir Stacy Webb.

A. R. Bowman Memorial Museum: 246 N Main St, Prineville, OR 97754; tel. (541) 447-3715; e-mail bowmuse@netscape.net; internet www.bowmanmuseum.org; f. 1971; historical and genealogical exhibits and research; Exec. Dir Gordon Gillespie.

Albany Regional Museum: 136 Lyon St S, Albany, OR 97321; tel. (541) 967-7122; e-mail armuseum@peak.org; internet www.armuseum.com; f. 1980; artefacts, documents and photographs depicting history and culture of Albany, Oregon, and its immediate surroundings; Chair. LARRY BARDELL; Sec. MARY JACQ BURCK; Treas. MICHAEL KOK.

Classic Aircraft Aviation Museum, Inc.: POB 91430, Portland, OR 97291-0430; 3005 NE Cornell Rd, Hillsboro, OR 97125; tel. (503) 693-1414; internet www.classicaircraft .org; acquisition, restoration and operation of classic military aircraft and aviation artefacts; educational programmes about the jet age and cold-war period; aerospace technology; Dir Dr DOUG DONKEL.

Coos Art Museum: 235 Anderson Ave, Coos Bay, OR 97420; tel. (541) 267-3901; e-mail info@coosart.org; internet www.coosart.org; f. 1950 as Coos Artist League; 550 pieces of artwork, incl. contemporary fine art prints and original works in all media by Pacific NW artists.

Grants Pass Museum of Art: POB 966, Grants Pass, OR 97528; 229 SW 'G' St, Grants Pass, OR 97526; tel. (541) 479-3290; e-mail museum@gpmuseum.com; internet www.gpmuseum.com; f. 1979 as Gallery One; Exec. Dir CHRIS PONDELICK; Pres. SUSAN EILEEN BURNES; Sec. ERVA ZABEL; Treas. DON STOCKING.

Jordan Schnitzer Museum of Art: 1223 Univ. of Oregon, Eugene, OR 97403-1233; 1430 Johnson Lane Eugene, Eugene, OR 97403; tel. (541) 346-3027; e-mail jsmadesk@uoregon.edu; internet jsma .uoregon.edu; f. 1933, present name 2005; attached to Univ. of Oregon; galleries featuring 13,000 objects of American, Chinese, European, Japanese, Korean, and S Asian art; Gordon Gilkey Research Center; animation classes, UO Geography Seminars and photography courses; Pres. GREG FITZ-GERALD; Exec. Dir JILL HARTZ.

Museum of Natural and Cultural History: 1680 E 15th Ave, Eugene, OR 97403-1224; tel. (541) 346-3024; e-mail mnh@ uoregon.edu; internet natural-history .uoregon.edu; f. 1935 as Oregon State Museum of Anthropology and UO Museum of Natural History; attached to Univ. of Oregon; 1m. ethnographic and archaeological objects; 100,000 fossils and biological specimens from Oregon, the Pacific Northwest and around the world; Native American cultural and archaeological artefacts, spanning 15,000 years; incl. cache of 10,000-year-old sagebrush bark sandals, extensive fossil collns, several hundred w Indian baskets made before 1900; Dir JON ERLANDSON; publ. *University of Oregon Anthropological Papers* (irregular).

Oregon Historical Society Museum: 1200 SW Park Ave, Portland, OR 97205; tel. (503) 222-1741; e-mail orhist@ohs.org; internet www.ohs.org; f. 1898; 85,000 artefacts of local history; library of 30,000 vols, 25,000 maps, 12,000 linear ft of MSS, 4,000 serials titles, 6,000 vertical files, 16,000 rolls of microfilm, 8.5m. ft of film and video cassettes, 10,000 oral history cassettes, 2.5m. photographs; Exec. Dir KERRY TYMCHUK; Pres. Dr JERRY E. HUDSON; Sec. Dr LESLEY HALLICK; Treas. PAT RITZ; publ. *Oregon Historical Quarterly* (4 a year).

Oregon Sports Hall of Fame and Museum: 8500 SE McLoughlin Blvd, Suite 101, Portland, OR 97222; tel. (503) 227-7466; e-mail info@oregonsportshall.org; internet www.oregonsportshall.org; f. 1978; Oregon's athletic history; seminars and programmes concerning history and participation in sports; presently closed for relocation; Exec. Dir MIKE ROSE; Pres. CHUCK RICHARDS; Sec. and Treas. GREG HITCHCOCK.

Pennsylvania

Academy of Natural Sciences: 1900 Benjamin Franklin Parkway, Philadelphia, PA 19103-1195; tel. (215) 299-1000; e-mail presidentsoffice@ansp.org; internet www .ansp.org; f. 1812; attached to Drextel Univ.; 17m. specimens; collns incl. butterflies and dinosaurs; dioramas; a fusion of art and science; library of 200,000 vols; Pres. and CEO GEORGE W. GEPHART, JR; publs *Notulae Naturae* (irregular), *Proceedings of the Academy of Natural Sciences of Philadelphia*, *Special Publications*.

American Philosophical Society Museum: Richardson Hall, Second Fl., 431 Chestnut St, Philadelphia, PA 19106; Philosophical Hall, 104 S Fifth St, Philadelphia, PA 19106; tel. (215) 440-3442; e-mail museum@amphilsoc.org; internet www .apsmuseum.org; 3,000 artefacts and fine art objects of 18th century; portraits of founding fathers; models of inventions; scientific instruments owned by or relating to David Rittenhouse and other early APS members; plant specimens collected by Lewis and Clark; Benjamin Franklin's personal belongings; Dir and Curator Dr SUE ANN PRINCE.

American Swedish Historical Museum: 1900 Pattison Ave, Philadelphia, PA 19145; tel. (215) 389-1776; e-mail info@ americanswedish.org; internet www .americanswedish.org; f. 1926; contributions by Swedes and Swedish-Americans since the mid-17th century; 12 galleries dedicated to all major historical and cultural aspects of Swedish accomplishments; exhibition on New Sweden Colony (1638–1655); colln of letters, documents and designs by John Ericsson; library of 11,000 vols, primary source genealogical documents and sources; Chair. JOHN MCCANN; Exec. Dir TRACEY BECK; Curator CARRIE HOGAN.

Barnes Foundation Gallery, Collections and Arboretum: 300 N Latch's Lane, Merion, PA 19066-1729; tel. (610) 667-0290; e-mail info@barnesfoundation.org; internet www.barnesfoundation.org; f. 1922; offers courses in visual literacy and the philosophy and appreciation of art; colln of 1,000 paintings, incl. works by El Greco, Titian, Goya, Rubens, Cézanne, Renoir, Modigliani, Soutine, Picasso, Matisse and Van Gogh; sculpture, antique furniture and wrought iron; Arboretum, school with courses in botany, horticulture and landscape design; Teacher Institute with courses in visual arts and environmental and horticultural studies; library of 4,000 vols; Chair. Dr BERNARD C. WATSON; Sec. JACQUELINE F. ALLEN; Treas. STEPHEN J. HARMELIN.

Berman Museum of Art: 601 E Main St, Collegeville, PA 19426-1000; tel. (610) 409-3500; internet www.ursinus.edu/ netcommunity; f. 1989; attached to Ursinus College; 4,000 paintings, prints, drawings, sculpture, decorative and cultural objects; paper colln of 1,500 pieces of art by Durer, Rembrandt, and Cézanne; early 20th-century New York and Philadelphia School artists; Op and Pop Art compositions; paintings and prints of Francoise Gilot; colln of Pennsylvania German art and artefacts; Dir LISA TREMPER HANOVER.

Brandywine River Museum: POB 141, Chadds Ford, PA 19317; tel. (610) 388-2700; e-mail inquiries@brandywine.org; internet www.brandywinemuseum.org; f. 1971; colln of works by 3 generations of Wyeths; colln of American illustration, still life and landscape painting; library of 3,500 vols, 22,000 items, incl. portfolios and scrapbooks, films and video cassettes, sound cassettes and phonograph records, historic calendars and posters, exhibition posters and brochures,

photographs, ephemera such as clippings, tear sheets, book jackets and archival materials related to various artists; Dir JAMES H. DUFF; Curator VIRGINIA H. O'HARA.

Carnegie Museum of Art: 4400 Forbes Ave, Pittsburgh, PA 15213-4080; tel. (412) 622-3131; e-mail cma-development@ carnegiemuseums.org; internet web.cmoa .org; f. 1895; 101,477 objects; contemporary art incl. film and video works; works of American art from the late 19th century, French impressionist and post-impressionist paintings and European and American decorative arts from the late 17th century to the present; Ailsa Mellon Bruce Galleries, Heinz Architectural Center, Hall of Architecture and Hall of Sculpture; Chair. WILLIAM E. HUNT; Dir LYNN ZELEVANSKY.

Carnegie Museum of Natural History: 4400 Forbes Ave, Pittsburgh, PA 15213; tel. (412) 622-3131; e-mail cmnhweb@ carnegiemnh.org; internet www .carnegiemnh.org; f. 1896; Alcoa Foundation Hall of American Indians; Benedum Hall of Geology; Bonehunters Quarry; Botany Hall; Discovery Basecamp; Hall of African Wildlife; Hall of N American Wildlife; Hillman Hall of Minerals and Gems; Ice Age Animals; PaleoLab; Polar World: Wyckoff Hall of Arctic Life; Walton Hall of Ancient Egypt; Wertz Gallery: Gems and Jewellery; spec. colln of Dinosaurs spanning the Mesozoic era; library of 132,000 vols, 5,400 periodical titles; Dir DAVID HILLENBRAND; publ. *Annals of Carnegie Museum* (4 a year).

Carnegie Science Center: 1 Allegheny Ave, Pittsburgh, PA 15212-5850; tel. (412) 237-3400; internet www .carnegiesciencecenter.org; f. 1991; 400 interactive exhibits; 3 live demonstration theatres; 4-storey Imax dome theatre; 36,000-sq. ft sport science exhibition; planetarium; Cold War submarine moored on Pittsburgh's Ohio River; model-railway display; working foundry; replicas of modules of the International Space Station; Tesla coil and Van de Graaff generator; interactive exhibits featuring robotics, cryogenics and lasers; Co-Dir RON BAILLIE; Co-Dir ANN METZGER.

Earth and Mineral Sciences Museum and Art Gallery: 16 Deike Bldg, University Park, PA 16802-5000; tel. (814) 865-6336; e-mail museum@ems.psu.edu; internet www .ems.psu.edu/outreach/museum; attached to College of Earth and Mineral Sciences, Pennsylvania State Univ. in State College; displays minerals incl. azurite and velvet malachite from Bisbee, Arizona; amazonite crystals from the Pikes' Peak, Colorado; 22,000 specimens of fossils, rocks and minerals; collns of glasses, ceramics, metals, plastics, synthetic materials, old mining and scientific equipment and archaeological artefacts; spec. colln: 100 mine safety lamps and scientific instruments and specimens of Frederick Augustus Genth; Chair. MARK PATZKOWSKY; Dir RUSS GRAHAM.

Everhart Museum of Natural History, Science and Art: 1901 Mulberry St, Scranton, PA 18510-2390; tel. (570) 346-7186; e-mail general.information@ everhart-museum.org; internet everhart-museum.org; f. 1908; colln of historic and contemporary American paintings; colln of Dorflinger glass; American folk art; works from Native American sources, pre-Columbian and S American objects, Africa, China, Japan, India, Indonesia, Korea and Tibet; colln of rocks, fossils, minerals, plant specimens, shell coral and a wet specimen; Chair. JOSEPH T. WRIGHT; Sec. MICHELE HUGHES; Treas. KEN M. MARQUIS.

Fort Pitt Museum: Point State Park, 101 Commonwealth Pl, Pittsburgh, PA 15222; tel. (412) 281-9285; e-mail membership@ heinzhistorycenter.org; internet www .heinzhistorycenter.org; f. 1969; attached to Senator John Heinz History Center; W Pennsylvania's early history through inter-active exhibits and artefacts; life-like museum figures; W Pennsylvania's role during the French and Indian War and the American Revolution; Dir ALAN GUTCHESS.

Franklin Institute Science Museum: 222 N 20th St, Philadelphia, PA 19103; tel. (215) 448-1200; e-mail guestservices@www.fi.edu; internet www.fi.edu; f. 1824 as The Franklin Institute of the State of Pennsylvania for the Promotion of the Mechanic Arts, moved to new bldg and adopted current name in 1934; flight simulator, sky bike, planetarium, Imax Theater, 3D theatre; exhibits and demonstrations on physical sciences and technology; camps, workshops and teacher training; Pres. and CEO Dr DENNIS M. WINT; publ. *Journal.*

Frick Art & Historical Center: 7227 Reynolds St, Pittsburgh, PA 15208; tel. (412) 371-0600; e-mail info@ thefrickpittsburgh.org; internet www .thefrickpittsburgh.org; f. 1881; fine and decorative arts, cars, carriages, bldgs and other items related to the Frick family's life in Pittsburgh; works on paper by Jean-François Millet, a group of Renaissance and Baroque bronzes; colln of early Renaissance painting and 18th-century French painting and decorative art; Frick Art museum, Clayton and Car and Carriage Museum; Dir BILL BODINE; Dir of Curatorial Affairs SARAH J. HALL; Chair. DAVID A. BROWNLEE; Sec. CAROL A. WORD; Treas. MATTHEW J. TEPLITZ.

Hoyt Institute of Fine Arts: 124 E Leasure Ave, New Castle, PA 16101; tel. (724) 652-2882; e-mail hoyt@hoytartcenter.org; internet www.hoytartcenter.org; Shenango China Colln, WPA Poster Colln and Louis J. G. Buehler colln; arts classes, workshops and annual exhibits; library of 1,000 vols; Exec. Dir KIMBERLY KOLLER-JONES.

Penn Museum–University of Pennsylvania Museum of Archaeology and Anthropology: 3260 South St, Philadelphia, PA 19104; tel. (215) 898-4000; e-mail info@ museum.upenn.edu; internet www.penn .museum; f. 1887; 1m. objects from Egypt, Mesopotamia, Canaan and Israel, Mesoamerica, Asia and the ancient Mediterranean world; artefacts from native peoples of the Americas and Africa; library of 100,000 vols, archives with 300,000 photographic items and more than 600m. of textual records; Dir Dr RICHARD HODGES; Chair. MICHAEL J. KOWALSKI; publ. *Expedition* (3 a year).

Pennsylvania Academy of the Fine Arts: 118–128 N Broad St, Philadelphia, PA 19102; tel. (215) 972-7600; internet www.pafa.org; f. 1805; 19th- and 20th-century American paintings, sculptures, and works on paper; Albert M. Greenfield American Art Resource; library of 16,000 vols, 55 current periodical subscriptions, 20,000 slides; Pres. and CEO DAVID R. BRIGHAM; Sr Curator ROBERT COZZOLINO; Chair. KEVIN F. DONOHOE; Sec. HERBERT S. RIBAND, JR; Treas. THOMAS L. BENNETT.

Philadelphia History Museum: 15 S Seventh St, Philadelphia, PA 19106; tel. (215) 685-4830; e-mail info@philadelphiahistory .org; internet www.philadelphiahistory.org; f. 1938; 10,500 objects and 800 paintings by Philadelphia artists like Charles Wilson Peale and his sons; portraits of local and nat. leaders: William Penn, Benjamin Franklin, and John Quincy Adams; spec. colln incl. objects from Balch Institute of Ethnic Stud-

ies and CIGNA; Exec. Dir and CEO CHARLES CROCE; Sr Curator JEFFREY R. RAY; Pres. JAMES J. MAZZARELLI, JR; Sec. LISA YANG; Treas. GREGORY KLEIBER.

Philadelphia Museum of Art: POB 7646, Philadelphia, PA 19101-7646; tel. (215) 763-8100; e-mail mpr@philamuseum.org; internet www.philamuseum.org; f. 1876; 230,000 works of art, incl. paintings, prints, sculpture and silver from medieval to contemporary times representing European, American, and Far Eastern art; library of 200,000 vols; Chair. CONTANCE H. WILLIAMS; Dir and CEO TIMOTHY RUB; publ. *Bulletin* (irregular)

Attached Museum:

> **Rodin Museum:** POB 7646, Benjamin Franklin Parkway, 22nd St, Philadelphia, PA 19101-7646; tel. (215) 568-6026; e-mail visitorservices@philamuseum.org; internet www.rodinmuseum.org; f. 1923, present status 1939; houses 130 sculptures; Chair. BARBARA ARONSON.

Reading Public Museum: 500 Museum Rd, Reading, PA 19611-1425; tel. (610) 371-5850; e-mail museum@readingpublicmuseum.org; internet www.readingpublicmuseum.org; f. 1904, present status 1992; colln of Pennsylvania German folk art; an Egyptian mummy; 25-acre arboretum; Neag Planetarium; Dir and CEO JOHN GRAYDON SMITH; Chair. KATHLEEN KLEPPINGER; Sec. LEIGH A. RYE; Treas. SOCRATES J. GEORGEADIS.

State Museum of Pennsylvania: 300 N St, Harrisburg, PA 17120-0024; tel. (717) 787-4980; e-mail bhager@state.pa.us; internet www.statemuseumpa.org; f. 1905; 4m. objects of archaeology, community and domestic life, fine arts, paleontology and geology, industry and technology, popular culture and political history and zoology and botany; incl. planetarium; Dir DAVID W. DUNN (acting).

Suzanne H. Arnold Art Gallery: Lebanon Valley College, 101 N College Ave, Annville, PA 17003-1400; tel. (717) 867-6445; e-mail gallery@lvc.edu; internet www.lvc.edu/ gallery; attached to Lebanon Valley College; works from the 16th century to the present: medieval MSS, Renaissance prints, Japanese woodcuts, and Pop Art, as well as installations, drawings; paper colln; African and Inuit art; Dir Dr BARBARA MCNULTY.

Westmoreland Museum of American Art: 221 N Main St, Greensburg, PA 15601; tel. (724) 837-1500; e-mail info@wmuseumaa .org; internet www.wmuseumaa.org; f. 1949; 3,400 objects, incl. American and SW Pennsylvania art; Dir and CEO JUDITH HANSEN O'TOOLE; Chief Curator BARBARA L. JONES.

Widener University Art Gallery: 1 University Pl., Chester, PA 19013; tel. (610) 499-1189; internet www.widener.edu/about/ artgallery; Alfred O. Deshong Colln of 19th-and 20th-century American paintings; 19th-century European paintings; 18th- and 19th-century Asian art; colln of African and Oceanic pottery and pre-Columbian pottery from Peru; Collns Man. REBECCA M. WARDA.

Woodmere Art Museum: 9201 Germantown Ave, Philadelphia, PA 19118; tel. (215) 247-0476; e-mail education@ woodmereartmuseum.org; internet www .woodmereartmuseum.org; f. 1940; 3,000 works of art incl. paintings, antique rugs, statuary, vases and objects of art dating from the 18th and 19th centuries; 9 galleries and salons; Dir and CEO Dr WILLIAM R. VALERIO; Curator Dr MATTHEW PALCZYNSKI.

Rhode Island

Annmary Brown Memorial: 21 Brown St, Providence, RI 02912; tel. (401) 863-2942;

e-mail barbara_schulz@brown.edu; internet library.brown.edu/about/amb; f. present status 1948; attached to Brown Univ.; European and American paintings dating from 17th to 20th century; 105 swords from Cyril and Harriet Mazansky British Sword Colln; Univ. Curator ROBERT EMLEN.

David Winton Bell Gallery: List Art Center, Brown Univ., 64 College St, Providence, RI 02912; tel. (401) 863-2932; internet www .brown.edu/bellgallery; f. 1971; attached to Brown Univ.; 4,000 works of art dating from 16th century to present; Dir JO-ANN CONKLIN; Curator Dr IAN ALDEN RUSSELL.

Haffenreffer Museum of Anthropology: 21 Prospect St, POB 1965, Brown Univ., Providence, RI 02912; tel. (401) 863-5700; e-mail haffenreffermuseum@brown.edu; internet brown.edu/facilities/haffenreffer; attached to Brown Univ.; 1m. ethnographic objects, archaeological specimens and images from all parts of the world, esp. the Americas, Africa and SE Asia; Herbert Spinden Photographic Archive of 20,000 images and documents on Central American archaeology and ethnography from the early 20th century; Kensinger Colln with 5,000 photographs and notes on Cashinahua of Peru; Conti Colln with 3,000 photos from the late 1950s to early 1970s on Apache and Navaho reservations; library of 10,000 vols; Dir ROBERT PREUCEL; Chief Curator KEVIN P. SMITH.

Museum of Art, Rhode Island School of Design: 224 Benefit St, Providence, RI 02903; tel. (401) 454-6500; e-mail museum@ risd.edu; internet www.risd.edu; f. 1877; 84,000 objects, incl. 19th-century American paintings, contemporary art paintings dating since 1960; decorative arts colln: European and American decorative arts from Medieval period to present, Asian Art spanning 5,000 years; Dir JOHN W. SMITH.

Museum of Primitive Art and Culture: 1058 Kingstown Rd, Suite 5, Peace Dale, RI 02879; tel. (401) 783-5711; internet www .primitiveartmuseum.org; f. 1892; 15,000 archaeological and ethnological objects; colln incl. chopping tool from E Africa that dates to 2m. years ago, prehistoric stone artefacts from New England, Stone Age artefacts from Europe; Curator SARAH PEABODY TURNBAUGH.

National Museum of American Illustration: Vernon Court, 492 Bellevue Ave, Newport, RI 02840; tel. (401) 851-8949; e-mail art@americanillustration.org; internet www .americanillustration.org; f. 1998; housed in Vernon Court, an adaptation of an 18th-century French château built in 1898; American Imagist Colln of 2,000 original works by Maxfield Parrish, Norman Rockwell, J. C. Leyendecker, Howard Pyle, N. C. Wyeth, Charles Dana Gibson, Henry Hutt, James Montgomery Flagg, Howard Chandler Christy, John Falter; comprises original art works, prints (open and ltd edns), as well as significant memorabilia, vintage materials, artefacts (such as Rockwell's first paint box and Parrish's stippling paint brushes) and photographic materials; Chair. LAURENCE S. CUTLER; Dir JUDY GOFFMAN CUTLER.

Newport Art Museum & Art Association: 76 Bellevue Ave, Newport, RI 02840; tel. (401) 848-8200; e-mail info@ newportartmuseum.org; internet www .newportartmuseum.org; f. 1912 as Art Asscn of Newport, present bldg 1916; colln on visual arts of Newport and SE New England; dating since late 18th century; Exec. Dir ELIZABETH A. GODDARD; Curator NANCY WHIPPLE GRINNELL; Curator TARA ECENARRO.

Pettaquamscutt Historical Society Museum: Old Washington County Jail, 2636 Kingstown Rd, Kingston, RI 02881; tel. (401) 783-1328; e-mail pettaquamscutt@

yahoo.com; internet www.pettaquamscutt .org; f. 1958; colln incl. artefacts and decorative arts, MSS and furniture dating from mid-19th to mid-20th century; Pres. H. GRAHAM NYE; Sec. SANDY MCCAW; Treas. MARY KEANE; Dir LORI URSO.

South Carolina

American Military Museum: 360 Concord St, Suite 9, Charleston, SC 29401; tel. (843) 577-7000; e-mail info@ americanmilitarymuseum.org; internet www .americanmilitarymuseum.org; f. 1987; artefacts from 14 American conflicts dating from Revolutionary War to ongoing conflicts in Iraq and Afghanistan; colln incl. headgear, edged weapons, guns, rifles, patches, insignia, personal equipment, medals, decorations, belts, flags and other military artefacts from the US Army, Navy, Air Force, Marines and Coast Guard.

Anderson County Museum: 202 E Greenville St, Anderson, SC 29624; tel. (864) 260-4737; internet andersoncountymuseum.org; 20,000 diverse artefacts incl. history of Anderson co.; library of 1,600 vols, 2,000 historic photos; Curator ALISON HINMAN.

Avery Research Center for African American History and Culture: College of Charleston, 66 George St, Charleston, SC 29424; tel. (843) 953-7609; e-mail averyresearchcenter@cofc.edu; internet avery.cofc.edu; f. 1985; attached to College of Charleston; colln incl. African and African-American history; Exec. Dir PATRICIA WILLIAMS-LESSANE.

Bob Campbell Geology Museum: 140 Discovery Lane, Clemson, SC 29634-0130; tel. (864) 656-4600; e-mail bcgm@clemson .edu; internet www.clemson.edu/public/ geomuseum; f. 1998; attached to Clemson Univ.; colln incl. 10,000 rocks, minerals, fossils, carvings, gemstones and artefacts such as Native American tools; Dir Dr PATRICK MCMILAN.

Bob Jones University Museum and Gallery: 1700 Wade Hampton Blvd, Greenville, SC 29614; tel. (864) 770-1331; e-mail contact@bjumg.org; internet bjumg.org; f. 1948; European old master paintings in America dating from 14th to 19th century; Russian Icon colln dating from 14th to 20th century; 200 pieces of Gothic to 19th century furniture; 1,000 ancient artefacts; educational satellite facility at Heritage Green.

Charleston Museum: 360 Meeting St, Charleston, SC 29403; tel. (843) 722-2996; e-mail info@charlestonmuseum.org; internet www.charlestonmuseum.org; f. 1773; colln incl. weaponry dating from 18th to 20th century, civil war artefacts and silver artefacts dating from colonial era to Victorian age; Heyward-Washington House, Joseph Manigault House, Dill Sanctuary; Pres. Dr JOHN RASHFORD; Dir Dr JOHN R. BRUMGARDT.

Cherokee County History & Arts Museum: Cherokee Historical and Preservation Society Inc., POB 8113, 301 College Dr., Gaffney, SC 29340; tel. (864) 489-3988; e-mail chaps@cherokeecountyhistory.org; internet www.cherokeecountyhistory.org; f. 2008; 2,000 exhibits on Native Americans, American revolution and geology.

Columbia Museum of Art: POB 2068, 1515 Main St, Columbia, SC 29202; tel. (803) 799-2810; internet www.columbiamuseum.org; f. 1950; 6,000 objects incl. European and American fine and decorative art spanning centuries, Asian art and antiquities; Exec. Dir KAREN BROSIUS; Chief Curator WILL SOUTH.

Florence Museum of Art, Science and History: 558 Spruce St, Florence, SC 29501; tel. (843) 662-3351; e-mail florencemuseum@ me.com; internet www.florencemuseum.org; African colln: weaponry, tools and vessels from tribal cultures; Civil War colln: 1,000 items incl. uniforms, battle swords and guns; antiques from Mesopotamia, ancient Egypt, Babylonia, ancient Greece and Rome; Exec. Dir ANDREW R. STOUT.

Gibbes Museum of Art: 135 Meeting St, Charleston, SC 29401; tel. (843) 722-2706; e-mail research@gibbesmuseum.org; internet www.gibbesmuseum.org; f. 1905 as Gibbes Memorial Art Gallery; 10,000 works of fine art, mainly American works with a Charleston or Southern connection; 18th-, 19th- and early 20th-century paintings, works on paper (prints, drawings, watercolours, photographs), miniature portraits and sculpture; Exec. Dir and Chief Curator ANGELA D. MACK.

Greenville County Museum of Art: 420 College St, Greenville, SC 29601; tel. (864) 271-7570; e-mail info@greenvillemuseum .org; internet www.greenvillemuseum.org; Southern colln of American art dating from colonial times to present; portraits from the 1700s and art from 19th and 20th centuries; contemporary art colln incl. features artists such as Josef Albers, Jasper Johns and Andy Warhol; Dir THOMAS W. STYRON.

McKissick Museum: 816 Bull St, Columbia, SC 29208; tel. (803) 777-7251; e-mail mckscal@mailbox.sc.edu; internet www.cas .sc.edu/mcks; f. 1976; attached to College of Arts and Sciences, Univ. of South Carolina; collns dating to 1801 incl. natural science specimens, traditional and contemporary crafts, textiles, political memorabilia, fine and decorative arts, art glass and material culture objects; Exec. Dir Dr JANE PRZYBYSZ.

Slave Relics Museum: 208 Carn St, Walterboro, SC 29488; tel. (843) 549-9130; e-mail info@slaverelics.org; internet www .slaverelics.org; colln incl. historical artefacts, documents, photographs and memorabilia on African American culture; artefacts used by enslaved Africans dating from 1750 to mid-1800s; Curator and Pres. DANNY DRAIN.

South Carolina Confederate Relic Room & Military Museum: 301 Gervais St, Columbia, SC 29201; tel. (803) 737-8095; internet www.crr.sc.gov; f. 1896, present status 1998; attached to South Carolina Budget and Control Board; military history museum of state; colln of military material of Revolutionary War, Mexican War, Civil War, Spanish-American War, First World War and Second World War; colln incl. images of troops stationed on Mexican Border in 1916, crew of Second World War light cruiser and USS Columbia CL-56; Dir ALLEN ROBERSON.

South Carolina State Museum: 301 Gervais St, Columbia, SC 29201; tel. (803) 898-4921; e-mail publicrelations@scmuseum.org; internet www.southcarolinastatemuseum .org; f. 1988; 70,000 artefacts; art, cultural history, natural history, science and technology; Stringer Discovery Center; travelling exhibits; Exec. Dir WILLIAM CALLOWAY.

South Dakota

Dacotah Prairie Museum: POB 395, Aberdeen, SD 57402-0395; 21 S Main St, Aberdeen, SD 57401; tel. (605) 626-7117; e-mail dpm@brown.sd.us; internet www .dacotahprairiemuseum.com; f. 1938 as Northern South Dakota History Museum, present name and status 1970; colln of 40,000 artefacts; works of local and regional artists; 55 mounted specimens from N America, Africa and India; Dir SUE GATES; Pres. NINA VILHAUER; Sec. JACIE SCHLEY.

Dakota Discovery Museum: 1300 McGovern Ave, Mitchell, SD 57301; tel. (605) 996-2122; e-mail info@dakotadiscovery.com; internet dakotadiscovery.com; f. 1939; sculptures of Merriwether Lewis and William Clark by James Earle Fraser; historic village complex; American Indian beadwork and porcupine quillwork incl. clothing, bags, ceremonial regalia, utilitarian objects, horse gear, dolls and missionary items; exhibit incl. Plains Indians, Fur Trade, Dakota Territory, Railroading, Farming and Ranching, 1930s Great Depression; Exec. Dir and Curator LORI HOLMBERG.

Deadwood's Adams Museum: 54 Sherman St, Deadwood, SD 57732; tel. (605) 578-1714; internet adamsmuseumandhouse.org/ adamsmuseum.php; f. 1930; artefacts, folk art colln, Lakota bead and quill work, Potato Creek Johnny's gold nugget, historic photographs and maps rep. of art and natural history of the Black Hills and Wild Bill, Calamity Jane and Deadwood Dick; Chair. Dr DAVID WOLFF; Sec. and Treas. CARLA CANEVA; Curator ARLETTE HANSEN.

Heritage Center: c/o Red Cloud Indian School, 100 Mission Dr., Pine Ridge, SD 57770; tel. (605) 867-8257; e-mail heritagecenter@redcloudschool.org; internet www.redcloudschool.org/museum; f. 1982 as museum; attached to Red Cloud Indian School; Native American fine arts and Lakota tribal arts and history; 2,000 paintings, drawings and sculptures; Dir PETER STRONG; Curator MARY BORDEAUX.

Journey Museum: 222 New York St, Rapid City, SD 57701; tel. (605) 394-6923; internet www.journeymuseum.org; incl. Museum of Geology on campus of the S Dakota School of Mines and Technology, S Dakota Historical Soc.'s Archeology Research Center, US Dept of Interior, Indian Arts and Craft Board's Sioux Indian Museum, Minnilusa Historical Asscn and City of Rapid City Duhamel Plains Indian Artifact Colln; colln of archaeology, geology, paleontology, space science, Sioux Indian Museum, W Native gardens and Duhamel Colln of Native American artefacts; Exec. Dir RAY SUMMERS.

Museum of the South Dakota State Historical Society: South Dakota Cultural Heritage Center, 900 Governors Dr., Pierre, SD 57501-2217; tel. (605) 773-3458; internet history.sd.gov/museum; f. 1901; attached to SD Dept of Tourism; 3 galleries of local history; travelling exhibitions; 29,000 artefacts; colln of Lakota materials and internationally significant objects that document European arrival on N plains; military colln; Dir JAY S. SMITH; Pres. BRAD TENNANT; Curator of Collns DANIEL BROSZ; Curator of Exhibits KATHRYN VANDEL; Curator of Interpretation RONETTE RUMPCA; publs *Hoofprints* (6 a year), *South Dakota History* (4 a year).

National Music Museum: c/o Univ. of South Dakota, 414 E Clark St, Vermillion, SD 57069; tel. (605) 677-5306; e-mail nmm@ usd.edu; internet orgs.usd.edu/nmm; f. 1973; attached to Univ. of South Dakota; 15,000 American, European and non-Western instruments; 2 18th-century grand pianos; 500 instruments made in late 19th and early 20th centuries; brass, woodwind and stringed instruments by 17th- and 18th-century Nürnberg craftsmen, incl. mems of the Haas and Oberlender families, Ernst Busch, Paul Hainlein and Jacob Denner; 17th- and 18th-century Dutch woodwind instruments by Richard Haka, Hendrik Richters, Philip Borkens and Abraham van Aardenberg; Witten-Rawlins Colln of early Italian stringed instruments; library of 5,000 vols, 20,000 periodicals; Exec. Dir Dr MARGARET DOWNIE BANKS; Chair. TOM LILLIBRIDGE; Sec. MARILYN NYBERG; Treas. JACK POWELL.

Pioneer Museum: POB 361, Hot Springs, SD 57747; 301 N Chicago St, Hot Springs, SD 57747; tel. (605) 745-5147; e-mail pioneer@pioneer-museum.com; internet www.pioneer-museum.com; f. 1961 as elementary school; attached to Fall River County Historical Soc.; 600 historical pieces of art by local artists, incl. paintings and sculpted sandstone, alabaster, marble pieces, historic photographs, tapestries and quilts; handcrafted tools, old washing machines, wood cook stoves and kerosene lamps; replica of 19th-century classroom and country store; Man. WANDA AABURG; Pres. JIM BINGHAM; Sec. CAROL SIDES; Treas. JOHN PENCE.

South Dakota Agricultural Heritage Museum: c/o South Dakota State Univ., 925 11th St, POB 601, Brookings, SD 57007; tel. (605) 688-6226; e-mail sdsu.agmuseum@sdstate.edu; internet www.sdstate.edu/agmuseum; attached to South Dakota State Univ.; exhibits incl. tractors and farm equipment, 1882 homestead claim shack, recreated 1915 farmhouse and historic photographs on S Dakota history, agricultural technology and rural life; Eugene Beckman Archive: original sales brochures, operators manuals, parts lists and sales premiums dating from the 1880s through the early 1960s; Dir MAC HARRIS.

South Dakota Art Museum: Medary Ave and Harvey Dunn St, POB 2250, Brookings, SD 57007; tel. (605) 688-5423; e-mail sdsu_sdam@sdstate.edu; internet www.sdstate.edu/southdakotaartmuseum; f. 1970; attached to South Dakota State Univ.; collns incl. paintings by Harvey Dunn, Native American Art (incl. clothing, quillwork, moccasins, headdresses, bags, beadwork, pipes, pottery, baskets and tools from N American Plains; pottery, jewellery and rugs from SW and baskets and carvings from NW Coast of N America), Marghab Linens of 1930s–70s, Paul Goble, Native American works by Oscar Howe; photographs, paintings, sculptures, ceramics, prints and textiles of South Dakota artists; temporary exhibitions; Dir LYNN VERSHOOR; Pres. MARILYN DeLONG; Sec. MAREE LARSON; Treas. JACK STENGEL.

University Art Galleries: c/o Univ. of South Dakota, 414 E Clark St, Vermillion, SD 57069; tel. (605) 677-3177; e-mail uag@usd.edu; internet www.usd.edu/uag; f. 1977; attached to Univ. of South Dakota; 1,600 pieces esp. of S Dakota artists, contemporary art, Northern Plains American Indian Art, Asian and African study collns; colln of Oscar Howe paintings; Dir ALISON ERAZMUS.

W. H. Over Museum of Natural and Cultural History: 1110 University St, Vermillion, SD 57069; tel. (605) 677-5228; e-mail whover@usd.edu; internet www.whovermuseum.org; f. 1912, present name 1949; attached to Univ. of South Dakota; colln of natural history materials of the state and region; Sioux artefacts, historic photographic portraits of legendary leaders and daily life of the tribes of the upper Missouri river; 500 stereographic cards of Stanley J. Morrow's photographs about the Indians, the US Army, the river trade and booming mining towns during the post-Civil War period; 182 mems; Pres. MAXINE JOHNSON; Sec. Dr HOWARD COKER; Treas. ROYCE MILLER.

Tennessee

American Museum of Science and Energy: 300 S Tulane Ave, Oak Ridge, TN 37830; tel. (865) 576-3200; e-mail information@amse.org; internet www.amse.org; f. 1949 as American Museum of Atomic Energy, present location 1975, present name 1978; attached to US Dept of Energy; operated by Enterprise Advisory Services, Inc.;

one of the world's largest energy exhibitions, with live demonstrations, computers and films on all energy forms and uses; Dir JAMES COMISH; Deputy Dir KEN MAYES.

Art Museum of University of Memphis (AMUM): 142 CFA Bldg, Memphis, TN 38152-3200; tel. (901) 678-2224; e-mail artmuseum@memphis.edu; internet www.memphis.edu/amum; f. 1981 as Univ. Gallery, present name and status 1994; attached to College of Communication and Fine Arts; Egyptian antiquities, 180 objects of Sub-Saharan African art, 1,000 works on paper; cultural artefacts incl. Japanese armour, flintlock duelling pistols, Ethiopian spear points, Navaho textiles and ancient Greco-Roman glass; Dir LESLIE LUEBBERS.

Beechcraft Heritage Museum: POB 550, 570 Old Shelbyville Highway, Tullahoma, TN 37388; tel. (931) 455-1974; e-mail info@beechcraftheritagemuseum.org; internet www.beechcraftheritagemuseum.org; f. 1973 Staggerwing Museum Foundation, present name 2007; aviation museum tracing lineage of Beechcraft airplanes; 30 airplane models, aviation artefacts and memorabilia.

Belz Museum of Asian & Judaic Art: 119 S Main St, Concourse Level, Memphis, TN 38103; tel. (901) 523-2787; e-mail info@belzmuseum.org; internet www.belzmuseum.org; f. 1998 as Peabody Place Museum; Asian art colln: 900 objects dating from 202BC to early 20th century incl. jades, ivories, sculptures, paintings, ceramics and textiles; colln of Judaica, Russian lacquer boxes, contemporary glass, Italian mosaics and mineral specimens; Dir BELINDA D. FISH; Chair and CEO JACK BELZ.

Cowan Railroad Museum: POB 53, 108 Front St, Cowan, TN 37318-0053; tel. (931) 967-3078; e-mail secretary@cowanrailroadmuseum.org; internet www.cowanrailroadmuseum.org; f. 1976; colln of 1000 historic railroad and Cowan city artefacts, period costumes, photographs, tools, documents, old maps and out-of-print railroad books; Pres. MARK LEDBETTER; Sec. MARYANN KNOWLES; Treas. DAVID ELLENBURG.

Dixon Gallery & Gardens: 4339 Park Ave, Memphis, TN 38117; tel. (901) 761-5250; internet www.dixon.org; f. 1976; 2,000 objects incl. French and American Impressionist paintings and significant holdings of German and English porcelain; Chair. STEPHEN C. REYNOLDS; Pres. D. STEPHEN MORROW; Sec. CHRISTINE P. RICHARDS; Treas. WILLIAM C. LOSCH; Dir KEVIN SHARP.

Frank H. McClung Museum of Natural History and Culture: Univ. of Tennessee, 1327 Circle Park Dr., Knoxville, TN 37996-3200; tel. (865) 974-2144; e-mail museum@utk.edu; internet mcclungmuseum.utk.edu; f. 1963; attached to Univ. of Tennessee; colln in anthropology, archaeology, decorative arts, local history and natural history; Dir JEFFERSON CHAPMAN.

Hunter Museum of American Art: 10 Bluff View, Chattanooga, TN 37403; tel. (423) 267-0968; internet www.huntermuseum.org; f. 1952 as George Thomas Hunter Gallery of Art, present name 1975; American art from Colonial period to present; colln incl. paintings, works on paper, sculpture, furniture and contemporary studio glass; Chair. NORMA P. MILLS; Sec. MARK A. RAMSEY; Treas. CRAIG HOLLEY; Exec. Dir DANIEL E. STETSON; Chief Curator ELLEN SIMAK.

Knoxville Museum of Art: 1050 World's Fair Park, Knoxville, TN 37916-1653; tel. (865) 525-6101; e-mail info@knoxart.org; internet www.knoxart.org; f. 1961, fmrly Dulin Gallery of Art, present location 1990; coll incl. 700 objects representing 20th- and

21st-century works on paper, paintings, mixed media works, sculpture and fine craft; Chair. JAY MCBRIDE; Exec. Dir DAVID L. BUTLER.

McMinn County Living Heritage Museum: POB 889, Athens, TN 37371; 522 W Madison Ave, Athens, TN 37303; tel. (423) 745-0329; internet www.livingheritagemuseum.com; colln of 7,000 artefacts on culture and history of SE Tennessee region from first settlers in the mid-1700s to the 1940s; Pres. LAURIE POWELL; Sec. BARRY WILLIS; Treas. TOM BIDDLE; Exec. Dir ASHLEY RUSH.

Memphis Brooks Museum of Art: 1934 Poplar Ave, Memphis, TN 38104; tel. (901) 544-6200; internet www.brooksmuseum.org; f. 1916 as Brooks Memorial Art Gallery, present name 1983, present status 1989; 8,500 works of art incl. Italian Renaissance and Baroque, British, French Impressionists and 20th-century artists; 19th- and 20th-century sculpture and decorative arts, incl. period furniture and textiles; ancient Greek and Mediterranean art; library of 5,000 vols; Pres. W. MARK PARKER; Sec. NATHAN A. BICKS; Dir CAMERON KITCHIN.

Reece Museum: POB 70660, East Tennessee State Univ., Johnson City, TN 37614-1701; tel. (423) 439-4392; e-mail reecemus@etsu.edu; internet www.etsu.edu/cass/reece; f. 1961; attached to East Tennessee State Univ.; colln on regional art and history; Civil War artefacts; Native American colln incl. stone axes; Dir THERESA BURCHETT.

Tennessee Museum of Aviation: POB 5587, Sevierville, TN 37864-5587; 135 Air Museum Way, Sevierville, TN 37862; tel. (865) 908-0171; e-mail info@tnairmuseum.com; internet www.tnairmuseum.com; f. 2001; exhibits tracing timeline of military aviation history and Tennessee aviation history; CEO and Chair. R. NEAL MELTON.

Tennessee State Museum: 505 Deaderick St, Nashville, TN 37243-1120; tel. (615) 741-2692; e-mail museuminfo@tnmuseum.org; internet www.tnmuseum.org; f. 1817; artefacts from Paleolithic, Archaic, Woodland and Mississippian periods; 15,000 years-old mastodon bones; 3,000 years old early ceremonial pottery; Civil War artefacts incl. uniforms, battle flags and weapons; Exec. Dir LOIS RIGGINS-EZZELL; Chief Curator DAN POMEROY.

West Tennessee Regional Art Center: 1200 Main St, Humboldt, TN 38343; tel. (731) 784-1787; internet www.wtrac.tn.org; f. 1994; Caldwell Colln: sculpture, watercolor paintings, drawings, prints and lithographs, pastels and silk-screens; Chair. CHARLES GUY; Sec. LOIS CURRIE; Treas. CAROLYN BARNETT; Curator BILL HICKERSON.

Texas

Amarillo Museum of Art: POB 447, Amarillo, TX 79178; 2200 S Van Buren St, Amarillo, TX 79109-2407; tel. (806) 371-5050; e-mail amoa@actx.edu; internet www.amarilloart.org; f. 1967; Asian art colln incl. rep. textiles from Middle East with examples from 8th to 20th century; early American modernist paintings; European paintings from 17th to 19th century; S and SE Asian sculpture incl. Buddhist and Hindu objects dating from 2nd century BC Gandharan works to 9th-century Java and 14th-century Khmer sculpture; Pres. SHERI BROSIER; Sec. MIKE LADD; Treas. RICHARD WALTON; Dir KIM MAHAN.

Amon Carter Museum of American Art: 3501 Camp Bowie Blvd, Fort Worth, TX 76107-2695; tel. (817) 738-1933; e-mail visitors@cartermuseum.org; internet www.cartermuseum.org; f. 1961; American paintings from 19th and 20th centuries; 100 sculptures by artists incl. Frederic Remington and Charles M. Russell; 5,700 prints from lithographs of Mexican War; library of 150,000 vols; Dir ANDREW J. WALKER.

Art Museum of Southeast Texas: 500 Main St, Beaumont, TX 77701; tel. (409) 832-3432; e-mail info@amset.org; internet www.amset.org; f. 1950 as Beaumont Art Museum, inc. 1950, present name and location 1987; 1,000 art works of modern and contemporary American art focusing on Texas and contemporary folk art (dating from 19th to 21st century); Exec. Dir LYNN CASTLE; Pres. J. MITCHELL SMITH; Sec. CARLA ALLEN; Treas. RUSS WADDILL.

Blanton Museum of Art: Univ. of Texas at Austin, 1 University Station D1303, Austin, TX 78712; Univ. of Texas at Austin, 200 E MLK, Austin, TX 78701; tel. (512) 471-7324; e-mail info@blantonmuseum.org; internet www.blantonmuseum.org; f. 1963 as Univ. Art Museum, present name 1997; attached to Univ. of Texas at Austin; 17,000 objects incl. 300 European paintings, predominantly Italian Renaissance and Baroque; American art colln incl. 4,000 paintings, prints, drawings and sculptures dating from 1875 to present; 2,000 works of Latin American art; Dir SIMONE J. WICHA; Chair. JUDY TATE.

Dallas Museum of Art: 1717 N Harwood, Dallas, TX 75201; tel. (214) 922-1200; e-mail mediarelations@dallasmuseumofart.org; internet www.dallasmuseumofart.org; f. 1903, present location 1984; more than 23,000 works of art from around the world; arts of Africa, Asia and Pacific; Indonesian textiles; architectural and shrine objects from S Asia; Egyptian antiquities; contemporary art since 1945; American art from pre-Columbian times to the mid-20th century; 19th-century and early modern European paintings and sculpture; N American and European decorative arts; Wendy and Emery Reves Colln, Faith and Charles Bybee Colln of American Furniture; prints, drawings, photographs; art works from c. 3000BC to the fall of the Roman Empire; library: reference library of 65,000 vols, spec. collns: ethnography, artists' files; Chair. DEEDIE ROSE; Dir MAXWELL L. ANDERSON; Pres. JOHN R. EAGLE; Sec. ANN V. HOBSON; Treas. VICTOR D. ALMEIDA.

Dishman Art Museum: POB 10027, Lamar Univ., Beaumont, TX 77710; tel. (409) 880-8959; internet dept.lamar.edu/cofac/deptart/dishman.asp; f. 1983; attached to Lamar Univ.; colln incl. 50 prints from European and American artists of late 19th and early 20th centuries; 19th-century African masks and ceramic vessels and figures from Mexico; Dir Dr JESSICA DANDONA.

Ellen Noël Art Museum of the Permian Basin: 4909 University Blvd, Odessa, TX 79762; tel. (432) 550-9696; internet www.noelartmuseum.org; f. 1985 as Art Institute for the Permian Basin, present name 1995; American art dating since 1860; 800 art works incl. paintings, sculptures, ceramics, glass, works on paper and photography; Exec. Dir LES REKER.

El Paso Museum of Art: One Arts Festival Plaza, El Paso, TX 79901; tel. (915) 532-1707; e-mail arts@elpasotexas.gov; internet www.elpasoartmuseum.org; f. 1959; 5,000 works of art incl. 12th–18th-century European art; 2,500 works on paper dating from 16th to 20th century; contemporary art focusing on SW region; American art dating from early 19th century to 20th century; Dir Dr MICHAEL A. TOMOR; Sr Curator Dr PATRICK SHAW CABLE.

Hall of State: c/o Dallas Historical Soc., POB 150038, Dallas, TX 75315-0038; 3939 Grand Ave, Dallas, TX 75210; tel. (214) 421-4500; internet www.dallashistory.org; f. 1936; attached to Dallas Historical Soc. (see Learned Societies); museum and archives of Texas and Dallas history; colln incl. 3,000,000 historic documents, 30,000 historic photographs, 10,000 garments; library of 14,000 vols, 15,000 museum artefacts and 3m. archival items; Exec. Dir JACK BUNNING; Dir JACK BUNNING; Collns Man. ALAN OLSON.

Kimbell Art Museum: 3333 Camp Bowie Blvd, Fort Worth, TX 76107-2792; tel. (817) 332-8451; e-mail curators@kimbellmuseum .org; internet www.kimbellart.org; f. 1972; colln of 350 works of art incl. Asian, European, African, pre-Columbian and Oceanic art dating from 3BC to mid-20th century; Dir ERIC M. LEE.

Longview Museum of Fine Arts: POB 3484, Longview, TX 75606; 215 E Tyler St., Downtown, Longview, TX 75606; tel. (903) 753-8103; e-mail fineart@lmfa.org; internet www.lmfa.org; f. 1958; 300 pieces of artwork incl. drawings, paintings, photographs, pottery, prints, sculpture, woodblock and paper works; Dir RENEE HAWKINS.

McNay Art Museum: 6000 N New Braunfels, POB 6069, San Antonio, TX 78209-0069; 6000 N New Braunfels, San Antonio, TX 78209; tel. (210) 824-5368; e-mail info@ mcnayart.org; internet www.mcnayart.org; f. 1950; Medieval and Renaissance art colln incl. paintings, fragments of altarpieces and portraits; 19th- and 20th-century European and American paintings and sculptures; 19th- and 20th-century French, American and Mexican prints and drawings; 2,000 rare books; Chair. TOM FROST; Pres. JOAN BUZZINI HURD; Sec. SARAH E. HARTE; Treas. BILL MCCARTNEY; Dir WILLIAM J. CHIEGO; Chief Curator RENE P. BARILLEAUX.

Meadows Museum: 5900 Bishop, Southern Methodist Univ., Dallas, TX 75205-0357; tel. (214) 768-2516; e-mail meadows@smu.edu; internet smu.edu/meadowsmuseum; f. 1962; attached to Southern Methodist Univ.; modern works by Picasso and Juan Gris; Renaissance altarpieces, monumental Baroque canvases, exquisite Rococo oil sketches, polychrome wood sculptures, Impressionist landscapes, modernist abstractions; Dir Dr MARK ROGLÁN.

Menil Collection: 1515 Sul Ross St, Houston, TX 77006; tel. (713) 525-9400; e-mail info@menil.org; internet www.menil.org; f. 1987; 16,000 paintings, sculptures, decorative objects, prints, drawings, photographs and rare books; library of 30,000 vols; Chair. LOUISA STUDE SAROFIM; Pres. HARRY C. PINSON; Sec. ADELAIDE DE MENIL CARPENTER; Dir JOSEF HELFENSTEIN.

Modern Art Museum of Fort Worth: 3200 Darnell St, Fort Worth, TX 76107; tel. (817) 738-9215; e-mail info@themodern.org; internet www.themodern.org; f. 1892; colln incl. 2,600 works of modern and contemporary int. art; Curator ANDREA KARNES.

Museum of Fine Arts Houston: 1001 Bissonnet St, Houston, TX 77005; tel. (713) 639-7300; e-mail guestservices@mfah.org; internet www.mfah.org; f. 1900; 63,000 artworks; art of the ancient world; European painting and sculpture; Far Eastern art; art of Africa, Oceania and the Americas; decorative arts; prints and drawings; film and video; modern art; photography; textiles and costume; 2 major museum bldgs, the Caroline Wiess Law Bldg and the Audrey Jones Beck Bldg; 2 facilities for the Glassell School of Art, the Studio School for Adults and the Glassell Jr School; 2 house museums that exhibit decorative arts, Bayou Bend Colln and Gardens and Rienzi; the Lillie and Hugh Roy Cullen Sculpture Garden; 18 acres of public gardens; library of 146,000 vols, 83,000 slides; Chair. MEREDITH J. LONG; Dir GWENDOLYN H. GOFFE; publ. *MFA Today* (6 a year).

San Angelo Museum of Fine Arts: 1 Love St, San Angelo, TX 76903; tel. (325) 653-3333; e-mail museum@samfa.org; internet www.samfa.org; f. 1981; 276 objects of American crafts since 1945, ceramic arts, Mexican and Mexican-American art of all eras and contemporary American ceramics; Dir HOWARD TAYLOR.

San Antonio Museum of Art: 200 W Jones Ave, San Antonio, TX 78215; tel. (210) 978-8100; e-mail info@samuseum.org; internet www.samuseum.org; f. 1981; colln incl. 17th–20th-century European art, Greek and Roman sculptures; contemporary colln incl. works of 20th century and 500 Asian objects; Latin American colln from Pre-Columbian to contemporary times; Dir Dr KATIE LUBER.

San Jacinto Museum of History: 1 Monument Circle, La Porte (Houston), TX 77571-9585; tel. (281) 479-2421; e-mail sjm@ sanjacinto-museum.org; internet www .sanjacinto-museum.org; f. 1939; attached to San Jacinto Museum of History Asscn and Texas State Parks and Wildlife Comm.; 17,000 items and 220 m of MSS from TX, New Spain, US and Mexico; documents since the 15th century; colln of Mayan, Aztec and Mexican artefacts; exhibits history of Texas region from 1519 to 1900; library of 30,000 vols, 250,000 documents and MSS; Chair. ROBERT B. HIXON; Pres. LARRY SPASIC; Dir J. C. MARTIN; Curator ELIZABETH APPLEBY.

Stark Museum of Art: 712 Green Ave, Orange, TX 77630-5721; tel. (409) 886-2787; e-mail info@starkmuseum.org; internet www .starkmuseum.org; f. 1978; colln incl. 19th- and 20th-century W American art and artefacts; decorative arts incl. glass and porcelain; rare books and MSS; Man. Dir Dr SARAH E. BOEHME.

Strake Jesuit Art Museum: 8900 Bellaire Blvd, Houston, TX 77036-4699; tel. (713) 490-8117; internet www.strakejesuit.org; f. 1996; attached to Strake Jesuit College Preparatory; 300 artworks incl. Egyptian antiquity and Mayan culture; Registrar PAM HOWARD.

Texas Memorial Museum: 2400 Trinity St, Austin, TX 78705; tel. (512) 471-1604; internet www.utexas.edu/tmm; f. 1936; attached to Univ. of Texas; natural history of Texas, the Southwest and Latin America, minerals, dinosaurs, fossils, palaeontology, vertebrate and invertebrate zoology, geology, entomology; Dir EDWARD C. THERIOT; publ. *Pearce-Sellards Series*.

Trammell & Margaret Crow Collection of Asian Art: 2010 Flora St, Dallas, TX 75201; tel. (214) 979-6430; internet www .crowcollection.org; f. 1998; colln incl. pieces from China, Japan, India and SE Asia spanning 3500BC to early 20th century; Dir AMY LEWIS HOFLAND; Curator Dr CARON SMITH.

Tyler Museum of Art: 1300 S Mahon Ave, Tyler, TX 75701; tel. (903) 595-1001; e-mail info@tylermuseum.org; internet www .tylermuseum.org; f. 1971; colln incl. 1,500 paintings, prints, photographs and sculpture; works by early and contemporary Texas artists; Dir KIMBERLEY BUSH TOMIO.

Utah

BYU Museum of Art: BYU Museum of Art, N Campus Dr., Provo, UT 84602; tel. (801) 422-8287; e-mail moa@byu.edu; internet cfacweb.byu.edu/departments/moa; attached to BYU College of Fine Arts and Communication, Brigham Young Univ.; 17,000 objects: on American art from the late 18th century to the present, incl. painting, photography, prints and sculpture; Hudson River School landscape paintings and American impressionism.

BYU Museum of Paleontology: 1683 N Canyon Rd, Provo, UT 84602-3300; tel. (801) 422-3680; internet cpms.byu.edu/esm; f. 1976; attached to Brigham Young Univ.; fossil vertebrate colln of over 17,000 specimens incl. Devonian fish (380m. years ago), Pleistocene mammoths and cave fossils (15,000 years ago), and dinosaurs from the Intermountain W; Curator and Man. Dr RODNEY D. SCHEETZ.

Chase Home Museum of Utah Folk Arts: 900 S 600E, Liberty Park, Salt Lake City, UT 84105-1519; tel. (801) 236-7548; state-owned colln of contemporary folk art; Ethnic Folk Arts Gallery, Native American Gallery, Occupational Folk Arts Gallery, Rural Folk Arts Gallery.

Orem Heritage Museum: SCERA Center for the Arts, 745 S State St, Second Fl., Orem, UT 84058; internet www.scera.org; f. 1933; attached to SCERA Center for the Arts; 30,000 artefacts depicting history of Orem; Pres. and CEO ADAM J. ROBERTSON.

USU Eastern Prehistoric Museum: 451 E 400N, Price, UT 84501; 155 E Main St, Price, UT; tel. (435) 613-5060; e-mail castlecountryvisitorinfo@gmail.com; internet www.ceu.edu/museum; f. 1961 as Carbon College Prehistoric Museum; attached to College of Eastern Utah, Utah State Univ.; colln of prehistoric artefacts; Museum Dir KEN CARPENTER; Chair. KEN FLECK.

Utah Museum of Fine Arts: Marcia and John Price Museum Bldg, 410 Campus Center Dr., Salt Lake City, UT 84112-0350; tel. (801) 581-7332; internet umfa.utah.edu; f. 1951; attached to Univ. of Utah; 18,000 original objects of African art, American art, American Indian art, ancient Greek and Roman art, art of the Pacific Islands, Austrian art, Cambodian art, Chinese art, decorative arts, Dutch art, Egyptian art, English art, Flemish art, French art, German art, Italian art, Japanese art, Nazi-era provenance research project, Pre-Columbian art, Scottish art, Spanish art, Thai art; Exec. Dir GRETCHEN DIETRICH.

Vermont

Bennington Museum: 75 Main St, Bennington, VT 05201-2885; tel. (802) 447-1571; e-mail info@benningtonmuseum.org; internet www.benningtonmuseum.org; f. 1852, present name and status 1954; colln incl. paintings and sculptures by Vermont artists, maps, books and military artefacts; artefacts dating from early 18th century to present; library of 8,000 vols; Chair. RAYMOND BOLTON; Sec. PATRICIA GUERERRO; Treas. LARAINE SMITH.

Dorset Historical Society: POB 52, Route 30, Kent Hill Rd, Dorset, VT 05251; tel. (802) 867-0331; e-mail info@dorsetvthistory.org; internet dorsetvthistory.org/museum; colln incl. Republic of Vermont coins dating 1785-1788 and iron tools dating 19th century; Pres. DICK HITTLE; Sec. RUTH STEWART; Treas. AL ECKHARDT; Curator JON MATHEWSON.

Fairbanks Museum and Planetarium: 1302 Main St, Saint Johnsbury, VT 05819; tel. (802) 748-2372; internet www .fairbanksmuseum.org; f. 1889; colln of 1,75,000 objects incl. 75,000 natural history specimens, 95,000 historical artefacts and 5,000 ethnological items representing Oceania, Africa, Egypt, Japan and native N America; archives colln incl. Civil War records, photographic materials, personal papers and institutional records; historical colln incl. 19th century agricultural, industrial and household objects; museum incl.

planetarium; Chair. ARTHUR S. BROOKS; Exec. Dir CHARLES C. BROWNE.

Henry Sheldon Museum of Vermont History: 1 Park St, Middlebury, VT 05753-1334; tel. (802) 388-2117; e-mail info@ henrysheldonmuseum.org; internet www .henrysheldonmuseum.org; f. 1882; colln on Vermont's furniture, paintings, documents and artefacts; colln incl. portraits, paintings, household objects; personal artefacts; textiles and clothing; Assoc. Dir MARY MANLEY.

Lake Champlain Maritime Museum: 4472 Basin Harbor Rd, Vergennes, VT 05491; tel. (802) 475-2022; e-mail info@ lcmm.org; internet www.lcmm.org; f. 1985; colln incl. original small watercraft built over last 150 years; shipwrecks and recovered artefacts; Chair. DARCEY HALE; Sec. FRANCES FOSTER; Treas. GARY FARRELL; Exec. Dir ARTHUR B. COHN.

Middlebury College Museum of Art: Mahaney Center for Arts, Route 30, Middlebury, VT 05753; tel. (802) 443-5007; internet museum.middlebury.edu; f. 1968 as Johnson Gallery, present name 1992; 2,500 works spanning from 4BC to the present; Asian art, American and European paintings and sculptures dating from Renaissance to 19th century; Asian art, antiques, photography, 19th-century European and American sculptures and contemporary prints; Dir RICHARD SAUNDERS; Chief Curator EMMIE DONADIO.

Robert Hull Fleming Museum: 61 Colchester Ave, Univ. of Vermont, Burlington, VT 05405; tel. (802) 656-0750; e-mail fleming@ uvm.edu; internet www.uvm.edu/~fleming; f. 1931; attached to Univ. of Vermont; 20,000 objects spanning history of civilization; art and artefacts from Ancient Egypt, Africa, Asia, Europe and America; Dir JANIE COHEN.

Shelburne Museum: POB 10, Shelburne, VT 05482; 6000 Shelburne Rd, Shelburne, VT 05482; tel. (802) 985-3346; e-mail info@ shelburnemuseum.org; internet shelburnemuseum.org; f. 1947; colln incl. decorative arts, design, 19th-century American folk art, 19th- and 20th-century decoys, quilts, carriages, artefacts dating from 17th-20th century; painting colln incl. French Impressionists and 400 American works dating from 18th to 20th century; Chair. JAMES PIZZAGALLI; Sec. ALICE COONEY FRELINGHUYSEN; Treas. PAUL PERRAULT.

Southern Vermont Arts Center: POB 617 West Rd, Manchester, VT 05254; 930 SVAC Dr., West Road, Manchester, VT 05254; tel. (802) 362-1405; e-mail info@svac.org; internet www.svac.org; colln of 800 art works from 9th and 20th century; colln incl. works by Luigi Lucioni; Pres. STANLEY S. STROUP; Exec. Dir JOSEPH M. MADEIRA.

Southern Vermont Natural History Museum: Route 9, Hogback Mountain, Marlboro, VT 05363; tel. (802) 464-0048; e-mail museum@sover.net; internet www .vermontmuseum.org; f. 1996; colln incl. 600 native New England birds and mammals in 150 small dioramas; Exec. Dir EDWARD METCALFE.

St Johnsbury Athenaeum: 1171 Main St, St Johnsbury, VT 05819; tel. (802) 748-8291; e-mail inform@stjathenaeum.org; internet www.stjathenaeum.org; f. 1873; colln incl. works from American and European artists dating from late 18th century to mid-19th century; Chair. WILLIAM MARSHALL; Sec. EILEEN BOLAND; Treas. BRENDA MARIE WILKINS; Exec. Dir MATTHEW POWERS.

Woodstock Historical Society: 26 Elm St, Woodstock, VT 05091; tel. (802) 457-1822; e-mail info@woodstockhistorical.org; internet woodstockhistorical.org; f. 1943; colln incl. exhibits of furniture, fine art, clothing, tex-

tiles, silver, ceramics, photographs and early American toys; Dir JACK ANDERSON.

Virginia

Chrysler Museum of Art: 245 W Olney Rd, Norfolk, VA 23510; tel. (757) 664-6200; e-mail museum@chrysler.org; internet www .chrysler.org; f. 1933, present name and status 1971; colln incl. 10,000 glass objects spanning 3,000 years, European painting and sculptures dating from Renaissance to present, American paintings and sculptures, contemporary art since 1945 and decorative art; library of 106,000 vols; Chair. MACON F. BROCK; Sec. MAURICE A. JONES; Dir WILLIAM HENNESSEY; Curator JEFF HARRISON.

Art Museums of Colonial Williamsburg: 326 West Francis St, Williamsburg, VA 23185; tel. (757) 220-7984; e-mail mcottrill@ cwf.org; internet www.colonialwilliamsburg .com/do/art-museums; f. 1957; Colonial Williamsburg incl. DeWitt Wallace Decorative Arts museum and Abby Aldrich Rockefeller Folk Art museum; colln incl. colonial and contemporary folk art; furniture, metals, ceramics, paintings and prints dating from 17th to 19th centuries; Pres. and CEO RONALD J. HURST.

Colonial Williamsburg Foundation: POB 1776, Williamsburg, VA 23187-1776; tel. (757) 229-1000; e-mail cwres@cwf.org; internet www.history.org; f. 1926; 301-acre outdoor living history museum with nearly 500 preserved, restored and reconstructed bldgs; 90 acres of period gardens and greens; demonstration of 18 historic trades; incl. DeWitt Wallace Decorative Arts Museum, Bassett Hall, Kimball Theatre and Abby Aldrich Rockefeller Folk Art Museum; library: John D. Rockefeller, Jr, Library of 75,000 vols, 45,000 MSS, 55,000 architectural plans; Pres. COLIN G. CAMPBELL; publ. *Colonial Williamsburg* (3 a year).

Danville Museum of Fine Arts and History: 975 Main St, Danville, VA 24541; tel. (434) 793-5644; internet www .danvillemuseum.org; f. 1974; colln incl. 19th-century art by artists like Jean Joseph Weertz, Edward Gay and Harvey Young, American Modern art, decorative arts and artefacts related to Civil War; Pres. GLENN N. SCARBORO; Treas. THOMAS W. FREEZE; Exec. Dir LYNNE BJARNESEN.

Eleanor D. Wilson Museum: POB 9679, 8009 Fishburn Dr., Roanoke, VA 24020-1679; tel. (540) 362-6532; e-mail wilsonmuseum@ hollins.edu; internet www.hollins.edu/ museum; attached to Hollins Univ.; colln incl. 1000 art objects incl. paintings, photographs and works on paper; Dir AMY MOOREFIELD.

Fredericksburg Area Museum and Cultural Center: 1001 Princess Anne St, Fredericksburg, VA 22401; tel. (540) 371-3037; e-mail info@famcc.org; internet www.famcc .org; f. 1986; colln incl. objects significant to Fredericksburg and surrounding areas of Stafford, Spotsylvania, King George and Caroline; colln incl. 8,000 individual objects and artefacts on Fredericksburg area history; Chair. ANDREW WITHERS; Pres. and CEO ELLEN KILLOUGH; Sec. TERESA D'ORAZIO; Treas. RICK PEARCE.

Gari Melchers Home and Studio: Belmont, 224 Washington St, Fredericksburg, VA 22405; tel. (540) 654-1015; e-mail garimelchers@umw.edu; internet garimelchers.umw.edu; f. 1955; colln incl. 1,677 paintings and drawings by Gari Melchers, 414 works by other artists, 3000 items of furniture, decorative objects and books; Dir DAVID BERRETH; Curator JOANNA CATRON.

Hampton University Museum: Hampton Univ., Hampton, VA 23668; tel. (757) 727-

5308; e-mail museum@hamptonu.edu; internet museum.hamptonu.edu; f. 1868; colln incl. 9,000 objects on African American fine arts, traditional African, native American, native Hawaiian, Pacific Island and Asian art; Dir NASHID MADYUN.

Hermitage Museum and Gardens: 7637 North Shore Rd, Norfolk, VA 23505; tel. (757) 423-2052; e-mail info@thehermitagemuseum .org; internet www.thehermitagemuseum .org; f. 1942; colln incl. 40,000 objects spanning 5,000 years of art history from over 30 countries; colln incl. fine and decorative art objects; Pres. K. MAXWELL DALE; Treas. F. NASH BILISOLY; Sec. ELEANOR A. LEWIS; Exec. Dir MELANIE MATHEWES.

Longwood Center for the Visual Arts (LCVA): 29 N Main St, Farmville, VA 23901; tel. (434) 395-2206; internet www.longwood .edu/lcva; f. 1978; attached to Longwood Univ.; colln incl. Ziegler and Brumfield colln of African art, Rowe colln of Chinese art, Cole colln of 19th-century Bohemian and European glass, English pottery and Meissen porcelain, American works by Thomas Sully and James McNeil Whistler and 19th-century decorative arts; Dir KATHY JOHNSON BOWLES.

Mariners' Museum: 100 Museum Dr., Newport News, VA 23606; tel. (757) 596-2222; e-mail frontdeskstaff@marinersmuseum.org; internet www.mariner.org; f. 1930; int. maritime colln of c. 35,000 artefacts; incl. Peter W. Ifland Colln of Navigation Instruments (169 navigation pieces covering 5 centuries), Edwin Levick Colln of 30,000 photographs (yachting events and America's Cup races), artefacts and archives of the Civil War ironclad USS Monitor; library: see Libraries and Archives; Chair. JOHN R. LAWSON, JR; Pres. and Chief Exec. WILLIAM B. COGAR; Chief Curator LYLES FORBES.

Muscarelle Museum of Art: College of William and Mary, POB 8795, Williamsburg, VA 23187-8795; tel. (757) 221-2700; e-mail muscarelle@wm.edu; internet web.wm.edu/ muscarelle; f. 1983; attached to College of William & Mary; colln incl. Colonial American, 17th- and 18th-century English portraits, prints and drawings from 16th to 20th centuries representing American and European artists, Japanese prints and German Expressionist works; Dir Dr AARON H. DE GROFT.

Taubman Museum of Art: 110 Salem Ave SE, Roanoke, VA 24011; tel. (540) 342-5760; internet www.taubmanmuseum.org; colln incl. 2,050 pieces incl. decorative arts, American art, 3,500-year-old Egyptian Ushabti ceramic figures and contemporary art works by Roanoke artists; Chair. PATRICIA P. KERMES; Sec. THOMAS L. McKEON; Treas. DAVID J. WINE; Exec. Dir DAVID MICKENBERG.

University of Virginia Art Museum: Thomas H. Bayly Bldg, 155 Rugby Rd, POB 400119, Charlottesville, VA 22904-4119; tel. (434) 924-3592; internet www.virginia.edu/ artmuseum; f. 1935; colln incl. 12,000 objects on American and European paintings, works on paper, sculptures dating from 15th to 20th centuries, ancient Mediterranean art and Asian art; Dir BRUCE BOUCHER.

Virginia Historical Society: POB 7311, Richmond, VA 23221-0311; tel. (804) 358-4901; internet www.warmuseum.org; f. 1831; colln incl. genealogical materials, maps, paintings, prints, postcards, weapons, militaria, glass plate negatives and 19th–21st century photographs; Chair. W. TAYLOR REVELEY, III.

Virginia Museum of Fine Arts: 200 North Blvd, Richmond, VA 23220-4007; tel. (804) 340-1400; internet www.vmfa.museum; f. 1936; state-wide network of local and regional arts orgs and loan programme offering exhibition material to affiliated groups; film programmes; permanent collns incl. Russian Imperial jewelled objects by Fabergé, ancient Greek, Roman and Byzantine objects and sculptures; Indian, Chinese, Japanese, medieval, renaissance, and baroque paintings and sculptures; Himalayan colln; Art Nouveau and Art Deco colln; European and American decorative arts, prints, sculpture and paintings; contemporary art; library of 134,500 vols; Assoc. Dir SANDRA C. RUSAK; publ. *Calendar* (6 a year).

Virginia War Museum: 9285 Warwick Blvd, Newport News, VA 23607; tel. (757) 247-8523; e-mail virginiawarmuseum@nngov .com; internet www.warmuseum.org; f. 1923; colln incl. uniforms, weapons and art work from Revolutionary War to Viet Nam War; overview of US military history from 1775 to present; Pres. WARREN SHINDLE; Sec. LAWRENCE MUNNIKHUYSEN, III; Treas. (vacant).

Washington

Aberdeen Museum of History: 111 E Third St, Aberdeen, WA 98520; tel. (360) 533-1976; e-mail museum@ aberdeen-museum.org; internet www .aberdeen-museum.org; f. 1981; housed in the Aberdeen Armory Bldg; colln of armoury.

Anacortes Museum: 1305 Eighth St, Anacortes, WA 98221; tel. (360) 293-1915; e-mail coa.museum@cityofanacortes.org; internet museum.cityofanacortes.org; f. 1958; Dir STEVE OAKLEY; Curator of Collns JUDY HAKINS.

Bainbridge Island Historical Museum: 215 Ericksen Ave, NE, Bainbridge Island, WA 98110; tel. (206) 842-2773; internet www .bainbridgehistory.org/museum.php; f. 1949; 3,500 artefacts and documents and more than 4,000 photographs that depict life on Bainbridge Island from 1854 to the present; Curator RICK CHANDLER; Exec. Dir HENRY R. (HANK) HELM.

Bellevue Arts Museum: 510 Bellevue Way, NE, Bellevue, WA 98004; tel. (425) 519-0770; e-mail info@bellevuearts.org; internet www .bellevuearts.org; f. 1947, present bldg 2001, present name 2005; Managing Dir LARRY WRIGHT; Dir of Curatorial Affairs STEFANO CATALANI.

National Museum of American Jewish History: 101 S Independence Mall E, Philadelphia, PA 19106-2517; tel. (215) 923-3811; internet www.nmajh.org; f. 1740 as Synagogue of the American Revolution; repository with more than 25,000 artefacts that relate to the daily occupational, domestic, religious and communal aspects of American Jewish life; Pres. and CEO MICHAEL ROSENZWEIG.

Seattle Art Museum: 1300 First Ave, Seattle, WA 98101-2003; tel. (206) 625-8900; e-mail pr@seattleartmuseum.org; internet www.seattleartmuseum.org; f. 1906; 23,000 objects: Aboriginal and Oceanic art, African art, American art, ancient Mediterranean and Islamic art, decorative arts, European arts, Japanese and Korean art, modern and contemporary art, Native and Mesoamerican art, textiles; 2 research libraries and a lending library for educators; Pres. WINNIE STRATTON; Sec. STEWART LANDEFEL; Treas. ROBERT STRONG.

Attached Museums:

Olympic Sculpture Park: 2901 W Ave, Seattle, WA 98121; tel. (206) 654-3100; f. 1999; waterfront site for exhibition of sculptures.

Seattle Asian Art Museum: 1400 E Prospect St, Volunteer Park, Seattle, WA 98112-3303; tel. (206) 654-3100; Chinese, S Asian and SE Asian Art.

Washington State History Museum: 1911 Pacific Ave, Tacoma, WA 98402; tel. (253) 272-3500; e-mail researchcenter@wshs.wa .gov; internet www.washingtonhistory.org/ wshm; f. 1996; attached to Washington State Historical Soc.; Great Hall of Washington History, History Lab Learning Center; Dir JENNIFER KILMER; publ. *Columbia* (1 a year).

West Virginia

Clay Center for the Arts and Sciences of West Virginia: 1 Clay Sq., Charleston, WV 25301; tel. (304) 561-3570; internet www .theclaycenter.org; f. 2003; Avampato Discovery Museum, Maier Foundation Performance Hall, Juliet Museum of Art and Walker Theater; 806 objects incl. works on paper by American artists from 19th and 20th centuries; outdoor sculptures; Chair. ELLEN CAPPELLANTI; Pres. and CEO Dr JUDITH L. WELLINGTON; Sec. FONDA ELLIOT; Treas. CHARLES M. AVAMPATO.

Harpers Ferry National Historical Park: POB 65, Harpers Ferry, WV 25425; tel. (304) 535-6029; internet www.nps.gov/hafe; historic photographs, technical drawings, rare postcards and contemporary images; E deciduous forest with different plant species, 170 bird and 30 mammal species; Superintendent REBECCA HARRIET.

Huntington Museum of Art: 2033 McCoy Rd, Huntington, WV 25701; tel. (304) 529-2701; internet www.hmoa.org; collns incl. folk art, prints, sculptures, silver, touma, glass; Herman P. Dean Firearms colln; Daywood Colln; art glass colln incl. Wilbur Myers Glass Colln; Dr Marion C. Korstanje Colln of Natural History Prints; Winslow Anderson Colln of Haitian Art (incl. 156 paintings, metal artefacts and wooden sculptures); Touma Near Eastern Colln (art objects from Middle E, Ottoman Turkey, Central Asian Republics, Indian sub-continent, N Africa and Moorish Spain); American colln (incl. Native American works from N, Central and S America); European paintings, sculptures, drawings and prints from mid-16th century to mid-20th century; incl. C. Fred Edwards Conservatory of subtropical plants; library of 20,000 vols in James D. Francis Art Library; Pres. LEE OXLEY; Sec. JOAN WEISBERG; Treas. BRANDON ROISMAN; Exec. Dir MARGARET MARY LAYNE; Sr Curator JENINE CULLIGAN.

Museum of American Glass in West Virginia: POB 574, Weston, WV 26452; 230 Main Ave, Weston, WV; tel. (304) 269-5006; e-mail wvmuseumofglass@aol.com; internet www.magwv.com; f. 1993; artefacts of handmade glass incl. bottles to lightening rod balls, telegraph insulators to glass used in automobiles, pressed to blown tableware of 18th century rep. of history of glass artists, places and competing companies.

Museums of Oglebay Institute: Oglebay Resort, Wheeling, WV; tel. (304) 242-7272; internet www.oionline.com/museums; f. 1930; Mansion Museum; Oglebay Institute Glass Museum of 3,000 artefacts of Wheeling Glass made from 1829–1939, incl. cut-lead crystal, Victorian art glass, Peachblow, pattern and depression and Northwood's carnival glass; Northwood Gallery incl. crystal, carnival, coloured and opalescent glassware; organizes history lectures, appraisal events and educational activities; Dir CHRISTIN BYRUM; Curator MEGAN CLARK.

Museum of the Berkeley Springs: POB 99, Berkeley Springs, WV 25411; e-mail history@museumoftheberkeleysprings.com; internet www.museumoftheberkeleysprings .com; colln on geology of Berkeley Springs: relief map and quartz crystals, tools, arrowheads and locator map of Native Americans telling 8,500 years of local history, sketches by Porte Crayon, historic swimsuits, photos and sit-up steam cabinet; bottle cappers and signs, silica products and photographs; artefacts from Washington Elm; Pres. JEANNE MOZIER; Exec. Dir BETH ROWLAND.

West Virginia State Museum at the Cultural Center: Capitol Complex, 1900 Kanawha Blvd E, Charleston, WV 25305-0300; tel. (304) 558-0220; internet www.wvculture.org/ agency/cultcenter.html; f. 1890 as West Virginia Historical and Antiquarian Soc., present bldg 1976; attached to West Virginia Div. of Culture and History; local art and history; also houses state archives and state museum; operates 6 historic sites and museums; Museum Dir CHARLES MORRIS, III; publ. *Artworks* (4 a year).

Wisconsin

Charles Allis Art Museum: 1801 N Prospect Ave, Milwaukee, WI 53202; tel. (414) 278-8295; internet www.charlesallis.org; f. 1911; 19th-century French and American Paintings, Chinese and Japanese porcelains, Renaissance bronzes, Japanese netsuke and antique furnishings; Exec. Dir MARIA COST-ELLO; Curator MARTHA MONROE.

Chazen Museum of Art: 800 University Ave, Madison, WI 53706; tel. (608) 263-2246; internet www.chazen.wisc.edu; f. 1970 as Elvehjem Art Center, present name 2005; attached to Univ. of Wisconsin–Madison; colln of 20,000 works of art incl. paintings, sculptures, drawings and watercolours; prints of American, European, Asian and ancient art; photography and applied and decorative arts incl. architectural decoration, beadwork, baskets and textiles, ceramics, glass and metalwork, medallic art and coins; Dir RUSSELL PANCZENKO.

Door County Maritime Museum: 120 N Madison Ave, Sturgeon Bay, WI 54235; tel. (920) 743-5958; e-mail info@dcmm.org; internet www.dcmm.org; exhibits shipyards producing fishing trawlers, Navy vessels, ore carriers and yachts; Cana Island Lighthouse and Gills Rock Museum; Sturgeon Bay Museum; Exec. Dir BOB DESH; Curator JOHN MOGA.

Haggerty Museum of Art: Marquette Univ., POB 1881, Milwaukee, WI 53201-1881; tel. (414) 288-1669; e-mail haggertym@marquette.edu; internet www .marquette.edu/haggerty; f. 1889; attached to Marquette Univ.; Dir WALLY MASON.

Kenosha Public Museums: 5500 First Ave, Kenosha, WI 53140; tel. (262) 653-4140; internet www.kenosha.org/museum/; f. 1933; 70,000 works, incl. 1,000 works in fine arts colln; decorative and fine arts, natural science specimens and cultural artefacts, related to world cultures, Native Americans, zoology, geology, fossils and fine and decorative arts; dinosaurs and associated flora and fauna; Civil War/Victorian era materials; consists of three museums: Kenosha Public Museum, Civil War Museum and Dinosaur Discovery Museum; library of 1,000 vols; Dir DANIEL JOYCE.

Leigh Yawkey Woodson Art Museum: 700 N 12th St, Franklin and 12th Sts, Wausau, WI 54403-5007; tel. (715) 845-7010; e-mail museum@lywam.org; internet www.lywam.org; f. 1976; colln of 2,000 works of art, incl. paintings, drawings and field sketches, prints (etchings, engravings, woodcuts, and screenprints), photographs, 125 Victorian glass baskets, 20th-century utilitarian and decorative glassware and porcelain, 100 Royal Worcester porcelain bird figurines and historic and contemporary glass vessel forms and sculptural objects; Dir KATHY FOLEY.

Madison Museum of Contemporary Art: 227 State St, Madison, WI 53703; tel. (608) 257-0158; e-mail flash@mmoca.org; internet www.mmoca.org; f. present location 2006; colln of 5,000 artworks incl. works of 20th and 21st centuries paintings, sculpture, photography, prints and drawings; Dir STEPHEN FLEISCHMAN; Pres. JIM YEHLE; Sec. WILLIAM DEATLEY; Treas. DAVID STEIN.

Milwaukee Art Museum: 700 N Art Museum Dr., Milwaukee, WI 53202; tel. (414) 224-3200; e-mail mam@mam.org; internet www.mam.org; f. 1957 as Milwaukee Art Center; 20,000 works of art, incl. collns of American decorative arts, German Expressionist prints and paintings, folk and Haitian art, and American art after 1960; George Mann Niedecken Archives; Landfall Press Archives; Rogovin Colln of photographs of working-class families; Herzfeld Foundation Print, Drawing, and Photography Study Center; library of 20,000 vols; Dir and CEO DANIEL T. KEEGAN; Chief Curator BRADY ROBERTS.

Milwaukee Public Museum: 800 W Wells St, Milwaukee, WI 53233-1478; tel. (414) 278-2702; e-mail museumnews@mpm.edu; internet www.mpm.edu; photographic colln of 300,000 images; anthropology colln of 120,000 artefacts of world cultural areas of the Americas, Africa and Oceania; geology colln of fossils, minerals and rocks; 250,000 specimens of preserved plants and plant material in botanical colln; 250,000 historical objects from Egyptian mummies to 20th-century Milwaukee clothing and manufactures; vertebrate and invertebrate zoology colln; planetarium; library of 100,000 vols; Chair. RICHARD A. MEEUSEN; Pres. and CEO JAY WILLIAMS; Sec. and Treas. CHARLES I. HENDERSON.

Museum of Wisconsin Art: 300 S 6th Ave, West Bend, WI 262-334-9638; tel. (262) 334-9638; internet wisconsinart.org; f. 1961 as West Bend Gallery of Fine Arts, present name 2007; Carl von Marr colln and Early Wisconsin Regional Art colln; 2,000 works of art; Wisconsin Art Archive with 8,000 files on Wisconsin art, artists and library of research material on state art and history; Exec. Dir THOMAS D. LIDTKE; Pres. DALE KENT; Sec. VIRGI DRISCOLL; Treas. RAYMOND LIPMAN.

Neville Public Museum: 210 Museum Place, Green Bay, WI 54303-2760; tel. (920) 448-4460; e-mail generalinfo@ nevillepublicmuseum.org; internet www .nevillepublicmuseum.org; f. 1915, present name and status 1927; 100,000 3-D historic and prehistoric artefacts; photograph colln of approx 1m. images and 4m. ft of news film; archival repository of MSS, public records, maps, newspapers and spec. collns library; Dir ROLF JOHNSON; Chair. KRAMER ROCK; Sec. DAVID PAMPERIN; Treas. DIANE FORD.

Oshkosh Public Museum: 1331 Algoma Blvd, Oshkosh, WI 54901; tel. (920) 236-5799; e-mail museum_info@ci.oshkosh.wi.us; internet www.oshkoshmuseum.org; f. 1924; colln of 250,000 objects incl. fine, folk and decorative arts, textiles, toys, natural history specimens, Native American objects and historic artefacts; 47,000 historic photographs and 1,078 linear ft of archival records; Dir BRAD LARSON; Curator DEBRA DAUBERT.

Racine Art Museum: POB 187, Racine, WI 53401-0187; 441 Main St, Racine, WI 53403; tel. (262) 638-8300; internet www.ramart .org; f. 1941 as Charles A. Wustum Museum of Fine Arts; 5,000 objects in ceramics, fibres, glass, metals and wood; Wustum Museum; Exec. Dir BRUCE W. PEPICH; Pres. STEPHANIE LAZZERONI; Sec. KRAIG BRYANT; Treas. JAMES WALKER.

Rahr—West Art Museum: 610 N Eight St, Manitowoc, WI 54220; tel. (920) 686-3090; e-mail rahrwest@manitowoc.org; internet www.manitowoc.org/index.aspx?nid=1006; 19th-, 20th- and 21st-century contemporary art and decorative arts with emphasis on American art and int. and regional US and Wisconsin art; Pres. AMY FRICKE WEIGEL; Dir GREG VADNEY.

Trout Museum of Art: Reigel Bldg, 111 W College Ave, Appleton, WI 54911; tel. (920) 733-4089; e-mail info@troutmuseum.org; internet www.troutmuseum.org; f. 1972 as Appleton Gallery of Art, present name 2010; colln of 150 works of art incl. American, European, Asian and African paintings, sculptures and decorative objects rep. of 400 years of art history; Exec. Dir TIMOTHY RILEY; Pres. MICHAEL CISLER; Sec. WENDY SCHMIDT; Treas. PRATEEK MEHROTRA.

Villa Terrace Decorative Arts Museum: 2220 N Terrace Ave, Milwaukee, WI 53202; tel. (414) 271-3656; internet projects.tsrnet .com/cavt/development/villa; f. 1923; furnishings and works of art from 15th to 18th centuries; Colnik colln of 200 pieces of ironwork; Renaissance Garden; Exec. Dir MARIA COSTELLO; Curator MARTHA MONROE.

Wisconsin Historical Museum: 30 N Carroll St, Madison, WI 53703; tel. (608) 264-6555; e-mail museum@wisconsinhistory.org; internet www.wisconsinhistoricalmuseum .org; attached to Wisconsin Historical Soc.; 110,000 historical objects and 400,000 archaeological artefacts documenting the history of Wisconsin from prehistoric times to the present; spec. collns incl. anthropology, business and technology, costumes and textiles, domestic life, political and military life; Dir JENNIFER KOLB; Chief Curator PAUL G. BOURCIER.

Wisconsin Maritime Museum: 75 Maritime Dr., Manitowoc, WI 54220; tel. (920) 684-0218; e-mail museum@ wisconsinmaritime.org; internet www .wisconsinmaritime.org; f. 1970 as Manitowoc Submarine Memorial Asscn; colln of model ships and boats, operating steam engine, displays of historic vessels and marine engines, and the Wisconsin Waterways and Little Lakefarer's Rooms; Second World War submarine USS Cobia; library of 8,000 vols, 40,000 photographs, 300 linear ft of MSS materials; Exec. Dir NORMA BISHOP; Curator JOHN LARNER.

Wisconsin Veterans Museum: 30 W Mifflin St, Madison, WI 53703; tel. (608) 267-1799; internet www.wisvetsmuseum.com; f. 1901; attached to Wisconsin Dept of Veterans Affairs; 23,000 artefacts incl. uniforms, equipment, armament, flags, insignia, decorations, personal items and souvenirs; battle flag colln and archives; Wisconsin Nat. Guard Museum; Dir MICHAEL TELZROW.

Wright Museum of Art: Beloit College, 700 College St, Beloit, WI 53511; tel. (608) 363-2702; e-mail wright@beloit.edu; internet www.beloit.edu/wright; f. 1930; attached to Beloit College; 6,000 works of art incl. American Impressionism, Modernist paintings, 19th-century plaster casts, German Expressionism, ancient art, Asian art, landscapes, portraiture and Japanese Modern print; Dir JOY ELIZABETH BECKMAN.

Wyoming

Buffalo Bill Historical Center: 720 Sheridan Ave, Cody, WY 82414; tel. (307) 587-4771; e-mail info@bbhc.org; internet www .bbhc.org; f. 1917 as Buffalo Bill Museum, present name 1950; incl. Whitney Gallery of Western Art (paintings, sculpture and prints of the American W from early 19th century through present), Plains Indian Museum (collns of Plains Indian art and artefacts), Cody Firearms Museum (colln of 5,000 American and European firearms on devt of firearms from 16th century to the present), McCracken Research Library and Draper Museum of Natural History (research on natural environment and human cultures of the American W, focusing on the Greater Yellowstone region); library of 30,000 vols, 300 MSS and 500,000 photographs; Chair. BARRON G. COLLIER, II; Exec. Dir and CEO BRUCE B. ELDREDGE.

Carbon County Museum: 904 W Walnut, Rawlins, WY 82301; tel. (307) 328-2740; e-mail carbonc@wyoming.com; internet www.carboncountymuseum.org; colln on the Union Pacific Railroad, pioneers, residents and outlaws, Native Americans and agriculture; Thomas Edison exhibit; Dir TIFFANY WILSON; Chair. GENE CARRICO (acting); Sec. DAVID THROGMORTON; Treas. LEON CORPUZ.

Cheyenne Frontier Days Old West Museum: 4610 Carey Ave, POB 2720, Cheyenne, WY 82003; tel. (307) 778-7290; e-mail info@oldwestmuseum.org; internet www.oldwestmuseum.org; f. 1978; 60,000 artefacts incl. paintings, sculptures, historic clothing dating to 1850 and artefacts related to art and material culture of the American W; Exec. Dir AIMEE REESE; Pres. Dr JIM MCSHANE; Sec. Dr RICK DAVIS; Treas. GENE ENGRAV.

Hulett Museum and Art Gallery: POB 103, Hulett, WY 82720; 115 Highway 24, Hulett, WY 82720; tel. (307) 467-5292; e-mail hulettmuseum@rtconnect.net; internet hulettmuseum.org; f. 2010; colln of prehistoric and historic artefacts related to history and culture of NE Wyoming; Dir MITCH MAHONEY.

Jim Gatchell Memorial Museum: POB 596, Buffalo, WY 82834; 100 Fort St, Buffalo, WY 82834; tel. (307) 684-9331; e-mail jmuseum@vcn.com; internet www .jimgatchell.com/jim_gatchell_memorial_museum; f. 1900 as Buffalo Pharmacy; 14,000 artefacts incl. documents, photographs, firearms, clothing and wagons related to history of Johnson Co. with emphasis on its Frontier Era; Dir JOHN GAVIN; Pres. DAVE OSMUNDSEN; Sec. BARBARA MADSEN; Treas. SALLY RAMSBOTTOM.

National Museum of Wildlife Art: 2820 Rungius Rd, Jackson Hole, WY 83002; tel. (307) 733-5771; e-mail info@wildlifeart.org; internet www.wildlifeart.org; f. 1987 as Wildlife of the American West Art Museum; 5,000 pieces of art portraying wildlife, dating from 2500BC to the present; European and American painting and sculpture; colln of American art from the 19th and 20th centuries recording European exploration of the American West; spec. collns incl. Carl Rungius Colln, John Clymer Colln, American Bison Colln, Dellenback Colln, JKM Colln; art library and archives; incl. Nat. Elk Refuge; Chair. STEPHANIE BRENNAN; Pres. and CEO Dr JAMES C. MCNUTT; Sec. JUDSON BALL; Treas. DAVID WALSH.

Nicolaysen Art Museum: 400 E Collins St, Casper, WY 82601; tel. (307) 235-5247; internet www.thenic.org; f. 1967; 6,265 objects, incl. paintings, sculptures, textiles, drawings, photographs, prints and works on paper; spec. collns: Conrad Schwiering Studies and Illustrations by Carl Link; Discovery ... Exec. Dir CONNIE GIBBONS; Chair. ... Sec. CRAIG VALDEZ; Curator ...

... Art Museum: ... WY 82072; tel. ... vo.edu; ...072;

can paintings, prints, sculpture and drawings; spec. collns of 18th- and 19th-century Japanese Ukiyo-e prints, 15th- through 19th-century Persian and Indian miniature paintings, 20th-century Haitian art, 20th-century Japanese netsuke, 20th-century and contemporary photography, and Rapa Nui, African and Native American artefacts; 15th-century Old Master prints, French Rococo, German Expressionism, Fauvism, Modernism, Surrealism, Abstract Expressionism and Contemporary Art; outdoor sculptures; Dir and Chief Curator SUSAN MOLDENHAUER; Pres. RUTH ARNOLD; Sec. and Treas. JACQUE BUCHANAN.

Wyoming Dinosaur Center & Dig Sites: 110 Carter Ranch Rd, POB 868, Thermopolis, WY 82443; tel. (307) 864-2997; e-mail wdinoc@wyodino.org; internet www.wyodino .org; museum with interpretive displays, dioramas, life-size dinosaur mounts, exhibits covering all facets of early life; colln incl. fossil fish from Scotland, flying reptiles from Brazil, marine reptiles from Russia and Switzerland and fossil dinosaur eggs from China and Argentina; fossil preparation laboratory; 80 dig sites in Warm Springs Ranch; Research Center; Casting Laboratory; Dir of Science SCOTT HARTMAN; Gen. Man. ANGIE GUYON.

Wyoming State Museum: Barrett Bldg, 2301 Central Ave, Fourth Fl., Cheyenne, WY 82002; tel. (307) 777-2416; e-mail wsm@ state.wy.us; internet wyomuseum.state.wy .us; f. 1895; themed galleries: Barber Gallery, Drawn to this Land, Hands-on History Room, Living in Wyoming, RIP–Rex in Pieces, Swamped with Coal, The Wild Bunch, Wyoming's Story; travelling exhibits; colln of structures, bldg furnishings, personal artefacts, tools and equipment, recreational artefacts, societal artefacts, ethnographic artefact, archaeology and natural history; Museum Supervisor MANNY VIGIL.

Universities and Colleges

(Arranged alphabetically by State)

ALABAMA

AIR UNIVERSITY

55 LeMay Plaza S, Maxwell AFB, Montgomery, AL 36112-6335

Telephone: (334) 953-2014
Internet: www.au.af.mil/au

Founded 1946
State control

Pres. and Cmdr: Lt Gen. DAVID S. FADOK
Vice-Pres. for Academic Affairs: Dr BRUCE MURPHY
Registrar: LLOYD L. WILSON
Library Dir: Dr JEFF LUZIUS
Library: 2.9m. vols, 530,000 military documents, 429,000 bound periodical vols, 433,000 maps and charts, 909,000 microforms
Number of students: 500

Publication: *Air and Space Power Journal* (4 a year)

ALABAMA AGRICULTURAL AND MECHANICAL UNIVERSITY

POB 908, Huntsville, AL 35762
4900 Meridian St, Huntsville, AL 35810-1015
Telephone: (256) 372-5000
E-mail: info@aamu.edu
Internet: www.aamu.edu

Founded 1875 as Huntsville Normal School, present name 1969
State control
Academic year: August to May

Pres.: Dr ANDREW HUGINE, JR
Exec. Vice-Pres. and Chief Operating Officer: Dr KEVIN ROLLE
Vice-Pres. for Academic Affairs and Provost: Dr DANIEL WIMS
Vice-Pres. for Business and Finance: RALPH JOHNSON
Vice-Pres. for Research and Devt: Dr ROSE M. YATES
Vice-Pres. for Student Affairs: JEFFERY T. BURGIN, JR
Registrar: CEDRIC ARRINGTON
Dir and Head of Public and Information Services: GARY BUSH (acting)
Library of 339,272 vols, 2,200 journals
Number of teachers: 350
Number of students: 5,800

DEANS

College of Agricultural and Environmental Studies: Dr ROBERT TAYLOR
College of Arts and Sciences: Dr MATTHEW EDWARDS
College of Business and Public Affairs: Dr AMIN SARKAR
College of Education, Humanities and Behavioral Sciences: Dr CURTIS E. MARTIN
College of Engineering, Technology and Physical Sciences: Dr TRENT MONTGOMERY
School of Graduate Studies: Dr VANN NEWKIRK
Univ. College: Dr JUARINE STEWART

ALABAMA STATE UNIVERSITY

915 S Jackson St, POB 271, Montgomery, AL 36101-0271

Telephone: (334) 229-4100
E-mail: wharris@alasu.edu
Internet: www.alasu.edu

Founded 1867 as Lincoln Normal School, present name and status 1969
State control
Academic year: September to May

Pres.: Dr WILLIAM H. HARRIS
Exec. Vice-Pres. and Chief Operating Officer: Dr JOHN F. KNIGHT, JR
Vice-Pres. for Academic Affairs and Provost: Dr ALFRED SMITH
Vice-Pres. for Admin. Services: Dr LEON FRAZIER
Vice-Pres. for Business and Finance: Dr FREDDIE GALLOT
Vice-Pres. for Institutional Advancement: ZILLAH FLUKER
Vice-Pres. for Student Affairs: Dr WILLIAM P. HYTCHE
Vice-Pres. for Univ. Relations: DANIELLE KENNEDY
Univ. Librarian and Learning Resources: Dr JANICE FRANKLIN
Library of 507,374 vols (incl. 304,944 books, 74,659 ebooks, 127,771 bound journals), 6,026 periodical titles (1,597 physical titles and 4,429 ejournals)
Number of teachers: 270
Number of students: 5,100

Publications: *ASU Today, Sciences@ASU*

DEANS

College of Business Administration: Dr LEQUITA BOOTH
College of Education: Dr JOHN GOODEN (acting)
College of Health Sciences: Dr STEVEN B. CHESBRO
College of Liberal Arts and Social Sciences: Dr LEON C. WILSON
College of Science, Mathematics and Technology: Dr CAJETAN M. AKUJUOBI

College of Visual and Performing Arts: Dr TOMMIE H. STEWART
Division of Aerospace Studies–Air Force ROTC: Lt Col DAWN DAVIS
School of Graduate Studies: Dr WILLIAM A. PERSON
School of Music: Dr HORACE B. LAMAR, Jr
University College: Dr EVELYN HODGE

AMRIDGE UNIVERSITY

POB 240240, Montgomery, AL 36117-3553
1200 Taylor Rd, Montgomery, AL 36117-3553
Telephone: (334) 387-7524
E-mail: admissions@amridgeuniversity.edu
Internet: www.amridgeuniversity.edu

Founded 1942 as Montgomery Bible School, present name 2008
Private control
Academic year: August to August

Pres.: Dr MICHAEL C. TURNER
Vice-Pres. for Academic Affairs: Dr STANLEY DOUGLAS PATTERSON
Registrar: ELAINE TARENCE
Librarian: TERENCE SHERIDAN
Library: 150,000 journals, 20m. monographs

DEANS

College of Business and Leadership: Dr KENYETTA MCCURTY
College of General Studies: ROGER SHEPHERD (acting)
School of Human Services: Dr KENYETTA MCCURTY
Turner School of Theology: Dr RODNEY CLOUD (acting)

ATHENS STATE UNIVERSITY

300 N Beaty St, Athens, AL 35611-1999
Telephone: (256) 233-8100
Internet: www.athens.edu

Founded 1822 as Athens Female Acad., present status 1975, present name 1988
State control
Academic year: August to July

Pres.: ROBERT K. GLENN
Provost and Vice-Pres. for Academic Affairs: RONALD CROMWELL
Vice-Pres. for Advancement: RICK MOULD
Vice-Pres. for Enrolment and Student Support Services: JIM HUTTO
Vice-Pres. for Financial Affairs: MIKE MCCOY
Dir of Admissions and Records: NECEDAH HENDERSON
Registrar: TERESA SUIT
Library Dir: Prof. Dr ROBERT BURKHARDT
Library of 100,000 vols
Number of teachers: 70
Number of students: 3,500

DEANS

College of Arts and Sciences: RONALD FRITZE
College of Business: Dr LINDA SHONESY
College of Education: Prof. DEBRA BAIRD

AUBURN UNIVERSITY

Auburn, AL 36849
Telephone: (334) 844-4000
E-mail: registrar@auburn.edu
Internet: www.auburn.edu

Founded 1856 as East Alabama Male College, current name and status 1960
public control
Academic year: August to July

Pres.: Dr JAY GOGUE
Exec. Vice-Pres. and Chief Financial Officer: Dr DONALD L. LARGE, JR
Vice-Pres. for Academic Affairs and Provost: Dr TIMOTHY BOOSINGER
Vice-Pres. for Devt: JANE PARKER

Vice-Pres. for Research and Assoc. Provost: Dr JOHN M. MASON, JR
Vice-Pres. for Student Affairs: JON WAGGONER
Registrar: LAURA ANN FOREST
Dean for Libraries: Dr BONNIE MACEWAN
Library of 4,317,592 bound vols, 2,720,297 microfilms, 39,318 current periodicals, 256,354 maps, govt documents
Number of teachers: 1,360
Number of students: 24,860

Publications: *Alabama Cooperative Extension System* (1 a year), *Auburn Magazine* (4 a year), *Auburn University Research* (1 a year), *AU Daily*, *Beyond Auburn* (4 a year), *Engineering Research Activities* (1 a year), *Facts and Figures* (every 2 years), *Glomerata* (1 a year), *Graduate & Undergraduate* (1 a year), *Southern Humanities Review* (4 a year), *The Auburn Pharmacist* (4 a year), *The Auburn Plainsman* (48 a year), *The Auburn Veterinarian* (4 a year), *The Circle* (4 a year), *Tiger Cub* (1 a year)

DEANS

College of Agriculture: Dr WILLIAM BATCHELOR
College of Architecture, Design and Construction: Dr VINI NATHAN
College of Education: Dr BETTY LOU WHITFORD
College of Human Sciences: Dr JUNE HENTON
College of Liberal Arts: Dr ANNE-KATRIN GRAMBERG
College of Sciences and Mathematics: Prof. Dr NICHOLAS GIORDANO
College of Veterinary Medicine: Dr CALVIN JOHNSON
Graduate School: Dr GEORGE FLOWERS
Harrison School of Pharmacy: Dr R. LEE EVANS
Raymond J. Harbert College of Business: Prof. Dr BILL C. HARDGRAVE
Samuel Ginn College of Engineering: Dr CHRISTOPHER ROBERTS
School of Forestry and Wildlife Sciences: Dr JAMES P. SHEPARD
School of Nursing: Prof. Dr GREGG E. NEWSCHWANDER

AUBURN UNIVERSITY AT MONTGOMERY

POB 244023, Montgomery, AL 36124-4023
Telephone: (334) 244-3000
E-mail: askaum@aum.edu
Internet: www.aum.edu

Founded 1967
State control
Academic year: August to August

Chancellor: Dr JOHN G. VERES, III
Vice-Chancellor for Advancement: CAROLYN C. GOLDEN
Vice-Chancellor for Financial Affairs: WANDA C. MEADOWS
Vice-Chancellor for Outreach and Strategic Initiatives: Dr KATHERINE A. JACKSON
Provost: Dr JENNIFER A. BROWN
Dean of Students: Dr JAN LYN
Registrar: ELIZABETH WARD
Dean of Libraries: LUCY FARROW
Library of 325,000 vols, 1,600 periodicals, 10,000,000 fed. govt documents, 15,000 journal titles
Number of students: 5,200

DEANS

School of Business: Dr W. RHEA INGRAM
School of Education: Dr SAMUEL FLYNT
School of Liberal Arts: Dr MICHAEL BURGER
School of Nursing: Dr GREGG NEWSCHWANDER
School of Sciences: Dr KAREN STINE

BIRMINGHAM—SOUTHERN COLLEGE

900 Arkadelphia Rd, Birmingham, AL 35254
Telephone: (205) 226-4600
Internet: www.bsc.edu

Founded 1918 by merger of Southern Univ. (f. 1856) and Birmingham College (f. 1898)
Private control
Academic year: August to August

Offers bachelors degree in arts, fine arts, music, musical arts, music education, science

Pres.: Gen. CHARLES C. KRULAK
Provost: Dr MARK S. SCHANTZ
Vice-Pres. for Admin.: LANE ESTES
Vice-Pres. for Communications: BILL WAGNON
Vice-Pres. for Enrolment Management: Dr KATHLEEN GREER ROSSMANN
Vice-Pres. for Finance: ELI PHILLIPS
Vice Pres. for Information Technology: ANTHONY HAMBEY
Vice Pres. for Institutional Advancement: PAT ANDERSON-FLOWERS
Vice-Pres. for Student Devt: Dr DAVID EBERHARDT
Library Dir: CHARLOTTE FORD
Library of 257,000 vols, 57,000 govt documents, 35,000 periodicals, 47,000 microfiches, 20,000 microfilms, audiovisual items, recordings, slides
Number of teachers: 110
Number of students: 1,500

CONCORDIA COLLEGE ALABAMA

POB 2470, Selma, AL 36703
1712 Broad St, Selma, AL 36701
Telephone: (334) 874-5700
E-mail: admissions@ccal.edu
Internet: www.ccal.edu

Founded 1922 as Alabama Luther College, current name adopted 1981, current status 1994
Private control
Language of instruction: English
Academic year: August to May

Pres.: Rev. Dr TILAHUN MEKONNEN MENDEDO
Dean for Institutional Advancement: RUTHIE ORSBORN
Dean for Instruction: Dr DOREEN MOYO
Library Dir: J. SCOTT WHITING
Library of 55,000 vols, 100 periodicals and 3,000 ebooks
Number of students: 650

FAULKNER UNIVERSITY

5345 Atlanta Highway, Montgomery, AL 36109
Telephone: (334) 386-7140
E-mail: admissions@faulkner.edu
Internet: www.faulkner.edu

Founded 1942 as Montgomery Bible College; present name 1985
Private control
Academic year: August to July
Campuses at Huntsville, Birmingham, Montgomery, Mobile

Pres.: Dr BILLY D. HILYER
Vice-Pres. for Academic Affairs: JACK TUCCI
Vice-Pres. for Advancement: BEN BRUCE
Vice-Pres. for Enrolment Management: KEITH MOCK
Vice-Pres. for Finance: WILMA PHILLIPS
Registrar: DON REYNOLDS
Dean of Students: FAIRES AUSTIN
Dir of Admissions: NEIL SCOTT
Dir of Libraries: BARBARA KELLY
Library of 100,000 vols

DEANS

College of Arts and Sciences: Prof. DAVE RAMPERSAD
College of Biblical Studies: Prof. CECIL MAY
College of Business: Prof. DAVE A. KHADANGA
College of Education: JENDIA GRISSETT
Jones School of Law Admin.: CHARLES NELSON

HERITAGE CHRISTIAN UNIVERSITY

POB HCU, Florence, AL 35630
3625 Helton Dr., Florence, AL 35630
Telephone: (256) 766-6610
E-mail: hcu@hcu.edu
Internet: www.hcu.edu
Founded 1971 as Int. Bible College; present name 2000
Private control
Academic year: August to July
Offers courses in Bible and theology
Pres.: DENNIS JONES
Vice-Pres. and Dean of Academic Affairs: Prof. Dr BILL BAGENTS
Vice-Pres. for Operations: PAT MOON
Vice-Pres. for Univ. Advancement: PHILIP GOAD
Dean of Students: BRAD McKINNON
Registrar: CHARLOTTE ORR
Librarian: JAMIE COX
Library of 61,000 vols

HUNTINGDON COLLEGE

1500 E Fairview Ave, Montgomery, AL 36106-2148
Telephone: (334) 833-4497
E-mail: admiss@huntingdon.edu
Internet: www.huntingdon.edu
Founded 1854 as Tuskegee Female College, current name adopted 1935
Private control
Academic year: August to July
Majors in accounting, art, biochemistry, biology, business administration, cell biology, chemistry, Christian education, communication studies, digital art, elementary education/collaborative special education, English, history, mathematics, music, music education, physical education, political science, psychology, religion, sport science, youth ministry
Pres.: J. CAMERON WEST
Provost and Dean of College: SIDNEY J. STUBBS
Treas. and Sr Vice-Pres. for Planning and Admin.: JAY A. DORMAN
Vice Pres. for College and Alumni Relations: ANTHONY J. LEIGH
Vice-Pres. for Enrolment Management: LAURA HINDS DUNCAN
Vice-Pres. for Student Life and Dean of Students: FRANK R. PARSONS, JR
Dir for Library: Prof. ERIC A. KIDWELL
Library of 113,364 vols
Number of teachers: 121
Number of students: 1,110

JACKSONVILLE STATE UNIVERSITY

700 Pelham Rd N, Jacksonville, AL 36265-1602
Telephone: (256) 782-5781
E-mail: info@jsu.edu
Internet: www.jsu.edu
Founded 1883 as Jacksonville State Normal School, present name and status 1966
State control
Academic year: August to July
Pres.: BILL MEEHAN
Provost and Vice-Pres. for Academic and Student Affairs: Dr REBECCA O. TURNER

Vice-Pres. for Admin. and Business Affairs: CLINT CARLSON (acting)
Vice-Pres. for Information Technology: VINSON HOUSTON
Vice-Pres. for Institutional Advancement: Dr CHARLES LEWIS
Dean of Library Services: JOHN-BAUER GRAHAM
Library of 600,000 vols
Number of teachers: 380 (265 full-time, 115 part-time)
Number of students: 9,100

DEANS

College of Arts and Sciences: Dr J. E. WADE
College of Commerce and Business Admin.: Dr BILL FIELDING
College of Education and Professional Studies: Dr JOHN HAMMETT
College of Graduate Studies and Continuing Education: Dr BILL CARR
College of Nursing and Health Sciences: Dr SARAH LATHAM

JUDSON COLLEGE

302 Bibb St, Marion, AL 36756
Telephone: (334) 683-5100
E-mail: admissions@judson.edu
Internet: www.judson.edu
Founded 1838 as Judson Female Institute, present name 1903
Private control
Academic year: August to July
Offers arts majors and programmes incl. medicine, dentistry, law and engineering
Pres.: DAVID EARL POTTS
Vice-Pres. and Academic Dean: SARA BLISS KISER
Vice-Pres. and Dean of Students: SANDRA S. FOWLER
Vice-Pres. for Admissions and Financial Aid: CHARLOTTE S. CLEMENTS
Vice-Pres. for Advancement and Gen. Counsel: JOSEPH W. MATHEWS, JR
Vice-Pres. for Business Affairs: DENNIS FRODSHAM
Registrar: ELEANOR C. DRAKE
Dir of Library Services: GEORGE WASHBURN
Library of 70,000 vols
Number of students: 300
Publications: *The Ivy Vine*, *The Scrimshaw* (1 a year)

MILES COLLEGE

POB 39800, Birmingham, AL 35208
5500 Myron Massey Blvd, Fairfield, AL 35064
Telephone: (205) 929-1000
E-mail: admissions@miles.edu
Internet: www.miles.edu
Founded 1898 as Miles Memorial College, present name 1941
Private control
Academic year: August to July
Academic divs: business and accounting, communications, education, humanities, natural sciences and mathematics, social and behavioural sciences
Pres.: Dr GEORGE T. FRENCH, JR
Sr Vice-Pres. of Finance and Admin.: DIANA KNIGHTON
Dean and Vice-Pres. of Academic Affairs: Dr EMMANUEL CHEKWA
Dean of Students Affairs: GRIENA KNIGHT
Dir of College Relations: Dr RICKY LEE
Dir of Institutional Planning and Devt: W. FRANK TOPPING
Library of 90,000 vols, 6,000 periodicals
Number of teachers: 135
Number of students: 1,800

OAKWOOD UNIVERSITY

7000 Adventist Blvd NW, Huntsville, AL 35896
Telephone: (256) 726-7000
E-mail: admission@oakwood.edu
Internet: www.oakwood.edu
Founded 1896 as Oakwood Industrial School, current name and status 2008
Private control
Academic year: July to June
Areas of study incl. allied health, biological sciences, business and information systems, chemistry, communication and fine arts, dietetics, elementary and secondary education, English and foreign languages, health and physical education, history and political science, mathematics and computer sciences, music, nursing, psychology, religion and theology, social work
Pres.: Dr LESLIE N. POLLARD
Provost and Sr Vice-Pres.: Dr R. TIMOTHY McDONALD
Vice-Pres. for Academic Admin.: Dr C. GARLAND DULAN
Dir for Admissions: NIKKI LAWSON
Dir for Library Services: PAULETTE MacLEAN JOHNSON
Library of 78,658 vols
Number of teachers: 180 (110 full-time, 70 part-time)
Number of students: 1,900 (1,860 undergraduate, 40 graduate)

SAMFORD UNIVERSITY

800 Lakeshore Dr., Birmingham, AL 35229
Telephone: (205) 726-2011
Internet: www.samford.edu
Founded 1841 as Howard College, present name and status 1965
Private control
Academic year: June to May
Pres.: ANDREW WESTMORELAND
Provost and Exec. Vice-Pres.: Dr J. BRADLEY CREED
Vice-Pres. for Business and Financial Affairs: HARRY B. BROCK, III
Vice-Pres. for Operations and Planning: SARAH C. LATHAM
Vice-Pres. for Student Affairs and Enrolment Management: R. PHIL KIMREY
Vice-Pres. for Univ. Advancement: W. RANDALL PITTMAN
Dean of Admission: JASON BLACK
Dean of Academic Services and Registrar: PAUL G. AUCOIN
Library Dir: KIMMETHA HERNDON
Number of teachers: 250
Number of students: 4,700
Publications: *American Journal of Trial Advocacy* (3 a year), *Cumberland Lawyer* (2 a year), *Cumberland Law Review* (3 a year), *Seasons Magazine* (4 a year, online), *Samford University Catalog* (1 a year, online), *The Beeson Journal* (1 a year), *The Educational Collaborative*

DEANS

Beeson Divinity School: Prof. Dr TIMOTHY F. GEORGE
Brock School of Business: HOWARD FINCH (acting)
Cumberland School of Law: Dr JOHN L. CARROLL
Howard College of Arts and Sciences: DAVID W. CHAPMAN
Ida V. Moffett School of Nursing: Prof. NENA F. SANDERS
McWhorter School of Pharmacy: Prof. Dr CHARLES D. SANDS, III
Orlean Bullard Beeson School of Education and Professional Studies: Prof. Dr JEANIE ANN BOX

School of Arts: JOSEPH HOPKINS

SOUTHEASTERN BIBLE COLLEGE

2545 Valleydale Rd, Birmingham, AL 35244-2083

Telephone: (205) 970-9200
E-mail: info@sebc.edu
Internet: www.sebc.edu
Founded 1935 as Birmingham School of the Bible, present name 1952, present status 1962
Private control
Academic year: August to May
Depts of arts and sciences, Biblical studies, education
Pres.: Dr DONALD W. HAWKINS
Provost and Vice-Pres. for Education: Dr VICKI L. WOLFE
Dean for Student Life: KRISTIE HARRICK
Registrar: JOEL WOLFE
Dir of Library Services: PAUL A. ROBERTS
Library of 35,000 vols

SPRING HILL COLLEGE

4000 Dauphin St, Mobile, AL 36608
Telephone: (251) 380-4000
E-mail: admit@shc.edu
Internet: www.shc.edu
Founded 1830
Private control
Language of instruction: English
Academic year: August to May
Pres.: Rev. RICHARD P. SALMI
Provost: Dr GEORGE E. SIMS
Vice-Pres. for Advancement: JEFFREY A. HILPERTS
Vice-Pres. for Business and Finance: RHONDA M. SHIRAZI
Vice-Pres. for Student Affairs and Dean of Students: JOSEPH W. DEIGHTON
Dir of Athletics and Recreation: JAMES K. HALL
Chief Information Officer: MARGARET G. MASSEY
Registrar: STUART MOORE
Dir of Library: GENTRY LANKEWICZ HOLBERT
Library of 196,451 vols
Number of teachers: 134 (78 full-time, 56 part-time)
Number of students: 1,328

DEANS

Biology: Dr DONALD E. CULBERSON
Business: Dr SERGIO CASTELLO
Chemistry, Physics and Engineering: Dr LESLI W. BORDAS
Communication Arts: Dr SHAREE L. BROUSSARD
English: Dr CATHERINE A. SWENDER
Fine and Performing Arts: Rev. STEPHEN F. CAMPBELL
Foreign Languages: Dr COLETTE J. WINDISH
History: Dr THOMAS J. WARD
Mathematics: Dr DANIEL S. CYPHERT
Nursing: Dr TERRAN A. MATHERS
Philosophy: Dr CHRISTOPHER R. DODSWORTH
Political Science and Law: Dr ROBERT C. HARDING
Psychology: Dr ROYCE G. SIMPSON
Sociology: Dr HAROLD E. DORTON
Teacher Education: Dr LORI P. AULTMAN
Theology: Rev. CHRISTOPHER J. VISCARDI

STILLMAN COLLEGE

POB 1430, Tuscaloosa, AL 35403-9990
3601 Stillman Blvd, Tuscaloosa, AL 35401
Telephone: (205) 349-4240
E-mail: admissions@stillman.edu
Internet: www.stillman.edu

Founded 1876 as Tuscaloosa Institute, present name 1948
Private control
Academic year: August to July
Pres.: Dr ERNEST MCNEALEY
Vice-Pres. for Academic Affairs: Dr CHRISTOPHER JEFFRIES
Vice-Pres. for External Affairs: EDDIE B. THOMAS
Vice-Pres. for Fiscal Affairs: SAMA MONDEH
Vice-Pres. for Retention: CHARLOTTE CARTER
Vice-Pres. for Student Affairs: Dr SHARON WHITTAKER-DAVIS
Dean of Enrolment Management: GEORGE LEE
Dean of the Library: ROBERT J. HEATH
Library of 117,550 vols, 410 periodicals
Number of teachers: 60
Number of students: 1,000

DEANS

Arts and Sciences: Dr MARY JANE KROTZER
Professional Education: LINDA BRADFORD

TALLADEGA COLLEGE

627 W Battle St, Talladega, AL 35160
Telephone: (256) 761-0206
E-mail: admissions@talladega.edu
Internet: www.talladega.edu
Founded 1867 as Swayne School, present name and status 1869
Private control
Academic year: August to May (2 semesters)
Pres.: Dr BILLY C. HAWKINS
Provost and Vice-Pres. for Academic Affairs: Dr EVELYN M. WHITE
Vice-Pres. for Admin. and Finance: Dr GERALD WILLIAMS
Vice-Pres. for Institutional Advancement: (vacant)
Vice-Pres. for Student Affairs: JACQUELINE PADDIO
Dean for Enrolment Management: (vacant)
Registrar: (vacant)
Library Dir: Dr JOSEPH MCDONALD
Library of 130,000 vols
Number of teachers: 35
Number of students: 1,202

DEANS

Div. of Business and Admin.: ERIC HELVY
Div. of Humanities and Fine Arts: JOHNNIE LINDSEY
Div. of Natural Sciences and Mathematics: Prof. Dr CHARLIE M. STINSON
Eunice Walker Div. of Social Sciences and Education: Dr LISA LONG

TROY UNIVERSITY

Troy, AL 36082
Telephone: (334) 670-3000
E-mail: ask@troy.edu
Internet: www.troy.edu
Founded 1887 as Troy State Normal School, present name 2004
Academic year: August to May
Colleges of arts and sciences, business, communication and fine arts, education, health and human services
Chancellor: Dr JACK HAWKINS, JR
Sr Vice-Chancellor for Student Services and Admin.: Dr JOHN R. DEW
Sr Vice-Chancellor for Academic Affairs: Dr EARL INGRAM
Sr Vice-Chancellor for Advancement and External Relations: JOHN W. SCHMIDT
Sr Vice-Chancellor for Finance and Business Affairs: JAMES M. BOOKOUT
Exec. Vice-Chancellor and Provost: Dr ED D. ROACH
Registrar: VICKIE MILES

Dean for Libraries: Dr HENRY R. STEWART
Dean for Student Services: HERBERT E. REEVES
Library of 334,000 vols
Number of teachers: 265
Number of students: 5,100 ...

CONSTITUENT UNIVERSITIES

Troy University, Dothan

500 Univ. Dr., Dothan, AL 36303
Telephone: (334) 9836556
E-mail: ask@troy.edu
Internet: dothan.troy.edu
Founded 1887 as Troy State Normal School, present name 2004
Academic year: August to August
Vice-Chancellor: Dr DON JEFFREY
Dean for Student Services: ROBERT G. WILLIS
Campus Registrar: LISA J. BOUTWELL
Dir for Library Services: CHRIS SHAFFER
Number of students: 1,855

DEANS

College of Arts and Sciences: Dr ROBERT SAUNDERS
College of Business Admin.: Dr ADAIR GILBERT
College of Education: Dr SANDRA LEE JONES

Troy University, Montgomery

231 Montgomery St, PO Drawer 4419, Montgomery, AL 361034419
Telephone: (334) 241-9576
E-mail: libweb@troy.edu
Internet: montgomery.troy.edu
Academic year: August to May
Vice-Chancellor: RAY WHITE
Dean for Student Services: Dr CHARLES WESTERN
Campus Registrar: LYNN LEWIS
Library Dir: KENT SNOWDEN
Library of 32,000 vols, 50,000 ebooks

DEANS

College of Arts and Sciences: Dr WILLIAM S. RICHARDSON
College of Business: Dr JAMES SIMPSON
College of Education: Dr LEN KITCHENS

Troy University, Phenix City

1 Univ. Pl., Phenix City, AL 36869
Telephone: (334) 448-5106
Internet: phenix.troy.edu
Academic year: August to August
Vice-Chancellor: Dr DAVE WHITE
Campus Registrar: CHRISTOPHER WAID
Dean for Student Services: JACK MILLER

DEANS

College of Business Admin.: Dr CHERIE FRETWELL
College of Counselling and Psychology: Dr KATHRYN NESS
College of Education: Dr LARRY THACKER

TUSKEGEE UNIVERSITY

Tuskegee, AL 36088
1200 W Montgomery Rd, Tuskegee Inst, AL 36088
Telephone: (334) 727-8011
E-mail: admissions@mytu.tuskegee.edu
Internet: www.tuskegee.edu
Founded 1881
Private control
Academic year: August to July
Pres.: Dr BRIAN L. JOHNSON
Provost and Vice-Pres. for Academic Affairs: Dr WALTER HILL
Vice-Pres. for Devt.: EARNELLE SEAY

Vice-Pres. for Finance and Chief Financial Officer: GLENN DICKERSON
Vice-Pres. for Student Affairs and Enrolment Management: Dr CYNTHIA D. SELLERS-SIMON
Dean for Students: PETER J. SPEARS
Registrar: EDRICE D. LEFTWICH
Dir for Library Services: JUANITA M. ROBERTS
Library of 380,000 vols, 1,000 periodicals
Number of teachers: 266
Number of students: 3,000

DEANS

Andrew F. Brimmer College of Business and Information Science: Dr TEJINDER SARA
College of Agriculture and Environmental and Natural Sciences: Dr WALTER H. HILL
College of Arts and Sciences: Dr FITZGERALD BRAMWELL
College of Education: Dr CARLTON E. MORRIS
College of Engineering, Architecture and Physical Science: Dr LEGAND L. BURGE, JR
College of Veterinary Medicine, Nursing and Allied Health: Dr RUBY PERRY
Robert R. Taylor School of Architecture and Construction Science: Dr RICHARD K. DOZIER

UNITED STATES SPORTS ACADEMY

One Academy Dr., Daphne, AL 36526
Telephone: (251) 626-3303
E-mail: academy@ussa.edu
Internet: www.ussa.edu
Founded 1972
Private control
Academic year: September to August
Offers degrees in sports science, sports management
Pres. and CEO: Dr THOMAS P. ROSANDICH
Vice-Pres.: Dr T. J. ROSANDICH
Exec. Sec.: CANELA STEINER
Dean of Admin. and Finance: HOLLY McLELLAN
Dir of Doctoral Studies: Dr FRED CROMARTIE
Dir of Student Services: Dr TIMOTHY FOLEY
Registrar: SARA COLE
Dir for Library and Archivist: GREG TYLER
Library: 1m. vols
Number of teachers: 30
Number of students: 875
Publications: *The Academy* (2 a year), *The Sport Digest* (4 a year, online, thesportdigest.com), *The Sport Journal* (4 a year, online, www.thesportjournal.org)

UNIVERSITY OF ALABAMA

POB 870100, Tuscaloosa, AL 35487-0134
Telephone: (205) 348-6010
E-mail: registrar@ua.edu
Internet: www.ua.edu
Founded 1831
State control
Academic year: August to May
Pres.: Dr JUDY L. BONNER
Provost and Vice-Pres. for Academic Affairs: Dr JUDY L. BONNER
Vice-Pres. for Financial Affairs and Treas.: Dr LYNDA GILBERT
Vice-Pres. for Research: JOE BENSON
Vice-Pres. for Student Affairs and Vice Provost for Academic Affairs: Dr MARK D. NELSON
Vice-Pres. for Univ. Advancement: Dr PAMELA H. PARKER
Exec. Sec.: MARGARET SMITH
Dean for Students: Dr TIM HEBSON
Dean for Libraries: Prof. LOUIS A. PITSCHMANN
Library: see under Libraries and Archives
Number of teachers: 1,501
Number of students: 31,747

Publications: *Alabama Alumni Magazine* (4 a year), *Alabama Business* (4 a year), *Alabama Heritage* (4 a year), *Alabama Law Review* (5 a year), *Alabama Research Magazine* (1 a year), *Alabama Review* (4 a year), *Law and Psychology Review* (1 a year)

DEANS

Capstone College of Nursing: Prof. SARA E. BARGER
College of Arts and Sciences: Dr ROBERT F. OLIN
College of Community Health Sciences: Dr THADDEUS P. M. ULZEN
College of Communication and Information Sciences: LOY SINGLETON
College of Continuing Studies: Dr CAROLYN DAHL
College of Education: Dr JAMES E. McLEAN
College of Engineering: CHARLES KARR
College of Human Environmental Sciences: Dr MILLA D. BOSCHUNG
Culverhouse College of Commerce and Business Admin.: Dr J. MICHAEL HARDIN
Graduate School: Dr DAVID A. FRANCKO
Honors College: Dr SHANE SHARPE
School of Law: Dr KENNETH RANDALL
School of Social Work: LUCINDA L. ROFF

UNIVERSITY OF ALABAMA AT BIRMINGHAM

1530 Third Ave S, Birmingham, AL 35294-1150
Telephone: (205) 934-4011
E-mail: president@uab.edu
Internet: www.uab.edu
Founded 1936, present name and status 1969
State control
Pres.: Dr CAROL Z. GARRISON
Provost: Dr LINDA LUCAS
Sr Vice-Pres.: Dr RAY L. WATTS
Vice-Pres. for Devt., Alumni and External Relations: Dr SHIRLEY SALLOWAY KAHN
Vice-Pres. for Financial Affairs and Admin.: RICHARD L. MARGISON
Vice-Pres. for Information Technology: Dr DOUG RIGNEY
Vice-Pres. Research and Economic Devt: Dr RICHARD B. MARCHASE
Library: 1m. vols (Mervyn H. Sterne Library), 358,858 vols (Lister Hill Library of the Health Sciences); 2,125 current periodicals (Sterne), 1,809 current periodicals (Lister Hill)
Number of teachers: 2,240 (2,090 full-time)
Number of students: 17,600
Publications: *UAB Magazine* (4 a year), *UAB Reporter* (52 a year)

DEANS

College of Arts and Sciences: THOMAS M. DiLORENZO
Graduate School: Dr BRYAN D. NOE
School of Business: Prof. Dr DAVID R. KLOCK
School of Dentistry: Dr MICHAEL S. REDDY
School of Education: Prof. DEBORAH L. VOLTZ
School of Engineering: Dr MELINDA LALOR
School of Health Professions: Dr HAROLD P. JONES
School of Medicine: Dr RAY L. WATTS
School of Nursing: Dr DOREEN C. HARPER
School of Optometry: Dr KELLY NICHOLS
School of Public Health: Prof. Dr MAX MICHAEL, III

UNIVERSITY OF ALABAMA IN HUNTSVILLE

301 Sparkman Dr., Huntsville, AL 35899
Telephone: (256) 824-1000
E-mail: uahadmissions@uah.edu
Internet: www.uah.edu

Founded 1950, present status 1969
State control
Academic year: August to July
Pres.: Dr ROBERT A. ALTENKIRCH
Provost and Exec. Vice-Pres. for Academic Affairs: Dr CHRISTINE CURTIS
Vice-Pres. for Diversity: DELOIS SMITH
Vice-Pres. for Finance and Admin.: RAY M. PINNER
Vice-Pres. for Research: Dr RAYFORD VAUGHN
Vice-Pres. for Univ. Advancement: ROBERT LYON
Dean for Students: Dr REGINA HYATT
Dir for Institutional Research: DEBBIE STOWERS
Dir for Library: Dr DAVID MOORE
Library of 284,264 vols, 27,625 current serial titles, 571,000 microforms, 2,677 audiovisual materials, 62,941 ebooks
Number of teachers: 460
Number of students: 7,400

DEANS

College of Business Administration: Dr CARON ST JOHN
College of Engineering: Dr SHANKAR MAHALINGAM
College of Liberal Arts: GLENN T. DASHER
College of Nursing: Dr C. FAY RAINES
College of Science: Dr JOHN D. FIX
Graduate Studies: Dr DAVID BERKOWITZ

UNIVERSITY OF MOBILE

5735 College Parkway, Mobile, AL 36613-2842
Telephone: (251) 675-5990
Internet: www.umobile.edu
Founded 1961 as Mobile College, present name 1993
Private control
Academic year: May to August
Pres.: Dr MARK R. FOLEY
Chancellor: Dr WILLIAM K. WEAVER, JR
Vice-Pres. for Academic Affairs: Dr AUDREY C. EUBANKS
Vice-Pres. for Business Affairs: J. STEPHEN LEE
Vice-Pres. for Devt and Institutional Advancement: BRIAN BOYLE
Vice-Pres. for Enrolment Management: KIM LEOUSIS
Vice-Pres. for Student Devt: KIMBERLY B. LEOUSIS
Dean of Academic Services and Registrar: Dr DONALD BERRY
Dir of Library Services: JEFFREY D. CALAMETTI
Library of 64,504 vols, 143,605 microfiches, 950 periodical titles
Number of teachers: 111 full-time
Number of students: 1,987

DEANS

College of Arts and Sciences: Dr DWIGHT STEEDLEY
Centre for Adult Programmes: Dr PAMELA S. BUCHANAN
Graduate Programmes: Dr ANNE LOWERY
School of Business: Dr JANE FINLEY
School of Christian Studies: Dr CECIL TAYLOR
School of Education: Dr PETER KINGSFORD
School of Nursing: RICHARD McELHANEY

UNIVERSITY OF MONTEVALLO

Montevallo, AL 35115
Telephone: (205) 665-6000
E-mail: registrar@montevallo.edu
Internet: www.montevallo.edu
Founded 1896 as Alabama Girls Industrial School, present name and status 1969
State control
Academic year: August to August

Pres.: JOHN W. STEWART, III
Vice-Pres. for Academic Affairs: Dr MARY BETH ARMSTRONG
Sr Vice-Pres. for Admin. Affairs: Dr MICHELLE R. JOHNSTON
Vice-Pres. for Business Affairs: DEANNA SMITH
Vice-Pres. for Student Affairs: Dr KIMBERLY BARRETT
Registrar: SHAYNE GERVAIS
Dir of Admissions: GREG EMBRY
Dir of Libraries: KATHLEEN LOWE
Library of 248,132 vols, 7,51,618 microfilms items, 2,523 audiovisual items, 868 current periodicals
Number of teachers: 210 (135 full-time and 75 part-time)
Number of students: 3,100

DEANS

College of Arts and Sciences: Dr MARY BETH ARMSTRONG
College of Education: ANNA MCEWAN
College of Fine Arts: WILLIAM T. CLOW
Stephens College of Business: Prof. Dr STEPHEN H. CRAFT

UNIVERSITY OF NORTH ALABAMA

1 Harrison Plaza, Florence, AL 35632-0001
Telephone: (256) 765-4608
E-mail: registrar@una.edu
Internet: www.una.edu
Founded 1830 as LaGrange College, present name and status 1872
State control
Academic year: August to July (2 semesters)
Pres.: WILLIAM G. CALE, JR
Provost and Vice-Pres. for Academic Affairs: Dr JOHN G. THORNELL
Vice-Pres. for Business and Financial Affairs: Dr STEVEN SMITH
Vice-Pres. for Student Affairs: Dr DAVID P. SHIELDS, JR
Vice-Pres. for Univ. Advancement: Dr ALAN MEDDERS
Registrar: TINA SHARP
Dir of Library Services: MELVIN D. DAVIS
Library of 328,456 vols, 900,000 microform items, 7,800 audiovisual items, 2,145 current periodicals, 200,000 ebooks
Number of teachers: 285 (201 full-time, 84 part-time)
Number of students: 7,100

DEANS

College of Arts and Sciences: Dr VAGN HANSEN
College of Business: Dr KERRY P. GATLIN
College of Education: Dr DONNA JACOBS
College of Nursing and Allied Health: Dr BIRDIE I. BAILEY

UNIVERSITY OF SOUTH ALABAMA

307 University Blvd, Mobile, AL 36688-0002
Telephone: (251) 460-6101
E-mail: admiss@usouthal.edu
Internet: www.southalabama.edu
Founded 1963
public control
Academic year: August to July (3 semesters)
Pres.: Dr JOHN SMITH
Sr Vice-Pres. for Academic Affairs: Dr DAVID JOHNSON
Vice-Pres. for Devt and Alumni Relations: Dr JOSEPH F. BUSTA, JR
Vice-Pres. for Financial Affairs: STEVE SIMMONS
Vice-Pres. for Research and Economic Devt: LYNNE CHRONISTER
Registrar: KELLY OSTERBIND
Dean for Students: Dr MICHAEL MITCHELL
Dean for Libraries: Dr RICHARD J. WOOD

Library of 453,829 vols
Number of teachers: 1,050 (760 full-time, 290 part-time)
Number of students: 14,600

DEANS

College of Arts and Sciences: Dr ANDRZEJ WIERZBICKI
College of Education: Dr RICHARD L. HAYES
College of Engineering: Dr JOHN W. STEADMAN
College of Medicine: Dr SAMUEL J. STRADA
College of Nursing: Dr DEBRA C. DAVIS
Covey College of Allied Health Professions: Dr RICHARD E. TALBOTT
Graduate School: Dr KEITH HARRISON
Mitchell College of Business: Dr CARL C. MOORE
School of Computing: Dr ALEC F. YASINSAC
School of Continuing Education and Special Programs: Dr VAUGHN S. MILLNER

UNIVERSITY OF WEST ALABAMA

Livingston, AL 35470
Telephone: (205) 652-3400
E-mail: admissions@uwa.edu
Internet: www.uwa.edu
Founded 1835, present name and status 1995
State control
Academic year: August to July
Pres.: Dr RICHARD D. HOLLAND
Provost: Dr DAVID M. TAYLOR
Vice-Pres. for Financial Affairs: T. RAIFORD NOLAND
Vice-Pres. for Institutional Advancement: CLEMIT W. SPRUIELL
Vice-Pres. for Student Affairs: DANNY BUCKALEW
School of Graduate Studies: Dr KATHY CHANDLER
Dir of Library: Prof. Dr NEIL SNIDER
Library of 250,000 vols
Number of teachers: 90
Number of students: 2,300

DEANS

College of Business: Dr KEN TUCKER
College of Education: Dr KATHY CHANDLER
College of Liberal Arts: Dr TIM EDWARDS
College of Natural Sciences and Mathematics: Dr VENKAT SHARMA

ALASKA

ALASKA BIBLE COLLEGE

POB 289, Glennallen, AK 99588
Telephone: (907) 822-3201
E-mail: info@akbible.edu
Internet: www.akbible.edu
Founded 1966
Private control
Academic year: August to May (2 semesters)
Pres.: NICK RINGGER
Vice-Pres. for Academic Affairs: KEVIN NEWMAN
Vice-Pres. for Student Devt: BOB WENDT
Librarian: PAM HORST
Registrar: CAROL REIMER
Library of 30,500 vols, over 200 magazines and periodicals
Number of teachers: 10
Number of students: 45

ALASKA PACIFIC UNIVERSITY

4101 University Dr., Anchorage, AK 99508
Telephone: (907) 561-1266
E-mail: infodesk@alaskapacific.edu
Internet: www.alaskapacific.edu
Founded 1957 as Alaska Methodist Univ., present name 1978

Academic year: September to August
Pres.: Dr DON BANTZ
Academic Dean: TRACY M. STEWART
Registrar: DONNA DOUGHERTY
Library of 400,000 vols, shared with Univ. of Alaska, Anchorage
Number of teachers: 80
Number of students: 690

ILISAGVIK COLLEGE

POB 749, 100 Stevenson St, Barrow, AK 99723
Telephone: (907) 852-3333
Internet: www.ilisagvik.cc
Founded 1986 as North Slope Higher Education Center
Private control
Pres.: Dr BROOKE GONDARA
Dean of Students and Institutional Devt: PEARL BROWER
Library Dir: DAVID ONGLEY

PRINCE WILLIAM SOUND COMMUNITY COLLEGE (PWSCC)

POB 97, 303 Lowe St, Valdez, AK 99686
Telephone: (907) 834-1600
Internet: www.pwscc.edu
Founded 1978
Private control
Academic year: May to August
Some of the Bachelors courses are provided in partnership with Univ. of Alaska Anchorage and Univ. of Alaska Southeast
Pres.: DOUG A. DESORCIE
Academic Advisor: ROBYN PAUL
Dir for Student Services: CHRISTOPHER WASHKO
Dir for Training: B. J. WILLIAMS
Head Librarian: MOLLIE GOOD
Number of students: 1,500 (incl. on-campus, distance, part-time and full-time)

UNIVERSITY OF ALASKA STATEWIDE SYSTEM

POB 757500, Fairbanks, AK 99775
Suite 206, Butrovich Bldg, Fairbanks, AK 99775
Telephone: (907) 450-8100
E-mail: syserve@alaska.edu
Internet: www.alaska.edu
Founded 1917 as Alaska Agricultural College and School of Mines; univ. status 1935; consists of 3 multi-campus 4-year univs, community college
Pres.: PATRICK K. GAMBLE
Vice-Pres. for Academic Affairs: DANIEL J. JULIUS
Vice-Pres. for Finance and Admin.: JOE TRUBACZ
Vice-Pres. for Research: Dr DANIEL J. JULIUS
Vice-Pres. for Univ. Relations: CARLA BEAM
Number of teachers: 2,300 (statewide)
Number of students: 32,700 (statewide)
Publs program catalogues from various units of the univ...

CONSTITUENT UNIVERSITIES

University of Alaska Anchorage: POB 141629, Anchorage, AK 99514-1629; tel. (907) 786-1480; e-mail enroll@uaa.alaska .edu; internet www.uaa.alaska.edu; Chancellor and CEO TOM CASE; 20,554 students.
University of Alaska Fairbanks: POB 757520, Fairbanks, AK 99775; tel. (907) 474-7211; e-mail admissions@uaf.edu; internet www.uaf.edu; Chancellor and CEO BRIAN ROGERS; 1,050 teachers; 11,000 students.

University of Alaska Southeast: 11120 Glacier Highway, Juneau, AK 99801; tel. (907) 796-6000; e-mail uas.info@uas.alaska .edu; internet www.uas.alaska.edu; Chancellor JOHN PUGH; Vice-Chancellor CAROL GRIFFIN

ARIZONA

AMERICAN INDIAN COLLEGE OF THE ASSEMBLIES OF GOD

10020 N 15th Ave, Phoenix, AZ 85021-2199

Telephone: (602) 944-3335

E-mail: aicadm@aicag.edu

Internet: www.aicag.edu

Founded 1957

Private control

Academic year: August to May

Depts of business admin., Christian ministry and education

Pres.: Dr DAVID L. DEGARMO

Vice-Pres. for Academic Affairs: Dr JOSEPH J. SAGGIO

Vice-Pres. for Financial Services: Rev. PAUL G. HENNING

Vice-Pres. for Student Devt: Rev. VINCENT R. ROUBIDEAUX

Dir for Enrollment Services: LARISSA GARMAN

Registrar: JENNIFER ROUBIDEAUX

Library Dir: Rev. JOHN S. ROSE

Library of 24,000 vols

Number of teachers: 20 (7 full-time, 13 part-time)

Number of students: 80

ARIZONA CHRISTIAN UNIVERSITY

2625 E Cactus Rd, Phoenix, AZ 85032

Telephone: (602) 489-5300

E-mail: info@arizonachristian.edu

Internet: arizonachristian.edu

Founded 1960 as Southwestern Conservative Baptist Bible College, present name and status 2011

Private control

Academic year: August to August

Depts of behavioural studies, biblical studies, business administration, Christian ministries, elementary education, secondary education, music ministry, pre-law and pre-med

Pres.: LEN MUNSIL

Provost and Sr Vice-Pres.: Dr GARY DAMORE

Sr Vice-Pres. and Chief Financial Officer: DIANE CATLIN

Academic Dean: Dr W. PERRY BAKER

Vice-Pres. for Enrolment and Marketing: HEATHER KIM

Dean for Students: CHUCK HUNTER

Registrar: LAMBERT CRUZ

Dir for Library Services: SEAN J. MCNULTY

Library of 25,000 vols, 20,000 ebooks, 13,900 ejournals and magazines

Number of teachers: 85 (18 full-time, 67 part-time)

ARIZONA STATE UNIVERSITY

University Dr. and Mill Ave Tempe, AZ 85287

Telephone: (480) 965-9011

E-mail: askasu@asu.edu

Internet: www.asu.edu

Founded 1885

State control

Pres.: Dr MICHAEL M. CROW

Exec. Vice-Pres. and Provost: ELIZABETH D. CAPALDI

Exec. Vice-Pres. and Chief Financial Officer: MORGAN OLSEN

Sr Vice-Pres. for Academic Affairs: Prof. Dr DAVID YOUNG

Sr Vice-Pres. for Educational Outreach and Student Services: JAMES RUND

Vice-Pres. and Chief of Staff: JAMES O'BRIEN

Vice-Pres. and Exec. Vice-Provost for Online and Extended Education: Dr MERNOY HARRISON

Registrar: LOU ANN DENNY

Univ. Librarian: SHERRIE SCHMIDT

Library: see under Libraries and Archives

Number of teachers: 1,800 (full-time)

Number of students: 72,254

Publications: *ASU Magazine* (4 a year), *Canyon Voices* (online —canyonvoices.asu.edu), *TRIVIA: Voices of Feminism* (online —www.triviavoices.com)

DEANS

Barrett, The Honors College: MARK JACOBS

College of Liberal Arts and Sciences: ROBERT E. PAGE, JR

College of Nursing and Health Innovation: Dr TERI BRITT PIPE

College of Public Programmes: JONATHAN KOPPELL

College of Technology and Innovation: MITZI MONTOYA

Graduate College: Dr MARIA T. ALLISON

Herberger Institute for Design and the Arts: KWANG-WU KIM

Ira A. Fulton Schools of Engineering: PAUL JOHNSON

Mary Lou Fulton Teachers College: Dr MARI KOERNER

New College of Interdisciplinary Arts and Sciences: Dr ELIZABETH LANGLAND

Sandra Day O'Connor College of Law: DOUGLAS SYLVESTER

School of Sustainability: SANDER VAN DER LEEUW

University College: Dr FREDERICK C. COREY

W. P. Carey School of Business: ROBERT MITTELSTAEDT

Walter Cronkite School of Journalism and Mass Communication: CHRISTOPHER CALLAHAN

DINÉ COLLEGE

1 Circle Dr., Route 12, Tsaile, AZ 86556-0067

Telephone: (928) 724-6600

E-mail: info@dinecollege.edu

Internet: www.dinecollege.edu

Founded 1968

Tribal control

Campuses at Chinle, Ganado, Kayenta, Tuba City, Window Rock in Arizona, Shiprock and Crownpoint in New Mexico

Pres.: Dr MAGGIE GEORGE

Vice-Pres. for Academic and Student Affairs: KY TRAVIS

Vice-Pres. for Admin. and Finance: RONALD R. BELLOLI

Library of 90,000 vols, 3,000 video cassettes and DVDs, 600 magazines, newspapers, journals and microforms

Number of teachers: 60

Number of students: 1,660

EVEREST COLLEGE PHOENIX

10400 N 25th Ave, Suite 190, Phoenix, AZ 85021

Telephone: (602) 942-4141

Internet: www.everestcollegephoenix.edu

Founded 1982 as Academy of Business College, present name 2009

Private control

Offers Bachelors degrees in criminal justice and business administration; campus in Mesa

Pres.: Dr EDWARD JOHNSON

Provost: Dr MICHAEL BERRY

Pres. for Phoenix Campus: TODD MCDONALD

Pres. for Mesa Campus: MARY RITTER

Academic Dean: JOELLYN SCHNURR

Dir for Admissions: NICK THORESON

Sr Registrar: ROSALIND PEREIRA

Librarian: DIANA FURMAN

FRANK LLOYD WRIGHT SCHOOL OF ARCHITECTURE

POB 4430, Scottsdale, AZ 85261

Telephone: (480) 860-2700

E-mail: info@taliesin.edu

Internet: taliesin.edu

Founded 1932 as Taliesin Fellowship, present name 1960

Private control

Pres. and CEO: ANNE MALEY

Dean: VICTOR SIDY

Dir of Academic Affairs: MADALENA MAESTRI

Dir for Admissions, Financial Aid and Registrar: PAMELA STEFANSSON

Dir for Libraries: ELIZABETH DAWSARI

Library of 27,000 vols

GRAND CANYON UNIVERSITY

POB 11097, Phoenix, AZ 85061-1097

3300 W Camelback Rd, Phoenix, AZ 85017-3030

Telephone: (602) 639-7500

Internet: www.gcu.edu

Founded 1949 as Grand Canyon College, present name 1989

Private control

Academic year: August to August

Pres.: Dr KATHY PLAYER

Provost and Chief Academic Officer: Dr CHERI ST ARNAULD

CEO: BRIAN MUELLER

Exec. Vice-Pres.: Dr STAN MEYER

Sr Vice-Pres. for Campus Devt: ROBERT MACHEN

Vice-Pres. for Academic Compliance and Univ. Registrar: JENNIFER LECH

Vice-Pres. for Student Services and Dean for Students: TIM GRIFFIN

Library of 155,000 vols

Number of students: 40,000

DEANS

College of Arts and Sciences: Dr MARK WOODEN

College of Doctoral Studies: Dr HANK RADDA

College of Education: Dr KIMBERLY A. LA PRADE

College of Fine Arts and Production: CLAUDE N. PENSIS

College of Nursing: Dr ANNE M. MCNAMARA

Ken Blanchard College of Business: Dr W. KEVIN BARKSDALE

NORTHCENTRAL UNIVERSITY

10000 E University Dr., Prescott Valley, AZ 86314

Telephone: (928) 541-7777

E-mail: information@ncu.edu

Internet: www.ncu.edu

Founded 1996

Private control

CEO: GEORGE A. BURNETT

Pres. and Provost: Dr CLINTON D. GARDNER

Vice-Provost: Dr SCOTT W. M. BURRUS

Dir for Library Services: ED SALAZAR

DEANS

Graduate School: Dr GREGORY T. BRADLEY

School of Behavioural and Health Sciences: Dr HEATHER FREDERICK

School of Business and Technology Management: Dr A. LEE SMITH

School of Education: Dr CINDY K. KNOTT

NORTHERN ARIZONA UNIVERSITY

S San Francisco St., Flagstaff, AZ 86011
Telephone: (928) 523-9011
Internet: www.nau.edu

Founded 1899
public control
Academic year: August to May

36 Campuses throughout Arizona

Pres.: Dr JOHN D. HAEGER
Provost and Vice-Pres. for Academic Affairs:
Dr LAURA HUENNEKE
Vice-Provost for Undergraduate Studies: Dr
KAREN PUGLIESI
Exec. Vice-Pres.: Dr M. J. McMAHON
Sr Vice-Pres. for Enrolment Management
and Student Affairs: DAVID BOUSQUET
Vice-Pres. for Admin. and Finance: JENNUS
BURTON
Vice-Pres. for Institutional Research: Dr
PATRICIA HAEUSER
Vice-Pres. for Research: Dr WILLIAM GRABE
Vice-Pres. for Univ. Advancement: MASON
GERETY
Dean and Univ. Librarian: CYNTHIA CHILD-
REY

Library: 1.4m. vols
Number of teachers: 900
Number of students: 26,000

Publication: *Horizons*

DEANS

College of Arts and Letters: Dr MICHAEL
VINCENT
College of Education: Dr MICHAEL R. SAMP-
SON
College of Engineering, Forestry and Natural
Sciences: Dr PAUL W. JAGODZINSKI
College of Health and Human Services: Dr
LESLIE SCHULZ
College of Social and Behavioural Sciences:
Dr STEPHEN WRIGHT
Graduate College: Dr RAMONA MELLOTT
W. A. Franke College of Business: Dr CRAIG
VAN SLYKE

PRESCOTT COLLEGE

220 Grove Ave, Prescott, AZ 86301
Telephone: (928) 350-2100
E-mail: admissions@prescott.edu
Internet: www.prescott.edu

Founded 1966
Private control
Academic year: September to August

Campus at Tuscon, Arizona; offers courses in
abstract art, agroecology, counselling psychology, creative writing, ecopsychology, education, environmental education and
interpretation, fine arts, human development, humanities, human ecology, management, outdoor adventure and teacher
education

Pres.: Dr KRISTIN R. WOOLEVER
Provost and Exec. Vice-Pres. for Academic
Affairs: Dr PAUL BURKHARDT
Chief Operating Officer: CATHERINE BOLAND
Registrar: MARY TREVOR
Library Dir: RICH LEWIS

Library of 23,900 vols
Number of teachers: 60 (full-time)
Number of students: 1,100

Publications: *Alligator Juniper* (1 a year,
print and online —www.prescott.edu/
experience/publications/alligatorjuniper),
Transitions

SOUTHWEST COLLEGE OF NATUROPATHIC MEDICINE & HEALTH SCIENCES

2140 E Broadway Rd, Tempe, AZ 85282
Telephone: (480) 858-9100

E-mail: admissions@scnm.edu
Internet: www.scnm.edu

Founded 1993
Private control

Pres. and CEO: Dr PAUL A. MITTMAN
Exec. Vice-Pres. for Academic and Clinical
Affairs: CHRISTINE L. GIRARD
Vice-Pres. for Devt: VONISE PETERSEN
Vice-Pres. for Finance and Admin.: MARION
DAVIS
Vice-Pres. for Student Affairs: MELISSA WIN-
QUIST
Dean for Medical Education: JONI OLEHAUSEN
Dean for Faculty and Curriculum Devt: Dr
BECKY B. CLARK

Library of 15,000 vols, 200 journal titles
Number of students: 340

Publication: *SCNM Now* (2 a year)

SOUTHWEST UNIVERSITY OF VISUAL ARTS

2525 N Country Club Rd, Tucson, AZ 85716
Telephone: (520) 325-0123
E-mail: admissions@suva.edu
Internet: www.suva.edu

Founded 1983 as Art Center Design College,
present name and status 2011
Private control

Campus at Albuquerque, New Mexico

Pres.: SHARMAN R. WOODS
Chief Academic Officer: MARVIN R. WOODS

Library of 5,000 vols, 250 video cassettes, 200
CD-ROMs, 80 magazine subscriptions, 3
newspaper subscriptions

THUNDERBIRD SCHOOL OF GLOBAL MANAGEMENT

1 Global Pl., Glendale, AZ 85306-6000
Telephone: (602) 9787000
E-mail: admissions@thunderbird.edu
Internet: www.thunderbird.edu

Founded 1946 as The American Institute for
Foreign Trade, present name 1997
Private control
Academic year: September to August

Campuses in China, Switzerland, Mexico and
Russia

Pres.: Prof. Dr ÁNGEL CABRERA
Sr Vice-Pres. for Exec. Education: Dr DENNIS
BALTZLEY
Vice-Pres. for Institutional Advancement
and and Chief Devt Officer: Dr JOAN NEICE
Chief Academic Officer and Dean for the
School: Prof. Dr DAVID BOWEN
Chief Financial Officer: TIM PROPP
Dean for Faculty: Dr DALE DAVISON
Dean for Research: Dr MANSOUR JAVIDAN
Registrar: DONNA METZGER
Dir for Library: CAROL HAMMOND
Number of students: 1,275

Publications: *Thunderbird Global Impact
Report* (1 a year), *Thunderbird Inter-
national Business Review* (6 a year),
Thunderbird Magazine (2 a year)

DEANS

Accounting: DALE L. DAVISON
Economics: JOHN F. MATHIS
Executive Education: DAVID BOWEN

PROFESSORS

Applied Accounting: DALE DAVISON
Applied Entrepreneurship: STEVEN STRALSER
Applied Family Business: ERNESTO POZA
Global Entrepreneurship: ROBERT HISRICH
Global Management: MARY TEAGARDEN
Int. Finance: JOHN F. MATHIS
Int. Studies: MARTIN SOURS
Management: DAVID BOWEN

ManagementManagement: ANDREW INKPEN,
MANSOUR JAVIDAN
Management: CHRISTINE PEARSON
Management: KANNAN RAMASWAMY
Marketing: ROBERT WIDING
Risk Management: JOHN O'CONNELL
Supply Chain Management: JOSEPH CAVI-
NATO

UNIVERSITY OF ADVANCING TECHNOLOGY

2625 W Baseline Rd, Tempe, AZ 85283-1056
Telephone: (602) 383-8228
E-mail: admissions@uat.edu
Internet: www.uat.edu

Founded 1983 as CAD Institute, present
name 2002
Private control
Academic year: September to August

Technology disciplines incl. advancing computer science, artificial life programming,
computer forensics, game design, game programming, human-computer interaction,
network security, robotics and embedded
systems, strategic technology development,
technology forensics, technology product
design, and web and social media technologies

Pres.: JASON D. PISTILLO
Provost and Dean: DAVID B. BOLMAN
Vice-Pres. for Finance: ROBERT L. WRIGHT
Dean for Academic Affairs: REBECCA R.
WHITEHEAD
Dean for Admissions and Student Support:
CHRYS PISTILLO
Dean for Online Education: MICHAEL ERWIN
Dean for Student and Employer Affairs:
MEREDITH BARHAM
Registrar: JUDITH DRAYER
Academic Librarian: SUSAN WHITE

Library of 10,000 books, CD-ROMs and video
cassettes
Number of teachers: 70 (full-time and part-
time)
Number of students: 1,050 (incl. 420 online,
64 graduates)

Publication: *Journal of Advancing Technology* (2 a year)

UNIVERSITY OF ARIZONA

Tucson, AZ 85721
Telephone: (520) 621-2211
E-mail: admissions@arizona.edu
Internet: www.arizona.edu

Founded 1885
State control
Academic year: August to May (2 terms)

Pres.: Dr EUGENE G. SANDER
Provost and Sr Vice-Pres. for Academic
Affairs: JACQUELINE MOK
Sr Vice-Pres. for Research: Dr KIMBERLY
ANDREWS ESPY
Vice-Pres. for External Relations: JAIME
GUTIERREZ
Vice-Pres. for Legal Affairs and Gen. Coun-
sel: LYNNE WOOD
Vice-Pres. for Research, Graduate Studies
and Economic Devt: LESLIE TOLBERT
Vice-Pres. for Student Affairs: MELISSO VITO
Dean for Admissions: Dr KASEY URQUIDEZ
Dean for Univ. Libraries: CARLA STOFFLE

Library: see Libraries and Archives
Number of teachers: 2,400 (f.t.e.)
Number of students: 38,057 (29,719 undergraduate, 6,962 graduate, 1,376 professional and medical)

Publications: *Arizona and the West* (history,
4 a year), *Arizona Law Review*, *Arizona
Quarterly* (literature), *Books of the Southwest*, *Business and Economic Review* (12 a

year), *Hispanic American Historical Review* (4 a year), *Record*

DEANS

College of Agriculture and Life Sciences: Dr SHANE C. BURGESS
College of Architecture and Landscape Architecture: JANICE CERVELLI
College of Education: Dr RONALD W. MARX
College of Engineering: Dr JEFFREY GOLDBERG
College of Fine Arts: JORY HANCOCK
College of Humanities: Dr MARY WILDNER-BASSETT
Colleges of Letters, Arts and Science: Dr JOAQUIN RUIZ (Exec. Dean)
College of Medicine: Dr STEVEN GOLDSCHMID
College of Nursing: Dr JOAN SHAVER
College of Optical Sciences: Dr THOMAS L. KOCH
College of Pharmacy: Dr J. LYLE BOOTMAN
College of Science: Dr JOAQUIN RUIZ
College of Social and Behavioural Sciences: Dr JOHN P. JONES, III
Eller College of Management: Dr LEONARD M. JESSUP
Graduate College: Dr ANDREW C. COMRIE
Honors College: Dr PATRICIA MACCORQUODALE
James E. Rogers College of Law: Dr LAWRENCE PONOROFF
Mel and Enid Zuckerman College of Public Health: Dr IMAN HAKIM
Outreach College: Dr MICHAEL A. PROCTOR
UA South: Dr JAMES SHOCKEY

PROFESSORS

College of Agriculture and Life Sciences:

ALLEN, R. E., Animal Science; Nutritional Sciences
AX, R. L., Animal Science; Obstetrics and Gynaecology
BEATTIE, B. R., Agricultural and Resource Economics
BOURQUE, D. P., Biochemistry; Molecular and Cellular Biology
BOWERS, W. S., Entomology
BRUSSEAU, M. L., Soil, Water and Environmental Sciences; Hydrology and Water Resources
BURAS, N., Hydrology and Water Resources
BYRNE, D. N., Entomology
CALDWELL, R. L., Soil, Water and Environmental Sciences; Communication
CATE, R. M., Family and Consumer Sciences
CHANDLER, V. L., Plant Science; Molecular and Cellular Biology
CHRISTENSON, J. A., Agricultural and Resource Economics
COATES, W. E., Arid Lands
COLBY, B. G., Agricultural and Resource Economics; Hydrology and Water Resources
COLLIER, R. J., Animal Science
COLLINS, J. K., Veterinary Science and Microbiology
CORY, D. C., Agricultural and Resource Economics
COX, D. E., Agriculture Education
DANIEL, T. C., Renewable Natural Resources; Psychology
DENISE, R. K., Animal Science
DENNEHY, T. J., Entomology
DESTEIGUER, J. E., Renewable Natural Resources
FFOLLIOTT, P. F., Watershed Management; Arid Lands
FOSTER, K. E., Arid Lands
GALBRAITH, D. W., Plant Science
GAY, L. W., Watershed Management
GERBA, C. P., Soil, Water and Environmental Sciences; Microbiology and Immunology

GIACOMELLI, G. A., Agricultural and Biosystems Engineering
GIMBLETT, H. R., Renewable Natural Resources; Landscape Architecture
GLENN, E. P., III, Soil, Water and Environmental Sciences; Wildlife and Fisheries Science
GOLL, D. E., Nutritional Sciences; Biochemistry
GUNATILAKA, L., Arid Lands
HAGEDORN, H. H., Entomology
HARTSHORNE, D. J., Nutritional Sciences; Biochemistry
HATCH, K. L., Agricultural and Biosystems Engineering
HAWES, M. C., Plant Pathology
HAWKINS, R. H., Watershed Management; Hydrology and Water Resources
HUETE, A. R., Soil, Water and Environmental Sciences
INNES, R. D., Agricultural and Resource Economics; Economics
JENSEN, M. H., Plant Science
JOENS, L. A., Veterinary Science and Microbiology
KALTENBACH, C., Animal Science
KENNEDY, C. K., Plant Pathology; Molecular and Cellular Biology
KNIGHT, J. A., Jr, Agriculture Education
LARKINS, B. A., Plant Science; Molecular and Cellular Biology
LEONARD, R. T., Plant Science
LIGHTNER, D. V., Veterinary Science and Microbiology
McCLARAN, M. P., Range Management
McCLURE, M. A., Plant Pathology
McDANIEL, R. G., Plant Science
McLAUGHLIN, S. P., Arid Lands
McPHERSON, G. R., Renewable Natural Resources
MAIER, R. M., Soil, Water and Environmental Sciences
MANNAN, R. W., Wildlife and Fisheries Science
MARCHELLO, J. A., Animal Science; Nutritional Sciences
MARSH, S. E., Arid Lands; Geography and Regional Development; Renewable Natural Resources
MILLER, G. M., Agriculture Education
MONKE, E. A., Agricultural and Resource Economics
MORAN, N. A., Ecology and Evolutionary Biology; Entomology
PEPPER, I. L., Soil, Water and Environmental Sciences
POE, S. E., Agricultural and Biosystems Engineering
RAY, D. T., Plant Science
REID, C. P., Renewable Natural Resources
RIDLEY, C. A., Family and Consumer Sciences; Psychology
ROHRBAUGH, M. J., Family and Consumer Sciences; Psychology
ROTH, R. L., Agricultural and Biosystems Engineering
ROWE, D. C., Family and Consumer Sciences; Psychology
RUYLE, G. B., Range Management
SANDER, E. G., Biochemistry; Nutritional Sciences
SCHOWENGERDT, R., Arid Lands; Electrical and Computer Engineering; Optical Sciences
SCHURG, W. A., Veterinary Science and Microbiology; Animal Science
SHAW, W. W., Wildlife and Fisheries Science
SHIM, S., Family and Consumer Sciences
SILVERTOOTH, J. C., Soil, Water and Environment Sciences; Plant Science
SLACK, D. C., Agricultural and Biosystems Engineering
SONGER, J. G., Veterinary Science and Microbiology

STERLING, C. R., Veterinary Science and Microbiology
TABASHNIK, B., Entomology
THOMPSON, G. D., Agricultural and Resource Economics
VANETTEN, H. D., Plant Pathology
VIERLING, E., Biochemistry; Molecular and Cellular Biology
WARRICK, A. W., Soil, Water and Environmental Sciences; Hydrology and Water Resources
WHEELER, D. E., Entomology
WIERENGA, P. J., Soil, Water and Environmental Sciences
WILSON, P. N., Agricultural and Resource Economics
WOLFE, F. H., Nutritional Sciences
ZWOLINSKI, M. J., Watershed Management

College of Architecture and Landscape Architecture:

ALBANESE, C. A., Architecture
CHALFOUN, N. V., Architecture
ERIBES, R. A., Planning; Architecture
MALO, A., Architecture
MATTER, F. S., Planning; Architecture
ROSENBLOOM, S., Planning; Architecture
SAN MARTIN, I. J., Architecture
STAMM, W. P., Architecture

College of Education:

ALEAMONI, L. M., Special Education, Rehabilitation and School Psychology
AMES, W. S., Teaching and Teacher Education
ANDERS, P. L., Language, Reading and Culture
ANTIA, S. D., Special Education, Rehabilitation and School Psychology
CARTER, K. J., Teaching and Teacher Education
DOYLE, W., Teaching and Teacher Education
GOOD, T. L., Educational Psychology
GOODMAN, Y. M., Language, Reading and Culture
GRIFFEY, D. C., Physical Education
LESLIE, L., Higher Education
LEVIN, J. R., Educational Psychology
LEVIN, J. S., Higher Education
McCARTY, T. L., Language, Reading and Culture
MAKER, C. J., Special Education, Rehabilitation and School Psychology
MISHRA, S. P., Special Education, Rehabilitation and School Psychology
MOLL, L. C., Language, Reading and Culture
MORRIS, R. J., Special Education, Rehabilitation and School Psychology
OBRZUT, J. E., Special Education, Rehabilitation and School Psychology
RHOADES, G. D., Higher Education (H)
RUIZ, R., Language, Reading and Culture
SABERS, D. L., Educational Psychology
SALES, A. P., Special Education, Rehabilitation and School Psychology
SHORT, K. G., Language, Reading and Culture
SLAUGHTER, S. A., Higher Education
STREITMATTER, J. L., Educational Psychology
TAYLOR, J. L., Educational Administration
UMBREIT, J., Special Education, Rehabilitation and School Psychology
VALMONT, W. J., Language, Reading and Culture
WOODARD, D. B., Higher Education

College of Engineering:

ARNOLD, R. G., Chemical Engineering
ASKIN, R. G., Systems and Industrial Engineering
BAHILL, A. T., Systems and Industrial Engineering
BALES, R. C., Hydrology and Water Resources

BALSA, T. F., Aerospace and Mechanical Engineering
BASSETT, R. L., Hydrology and Water Resources
BIRNIE, D. P., III, Materials Science and Engineering; Electrical and Computer Engineering
BREWS, J. R., Electrical and Computing Engineering
BUDHU, M., Civil Engineering and Engineering Mechanics
BURAS, N., Hydrology and Water Resources
CALVERT, P. D., Materials Science and Engineering
CELLIER, F. E., Electrical and Computer Engineering
CETAS, T. C., Aerospace and Mechanical Engineering; Electrical and Computer Engineering
CHAMPAGNE, F. H., Aerospace and Mechanical Engineering
CHEN, C. F., Aerospace and Mechanical Engineering
COLBY, B. G., Hydrology and Water Resources
CONTRACTOR, D., Civil Engineering and Engineering Mechanics
DAVENPORT, W. G., Materials Science and Engineering
DAVIS, D. R., Hydrology and Water Resources
DESAI, C., Civil Engineering and Engineering Mechanics
DEYMIER, P. A., Materials Science and Engineering
EHSANI, M. R., Civil Engineering and Engineering Mechanics
FASEL, H. F., Aerospace and Mechanical Engineering
FRANTZISKONIS, G. N., Civil Engineering and Engineering Mechanics
GANAPOL, B. D., Hydrology and Water Resources
HALDAR, A., Civil Engineering and Engineering Mechanics
HAWKINS, R. H., Hydrology and Water Resources
HEINRICH, J. C., Aerospace and Mechanical Engineering
HIGLE, J. L., Systems and Industrial Engineering
HISKEY, J. B., Materials Science and Engineering
JACKSON, K. A., Materials Science and Engineering; Optical Sciences
KECECIOGLU, D. B., Aerospace and Mechanical Engineering
KERSCHEN, E. J., Aerospace and Mechanical Engineering
KOSTUK, R. K., Electrical and Computer Engineering; Optical Sciences
KULATILAKE, P., Mining and Geological Engineering
KUNDU, T., Civil Engineering and Engineering Mechanics
LOURI, A., Electrical and Computer Engineering
LYNCH, D. C., Materials Science and Engineering
MADDOCK, T., III, Hydrology and Water Resources
MADENCI, E., Aerospace and Mechanical Engineering
MARCELLIN, M. W., Electrical and Computer Engineering
MIRCHANDANI, P. B., Systems and Industrial Engineering; Electrical and Computer Engineering
NEUMAN, S. P., Hydrology and Water Resources
NIKRAVESH, P. E., Aerospace and Mechanical Engineering
OHANLON, J. F., Electrical and Computer Engineering
PALUSINSKI, O. A., Electrical and Computer Engineering

PETERSON, T. W., Chemical and Environmental Engineering (H)
POIRIER, D. R., Materials Science and Engineering
PRINCE, J. L., III, Electrical and Computer Engineering
RAGHAVAN, S., Materials Science and Engineering
RAMBERG, J. S., Systems and Industrial Engineering
RAMOHALLI, K. N., Aerospace and Mechanical Engineering
REAGAN, J. A., Electrical and Computer Engineering; Optical Sciences
ROZENBLIT, J. W., Electrical and Computer Engineering
SAADATMANESH, H., Civil Engineering and Engineering Mechanics
SCHOOLEY, L. C., Electrical and Computer Engineering
SCHOWENGERDT, R., Electrical and Computer Engineering; Optical Sciences
SEN, S., Systems and Industrial Engineering
SHADMAN, F., Chemical Engineering
SHUTTLEWORTH, W. J., Hydrology and Water Resources
SIMMONS, J. H., Materials Science and Engineering; Optical Sciences
SIMON, B. R., Aerospace and Mechanical Engineering
SOROOSHIAN, S., Hydrology and Water Resources; Systems and Industrial Engineering
STERNBERG, B. K., Mining and Geological Engineering
STRICKLAND, R. N., Electrical and Computer Engineering; Optical Sciences
SUNDARESHAN, M. K., Electrical and Computer Engineering
SZIDAROVSZKY, F., Systems and Industrial Engineering; Hydrology and Water Resources
SZILAGYI, M. N., Electrical and Computer Engineering
UHLMANN, D. R., Materials Science and Engineering; Optical Sciences
VALDES, J. B., Civil Engineering and Engineering Mechanics; Hydrology and Water Resources
VARADY, R. G., Hydrology and Water Resources
VRUDHULA, S. B. K., Electrical and Computer Engineering
WANG, F., Systems and Industrial Engineering
WEINBERG, M. C., Materials Science and Engineering
WENDT, J. O. L., Chemical and Environmental Engineering
WILLIAMS, J. G., Nuclear and Energy Engineering
WILLIAMS, S. K., Materials Science and Engineering
WYGNANSKI, I. J., Aerospace and Mechanical Engineering
YEH, T.-C. J., Hydrology and Water Resources
ZEIGLER, B. P., Electrical and Computer Engineering
ZIOLKOWSKI, R. W., Electrical and Computer Engineering

College of Fine Arts:
ASIA, D. I., Music
BOELTS, J. G., Art
CALDWELL, C. B., Media Arts
CHABOT, A. M., Art
CHAMBERLAIN, B. B., Music
COOK, G. D., Music
CROFT, M. F., Art
CUTIETTA, R. A., Music
DEMING, C. J., Media Arts
DIETZ, W. D., Music
DIXON, H. W., Theatre Arts
ERVIN, T. R., Music

FAN, P., Music
FERNANDEZ, N., Music
GEOFFRION, M. M., Art
GREER, W. D., Art
HAMMAN, D. L., Music
HAMMOND, H., Art
HANCOCK, J. L., Dance
HANSON, G. I., Music
HASKELL, J. R., Music
HEDDEN, S. K., Music
HITNER, C. V., Art
JONES, H. H., Art
KASHY, J. L., Music
KIRKBRIDE, J. E., Music
KOLOSICK, J. T., Music
LOWE, M., Dance
McLAUGHLIN, C. M., Music
MURPHY, E. W., Music
O'BRIEN, J. P., Music
PARRY, E. C., III, Art
PATTERSON, R. T., Music
POLK, A. W., Art
POWELL, G. C., Music
QUIROZ, A. J., Music
ROE, C. R., Music
ROGERS, B. J., Art
SEVIGNY, M. J., Art
TUCCI, A. D., Theatre Arts
TUNKARA, M. S., Art
WIMMER, G. E., Art
WINSLOW, D. J., Theatre Arts
ZUMBRO, N. L., Music

College of Humanities:
AIKEN, S. H., English
ARIEW, R. A., French and Italian
BABCOCK, B. A., English
BECK, J., French and Italian
BOWEN, R., English
CANFIELD, J. D., English
CHANDOLA, A. C., East Asian Studies
CHISHOLM, D. H., German Studies
CLASSEN, A., German Studies
COMPITELLO, M. A., Spanish and Portuguese
DAHOOD, R., English
DAYAN, J., English
DRYDEN, E. A., English
ENOS, T., English
EPSTEIN, W. H., English
EVANS, E. J., English
EVERS, L. J., English
FIELDER, G. E., Russian and Slavic Languages
FIORE, R. L., Spanish and Portuguese
GARRARD, J. G., Russian and Slavic Languages
GILABERT, J. J., Spanish and Portuguese
GONZALEZ, R. D., English
GUTSCHE, G. J., Russian and Slavic Languages
GYURKO, L. A., Spanish and Portuguese
HOGLE, J. E., English
HOUSTON, R. W., English
KIEFER, F. P., Jr, English
KINKADE, R. P., Spanish and Portuguese
KOLODNY, A., English
KUNNIE, J. E., African-American Studies
LEONARD, A., Jr, Classics; Near Eastern Studies
McKNIGHT, B. E., East Asian Studies
MARTINSON, S. D., German Studies
MEDINE, P. E., English
MILLER, J. R., English
MILLER, T. P., English
MOMADAY, N. S., English
MONSMAN, G. C., English
NANTELL, J. A., Spanish and Portuguese
ORLEN, S. L., English
PENNER, J. D., English
PIALORSI, F. P., English
POVERMAN, C. E., English
PROMIS, J. M. O., Spanish and Portuguese
RAVAL, S. S., English
RIVERO, E. S., Spanish and Portuguese

SALDATE, M., IV, Education Foundations and Administration
SAVILLE-TROIKE, M., English
SCHULZ, R. A., German Studies
SCRUGGS, C. W., English
SHELTON, R. W., English
SKINNER, M. B., Classics
SOLOMON, J., Classics
SOREN, H. D., Classics
TAO, C-L. P., East Asian Studies
TAO, J-S., East Asian Studies
TAPAHONSO, L., American Indian Studies
TATUM, C. M., Spanish and Portuguese
TERPENING, R. H., French and Italian
TROIKE, R. C., English
ULREICH, J. C., Jr, English
VANCE, T. J., East Asian Studies
VOYATZIS, M. E., Classics
WAUGH, L. R., French and Italian
WILD, P. T., English
WITTIG, M. M., French and Italian; Women's Studies

Eller College of Business and Public Administration:

BLOCK, M. K., Economics
BRUCKS, M. L., Marketing
BURGOON, J. K., Communication
CHEN, H., Management Information Systems
CONNOLLY, T., Management and Policy
COX, J. C., Economics
DROR, M., Management Information Systems
DYL, E. A., Finance
FELIX, W. L., Accounting
FISHBACK, P. V., Economics
GILLILAND, S. W., Management and Policy
HECKLER, S. E., Marketing
IACOBUCCI, D. M., Marketing
ISAAC, M. R., Economics
KANTOR, S. E., Economics
LIBECAP, G. D., Economics
MCCABE, K. A., Economics
MILWARD, H. B., Public Administration and Policy; Management and Policy
NUNAMAKER, J. F., Jr, Management Information Systems
OAXACA, R. L., Economics
RAM, S., Management Information Systems
RAPORPORT, A., Management and Policy
SHENG, O. R. L., Management Information Systems
SILVERS, A. L., Public Administration and Policy
SMITH, K. R., Economics
TAYLOR, L. D., Economics
WALKER, M. A., Economics
WALLENDORF, M., Marketing
WALLER, W. S., Accounting
ZUPAN, M. A., Economics

James E. Rogers College of Law:

ANAYA, S. J.
ANDREWS, A. W.
ATWOOD, B. A.
AUSTIN, G. W.
BRAUCHER, J.
CHIORAZZI, M. G.
DOBBS, D. B.
GANTZ, D. A.
GLENNON, R. J., Jr, Law and Public Policy
HEGLAND, K. F.
HENDERSON, R. C.
KORN, J. B.
KOZOLCHYK, B.
MASSARO, T. M.
MAUET, T. A.
OBIORA, L. A.
RATNER, J. R.
SCHNEYER, T. J.
SCHUESSLER, T. L.
SILVERMAN, A.
SPECE, R. G., Jr
WEISS, E. J.
WILLIAMS, R. A., Jr

WOODS, W. D., Jr

College of Medicine:

AHMANN, F. R., Medicine; Surgery
AKPORIAYE, E., Microbiology and Immunology
ALBERTS, D. S., Medicine; Pharmacology; Public Health
ALECK, K. A., Clinical Paediatrics
ALPERT, J. S., Medicine
AMPEL, N. M., Medicine
ATWATER, A. E., Physiology
BALDWIN, A. L., Physiology
BARANKO, P. V., Clinical Professor
BARKER, S. J., Anaesthesiology
BARNES, G. R., Jr, Clinical Professor
BARRETT, H. H., Optical Sciences; Radiology
BARTON, L. L., Paediatrics
BERG, R. A., Paediatrics
BERNSTEIN, H., Microbiology and Immunology
BOWDEN, G. T., Radiation Oncology; Pharmacology and Toxicology
BOYWER, T. D., Medicine
BRANDENBURG, R. O., Medicine
BRAUN, E. J., Physiology
BUCHSBAUM, H. W., Clinical Neurology
BURT, J. M., Physiology; Surgery
BUXER, J. B., Clinical Professor
CANFIELD, L. M., Public Health
CARMONA, R. H., Clinical Surgery
CARTER, D. E., Pharmacology and Toxicology
CETAS, T. C., Radiation Oncology
CHAMBLISS, L., Clinical Obstetrics and Gynaecology
CLEWELL, W. H., Clinical Professor
COULL, B. M., Neurology; Medicine
COULTHARD, S. W., Clinical Surgery
CRAIG, A. D., Jr, Cell Biology and Anatomy
CROSS, H. E., Clinical Ophthalmology
CUNNIFF, C. M., Paediatrics; Clinical Obstetrics and Gynaecology
CUNNINGHAM, J. T., Clinical Medicine
DALLAS, W. J., Optical Sciences; Radiology
DALTON, W. S., Medicine
DANTZLER, W. H., Physiology
DASPIT, C. P., Clinical Surgery
DAVIS, T. P., Pharmacology
DELLON, A. L., Clinical Professor
DEMEURE, M. J., Surgery
DORR, R. T., Pharmacology
DRESNER, M. L., Clinical Surgery
DRYDEN, R. M., Clinical Opthalmology
DUCKWORTH, W. C., Clinical Medicine
DUNCAN, B. R., Paediatrics; Public Health
ELLIOT, J., Clinical Obstetrics and Gynaecology
ERENBERG, A., Clinical Paediatrics
ESCOBAR, P. L., Clinical Medicine
EWY, G. A., Medicine
FAGAN, T. C., Medicine
FELICETTA, J. V., Clinical Medicine
FISHBURNE, J. I., Jr, Clinical Obstetrics and Gynaecology
FLINK, I. L., Medicine
FREGOSI, R. F., Physiology
FRENCH, E. D., Pharmacology
FREUNDLICH, I. M., Clinical Professor
FRIEDMAN, R. L., Microbiology and Immunology
GALGIANI, J. N., Medicine
GANDOLFI, A. J., Anaesthesiology; Pharmacology and Toxicology
GAREWAL, H. S., Medicine
GATENBY, R. A., Radiology
GELENBERG, A. J., Psychiatry
GERNER, E. W., Radiation Oncology
GHISHAN, F. K., Paediatrics; Physiology
GILLIES, R. J., Radiology
GLATTKE, T. J., Surgery
GLEASON, D. M., Clinical Surgery
GLICKMAN, S. I., Clinical Surgery
GMITRO, A. F., Radiology; Optical Sciences
GOLDMAN, S., Surgery; Medicine

GORE, R. W., Physiology; Cell Biology and Anatomy
GRAHAM, A. R., Pathology
GRANA, W. A., Orthopaedic Surgery
GREEN, S. A., Public Health
GROGAN, T. M., Pathology
GROSS, R. A., Clinical Medicine
GROSSMAN, M., Clinical Medicine
GRUENER, R. P., Physiology
HABIB, M. P., Clinical Medicine
HADJIPAVLOU, A. G., Clinical Surgery
HALE, F. A., Clinical Family and Community Medicine
HALONEN, M. J., Pharmacology; Microbiology; Medicine
HAMEROFF, S. R., Anaesthesiology
HAMILTON, A. J., Surgery; Clinical Radiation Oncology; Psychology
HANSEN, R. C., Medicine; Paediatrics
HARRIS, D. T., Microbiology and Immunology
HATCH, K. D., Obstetrics and Gynaecology
HAUSSLER, M. R., Biochemistry
HAYNES, R. J., Clinical Surgery
HEINE, M. W., Obstetrics and Gynaecology
HENDIN, B. A., Clinical Neurology
HERMAN, R. M., Pharmacology
HERSH, E. M., Medicine; Microbiology and Immunology
HOYER, P. B., Physiology
HUNT, K. R., Clinical Radiology
HUNTER, T. B., Radiology
HUTTER, J. J., Paediatrics
ISERSON, K. V., Emergency Medicine
JOHNSON, D. G., Medicine; Pharmacology
KALIVAS, J., Clinical Medicine
KAPLAN, A. M., Clinical Paediatrics
KATZ, M. A., Medicine; Physiology
KAY, M., Microbiology and Immunology; Medicine
KERN, K. B., Medicine
KLOTZ, S. A., Medicine
LANCE, M. P., Medicine
LANE, R. D., Psychiatry
LEIBOWITZ, A. I., Clinical Medicine
LESLIE, J. B., Clinical Anaesthesiology
LEVINE, B. E., Clinical Medicine
LEVINE, N., Medicine
LEVINE, R. B., Neurobiology; Physiology
LEVY, P., Clinical Medicine
LIEN, Y-H. H., Medicine; Physiology
LISSE, J. R., Medicine
LOHMAN, T. G., Physiology
LUKAS, R. J., Pharmacology
MCCARTY, R. J., Clinical Medicine
MCCLURE, C. L., Clinical Family and Community Medicine
MCCUSKEY, R. S., Cell Biology and Anatomy; Physiology
MCDONAGH, P. F., Surgery; Physiology
MCLOONE, J. B., Clinical Psychiatry
MCMULLEN, N. T., Cell Biology and Anatomy; Neurology
MALAN, T. P., Anaesthesiology
MALONE, J. M., Clinical Surgery
MARCHALONIS, J. J., Microbiology and Immunology; Pathology; Medicine
MARSHALL, J. R., Public Health; Medicine
MARSHALL, W. N., Jr, Clinical Paediatrics
MARTINEZ, F., Paediatrics
MATTOX, J. H., Public Health; Clinical Obstetrics and Gynaecology
MEISLIN, H. W., Emergency Medicine
MICHAEL, U. F., Clinical Medicine
MILLER, J. M., Ophthalmology; Optical Sciences
MILLER, T. P., Medicine
MILLS, J. L., Surgery
MOHER, L. M., Clinical Family and Community Medicine
MORGAN, W. J., Paediatrics; Physiology
MORKIN, E., Medicine; Physiology; Pharmacology
MORRISON, D. A., Medicine; Radiology
NAGLE, R. B., Pathology; Cell Biology and Anatomy; Surgery

NOLTE, J., Cell Biology and Anatomy
OBER, R. R., Clinical Ophthalmology
OLESON, J. R., Radiation Oncology
ORTIZ, A., Public Health
OTTO, C. W., Anaesthesiology
OUTWATER, E. K., Radiology
OVITT, T. W., Radiology
PALMER, C. M., Clinical Anaesthesiology
PAYNE, C. M., Microbiology and Immunology
PEIRCE, J. C., Clinical Medicine
PELLETIER, K. R., Clinical Professor
PENG, Y-M., Medicine
PETERSEN, E. A., Medicine; Family and Community Health; Public Health
PETERSEN, S. R., Clinical Professor
PHIBBS, B. P., Clinical Medicine
PINNAS, J. L., Clinical Professor
PORRECA, F., Pharmacology; Anaethesiology
PORTER, J. M., Clinical Surgery
POTTER, R. L., Psychiatry
POWIS, G., Pathology; Pharmacology
PURDON, T. F., Clinical Obstetrics and Gynaecology
PUST, R. E., Family and Community Medicine; Public Health
PUTNAM, C. W., Surgery; Pharmacology
QUAN, S. F., Medicine; Anaesthesiology
RACY, J. C., Psychiatry
RAMSAY, E. G., Surgery
RANCE, N. E., Pathology; Neurology; Cell Biology and Anatomy
RAY, C. G., Clinical Pathology
REED, K. L., Obstetrics and Gynaecology
REICHLIN, S., Medicine
REIMAN, E. M., Psychiatry
REKATE, H. L., Clinical Surgery
REYNA, V. F., Surgery; Medicine
RIMSZA, M. E., Clinical Paediatrics
RIZKALLAH, T. H., Clinical Obstetrics and Gynaecology
ROBBINS, R. A., Medicine
ROEHRIG, H., Radiology
ROESKE, W. R., Medicine; Pharmacology
ROSENFELD, P. A., Clinical Obstetrics and Gynaecology
RUNYAN, R. B., Cell Biology and Anatomy
RYAN, K. J., Pathology; Microbiology and Immunology
SABBAGH, A. H., Clinical Professor
SAMPLINER, R. E., Medicine
SANDERS, A. B., Emergency Medicine
SANOWSKI, R. A., Clinical Medicine
SATTENSPIEL, E., Clinical Obstetrics and Gynaecology
SCHIFF, M., Clinical Surgery
SCHILLER, W. R., Clinical Surgery
SCHMITZ, G. L., Clinical Surgery
SCHORR, W. F., Clinical Medicine
SCHUMACHER, M. J., Paediatrics; Medicine
SECOMB, T. W., Physiology
SEEGER, J. F., Radiology
SETHI, G. K., Surgery
SHAH, J. H., Medicine; Radiology
SHAPIRO, W. R., Clinical Neurology
SHEHAB, Z. M., Clinical Paediatrics; Clinical Pathology
SHISSLAK, C. M., Public Health; Family and Community Medicine, Psychology
SIBLEY, W. A., Neurology
SILVERMAN, H. D., Clinical Family and Community Medicine
SIPES, I. G., Pharmacology and Toxicology; Anaesthesiology
SKINNER, P. H., Family and Community Medicine
SLOVITER, R. S., Pharmacology; Neurology
SNYDER, R. W., Ophthalmology
SOBONYA, R. E., Pathology
SONNTAG, V. K. H., Clinical Surgery
SPAITE, D. W., Emergency Medicine
SPETZLER, R. F., Surgery
STERN, L. Z., Medicine
STERN, R. G., Clinical Radiology
STONE, H. H., Clinical Surgery

STUART, D. G., Physiology
SURWIT, E. A., Clinical Obstetrics and Gynaecology
SZIVEK, J. A., Orthopaedic Surgery
TAETLE, R., Medicine
TISCHLER, M. E., Biochemistry; Medicine; Physiology
TOLBERT, L. P., Neurobiology; Cell Biology and Anatomy
ULMER, D. D., Clinical Medicine
UNGER, E. C., Radiology
VALENZUELA, T. D., Emergency Medicine
VAN WYCK, D., Medicine
VILLAR, H. V., Surgery; Radiation Oncology
WEIL, A. T., Clinical Public Health
WEINSTEIN, R. S., Pathology
WEISS, B. D., Clinical Family and Community Medicine
WEISS, J. C., Clinical Paediatrics
WHITNEY, P. J., Clinical Surgery
WILLIAMS, C. L., Surgery
WILLIAMS, R. L., Clinical Paediatrics
WILLIAMS, S. K., Surgery; Physiology
WITTE, C. L., Surgery
WITTE, M. H., Surgery
WITTEN, M. L., Paediatrics
WOOLFENDEN, J. M., Radiology
WOOSLEY, R. L., Pharmacology; Medicine
WRIGHT, S. H., Physiology
YAMAMURA, H. I., Pharmacology; Biochemistry; Psychiatry
YATES, A., Clinical Family and Community Medicine
YUDELL, A., Clinical Neurology

College of Nursing:

BADGER, T. A.
GLITTENBERG, J. E.
ISENBERG, M. A.
MOORE, I. M.
PARSONS, L. C.
PHILLIPS, L. R.
REED, P. G.
VERRAN, J. A.
WOODTLI, M. A.

College of Pharmacy:

BOOTMAN, J. L., Pharmacy Practice and Science; Pharmaceutical Sciences; Public Health
CARTER, D. E., Pharmacology and Toxicology
COLE, J. R., Medicinal Chemistry; Pharmaceutical Sciences
CONSROE, P. F., Pharmacology and Toxicology
COONS, S. J., Pharmacy Practice and Science; Public Health
DRAUGALIS, J., Pharmacy Practice and Science; Pharmaceutical Sciences
GANDOLFI, A. J., Pharmacology; Pharmacology and Toxicology
HURLEY, L., Medicinal Chemistry–Pharmacology and Toxicology; Medicinal Chemistry–Pharmaceutical Sciences
JACOBSON, E. L., Pharmacology and Toxicology
JACOBSON, M. K., Medicinal Chemistry–Pharmacology and Toxicology
LIEBLER, D. C., Pharmacology and Toxicology
McQUEEN, C. A., Pharmacology and Toxicology
MAYERSOHN, M., Pharmaceutical Sciences
MURPHY, J. E., Pharmacy Practice and Science; Pharmaceutical Sciences
NOLAN, P. E., Pharmacy Practice and Science; Pharmaceutical Sciences
REGAN, J. W., Pharmacology and Toxicology
SCHRAM, K. H., Pharmaceutical Sciences
SIPES, I. G., Pharmacology and Toxicology
SLOVITER, R. S., Pharmacology
TIMMERMANN, B., Pharmacology and Toxicology; Pharmaceutical Sciences
TONG, T. G., Pharmacy Practice and Science; Pharmacology and Toxicology

YALKOWSKY, S. H., Pharmaceutical Sciences

College of Science:

ADAMOWICZ, L., Chemistry
ANDREWS, G. R., Computer Science
ANGEL, J. R. P., Astronomy; Optical Sciences
APOSHIAN, H. V., Molecular and Cellular Biology; Pharmacology
ARMSTRONG, N. R., Chemistry; Optical Sciences
ARNETT, W. D., Astronomy
ATKINSON, G. H., Chemistry; Optical Sciences
BALDWIN, T. O., Biochemistry
BARRETT, B. R., Physics
BARTON, M. D., Geosciences
BAYLES, K. A., Speech and Hearing Science
BECK, S. L., Geosciences
BETTERTON, E. A., Atmospheric Sciences
BICKEL, W. S., Physics
BIRKY, C. W., Jr, Ecology and Environmental Biology
BOURQUE, D. P., Biochemistry; Molecular and Cellular Biology
BOWDEN, G. T., Radiation Oncology; Pharmacology and Toxicology; Molecular and Cellular Biology
BOYNTON, W. V., Lunar and Planetary Laboratory; Planetary Sciences
BREDAS, J-L. E., Chemistry
BRILLIANT, M. H., Paediatrics; Molecular and Cellular Biology
BROWER, D. L., Molecular and Cellular Biology; Biochemistry
BROWN, M. F., Chemistry; Biochemistry
BROWN, R. H., Planetary Sciences; Lunar and Planetary Laboratory; Astronomy
BURD, G. D., Molecular and Cellular Biology; Cell Biology and Anatomy; International Studies
BURROWS, A. S., Physics; Astronomy
BUTLER, R. F., Geosciences; Arizona Research Laboratories
CALDER, W. A., III, Ecology and Evolutionary Biology
CHANDLER, V. L., Plant Science; Molecular and Cellular Biology
CHASE, C. G., Geosciences
COHEN, A. S., Geosciences; Ecology and Environmental Biology
CRANFIELD, L. M., Biochemistry; Public Health
CRESS, A. E., Radiation Oncology; Molecular and Cellular Biology
CUSANOVICH, M. A., Biochemistry; Chemistry
CUSHING, J. M., Mathematics
DAVIES, R., Atmospheric Sciences
DAVIS, O. K., Geosciences
DEAN, J. S., Dendrochronology; Anthropology
DEBRAY, S. K., Computer Science
DECELLES, P. G., Geosciences
DENTON, M. B., Chemistry; Geosciences
DIECKMANN, C. L., Biochemistry; Molecular and Cellular Biology
DOWNEY, P. J., Computer Science
DRAKE, M. J., Planetary Sciences; Lunar and Planetary Laboratory; Arizona Research Laboratories; Geosciences
ENEMARK, J. H., Chemistry
ERCOLANI, N. M., Mathematics
ERICKSON, R. P., Paediatrics; Molecular and Cellular Biology
FANG, L.-Z., Physics
FARIS, W. G., Mathematics
FINK, U., Lunar and Planetary Laboratory; Planetary Sciences
FLASCHKA, H., Mathematics
FLESSA, K. W., Geosciences
FORSTER, K. I., Psychology
FRIEDLANDER, L., Mathematics
GANGULY, T., Geosciences
GARCIA, J. D., Physics

GAY, D. A., Mathematics
GEHRELS, A. M. J. T., Lunar and Planetary Laboratory; Planetary Sciences
GEHRELS, G. E., Geosciences
GLASS, R. S., Chemistry
GLATTKE, T. J., Speech and Hearing Science; Surgery
GREENBERG, R. J., Planetary Sciences; Teaching and Teacher Education
GREENLEE, W. M., Mathematics
GRIMES, W. J., Biochemistry; Molecular and Cellular Biology
GROVE, L. C., Mathematics
GUPTA, R., Computer Science
HALLICK, R. B., Biochemistry
HAUSSLER, M. R., Biochemistry
HAYNES, C. V., Geosciences
HERMAN, B. M., Atmospheric Sciences
HILDEBRAND, J. G., Neurobiology; Biochemistry
HOLLAND, A. L., Speech and Hearing Science
HRUBY, V. J., Chemistry; Arizona Research Laboratories; Biochemistry
HSIEH, K. C., Physics
HUBBARD, W. B., Lunar and Planetary Laboratory; Planetary Sciences
HUGHES HALLETT, D. J., Mathematics
HUGHES, M. K., Dendrochronology; Watershed Management
IMPEY, C. D., Astronomy
JOHNS, K. A., Physics
JOHNSON, R. A., Geosciences
JOKIPII, J. R., Planetary Sciences; Lunar and Planetary Laboratory; Astronomy
KELLER, P. C., Chemistry
KENNEDY, C. K., Plant Pathology; Molecular and Cellular Biology
KENNEDY, T. G., Mathematics; Physics
KENNICUTT, R. C., Astronomy
KRIEG, P. A., Cell Biology and Anatomy; Molecular and Cellular Biology
KUKOLICH, S. G., Chemistry
LARSON, H. P., Lunar and Planetary Laboratory; Planetary Sciences
LEAVITT, S. W., Dendrochronology
LEVERMORE, C. D., Mathematics
LEWIS, J. S., Lunar and Planetary Laboratory; Planetary Sciences
LICHTENBERGER, D. L., Chemistry
LIEBERT, J. W., Astronomy
LITTLE, J. W., Biochemistry; Molecular and Cellular Biology
LOMEN, D. O., Mathematics
LOVELOCK, D., Mathematics
LUNINE, J. I., Planetary Sciences; Lunar and Planetary Laboratory; Arizona Research Laboratories; Physics
MCCALLUM, W. G., Mathematics
MCCULLEN, J. D., Physics
MCINTYRE, L., Jr, Physics
MAIER, R., Mathematics; Physics
MARDER, S. R., Chemistry; Optical Sciences
MARKOW, T. A., Ecology and Environmental Biology
MASH, E. A., Jr., Chemistry
MAZUMDAR, S., Physics; Optical Sciences
MELIA, F., Physics; Astronomy
MELOSH, H. J., Lunar and Planetary Laboratory; Planetary Sciences; Geosciences
MENDELSON, N. H., Molecular and Cellular Biology
MICHOD, R. E., Ecology and Evolutionary Biology
MIESFELD, R. L., Biochemistry; Molecular and Cellular Biology
MITTAL, Y. D., Mathematics
MOLONEY, J. V., Mathematics; Optical Sciences
MORAN, N. A., Ecology and Environmental Biology; Entomology
MOUNT, D. W., Molecular and Cellular Biology; Ecology and Environmental Biology; Biochemistry

MULLEN, S. L., Atmospheric Sciences; Hydrology and Water Resources
MYERS, E. W., Jr, Computer Science; Molecular and Cellular Biology
NEWELL, A. C., Mathematics; Arizona Research Laboratories
O'BRIEN, D. F., Chemistry; Biochemistry
OCHMAN, H., Biochemistry; Ecology and Environmental Biology; Molecular and Cellular Biology
OVERPECK, J. T., Geosciences
PALMER, J. N., Mathematics
PARKER, R. R., Molecular and Cellular Biology; Biochemistry
PARRISH-JONES, J. T., Geosciences
PATCHETT, P. J., Geosciences; Arizona Research Laboratories
PATRASCIOIU, A. N., Physics
PEMBERTON, J. E., Chemistry
POLT, R. L., Chemistry
POMEAU, Y., Mathematics
RAFELSKI, J., Physics; Arizona Research Laboratories
RIEKE, G. H., Astronomy; Planetary Sciences; Lunar and Planetary Laboratory
RIEKE, M. J., Astronomy
ROSENZWEIG, M. L., Ecology and Evolutionary Biology
RUIZ, J., Geosciences
RUTHERFOORD, J. P., Physics
RYCHLIK, M. R., Mathematics
SALZMAN, W. R., Chemistry
SARCEVIC, I., Physics
SCADRON, M. D., Physics
SCHAFFER, W. M., Ecology and Evolutionary Biology
SCHLICHTING, R. D., Computer Science
SCHMIDT, G. D., Astronomy
SHAKED, M., Mathematics
SHUPE, M. A., Physics
SMITH, M. A., Chemistry
SNODGRASS, R. T., Computer Science
STEIN, D. L., Physics
STEVENSON, F. W., Mathematics
STRITTMATTER, P. A., Astronomy
SWETNAM, T. W., Dendrochronology
SWINDLE, T. D., Lunar and Planetary Laboratory; Planetary Sciences; Geosciences
TABOR, M., Mathematics; Applied Mathematics; Physics
THAKUR, D. S., Mathematics
THOMPSON, R. I., Astronomy
TIFFT, W. G., Astronomy
TISCHLER, M. E., Biochemistry; Medicine; Physiology
TITLEY, S. R., Geosciences
TOMASKO, M. G., Lunar and Planetary Laboratory
TOUBASSI, E., Mathematics
TOUSSAINT, W. D., Physics
VANETTEN, H. D., Plant Pathology; Molecular and Cellular Biology
VELEZ, W. Y., Mathematics
VENABLE, D. L., Ecology and Evolutionary Biology
VIERLING, E., Biochemistry; Molecular and Cellular Biology
VON HOFF, D. D., Medicine; Pathology; Molecular and Cellular Biology
WALKER, F. A., Chemistry; Biochemistry
WALLACE, T. C., Jr, Geosciences
WARD, S., Molecular and Cellular Biology; Ecology and Environmental Biology
WELLS, M. A., Biochemistry
WILLOUGHBY, S. S., Mathematics
WINFREE, A. T., Ecology and Environmental Biology
WING, W. H., Physics; Optical Sciences; Arizona Research Laboratories; International Studies
WOJTKOWSKI, M. P., Mathematics
WOOLF, N. J., Astronomy
WYSOCKI, V. H., Chemistry; Biochemistry
YELLE, R. V., Planetary Sciences; Lunar and Planetary Laboratory

ZAKHAROV, V. E., Mathematics
ZANDT, G., Geosciences
ZIURYS, L. M., Chemistry; Astronomy

College of Social and Behavioural Sciences:
ADAMS, E. C., Anthropology
ANDERSON, K. S., History
ANNAS, J. E., Philosophy
BARNES, C. A., Psychology
BASSO, E. B., Anthropology
BECHTEL, R. B., Psychology; Renewable Natural Resources
BECKER, J. V., Psychology; Psychiatry
BEEZLEY, W. H., History
BERGENSEN, A. J., Sociology
BERNSTEIN, A. E., History
BERNSTEIN, G. L., History
BEVER, T. G., Psychology; Linguistics; Cognitive Science
BONINE, M. E., Near Eastern Studies; Geography and Regional Development
BOOTZIN, R. R., Psychology; Psychiatry
BUCHANAN, A. E., Philosophy
CHALMERS, D. J., Philosophy
CHAVES, M. A., Sociology
CLARKE, J. W., Political Science
COSGROVE, R. A., History
DANIEL, T. C., Psychology; Renewable Natural Resources
DE LA TORRE, A. I., Mexican American Studies–Public Health
DEAN, J. S., Dendrochronology; Anthropology
DEMERS, R. A., Linguistics
DEUTSCH, S. J., History
DEVER, W. G., Near Eastern Studies
DINNERSTEIN, L., History
DINNERSTEIN, M., Women's Studies
DOBSON, M. V., Ophthalmology
EATON, R. M., History
ESTRADA, A. L., Mexican American Studies
FERNANDEZ, C., Sociology
FINAN, T. J., Anthropology
FISH, P. R., Anthropology
FORSTER, K. I., Psychology
FUCHS, E., Near Eastern Studies; Judaic Studies
GALASKIEWICZ, J. J., Sociology
GAMAL, A. S., Near Eastern Studies
GARCIA, J. A., Political Science
GARCIA, J. R., History
GARRETT, M. F., Psychology; Linguistics; Speech and Hearing Studies
GIBSON, L. J., Geography
GLISKY, E. L., Psychology
GLITTENBERG, J. E., Nursing; Psychiatry; Anthropology
GOLDMAN, A. I., Philosophy
GREENBERG, J. B., Anthropology
GUMERMAN, G. J., Anthropology
HAMMOND, M., Linguistics
HARNISH, R. M., Philosophy; Linguistics
HEALEY, R. A., Philosophy
HILL, J. H., Anthropology
HURT, C. D., Information Resources and Library Science; Communication
JACOB, C. S., Communication
JOHNSON, J. W., Journalism
KARANT-NUNN, S. C., History
KASZNIAK, A. W., Psychology; Psychiatry; Neurology
KENNEDY, E. J., Women's Studies; Anthropology
KING, J. E., Psychology; Anthropology
KRAMER, C., Anthropology
LANGENDOEN, D. T., Linguistics
LANSING, J. S., Anthropology
LONGACRE, W. A., Anthropology
MCNAUGHTON, B. L., Psychology; Physiology
MCPHERSON, J. M., Sociology
MALONEY, J. C., Philosophy
MARSH, S. E., Arid Lands; Geography and Regional Development
MARSTON, S., Geography and Regional Development

MARTINEZ, O., History
MISHLER, W. T., II, Political Science
MOLM, L. D., Sociology
MORBECK, M. E., Anthropology
MORILL, C. K., Sociology; Psychology; Communication
MULLIGAN, G. F., Geography and Regional Development
NADEL, L., Psychology
NADER, H., History
NICHOLS, R. L., History
NICHTER, M., Anthropology; Public Health
NORRANDER, B., Political Science
OLSEN, J. W., Anthropology
PAREZO, N. J., American Indian Studies; Anthropology
PETERSON, M. A., Psychology
PHILIPS, S. U., Anthropology
PIATTELLI-PALMARINI, M., Cognitive Science
PLANE, D., Geography and Regional Development
POLLOCK, J. L., Philosophy
RAGIN, C. C., Sociology
REID, J. J., Jr, Anthropology
ROHRBAUGH, M. J., Psychology; Family and Consumer Sciences
ROWE, D. C., Family and Consumer Sciences; Psychology
SALES, B. D., Psychology; Psychiatry; Law
SCHIFFER, M. B., Anthropology
SCHLEGEL, A. E., Anthropology
SCHMIDTZ, D. J., Philosophy; Economics
SCHWARTZ, G. E., Psychology; Psychiatry; Neurology; Medicine
SCHWARTZ, J. E., Political Science
SECHREST, L., Psychology
SHARKEY, J. E., Journalism
SHELDON, B. E., Information Resources and Library Science
SHERIDAN, T. E., Anthropology
SHOHAM, V., Psychology
SILVERS, A. L., Public Administration and Policy
SMITH, C. D., Jr, Near Eastern Studies
SMITH-LOVIN, D. L., Sociology
SNOW, D. A., Sociology
STEVENS, S. J., Research Professor
STINI, W. A., Anthropology; Family and Community Medicine; Public Health
SULLIVAN, M. P., Political Science
VOLGY, T. J., Political Science
WALKER, H. A., Sociology
WEINER, D. R., History
WELSH, W. A., Political Science; Family and Consumer Medicine
WENK, G. L., Psychology; Neurology
WILLIAMS, E. J., Political Science
WILLIAMS, J. M., Psychology
ZEGURA, S. L., Anthropology
ZEPEDA, O., Linguistics

Arizona International College:
AMEGAGO, M. M. K.
BIXBY, B. R.
BUKHARDT, P. E.
BURGESS, K. H.
CONTERIS, H. J.
DURAN-CERDA, D. M.
FERNANDO, J. L.
GRIJALVA, M. A.
HELGERT, J. P.
PELTIER, J.
POPE, E. R.
SCOTT, A. G.
SHERMAN, P. M.
SPATARO, L. P.
TAL, K.

Optical Sciences Center:
DERENIAK, E. L., Optical Sciences; Electrical and Computer Engineering
FALCO, C. M., Optical Sciences; Arizona Research Laboratories
FRIEDEN, B. R., Optical Sciences
GIBBS, H. M., Optical Sciences
MANSURIPUR, M., Optical Sciences
MARATHAY, A. S., Optical Sciences

MEYSTRE, P., Optical Sciences; Physics
PEYGHAMBARIAN, N. N., Optical Sciences; Materials Science and Engineering
POWELL, R. C., Optical Sciences; Materials Science and Engineering
SARGENT, M., III, Optical Sciences
SARID, D., Optical Sciences; Arizona Research Laboratories
SASIAN, J. M., Optical Sciences; Astronomy
SHACK, R. V., Optical Sciences
SHOEMAKER, R. L., Optical Sciences; Chemistry; Radiology
WRIGHT, E. M., Optical Sciences; Physics
WYANT, J. C., Optical Sciences; Electrical and Computer Engineering

Other academic units:
ACOSTA, J. J., Military Science Tactics
CHRISTMAN, W. E., Naval Science
DYCHE, D. D., Military Aerospace Studies
WILKINSON, R. H., Humanities Programme.

ATTACHED RESEARCH INSTITUTE
Mount Graham International Observatory: operated by Steward Observatory, the research arm of the Dept of Astronomy; see separate entry under Research Institutes

UNIVERSITY OF PHOENIX

1625 W Fountainhead Parkway, Tempe, AZ 85282-2371

Telephone: (480) 966-9577
Internet: www.phoenix.edu

Founded 1976
Private control

163 Campuses and learning centres in the USA, Canada and Puerto Rico; internet-based degree courses

Pres.: TIMOTHY P. SLOTTOW
Provost and Sr Vice-Pres.: ALAN DRIMMER
Sr Vice-Pres. for Academic Research: ADAM HONEA
Vice-Pres. for Academic Admin.: LEE FINKEL
Vice-Pres. for Academic Operations: RUSS PADEN

Number of teachers: 32,000
Number of students: 470,800

DEANS

College of Criminal Justice and Security: Dr JAMES J. NESS
College of Education: Dr MEREDITH CURLEY
College of Humanities: Dr BARB BADERMAN
College of Information Systems and Technology: Dr BLAIR SMITH
College of Natural Sciences: Dr HINRICH EYLERS
College of Nursing: Dr PAMELA FULLER
College of Social Sciences: Dr LYNN HALL
School of Advanced Studies: Dr JEREMY MORELAND
School of Business: Dr BILL BERRY

WESTERN INTERNATIONAL UNIVERSITY

9215 N Black Canyon Highway, Phoenix, AZ 85021

Telephone: (602) 943-2311
E-mail: wiuinfo@apollogrp.edu
Internet: www.west.edu

Founded 1978
Private control

Campuses at Scottsdale, Chandler, Tempe, and Peoria in Arizona, and in China, India and Netherlands; offers bachelors degrees and MBA in business admin., management, information technology, finance, marketing and int. business

Pres.: TRACY LORENZ
Provost: Dr BARBARA BADERMAN
Vice-Pres. for Information Technology

Vice-Pres. for Strategy and Devt: ALLYSON POOLEY
Vice-Pres. for Univ. Services: KRIS McCALL
Sr Dir for Finance: HEIDI PHIPPS
Dir for Enrolment: AMY KWIATKOWSKI
Dir for Enrolment: MELISSA MACHUCA
Registrar: HUE HASLIM

ARKANSAS

ARKANSAS BAPTIST COLLEGE

1621 Dr Martin Luther King Dr., Little Rock, AR 72202

Telephone: (501) 370-4000
E-mail: admissions@arkansasbaptist.edu
Internet: www.arkansasbaptist.edu

Founded 1884 as Minister's Institute, present name 1885
Private control

Schools of arts and sciences, business and religious studies

Pres.: Dr O. FITZGERALD HILL
Exec. Vice-Pres. and Chief Financial Officer: BILLY OWENS
Vice-Pres. for Academic Affairs: Dr HOWARD O. GIBSON
Registrar: FREDDIE FOX
Library Dir: JOYCE CAMPBELL

DEANS

School of Business: Dr HOWARD O. GIBSON

ARKANSAS STATE UNIVERSITY

POB 179, 2105 Aggie Rd, Admin. Bldg, Room 202, State Univ., AR 72467

Telephone: (870) 972-2100
E-mail: admissions@astate.edu
Internet: www.astate.edu

Founded 1909 as a regional agricultural training school, present name and status 1967
State control

Academic year: August to July

Main campus in Jonesboro, also campuses in Beebe, Mountain Home, Newport, Heber Springs and Paragould; Technical Center at Marked Tree

Pres.: Dr CHARLES L. WELCH
Chancellor: Dr G. DANIEL HOWARD
Exec. Vice Chancellor and Provost: Dr GLEN JONES
Vice-Chancellor for Finance and Admin.: ED KREMERS
Vice-Chancellor for Student Affairs: Dr WILLIAM R. STRIPLING
Vice-Chancellor for Univ. Advancement: Dr JASON PENRY
Registrar: TRACY FINCH
Dean for Library and Information Services: JEFF BAILEY
Library of 536,900 vols, 531,307 fed. and state documents, 482,122 microforms
Number of teachers: 630
Number of students: 21,800 (ASU System)

DEANS

College of Agriculture and Technology: Dr DAVID BEASLEY
College of Business: Dr LEN FREY
College of Communications: Dr OSA AMIENYI
College of Education: Dr GREGORY MEEKS
College of Engineering: Dr DAVID B. BEASLEY
College of Fine Arts: Dr DALE MILLER
College of Humanities and Social Sciences: Dr CAROL O'CONNOR
College of Nursing and Health Professions: Dr SUSAN N. HANRAHAN
College of Sciences and Mathematics: Dr ANDREW NOVOBILSKI
Continuing Education and Community Outreach: Dr BEVERLY GILBERT

Graduate School: Dr ANDREW SUSTICH
Honors College: Dr ANDREW SUSTICH
Univ. College: Dr LYNITA COOKSEY

ARKANSAS TECH UNIVERSITY

1605 Coliseum Dr., Russellville, AR 72801
Telephone: (479) 968-0389
E-mail: tech.enroll@atu.edu
Internet: www.atu.edu

Founded 1909, present name and status 1976
Pres.: Dr ROBERT CHARLES BROWN
Vice-Pres. for Academic Affairs: Dr JOHN W. WATSON
Sr Vice-Pres. for Admin. and Finance: DAVID C. MOSELEY
Vice-Pres. for Devt: JAYNE W. JONES
Vice-Pres. for Student Services and Univ. Relations: SUSIE NICHOLSON
Chancellor for Ozark Campus: Dr JO ALICE BLONDIN
Registrar: TAMMY RHODES
Dir for Library: WILLIAM A. PARTON
Library of 160,000 vols, 810,000 microforms, 110,000 govt documents, 10,000 multimedia titles and 1,245 current periodicals
Number of teachers: 400
Number of students: 9,800

DEANS

College of Applied Sciences: Prof. Dr WILLIAM HOEFLER
College of Arts and Humanities: Prof. Dr H. MICHEAL TARVER
College of Business: Dr ED BASHAW
College of Education: Prof. ELDON CLARY
College of Natural and Health Sciences: JEFF ROBERTSON
College of Professional Studies and Community Outreach: MARY ANN ROLLANS
Graduate College: Dr MARY B. GUNTER

CENTRAL BAPTIST COLLEGE

1501 College Ave, Conway, AR 72034
Telephone: (501) 329-6872
E-mail: info@cbc.edu
Internet: www.cbc.edu

Founded 1952 as Conway Baptist College, present name 1962
Private control
Depts of behavioural sciences, Bible, business, fine arts, health and physical education, literature and language arts, maths and science, and social studies
Pres.: TERRY KIMBROW
Vice-Pres. for Academic Affairs: Dr GARY MCALLISTER
Vice-Pres. for Advancement: SANCY FAULK
Vice-Pres. for Financial Affairs: DONNA GRAY
Dir for Student Services: BOBBY SULLIVAN
Registrar: PHYLIS HOFFMANN
Library Dir: RACHEL WHITTINGHAM
Library of 40,000 vols
Number of teachers: 50 (full-time and part-time)
Number of students: 740

CROWLEY'S RIDGE COLLEGE

100 College Dr., Paragould, AR 72450
Telephone: (870) 236-6901
Internet: www.crc.edu

Founded 1964
Private control
Offers courses in Biblical studies and business administration
Pres.: KEN HOPPE
Vice-Pres. for Academic Affairs: PHIL WILKERSON
Vice-Pres. for Advancement: RICHARD JOHNSON
Vice-Pres. for Student Affairs: ART SMITH

Dir for Admissions: NANCY JONESHILL
Registrar: PAUL MCFADDEN
Library of 12,000 vols
Publication: *CRC Insider* (2 a year)

HARDING UNIVERSITY

915 E Market Ave, Searcy, AR 72143
Telephone: (501) 279-4000
E-mail: admissions@harding.edu
Internet: www.harding.edu

Founded 1924 as Harding College, by merger of Arkansas Christian College with Harper College, present name 1979
Private control
Pres.: DAVID B. BURKS
Provost and Vice-Pres. for Academic Affairs: Prof. Dr LARRY L. LONG
Vice-Pres. for Univ. Advancement: MIKE WILLIAMS
Vice-Pres. and Dean of Students: Dr DAVID COLLINS
Registrar: JANICE HURD
Dir for Library: ANN DIXON
Library of 373,133 vols, 4,951 cassettes, 817 CDROMs, 688 maps, 837 periodical subscriptions
Number of teachers: 300
Number of students: 7,160
Publication: *Harding Magazine*

DEANS

College of Arts and Humanities: Dr J. WARREN CASEY
College of Bible and Religion: Dr MONTE COX
College of Business Administration: Dr BRYAN D. BURKS
College of Education: Prof. Dr LEWIS FINLEY
College of Nursing: Prof. Dr CATHLEEN M. SCULTZ
College of Pharmacy: Dr JULIE HIXSON-WALLACE
College of Sciences: Prof. Dr TRAVIS THOMPSON
Honors College: Dr J. WARREN CASEY
International Programmes: Dr JEFFREY T. HOPPER

HENDERSON STATE UNIVERSITY

1100 Henderson St, Arkadelphia, AR 71999-0001
Telephone: (870) 230-5000
Internet: www.hsu.edu

Founded 1890 as Arkadelphia Methodist College, present status 1929
State control
Academic year: August to May
Pres.: BOBBY G. JONES
Provost and Vice-Pres. for Academic Affairs: Dr VERNON G. MILES
Vice-Pres. for Finance and Admin.: LECIA FRANKLIN
Vice-Pres. for Student Services: CHAD FIELDING
Dir for Univ. Relations and Admissions: VIKITA HARDWRICK
Registrar: TOM GATTIN
Dir for Library: ROBERT YEHL
Library of 300,000 vols
Number of teachers: 170 (full-time)
Number of students: 3,780
Publication: *FORGE* (1 a year)

DEANS

Ellis College of Arts and Sciences: Dr MARALYN SOMMER
Graduate School: Dr KENNETH D. TAYLOR
School of Business: Dr JEFFREY L. HAMM
Teachers College: Dr JUDY HARRISON

HENDRIX COLLEGE

1600 Washington Ave, Conway, AR 72032
Telephone: (501) 329-6811
Internet: www.hendrix.edu

Founded 1876 as Central Institute, present name 1889
Private control
Language of instruction: English
Academic year: August to May
Depts of humanities, interdisciplinary and pre-professional programmes, natural sciences, social sciences
Pres.: Dr J. TIMOTHY CLOYD
Provost and Dean for the College: Dr ROBERT ENTZMINGER
Exec. Vice-Pres. and Dean for Advancement: ELLIS ARNOLD
Vice-Pres. for Enrolment and Dean for Admissions: KAREN FOUST
Vice-Pres. for Student Affairs: JIM WILTGEN
Registrar: XINYING WANG
Library Dir: AMANDA MOORE
Library of 225,000 bound vols, 20,000 govt documents, 45,000 electronic journals
Number of teachers: 110 (full-time)
Number of students: 1,400

JOHN BROWN UNIVERSITY

2000 W University St, Siloam Springs, AR 72761
Telephone: (479) 5249500
E-mail: jbuinfo@jbu.edu
Internet: www.jbu.edu

Founded 1919 as Southwestern Collegiate Institute, renamed to John E. Brown College in 1920, univ. established in 1934
Private control
Academic year: July to June
3 Locations: Fort Smith, Rogers and Siloam Springs; Undergraduate academic divs: art and design, biblical studies, business, communication, education, engineering and construction management, general studies, humanities and social sciences, natural sciences, music; depts in the graduate studies division: Christian ministry, counselling, leadership and ethics
Pres.: Dr CHARLES POLLARD
Vice-Pres. for Academic Affairs: Dr ED ERICSON, III
Vice-Pres. for Enrolment Management: DON CRANDALL
Vice-Pres. for Finance and Administration: KIM HADLEY
Vice-Pres. for Student Development: Dr STEPHEN BEERS
Vice-Pres. for Univ. Advancement: Dr JAMES KRALL
Dean of the Graduate School: Dr J. RICHARD ELLIS
Dean of Undergraduate Studies: Dr ROB NORWOOD
Dean of Degree Completion: SUSAN DEWOODY
Registrar: Dr REBECCA LAMBERT
Library Dir: MARY HABERMAS
Library of 120,000 items, incl. 6,000 periodicals, 11,000 ebooks
Number of teachers: 160 (85 full time, 75 adjunct)
Number of students: 2,200

LYON COLLEGE

POB 2317, 2300 Highland Rd, Batesville, AR 72503-2317
Telephone: (870) 307-7000
E-mail: admissions@lyon.edu
Internet: www.lyon.edu

Founded 1872 as Arkansas College, present name 1994
Private control

Academic year: August to May

Divs of business and economics, fine arts, humanities, language and literature, math and science, social science, international programmes

Pres.: Prof. Dr DONALD V. WEATHERMAN
Vice-Pres. for Academic Services and Dean for Faculty: Dr VIRGINIA F. WRAY
Vice-Pres. for Admin.: DAVID L. HERINGER
Vice-Pres. for Business and Finance: KENNETH J. RUETER
Vice-Pres. for Enrolment Services: DENNY G. BARDOS
Vice-Pres. for Institutional Advancement: TIMOTHY L. BRUNER
Vice-Pres. for Student Life and Dean of Students: Dr F. BRUCE JOHNSTON
Registrar: DONALD R. TAYLOR
Library Dir: DEAN COVINGTON
Library of 215,000 vols, 20,000 periodical subscriptions
Number of teachers: 45
Number of students: 650

Publication: *Piper Magazine*

OUACHITA BAPTIST UNIVERSITY

410 Ouachita St, Arkadelphia, AR 71998
Telephone: (870) 245-5000
Internet: www.obu.edu
Founded 1886 as Ouachita Baptist College, current name and status 1965
Private control
Academic year: June to May
Pres.: Dr REX M. HORNE, JR
Vice-Pres. for Academic Affairs: Prof. STAN POOLE
Vice-Pres. for Admin. Services: BRETT POWELL
Vice-Pres. for Communications: TRENNIS HENDERSON
Vice-Pres. for Devt: TERRY PEEPLES
Vice-Pres. for Institutional Advancement: KELDON HENLEY
Vice-Pres. for Student Services and Dean of Students: WESLEY KLUCK
Chancellor: BEN ELROD
Registrar and Dir for Admissions: JUDY JONES
Dir for Library Services: Prof. Dr RAY GRANADE
Library of 845,042 vols, 9,321 current serial titles
Number of teachers: 100 (full-time)
Number of students: 1,550

DEANS

Chesley and Elizabeth Pruet School of Christian Studies: J. DANIEL HAYS
Frank D. Hickingbotham School of Business: BRYAN MCKINNEY
J. D. Patterson School of Natural Sciences: TIM KNIGHT
Michael D. Huckabee School of Education: MERRIBETH D. BRUNING
School of Fine Arts: D. SCOTT HOLSCLAW
School of Humanities: JEFF ROOT
School of Interdisciplinary Studies: STAN POOLE
W. H. Sutton School of Social Sciences: RANDALL D. WIGHT

PHILANDER SMITH COLLEGE

900 W Daisy L. Gatson Bates Dr., Little Rock, AR 72202
Telephone: (501) 375-9845
E-mail: info@philander.edu
Internet: www.philander.edu
Founded 1877 as Walden Seminary, present name 1882
Private control
Academic year: August to July

Divs of business and economics, education, humanities, natural and physical sciences, and social sciences
Pres.: Dr WALTER M. KIMBROUGH
Vice-Pres. for Academic Affairs: Dr FRANK JAMES
Vice-Pres. for Enrolment Management: DAVID D. PAGE
Vice-Pres. for Fiscal Affairs: TERRY WALLACE
Vice-Pres. for Institutional Advancement: Dr SHANNON FLEMING
Vice-Pres. for Student Affairs: Dr STACY DOWNING
Registrar: BERTHA OWENS
Head Librarian: TERESA OJEZUA
Library of 46,000 vols

SOUTHERN ARKANSAS UNIVERSITY

100 E University, Magnolia, AR 71753-5000
Telephone: (870) 235-4000
Internet: www.saumag.edu
Founded 1911 as Third District Agricultural School, present name 1976
State control
Academic year: August to July
Pres.: Prof. Dr DAVID F. RANKIN
Vice-Pres. for Academic Affairs: Dr DAVID L. CROUSE
Vice-Pres. for Admin. and Gen. Counsel: ROGER W. GILES
Vice-Pres. for Facilities: CHARLES J. LEWIS
Vice-Pres. for Finance: DARRELL MORRISON
Vice-Pres. for Student Affairs: Dr DONNA Y. ALLEN
Dean for Students: SANDRA SMITH
Dean for Enrolment Services: SARAH JENNINGS
Registrar: Dr ED NIPPER
Library Dir: DANIEL PAGE
Library of 150,000 vols
Number of students: 3,400 (2,944 undergraduate, 435 graduate)

DEANS

College of Business: Dr LISA TOMS
College of Education: Prof. Dr ZAIDY MOHD-ZAIN
College of Liberal and Performing Arts: Prof. Dr TREY BERRY
College of Science and Technology: Prof. Dr SCOTT MCKAY
School of Graduate Studies: Prof. Dr KIM BLOSS-BERNARD

UNIVERSITY OF ARKANSAS SYSTEM

2404 N University Ave, Little Rock, AR 72207
Telephone: (501) 686-2500
Internet: www.uasys.edu
Founded 1871 as Arkansas Industrial Univ., present name 1899
State control
Pres.: DONALD R. BOBBITT
Vice-Pres. for Academic Affairs: DANIEL E. FERRITOR
Vice-Pres. for Admin.: ANN KEMP
Vice-Pres. for Finance: BARBARA A. GOSWICK
Vice-Pres. for Univ. Relations: MELISSA K. RUST
Gen. Counsel: FRED HARRISON
Number of students: 70,000 ...

CONSTITUENT UNIVERSITIES

University of Arkansas at Little Rock

2801 S University Ave, Little Rock, AR 72204
Telephone: (501) 569-3000
Internet: ualr.edu
Founded 1927, present name and status 1969
Chancellor: Dr JOEL E. ANDERSON

Provost and Vice-Chancellor for Academic Affairs: Dr SANDRA ROBERTSON
Vice-Chancellor for Educational, Student Services and Student Life: Dr CHARLES W. DONALDSON
Vice-Chancellor for Finance and Admin.: Dr ROBERT ADAMS
Vice-Chancellor for Univ. Advancement: BILL WALKER
Dean for Library: WANDA DOLE
Library of 500,000 vols, 11,000 ebooks, 28,000 journals, 3,600 periodicals
Number of teachers: 1,202 (675 full-time, 527 part-time)
Number of students: 13,000
Publications: *Arkansas Journal of Social Change and Public Service, The Journal of Appellate Practice and Process, UALR Law Review* (4 a year, online —ualr.edu/lawreview)

DEANS

College of Arts, Humanities and Social Sciences: Dr DEBORAH BALDWIN
College of Business: Dr JANE WAYLAND
College of Education: Dr ANGELA MAYNARD SEWALL
College of Professional Studies: Dr ANGELA BRENTON
College of Science and Mathematics: Dr MICHAEL A. GEALT
Donaghey College of Engineering and Information Technology: Dr ERIC SANDGREN
Graduate School: Dr PATRICK J. PELLICANE
William H. Bowen School of Law: Prof. JOHN DIPIPPA

University of Arkansas at Monticello

Monticello, AR 71655
Telephone: (870) 460-1026
Internet: www.uamont.edu
Founded 1909, present status 2003
Chancellor: H. JACK LASSITER
Provost and Vice-Chancellor for Academic Affairs: Dr R. DAVID RAY
Vice-Chancellor for Advancement and Univ. Relations: CLAY BROWN
Vice-Chancellor for Finance and Admin.: JAY JONES
Vice-Chancellor for Student Affairs: JAY HUGHES
Vice-Chancellor for UAM College of Technology Crossett: LINDA RUSHING
Vice-Chancellor for UAM College of Technology McGehee: BOB WARE
Dean for Students: SCOTT KUTTENKULER
Dean for Enrolment Management and Dir for Admissions: MARY WHITING
Registrar: Dr DEBBIE K. BRYANT
Library Dir: SANDRA CAMPBELL
Library of 500,000 vols (incl. 1,200 current periodicals)
Number of teachers: 100
Number of students: 3,638 (3,506 undergraduate, 132 graduate)

DEANS

School of Agriculture: Dr KELLY BRYANT
School of Arts and Humanities: MARK SPENCER
School of Business: Dr LOUIS JAMES
School of Computer Information Systems: BRIAN HAIRSTON
School of Education: Dr PEGGY DOSS
School of Forest Resources: Dr PHIL TAPPE
School of Mathematics and Natural Sciences: MORRIS BRAMLETT
School of Nursing: PAM GOUNER
School of Social and Behavioural Sciences: Dr THOMAS SPRINGER

University of Arkansas at Pine Bluff

1200 N University Dr., Pine Bluff, AR 71601
Telephone: (870) 575-8000
Internet: www.uapb.edu

Founded 1873, present status 1972
Chancellor: LAWRENCE A. DAVIS, JR
Vice-Chancellor for Academic Affairs: Dr
MARY E. BENJAMIN
Vice-Chancellor for Finance and Admin.:
PAULINE THOMAS
Registrar: ERICA W. FULTON
Library Dir: EDWARD J. FONTENETTE
Library of 362,653 vols, 466 journals
Number of students: 3,710

DEANS

Honors College: Dr CAROLYN F. BLAKELY
School of Agriculture, Fisheries and Human
Sciences: Dr JAMES O. GARNER, JR
School of Business and Management: CARLA
M. MARTIN
School of Education: Dr CALVIN JOHNSON
University College: Dr JEWELL M. WALKER

University of Arkansas, Fayetteville

1 Univ. of Arkansas, Fayetteville, AR 72701
Telephone: (479) 575-2000
E-mail: uofa@uark.edu
Internet: www.uark.edu

Founded 1871
Academic year: August to May

Chancellor: Dr G. DAVID GEARHART
Provost and Vice-Chancellor for Academic
Affairs: SHARON GABER
Vice-Provost for Enrolment Management
and Dean for Admissions: SUZANNE
MCCRAY
Vice-Chancellor for Advancement: BRADFORD
E. CHOATE
Vice-Chancellor for Finance and Admin.: Dr
DONALD O. PEDERSON
Vice-Chancellor for Govt and Community
Relations: RICHARD B. HUDSON
Vice-Chancellor for Student Affairs and
Dean for Students: Dr DANIEL PUGH
Registrar: DAVE DAWSON
Dean for Libraries: CAROLYN HENDERSON
ALLEN
Library: see under Libraries and Archives
Number of teachers: 989
Number of students: 23,199 (19,027 under-
graduate, 3,773 graduate, 399 law)
Publications: *Arkansas Land & Life Maga-
zine* (2 a year), *Arkansas Law Notes* (1 a
year, online, lawnotes.law.uark.edu),
Arkansas Law Record (2 a year), *Arkansas
Law Review* (4 a year, print and online,
lawreview.law.uark.edu), *Bumpers College
Alumni Magazine, Discovery, Inquiry: The
Undergraduate Research Journal* (online,
inquiry.uark.edu), *Journal of Food Law &
Policy, Journal of Islamic Law & Culture*
(2 a year), *Research Frontiers* (2 a year,
online, researchfrontiers.uark.edu)

DEANS

Clinton School of Public Service: JAMES L.
RUTHERFORD
College of Education and Health Professions:
Prof. Dr TOM E. C. SMITH
College of Engineering: Prof. ASHOK SAXENA
Dale Bumpers College of Agricultural, Food
and Life Sciences: MICHAEL E. VAYDA
Fay Jones School of Architecture: PETER
MACKEITH
Graduate School and Int. Education: TODD G.
SHIELDS
Honors College: BOB MCMATH
J. W. Fulbright College of Arts and Sciences:
Prof. Dr ROBIN A. ROBERTS
Sam M. Walton College of Business: Dr DAN
L. WORRELL

School of Continuing Education and Academic Outreach: Dr PAULINE RANKIN
School of Law: Dr STACY L. LEEDS

University of Arkansas for Medical Sciences

4301 W Markham St, Little Rock, AR 72205
Telephone: (501) 686-7000
Internet: www.uams.edu

Founded 1879, present status 1911
Chancellor: Dr DAN RAHN
Vice-Chancellor for Academic Affairs and
Chief Academic Officer: Dr JEANNE K.
HEARD
Vice-Chancellor for Admin. and Governmen-
tal Affairs: TOM S. BUTLER
Vice-Chancellor for Campus Operations:
MARK KENNEDAY
Vice-Chancellor for Devt and Alumni Affairs:
LANCE BURCHETT
Vice-Chancellor for Information Technology
and Chief Information Officer: DAVID L.
MILLER
Vice-Chancellor for Regional Programmes:
Dr MARK MENGEL
Vice-Chancellor for Research: Dr LARRY
CORNETT
Dir for Admissions: MARY MCCLAIN
Registrar: KRISTINE STUMP
Library Dir: MARY L. RYAN
Library of 42,038 vols (incl. 35,342 titles)
Number of teachers: 1,354
Number of students: 2,820
Publications: *Seek* (4 a year), *UAMS Journal*,
UAMS Medical Center Magazine

DEANS

College of Health Related-Professions: Dr
DOUGLAS L. MURPHY
College of Medicine: Dr DEBRA FISER
College of Nursing: Dr LORRAINE FRAZIER
College of Pharmacy: Dr STEPHANIE GARDNER
College of Public Health: Dr JAMES M.
RACZYNSKI
Graduate School: Dr ROBERT E. MCGEHEE

University of Arkansas—Fort Smith

5210 Grand Ave, POB 3649, Fort Smith, AR
72913-3649
Telephone: (479) 788-7000
Internet: www.uafs.edu

Founded 1928, present status 2002
Chancellor: Dr PAUL B. BERAN
Provost and Sr Vice-Chancellor: Dr RAY
WALLACE
Vice-Chancellor for Operations: Dr KYLE
PARKER
Vice-Chancellor for Student Affairs: Dr LEE
KREHBIEL
Vice-Chancellor for Univ. Advancement: Dr
MARY LACKIE
Vice-Chancellor for Univ. Relations: MARK
HORN
Dir for Admissions: MARK LLOYD
Dir for Library Services: ROBERT FRIZZELL
Number of students: 7,587
Publications: *Azahares*, *Bell Tower* (2 a year)

DEANS

College of Applied Science and Technology:
Dr GEORGIA M. HALE
College of Business: Prof. Dr STEVE WILLIAMS
College of Education: JOHN R. JONES
College of Health Sciences: Prof. Dr CAROLYN
MOSLEY
College of Humanities and Social Sciences:
Dr HENRY Q. RINNE
College of Languages and Communication:
Dr JOE HARDIN
College of Science, Technology, Engineering
and Mathematics: MARK ARANT
College of Student Success: DIANA ROWDEN

UNIVERSITY OF CENTRAL ARKANSAS

201 Donaghey Ave, Conway, AR 72035
Telephone: (501) 450-5000
E-mail: admissions@uca.edu
Internet: www.uca.edu

Founded 1907 as Arkansas State Normal
School, present name 1975
State control
Academic year: August to August

Pres. and Gen. Counsel: TOM COURTWAY
Provost and Vice-Pres. for Academic Affairs:
Dr LANCE R. GRAHN
Vice-Pres. for Enrolment Management: Dr
ROBERT W. PARRENT
Vice-Pres. for Finance and Admin.: DIANE
NEWTON
Vice-Pres. for Institutional Advancement
and Devt: SHELLEY MEHL
Vice-Pres. for Student Services: RONNIE WIL-
LIAMS
Vice-Pres. for Univ. and Govt Relations: JEFF
PITCHFORD
Dean for Students: Dr GARY ROBERTS
Registrar: ANTHONY D. SITZ
Library Dir: ART LICHTENSTEIN
Library of 400,000 vols
Number of teachers: 380 (full-time)
Number of students: 11,200

DEANS

College of Business: Dr PATRICIA CANTRELL
College of Education: Dr DIANA POUNDER
College of Fine Arts and Communication: Dr
ROLLIN POTTER
College of Health and Behavioural Sciences:
Dr NEIL W. HATTLESTAD
College of Liberal Arts: Dr MAURICE A. LEE
College of Natural Science and Mathematics:
Dr STEPHEN ADDISON
Graduate School: Dr ELAINE MCNIECE
Honors College: Prof. Dr RICK SCOTT
Undergraduate Studies: Dr T. CLAY ARNOLD

UNIVERSITY OF THE OZARKS

415 N College Ave, Clarksville, AR 72830-
2880
Telephone: (501) 979-1000
E-mail: admiss@ozarks.edu
Internet: www.ozarks.edu

Founded 1834 as Cane Hill School, present
location 1891, present name 1987
Private control

Divs of business, communications and government, education, humanities and fine
arts, sciences and mathematics

Pres.: RICHARD L. DUNSWORTH
Provost and Vice-Pres. for Academic Affairs:
Dr DANIEL TADDIE
Exec. Vice-Pres.: STEVE EDMISTEN
Dean for Admissions and Financial Aid: JANA
HART
Dean for Enrolment Management: KIM MYR-
ICK (acting)
Dean for Students: JOE HOING
Registrar: WILMA HARRIS
Library Dir: STUART STELZER
Library of 80,000 vols, 40,000 govt docu-
ments, 10,000 microfilms, 12,000 bound
periodicals, 480 current periodicals
Number of teachers: 50
Number of students: 630

WILLIAMS BAPTIST COLLEGE

60 W Fulbright Ave, Walnut Ridge, AR 72476
Telephone: (870) 886-6741
E-mail: admissions@wbcoll.edu
Internet: www.wbcoll.edu

Founded 1941 as Southern Baptist College,
present name 1991
Private control

Depts of art, business, Christian ministries, education, English, history, music, natural science and psychology
Pres.: Dr THOMAS JONES
Vice-Pres. for Academic Affairs: Prof. Dr KENNETH M. STARTUP
Vice-Pres. for Enrolment Management and Student Affairs: ANGELA FLIPPO
Vice-Pres. for Institutional Advancement and Alumni Affairs: ERIC TURNER
Dir for Admissions: AARON ABBOTT
Dean for Students: SUSAN WATSON
Registrar: TONYA BOLTON
Dir for Library Services: PAMELA MERIDITH
Library of 75,000 vols
Number of students: 690

CALIFORNIA

ACADEMY OF ART UNIVERSITY

79 New Montgomery St, San Francisco, CA 94105-3410

Telephone: (415) 274-2208
E-mail: info@academyart.edu
Internet: www.academyart.edu

Founded 1929 as Acad. of Art College, current name adopted 2004
Private control
Academic year: September to August

Schools of acting, advertising, animation and visual effects, architecture, art education, art history, art teaching credential, fashion, fashion journalism, fashion styling, fine art, game design, graphic design, illustration, industrial design, interior architecture and design, jewellery and metal arts, landscape architecture, motion pictures and television, multimedia communications, music production and sound design for visual media, photography, visual development, web design and new media
Pres.: Dr ELISA STEPHENS
Library Dir: AUDREY FERRIE (acting)
Library of 47,800 vols, 275 periodicals
Number of teachers: 1,500
Number of students: 16,000

ALLIANT INTERNATIONAL UNIVERSITY

10455 Pomerado Rd, San Diego, CA 92131-1799

Telephone: (866) 825-5426
E-mail: admissions@alliant.edu
Internet: www.alliant.edu

Founded 2001 by merger of California School of Professional Psychology (f. 1969) and United States Int. Univ. (f. 1927)
Private control
Academic year: August to May

6 Campuses in Fresno, Irvine, Los Angeles, Sacramento, San Diego, San Francisco; also in Mexico (Mexico City)
Pres.: Dr GEOFFREY COX
Provost and Vice-Pres. for Academic Affairs: Dr RUSS NEWMAN
Vice-Pres. for Admin. and Gen. Counsel: JENNIFER TREESE WILSON
Vice-Pres. for Devt and Univ. Relations: JOHN DE MICHELE
Vice-Pres. for Finance and CFO: JEANINE HAWK
Vice-Pres. for Int. Relations: TERENCE BARBER
Vice-Pres. for Undergraduates: Dr ERIC GRAVENBERG
Chief Human Resources Officer: KRISTINA COMBS
Dir of Communications: NICOLETTE TOUSSAINT
Dean for Students: Dr CRAIG BREWER
Univ. Librarian: SCOTT ZIMMER

Library of 136,471 vols, 10,065 online vols, 375 print journals, 4,945 electronic journals, 55 research databases, 3,007 video cassettes and DVDs, 892 audio cassettes, 4,463 psychological tests
Number of teachers: 200
Number of students: 4,236

DEANS

Alliant School of Management: Dr CHESTER HASKELL
California School of Forensic Studies: Dr ERIC HICKEY
California School of Professional Psychology: Dr MORGAN SAMMONS
Hufstedler School of Education: Dr KAREN SCHUSTER WEBB
San Francisco Law School: JANE GAMP

AMERICAN BAPTIST SEMINARY OF THE WEST

2606 Dwight Way, Berkeley, CA 94704-3029

Telephone: (510) 841-1905
E-mail: admissions@absw.edu
Internet: www.absw.edu

Founded 1871 as California College, present name 1968, present location 1974
Private control (part of the Graduate Theological Union)

Graduate areas of study: biblical studies, theology, ethics, church history, arts of ministry, history, social sciences, foreign languages, social theory, psychology, art, liturgical studies, Christian spirituality
Pres.: Dr PAUL M. MARTIN
Vice-Pres.: MICHELLE M. HOLMES
Dean of Faculty: JUDY YATES SIKER
Registrar and Dir for Student Services: NANCY SVENSSON

AMERICAN CONSERVATORY THEATER

30 Grant Ave, 6th Fl., San Francisco, CA 94108-5800

Telephone: (415) 834-3200
E-mail: hr@act-sf.org
Internet: www.act-sf.org

Founded 1965
Private control
Language of instruction: English
Academic year: September to May

Graduate area of study: fine arts
Chair.: NANCY LIVINGSTON
Pres.: RUSTY REUFF
Artistic Dir: CAREY PERLOFF
Conservatory Dir: MELISSA SMITH
Exec. Dir: ELLEN RICHARD
Library of 10,000 vols (incl. playscripts, books, video cassettes, language and music compact discs and tapes, music scores, and theatre journals)
Number of students: 3,000

AMERICAN FILM INSTITUTE

2021 N Western Ave, Los Angeles, CA 90027-1657

Telephone: (323) 856-7600
E-mail: information@afi.com
Internet: www.afi.com

Founded 1967
Private control

Depts of cinematography, directing, editing, producing, production design, screenwriting, sound, stage and post-production facilities
Pres. and CEO: BOB GAZZALE
Chair.: HOWARD STRINGER
Dean: ROBERT MANDEL
Artistic Dir: ROGER BIRNBAUM
Artistic Dir: FRANK PIERSON
Exec. Vice-Dean: JOE PETRICCA

Vice-Dean for Fellow Affairs: CAROLYN BROOKS
Vice-Dean for Production and Post-Production: PHILLIP LINSON

Library of 10,000 vols, 100 journals, 5,000 film scripts, 4,000 television scripts, 2,500 DVDs; spec. collns Martin Scorsese, Fritz Lang, Robert Aldrich, Charles Feldman

AMERICAN JEWISH UNIVERSITY

15600 Mulholland Dr., Bel Air, CA 90077

Telephone: (310) 476-9777
E-mail: admissions@ajula.edu
Internet: www.ajula.edu

Founded 2007 by merger of Brandeis-Bardin Institute (f. 1941) with Univ. of Judaism (f. 1947)
Private control
Academic year: August to May
Campus at Brandeis
Pres.: Dr ROBERT D. WEXLER
Provost: Dr STUART J. SIGMAN
Sr Vice-Pres. and Chief Advancement Officer: JAY A. STREAAR
Vice-Pres. for Academic Affairs: Dr LOIS HECHT OPPENHEIM
Vice-Pres. for Business, Admin. and Technology: ZOFIA YALOVSKY
Vice-Pres. for Devt: JAY STREAR
Vice-Pres. for Finance, Admin. and Technology: ZOFIA YALOVSKY
Rector: Dr ELLIOT DORFF
Dir of Sigi Ziering Institute: Dr MICHAEL BERENBAUM
Registrar: ARNIE WEISBERG
Library Dir: PAUL MILLER

Library of 120,000 vols

Publication: *Vision Magazine* (1 a year)

DEANS

College of Arts and Sciences: Dr STUART J. SIGMAN
Graduate Center for Education: Dr MIRIAM HELLER STERN
Graduate School of Nonprofit Management: NINA LIEBERMAN
Whizin Center for Continuing Education: Dr GADY LEVY
Ziegler School of Rabbinic Studies: BRADLEY SHAVIT ARTSON

ARGOSY UNIVERSITY

601 S Lewis St, Orange, CA 92868

Telephone: (714) 620-3700
Internet: www.argosy.edu

Founded 2001 by merger of American Schools of Professional Psychology, Medical Institute of Minnesota and Univ. of Sarasota

Campuses: Atlanta, GA; Chicago, IL; Dallas, TX; Denver, CO; Honolulu, HI; Nashville, TN; Orange County, CA; Phoenix, AZ; San Diego, CA; Santa Monica, FL; Schaumburg, IL; Seattle, WA; Tampa, FL; Twin Cities (Minneapolis and St Paul), MN; Washington, DC
State control

Chancellor: Dr CRAIG D. SWENSON
Exec. Vice-Pres.: Dr ERIC EVENSON
Vice-Pres. for Academic Affairs: Dr KATHRYN J. TOOREDMAN
Vice-Pres. for Admissions: JEFF CROSS
Vice-Pres. for Finance: KEN STEVENS
Dir for Library Services: CLARA WILLIAMS

DEANS

College of Business: Dr CYNTHIA LARSON
College of Education: Dr CYNTHIA KUCK
College of Health Sciences: Dr KRISTIN BENSON

College of Psychology and Behavioural Sciences: Dr SUSAN SANCES
College of Undergraduate Studies: Dr RUKMANI JAYARAMAN

ART CENTER COLLEGE OF DESIGN

1700 Lida St, Pasadena, CA 91103
Telephone: (626) 396-2200
E-mail: proffice@artcenter.edu
Internet: www.artcenter.edu

Founded 1930, current name adopted 1965
Private control
Language of instruction: English
Academic year: September to August
Undergraduate courses in advertising, environmental design, film, fine art media, graphic design, illustration, interaction design, photography and imaging, product design, transportation design; graduate courses in art, environmental design, film, industrial design, media design, transportation design
Pres. and CEO: LORNE BUCHMAN
Provost: FRED FEHLAU
Vice-Pres. and Chief Financial Officer: RICHARD HALUSCHAK
Vice-Pres. for Admissions: KIT BARON
Vice-Pres. for Int. Initiatives: MARIANA AMATULLO
Sr Vice-Pres. for Real Estate and Operations: GEORGE FALARDEAU
Vice-Pres. for Marketing and Communications: ARWIN DUFFY
Chief Human Resources Officer: NANCY DUGGAN
Vice-Pres. for Student Gallery: STEPHEN L. NOWLIN
Dir for Academics: LESLIE JOHNSON
Chief Officer for Student Affairs: (vacant)
Vice-Pres. and Library Dir: (vacant)
Registrar: WILLIAM GARTRELL

Number of teachers: 375
Number of students: 1,986

AZUSA PACIFIC UNIVERSITY

901 East Alosta Ave, POB 7000, Azusa, CA 91702-7000
Telephone: (626) 969-3434
Internet: www.apu.edu

Founded 1899 as Training School for Christian Workers, present name and status 1981
Private control
Pres. and CEO: Dr JON R. WALLACE
Pres. for Legal Affairs and Community Relations: Dr MARK S. DICKERSON
Exec. Vice-Pres.: DAVID E. BIXBY
Exec. Vice-Pres.: JOHN C. REYNOLDS
Sr Vice-Pres. for Student Life and Dean of Students: Dr TERRY A. FRANSON
Vice-Pres. for Enrolment Management: DAVID HUNTER
Provost: Dr MARK STATON (acting)
Vice-Provost for Graduate Programmes and Research: PAUL W. GRAY
Vice-Provost for Undergraduate Programmes: DIANE J. GUIDO
Library of 240,000 vols, media items, 703,000 microforms, 1,900 serial titles, 140 online databases, 46,000 electronic titles
Number of teachers: 1,074 (incl. 354 full-time, 41 part-time, 679 adjunct)
Number of students: 9,300

DEANS

Center for Adult and Professional Studies: FRED GARLETT
College of Liberal Arts and Sciences: DAVID L. WEEKS
School of Behavioural and Applied Sciences: ROSEMARY LIEGLER

School of Business and Management: ILENE L. SMITH-BEZJIAN
School of Education: HELEN EASTERLING WILLIAMS
School of Music: DONALD NEUFELD (acting)
School of Nursing: AJA TULLENERS LESH
School of Theology: T. SCOTT DANIELS

BIOLA UNIVERSITY

13800 Biola Ave, La Mirada, CA 90639-0001
Telephone: (562) 903-6000
E-mail: president@biola.edu
Internet: www.biola.edu

Founded 1908, present status 1981
Private control
Pres.: Dr BARRY COREY
Provost and Sr Vice-Pres.: DAVID P. NYSTROM
Vice-Provost for Faculty Devt and Univ. Assessment: CHRIS GRACE
Vice-Provost for Undergraduate Education: CAROL TAYLOR
Vice-Pres. for Business and Financial Affairs: MICHAEL PIERCE
Vice-Pres. for Univ. Advancement: ADAM MORRIS
Vice-Pres. for Univ. Services: GREG BALSANO
Dean of Student Affairs: JOHN W. BACK
Sr Director for Enrollment Management: GREGORY VAUGHAN
Library of 270,000 vols, 1,100 current periodicals
Number of teachers: 250
Number of students: 3,500

DEANS

Cook School of Intercultural Studies: Dr F. DOUGLAS PENNOYER
Crowell School of Business: LARRY D. STRAND
Fine Arts and Communication: DOUG TARPLEY
Humanities and Social Sciences: CASSANDRA VAN ZANDT
Rosemead School of Psychology: Dr CLARK D. CAMPBELL
School of Education: Dr JUNE HETZEL
Sciences: WALT STANGL
Talbot School of Theology: Dr DENNIS H. DIRKS

BROOKS INSTITUTE

27 E Cota St, Santa Barbara, CA 93101
Telephone: (805) 585-8000
E-mail: admissions@brooks.edu
Internet: www.brooks.edu

Founded 1945
Private control
Areas of study: photography, visual communications, visual journalism, film and video production
Pres.: JOHN CALMAN

CALIFORNIA BAPTIST UNIVERSITY

8432 Magnolia Ave, Riverside, CA 92504
Telephone: (951) 689-5771
E-mail: admissions@calbaptist.edu
Internet: www.calbaptist.edu

Founded 1950
Private control
Language of instruction: English
Academic year: September to May
Pres.: Dr RONALD L. ELLIS
Provost and Vice-Pres. for Academic Affairs: Dr JONATHAN K. PARKER
Vice-Pres. for Enrolment and Student Services: KENT DACUS
Vice-Pres. for Finance and Admin.: MARK HOWE
Vice-Pres. for Global Initiatives: Dr LARRY LINAMEN

Vice-Pres. for Institutional Advancement: Dr ARTHUR CLEVELAND
Vice-Pres. for Marketing and Communication: Dr MARK A. WYATT
Vice-Pres. for Online and Professional Studies: Dr DAVID POOLE
Vice-Pres. and Gen. Counsel: ADAM BURTON
Dean for Students: ANTHONY LAMMONS
Registrar: SHAWNN KONING
Library Dir: Dr STEVE EMERSON

Library of 257,000 vols, 277 print journals; 921 classical music CDs; and 1,241 DVDs
Number of teachers: 270 full-time
Number of students: 7,140

DEANS

College of Allied Health: Dr CHUCK SANDS
College of Architecture, Visual Arts and Design: MARK ROBERSON
College of Arts and Sciences: Dr GAYNE ANACKER
College of Engineering: Dr ANTHONY DONALDSON
Dr Bonnie G. Metcalfe School of Education: Dr JOHN SHOUP
Dr Robert K. Jabs School of Business: Dr FRANCO GANDOLFI
School of Behavioural Sciences: Dr GARY COLLINS
School of Christian Ministries: Dr CHRIS MORGAN
School of Nursing: Dr GENEVA OAKS
Shelby and Ferne Collinsworth School of Music: Dr JUDD BONNER

CALIFORNIA COLLEGE OF THE ARTS

1111 Eighth St, San Francisco, CA 94107-2247
Telephone: (415) 703-9500
E-mail: info@cca.edu
Internet: www.cca.edu

Founded 1907
Academic year: September to May
Campuses in Oakland and San Francisco
Pres.: STEPHEN BEAL
Provost: MARK BREITENBERG
Sr Vice-Pres. of Advancement: SUSAN AVILA
Vice-Pres. of Communications: CHRIS BLISS
Vice-Pres. of Enrolment Management: SHERI MCKENZIE
Dean of Students: LIZ POINTER
Dir of Libraries: JANICE WOO
Library of 73,000 vols, 2,500 online periodicals, 500,000 images and 150,000 slides
Number of teachers: 326
Number of students: 1,860
Publications: *Design Book Review* (4 a year), *Glance* (2 a year)..

ATTACHED INSTITUTES

Center for Art and Public Life: tel. (510) 594-3757; e-mail center@cca.edu; internet center.cca.edu; f. 1998; Dir SANJIT SETHI.

Wattis Institute for Contemporary Arts: tel. (415) 551-9210; e-mail wattis@cca.edu; internet www.wattis.org; f. 1998; forum for presentation and discussion of local, nat. and int. contemporary culture; Dir JENS HOFFMAN

CALIFORNIA INSTITUTE OF INTEGRAL STUDIES

1453 Mission St, San Francisco, CA 94103
Telephone: (415) 575-6100
E-mail: registrar@ciis.edu
Internet: www.ciis.edu

Founded 1968
Pres.: JOSEPH L. SUBBIONDO
Academic Vice-Pres.: JUDIE WEXLER
Dean for Students and Alumni: RICHARD BUGGS

Dir for Communications and Marketing: VALERIE BUSH
Dir for Devt: DOROTEA REYNA
Dir for Diversity and Human Resources: L'ESA GUILIAN
Dir for Facilities and Operations: JONATHAN MILLS
Dir for Finance: KEN ABIKO
Dir for Financial Aid: MICHAEL SZKOTAK
Dir for IT Services: SCOTT CILIBERTI
Dir for Public Programmes: KARIM BAER
Dir for Undergraduate Studies: MICHELLE ENG
Registrar: NANCY HAGER
Library Dir: LISE DYCKMAN
Library of 35,000 vols, 300 periodicals, 1,300 audiovisual titles
Number of teachers: 55 full-time, 11 part-time
Number of students: 1,005

CALIFORNIA INSTITUTE OF TECHNOLOGY

Mail Code 206-31, Pasadena, CA 91125
1200 East California Blvd, Pasadena, CA 91125
Telephone: (626) 395-6811
Internet: www.caltech.edu

Founded 1891 as Throop University, present name 1921
Private control
Academic year: September to June

Pres.: Dr JEAN-LOU CHAMEAU
Provost: Dr EDWARD STOLPER
Vice-Provost: Dr MORY GHARIB
Vice-Provost: Dr MELANY HUNT
Gen. Counsel: VICTORIA STRATMAN
Vice-Pres. for Business and Finance: DEAN W. CURRIE
Vice-Pres. for Devt and Institute Relations: PETER B. DERVAN
Vice-Pres. for Marketing and Communications: (vacant)
Vice-Pres. for Student Affairs: Prof. ANNEILA SARGENT (acting)
Dir of Admissions: JARRID WHITNEY
Dean of Graduate Studies: Prof. JOSEPH E. SHEPHERD
Controller and Chief Financial Accountant: MATTHEW BREWER
Sec.: MARY L. WEBSTER
Registrar: MARY NEARY MORLEY
Univ. Librarian: KIMBERLY DOUGLAS
Library of 825,498 vols
Number of teachers: 489 (incl. professorial, visiting, research)
Number of students: 2,175
Publication: *Engineering and Science*

CHAIRMEN OF DIVISIONS

Biology: STEPHEN L. MAYO
Chemistry and Chemical Engineering: JACQUELINE K. BARTON
Engineering and Applied Science: ARES J. ROSAKIS
Geological and Planetary Sciences: KENNETH A. FARLEY
Humanities and Social Sciences: JONATHAN N. KATZ
Physics, Mathematics and Astronomy: B. THOMAS SOIFER

PROFESSORS

ABELSON, J. N.
ABU-MOSTAFA, Y. S., Electrical Engineering and Computer Science
ADOLPHS, R., Psychology and Neuroscience and Biology
ALLMAN, J. M., Neurobiology
ALVAREZ, R. M., Political Science
ANDERSEN, R. A., Neuroscience
ANDERSON, D. J., Biology
ANTONSSON, E. K., Mechanical Engineering

ARNOLD, F. H., Chemical Engineering and Biochemistry
ASCHBACHER, M., Mathematics
ATTARDI, G., Molecular Biology
ATWATER, H. A., Jr, Applied Physics and Materials Science
AVOUAC, J., Geology
BALTIMORE, D., Biology
BARR, A. H., Computer Science
BARTON, J. K., Chemistry
BEAUCHAMP, J. L., Chemistry
BECK, J. L., Engineering and Applied Science
BELLAN, P. M., Applied Physics
BERCAW, J. E., Chemistry
BHATTACHARYA, K., Mechanics and Materials Science
BJORKMAN, P. J., Biology
BLAKE, G. A., Cosmochemistry, Planetary Sciences, Chemistry
BORDER, K. C., Economics
BORODIN, A., Mathematics
BOSSAERTS, P. L., Finance
BRADY, J. F., Chemical Engineering and Mechanical Engineering
BRENNEN, C. E., Mechanical Engineering
BREWER, J., History and Literature
BRONNER-FRASER, M., Biology
BROWN, M. E., Astronomy
BRUCK, J., Computation and Neural Systems and Electrical Engineering
BRUNO, O. P., Applied and Computational Mathematics
BUCHWALD, J. Z., History
BURDICK, J. W., Mechanical Engineering and Bioengineering
CALEGARI, D., Mathematics
CAMERER, C. F., Economics
CAMPBELL, J. L., Chemistry and Biology
CANDES, E. J. D., Applied and Computational Mathematics
CHAMEAU, J., Civil Engineering, Environmental Science and Engineering, Mechanical Engineering
CHANDY, K. M., Computer Science
CLAYTON, R. W., Geophysics
COHEN, J. G., Astronomy
COLONIUS, T. E., Mechanical Engineering
CROSS, M. C., Theoretical Physics
CVITANIC, J., Mathematical Finance
DAVIDSON, E. H., Cell Biology
DAVIS, M. E., Chemical Engineering
DERVAN, P. B., Chemistry
DESHAIES, R., Biology
DICKINSON, M. H., Bioengineering
DIMOTAKIS, P. E., Aeronautics, Applied Physics
DJORGOVSKI, S. G., Astronomy
DOUGHERTY, D. A., Chemistry
DOYLE, J. C., Control and Dynamical Systems, Electrical Engineering and Bioengineering
DUBIN, J. A., Economics
DUNPHY, W. G., Biology
EFFROS, M., Electrical Engineering
EILER, J. M., Geochemistry
EISENSTEIN, J. P., Physics, Applied Physics
ELACHI, C., Electrical Engineering and Planetary Science
ELLIS, R. S., Astronomy
ENSMINGER, J. E., Anthropology
FARLEY, K. A., Geochemistry
FEINGOLD, M., History
FILIPPONE, B. W., Physics
FLACH, M., Mathematics
FLAGAN, R. C., Chemical Engineering, Environmental Science and Engineering
FRASER, S. E., Biology, Bioengineering
FULTZ, B. T., Materials Science and Applied Physics
GHARIB, M., Aeronautics and Bioengineering
GODDARD, W. A., III, Chemistry, Materials Science and Applied Physics
GOEREE, J. K., Economics
GOODSTEIN, D. L., Physics and Applied Physics

GOODWIN, D. G., Mechanical Engineering and Applied Physics
GRAY, H. B., Chemistry
GRETHER, D. M., Economics
GROTZINGER, J. P., Geology
GRUBBS, R. H., Chemistry
GURNIS, M. C., Geophysics
HAILE, S. M., Materials Science and Chemical Engineering
HAJIMIRI, S., Electrical Engineering
HALL, J. F., Civil Engineering
HARRISON, F. A., Physics and Astronomy
HEATH, J. R., Chemistry
HEATON, T. H., Engineering Seismology
HELMBERGER, D. V., Geophysics
HERING, J. G., Environmental Science and Engineering
HITCHCOCK, C. R., Philosophy
HITLIN, D. G., Physics
HOFFMAN, P. T., History and Social Science
HOFFMANN, M. R., Environmental Science
HOU, Y. T., Applied and Computational Mathematics
HUGHES, E. W., Physics
HUNT, M. L., Mechanical Engineering
INGERSOLL, A. P., Planetary Science
JOHNSON, W. L., Engineering and Applied Science
KAMIONKOWSKI, M., Theoretical Physics and Astrophysics
KATZ, J. N., Political Science
KECHRIS, A. S., Mathematics
KENNEDY, M. B., Biology
KIEWIET, D. R., Political Science
KIMBLE, H. J., Physics
KIRSCHVINK, J. L., Geobiology
KITAEV, A., Theoretical Astrophysics and Computer Science
KOCH, C., Computation and Neural Systems
KONISHI, M., Behavioural Biology
KORMOS-BUCHWALD, D. L., History
KORNFIELD, J. A., Chemical Engineering
KOUSSER, J. M., History and Social Science
KULKARNI, S. R., Astronomy and Planetary Science
KUPPERMANN, A., Chemical Physics
LA BELLE, J., English
LANGE, A. E., Physics
LAURENT, G. J., Biology and Computation and Neural Systems
LEDYARD, J. O., Economics and Social Sciences
LESTER, H. A., Biology
LEWIS, N. S., Chemistry
LIBBRECHT, K. G., Physics
LORDEN, G. A., Mathematics
LOW, S., Computer Science and Electrical Engineering
MCAFEE, R. P., Business Economics and Management
MCELIECE, R. J., Electrical Engineering
MCGILL, T. C., Applied Physics
MCKEOWN, R. D., Physics
MCKOY, B. V., Theoretical Chemistry
MACMILLAN, D. W. C., Chemistry
MAKAROV, N. G., Mathematics
MARCUS, R. A., Chemistry
MARSDEN, J. E., Engineering and Control and Dynamical Systems
MARTIN, A. J., Computer Science
MARTIN, D. C., Physics
MAYO, S. L., Biology and Chemistry
MEIRON, D. I., Applied and Computational Mathematics and Computer Science
MEYEROWITZ, E. M., Biology
MURRAY, R. M., Control and Dynamical Systems
NEWMAN, D. K., Geobiology and Biology
NEWMAN, H. B., Physics
OGURI, H., Theoretical Physics
OH, H., Mathematics
OKUMURA, M., Chemical Physics
ORDESHOOK, P. C., Political Science
ORTIZ, M., Aeronautics and Mechanical Engineering

PALFREY, T. R., III, Economics and Political Science
PARKER, C. S., Biochemistry
PATTERSON, P. H., Biology
PERONA, P., Electrical Engineering
PETERS, J. C., Chemistry
PHILLIPS, R., Applied Physics and Mechanical Engineering
PHILLIPS, T. G., Physics
PHINNEY, E. S., III, Theoretical Astrophysics
PIGMAN, G. W., III, English
PINE, J., Physics
PLOTT, C. R., Economics and Political Science
POLITZER, H. D., Theoretical Physics
PORTER, F. C., Physics
PRESKILL, J. P., Theoretical Physics
PRINCE, T. A., Physics
PSALTIS, D., Electrical Engineering
PULLIN, D. I., Aeronautics
RAMAKRISHNAN, D., Mathematics
RAVICHANDRAN, G., Aeronautics and Mechanical Engineering
READHEAD, A. C. S., Astronomy
REES, D. C., Chemistry
RICHARDS, J. H., Organic Chemistry and Biochemistry
ROSAKIS, A. J., Aeronautics and Mechanical Engineering
ROSENSTONE, R. A., History
ROSENTHAL, J., Economics
ROSSMAN, G. R., Mineralogy
ROTHENBERG, E., Biology
ROUKES, M. L., Physics, Applied Physics and Bioengineering
RUTLEDGE, D. B., Electrical Engineering
SALEEBY, J. B., Geology
SARGENT, A. I., Astronomy
SARGENT, W. L. W., Astronomy
SCHERER, A., Electrical Engineering, Applied Physics, and Physics
SCHRODER, P., Computer Science and Applied and Computational Mathematics
SCHULMAN, L. J., Computer Science
SCHUMAN, E. M., Biology
SCHWARZ, J. H., Theoretical Physics
SCOVILLE, N. Z., Astronomy
SEINFELD, J. H., Chemical Engineering
SHEPHERD, J. E., Aeronautics and Mechanical Engineering
SHERMAN, R. P., Economics and Statistics
SHIMOJO, S., Biology
SIEH, K. E., Geology
SIMON, B. M., Mathematics and Theoretical Physics
SOIFER, B. T., Physics
SPITZER, M. L., Law and Social Science
STEIDEL, C. C., Astronomy
STERNBERG, P. W., Biology
STEVENSON, D. J., Planetary Science
STOCK, J. M., Geology and Geophysics
STOLPER, E. M., Geology
STOLTZ, B. M., Chemistry
STONE, E. C., Physics
STRAUSS, J. H., Biology
TAI, Y., Electrical Engineering and Mechanical Engineering
THORNE, K. S., Theoretical Physics
TIRRELL, D. A., Chemistry and Chemical Engineering
TOMBRELLO, T. A., Physics
TROIAN, S., Applied Physics, Aeronautics, and Mechanical Engineering
TROMP, J., Geophysics
VAHALA, K. J., Applied Physics
VAIDYANATHAN, P. P., Electrical Engineering
VARSHAVSKY, A. J., Cell Biology
WALES, D. B., Mathematics
WANG, Z., Chemical Engineering
WEINSTEIN, A. J., Physics
WEINSTEIN, C., English
WEITEKAMP, D. P., Chemical Physics
WENNBERG, P. O., Atmospheric Chemistry and Environmental Science and Engineering
WERNICKE, B. P., Geology
WILSON, R. M., Mathematics

WISE, M. B., High Energy Physics
WOLD, B. J., Molecular Biology
WOODWARD, J. F., Philosophy
YARIV, A., Applied Physics and Electrical Engineering
YEH, N., Physics
YUNG, Y. L., Planetary Science
ZEWAIL, A. H., Chemical Physics, Physics
ZINN, K., Biology
ZMUIDZINAS, J., Physics

CALIFORNIA INSTITUTE OF THE ARTS

24700 McBean Parkway, Valencia, CA 91355-2397

Telephone: (661) 255-1050
E-mail: info@calarts.edu
Internet: www.calarts.edu

Founded 1961 by merger of Los Angeles Conservatory of Music (f. 1883) and Chouinard Art Institute (f. 1921)
Academic year: September to May

Pres.: STEVEN D. LAVINE
Vice-Pres. for Admin.: D. DEAN HOUCHIN
Vice-Pres. and Chief Advancement Officer: BIANCA ROBERTS
Vice-Pres. for Spec. Projects: LYNN R. ROSENFELD
Provost: JAQUELINE ELAM (acting)
Registrar: NANCY WHITTEMORE
Vice Pres. for Int. Relations: CAROL KIM
Dean of Library and Information Resources: JEFFREY GATTEN
Dean of Students: YVONNE GUY

Library of 90,000 vols
Number of teachers: 310
Number of students: 1,500

Publications: *Black Clock* (2 a year), *CalArts Magazine* (2 a year)

DEANS

Herb Alpert School of Music at CalArts Richard Seaver Distinguished Chair in Music: DAVID ROSENBOOM
School of Art: THOMAS LAWSON
School of Critical Studies: MICHAEL BRYANT, JANET SARBANES (acting)
School of Film and Video: STEVE ANKER
School of Theatre: TRAVIS PRESTON
Sharon Disney Lund School of Dance: STEPHAN KOPLOWITZ

CALIFORNIA LUTHERAN UNIVERSITY

60 West Olsen Rd, Thousand Oaks, CA 91360-2787

Telephone: (805) 493-3820
E-mail: media@callutheran.edu
Internet: www.callutheran.edu

Founded 1959; attached to Evangelical Lutheran Church in America
Private control

Pres.: Dr CHRIS KIMBALL
Provost and Vice-Pres. for Academic Affairs: LEANNE NEILSON
Vice-Pres. for Admin. and Finance: KAREN DAVIS
Vice-Pres. for Student Affairs and Dean of Students: WILLIAM ROSSER
Vice-Pres. for Univ. Advancement: R. STEPHEN WHEATLY
Registrar: MARIA KOHNKE
Librarian: KENNETH PFLUEGER

Library of 110,416 vols
Number of teachers: 260 (120 full-time, 140 part-time)
Number of students: 3,000

DEANS

College of Arts and Sciences: Dr JOAN L. GRIFFIN

Graduate School of Education: Prof. GEORGE J. PETERSEN
School of Management: Dr CHARLES MAXEY

CALIFORNIA MARITIME ACADEMY

200 Maritime Academy Dr., Vallejo, CA 94590

Telephone: (707) 654-1000
E-mail: humanresources@csum.edu
Internet: www.csum.edu

Founded 1929 as California Nautical School, present name 1938; attached to specialized campus of California State Univ.
State control
Academic year: September to May

Degrees in marine transportation, global studies and maritime affairs, marine engineering technology, mechanical engineering, facilities engineering technology, business admin., int. business and logistics

Pres.: Dr THOMAS A. CROPPER
Provost and Vice-Pres. for Academic Affairs: Dr GERALD S. JACUBOWSKI
Vice-Pres. for Admin. and Finance: KURT LOHIDE
Vice Pres. for Advancement and Executive Dir: BEVERLY BYL
Academic Dean: NAEL ALY

Library of 35,000 vols, 270 periodicals
Number of students: 1,000

Publication: *Cal Maritime Magazine* (2 a year)

CALIFORNIA POLYTECHNIC STATE UNIVERSITY

1 Grand Ave, San Luis Obispo, CA 93407

Telephone: (805) 756-1111
E-mail: admissions@calpoly.edu
Internet: www.calpoly.edu

Founded 1901 as California Polytechnic School, present name 1972
Academic year: September to June

Pres.: JEFFREY D. ARMSTRONG
Provost and Vice-Pres. for Academic Affairs: Dr ROBERT D. KOOB
Vice-Pres. for Student Affairs: CORNEL MORTON
Vice-Pres. for Univ. Advancement: SANDRA OGREN
Dean of Library Services: MICHAEL D. MILLER

Library of 600,000 books, 45,000 online journals, 750 print journals, 195 article databases
Number of teachers: 1,047
Number of students: 19,325

Publications: *Cal Poly Today* (4 a year), *Mustang Daily*

DEANS

College of Agriculture, Food and Environmental Sciences: Dr DAVID J. WEHNER
College of Architecture and Environmental Design: R. THOMAS JONES
College of Engineering: Dr ERLING SMITH
College of Liberal Arts: LINDA HALISKY
College of Science and Mathematics: PHILIP S. BAILEY
Orfalea College of Business: DAVE CHRISTY
School of Education: Dr ROBERT DETWEILER

CALIFORNIA STATE POLYTECHNIC UNIVERSITY, POMONA

3801 W Temple Ave, Pomona, CA 91768

Telephone: (909) 869-7659
Internet: www.csupomona.edu

Founded 1938

Pres.: J. MICHAEL ORTIZ
Provost and Vice-Pres. for Academic Affairs: Dr MARTEN L. denBOER

Vice-Pres. for Admin. Affairs and Chief Financial Officer: Dr EDWIN A. BARNES
Vice-Pres. for Student Affairs: Dr DOUGLAS R. FREER
Vice-Pres. for Univ. Advancement: SCOTT WARRINGTON
Chief Information Officer Instructional and Information Technology: STEPHANIE DODA
Registrar: MARIA L. MARTINEZ
Library Dean: Dr RAY WANG
Library: 2.4m. books, microfilms, maps, 3,000 periodicals, 2,800 online journals
Number of teachers: 3,000
Number of students: 21,000
Publication: *Panorama* (1 a year)

DEANS

College of Agriculture: LESTER C. YOUNG
College of Business Admin.: RICHARD S. LAPIDUS
College of Education and Integrative Studies: Dr PEGGY KELLY
College of Engineering: Dr MAHYAR AMOUZEGAR
College of Environmental Design: MICHAEL WOO
College of Letters, Arts and Social Sciences: Dr SHARON HILLES
College of Science: MANDAYAM SRINIVAS
College of the Extended Univ.: Dr UEI-JIUN FAN
Collins School of Hospitality Management: ANDREW FEINSTEIN

CALIFORNIA STATE UNIVERSITY SYSTEM

401 Golden Shore, Long Beach, CA 90802-4210
Telephone: (562) 951-4000
Internet: www.calstate.edu
Coordinating HQ for 23 state univs
Chancellor: TIMOTHY P. WHITE
Exec. Vice-Chancellor And Chief Financial Officer: STEVE RELYEA
Number of teachers: 43,000
Number of students: 412,000
Publications: *Annual Fact Book* (1 a year), *CSU Leader* (12 a year)

CALIFORNIA STATE UNIVERSITY, BAKERSFIELD

9001 Stockdale Highway, Bakersfield, CA 93311-1022
Telephone: (661) 654-2456
E-mail: excellence@csub.edu
Internet: www.csub.edu
Founded 1970
Academic year: September to June
Pres.: Dr HORACE MITCHELL
Provost and Vice-Pres. for Academic Affairs: SORAYA M. COLEY
Vice-Pres. for Business and Admin. Services: MICHAEL A. NEAL
Vice-Pres. for Student Affairs: Dr JOHN HULTSMAN
Vice-Pres. for Univ. Advancement: SORAYA M. COLEY
Dean for Libraries: RODNEY M. HERBSBERGER
Library of 521,199 vols, 30,000 ejournals and ebooks
Number of teachers: 470
Number of students: 7,800

DEANS

School of Arts and Humanities: RICHARD COLLINS
School of Business and Public Administration: Dr JOHN EMERY
School of Natural Sciences, Mathematics and Engineering: Dr JULIO R. BLANCO

School of Social Sciences and Education: Dr KATHLEEN M KNUTZEN

CALIFORNIA STATE UNIVERSITY, CHICO

400 West First St, Chico, CA 95929
Telephone: (530) 898-4636
Internet: www.csuchico.edu
Founded 1889 as Chico Normal School, present name 1972
Pres.: Dr PAUL J. ZINGG
Provost and Vice-Pres. for Academic Affairs: SANDRA M. FLAKE
Vice-Pres. for Business and Finance: LORRAINE B. HOFFMAN
Vice-Provost for Information Resources: WILLIAM POST
Vice-Pres. for Student Affairs: DREW CALANDRELLA
Vice-Pres. for Univ. Advancement: RICHARD ELLISON
Library Services Dir: CAROLYN DUSENBURY
Library of 634,000 vols, 2m. documents
Number of teachers: 960
Number of students: 15,500

DEANS

College of Agriculture: Dr JENNIFER RYDER FOX
College of Behavioural and Social Sciences: Dr GAYLE E. HUTCHINSON
College of Business: Dr MIKE WARD
College of Communication and Education: MAGGIE PAYNE
College of Engineering, Computer Science and Construction Management: Dr MIKE WARD
College of Humanities and Fine Arts: Dr JOEL ZIMBELMAN
College of Natural Sciences: Dr FREDERIKA (FRAKA) HARMSEN
Graduate Studies: E. K. PARK

CALIFORNIA STATE UNIVERSITY, DOMINGUEZ HILLS

1000 E Victoria St, Carson, CA 90747
Telephone: (310) 243-3696
Internet: www.csudh.edu
Founded 1960 as South Bay State College
Pres.: Dr WILLIE J. HAGAN
Provost and Vice-Pres. for Academic Affairs: Dr ELLEN JUNN
Vice-Pres. for Admin. and Finance: ROBERT LOVITT
Vice-Pres. for Enrolment Management and Student Affairs: Dr SUSAN E. BORREGO
Vice-Pres for IT: CHRIS MARIQUEZ
Vice-Pres. for Univ. Advancement: CARRIE STEWART
Dean for Univ. Library: SANDRA PARHAM
Library of 440,000 vols, 687,800 microfilms, 2,200 current periodicals
Number of teachers: 841 (incl. 229 full-time, 612 part-time)
Number of students: 14,670

DEANS

College of Arts and Humanities: Dr MUNASHE FURUSA (acting)
College of Business Administration and Public Policy: JOSEPH WEN (acting)
College of Education: ANN CHLEBICKI (acting)
College of Extended and International Education: Dr JOANNE ZITELLI (acting)
College of Health and Human Services: ANUPAMA JOSHI (acting)
College of Natural Behavioural Sciences: Dr ROD HAY

CALIFORNIA STATE UNIVERSITY, EAST BAY

25800 Carlos Bee Blvd, Hayward, CA 94542-3000
Telephone: (510) 885-3000
E-mail: admissions@csueastbay.edu
Internet: www20.csueastbay.edu
Founded 1957
Also has a Concord Campus and a Oakland Center
Pres.: LEROY M. MORISHITA
Provost and Vice-Pres. for Academic Affairs: Dr JAMES L. J. HOUPIS
Vice-Pres. for Admin. and Finance: BRAD WELLS
Vice-Pres. for Planning and Enrollment Management and Student Affairs: Dr LINDA DALTON
Vice-Pres. for Univ. Advancement: ROBERT BURT
Chief Information Officer: (vacant)
Univ. Librarian: MYOUNG-JA LEE KWON
Library of 700,000 vols
Number of teachers: 500
Number of students: 12,890

DEANS

College of Business and Economics: TERRI SWARTZ
College of Education and Allied Studies: Dr CAROLYN NELSON
College of Letters, Arts and Social Sciences: KATHELEEN ROUNTREE
College of Science: MICHAEL LEUNG

CALIFORNIA STATE UNIVERSITY, FRESNO

5241 N Maple Ave, Fresno, CA 93740-8027
Telephone: (559) 278-4240
E-mail: outreach@listserv.csufresno.edu
Internet: www.csufresno.edu
Founded 1911 as Fresno State Normal School
Academic year: August to December, January to May (2 semesters)
Pres.: Dr JOHN D. WELTY
Provost and Vice-Pres. for Academic Affairs: Dr WILLIAM A. COVINO
Vice-Pres. for Admin. and Chief Financial Officer: CYNTHIA TENIENTE-MATSON
Vice-Pres. for Student Affairs: FRANK R. LAMAS
Vice-Pres. for Univ. Advancement: (vacant)
Assoc. Vice-Pres. and Dean for Undergraduate Studies: Dr DENNIS NEF
Dean for Library Services: PETER McDONALD
Library: 1m. vols, 60,000 ejournals, magazines and newspapers, colln of ebooks
Number of teachers: 1,100 (incl. full-time and part-time)
Number of students: 21,500

DEANS

College of Arts and Humanities: Dr VIDA SAMIIAN
College of Health and Human Services: Dr ANDREW HOFF
College of Science and Mathematics: Dr ANDREW HOFF
College of Social Sciences: LUZ GONZALEZ
Craig School of Business: ROBERT HARPER
Jordan College of Agricultural Sciences and Technology: CHARLES BOYER
Kremen School of Education and Human Development: PAUL BEARE
Lyles College of Engineering: Dr RAM NUNNA

CALIFORNIA STATE UNIVERSITY, FULLERTON

POB 34080 Fullerton, CA 92834-9480
800 N College Blvd, Fullerton, CA 92831-3599
Telephone: (657) 278-2011
E-mail: outreach@fullerton.edu
Internet: www.fullerton.edu
Founded 1957
Pres.: MILTON A. GORDON
Exec. Vice-Pres.: JUDITH A. ANDERSON
Vice-Pres. for Academic Affairs: STEVEN N. MURRAY (acting)
Vice-Pres. for Admin. and Finance: WILLIE J. HAGAN
Vice-Pres. for Student Affairs: SILAS H. ABREGO (acting)
Vice-Pres. for Univ. Advancement: PAMELA HILLMAN
Vice-Pres. for Information and Technology: AMIR DABIRIAN
Registrar: MELISSA WHATLEY
Univ. Librarian: RICHARD C. POLLARD
Library of 1,279,172 vols, 1,149,348 microforms, 10,049 maps, 8,087 films and video cassettes
Number of teachers: 2,000 (incl. full-time and part-time)
Number of students: 34,912

DEANS

College of the Arts: JOE ARNOLD
College of Communications: WILLIAM BRIGGS
College of Education: Dr CLAIRE C. CAVALLARO (acting)
College of Engineering and Computer Science: RAMAN UNNIKRISHNAN
College of Health and Human Development: Dr SHARI G. McMAHAN
College of Humanities and Social Sciences: Dr ANGELA DELLA VOLPE
College of Natural Sciences and Mathematics: Dr ROBERT A. KOCH (acting)
Mihaylo College of Business and Economics: ANIL K. PURI

CALIFORNIA STATE UNIVERSITY, LONG BEACH

1250 Bellflower Blvd, Long Beach, CA 90840-0115
Telephone: (562) 985-4111
Internet: www.csulb.edu
Founded 1949 as Los Angeles-Orange County State College, present name 1972
State control
Pres.: F. KING ALEXANDER
Provost and Sr Vice-Pres. for Academic Affairs: Dr DONALD J. PARA
Vice-Pres. for Admin. and Finance: MARY STEPHENS
Vice-Pres. for Student Services: Dr DOUGLAS W. ROBINSON
Vice-Pres. for Univ. Relations and Devt: ANDREA TAYLOR
Dean of Library Services: ROMAN KOCHAN
Library of 1,096,089 vols, 1,503,457 microfilms, 35,080 non-book materials, 2,110 current periodicals
Number of teachers: 2,100 (948 full-time, 1,180 part-time)
Number of students: 33,400

DEANS

College of the Arts: RAYMOND TORRES-SANTOS
College of Business Administration: MICHAEL E. SOLT
College of Continuing and Professional Education: JEET JOSHEE
College of Education: MARQUITA GRENOT-SCHEYER
College of Engineering: FOROUZAN GOLSHANI

College of Health and Human Services: KENNETH I. MILLAR
College of Liberal Arts: GERRY RIPOSA
College of Natural Sciences and Mathematics: LAURA KINGSFORD

CALIFORNIA STATE UNIVERSITY, LOS ANGELES

5151 State University Dr., Los Angeles, CA 90032-8530
Telephone: (323) 343-3901
E-mail: admission@calstatela.edu
Internet: www.calstatela.edu
Founded 1947
Pres.: JAMES M. ROSSER
Provost and Vice-Pres. for Academic Affairs: Dr ASHISH VAIDYA
Vice-Pres. for Admin. and Chief Financial Officer: LISA CHAVEZ
Vice-Pres. for Information Technology Services: PETER QUAN
Vice-Pres. for Institutional Advancement: KYLE C. BUTTON
Vice-Pres. for Student Affairs: ANTHONY R. ROSS
Dean of Graduate Studies and Research: ALAN E. MUCHLINSKI
Dean of Undergraduate Studies: ALFREDO G. GONZALEZ (acting)
Univ. Librarian: ALICE KAWAKAMI (acting)
Library: 1m. vols, 200 historical and geographical atlases, 4,500 periodicals and newspapers
Number of teachers: 890
Number of students: 18,000

DEANS

College of Arts and Letters: Dr PETER McALLISTAR
College of Business and Economics: JAMES A. GOODRICH
Charter College of Education: Dr MARY FALVEY
College of Engineering, Computer Science and Technology: Dr H. KEITH MOO-YOUNG
College of Health and Human Services: Dr BEATRICE YORKER (acting)
College of Natural and Social Sciences: Dr JIM HENDERSON

CALIFORNIA STATE UNIVERSITY, MONTEREY BAY

100 Campus Center, Seaside, CA 93955-8001
Telephone: (831) 582-3000
E-mail: moreinfo_prospective@csumb.edu
Internet: csumb.edu
Founded 1994
Academic year: August to May
Pres.: Dr DIANE F. HARRISON
Provost and Vice-Pres. for Academic Affairs: Dr KATHRYN CRUZ-URIBE
Vice-Pres. for Admin. and Finance: KEVIN SAUNDERS
Vice-Pres. for Devt: Dr CHRIS HASEGAWA
Vice-Pres. for Student Affairs: Dr RONNIE HIGGS
Vice-Pres. for Univ. Advancement: Dr PATTI HIRAMOTO
Dir of the Library: BILL ROBNETT
Library of 65,000 vols
Number of teachers: 280
Number of students: 4,790

DEANS

College of Arts, Humanities, and Social Sciences: Dr RENEE R. CURRY
College of Professional Studies: Dr BRIAN SIMMONS
College of Science, Media Arts, and Technology: Dr MARSHA MOROH
College of Univ. Studies and Programmes: Dr CHRIS HASEGAWA (acting)

CALIFORNIA STATE UNIVERSITY, NORTHRIDGE

18111 Nordhoff St, Northridge, CA 91330
Telephone: (818) 677-1200
E-mail: admissions@csun.edu
Internet: www.csun.edu
Founded 1958 as Los Angeles State College, present name 1972
Academic year: August to to May
Pres.: Dr JOLENE KOESTER
Provost and Vice-Pres. for Academic Affairs: Dr HARRY HELLENBRAND
Vice-Pres. for Admin. and Finance: THOMAS McCARRON
Vice-Pres. for Information Technology: HILARY BAKER
Vice-Pres. for Operations: JULIE WANKE
Vice-Pres. for Student Affairs: Dr WILLIAM WATKINS
Vice-Pres. for Univ. Advancement: Dr VANCE T. PETERSON
Dir for Admissions and Records: ERIC FORBES
Dean for Univ. Library: Dr MARK STOVER
Library: 1.4m vols (incl. 1.1m books, 250,000 periodicals), 3.2m. microforms, 53,000 ejournals, 274,713 ebooks, 2,300 print journals, 14,200 sound recordings, 12,700 film and video recordings, 60,000 photographs
Number of teachers: 4,000
Number of students: 36,000

DEANS

College of Business and Economics: Dr WILLIAM JENNINGS
College of Engineering and Computer Science: Dr S. K. RAMESH
College of Extended Learning: JOYCE FEUCHT-HAVIAR
College of Health and Human Development: Dr SYLVIA A. ALVA
College of Humanities: Dr ELIZABETH SAY
College of Science and Mathematics: JERRY STINNER
College of Social and Behavioural Sciences: STELLA THEODOULOU
Michael D. Eisner College of Education: MICHAEL D. SPAGNA
Mike Curb College of Arts, Media and Communication: W. ROBERT BUCKER
Tseng College: JOYCE FEUCHT-HAVIAR

CALIFORNIA STATE UNIVERSITY, SACRAMENTO

6000 J St, Sacramento, CA 95819-6056
Telephone: (916) 278-6011
E-mail: infodesk@csus.edu
Internet: www.csus.edu
Founded 1947 as Sacramento State College
Academic year: September to May
Pres.: ALEXANDER GONZALEZ
Provost and Vice-Pres. for Academic Affairs: JOSEPH F. SHELEY
Vice-Pres. for Admin.: STEPHEN G. GARCIA
Vice-Pres. for Student Affairs: Dr LORI VARLOTTA
Vice-Pres. for Univ. Affairs: CAROLE HAYASHINO
Dir of Library Systems: CARLOS RODRIGUEZ
Library: 2m. vols
Number of teachers: 1,300
Number of students: 27,000
Publications: *Calaveras Station* (1 a year), *Capitol University Journal* (2 a year)

DEANS

College of Arts and Letters: EDWARD S. INCH
College of Business Administration: Dr SANJAY VARSHNEY
College of Continuing Education: Dr ALICE TOM
College of Education: VANESSA SHEARED

College of Engineering and Computer Science: EMIR JOSÉ MACARI
College of Health and Human Services: Dr FRED D. BALDINI
College of Natural Sciences and Mathematics: Dr JILL M. TRAINER
College of Social Sciences and Interdisciplinary Studies: Dr CHARLES GOSSETT

CALIFORNIA STATE UNIVERSITY, SAN BERNARDINO

5500 University Parkway, San Bernardino, CA 92407-2318

Telephone: (909) 537-5000
E-mail: moreinfo@csusb.edu
Internet: www.csusb.edu

Founded 1960 as San Bernardino-Riverside State College, current name adopted 1972 public control
Academic year: September to June
Liberal arts college with several applied programmes offering a broad range of first degrees, several teaching credentials and Masters degrees in selected fields
Pres.: Dr TOMÁS MORALES
Provost and Vice-Pres. for Academic Affairs: Dr ANDREW BODMAN
Vice-Pres. for Admin. and Finance: BOB GARDNER
Vice-Pres. for Information Resources and Technology: Dr SAMUEL SUDHAKAR
Vice-Pres. for Student Affairs: Dr BRIAN HAYNES
Vice-Pres. for Univ. Advancement: Dr RON FREMONT
Univ. Librarian: CEASAR CABALLERO
Library of 720,000 vols, 2,400 current periodicals and serial publs, also maps, microfilms, musical scores, CD-ROMs; depository for CA state and fed. govt documents
Number of teachers: 2,100
Number of students: 18,400

DEANS

College of Arts and Letters: Dr TERRY BALLMAN
College of Business and Public Administration: Dr LAWRENCE C. ROSE
College of Education: Dr JAY FIENE
College of Extended Learning: Dr TATIANA KARMANOVA
College of Natural Sciences: KIRSTY FLEMING
College of Social and Behavioural Sciences: Dr JAMAL R. NASSAR

CALIFORNIA STATE UNIVERSITY, SAN MARCOS

333 S Twin Oaks Valley Rd, San Marcos, CA 92096-0001

Telephone: (760) 750-4000
E-mail: registrar@csusm.edu
Internet: www.csusm.edu
Founded 1979
Academic year: September to May
Pres.: Dr KAREN S. HAYNES
Chancellor: CHARLES B. REED
Provost and Vice-Pres. for Academic Affairs: EMILY F. CUTRER
Vice-Pres. for Community Engagement: Dr JAN JACKSON
Vice-Pres. for Finance and Admin.: LINDA HAWK
Vice-Pres. for Student Affairs: Dr ELOISE STIGLITZ
Vice-Pres. for Univ. Advancement: NEAL HOSS
Dean of Library: BARBARA PREECE
Library of 290,444 vols (incl. books, periodicals and documents), 38,955 ejournals, 47,068 ebooks, 3,798 sound recordings, 8,192 film and video recordings

Number of teachers: 230
Number of students: 9,700

DEANS

College of Business Administration: Dr REGINA EISENBACH
College of Education, Health and Human Services: Dr DON CHU
College of Science and Mathematics: Dr KATHERINE KANTARDJIEFF
Extended Learning: MIKE SCHRODER
Graduate Studies: Dr GERARDO M. GONZÁLEZ
School of Nursing: JUDY PAPENHAUSEN

CALIFORNIA STATE UNIVERSITY, STANISLAUS

1 University Circle, Turlock, CA 95382
Telephone: (209) 667-3122
Internet: www.csustan.edu
Founded 1960
Pres.: Dr HAMID SHIRVANI
Provost and Vice-Pres. for Academic Affairs: Dr JAMES T STRONG
Vice-Pres. for Business and Finance: RUSS GIAMBELLUCA
Vice-Pres. for Univ. Advancement: SUSANA GAJIC-BRUEYA
Vice-Pres. for Faculty Affairs and Human Resources: DENNIS W. SHIMEK
Assoc. Vice-Pres. for Enrolment and Student Affairs: Dr SUZANNE ESPINOZA
Dean of Admissions and Registrar: LISA BERNARDO
Dean of Library Services: ANNIE HOR
Library of 361,000 vols, 2,000 current periodicals, 1.3m. microfilms, 4,700 sound and video recordings, govt documents, special colln of children's literature
Number of teachers: 443 (incl. 265 full-time and 178 part-time)
Number of students: 8,305

DEANS

College of the Arts: Dr DARYL JOSEPH MOORE
College of Business Administration: Dr LINDA NOWAK
College of Education: Dr KATHY NORMAN
College of Human and Health Sciences: Dr JUNE BOFFMAN
College of Humanities and Social Sciences: Dr JAMES A. TUEDIO
College of Natural Sciences: Dr ROBERT MARINO

CHAPMAN UNIVERSITY

1 University Dr., Orange, CA 92866
Telephone: (714) 997-6815
Internet: www.chapman.edu
Founded 1861 as Hesperian College in Woodland
Private (Disciples of Christ) Liberal Arts
Pres.: Dr JAMES L. DOTI
Provost and Exec. Vice-Pres.: Dr DANIELE STRUPPA
Exec. Vice-Pres. for Finance and Admin.: GARY BRAHM
Vice-Chancellor and Dean for Enrollment Management: MIKE PELLY
Vice-Chancellor for Student Affairs and Dean of Students: Dr JERRY PRICE
Exec. Vice-Pres. for Univ. Advancement: SHERYL BOURGEOIS
Registrar: Dr JACK F. FARRELL
Dean of the Libraries: CHARLENE BALDWIN
Library of 593,000 vols
Number of teachers: 650 (350 full-time, 300 part-time)
Number of students: 6,400

DEANS

College of Educational Studies: Dr DON N. CARDINAL

College of Performing Arts: WILLIAM HALL (acting)
George L. Argyros School of Business and Economics: Dr ARTHUR KRAFT
Lawrence and Kristina Dodge College of Film and Media Arts: BOB BASSETT
Schmid College of Science and Technology: Dr MENAS KAFATOS
School of Law: SCOTT HOWE
Wilkinson College of Humanities and Social Sciences: PATRICK QUINN

CHURCH DIVINITY SCHOOL OF THE PACIFIC

2451 Ridge Rd, Berkeley, CA 94709-1217
Telephone: (510) 204-0700
E-mail: info@cdsp.edu
Internet: www.cdsp.edu
Founded 1893
Private control (part of the Graduate Theological Union)
Academic year: August to May
Areas of study: divinity, theological studies, arts, ministry
Pres. and Dean: Rev. Dr W. MARK RICHARDSON
Vice-Pres. for Admin.: STEVE ARGYRIS
Vice-Pres. for Advancement: JERRY CAMPBELL
Dean of Academic Affairs: Dr LINDA L. CLADER
Dean of School for Deacons: RODERICK B. DUGLISS
Dean of Students: L. ANN HALLISEY
Registrar: MARGO WEBSTER

CLAREMONT GRADUATE UNIVERSITY

150 E 10th St, Claremont, CA 91711
Telephone: (909) 621-8000
E-mail: information@cgu.edu
Internet: www.cgu.edu
Founded 1925
Masters and doctoral degrees in 22 professional and academic disciplines
Pres.: DEBORAH A. FREUND
Provost and Exec. Vice-Pres. for Academic Affairs: JACOB ADAMS
Asst Vice-Pres. for Advancement: MIKE AVILA
Sr Vice-Pres. for Finance and Admin.: Dr STEVEN N. GARCIA
Library: 2m. vols (incl. ebooks and journals)
Number of teachers: 170 (80 full-time, 90 part-time)
Number of students: 2,200

DEANS

Peter F. Drucker and Masatoshi Ito Graduate School of Management: LAWRENCE CROSBY
School of the Arts and Humanities: JANET FARRELL BRODIE
School of Behavioural and Organizational Sciences: Dr STEWART I. DONALDSON
School of Community and Global Health: C. ANDERSON JOHNSON
School of Educational Studies: MARGARET GROGAN
School of Information Systems and Technology: Dr THOMAS A. HORAN
School of Mathematical Sciences: ELLIS CUMBERBATCH
School of Politics and Economics: JEAN SCHROEDEL
School of Religion: TAMMI J. SCHNEIDER

CLAREMONT MCKENNA COLLEGE

500 E Ninth St, Claremont, CA 91711-6400
Telephone: (909) 621-8000
E-mail: deanofstudents@cmc.edu
Internet: www.cmc.edu

Founded 1946
Academic year: August to May (2 semesters)
Liberal arts college with emphasis on business and public affairs; mem. of the Claremont Colleges
Pres.: Prof. PAMELA BROOKS GANN
Dean of the Faculty and Vice-Pres. for Academic Affairs: GREGORY D. HESS
Vice-Pres. for Business and Admin. and Treas.: ROBIN J. ASPINALL
Vice-Pres. for Devt and External Relations: ERNIE ISEMINGER
Vice-Pres. for Student Affairs: JEFFERSON HUANG
Assoc. Vice-Pres. for Devt: STEVE SIEGEL
Dean for Students: MARY SPELLMAN
Registrar and Dir for Institutional Research: ELIZABETH MORGAN
Chief Technology Officer: CYNTHIA HUMES

Library: 2m. vols
Number of teachers: 130
Number of students: 1,200

CLAREMONT SCHOOL OF THEOLOGY

1325 N College Ave, Claremont, CA 91711-3199

Telephone: (909) 447-2500
E-mail: president@cst.edu
Internet: www.cst.edu

Founded 1885 as Maclay College of Theology, present location 1957
Private control
Academic year: September to May
Pres.: Dr JERRY D. CAMPBELL
Vice-Pres. for Academic Affairs and Dean of Faculty: Dr PHILIP CLAYTON
Vice Pres. for Admin. and Finance: LYNN O'LEARY-ARCHER
Vice Pres. for Devt: DUANE DYER
Chief Financial Officer: JOAN FROST
Registrar: JENNIE J. ALLEN
Dir for the Library: JOHN DICKASON

Library of 210,000 vols, 650 print subscriptions, 6,000 ejournals

Publication: *Claremont Journal of Religion* (online)

CLEVELAND CHIROPRACTIC COLLEGE

10850 Lowell Ave, Overland Park, KS 66210
Telephone: (913) 234-0600
E-mail: la.admissions@cleveland.edu
Internet: www.cleveland.edu

Founded 1911, present status 2011
Academic year: September to August
Private control

Depts of basic sciences, diagnostic sciences, chiropractic sciences, clinical sciences, humanities and social sciences, physical and life sciences
Pres.: Dr CARL S. CLEVELAND, III
Provost: ASHLEY E. CLEVELAND
Chief Operating Officer: JEFF KARP
Vice-Pres. for Campus Relations: D. CLARK BECKLEY
Dir for Student Services: JALONNA BOWIE
Dir for Admissions: MELISSA DENTON
Dir for Library: MARCIA THOMAS

Library of 15,000 vols, 350 journal subscriptions, 7,000 ejournals, 75,000 microfiche files
Number of students: 568

Publication: *Clevelander*

COGSWELL POLYTECHNICAL COLLEGE

1175 Bordeaux Dr., Sunnyvale, CA 94089-9772
Telephone: (408) 541-0100

E-mail: info@cogswell.edu
Internet: www.cogswell.edu

Founded 1887
Private control
Academic year: January to August
Areas of study: 3-D animation, 3-D modelling, computer engineering, digital arts engineering, digital audio, entertainment design, game design, software engineering
Chancellor: CHARLES H. HOUSE
Pres.: LISA. KEMP
Vice-Pres. for Finance and Admin.: REJINO CASTANEDA
Vice-Pres. for Information Technology: Dr ANDREY FEDIN
Dean for College: MICHAEL MARTIN
Dean of Information Technology: Dr ANDREY FEDIN
Dean for Institutional Advancement: BONNIE PHELPS
Dean for Student Life: BARB BLOOM
Registrar: JILL MUSICK
Librarian: BRUCE DAHMS
Number of teachers: 55 (12 full-time, 43 part-time)
Number of students: 288 (182 full-time, 106 part-time)
Library of 12,000 vols, 100 periodicals

COLEMAN UNIVERSITY

8888 Balboa Ave, San Diego, CA 92123-1506
Telephone: (858) 499-0202
E-mail: admissions@coleman.edu
Internet: www.coleman.edu

Founded 1963 as Coleman College, present name 2008
Private control

Depts of bioinformatics, graphic design, information systems, networks and security; campus: San Marcos
Pres.: PAUL PANESAR
Vice-Pres. for Academics: SHERYL RIDENS
Vice-Pres.: DARLENE ANKTON
Registrar: KAREN ABEL
Librarian (San Diego): MANNY BERNAD
Number of students: 1,000

COLUMBIA COLLEGE HOLLYWOOD

18618 Oxnard St, Tarzana, CA 91356-1411
Telephone: (818) 345-8414
E-mail: info@columbiacollege.edu
Internet: www.columbiacollege.edu

Founded 1951
Private control
Language of instruction: English
Academic year: September to June
Areas of study: cinema, television and video production
Pres.: RICHARD KOBRITZ
Dean for College: ALAN L. GANSBERG
Dean for Student Services: Dr YOLANDA DAWSON
Sr. Dir for Finance: RICHARD CROWE
Dir for Admissions: CARMEN MUNOZ
Dir for Information Technology and Production Services: RONALD REEVES
Registrar: CARMELA CHANEY
Librarian: CHERICE HALL

Library of 10,000 vols
Number of students: 350

CONCORDIA UNIVERSITY IRVINE

1530 Concordia W, Irvine, CA 92612-3203
Telephone: (949) 854-8002
E-mail: info@cui.edu
Internet: www.cui.edu

Founded 1973 as Christ College Irvine, present name 1993
Private control

Academic year: August to May
Pres.: Dr KURT KRUEGER
Provost and Exec. Vice-Pres.: Dr MARY. SCOTT
Assoc. Provost and Vice-Pres. for Academic Affairs: Dr PETER SENKBEIL
Exec. Vice-Pres. for Univ. Advancement: TIM JAEGER
Exec. Vice Pres. for External Relations: STEPHEN CHRISTENSEN
Vice-Pres. for Business Operations and Information Technology: ALAN K. RUDI
Vice-Pres. for Student Services: Dr GARY R. McDANIEL
Dean for Academic Records and Registrar: Prof. KENNETH CLAVIR
Dean for Students: Dr DEREK VERGARA
Dir for Library Services: CAROLINA BARTON

Library of 92,000 vols
Number of teachers: 100 (full-time)
Number of students: 3,362

Publication: *Concordia Today* (online)

DEANS

Christ College: Dr STEVEN P. MUELLER
School of Arts and Sciences: Dr TIMOTHY L. PREUSS
School of Business and Professional Studies: Dr TIMOTHY C. PETERS (acting)
School of Education: Dr JANICE E. NELSON

DOMINICAN SCHOOL OF PHILOSOPHY & THEOLOGY

2301 Vine St, Berkeley, CA 94708
Telephone: (510) 849-2030
E-mail: info@dspt.edu
Internet: www.dspt.edu

Founded 1851, present name 1976
Private control
Language of instruction: English
Academic year: August to June
Pres.: Rev. MICHAEL SWEENEY
Vice-Pres. for Admin.: PETER MacLEOD
Academic Dean: CHRISTOPHER RENZ
Registrar: TERESA OLSON

Library of 440,000 vols, 1,500 periodical subscriptions and 292,000 non-book holdings
Number of teachers: 20 (14 full-time, 6 part-time)
Number of students: 100

Publication: *Ad Gentes*

DOMINICAN UNIVERSITY OF CALIFORNIA

50 Acacia Ave, San Rafael, CA 94901-2298
Telephone: (415) 457-4440
E-mail: chilly@dominican.edu
Internet: www.dominican.edu

Founded 1890 as a women's college, present name 2000
Private control
Academic year: August to May
Br. campus: Ukiah Center
Pres.: Dr MARY B. MARCY
Provost: Dr KENNETH J. PORADA
Exec. Vice-Pres. and Chief Academic Officer: Dr LUÍS MARÍA R. CALINGO
Exec. Dir for Library: GARY GORKA

Library of 100,000 vols, 375 periodicals
Number of teachers: 220
Number of students: 2,280

DEANS

School of Arts, Humanities and Social Sciences: Dr NICOLA PITCHFORD
School of Business and Leadership: Dr DAN MOSHAVI
School of Education and Counseling Psychology: Dr EDWARD KUJAWA

School of Health and Natural Sciences: Dr MARTHA A. NELSON

FIELDING GRADUATE UNIVERSITY

2112 Santa Barbara St, Santa Barbara, CA 93105-3538
Telephone: (805) 687-1099
E-mail: admissions@fielding.edu
Internet: www.fielding.edu
Founded 1974
Private control
Pres.: Dr RICHARD S. MEYERS
Provost and Sr Vice-Pres.: Dr GLORIA J. WILLINGHAM
Assoc. Provost for Enrolment Management: MONIQUE SNOWDEN
Assoc. Provost for Research and Learning: Dr DANIEL R. SEWELL
Vice-Pres.: LISA LEWIS
Vice-Pres. for Univ. Advancement and Devt: Dr DAVID EDELMAN
Vice-Pres. for Human Resources and Admin.: Dr ANNA J. McDONALD
Dir for Library Services: LESLIE MATHEWS
Number of teachers: 131 (75 full-time, 56 part-time)
Number of students: 1,300
Publication: *Fielding Focus*

DEANS

School of Educational Leadership and Change: Dr MURIO BORUNDA
School of Human and Organization Development: Dr CHARLES McCLINTOCK
School of Psychology: Dr GERARDO RODRI-QUEZ-MENENDEZ

FIVE BRANCHES UNIVERSITY

200 Seventh Ave, Santa Cruz, CA 95062
Telephone: (831) 476-9424
E-mail: receptionist@fivebranches.edu
Internet: www.fivebranches.edu
Founded 1984
Private control
Languages of instruction: Chinese, English, Korean
Areas of study: acupuncture, Chinese herbology, traditional Chinese medicine, Western medicine and natural sciences; campuses at San Jose and Santa Cruz
Pres.: RON ZAIDMAN
Vice-Pres. for Academic Affairs and Academic Dean: JOANNA ZHAO
Dir for Admissions: ELEONOR MENDELSON
Registrar and Dir for Student Services: ANA LOBATO
Library of 7,000 vols
Number of teachers: 200
Number of students: 500

DEANS

Traditional Chinese Medicine: JOANNA ZHAO

FRANCISCAN SCHOOL OF THEOLOGY

1712 Euclid Ave, Berkeley, CA 94709-1294
Telephone: (510) 848-5232
E-mail: info@fst.edu
Internet: www.fst.edu
Founded 1854 as Mission Santa Barbara, present name 1968
Private control
Offers Masters in arts, divinity, ministry, theology; continuing education programme
Pres. and Rector: Fr JOSEPH P. CHINNICI
Academic Dean: Prof. WILLIAM J. SHORT
Chief Financial Officer: CAROLYN RODKIN
Number of students: 100

FRESNO PACIFIC BIBLICAL SEMINARY

1717 S Chestnut Ave, Fresno, CA 93702
Telephone: (559) 453-2317
E-mail: fresno@mbseminary.edu
Internet: seminary.fresno.edu
Founded 1955; attached to Fresno Pacific Univ.
Private control
Academic year: August to August
MAs in Christian ministry, divinity, intercultural mission, marriage, family and child counselling, New Testament, Old Testament, theology; diplomas in Anglican studies, Christian studies, congregational care, evangelism and church planting, integration, Presbyterian studies, women in ministry; campuses at Langley and Winnipeg in Canada
Pres.: JIM HOLM
Academic Dean: LYNN JOST
Dean for Students: RICK BARTLETT
Chief Financial Officer: LINDA BOWMAN
Registrar: LORI JAMES
Librarian: RICHARD RAWLS
Library of 150,000 vols
Number of teachers: 10
Number of students: 140

FRESNO PACIFIC UNIVERSITY

1717 S Chestnut Ave, Fresno, CA 93702-4709
Telephone: (209) 453-2000
Internet: www.fresno.edu
Founded 1944 as Pacific Bible Institute, present name 1997
Private control
Academic year: August to May
Campuses at Bakersfield, N Fresno, Visalia, Merced and Fresno
Pres.: Dr D. MERRILL EWERT
Provost and Vice-Pres. for Enrolment Management: Dr STEVE VARVIS
Vice-Pres. and Chief Information Officer: ALAN OURS
Vice-Pres. for Advancement and Univ. Relations: MARK DEFFENBACHER
Vice-Pres. for Finance and Business Affairs: DIANE CATLIN
Library Dir: KEVIN ENNS-REMPEL
Library of 145,000 vols
Number of teachers: 70
Number of students: 1,450

DEANS

School of Business: DENNIS LANGHOFER
School of Education: GARY GRAMENZ
School of Humanities, Religion and Social Sciences: Dr KEVIN REIMER
School of Natural Sciences: Dr KAREN CIANCI

FULLER THEOLOGICAL SEMINARY

135 N Oakland Ave, Pasadena, CA 91182
Telephone: (626) 584-5200
E-mail: admissions@fuller.edu
Internet: www.fuller.edu
Founded 1947
Private control
Regional campuses: California Coast, Northern California, Northwest, Southwest, Colorado and Texas
Pres.: Dr RICHARD J. MOUW
Provost and Sr. Vice-Pres.: C. DOUGLAS McCONNELL
Vice-Pres. for Enrolment and Student Affairs: WENDY WAKEMAN
Vice-Pres. for Finance: JOHN W. WARD
Vice-Pres. for Seminary Advancement: JOE B. WEBB
Registrar: DAVID E. KIEFER
Library Dir: MICHAEL D. MURRAY

Library of 500,000 vols, 10,000 ejournals, 10,000 ebooks, 3,400 print periodicals, 900 nat. and int. journals and 800 monographic serials
Number of teachers: 80
Number of students: 4,500

DEANS

School of Intercultural Studies: Dr C. DOUGLAS McCONNELL
School of Psychology: Dr WINSTON E. GOODEN
School of Theology: Dr HOWARD LOEWEN

GOLDEN GATE BAPTIST THEOLOGICAL SEMINARY

201 Seminary Dr., Mill Valley, CA 94941-3163
Telephone: (415) 380-1300
E-mail: admissions@ggbts.edu
Internet: www.ggbts.edu
Founded 1944
Private control
Language of instruction: English, Korean
Academic year: August to August
Br. campuses: Northern California Campus, CA; Southern California Campus, CA; Pacific Northwest Campus, WA; Arizona Campus, AZ; Rocky Mountain Campus, CO
Pres.: Dr JEFF IORG
Vice-Pres. for Academic Affairs: Dr D. MICHAEL MARTIN
Vice-Pres. for Business and Finance: GARY GROAT
Vice-Pres. for Institutional Advancement: (vacant)
Vice-Pres. for Enrollment and Student Services: Dr ADAM GROZA
Registrar: JENNIFER PEACH
Dir of Library Services: KELLY CAMPBELL
Number of teachers: 20 full-time
Number of students: 2,060

GOLDEN GATE UNIVERSITY

536 Mission St, San Francisco, CA 94105-2968
Telephone: (415) 442-7000
Internet: www.ggu.edu
Founded 1901
Private control
Campuses: Silicon Valley, Los Angeles and San Francisco (California), and Seattle (Washington)
Pres.: Dr DAN ANGEL
Vice-Pres. for Academic Affairs: Dr BARBARA H. KARLIN
Vice-Pres. for Finance: SWAGAT KAJALE
Vice-Pres. for Operations: BOB HITE
Dir for Enrolment Services: LOUIS D. RICCARDI
Dir for Univ. Library: JANICE CARTER
Library of 75,000 vols, 75,000 ebook vols
Number of teachers: 264 (incl. full-time and part-time)
Number of students: 3,605
Publication: *GGU magazine* (3 a year)

DEANS

Edward S. Ageno School of Business: PAUL FOUTS
School of Accounting: Dr MARY P. CANNING
School of Law: Dr DRUCILLA STENDER RAMEY
School of Taxation: Dr MARY P. CANNING
Undergraduate Programmes: CHERRON HOPPES

HARVEY MUDD COLLEGE

301 Platt Blvd, Claremont, CA 91711-5901
Telephone: (909) 621-8000
E-mail: president@hmc.edu
Internet: www.hmc.edu

Founded 1955
Private control
Academic year: August to May
Liberal arts college; mem. of Claremont Univ. Consortium; depts of biology, chemistry, computer science, engineering, humanities, social sciences and arts, mathematics, physics
Pres.: MARIA KLAWE
Vice-Pres. and Chief Information Officer: JOSEPH VAUGHAN
Vice-Pres. for Academic Affairs and Dean for Faculty: ROBERT CAVE
Vice-Pres. for Admin. and Finance: ANDREW DORANTES
Vice-Pres. for Admission and Financial Aid: THYRA BRIGGS
Vice-Pres. for College Advancement: DAN MACALUSO
Vice-Pres. for Computing and Information Services and Chief Information Officer: JOSEPH VAUGHAN
Vice-Pres. for Student Affairs and Dean for Students: MAGGIE BROWNING
Registrar: NOEL KELLER
Librarian: JOHN MCDONALD
Library: 1m. vols (shared with the Claremont Colleges)
Number of teachers: 82 (full-time and part-time)
Number of students: 756

HOLY NAMES UNIVERSITY

3500 Mountain Blvd, Oakland, CA 94619-1699
Telephone: (510) 436-1000
E-mail: admissions@hnu.edu
Internet: www.hnu.edu
Founded 1868
Private control
Academic year: August to July
Coeducational liberal arts college
Pres.: Dr WILLIAM J. HYNES
Vice-Pres. for Academic Affairs and Dean of Faculty: BETH MARTIN
Vice-Pres. for Finance and Admin.: STUART KOOP
Vice-Pres. for Institutional Advancement: DAV CVITKOVIC
Vice-Pres. for Mission Effectiveness: Sr CAROL SELLMAN
Vice-Pres. for Student Affairs and Enrolment Services: MICHAEL MILLER
Vice-Pres. for Univ. Advancement: RICHARD ORTEGA
Dir for Library Services: KAREN SCHEINDER
Library of 30,000 vols, 50,000 e-books
Number of teachers: 120
Number of students: 1,330

HOPE INTERNATIONAL UNIVERSITY

2500 E Nutwood Ave, Fullerton, CA 92831
Telephone: (714) 879-3901
E-mail: gradinfo@hiu.edu
Internet: www.hiu.edu
Founded 1928 as Pacific Bible Seminary, present name 1997
Private control
Academic year: August to March
Educational centres at Corona and Orange (California), and Everett (Washington)
Pres.: Dr JOHN DERRY
Vice-Pres. for Academic Affairs: Dr PAUL ALEXANDER
Vice-Pres. for Business and Finance: FRANK SCOTTI
Vice-Pres. for Enrolment Management: TERESA SMITH
Vice-Pres. for Institutional Advancement: MICHAEL MULRYAN

Vice-Pres. for Student Affairs: MARK COMEAUX
Registrar: RON ARCHER
Dir for Library Services: ROBIN HARTMAN
Library of 65,000 vols
Number of teachers: 165
Number of students: 1,300

DEANS

College of Arts and Science: Dr STEVEN D. EDGINGTON
College of Business and Management: Dr JAMES D. WOEST
College of Education: Dr GEORGE E. WEST
College of Ministry and Biblical Studies: Dr JOE GRANA
College of Psychology and Counseling: Dr LAURA L. STEELE
Pacific Christian College: STEVEN D. EDGINGTON

HUMBOLDT STATE UNIVERSITY

One Harpst St, Arcata, CA 95521-8299
Telephone: (707) 826-3011
E-mail: welcome@humboldt.edu
Internet: www.humboldt.edu
Founded 1913
Academic year: August to May
Pres.: ROLLIN C. RICHMOND
Provost and Vice-Pres. for Academic Affairs: ROBERT SNYDER
Vice-Pres. for Admin. Affairs: BURT NORDSTROM
Vice-Pres. for Student Affairs: Dr PEG L. BLAKE
Vice-Pres. for Univ. Advancement: FRANK WHITLATCH
Dean of Enrolment Management: JEAN BUTLER
Dir for Institutional Research and Planning: JACQUELINE NAGATSUKA
Registrar: HILARY DASHIELL
Dean for the Library: TERESA L. GRENOT
Library of 560,000 vols, 650 atlases, 8,000 CDs, 6,000 VHS, 1,000 DVDs
Number of teachers: 520
Number of students: 7,900

DEANS

College of Arts, Humanities and Social Sciences: KEN AYOOB
College of Natural Resources and Sciences: STEVE SMITH
College of Professional Studies: JOHN LEE

HUMPHREYS COLLEGE

6650 Inglewood Ave, Stockton, CA 95207
Telephone: (209) 478-0800
E-mail: college_president@humphreys.edu
Internet: www.humphreys.edu
Founded 1896 as Stockton Business College, present name 1947
Private control
Academic year: September to September
Campuses in Modesto and Stockton
Pres.: Dr ROBERT G. HUMPHREYS
Dean for Admin.: WILMA OKAMOTO-VAUGHN
Dean for Instruction: JESS BONDS
Registrar: MARIA J. GARCIA-MILLER
Librarian: STANISLAV PERKNER
Number of students: 1,172

DEANS

Laurence Drivon School of Law: L. PATRICK PIGGOTT

ITT TECHNICAL INSTITUTE

9680 Granite Ridge Dr., San Diego, CA 92123
Telephone: (858) 571-8500
Internet: itt-tech.edu

Founded 1969
Private control
Academic year: September to September
140 Campuses in 38 states; Breckinridge School of Nursing, School of Business, School of Criminal Justice, School of Drafting and Design, School of Electronics Technology, School of Health Sciences, School of Information Technology
Dir: JOHN A. BYERS
Dean: CORNELL R. HOKE
Registrar: COLLEEN HEBDING
Number of students: 70,000

JOHN F. KENNEDY UNIVERSITY

100 Ellinwood Way, Pleasant Hill, CA 94523-4817
Telephone: (925) 969-3450
E-mail: proginfo@jfku.edu
Internet: www.jfku.edu
Founded 1964
Private control
Affiliate of Nat. Univ. System; campuses at: Pleasant Hill, San Jose, Berkeley and Costa Mesa
Chancellor: Dr JERRY C. LEE
Pres.: Dr STEVEN STARGARDTER
Provost: DIANA PAQUE
Academic Vice-Pres.: IRVING BERKOWITZ
Vice-Pres. for Academic Affairs: DONALD CAMPBELL
Vice-Pres. for Advancement: ANNE MARIE TAYLOR
Vice-Pres. for Enrolment Services: K. SUE DUNCAN
Vice-Pres. for Institutional Research, Planning and Assessment: SANDI TATMAN
Dir for Human Resources: THERESA RODGERS
Registrar: MICHAEL RAINE
Univ. Librarian: CLAUDIA CHESTER
Library of 100,000 vols, 1,000 print journals, 18,000 ejournals and 50,000 ebooks
Number of teachers: 690
Number of students: 2,000

DEANS

College of Continuing Education: Dr JOSHUA LACHS
College of Graduate and Professional Studies: RUTH FASSINGER
College of Law: BARBIERI
College of Undergraduate Studies: MICHAEL GRANEY-MULHOLLAND
Extended University: JOSHUA LACHS

LA SIERRA UNIVERSITY

4500 Riverwalk Parkway, Riverside, CA 92515
Telephone: (951) 785-2000
E-mail: info@lasierra.edu
Internet: www.lasierra.edu
Founded 1922 as La Sierra Acad., present name 1990
Private Control
Academic year: September to June
Pres.: Dr RANDAL R. WISBEY
Provost: Dr STEVE PAWLUK
Vice-Pres. for Advancement and Univ. Relations: Dr NORMAN YERGEN
Vice-Pres. for Enrolment Services: DAVID LOFTHOUSE
Vice-Pres. for Financial Admin.: DAVID GERIGUIS
Vice-Pres. for Student Life: YAMI BAZAN
Registrar: FAYE SWAYZE
Library Dir: KITTY SIMMONS
Library of 260,395 vols, 646,289 audiovisual material, 50,121 electronic books
Number of teachers: 110 (full-time)
Number of students: 2,200

Publications: *Adventist Heritage* (4 a year), *La Sierra University*

DEANS

College of Arts and Sciences: Dr ADENY SCHMIDT
School of Business: Dr JOHN THOMAS
School of Education: Dr ED BOYATT
School of Religion: Dr JOHN W. WEBSTER

LIFE CHIROPRACTIC COLLEGE WEST

25001 Industrial Blvd, Hayward, CA 94545
Telephone: (510) 780-4500
Internet: www.lifewest.edu
Founded 1976 as Pacific States Chiropractic College, present name 1981
Private control
Academic year: September to June

Pres.: Dr BRIAN D. KELLY
Chief Financial Officer: REZA BADIEE
Dean for College: Dr JOSEPH FERGUSON
Dean for Health Center: Dr SCOTT DONALD-SON
Exec. Dir for Enrolment: CARLOS R. ALICEA
Dir for Financial Aid: BRENDA R. JOHNSON
Dir for Research: Dr DALE JOHNSON
Dir for Student Services, Job Location and Devt: JACKIE BIRON
Registrar: ROBBIE SHERWOOD
Library Dir: ANNETTE OSENGA

LIFE PACIFIC COLLEGE

1100 W Covina Blvd, San Dimas, CA 91773
Telephone: (909) 599-5433
E-mail: info@lifepacific.edu
Internet: www.lifepacific.edu
Founded 1923, L.I.F.E. Bible College
Private control
Academic year: August to May

Pres.: Dr ROBERT FLORES
Vice-Pres. for Academic Affairs: Dr TERRY SAMPLES
Dir for Advancement: LYNNETTE LOZOYA
Dir for Institutional Research: BRUCE PRIM-ROSE
Chief Financial Officer: Rev. JARROD KULA
Dean for Students: J. J. PETERSON
Registrar: BRITTANY ADAMS
Librarian: KEITH DAWSON

LOMA LINDA UNIVERSITY

Loma Linda, CA 92350
Telephone: (909) 558-1000
E-mail: admissions.app@llu.edu
Internet: www.llu.edu
Founded 1905
Private control

Pres. and CEO: Dr RICHARD H. HART
Sr Vice-Pres. for Clinical Faculty: RICARDO PEVERINI
Sr Vice-Pres. for Educational Affairs: RONALD L. CARTER
Sr Vice-Pres. for Faculty Practice: DAVID WREN
Sr Vice-Pres. for Finance: STEVEN MOHR
Sr Vice-Pres. for Health Admin.: DANIEL FONTOURA
Sr Vice-Pres. for Human Resource Management and Risk Management: MARK L. HUBBARD
Sr Vice-Pres. for Managed Care: ZAREH SARRAFIAN
Sr Vice-Pres. for Strategic Planning: MICHAEL H. JACKSON
Exec. Vice-Pres. for Finance and Admin. and Chief Financial Officer: KEVIN J. LANG
Exec. Vice-Pres. for Hospital Affairs: RUTHITA J. FIKE
Exec. Vice-Pres. for Medical Affairs: H. ROGER HADLEY

Exec. Vice-Pres. for Univ. Affairs: RICHARD H. HART
Vice-Pres. and CIO for Academia: DAVID P. HARRIS
Vice-Pres. and CIO for Health Ministries: RICHARD HERGERT
Vice-Pres. for Allied Health Professions Education: CRAIG R. JACKSON
Vice-Pres. for Dentistry: CHARLES J. GOOD-ACRE
Vice-Pres. for Diversity: LESLIE N. POLLARD
Vice-Pres. for Finance: ROD NEAL
Vice-Pres. for Graduate Medical Education: DANIEL W. GIANG
Vice-Pres. for Graduate Studies Education: ANTHONY J. ZUCCARELLI
Vice-Pres. for Healthcare Business Devt and Govt Relations: MEL SAUDER
Vice-Pres. for Nursing Education: MARILYN M. HERMANN
Vice-Pres. for Patient Care Services: ELIZA-BETH J. DICKINSON
Vice-Pres. for Public Affairs: W. AUGUSTUS CHEATHAM
Vice-Pres. for Quality: Dr JAMES PAPPAS
Vice-Pres. for Religious Education: Dr JON PAULIEN
Vice-Pres. for Spiritual Life and Wholeness: Dr GERALD R. WINSLOW
Dir of Libraries: CARLENE DRAKE
Library of 317,368 vols
Number of teachers: 1,393 (full-time)
Number of students: 4,212

DEANS

School of Allied Health Professions: Dr CRAIG R. JACKSON
School of Dentistry: Dr CHARLES J. GOODACRE
School of Medicine: Dr ROGER HADLEY
School of Nursing: Dr MARILYN H. HERMANN
School of Pharmacy: Dr W. WILLIAM HUGHES
School of Public Health: Dr JAMES KYLE
School of Religion: Dr JON PAULIEN
School of Science and Technology: BEVERLY J. BUCKLES

LOYOLA MARYMOUNT UNIVERSITY

1 LMU Dr., Los Angeles, CA 90045-2659
Telephone: (310) 338-2700
E-mail: admissions@lmu.edu
Internet: www.lmu.edu
Founded 1911, present name 1973
Private control
Academic year: August to May

Pres.: DAVID W. BURCHAM
Chancellor: PATRICK J. CAHALAN
Sr Vice-Pres.: DAVID W. BURCHAM
Sr Vice-Pres. for Academic Affairs and Chief Academic Officer: Dr JOSEPH HELLIGE
Sr Vice-Pres. for Admin.: EVELYNNE B. SCAR-BOROUGH
Sr Vice-Pres. for Business and Finance: THOMAS FLEMING
Sr Vice-Pres. for Student Affairs: Dr ELENA M. BOVE
Sr Vice-Pres. for Univ. Relations: DENNIS SLON
Vice-Pres. for Communications and Govt Relations: KATHLEEN FLANAGAN
Vice-Pres. for Devt and Alumni Relations: BEDFORD MCINTOSH
Dir of Graduate Admissions: CHAKÉ KOUYOUMJIAN
Dean of Univ. Libraries: KRISTINE BRANCO-LINI
Library of 561,498 vols (289,201 main campus; 272,297 Law School)
Number of teachers: 500 (full-time)
Number of students: 9,070 (5,797 undergraduate, 1,961 graduate and 1,312 Law School)

DEANS

Bellarmine College of Liberal Arts: PAUL TIYAMBE ZELEZA
College of Business Administration: Dr DEN-NIS W. DRAPER
College of Communication and Fine Arts: Prof. BARBARA J. BUSSE
Frank R. Seaver College of Science and Engineering: Dr RICHARD G. PLUMB
Loyola Law School: Dr VICTOR J. GOLD
School of Education: Dr SHANE P. MARTIN
School of Film and Television: STEPHEN UJLAKI

MASTER'S COLLEGE

21726 Placerita Canyon Rd, Santa Clarita, CA 91321
Telephone: (661) 259-3540
E-mail: admissions@masters.edu
Internet: www.masters.edu
Founded 1927 as Los Angeles Baptist Theological Seminary, present name 1985
Private control

Areas of study: biblical counselling, biblical studies, biological and physical science, business, communication, computer and information sciences, English, history and political studies, home economics, liberal studies, mathematics, music, physical education, teacher education, divinity, theology

Pres.: Dr JOHN MACARTHUR
Exec. Vice-Pres. and Provost: Dr MARK TATLOCK
Vice-Pres. for Academic Affairs: Dr JOHN HUGHES
Vice-Pres. of Advancement: MARK AYDELOTTE
Vice-Pres. for Enrolment Management: Dr PAUL BERRY
Vice-Pres. for Finance: JASON HARTUNG
Vice-Pres. for Operations: ROBERT L. HOTTON
Dean for Student Life: JOE KELLER
Chief Operating Officer and Chief Information Officer: NATE PRINCE
Dir for Library Services: JOHN STONE
Library of 143,000 vols
Number of teachers: 70
Number of students: 1,100

MENLO COLLEGE

1000 El Camino Real, Atherton, CA 94027-4301
Telephone: (650) 543-3887
E-mail: advancement@menlo.edu
Internet: www.menlo.edu
Founded 1927 as Menlo Junior College, present name 1949
Private control

Depts of communication, liberal arts and management

Pres.: Dr JAMES KELLY
Provost: Dr JIM WOOLEVER
Vice-Pres. for Student Services: DAVID PLA-CEY
Academic Dean: LOWELL PRATT
Dean for Arts and Sciences: MARILYN THOMAS
Dean for Business and Academic Affairs: DALE HOCKSTRA
Sr Assoc. Dir for Admissions: BOB WILMS
Dir for Financial Aid: ANNE HEATON-DUNLAP
Dir for Enrolment Management: CINDY MCGREW
Dean for Library and Information Services: C. BRIGID WELCH
Number of students: 750
Publication: *Advantage*

MILLS COLLEGE

5000 MacArthur Blvd, Oakland, CA 94613
Telephone: (510) 430-2255
E-mail: admission@mills.edu

Internet: www.mills.edu

Founded 1852 as Young Ladies' Seminary, as a college 1885

Private control

Academic year: August to May

Liberal arts college for women; co-educational graduate programmes

Pres.: Dr ALECIA A. DeCOUDREAUX

Provost and Dean of the Faculty: SANDRA GREER

Vice-Pres. and Gen. Counsel: THERESE LEONE

Vice-Pres. for Admin. and Human Resources: LESA HAMMOND

Vice-Pres. for Finance and Treas.: JAMIE NICKEL

Vice-Pres. for Institutional Advancement: CYNTHIA BRANDT STOVER

Vice-Pres. for Operations and Chief of Staff: RENÉE JADUSHLEVER

Dean for Student Life: JOI D. LEWIS

Dean for Undergraduate Admission: GIULIETTA AQUINO

Library of 240,000 vols; spec. collns 12,000 vols and 10,000 MSS, incl. Shakespeare's First Folio, a Mozart MSS, leaf from a Gutenberg Bible and 3,100 journals

Number of teachers: 200 (100 full-time, 100 part-time)

Number of students: 1,550

Publications: *580 Split* (1 a year), *Mills Academic Research Journal* (1 a year, online), *The Walrus* (1 a year), *Womanist, A Women of Color Journal* (1 a year)

DEANS

Fine Arts: MARY-ANN MILFORD

Graduate Literary Studies: CYNTHIA SCHEINBERG

Letters: RUTH SAXTON

Lorry I. Lokey Graduate School of Business: Dr DEBORAH MERRILL-SANDS

Natural Sciences and Education: LINDA KROLL

School of Education: KATHERINE SCHULTZ

Social Sciences: LAURA NATHAN

MONTEREY INSTITUTE OF INTERNATIONAL STUDIES: A GRADUATE SCHOOL OF MIDDLEBURY COLLEGE

460 Pierce St, Monterey, CA 93940

Telephone: (831) 647-4123

E-mail: info@miis.edu

Internet: www.miis.edu

Founded 1955 as Monterey Institute of Foreign Studies, present name 2010

Academic year: September to June

Pres.: SUNDER RAMASWAMY

Provost: AMY SANDS

Dean for Student Services: TATE MILLER

Exec. Dir for Institutional Advancement: KEVIN WASBAUER

Exec. Dir for Finance: JAI SHANKAR

Exec. Dir for Strategic Planning and Technology: AMY McGILL

Exec. Dir for Communications: JASON WARBURG

Library Dir: PETER LIU

Library of 100,000 vols, 500 print periodicals

Number of teachers: 120 (70 full-time, 50 part-time)

Number of students: 780

DEANS

Graduate School of International Policy and Management: YUWEI SHI

Graduate School of Translation, Interpretation and Language Education: RENEE JOURDENAIS

MOUNT ST MARY'S COLLEGE

Chalon Campus: 12001 Chalon Rd, Los Angeles, CA 90049-1599

Telephone: (310) 954-4000

E-mail: mountnews@msmc.la.edu

Internet: www.msmc.la.edu

Founded 1925

Private control

Academic year: June to May

Liberal arts and sciences college primarily for women; depts of American studies, art, biological sciences, business admin., education, English, film and social justice, gerontology, history, humanities, language and culture, music, nursing, philosophy, physical sciences and mathematics, physical therapy, political science, psychology, religious studies, social work, sociology; campus in Doheny

Pres.: Dr ANN McELANEY-JOHNSON

Provost and Academic Vice-Pres.: Dr ELEANOR SIEBERT

Vice-Pres. for Admin. and Finance: CHRIS K. McALARY

Vice-Pres. for Information Support Service and Enrolment Management: LARRY SMITH

Vice-Pres. for Institutional Advancement: Dr STEPHANIE CUBBA

Vice-Pres. for Student Affairs: Dr JANE LINGUA

Dir of Libraries: CLAUDIA REED

Library of 140,000 vols

Number of teachers: 190

Number of students: 2,480 (1,980 undergraduates, 500 graduates)

Publication: *Mount Magazine* (2 a year)

NATIONAL UNIVERSITY

11255 N Torrey Pines Rd, La Jolla, CA 92037-1011

Telephone: (858) 642-8000

E-mail: advisor@nu.edu

Internet: www.nu.edu

Founded 1971

Private control

Academic year: August to January

26 Learning centres throughout California; campuses at Carlsbad, La Mesa, Mission Valley, Rancho Bernardo, South Bay, Spectrum Business Park

Pres.: PATRICIA E. POTTER

Provost: Dr EILEEN D. HEVERON

Chancellor: Dr JERRY C. LEE

Exec. Vice-Pres.: Dr JOHN F. CADY

Exec. Vice-Pres. for Business and Regional Operation: RICHARD E. CARTER

Vice-Chancellor for Organizational Devt: Dr GARY FROST

Vice-Pres. for Admin and Business: KEVIN CASEY

Vice-Pres. for Advancement and Alumni Relations: MAGGIE T. WATKINS

Vice-Pres. for Regional Operations and Marketing: VIRGINIA BENEKE

Vice-Pres. for Strategic Planning: RICHARD C. JOY

Vice-Pres. for Student Services: Dr JOSEPH ZAVALA

Vice-Pres. for Univ. Relations: ROBERT FREELEN

Dean for Graduate Studies: (vacant)

Library Dir: ANNE MARIE SECORD

Library of 200,000 vols

Number of teachers: 1,100 (140 full-time, 85 assoc., 875 adjunct)

Number of students: 17,090 (full-time)

DEANS

College of Letters and Sciences: Dr MICHAEL McANEAR

School of Business and Management: Dr RONALD UHLIG

School of Education: Dr KEN FAWSON

School of Engineering, Technology and Media: Dr JOHN A. CICERO

School of Health and Human Services: MICHAEL LACOURSE

NAVAL POSTGRADUATE SCHOOL

Public Affairs Office, Code 004, 1 University Circle, Monterey, CA 93943-5001

Telephone: (831) 656-2023

E-mail: pao@nps.edu

Internet: www.nps.edu

Founded 1909 as School of Marine Engineering, present name 1919, present location 1951

State control

Academic year: October to September

Pres.: Vice-Admiral DANIEL T. OLIVER

Exec. Vice-Pres. and Provost: Dr LEONARD A. FERRARI

Vice-Provost for Academic Affairs: Dr DOUG MOSES

Vice-Pres. for Finance and Admin.: COLLEEN NICKLES

Vice-Pres. for Information Resources and Chief Information Officer: Dr CHRISTINE M. HAKSA

Vice-Pres. and Dean for Research: Dr KARL VAN BIBBER

Dean for Students: ALAN G. POINDEXTER

Univ. Librarian: ELEANOR UHLINGER

Library of 1,063,696 vols (incl. microform)

Number of teachers: 360

Number of students: 2,400

DEANS

Graduate School of Business and Public Policy: Dr WILLIAM R. GATES

Graduate School of Engineering and Applied Sciences: Dr PHILIP DURKEE

Graduate School of Operational Information Sciences: Dr PETER PURDUE

School of International Graduate Studies: Dr JAMES J. WIRTZ

NOTRE DAME DE NAMUR UNIVERSITY

1500 Ralston Ave, Belmont, CA 94002

Telephone: (650) 508-3500

E-mail: pr@ndnu.edu

Internet: www.ndnu.edu

Founded 1851, chartered 1868, present location 1923

Private control

Pres.: Dr JUDITH MAXWELL GREIG

Provost: Dr DIANA DEMETRULIAS

Vice-Pres. for Advancement: MICHAEL J. ROMO

Vice-Pres. for Campus Life: RAYMOND JONES

Vice-Pres. for Enrolment Management: HERNAN BUCHELI

Vice-Pres. for Finance and Admin.: HENRY ROTH

Dean for Enrolment: JARRID WHITNEY

Librarian: Dr KLAUS MUSMANN

Registrar: SANDRA LEE

Library of 120,000 vols, 300 periodicals

Number of teachers: 100 (full-time)

Number of students: 1,790 (full-time and part-time)

DEANS

College of Arts and Sciences: Dr JOHN LEMMON

School of Business and Management: Dr BARBARA CAULLEY

School of Education and Leadership: Dr JOANNE ROSSI

OCCIDENTAL COLLEGE

1600 Campus Rd, Los Angeles, CA 90041

Telephone: (323) 259-2500

E-mail: admission@oxy.edu
Internet: www.oxy.edu
Founded 1887
Private control
Academic year: August to May

Courses in American studies, art history and visual arts, Asian studies, biochemistry, biology, chemistry, cognitive science, critical theory and social justice, diplomacy and world affairs, economics, education, English and comparative literary studies, English writing, environmental programmes, geology, German, Russian, and classical studies, global affairs, history, kinesiology, mathematics, music, philosophy, physics, politics, psychobiology, psychology, religious studies, sociology, Spanish and French literary studies, Theatre, women's studies/gender studies

Pres.: Dr JONATHAN VEITCH
Vice-Pres. for Academic Affairs and Dean for the College: Dr JORGE GONZALEZ
Vice-Pres. for Admin.: MICHAEL P. GROENER
Vice-Pres. for Finance and Planning: AMOS HIMMELSTEIN
Vice-Pres. for Information Resources and Chief Information Officer: PAMELA MCQUESTEN
Vice-Pres. for Legal Affairs and Gen. Counsel: Dr SANDRA COOPER
Vice-Pres. for Student Affairs and Dean for Students: BARBARA J. AVERY
Vice-Pres. and Dean for Admission and Financial Aid: VINCE CUSEO
Sr. Vice-Pres. for Institutional Advancement and External Relations: DENNIS COLLINS
Registrar: VICTOR T. EGITTO
Librarian: EMILY BERGMAN
Library of 500,000 items (books, video and audio recordings and microfilms) and 1,255 current periodicals
Number of teachers: 170
Number of students: 2,100

OTIS COLLEGE OF ART AND DESIGN

9045 Lincoln Blvd, Los Angeles, CA 90045
Telephone: (310) 665-6800
E-mail: admissions@otis.edu
Internet: www.otis.edu

Founded 1918

Bachelors in architecture/landscape/interiors, communication arts, digital media, fashion design, fine arts, interactive product design, toy design; Masters in fine arts, public practice, writing

Pres.: SAMUEL HOI
Provost: KERRY WALK
Vice-Pres. for Administrative and Financial Services: WILLIAM SCHAEFFER
Vice-Pres. for Enrolment Management: MARC MEREDITH
Vice-Pres. of Institutional Advancement: CARRIE STEWART
Dean for Admissions: YVETTE SOBKY
Dean for Student Affairs: LAURA KIRALLA
Registrar: ANNA MANZANO
Dir for Library: SUE MABERRY
Library of 25,000 vols, 5,000 video cassettes and DVDs, 150 periodicals
Number of teachers: 200
Number of students: 1,200

PACIFIC LUTHERAN THEOLOGICAL SEMINARY

2770 Marin Ave, Berkeley, CA 94708
Telephone: (510) 524-5264
E-mail: seminaryrelations@plts.edu
Internet: plts.edu
Founded 1950
Private control

MAs in Christian ministry, divinity and theological studies; partnership with Luther Seminary in St Paul, Minnesota
Academic year: September to May

Pres.: Dr PHYLIS ANDERSON
Vice-Pres. for Advancement: CINDY CARROLL
Academic Dean: MICHAEL AUNE
Dir for Admissions: Dr Rev. STEVEN CHURCHILL
Dean for Faculty: MICHAEL B. AULNE
Dean for Students and Registrar: CHERYL HEUER
Library Dir: ROBERT BENEDETTO
Library of 450,000 vols, 1,500 journal subscriptions, 290,000 other media holdings
Number of teachers: 150
Number of students: 1,350

PACIFIC OAKS COLLEGE

55 Eureka St, Pasadena, CA 91103
Telephone: (626) 529-8500
E-mail: president@pacificoaks.edu
Internet: www.pacificoaks.edu

Founded 1945
Private control

Courses in human devt, marital and family therapy, teacher education programmes

Pres.: EZAT PARNIA
Provost: Dr MICHAEL HOROWITZ
Vice-Pres. for Institutional Advancement: KERRY NEAL
Registrar: MARSHA FRANKER
Librarian: NERMINE HANNA
Library of 17,000 vols
Number of teachers: 70
Number of students: 1,280
Publication: Voices (2 a year)

DEANS

College of Education: Dr KALANI BEYER
College of Human Development and Family Studies: Dr KALANI BEYER
Online Learning: Dr MARCIA MOODY

PACIFIC SCHOOL OF RELIGION

1798 Scenic Ave, Berkeley, CA 94709-1323
Telephone: (510) 849-8200
E-mail: psrinfo@psr.edu
Internet: www.psr.edu

Founded 1866 as Pacific Theological Seminary, present name 1916; attached to Graduate Theological Union
Private control
Academic year: September to May

Pres.: RIESS POTTERVELD
Vice-Pres. for Academic Affairs and Dean: Dr TAT-SIONG BENNY LIEW
Vice-Pres. for Institutional Advancement: KATHI MCSHANE
Chief Financial Officer: STEVE ARGYRIS
Registrar: DELPHINE HWANG
Dir for Badè Museum: AARON BRODY
Library Dir: ROBERT BENETTO
Library of 700,000 vols
Number of teachers: 40 (20 core, 20 adjunct)
Number of students: 250

PACIFIC UNION COLLEGE

One Angwin Ave, Angwin, CA 94508
Telephone: (707) 965-6336
E-mail: pr@puc.edu
Internet: www.puc.edu

Founded 1882
Private control
Academic year: September to June

Liberal arts college; depts of aviation, biology, business administration and economics, chemistry, communication, computer science, education, English, exercise science,

health and nutrition, history, honours, mathematics, modern languages, music, nursing, physics, psychology and social work, religion, visual arts

Pres.: Dr HEATHER KNIGHT
Vice-Pres. for Academic Admin. and Academic Dean: Dr NANCY LECOURT
Vice-Pres. for Advancement: WALTER COLLINS
Vice-Pres. for Financial Admin. and Chief Financial Officer: Dr DAVE LAURENCE
Vice-Pres. for Student Services: Dr LISA BISSELL PAULSON
Registrar: MARLO WATERS
Chair of Library Services: ADUGNAW WORKU
Library of 153,898 vols
Number of teachers: 135 (94 full-time, 41 part-time)
Number of students: 1,530
Publication: PUC Viewpoint (4 a year)

PACIFICA GRADUATE INSTITUTE

249 Lambert Rd, Carpinteria, CA 93013
Telephone: (805) 969-3626
E-mail: contact@pacifica.edu
Internet: www.pacifica.edu

Founded 1976

Depts of clinical psychology, counselling psychology, depth psychology, depth psychotherapy, humanities, mythological studies

Chancellor: Dr STEPHEN AIZENSTAT
Pres.: Dr CAROL S. PEARSON
Provost: Dr PATRICIA KATSKY
Chief Financial Officer: DAVID HENKEL
Dean for Academic Affairs: Dr CINDY CARTER
Dir for Admissions: WENDY OVEREND
Dir for Institutional Advancement and Public Relations: ERIK H. DAVIS
Dir for Library Services: ALAIN DUSSERT
Registrar: FRANCINE MATAS

PALO ALTO UNIVERSITY

1791 Arastradero Rd, Palo Alto, CA 94304
Telephone: (800) 818-6136
E-mail: admissions@paloaltou.edu
Internet: www.paloaltou.edu

Founded 1975 as Pacific Graduate School of Psychology, present name 2009
Private control

Undergraduate and graduate and doctoral programmes; offers business psychology, clinical psychology, neuropsychology; psychology and social action; mental health counselling

Pres.: Dr ALLEN D. CALVIN
Vice-Pres. for Academic Affairs: Dr WILLIAM FROMING
Registrar: NORA MARQUEZ

PARDEE RAND GRADUATE SCHOOL

1776 Main St, Santa Monica, CA 90407-2138
Telephone: (310) 393-0411
E-mail: prgs@prgs.edu
Internet: www.prgs.edu

Founded 1970
Private control

Areas of study: economics, empirical analysis, modelling and computational methods, policy analysis, science and technology, social and behavioural sciences

Dean: Dr SUSAN L. MARQUIS
Number of teachers: 150
Number of students: 110

PATTEN UNIVERSITY

2433 Coolidge Ave, Oakland, CA 94601
Telephone: (510) 261-8500
E-mail: admissions@patten.edu
Internet: www.patten.edu

Founded 1944

Private control

Depts of art, biblical studies, Christian leadership, church ministries, communications, education, liberal studies for teaching, music, organizational management, pastoral studies, psychology, urban missions, youth ministry

Pres.: Dr GARY R. MONCHER

Academic Vice-Pres. and Provost: Dr KENNETH ROMINES

Vice-Pres. for Finance and Admin.: ANDREW M. GANES

Vice-Pres. for Univ. Services: DARLA E. CUADRA

Dean for Enrolment Services: ROBERT OLIVERA

Dean for Student Services: SHARON BARTA

Library Dir: ANN ZEMENS

Library of 35,000 vols, 180 periodicals

PEPPERDINE UNIVERSITY

24255 Pacific Coast Highway, Malibu, CA 90263

Telephone: (310) 506-4000

Internet: www.pepperdine.edu

Founded 1937 as college, present status 1970

Private control

Pres. and Chief Exec. Officer: ANDREW K. BENTON

Chancellor: Dr CHARLES B. RUNNELS

Provost and Chief Academic Officer: Dr DARRYL TIPPENS

Exec. Vice-Pres. and Chief Operating Officer: GARY HANSON

Sr Vice-Pres. for Investments and Chief Investment Officer: JEFF PIPPIN

Sr Vice-Pres. for Planning, Information and Technology: Dr NANCY MAGNUSSON

Vice-Pres. for Advancement and Public Affairs: KEITH HINKLE

Dean for Admission and Enrolment Management: PAUL A. LONG

Dean for Int. Programmes: CHARLES HALL

Dean for Libraries: MARK S. ROOSA

Dean for Student Affairs: MARK DAVIS

Registrar: HUNG V. LE

Library: 7 libraries with a combined colln of 1m. vols

Number of teachers: 300 (full-time)

Number of students: 7,700

Publication: *Pepperdine People Magazine*

DEANS

Frank R. Seaver College of Letters, Arts, and Sciences: RICK MARRS

George L. Graziadio School of Business and Management: LINDA A. LIVINGSTONE

Graduate School of Education and Psychology: MARGARET WEBER

School of Law: DEANELL REECE TACHA

School of Public Policy: JAMES R. WILBURN

PROFESSORS

Frank R. Seaver College of Letters, Arts, and Sciences:

ADJEMIAN, C., Mathematics
ADLER, R., Marketing
ARDOIN, B., Communication
BAIM, D., Economics and Finance
BAIRD, D., History
BANKS, J., Management and Organizational Behaviour
BATCHELDER, R., Economics
BUCHANAN, R. W., Communication
CALDWELL, D. E., Social Sciences
CARROLL, L. A., English
CASEY, M. W., Communication
CHANDLER, R., Communication
CHESNUTT, R. D., Religion
CLEGG, C., English
CLOUD, D. C., Accounting

COBB, G., Music
COLLINGS, M. R., English
DAVIS, S., Biology
DOWDEY, D., German
DUNPHY, M., Physical Education
FALKNER, A., Art
FELTNER, M., Sports Medicine
GAMBILL, K., English
GANSKE, J., Chemistry
GIBONEY, S., Education
GIBSON, D., Philosophy
GOSE, M. D., Education
GREEN, D. B., Chemistry
HANCOCK, D. L., Mathematics
HART, G. W., English
HENDERSON, J., Theatre
HUGHES, R. T., Religion
KATS, L., Biology
LANGFORD, M., French
LOVE, S., Religion
LOWRY, D. N., Communication
MacRAE, H., Sports Medicine
MacRAE, P., Sports Medicine
MADDOX, R. B., Mathematics
MARRS, R. R., Religion
MARTIN, K. L., Biology
MONSMA, S., Political Science
MURRIE, M., Telecommunications
MYERS, V., English
NEILSON, G., Theatre
PARKENING, C., Music
PAYNE-PALACIO, J., Nutritional Science
PHILLIPS, W., Physics
PIASENTIN, J., Art
PULLEN, M., Music
REINECK, L., English
SESHAN, V., Management
SEXTON, R. L., Social Sciences
SHATZER, M., Communication
SHORES, D., Broadcasting
STRACHE, C. V., Physical Education
SUMMERS, M. R., Business Administration
SWARTZENDRUBER, D., Biology
THOMAS, J., English
THOMASON, P. B., Spanish
THOMPSON, D., Mathematics
TYLER, R. L., Religion
WARFORD, S., Computer Science
WEBB, G. T., Japanese Cultural History
WHITE, J. B., Chemistry
WILSON, J. F., New Testament
YATES, J. E., Organizational Behaviour and Management

George L. Graziadio School of Business and Management:

BLEUEL, W. H., Quantitative Methods
BUSKIRK, B. D., Marketing
DARDEN, C. E., Organization and Management
DUDLEY, T. J., Quantitative Methods
FLIEGE, S., Quantitative Methods
FOJTIK, C. W., Marketing
GERTMENIAN, W., Economics
GOODRICH, J., Int. Business
HAGAN, A. J., Economics
HALL, O. P., Jr, Quantitative Methods
HESSE, R., Quantitative Methods
HITCHIN, D. E., Management
HOISMAN, A. J., Behavioural Science
HUNT, C. J., Jr, Business Law
LARSON, W. G., Business Law
MALLINGER, M., Organization Behaviour
MARTINOFF, J. T., Finance
MOTAMEDI, K. K., Organization and Management
NICKLES, M. D., Economics
PENDERGHAST, T. F., Quantitative Methods
PETRO, F. A., Accounting
REISMAN, G., Economics
RICHARDSON, J. E., Marketing
RIERDAN, R. C., Behavioural Science
ROCKEY, E., Behavioural Science
SAMUELSON, B. A., Accounting
SANFORD, E., Economics
SHAFER, W., Accounting

SIEGEL, S., Technology Management
STANLEY, D. J., Finance and Accounting
STROM, W. L., Behavioural Science
VARDIABASIS, D., Economics
YOUNG, T. W., Economics

School of Education and Psychology:

ASAMEN, J. K., Psychology
COZOLINO, L. J., Psychology
FOY, D., Psychology
GARCIA, C. L., Education
HARRELL, S. P., Psychology
HEDGESPETH, J., Psychology
HIATT-MICHAEL, D., Education
HIBBS, C., Psychology
INGRAM, B., Psychology
LEVY, D. A., Psychology
LOWE, D. W., Psychology
McCALL, C., Research Methods
McMANUS, J. F., Education
MARTINEZ, T., Psychology
NEELY, F. W., Psychology
PAULL, R., Education
POLIN, L. G., Education
ROWE, D., Psychology
SÁNCHEZ, M., Education
SCHMIEDER-RAMIREZ, J., Education
SHAFRANSKE, E. P., Psychology
STEPHENS, R., Education

School of Law:

ALFORD, R. P.
BOST, T. G.
BOYD, K. L.
BUCHAN, L.
CALDWELL, H. M.
CHASE, C. A.
COCHRAN, R. F., Jr
COE, J. J., Jr
GAFFNEY, E. M., Jr
GASH, J. A.
GOODMAN, C. C.
GRADISHER, M. R.
GRAFFY, C. P.
JAMES, B.
KERR, C. L.
KERR, J. E.
KNAPLUND, K. S.
LEVINE, S. J.
LOWRY, L. R.
McCRORY, J. P.
McDERMOTT, A. X.
McDONALD, B. P.
McGOLDRICK, J. M., Jr
MARTIN, D. W.
MENDOZA, A.
MILLER, A.
NELSON, C. I.
OGDEN, G. L.
PERRIN, L. T.
POPOVICH, R.
PUSHAW, R. J.
ROBINSON, P.
SAXER, S. R.
SCARBERRY, M. S.
SEYMOUR, A. D.
SMITH, M. L.
WENDEL, P. T.
WESTON, M. A.

School of Public Policy:

LLOYD, G., Public Policy
McALLISTER, E., Public Policy
MONSMA, S. V., Political Science
SEXTON, R., Economics
VAN EATON, C., Public Policy
VARDIABASIS, D., Economics
WILSON, J. Q., Public Policy

PITZER COLLEGE

1050 N Mills Ave, Claremont, CA 91711-6110

Telephone: (909) 621-8000

E-mail: admission@pitzer.edu

Internet: www.pitzer.edu

Founded 1963; attached to Claremont Colleges

Private control
Language of instruction: English
Academic year: August to May

Pres.: Dr LAURA SKANDERA TROMBLEY
Vice-Pres. for Academic Affairs and Dean for Faculty: ALAN JONES
Vice-Pres. for Admin. and Treas.: YUET LEE
Vice-Pres. and Dean for Admission and Financial Aid: ANGEL B. PÉREZ
Vice-Pres. for College Advancement: ADRIAN STEVENS
Vice-Pres. for Marketing and Public Relations and Marketing: ANNA CHANG
Vice-Pres. for Student Affairs: JIM MARCHANT
Registrar: EVA PETERS
Librarian: ALBERTA WALKER
Library: 2m. vols, 70,000 periodicals
Number of teachers: 75
Number of students: 1,000

POINT LOMA NAZARENE UNIVERSITY

3900 Lomaland Dr., San Diego, CA 92106-2810

Telephone: (619) 849-2200
E-mail: admissions@ptloma.edu
Internet: www.pointloma.edu

Founded 1902 as Pacific Bible College, present name 1998
Private control
Academic year: August to May

Depts of art and design, biology, chemistry, communication and theatre, family and consumer sciences, history and political science, kinesiology, literature, journalism and modern languages, mathematics, information and computer sciences, music, physics and eng., psychology, sociology and social work; campuses in Arcadia, Bakersfield and Mission Valley

Pres.: Dr BOB BROWER
Provost and Chief Academic Officer: Dr KERRY D. FULCHER
Vice-Pres. for External Relations: JOSEPH E. WATKINS, III
Vice-Pres. for Financial Affairs: GEORGE R. LATTER
Vice-Pres. for Spiritual Devt: MICHAEL A. PITTS
Vice-Pres. for Student Devt: CAYE BARTON SMITH
Vice-Pres. for Univ. Advancement: DANIEL J. MARTIN
Dir for Admissions: SCOTT SHOEMAKER
Dir for Learning Services: Dr FRANK QUINN
Number of students: 3,500

DEANS

Fermanian School of Business: Dr KEN ARMSTRONG
School of Education: Dr GARY L. RAILSBACK
School of Nursing: Dr BARB TAYLOR
School of Theology and Christian Ministry: Dr RON BENEFIEL

POMONA COLLEGE

550 N College Ave, Claremont, CA 91711
Telephone: (909) 621-8000
Internet: www.pomona.edu

Founded 1887
Private control

Coeducational, nonsectarian, undergraduate college of liberal arts and sciences

Pres.: DAVID W. OXTOBY
Vice-Pres. for Academic Affairs and Dean of the College: JANICE HUDGINGS
Vice-pres. for Advancement: CHRISTOPHER PONCE
Vice-Pres. for Devt: CHRIS PONCE
Vice-Pres. and Dean for Students: MIRIAM FELDBLUM

Vice-Pres. for Planning: RICHARD FASS
Vice-Pres. and Treas.: KAREN SISSON
Dean for Admissions and Financial Aid: SETH ALLEN
Registrar: MARGARET ADORNO
Library: 2.2m. vols
Number of teachers: 190
Number of students: 1,590
Publication: *Pomona College Magazine* (3 a year)

SAINT MARY'S COLLEGE OF CALIFORNIA

1928 St Mary's Rd, Moraga, CA 94556
Telephone: (925) 631-4000
E-mail: smcadmit@stmarys-ca.edu
Internet: www.stmarys-ca.edu

Founded 1863
Private control

Pres.: Dr RONALD GALLAGHER
Provost and Vice-Pres. for Academic Affairs: Dr BETHAMI DOBKIN
Vice-Pres. for Advancement and Planning: Bro. STANISLAUS SOBCZYK
Vice-Pres. for College Communications and Vice-Provost for Enrollment: MICHAEL BESEDA
Vice-Pres. for Devt: Dr KEITH E. BRANT
Vice-Pres. for Finance: PETER A. MICHELL
Dean of Academic Resources: PAT KREITZ
Vice-Provost for Academic Affairs: FRANCES SWEENEY
Vice-Provost for Student Life: Dr JANE CAMARILLO
Library of 200,000 vols, 1,100 current periodicals
Number of teachers: 190 (full-time)
Number of students: 4,000

DEANS

Kalmanovitz School of Education: Dr PHYLLIS METCALF-TURNER
School of Economics and Business Administration: Dr ZHAN LI
School of Liberal Arts: Dr STEPHEN WOOLPERT
School of Science: Dr Prof. ROY WENSLEY

SAMRA UNIVERSITY OF ORIENTAL MEDICINE

3545 Wilshire Blvd., Suite 355, Los Angeles, CA 90010
Telephone: (213) 381-1700
E-mail: samrauc@gmail.com
Internet: www.samra.edu

Founded 1965
Private control
Languages of instruction: English, Chinese, Korean
Academic year: October to September

Areas of study: acupuncture theory; anatomy; basic sciences; Chinese herbology; Chinese medical theory; Oriental medicine; physiology

Pres.: Dr TAE CHEONG CHOO
Vice-Pres.: Dr BYUNG S. HONG
Provost: Dr KAATSUYUKI SAKAMOTO
Academic Dean: DEANNIE JANOWITZ
Registrar: ELIZABETH GOMEZ
Librarian: GAN YE
Library of 7,000 items

SAMUEL MERRITT UNIVERSITY

3100 Telegraph Ave, Oakland, CA, 94609
Telephone: (510) 869-6511
E-mail: information@samuelmerritt.edu
Internet: www.samuelmerritt.edu

Founded 1909, current name adopted 2009
Campuses in Oakland, Sacramento, San Francisco and San Mateo

Pres. and CEO: SHARON DIAZ
Academic Vice-Pres. and Provost: Dr SCOT FOSTER
Vice-Pres. for Enrolment and Student Services: JOHN GARTEN-SHUMAN
Vice-Pres. for Finance and Admin.: GREGORY GINGRAS
Library Dir: MARCUS BANKS
Library of 13,896 vols, 26,697 bound journals, 474 current periodicals
Number of teachers: 250 (110 full-time, 140 part-time)
Number of students: 1,400

DEANS

School of Nursing: Dr AUDREY BERMAN
School of Podiatric Medicine: Dr JOHN N. VENSON

SAN DIEGO CHRISTIAN COLLEGE

2100 Greenfield Dr., El Cajon, CA 92019
Telephone: (619) 201-8700
E-mail: admissions@sdcc.edu
Internet: www.sdcc.edu

Founded 1970 as Christian Heritage College, present name 2005
Private control
Academic year: September to May

Depts of aviation, adult professional studies (degree completion), biblical studies, business, communication, education, English, history and social science, kinesiology, mathematics, music, psychology, biological science

Pres.: Dr PAUL AGUE
Vice-Pres. of Academic Affairs: JON DEPRIEST
Vice-Pres. for Admin. and Finance: KEN YODER
Vice-Pres. for Enrolment and Marketing: MITCH FISK
Vice-Pres. for Student Life: JON DEPRIEST
Dean for Admin. and Finance: ROBERT JENSEN
Dean for Students: STEVE JENKINS
Registrar: SUSIE PARKS
Dir for Library Services: RUTH MARTIN
Library of 119,850 vols
Number of students: 400
Publication: *IMPACT* (1 a year)

SAN DIEGO STATE UNIVERSITY

5500 Campanile Dr., San Diego, CA 92182-8000
Telephone: (619) 594-5200
Internet: www.sdsu.edu

Founded 1897 as San Diego Normal School, present name 1970
Academic year: May to May

Pres.: ELLIOT HIRSHMAN
Provost for Academic Affairs: NANCY A. MARLIN
Vice-Pres. for Business and Financial Affairs: SALLY F. ROUSH
Vice-Pres. for Research and Dean of Graduate Affairs: STEPHEN WELTER
Vice-Pres. for Student Affairs: JAMES R. KITCHEN
Vice-Pres. for Univ. Relations and Devt: MARY RUTH CARLETON
Exec. Dir for Enrolment Services: SANDRA COOK
Dean of Library: GALE ETSCHMAIER
Library of 1,342,735 vols, 644,028 govt documents
Number of teachers: 1,800 (990 full-time, 810 part-time)
Number of students: 30,000 (24,590 undergraduate, 5,410 graduate)
Publications: *360: The Magazine of San Diego State University*, *Fiction International* (1 a year), *Journal of Borderlands Studies* (2 a year), *Mobilization* (3 a year),

Pacific Coast Council on Latin-American Studies (2 a year), *Pacific Review: A West Coast Arts Review Annual, Poetry International* (1 a year)

DEANS

College of Arts and Letters: PAUL WONG
College of Business Admin.: MICHAEL R. CUNNINGHAM
College of Education: Dr RIC A. HOVDA
College of Engineering: Dr DAVID T. HAYHURST
College of Extended Studies: JOE SHAPIRO
College of Health and Human Services: MARILYN NEWHOFF
College of Professional Studies and Fine Arts: JOYCE M. GATTAS
College of Sciences: STANLEY MALOY
Graduate Division: STEVEN WELTER
Imperial Valley Campus: DAVID PEARSON
Undergraduate Division: GEOFFREY W. CHASE

SAN FRANCISCO ART INSTITUTE

800 Chestnut St, San Francisco, CA 94133

Telephone: (415) 771-7020
E-mail: admissions@sfai.edu
Internet: www.sfai.edu
Founded 1871 as San Francisco Art Asscn, present name 1961
Private control
Academic year: August to May
Areas of study: design and technology, filmmaking, liberal arts, new genres, painting, photography, printmaking, sculpture
Pres.: CHARLES DESMARAIS
Sr Vice-Pres. for Finance and Admin.: JUDY LOGAN
Vice-Pres. and Dean for Academic Affairs: Dr JEANNENE PRZYBLYSKI
Vice-Pres. for Academic Planning and Facilities: JENNIFER STEIN
Vice-Pres. for Advancement: KATHY LOWRY
Vice-Pres. for Devt and Alumni Relations: CYNTHIA PERRY COLEBROOK
Vice-Pres. for Enrolment: ELIZABETH O'BRIEN
Dean for Students: YUNNY YIP
Library of 26,000 vols

SAN FRANCISCO CONSERVATORY OF MUSIC

50 Oak St, San Francisco, CA 94102-6011

Telephone: (415) 864-7326
Internet: www.sfcm.edu
Founded 1917 as Ada Clement Piano School, present name 1923
Private control
Depts of brass, chamber music, conducting, composition, guitar, keyboards, percussion, strings, voice, woodwinds; undergraduate and graduate degrees, postgraduate diplomas
Pres.: COLIN MURDOCH
Vice-Pres. for Advancement: BESS TOUMA
Vice-Pres. for Finance and Admin.: KATHRYN WITTENMYER
Dean: MARY ELLEN POOLE
Dir for Admission: MELISSA COCCO-MITTEN
Registrar: JONAS WRIGHT
Head Librarian: KEVIN MCLAUGHLIN
Library of 60,000 vols, incl. 38,000 scores and parts, 15,000 audiovisual items, 12,500 books and 77 periodicals
Number of teachers: 110 (30 full-time, 80 part-time)
Number of students: 400

SAN FRANCISCO STATE UNIVERSITY

1600 Holloway Ave, San Francisco, CA 94132
Telephone: (415) 338-1111

E-mail: sfsuinfo@sfsu.edu
Internet: www.sfsu.edu
Founded 1899 as San Francisco State Normal School
Academic year: August to DecemberJanuary to MayJune to August (3 semesters)
Pres.: Dr ROBERT A. CORRIGAN
Provost and Vice-Pres. for Academic Affairs: Dr SUE V. ROSSER
Exec. Vice-Pres. for Admin. and Finance and Chief Financial Officer: LEROY M. MORISHITA
Vice-Pres. for Student Affairs and Dean of Students: J. E. (PENNY) SAFFOLD
Vice-Pres. for Univ. Advancement: ROBERT J. NAVA (acting)
Registrar: SUZANNE DMYTRENKO
Univ. Librarian: DEBORAH C. MASTERS
Library of 1,160,869 items, incl; 2,557,985 microforms, 193,202 audiovisual items, 17,119 subscription periodicals
Number of teachers: 1,600
Number of students: 29,700
Publication: *SF State Magazine*

DEANS

College of Arts and Humanities: PAUL SHERWIN
College of Behavioural and Social Sciences: JOEL KASSIOLA
College of Business: CARAN COLVIN
College of Ethnic Studies: KENNETH P. MONTEIRO
College of Extended Learning: GAIL WHITAKER
College of Health and Human Services: DON TAYLOR (acting)
College of Science and Engineering: SHELDON AXLER
Graduate College of Education: Dr JACOB E. PEREA

SAN FRANCISCO THEOLOGICAL SEMINARY

105 Seminary Rd, San Anselmo, CA 94960

Telephone: (415) 451-2800
E-mail: info@sfts.edu
Internet: www.sfts.edu
Founded 1871; attached to Graduate Theological Union
Private control
Pres.: Dr Rev. JAMES L. MCDONALD
Vice-Pres. for Academic Affairs and Dean for the Seminary: Dr ELIZABETH LIEBERT
Vice-Pres. for Admin. and Finance and Chief Financial Officer: BARBARA BRENNER BUDER
Vice-Pres. for Institutional Advancement: Rev. SCOTT SHELDON
Dean: Dr ELIZABETH LIEBERT
Registrar: Dr POLLY COOTE
Library Dir (GTU): ROBERT BENETTO
Librarian (SFTS): MICHAEL PETERSON
Library of 100,000 vols

SAN JOSÉ STATE UNIVERSITY

1 Washington Sq., San José, CA 95192

Telephone: (408) 924-1000
Internet: www.sjsu.edu
Founded 1857
Pres.: MOHAMMAD QAYOUMI
Provost and Vice-Pres. for Academic Affairs: Dr ELLEN JUNN
Vice-Pres. for Admin. and Finance: SHAWN BIBB
Vice-Pres. for Student Affairs: WILLIAM NANCE
Vice-Pres. for Univ. Advancement: NANCY BUSSANI
Librarian: ROBERT BRUCE
Library of 900,000 vols, 3,500 periodical titles

Number of teachers: 630 (full-time)
Number of students: 30,200

DEANS

Charles W. Davidson College of Engineering: Dr BELLE WEI
College of Applied Sciences and Arts: Dr CHARLES BULLOCK
College of Business: Dr DAVID M. STEELE
College of Humanities and the Arts: KARL TOEPFER
College of Science: J. MICHAEL PARRISH
College of Social Sciences: SHEILA BIENENFELD
Connie L. Lurie College of Education: ELAINE CHIN
Continuing Education: MARK NOVAK

SANTA CLARA UNIVERSITY

500 El Camino Real, Santa Clara, CA 95053

Telephone: (408) 554-4000
Internet: www.scu.edu
Founded 1851 as Santa Clara College, present name 1985
Private control
Academic year: September to June
Chancellor: WILLIAM REWAK
Pres.: MICHAEL ENGH
Provost: DENNIS C. JACOBS
Vice-Pres. for Admin. and Finance: ROBERT WARREN
Vice-Pres. for Enrolment Management: MICHAEL SEXTON
Vice-Pres. for Univ. Relations: ROBERT GUNSALUS
Gen. Counsel: JOHN OTTOBONI
Registrar: MONICA AUGUSTIN
Univ. Librarian: ELIZABETH SALZER
Library of 800,000 vols, law library of 370,000 vols
Number of teachers: 850 (460 full-time, 390 part-time)
Number of students: 8,850
Publications: *Explore* (2 a year), *Santa Clara Law* (2 a year), *Santa Clara Magazine* (4 a year), *STS Nexus* (2 a year)

DEANS

College of Arts and Sciences: W. ATOM YEE (acting)
Jesuit School of Theology: KEVIN F. BURKE
Leavey School of Business: Dr DREW STARBIRD
School of Education and Counselling Psychology: ATOM YEE
School of Engineering: GODFREY MUNGAL
School of Law: DONALD J. POLDEN

SAYBROOK UNIVERSITY

747 Front St, Third Fl., San Francisco, CA 94111-1920

Telephone: (415) 433-9200
E-mail: info@saybrook.edu
Internet: www.saybrook.edu
Founded 1971 as Saybrook Graduate School and Research Center
Academic year: September to July
Pres.: Dr MARK SCHULMAN
Exec. Vice-Pres.: Dr ARTHUR C. BOHART, Jr
Vice-Pres. for Academic Affairs: Dr DANIEL SEWELL
Vice-Pres. for Marketing and Enrolment Management: SIGRID BADINELLI
Vice-Pres. for Operations and CFO: MICHAEL CAIRNS
Dir for Admissions: CATHLEEN FUSCO
Dir for Research and Library Services: NOAH LOWENSTEIN
Registrar: AARON HIATT
Number of teachers: 110 (20 executive, 20 consulting, 70 part-time)
Number of students: 600

Publication: *International Journal of Transpersonal Studies* (1 a year)

DEANS

Graduate College of Mind-Body Medicine: JAMES S. GORDON
Graduate College of Psychology and Humanistic Studies: Dr ROBERT SCHMITT
LIOS Graduate College of Leadership Studies: CYNTHIA FITZGERALD

SCRIPPS COLLEGE

1030 Columbia Ave, Claremont, CA 91711
Telephone: (909) 621-8000
Internet: www.scrippscollege.edu
Founded 1926; attached to Claremont Colleges
Private control
Pres.: LORI BETTISON-VARGA
Vice-Pres. and Dean of Admission and Financial Aid: PATRICIA F. GOLDSMITH
Vice-Pres. and Dean of Faculty: Dr AMY MARCUS-NEWHALL
Vice-Pres. for Devt and College Relations: MARTHA H. KEATES
Vice-Pres. for Enrolment: VICTORIA ROMERO
Vice-Pres. for Financial and Business Affairs: JOANNE M. COVILLE
Vice-Pres. for Institutional Advancement: MIKE ARCHIBALD
Vice-Pres. for Student Affairs and Dean of Students: REBECCA R. LEE
Librarian: JUDY HARVEY SAHAK
Library of 110,000 vols in Denison Library and 10,000 in Rare Book Room
Number of teachers: 100 (70 full-time and 30 part-time)
Number of students: 860

SIMPSON UNIVERSITY

2211 College View Dr., Redding, CA 96003
Telephone: (530) 224-5600
E-mail: registrar@simpsonu.edu
Internet: www.simpsonu.edu
Founded 1921 as Simpson Bible Institute, Simpson College 1971
Private control
Academic year: September to July
Pres.: Dr LARRY J. MCKINNEY
Provost: Dr STANLEY CLARK
Exec. Vice-Pres. and and Treas. and Chief Financial Officer: BRADLEY E. WILLIAMS
Vice-Pres. for Advancement: GORDON B. FLINN
Vice-Pres. for Enrolment Management: Dr HERB TOLBERT
Vice-Pres. for Student Devt: Dr RICHARD BROWN
Dean for Education: GLEE R. BROOKS
Dir ASPIRE Programme: PATTY TAYLOR
Registrar: WENDY RIDDLE
Dir for Library Services: LARRY L. HAIGHT
Library of 70,000 vols
Number of students: 1,220

DEANS

A. W. Tozer Theological Seminary: Dr SARAH SUMNER
School of Continuing Studies: PATTY TAYLOR
School of Education: Dr GLEE BROOKS
School of Traditional Undergraduate Studies: ROBIN DUMMER

SONOMA STATE UNIVERSITY

1801 E Cotati Ave, Rohnert Park, CA 94928-3609
Telephone: (707) 664-2880
Internet: www.sonoma.edu
Founded 1960 as Sonoma State College, present name and status 1978

Academic year: August to June
Pres.: Dr RUBEN ARMIÑANA
Provost and Vice-Pres. for Academic Affairs: Dr ANDREW ROGERSON
Chief Financial Officer and Vice-Pres. for Admin. and Finance: Dr LAURENCE FURU-KAWA-SCHLERETH
Vice-Pres. for Student Affairs and Enrolment Management: MATTHEW LOPEZ-PHILLIPS
Vice-Pres. for Univ. Affairs: DAN CONDRON
Vice-Pres. for Univ. Devt: ERIK GREENY
Library Dean: Dr BARBARA BUTLER
Library of 670,000 vols, 35,000 periodicals and 275,000 items
Number of teachers: 1,500
Number of students: 9,000

DEANS

School of Arts and Humanities: Dr THAINE STEARNS
School of Business and Economics: Dr WILLIAM SILVER
School of Education: Dr CARLOS AYALA
School of Extended Education: Dr MARK MERICKEL
School of Science and Technology: Dr LYNN STAUFFER
School of Social Sciences: Dr ELAINE LEEDER

SOUTHERN CALIFORNIA COLLEGE OF OPTOMETRY

2575 Yorba Linda Blvd, Fullerton, CA 92831-1699
Telephone: (714) 870-7226
Internet: www.scco.edu
Founded 1904
Private control
Pres.: Dr KEVIN L. ALEXANDER
Vice-Pres. and Dean for Academic Affairs: Dr Prof. MORRIS S. BERMAN
Vice-Pres. and Dean for Clinical Affairs: Dr JULIE A. SCHORNACK
Vice-Pres. for Advancement and Marketing: PAUL A. STOVER
Vice-Pres. for Financial Affairs and Chief Financial Officer: LISA K. ALBERS
Vice-Pres. for Student Affairs: Dr LORRAINE I. VOORHEES
Librarian: DONNA JEAN MATTHEWS
Library of 10,000 vols, 6,500 bound journals and 300 current periodicals
Number of teachers: 80 (full-time and part-time)
Number of students: 380
Publications: *Alumniscope* (2 a year), *SCCO Admissions Catalog* (every 2 years)

SOUTHERN CALIFORNIA UNIVERSITY OF HEALTH SCIENCES

16200 E Amber Valley Dr., Whittier, CA 90604-4051
Telephone: (562) 947-8755
E-mail: admissions@scuhs.edu
Internet: www.scuhs.edu
Founded 1911 as Los Angeles College of Chiropractic
Pres.: Dr JOHN SCARINGE
Vice-Pres. for Academic Affairs: TODD KNUDSEN
Vice-Pres. of Admin. and Finance: THOMAS ARENDT
Vice-Pres. for Institutional Advancement: REGINA WEBSTER
Assoc. Vice-Pres. for Student Affairs: GEOFFREY JOWETT
Chief Financial Officer: ROGER JENKINS

DEANS

College of Acupuncture and Oriental Medicine: Dr WEN-SHUO WU

Los Angeles College of Chiropractic: MICHAEL SACKETT

SOUTHWESTERN LAW SCHOOL

3050 Wilshire Blvd, Los Angeles, CA 90010
Telephone: (213) 738-6700
E-mail: admissions@swlaw.edu
Internet: www.swlaw.edu
Founded 1911
Private control
Academic year: August to July
Dean and CEO: AUSTEN L. PARRISH
Vice-Dean for Academic Affairs: ANAHID GHARAKHANIAN
Sr Assoc. Dean for Academic Admin.: DOREEN E. HEYER
Assoc. Dean for Career Services: GARY J. GREENER
Assoc. Dean for Institutional Advancement: DEBRA L. LEATHERS
Assoc. Dean for Library Services: LINDA WHISMAN
Assoc. Dean for Public Affairs: LESLIE R. STEINBERG
Assoc. Dean for Research: ARTHUR F. McEVOY
Assoc. Dean for Students and Diversity Affairs: H. NYREE GRAY
Assoc. Dean and Gen. Counsel: PATRICK PYLE
Asst Dean for Financial Aid: WAYNE MAHONEY
Asst Dean for Registration and Academic Records: CAROLYN HAITH
Asst Dir for Admissions: LISA M. GEAR
Chief Financial Officer: PAUL KALUSH
Chief Information Systems Officer: BO SUZOW
Chief Operating Officer: JANICE A. MANIS
Library of 500,000 vols
Number of teachers: 65 (full-time)
Number of students: 1,050
Publications: *Journal of International Media and Entertainment Law* (print and online —www.swlaw.edu/academics/entertainmentlaw/journal), *Southwestern Journal of International Law* (print and online — www.swlawjournal.org), *Southwestern Law Review* (print and online —www.swlawreview.org)

SAINT MARY'S COLLEGE OF CALIFORNIA

1928 St Mary's Rd, Moraga, CA 94556
Telephone: (925) 631-4000
E-mail: smcadmit@stmarys-ca.edu
Internet: www.stmarys-ca.edu
Founded 1863
Private control
Pres.: Dr RONALD GALLAGHER
Provost and Vice-Pres. for Academic Affairs: Dr BETHAMI DOBKIN
Vice-Pres. for Advancement and Planning: Bro. STANISLAUS SOBCZYK
Vice-Pres. for College Communications and Vice-Provost for Enrollment: MICHAEL BESEDA
Vice-Pres. for Devt: Dr KEITH E. BRANT
Vice-Pres. for Finance: PETER A. MICHELL
Dean of Academic Resources: PAT KREITZ
Vice-Provost for Academic Affairs: FRANCES SWEENEY
Vice-Provost for Student Life: Dr JANE CAMARILLO
Library of 200,000 vols, 1,100 current periodicals
Number of teachers: 190 (full-time)
Number of students: 4,000

DEANS

Kalmanovitz School of Education: Dr PHYLLIS METCALF-TURNER
School of Economics and Business Administration: Dr ZHAN LI

School of Liberal Arts: Dr STEPHEN WOOLPERT
School of Science: Dr Prof. ROY WENSLEY

ST PATRICK'S SEMINARY & UNIVERSITY

320 Middlefield Rd, Menlo Park, CA 94025
Telephone: (650) 325-5621
E-mail: info@stpatricksseminary.org
Internet: www.stpatricksseminary.org

Founded 1898
Private control
Academic year: September to May

Chancellor: Dr Rev. GEORGE H. NIEDERAUER
Pres., Rector and Vice-Chancellor: Dr Rev. JAMES L. MCKEARNEY
Vice-Pres. and Sec.: Rev. JOHN C. WESTER
Vice-Pres. for Advancement: CHRISTOPHER GRASSO
Vice-Pres. for Business and Finance: JENNIFER MORRIS
Academic Dean: Rev. GLADSTONE STEVENS
Dean for Students: Rev. VINCENT D. BUI
Registrar: NURIA ORTIZ
Library Manager: LAUREN JOHN

Library of 100,000 vols, 250 periodicals

STANFORD UNIVERSITY

450 Serra Mall, Stanford, CA 94305-2004
Telephone: (650) 723-2300
Internet: www.stanford.edu

Founded 1885
Private control
Academic year: September to June

Pres.: Dr JOHN HENNESSY
Provost: Dr JOHN ETCHEMENDY
Vice-Pres. and Gen. Counsel: DEBRA L. ZUMWALT
Vice-Pres. for Alumni Affairs: HOWARD WOLF
Vice-Pres. for Business Affairs and CFO: RANDALL S. LIVINGSTON
Vice-Pres. for Devt: MARTIN SHELL
Vice-Pres. for Land, Bldgs and Real Estate: ROBERT REIDY
Vice-Pres. for Public Affairs: DAVID DEMAREST
Vice-Pres., Stanford Linear Accelerator Center: WILLIAM J. MADIA
Registrar: THOMAS C. BLACK
Vice-Provost for Graduate Education: PATRICIA GUMPORT
Vice-Provost for Undergraduate Education: HARRY ELAM
Vice-Provost and Dean of Research: ANN ARVIN
Univ. Librarian: MICHAEL A. KELLER

Library: see under Libraries and Archives
Number of teachers: 2,000
Number of students: 15,900 (7,000 undergraduate and 8900 graduate)
Publications: *Journal of Law, Business and Finance* (2 a year), *Stanford Environmental Law Journal* (2 a year), *Stanford Humanities Review* (2 a year), *Stanford Journal of International Law* (2 a year), *Stanford Law Review* (6 a year), *Stanford Social Innovation Review* (4 a year)

DEANS

Continuing Studies: CHARLES JUNKERMAN
Graduate School of Business: GARTH SALONER
School of Earth Sciences: PAMELA A. MATSON
School of Education: CLAUDE STEELE
School of Engineering: JAMES D. PLUMMER
School of Humanities and Sciences: RICHARD SALLER
School of Law: ELIZABETH MAGILL
School of Medicine: Dr LLOYD MINOR

PROFESSORS

AAKER, J. L., Graduate School of Business
ADLER, J. R., Jr, Neurosurgery
ADMATI, A. R., Graduate School of Business

ALBANESE, C., Surgery
ALBERS, G. W., Neurology
ALDRICH, R. W., Molecular and Cell Physiology
ALEXANDER, J. C., Law
ALEXANDER, S. R., Paediatrics
AMEMIYA, T., Economics
ANDERSEN, H., Chemistry
ANDERSON, R. U., Jr, Urology
ANDRIACCHI, T. P., Mechanical Engineering
APOSTOLIDES, J.-M., French and Italian
ARBER, D., Pathology
ARIAGNO, R. L., Paediatrics
ARVIN, A. M., Paediatrics
ATHEY, S. C., Economics
ATLAS, S. W., Radiology
ATTANASAIO, O., Economics
AYDIN, A., Geology and Environmental Sciences
AZIZ, K., Petroleum Engineering
BABCOCK, B., Law
BACHRACH, L. K., Paediatrics
BAER, U., German Studies
BAKER, B. S., Biological Sciences
BAKER, K., History
BAMBOS, N., Management Science and Engineering
BANDURA, A., Psychology
BANKMAN, A. J., Law
BARCHIESI, A., Classics
BARLEY, S., Management Science and Engineering
BARNETT, D., Materials Science and Engineering
BARNETT, W., Graduate School of Business
BARON, D. P., Graduate School of Business
BARON, E. J., Pathology
BARON, J. N., Graduate School of Business
BARRES, B. A., Neurobiology
BARSH, G. S., Paediatrics
BARTH, M. E., Graduate School of Business
BARTH, R. A., Radiology
BAUGH, J., Education
BEACH, D., Mechanical Engineering
BEASLEY, M., Applied Physics
BEAVER, W. H., Graduate School of Business
BEININ, J. S., History
BENDER, J., English
BENDOR, J., Graduate School of Business
BENITZ, W. E., Paediatrics
BERGER, K., Music
BERMAN, R. A., German Studies
BERNHARDT, E., German Studies
BERNHEIM, B. D., Economics
BERNSTEIN, B., History
BERNSTEIN, D., Paediatrics
BEROZA, G. C., Geophysics
BETTINGER, J. R., Communication
BIELEFELDT, C. W., Religious Studies
BIENENSTOCK, A. I., Stanford Synchrotron Radiation Laboratory
BIRD, D. K., Geological and Environmental Sciences
BLACK, B. S., Law
BLAND, R. D., Paediatrics
BLANDFORD, R., Stanford Linear Acceleration Center
BLASCHKE, T., Medicine
BLAU, H. M., Molecular Pharmacology
BLOCH, D. A., Health Research and Policy
BLOCK, S. M., Applied Physics
BLOOM, E., Stanford Linear Accelerator Center
BLUMENKRANZ, M. S., Ophthalmology
BOBO, L., Sociology
BOOTHROYD, J. C., Microbiology and Immunology
BORJA, R. I., Civil and Environmental Engineering
BOSKIN, M., Economics
BOWER, G. H., Psychology
BOWMAN, C., Mechanical Engineering
BOXER, S., Chemistry
BOYD, S. P., Electrical Engineering
BOYER, A. L., Radiation Oncology
BRADY, D., Graduate School of Business

BRANDEAU, M. L., Management Science and Engineering
BRATMAN, M., Philosophy
BRAUMAN, J. J., Chemistry
BRAUND, S., Classics
BRAVMAN, J. C., Materials Science and Engineering
BREIDENBACH, M., Stanford Linear Accelerator Center
BRESNAHAN, T., Economics
BRESNAN, J., Linguistics
BROCK-UTNE, J. G., Anaesthesia
BRODSKY, J. B., Anaesthesia
BRODSKY, S., Stanford Linear Accelerator Center
BROTHERSTON, J. G., Spanish and Portuguese
BROWN, G. H., English
BROWN, J. M., Radiation Oncology
BROWN, P. O., Biochemistry
BRUMFIEL, G., Mathematics
BRUNGER, A. T., Molecular and Cellular Physiology
BRUTLAG, D. L., Biochemistry
BRYK, A., Education
BUC, P. C., History
BULOW, J. I., Graduate School of Business
BUMP, D. W., Mathematics
BURCHAT, P. R., Physics
BURGELMAN, R. A., Graduate School of Business
BURKE, D. L., Stanford Linear Accelerator Center
BUTCHER, E. C., Pathology
BYER, R., Applied Physics
BYERS, T. H., Management Science and Engineering
CABRERA, B., Physics
CALLAN, E., Education
CAMARILLO, A. M., History
CAMPBELL, A. M., Biological Sciences
CANTWELL, B., Aeronautics, Astronautics
CARLSON, R., Management Science and Engineering
CARLSON, R. W., Medicine
CARLSSON, G., Mathematics
CARNOY, M., Education
CARRAGEE, E. J., Orthopaedic Surgery
CARROLL, G. R., Graduate School of Business
CARSON, C., History
CARSTENSEN, L. L., Psychology
CARTER, D., Mechanical Engineering
CARTER, S., Asian Languages
CASEY, E. B., English
CASPER, G., Law
CASPER, R., Psychiatry
CASTLE, T., English
CHAFE, C. D., Music
CHAMBERLAIN, C. P., Geological and Environmental Sciences
CHAN, P. H., Neurosurgery
CHANG, F. K., Aeronautics and Astronautics
CHAO, A. W., Stanford Linear Accelerator Center
CHERITON, D. R., Computer Science
CHIEN, Y. K., Microbiology and Immunology
CHRISTENSEN, R. M., Aeronautics and Astronautics
CHU, G., Medicine
CHU, S., Physics
CIOFFI, J. M., Electrical Engineering
CLAERBOUT, J. F., Geophysics
CLARK, E., Linguistics
CLARK, H. H., Psychology
CLAYBERGER, C. A., Paediatrics
CLEARY, M. L., Pathology
CLEMENS, B. M., Materials Science and Engineering
COHEN, H. J., Paediatrics
COHEN, M., French and Italian
COHEN, P. J., Mathematics
COHEN, R. L., Mathematics
COHEN, S. E., Anaesthesia
COHEN, S. N., Genetics
COLE, G. M., Law
COLLMAN, J. P., Chemistry
CONTI, M., Gynaecology and Obstetrics

COOK, K. S., Sociology
COOKE, J. P., Medicine
COOPER, A., Medicine
CORK, L., Comparative Medicine
CORN, W., Art, Art History
CORNELL, C. A., Civil and Environmental Engineering
COTTLE, R. W., Management Science and Engineering
COVER, T. M., Electrical Engineering
COX, D., Electrical Engineering
COX, K. L., Paediatrics
CRABTREE, G., Pathology
CRASWELL, R., Law
CROSS, P. C., Structural Biology
CUTKOSKY, M. R., Mechanical Engineering
DAHL, G. V. H., Paediatrics
DAINES, R., Law
DALLY, W. J., Electrical Engineering
DAMON, W., Education
DARLING-HAMMOND, L., Education
DAUSKARDT, R. H., Materials Science and Engineering
DAVID, P. A., Economics
DAVIS, M. M., Microbiology and Immunology
DAVIS, R., Biochemistry
DEIERLEIN, G. G., Civil and Environmental Engineering
DE KRUYFF, R. H., Paediatrics
DE MARZO, P. M., Graduate School of Business
DEMBO, A., Mathematics
DEMENT, W. C., Psychiatry
DE MICHELI, G., Electrical Engineering
DENNY, M. W., Biological Sciences
DEVINE, A., Classics
DIACONIS, P., Statistics
DILL, D. L., Computer Science
DIMOPOULOS, S., Physics
DIRZO, R., Biological Sciences
DIXON, L. J., Stanford Linear Accelerator Center
DOLAN, J., Drama
DONALDSON, S., Radiation Oncology
DONIACH, S., Applied Physics
DONOHO, D., Statistics
DORFAN, J., Stanford Linear Accelerator Center
DORFMAN, L., Neurology
DRELL, P. S., Stanford Linear Accelerator Center
DRUZIN, M. L., Obstetrics and Gynaecology
DUFFIE, J. D., Graduate School of Business
DUNBAR, R. B., Geological and Environmental Sciences
DUPUY, J.-P., French and Italian
DURBIN, P. A., Mechanical Engineering
DURHAM, W., Anthropological Sciences
DURLOFSKY, L. J., Petroleum Engineering
DUTTON, R., Electrical Engineering
EATON, J. K., Mechanical Engineering
ECKERT, P., Linguistics
EFRON, B., Statistics
EGBERT, P., Ophthalmology
EHRLICH, P. R., Biological Sciences
EISEN, A. M., Religious Studies
EISENHARDT, K. M., Management Science and Engineering
EISNER, E. W., Education
EL GAMAL, A., Electrical Engineering
ELAM, H. J., Jr, Drama
ELIASHBERG, Mathematics
ENGE, P. K., Aeronautics and Astronautics
ENGLAND, P., Sociology
ENGLEMAN, E., Pathology
EPEL, D., Biological Sciences
ERNST, W. G., Geology, Environmental Sciences
ESQUIVEL, C., Surgery
ETCHEMENDY, J. W., Philosophy
EVANS, J. M., English
EVERITT, C. W. F., Hansen Laboratory
FAINSTAT, T., Obstetrics and Gynaecology
FAJARDO, L., Pathology
FALKOW, S., Microbiology and Immunology
FARHAT, C., Mechanical Engineering

FATHMAN, C., Medicine
FAURE, B. R., Religious Studies
FAYER, M., Chemistry
FEARON, J. D., Political Science
FEE, W., Surgery
FEINSTEIN, C. B., Psychiatry
FEJER, M. M., Applied Physics
FELDMAN, D., Medicine
FELDMAN, M. W., Biological Sciences
FELSTINER, J., English
FEREJOHN, J. A., Political Science
FERGUSON, J., Cultural and Social Anthropology
FERNALD, R. D., Psychology
FERNEYHOUGH, B., Music
FERRELL, J. E., Jr, Molecular Pharmacology
FETTER, A. L., Physics
FIELD, C., Biological Sciences
FIELDS, K., English
FIKES, R. E., Computer Science
FINDLEN, P., History
FIORINA, M. P., Political Science
FIRE, A., Pathology
FISH, K. J., Anaesthesia
FISHER, G., Law
FISHER, R. S., Neurology
FISHKIN, J., Communication
FISHKIN, S. F., English
FLANAGAN, R., Graduate School of Business
FLEISHMAN, L., Slavic Languages and Literature
FLIEGELMAN, J. W., English
FOLLESDAL, D., Philosophy
FORD, J. M., Psychiatry
FORD, R. T., Law
FORTMANN, S. P., Medicine
FOSTER, G., Graduate School of Business
FOWLER, M. B., Medicine
FRANCKE, U., Genetics
FRANK, C., Chemical Engineering
FREEDMAN, E., History
FREIDIN, G., Slavic Languages and Literature
FRIED, B., Law
FRIEDLANDER, L., English
FRIEDMAN, J. H., Statistics
FRIEDMAN, L. M., Law
FRIEDMAN, M., Philosophy
FRIES, J. F., Medicine
FROELICHER, V. F., Medicine
FULLER, G. G., Chemical Engineering
FULLER, M. T., Developmental Biology
FURTHMAYR, H., Pathology
GABA, D. M., Anaesthesia
GABRIELLI, J., Psychology
GALLI, S. J., Pathology
GAMBHIR, S., Radiology
GAMBLE, J. G., Orthopaedic Surgery
GARBER, A. M., Medicine
GARCIA-MOLINA, H., Computer Science
GARNER, C. C., Psychiatry
GARWIN, E. L., Stanford Linear Accelerator Center
GELLER, E., Anaesthesia
GIACCIA, A. J., Radiation Oncology
GIACOMINI, J. C., Medicine
GIBBONS, J. F., Electrical Engineering
GILLY, W. F., Biological Sciences
GILSON, R. J., Law
GIROD, B., Electrical Engineering
GIUDICE, L. C., Obstetrics and Gynaecology
GLADER, B. E., Paediatrics
GLASSER, T. L., Communication
GLAZER, G. M., Radiology
GLICK, I., Psychiatry
GLOVER, G. H., Radiology
GLYNN, P. W., Management Science and Engineering
GOLDSTEIN, J. L., Political Science
GOLDSTEIN, P. L., Law
GOLUB, G. H., Computer Science
GOODE, R., Surgery
GOODMAN, S. B., Functional Restoration
GORDON, D. M., Biological Sciences
GORELICK, S. M., Geological and Environmental Sciences
GORIS, M., Radiology

GOSLING, J. A., Surgery
GOTLIB, I. H., Psychology
GOULD, J., Paediatrics
GOULDER, L. H., Economics
GRAHAM, S. A., Geological and Environmental Sciences
GRANOVETTER, M., Sociology
GRAY, R., Electrical Engineering
GRECO, R. S., Surgery
GREELY, H. T., Law
GREENBERG, H., Medicine
GREENBERG, P., Medicine
GREENE, R., English
GREGG, R. C., Religious Studies
GREIF, A., Economics
GRENADIER, S. R., Graduate School of Business
GREY, T. C., Law
GROSSMAN, P. L., Education
GRUENFELD, D. H., Graduate School of Business
GRUMET, F. C., Pathology
GRUNDFEST, J. A., Law
GRUSKY, D. B., Sociology
GUIBAS, L. J., Computer Science
GUILLEMINAULT, C., Psychiatry
GUMBRECHT, J. U., French and Italian
GUMPORT, P. J., Education
HABER, S. H., History
HAERTEL, E. H., Education
HAKUTA, K., Education
HALL, R., Economics
HAMMER, L. D., Paediatrics
HAMMOND, P., Economics
HANAWALT, P. C., Biological Sciences
HANCOCK, S. L., Radiation Oncology
HANLEY, F. L., Cardiothoracic Surgery
HANNAH, D., Art, Art History
HANNAN, M., Graduate School of Business
HANRAHAN, P. M., Computer Science
HANSON, R., Mechanical Engineering
HARO, M.-P., Spanish and Portuguese
HARRIS, J. M., Geophysics
HARRIS, J. S., Electrical Engineering
HARRIS, S. E., Electrical Engineering
HARRISON, J. M., Graduate School of Business
HARRISON, R. P., French and Italian
HARSH, G. R. IV, Neurosurgery
HASTIE, T. J., Statistics
HAUSMAN, W., Management Science and Engineering
HEDMAN, G.-B., Stanford Synchrotron Radiation Laboratory
HELLER, H. C., Biological Sciences
HELLER, T. C., Law
HENDRICKSON, M. R., Pathology
HENNESSY, J., Electrical Engineering
HENSLER, D. R., Law
HENTZ, V. R., Surgery
HERFKENS, R. J., Radiology
HERSCHLAG, D., Biochemistry
HERTZENBERG, L. A., Genetics
HERZOG, T., History
HESSELINK, L., Electrical Engineering
HIMEL, T. M., Stamford Linear Accelerator Center
HINTON, S., Music
HINTZ, R., Paediatrics
HLATKY, M. A., Health Research and Policy
HODDER, I., Cultural and Social Anthropology
HODGSON, K., Chemistry
HOFFMAN, A. R., Medicine
HOLLOWAY, D., Political Science
HOPPE, R., Radiation Oncology
HORNE, R. N., Petroleum Engineering
HORNING, S. J., Medicine
HOROWITZ, L., Psychology
HOROWITZ, M. A., Electrical Engineering
HOTSON, J. R., Neurology
HOWARD, R. A., Management Science and Engineering
HOYME, H. E., Paediatrics
HSUEH, A., Obstetrics and Gynaecology
HUESTIS, W., Chemistry
HUNT, S., Medicine

INAN, U. S., Electrical Engineering
INGLE, J., Geological and Environmental Sciences
ISHII, K., Mechanical Engineering
IYENGAR, S., Communication
JACKLER, R., Otolaryngology and HNS
JACOBS, C. D., Medicine
JAFFE, R. A., Anaesthesia
JAMESON, A., Aeronautics and Astronautics
JARDETZKY, O., Molecular Pharmacology
JARDETZKY, T., Structural Biology
JAROS, J. A., Stanford Linear Accelerator Center
JEFFREY, R. B., Radiology
JOHNSTONE, I. M., Statistics
JONES, P., Biological Sciences
JOURNEL, A., Petroleum Engineering
JUEL, C., Education
KAHN, J., Electrical Engineering
KAHN, M. S., Art, Art History
KAHN, S., Stanford Linear Accelerator Center
KAISER, A. D., Biochemistry
KALLOSH, R., Physics
KAMAE, T., Stanford Linear Accelerator Center
KAPITULNIK, A., Applied Physics
KAPP, D. S., Radiation Oncology
KARL, T. L., Political Science
KARLAN, P., Law
KASEVICH, M., Physics
KATZNELSON, Y., Mathematics
KAY, M., Linguistics
KAY, M. A., Paediatrics
KAZOVSKY, L. G., Electrical Engineering
KEEFFE, E. B., Medicine
KELLEY, D. M., Mechanical Engineering
KELMAN, M. G., Law
KENDIG, J., Anaesthesia
KENNEDY, D. M., History
KERCKHOFF, S. P., Mathematics
KERNER, J. A., Paediatrics
KESSLER, D. P., Graduate School of Business
KESSLER, R., Urology
KHATIB, O., Computer Science
KHAVARI, P. A., Dermatology
KHOSLA, C. S., Chemical Engineering
KILLEN, J. D., Medicine
KIM, S. K., Developmental Biology
KING, A. C., Health Research and Policy
KINGSLEY, D. M., Developmental Biology
KIPARSKY, P., Linguistics
KIREMIDJIAN, A. S., Civil and Environmental Engineering
KIRKEGAARD, K, Microbiology and Immunology
KIRST, M., Education
KITANIDIS, P. K., Civil and Environmental Engineering
KLAUSNER, M., Law
KLEIN, R. G., Anthropological Studies
KLENOW, P., Economics
KNIGHT, R., Geophysics
KNUDSEN, E. I., Neurobiology
KOBILKA, B. K., Medicine
KOCHERLAKOTA, N., Economics
KOLLMAN, N. S., History
KOOL, E. T., Chemistry
KOPITO, R. R., Biological Sciences
KORAN, L. M., Psychiatry
KORNBERG, R. D., Structural Biology
KOSEFF, J. R., Civil and Environmental Engineering
KOSEK, J., Pathology
KOVACH, R. L., Geophysics
KRAEMER, F. B., Medicine
KRAEMER, H., Psychiatry
KRAMER, R. M., Graduate School of Business
KRANE, E. J., Anaesthesia
KRASNER, S., Political Science
KRASNOW, M. A., Biochemistry
KRAWINKLER, H., Civil and Environmental Engineering
KRAWITZ, J., Communication
KREHBIEL, K., Graduate School of Business
KRENSKY, A. M., Paediatrics
KREPS, D., Graduate School of Business

KROO, I. M., Aeronautics and Astronautics
KROSNICK, J. A., Communication
KRUGER, C. H., Mechanical Engineering
KRUMBOLTZ, J. D., Education
KRUMMEL, T. M., Surgery
KURZ, M., Economics
LABAREE, D., Education
LAI, T. L., Statistics
LAITIN, D., Political Science
LAM, M. S., Computer Science
LANE, A. T., Dermatology
LANE, B., Radiology
LATOMBE, J.-C., Computer Science
LATTIN, J. M., Graduate School of Business
LAU, L. J., Economics
LAUGHLIN, R., Physics
LAVORI, P. W., Health Research and Policy
LAW, K. H., Civil and Environmental Engineering
LAZEAR, E. P., Graduate School of Business
LECKIE, J., Civil and Environmental Engineering
LEE, H. L., Graduate School of Business
LEHMAN, I. R., Biochemistry
LEIFER, L., Mechanical Engineering
LEITH, D., Stanford Linear Accelerator Center
LEIVICK, J. R., Art and Art History
LELE, S. K., Aeronautics and Astronautics
LEMLEY, M., Law
LENOIR, T., History
LEPPER, M., Psychology
LERER, S., English
LESSIG, L., Law
LEUNG, L. L., Medicine
LEVIN, B., Linguistics
LEVITT, L. J., Medicine
LEVITT, M., Structural Biology
LEVITT, R. E., Civil and Environmental Engineering
LEVY, R., Medicine
LEVY, S., Medicine
LEWIS, M. E., Asian Languages
LI, J., Mathematics
LINDE, A., Physics
LINK, M., Paediatrics
LIOU, J., Geological and Environmental Sciences
LIPSICK, J., Pathology
LITT, I., Paediatrics
LIU, T.-P., Mathematics
LOAGUE, K., Geological and Environmental Sciences
LOEW, G. A., Stanford Linear Accelerator Center
LONG, S., Biological Sciences
LONGAKER, M. T., Surgery
LORIG, K., Medicine
LOUGEE CHAPPELL, C., History
LOWE, D. R., Geological and Environmental Sciences
LUENBERGER, D. G., Management Science and Engineering
LUNSFORD, A., English
LUTH, V., Stanford Linear Acceleration Center
LUTHY, R. G., Civil and Environmental Engineering
MCADAM, D., Sociology
MCCALL, M., Classics
MCCLUSKEY, E. J., Electrical Engineering
MCCONNELL, S. K., Biological Sciences
MACCORMACK, R., Aeronautics and Astronautics
MCDERMOTT, R., Education
MCDEVITT, H. O., Microbiology and Immunology
MCDONALD, J. G., Graduate School of Business
MCDOUGALL, I. R., Radiology
MCGINN, R. E., Management Science and Engineering
MCGUIRE, J., Dermatology
MCKAY, D., Structural Biology
MCKINNON, R. I., Economics
MCLAUGHLIN, M. W., Education

MCMAHAN, U. J., Neurobiology
MCMILLAN, R. J., Graduate School of Business
MCNICHOLS, M., Graduate School of Business
MCNUTT, M. K., Geophysics
MACURDY, T., Economics
MADIX, R. J., Chemical Engineering
MAHOOD, G. A., Geological and Environmental Sciences
MALENKA, R. C., Psychiatry
MANCALL, M., History
MANNA, Z., Computer Science
MARINA, N., Paediatrics
MARKMAN, E., Psychology
MARKUS, H., Psychology
MARMOR, M., Ophthalmology
MARTIN, J., Graduate School of Business
MARTIN, R. P., Classics
MATHESON, G. O., Orthopaedic Surgery
MATHEWS, M. V., Music
MATIN, A., Microbiology and Immunology
MATSON, P. A., Geological and Environmental Sciences
MAVKO, G. M., Geophysics
MAZZEO, R. R., Mathematics
MENDELSON, H., Graduate School of Business
MENDEZ, M. A., Law
MENDOZA, F. S., Paediatrics
MENG, T. H.-Y., Electrical Engineering
MERIGAN, T., Medicine
MEYER, T. W., Medicine
MICHELSON, P. F., Physics
MIGNOT, E., Psychiatry
MIHM, F. G., Anaesthesia
MILGRAM, R. J., Mathematics
MILGROM, P., Economics
MILLER, D. A. B., Electrical Engineering
MILLER, D. C., Cardiothoracic Surgery
MILLER, D. T., Graduate School of Business
MILLER, E., Geological and Environmental Sciences
MINTS, G., Philosophy
MITCHELL, J. C., Computer Science
MITCHELL, R. S., Cardiothoracic Surgery
MOBLEY, W. C., Neurology
MOCARSKI, E. S., Microbiology and Immunology
MOCHLY-ROSEN, D., Molecular Pharmacology
MOE, T. M., Political Science
MOERNER, W. E., Chemistry
MOIN, P., Mechanical Engineering
MOLDOWAN, J. M., Geological and Environmental Sciences
MONISMITH, S. G., Civil and Environmental Engineering
MOONEY, H. A., Biological Sciences
MOOS, R. H., Psychiatry
MORA-MANGANO, C., Anaesthesia
MORAVCSIK, J. M., Philosophy
MORETTI, F., English
MORRIS, I., Classics
MORRIS, R. E., Cardiothoracic Surgery
MOSS, R. B., Paediatrics
MOTWANI, R., Computer Science
MUNGAL, M. G., Mechanical Engineering
MURRAY, W., Management Science and Engineering
MUSEN, M. A., Medicine
MYERS, B., Medicine
MYERS, R. M., Genetics
NAIMARK, N., History
NAPEL, S. A., Radiology
NASS, C. I., Communications
NEALE, M. A., Graduate School of Business
NELSON, D. V., Mechanical Engineering
NELSON, W. J., Molecular and Cell Physiology
NETZ, R., Classics
NEWSOME, W. T., III, Neurobiology
NISHI, Y., Electrical Engineering
NISHIMURA, D. G., Electrical Engineering
NOLL, R., Economics
NUR, A., Geophysics
NUSSE, R., Developmental Biology
OAKES, D. D., Surgery
OI, J., Political Science
OKIMOTO, D. I., Political Science

OLCOTT, C., IV, Surgery
OLKIN, I., Statistics
OLSHEN, R., Health Research and Policy
OLZAK, S., Sociology
OMARY, M. B., Medicine
O'REILLY, C. A., III, Graduate School of Business
ORGEL, S., English
ORNSTEIN, D., Mathematics
ORR, F., Petroleum Engineering
ORTOLANO, L., Civil and Environmental Engineering
OSGOOD, B. G., Electrical Engineering
OSHEROFF, D., Physics
OWEN, A. B., Statistics
OYER, P. E., Cardiothoracic Surgery
PADILLA, A., Education
PALUMBI, S., Biological Sciences
PALUMBO-LIU, D. J., Comparative Literature
PAPANICOLAOU, G. C., Mathematics
PARHAM, P., Structural Biology
PARKER, G. G. C., Graduate School of Business
PARKER, P., English
PARNES, J. R., Medicine
PATE-CORNELL, E., Management Science and Engineering
PATELL, J., Graduate School of Business
PATERSON, J., Stanford Linear Accelerator Center
PAULRAJ, A., Electrical Engineering
PAULSON, B., Civil and Environmental Engineering
PEA, R., Education
PEARL, R., Anaesthesia
PEASE, R., Electrical Engineering
PECORA, R., Chemistry
PELC, N. J., Radiology
PENCAVEL, J., Economics
PERKASH, I., Urology
PERLROTH, M. G., Medicine
PERRY, J., Philosophy
PERRY, W., Management Science and Engineering
PESKIN, M., Stanford Linear Accelerator Center
PETERS, P. S., Linguistics
PETERSEN, J., Medicine
PETROSIAN, V., Physics
PFEFFER, J., Graduate School of Business
PFEFFER, S. R., Biochemistry
PFEFFERBAUM, A., Psychiatry
PFLEIDERER, P., Graduate School of Business
PHELAN, P., Drama
PHILIP, A. G. S., Paediatrics
PHILLIPS, D., Education
PHIZACKERLEY, R. P., Stanford Synchrotron Radiation Laboratory
PIANETTA, P., Stanford Synchrotron Radiation Laboratory
PINSKY, P. M., Mechanical Engineering
PIZZO, P. A., Paediatrics
PLUMMER, J., Electrical Engineering
POLAN, M., Obstetrics and Gynaecology
POLHEMUS, R., English
POLINSKY, A., Law
POLLARD, D. D., Geological and Environmental Sciences
POPP, R., Medicine
PORTEUS, E., Graduate School of Business
POWELL, W. W., Education
PRATT, M., Spanish and Portuguese
PREDMORE, M., Spanish and Portuguese
PRESCOTT, C., Stanford Linear Accelerator Center
PRINCE, D. A., Neurology
PRINZ, F. B., Mechanical Engineering
PROBER, C. G., Paediatrics
PROCTOR, R., History
QUERTERMOUS, T., Medicine
QUINN, H., Stanford Linear Accelerator Center
RABIN, R. L., Law
RABINOVITCH, M., Paediatrics
RADIN, M., Law
RAJAN, M. V., Graduate School of Business

RAKOVE, J., History
RAMIREZ, F., Education
RAMPERSAD, A., English
RAMSAUR, M. F., Drama
RECHT, L., Neurology
REEVES, B., Communication
REHM, M. R., Drama
REICHELSTEIN, S. J., Graduate School of Business
REINHARD, M., Civil and Environmental Engineering
REISS, A. L., Psychiatry
REISS, P. C., Graduate School of Business
REITZ, B., Cardiothoracic Surgery
REMINGTON, J. S., Medicine
RHINE, W. D., Paediatrics
RHODE, D. L., Law
RICE, C., Political Science
RICHTER, B., Stanford Linear Accelerator Center
RICKFORD, J., Linguistics
RIDGEWAY, C., Sociology
RIGGS, D., English
RINSKY, L. A., Orthopaedic Surgery
RISCH, N. J., Genetics
RIVERS, D., Political Science
RIZK, N. W., Medicine
ROBERTS, D. F., Communication
ROBERTS, D. J., Graduate School of Business
ROBERTS, E. S., Computer Science
ROBERTS, R. L., History
ROBERTSON, C. R., Chemical Engineering
ROBINSON, J. A., Political Science
ROBINSON, O. W., III, German Studies
ROBINSON, P., History
ROCK, S. M., Aeronautics and Astronautics
RODRIGUE, A., History
ROMANO, J., Statistics
ROMER, P., Graduate School of Business
RORTY, R., Comparative Literature
ROSALDO, R. I., Jr, Cultural and Social Anthropology
ROSENTHAL, M. H., Anaesthesia
ROSS, L., Psychology
ROTH, B., Mechanical Engineering
ROTH, R. A., Molecular Pharmacology
ROTH, W., Psychiatry
ROUGHGARDEN, J., Biological Sciences
ROUSE, R. V., Pathology
RUBIN, K., Mathematics
RUDD, P., Medicine
RUFFINELLI-ALTESOR, J., Spanish and Portuguese
RUMELHART, D. E., Psychology
RUTH, R. D., Stanford Linear Accelerator Center
SAG, I. A., Linguistics
SAGAN, S. D., Political Science
SAIDMAN, L. J., Anaesthesia
SALDIVAR, R., English
SALISBURY, J. K., Computer Science
SALONER, G., Graduate School of Business
SALVATIERRA, O., Jr, Surgery
SAMUELSON, K., Communication
SAPOLSKY, R. M., Biological Sciences
SARASWAT, K., Electrical Engineering
SARGENT, T. J., Economics
SARNOW, P., Microbiology and Immunology
SAUNDERS, M. A., Management Science and Engineering
SAUSSY, C. P. H., Comparative Literature
SCANDLING, J., Medicine
SCHATZBERG, A., Psychiatry
SCHEIDEL, W., Classics
SCHENDEL, S. A., Surgery
SCHERRER, P. H., Physics
SCHIEBERGER, L., History
SCHINDLER, R., Stanford Linear Accelerator Center
SCHNAPP, J. T., French and Italian
SCHNEIDER, S., Biological Sciences
SCHNITTGER, I., Medicine
SCHOEN, R., Mathematics
SCHOOLNIK, G. K., Medicine
SCHROEDER, J. S., Medicine

SCHUPBACH, Slavic Languages and Literatures
SCHURMAN, D., Functional Restoration
SCOTT, M. P., Developmental Biology
SEGAL, I. R., Economics
SEGALL, P., Geophysics
SELLS, P., Linguistics
SERRES, M., French and Italian
SHAFER, S. L., Anaesthesia
SHANKS, M., Classics
SHAPIRO, L., Developmental Biology
SHAQFEH, E. S. G., Chemical Engineering
SHAVELSON, R., Education
SHAW, K., Graduate School of Business
SHEEHAN, J. J., History
SHEEHAN, T., Religious Studies
SHEIKH, J. T., Psychiatry
SHEN, Z.-X., Applied Physics
SHENKER, S. H., Physics
SHORTLIFFE, L., Urology
SHOVEN, J., Economics
SHUER, L. M., Neurosurgery
SIBLEY, R. K., Pathology
SIEGMUND, D. O., Statistics
SIEMANN, R., Stanford Linear Accelerator Center
SIKIC, B. I., Medicine
SILVERBERG, G. D., Neurosurgery
SILVERMAN, N., Paediatrics
SIMON, L., Mathematics
SIMONI, R., Biological Sciences
SIMONSON, I., Graduate School of Business
SINCLAIR, R., Materials Science and Engineering
SINGH, K., Ophthalmology
SINGLETON, K., Graduate School of Business
SKEFF, K. M., Medicine
SLEEP, N., Geophysics
SMITH, S. J., Molecular and Cell Physiology
SMITH, T. I., Physics
SNIDERMAN, P., Political Science
SNIPP, C. M., Sociology
SO, S. K. S., Surgery
SOLOMON, E., Chemistry
SOMERO, G., Biological Sciences
SOMERVILLE, C., Biological Sciences
SOMMER, F. G., Radiology
SPAIN, D., Surgery
SPIEGEL, D., Psychiatry
SPRINGER, G., Aeronautics and Astronautics
SPUDICH, J. A., Biochemistry
SRINIVASAN, V., Graduate School of Business
STAMEY, T. A., Urology
STANSKI, D. R., Anaesthesia
STANSKY, P. D. L., History
STEBBINS, J., Geological and Environmental Sciences
STEELE, C. M., Psychology
STEFANICK, M., Medicine
STEINBERG, G. K., Neurosurgery
STEINER, H., Psychiatry
STEINMAN, L., Neurology
STEPHENS, S., Classics
STEVENS, D., Medicine
STEVENSON, D., Paediatrics
STIPEK, D. J., Education
STOHR, J., Stanford Synchrotron Radiation Laboratory
STREET, R. L., Civil and Environmental Engineering
STRNAD, J. F., Law
STROBER, M., Education
STROBER, S., Medicine
SULLIVAN, K., Law
SUSSKIND, L., Physics
SUSSMAN, H., Pathology
SUTTON, R. I., Management Science and Engineering
SWAIN, J., Medicine
SWARTZ, J. R., Chemical Engineering
SWEENEY, J., Management Science and Engineering
SWITZER, P., Statistics
TAKEUCHI, M. R., Art and Art History
TALLENT, E., English

TATUM, C. B., Civil and Environmental Engineering
TAYLOR, C., Psychiatry
TAYLOR, J. B., Economics
TAYLOR, K. A., Philosophy
TESSIER-LAVIGNE, M., Biological Sciences
THOMAS, E. A. C., Psychology
THOMPSON, B. H., Jr, Law
THOMPSON, D. G., Psychiatry
THOMPSON, S., Biological Sciences
TIBSHIRANI, R. J., Health Research and Policy
TINKLENBERG, J., Psychiatry
TOBAGI, F., Electrical Engineering
TOMPKINS, L., Medicine
TRIADAFILOPOULOS, G., Medicine
TROST, B., Chemistry
TRUDELL, J. R., Anaesthesia
TSIEN, R., Molecular and Cellular Physiology
TULJAPURKAR, S., Biological Sciences
TUMA, N., Sociology
TURNER, P., Art and Art History
TVERSKY, B., Psychology
TYLER, G., Electrical Engineering
UMETSU, D. T., Paediatrics
VALANTINE, H. A., Medicine
VALDES, G., Education
VAN BENTHEM, J. F., Philosophy
VAN DAM, J., Medicine
VAN HORNE, J. C., Graduate School of Business
VAN MEURS, K. P., Paediatrics
VEINOTT, A. F., Jr, Management Science and Engineering
VINOGRAD, R. E., Art and Art History
VITOUSEK, P., Biological Sciences
WAGONER, R. V., Physics
WALBOT, V., Biological Sciences
WALD, M. S., Law
WALDER, A. G., Sociology
WALDRON, K. J., Mechanical Engineering
WALKER, D., Education
WANDELL, B. A., Psychology
WANG, J., Asian Languages
WANG, P., Medicine
WANG, T. S.-F., Pathology
WARNKE, R., Pathology
WASOW, T., Linguistics
WATT, W., Biological Sciences
WAYMOUTH, R. M., Chemistry
WEBER, C., Drama
WEIN, L. M., Graduate School of Business
WEINGAST, B. R., Political Science
WEISBERG, R., Law
WEISSMAN, I., Pathology
WENDER, P., Chemistry
WEYANT, J. P., Management Science and Engineering
WHANG, S., Graduate School of Business
WHITE, B., Mathematics
WHITE, R., History
WHITMORE, I., Surgery
WHITTEMORE, A., Health Research and Policy
WHYTE, R. I., Cardiothoracic Surgery
WIDROW, B., Electrical Engineering
WILSON, D. M., Paediatrics
WINE, J., Psychology
WINEBERG, S., Education
WINOGRAD, T., Computer Sciences
WOJCICKI, S. G., Physics
WOLAK, F. A., Economics
WOLF, A., Anthropological Sciences
WOLF, B. J., Art and Art History
WOLFF, T., English
WONG, H.-S., Electrical Engineering
WONG, S.-W. S., Electrical Engineering
WOOD, A. W., Philosophy
WOOD, R., Philosophy
WOOLEY, B. A., Electrical Engineering
WRIGHT, G., Economics
XIE, Y., Sociology
YAMAMOTO, Y., Electrical Engineering
YANAGISAKO, S. J., Cultural and Social Anthropology
YARBRO-BEJARANO, Y., Spanish and Portuguese
YAU, H.-T., Mathematics

YE, Y., Management Science and Engineering
YEARLEY, L., Religious Studies
YESAVAGE, J., Psychiatry
YOCK, P. G., Medicine
ZARE, R. N., Chemistry
ZARINS, C. K., Surgery
ZHANG, S., Physics
ZIPPERSTEIN, S. J., History
ZOBACK, M., Geophysics

STARR KING SCHOOL FOR THE MINISTRY

2441 LeConte Ave, Berkeley, CA 94709-1209
Telephone: (510) 845-6232
E-mail: starrking@sksm.edu
Internet: www.sksm.edu

Founded 1904 as Pacific Unitarian School for the Ministry, present name 1941; attached to Graduate Theological Union
Private control
Academic year: September to May

Pres.: Dr Rev REBECCA A. PARKER
Provost: IBRAHIM ABDURRAHMAN FARAJAJÉ
Vice-Pres. for Academic Affairs and Dean of Faculty: Rev. Dr DORSEY BLAKE
Vice-Pres. for Advancement: KELLY FLOOD
Vice-Pres. for Finance and Admin.: THOMAS SMITH
Dean for Students: BECKY LEYSER
Dir for Continuing and Online Education: CATHLEEN YOUNG
Library Dir: BONNIE HARDWICK
Registrar: KATRINA CROSWELL
Library of 365,000 vols

THOMAS AQUINAS COLLEGE

10,000 N Ojai Rd, Santa Paula, CA 93060
Telephone: (805) 525-4417
E-mail: admissions@thomasaquinas.edu
Internet: www.thomasaquinas.edu

Founded 1971
Private control
Offers Bachelors degrees in liberal arts
Private control
Academic year: September to June

Pres.: Dr MICHAEL F. MCLEAN
Vice-Pres.: JOHN W. NEUMAYR
Vice-Pres. for Devt and General Counsel: JOHN QUINCY MASTELLER
Vice-Pres. for Finance and Admin.: PETER L. DELUCA
Dean: Dr BRIAN T. KELLY
Registrar: MARK KRETSCHMER
Librarian: VILTIS JATULIS
Library of 72,000 vols
Number of teachers: 40
Number of students: 360

Publication: *The Aquinas Review* (2 a year)

THOMAS JEFFERSON SCHOOL OF LAW

1155 Island Ave, San Diego, CA 92101
Telephone: (619) 297-9700
E-mail: admissions@tjsl.edu
Internet: www.tjsl.edu

Founded 1969
Private control
Academic year: June to August

Pres. and Dean: RUDY HASL
Library Dir: PATRICK MEYER
Library of 200,000 vols

UNIVERSITY OF CALIFORNIA

Office of the Pres., 12th Fl., 1111 Franklin St, Oakland, CA 94607-5200
E-mail: ucinfo@ucapplication.net
Internet: www.universityofcalifornia.edu

Founded 1869
10 Campuses

Pres.: JANET NAPOLITANO
Provost and Exec. Vice-Pres. for Academic Affairs: Dr WYATT R. HUME
Exec. Vice-Pres. for Univ. Affairs: BRUCE B. DARLING
Vice-Pres. for Agriculture and Natural Resources: W. R. GOMES
Vice-Pres. for Budget: LARRY HERSHMAN
Vice-Pres. for Clinical Services Devt: WILLIAM H. GURTNER
Vice-Pres. for Financial Management: ANNE BROOME
Vice-Pres. for Health Affairs: RORY HUME
Vice-Pres. for Investments: MARIE N. BERGREN
Vice-Pres. for Laboratory Admin.: S. ROBERT FOLEY
Vice-Pres. for Legal Affairs: CHARLES F. ROBINSON
Vice-Pres. for Student Affairs: JUDY K. SAKAKI

Library: see Libraries and Archives
Number of teachers: 8,776
Number of students: 220,000 ...

CONSTITUENT CAMPUSES

University of California, Berkeley

Berkeley, CA 94720
Telephone: (510) 642-6000
Internet: www.berkeley.edu

Founded 1868
State control

Chancellor: ROBERT J. BIRGENEAU
Exec. Vice-Chancellor and Provost: CLAUDE STEELE
Vice-Chancellor for Admin. and Finance: JOHN WILTON
Vice-Chancellor for Equity and Inclusion: GIBOR BASRI
Vice-Chancellor for Facilities Services: EDWARD J. DENTON
Vice-Chancellor for Research: GRAHAM FLEMING
Vice-Chancellor for Student Affairs: HARRY LE GRANDE
Vice-Chancellor for Univ. Relations: SCOTT BIDDY
Univ. Librarian: THOMAS C. LEONARD
Number of teachers: 2,082 (1,582 full-time, 500 part-time)
Number of students: 36,142 (25,885 undergraduate, 10,257 graduate)

DEANS

College of Chemistry: RICHARD A. MATHIES
College of Engineering: SHANKAR SASTRY
College of Environmental Design: JENNIFER WOLCH
College of Letters and Science: MARK RICHARDS
College of Natural Resources: J. KEITH GILLESS
Graduate School of Education: JUDITH WARREN LITTLE
Graduate School of Journalism: NEIL HENRY
Richard and Rhoda Goldman School of Public Policy: HENRY BRADY
School of Information: ANNALEE SAXENIAN
School of Law: CHRISTOPHER F. EDLEY, Jr
School of Optometry: DENNIS LEVI
School of Public Health: STEPHEN SHORTELL (acting)
School of Social Welfare: LORRAINE MIDANIK
Walter A. Haas School of Business: RICHARD K. LYONS

University of California, Davis

1 Shields Ave, Davis, CA 95616
Telephone: (530) 752-1011
Internet: www.ucdavis.edu

Founded 1905
State control
Academic year: September to June
Chancellor: LINDA KATEHI
Provost and Exec. Vice-Chancellor: RALPH HEXTER
Vice-Chancellor for Admin. and Resource Management: JOHN A. MEYER
Vice-Chancellor for Human Health Sciences: CLAIRE POMEROY
Vice-Chancellor for Research: HARRIS LEWIN
Vice-Chancellor for Student Affairs: FRED WOOD
Vice-Chancellor for Univ. Relations: BEVERLY SANDEEN
Vice-Provost for Academic Personnel: MAUREEN STANTON
Vice-Provost for Information and Educational Technology: PETER SIEGEL
Vice-Provost for Undergraduate Studies: PATRICA TURNER
Vice-Provost for Univ. Outreach and Int. Programs: WILLIAM B. LACY
Univ. Librarian: RANDOLPH SIVERSON (acting)
Library: see Libraries and Archives
Number of teachers: 2,558
Number of students: 32,153

Publications: *BizLawJournal.com* (online), *CA&ES Outlook* (2 a year), *Environs* (2 a year), *Journal of International Law Policy* (2 a year), *Journal of Juvenile Law and Policy* (2 a year), *Migration News* (12 a year), *The Horse Report* (4 a year), *UC Davis Law Review* (4 a year)

DEANS

Betty Irene Moore School of Nursing: HEATHER YOUNG
College of Agricultural and Environmental Sciences: NEAL K. VAN ALFEN
College of Biological Sciences: JAMES E. K. HILDRETH
College of Education: HAROLD G. LEVINE
College of Engineering: ENRIQUE LAVERNIA (acting)
Div. of Humanities, Arts and Cultural Studies: JESSIE ANN OWENS
Div. of Mathematics and Physical Sciences: WINSTON KO
Div. of Social Sciences: GEORGE R. MANGUN
Graduate School of Management: STEVEN CURRALL
Graduate Studies: JEFFERY C. GIBELING
School of Law: KEVIN JOHNSON
School of Medicine: CLAIRE POMEROY
School of Veterinary Medicine: MICHAEL D. LAIRMORE
Univ. Extension: DENNIS F. PENDLETON

PROFESSORS

College of Agricultural and Environmental Sciences (150 Mrak Hall, 1 Shields Ave, Davis, CA 95616; tel. (530) 752-0107; internet www.aes.ucdavis.edu):

Faculty of Agricultural and Resource Economics:

ALSTON, J. M.
CAPUTO, M. R.
CARMAN, H.
CARTER, C. A.
CHALFANT, J. A.
FARZIN, Y. H.
GREEN, R. D.
HAVENNER, A.
HEIEN, D. M.
HOWITT, R. E.
JARVIS, L. S.
MARTIN, P. L.
MORRISON PAUL, C. J.
PARIS, Q.
ROZELLE, S.
SEXTON, R. J.
SUMNER, D. A.
TAYLOR, J. E.

VOSTI, S. A.
WILEN, J. E.
WILLIAMS, J.

Faculty of Agronomy and Range Science:

DEMMENT, M. W.
DENISON, R. F.
DVORAK, J.
FOIN, T. C.
GENG, S.
GEPTS, P. L.
JERNSTEDT, J.
PHILLIPS, D. A.
PLANT, R. E.
RAINS, D. W.
RICE, K. J.
TEUBER, L. R.
TRAVIS, R. L.
VAN KESSEL, C.
WILKENS, T.

Faculty of Animal Science:

ADAMS, T. E.
ANDERSON, G. B.
BERGER, T. J.
CALVERT, C. C.
DE PETERS, E. J.
DOROSHOV, S. I.
FADEL, J. G.
FAMULA, T. R.
GALL, G. A.
HUNG, S. S.
KING, A. J.
KLASING, K. C.
LEE, Y. B.
MEDRANO, J. F.
MENCH, J. A.
MILLAM, J. R.
OBERBAUER, A. M.
PRICE, E. O.
ROSER, J. F.
WEATHERS, W. W.
WILSON, B. W.
ZINN, R. A.

Faculty of Biological and Agricultural Engineering under the College of Agricultural and Environmental Sciences:

PIEDRAHITA, R. H.
UPADHYAYA, S. K.

Faculty of Entomology:

CAREY, J. R.
CRANSTON, P. S.
DINGLE, H.
EDMAN, J. D.
EHLER, L. E.
GRANETT, J.
GULLAN, P. J.
HAMMOCK, B. D.
KARBAN, R.
KAYA, H. K.
KIMSEY, L. S.
LEAL, W. S.
PAGE, R. E.
PARRELA, M. P.
PENG, Y. S. C.
ROSENHEIM, J. A.
SCOTT, T. W.
ULLMAN, D. E.
WARD, P. S.

Faculty of Environmental Design:

GOTELLI, D. E.
HARRISON, P.
LAKY, G.
RIVERS, V. Z.
SHAWCROFT-GUARINO, B.

Faculty of Environmental Horticulture:

BARBOUR, M. G.
BERRY, A. M.
BURGER, D. W.
DURZAN, D. J.
HARDING, J. A.
LIETH, J. H.
REID, M. S.
WU, L. L.

Faculty of Environmental Science and Policy:

GOLDMAN, C. R.
HARRISON, S. P.
HASTINGS, A. M.
JOHNSTON, R. A.
ORLOVE, B. S.
QUINN, J. F.
REJMANKOVA, E.
RICHERSON, P. J.
SABATIER, P. A.
SIH, A.
WILLIAMS, S. L.

Faculty of Environmental Toxicology:

CHERR, G. N.
DENISON, M. S.
KADO, N. Y.
KNEZOVICH, J. P.
MATSUMURA, F.
MILLER-SEARS, M. G.
RICE, R. H.
SHIBAMOTO, T.
TJEERDEMA, R. S.

Faculty of Food Science and Technology:

BAMFORTH, C. W.
BANDMAN, E.
DUNGAN, S. R.
GERMAN, J. B.
GUINARD, J.
HAARD, N. F.
KROCHTA, J. M.
MCCARTHY, M. J.
OGRYDZIAK, D. M.
O'MAHONY, M. A.
PRICE, C. W.
REID, D. S.
SHOEMAKER, C. F.
SINGH, R. P.
SMITH, G. M.

Faculty of Human and Community Development:

ALDWIN, C.
BARTON, K.
BRUSH, S. B.
BRYANT, B. K.
CONGER, R. D.
GE, X.
HARPER, L. V.
KENNEY, M. F.
LACY, W. B.
MOMSEN, J.
OBER, B. A.
SMITH, M. P.
WELLS, M. J.

Faculty of Land, Air and Water Resources:

BAHRE, C. J.
BLEDSOE, C. S.
CARROLL, J. J.
CASEY, W. H.
DAHLGREN, R. A.
FLOCCHINI, R. G.
FOGG, G. E.
GRISMER, M. E.
GROTJAHN, R.
HOPMANS, J. W.
HSIAO, T. C.
LAUCHLI, A. E.
NATHAN, T. R.
PAW U, K. T.
RECK, R. A.
RICHARDS, J. M.
ROLSTON, D. E.
SCOW, K. M.
SHELTON, M. L.
SILK, M. W.
SINGER, M. J.
SOUTHARD, R. J.
USTIN, S. L.
WEARE, B. C.
ZASOSKI, R. J.

Faculty of Landscape Architecture:

ALLAN, N.
FRANCIS, M.
MACCANNELL, E. D.

Faculty of Nematology:

CASWELL-CHAN, E. P.
FERRIS, H.
JAFFEE, B. A.
NADLER, S. A.
WILLIAMSON, V. M.

Faculty of Nutrition:

ALLEN, L. H.
BROWN, K. G.
CLIFFORD, A. J.
DEWEY, K. G.
GRIVETTI, L. E.
KEEN, C. L.
LONNERDAL, B. L.
MCDONALD, R. B.
RUCKER, R. B.
SCHNEEMAN, B. O.
STERN, J. S.

Faculty of Plant Pathology:

BOSTOCK, R. M.
BRUENING, G.
COOK, D. R.
DAVIS, R. M.
DUNIWAY, J. M.
FALK, B. W.
GILBERTSON, R. L.
GILCHRIST, D. G.
GORDON, T. R.
KADO, C. I.
KIRKPATRICK, B. C.
MACDONALD, J. D.
RONALD, P. C.
TYLER, B. M.
VAN ALFEN, N.
WEBSTER, R. K.

Faculty of Pomology:

BLUMWALD, E.
BROWN, P. H.
DANDEKAR, A. M.
DEJONG, T. M.
GRADZIEL, T. M.
KADER, A. A.
LABAVITCH, J. M.
POLITO, V. S.
SHACKEL, K. A.
SHAW, D. V.
SUTTER, E. G.
WEINBAUM, S.

Faculty of Textiles and Clothing:

HSIEH, Y.
KAISER, S. B.
PAN, N.
RUCKER, M. H.

Faculty of Vegetable Crops:

BAYER, D. E.
BLOOM, A. J.
BRADFORD, K. J.
JACKSON, L. E.
MICHELMORE, R. W.
NEVINS, D. J.
QUIROS, C. F.
SALTVEIT, M. E.
YODER, J. I.

Faculty of Viticulture and Oenology:

BISSON, L. F.
BOULTON, R. B.
HEYMANN, H.
MATTHEWS, M. A.
MEREDITH, C. P.
NOBLE, A. C.
WALKER, M. A.
WATERHOUSE, A. L.
WILLIAMS, L. E.

Faculty of Wildlife, Fish and Conservation Biology:

ANDERSON, D. W.
BOTSFORD, L. W.
CARO, T. M.
CECH, J. J.
EADIE, J. M.
ELLIOTT-FISK, D. L.
MOYLE, P. B.

VAN VUREN, D.

School of Education (2077 Academic Surge Bldg, 1 Shields Ave, Davis, CA 95616; tel. (530) 752-8019):

DUGDALE, S. S.
FIGUEROA, R. A.
GANDARA, P.
LEVINE, H. G.
MERINO, B. J.
MURPHY, S.
SANDOVAL, J. H.
WAGNER, J. C.
WATSON-GEGEO, K. A.
YOUNG, I. P.

College of Engineering (1050 Engineering Unit II, 1 Shields Ave, Davis, CA 95616; tel. (530) 752-0553; internet engineering.ucdavis.edu):

Faculty of Biological and Agricultural Engineering under the College of Engineering:

DELWICHE, M. J.
GILES, D. K.
HARTSOUGH, B. R.
HILLS, D. J.
JENKINS, B. M.
MCCARTHY, K. L.
MILES, J. A.
RUMSEY, T. R.
SLAUGHTER, D. C.
UPADHYAYA, S. K.
WALLENDER, W. W.

Faculty of Biomedical Engineering:

BENHAM, C. J.
CHERRY, S. R.
FERRARA, K. W.
INSANA, M. F.
SAVAGEAU, M. A.
SIMON, I.

Faculty of Chemical Engineering and Materials Science:

BROWNING, N. D.
GATES, B. C.
GIBELING, J. C.
GROZA, J. R.
HIGGINS, B. G.
HOWITT, D. G.
JACKMAN, A. P.
MCCOY, B. J.
MCDONALD, K. A.
MUKHERJEE, A. K.
NAVROTSKY, A.
PALAZOGLU, A. N.
PHILLIPS, R. J.
POWELL, R. L.
RISBUD, S. H.
RYU, D. D. Y.
SHACKELFORD, J. F.
STROEVE, P.
WHITAKER, S.

Faculty of Civil and Environmental Engineering:

ARULANANDAN, K.
BOULANGER, R.
CHANG, D. P.
DAFALIAS, Y. F.
DARBY, J. L.
GINN, T.
IDRISS, I. M.
KAVVAS, M. L.
KUTTER, B. L.
LAROCK, B. E.
LUND, J. R.
MARINO, M. A.
MOKHTARIAN, P. L.
NIEMEIER, D. A.
RAMEY, M. R.
RUNDLE, J. B.
SPERLING, D.
YOUNIS, B.

Faculty of Computer Science:

BAI, Z.

BRUNO, J.
FARRENS, M. K.
GUSFIELD, D.
HAMANN, B.
JOY, K. I.
LEVITT, K. N.
MARTEL, C. U.
MATLOFF, N. S.
MUKHERJEE, B.
OLSSON, R. A.
ROGAWAY, P. W.
RUSCHITZKA, M. G.

Faculty of Electrical and Computer Engineering:

ABDEL-GHAFFAR, K. A.
BRANNER, G. R.
CHANG, T. S.
COLINGE, J. P.
CURRENT, K. W.
DING, Z.
FEHER, K.
FORD, G. E.
HALEY, S. B.
HERITAGE, J. P.
HUNT, C. E.
HURST, P. J.
KNOESEN, A.
LEVY, B. C.
LEWIS, S. H.
OKLOBDZIJA, V. G.
REDINBO, G. R.
REED, T. R.
SMITH, R. L.
SPENCER, R. R.
TIEN, N. C.
WANG, S.
YOO, S. B.

Faculty of Engineering:

MUNIR, Z. A.

Faculty of Engineering—Applied Science:

BALDIS, H. A.
CRAMER, S. P.
FREEMAN, R. R.
HWANG, D. Q.
JENSEN, N. G.
KOLNER, B. H.
KROL, D.
LAUB, A. J.
LUHMANN, N. C.
MAX, N. L.
MCCURDY, W. C.
MILLER, G. H.
OREL, A. E.
ROCKE, D. M.
RODRIGUE, G.
VEMURI, V.
YEH, Y.

Faculty of Mechanical and Aeronautical Engineering:

BAUGHN, J. W.
CHATTOT, J. J.
DAVIS, R. J.
DWYER, H. A.
FAROUKI, R. T.
FRANK, A. A.
HAFEZ, M. M.
HESS, R. A.
HUBBARD, M.
HULL, M. L.
KARNOPP, D. C.
KENNEDY, I. M.
KOLLMANN, W.
MARGOLIS, D. L.
RAVANI, B.
REHFIELD, L. W.
SARIGUL-KLIJN, N.
SHAW, B. D.
VAN DAM, C. P.
VELINSKY, S. A.
WEXLER, A. S.
WHITE, B. R.
YAMAZAKI, K.

School of Law (1013 King Hall, 1 Shields Ave, Davis, CA 95616; tel. (530) 752-0243; internet www.kinghall.ucdavis.edu):

AMANN, D. M.
AYER, J. D.
BROWNSTEIN, A. E.
DOBRIS, J. C.
DOREMUS, H.
FEENEY, F. F.
GANDARA, A.
GLENNON, M. J.
GROSSMAN, G. S.
HILLMAN, R. W.
IMWINKELRIED, E. J.
JOHNSON, K. R.
JOO, T. W.
KURTZ, L. A.
LEWIS, E. A.
OAKLEY, J. B.
PERSCHBACHER, R. R.
POULOS, J. W.
REYNOSO, C.
SIMMONS, D. L.
WEST, M. S.
WOLK, B. A.
WYDICK, R. C.

College of Letters and Science (200 Social Sciences and Humanities Bldg, 1 Shields Ave, Davis, CA 95616; tel. (530) 752-0392; internet www.ls.ucdavis.edu):

Faculty of African American and African Studies:

OLUPONA, J. K.
STEWART, J. O.
TURNER, P. A.

Faculty of American Studies:

BLAIR, C.
FRANKENBERG, R.
MECHLING, J. E.
SMITH, M.

Faculty of Anthropology:

BETTINGER, R. L.
BORGERHOFF-MULDER, M.
DONHAM, D. L.
HARCOURT, A. H.
JOSEPH, S.
MCHENRY, H. M.
RODMAN, P. S.
SMITH, C. A.
SMITH, D. G.
SMITH, J. S.
SRINIVAS, S.
WINTERHALDER, B. P.
YENGOYAN, A. A.

Faculty of Art History and Art Studio:

ATKINSON, C.
BILLS, T. B.
COLLINS, H. M.
HENDERSON, W.
HERSHMAN, L.
HOLLOWELL, D.
MACLEOD, D. S.
PULS, L. A.
RUDA, J.
WERFEL, G. S.

Faculty of Asian American Studies:

HAMAMOTO, D. Y.
HING, B. O.
SUE, S.

Faculty of Chemistry:

BALCH, A. L.
BRITT, R. D.
FAWCETT, W. R.
FINK, W. H.
GERVAY HAGUE, J.
JACKSON, W. M.
KAUZLARICH, S.
KELLY, P. B.
KURTH, M. J.
LAMAR, G. N.
LEBRILLA, C. B.
MEARES, C. F.

MOLINSKI, T.
NANTZ, M
NG, C. Y.
POWER, P. P.
ROCK, P. A.
SCHORE, N. E.
STUCHEBRUKHOV, A.
TINTI, D. S.
TRUE, N. S.
TUCKER, S. C.

Faculty of Chicana/o Studies:

CHABRAM-DERNE, A.
DE LA TORRE, A.
MONTOYA, M.

Faculty of Communication:

BELL, R. A.
BERGER, C. R.
MOTLEY, M. T.

Faculty of Comparative Literature:

BLANCHARD, M. E.
FINNEY, G.
LARSEN, N. A.
LU, S. H.
MURAV, H. L.
SCHEIN, S. L.
SCHIESARI, J.
SCHILDGEN, B. P.
TORRANCE, R. M.

Faculty of Comparative Research:

SKINNER, G. W.

Faculty of East Asian Languages and Cultures:

BORGEN, R.
YEH, M.

Faculty of Economics:

BONANNO, G.
CAMERON, A.
CLARK, G.
FEENSTRA, R. C.
HOOVER, K. D.
LINDERT, P. H.
MAKOWSKI, L.
OLMSTEAD, A. L.
QUINZII, M.
SHEFFRIN, S. M.
SILVESTRE, J.
WALTON, G. M.
WOO, W. T.

Faculty of English:

ABBOTT, D. P.
BYRD, W. M.
DALE, P. A.
DIEHL, J. F.
FERGUSON, M. W.
FREED, L. R.
GILBERT, S. M.
HAYS, P. L.
LANGLAND, E.
LEVIN, R. A.
LOKKE, K.
MCPHERSON, S. J.
MAJOR, C.
MORRIS, L. A.
OSBORN, M.
OWENS, L. D.
ROBERTSON, D. A.
SCHLEINER, W.
SIMMONS, S.
SIMPSON, D. E.
SNYDER, G. S.
VAN LEER, D. M.
WADDINGTON, R. B.
WATKINS, E. P.
WILLIAMSON, A. B.
ZENDER, K. F.

Faculty of French and Italian:

BLANCHARD, M. E.
CANNON, J.
DUTSCHKE, D. J.
MANOLIU, M. I.
VAN DEN ABBEELE, G.

Faculty of Geology:

CARLSON, S. J.
DAY, H. W.
DEWEY, J. F.
KELLOGG, L. H.
LESHER, C. E.
MONTAÑEZ, I. P.
MOORES, E. M.
MOUNT, J. F.
SCHIFFMAN, P.
SPERO, H. J.
TURCOTTE, D. L.
TWISS, R. J.
VERMEIJ, G.
VEROSUB, K. L.
ZIERENBERG, R. A.

Faculty of German and Russian:

BERND, C. A.
DRUZHNIKOV, Y.
MCCONNELL, W.
MENGES, K. R.
RANCOUR-LAFERRIERE, D.
SCHAEFFER, P. M.

Faculty of History:

BAUER, A. J.
BIALE, D.
BRANTLEY, C. L.
BROWER, D. R.
CADDEN, J.
HAGEN, W. W.
HALTTUNEN, K.
HOLLOWAY, T. H.
KUDLICK, C. J.
LANDAU, N. B.
MANN, S. L.
MARGADANT, T. W.
METCALF, B. O.
PRICE, D. C.
ROSEN, R. E.
SMITH, M.
SPYRIDAKIS, S.
TAYLOR, A. S.
WALKER, C. E.

Faculty of Linguistics:

BENWARE, W. A.
OJEDA, A. E.
TIMM, L. A.

Faculty of Mathematics:

BORGES, C. R.
BRAMSON, M. D.
CHEER, A. Y.
DIEDERICH, J. R.
EDELSON, A. L.
FUCHS, D. B.
GRAVNER, J.
HAAS, J.
HUNTER, J. K.
KRENER, A. J.
KUPERBERG, G. J.
MILTON, E. O.
MOGILNER, A.
MULASE, M.
NACHTERGAELE, B.
PUCKETT, E. G.
SAITO, N.
SALLEE, G. T.
SCHWARZ, A.
SHKOLLER, S.
SILVIA, E. M.
TEMPLE, J. B.
THOMPSON, A. A.
THURSTON, W. P.
TRACY, C. A.
WETS, R. J.

Faculty of Music:

BAUER, R.
BUSSE BERGER, A. M.
FRANK, A. D.
HOLOMAN, D. K.
NUTTER, D. A.
ORTIZ, P. V.
REYNOLDS, C. A.

Faculty of Native American Studies:

HERNANDEZ-AVILA, I.
LONGFISH, G. C.
MACRI, M. J.
MONTEJO, V. D.
VARESE, S.

Faculty of Philosophy:

CUMMINS, R. C.
DWORKIN, G.
GRIESEMER, J. R.
JUBIEN, M.
KING, J. C.
NEANDER, K. L.
TELLER, P.
WEDIN, M. V.
WILSON, G. M.

Faculty of Physics:

ALBRECHT, A. J.
BECKER, R. H.
CARLIP, S.
CHAU, L.
CHIANG, S.
CORRUCCINI, L. R.
COX, D. L.
FADLEY, C. S.
FONG, C.
GUNION, J. F.
KISKIS, J. E.
KLEIN, B. M.
KO, W. T.
LANDER, R.
PELLETT, D. E.
PICKETT, W. E.
SCALETTAR, R. T.
SINGH, R. R.
TRIPATHI, S. M.
YAGER, P. M.
ZHU, X.
ZIMANYI, G.

Faculty of Political Science:

HUCKFELDT, R. R.
JACKMAN, R. W.
NINCIC, M.
PETERMAN, L. I.
ROTHCHILD, D. S.
SIVERSON, R. M.
STONE, W. J.
WADE, L. L.

Faculty of Psychology:

ACREDOLO, L. P.
CAPITANIO, J. P.
COSS, R. G.
ELMS, A. C.
EMMONS, R. A.
ERICKSEN, K. P.
GOODMAN, G. S.
HARRISON, A. A.
HENRY, K. R.
HEREK, G. M.
JOHNSON, J. T.
KROLL, N. E.
KRUBITZER, L. A.
LONG, D. L.
MANGUN, G. R.
MENDOZA, S. P.
OWINGS, D. H.
PARKS, T. E.
POST, R. B.
SHAVER, P. R.
SIMONTON, D. K.
SOMMER, R.
WIDAMAN, K. F.

Faculty of Religious Studies:

JANOWITZ, N.
LAI, W. W.

Faculty of Sociology:

BLOCK, F.
COHEN, L. E.
CRAMER, J. C.
FELMLEE, D. H.
GOLDSTONE, J. A.
HALL, J. R.

JACKMAN, M. R.
JOFFE, C.
LOFLAND, L. H.
McCARTHY, W. D.
SMITH, V. A.
WALTON, J. T.
WOLF, D. L.

Faculty of Spanish and Classics:

ARMISTEAD, S. G.
BLAKE, R. J.
GONZÁLEZ, C.
LARSEN, N. A.
ROLLER, L. E.
SCARI, R. M.
TRAILL, D. A.
VERANI, H. J.

Faculty of Statistics:

BERAN, R. J.
BURMAN, P.
JOHNSON, W. O.
MACK, Y. P.
MUELLER, H. G.
ROUSSAS, G. G.
SAMANIEGO, F. J.
SHUMWAY, R. H.
UTTS, J. M.
WANG, J.-L.

Faculty of Theatre and Dance:

ANDERSON, S. P.
IACOVELLI, J. C.
SELLERS-YOUNG, B. A.
SHANNON, P.

Faculty of Women and Gender Studies:

KUHN, A. K.
NEWTON, J.
RABINE, L. W.

Division of Biological Sciences (202 Life Sciences Addition, 1 Shields Ave, Davis, CA 95616; tel. (530) 752-0410; internet www.dbs .ucdavis.edu):

Biological Science:

CHANG, E. S.

Evolution and Ecology:

CHESSON, P. L.
DOYLE, J. A.
GILLESPIE, J. H.
GOTTLIEB, L. D.
GREY, R. D.
GROSBERG, R. K.
LANGLEY, C. H.
PEARCY, R. W.
REJMANEK, M.
SANDERSON, M. J.
SCHOENER, T. W.
SHAFFER, H. B.
SHAPIRO, A. M.
STAMPS, J. A.
STANTON, M. L.
STRONG, D. R.
TOFT, C. A.
TURELLI, M.
WAINWRIGHT, P. C.

Microbiology:

ARTZ, S. W.
BAUMANN, P.
HEYER, W. D.
KOWALCZYKOWSKI, S. C.
MANNING, J. S.
MEEKS, J. C.
NELSON, D. C.
PRIVALSKY, M. L.
STEWART, V. J.
ROTH, J. R.

Molecular and Cellular Biology:

ARMSTRONG, P. B.
BASKIN, R. J.
BURTIS, K. C.
CALLIS, J.
CLEGG, J. S.
CROWE, J. H.
DAHMUS, M. E.

DOI, R. H.
ERICKSON, C. A.
ETZLER, M. E.
GASSER, C. S.
HEDRICK, J. L.
HJELMELAND, L. M.
KIGER, J. A.
LAGARIAS, J. C.
MYLES, D.
RODRIGUEZ, R. L.
SCHMID, C. W.
SHOLEY, J. M.
SEGEL, I. H.

Neurobiology, Physiology and Behaviour:

CARSTENS, E. E.
FULLER, C. A.
HORWITZ, B. A.
ISHIDA, A. T.
MULLONEY, B.
PAPPONE, P. A.
SILLMAN, A. J.
WEIDNER, W. J.
WILSON, M. C.
WOOLLEY, D. E.

Plant Biology:

DELMER, D. P.
HARADA, J. J.
LUCAS, W. J.
MURPHY, T. M.
O'NEILL, S. D.
ROST, T. L.
SINHA, N.
STEMLER, A. J.
SUNDARESEN, V.
THEG, S. M.
VANDERHOEF, L. N.

Graduate School of Management (106 AOB4, 1 Shields Ave, Davis, CA 95616; tel. (530) 752-7399; e-mail gsm@ucdavis.edu; internet www.gsm.ucdacvis.edu):

BARBER, B.
BIGGART, N. W.
BUNCH, D. S.
CLARK, P. K.
GERSTNER, E.
GRIFFIN, P. A.
MAHER, M.
PALMER, D.
SMILEY, R. H.
SWAMINATHAN, A.
TOPKIS, D. M.
TSAI, C.-L.
WOODRUFF, D.

School of Medicine (Med Sci 1c, Room 102 Campus, 1 Shields Ave, Davis, CA 95616; tel. (530) 752-4028; internet www-med.ucdavis .edu):

Department of Anaesthesiology and Pain Medicine:

ANTOGNINI, J. F.

Department of Biological Chemistry:

BRADBURY, E. M.
HAGERMAN, P. J.
HERSHEY, J. W.
HJELMELAND, L. M.
HOLLAND, M. J.
JUE, T.
KUNG, H.-J.
TROY LI, F. A.

Department of Cell Biology and Human Anatomy:

ERICKSON, K. L.
FITZGERALD, P.
KUMARI, V.
MEIZEL, S.
PRIMAKOFF, P.
TUCKER, R. P.

Department of Dermatology:

GRANDO, S. A.
HUNTLEY, A. C.
ISSEROFF, R. R.
LIU, F.-T.

ZIBOH, V. A.

Department of Epidemiology and Preventive Medicine:

BECKETT, L. A.
CHEN, M. S.
GOLD, E. B.
LEIGH, J. P.
SCHENKER, M. B.
WINTEMUTE, G. J.

Department of Family and Community Medicine:

BERTAKIS, K. D.
CALLAHAN, E. J.
FRANKS, P.
MELNIKOW, J.
NESBITT, T. S.
NUOVO, J.

Department of Human Physiology:

CALA, P. M.
CARLSEN, R. C.
CURRY, F. E.
O'DONNELL, M. E.
TURGEON, J. L.
WIDDICOMBE, J.
WISE, P.

Department of Internal Medicine:

ALBERTSON, T. E.
AMSTERDAM, E. A.
AOKI, T.
BERGLUND, L.
BONHAM, A. C.
COHEN, S. H.
CROSS, C. E.
DEGREGORIO, M.
DENARDO, S. J.
DEPNER, T. A.
FITZGERALD, F. T.
GANDARA, D. R.
GERSHWIN, M. E.
HALSTED, C. H.
HINSHAW, V. S.
KAPPAGODA, C. T.
KARAKAS, S. E.
KAUFMAN, M. P.
KAYSEN, G.
KRAVITZ, R.
LAM, K.
LAST, J. A.
LEUNG, J.
LOEWY, E.
MARTIN, R. B.
MATTHEWS, H. R.
MEYERS, F. J.
PARSONS, G. H.
PIMSTONE, N. R.
POLLARD, R. B.
POWELL, J. S.
PRINDIVILLE, T. P.
REDDI, A. H.
RICHMAN, C. M.
ROBBINS, J. A.
ROBBINS, R. L.
RUTLEDGE, J. C.
SCHAEFER, S.
SIEGEL, D.
SILVA, J.
STEBBINS, C. L.
ZERN, M.

Department of Medical Microbiology and Immunology:

BEAMAN, B. L.
DANDEKAR, S.
PAPPAGIANIS, D.
SYVANEN, M.
THEIS, J. H.

Medicine:

ANDERS, T. F.
SELDIN, M. F.

Department of Neurological Surgery:

BERMAN, R. F.
BOGGAN, J. E.
LYETH, B. G.

MATTHEWS, D. L.
MUIZELAAR, J. P.
SCHWARTZKROIN, P. A.

Department of Neurology:

DE CARLI, C.
GORIN, F. A.
JAGUST, W. J.
KWEE, I.
MANGUN, G. R.
MASELLI, R. A.
REMLER, M. P.
RICHMAN, D. P.
SEYAL, M.

Department of Obstetrics and Gynaecology:

BOYERS, S.
GILBERT, W. M.
OVERSTREET, J. W.
SMITH, L. H.

Department of Ophthalmology:

CHALUPA, L. M.
KELTNER, J. L.
MANNIS, M. J.
WERNER, J. S.

Department of Orthopaedic Surgery:

BENSON, D. R.
RAB, G. T.
RODRIGO, J. J.
SZABO, R. M.

Department of Otolaryngology:

DONALD, P. J.

Department of Paediatrics:

HAGERMAN, R. J.
JOAD, J. P.
MAKKER, S. P.
PHILIPPS, A. F.
SHERMAN, M. P.
STYNE, D. M.
TARANTAL, A. F.
WENMAN, W. M.

Department of Pathology:

CARDIFF, R. D.
ELLIS, W. G.
GREEN, R.
JIALAL, I.
KOST, G. J.
LARKIN, E. C.
LUCIW, P. A.

Department of Pharmacology:

BONHAM, A. C.
CHUANG, R. Y.
HENDERSON, G. L.

Department of Plastic Surgery:

STEVENSON, T. R.

Department of Psychiatry:

AMARAL, D. G.
HENDREN, R. L.
JONES, E. G.
KNAPP, P. K.
MADDOCK, R. J.
MORRISON, T. L.
ROGERS, S. J.

Department of Radiation Oncology:

BOGREN, H. G.
BOONE, J. M.
BRUNBERG, J. A.
BUONOCORE, M. H.
KATZBERG, R. W.
KUBO, H.
LATCHAW, R. E.
LINK, D. P.
MCGAHAN, J. P.
MOORE, E. H.
ROSENQUIST, C. J.
SEIBERT, J. A.
STADAINIK, R. C.
VIJAYAKUMAR, S.

Department of Surgery:

FOLLETTE, D. M.
GREENHALGH, D. G.
HOLCROFT, J. W.

SEGEL, L. D.
WISNER, D. H.
WOLFE, B. M.

Department of Urology:

DE VERE WHITE, R. W.
STONE, A. R.

School of Veterinary Medicine (tel. (530) 752-1360; internet www.vetmed.ucdavis.edu):

Faculty of Anatomy, Physiology and Cell Biology:

BRUSS, M. L.
GIETZEN, D. W.
HART, B. L.
HYDE, D. M.
PINKERTON, K. E.
PLOPPER, C. G.
RAYBOULD, M. J.
STOVER, S. M.
TABLIN, F.
WU, R.

Faculty of Medicine and Epidemiology:

ARDANS, A. A.
CARLSON, G. P.
CARPENTER, T. E.
COWGILL, L. D.
FELDMAN, E. C.
GARDNER, I.
GEORGE, L. W.
HEDRICK, R. P.
HIRD, D. W.
IHRKE, P. J.
KITTLESON, M. D.
LING, G. V.
MADIGAN, J. E.
NELSON, R. W.
PEDERSEN, N. C.
SMITH, B. P.
THOMAS, W. P.
THURMOND, M. C.
WALSH, D. A.
WHITE, S. D.
WILSON, W. D.

Faculty of Molecular Biosciences:

BUCKPITT, A. R.
CORTOPASSI, G. I.
GIRI, S. N.
HANSEN, R. J.
PESSAH, I. N.
ROGERS, Q. R.
SEGALL, H. J.
VULLIET, P. R.

Faculty of Pathology, Microbiology and Immunology:

BARTHOLD, S. W.
BOYCE, W. M.
CHRISTOPHER, M. W.
CONRAD, P. A.
GERSHWIN, L. J.
HIGGINS, R. J.
LEFEBVRE, R. B.
LOWENSTINE, L. J.
MACLACHLAN, N. J.
MILLER, C. J.
MOORE, P. F.
MUNSON, L.
MURPHY, F. A.
OSBURN, B. I.
STOTT, J. L.
WILSON, D. W.
YILMA, T.
ZINKL, J. G.

Faculty of Population Health and Reproduction:

BALL, B. A.
BONDURANT, R. H.
CHOMEL, B. B.
CLIVER, D. O.
CULLOR, J. S.
FARVER, T. B.
HART, L. A.
LAM, K. M.
LASLEY, W. L.

LIU, I. K.
MURRAY, J. D.
TANNENBAUM, J.
  Faculty of Surgical and Radiological
    Sciences:
BUYUKMIHCI, N. C.
GREGORY, C. R.
HASKINS, S. C.
HILDEBRAND, S. V.
HORNOF, W. J.
ILKIW, J.
JONES, J. H.
LECOUTEUR, R. A.
MADEWELL, B. R.
NYLAND, T. G.
O'BRIEN, T. R.
PASCOE, J. R.
PASCOE, P. J.
SNYDER, J. R.
STEFFEY, E. P.
THEON, A. P.
VASSEUR, P.
VERSTRAETE, F. J. M.
WISNER, E. R.

University of California, Irvine

Irvine, CA 92697

Telephone: (949) 824-5011
Internet: www.uci.edu

Founded 1965
State control

Chancellor: MICHAEL V. DRAKE
Exec. Vice-Chancellor and Provost: MICHAEL R. GOTTFREDSON
Vice-Chancellor for Admin. and Business Services: WENDELL C. BRASE
Vice-Chancellor for Planning and Budget: MEREDITH MICHAELS
Vice-Chancellor for Research: JOHN C. HEMMINGER
Vice-Chancellor for Student Affairs: THOMAS A. PARHAM
Vice-Chancellor for Univ. Advancement: GREGORY R. LEET
Univ. Librarian (vacant)

Library of 2,250,000 vols and 22,000 current periodicals
Number of teachers: 1,500
Number of students: 27,000

Publication: *UCI* Gen. Catalogue (1 a year)

DEANS

Claire Trevor School of the Arts: JOSEPH S. LEWIS, III
Donald Bren School of Information and Computer Sciences: HAL STERN (acting)
Henry Samueli School of Engineering: GREGORY WASHINGTON
Paul Merage School of Business: ANDREW J. POLICANO (acting)
School of Biological Sciences: ALBERT BENNETT
School of Humanities: VICKI L. RUIZ
School of Law: ERWIN CHEMERINSKY
School of Medicine: RALPH V. CLAYMAN
School of Physical Sciences: KENNETH C. JANDA
School of Social Ecology: VALERIE JENNESS
School of Social Sciences: BARBARA DOSHER

University of California, Los Angeles (UCLA)

405 Hilgard Ave, Los Angeles, CA 90095-9000

Telephone: (310) 825-4321
Internet: www.ucla.edu

Founded 1919

Chancellor: GENE D. BLOCK
Exec. Vice-Chancellor and Provost: SCOTT WAUGH
Vice-Chancellor for Academic Personnel: CAROLE GOLDBERG

Vice-Chancellor for Admin. Affairs: JACK POWAZEK
Vice-Chancellor for External Affairs: RHEA TURTELTAUB
Vice-Chancellor for Finance, Budget and Capital Programmes: STEVEN A. OLSEN
Vice-Chancellor for Graduate Studies and Dean of Graduate Division: ROBIN L. GARRELL
Vice-Chancellor for Health Sciences: A. EUGENE WASHINGTON
Vice-Chancellor for Legal Affairs: KEVIN REED
Vice-Chancellor for Research: JAMES STEVEN ECONOMOU
Vice-Chancellor for Student Affairs: JANINA MONTERO
Univ. Librarian: VIRGINIA STEEL

Library: 8m. vols, 90,000 periodicals
Number of teachers: 4,016
Number of students: 39,252

DEANS

Anderson School of Management: JUDY OLIAN
Continuing Education and UCLA Extension: CATHY SANDEEN
David Geffen School of Medicine: A. EUGENE WASHINGTON
Graduate Division: ROBIN L. GARRELL
Graduate School of Education and Information Studies: MARCELO SUAREZ-OROZCO
Henry Samueli School of Engineering and Applied Science: VIJAY DHIR
School of the Arts and Architecture: CHRISTOPHER WATERMAN
School of Dentistry: NO-HEE PARK
School of Law: RACHEL F. MORAN
School of Nursing: COURTNEY LYDER
School of Public Affairs: FRANKLIN GILLIAM, JR
School of Public Health: JODY HEYMANN
School of Theater, Film and Television: TERI SCHWARTZ

University of California, Merced

POB 2039, Merced, CA 95344
5200 N Lake Rd., Merced, CA 95343

Telephone: (209) 228-4400
Internet: www.ucmerced.edu

Founded 2005

Chancellor: DOROTHY LELAND
Provost and Exec. Vice-Chancellor: TOM PETERSON
Vice-Chancellor for Admin.: MARY E. MILLER
Vice-Chancellor for Devt and Alumni Relations: KYLE HOFFMAN
Vice-Chancellor for Research: CHRIS KELLO
Vice-Chancellor for Student Affairs: JANE FIORI LAWRENCE
Chief Information Officer: FAUST GORHAM
Univ. Librarian: DONALD BARLCAY

Number of teachers: 80
Number of students: 5,200

DEANS

Graduate Studies: SAMUEL TRAINA
School of Engineering: E. DANIEL HIRLEMAN
School of Natural Sciences: JUAN MEZA
School of Social Sciences, Humanities and Arts: MARK ALDENDERFER

University of California, Riverside

900 University Ave, Riverside, CA 92521

Telephone: (909) 787-1012
Internet: www.ucr.edu

Founded 1954
State control
Academic year: September to June

Chancellor: Dr TIMOTHY P. WHITE
Exec. Vice-Chancellor and Provost: DALLAS RABENSTEIN
Vice-Chancellor Finance and Business Operations: GRETCHEN BOLAR
Vice-Chancellor for Admin.: AL DIAZ

Vice-Chancellor for Public Service and Int. Programmes: JOHN F. AZZARETTO
Vice-Chancellor for Research: Dr CHARLES F. LOUIS
Vice-Chancellor for Student Affairs: JAMES W. SANDOVAL
Vice-Chancellor for Univ. Advancement: PETER A. HAYASHIDA
Registrar: ELIZABETH C. BENNETT
Univ. Librarian: Dr RUTH JACKSON

Library of 2,368,843 vols, 2,151 serial subscriptions and 1,772,053 microforms
Number of teachers: 600 (f.t.e.)
Number of students: 19,000

DEANS

Bourns College of Engineering: REZA ABBASCHIAN
College of Humanities, Arts and Social Sciences: STEPHEN CULLENBERG
College of Natural and Agricultural Sciences: MARYLYNN V. YATES
Div. of Biomedical Sciences: Dr CRAIG V. BYUS
Graduate Div.: JOSEPH W. CHILDERS
Graduate School of Education: DOUG MITCHELL
School of Business Administration: YUNZENG WANG

University of California, San Diego

9500 Gilman Dr., La Jolla, CA 92093

Telephone: (858) 534-2230
Internet: ucsd.edu
State control
Academic year: September to June

Chancellor: PRADEEP K. KHOSLA
Exec. Vice-Chancellor for Academic Affairs: SURESH SUBRAMANI
Vice-Chancellor for External and Business Affairs: STEVEN W. RELYEA
Vice-Chancellor for Health Sciences: DAVID A. BRENNER
Vice-Chancellor for Marine Sciences and Dir of Scripps Institution of Oceanography: TONY D. HAYMET
Vice-Chancellor for Research: SANDRA A. BROWN
Vice-Chancellor for Resource Management and Planning: GARY MATTHEWS
Vice-Chancellor for Student Affairs: PENNY RUE
Provost of Earl Warren College: STEVEN ADLER
Provost of Eleanor Roosevelt College: ALAN HOUSTON
Provost of John Muir College: SUSAN SMITH (acting)
Provost of Revelle College: DON WAYNE
Provost of Sixth College: JIM LIN
Provost of Thurgood Marshall College: ALLAN HAVIS
Registrar: GABRIEL OLSEZEWSKI
Librarian: BRIAN SCHOTTLAENDER

Number of teachers: 1,200
Number of students: 29,300

Publication: *USCD Perspectives*

DEANS

Div. of Arts and Humanities: SETH LERER
Div. of Biological Sciences: STEVE KAY
Div. of Physical Sciences: MARK THIEMENS
Div. of Social Sciences: JEFFREY L. ELMAN
Jacobs School of Engineering: FRIEDER SEIBLE
Rady School of Management: ROBERT S. SULLIVAN
School of Int. Relations and Pacific Studies: PETER COWHEY
School of Medicine: DAVID A. BRENNER
Scripps Instn of Oceanography: TONY HAYMET
Skaggs School of Pharmacy and Pharmaceutical Sciences: PALMER TAYLOR

University of California, San Francisco

Third and Parnassus Ave, San Francisco, CA 94143

Telephone: (415) 476-9000
Internet: www.ucsf.edu

Founded 1864

Chancellor (vacant)
Exec. Vice-Chancellor and Provost: Dr JEFFREY BLUESTONE
Sr Vice-Chancellor: STEVE BARCLAY
Sr Vice-Chancellor for Finance and Admin.: JOHN E. PLOTTS
Sr Vice-Chancellor for Strategic Communications and Univ. Relations: BARBARA J. FRENCH
Vice-Chancellor for Medical Affairs: DAVID KESSLER
Exec. Dir Institute for Biomedical Research: REGIS KELLY
Registrar: DOUGLAS CARLSON
Librarian: KAREN BUTTER

Library of 821,492 vols
Number of teachers: 2,400
Number of students: 4,050

DEANS

Graduate Div.: Dr JOSEPH CASTRO
School of Dentistry: Dr JOHN FEATHERSTONE
School of Medicine: Dr SAM HAGWOOD
School of Nursing: Dr DAVID VLAHOV
School of Pharmacy: MARY-ANNE KODA-KIMBLE

University of California, Santa Barbara

Santa Barbara, CA 93106

Telephone: (805) 893-8000
Internet: www.ucsb.edu

Founded 1909, present status 1944
Academic year: September to June

Chancellor: HENRY T. YANG
Exec. Vice-Chancellor: GENE LUCAS
Vice-Chancellor for Admin. Services: DONNA J. CARPENTER
Vice-Chancellor for Institutional Advancement: JOHN M. WIEMANN
Vice-Chancellor for Research: MICHAEL S. WITHERELL
Vice-Chancellor for Student Affairs: MICHAEL D. YOUNG
Asst Chancellor for Budget and Planning: TODD G. LEE
Registrar: MARSHA BANKSTON (acting)
Univ. Librarian: DENISE STEPHENS

Library: 3m. vols, 540,000 maps, 4,100 MSS collns, 5m. cartographic images and aerial photos
Number of teachers: 1,050
Number of students: 21,700

DEANS

Bren School of Environmental Science and Management: STEVEN D. GAINES
College of Creative Studies: BRUCE TIFFNEY
College of Engineering: ROD C. ALFERNESS
College of Letters and Science: DAVID MARSHALL
Gevirtz Graduate School of Education: JANE CLOSE CONOLEY
Graduate Division: GALE M. MORRISON
Humanities and Fine Arts: Dr DAVID MARSHALL
Science: PIERRE WILTZIUS
Social Sciences: Dr MELVIN L. OLIVER
Undergraduate Education: MARY NISBET (acting)

University of California, Santa Cruz

1156 High St, Santa Cruz, CA 95064

Telephone: (831) 459-2131
E-mail: admissions@ucsc.edu
Internet: www.ucsc.edu

Founded 1962

Academic year: September to June
Chancellor: GEORGE R. BLUMENTHAL (acting)
Campus Provost and Exec. Vice-Chancellor: Dr ALISON GALLOWAY
Vice-Provost for Academic Affairs: HERBERT LEE
Vice-Provost and Dean of Undergraduate Education: WILLIAM A. LADUSAW
Vice-Provost and Dean of Univ. Extension: MARK CIOC
Vice-Chancellor for Business and Admin. Services: CHRISTINA L. VALENTINO
Vice-Chancellor for Planning and Budget: MEREDITH MICHAELS
Vice-Chancellor for Research: BRUCE H. MARGON
Vice-Chancellor for Student Affairs: SUSAN HANSEN (acting)
Vice-Chancellor for Univ. Relations: DONNA M. MURPHY
Exec. Director of Admissions and Univ. Registrar: KEVIN BROWNE
Univ. Librarian: VIRGINIA STEEL

Library of 1,350,000 vols, 15,000 periodicals, 800,000 microforms, 500 other items (maps, slides, audio and visual recordings)
Number of teachers: 550 (ladder-rank faculty)
Number of students: 16,300

DEANS

Div. of Arts: DAVID YAGER
Div. of Humanities: WILLIAM A. LADUSAW
Div. of Physical and Biological Sciences: PAUL KOCH
Div. of Social Sciences: SHELDON KAMIENIECKI
Jack Baskin School of Engineering: ARTHUR RAMIREZ

UNIVERSITY OF LA VERNE

1950 Third St, La Verne, CA 91750

Telephone: (909) 593-3511
E-mail: commdept@laverne.edu
Internet: laverne.edu

Founded 1891 as Lordsburg College, present name 1977
Private control
Academic year: September to June

9 Regional campuses

Provost and Chief Academic Officer: Dr JONATHAN L. REED
Pres.: DEVORAH LIEBERMAN
Provost and Vice-Pres. for Academic Affairs: ROBERT NEHER
Exec. Vice-Pres.: PHILIP A. HAWKEY
Vice-Pres. for Enrolment Management: HOMA SHABAHANG
Vice-Pres. for Univ. Relations: JEAN BJERKE
Registrar: MARILYN DAVIES
Dean of Student Affairs: LORETTA RAHMANI
Librarian: TAYLOR RUHL

Library of 337,000 vols
Number of teachers: 220 (85 full-time, 135 part-time)
Number of students: 7,500

DEANS

College of Arts and Sciences: FELICIA BEARDSLEY
College of Business and Public Management: Dr ABE HELOU
College of Education and Organization Leadership: Dr MARK GOOR
College of Law: Prof. ALLEN K. EASLEY

UNIVERSITY OF REDLANDS

POB 3080, 1200 E Colton Ave, Redlands, CA 92373-0999

Telephone: (909) 793-2121
Internet: www.redlands.edu

Founded 1907
Private control

Pres.: Dr JAMES R. APPLETON
Vice-Pres. and Dean for Student Life: CHARLOTTE G. BURGESS
Vice-Pres. for Academic Affairs: DAVID FITE
Sr Vice-Pres. for Finance and Admin.: PHILLIP DOOLITTLE
Vice-Pres. for Univ. Relations: NEIL MACREADY
Registrar: CHARLOTTE LUCEY
Library Dir: JEAN SWANSON

Library of 280,000 vols
Number of teachers: 550
Number of students: 4,100

Publication: *Redlands*

DEANS

College of Arts and Sciences: Dr KATHY OGREN
School of Business: Dr STUART NOBLE-GOODMAN
School of Education: Dr JAMES VALADEZ
School of Music: Dr ANDREW R. GLENDENING

UNIVERSITY OF SAN DIEGO

5998 Alcala Park, San Diego, CA 92110

Telephone: (619) 260-4600
E-mail: admissions@sandiego.edu
Internet: www.sandiego.edu

Founded 1949
Private control
Language of instruction: English
Academic year: September to May

Pres.: Dr MARY E. LYONS
Exec. Vice-Pres. and Provost: Dr JULIE H. SULLIVAN
Vice-Pres. for Business and Admin.: RUSSELL C. THACKSTON
Vice-Pres. for Mission and Ministry: DANIEL J. DILLABOUGH
Vice-Pres. for Student Affairs: CARMEN M. VAZQUEZ
Vice-Pres. for Univ. Relations: Dr TIMOTHY L. O'MALLEY
Librarian: THERESA BYRD

Library of 500,000 vols and 2,200 current periodicals
Number of teachers: 880 (405 full-time, 475 part-time)
Number of students: 8,100

Publications: *Journal of Contemporary Legal Issues* (2 a year), *Law Review* (4 a year), *San Diego International Law Journal* (2 a year)

DEANS

College of Arts and Sciences: Dr MARY K. BOYD
Hahn School of Nursing and Health Sciences: Dr SALLY BROSZ HARDIN
Joan B. Kroc School of Peace Studies: Dr EDWARD LUCK
School of Business Administration: Dr DAVID PYKE
School of Law: Dr STEPHEN FERRUOLO
School of Leadership and Education Sciences: Dr PAULA A. CORDEIRO

UNIVERSITY OF SAN FRANCISCO

2130 Fulton St, San Francisco, CA 94117-1080

Telephone: (415) 422-5555
Internet: www.usfca.edu

Founded 1855
Private control
Academic year: September to May

Pres.: Dr Rev. STEPHEN A. PRIVETT
Provost and Vice-Pres. for Academic Affairs: Dr JENNIFER E. TURPIN
Chancellor: Rev. JOHN LO SCHIAVO
Vice-Pres. for Business and Finance: CHARLIE CROSS

Vice-Pres. for Int. Relations: STANLEY D. NEL

Vice-Pres. for Univ. Advancement: DAVID F. MACMILLAN

Vice-Pres. for Univ. Life: Dr MARGARET M. HIGGINS

Gen. Counsel: DONNA DAVIS

Dean for Academic and Enrolment Services: ELIZABETH J. JOHNSON

Dean for the Univ. Library: TYRONE H. CANNON

Library of 593,543 vols
Number of teachers: 290
Number of students: 8,570

Publications: *Maritime Law Journal* (2 a year), *USF Law Review* (4 a year)

DEANS

Colleges of Arts and Sciences: Dr MARCELO CAMPERI

School of Education: Dr WALTER GMELCH

School of Law: Dr JEFFREY S. BRAND

School of Management: Dr MICHAEL J. WEBBER

School of Nursing and Health Professions: Dr JUDITH F. KARSHNER

UNIVERSITY OF SOUTHERN CALIFORNIA

University Park Campus, Los Angeles, CA 90089

Telephone: (213) 740-2311

Internet: www.usc.edu

Founded 1880
Academic year: August to May
Private control

Pres.: C. L. MAX NIKIAS

Provost and Sr Vice-Pres. for Academic Affairs: ELIZABETH GARRETT

Sr Vice-Pres. for Admin.: TODD R. DICKEY

Sr Vice-Pres. for Finance and Chief Financial Officer: ROBERT ABELES

Sr Vice-Pres. for Univ. Advancement: ALBERT R. CHECCIO

Vice-Pres. for Admissions and Planning: KATHERINE HARRINGTON

Gen. Counsel and Sec.: CAROL MAUCH AMIR

Dean of Libraries: CATHERINE QUINLAN

Library: see Libraries and Archives
Number of teachers: 3,400 (full-time)
Number of students: 38,000

Publications: *USC Chronicle, USC Trojan Family* (4 a year)

DEANS

Annenberg School for Communication and Journalism: ERNEST J. WILSON, III

Davis School of Gerontology: GERALD C. DAVISON

Dornsife College of Letters, Arts and Sciences: HOWARD GILLMAN

Gould School of Law: ROBERT K. RASMUSSEN

Herman Ostrow School of Dentistry: AVISHAI SADAN

Keck School of Medicine: CARMEN A. PULIAFITO

Leventhal School of Accounting: JAMES G. ELLIS

Marshall School of Business: JAMES G. ELLIS

Roski School of Fine Arts: ROCHELLE STEINER

Rossier School of Education: KAREN SYMMS GALLAGHER

School of Architecture: QINGYUN MA

School of Cinematic Arts: ELIZABETH M. DALEY

School of Pharmacy: R. PETE VANDERVEEN

School of Social Work: MARILYN L. FLYNN

School of Theatre: MADELINE PUZO

Sol Price School of Public Policy: JACK H. KNOTT

Thornton School of Music: ROBERT A. CUTIETTA

Viterbi School of Engineering: YANNIS C. YORTSOS

PROFESSORS

Distinguished and University Professors:

ARBIB, MICHAEL A., Biological Sciences and Biomedical Engineering

ARMSTRONG, LLOYD, Jr, Physics and Education

BENNIS, WARREN, Business Admin.

BRAUDY, LEO B., English and American Literature

CAPRON, ALEXANDER M., Law and Medicine

COHEN, MARSHALL, Emeritus of Philosophy and Law

COWAN, GEOFFREY, Communication Leadership

EASTERLIN, RICHARD A., Economics

FINCH, CALEB, Gerontology and Biological Sciences

GOLOMB, SOLOMON W., Electrical Engineering and Mathematics

HELLWARTH, ROBERT W., Physics

JORDAN, THOMAS, Geophysics and Earth Sciences

KINDER, MARSHA, Comparative Literature

PIKE, MALCOLM CECIL, Preventive Medicine

SHIH, JEAN C., Cell and Neurobiology

STARR, KEVIN O., History and Policy, Planning and Devt

TIERNEY, WILLIAM G., Higher Education

TOULMIN, STEPHEN E., Anthropology, Int. Relations and Religion

WATERMAN, MICHAEL S., Biological Sciences and Mathematics

ARNHEIM, NORMAN, Biological Sciences

BENNIS, WARREN, English

CORAGHESSAN BOYLE, T., English

EVERETT, PERCIVAL, Cinematic Arts

HARRIS, MARK JONATHAN, Theory and Composition

HARTKE, STEPHEN, Preventive Medicine

HENDERSON, BRIAN E., Biochemistry and Molecular Biology

JONES, PETER A., Paediatrics

KAUFMAN, FRANCINE R., Molecular Microbiology and Immunology

LAI, MICHAEL M. C., Business

LAWLER, EDWARD E., III, Medicine

LEVINE, ALEXANDRA M., Chemistry

OLAH, GEORGE A., Medicine

RAHIMTOOLA, SHAHBUDIN H., Cardiothoracic Surgery

STARNES, VAUGHN A., Pharmaceutical Sciences

WOLF, MICHAEL A., Biological Sciences and Biomedical Engineering

School of Gerontology:

BENGTSON, V. L.
BONDAREFF, W.
CRIMMINS, E.
DAVIES, K.
FINCH, C.
GATZ, M.
KNIGHT, R.
PYNOOS, J.
SCHNEIDER, E. L.
SCHNEIDER, L.
SILVERSTEIN, M.
WILBER, K.
ZELINSKI, E.

School of Law:

ALTMAN, S. A.
ARMOUR, J. D.
BICE, S. H.
BRECHT, A. O.
CAPRON, A. M.
COWAN, G.
CRUZ, D. B.
DUDZIAK, M. L.
ESTRICH, S.
FINEGAN, E. J.
GARET, R. R.
GARRETT, E.
GILLMAN, H.
GRIFFITH, T. D.
GROSS, A. J.

HADFIELD, G.
KEATING, G. C.
KLERMAN, D. M.
KURAN, T.
LEFCOE, G.
LEVINE, M. L.
LYON, T. D.
McCAFFERY, E. J.
MARMOR, A.
MURPHY, K. J.
SAKS, E. R.
SCHOR, H. M.
SHAPIRO, M. H.
SIMON, L. G.
SLAWSON, W. D.
SMITH, E. M.
SPITZER, M. L.
STOLZENBERG, N. M.
STONE, C. D.
TALLEY, E. L.
WHITEBREAD, C. H.

School of Medicine:

ADLER, R.
AHMADI, J.
AKMAL, M.
ALKANA, R.
ANDERSON, W.
ANN, D.
APUZZO, M.
ASKANAS, V.
AZEN, S.
BAEHNER, R.
BALLARD, C.
BEART, R., Jr
BERGMAN, R.
BERNE, T.
BERNSTEIN, L.
BEYDOUN, S.
BONDAREFF, W.
BOYD, S.
BREMNER, C.
BRENNER, P.
BRINTON, R.
BROEK, D.
BUCHANAN, T.
CADENAS, E.
CAMPESE, V.
CHANDRASOMA, P.
CHUI, H.
CHUONG, C.-M.
CLARK, F.
COLLETTI, P.
CONTI, P.
COSTIN, G.
COTE, R.
CRAFT, C.
CRANDALL, E.
DANENBERG, P.
DE JUAN, E., Jr
DE MEESTER, T.
DECLERCK, Y.
DEMETRIADES, D.
DENNERT, G.
DIZEREGA, G.
DUBEAU, L.
DWYER, J.
ELKAYAM, U.
EL-SHAHAWY, M.
ENGEL, W.
EPSTEIN, A.
FARLEY, R.
FEINSTEIN, D.
FRANK, G.
GAYNON, P.
GEFFNER, M.
GIANNOTTA, S.
GILL, P.
GILLES, F.
GILLILAND, F.
GILSANZ, V.
GOMER, C.
GONG, H., Jr
GOODWIN, T.
GORAN, M.
GOVINDARAJAN, S.

GRANT, E.
GROFFEN, J.
GRUSHKIN, C.
HAHN, R.
HAILE, R.
HALLS, J.
HAMMOND, G.
HAYS, D.
HAYWOOD, L.
HEISTERKAMP, N.
HENDERSON, B.
HILL, A.
HINTON, D.
HODGMAN, J.
HODIS, H.
HOFMAN, F.
HOHN, A.
HORWITZ, D.
HSIEH, C.-L.
HUANG, H.
HUMAYUN, M.
HURVITZ, R.
ISRAEL, R.
IWAKI, Y.
JACOBS, R.
JELLIFFE, R.
JOHNSON, C.
JOHNSON, C.
JOHNSON, D.
JONES, P.
KALRA, V.
KAPLOWITZ, N.
KAPTEIN, E.
KAST, W. M.
KATKHOUDA, N.
KAUFMAN, F.
KEANE, J.
KEDES, L.
KEENS, T.
KILBURN, K.
KLONER, R.
KOHN, D.
KORSCH, B.
KOSS, M.
LAINE, L.
LAMB, H.
LAUG, W.
LAWLOR, M.
LEE, A.
LEVINE, A.
LEVY, D.
LEWIS, A.
LIEBER, M.
LIESKOVSKY, G.
LU, S.
LUMB, P.
McCOMB, J.
McDONOUGH, A.
McMILLAN, M.
McNEILL, T.
MACK, T.
MAHOUR, G.
MARKLAND, F.
MARTIN, W.
MATTINGLY, C.
MAXSON, R.
MEISELMAN, H.
MENDEZ, R.
MILLER, C.
MINCKLER, D.
MIRCHEFF, A.
MISHELL, D., Jr
MISHRA, S.
MORROW, C.
MULL, J.
MURPHREE, A.
NATHWANI, B.
NELSON, M.
NEWTH, C.
NICOLOFF, J.
NIMNI, M.
O'LEARY, D.
OU, J.-H.
PARKMAN, R.
PATTENGALE, P.
PATZAKIS, M.

PAULSON, R.
PENTZ, M.
PETERS, J. M.
PIKE, M.
PLATZKER, A.
PORTNOY, B.
POWARS, D.
PRESS, M.
PRESTON-MARTIN, S.
QUISMORIO, F.
RADIN, D.
RAHIMTOOLA, S.
RALLS, P.
RAO, N.
RASHEED, S.
REYNOLDS, C.
RICE, D.
RICHARDSON, J.
ROSS, R.
ROY, S.
ROY-BURMAN, P.
RUDE, R.
RYAN, S., Jr
SADUN, A.
SATTLER, F.
SCHECHTER, J.
SCHNEIDER, L.
SEEGER, R.
SEGALL, H.
SELBY, R.
SENER, S.
SHARMA, O.
SHERWIN, R.
SHIBATA, D.
SHIH, J.
SHOUPE, D.
SHRIVASTAVA, P.
SHULMAN, I.
SIEGEL, M.
SIEGEL, S.
SILBERMAN, H.
SILKA, M.
SILVERSTEIN, M.
SINATRA, F.
SINGH, M.
SKINNER, D.
SMITH, R.
SOHAL, R.
SOKOL, R.
STALLCUP, M.
STANLEY, P.
STARNES, V.
STELLWAGEN, R.
STOHL, W.
STOHLMAN, S.
STRAM, D.
SUSSMAN, S.
TAKAHASHI, M.
TAYLOR, C.
TENG, E.
THOMAS, D.
THORDARSON, D.
TOKES, Z.
TOLO, V.
TRICHE, T.
TSUKAMOTO, H.
VANGSNESS, T., Jr
VARMA, R.
VESELY, L.
WARBURTON, D.
WEAVER, F.
WEBER, J.
WEINBERG, K.
WEINER, L.
WEISS, M.
WETZEL, R.
WILLIAMS, R.
WOOD, B.
WOODLEY, D.
WU, P.
WU-WILLIAMS, A.
YELLIN, A.
YING, S.-Y.
YU, M.
ZEE, C.-S.
ZEIDLER, A.

ZELMAN, V.

School of Music:
BEER, H., Conducting
BERG, S., Jazz Studies
BROWN, B. A., Music History
CRAVENS, T., Winds and Percussion
CROCKETT, D., Composition
DEHNING, W., Choral and Sacred Music
GLAZE, G., Vocal Arts
GORDON, S., Keyboard Studies
HARTKE, S. N., Composition
HOPKINS, J. F., Composition
LAURIDSEN, M., II, Composition
LEONARD, R., Strings
LESEMANN, F., Composition
LIVINGSTON, L., Conducting
MASON, T. D., Jazz Studies
McCURDY, R. C., Jazz Studies
McINNES, D., Strings
PERRY, J., Keyboard Studies
POLLACK, D., Keyboard Studies
SCHOENFELD, E., Strings
SIMMS, B., Music History
THOMAS, W. E. L., Electro-Acoustic Media
TICHELI, F., IV, Composition
TYLER, J., Early Music Performance, Music
  History

School of Pharmacy:
ALKANA, R. L.
ANN, D.
BRINTON, R.
BURCKHART, G.
CADENAS, E.
CHAN, T. M.
JOHNSON, D.
SHEN, W.-C.
SHIH, J. C.
SOHAL, R.
STIMMEL, G. L.
WOLF, W.

School of Policy, Planning and Development:
BANERJEE, T.
CAIDEN, G.
COOPER, T.
FERRIS, J. M.
GABRIEL, S. A.
GIULIANO, G.
GORDON, P.
GRADDY, E.
GREENWALD, H.
HEIKKILA, E.
KREIGER, M. H.
LOPEZ-LEE, D.
MAZMANIAN, D.
MELNICK, G.
MYERS, D.
MYRTLE, R.
NEWLAND, C.
PACHON, H.
PETAK, W.
RICHARDSON, H.
SLOANE, D.
SUNDEEN, R., Jr
TANG, S.-Y.
VON WINTERFELDT, D.
WHOLEY, J. S.

School of Social Work:
BREKKE, J.
CHI, I.
ELL, K.
FLYNN, M.
JANSSON, B.
McCROSKEY, J.
MONDROS, J.
MOR-BARAK, M.
STONER, M.
TRICKETT, P.

School of Theatre:
CARNICKE, S. M.
HOUSTON, V.
PUZO, M.

UNIVERSITY OF THE PACIFIC

3601 Pacific Ave, Stockton, CA 95211
Telephone: (209) 946-2211
E-mail: admission@pacific.edu
Internet: www.pacific.edu

Founded 1851 as California Wesleyan College, present name 1961
Private control
Academic year: August to May
Main campus in Stockton; Pacific McGeorge School of Law in Sacramento; Arthur A. Dugoni School of Dentistry in San Francisco
Pres.: PAMELA A. EIBECK
Provost: Dr MARIA G. PALLAVICINI
Vice-Pres. for Business and Finance: PATRICK CAVANAUGH
Vice-Pres. for Devt: CHRISTOPHER JOHNSTON
Vice-Pres. for External Relations: TED LELAND
Vice-Pres. for Student Life: Dr ELIZABETH GRIEGO
Dean for the Library: C. BRIGID WELCH
Library of 281,769 vols, 1,361 periodicals, 689,462 microforms
Number of teachers: 440 (all campuses)
Number of students: 7,000 (all campuses)
Publications: *Contact Point* (3 a year), *De Minimis*, *Pacifican*, *Pacific Historian*, *Pacific Law*, *Pacific Review*

DEANS

Arthur A. Dugoni School of Dentistry: Dr PATRICK J. FERRILLO, JR
College of the Pacific: Dr THOMAS W. KRISE
Conservatory of Music: GIULIO M. ONGARO
Eberhardt School of Business: LEWIS R. GALES
Gladys L. Benerd School of Education: LYNN BECK
McGeorge School of Law: ELIZABETH RINDSKOPF PARKER
School of Engineering and Computer Science: Dr RAVI JAIN
School of International Studies: Dr CYNTHIA WAGNER WEICK
Research and Graduate Studies: Dr JIN K. GONG
Thomas J. Long School of Pharmacy and Health Sciences: PHILIP OPPENHEIMER

UNIVERSITY OF WEST LOS ANGELES

9800 S La Cienega Blvd, 12th Fl., Inglewood, CA 90301-4423
Telephone: (310) 342-5200
E-mail: admissions@uwla.edu
Internet: www.uwla.edu

Founded 1966
Private control
Campuses in LAX area and the San Fernando Valley
Pres.: ROBERT W. BROWN
Dean: JAY P. FRYKBERG
Assoc. Dean: JOHN MCTEAGUE
Dir for Admissions and Recruitment: GINA WONG
Dir for Facilities: RON BEATTY
Dir for Operations (San Fernando Valley Campus): PAT GALASSO
Registrar: NAILAH SMITH
Librarian: JESSE ALDAVA
Library of 34,000 vols
Number of teachers: 40 (3 full-time, 37 adjunct)
Number of students: 350
Publication: *UWLA Law Review* (2 a year)

DEANS

School of Graduate Studies: KIMBERLY JOHNSON
School of Law: JAY P. FRYKBERG

VANGUARD UNIVERSITY OF SOUTHERN CALIFORNIA

55 Fair Dr., Costa Mesa, CA 92626-9601
Telephone: (714) 556-3610
E-mail: kanolf@vanguard.edu
Internet: www.vanguard.edu

Founded 1920 as Southern California Bible School, present name and status 1999
Private control
Courses incl. business and management, communication and arts, education, humanities, natural sciences and mathematics, psychology and religion
Pres.: Dr CAROL A. TAYLOR
Provost and Vice-Pres. for Academic Affairs: Dr JEFF HITTENBERGER
Vice-Pres. for Business and Finance: LETTIE COWIE
Vice-Pres. for Enrolment Management: KIM JOHNSON
Vice-Pres. for Student Affairs: ANN HAMILTON
Vice-Pres. for Univ. Advancement: KELLY KANNWISCHER
Dean of Students: LINDA HARTZELL
Registrar: JUDY K. HAMILTON
Head Librarian: ALISON ENGLISH
Library of 135,500 vols, 1,053 periodicals
Number of teachers: 175 (62 full-time, 113 part-time)
Number of students: 2,000
Publication: *Vanguard Magazine* (4 a year)

DEANS

School for Professional Studies: Dr PAUL COX

WESTERN STATE UNIVERSITY COLLEGE OF LAW

1111 N State College Blvd, Fullerton, CA 92831-3014
Telephone: (714) 738-1000
E-mail: adm@wsulaw.edu
Internet: www.wsulaw.edu

Founded 1966
Private control
Academic year: August to May
Criminal Law Practice Center, Business Law Center, Legal Clinic and Trial Practice Programme
Dean and Pres.: WILLIAM E. ADAMS
Assoc. Dean of Academic Affairs: SUSAN KELLER
Dir of Criminal Law Practice Center: DAVID FRAKT
Dir of Legal Clinic: TERENCE W. ROBERTS
Library Dir: PATRICIA HARRIS O'CONNOR (acting)
Number of teachers: 60 (28 full-time, 34 adjunct)
Number of students: 500

WESTERN UNIVERSITY OF HEALTH SCIENCES

309 East Second St, Pomona, CA 91766-1854
Telephone: (909) 6236116
E-mail: admissions@westernu.edu
Internet: www.westernu.edu

Founded 1977 as College of Osteopathic Medicine of the Pacific, present name 1996
Private control
Pres.: Dr PHILIP PUMERANTZ
Provost and Chief Operating Officer: GARY M. GUGELCHUK
Treas. and Chief Financial Officer: KEVIN D. SHAW
Vice-Pres. for Enrolment Management and Student Affairs: BEVERLY A. GUIDRY
Vice-Pres. for Human Resources: HOWARD M. PARDUE
Vice-Pres. for Research and Biotechnology: STEVEN J. HENRIKSEN

Library Dir: PATRICIA VADER
Number of students: 1,400

DEANS

College of Allied Health Professions: Dr STEPHANIE D. BOWLIN
College of Biomedical Sciences: Dr MICHEL BAUDRY
College of Dental Medicine: Dr STEVEN W. FRIEDRICHSEN
College of Graduate Nursing: KAREN HANFORD
College of Optometry: Dr ELIZABETH HOPPE
College of Osteopathic Medicine of the Pacific: CLINTON E. ADAMS
College of Podiatric Medicine: Dr LAWRENCE B. HARKLESS
College of Pharmacy: Dr DANIEL ROBINSON
College of Veterinary Medicine: Dr PHILLIP D. NELSON

WESTMINSTER SEMINARY CALIFORNIA

1725 Bear Valley Parkway, Escondido, CA 92027
Telephone: (760) 480-8474
E-mail: info@wscal.edu
Internet: www.wscal.edu

Founded 1979
Private control
Academic year: September to May
Offers MDiv and MA in biblical studies, theological studies, historical theology, Christian studies
Pres.: Dr W. ROBERT GODFREY
Exec. Vice-Pres.: STEVEN OEVERMAN
Vice-Pres. for Advancement: DAWN G. DOORN
Academic Dean: Dr J. V. FESKO
Dean of Students: Dr JULIUS J. KIM
Registrar: BRIAN J. MILLS
Library Dir: JOHN BALES
Library of 120,000 vols, 260 periodicals
Number of teachers: 25 (12 full-time)
Number of students: 150

WHITTIER COLLEGE

POB 634, 13406 E Philadelphia, Whittier, CA 90608-4413
Telephone: (562) 907-4200
E-mail: president@whittier.edu
Internet: www.whittier.edu

Founded 1887
Private control
Liberal arts, business and law
Pres.: Dr SHARON D. HERZBERGER
Vice-Pres. and Dean of Students: JEANNE ORTIZ
Vice-Pres. for Academic Affairs and Dean of the Faculty: CHARLOTTE BORST
Vice-Pres. for Advancement: ELIZABETH POWER ROBISON
Vice-Pres. for Enrolment: LISA MEYER
Vice-Pres. for Finance and Admin.: JAMES DUNKELMAN
Registrar: WILLIAM GARTRELL
Assoc. Library Dir: LAUREL CRUMP
Library of 250,000 vols, 44,000 microfilms, 300 current periodicals; spec. collns: John Greenleaf Whittier, Quakers
Number of teachers: 100 (full-time)
Number of students: 1,500
Publications: *The Rock* (3 a year), *Whittier Law Review*

DEANS

Whittier Law School: PENELOPE BRYAN

WILLIAM JESSUP UNIVERSITY

333 Sunset Blvd, Rocklin, CA 95765
Telephone: (916) 577-2200

E-mail: information@jessup.edu
Internet: www.jessup.edu
Founded 1939 as San Jose Bible College, present name and status 2004
Private control
Academic year: September to May
Areas of study: Bible and theology, business administration, Christian education, English, history, intercultural studies, liberal studies, music, pastoral ministry, psychology, public policy and youth ministry; br. campus at San Jose
Pres.: JOHN JACKSON
Vice-Pres. for Academic Affairs: Dr DENNIS JAMESON
Vice-Pres. for Advancement: JOSEPH D. WOMACK
Vice-Pres. for Finance and Admin.: GENE DE YOUNG
Vice-Pres. for Student Devt: PAUL BLEZIEN
Registrar: TINA PETERSEN
Library Dir: KEVIN PISCHKE
Library of 34,000 vols
Number of students: 900

WOODBURY UNIVERSITY

7500 Glenoaks Blvd, Burbank, CA 91510-7846
Telephone: (818) 767-0888
E-mail: info@woodbury.edu
Internet: www.woodbury.edu
Founded 1884 as Woodbury Business College; present name 1974
Private control
Academic year: August to August
Br. campus at San Diego
Pres.: Dr LUIS CALINGO
Vice-Pres. for Academic Affairs: DAVID M. ROSEN
Vice-Pres. for Enrolment Management and Univ. Marketing: DON E. ST. CLAIR
Vice-Pres. for Finance and Admin.: KEN JONES
Vice-Pres. for Information Technology and Planning: STEVE DYER
Vice Pres. for Student Devt: PHYLLIS CREMER
Vice-Pres. for Univ. Advancement: RICHARD M. NORDIN
Dir for Library Services: NEDRA PETERSON
Number of students: 1,500

DEANS

Institute of Transdisciplinary Studies: Dr DOUGLAS J. CREMER
School of Architecture: NORMAN MILLAR
School of Business: Dr ANDRÈ B. VAN NIEKERK
School of Media, Culture and Design: Dr EDWARD M. CLIFT

WRIGHT INSTITUTE

2728 Durant Ave, Berkeley, CA 94704
Telephone: (510) 841-9230
E-mail: info@wi.edu
Internet: www.wi.edu
Founded 1968
Private control
Academic year: September to June
Area of study: clinical psychology
Pres.: PETER DYBWAD
Vice-Pres. for Finance and Admin. Affairs: TRICIA O'REILLY
Dean: Dr CHUCK ALEXANDER
Dir of Clinical Services: CRYSTAL A. JOHNSON
Dir for Clinical Training: GILBERT NEWMAN
Registrar: GINNY MORGAN
Library Dir: JASON STRAUSS
Library of 10,000 items, 1,100 journals

COLORADO

ADAMS STATE COLLEGE

208 Edgemont Blvd, Alamosa, CO 81101
Telephone: (719) 587-7011
E-mail: ascadmit@adams.edu
Internet: www.adams.edu
Founded 1921
State control
Depts of art, biology, business administration, chemistry, communications, computer science, earth sciences, English, history/government/philosophy, human performance and physical education, interdisciplinary studies, mathematics, music, nursing, physics, psychology, sociology, Spanish, teacher education, theatre
Pres.: Dr DAVID P. SVALDI
Vice-Pres. for Academic Affairs: Dr FRANK NOVOTNY
Sr Vice-Pres. for Enrolment Management and Programme Devt: Dr MICHAEL MUMPER
Vice-Pres. for Finance and Govt Relations: BILL MANSHEIM
Asst Vice-Pres. for Student Affairs: KENNETH MARQUEZ
Dir for Student Support Services: DEBORAH WHITE
Registrar: M. BELEN MAESTAS
Dir for Library: DAVID GOETZMAN
Library of 127,024 vols, 1,350 maps, 2,748 video cassettes and DVDs, 13,577 microfilm reels, 338 periodical subscriptions, 119,289 unique titles and editions
Number of teachers: 120 (full-time and part-time)
Number of students: 3,700

COLLEGE FOR FINANCIAL PLANNING

8000 E Maplewood Ave, Suite 200, Greenwood Village, CO 80111
Telephone: (303) 220-1200
E-mail: cffpenrollmentgroup@apollogrp.edu
Internet: www.cffp.edu
Founded 1972
Private control
Pres.: JOHN SEARS
Vice-Pres. for Academic Affairs: Dr JESSE B. ARMAN

COLORADO CHRISTIAN UNIVERSITY

8787 W Alameda Ave, Lakewood, CO 80226
Telephone: (303) 963-3000
E-mail: admission@ccu.edu
Internet: www.ccu.edu
Founded 1989 by merger of Colorado Christian College and Colorado Baptist Univ.
Private control
Academic year: August to August
Pres.: WILLIAM L. ARMSTRONG
Vice-Pres. for Academic Affairs: Dr CHERRI PARKS
Vice-Pres. for Business Affairs and Chief Financial Officer: DANIEL L. COHRS
Vice-Pres. for Devt: PAUL J. ELDRIDGE
Vice-Pres. for Student Devt: JAMES S. McCORMICK
Asst Vice-Pres. for Admin. Services: RON W. BENTON
Registrar: LINDA PERCIANTE
Library Dir: GAYLE C. GUNDERSON
Library of 100,000 vols, 9,300 reference titles, 1,500 video cassettes, 200 audio cassettes, 2,500 music CDs
Number of teachers: 330
Number of students: 4,000

DEANS

College of Adult and Graduate Studies, Business and Technology Division: Dr MELLANI J. DAY
College of Adult and Graduate Studies, Curriculum and Instruction Education Division: Dr WENDY ELLIOT WENDOVER
College of Adult and Graduate Studies, Nursing and Sciences Division: Dr BARBARA J. WHITE
College of Adult and Graduate Studies, Social Sciences and Humanities Division: Prof. Dr LAVERNE K. JORDAN
School of Business and Leadership: Dr GARY W. EWEN
School of Education: Dr SARA DALLMAN
School of Humanities and Sciences: Dr WILLIAM R. SAXBY
School of Music: STEVEN T. TAYLOR
School of Theology: Dr SID BUZZELL

COLORADO COLLEGE

14 E Cache La Poudre St, Colorado Springs, CO 80903
Telephone: (719) 389-6000
E-mail: communications@coloradocollege.edu
Internet: www.coloradocollege.edu
Founded 1874
Private control
American cultural studies, anthropology, art, Asian studies, biology, chemistry, classics, comparative literature, drama and dance, E Asian languages, economics and business, education, English, environmental science, feminist and gender studies, geology, German, history, mathematics and computer science, music, philosophy, physics, political science, psychology, religion, Romance languages, Russian, sociology, sport science, Southwest studies
Pres.: JILL TIEFENTHALER
Vice-Pres. for Advancement: STEPHEN ELDER
Vice-Pres. for Finance and Admin. and Treas.: ROBERT MOORE
Vice-Pres. for Enrolment Management: MARK HATCH
Vice-Pres. for Information Management: DAVE ARMSTRONG
Vice-Pres. for Student Life: MIKE EDMONDS
Dean for College and Faculty: SUSAN ASHLEY
Registrar: PHIL APODOCA
Library Dir: CAROL DICKERSON
Number of teachers: 140
Number of students: 2,040

COLORADO MESA UNIVERSITY

1100 N Ave, Grand Junction, CO 81501-3122
Telephone: (970) 248-1020
Internet: www.coloradomesa.edu
Founded 1925 as Grand Junction Junior College, present name 2011
State control
Academic year: August to May
Depts of art, biological sciences, business, computer science, mathematics and statistics, health sciences, kinesiology, languages, literature and mass communication, mechanical engineering partnership programme, physical and environmental sciences, social and behavioural sciences, teacher education and theatre; campuses in Montrose and Grand Junction in Colorado
Pres.: TIMOTHY E. FOSTER
Vice-Pres. for Academic Affairs: Dr CAROL FUTHEY
Vice-Pres. for Admin. Services and Finance: PATRICK DOYLE
Vice-Pres. for Student Services: JOHN MARSHALL
Dir of Admissions: JARED MEIER

Registrar: HOLLY TEAL

Dir of Library: ELIZABETH BRODAK (acting)

Library of 395,200 vols, 59,300 current journals, 30,500 ebooks and documents, 82,375 govt docs, 12,248 audiovisual items, 17,390 maps

Number of teachers: 230 (full-time)

Number of students: 8,800 (8,720 undergraduate, 60 graduate, 20 exclusively extended studies)

COLORADO MOUNTAIN COLLEGE

802 Grand Ave, Glenwood Springs, CO 81601

Telephone: (970) 945-8691

E-mail: joinus@coloradomtn.edu

Internet: www.coloradomtn.edu

Founded 1967

State control

Academic year: May to April

Offers Bachelors degrees in business administration and sustainability studies; 11 campuses

Pres.: Dr STANLEY JENSEN

Sr Vice-Pres.: Dr JILL BOYLE

Sr Vice-Pres. for Academic Affairs: Dr BRAD TYNDALL

Vice-Pres. for Institutional Effectiveness: Dr MEETA GOEL

Vice-Pres. for Student Affairs: BRAD BANKHEAD

Vice-Pres. and Chief Information Officer: SCOTT COWDREY

Number of students: 25,000

COLORADO SCHOOL OF MINES

1500 Illinois St, Golden, CO 80401-1887

Telephone: (303) 273-3000

E-mail: presoffice@mines.edu

Internet: www.mines.edu

Founded 1874

State control

Engineering education and applied science related to earth, energy, materials and environment

Pres.: BILL SCOGGINS

Provost and Exec. Vice-Pres.: Dr TERENCE PARKER

Exec. Vice-Pres. for Finance and Admin.: KIRSTEN VOLPI

Exec. Vice-Pres. for Univ. Advancement: BRIAN WINKELBAUER

Vice-Pres. for Research and Technology Transfer: Dr JOHN POATE

Vice-Pres. for Student Life: Dr DANIEL FOX

Dean for Graduate Studies: Dr THOMAS M. BOYD

Dir for Enrolment Management: HEATHER BOYD

Chief Information Officer: DEREK WILSON

Dir for Library: JOANNE LERUD HECK

Library of 200,000 vols, 900 print journals, 60,000 ejournals, 30,000 ebooks, 500,000 govt publs, 453,000 microforms and 172,000 maps

Number of teachers: 200

Number of students: 5,000

Publications: *Energy and the Earth*, *High Grade* (online, highgrade.mines.edu), *Mines Magazine* (3 a year, online, minesmagazine.com)

COLORADO STATE UNIVERSITY

Fort Collins, CO 80523

Telephone: (970) 491-6444

E-mail: presofc@lamar.colostate.edu

Internet: www.colostate.edu

Founded 1870 as Colorado Agricultural College, current name adopted 1957

State control

Pres.: Dr TONY FRANK

Provost and Exec. Vice-Pres.: Prof. Dr RICK MIRANDA

Vice-Pres. for Advancement: BRETT ANDERSON

Vice-Pres. for Enrolment and Access: Dr ROBIN BROWN

Vice-Pres. for Information Technology and Dean for Libraries: Dr PATRICK J. BURNS

Vice-Pres. for Research: WILLIAM H. FARLAND

Vice-Pres. for Student Affairs: Dr BLANCHE M. HUGHES

Vice-Pres. for Univ. Operations: AMY PARSONS

Library: see under Libraries and Archives

Number of teachers: 1,540

Number of students: 30,450

DEANS

College of Agricultural Sciences: Dr CRAIG BEYROUTY

College of Applied Human Sciences: Dr JEFF McCUBBIN

College of Business: Dr AJAY MENON

College of Engineering: Dr SANDRA WOODS

College of Liberal Arts: Dr ANN M. GILL

College of Natural Sciences: Prof. JANICE L. NERGER

College of Veterinary Medicine and Biomedical Sciences: Dr LANCE PERRYMAN

Warner College of Natural Resources: JOHN P. HAYES

COLORADO STATE UNIVERSITY—PUEBLO

2200 Bonforte Blvd, Pueblo, CO 81001-4901

Telephone: (719) 549-2100

E-mail: info@colostate-pueblo.edu

Internet: www.colostate-pueblo.edu

Founded 1933 as S Colorado Junior College, present status 1965, present name 2003

State control

Pres.: LESLEY A. DI MARE

Provost and Vice-Pres. for Academic Affairs: Dr RICK KREMINSKI

Dean for Student Affairs: Dr ZAV DADABHOY

Dean for Univ. Library: RHONDA GONZALES

Library of 350,000 vols, 12,000 CDs, DVDs and video cassettes, 40,000 print and online journals

Number of teachers: 400 (190 full-time, 210 part-time)

Number of students: 5,250

DEANS

College of Education, Engineering and Professional Studies: Prof. HECTOR R. CARRASCO

College of Humanities and Social Sciences: ROY B. SONNEMA

College of Science and Mathematics: Dr DAVID W. LEHMPUHL

Division of Continuing Education: Dr JAMES MALM

Graduate Studies: Dr MEL DRUELINGER

Hasan School of Business: SUE HANKS

COLORADO TECHNICAL UNIVERSITY

4435 N Chestnut St, Colorado Springs, CO 80907

Telephone: (719) 598-0200

E-mail: help@coloradotech.edu

Internet: www.coloradotech.edu

Founded 1965

Private control

Academic year: October to September

Campuses in Colorado Springs, Denver, Kansas City, Pueblo and Sioux Falls

CEO: JEREMY WHEATON

Chancellor and Chief Academic Officer: Dr DAVID LEASURE

Provost: Dr CONNIE JOHNSON

Vice-Provost: Dr CHRIS DAVIS

Vice-Pres. for Admissions: KEITH ARMSTRONG

Vice-Pres. for Finance: JENNIFER BRIAR

Vice-Pres. for Operations: ERIC STORTZ

Vice-Pres. for Student Affairs: MARK GASCHE

Registrar: ROLAND RUDAS

Librarian: KAY BURMAN

DEANS

College of Business and Management: JOSEPH HEINZMAN, JR

College of Engineering and Computer Science: Dr BRUCE HARMON

DENVER SEMINARY

6399 S Santa Fe Dr., Littleton, CO 80120

Telephone: (303) 761-2482

E-mail: info@denverseminary.edu

Internet: www.denverseminary.edu

Founded 1950

Private control

Academic year: September to May

Pres.: Dr MARK YOUNG

Chancellor: GORDON MACDONALD

Provost and Dean: Dr RANDY MACFARLAND

Vice-Pres. for Advancement: Dr JIM HOWARD

Vice-Pres. for Enrolment Management: BOB FOMER

Vice-Pres. of Finance: DEBBIE KELLAR

Vice-Pres. for Student Services: ROBERT JONES

Dir for Admissions: CHRISTINE MULLER

Registrar: PAM BETKER

Dir for Library: Dr KEITH P. WELLS

Library of 175,000 vols, 250 periodical subscriptions

Number of teachers: 30

Number of students: 1,000

Publications: *Denver Seminary Magazine*, *The Denver Journal*

FORT LEWIS COLLEGE

1000 Rim Dr., Durango, CO 81301-3999

Telephone: (970) 247-7010

E-mail: admission@fortlewis.edu

Internet: www.fortlewis.edu

Founded 1911

State control

Pres.: Dr DENE KAY THOMAS

Provost and Vice-Pres. for Academic Affairs: Dr BARBARA MORRIS

Vice-Pres. for Finance and Admin.: STEVEN SCHWARTZ

Vice-Pres. for Student Affairs: Dr GLENNA WITT SEXTON

Dir for Admission and Advising: ANDREW BURNS

Registrar: KATHY KENDALL

Dir for Library: ASTRID OLIVER

Library of 175,000 vols

Number of teachers: 260

Number of students: 3,700

DEANS

School of Arts, Humanities and Social Sciences: Dr LINDA SCHOTT

School of Business Administration: Dr GARY LINN

School of Natural and Behavioural Sciences: Dr MAUREEN BRANDON

ILIFF SCHOOL OF THEOLOGY

2201 S University Blvd, Denver, CO 80210-4798

Telephone: (303) 744-1287

E-mail: info@iliff.edu

Internet: www.iliff.edu

Founded 1892

Private control

Academic year: September to August

Pres.: DAVID TRICKETT
Academic Vice-Pres. and Dean for Faculty: ALBERT HERNANDEZ
Vice-Pres. for Institutional Advancement: PEGGY SANDGREN
Dean for Enrolment and Student Services: DAVID WORLEY
Registrar: CARMEN BACA DOSTER
Dir for Library and Information Services: Dr DEBORAH CREAMER

Library of 248,000 vols, 900 periodical subsriptions, 56,000 microforms
Number of teachers: 20
Number of students: 300

JONES INTERNATIONAL UNIVERSITY

9697 E Mineral Ave, Centennial, CO 80112
Telephone: (303) 784-8904
E-mail: info@jonesinternational.edu
Internet: www.jiu.edu

Founded 1993
Private control

Pres.: RICHARD COX, JR
Chancellor: GLENN R. JONES
Exec. Vice-Chancellor: BRUCE CUNNINGHAM
Sr Vice-Pres., Admin. and Human Resources: AMY THRALL
Chief Academic Officer: MARIJANE AXTELL PAULSEN
Chief Information Officer: JOHN E. JENNINGS

Library of 45,000 vols of ebooks

DEANS

School of Business: Dr DANETTE LANCE
School of Education: Dr JOANNE MAYPOLE

METROPOLITAN STATE COLLEGE OF DENVER

Auraria Campus, Speer Blvd and Colfax Ave, Denver, CO 80217
Telephone: (303) 556-2400
Internet: www.mscd.edu
State control
Academic year: August to May

Pres.: Dr STEPHEN M. JORDAN
Provost and Vice-Pres. for Academic Affairs: Dr VICKI GOLICH
Vice-Pres. for Admin. and Finance: NATALIE LUTES
Vice-Pres. for Institutional Advancement: Dr ERIN TRAPP
Vice-Pres. for Student Services: Dr KATHLEEN MACKAY
Vice-Pres. for Information Technology: Dr STEVE BEATY
Registrar: PAULA. MARTINEZ
Dean of Library: DAVID GLEIM

Library of 1,000,000 traditional print and media items
Number of teachers: 450 (540 full-time, 910 part-time)
Number of students: 23,600

Publication: *Metrosphere* (1 a year)

DEANS

School of Business: Dr ANN MURPHY
School of Letters, Arts and Sciences: Dr JOAN LAURA FOSTER
School of Professional Studies: Dr SANDRA D. HAYNES.

BRANCH CAMPUSES

MSU Denver North Campus: Suite 102, 11990 Grant St, Northglenn, CO 80233; tel. (303) 450-5111.

MSU Denver South Campus: Suite 100, 5660 Greenwood Plaza Blvd, Greenwood Village, CO 80111; tel. (303) 721-1313

NAROPA UNIVERSITY

2130 Arapahoe Ave, Boulder, CO 80302
Telephone: (303) 444-0202
E-mail: infodesk@naropa.edu
Internet: www.naropa.edu

Founded 1974 as Naropa Institute
Private control
Academic year: August to July (3 semesters)

BAs in contemplative psychology, early childhood education, environmental studies, interdisciplinary studies, music, religious studies, traditional eastern arts, visual arts and writing and literature, fine arts in performance; MAs in contemplative education, creative writing, divinity, environmental leadership, fine arts, Indo-Tibetan Buddhism, religious studies, counselling psychology (contemplative, somatic transpersonal), writing and poetics

Pres.: JOHN WHITEHOUSE COBB (acting)
Provost and Vice-Pres. for Academic Affairs: Dr CAROL A. BLACKSHIRE-BELAY
Vice-Pres. for Student Affairs and Enrolment Management: CHERYL BARBOUR
Dir for Library and Archives: NICHOLAS WEISS

Library of 26,000 vols, 100 periodicals; spec. collns incl. 15,000 original Tibetan texts in 2,200 vols, 6,000 audiocassette recordings of events held at Naropa Univ.
Number of students: 1,060 445 undergraduate, 618 graduate)

NATIONAL THEATRE CONSERVATORY

1101 13th St, Denver, CO 80204-2154
Telephone: (303) 893-4000
E-mail: ntc@dcpa.org
Internet: www.denvercenter.org

Founded 1984; attached to Denver Center for the Performing Arts
Private control

Area of study: fine arts

Pres. of Denver Center for the Performing Arts: RANDY WEEKS
Dir for Education and Dean: DANIEL RENNER
Registrar: KATE AMBERG
Librarian: LINDA ELLER

Library of 30,000 single scripts and anthologies

NAZARENE BIBLE COLLEGE

1111 Academy Park Loop, Colorado Springs, CO 80910-3704
Telephone: (719) 884-5000
E-mail: info@nbc.edu
Internet: www.nbc.edu

Founded 1964
Private control
Languages of instruction: English, Spanish
Academic year: September to May

Pres.: Dr HAROLD B. GRAVES, JR
Vice-Pres. for Academic Affairs: Dr GARY W. STREIT
Vice-Pres. for Finance: J. MIKE ARRAMBIDE
Dean for Online Education: Dr ALAN D. LYKE
Registrar: Dr JAY W. OTT
Library Dir: Prof. ANN M. ATTIG

Number of teachers: 155 (9 full-time, 146 part-time)
Number of students: 3,020 (1,410 online, 1,610 on campus)

Publication: *Voice and Vision*

REGIS UNIVERSITY

3333 Regis Blvd, Denver, CO 80221-1099
Telephone: (303) 458-4126
E-mail: enrolsvc@regis.edu
Internet: www.regis.edu

Founded 1877 as Las Vegas College, present name 1921
Private control
Academic year: August to August
Campuses in Aurora, Broomfield, Colorado Springs, Englewood, Fort Collins and Longmont in Colorado, and Las Vegas in Nevada

Pres.: MICHAEL J. SHEERAN
Vice-Pres. for Academic Affairs: PATRICIA LADEWIG
Vice-Pres. for Univ. Relations: JULIE CROCKETT
Dir for Admissions: VIC DAVOLT
Dean for Libraries: IVAN GAETZ

Library of 260,000 vols, 2,500 periodicals
Number of teachers: 270
Number of students: 14,600 (7,119 undergraduate, 7,490 graduate)

Publications: *Human Development Magazine* (2 a year), *Regis University Magazine* (2 a year)

DEANS

College for Professional Studies: Dr HEINZ BUSCHANG (acting)
Regis College: PAUL D. EWALD
Rueckert-Hartman College for Health Professions: Prof. Dr JANET L. HOUSER

ROCKY MOUNTAIN COLLEGE OF ART AND DESIGN

1600 Pierce St, Denver, CO 80214
Telephone: (303) 753-6046
E-mail: admissions@rmcad.edu
Internet: www.rmcad.edu

Founded 1963
Private control

Courses in animation, art education, communications design (graphic design), fine arts, game art, illustration, interior design; online degree programmes

Pres. and Provost: Dr MARIA PUZIFERRO
Dean for Academics: Dr KIKI GILDERHUS

Library of 14,000 vols, 8,700 digital images, 100,000 digital art and design images, 1,700 DVDs
Number of teachers: 45 (full-time)
Number of students: 600

UNITED STATES AIR FORCE ACADEMY

2304 Cadet Dr., Suite 320, Colorado Springs, CO 80840-5016
Telephone: (719) 333-2990
Internet: www.usafa.af.mil

Founded 1954
State control

Divs of basic sciences, engineering, humanities, social sciences

Superintendent: Lt Gen. MICHAEL C. GOULD
Vice-Superintendent: Col TAMRA RANK
Dean for Faculty: Brig. Gen. DANA H. BORN

Library of 1,898,549 vols
Number of teachers: 600
Number of students: 4,000

UNIVERSITY OF COLORADO

1800 Grant St, Suite 800, Denver, CO 80203
Telephone: (303) 860-5600
E-mail: officeofthepresident@cu.edu
Internet: www.cu.edu

Founded 1876
State control

Pres.: BRUCE D. BENSON
Sr Vice-Pres. and Chief of Staff: LEONARD DINEGAR
Vice-Pres. and Academic Affairs Officer: KATHLEEN BOLLARD

Vice-Pres. and Chief Financial Officer: KELLY FOX
Vice-Pres. and Univ. Counsel: DANIEL J. WILKERSON
Vice-Pres. for Communication: KEN MCCON-NELLOGUE
Vice-Pres. for Govt Relations: TANYA MARES KELLY-BOWRY

Number of teachers: 4,300
Number of students: 57,739 (all campuses)...

CONSTITUENT CAMPUSES

University of Colorado at Boulder

Boulder, CO 80309
Telephone: (303) 492-1411
E-mail: homepage@colorado.edu
Internet: www.colorado.edu
Founded 1877

Chancellor: PHILIP P. DiSTEFANO
Provost and Exec. Vice-Chancellor for Academic Affairs: RUSSELL MOORE
Sr Vice-Chancellor and Chief Financial Officer: RIC PORRECA
Vice-Chancellor for Admin.: JEFFREY LIPTON
Vice-Chancellor for Diversity, Equity and Community Engagement: ROBERT BOSWELL
Vice-Chancellor for Research: STEIN STURE
Vice-Chancellor for Student Affairs: DEB COFFIN
Registrar: BARBARA TODD
Dean for Students: KAREN RAFORTH
Dean for Libraries: JAMES WILLIAMS, II
Library: see Libraries and Archives
Number of teachers: 3,800 (2,723 full-time, 1,076 part-time)
Number of students: 29,900 (24,770 undergraduate, 5,130 graduate)
Publications: *Arctic and Alpine Research* (4 a year), *Colorado Alumnus* (10 a year), *Colorado Arts & Sciences Magazine* (4 a year, online (artsandsciences.colorado.edu/magazine)), *Colorado Business Review* (12 a year), *Colorado Engineer*, *Colorado Journal of International Environmental Law and Policy* (2 a year), *English Language Notes*, *Journal on Telecommunications and High Technology Law*, *University of Colorado Law Review* (4 a year)

DEANS

College of Architecture and Planning: MARK GELERNTER
College of Arts and Sciences: TODD GLEESON
College of Engineering and Applied Science: ROBERT DAVIS
College of Music: DANIEL SHER
Continuing Education and Professional Studies: ANNE HEINZ
Graduate School: JOHN A. STEVENSON
Leeds School of Business: DAVID IKENBERRY
School of Education: LORRIE SHEPARD
School of Law: PHILIP J. WEISER

University of Colorado at Colorado Springs

1420 Austin Bluffs Pkwy, Colorado Springs, CO 80918
Telephone: (719) 255-8227
E-mail: ugapp@uccs.edu
Internet: www.uccs.edu

Chancellor: Prof. Dr PAMELA S. SHOCKLEY-ZALABAK
Provost and Exec. Vice-Chancellor for Academic Affairs: MARGARET A. BACON
Vice-Chancellor for Admin. and Finance: BRIAN D. BURNETT
Vice-Chancellor for Student Success and Enrolment Management: HOMER WESLEY
Vice-Chancellor for Univ. Advancement: MARTIN WOOD
Registrar: JOHN SALNAITIS
Dean for Library: Prof. TERI R. SWITZER

Library of 408,018 vols, 451,923 microforms, 396,572 govt documents/maps, 9,720 audiovisual items
Number of teachers: 510
Number of students: 13,500

DEANS

Beth-El College of Nursing and Health Sciences: Dr NANCY SMITH
College of Business and Administration: Dr VENKATESHWAR REDDY
College of Education: Dr MARY L. SNYDER
College of Engineering and Applied Science: Dr R. DANDAPANI
College of Letters, Arts and Sciences: Dr THOMAS M. CHRISTIENSEN
Graduate School: Dr JENENNE P. NELSON

University of Colorado at Denver and Health Sciences Center

POB 173364, Denver, CO 80217-3364
1250 14th St, Denver, CO 80217
Telephone: (303) 556-2400
E-mail: registrar@ucdenver.edu
Internet: www.ucdenver.edu
Founded 1912, present name and status 2009

Chancellor: JERRY WARTGOW
Exec. Vice-Chancellor for Anschutz Medical Campus: LILLY MARKS
Provost and Vice-Chancellor for Academic and Student Affairs: RODERICK NAIRN
Vice-Chancellor for Admin. and Finance: JEFFREY PARKER
Vice-Chancellor for Research: RICHARD J. TRAYSTMAN
Dean for Faculty: J. C. BOSCH
Univ. Librarian: MARY M. SOMERVILLE
Number of teachers: 4,500
Number of students: 29,000 (incl. Denver, Aurora and online)
Publication: *The EDition*

DEANS

Business School: SUEANN AMBRON
College of Architecture and Planning: Prof. MARK GELERNTER
College of Arts and Media: Dr DAVID DYNAK
College of Engineering and Applied Science: Dr MARC INGBER
College of Liberal Arts and Sciences: Prof. Dr DANIEL J. HOWARD
College of Nursing: Dr PATRICIA MORITZ
Colorado School of Public Health: Dr JUDITH ALBINO
Graduate School: BARRY SHUR
School of Dental Medicine: Dr DENISE KASSE-BAUM
School of Education and Human Development: Dr REBECCA KANTOR
School of Medicine: Dr RICHARD D. KRUGMAN
Skaggs School of Pharmacy and Pharmaceutical Sciences: RALPH ALTIERE
School of Public Affairs: Prof. PAUL TESKE

UNIVERSITY OF DENVER

2199 S University Blvd, Denver, CO 80208
Telephone: (303) 871-2000
Internet: www.du.edu
Founded 1864 as Colorado Seminary, present name 1880
Private control
Academic year: September to May

Chancellor: ROBERT COOMBE
Provost: GREGG KVISTAD
Vice-Chancellor for Business and Financial Affairs: CRAIG W. WOODY
Vice-Chancellor for Enrolment Services: THOMAS F. WILLOUGHBY
Vice-Chancellor for Univ. Advancement: SCOTT LUMPKIN
Vice-Chancellor for Univ. Communications: KEVIN CARROLL

Registrar: DENNIS BECKER
Dean and Dir for Library: NANCY ALLEN
Library of 1,897,000 vols
Number of teachers: 640 (full-time)
Number of students: 11,800 (5,450 undergraduate, 6,350 graduate)
Publications: *Denver Law Journal* (4 a year), *Denver Law Journal of International Law and Policy* (4 a year, online —djilp.org), *Family Law Quarterly*, *GSSW Magazine* (2 a year), *The Centre Report* (4 a year), *The University of Denver Law Review*, *The University of Denver Water Law Review* (2 a year, online —law.du.edu/index.php/university-of-denver-water-law-review), *Transportation Law Journal* (3 a year, online —law.du.edu/index.php/transportation-law-journal), *University of Denver Magazine* (4 a year, print and online —blogs.du.edu/today/content/magazine)

DEANS

Daniels College of Business: Prof. Dr CHRISTINE RIORDAN
Division of Arts, Humanities and Social Sciences: ANNE MCCALL
Division of Natural Sciences and Mathematics: ANDREI KUTATELADZE
Graduate School of Professional Psychology: Prof. PETER BUIRSKI
Graduate School of Social Work: Dr JAMES HERBERT WILLIAMS
Josef Korbel School of International Studies: CHRISTOPHER ROBERT HILL
Morgridge College of Education: Dr GREGORY ANDERSON
School of Engineering and Computer Science: MICHAEL KEABLES
Sturm College of Law: MARTIN J. KATZ
University College of Professional and Continuing Education: JAMES R. DAVIS
Women's College: Dr LYNN M. GANGONE

UNIVERSITY OF NORTHERN COLORADO

501 20 St, Greeley, CO 80639
1862 10th Ave, Greeley, CO 80639
Telephone: (970) 351-1890
E-mail: admissions@unco.edu
Internet: www.unco.edu
Founded 1889 as State Normal School, present name 1970
State control
Academic year: August to May (2 semesters)

Pres.: KAY NORTON
Provost and Sr Vice-Pres.: ROBBYN WACKER (acting)
Sr Vice-Pres. for Finance and Admin.: MICHELLE QUINN
Vice-Pres. for Devt and Alumni Relations: VICTORIA L. GORRELL
Vice-Pres. and Gen. Counsel: DAN SATRIANA
Vice-Pres. for Univ. Relations: CHARLES LEONHARDT
Dean for Students: Dr KATRINA RODRIGUEZ
Registrar: CHARLIE COUCH
Dean for Libraries: HELEN REED
Library: 1.5m. vols
Number of teachers: 700 (490 full-time, 210 part-time)
Number of students: 12,500 (10,231 undergraduate, 2,269 graduate)

DEANS

College of Education and Behavioural Sciences: Dr EUGENE P. SHEEHAN
College of Humanities and Social Sciences: DAVID CALDWELL
College of Natural and Health Sciences: DENISE A. BATTLES
College of Performing and Visual Arts: Dr ANDREW JAY SVEDLOW

Monfort College of Business: DONALD GUD-
MUNDSON
University College: Dr THOMAS SMITH

UNIVERSITY OF THE ROCKIES

555 E Pikes Peak Ave, Colorado Springs, CO
80903-3612

Telephone: (719) 442-0505
E-mail: admissions@rockies.edu
Internet: www.rockies.edu

Founded 1998 as Colorado School of Profes-
sional Psychology, present name 2007
Private control
Pres.: Dr CHARLITA SHELTON
Provost: Dr TINA J. PARSCAL
Vice-Pres.: Dr ROBERT EDELBROCK
Vice-Pres. for Academic Affairs, Online: Dr
LINDA HIEMER
Dir for Online Admissions: ADAM FORREST
Dean for Research: DEBORA SCHEFFEL
Dir for Student Services: Dr SERENE PRITCH-
ETT
Registrar: ERIK GASKILL
Library Dir: TRINA PURCELL

Library of 3,000 vols

DEANS

School of Organizational Leadership: Dr J.
STEPHEN KIRKPATRICK
School of Professional Psychology: Dr DAVID
STEPHENS

WESTERN STATE COLLEGE OF COLORADO

600 N Adams St, Gunnison, CO 81231

Telephone: (970) 943-0120
E-mail: admissions@western.edu
Internet: www.western.edu

Founded 1901, fmrly Colorado State Normal
School, present name 1923
State control

Depts of accounting, anthropology, art, biology, business administration, chemistry,
communication and theatre, computer infor-
mation science, economics, education, Eng-
lish, environmental studies, exercise and
sport science, French, geography, geology,
history, mathematics, music, philosophy,
physics, politics and government, psychology,
recreation and outdoor education, sociology,
Spanish
Pres.: Dr JAY W. HELMAN
Vice-Pres. for Academic Affairs: Prof. JESSICA
YOUNG
Vice-Pres. for Finance and Admin.: BRAD
BACA
Vice-Pres. for Student Affairs and Dean for
Students: GARY PIERSON
Dir for Admissions and Assoc. Vice-Pres. for
Enrolment Services: TIM ALBERS
Registrar: DEBRA CLARK
Library Dir: NANCY GAUSS

Library of 435,000 vols, 700 periodicals,
1,461 video cassettes; spec. colln of books
and govt documents about Colorado
Number of teachers: 145
Number of students: 2,300

CONNECTICUT

ALBERTUS MAGNUS COLLEGE

700 Prospect St, New Haven, CT 06511-1189
Telephone: (203) 773-8550
E-mail: admissions@albertus.edu
Internet: www.albertus.edu
Founded 1925
Private control
Academic year: August to May

Offers bachelor degree in arts, science, fine
arts; graduate programmes incl. art therapy,
business and management, education, lead-
ership, liberal studies
Pres.: Dr JULIA M. MCNAMARA
Provost and Vice-Pres. for Academic Affairs:
Dr JOHN J. DONOHUE
Vice-Pres. for Devt and Alumni Relations:
CAROLYN BEHAN KRAUS
Vice-Pres. for Finance and Treas.: JEANNE
MANN
Vice-Pres. for Institutional Advancement
and Planning: ROBERT J. BUCCINO
Dean for Admissions and Financial Aid:
RICHARD J. LOLATTE
Dean for Student Services: MAUREEN V.
MORRISON
Registrar: CLAUDIA A. SCHIAVONE
Dir for Library and Information Services:
ANNE LEENEY-PANAGROSSI
Library of 100,000 vols, 650 periodical titles,
2,000 audiovisual titles, 24,316 ejournals,
54,108 ebooks
Number of teachers: 75
Number of students: 2,250

CENTRAL CONNECTICUT STATE UNIVERSITY

1615 Stanley St, New Britain, CT 06050
Telephone: (860) 832-2278
E-mail: admissions@ccsu.edu
Internet: www.ccsu.edu
Founded 1849 as New Britain Normal
School, present name and status 1983
State control
Academic year: September to May
Pres.: Prof. Dr JACK W. MILLER
Provost and Vice-Pres. for Academic Affairs:
Dr CARL R. LOVITT
Vice-Pres. for Institutional Advancement:
CHRISTOPHER J. GALLIGAN
Vice-Pres. for Student Affairs: Dr LAURA
TORDENTI
Chief Admin. Officer: Dr RICHARD R. BACHOO
Chief Financial Officer: CHARLENE CASA-
MENTO
Chief Information Officer: JAMES ESTRADA
Dean of Students: JANE M. HIGGINS
Registrar: SUSAN PETROSINO
Dir of Library Services: CARL ANTONUCCI
Library of 665,605 vols, 3,000 periodicals,
govt docs, Polish Heritage Colln of 17,000
vols
Number of teachers: 970 (440 full-time, 530
part-time)
Number of students: 12,500 (10,080 under-
graduate, 2,420 graduate)

DEANS

Carol A. Ammon School of Arts and Sciences:
Dr SUSAN E. PEASE
School of Business: Dr SIAMACK SHOJAI (act-
ing)
School of Education and Professional Stud-
ies: Dr MITCHELL SAKOFS
School of Engineering and Technology: Prof.
Dr ZDZISLAW B. KREMENS
School of Graduate Studies: Prof. Dr PAUL-
ETTE A. LEMMA

CHARTER OAK STATE COLLEGE

55 Paul J. Manafort Dr., New Britain, CT
06053-2150
Telephone: (860) 515-3800
E-mail: admissions@charteroak.edu
Internet: www.cosc.edu
Founded 1973
State control
Offers bachelors degree in arts and science,
business, health care, public safety, informa-
tion systems

Pres.: ED KLONOSKI
Provost: Dr SHIRLEY M. ADAMS
Chief Financial and Admin. Officer: CLIFFORD
S. WILLIAMS
Academic Dean of Undergraduate Pro-
grammes: Dr DANA A. WILKIE
Dean of Marketing and Enrolment Services:
HARRY E. WHITE
Dean and Chief Information Officer: GEORGE
F. CLAFFEY, JR
Registrar: JENNIFER WASHINGTON
Number of students: 2,300

CONNECTICUT COLLEGE

270 Mohegan Ave, New London, CT 06320-
4196
Telephone: (860) 447-1911
E-mail: admission@conncoll.edu
Internet: www.conncoll.edu
Founded 1911
Academic year: August to May
Centres of arts and technology, environment,
int. studies and liberal arts, public policy and
community action, race and ethnicity
Pres.: Dr KATHERINE BERGERON
Vice-Pres. for Admin.: ULYSSES B. HAMMOND
Vice-Pres. for Advancement: CLAIRE GADROW
(acting)
Vice-Pres. for College Relations: PATRICIA M.
CAREY
Vice-Pres. for Information Services and Col-
lege Librarian: Dr W. LEE HISLE
Vice-Pres. for Finance: PAUL MARONI
Provost and Dean for the Faculty: Prof.
ROGER BROOKS
Dean for Admissions and Financial Aid:
MARTHA C. MERRILL
Dean for College: CAROLYN DENARD
Dean for Freshman: ANDREA REDER-ROSSI
Dean for Multicultural Affairs: ELIZABETH
GARCIA
Dean for Religious and Spiritual Life: CLAU-
DIA HIGHBAUGH
Dean for Sophomores and Int. Student
Adviser: CARMELA PATTON
Dean for Student Life: VICTOR ARCELUS
Dean for Studies: THERESA AMMIRATI
Registrar: BETH LABRIOLA
Library of 555,578 vols, 438,170 govt docu-
ments, 94,710 audiovisual items, 1,325
journals and 6,675 ejournals
Number of teachers: 180 (full-time)
Number of students: 1,900
Publication: CC (4 a year)

EASTERN CONNECTICUT STATE UNIVERSITY

83 Windham St, Willimantic, CT 06226-2295
Telephone: (860) 465-5000
E-mail: admissions@easternct.edu
Internet: www.easternct.edu
Founded 1889, refounded as Willimantic
State College 1959, present name 1983
State control
Academic year: August to May
Pres.: Dr ELSA M. NÚÑEZ
Exec. Vice-Pres.: Dr MICHAEL PERNAL
Vice-Pres. for Academic Affairs: Dr RHONA
FREE
Vice-Pres. for Finance and Admin.: JAMES R.
HOWARTH
Vice-Pres. for Institutional Advancement:
KENNETH J. DELISA
Vice-Pres. for Student Affairs: Dr KENNETH
M. BEDINI
Dean of Students: WALTER DIAZ
Registrar: JENNIFER HUOPPI
Dir of Admissions: CHRISTOPHER DORSEY
Dir of Library Services: PATRICIA S. BANACH
Library of 311,320 vols

Number of teachers: 360 (184 full-time, 176 part-time)
Number of students: 5,600

DEANS

School of Arts and Sciences: Prof. Dr CARMEN R. CID
School of Continuing Education: Dr SHELLY GIMÉNEZ
School of Educational and Professional Studies: Dr JAIME GOMEZ

FAIRFIELD UNIVERSITY

1073 N Benson Rd, Fairfield, CT 06824-5171
Telephone: (203) 254-4000
E-mail: admis@fairfield.edu
Internet: www.fairfield.edu

Founded 1942
Private control
Language of instruction: English
Academic year: September to May

Pres.: Rev. JEFFREY P. VON ARX
Sr Vice-Pres. for Academic Affairs: Dr PAUL J. FITZGERALD
Sr Vice-Pres. for Admin. and Chief of Staff: Dr MARK C. REED
Vice-Pres. for Finance and Treas.: MICHAEL TRAFECANTE
Vice-Pres. for Student Affairs: Dr THOMAS C. PELLEGRINO
Exec. Vice-Pres.: KEVIN LAWLOR
Dean for Admissions: KAREN PELLEGRINO
Dean for Students: KAREN DONOGHUE
Registrar: ROBERT C. RUSSO
Dir for Library Services and Librarian: JOAN OVERFIELD

Library of 376,085 vols, 945,121 microforms, 22,539 audiovisual items, 72,132 periodicals
Number of teachers: 590 (254 full-time, 336 part-time)
Number of students: 4,900 (3,860 undergraduates, 1,040 graduates)

DEANS

Charles F. Dolan School of Business: Dr DONALD E. GIBSON
College of Arts and Sciences: Dr ROBBIN CRABTREE
Graduate School of Education and Allied Professions: Dr FAITH-ANNE DOHM
School of Engineering: Dr BRUCE W. BERDANIER
School of Nursing: Dr LYNN BABINGTON

PROFESSORS

Charles F. Dolan School of Business:
  CAMPBELL, G., Information Systems
  CASTER, P., Accounting
  CHAUDHURI, A., Marketing
  CONINE, T., Finance
  DAY, R., Management
  HE, J., Information Systems
  KOUTMOS, G., Finance
  MAINIERO, L., Management
  MASSEY, D., Accounting
  MCEVOY, S., Management
  SCHERAGA, C., Management
  SOLOMON, N., Management
  TROMLEY, C., Management
  TUCKER, M., Finance
  VAN HISE, J., Accounting
College of Arts and Sciences:
  BERNHARDT, C., Mathematics and Computer Science
  BOQUET, E., English
  BOWEN, B., English
  BRAGINSKY, D., Psychology
  BRAUN, P., Biology
  BROUSSEAU, D., Biology
  BUCKI, C., History
  CAMPOS, J., Modern Languages
  CASSIDY, K., Politics

COLEMAN, M., Mathematics and Computer Science
DENNIN, J., Mathematics and Computer Science
DEWITT, W., Philosophy
ELIASOPH, P., Visual and Performing Arts
FINE, B., Mathematics and Computer Science
FRANCESCHI, D., Economics
GANNETT, C., English
HENKEL, L., Psychology
HODGSON, D., Sociology
HUMPHREY, H., Religious Studies
KEENAN, D., Philosophy
LAKELAND, P., Religious Studies
LEATHERMAN, J., Politics
LECLAIR, M., Economics
LI, D., History
LOMONACO, M., Visual and Performing Arts
LONG, R., Philosophy
MCFADDEN, D., History
MINERS, L., Economics
MULVEY, I., Mathematics and Computer Science
NANTZ, K., Economics
O'CONNELL, E., Chemistry
O'CONNOR, L., English
PATTON, M., Politics
PHELAN, S., Biology
PRIMAVERA, J., Psychology
RAJAN, G., English
ROSENFELD, G., History
ROSIVACH, V., Classical Studies
SALAFIA, W., Psychology
SAWIN, S., Mathematics and Computer Science
SCHLICHTING, K., Sociology
SCHWAB, K., Visual and Performing Arts
SIMON, J., English
THIEL, J., Religious Studies
TORFF, B., Visual and Performing Arts
UMANSKY, E., Religious Studies
WEISS, J., Mathematics and Computer Science
WHITE, M., English
WILLIAMS, Y., History
WINN, D., Physics
YARRINGTON, K., Visual and Performing Arts
Graduate School of Education and Allied Professions:
  CALDERWOOD, P., Education Studies and Teacher Preparation
  DOHM, F., Psychology and Education Consultation
  HULSE, D., Counsellor Education
  KOHLI, W., Curriculum and Instruction
School of Engineering:
  HADJIMICHAEL, E.
  HOFFMAN, H.
  LYON, D.
  ZABINSKI, M.
School of Nursing:
  GROSSMAN, S.
  HOFFMAN, H.
  MURPHY, M.
  WHEELER, K.

GOODWIN COLLEGE

1 Riverside Dr., East Hartford, CT 06118
Telephone: (860) 528-4111
Internet: www.goodwin.edu

Founded 1999, present status 2004
Private control
Language of instruction: English
Academic year: August to August

Offers bachelor programmes in business administration, child study, environmental studies, health science, human services, nursing, organizational studies

Pres.: MARK SCHEINBERG

Exec. Vice-Pres. and Provost: ANN CLARK
Vice-Pres. for Academic Affairs: JUDITH D. ZIMMERMAN
Vice-Pres. for Enrolment Services: DANIEL NOONAN
Vice-Pres. for Finance and Chief Financial Officer: JERRY EMLET
Vice-Pres. for Governmental Relations: TODD ANDREWS
Vice-Pres. for Institutional Advancement: BROOKE PENDERS
Vice-Pres. for Institutional Effectiveness: JANET JEFFORD
Registrar: ALLISON MISKY
Dean for Faculty: Dr HENRIETTE PRANGER
Dean for Students: Dr SANDY WIRTH
Library Dir: MARILYN NOWLAN

Number of teachers: 290 (65 full-time, 225 part-time)
Number of students: 3,300

Publication: *Goodwin Magazine*

HARTFORD SEMINARY

77 Sherman St, Hartford, CT 06105-2260
Telephone: (860) 509-9500
E-mail: info@hartsem.edu
Internet: www.hartsem.edu

Founded 1913 by merger of Hartford Theological Seminary, Hartford School of Religious Education and Kennedy School of Missions; present name 1981
Private control
Academic year: September to June

Hartford Institute for Religion Research, Duncan Black Macdonald Center for the Study of Islam and Christian-Muslim Relations

Pres.: Dr HEIDI HADSELL
Dean: Dr URIAH KIM
Academic Dean: Prof. Dr JAMES NIEMAN
Chief Devt Officer: JONATHAN LEE
Registrar and Dir of Academic Services: KAREN ROLLINS
Library Dir: Dr STEVEN BLACKBURN

Library of 72,000 vols, 305 periodicals

Publication: *The Muslim World* (4 a year)

HOLY APOSTLES COLLEGE & SEMINARY

33 Prospect Hill Rd, Cromwell, CT 06416-2027
Telephone: (860) 632-3010
E-mail: admissions@holyapostles.edu
Internet: www.holyapostles.edu

Founded 1956 as Holy Apostles Seminary; present name 1972
Private control
Academic year: August to May

Offers BA degree programmes in liberal arts, MA degree in pastoral studies, philosophy, theology

Chancellor: Most Rev. MICHAEL R. COTE
Pres. and Rector: Very Rev. DOUGLAS L. MOSEY
Vice-Rector: Rev. Dr JOHN HILLIER
Vice-Pres. for Academic Affairs: Rev. Dr GREGOIRE J. FLUET
Vice-Pres. for Admin. Affairs: Dr JAMES F. PAPILLO
Registrar: Dr CYNTHIA TOOLIN
Dir of Library Services: CLARE ADAMO

Library of 60,000 vols, 200 newspapers, journals and periodicals

LINCOLN COLLEGE OF NEW ENGLAND

2279 Mt Vernon Rd, Southington, CT 06489
Telephone: (860) 628-4751
Internet: www.lincolncollegene.edu

Founded 2009 by merger of Clemens College and Briarwood College

Private control

Academic year: August to August

Campuses in Hartford, Suffield; offers bachelor degree programmes in criminal justice, funeral service management, health information admin.

Pres.: Dr KATHRYN S. REGJO

Vice-Pres. for Academic Affairs: Dr VINCE BEACH

Vice-Pres. for Career Services: BOB McNAMARA

Vice-Pres. for Operations and Student Affairs: SPENCER W. McNIVEN

Assoc. Dean for Academic Affairs: MARK ANDERSON

Dir for Admissions: JOHN J. ALONSO

Chief Financial Officer: DENISE LEWICKI

Registrar: STEPHANIE CROMBIE

Number of students: 720

LYME ACADEMY COLLEGE OF FINE ARTS

84 Lyme St, Old Lyme, CT 06371

Telephone: (860) 434-5232

E-mail: admissions@lymeacademy.edu

Internet: www.lymeacademy.edu

Founded 1976

Private control

Academic year: August to May

Offers bachelor of fine arts degrees in drawing, illustration, painting, sculpture

Pres. and CEO: SCOTT COLLEY

Vice-Pres. for Academic Affairs and Interim Dean: SALLY SEAMAN

Vice-Pres. for Devt: FRITZ JELLINGHAUS

Registrar: STEVE PODESZWA

Dir for Admissions: MICHAEL HAYES

Number of students: 85

MITCHELL COLLEGE

437 Pequot Ave, New London, CT 06320

Telephone: (860) 701-5000

E-mail: admissions@mitchell.edu

Internet: www.mitchell.edu

Founded 1938

Private control

Academic year: August to May

Offers bachelors degree in arts, science

Pres.: Dr MARY ELLEN JUKOSKI

Vice-Pres. for Academic Affairs and Dean of College: Dr LAURENCE M. CONNER

Vice-Pres. for Student Affairs and Dean of Students: DIANE MILLER

Registrar: KEVIN P. KELLY

Dir of Library and Information Services: SUZANNE BARTELS

Number of students: 950 (805 full-time, 145 part-time)

PAIER COLLEGE OF ART, INC.

20 Gorham Ave Hamden, CT 06514-3902

Telephone: (203) 287-3031

E-mail: admissions@paiercollegeofart.edu

Internet: www.paiercollegeofart.edu

Founded 1946 as Paier School of Applied Art, present name and status 1982

Private control

Academic year: August to May (2 semesters)

Courses incl. fine arts, graphic design, illustration, interior design, photography

Pres.: JONATHAN E. PAIER

Vice-Pres. and Dean of Admissions: DANIEL LEWIS PAIER

Dean of College: FRANCIS REXFORD COOLEY

Dir for Admin. Services: ANGELA DeROSE

Librarian: BETH R. HARRIS

POST UNIVERSITY

POB 2540, 800 Country Club Rd, Waterbury, CT 06723-2540

Telephone: (203) 596-4500

E-mail: admissions@post.edu

Internet: www.post.edu

Founded 1890 as Matoon Shorthand School, present name and status 2004

Private control

Academic year: September to May

Pres. and CEO: Dr TOM SAMPH

Provost: Dr DONALD MROZ

Vice-Pres. for Academic Affairs: Dr WILLIAM H. McDONALD

Vice-Pres. for Finance and Admin.: SCOTT T. ALLEN

Dean of Students: ERICA KLUGE

Dir for Admissions: JAY E. MURRAY

Registrar: KEITH GAUVIN

Library Dir: TRACY A. RALSTON

Library of 61,116 vols, 10,943 govt documents, 400 periodicals

Number of teachers: 220 (40 full-time, 180 part-time)

Number of students: 860

DEANS

John P. School of Public Service: RICHARD STROMPF

Post College: JAMES F. NARDOZZI (acting)

School of Business: Dr DONALD MROZ

School of Education: JANE BAILEY

QUINNIPIAC UNIVERSITY

275 Mount Carmel Ave, Hamden, CT 06518-1908

Telephone: (203) 582-8600

E-mail: admissions@quinnipiac.edu

Internet: www.quinnipiac.edu

Founded 1929

Private control

Academic year: June to May

Pres.: JOHN L. LAHEY

Sr Vice-Pres. for Academic and Student Affairs: MARK THOMPSON

Sr Vice-Pres. for Admin.: RICHARD FERGUSON

Sr Vice-Pres. for Finance: PATRICK HEALY

Vice-Pres. and Dean of Admissions: JOHN ISAAC MOHR

Vice-Pres. and Dean of Students: MANUEL CARREIRO

Vice-Pres. for Devt and Alumni Affairs: DONALD WEINBACH

Vice-Pres. for Public Affairs: LYNN BUSHNELL

Registrar: DOROTHY LAURIA

Dean of Graduate Student Affairs: GINA FRANK

Library Dir: CHARLES M. GETCHELL, JR

Library of 466,000 vols

Number of teachers: 670 (350 full-time, 320 part-time)

Number of students: 8,400

Publications: *Quinnipiac Magazine* (2 a year), *Quinnipiac Law Magazine* (2 a year), *Quinnipiac University Business Magazine* (2 a year)

DEANS

College of Arts and Sciences: Dr JOHANNES BERGMANN

Frank H. Netter, M. D., School of Medicine: Dr BRUCE KOEPPEN

School of Business: MATTHEW L. O'CONNOR

School of Communications: LEE KAMLET

School of Education: CYNTHIA DUBEA

School of Health Sciences: Dr EDWARD R. O'CONNOR

School of Law: Dr BRAD SAXTON

School of Nursing: Dr JEAN LANGE

RENSSELAER AT HARTFORD

275 Windsor St, Hartford, CT 06120-2910

Telephone: (860) 548-2400

E-mail: info@ewp.rpi.edu

Internet: www.ewp.rpi.edu

Founded 1955; attached to Rensselaer Polytechnic Institute, New York

Private control

Academic year: September to July (3 terms)

Offers MA in computer science, engineering and information technology, management; computer science and engineering graduate certificate programmes

Vice-Pres. and Dean: JOHN A. MINASIAN

Vice-Provost and Dean: LESTER GERHARDT

Dean for Admin.: Dr DAVID L. RAINEY (acting)

Registrar: DORIS M. MATSIKAS

Library Dir: MARY S. DIXEY

Library of 44,000 vols, 490 periodicals, 400 journals and 36,000 ejournals

Number of teachers: 135 (35 full-time, 100 part-time)

Number of students: 2,100

SACRED HEART UNIVERSITY

5151 Park Ave, Fairfield, CT 06825-1000

Telephone: (203) 371-7999

E-mail: enroll@sacredheart.edu

Internet: www.sacredheart.edu

Founded 1963

Private control

Campuses in Fairfield, Griswold, Ireland, Luxembourg, Stamford, Trumbull

Pres.: Dr JOHN J. PETILLO

Sr Vice-Pres. for Finance and Admin.: MICHAEL J. KINNEY

Sr Vice-Pres. for Student Affairs and Athletics: JAMES M. BARQUINERO

Provost and Vice-Pres. for Academic Affairs: Dr LAURA NIESEN DE ABRUNA

Vice-Pres. for Strategic Planning and Admin.: Dr DAVID L. COPPOLA

Vice-Pres. for Univ. Advancement: MEGAN ROCK

Dean of Students: LARRY WIELK

Registrar: DONNA J. PERRONE

Univ. Librarian: Dr PETER GAVIN FERRIBY

Library of 180,000 vols

Number of teachers: 620 (220 full-time, 400 part-time)

Number of students: 6,400 (incl. 3,488 full-time undergraduates, 685 part-time undergraduates, 2,234 graduates)

DEANS

College of Arts and Sciences: Dr SEAMUS CAREY

College of Health Professions: Dr PATRICIA W. WALKER

Isabelle Farrington College of Education: PATRICIA W. WALKER

John F. Welch College of Business: Dr RUPENDRA PALIWAL

Univ. College: MARY LOU DeROSA

ST VINCENT'S COLLEGE

2800 Main St, Bridgeport, CT 06606

Telephone: (203) 576-5278

E-mail: registrar@stvincentscollege.edu

Internet: www.stvincentscollege.edu

Founded 1905

Private control

Academic year: August to May (2 semesters)

Degree programmes incl. general studies, medical assisting, nursing, radiography

Pres. and CEO: Dr MARTHA K. SHOULDIS

Sr Vice-Pres. for Finance and Interim Chief Financial Officer: JOHN GLECKER

Vice-Pres. and Dean: JOANNE R. WOLFERTZ

Dean of Academic Services: SUSAN CAPASSO

Dir of Admin. Services: JANICE N. FAYE
Dir of Admissions: JOSEPH P. MARRONE
Registrar: JOSEPH MACIONUS
Librarian: VICKY JACOBSON
Number of students: 580

SOUTHERN CONNECTICUT STATE UNIVERSITY

501 Crescent St, New Haven, CT 06515-1355
Telephone: (203) 392-5200
E-mail: gradinfo@southernct.edu
Internet: www.southernct.edu

Founded 1893, present name 1959
State control
Academic year: August to May
Pres.: Prof. MARY A. PAPAZIAN
Exec. Vice-Pres.: JAMES E. BLAKE
Vice-Pres. for Academic Affairs and Interim Provost: MARIANNE KENNEDY
Vice-Pres. for Institutional Advancement: GREGG CRERAR
Vice-Pres. for Student and Univ. Affairs: PETER TROIANO
Registrar: KIMBERLY LAING
Dir of Library Services: CHRISTINA D. BAUM
Library of 300,000 vols
Number of teachers: 1,053 (438 full-time, 615 part-time)
Number of students: 11,769 (incl. 8,496 undergraduates, 3,273 graduates)

DEANS

School of Arts and Sciences: DONNA JEAN FREDEEN
School of Business: ELLEN DURNIN
School of Education: MICHAEL SAMPSON
School of Graduate Studies: HOLLY CRAWFORD
School of Health and Human Services: GREGORY J. PAVEZA

TRINITY COLLEGE

300 Summit St, Hartford, CT 06106-3100
Telephone: (860) 297-2000
E-mail: registrar.office@trincoll.edu
Internet: www.trincoll.edu

Founded 1823
Private control
Academic year: August to May
American studies, anthropology, art history, biology, chemistry or biochemistry, classics, computer science, economics, educational studies, engineering, English, environmental science, history, int. studies, Jewish studies, mathematics, modern languages and literature, music, neuroscience, philosophy, physics, political science, psychology, public policy and law, religion, sociology, studio arts, theatre and dance, women, gender and sexuality
Pres.: JAMES F. JONES, JR
Vice-Pres. for Academic Affairs and Dean of the Faculty: Prof. Dr RENA FRADEN
Vice-Pres. for College Advancement: RONALD A. JOYCE
Vice-Pres. for Finance and Operations and Treas.: PAUL MUTONE
Vice-Pres. for Strategic Planning, Admin. and Affirmative Action: PAULA A. RUSSO
Dean of Admissions and Financial Aid: LARRY DOW
Dean of Multicultural Affairs: KARLA SPURLOCK-EVANS
Dean of Students: FREDERICK ALFORD
Registrar: PATRICIA MCGREGOR
Librarian: Prof. RICHARD S. ROSS
Library: 1m. vols, 7,00,000 items incl. microforms, 13,000 current periodicals, 21,852 audiovisual materials, govt documents
Number of teachers: 185 (full-time)
Number of students: 2,248 (2,144 undergraduate, 104 graduate)

Publications: *Reporter*, *Review*, *Trinity Papers*, *Trinity Reporter* (3 a year), *Tripod*

UNITED STATES COAST GUARD ACADEMY

31 Mohegan Ave, New London, CT 06320-8103
Telephone: (860) 444-8444
Internet: www.uscga.edu

Founded 1876 as School of Instruction for the Revenue Marine; present name 1915
State control
Faculties of engineering, humanities, management, mathematics, science
Superintendent: Rear Admiral SANDRA L. STOSZ
Dean of Academics: Dr KURT J. COLELLA
Dir of Admissions: STEVE FINTON
Registrar: DONALD E. DYKES
Library Dir: (vacant)
Library of 178,000 vols, 55,000 periodicals
Number of teachers: 120
Number of students: 1,040

UNIVERSITY OF BRIDGEPORT

126 Park Ave, Bridgeport, CT 06604-5620
Telephone: (203) 576-4552
E-mail: admit@bridgeport.edu
Internet: www.bridgeport.edu

Founded 1927 as Junior College of Connecticut, current name and status 1947
Private control
Academic year: September to May
Pres.: NEIL ALBERT SALONEN
Provost and Vice-Pres. for Academic Affairs: Dr HANS VAN DER GIESSEN
Vice-Pres. for Admin. and Finance: Dr SUSAN D. WILLIAMS
Vice-Pres. for Facilities: GEORGE ESTRADA
Vice-Pres. for Graduate Studies and Research: Dr TAREK M. SOBH
Vice-Pres. for Int. Programmes: Dr THOMAS J. WARD
Vice-Pres. for Univ. Relations: MARY-JANE FOSTER
Dean for Admissions: KARISSA PECKHAM
Dean for Student Affairs: EDINA OESTREICHER
Registrar: CHRISTIAN HANSEN
Univ. Librarian: DEBORAH DULEPSKI
Library of 243,586 vols, 1,051,159 microforms, 3,342 audiovisual items, 45,712 serial subscriptions
Number of teachers: 121 (full-time)
Number of students: 4,842

DEANS

Acupuncture Institute: Dr JENNIFER BRETT
College of Chiropractice: DAVID J. WICKES
College of Naturopathic Medicine: MIKYLE S. BYRD-VAUGHNL (acting)
College of Public and Int. Affairs: Dr THOMAS J. WARD
Fones School of Dental Hygiene: Dr MARCIA H. LORENTZEN
Nutrition Institute: Dr DAVID M. BRADY
Physician Assistant Institute: Dr DANIEL CERVONKA
School of Arts and Sciences: Dr LAURENCE M CONNER
School of Business: Dr LLOYD G GIBSON
School of Continuing and Professional Studies: MICHAEL J. GIAMPAOLI
School of Education: Dr ALLEN P. COOK
School of Engineering: Dr TAREK M. SOBH
Shintaro Akatsu School of Design: RICHARD W. YELLE

UNIVERSITY OF CONNECTICUT

352 Mansfield Rd, Storrs, CT 06269
Telephone: (860) 486-2000

Internet: www.uconn.edu

Founded 1881 as The Storrs Agricultural School, present name 1939
State control
Academic year: September to May
Campuses in Avery Point, Greater Hartford, Stamford, Torrington, Waterbury
Pres.: Prof. Dr SUSAN HERBST
Provost and Exec. Vice-Pres. for Academic Affairs: MUN CHOI
Sr Vice-Provost and Vice-Pres. for Research: SUMAN SINGHA
Vice-Pres. and Chief Financial Officer: RICHARD GRAY
Vice-Pres.for Economic Devt: MARY HOLZ-CLAUSE
Vice-Pres. for Enrolment Planning and Management: WAYNE LOCUST
Vice-Pres. for Health Affairs: PHILIP E. AUSTIN
Vice-Pres. for Student Affairs: Dr JOHN R. SADDLEMIRE
Library: see under Libraries and Archives
Number of teachers: 1,330
Number of students: 30,500

Publications: *Connecticut Insurance Law Journal* (2 a year), *Connecticut Journal of International Law* (2 a year), *Connecticut Law Review* (4 a year), *Connecticut Public Interest Law Journal* (online), *MELUS* (4 a year), *The Connecticut Economy* (4 a year), *UConn Magazine* (3 a year), *University Today* (52 during academic year, online)

DEANS

College of Agriculture and Natural Resources: GREGORY J. WEIDEMANN
College of Liberal Arts and Sciences: Dr JEREMY TEITELBAUM
Graduate School: KENT HOLSINGER
Neag School of Education: THOMAS C. DEFRANCO
School of Business: JOHN A ELLIOTT
School of Dental Medicine: Dr R. LAMONT MACNEIL
School of Engineering: KAZEM KAZEROUNIAN
School of Fine Arts: Dr BRID GRANT
School of Law: Prof. JEREMY R. PAUL
School of Medicine: Dr FRANK M TORTI
School of Nursing: Dr REGINA CUSSON
School of Pharmacy: JOHN B. MORRIS
School of Social Work: Prof. Dr SALOME RAHEIM

PROFESSORS

College of Agriculture and Natural Resources (1376 Storrs Rd, Unit 4066, Storrs, CT 06269-4066; tel. (860) 486-2917; e-mail canrdean@uconn.edu; internet www.canr.uconn.edu):

ADAMS, R. G., Jr, Entomology
BERKOWITZ, G., Plant Science
BLASIAK, M. M., Plant Science
BRAND, M. H., Plant Science
BRAVO-URETA, B. E., Agricultural Economics
BULL, N. H., Extension
BUSHMICH, S., Pathobiology
CIVCO, D. L., Natural Resources Management
CLARK, R. M., Nutritional Sciences
CLAUSEN, J. C., Natural Resources Management and Engineering
COTTERILL, R. W., Agricultural Economics
DARRE, M. J., Animal Science
FAUSTMAN, L. C., Animal Science
FERNANDEZ, M. L., Nutritional Sciences
FLETCHER, D., Animal Science
FREAKE, H. C., Nutritional Sciences
GARMENDIA, A., Pathobiology
GEARY, S. J., Pathobiology
GREGER, J., Nutritional Sciences
GUILLARD, K., Plant Science
HART, I. C., Animal Science

HOAGLUND, T. A., Animal Science
KERR, K. M., Pathobiology
KHAN, M. I., Pathology
KOO, S. I., Nutritional Sciences
LEE, L. K., Agriculture and Resource Economics
LI, Y., Plant Science
LOPEZ, R. A., Agricultural Economics
LOVE, C., Extension
MCAVOY, R. J., Plant Science
PAGOULATOS, E., Agricultural Economics
PEREZ-ESCAMILLA, R., Nutritional Sciences
POMEROY, R., Agricultural and Resource Economics
ROBBINS, G. A., Natural Resources
RODRIGUEZ, N., Nutritional Sciences
SILBART, L. K., Allied Health Sciences
SINGHA, S., Horticulture
VAN KRUININGEN, H. J., Pathobiology
WARNER, G., Natural Resources Management and Engineering
YANG, X., Animal Science
YANG, X. (H.), Natural Resources Management and Engineering
ZINN, S. A., Animal Science

College of Liberal Arts and Sciences (215 Glenbrook Rd, Unit 4098, Storrs, CT 06269-4098; tel. (860) 486-2713; internet www.clas.uconn.edu):

ABE, K., Mathematics
ABIKOFF, W., Mathematics
ADAMS, E., Ecology and Evolutionary Biology
ALBERT, A. D., Molecular and Cell Biology
ANDERSON, G. J., Ecology and Evolutionary Biology
ANDERSON, S., Human Development and Family Studies
ANDERSON, S. L., Philosophy
ANSELMENT, R. A., English
AUSTIN, P. E., Economics
AZIMI, F., History
BAILEY, W. F., Chemistry
BARNES-FARRELL, J., Psychology
BARRECA, R. R., English
BASS, R., Mathematics
BASU, A. K., Chemistry
BAXTER, D. L., Philosophy
BEALL, J. C., Philosophy
BENSON, C. D., English
BENSON, D. R., Molecular and Cell Biology
BERENTSON, W., Geography
BERTHELOT, A., Modern and Classical Languages (French)
BEST, P. E., Physics
BIGGS, F., English
BIRGE, R. R., Physics
BLANK, T. O., Human Development and Family Studies
BLEI, R. C., Mathematics
BLOOM, L. Z., English
BOBALJIK, J., Linguistics
BOHLEN, W. F., Marine Sciences
BOHN, R. K., Chemistry
BOSKOVIC, Z., Linguistics
BOSTER, J. S., Anthropology
BOYER, M. A., Political Science
BRADFIELD, S., English
BROADHEAD, R. S., Sociology
BROWN, R. D., History
BUCK, R. W., Communication Sciences
BUCKLEY, R. N., History
BUCKLIN, A., Marine Sciences
CAIRA, J. N., Ecology and Evolutionary Biology
CALABRESE, A., Linguistics
CARELLO, C. A., Psychology
CARSTENSEN, F. V., Economics
CELESTIN, R., Modern and Classical Languages (French)
CHAFFIN, R., Psychology
CHAPPLE, W. D., Physiology and Neurobiology
CHAZDON, R. L., Ecology and Environmental Biology

CHEN, M. H., Statistics
CHEN, T. T., Molecular and Cell Biology
CHOI, Y. S., Mathematics
CLARK, A., Philosophy
CLIFFORD, J. G., Political Science
COELHO, C. A., Communication Sciences
COLWELL, R. K., Ecology and Evolutionary Biology
COMPRONE, J. J., English
CORMIER, V. F., Physics
COSGEL, M. M., Economics
COSTIGLIOLA, F., History
COTE, R., Physics
CRAWFORD, M., Psychology
CRIVELLO, J. F., Physiology and Neurobiology
CROMLEY, E. K., Geography
CROMLEY, R. G., Geography
CROTEAU, M. E., Journalism
DALMOLIN, E. F., Modern and Classical Languages (French)
DAM, H. G., Marine Sciences
D'ANDRELE, R., Anthropology
DASHEFSKY, A. M., Sociology
DAVID, C. W., Chemistry
DAVIS, J. A., History
DEBLAS, A. L., Physiology and Neurobiology
DESCH, C. E., Jr, Ecology and Evolutionary Biology
DEY, D. K., Statistics
DULACK, T., English
DUNNE, G. V., Physics
DUSSART, J. T., Psychology
DUTTA, N. K., Physics
EBY, C. V., English
ELDER, C. L., Philosophy
ERICKSON, P. I., Anthropology
EYLER, E. E., Physics
FARNEN, R. F., Political Science
FEIN, D. A., Psychology
FISHER, J. D., Psychology
FITZGERALD, W. F., Marine Sciences
FOWLER, C. A., Psychology
FRANK, H. A., Chemistry
FRANKLIN, W., English
FULLERTON, R. J., Jr, Aerospace Studies
GAI, M., Physics
GALLO, R. V., Physiology and Neurobiology
GIBSON, G. N., Physics
GILBERT, H. R., Communication Sciences
GINE, E., Mathematics
GLASBERG, D. S., Sociology
GLAZ, J., Statistics
GLAZ, S., Mathematics
GOGARTEN, J. P., Molecular and Cell Biology
GOMES, M. A., Modern and Classical Languages (Spanish)
GOODHEART, L. B., History
GOODSTEIN, L., Sociology
GORDON, R. B., Modern and Classical Languages (French)
GOULD, P. L., Physics
GREEN, J. A., Psychology
GROSS, R. A., History
GUENOUN, S., Modern and Classical Languages (French)
GUI, C., Mathematics
HAAS, A. H., Mathematics
HALLWOOD, C. P., Economics
HAMILTON, D. S., Physics
HANDWERKER, W. P., Anthropology
HANINK, D. M., Geography
HANSON, B. C., Political Science
HARKNESS, S., Human Development and Family Studies
HARRIS, S., English
HARVEY, C., Military Science
HASENFRATZ, R., English
HEFFLEY, D. R., Economics
HENRY, C. S., Ecology and Evolutionary Biology
HIGONETT, M. R., English
HISKES, R. P., Political Science
HOGAN, P. C., English

HOLLENBERG, D. C., English
HOLSINGER, K. E., Ecology and Evolutionary Biology
HOLZWORTH, J., Psychology
HOWELL, A. R., Chemistry
JAVANAINEN, J. M., Physics
JOESTEN, R. L., Chemistry
JOHNSON, B. T., Psychology
JONES, S. P., English
KALICHMAN, S., Psychology
KAPPERS, L. A., Physics
KENDALL, D. A., Molecular and Cell Biology
KENNY, D. A., Psychology
KHARCHENCO, V., Physics
KNECHT, D. A., Molecular and Cell Biology
KNOBLAUCH, V. L., Economics
KOLTRACHT, I., Mathematics
KOVNER, A., Physics
KREMER, J. N., Marine Sciences
KUMAR, C. V., Chemistry
KUO, L., Statistics
KUPPERMAN, J. J., Philosophy
LANGLOIS, R. N., Economics
LES, D. H., Ecology and Environmental Biology
LEWIS, C. W., Political Science
LILLO-MARTIN, D. C., Linguistics
LIN, C. A., Communication Sciences
LINNEKIN, J. S., Anthropology
LOTURCO, J. J., Physiology and Neurobiology
LOWE, C. A., Psychology
LUYSTER, R. W., Philosophy
LYNCH, M. P., Philosophy
LYNES, M. A., Molecular and Cell Biology
MCBREATY, S. A., Anthropology
MCBREEN, E., Human Development and Family Studies
MCKENNA, P. J., Mathematics
MACKINNON, R. D., Geography
MACLEOD, G. G., English
MCMANUS, G. B., Marine Sciences
MADYCH, W. R., Mathematics
MAKOWSKY, V. A., English
MALLETT, R. L., Physics
MANNHEIM, P. O., Physics
MARCUS, P. I., Molecular and Cell Biology
MARKUS, E., Psychology
MARSDEN, J., English
MASCIANDARO, F., Modern and Classical Languages (Italian)
MASON, R., Marine Sciences
MAXSON, S. C., Psychology
MEYER, M., English
MEYERS, D. T., Philosophy
MICELI, T. J., Economics
MICHEL, R. G., Chemistry
MILLER, D. B., Psychology
MILLER, R. L., English
MILLER, S. S., Modern and Classical Languages (Classics and Hebrew)
MOISEFF, A., Physiology and Neurobiology
MUKHOPADHYAY, N., Statistics
MURPHY, B., English
MUSIEK, F., Communication Sciences
NAIGLES, L. R., Psychology
NAPLES, N., Sociology
NEUMANN, M., Mathematics
NOLL, K. M., Molecular and Cell Biology
O'DONNELL, J., Marine Sciences
OLSHEVASKY, V., Mathematics
OSLEEB, J. P., Geography
PAPADIMITRAKOPOULOUS, F., Chemistry
PEASE, D. M., Physics
PETERSON, C. W., Physics
PETERSON, R. S., English
PHILLIPS, R. L., Philosophy
PICKERING, S. F., English
PRATTO, F., Psychology
RAVISHANKER, N., Statistics
RAWITSCHER, G. H., Physics
RAY, S. C., Economics
REITER, H. L., Political Science
RENFRO, J. L., Physiology and Neurobiology
RICKARDS, J. P., Psychology

RIGAZIO-DIGILIO, S., Human Development and Family Studies
ROBINSON, J., Human Development and Family Studies
ROCKWELL, R. C., Sociology
ROE, S. A., History
ROSS, S. L., Economics
RUSLING, J. F., Chemistry
SABATELLI, R., Human Development and Family Studies
SALAMONE, J. D., Psychology
SANDERS, C. R., Sociology
SCHAEFER, C. W., Ecology and Evolutionary Biology
SCHLICHTING, C. D., Ecology and Environmental Biology
SCHWENK, K., Ecology and Environmental Biology
SEGERSON, K., Economics
SEHULSTER, J. R., Psychology
SHOEMAKER, N., History
SIDNEY, S. J., Mathematics
SILANDER, J. A., Ecology and Evolutionary Biology
SILVESTRINI, B. G., History
SIMON, C. M., Ecology and Environmental Biology
SIMONSEN, W., Public Policy
SMITH, M. B., Chemistry
SMITH, W. W., Physics
SNYDER, L. B., Communication Sciences
SONSTROEM, D. A., English
SPALDING, K., History
SPIEGEL, E. S., Mathematics
STRAUSBAUGH, L. D., Molecular and Cell Biology
STWALLEY, W. C., Physics
SUIB, S. L., Chemistry
SUNG, C. S. P., Chemistry
SUPER, C. M., Human Development and Family Studies
SWADLOW, H. A., Psychology
SWANSON, M. S., Physics
TAYLOR, R. L., Sociology
TEITELBAUM, J., Mathematics
TESCHKE, C., Molecular and Cell Biology
THORSON, R. M., Ecology and Evolutionary Biology
TOLLEFSON, J. L., Mathematics
TORGERSEN, T. L., Marine Sciences
TROYER, L., Sociology
TRUMBO, S., Ecology and Evolutionary Biology
TUCHMAN, G., Sociology
TURCHIN, P., Ecology and Environmental Biology
TURVEY, M. T., Psychology
VAN DER HULST, H. G., Linguistics
VILLEMEZ, W. J., Sociology
VITALE, R. A., Statistics
WAGNER, D., Ecology and Evolutionary Biology
WALLACE, M., Sociology
WALLER, A. L., History
WANG, Y., Statistics
WEAKLIEM, D. L., Sociology
WELLS, K. D., Ecology and Evolutionary Biology
WHEELER, S. C., Philosophy
WHITLATCH, R. B., Marine Sciences
WILKENFELD, R. B., English
WILSON, R. A., Anthropology
WISENSALE, S., Human Development and Family Studies
WORCESTER, W. A., Journalism
YARISH, C., Ecology and Evolutionary Biology
YEAGLE, P. L., Molecular and Cell Biology
ZIRAKZADEH, C. E., Political Science

Neag School of Education (249 Glenbrook Rd, Unit 2064C, Storrs, CT 06269-2064; tel. (860) 486-3813; internet www.education.uconn .edu):

ARMSTRONG, L. E., Kinesiology
BONANNON, R., Physical Therapy

BRAY, M., Educational Psychology
BROWN, S. W., Educational Psychology
DEFRANCO, T., Curriculum and Instruction
DENEGAR, C. R., Physical Therapy
DOYLE, M. A., Curriculum and Instruction
GOODKIND, T. B., Curriculum and Instruction
HASSON, S. M., Physical Therapy
JUNDA, M. E., Educational Leadership
KARAN, O. C., Educational Psychology
KEHLE, T. J., Educational Psychology
KRAEMER, W. J., Kinesiology
LEU, D. J., Curriculum and Instruction
MCGUIRE, J. M., Educational Psychology
MARESH, C. M., Kinesiology
REAGAN, T. G., Curriculum and Instruction
REIS, S. M., Educational Psychology
SCHWAB, R. L., Educational Leadership
SHECKLEY, B. G., Educational Leadership
SMEY, J. W., Physical Therapy
STEPHENS, R., Educational Leadership
SUGAI, G., Educational Psychology
SWAMINATHAN, H., Educational Psychology

Ratcliffe Hicks School of Agriculture (1376 Storrs Rd, Unit 4090, Storrs, CT 06269-4090; tel. (860) 486-2920; e-mail acadprog@uconn .edu; internet www.cag.uconn.edu/rh/rh).

School of Business (2100 Hillside Rd, Unit 1041, Storrs, CT 06269-1041; tel. (860) 486-2314; e-mail contact@business.uconn.edu; internet www.sba.uconn.edu):

BIGGS, S. F., Accounting
CARRAFIELLO, V. A., Business Law
CLAPP, J. M., Finance
COULTER, R. H., Marketing
EARLEY, P. C., Management
FOX, K. H., Business Law
GARFINKEL, R. S., Operations Research and Information Management
GHOSH, C., Finance
GIACOTTO, C., Finance
GOES, P. B., Operations and Information Management
GOPAL, R., Operations Research and Information Management
HARDING, J., Finance
HEGDE, S. P., Finance
HUSSEIN, M. E., Accounting
JAIN, S. C., Marketing
KLEIN, L. S., Finance
KUMAR, V., Marketing
LUBATKIN, M. J., Management
MARSDEN, J. R., Operations Research and Information Management
MATHIEU, J. E., Management
NAIR, S. K., Operations Research and Information Management
O'BRIEN, T. J., Finance
POWELL, G. N., Management
SANTERRE, R., Finance
SEWALL, M. A., Marketing
SIRMANS, C. F., Finance and Real Estate
VEIGA, J. F., Management
WILLENBORG, M., Accounting

School of Dental Medicine (263 Farmington Ave, Farmington, CT 06030; tel. (860) 679-2000; internet sdm.uchc.edu):

AGAR, J., Reconstructive Sciences
BEAZOGLOU, T., Craniofacial Sciences
D'AMBROSIO, J., Oral Health and Diagnostic Services
DEALY, C., Reconstructive Sciences
DONGARI-BAGTZOGLOU, A., Oral Health and Diagnostic Services
EISENBERG, E., Oral Health and Diagnostic Sciences
FRANK, M. E., Oral Health and Diagnostic Sciences
FREILICH, M., Reconstructive Sciences
GOLDBERG, A. J., Reconstructive Sciences
GOUPIL, M., Craniofacial Sciences
HAND, A., Craniofacial Sciences
KAZEMI, R., Reconstructive Sciences
KELLY, J. R., Reconstructive Sciences

KOSHER, R., Reconstructive Sciences
LITT, M. D., Oral Health and Diagnostic Sciences
LURIE, A. G., Oral Health and Diagnostic Sciences
MACNEIL, R., Oral Health and Diagnostic Sciences
MEIERS, J., Reconstructive Sciences
MINA, M., Craniofacial Sciences
NANDA, R., Craniofacial Sciences
NEWITTER, D., Reconstructive Sciences
NICHOLS, F., Oral Health and Diagnostic Sciences
PENDRYS, D., Oral Health and Diagnostic Services
PETERSON, D. E., Oral Health and Diagnostic Sciences
REISINE, S., Oral Health and Diagnostic Sciences
ROBINSON, P., Oral Health and Diagnostic Sciences
ROSSOMANDO, E. P., Craniofacial Sciences
SAFAVI, K., Craniofacial Sciences
SHAFER, D., Craniofacial Sciences
SPANGBERG, L. S. W., Oral Health and Diagnostic Sciences
TANZER, J. M., Oral Health and Diagnostic Sciences
TAYLOR, T., Reconstructive Sciences
TRUMMEL, C. L., Oral Health and Diagnostic Sciences
UPHOLT, W., Reconstructive Sciences
ZHU, Q., Craniofacial Sciences

School of Engineering (261 Glenbrook Rd, Unit 2237, Storrs, CT 06269-2237; tel. (860) 486-2221; internet www.engr.uconn.edu):

ACCORSI, M. L., Civil and Environmental Engineering
ACHENIE, L. E., Chemical, Materials and Biomolecular Engineering
AINDOW, M., Chemical, Materials and Biomolecular Engineering
AMMAR, R. A., Computer Science and Engineering
ANWAR, A. F. M., Electrical and Computer Engineering
BAGTZOGLOU, A., Civil and Environmental Engineering
BANSAL, R., Electrical and Systems Engineering
BAR-SHALOM, Y., Electrical and Computer Engineering
BARKER, K., Computer Science and Engineering
BERGMAN, T. L., Mechanical Engineering
BRODY, H. D., Chemical, Materials and Biomolecular Engineering
CETEGEN, B., Mechanical Engineering
COOPER, D. J., Chemical, Materials and Biomolecular Engineering
DEMURJIAN, S. A., Computer Science and Engineering
DEWOLF, J. T., Civil and Environmental Engineering
ENDERLE, J. D., Electrical and Computer Engineering
ENGEL, G. L., Computer Science and Engineering and Electrical and Systems Engineering
EPSTEIN, H. I., Civil and Environmental Engineering
ERKEY, C., Chemical, Materials and Biomolecular Engineering
FAGHIRI, A., Mechanical Engineering
FOX, M. D., Electrical and Computer Engineering
FRANTZ, G. C., Civil and Environmental Engineering
IVAN, J. N., Civil Engineering
JAIN, F. C., Electrical and Computer Engineering
JAVIDI, B., Electrical and Computer Engineering
JORDAN, E. H., Mechanical Engineering

KATTAMIS, T. Z., Materials Science and Engineering
KAZEROUNIAN, K., Mechanical Engineering
LUH, P. B., Electrical and Computer Engineering
MAGNUSSON, R., Electrical and Computer Engineering
MARCUS, H. L., Chemical, Materials and Biomolecular Engineering
OLGAC, N., Mechanical Engineering
OR, D., Civil and Electrical Engineering
PATTIPATI, K. R., Electrical and Computer Engineering
PETERS, T. J., Computer Science and Engineering
PITCHUMANI, R., Mechanical Engineering
RAJASEKARAN, S., Computer Science and Engineering
REIFSNIDER, K. L., Mechanical Engineering
SAMMES, N. M., Mechanical Engineering
SHAW, L. L., Chemical, Materials and Biomolecular Engineering
SHAW, M. T., Chemical, Materials and Biomolecular Engineering
SHIN, D. G., Computer Science and Engineering
SMITH, E., Civil and Environmental Engineering
TAYLOR, G. W., Electrical and Computer Engineering
WEISS, R. A., Chemical, Materials and Biomolecular Engineering
WILLETT, P. K., Electrical and Computer Engineering
ZHANG, B., Mechanical Engineering
ZHU, Q., Electrical and Computer Engineering

School of Fine Arts (830 Bolton Rd, Unit 1128, Storrs, CT 06269-1128; tel. (860) 486-3016; internet www.sfa.uconn.edu):

ARM, T. E., Music
BASS, W. R., Music
CROW, L. J., Dramatic Arts
ENGLISH, G. M., Dramatic Arts
FRANKLIN, J. F., Dramatic Arts
FROGLEY, A., Music
FUCHS, K., Music
GIVENS, J., Art and Art History
MCDONALD, R. A., Dramatic Arts
MARTINEZ, A., Art
MAZZOCCA, A. N., Art
MILLER, R. F., Music
MILLS, D. L., Music
MOLETTE, C. W., Dramatic Arts
MUIRHEAD, D. D., Art
MYERS, K. M., Art and Art History
OGUIBE, O., Art and Art History
RENSHAW, J. H., Music
ROCCOBERTON, B. P., Jr, Dramatic Arts
RYKER, K., Dramatic Arts
SABATINE, J., Dramatic Arts
STANLEY, G., Music
STERN, A. S., Dramatic Arts
TALVACCHIA, B. L., Art
THORPE, J. K., Art
WOODS, D. G., Music

School of Law (65 Elizabeth St, Hartford, CT 06105-2290; tel. (860) 570-5000; internet www.law.uconn.edu):

BAKER, T. E.
BARNES, R. D.
BECKER, L. E., Jr
BERGER, B.
BERMAN, P. S.
BIRMINGHAM, R. L.
CALLOWAY, D. A.
DAILEY, A. C.
DICKERSON, L.
FERNOW, T. O.
FISCHL, R. M.
GUSTAFSON, K.
JANIS, M. W.
KAY, R. S.
KIRK, D.
KURLANTZICK, L. S.

LEVIN, L. C.
LINDSETH, P.
MCCOY, P.
MCLEAN, W. E.
MORAWETZ, T. H.
OQUENDO, A. R.
ORLAND, L.
PARKER, R. W.
PAUL, J.
POMP, R. D.
SIEGELMAN, P.
STARK, J. H.
STRASSER, K. A.
TONDRO, T. J.
UTZ, S. G.
WEISBROD, C. A.
WHITMAN, R.
WILF, S.

School of Medicine (263 Farmington Ave, Farmington, CT 06030-1912; tel. (860) 679-2000; internet medicine.uchc.edu):

ALBERTSON, P. C., Surgery
ALTMAN, A. J., Paediatrics
ARNOLD, A., Medicine
BABOR, T. F., Community Medicine and Health Care
BARBARESE, E., Neuroscience
BAUER, L. O., Psychiatry
BENN, P. A., Genetics and Developmental Biology
BERNSTEIN, L., Neuroscience
BIGAZZI, P. E., Pathology and Laboratory Medicine
BROWNER, B. O., Orthopaedic Surgery
BRUDER, M. E., Paediatrics
CAMPBELL, W. A., Obstetrics and Gynaecology
CARMICHAEL, G. G., Genetics and Developmental Biology
CARSON, J. H., Molecular, Microbial and Structural Biology
CHERNIAK, M. G., Medicine
CLOUTIER, M., Paediatrics
CONE, R. E., Immunology
CUSHMAN, R. A., Family Medicine
DAS, A. K., Molecular, Microbial and Structural Biology
DAS, D. K., Surgery
DECKERS, P. J., Surgery
EIPPER, E. A., Molecular, Microbial and Structural Biology
EISENBERG, S., Molecular, Microbial and Structural Biology
FEDER, H. M., Jr, Family Medicine
FEIN, A., Cell Biology
FEINSTEIN, M. B., Cell Biology
FIFIELD, J., Family Medicine
FOROUHAR, F., Pathology and Laboratory Medicine
FORTINSKY, R. H., Medicine
GOLDSCHNEIDER, I., Immunology
GRANT-KELS, J. M., Dermatology
GRASSO, J. A., Cell Biology
GREENSTEIN, R. M., Genetics and Developmental Biology
GRONOWICZ, G. F., Surgery
GROSS, J. B., Anaesthesiology
HANSEN, M., Medicine
HESSELBROCK, V. M., Psychiatry
HLA, T. R., Cell Biology
HUEY, L., Psychiatry
HURLEY, M. M., Medicine
JAFFE, L., Cell Biology
KADDEN, R. M., Psychiatry
KIM, D. O., Neuroscience
KING, S. M., Molecular, Microbial and Structural Biology
KLOBUTCHER, L. A., Molecular, Microbial and Structural Biology
KOEPPEN, B. M., Medicine
KOPPEL, D. E., Molecular, Microbial and Structural Biology
KRANZLER, H. R., Psychiatry
KREAM, B., Medicine
KREUTZER, D. L., Pathology

KUCHEL, G., Medicine
KUWADA, S., Neuroscience
LALANDE, M., Genetics and Developmental Biology
LE FRANCOIS, L., Medicine
LEVINE, J. B., Medicine
LIANG, B. T., Medicine
LIEBERMAN, J., Orthopaedic Surgery
LOEW, L. M., Cell Biology
LORENZO, J. A., Medicine
MAINS, R. E., Neuroscience
MAULIK, N., Surgery
MAXWELL, G. D., Neuroscience
MAYER, B., Genetics and Developmental Biology
MOREST, D. K., Neuroscience
MUKHOPADHYAY, B., Medicine
OLIVER, D. L., Neuroscience
O'ROURKE, J. T., Immunology
OZOLS, J., Molecular, Microbial and Structural Biology
PACHTER, J., Cell Biology
PAPPANO, A. J., Cell Biology
PELUSO, J. J., Cell Biology
PETRY, N., Psychiatry
POTASHNER, S. J., Neuroscience
RADOLF, J. D., Medicine
RAJAN, T. V., Pathology and Laboratory Medicine
RATZAN, S. K., Paediatrics
ROSENBERG, D., Medicine
RUNOWICZ, C. D., Obstetrics and Gynaecology
SANDERS, M. M., Pathology and Laboratory Medicine
SARFARAZI, M., Surgery
SCHENSUL, S., Community Medicine and Health Care
SETLOW, P., Molecular, Microbial and Structural Biology
SIMON, R. H., Surgery
SRIVASTAVA, P. K., Immunology
STEVENS, R., Community Medicine and Health Care
TENNEN, H., Community Medicine and Health Care
TRAHIOTIS, C., Neuroscience
TRESTMAN, R., Medicine
TSIPOURAS, P., Genetics and Developmental Biology
WELLER, S. K., Molecular, Microbial and Structural Biology
WHITE, B. A., Cell Biology
WHITE, W. B., Medicine
WIKEL, S. K., Immunology
WINOKUR, A., Psychiatry
WOLFSON, L. I., Neurology
WU, C. H., Medicine
WU, G. Y., Medicine

School of Nursing (231 Glenbrook Rd, Storrs, CT 06269-2026; tel. (860) 486-3716; internet www.nursing.uconn.edu):

BAVIER, A., Nursing
BECK, C. L., Nursing
CUSSON, R., Nursing
KOERNER, B. L., Nursing
NEAFSEY, P. J., Nursing

School of Pharmacy (69 N Eagleville Rd, Storrs, CT 06268; tel. (860) 486-2121; internet pharmacy.uconn.edu):

BURGESS, D. J., Pharmaceutics
GERALD, M. C., Pharmacology
LANGNER, R. O., Pharmacology
MCCARTHY, R. L., Pharmacy Practice
MORRIS, J. B., Toxicology
PIKAL, M. J., Pharmaceutics
WHITE, C. M., Pharmacy Practice

School of Social Work (1798 Asylum Ave, West Hartford, CT 06117-2698; tel. (860) 570-9118; e-mail swadmission@uconn.edu; internet www.ssw.uconn.edu):

DAVIDSON, K. W.
FISHER, R.
GITTERMAN, A.

HEALY, L. M.
HESSELBROCK, M. N.
HUMPHREYS, N. A.
JOHNSON, H. C.

Whetten Graduate Center (438 Whitney Rd Ext., Storrs, CT 06269-1152; tel. (860) 486-3617; e-mail gradschool@uconn.edu; internet www.grad.uconn.edu).

UNIVERSITY OF HARTFORD

200 Bloomfield Ave, West Hartford, CT 06117-1599

Telephone: (860) 768-4100
E-mail: uofhart@hartford.edu
Internet: www.hartford.edu

Founded 1957 by merger of Hartford Art School, Hartt College of Music, Hillyer College
Private control
Academic year: September to August (2 semesters)

Pres.: Dr WALTER HARRISON
Provost: SHARON L. VASQUEZ
Vice-Pres. for Finance and Admin.: AROSHA JAYAWICKREMA
Vice-Pres. for Institutional Advancement: CHRISTINE PINA
Vice-Pres. for Student Affairs: J. LEE PETERS
Vice-Pres. for Univ. Relations: JOHN J. CARSON
Dean of Admissions: RICHARD A. ZEISER
Dean of Graduate Studies: PETER DIFFLEY
Asst Provost and Dean of Faculty Devt: H. FREDERICK SWEITZER
Assoc. Provost and Dean of Undergraduate Studies: GUY CHARLES COLARULLI
Registrar: DOREEN LAY
Dir of Univ. Libraries: RANDI ASHTON-PRITTING
Library of 606,154 vols
Number of teachers: 850 (350 full-time, 500 part-time)
Number of students: 7,400

DEANS

Barney School of Business: Dr JAMES W. FAIRFIELD-SONN
College of Arts and Sciences: Dr JOSEPH C. VOELKER
College of Education, Nursing and Health Professions: Prof. Dr RALPH O. MUELLER
College of Engineering, Technology and Architecture: Dr LOUIS T. MANZIONE
Hartford Art School: NANCY M. STAURT (acting)
Hartt School: Dr AARON A. FLAGG
Hillyer College: Dr DAVID H. GOLDENBERG

UNIVERSITY OF NEW HAVEN

300 Boston Post Rd, West Haven, CT 06516

Telephone: (203) 932-7000
E-mail: adminfo@newhaven.edu
Internet: www.newhaven.edu

Founded 1920
Private control
Academic year: August to May

Pres.: Prof. Dr STEVEN H. KAPLAN
Provost and Sr Vice-Pres. for Academic and Student Affairs: Dr DAVID P. DAUWALDER
Vice-Pres. for Enrolment Management: Dr JAMES MCCOY
Vice-Pres. for Finance and Treas.: GEORGE S. SYNODI
Vice-Pres. for Univ. Advancement: RICHARD J. TUCHMAN
Assoc. Vice-Pres. for Facilities: LOUIS ANNINO
Dean of Students and Assoc. Vice-Pres. of Student Affairs: REBECCA JOHNSON
Registrar: LYNN M. KOHRN
Librarian: HANKO DOBI
Library of 231,414 vols, 144,120 print documents

Number of teachers: 600 (170 full-time, 430 part-time)
Number of students: 5,540 (4,600 undergraduates, 1,780 graduates)
Publication: *Essays in Arts and Sciences*

DEANS

College of Arts and Sciences: Dr LOURDES ALVAREZ
College of Business and Arts: LAWRENCE FLANAGAN
Henry C. Lee College of Criminal Justice and Forensic Sciences: Dr MARIO THOMAS GABOURY
Tagliatela College of Engineering: Dr RONALD S. HARICHANDRAN
Univ. College: MARSHA HAM

UNIVERSITY OF SAINT JOSEPH

1678 Asylum Ave, West Hartford, CT 06117

Telephone: (860) 232-4571
E-mail: admissions@sjc.edu
Internet: www.usj.edu

Founded 1932
Private control
Academic year: September to August

Pres.: Dr PAMELA TROTMAN REID
Provost: Dr MICHELLE KALIS
Vice-Pres. for Enrolment Management: GARY L. SHERMAN
Vice-Pres. for Finance and Admin.: SHAWN HARRINGTON
Vice-Pres. for Institutional Advancement: DOUGLAS NELSON
Vice-Pres. for Student Affairs and Dean for Students: Dr CHERYL A. BARNARD
Registrar: ALLISON MISKY
Dir for Library: LINDA GEFFNER
Library of 141,600 vols (incl. books, ebooks and cjournals)
Number of teachers: 110 (full-time)
Number of students: 2,600

DEANS

School of Education: Dr KATHLEEN A. BUTLER
School of Graduate and Professional Studies: Dr DANIEL NUSSBAUM
School of Health and Natural Sciences: Dr SANDRA AFFENITO
School of Humanities and Social Sciences: Dr WAYNE STEELY
School of Pharmacy: Dr JOSEPH R. OFOSU

WESLEYAN UNIVERSITY

45 Wyllys Ave, Middletown, CT 06459

Telephone: (860) 685-2000
E-mail: admission@wesleyan.edu
Internet: www.wesleyan.edu

Founded 1831
Private control
Academic year: September to May

Pres.: Dr MICHAEL S. ROTH
Provost and Vice-Pres. for Academic Affairs: Prof. Dr ROB ROSENTHAL
Vice-Pres. for Finance and Admin.: JOHN C. MEERTS
Vice-Pres. for Student Affairs: MICHAEL J. WHALEY
Vice-Pres. for Univ. Relations: BARBARA-JAN WILSON
Registrar: ANNA C. G. VAN DER BURG
Dean of Admissions and Financial Aid: NANCY HARGRAVE MEISLAHN
Univ. Librarian: PATRICIA TULLY
Library: 1.2m. vols
Number of teachers: 375
Number of students: 3,400 (undergraduates and postgraduates)
Publication: *History and Theory*

DEANS

Arts and Humanities: Prof. ANDREW CURRAN
Natural Sciences and Mathematics: Prof. ISHITA MUKERJI
Social Sciences and Interdisciplinary Programmes: Prof. GARY SHAW

WESTERN CONNECTICUT STATE UNIVERSITY

181 White St, Danbury, CT 06810

Telephone: (203) 837-8210
E-mail: admissions@wcsu.edu
Internet: www.wcsu.edu

Founded 1903
State control
Academic year: August to May

Pres.: JAMES W. SCHMOTTER
Provost and Vice-Pres. for Academic Affairs: Dr JANE MCBRIDE GATES
Vice-Pres. for Finance and Admin.: PAUL REIS
Vice-Pres. for Student Affairs: WALTER B. BERNSTEIN
Chief Information Officer: LORRAINE CAPOBIANCO
Dean of Graduate Studies and External Programs: Dr BURTON PERETTI
Dean of Student Affairs: WALTER CRAMER
Registrar: LOURDES CRUZ
Dir of Library Services: Dr ED O'HARA
Number of teachers: 530 (224 full-time and 300 part-time)
Number of students: 6,400 (4,840 full-time and 1,560 part-time)

DEANS

Ancell School of Business: ALLEN D. MORTON
School of Arts and Sciences: Dr ABBEY ZINK
School of Professional Studies: MARYANN ROSSI
School of Visual and Performing Arts: Prof. Dr DANIEL GOBLE

YALE UNIVERSITY

POB 208234, New Haven, CT 06520-8234

Telephone: (203) 432-2550
E-mail: student.questions@yale.edu
Internet: www.yale.edu

Founded 1701, named Yale College 1718, present name and status 1861
Private control

Pres.: Dr RICHARD CHARLES LEVIN
Provost: Dr PETER SALOVEY
Vice-Pres. and Gen. Counsel: Dr DOROTHY KATHRYN ROBINSON
Vice-Pres. and Sec.: Dr LINDA KOCH LORIMER
Vice-Pres. for Devt: INGE THERESIA REICHENBACH
Vice-Pres. for Finance and Business Operations: SHAUNA RYAN KING
Vice-Pres. for Human Resources and Admin.: MICHAEL ALLAN PEEL
Vice-Pres. for New Haven and State Affairs and Campus Devt: Dr BRUCE D. ALEXANDER
Vice-Pres. for West Campus Planning and Program Devt: Dr SCOTT ALLAN STROBEL
Univ. Registrar: GABRIEL G. OLSZEWSKI
Librarian: Dr SUSAN GIBBONS
Library: see under Libraries and Archives
Number of teachers: 3,800
Number of students: 13,650 (incl. 5,280 undergraduate, 6,380 graduate

Publications: *American Journal of Science, American Scientist, Journal of American Oriental Society, Journal of Biological Chemistry, Journal of Industrial Ecology* (4 a year), *Journal of Music Theory, Journal of the History of Medicine and Allied Sciences, Theatre Magazine* (3 a year), *Yale Alumni Magazine* (1 a year), *Yale French Studies, Yale Human Rights and Development Law Journal* (1 a year), *Yale Journal of Biology and Medicine* (4 a year), *Yale Journal of Health Policy, Law and Ethics* (2 a year), *Yale Journal of International Law* (2 a year), *Yale Journal of Law and Feminism* (2 a year), *Yale Journal of Law and the Humanities* (2 a year), *Yale Journal on Regulation, Yale Law and Policy Review, Yale Law Journal* (8 a year), *Yale Literary Magazine* (2 a year), *Yale Review, Yale Scientific Magazine* (4 a year)

DEANS

School of Architecture: ROBERT A. M. STERN
School of Art: ROBERT STORR
Divinity School: HAROLD W. ATTRIDGE
School of Drama: JAMES BUNDY
School of Engineering and Applied Science: T. KYLE VANDERLICK
School of Forestry and Environmental Studies: PETER CRANE
Law School: ROBERT C. POST
School of Management: EDWARD A. SNYDER
School of Medicine: ROBERT J. ALPERN
School of Music: ROBERT BLOCKER
School of Nursing: MARGARET GREY
School of Public Health: PAUL D. CLEARY
Graduate School of Arts and Sciences: THOMAS D. POLLARD
Yale College: MARY MILLER

PROFESSORS
(Some staff serve in more than one faculty)

School of Architecture:

ALEXLEY, J. W.
BEEBY, T. H., Architectural Design
BLOOMER, K. C., Architectural Design
GARVIN, A., Urban Planning and Devt
HAYDEN, D., Architecture and Urbanism
KOETTER, F. H.
PLATTUS, A. J.
PURVES, A., Architectural Design
STERN, R. A. M.

School of Art:

BARTH, F., Painting and Printmaking
BENSON, R. M., Photography
DE BRETTEVILLE, S. L., Graphic Design
LYTLE, W. R., Painting
PAPAGEORGE, T., Photography
REED, R. J., Jr, Painting and Printmaking
STOCKHOLDER, J., Sculpture

Faculty of Arts and Sciences (Yale College and Graduate School):

ACKERMAN, B., Law and Political Science
ADAIR, R. K., Physics
ADAMS, M. McC., Philosophy, Religious Studies
ADAMS, R. M., Philosophy
ADORNO, R., Spanish
AGNEW, J.-C., American Studies and History
ALEXANDER, J. C., Sociology
ALEXANDROV, V. E., Slavic Languages and Literatures
ALHASSID, Y., Physics
ALTMAN, S., Biology
ALTONJI, J., Economics
AMANAT, A., History
ANDERSON, S. R., Linguistics
ANDREW, D., Comparative Literature, Film Studies
ANDREWS, D. W. K., Economics and Statistics
ANGULIN, D., Computer Science
APPADURAI, A., Int. Studies
APPELQUIST, T. W., Physics
AUSTIN, D. J., Chemistry
AVNI, O., French
BAILYN, C., Astronomy, Physics
BALTAY, C., Physics and Astronomy
BANAC, I., History
BARRON, A., Statistics
BATISTA, V. S., Chemistry
BEALS, R. W., Mathematics
BENHABIB, S., Philosophy, Political Science

BERCOVICI, D., Geology and Geophysics
BERNER, R. A., Geology and Geophysics
BERNSTEIN, I. B., Mechanical Engineering and Physics
BERRY, S. T., Economics
BERS, V., Classics
BEWLEY, T. F., Economics
BLOCH, R. H., French
BLOOM, H. I., English Language and Literature
BLOOM, P., Psychology and Linguistics
BOBZIEN, S., Philosophy
BOORMAN, S. A., Sociology
BÖWERING, G. H., Religious Studies
BRACKEN, P., Management and Political Science
BRAINARD, W. C., Economics
BRAUND, S. M., Classics
BRISMAN, L., English Language and Literature
BRODHEAD, R. H., American Studies, English Language and Literature
BROMLEY, D. A., Physics
BROMWICH, D., English Language and Literature
BROOKS, P., Comparative Literature and French
BROWN, D. J., Economics
BROWN, T. H., Psychology and Physiology
BROWNELL, K. D., Psychology
BRUDVIG, G., Chemistry
BURGER, R. L., Anthropology
BUSHKOVITCH, P. A., History
BUSS, L. W., Ecology and Evolutionary Biology, Geology and Geophysics
BUTLER, J., History and American Studies, Religious Studies
CAMERON, D. R., Political Science
CAMPBELL, J., English Language and Literature
CARBY, H. V., African American Studies and American Studies
CASSON, A. W., Mathematics
CASTEN, R., Physics
CHANG, J. T., Statistics
CHANG, K.-I. S., East Asian Languages and Literatures
CHANG, R. K., Applied Physics, Physics and Electrical Engineering
CHU, B.-T., Mechanical Engineering
CLARK, K., Comparative Literature and Slavic Languages and Literatures
COIFMAN, R. R., Mathematics and Computer Science
COLEMAN, J., Philosophy
CRABTREE, R. H., Chemistry
CROSS, R. J., Jr, Chemistry
CROTHERS, D. M., Chemical Engineering, Chemistry and Molecular Physics and Biochemistry
DAVIS, D., Sociology
DE LA MORA, J. F., Mechanical Engineering
DELLAPORTA, S., Biology
DEMOS, J. P., Religious Studies, Near Eastern Languages and Civilizations, and History
DENNING, M., American Studies
DE ROSE, K., Philosophy
DEVORET, M., Applied Physics and Physics
DIMOCK, W. C., American Studies, English Language and Literature
DONOGHUE, M. J., Ecology and Environmental Biology
DORSEY, J., Computer Science
DOUDNA, J., Molecular Biophysics and Biochemistry
DUDLEY, K., American Studies
DUNCAN, J., Diagnostic Radiology, Electrical Engineering
DUVAL, E. M., French
EIRE, C. M. N., History and Religious Studies
EISENSTAT, S. C., Computer Science
ELIMELECH, M., Chemical Engineering
ENGEL, E., Economics

ENGELMAN, D. M., Molecular Biophysics and Biochemistry
ENGELSTEIN, L., History
ERRINGTON, J. J., Anthropology, East Asian Languages and Literatures
EVENSON, R. E., Economics
FAIR, R. C., Economics
FALLER, J. W., Jr, Chemistry
FARAGHER, J. M., American Studies, History
FEIGELBAUM, J., Computer Science
FEIT, W., Mathematics
FELMAN, S., French and Comparative Literature
FISCHER, M. J., Computer Science
FLAVELL, R. A., Immunobiology and Biology
FLEURY, P., Engineering and Applied Physics, Physics
FOLTZ, W. J., African Studies and Political Science
FOSTER, B. R., Near Eastern Languages and Civilizations
FRAADE, S. D., Religious Studies
FRANK, R., English Language and Literature
FREEDMAN, P. H., History
FRENKEL, I. B., Mathematics
FRY, P. H., English Language and Literature
GADDIS, J. L., History
GAREN, A., Molecular Biophysics and Biochemistry
GARLAND, H., Mathematics
GAUTHIER, J. A., Geology and Geophysics
GEANAKOPLOS, J., Economics
GELERNTNER, D., Computer Science
GERBER, A., Political Science
GHOSH, S., Molecular Biophysics and Biochemistry
GILMORE, G., African American Studies, History
GILROY, P., Sociology and African American Studies
GIRVIN, S. M., Physics and Applied Physics
GLIER, I., Germanic Languages and Literatures
GOLDBERG, P., Economics
GOLDBLATT, H., Medieval Slavic Languages and Literatures
GOLDSMITH, M. H., Biology
GOLDSMITH, T. H., Biology
GOLDSTEIN, L. M., Linguistics
GOMEZ, A., Mechanical Engineering
GONZÁLEZ ECHEVERRÍA, R. O., Hispanic and Comparative Literatures
GOODYEAR, S. S., English Language and Literature
GORDON, R. B., Geology and Geophysics
GORDON, R. W., History, Law
GRAEDEL, T., Geology and Geophysics
GREEN, D., Political Science
GRIFFITH, E. H., African and African American Studies
GRINDLEY, N. D. F., Molecular Biophysics and Biochemistry
GROBER, R., Applied Physics and Physics
GRUENDLER, B., Near Eastern Languages and Civilizations
GUICHARNAUD, J. E., French
GUINNANE, T., Economics and History
GUTAS, D., Near Eastern Languages and Civilizations
HALLER, G. L., Chemical Engineering and Chemistry
HAMADA, K., Economics
HAMILTON, A. D., Chemistry
HAMLIN, C., Germanic Languages and Literatures and Comparative Literature
HAMMER, L., English Language and Literature
HANSEN, V., History
HARMS, R. W., African Studies, History
HARRIES, K., Philosophy
HARRIS, J., Physics
HARSHAV, B., Comparative Literature

HARTIGAN, J. A., Statistics
HARTWIG, J. F., Chemistry
HAYDEN, D., American Studies
HAYES, C., Religious Studies
HENRICH, V. E., Applied Sciences, Physics
HERSEY, G. L., History of Art
HICKEY, L. J., Geology and Geophysics
HILL, A., Anthropology
HOLE, F., Anthropology
HOLFORD, T., Public Health and Statistics
HOLLOWAY, J. S., History
HOLMES, F. L., History
HOMANS, M. B., English, Women's and Gender Studies
HORN, L. R., Linguistics
HORVÁTH, C. G., Chemical Engineering
HUDAK, P., Computer Science
HYMAN, P. E., Modern Jewish History
IACHELLO, F., Physics and Chemistry
INSLER, S., Linguistics
JACKSON, K. D., Spanish and Portuguese
JACOBS, C., Comparative Literature
JACOBSON, M. F., African American Studies, American Studies, History
JAYNES, G. D., Economics, African Studies and African American Studies
JESHION, R., Philosophy
JOHNSON, M. A., Chemistry
JOHNSON, M. K., Psychology
JONES, P. W., Mathematics
JORGENSEN, W. L., Chemistry
JOSEPH, G. M., History
KAGAN, D., Classics and History
KAGAN, S., Classics, Philosophy
KAMENS, E., East Asian Languages and Literatures
KANKEL, D. R., Biology
KARATO, S., Geology and Geophysics
KAVANAGH, T., French
KAZDIN, A. E., Psychology
KEANE, M., Economics
KEIL, F. C., Psychology and Linguistics
KELLY, W. W., Anthropology
KENNEDY, P. M., History
KENNEY, J., Astronomy
KEVLES, D. J., History
KIERNAN, B. F., History
KLEIN, M. J., History of Science and Physics
KLEINER, D. E. E., Classics and History of Art
KLEVORICK, A. K., Economics
KONIGSBERG, W., Molecular Biophysics and Biochemistry
KUTZINSKY, V. M., English Language and Literature, African American Studies and American Studies
LAFRANCE, M., Psychology, Women's and Gender Studies
LANG, S., Mathematics
LARSON, R. B., Astronomy
LAWLER, T., English Language and Literature
LAYTON, B. R., Religious Studies and Near Eastern Languages and Civilizations
LEE, R., Mathematics
LEVIN, R. C., Economics
LIFTON, R., Medicine, Genetics, Molecular Biophysics and Biochemistry
LONG, M. B., Mechanical Engineering and Applied Physics
MA, T.-P., Electrical Engineering and Applied Physics
MCDERMOTT, D. V., Computer Science
MACDOWELL, S. W., Physics
MACNAB, R. M., Molecular Biophysics and Biochemistry
MANDELBROT, B. B., Mathematics
MANLEY, L. G., English Language and Literature
MARCUS, I. G., Jewish History
MARGULIS, G. A., Mathematics
MARMOR, T., Public Management and Political Science
MARTIN, D., Religious Studies
MATTHEWS, J. F., History and Classics

MAYER, E., Anthropology
MAYHEW, D. R., Political Science
MAZZOTTA, G., Italian
MENDELSOHN, R., Economics, Forestry and Enviromental Studies, Management
MENOCAL, M. R., Spanish
MERRIMAN, J. M., History
MILLER, C. L., French, and African and African American Studies
MILLER, G., Molecular Bophysics and Biochemistry
MOCHRIE, S., Physics and Applied Physics
MONTGOMERY, D., History
MOORE, P. B., Chemistry and Molecular Biophysics and Biochemistry
MOOSEKER, M. S., Biology and Cell Biology
MORGAN, R. P., Theory of Music
MORRIS, S., Economics
MORSE, A. S., Computer Science, Electrical Engineering
MUSSER, C., American Studies, Film Studies
NALEBUFF, B., Economics
NARENDRA, K. S., Electrical Engineering
NOVICK, A., Ecology and Environmental Biology
ORNSTON, L. N., Biology
ORSZAG, S. A., Mathematics
OUTKA, G., Philosophy and Christian Ethics
PARK, J., Geology and Geophysics
PARKER, P. D. M., Physics
PATTERSON, A., English Language and Literature
PATTERSON, L., English Language and Literature
PEARCE, D. G., Economics
PETERSON, L. H., English Language and Literature
PEUCKER, B., Germanic Languages and Literatures
PFEFFERLE, L. D., Chemical Engineering
PHILLIPS, P. C. B., Economics and Statistics
PIATETSKI-SHAPIRO, I., Mathematics
PLANTINGA, L. B., History of Music
POLAK, B., Economics
POLLARD, D. B., Statistics and Mathematics
POWELL, J. R., Ecology and Environmental Biology
PROBER, D. E., Applied Physics, Physics
QUINT, D. L., English and Comparative Literature
RAE, D. W., Political Science and Management
RANIS, G., Int. Economics
RAWSON, C., English Language and Literature
READ, N., Physics and Applied Physics
REED, M. A., Electrical Engineering and Applied Physics
REGAN, L. J., Molecular Biophysics and Biochemistry
RILEY, M. A., Ecology and Environmental Biology
ROACH, J. R., Theatre and English
ROBINSON, F. C., English
ROEDER, S., Biology
ROEMER, J. E., Economics, Political Science
ROGERS, J., English Language and Literature
ROKHLIN, V., Computer Science and Mathematics
ROSE-ACKERMAN, S., Jurisprudence, Law and Political Science
ROSENBAUM, J. L., Biology
ROSENBLUTH, F. M., Political Science
ROSNER, D. E., Chemical Engineering
RUDDLE, F. H., Biology and Genetics
RUSSETT, B. M., Political Science and Int. Relations
RUSSETT, C. E., History
RYE, D. M., Geology and Geophysics
SACHDEV, S., Physics and Applied Physics
SALOVEY, P., Epidemiology and Public Health, Psychology
SALTZMAN, W. M., Chemical Engineering

SAMMONS, J. L., Germanic Languages and Literatures
SANDWEISS, J., Physics
SANNEH, L., History, Divinity
SAUNDERS, M., Chemistry
SCARF, H. E., Economics
SCHEFFLER, H. W., Anthropology
SCHEPARTZ, A., Chemistry
SCHMIDT, M. P., Physics
SCHULTZ, M. H., Computer Science
SCHULZ, T. P., Economics and Demography
SCHWARTZ, S. B., History
SCOTT, J. C., Political Science and Anthropology
SEILACHER, A., Geology and Geophysics
SHANKAR, R., Physics and Applied Physics
SHAPIRO, I., Political Science
SHIN, S.-J., Philosophy
SHUBIK, M., Economics
SHULMAN, R. G., Chemistry, Molecular Biophysics and Biochemistry
SILBERSCHATZ, A., Computer Science
SIMPSON, W. K., Near Eastern Languages and Civilizations
SINGER, J. L., Psychology
SIU, H. F., Anthropology
SKINNER, B. J., Geology and Geophysics
SKOWRONEK, S., Political Science and Social Science
SMITH, R. B., Geology and Geophysics
SMITH, S. B., Political Science
SMOOKE, M. D., Mechanical Engineering
SNYDER, M., Molecular Biophysics and Biochemistry
SOFIA, S., Astronomy
SÖLL, D. G., Molecular Biophysics and Biochemistry, Biology and Chemistry
SOMMERFIELD, C. M., Physics
SPENCE, J. D., History
SREENIVASAN, K. R., Mechanical Engineering, Physics and Applied Physics
SRINIVASAN, T. N., Economics
STEITZ, T. A., Chemistry, Molecular Biophysics and Biochemistry
STEPTO, R. B., English, African American Studies, American Studies
STERNBERG, R. J., Psychology and Education
STIMSON, H. M., Linguistics, East Asian Languages and Literatures
STONE, A. D., Physics and Applied Physics
STOUT, H. S., History, Religious Studies and American Studies, American Christianity
STROBEL, S., Molecular Biophysics and Biochemistry
SUMMERS, W. C., History of Medicine and Science, Molecular Biophysics and Biochemistry, Therapeutic Radiology
SUNDER, S., Accounting, Economics and Finance
SZELENYI, I., Sociology
SZWED, J. F., Anthropology, African and African American Studies and American Studies
THOMPSON, R. F., African American Studies and History of Art
TREAT, J., East Asian Languages and Literatures
TRUMPENER, K., English and Comparative Literature
TULLY, J. C., Chemistry, Physics and Applied Physics
TUREKIAN, K. K., Geology and Geophysics
TURNER, F. M., History
TURNER, H. A., Jr, History
UDRY, C., Economics
URRY, C. M., Physics and Astrophysics
VACCARO, P. H., Chemistry
VAISNYS, J. R., Ecology and Environmental Biology, Electrical Engineering
VALENTINE, A. M., Chemistry
VALESIO, P., Italian
VALIS, N., Spanish and Portuguese
VAN ALTENA, W. F., Astronomy

VENCLOVA, T., Slavic Languages and Literatures
VERONIS, G., Geology and Geophysics
VRBA, E. S., Geology and Geophysics
WAGNER, A. R., Psychology
WAGNER, G. P., Ecology and Environmental Biology
WALZ, J. Y., Chemical Engineering
WARD, D. C., Genetics, Molecular Biophysics and Biochemistry
WARNER, J. H., American Studies, History, History of Medicine
WATTS, D. P., Anthropology
WEINSTEIN, S., Religious Studies, Buddhist Studies and East Asian Languages and Literatures
WEISS, H., Near Eastern Archaeology, Near Eastern Languages and Civilizations, and Anthropology
WELSH, A., English Language and Literature
WETTLAUFER, J., Geology and Geophysics, Physics
WEXLER, L., American Studies
WHEELER, S., Law and the Social Sciences
WIKSTROM, L. L., Chemical Engineering
WILSON, R., Religious Studies
WINTER, J., History
WOOD, J. L., Chemistry
WOODALL, J. M., Electrical Engineering
WRIGHT, C. M., History of Music
WRIGHTSON, K., History
WYMAN, R. J., Biology
WYNN, K., Psychology
YEAZELL, R. B., English Language and Literature
ZELLER, M. E., Physics
ZIEGLER, F. E., Chemistry
ZIGLER, E. F., Psychology
ZILM, K. W., Chemistry
ZINN, R. J., Astronomy
ZUCKER, S. W., Computer Science and Electrical Engineering
ZUCKERMAN, G. J., Mathematics

Divinity School:

ADAMS, M. MC., Historical Theology
ATTRIDGE, H. W., New Testament
BARTLETT, D. L., Preaching and Christian Communication
COLLINS, A. Y., Old Testament Interpretation and Criticism
DITTES, J. E., Pastoral Theology and Psychology
FARLEY, M. A., Christian Ethics
FASSLER, M. E., Music History and Liturgy
KELSEY, D. H., Theology
MURRAY, T., Organ
OGLETREE, T. W., Theological Ethics
OUTKA, G., Philosophy and Christian Ethics
SANNEH, L. O., Missions and World Christianity and History
SPINKS, B. D., Liturgical Studies
STOUT, H. S., American Religious History
VOLF, M., Systematic Theology
WILSON, R. R., Old Testament and Religious Studies

School of Drama:

BUNDY, J.

School of Forestry and Environmental Studies:

ASHTON, M. S., Silviculture and Forest Ecology
BERLYN, G. P., Anatomy and Physiology of Trees
BREWER, G. D., Resource Policy and Management
BURCH, W. R., Jr, Natural Resource Management
DOVE, M. R., Social Ecology
ESTY, D. C., Environmental Law and Policy
GRAEDEL, T. E., Industrial Ecology
GREGOIRE, T. G., Forest Management
KELLERT, S. R., Social Ecology

LYONS, J. R., Natural Resource Management
MENDELSOHN, R., Forest Policy
MONTAGNINI, F., Tropical Forestry
OLIVER, C. D., Forest Policy
REPETTO, R., Economics and Sustainable Devt
SCHMITZ, O. J., Population and Community Ecology
SICCIAMA, T. G., Forest Ecology
SPETH, J. G., Environmental Policy and Sustainable Devt
WARGO, J. P., Environmental Risk Analysis, Political Science

School of Law:

ACKERMAN, B. A., Law and Political Science
AMAR, A. R., Law
AYRES, I., Law
BALKIN, J. M., Constitutional Law and the First Amendment
BRILMAYER, L., Int. Law
BURT, R. A., Law
CARTER, S. L., Law
CHUA, A. L., Law
COLEMAN, J. L., Jurisprudence and Philosophy
CURTIS, D. E., Law
DALTON, H. L., Law
DAMASKA, M. R., Law
DAYS, D. S., III, Law
DEUTSCH, J. G., Law
DIGNAM, B., Law
DUKE, S. B., Law
ELLICKSON, R. C., Property and Urban Law
ESTY, D. C., Environmental Law and Policy
FISS, O. M., Law
GEWIRTZ, P. D., Constitutional Law
GOLDSTEIN, A. S., Law
GORDON, R. W., Law and Legal History
GRAETZ, M. J., Law
HANSMANN, H. B., Law
KAHAN, D. M., Law
KAHN, P. W., Law and the Humanities
KLEVORICK, A. K., Law and Economics
KOH, H. H., Int. Law
LANGBEIN, J. H., Law and Legal History
LUCHT, C. L., Law
MASHAW, J. L., Law
PETERS, J. K., Law
POTTENGER, J. L., Law
PRIEST, G. L., Law and Economics
REISMAN, W. M., Int. Law
RESNIK, J., Law
ROMANO, R., Law
ROSE, C. M., Law and Organization
ROSE-ACKERMAN, S., Jurisprudence (Law School and Dept of Political Science)
RUBENFELD, J., Law
SCHUCK, P. H., Law
SCHULTZ, V., Law and Social Sciences
SIEGEL, R., Law
SIMON, J. G., Law
SOLOMON, R. A., Law
STITH, K., Law
WEDGWOOD, R., Law
WHITMAN, J. Q., Comparative and Foreign Law
WIZNER, S., Law
YOSHINO, K., Law

Yale School of Management:

BRACKEN, P., Management and Political Science
BREWER, G. D., Resource Policy and Management
CHEN, ZH., Finance
CHEVALIER, J. A., Finance and Economics
DHAR, R., Marketing
FEINSTEIN, J., Economics
GARSTKA, S., Practice of Management
GARTEN, J. E., Practice of Int. Trade and Finance
GOETZMANN, W., Management and Finance Studies
IBBOTSON, R., Practice of Finance
INGERSOLL, J. E., Jr, Int. Trade and Finance

KAPLAN, E., Management Sciences, Public Health
LI, L., Production Management
LÓPEZ-DE-SILANES, F., Finance and Economics
MACAVOY, P., Management Studies
MARMOR, T. R., Public Policy and Management
NALEBUFF, B., Economics and Management
OSTER, S. M., Management and Entrepreneurship
POLAK, B., Economics and Management
RAE, D. W., Management
ROUWENHORST, K. G., Finance
SCOTT MORTON, F. M., Economics
SEN, S. K., Organization, Management and Marketing
SHUBIK, M. S., Mathematical Institutional Economics
SPIEGEL, M., Finance
SUNDER, S., Accounting, Economics and Finance
SWERSEY, A. J., Operations Research
VROOM, V. H., Organization and Management, Psychology
WELCH, I., Finance
WITTINK, D. R., Management and Marketing

School of Medicine:

AGHAJANIAN, G. K., Psychiatry and Pharmacology
ANDERSON, K. S., Pharmacology
ANDIMAN, W. A., Paediatrics and Epidemiology and Public Health
ANDREWS, N. W., Cell Biology, Microbial Pathogenesis
ANDRIOLE, V. T., Internal Medicine
ANYAN, W. R., Paediatrics
ARONSON, P. S., Internal Medicine and Cellular and Molecular Physiology
ASKENASE, P. W., Internal Medicine
BAKER, M. D., Emergency Medicine, Paediatrics
BALTIMORE, R. S., Paediatrics, Infectious Diseases and Epidemiology and Public Health
BARASH, P. G., Anaesthesiology
BARNSTABLE, C. J., Neurobiology, Ophthalmology and Visual Science
BARON, R., Orthopaedics and Rehabilitation, Internal Medicine and Cell Biology
BARTOSHUK, L. M., Surgery
BATSFORD, W. P., Internal Medicine
BEARDSLEY, G. P., Paediatric Haematology and Pharmacology
BEHRMAN, H. R., Obstetrics and Gynaecology
BELSKY, J. L., Internal Medicine
BERLINER, N., Genetics and Internal Medicine
BIA, F. J., Medicine and Laboratory Medicine
BIA, M. J., Medicine
BINDER, H. J., Cellular and Molecular Physiology, Digestive Diseases and Internal Medicine
BLATT, S. J., Psychiatry and Psychology
BOLOGNIA, J. L., Dermatology
BOOSS, J., Neurology and Laboratory Medicine
BORON, W. F., Cellular and Molecular Physiology
BOTHWELL, A., Immunobiology
BOTTOMLY, H. K., Immunobiology and Molecular, Cellular and Developmental Biology
BOULPAEP, E. L., Cellular and Molecular Physiology
BOWERS, M. B., Jr, Psychiatry
BOYER, J. L., Digestive Diseases, Internal Medicine
BRACKEN, M. B., Epidemiology and Public Health, Chronic Disease Epidemiology, Neurology

BRASH, D. E., Genetics, Therapeutic Radiology

BRAVERMAN, I. M., Dermatology

BROADUS, A. E., Internal Medicine and Cellular and Molecular Physiology

BROWN, T. H., Cellular and Molecular Physiology, Psychology

BUCALA, R., Medicine

BUNNEY, B. S., Psychiatry and Pharmacology

BURRELL, M. I., Diagnostic Radiology

BURROW, G. N., Obstetrics and Gynaecology

BYRNE, T. N., Neurology and Medicine

CABIN, H., Internal Medicine

CADMAN, E. C., Internal Medicine

CAPLAN, M., Cellular and Molecular Physiology

CARPENTER, T. O., Endocrinology, Paediatrics

CARTER, D., Pathology

CENTRELLA, M., Surgery

CHAMBERS, S. K., Obstetrics and Gynaecology

CHANDLER, W. K., Cellular and Molecular Physiology

CHASE, H. S., Jr, Medicine

CHENG, Y.-C., Pharmacology

CHOI, Y., Laboratory Medicine, Pathology

CLEARY, J. P., Internal Medicine

CLEMAN, M., Internal Medicine

COCA-PRADOS, M., Ophthalmology and Visual Science

COHEN, L. B., Cellular and Molecular Physiology

COHEN, L. S., Internal Medicine

COLEMAN, D., Medicine

COLLINS, J. G., Anaesthesiology

COOLEY, L., Cell Biology, Genetics

COONEY, L. M., Jr, Internal Medicine

COSTA, J. C., Pathology

CRAFT, J., Immunobiology, Medicine

CRESSWELL, P., Immunobiology

CULLEN, M. R., Medicine, Occupational and Environmental Medicine, Public Health

CURTIS, A. M., Diagnostic Radiology

DANNIES, P. S., Pharmacology

DAW, N. W., Ophthalmology and Visual Science

DE CAMILLI, P. V., Cell Biology

DEISSEROTH, A. B., Internal Medicine

DE LUCA, V. A., Internal Medicine

D'ESCOPO, N. D., Internal Medicine

DE VITA, V. T., Internal Medicine

DI MAIO, D., Genetics

DOBBINS, J. W., Internal Medicine

DONABEDIAN, R. K., Laboratory Medicine

DU BOIS, A. B., Epidemiology and Public Health, and Cellular and Molecular Physiology

DUFFY, T. P., Internal Medicine

DUNCAN, C. C., Neurosurgery and Paediatrics

DUNCAN, J., Diagnostic Radiology

EDBERG, S. C., Internal Medicine, Laboratory Medicine

EHRENKRANZ, R. A., Neonatology, Obstetrics and Gynaecology, Paediatrics

EHRENWERTH, J., Anaesthesiology

EHRLICH, B., Pharmacology and Cellular and Molecular Biology

ELEFTERIADES, J. A., Surgery

ELIAS, J. A., Medicine

FARBER, L. R., Internal Medicine

FERRO-NOVICK, S., Cell Biology

FINKELSTEIN, F. O., Internal Medicine

FISCH, D., Epidemiology of Microbial Diseases

FISCHER, D. S., Internal Medicine

FISCHER, J. J., Therapeutic Radiology

FLAVELL, R., Immunobiology, Molecular, Cellular and Developmental Biology

FLOCH, M. H., Internal Medicine

FLYNN, S. D., Pathology, Surgery

FORBUSH, B., III, Cellular and Molecular Physiology

FORGET, B. G., Medicine and Genetics

FORMAN, B. H., Internal Medicine

FORREST, J. N., Jr, Medicine

FRIEDLAENDER, G. E., Orthopaedics and Rehabilitation

FRIEDLAND, G. H., Epidemiology, Medicine

GALÁN, J., Cell Biology, Microbial Pathogenesis

GEIBEL, J. P., Surgery

GENEL, M., Paediatrics

GHOSH, S., Immunobiology, Molecular Biophysics and Biochemistry, Molecular, Cellular and Developmental Biology

GIEBISCH, G. H., Cellular and Molecular Physiology

GIFFORD, R. H., Internal Medicine

GLAZER, P. M., Therapeutic Radiology and Genetics

GLICKMAN, M. G., Diagnostic Radiology and Surgery

GOLDMAN-RAKIC, P., Neurobiology, Neurology

GOLDSTEIN, S. A. N., Cellular and Molecular Physiology, Paediatrics

GONZALEZ, C., Ophthalmology and Visual Science, Paediatrics

GORE, J. C., Diagnostic Radiology

GORELICK, F., Internal Medicine, Digestive Diseases and Cell Biology

GREEN, B., Surgery

GREENFELD, D. G., Psychiatry

GREER, C., Neurobiology, Neurosurgery

GRIFFITH, B., Laboratory Medicine

GRIFFITH, E. E. H., Psychiatry

GROSS, I., Neonatology, Obstetrics and Gynaecology, Paediatrics

GROSZMANN, R. J., Digestive Diseases, Internal Medicine

GUSBERG, R. J., Surgery

HAFFTY, B. G., Therapeutic Radiology

HAYSLETT, J. P., Medicine

HEALD, P. W., Dermatology

HEBERT, S. C., Cellular and Molecular Physiology, Medicine

HENDLER, E. D., Internal Medicine

HENINGER, G. R., Psychiatry

HERBERT, P. N., Internal Medicine

HIERHOLZER, W. J., Internal Medicine and Epidemiology

HINES, R. L., Anaesthesiology

HOCKFIELD, S., Neurology

HOFFER, P. B., Diagnostic Radiology

HOFFMAN, J. F., Cellular and Molecular Physiology

HOLBROOK, N. J., Geriatrics

HOLFORD, T. R., Epidemiology and Public Health

HORWICH, A. L., Genetics and Paediatrics

HOSTETTER, M. K., Paediatrics

IANNINI, P. B., Internal Medicine

INNIS, R. B., Psychiatry and Pharmacology

INOUYE, S. K., Geriatrics

INSOGNA, K. L., Internal Medicine

JACOBS, S. C., Psychiatry

JACOBY, R. O., Comparative Medicine

JAFFE, C. C., Diagnostic Radiology and Internal Medicine

JAMIESON, J. D., Cell Biology

JANEWAY, C., Immunobiology and Molecular, Cellular and Developmental Biology

JATLOW, P. I., Laboratory Medicine and Psychiatry

JOINER, K. A., Internal Medicine, Cell Biology and Infectious Diseases

JOKL, P., Orthopaedics and Rehabilitation

KACZMAREK, L. K., Cellular and Molecular Physiology and Pharmacology

KAETZ, H. W., Internal Medicine

KAIN, Z., Anaesthesiology, Paediatrics

KANTOR, F. S., Internal Medicine

KAPADIA, C. R., Internal Medicine

KASHGARIAN, M., Pathology and Molecular, Cellular and Developmental Biology

KASL, S. V., Chronic Disease Epidemiology

KAVATHAS, P., Genetics, Immunobiology, Laboratory Medicine

KELLER, M. S., Diagnostic Radiology and Paediatrics

KENNEY, J. D., Internal Medicine

KICKBUSCH, I. S., Epidemiology and Public Health

KIDD, K. K., Genetics, Molecular, Cellular and Developmental Biology, and Psychiatry

KIER, E. L., Diagnostic Radiology

KIM, J. H., Pathology

KINDER, B. K., Surgery

KLIGER, A. S., Internal Medicine

KOCSIS, J. D., Neurology

KOPF, G. S., Surgery

KOSTEN, T. R., Psychiatry

KRUMHOLZ, H. M., Epidemiology and Public Health, Internal Medicine

KRYSTAL, J. H., Psychiatry

LAMOTTE, R. H., Anaesthesiology

LANDRY, M., Laboratory Medicine

LANNIN, D. R., Surgery

LAWSON, J. P., Diagnostic Radiology, Orthopaedics and Rehabilitation

LEADERER, B. P., Public Health, Environmental Studies

LEDER, S. B., Surgery

LEFFELL, D. J., Dermatology

LENTZ, T. L., Cell Biology

LESSER, R. L., Neurology, Ophthalmology and Visual Science

LEVANTHAL, J. M., Nursing, Paediatrics and Child Study Center

LEVINE, R. A., Laboratory Medicine

LEVINE, R. J., Internal Medicine

LEVITIN, H., Internal Medicine

LEVY, L. L., Neurology

LEVY, S. R., Neurology

LIFTON, R. P., Medicine and Genetics

LISTER, G., Jr, Paediatrics and Anaesthesiology

LORBER, M. I., Surgery

LYTTON, B., Surgery, Urology

MCCARTHY, P., Paediatrics, Nursing

MCCARTHY, S., Diagnostic Radiology

MCCLENNAN, B. L., Diagnostic Radiology

MCCORMICK, D., Neurology

MCGLASHAN, T. H., Psychiatry

MCMAHON-PRATT, D., Epidemiology of Microbial Diseases

MCPHEDRAN, P., Laboratory Medicine and Internal Medicine

MADRI, J. A., Pathology

MAHNENSMITH, R., Medicine

MAHONEY, M. J., Genetics, and Obstetrics and Gynaecology, and Paediatrics

MAKUCH, R. W., Epidemiology and Public Health

MALAWISTA, S. E., Medicine

MARCHESI, S. L., Pathology and Laboratory Medicine

MARCHESI, V. T., Pathology, Cell Biology

MARIEB, N. J., Internal Medicine

MARKS, L. E., Environmental Health Sciences

MARSH, J. C., Internal Medicine

MATTHAY, R. A., Medicine

MAZURE, C. M., Psychiatry

MELLMAN, I. S., Cell Biology and Immunobiology

MENT, L. R., Paediatrics and Neurology

MERIKANGAS, K. R., Chronic Disease Epidemiology, Psychiatry

MERSON, M. H., Epidemiology and Public Health

MILLER, I. G., Jr, Epidemiology and Public Health, Molecular Biophysics and Biochemistry, Paediatrics

MILLER, P. L., Anaesthesiology

MILSTONE, L. M., Dermatology

MOCZYDLOWSKI, E. G., Cellular and Molecular Physiology, Pharmacology

MODLIN, I. M., Surgery

MOGHADDAM, B., Neurobiology, Psychiatry

MOOSEKER, M., Cell Biology

MORROW, J. S., Molecular, Cellular and Developmental Biology, Pathology

MOSER, M., Internal Medicine
MOYER, M. S., Paediatrics
NAIM, A., Psychiatry
NAIR, S., Internal Medicine
NATH, R., Therapeutic Radiology
NOVICK, P., Cell Biology
O'MALLEY, S. S., Psychiatry
PATTON, C. L., Epidemiology of Microbial Diseases
PELKER, R. R., Orthopaedics and Rehabilitation
PERILLIE, P. E., Internal Medicine
PERSING, J. A., Surgery and Neurosurgery
PESCHEL, R. E., Therapeutic Radiology
PEZZIMENTI, J. F., Internal Medicine
PIEPMEIER, J. M., Neurosurgery
POBER, J. S., Pathology, Dermatology and Immunobiology
QUAGLIARELLO, V. J., Medicine
RABINOVICI, R., Surgery
RADDING, C. M., Genetics and Molecular Biophysics and Biochemistry
RAFFERTY, T. D., Anaesthesiology
RAKIC, P., Neurology and Neurobiology
RAPPEPORT, J., Internal Medicine
RASTEGAR, A., Medicine
REDMOND, D. E., Jr, Psychiatry and Neurosurgery
RENSHAW, T., Orthopaedics and Rehabilitation
RICHARDS, F. F., Internal Medicine
RISCH, H. A., Chronic Disease Epidemiology
ROCKWELL, S. C., Pharmacology, Therapeutic Radiology
ROEDER, S., Genetics, Molecular, Cellular and Developmental Biology
ROSE, J. K., Pathology and Cell Biology
ROSENBAUM, S., Anaesthesiology
ROSENFIELD, A. T., Diagnostic Radiology
ROSENHECK, R. A., Epidemiology and Public Health, Psychiatry
ROTH, R. H., Jr, Psychiatry and Pharmacology
ROUNSAVILLE, B. J., Psychiatry
RUDDLE, F., Genetics, Molecular, Cellular and Developmental Biology
RUDDLE, N. H., Epidemiology of Microbial Diseases, Immunobiology
RUDNICK, G., Pharmacology
SACKS, F. L., Internal Medicine
SANTOS-SACCHI, J., Surgery
SARTORELLI, A. C., Pharmacology
SASAKI, C. T., Surgery
SCHATZ, D., Immunobiology
SCHLESSINGER, J., Pharmacology
SCHOEN, R., Internal Medicine
SCHOTTENFELD, R. S., Psychiatry
SCHWARTZ, I. R., Surgery
SCHWARTZ, P. E., Obstetrics and Gynaecology
SEASHORE, J. H., Surgery
SEASHORE, M. R., Genetics, Paediatrics
SEGAL, S. S., Cellular and Molecular Physiology
SESSA, W. C., Pharmacology
SHAPIRO, E. D., Epidemiology and Public Health, Paediatrics, Nursing
SHAW, C., Diagnostic Radiology
SHAYWITZ, A. E., Neurology, Paediatrics
SHAYWITZ, S. E., Paediatrics
SHERTER, C. B., Internal Medicine
SHERWIN, R. S., Internal Medicine
SHULMAN, G. I., Internal Medicine, and Cellular and Molecular Physiology
SIEGEL, N. J., Medicine, Paediatrics
SIGWORTH, F. J., Cellular and Molecular Physiology
SILVERMAN, D., Anaesthesiology
SINATRA, R., Anaesthesiology
SIVARAJAN, M., Anaesthesiology
SLAYMAN, C. L., Cellular and Molecular Physiology
SLAYMAN, C. W., Genetics and Cellular and Molecular Physiology
SLEDGE, W. H., Psychiatry

SMITH, B. R., Internal Medicine, Laboratory Medicine, Paediatrics
SNOW, D. L., Psychiatry
SNYDER, E. L., Laboratory Medicine
SPENCER, D. D., Neurosurgery
SPENCER, S. S., Neurology
SPIRO, H. M., Internal Medicine
STERN, D. F., Pathology
STITT, J. T., Cellular and Molecular Physiology, Epidemiology and Environmental Health Sciences
STRITTMATTER, S. M., Neurobiology, Neurology
SULAVIK, S. B., Internal Medicine
SUMMERS, W. C., Therapeutic Radiology, Molecular Biophysics and Biochemistry, and Genetics
SUMPIO, B. E., Surgery
TAMBORLANE, W. V., Paediatrics
TATTERSALL, P., Laboratory Medicine and Genetics
TAYLOR, K. J., Diagnostic Radiology
TIGELAAR, R. E., Dermatology and Immunobiology
TINETTI, M., Medicine, Epidemiology and Public Health
TOULOUKIAN, R. J., Paediatrics, Surgery
TRAUBE, M., Digestive Diseases, Internal Medicine
UDELSMAN, R., Surgery
ULLU, E., Cell Biology, Medicine
VAN DEN POL, A., Neurosurgery
WACKERS, F. J., Diagnostic Radiology and Medicine
WALSH, T. J., Neurology, Ophthalmology and Visual Science
WARD, D. C., Genetics, Molecular Biophysics and Biochemistry
WARDLAW, S. C., Laboratory Medicine
WARREN, G., Cell Biology
WAXMAN, S. G., Neurology, Neurobiology
WEISS, R. M., Surgery, Urology
WEISSMAN, S. M., Genetics and Internal Medicine
WESTCOTT, J. A., Diagnostic Radiology
WHITE, R. I., Jr, Diagnostic Radiology
WRIGHT, F. S., Internal Medicine and Cellular and Molecular Physiology
ZARET, B. L., Diagnostic Radiology, Medicine
ZELTERMAN, D., Epidemiology and Public Health
ZONANA, H. V., Psychiatry

School of Music:

AGAWU, K., Theory of Music
AKI, S., Violin
BERMAN, B., Piano
BRESNICK, M. I., Composition
CHOOKASIAN, L., Voice and Opera
DUFFY, T. C.
FASSLER, M. E.
FORTE, A., Theory of Music
FRANK, C., Piano
GOTTLIEB, G., Percussion
HARTH, S., Violin
HAWKSHAW, P., History of Music
LADERMAN, E., Composition
LEVINE, J., Viola
MURRAY, T., Organ
OUNDJIAN, P., Violin
PARISOT, A. S.
REPHANN, R.
ROSAND, E., History of Music
ROSEMAN, R., Oboe
RUFF, W. H., Jr.
SHIFRIN, D., Clarinet
SMITH, L. L.
SWALLOW, J. W., Brass and Ensemble Performance
TIRRO, F. P.
YARICK-CROSS, D., Voice

School of Nursing:

BURST, H. V., Nursing
DIERS, D. K., Nursing
DIXON, J. K., Nursing

FUNK, M., Nursing
GILLISS, C. L., Nursing
GREY, M., Nursing
KNAFL, K. A., Nursing
KNOPF, M. T., Oncology Nursing
KRAUSS, J. B., Nursing
MILONE-NUZZO, P., Nursing
MINARKI, P., Nursing
WILLIAMS, A., Nursing

DELAWARE

DELAWARE STATE UNIVERSITY

1200 N Dupont Highway, Dover, DE 19901-2277

Telephone: (302) 857-6290
E-mail: admissions@desu.edu
Internet: www.desu.edu

Founded 1891 as State College for Colored Students, present name and status 1993
State control
Academic year: August to DecemberJanuary to May (2 semesters)
2 Satellite campuses: Sussex County campus and Wilmington campus
Pres.: Dr HARRY LEE WILLIAMS (acting)
Provost and Vice-Pres. for Academic Affairs: Dr ALTON THOMAS
Vice-Pres. for Finance and Admin.: AMIR. MOHAMMADI
Vice-Pres. for Institutional Advancement: CAROLYN CURRY
Vice-Pres. for Research: NOUREDDINE MELIKECHI
Vice-Pres. for Student Affairs: KEMAL M. ATKINS
Dean for Univ. Libraries: Dr REBECCA BATSON
Registrar: TERELL D. HOLMES
Dir for Admissions: LAWITA G. CHEATHAM
Library: see under Libraries and Archives
Number of teachers: 200
Number of students: 3,820

DEANS

College of Agriculture and Related Sciences: Dr DYREMPLE B. MARSH
College of Arts Humanities and Social Sciences: Prof. MARSHALL STEVENSON
College of Business: Dr SHELTON RHODES
College of Education, Health and Public Policy: Dr JOHN N. AUSTIN
College of Mathematics, Natural Science and Technology: Dr NOUREDDINE MELIKECHI
School of Graduate Studies and Research: Dr MICHAEL CASSON

GOLDEY-BEACOM COLLEGE

4701 Limestone Rd, Wilmington, DE 19808
Telephone: (302) 998-8814
E-mail: gbc@gbc.edu
Internet: www.gbc.edu

Founded 1886 as Wilmington Commercial College, present name 1951
Private control
Academic year: August to May
Areas of study: business, computer information systems, criminal justice, economics, English and psychology
Pres.: MOHAMMAD ILYAS
Vice-Pres.: GARY L. WIRT
Vice-Pres. for Admin. and Finance: KRISTINE M. SANTOMAURO
Academic Dean: ALISON BOORD WHITE
Dean for Enrolment Management: JANE H. LYSLE
Dean for Student Affairs: BERNADETTE H. WIMBERLEY
Dir for Admissions: LARRY EBY
Dean for Information Technology: EMILY JACKSON

Number of students: 1,600

UNIVERSITY OF DELAWARE

Newark, DE 19716
Telephone: (302) 831-2792
E-mail: registrar@udel.edu
Internet: www.udel.edu
Founded 1743 as Free School, present status and name 1921
State control
Academic year: June to May
Pres.: Dr PATRICK T. HARKER
Provost: TOM APPLE (acting)
Sr Vice-Provost for Research and Strategic Initiatives: MARK A. BARTEAU
Deputy Provost: NANCY BRICKHOUSE
Exec. Vice-Pres. and Univ. Treas.: SCOTT R. DOUGLASS
Vice-Pres. and Chief of Staff: PATRICIA PLUMMER WILSON
Vice-Pres. and Gen. Counsel: LAWRENCE WHITE
Vice-Pres. and Univ. Sec.: PIERRE D. HAYWARD
Vice-Pres. for Devt and Alumni Relations: MONICA M. TAYLOR
Vice-Pres. for Facilities and Auxiliary Services: DAVID SINGLETON
Vice-Pres. for Finance and Admin.: JENNIFER J. J. DAVIS
Vice-Pres. for Information Technologies: CARL JACOBSON
Vice-Pres. for Student Life: MICHAEL A. GILBERT
Dean for Library Services: MATHEW SIMON
Library: see Libraries and Archives
Number of teachers: 1,130
Number of students: 21,500 (17,100 undergraduate, 3,600 graduate and 800 professional)
Publications: *DEconstruction*, *UD Research* (online, www.udel.edu/researchmagazine)

DEANS

Alfred Learner College of Business and Economics: Prof. BRUCE WEBBER
College of Agriculture and Natural Resources: Prof. ROBIN MORGAN
College of Arts and Science: Prof. GEORGE WATSON
College of Earth, Ocean and Environment: NANCY TARGETT
College of Education and Human Development: Prof. LYNN OKAGAKI (acting)
College of Engineering: BABATUNDE A. OGUNNAIKE
College of Health Sciences: Dr KATHLEEN S. MATT

PROFESSORS

ABRAMS, B. A., Economics
ACKERMAN, B. P., Psychology, Linguistics
ADAMS, F., Philosophy
ADVANI, S. G., Mechanical Engineering
AGARWAL, S. K., Mechanical Engineering
AGUIRRE, B. E., Sociology and Criminal Justice
ALCHON, S. A., History
ALLEN, H. E., Civil Engineering
ALLMENDINGER, D. F., Jr, History
AMER, P. D., Computer and Information Sciences, Electrical and Computer Engineering
AMES, D. L., Urban Affairs and Public Policy, Geography
ANDERSEN, M. L., Sociology and Criminal Justice, Women's Studies
ANDERSON, L. G., Marine Studies, Economics
ANDREWS, D. C., English
ANGELL, T. S., Mathematical Sciences
ARCE, G. R., Electrical and Computer Engineering, Marine Studies
ARDIS, A. L., English

ARENSON, M. A., Music
ATHANASSOGLOU-KALLMYER, N., Art History
BACH, R. D., Chemistry and Biochemistry
BACHMAN, R, Sociology and Criminal Justice
BADIEY, M., Marine Studies
BARNEKOV, T. K., Urban Affairs and Public Policy
BAROUDI, J., Accounting and Management Information Systems
BARR, S. M., Bartol Research Institute
BARTEAU, M. A., Chemical Engineering, Chemistry and Biochemistry
BEAR, G. G., Education
BEASLEY, J. C., English
BEEBE, T. P., Jr, Chemistry and Biochemistry
BELLAMY, D. P., Mathematical Sciences
BENNETT, J., English
BENNETT, R. B., English
BERIS, A. N., Chemical Engineering
BERNHARDT, S. A., Writing
BERNSTEIN, J. A., History
BEST, J., Sociology and Criminal Justice
BIEBER, J. W., Bartol Research Institute
BIEDERMAN, K., Finance
BILINSKY, Y., Political Science and International Relations
BINDER-MACLEOD, S. A., Physical Therapy
BLITS, J. H., Education, Political Science and Int. Relations
BOLTON, R. C., Art
BONCELET, C. G., Electrical and Computer Engineering
BOULD, S., Sociology and Criminal Justice, Individual and Family Studies, Women's Studies
BOYER, J. S., Marine Biochemistry and Biophysics, Plant and Soil Sciences
BOYLAN, A. M., History, Women's Studies
BRAUN, T. E. D., Comparative Literature, Foreign Languages and Literatures
BRICKHOUSE, N., Education
BRILL, T. B., Chemistry and Biochemistry
BROADBRIDGE, P., Mathematical Sciences
BROCK, D. H., English
BROCKMANN, R. J., English
BROWN, F., English
BROWN, H. E., Art, Art Conservation, Art History, Museum Studies
BROWN, J. L., Foreign Languages and Literatures
BROWN, R. F., Philosophy
BROWN, R. P., Theatre
BROWN, S. D., Chemistry and Biochemistry
BROWNING, J. E., Theatre
BROWNING, W. L., Theatre
BUCHANAN, T. S., Mechanical Engineering
BUCKMASTER, D. A., Accounting and Management Information Systems
BURMEISTER, J. L., Chemistry and Biochemistry
BURNSIDE, J., Animal and Food Sciences, Biological Sciences
BUTKIEWICZ, J. L., Economics
BYRNE, J. M., Urban Affairs and Public Policy, Marine Studies
CALLAHAN, D. F., History
CALLAHAN, R. A., History
CAMPBELL, L. L., Biological Sciences
CARBERRY, M. S., Computer and Information Sciences, Linguistics
CARON, D. M., Entomology and Applied Ecology
CAROTHERS, M. L., Art
CARR, C. L., Music
CARROLL, R. B., Plant and Soil Sciences
CARSON, D., Biological Sciences
CASE, J., Computer and Information Sciences
CAVINESS, B. F., Computer and Information Sciences, Mathematical Sciences
CHAJES, M. J., Civil and Environmental Engineering
CHAPMAN, H. P., Art History
CHEN, J. G., Chemical Engineering, Materials Science and Engineering
CHOU, T. W., Mechanical Engineering
CHUI, S.-T., Bartol Research Institute

CHURCH, T. M., Marine Studies, Chemistry and Biochemistry
CICALA, G. A., Psychology
CINCIN-SAIN, B., Marine Studies, Political Science and International Relations, Urban Affairs and Public Policy
COGBURN, L. A., Animal and Food Sciences
COHEN, L. H., Psychology
COLE, P., Linguistics
COLLINS, G. E., Computer and Information Sciences
COLLINS, N. E., Bioresources Engineering
COLMAN, R. F., Chemistry and Biochemistry
COLTON, D. L., Mathematical Sciences
COOK-IOANNIDIS, P., Mathematical Sciences
CORNELL, H. V., Biological Sciences
COTUNGA, N., Nutrition and Dietetics
COURTRIGHT, J. A., Communications
CURTIS, J. C., History
CURTIS, L. A., Biological Sciences, Marine Studies
CUSTER, J. F., Anthropology
DAVIS, S., Political Science and International Relations
DAVISON, R. A., English
DAWSON, C., English
DEAN, J. M., English
DEBESSAY, A., Accounting and Management Information Systems
DEINER, P. L., Individual and Family Studies
DE LEON, P. A., Biological Sciences
DEL FATTORE, J., English, Legal Studies
DEMICCIO, F. J., Hotel, Restaurant and Institutional Management
DENSON, C. D., Chemical Engineering
DENTEL, S. K., Civil and Environmental Engineering
DEXTER, S. C., Marine Studies, Materials Science and Engineering
DHURJATI, P., Chemical Engineering
DI LORENZO, T. M., Psychology
DIRENZO, G., Sociology and Criminal Justice
DOHMS, J. E., Immunology and Microbiology
DONALDSON-EVANS, M. P., Foreign Languages and Literatures
DOREN, D. J., Chemistry and Biochemistry
DUGGAN, L. G. J., History
DURBIN, P. T., Philosophy, Urban Affairs and Public Policy
DYBOWSKI, C. R., Chemistry and Biochemistry
EBERT, G. L., Mathematical Sciences
EISENBERGER, R. W., Psychology
ELIAS, J. G., Electrical and Computer Engineering
ELSON, C. M., Legal Studies, Corporate Governance
EPIFANIO, C., Marine Studies
ERMANN, M. D., Sociology and Criminal Justice
EVANS, D. H., Chemistry and Biochemistry
EVENSON, P. A., Bartol Research Institute
FAGHRI, A., Civil and Environmental Engineering
FANELLI-KUCZMARSKI, M. T., Nutrition and Dietetics
FARACH-CARSON, M. C., Biological Sciences
FERRETTI, R., Education, Psychology
FITZMAURICE, C., Theatre
FLYNN, P. D., English
FOU, C.-M., Physics and Astronomy
FRETT, J. J., Plant and Soil Sciences
FUHRMANN, J. J., Plant and Soil Sciences
GAERTNER, S. L., Psychology
GAFFNEY, P. M., Marine Studies
GAISSER, T. K., Bartol Research Institute
GALLAGHER, J. L., Marine Studies
GALVIN, M. E., Materials Science and Engineering
GAO, G.-R., Electrical and Computer Engineering
GARLAND, H., Business Administration
GARVINE, R. W., Marine Studies, Civil and Environmental Engineering
GATES, B. T., English, Women's Studies
GEHRLEIN, W. V., Business Administration

GELB, J., Jr, Animal and Food Sciences
GEMPESHAW, C. M., II, Economics, Food and Resource Economics
GIBSON, A. E., Art History
GILBERT, R. P., Mathematical Sciences, Marine Studies, Computer and Information Sciences
GILLESPIE, J. W., Jr, Materials Science and Engineering
GINZBERG, M. J., Accounting and Management Information Systems, Business Administration
GLASS, B. P., Geology, Marine Studies
GLUTTING, J. J., Education
GLYDE, H. R., Physics and Astronomy
GOLDSTEIN, L. F., Political Science and Int. Relations
GOLINKOFF, R. M., Education, Linguistics, Psychology
GOODMAN, S., English
GREEN, P., Plant and Soil Sciences
GREENBERG, M. D., Mechanical Engineering
GRIFFITHS, L., Animal and Food Sciences
GRUBB, F., Economics, History
HAAS, K. C., Sociology and Criminal Justice
HABER, C., History
HADJIPANAYIS, G., Physics and Astronomy
HALIO, J. L., Communications, Comparative Literature, English, Theatre
HALL, H. B., Philosophy
HALL, S. J., Health and Exercise Sciences
HALLENBECK, D. J., Mathematical Sciences
HALPRIN, A., Physics and Astronomy
HAMILTON, C., Nutrition and Dietetics
HAMPEL, R., Education
HANEY, M. H., Electrical and Computer Engineering
HANS, V. P., Sociology and Criminal Justice
HAREVEN, T. K., Individual and Family Studies, History
HASLETT, B. J., Communications, Psychology, Women's Studies
HASLETT, D. W., Philosophy
HASTINGS, S. E., Food and Resource Economics
HAUS, H.-U., Theatre
HAWK, J. A., Plant and Soil Sciences
HAYES, E. R., Nursing
HELMLING, S., English
HERMAN, B. L., Art History, History
HERMAN, D., Music
HEWITT, K. H., Military Science
HEYRMAN, C. L., History
HIEBERT, J., Education
HIGGINBOTHAM, E., Sociology and Criminal Justice
HILDEBRANDT, D. J., Music
HOFFECKER, C. E., History
HOFFMAN, J. E., Psychology
HOFFMAN, S. D., Economics, Women's Studies
HOFSTETTER, F., Education
HOLMES, L. W., Art
HOOVER, D. G., Animal and Food Sciences
HOUGH-GOLDSTEIN, J. A., Entomology and Applied Ecology
HSIAO, G. C., Mathematical Sciences
HUANG, C. P., Civil and Environmental Engineering, Marine Studies
HUDDLESTON, M. W., Political Science and Interntional Relations, Urban Affairs and Public Policy
HUNSPERGER, R. G., Electrical and Computer Engineering
HURT, J. J., History
IH, C. S., Electrical and Computer Engineering, Marine Studies
ILVENTO, T. W., Food and Resource Economics
INCIARDI, J. A., Sociology and Criminal Justice
INGERSOLL, D. E., Political Science and International Relations
INTRAUB, H., Psychology
IZARD, C., Psychology
JACKSON, M. D., English
JAIN, M. K., Chemistry and Biochemistry

JOHNSON, H. B., Black American Studies, History
JOHNSON, M. V., Chemistry and Biochemistry
JONES, J. M., Psychology
JONES, S. K., Accounting and Management Information Systems
JORDAN, R. R., Geology
KALER, E. W., Chemical Engineering
KALKSTEIN, L. S., Geography
KALLAL, M. J., Consumer Studies
KAPLAN, D. W., Education
KARLSON, R. H., Biological Sciences
KEELER, C., Animal and Food Sciences
KENNEDY, J. A., Mathematical Sciences
KERR, A. D., Civil and Environmental Engineering
KERRANE, K., English
KIKUCHI, S., Civil and Environmental Engineering
KIRBY, J. T., Civil and Environmental Engineering, Marine Studies
KIRCHMAN, D. L., Marine Studies
KIRWAN, A. D., Jr, Marine Studies
KITTO, S. L., Plant and Soil Sciences
KLEMAS, V. V., Marine Studies, Electrical and Computer Engineering
KLINZING, D. G., Individual and Family Studies
KLOCKARS, C. B., Sociology and Criminal Justice
KMIEC, E. B., Biological Sciences
KOBAYASHI, N., Civil and Environmental Engineering, Marine Studies
KOFORD, K. J., History, Economics, Political Science and International Relations
KOLCHIN, P. R., History
KOLODZEY, J., Electrical and Computer Engineering
KRAFT, J. C., Geology, Marine Studies
KUNG, L., Animal and Food Sciences
KUSHMAN, J. E., Consumer Studies
LAMBRECHT, M., Nursing
LANE, R., Art
LATHROP, T. A., Foreign Languages and Literatures
LAZENBIK, F., Mathematical Sciences
LEATHERS, D. J., Geography
LEAVENS, P. B., Geology
LEITCH, T. M., English
LEJA, M., English
LEMIEUX, B., Plant and Soil Sciences
LENHOFF, A. M., Chemical Engineering
LESHCHINSKY, P. E., Civil and Environmental Engineering
LEUNG, C. N., Physics and Astronomy
LEWIS, K. A., Business
LI, W., Mathematical Sciences
LINK, C. R., Economics
LLOYD, E. L., Computer and Information Sciences
LUTHER, G. W., Marine Studies, Chemistry and Biochemistry, Civil and Environmental Engineering
MacDONALD, J., Physics and Astronomy
MAGEE, J., Political Science and International Relations
MANGONE, G. J., Legal Studies, Marine Studies
MANRAI, A. K., Business Administration
MANRAI, L., Business Administration
MARKS, C. C., Black American Studies, Sociology and Criminal Justice
MARTIN, R. E., Geology
MASON, C. E., Entomology and Applied Ecology
MASON, D. M., Food and Resource Economics
MASTERSON, F. A., Psychology
MATTHAEUS, W. H., Bartol Research Institute
MAY, G., History
MELL, D. C., English
MEYER, D. H., History
MEYER, W. H., Political Science and International Relations
MILLER, G. E., English
MILLER, J. B., Economics

MILLER, M. J., Political Science and International Relations
MILLER, S., Sociology and Criminal Justice, Women's Studies
MILLS, D. L., Electrical and Computer Engineering
MONK, P. B., Mathematics
MOODY, W. B., Education, Mathematical Sciences
MORGAN, R. W., Agriculture and Food Sciences, Biology, Chemistry and Biochemistry
MORRISON, J. L., Consumer Studies
MULLAN, D. J., Bartol Research Institute
MULLIGAN, J., Economics
MUNSON, M. S. B., Chemistry and Biochemistry
MURRAY, F. B., Education, Psychology
NANDAKUMAR, R., Education
NASHED, M. Z., Mathematical Sciences, Electrical Engineering
NEES, L. P., Art History
NEEVES, R. E., Health and Exercise Science
NELSON, F. E., Geography
NELSON, M., English
NELSON, P., Food and Resource Economics
NESS, N. F., Bartol Research Institute
NEWTON, J. E., Black American Studies
NICHOLS, R. D., Art
NIGG, J. M., Sociology and Criminal Justice
NORTHMORE, D. P. M., Psychology
OLIVER, J. K., Political Science and International Relations, Marine Studies
O'NEILL, J. B., Economics
OPILA, R. L., Materials Science and Engineering
OWOCKI, S. P., Bartol Research Institute
PALKOVITZ, R. J., Individual and Family Studies
PALLEY, M. L., Political Science and International Relations, Women's Studies
PALMER, L. M., Philosophy, Women's Studies
PARSONS, G. R., Marine Studies, Economics
PAULANKA, B. J., Nursing
PAULY, T. H., English
PERSE, E. M., Communications
PETERS, D. L., Individual and Family Studies, Urban Affairs and Public Policy
PETERSON, L. W., Music
PFAELZER, J., English
PIFER, E. I., Communications, Comparative Literature, English
PIKA, J. A., Political Science and International Relations
PILL, W. G., Plant and Soil Sciences
PITTEL, S., Bartol Research Institute
PIZZOLATO, T. D., Plant and Soil Sciences
PIZZUTO, J. E., Geology
PONG, D., History
POPE, C. R., Animal and Food Sciences
POTTER, L. D., English
PRODAN, J. C., Music
PURNELL, L., Nursing
RABOLT, J. F., Materials Science and Engineering
RAFFEL, J. A., Urban Affairs and Public Policy, Political Science and International Relations
RATHS, J., Education
REEDY, C. L., Museum Studies, Art History, Urban Affairs and Public Policy
REIDEL, L., Theatre
REYNOLDS, H. T., Political Science and International Relations, Urban Affairs and Public Policy
RHEINGOLD, A. L., Chemistry and Biochemistry
RICH, D., Urban Affairs and Public Policy, Political Science and International Relations
RICHARDS, J. G., Health and Exercise Sciences
RICHARDS, M. P., English
RIDGE, D., Chemistry and Biochemistry
RITTER, W. F., Bioresources Engineering
ROBBINS, C., Sociology and Criminal Justice

ROBBINS, S. L., Theatre
ROBINSON, C. E., English
ROE, P. G., Anthropology
ROSELLE, D. P., Mathematics
ROSENBERGER, J. K., Microbiology
ROTH, R. R., Entomology and Applied Ecology
RUARK, G., English
RUSSELL, T. W. F., Chemical Engineering
SAFER, E. B., English
SANDLER, S. I., Chemical Engineering, Chemistry and Biochemistry
SANIGA, E. M., Business Administration
SATINOFF, E., Psychology
SAUNDERS, B. D., Computer and Information Sciences, Mathematical Sciences
SAYDAM, T., Computer and Information Sciences
SCARPITTI, F. R., Sociology and Criminal Justice
SCHWARTZ, L. W., Mechanical Engineering, Mathematical Sciences
SCHWARTZ, N. B., Anthropology
SCHWEDA-NICHOLSON, N. L., Legal Studies, Linguistics
SCHWEITZER, R. L., Economics
SEIDMAN, L. S., Economics
SELEKMAN, J. A., Nursing
SETHI, A. S., Computer and Information Sciences
SETTLE, R. F., Economics
SETTLES, B. H., Individual and Family Studies
SHAFI, M., Foreign Languages and Literatures
SHAFI, Q., Bartol Research Institute
SHARNOFF, M., Physics and Astronomy
SHARP, J. H., Marine Studies
SHIPMAN, H. L., Physics and Astronomy
SIDEBOTHAM, S. E., History
SIGNORIELLI, N., Communications
SIMMONS, D. T., Biological Sciences
SIMONS, R. F., Psychology
SIMS, J. T., Plant and Soil Sciences
SKOPIK, S. D., Biological Sciences
SLOYER, C. W., Jr, Mathematical Sciences
SMITH, J. L., Nutrition and Dietetics
SNIDER, O. S., Animal and Food Sciences
SNYDER-MACKLER, L., Physical Therapy, Philosophy
SOLES, J. R., Political Science and International Relations
SPARKS, D. L., Civil and Environmental Engineering, Chemistry and Biochemistry, Plant and Soil Sciences
SPINSKI, V., Art
STANEV, T., Bartol Research Institute
STARK, C., English
STARK, R. M., Mathematical Sciences, Civil and Environmental Engineering
STETSON, M. H., Biological Sciences
STONER, J. H., Art Conservation
ST PIERRE, E. K., Accounting and Management Information Systems
STRAIGHT, R., Arts
STRASSER, S., History
STRECKFUSS, R. J., Music
SVENDSEN, I. A., Civil and Environmental Engineering, Marine Studies
SWASEY, J. E., Plant and Soil Sciences
SWEENEY, S. R., Theatre
SYLVES, R. T., Political Science and Int. Relations, Marine Studies, Urban Affairs and Public Policy
SZALEWICZ, K., Physics and Astronomy
SZERI, A. Z., Mechanical Engineering
TABER, D. F., Chemistry and Biochemistry
TALLAMY, D. W., Entomology and Applied Ecology
TARGETT, N. M., Marine Studies
TARGETT, T. E., Marine Studies
THEOPOLD, K. H., Chemistry and Biochemistry
THIBAULT, B., Foreign Languages and Literatures
THORPE, C., Chemistry and Biochemistry

TIERNEY, K. J., Sociology and Criminal Justice
TILMON, H. D., Food and Resource Economics
TOENSMEYER, U. C., Food and Resource Economics
TOLLES, B. F., Jr, Art History, History, Museum Studies
TURKEL, G. M., Sociology and Criminal Justice
ULLMAN, W. J., Marine Studies, Geology
UNGER, D. G., Individual and Family Studies
UNRUH, K., Physics and Astronomy
VARMA, R. D., Economics
VASILAS, B. L., Plant and Soil Sciences
VENEZKY, R., Education, Computer and Information Sciences, Linguistics
VICKERY, C. E., Nutrition and Dietetics
VINSON, J. R., Mechanical Engineering; Marine Studies
VUKELICH, C., Individual and Family Studies
WAGNER, N. J., Chemical Engineering
WAGNER, R. C., Biological Sciences
WALKER, J. H., Theatre
WALKER, J. M., English
WARREN, R., Urban Affairs and Public Policy; Political Science and International Relations
WATSON, G. H., Physics and Astronomy
WEBSTER, F., Marine Studies
WEDEL, A. R., Communications, Linguistics, Foreign Languages and Literatures
WEHMILLER, J. F., Geology, Marine Studies
WEISS, J. J., Art
WHITE, C. E., Jr, Accounting and Management Information Systems
WHITE, H. B., III, Chemistry and Biochemistry
WILDER, M. S., Urban Affairs and Public Policy
WILKINS, D. J., Mechanical Engineering
WILLMOTT, C. J., Geography, Marine Studies
WIRTH, M. J., Chemistry and Biochemistry
WOLTERS, R. B., History
WONG, K.-C., Marine Studies
WOOD, T. K., Entomology and Applied Ecology
WOOL, R. P., Chemical Engineering
YAGODA, B., English
YAN, X.-H., Marine Studies
ZINN, M. A., Music
ZIPSER, R. A., Foreign Languages and Literatures
ZUCKERMAN, M., Psychology

WESLEY COLLEGE

120 N State St, Dover, DE 19901
Telephone: (302) 736-2300
E-mail: info@wesley.edu
Internet: www.wesley.edu
Founded 1873 as Wilmington Conf. Acad., present name 1918
Private control
Academic year: August to May
2 Campuses: New Castle and Dover Air Force Base
Pres.: Dr WILLIAM N. JOHNSTON
Exec. Vice-Pres. and Provost: Dr BETTE S. COPLAN
Vice-Pres. for Academic Affairs: Dr PATRICIA DWYER
Vice-Pres. for Finance and Dir of Human Resources: ERIC R. NELSON
Vice-Pres. for Institutional Advancement: CHRIS A. WOOD
Dean for Enrolment Management: Dr HOWARD BALLENTINE
Dean for Students: MARY-ALICE OZECHOSKI
Registrar: RAYANN FRYATT
Library Dir: ROGER GETZ
Library of 100,000 vols 20,000 ejournals
Number of students: 2,500
Publication: *Wesley Magazine* (2 a year)

WIDENER UNIVERSITY SCHOOL OF LAW

Delaware Campus: POB 7474, 4601 Concord Pike, Wilmington, DE 19803-0474
Harrisburg Campus: POB 69381, 3800 Vartan Way, Harrisburg, PA 17106-9381
Telephone: (302) 477-21703 (Delaware)
E-mail: lawadmissions@widener.edu
Internet: law.widener.edu
Founded 1971
Private control
Academic year: August to May
Pres.: JAMES HARRIS
Assoc. Provost and Dean for Law School: LINDA L. AMMONS
Dean for Student Affairs: KEITH E. SEALING
Asst Dean forBusiness and Admin.: VERNE R. SMITH
Dir for Information Technology: SHARON BUCZALA
Dir for Admissions: ERIC M. KNISKERN
Registrar: DOROTHY HEMPHILL
Number of teachers: 200 (80 full-time, 120 part-time)
Number of students: 1,600
Publications: *Delaware Journal of Corporate Law* (2 a year), *Widener Journal of Law, Economics and Race* (online, www.wjler.org), *Widener Law Journal* (1 a year), *Widener Law Review* (1 a year)

WILMINGTON UNIVERSITY

320 N DuPont Highway, New Castle, DE 19720-6491
Telephone: (302) 356-4636
E-mail: infocenter@wilmu.edu
Internet: www.wilmu.edu
Founded 1968 as Wilmington College, present name 2007
Private control
Academic year: 3 semesters
Campuses: Wilson Graduate Center, Middletown, Dover, Dover Air Force Base, Georgetown, Rehoboth Beach and N Wilmington, New Jersey
Pres.: Dr JACK P. VARSALONA
Provost and Vice-Pres. for Academic Affairs: BETTY J. CAFFO
Chief Financial Officer and Vice-Pres. for Financial Affairs: HEATHER A. O'CONNELL
Vice-Pres. for Admin. Affairs: CAROLE D. PITCHER
Vice-Pres. for Student Affairs: LAVERNE T. HARMON
Librarian: JAMES A. BRADLEY
Registrar: ELIZABETH P. JORDAN
Library of 117,000 vols
Number of students: 15,000
Publication: *WilmU* (2 a year)

DEANS

College of Arts and Sciences: Dr DOREEN TURNBO
College of Business: Dr DONALD W. DURANDETTA
College of Education: Dr JOHN C. GRAY
College of Health Professions: Dr DENISE Z. WESTBROOK
College of Social and Behavioral Sciences: CHRISTIAN A. TROWBRIDGE
College of Technology: Dr EDWARD L. GUTHRIE

DISTRICT OF COLUMBIA

AMERICAN UNIVERSITY

4400 Massachusetts Ave, NW, Washington, DC 20016
Telephone: (202) 885-1000
E-mail: admissions@american.edu

Internet: www.american.edu
Private control
Academic year: August to December, January to July (2 semesters)
Liberal arts curriculum; doctoral instn
Pres.: NEIL KERWIN
Provost: SCOTT A. BASS
Vice Pres., Chief Legal Counsel and Sec.: MARY E. KENNARD
Vice-Pres. for Campus Life and Dean of Students: GAIL SHORT HANSON
Vice-Pres. for Communications: TERESA FLANNERY
Vice-Pres. for Devt and Alumni Relations: THOMAS J. MINAR
Vice-Pres. for Finance and Treas.: DONALD L. MYERS
Dean for Academic Affairs: Dr PHYLLIS PERES (acting)
Registrar: ALICE POEHLS
Univ. Librarian: BILL MAYER
Library of 701,518 vols, 20,000 ebooks, 258,000 digitized primary source materials, 41,000 media and sound recordings and 14,245 musical scores
Number of teachers: 750 (full-time)
Number of students: 12,000 (6,650 undergraduates, 3,600 graduates, 1,750 law)
Publications: *Folio, Intercultural Management Quarterly, Journal of International Service* (2 a year), *Pharmakon*

DEANS

College of Arts and Sciences: PETER STARR
Kogod College of Business Administration: MICHAEL J. GINZBERG
School of Communication: LARRY KIRKMAN
School of International Service: JAMES GOLDGEIER
School of Public Affairs: WILLIAM M. LEO-GRANDE (acting)
Washington College of Law: CLAUDIO M. GROSSMAN

CATHOLIC UNIVERSITY OF AMERICA

620 Michigan Ave, NE, Washington, DC 20064

Telephone: (202) 319-5000
Internet: www.cua.edu
Founded 1887
Private control
Academic year: September to August
Pres.: JOHN H. GARVEY
Provost: Dr JAMES BRENNAN
Vice-Pres. for Enrolment Management: Dr W. MICHAEL HENDRICKS
Vice-Pres. for Finance and Treas.: CATHY R. WOOD
Vice-Pres. for Institutional Advancement: JOHN L. HANNAN
Vice-Pres. for Student Affairs: Dr MIKE ALLEN
Vice-Pres. for Univ. Relations and Chief of Staff: FRANK G. PERSICO
Assoc. Vice-Pres. for Enrolment Services and Univ. Registrar: JULIE ISHA
Gen. Counsel: Dr LAWRENCE MORRIS
Univ. Librarian: STEPHEN CONNAGHAN
Library: 4.1m. vols (incl. books, ebooks, microforms and audiovisual materials).
Number of teachers: 825
Number of students: 6,725 (3,713 undergraduate, 3,012 graduate)
Publications: *Catholic University Law Review, CommLaw Conspectus: Journal of Communications Law and Policy, Journal of Contemporary Health Law and Policy, Journal of Law, Philosophy and Culture, Pierre d'angle, Review of Metaphysics, The Catholic Historical Review* (4 a year), *The Jurist: Studies in Church Law and Ministry, U.S. Catholic Historian*

DEANS

Benjamin T. Rome School of Music: Dr GRAYSON WAGSTAFF
Columbus School of Law: DANIEL F. ATTRIDGE
Metropolitan School of Professional Studies: Dr SARA THOMPSON
National School of Social Service: Dr WILL RAINFORD
School of Architecture and Planning: RANDALL OTT
School of Arts and Sciences: Dr CLAUDIA BORNHOLDT (acting)
School of Business and Economics: Dr ANDREW ABELA
School of Canon Law: Rev. ROBERT KASLYN
School of Engineering: Dr CHARLES C. NGUYEN
School of Nursing: Dr PATRICIA McMULLEN
School of Philosophy: Dr JOHN C. McCARTHY
School of Theology and Religious Studies: Rev. MARK MOROZOWICH

CORCORAN COLLEGE OF ART AND DESIGN

500 17th St, NW, Washington, DC 20006-4804

Telephone: (202) 639-1800
E-mail: admissions@corcoran.org
Internet: www.corcoran.edu
Founded 1890
Private control
Academic year: August to December, January to May (2 semesters)
Campuses in Downtown and Georgetown
Provost and Chief Academic Officer: CATHERINE ARMOUR
Dean for Enrolment: Dr CHRISTINE LEICHLITER
Dean for Students: JOHN DICKSON
Dean for Undergraduate Studies: ANDY GRUNDBERG
Registrar: CURREN McLANE
Library Dir: MARIO ASCENCIO
Library of 35,000 vols, 32,000 slides, 1,200 DVDs, 190 periodicals subscription
Number of students: 615 (347 undergraduate, 268 graduate)

GALLAUDET UNIVERSITY

800 Florida Ave, NE, Washington, DC 20002-3695

Telephone: (202) 651-5000
E-mail: public.relations@gallaudet.edu
Internet: www.gallaudet.edu
Founded 1864 as Columbia Instn for the Instruction of the Deaf and Dumb and Blind, present name 1954
Academic year: August to May
Liberal education and career devt for deaf and hard-of-hearing students; incl. a museum
Pres.: Dr ALAN HURWITZ
Provost: Dr STEPHEN WEINER
Vice-Pres. for Admin. and Finance: PAUL KELLY
Vice-Pres. for Devt and Alumni Relations: Dr LYNNE MURRAY
Chief Enrolment and Management Officer: CHARITY REEDY-HINES
Dean for Student Affairs: DWIGHT BENEDICT
Dir for Library Services: SARAH HAMRICK
Library of 200,000 vols
Number of teachers: 235
Number of students: 1,800 (1,100 undergraduate, 440 graduate, 200 professional studies and 60 English Language Institute)
Publications: *Gallaudet Today* (2 a year), *Perspectives in Education and Deafness* (4 a year)

DEANS

College of Liberal Arts, Sciences and Technologies: Dr ISAAC AGBOOLA
Graduate School and Professional Programmes: Dr CAROL ERTING

GEORGE WASHINGTON UNIVERSITY

2121 I St, NW, Washington, DC 20052

Telephone: (202) 994-1000
Internet: www.gwu.edu
Founded 1821 as Columbian College, current name adopted 1994
Private control
Academic year: September to May
3 Campuses: Foggy Bottom and Mount Vernon in Washington, DC, and the GW Virginia Science and Technology Campus in Ashburn, Virginia
Pres.: STEVEN KNAPP
Provost and Exec. Vice-Pres. for Academic Affairs: Dr STEVEN R. LERMAN
Sr Vice-Provost for Academic Affairs and Planning: FORREST MALTZMAN
Sr Vice-Pres. and Sr Vice-Provost for Student and Academic Support Services: ROBERT A. CHERNAK
Sr Vice-Pres. and Gen. Counsel: BETH NOLAN
Exec. Vice-Pres. and Treas.: LOUIS H. KATZ
Vice-Pres. for Advancement: MICHAEL MORSBERGER
Vice-Pres. for Devt and Alumni Relations: MICHAEL J. MORSBERGER
Vice-Pres. for External Relations: LORRAINE VOLES
Vice-Pres. for Research: LEO M. CHALUPA
Vice-Pres. and Sec.: ARISTIDE J. COLLINS, JR
Registrar: ELIZABETH AMUNDSON
Univ. Librarian: GENEVA HENRY
Library: see under Libraries and Archives
Number of teachers: 2,220
Number of students: 25,300
Publications: *GW Review* (2 a year), *The American Intellectual Property Law Association Quarterly Journal, The Federal Circuit Bar Journal (FCBJ)* (4 a year), *The George Washington International Law Review* (4 a year), *The George Washington Law Review* (6 a year), *The Journal of Energy and Environmental Law* (2 a year), *The Public Contract Law Journal* (4 a year), *Wooden Teeth* (2 a year)

DEANS

College of Professional Studies: Dr ALI ESKANDARIAN
Columbian College of Arts and Sciences: BEN VINSON
Elliott School of International Affairs: MICHAEL E. BROWN
Graduate School of Education and Human Development: MICHAEL J. FEUER
Law School: PAUL SCHIFF BERMAN
School of Business: Dr D. CHRISTOPHER KAYES
School of Engineering and Applied Science: Dr DAVID S. DOLLING
School of Medicine and Health Sciences: JEFFREY S. AKMAN
School of Public Health and Health Services: Dr LYNN R. GOLDMAN
School of Nursing: Dr JEAN JOHNSON

PROFESSORS

(Some professors serve in more than one school)

Columbian School of Arts and Sciences and Elliott School of International Affairs:

ABRAMSON, F. P., Pharmacology, Chemistry
ABRAVANEL, E., Psychology
ADAMS, G. M., International Affairs
ALBRIGHT, J. W., Microbiology and Immunology

ALLEN, C. J., Anthropology, International Affairs
ANDERSON, J. C., Art
ARNDT, R. A., Physics
ARTERTON, F. C., Political Management
ASKARI, H. G., Business, International Affairs
ATKIN, M. A., History
AUSTIN, J. F., Sociology
AZAR, I., Spanish and Human Sciences
BAGINSKI, F. E., Mathematics
BAILEY, J. M., Biochemistry and Molecular Biology
BECKER, W. H., History and International Affairs
BELL, D., Anthropology
BERKOWITZ, E. D., History
BERMAN, B. L., Physics
BHALA, R., Law, International Affairs
BLACK, A. M., History and International Affairs
BLOSSOM, N. H., Interior Design
BORRIELLO, J., Psychology
BOULIER, B. L., Economics
BRADLEY, M. D., Economics, International Affairs
BRISCOE, W. J., Physics
BROCK, G. W., Telecommunications
BROWN, N. J., Political Science, International Affairs
BURNS, J. R., Zoology
CARESS, E. A., Chemistry
CAWS, P. J., Philosophy
CHAVES, J., Chinese
CHIAPPINELLI, V. A., Basic Science, Pharmacology, Neurological Surgery
CHURCHILL, R. P., Philosophy
CORDES, J. J., Economics and International Affairs
COSTIGAN, C. C., Design
COTTROL, R. J., Law, History, Sociology
DAVIS, H., Strategic Management and International Affairs
DEERING, C. J., Political Science
DONALDSON, R. P., Biology
DUNNING, Jr, R. M., Economics
EAST, M. A., International Affairs and Political Science
ETZIONI, A., Sociology
FALK, J. E., Operations Research
FEIGELBAUM, H. B., Political Science, International Affairs
FERRER, Jr, J., Business, International Affairs
FISHER, E. A., Classics
FRIEDLER, G., Engineering and Applied Science, Statistics
FUERTH, L., International Affairs
GALLO, L. L., Biochemistry and Molecular Biology
GANZ, Jr, R. N., English
GARNER, N. C., Theatre
GASTWIRTH, J. L., Statistics and Economics
GLICK, I. I., Mathematics
GOLDFARB, R. S., Economics
GOLDSTEIN, A. L., Biochemistry and Molecular Biology
GOW, D. D., Anthropology, International Affairs
GRIFFITH, W. B., Philosophy
GRINKER, R. R., Anthropology, International Affairs, Human Sciences
GUENTHER, R. J., Music
GUPTA, M. M., Mathematics
HARDING, H., International Affairs, Political Science
HARTMANN, H., Women's Studies
HENIG, J. R., Political Science
HILTEBEITEL, A. J., Religion, Human Sciences
HOLMES, D. E., Clinical Psychology
HORTON, J. O., American Civilization and History
HOTEZ, P. J., Microbiology, Tropical Medicine, Global Health, International Affairs

HOWE, G. W., Psychology
INDERFURTH, K. F., International Affairs
JACOBSON, L. B., Theatre
JOHNSON, K. E., Anatomy
JUDSON, H. F., History
JUNGHENN, H. D., Mathematics
KAMINSKI, G. L., Economics, International Affairs
KATZ, I. J., Mathematics
KENNEDY, D. K., History, International Affairs
KENNEDY, K. A., Pharmacology and Genetics
KENNEDY, Jr, R. E., European History
KIM-RENAUD, Y. K., Korean Language and Culture, International Affairs
KING, M. M., Chemistry
KLAMER, A., Economics, International Affairs
KLARÉAN, P. F., History, International Affairs
KNOWLTON, R. E., Biology
KUIPERS, J. C., Anthropology, International Affairs, Human Sciences
KUMAR, A., Biochemistry, Molecular Biology and Genetics
KWOKA, Jr, J. E., Economics
LABADIE, P. A., Economics
LACHIN, III, J. M., Statistics, Biostatistics
LADER, M. P., Art
LADISCH, S., Paediatrics, Biochemistry and Molecular Biochemistry
LAKE, J. L., Photography
LEHMAN, D. R., Physics
LENGERMANN, P. M., Sociology
LEWIS, J. F., Geology
LILLIEFORS, H. W., Statistics
LINEBAUGH, C. W., Speech and Hearing, Medicine
LIPSCOMB, D. L., Biology
LOGSDON, J. M., Political Science, International Affairs
LONGSTRETH, R. W., American Civilization
LUDLOW, G., French, International Affairs
McALEAVEY, D. W., English
McCLINTOCK, C., Political Science, International Affairs
McGRATH, Jr, D. C., Geography, Urban and Regional Planning
MADDOX, J. H., English
MAHMOUD, H. M., Statistics
MANDEL, H. G., Pharmacology
MANHEIM, J. B., Political Communications and Political Science
MAXIMON, L. C., Physics
MAZZUCHI, T. A., Operations Research, Engineering Management
MERGEN, B. M., American Civilization
MILLAR, J. R., Economics and International Affairs
MILLER, B. D., Anthropology, International Affairs
MILLER, J. A., English, American Studies
MILLER, J. C., Psychology
MILLER, J. H., Chemistry
MOLINA, S. B., Art
MUFTIC, S., Computer Science
NASR, S. H., Islamic Studies
NAU, H. R., Political Science and International Affairs
NAYAK, T. K., Statistics
OFFERMAN, L. R., Psychology
OZDOGAN, T., Ceramics
PACKER, R. K., Biology
PALMER, P. M., American Civilization, Women's Studies
PARKE, W. C., Physics
PARSONS, D. O., Economics
PASTER, G. K., English
PATIERNO, S. R., Pharmacology, Genetics
PECK, L. L., History
PELZMAN, J., Economics and International Affairs
PERRY, D. C., Pharmacology
PETERSON, R. A., Psychology, Psychiatry and Behavioural Sciences

PEUSNER, K. D., Anatomy
PLOTZ, J. A., English, Human Sciences
POPPEN, P. J., Psychology
POST, J. M., Psychiatry, Political Psychology, International Affairs
PRZYTYCKI, J. H., Mathematics
RAMAKER, D. E., Chemistry
RASKIN, M., Policy Studies
REDDAWAY, P., Political Science and International Affairs
REICH, B., Political Science and International Affairs
REICH, W., International Affairs, Ethics and Human Behaviour
REISS, D., Psychiatry and Behavioural Science, Medicine, Psychology
RIBUFFO, L. P., History
ROBINSON, Jr, E. A., Mathematics
ROBINSON, L. F., Art
ROBLES, F., International Marketing, International Affairs
ROSENAU, J. N., International Affairs
ROTHBLAT, L. A., Psychology, Anatomy
ROWE, W. F., Forensic Sciences
ROWLEY, D. A., Chemistry
RYCROFT, R. W., International Science and Technology Policy, International Affairs
SACHAR, H. M., History, International Affairs
SALAMON, L. B., English, Human Sciences
SAPERSTEIN, M. E., Jewish History
SASHKIN, M., Human Resource Development
SCHAFFNER, R. F., Medical Humanities, Philosophy
SCHWANDT, D. R., Human Resource Development
SCOTT, D. W., Microbiology and Immunology, Anatomy and Cell Biology
SEAVEY, O. A., English
SHAMBAUGH, D. L., Political Science and International Affairs
SHAO, X.-Q., Anthropology
SIGELMAN, C. K., Psychology
SIGELMAN, L., Political Science
SINGPURWALLA, N. D., Operations Research, Statistics
SMITH, S. C., Economics, International Affairs
SODARO, M. J., Political Science and International Affairs
SOLAND, R. M., Operations Research
SPECTOR, R. H., History and International Affairs
SQUIRES, G. D., Sociology
STEINHARDT, R., Law, International Affairs
STEN, C. W., English
STEPHENS, G. C., Geology
STERLING, C. H., Media and Public Affairs, Telecommunication
THIBAULT, J. F., French, Human Sciences
THORNTON, R. C., History and International Affairs
TROPEA, J. L., Sociology
TROST, R. P., Economics
TUCH, S. A., Sociology
ULLMAN, D. H., Mathematics
VANDERHOEK, J. Y., Biochemistry and Molecular Biology
VERTER, J. L., Statistics
VLACH, J. M., American Civilization, Anthropology
VON BARGHAHN-CALVETTI, B. A., Art
WADE, A. G., Theatre
WALLACE, Jr, D. D., Religion
WALLACE, R. A., Sociology
WALSH, R. J., Anatomy and Cell Biology
WARREN, C., Communication
WATSON, H. S., Economics
WEGLICKI, W. B., Medicine, Physiology
WEINER, R. J., International Business, International Affairs
WEITZER, R., Sociology
WERLING, L. L., Pharmacology
WILLIAMS, R. L., Naval Science
WINSLOW, E. K., Behavioural Sciences

WIRTZ, P. W., Management Science, Psychology
WITHERS, M. R., Dance
WOLCHIK, S. L., Political Science and International Affairs
WOOD, B., Human Origins, Human Evolutionary Anatomy
WOODWARD, W. T., Painting
WRIGHT, Jr, J. F., Drawing and Graphics
YEIDE, Jr, H. E., Religion
YEZER, A., Economics
ZIOLKOWSI, J. E., Classics

School of Business and Public Management:
ACHROL, R. S., Marketing
ADAMS, W. C., Public Administration
ARTERTON, F. C., Political Management
BABER, W. R., Accountancy
BAGCHI, P. K., Business Administration
BARNHILL, T. M., Finance
CARSON, J. H., Management Science
CHERIAN, E. J., Information Systems
CHITWOOD, S. R., Public Administration
COYNE, J. P., Management Science
DAVIS, H. J., Strategic Management
DIVITA, S. F., Marketing
DYER, R. F., Business Administration
FOLKERTS, J., Media and Public Affairs
FORMAN, E. H., Management Science
GLASCOCK, J. L., Finance
GRANGER, M. J., Management Science
HALAL, W. E., Management Science
HANDORF, W. C., Finance
HARMON, M. M., Public Administration
HARVEY, J. B., Management Science
HAWKINS, D. E., Tourism Studies, Tourism Policy, Medicine
HILMY, J., Accountancy
INFELD, D. L., Public Administration, Health Services Management and Policy
JAQUES, E., Management Science
KEE, J. E., Public Administration
KLOCK, M. S., Finance
KUMAR, K. R., Accountancy
LAUTER, G. P., International Business
LENN, D. J., Strategic Management and Public Policy
LOBUTS, Jr, J. F., Management Science
McSWAIN, C. J., Public Administration
MADDOX, L. M., Business Administration
MANHEIM, J. B., Media and Public Affairs, Political Science
NEWCOMER, K. E., Public Administration
PAIK, C.-M., Accountancy and Quantitative Methods
PARK, Y. S., International Business
PERRY, Jr, J. H., Business Administration
PHILLIPS, S. M., Finance
RAU, P. A., Business Administration
ROBERTS, S. V., Media and Public Affairs
ROBLES, F., International Marketing and International Affairs
SHELDON, D. R., Accountancy
SOYER, R., Management Science
STERLING, C. H., Media and Public Affairs, Telecommunication
STERN, C., Media and Public Affairs
TRACHTENBERG, S. J., Public Administration
UMPLEBY, S. A., Management Science
WEINER, R. J., International Business and International Affairs
WIRTZ, P. W., Management Science, Psychology
WORTH, M. J., Nonprofit Management

School of Engineering and Applied Science:
BERKOVICH, S. Y., Engineering and Applied Science
BOCK, P. S., Engineering
BRIER, G. R., Engineering Management
CARROLL, Jr, R. L., Engineering and Applied Science
CHOI, H.-A., Engineering and Applied Science
COOPER, P. A., Engineering

DEASON, J. P., Engineering Management, Systems Engineering
DELLA TORRE, E., Engineering and Applied Science
DIGGES, K. H., Engineering and Applied Science
EDELSON, B. L., Engineering
EISNER, H., Engineering Management
FELDMAN, M. B., Engineering and Applied Science
FRIEDER, G., Engineering and Applied Science, Statistics
GARRIS, C. A., Engineering
GILMORE, C. M., Engineering and Applied Science
HAQUE, M. I., Engineering and Applied Science
HARRALD, J. R., Engineering Management
HARRINGTON, R. J., Engineering and Applied Science
HELGERT, H. J., Engineering and Applied Science
HELLER, R. S., Engineering and Applied Science
HOFFMAN, L. J., Engineering and Applied Science
JONES, D. L., Engineering
KAHN, W. K., Engineering and Applied Science
KAUFMAN, R. E., Engineering
KYRIAKOPOULOS, N., Engineering
LANG, R. H., Engineering and Applied Science
LEE, J. D.-Y., Engineering and Applied Science
LIEBOWITZ, H., Engineering and Applied Science
LOEW, M. H., Engineering
MAHMOOD, K., Engineering
MARTIN, C. D., Engineering and Applied Science
MAURER, W. D., Engineering and Applied Science
MAZZUCHI, T. A., Operations Research, Engineering Management
MELTZER, A. C., Engineering and Applied Science
MURPHREE, Jr, E. L., Engineering Management, Systems Engineering
MYERS, M. K., Engineering and Applied Science
NAGEL, D. J., Engineering
NARAHARI, B., Engineering and Applied Science
PARDAVI-HORVATH, M., Engineering and Applied Science
PELTON, J. N., Engineering
PICKHOLTZ, R. L., Engineering and Applied Science
POST, J. M., Engineering Management, Political Psychology, International Affairs, Psychiatry and Behavioural Sciences
ROPER, W. E., Engineering and Applied Science
SANDUSKY, Jr, R. R., Engineering and Applied Science
SARKANI, S., Engineering Management, Systems Engineering
SIBERT, J. L., Engineering and Applied Science
SZU, H., Engineering
TOLSON, R. H., Engineering and Applied Science
TONG, T. W., Mechanical Engineering
VOJCIC, B. R., Engineering and Applied Science
WASYLKIWSKYJ, W., Engineering and Applied Science
WATERS, R. C., Engineering Management
YOUSSEF, A., Engineering and Applied Science
ZAGHLOUL, M. E., Engineering and Applied Science

Law School:
ADELMAN, M. J.
BANZHAF, III, J. F.
BARRON, J. A.
BENITEZ, A. M.
BHALA, R.
BLOCK, C. D.
BRATTON, W. W.
BROWN, K. B.
BUTLER, P.
CAHN, N. R.
CARTER, W. B.
CHEH, M. M.
CLARK, B. R.
CRAVER, C. B.
CUNNINGHAM, L. E.
DIENES, C. T.
FRIEDENTHAL, J. H.
GABALDON, T. A.
GUTMAN, J. S.
IZUMU, C. L.
JOHNSTON, G. P.
JONES, S. R.
KOVACIC, W. E.
LEE, C.
LEES, F. J.
LERNER, R. L.
LUPU, I. C.
LYMAN, J. P.
MAGGS, G. E.
MEIER, J. S.
MEYER, P. H.
MITCHELL, L. E.
MORGAN, T. D.
PAGEL, S. B.
PARK, R. E.
PERONI, R. J.
PETERSON, T. D.
PIERCE, Jr, R. J.
RAVEN-HANSEN, P.
REITZE, Jr, A. W.
ROBINSON, Jr, D.
SALTZBURG, S. A.
SCHECHTER, R. E.
SCHWARTZ, J. I.
SELMI, M.
SIEGEL, J. R.
SIRULNIK, E. S.
SOHN, L. B.
SOLOMON, L. D.
SPANOGLE, J. A.
STEINHARDT, R. G.
STRAND, J. H.
TRANGSRUD, R. H.
TURLEY, J. R.
TUTTLE, R.
WILMARTH, Jr, A. E.
YOUNG, M. K.
ZUBROW, L. E.

School of Medicine and Health Sciences:
ABRAMSON, F. P., Pharmacology, Chemistry
ADELSON, E., Medicine
ADVANI, M., Psychiatry and Behavioural Sciences
AHLGREN, J. D., Medicine, Pharmacology
ALBERT, M., Medicine
ALBRIGHT, J., Microbiology and Tropical Medicine
AMIRI, S., Paediatrics
AMMERMAN, B., Neurological Surgery
APUD, J., Psychiatry and Behavioural Sciences
ARLING, B., Medicine
ARONS, B., Psychiatry and Behavioural Sciences
ASCENSAO, J., Medicine
AUGUST, G. P., Paediatrics
BACHMAN, L., Anaesthesiology, Critical Care Medicine, Paediatrics
BAILEY, J. M., Biochemistry and Molecular Biology
BANK, W. O., Radiology and Neurological Surgery
BARAF, H., Medicine
BARNHILL, R., Dermatology, Pathology

BARR, N., Surgery, Health Care Sciences
BARRY, P., Medicine, Health Care Sciences
BARTH, W. F., Medicine
BATSHAW, M., Paediatrics
BATTEY, J., Surgery
BATTLE, C., Paediatrics
BECKER, A., Obstetrics and Gynaecology
BECKER, K. L., Medicine and Physiology, Experimental Medicine
BELMAN, A. B., Urology and Paediatrics
BENNETT, H., Paediatrics
BERBERIAN, B. J., Dermatology
BERENSON, R., Health Care Sciences
BERNAD, P., Neurology
BERNSTEIN, L., Medicine
BERRY, G., Paediatrics
BIGELOW, L., Psychiatry and Behavioural Sciences
BLANK, A., Psychiatry and Behavioural Sciences
BORENSTEIN, D., Medicine
BORUM, M., Medicine
BOWLES, L. T., Surgery
BRAUN, M., Dermatology
BRILL, D., Medicine
BRILL, W., Medicine
BRONSTHER, O., Surgery
BROWN, B., Psychiatry and Behavioural Sciences
BROWN, H., Ophthalmology
BUKRINSKY, M., Microbiology and Tropical Medicine
BULAS, D., Radiology, Paediatrics
BURMAN, K., Medicine
BURNS, W., Pathology
BURRIS, B., Psychiatry
BYRNE, J., Paediatrics, Epidemiology and Biostatistics
BYRON, H., Ophthalmology
CAHAN, J., Surgery, Health Care Sciences
CALLENDER, C., Surgery
CAMPOS, J. M., Paediatrics, Pathology, Microbiology and Tropical Medicine
CANTER, J., Surgery
CAPUTY, A., Neurological Surgery
CARLSON, D., Obstetrics and Gynaecology
CAWLEY, J., Prevention and Community Health, Health Care Sciences
CHAMBERLAIN, J., Paediatrics
CHANDRA, R., Pathology, Paediatrics
CHANG, P., Medicine
CHATOOR-KOCH, I. M., Psychiatry and Behavioural Sciences and Paediatrics
CHENG, T. O., Medicine
CHERTOFF, J., Psychiatry and Behavioural Sciences
CHIAPPINELLI, V., Pharmacology and Neurological Surgery
CHIN, M., Anaesthesiology and Critical Care Medicine
CHODOFF, P., Psychiatry and Behavioural Sciences
CHUSED, J., Psychiatry and Behavioural Sciences, Paediatrics
COGEN, P., Neurological Surgery, Paediatrics
COHEN, G. D., Health Care Sciences, Psychiatry and Behavioural Sciences
COHEN, L., Paediatrics
COHEN, M., Surgery
COHEN-MANSFIELD, J., Health Care Sciences, Prevention and Community Health
COLBERG-POLEY, A., Paediatrics, Biochemistry and Molecular Biology
COLEMAN, R., Paediatrics
COLEMAN, R., Psychiatry and Behavioural Sciences
COLICE, G., Medicine
COMAS-DIAZ, L., Psychiatry and Behavioural Sciences
COOK, C., Pathology
COONEY, F., Neurological Surgery
COOPER, B., Medicine
CORSO, P., Surgery

COTLOVE, E., Psychiatry and Behavioural Sciences
COWAN, C., Ophthalmology
COX, G., Emergency Medicine
CYTRYN, L., Psychiatry and Behavioural Sciences
D'ANGELO, L. J., Paediatrics, Prevention and Community Health, Medicine
DANIEL, D., Psychiatry and Behavioural Sciences
DANOVITCH, S., Medicine
DAVIS, D., Psychiatry and Behavioural Sciences
DAVIS, D. O., Radiology, Neurology and Neurological Surgery
DAVIS, G., Microbiology and Tropical Medicine
DENNIS, M., Neurological Surgery
DEPALMA, L., Pathology, Anatomy and Cell Biology
DIAMOND, D., Psychiatry and Behavioural Sciences
DIAMOND, R., Medicine
DLUHY, J., Psychiatry and Behavioural Sciences
DOMAN, D., Medicine
DOPPELHEUER, J., Obstetrics and Gynaecology
DOSA, S., Medicine
DRUY, E. M., Radiology
DUBEY, A., Obstetrics and Gynaecology
DUFOUR, D. R., Pathology
DYER, C., Psychiatry and Behavioural Sciences
EATON, J., Psychiatry and Behavioural Sciences
ECONOMOPOULOS, B., Anaesthesiology and Critical Care Medicine
EDELSON, R., Neurology
EDELSTEIN, S., Emergency Medicine, Anaesthesiology and Critical Care Medicine
EICHELBERGER, M. R., Surgery and Paediatrics
EIG, B., Paediatrics
EIN, D., Medicine
EIN, T., Obstetrics and Gynaecology
EIST, H., Psychiatry and Behavioural Sciences
ELLWOOD, L., Health Care Sciences
EL-MOHANDES, A., Prevention and Community Health, Paediatrics, Obstetrics and Gynaecology
ERSHLER, W., Medicine
EVANS, F. B., Psychiatry and Behavioural Sciences
FAIRBANKS, D., Surgery
FALK, N., Medicine, Health Care Sciences
FALK, R., Obstetrics and Gynaecology
FEIGIN, D., Radiology
FELDMAN, B., Surgery, Health Care Sciences, Paediatrics
FELDMAN, I., Surgery
FIELDS, A., Anaesthesiology and Critical Care Medicine
FINKELSTEIN, J. D., Medicine
FISCHER, R., Medicine
FRAM, D., Psychiatry and Behavioural Sciences
FRANK, J., Psychiatry and Behavioural Sciences
FRASER, C., Pharmacology, Microbiology and Tropical Medicine
FUCHS, M., Medicine
GAARDER, K., Psychiatry and Behavioural Sciences
GAASTERLAND, D., Ophthalmology
GAHRES, E., Obstetrics and Gynaecology
GALLO, L., Biochemistry and Molecular Biology
GALLO, V., Paediatrics, Pharmacology
GEELHOED, G. W., International Medicine and Surgery
GEORGE, D., Psychiatry and Behavioural Sciences
GERSHEN, B., Medicine

GIAUME, C., Anatomy and Cell Biology
GILBERT, C., Obstetrics and Gynaecology
GILLANDERS, R., Obstetrics and Gynaecology
GILLMAN, R., Psychiatry and Behavioural Sciences
GINDOFF, P. R., Obstetrics and Gynaecology
GINSBERG, A. L., Medicine
GIORDANO, J. M., Surgery
GLASER, B., Ophthalmology
GLASSMAN, L., Radiology
GLATT, M., Paediatrics, Psychiatry and Behavioural Sciences
GOLD, M., Medicine
GOLDSTEIN, A., Biochemistry and Molecular Biology
GOLDSTEIN, H., Medicine
GOLDSTEIN, K., Medicine
GOLDSTEIN, S., Medicine
GOODENHOUGH, D. J., Radiology
GOODMAN, S., Psychiatry and Behavioural Sciences
GOODWIN, F., Psychiatry and Behavioural Sciences
GORDIN, F., Medicine
GORDON, G., Psychiatry and Behavioural Sciences
GORELICK, K., Psychiatry and Behavioural Sciences
GRAETER, J., Orthopaedic Surgery
GRANATIR, W., Psychiatry and Behavioural Sciences
GRAVITZ, M., Psychiatry and Behavioural Sciences
GREENBERG, L. W., Paediatrics
GREENE, C., Paediatrics
GREENSPAN, S., Psychiatry and Behavioural Sciences, Paediatrics
GRIFFITH, J. L., Psychiatry and Behavioural Sciences, Neurology
GROSS, P., Urology
GROSS, R., Psychiatry and Behavioural Sciences
GROSSMAN, J. H., Obstetrics and Gynaecology, Microbiology and Tropical Medicine, Prevention and Community Health
GUIDOTTI, T., Environmental Occupational Health, Medicine
GULYA, A., Surgery
GUNTHER, S. F., Orthopaedic Surgery
GUTIERREZ, G., Medicine, Anaesthesiology and Critical Care Medicine
HAAS, M., Psychiatry and Behavioural Sciences
HAAS, S., Orthopaedic Surgery
HAIDER, R., Medicine
HANNALLAH, R. S., Anaesthesiology and Critical Care Medicine, Paediatrics
HARISIADIS, L. A., Radiology
HARSHBARGER, J., Pathology
HARTMAN, G., Surgery, Paediatrics
HASSAN, M., Obstetrics and Gynaecology
HAUDENSCHILD, C. C., Pathology and Medicine
HAWLEY, R., Anatomy and Cell Biology
HECKMAN, B., Medicine
HEINTZE, A., Obstetrics and Gynaecology
HELLER, N., Psychiatry and Behavioural Sciences
HELMKAMP, B., Obstetrics and Gynaecology
HENSON, D., Pathology
HERER, G. R., Paediatrics
HERSH, S., Psychiatry and Behavioural Sciences, Paediatrics
HILL, M. C., Radiology
HOFFMAN, D., Epidemiology and Biostatistics, Global Health
HOFFMAN, E., Paediatrics, Biochemistry and Molecular Biology
HOLBROOK, P. R., Anaesthesiology and Critical Care Medicine, Paediatrics
HOLLAND, C. A., Paediatrics
HOPPING, S., Surgery

HOTEZ, P., Microbiology and Tropical Medicine, Global Health, Epidemiology and Biostatistics
HOWARD, W. J., Medicine
HOWE, G., Psychiatry and Behavioural Sciences
HSIA, J., Medicine
HURLEY, J., Paediatrics
HUTTON, J., Surgery
ISSA, F., Psychiatry and Behavioural Sciences
JAAFAR, M., Ophthalmology, Paediatrics
JACOBSEN, F., Psychiatry and Behavioural Sciences
JACOBSON, J., Neurological Surgery
JAFFE, E., Pathology
JANATI, A., Neurology
JEROME, M., Obstetrics and Gynaecology
JOHNSON, F., Pathology
JOHNSON, K., Anatomy and Cell Biology, Obstetrics and Gynaecology
JOSEPH, D., Psychiatry and Behavioural Sciences
JOSEPH, J., Paediatrics, Epidemiology and Biostatistics
JOSHI, P., Psychiatry and Behavioural Sciences, Paediatrics
KAFKA, J., Psychiatry and Behavioural Sciences
KALINER, M., Medicine
KAMANI, N., Paediatrics
KAO, G., Dermatology
KAPIKIAN, A., Paediatrics
KAPLAN, K., Psychiatry and Behavioural Sciences, Paediatrics
KAPLAN, R., Anaesthesiology and Critical Care Medicine, Paediatrics
KARCHER, D., Pathology
KATZ, A., Pathology
KATZ, B., Ophthalmology
KATZ, N., Surgery
KATZ, R., Dermatology, Paediatrics
KATZ, R. J., Medicine and Emergency Medicine
KATZ, S., Urology
KAUFMAN, R., Engineering, Anatomy and Cell Biology
KAUFMAN, R., Medicine
KELLEHER, J., Physiology and Experimental Medicine
KELLY, J. J., Neurology and Neurological Surgery
KENNEDY, K., Pharmacology, Genetics
KESHISHIAN, J., Surgery
KHOURY, A., Obstetrics and Gynaecology
KIMMEL, P. L., Medicine
KIRBY, E., Psychiatry and Behavioural Sciences
KIRKPATRICK, J., Surgery
KLINE, P., Medicine
KNELLER, M., Radiology
KNOLL, S., Surgery
KOBRINE, A., Neurological Surgery
KOCH, E., Obstetrics and Gynaecology
KOENIG, K., Emergency Medicine
KOVAL, N., Medicine
KOZLOFF, L., Surgery
KREBS, H., Obstetrics and Gynaecology
KRESSEL, B., Medicine
KUEHL, K., Paediatrics
KUMAR, A., Biochemistry and Molecular Biology, Genetics
KUSHNER, D. C., Radiology and Paediatrics
KUSHNER, E., Psychiatry and Behavioural Sciences
LACHER, D., Pathology
LADISCH, S., Paediatrics, Biochemistry and Molecular Biology
LAKSHMAN, R., Medicine, Biochemistry and Molecular Biology
LANDAU, B., Psychiatry and Behavioural Sciences, Paediatrics
LANDO, H., Medicine
LANE, H., Medicine
LARSEN, Jr, J. W., Obstetrics and Gynaecology

LAURENO, R., Neurology
LAWS, E., Neurological Surgery
LAZAR, S., Psychiatry and Behavioural Sciences
LAZARUS, A., Obstetrics and Gynaecology
LE GOLVAN, P., Pathology
LEATHERBURY, L., Paediatrics
LEFKOWITZ, L., Paediatrics, Health Care Sciences
LEMP, M., Ophthalmology
LEVI, L., Psychiatry and Behavioural Sciences
LEVINE, P., Epidemiology and Biostatistics, Medicine
LEVITT, R., Obstetrics and Gynaecology
LEVY, L., Radiology
LEW, S., Medicine
LEWIS, J., Medicine
LEWIS, R., Orthopaedic Surgery
LIEBERMAN, E., Psychiatry and Behavioural Sciences
LIEBERMAN, M., Medicine
LINDSAY, J., Medicine
LIOTTA, L., Pathology
LIPSIUS, S., Psychiatry and Behavioural Sciences, Obstetrics and Gynaecology
LIPSON, A., Medicine
LITOVITZ, T., Emergency Medicine
LITTMAN, B., Obstetrics and Gynaecology
LOO, T., Pharmacology
LOWE, J., Paediatrics
LUBAN, N. C., Paediatrics and Pathology
LUKE, J., Pathology
LURIE, N., Medicine
LYNN, D. J., Health Care Sciences and Medicine
MCAFEE, J., Radiology
MACDONALD-GINZBURG, M. G., Paediatrics
MCDOWELL, R., Paediatrics
MCGILL, W. A., Anaesthesiology and Critical Care Medicine, Paediatrics
MACHT, S., Surgery
MCKNEW, D., Paediatrics
MADDOX, J., Obstetrics and Gynaecology
MAHDAVI, I., Paediatrics
MAJD, M., Radiology and Paediatrics
MALAWER, M. M., Orthopaedic Surgery
MANDEL, H. G., Pharmocology
MANDLER, R., Neurology and Neurological Surgery
MANYAK, M. J., Urology, Microbiology and Tropical Medicine
MARINOFF, S., Obstetrics and Gynaecology
MARLOW, J., Obstetrics and Gynaecology
MARTIN, D., Obstetrics and Gynaecology
MARTIN, G. R., Paediatrics
MASTERS, E. C., Obstetrics and Gynaecology
MASTROYANNIS, C., Obstetrics and Gynaecology
MASUR, H., Medicine
MAYER, T., Emergency Medicine
MECKLENBURG, F., Obstetrics and Gynaecology
MERIKANGAS, J., Psychiatry and Behavioural Science
MEYER, J., Medicine
MIDGLEY, F. M., Surgery and Paediatrics
MILLER, G., Psychiatry and Behavioural Sciences
MILOWE, I., Paediatrics
MOAK, J. P., Paediatrics
MONDZAC, A., Medicine
MOODY, S., Anatomy and Cell Biology
MOSKOVITZ, P., Orthopaedic Surgery, Neurological Surgery
MUFARRIJ, I., Obstetrics and Gynaecology
MULLAN, F., Health Care Sciences, Paediatrics, Prevention and Community Health
MURPHY, R., Ophthalmology
NACHNANI, G., Medicine
NASHEL, D., Medicine
NASR, M., Psychiatry and Behavioural Sciences
NAWAB, E., Obstetrics and Gynaecology

NEVIASER, R. J., Orthopaedic Surgery
NEWMAN, K., Surgery, Paediatrics
NEWMAN, M., Medicine
NG, L., Neurology
NICKLAS, R., Medicine
NICOLAS, J., Paediatrics, Pharmacology
NIERMAN, W., Biochemistry and Molecular Biology
NIGRA, T., Dermatology, Paediatrics
NOWAK, J., Psychiatry and Behavioural Sciences
OBOLER, A., Medicine
OCHSENSCHLAGER, D. W., Paediatrics and Emergency Medicine
O'KIEEFE, D., Medicine
OLDFIELD, E., Neurological Surgery
OMMAYA, A., Neurological Surgery
O'NEILL, J., Ophthalmology
ORENSTEIN, J., Pathology
ORKIN, B., Surgery
PACKER, R. J., Neurology and Paediatrics
PALOMBI, J., Psychiatry and Behavioural Sciences, Paediatrics
PAN, J., Obstetrics and Gynaecology
PARENTI, D., Medicine, Microbiology and Tropical Medicine
PARKER, P., Paediatrics
PARKS, M., Ophthalmology, Paediatrics
PATEL, R. I., Anaesthesiology and Critical Care Medicine, Paediatrics
PATIERNO, S., Pharmacology, Genetics, Environmental Occupational Health
PAWLSON, L. G., Healthcare Sciences, Medicine, Health Services Management and Policy
PEDREIRA, F., Paediatrics
PEEBLES, P., Paediatrics
PEELE, R., Psychiatry and Behavioural Sciences
PERMAN, G., Psychiatry and Behavioural Sciences
PERRY, D., Pharmacology
PETROVITCH, C., Anaesthesiology and Critical Care Medicine
PEUSNER, K., Anatomy and Cell Biology
PHILLIPS, M., Medicine
PILLAI, M., Medicine
PLATIA, E. V., Medicine
POLIS, M., Emergency Medicine
POLLACK, M. M., Anaesthesiology and Critical Care Medicine, Paediatrics
POST, J., Psychiatry and Behavioural Sciences
POTOLICCHIO, S. J., Neurology and Neurological Surgery
POTTER, B. M., Radiology and Paediatrics
POVAR, G., Health Care Sciences, Medicine
POWERS, D., Obstetrics and Gynaecology
PRINCIPATO, J., Surgery
PROTOS, P., Obstetrics and Gynaecology
PULASKI, P., Neurology
PUMPHREY, R., Surgery
PUTNAM, J., Medicine
PYATT, R., Radiology
RABSON, A., Pathology
RAIS-BAHRMANI, K., Paediatrics
RANKIN, J., Psychiatry and Behavioural Sciences
RANKIN, R., Psychiatry and Behavioural Sciences
RAPOPORT, J., Psychiatry and Behavioural Sciences, Paediatrics
RATNER, R., Psychiatry and Behavioural Sciences
REAMAN, G. H., Paediatrics
REICH, W., Psychiatry and Behavioural Sciences
REISS, D., Psychiatry and Behavioural Sciences, Medicine and Psychology
RESTAK, R., Neurology
RICKLES, F., Medicine, Paediatrics
RIEGELMAN, R., Epidemiology and Biostatistics, Medicine, Health Care Sciences
RIEGER, R., Paediatrics, Psychiatry and Behavioural Sciences
ROBBINS, D. C., Medicine

ROBERTSON, W. W., Orthopaedic Surgery

ROBINOWITZ, C., Psychiatry and Behavioural Sciences

ROBINSON, L., Psychiatry and Behavioural Sciences

RODRIGUEZ-GARCIA, R., Global Health, Prevention and Community Health, International Affairs

ROSENBAUM, S., Health Policy, Health Services Management and Leadership, Health Care Sciences

ROSENBERG, J., Medicine

ROSENBLUM, S., Psychiatry and Behavioural Sciences

ROSENQUIST, G. C., Paediatrics

ROSENSTEIN, J., Anatomy and Cell Biology, Neurological Surgery

ROSS, M., Obstetrics and Gynaecology

ROTHMAN, B., Obstetrics and Gynaecology

ROTSZTAIN, A., Medicine

RUBOVITS-SEITZ, P., Psychiatry and Behavioural Sciences

RUCKMAN, R. N., Paediatrics

RUDZKI, C., Medicine

RUSHTON, H. G., Urology and Paediatrics

SADIN, H., Medicine

SARIN, P., Environmental Occupational Heath, Biochemistry and Molecular Biology

SCALETTAR, R., Medicine

SCHECHTER, G. P., Medicine

SCHEER, J., Health Care Sciences

SCHLEIN, P., Medicine

SCHNEIDER, M., Medicine

SCHWARTZ, A., Pathology

SCHWARTZ, R., Paediatrics, Health Care Sciences

SCOTT, D., Immunology, Anatomy and Cell Biology

SCOTT, J., Emergency Medicine

SCOTT, S., Medicine

SEIBEL, N., Paediatrics

SEIDES, S., Medicine

SEKHAR, L. N., Neurological Surgery

SEMERJIAN, H., Urology

SEVER, J. L., Paediatrics, Microbiology and Tropical Medicine, Obstetrics and Gynaecology

SHARGEL, M., Medicine

SHESSER, R. F., Emergency Medicine, Medicine, Environmental Occupational Health

SHORE, M., Paediatrics

SHORT, B. L., Paediatrics

SHRIER, D., Psychiatry and Behavioural Sciences, Paediatrics

SIDAWY, A. N., Surgery

SIDAWY, M., Pathology

SILBER, T. J., Paediatrics, Global Health, Prevention and Community Health

SILVA, C., Surgery

SILVER, S., Pathology, Prevention and Community Health, Medicine

SIMON, D., Medicine

SIMON, G. L., Medicine, Biochemistry and Molecular Biology, Microbiology and Tropical Medicine

SIMON, J., Obstetrics and Gynaecology

SINGH, N., Paediatrics, Health Care Sciences, Global Health

SLUZKI, C., Psychiatry and Behavioural Sciences

SLY, R. M., Paediatrics

SMITH, L., Surgery

SMITH, M., Emergency Medicine

SMOLLER, B., Psychiatry and Behavioural Sciences

SOLDIN, S. J., Paediatrics, Pathology

SOLOMON, F., Psychiatry and Behavioural Sciences

SOREL, E., Psychiatry and Behavioural Sciences

SOUTHBY, R., Global Health, Health Care Sciences, Health Policy

SPAGNOLO, S. V., Medicine

STAR, R., Medicine

STARK, W., Psychiatry and Behavioural Sciences, Paediatrics

STEIN, M., Psychiatry and Behavioural Sciences, Paediatrics

STEINBERG, W. M., Medicine

STEINFELD, H., Medicine

STERN, M., Psychiatry and Behavioural Sciences

STEVENS, C., Psychiatry and Behavioural Sciences

STOCK, M., Medicine and Health Care Sciences

STOCKTON, W., Psychiatry and Behavioural Sciences

STONE, A., Health Care Sciences, Medicine

STOPAK, B., Neurological Surgery

STOPAK, S., Ophthalmology

STRASSBURGER, F., Paediatrics

STRICKLAND, D., Biochemistry and Molecular Biology

TAUBER, L., Neurological Surgery

TAUBIN, J., Medicine, Health Care Sciences

TAVASSOLI, F., Pathology

TAYLOR, D., Psychiatry and Behavioural Sciences

TETTE, A., Surgery

THOMAS, J., Psychiatry and Behavioural Sciences

THOMPSON, A., Medicine

TIEVSKY, G., Radiology

TRAMONT, E., Medicine

TROUT, H., Surgery

TRUJILLO, N., Medicine

TSOKOS, G., Paediatrics

TUAZON, C. U., Medicine

TUCHMAN, M., Paediatrics, Biochemistry and Molecular Biology

TURNER, M., Dermatology

USHER, M., Psychiatry and Behavioural Sciences

VAN BREDA, A., Radiology

VANDERHOEK, J., Biochemistry and Molecular Biology

VARGHESE, P. J., Medicine and Paediatrics

VELASQUEZ, M. T., Medicine

VENBRUX, A., Radiology, Surgery

VIRMANI, R., Pathology

WALETZKY, J., Psychiatry and Behavioural Sciences

WALKER, G., Biochemistry and Molecular Biology

WALSH, R., Anatomy and Cell Biology, Neurological Surgery

WARGOTZ, E., Pathology

WARREN, N., Dermatology

WARTOFSKY, L., Medicine

WATKIN, D., Medicine

WEGLICKI, W. B., Medicine, Physiology and Experimental Medicine

WEINBERGER, D., Psychiatry and Behavioural Sciences

WEINSTEIN, S., Neurology, Paediatrics

WEISS, H., Medicine

WEISS, L., Medicine

WELBORN, L. G., Anaesthesiology and Critical Care Medicine, Paediatrics

WERLING, L., Pharmacology, Neurological Surgery

WHERRY, D., Surgery

WHITE, P. H., Medicine and Paediatrics

WILKINSON, R., Medicine

WILLIAMS, C. M., Dermatology and Pathology

WILLIAMS, J. F., Anaesthesiology and Critical Care Medicine, Health Services Management and Policy

WILLIAMS, M., Pathology

WILLIAMS, S., Obstetrics and Gynaecology

WINKLES, J., Biochemistry and Molecular Biology

WISNESKI, L., Medicine

WITTENBERG, R., Psychiatry and Behavioural Sciences

WOLFE, M., Medicine

WOLIN, S., Psychiatry and Behavioural Sciences

WOLMAN, S., Pathology

WOOD, B., Anthropology, Anatomy and Cell Biology

WRIGHT, D. C., Neurological Surgery

YODAIKEN, R., Pathology, Health Care Sciences

YOO, D., Medicine

YU, G., Urology

ZAJTCHUK, R., Surgery

ZALAL, G. H., Surgery and Paediatrics

ZALESKE, D., Orthopaedic Surgery, Paediatrics

ZEMAN, R., Radiology

ZIMMERMAN, M., Ophthalmology

ZINNER, J., Psychiatry and Behavioural Sciences

School of Public Health and Health Services:

BILES, B., Health Policy

BORZI, P., Health Policy

BOYD, N. R., Prevention and Community Health

CAWLEY, J. F., Prevention and Community Health

D'ANGELO, L. J., Prevention and Community Medicine

DARR, K. J., Health Services Management and Leadership

EASTAUGH, S. R., Health Services Management and Leadership

EL-MOHANDES, A., Prevention and Community Medicine

GREENBERG, W., Health Economics

GUIDOTTI, T. L., Environmental and Occupational Health

HIDALGO, J., Health Policy

HIRSCH, R. P., Epidemiology and Biostatistics

LACHIN, J., Epidemiology and Biostatistics

LEVINE, P. H., Epidemiology and Biostatistics, Environmental and Occupational Health

MICHAELS, D., Environmental and Occupational Health

MILLER, W. C., Exercise Science

PAUP, D. C., Exercise Science

RIEGELMAN, R. K., Epidemiology and Biostatistics

RODRIGUEZ-GARCIA, R., International Health

ROSSELLO, P., Global Health

SARIN, P., Environmental and Occupational Health

SOUTHBY, R. M. F., Global Health, Health Policy

SULLIVAN, P. A., Exercise Science

WINDSOR, R. A., Prevention and Community Medicine

Graduate School of Education and Human Development:

CASTLEBERRY, M. S., Special Education

CONFESSORE, G. J., Higher Education Administration

CUMMINGS, W. K., International Education

DEW, D. W., Counselling, Psychiatry and Behavioural Sciences

EL-KHAWAS, E. H., Education Policy

FERRANTE, R., Education

FREUND, M. B., Special Education

FUTRELL, M. H., Education

HEDDESHEIMER, J. C., Counselling, Psychiatry and Behavioural Sciences

HOARE, C. H., Human Development and Human Resource Development

HOLMES, D. H., Education

HOWERTON, Jr, E. B., Education

IANACONE, R. N., Special Education

KOCHHAR-BRYANT, C. A., Special Education

LINKOWSKI, D. C., Counselling, Psychology and Behavioural Sciences

LYNCH, S. H., Teacher Preparation, Special Education

MAZUR, A. J., Special Education

MULLER, R. O., Educational Research

PALEY, N. B., Elementary Education

PARATORE, S. R., Education

ROTBERG, I. C., Education Policy
SASHKIN, M., Human Resource Development
SCHWANDT, D. R., Human Resource Development
SHOTEL, J. R., Special Education
TAYMANS, J. H., Special Education
WATSON, A., Higher Education Administration
WEST, L. L., Special Education
WHITAKER, R., Higher Education

GEORGETOWN UNIVERSITY

37th and O Sts, NW, Washington, DC 20057

Telephone: (202) 687-0100

E-mail: gucomm@georgetown.edu

Internet: www.georgetown.edu

Private control

Founded 1789

First Catholic and Jesuit Univ. in the USA; 4 undergraduate, 3 graduate and professional schools, professional devt programmes and certificates; medical residencies; courses in arts, humanities, sciences and business

Pres.: Dr JOHN J. DEGIOIA

Chair.: PAUL TAGLIABUE

Provost: Dr ROBERT M. GROVES

Sr Vice-Pres. and COO: CHRIS AUGUSTINI

Sr Vice-Pres. and Chief Tech. Officer: SPIROS DIMOLITSAS

Exec. Vice-Pres. for Health Sciences: HOWARD FEDEROFF

Exec. Vice-Pres. for Law Center Affairs: WILLIAM TREANOR

Vice-Pres. for Advancement: R. BARTLEY MOORE

Vice-Pres. and Gen. Counsel: LISA BROWN

Vice-Pres. for Information Services and Chief Information Officer: LISA DAVIS

Vice-Pres. for Institutional Diversity and Equity: ROSEMARY KILKENNY

Vice-Pres. for Mission and Ministry: Fr KEVIN O'BRIEN

Vice-Pres. for Public Affairs: ERIK SMULSON

Librarian: ARTEMIS G. KIRK

Library: 2.4m. vols

Number of teachers: 2,100 (1300 full-time, 800 part-time)

Number of students: 12,600

Publications: *Blue and Gray* (24 a year, online), *Georgetown Business* (2 a year), *Georgetown Law* (6 a year), *Georgetown Magazine* (6 a year, online), *Georgetown Medicine* (6 a year), *Georgetown Today* (12 a year, online), *Health Care Horizons* (2 a year, print and online), *Lombardi Magazine* (3 a year)

DEANS

Edmund A. Walsh School of Foreign Service: CAROL LANCASTER

Georgetown College: CHESTER L. GILLIS

Georgetown Public Policy Institute: EDWARD MONTGOMERY

Georgetown University Medical Center, Medical Education: Dr STEPHEN RAY MITCHELL

Georgetown University Medical Center, Research: Dr ROBERT CLARKE

Graduate School of Arts and Sciences: Dr GERALD M. MARA

Law Center: WILLIAM M. TREANOR

McDonough School of Business: Prof. DAVID A THOMAS

School of Continuing Studies: WALTER RANKIN

School of Foreign Service, Qatar: Dr GERD NONNEMAN

School of Medicine: Dr HOWARD FEDEROFF

School of Nursing and Health Studies: Dr MARTIN Y. IGUCHI

PROFESSORS

Edmund A. Walsh School of Foreign Service:

ABI-MERSHED, O. W.
ADELY, F.
AKSAKAL, M.
ALBRIGHT, M.
ANDERSON, J. R.
AREND, A. C.
BAILEY, J. J.
BALZER, H.
BANCHOFF, T.
BAUMANN, H.
BEACH, T.
BELK, P.
BENEDICT, C.
BENNETT, A.
BERLINERBLAU, J. D.
BROWN, J. A.
BUSCH, M. L.
BYMAN, D. L.
CHA, V.
CHAUDHURI, A.
CHERNICK, M.
CIDDI, S.
CROCKER, C.
CUMBY, R. E.
DAHLMAN, C. J.
DANIEL, D. C. F.
DAVID-FOX, M.
DAVIS, R. A.
DELETANT, D. J.
DESAI, R.
DUNKLEY, P.
EDELSTEIN, D. M.
EGNELL, R.
ESPOSITO, J. L.
FAIR, C. C.
FARR, T. F.
GRAGLIA, P.
GREEN, M. J.
HADDAD, Y. Y.
HARRISON, R.
HOFFMAN, B.
KRUPAR, S. R.
KUPCHAN, C. A.
LAGON, M. P.
LANCASTER, C. J.
KLINE, J. M.
LANGAN, J. P.
LANGER, E. D.
LESTER, G.
LEWIS, J. I.
LEWIS, M.
LIEBER, K. A.
LIEBER, R. J.
LOONEY, K.
LUDEMA, R.
MADAVO, C. E.
MARSHALL, K.
MARTIN, S.
MAYDA, A.
McHENRY, D.
McKITTRICK, M.
McMANUS, D.
McMORROW, M.
McNAMARA, K.
McNAUGHER, T.
McNEILL, J.
MIKELL, G.
MILLWARD, J.
MORAN, T.
MORFIT, M.
MUJAL-LEON, E.
NEWMAN, A.
NEXON, D.
O'BRIEN, P.
OLDENSKI, L.
OLESKO, K.
OLOFSGARD, A.
PAINTER, D.
PATEL, P.
PONSATI, C.
RADELET, S.
REARDON-ANDERSON, J.
ROMAN, A.

ROSS, D.
SASSOON, J.
SHAMBAUGH, G.
SHEHATA, S.
SIEG, K.
SMITH, L.
SMITH, K.
SONBOL, A.
STANLEY, E.
STEINBERG, D.
STENT, A.
STEPHEN, E.
TAYLOR, S.
TIDWELL, A.
TUCKER, J.
TUTINO, J.
UDOMSAPH, C.
VALENZUELA, A.
VAN DUSEN, A.
VOETEN, E.
VOLL, J.
VON DER GOLTZ, A.
VREELAND, J.
WAGNER, M.
WEISS, C.
WISE, H.
WOLF, H.

Law Center:

ABERNATHY, C.
ABU-ODEH, L.
AIKEN, J.
ALEINIKOFF, T.
AREEN, J.
BABCOCK, H.
BARALE-CEURVORST, L.
BARNETT, R.
BAUMAN, J.
BLOCH, S.
BLOCHE, M.
BONNEAU, S.
BROOKS, R.
BRUMMER, C.
BYRNE, J.
CAMPBELL, A.
CARTER, B.
CASHIN, S.
COHEN, J.
COHEN, S.
COHN, S.
COLE, D.
COOK, A.
COPACINO, J.
DELAURENTIS, F.
DIAMOND, M.
DIAMOND, R.
DINH, V.
DONAHOE, D.
DORAN, M.
EDELMAN, P.
EPSTEIN, D.
ERNST, D.
FEINERMAN, J.
FELDBLUM, C.
FELDMAN, H.
GIRARD, V.
GOLDBLATT, S.
GOLDEN, M.
GOSTIN, L.
GOTTESMAN, M.
GUSTAFSON, C.
HEINZERLING, L.
HENNING, K.
HOFFMAN, C.
HUNTER, N.
JACKSON, J.
JORDAN, E.
KATYAL, N.
KING, P.
KLASS, G.
KOPLOW, D.
LANGEVOORT, D.
LAWRENCE, C.
LEDERMAN, M.
LEVITIN, A.
LUBAN, D.

MENKEL-MEADOW, C.
MEZEY, N.
MIKHAIL, J.
MLYNIEC, W.
MOLOT, J.
NORTON, E.
OLDHAM, J.
O'SULLIVAN, J.
PAGE, J.
PELLER, G.
PITOFSKY, R.
REGAN, M.
ROE, R.
ROSENKRANZ, N.
ROSS, J.
ROSS, S.
ROTHSTEIN, P.
RUBIN, P.
SALOP, S.
SAULSKI, P.
SCHRAG, P.
SEIDMAN, L.
SHELANSKI, H.
SHERMAN, N.
SMITH, A.
SPANN, G.
STROMSETH, J.
STUMBERG, R.
TAGUE, P.
THOMAS, J.
TISCIONE, K.
TREANOR, W.
TUSHNET, R.
VAZQUEZ, C.
VLADECK, D.
WASSERSTROM, S.
WEISS, E.
WERRO, F.
WEST, R.
ZEILER, K.

McDonough School of Business:
AGGARWAL, R.
ALMEIDA, P.
ANDERSON, K.
ANDREASEN, A.
BABER, W.
BALI, T.
BAMOSSY, G.
BIES, R.
BRENKERT, G.
CYPHER, M.
DALY, G.
DROMS, W.
DUGAN, S.
EBERHART, A.
ERNST, R.
EVANS, M.
JENSEN, J.
JOHANSSON, J.
KAMRAD, B.
MAYO, J.
McCABE, D.
MICELI, M.
NOLLEN, S.
ORD, K.
QUINN, D.
REINSCH, L.
RIVOLI, P.
ROMANELLI, E.
RONKAINEN, I.
SWEENEY, R.
TAN, D.
THOMAS, R.
TINSLEY, C.
WALKER, D.
WILLIAMSON, R.

School of Nursing and Health Studies:
COLLMANN, J.
HORAK, B.
IGUCHI, M.
JACOBS, B.
TAYLOR, C.

Undergraduate School:
AGGARWAL, R., School of Business

ALATIS, J. E., Linguistics and Modern Greek
ALBRECHT, J. W., Economics
ALBRIGHT, M. K., Practice of Diplomacy
ANDERLINI, L., Economics
ANDREASEN, A. R., School of Business
ASTARITA, T., History
BABB, V., English
BAIGIS, J., Nursing
BAILEY, J. J., Government and School of Foreign Service
BARNES, S. H., Government and School of Foreign Service
BARROWS, E. M., Biology
BATES, R. D., Jr, Chemistry
BEAUCHAMP, T. L., Philosophy
BENKE, G., Mathematics
BENSKY, R. D., French
BETZ, P. F., English
BIES, R. J., School of Business
Rev. BRADLEY, D. J. M., Philosophy
BRENKERT, G. G., School of Business
BROUGH, J. B., Philosophy
BROWN, D. M., History
BYRNES, A. S., German
CALVERT, S., Psychology
CALVEZ, J.-Y., Government
CANZONERI, M. B., Economics and School of Foreign Service
CAREY, G. W., Government
CHANG, D.-C., Mathematics
CHAPMAN, G. B., Biology
CHAPMAN, T., School of Nursing and Health Studies
CHICKERING, R., History and School of Foreign Service
CIMA, G. G., English
COLLINS, J. B., History
COLLINS, S. M., Economics
COOKE, T. B., School of Business
CROCKER, C. A., Strategic Studies in School of Foreign Service
CUDDINGTON, J. T., Economics and School of Foreign Service
CUMBY, R. E., International Business Diplomacy
CURRAN, R. E., History
CURRIE, J. F., Physics
DAVIS, W., Philosophy
DENNING, D. E., Computer Science
DROMS, W.M G., School of Business
ENGLER, H., Mathematics
ERNST, R., School of Business
ESPOSITO, J. L., Center for Muslim–Christian Understanding
EVANS, M. D., Economics
FASOLD, R. H W., Linguistics
FEKRAT, M. A., School of Business
FERDOWS, K.A, School of Business
FILERMAN, G., Health Studies
FINKEL, N. J., Psychology
GALE, I., Economics
GALLUCCI, R. L., School of Foreign Service
GIBERT, S. P., Government
GLAVIN, J. J., English
GODSON, R., Government
GOLDFRANK, D. M., History
GOMEZ-LOBO, A., Philosophy
GOODMAN, A. E., School of Foreign Service
GORMLEY, W. T., Government and Public Policy
GRANT, R. M., School of Business
GUSTAFSON, T., Government
HADDAD, Y. Y., School of Foreign Service
HALL, C. M., Sociology
HAUGHT, J. F., Theology
HEELAN, P. A., Philosophy
HENDERSON, E. J., Biology
HILTON, A. H., Art
HIRSH, J. C., English
HOLMER, J. M., English
HOWARD, D. V., Psychology
HUDSON, M. C., Arab Studies
IKENBERRY, G. J., School of Foreign Service
IRIZARRY, E. D., Spanish
JANKOWSKY, K. R., German

JOHANSSON, J. K., School of Business
JOHNSON, R. M., History
JOYNER, C. C., Government
KALYANASUNDARAM, B., Computer Science
KAZIN, M., History
KELTNER, B., School of Nursing and Health Studies
KERTESZ, M., Chemistry
KING, T. M., Theology
KIRKPATRICK, J. J.
KLINE, J. M., School of Foreign Service
KONÉ, A., French
KORD, S. T., German
KROGH, P. F., School of Foreign Service
KUHN, S. T., Philosophy
LAGNESE, J. E., Mathematics
LAKE, A., School of Foreign Service
LARUBIA-PRADO, F., Spanish
LEVY, M. B., School of Business
LIEBER, R. J., Government
McAULIFFE, J. D., Georgetown College
McCABE, D. M., School of Business
McDONALD, W. F., Sociology
McHENRY, D. F., School of Foreign Service
McKEOWN, E., Theology
McNAMARA, D., Sociology
McNEILL, J. R., School of Foreign Service and History
McNELIS, P. D., Economics and School of Foreign Service
MADDOX, L. B., English
MARTIRE, D. E., Chemistry
MARULLO, S., Sociology
MASSOUD-MOGHADDAM, F., Psychology
MAZZOLA, J. B., School of Business
MICELI, M. P., School of Business
MIKELL, G., Sociology and School of Foreign Service
MORAN, T. H., Int. Business Diplomacy
MORRIS, M. A., Slavic Languages
MUJICA, B. L., Spanish
MURPHY, G. R., German
NEALE, J. H., Biology
NISHIOKA, D. J., Biology
NOLLEN, S. D., School of Business
O'BRIEN, G., English
ORD, J. K., School of Business
PARKER, R. S., School of Business
PARROTT, W. G., Psychology
PFORDRESHER, J. C., English
PHILLIPS, D. A., Psychology
POPE, M. T., Chemistry
PRELINGER, E. A., Art
PUTO, C. P., School of Business
QUINN, D., School of Business
RAGUSSIS, M., English
RAMEY, C. T., School of Nursing and Health Studies
RAMEY, S. L., School of Nursing and Health Studies
RAPPAPORT, J., Spanish and School of Foreign Service
REARDON-ANDERSON, J., School of Foreign Service
REINSCH, N. LAMAR, Jr, School of Business
ROBINSON, D. N., Psychology
ROSENBLATT, J. P., English
ROSHWALD, A., History
RUEDY, J. D., History
RYDING, K. C., Arabic
SANDEFUR, J. T., Jr, Mathematics
SCHALL, J. V., Government
SCHIFFRIN, D., Linguistics
SCHURER, W., School of Business
SCHWARTZ, M., Economics
SCOLLON, R. T., Linguistics
SERENE, J. W., Physics
SEVERINO, R., Italian
SHAHID, I., Arabic
SHERMAN, N.
SITTERSON, J. C., Jr, English
SLEVIN, J. F., English
SMITH, B. R., English
STEINBERG, D. I., School of Foreign Service
STENT, A., Government

STITES, R., History and School of Foreign Service

STOWASSER, B., Arabic and School of Foreign Service

SWEENEY, R. J., School of Business

SZITTYA, P. R., English

TAMBASCO, A. J., Theology

TANNEN, D.

TAYLOR, D. W., Biology

THOMAS, R. J., School of Business

TUCKER, J. E., History

TUCKER, N. B., School of Foreign Service and History

VALENZUELA, A., Government

VEATCH, R. M., Philosophy

VELAUTHAPILLAI, M., Computer Science

VERECKE, W., Philosophy

VIKSNINS, G. J., Economics and School of Foreign Service

VOLL, J. O., School of Foreign Service and History

VROMAN, S., Economics

WALKER, D. A., School of Business

WALTERS, L. B., Jr, Philosophy

WAYNE, S. J., Government

WEISS, C., School of Foreign Service

WEISS, R. G., Chemistry

WILCOX, W. C., Government

WINTERS, F. X., School of Foreign Service

YANG, D. C., Chemistry

YOST, C. A., School of Foreign Service.

ATTACHED INSTITUTES

Center for Applied Research in the Apostolate: email cara@georgetown.edu2300 Wisconsin Ave, NW, Washington, DC; tel. (202) 687-8080; e-mail cara@georgetown.edu; internet cara.georgetown.edu; Chair. GERALD F. KICANAS; Exec. Dir THOMAS P. GAUNT, SJ; publ. *The CARA Report* (4 a year).

Center for Australian and New Zealand Studies: Dir ALAN C. TIDWELL.

Center for Business and Public Policy: Dir Prof. JOHN W. MAYO.

Center for Clinical Bioethics: Dir G. KEVIN DONOVAN.

Center for Contemporary Arab Studies: e-mail ccasinfo@georgetown.edu; Dir OSAMA ABI-MERSHED.

Center for Democracy and Civil Society: e-mail jjh76@georgetown.edu; Dir BARAK D. HOFFMAN.

Center for Continuing and Professional Education: Dir EDWIN W. SCHMIERER.

Center for Electronic Projects in American Culture Studies: Dir RANDY BASS.

Center for Eurasian, Russian and East European Studies: e-mail ceres@georgetown.edu; Dir ANGELA E. STENT (acting).

Center for Hypertension and Renal Disease Research: Chair. ALMA GILDENHORN.

Center for Intercultural Education and Development: e-mail cied@georgetown.edu; Dir CHANTAL SANTELICES.

Center for Latin American Studies: Dir ERICK LANGER.

Center for Multicultural Equity and Access: e-mail cmea@georgetown.edu; Dir CHARLENE BROWN-MCKENZIE.

Prince Alwaleed Bin Talal Center for Muslim–Christian Understanding: Dir JOHN L. ESPOSITO.

Center for Neural Injury and Recovery: Dir JEAN WRATHALL; Dir KATHLEEN MAGUIRE-ZEISS.

Center for New Designs in Learning and Scholarship: e-mail cndls@georgetown.edu; Dir RANDALL BASS.

Center for Peace and Security Studies: e-mail securitystudies@georgetown.edu; Dir BRUCE HOFFMAN.

Center for Public and Non-Profit Leadership: Dir KATHY POSTEL KRETMAN.

Center for Research on Children in the United States: Dir DEBORAH A. PHILLIPS; Dir WILLIAM T. GORMLEY.

Center for Social Justice: e-mail getinvolved@georgetown.edu; Dir WILLIAM T. GORMLEY; Dir DEBORAH A. PHILLIPS.

Center for the Brain Basis of Cognition: Dirs CRISTINA SANZ, MICHAEL ULLMAN.

Center for the Environment: Dir EDWARD M. BARROWS.

Center for the Study of Learning: Dir GUINEVERE EDEN.

Center for the Study of Sex Differences in Health, Aging, and Disease: e-mail csdgu@georgtown.edu; Dir KATHRYN SANDBERG.

Center on an Aging Society: e-mail info@aging-society.org; Dir ROBERT B. FRIEDLAND.

Institute for the Study of Diplomacy: Dir JAMES P. SEEVERS.

Kennedy Institute of Ethics: e-mail kennedyinstitute@georgetown.edu; Dir MARGARET OLIVIA LITTLE

HOWARD UNIVERSITY

2400 Sixth St, NW, Washington, DC 20059

Telephone: (202) 806-6100

Internet: www.howard.edu

Founded 1867

Private control

Academic year: August to May (2 terms)

Pres.: Dr SIDNEY A. RIBEAU

Provost and Sr Vice-Pres. for Academic Affairs and Health Sciences: Dr LASALLE LEFFALL

Sr Vice-Pres. and Sec.: Dr ARTIS HAMPSHIRE-COWAN

Sr Vice-Pres., Chief Financial Officer and Treas.: ROBERT TAROLA

Sr Vice-Pres. and Exec. Dean for Health Sciences: Dr EVE J. HIGGINBOTHAM

Sr Vice-Pres. for Strategic Planning and External Affairs: Dr HASSAN MINOR

Sr Vice-Pres. and Sec.: ARTIS G. HAMPSHIRE-COWAN

Exec. Vice-Pres. and Chief Operating Officer: TROY A. STOVALL

Vice-Pres. for Research and Compliance: Dr FLORENCE BONNER

Vice-Pres. for Devt and Alumni Relations: NESTA BERNARD

Vice-Pres. for Student Affairs: Dr BARBARA GRIFFIN

Gen. Counsel: NORMA LEFTWICH

Dir for Libraries: ARTHUREE R. WRIGHT

Library: see Libraries and Archives

Number of teachers: 1,300 (1,100 full-time, 200 part-time)

Number of students: 10,600

Publications: *Howard Journal of Communications* (4 a year), *Howard Law Journal* (1 year), *Howard Magazine*, *Human Rights and Globalization Law Review*, *Journal of Negro Education* (4 a year), *Journal of Religious Thought* (2 a year), *The Jurist* (2 a year)

DEANS

College of Arts and Sciences: Dr JAMES DONALDSON

College of Dentistry: Dr LEO E. ROUSE

College of Medicine: Dr MARK S. JOHNSON

College of Nursing and Allied Health Sciences: Dr MARY HILL

College of Pharmacy: Dr ANTHONY K. WUTOH

Graduate School: Dr CHARLES L. BETSEY

School of Business: Dr BARRON HARVEY

School of Communications: Dr CHUKA ONWU-MECHILI

School of Divinity: Dr ALTON POLLARD, III

School of Education: Dr LESLIE FENWICK

School of Engineering, Architecture and Computer Sciences: Dr JAMES MITCHELL

School of Law: Dr KURT L. SCHMOKE

School of Social Work: Dr CUDORE L. SNELL

INSTITUTE OF WORLD POLITICS

1521 16th St, NW, Washington, DC 20036-1464

Telephone: (202) 462-2101

E-mail: info@iwp.edu

Internet: www.iwp.edu

Founded 1990, present status 2005

Private control

Academic year: September to July

Offers Master's degrees in statecraft and nat. security affairs, statecraft and int. affairs and strategic intelligence studies

Pres.: Dr JOHN LENCZOWSKI

Exec. Vice-Pres.: DOUGLAS MILLS

Vice-Pres. for Academic Affairs and Academic Dean: Dr CHARLES ROGER SMITH

Vice-Pres. for Finance and Admin.: JIM HOLMES

Vice-Pres. for Institutional Advancement: TRICIA LLOYD

Dir for Libraries and Information Services: JAMES STAMBAUGH

Registrar: HASANNA BENSON-TYUS

Library of 30,000 vols

NATIONAL INTELLIGENCE UNIVERSITY

200 MacDill Blvd, Washington, DC 20340-5100

Telephone: (202) 231-3319

E-mail: niuadmit@ni-u.edu

Internet: www.ni-u.edu

Founded 1962 as Defense Intelligence School, present name 2011

State control

Academic year: August to July

Pres.: DAVID R. ELLISON

Provost: Dr SUSAN M. STUDDS

Registrar: ERIC H. STUPAR

Dir for Library: DENISE M. CAMPBELL

Library of 70,000 vols, 550 journals

Number of teachers: 80 (40 full-time, 40 part-time)

Number of students: 630

DEANS

College of Strategic Intelligence: Dr VANCE R. SKARSTEDT

School of Science and Technology Intelligence: Dr BRIAN R. SHAW

NATIONAL DEFENSE UNIVERSITY

300 Fifth Ave SW, Marshall Hall, Fort Lesley J. McNair, Washington, DC 20319-5066

Telephone: (202) 685-4700

Internet: www.ndu.edu

Founded 1924 as Army Industrial College

State control

Academic year: August to July

5 Colleges: College of Int Security Affairs, Industrial College of the Armed Forces, Information Resources Management College, Jt Forces Staff College and Nat. War College

Pres.: Vice-Admiral ANN E. RONDEAU

Sr Vice-Pres. for Int. Programmes and Outreach: NANCY MCELDOWNEY

Vice-Pres. for Academic Affairs: Dr JOHN W. YAEGER

Vice-Pres. for Research: Dr HANS BINNENDIJK

Number of teachers: 350
Number of students: 4,100
Publications: *Joint Force Quarterly*, *Prism* (4 a year)

PONTIFICAL FACULTY OF THE IMMACULATE CONCEPTION AT THE DOMINICAN HOUSE OF STUDIES

487 Michigan Ave, NE, Washington, DC 20017-1585
Telephone: (202) 495-3820
E-mail: registrar@dhs.edu
Internet: www.dhs.edu
Founded 1902 as The College of the Immaculate Conception, current name adopted 1988
Private control
Languages of instruction: Greek, Latin
Academic year: August to May
Chancellor: Very Rev. BRUNO CADORÉ
Vice-Chancellor: Very Rev. BRIAN MULCAHY
Pres.: Very Rev. Prof. JOHN LANGLOIS
Vice-Pres. and Academic Dean: Rev. Prof. THOMAS PETRI
Registrar: Rev. ALBERT TRUDEL
Treas.: SHAUNA ROYE
Librarian: Rev. JOHN MARTIN RUIZ
Library of 56,500 vols, 2,500 titles in specialized reference, Dominican and rare books collns
Number of teachers: 25
Number of students: 97
Publication: *The Thomist* (online, www.thomist.org)

POTOMAC COLLEGE

4000 Chesapeake St, NW, Washington, DC 20016
Telephone: (202) 686-0876
E-mail: admissions@potomac.edu
Internet: www.potomac.edu
Founded 1991
Private control
Academic year: January to December
Courses in accounting, business management, international business, information systems management, network security management; campus in N Virginia
Pres.: C. CATHLEEN RAFFAELI
Vice-Pres. for Academic Affairs: Dr CATHY EBERHART
Vice-Pres. for Human Resources and Student Affairs: DEEDY GIBBS
Library of 6,500 vols, 60 print periodicals, 50,000 ebooks

TRINITY WASHINGTON UNIVERSITY

125 Michigan Ave, NE, Washington, DC 20017
Telephone: (202) 884-9000
E-mail: president@trinitydc.edu
Internet: www.trinitydc.edu
Founded 1897
Private control
Pres.: Dr PATRICIA McGUIRE
Provost and Vice-Pres. for Academic Affairs: Dr VIRGINIA BROADDUS
Chief Financial Officer: BARBARA LETTIERE
Vice-Pres. for Institutional Advancement: ANN PAULEY
Dean for Education: SUELLEN MEARA
Dean for Student Services: MEECHIE BOWIE
Registrar: MARVA BOSWELL
Dir for Library: JACOB BERG
Library of 200,000 vols
Number of teachers: 60 full-time
Number of students: 2,550
Publications: *Trinilogue*, *Trinity Magazine* (3 a year), *Trinity Times*

DEANS
College of Arts and Sciences: Dr ELIZABETH CHILD
School of Education: Dr SUELLEN MEARA
School of Nursing and Health Professions: Dr MARY ROMANELLO
School of Professional Studies: Dr TELAEKAH BROOKS

UNIVERSITY OF THE DISTRICT OF COLUMBIA

4200 Connecticut Ave, NW, Washington, DC 20008
Telephone: (202) 274-5000
E-mail: udcadmission@udc.edu
Internet: www.udc.edu
Founded 1851 as Miner Normal School
Academic year: August to May
Pres.: Dr ALLEN L. SESSOMS
Provost and Vice-Pres. for Academic Affairs: Dr KEN BAIN
Vice-Pres. for Facilities Management: BARBARA JUMPER
Vice-Pres. for Govt Relations: AIMEE OCCHETTI
Vice-Pres. for Student Affairs: Dr VALERIE L. EPPS (acting)
Vice-Pres. for Univ. Relations and Public Affairs: ALAN ETTER
Gen. Counsel: Dr CRAIG W. PARKER
Chief of Staff and Vice-Pres. of Operations: STAN JACKSON
Dean for Library: ALBERT J. CASCIERO
Number of students: 9,700

DEANS
College of Agriculture, Urban Sustainability and Environmental Sciences: Dr GLORIA WYCHE MOORE
College of Arts and Sciences: (vacant)
David A. Clarke School of Law: Dr KATHERINE S. BRODERICK
School of Business and Public Admin.: Dr RICHARD F. BEBEE
School of Engineering and Applied Sciences: BEVERLY HARTLINE (acting)

WASHINGTON THEOLOGICAL UNION

6896 Laurel St, NW, Washington, DC 20012
Telephone: (202) 726-8800
E-mail: info@wtu.edu
Internet: www.wtu.edu
Founded 1968 as Coalition of Religious Seminaries, present name 1969
Private control
Academic year: August to May
Pres.: Very Rev. FREDERICK J. TILLOTSON
Academic Dean: ANNE E. McLAUGHLIN (acting)
Dir for Enrolment Services: CYNTHIA CAMERON
Dir for Institutional Advancement: JOAN KNETEMANN
Registrar: Rev. BARTHOLOMEW J. MERELLA
Dir for Library: (vacant)
Library of 130,000 vols
Number of students: 250

WESLEY THEOLOGICAL SEMINARY

4500 Massachusetts Ave NW, Washington, DC 20016
Telephone: (202) 885-8600
E-mail: admiss@wesleysem.edu
Internet: www.wesleyseminary.edu
Founded 1882 as Westminster Theological Seminary, present name and location 1958
Private control
Academic year: August to May
2 Campuses
Pres.: Rev. Dr DAVID F. McALLISTER-WILSON

Vice-Pres. for Devt: Dr MICHAEL T. BRADFIELD
Vice-Pres. for Finance and Admin.: JUNE R. STOWE
Vice-Pres. for Int. Relations: KYUNGLIM SHIN LEE
Dean: AMY ODEN
Dean: BRUCE C. BIRCH
Registrar: ELEANOR GEASE
Dir of Library: DAVID WILLIAM FAUPEL
Library of 175,000 vols, 400 journals subscriptions
Number of students: 1,000

FLORIDA

AVE MARIA SCHOOL OF LAW

1025 Commons Circle, Naples, FL 34119
Telephone: (239) 687-5300
E-mail: info@avemarialaw.edu
Internet: www.avemarialaw.edu
Founded 1999 at Ann Arbor, Michigan, present location 2009
Private control
Academic year: August to May
Pres. and Dean: Prof. Dr EUGENE R. MILHIZER
Assoc. Dean of Academic Affairs: PATRICK QUIRK
Assoc. Dean for Student Affairs: KAYE A. CASTRO
Dir of Admissions: MICHELE CONNOR
Dir of Devt and External Affairs: JOHN KNOWLES
Dir of Finance and Admin.: VIRGINIA TRAVER
Registrar: ANGELA KOJIRO
Dir of Law Library: ROBERTA STUDWELL
Library of 400,000 vols
Publications: *International Law Journal*, *Law Review*

AVE MARIA UNIVERSITY

5050 Ave Maria Blvd, Ave Maria, FL 34142-9505
Telephone: (239) 280-2500
E-mail: admissions@avemaria.edu
Internet: www.avemaria.edu
Founded 1998 as Ave Maria Institute
Private control
Academic year: August to July
Depts of biology and chemistry, economics, history, literature, mathematics and physics, philosophy, politics, sacred music, theology
Pres. and CEO: H. JAMES TOWEY
Chancellor: THOMAS S. MONAGHAN
Chief Financial Officer: PAUL R. RONEY
Sr Vice-Pres. for Academic Affairs: JOHN E. SITES
Vice-Pres. for Enrolment and Marketing: DENNIS GRACE
Vice Pres. for Institutional Advancement: Dr LOUIS TRAINA
Vice-Pres. for Student Affairs and Dean of Students: Dr DANIEL DENTINO
Vice-Pres. for Univ. Relations: (vacant)
Dean of Faculty: Dr MICHAEL A. DAUPHINAIS
Dir of Admission: JASON FABAZ
Registrar: STEPHANIE E. NEGIP
Dir of Library Services: TERENCE GALLAGHER (acting)
Library of 200,000 vols, 25,000 bound periodicals, 10,000 rare books colln
Number of teachers: 30 (13 full-time, 17 adjunct)
Number of students: 110

BAPTIST COLLEGE OF FLORIDA

5400 College Dr., Graceville, FL 32440-1898
Telephone: (850) 328-2660
E-mail: admissions@baptistcollege.edu
Internet: www.baptistcollege.edu

Founded 1943 as Florida Baptist Institute, current name and status 2000
Private control
Academic year: August to July
Pres.: Dr THOMAS A. KINCHEN
Vice-Pres. for Devt: CHARLES R. PARKER
Dean for Faculty: Dr ROBIN JUMPER
Dean for Students: Dr ROGER RICHARDS
Dir for Marketing and Admissions: SANDRA RICHARDS
Registrar: STEPHANIE W. ORR
Number of students: 625
Publication: *Echoes* (4 a year)

BARRY UNIVERSITY

11300 NE Second Ave, Miami Shores, FL 33161-6695
Telephone: (305) 899-3000
E-mail: admissions@mail.barry.edu
Internet: www.barry.edu
Founded 1940
Private control
Academic year: August to May
Pres.: Sis. Dr LINDA BEVILACQUA
Gen. Counsel: DAVID DUDGEON
Provost: Dr LINDA M. PETERSON
Vice-Pres. for Business and Finance: D. BRUCE EDWARDS
Vice-Pres. for Institutional Advancement: (vacant)
Vice-Pres. for Legal Affairs: JOHN WALKER
Vice-Pres. for Student Affairs: Dr SCOTT SMITH
Registrar: CYNTHIA CHRUSZCZYK
Library Dir: TOM MESSNER
Library of 950,000 vols, 2,880 periodicals, 1,200 journals and 541,560 microforms
Number of teachers: 310 full-time
Number of students: 6,900

DEANS

Adrian Dominican School of Education: Dr TERRY PIPER
College of Arts and Sciences: Dr KAREN A. CALLAGHAN
College of Health Sciences: Dr PEGGE BELL
D. Inez Andreas School of Business: Dr TOMISLAV MANDAKOVIC
Dwayne O. Andreas School of Law: Dr LETICIA M. DIAZ
Ellen Whiteside McDonnell School of Social Work: Dr PHYLLIS SCOTT
Frank J. Rooney School of Adult and Continuing Education: Dr CAROL-RAE SODANO
School of Human Performance and Leisure Sciences: Dr DARLENE KLUKA
School of Podiatric Medicine: Dr JEFFREY JENSEN

BEACON COLLEGE

105 E Main St, Leesburg, FL 34748
Telephone: (352) 787-7660
E-mail: admissions@beaconcollege.edu
Internet: www.beaconcollege.edu
Founded 1989
Private control
Academic year: August to June
Offers academic degree programmes to students with learning disabilities; offers bachelor degrees in computer information systems, human services, liberal studies
Pres.: Dr JOHN M. HUTCHINSON
Vice-Pres. for Academic Affairs: Dr SHELLY CHANDLER
Vice-Pres. for Finance and Admin.: CALVIN SANSON
Vice-Pres. for Institutional Advancement and Alumni Relations: Dr WALTER ZIELINSKI
Vice-Pres. for Student Services: Dr ROBERT BRIDGEMAN

Dir of Admissions: BRENDA MELI
Registrar: DAVID BROWN
Dir of Library Resources: DIANNA WADE
Library of 23,000 vols, 38,000 ebooks, 100 periodicals, 1000 audiovisuals and 600 items in learning disabilities colln
Number of students: 130

BETHUNE—COOKMAN COLLEGE

640 Dr Mary McLeod Bethune Blvd, Daytona Beach, FL 32114-3099
Telephone: (386) 481-2000
E-mail: bronson@cookman.edu
Internet: www.cookman.edu
Founded 1904 as Daytona Educational and Industrial Training School, present name 1924, present status 2007
Private control
Academic year: August to April
Pres.: Dr TRUDIE KIBBE REED
Vice-Pres. for Academic Affairs: Dr DORCAS McCOY
Vice-Pres. for Institutional Advancement: Dr HIRAM POWELL
Vice-Pres. for Institutional Effectiveness: Dr RAY SHACKELFORD
Vice-Pres. for Student Affairs: DWAUN J. WARMACK (acting)
Chief Financial Officer: Dr RONALD DOWDY
Chief Information Officer: FRANKLIN E. PATTERSON
Registrar: ANNIE REDD
Dir of Library Learning: Dr TASHA LUCAS-YOUMANS
Library of 130,000 vols
Number of teachers: 360 (full-time)
Number of students: 3,600
Publication: *Undergraduate Research Journal* (1 a year)

DEANS

School of Arts and Humanities: Dr JAMES BROOKS
School of Business: Dr AUBREY E. LONG
School of Education: Dr CAROL JOHNSON
School of Graduate and Professional Studies: Dr DARRYL FRAZIER
School of Nursing: Dr WILLIE MAE SESSION
School of Science, Engineering and Mathematics: Dr HERBERT THOMPSON
School of Social Sciences: Dr IAN PAYTON

BROWARD COLLEGE

111 E Las Olas Blvd, Fort Lauderdale, FL 33301
Telephone: (954) 201-7350
Internet: www.broward.edu
Founded 1960, present name and status 2008
State control
Academic year: August to August
Campuses: Judson A. Samuels S campus, N campus; offers bachelor of applied science degree in information technology, nursing, supervision and management, teacher education, technology management
Pres.: Dr J. DAVID ARMSTRONG, JR
Provost and Sr Vice-Pres. for Academic Affairs and Student Success: Dr LINDA HOWDYSHELL
Sr Vice-Pres. for Admin.: THOMAS W. OLLIFF
Vice-Pres. for Advancement: NANCY R. BOTERO
Vice-Pres. for Finance: JAYSON IROFF
Vice-Pres. for Information Technology and Institutional Effectiveness: PATTI BARNEY
Vice-Pres. for Student Affairs and Enrolment Management: ANGELIA N. MILLENDER
Dean of Student Affairs: DAVID ASENCIO
Registrar and Assoc. Vice-Pres. for Student Affairs: WILLIE J. ALEXANDER

Dean of Univ. and College Library: MIGUEL MENENDEZ
Publication: *P'an Ku*

CARLOS ALBIZU UNIVERSITY

2173 NW 99th Ave, Miami, FL 33172-2209
Telephone: (305) 593-1223
E-mail: admissions@albizu.edu
Internet: mia.albizu.edu
Founded 1966, present name and status 2000
Private control
Campus in San Juan; offers degree courses in business admin., education, English, psychology
Pres.: Dr ILEANA RODRIGUEZ-GARCIA
Chancellor of Miami campus: Dr CARMEN S. ROCA
Chancellor of San Juan campus: Dr JOSÉ J. CABIYA
Dir of Finance: EUNICE PIERRE-LOUIS
Dir of Student Services: PETER RUBIO
Registrar: FINA CAMPA
Library Dir: MARY BISHOP

CHIPOLA COLLEGE

3094 Indian Circle, Marianna, FL 32446
Telephone: (850) 526-2761
Internet: www.chipola.edu
Founded 1947 as Chipola Jr College, present name and status 2003
Courses incl. BSc in nursing and bachelor of business admin.
State control
Academic year: August to August
Pres.: Dr GENE PROUGH
Sr Vice-Pres. for Instruction: Dr SARAH CLEMMONS
Vice-Pres. for Finance: STEVE YOUNG
Vice-Pres. for Student Affairs: Dr JAYNE ROBERTS
Dean of Institutional Devt and Planning: GAIL HARTZOG
Registrar: KATHY REHBERG
Dir of Library Services and Distance Learning: Dr LOU KIND
Number of students: 2,000

DEANS

School of Business and Technology: Dr JAMES P. FROH
School of Education: Dr LOU CLEVELAND
School of Health Sciences: VICKIE W. STEPHENS

CLEARWATER CHRISTIAN COLLEGE

3400 Gulf-to-Bay Blvd, Clearwater, FL 33759-4595
Telephone: (727) 726-1153
E-mail: admissions@clearwater.edu
Internet: www.clearwater.edu
Founded 1966, present status 2008
Private control
Academic year: August to May
Areas of study incl. biblical studies, business, education, fine arts, humanities, sciences
Pres.: Prof. Dr JACK KLEM
Vice-Pres. for Academic Affairs: Prof. Dr MARY C. DRAPER
Vice-Pres. for Financial Affairs: RANDY T. LIVINGSTON
Vice-Pres. for Institutional Advancement: TERRY D. WILD
Vice-Pres. for Student Life: RYAN DUPEE
Registrar: THOMAS CANNON, JR
Dean of Students: TODD BARTON
Dir of Library: ELIZABETH WERNER
Library of 100,000 vols
Number of teachers: 50 (incl. 32 full-time)
Number of students: 560

COLLEGE OF CENTRAL FLORIDA

3001 SW College Rd, Ocala, FL 34474-4415

Telephone: (352) 873-5800
E-mail: library@cf.edu
Internet: www.cf.edu

Founded 1966 by merger of Hampton Jr College and Central Florida Jr College, present name and status 2010
State control
Academic year: August to August

Campuses: Citrus, Levy centre, Hampton centre; offers bachelor degrees courses in applied science, science

Interim Pres. and Sr Vice-Pres. for Admin. and Finance: Dr JAMES D. HARVEY
Vice-Pres. for Citrus Campus: Dr VERNON LAWTER
Vice-Pres. for Institutional Advancement: JOAN M. STEARNS
Vice-Pres. for Instructional Affairs: Dr MARK PAUGH
Vice-Pres. for Student Affairs: Dr TIMOTHY G. WISE
Dean of Enrolment Management: LYN POWELL
Dean of Student Services: HENRI BENLOLO
Dean of Learning Resource Centre: RICHARD BAZILE

Library of 65,000 vols
Number of teachers: 120
Number of students: 18,800

Publications: *CF Connection* (2 a year), *Imprints* (1 a year), *In The Write Mind* (1 a year)

DAYTONA STATE COLLEGE

1200 W Int. Speedway Blvd, Daytona Beach, FL 32114-2817

Telephone: (386) 506-3000
Internet: www.daytonastate.edu

Founded 1957 as Daytona Beach Jr College, present status 2006, present name 2008
State control
Academic year: August to June

Campuses in DeLand, Flagler/Palm Coast, New Smyrna Beach-Edgewater

Pres.: Dr CAROL W. EATON
Exec. Vice-Pres. and Gen. Counsel: BRIAN BABB
Sr Vice-Pres. for Academic Affairs: Dr MICHAEL VITALE
Sr Vice-Pres. for Admin. and Accounting and Chief Financial Officer: DENNIS MICARE
Sr Vice-Pres. for Enrolment, Student Devt and Marketing: Dr THOMAS LOBASSO
Dean of Institutional Research: SUSAN ANTILLON

Number of students: 35,000

Publication: *Ole' Literary Magazine*

DEANS

College of Online Studies: ROBERT SAUM
Mori Hosseini College of Hospitality Management: COSTA MAGOULAS
School of Adult Education: KATRINA BELL
School of Health and Wellness: WILLIAM DUNNE

ECKERD COLLEGE

4200 54th Ave S, St Petersburg, FL 33711

Telephone: (727) 867-1166
E-mail: admissions@eckerd.edu
Internet: www.eckerd.edu

Founded 1958 as Florida Presbyterian College, present name and status 1972
Private control
Academic year: August to May

Liberal arts college; courses incl. bachelor degrees in arts, chemistry, science

Pres.: Dr DONALD R. EASTMAN, III

Vice-Pres. and Dean of Special Programmes: JAMES E. DEEGAN
Vice-Pres. and Sec. of College: LISA METS
Vice-Pres. for Academic Affairs and Dean of Faculty: Dr BETTY H. STEWART
Vice-Pres. for Advancement: MATTHEW S. BISSET
Vice Pres. for Business and Finance: CHRISTOPHER P. BRENNAN
Vice-Pres. for Student Life and Dean of Students: Dr JAMES J. ANNARELLI
Dir of Admissions: MARIA FURTADO
Dean of Admissions and Financial Aid: JOHN F. SULLIVAN
Registrar: LINDA SWINDALL
Dir of Library Services: JAMIE GILL

Library of 150,000 vols, 20,000 journals
Number of teachers: 160 (110 full-time, 50 part-time)
Number of students: 1,830

EDISON STATE COLLEGE

8099 College Parkway, Fort Myers, FL 33919

Telephone: (239) 489-9300
E-mail: president@edison.edu
Internet: www.edison.edu

Founded 1962, present name 2008
State control
Academic year: August to June

Campuses in Charlotte co, Collier co, Hendry/Glades centre

District Pres.: KENNETH P. WALKER
Gen. Counsel: MARK LUPE
Vice-Pres. for Academic Affairs: Dr ERIN HARREL
Vice-Pres. for Financial Services: GINA DOEBLE
Vice-Pres. for Strategic Initiatives: EDITH PENDLETON
Charlotte Campus Pres.: Dr PATRICIA LAND
Vice-Pres. and Provost of Henry/Glades Centre and Interim Collier Campus Pres.: Dr ROBERT R. JONES
Registrar: BILLEE SILVA
Dean of Student Services: PATRICIA NEWELL
District Dean of Learning Resources and Vice-Pres. for Strategic Initiatives: Dr EDITH PENDELTON

Number of teachers: 130 (full-time)
Number of students: 25,000

DEANS

School of Education and Charter Schools: ERIN HARREL
School of Health Sciences: (vacant)
School of Nursing: (vacant)

EDWARD WATERS COLLEGE

1658 Kings Rd, Jacksonville, FL 32209-6199

Telephone: (904) 470-8000
Internet: www.ewc.edu

Founded 1866, present name 1892
Private control
Academic year: August to May

Liberal arts college; degree programmes incl. biology, business admin., communications, criminal justice, elementary education, mathematics, music

Pres.: Dr NATHANIEL GLOVER, JR
Exec. Vice-Pres.: Dr EURMON HERVEY, JR
Vice-Pres. for Academic Affairs: Dr BERTHA D. MINUS
Vice-Pres. for Business and Finance: RANDOLPH MITCHELL
Vice-Pres. for Student Affairs and Enrolment Management: Dr JAMES B. EWERS, JR
Dean of Faculty: Dr REUBEN PERECHI
Registrar: LINDSEY BARNETTE
Library Dir: CARMELLA MARTIN

Library of 30,000 vols, 147 periodicals
Number of students: 840

EMBRY-RIDDLE AERONAUTICAL UNIVERSITY

600 S Clyde Morris Blvd, Daytona Beach, FL 32114-3900

Telephone: (386) 226-6000
E-mail: dbadmit@erau.edu
Internet: www.erau.edu

Founded 1926 as Embry-Riddle School of Aviation; present name 1970
Private control
Academic year: September to August

Pres.: Dr JOHN P. JOHNSON
Sr Exec. Vice-Pres. for Academics and Research: CHRISTINA FREDERICK-RECASCINO
Sr Exec. Vice-Pres. and Chief Financial Officer: ERIC WEEKES
Vice-Pres. for Institutional Advancement: DANIEL MONTPLAISIR
Vice-Pres. for Devt: PAT RAMSEY
Chief Information Officer: CINDY BIXLER
Exec. Vice-Pres. and Chief Academic Officer for Daytona Beach Campus: Dr RICHARD HEIST
Library Dir: Dr ANNE MARIE CASEY

Library of 116,227 vols, 2,078 periodicals
Number of teachers: 340 (249 full-time, 91 part-time)
Number of students: 9,600 (4,500 undergraduates, 5,100 graduates)

DEANS

College of Arts and Sciences: Dr BILL GRAMS
College of Aviation: Dr TIM BRADY
College of Business: Dr MICHAEL WILLIAMS
College of Engineering: Dr MAJ MIRMIRANI.

CAMPUSES

Embry-Riddle Aeronautical University—Daytona Beach, Florida, Campus

600 S Clyde Morris Blvd, Daytona Beach, FL 32114

Telephone: (386) 226-6100
E-mail: dbadmit@erau.edu
Internet: db.erau.edu

Founded 1925
Private control
Academic year: September to August

Number of teachers: 410
Number of students: 5,300

Embry-Riddle Aeronautical University—Worldwide

600 S Clyde Morris Blvd, Daytona Beach, FL 32114-3900

Telephone: (386) 226-6910
E-mail: worldwide@erau.edu
Internet: worldwide.erau.edu

Comprises Centre for Distance Learning, College of Career Education; operates in the USA, Europe

Exec. Vice-Pres. and Chief Academic Officer for Worldwide Campus: Dr JOHN R. WATRET
Dean of Academic Affairs for Central Region: Dr MARK FRIEND
Dean of Academic Affairs for Eastern Region: Dr BERNARD CORDIAL
Dean of Academic Affairs for Int. Region: BILL MULDOON
Dean of Academic Affairs for Western Region: Dr KATHERINE MORAN
Registrar: EDWARD TROMBLEY, III
Library Dir: ANNE MARIE CASEY

Library of 116,227 vols, 2,078 periodicals
Number of teachers: 2,500 (100 full-time, 2,400 part-time)
Number of students: 27,300 (20,100 undergraduate, 7,200 graduate)

EVEREST UNIVERSITY

Suite 400, 6 Hutton Centre Dr., Santa Ana, FL 92707

Telephone: (714) 427-3000
Internet: www.everest.edu

Founded 1890, fmrly Florida Metropolitan Univ., present name and status 2007
Private control

Campuses in Brandon, Lakeland, Jacksonville, Largo, Melbourne, Orange Park, S Orlando, N Orlando, Pompano Beach, Tampa

Chair. and CEO: DAVID G. MOORE

Pres. and Chief Operating Officer: ANTHONY DIGIOVANNI

Sr Vice-Pres. for Academic Affairs: Dr MARY H. BARRY

Number of students: 11,000 (all campuses)

FLAGLER COLLEGE

74 King St, St Augustine, FL 32084

Telephone: (904) 829-6481
E-mail: admissions@flagler.edu
Internet: www.flagler.edu

Founded 1968
Private control
Academic year: August to June (2 semesters)
Language of instruction: English

Offers bachelors degree in arts, fine arts, public admin.

Chancellor: Dr WILLIAM T. PROCTOR
Pres.: Dr WILLIAM T. ABARE, JR
Vice-Pres. for Business Services: KENNETH S. RUSSOM
Vice-Pres. for Enrolment Management: MARC G. WILLIAR
Vice-Pres. for Institutional Advancement: F. MARK WHITTAKER
Dean of Academic Affairs: Dr ALAN WOOLFOLK
Dean of Student Services: DANIEL P. STEWART
Registrar: MIRIAM ROBERSON
Dir for Library Services: JENNIFER M. EASON

Library of 92,010 vols, 132,994 ebooks, 1,877 microform, 4,922 audiovisual material, 533 periodicals
Number of students: 2,700

FLORIDA AGRICULTURAL AND MECHANICAL UNIVERSITY

1601 Martin Luther King Jr Blvd, Tallahassee, FL 32307

Telephone: (850) 599-3000
Internet: www.famu.edu

Founded 1887, current name adopted 1909
State control
Academic year: August to June

Pres.: Dr ELMIRA MANGUM
Provost and Vice-Pres. for Academic Affairs: CYNTHIA HUGHES HARRIS
Gen. Counsel: AVERY D. McKNIGHT
Vice-Pres. for Admin. and Financial Services: TERESA HARDEE
Vice-Pres. for Devt: CARLA S. WILLIS
Vice-Pres. for Student Affairs: WILLIAM HUDSON, JR
Vice-Pres. for Univ. Relations: SHARON P. SAUNDERS
Chief Communications Officer: SHARON SAUNDERS
Dir of Libraries: LAUREN B. SAPP

Library: 1m. vols, 98,538 current periodicals, 192,000 microforms, 76,000 non-print items
Number of teachers: 532
Number of students: 12,161

DEANS

School of Architecture: RODNER WRIGHT
College of Arts and Sciences: Dr RALPH W. TURNER

College of Education: GENNIVER C. BELL
College of Engineering Sciences, Technology and Agriculture: Dr MAKOLA ABDULLAH
College of Law: LEROY PERNELL
College of Pharmacy and Pharmaceutical Sciences: HENRY LEWIS, III
FAMU/FSU College of Engineering: Dr CHING-JEN CHEN
School of Allied Health Sciences: Dr BARBARA MOSLEY
School of Business and Industry: Dr SHAWNTA FRIDAY-STROUD
School of Gen. Studies: Dr DOROTHY HENDERSON
School of Graduate Studies, Research and Continuing Education: Dr CHANTA M. HAYWOOD
School of Journalism and Graphic Communication: Dr JAMES E. HAWKINS
School of Nursing: Dr RUENA NORMAN

FLORIDA ATLANTIC UNIVERSITY

777 Glades Rd, POB 3091, Boca Raton, FL 33431

Telephone: (561) 297-3000
E-mail: admissions@fau.edu
Internet: www.fau.edu

Founded 1964
State control

Campuses in Boca Raton, Dania Beach, Davie, Fort Lauderdale, Jupiter, Treasure Coast; also Open Univ. and Continuing Education Div. (Fort Lauderdale), Harbor Br. Marine Sciences Bldg (Fort Pierce) and SeaTech (ocean engineering research and graduate education centre, Dania Beach)

Pres.: Dr MARY JANE SAUNDERS
Univ. Provost and Chief Academic Officer: Dr BRENDA CLAIBORNE
Sr Vice-Pres. for Student Affairs: Dr CHARLES BROWN
Vice-Pres. for Research: Dr BARRY T. ROSSON
Vice-Pres. for Univ. Advancement: RANDY TALBOT
Univ. Registrar: HARRY E. DeMIK
Dean of Univ. Libraries: Dr WILLIAM MILLER

Library: 2.5m. vols incl. books, periodicals, govt documents, microforms, maps, media and other materials, 200,000 ebooks, 20,000 ejournals
Number of teachers: 1,100 (1,060 full-time, 40 part-time)
Number of students: 28,300 (15,830 full-time, 12,470 part-time)

Publications: *Coastlines Literary Magazine, Florida Atlantic Comparative Studies Journal, Journal of the Fantastic in the Arts*

DEANS

Charles E. Schmidt College of Medicine: Dr DAVID J. BJORKMAN
Charles E. Schmidt College of Science: Dr GARY W. PERRY
Christine E. Lynn College of Nursing: Dr MARLAINE SMITH
College of Business: Dr J. DENNIS COATES
College for Design and Social Inquiry: Dr ROSALYN CARTER
College of Education: Dr VALERIE J. BRISTOR
College of Engineering and Computer Science: Dr MOHAMMAD ILYAS
Dorothy F. Schmidt College of Arts and Letters: Prof. Dr HEATHER COLTMAN
Graduate College: Dr BARRY T. ROSSON
Harriet L. Wilkes Honors College: Dr JEFFREY BULLER

FLORIDA CHRISTIAN COLLEGE

1011 Bill Beck Blvd, Kissimmee, FL 34744

Telephone: (407) 847-8966
E-mail: fcc@fcc.edu

Internet: www.fcc.edu

Founded 1975, present name 1981
Private control
Academic year: August to May

Bachelors programmes incl. Bible, Bible and humanities, children's min. Christian min., counselling, cross-cultural min., educational leadership, elementary education, musical arts, music and worship min., organizational leadership, non-profit management, preaching, youth and family min.

Pres.: WILLIAM K. BEHRMAN
Exec. Vice-Pres.: Dr TERRY ALLCORN
Vice-Pres. for Academics: Dr BRIAN D. SMITH
Vice-Pres. for Finance: RENEE COOK
Dir of Institutional Research: BRUCE DUSTERHOFT
Registrar: DIANE ADAMS
Librarian: LINDA STARK

Number of teachers: 16
Number of students: 380

Publication: *Sonlife* (2 a year)

FLORIDA COLLEGE

119 N Glen Arven Ave, Temple Terrace, FL 33617-5578

Telephone: (813) 988-5131
E-mail: admissions@floridacollege.edu
Internet: www.floridacollege.edu

Founded 1946 as Florida Christian College, present name 1963
Private control
Academic year: August to May

Offers degree programmes in business admin., communication, education, music

Pres.: Dr H. E. PAYNE, JR
Vice-Pres. for Academic and Student Affairs: DOUGLAS H. C. NORTHCUTT
Dir of Enrolment Management: PAUL J. CASEBOLT
Dir of Institutional Devt: DOUGLAS R. NERLAND
Academic Dean: DANIEL W. PETTY
Dean of Student Services: BRIAN CRISPELL
Registrar: BETH ANN GRANT
Library Dir: WANDA D. DICKEY

Library of 150,000 vols, 22,000 periodicals

Publication: *Florida College Magazine*

FLORIDA GULF COAST UNIVERSITY

10501 FGCU Blvd S, Fort Myers, FL 33965-6565

Telephone: (239) 590-1000
E-mail: admissions@fgcu.edu
Internet: www.fgcu.edu

Founded 1991
State control
Academic year: August to May

Pres.: Dr WILSON G. BRADSHAW
Provost and Vice-Pres. for Academic Affairs: Dr RONALD B. TOLL
Vice-Pres. for Admin. Services and Finance: STEVE L. MAGIERA
Vice-Pres. for Student Affairs: Dr J. MICHAEL ROLLO
Vice-Pres. for Univ. Advancement: Dr ROSEMARY M. THOMAS
Dir for Graduate Studies: Dr GREG TOLLEY
Dean for Students: Dr MICHELE YOVANOVICH
Gen. Counsel: VEE LEONARD
Univ. Registrar: SUSAN BYARS
Library Dean: Dr KATHLEEN F. MILLER

Library of 314,785 vols, 123,917 govt publs, 40,863 periodicals, 23,968 ebooks, 94,211 ejournals
Number of teachers: 3,100
Number of students: 12,000

DEANS

College of Arts and Sciences: Prof. Dr DONNA HENRY
College of Education: Prof. Dr MARCI GREENE
College of Health Professions: Prof. Dr MITCHELL L. CORDOVA
College of Professional Studies: TONY A. BARRINGER
Lutgert College of Business: Dr HUDSON ROGERS
U. A. Whitaker College of Engineering: Prof. Dr SUSAN M. BLANCHARD

FLORIDA HOSPITAL COLLEGE OF HEALTH SCIENCES

671 Winyah Dr., Orlando, FL 32803-1226
Telephone: (407) 303-5619
Internet: www.fhchs.edu
Founded 1992, present status 2008
Private control
Academic year: August to August (3 semesters)

Courses in nuclear medicine technology, nursing, occupational therapy, radiological sciences

Pres.: Dr DAVID E. GREENLAW
Sr Vice-Pres. for Academic Admin.: Dr DONALD E. WILLIAMS
Sr Vice-Pres. for Financial Admin.: ROBERT CURREN
Vice Pres. for Academic Admin. for Educational Technology and Distance Education: Dr DAN LIM
Vice-Pres. for Operations: RUBEN MARTINEZ
Vice-Pres. for Student Services: STEPHEN ROCHE
Library Dir: DEANNA FLORES

FLORIDA INSTITUTE OF TECHNOLOGY

150 W University Blvd, Melbourne, FL 32901-6975
Telephone: (321) 674-8030
E-mail: admission@fit.edu
Internet: www.fit.edu
Founded 1958, current name and status 1966
Private control
Academic year: August to May

Pres. and Chief Exec. Officer: Dr ANTHONY JAMES CATANESE
Sr Vice-Pres. and Chief Devt Officer: SUSAN ST. ONGE
Sr Vice-Pres. and Chief Financial Officer: Dr ROBERT E. NIEBUHR
Sr Vice-Pres. for External Relations: Capt. WINSTON SCOTT
Exec. Vice-Pres. and Chief Operating Officer: Dr T. DWAYNE McCAY
Vice-Pres. for Academic Affairs: Dr SEMEN KOKSAL
Vice-Pres. for Research: FRANK KINNEY
Vice-Pres. for Student Affairs: Dr RANDALL L. ALFORD
Registrar: CHARLOTTE YOUNG
Dir for Undergraduate Admission: MICHAEL J. PERRY
Dean for Students: RODNEY B. BOWERS
Dean for Libraries: Dr SOHAIR WASTAWY
Library of 527,223 vols, 228,000 govt documents, 32,000 journals
Number of teachers: 687 (271 full-time, 416 part-time)
Number of students: 9,110

DEANS

College of Aeronautics: Dr KORHAN OYMAN
College of Engineering: Dr MARTIN GLICKSMAN
College of Psychology and Liberal Arts: Dr MARY BETH KENKEL
College of Science: Dr HAMID K. RASSOUL

Nathan M. Bisk College of Business: Dr S. ANN BECKER

FLORIDA INTERNATIONAL UNIVERSITY

11200 SW Eighth St, Miami, FL 33199
Telephone: (305) 348-2000
Internet: www.fiu.edu
Founded 1965
State control
Academic year: August to August

Campuses: Biscayne Bay, FIU Broward-Pines Centre, Engineering Centre, FIU Downtown, FIU College of Architecture and Arts, Wolfsonian-FIU

Pres.: Dr MARK B. ROSENBERG
Provost, Exec. Vice-Pres. and Chief Operating Officer: Dr DOUGLAS WARTZOK
Sr Vice-Pres. for Admin. and Chief Financial Officer: Dr KENNETH A. JESSELL
Sr Vice-Pres. for Information Technology and Chief Information Officer: ROBERT GRILLO
Sr Vice-Pres. for Univ. Advancement: HOWARD R. LIPMAN
Sr Vice-Pres. for External Relations: SANDRA B. GONZALEZ-LEVY
Vice-Pres. for Research: Dr ANDRÉS G. GIL
Vice-Pres. for Student Affairs: Dr ROSA L. JONES
Gen. Counsel: M. KRISTINA RAATTAMA
Dean of Univ. Libraries: LAURA K. PROBST
Library: 1.7m. vols, 9,700 current periodicals, maps, microforms, govt documents, archives, rare books
Number of teachers: 1,100 (full-time)
Number of students: 46,000

DEANS

Chaplin School of Hospitality and Tourism Management: Dr MIKE HAMPTON
College of Architecture and Arts: BRIAN SCHRINER
College of Arts and Sciences: Dr KENNETH G. FURTON
College of Business Admin.: Dr JOYCE J. ELAM
College of Education: DELIA C. GARCIA
College of Engineering and Computing: Prof. Dr AMIR MIRMIRAN
College of Law: R. ALEXANDER ACOSTA
College of Nursing and Health Sciences: Prof. Dr ORA STRICKLAND
Herbert Wertheim College of Medicine: Dr JOHN A. ROCK
Honors College: Dr LESLEY A. NORTHUP
Robert Stempel College of Public Health and Social Work: MICHELE CICCAZZO
School of Journalism and Mass Communication: Prof. Dr RAUL REIS
Univ. College: JOYCE J. ELAM
Univ. Graduate School: Dr LAKSHMI N. REDDI

FLORIDA MEMORIAL UNIVERSITY

15800 N W 42nd Ave, Miami Gardens, FL 33054-6155
Telephone: (305) 626-3600
E-mail: admit@fmuniv.edu
Internet: www.fmuniv.edu
Founded 1941 by merger of Florida Baptist Institute and Florida Baptist Acad., present name and status 2006
Private control
Academic year: August to July
Pres.: Dr HENRY LEWIS, III
Provost and Vice-Pres. for Academic Affairs: Dr MAKOLA M. ABDULLAH
Vice-Pres. for Admin.: Dr HAROLD R. CLARKE, JR
Vice-Pres. for Business and Fiscal Affairs: TONY VALENTINE
Vice-Pres. for Institutional Advancement: Dr ADRIENE B. WRIGHT

Vice-Pres. for Student Affairs: Dr DANNEAL JONES, JR
Registrar: LELIA ALLEN-EFFORD
Dir of Library: GLORIA OSWALD
Library of 127,000 vols, 700 current periodicals
Number of teachers: 90 (full-time)
Number of students: 2,200

DEANS

School of Arts and Sciences: WILLIAM E. HOPPER, JR
School of Business: Prof. Dr ABBASS ENTESSARI
School of Education: Prof. Dr MILDRED E. BERRY

FLORIDA NATIONAL COLLEGE

4425 W Jose Regueiro 20th Ave, Hialeah, FL 33012
Telephone: (305) 821-3333
E-mail: admissions@mm.fnc.edu
Internet: www.fnc.edu
Founded 1988 as Florida Int. Institute, present name 1989
Private control
Academic year: August to August (3 semesters)
Academic divs incl. allied health, business and economics, English, humanities and fine arts, nursing
Pres.: Dr MARÍA CRISTINA REGUEIRO
Vice-Pres. for Academic Affairs: CARIDAD SÁNCHEZ
Vice-Pres. for Assessment and Research and Dir of Financial Aid: OMAR SÁNCHEZ
Vice-Pres. for Operations: FRANK ANDREU
Dir of Admission: GUILLERMO ARAYA
Dir of Student Services: MAKEDA MEEKS
Registrar: JOSE LUIS VALDES
Library Dir: PATRICK BYRNES
Library of 32,045 vols

FLORIDA SOUTHERN COLLEGE

111 Lake Hollingsworth Dr., Lakeland, FL 33801-5698
Telephone: (863) 680-4111
E-mail: fscadm@flsouthern.edu
Internet: www.flsouthern.edu
Founded 1883 as South Florida Institute, present name 1935
Private control
Academic year: August to July
Pres.: Dr ANNE B. KERR
Provost and Vice-Pres. for Academic Affairs: Dr KYLE FEDLER
Vice-Pres. for Advancement: Dr MATTHEW R. THOMPSON
Vice-Pres. for Enrolment Management: Dr JOHN P. GRUNDIG
Vice-Pres. for External Relations: Dr ROBERT H. TATE
Vice-Pres. for Finance and Admin.: V. TERRY DENNIS
Vice-Pres. for Student Life: Dr CAROLE R. OBERMEYER
Dir of Library: RANDALL M. MacDONALD
Library of 175,213 vols, 15,412 audiovisuals
Number of teachers: 110
Number of students: 2,300 (2,170 undergraduates, 130 graduates)

DEANS

Barney Barnett School of Business and Economics: Dr WILLIAM L. RHEY
School of Arts and Sciences: Dr JAMES T. BYRD
School of Education: TRACY D. TEDDER
School of Nursing and Health Sciences: Prof. Dr JOHN M. WELTON

FLORIDA STATE COLLEGE AT JACKSONVILLE

501 W State St, Jacksonville, FL 32202-4076

Telephone: (904) 633-5950

E-mail: justask@fscj.edu

Internet: www.fscj.edu

Founded 1966, present name 2009

State control

Academic year: August to August

Schools of arts and sciences, aviation, business, construction, manufacturing and architecture, culinary arts and hospitality, digital media and entertainment technology, education, health sciences, information technology, public safety and security, transportation

Pres.: Dr STEVEN R. WALLACE

Vice-Pres. and Provost: JUDITH BILSKY

Exec. Vice-Pres. for Instruction and Student Services: Dr DONALD W. GREEN, JR

Vice-Pres. for Admin. Services: STEVEN P. BOWERS

Vice-Pres. for Institutional Advancement: ROBERT STAMP

Vice-Pres. for Student Devt and Community Education: Dr TRACY A. PIERCE

Gen. Counsel and Vice-Pres. for Strategic Initiatives: JEANNE MILLER

Academic Dean: WENDY NORFLEET

Library of 257,473 vols, 23,320 audiovisual colln

Number of teachers: 2,150 (395 full-time, 1,750 part-time)

Number of students: 80,000

FLORIDA STATE UNIVERSITY

600 W College Ave, Tallahassee, FL 32306

Telephone: (850) 644-6200

E-mail: admissions@admin.fsu.edu

Internet: www.fsu.edu

Founded 1851 as Seminary W of Suwannee River, present name and status 1947

State control

Academic year: August to April (2 semesters)

Satellite campus in Panama city, Florida

Chancellor of the State Univ. System: CHARLES REED

Pres.: Dr ERIC J. BARRON

Provost and Exec. Vice-Pres. for Academic Affairs: Dr GARNETT S. STOKES

Sr Vice-Pres. for Finance and Admin.: JOHN R. CARNAGHI

Vice-Pres. for Planning and Programmes: Dr ROBERT B. BRADLEY

Vice-Pres. for Research: Prof. Dr KIRBY W. KEMPER

Vice-Pres. for Student Affairs: MARY B. COBURN

Vice-Pres. for Univ. Relations: ELIZABETH MARYANSKI

Dean of the Faculties and Deputy Provost: Dr JENNIFER N. BUCHANAN

Dean of Graduate School: NANCY MARCUS (acting)

Dean of Students: Dr JEANINE WARD-ROOF

Dean of Undergraduate Studies: KAREN L. LAUGHLIN

Registrar: MAXWELL CARRAWAY

Dean of Univ. Libraries: JULIA ZIMMERMAN

Library: see Libraries and Archives

Number of teachers: 1,950

Number of students: 40,000

DEANS

College of Applied Studies: DONALD FOSS

College of Arts and Sciences: SAM HUCKABA

College of Business: Prof. CARYN L. BECK-DUDLEY

College of Communication and Information: Dr LAWRENCE C. DENNIS

College of Criminology and Criminal Justice: Prof. Dr THOMAS BLOMBERG

College of Education: Prof. Dr MARCY P. DRISCOLL

College of Engineering: Prof. JOHN COLLIER

College of Human Sciences: Dr BILLIE J. COLLIER

College of Law: Prof. DONALD J. WEIDNER

College of Medicine: Prof. Dr JOHN P. FOGARTY

College of Motion Picture Arts: Prof. Dr FRANK PATTERSON

College of Music: Prof. Dr DON GIBSON

College of Nursing: Prof. Dr DIANNE SPEAKE

College of Social Sciences and Public Policy: Prof. Dr DAVID W. RASMUSSEN

College of Social Work: Prof. Dr NICHOLAS F. MAZZA

College of Visual Arts, Theatre and Dance: Dr SALLY E. McRORIE

GULF COAST STATE COLLEGE

5230 W Highway 98, Panama City, FL 32401

Telephone: (850) 769-1551

Internet: www.gulfcoast.edu

Founded 1957, present name 2011

State control

Academic year: August to May

Campus in Gulf; academic divs incl. business and technology, business, continuing and community education, health sciences, language and literature, mathematics, natural sciences, public safety, social sciences, visual and performing arts, wellness and athletics

Pres.: Dr JIM KERLEY

Vice-Pres. for Academic Affairs: GEORGE BISHOP

Vice-Pres. for Admin. and Finance: JOHN MERCER

Dir of Enrolment Services: SHARON TODD

Dir of Library Services: LORI DRISCOLL

Library of 100,000 vols, 275 journals, magazines and newspapers

HOBE SOUND BIBLE COLLEGE

11298 SE Gomez Ave, POB 1065, Hobe Sound, FL 33455-1065

Telephone: (772) 546-5534

E-mail: info@hsbc.edu

Internet: www.hsbc.edu

Founded 1960

Private control

Academic year: August to May

Offers bachelors of art in ministerial studies

Pres.: P. DANIEL STETLER

Academic Dean: Dr CLIFFORD W. CHURCHILL

Dir of Admin. Services: WESLEY HOLDEN

Dir of Admissions: JOANNA WETHERALD

Dir of Advancement: JONATHAN HEATH

Dir of Finances: KENDALL STRAIGHT

Dir of Institutional Advancement: JONATHAN HEATH

Dean of Students: JOHN S. JONES

Registrar: ANN FRENCH

Librarian: KELLY CASTORO

Library of 30,000 vols

HODGES UNIVERSITY

2655 Northbrooke Dr., Naples, FL 34119

Telephone: (239) 513-1122

E-mail: admissions@hodges.edu

Internet: www.hodges.edu

Founded 1990 as Int. College, current name and status 2007

Private control

Academic year: September to August

Campus in Fort Myers

Pres.: Dr JEANETTE BROCK

Provost and Exec. Vice-Pres. for Academic Affairs: Dr KIM SPIEZIO

Exec. Vice-Pres. for Admin.: Dr JOSEPH PEPE

Vice-Pres. for IT and Facilities Management: DAVE RICE

Vice-Pres. for Student Enrolment Management: Dr JOSEPH PEPE

Vice-Pres. for Student Records Management: CAROL MORRISON

Vice-Pres. for Univ. Advancement: PHIL MEMOLI

Dean for Students: Dr MARCIA TURNER

Registrar: JENNA KAISER

Dir for Library: CAROLYNN VOLZ

Library of 30,000 vols, 59,000 ebooks

Number of teachers: 160 (80 full-time, 80 part-time)

Number of students: 2,640

DEANS

Fisher School of Technology: Dr AL BALL

Johnson School of Business: Dr NANCEY WYANT

Liberal Arts: ELSA ROGERS

Nichols School of Professional Studies: Dr KAREN LOCKLEAR

School of Allied Health: Dr CARLENE HARRISON

INDIAN RIVER STATE COLLEGE

3209 Virginia Ave, Fort Pierce, FL 34981-5596

Telephone: (772) 462-4772

E-mail: admissions-info@irsc.edu

Internet: www.irsc.edu

Founded 1959, present name and status 1970

State control

Academic year: August to August

Campuses in Chastain, Dixon Hendry, Mueller, St Lucie W; offers bachelor degree courses in applied science, biology, digital media, education, nursing

Pres.: Dr EDWIN R. MASSEY

Vice-Pres. for Academic Affairs: ANTHONY IACONO

Vice-Pres. for Admin. and Finance: BARRY A. KEIM

Vice-Pres. for Institutional Effectiveness: Dr CHRISTINA T. HART

Vice-Pres. for Instructional Services: Dr MARY G. LOCKE

Vice-Pres. for Student Affairs: FRANK L. WATKINS, JR

Number of students: 34,000

JACKSONVILLE UNIVERSITY

2800 University Blvd N, Jacksonville, FL 32211-3394

Telephone: (904) 256-8000

E-mail: admissions@ju.edu

Internet: www.ju.edu

Founded 1934, present name and status 1958

Private control

Academic year: 3 semesters

Pres.: Dr KERRY D. ROMESBURG

Sr Vice-Pres. for Academic Affairs: Dr LOIS S. BECKER

Sr Vice-Pres. for Enrolment Management: TERRY WHITTUM

Vice-Pres. for Finance and Admin.: Dr GEORGE SCADUTO

Vice-Pres. for Student Life: Dr JOHN BALOG

Vice-Pres. for Univ. Advancement: MICHAEL HOWLAND

Dean of Students: Dr BRYAN COKER

Registrar: CAROLYN A. BARRETT

Dir of Library: DAVID JONES

Library of 572,000 vols

Number of teachers: 270 (165 full-time, 105 part-time)

Number of students: 3,550

Publication: *Wave* (2 a year)

DEANS

College of Arts and Sciences: Dr Douglas M. Hazzard
College of Fine Arts: Bill Hill
Davis College of Business: Dr William M. Crosby
School of Education: Dr Christina Ramirez-Smith
School of Nursing: Dr Judith Erickson

JONES COLLEGE

5353 Arlington Expressway, Jacksonville, FL 32211-5588

Telephone: (904) 743-1122
E-mail: info@jones.edu
Internet: www.jones.edu

Founded 1918
Private control
Academic year: September to August (3 semesters)

Areas of study incl. allied health management, business admin., computer information systems; offers bachelors degree in allied health management, business admin., computer information systems, elementary education, interdisciplinary studies, legal assistant

Pres.: Dr Frank McCafferty
Dean of College: Dee Thornton
Dir of Admissions: Linda Vaughn

KEISER UNIVERSITY

1500 NW 49th St, Fort Lauderdale, FL 33309

Telephone: (954) 776-4456
E-mail: admissions@keiseruniversity.edu
Internet: www.keiseruniversity.edu

Founded 1977 as Keiser School, present name and status 2006
Private control

Campuses in Daytona Beach, Fort Myers, Jacksonville, Lakeland, Melbourne, Miami, Orlando, Pembroke Pines, Port St. Lucie, Sarasota, Tallahassee, Tampa, West Palm Beach.

Chancellor and CEO: Dr Arthur Keiser
Vice-Chancellor for Academic Affairs: Dr William Ritchie
Vice-Chancellor for Student Advancement and Community Relations: Belinda Keiser
Library of 111,740 vols
Number of students: 13,000

LYNN UNIVERSITY

3601 N Military Trail, Boca Raton, FL 33431-5598

Telephone: (561) 237-7000
E-mail: admission@lynn.edu
Internet: www.lynn.edu

Founded 1962 as Marymount College, present name 1991
Private control
Academic year: September to May
Pres. and CEO: Dr Kevin McAndrew Ross
Chief Information Officer: Dr Christian G. Boniforti
Sr Vice-Pres. for Admin.: Gregory Malfitano
Vice-Pres. for Academic Affairs: Prof. Dr Gregg Cox
Vice-Pres. for Devt and Alumni Affairs: Judi Nelson
Vice-Pres. for Student Life: Dr Phil Riordan
Gen. Counsel: Margaret E. Ruddy
Library Dir: Charles L. Kuhn
Library of 270,000 vols (incl. books, periodicals, video cassettes, microforms)
Number of students: 2,100 (1,650 undergraduate, 450 graduate)

DEANS

College of Business and Management: Dr Thomas Kruczek
College of Education: Dr Craig A. Mertler
College of Hospitality Management: Dr Joseph A. Rooney
College of Int. Communication: Prof. Dr David L. Jaffe
College of Liberal Education: Dr Katrina Carter-Tellison
Conservatory of Music: Prof. Dr Jon Robertson
School of Aeronautics: Major Dr Jeffrey C. Johnson

MIAMI DADE COLLEGE

300 N E Second Ave, Miami, FL 33132-2204

Telephone: (305) 237-8888
E-mail: mdcinfo@mdc.edu
Internet: www.mdc.edu

Founded 1960 as Dade County Jr College, present name and status 2003
State control
Academic year: August to April

Campuses in Doral, Hialeah, Homestead, Miami; offers bachelors degree courses in applied science, science

Pres.: Dr Eduardo J. Padrón
Provost: Dr Rolando Montoya
Vice-Provost For Education: Dr Pamela G. Menke
Exec. Dir and CEO: Glenn Kaufhold
Number of teachers: 670
Number of students: 174,000
Publication: *MCD Magazine*

MIAMI INTERNATIONAL UNIVERSITY OF ART & DESIGN

1501 Biscayne Blvd, Suite 100, Miami, FL 33132-1418

Telephone: (305) 428-5700
E-mail: aimiuadm@aii.edu
Internet: www.artinstitutes.edu/miami

Founded 1965
Private control
Academic year: July to June
Courses incl. BA, science and MA, fine arts
Pres.: Erika Fleming
Vice-Pres. for Admin and Financial Services: Joe Giannattasio
Dean for Academic Affairs: Paul Cox
Dean for Student Affairs: John Osborne
Sr Dir for Admissions: Kevin Ryan
Library of 23,000 vols, 200 periodicals

NEW COLLEGE OF FLORIDA

5800 Bay Shore Rd, Sarasota, FL 34243-2109

Telephone: (941) 487-5000
E-mail: admissions@ncf.edu
Internet: www.ncf.edu

Founded 1960
State control
Academic year: August to May (2 semesters)
Pres.: Prof. Dr Gordon E. Michalson, jr
Provost and Vice-Pres. of Academic Affairs: Prof. Dr Stephen Miles
Vice-Pres. for Admin. and Finance: John U. Martin
Dean of Students: Wendy Bashant
Dean of Enrolment Services and Information Technology: Kathleen Killion
Registrar: Kathleen Allen
Dean of the Library: Dr Brian Doherty
Library of 285,897 vols, 1,174 current serials received, 540,234 microforms, 165 ebooks, 8,400 audiovisual, 4,210 video cassettes
Number of teachers: 70 (full-time)
Number of students: 800

PROFESSORS

Division of Humanities:
Carrasco, M. E., Art History
Cuomo, G. R., German Language and Literature
Edidin, A. Z., Philosophy
Hassold, C., Art History
Langston, D. C., Philosophy and Religion
Michalson, G. E., Humanities

Division of Natural Sciences:
Beulig, A., Biology
Demski, L. S., Biology
Gilchrist, S., Biology
Lowman, M., Biology and Environmental Studies
Ruppeiner, G., Physics
Scudder, P., Chemistry

Division of Social Sciences:
Anthony, A. P., Art History
Doenecke, J., History
Elliott, C., Economics
Lewis, E., Political Science
Strobel, F., Economics
Vesperi, M. D., Anthropology

NORTHWEST FLORIDA STATE COLLEGE

100 College Blvd, Niceville, FL 32578-1295

Telephone: (850) 678-5111
E-mail: registrar@nwfsc.edu
Internet: www.nwfsc.edu

Founded 1964 as Okaloosa-Walton Jr College, present name and status 2008
State control
Academic year: August to May (3 semesters)

Campuses in Chautauqua Centre, Fort Walton Beach, Eglin AF Base Centre, Hurlburt Field Centre, Robert L. F. Sikes Education Centre, S Walton Centre; depts of adult gen. education, advanced technology and design, athletics, health and fitness, business and computer technology, English and communications, humanities, fine and performing arts, mathematics, nursing and allied health, public safety

Pres.: Dr Ty Handy
Vice-Pres. for Academic Affairs: Dr Sasha L. Jarrell
Vice-Pres. for Admin. Services: Dr Gary Yancey
Registrar and Dean of Enrolment Services: Christine C. Bishop
Library Dir: Janice Henderson
Library of 106,260 vols, 5,701 audiovisuals, 30,000 ebooks
Number of teachers: 310 (95 full-time and 215 part-time)
Number of students: 17,000

NOVA SOUTHEASTERN UNIVERSITY

3301 College Ave, Fort Lauderdale-Davie, FL 33314-7796

Telephone: (954) 262-8000
E-mail: admissions@nova.edu
Internet: www.nova.edu

Founded 1994, by merger of Nova Univ., Southeastern Univ. of Health Sciences
Private control
Academic year: July to June
Pres. and CEO: Dr George L. Hanbury, II
Chancellor of Health Professions Div.: Dr Frederick Lippman
Provost and Exec. Vice-Pres. for Academic Affairs: Dr Frank De Piano
Exec. Vice-Pres. and Chief Operating Officer: Jacqueline A. Travisano
Vice-Pres. for Community and Govt Affairs: Dr Larry A. Calderon
Vice-Pres. for Enrolment and Student Services: Stephanie G. Brown

Vice-Pres. for Financial Operations: W. DAVID HERON

Vice-Pres. for Information Services and Univ. Librarian: DONALD E. RIGGS

Vice-Pres. for Institutional Advancement: Dr JOE PINEDA

Vice Pres. for Institutional Effectiveness: Dr RONALD CHENAIL

Exec. Dir for Univ. Relations: DAVID C. DAWSON

Dean for Student Affairs: Dr BRAD A. WILLIAMS

Registrar: ELAINE POFF

Library: 1.4m. vols
Number of teachers: 720
Number of students: 29,000

Publications: *Digressions* (1 a year), *Farquhar Student Journal* (2 a year (online)), *ILSA Journal of International and Comparative Law* (3 a year), *International Travel Law Journal* (3 a year), *Internet Journal of Allied Health Sciences and Practice* (6 a year), *Nova Law Review* (3 a year), *Nova Lawyer* (1 a year), *Peace and Conflict Studies* (2 a year), *The Qualitative Report* (4 a year), *Viewpoint* (3 a year)

DEANS

Abraham S. Fischler School of Education: Dr H. WELLS SINGLETON

Center for Psychological Studies: Dr KAREN S. GROSBY

College of Dental Medicine: Dr ROBERT UCHIN

College of Health Care Sciences: Dr RICHARD E. DAVIS

College of Medical Sciences: Dr HAROLD E. LAUBACH

College of Nursing: Dr MARCELLA RUTHERFORD

College of Optometry: Dr DAVID S. LOSHIN

College of Osteopathic Medicine: Dr ANTHONY J. SILVAGNI

College of Pharmacy: Dr ANDRÉS MALAVÉ

Farquhar College of Arts and Sciences: Dr DONALD ROSENBLUM

Fischler School of Education and Human Services: Dr H. WELLS SINGLETON (Dean and Provost)

Graduate School of Computer and Information Sciences: Dr ERIC S. ACKERMAN

Graduate School of Humanities and Social Sciences: Dr HONGGANG YANG

H. Wayne Huizenga School of Business and Entrepreneurship: Dr J. PRESTON JAMES

Mailman Segal Centre for Human Development: Dr RONI COHEN LIEDERMAN

Oceanographic Center: Prof. Dr RICHARD E. DODGE

School of Humanities and Social Sciences: Dr HONGGANG YANG

Shepard Broad Law Center: Prof. ATHORNIA STEELE

Univ. School: Dr JEROME S. CHERMAK

PALM BEACH ATLANTIC UNIVERSITY

POB 24708, West Palm Beach, FL 33416-4708

901 S Flagler Dr., West Palm Beach, FL 33401

Telephone: (561) 803-2000
E-mail: admit@pba.edu
Internet: www.pba.edu

Founded 1968

Campuses in Orlando, Wellington
Private control
Academic year: August to May

Pres.: Dr WILLIAM M. B. FLEMING, JR
Provost: Prof. Dr JOSEPH A. KLOBA
Vice-Pres. and Chief Financial Officer: GEORGE GALL
Vice-Pres. for Enrolment Services: BUCKLEY A. JAMES

Vice-Pres. for Student Devt: Dr MARY ANN SEARLE
Dean of Students: KEVIN ABEL
Registrar: AUDREY SCHOFIELD
Library Dean: STEVEN BAKER

Library of 350,000 vols
Number of teachers: 150 (full-time)
Number of students: 3,660

DEANS

Catherine T. MacArthur School of Leadership: Prof. Dr JIM LAUB

Gregory School of Pharmacy: Prof. Dr MARY FERRILL

Rinker School of Business: Prof. Dr LESLIE TURNER

School of Arts and Sciences: Prof. Dr BARTON STARR

School of Communication and Media: Dr DUANE MEEKS

School of Education and Behavioural Studies: Dr GENE SALE

School of Ministry: Prof. Dr RANDY RICHARDS

School of Music and Fine Arts: Prof. Dr LLOYD MIMS

School of Nursing: Prof. Dr JOANNE MASELLA

PALM BEACH STATE COLLEGE

4200 Congress Ave, Lake Worth, FL 33461-4796

Telephone: (561) 868-3350
E-mail: enrollmt@palmbeachstate.edu
Internet: www.palmbeachstate.edu

Founded 1933 as Palm Beach Jr College, present status 2009, present name 2010
State control
Academic year: August to August

Campuses in Belle Glade, Boca Raton, Palm Beach Gardens, W Palm Beach; offers bachelors degree courses in applied sciences, sciences

Pres.: Dr DENNIS P. GALLON
Vice-Pres. for Academic Affairs: Dr SHARON A. SASS
Vice-Pres. for Admin. and Business Services: RICHARD A. BECKER
Vice-Pres. for Student Services and Enrolment Management: PATRICIA J. ANDERSON
Provost: Dr MARÍA M. VALLEJO
Gen. Counsel: DENISE WALLACE
Registrar: EDWARD MUELLER

Library of 10,000 vols, 2,000 journals and periodicals
Number of students: 51,250

PENSACOLA STATE COLLEGE

1000 College Blvd, Pensacola, FL 32504
Telephone: (850) 484-1000
E-mail: askus@pensacolastate.edu
Internet: www.pensacolastate.edu

Founded 1948 as Pensacola Jr College, present name and status 2010
State control
Academic year: August to August

Campuses in Pensacola, Milton, Warrington; depts of allied health, biological sciences, education, engineering, English and communications, health science, history, languages and social sciences, mathematics, nursing, performing arts, physical sciences, visual arts

Pres.: Dr C. EDWARD MEADOWS
Vice-Pres. for Academic Affairs: Dr ERIN SPICER
Vice-Pres. for Business Affairs: GEAN ANN EMOND
Vice-Pres. for Instructional Affairs: Dr MARTIN GONZALEZ
Vice-Pres. for Student Affairs and Gen. Counsel: THOMAS J. GILLIAM, JR
Dean of Milton Campus: Dr ANTHEA AMOS

Number of teachers: 580 (180 full-time, 400 part-time)
Number of students: 28,000

POLK STATE COLLEGE

999 Ave H NE, Winter Haven, FL 33881-4299

Telephone: (863) 297-1000
E-mail: registrar@polk.edu
Internet: www.polk.edu

Founded 1964, present name and status 2009
State control
Academic year: August to August

Campuses in Lakeland, Winter Haven; offers bachelors degree in applied science

Pres.: Dr EILEEN HOLDEN
Vice-Pres. for Academic and Student Services: Dr KENNETH ROSS
Vice-Pres. for Admin. and Chief Financial Officer: PETER S. ELLIOTT
Provost for Lakeland Campus: STEVE HULL
Provost for Winter Haven Campus: Dr SHARON E. MILLER
Dir of Financial Services: (vacant)
Dir of Institutional Research, Effectiveness and Planning: PETER USINGER

Library of 93,000 vols
Number of teachers: 100 (full-time)
Number of students: 12,900

RINGLING COLLEGE OF ART AND DESIGN

2700 N Tamiami Trail, Sarasota, FL 34234-5895

Telephone: (941) 3515100
E-mail: info@ringling.edu
Internet: www.ringling.edu

Founded 1931
Private control
Academic year: August to May

Courses incl. advertising design, business of art and design, computer animation, digital filmmaking, gen. fine arts, game art and design, graphic and interactive communication, illustration, interior design, motion design, photography and digital imaging

Pres.: Dr LARRY R. THOMPSON
Vice-Pres. for Academic Affairs: MELODY WEILER
Vice-Pres. for Finance and Admin.: TRACY A. WAGNER
Vice-Pres. for Institutional Advancement: (vacant)
Vice-Pres. for Student Life and Dean of Students: Dr TAMMY S. WALSH
Dean of Admissions: JAMES H. DEAN
Dir of Library Services: KATHLEEN LIST

Library of 55,000 vols, 6,100 DVDs and audiovisual items, 350 periodicals, 127,000 35-mm slides
Number of teachers: 130
Number of students: 1,300

ROLLINS COLLEGE

1000 Holt Ave, Winter Park, FL 32789-4499
Telephone: (407) 646-2000
E-mail: admission@rollins.edu
Internet: www.rollins.edu

Founded 1885
Private control
Academic year: September to May

Pres.: Dr LEWIS M. DUNCAN
Provost and Vice-Pres. for Academic Affairs: Dr CAROL M. BRESNAHAN
Vice-Pres. for Business and Finance and Treas.: JEFFREY G. EISENBARTH
Vice-Pres. for Institutional Advancement: RONALD J. KORVAS
Vice-Pres. for Planning and Dean of College: Dr LAURIE M. JOYNER

Dean of Admissions and Enrolment: DAVID G. ERDMANN
Dean of Faculty: Dr ROBERT SMITHER
Dean of Student Affairs: Dr KAREN L. HATER
Library Dir: JONATHAN MILLER
Library of 303,000 vols, 1,600 current periodicals
Number of teachers: 210
Number of students: 3,300 (2,630 undergraduate, 670 graduate).
Publications: *Alumni Record* (4 a year), *Brushing* (1 a year)

DEANS

College of Arts and Sciences: Dr ROBERT SMITHER
College of Professional Studies: Dr DEBRA K. WELLMAN
Crummer Graduate School of Business: CRAIG M. MCALLASTER
Hamilton Holt School: Dr DEBRA K. WELLMAN

SAINT LEO UNIVERSITY

33701 State Rd 52, POB 6665, Saint Leo, FL 33574-6665

Telephone: (352) 588-8200
E-mail: news@saintleo.edu
Internet: www.saintleo.edu

Founded 1889, present name and status 1999
Private control
Academic year: August to April (2 semesters)
Pres.: Dr ARTHUR F. KIRK, JR
Vice-Pres. for Academic Affairs: Dr MARIBETH DURST
Vice-Pres. for Business Affairs and Chief Financial Officer: FRANK MEZZANINI
Vice-Pres. for Enrolment and Online Programs: KATHRYN MCFARLAND
Vice-Pres. for Student Services: Dr EDWARD DADEZ
Dir of Univ. Advancement: DAVID OSTRANDER
Registrar: KAREN HATFIELD
Dir of Library Services: BRENT SHORT
Library of 152,584 vols
Number of teachers: 1,300
Number of students: 15,600

DEANS

Donald R. Tapia School of Business: Dr MICHAEL NASTANSKI
School of Arts and Sciences: Dr MARY T. SPOTO
School of Education and Social Services: Dr CAROL G. WALKER

ST JOHNS RIVER STATE COLLEGE

5001 St Johns Ave, Palatka, FL 32177-3807
Telephone: (386) 312-4200
E-mail: bachelorsprograms@sjrstate.edu
Internet: www.sjrstate.edu

Founded 1958 as St Johns River Jr College, present name and status 2010
State control
Academic year: August to August
Campuses in Orange Park, Palatka, St Augustine
Pres. and Chair.: JOE H. PICKENS
Exec. Vice-Pres.: MELISSA C. MILLER
Vice-Pres. for Academic Affairs: Dr MELANIE A. BROWN
Vice-Pres. for Admin. Affairs: ANNETTE W. BARRINEAU
Vice-Pres. for Business Affairs: ALBERT P. LITTLE
Vice-Pres. for Devt and External Affairs: CAROLINE D. TINGLE
Vice-Pres. for Finance and Admin.: ALBERT P. LITTLE
Vice-Pres. for Research and Institutional Effectiveness: Dr ROSALIND M. HUMERICK

Vice-Pres. for Student Affairs: Dr GILBERT L. EVANS, JR
Chief Information Officer: PAUL M. HAWKINS
Provost for St Augustine Campus: Dr GREGORY K. MCLEOD
Provost for Orange Park Campus: JAMES C. ROY
Dir of Admissions and Records: SUSANNE LINEBERGER
Dean of Library Services: CARMEN M. CUMMINGS
Library of 65,000 vols, 3,000 journals, 30,000 ebooks
Number of teachers: 110 (full-time)
Number of students: 7,500 (2,500 full-time, 5,000 part-time)

DEANS

Allied Health: Dr THOMAS D. BAXTER
Arts and Sciences: Dr LAURA L. BOILINI
Florida School of Arts: ALAN R. HENTSCHEL
Nursing: Dr MARY ANNE LANEY

ST JOHN VIANNEY COLLEGE SEMINARY

2900 SW 87th Ave, Miami, FL 33165-3244
Telephone: (305) 223-4561
E-mail: sjvcsadmin@gmail.com
Internet: www.sjvcs.edu

Founded 1959 as St John Vianney Seminary; present name 1977
Private control
Offers Catholic education, priestly formation
Rector and Pres.: Rev. ROBERTO GARZA
Dean of Students: Rev. LUCIEN E. PIERRE
Academic Dean: Dr RAMÓN J. SANTOS
Registrar: BONNIE DE ANGULO
Library Dir: MARIA RODRIGUEZ
Library of 50,000 vols
Number of teachers: 20

ST PETERSBURG COLLEGE

POB 13489, St Petersburg, FL 33733-3489
Telephone: (727) 341-4772
E-mail: information@spcollege.edu
Internet: www.spcollege.edu

Founded 1927 as St Petersburg Jr College, present name and status 2002
State control
Academic year: August to July
Pres.: Dr WILLIAM D. LAW, JR
Sr Vice-Pres. for Academic and Student Affairs: Dr ANNE M. COOPER
Sr Vice-Pres. for Admin., Business Services and Information Technology: Dr DOUGLAS S. DUNCAN
Vice-Pres. for Economic Devt and Innovative Projects: DENNIS L. JONES
Vice-Pres. for Institutional Advancement: FRANCES Z. NEU
Gen. Counsel: SUZANNE GARDNER (acting)
Dir for Learning Resources: JOSEPH LEOPOLD
Library of 250,000 vols, 25,000 ejournals and periodicals and 57,000 ebooks
Number of teachers: 1,740 (310 full-time, 1,430 part time)
Number of students: 33,900

DEANS

College of Education: KIMBERLY HARTMAN
College of Health Sciences: TAMI J. GRZESIKOWSKI
College of Nursing: SUSAN BAKER (acting)
College of Public Safety Admin.: BRIAN FRANK
College of Technology and Management: GREGORY NENSTIEL
Paralegal Studies: SUSAN DEMERS
School of Veterinary Technology: Dr RICHARD M. FLORA

ST THOMAS UNIVERSITY

16401 NW 37th Ave, Miami Gardens, Miami, FL 33054-6459

Telephone: (305) 628-6546
E-mail: signup@stu.edu
Internet: www.stu.edu

Founded 1961 as Biscayne College, present name and status 1984
Private control
Academic year: August to May
Pres.: Rev. FRANKLYN M. CASALE
Provost and Chief Academic Officer: Dr GREGORY S. CHAN
Vice-Pres. for Admin. and Chief Financial Officer: TERRENCE L. O'CONNOR
Vice-Pres. for Planning and Enrolment: Dr BEATRIZ GONZALEZ ROBINSON
Vice-Pres. for Student Affairs: Dr SARAH SHUMATE
Vice-Pres. for Univ. Advancement: BEVERLY S. BACHRACH
Dean of Academic Support: BARBARA SINGER
Dean of Enrolment: ANDRE LIGHTBOURN
Dean of Graduate Studies: Dr JOSEPH A. IANNONE
Dean of Undergraduate Studies: Dr GUIYOU HUANG
Dean of Students: ISSAC M. CARTER
Registrar: IRAIDA ACEBO
Library Admin.: JONATHAN C. ROACH
Library of 275,106 vols, 99,000 ebooks, 600 print journal, newspaper titles
Number of teachers: 115 (55 full-time, 60 part-time)
Number of students: 2,500
Publications: *Journal of Multidisciplinary Research*, *St Thomas Law Review* (1 a year)

DEANS

Biscayne College of Liberal Arts and Social Sciences: Prof. Dr SCOTT C. ZEMAN
School of Business: Prof. Dr J. ANTONIO VILLAMIL
School of Law: Prof. Dr DOUGLAS E. RAY
School of Leadership Studies: Dr SUSAN B. ANGULO
School of Science, Technology and Engineering Management: Dr WIM F. A. STEELANT
School of Theology and Ministry: MARY CARTER WAREN

ST VINCENT DE PAUL REGIONAL SEMINARY

10701 S Military Trail, Boynton Beach, FL 33436-4899

Telephone: (561) 732-4424
Internet: www.svdp.edu

Founded 1963
Private control
Academic year: August to May (2 semesters)
Offers master of art, divinity
Rector, Pres. and Dean of Formation: Rev. KEITH BRENNAN
Vice-Rector and Dean of Human Formation: Rev. JOSÉ N. ALFARO
Academic Dean: Rev. Dr DEACON DENNIS T. DEMES
Dean of Pastoral Formation: Rev. LOUIS GUERIN
Dean of Spiritual Formation: Rev. STEPHEN OLDS
Treas. and Campus Admin.: KEITH PARKER
Library Dir: ARTHUR G. QUINN
Library of 81,000 vols, 3,000 bound periodicals, 1,500 audiovisuals
Number of teachers: 30
Publication: *St Vincent's* (2 a year)

SCHILLER INTERNATIONAL UNIVERSITY—FLORIDA

(For general information, see entry for Schiller International University in Germany chapter)

8560 Ulmerton Rd, Largo, FL 33771

Telephone: (727) 474-4080

E-mail: admissions@schiller.edu

Internet: www.schiller.edu

Founded 1964

Private control

Academic year: September to June (3 semesters)

Int. campuses in France, Germany, Spain; offers degrees in business admin., financial planning, interdisciplinary studies, int. business, int. economics, int. hospitality and tourism, int. management, int. relations and diplomacy, management of information technology

Pres.: MICHELE GEIGLE

Provost: ANGELA CARNEY

Registrar: STEPHANIE HAGEN

Librarian: JEANNE GROSSMAN

Number of teachers: 40

Number of students: 250

SEMINOLE STATE COLLEGE OF FLORIDA

100 Weldon Blvd, Sanford, FL 32773-6199

Telephone: (407) 708-2106

E-mail: admissions@seminolestate.edu

Internet: www.seminolestate.edu

Founded 1966 as Seminole Jr College, present name and status 2009

State control

Academic year: August to July

Campuses in Altamonte Springs, Heathrow, Oviedo, Sanford/Lake Mary; offers bachelor degrees in applied science, science

Pres.: Dr E. ANN McGEE

Exec. Vice-Pres. for Admin. Services and Chief Financial Officer: Dr JOE SARNOVSKY

Vice-Pres. for Academic Affairs and Chief Academic Officer: JIM HENNINGSEN

Vice-Pres. for Information Technology and Resources and Chief Information Officer: DICK HAMANN

Vice-Pres. for Student Affairs and Chief Student Affairs Officer: Dr MARCIA ROMAN

Dean of Libraries and Learning Technology: PATRICIA S. DeSALVO

Number of teachers: 780 (550 full-time, 230 part-time)

Number of students: 32,770

SOUTHEASTERN UNIVERSITY

1000 Longfellow Blvd, Lakeland, FL 33801

Telephone: (863) 667-5000

E-mail: info@seu.edu

Internet: www.seu.edu

Founded 1935 as South-Eastern Bible Institute, present name and status 2005

Private control

Academic year: August to May (3 semesters)

Pres.: Dr KENT INGLE

Exec. Vice-Pres.: DEL CHITTIM

Vice-Pres. for Academic Affairs: Prof. Dr WILLIAM HACKETT

Vice-Pres. for Enrolment Management: ROY ROWLAND, IV

Vice-Pres. for Finance and Admin.: DAN MORTENSEN

Vice-Pres. for Student Devt: CHRIS OWENS

Vice-Pres. for Univ. Advancement: BRIAN C. CARROLL

Registrar: LINDA KELSO

Dir for Admission: BETANIA TORRES

Dean of Student Services: DARRELL HARDT

Dean of Library Services: GRACE VEACH

Library of 100,000 vols, 800 periodicals, 32,000 ebooks

Number of teachers: 100

Number of students: 2,900

DEANS

College of Arts and Sciences: Dr GORDON MILLER

College of Business and Legal Studies: Dr R. JOSEPH CHILDS

College of Christian Ministries and Religion: Dr ROBERT HOULIHAN

College of Education: Dr DOUG ROTH

STATE COLLEGE OF FLORIDA, MANATEE—SARASOTA

POB 1849, Bradenton, FL 34206

5840 26 St W, Bradenton, FL 34207

Telephone: (941) 752-5000

E-mail: admissions@scf.edu

Internet: www.scf.edu

Founded 1957 as Manatee Jr College, present name and status 2009

State control

Academic year: August to August (3 semesters)

Campuses in Lakewood Ranch, Venice

Pres.: Dr CAROL F. PROBSTFELD

Vice-Pres. for Academic Affairs: GARY T. RUSSELL

Vice-Pres. for Baccalaureate Programmes: Dr MICHAEL J. MEARS

Vice-Pres. for Educational and Student Services: Dr DONALD R. BOWMAN

Library Dir: TRACY ELLIOTT

Library of 96,670 vols, 292 periodicals and 34,319 ebooks,

Number of teachers: 130 (full-time)

Number of students: 27,000

DEANS

Nursing and Health Professions: Dr BEVERLY HINDENLANG

STETSON UNIVERSITY

421 N Woodland Blvd, DeLand, FL 32723

Telephone: (386) 822-7100

E-mail: admissions@stetson.edu

Internet: www.stetson.edu

Founded 1883 as DeLand Acad., DeLand Univ. 1887, present name 1889

Private control

Academic year: August to July

Campus in St Petersburg; satellite centres in Celebration, Tampa

Pres.: Dr WENDY B. LIBBY

Provost and Vice-Pres. for Academic Affairs: Dr ELIZABETH PAUL

Vice-Pres. for Business and Chief Operating Officer: Dr F. ROBERT HUTH, JR

Vice-Pres. for Campus Life: RINA TOVAR

Vice-Pres. for Enrolment Management: JOEL BAUMAN

Vice-Pres. for Students Affairs and Dean of Students: CHRISTOPHER M. KANDUS-FISHER

Vice-Pres. for Univ. Relations: CAROL L. JULIAN

Dean for Admissions: REBECCA R. ECKSTEIN

Registrar: TERRI M. RICHARDS

Library of 330,000 vols and 245,000 govt documents

Number of teachers: 195 (full-time, DeLand campus)

Number of students: 3,250 (2,500 in DeLand, 750 at College of Law in St Petersburg)

Publications: *Alumni Magazine*, *Stetson Lawyer-Alumni Magazine* (2 a year), *Stetson University Magazine* (2 a year), *The Cupola* (2 a year), *Touchstone* (1 a year), *Visual* (2 a year)

DEANS

College of Arts and Sciences: Dr GRADY W. BALLENGER

College of Law: Prof. Dr ROYAL C. GARDNER

School of Business Administration: Dr STUART MICHELSON

School of Music: Prof. Dr JEAN OHLSSON WEST

UNIVERSITY OF CENTRAL FLORIDA

POB 160000, Orlando FL 32816

4000 Central Florida Blvd, Orlando, FL 32816

Telephone: (407) 823-2000

E-mail: admission@mail.ucf.edu

Internet: www.ucf.edu

Founded 1963 as Florida Technological Univ., present name 1978

State control

Academic year: August to August (3 semesters)

Pres.: Dr JOHN C. HITT

Provost and Exec. Vice-Pres.: Dr TONY WALDROP

Vice-Pres. and Chief of Staff: Dr JOHN F. SCHELL

Vice-Pres. for Admin. and Finance: WILLIAM F. MERCK, II

Vice-Pres. for Devt and Alumni Relations: ROBERT J. HOLMES, JR

Vice-Pres. for Research and Commercialization: Dr M. J. SOILEAU

Vice-Pres. for Student Devt and Enrolment Services: Dr MARIBETH EHASZ

Vice-Pres. for Univ. Relations: Dr DANIEL C. HOLSENBECK

Dean of Undergraduate Studies and Vice-Provost: Dr ELLIOT VITTES

Registrar: Dr DENNIS J. DULNIAK

Dir of Univ. Libraries: BARRY B. BAKER

Library: 2m. vols, 593,000 ebooks, 326,310 govt. documents, 29,659 current periodicals, 3,092,514 microforms, 50,517 audiovisual items

Number of teachers: 1,830

Number of students: 58,600

DEANS

Burnett Honors College: Prof. Dr ALVIN WANG

College of Arts and Humanities: Dr JOSÉ FERNÁNDEZ

College of Business Admin.: Dr FOARD F. JONES

College of Education: Dr SANDRA L. ROBINSON

College of Engineering and Computer Science: Dr MARWAN A. SIMAAN

College of Graduate Studies: PATRICIA BISHOP

College of Health and Public Affairs: Dr MICHAEL L. FRUMKIN

College of Medicine: Dr DEBORAH C. GERMAN

College of Nursing: JEAN D'MEZA LEUNER

College of Optics and Photonics: Prof. Dr BAHAA E. A. SALEH

College of Sciences: Prof. Dr MICHAEL D. JOHNSON

Rosen College of Hospitality Management: Dr ABRAHAM PIZAM

UNIVERSITY OF FLORIDA

Gainesville, FL 32611-3150

Telephone: (352) 392-3261

E-mail: gradschool@ufl.edu

Internet: www.ufl.edu

Founded 1853, present name 1905

State control

Academic year: August to September

Pres.: Dr JAMES BERNARD MACHEN

Provost and Sr Vice-Pres. for Academic Affairs: Dr JOE GLOVER

Sr Vice-Pres. for Health Affairs: Dr DAVID S. GUZICK

Sr Vice Pres. and Chief Operating Officer: CHARLES E. LANE
Vice-Pres. and Chief Information Officer: Dr ELIAS ELDAYRIE
Vice-Pres. and Gen. Counsel: JAMIE LEWIS KEITH
Vice-Pres. for Business Affairs and Economic Devt: CURTIS REYNOLDS
Vice-Pres. for Devt and Alumni Affairs: THOMAS J. MITCHELL
Vice-Pres. and Chief Financial Officer: MATTHEW FAJACK
Vice-Pres. for Enrolment Management and Assoc. Provost: Dr ZINA EVANS
Vice-Pres. for Research: WINFRED M. PHILLIPS
Vice-Pres. for Student Affairs: DAVE KRATZER
Vice-Pres. for Univ. Relations: JANE ADAMS
Univ. Registrar: STEPHEN J. PRITZ, JR
Dean of Students: Dr JEN DAY SHAW
Dean of Univ. Libraries: JUDITH RUSSELL
Library: see under Libraries and Archives
Number of teachers: 5,430
Number of students: 52,300 (36,400 undergraduate, 15,900 graduate)
Publications: *Florida Historical Quarterly, Journal of Politics, Southern Folklore Quarterly, University of Florida Law Review, UF Law*

DEANS

College of Agricultural and Life Sciences: Dr TERESA BALSER
College of Dentistry: Prof. Dr TERESA A. DOLAN
College of Design, Construction and Planning: Prof. Dr CHRISTOPHER SILVER
College of Education: Prof. Dr GLENN E. GOOD
College of Engineering: CAMMY R. ABERNATHY
College of Fine Arts: LUCINDA LAVELLI
College of Health and Human Performance: Prof. Dr STEVE M. DORMAN
College of Journalism and Communications: Prof. Dr JOHN W. WRIGHT, II
College of Liberal Arts and Sciences: PAUL J. D'ANIERI
College of Medicine: Dr MICHAEL L. GOOD
College of Nursing: Dr KATHLEEN ANN LONG
College of Pharmacy: Prof. JULIE JOHNSON
College of Public Health and Health Professions: Dr MICHAEL G. PERRI
College of Veterinary Medicine: Dr GLEN F. HOFFSIS
Graduate School: Dr HENRY FRIERSON
Institute of Food and Agricultural Sciences: Dr MILLIE FERRER-CHANCY
Levin College of Law: (vacant)
Warrington College of Business Admin.: JOHN KRAFT

UNIVERSITY OF MIAMI

Coral Gables, FL 33124
Telephone: (305) 284-2211
E-mail: admission@miami.edu
Internet: www.miami.edu
Founded 1925
Private control
Academic year: September to May (2 terms)
Pres.: DONNA E. SHALALA
Provost and Exec. Vice-Pres.: Dr THOMAS J. LEBLANC
Sr Vice-Pres. for Business and Finance and Chief Financial Officer: JOSEPH T. NATOLI
Sr Vice-Pres. for Medical Affairs: Dr PASCAL J. GOLDSCHMIDT
Sr Vice-Pres. for Univ. Advancement and External Affairs: SERGIO M. GONZALEZ
Vice-Pres., Gen. Counsel and Sec. of the Univ.: AILEEN M. UGALDE
Vice-Pres. for Enrolment Management and Continuing Studies: PAUL M. OREHOVEC
Vice-Pres. for Finance and Treas.: JOHN R. SHIPLEY

Vice-Pres. for Govt Affairs: RODOLFO J. FERNANDEZ
Vice-Pres. for Information Technology and Chief Information Officer: STEVE CAWLEY
Vice-Pres. for Student Affairs: PATRICIA A. WHITELY
Dean for Undergraduate Education and Sr Vice-Provost: WILLIAM SCOTT GREEN
Dean for Libraries: CHARLES ECKMAN
Library: 4.1m. vols, 86,740 current serials titles, 83,789 ejournals, 630,755 ebooks, 4m. microforms, 176,052 audiovisual materials
Number of teachers: 3,100 (2,625 full-time, 475 part-time)
Number of students: 16,100 (14,750 full-time, 1,350 part-time)
Publications: *Journal of Inter-American Studies* (4 a year), *Medicine* (3 a year), *Miami* (3 a year), *World Affairs* (4 a year)

DEANS

College of Arts and Sciences: Dr LEONIDAS G. BACHAS
College of Engineering: Dr JAMES M. TIEN
Graduate School: Dr TERRI A. SCANDURA
Miller School of Medicine: Dr PASCAL J. GOLDSCHMIDT
Phillip and Patricia Frost School of Music: Dr SHELTON G. BERG
Rosenstiel School of Marine and Atmospheric Sciences: Dr RONI AVISSAR
School of Architecture: ELIZABETH PLATER-ZYBERK
School of Business Admin.: Dr EUGENE W. ANDERSON
School of Communication: GREGORY J. SHEPHERD
School of Education: Dr ISAAC PRILLELTENSKY
School of Law: Dr PATRICIA D. WHITE
School of Nursing and Health Studies: NILDA P. PERAGALLO

UNIVERSITY OF NORTH FLORIDA

1 UNF Dr, Jacksonville, FL 32224-2645
Telephone: (904) 620-1000
E-mail: admissions@unf.edu
Internet: www.unf.edu
Founded 1972
State control
Academic year: August to August
Pres.: Prof. JOHN A. DELANEY
Provost and Vice-Pres. for Academic Affairs: Dr MARK E. WORKMAN
Vice-Pres. and Chief of Staff: Dr THOMAS S. SERWATKA
Vice-Pres. and Gen. Counsel: KAREN J. STONE
Vice-Pres. for Admin. and Finance: SHARI SHUMAN
Vice-Pres. for Institutional Advancement: Dr PIERRE N. ALLAIRE
Vice-Pres. for Student and Int. Affairs: Dr MAURICIO GONZALEZ
Dean of Continuing Education: ROBERT L. WOOD
Dean of Graduate School: Dr LEN ROBERSON
Dean for Undergraduate Studies: Dr JEFFREY COKER
Dean for Library: Dr SHIRLEY HALLBLADE
Library of 840,423 vols, 2,800 serial journals, 32,875 ejournals, 53,252 ebooks, 21,521 audio items, 8,753 video materials, 8,528 maps, 1.5m. microforms
Number of teachers: 510 (full-time)
Number of students: 16,300 (13,700 undergraduate, 1,800 graduate)

DEANS

Brooks College of Health: Prof. Dr PAMELA S. CHALLY
Coggin College of Business Admin.: Prof. Dr AJAY SAMANT

College of Arts and Sciences: Dr BARBARA A. HETRICK
College of Computing, Engineering and Construction: Dr MARK A. TUMEO
College of Education and Human Services: Dr LARRY DANIEL

UNIVERSITY OF SOUTH FLORIDA

4202 E Fowler Ave, Tampa, FL 33620
Telephone: (813) 974-2011
E-mail: info@admin.usf.edu
Internet: www.usf.edu
Founded 1956
State control
Academic year: August to July (3 semesters)
Campuses in Lakeland, Sarasota-Manatee, St Petersburg
Pres.: Dr JUDY LYNN GENSHAFT
Provost and Exec. Vice-Pres.: Dr RALPH WILCOX
Sr Vice-Pres. for Research, Innovation and Global Affairs: Dr KAREN A. HOLBROOK
Sr Vice-Pres. for Univ. Advancement: JOEL MOMBERG
Vice-Pres. for Admin. Affairs: SANDY LOVINS
Vice-Pres. for Student Affairs: Dr JENNIFER MENINGALL
Chief Operating Officer: JOHN LONG
Regional Chancellor and Campus Chief Exec. Officer for Lakeland: Dr MARSHALL GOODMAN
Regional Chancellor and Campus Chief Exec. Officer for Sarasota-Manatee: Dr ARTHUR M. GUILFORD
Regional Chancellor and Campus Chief Exec. Officer for St Petersburg: Dr MARGARET SULLIVAN
Dean for Graduate School: Dr KAREN LILLER
Dean for Undergraduate Studies: Dr W. ROBERT SULLINS
Exec. Dir for Univ. College: Dr SANDRA COOPER
Registrar: LINDA ERICKSON
Dean for Libraries: WILLIAM A. GARRISON
Library of 2,556,031 vols, 82,706 serials
Number of teachers: 1,820 (1,679 full-time, 141 part-time)
Number of students: 44,632 (35,799 undergraduate, 8,833 graduate)

DEANS

College of Arts and Sciences: Prof. Dr ERIC EISENBERG
College of Behavioural and Community Sciences: Dr CATHERINE BATSCHE
College of Business: Dr ROBERT L. FORSYTHE
College of Education: Dr COLLEEN S. KENNEDY
College of Engineering: Prof. Dr JOHN M. WIENCEK
College of Graduate Studies: Dr KAREN LILLER
College of Marine Science: Dr JACQUELINE E. DIXON
College of Nursing: Dr PATRICIA A. BURNS
College of Public Health: Dr DONNA PETERSEN
College of the Arts: Dr BARTON LEE
Honors College: Dr STUART SILVERMAN
Morsani College of Medicine: Dr CHARLES LOCKWOOD (acting)

UNIVERSITY OF SOUTH FLORIDA ST. PETERSBURG

140 Seventh Ave S, St Petersburg, FL 33701
Telephone: (727) 873-4873
E-mail: admissions@usfsp.edu
Internet: www.usfsp.edu
Founded 1965, present name and status 1968
State control
Academic year: September to August
Regional Chancellor and CEO: Dr MARGARET SULLIVAN

Regional Vice-Chancellor for Academic Affairs: NORINE NOONAN
Regional Vice-Chancellor for Admin. and Financial Services: ASHOK K. DHINGRA
Regional Vice-Chancellor for External Affairs: HELEN LEVINE
Dean of Library: CAROL HIXSON

Library of 204,839 vols
Number of teachers: 160 (full-time)
Number of students: 4,000

DEANS

College of Arts and Sciences: Dr FRANK A. BIAFORA
College of Business: Dr MALING EBRAHIMPOUR
College of Education: Dr BILL HELLER
College of Marine Science: Dr JACQUELINE E. DIXON

UNIVERSITY OF TAMPA

401 W Kennedy Blvd, Tampa, FL 33606-1490
Telephone: (813) 253-3333
E-mail: admissions@ut.edu
Internet: www.ut.edu

Founded 1931, current name and status 1933
Private control
Academic year: August to July

Pres.: Dr RONALD L. VAUGHN
Provost and Vice Pres. for Academic Affairs: Dr DAVID STERN
Vice-Pres. for Admin. and Finance: RICHARD W. OGOREK
Vice-Pres. for Devt and Univ. Relations: DANIEL T. GURA
Vice-Pres. for Enrolment: DENNIS NOSTRAND
Vice-Pres. for Operations and Planning: Dr LINDA W. DEVINE
Dean for Students: STEPHANIE RUSSELL KREBS
Registrar: MICHELLE PELAEZ
Dir for Macdonald-Kelce Library: MARLYN R. PETHE

Library of 243,334 vols, 56,220 print and electronic periodicals, 65,230 microforms, 11,309 audiovisual items; partial depository for US govt documents
Number of teachers: 593
Number of students: 6,912
Publications: *Pinter Review* (2 a year), *Tampa Review* (2 a year), *UT Journal* (3 a year)

DEANS

College of Arts and Letters: Dr HAIG MARDIROSIAN
College of Natural and Health Sciences: Dr JAMES GORE
College of Social Sciences, Mathematics and Education: Dr JACK GELLER
John H. Sykes College of Business: Dr F. FRANK GHANNADIAN

UNIVERSITY OF WEST FLORIDA

Bldg 10, 11000 Univ. Parkway, Pensacola, FL 32514-5750
Telephone: (850) 474-2000
E-mail: admissions@uwf.edu
Internet: www.uwf.edu

Founded 1965
State control
Academic year: August to August

Pres.: Dr JUDY BENSE
Vice-Pres. for Academic Affairs and Interim Provost: DAVID MARKER
Gen. Counsel: LEE GORE
Exec. Vice-Pres.: HAROLD M. WHITE, JR
Vice-Pres. for Admin. Affairs: Dr MATTHEW ALTIER
Vice-Pres. for Student Affairs: Dr KEVIN W. BAILEY
Vice-Pres. for Univ. Advancement: Dr KYLE MARRERO
Registrar: ANN H. DZIADON

Dean of Libraries: ROBERT DUGAN

Library of 840,125 vols, 4,588 serial subscriptions, 1,693,620 microforms, 714,729 govt. documents, 3,811 maps, 108,195 ebooks
Number of teachers: 340
Number of students: 12,000

DEANS

College of Arts and Sciences: Prof. Dr JANE HALONEN
College of Business: Prof. Dr EDWARD RANELLI
College of Professional Studies: Dr PAM NORTHRUP

WARNER UNIVERSITY

13895 Highway 27, Lake Wales, FL 33859
Telephone: (863) 638-1426
E-mail: admissions@warner.edu
Internet: www.warner.edu

Founded 1968 as Warner Southern College, present name and status 2008
Private control
Academic year: August to May

Pres.: Dr GREGORY V. HALL
Vice-Pres. and Chief Academic Officer: Prof. Dr JAMES MOYER
Vice-Pres. for Advancement: DORIS B. GUKICH
Vice-Pres. for Enrolment Management and Marketing: DAWN RAFOOL
Dean for Students: Dr WENDI SANTEE
Registrar: SARA FASEL KANE
Dir of Learning Resource Centre: SHERILL HARRIGER

Library of 95,000 vols and 8,000 periodicals
Number of teachers: 120
Number of students: 1,000

DEANS

School of Business: Prof. Dr CATHY LEWIS-BRIM
School of Education: Prof. Dr BILL RIGEL
School of Ministry, Arts and Sciences: Prof. Dr STEVEN DARR

WEBBER INTERNATIONAL UNIVERSITY

POB 96, Babson Park, FL 33827
1201 N Scenic Highway, Babson Park, FL 33827
Telephone: (836) 638-1431
E-mail: admissions@webber.edu
Internet: www.webber.edu

Founded 1927
Private control
Academic year: June to May (4 semesters)
Offers bachelors in business admin, gen. business studies; masters in business admin.

Pres.: Dr KEITH WADE
Vice-Pres. for Enrolment and Student Record Services: KATHY WILSON
Vice-Pres. for Finance: CHRISTINA JORDON
Vice-Pres. for Institutional Advancement: STEVE WARNER
Academic Dean: Dr CHARLES SHIEH
Dean for Student Life: Dr JOHANNA DE VERTEUIL
Registrar and Dir for Financial Aid: KATHY WILSON
Head Librarian: SUE DUNNING

Number of teachers: 45 (20 full-time, 25 adjunct)
Number of students: 720 (670 undergraduate, 50 graduate)

ABRAHAM BALDWIN AGRICULTURAL COLLEGE

2802 Moore Highway, Tifton, GA 31793-2601
Telephone: (229) 391-5001
E-mail: abacinfo@abac.edu
Internet: www.abac.edu

Founded 1908, present name and status 1933
State control
Academic year: August to July (2 semesters)

Pres.: Dr DAVID C. BRIDGES
Vice-Pres. for Academic Affairs: Dr NILES M. REDDICK
Vice-Pres. for External Affairs and Advancement: KEITH D. BARBER
Dir for Enrolment Management: DONNA WEBB
Library Dir: MARIE DAVIS
Number of students: 3,300

Publication: *Pegasus* (1 a year)

DEANS

School of Agriculture and Natural Resources: Prof. Dr TIMOTHY MARSHALL
School of Business: Prof. Dr JEFF GIBBS
School of Human Sciences: Dr DARBY T. SEWELL
School of Liberal Arts: Prof. Dr BOBBIE ROBINSON
School of Nursing and Health Sciences: Dr WANDA GOLDEN
School of Science and Mathematics: Prof. Dr RAY N. BARBER

AGNES SCOTT COLLEGE

141 E College Ave, Decatur, GA 30030
Telephone: (404) 471-6000
E-mail: admission@agnesscott.edu
Internet: www.agnesscott.edu

Founded 1889
Private control
Academic year: August to May

Depts of Africana studies, anthropology, art and art history, Asian studies, biochemistry and molecular biology, biology, chemistry, classics, economics, education, English, environmental and sustainability studies, film and media studies, French and German, history, human rights, international relations, mathematics, music, neuroscience, philosophy, physical education and athletics, physics and astronomy, political science, psychology, public health, religious studies, sociology and anthropology, Spanish, theatre and dance, women's studies

Pres.: Dr ELIZABETH KISS
Vice-Pres. for Academic Affairs and Dean of College: Prof. Dr CAROLYN J. STEFANCO
Vice-Pres. for Business and Finance: JOHN P. HEGMAN
Vice-Pres. for College Advancement: Dr ROBERT J. PARKER
Vice-Pres. for Enrolment and Dean of Admission: LAURA E. MARTIN
Vice-Pres. for Student Life and Dean of Students: DONNA A. LEE
Dir for Admissions: ALEXA WOOD GAETA
Registrar: GAIL MEIS
Dir of Library Services: ELIZABETH BAGLEY

Library of 236,551 vols, 54,126 ebooks, 26,731 audiovisual items, 40,072 current periodicals
Number of teachers: 100
Number of students: 900

ALBANY STATE UNIVERSITY

504 College Dr., Albany, GA 31705
Telephone: (229) 430-4600
E-mail: enrollmentservices@asurams.edu
Internet: www.asurams.edu

Founded 1903 as Albany Bible and Manual Training Instn, present name and status 1996
Pres.: Dr EVERETTE J. FREEMAN
Vice-Pres. for Academic Affairs: Dr ABIODUN OJEMAKINDE
Vice-Pres. for Fiscal Affairs: LARRY WAKEFIELD
Vice-Pres. for Institutional Advancement: CLIFFORD PORTER
Vice-Pres. for Student Affairs: Dr EDGAR L. BERRY
Dir for Enrolment Services: JAMES BURRELL
Dean for Graduate School: RANI GEORGE
Registrar: ARNA ALBRITTEN
Dir for Library Services: Dr LaVERNE L. McLAUGHLIN
Library of 900,000 vols
Number of teachers: 150 (full-time)
Number of students: 6,700

DEANS

College of Arts and Humanities: Dr LEROY E. BYNUM, JR
College of Business: KATHALEENA MONDS
College of Education: Dr KIMBERLY KING-JUPITER
College of Sciences and Health Professions: JOYCE JOHNSON

ARMSTRONG ATLANTIC STATE UNIVERSITY

11935 Abercorn St, Savannah, GA 31419
Telephone: (912) 344-2576
E-mail: adm-info@armstrong.edu
Internet: www.armstrong.edu
Founded 1935 as Armstrong Jr College, present name and status 1996
State control
Academic year: August to May
Pres.: Dr LINDA M. BLEICKEN
Vice-Pres. for Academic Affairs and Dean of Faculty: Dr ANNE THOMPSON
Vice-Pres. for Advancement: SCOTT JOYNER
Vice-Pres. for Business and Finance: DAVID CARSON
Vice-Pres. for Student Affairs: Dr KEITH BETTS
Registrar: JUDY GINTER
Librarian: DOUG FRAZIER
Library of 200,000 vols, 1,000 journals, 18,000 audiovisual items
Number of teachers: 260 (full-time)
Number of students: 7,500 (6,820 undergraduate, 680 graduate)
Publications: *AMT Marquee* (1 a year), *Calliope*

DEANS

College of Education: Dr PATRICIA WACHHOLZ
College of Health Professions: DONNA BROOKS
College of Liberal Arts: LAURA BARRETT
College of Science and Technology: Dr ROBERT GREGERSON

ART INSTITUTE OF ATLANTA

6600 Peachtree Dunwoody Rd, NE, 100 Embassy Row, Atlanta, GA 30328-1649
Telephone: (770) 394-8300
E-mail: aiaadm@aii.edu
Internet: www.artinstitutes.edu/atlanta
Founded 1949 as Massey Business College, current name adopted 1975
Private control
Academic year: October to September
Br. campuses in Charleston, N Virginia, Tennessee, Virginia Beach, Washington; degree programmes in culinary arts, design, fashion, general education, media arts
Pres.: JO ANN KOCH

Vice-Pres. for Human Resources: JOSELYN C. CASSIDY
Sr Dir for Admissions: JOY McCLURE
Dir for Admin. and Financial Services: CHRIS SCHWARZER
Dean for Academic Affairs: Dr DAN GARLAND
Dean for Student Affairs: Dr APRIL SHAVKIN
Registrar: DIANA HILL
Library Dir: GAYLE MEIER
Library of 40,000 vols, 4,000 video materials, 150 periodicals
Number of teachers: 250
Number of students: 3,300

AUGUSTA STATE UNIVERSITY

2500 Walton Way, Augusta, GA 30904-2200
Telephone: (706) 737-1444
E-mail: admissions@aug.edu
Internet: www.aug.edu
Founded 1783 as Acad. of Richmond County, present name and status 1996
State control
Academic year: August to July
Pres.: Dr WILLIAM A. BLOODWORTH, JR
Vice-Pres. for Academic Affairs: CAROL J. RYCHLY (acting)
Vice-Pres. for Business Operations: THERESE ROSIER
Vice-Pres. for Student Services and Dean of Students: Dr JOYCE A. JONES
Registrar and Dir of Admissions: KATHERINE H. SWEENEY
Library Dir: Dr CAMILLA REID
Library of 435,000 vols incl. 50,000 ebooks
Number of teachers: 200 (full-time)
Number of students: 6,500

DEANS

College of Arts and Sciences: Prof. Dr ROBERT R. PARHAM
College of Education: Prof. Dr GORDON EISENMAN
Hull College of Business Administration: Prof. Dr MARC D. MILLER,
Pamplin College of Arts and Sciences: Dr ROBERT PARHAM (acting)

BAUDER COLLEGE

384 Northyards Blvd, NW, Suites 190 and 400, Atlanta, GA 30313
Telephone: (404) 237-7573
E-mail: admissions@bauder.edu
Internet: atlanta.bauder.edu
Founded 1964
Private control
Programmes in BSc incl. business admin., criminal justice, information technology, paralegal studies
Pres.: Dr CHARLES A. TAYLOR
Head Librarian: MARY KAYE HOOKER
Library of 12,000 vols, 150 journals, 52,000 ebooks

BERRY COLLEGE

2277 Martha Berry Highway, NW, Mount Berry, GA 30149
Telephone: (706) 232-5374
E-mail: admissions@berry.edu
Internet: www.berry.edu
Founded 1902 as Boys' Industrial School
Private control
Academic year: August to August (3 semesters)
Pres.: Dr STEPHEN R. BRIGGS
Provost: Dr KATHERINE M. WHATLEY
Vice-Pres. for Advancement: BETTYANN M. O'NEILL
Vice-Pres. for Enrolment Management: Dr GARY WATERS
Vice-Pres. for Finance: BRIAN ERB

Vice-Pres. for Student Affairs and Dean for Students: DEBBIE E. HEIDA
Dir for Admissions: BRETT E. KENNEDY
Registrar: LINDA A. TENNANT
Library Dir: SHERRE L. HARRINGTON
Library of 700,000 vols incl. print and microform, 1,700 journals, 104,871 govt documents
Number of teachers: 125
Number of students: 2,100 (1,950 undergraduate, 150 graduate)

DEANS

Campbell School of Business: Dr JOHN R. GROUT
Charter School of Education and Human Sciences: Prof. Dr JACQUELINE M. McDOWELL
Evans School of Humanities, Arts and Social Sciences: Prof. Dr THOMAS D. KENNEDY
School of Mathematical and Natural Sciences: Prof. Dr D. BRUCE CONN

BEULAH HEIGHTS UNIVERSITY

POB 18145, 892 Berne St, SE, Atlanta, GA 30316
Telephone: (404) 627-2681
E-mail: admissionsinfo@beulah.org
Internet: www.beulah.org
Founded 1918 as Beulah Heights Bible Institute, present name and status 2006
Private control
Academic year: August to May (3 semesters)
Bachelors of arts in leadership studies, religious studies, masters of business admin., divinity
Pres.: Dr BENSON M. KARANJA
Vice-Pres. for Academic Programme Devt: Dr ANGELITA HOWARD
Vice-Pres. and Dean of Academic Affairs: Dr JAMES B. KEILLER
Vice-Pres. for Finance: TAMMY GUELFO
Vice-Pres. for Student Life and Enrolment Management: SHAWN ADAMS
Registrar: JACQUELYN B. ARMSTRONG
Dir of Admissions: JOHN DREHER
Dir of Library Service: PRADEEP K. DAS
Library of 45,000 vols
Number of teachers: 35
Number of students: 2,100

BRENAU UNIVERSITY

500 Washington St, SE, Gainesville, GA 30501
Telephone: (770) 534-6100
E-mail: admissions@brenau.edu
Internet: www.brenau.edu
Founded 1878 as Georgia Baptist Female Seminary, present name and status 1992
Private control
Academic year: July to August
Campuses in Augusta, Kings Bay, N Atlanta, S Atlanta
Pres.: Dr ED L. SCHRADER
Provost and Vice-Pres. for Academic Affairs: Dr NANCY KRIPPEL
Exec. Vice-Pres. and Chief Financial Officer: Dr WAYNE DEMPSEY
Sr Vice-Pres. for Enrolment Management and Student Services: SCOTT BRIELL
Sr Vice-Pres. for Institutional Devt: JIM BARCO
Vice-Pres. for External Relations: MATT THOMAS
Registrar and Dir of Student Records: BARBARA WILSON
Dean of Library Services: MARLENE GIGUERE
Library of 85,000 vols, 60,000 ebooks, 16,000 ejournals and magazines
Number of students: 2,800
Publication: *The Window* (4 a year)

DEANS

College of Business and Mass Communication: Dr BILL LIGHTFOOT
College of Education: Prof. Dr DAVID L. BARNETT
College of Fine Arts and Humanities: Dr ANDREA BIRCH
College of Health and Science: Prof. Dr GALE HANSEN STARICH
Graduate School: Dr GALE HANSEN STARICH

BREWTON-PARKER COLLEGE

Highway 280, 201 David-Eliza Fountain Circle, POB 197, Mount Vernon, GA 30445
Telephone: (912) 583-2241
E-mail: admissions@bpc.edu
Internet: www.bpc.edu

Founded 1904 as Union Baptist Institute, current name adopted 1978
Private control
Academic year: August to June
Divs of arts and letters, business, education, religion and philosophy
Pres.: Dr MIKE SIMONEAUX
Exec. Vice-Pres.: RANDY MINTON
Vice-Pres. for Academic Services: Dr TIM SEARCY
Vice-Pres. for Enrolment Services: JIM BEALL
Vice-Pres. for Student Services: Dr CHARLIE BASS
Registrar: SARA CROWE
Dir of Library: ANN C. HUGHES
Library of 80,000 vols
Number of teachers: 85 (31 full-time, 54 part-time)
Number of students: 630

Publication: *Oracle* (1 a year)

CLARK ATLANTA UNIVERSITY

223 James P. Brawley, Atlanta, GA 30314-4389
Telephone: (404) 880-8000
E-mail: cauadmissions@cau.edu
Internet: www.cau.edu

Founded 1988 by merger of Atlanta Univ. (f. 1865) and Clark College (f. 1869)
Private control
Academic year: August to July (3 semesters)
Pres.: Dr CARLTON E. BROWN
Provost and Vice-Pres. for Academic Affairs: Dr JOSEPH H. SILVER, SR
Vice-Pres. for Enrolment Services and Student Affairs: Dr CARL E. JONES
Vice-Pres. for Finance and Business Services and Chief Financial Officer: LUCILLE MAUGÉ
Vice-Pres. for Institutional Advancement and Univ. Relations: (vacant)
Vice-Pres. for Research and Sponsored Programmes: Dr MARCUS W. SHUTE
Gen. Counsel: LANCE DUNNINGS
Dean of Graduate Studies: Dr BETTYE CLARK
Dean of Undergraduate Studies: Dr ALEXA B. HENDERSON
Dir of Library Services: LORETTA PARHAM
Library: 1.6m. vols incl. 43,000 ebooks, 867,000 microforms, 314,000 govt documents, 17,000 theses and dissertations, 35,000 bound periodicals, 1,500 current periodicals, 7,000 audiovisual material
Number of teachers: 300 (175 full-time)
Number of students: 3,950 (3,270 undergraduate, 680 graduate)

DEANS

School of Arts and Sciences: Dr SHIRLEY WILLIAMS-KIRKSEY
School of Business Admin.: Prof. Dr LYDIA FLOYD
School of Education: Dr SEAN S. WARNER

Whitney M. Young, Jr School of Social Work: Prof. Dr VIMALA PILLARI

CLAYTON STATE UNIVERSITY

2000 Clayton State Blvd, Morrow, GA 30260
Telephone: (678) 466-4000
E-mail: registrar@clayton.edu
Internet: www.clayton.edu

Founded 1969 as Clayton Jr College, present name and status 2005
State control
Academic year: August to May
Pres.: Prof. Dr THOMAS J. HYNES, JR
Provost and Vice-Pres. for Academic Affairs: Dr MICHEAL CRAFTON
Vice-Pres. for Business and Operations: CORLIS CUMMINGS
Vice-Pres. for External Relations: STEVE STEPHENS
Vice-Pres. for Information Technology and Services: Dr JOHN BRYAN (acting)
Vice-Pres. for Student Affairs: Dr BRIAN HAYNES
Registrar: REBECCA GMEINER
Dean of Library: Dr GORDON N. BAKER
Library of 116,201 vols, 372 journals, 27,693 ebooks
Number of teachers: 210 (195 full-time)
Number of students: 6,900

DEANS

College of Arts and Sciences: Prof. Dr NASSER MOMAYEZI
College of Business: Prof. Dr ALPHONSO OGBUEHI
College of Health: Dr LISA EICHELBERGER
College of Information and Mathematical Sciences: Prof. Dr LILA F. ROBERTS
School of Graduate Studies: GWENDOLYN JONES HAROLD

COLLEGE OF COASTAL GEORGIA

One College Dr., Brunswick, GA 31520
Telephone: (912) 279-5700
E-mail: admiss@ccga.edu
Internet: www.ccga.edu

Founded 1961 as Brunswick College, present name and status 2008
State control
Academic year: August to May (2 semesters)
Pres.: Dr VALERIE A. HEPBURN
Vice-Pres. for Academic Affairs: Dr PHILIP J. MASON
Vice-Pres. for Student Affairs: Dr GERALD KIEL
Vice-Pres. for Business Affairs: JEFF PRESTON
Chief Advancement Officer: ELIZABETH K. WEATHERLY
Chief Information Officer: GERI CHAPMAN CULBREATH
Dir for Admissions and Orientation: (vacant)
Registrar: LISA LESSEIG
Dean of Library Science: DEBORAH HOLMES
Number of teachers: 90
Number of students: 3,500

Publications: *College of Coastal Georgia, Pulse of Camden* (1 a year), *Seaswells* (1 a year)

DEANS

School of Arts, Humanities and Social Sciences: Prof. Dr M. KAREN HAMBRIGHT
School of Business and Public Affairs: Prof. Dr WILLIAM STEWART MOUNTS, JR
School of Education and Teacher Preparation: Dr KENT LAYTON
School of Mathematics and Natural Sciences: Dr KEITH E. BELCHER
School of Nursing and Health Sciences: Dr PATRICIA KRAFT

COLUMBIA THEOLOGICAL SEMINARY

POB 520, Decatur, GA 30031-0520
701 S Columbia Dr., Decatur, GA 30030-4118
Telephone: (404) 378-8821
E-mail: admissions@ctsnet.edu
Internet: www.ctsnet.edu

Founded 1828, current name adopted 1925
Private control
Academic year: September to May
Offers MA in divinity, educational ministry, ministry, practical theology, theological studies, theology
Pres.: Dr STEPHEN A. HAYNER
Exec. Vice-Pres. and Dean of Faculty: Dr DEBORAH F. MULLEN
Vice-Pres. for Business and Finance: J. MARTIN SADLER
Vice-Pres. for Institutional Advancement: DOUG TAYLOR
Dean for Students and Vice-Pres. for Student Services: Dr JOHN E. WHITE
Registrar: MIKE MEDFORD
Dir for Advancement Services: C. J. DRYMON
Library Dir: Dr SARA MYERS
Library of 165,000 vols, 878 current periodicals, 41,000 microforms
Number of teachers: 40
Number of students: 500

Publication: *Journal for Preachers* (4 a year)

COLUMBUS STATE UNIVERSITY

4225 University Ave, Columbus, GA 31907
Telephone: (706) 507-8800
E-mail: pr@colstate.edu
Internet: www.columbusstate.edu

Founded 1958
State control
Academic year: August to June
Pres.: Dr TIMOTHY S. MESCON
Provost and Vice-Pres. for Academic Affairs: Dr TOM HACKETT
Vice-Pres. for Business and Finance: TOM HELTON
Vice-Pres. for Student Affairs and Enrolment Management: Dr GINA L. SHEEKS
Vice-Pres. for Univ. Advancement: REX WHIDDON
Chief Information Officer: ABRAHAM GEORGE
Dean for Students: AARON REESE
Registrar: JOHN BROWN
Dean for Libraries: MARK FLYNN
Library of 375,000 vols, 11,400 multimedia materials, 1.3m. microfilm and microfiche
Number of teachers: 480 (295 full-time, 185 part-time)
Number of students: 8,300

DEANS

College of Arts: Dr RICHARD BAXTER, JR
College of Business and Computer Science: Dr LINDA U. HADLEY
College of Education and Health Professions: Dr BARBARA BUCKNER
College of Letters and Sciences: Dr DAVID J. LANOUE
D. Abbott Turner College of Business and Computer Science: Dr LINDA HADLEY

COVENANT COLLEGE

14049 Scenic Highway, Lookout Mountain, GA 30750-4164
Telephone: (706) 820-1560
E-mail: info@covenant.edu
Internet: www.covenant.edu

Founded 1955
Private control
Academic year: August to May (2 semesters)
Pres.: Dr NIEL NIELSON

Vice-Pres. for Academic Affairs: Dr JEFFREY B. HALL
Vice-Pres. for Advancement: TROY DUBLE
Vice-Pres. for Student Devt and Dean for Students: BRAD VOYLES
Registrar and Dean for Records: RODNEY MILLER
Dir for Admissions and Church Relations: MATTHEW BRYANT
Dir for Library Services: TAD MINDEMAN
Library of 100,000 vols, 90,000 ebooks, 10,000 ejournals, magazines and newspapers
Number of teachers: 60 (full-time)
Number of students: 1,030
Publication: *The View*

DEANS

Education and Social Science: Prof. Dr JAMES L. DREXLER
Humanities: Prof. Dr PAUL J. MORTON
Organizational Management and Instructional Technology: Dr GINNER W. HUDSON
Sciences: Prof. Dr JEROME D. WENGER

DALTON STATE COLLEGE

650 College Dr., Dalton, GA 30720
Telephone: (706) 272-4436
E-mail: admissions@daltonstate.edu
Internet: www.daltonstate.edu
Founded 1963 as Dalton Jr College, present name and status 1998
State control
Academic year: August to May (2 semesters)
Pres.: Dr JOHN O. SCHWENN
Vice-Pres. for Academic Affairs: Dr SANDRA STONE
Vice-Pres. for Enrolment and Student Services: Dr JODI S. JOHNSON
Vice-Pres. for Fiscal Affairs: SCOTT A. BAILEY
Registrar: PATRICIA A. KRESL
Library Dir: LYDIA F. KNIGHT
Library of 135,597 vols, 200 current periodicals, 59,609 ebooks
Number of teachers: 250 (170 full-time, 80 part-time)
Number of students: 5,500

DEANS

School of Business: Prof. Dr DONNA MAYO
School of Education: Prof. Dr CALVIN MEYER
School of Liberal Arts: Prof. Dr MARY NIELSEN
School of Sciences and Mathematics: Dr RANDALL GRIFFUS
School of Nursing: Prof. Dr CORDIA STARLING
School of Social Work: Prof. Dr SPENCER ZEIGER
School of Technology: Prof. Dr CHARLES DAVID JOHNSON

EMMANUEL COLLEGE

POB 129, Franklin Springs, GA 30639-0129
181 Springs St, Franklin Springs, GA 30639
Telephone: (706) 245-2874
E-mail: admissions@ec.edu
Internet: www.ec.edu
Founded 1919 as Franklin Springs Institute; present name and status 1939
Private control
Academic year: August to May (3 semesters)
Pres.: Dr MICHAEL S. STEWART
Vice-Pres. for Academic Affairs: Dr JOHN R. HENZEL
Vice-Pres. for Devt: BRIAN JAMES
Vice-Pres. for Enrolment and Marketing: WENDY D. VINSON
Vice-Pres. for Finance: KEVIN L. CRAWFORD
Vice-Pres. for Student Life: JASON L. CROY
Dean of Students: TIM HARRISON
Registrar: DEBRA F. GRIZZLE

Library Dir: JOY SLIFE
Library of 95,000 vols
Number of students: 800

DEANS

School of Arts and Sciences: Dr LESLIE BOUCHER
School of Business: JENNIFER LESTER-BENSON
School of Christian Ministries: Rev. TRACY REYNOLDS
School of Education: Dr VICKI HOLLINSHEAD

EMORY UNIVERSITY

Atlanta, GA 30322
Telephone: (404) 727-6123
E-mail: admiss@learnlink.emory.edu
Internet: www.emory.edu
Founded 1836 as Emory College, present name and status 1915
Private control
Academic year: August to May
Pres.: JAMES W. WAGNER
Provost and Exec. Vice-Pres. for Academic Affairs: Dr EARL LEWIS
Vice-Provost for Academic Affairs: LISA A. TEDESCO
Exec. Vice-Pres. for Finance and Admin.: MICHAEL J. MANDL
Exec. Vice-Pres. for Health Affairs: Dr S. WRIGHT CAUGHMAN
Sr Vice-Pres. and Gen. Counsel: STEPHEN D. SENCER
Sr Vice-Pres. and Dean of Campus Life: JOHN L. FORD
Sr Vice-Pres. for Devt and Alumni Relations: SUSAN CRUSE
Vice-Pres. and Deputy to the Pres.: Dr GARY S. HAUK
Vice-Pres. and Sec. of the Univ.: Dr ROSEMARY M. MAGEE
Vice-Pres. for Communications and Marketing: RON SAUDER
Vice-Provost and Dean of the Graduate Study: LISA A. TEDESCO
Registrar: TOM MILLEN
Vice-Provost and Dir of Libraries: RICHARD E. LUCE
Library of 3,662,882 vols
Number of teachers: 305 (full-time)
Number of students: 13,900 (12,800 full-time, 1,100 part-time)
Publications: *Academic Exchange* (6 a year), *Emory Bankruptcy Developments Journal* (2 a year), *Emory Health* (4 a year), *Emory International Law Review* (2 a year), *Emory Law Journal* (6 a year), *Emory Lawyer* (2 a year), *Emory Magazine* (4 a year), *Emory Medicine* (3 a year), *Emory Nursing* (2 a year), *Goizueta Business Magazine* (3 a year), *Methodist Review* (1 a year), *New Vico Studies* (1 a year), *Practical Matters*, *Public Health Magazine* (2 a year), *Quadrangle* (2 a year)

DEANS

Candler School of Theology: Prof. Dr JANICE LOVE
Emory College of Arts and Sciences: Prof. Dr ROBIN FORMAN
Goizueta Business School: Prof. Dr LAWRENCE M. BENVENISTE
Graduate School: LISA A. TEDESCO
Nell Hodgson Woodruff School of Nursing: Prof. Dr LINDA A. McCAULEY
Oxford College: Prof. Dr STEPHEN H. BOWEN
Rollins School of Public Health: Dr JAMES W. CURRAN
School of Law: Prof. Dr ROBERT A. SCHAPIRO
School of Medicine: Dr THOMAS J. LAWLEY

PROFESSORS

AABERG, T. M., Ophthalmology
ABRAMOWITZ, A., Political Science

ABRAMOWSKY, C. R., Pathology
ABRAMS, H. E., Law
ADAMSON, W. L., History
AGNEW, R. S., Sociology
ALARCON, R., Psychiatry/Behavioural Sciences
ALAVI, M., Information Strategy
ALBRECHT, T. E., Music
ALDRIDGE, D. P., Sociology
ALEXANDER, F. S., Law
ALEXANDER, G. E., Neurology
ALEXANDER, R. W., Medicine
ALLITT, P., History
AN-NA'IM, A., Law
ANSARI, A. A., Pathology
ANSEL, J. C., Dermatology
ARMELAGOS, G., Anthropology
ARTHUR, T. C., Law
AUSTIN, H., Epidemiology
BAJAJ, K., Physics
BARLETT, P., Anthropology
BARON, M., Radiology
BARROW, D., Neurosurgery
BARSALOU, L., Psychology
BAUERLEIN, M., English
BAUMGARTNER, B. R., Radiology
BEARD, L., Accounting
BECKER, E. R., Health Policy and Management
BEDERMAN, D. J., Law
BEIK, W., History
BENSTON, G. J., Finance
BERMAN, H. J., Law
BERNSTEIN, A., Law
BERNSTEIN, K. E., Pathology
BERRY, A. J., Anaesthesiology
BESSEMBINDER, H., Finance
BLACK, M., Political Science
BLAKE, D. A., Pharmacology
BLUMENTHAL, D. R., Judaic Studies
BONDI, R. C., Church History
BONNEFIS, P., French and Italian
BOOTHE, R., Psychology
BORING, J. R., III, Epidemiology
BOSS, J., Microbiology/Immunology
BOSTWICK, J., III, Plastic Surgery
BOSWELL, T. E., Sociology
BRACHMAN, P., International Health
BRAITHWAITE, R., Behavioural Science and Health Education
BRANCH, W. T., General Medicine
BRANN, A. W., Neurology, Paediatrics
BRIGHT, D. F., Classics and Comparative Literature
BROGAN, D. J., Biostatistics
BROWN, P. J., Anthropology
BROWN, W. V., Medicine (Lipids)
BROWNLEY, M. W., English
BRYAN, J. A., Pathology
BUGGE, J. M., English
BUSS, M. J., Religion
BUZBEE, W., Law
CALABRESE, R., Biology
CARNEY, W. J., Law
CARPENTER, L., English
CARR, D., Philosophy
CARTER, E. B., Biology
CARUTH, C., English
CASARELLA, W. J., Radiology
CATLIN, P. A., Rehabilitation Medicine
CAUGHMAN, S. W., Dermatology
CHAKRABORTY, H., Biostatistics
CHEN, R. L., Physics
CHENG, X., Biochemistry
CHIMOWITZ, M. I., Neurology
CHIRINKO, R., Economics
CHOPP, R., Systematic Theology
CHURCH, R., Ophthalmology
CLEMENTS, S. D., Cardiology
CLOUD, A. M., Law
COHEN, C., Pathology
COLE, J. A., Anthropology
COMPANS, R. W., Microbiology/Immunology
CONN, D. L., Rheumatology
CONN, P. J., Pharmacology
COOK, D. A., Film Studies

COOPER, R., Practice of Cost Management, Accounting
COPE, T., Physiology
CORNISH, J. D., Paediatrics
COURTRIGHT, P., Asian Studies
CRAVER, J. M., Cardiothoracic Surgery
CURRAN, J. M., Public Health
DANNER, D. J., Genetics
DAVIS, D. C., Medicine
DAVIS, L. W., Oncology
DAVIS, M., Psychiatry/Behavioural Sciences
DAVIS, P., Radiology
DE WAAL, F. B. M., Psychology, Primate Behaviour
DEANGRADE, J. R., Orthopaedics
DECONCINI, B., Religion
DELONG, M. R., Neurology
DICLEMENTE, R. J., Behavioural Science and Health Education
DIGIROLAMO, M., Medicine (Geriatrics)
DILORIO, C., Behavioural Science and Health Education
DINGLEDINE, R. J., Pharmacology
DOERNBERG, R. L., International Legal Studies
DOETSCH, P., Biochemistry
DONHAM, D. L., Anthropology
DOUGLAS, J. S., Medicine (Cardiology)
DUFFUS, D. A., Mathematic and Computer Science
DUKE, M., Psychology
DUNBAR, S., Adult and Elder Health
DUNCAN, M., Law
EATON, D. C., Physiology
ECKMAN, J. R., Haematology/Oncology
EDELHAUSER, H., Ophthalmology
EDMONDSON, D. E., Biochemistry
ELMER, W. A., Biology
ELSAS, L. J., II, Medical Genetics, Paediatrics
EMORY, E., Psychology
ENGELHARD, G., Educational Studies
ENGLAND, P., Physical Education
ENGLISH, A. W., Cell Biology
EPSTEIN, M., Russian and East Asian Languages and Culture
FALEK, A., Psychiatry/Behavioural Sciences
FAMILY, F., Physics
FARLEY, M. M., Infectious Diseases
FELICIANO, D. V., Surgery, Trauma/Critical Care
FELNER, J. M., Medicine (Cardiology)
FINK, A. S., General Surgery
FINNERTY, V. M., Biology
FIVUSH, R., Psychology
FLANDERS, W. D., Epidemiology
FLANNERY, J., Performing Arts
FLEMING, L. L., Orthopaedics
FLYNN, T. R., Philosophy
FONG, P., Physics
FOSTER, F. S., English
FOTION, N., Philosophy
FOWLER, J., Theology
FOX-GENOVESE, E., History
FRANCH, R., Medicine (Cardiology)
FRANKEL, B., Psychiatry/Behavioural Sciences
FREER, R. D., Law
FYFE, D., Paediatrics
GARCIA, E. V., Radiology
GARROW, D. J., Law
GELLER, R. J., Paediatrics
GIDDENS, D., Medical School Administration
GILES, M. W., Political Science
GOLDSMITH, D., Chemistry
GOODING, L. R., Microbiology/Immunology
GOODMAN, M., Radiology
GOULD, K., Primate Research
GOULD, R., Mathematic and Computer Science
GOUZOULES, H., Psychology
GOZANSKY, N. E., Law
GRAVANIS, M. B., Pathology
GREENAMYRE, T. J., Neurology
GREENE, D. K., History
GRIFFIN, J. B., Psychiatry/Behavioural Sciences

GRINDON, A. J., Pathology
GROSSNIKLAUS, H., Ophthalmology
GRUBER, W., English
GUNN, R. B., Physiology
GUNNEMANN, J., Social Ethics, Theology
GUTTERMAN, M., Law
GUTTIERREZ-MOUAT, R., Spanish
GUYTON, R., Cardiothoracic Surgery
HABER, M. J., Biostatistics
HAHN, C., Educational Studies
HALLORAN, M. E., Biostatistics
HANSON, S. R., Biomedical Engineering
HARARI, J., French and Italian
HARTGRAVES, A., Accounting
HARTLE, A., Philosophy
HARTZELL, H. C., Cell Biology
HATCHER, R. A., Gynaecology/Obstetrics
HAY, P., Law
HAYES, J. H., Theology (Old Testament)
HEAVEN, M., Chemistry
HERMAN, C., Pathology
HERRON, C., French and Italian
HICKS, A., Sociology
HILL, C. L., Chemistry
HOGUE, C., Epidemiology
HOLIFIELD, E. B., Theology
HOLLADAY, C. R., Theology (New Testament)
HOLLAND, B., Psychiatry/Behavioural Sciences
HOLTZMAN, S. G., Pharmacology
HOPKINS, L. C., Neurology
HOROWITZ, I. R., Gynaecology/Obstetrics
HUDSON, T., Radiology
HUG, C. C., Academic Affairs
HUMPHREY, D. R., Physiology
HUNTER, H. O., Law
HUNTER, R. J., Theology
HUTTON, W. C., Orthopaedics
HUYNH, B. H., Physics
INSEL, T. R., Psychiatry/Behavioural Sciences
IRVINE, J., Educational Studies
IUVONE, P. M., Pharmacology
JAFFE, S. L., Psychiatry/Behavioural Sciences
JENSEN, P., Pathology
JINKS-ROBERTSON, S., Biology
JOHNSON, L. T., Theology
JOHNSON, R., Chemistry
JOHNSON, T. C., Health, Physical Education and Dance
JOHNSTON, J. H., English
JONES, D. P., Biochemistry
JONES, E., Cardiothoracic Surgery
JONES, G., Biology
JORDAN, M., Religion
JOSEPH, R., Political Science
JOYNER, R. W., Paediatrics
JUDOVITZ, D., French and Italian
JUSTICE, J. B., Chemistry
KAHN, R. A., Biochemistry
KALAIDJIAN, W., English
KANTER, K. R., Cardiothoracic Surgery
KAPP, J., Ophthalmology
KARP, I., Liberal Arts, African Studies
KASLOW, N., Psychiatry/Behavioural Sciences
KAUFMAN, M. J., Chemistry
KAUFMAN, S., Radiology
KELLER, J. W., Radiation Oncology
KELLERMANN, A., Emergency Medicine
KERTZ, C. L., Accounting
KINKADE, J. M., Biochemistry
KLEHR, H., Politics and History
KLEIN, L., Gynaecology/Obstetrics
KLEINBAUM, D., Epidemiology
KLUGMAN, K. P., International Health
KNAUFT, B. M., Anthropology
KOHLI, A., Marketing
KONNER, M. J., Anthropology
KONSYNSKI, B., Business
KOVAC, S. R., Gynaecology/Obstetrics
KUHAR, M. J., Pharmacology
KULL, A., Law
KUSHNER, H., Science and Society
KUTNER, M., Biostatistics
KUTNER, N., Rehabilitation Medicine
LAMBETH, J. D., Biochemistry

LANGBERG, J. J., Cardiology, Electrophysiology
LAUER, S., Oncology, Paediatrics
LAWLEY, T. J., Medical School Administration
LAWRENCE, E. C., Medicine
LESSER, J., History, Latin American and Caribbean Studies
LETZ, R., Behavioural Science and Health Education
LEVEY, A. I., Neurology
LEVIN, B., Biology
LEVINSON, R. M., Medicine
LEVY, R., Psychiatry/Behavioural Sciences
LEWIS, W., Pathology
LIEBESKIND, L. S., Chemistry
LIN, M. C., Physical Chemistry
LINVILLE, K. B., Academic Affairs
LIOTTA, D. C., Chemistry
LIPSTADT, D., Judaic Studies
LIVINGSTON, D., Philosophy
LOLLAR, J. S., Haematology/Oncology
LONG, R. A., African Studies
LONG, T., Theology
LONGINI, I. M., Biostatistics
LOWE, W. J., Theology
LUCCHESI, J., Biology
LUSKIN, M. B., Cell Biology
LUTZ, L. J., Family and Preventive Medicine
LYNN, D., Chemistry
MABERLY, G., International Health
MCCAREY, B. E., Ophthalmology
MCCAULEY, R., Philosophy
MCDOWELL, J. J., Psychology
MCGINLEY, P. H., Radiation/Oncology
MCGOWAN, J. E., Epidemiology
MACON, E. J., Medicine
MCQUAIDE, M. M., Sociology
MADARA, J. L., Pathology
MAHAVIER, W. S., Mathematics and Computer Science
MAJMUDAR, B., Pathology
MAKKREEL, R. A., Philosophy
MANDELL, A. J., Psychiatry/Behavioural Sciences
MANSOUR, K., Cardiothoracic Surgery
MARSHALL, F. F., Urology
MARTIN, L. G., Radiology
MARTIN, R. C., Religion
MARTORELL, R., International Health
MARZILLI, L. G., Chemistry
MATTOX, D. E., Otolaryngology
MAYTON, W. T., Law
MEINERT, W. J., Family and Preventive Medicine
MERRILL, A. H., Biochemistry
MILLER, J. I., Cardiothoracic Surgery
MILLER, M., Law
MILLER, S. B., General Medicine
MINNEMAN, K. P., Pharmacology
MITCH, W. E., Medicine (Renal)
MOHANTY, J. N., Philosophy
MORAN, C., Microbiology/Immunology
MORGAN, E. T., Pharmacology
MOROKUMA, K., Chemistry
MORRIS, D. C., Cardiology
MURRAY, J., Adult and Elder Health
MUTH, R. D., Economics
NAHMIAS, A. J., Infectious Diseases, Paediatrics
NASSAR, V. H., Pathology
NAURIGHT, L. P., Adult and Elder Health
NEILL, D. B., Psychology
NEMEROFF, C., Psychiatry/Behavioural Sciences
NEWBY, G., Middle Eastern Studies
NEWSOM, C. A., Old Testament
NEYLAN, J. F., Medicine
NICHOLS, T. R., Physiology
NOE, B., Cell Biology
NOWICKI, S., Psychology
O'DAY, G. R., Theology
OLIKER, V., Mathematics and Computer Science
OLIVER, H. P., Religion
O'SHEA, H. S., Adult and Elder Health
OUSLANDER, J. G., Geriatric Medicine

PACKARD, R., International Health, History
PADWA, A., Chemistry
PARTIN, C., Health, Physical Education and Dance
PASCAL, R. R., Pathology
PASTOR, R., International Relations/Political Science
PATTERSON, R., Philosophy
PATTERSON, R. E., Cardiology
PEDERSON, L., English
PENNELL, J. N., Law
PERKOWITZ, S., Physics
PESKOWITZ, M., Religion
PETERSEN, K. W., Cell Biology
PETTIGREW, R., Radiology
PHILLIPS, L. S., Endocrinology
PINTER, M., Physiology
PLOTSKY, P. M., Psychiatry/Behavioural Sciences
PLUMMER, A., Medicine
POHL, J., Medicine
POLING, C. V., Art History
POLLET, R. J., Medicine
POMERANTZ, G., Journalism
POWELL, M. L., Nursing
POWNALL, G., Accounting
RAMBUSS, R., English
RAMOS, H. S., General Medicine
RANDALL, H. W., Gynaecology/Obstetrics
REAL, L., Biology
RECTOR, A. M., Law
REED, W. L., English
REMINGTON, T. F., Political Science
RICHEY, R., Theology
RICKETTS, R., Surgery, Paediatrics
RIMLAND, D., Infectious Diseases
ROARK, J., History
ROBBINS, V., Religion
ROCHAT, P., Psychology
ROCK, J. A., Gynaecology/Obstetrics
RODL, V., Mathematics and Computer Science
ROSENBERG, A., Psychiatry/Behavioural Sciences
ROTHENBERG, R. B., Family and Preventive Medicine
RUBIN, P. H., Economics
RUBINSON, R., Sociology
RUSCHE, H., English
RYAN, P. B., Environmental and Occupational Health
SALAM, A., Surgery (Vascular)
SALE, W. S., Cell Biology
SALIERS, D. E., Theology
SALMON, M. E., Nursing
SALTMAN, R. B., Health Policy and Management
SANDS, J. M., Medicine
SARAL, R., Medicine
SCHAFFER, B. K., Economics
SCHINAZI, R. F., Paediatrics
SCHISLER, C., Music History
SCHMID, R., Mathematics and Computer Science
SCHUCHARD, R., English
SCOTT, J., Cell Biology
SCOTT, J. R., Microbiology/Immunology
SEBEL, P., Anaesthesiology
SEWELL, C. W., Pathology
SHAFER, W. M., Microbiology/Immunology
SHANOR, C. A., Law
SHAPIRO, M. M., Psychology
SHAPIRO, W., Political Science
SHAPPELL, R., Physical Education
SHARP, E., Nursing
SHERMAN, S., Genetics
SHETH, J., Marketing
SHORE, B., Anthropology
SHULMAN, J. A., Medicine
SHURE, D., Biology
SIDELL, N., Gynaecology/Obstetrics
SILVERMAN, M. E., Medicine
SIMONS, J. W., Medicine
SITTER, J. E., English
SKANDALAKIS, J. E., Surgical Anatomy and Techniques

SLATER, N. W., Classics
SMITH, G. R., Law
SMITH, K., Haematology/Oncology
SMITH, L. E., Theology
SMITH, R. B., III, Surgery
SNAREY, J., Human Development and Ethics, Psychology
SOCOLOW, S. M., History, Latin American and Caribbean Studies
SOLOMON, A. R., Dermatology
SPITZNAGEL, J. K., Microbiology/Immunology
SPRAWLS, P., Radiological Services
SRIVASTAVA, R., Marketing
STEIN, D., Emergency Medicine
STEIN, D. G., Psychology
STEIN, K. W., Middle East Research
STERK, C. E., Behavioural Science and Health Education
STERN, B. J., Neurology
STERNBERG, P., Ophthalmology
STOKES, D., Biology
STONE, J., Medicine
STRICKLAND, O., Nursing
STULTING, R. D., Ophthalmology
SUNDERAM, V. S., Mathematics and Computer Science
SUNG, Y. F., Anaesthesiology
SYBERS, R. G., Radiology
SYMBAS, P., Cardiothoracic Surgery
TARCAN, Y., Radiology
TAYLOR, A., Nuclear Medicine, Radiology
TERRELL, T. P., Law
THOMAS, L.-G., III, Business Organization and Management
THORPE, K. E., Health Policy and Management
TIPTON, S. M., Theology
TORRES, W. E., Radiology
TUNE, L., Psychiatry/Behavioural Sciences
TUSA, R., Neurology
VAN DER VYVER, J., International Law
VANDALL, F. J., Law
VARADY, T., Law
VERENE, D. P., III, Philosophy
VINTEN-JOHANSEN, J., Cardiothoracic Surgery
VON WURTTEMBERG, A., Sanskrit
WAINER, B. E., Pathology, Geriatric Medicine
WALKER, E., Psychology
WALKER, H. K., Medicine
WALKER, T. G., Political Science
WALLEN, K., Psychology, Primate Research
WALLER, J. L., Anaesthesiology
WALTER, P. F., Medicine
WALTMAN, P., Mathematics and Computer Science
WARING, G. O., Ophthalmology
WARREN, S., Genetics
WATTS, N. B., Endocrinology
WATTS, R. L., Neurology
WAYMIRE, G., Marketing
WEATHERS, D. R., Pathology
WEBER, C. J., General Surgery
WEINTRAUB, W. S., Medicine
WEISS, B., Pathology
WEISS, J., Psychiatry/Behavioural Sciences
WEISS, S. A., Pathology
WENGER, N. K., Medicine
WHITE, D. F., Liberal Arts
WHITE, S., History
WHITESIDES, T. E., Orthopaedics
WILCOX, W. D., Paediatrics
WILKINSON, K. D., Biochemistry
WILLIAMS, W. H., Cardiothoracic Surgery
WILSON, M., Primate Research
WINOGRAD, E., Psychology
WITTE, J., Law
WOLF, S. L., Rehabilitation Medicine
WOOD, J. G., Cell Biology
WOOD, W. C., Surgical Oncology
WORKOWSKI, K. A., Infectious Diseases
WORTHMAN, C., Anthropology
YOUNG, J., Epidemiology
YOUNG, L., Physiology
ZAIDAN, J. R., Anaesthesiology
ZIEGLER, H. K., Microbiology/Immunology
ZUMPE, D., Psychiatry/Behavioural Sciences

FORT VALLEY STATE UNIVERSITY

1005 State University Dr., Fort Valley, GA 31030-4313

Telephone: (478) 825-6211
E-mail: registrar1@fvsu.edu
Internet: www.fvsu.edu

Founded 1895 as Fort Valley High and Industrial School, present name and status 1996
State control
Academic year: July to June

Pres.: Prof. Dr LARRY EUGENE RIVERS
Exec. Vice-Pres. and Chief Legal Officer: Dr CANTER BROWN
Vice-Pres. for Academic Affairs: Dr JULIUS SCIPIO
Vice-Pres. for Business and Finance: HENRY SPINKS
Vice-Pres. for External Affairs: Dr MELODY L. CARTER
Vice-Pres. for Student Affairs and Enrolment Management: WILLIE L. WILLIAMS
Dir of Admissions: DONAVON COLEY
Registrar: SHAREE J. LAWRENCE
Librarian: Dr ANNIE M. PAYTON

Library of 191,806 vols
Number of teachers: 200 (150 full-time, 50 part-time)
Number of students: 3,500

DEANS

College of Agriculture, Family Sciences and Technology: Dr GOVINDARAJAN KANNAN
College of Arts and Sciences: Dr B. KEITH MURPHY
College of Education: Dr EDWARD HILL
College of Graduate Studies and Extended Education: Dr ANNA R. HOLLOWAY

GAINESVILLE STATE COLLEGE

POB 1358, Gainesville, GA 30503
3820 Mundy Mill Rd, Oakwood, GA 30566

Telephone: (678) 717-3639
E-mail: info@gsc.edu
Internet: www.gsc.edu

Founded 1966 as Gainesville Jr College, present name and status 2005
State control

Campus in Oconee

Pres.: Dr MARTHA T. NESBITT
Vice-Pres. and CEO for Oconee Campus: Dr MARGARET VENABLE
Vice-Pres. for Academic Affairs: Dr AL PANU
Vice-Pres. for Business and Finance: PAUL GLASER
Vice-Pres. for Institutional Advancement: MARY TRANSUE
Vice-Pres. for Student Affairs: Dr TOM G. WALTER
Chief Information Officer: BRANDON E. HAAG
Dean of Students and Assoc. Vice-Pres.: ALICIA CAUDILL
Registrar: JANICE C. HARTSOE
Dean of Libraries: Dr DEBORAH PROSSER
Number of students: 8,600 (5,250 full-time, 3,350 part-time)

DEANS

School of Business, Education, Health and Wellness: Dr MARYELLEN S. COSGROVE
School of Humanities and Fine Arts: Prof. Dr ERIC SKIPPER
School of Science, Technology, Engineering and Mathematics: Dr DANNY LAU (acting)
School of Social Sciences: Dr H. LEE CHEEK, JR

GEORGIA COLLEGE AND STATE UNIVERSITY

231 W Hancock St, Milledgeville, GA 31061
Telephone: (478) 445-5004

E-mail: admissions@gcsu.edu

Internet: www.gcsu.edu

Founded 1889 as Georgia Normal and Industrial College, present name and status 1996

State control

Pres.: Dr STANLEY PRECZEWSKI

Provost and Vice-Pres. for Academic Affairs: Dr SANDRA JORDAN

Gen. Counsel: MARC CARDINALLI

Vice-Pres. for Admin. and Operations: Dr PAUL JONES

Vice-Pres. for External Relations and Univ. Advancement: AMY AMASON

Vice-Pres. for Institutional Research and Enrolment Management: Dr PAUL JONES

Vice-Pres. for Student Affairs and Dean for Students: Dr BRUCE HARSHBARGER

Dir of Libraries: NANCY DAVIS BRAY

Library of 200,000 vols, 37,118 journals, 37,920 federal documents, 23,500 print and electronic periodicals, partial depository for US govt documents

Number of teachers: 320 (full-time)

Number of students: 6,750 (5,725 undergraduate, 1,025 graduate)

DEANS

College of Arts and Sciences: KENNETH J. PROCTER

College of Health Sciences: Dr SANDRA GANGSTEAD

J. Whitney Bunting College of Business: Dr MATTHEW LIAO-TROTH

John H. Lounsbury College of Education: Dr JANE HINSON

GEORGIA HEALTH SCIENCES UNIVERSITY

1120 15th St, Augusta, GA 30912

Telephone: (706) 721-0211

E-mail: admissions@georgiahealth.edu

Internet: www.georgiahealth.edu

Founded 1828 as Medical Academy of Georgia, current name adopted 2011

State control

Pres.: Dr RICARDO AZZIZ

Provost and Exec. Vice-Pres. for Academic Affairs: Dr GRETCHEN CAUGHMAN

Sr Vice-Pres. for Admin. and Chief Admin. Officer: Dr WILLIAM BOWES

Sr Vice-Pres. for Advancement and Community Relations and Chief Devt Officer: SUSAN L. BARCUS

Sr Vice-Pres. for Finance and Chief Financial Officer: DENNIS ROEMER

Sr Vice-Pres. for Research: Dr MARK HAMRICK

Vice-Pres. for Institutional Effectiveness: BETH BRIGDON

Vice-Pres. for Instruction and Enrolment Management and Assoc. Provost: Dr ROMAN CIBIRKA

Vice-Pres. for Student Services and Devt: KEVIN FRAZIER

Chief Information Officer: HELEN THOMPSON

Registrar: HEATHER METRESS, RITA GARNER

Dir for Libraries: Prof. Dr DAVID KING

Library of 164,984 vols, 4,000 periodicals

Number of teachers: 1,030 (650 full-time)

Number of students: 2,500

Publications: *GHSU Today Magazine* (3 a year), *MCG Tomorrow* (1 a year), *Scope, Word of Mouth Magazine* (3 a year)

DEANS

College of Allied Health Sciences: Prof. Dr ANDREW BALAS

College of Dental Medicine: Dr CONNIE L. DRISKO

College of Graduate Studies: Dr EDWARD INSCHO

College of Nursing: Prof. Dr LUCY MARION

Medical College of Georgia: Dr PETER F. BUCKLEY

GEORGIA INSTITUTE OF TECHNOLOGY

225 North Ave NW, Atlanta, GA 30332

Telephone: (404) 894-2000

Internet: www.gatech.edu

Founded 1885, current name adopted 1948

State control

Academic year: August to May

Pres.: Dr G. P. PETERSON

Provost and Exec. Vice-Pres. for Academic Affairs: Dr RAFAEL L. BRAS

Sr Vice Provost for Academic Affairs: ANDERSON D. SMITH

Exec. Vice-Pres. for Admin. and Finance: STEVEN G. SWANT

Exec. Vice-Pres. for Research: Dr STEPHEN E. CROSS

Vice-Pres. for Devt: BARRETT H. CARSON

Vice-Pres. for Institute Diversity: Dr ARCHIE W. ERVIN

Vice-Pres. for Student Affairs: Dr WILLIAM D. SCHAFER

Exec. Dir of Govt and Community Relations: DENE H. SHEHEANE

Registrar: RETA PIKOWSKY

Dean of Libraries: CATHERINE MURRARY-RUST

Library of 2,549,845 vols (incl. books, serial backfiles and govt documents), 4,668,536 microforms, 325,350 audiovisual materials, 46,017 current serial subscriptions

Number of teachers: 1,100

Number of students: 21,000

Publications: *Blue Print, Research Horizons, The Technique*

DEANS

College of Architecture: Prof. ALAN BALFOUR

College of Computing: Prof. ZVI GALIL

College of Engineering: Prof. GARY S. MAY

College of Management: Prof. STEVE SALBU

College of Sciences: Prof. Dr PAUL HOUSTON

Ivan Allen College of Liberal Arts: Prof. JACQUELINE JONES-ROYSTER

GEORGIA SOUTHERN UNIVERSITY

POB 8024, Statesboro, GA 30460

1332 S Dr., Statesboro, GA 30458

Telephone: (912) 478-4636

E-mail: admissions@georigasouthern.edu

Internet: www.georgiasouthern.edu

Founded 1906

State control

Academic year: August to July

Pres.: Prof. Dr BROOKS A. KEEL

Provost: Dr WILLIAM T. MOORE

Vice-Pres. for Business and Finance: Dr RONALD J. CORE

Vice-Pres. for Research: Dr CHARLES E. PATTERSON

Vice-Pres. for Student Affairs and Enrolment Management: Dr TERESA ELAINE THOMPSON

Vice-Pres. for Univ. Advancement: SALINDA ARTHUR

Registrar: T. MICHAEL DEAL

Dean of the Library: W. BEDE MITCHELL

Library of 1,579,038 vols incl. 761,163 govt documents, 896,011 microforms

Number of teachers: 785 (750 full-time)

Number of students: 19,700 (17,050 undergraduate, 2,650 graduate)

DEANS

Allen E. Paulson College of Science and Technology: Dr BRET DANILOWICZ

College of Business Administration: Dr RONALD SHIFFLER

College of Education: Dr THOMAS R. KOBALLA, JR

College of Engineering and Information Technology: MUHAMMAD DAVOUD

College of Health and Human Sciences: Prof. Dr JEAN BARTELS

College of Liberal Arts and Social Sciences: Dr MICHAEL R. SMITH

Jack N. Averitt College of Graduate Studies: Dr CHARLES PATTERSON

Jiann-Ping Hsu College of Public Health: Prof. Dr LYNN D. WOODHOUSE

GEORGIA SOUTHWESTERN STATE UNIVERSITY

800 GSW State Univ. Dr., Americus, GA 31709

Telephone: (229) 928-1273

E-mail: gswapps@canes.gsw.edu

Internet: www.gsw.edu

Founded 1906 as Third Agricultural and Mechanical School, current name adopted 1996

State control

Academic year: August to May

Pres.: Dr KENDALL BLANCHARD

Vice-Pres. for Academic Affairs and Dean of Faculty: Dr BRIAN U. ADLER

Vice-Pres. for Business and Finance: W. CODY KING

Vice-Pres. for Enrolment Management: Dr GAYE S. HAYES

Vice-Pres. for Student Affairs: Dr SAMUEL T. MILLER

Vice-Pres. for Univ. Relations: (vacant)

Registrar: KRISTA SMITH

Dean of the Library: VERA J. WEISSKOPF

Library of 190,000 vols

Number of teachers: 110

Number of students: 3,050 (2,815 undergraduate, 235 graduate)

DEANS

College of Arts and Sciences: Dr KELLY McCOY

School of Business Administration: Dr LIZ WILSON

School of Computing and Mathematics: Dr BORIS V. PELTSVERGER

School of Education: Prof. Dr LETTIE J. WATFORD

School of Nursing: Prof. Dr SANDRA DANIEL

GEORGIA STATE UNIVERSITY

POB 3965, Atlanta, GA 30302-3965

Telephone: (404) 651-2500

E-mail: admissions@gsu.edu

Internet: www.gsu.edu

Founded 1913

State control

Academic year: August to May

Pres.: Dr MARK P. BECKER

Provost and Sr Vice-Pres. for Academic Affairs: Dr RISA PALM

Sr Vice-Pres. for Finance and Admin.: JERRY RACKLIFFE

Vice-Pres. for Devt: WALTER MASSEY

Vice-Pres. for Research and Economic Devt: JAMES WEYHENMEYER

Vice-Pres. for Student Affairs: Dr DOUGLASS F. COVEY

Registrar: SHARI PIOTROWSKI SCHWARTZ

Dean of Libraries: NANCY H. SEAMANS

Library of 3,444,343 vols

Number of teachers: 1,140 (full-time)

Number of students: 32,000

Publications: *GSU Magazine* (4 a year), *Health and Human Review* (2 a year), *Law Review* (4 a year), *State of Business Magazine* (2 a year), *The Forecast for the Nation* (4 a year)

DEANS

Andrew Young School of Policy Studies: MARY BETH WALKER (acting)

Byrdine F. Lewis School of Nursing and Health Professions: Dr MARGARET C. WILMOTH

College of Arts and Sciences: Dr WILLIAM J. LONG

College of Education: Prof. Dr RANDY W. KAMPHAUS

College of Law: Dr PAUL ALBERTO (acting)

Honors College: Dr LARRY BERMAN

J. Mack Robinson College of Business: (vacant)

GORDON COLLEGE

419 College Dr., Barnesville, GA 30204

Telephone: (678) 359-5555

E-mail: gordon@gdn.edu

Internet: www.gdn.edu

Founded 1852 as Barnesville Male and Female High School, present name and status 2006

State control

Academic divs incl. business and social science, humanities, mathematics and natural sciences, nursing and health sciences, teacher education

Pres.: Dr MAX BURNS

Vice-Pres. for Academic Affairs: ED WHEELER

Vice-Pres. for Business Affairs: Dr LEE FRUITTICHER

Vice-Pres. for Institutional Advancement: RHONDA TOON

Vice-Pres. for Student Affairs: Dr DENNIS R. CHAMBERLAIN

Dir for Admissions: BENNETT FERGUSON

Registrar: JANET BARRAS

Library Dir: NANCY ANDERSON

Library of 102,757 vols, 27,417 ebooks, 9,637 microfilms, 4,785 audiovisual materials

Number of teachers: 230 (115 full-time, 115 part-time)

Number of students: 5,000

INTERDENOMINATIONAL THEOLOGICAL CENTER

700 Martin Luther King, Jr Dr., SW, Atlanta, GA 303144143

Telephone: (404) 527-7700

E-mail: info@itc.edu

Internet: www.itc.edu

Founded 1958

Private control

Academic year: September to May

Pres.: Rev. Dr RONALD EDWARD PETERS

Provost and Exec. Vice-Pres. for Academic Services: Dr TEMBA MAFICO

Vice-Pres. for Financial and Admin. Services: ELIZABETH LITTLEJOHN

Dir of Institutional Advacement: Dr GEORGE THOMPSON

Registrar: BOBBIE HALL

Library Dir: LORETTA PARHAM

Library of 383,000 vols, 43,000 ebooks, 867,000 microforms, 3,14,000 govt documents, 17,000 theses and dissertations, 35,000 bound periodicals, 1,500 current periodical subscriptions

Publications: *Journal of the Interdenominational Theological Center* (2 a year), *The Lantern* (1 a year)

DEANS

Charles H. Mason Theological Seminary: HAROLD D BENNETT

Gammon Theological Seminary: ALBERT MOSLEY

Johnson C. Smith Theological Seminary: PAUL T. ROBERTS

Morehouse School of Religion: G. MARTIN YOUNG

Phillips School Of Theology: MARVIN FRANK THOMAS

Turner Theological Seminary: JOHN FRANK GREEN

KENNESAW STATE UNIVERSITY

1000 Chastain Rd, Kennesaw, GA 30144

Telephone: (770) 423-6000

E-mail: ksuadmit@kennesaw.edu

Internet: www.kennesaw.edu

Founded 1966 as Kennesaw Jr College, current name adopted 1996

State control

Academic year: August to May

Pres.: Dr DANIEL S. PAPP

Provost and Vice-Pres. for Academic Affairs: Prof. Dr WILLIAM KEN HARMON

Vice-Pres. for External Affairs: ARLETHIA PERRY-JOHNSON

Vice-Pres. for Research and Dean of Graduate Studies: Dr CHARLES AMLANER

Vice-Pres. for Student Success: Dr JEROME RATCHFORD

Vice-Pres. for Univ. Advancement: JOE MEEKS

Registrar and Assoc. Vice-Pres. for Enrolment Services: KIM WEST

Library Dir: BETTY CHILDRES

Library of 600,000 vols and govt publs

Number of teachers: 1,280 (740 full-time, 540 part-time)

Number of students: 23,450 (21,465 undergraduate, 1,985 graduate)

DEANS

Bagwell College of Education: Dr ARLINDA J. EATON

Coles College of Business: Dr KATHY SCHWAIG

College of Continuing and Professional Education: BARBARA S. CALHOUN

College of Health and Human Services: Dr RICHARD L. SOWELL

College of Humanities and Social Sciences: Dr RICHARD VENGROFF

College of Science and Mathematics: Prof. Dr RONALD H. MATSON

College of the Arts: Prof. JOSEPH D. MEEKS

University College: Prof. Dr RALPH J. RASCATI

LAGRANGE COLLEGE

601 Broad St, LaGrange, GA 30240-2999

Telephone: (706) 880-8000

Internet: www.lagrange.edu

Founded 1831, current name adopted 1934

Private control

Academic year: September to May

Major areas of study incl. accountancy, art and design, biochemistry, biology, business management, chemistry, computer science, early childhood education, English, exercise science, history, mathematics, music, nursing, political science, psychology, religion, sociology, Spanish, theatre arts

Pres.: Dr DAN McALEXANDER

Provost and Chief Academic Officer: Prof. Dr DAVID L. GARRISON

Exec. Vice-Pres. for Admin.: PHYLLIS D. WHITNEY

Vice-Pres. for Academic Affairs and Dean: Dr JAY K. SIMMONS

Vice-Pres. for Advancement: WILLIAM JONES

Vice-Pres. for Finance and Operations: MARTIN E. PIRRMAN

Dir for Enrolment Management and Admissions: RICHARD DANA PAUL

Dean for Students: Prof. Dr JACK C. SLAY, JR

Registrar: JIMMY HERRING

Library Dir: LOREN PINKERMAN

Library of 190,000 vols

Number of teachers: 75

Number of students: 1,000

LIFE UNIVERSITY

1269 Barclay Circle, Marietta, GA 30060

Telephone: (770) 426-2600

E-mail: admissions@life.edu

Internet: www.life.edu

Founded 1974 as Life Chiropractic College. present name and status 1996

Private control

Pres.: Dr GUY F. RIEKEMAN

Provost and Exec. Vice-Pres.: Dr BRIAN J. McAULAY

Vice-Pres. for Operations and Finance: WILLIAM D. JARR

Vice-Pres. for Univ. Advancement: GREG HARRIS

Exec. Dir for Enrolment Management: Dr GARY SULLENGER

Exec. Dir for Student Services: MARC SCHNEIDER

Registrar: BRIAN SHERES

Library Dir: SUSAN A. STEWART

Number of teachers: 125

Number of students: 2,600

Publications: *Today's Chiropractic LifeStyle* (6 a year), *Your Extraordinary LIFE* (3 a year)

DEANS

College of Chiropractic Science: Dr LESLIE KING

College of Graduate Studies and Research: Dr CATHERINE FAUST

College of Undergraduate Studies: Dr MICHAEL SMITH

MACON STATE COLLEGE

100 College Station Dr., Macon, GA 31206-5145

Telephone: (478) 471-2700

E-mail: mscinfo@maconstate.edu

Internet: www.maconstate.edu

Founded 1968 as Macon Jr College, present name and status 1997

State control

Campus in Warner Robins

Pres.: Dr JEFFERY S. ALLBRITTEN

Provost and Vice-Pres. for Academic Affairs: Dr MARTHA VENN

Vice-Pres. for External Affairs and Continuing Studies: ALBERT J. ABRAMS

Vice-Pres. for Fiscal Affairs: NANCY STROUD

Vice-Pres. for Student Affairs and Enrolment Management: Dr MELANIE McCLELLAN

Chief Information Officer: ROGER DIXON

Dean for Students: LYNN W. McCRANEY

Registrar: TOM WAUGH

Library Dir: PAT BORCK

Library of 7,373 vols

Number of teachers: 200

Number of students: 5,700

DEANS

School of Arts and Sciences: Dr RONALD WILLIAMS

School of Business: Dr VARKEY K. TITUS

School of Education: Dr M. ANN LEVETT (acting)

School of Information Technology: Dr ALEX KOOHANG

School of Nursing and Health Sciences: Dr REBECCA CORVEY

MERCER UNIVERSITY

1400 Coleman Ave, Macon, GA 31207-0001

Telephone: (478) 301-2500

E-mail: info@mercer.edu

Internet: mercer.edu

Founded 1833, present name and status 1838

Private control
Academic year: August to May
Campuses in Atlanta, Savannah
Pres.: Dr WILLIAM D. UNDERWOOD
Provost: Dr D. SCOTT DAVIS
Exec. Vice-Pres. for Admin. and Finance: Dr JAMES S. NETHERTON
Sr Vice-Pres. and Gen. Counsel: Dr WILLIAM G. SOLOMON, IV
Sr Vice-Pres. for Atlanta Campus: Dr RICHARD V. SWINDLE
Sr Vice-Pres. for Enrolment Management: Dr PENNY L. ELKINS
Sr Vice-Pres. for Univ. Advancement: JOHN A. PATTERSON
Vice-Pres. and Dean of Students: Dr DOUGLAS R. PEARSON
Dean of Students for Atlanta Campus: CLAIRE CORDELL DYES
Vice-Provost: Dr MARILYN MINDINGALL
Dean for Univ. Libraries: ELIZABETH D. HAMMOND
Library of 754,700 vols, 100,452 ebooks, 2,460,731 microforms, 12,446 audiovisual materials
Number of teachers: 736
Number of students: 8,351
Publications: *Dulcimer, Inside Mercer, Mercer Lawyer* (2 a year), *The Business Advisor, The Law Letter* (2 a year), *The Mercer Cluster* (online, mercercluster.com), *The Mercer Engineer, The Mercerian* (2 a year, print and online, mercerian.mercer.edu)

DEANS

College of Continuing and Professional Studies: Dr PRISCILLA R. DANHEISER
College of Liberal Arts: Dr LAKE LAMBERT
College of Pharmacy and Health Sciences: Prof. Dr HEWITT W. MATTHEWS
Eugene W. Stetson School of Business and Economics: Dr SUSAN GILBERT
Georgia Baptist College of Nursing: Prof. Dr LINDA A. STREIT
James and Carolyn McAfee School of Theology: Prof. R. ALAN CULPEPPER
School of Engineering: Prof. Dr WADE H. SHAW
School of Medicine: Dr WILLIAM F. BINA, III
Tift College of Education: Dr PAIGE TOMPKINS
Townsend School of Music: Dr DAVID KEITH
Walter F. George School of Law: Prof. DAISY FLOYD

MIDDLE GEORGIA COLLEGE

1100 Second St, SE, Cochran, GA 31014
Telephone: (478) 934-6221
E-mail: admissions@mgc.edu
Internet: www.mgc.edu
Founded 1884 as Middle Georgia Agricultural and Mechanical Jr College, present name and status 1929
State control
Academic year: May to May
Campuses in Dublin, Eastman; academic divs incl. aviation management, business, fiscal affairs, humanities, science, mathematics and engineering, social science education
Pres.: Dr W. MICHAEL STOY
Vice-Pres. for Academic Affairs: Dr MARY LOU FRANK
Vice-Pres. for Fiscal Affairs: LYNN HOBBS
Vice-Pres. for Student and Public Affairs: JENNIFER BRANNON
Registrar and Dir of Admissions: JOHN EDGE
Dir of Library Resources: PAUL E. ROBARDS
Library of 55,000 vols, 933 periodicals

MOREHOUSE COLLEGE

830 Westview Dr., SW, Atlanta, GA 30314
Telephone: (404) 681-2800
E-mail: admissions@morehouse.edu
Internet: www.morehouse.edu
Founded 1867 as Augusta Institute, present name and status 1913
Private control
Pres.: Prof. Dr ROBERT M. FRANKLIN, JR
Provost and Sr Vice-Pres. for Academic Affairs: WELDON JACKSON
Vice-Pres. for Business and Finance: SHEILA JACOBS
Vice-Pres. for Campus Operations: ANDRÉ BERTRAND
Vice-Pres. for Institutional Advancement: PHILLIP HOWARD
Vice-Pres. for Student Services: WILLIAM BYNUM, JR
Dean for Admissions: KEVIN L. WILLIAMS
Library Dir: LORETTA PARHAM
Library of 404,000 vols, 31,000 bound journals, 1,500 current serials, 7,600 audiovisual materials
Number of teachers: 220 (165 full-time, 55 part-time)
Number of students: 2,800
Publications: *Inside Morehouse, Journal of Negro History, Morehouse Magazine* (1 a year)

DEANS

Div. of Business and Economics: JOHN E. WILLIAMS
Div. of Humanities and Social Science: Dr TOBE JOHNSON
Div. of Science and Mathematics: Dr JOHN K. HAYNES

MOREHOUSE SCHOOL OF MEDICINE

720 Westview Dr., SW, Atlanta, GA 30310-1495
Telephone: (404) 752-1500
Internet: www.msm.edu
Founded 1975 as School of Medicine at Morehouse College, current name adopted 1981
Private control
Academic year: July to May
Depts of community health and preventive medicine, family medicine, internal medicine, medical education, microbiology, biochemistry and immunology, neurobiology, obstetrics and gynaecology, pathology and anatomy, paediatrics, pharmacology and toxicology, physiology, psychiatry and behavioural sciences, surgery
Pres.: Dr JOHN E. MAUPIN, JR
Dean and Exec. Vice-Pres.: Dr VALERIE MONTGOMERY RICE
Sr Vice-Pres. for Admin. and Chief Financial Officer: DONNETTA S. BUTLER
Vice-Pres. for Institutional Advancement: SALLY DAVIS
Vice-Pres. and Sr Assoc. Dean: Dr SANDRA HARRIS-HOOKER
Chief Information Officer: CIGDEM DELANO
Gen. Counsel: HAROLD JORDAN
Registrar: DERRECK PRESSLEY
Library Dir: JOE SWANSON, JR
Library of 80,000 vols
Number of teachers: 200
Number of students: 350
Publication: *MSM Magazine* (1 a year)

NORTH GEORGIA COLLEGE AND STATE UNIVERSITY

82 College Circle, Dahlonega, GA 30597
Telephone: (706) 864-1400
E-mail: admissions@northgeorgia.edu

Internet: www.northgeorgia.edu
Founded 1873 as North Georgia Agricultural College, present name and status 1996
State control
Academic year: August to May
Pres.: Prof. Dr BONITA JACOBS
Vice-Pres. for Academic Affairs: Dr PATRICIA DONAT (acting)
Vice-Pres. for Business and Finance: FRANK J. McCONNELL
Vice-Pres. for Exec. Affairs: BILLY WELLS
Vice-Pres. for Institutional Advancement: Dr ANDREW J. LEAVITT
Vice-Pres. for Student Affairs: Col. TOM PALMER
Chief Information Officer: Dr BRYSON PAYNE
Registrar: JILL BRADY
Dir for Library Services: SHAWN TONNER
Library of 180,000 vols (incl. print and ebooks), 40,000 electronic and print periodicals
Number of teachers: 360
Number of students: 6,100
Publications: *Honores: The NGCSU Journal of Undergraduate Research* (2 a year), *North Georgia Leader* (2 a year)

DEANS

Mike Cottrell School of Business: Dr RICHARD OATES
School of Arts and Letters: Dr CHRISTOPHER JESPERSEN
School of Education: Dr ROBERT O. MICHAEL
School of Science and Health Professions: Prof. Dr MICHAEL S. BODRI

OGLETHORPE UNIVERSITY

4484 Peachtree Rd, NE, Atlanta, GA 30319
Telephone: (404) 261-1441
E-mail: admission@oglethorpe.edu
Internet: www.oglethorpe.edu
Founded 1835
Private control
Academic year: September to May
Offers BA, science
Pres.: Dr LAWRENCE M. SCHALL
Provost and Vice-Pres. for Academic Affairs: Dr DENISE VON HERRMANN
Vice-Pres. for Business and Finance: MIKE HORAN
Vice-Pres. for Devt and Alumni Relations: PETER A. ROONEY
Vice-Pres. for Enrolment and Financial Aid: LUCY LEUSCH
Registrar: GAIL MEIS
Dir of Library: ANNE A. SALTER
Library of 150,000 bound vols, 1,600 DVDs
Number of teachers: 120
Number of students: 1,230
Publications: *Telefunkin', The Flying Petrel* (4 a year), *The Tower* (2 a year), *Yamacraw* (1 a year)

PAINE COLLEGE

1235 15th St, Augusta, GA 30901-3182
Telephone: (706) 821-8200
Internet: www.paine.edu
Founded 1882, present name and status 1903
Private control
Academic year: August to May
Pres.: Dr GEORGE C. BRADLEY
Provost and Vice-Pres. for Academic Affairs: MARCUS TILLERY
Vice-Pres. and Dean for Student Affairs: TINA CARDENAS
Vice-Pres. for Admin. and Fiscal Affairs: LeRoy SUMMERS, JR
Vice-Pres. for Institutional Devt: BRANDON BROWN
Registrar: CASTINE RHOADES WILLIAMS
Dir of Library: LYN DENNISON

Library of 122,752 vols, periodicals, electronic resources
Number of teachers: 130 (60 full-time)
Number of students: 925
Publications: *The Lion* (1 a year), *The Paine Magazine* (4 a year)

DEANS

School of Arts and Sciences: Dr EMILY ALLEN WILLIAMS
School of Professional Studies: Dr STEVEN L. THOMAS

PIEDMONT COLLEGE

POB 10, 165 Central Ave, Demorest, GA 30535
Telephone: (706) 778-3000
E-mail: ugrad@piedmont.edu
Internet: www.piedmont.edu
Founded 1897 as J. S. Green Collegiate Institute, current name adopted 1903
Private control
Academic year: August to May
Campus in Athens
Pres.: Dr JAMES F. MELLICHAMP
Vice-Pres. for Academic Affairs: Dr PERRY RETTIG
Dean for Admissions: CINDY PETERSON
Registrar: CARLA EDENFIELD
Dean for Libraries and College Librarian: ROBERT GLASS
Library of 95,000 vols
Number of teachers: 130
Number of students: 2,700

DEANS

School of Arts and Sciences: Dr STEVEN NIMMO
School of Business: Dr JOHN M. MISNER
School of Education: Dr DON GNECCO
School of Nursing: Dr LINDA SCOTT

POINT UNIVERSITY

2605 Ben Hill Rd, East Point, GA 30344
Telephone: (404) 761-8861
Internet: point.edu
Founded 1937 as Atlanta Christian College, current name adopted 2011
Private control
Academic year: August to May
Depts of Biblical studies, business, counselling and human services, education, fine arts, humanities and general studies, math and science
Pres.: DEAN C. COLLINS
Chief Academic Officer and Vice-Pres. for Adult and Professional Studies: Dr W. DARRYL HARRISON
Vice-Pres. for Academic Affairs: Dr KIMBERLY C. MACENCZAK
Vice-Pres. for Admin. and Chief Financial Officer: JEFF HAVERLY
Vice-Pres. for Advancement: EMMA W. MORRIS
Vice-Pres. for Business and Finance: JEFFREY A. HAVERLY
Vice-Pres. for Enrolment Management: STACY BARTLETT
Vice-Pres. for Institutional Effectiveness: Dr DENNIS E. GLENN
Vice-Pres. for Student Devt and Dean of Chapel: SAMUEL W. HUXFORD
Dir of Admission: TIFFANY SCHOENOFF
Registrar: LISA SELLERS
Library Dir: Prof. MICHEAL L. BAIN
Library of 80,000 vols
Number of teachers: 30 (full-time)
Number of students: 1,300

REINHARDT UNIVERSITY

7300 Reinhardt Circle, Waleska, GA 30183-2981
Telephone: (770) 720-5600
E-mail: admissions@reinhardt.edu
Internet: www.reinhardt.edu
Founded 1883 as Reinhardt Acad., present name and status 2010
Private control
Academic year: August to May
Pres.: Dr J. THOMAS ISHERWOOD
Vice-Pres. and Dean for Academic Affairs: Dr MARK A. ROBERTS
Vice-Pres. for Advancement: JoELLEN B. WILSON
Vice-Pres. for Finance and Admin.: ROBERT G. McKINNON
Vice-Pres. for Student Affairs and Dean for Students: Dr ROGER R. LEE
Dir for Admissions: JULIE C. FLEMING
Registrar: JANET M. RODNING
Dir for Library Services: JOEL C. LANGFORD
Library of 72,795 books, periodicals, microfilm, microfiche, cassettes, CDs, DVDs; 150,000 ebooks, 35,000 digital full-text periodicals, 300 databases
Number of teachers: 75 (full-time)
Number of students: 1,300

DEANS

McCamish School of Business: Dr DONALD D. WILSON, JR
Price School of Education: Dr JAMES L. CURRY, JR
School of Arts and Humanities: Dr A. WAYNE GLOWKA
School of Mathematics and Sciences: Dr WILLIAM J. DE ANGELIS
School of Music: Dr DENNIS K. McINTIRE
School of Professional Studies: LESTER W. DRAWDY, III

RICHMONT GRADUATE UNIVERSITY

1815 McCallie Ave, Chattanooga, GA 37404-3026
Telephone: (423) 266-4574
E-mail: admissions@richmont.edu
Internet: richmont.edu
Founded 2000 by merger of Chattanooga Bible Institute (f. 1933) with Psychological Studies Institute; present name and status 2003
Private control
Academic year: August to August
Campus in Atlanta
Pres.: Dr C. JEFFREY TERRELL
Academic Dean: Dr PHILIP A. COYLE
Exec. Vice-Pres.: BOB RODGERS
Vice-Pres. for Advancement: GEORGE DEMPSEY
Chief Financial Officer: WILLIAM J. MUELLER
Dean of Students: Dr DEANNE TERRELL
Dir of Admissions: NOVELL BLAIN
Dir of Libraries: JOHN L. HUGHES
Library of 37,000 vols, 15,000 ebooks

DEANS

Clinical Affairs: Dr EVALIN RHODES HANSHEW
School of Counseling: Dr KENY FELIX
School of Ministry: Dr LELAND ELIASON

SAVANNAH COLLEGE OF ART AND DESIGN

POB 77300, Atlanta, GA 30357-1300
1600 Peachtree St, NE, Atlanta, GA 30309
Telephone: (404) 253-2700
E-mail: scadatl@scad.edu
Internet: www.scad.edu
Founded 1978
Private control
Academic year: August to May

Campuses in Hong Kong, Lacoste, Savannah
Pres. and Co-Founder: PAULA S. WALLACE
Chief Academic Officer: TOM FISCHER
Vice-Pres. for Academic Support: Dr GOKHAN OZAYSIN
Vice-Pres. for Business and Finance: DAVID LEOPARD
Vice-Pres. for Enrolment Management: SCOTT LINZEY
Vice-Pres. for Student Success: PHIL ALLETTO
Exec. Dir of Institutional Advancement: McLEAN HOOFF
Dean of Library Services: DEBORAH IRENE PROSSER
Library of 40,000 vols, 370 periodicals
Number of teachers: 720
Number of students: 11,000

DEANS

School of Building Arts: CHRISTIAN SOTTILE
School of Communication Arts: JOHN LOWE
School of Design: VICTOR ERMOLI
School of Fashion: MICHAEL FINK
School of Film, Digital Media and Performing Arts: PETER WEISHAR
School of Fine Arts: STEVE BLISS
School of Foundation Studies: MAUREEN GARVIN
School of Liberal Arts: ROBERT EISINGER

SAVANNAH STATE UNIVERSITY

3219 College St, Savannah, GA 31404
Telephone: (912) 3568-4778
E-mail: registrar@savannahstate.edu
Internet: www.savannahstate.edu
Founded 1890 as Georgia State Industrial College, present name and status 1996
State control
Academic year: August to May
Pres.: Dr CHERYL DAVENPORT DOZIER
Vice-Pres. for Academic Affairs: Dr MOSTAFA SARHAN
Vice-Pres. for Business and Financial Affairs: EDWARD B. JOLLEY, JR
Vice-Pres. for Univ. Advancement: (vacant)
Vice-Pres. for Student Affairs: Dr IRVIN CLARK
Library Dir: MARY JO FAYOYIN
Library of 190,209 vols, 30,000 bound periodicals, 548,273 microforms and print periodical subscriptions, 4,000 audiovisuals
Number of teachers: 200 (155 full-time, 45 part-time)
Number of students: 4,080

DEANS

College of Business Admin.: Prof. Dr MOSTAFA SARHAN
College of Liberal Arts And Social Sciences: Dr MICHAEL SCHROEDER
College of Sciences And Technology: Dr DERREK B. DUNN

SHORTER UNIVERSITY

315 Shorter Ave, Rome, GA 30165-4298
Telephone: (706) 291-2121
E-mail: admissions@shorter.edu
Internet: www.shorter.edu
Founded 1873 as Cherokee Baptist Female College, current name adopted 2010
Private control
Academic year: August to May (2 semesters)
Pres.: Dr DONALD V. DOWLESS
Provost: Dr L. CRAIG SHULL
Vice-Pres. for Advancement: BERT EPTING
Vice-Pres. for Devt and Alumni: SUZANNE SCOTT (acting)
Vice-Pres. for Enrolment Management: Dr JOHN HEAD
Vice-Pres. for Finance and Chief Financial Officer: STEPHANIE OWENS

Vice-Pres. for Student Affairs and Dean for Students: Dr DEBRA FAUST
Vice-Pres. for Univ. Management: BERT EPTING
Dir for Admissions: PATRICK MCELHANEY
Registrar: BRANDI BERGER
Dir for Libraries: DEWAYNE WILLIAMS
Library of 144,673 vols, 8,230 microforms, 65,397 audiovisual materials, 51,199 ebooks
Number of teachers: 420 (100 full-time, 320 part-time)
Number of students: 3,800
Publications: *Shorter Magazine* (1 a year), *The Chimes* (1 a year)

DEANS

College of Adult and Professional Programs: Dr BARBARA FINN
College of Arts and Sciences: Dr SABRENA R. PARTON
Robert H. Ledbetter College of Business: Dr ROBERT DARVILLE, III
School of Education: Dr SANDRA LESLIE
School of Fine and Performing Arts: Dr ALAN WINGARD
School of Nursing: Dr VANICE W. ROBERTS
School of Science and Mathematics: Dr CRAIG ALLEE

SOUTH UNIVERSITY

709 Mall Blvd, Savannah, GA 31406-4805
Telephone: (912) 201-8000
E-mail: susavadm@southuniversity.edu
Internet: www.southuniversity.edu
Founded 1899 as Draughon's Practical Business College, present name and status 2001
Private control
Academic year: September to September
Campuses in Alabama, Austin, Florida, Michigan, Ohio, South Carolina, Texas, Virginia
Chancellor: JOHN T. SOUTH, III
Vice-Chancellor for Academic Affairs: Dr STEVEN K. YOHO
Vice-Chancellor for Finance: CHAD THOMPSON
Vice-Chancellor for South Univ. Campuses: Dr DAN PETERSON
Vice-Pres. for Academic Affairs: Dr LESLIE BAUGHMAN
Registrar: ANITA MACIAS
Dir of Univ. Libraries: KATE SAWYER
Number of students: 23,800

DEANS

College of Arts and Sciences: Dr JOHN MICHAEL BROOKS
College of Business: Dr STEVEN K. YOHO (acting)
College of Creative Art and Design: Dr LESLIE BAUGHMAN
College of Health Professions: Dr A. WILLIAM PAULSEN
College of Nursing: Dr MARY WALKER
School of Pharmacy: Prof. Dr JAMES E. WYNN

SOUTHERN POLYTECHNIC STATE UNIVERSITY

1100 S Marietta Parkway, Marietta, GA 30060-2896
Telephone: (678) 915-7778
E-mail: admiss@spsu.edu
Internet: www.spsu.edu
Founded 1948 as Technical Institute, current name and status 1996
public control
Academic year: August to August
Pres.: Dr LISA A. ROSSBACHER
Vice-Pres. for Academic Affairs: Dr ZVI SZAFRAN

Vice-Pres. for Advancement: Dr RON DEMPSEY
Vice-Pres. for Business and Finance: MICHAEL FOXMAN
Vice-Pres. for Student and Enrolment Services: Dr RON R. KOGER
Dir for Admissions: GARY BUSH
Library Dir: Dr NANCY COLYAR
Library of 129,954 vols, 994 periodicals and newspapers, 3,490 microforms, 330 audiovisual materials
Number of teachers: 200 (full-time)
Number of students: 6,550

DEANS

School of Architecture and Construction Management: RICHARD COLE
School of Arts and Sciences: Dr THOMAS NELSON
School of Computing and Software Engineering: Dr HAN REICHGELT
School of Engineering Technology and Management: Dr JEFFREY RAY

SPELMAN COLLEGE

350 Spelman Lane, SW, Atlanta, GA 30314-4399
Telephone: (404) 681-3642
Internet: www.spelman.edu
Founded 1881 as Atlanta Baptist Female Seminary, current name adopted 1924
Private control
Academic year: August to May
Offers BA, science
Pres.: Dr BEVERLEY DANIEL TATUM
Provost and Vice-Pres. for Academic Affairs: Dr JOHNNELLA E. BUTLER
Vice-Pres. for Business and Financial Affairs and Treas.: ROBERT D. FLANIGAN, JR
Vice-Pres. for Devt: KASSANDRA JOLLEY
Vice-Pres. for Enrolment Management: ARLENE CASH
Vice-Pres. for Institutional Advancement: KASSANDRA JOLLEY
Vice-Pres. for Student Affairs: Dr DARNITA KILLIAN
Academic Dean: Dr CYNTHIA NEAL SPENCE
Dean for Undergraduate Studies: Dr DESIREE S. PEDESCLEAUX
Registrar: Dr FREDERICK A. FRESH
Library Dir: LORETTA PARHAM
Library of 383,000 vols, 3,000 ebooks, 867,000 microforms, 314,000 govt documents, 17,000 theses and dissertations, 35,000 bound periodicals, 1,500 current periodicals
Number of teachers: 150
Number of students: 2,200

THOMAS UNIVERSITY

1501 Millpond Rd, Thomasville, GA 31792-7636
Telephone: (229) 226-1621
E-mail: admissions@thomasu.edu
Internet: www.thomasu.edu
Founded 1950 as Birdwood Jr College, current name adopted 2000
Private control
Academic year: August to May
Depts of arts and sciences, business, education, human services, nursing, social work
Pres.: Dr GARY BONVILLIAN
Provost and Vice-Pres. for Academic Affairs: ANN LANDIS
Vice-Pres. for Finance and Admin.: TIM KLOCKO
Vice-Pres. for Institutional Advancement: RICHARD A. MUNROE
Exec. Dir for Enrolment Management and Student Affairs: MICKY WEST
Dir for Admissions: KERRI KNIGHT

Registrar: LACEY HARRISON
Dir for Library Services: AMBER BROCK
Library of 31,000 vols, 160 periodicals and newspapers
Number of teachers: 120 (50 full-time, 70 part-time)
Number of students: 1,100 (850 undergraduate, 250 graduate)

TOCCOA FALLS COLLEGE

107 N Chapel Dr., POB 800777, Toccoa Falls, GA 30598
Telephone: (706) 886-6831
E-mail: admissions@tfc.edu
Internet: www.tfc.edu
Founded 1907
Private control
Academic year: August to May
Pres.: Dr W. WAYNE GARDNER
Provost: Dr BARBARA K. BELLEFEUILLE
Vice-Pres. for Academic Affairs: Dr W. BRIAN SHELTON
Vice-Pres. for Advancement: JAMES HANSEN
Vice-Pres. for Business and Finance: GREGG SCHULTE
Vice-Pres. for Institutional Advancement: JAMES HANSEN
Vice-Pres. for Student Devt: LEE YOWELL
Registrar: KELLY G. VICKERS
Dir for Information Services: PATRICIA FISHER
Library of 150,000 vols and 175 current subscriptions
Number of teachers: 70
Number of students: 750

DEANS

School of Arts and Sciences: Prof. Dr KIERAN CLEMENTS
School of Christian Ministries: Dr W. BRIAN SHELTON
School of Professional Studies: Prof. Dr THOMAS COUNCIL

TRUETT MCCONNELL COLLEGE

100 Alumni Dr., Cleveland, GA 30528
Telephone: (706) 865-2134
E-mail: admissions@truett.edu
Internet: www.truett.edu
Founded 1947
Private control
Academic year: August to July (2 semesters)
Degree programmes incl. BA in business admin., world missions; BSc in education, psychology
Pres.: Dr EMIR FETHI CANER
Vice-Pres. for Academic Services: Dr BRAD REYNOLDS
Vice-Pres. for Advancement: Dr DANIEL MOOSBRUGGER
Vice-Pres. for Business Admin.: Dr DAVID ARMSTRONG
Vice-Pres. for Student Services and Athletic Dir: CHRIS EPPLING
Dir of Admissions: NATHAN RAYNOR
Registrar: MELISSA FORTNER
Library Dir: JANICE WILSON

UNIVERSITY OF GEORGIA

Athens, GA 30602
Telephone: (706) 542-3000
E-mail: reghelp@uga.edu
Internet: www.uga.edu
Founded 1785
State control
Pres.: Prof. Dr JERE W. MOREHEAD
Provost and Sr Vice-Pres. for Academic Affairs: Prof. PAMELA S. WHITTEN
Sr Vice-Pres. for External Affairs: THOMAS S. LANDRUM

Sr Vice-Pres. for Finance and Admin.: TIMOTHY P. BURGESS
Vice-Pres. for Instruction: Dr LAURA D. JOLLY
Vice-Pres. for Public Service and Outreach: Dr JENNIFER FRUM
Vice-Pres. for Research: Dr DAVID C. LEE
Vice-Pres. for Student Affairs: Dr RODNEY D. BENNETT
Registrar: JAN HATHCOTE
Univ. Librarian: Dr WILLIAM GRAY POTTER
Library: 4.7m. vols
Number of teachers: 2,807
Number of students: 34,765 (26,571 undergraduate, 8,194 graduate)
Publications: *Environmental Ethics* (4 a year), *Georgia Economic Outlook* (1 a year), *Georgia Historical Quarterly* (4 a year), *Georgia Journal of College Student Affairs* (2 a year), *Georgia Journal of Ecological Anthropology* (1 a year), *Georgia Journal of International and Comparative Law* (3 a year), *Georgia Magazine* (4 a year), *Georgia Pharmacist Magazine* (1 a year), *Georgia Pharmacist Quarterly* (4 a year), *Georgia Preceptor* (4 a year), *Georgia Science Teacher* (3 a year), *Impact Interactive* (a service-learning magazine project, 1 a year), *Journal of Agribusiness* (2 a year), *Journal of Business Research* (12 a year), *Journal of Public Service and Outreach* (3 a year), *Journal of Research and Development in Education* (4 a year), *State and Local Government Review* (3 a year), *Teaching Georgia Government* (3 a year), *The Aesculapian* (4 a year), *The Georgia Advocate* (3 a year), *The Georgia Review* (4 a year), *Toxicology Digest* (4 a year)

DEANS

College of Agricultural and Environmental Sciences: Dr JAY SCOTT ANGLE
College of Education: Dr ARTHUR M. HORNE
College of Environment and Design: Dr DANIEL NADENICEK
College of Family and Consumer Sciences: Dr LINDA KIRK FOX
College of Pharmacy: Dr SVEIN ØIE
College of Public Health: Dr PHILLIP L. WILLIAMS
Franklin College of Arts and Sciences: Dr HUGH RUPPERSBURG
Graduate School: Dr MAUREEN GRASSO
Grady College of Journalism and Mass Communication: Dr E. CULPEPPER CLARK
Odum School of Ecology: Dr JOHN GITTLEMAN
School of Law: Prof. Dr REBECCA H. WHITE
School of Public and Int. Affairs: Dr THOMAS P. LAUTH
School of Social Work: Prof. Dr MAURICE C. DANIELS
School of Veterinary Medicine: Dr SHEILA W. ALLEN
Terry College of Business: Dr ROBERT SUMICHRAST
Warnell School of Forestry and Natural Resources: Prof. Dr MICHAEL CLUTTER

UNIVERSITY OF WEST GEORGIA

1601 Maple St, Carrollton, GA 30118
Telephone: (678) 839-5600
E-mail: admiss@westga.edu
Internet: www.westga.edu
Founded 1906, present status 1995, current name adopted 2005
State control
Language of instruction: English
Academic year: July to August
Pres.: Dr KYLE MARRERO
Provost and Vice-Pres. for Academic Affairs: Dr MICHAEL HORVATH
Vice-Pres. for Business and Finance: JAMES SUTHERLAND

Vice-Pres. for Student Affairs and Enrolment Management: Dr SCOT LINGRELL
Vice-Pres. for Univ. Advancement: Dr BILL ESTES
Chief Information Officer: KATHY KRAL
Registrar: DONNA HALEY
Dir for Admissions: JUSTIN BARLOW
Dir for Institutional Research and Planning: (vacant)
Library of 671,683 vols, 77,717 current serials subscriptions (paper, microform and electronic), 21,052 microforms, 23,935 audiovisual items, 101,073 ebooks
Number of teachers: 650 (450 full-time, 200 part-time)
Number of students: 11,800 (10,000 undergraduate, 1,800 graduate)
Publications: *Just the Facts*, *Studies in the Social Sciences* (1 a year), *West Georgia College Faculty Research Review* (1 a year)

DEANS

College of Arts and Humanities: Dr RANDY J. HENDRICKS
College of Education: Dr KIM METCALF
College of Science and Mathematics: Dr BRUCE LANDMAN
College of Social Sciences: Prof. Dr N. JANE McCANDLESS
Graduate School: Dr CHARLES W. CLARK
Honors College: Dr MICHAEL HESTER
Richards College of Business: Dr FAYE McINTYRE
School of Nursing: Prof. Dr KATHRYN M. GRAMS

VALDOSTA STATE UNIVERSITY

1500 N Patterson St, Valdosta, GA 31698
Telephone: (229) 333-5791
E-mail: admissions@valdosta.edu
Internet: www.valdosta.edu
Founded 1906, current name and status 1993
State control
Academic year: January to December
Pres.: Dr WILLIAM McKINNEY
Provost and Vice-Pres. for Academic Affairs: Dr DAVID DANAHAR
Vice-Pres. for Enrolment, Marketing, and Communications: ANDY CLARK
Vice-Pres. for Finance and Admin.: TRAYCEE MARTIN
Vice-Pres. for Student Affairs and Dean for Students: RUSSELL MAST
Vice-Pres. for Univ. Advancement: JOHN D. CRAWFORD (acting)
Registrar: STANLEY JONES
Library Dir: Dr ALAN BERNSTEIN
Library of 549,683 vols
Number of teachers: 616
Number of students: 11,885
Publication: *The Journal of Southwest Georgia History* (4 a year)

DEANS

College of Arts and Sciences: Dr CONNIE L. RICHARDS
College of Nursing and Health Sciences: Dr ANITA HUFFT
Graduate School: Dr JAMES LaPLANT
Harley Langdale, Jr College of Business Admin.: Dr L. WAYNE PLUMLY, JR
Honors College: MICHAEL SAVOIE
James L. and Dorothy H. Dewar College of Education: Dr BRIAN GEBER

WESLEYAN COLLEGE

4760 Forsyth Rd, Macon, GA 31210
Telephone: (478) 477-1110
Internet: www.wesleyancollege.edu
Founded 1836 as Georgia Female College, current name adopted 1917
Private control

Academic year: August to May
Divs of fine arts, humanities, natural sciences and mathematics, professional studies, social and behavioural sciences
Pres.: Dr RUTH AUSTIN KNOX
Vice-Pres. for Academic Affairs and Dean of College: VIVIA L. FOWLER
Vice-Pres. for Business and Fiscal Affairs and Treas.: RICHARD P. MAIER
Vice-Pres. for Enrolment Services: CHARLES STEPHEN FARR
Vice-Pres. for Institutional Advancement: SUSAN T. WELSH
Vice-Pres. for Student Affairs: PATRICIA M. GIBBS
Registrar: PATRICIA R. HARDEMAN
Library Dir: SYBIL McNEIL
Library of 142,579 vols, 33,000 microforms, 500 periodicals
Number of teachers: 80
Number of students: 700

YOUNG HARRIS COLLEGE

One College St, POB 68, Young Harris, GA 30582
Telephone: (706) 379-5125
E-mail: admissions@yhc.edu
Internet: www.yhc.edu
Founded 1886
Private control
Academic year: June to May
Pres.: Dr CATHY COX
Sr Vice-Pres. for Finance and Admin.: DAVID LEOPARD
Vice-Pres. for Academic Affairs: Dr RONALD ROACH
Vice-Pres. for Advancement: JAY T. STROMAN
Vice-Pres. for Business and Controller: WADE BENSON
Vice-Pres. for Enrolment Management and External Relations: CLINTON G. HOBBS
Vice-Pres. for Planning and Assessment: ROSEMARY ROYSTON
Vice-Pres. for Student Devt: SUSAN ROGERS
Registrar: TAMMY GIBSON
Dean for Library Services: DAWN LAMADE
Library of 50,000 vols, 50,000 ebooks
Number of students: 900
Publications: *Communique* (1 a year), *Echoes Magazine* (1 a year), *Legacy* (1 a year)

DEANS

Div. of Fine Arts: Prof. Dr KEITH DeFOOR
Div. of Humanities: Prof. Dr RUTH B. LOOPER
Div. of Mathematics and Science: Prof. Dr PAUL T. ARNOLD
Div. of Social and Behavioural Science: Prof. Dr B. LEE MARCH

HAWAII

BRIGHAM YOUNG UNIVERSITY, HAWAII CAMPUS

55–220 Kulanui St, Laie, Oahu, HI 96762
Telephone: (808) 675-3211
Internet: www.byuh.edu
Founded 1875 as Brigham Young Acad.
Private control
Pres.: Dr STEVEN C. WHEELWRIGHT
Vice-Pres. for Academics: Dr MAX L. CHECKETTS
Vice-Pres. for Admin. Services: MICHAEL B. BLISS
Vice-Pres. for Student Devt and Services: Dr DEBBIE HIPPOLITE WRIGHT
Vice-Pres. for Univ. Advancement: V. NAPUA BAKER
Chief Information Officer: JIM NILSON
Registrar: VERNELLE LAKATANI
Univ. Librarian: MICHAEL ALDRICH

Library of 163,000 vols
Number of teachers: 100
Number of students: 2,800

DEANS

College of Business, Computing and Government: Dr GLADE TEW
College of Human Development: JOHN BAILEY
College of Language, Culture and Art: PHILLIP MCARTHUR
College of Mathematics and Sciences: JEFF BURROUGHS

CHAMINADE UNIVERSITY

3140 Waialae Ave, Honolulu, HI 96816-1578
Telephone: (808) 735-4711
E-mail: admissions@chaminade.edu
Internet: www.chaminade.edu
Founded 1955
Private control
Academic year: August to May
Pres.: Bro. BERNARD PLOEGER
Provost: Dr LARRY OSBORNE
Vice-Pres. for Finance and Facilities: Dr DANIEL GILMORE
Dean for Enrolment Management: JOY BOUEY
Dean for Students: GRISSEL BENITEZ-HODGE
Dir for Information Services and Library: SHARON LEPAGE
Registrar: JOHN MORRIS
Library of 75,000 vols
Number of teachers: 75 full-time
Number of students: 2,800
Publications: *Aulama, Chaminade Literary Review* (2 a year)

DEANS

Division of Behavioral Sciences: Dr ROBERT SANTEE
Division of Business and Communication: Dr BARBARA POOLE-STREET (acting)
Division of Education: Dr DAVID GROSSMAN
Division of Humanities and Fine Arts: Dr DAVID L. COLEMAN
Division of Natural Sciences and Mathematics: Dr HELEN TURNER

HAWAII PACIFIC UNIVERSITY

1164 Bishop St, Honolulu, HI 96813
Telephone: (808) 544-0200
E-mail: hr@hpu.edu
Internet: www.hpu.edu
Founded 1965 as Hawai'i Pacific College, current name adopted 1990
Private control
Academic year: September to June
Windward campus and Downtown campus
Pres.: Dr GEOFFREY. BANNISTER
Sr Vice-Pres. for Academic Affairs: Dr JOHN KEARNS
Vice-Pres. for Community Relations: NANCY ELLIS
Vice-Pres. for Enrolment Management: SCOTT STENSRUD
Vice-Pres. for Human Resources: CLAIRE COOPER
Vice-Pres. for Institutional Research and Academic Support: LESLIE CORREA
Vice-Pres. for Student Support Services: JEFFREY PHILPOTT
Registrar: KELLY NASHIRO-YOSHIDA
Librarian: KATHLEEN CHEE
Library of 180,000 vols, 11,000 periodicals
Number of teachers: 600
Number of students: 7,800
Publications: *Hawaii Pacific Review* (1 a year), *Kalamalama* (12 a year), *The Voice* (2 a year), *Wanderlust* (1 a year)

DEANS

College of Business Administration: Dr DEBORAH CROWN
College of Humanities and Social Sciences: Dr STEVEN C. COMBS
College of Natural and Computational Sciences: Dr ANDREW M. BRITTAIN
College of Nursing and Health Sciences: Dr RANDY M. CAINE

UNIVERSITY OF HAWAI'I SYSTEM

2444 Dole St, Honolulu, HI 96822
Telephone: (808) 956-8111
Internet: www.hawaii.edu
Founded 1907 as College of Agriculture and Mechanic Arts
State control
Academic year: January to December
10 Campuses: 3 univs and 7 community colleges in Hawai'i, Honolulu, Kapiolani, Kauai, Leeward, Maui, Windward
Academic year: August to May
Pres.: M. R. C. GREENWOOD
Provost and Exec. Vice-Pres. for Academic Affairs: LINDA JOHNSRUD
Vice-Pres. for Admin.: SAM CALLEJO
Vice-Pres. for Budget and Finance: HOWARD TODO
Vice-Pres. for Information Technology: DAVID LASSNER
Vice-Pres. for Legal Affairs and Univ. Gen. Counsel: DAROLYN LENDIO
Vice-Pres. for Research: JAMES GAINES
Vice-Pres. for Student Affairs and Univ. Relations: ROCKNE FREITAS
Librarian: DIANE PERUSHEK
Library: 3.5m. vols
Number of teachers: 3,300
Number of students: 60,000
Publications: *Asian Perspectives* (2 a year, archaeology for Asia and the Pacific), *Asian Theatre Journal* (2 a year, journal of the Asscn for Asian Performance), *Buddhist–Christian Studies* (1 a year, journal of the Soc. for Buddhist–Christian Studies), *Biography* (4 a year, interdisciplinary biographical scholarship), *The Contemporary Pacific* (2 a year, island affairs), *China Review International* (2 a year, reviews of scholarly literature in Chinese studies), *Journal of World History* (4 a year, journal of the World History Asscn), *Ka Ho'oilina* (2 a year, journal of Hawaiian language sources), *Korean Studies* (2 a year, multidisciplinary journal on Korea and Koreans abroad), *Manoa* (2 a year, new writing from America, the Pacific and Asia), *Oceanic Linguistics* (2 a year, current research on languages of the Oceanic area), *Pacific Science* (4 a year, biological and physical sciences of the Pacific region), *Philosophy East & West* (4 a year, comparative philosophy), *Journal of Modern Literature in Chinese* (2 a year, bilingual), *Yearbook of the Association of Pacific Coast Geographers* (1 a year), *Yishu* (4 a year, contemporary Chinese art)...

CONSTITUENT CAMPUSES

University of Hawai'i at Hilo

200 W Kawili St, Hilo, HI 96720-4091
Telephone: (808) 974-7414
E-mail: uhhadm@hawaii.edu
Internet: www.hilo.hawaii.edu
Founded 1947 as Hawaii Vocational School, current name adopted 1970
Academic year: August to May
Chancellor: Dr DONALD STRANEY
Number of teachers: 230
Number of students: 4,100

DEANS

College of Agriculture, Forestry and Natural Resource Management: BRUCE MATHEWS
College of Arts and Sciences: RANDY Y. HIROKAWA
College of Business and Economics: HARRY HENNESSEY
College of Pharmacy: Dr JOHN M. PEZZUTO

University of Hawai'i at Manoa

2500 Campus Rd, Honolulu, HI 96822
Telephone: (808) 956-8111
E-mail: uhmanoa.admissions@hawaii.edu
Internet: manoa.hawaii.edu
Founded 1907
Academic year: August to May
Chancellor: Dr VIRGINIA S. HINSHAW
Number of teachers: 1,200
Number of students: 20,300

DEANS

College of Arts and Humanities: THOMAS BINGHAM
College of Education: Dr CHRISTINE K. SORENSEN
College of Engineering: Dr PETER E. CROUCH
College of Languages, Linguistics and Literature: ROBERT . BLEY-VROMAN
College of Natural Sciences: WILLIAM L. DITTO
College of Social Sciences: DENISE E. KONAN
College of Tropical Agriculture and Human Resources: SYLVIA YUEN
Graduate Division: PATRICIA COOPER
Hawai'inuiākea School of Hawaiian Knowledge: MAENETTE AH NEE-BENHAM
John A. Burns School of Medicine: Dr JERRIS HEDGES
Myron B. Thompson School of Social Work: Dr NOREEN MOKUAU
Outreach College: WILLIAM G. CHISMAR
School of Architecture: CLARK E. LLEWELLYN
School of Nursing and Dental Hygiene: Dr MARY G. BOLAND
School of Ocean and Earth Science and Technology: BRIAN TAYLOR
School of Pacific and Asian Studies: EDWARD J. SHULTZ
School of Travel Industry Management: Dr JUANITA LIU
Shidler College of Business: V. VANCE ROLEY
William S. Richardson School of Law: Prof. AVI SOIFER

University of Hawai'i—West O'ahu

96–129 Ala Ike, Pearl City, HI 96782
Telephone: (808) 454-4700
E-mail: info@uhwo.hawaii.edu
Internet: westoahu.hawaii.edu
Founded 1976
Academic year: August to May
Divs of humanities, professional studies, social sciences
Chancellor: GENE I. AWAKUNI
Number of teachers: 40
Number of students: 1,470

IDAHO

BOISE BIBLE COLLEGE

8695 W Marigold St, Boise, ID 83714
Telephone: (208) 376-7731
Internet: www.boisebible.edu
Founded 1945
Private control
Academic year: July to June
Chancellor: Dr CHARLES A. CRANE
Pres.: Dr TERRY E. STINE
Academic Dean: CHARLES H. FABER
Dean for Students: TRAVIS JACOB

Dir for Admissions: RUSSELL GROVE
Dir for Devt: DAVID DAVOLT
Dir for Enrolment Services: ROSS A. KNUDSEN
Librarian: GLENNIS THOMAS
Library of 35,500 vols
Number of teachers: 15
Number of students: 175

BOISE STATE UNIVERSITY

1910 Univ. Dr., Boise, ID 83725
Telephone: (208) 426-1000
E-mail: communications@boisestate.edu
Internet: www.boisestate.edu
Founded 1932
State control
Pres.: Dr BOB KUSTRA
Provost and Vice-Pres. for Academic Affairs:
Dr MARTIN SCHIMPF
Vice-Pres. for Finance and Admin.: STACY A.
PEARSON
Vice-Pres. for Student Affairs: Dr LISA HAR-
RIS
Vice-Pres. for Univ. Advancements: ROSE-
MARY REINHARDT
Registrar: KRIS MARIE COLLINS
Dean for Univ. Libraries: Dr MARILYN MOODY
Library of 573,452 vols, 10,097 reference
books, 94,459 bound periodicals, 51,399
ebooks, 88,362 periodicals, newspapers,
and serials, 1,443,488 microforms, 19,490
non-print materials, 92,459 maps, 7,047
MSS
Number of teachers: 2,100
Number of students: 20,000

DEANS

College of Applied Technology: VERA
MCCRINK
College of Arts and Sciences: Dr TONY ROARK
College of Business and Economics: Dr
PATRICK SHANNON
College of Education: RICHARD OSGUTHORPE
College of Engineering: Dr AMY J. MOLL
College of Health Science: Dr TIM DUNNAGAN
College of Social Sciences and Public Affairs:
Dr MELISSA LAVITT
Extended Studies: MARK WHEELER
Graduate College: Dr JOHN R. PELTON

BRIGHAM YOUNG UNIVERSITY— IDAHO

525 S Center St, Rexburg, ID 83460
Telephone: (208) 496-1411
E-mail: ask@byui.edu
Internet: www.byui.edu
Founded 1888 as Bannock Stake Acad.
Private control
Academic year: 3 semesters
Pres.: KIM B. CLARK
Academic Vice-Pres.: FENTON L. BROADHEAD
Vice-Pres. for Advancement: HENRY J. EYR-
ING
Vice-Pres. for Student Services and Activ-
ities: KEVIN MIYASAKI
Vice-Pres. for Univ. Resource: CHARLES N.
ANDERSEN
Dean for Students: KIP HARRIS
Institutional Research and Assessment Dir:
SCOTT BERGSTROM
Chief Information Officer: SPALDING JUGGA-
NAIKLO
Library Dir: MARTIN H. RAISH
Registrar: KYLE MARTIN
Library of 200,000 vols, 330,000 ebooks,
100,000 ejournals, 10,000 video cassettes
and DVDs
Number of students: 15,000

DEANS

College of Agriculture and Life Sciences: VAN
CHRISTMAN

College of Business and Communication:
ROBYN BERGSTROM
College of Education and Human Develop-
ment: STEVE DENNIS
College of Language and Letters: JOHN IVERS
College of Performing and Visual Arts: KEVIN
BROWER
College of Physical Sciences and Engineer-
ing: KENDALL PECK
Continuing Education: CHAD PRICE
Foundations and Interdisciplinary Studies:
JON LINFORD

COLLEGE OF IDAHO

2112 Cleveland Blvd, Caldwell, ID 83605
Telephone: (208) 459-5011
E-mail: admissions@albertson.edu
Internet: www.collegeofidaho.edu
Founded 1891 as College of Idaho, current
name adopted 2007
Private control
Academic year: September to June
Pres.: Dr MARVIN HENBERG
Vice-Pres. for Academic Affairs and Dean for
Faculty: Dr MARK SMITH
Vice-Pres. for Advancement: MICHAEL VAN-
DERVELDEN
Vice-Pres. for Finance and Admin.: PETRA
CARVER
Vice-Pres. for Student Affairs and Dean for
Students: PAUL BENNION
Dir for Admissions: BRUCE SMITH
Exec. Dir for Devt: MICHAEL VANDERVELDEN
Library Dir: CHRISTINE SCHUTZ
Library of 185,000 vols, 10,000 journals,
magazines and newspapers; 75,000 govt
documents
Number of teachers: 60 (full-time)
Number of students: 1,050
Publications: Catalog (1 a year), Quest (3 a
year)

IDAHO STATE UNIVERSITY

921 S Eighth Ave, Pocatello, ID 83209
Telephone: (208) 236-0211
Internet: www.isu.edu
Founded 1901
State control
Pres.: ARTHUR C. VAILAS
Provost and Vice-Pres. for Academic Affairs:
Dr BARBARA ADAMCIK
Vice-Pres. for Finance and Admin.: JAMES
FLETCHER
Vice-Pres. for Student Affairs: Dr PATRICIA
TERRELL
Vice-Pres. for Univ. Advancement: Dr KENT
TINGLEY
Registrar: ROSS RUCHTI
Librarian: KAY FLOWERS
Library of 995,525 vols (incl. books, bound
periodicals and govt documents), 34,428
microfilms, 1,847,083 microfiches and
microcards, 44,257 maps and 2,938 current
periodicals
Number of teachers: 770
Number of students: 14,500

DEANS

College of Arts and Letters: KANDI TURLEY-
AMES
College of Business: Dr KREGG AYTES
College of Education: DEBORAH L. HEDEEN
College of Pharmacy: Dr PAUL CADY
College of Science and Engineering: Dr
GEORGE IMEL
College of Technology: Dr MARILYN E. DAVIS
Graduate School: Dr NICOLE R. HILL

LEWIS-CLARK STATE COLLEGE

500 Eighth Ave, Lewiston, ID 83501
Telephone: (208) 792-5272
E-mail: registrar@lcsc.edu
Internet: www.lcsc.edu
Founded 1893 as Lewiston State Normal
School, current name adopted 1971
State control
Academic year: August to May
Pres.: J. ANTHONY FERNÁNDEZ
Provost and Vice-Pres. for Academic Affairs:
Dr CARMEN SIMONE
Vice-Pres. for Finance and Admin.: CHET
HERBST
Dean for Academic Programmes: (vacant)
Dean for Community Programmes: KATHY
MARTIN
Dean for Professional-Technical Pro-
grammes: Dr ROB LOHRMEYER
Dean for Student Services: ANDREW HANSON
Registrar: NIKOL LUTHER
Dir for Library Services: SUSAN NIEWENHOUS
Library of 251,000 vols
Number of teachers: 180
Number of students: 4,200

NORTHWEST NAZARENE UNIVERSITY

623 S. University Blvd, Nampa, ID 83686-
5897
Telephone: (208) 467-8011
Internet: www.nnu.edu
Founded 1913
Private control
Pres.: Dr DAVID ALEXANDER
Vice-Pres. for Academic Affairs: Dr BURTON
J. WEBB
Vice-Pres. for Enrolment and Marketing:
STACEY BERGGREN
Vice-Pres. for Financial Affairs: DAVE PETER-
SON
Vice-Pres. for Spiritual and Leadership Devt:
FRED FULLERTON
Vice-Pres. for Student Devt: CAREY COOK
Registrar: NANCY AYERS
Dir of Library Services: SHARON I. BULL
Library of 120,000 vols, 850 current period-
icals, 600,000 vols of microforms, non-print
materials and govt documents
Number of teachers: 105 (full-time)
Number of students: 2,020 (1,322 under-
graduate, 698 graduate)

DEANS

School of Arts, Humanities and Social Sciences: RON E. PONSFORD
School of Business, Economics and Leadership: Dr STEVE MOUNTJOY
School of Education, Social Work and Counseling: JIM BADER

UNIVERSITY OF IDAHO

875 Perimeter Dr., Moscow, ID 83844
Telephone: (208) 885-6326
E-mail: registrar@uidaho.edu
Internet: www.uidaho.edu
Founded 1889
Pres.: CHUCK STABEN
Provost and Exec. Vice-Pres.: DOUGLAS D.
BAKER
Vice-Pres. for Finance and Admin.: RON
SMITH
Vice-Pres. for Research and Economic Devt:
JOHN K. MCIVER
Vice-Pres. for Univ. Advancement: CHRIS
MURRAY
Registrar: RETA PIKOWSKY
Dean for Students: Dr BRUCE PITMAN
Dean for the Library: LYNN BAIRD

Library of 936,738 vols, 105,493 microforms, 642,199 govt documents, 786,882 govt documents on microfiche, 207,087 maps and 5,305 current periodicals
Number of teachers: 3,150
Number of students: 12,300

DEANS

College of Agriculture and Life Sciences: Dr JOHN HAMMEL
College of Art and Architecture: MARK HOVERSTEN
College of Business and Economics: Dr JOHN MORRIS
College of Education: Dr CORI MANTLE-BROMLEY
College of Engineering: LARRY STAUFFER
College of Graduate Studies: Dr JIE CHEN
College of Law: MARK ADAMS
College of Letters, Arts and Social Sciences: KATHERINE G. AIKEN
College of Natural Resources: KURT PREGITZER
College of Science: SCOTT A. WOOD

ILLINOIS

ADLER SCHOOL OF PROFESSIONAL PSYCHOLOGY

17 N Dearborn St, Chicago, IL 60602
Telephone: (312) 662-4000
E-mail: information@adler.edu
Internet: www.adler.edu
Founded 1952 as Alfred Adler Institute of Chicago, present name 1991
Private control
Academic year: June to June
Campus in Vancouver, Canada
Pres.: Dr RAYMOND E. CROSSMAN
Vice-Pres. for Academic Affairs: Dr MARTHA CASAZZA
Vice-Pres. for Admin.: JO BETH CUP
Vice-Pres. for Finance and Technology: JEFFREY GREEN
Vice-Pres. for Institutional Advancement: ANTHONY CHIMERA
Dean for Vancouver Campus: Dr LARRY AXELROD
Dir for Library Services: KERRY COCHRANE
Library of 10,000 vols, 350 audiovisual materials
Number of teachers: 30
Publication: *Gemeinschaftsgefühl* (1 a year, Social Interest)

AMERICAN INTERCONTINENTAL UNIVERSITY

231 N Martingale Rd, 6th Floor, Schaumburg, IL 60173
Telephone: (877) 701-3800
E-mail: aiuaadministration@aiuniv.edu
Internet: www.aiuniv.edu
Founded 1970
Private control
Schools of business, criminal justice, design, education and information technology; campuses in Atlanta (Georgia), Houston (Texas), Weston (Florida); int. campus in London (UK)
Pres. and Chancellor: Dr GEORGE MILLER
Provost and Chief Academic Officer: GREGORY G. WASHINGTON
Vice-Provost: Dr JOHN CAMPBELL
Sr Vice-Pres. for Finance and Admin.: NATE SWANSON
Vice-Pres. for Student Affairs: LEON KELLEY
Registrar: Dr RAGINI BILOLIKAR

AUGUSTANA COLLEGE

639 38th St, Rock Island, IL 61201
Telephone: (309) 794-7000
Internet: www.augustana.edu
Founded 1860
Private control
Academic year: September to May
Liberal arts and sciences college; courses in accounting, art, art education, art history, biochemistry, biology, business administration, chemistry, classics, computer science/mathematics, communication sciences and disorders, earth science teaching, economics, elementary and secondary education, English, French, geography, geology, German, history, mathematics, pre-medicine, music, music education, music performance, philosophy, physics, political science, psychology, religion, Scandinavian, sociology, Spanish, speech communication, studio art, and theatre
Pres.: STEVEN C. BAHLS
Dean of the College: PAREENA LAWRENCE
Dean for Students: EVELYN S. CAMPBELL
Registrar: LIESL FOWLER
Dir of the Library: CARLA TRACY
Library of 244,368 vols
Number of teachers: 185 (135 full-time, 50 part-time)
Number of students: 2,500

AURORA UNIVERSITY

347 S Gladstone Ave, Aurora, IL 60506-4892
Telephone: (630) 892-6431
E-mail: admission@aurora.edu
Internet: www.aurora.edu
Founded 1893 as Mendota Seminary, present name 1985
Private control
Academic year: September to May
Campus at Williams Bay, Wisconsin
Pres.: Dr REBECCA L. SHERRICK
Provost: Dr ANDREW P. MANION
Exec. Vice-Pres. for Advancement: THEODORE PARGE
Sr Vice-Pres. for George Williams Campus: Dr JOHN PYLE
Vice-Pres. for Admin.: THOMAS HAMMOND
Vice-Pres. for Community Relations: SARAH RUSSE
Vice-Pres. for Devt and Alumni Relations: TERI TOMASZKIEWICZ
Vice-Pres. for Enrolment: Dr DONNA DeSPAIN
Vice-Pres. for Finance: BETH REISSENWEBER
Vice-Pres. for Student Life: LORA DE LACEY
Vice-Pres. for Univ. Communications: STEVEN McFARLAND
Registrar: KATE MALE
Dir for Univ. Library: JOHN LAW
Library of 99,000 vols, 7,000 multimedia materials, 210 periodical subscriptions
Number of teachers: 155
Number of students: 4,400

DEANS

College of Arts and Sciences: Dr SAIB OTHMAN
College of Education: Dr DONALD C. WOLD
College of Professional Studies: Dr JODI KOSLOW-MARTIN
School of Continuing Education: Dr LINDA OLBINSKI

BENEDICTINE UNIVERSITY

5700 College Rd, Lisle, IL 60532-0900
Telephone: (630) 829-6000
E-mail: admissions@ben.edu
Internet: www.ben.edu
Founded 1887 as St Procopius College
Private control
Academic year: September to May

Br. campuses at Springfield, IL and Mesa, AZ
Pres.: Dr WILLIAM J. CARROLL
Provost and Vice-Pres. for Academic Affairs: Dr MARIA DE LA CÁMARA
Exec. Vice-Pres.: CHARLES GREGORY
Vice-Pres. for Enrolment Services: KARI GIBBONS
Dir for Undergraduate Enrolment: ANTHONY SCOLA
Registrar: BETTY MORRISON
Univ. Librarian: JACK FRITTS
Library of 100,000 vols, 15,000 periodicals, 120 databases
Number of teachers: 598 (117 full-time, 7 part-time, 474 adjunct)
Number of students: 6,164 (3,830 undergraduate, 2,334 graduate)
Publication: *Voices Magazine* (3 a year)

DEANS

College of Business: Dr SANDRA L. GILL
College of Education and Health Services: Dr ETHEL RAGLAND
College of Liberal Arts: (vacant)
College of Science: Dr BART NG
Global College: Dr ALAN GORR

BLACKBURN COLLEGE

700 College Ave, Carlinville, IL 62626
Telephone: (217) 854-3231
E-mail: info@blackburn.edu
Internet: www.blackburn.edu
Founded 1837
Private control
Academic year: August to May
Depts of accounting, art, biology, business and economics, chemistry, communications, computer science, criminal justice, education, engineering, English, history, mathematics, medical technology, performing arts, philosophy and religion, physical education, physics, political science, pre-law, pre-professional, psychology, Spanish
Pres.: MIRIAM R. PRIDE
Provost: Dr JEFFERY P. APER
Vice-Pres. for Admin. and Finance: HEATHER BIGARD
Dir for Admissions: ALISHA KAPP
Dean for Students: HEIDI HEINZ
Registrar: DIANNA M. RUYLE
Head Librarian: CAROL SCHAEFER
Library of 70,000 vols
Number of teachers: 55 (40 full-time, 15 part-time)
Number of students: 600

BRADLEY UNIVERSITY

1501 W Bradley Ave, Peoria, IL 61625
Telephone: (309) 676-7611
E-mail: admissions@bradley.edu
Internet: www.bradley.edu
Founded 1897, present name and status 1946
Private control
Pres.: JOANNE K. GLASSER
Provost and Vice-Pres. for Academic Affairs: Dr DAVID GLASSMAN
Vice-Pres. for Advancement: PATRICK VICKERMAN
Vice-Pres. for Business Affairs: GARY ANNA
Vice-Pres. for Student Affairs: Dr ALAN GALSKY
Registrar: KATHERINE M. BEATY
Exec. Dir for Library: BARBARA A. GALIK
Library: 1.2m. vols (incl. 510,297 books, bound periodicals and govt documents, 787,169 microforms)
Number of teachers: 350 (full-time)
Number of students: 6,000 (5,200 undergraduate, 800 graduate)
Publications: *Bradley Hilltopics* (4 a year), *Bradley Works*

DEANS

College of Education and Health Sciences: Dr JOAN SATTLER

College of Engineering and Technology: Dr RICHARD T. JOHNSON

College of Liberal Arts and Sciences: Dr CLAIRE ETAUGH

Foster College of Business Administration: Dr ROBERT SCOTT

Graduate School: Dr ALBERTO DELGADO

Slane College of Communications and Fine Arts: Dr JEFFREY H. HUBERMAN

CATHOLIC THEOLOGICAL UNION

5401 S Cornell Ave, Chicago, IL 60615-5698

Telephone: (773) 371-5400

E-mail: admissions@ctu.edu

Internet: www.ctu.edu

Founded 1968

Private control

Academic year: September to June

Depts of biblical literature and languages, historical and doctrinal studies, intercultural studies and ministries, spirituality and pastoral ministry, and word and worship

Pres.: Rev. DONALD SENIOR

Vice-Pres. and Academic Dean: Sis. BARBARA REID

Vice-Pres. for Admin. and Finance: MICHAEL W. CONNORS

Registrar: MARÍA DE JESÚS LEMUS

Library Dir: MELODY LAYTON MCMAHON

Library of 150,000 vols, 500 periodicals

Publication: *New Theology Review*

CHAMBERLAIN COLLEGE OF NURSING

3005 Highland Parkway, Downers Grove, IL 60515

E-mail: info@chamberlain.edu

Internet: www.chamberlain.edu

Founded 1889

Private control

Campuses in Florida, Arizona, Texas, Illinois, Virginia, Missouri, Ohio and Indiana

Pres.: Dr SUSAN L. GROENWALD

Vice-Pres. for Academic Affairs: Dr WILLIAM RICHARD COWLING, III

Vice-Pres. for Campus Operations: MARIE HALLINAN

Dir for Admissions: LARRY VEENEMAN

Dir for Finance: TAE KANG

Dir for Online Programmes: BRENDA HAMMERSLEY

Dir for Student Services: JUNE MARLOWE

CHICAGO SCHOOL OF PROFESSIONAL PSYCHOLOGY

325 N Wells St, Chicago, IL 60654-1822

Telephone: (312) 329-6600

E-mail: admissions@thechicagoschool.edu

Internet: www.thechicagoschool.edu

Founded 1979

Private control

Academic year: June to May

Campuses in Chicago, Los Angeles, Irvine, Westwood, Washington, DC; courses in applied behaviour analysis, clinical psychology graduate programme, continuing professional education, counselling psychology graduate programmes, forensic psychology graduate programmes, industrial organizational and business psychology programmes, school psychology; online courses

Pres.: Dr MICHELE NEALON-WOODS

Pres. (Chicago Campus): Dr PATRICIA ARREDONDO

Pres. (Washington, DC Campus): Dr ORLANDO TAYLOR

Vice-Pres. for Academic Affairs: Dr JAY FINKELMAN

Vice-Pres. for Admissions: MAGDALEN KELLOGG

Vice-Pres. for Finance and Admin.: CAROLE ROBERTSON

Vice-Pres. for Online-Blended Learning: Dr GINO NATALICCHIO

Vice-Pres. for Student Affairs: Dr JENNIFER STRIPE PORTILLO

Chief of Staff: MATTHEW NEHMER

Registrar: ANA DEL CASTILLO

Dir for Library Services: INDU AGGARWAL

Number of students: 4,300

Publication: *INSIGHT* (2 a year)

CHICAGO STATE UNIVERSITY

9501 S King Dr., Chicago, IL 60628-1598

Telephone: (773) 995-2000

E-mail: ug-admisssions@csu.edu

Internet: www.csu.edu

Founded 1867 as a teacher training school, present name 1971

State control

Academic year: August to May (2 terms)

Pres.: Dr WAYNE WATSON

Provost and Sr Vice-Pres. for Academic Affairs: Dr SANDRA WESTBROOKS

Sr Vice-Pres. for Admin. and Finance: GLEN MEEKS

Vice-Pres. for Enrolment Management: ANDRE BELL

Dir for Admissions: MATTHEW HARRISON

Registrar: CARNICE HILL

Dean for Library and Learning Resources: Dr RICHARD DARGA (acting)

Number of teachers: 470 (350 full-time, 120 part-time)

Number of students: 7,000

Publications: *CSU Excellence Magazine* (2 a year), *Illinois Schools Journal* (1 a year), *Reflections* (12 a year)

DEANS

College of Arts and Sciences: Dr DAVID KANIS

College of Business: Dr DERRICK K. COLLINS

College of Education: Dr SYLVIA GIST

College of Health Sciences: Dr JOSEPH BALOGUN

College of Pharmacy: Dr MIRIAM A. MOBLEY SMITH

Continuing Education and Non-Traditional Degree Programmes: NELLIE MAYNARD

Honors College: Dr RICHARD G. MILO

School of Graduate and Professional Studies: Dr JUSTIN K. AKUJIEZE

CHICAGO THEOLOGICAL SEMINARY

1407 E 60th St, Chicago, IL 60637

Telephone: (773) 896-2400

E-mail: admissions@ctschicago.edu

Internet: www.ctschicago.edu

Founded 1855

Private control

Academic year: September to May

Postgraduate courses in arts, divinity, religious leadership, sacred theology; doctoral courses in ministry, philosophy

Pres.: Dr ALICE HUNT

Vice-Pres. for Devt: MEGAN DAVIS-OCHI

Vice-Pres. for Finance and Admin.: STEPHEN MANNING

Academic Dean: Prof. Dr KEN STONE

Dir for Enrolment Management: LISA SEIWERT

Registrar: ELENA JIMENEZ

Library of 50,500 vols, 100 periodicals

COLUMBIA COLLEGE CHICAGO

600 S Michigan Ave, Chicago, IL 60605

Telephone: (312) 663-1600

E-mail: admissions@colum.edu

Internet: www.colum.edu

Founded 1890 as Columbia School of Oratory, current name adopted 1997

Private control

Pres.: Dr WARWICK L. CARTER

Sr Vice-Pres. and Provost: STANLEY T. WEARDEN

Vice-Pres. and Gen. Counsel: ANNICE M. KELLY

Vice-Pres. for Academic Affairs and Interim Provost: Dr LOUISE LOVE

Vice-Pres. for Campus Environment: ALICIA BERG

Vice-Pres. for Institutional Advancement: Dr ERIC WINSTON

Vice-Pres. for Student Affairs: MARK KELLY

Dean for Students: SHARON WILSON-TAYLOR

Dean for the Library: JO CATES (acting)

Library of 306,807 vols, 1,255 print serials, 46,978 ebooks, 58,375 ejournals, 37,888 multimedia materials

Number of teachers: 1,150

Number of students: 11,900 (11,400 undergraduate, 500 graduate)

Publications: *@LAS* (1 a year), *Court Green* (1 a year), *DEMO*, *Echo magazine* (2 a year), *Fictionary*, *Hair Trigger* (1 a year), *South Loop Review: Creative Nonfiction+Art* (1 a year)

DEANS

School of Fine and Performing Arts: Dr ELIZA NICHOLS

School of Liberal Arts and Sciences: Dr DEBORAH H. HOLDSTEIN

School of Media Arts: Dr ROBIN BARGAR

CONCORDIA UNIVERSITY CHICAGO

7400 Augusta St, River Forest, IL 60305-1402

Telephone: (708) 771-8300

E-mail: admission@cuchicago.edu

Internet: www.cuchicago.edu

Founded 1864

Private control

Academic year: August to May (2 semesters)

Pres.: Rev. Dr JOHN F. JOHNSON

Sr Vice-Pres. for Academics: Dr MANFRED B. BOOS

Sr Vice-Pres. for Univ. Advancement: Dr ALAN C. KLAAS

Sr Vice-Pres. for Univ. Planning and Research: ALAN E. MEYER

Vice-Pres. for Admin.: Dr DENNIS WITTE

Vice-Pres. for Enrolment and Marketing: EVELYN BURDICK

Vice-Pres. for Student Life and Leadership and Dean for students: JEFFREY C. HYNES

Registrar: CONSTANCE K. PETTINGER

Dir for Library Services: YANA V. SERDYUK

Library of 160,000 vols, 140 periodical subscriptions, 480,000 ERIC microfiche documents

Number of students: 5,130 (1,450 undergraduate, 3,680 graduate)

Publication: *Forester Magazine*

DEANS

College of Arts and Sciences: Dr GARY E. WENZEL

College of Business: Dr GEORGE VUKOTICH

College of Education: Dr KEVIN BRANDON

College of Graduate and Innovative Programmes: Prof. Dr THOMAS P. JANDRIS

DEPAUL UNIVERSITY

1 E Jackson Blvd, Chicago, IL 60604

Telephone: (312) 362-8000
E-mail: dpcl@depaul.edu
Internet: www.depaul.edu

Founded 1898, present name and status 1907
Private control

Campuses at Lincoln Park, Loop, Naperville, O'Hare, Oak Forest and Rolling Meadows

Pres.: Rev. Dr DENNIS H. HOLTSCHNEIDER
Chancellor: Rev. JOHN T. RICHARDSON
Provost: Dr HELMUT P. EPP
Exec. Vice-Pres.: Dr ROBERT L. KOZOMAN
Sr Vice-Pres. for Advancement: MARY C. FINGER
Sr Vice-Pres. for Enrolment Management and Marketing: Dr DAVID H. KALSBEEK
Vice-Pres. and Gen. Counsel: JOSÉ D. PADILLA
Vice-Pres. for Community, Govt and Int. Affairs: J. D. BINDENAGEL
Vice-Pres. for Devt: DAVID LIVELY
Vice-Pres. for Finance: BONNIE FRANKEL
Vice-Pres. for Institutional Diversity and Equity: ELIZABETH F. ORTIZ
Vice-Pres. for Student Affairs: JAMES R. DOYLE
Registrar: NANCY GALL
Dir for Libraries: JAMES GALBRAITH

Library of 799,756 vols, 28,319 ebooks, 100,774 microforms, 2,168 ft archives, 47,056 ejournals, 31,237 spec. collns
Number of teachers: 940 (full-time)
Number of students: 25,400 (16,385 undergraduates, 7,985 graduate, 1,030 law)

Publications: *Business & Commercial Law Journal* (2 a year, online, laworgs.depaul.edu/journals/bclj), *DePaul Journal of Art, Technology and Intellectual* (2 a year), *De Paul Magazine* (4 a year), *Journal for Social Justice* (online, laworgs.depaul.edu/journals/social_justice), *Journal of Health and Hospital Law* (12 a year), *Law Review* (4 a year, online, laworgs.depaul.edu/journals/lawreview), *Philosophy Today* (4 a year)

DEANS

College of Computing and Digital Media: Dr DAVID MILLER
College of Communication: Dr JACQUELINE TAYLOR
College of Education: Dr PAUL ZIONTS
College of Law: Dr GREGORY MARK
College of Liberal Arts and Social Sciences: Dr CHARLES S. SUCHAR
College of Science and Health: Dr JERRY CLELAND
Driehaus College of Business: Dr RAY WHITTINGTON
School for New Learning: Dr MARISA ALICEA
School of Music: Dr DONALD E. CASEY
Theatre School: JOHN CULBERT

DEVRY UNIVERSITY

Highland Landmark V, 3005 Highland Parkway, Downers Grove, IL 60515-5683

Telephone: (602) 216-7700
E-mail: info@devry.edu
Internet: www.devry.edu

Founded 1931 as DeForest Training School, present name and status 2002
Private control
Academic year: November to October

90 Campus locations in the USA and Canada

Pres.: DAVID J. PAULDINE
Provost and Vice-Pres. for Academic Affairs: Dr DONNA M. LORAINE
Vice-Pres. for Enrolment Management: ERIKA R. ORRIS
Vice-Pres. for Student and Career Services: CLAUDE TOLAND

Univ. Librarian: GLENN FERDMAN

Library of 375,000 vols, 80,000 ebook titles (25 campus libraries)
Number of teachers: 700 (full-time)
Number of students: 85,000 (incl. online)

DEANS

College of Business and Management: Dr OSCAR GUTIERREZ
College of Engineering and Information Science: JOHN GIANCOLA
College of Health Sciences: Dr JOSEPH YORK
College of Liberal Arts and Sciences: Dr DONNA REKAU
College of Media Arts and Technology: Dr BRIAN BETHUNE
Keller Graduate School of Management: Dr DONNA M. LORAINE

DOMINICAN UNIVERSITY

7900 W Div. St, River Forest, IL 60305

Telephone: (708) 366-2490
Internet: www.dom.edu

Founded 1901 as St Clara College in Wisconsin, current name adopted 1997
Private control
Academic year: May to April

Pres.: DONNA M. CARROLL
Sr Vice-Pres. for Admin.: AMY McCORMACK
Provost and Vice-Pres. for Academic Affairs: CHERYL JOHNSON-ODIM
Vice-Pres. for Enrolment Management: MARY ANN ROWAN
Vice-Pres. for Univ. Advancement: GRACE CICHOMSKA
Vice-Pres. for Mission and Min.: DIANE KENNEDY
Dean for Students: TRUDI GOGGIN
Registrar: MICHAEL P. MILLER
Univ. Librarian: Dr INEZ RINGLAND

Library of 250,000 vols, 30,000 periodicals
Number of teachers: 400 (150 full-time, 250 part-time)
Number of students: 3,600 (1,950 undergraduate, 1,650 graduate)

Publications: *Dominican* (online, www.dom.edu/magazine), *World Libraries* (2 a year)

DEANS

Brennan School of Business: Dr ARVID C. JOHNSON
Graduate School of Library and Information Science: Prof. Dr SUSAN ROMAN
Graduate School of Social Work: Dr CHARLIE STOOPS (acting)
Rosary College of Arts and Sciences: Prof. Dr JEFFREY CARLSON
School of Education: Dr COLLEEN REARDON

EASTERN ILLINOIS UNIVERSITY

600 Lincoln Ave, Charleston, IL 61920-3099

Telephone: (217) 581-5000
E-mail: international@eiu.edu
Internet: www.eiu.edu

Founded 1895
State control
Academic year: August to June

Pres.: Dr WILLIAM L. PERRY
Provost and Vice-Pres. for Academic Affairs: Dr BLAIR M. LORD
Vice-Pres. for Student Affairs: Dr DANIEL P. ADLER
Vice-Pres. for Univ. Advancement: BOB MARTIN
Dean for Enrolment Management: FRANK HOHENGARTEN
Registrar: G. SUE HARVEY
Dean for Library Services: Dr ALLEN LANHAM

Library of 978,209 vols, 1.2m. microtexts, maps, music scores and pamphlets

Number of teachers: 750 (610 full-time, 140 part-time)
Number of students: 11,630 (9,970 undergraduate, 1,660 graduate)

DEANS

College of Arts and Humanities: BONNIE IRWIN
College of Education and Professional Studies: DIANE H. JACKMAN
College of Sciences: GODSON OBIA
Graduate School: Dr ROBERT M. AUGUSTINE
Honors College: JOHN STIMAC
Lumpkin College of Business and Applied Sciences: Dr MAHYAR IZADI
School of Continuing Education: Dr WILLIAM C. HINE

EAST-WEST UNIVERSITY

816 S Michigan Ave, Chicago, IL 60605

Telephone: (312) 939-0111
E-mail: info@eastwest.edu
Internet: www.eastwest.edu

Founded 1980
Private control
Academic year: September to August

Depts of behavioural and social sciences, biology, business administration, computer and information science, English and communications, electronics engineering technology, mathematics, office administration

Chancellor: Dr M. WASIULLAH KHAN
Provost: Dr MADHU JAIN
Dean for Enrolment Management: MAZIN SAFAR
Dir for Devt: JUDY BACON
Registrar: AMAL MATARI
Librarian: Dr EKKEHARD-TEJA WILKE

Library of 26,000 vols, 2,500 films, 150 periodical subscriptions, 30 ebook reference sets
Number of teachers: 45 (full-time)
Number of students: 1,170

ELMHURST COLLEGE

190 Prospect Ave, Elmhurst, IL 60126-3296

Telephone: (630) 617-3500
E-mail: admit@elmhurst.edu
Internet: public.elmhurst.edu

Founded 1871, current name adopted 1924
Private control
Academic year: August to May

Depts of art, biology, business and economics, chemistry, communication arts and sciences, computer science and information systems, education, English, foreign languages and literatures, geography and geosciences, history, kinesiology, mathematics, music, nursing, philosophy, physics, political science, psychology, sociology, theology and religion, urban studies

Pres.: Dr S. ALAN RAY
Sr Vice-Pres. for Finance and Admin.: DENISE JONES
Vice-Pres. for Academic Affairs and Dean for Faculty: ALZADA J. TIPTON
Vice-Pres. and Chief Information Officer: JAMES KULICH
Vice-Pres. for Communications and Public Affairs: JAMES W. WINTERS
Vice-Pres. for Devt and Alumni Relations: JOSEPH R. EMMICK
Dean for Admission: GARY ROLD
Dean for Students: EILEEN SULLIVAN
Dir for Library: SUSAN SWORDS STEFFEN

Library of 320,000 vols
Number of teachers: 135 (full-time)
Number of students: 3,410

EUREKA COLLEGE

300 E College Ave, Eureka, IL 61530-1500
Telephone: (309) 467-3721
E-mail: admissions@eureka.edu
Internet: www.eureka.edu
Founded 1855
Private control
Academic year: August to May

Divs of education, fine and performing arts, humanities, science and mathematics, social sciences and business

Pres.: Dr J. DAVID ARNOLD
Provost and Dean for College: Dr DANIEL BLANKENSHIP
Vice-Pres. for Admissions, Communications and Integrated Marketing: Dr BRIAN SAJKO
Vice-Pres. for Devt and Alumni Relations: MARC PASTERIS
Dean for Admissions and Financial Aid: KURT KRILE
Dean for Students: BROOKE CAMPBELL
Library Dir: ANTHONY GLASS

Library of 80,000 vols, 300 periodical subsriptions
Number of teachers: 45
Number of students: 800

GARRETT-EVANGELICAL THEOLOGICAL SEMINARY

2121 Sheridan Rd, Evanston, IL 60201
Telephone: (847) 866-3900
E-mail: seminary@garrett.edu
Internet: www.garrett.edu
Founded 1853 as Garrett Biblical Institute, present name and status 1974
Private control
Academic year: September to July

Masters degrees in art and music ministry, Christian education and pastoral care, divinity, theological studies; doctoral degrees in Christian education and congregational studies, ethics and history, liturgical studies and Biblical studies, pastoral theology, personality and culture, theology

Pres.: PHILIP AMERSON
Academic Dean and Vice-Pres. for Academic Affairs: Dr LALLENE RECTOR
Vice-Pres. for Devt: DAVID HEETLAND
Dean for Students: Rev. CYNTHIA A. WILSON
Dir for Academic Studies and Registrar: VINCE McGLOTHIN-ELLER
Library Dir: Dr BETH SHEPPARD

Library of 300,000 vols
Number of teachers: 35
Number of students: 400

Publication: *Aware Magazine* (4 a year)

GOVERNORS STATE UNIVERSITY

1 University Parkway, University Park, IL 60466-0975
Telephone: (708) 534-5000
E-mail: gsunow@govst.edu
Internet: www.govst.edu
Founded 1969
State control

Pres.: ELAINE P. MAIMON
Provost and Vice-Pres. for Academic Affairs: TERRY ALLISON
Exec. Vice-Pres., Chief of Staff and Treas.: Dr GEBEYEHU EJIGU
Vice-Pres. for Institutional Advancement: JOAN VAUGHAN
Vice-Pres. and Gen. Counsel: ALEXIS KENNEDY
Registrar: MICHELLE SMITH-WILLIAMS
Dean for Library Services: DIANE DATES CASEY

Library of 459,994 vols, 28,930 audiovisual materials, 449 linear ft MSS.
Number of teachers: 300

Number of students: 7,800

DEANS

College of Arts and Sciences: Prof. REINHOLD HILL
College of Business and Public Administration.: Dr ELLEN FOSTER-CURTIS
College of Education: DEBORAH BORDELON
College of Health and Human Services: Dr ELIZABETH CADA

GREENVILLE COLLEGE

315 E College Ave, Greenville, IL 62246-1145
Telephone: (618) 664-2800
Internet: www.greenville.edu
Founded 1892
Private control
Academic year: July to June

Pres.: Dr LARRY LINAMEN
Provost: Dr RANDALL BERGEN
Vice-Pres. for Advancement: WALTER FENTON
Vice-Pres. for Enrolment: MICHAEL RITTER
Vice-Pres. for Finance: DANA FUNDERBURK
Vice-Pres. and Dean for Student Devt: Dr NORMAN HALL
Registrar: MICHELLE SUSSENBACH
Dir for Library: JANE HOPKINS

Library of 114,059 vols
Number of teachers: 160 (65 full-time, 95 part-time)
Number of students: 1,600

Publication: *Record* (2 a year)

DEANS

School of Arts and Sciences: Dr BRADLEY S. SHAW
School of Education: Dr VICKIE COOK
School of Professional Studies: Dr DAVE HOLDEN

HARRINGTON COLLEGE OF DESIGN

2nd Floor, 200 W Madison St, Chicago, IL 60606-3433
Telephone: (877) 939-4975
Internet: www.harrington.edu
Founded 1931, fmrly Harrington Institute of Interior Design, current name adopted 2003
Private control

Courses in communication design, digital photography and interior design

Pres.: BOB NACHTSHEIM
Sr Dir for Admissions: BRYAN LAMBERT
Registrar: SAM DELAROSA
Dir for Library Services: LEIGH GATES

Library of 27,000 vols, 16,000 ebooks, 125 journal and newspaper titles, 35,000 digital images, 500 video cassettes, DVDs and CDs
Number of teachers: 70
Number of students: 500

HEBREW THEOLOGICAL COLLEGE

7135 N Carpenter Rd, Skokie, IL 60077
Telephone: (847) 982-2500
E-mail: htc@htc.edu
Internet: www.htc.edu
Founded 1919, present name 1921
Private control

Chancellor: Dr JEROLD ISENBERG
Vice-Pres. for Admin.: SENDER KUTNER
Dir for Admissions: JOSHUA ZISOOK
Dir for Devt: GERSHON SEIF
Registrar and Financial Aid Officer: SHMUEL LEIB SCHUMAN

Library of 70,000 vols

DEANS

Blitstein Institute for Women: Dr ESTHER SHKOP
Men's College Division: MICHAEL A. MYERS

ILLINOIS COLLEGE

1101 W College Ave, Jacksonville, IL 62650
Telephone: (217) 245-3000
E-mail: info@ic.edu
Internet: www.ic.edu
Founded 1829
Private control

Divs of humanities, natural science, social sciences

Pres.: Dr AXEL D. STEUER
Vice-Pres. for Academic Affairs and Dean for College: Dr ELIZABETH H. TOBIN
Vice-Pres. for Business Affairs: FRANK G. WILLIAMS
Vice-Pres. for Devt and Alumni Relations: PHILIP HOOD
Vice-Pres. for Enrolment Management and College Marketing: STEPHANIE ELPERS CHIPMAN
Vice-Pres. for Student Affairs and Dean for Students: Dr MALINDA L. CARLSON
Registrar: Dr GLEN W. CLATTERBUCK
Librarian: MARTIN H. GALLAS

Library of 143,000 vols, 600 journal subscriptions, 10,000 microfilm and microfiche items
Number of teachers: 50
Number of students: 1,000

ILLINOIS COLLEGE OF OPTOMETRY

3241 S Michigan Ave, Chicago, IL 60616-3878
Telephone: (312) 949-7400
E-mail: admissions@ico.edu
Internet: www.ico.edu
Founded 1872
Private control
Academic year: August to May

Degree offered: Doctor of Optometry

Pres.: Dr AROL AUGSBURGER
Vice-Pres. and Dean for Academic Affairs: STEPHANIE MESSNER
Vice-Pres. for Student, Alumni and College Devt: Dr MARK COLIP
Registrar: LAVERN YOUNG

Library of 22,000 vols
Number of teachers: 93 (55 full-time, 38 part-time)
Number of students: 624

Publication: *ICO Matters* (3 a year)

ILLINOIS INSTITUTE OF ART— CHICAGO

350 N Orleans St, Chicago, IL 60654
Telephone: (312) 280-3500
Internet: www.artinstitutes.edu/chicago
Founded 1916 as Commercial Arts School, present name and status 1995
Private control

Depts of culinary, design, fashion, general education, media arts

Pres.: JOHN BALESTER JENKINS
Vice-Pres. for Academic Affairs: VESNA GRBO-VIC
Vice-Pres. and Sr Dir for Admissions: JANIS K. ANTON
Dean for Student Affairs: BETTY KOURASIS
Registrar: LaVONDRA L. LACEY
Library Dir: JULIET S. TEIPEL

Library of 33,000 vols, 600,000 images

ILLINOIS INSTITUTE OF TECHNOLOGY

3300 S Federal St, Chicago, IL 60616-3793

Telephone: (312) 567-3000

Internet: www.iit.edu

Founded 1940 by merger of Armour Institute of Technology (f. 1892) with Lewis Institute (f. 1896)

Private control

Pres.: Dr JOHN L. ANDERSON

Provost and Sr Vice-Pres. for Academic Affairs: ALAN W. CRAMB

Vice-Pres. and Gen. Counsel: MARY ANN SMITH

Vice-Pres. for External Affairs: DAVID BAKER

Vice-Pres. for Finance and Admin.: PATRICIA LAUGHLIN

Vice-Pres. for Institutional Advancement: ELIZABETH J. HUGHES

Vice-Pres. for Int. Affairs: Prof. DARSH WASAN

Dean for Student Affairs: KATHERINE MURPHY STETZ

Registrar: REBECCA NICHOLES

Dean for Libraries: CHRISTOPHER STEWART

Library: see under Libraries and Archives

Number of teachers: 550 (295 full-time, 255 part-time)

Number of students: 7,800

Publications: *ece@iit* (1 a year), *Employee Rights and Employment Policy*, *iitmagazine* (3 a year), *Seventh Circuit Review* (2 a year), *Vectors* (1 a year)

DEANS

Armour College of Engineering: NATACHA DEPAOLA

Chicago-Kent College of Law: Prof. HAROLD J. KRENT

College of Architecture: DONNA V. ROBERTSON

College of Psychology: Dr M. ELLEN MITCHELL

College of Science and Letters: R. RUSSELL BETTS

Institute of Design: PATRICK WHITNEY

School of Applied Technology: C. ROBERT CARLSON

Stuart School of Business: Dr HARVEY KAHALAS

ILLINOIS STATE UNIVERSITY

Normal, IL 61790

Telephone: (309) 438-2111

E-mail: admissions@illinoisstate.edu

Internet: illinoisstate.edu

Founded 1857

State control

Pres.: Dr AL BOWMAN

Provost and Vice-Pres. for Academic Affairs: Dr SHERI NOREN EVERTS

Vice-Pres. for Finance and Planning: Dr DANIEL LAYZELL

Vice-Pres. for Student Affairs: Dr LARRY DIETZ

Vice-Pres. for Univ. Advancement: ERIN MINNÉ

Registrar: JESS RAY

Dean for Univ. Libraries: Dr SOHAIR F. WASTAWY

Library of 1,610,271 vols, 38,395 ejournals, 48,527 multimedia titles, 2,541 print journals

Number of teachers: 1,200

Number of students: 21,080 (18,535 undergraduate, 2,545 graduate; on-campus)

DEANS

College of Applied Science and Technology: Dr JEFFERY A. WOOD

College of Arts and Sciences: GREGORY B. SIMPSON

College of Business: Dr SCOTT D. JOHNSON

College of Education: Dr DEBORAH J. CURTIS

College of Fine Arts: Dr JAMES MAJOR (acting)

Mennonite College of Nursing: Prof. Dr JANET WESSEL KREJCI

ILLINOIS WESLEYAN UNIVERSITY

1312 Park St, Bloomington, IL 61702

Telephone: (309) 556-1000

E-mail: iwuadmit@iwu.edu

Internet: www.iwu.edu

Founded 1850

Private control

Language of instruction: English

Academic year: September to May

College of liberal arts; college of fine arts with schools of music, theatre arts and art; school of nursing

Pres.: RICHARD F. WILSON

Provost and Dean for Faculty: JONATHAN GREEN

Vice-Pres. for Advancement: MARTIN W. SMITH

Vice-Pres. for Business and Finance: DANIEL KLOTZBACH

Vice-Pres. for Communications: MATTHEW KURZ

Vice-Pres. for Student Affairs and Dean for Students: KARLA CARNEY-HALL

Dean for Admissions: TONY BANKSTON

Dean for Enrolment Management: BOB MURRAY

Registrar: LESLIE BETZ

Univ. Librarian: KAREN SCHMIDT

Library of 368,317 vols

Number of teachers: 182 (full-time)

Number of students: 2,090

Publication: *Illinois Wesleyan University Magazine* (4 a year)

INSTITUTE FOR CLINICAL SOCIAL WORK

Robert Morris Center, 401 S State St, Suite 822, Chicago, IL 60605

Telephone: (312) 935-4232

E-mail: info@icsw.edu

Internet: www.icsw.edu

Founded 1981

Private control

Pres.: Dr MARTIN LAUB

Dean: Dr AMY ELDRIDGE

Dir for Student Affairs: KAREN BLOOMBERG

Librarian: SCOT AUSBORN

Number of teachers: 45

Number of students: 90

JOHN MARSHALL LAW SCHOOL

315 S Plymouth Court, Chicago, IL 60604

Telephone: (312) 427-2737

E-mail: admission@jmls.edu

Internet: www.jmls.edu

Founded 1899

Private control

Academic year: August to May

Advocacy and dispute resolution, global legal studies, tax, employee benefits, fair housing, information technology and privacy, intellectual property, international business and trade, real estate

Dean: JOHN E. CORKERY (acting)

Assoc. Dean for Academic Affairs: RALPH RUEBNER

Assoc. Dean for Admission and Student Affairs: Dr WILLIAM B. POWERS

Assoc. Dean for Advanced Studies and Research: KATHRYN J. KENNEDY

Assoc. Dean for Outreach and Planning: RORY DEAN SMITH

Exec. Dir for Institutional Affairs: ANNA KRUG

Chief Financial Officer: CYNTHIA SAH

Registrar: ANNA JOHNSON

Library Dir: JUNE HSIAO LIEBERT (acting)

Library of 254,585 vols

Number of teachers: 70

Number of students: 1,550 (1,150 undergraduate, 400 graduate)

Publications: *Journal of Computer and Information Law*, *The John Marshall Law Review*, *The John Marshall Law School Review of Intellectual Property Law*

JUDSON UNIVERSITY

1151 N State St, Elgin, IL 60123-1498

Telephone: (847) 628-2500

E-mail: askthecabinet@judsonu.edu

Internet: www.judsonu.edu

Founded 1913 as undergraduate div. of Northern Seminary, present name and status 2007

Private control

Campus at Rockford, Illinois

Pres.: Dr JERRY B. CAIN

Provost and Vice-Pres. for Academic Affairs: Dr DALE H. SIMMONS

Vice-Pres. for Business Affairs: JOHN POTTER

Vice-Pres. for External Relations: TORY GUM

Vice-Pres. and Dean for Student Affairs: LeANN PAULEY HEARD

Exec. Dir for Enrolment Services: NANCY BINGER

Registrar: VIRGINIA L. GUTH

Library Dir: LARRY C. WILD

Library of 91,000 vols

Number of teachers: 100 (40 full-time, 60 part-time)

Number of students: 1,200

Publication: *Judson today* (online, www.judsonu.edu/judsontoday)

DEANS

College of Liberal Arts and Sciences: Dr LANETTE POTEETE-YOUNG

School of Art, Design and Architecture: Dr CURTIS J. SARTOR

School of Education: Dr KATHLEEN E. MILLER

School of Leadership and Business: Dr THOMAS H. BERLINER

KENDALL COLLEGE

900 N North Branch St, Chicago, IL 60642

Telephone: (312) 752-2000

E-mail: kendalladmissions@kendall.edu

Internet: www.kendall.edu

Founded 1934 as Evanston Collegiate Institute, present name 1950

Private control

Academic year: November to October

Pres.: EMILY WILLIAMS KNIGHT

Provost: Dr GWEN HILLESHEIM

Dean for Student Affairs: KIMBERLY SKARR

Registrar: ALEX UNDERWOOD

Dir for Library Services: IVA FREEMAN

Library of 35,000 vols

Number of teachers: 32

Number of students: 4,155

DEANS

School of Business: MICHELLE COUSSENS

School of Culinary Arts: RENEE ZONKA

School of Education: Dr PAUL T. BUSCENI

School of Hospitality Management: JEFFREY CATRETT

KNOWLEDGE SYSTEMS INSTITUTE

3420 Main St, Skokie, IL 60076

Telephone: (847) 679-3135

E-mail: info@ksi.edu

Internet: www.ksi.edu

Founded 1978
Private control
Offers Masters degree in information technology and computer science
Chancellor: Dr SHI-KUO CHANG
Dean for Academic Affairs: Dr FREDERICK THULIN
Exec. Dir: JUDY PAN
Dir for Research: Dr HUBERT KORDYLEWSKI
Library Dir: JILL FRANKLIN

KNOX COLLEGE

2 E South St, Galesburg, IL 61401-4999
Telephone: (309) 341-7000
E-mail: admission@knox.edu
Internet: www.knox.edu
Founded 1837
Private control
Programmes in arts, humanities, sciences and social sciences
Pres.: Dr TERESA L. AMOTT
Vice-Pres. for Academic Affairs and Dean for College: Prof. LAWRENCE B. BREITBORDE
Vice-Pres. for Advancement: BEVERLY HOLMES
Vice-Pres. for Enrolment and Dean for Admission: PAUL STEENIS
Vice-Pres. for Finance and Admin. Services: THOMAS B. AXTELL
Dean for Students: DEBRA SOUTHERN
Library Dir: JEFFREY DOUGLAS
Library of 350,000 vols, 14,000 periodicals
Number of teachers: 120 (104 full-time, 16 part-time)
Number of students: 1,420 (undergraduate)
Publications: *Catch* (2 a year), *Knox Magazine* (4 a year)

LAKE FOREST COLLEGE

555 N Sheridan Rd, Lake Forest, IL 60045
Telephone: (847) 234-3100
E-mail: president@lakeforest.edu
Internet: www.lakeforest.edu
Founded 1857 as Lake Forest Univ.
Private control
Academic year: August to May
Liberal arts college
Pres.: STEPHEN D. SCHUTT
Provost and Dean for Faculty: MICHAEL T. ORR
Vice-Pres. for Admissions and Career Services: WILLIAM J. MOTZER, JR
Vice-Pres. for Business Affairs: LESLIE T. CHAPMAN
Vice-Pres. for Devt and Alumni Relations: RICH BARTOLOZZI
Dean for Students: ROB FLOT
Registrar: RUTHANE BOPP
Dir for Library and Information Technology: JAMES R. CUBIT
Library of 281,079 vols, 2,540 journals, magazines and newspapers, 4,778 video cassettes and DVDs, 1,904 music recordings
Number of teachers: 120
Number of students: 1,500
Publications: *Collage, Tusitala*

LAKE FOREST GRADUATE SCHOOL OF MANAGEMENT

Conway Park, 1905 W Field Court, Lake Forest, IL 60045-4824
Telephone: (847) 234-5005
E-mail: question@lfgsm.edu
Internet: www.lakeforestmba.edu
Founded 1946
Private control
Academic year: August to June

Campuses at Chicago and Schaumburg in Illinois
Pres. and CEO: JOHN N. POPOLI
Vice-Pres. for Devt: STASIA ZWISLER
Vice-Pres. for Finance and Admin.: MALCOLM C. DOUGLAS
Vice-Pres. for Information Technology: GREG KOZAK
Vice-Pres. for Research, Devt and Innovation: KATHY M. LECK
Dir for Admissions: CAROLYN BRUNE
Registrar: CHRISTINE L. PERLSTROM
Number of teachers: 120 (all adjunct faculty)
Number of students: 825

LEWIS UNIVERSITY

1 University Parkway, Romeoville, IL 60446-2200
Telephone: (815) 838-0500
E-mail: admissions@lewisu.edu
Internet: www.lewisu.edu
Founded 1932
Private control
Pres.: Bro. JAMES GAFFNEY
Provost: Dr STEPHANY SCHLACHTER
Exec. Vice-Pres.: WAYNE DRAUDT
Sr Vice-Pres. for Enrolment Management: RAYMOND KENNELLY
Sr Vice-Pres. for Finance and Facilities: ROBERT C. DEROSE
Vice-Pres. for Student Services: JOSEPH FALESE
Vice-Pres. for Univ. Advancement: LEONARD BERTOLINI
Dir for Admissions: RYAN COCKERILL
Registrar: ROBERT KEMPIAK
Library Dir: Dr JULIE KRAHL
Library of 145,000 vols, 600 current periodicals, 2,500 video cassettes
Number of teachers: 200 (full-time)
Number of students: 6,500

DEANS

College of Arts and Sciences: Dr BONNIE BONDAVALLI
College of Business: Dr RAMI KHASAWNEH
College of Education: Dr JEANETTE M. MINES
College of Nursing and Health Professions: Dr PEGGY RICE
School for Professional and Continuing Education: Dr WALTER PEARSON

LEXINGTON COLLEGE

310 S Peoria St, Chicago, IL 60607
Telephone: (312) 226-6294
E-mail: admissions@lexingtoncollege.edu
Internet: www.lexingtoncollege.edu
Private control
Academic year: August to May
Women's college
Pres.: KELLY O'LEARY
Academic Dean: Dr JOLENE BIRMINGHAM
Dir for Financial Aid: MARIA LEBRON-CARDONA
Registrar: CRISTY ACOSTA
Librarian: JOSEPHINE KUJAWA
Library of 3,000 vols

LINCOLN CHRISTIAN UNIVERSITY

100 Campus View Dr., Lincoln, IL 62656
Telephone: (217) 732-3168
E-mail: admissions@lincolnchristian.edu
Internet: www.lincolnchristian.edu
Founded 1944
Private control
Academic year: August to May
Campuses at Lincoln and Normal in Illinois, and Henderson in Nevada; offers doctoral degrees in ministry

Pres.: Dr KEITH H. RAY
Provost: Dr CLAY ALAN HAM
Vice-Pres. for Enrolment Management: KRISTA J. BROOKS
Vice-Pres. for Finance: ANDREA SHORT
Vice-Pres. for Student Devt: BRIAN MILLS
Vice-Pres. for Univ. Advancement: GORDON VENTURELLA
Registrar: SHAWN SMITH
Library Dir: NANCY J. OLSON
Library of 189,293 vols
Number of teachers: 45
Number of students: 1,050

DEANS

Hargrove School of Adult and Graduate Studies: Dr DON GREEN
Seminary: Dr DINELLE FRANKLAND
Undergraduate Studies: Dr JAMES ESTEP

LOYOLA UNIVERSITY CHICAGO

1032 W Sheridan Rd, Chicago, IL 60660
Telephone: (773) 274-3000
E-mail: admission@luc.edu
Internet: www.luc.edu
Founded 1870 as St Ignatius College, present name and status 1909
Private control
Academic year: August to May
3 Campuses in Chicago and Maywood, Illinois, and 1 in Italy
Pres.: Rev. MICHAEL J. GARANZINI
Provost: Dr JOHN PELISSERO
Sr Vice-Pres. and Gen. Counsel: ELLEN KANE MUNRO
Sr Vice-Pres. for Admin. Services: THOMAS M. KELLY
Sr Vice-Pres. for Advancement: JONATHAN HEINTZELMAN
Vice-Pres. for Facilities: PHILIP KOSIBA
Vice-Pres. for Information Services and Chief Information Officer: SUSAN M. MALISCH
Vice-Pres. for Student Devt: Dr ROBERT D. KELLY
Registrar: CLARE KORINEK
Dean of Libraries: ROBERT SEAL
Library of 900,000 vols, 3,600 periodical subscriptions
Number of teachers: 650 (full-time)
Number of students: 16,000
Publications: *Children's Legal Rights Journal* (4 a year), *International Law Review* (2 a year), *Loyola Law* (2 a year), *Loyola Magazine, Loyola World, Stritch M.D.*

DEANS

College of Arts and Sciences: Dr FRANK FENNELL (acting)
Graduate School: Dr SAMUEL ATTOH
Graduate School of Business: Dr KATHLEEN A. GETZ
Marcella Niehoff School of Nursing: Dr VICKI A. KEOUGH
School of Business Administration: Dr KATHLEEN A. GETZ
School of Communication: Dr DON HEIDER
School of Continuing and Professional Studies: Dr JANET V. DEATHERAGE (acting)
School of Education: Dr DAVID PRASSE
School of Law: DAVID N. YELLEN
School of Social Work: Prof. Dr DARRELL P. WHEELER
Stritch School of Medicine: Dr LINDA BRUBAKER

LUTHERAN SCHOOL OF THEOLOGY AT CHICAGO

1100 E 55th St, Chicago, IL 60615
Telephone: (773) 256-0700
E-mail: admissions@lstc.edu
Internet: www.lstc.edu

Founded 1962 by merger of Augustana Theological Seminary, Grand View Seminary, Chicago Lutheran Theological Seminary and Suomi Theological Seminary
Private control
Language of instruction: English, Spanish
Academic year: September to May
Areas of study incl. biblical studies, Church history, environmental ministry, interfaith relations, multicultural ministry, religion and science, systematic theology, urban ministry
Pres.: JAMES NIEMAN
Vice-Pres. for Advancement: MARK VAN SCHARREL
Vice-Pres. for Operations: BOB BERRIDGE
Dean and Vice-Pres. for Academic Affairs: ESTHER MENN
Dean for Students: TERRY BAEDER
Dir for Admissions: SCOTT CHALMERS
Dir for Advanced Studies: JOSE RODRIGUEZ
Registrar: PATRICIA A. BARTLEY
Dir for Library: CHRISTINE WENDEROTH
Library of 400,000 vols
Number of teachers: 19
Number of students: 261
Publications: *Currents in Theology and Mission* (6 a year), *Epistle* (3 a year)

MCCORMICK THEOLOGICAL SEMINARY

5460 S University Ave, Chicago, IL 60615
Telephone: (773) 947-6300
E-mail: admit@mccormick.edu
Internet: mccormick.edu
Founded 1829 as Indiana Seminary, current name adopted 1884
Private control
Academic year: September to June
Doctoral degree in ministry programmes and Masters degree in discipleship development, theology, urban ministry and divinity
Pres.: FRANK M. YAMADA
Vice-Pres. for Academic Affairs and Dean for Faculty: LUIS RIVERA
Vice-Pres. for Admin. and Finance: DAVID CRAWFORD
Vice-Pres. for Student Affairs and Dean for Students: CHRISTINE VOGEL
Sr Dir for Seminary Relations and Devt: SAM EVANS
Registrar: JIM COURTNEY
Dir for Library: CHRISTINE WENDEROTH
Library of 400,000 vols
Number of teachers: 15 (full-time)
Number of students: 150

MCKENDREE UNIVERSITY

701 College Rd, Lebanon, IL 62254
Telephone: (618) 537-4481
E-mail: info@mckendree.edu
Internet: www.mckendree.edu
Founded 1828 as Lebanon Seminary, present name and status 2007
Private control
Academic year: August to May
College of arts and sciences; schools of business, education, and nursing and health professions; campuses at Scott AFB, Illinois, and Louisville and Radcliff in Kentucky
Pres.: Dr JAMES M. DENNIS
Provost and Dean for Univ.: Dr CHRISTINE BAHR
Sr Vice-Pres.: VICTORIA DOWLING
Vice-Pres. for Admin. and Finance: SALLY MAYHEW
Vice-Pres. for Admission and Financial Aid: CHRISTOPHER HALL
Vice-Pres. for Research, Planning and Technology: Dr MARY BORNHEIMER

Vice-Pres. for Student Affairs and Dean for Students: Dr JONI BASTIAN
Exec. Dir for Kentucky Campuses: Dr DARREL HARDT
Registrar: DEBORAH L. LARSON
Dir for Library: REBECCA L. SCHREINER
Library of 70,000 vols
Number of teachers: 100 (full-time)
Number of students: 3,220 (2,355 undergraduate, 865 graduate)

DEAN

Graduate School: Dr JOSEPH CIPFL

MACMURRAY COLLEGE

447 E College Ave, Jacksonville, IL 62650
Telephone: (217) 479-7000
E-mail: publicinformation@mac.edu
Internet: www.mac.edu
Founded 1846 as Illinois Conf. Female Acad., present name and status 1955
Private control
Divs of business and social sciences, education, fine arts and humanities, interdisciplinary and pre-professional programmes, and natural and health sciences
Pres.: Dr COLLEEN HESTER
Vice-Pres. for Academic and Student Affairs: JOHN L. BAILEY
Dean for Students: MARTIN SABOLO
Dir for Admissions: ALICIA ZEONE
Registrar: Prof. Dr ALLAN A. METCALF
Library Dir: SUSAN EILERING
Library of 130,000 vols, 125 periodicals
Number of teachers: 50
Number of students: 550
Publications: *Mac News* (2 a year), *Montage* (1 a year)

MEADVILLE LOMBARD THEOLOGICAL SCHOOL

610 S Michigan Ave, Chicago, IL 60605
Telephone: (773) 256-3000
Internet: www.meadville.edu
Founded 1844
Private control
Academic year: September to June
Pres.: Prof. LEE BARKER
Provost: Prof. SHARON WELCH
Vice-Pres. for Finance and Admin.: DEBORAH BIEBER
Registrar: (vacant)
Dean for Library: Rev. Dr NEIL W. GERDES
Library of 140,000 vols, 120 periodicals
Number of teachers: 10
Number of students: 100

MEDICINE SHIELD COLLEGE PROGRAM—AMERICAN INDIAN ASSOCIATION OF ILLINOIS/NATIVE AMERICAN EDUCATIONAL SERVICES

6554 N Rockwell, Chicago, IL 60659
Telephone: (773) 338-8320
E-mail: dpwiese@aol.com
Internet: www.chicago-american-indian-edu.org
Founded 1974, present name and status 2007; attached to Eastern Illinois Univ.
Private control
Languages of instruction: English, Ojibwe, Lakota
Academic year: August to May
Areas of study: general studies, public policy, with emphasis on tribal knowledge, community service, community developmentt and leadership
Pres.: DORENE WIESE
Dean of AIAI Campus: LOLA HILL
Registrar: Dr MELANIE CLOUD

Head Librarian: MELANIE CLOUD
Library of 10,000 vols
Number of teachers: 8
Number of students: 30

METHODIST COLLEGE

415 NE St Mark Ct, Peoria, IL 61603
Telephone: (309) 672-5513
E-mail: admissions@methodistcol.edu
Internet: www.methodistcol.edu
Founded 1900
Private control
Academic year: August to May
Pres.: Dr KIMBERLY A. JOHNSTON
Dean for Academic Affairs: Dr LINDA PENDERGAST
Dean for Enrolment Management: Dr KEITH BRANHAM
Dean for Nursing: Dr PAM FERGUSON
Registrar: ANN GAREY
Library Coordinator: TRAVIS DUDLEY
Number of teachers: 60
Number of students: 600

MIDSTATE COLLEGE

411 W Northmoor Rd, Peoria, IL 61614-3558
Telephone: (309) 692-4092
E-mail: midstate@midstate.edu
Internet: www.midstate.edu
Founded 1888, current name adopted 1970
Private control
Depts of business administration, health information technology, allied health, general studies, realtime reporting, accounting, paralegal services and administration professional
Pres. and CEO: MEREDITH N. BUNCH
Chief Academic Dean: MARGARET STARR
Dir for Student Affairs: RHONDA URBAN
Dir for Library Services: ZACHARY BROWN
Number of teachers: 80

MIDWESTERN UNIVERSITY

555 31st St, Downers Grove, IL 60515
Telephone: (630) 515-6171
E-mail: admissil@midwestern.edu
Internet: www.midwestern.edu
Founded 1900 as American College of Osteopathic Medicine and Surgery, present name and status 1993
Private control
Academic year: September to May
Campus at Glendale, AZ
Pres. and CEO: Dr KATHLEEN H. GOEPPINGER
Exec. Vice-Pres. and Chief Operating Officer: Dr ARTHUR G. DOBBELEARE
Sr Vice-Pres. and Chief Financial Officer: GREGORY J. GAUS
Vice-Pres. for Clinical Education: GEORGE T. CALEEL
Vice-Pres. for Human Resources and Admin.: ANGELA L. MARTY
Vice-Pres. for Univ. Relations: Dr KAREN D. JOHNSON
Dean for Student Services: Dr TERESA DOMBROWSKI
Registrar: SUE HARDWIDGE
Dir for Library Services: NATALIE REED
Number of students: 4,400

DEANS

Arizona College of Optometry: DONALD E. JARNAGIN
Arizona College of Osteopathic Medicine: LORI A. KEMPER
Basic Sciences: Dr JOHN R. BURDICK
Chicago College of Osteopathic Medicine: KAREN J. NICHOLS

Chicago College of Pharmacy: Dr NANCY FJORTOFT

College of Pharmacy—Glendale Campus: Dr DENNIS J. MCCALLIAN

College of Dental Medicine—Downers Grove Campus: M. A. J. MACNEIL

College of Dental Medicine—Glendale Campus): Dr RUSSELL GILPATRICK

College of Health Sciences—Downers Grove Campus: Dr FRED D. ROMANO

College of Health Sciences—Glendale Campus: Dr JACQUELYN M. SMITH

MILLIKIN UNIVERSITY

1184 W Main St, Decatur, IL 62522-2084

Telephone: (217) 424-6211

Internet: www.millikin.edu

Founded 1901

Private control

Academic year: August to May

Pres.: Dr HAROLD G. JEFFCOAT

Vice-Pres. for Academic Affairs: BARRY PEARSON

Vice-Pres. for Enrolment: Dr RICHARD DUNSWORTH

Vice-Pres. for Finance and Business Affairs: RICK RIEDER

Vice-Pres. for Univ. Devt: PEGGY S. LUY

Dean for Admission and Financial Aid: STACEY HUBBARD

Dean for Student Devt: RAPHAELLA PRANGE (acting)

Registrar: WALT WESSELL

Dir for Library: CYNTHIA FULLER

Library of 189,000 vols, 1,000 periodicals, 53,000 ejournals, 82,000 ebooks

Number of teachers: 250

Number of students: 2,340 (2,300 undergraduate, 40 graduate)

Publications: *Collage* (1 a year), *Millikin University Quarterly*, *Quarterly Economic and Financial Forecast*

DEANS

College of Arts and Sciences: Dr RANDY BROOKS

College of Fine Arts: LAURA LEDFORD

College of Professional Studies: Dr DEBORAH SLAYTON (acting)

Tabor School of Business: Dr JAMES G. DAHL

MONMOUTH COLLEGE

700 E Broadway, Monmouth, IL 61462-1998

Telephone: (309) 457-2131

E-mail: info@monmouthcollege.edu

Internet: www.monmouthcollege.edu

Founded 1853

Private control

Languages of instruction: English, French, German, Greek, Japanese, Latin, Spanish

Academic year: August to May

Pres.: Dr MAURI A. DITZLER

Vice-Pres. for Devt and College Relations: MOLLY A. BALL

Vice-Pres. for Enrolment Management: OMAR G. CORREA

Vice-Pres. for Finance and Business: DONALD GLADFELTER

Vice-Pres. for Student Life and Dean for Students: JACQUELYN CONDON

Dean for Faculty: DAVID M. TIMMERMAN

Registrar: CHRISTINE JOHNSTON

Library Dir: J. RICHARD SAYRE

Library of 333,000 vols

Number of teachers: 120 (85 full-time, 35 part-time)

Number of students: 1,300

Publication: *Monmouth College Magazine* (2 a year)

MOODY BIBLE INSTITUTE

820 N LaSalle Blvd, Chicago, IL 60610

Telephone: (312) 329-4000

E-mail: pr@moody.edu

Internet: www.moody.edu

Founded 1886 as Chicago Evangelization Soc., current name adopted 1900

Private control

Academic year: August to May

Br. campuses in Spokane, Washington, and Plymouth, Michigan

Pres.: Dr PAUL NYQUIST

Provost and Dean of Education: JUNIAS VENUGOPAL

Exec. Vice-Pres. and Chief Operating Officer: STEVEN MOGCK

Vice-Pres. and Gen. Counsel: STEPHEN OAKLEY

Vice-Pres. for Educational Resources: WILLIAM W. BLOCKER

Vice-Pres. for Information Systems: FRANK W. LEBER, JR

Vice-Pres. for Student Services: THOMAS SHAW

Registrar: TIMOTHY C. WIEGERT

Library Dir: JAMES PRESTON

Library of 216,318 vols

Number of teachers: 80 (full-time)

DEANS

Education: JUNIAS VENUGOPAL

Moody Theological Seminary: JOHN JELINEK

Undergraduate School: LARRY DAVIDHIZAR

NATIONAL LOUIS UNIVERSITY

Chicago Campus, 122 S Michigan Ave, Chicago, IL 60603-3032

Telephone: (312) 621-9650

E-mail: nluinfo@nl.edu

Internet: www.nl.edu

Founded 1886 as Miss Harrison's Training School, current name adopted 1990

Private control

Campuses in Skokie, Lisle, Wheeling and Elgin (Illinois), Milwaukee and Beloit (Wisconsin), Tampa (Florida) and Nowy Sacz (Poland)

Pres.: Dr NIVINE MEGAHED

Provost: Dr CHRISTINE QUINN

Vice-Pres. for Devt: REBECCA STIMSON

Vice-Pres. for Enrolment Management: BOBBI BIRINGER

Vice-Pres. for Finance and Admin.: KENT KAY

Vice-Pres. for Institutional Advancement: (vacant)

Dir for Admissions: KEN KASPRZAK

Vice-Pres. for Operational Services: WILLIAM ROBERTS

Registrar: KENNETH GILSON

Dean for Library: KATHLEEN WALSH

Library of 125,000 vols

Number of teachers: 250

Number of students: 10,100 (2,250 undergraduate, 7,850 graduate)

Publication: *nlu today*

DEANS

College of Arts and Sciences: STEPHEN THOMPSON

College of Management and Business: WALTER ROETTGER

National College of Education: Dr ALISON HILSABECK

NATIONAL UNIVERSITY OF HEALTH SCIENCES

200 E Roosevelt Rd, Lombard, IL 60148

Telephone: (630) 629-2000

Internet: www.nuhs.edu

Founded 1906 as Nat. School of Chiropractic, present name 2000

Private control

Br. campuses in Florida

Pres.: Dr JAMES F. WINTERSTEIN

Vice-Pres. for Academic Services: VINCENT DEBONO

Vice-Pres. for Admin. Services: TRACY MCHUGH

Vice-Pres. for Business Services: RONALD MENSCHING

Dean for Students: DANIEL DRISCOLL

Registrar: YESENIA MALDONADO

Chair. for Learning Resource Centre: JOYCE WHITEHEAD

Library of 15,000 vols

Publications: *Journal of Chiropractic Humanities* (online), *Journal of Chiropractic Medicine* (4 a year), *Journal of Manipulative and Physiological Therapeutics*

DEANS

College of Allied Health Sciences: Dr RANDY SWENSON

College of Professional Studies—Florida Campus: Dr JOSEPH STIEFEL

College of Professional Studies—Lombard Campus: Dr NICHOLAS TRONGALE

Lincoln College of Post-Professional, Graduate and Continuing Education: Dr JONATHAN SOLTYS

NORTH CENTRAL COLLEGE

30 N Brainard St, Naperville, IL 60540

Telephone: (630) 637-5100

E-mail: admissions@noctrl.edu

Internet: www.northcentralcollege.edu

Founded 1861, fmrly Plainfield College

Private control

Academic year: September to June

Liberal arts college; offers graduate programmes in business administration, education, leadership studies, liberal studies, management information systems, web and internet applications

Pres.: Dr TROY HAMMOND

Vice-Pres. for Academic Affairs and Dean for Faculty: Dr R. DEVADOSS PANDIAN

Vice-Pres. for Business Affairs: PAUL H. LOSCHEIDER

Vice-Pres. for Enrolment Management, Athletics and Student Affairs: LAURIE HAMEN

Vice-Pres. for Institutional Advancement: RICK SPENCER

Registrar: JONATHAN PICKERING

Dir for Library Services: JOHN J. SMALL

Library of 145,000 vols, 3,400 journals

Number of teachers: 250 (140 full-time, 110 part-time)

Number of students: 3,050 (2,755 undergraduate, 295 graduate)

NORTH PARK UNIVERSITY

3225 W Foster Ave, Chicago, IL 60625-4895

Telephone: (773) 244-6200

E-mail: admissions@northpark.edu

Internet: www.northpark.edu

Founded 1891, present name and status 1997

Private control

Pres.: Dr DAVID L. PARKYN

Provost: Dr JOSEPH JONES

Exec. Vice-Pres. and Chief Financial Officer: CARL BALSAM

Vice-Pres. for Devt and Alumni Affairs: MARY SURRIDGE

Vice-Pres. for Enrolment and Marketing: NATHAN MOUTTET

Vice-Pres. for Student Devt and Dean for Students: Dr ANDREA NEVELS

Registrar: AARON SCHOOF

Library Dir: SARAH ANDERSON

Library of 443,665 vols, 995 journals, 28 newspapers
Number of teachers: 125 (full-time)
Number of students: 3,130 (1,855 undergraduate, 1,000 graduate/seminary, 275 continuing studies)

DEANS

College of Arts and Sciences: CHARLES PETERSON
School of Adult Learning: Dr BRYAN J. WATKINS
School of Business and Non-profit Management: Prof. Dr WESLEY E. LINDAHL
School of Education: Dr REBECCA NELSON
School of Music: CRAIG JOHNSON
School of Nursing: Prof. LINDA DUNCAN
Theological Seminary: LINDA CANNELL

NORTHEASTERN ILLINOIS UNIVERSITY

5500 N St Louis Ave, Chicago, IL 60625-4699

Telephone: (773) 583-4050
E-mail: admrec@neiu.edu
Internet: www.neiu.edu

Founded 1867 as a teacher training instn
State control

Pres.: SHARON K. HAHS
Provost and Vice-Pres. for Academic Affairs: VICKI ROMAN-LAGUNAS (acting)
Vice-Pres. for Finance and Admin.: MARK D. WILCOCKSON
Vice-Pres. for Institutional Advancement: MELBA RODRIGUEZ
Vice-Pres. for Student Affairs: Dr FRANK E. ROSS
Dir for Admissions: CLAUDIA MERCADO
Dean for Students: Dr MICHAEL T. KELLY
Registrar: DANIEL R. WEBER
Univ. Librarian: BRADLEY F. BAKER

Library of 651,005 vols (and Regional Archives Depository)
Number of teachers: 500 (325 full-time, 175 part-time)
Number of students: 11,000

DEANS

College of Arts and Sciences: Dr WAMUCII NJOGU
College of Business and Management: Dr AMY B. HIETAPELTO
College of Education: Dr MAUREEN D. GILLETTE
Graduate College: Dr MARCELO SZTAINBERG

NORTHERN SEMINARY

660 E Butterfield Rd, Lombard, IL 60148
Telephone: (630) 620-2180
E-mail: admissions@seminary.edu
Internet: www.seminary.edu

Founded 1913
Private control

Campuses at Lombard and Chicago; online programmes

Pres.: Dr ALISTAIR BROWN
Dir for Admissions: RANDY TUMBLIN
Registrar and Dir for Student Services: MARILYN MAST HEWITT
Chief Academic Officer: Rev. Dr KAREN WALKER FREEBURG
Dir for Library: BLAKE WALTER

Library of 55,000 vols, 175 journals, 8,000 ebooks
Number of teachers: 32
Number of students: 200

NORTHERN ILLINOIS UNIVERSITY

1425 W Lincoln Highway, DeKalb, IL 60115-2828

Telephone: (815) 753-1000

E-mail: admissions@niu.edu
Internet: www.niu.edu

Founded 1895, fmrly Northern Illinois State Normal School, present name and status 1957
State control

Academic year: August to May

Pres.: JOHN G. PETERS
Exec. Vice-Pres. and Provost: RAYMOND W. ALDEN, III
Exec. Vice-Pres. for Finance and Facilities: EDDIE R. WILLIAMS
Vice-Pres. for Outreach, Engagement and Information Technologies: ANNE C. KAPLAN
Vice-Pres. for Research and Graduate Studies: LISA C. FREEMAN
Vice-Pres. for Student Affairs and Enrolment Management: Dr BRIAN O. HEMPHILL
Vice-Pres. for Univ. Advancement: MICHAEL P. MALONE
Vice-Pres. for Univ. Relations: KATHY BUETTNER
Dean for Univ. Libraries: PATRICK J. DAWSON

Library: 2m. vols, 1,343,933 govt documents, 21,267 current periodicals, 3,000,087 microfilm units, 6,000 ejournals
Number of teachers: 1,200
Number of students: 23,000 (17,310 undergraduate, 5,370 graduate, 320 law)

Publications: Applied and Computational Control, Signals and Circuits (1 a year), Crossroads: An Interdisciplinary Journal of Southeast Asian Studies (2 a year), George Eliot—George Henry Lewes Studies (1 or 2 a year), International Economic Journal (4 a year), International Journal of Sociology of the Family (2 a year), International Review of Modern Sociology (2 a year), Journal of Political and Military Sociology (2 a year), Names: A Journal of Onomastics (4 a year), Popular Music and Society (4 a year), Style Journal (4 a year), The Journal of Burma Studies (1 a year), Thresholds in Education (4 a year)

DEANS

College of Business: DENISE D. SCHOENBACHLER
College of Education: Dr LA VONNE I. NEAL
College of Engineering and Engineering Technology: PROMOD VOHRA
College of Health and Human Sciences: MARY PRITCHARD
College of Law: JENNIFER ROSATO
College of Liberal Arts and Sciences: CHRISTOPHER K. MCCORD
College of Visual and Performing Arts: RICHARD HOLLY
Graduate School: Dr BRADLEY G. BOND (acting)

NORTHWESTERN UNIVERSITY

633 Clark St, Evanston, IL 60208
Telephone: (847) 491-3741
E-mail: ug-admission@northwestern.edu
Internet: www.northwestern.edu

Founded 1851
Private control
Academic year: September to June

Campuses at Evanston and Chicago in Illinois, and Doha in Qatar

Pres.: MORTON O. SCHAPIRO
Provost: DANIEL I. LINZER
Sr Vice-Pres. for Business and Finance: EUGENE S. SUNSHINE
Vice-Pres. and Chief Investment Officer: WILLIAM H. MCLEAN
Vice-Pres. and Gen. Counsel: THOMAS G. CLINE
Vice-Pres. for Admin. and Planning: MARILYN MCCOY
Vice-Pres. for Alumni Relations and Devt: ROBERT MCQUINN

Vice-Pres. for Information Technology and Chief Information Officer: SEAN REYNOLDS
Vice-Pres. for Research: JOSEPH T. WALSH, JR
Vice-Pres. for Student Affairs: PATRICIA TELLES-IRVIN
Vice-Pres. for Univ. Relations: ALAN K. CUBBAGE
Registrar: JACQUALYN CASAZZA
Dean for Libraries: SARAH M. PRITCHARD

Library: see under Libraries and Archives
Number of teachers: 2,500 (full-time)
Number of students: 16,500 (8,400 undergraduate, 8,100 graduate)

Publications: Journal of Criminal Law and Criminology (4 a year, online, www.law.northwestern.edu/jclc), Journal of International Human Rights (online, www.law.northwestern.edu/journals/jihr), Journal of International Law and Business (3 a year, online, www.law.northwestern.edu/journals/jilb), Journal of Law and Social Policy (online, www.law.northwestern.edu/journals/njlsp), Northwestern Journal of Technology and Intellectual Property (online, scholarlycommons.law.northwestern.edu/njtip), Northwestern Perspective (4 a year), Northwestern University Journal of International Law and Business (3 a year, online, www.law.northwestern.edu/journals/jilb), Northwestern University Law Review (4 a year, online, www.law.northwestern.edu/journals/lawreview), Tri-Quarterly (3 a year, online, triquarterly.org), The Reporter (4 a year)

DEANS

Feinberg School of Medicine: ERIC G. NEILSON
Graduate School: DWIGHT A. MCBRIDE
Henry and Leigh Bienen School of Music: TONI-MARIE MONTGOMERY
J. L. Kellogg School of Management: SALLY BLOUNT
Judd A. and Marjorie Weinberg College of Arts and Sciences: SARAH MANGELSDORF
Medill School of Journalism, Media, Integrated Marketing Communications: JOHN LAVINE
Northwestern Univ. in Qatar: EVERETTE DENNIS
Robert R. McCormick School of Engineering and Applied Science: JULIO OTTINO
School of Communication: BARBARA J. O'KEEFE
School of Continuing Studies: THOMAS F. GIBBONS
School of Education and Social Policy: PENELOPE L. PETERSON
School of Law: DANIEL B. RODRIGUEZ

OLIVET NAZARENE UNIVERSITY

1 University Ave, Bourbonnais, IL 60914-2345

Telephone: (815) 939-5011
E-mail: admissions@olivet.edu
Internet: www.olivet.edu

Founded 1907, fmrly Illinois Holiness Univ., present name 1986
Private control

Pres.: Dr JOHN C. BOWLING
Vice-Pres. for Academic Affairs and Academic Dean: Dr GREGG CHENOWETH
Vice-Pres. for Finance: Dr DOUGLAS PERRY
Vice-Pres. for Graduate and Continuing Education: Dr RYAN D. SPITTAL
Vice-Pres. for Institutional Advancement: Dr BRIAN ALLEN
Vice-Pres. for Student Devt and Dean for Students: Rev. Dr WALTER (WOODY) WEBB
Dir for Admissions: SUSAN WOLFF
Registrar: JIM KNIGHT
Library Dir: KATHY BOYENS

Library of 160,000 vols, 900 current periodicals, 100,000 other items (maps, pamphlets, sheet-music, microforms, govt documents)
Number of teachers: 100
Number of students: 4,600

DEANS

College of Arts and Sciences: Dr JANNA MCLEAN
School of Education: Dr JAMES UPCHURCH
School of Graduate and Continuing Studies: Dr JEFFREY WILLIAMSON
School of Professional Studies: Dr DENNIS CROCKER
School of Theology and Christian Ministry: Dr CARL LETH

PRINCIPIA COLLEGE

1 Maybeck Pl., Elsah, IL 62028-9720
Telephone: (618) 374-2131
E-mail: registrar@principia.edu
Internet: www.principiacollege.edu

Founded 1910, present status 1932
Private control

Liberal arts courses

Pres.: Prof. Dr JONATHAN PALMER
Dean for Academics: Prof. Dr SCOTT SCHNEBERGER
Dean for Enrolment Management: BRIAN MCCAULEY
Dean for Students: DORSIE GLEN
Registrar: PATRICIA W. LANGTON
Library Dir: LISA ROBERTS

Library of 125,000 vols
Number of teachers: 100
Number of students: 525

QUINCY UNIVERSITY

1800 College Ave, Quincy, IL 62301-2699
Telephone: (217) 222-8020
E-mail: admissions@quincy.edu
Internet: www.quincy.edu

Founded 1860, present name and status 1993
Private control

Divs of behavioural and social sciences, fine arts and communication, humanities and science and technology

Pres.: Dr ROBERT A. GERVASI (acting)
Vice-Pres. for Academic Affairs: Dr TERESA I. REED
Vice-Pres. for Business and Finance: TIM WEIS
Vice-Pres. for Enrolment Management: SYNDI L. PECK
Vice-Pres. for Mission and Min.: Fr JOHN DOCTOR
Vice-Pres. for Student Affairs: Dr TIFFANY QUINZE
Registrar: BARBARA WELLMAN
Dean for Library and Information Resources: PATRICIA TOMCZAK

Library of 210,000 vols
Number of teachers: 150
Number of students: 1,450

Publications: *Communication Magazine*, *QUniverse Magazine*

DEANS

School of Business: Dr CYNTHIA HALIEMUN
School of Education: Dr ANN BEHRENS

RESURRECTION UNIVERSITY

3 Erie Court, Third Fl., Oak Park, IL 60302
Telephone: (708) 763-6530
E-mail: admissions@resu.edu
Internet: www.resu.edu

Founded 1914 as West Suburban School of Nursing, present name 2010
Private control

Offers BSc in health informatics and information management, nursing; MSc in nursing

Pres.: Dr BETH A. BROOKS
Chief Financial Officer: Dr THERESA SCANLAN
Exec. Dir for Marketing and Admissions: DESLA MANCILLA
Dir for Student Services: CARMELITA GEE
Dean for Nursing: Prof. Dr SANDIE SOLDWISCH
Registrar: EDY COOPER
Librarian: ERIC HERNANDEZ
Number of students: 230

ROBERT MORRIS UNIVERSITY

401 S State St, Chicago, IL 60605
Telephone: (312) 935-6800
E-mail: enroll@robertmorris.edu
Internet: www.robertmorris.edu

Founded 1965, present name and status 2005
Private control

Campuses at Aurora, Bensenville, Chicago, Elgin, Orland Park, Peoria, Schaumburg, Springfield and Waukegan

Pres.: MICHAEL P. VIOLLT
Provost: MABLENE KRUEGER
Sr Vice-Pres. for Enrolment Management: NICOLE FARINELLA
Sr Vice-Pres. for Resource Admin.: DEBORAH BRODZINSKI
Vice-Pres. for Academic Admin.: KATHLEEN SUHAJDA
Vice-Pres. for Business Affairs: RONALD M. ARNOLD
Vice-Pres. for External Affairs: MARIE GIACOMELLI
Vice-Pres. for Information Systems: LISA CONTRERAS
Vice-Pres. for Student Affairs: ANGELA JORDAN
Registrar: STELLA MACH
Library Dir: SUE DUTLER

Library of 190,000 vols (incl. all campuses)
Number of students: 3,500

Publications: *egg* (1 a year), *Full Bleed*, *Radius*, *SCOPE*

DEANS

College of Liberal Arts: PAULA DIAZ
College of Nursing and Health Studies: Dr JANET HAGGERTY DAVIS
Institute of Art and Design: JANICE KAUSHAL
Institute of Technology and Media: BASIM KHARTABIL
Morris Graduate School of Management: Dr KAYED AKKAWI
School of Business Administration: LARRY NIEMAN

ROCKFORD COLLEGE

5050 E State St, Rockford, IL 61108
Telephone: (815) 226-4000
Internet: www.rockford.edu

Founded 1847, current name adopted 1892
Private control

Divs of arts and humanities; science, mathematics and nursing; social and behavioural sciences and education

Pres.: Dr ROBERT HEAD
Exec. Vice-Pres. and Dean of College: Dr STEVE SICONOLFI
Vice-Pres. for College Devt: JOHN MCNAMARA
Vice-Pres. for Enrolment Management: ERIC FULCOMER
Vice-Pres. for Institutional Advancement: BERNARD SUNDSTEDT
Dean for Students: BRADLEY KNOTTS
Registrar: ANNA JATTKOWSKI-HUDSON
Library Dir: KELLY JAMES

Library of 138,000 vols and 203 current periodicals, 795 linear ft archives

Number of teachers: 70 (full-time)
Number of students: 1,300

Publications: *Decus* (3 a year), *Rockford College Literary Magazine (RCLM)*

ROOSEVELT UNIVERSITY

Wabash Bldg, Room 116, 425 S Wabash Ave, Chicago, IL 60605
Telephone: (312) 341-3500
E-mail: gradadmission@roosevelt.edu
Internet: www.roosevelt.edu

Founded 1945 as Thomas Jefferson College, present name and status 1959
Private control

Campuses at Chicago and Schaumburg in Illinois

Pres.: Dr CHARLES R. MIDDLETON
Provost and Exec. Vice-Pres.: Dr JAMES GANDRE
Sr Vice-Pres. for Finance and Admin.: MIROSLAVA MEJIA KRUG
Vice-Pres. for Enrolment Management and Student Services: Dr SALLYE MCKEE
Vice-Pres. for Government Relations and Univ. Outreach: LESLEY D. SLAVITT
Vice-Pres. for Institutional Advancement and Chief Advancement Officer: PATRICK M. WOODS
Sr Dir for Admission: JOANNE CANYON-HELLER
Registrar: SHELIA COFFIN
Univ. Librarian: RICHARD M. UTTICH

Library of 374,000 vols
Number of teachers: 500
Number of students: 6,600

Publications: *Business and Society*, *Roosevelt University Magazine*

DEANS

Chicago College of Performing Arts: HENRY FOGEL
College of Arts and Science: Dr LYNN Y. WEINER
College of Education: HOLLY STADLER
College of Pharmacy: Dr GEORGE E. MACKINNON, III
Evelyn T. Stone College of Professional Studies: GREG BUCKLEY
Walter E. Heller College of Business: TERRI FRIEL

ROSALIND FRANKLIN UNIVERSITY OF MEDICINE AND SCIENCE

3333 Green Bay Rd, N Chicago, IL 60064
Telephone: (847) 578-3000
E-mail: helpdesk@rosalindfranklin.edu
Internet: www.rosalindfranklin.edu

Founded 1912 as Chicago Hospital-College of Medicine
Private control

Academic year: July to June

Pres. and CEO: K. MICHAEL WELCH
Exec. Vice-Pres. and Chief Operating Officer: MARGOT A. SURRIDGE
Vice-Pres. for Academic Affairs: Dr WENDY RHEAULT
Vice-Pres. for Faculty Affairs: Dr TIMOTHY HANSEN
Vice-Pres. for Institutional Advancement: TINA M. ERICKSON
Vice-Pres. for Research: Dr RONALD KAPLAN
Chief Financial Officer: ROBERTA LANE
Registrar: CINDY FRIESEN
Dir of Library: BONNIE J. WATTERSON

Library of 119,000 vols, 2,000 biomedical journals
Number of teachers: 1,000 (160 full-time, 100 part-time, 740 volunteer)
Number of students: 2,000

DEANS

Chicago Medical School: Dr RUSSELL ROBERT-
SON
College of Health Professions: Dr WENDY
RHEAULT
College of Pharmacy: Dr GLORIA MEREDITH
Dr William M. Scholl College of Podiatric
Medicine: Dr NANCY PARSLEY
School of Graduate and Postdoctoral Studies:
Dr JOSEPH X. DiMARIO

RUSH UNIVERSITY

Suite 440, 600 S Paulina St, Chicago, IL
60612

Telephone: (312) 942-5000
E-mail: rush_admissions@rush.edu
Internet: www.rushu.rush.edu

Founded 1972
Private control
Academic year: September to June (3 terms)

Pres. and Chief Operating Officer: PETER W.
BUTLER
CEO: Dr LARRY J. GOODMAN
Provost: THOMAS A. DEUTSCH
Vice-Provost: Dr LOIS K. HALSTEAD
Registrar: WILLIAM F. KARNOSCAK
Library Dir: CHRISTINE D. FRANK

Library of 108,380 vols, 41,228 book titles,
253 ebooks, 4,300 ejournals
Number of teachers: 2,900
Number of students: 2,000

DEANS

College of Health Sciences: DAVID SHELLEDY
(acting)
College of Nursing: Dr MELANIE C. DREHER
Graduate College: Dr PAUL M. CARVEY
Rush Medical College: Dr THOMAS A.
DEUTSCH

SAINT ANTHONY COLLEGE OF NURSING

5658 E State St, Rockford, IL 61108-2468

Telephone: (815) 395-5091
E-mail: info@sacn.edu
Internet: www.sacn.edu

Founded 1915 as Saint Anthony School of
Nursing, current name adopted 1990
Private control
Academic year: August to May

Pres.: Dr TERESE ANN BURCH
Dean for Graduate Affairs and Research: Dr
SHANNON LIZER
Dean for Undergraduate Affairs: Dr BETH M.
CARSON
Assoc. Dean for Support Services: NANCY
SANDERS
Dir for Learning Resource Centre: HEATHER
KLEPITSCH
Librarian: MARY DUMAR

Library of 2,700 vols, 200 print and 1,000
online periodicals
Number of teachers: 20 (f.t.e.)
Number of students: 230 (185 undergraduate, 45 graduate)

ST AUGUSTINE COLLEGE

1345 W Argyle St, Chicago, IL 60640

Telephone: (773) 878-7989
Internet: www.staugustine.edu

Founded 1980
Private control

4 Campuses in Chicago; offers Bachelors
degree in social work

Pres.: ANDREW SUND
Vice-Pres. for Institutional Advancement:
ALFREDO CALIXTO
Vice-Pres. for Technology, Research and
Systems: PAUL HECK

Dean for Academic and Student Affairs: Dr
BRUNO BONDAVALLI
Dean for Instruction: LEE MALTBY
Dir for Financial Aid: MARIA ZAMBONINO
Number of teachers: 100

SAINT FRANCIS MEDICAL CENTER COLLEGE OF NURSING

511 NE Greenleaf St, Peoria, IL 61603-3783

Telephone: (309) 655-2201
E-mail: conadmissions@osfhealthcare.org
Internet: www.sfmccon.edu

Founded 1905 as St Francis Hospital School
of Nursing, current name adopted 1985
Private control
Academic year: August to May

Pres.: Dr PATRICIA A. STOCKERT
Dean for Graduate Programme: Dr JANICE F.
BOUNDY
Dean for Undergraduate Programme: Dr
SUZANNE BROWN
Assoc. Dean for Institutional Research: Dr
MARY C. SHOEMAKER
Asst Dean for Support Services: KEVIN
STEPHENS
Dir for Admissions and Registrar: JANICE
FARQUHARSON
Librarian: LESLIE E. MENZ

Library of 7,556 vols, 1,840 periodicals, 123
professional journals
Number of teachers: 45 (32 full-time, 13
part-time)
Number of students: 450 (330 undergraduate, 120 graduate)

ST JOHN'S COLLEGE

729 E Carpenter St, Springfield, IL 62702

Telephone: (217) 525-5628
E-mail: information@
stjohnscollegespringfield.edu
Internet: www.stjohnscollegespringfield.edu

Founded 1886
Private control

Depts of continuing education and nursing

Chancellor and Dean: Prof. Dr BRENDA
RECCHIA JEFFERS
Student Devt Officer: BETH BEASLEY
Admissions Officer and Registrar: ANNE
KLINGBORG
Library Dir: KITTY WRIGLEY

Number of teachers: 20
Number of students: 120

SAINT XAVIER UNIVERSITY

3700 W 103rd St, Chicago, IL 60655

Telephone: (773) 298-3000
E-mail: admission@sxu.edu
Internet: www.sxu.edu

Founded 1846, present name and status 1992
Private control
Academic year: August to May

Campus at Orlando Park, Illinois

Pres.: Dr CHRISTINE M. WISEMAN
Provost: Dr ANGELA DURANTE
Vice-Pres. for Business and Finance: RAY-
MOND P. CATANIA
Vice-Pres. for Student Affairs: JOHN P.
PELRINE, JR
Vice-Pres. for Student Recruitment and
Enrolment Planning: Dr KATHLEEN CARL-
SON
Vice-Pres. for Univ. Advancement: Dr STE-
VEN J. MURPHY
Vice-Pres. for Univ. Mission and Heritage:
Dr SUSAN M. SANDERS
Vice-Pres. for Univ. Relations: ROBERT C.
TENCZAR, JR
Librarian and Library Dir: MARK A. VARGAS

Library of 120,000 vols, 5,000 DVDs, 45,000
journals, 8,000 music scores, 7,000 music
albums and 6,000 video cassettes
Number of teachers: 450 (190 full-time, 14
part-time, 256 adjunct)
Number of students: 4,700 (2,990 undergraduate, 1,710 undergraduate)
Publication: Saint Xavier Magazine (2 a
year)

DEANS

College of Arts and Sciences: Prof. Dr
KATHLEEN ALAIMO
Graham School of Management: Prof. Dr
ASGHAR SABBAGHI
School for Continuing and Professional Stud-
ies: Dr LESLIE M. PETTY
School of Education: Dr BEVERLY GULLEY
School of Nursing: Dr GLORIA JACOBSON

SCHOOL OF THE ART INSTITUTE OF CHICAGO

37 S Wabash Ave, Chicago, IL 60603

Telephone: (312) 629-6100
E-mail: admiss@saic.edu
Internet: www.saic.edu

Founded 1866 as Chicago Acad. of Design
Private control
Academic year: September to May

Depts of architecture, art education, art
history, art and technology studies, ceramics,
design for emerging technologies, fashion
design, fibre and material studies, film, video
and new media, liberal arts, painting and
drawing, performance, photography, print
media, sculpture, sound, visual communication, visual and critical studies and writing

Pres.: Dr WALTER E. MASSEY
Provost: ELISSA TENNY
Vice-Provost: PAUL COFFEY
Vice-Pres. for Enrolment Management: ROSE
MILKOWSKI
Dean for Faculty: LISA WAINWRIGHT
Dean for Graduate Studies: CANDIDA ALVAREZ
Dean for Undergraduate Studies: TIFFANY
HOLMES

Library of 400,000 vols, 1,200 current serial
subscriptions
Number of teachers: 570 (140 full-time, 430
part-time)
Number of students: 3,200 (2,472 undergraduate, 728 graduate)

SEABURY-WESTERN THEOLOGICAL SEMINARY

8765 W Higgins Rd, Evanston, IL 60631

Telephone: 773-380-6780
E-mail: seabury@seabury.edu
Internet: www.seabury.edu

Founded 1933 by merger of Seabury Divinity
School (f. 1858) with Western Theological
Seminary (f. 1883)
Private control
Academic year: September to June

Dean and Pres.: ROBERT G. BOTTOMS
Vice-Pres. and Chief Operating Officer: ELI-
ZABETH BUTLER JAMESON
Academic Dean: Prof. ELLEN K. WONDRA
Dir for Finance and Admin.: MARK MILIOTTO
Registrar: PEGGY PEARSON
Dir for Library: BETH SHEPPARD

Library of 300,000 vols
Number of students: 100

SHIMER COLLEGE

3424 S State St, Chicago, IL 60616

Telephone: (312) 235-3500
Internet: www.shimer.edu

Founded 1853
Private control

Courses in liberal arts: humanities, natural sciences and social sciences

Pres.: EDWARD NOONAN
Vice-Pres. for Academic Affairs and Dean for College: BARBARA STONE
Vice-Pres. for Enrolment Management and Student Services and Dean for Students: B. DAVID GALT
Chief Financial Officer: SANDRA COLLINS
Dir for Devt: MARY PAT BARBARIE
Registrar: JIM ULRICH
Library Dir: COLLEEN MCCARROLL

Library of 20,000 vols
Number of teachers: 15 (12 full-time, 3 part-time)
Number of students: 100 (undergraduate)

SOUTHERN ILLINOIS UNIVERSITY CARBONDALE

Carbondale, IL 62901-6899
Telephone: (618) 453-2121
E-mail: joinsiuc@siu.edu
Internet: www.siuc.edu

Founded 1869
State control

Chancellor: Dr RITA CHENG
Pres.: RANDY J. DUNN
Provost and Vice-Chancellor: Dr JOHN NICK-LOW
Vice-Chancellor for Admin. and Finance: KEVIN D. BAME
Vice-Chancellor for Institutional Advancement: (vacant)
Vice-Chancellor for Research and Graduate Dean: JOHN A. KOROPCHAK
Dean for Students: PETER GITAU
Dean for Library: DAVID H. CARLSON

Library of 3,203,455 vols, 58,246 current serials, 4,633,365 microform units, 312,153 govt documents, 89,050 rare books, 18,610 linear ft MSS and archives
Number of teachers: 1,598 (full-time and part-time)
Number of students: 19,817

DEANS

College of Agricultural Sciences: TODD A. WINTERS
College of Applied Sciences and Arts: TERRY A. OWENS
College of Business: J. DENNIS CRADIT
College of Education and Human Services: JOHN BENSHOFF
College of Engineering: JOHN J. WARWICK
College of Liberal Arts: KIMBERLY KEMPF-LEONARD
College of Mass Communication and Media Arts: GARY P. KOLB
College of Science: Dr JAY C. MEANS
Graduate School: JOHN A. KOROPCHAK
School of Law: CYNTHIA FOUNTAINE
School of Medicine: Dr J. KEVIN DORSEY

SOUTHERN ILLINOIS UNIVERSITY EDWARDSVILLE

Edwardsville, IL 62026-1151
Telephone: (618) 650-2000
Internet: www.siue.edu

Founded 1957
public control
Academic year: August to May

Chancellor: Dr JULIE FURST-BOWE
Pres.: RANDY J. DUNN
Provost and Vice-Chancellor for Academic Affairs: Dr ANN M. BOYLE
Vice-Chancellor for Admin.: KENNETH R. NEHER
Vice-Chancellor for Student Affairs: Dr NARBETH R. EMMANUEL
Vice-Chancellor for Univ. Advancement: RACHEL C. STACK
Dean for Students: Dr JAMES KLENKE

Dean for Library and Information Services: Dr REGINA MCBRIDE

Library of 808,188 vols, 1,678,044 microforms, 29,222 current periodicals, 33,527 audiovisual items
Number of teachers: 900 (620 full-time, 280 part-time)
Number of students: 13,850

Publications: *Papers on Language and Literature* (4 a year, online, www.siue.edu/PLL), *Sou'wester* (2 a year, online, www.souwester.org)

DEANS

College of Arts and Sciences: Dr ALDEMARO ROMERO
Graduate School: Dr JERRY WEINBERG
School of Business: Dr JOHN NAVIN
School of Dental Medicine: Dr BRUCE E. ROTTER
School of Education: Dr BETTE S. BERGERON
School of Engineering: Dr HASAN SEVIM
School of Nursing: Dr ANNE G. PERRY
School of Pharmacy: Dr GIREESH V. GUPCHUP

SPERTUS—A CENTER FOR JEWISH LEARNING & CULTURE

610 S Michigan Ave, Chicago, IL 60605
Telephone: (312) 322-1700
E-mail: info@spertus.edu
Internet: www.spertus.edu

Founded 1924
Private control
Academic year: September to August

Pres. and CEO: Prof. Dr HAL M. LEWIS
Dean and Chief Academic Officer: Prof. Dr DEAN P. BELL

Library of 110,000 vols; spec. colln: 1,500 rare books dating from 15th–20th centuries; Chicago Jewish Archives
Number of teachers: 50
Number of students: 300

TELSHE YESHIVA–CHICAGO

3535 W Foster Ave, Chicago, IL 60625
Telephone: (773) 463-7738
Private control

Areas of study: rabbinical and Talmudic education

Pres.: Rabbi AVRAHAM LEVIN
Number of students: 75

TRINITY CHRISTIAN COLLEGE

6601 W College Dr., Palos Heights, IL 60463-0929
Telephone: (708) 597-3000
E-mail: admissions@trnty.edu
Internet: www.trnty.edu

Founded 1959
Private control
Academic year: August to May

Programmes of study in accounting, art and design, biology, business, business communication, chemistry, church and ministry leadership, communication arts, computer science, economics, education, English, exercise science, geology, Greek, history, information systems, mathematics, music, nursing, philosophy, physical education, physics, political science, psychology, science, social work, sociology, Spanish, special education, theology

Pres.: Dr STEVEN TIMMERMANS
Provost: Dr ELIZABETH A. RUDENGA
Vice-Pres. for Admissions and Marketing: PETER HAMSTRA
Vice-Pres. for Business and Finance: JAMES BELSTRA
Vice-Pres. for Campus Devt: Dr GEORGE VANDER VELDE

Vice-Pres. for Devt: LARRYL HUMME
Vice-Pres. for Student Devt: GINNY CARPENTER
Registrar: CHRISTOPHER HUANG
Library Dir: MARCILLE FREDERICK

Library of 68,000 vols, 30,000 journals, magazines and newspapers
Number of students: 1,470

TRINITY COLLEGE OF NURSING & HEALTH SCIENCES

2122 25th Ave, Rock Island, IL 61201
Telephone: (309) 779-7700
E-mail: admissions@trinitycollegeqc.edu
Internet: www.trinitycollegeqc.edu

Founded 1898
Private control

Chancellor: Dr SUSAN C. WAJERT
Dir for Student Services and External Relations: JOANN M. LAY
Dean for Nursing and Health Sciences: TRACY L. POELVOORDE
Registrar: CARA BANKS
Librarian: MARY VICKREY
Number of students: 240

TRINITY INTERNATIONAL UNIVERSITY

2065 Half Day Rd, Deerfield, IL 60015
Telephone: (847) 945-8800
Internet: www.tiu.edu

Founded 1897, present name and status 1995
Private control

Campuses in California, Florida, Illinois; online programmes

Chancellor: KENNETH L. MEYER
Pres.: DAVID DOCKERY
Provost and Exec. Vice-Pres.: JEANETTE L. HSIEH
Sr Vice-Pres. for Academic Affairs: Dr ROBERT HERRON
Sr Vice-Pres. for Business and Finance and Chief Financial Officer: J. MICHAEL PICHA
Sr Vice-Pres. for Education: Dr TITE TIÉNOU
Sr Vice-Pres. for Enrolment: ROGER L. KIEFFER
Sr Vice-Pres. for Information Technology and Planning: STEVE GEGGIE
Sr Vice-Pres. for Student Affairs and Dean of Students: Dr WILLIAM O. WASHINGTON
Sr Vice-Pres. for Univ. Advancement: Dr DAVID HOAG
Registrar: ROBERT M. BOSANAC
Univ. Librarian: ROBERT H. KRAPOHL

Library of 233,000 bound vols, 170,000 microform vols, 2,000 current periodicals, 2 microform collns of English literature from 15th–17th centuries, items from collns of Dr Carl F. H. Henry and Dr Wilbur Smith
Number of teachers: 100
Number of students: 2,864 (1,280 undergraduate, 1,584 graduate)

Publications: *The Trillium* (2 a year), *Trinity Journal* (2 a year), *Trinity Magazine* (2 a year)

DEANS

Trinity College: Dr ROBERT W. HERRON
Trinity Evangelical Divinity School: Prof. Dr TITE TIÉNOU
Trinity Graduate School: Dr ROBERT W. HERRON
Trinity Law School: MYRON STEEVES.

CONSTITUENT COLLEGES

Trinity College

E-mail: tcadmissions@tiu.edu
Internet: undergrad.tiu.edu

PROFESSORS
GRADDY, W. E., English
MOULDER, W. J., Biblical Studies
POINTER, S. R., History
SATRE, P. J., Music

Trinity Evangelical Divinity School

E-mail: tedsadm@tiu.edu
Internet: www.teds.edu

PROFESSORS
AVERBECK, R. E., Old Testament and Semitic
  Languages
BEITZEL, B. J., Old Testament and Semitic
  Languages
CANNELL, L. M., Educational Mins
CARSON, D. A., New Testament
COLE, G. A., Biblical and Systematic The-
  ology
ELMER, D. H., Educational Ministries
FEINBERG, P. D., Biblical and Systematic
  Theology
HIEBERT, P. G., Mission and Anthropology
HOFFMEIER, J. K., Old Testament and
  Ancient Near Eastern History and Archae-
  ology
KILNER, J. F., Bioethics and Contemporary
  Culture
NETLAND, H. A., Mission and Evangelism
NYQUIST, J. W., Mission and Evangelism
OSBORNE, G. R., New Testament
SENTER, M. H., Educational Mins
VAN GEMEREN, W. A., Old Testament and
  Semitic Languages
WOODBRIDGE, J. D., Church History and the
  History of Christian Thought
YOUNGER, K. L., Jr, Old Testament, Semitic
  Languages and Near Eastern History

Trinity Graduate School

E-mail: tgsadm@tiu.edu
Internet: graduate.tiu.edu

PROFESSORS
KILNER, J. F., Bioethics and Contemporary
  Culture
TIÉNOU, T., Theology of Mission

UNIVERSITY OF CHICAGO

5801 S Ellis Ave, Chicago, IL 60637
Telephone: (773) 702-1234
E-mail: infocenter@uchicago.edu
Internet: www.uchicago.edu
Founded 1890
Private control
Academic year: September to June

Pres.: ROBERT J. ZIMMER
Provost: THOMAS F. ROSENBAUM
Exec. Vice-Pres.: DAVID A. GREENE
Vice-Pres. and Chief Investment Officer:
  MARK A. SCHMID
Vice-Pres. and Dean for College Admissions
  and Financial Aid: JAMES G. NONDORF
Vice-Pres. and Gen. Counsel: BETH A. HARRIS
Vice-Pres. and Sec. for Univ.: DAVID B.
  FITHIAN
Vice-Pres. for Admin. and Chief Financial
  Office: NIM CHINNIAH
Vice-Pres. for Alumni Relations and Devt:
  THOMAS J. FARRELL
Vice-Pres. for Campus Life and Dean for
  Students: KIMBERLY M. GOFF-CREWS
Vice-Pres. for Research and Nat. Laborator-
  ies: DONALD H. LEVY
Registrar: ANDREW HANNAH
Dir for Libraries and Univ. Librarian: JUDITH
  NADLER
Library: see under Libraries and Archives
Number of teachers: 2,200 (full-time)

Number of students: 15,600 (5,124 undergraduate, 10,476 graduate, professional
  and other)
Publications: *American Art: Smithsonian
  American Art Museum* (3 a year), *American Journal of Education* (4 a year),
  American Journal of Human Genetics (12
  a year), *American Journal of Sociology* (6 a
  year), *American Naturalist* (12 a year),
  Astronomical Journal (12 a year), *Astro-
  physical Journal* (36 a year and 12 sup-
  plements a year), *Chicago Journal of
  International Law* (2 a year, online, cjil.u-
  chicago.edu), *Classical Philology* (4 a year),
  Clinical Infectious Diseases (24 a year),
  Comparative Education Review (4 a year),
  Crime and Justice (1 a year), *Critical
  Inquiry* (4 a year), *Current Anthropology*
  (5 a year), *Economic Development and
  Cultural Change* (4 a year), *Elementary
  School Journal* (5 a year), *Ethics: An
  International Journal of Social, Political
  and Legal Philosophy* (4 a year), *History of
  Religions* (4 a year), *International Journal
  of American Linguistics* (4 a year), *Inter-
  national Journal of Plant Sciences* (6 a
  year), *Isis* (4 a year, plus *Current Bibliography* as 5th issue), *Journal of Accounting
  Research* (online, www.chicagobooth.edu/
  jar), *Journal of British Studies* (4 a year),
  Journal of Business (4 a year), *Journal of
  Consumer Research: An Interdisciplinary
  Quarterly*, *Journal of Econometrics*
  (online, www.journals.elsevier.com/jour-
  nal-of-econometrics), *Journal of Geology*
  (6 a year), *Journal of Infectious Diseases*
  (24 a year), *Journal of Labor Economics* (4
  a year), *Journal of Law & Economics* (2 a
  year), *Journal of Legal Studies* (2 a year),
  Journal of Modern History (4 a year),
  Journal of Near Eastern Studies (4 a
  year), *Journal of Political Economy* (6 a
  year), *Journal of Religion* (4 a year),
  *Journal of the American Musicological
  Society* (3 a year), *Law & Social Inquiry*
  (4 a year), *Library Quarterly*, *Modern
  Philology* (4 a year), *Ocean Yearbook* (1 a
  year), *Osiris* (1 a year), *Philosophy of
  Science* (5 a year), *Physiological and Biochemical Zoology* (6 a year), *Publications of
  the Astronomical Society of the Pacific* (12 a
  year), *Quantitative Marketing and Economics*, *Quarterly Review of Biology*,
  *Signs: Journal of Women in Culture and
  Society* (4 a year), *Social Service Review* (4
  a year), *Supreme Court Economic Review*
  (1 a year), *Supreme Court Review* (1 a
  year), *University of Chicago Law Review* (4
  a year, online, lawreview.uchicago.edu),
  University of Chicago Legal Forum (1 a
  year, online, legal-forum.uchicago.edu),
  *Winterthur Portfolio: A Journal of Ameri-
  can Material Culture* (3 a year)

DEANS
Biological Sciences Division and the Pritzker
  School of Medicine: KENNETH S. POLONSKY
Chicago Booth School of Business: SUNIL
  KUMAR
Divinity School: MARGARET M. MITCHELL
Division of Humanities: MARTHA T. ROTH
Division of the Physical Sciences: ROBERT A.
  FEFFERMAN
Division of the Social Sciences: JOHN MARK
  HANSEN
Graham School of Continuing Liberal and
  Professional Studies: DANIEL W. SHANNON
Harris School of Public Policy Studies: COLM
  O'MUIRCHEARTAIGH
Law School: MICHAEL H. SCHILL
School of Social Service Administration: NEIL
  B. GUTERMAN
The College: JOHN W. BOYER

UNIVERSITY OF ILLINOIS

Urbana, IL 61801
Telephone: (217) 333-1000
E-mail: infosource@uillinois.edu
Internet: www.uillinois.edu
Founded 1867
State control
Pres.: Prof. Dr ROBERT A. EASTER
Vice-Pres. and Chief Financial Officer: WAL-
  TER K. KNORR
Vice-Pres. for Academic Affairs: CHRISTOPHE
  PIERRE
Vice-Pres. for Health Affairs.: JOE G. N.
  GARCIA
Vice-Pres. for Research: Dr LAWRENCE B.
  SCHOOK
Number of teachers: 5,650 (f.t.e.)
Number of students: 77,600 (3 campuses)

CONSTITUENT CAMPUSES

University of Illinois at Chicago

601 S Morgan St, Chicago, IL 60607-7113
Telephone: (312) 413-3350
Internet: www.uic.edu
Founded 1982 by merger of Medical Center
  campus with Chicago Circle campus
Chancellor: PAULA ALLEN-MEARES
Provost and Vice-Chancellor for Academic
  Affairs: LON S. KAUFMAN
Vice-Chancellor for Administrative Services:
  MARK DONOVAN
Vice-Chancellor for Devt: PENELOPE HUNT
Vice-Chancellor for External Affairs: WARREN
  CHAPMAN
Vice-Chancellor for Human Resources: JOHN
  LOYA
Vice-Chancellor for Research: MITRA DUTTA
Vice-Chancellor for Student Affairs: BARBARA
  HENLEY
Univ. Librarian: MARY CASE (acting)
Library: 1.9m. vols
Number of teachers: 2,600 (f.t.e.)
Number of students: 27,580 (16,911 under-
  graduate, 8,012 graduate, 2,657 profes-
  sional)

DEANS
College of Applied Health Sciences: BO
  FERNHALL
College of Architecture and the Arts: JUDITH
  R. KIRSHNER
College of Business Administration: MICHAEL
  PAGANO
College of Dentistry: BRUCE GRAHAM
College of Education: VICTORIA CHOU
College of Engineering: PETER C. NELSON
College of Liberal Arts and Sciences: ASTRIDA
  TANTILLO
College of Medicine: DIMITRI T. AZAR
College of Medicine at Peoria: SARA L. RUSCH
  (Regional Dean)
College of Medicine at Rockford: MARTIN
  LIPSKY (Regional Dean)
College of Nursing: TERRI E. WEAVER
College of Pharmacy: JERRY L. BAUMAN
College of Urban Planning and Public
  Affairs: MICHAEL PAGANO
Graduate College: KAREN J. COLLEY
Honors College: BETTE L. BOTTOMS
Jane Addams College of Social Work: CREASIE
  FINNEY HAIRSTON
School of Public Health: PAUL BRANDT-RAUF

University of Illinois at Springfield

1 University Plaza, Springfield, IL 62703-
5407
Telephone: (217) 206-6600
E-mail: admissions@uis.edu
Internet: www.uis.edu
Founded 1969 as Sangamon State Univ.,
  present name and status 1995

Chancellor: SUSAN J. KOCH
Vice-Chancellor for Academic Affairs: LYNN PARDIE
Vice-Chancellor for Student Affairs: TIMOTHY L. BARNETT
Registrar: BRIAN CLEVENGER
Dean for Library and Univ. Librarian: JANE TREADWELL
Library of 566,000 vols, 30,000 ebooks, 4,848 films, DVDs and video cassettes, 1,863,000 microforms, 200,000 govt documents
Number of students: 5,175 (3,197 undergraduate, 1,978 graduate)
Publication: *Illinois Issues* (12 a year, online, illinoisissues.uis.edu)

DEANS

College of Business and Management: RONALD D. MCNEIL
College of Education and Human Services: JAMES W. ERMATINGER
College of Liberal Arts and Sciences: JAMES W. ERMATINGER
College of Public Affairs and Administration: PINKY S. WASSENBERG

University of Illinois at Urbana-Champaign

901 W Illinois St, Urbana, IL 61801
Telephone: (217) 333-1000
E-mail: admissions@illinois.edu
Internet: www.uiuc.edu

Founded 1867, current name adopted 1885
More than 80 centres, laboratories, and institutes on the Urbana-Champaign campus that perform research for govt agencies and industry

Chancellor: PHYLLIS M. WISE
Provost and Vice-Chancellor for Academic Affairs: RICHARD WHEELER
Vice-Chancellor for Institutional Advancement: JAMES SCHROEDER
Vice-Chancellor for Public Engagement: STEVEN SONKA
Vice-Chancellor for Research: ROBERT EASTER
Vice-Chancellor for Student Affairs: C. RENEE ROMANO
Library: see under Libraries and Archives
Number of teachers: 3,100
Number of students: 42,600
Publications: *Creating Engineers for the 21st Century, Health Care, Transportation and Security, Illinois Journal of Mathematics, LASNews* (online, www.las.illinois.edu/alumni/magazine), *Water Energy Food*

DEANS

College of Agricultural, Consumer and Environmental Sciences: ROBERT J. HAUSER
College of Applied Health Sciences: TANYA M. GALLAGHER
College of Business: LARRY DEBROCK
College of Education: MARY KALANTZIS
College of Engineering: Prof. ILESANMI ADESIDA
College of Fine and Applied Arts: ROBERT B. GRAVES
College of Law: Prof. BRUCE P. SMITH
College of Liberal Arts and Sciences: Dr RUTH V. WATKINS
College of Media: Prof. JAN SLATER
College of Medicine at Urbana-Champaign: Dr URETZ J. OLIPHANT
College of Veterinary Medicine: HERB WHITELEY
Graduate College: DEBASISH DUTTA
Graduate School of Library and Information Science: JOHN UNSWORTH
School of Labour and Employment Relations: Prof. JOEL CUTCHER-GERSHENFELD
School of Social Work: Prof. WYNNE KORR

PROFESSORS

College of Agricultural, Consumer and Environmental Sciences:
AHERIN, R. A., Farm Safety
ANSELIN, L. E., Econometrics, Regional Economics
BAHR, J. M., Reproductive Physiology
BAIANU, I. C., Food Chemistry
BANWART, W. L., Soil Chemistry
BARRICK, R. K., Human and Community Devt
BARRY, P. J., Agricultural Finance
BELLER, A. H., Family Economics
BELOW, F. E., Plant Physiology
BERENBAUM, M. R., Insect Ecology
BERGER, L. L., Ruminant Nutrition
BLASCHEK, H. P., Food Microbiology
BOAST, C. W., Soil Physics
BODE, L. E., Power and Machinery
BOHNERT, H. J., Molecular Biology and Genomics of Plant Stress
BRADEN, J. B., Natural Resource and Environmental Economics
BREWER, M. S., Food Science
BRISKIN, D. P., Plant Physiology, Plant Biochemistry
BULLOCK, D. G., Crop Production and Biometry
BURIAK, P., Technical Systems Management
CAMPION, D. R., Animal Growth and Devt
CARR, T. R., Meat Science
CHASSY, B. M., Food Microbiology and Biotechnology
CHERYAN, M., Processing, Food and Biochemical Engineering
CHICOINE, D. L., State and Local Govt Finance
CHOW, P., Wood Science
CHRISTIANSON, L. L., Structures and Environment
CLARK, J. H., Ruminant Nutrition
COOKE, P. S., Veterinary Biosciences, Morphology
D'ARCY, C. J., Virology
DARMODY, R. G., Pedology
DAVID, M. B., Biogeochemistry
DAWSON, J. O., Tree Physiology
DIAMOND, A. M., Human Nutrition
DOCAMPO, R., Microbiology and Immunology
DONG, F. M., Food Science and Human Nutrition
DONOVAN, S. M., Nutrition
DRACKLEY, J. K., Nutrition
DUDLEY, J. W., Plant Genetics
EASTER, R. A., Animal Nutrition
ECKHOFF, S. R., Food and Bioprocess Engineering
ELLIS, M., Swine Nutrition
ENDRESS, A. G., Environmental Stress Physiology
ERDMAN, J. W., Nutrition
FAHEY, G. C., Animal Sciences, Nutritional Biochemistry
FARRAND, S. K., Molecular Biology
FAULKNER, D. B., Beef Extension
GARCIA, P., Agricultural Marketing and Price Analysis
GASKINS, H. R., Animal Sciences
GERTNER, G. Z., Forest Biometrics
GOOD, D. L., Agricultural Marketing
GRAY, M. E., Integrated Pest Management and Extension
GROSSMAN, M., Genetics
GROSSMAN, M. R., Agricultural Law
HANSEN, L. G., Pharmacology and Toxicology
HARPER, J. G., Agricultural Education
HAUSER, R. J., Agricultural Marketing and Price Analysis
HEICHEL, G. H., Plant Physiology
HELFERICH, W. G., Nutrition, Food Toxicology
HESS, R. A., Morphology/Toxicology

HIRSCHI, M. C., Soil and Water Extension
HOEFT, R. G., Soil Fertility and Extension
HOLLIS, G. R., Swine Extension
HURLEY, W. L., Lactation
HUTJENS, M. F., Dairy Extension
HYMOWITZ, T., Plant Genetics and Genetic Engineering
IRWIN, M. E., Entomology
IRWIN, S. H., Agricultural Marketing and Price Analysis
ISSERMAN, A. M., Rural Economic Devt
JEFFERY, E. H., Toxicology, Food Science and Human Nutrition, Veterinary Biosciences
JONES, R. L., Soil Mineralogy and Ecology
JUVIK, J. A., Plant Genetics
KALITA, P. K., Soil and Water Association
KELLEY, K. W., Animal Sciences
KESLER, D. J., Reproductive Physiology
KOLB, F. L., Small Grain Breeding and Genetics
KORBAN, S. S., Plant Genetics
KRAMER, L. F., Applied Family Studies
KUHLENSCHMIDT, M. S., Microbiology
LARSON, R. A., Environmental Chemistry
LARSON, R. W., Family Ecology
LAYMAN, D. K., Nutrition
LEWIN, H. A., Biotechnology
LILA, M. A., Plant Physiology
LINS, D. A., Finance
LITCHFIELD, J. B., Food and Bioprocess Engineering
LONG, S. P., Photosynthesis and Environmental Sciences
MCKEITH, F. K., Meat Science
MACKIE, R. I., Animal Sciences, Microbiology
MARTIN, S. E., Food Microbiology
MERCHEN, N. R., Animal Sciences, Ruminant Nutrition
MILLER, G. Y., Veterinary Pathobiology
MORGANOSKY, M. A., Consumer and Retail Marketing
MORRIS, S. A., Processing Association
MULVANEY, R. L., Soil Fertility, Soil Chemistry, Soil Microbiology
MURPHY, M. R., Animal Sciences, Ruminant Nutrition
NAFZIGER, E. D., Crop Production and Extension
NELSON, R. L., Plant Genetics
NIBLACK, T. L., Cyst Nematode Management and Extension
NOEL, G. R., Nematology
NOVAKOFSKI, J. E., Animal Sciences, Meat Science
O'BRIEN, W. D., Electrical and Computer Engineering
OLSON, K. R., Soil Conservation, Soil Management, Pedology
ORT, D. R., Plant Physiology
PARRETT, D. F., Meat Animal Evaluation
PARSONS, C. M., Poultry Nutrition and Management
PATAKY, J. K., Epidemiology
PAUL, A. J., Small Animal Extension and Medicine
PAULSEN, M. R., Food and Bioprocess Engineering
PECK, T. R., Soil Chemistry and Extension
PERLMAN, A. L., Speech and Hearing
PERSHING, R. L., Power and Machinery
PETTIGREW, J. E., Animal Sciences, Swine Nutrition
PLECK, E. H., Human and Community Devt, History
PLECK, J. H., Human Devt and Family Studies
PLEWA, M. J., Plant Genetics/Environmental Mutagens
PORTIS, A. R., Plant Biochemistry
PUEPPKE, S. G., Plant Pathology
RAHEEL, M., Textiles and Clothing
REBEIZ, C. A., Plant Biochemistry and Plant Physiology

ROLFE, G. L., Forest Ecology and Environmental Studies

SALAMON, S. B., Community Studies, Family Studies

SCHMIDT, S. J., Food Chemistry

SCHOOK, L. B., Comparative Genomics

SHANKS, R. D., Genetics

SHAPIRO, C. H., Human and Community Devt

SINGLETARY, K. W., Nutrition

SKIRVIN, R. M., Horticulture

SMITH, R. D., Epidemiology and Preventive Medicine

SOFRANKO, A. J., Rural Sociology

SONKA, S. T., Agricultural Management

SPOMER, L. A., Plant Physiology

STEFFEY, K. L., Forage and Field Crop Insects and Extension

STUCKI, J. W., Soil Chemistry

SWANSON, B. E., International Agricultural Education, International Extension Technology Transfer

TIAN, L., Power and Machinery Association

TRUPIN, S. R., Obstetrics and Gynaecology

UCHTMANN, D. L., Agricultural Law

UNNEVEHR, L. J., Agricultural Marketing and Policy

VAN ES, J. C., Rural Sociology

VODKIN, L. O., Soybean Genetics and Genetic Engineering

WALLIG, M. A., Veterinary Pathobiology

WANSINK, B. C., Marketing and Agricultural Economics

WAX, L. M., Plant Physiology and Weed Science

WEATHERHEAD, P. J., Behavioural Ecology

WEIGEL, R. M., Epidemiology and Preventive Medicine

WEINZIERL, R. A., Fruit, Vegetable, and Livestock Insects

WHEELER, M. B., Reproductive Physiology

WHITE, B. A., Microbiology

WHITE, D. G., Fungal Diseases of Corn

WIDHOLM, J. M., Plant Physiology and Genetic Engineering

WILKINSON, H. T., Turfgrass Diseases

WILLIAMS, D. J., Horticulture

ZHANG, Q., Power and Machinery Association

College of Applied Health Studies:

BOILEAU, R. A., Kinesiology

CHAMBERS, R. D., Speech and Hearing Science

CHODZKO-ZAJKO, W., Kinesiology

FESENMAIER, D. R., Leisure Studies

GALLAGHER, T. M., Speech and Hearing Science

GOOLER, D. M., Speech and Hearing Science

HENGST, J., Speech and Hearing Science

IWAMOTO, G., Kinesiology

JOHNSON, C. J., Speech and Hearing Science

KUEHN, D. P., Speech and Hearing Science

LANSING, C. R., Speech and Hearing Science

MCAULEY, E., Kinesiology

O'ROURKE, T., Community Health

PERLMAN, A. L., Speech and Hearing Science

PROCTOR, F. A., Speech and Hearing Science

REIS, J., Community Health

SCHIRO-GEIST, C., Community Health

WATKIN, K. L., Speech and Hearing Science

WATKINS, R. V., Speech and Hearing Science

YAIRI, E., Speech and Hearing Science

College of Business:

ABDEL-KHALIK, A. R., Accountancy

ALSTON, L. J., Economics

ARNOULD, R. J., Economics

BAER, W., Economics

BECK, P. J., Accountancy

BERA, A. K., Economics

BERNHARDT, D., Economics

BLAIR, C., Management Science/Process Management

BLAIR, C. E., Business Administration

BROWN, C. E., Accountancy

BRUECKNER, J. K., Economics

CHAN, L. K. C., Finance

CHENG, J. L., Business Administration, International Business

CHHAJED, D., Business Administration, Programme Management Science/Process Management

CHO, I. K., Economics

COLWELL, P. F., Finance and Real Estate Research

CONLEY, J. P., Economics

D'ARCY, S. P., Finance

DEBROCK, L., Economics

ENGELBRECHT-WIGGANS, R., Business Administration, Management Science/Process Management

FINNERTY, J. E., Finance

GAHVARI, F., Economics

GENTRY, J. A., Finance

GIERTZ, J. F., Economics

GOTTHEIL, F. M., Economics

GRIFFIN, A., Business Administration, Marketing

GRINOLS, E. L., Economics

HALPERIN, R. M., Accountancy

HESS, J. D., Business Administration

IKENBERRY, D., Finance

JEGADEESH, N., Finance

KAHN, C. M., Finance and Economics

KANNAN, S., Finance

KINDT, J., Business Law

KLEINMUNTZ, D. N., Business Administration, Strategic Management

KOENKER, R., Economics

KRASA, S., Economics

KWON, Y. K., Accountancy

LAKONISHOK, J., Finance

LANSING, P., Business Administration, Business Law

LEBLEBICI, H., Business Administration, Organizational Behaviour

LINS, D. A., Finance, Agricultural and Consumer Economics

LYNGE, M. J., Jr, Finance

MONAHAN, G. E., Business Administration, Management Science/Process Management

MONROE, K. B., Marketing

NEAL, L. D., Economics

NEUMANN, F. L., Accountancy Executive Leadership

NORTHCRAFT, G., Organizational Behaviour

OLDHAM, G., Organizational Behaviour

PEARSON, N. D., Finance

PENNACCHI, G. G., Finance

QUALLS, W. J., Business Administration, Marketing

RASHID, S., Economics

RESEK, R. W., Economics

ROSZKOWSKI, M. E., Business Administration, Business Law

SETH, A., Business Administration, Strategic Management

SHAFER, W. J., Economics

SHAVITT, S., Business Administration, Marketing

SHAW, M. J., Commerce and Business Administration, Marketing

SOLOMON, I., Accountancy

SUDHARSHAN, D., Business Administration, Marketing

TAUB, B., Economics

VILLAMIL, A. P., Economics

WANSINK, B., Marketing

WEISBACH, M. S., Finance

WILLIAMS, S. R., Economics

WON, Y., Accountancy

YANNELIS, N. C., Economics

ZIEBART, D. A., Accountancy

College of Communications:

BREWER, W. F., Psychology

CHRISTIANS, C., Communications

DASH, L., Journalism

DAVIS, S., Folklore and Folklife

DELIA, J. G., Communication and Human Relations

DENZIN, N., Sociology

DESSER, D., Cinema Studies, Speech Communication

GAINES, W., Journalism

HARRINGTON, W., Journalism

HELLE, S., Advertising and Journalism

LIEBOVICH, L. W., Mass Communications

MCCARTHY, C., Education, Curriculum Theory

MCCHESNEY, R. W., Library and Information Science

MERRITT, R. L., International Relations, Political Science

NERONE, J., Media Studies

O'GUINN, T., Advertising and Business Administration

PRESS, A., Media Studies, Speech Communication

RICH, R., Law, Political Science

ROTZOLL, K., Advertising

SCHILLER, D., Communication, Library and Information Science

SRULL, T., Advertising

TREICHLER, P. A., Linguistics, Criticism and Interpretive Theory

WILLIAMS, B., Political Science

YATES, R., Journalism

College of Education:

ALEXANDER, K.

ANDERSON, R.

ANDERSON, T.

ARMBRUSTER, B.

BAROODY, A.

BARRERA, R.

BRAGG, D.

BRESLER, L.

BURBULES, N.

CHADSEY, J.

CLIFT, R.

CORDOVA-WENTLING, R. M.

CZIKO, G.

FEINBERG, W.

GARCIA, G.

GREENE, J.

HALLE, J.

HARRIS, V.

HUNTER, R.

IKENBERRY, S. R.

JOHNSON, S.

LEVIN, J.

LOEB, J.

MCCLURE, E.

MCCOLLUM, J.

MCCONKIE, G.

MIRON, L.

PERRY, M.

RENZAGLIA, A.

RIZVI, F.

ROUNDS, J.

RUSCH, F.

SCHWANDT, T.

STAHL, S.

TRAVERS, K.

TRENT, W.

WARD, J.

WESTBURY, I.

WILLIS, A.

College of Engineering:

ABELSON, J. R., Materials Science and Engineering

ADRIAN, R. J., Mechanical and Industrial Engineering, Theoretical and Applied Mechanics

AGHA, G., Computer Science

AHERIN, R., Agricultural Engineering

AHUJA, N., Engineering

ALKIRE, R. C., Chemical and Biomolecular Engineering
AREF, H., Physics, Theoretical and Applied Mechanics
AVERBACK, R. S., Materials Science and Engineering
AXFORD, R., Nuclear, Plasma and Radiological Engineering
BALACHANDAR, S. B., Theoretical and Applied Mechanics
BASAR, T., Electrical and Computer Engineering
BAYM, G. A., Physics
BECK, D. H., Physics
BERGMAN, L. A., Aeronautical and Astronautical Engineering
BLAHUT, R., Electrical and Computer Engineering
BRAATZ, R. D., Chemical and Biomolecular Engineering
BRAGG, M. B., Aeronautical and Astronautical Engineering
BREWSTER, M. Q., Mechanical and Industrial Engineering
BUCKIUS, R. O., Mechanical and Industrial Engineering
BUCKMASTER, J. D., Aeronautical and Astronautical Engineering, Theoretical and Applied Mechanics
BULLARD, C. W., Mechanical and Industrial Engineering
BURIAK, P., Agricultural Engineering
BURTON, R. L., Aeronautical and Astronautical Engineering
CAHILL, D. G., Materials Science and Engineering
CAMPBELL, E., Computer Science
CARLSON, D. E., Theoretical and Applied Mechanics
CEPERLEY, D. M., Physics
CHANG, Y.-C., Physics
CHEW, W., Engineering
CHIANG, T.-C., Physics
CHRISTIANSON, L., Agricultural Engineering
CLEGG, R. M., Physics
COLEMAN, J., Electrical and Computer Engineering
CONRY, T. F., General Engineering
CONWAY, B. A., Aeronautical and Astronautical Engineering
COOK, H. E., Gen. Engineering
COOPER, S. L., Physics
CRAIG, J., Mechanical and Industrial Engineering
DANTZIG, J. A., Mechanical and Industrial Engineering
DAVIS, W. J., Gen. Engineering
DEBEVEC, P. T., Physics
DEJONG, G., Computer Science
DEVOR, R. E., Mechanical and Industrial Engineering
ECKHOFF, S., Agricultural Engineering
ECKSTEIN, J. N., Physics
ECONOMY, J., Materials Science and Engineering
EHRLICH, G., Materials Science and Engineering
ERREDE, S. M., Physics
FENG, M., Electrical and Computer Engineering
FERREIRA, P. M., Mechanical and Industrial Engineering
FLYNN, C. P., Physics
FRADKIN, E. H., Physics
GEIL, P. H., Materials Science and Engineering
GEORGIADIS, J. G., Mechanical and Industrial Engineering
GLADDING, G. E., Physics
GOLDBART, P. M., Physics, Gen. Engineering
GOLDENFELD, N. D., Physics
GOLLIN, G. D., Physics

GRANICK, S., Chemical and Biomolecular Engineering, Materials Science and Engineering, Physics
GRATTON, E., Physics
GREENE, J. E., Materials Science and Engineering, Physics
GREENE, L. H., Physics
GRUEBELE, M. H., Physics
HABER, R. B., Theoretical and Applied Mechanics
HAJEK, B., Engineering
HAN, J., Computer Science
HEATH, M. T., Computer Science
HERTZOG, D. W., Physics
HESS, K., Physics
HIGDON, J. J. L., Chemical and Biomolecular Engineering
HIRSCHI, M., Agricultural Engineering
HODDESON, L., Physics
HOLONYAK, N., Physics
HRNJAK, P. S., Mechanical and Industrial Engineering
HUANG, T., Electrical Engineering
HUANG, Y. Y., Mechanical and Industrial Engineering, Theoretical and Applied Mechanics
HWU, W.-M., Electrical and Computer Engineering
IYER, R., Engineering
JACOBI, A. M., Mechanical and Industrial Engineering
JACOBSON, S. H., Mechanical and Industrial Engineering
JAMISON, R. D., Materials Science and Engineering
JONES, B. G., Nuclear, Plasma and Radiological Engineering, Mechanical and Industrial Engineering
KALE, L., Computer Science
KAPOOR, S. G., Mechanical and Industrial Engineering
KATZ, S., Physics
KERKHOVEN, T., Computer Science
KIM, K., Nuclear, Plasma and Radiological Engineering
KLEIN, M. V., Physics
KOGUT, J. B., Physics
KRIER, H., Mechanical and Industrial Engineering
KRIVEN, W. M., Materials Science and Engineering
KUMAR, P., Electrical and Computer Engineering
KUSHNER, M., Engineering
KUSHNER, M. J., Physics
KUSHNER, M. K., Chemical and Biomolecular Engineering
KWIAT, P. G., Physics
LAMB, F. K., Physics
LAWRENCE, F. V., Jr, Materials Science and Engineering
LECKBAND, D. E., Chemical and Biomolecular Engineering
LEE, K. D., Aeronautical and Astronautical Engineering
LEGGETT, A. J., Physics
LISS, TONY M., Physics
LOTH, E., Aeronautical and Astronautical Engineering
MAKRI, N., Physics
MARTIN, R. M., Physics
MASEL, R. I., Chemical and Biomolecular Engineering
MEDANIC, J. V., Gen. Engineering
MESEGUER, J., Computer Science
MILEY, G. H., Nuclear, Plasma and Radiological Engineering
MOSER, R. D., Theoretical and Applied Mechanics
MOUSCHOVIAS, T. C., Physics
MUNSON, D., Jr, Electrical and Computer Engineering
NAHRSTEDT, K., Computer Science
NAMACHCHIVAYA, N. S., Aeronautical and Astronautical Engineering
NAYFEH, M. H., Physics

NEWELL, T. A., Mechanical and Industrial Engineering
OONO, Y., Physics
PADUA, D., Computer Science
PANDHARIPANDE, V. R., Physics
PATEL, J., Engineering
PAULSEN, M., Agricultural Engineering
PAYNE, D. A., Materials Science and Engineering
PEARLSTEIN, A. J., Mechanical and Industrial Engineering, Theoretical and Applied Mechanics
PENG, J.-C., Physics
PHILLIPS, J. W., Theoretical and Applied Mechanics
PHILLIPS, P. W., Physics
PHILLIPS, W. R. C., Theoretical and Applied Mechanics
PINES, D., Physics
PITT, L., Computer Science
PONCE, J., Computer Science
PRICE, R. L., Gen. Engineering
PRUSSING, J. E., Aeronautical and Astronautical Engineering
REED, D., Computer Science
REIS, H. L. M., Gen. Engineering
RIAHI, D. N., Theoretical and Applied Mechanics
ROBERTSON, I. M., Materials Science and Engineering
ROBINSON, I. K., Physics
ROCKETT, A., Materials Science and Engineering
ROGERS, J. A., Materials Science and Engineering
RUZIC, D. N., Nuclear, Plasma and Radiological Engineering
SALAMON, M. B., Physics
SCHULTEN, K. J., Physics
SCHWEIZER, K. S., Chemical and Biomolecular Engineering, Materials Science and Engineering
SEEBAUER, E. G., Chemical and Biomolecular Engineering
SEHITOGLU, H., Mechanical and Industrial Engineering
SELEN, M. A., Physics
SENTMAN, L. H., Aeronautical and Astronautical Engineering
SHA, L., Computer Science
SHAPIRO, S. L., Physics
SINGER, C., Nuclear, Plasma and Radiological Engineering
SKEEL, R. D., Computer Science
SLICHTER, C. P., Physics
SNIR, M., Computer Science
SOCIE, D. F., Mechanical and Industrial Engineering
SOTTOS, N. R., Theoretical and Applied Mechanics
SPONG, M. W., Gen. Engineering
STACK, J. D., Physics
STEWART, D. S., Theoretical and Applied Mechanics
STONE, M., Physics
STUBBINS, J. F., Nuclear, Plasma and Radiological Engineering
SULLIVAN, J. D., Physics
THALER, J. J., Physics
THOMAS, B. G., Mechanical and Industrial Engineering
THURSTON, D. L., Gen. Engineering
TORRELLAS, J., Computer Science
TORTORELLI, D. A., Mechanical and Industrial Engineering, Theoretical and Applied Mechanics
TUCKER, C. L., III, Mechanical and Industrial Engineering
VAN HARLINGEN, D. J., Physics
VANKA, S. P., Mechanical and Industrial Engineering
WAH, B., Electrical and Computer Engineering
WALKER, J. S., Mechanical and Industrial Engineering
WATSON, W. D., Physics

WEAVER, J. H., Materials Science and Engineering, Physics
WEAVER, R. L., Theoretical and Applied Mechanics
WEISSMAN, M. B., Physics
WHITE, S. R., Aeronautical and Astronautical Engineering
WILTZIUS, P., Materials Science and Engineering, Physics
WISS, J. E., Physics
WOLFE, J. P., Physics
ZUKOSKI, C. F., Chemical and Biomolecular Engineering

College of Fine and Applied Arts:

ALBRECHT, J. G., Architecture
ALEXANDER, R., Music
ALI, M. M., Architecture
ANDERSON, J. R., Architecture
ANTHONY, K. H., Architecture
ARENDS, M., Industrial Design
BASKINGER, M., Graphic Design
BELLAFIORE, V., Landscape Architecture
BOGNAR, B., Architecture
BULLOCK, W., Industrial Design
CAMERON, M., Music
CARLSON, W., Glass
CONLIN, K. F., Theatre
DALHEIM, E., Music
DI VIRGILIO, N., Music
DRY, C., Architecture
EWALD, M., Music
FINEBERG, J., Art History
FORREST, C. W., Urban and Regional Planning
GARNER, J. S., Architecture
GOGGIN, N., Narrative Media
GRAVES, R., Theatre
GRUCZA, L., Painting
HARKNESS, T., Landscape Architecture
HARRIS, J. B., Theatre
HEDEMAN, A. D., Art History
HEDLUND, R., Music
HEILES, W., Music
HILL, J. W., Music
HOBSON, I., Music
HOPKINS, L., Landscape Architecture
HOPKINS, L. D., Urban and Regional Planning
HOSTETTER, E., Art History
ISSERMAN, A., Urban and Regional Planning
JAKLE, J., Landscape Architecture
KEENE, J. F., Music
KENDRICK, B., Painting
KEYS, H., Theatre
KIM, M. K., Architecture
KIM, T. J., Urban and Regional Planning
KINDERMAN, W., Music
KNAAP, G. J., Urban and Regional Planning
KOVATCH, R., Ceramics
KRAMER, K., Music
McFARQUHAR, R., Theatre
MACHALA, K., Music
MARTENS, C., Foundation
METTEM, A., Foundation
NETTLES, B., Photography
OUSTERHOUT, R. G., Architecture
PERKINS, K. A., Theatre
PLUMMER, H. S., Architecture
RICHTMEYER, D., Music
ROMM, R., Music
ROWAN, D., Printmaking
SCHAFFER, P., Music
SCHWARTZ, R., Painting
SIENA, J., Music
SILVER, C., Urban and Regional Planning
SOCHA, D., Printmaking
SQUIERM, J., Narrative Media
STOLTZFUS, F., Music
STONE, S., Music
SULLIVAN, D., Theatre
THEIDE, B. J., Metals
TIPEI, S., Music
TURINO, T., Music

VAN LAARM, T., Painting
WADLEIGH, R., Dance
WARD, T. R., Music
WARFIELD, J. P., Architecture
WESCOAT, J. L., Landscape Architecture
WILLIAMS, B., Urban and Regional Planning
WYATT, S. A., Music

College of Law:

BALL, C. A.
BELL, G.
BOYLE, F. A.
COLOMBO, J. D.
DAVEY, W. J.
FINKIN, M. W.
FREYFOGLE, E. T.
GEERDES, C. E.
HARRIS, O. F., Jr
HURD, H. M.
KAPLAN, R. L.
KINPORTS, K.
LEIPOLD, A. D.
McADAMS, R. H.
MAGGS, P. B.
MEYER, D. D.
PAINTER, R. W.
PFANDER, J. E.
REYNOLDS, L. A.
RIBSTEIN, L. E.
RICH, R. F.
ROSS, S. F.
SHOBEN, E. W.
TABB, C. J.
TARR, N. W.
TERRY, C. T.
ULEN, T. S.

College of Liberal Arts and Sciences:

ACCAD, E., French
ADELMAN, G., English
ALEXANDER, S., Mathematics
ALKIRE, R. C., Chemical and Biomolecular Engineering
ANGIONE, R. J., Astronomy
AUGSPURGER, C., Animal Biology, Plant Biology
BAILLARGEON, R., Psychology
BARON, D., English
BASS, J. D., Geology
BASSETT, T. J., Geography
BATZLI, G. O., Animal Biology
BAYM, G. A., Physics
BAYM, N., English
BEAK, P., Chemistry
BEARD, K., Atmospheric Sciences
BELFORD, R. L., Chemistry
BELMONT, A. S., Cell and Structural Biology, Biophysics
BERENBAUM, M. R., Entomology
BERNDT, B. C., Mathematics
BEST, P. M., Molecular and Integrative Physiology, Biophysics, Neuroscience and Bioengineering
BETHKE, C. M., Geology
BLAKE, D. B., Geology
BLAKE, N., Comparative Literature, Slavic Languages and Literature
BOCK, J. K., Psychology
BOHN, P. W., Chemistry
BOHNERT, H., Plant Biology and Crop Sciences
BOURGAIN, J., Mathematics
BRAATZ, R. D., Chemical and Biomolecular Engineering
BRECHIN, S., Sociology
BREWER, D. J., Anthropology
BREWER, W. F., Psychology
BRISKIN, D., Natural Resources and Environmental Sciences, Plant Biology
BRISTOL, E., Slavic Languages and Literature
BROWNE, G. M., Classics
BUDESCU, D., Psychology
BUSH, D. R., Plant Biology
CALDER, W. M., III, Classics
CAPWELL, C., Music

CARMEN, I. H., Political Science
CARRINGER, R. L., Cinema Studies, English
CASSELL, A. K., Italian and Comparative Literature
CHAI, L., English
CHEESEMAN, J., Plant Biology
CHEN, W.-P., Geology
CHENG, C-C., East Asian Languages and Culture
CHU, Y.-H., Astronomy
CLARK, R. A., Speech Communication
CLEGG, R. M., Physics and Biophysics
COATES, R. M., Chemistry
COHEN, N. J., Psychology
CONLEY, T. M., Speech Communication
CONTRACTOR, N., Speech Communication
CROFTS, A. R., Biochemistry
CRONAN, J. E., Microbiology, Biochemistry
DADE, E. C., Mathematics
D'ANGELO, J. P., Mathematics
DELCOMYN, F., Entomology
DELEY, H., French
DELIA, J. G., Speech Communication
DELL, G. S., Psychology
DeLUCIA, E., Plant Biology
DENMARK, S. E., Chemistry
DENZIN, N., Cinema Studies
DESSER, D., Cinema Studies
DeVRIES, A. L., Animal Biology
DIENER, E. F., Psychology
DLOTT, D. D., Chemistry
DRASGOW, F., Psychology
DUTTA, S., Mathematics
FAGYAL, Z., French
FENG, A. S., Molecular and Integrative Physiology, Biophysics, Bioengineering, and Neuroscience
FITZGERALD, L., Psychology
FOSSUM, R. M., Mathematics
FRANCIS, G. K., Mathematics
FRAZZETTA, T. H., Animal Biology
FRIEDMAN, P., English
FRITZSCHE, P., History
FÜREDI, Z., Mathematics
GABRIEL, M., Psychology
GARBER, P. A., Anthropology
GARCIA, P., Agricultural Economics
GARRETT, P., English
GENNIS, R. B., Biochemistry, Chemistry, Biophysics
GERLACH, U. H., Germanic Languages and Literature
GERLT, J. A., Biochemistry, Chemistry and Biophysics, Basic Medical Science
GEWIRTH, A. A., Chemistry
GIROLAMI, G. S., Chemistry
GLASER, M., Biochemistry, Basic Medical Sciences
GOLATO, P., French
GOLD, P. E., Psychology
GOODMAN, D. G., East Asian Languages and Culture
GOTTLIEB, A., Anthropology
GRAHAM, P., English
GRANICK, S., Chemical and Biomolecular Engineering
GRAY, M. E., Entomology
GRAYSON, D. R., Mathematics
GREENOUGH, W. T., Psychology
GROVE, D., Anthropology
GRUEBELE, M., Chemistry
GUIBBOR, A., English
GUMPORT, R. I., Biochemistry, Basic Medical Sciences
HABOUSH, W., Mathematics
HADLEY, A. O., French
HANNON, B. M., Geography
HAWISHER, G. E., English
HE, X., Statistics
HELLER, W., Psychology
HELMAN, S. I., Molecular and Integrative Physiology, Biophysics, and Bioengineering
HENSON, C. W., Mathematics
HEWINGS, G. J. D., Geography

HIGDON, J. J. L., Chemical and Biomolecular Engineering
HILDEBRAND, A. J., Mathematics
HINKKANEN, A., Mathematics
HITCHINS, K., History
HOCK, H. H., Linguistics
HSUI, A. T., Geology
HUALDE, J. I., Linguistics and Spanish, Italian, and Portuguese
HUBERT, L., Psychology
IBEN, I., Jr, Physics
IMREY, P., Statistics
IRWIN, D., Psychology
IRWIN, M. E., Entomology
IVANOV, S. V., Mathematics
JACOBSON, H., Classics
JAEGER, C. S., Cinema Studies
JAEGER, S., Comparative Literature
JAHER, F. C., Cinema Studies
JAHIEL, E., Cinema Studies, French
JAKLE, J. A., Geography
JAKOBSSON, E., Molecular and Integrative Physiology, Biochemistry, Biophysics, Bioengineering, and Neuroscience
JOCKUSCH, C. G., Mathematics
JOHNSON, D. L., Geography
JURASKA, J., Psychology
KALINKE, M. E., Germanic Languages and Literature
KATZ, S., Mathematics
KATZENELLENBOGEN, B. S., Molecular and Integrative Physiology
KATZENELLENBOGEN, J. A., Chemistry
KELLER, J. D., Anthropology
KELLY, B., English
KEMPER, B. W., Molecular and Integrative Physiology, Cell and Structural Biology
KIBBEE, D., French
KIM, C. W., Linguistics, East Asian Languages and Culture
KIRKPATRICK, R. J., Geology
KLEMPERER, W. G., Chemistry
KLEPINGER, L. L., Anthropology
KLUEGEL, J., Sociology
KNOTT, J. H., Political Science
KOENKER, D. P., History
KOSTOCHKA, A. V., Mathematics
KRAMER, A., Psychology
KRANZ, D. M., Biochemistry
KUKLINSKI, J. H., Political Science
LAMB, F. K., Physics
LAUGHLIN, P. R., Psychology
LAUTERBUR, P. C., Chemistry
LECKBAND, D. E., Chemistry, Chemical and Biomolecular Engineering
LEHMAN, F. K., Anthropology
LEWIS, R. B., Anthropology
LIEBERMAN, L., English
LISY, J. M., Chemistry
LOEB, P. A., Mathematics
LOTZ, H. P., Mathematics
LOVE, J. L., History
McCARTHY, T., Philosophy
McDONALD, J. D., Chemistry
McDONALD, R., Psychology
McKIM, R., Religious Studies, Philosophy
McLAFFERTY, S., Geography
McLINDEN, L., Mathematics
McMAHAN, J., Philosophy
MAHER, P., Philosophy
MAK, M., Atmospheric Sciences
MAKRI, N., Chemistry
MALL, L., French
MALPELI, J. G., Psychology
MANGELSDORF, S., Psychology
MARDEN, J., Statistics
MARSHAK, S., Geology
MARTINSEK, A., Statistics
MASEL, R. I., Chemical and Biomolecular Engineering
MATHY, J.-P., French, Comparative Literature
MICHELSON, B., English
MILES, J. B., Mathematics
MILLER, G., Psychology
MILLER, P., Psychology

MILLER, P. J., Speech Communication
MOHR, R., Philosophy
MOORE, J. S., Chemistry
MORGAN, J. L., Linguistics
MORRISSEY, J. H., Biochemistry
MORTIMER, A., French
MOUSCHOVIAS, T., Physics and Astrophysics
MURAV, H., Slavic Languages and Literature, Comparative Literature
MUSUMECCI, A., Italian
NARDULLI, P. F., Political Science
NEDERVEEN-PIETERSE, J., Sociology
NEELY, C., English
NIKOLAEV, I., Mathematics
NUZZO, R., Chemistry
O'KEEFE, D. J., Speech Communication
OLDFIELD, E., Chemistry
ONO, K., Asian American Studies
ORDAL, G. W., Biochemistry, Basic Medical Science
ORT, D. R., Plant Biology
PACKARD, J., East Asian Languages and Culture
PAHRE, R., Political Science
PAIGE, K. N., Animal Biology
PALENCIA-ROTH, M., Comparative Literature
PALMORE, J. I., Mathematics
PANDHARIPANDE, R., Linguistics, Religious Studies, Sanskrit, Comparative Literature
PANDHARIPANDE, V., Physics
PARK, D., Psychology
PARKER, R. D., English
PHILLIPS, P. W., Physics
PHILLIPS, T. L., Plant Biology
PILLAY, A., Mathematics
PINDERHUGHES, D. M., Political Science, African-American Studies
PINES, D., Physics and Electrical and Computer Engineering
PITARD, W. T., Religious Studies
PORTON, G. G., Religious Studies, History, Comparative Literature
POWERS, R., English
PRESS, A., Speech Communication
QUIRK, P. J., Political Science
RAPPAPORT, J., Psychology
RAUBER, R., Atmospheric Sciences
RAUCHFUSS, T. B., Chemistry
REZNICK, B., Mathematics
RHOADS, B. L., Geography
RICH, R. F., Political Science
ROBERTSON, H. M., Entomology
ROBINSON, D. J. S., Mathematics
ROBINSON, G. E., Entomology, Political Science
ROBINSON, S. K., Animal Biology
ROBINSON, W., Atmospheric Sciences
ROEDIGER, D., African-American Studies
ROGERS, J. A., Chemistry
RONCADOR, S. M., Brazilian, Portuguese and Lusophone Literatures
ROSENBLATT, J., Mathematics
ROSS, B., Psychology
ROTMAN, J., Mathematics
ROY, E., Psychology
RUAN, Z.-J., Mathematics
SAHINIDIS, N. V., Chemical and Biomolecular Engineering
SANSONE, D., Classics
SCHACHT, R., Philosophy
SCHEELINE, A., Chemistry
SCHEHR, L., French
SCHLESINGER, M., Atmospheric Sciences
SCHULER, M. A., Cell and Structural Biology, Biochemistry
SCHULTEN, K., Chemistry
SCHUPP, P., Mathematics
SCHWEIZER, K. S., Chemistry, Chemical and Biomolecular Engineering
SEEBAUER, E. G., Chemical and Biomolecular Engineering
SEIGLER, D. S., Plant Biology
SHAFTER, A. W., Astronomy
SHAPIRO, M., English

SHAPIRO, S. L., Physics and Astronomy
SHAPLEY, J. R., Chemistry
SHAPLEY, P. A., Chemistry
SHEARER, C. A., Plant Biology
SHERWOOD, O. D., Molecular and Integrative Physiology
SHOBEN, E. J., Psychology
SIMPSON, D., Statistics
SLIGAR, S. G., Chemistry
SMITH, S. G., Chemistry
SNIEZEK, J. A., Psychology
SOFFER, O., Anthropology
SOUSA, R., Portuguese, Spanish and Comparative Literature
SRULL, T. K., Psychology
STEFFEY, K. L., Entomology
STILLINGER, N. B., English
STOLARSKY, K. B., Mathematics
SULLIVAN, Z., English
SUSLICK, K. S., Chemistry
SWANSON, D. L., Political Science, Speech Communication
SWEEDLER, J. V., Chemistry
TALBOT, E. J., French
TEARE, S., Electrical Engineering
THOMPSON, L. A., Astronomy
THOMPSON, J., English
TOBY, R. P., East Asian Languages and Culture
TODOROVA, M., History
TUMANOV, A. E., Mathematics
ULLOM, S. V., Mathematics
UNNEVEHR, L., Agricultural and Consumer Economics
VALENTE, J., English
VAN DEN DRIES, L., Mathematics
WALLACE, J., Philosophy
WALSH, J., Atmospheric Sciences
WASSERMAN, S., Psychology, Statistics
WATSON, W. D., Physics and Astronomy
WATTS, E., English
WEATHERHEAD, P. J., Animal Biology, Natural Resources, Environmental Sciences
WEBBINK, R. F., Astronomy
WEINZIERL, R. A., Entomology
WEISSBERG, R., Political Science
WEST, D. B., Mathematics
WHITT, G. S., Animal Biology
WHITTEN, N. E., Jr, Anthropology
WICKENS, C., Psychology
WIECKOWSKI, A., Chemistry
WILCOX, J., Spanish
WILHELMSON, R., Atmospheric Sciences
WILSON, B. J., Speech Communication
WOESE, C. I., Microbiology and Animal Biology
WRAIGHT, C. A., Biochemistry and Plant Biology
WRIGHT, D., English
WRIGHT, R., Germanic Languages and Literature, Cinema Studies
WU, J.-M., Mathematics
WUEBBLES, D. J., Atmospheric Sciences
YU, G. T., Political Science
ZIMMERMAN, S. C., Chemistry
ZINNES, D., Political Science
ZUKOSKI, C. F., Chemical and Biomolecular Engineering

College of Medicine:

BAKER, D. H., Internal Medicine
BELMONT, A. S., Cell and Structural Biology
BEST, P. M., Molecular and Integrative Physiology, Physiology, Biophysics, Bioengineering and Neuroscience
BOILEAU, R. A., Internal Medicine
BUETOW, M. K., Paediatrics and Adolescent Health
CLEGG, R. M., Physics and Biophysics
CRASS, J. R., Internal Medicine
CROFTS, A. R., Biochemistry and Biophysics
CRONAN, J. E., Microbiology, Biochemistry and Microbiology
DONCHIN, E., Internal Medicine

ENSRUD, E. R., Internal Medicine
ERDMAN, J. W., Jr, Internal Medicine
ESSEX-SORLIE, D. L., Internal Medicine
FARRAND, S., Microbiology and Plant Pathology
FENG, A. S., Physiology, Biophysics, Bioengineering and Neuroscience
FREEDMAN, P., Internal Medicine
GARDNER, J. F., Microbiology
GELFAND, V. I., Cell and Structural Biology
GENNIS, R. B., Biochemistry, Chemistry, Biophysics
GERLT, J. A., Biochemistry, Chemistry and Biophysics, Basic Medical Sciences
GILLETTE, M. U., Cell and Structural Biology
GILLETTE, R., Molecular and Integrative Physiology, Biophysics
GLASER, M., Biochemistry and Biophysics
GREENOUGH, W. T., Psychiatry, Cell and Structural Biology, Psychology and Psychiatry
GUMPORT, R. I., Biochemistry, Basic Medical Sciences
HELMAN, S. I., Physiology, Biophysics and Bioengineering
JAKOBSSON, E., Physiology, Biochemistry, Biophysics
JEFFERY, E., Pharmacology
KATZENELLENBOGEN, B. S., Cell and Structural Biology, Molecular and Integrative Physiology
KAUFMAN, S. J., Cell and Structural Biology
KEMPER, B. W., Cell and Structural Biology, Pharmacology, Molecular and Integrative Physiology
KIRBY, R. W., Internal Medicine
KRANZ, D. M., Biochemistry
LAYMAN, D. K., Internal Medicine
LEVY, A., Pathology
MARSHALL, W. P., Internal Medicine
MILLER, C. G., Microbiology
MILLER, G. A., Psychiatry
MORRISSEY, J. H., Biochemistry
NELSON, R. A., Internal Medicine
OLSEN, G., Microbiology and Biophysics
ORDAL, G. W., Biochemistry, Basic Medical Science
POLLARD, J. W., Internal Medicine
PRABHUDESAI, M., Pathology
RAMIREZ, V. D., Physiology and Neuroscience
ROBBINS, A. W., Internal Medicine
ROBERTSON, H. M., Cell and Structural Biology, Entomology
ROBINSON, G. E., Cell and Structural Biology, Entomology
RUEDA, J. L., Psychiatry
SALYERS, A., Microbiology
SCHULER, M. A., Cell and Structural Biology, Biochemistry, Plant Biology
SCHWARTZ, B. S., Biochemistry
SHAPIRO, D. J., Biochemistry
SHERWOOD, O. D., Physiology
SIEGEL, I. A.
SLIGAR, S. G., Biochemistry, Chemistry, Physiology and Biophysics, Medicine
SWITZER, R. L., Biochemistry, Basic Medical Sciences
WEYHENMEYER, J., Pathology
WILLIAMS, B., Pathology
WOESE, C. R., Microbiology
WRAIGHT, C. A., Biochemistry, Biophysics, Plant Biology

College of Veterinary Medicine:

ANDREWS, J. J., Veterinary Pathobiology
ARDEN, W. A., Veterinary Clinical Medicine
BEASLEY, V. R., Veterinary Biosciences
BENSON, G. J., Veterinary Clinical Medicine, Veterinary Anaesthesiology and Comparative Medicine
CAMPBELL, K. L., Veterinary Clinical Medicine

CLARKSON, R. B., Veterinary Clinical Medicine, Veterinary Biosciences
COOKE, P. S., Veterinary Biosciences
DOCAMPO, R., Veterinary Pathobiology
GOETZ, T. E., Veterinary Clinical Medicine
GROSS, D. R., Veterinary Biosciences
HANSEN, L. G., Veterinary Biosciences
HASCHEK-HOCK, W. M., Veterinary Pathobiology
HESS, R. A., Veterinary Biosciences
JOHNSON, A. L., Veterinary Clinical Medicine
KITRON, U. D., Veterinary Pathobiology
KUHLENSCHMIDT, M. S., Veterinary Pathobiology
LOCK, T. F., Veterinary Clinical Medicine
MANOHAR, M., Veterinary Biosciences
MARRETTA, S. M., Veterinary Clinical Medicine
MEERDINK, G. L., Toxicology
MILLER, G. Y., Veterinary Pathobiology, Veterinary Clinical Medicine
OTT, R. S., Veterinary Clinical Medicine, Veterinary Medicine Administration
PAUL, A. J., Veterinary Pathobiology
RAFFE, M. R., Veterinary Clinical Medicine
SCHANTZ, S. L., Veterinary Biosciences
SEGRE, M., Veterinary Pathobiology
SISSON, D. D., Veterinary Clinical Medicine
SMITH, R. D., Veterinary Pathobiology
TRANQUILLI, W. J., Veterinary Clinical Medicine
TROUTT, H. F., Veterinary Clinical Medicine
VALLI, V. E. O., Veterinary Pathobiology
VIMR, E. R., Veterinary Pathobiology
WALLIG, M. A., Veterinary Pathobiology
WEIGEL, R. M., Veterinary Pathobiology
WHITELEY, H. E., Veterinary Pathobiology
ZACHARY, J. F., Veterinary Pathobiology

School of Labour and Employment Relations:

DRASGOW, F.
FEUILLE, P.
LAWLER, J.
LEROY, M.
MARTOCCHIO, J.
NORTHCRAFT, G.
OLDHAM, G.
OLSON, C.

UNIVERSITY OF ST FRANCIS

500 Wilcox St, Joliet, IL 60435

Telephone: (815) 740-3400
E-mail: information@stfrancis.edu
Internet: www.stfrancis.edu

Founded 1920
Private control
Language of instruction: English
Academic year: August to May

Pres.: Dr ARVID C. JOHNSON
Provost and Vice-Pres. for Academic Affairs: Dr FRANK PASCOE
Vice-Pres. for Admin. and Finance: ELIZABETH LAKEN
Vice-Pres. for Admissions, Marketing and Enrolment Services: CHARLES M. BEUTEL
Vice-Pres. for Mission Integration and Min.: Sis. MARY ELIZABETH IMLER
Vice-Pres. for Student and Alumni Affairs: DAMON SLOAN
Chief Information Officer for IT and Library Services: TERRY COTTRELL

Library of 142,761 vols
Number of teachers: 313
Number of students: 3,764 (1,780 undergraduate, 1,984 graduate)

DEANS

College of Arts and Sciences: Dr ROBERT W. KASE
College of Business and Health Administration: Dr CHRISTOPHER CLOTT
College of Education: Dr JOHN GAMBRO

Leach College of Nursing: Dr CAROL J. WILSON

UNIVERSITY OF SAINT MARY OF THE LAKE—MUNDELEIN SEMINARY

1000 E Maple Ave, Mundelein, IL 60060

Telephone: (847) 566-6401
E-mail: info@usml.edu
Internet: www.vocations.org

Founded 1844 as Saint Mary's College, current name adopted 2000
Private control

Offers Masters degrees in divinity, liturgy and liturgical studies; doctoral degree in ministry

Rector and Pres.: Very Rev. DENNIS J. LYLE
Provost: Rev. THOMAS FRANZMAN
Vice-Rector for Academic Affairs: Rev. THOMAS A. BAIMA
Vice-Rector for Seminary Admin.: Rev. JAMES PRESTA
Vice-Pres. for Facilities: STAN RYS
Vice-Pres. for Finance: JOHN LEHOCKY
Vice-Pres. for Institutional Advancement: MARK J. TERESI
Dean for Formation: Rev. KEVIN J. FEENEY
Library Dir: LORRAINE OLLEY

Library of 200,000 vols, 434 periodicals

Publications: *Chicago Studies* (3 a year, online, www.chicagostudies.org), *Interconnections: Journal of Catholic Seminary Studies* (online, www.usml.edu/journal), *The Bridge* (print and online, www.usml.edu/publications/bridge)

VANDERCOOK COLLEGE OF MUSIC

3140 S Federal St, Chicago, IL 60616-3731

Telephone: (312) 225-6288
E-mail: vandercook@vandercook.edu
Internet: www.vandercook.edu

Founded 1909
Private control

Pres.: Dr CHARLES T. MENGHINI
Dean for Graduate Studies: RUTH RHODES
Dean for Undergraduate Studies: KAYE CLEMENTS
Dir for Admissions and Retention: AMY LENTING
Registrar: CAROLYN BERGHOFF
Head Librarian: ROB DELAND

Library of 14,653 vols
Number of teachers: 5
Number of students: 230

WESTERN ILLINOIS UNIVERSITY

1 University Circle, Macomb, IL 61455-1380

Telephone: (309) 298-1414
E-mail: info@wiu.edu
Internet: www.wiu.edu

Founded 1899
State control
Academic year: August to May

Pres.: Dr JACK THOMAS
Provost and Academic Vice-Pres.: Dr KENNETH S. HAWKINSON
Vice-Pres. for Admin. Services: JULIE DEWEES
Vice-Pres. for Advancement and Public Services: BRAD BAINTER
Vice-Pres. for Student Services: Dr GARY BILLER
Registrar: ANGELA NICOLE LYNN
Dean for Univ. Libraries: Dr PHYLIS C. SELF

Library of 1,150,000 vols
Number of teachers: 620 (full-time)
Number of students: 12,600

Publications: *Essays in Literature, Western Illinois Magazine*

DEANS

College of Arts and Sciences: Dr SUSAN MARTINELLI-FERNANDEZ

College of Business and Technology: Dr TOM EREKSON

College of Education and Human Services: Dr STERLING SADDLER

College of Fine Arts and Communication: Dr SHARON EVANS

WHEATON COLLEGE

501 College Ave, Wheaton, IL 60187-5593

Telephone: (630) 752-5000

Internet: www.wheaton.edu

Founded 1860

Private control

Academic year: August to May

Pres.: Dr PHILIP G. RYKEN

Provost: Dr STANTON JONES

Vice-Pres. for Advancement and Alumni Relations: CINDRA STACKHOUSE TAETZSCH

Vice-Pres. for Finance and Treas.: Dr DALE A. KEMP

Vice-Pres. for Student Devt: Dr PAUL CHELSEN

Registrar: PEGGY KING

Librarian: LISA RICHMOND

Library of 1,113,924 vols (incl. 370,000 books), 7,833 current periodicals

Number of teachers: 290 (197 full-time, 93 part-time)

Number of students: 3,000 (2,450 undergraduate, 550 graduate)

Publication: *Kodon Literary Magazine* (3 a year)

DEANS

Conservatory, Arts and Communication: Dr MICHAEL WILDER

Graduate School: Dr NICHOLAS PERRIN

Humanities and Theological Studies: Dr JILL PELÁEZ BAUMGAERTNER

Information and Technology: Dr GARY N. LARSON

Natural and Social Sciences: Prof. Dr DOROTHY F. CHAPPELL

INDIANA

AMERICAN COLLEGE OF EDUCATION

101 W Ohio St, Suite 1200, Indianapolis, IN 46204

Telephone: (800) 280-0307

E-mail: ace.admissions@ace.edu

Internet: www.ace.edu

Founded 2005, fmrly Barat College (f. 1858)

Private control

Offers online Masters degree in education

Pres.: Dr SANDRA DORAN

Assoc. Provost and Sr Vice-Pres. for Institutional Effectiveness and Assessment: Dr SHAWNTEL LANDRY

Vice-Pres. for Curriculum and Devt: LANA SLOAN

Vice-Pres. for Enrolment and Student Services: AMY LANGFORD

Vice-Pres. for Online Learning and Technology: CHANCE SPIKER

Vice-Pres. for Professional Devt: Dr STACEY HUGHES

Academic Dean: Dr MARY BOLD

Chief Financial Officer: MICHAEL BRISKEY

Registrar: LYNDIA WAGNER

Dir for Library: Dr SANDRA AL-ABDULMUNEM

ANDERSON UNIVERSITY

1100 E Fifth St, Anderson, IN 46012

Telephone: (765) 649-9071

E-mail: info@anderson.edu

Internet: www.anderson.edu

Founded 1917

Private control

Academic year: August to May

Pres.: Dr JAMES L. EDWARDS

Provost and Vice-Pres. for Academic Affairs and Dean: Dr MARIE S. MORRIS

Vice-Pres. for Advancement: ROBERT L. COFFMAN

Vice-Pres. for Finance and Treas.: DANA S. STUART

Vice-Pres. for Student Affairs: Dr BRENT BAKER

Dir for Admissions: JOE DAVIS

Registrar: ARTHUR J. LEAK

Dir for Univ. Libraries: Dr JANET BREWER

Library of 285,144 vols, 56,925 microfiche, 25,926 periodicals, 17,968 govt documents, 6,633 ebooks, 2,342 video cassettes, 1,162 DVDs, 7,789 reference books

Number of teachers: 200 (140 full-time, 60 part-time)

Number of students: 2,550 (2,020 undergraduate, 530 graduate)

DEANS

College of Science and Humanities: Dr D. BLAKE JANUTOLO

College of the Arts: Dr JEFFREY E. WRIGHT

Falls School of Business: TERRY TRUITT

School of Adult Learning: Dr ALEZA D. BEVERLY

School of Education: Dr JAN FULKERSON

School of Nursing: KAREN WILLIAMS

School of Theology: Dr DAVID L. SEBASTIAN

ASSOCIATED MENNONITE BIBLICAL SEMINARY

3003 Benham Ave, Elkhart, IN 46517-1999

Telephone: (574) 295-3726

E-mail: admissions@ambs.edu

Internet: www.ambs.edu

Founded 1958

Private control

Courses in Christian formation, divinity, peace studies and theological studies; br. campus at North Newton (Kansas)

Pres.: Dr SARA WENGER SHENK

Vice-Pres. for Advancement Admin.: RON RINGENBERG

Academic Dean: REBECCA SLOUGH

Dir for Enrolment and Student Services: S. ROBERT ROSA

Dir for Devt: MISSY KAUFFMAN SCHROCK

Registrar: SCOTT JANZEN

Dir for Library Services: EILEEN K. SANER

Library of 109,000 vols

Number of teachers: 20

Number of students: 180

Publication: *Vision: A Journal for Church and Theology* (2 a year)

BALL STATE UNIVERSITY

2000 W University Ave, Muncie, IN 47306

Telephone: (765) 289-1241

E-mail: askus@bsu.edu

Internet: www.bsu.edu

Founded 1918 as Indiana State Normal School E Div., current name adopted 1965

State control

Academic year: August to May

Pres.: JO ANN M. GORA

Provost and Vice-Pres. for Academic Affairs: TERRY KING

Vice-Pres. for Business Affairs and Treas.: RANDY HOWARD

Vice-Pres. for Enrolment, Marketing and Communications: TOM TAYLOR

Vice-Pres. for Information Technology: PHILIP REPP

Vice-Pres. for Student Affairs and Dean for Students: KAY BALES

Vice-Pres. for Univ. Advancement: Dr HUDSON AKIN

Registrar: NANCY CRONK

Dean for Univ. Libraries: ARTHUR W. HAFNER

Library: 1.5m. vols (incl. microfilms and audiovisual items), 4,000 current periodicals

Number of teachers: 840 (full-time)

Number of students: 22,150

Publications: *Ball State Alumnus* (6 a year), *Indiana Mathematics Teacher* (2 a year), *International Journal of Social Education*, *Odyssey* (1 a year), *Proceedings of the Indiana Academy of Social Sciences* (1 a year), *Teacher Educator* (4 a year)

DEANS

College of Applied Sciences and Technology: Prof. MITCHELL WHALEY

College of Architecture and Planning: Prof. GUILLERMO VASQUEZ DE VELASCO

College of Communication, Information and Media: ROGER LAVERY

College of Fine Arts: Prof. ROBERT A. KVAM

College of Sciences and the Humanities: Dr MICHAEL MAGGIOTTO

Honors College: Prof. JAMES RUEBEL

Miller College of Business: RAJIB SANYAL

Teachers' College: Prof. JOHN JACOBSON

University College: Dr MARILYN BUCK

BETHANY THEOLOGICAL SEMINARY

615 National Rd W, Richmond, IN 47374-4019

Telephone: (765) 983-1800

E-mail: contactus@bethanyseminary.edu

Internet: www.bethanyseminary.edu

Founded 1905 as Bethany Bible School, current name adopted 1963

Private control

Academic year: August to May

Masters degree in arts and divinity

Pres.: JEFF CARTER

Academic Dean: STEVEN SCHWEITZER

Exec. Dir for Institutional Advancement: LOWELL FLORY

Exec. Dir for Student and Business Services and Treas.: BRENDA REISH

Dir for Academic Services and Registrar: APRIL VANLONDEN

Dir for Admissions: TRACY PRIMOZICH

Dir for Student Devt: AMY GALL RITCHIE

Number of teachers: 10

Number of students: 60

Publication: *Wonder & Word* (2 a year)

BETHEL COLLEGE

1001 Bethel Circle, Mishawaka, IN 46545

Telephone: (574) 807-7000

E-mail: info@bethelcollege.edu

Internet: www.bethelcollege.edu

Founded 1947

Private control

Academic year: August to May

Br. campuses at Elkhart, Fort Wayne, Winona Lake (Indiana); extension centres in Michigan

Pres.: Dr STEVEN R. CRAMER

Sr Vice-Pres.: Prof. Dr DENNIS D. ENGBRECHT

Vice-Pres. for Academic Services: Dr BRADLEY D. SMITH

Vice-Pres. for College Relations: Dr C. ROBERT LAURENT

Vice-Pres. for Devt: TERRY A. ZEITLOW

Vice-Pres. for Student Devt: Dr SHAWN M. HOLTGREN

Registrar: JEANNE FOX

Dir for Library Services: Dr CLYDE R. ROOT

Number of teachers: 220

Number of students: 2,100

DEANS

Division of Arts and Humanities: Dr TOM VISKER
Division of Professional and Graduate Studies: Dr BRADLEY SMITH
Division of Sciences: Dr ROB MYERS
School of Nursing: Dr CAROL DOROUGH

BUTLER UNIVERSITY

4600 Sunset Ave, Indianapolis, IN 46208
Telephone: (317) 940-6000
E-mail: info@butler.edu
Internet: www.butler.edu
Founded 1855
Private control
Pres.: JAMES M. DANKO
Provost and Vice-Pres. for Academic Affairs: KATHRYN MORRIS
Vice-Pres. for Enrolment Management: TOM WEEDE
Vice-Pres. for Operations: GERALD CARLSON
Vice-Pres. for Student Affairs: LEVESTER JOHNSON
Vice-Pres. for Univ. Advancement: MARK HELMUS
Registrar: SONDREA OZOLINS
Dean for Libraries: LEWIS MILLER
Library of 330,000 vols, 20,000 ebooks, 35,000 ejournal subscriptions, 16,000 audiovisual materials, 17,000 musical scores
Number of teachers: 340 (full-time)
Number of students: 4,700
Publication: *Real*

DEANS

College of Business: CHUCK WILLIAMS
College of Communication: Prof. WILLIAM NEHER
College of Education: Dr ENA SHELLEY
College of Liberal Arts and Sciences: Dr JAY R. HOWARD
College of Pharmacy and Health Sciences: MARY H. ANDRITZ
Jordan College of Fine Arts: Dr RONALD CALTABIANO

CALUMET COLLEGE OF ST JOSEPH

2400 New York Ave, Whiting, IN 46394
Telephone: (219) 473-4215
E-mail: admissions@ccsj.edu
Internet: www.ccsj.edu
Founded 1951
Private control
Academic year: September to August
Divs of liberal arts and professional studies
Pres.: Dr DANIEL LOWERY
Vice-Pres. for Academic Affairs: Dr JOI PATTERSON
Vice-Pres. for Student Life and Dean for Students: MELISHA HENDERSON
Dir for Devt: MICHAEL SPICCIA
Dir for Enrolment Management: MARY SEVERA
Registrar: DIANA FRANCIS
Library Dir: MARCIA KEITH
Library of 110,000 vols, 74 periodicals, 1,417 multimedia items
Number of teachers: 60
Number of students: 1,260

CHRISTIAN THEOLOGICAL SEMINARY

1000 W 42nd St, Indianapolis, IN 46208
Telephone: (317) 924-1331
E-mail: admissions@cts.edu
Internet: www.cts.edu

Founded 1910 as Butler School of Religion, present name and status 1958
Private control
Academic year: September to May
Pres.: MATTHEW MYER BOULTON
Vice-Pres. and Co-Academic Dean: Dr HOLLY HEARON
Vice-Pres. and Co-Academic Dean: Dr K. BERNIE LYON
Vice-Pres. for Seminary Advancement: MELISSA HICKMAN
Registrar: MATT SCHLIMGEN
Library Dir: LORNA A. SHOEMAKER
Library of 210,000 vols (incl. 1,000 periodicals)
Number of teachers: 45
Number of students: 300
Publications: *Encounter*, *Link*

CONCORDIA THEOLOGICAL SEMINARY

6600 N Clinton St, Fort Wayne, IN 46825-4996
Telephone: (260) 452-2100
E-mail: info@ctsfw.edu
Internet: www.ctsfw.edu
Founded 1846
Private control
Academic year: September to May
Masters and doctoral degrees in divinity, ministry, sacred theology
Pres.: Rev. Dr LAWRENCE R. RAST, JR
Vice-Pres. for Resource Devt: Rev. JON SCICLUNA
Academic Dean: Rev. Dr CHARLES A. GIESCHEN
Dir for Enrolment Management and Dean for Students: THOMAS P. ZIMMERMAN
Dean for Graduate Studies: Dr K. DETLEV SCHULZ
Registrar: BARBARA A. WEGMAN
Dir of Library Services: Rev. Prof. ROBERT V. ROETHEMEYER
Library of 152,000 vols
Number of teachers: 25
Number of students: 320
Publications: *Concordia Theological Quarterly* (4 a year), *For the Life of the World*

DEPAUW UNIVERSITY

POB 37, Greencastle, IN 46135-0037
Telephone: (765) 658-4800
E-mail: admission@depauw.edu
Internet: www.depauw.edu
Founded 1837 as Indiana Asbury Univ., current name adopted 1884
Private control
Academic year: August to May
Liberal arts programmes and interdisciplinary study programmes
Pres.: Dr BRIAN W. CASEY
Exec. Vice-Pres. and Dean of the Faculty: Dr NEAL ABRAHAM
Vice-Pres. for Academic Affairs: Prof. Dr DAVID THORP HARVEY
Vice-Pres. for Admission and Financial Aid: DANIEL LEE MEYER
Vice-Pres. for Advancement: MARCIA SLOAN LATTA
Vice-Pres. for Finance and Admin.: BRADLEY ALAN KELSHEIMER
Vice-Pres. for Student Life and Dean for Students: CINDY BABINGTON
Registrar: Dr KENNETH J. KIRKPATRICK
Dir for Libraries: RICK PROVINE
Library of 400,000 vols
Number of teachers: 235
Number of students: 2,400
Publication: *DePauw Magazine*

EARLHAM COLLEGE

801 National Rd W, Richmond, IN 47374-4095
Telephone: (765) 983-1200
E-mail: admissions@earlham.edu
Internet: www.earlham.edu
Founded 1847, present name and status 1859
Private control
Academic year: August to May
Liberal arts college
Pres.: DAVID DAWSON
Provost: NELSON BINGHAM
Vice-Pres. for Academic Affairs and Academic Dean: GREG MAHLER
Vice-Pres. for Finance and Operations: SENA LANDEY
Vice-Pres. for Institutional Advancement: JAMES McKEY
Vice-Pres. and Dean for Enrolment, Financial Aid and Communications: JONATHAN STROUD
Vice-Pres. and Dean for Student Devt: LAURA HUTCHINSON
Registrar: BONITA WASHINGTON-LACEY
Dir for Library: NEAL BAKER
Library of 400,834 vols
Number of teachers: 120 (103 full-time, 17 part-time)
Number of students: 1,100 (undergraduate)
Publication: *The Earlhamite* (2 a year)

FRANKLIN COLLEGE

101 Branigin Blvd, Franklin, IN 46131-2623
Telephone: (317) 738-8000
E-mail: admissions@franklincollege.edu
Internet: www.franklincollege.edu
Founded 1834
Private control
Academic year: August to May
Divs of business, computing and mathematics, education, fine arts, humanities, journalism, natural sciences and social sciences
Chancellor: (vacant)
Pres.: Dr JAMES G. MOSELEY
Vice-Pres. for Academic Affairs and Dean for College: Dr DAVID G. BRAILOW
Vice-Pres. for Enrolment and Student Affairs: ALAN P. HILL
Vice-Pres. for Institutional Advancement: JAMES B. MEYER
Dean for Students: ELLIS F. HALL
Registrar: MATTHEW R. JONES
Dir for Library: RONALD L. SCHUETZ
Library of 107,000 vols, 6,000 video cassettes, 300 journal subscriptions, 17,000 ejournals and newspapers
Number of teachers: 65 (full-time)
Number of students: 1,060

GOSHEN COLLEGE

1700 S Main St, Goshen, IN 46526
Telephone: (574) 535-7000
E-mail: info@goshen.edu
Internet: www.goshen.edu
Founded 1894 as Elkhart Institute of Science
Private control
Liberal arts courses
Pres.: Dr JAMES E. BRENNEMAN
Vice-Pres. for Academic Affairs and Academic Dean: Dr ANITA STALTER
Vice-Pres. for Finance: JIM HISTAND
Vice-Pres. for Institutional Advancement: JIM CASKEY
Vice-Pres. for Student Life and Dean for Students: WILLIAM J. BORN
Registrar: STANLEY W. MILLER
Library Dir: LISA GUEDEA CARREÑO
Library of 135,000 vols, 400 periodical subscriptions

Number of teachers: 110 (80 full-time, 30 part-time)

Number of students: 1,000

Publication: *Mennonite Quarterly Review* (4 a year, online, www.goshen.edu/mqr)

GRACE COLLEGE AND SEMINARY

200 Seminary Dr., Winona Lake, IN 46590

Telephone: (574) 372-5100

E-mail: admissions@grace.edu

Internet: www.grace.edu

Founded 1937, present status 1994

Private control

Academic year: August to July

Pres.: Dr RONALD E. MANAHAN

Provost: Dr WILLIAM J. KATIP

Vice-Pres. for Academic and Student Services: Dr JAMES E. SWANSON

Vice-Pres. for Advancement: Dr JOHN R. BOAL

Chief Financial Officer: G. STEPHEN POPENFOOSE

Dean for Enrolment Management: CINDY N. SISSON

Dir for Admissions: MARK POHL

Registrar: STEVEN T. CARLSON

Dir for Library Services: TONYA FAWCETT

Library of 150,000 vols

Number of teachers: 120

Number of students: 1,700

DEANS

School of Adult and Community Education: Prof. Dr STEPHEN A. GRILL

School of Arts and Sciences: Prof. Dr MARK M. NORRIS

School of Behavioural Science: Prof. E. MICHAEL GRILL

School of Business: Prof. JEFFREY K. FAWCETT

School of Education: LAURINDA A. OWEN

School of Ministry Studies: Prof. Dr JEFFREY GILL

HANOVER COLLEGE

POB 108, Hanover, IN 47243

484 Ball Dr., Hanover, IN 47243

Telephone: (812) 866-7000

E-mail: info@hanover.edu

Internet: www.hanover.edu

Founded 1827

Private control

Divs of arts and letters, natural sciences, humanities and social sciences

Pres.: Dr SUE DEWINE

Vice-Pres. for Academic Affairs and Dean for Faculty: STEVE JOBE

Vice-Pres. for College Advancement: DENNIS HUNT

Vice-Pres. for Enrolment Management: JON RIESTER

Vice-Pres. and Dean for Student Life: DAVID YEAGER

Dean for Admission: CHRISTOPHER GAGE

Registrar: KEN PRINCE

Dir for Library: KENNETH E. GIBSON

Library of 3,000 vols, 314,000 govt documents, 6,700 audiovisual items, 52,000 microforms, 2,000 periodicals

Number of teachers: 70

Number of students: 1,100

Publication: *The Hanoverian*

HOLY CROSS COLLEGE

54515 State Rd, 933N, POB 308, Notre Dame, IN 46556

Telephone: (574) 239-8377

E-mail: admissions@hcc-nd.edu

Internet: www.hcc-nd.edu

Founded 1966

Private control

Pres.: Dr JOHN R. PAIGE

Exec. Vice-Pres.: Dr TINA HOLLAND

Vice-Pres. for Mission Advancement: ROBERT KLOSKA

Vice-Pres. for Operations: DANIEL HAVERTY

Dean for Admissions and Enrolment Management: MARIE E. BENSMAN

Dean for Students: DANIEL COCHRAN

Dir for Library Services: MARY ELLEN HEGEDUS

Library of 20,000 vols, 140 periodicals, 8,000 journals and newspapers

Number of students: 500

HUNTINGTON UNIVERSITY

2303 College Ave, Huntington, IN 46750

Telephone: (219) 356-6000

E-mail: admissions@huntington.edu

Internet: www.huntington.edu

Founded 1897

Private control

Academic year: September to May

Liberal arts courses

Pres.: Dr G. BLAIR DOWDEN

Sr Vice-Pres. for Academic Affairs and Dean for Faculty: Dr A. NORRIS FRIESEN

Sr Vice-Pres. for Strategy and Graduate and Adult Programmes: Dr ANN C. McPHERREN

Vice-Pres. for Enrolment Management and Marketing: JEFFREY C. BERGGREN

Vice-Pres. for Student Life: Dr RONALD L. COFFEY

Vice-Pres. for Univ. Relations: JOHN W. PAFF

Registrar: SARAH J. HARVEY

Dir for Library Services: ANITA GRAY

Library of 200,000 vols, 60,000 ebooks

Number of teachers: 70

Number of students: 1,300

INDIANA INSTITUTE OF TECHNOLOGY

1600 E Washington Blvd, Fort Wayne, IN 46803

Telephone: (260) 422-5561

E-mail: admissions@indianatech.edu

Internet: www.indianatech.edu

Founded 1930, current name adopted 1963

Private control

Campuses at Fishers, Greenwood, Huntington, Kendallville, Mishawaka, Munster, Plainfield, Shelbyville and Warsaw

Pres.: Dr ARTHUR E. SNYDER

Vice-Pres. for Academic Affairs: Dr DOUGLAS PERRY

Vice-Pres. for Enrolment Management: ALLISON CARNAHAN

Vice-Pres. for Institutional Advancement: MARK RICHTER

Library Dir: CONNIE SCOTT

Library of 33,000 vols

Number of teachers: 50

Number of students: 5,000

DEANS

College of Business: Dr JEFFREY A. ZIMMERMAN

College of Engineering: DAVE ASCHLIMAN

College of General Studies: Dr DOTY LATUSZEK

School of Computer Sciences: DAVE ASCHLIMAN

INDIANA STATE UNIVERSITY

200 N Seventh St, Terre Haute, IN 47809-1902

419 Rankin Hall, 210 N Seventh St, Terre Haute, IN 47809

Telephone: (812) 237-6311

E-mail: admissions@indstate.edu

Internet: www.indstate.edu

Founded 1865 as Indiana State Normal School, present name and status 1965

State control

Academic year: August to May

Pres.: Dr DANIEL J. BRADLEY

Provost and Vice-Pres. for Academic Affairs: C. JACK MAYNARD

Gen. Counsel and Sec. of the Univ.: MELONY A. SACOPULOS

Vice-Pres. for Enrolment Management, Marketing and Communication: JOHN E. BEACON

Vice-Pres. for Student Affairs and Dean for Students: CARMEN TILLERY

Registrar: APRIL HAY

Dean for Library Services: ALBERTA D. COMER

Library of 1,344,592 vols

Number of teachers: 450 (full-time)

Number of students: 11,500

Publications: *Cognitive Technology* (2 a year), *Folklore Historian* (1 a year), *Grassland* (1 a year), *Hoosier Folklore*, *Indiana English* (3 a year), *Indiana State University Magazine* (3 a year, online, www.isu-magazine.com), *Midwestern Folklore* (2 a year), *Snowy Egret*, *The Hoosier Science Teacher* (4 a year, online, www.indstate.edu/scied/thstforms.htm), *The Indiana Council of Teachers of Mathematics Journal—Mathematics Teacher* (2 a year), *Tonic* (1 a year), *Via Solaris*

DEANS

Bayh College of Education: Dr BRADLEY V. BALCH

College of Arts and Sciences: Dr JOHN D. MURRAY

College of Graduate and Professional Studies: Dr JAY D. GATRELL

College of Nursing, Health and Human Services: Dr RICHARD WILLIAMS

College of Technology: Prof. ROBERT ENGLISH

Scott College of Business: Dr NANCY J. MERRITT

INDIANA UNIVERSITY

107 S. Indiana Ave, Bloomington, IN 47405-7000

Telephone: (812) 855-4848

Internet: www.iu.edu

Founded 1820 as a state seminary, present status 1852

State control

Pres.: MICHAEL A. McROBBIE

Exec. Vice-Pres.: CHARLES R. BANTZ

Exec. Vice-Pres.: KAREN HANSON

Exec. Vice-Pres. for Univ. Regional Affairs, Planning and Policy: JOHN APPLEGATE

Vice-Pres. and Chief Financial Officer: NEIL D. THEOBALD

Vice-Pres. and Gen. Counsel: DOROTHY J. FRAPWELL

Vice-Pres. for Diversity, Equity and Multicultural Affairs: EDWIN C. MARSHALL

Vice-Pres. for Information Technology and Chief Information Officer: BRADLEY C. WHEELER

Vice-Pres. for Public Affairs and Govt Relations: MIKE SAMPLE

Vice-Pres. for Research: JORGE JOSÉ

Dean for Univ. Libraries: BRENDA JOHNSON

Number of teachers: 8,700 (all campuses)

Number of students: 110,000 (all campuses)

Publication: *Research & Creative Activity...*

CONSTITUENT CAMPUSES

Indiana University Bloomington

107 S Indiana Ave, Bloomington, IN 47405-7000

Telephone: (812) 855-4848

E-mail: iuadmit@indiana.edu

Internet: www.iub.edu

Founded 1820 as a state seminary, current name adopted 1838

Provost and Chief Academic Officer: KAREN HANSON

Vice-Provost for Enrolment Management: Dr DAVID B. JOHNSON

Vice-Provost for Faculty and Academic Affairs: THOMAS GIERYN

Vice-Provost for Research: P. SARITA SONI

Vice-Provost for Undergraduate Education: SONYA STEPHENS

Dir for Admissions: MARY ELLEN ANDERSON

Dean for Students: Dr HAROLD GOLDSMITH

Registrar: MARK MCCONAHAY

Dean for Univ. Libraries: BRENDA JOHNSON

Library: see under Libraries and Archives

Number of teachers: 3,000

Number of students: 42,500

Publications: *American Historical Review* (5 a year), *American Journal of Semiotics* (4 a year), *Anthropological Linguistics* (4 a year, online, www.indiana.edu/~anthling), *Business Horizons* (6 a year), *Indiana Business Review* (4 a year, online, www.ibrc.indiana.edu/ibr), *Indiana Law Journal* (4 a year, online, ilj.law.indiana.edu), *Indiana Magazine of History* (4 a year, online, www.indiana.edu/~imaghist), *Indiana Slavic Studies* (1 a year), *Indiana University Mathematics Journal* (4 a year), *Journal of American History* (4 a year), *Journal of Asian History* (2 a year), *Journal of Chemical Physics* (52 a year), *Journal of Folklore Research* (3 a year, print and online, scholarworks.iu.edu/journals/index.php/jfr), *Journal of Mathematical Physics* (12 a year), *Journal of Slavic Linguistics* (2 a year), *Journal of the Experimental Analysis of Behavior* (6 a year), *Kelley Magazine* (2 a year), *Phi Delta Kappan* (10 a year), *SPEA Magazine*, *Teaching & Learning* (2 a year), *Victorian Studies* (4 a year)

DEANS

College of Arts and Sciences: LARRY SINGELL

Hutton Honors College: MATTHEW AUER

Jacobs School of Music: GWYN RICHARDS

Kelley School of Business: DANIEL C. SMITH

Maurer School of Law: Prof. AUSTEN L. PARRISH (acting)

School of Continuing Studies: Prof. DANIEL CALLISON

School of Education: Prof. GERARDO GONZÁLEZ

School of Health, Physical Education and Recreation: MOHAMMED R. TORABI

School of Informatics and Computing: ROBERT B. SCHNABEL

School of Journalism: Prof. BRADLEY HAMM

School of Library and Information Science: Prof. Dr DEBORA SHAW

School of Nursing: MARION BROOME

School of Optometry: Dr JOSEPH A. BONANNO

School of Public and Environmental Affairs: Dr JOHN D. GRAHAM

School of Social Work: Dr MICHAEL A. PATCHNER

University Graduate School: JAMES WIMBUSH

Indiana University East

2325 Chester Blvd, Richmond, IN 47374-1289

Telephone: (765) 973-8200

E-mail: eawelcc@indiana.edu

Internet: www.iue.edu

Chancellor: Dr KATHRYN CRUZ-URIBE

Exec. Vice-Chancellor for Academic Affairs: LARRY RICHARDS

Vice-Chancellor for Admin. and Finance: DAN DOOLEY

Dean for Students: MARY BLAKEFIELD

Library Dir: FRANCES YATES

Library of 85,000 vols

Number of teachers: 200 (85 full-time, 115 part-time)

Number of students: 3,825 (3,725 undergraduate, 100 graduate)

DEANS

School of Business and Economics: DAVID W. FRANTZ

School of Education: MARILYN WATKINS

School of Humanities and Social Sciences: KATHERINE FRANK

School of Natural Science and Mathematics: NEIL SABINE

School of Nursing: KAREN CLARK

Indiana University Kokomo

2300 S Washington St, Kokomo, IN 46904-9003

Telephone: (317) 453-2000

E-mail: iuadmis@iuk.edu

Internet: www.iuk.edu

Founded 1932 as Kokomo Junior College, present status 1970

Chancellor: SUSAN SCIAME-GIESECKE

Exec. Vice-Chancellor for Academic Affairs: SUE SCIAME-GIESECKE

Vice-Chancellor for Admin. and Finance: ROY TAMIR

Vice-Chancellor for Public Affairs and Advancement: PENNY LEE

Vice-Chancellor for Student Affairs: JACK THARP

Dean for Library: RHONDA ARMSTRONG

Library of 112,000 vols, 5,000 multimedia items

Number of teachers: 170

Number of students: 3,100

DEANS

School of Arts and Sciences: Dr ERV BOSCHMANN

School of Business: Dr FRANK WADSWORTH

School of Education: Dr PAUL C. PAESE

School of Nursing: Dr LINDA WALLACE

School of Public and Environmental Affairs: Dr ROBERT DIDIE

Indiana University Northwest

3400 Broadway, Gary, IN 46408-1197

Telephone: (219) 980-6500

E-mail: admit@iun.edu

Internet: www.iun.edu

Founded 1963

Chancellor: Dr WILLIAM J. LOWE

Exec. Vice-Chancellor for Academic Affairs: Dr DAVID J. MALIK

Vice-Chancellor for Admin.: JOSEPH PELLICCIOTTI

Vice-Chancellor for Student Services Admin.: ERNEST SMITH

Dir for Admissions: LINDA TEMPLETON

Registrar: JEFF JOHNSTON

Dir for Library Services: TIMOTHY SUTHERLAND

Library of 200,000 vols (incl. books and periodicals), 200,000 govt documents

Number of teachers: 360 (160 full-time, 200 part-time)

Number of students: 6,000

DEANS

College of Arts and Sciences: Dr MARK S. HOYERT

College of Health and Human Services: Dr PATRICK BANKSTON

School of Business and Economics: ANNA S. ROMINGER

School of Continuing Studies: Dr DANIEL J. CALLISON

School of Education: Dr STANLEY E. WIGLE

Indiana University—Purdue University at Fort Wayne

2101 E Coliseum Blvd, Fort Wayne, IN 46805-1499

Telephone: (260) 481-6812

Internet: www.ipfw.edu

Founded 1964

Academic year: August to May

Chancellor: MICHAEL A. WARTELL

Vice-Chancellor for Academic Affairs: WILLIAM J. McKINNEY

Vice-Chancellor for Advancement: WENDY KOBLER

Vice-Chancellor for Financial Affairs: WALTER J. BRANSON

Vice-Chancellor for Student Affairs: GEORGE S. McCLELLAN

Dir for Admissions: CAROL B. ISAACS

Registrar: PATRICK A. McLAUGHLIN

Library Dean: CHERYL TRUESDELL

Library of 311,094 vols, 1,500 current periodicals, 106,114 govt publs, 537,778 microforms, audiovisual items

Number of teachers: 400 (full-time)

Number of students: 14,000

DEANS

College of Arts and Sciences: Dr CARL N. DRUMMOND

College of Education and Public Policy: Prof. BARRY KANPOL

College of Engineering, Technology and Computer Science: Prof. MAX YEN

College of Health and Human Services: Prof. ANN OBERGFELD

College of Visual and Performing Arts: CHUCK O'CONNOR

Richard T. Doermer School of Business: Dr OTTO H. CHANG

Indiana University—Purdue University at Indianapolis

420 University Blvd, Indianapolis, IN 46202

Telephone: (317) 274-5555

E-mail: apply@iupui.edu

Internet: www.iupui.edu

Founded 1969

Chancellor: CHARLES R. BANTZ (acting)

Exec. Vice-Chancellor and Dean for Faculties: UDAY P. SUKHATME

Vice-Chancellor for External Affairs: AMY CONRAD WARNER

Vice-Chancellor for Finance and Admin.: DAWN RHODES

Vice-Chancellor for Research: KODY VARAHRAMYAN

Vice-Chancellor for Student Life: ZEBULUN DAVENPORT

Sr Assoc. Vice-Chancellor for Academic Affairs: MELISSA LAVITT

Dean for Univ. Library: DAVID LEWIS

Library of 650,000 vols, 4,000 periodicals and journals

Number of teachers: 2,500

Number of students: 30,600

DEANS

Herron School of Art: VALERIE EICKMEIER

Honors College: JANE LUZAR

Kelley School of Business: Prof. DANIEL C. SMITH

Purdue School of Engineering and Technology: Dr DAVID J. RUSSOMANNO

Robert H. McKinney School of Law: Prof. GARY R. ROBERTS

School of Allied Health and Rehabilitation Sciences: Dr AUGUSTINE AGHO

School of Dentistry: Prof. JOHN N. WILLIAMS, JR

School of Education: GERARDO M. GONZALEZ

School of Informatics: ROBERT B. SCHNABEL

School of Journalism: Prof. JAMES W. BROWN

School of Liberal Arts: Prof. WILLIAM BLOM-
QUIST
School of Library and Information Science:
Prof. Dr DEBORA SHAW
School of Medicine: Prof. D. CRAIG BRATER
School of Nursing: Dr MARION E. BROOME
School of Physical Education and Tourism
Management: Dr JAY GLADDEN
School of Public and Environmental Affairs:
Dr JOHN D. GRAHAM
School of Science: Prof. Dr SIMON J. RHODES
School of Social Work: Dr MICHAEL A.
PATCHNER
University College: Prof. Dr KATHY E. JOHN-
SON

Indiana University South Bend

1700 Mishawaka Ave, POB 7111, South
Bend, IN 46614-7111
Telephone: (574) 520-5005
Internet: www.iusb.edu
Founded 1916
State control
Academic year: August to May
Chancellor: Dr TERRY ALLISON
Exec. Vice-Chancellor for Academic Affairs:
Dr JANN JOSEPH
Vice-Chancellor for Admin. and Fiscal
Affairs: WILLIAM O'DONNELL
Vice-Chancellor for Public Affairs and Univ.
Advancement: ILENE SHEFFER
Assoc. Vice-Chancellor for Enrolment Ser-
vices: CATHY BUCKMAN
Assoc. Vice Chancellor for Student Services:
KAREN WHITE
Chief Information Officer: BETH VAN GORDON
Dean for Library Services: VICKI BLOOM
Library of 511,516 vols
Number of teachers: 585 (300 full-time, 285
part-time)
Number of students: 8,500

DEANS

College of Health Sciences: Dr MARIO ORTIZ
College of Liberal Arts and Sciences: Dr
ELIZABETH DUNN
Judd Leighton School of Business and Eco-
nomics: Dr ROBERT DUCOFFE
Raclin School of the Arts: Dr MARVIN CURTIS
School of Education: Dr MARVIN LYNN
School of Social Work: CAROL MASSAT (Dir)

Indiana University Southeast

4201 Grant Line Rd, New Albany, IN 47150
Telephone: (812) 941-2000
E-mail: admissions@ius.edu
Internet: www.ius.edu
Founded 1941, present name and status 1968
Academic year: August to May
Chancellor: Dr SANDRA R. PATTERSON-RAN-
DLES
Vice-Chancellor for Academic Affairs: Dr
GILBERT W. ATNIP
Vice-Chancellor for Admin. and Finance:
DANA C. WAVLE
Vice-Chancellor for Student Affairs: Dr RUTH
C. GARVEY-NIX
Registrar: BRITTANY HUBBARD
Dir for Library Services: C. MARTIN ROSEN
Library of 585,000 vols (incl. microforms),
1,200 current periodicals
Number of students: 7,200
Publication: *Journal of Business Disciplines*

DEANS

School of Arts and Letters: SAMANTHA EARLEY
School of Business: Dr ALAN JAY WHITE
School of Education: Dr GLORIA MURRAY
School of Natural Sciences: EMMANUEL OTU
School of Nursing: MIMI MCKAY
School of Social Sciences: JOE WERT

INDIANA WESLEYAN UNIVERSITY

4201 S Washington St, Marion, IN 46953
Telephone: (765) 674-6901
E-mail: admissions@indwes.edu
Internet: www.indwes.edu
Founded 1920 as Marion College, present
name and status 1998
Private control
Academic year: September to April
Education centres in Indiana, Kentucky and
Ohio
Pres.: Dr HENRY L. SMITH
Provost and Chief Academic Officer: Dr
DAVID WRIGHT
Exec. Vice-Pres.: Dr KEITH NEWMAN
Vice-Pres. for Enrolment Management: KRIS
DOUGLAS
Vice-Pres. for Student Devt: MICHAEL MOF-
FITT
Vice-Pres. for Wesley Seminary: WAYNE
SCHMIDT
Registrar: KIMBERLY NICHOLSON
Library Dir: SHEILA CARLBLOM
Library of 133,396 vols
Number of teachers: 1,000 (f. t. e.)
Number of students: 15,900

DEANS

College of Adult and Professional Studies: Dr
BRIDGET AITCHISON
College of Arts and Sciences: Dr DARLENE
BRESSLER
Graduate School: Dr JIM FULLER
School of Nursing: Dr BARBARA IHRKE

ITT TECHNICAL INSTITUTE

9511 Angola Court, Indianapolis, IN 46268-
1119
Telephone: (317) 875-8640
Internet: www.itt-tech.edu
Founded 1956
Private control
Areas of study: automated manufacturing
technology, computer and electronics engineering technology, computer drafting and
design, computer visualization technology,
computer-aided drafting and design technology, electronics engineering technology,
information systems security, information
technology–computer network systems,
information technology–multimedia, infor-
mation technology–software applications
and programming, information technology–
web development, technical project management for electronic commerce; 130 campuses
in 35 states
Pres.: Dr EUGENE W. FEICHTNER
Sr Vice-Pres. and Chief Academic Officer: Dr
P. MICHAEL LINZMAIER
Vice-Pres. for Learning Technologies: JOHN
P. TRIMBLE
Vice-Pres. for Student Services: JONATHAN H.
PATTERSON
Registrar: HARRIET ALLEN
Librarian: ANN C. LEE
Number of students: 80,000 (all campuses)

MANCHESTER COLLEGE

604 E College Ave, N Manchester, IN 46962
Telephone: (260) 982-5000
E-mail: admitinfo@manchester.edu
Internet: www.manchester.edu
Founded 1860 as Roanoke Classical Semin-
ary, current name adopted 1889, present
status 1932
Private control
Liberal arts and professional courses
Pres.: JO YOUNG SWITZER
Exec. Vice-Pres.: Dr DAVID F. MCFADDEN

Vice-Pres. and Dean for Academic Affairs:
GLENN SHARFMAN
Vice-Pres. for College Advancement:
MICHAEL EASTMAN
Vice-Pres. for Student Devt: BETH SWEITZER-
RILEY
Dir for Admissions: ADAM HOHMAN
Registrar: LILA D. HAMMER
Dir for Library: ROBIN J. GRATZ
Library of 160,000 vols
Number of teachers: 75 (full-time)
Number of students: 1,300
Publication: *Manchester Magazine* (4 a week)

MARIAN UNIVERSITY

3200 Cold Spring Rd, Indianapolis, IN 46222-
1997
Telephone: (317) 955-6000
E-mail: admissions@marian.edu
Internet: www.marian.edu
Founded 1851 as St Francis Normal, present
name and status 2009
Private control
Academic year: August to May
Pres.: Dr DANIEL J. ELSENER
Exec. Vice-Pres. and Provost: Dr THOMAS J.
ENNEKING
Vice-Pres. for Admin. and Gen. Counsel:
DEBORAH A. LAWRENCE
Vice-Pres. for Institutional Advancement:
JOHN FINKE
Vice-Pres. for Student Affairs and Dean for
Students: RUTH RODGERS
Dean for Academic Affairs: WILLIAM B.
HARTING
Registrar: JACK HILL
Librarian: KELLEY F. GRIFFITH
Library of 135,000 vols
Number of teachers: 155 (93 full-time, 62
part-time)
Number of students: 2,300

DEANS

Clark H. Byrum School of Business: Dr RUSS
KERSHAW
College of Osteopathic Medicine: PAUL EVANS
School of Education: Dr LINDAN B. HILL
School of Liberal Arts: Dr JAMES NORTON, III
School of Mathematics and Sciences: Dr
LOREN BERTOCCI
School of Nursing: Prof. ANITA SICCARDI

MARTIN UNIVERSITY

2171 Avondale Pl., Indianapolis, IN 46218
Telephone: (317) 543-3235
E-mail: president@martin.edu
Internet: www.martin.edu
Founded 1977 as Martin Center College,
present name and status 1990
Private control
Academic year: August to July
Pres.: Dr GEORGE E. MILLER, III
Exec. Vice-Pres.: RUBY BOWMAN
Vice-Pres. for Academic Affairs: Dr MARTIN
GREENAN
Vice-Pres. for Advancement.: LAURA-LEE
DAVIDSON
Vice-Pres. for Fiscal Affairs: MICHAEL MOOS
Vice-Pres. for Student Services: Dr STANLEY
SINGLETON
Dir for Admissions: THERESA BUTLER
Registrar: RUDELL MOORE
Number of teachers: 50 (30 full-time, 20
adjunct)
Number of students: 1,400

DEANS

School of Business: JESSE BROWN
School of Liberal Arts and Social Sciences: Dr
DENNIS JACKSON

School of Science and Technology: Dr MAMTA SINGH

OAKLAND CITY UNIVERSITY

138 N Lucretia St, Oakland City, IN 47660
Telephone: (800) 737-5125
E-mail: ocuadmit@oak.edu
Internet: www.oak.edu
Founded 1885 as Oakland City College, present name and status 1995
Private control
Academic year: August to May
Pres.: Dr RAY G. BARBER
Provost: Dr MICHAEL J. ATKINSON
Vice-Pres. for Admin. and Finance: Dr ROBERT E. YEAGER
Dir for Admissions: KIM HELDT
Dir for Devt and Advancement: BRIAN BAKER
Registrar: BETTY BURNS
Library Dir: Dr DENISE J. PINNICK
Number of teachers: 65
Number of students: 1,500 (1,350 undergraduate, 150 graduate and professional)
Publication: *The Connection* (4 a year)

DEANS

Chapman School of Religious Studies: DANNY DUNIVAN
School of Arts and Sciences: Dr CLAUDINE D. CUTCHINE
School of Business: MICHAEL J. BURCH
School of Education: Dr MARY JO BEAUCHAMP

PURDUE UNIVERSITY

1031 Hovde Hall, West Lafayette, IN 47907-1031
Telephone: (765) 494-4600
E-mail: admissions@purdue.edu
Internet: www.purdue.edu
Founded 1869
State control
Academic year: August to May
Chancellor: MICHAEL A. WARTELL
Pres.: FRANCE A. CÓRDOVA
Exec. Vice-Pres. for Academic Affairs and Provost: TIMOTHY D. SANDS
Vice-Pres. for Devt: LISA D. CALVERT
Vice-Pres. for Ethics and Compliance: ALYSA CHRISTMAS ROLLOCK
Vice-Pres. for Information Technology and Chief Information Officer: GERARD MCCARTNEY
Vice-Pres. for Research: RICHARD O. BUCKIUS
Vice-Pres. for Student Affairs: MELISSA EXUM
Registrar: ROBERT A. KUBAT
Dean for Libraries: JAMES L. MULLINS
Library: see under Libraries and Archives
Number of teachers: 5,100 (system wide)
Number of students: 74,800 (system wide)
Publications: *Engineering Impact, Innovation, Inside Purdue, Perspective, THiNK* (1 a year)

DEANS

College of Agriculture: JAY T. AKRIDGE
College of Education: MARYANN SANTOS DE BARONA
College of Engineering: LEAH H. JAMIESON
College of Health and Human Sciences: CHRISTINE M. LADISCH
College of Liberal Arts: IRWIN H. WEISER
College of Pharmacy: CRAIG K. SVENSSON
College of Science: JEFFREY T. ROBERTS
College of Technology: GARY BERTOLINE
Graduate School: MARK J. T. SMITH
Krannert Graduate School of Management: P. CHRISTOPHER EARLEY
School of Veterinary Medicine: WILLIE M. REED.

UNIVERSITY BRANCHES

Purdue University Calumet

2200 169th St, Hammond, IN 463232094
Telephone: (219) 989-2400
E-mail: adms@calumet.purdue.edu
Internet: www.purduecal.edu
State control
Chancellor: Dr THOMAS L. KEON
Vice-Chancellor for Academic Affairs: Dr RALPH V. ROGERS
Vice-Chancellor for Admin. Services: JAMES K. JOHNSTON
Vice-Chancellor for Advancement: DANIEL HENDRICKS
Vice-Chancellor for Student Affairs: SARAH HOWARD
Vice-Chancellor for Information Services: FRANK CERVONE
Registrar: ANNE AGOSTO-SEVERA
Dir for Learning and Research Services: TAMMY S. GUERRERO
Library of 264,000 vols
Number of teachers: 600
Number of students: 9,800 (8,660 undergraduate, 1,140 graduate)

DEANS

School of Education: Dr ALICE G. ANDERSON
School of Engineering, Mathematics and Science: Dr MICHAEL C. HENSON
School of Liberal Arts and Social Sciences: Dr RON CORTHELL
School of Management: Dr MARTINE DUCHA-TELET
School of Nursing: Dr PEGGY GERARD
School of Technology: Dr NIAZ LATIF

Purdue University North Central

1401 S U.S. 421, Westville, IN 46391
Telephone: (219) 872-0527
E-mail: admissions@pnc.edu
Internet: www.pnc.edu
Founded 1967
State control
Chancellor: Dr JAMES B. DWORKIN
Vice-Chancellor for Academic Affairs: KAREN SCHMID
Vice-Chancellor for Admin.: STEPHEN R. TURNER
Vice-Chancellor for Enrolment Management and Student Services: PAUL MCGUINNESS
Registrar: GEORGE ROYSTER
Librarian: K. R. JOHNSON
Number of teachers: 300 (130 full-time, 170 part-time)
Number of students: 5,300

DEANS

College of Business: Prof. Dr ALAN G. KRABBENHOFT
College of Engineering and Technology: Prof. Dr LARRYL MATTHEWS
College of Liberal Arts: Prof. Dr S. REX MORROW
College of Science: Prof. Dr KEITH SCHWIN-GENDORF

ROSE—HULMAN INSTITUTE OF TECHNOLOGY

5500 Wabash Ave, Terre Haute, IN 47803
Telephone: (812) 877-1511
E-mail: admissions@rose-hulman.edu
Internet: www.rose-hulman.edu
Founded 1874 as Rose Polytechnic Institute, current name adopted 1971
Private control
Depts of applied biology and biomedical engineering, chemical engineering, chemistry and biochemistry, civil engineering, computer science and software engineering, electrical and computer engineering, engin-

eering management, humanities and social sciences, mathematics, mechanical engineering and physics and optical engineering
Pres.: MATT BRANAM
Vice-Pres. and Chief Admin. Officer: ROBERT A. COONS
Vice-Pres. for Academic Affairs: PHILLIP J. CORNWELL
Vice-Pres. for Enrolment Management: JAMES A. GOECKER
Vice-Pres. for Institutional Advancement: RICKEY N. MCCURRY
Vice-Pres. for Student Affairs and Dean for Students: PETER A. GUSTAFSON
Dean for Faculty: WILLIAM KLINE
Dir for Admissions: LISA NORTON
Registrar: TIMOTHY J. PRICKEL
Library Dir: RICHARD BERNIER
Library of 70,000 vols, 22,000 vols of periodicals, 1,500 NASA and NATO documents
Number of teachers: 180 (165 full-time, 15 part-time)
Number of students: 1,980 (1,910 undergraduate, 90 graduate)
Publication: *Echoes*

SAINT JOSEPH'S COLLEGE

POB 870, Rensselaer, IN 47978
1498 S College Ave, Rensselaer, IN 47978
Telephone: (219) 866-6000
E-mail: admissions@saintjoe.edu
Internet: www.saintjoe.edu
Founded 1889
Private control
Liberal arts courses
Pres.: Dr F. DENNIS RIEGELNEGG
Vice-Pres. for Academic Affairs: Dr DANIEL J. BLANKENSHIP
Vice-Pres. for Institutional Advancement and Marketing: Dr MAUREEN V. EGAN
Dean for Students: Dr LESLIE FRERE
Registrar: CAROL A. BURNS
Library Dir: CATHERINE SAYLERS
Library of 134,628 vols, 22,096 audiovisual items, 67,069 microforms, 2,500 ebooks
Number of teachers: 100 (full-time and part-time)
Number of students: 1,030
Publication: *Contact*

SAINT MARY-OF-THE-WOODS COLLEGE

1 St Mary of Woods College, Saint Mary-of-the-Woods, IN 47876
Telephone: (812) 535-5151
E-mail: smwc@smwc.edu
Internet: www.smwc.edu
Founded 1840
Private control
Academic year: August to May
Liberal arts courses
Pres.: Dr DOTTIE L. KING
Co-Chancellor: Dr BARBARA DOHERTY
Co-Chancellor: Dr JEANNE KNOERLE
Vice-Pres. for Academic Affairs: Dr JANET CLARK
Vice-Pres. for Finance and Admin.: GORDON AFDAHL
Vice-Pres. for Student Life: VICKI KOSOWSKY
Registrar: SUSAN MEIER
Library Dir: JUDITH TRIBBLE
Library of 150,000 vols
Number of teachers: 70
Number of students: 1,700
Publication: *Aurora* (2 a year)

SAINT MARY'S COLLEGE

Notre Dame, IN 46556
Telephone: (219) 284-4000

E-mail: admission@saintmarys.edu
Internet: www.saintmarys.edu

Founded 1844
Private control
Liberal arts courses
Pres.: CAROL ANN MOONEY
Sr Vice-Pres. and Dean for Faculty: PATRICIA
  FLEMING
Vice-Pres. for College Relations: SHARI RODRI-
  GUEZ
Vice-Pres. for Enrolment Management:
  MONA C. BOWE
Vice-Pres. for Finance and Admin.: RICHARD
  SPELLER
Vice-Pres. for Mission: VERONIQUE WIEDOWER
Vice-Pres. for Student Affairs: KAREN JOHN-
  SON
Dir for Admission: KRISTIN MCANDREW
Registrar: TODD NORRIS
Library Dir: JANET FORE

Library of 260,000 vols, 2,000 journals
Number of students: 1,500 (full-time)

Publications: *Chimes* (1 a year), *Courier*
  (online, www3.saintmarys.edu/courier),
  The Avenue

SAINT MEINRAD SEMINARY AND SCHOOL OF THEOLOGY

200 Hill Dr., St Meinrad, IN 47577
Telephone: (812) 357-6611
E-mail: theology@saintmeinrad.edu
Internet: www.saintmeinrad.edu

Founded 1857
Private control
Language of instruction: English
Academic year: August to July (2 semesters)
Offers Masters in divinity, Catholic philo-
  sophical studies, pastoral theology, theology
Pres. and Rector: Rev. DENIS ROBINSON
Vice-Rector: Rev. TOBIAS COLGAN
Academic Dean: Dr ROBERT ALVIS
Dir for Enrolment: Rev. BRENDAN MOSS
Library Dir: DAN KOLB

Library of 170,000 vols, 300 periodicals,
  2,000 rare books
Number of teachers: 30
Number of students: 150

TAYLOR UNIVERSITY

236 W Reade Ave, Upland, IN 46989-1001
Telephone: (317) 998-2751
E-mail: admissions@taylor.edu
Internet: www.taylor.edu

Founded 1846
Private control
Academic year: September to May (3 terms)
Pres.: Dr GENE B. HABECKER
Chancellor: Dr JAY KESLER
Provost: Dr STEPHEN S. BEDI
Vice-Pres. for Enrolment Management and
  Marketing: STEPHEN MORTLAND
Vice-Pres. for Student Devt and Dean for
  Students: Dr SKIP TRUDEAU
Vice-Pres. for Univ. Advancement: Dr BEN
  SELLS
Dir for Admissions: AMY BARNETT
Registrar: JANET SHAFFER
Univ. Librarian: DAN BOWELL

Library of 235,114 vols
Number of teachers: 140 (full-time)
Number of students: 2,400

Publications: *Parnassus*, *Profile*, *Taylor University Magazine*

DEANS

School of Business: Dr LAWRENCE BELCHER
School of Liberal Arts: Dr THOMAS JONES
School of Natural and Applied Sciences: Dr
  MARK BIERMANN

School of Professional and Graduate Studies:
Dr CONNIE LIGHTFOOT

TCM INTERNATIONAL INSTITUTE

POB 24560, 6337 Hollister Dr., Indianapolis,
IN 46224
Telephone: (317) 299-0333
E-mail: tcm@tcmi.org
Internet: www.tcmi.edu

Founded 1982 as Summer Seminary
Private control
Campus in Austria; provides courses in
Belarus, Bulgaria, Czech Republic, Estonia,
Hungary, Moldova, Poland, Romania, Russia
and Ukraine
Pres. and CEO: Dr DONALD ANTHONY TWIST
N American Vice-Pres.: DAVID WRIGHT
Dir for Academic Services: SUE ABEGGLEN
Dir for Assessment: RICHARD JUSTICE
Dir for Global Outreach: DEBBIE POER
Dir for Operations: CAROL FIELDS

Library of 16,000 vols

TRINE UNIVERSITY

1 University Ave, Angola, IN 46703-1764
Telephone: (260) 665-4100
E-mail: admit@trine.edu
Internet: www.trine.edu

Founded 1884 as Tri-State Normal College,
  current name adopted 2008
Private control
Campuses at Angola, Fort Wayne, Scherer-
  ville, South Bend/Mishawaka, Columbus,
  Logansport and Indianapolis
Pres.: Dr EARL D. BROOKS, II
Sr Vice-Pres.: MICHAEL R. BOCK
Vice-Pres. for Academic Affairs: Dr DAVID R.
  FINLEY
Vice-Pres. for Alumni and Devt: KENT
  STUCKY
Vice-Pres. for Enrolment Management:
  SCOTT J. GOPLIN
Vice-Pres. for Finance: JODY GREER
Vice-Pres. for Student Services: RANDY
  WHITE
Registrar: DEBBIE HELMSING
Dir for Library and Information Services:
  KRISTINA BREWER

Number of teachers: 70
Number of students: 2,400

Publications: *Discover*, *Trine Magazine*

DEANS

Allen School of Engineering and Technology:
  Dr V. K. SHARMA
Franks School of Education: Dr SUZANNE VAN
  WAGNER
Jannen School of Arts and Sciences: Dr JOHN
  SHANNON
Ketner School of Business: Dr V. K. SHARMA
School of Professional Studies: DAVID W.
  WOOD

UNIVERSITY OF EVANSVILLE

1800 Lincoln Ave, Evansville, IN 47722
Telephone: (812) 488-2000
E-mail: admission@evansville.edu
Internet: www.evansville.edu

Founded 1854 as Moores Hill Male and
  Female Collegiate Institute, present name
  and status 1967
Private control
Academic year: August to May
Pres.: Dr THOMAS A. KAZEE
Sr Vice-Pres. for Academic Affairs: Dr JOHN
  MOSBO
Vice-Pres. for Enrolment Services: Dr TOM
  BEAR

Vice-Pres. for Institutional Advancement:
  JOHN BARNER
Vice-Pres. for Fiscal Affairs and Admin.:
  JEFFREY WOLF
Vice-Pres. for Students Affairs and Dean for
  Students: DANA CLAYTON
Dir for Univ. Relations: LUCY HIMSTEDT
Dean for Admission: DON VOS
Registrar: AMY BRANDEBURY
Univ. Librarian: WILLIAM LOUDEN

Library of 274,123 vols, 678 journals, 14,000
  ejournals, 472,469 microform units, 12,687
  audiovisual items
Number of teachers: 200
Number of students: 3,000

DEANS

College of Arts and Sciences: JEAN BECKMAN
College of Education and Health Sciences: Dr
  LYNN R. PENLAND
College of Engineering and Computer Sci-
  ence: Dr PHILIP GERHART
Schroeder Family School of Business Admin-
  istration: Dr STEPHEN STANDIFIRD

UNIVERSITY OF INDIANAPOLIS

1400 E Hanna Ave, Indianapolis, IN 46227
Telephone: (317) 788-3368
Internet: www.uindy.edu

Founded 1902, current name adopted 1986
Private control
Academic year: September to August (2
  semesters)
Campus in Athens, Greece; partnership sites
  in Asia and Central America
Pres.: Dr BEVERLEY J. PITTS
Exec. Vice-Pres. and Provost: Dr DEBORAH
  BALOGH
Vice-Pres. for Research, Planning and Int.
  Partnership: Dr MARY MOORE
Vice-Pres. for Student Affairs and Enrol-
  ment: MARK WEIGAND
Vice-Pres. for Univ. Advancement: JAMES
  SMITH
Dir for Admissions: RON WILKS
Registrar: Dr MARY BETH BAGG
Library Dir: FRANCESCA BUSCH

Library of 150,000 vols, 600 periodicals
Number of teachers: 500 (full-time and part-
  time)
Number of students: 5,400 (main campus)

DEANS

College of Arts and Sciences: Dr JENNIFER
  DRAKE (acting)
College of Health Sciences: Dr STEPHANIE
  KELLY
Ecumenical Programmes: Dr MICHAEL CART-
  WRIGHT
School for Adult Learning: Dr PATRICIA
  JEFFERSON
School of Business: Dr SHEELA YADAV
School of Education: Dr KATHRYN MORAN
School of Nursing: Dr ANNE THOMAS
School of Psychological Sciences: Dr RICK
  HOLIGROCKI

UNIVERSITY OF NOTRE DAME

300 Main Bldg, Notre Dame, IN 46556
Telephone: (574) 631-5000
E-mail: admissions@nd.edu
Internet: www.nd.edu

Founded 1842 as l'Université de Notre Dame
  du Lac
Private control
Academic year: August to May
Pres.: Rev. JOHN I. JENKINS
Provost: Dr THOMAS G. BURISH
Exec. Vice-Pres.: JOHN F. AFFLECK-GRAVES
Vice-Pres. and Chief Information Officer:
  RONALD D. KRAEMER
Vice-Pres. and Gen. Counsel: MARIANNE CORR

Vice-Pres. for Research: ROBERT J. BERNHARD
Vice-Pres. for Student Affairs: Rev. THOMAS P. DOYLE
Vice-Pres. for Univ. Relations: LOUIS M. NANNI
Dir for Admissions: ROBERT MUNDY
Registrar: CHUCK HURLEY
Univ. Librarian: DIANE P. WALKER
Library: see under Libraries and Archives
Number of teachers: 1,100 (990 full time, 110 part-time)
Number of students: 12,000

Publications: *Academy of Management Review, Acroterion* (1 a year), *American Journal of Jurisprudence* (print and online, www.nd.edu/~ndlaw/ajj), *American Midland Naturalist: An International Journal of Ecology, Evolution and Environment* (online, www.nd.edu/~ammidnat), *Journal of College and University Law* (online, www.nd.edu/~jcul), *Journal of Legislation* (online, www.nd.edu/~ndlaw/jleg), *Journal of Multicultural Counseling and Development, Juggler* (2 a year, online, www.nd.edu/~juggler), *Nineteenth-Century Contexts* (online, www.nd.edu/~ncc), *Notre Dame Journal of Formal Logic* (online, www.nd.edu/~ndjfl), *Notre Dame Journal of Law, Ethics and Public Policy* (2 a year, print and online, www.nd.edu/~ndlaw/jlepp), *Notre Dame Law Review* (online, ndlawreview.org), *Notre Dame Magazine* (4 a year, online, magazine.nd.edu), *Notre Dame Philosophical Review* (online, ndpr.nd.edu/recentreviews), *Notre Dame Review* (print and online, ndreview.nd.edu), *Religion and Literature* (3 a year, online, religionandlit.nd.edu), *Review of Politics* (online, www.nd.edu/~rop), *Technical Review*

DEANS

College of Arts and Letters: JOHN T. MCGREEVY
College of Engineering: PETER K. KILPATRICK
College of Science: GREGORY P. CRAWFORD
First Year of Studies: HUGH R. PAGE, Jr
Graduate School: GREGORY E. STERLING
Law School: NELL JESSUP NEWTON
Mendoza College of Business: Dr CAROLYN Y. WOO
School of Architecture: MICHAEL N. LYKOUDIS

PROFESSORS

College of Arts and Letters:

ALDOUS, J., Sociology
AMERIKS, K., Philosophy
ANADON, J., Romance Languages and Literature
APPLEBY, R. S., History
ARNOLD, P., Political Science
AUNE, D. E., Theology
AYO, N., Liberal Studies
BARBER, S. A., Political Science
BARTELL, E., Economics
BIDDICK, K., History
BLACHLY, A., Music
BLANTZ, T. E., History
BOBIK, J., Philosophy
BORKOWSKI, J. G., Psychology
BOULTON, M. B., Romance Languages and Literatures
BOWER, C., Music
BRADLEY, K. R., Classics
BRADSHAW, P. F., Theology
BROGAN, J. V., English
BRUNS, G. L., English
BURRELL, D. B., Philosophy
BUSTAMANTE, J. A., Psychology, Sociology
BUTTIGIEG, J. A., English
CACHEY, T., Romance Languages and Literatures
CARDENAS, G., Psychology
CRAFTON, D., Film, Television and Theatre
CRAMER, C., Music

CUMMINGS, E. M., Psychology
CUNNINGHAM, L. S., Theology
DALEY, S. J., Theology
DALLMAYR, F., Political Theory
DAMATTA, R., Anthropology
DAVID, M., Philosophy
DAY, J. D., Psychology
DELANEY, C. F., Philosophy
DEPAUL, M., Philosophy
DETLEFSEN, M., Philosophy
DOODY, M. A., English Literature
DOUGHERTY, J. P., English
DOUTHWAITE, J., Romance Languages and Literatures
DOWTY, A., Political Science
DUNNE, J. S., Theology
DUTT, A., Economics
DYE, K., Music
EMERY, K., Jr, Programme of Liberal Studies
FLINT, T., Philosophy
FOX, C. B., English
FRANCIS, M. J., Political Science
FREDDOSO, A. J., Philosophy
FREDMAN, S., English
FRESE, D., English
GERNES, S. G., English
GERSH, S., Medieval Studies
GIBBONS, L., English, Film, Television and Theatre
GODMILOW, J., Film, Television and Theatre
GUTTING, G., Philosophy
HAIMO, E. T., Music
HALLINAN, M. W., Sociology
HALTON, E., Sociology
HAMBURG, G., History
HAMLIN, C., History
HART, K., English
HERO, R. E., Political Science
HIGGINS, P., Music
HOLLAND, P. D., Film, Television and Theatre
HÖSLE, V., German and Russian Languages and Literatures
HOWARD, D. A., Philosophy
HOWARD, G. S., Psychology
JAKSIC, I., History
JEMIELITY, T. J., English
JENSEN, R., Economics
JOHANSEN, R. C., Political Science
JOHNSON, M., Theology
JOY, L. S., Philosophy
KAVENY, M., Theology
KIM, K., Economics
KLINE, E. A., English
KOMMERS, D. P., Political Science
KREMER, W. J., Art, Art History and Design
KRIEG, R. A., Theology
KSELMAN, T., History
LAPIDGE, M., English
LEAHY, W. H., Economics
LOPEZ, G., Political Science
LOUX, M. J., Philosophy
MCADAMS, A. J., Political Science
MCBRIEN, R. P., Theology
MCINERNY, R., Philosophy
MCKENNA, J. J., Anthropology
MAINWARING, S., Political Science
MANIER, E., Philosophy
MANN, G. L., English
MARSDEN, G. M., History
MARULLO, T., German and Russian Languages and Literature
MATTHIAS, J. E., English
MAXWELL, S. E., Psychology
MEIER, J. P., Theology
MOODY, P., Political Science
MURRAY, D., History
NEYREY, S. J., Theology
NICGORSKI, W. J., Political Science, Programme of Liberal Studies
NOBLE, T., Medieval Institute
NORTON, R. E., German and Russian Languages and Literatures
O'BRIEN O'KEEFFE, K., English

O'DONNELL, G., Political Science
O'REGAN, C., Theology
O'ROURKE, W. A., English
PILKINTON, M. C., Film, Television and Theatre
PLANTINGA, A., Philosophy
POPE-DAVIS, D., Psychology
POWER, F. C., Liberal Studies, Psychology
PROFIT, V. B., German and Russian Languages and Literatures
ROCHE, M., German Language and Literature, Philosophy
ROOS, J., Political Science
ROS, J., Economics
ROSENBERG, C., Art, Art History and Design
SAYERS, V., English
SAYRE, K. M., Philosophy
SCHLERETH, T. J., American Studies
SCHMUHL, R., American Studies
SCULLY, T. R., Political Science
SEIDENSPINNER-NÚÑEZ, D., Romance Languages and Literatures
SHEERIN, D., Classics, Theology
SHRADER-FRECHETTE, K., Philosophy, Biological Sciences
SKURSKI, R., Economics
SLAUGHTER, T., History
SLOAN, P. R., Liberal Studies
SMYTH, J., History
STERBA, J., Philosophy
STERLING, G. E., Theology
SWARTZ, T., Economics
TURNER, J., History
ULRICH, E., Theology
VALENZUELA, J. S., Sociology
VANDEN BOSSCHE, C., English
VANDERKAM, J. C., Theology
VAYRYNEN, R., Political Science
WALSHE, A. P., Political Science
WALTON, J., English
WATSON, S., Philosophy
WEGS, R., History
WEIGERT, A., Sociology
WEITHMAN, P., Philosophy
WELLE, J., Romance Languages and Literatures
WERGE, T., English
WHITMAN, T., Psychology
YOUENS, S., Music
ZIAREK, E., English

College of Engineering

Department of Aerospace and Mechanical Engineering:

ATASSI, H. M., Aero-acoustics
BATILL, S. M., Design
CORKE, T. C., Fluid Mechanics
DUNN, P. F., Particle Dynamics
INCROPERA, F. P., Heat Transfer
JUMPER, E. J., Aerodynamics
MUELLER, T. J., Fluid Mechanics
NELSON, R. C., Aerodynamics
OVAERT, T., Manufacturing
PAOLUCCI, S., Fluid Mechanics
RENAUD, J. E., Design
SEN, M., Heat Transfer
SKAAR, S. B., Control
THOMAS, F. O., Fluid Mechanics

Department of Chemical Engineering:

BRENNECKE, J. F.
CHANG, H.-C.
KANTOR, J. C.
LEIGHTON, D. T.
MCCREADY, M. J.
MCGINN, P. J.
MILLER, A. E.
SCHMITZ, R. A.
STADTHERR, M. A.
STRIEDER, W. C.
VARMA, A.
WOLF, E. E.

Department of Civil Engineering and Geological Sciences:

BURNS, P. C.

KAREEM, A.
SILLIMAN, S. E.
TAYLOR, J. I.

Department of Computer Science and Engineering:

BOWYER, K.
CHEN, D. Z.
KOGGE, P. M.
UHRAN, J., Jr

Department of Electrical Engineering:

ANTSAKLIS, P. J.
BAUER, P. H.
BERNSTEIN, G. H.
COLLINS, O.
COSTELLO, D. J.
FUJA, T. E.
HUANG, Y.-F.
LENT, C. S.
MERZ, J. L.
POROD, W.
ROSENTHAL, J.
SAIN, M. K.
SEABAUGH, A. C.
STEVENSON, R. L.

College of Science:

ALBER, M. S., Mathematics
APRAHAMIAN, A., Physics
ARNOLD, G. B., Physics
ASMUS, K.-D., Chemistry and Biochemistry
BARABASI, A.-L., Physics
BASU, S. C., Chemistry and Biochemistry
BELOVSKY, G. E., Biological Sciences
BENDER, H. A., Biological Sciences
BERRY, H. G., Physics
BESANSKY, N. J., Biological Sciences
BIGI, I. I., Physics
BLACKSTEAD, H. A., Physics
BOTTEI, R. S., Chemistry and Biochemistry
BUECHLER, S. A., Mathematics
BUNKER, B. A., Physics
CAO, J., Mathematics
CASON, N. M., Physics
COLLINS, F. H., Biological Sciences
CONNOLLY, F. X., Mathematics
CREARY, X., Chemistry and Biochemistry
DOBROWOLSKA-FURDYNA, M., Physics
DUMAN, J., Biological Sciences
DWYER, W. G., Mathematics
FAYBUSOVICH, L. E., Mathematics
FEHLNER, T. P., Chemistry and Biochemistry
FRASER, M. J., Jr, Biological Sciences
FRAUENDORF, S. G., Physics
FURDYNA, J. K., Physics
GARG, U., Physics
GOERRES, J., Physics
HAHN, A. J., Mathematics
HELLENTHAL, R., Biological Sciences
HELQUIST, P., Chemistry and Biochemistry
HIMONAS, A. A., Mathematics
HOWARD, A., Mathematics
HU, B., Mathematics
HYDE, D. R., Biological Sciences
HYDER, A. K., Research Physics
JACOBS, D. C., Chemistry and Biochemistry
JOHNSON, A. L., Biological Sciences
JOHNSON, W. R., Physics
JONES, G. L., Physics
KNIGHT, J. F., Mathematics
KOLATA, J. J., Physics
KULPA, C. F., Biological Sciences
LAMBERTI, G. A., Biological Sciences
LAPPIN, A. G., Chemistry and Biochemistry
LEPRAPPIER, F., Mathematics
LIVINGSTON, A. E., Physics
LODGE, D. M., Biological Sciences
LOSECCO, J. M., Physics
MARINO, J. P., Chemistry and Biochemistry
MATHEWS, G. J., Physics
MEISEL, D., Chemistry and Biochemistry
MERZ, J. L., Physics
MIGLIORE, J. C., Mathematics
MILLER, M. J., Chemistry and Biochemistry

NEWMAN, K. E., Physics
NOWAK, T. L., Chemistry and Biochemistry
O'TOUSA, J. E., Biological Sciences
PAONI, N., Chemistry and Biochemistry
RETTIG, T. W., Physics
ROSENTHAL, J. J., Mathematics
RUCHTI, R. C., Physics
SAPIRSTEIN, J. R., Physics
SCHEIDT, W. R., Chemistry and Biochemistry
SERIANNI, A. S., Chemistry and Biochemistry
SEVERSON, D. W., Biological Sciences
SEVOV, S., Chemistry and Biochemistry
SHAW, M.-C., Mathematics
SHEPHARD, W. D., Physics
SHRADER-FRECHETTE, K., Biological Sciences
SMITH, B. D., Chemistry and Biochemistry
SMYTH, B., Mathematics
SNOW, D. M., Mathematics
SOMMESE, A. J., Mathematics
STANTON, N. K., Mathematics
STOLZ, S. A., Mathematics
TAYLOR, L. R., Mathematics
TENNISWOOD, M. P., Biological Sciences
WARCHOL, J., Physics
WAYNE, M. R., Physics
WELSH, J. E. J., Biological Sciences
WIESCHER, M. C. F., Physics
WILLIAMS, E. B., Mathematics
WONG, P.-M., Mathematics
XAVIER, F., Mathematics

Law School:

BARRETT, M.
BAUER, J. P.
BENNETT, G.
BLAKEY, G. R.
BRADLEY, G. V.
DUTILE, F. N.
GUNN, A.
GURULE, J.
JACOBS, R. F.
KAVENY, M. C.
KELLENBERG, C. L.
KOMMERS, D. P.
MENDEZ, J. E.
MOONEY, C. A.
O'HARA, P.
PHELPS, T. G.
PRATT, W. F., Jr
RODES, R. E., Jr
SECKINGER, J. H.
SHELTON, D. L.
SMITHBURN, E.
TIDMARSH, J.

Mendoza College of Business:

AFFLECK-GRAVES, J., Finance and Business Economics
BRETZ, R., Management and Administrative Sciences
CONLON, E. J., Management and Administrative Sciences
COSIMANO, T. F., Finance and Business Economics
ENDERLE, G., Marketing
ETZEL, M. J., Marketing
FRECKA, T. J., Accountancy
GRESIK, T., Finance and Business Economics
GUILTINAN, J. P., Marketing
GUNDLACH, G. T., Marketing
HARTVIGSEN, D. B., Management and Administrative Sciences
HUANG, R. D., Finance and Business Economics
KEANE, J. G., Management and Administrative Sciences
KEATING, B. P., Finance and Business Economics
KENNEDY, J. J., Marketing
KRAJEWSKI, L., Management and Administrative Sciences
McDONALD, W. D., Finance and Business Economics

MATTA, K. F., Management and Administrative Sciences
MILANI, K. W., Accountancy
MITTELSTAEDT, H. F., Accountancy
MORRIS, M. H., Accountancy
MURPHY, P. E., Marketing
NICHOLS, W. D., Accountancy
RAMANAN, R., Accountancy
REILLY, F. K., Finance and Business Economics
RICCHIUTE, D. N., Accountancy
RUESCHHOFF, N. G., Accountancy
SCHAEFER, T., Accountancy
SCHULTZ, P., Finance and Business Economics
SHEEHAN, R. G., Finance and Business Economics
SIMON, D. T., Accountancy
TAVIS, L. A., Finance and Business Economics
URBANY, J., Marketing
VECCHIO, R. P., Management and Administrative Sciences
WILKIE, W. L., Marketing
WITTENBACH, J. L., Accountancy

School of Architecture:

AMICO, R.
CROWE, N.
LYKOUDIS, M.
SMITH, T. G.
WESTFALL, C. W.

UNIVERSITY OF SAINT FRANCIS

2701 Spring St, Fort Wayne, IN 46808-3994

Telephone: (260) 399-7999
E-mail: admis@sf.edu
Internet: www.sf.edu

Founded 1890 as Saint Francis College, current name and status 1998
Private control
Academic year: August to May

Pres.: Sis. M. ELISE KRISS
Exec. Vice-Pres.: Dr STACY J. ADKINSON
Vice Pres. for Academic Affairs: Dr J. ANDREW PRALL
Vice-Pres. for Finance and Operations: RICHARD BIENZ
Vice-Pres. for Univ. Relations: Dr MATTHEW SMITH
Dean for Crown Point Site: MARSHA KING
Dean for Students: DONALD APPIARIUS
Registrar: FRANK CONNOR
Exec. Dir for Information and Instructional Service: KARLA ALEXANDER

Library of 68,000 vols, 450 periodical subscriptions
Number of teachers: 140
Number of students: 2,300

DEANS

Keith Busse School of Business and Entrepreneurial Leadership: ROBERT LEE
School of Arts and Sciences: Dr EARL KUMFER
School of Creative Arts: RICK CARTWRIGHT
School of Health Sciences: Dr MINDY YODER

UNIVERSITY OF SOUTHERN INDIANA

8600 University Blvd, Evansville, IN 47712-3596

Telephone: (812) 464-8600
E-mail: enroll@usi.edu
Internet: www.usi.edu

Founded 1965 as the Evansville Campus of Indiana State Univ., present name and status 1985
State control
Academic year: August to May

Pres.: Prof. Dr LINDA L. M. BENNETT
Provost and Vice-Pres. for Academic Affairs: Dr RONALD S. ROCHON
Vice-Pres. for Finance and Admin.: MARK ROZEWSKI

Vice-Pres. for Govt and Univ. Relations: CYNTHIA S. BRINKER
Registrar: SANDY FRANK
Dir for Library: MARTHA NIEMEIER
Library of 244,622 vols, 88,720 vols of govt documents, 576,304 microform units, 33,946 ejournals, 975 linear ft MSS
Number of teachers: 660 (339 full-time, and 321 part-time)
Number of students: 10,800
Publication: *USI Magazine* (online, www. usi.edu/magazine)

DEANS

College of Business: Dr MUHAMMAD KHAYUM
College of Liberal Arts: MICHAEL K. AAKHUS
College of Nursing and Health Professions: Dr NADINE A. COUDRET
Pott College of Science and Engineering: Dr SCOTT A. GORDON

VALPARAISO UNIVERSITY

Valparaiso, IN 46383-6493
Telephone: (219) 464-5000
E-mail: university.relations@valpo.edu
Internet: www.valpo.edu
Founded 1859, present name and status 1906
Private control
Pres.: Dr MARK A. HECKLER
Provost and Exec. Vice-Pres. for Academic Affairs: Dr MARK R. SCHWEHN
Vice-Pres. for Admin. and Finance: CHARLEY E. GILLESPIE
Vice-Pres. for Enrolment Management: MICHAEL JOSEPH
Vice-Pres. for Institutional Advancement: LISA HOLLANDER
Vice-Pres. for Student Affairs: Dr BONNIE L. HUNTER
Dean for Library Services: BRAD EDEN
Library of 451,000 vols, 262,068 printed monographic vols, 78,563 journals, 3,536 films
Number of teachers: 220 (full-time)
Number of students: 4,000
Publication: *Valpo Magazine*

DEANS

Christ College (The Honors College): Dr MEL PIEHL
College of Arts and Sciences: Dr JON T. KILPINEN
College of Business: Dr ROY AUSTENSEN (acting)
College of Engineering: Dr KRAIG J. OLEJNICZAK
College of Nursing: Dr JANET BROWN
Graduate School and Continuing Education: JENNIFER A. ZIEGLER
School of Law: JAY CONISON

VINCENNES UNIVERSITY

1002 N First St, Vincennes, IN 47591
Telephone: (800) 742-9198
E-mail: vuadmit@vinu.edu
Internet: www.vinu.edu
Founded 1801
State control
Pres.: Dr DICK HELTON
Provost and Vice-Pres. for Instructional Services and Dean for Faculty: Dr RONALD M. DAVIS
Dean for Students: JOHN LIVERS
Dir for Admissions: CHRISTIAN BLOME
Registrar: DONNA JO WEAVER
Dean for Learning Resources Centre: ROBERT A. SLAYTON

DEANS

Business and Public Service: NICOLAS SPINA
Extended Studies: DON KAUFMAN

Health Sciences and Human Performance: JANA VIECK
Humanities: CHARLES W. REINHART
Science and Mathematics: PETER IYERE
Social Sciences and Performing Arts: ERIC MARGERUM
Technology and Aviation Technology Centre: ARTHUR H. HAASE

WABASH COLLEGE

301 W Wabash Ave, Crawfordsville, IN 47933
Telephone: (765) 361-6100
E-mail: admissions@wabash.edu
Internet: www.wabash.edu
Founded 1832
Private control
Liberal arts courses
Pres.: Dr PATRICK E. WHITE
Dean for Admissions and Financial Aid: STEVEN J. KLEIN
Dean for College: Dr GARY A. PHILLIPS
Dean for College Advancement: JOSEPH R. EMMICK
Dean for Students: MICHAEL P. RATERS
Registrar: Dr JULIE A. OLSEN
Librarian: JOHN LAMBORN
Library of 434,460 vols, 5,530 current periodicals, 162,000 govt documents, 11,151 audiovisual titles
Number of teachers: 90
Number of students: 900
Publication: *Columns*

IOWA

AIB COLLEGE OF BUSINESS

2500 Fleur Dr., Des Moines, IA 50321
Telephone: (515) 244-4221
E-mail: admissions@aib.edu
Internet: www.aib.edu
Founded 1921 as American Institute of Business
Private control
Academic year: September to August
Pres.: NANCY WILLIAMS
Vice-Pres. for Academic Affairs: Dr SUSAN CIGELMAN
Vice-Pres. for Student Life: TERRY WILSON
Chief Academic Officer: CHRISTY ROLAND
Chief Financial Officer: PAUL WINGET
Dir for Admissions: STEVE OLSEN
Registrar: RANDY TERRONEZ
Library Dir: LESLIE BINTNER
Number of teachers: 70 (20 full-time, 50 part-time)
Number of students: 1,000

ALLEN COLLEGE

1825 Logan Ave, Waterloo, IA 50703
Telephone: (319) 226-2000
E-mail: allencollegeadmissions@ihs.org
Internet: www.allencollege.edu
Founded 1925 as Allen Memorial Hospital School of Nursing, current name adopted 1996
Private control
Academic year: August to May (2 semesters)
Chancellor: Prof. Dr JERRY D. DURHAM
Vice-Chancellor for Academic Affairs: Dr NANCY KRAMER
Dir for Student Services: JOANNA RAMSDEN-MEIER
Coordinator for Library/Media Services: Dr RUTH LINGXIN YAN
Number of teachers: 25
Number of students: 500

DEANS

School of Health Sciences: Prof. Dr PEGGY FORTSCH
School of Nursing: Prof. Dr KENDRA WILLIAMS-PEREZ

ASHFORD UNIVERSITY

400 N Bluff Blvd, Clinton, IA 52732
Telephone: (563) 242-4023
E-mail: admissions@ashford.edu
Internet: www.ashford.edu
Founded 1918 as Mount St Clare College, present name and status 2005
Private control
Pres.: Dr ELIZABETH TICE
Provost: REBECCA WARDLOW
Vice-Pres. for Admissions: ALICE PARENTI
Univ. Registrar: KIRK MORRISON
Library Dir: FLORA S. LOWE
Library of 101,000 vols, 650 periodicals and journals, 70,000 microforms, 700 audiovisual titles
Number of teachers: 50 (25 full-time, 25 part-time)
Number of students: 500 (460 undergraduate, 40 graduate)

DEANS

College of Business and Professional Studies: Dr CHARLES R. MINNICK
College of Education: Dr JOEN ROTTLER
College of Health, Human Services and Science: Dr BARBARA PHILIBERT
College of Liberal Arts: Dr WILLIAM C. LOWE

BRIAR CLIFF UNIVERSITY

POB 2100, Sioux City, IA 51104-0100
3303 Rebecca St, Sioux City, IA 51104-2324
Telephone: (712) 279-5200
E-mail: admissions@briarcliff.edu
Internet: www.briarcliff.edu
Founded 1930 as Briar Cliff College, current name adopted 2001
Private control
Academic year: September to May
Programmes in accounting, art, biology, business administration, chemistry, computer science, criminal justice, elementary education, English, environmental science, graphic design, health, physical education, and recreation, history, human resource management, mass communications, management information systems, mathematics, medical technology, music, new media, nursing, political science, psychology, radiological technology, secondary education, social research, social work, Spanish, sports science, theatre, theology, writing
Pres.: BEVERLY A. WHARTON
Provost, Vice-Pres. for Academic Affairs and Academic Dean: Dr WILLIAM T. MANGAN
Vice-Pres. for Enrolment Management: SHARISUE WILCOXON
Vice-Pres. for Institutional Advancement: CRAIG MCGARRY
Vice-Pres. for Student Devt: STEVEN JANOWIAK
Registrar: DEIDRE ENGEL
Library Dir: DEB ROBERTSON
Library of 100,000 vols
Number of teachers: 50
Number of students: 1,100
Publications: *Briar Cliff University Magazine*, *The Briar Cliff Review*

BUENA VISTA UNIVERSITY

610 W Fourth St, Storm Lake, IA 50588
Telephone: (712) 749-2351
Internet: www.bvu.edu
Founded 1891, present name and status 1995

Private control
Academic year: September to May
Pres.: FREDERICK V. MOORE
Vice-Pres. for Academic Affairs and Dean for Faculty: Dr DAVID EVANS
Vice-Pres. for Enrolment Management: JOHN KLOCKENTAGER
Vice-Pres. for Institutional Advancement: KENNETH CONVERSE
Vice-Pres. for Student Services and Dean for Students: Dr MARY GILL
Registrar: NILA HOUSKA
Univ. Librarian: JAMES R. KENNEDY
Library of 147,000 vols, 29,000 periodicals
Number of teachers: 80 (full-time)
Number of students: 2,600

DEANS

Harold Walters Siebens School of Business: Dr ELIZABETH THROOP
School of Communication and Arts: Prof. Dr MICHAEL WHITLATCH
School of Education and Exercise Science: (vacant)
School of Science: BENJAMIN DONATH
School of Social Science, Philosophy and Religion: Prof. Dr DIXEE BARTHOLOMEW-FEIS

CENTRAL COLLEGE

812 University, Pella, IA 50219
Telephone: (877) 462-3687
E-mail: admission@central.edu
Internet: www.central.edu
Founded 1853; attached to Reformed Church
Private control
Academic year: August to May

Programmes in accounting, actuarial science, anthropology, art, athletic training, biology, business management, chemistry, communication studies, computer science, economics, elementary education, English, environmental studies, exercise science, french, general studies, German studies, history, information systems, international management, international studies, linguistics, mathematics, mathematics/computer science, music, music education, natural science, philosophy, physics, political science, psychology, religion, secondary education, social science, sociology, Spanish, theatre; pre-professional programmes: architecture, chiropractics, dentistry, engineering, law, medicine, nursing, occupational therapy, optometry, pharmacy, physical therapy, podiatric medicine, veterinary medicine; overseas study centres in France, Austria, Spain, Wales, England, Yucatan, China and the Netherlands
Pres.: Dr MARK PUTNAM
Vice-Pres. for Academic Affairs and Dean for Faculty: Dr MARY MORTON-STREY
Vice-Pres. for Advancement: DAVE SUTPHEN
Vice-Pres. for Finance and Admin. and Treas.: MARGARET TUNGSETH
Vice-Pres. for Student Enrolment Management: CAROL WILLIAMSON
Dean for Student Life: ERIC JONES
Registrar: STEPHANIE HENNING
Library Dir: NATALIE H. HUTCHINSON
Library of 200,000 vols, 4,000 music scores and anthologies
Number of teachers: 90 (full-time)
Number of students: 1,600

Publication: *The Central Ray*

CLARKE UNIVERSITY

1550 Clarke Dr., Dubuque, IA 52001-3198
Telephone: (563) 588-6300
E-mail: clarke-info@clarke.edu
Internet: www.clarke.edu
Founded 1843, present name and status 2010

Private control
Academic year: August to May
Depts of accounting and business admin., art and art history, athletic training, biology, chemistry, communication, computer science, drama and speech, education, history/political science, language and literature, mathematics, music, nursing, philosophy, physical therapy, psychology, religious studies and social work
Pres.: Dr JOANNE M. BURROWS
Provost and Vice-Pres. for Academic Affairs: JOAN LINGEN
Vice-Pres. for Institutional Advancement: BILL BIEBUYCK
Vice-Pres. for Enrolment Management: BETH TRIPLETT
Vice-Pres. for Student Life: KATHLEEN ZANGER
Registrar: KRISTI DROESSLER
Library Dir: SUE LEIBOLD
Library of 121,000 vols
Number of teachers: 120
Number of students: 1,250

Publications: *Catalyst* (1 a year), *CLARKE: The Magazine of Clarke University*, *Tenth Muse* (1 a year)

COE COLLEGE

1220 First Ave, NE, Cedar Rapids, IA 52402
Telephone: (319) 399-8500
E-mail: admission@coe.edu
Internet: www.coe.edu
Founded 1851 as School for the Prophets, current name adopted 1881
Private control
Academic year: August to May

Majors in accounting, African-American studies, American studies, art, Asian studies, athletic training, biochemistry, biology, business administration, chemistry, communication studies, computer science, economics, education, English, English as a second language, environmental science, environmental studies, film studies, French, French studies, gender studies, general science, German, German studies, historical studies, history, interdisciplinary, literature, mathematics, molecular biology, music, nursing, philosophy, physical education, physics, political science, pre-professional programmes, psychology, public relations, religion, sociology, Spanish, Spanish studies, speech, theatre arts, writing
Pres.: Dr JAMES R. PHIFER
Vice-Pres. for Academic Affairs and Dean for Faculty: Dr MARIE BAEHR
Vice-Pres. for Admin. and Enrolment Services: MICHAEL WHITE
Vice-Pres. for Advancement: RICHARD MEISTERLING
Vice-Pres. for Student Affairs: LOU STARK
Dean for Admission: JULIE STAKER
Registrar: Dr EVELYN MOORE
Dir for Library Services: JILL JACK
Library of 300,000 vols, 1,100 current periodicals, 10,000 microforms, 16,000 audiovisual items, 33,500 print and online periodicals
Number of teachers: 140 (80 full-time, 60 part-time)
Number of students: 1,350

Publication: *Courier* (4 a year)

CORNELL COLLEGE

600 First St, SW, Mount Vernon, IA 52314-1098
Telephone: (319) 895-4000
E-mail: admission@cornellcollege.edu
Internet: www.cornellcollege.edu

Founded 1853 as Iowa Conf. Seminary, current name adopted 1857
Private control
Depts of art, biology, chemistry, computer science, economics and business, education, English, geology, history, kinesiology, languages, mathematics, music, philosophy, physics, politics, psychology, religion, sociology and anthropology, theatre and communications studies
Pres.: JONATHAN BRAND
Vice-Pres. for Academic Affairs and Dean for College: R. JOSEPH DIEKER
Vice-Pres. for Alumni and College Advancement: PETER WILCH
Vice-Pres. for Enrolment and Dean for Admissions: JONATHAN STROUD
Vice-Pres. for Student Affairs: JOHN HARP
Registrar: JONNA HIGGINS-FREESE
Dir for Library: PAUL WAELCHLI
Library of 190,000 vols
Number of teachers: 80
Number of students: 1,200

DES MOINES UNIVERSITY

3200 Grand Ave, Des Moines, IA 50312-4198
Telephone: (515) 271-1400
E-mail: info@dmu.edu
Internet: www.dmu.edu
Founded 1898 as Dr S. S. Still College of Osteopathy, current name adopted 1999
Private control
Pres. and CEO: Dr ANGELA L. WALKER FRANKLIN
Provost: Dr KAREN MCLEAN
Vice-Pres. for Admin. Services: STEPHEN DENGLE
Vice-Pres. for Institutional Advancement: SUE HUPPERT
Vice-Pres. for Student Services: MARY ANN ZUG
Registrar: KATHY L. SCAGLIONE
Library Dir: LARRY D. MARQUARDT
Library of 26,000 medical vols, 30,000 bound journals, 3,000 ejournals
Number of students: 1,700

Publication: *DMU Magazine* (4 a year)

DEANS

College of Health Sciences: Dr JODI L. CAHALAN
College of Osteopathic Medicine: Dr KENDALL REED
College of Podiatric Medicine and Surgery: Dr ROBERT M. YOHO
University Research: Dr JEFFREY GRAY

DIVINE WORD COLLEGE

102 Jacoby Dr. SW, POB 380, Epworth, IA 52045-0380
Telephone: (319) 876-3353
E-mail: dwcinfo@dwci.edu
Internet: www.dwci.edu
Founded 1931 as St Paul's Mission House, current name adopted 1964
Private control
Academic year: August to May

Courses in cross-cultural studies, philosophy and religious studies
Pres.: Rev. TIMOTHY LENCHAK
Vice-Pres. for Academic Affairs: Dr MATHEW KANJIRATHINKAL
Vice-Pres. for Devt: TERRY SYKORA
Vice-Pres. for Formation and Dean for Students: Rev. KHIEN MAI LUU
Vice-Pres. for Recruitment and Admissions: LEN UHAL
Registrar: DEBORAH HIRSCH
Library Dir: DANIEL BOICE
Library of 90,000 vols, 350 magazines

DORDT COLLEGE

498 Fourth Ave, NE, Sioux Center, IA 51250
Telephone: (712) 722-6000
E-mail: admissions@dordt.edu
Internet: www.dordt.edu

Founded 1955
Private control
Languages of instruction: English, Dutch, Latin, Spanish
Academic year: August to May
Liberal arts courses

Pres.: Dr CARL E. ZYLSTRA
Provost: Dr ERIK HOEKSTRA
Vice-Pres. for Academic Affairs: Dr ROCKNE MCCARTHY
Vice-Pres. for College Advancement: JOHN BAAS
Vice-Pres. for Student Services: KEN BOERSMA
Exec. Dir for Admissions: QUENTIN VAN ESSEN
Registrar: JIM BOS
Dir for Library Services: SHERYL TAYLOR

Library of 285,000 vols, 300 journals, magazines and newspapers, 58,500 etitles
Number of teachers: 80 (full-time)
Number of students: 1,400

Publication: *Pro Rege* (4 a year)

DRAKE UNIVERSITY

2507 University Ave, Des Moines, IA 50311-4505
Telephone: (515) 271-2011
E-mail: admission@drake.edu
Internet: www.drake.edu

Founded 1881
Private control
Academic year: September to May (2 semesters)

Pres.: Dr DAVID E. MAXWELL
Provost: SUE WRIGHT
Vice-Pres. for Admission and Financial Aid: TOM DELAHUNT
Vice-Pres. for Alumni and Devt: JOHN SMITH
Dean for Students: Dr SENTWALI BAKARI
Registrar: NANCY GEIGER
Dean for Cowles Library: RODNEY HENSHAW
Dir for Law Library: JOHN EDWARDS

Library of 514,886 vols, 1,900 journals, 107,995 govt documents, 2,500 audiovisual items, 35,703 ebooks
Number of teachers: 420 (240 full-time, 180 part-time)
Number of students: 4,400 (3,225 undergraduate, 1,175 graduate)

Publications: *Drake Blue* (online, www.drake.edu/magazine), *Drake Law Review*, *Drake Update*

DEANS

College of Arts and Sciences: Dr JOSEPH LENZ
College of Business and Public Administration: CHARLES C. EDWARDS, JR
College of Pharmacy and Health Sciences: RAYLENE ROSPOND
Drake Law School: BENJAMIN B. ULLEM
School of Education: JANET MCMAHILL
School of Journalism and Mass Communication: CHARLES C. EDWARDS, JR

EMMAUS BIBLE COLLEGE

2570 Asbury Rd, Dubuque, IA 52001
Telephone: (563) 588-8000
E-mail: info@emmaus.edu
Internet: www.emmaus.edu

Founded 1941
Private control
Language of instruction: English
Academic year: August to May

Depts of Bible and theology, business, Christian education, computer studies, counselling, general education, intercultural studies, nursing, teacher education

Pres.: WILLIAM J. MOORE
Chancellor: Dr DANIEL H. SMITH
Vice-Pres. for Academic Affairs: LISA L. BEATTY
Vice-Pres. for Admin. and Finance: Dr MARK A. PRESSON
Vice-Pres. for Advancement: Dr JON W. GLOCK
Registrar: KATHRYN L. VAN DINE
Librarian: JOHN H. RUSH

Library of 120,000 vols
Number of teachers: 25
Number of students: 200

Publications: *Journey Magazine* (2 a year), *The Emmaus Journal* (2 a year, print and online, www.emmaus.edu/ministry/the-emmaus-journal)

FAITH BAPTIST BIBLE COLLEGE AND THEOLOGICAL SEMINARY

1900 NW Fourth St, Ankeny, IA 50023
Telephone: (515) 964-0601
E-mail: admissions@faith.edu
Internet: www.faith.edu

Founded 1921 as Omaha Bible Institute, current name adopted 1967
Private control
Academic year: August to May
Divs of Bible and theology, Christian studies, general education

Pres.: Dr ERNEST SCHMIDT
Vice-Pres. for Academic Services: Dr PAUL HARTOG
Dean of the Seminary: Dr DOUGLAS BROWN
Dir for Enrolment: MARK DAVIS
Dean for Students: LANCE AUGSBURGER
Registrar: DAVID STOUT
Head Librarian: Dr JOHN HARTOG, II

Library of 69,000 vols, 395 periodicals, 2,000 video cassettes and DVDs, 4,800 audio cassettes and CDs, 4,800 microfiche
Number of teachers: 28
Number of students: 229

Publication: *Faith Pulpit*

GRACELAND UNIVERSITY

1 University Pl., Lamoni, IA 50140
Telephone: (641) 784-5423
E-mail: admissions@graceland.edu
Internet: www.graceland.edu

Founded 1895
Private control
Academic year: August to May
Campus at Independence (Missouri)

Pres.: Dr JOHN D. SELLARS
Vice-Pres. for Academic Affairs and Dean for Faculty: PARRIS R. WATTS
Vice-Pres. for Business and Admin. Services: JANICE K. TIFFANY
Vice-Pres. for Enrolment Management: LOUISE CUMMINGS-SIMMONS
Vice-Pres. for Institutional Advancement: KELLY W. EVERETT
Vice-Pres. for Institutional Effectiveness: Dr KATHLEEN M. CLAUSON BASH
Dir for Admissions: KEVIN BROWN
Dean for Students: MARIAN KILLPACK
Registrar: JOYCE LIGHTHILL
Dir for Library Services: FRANCIS ACLAND

Library of 119,233 vols, 526 periodical and newspaper subscriptions, 2,139 records, cassettes and CDs, 618 DVDs and video cassettes
Number of teachers: 80 (full-time)
Number of students: 2,270 (1,710 full-time, 560 part-time)

DEANS

C. H. Sandage School of Business: Dr STEVEN L. ANDERS
College of Liberal Arts and Studies: Dr GARY HEISSERER
Edmund J. Gleazer School of Education: Dr TAMMY E. EVERETT
School of Nursing: Dr CLAUDIA D. HORTON
Seminary: Dr DON COMPIER

GRAND VIEW UNIVERSITY

1200 Grandview Ave, Des Moines, IA 50316
Telephone: (515) 263-2800
E-mail: admissions@grandview.edu
Internet: www.grandview.edu

Founded 1896, present name and status 2008
Private control
Academic year: August to May (2 semesters)
Divs of humanities, natural science, nursing and social science

Pres.: KENT L. HENNING
Provost and Vice-Pres. for Academic Affairs: Dr MARY ELIZABETH STIVERS
Vice-Pres. for Admin. and Finance: ADAM J. VOIGTS
Vice-Pres. for Advancement: WILLIAM BURMA
Vice-Pres. for Enrolment Management: DEBBIE M. BARGER
Vice-Pres. for Student Affairs: Dr JAY PRESCOTT
Dir for Admissions: DIANE JOHNSON SCHAEFER
Registrar: DEBORAH GANNON
Library Dir: PAMELA REES

Number of teachers: 190 (90 part-time, 100 part-time)
Number of students: 2,230

GRINNELL COLLEGE

1121 Park St, Grinnell, IA 50112-1690
Telephone: (641) 269-4000
E-mail: askgrin@grinnell.edu
Internet: www.grinnell.edu

Founded 1846
Private control
Divs of humanities, science and social studies

Pres.: RAYNARD S. KINGTON
Vice-Pres. for Academic Affairs and Dean for College: PAULA V. SMITH
Vice-Pres. for College Services: JOHN W. KALKBRENNER
Vice-Pres. for Devt and Alumni Relations: BETH HALLORAN
Vice-Pres. for Student Affairs: W. HOUSTON DOUGHARTY
Dean for Admission: DOUG BADGER (acting)
Registrar: CHERYL CHASE
Librarian: RICHARD FYFFE

Library of 817,849 vols, 39,745 audiovisual materials, 2,000 periodicals and journals, 140,000 ebooks
Number of teachers: 215 (161 full-time, 54 part-time)
Number of students: 1,600

IOWA STATE UNIVERSITY

Ames, IA 50011
Telephone: (515) 294-4111
E-mail: contact@iastate.edu
Internet: www.iastate.edu

Founded 1858 as Iowa Agricultural College and Model Farm, present status 1959
State control
Academic year: August to July

Pres.: Prof. STEVEN LEATH
Sr Exec. Vice-Pres. and Provost: JONATHAN WICKERT
Sr Vice-Pres. for Business and Finance: WARREN MADDEN

Sr Vice-Pres. for Student Affairs: THOMAS L. HILL

Vice-Pres. for Extension and Outreach: CATH-ANN KRESS

Vice-Pres. for Research and Economic Devt: DAVID OLIVER

Registrar: LAURA DOERING

Dean for Library Services: OLIVIA M. MADISON

Library: see under Libraries and Archives

Number of teachers: 1,700

Number of students: 31,040

Publications: *Ethos* (2 a year, print and online, www.ethosmagazine.org), *Inquiry*, *Iowa State University Veterinarian*, *IVisions*, *Marston Muses*, *Outlook*, *The Agriculturist*, *The Gentle Doctor* (2 a year), *The Iowa Engineer*

DEANS

College of Agriculture and Life Sciences: WENDY WINTERSTEEN

College of Business Administration: DAVID SPALDING

College of Design: LUIS RICO-GUTIERREZ

College of Engineering: SARA RAJALA

College of Human Sciences: PAMELA WHITE

College of Liberal Arts and Sciences: BEATTE SCHMITTMAN

College of Veterinary Medicine: Dr LISA K. NOLAN

Graduate College: DAVID K. HOLGER

IOWA WESLEYAN COLLEGE

601 N Main St, Mount Pleasant, IA 52641

Telephone: (319) 385-8021

E-mail: admit@iwc.edu

Internet: www.iwc.edu

Founded 1842, current name adopted 1912

Private control

Divs of business, education, fine arts, human studies, language and literature, nursing, science, mathematics and computer studies

Pres.: Dr JAY K. SIMMONS

Vice-Pres. and Dean for Student Life: Dr LINDA BUCHANAN

Vice-Pres. for Academic Affairs: Dr NANCY ERICKSON

Vice-Pres. for Institutional Relations: JERRY THOMAS

Dean for Admissions: MARK PETTY

Registrar: PATTY BROKKEN

Library Dir: PAULA KINNEY

Library of 108,427 vols

Number of teachers: 45

Number of students: 865

Publication: *Purple & White*

KAPLAN UNIVERSITY

1801 E Kimberly Rd, Suite one, Davenport, IA 52807

Telephone: (563) 355-3500

E-mail: infoku@kaplan.edu

Internet: portal.kaplanuniversity.edu

Founded 1937 as American Institute of Commerce, present name and status 2004

Private control

Campuses in Maryland, Maine and Nebraska; learning centres in Indiana, Maryland, Missouri and Wisconsin

Pres. for Kaplan Univ. Group: GREGORY MARINO

Pres.: Dr WADE DYKE

Provost: Dr GERI MALANDRA

Vice-Provost for Academic Affairs: Dr KARA VANDAM

Vice-Provost for Governance and Admin.: Dr KEITH SMITH

Dir for Library Services: JENNIE VER STEEG

Library of 50,000 vols of ebooks

Number of teachers: 4,500

Number of students: 61,000 (online and campus-based)

DEANS

College of Arts and Sciences: Dr SARA SANDER

Concord Law School: GREG BRANDES

School of Business and Management: Dr THOMAS C. BOYD

School of Criminal Justice: TIM PARDUE

School of General Education: Dr JODY DEKORTE

School of Graduate Education: Dr DREW ROSS

School of Health Sciences: Dr GINGER CAMERON

School of Information Systems and Technology: Dr DAVID DeHAVEN

School of Legal Studies: FRANK DiMARINO

School of Nursing: SHELIA BURKE

LORAS COLLEGE

1450 Alta Vista St, Dubuque, IA 52004-0178

Telephone: (563) 588-7100

E-mail: admissions@loras.edu

Internet: www.loras.edu

Founded 1839, current name adopted 1939

Private control

Courses in accounting, art-studio, athletic training, archaeology/cultural interpretation, biochemistry, biology, business, business finance, business management, business marketing, Catholic studies, chemistry, computer science, criminal justice, economics, electromechanical engineering, elementary education, English literature, English writing, gender studies, Greek and Roman studies, history, integrated visual arts, international studies, management information systems, mathematics, media studies, music/music education, philosophy, physics-applied, politics, psychology, public relations, publishing, religious studies, social work, sociology, Spanish, sport management, sport science, theatre, world literature

Pres.: JAMES E. COLLINS

Provost: Dr CHERYL R. JACOBSEN

Vice-Pres. for Finance and Admin. Services: STEPHEN J. SCHMALL

Vice-Pres. for Institutional Advancement: PAMELA S. GERAD

Dean for Students: ARTHUR W. SUNLEAF

Registrar: J. T. BROWN

Library Dir: JOYCE MELDREM

Library of 440,000 vols, 8,000 current periodicals

Number of teachers: 140

Number of students: 1,580

Publication: *Loras College Magazine* (print and online, www.loras.edu/magazine)

LUTHER COLLEGE

700 College Dr., Decorah, IA 52101-1045

Telephone: (563) 387-2000

E-mail: admissions@luther.edu

Internet: www.luther.edu

Founded 1861

Private control

Academic year: September to July (2 semesters)

Majors/minors in accounting, African studies, anthropology, art, arts management, athletic training, biblical languages, biology, business (management), chemistry, classical studies, classics, communication studies, computer science, economics, education, English, environmental studies, French, German, Greek, health, history, int. management studies, Latin, Latin American studies, management, management information systems, mathematics, management information systems, mathematics, museum studies, music, music management, nursing, philosophy, physical education, physics, political science, psych-

ology, religion, resource management, Russian studies, Scandinavian studies, social work, sociology, Spanish, speech/theatre, sports management, theatre/dance management, women's and gender studies

Pres.: Dr PAULA J. CARLSON

Vice-Pres. and Dean for Student Life: Dr ANN HIGHUM

Vice-Pres. for Academic Affairs and Dean for Faculty: Dr KEVIN KRAUS

Vice-Pres. for Devt: KEITH J. CHRISTENSEN

Vice-Pres. for Enrolment Management: (vacant): SCOT SCHAEFFER

Vice-Pres. for Finance and Admin.: DIANE TACKE

Dir for Admissions: DEREK HARTL

Registrar: DOUGLAS KOSCHMEDER

Library Head: ANDREA BECKENDORF

Library of 340,000 vols, 800 periodicals, 63,000 ebooks

Number of teachers: 180 (full-time)

Number of students: 2,500

MAHARISHI UNIVERSITY OF MANAGEMENT

Fairfield, IA 52557

Telephone: (641) 472-7000

E-mail: admissions@mum.edu

Internet: www.mum.edu

Founded 1971 as Maharishi International Univ., current name adopted 1995

Private control

Academic year: August to June

Pres.: Dr BEVAN MORRIS

Exec. Vice-Pres.: Dr CRAIG PEARSON

Chief Admin. Officer: Dr DAVID STREID

Dean for Admissions: BRADFORD MYLETT

Dean for Faculty: Dr CATHERINE GORINI

Dean for Student Life: ROD EASON

Registrar: TOM ROWE

Library Dir: MARTIN SCHMIDT

Library of 144,000 vols

Number of teachers: 80

Number of students: 1,238

Publications: *Consciousness Based Education Series*, *Modern Science and Vedic Science*

DEANS

College of Arts and Sciences: Dr CHRIS JONES

College of Computer Science and Mathematics: Dr GREGORY GUTHRIE

Graduate School: Dr FRED TRAVIS

MERCY COLLEGE OF HEALTH SCIENCES

928 Sixth Ave, Des Moines, IA 50309-1239

Telephone: (515) 643-3180

E-mail: admissions@mchs.edu

Internet: www.mchs.edu

Founded 1899 as Mercy Hospital Training School, present name and status 1995

Private control

Pres.: BARBARA Q. DECKER

Provost and Vice-Pres. for Academic Affairs: ELIZABETH RITT

Vice-Pres. for Admissions and Advancement: BRIAN TINGLEFF

Registrar: CAROLYN BUCKLIN

Library Dir: EILEEN HANSEN

Library of 14,738 vols, 158 journals

Number of students: 730

Publications: *Mercy Messenger* (12 a year, online, www.mchs.edu/mercy-messenger.cfm), *VitalSigns* (2 a year)

DEANS

School of Allied Health: THERESA SMITH

School of Liberal Arts and Sciences: Dr JEANNINE MATZ

School of Nursing: Dr SHIRLEY BEAVER

MORNINGSIDE COLLEGE

1501 Morningside Ave, Sioux City, IA 51106

Telephone: (712) 274-5000
E-mail: msadm@morningside.edu
Internet: www.morningside.edu

Founded 1894
Private control

Depts of art, biology, business administration, chemistry, computer and application programming, computer science, corporate communication, education, engineering physics, English, history, mass communication, mathematics, music, nursing, philosophy, political science, psychology, religious studies, Spanish and theatre

Pres.: JOHN C. REYNDERS
Vice-Pres. for Academic Affairs and Dean for College: Dr WILLIAM C. DEEDS
Vice-Pres. for Institutional Advancement: TOM RICE
Vice-Pres. for Student Services and Admissions: TERRI CURRY
Dean for Enrolment: ROBBIE ROHLENA
Registrar: MARY PESHEK
Dir for Library Services: DARIA BOSSMAN

Library of 117,330 vols, 3,575 sound recordings, 8,869 micofilms, 76,285 microfiche
Number of teachers: 75
Number of students: 1,200

Publications: *Student Health 101*, *The Kiosk*, *The Morningsider*

MOUNT MERCY UNIVERSITY

1330 Elmhurst Dr., NE, Cedar Rapids, IA 52402-4798

Telephone: (319) 363-8213
E-mail: admission@mtmercy.edu
Internet: www.mtmercy.edu

Founded 1924 as Mount Mercy Acad., present name and status 2010
Private control
Academic year: August to May

Depts of business, communications, education, history, literature and arts, natural and applied sciences, nursing and psychology, politics and justice, philosophy, religion and campus ministry, sociology and social work

Pres.: LAURIE HAMEN
Provost and Vice-Pres. for Academic Affairs: Dr MELODY GRAHAM (acting)
Vice-Pres. for Devt: DUFF RIDGEWAY
Vice-Pres. for Enrolment and Student Life: Dr SUE OATEY
Registrar: JASON CLAPP
Dir for Library Services: MARILYN MURPHY

Library of 140,000 vols
Number of teachers: 150 (80 full-time, 70 part-time)
Number of students: 1,825

NORTHWESTERN COLLEGE

101 Seventh St, SW, Orange City, IA 51041-1996

Telephone: (712) 707-7100
E-mail: admissions@nwciowa.edu
Internet: www.nwciowa.edu

Founded 1882, present name and status 1960
Private control
Academic year: August to May

Depts of art, biology, business/economics, chemistry, communications, computer science, education, English/writing and rhetoric, foreign languages, history, humanities, kinesiology, mathematics, music, nursing, philosophy, physics, political science, psychology, religion/Christian education, social work, sociology, theatre and speech

Pres.: GREGORY E. CHRISTY
Provost: Dr JASPER LESAGE
Vice-Pres. for Advancement: JAY WIELENGA

Dean for Enrolment Management: KENTON PAULS
Dean for Faculty: Dr ADRIENNE FORGETTE
Dean for Student Life: Dr JOHN G. BROGAN
Registrar: SANDY VAN KLEY
Dir for Library: Dr TIM SCHLAK

Library of 129,000 vols
Number of teachers: 135 (85 full-time, 50 part-time)
Number of students: 1,200

PALMER COLLEGE OF CHIROPRACTIC

1000 Brady St, Davenport, IA 52803

Telephone: (563) 884-5000
E-mail: admissions.ia@palmer.edu
Internet: www.palmer.edu

Founded 1897

Campuses at Port Orange (Florida) and San Jose (California)

Chancellor: Dr DENNIS M. MARCHIORI
Vice-Chancellor for Academics: ROBERT E. PERCUOCO
Vice-Chancellor for Admin.: THOMAS L. TIEMEIER
Vice-Chancellor for Advancement: Dr ROBERT E. LEE
Vice-Chancellor for Clinic Affairs: KURT WOOD
Vice-Chancellor for Enrolment: Dr J. MICHAEL NOVAK
Vice-Chancellor for Research and Health Policy: Dr CHRISTINE GOERTZ
Vice-Chancellor for Student Affairs: Dr KEVIN A. CUNNINGHAM
Vice-Chancellor for Support Services: ROBERT E. LEE
Pres. for W Campus: Dr WILLIAM C. MEEKER
Pres. for Florida Campus: Dr PETER A. MARTIN
Provost for Davenport Campus: DAN WEINTERT
Registrar: MINDY LEAHY
Dir for Libraries: DENNIS PETERSON

Library of 85,000 vols
Number of students: 2,340

Publication: *Streams from the Fountainhead* (2 a year)

ST AMBROSE UNIVERSITY

518 W Locust St, Davenport, IA 52803-2898

Telephone: (319) 333-6000
E-mail: admit@sau.edu
Internet: www.sau.edu

Founded 1882, present name and status 1987
Private control
Academic year: August to May

Pres.: Dr JOAN LESCINSKI
Vice-Pres. for Academic and Student Affairs: Dr PAUL KOCH
Vice-Pres. for Advancement: JAMES STANGLE
Vice-Pres. for Enrolment Management: JOHN COOPER
Library Dir: MARY HEINZMAN

Library of 165,000 vols
Number of teachers: 360
Number of students: 3,670 (2,793 undergraduate, 877 graduate)
Publication: *Scene Magazine*

DEANS

College of Arts and Sciences: Dr ARON R. AJI
College of Business: Dr DAVID O'CONNELL
College of Education and Health Sciences: Dr SANDRA CASSADY
Graduate and Adult Education: Dr REGINA MATHESON

SIMPSON COLLEGE

701 North C St, Indianola, IA 50125-1297

Telephone: (515) 961-6251
E-mail: admiss@simpson.edu
Internet: www.simpson.edu

Founded 1860
Private control
Academic year: August to May

Campuses at West Des Moines and Ankeny; depts of art, biology and environmental science, business administration and economics, chemistry and physics, communication studies, computer science, education, English, history, mathematics, music, philosophy, political science, psychology, social sciences, sport science and health education, theatre arts, world language and culture studies and women's and gender studies

Pres.: JOHN W. BYRD
Vice-Pres. for Academic Affairs and Academic Dean: STEVE GRIFFITH
Vice-Pres. for College Advancement: BOB LANE
Vice-Pres. for Enrolment: DEB TIERNEY
Vice-Pres. for Student Devt and Dean for Students: JAMES THORIUS
Registrar: JODY RAGAN
Librarian: CYNTHIA M. DYER

Library of 155,761 vols
Number of teachers: 90
Number of students: 2,040 (1,490 full-time, 550 part-time)

Publication: *The Simpson Magazine* (4 a year)

UNIVERSITY OF DUBUQUE

2000 University Ave, Dubuque, IA 52001

Telephone: (563) 589-3000
Internet: www.dbq.edu

Founded 1852
Private control
Language of instruction: English
Academic year: August to May

Schools of business, liberal arts, professional programmes and theology

Pres.: Rev. Dr JEFFREY F. BULLOCK
Vice-Pres. and Dean of Seminary: Dr BRADLEY LONGFIELD
Vice-Pres. for Academic Affairs and Dean of College: Dr MARK WARD
Vice-Pres for Enrolment Management, Marketing and Univ. Relations: SUSAN SMITH
Vice-Pres. and Dean for Student Life: Dr MICHAEL MIYAMOTO
Dean for Admission: JESSE JAMES
Registrar: LIZ OLSEN
Univ. Librarian: MARY ANN KNEFEL

Library of 182,502 vols, 3,051 multimedia items, 417 periodicals
Number of teachers: 80
Number of students: 2,000

UNIVERSITY OF IOWA

1 Jessup Hall, Iowa City, IA 52242-1316
2222 Old Highway 218S, Iowa City, IA 52242-1602

Telephone: (319) 335-3500
E-mail: admissions@uiowa.edu
Internet: www.uiowa.edu

Founded 1847
State control
Academic year: August to May (2 terms and summer session)

Pres.: SALLY MASON
Exec. Vice-Pres. and Provost: P. BARRY BUTLER
Sr Vice-Pres. and Treas.: DOUGLAS K. TRUE
Vice-Pres. for Research and Economic Devt: JORDEN COHEN

Vice-Pres. of Student Life: THOMAS R. ROCK-LIN
Dir for Admissions: MICHAEL BARRON
Registrar: LAWRENCE J. LOCKWOOD
Univ. Librarian: NANCY L. BAKER
Library: see under Libraries and Archives
Number of teachers: 1,700
Number of students: 30,900 (21,570 undergraduate, 5,618 graduate, 3,712 professional)

Publications: *Journal of Communication Inquiry* (4 a year), *Iowa Law Review* (5 a year, online, www.uiowa.edu/~ilr), *Syllecta Classica* (1 a year, online, www.uiowa.edu/~classics/syllecta), *The Iowa Review* (3 a year, online, iowareview.uiowa.edu), *Walt Whitman Quarterly Review* (4 a year, print and online, ir.uiowa.edu/wwqr)

DEANS

College of Dentistry: DAVID C. JOHNSEN
College of Education: MARGARET S. CROCCO
College of Engineering: ALEC B. SCRANTON
College of Law: GAIL B. AGRAWAL
College of Liberal Arts and Sciences: LINDA MAXSON
College of Nursing: RITA FRANTZ
College of Pharmacy: DONALD LETENDRE
College of Public Health: SUSAN CURRY
Graduate College: JOHN C. KELLER
Henry B. Tippie College of Business: WILLIAM C. HUNTER
Roy J. and Lucille A. Carver College of Medicine: PAUL ROTHMAN

UNIVERSITY OF NORTHERN IOWA

1227 W 27th St, Cedar Falls, IA 50614
Telephone: (319) 273-2311
E-mail: admissions@uni.edu
Internet: www.uni.edu

Founded 1876
State control
Academic year: July to June
Pres.: Dr BENJAMIN J. ALLEN
Exec. Vice-Pres. and Provost: Dr GLORIA J. GIBSON
Vice-Pres. for Admin. and Financial Services: MICHAEL HAGER
Vice-Pres. for Student Affairs: Dr TERRENCE HOGAN
Exec. Dir for Univ. Relations: JAMES E. O'CONNOR
Dir for Admissions: CHRISTIE M. KANGAS
Dean for Students: LESLIE WILLIAMS
Registrar: PHILIP L. PATTON
Dean for Library: CHRISTOPHER COX
Library of 1,642,097 vols, 230,393 govt documents, 1,124,486 microform units, 41,567 maps, 3,652 audiovisual materials, 176,824 periodicals, 50,909 ejournals, 14,245 ebooks
Number of teachers: 790 (603 full-time, 187 part-time)
Number of students: 12,300

Publications: *American Journal of Undergraduate Research* (4 a year), *Argumentation and Advocacy* (4 a year), *Iowa Council for the Social Studies (ICSS) Journal* (1 a year), *Iowa Journal of Communication* (4 a year, online, www.uni.edu/commstudies/ica/journal/journal.htm), *Journal of Assessment and Accountability in Educator Preparation*, *Journal of Contemporary Ethnography* (2 a year), *Journal of Economics (MVEA)* (2 a year), *The North American Review* (4 a year), *Universitas* (2 a year, online, www.uni.edu/universitas)

DEANS

College of Business Administration: Dr FARZAD MOUSSAVI
College of Education: Dr DWIGHT C. WATSON

College of Humanities, Arts and Sciences: Dr JOEL K. HAACK
College of Social and Behavioural Science: Dr PHILIP MAUCERI
Continuing Education and Special Programmes: KENT M. JOHNSON
Graduate College: Dr MIKE LICARI

UPPER IOWA UNIVERSITY

POB 1857, 605 Washington St, Fayette, IA 52142
Telephone: (563) 425-5200
E-mail: info@uiu.edu
Internet: www.uiu.edu

Founded 1857
Private control
Academic year: August to May
Divs of business, education, liberal arts and science and mathematics
Pres.: Dr ALAN G. WALKER
Sr Vice-Pres. and Chief Academic Officer: Dr DAVID CHOWN
Sr Vice-Pres. for Academic Extension: Dr WILLIAM DUFFY
Sr Vice-Pres. for External Affairs: ANDREW WENTHE
Vice-Pres. for Admissions and Financial Aid: JOBYNA JOHNSTON
Vice-Pres. for Advancement, Devt and Alumni Relations: WENDELL SNODGRASS
Registrar: HOLLY STREETER
Dir for Library Services: BECKY WADIAN
Library of 155,108 vols
Number of teachers: 575
Number of students: 6,600

WALDORF COLLEGE

106 S Sixth St, Forest City, IA 50436
Telephone: (641) 585-2450
E-mail: admissions@waldorf.edu
Internet: www.waldorf.edu

Founded 1903, present status 2001
Private control
Academic year: August to July
Liberal arts courses; online degree programmes
Pres.: Dr BOB ALSOP
Vice-Pres. for Academic Affairs and Dean for College: SCOTT SEARCY
Vice-Pres. for Operations: RICK COOPER
Dir for Admissions: SCOTT PITCHER
Dean for Students: JASON RAMAKER
Registrar: TWYLAH KRAGEL
Library Dir: AMY HILL
Library of 90,000 vols
Number of students: 600

WARTBURG COLLEGE

100 Wartburg Blvd, Waverly, IA 50677
Telephone: (319) 352-8200
E-mail: admissions@wartburg.edu
Internet: www.wartburg.edu

Founded 1852
Private control
Academic year: September to June
Depts of accounting, art, art education, biochemistry, biology, business admin., chemistry, church music, communication arts, communication design, communication studies, community sociology, computer information systems, computer science, economics, education, engineering science, English, exploring, fitness management, history, interdepartmental major, int. relations, mathematics, medical technology, modern languages, music education, music performance, music therapy, philosophy, physical education, physics, political science, psychology, religion, social work, sociology, writing

Pres.: Dr DARREL D. COLSON
Vice-Pres. for Academic Affairs and Dean for Faculty: Dr FRED RIBICH
Vice-Pres. for Enrolment Management: Dr EDITH J. WALDSTEIN
Vice-Pres. for Institutional Advancement: SCOTT LEISINGER
Vice-Pres. for Student Life and Dean for Students: Dr DEBORAH LOERS
Registrar: SHEREE COVERT
Librarian: CHRIS SCHAFER
Library of 130,000 vols
Number of teachers: 110 (full-time)
Number of students: 1,800
Publication: *Wartburg Magazine* (3 a year, print and online, www.wartburg.edu/magazine)

WARTBURG THEOLOGICAL SEMINARY

POB 5004, Dubuque, IA 52004-5004
333 Wartburg Pl., Dubuque, IA 52003-7797
Telephone: (563) 589-0200
E-mail: admissions@wartburgseminary.edu
Internet: www.wartburgseminary.edu

Founded 1854
Private control
Offers Masters in arts, diaconal ministry, divinity and theology
Pres.: Dr STANLEY N. OLSON
Vice-Pres. for Mission Support: Rev. Dr LEN HOFFMANN
Academic Dean: Prof. Dr CRAIG NESSAN
Dir for Admissions: Rev. KARLA WILDBERGER
Registrar: Dr KEVIN ANDERSON
Dir for Library: SUSAN EBERTZ
Library of 92,000 vols
Number of teachers: 20
Number of students: 190

WILLIAM PENN UNIVERSITY

201 Trueblood Ave, Oskaloosa, IA 52577
Telephone: (641) 673-1076
E-mail: admissions@wmpenn.edu
Internet: www.wmpenn.edu

Founded 1873 as Penn College, present name and status 2000
Private control
Academic year: August to May
Pres.: Dr ANN M. FIELDS
Vice-Pres. for Academic Affairs: Dr MARJORIE WELCH
Vice-Pres. for Advancement: SHERRI L. TAYLOR
Vice-Pres. for Student Services and Enrolment Management: JOHN OTTOSSON
Registrar: PATRICK MCADAMS
Librarian: JULIE HANSEN
Number of teachers: 55
Number of students: 1,650
Publication: *Penn & Ink* (2 a year)

DEANS

College of Arts, Sciences and Professional Studies: Dr NOEL STAHLE
College for Working Adults: Dr MARJORIE WELCH

KANSAS

BAKER UNIVERSITY

POB 65, Baldwin City, KS 66006-0065
618 Eighth St, Baldwin City, KS 66006
Telephone: (785) 594-6451
E-mail: admission@bakeru.edu
Internet: www.bakeru.edu

Founded 1858 (chartered)
Private control

Pres.: Dr PATRICIA N. LONG
Exec. Vice-Pres. for Admin. Services: SUSAN LINDAHL
Vice-Pres. for Enrolment Management and Student Devt: MARK BANDRE
Vice-Pres. for Univ. Advancement: LYN LAKIN
Dean for Students: CASSY BAILEY
Univ. Registrar: RUTH MILLER
Dir for Library Services: KATHLEEN R. BRADT
Library of 108,652 vols, 399 periodicals
Number of teachers: 160 (75 full-time, 85 part-time)
Number of students: 3,540

DEANS

College of Arts and Sciences: Dr RAND ZIEGLER
School of Education: Dr PEGGY HARRIS
School of Nursing: Dr KATHLEEN HARR
School of Professional and Graduate Studies: Dr PEGGY HARRIS

BARCLAY COLLEGE

607 N Kingman, Haviland, KS 67059
Telephone: (620) 862-5252
E-mail: admissions@barclaycollege.edu
Internet: www.barclaycollege.edu
Founded 1917 as Kansas Central Bible Training School, present name 1990
Private control
Divs of biblical studies, general studies and liberal arts
Pres.: Dr ROYCE FRAZIER
Provost: Dr ADRIAN HALVERSTADT
Vice-Pres. for Student Services: KEVIN LEE
Dir for Library Services: PAT HALL
Library of 62,000 vols
Number of teachers: 30
Number of students: 250

BENEDICTINE COLLEGE

1020 N Second St, Atchison, KS 66002-1499
Telephone: (913) 367-5340
Internet: www.benedictine.edu
Founded 1858, current name adopted 1971
Private control
Academic year: August to May
Depts of arts and communication, business and public policy, education, health, humanities, science and mathematics, social and behavioural science
Pres.: STEPHEN D. MINNIS
Vice-Pres. for Academic Affairs and Dean of College: Dr KIMBERLY J. SHANKMAN
Vice-Pres. for Advancement: KELLY J. VOWELS
Vice-Pres. for Student Life: LINDA HENRY
Dean for Enrolment Management: PETE HELGESEN
Registrar: LINDA HERNDON
Library Dir: STEVEN GROMATZKY
Library of 320,000 vols, 340 current periodicals
Number of teachers: 50
Number of students: 1,900
Publications: *Loomings* (1 a year), *Raven Review*

BETHANY COLLEGE

335 E Swensson St, Lindsborg, KS 67456-1895
Telephone: (785) 227-3380
E-mail: admissions@bethanylb.edu
Internet: www.bethanylb.edu
Founded 1881 as Bethany Acad., present name and status 1889
Private control
Academic year: August to May

Depts of accounting, art, athletic training, biology, business, chemistry, Christian min., coaching, communication, computer applications, criminal justice, economics, education, engineering, English, finance, foreign, language, forensic, science, global studies, health sciences, history, int. management, management, marketing, mathematics, multicultural studies, music, philosophy, physical education, physics, political science, psychology, religion, spec. education, sports management, theatre
Pres.: Dr EDWARD F. LEONARD, III
Provost and Dean for College: Dr EUGENE BALES
Vice-Pres. for Advancement: JIM RUBLE
Dean for Student Life: FREDA STRACK
Registrar: JILL MEGREDY
Dir for Library Services: DENISE CARSON
Library of 115,000 vols
Number of teachers: 55
Number of students: 620

BETHEL COLLEGE

300 E 27th St, N Newton, KS 67117-1716
Telephone: (316) 283-2500
E-mail: admissions@bethelks.edu
Internet: www.bethelks.edu
Founded 1887
Private control
Courses in arts, nursing, sciences, social work
Pres.: PERRY WHITE
Vice-Pres. for Academic Affairs: Dr BRAD BORN
Vice-Pres. for Admissions: TODD MOORE
Vice-Pres. for Advancement: SONDRA KOONTZ
Vice-Pres. for Student Life: WELDON MARTENS
Registrar: RODNEY FREY
Co-Dir for Libraries: GAIL NILES STUCKY
Co-Dir for Libraries: BARBARA THIESEN
Co-Dir for Libraries: JOHN THIESEN
Library of 125,000 vols
Number of teachers: 60 (36 full-time, 24 part-time)
Number of students: 525
Publications: *Context*, *Mennonite Life* (4 a year)

CENTRAL BAPTIST THEOLOGICAL SEMINARY

6601 Monticello Rd, Shawnee, KS 66226-3513
Telephone: (913) 667-5700
E-mail: info@cbts.edu
Internet: www.cbts.edu
Founded 1901
Private control
Academic year: June to May
Doctoral and Masters degree in divinity, ministry, theological studies
Pres.: Prof. Dr MOLLY T. MARSHALL
Exec. Vice-Pres.: GEORGE N. TOWNSEND
Vice-Pres. for Institutional Advancement: JOHN W. GRAVLEY
Dean for Seminary: Prof. Dr ROBERT E. JOHNSON
Library Dir: VANCE THOMAS

CENTRAL CHRISTIAN COLLEGE OF KANSAS

1200 S Main St, POB 1403, McPherson, KS 67460
Telephone: (620) 241-0723
E-mail: admissions@centralchristian.edu
Internet: www.centralchristian.edu
Founded 1884 as Orleans Seminary, present name 1999

Private control
Offers Bachelors of science in ministry and business
Pres.: HAL HOXIE
Vice-Pres. for Academics: Dr LEONARD F. FAVARA
Vice-Pres. for Advancement: CALVIN HAWKINS
Vice-Pres. for Finance and Admissions: J. DAVID FERRELL
Registrar: BEV KELLEY
Library Dir: JUDY STOCKSTILL

DONNELLY COLLEGE

608 N 18th St, Kansas City, KS 66102
Telephone: (913) 621-8700
E-mail: admissions@donnelly.edu
Internet: www.donnelly.edu
Founded 1949
Private control
Academic year: August to June (3 semesters)
Offers Bachelors in arts and applied sciences in organizational leadership
Pres.: Dr STEVE LaNASA
Vice-Pres. for Institutional Effectiveness: FRANCES SANDERS
Vice-Pres. for Student Affairs: DONETTE ALONZO
Registrar: AMBER BLOOMFIELD-MARTINEZ
Number of students: 1,100

EMPORIA STATE UNIVERSITY

1200 Commercial St, Emporia, KS 66801-5087
Telephone: (620) 341-1200
E-mail: go2esu@emporia.edu
Internet: www.emporia.edu
Founded 1863, present status 1976, current name adopted 1977
State control
Pres.: Dr H. EDWARD FLENTJE
Provost and Vice-Pres. for Academic Affairs and Student Life: TERESA MEHRING
Assoc. Provost for Enrolment Management: JAMES E. WILLIAMS
Vice-Pres. for Admin. and Fiscal Affairs: RAYMOND A. HAUKE
Registrar: ELAINE HENRIE
Dean for Univ. Libraries and Archives: JOHN B. SHERIDAN
Library of 711,000 vols
Number of teachers: 255
Number of students: 6,000 (3,860 undergraduate, 2,140 postgraduate)
Publications: *ESU Business World* (4 a year), *Flint Hills Review* (1 a year), *Kansas School Naturalist* (4 a year), *Spotlight* (4 a year)

DEANS

College of Liberal Arts and Sciences: BRENT THOMAS
Graduate School: KATHY ERMLER
School of Business: Dr JOSEPH WEN
School of Library and Information Management: Dr GWEN ALEXANDER
Teachers College: Dr PHIL BENNETT

FORT HAYS STATE UNIVERSITY

Sheridan Hall 204, 600 Park St, Hays, KS 67601-4099
Telephone: (785) 628-4000
E-mail: tigerinfo@fhsu.edu
Internet: www.fhsu.edu
Founded 1902
State control
Academic year: August to May
Pres.: (vacant)
Provost: LAWRENCE V. GOULD (acting)

Vice-Pres. for Admin. and Finance: MIKE BARNETT
Vice-Pres. for Student Affairs: Dr TISA MASON
Dir for Admissions: TRICIA CLINE
Registrar: Dr JOEY LINN
Library Dir: JOHN ROSS
Library of 300,000 vols, 500,000 vols in govt document section
Number of teachers: 300
Number of students: 12,800

DEANS

College of Arts and Sciences: PAUL W. FABER
College of Business and Leadership: MARK BANNISTER
College of Education and Technology: ROBERT F. SCOTT
College of Health and Life Sciences: JEFF BRIGGS
Graduate Studies and Research: TIM CROWLEY
Virtual College: DENNIS KING

FRIENDS UNIVERSITY

2100 W University Ave, Wichita, KS 67213
Telephone: (316) 295-5000
E-mail: learn@friends.edu
Internet: www.friends.edu
Founded 1898
Private control
Academic year: July to June
Pres.: Prof. Dr T. J. ARANT
Vice-Pres. for Academic Affairs: Dr JOHN YODER
Vice-Pres. for Admin. and Finance: RANDALL C. DOERKSEN
Vice-Pres. for Student Affairs: CAROLE OBERMEYER
Vice-Pres. for Univ. Relations: HERVEY W. WRIGHT, III
Registrar: HEIDI HOSKINSON
Library Dir: Prof. MAX BURSON
Library of 100,000 vols
Number of teachers: 80
Number of students: 2,800
Publication: *Focus* (4 a year)

DEANS

College of Adult and Professional Studies: Dr JO LOBERTINI
College of Business, Arts, Sciences and Education: Dr STEVEN PETERS
Graduate School: Dr EVELYN C. HUME

HASKELL INDIAN NATIONS UNIVERSITY

155 Indian Ave, Lawrence, KS 66046
Telephone: (785) 749-8404
Internet: www.haskell.edu
Founded 1884 as United States Indian Industrial Training School, present name 1993
Tribal control
Academic year: August to May
Divs of arts and sciences, business, education
Pres.: CHRIS REDMAN
Vice-Pres. for Academic Affairs: Dr VENIDA CHENAULT
Vice-Pres. for Univ. Services: CLYDE PEACOCK
Dir for Admissions: DOROTHY D. STITES
Registrar: MANNY KING
Library Dir: Dr MARILYN RUSSELL
Number of students: 900

KANSAS STATE UNIVERSITY

Manhattan, KS 66506
Telephone: (785) 532-6011
E-mail: k-state@k-state.edu
Internet: www.k-state.edu

Founded 1863
State control
Academic year: August to May
Pres.: Dr KIRK H. SCHULZ
Provost and Sr Vice-Pres.: APRIL MASON
Sr Vice-Provost for Academic Affairs: RUTH DYER
Vice-Pres. for Admin. and Finance: BRUCE A. SHUBERT
Vice-Pres. for Communications and Marketing: JEFFERY B. MORRIS
Vice-Pres. for Research: Prof. R. W. TREWYN
Vice-Pres. for Student Life and Dean for Students: PAT BOSCO
Chief of Staff and Dir for Community Relations: JACKIE L. HARTMAN
Dir for Governmental Relations: SUE PETERSON
Library: see under Libraries and Archives
Number of teachers: 1,250
Number of students: 24,380
Publications: *K-Stater Alumni Magazine*, *Perspectives Research Magazine* (5 a year)

DEANS

College of Agriculture: JOHN FLOROS
College of Architecture, Planning and Design: TIMOTHY DE NOBLE
College of Arts and Sciences: PETER DORHOUT
College of Business Administration: Prof. ALI R. MALEKZADEH
College of Education: MICHAEL C. HOLEN
College of Engineering: Dr JOHN ENGLISH
College of Human Ecology: Dr VIRGINIA MOXLEY
College of Technology and Aviation: DENNIS KUHLMAN
College of Veterinary Medicine: RALPH C. RICHARDSON
Continuing Education: SUE MAES
Graduate School: Dr CAROL SHANKLIN

KANSAS WESLEYAN UNIVERSITY

100 E Claffin Ave, Salina, KS 67401-6196
Telephone: (785) 827-5541
E-mail: admissions@kwu.edu
Internet: www.kwu.edu
Founded 1886
Private control
Divs of applied arts and sciences, fine arts, humanities, nursing, social sciences
Pres. and CEO: Dr FLETCHER M. LAMKIN
Provost and Exec. Vice-Pres.: Dr WAYNE LOWEN
Vice-Pres. for Admissions: WILLIAM P. TANNER
Vice-Pres. for Finance and Admin.: WAYNE SCHNEIDER
Dir for Admissions: STEVE BERRY
Dir for Enrolment and Financial Services: GLENNA ALEXANDER
Registrar: DENISE HOEFFNER
Dir for Library Services: JAMES CORBLY
Library of 75,938 vols
Number of teachers: 45 (40 full-time, 5 part-time)
Number of students: 825

MCPHERSON COLLEGE

POB 1402, 1600 E Euclid, McPherson, KS 67460
Telephone: (620) 242-0400
E-mail: admiss@mcpherson.edu
Internet: www.mcpherson.edu
Founded 1887 as McPherson College and Institute, present name 1898
Private control
Academic year: September to May
Depts of art, behavioural science, business, English, health, physical education and recreation, history, mathematics and informa-

tion technology, modern language, music, natural sciences, philosophy and religion, teacher education, technology, theatre
Pres.: MICHAEL P. SCHNEIDER
Provost: Dr KENT EATON
Vice-Pres. for Academic Affairs: Dr KENT EATON
Vice-Pres. for Admissions: DAVID BARRETT
Vice-Pres. for Advancement: AMANDA GUTIERREZ
Dean for Students: LAMONTE ROTHROCK
Dir for Library Services: MARY HESTER
Number of teachers: 40
Number of students: 620

MANHATTAN CHRISTIAN COLLEGE

1415 Anderson Ave, Manhattan, KS 66502
Telephone: (785) 539-3571
E-mail: admit@mccks.edu
Internet: www.mccks.edu
Founded 1927 as Christian Workers Univ., current name adopted 1971
Private control
Academic year: August to May
Depts of Bible and theology, general studies, practical ministries
Pres.: KEVIN INGRAM
Vice-Pres. for Academic Affairs: RANDY INGMIRE
Vice-Pres. for Institutional Advancement: VERN HENRICKS
Vice-Pres. for Student Life: Dr RICK L. WRIGHT
Dir for Library Services: MARY ANN BUHLER
Library of 40,000 vols, 2,600 journals, 3,000 ebooks
Number of teachers: 20
Number of students: 400

MIDAMERICA NAZARENE UNIVERSITY

2030 E College Way, Olathe, KS 66062-1899
Telephone: (913) 782-3750
E-mail: info@mnu.edu
Internet: www.mnu.edu
Founded 1966
Private control
Academic year: August to April
Divs of business, Christian ministry and formation, education and counselling, liberal arts and sciences, nursing and health science
Pres.: JAMES H. DIEHL
Vice-Pres. for Academic Affairs: Dr STEPHEN W. RAGAN
Vice-Pres. for Enrolment Devt: (vacant)
Vice-Pres. for Student Devt: RANDY BECKUM
Vice-Pres. for Univ. Advancement: JON D. NORTH
Dir for Admissions: WARREN ROGERS
Registrar: JAMES GARRISON
Librarian: Dr RODNEY BIRCH
Library of 400,000 vols
Number of teachers: 120
Number of students: 1,780

NEWMAN UNIVERSITY

3100 McCormick Ave, Wichita, KS 67213-2097
Telephone: (316) 942-4291
E-mail: admissions@newmanu.edu
Internet: www.newmanu.edu
Founded 1933 as Sacred Heart Junior College, current name adopted 1998
Private control
Offers courses in Colorado, Oklahoma, SE Kansas and W Kansas
Pres.: Dr NOREEN M. CARROCCI
Provost and Vice-Pres. for Academic Affairs: MICHAEL AUSTIN

Vice-Pres. for Finance and Admin.: MARK B. DRESSELHAUS

Vice-Pres. for Institutional Advancement: THOMAS E. BORREGO

Dean for Admissions: JOHN CLAYTON

Dean for Students: LAURA NICHOLAS

Registrar: SHIRLEY RUEB

Dir for Library Services: JOSEPH FORTE

Number of teachers: 190

Number of students: 2,070

Publications: *Challenge* (online, challenge.newmanu.edu), *Sheridan Edwards Review* (1 a year)

DEANS

College of Graduate and Continuing Studies: Dr AUDREY CURTIS HANE

College of Undergraduate Studies: Dr DAVID SHUBERT

OTTAWA UNIVERSITY

1001 S Cedar St, Ottawa, KS 66067

Telephone: (785) 242-5200

E-mail: admiss@ottawa.edu

Internet: www.ottawa.edu

Founded 1865

Private control

Academic year: June to May

Campuses at Mesa, Phoenix and Tempus (Arizona), Indiana, Kansas City, Wisconsin; divs of arts and sciences, business and education

Pres.: KEVIN C. EICHNER

Provost and Chief Academic Officer: Dr TERRY HAINES

Vice-Pres. for Admin.: J. CLARK RIBORY

Vice-Pres. for Univ. Advancement: PAUL BEAN

Vice-Pres. and Provost for College: Dr DENNIS TYNER

Asst Vice-Pres. for Enrolment Management: BILL HAMMOND

Registrar: KAREN ADAMS

Dir for Library Services: GLORIA CREED-DIKEOGU

Library of 84,000 vols, 186 periodicals

Number of teachers: 60

Number of students: 2,500 (full-time)

PITTSBURG STATE UNIVERSITY

1701 S Broadway, Pittsburg, KS 66762

Telephone: (620) 231-7000

E-mail: psuinfo@pittstate.edu

Internet: www.pittstate.edu

Founded 1903

State control

Pres.: Dr STEVEN A. SCOTT

Provost and Vice-Pres. for Academic Affairs: Dr LYNETTE J. OLSON

Vice-Pres. for Admin. and Campus Life: JOHN D. PATTERSON

Vice-Pres. for Univ. Advancement: J. BRADFORD HODSON

Dean for Enrolment Management: WILLIAM A. IVY

Registrar: DEBBIE GREVE

Dean for Library Services: DAVID P. BUNNELL

Library of 350,000 vols, 71,000 ebooks, 4,900 periodicals, 23,000 e-periodicals

Number of teachers: 325

Number of students: 7,000

DEANS

College of Arts and Sciences: Prof. Dr KARL KUNKEL

College of Education: Prof. Dr HOWARD W. SMITH

College of Technology: Dr BRUCE DALLMAN

Gladys A. Kelce College of Business: Dr PAUL W. GRIMES

Graduate School: Dr PEGGY SNYDER

SOUTHWESTERN COLLEGE

100 College St, Winfield, KS 67156-2499

Telephone: (620) 229-6000

E-mail: scadmit@sckans.edu

Internet: www.sckans.edu

Founded 1885

Private control

Academic year: August to May

Courses in business, education, liberal arts, music

Pres.: Dr W. RICHARD MERRIMAN, JR

Vice-Pres. for Academic Affairs and Dean for Faculty: Dr J. ANDREW SHEPPARD

Vice-Pres. for Institutional Advancement: MIKE FARRELL

Vice-Pres. for Student Life: DAWN PLEAS-BAILEY

Dir for Admission: MARLA SEXSON

Registrar: STACY TOWNSLEY

Library Dir: VERONICA MCASEY

Library of 50,000 vols, 100,000 ebooks, 5,000 DVDs and CDs, 35,000 journal subscriptions

Number of teachers: 48 (full-time)

Number of students: 1,401 (691 full-time, 710 part-time)

STERLING COLLEGE

125 W Cooper, Sterling, KS 67579

Telephone: (620) 278-2173

E-mail: admissions@sterling.edu

Internet: www.sterling.edu

Founded 1887 as Cooper Memorial College, present name 1920

Private control

Majors incl. art and graphic design, athletic training, biology, business admin., chemistry, Christian ministries, communication and theatre arts, culinary arts, elementary education, English, exercise science, graphic design and effects, history, ind. interdisciplinary, mathematics, music, music education, psychology, religious and philosophical studies

Pres.: Dr SCOTT RICH

Vice-Pres. for Academic Affairs: Dr GREG KERR

Vice-Pres. for Institutional Advancement: MARVIN DEWEY

Vice-Pres. for Student Life: TINA WOHLER

Registrar: JANET CAYWOOD

Library Dir: VALORIE STARR

Library of 85,000 vols

Number of teachers: 32

Number of students: 736

Publication: *Sterling*

TABOR COLLEGE

400 S Jefferson, Hillsboro, KS 67063

Telephone: (620) 947-3121

E-mail: admissions@tabor.edu

Internet: www.tabor.edu

Founded 1908

Private control

Academic year: August to May

Divs of education, humanities, natural and mathematical sciences, pre-professional programmes, social science and applied arts

Pres.: Dr JULES GLANZER

Vice-Pres. for Academic Affairs and Academic Dean: Dr FRANK E. JOHNSON

Vice-Pres. for Advancement: JAMES ELLIOTT

Vice-Pres. for Enrolment Management: RUSTY ALLEN

Vice-Pres. for Student Life, Learning and Formation: JIM PAULUS

Registrar: DEANNE DUERKSEN

Dir for Library Services: ROBIN OTTOSON

Library of 53,000 vols, 150 periodicals

Number of teachers: 65

Number of students: 721

Publication: *Connection*

UNITED STATES ARMY COMMAND AND GENERAL STAFF COLLEGE

100 Stimson Ave, Fort Leavenworth, KS 66027-1352

Telephone: (913) 684-7313

E-mail: usarmy.leavenworth.tradoc.mbx.cgsc-ussd@mail.mil

Internet: usacac.army.mil/cac2/cgsc

Founded 1882 as School of Application for Cavalry and Infantry, present name 1947; attached to Combined Arms Center-Leader Devt and Education

State control

Academic year: August to June

Depts of army tactics, command and leadership, distance education, joint, inter-agency and multinational operations, logistics and resource operations and military history; 3 satellite campuses: Fort Belvoir and Fort Lee in Virginia and Fort Gordon in Georgia

Commanding Gen.: Lt Gen. DAVID G. PERKINS

Deputy Commandant: Col MICHAEL J. JOHNSON (acting)

Dean for Academics: Dr WENDELL CHRISTOPHER KING

UNIVERSITY OF KANSAS

Room 230, 1450 Jayhawk Blvd, Lawrence, KS 66045

Telephone: (785) 864-2700

E-mail: chancellor@ku.edu

Internet: www.ku.edu

Founded 1864

State control

Academic year: August to May

Chancellor: BERNADETTE GRAY-LITTLE

Provost and Exec. Vice-Chancellor: JEFFREY S. VITTER

Sr Vice-Provost for Academic Affairs: SARA THOMAS ROSEN

Vice-Provost for Admin. and Finance: DIANE GODDARD

Vice-Provost for Enrolment Management: MATT MELVIN

Vice-Provost for Faculty Devt: MARY LEE HUMMERT

Vice-Provost for Student Success: TAMMARA DURHAM

Vice-Chancellor and Dean for Edwards Campus: Dr ROBERT M. CLARK

Vice-Chancellor for Research and Graduate Studies: MARY LEE HUMMERT

Chief Information Officer: BOB LIM

Dean for Libraries: LORRAINE HARICOMBE

Library: see under Libraries and Archives

Number of teachers: 2,530

Number of students: 29,460

Publications: *American Studies Journal* (4 a year, online, journals.ku.edu/index.php/amerstud), *Auslegung* (2 a year), *Biodiversity Informatics*, *Chimères* (online, www2.ku.edu/~chimeres), *Folklorica*, *Indigenous Nations Studies Journal*, *Journal of Applied Behavior Analysis*, *Journal of Dramatic Theory and Criticism* (2 a year), *Journal of Kansas Entomological Society*, *Journal of Public Administration Research and Theory*, *Journal of Social and Clinical Psychology*, *Kansas Academy of Science Transactions*, *Kansas Journal of Law and Public Policy* (3 a year), *Kansas Law Review* (5 a year), *KU Law Magazine* (2 a year), *La Coronica: A Journal of Medieval Spanish Language and Literature*, *Latin American Theatre Review* (2 a year), *Middle School Journal*, *Paleontological Contributions* (online, paleo.ku.edu/

contributions.html), *Research Opportunities in Renaissance Drama, Russkij Tekst, Slovene Linguistic Studies, Social Thought and Research, The Nabokovian, Treatise on Invertebrate Paleontology, Yearbook of German-American Studies*

DEANS

College of Liberal Arts and Sciences: DANNY J. ANDERSON
Graduate Studies: SARA ROSEN
School of Architecture, Design and Planning: JOHN C. GAUNT
School of Business: NEELI BENDAPUDI
School of Education: RICK GINSBERG
School of Engineering: Dr STUART R. BELL
School of Journalism and Mass Communications: ANN M. BRILL
School of Law: STEPHEN MAZZA
School of Music: ROBERT L. WALZEL, JR
School of Pharmacy: KENNETH L. AUDUS
School of Social Welfare: MARY ELLEN KONDRAT.

ATTACHED MEDICAL CENTRE

University of Kansas Medical Center

3901 Rainbow Blvd, Kansas City, KS 66160
Telephone: (913) 588-5000
Internet: www.kumc.edu

Founded 1905

Exec. Vice-Chancellor: Dr BARBARA F. ATKINSON
Sr Vice-Chancellor for Academic and Student Affairs: Dr KAREN MILLER
Vice-Chancellor for Admin.: EDWARD PHILLIPS
Vice-Chancellor for Research: Dr PAUL TERRANOVA
Dean for Student Services: Dr DOROTHY KNOLL
Registrar: Dr CHRIS MEIERS
Number of teachers: 890
Number of students: 3,180

DEANS

Graduate Studies: Dr ALLEN B RAWITCH
School of Allied Health: Prof. KAREN MILLER
School of Medicine: Dr H. DAVID WILSON
School of Nursing: Dr KAREN MILLER

UNIVERSITY OF SAINT MARY

4100 S Fourth St, Leavenworth, KS 66048-5082
Telephone: (913) 682-5151
E-mail: admissions@stmary.edu
Internet: www.stmary.edu

Founded 1923, present name and status 2003
Private control
Academic year: August to July

Campuses at Overland Park, Shawnee and Wyandotte County in Kansas; depts of behavioural sciences, criminology and psychology, business, account and sport management, education, fine arts, history, political science and global studies, information systems and technology and healthcare informatics, language and literature, natural sciences, nursing, physical therapy and theology, philosophy, pastoral ministry

Pres.: Dr DIANE STEELE
Vice-Pres. for Academic Affairs: Dr BRYAN F. LE BEAU
Vice-Pres. for Finance and Admin. Services: DALE L. CULVER
Dir for Enrolment Management: KEN WUERZBERGER
Dean for Students: Dr LISA BECKENBAUGH
Registrar: MARY PAT DUTTON
Dir for Library: PENELOPE LONERGAN
Library of 118,195 vols
Number of teachers: 30 (full-time)
Number of students: 1,000

Publication: *Aspire*

WASHBURN UNIVERSITY

1700 SW College Ave, Topeka, KS 66621
Telephone: (785) 670-1010
E-mail: admissions@washburn.edu
Internet: www.washburn.edu

Founded 1865 as Lincoln College, present name and status 1952
State control
Academic year: August to May

Pres.: Dr JERRY B. FARLEY
Provost and Vice-Pres. for Academic Affairs: Dr RANDALL PEMBROOK
Vice-Pres. for Admin. and Treas.: RICHARD L. ANDERSON
Vice-Pres. for Student Life: Dr DENISE C. OTTINGER
Registrar: Dr WANDA DOLE
Dean for Univ. Libraries: Dr ALAN BEARMAN
Library of 320,000 vols, 1,700 periodicals
Number of teachers: 300
Number of students: 7,230

Publications: *Alumni Magazine* (4 a year), *Circuit Rider, KAW, Washburn Update*

DEANS

College of Arts and Sciences: Dr GORDON D. MCQUERE
School of Applied Studies: Dr WILLIAM S. DUNLAP
School of Business: Dr DAVID SOLLARS
School of Law: THOMAS J. ROMIG
School of Nursing: Prof. Dr MONICA SCHEIBMEIR

WICHITA STATE UNIVERSITY

1845 Fairmont St, Wichita, KS 67260
Telephone: (316) 978-3456
Internet: www.wichita.edu

Founded 1894 as Fairmount College (Congregational), present status 1964
State control

Pres.: Dr DONALD L. BEGGS
Provost: Prof. KEITH H. PICKUS
Vice-Pres. and Gen. Counsel: TED D. AYRES
Vice-Pres. for Admin. and Finance: MARY L. HERRIN
Vice-Pres. for Campus Life and Univ. Relations: WADE A. ROBINSON
Registrar: WILLIAM E. WYNNE
Dean for Univ. Libraries: DONALD GILSTRAP

Library of 1,243,272 vols, 1,187,960 microfilms and microfiche, 528,592 govt documents, 4,759 linear ft of archives and MSS
Number of teachers: 550
Number of students: 15,100

Publications: *Mikrokosmos* (1 a year), *The Shocker* (print and online, webs.wichita.edu/dt/shockermag/show)

DEANS

College of Education: Dr SHARON IORIO
College of Engineering: Dr ZULMA TORO-RAMOS
College of Fine Arts: Dr RODNEY E. MILLER
College of Health Professions: Prof. Dr PETER A. COHEN
Fairmount College of Liberal Arts and Sciences: Dr WILLIAM D. BISCHOFF
Graduate School: Dr J. DAVID MCDONALD
W. Frank Barton School of Business: Dr DOUGLAS HENSLER

KENTUCKY

ALICE LLOYD COLLEGE

100 Purpose Rd, Pippa Passes, KY 41844
Telephone: (606) 368-6000

E-mail: admissions@alc.edu
Internet: www.alc.edu

Founded 1923 as Caney Jr College, present status 1982
Private control
Academic year: August to May

Offers BA, science

Pres.: JOE A. STEPP
Exec. Vice-Pres.: JAMES STEPP
Vice-Pres. for Academic Affairs and Academic Dean: Prof. CLAUDE L. CRUM
Vice-Pres. for Business Affairs: DAVID JOHNSON
Dean of Student and Community Life: SCOTT CORNETT
Dir of Admissions: ANGELA PHIPPS
Registrar: THELMARIE THORNSBERRY
Library Dir: ANDREW BUSROE

Library of 3,000 vols in Appalachian colln
Number of teachers: 30
Number of students: 510

ASBURY THEOLOGICAL SEMINARY

204 N Lexington Ave, Wilmore, KY 40390
Telephone: (859) 858-3581
E-mail: admissions.office@asburyseminary.edu
Internet: www.asburyseminary.edu

Founded 1923
Private control
Academic year: September to May
Campus in Florida Dunnam

Pres.: Prof. Dr TIMOTHY C. TENNENT
Provost and Vice-Pres. for Academic Affairs: Dr LESLIE A. ANDREWS
Vice-Pres. for Community Formation: Dr MARILYN ELLIOTT
Vice-Pres. for Enrolment Management and Student Services: KEVIN BISH
Vice-Pres. for Finance and Admin.: BRYAN BLANKENSHIP
Vice-Pres. for Florida Campus: Dr GENEVA SILVERNAIL
Vice-Pres. for Seminary Advancement and Communications: JAY MANSUR
Vice-Pres. for Florida Dunnam Campus: Dr GENEVA SILVERNAIL
Exec. Dir of Libraries: PAUL A. TIPPEY
Library of 247,000 vols
Number of teachers: 60
Number of students: 1,780

Publications: *The Asbury Herald* (3 a year), *The Asbury Journal*

DEANS

Beeson International Center for Biblical Preaching and Church Leadership: Dr THOMAS F. TUMBLIN
E. Stanley Jones School of World Mission and Evangelism: Dr TERRY C. MUCK
School of Biblical Interpretation: Dr DAVID R. BAUER
School of Practical Theology: Dr ANNE K. GATOBU
School of Theology and Formation: Dr JAMES R. THOBABEN
School of Urban Ministries: Dr ZAIDA MALDONADO PÉREZ

ASBURY UNIVERSITY

One Macklem Dr., Wilmore, KY 40390
Telephone: (859) 858-3511
E-mail: admissions@asbury.edu
Internet: www.asbury.edu

Founded 1890 as Kentucky Holiness College, present name and status 2010
Private control
Academic year: August to May
Campus in Florida

Pres.: Prof. Dr SANDRA C. GRAY

Provost and Chief Academic Officer: Dr JONATHAN S. KULAGA

Vice-Pres. for Business Affairs and Treas.: Dr CHARLIE D. FISKEAUX

Vice-Pres. for Institutional Advancement and Gen. Counsel: GREG SWANSON

Vice-Pres. for Student Devt: Dr MARK TROYER

Academic Dean: Prof. Dr BONNIE BANKER

Registrar: WILLIAM A. HALL

Dir of Library Services: MORGAN A. TRACY

Library of 150,000 vols

Number of teachers: 160

Number of students: 1,640

Publication: *The Ambassador*

DEANS

College of Arts and Sciences: Dr STEVE K. CLEMENTS

School of Communication Arts: Dr JAMES R. OWENS

School of Education: Dr VERNA J. LOWE

School of Graduate and Professional Studies: Dr JONATHAN S. KULAGA (acting)

BELLARMINE UNIVERSITY

2001 Newburg Rd, Louisville, KY 40205-0671

Telephone: (502) 272-8000

E-mail: admissions@bellarmine.edu

Internet: www.bellarmine.edu

Founded 1950 as Bellarmine College, present name and status 2000

Private control

Academic year: August to May

Pres.: Dr JOSEPH J. MCGOWAN, JR

Provost: Dr DORIS A. TEGART

Vice-Pres. for Academic Affairs: Dr CAROLE C. PFEFFER

Vice-Pres. for Admin. and Finance: ROBERT L. ZIMLICH

Vice-Pres. for Admin. and Student Services: Dr ROBERT L. ZIMLICH

Vice-Pres. for Devt and Alumni Relations: GLENN F. KOSSE

Vice-Pres. for Enrolment Management: SEAN J. RYAN

Vice-Pres. for Student Affairs: Dr FRED W. RHODES

Dean of Graduate Admissions: Dr SARA Y. PETTINGILL

Dean of Students: HELEN-GRACE RYAN

Dean of Undergraduate Admissions: TIMOTHY A. STURGEON

Registrar: ANN OLSEN

Library Dir: Dr JOHN K. STEMMER

Library of 118,000 vols, 350 periodical subscriptions, 47,000 ebooks

Number of teachers: 150 (full-time)

Number of students: 3,250

Publication: *Bellarmine Magazine* (4 a year)

DEANS

Annsley Frazier Thornton School of Education: Prof. Dr ROBERT B. COOTER, JR

Bellarmine College: Dr WILLIAM E. FENTON

Donna and Allan Lansing School of Nursing and Health Sciences: Dr SUSAN H. DAVIS

Regional Center for Environmental Studies: Dr ROBERT W. KINGSOLVER

School of Communication: Dr LARA NEEDHAM

School of Continuing and Professional Studies: Dr MICHAEL D. MATTEI

W. Fielding Rubel School of Business: Prof. Dr DANIEL L. BAUER

BEREA COLLEGE

101 Chestnut St, Berea, KY 40404

Telephone: (859) 985-3000

E-mail: askadmissions@berea.edu

Internet: www.berea.edu

Founded 1855 as dist. school, present name and status 1869

Private control

Academic year: August to May

BA, sciences in 32 majors

Pres.: Dr LYLE D. ROELOFFS

Academic Vice-Pres. and Dean of Faculty: Prof. Dr CHAD BERRY

Vice-Pres. for College Relations and Devt: MICHELLE JANSSEN

Vice-Pres. for Finance: JEFFREY AMBURGEY

Vice-Pres. for Operations and Sustainability: STEVE KARCHER

Dir of Library Services: ANNE CHASE

Library of 450,000 vols

Number of teachers: 140

Number of students: 1,500

Publications: *Apollon—The Undergraduate eJournal* (apollonejournal.org), *Berea College Magazine* (1 a year)

BRESCIA UNIVERSITY

717 Frederica St, Owensboro, KY 42301-3023

Telephone: (270) 685-3131

E-mail: admissions@brescia.edu

Internet: www.brescia.edu

Founded 1950, current name adopted 1998

Private control

Academic year: August to May

Divs of fine arts, humanities, mathematics and natural science; schools of business, education, social and behavioural sciences

Pres.: Rev. LARRY HOSTETTER

Vice-Pres. and Dean of Student Devt: JAMES FITZPATRICK

Vice-Pres. for Academic Affairs: SIS. CHERYL CLEMONS

Vice-Pres. for Business and Finance: DALE CECIL

Vice-Pres. for Enrolment: CHRISTOPHER HOUK

Vice-Pres. for Institutional Advancement: TODD BROCK

Registrar: SIS. HELENA FISCHER

Dir of Library Services: SIS. JUDITH NELL RINEY

Number of teachers: 60

Number of students: 700

CAMPBELLSVILLE UNIVERSITY

1 University Dr., Campbellsville, KY 42718-2799

Telephone: (270) 789-5000

E-mail: admissions@campbellsville.edu

Internet: www.campbellsville.edu

Founded 1906

Private control

Academic year: August to July

Pres.: Dr MICHAEL V. CARTER

Vice-Pres. for Academic Affairs: Dr FRANKLIN D. CHEATHAM

Vice-Pres. for Admissions and Student Services: DAVID WALTERS

Vice-Pres. for Church and External Relations: JOHN E. CHOWNING

Vice-Pres. for Devt: J. BENJI KELLY

Vice-Pres. for Finance and Admin.: OTTO TENNANT

Vice-Pres. for Regional and Professional Education: Dr H. KEITH SPEARS

Dean of Student Services: JOSH ANDERSON

Dir of Library Services: Dr JOHN RUSSELL BIRCH

Library of 95,000 vols

Number of teachers: 350

Number of students: 1,800

DEANS

Carver School of Social Work and Counselling: Dr DARLENE EASTRIDGE

College of Arts and Sciences: Dr MARY WILGUS

Porter and Bouvette School of Business and Economics: Prof. Dr PATRICIA H. COWHERD

School of Education: Dr BRENDA A. PRIDDY

School of Music: Dr J. ROBERT GADDIS

School of Nursing: Prof. Dr ROBERT J. WADE

School of Theology: Prof. Dr JOHN HURTGEN

CENTRE COLLEGE

600 W Walnut St, Danville, KY 40422

Telephone: (859) 238-5200

E-mail: admission@centre.edu

Internet: www.centre.edu

Founded 1819

Private control

Academic year: August to May

Major courses incl. anthropology, sociology art history, art (studio), behavioural neuroscience, biochemistry and molecular biology, biology, chemical physics, chemistry, classical studies, computer science, dramatic arts, economics, education, English, financial economics, French, German studies, government, history, international studies, mathematics, music, philosophy, physics, psychology, religion, Spanish

Pres.: JOHN ALLEN ROUSH

Vice-Pres. for Academic Affairs and Dean of College: Prof. Dr STEPHANIE L. FABRITIUS

Vice-Pres. and Dean for Student Life: RANDY HAYS

Vice-Pres. for College Relations: Dr RICHARD W. TROLLINGER

Vice-Pres. for Finance and Treas.: JOHN E. CUNY

Dean for Admission and Student Financial Planning: ROBERT M. NESMITH

Registrar: TIMOTHY P. CULHAN

Library Dir: STANLEY R. CAMPBELL

Library of 375,000 vols, 28,000 ejournals and 32,000 ebooks

Number of teachers: 120

Number of students: 1,300

CLEAR CREEK BAPTIST BIBLE COLLEGE

300 Clear Creek Rd, Pineville, KY 40977

Telephone: (606) 337-3196

E-mail: ccbbc@ccbbc.edu

Internet: www.ccbbc.edu

Founded 1926 as Clear Creek Mountain Springs, Inc., present name and status 1986

Private control

Academic year: August to May

Offers BA in Church ministries and leadership, missions and Evangelism, pastoral ministry

Pres.: Dr DONNIE FOX

Academic Dean: Prof. Dr MALCOLM HESTER

Dean of Institutional Advancement: Dr JAY SULFRIDGE

Dean of Student Affairs: DAVID WADE

Dir of Admissions: BILLY HOWELL

Registrar: BRENDA HESTER

Dir of Library Services: MARGE CUMMINGS

Library of 37,000 vols, 42,000 monographs, 230 print periodicals

Number of teachers: 20

Number of students: 190

EASTERN KENTUCKY UNIVERSITY

521 Lancaster Ave, Richmond, KY 40475

Telephone: (859) 622-1000

E-mail: publicrelations@eku.edu

Internet: www.eku.edu

Founded 1906 as Eastern Kentucky State Normal School, present name and status 1966

State control

Language of instruction: English

Academic year: August to May

Pres.: Dr DOUG WHITLOCK

Provost and Vice-Pres. for Academic Affairs: Dr JANNA VICE
Vice-Pres. for Admin.: JAMES STREET
Vice-Pres. for Enrolment Management, Marketing and Univ. Relations: LIBBY WACHTEL (acting)
Vice-Pres. for Financial Affairs: BARRY POYNTER
Vice-Pres. for Student Affairs: Dr JAMES CONNEELY
Vice-Pres. for Univ. Advancement: JOSEPH FOSTER
Exec. Dir of Govt Relations: JIM CLARK
Registrar: TINA DAVIS
Dean of Libraries: BETINA GARDNER

Library of 837,945 vols, 3,565 current periodicals, 1,410,522 current periodicals
Number of teachers: 670 (full-time)
Number of students: 15,000
Publication: *The Eastern Magazine*

DEANS

College of Arts and Sciences: Dr JOHN WADE
College of Business and Technology: Prof. Dr ROBERT B. ROGOW
College of Education: Dr BILL PHILIPS
College of Health Sciences: Dr DEBORAH WHITEHOUSE (acting)
College of Justice and Safety: Dr ALLEN AULT

FRONTIER NURSING UNIVERSITY

POB 528, 195 School St, Hyden, KY 41749
Telephone: (606) 672-2312
E-mail: fnu@frontier.edu
Internet: www.frontierschool.edu

Founded 1939 as Frontier Graduate School of Midwifery, present name and status 2011
Private control

Offers MSc in nursing

Pres. and Dean: SUSAN STONE
Assoc. Dean of Academic Affairs: JOYCE KNESTRICK
Assoc. Dean of Family Nursing: JULIE MARFELL
Assoc. Dean of Midwifery and Women's Health: SUZAN ULRICH
Assoc. Dean of Research: JANET ENGSTROM
Dir of Library Services: BILLIE ANNE GEBB

GEORGETOWN COLLEGE

400 East College St, Georgetown, KY 40324-1696
Telephone: (502) 863-8000
E-mail: greene@georgetowncollege.edu
Internet: www.georgetowncollege.edu

Founded 1787, current status 1829
Private control
Academic year: August to July

Pres.: Dr M. DWAINE GREENE
Provost and Academic Dean: Dr ROSEMARY A. ALLEN
Vice-Pres., Chief Financial Officer and Treas.: JAMES A. MOAK, JR
Vice-Pres. for Enrolment Management: MICHELLE LYNCH
Vice-Pres. for Student Life and Dean for Students: LAURA WYLY
Dean for Education: Dr YOLANDA CARTER
Registrar: WINNIE BRATCHER
Library Dir: SUSAN MARTIN

Library of 185,592 vols, 314 current periodicals, 162,363 ebooks, 10,922 audiovisual items, 149,318 monographs
Number of teachers: 150 (109 full-time, 41 part-time)
Number of students: 1,400 (1044 undergraduate, 356 graduate)

KENTUCKY CHRISTIAN UNIVERSITY

100 Academic Parkway, Grayson, KY 41143-2205
Telephone: (606) 474-3000
E-mail: knights@kcu.edu
Internet: www.kcu.edu

Founded 1919 as Christian Normal Institute, present name and status 2004
Private control
Academic year: August to May

Chancellor: Dr KEITH P. KEERAN
Pres.: Dr JEFFREY K. METCALF
Exec. Vice-Pres.: JOHN L. DUNDON
Sr Vice-Pres. and Provost: Dr JEFF METCALF
Vice-Pres. for Academic Affairs: Dr PERRY STEPP
Vice-Pres. for Business and Finance: BILL BONDURANT
Vice-Pres. for Univ. Advancement: LARRY MONROE
Dean of Student Services: RON ARNETT
Dir of Admissions: SHEREE GREER
Registrar: ANDREA STAMPER
Library Dir: NAULAYNE ENDERS

Library of 100,000 vols, 200 print journals, 100,000 ebooks, 17,000 ejournal titles
Number of teachers: 30
Number of students: 580

DEANS

Graduate School: DAVID FIENSY
Keeran School of Education: Dr KAREN FORD
Sack School of Bible and Ministry: Prof. Dr DAVID FIENSY
School of Arts and Sciences: Dr JOHN WINELAND
School of Business: Prof. Dr TIM NISCHAN
School of Music: Dr WES GOLIGHTLY
School of Social Work and Human Services: MARGARET MCLAUGHLIN
Yancey School of Nursing: ABIGAIL LEIGH BECK

KENTUCKY MOUNTAIN BIBLE COLLEGE

POB 10, Vancleve, KY 41385-0010
855 Kentucky Highway 541, Vancleve, KY 41339
Telephone: (606) 693-5000
E-mail: kmbc@kmbc.edu
Internet: www.kmbc.edu

Founded 1931 as Kentucky Mountain Bible Institute; present name and status 1989
Private control
Academic year: August to May

Study programmes incl. Christian education, Christian min., communication, elementary education, ministerial, missions, music ministry, nursing

Pres.: Dr PHILIP SPEAS
Exec. Vice-Pres. and Vice-Pres. for Academic Affairs: THOMAS H. LORIMER
Vice-Pres. for Business Affairs: DOUG DUNN
Vice-Pres. for Devt: Dr JOHN ELDON NEIHOF
Dean of Students: JAMES NELSON
Registrar: RICHARD ENGLEHARDT
Librarian: PATRICIA ANN BOWEN

Library of 30,000 vols
Number of teachers: 20
Number of students: 90

KENTUCKY STATE UNIVERSITY

400 East Main St, Frankfort, KY 40601
Telephone: (502) 597-6000
E-mail: admissions@kysu.edu
Internet: www.kysu.edu

Founded 1886 as State Normal School for Colored Persons, present name and status 1972
State control
Academic year: August to May

Pres.: Dr MARY EVANS SIAS
Vice-Pres. for Academic Affairs and Interim Provost: Dr MAC A. STEWART
Vice-Pres. for Admin., External Relations and Devt: HINFRED MCDUFFIE
Vice-Pres. for Finance and Business Affairs: ALICE BURSEY JOHNSON
Vice-Pres. for Student Affairs and Enrolment Management: Dr RUBYE WILLIAM JONES
Gen. Counsel: LORI A. DAVIS
Registrar: JOHN B. MARTIN
Dir of Libraries: SHEILA A. STUCKEY

Library of 700,000 vols
Number of teachers: 150
Number of students: 2,310

DEANS

College of Agriculture, Food Science and Sustainable Systems: Dr TEFERI TSEGAYE
College of Arts, Social Sciences and Interdisciplinary Studies: Dr SAM O. OLEKA
College of Business and Computer Science: Dr TSEHAI ALEMAYEHU
College of Mathematics, Science, Technology and Health: Dr CHARLES BENNETT
College of Professional Studies: Dr GASHAW LAKE

KENTUCKY WESLEYAN COLLEGE

3000 Frederica St, Owensboro, KY 42301
Telephone: (270) 926-3111
E-mail: admissions@kwc.edu
Internet: www.kwc.edu

Founded 1858
Private control
Academic year: August to May

Depts of behavioural sciences, biology and zoology, centre for business studies, chemistry, communication arts, cross disciplinary, education, English, history and political science, kinesiology and health promotion, mathematics and physics, modern languages, pre-professional programmes, religion and philosophy

Pres.: Prof. Dr CRAIG TURNER
Vice-Pres. for Academic Affairs and Dean of College: Dr PAULA DEHN
Vice-Pres. for Finance and Treas.: CINDRA K. STIFF
Vice-Pres. for Student Services: SCOTT KRAMER
Dir for Admissions: RASHAD SMITH
Registrar: JENNIFER VAUGHAN
Dir for Library: PATRICIA MCFARLING

Library of 150,000 vols incl. books, periodicals, govt documents, audiovisual materials
Number of teachers: 80
Number of students: 680

LEXINGTON THEOLOGICAL SEMINARY

631 S Limestone St, Lexington, KY 40508
Telephone: (859) 252-0361
E-mail: admissions@lextheo.edu
Internet: www.lextheo.edu

Founded 1865 as College of the Bible, current name adopted 1965
Private control

Offers Masters programmes in divinity, arts, pastoral studies, ministry

Pres.: CHARISSE GILLETT
Vice-Pres. for Academic Affairs: Prof. Dr RICH WEIS
Vice-Pres. for Advancement: JAMES M. WRAY, JR
Chief Financial Officer: LAURA DAVIS
Dir of Admissions: ERIN CASH
Registrar: WINDY KIDD
Librarian: DOLORES YILIBUW

Library of 165,000 vols, 200 periodicals

Number of teachers: 20
Number of students: 60

Publication: *Lexington Theological Quarterly* (4 a year)

LINDSEY WILSON COLLEGE

210 Lindsey Wilson St, Columbia, KY 42728

Telephone: (270) 384-2126
E-mail: info@lindsey.edu
Internet: www.lindsey.edu

Founded 1903 as Lindsey Wilson Training School; current name adopted 1923, present status 1986
Private control
Academic year: August to May

Liberal arts college; Kentucky campuses: Ashland, Big Stone Gap, Cincinnati, Columbia, Cumberland, Danville, Elizabethtown, Florence, Gallatin, Hazard, Henderson, Hilsboro, Hopkinsville, Lexington, Mount Gay, London, Louisville, Madisonville, Maysville, Paducah, Prestonsburg, Radcliff, WythevilleScottsville, Shelbyville and Somerset; Virginia campuses: Wytheville, Richlands

Pres.: WILLIAM T. LUCKEY, JR
Chancellor: JOHN B. BEGLEY
Vice-Pres. for Academic Affairs: BETTIE STARR
Vice-Pres. for Admin. and Finance: ROGER DRAKE
Vice-Pres. for Development: KEVIN A. THOMPSON
Vice-Pres. for Educational Outreach and Student Financial Services: DENISE FUDGE
Vice-Pres. for Student Services and Enrolment Management: L. DEAN ADAMS
Dean of Admissions: TRACI POOLER
Dean of Students: CHRISTOPHER SCHMIDT
Registrar: SUE COOMER
Library Dir: PHILIP HANNA

Library of 500,000 vols
Number of teachers: 110
Number of students: 2,310

LOUISVILLE PRESBYTERIAN THEOLOGICAL SEMINARY

1044 Alta Vista Rd, Louisville, KY 40205

Telephone: (502) 895-3411
E-mail: admissions@lpts.edu
Internet: www.lpts.edu

Founded 1901 by merger of Danville Theological Seminary and Louisville Presbyterian Seminary
Private control
Academic year: August to May

Programmes offered incl. doctor of ministry, MA in spirituality, master of divinity

Pres.: Prof. Dr MICHAEL JINKINS
Vice-Pres. for Academic Affairs and Dean of Seminary: Dr SUSAN R. GARRETT
Vice-Pres. for Finance and Chief Financial Officer: PATRICK A. CECIL
Dean of Students: SUSAN R. GARRETT
Dir of Admissions and Recruitment: CHERI HARPER
Registrar: DAVID GRAY
Dir of Library and Information Technology Services: Prof. ANGELA MORRIS (acting)

Library of 175,000 vols, 12,000 microforms and 7,000 audiovisual items
Number of teachers: 20
Number of students: 230

PROFESSORS

ADENEY, F., Evangelism and Global Mission
BOS, J., Bible and Old Testament
BROGDON, L., New Testament and Black Church Studies
COOK, C., Pastoral Care and Counselling
CRAIGO-SNELL, S., Theology
ELWOOD, C., Historical Theology

GARRETT, S., New Testament
HESTER, D., Pastoral Theology
JINKINS, M., Theology
JOHNSON, K., Historical Theology and Church History
KIRKPATRICK, C., Ecumenical Studies and Global Ministries
MUMFORD, D., Homiletics
PAUW, A., Doctrinal Theology
REISTROFFER, D., Ministry
SOARDS, M., New Testament
TOWNSEND, L., Pastoral Ministry and Pastoral Care and Counselling
WALKER, E. J., Pastoral Care and Counseling
WIGGER, J., Christian Education
WILLIAMSON, S., Theological Ethics

MIDWAY COLLEGE

512 East Stephens St, Midway, KY 40347

Telephone: (859) 846-4421
Internet: www.midway.edu

Founded 1847 as Kentucky Female Orphan School; current name adopted 1978
Private control
Academic year: August to May

Pres.: Dr WILLIAM B. DRAKE, JR
Vice-Pres. for Academic Affairs: (vacant)
Vice-Pres. for Business Affairs: LYEN CREWS
Vice-Pres. for College Relations and Devt: JUDY MARCUM
Vice-Pres. and Dean of Enrollment Management: Dr JAMES WOMBLES
Vice-Pres. and Assoc. Dean of School for Career Devt: Dr WILLIAM BROWN
Provost and Dean of Women's College: SARAH H. LAWS
Registrar: P. EDWARD PRESLER
Dir of Library Services: CATHY REILENDER

Number of teachers: 50 (full-time)
Number of students: 1,200

MOREHEAD STATE UNIVERSITY

150 University Blvd, Morehead, KY 40351

Telephone: (606) 783-2221
E-mail: admissions@moreheadstate.edu
Internet: www.moreheadstate.edu

Founded 1887 as Morehead Normal School, present name and status 1966
State control
Academic year: August to May

Pres.: Dr WAYNE D. ANDREWS
Provost and Vice-Pres. for Academic Affairs: KARLA HUGHES
Vice-Pres. for Admin. and Fiscal Services: MICHAEL R. WALTERS
Vice-Pres. for Devt: BARBARA A. ENDER
Vice-Pres. for Planning and Budgets: BETH G. PATRICK
Vice-Pres. for Student Life: MADONNA WEATHERS
Vice-Pres. for Univ. Advancement: JAMES SHAW
Registrar: ROSLYN PERRY
Dean of Library Services: Dr DAVID GREGORY (acting)

Library: 5m. vols, 2,500 periodicals
Number of teachers: 440 (320 full-time, 120 part-time)
Number of students: 10,000
Publication: *Inscape* (2 a year)

DEANS

Caudill College of Arts, Humanities and Social Sciences: Dr M. SCOTT MCBRIDE
College of Business and Public Affairs: Dr ROBERT ALBERT
College of Education: Dr CATHY GUNN
College of Science and Technology: Dr ROGER MCNEIL
Institute for Regional Analysis and Public Policy: Dr DAVID RUDY

MURRAY STATE UNIVERSITY

102 Curris Centre, Murray, KY 42071

Telephone: (270) 809-3011
E-mail: msu.admissions@murraystate.edu
Internet: www.murraystate.edu

Founded 1922
State control
Language of instruction: English
Academic year: August to May

Pres.: Dr RANDY J. DUNN
Provost and Vice-Pres. for Academic Affairs: Prof. Dr BONNIE S. HIGGINSON
Vice-Pres. for Finance and Admin. Services: THOMAS W. DENTON
Vice-Pres. for Institutional Advancement: JAMES F. CARTER
Vice-Pres. for Student Affairs: Dr DONALD E. ROBERTSON
Gen. Counsel: JOHN P. RALL
Dean of Libraries: ADAM L. MURRAY

Library of 401,663 vols of monographs, 124,147 vols of periodicals, 215,649 govt documents
Number of teachers: 580 (422 full-time, 158 part-time)
Number of students: 10,620 (8,662 undergraduate, 1,958 graduate)
Publications: *Blue and Gold* (alumni magazine), *Chrysalis, JMC Journal, New Madrid, Notations*

DEANS

Academic Outreach and Continuing Education: Dr BRIAN VAN HORN
Arthur J. Bauernfeind College of Business: Dr TIMOTHY S. TODD
College of Education: Dr DAVID WHALEY
College of Health Sciences and Human Services: Dr SUSAN MULLER
College of Humanities and Fine Arts: Dr TED BROWN
College of Science, Engineering and Technology: Dr STEPHEN H. COBB
Hutson School of Agriculture: Dr TONY BRANNON
School of Nursing: Dr MARCIA B. HOBBS

NORTHERN KENTUCKY UNIVERSITY

Nunn Dr., Highland Heights, KY 41099

Telephone: (859) 572-5100
E-mail: gradprog@nku.edu
Internet: www.nku.edu

Founded 1968 as Northern Kentucky State College; current name adopted 1976, present status 1973
State control
Academic year: August to May

Pres.: Dr JAMES C. VOTRUBA
Vice-Pres. for Academic Affairs and Provost: Dr GAIL W. WELLS
Vice-Pres. for Admin. and Financeand Treas.: KENNETH H. RAMEY
Vice-Pres. for Legal Affairs and Gen. Counsel: SARA L. SIDEBOTTOM
Vice-Pres. for Student Affairs: Dr LISA B. RHINE
Vice-Pres. for Univ. Advancement: GERARD A. ST AMAND
Dean of Students: Dr JEFFREY N. WAPLE
Registrar: KIMBERLY K. TAYLOR
Assoc. Provost of Libraries: ARNE ALMQUIST

Library of 814,318 vols, 37,037 ebooks
Number of teachers: 530 (full-time)
Number of students: 15,750 (10,713 full-time, 5,037 part-time)
Publication: *Northern* (2 a year)

DEANS

College of Arts and Sciences: Prof. Dr SAMUEL J. ZACHARY
College of Education and Human Services: MARK WASICSKO

College of Health Professions: Prof. Dr DENISE ROBINSON
College of Informatics: Dr KEVIN KIRBY
Haile/US Bank College of Business: Prof. Dr RICHARD H. KOLBE
Salmon P. Chase College of Law: Prof. Dr DENNIS HONABACH

SAINT CATHARINE COLLEGE

2735 Bardstown Rd, St Catharine, KY 40061
Telephone: (859) 336-5082
E-mail: admissions@sccky.edu
Internet: www.sccky.edu
Founded 1931
Private control
Pres.: WILLIAM D. HUSTON
Exec. Vice-Pres.: ROGER MARCUM
Vice-Pres. for Academic Affairs: Dr DON GILES
Vice-Pres. for Advancement: JENNA COPPLE
Vice-Pres. for Enrolment Management and Dean of Students: Dr VICTORIA GUTHRIE
Vice-Pres. for Finance and Admin.: GARY ROBINSON
Registrar: ANITA FOSTER
Dir of Admissions: PAUL PRESTA
Dir of Library Services: ILONA BURDETTE
Library of 22,000 vols, 100 journals and periodicals, 1,000 audiovisual items
Number of students: 850

DEANS

Graduate School: Dr SIS. MARY ANGELA SHAUGHNESSY
School of Arts and Sciences: Rev. Dr ROBERT SLOCUM
School of Health and Human Sciences: Dr HARRY NICKENS
School of Professional Studies: Dr DAVID ARNOLD

SOUTHERN BAPTIST THEOLOGICAL SEMINARY

2825 Lexington Rd, Louisville, KY 40280
Telephone: (502) 897-4011
E-mail: admissions@sbts.edu
Internet: www.sbts.edu
Founded 1859
Private control
Academic year: August to May
Pres.: Prof. Dr R. ALBERT MOHLER, JR
Sr Vice-Pres. for Academic Admin.: Dr RUSSELL D. MOORE
Sr Vice-Pres. for Institutional Admin.: DAN S. DUMAS
Sr Vice-Pres. for Institutional Advancement: JASON K. ALLEN
Vice-Pres. for Academic Innovation: Dr RANDY L. STINSON
Vice-Pres. for Business Services: R. CRAIG PARKER
Vice-Pres. for Extension Education: Prof. Dr MARK T. COPPENGER
Vice-Pres. for Research and Assessment: Prof. Dr GREGORY A. WILLS
Vice-Pres. for Student Services: DANIEL E. HATFIELD
Dean of Students: LAWRENCE A. SMITH
Registrar: NORMAN CHUNG
Librarian and Assoc. Vice-Pres. for Academic Resources: BRUCE L. KEISLING
Library: 1m. vols incl. 384,500 vols of books, periodicals, audiovisual items
Number of teachers: 130
Number of students: 2,890
Publications: *Southern Baptist Journal of Theology* (4 a year), *Southern Seminary Magazine* (4 a year)

DEANS

Billy Graham School of Missions and Evangelism: Dr ZANE G. PRATT

Boyce College: Dr DAN DeWITT
School of Church Ministries: Dr RANDY L. STINSON
School of Theology: Prof. Dr RUSSELL D. MOORE

SPALDING UNIVERSITY

845 S Third St, Louisville, KY 40203
Telephone: (502) 585-9911
E-mail: admissions@spalding.edu
Internet: www.spalding.edu
Founded 1814, present name and status 1984
Private control
Academic year: July to June
Pres.: Dr TORI MURDEN McCLURE
Provost: Prof. Dr LEWIS RANDY STRICKLAND
Vice-Pres. for Univ. Advancement: JEFFREY L. ASHLEY
Dean of Enrolment Management: CHRISTOPHER HART
Dean of Students, Student Devt and Campus Life: Dr RICHARD HUDSON
Dir of Admissions: PATRICIA GOODMAN
Chief Financial Officer: MARK HOHMANN
Registrar: JENNIFER GOHMANN
Library Dir: JACQUELINE YOUNG
Library of 200,000 vols, 22,000 bound journals, 450 current periodical subscriptions
Number of teachers: 250
Number of students: 2,400

DEANS

College of Business and Communication: Dr DIANE TOBIN
College of Education: Dr BEVERLY KEEPERS
College of Health and Natural Sciences: JOANNE BERRYMAN
College of Social Sciences and Humanities: Dr JOHN JAMES

SULLIVAN UNIVERSITY

3101 Bardstown Rd, Louisville, KY 40205
Telephone: (502) 456-6505
E-mail: admissions@sullivan.edu
Internet: www.sullivan.edu
Founded 1962 as Sullivan Business College, present name and status 2000
Private control
Academic year: September to September (4 quarters)
Campuses in Fort Knox, Lexington
Chancellor: A. R. SULLIVAN
Pres.: Dr GLENN D. SULLIVAN
Exec. Vice-Pres.: Dr BILL NOEL
Sr Vice-Pres.: TOM DAVISSON
Vice-Pres. for Academic Affairs and Chief Academic Officer: JAY MARR
Vice-Pres. for Enrolment Management: JIM CRICK
Vice-Pres. for Finance: SHELTON BRIDGES
Vice-Pres. for Student Services and Dean of Students: CHRIS ERNST
Dean of Graduate School: Prof. Dr ERIC S. HARTER
Registrar: LESLEY CASH
Dir of Libraries: Prof. CHARLES BROWN
Library of 20,000 vols
Number of teachers: 40
Number of students: 2,000

DEANS

College of Business and Administration: KEN MORAN
College of Information and Computer Technology: VIRGINIA GODWIN
College of Pharmacy: Dr CINDY STOWE
General Education: MARGIE GALLO
Institute for Legal Studies: NICK RIGGS
National Center for Hospitality Studies: KEITH LERNE
School of Accountancy: TIM SWENSON

THOMAS MORE COLLEGE

333 Thomas More Parkway, Crestview Hills, KY 41017-3495
Telephone: (859) 341-5800
E-mail: admissions@thomasmore.edu
Internet: www.thomasmore.edu
Founded 1921 as Villa Madonna College, current name adopted 1968
Private control
Language of instruction: English
Academic year: June to May
Programmes of study incl. accountancy, art, art history, athletic training, biology, business admin., chemistry, communication, computer information systems, criminal justice, economics, education, English, environmental science, forensic science, French, gerontology, health care management, history, humanities, international studies, management, mathematics, medical laboratory science, music, nursing, philosophy, physics, political science, pre-legal studies, psychology, sociology, Spanish, sports and entertainment marketing, theatre, theology, web design
Pres.: DAVID A. ARMSTRONG
Vice-Pres. for Academic Affairs: Dr BRADLEY A. BIELSKI
Vice-Pres. for Institutional Advancement: CATHY L. SILVERS
Vice-Pres. for Operations and Community Affairs: MATTHEW H. WEBSTER
Dean for Students: EBONY GRIGGS-GRIFFIN
Exec. Dir for Enrolment Management: KRISTIN A. LEHMER
Chief Financial Officer: THOMAS E. PRICE
Registrar: KELLY FRENCH
Dir for Library: JAMES M. McKELLOGG
Library of 114,230 vols
Number of teachers: 170 (70 full-time, 100 part-time)
Number of students: 1,600

TRANSYLVANIA UNIVERSITY

300 N Broadway, Lexington, KY 40508-1797
Telephone: (859) 233-8300
E-mail: admissions@transy.edu
Internet: www.transy.edu
Founded 1780 as Transylvania Seminary, present name and status 1908
Private control
Academic year: August to July
Academic divs incl. business and economics, education, physical education and exercise science, fine arts, humanities, natural sciences and mathematics, social sciences
Pres.: Dr R. OWEN WILLIAMS
Vice-Pres. and Dean of the College: WILLIAM F. POLLARD
Vice-Pres. for Advancement: KIRK PURDOM
Vice-Pres. for Finance and Business: MARC A. MATHEWS
Vice-Pres. for Enrolment and Dean of Admissions: BRADLEY L GOAN
Vice-Pres. for Student Affairs and Dean of Students: MICHAEL K. VETTER
Registrar: JIM MONAGHAN MILLS
Dir of Library: SUSAN M. BROWN
Library of 130,000 vols
Number of teachers: 100
Number of students: 1,100

UNION COLLEGE

310 College St, Barbourville, KY 40906-1499
Telephone: (606) 546-4151
Internet: www.unionky.edu
Founded 1795
Private control
Academic year: July to June

Depts of business, educational studies, English and communications, history, religious studies, languages, fine and performing arts, natural sciences, nursing and health sciences, psychology, social and behavioural sciences, wellness, human performances and recreation management

Pres.: Dr THOMAS J. MCFARLAND (acting)
Academic Dean: Dr LARRY INKSTER (acting)
Vice-Pres. for Advancement: DENISE WAINSCOTT
Vice-Pres. for Business and Financial Services: STEVE HOSKINS
Dean of Admissions and Financial Aid: ANDRE WASHINGTON
Dean of Education: Dr ROBERT SWANSON
Dean of Enrolment Management: JERRY JACKSON
Dean of Student Life: DEBBIE D'ANNA
Registrar: KATHY WEBB
Dir of Library Services: TARA L. COOPER
Library of 162,646 vols, 439,794 microforms
Number of teachers: 210
Number of students: 2,130

UNIVERSITY OF KENTUCKY

Lexington, KY 40506
Telephone: (859) 257-9000
E-mail: admissions@uky.edu
Internet: www.uky.edu
Founded 1865 as Agricultural and Mechanical College of Kentucky Univ., current name adopted 1916
State control
Academic year: August to May
Pres.: Dr ELI CAPILOUTO
Provost: KUMBLE R. SUBBASWAMY (acting)
Exec. Vice-Pres. for Devt: D. MICHAEL RICHEY
Exec. Vice-Pres. for Finance and Admin.: FRANK A. BUTLER
Vice-Pres. for Facilities Management: BOB WISEMAN
Vice-Pres. for Institutional Diversity: JUDY JACKSON
Vice-Pres. for Institutional Research, Planning and Effectiveness: HEIDI ANDERSON
Vice-Pres. for Student Affairs: ROBERT C. MOCK, JR
Vice-Pres. for Univ. Relations: THOMAS W. HARRIS
Gen. Counsel: BARBARA W. JONES (acting)
Chief Information Officer: VINCE J. KELLEN
Dir of Admissions and Registrar: DONALD E. WITT
Dean of Libraries: TERRY BIRDWHISTELL
Library: see under Libraries and Archives
Number of teachers: 2,170 full-time
Number of students: 27,110
Publications: *Alzheimer's Disease Review* (4 a year), *Colloquia Germanica* (4 a year), *Disclosure (Lexington)* (1 a year), *Growth and Change* (urban and regional policy, 4 a year), *Kentucky Law Journal* (4 a year), *Kentucky Review* (2 a year), *L'Esprit Createur* (4 a year), *Retiarius: commentarii periodici Latini* (1 a year)

DEANS

College of Agriculture, Food and Environment: NANCY COX
College of Arts and Sciences: Prof. Dr MARK LAWRENCE KORNBLUH
College of Communications and Information Studies: Dr DAN O'HAIR
College of Dentistry: Dr SHARON P. TURNER
College of Design: MICHAEL A. SPEAKS
College of Education: Prof. Dr MARY JOHN O'HAIR
College of Engineering: Dr THOMAS W. LESTER
College of Fine Arts: Dr MICHAEL S. TICK
College of Health Sciences: Dr SHARON R. STEWART

College of Law: Prof. DAVID A. BRENNEN
College of Medicine: Dr FREDERICK C. DE BEER
College of Nursing: Prof. Dr JANE M. KIRSCHLING
College of Pharmacy: Prof. Dr TIMOTHY S. TRACY
College of Public Health: Dr STEPHEN W. WYATT
College of Social Work: Prof. Dr JAMES P. ADAMS, JR
Gatton College of Business and Economics: Prof. Dr DAVID W. BLACKWELL
Graduate School: JEANNINE BLACKWELL

UNIVERSITY OF LOUISVILLE

2301 S Third St, Louisville, KY 40292
Telephone: (502) 852-5555
E-mail: admitme@louisville.edu
Internet: www.louisville.edu
Founded 1798 as Jefferson Seminary, present name and status 1846
State control
Academic year: August to May
Pres.: Dr JAMES R. RAMSEY
Provost: Dr SHIRLEY C. WILLIHNGANZ (acting)
Vice-Pres. for External Affairs: Dr DAN HALL
Vice-Pres. for Finance: MICHAEL J. CURTIN
Exec. Vice-Pres. for Research and Innovation: Dr WILLIAM M. PIERCE, JR
Vice-Pres. for Student Affairs: Dr TOM JACKSON, JR (acting)
Vice-Pres. for Univ. Advancement: A. KEITH INMAN
Registrar: SCOTT BURKS (acting)
Dean of Univ. Libraries: Prof. ROBERT FOX (acting)
Library of 2,275,328 vols, 30,650 ebooks, 10,814 audiovisual items, 2,230,500 microforms, 12,118 current serial titles
Number of teachers: 2,320 (1,659 full-time, 661 part-time)
Number of students: 22,250 (16,925 full-time, 5,325 part-time)
Publications: *The Cardinal*, *Inside U of L*

DEANS

College of Arts and Sciences: Prof. Dr J. BLAINE HUDSON
College of Business: R. CHARLES MOYER
College of Education and Human Devt: Dr W. BLAKE HASELTON
J. B. Speed School of Engineering: Dr NEVILLE G. PINTO
Louis D. Brandeis School of Law: Prof. JIM CHEN
Raymond A. Kent School of Social Work: TERRY L. SINGER
School of Dentistry: Dr JOHN J. SAUK
School of Interdisciplinary and Graduate Studies: Dr BETH A. BOEHM
School of Medicine: Dr TONI GANZEL
School of Music: Prof. Dr CHRISTOPHER P. DOANE
School of Nursing: Prof. Dr MARCIA J. HERN
School of Public Health and Information Sciences: Dr RICHARD D. CLOVER (acting)

UNIVERSITY OF PIKEVILLE

147 Sycamore St, Pikeville, KY 41501
Telephone: (606) 218-5250
Internet: www.upike.edu
Founded 1889, current name and status 2011
Private control
Academic year: August to July
Pres.: Dr JAMES HURLEY
Vice-Pres. for Academic Affairs: THOMAS R. HESS
Vice-Pres. for Devt: Dr ERIC A. BECHER
Vice-Pres. for Finance and Business Affairs: DOUGLAS LANGE

Vice-Pres. for Student Services and Dean for Students: RONALD D. DAMRON
Dir for Admissions: GARY JUSTICE
Registrar: GIA POTTER
Library Dir: KAREN S. EVANS
Library of 72,673 vols
Number of teachers: 60
Number of students: 1,510 (1,201 undergraduate, 309 postgraduate)

DEANS

College of Arts and Science: THOMAS R. HESS
Kentucky College of Osteopathic Medicine: Dr BOYD R. BUSER

UNIVERSITY OF THE CUMBERLANDS

6191 College Station Dr., Williamsburg, KY 40769
Telephone: (606) 549-2200
E-mail: admiss@ucumberlands.edu
Internet: www.ucumberlands.edu
Founded 1889 as Williamsburg Institute, present name and status 2005
Private control
Academic year: August to August
Areas of study incl. business admin., education, public relations, religion, science, theatre arts and journalism
Pres.: JIM TAYLOR
Vice-Pres. for Academic Affairs: Dr LARRY COCKRUM
Vice-Pres. for Business Services: STEVE MORRIS
Vice-Pres. for Institutional Advancement: SUE WAKE
Vice-Pres. for Student Services: Dr MICHAEL COLGROVE
Registrar: CHUCK DUPIER
Dir of the Library: JANICE WREN
Library of 155,000 vols
Number of teachers: 110
Number of students: 3,300 (1,746 undergraduate, 1,554 graduate)

WESTERN KENTUCKY UNIVERSITY

1906 College Heights Blvd, Bowling Green, KY 42101
Telephone: (270) 745-0111
E-mail: wku@wku.edu
Internet: www.wku.edu
Founded 1907, present name and status 1966
State control
Academic year: August to July
Pres.: Dr GARY A. RANSDELL
Provost and Vice-Pres. for Academic Affairs: Dr A. GORDON EMSLIE
Vice-Pres. for Devt and Alumni Relations: KATHRYN R. COSTELLO
Vice-Pres. for Finance and Admin.: K. ANN MEAD
Vice-Pres. for Information Technology: Dr ROBERT OWEN
Vice-Pres. for Institutional Advancement: THOMAS S. HILES
Vice-Pres. for Research: Dr GORDON C. BAYLIS
Vice-Pres. for Student Affairs: HOWARD BAILEY
Registrar: (vacant)
Dir for Admissions: SCOTT GORDON
Dean for Libraries: CONNIE FOSTER
Library of 729,070 vols, 161,463 bound periodicals, 936,779 govt documents, 2,236,014 microforms, 6,984 MSS, 29,906 audiovisual items
Number of teachers: 750 (full-time)
Number of students: 20,900

DEANS

College of Education and Behavioural Sciences: Prof. Dr SAM EVANS

College of Health and Human Services: Dr JOHN A. BONAGURO

Gordon Ford College of Business: Dr JEFF KATZ

Ogden College of Science and Engineering: Dr BLAINE FERRELL

Potter College of Arts and Letters: Dr DAVID LEE

Univ. College: Dr DENNIS K. GEORGE

LOUISIANA

CENTENARY COLLEGE OF LOUISIANA

POB 41188, Shreveport, LA 71134-1188
2911 Centenary Blvd, Shreveport, LA 71104
Telephone: (318) 869-5011
E-mail: president@centenary.edu
Internet: www.centenary.edu

Founded 1845 by merger of College of Louisiana and Centenary College
Private control
Academic year: June to May

Pres.: Dr B. DAVID ROWE
Provost and Dean of College: Dr MICHAEL HEMPHILL
Vice-Pres. for Advancement: SCOTT RAWLES
Vice-Pres. for Finance and Admin.: BILL BALLARD
Vice-Pres. for Enrolment Services: MONTY CURTIS
Vice-Pres. for Student Devt: BETSY EAVES
Dean of Students: MARK MILLER
Dir of Admissions: GAIL ROBINSON
Registrar: Dr GARY YOUNG
Dir of Library Services: CHRISTY J. WRENN

Library of 251,477 vols, 179,934 online journal, 358 print journals
Number of teachers: 60 (full-time)
Number of students: 800 (undergraduate)
Publication: *Pandora*

DEANS

Frost School of Business: Dr CHRISTOPHER L. MARTIN
Hurley School of Music: Prof. GALE ODOM

DILLARD UNIVERSITY

2601 Gentilly Blvd, New Orleans, LA 70122
Telephone: (504) 283-8822
E-mail: admissions@dillard.edu
Internet: www.dillard.edu

Founded 1930 by merger of New Orleans Univ. and Straight College
Private control
Academic year: June to May

Pres.: Dr JAMES E. LYONS, SR
Provost and Sr Vice-Pres. for Academic Affairs: Dr PHYLLIS DAWKINS
Exec. Vice-Pres.: Dr WALTER L. STRONG
Provost and Sr Vice-Pres. for Academic Affairs: Dr PHYLLIS WORTHY DAWKINS
Chief Financial Officer: WANDA BROOKS
Vice-Pres. for Student Affairs: Dr CHRISTOPHER CAMERON
Registrar: PAMELA ENGLAND
Dean of Library: CYNTHIA J. CHARLES

Library of 105,128 vols, 295 current periodicals, 1,150 microfilms, 320 audiovisual items, 88,000 ebooks
Number of teachers: 130 (84 full-time, 46 part-time)
Number of students: 1,250
Publication: *Dillard Today* (1 a year)

DEANS

College of Arts and Sciences: Prof. Dr ROBERT A. COLLINS
College of Business: Prof. Dr CHRISTIAN V. FUGAR

College of General Studies: Dr DOROTHY SMITH
College of Professional Studies: Dr LAURA V. ROUZAN
School of Science, Technology, Engineering and Mathematics: Prof. Dr JOHN E. WILSON

LOUISIANA COLLEGE

1140 College Dr., Pineville, LA 71359
Telephone: (318) 487-7259
E-mail: admissions@lacollege.edu
Internet: www.lacollege.edu

Founded 1906
Private control
Academic year: August to August

Pres.: Dr JOE AQUILLARD
Exec. Vice-Pres.: Dr TIMOTHY L. JOHNSON
Vice-Pres. for Academic Affairs: Dr TIM SEARCY
Vice-Pres. for Business Affairs and Chief Financial Officer: RANDALL HARGIS
Vice-Pres. for Institutional Advancement: Rev. TIMOTHY JOHNSON
Vice-Pres. for Student Devt and Dean for Students: Dr PEGGY PACK
Registrar: CAROLYN DENNIS
Dir for Library: W. TERRY MARTIN

Library of 135,000 vols, 199,000 govt documents, 75,000 microfilm, 500 journals, 41,000 ebooks, 13,200 ejournals
Number of teachers: 110
Number of students: 1,460

DEANS

Caskey School of Divinity: Prof. Dr CHARLES QUARLES
Division of Fine Arts and Media: Dr FRED GUILBERT
Judge Paul Pressler School of Law: J. MICHAEL JOHNSON
School of Education: Dr RANDALL E. ESTERS
School of Nursing and Allied Health: Prof. Dr KIMBERLY J. SHARP

LOUISIANA STATE UNIVERSITY SYSTEM

3810 W Lakeshore Dr., Baton Rouge, LA 70808
Telephone: (225) 578-2111
Internet: www.lsusystem.edu

Founded 1860
Academic year: August to July

Pres.: Dr WILLIAM L. JENKINS
Vice-Pres. for Academic Affairs and Technology Transfer: CAROLYN H. HARGRAVE
Vice-Pres. for Student and Academic Support Services and Chief of Staff: MIKE GARGANO
Chief Financial Officer and Asst Vice-Pres. for Budget and Finance: WENDY SIMONEAUX...

CONSTITUENT UNIVERSITIES

Louisiana State University

Baton Rouge, LA 70803
Telephone: (225) 578-6977
E-mail: admissions@lsu.edu
Internet: www.lsu.edu

Founded 1860
State control
Academic year: August to August

Chancellor: Dr MICHAEL V. MARTIN
Exec. Vice-Chancellor and Provost: Dr JOHN MAXWELL HAMILTON
Vice-Chancellor and Chief Financial Officer: ERIC MONDAY
Vice-Chancellor for Research and Economic Devt: Dr THOMAS R. KLEI
Vice-Chancellor for Strategic Initiatives: Dr ISIAH M. WARNER

Vice-Chancellor for Student Life and Enrolment: Dr KURT KEPPLER
Exec. Dir of Univ. College: PAUL IVEY
Dean for Students and Assoc. Vice-Chancellor: Dr K. C. WHITE
Dean for Univ. Libraries: JENNIFER CARGILL
Registrar: ROBERT K. DOOLOS

Library of 3,664,826 vols, 6,778,517 microforms, 12m. MSS, 25,900 audiovisual, 549,153 maps, 1,01,615 current periodicals, 3,68,604 ebooks, 97,105 eperiodicals
Number of teachers: 1,240 (1,178 full-time, 62 part-time)
Number of students: 28,770 (23,685 undergraduate, 5,085 graduate)

DEANS

College of Agriculture: Dr KENNETH KOONCE
College of Art and Design: KENNETH E. CARPENTER
College of Education: Prof. LAURA F. LINDSAY
College of Engineering: Dr RICHARD KOUBEK
College of Humanities and Social Sciences: Prof. Dr GAINES M. FOSTER
College of Music and Dramatic Arts: LAURENCE KAPTAIN
College of Science: Prof. Dr KEVIN R. CARMAN
E. J. Ourso College of Business Admin.: Prof. ELI JONES
Graduate School: Prof. GARY L. BYERLY
Honors College: Dr NANCY CLARK
Manship School of Mass Communication: Prof. JERRY CEPPOS
School of Coast and Environment: Prof. CHRIS D'ELIA
School of Library and Information Science: Dr BETH M. PASKOFF
School of Social Work: Dr DAPHNE S. CAIN
School of Veterinary Medicine: Dr PETER F. HAYNES

Louisiana State University, Alexandria

8100 Highway 71S, Alexandria, LA 71302-9121
Telephone: (318) 473-6417
E-mail: contact@lsua.edu
Internet: www.lsua.edu

Founded 1960, present status 2002
State control
Academic year: August to May

Offers bachelor degrees in biology, business administration, communication studies, criminal justice, elementary education, English, history, mathematics, nursing, psychology

Chancellor: Dr DAVID P. MANUEL
Provost and Vice-Chancellor for Academic and Student Affairs: Dr BARBARA S. HATFIELD
Vice-Chancellor for Finance and Admin. Services: DAVID WESSE
Registrar: TERESA SEYMOUR
Dir for the Library: Dr BONNIE HINES

Library of 166,700 vols, 19,000 microfilms
Number of teachers: 110 (full-time)
Number of students: 2,610

Louisiana State University, Shreveport

One University Pl., Shreveport, LA 71115
Telephone: (318) 797-5000
Internet: www.lsus.edu

Founded 1967
State control
Academic year: August to May (2 semesters)

Chancellor: Dr VINCENT J. MARSALA
Provost and Vice-Chancellor for Academic Affairs: Dr PAUL D. SISSON
Vice-Chancellor for Business Affairs: MICHAEL T. FERRELL
Vice-Chancellor for Student Affairs: Dr GLORIA W. RAINES
Vice-Chancellor for Univ. Devt: Dr JOHNETTE H. MAGNER

Registrar and Dean of Enrolment Services: MICKY P. DIEZ

Dean for Student Affairs: Dr RANDY R. BUTTERBAUGH

Dean for Library: Dr ALAN D. GABEHART

Library of 250,000 vols, 2,000 periodicals, 68,000 ebooks, 45,000 ejournals

Number of teachers: 140 (full-time)

Number of students: 4,560

Publications: *Bulletin of the Museum of Life Sciences* (2 a year), *LSUS Magazine*, *Spectra* (1 a year), *North Louisiana Historical Journal* (3 a year)

DEANS

College Arts and Sciences: Dr LAWRENCE E. ANDERSON

College of Business, Education and Human Devt: Dr DAVID GUSTAVSON

Continuing Education and Public Service: TISHA SAMHAM

Graduate Studies: (vacant)..

OTHER CONSTITUENT INSTITUTIONS

Louisiana State University Health Sciences Center, New Orleans

433 Bolivar St, New Orleans, LA 70112

Telephone: (504) 568-4808

E-mail: registrar@lsuhsc.edu

Internet: www.lsuhsc.edu

Founded 1931

State control

Academic year: August to August

Chancellor: Dr LARRY H. HOLLIER

Vice-Chancellor For Academic Affairs: Dr JOSEPH M. MOERSCHBAECHER, III

Vice-Chancellor For Admin. And Finance: RONALD E. SMITH

Registrar: W. BRYANT FAUST, IV

Dir for Libraries: DEBORAH SIBLEY

Library of 238,000 vols, 3,000 audiovisual titles, 200 print journals

Number of students: 2,500

DEANS

School of Allied Health Professions: Dr J. M. CAIRO

School of Dentistry: Prof. Dr HENRY A. GREMILLION

School of Graduate Studies: Prof. JOSEPH M. MOERSCHBAECHER, III

School of Medicine: Prof. Dr STEVE NELSON

School of Nursing: Prof. Dr DEMETRIUS J. PORCHE

School of Public Health: Dr ELIZABETH T. H. FONTHAM

Louisiana State University Health Sciences Center, Shreveport

1501 Kings Highway, POB 33932, Shreveport, LA 71103-3932

Telephone: (318) 675-5000

E-mail: shvreg@lsuhsc.edu

Internet: www.lsuhscshreveport.edu

Founded 1976 as Univ. hospital, present status 1978, current name adopted 1999

State control

Academic year: June to June

Chancellor: Dr ROBERT A. BARISH

Vice-Chancellor for Admin.: JOHN T. DAILEY

Registrar: KIMBERLY CARMEN

Library Dir: MARIANNE COMEGYS

Library of 190,000 vols, 1,017 ebooks

Number of students: 830

DEANS

School of Allied Health Professions: Dr JOSEPH MCCULLOCH

School of Graduate Studies: Dr SANDRA C. ROERIG

School of Medicine: Dr ANDREW L. CHESSON, JR

Paul M. Hebert Law Center

One E Campus Dr., Louisiana State Univ., Baton Rouge, LA 70803-1000

Telephone: (225) 578-8646

E-mail: info@law.lsu.edu

Internet: www.law.lsu.edu

Founded 1906 as LSU Law School, current name adopted 1979; attached to Louisiana State Univ.

State control

Academic year: August to July (3 semesters)

Programmes incl. civil and int. law, intellectual property law, environmental law

Chancellor: Prof. JACK M. WEISS

Vice-Chancellor: Prof. CHRISTOPHER PIETRUSZKIEWICZ

Vice-Chancellor for Academic Affairs: Prof. ERICK V. ANDERSON

Vice-Chancellor for Faculty Devt and Institutional Assessment: Prof. RAYMOND T. DIAMOND

Vice-Chancellor for Finance and Business Affairs: Prof. N. GREGORY SMITH

Dir for Admissions: JAKE T. HENRY, III

Dir for Student Affairs and Registrar: MICHELE FORBES

Dir for Library and Information Services: BETH WILLIAMS

Library of 850,000 vols, 160,000 vols of court records

Number of teachers: 40 (full-time)

Publications: *LSU Law*, *Louisiana Law Review*

LOYOLA UNIVERSITY NEW ORLEANS

6363 St Charles Ave, New Orleans, LA 70118

Telephone: (504) 865-3240

E-mail: admit@loyno.edu

Internet: www.loyno.edu

Founded 1904 as Loyola College, present status 1912, current name adopted 1996

Private control

Academic year: August to July

Pres.: Rev. Dr KEVIN W. WILDES

Provost and Vice-Pres. for Academic Affairs: Dr EDWARD J. KVET

Vice-Pres. for Enrolment Management: SALVADORE A. LIBERTO

Vice-Pres. for Finance and Admin.: JAY CALAMIA

Vice-Pres. for Institutional Advancement: WILLIAM BISHOP

Vice-Pres. for Student Affairs: Dr M. L. PETTY

Dir of Admissions: KEITH E. GRAMLING

Dean of Libraries: DEBORAH POOLE

Library of 371,000 vols, 36,000 journals, 27,000 ebooks

Number of teachers: 280

Number of students: 4,980 (2,963 undergraduates)

Publications: *JustSouth Quarterly* (4 a year), *Loyola Executive* (2 a year), *Loyola Law Review* (4 a year), *Loyola Lawyer* (2 a year), *Loyola Magazine* (4 a year), *New Orleans Review* (4 a year)

DEANS

College of Business: Dr WILLIAM B. LOCANDER

College of Humanities and Natural Sciences: Dr JO ANN MORAN CRUZ, JR

College of Law: Prof. Dr MARÍA PABÓN LÓPEZ

College of Music and Fine Arts: Prof. Dr DONALD BOOMGAARDEN

College of Social Sciences: Prof. Dr LUIS MIRÓN

NEW ORLEANS BAPTIST THEOLOGICAL SEMINARY

3939 Gentilly Blvd, New Orleans, LA 70126

Telephone: (504) 282-4455

E-mail: nobts@nobts.edu

Internet: www.nobts.edu

Founded 1917 as Baptist Bible Institute, present name 1946

Private control

Pres.: Dr CHARLES S. KELLEY, JR

Provost: Dr STEVE W. LEMKE

Vice-Pres. for Business Affairs: L. CLAY CORVIN

Dean of Admissions and Registrar: Dr PAUL GREGOIRE

Dean of Libraries: Dr JEFF GRIFFIN

Library of 290,000 vols

Number of teachers: 70

Number of students: 3,000 (1926 full-time)

DEANS

Graduate Studies: Prof. JERRY BARLOW

Leavell College: Prof. Dr L. THOMAS STRONG, III

NOTRE DAME SEMINARY

2901 S Carrolton Ave, New Orleans, LA 70118-4391

Telephone: (504) 866-7426

E-mail: registrar@nds.edu

Internet: www.nds.edu

Founded 1923

Private control

Academic year: August to May

Divinity, theological studies; hispanic ministry programme, human formation, pastoral dept, spiritual formation

Chancellor: ARCHBISHOP OF NEW ORLEANS

Pres. and Rector: Rev. JOSÉ I LAVASTIDA

Academic Dean: MINH PHAN

Registrar: CYNTHIA GARRITY

Dir of Library: THOMAS B. BENDER, IV

Library of 95,000 vols incl. 12,000 bound periodicals, 165 periodicals

Number of teachers: 30

Number of students: 150 (full-time)

OUR LADY OF HOLY CROSS COLLEGE

4123 Woodland Dr., New Orleans, LA 70131-7399

Telephone: (504) 394-7744

E-mail: admissions@olhcc.edu

Internet: www.olhcc.edu

Founded 1916 as Holy Cross Normal, current name adopted 1960

Private control

Academic year: August to July

Undergraduate programmes incl. allied health, biology, business admin., counselling and behavioural sciences, education, English, general studies, history, nursing, social sciences, theology; offers masters degree in arts, education, theology

Pres.: Dr RONALD M. AMBROSETTI

Provost: Prof. Dr PATRICIA PRECHTER

Vice-Pres. for Finance and Operations: Sis. MARJORIE A. HEBERT

Registrar: ROBERT MITCHELL

Dean of Admissions and Student Affairs: KATHARINE GONZALES

Dir of Library Services: Sis. HELEN FONTENOT

Library of 201,807 vols

Number of teachers: 150 (50 full-time, 100 part-time)

Number of students: 1,260 (997 undergraduate, 263 graduate)

OUR LADY OF LAKE COLLEGE

7434 Perkins Rd, Baton Rouge, LA 70808

Telephone: (225) 768-1700

E-mail: registrar@ololcollege.edu

Internet: www.ololcollege-edu.org

Founded 1923, present name and status 1995
Private control
Academic year: August to July (3 semesters)
Pres.: Prof. Dr SANDRA S. HARPER
Exec. Vice-Pres. for Academic and Student Affairs: Prof. Dr DAVID ENGLAND
Vice-Pres. for Finance and Admin.: HOA T. NGUYEN
Vice-Pres. for Planning and Institutional Effectiveness: TRACY W. MOLIDOR
Dean of Student Services: Dr PHYLLIS L. SIMPSON
Dir of Enrolment Management: REBECCA CANNON
Registrar: RYAN F. GARRITY
Dean of Library: TRAVIS DUDLEY
Library of 30,000 print and ebook vols, 300 periodicals, 1,700 audiovisual items
Number of teachers: 80 (full-time)
Number of students: 1,860

DEANS

School of Arts, Sciences and Health Professions: Dr KATHERINE H. KRIEG
School of Nursing: Dr JENNIFER BECK

SAINT JOSEPH SEMINARY COLLEGE

75376 River Rd, St Benedict, LA 70457
Telephone: (985) 867-2299
E-mail: acsec@sjasc.edu
Internet: www.sjasc.edu
Private control
Programmes offered incl. Bachelors in philosophy and liberal arts, philosophy and theological studies
Pres.-Rector: Rev. GREGORY M. BOQUET
Dean of Academic Affairs: Dr JUDE LUPINETTI
Dean of Students: Rev. JUDE ISRAEL
Registrar: CASEY EDLER
Library Dir: BONNIE BESS WOOD
Library of 50,000 vols, 10,000 bound serials, 137 current serial titles, 1,500 audiovisual materials
Number of teachers: 30
Number of students: 100

SOUTHERN UNIVERSITY SYSTEM

J. S. Clark Admin. Bldg, Fourth Fl., Baton Rouge, LA 70813
Telephone: (225) 771-4500
Internet: www.sus.edu
Founded 1880
State control
Pres.: Dr RONALD MASON, JR
Vice-Pres. for Academic and Student Affairs: KASSIE FREEMAN
Vice-Pres. for Finance and Business Affairs: KEVIN APPLETON
Vice-Pres. for Information and Technology Management: TONY MOORE
Vice-Pres. for Institutional Advancement: ERNIE TROY HUGHES...

CONSTITUENT INSTITUTIONS

Southern University and A & M College

POB 9374, Baton Rouge, LA 70813
Telephone: (225) 771-4500
Internet: web.subr.edu
Founded 1880
State control
Academic year: August to May (2 semesters)
Chancellor (vacant)
Exec. Vice-Chancellor and Interim Provost: Dr JANET RAMI
Vice-Chancellor for Finance and Admin.: FLANDUS MCCLINTON, JR
Vice-Chancellor for Research and Strategic Initiatives: Dr MICHAEL STUBBLEFIELD
Vice-Chancellor for Student Affairs: Dr BRANDON DUMAS (acting)

Registrar: D'ANDREA LEE
Dean of Libraries: Prof. EMMA BRADFORD PERRY
Library of 112,858 vols, 744,000 microforms, 34,380 audiovisual materials
Number of teachers: 350
Number of students: 7,630
Publication: *The Southern Digest*

DEANS

College of Agricultural, Family and Consumer Sciences: Dr DEWITT JONES
College of Arts and Humanities: Dr JOYCE O'ROURKE
College of Business: Dr DONALD ANDREWS
College of Education: Dr VERJANIS ANDREWS PEOPLES
College of Engineering: Dr HABIB P. MOHAMADIAN
College of Sciences: Dr ROBERT H. MILLER, JR
Graduate School: Dr MWALIMU SHUJAA
Honors College: Dr ELLA KELLEY
Nelson Mandela School of Public Policy and Urban Affairs: Dr WILLIAM ARP, III
School of Architecture: LONNIE WILKINSON
School of Nursing: Dr CHERYL TAYLOR

Southern University at New Orleans

6400 Press Dr., New Orleans, LA 70126
Telephone: (504) 286-5000
Internet: www.suno.edu
Founded 1956
State control
Academic year: August to May (2 semesters)
Chancellor: Dr VICTOR UKPOLO
Vice-Chancellor for Academic Affairs: Dr DAVID ADEGBOYE
Vice-Chancellor for Admin. and Finance: WOODIE WHITE
Vice-Chancellor for Enrolment Services and Student Affairs: Dr DONNA GRANT
Vice-Chancellor for Univ. Advancement: GLORIA BARTLEY MOULTRIE
Registrar: GILDA DAVIS
Library Dir: SHATIQUA MOSBY-WILSON
Library of 9,000 ebooks
Number of students: 3,170
Publication: *The Journal of Urban Education*

DEANS

College of Arts and Sciences: Dr HENRY EFESOA-MOKOSSO
College of Business and Public Administration: Dr IGWE UDEH
College of Education and Human Development: Dr LOUISE S. KALTENBAUGH
School of Graduate Studies: Dr IRA NEIGHBORS
School of Social Work: Dr BEVERLY C. FAVRÉ

TULANE UNIVERSITY

6823 St Charles Ave, New Orleans, LA 70118
Telephone: (504) 865-8000
E-mail: pr@tulane.edu
Internet: tulane.edu
Founded 1834 as Medical College of Louisiana; present name and status 1884
Private control
Academic year: August to May (2 semesters)
Pres.: SCOTT S. COWEN
Provost and Sr Vice-Pres. for Academic Affairs: MICHAEL A. BERNSTEIN
Exec. Vice-Pres. for Univ. Relations and Devt: YVETTE M. JONES
Sr Vice-Pres.: BENJAMIN P. SACHS
Sr Vice-Pres. for Operations and Chief Financial Officer: ANTHONY P. LORINO
Chief of Staff and Vice-Pres.: ANNE P. BAÑOS
Vice-Pres. for Enrolment Management and Univ. Registrar: EARL RETIF
Vice-Pres. for Student Affairs and Dean of Students: MICHAEL H. HOGG

Gen. Counsel: VICTORIA D. JOHNSON
Dean of Libraries and Academic Information Resources: LANCE D. QUERY
Library: see under Libraries and Archives
Number of teachers: 1,140
Number of students: 13,490 (8,427 undergraduate)

DEANS

A. B. Freeman School of Business: Prof. Dr IRA SOLOMON
Graduate School: MICHAEL HERMAN
Law School: DAVID D. MEYER
Newcomb-Tulane College: JAMES MACLAREN
School of Architecture: KENNETH SCHWARTZ
School of Continuing Studies and Tulane Summer School: Dr RICHARD A. MARKSBURY
School of Liberal Arts: Prof. Dr CAROLE R. HABER
School of Medicine: Prof. BENJAMIN P. SACHS
School of Public Health and Tropical Medicine: Prof. Dr PIERRE M. BUEKENS
School of Science and Engineering: Prof. Dr NICHOLAS J. ALTIERO
School of Social Work: Dr RONALD E. MARKS

UNIVERSITY OF LOUISIANA SYSTEM

1201 N Third St, Suite 7-300, Baton Rouge, LA 70802
Telephone: (225) 342-6950
E-mail: rmoffett@uls.state.la.us
Internet: www.ulsystem.net
Founded 1974 as Board of Trustees for State Colleges and Universities, current name adopted 1995
Pres.: Dr SANDRA K. WOODLEY
Provost and Exec. Vice-Pres.: Dr KARLA HUGHES
Provost and Vice-Pres. for Academic and Student Affairs: Dr BRAD O'HARA
Vice-Pres. for Admin. and Gen. Counsel: DIANNE IRVINE
Vice-Pres. for Business and Finance: ROBBIE ROBINSON
Vice-Pres. for Research and Performance Assessment: Dr BEATRICE BALDWIN
Number of students: 83,000 at 8 univs...

CONSTITUENT INSTITUTIONS

Grambling State University

403 Main St, Grambling, LA 71245
Telephone: (318) 247-3811
E-mail: admissions@gram.edu
Internet: www.gram.edu
Founded 1901
State control
Academic year: August to May
Pres.: Dr FRANK G. POGUE
Provost and Vice-Pres. for Academic Affairs: Dr CONNIE WALTON
Vice-Pres. of Finance: LEON SANDERS
Vice-Pres. for Institutional Advancement: Dr KENOYE EKE
Registrar: PATRICIA J. HUTCHERSON
Dir for Library Services: FELIX E. UNAEZE (acting)
Library of 294,000 vols
Number of teachers: 240
Number of students: 4,990

DEANS

College of Arts and Sciences: Dr EVELYN WYNN
College of Business: Dr CARL N. WRIGHT
College of Education: Dr WYNETTA Y. LEE
College of Professional Studies: Dr RAMA M. TUNUGUNTLA
School of Graduate Studies and Research: Dr JANET GUYDEN

Louisiana Tech University

Ruston, LA 71272

Telephone: (318) 257-0211
E-mail: iso@latech.edu
Internet: www.latech.edu

Founded 1894 as Louisiana Industrial Institute and College, present name and status 1970

State control
Academic year: June to May (2 semesters)

Pres.: Dr DANIEL D. RENEAU
Exec. Vice-Pres.: Dr TERRY M. MCCONATHY
Vice-Pres. for Academic Affairs: Dr KENNETH W. REA
Vice-Pres. for Admin. Affairs: Dr KENNETH W. REA
Vice-Pres. for Finance and Admin.: JOSEPH R. THOMAS, JR
Vice-Pres. for Research and Devt: Dr LESLIE K. GUICE
Vice-Pres. for Student Affairs: Dr JAMES M. KING
Vice-Pres. for Univ. Advancement: CORRE STEGALL
Dean of Enrolment Management: PAMELA R. FORD
Registrar: ROBERT D. VENTO
Dean of Library Services: MICHAEL DiCARLO

Library of 3,715,805 vols incl. 462,696 bound vols, 62,931 ebooks, 1,933 periodical titles, 578,081 microforms, 2,269,644 govt documents, 396 audiovisual materials, 40,124 maps
Number of teachers: 370
Number of students: 11,580

DEANS

College of Applied and Natural Sciences: Prof. Dr JAMES D. LIBERATOS
College of Business: Dr JAMES R. LUMPKIN
College of Education: Dr DAVID GULLATT
College of Engineering and Science: Prof. Dr STAN A. NAPPER, Jr
College of Liberal Arts: Dr DONALD P. KACZVINSKY
Graduate School and Univ. Research: Dr TERRY M. MCCONATHY

McNeese State University

4205 Ryan St, Lake Charles, LA 70609

Telephone: (337) 475-5000
E-mail: amillet@mcneese.edu
Internet: www.mcneese.edu

Founded 1939 as Lake Charles Jr College, present name and status 1970

State control
Academic year: August to May

Pres.: Dr PHILLIP C. WILLIAMS
Provost and Vice-Pres. for Academic and Student Affairs: Dr JEANNE DABOVAL
Vice-Pres. for Admin. and Student Affairs: Dr KALIL LEYOUB
Vice-Pres. for Business Affairs: Dr EDDIE P. MECHE
Vice-Pres. for Univ. Advancement: RICHARD REID
Dean of Enrolment Management: STEPHANIE TARVER
Dean of Student Services: Dr TOBY W. OSBURN
Dir of Admissions: KARA SMITH
Registrar: APRIL MILLET
Library Dir: DEBBIE JOHNSON-HOUSTON

Library of 400,000 vols
Number of teachers: 320 (full-time)
Number of students: 8,940

Publications: *The Log* (1 a year), *The McNeese Arena* (1 a year), *The McNeese Review* (1 a year), *The McNeese Update* (3 a year)

DEANS

Burton College of Education: Dr WAYNE FETTER
College of Business: Dr MITCHELL ADRIAN
College of Engineering and Engineering Technology: Dr NIKOS KIRITSIS
College of Liberal Arts: Dr RAY MILES
College of Nursing: Dr PEGGY L. WOLFE
College of Science: Dr GEORGE MEAD, JR
William J. Doré, Sr. School of Graduate Studies: Dr GEORGE MEAD

Nicholls State University

Thibodaux, LA 70310

Telephone: (985) 446-8111
E-mail: info@nicholls.edu
Internet: www.nicholls.edu

Founded 1948 as Francis T. Nicholls Jr College of Louisiana State Univ., present name and status 1970

State control
Academic year: January to December (2 semesters)

Pres.: Dr BRUCE T. MURPHY
Exec. Vice-Pres.: LAWRENCE HOWELL
Vice-Pres. for Academic Affairs: Dr ALLAYNE BARRILLEAUX
Vice-Pres. for Student Affairs and Enrolment Services: Dr EUGENE A. DIAL, JR
Dir for Graduate Studies: Dr DESLEY PLAISANCE
Registrar: KELLY J. RODRIGUE
Library Dir: Dr ROBERT J. BREMER

Library of 450,000 vols and periodicals, 350,000 catalogued fed. and state documents, 40,000 ebooks, 380,000 microforms
Number of teachers: 260 (full-time)
Number of students: 6,540

DEANS

College of Arts and Sciences: Dr JOHN P. DOUCET
College of Business Administration: Dr SHAWN MAULDIN
College of Education: Dr LESLIE JONES
College of Nursing and Allied Health: Dr SUE WESTBROOK
Univ. College and John Folse Culinary Institute: Dr ALBERT DAVIS

Northwestern State University of Louisiana

Natchitoches, LA 71497-0002

Telephone: (318) 357-6011
E-mail: academicservices@nsula.edu
Internet: www.nsula.edu

Founded 1884 as state normal school, present name and status 1970

State control
Academic year: August to August

Pres.: Dr RANDALL J. WEBB
Vice-Pres. for Academic and Student Affairs and Acting Provost: Dr LISA ABNEY
Vice-Pres. for Business Affairs and Controller: CARL JONES
Vice-Pres. for External Affairs: JERRY D. PIERCE
Vice-Pres. for Technology, Research and Economic Devt: Dr DARLENE WILLIAMS
Vice-Pres. for Univ. Affairs: Dr MARCUS JONES
Dean for Students and Dir for Student Services: Dr FRANCES CONINE
Registrar: LILLIE FRAZIER BELL
Dir of Libraries: ABBIE LANDRY

Library of 322,270 vols, incl. books and serial vols, 295,166 print material and 27,104 ebooks, 458,000 govt documents, 5,500 audiovisual items, 50,000 journals, newspapers and magazines
Number of teachers: 280 (full-time)
Number of students: 9,190

Publication: *Southern Studies* (4 a year)

DEANS

College of Arts, Letters, Graduate Studies and Research and Graduate School: Dr STEVE HORTON
College of Business: Dr MARGARET KILCOYNE
College of Education and Human Development: Dr VICKIE S. GENTRY
College of Nursing and Allied Health: Dr NORANN Y. PLANCHOCK
College of Science, Technology and Business: Dr AUSTIN L. TEMPLE, JR

Southeastern Louisiana University

SLU 10784, Hammond, LA 70402

Telephone: (985) 549-2000
E-mail: admissions@selu.edu
Internet: www.selu.edu

Founded 1925 as Hammond Jr College, present status 1970

State control
Academic year: June to May

Pres.: Dr JOHN L. CRAIN
Provost and Vice-Pres. for Academic Affairs: Dr TAMMY BOURG
Vice-Pres. for Admin. and Finance: SAM DOMIANO
Vice-Pres. for Student Affairs: Dr MARVIN L. YATES
Vice-Pres. for Univ. Advancement: WENDY J. LAUDERDALE
Library Dir: ERIC JOHNSON
Chief Information Officer: Dr MIKE ASOODEH

Library of 377,256 vols, 3,561 serial subscriptions, 816,340 microforms, 44,492 audiovisual materials, 73,440 ebooks, 421,933 govt documents
Number of teachers: 630 (500 full-time, 130 part-time)
Number of students: 14,950 (10,360 full-time, 4,590 part-time)

Publications: *Economic Reporter* (4 a year), *Louisiana Literature* (2 a year), *Nineteenth Century Studies* (1 a year), *The Pick* (2 a year)

DEANS

College of Arts, Humanities and Social Sciences: Dr KAREN FONTENOT
College of Business: Dr TONI PHILLIPS
College of Education: Dr SHIRLEY JACOB
College of Nursing and Health Studies: Dr ANN K. CARRUTH
College of Science and Technology: Dr DANIEL MCCARTHY

PROFESSORS

ADAMS, N., Educational Leadership and Technology
ALESSI, H., Health and Human Sciences
ALKADI, G., Computer Science and Industrial Technology
BALLARD, M., Health and Human Sciences
BEAUBOUEF, T., Computer Science and Industrial Technology
BEDELL, J., English
BELL, J., History and Political Science
BLACKWOOD, C., Fine and Performing Arts
BOND, E., Nursing
BONNETTE, J., Computer Science and Industrial Technology
BOSTIC, M., Computer Science and Industrial Technology
BOULAHANIS, J., Sociology and Criminal Justice
BRAUN, R., Accounting and Finance
BUDDEN, M., Marketing and Supply Chain Management
BURNS, J., Languages and Communication
CANNON, G., Mathematics
CAPPEL, S., Management
CARRUTH, P., Accounting and Finance
CHILDERS, G., Biology
COPE, R., Marketing and Supply Chain Management

CROTHER, B., Biology
DeALWIS, T., Mathematics
DeVANEY, T., Educational Leadership and Technology
DOUGHTY, M., Chemistry and Physics
DRANGUET, C., History and Political Science
DUGGAL, R., Accounting and Finance
ECHOLS, C., Teaching and Learning
FAUST, J., English
FELLOM, M., Fine and Performing Arts
FICK, T., English
FORREST, B., History and Political Science
FREDELL, J., English
GERMAN, H., English
GOLD, E., English
GONZALEZ-PEREZ, M., History and Political Science
GUTTHY, A., Languages and Communication
HEMBERGER, G., Fine and Performing Arts
HOLLANDER, D., Kinesiology and Heath Studies
HSING, Y., Management
JAMAL, A., Marketing and Supply Chain Management
JOHANSEN, D., Fine and Performing Arts
JOHNSON, D., Health and Human Sciences
JONES, M., Marketing and Supply Chain Management
KABZA, L., Mathematics
KEARNEY, M., English
KEOWN, G., Fine and Performing Arts
KING, P., Management
KOUTSOUGERAS, C., Computer Science and Industrial Technology
KRAEMER, R., Kinesiology and Health Studies
LANE, K., Educational Leadership and Technology
LAVER, H., History and Political Science
LI, S., Mathematics
LONGMAN, D., General Studies
LOUTH, R., English
McKAY, S., Marketing and Supply Chain Management
MEEKER, B., Nursing
MERINO, D., Mathematics
MIRANDO, J., Languages and Communication
MUNCHAUSEN, L., Chemistry and Physics
NAQUIN, M., Kinesiology and Health Studies
NELSON, E., Biology
NORTON, W., Biology
PEDERSEN, K., Mathematics
PHILLIPS, C., Management
PRYOR, S., Nursing
REYES, E., Mathematics
RIEDEL, M., Sociology and Criminal Justice
ROLLING, P., Health and Human Sciences
ROSSANO, M., Psychology
RUSHING, S., Fine and Performing Arts
SCHEPKER, S., Fine and Performing Arts
SCHULDT, B., Marketing and Supply Chain Management
SEVER, D., Biology
SHAFFER, G., Biology
SIPIORSKI, D., Fine and Performing Arts
STIEGLER, L., Health and Human Sciences
SUBER, S., Fine and Performing Arts
SUGHRUE, J., Educational Leadership and Technology
SYNOVITZ, L., Kinesiology and Health Studies
TITARD, P., Accounting and Finance
TRAVER, A., History and Political Science
TROWBRIDGE, J., Teaching and Learning
VOLDMAN, Y., Fine and Performing Arts
WADLINGTON, E., Teaching and Learning
WAIKAR, A., Marketing and Supply Chain Management
WHITE, M., Biology
WOOD, R., Kinesiology and Heath Studies
WYLD, D., Management
YEARGAIN, J., Accounting and Finance
YOSHIDA, S., Chemistry and Physics
ZHANG, W., Computer Science and Industrial Technology

University of Louisiana at Lafayette

104 University Circle, Lafayette, LA 70504-1732

Telephone: (337) 482-1000
E-mail: enroll@louisiana.edu
Internet: www.louisiana.edu

Founded 1898 as Southwestern Louisiana Industrial Institute, present status 1960, current name adopted 1999
State control
Academic year: June to May
Pres.: Dr E. JOSEPH SAVOIE
Provost and Vice-Pres. for Academic affairs: Dr STEVE LANDRY
Vice-Pres. for Admin. and Finance: JERRY L. LeBLANC
Vice-Pres. for Enrolment Management and Registrar: Dr DeWAYNE BOWIE
Vice-Pres. for Research and Graduate Studies: Dr ROBERT E. TWILLEY
Vice-Pres. for Student Affairs: RAYMOND BLANCO
Vice-Pres. for Univ. Advancement: KENNETH ARDOIN
Dean of Students: EDWARD PRATT
Dir for Library: Dr CHARLES TRICHE
Library: 1m. vols, 2m. microforms, 6,000 serial titles
Number of teachers: 700 (600 full-time, 100 part-time)
Number of students: 16,890 (15,324 undergraduates, 1,566 graduates)
Publications: *Attakapas Gazette* (4 a year), *Louisiana History* (4 a year), *Southwestern Review* (1 a year)

DEANS

B. I. Moody III College of Business Administration: Dr JOBY JOHN (acting)
College of Education: Dr GERALD CARLSON
College of Engineering: Dr MARK E. ZAPPI
College of General Studies: Dr PHEBE A. HAYES
College of Liberal Arts: Dr DAVID BARRY
College of the Arts: H. GORDON BROOKS, II
College of Nursing and Allied Health Professions: Dr GAIL POIRRIER
Graduate School: Dr DAVID BREAUX
Ray P. Authement College of Sciences: Dr BRADD CLARK

University of Louisiana at Monroe

700 University Ave, Monroe, LA 71209

Telephone: (318) 342-1000
E-mail: recruit@ulm.edu
Internet: www.ulm.edu

Founded 1931 as Ouachita Parish Jr College, present status 1970, current name adopted 1999
State control
Academic year: May to June
Pres.: Dr NICK J. BRUNO
Exec. Vice-Pres.: Dr STEPHEN RICHTERS
Vice-Pres. for Academic Affairs: Dr ERIC PANI
Vice-Pres. for Business Affairs: DAVE NICKLAS
Vice-Pres. for Student Affairs: Dr WAYNE BRUMFIELD
Vice-Pres. for Univ. Advancement: Dr DON SKELTON
Dir of Admissions: JENNIFER MALONE
Registrar: ANTHONY MALTA
Dean of the Library: DONALD R. SMITH
Library of 633,818 vols, incl. 193,935 govt documents, 2,939 current periodicals, 555,603 microform vols
Number of teachers: 520
Number of students: 8,600

DEANS

College of Arts and Sciences: Dr MICHAEL CAMILLE

College of Business Administration: Dr RONALD BERRY
College of Education and Human Development: Dr SANDRA M. LEMOINE
College of Health Sciences: Dr DENNY RYMAN
College of Pharmacy: Dr BENNY L. BLAYLOCK

University of New Orleans

2000 Lakeshore Dr., New Orleans, LA 70148

Telephone: (504) 280-6000
E-mail: admissions@uno.edu
Internet: www.uno.edu

Founded 1958 as Louisiana State Univ. in New Orleans, current name adopted 1974
State control
Academic year: August to May (2 semesters)
Pres.: PETER J. FOS
Provost and Vice-Chancellor for Academic and Student Affairs: Dr LOUIS V. PARADISE
Vice-Chancellor for Campus Services (vacant)
Vice-Chancellor for External Affairs: RACHEL A. KINCAID
Vice-Chancellor for Financial Services, Comptroller and Chief Financial Officer: LINDA K. ROBISON
Vice-Chancellor for Governmental and Community Affairs: RACHEL A. KINCAID
Vice-Chancellor for Research and Sponsored Programs: Dr SCOTT WHITTENBURG
Univ. Registrar: ALEX ARCENEAUX
Dir for Admissions: ANDY J. BENOIT
Dean of Library Services: Dr SHARON MADER
Library of 800,000 vols, 3,000 current periodicals, 2m. microforms, 91,000 print and electronic journals, 139,000 ebooks
Number of teachers: 600
Number of students: 11,280 (8,347 undergraduate, 2,933 graduate)
Publications: *Metropolitan Report* (4 a year), *New Orleans Real Estate Market Survey* (2 a year), *Review of Business and Economics Research* (2 a year), *Statistical Abstract of Louisiana* (3 a year), *UNO Magazine* (4 a year)

DEANS

College of Business Admininstration: Dr JOHN A. WILLIAMS
College of Education and Human Development: Dr APRIL WHATLEY BEDFORD, JR
College of Engineering: Dr NORMA JEAN MATTEI
College of Liberal Arts: Prof. Dr SUSAN KRANTZ
College of Sciences: Dr STEVEN G. JOHNSON
Graduate School: Dr SCOTT WHITTENBURG

XAVIER UNIVERSITY OF LOUISIANA

One Drexel Dr., New Orleans, LA 70125

Telephone: (504) 486-7411
E-mail: apply@xula.edu
Internet: www.xula.edu

Founded 1925
Private control
Academic year: August to May (2 semesters)
Pres.: Dr NORMAN C. FRANCIS
Sr Vice-Pres. for Academic Affairs: Dr LOREN JAMES BLANCHARD
Sr Vice-Pres. for Admin.: CALVIN S. TREGRE
Vice-Pres. for Fiscal Affairs: EDWARD J. PHILLIPS
Vice-Pres. for Institutional Advancement: Dr KENNETH ANTHONY ST CHARLES
Vice-Pres. for Student Services: JOSEPH K. BYRD
Dean of Admissions: WINSTON D. BROWN
Registrar: AVIS M. STUARD
Librarian: ROBERT E. SKINNER
Library of 200,000 vols, 30,000 ebooks, 1,900 periodicals and newspapers 721,000 microforms

Number of teachers: 240 (full-time)
Number of students: 3,400
Publication: *Xavier Gold* (1 a year)

DEANS

College of Arts and Sciences: Dr ANIL KUKREJA
College of Pharmacy: Dr KATHLEEN B. KENNEDY
Graduate School: Dr ALVIN J. RICHARD

MAINE

BANGOR THEOLOGICAL SEMINARY

Two College Circle, POB 411, Bangor, ME 04402-0411
Telephone: (207) 942-6781
E-mail: ajaehnig@bts.edu
Internet: www.bts.edu
Founded 1814
Private control
Academic year: September to May
Campus in Portland; graduate programmes incl. MA, divinity, ministry
Pres.: Rev. Dr ROBERT S. GROVE-MARKWOOD
Vice-Pres. for Advancement: REBECCA WRIGHT
Academic Dean: STEVEN LEWIS
Dir of Admissions: ADREA JAEHNIG
Registrar: DANIELLE R. LAVINE
Library Dir: LORRAINE McQUARRIE
Library of 124,000 vols
Number of teachers: 50
Number of students: 160 (full-time)

BATES COLLEGE

Two Andrews Rd, Lewiston, ME 04240-6028
Telephone: (207) 786-6255
E-mail: admission@bates.edu
Internet: www.bates.edu
Founded 1855
Private control
Academic year: September to May (2 semesters)
Major academic programmes incl. anthropology, art and visual culture, biology, chemistry, dance, economics, English, French, geology, German, history, mathematics, music, philosophy, physics, politics, psychology, religious studies, rhetoric, Russian, sociology, Spanish, theatre
Pres.: NANCY J. CABLE
Vice-Pres. for Academic Affairs and Dean of Faculty: Dr PAMELA J. BAKER
Vice-Pres. for College Advancement: KELLY K. KERNER
Vice-Pres. and Dean for Enrolment and External Affairs: Dr NANCY J. CABLE
Vice-Pres. for Finance and Admin. and Treas.: TERRY J. BECKMANN
Vice-Pres. for Information and Library Services and Librarian: Dr EUGENE LEE WIEMERS
Dean for Admissions: (vacant)
Dean for Students: TEDD R. GOUNDIE
Registrar: MARY K. MESERVE
Library of 610,000 vols, 184,000 ebooks, 52,500 ejournals
Number of teachers: 210
Number of students: 1,730

BOWDOIN COLLEGE

3900 College Station, Brunswick, ME 04011
Telephone: (207) 725-3000
E-mail: admissions@bowdoin.edu
Internet: www.bowdoin.edu
Founded 1794
Private control
Academic year: August to July

Liberal arts college; academic programmes incl. anthropology, arts, computer science, mathematics, economics, education, French, German, govt and legal studies, Italian, neuroscience, Russian, science, Spanish, theatre, visual arts
Pres.: BARRY MILLS
Sr Vice-Pres. for Finance and Admin. and Treas.: S. CATHERINE LONGLEY
Sr Vice-Pres. for Planning and Devt and Sec.: WILLIAM A. TORREY
Vice-Pres. for Institutional Planning and Assessment: REBECCA BRODIGAN
Chief Information Officer: MITCHEL W. DAVIS
Dean for Academic Affairs: CRISTLE COLLINS JUDD
Dean of Admissions and Financial Aid: SCOTT A. MEIKLEJOHN
Dean of Student Affairs: TIMOTHY W. FOSTER
Registrar: JAN BRACKETT
Librarian: SHERRIE BERGMAN
Library of 1,034,168 vols, 29,864 audiovisual items, 915 microform, periodical titles
Number of teachers: 220
Number of students: 1,780
Publications: *Bowdoin Magazine* (4 a year), *Bowdoin Forum* (int. affairs, 1 a year)

COLBY COLLEGE

4000 Mayflower Hill, Waterville, ME 04901-8840
Telephone: (207) 859-4000
E-mail: admissions@colby.edu
Internet: www.colby.edu
Founded 1813 as Maine Literary and Theological Instn, present name 1896
Private control
Academic year: September to May
Languages of instruction: French, Spanish, Italian
Depts of administration, humanities, interdisciplinary studies, natural sciences, social sciences
Pres.: Dr WILLIAM D. ADAMS
Vice-Pres. for Academic Affairs and Dean of Faculty: LORI G. KLETZER
Vice-Pres. for Admin. and Treas.: DOUGLAS C. TERP
Vice-Pres. and Dean of Admissions and Financial Aid: TERESA E. COWDRY
Vice-Pres. for College Relations: MICHAEL D. KISER
Vice-Pres. for Devt and Alumni Relations: DEBORAH DUTTON COX
Vice-Pres. of Student Affairs and Dean of Students: JAMES S. TERHUNE
Registrar: ELIZABETH N. SCHILLER
Dir for Libraries: CLEMENT P. GUTHRO
Library of 489,436 vols, 37,839 serial titles, 24,768 audiovisual items, 61,000 microforms 750,663 ebooks
Number of teachers: 200 (162 full-time, 38 part-time)
Number of students: 1,815
Publications: *Colby* (4 a year), *Colby Library Quarterly*, *Colby Perspective*

COLLEGE OF THE ATLANTIC

105 Eden St, Bar Harbor, ME 04609
Telephone: (207) 288-5015
E-mail: inquiry@coa.edu
Internet: www.coa.edu
Founded 1969
Private control
Academic year: September to June
Academic areas incl. arts and design, environmental sciences, human studies
Pres.: DAVID HALES
Academic Dean: KEN HILL
Dean of Admission: SARAH BAKER
Dean of Devt: LYNN BOULGER

Admin. Dean: ANDREW GRIFFITHS
Registrar: JUDITH ALLEN
Library Dir: JANE HULTBERG
Library of 36,000 vols, 475 periodicals
Number of teachers: 40 (27 full-time, 13 part-time)
Number of students: 360
Publication: *COA* (2 a year)

HUSSON UNIVERSITY

1 College Circle, Bangor, ME 04401
Telephone: (207) 941-7100
E-mail: admit@husson.edu
Internet: www.husson.edu
Founded 1898, present name and status 2008
Private control
Academic year: September to May
Pres. and CEO: Dr ROBERT A. CLARK
Provost and Chief Academic Officer: LYNNE COY-OGAN
Exec. Vice-Pres.: BEN HASKELL
Vice-Pres. for Admin. and Finance and Chief Financial Officer: CRAIG HADLEY
Vice-Pres. for Admin.: JOHN RUBINO
Vice-Pres. for Advancement: THOMAS MARTZ
Assoc. Provost of Enrolment Management: JONATHAN HENRY
Dir of Admissions: CARLENA BEAN
Dean of Students: SHARON WILSON-BARKER
Registrar: NANCY FENDERS
Head Librarian: AMY AVERRE
Number of teachers: 90
Number of students: 2,600
Publications: *Crosscut* (1 a year), *The Ledger*

DEANS

College of Business: RONALD NYKIEL
College of Health and Education: BARBARA HIGGINS
New England School of Communications: BEN HASKELL
School of Graduate Studies: MICHAEL W. MULLANE
School of Pharmacy: RODNEY LARSON
School of Science and Humanities: FRANCIS A. HUBBARD

MAINE COLLEGE OF ART

522 Congress St, Portland, ME 04101
Telephone: (207) 775-3052
E-mail: info@meca.edu
Internet: www.meca.edu
Founded 1882 as part of Portland Soc. of Art, present status 1982, current name adopted 1992
Private control
Academic year: August to May
Academic programmes incl. art history, ceramics, new media, foundation, painting, photography, graphic design, printmaking, illustration, public engagement, liberal arts, sculpture, metalsmithing and jewellery, woodworking and furniture design
Pres.: DONALD TUSKI
Exec. Vice-Pres.: BETH ELICKER
Vice-Pres. for Academic Affairs and Dean of College: IAN ANDERSON
Vice-Pres. for Advancement and College Relations: TIMOTHY W. KANE
Vice-Pres. for Enrolment: RICK LONGO
Registrar: ANNE DENNISON
Dir of Admissions: GRACE HOPKINS-LISLE
Library Dir: MOIRA STEVEN
Library of 33,000 vols, 100 periodicals, 52,000 slides
Number of teachers: 50
Number of students: 380 (350 undergraduate, 30 graduate)

MAINE MARITIME ACADEMY

Castine, ME 04420-5000
Telephone: (207) 326-2206
E-mail: admissions@mma.edu
Internet: www.mainemaritime.edu

Founded 1941
State control
Academic year: September to April

Depts of arts and sciences, engineering, physical education; Corning School of Ocean Studies; Loeb-Sullivan School of Int. Business and Logistics

Pres.: Dr WILLIAM J. BRENNAN
Vice-Pres. for Academic Affairs and Academic Dean: Dr JOHN BARLOW
Vice-Pres. for Enrolment Management: JEFF LOUSTAUNAU
Vice-Pres. for Finance, Admin. and Govt Affairs: RICHARD R. ERICSON
Chief Advancement Officer: ELEANOR WILLMANN
Dean of Student Services: DEIDRA DAVIS
Dir of Admissions: JEFFREY C. WRIGHT
Registrar: CHRISTINA STEPHENS
Dir of Library Services: BRENT HALL

Library of 99,614 vols, 326 periodicals, 5,093 maps
Number of teachers: 120
Number of students: 970

SAINT JOSEPH'S COLLEGE OF MAINE

278 Whites Bridge Rd, Standish, ME 04084-5263
Telephone: (855) 752-4636
E-mail: info@sjcme.edu
Internet: www.sjcme.edu

Founded 1912
Private control
Academic year: June to May (2 semesters)

Pres.: Dr JAMES DLUGOS
Vice-Pres. and Chief Learning Officer: Dr MICHAEL PARDALES
Vice-Pres. and Chief Financial Officer: YVONNE BERRY
Vice-Pres. for Enrolment: KATHLEEN DAVIS
Dean for Admissions: KATHLEEN DAVIS
Dean for Online College: LYNNE ROBINSON
Dean for Student Life: REIS HAGERMAN
Dir for Institutional Research: Dr PAUL WOODWARD
Dir for Library Services: SHELLY DAVIS

Library: over 100,000 vols, 120,000 ebooks, 50,000 ejournals
Number of teachers: 295
Number of students: 4,066

THOMAS COLLEGE

180 West River Rd, Waterville, ME 04901-5097
Telephone: (207) 859-1111
E-mail: info@thomas.edu
Internet: www.thomas.edu

Founded 1894 as Keist Business College, current name adopted 1962, present status 1963
Private control
Academic year: September to May

Academic programmes incl. business and management, communications, criminal justice, finance, forensic psychology

Pres.: Dr GEORGE R. SPANN
Provost and Vice-Pres. for Academic Affairs: Prof. Dr THOMAS EDWARDS
Sr Vice-Pres. and Chief Financial Officer: BETH B. GIBBS
Vice-Pres. for Advancement: ROBERT MOORE
Vice-Pres. for Enrolment Management: ROBERT CALLAHAN

Vice-Pres. for Information Services: CHRISTOPHER H. RHODA
Vice-Pres. for Student Affairs: LISA DESAUTELS-POLIQUIN
Dean of Institutional Advancement: FRAN DAY
Registrar: MEGHAN REITCHEL
Library Dir: LISA AURIEMMA

Library of 30,000 vols
Number of students: 594
Publication: Thomas Magazine

UNITY COLLEGE

90 Quaker Hill Rd, Unity, ME 04988
Telephone: (207) 948-3131
E-mail: admissions@unity.edu
Internet: www.unity.edu

Founded 1965

Divs incl. environmental programmes, wildlife conservation, marine biology and liberal studies
Private control
Academic year: September to May

Pres.: STEPHEN MULKEY
Sr Vice-Pres. for Academic Affairs: Dr WILLIAM R. TRUMBLE
Vice-Pres. for College Devt: JOSEPH GALLI
Vice-Pres. for Finance and Admin.: DEBORAH CRONIN
Dean of Enrolment Management: ALISA JOHNSON
Dean for Student Affairs: GARY ZANE
Dir of Admissions: KAY FIEDLER
Registrar: HOLLY A. HEIN
Library Dir: MELORA R. NORMAN

Library of 50,000 vols, 400 periodicals
Number of teachers: 50 (30 full-time, 20 part-time)
Number of students: 580

UNIVERSITY OF MAINE SYSTEM

16 Central St, Bangor, ME 04401
Telephone: (207) 973-3201
E-mail: moreinfo@maine.edu
Internet: www.maine.edu

Founded 1968

Chancellor: JAMES H. PAGE
Vice-Chancellor for Academic and Student Affairs: JAMES BREECE
Vice-Chancellor for Admin. and Finance: REBECCA WYKE
Exec. Dir: ROSA REDONNETT

Number of teachers: 1,330
Number of students: 30,080 (total across 7 univs)...

CONSTITUENT INSTITUTIONS

University of Maine

Orono, ME 04469
Telephone: (207) 581-1865
E-mail: um-admit@maine.edu
Internet: www.umaine.edu

Founded 1862 as Maine College of Agriculture and Mechanic Arts, present name and status 1897
State control
Academic year: September to May (2 semesters)

Pres.: PAUL W. FERGUSON
Provost and Sr Vice-Pres. for Academic Affairs: Dr SUSAN J. HUNTER
Vice-Pres. for Admin. and Finance: JANET E. WALDRON
Vice-Pres. for Devt: ERIC ROLFSON
Vice-Pres. for Research: Dr MICHAEL J. ECKARDT
Vice-Pres. for Student Affairs and Dean of Students: ROBERT Q. DANA

Dean of Graduate Studies: DANIEL H. SANDWEISS
Dean of Libraries: JOYCE RUMERY

Library of 1,171,107 vols, 17,480 periodicals, 1.67m. microforms, 2.37m. govt documents, spec. colln on marine studies incl. 13,300 books and journals
Number of teachers: 610
Number of students: 11,170

Publications: Agricultural Experimental Station Publications, Maine Studies, UMaine Today Magazine (4 a year), Technology Experiment Station Publications

DEANS

College of Education and Human Devt: ANNE E. POOLER
College of Engineering: Prof. DANA HUMPHREY
College of Liberal Arts and Sciences: Prof. Dr JEFF HECKER
College of Natural Sciences, Forestry and Agriculture: EDWARD ASHWORTH
Honors College: CHARLIE SLAVIN
Maine Business School: Prof. Dr IVAN MANEV

University of Maine at Augusta

46 University Dr., Augusta, ME 04330-9410
Telephone: (207) 621-3000
E-mail: uma-info@maine.edu
Internet: www.uma.edu

Founded 1965, present status 1971
State control
Academic year: August to May (2 semesters)

Campus in Bangor

Pres.: Dr ALLYSON HUGHES HANDLEY
Provost and Interim Vice-Pres. for Academic Affairs: Dr JOSEPH SZAKAS
Vice-Pres. for Enrolment Services: JONATHAN H. HENRY
Vice-Pres. for Finance and Admin.: ELLEN J. SCHNEITER
Exec. Dir of Admin. Services: SHERI STEVENS
Dean of Extended Campus Learning: Dr THOMAS E. ABBOTT
Dean of Students: KATHLEEN DEXTER
Registrar: ANN CORBETT
Dean of Libraries and Distance Learning: Dr THOMAS E. ABBOTT

Library of 81,000 vols
Number of teachers: 100 (full-time)
Number of students: 5,000

DEANS

College of Arts and Sciences: GILLIAN JORDAN
College of Professional Studies: Dr BRENDA McALEER

University of Maine at Machias

116 O'Brien Ave, Machias, ME 04654-1397
Telephone: (207) 255-1200
E-mail: ummadmissions@maine.edu
Internet: www.umm.maine.edu

Founded 1909
public control
Academic year: September to May

Pres.: Dr CYNTHIA E. HUGGINS
Provost and Vice-Pres. for Academic Affairs: STUART G. SWAIN
Vice-Pres. for Admin. and Finance: THOMAS L. POTTER
Dean of Enrolment Management: MELVIN ADAMS III
Registrar: MARY STOVER
Dir of Library: MARIANNE THIBODEAU

Library of 94,000 vols, 15,000 journals
Number of teachers: 40
Number of students: 1,000

DEANS

Environmental and Biological Sciences: WILLIAM OTTO

University of Maine at Presque Isle

181 Main St, Presque Isle, ME 04769-2888
Telephone: (207) 768-9400
E-mail: admissions@umpi.edu
Internet: www.umpi.edu
Founded 1903 as Aroostook State Normal School, present name and status 1971
State control
Academic year: September to May
Colleges of arts and sciences, education, professional programmes
Pres.: Prof. Dr LINDA SCHOTT
Provost and Vice-Pres. for Academic Affairs: Dr MICHAEL SONNTAG
Vice-Pres. for Admin. and Finance: MARTY PARSONS
Dean for Students and Interim Vice-Pres. for Student Affairs: JAMES STEPP
Dir for Admissions: ERIN BENSON
Dir for Student Records: KATHY DAVIS
Library Dir: JoANNE WALLINGFORD
Library of 458,500 vols
Number of teachers: 110
Number of students: 1,460
Publication: *Upcountry* (online)

University of Maine, Farmington

246 Main St, Farmington, ME 04938
Telephone: (207) 778-7000
E-mail: umfadmit@maine.edu
Internet: www.umf.maine.edu
Founded 1864 as Western State Normal School, present name and status 1970
State control
Academic year: August to May (2 semesters)
Pres.: THEODORA J. KALIKOW
Vice-Pres. for Academic Affairs and Provost: Prof. DANIEL P. GUNN
Vice Pres. for Admin.: RYAN LOW
Vice Pres. for Enrolment Management and Marketing: ROBERTO NOYA
Vice-Pres. for Student and Community Services: F. CELESTE BRANHAM
Dir of Admissions: JAMIE MARCUS
Dir of Library: FRANKLIN D. ROBERTS
Library of 105,000 vols
Number of teachers: 130
Number of students: 2,000

DEANS

College of Arts and Sciences: ROBERT L. LIVELY
College of Education, Health and Rehabilitation: KATHERINE W. YARDLEY

University of Maine, Fort Kent

23 University Dr., Fort Kent, ME 04743
Telephone: (207) 834-7500
E-mail: umfkadm@maine.edu
Internet: www.umfk.edu
Founded 1878 as Madawaska Training School, present name and status 1970
State control
Academic year: September to May
Academic divs incl. arts and humanities, education, natural and behavioural sciences, nursing
Pres.: WILSON G. HESS
Vice-Pres. for Academic Affairs and Dean of Faculty: Dr RACHEL E. ALBERT
Vice-Pres. for Admin. and Interim Dean of Enrolment Management: JOHN D. MURPHY
Registrar: DONALD M. RAYMOND
Dir of Admissions: JILL M. CAIRNS
Dir of Information Services: LESLIE E. KELLY
Library of 48,280 vols, 118,452 ebooks, 183 periodicals, 6,024 microforms, 40,088 ejournals
Number of teachers: 70
Number of students: 1,110

University of Southern Maine

POB 9300, Portland, ME 04104-9300
Telephone: (207) 780-4141
E-mail: usmadm@usm.maine.edu
Internet: www.usm.maine.edu
Founded 1878
Campuses in Gorham, Lewiston-Auburn
State control
Academic year: September to May
Pres.: Dr SELMA BOTMAN
Provost and Vice-Pres. for Academic Affairs: Dr JOHN R. WRIGHT
Vice-Pres. for Univ. Advancement: MEG WESTON
Dir of Admission: SCOTT STEINBERG
Dean of Graduate Studies: DAHLIA LYNN
Registrar: STEVEN G. RAND
Librarian: DAVID NUTTY
Library of 484,000 vols
Number of teachers: 350
Number of students: 9,560

DEANS

College of Arts, Humanities and Sciences: Dr LYNN M. KUZMA
College of Management and Human Services: Prof. Dr JOSEPH McDONNELL
College of Science, Technology and Health: Prof. ANDREW ANDERSON
Lewiston-Auburn College: Dr JOYCE GIBSON
School of Law: PETER PITEGOFF

UNIVERSITY OF NEW ENGLAND

11 Hills Beach Rd, Biddeford, ME 04005
Telephone: (207) 283-0171
E-mail: admissions@une.edu
Internet: www.une.edu
Founded 1939 as College Séraphique; present name and status 1978; merged with Westbrook College (f. 1831) 1996
Campus in Portland
Private control
Academic year: September to May
Pres.: Dr DANIELLE N. RIPICH
Provost and Vice-Pres. for Academic Affairs: Dr JOHN L. WILLIAMS
Vice-Pres. for Campus Services: WILLIAM J. BOLA
Vice-Pres. for Fiscal Affairs: NICOLE TRUFANT
Vice-Pres. for Institutional Advancement: THOMAS E. WHITE
Vice-Pres. for Operations: BILL J. BOLA
Vice-Pres. for Research and Dean of Graduate Studies: Dr TIMOTHY FORD
Vice-Pres. for Student Affairs: CYNTHIA SMITH FORREST
Dean of Enrolment Management: S. GATO
Dean of Students: MARK NAHORNEY
Registrar: JOAN M. MONAHAN
Dean of Library Services: ANDREW J. GOLUB
Number of teachers: 148
Number of students: 7,330

DEANS

College of Arts and Sciences: Dr JEANNE A. K. HEY
College of Dental Medicine: Dr JAMES J. KOELBL
College of Osteopathic Medicine: Dr MARC B. HAHN
College of Pharmacy: Dr GAYLE A. BRAZEAU
Westbrook College of Health Professions: Dr DAVID M. WARD

MARYLAND

CAPITOL COLLEGE

11301 Springfield Rd, Laurel, MD 20708
Telephone: (301) 369-2800
E-mail: admissions@capitol-college.edu
Internet: www.capitol-college.edu
Founded 1927 as Capitol Radio Engineering Institute, present location 1980
Private control
Pres. and CEO: Dr MICHAEL T. WOOD
Vice-Pres. for Academic Affairs and Chief Academic Officer: Dr WILLIAM MACONACHY
Vice-Pres. for College Advancement and Chief Advancement Officer: MICHAEL GIBBS
Vice-Pres. for Finance and Admin. and Chief Financial Officer: DERICK VEENSTRA
Vice-Pres. for Planning and Assessment and Chief Technical Officer: DIANNE VEENSTRA
Dean for Student Life: MELINDA BUNNELL-RHYNE
Dir for Library Services: RICK A. SAMPLE
Library of 10,000 vols
Number of teachers: 60
Number of students: 800 (630 undergraduate, 170 graduate)

DEANS

School of Business and Information Sciences: Dr HELEN G. BARKER

GOUCHER COLLEGE

1021 Dulaney Valley Rd, Baltimore, MD 21204-2794
Telephone: (410) 337-6000
E-mail: admissions@goucher.edu
Internet: www.goucher.edu
Founded 1885
Private control
Academic year: August to May
Pres.: SANFORD J. UNGAR
Provost: MARC ROY
Vice-Pres. and Dean of Students: GAIL NEVERDON EDMONDS
Vice-Pres. for Devt and Alumni Affairs: JANET WILEY
Vice-Pres. for Enrolment Management: MICHAEL O'LEARY
Vice-Pres. for Finance: TOM PHIZACKLEA
Vice-Pres for Govt and Community Relations: WENDY BELZER LITZKE
Registrar: ANDREW WESTFALL
Librarian: NANCY MAGNUSON
Number of teachers: 170 (full-time and part-time)
Number of students: 2,350
Publications: *Donnybrook Fair* (1 a year), *Preface, Quindecim, The Goucher Quarterly*

HOOD COLLEGE

401 Rosemont Ave, Frederick, MD 21701-8575
Telephone: (301) 663-3131
Internet: www.hood.edu
Founded 1893 as Woman's College of Frederick, current name adopted 1912
Academic year: August to May
Pres.: Dr RONALD J. VOLPE
Provost and Vice-Pres. for Academic Affairs: Dr KATHERINE CONWAY-TURNER
Sr Vice-Pres. for Finance and Treas.: CHARLES MANN
Vice-Pres. for Institutional Advancement: NANCY GILLECE
Vice-Pres. for Student Life and Dean of Students: OLIVIA G. WHITE
Vice-Pres. for Undergraduate and Graduate Enrolment Management: Dr KATHLEEN C. BANDS
Dean for Graduate School: ALLEN FLORA
Registrar: NANETTE MARKEY
Library Dir: JAN SAMET O'LEARY
Library of 185,000 vols
Number of teachers: 140 (109 full-time, 31 part-time)
Number of students: 2,440

Publication: *Hood Magazine* (4 a year)

JOHNS HOPKINS UNIVERSITY

3400 N Charles St, Baltimore, MD 21218
Telephone: (410) 516-8000
E-mail: intlhelp@jhu.edu
Internet: www.jhu.edu

Founded 1876
Private control
Academic year: September to June
Pres.: RONALD J. DANIELS
Provost and Sr Vice-Pres. for Academic Affairs: LLOYD B. MINOR
Sr Vice-Pres. for External Affairs and Devt: MICHAEL C. EICHER
Sr Vice-Pres. for Finance and Admin.: DANIEL G. ENNIS
Sr Vice-Pres. and Chief of Staff: CLARENCE D. ARMBRISTER
Vice-Pres. and Gen. Counsel: STEPHEN S. DUNHAM
Vice-Pres. for Communications and Public Affairs: GLENN M. BIELER
Vice-Pres. for Devt and Alumni Relations: FRITZ W. SCHROEDER
Vice-Pres. for Finance and Treas.: (vacant)
Vice-Pres. for Govt and Community Affairs: THOMAS S. LEWIS
Vice-Pres. for Human Resources: CHARLENE MOORE HAYES
Vice-Pres. for Medicine: EDWARD D. MILLER
Registrar: HEDY SCHAEDEL
Dean for Univ. Libraries: WINSTON TABB
Library: see under Libraries and Archives
Number of teachers: 520
Number of students: 6,970 (5,037 undergraduate, 1,933 graduate)
Publications: *Cardiovascular Report* (4 a year), *Conquest, HeadLines, Hopkins BrainWise* (3 a year), *Hopkins Children's, Hopkins Medicine Magazine, Johns Hopkins Medicine Magazine, NeuroNow, On Target, Promise and Progress*

DEANS

Bloomberg School of Public Health: MICHAEL J. KLAG
Carey Business School: PHILLIP PHAN
School of Advanced International Studies: Dr JESSICA P. EINHORN (acting)
School of Education: DAVID ANDREWS
School of Medicine: EDWARD D. MILLER
School of Nursing: MARTHA N. HILL (acting)
Whiting School of Engineering: Prof. T. E. SCHLESINGER
Zanvyl Krieger School of Arts and Sciences: KATHERINE NEWMAN

PROFESSORS

Bloomberg School of Public Health:
ALEXANDER, C. S., Population and Family Health Sciences
ANDERSON, G. F., Health Policy and Management
ANTHONY, J. C., Mental Hygiene
ARMENIAN, H. K., Epidemiology
BAKER, S. P., Health Policy and Management
BAKER, T. D., International Health
BEATY, T. H., Epidemiology
BECKER, S., Population and Family Health Sciences
BERTRAND, J. T., Population and Family Health Sciences
BLACK, R., International Health
BREITNER, J. C. S., Mental Hygiene
BRENNER, M. H., Health Policy and Management
BREYSSE, P., Environmental Health Sciences
BROOKMEYER, R., Biostatistics
BROWN, T. R., Biochemistry and Molecular Biology

BRYANT, F. R., Biochemistry and Molecular Biology
BURKE, D. S., International Health
CABALLERO, B., International Health
CELENTANO, D., Epidemiology
CHANDRASEGARAN, S., Environmental Health Sciences
CHOW, L., Population and Family Health Sciences
COHEN, B. H., Epidemiology
COMSTOCK, G. W., Epidemiology
CULOTTA, V., Environmental Health Sciences
DANNENBERG, A. M., Environmental Health Sciences
DIENER-WEST, M., Biostatistics
EATON, W. W., Mental Hygiene
ENSMINGER, M. E., Health Policy and Management
FADEN, R., Health Policy and Management
FEINLEIB, M., Epidemiology
FITZGERALD, R. S., Environmental Health Sciences
GIELEN, A., Health Policy and Management
GILMAN, R., International Health
GOLDBERG, A. M., Environmental Health Sciences
GOLDMAN, L., Environmental Health Sciences
GORDIS, L., Epidemiology
GOSTIN, L., Health Policy and Management
GRAY, R. H., Population and Family Health Sciences
GRIFFIN, D. E., Molecular Microbiology and Immunology
GROOPMAN, J. D., Environmental Health Sciences
GROSSMAN, L., Biochemistry and Molecular Biology
GUILARTE, T. R., Environmental Health Sciences
GUYER, B., Population and Family Health Sciences
HALSEY, N., International Health
HARDWICK, J. M., Molecular Microbiology and Immunology
HELZLSOUER, K., Epidemiology
HENDERSON, D. A., International Health
HILL, K. H., Population and Family Health Sciences
HUANG, P. C., Biochemistry
JAKAB, G. J., Environmental Health Sciences
KASPER, J. A., Health Policy and Management
KATZ, J., International Health
KENSLER, T. W., Environmental Health Sciences
KETNER, G. W., Molecular Microbiology and Immunology
KIM, Y. J., Population and Family Health Sciences
KLEEBURGER, S., Environmental Health Sciences
KRAG, S. S., Biochemistry and Molecular Biology
KUMAR, N., Molecular Microbiology and Immunology
LAWRENCE, R. S., Health Policy and Management
LEAF, P. J., Mental Hygiene
LEVIN, D. E., Biochemistry
LIANG, K. Y., Biostatistics
LINKS, J. M., Environmental Health Sciences
MACKENZIE, E. J., Health Policy and Management
McMACKEN, R., Biochemistry and Molecular Biology
MARGOLIK, J., Molecular Microbiology and Immunology
MARKHAM, R., Molecular Microbiology and Immunology
MATANOSKI, G. M., Epidemiology
MEINERT, C. L., Epidemiology

MILLER, P. S., Biochemistry and Molecular Biology
MITZNER, W. A., Environmental Health Sciences
MORLOCK, L., Health Policy and Management
MORROW, R., International Health
MOSLEY, W. H., Population and Family Health Sciences
MUÑOZ, A., Epidemiology
NATHANSON, C. A., Population and Family Health Sciences
NAVARRO, V., Health Policy and Management
NELSON, K., Epidemiology
PAIGE, D. M., Population and Family Health Sciences
PICKART, C. M., Biochemistry
PIERCE, N. F., International Health
PIOTROW, P. T., Population and Family Health Sciences
POWE, N. R., Epidemiology
REINKE, W. A., International Health
RISBY, T., Environmental Health Sciences
ROHDE, C. A., Biostatistics
ROSE, N. R., Molecular Microbiology and Immunology
ROTER, D., Health Policy and Management
ROYALL, R. M., Biostatistics
SACK, D., International Health
SACK, R. B., International Health
SALKEVER, D. S., Health Policy and Management
SAMET, J., Epidemiology
SANTOSHAM, M., International Health
SCHOENRICH, E. H., Health Policy and Management
SCHWARTZ, B., Environmental Health Sciences
SCOCCA, J. J., Biochemistry
SCOTT, A. L., Molecular Microbiology and Immunology
SHAH, K. V., Molecular Microbiology and Immunology
SOMMER, A., Epidemiology
SPANNHAKE, E., Environmental Health Sciences
STARFIELD, B., Health Policy and Management
STEINHOFF, M., International Health
STEINWACHS, D. M., Health Policy and Management
STRICKLAND, P. T., Environmental Health Sciences
STROBINO, D. M., Population and Family Health Sciences
SZKLO, M., Epidemiology
TERET, S. P., Health Policy and Management
TIELSCH, J. M., International Health
TONASCIA, J., Biostatistics
TRPIS, M., Molecular Microbiology and Immunology
TRUSH, M. A., Environmental Health Sciences
TS'O, P. O. P., Biochemistry and Molecular Biology
TSUI, A. O., Population and Family Health Sciences
WAGNER, H. N., Environmental Health Sciences
WANG, M., Biostatistics
WEINER, J. P., Health Policy and Management
WEST, K., International Health
WRIGHT, W. W., Biochemistry and Molecular Biology
YAGER, J., Environmental Health Sciences
ZABIN, L. S., Population and Family Health Sciences
ZEGER, S., Biostatistics
ZIRKIN, B., Biochemistry and Molecular Biology

Carey School of Business:
AGRESTI, W., Business Studies

ANIKEEF, M., Business Studies
DADA, M., Business Studies
LIEBOWITZ, J., Business Studies
PHAN, P., Business Studies

School of Medicine:
ABELOFF, M. D., Oncology, Medicine
ACHUFF, S. C., Medicine
ADKINSON, N. F., Jr, Medicine
ADLER, R., Ophthalmology and Neuroscience
AGNEW, W. S., Physiology and Neuroscience
AGRE, P. C., Biological Chemistry and Medicine
AMBINDER, R. F., Oncology, Pathology, Pharmacology and Molecular Science
AMZEL, L. M., Biophysics and Biophysical Chemistry
ANHALT, G. J., Dermatology and Pathology
ASKIN, F. B., Pathology
ATOR, N. A., Psychiatry
AUGUST, J. T., Pharmacology and Molecular Sciences, Oncology
BARBARAN, J. M., Neuroscience, Psychiatry
BARKER, L. R., Medicine
BARTLETT, J. G., Medicine
BAUGHMAN, K. L., Medicine
BAUMGARTNER, W. A., Surgery and Cardiac Surgery
BAYLESS, T. M., Medicine
BAYLIN, S. B., Oncology and Medicine
BEACHY, P. A., Molecular Biology and Genetics
BECKER, D. M., Medicine
BECKER, L. C., Medicine
BELL, W. R., Medicine
BERG, J. M., Biophysics and Biophysical Chemistry
BIGELOW, G. E., Psychiatry and Behavioural Sciences
BOCHNER, B. S., Medicine
BOEKE, J. D., Molecular Biology and Genetics
BOITNOTT, J. K., Pathology
BOROWITZ, M. J., Pathology, Oncology
BOTTOMLEY, P. A., Radiology and Radiological Science, Nuclear Magnetic Resonance Research, Biomedical Engineering and Medicine
BRANDT, J., Psychiatry
BREAKEY, W. R., Psychiatry
BREM, H., Neurological Surgery, Oncology
BRESSLER, N. M., Ophthalmology
BRESSLER, S. B., Ophthalmology
BRIEGER, G. H., History of Science, Medicine and Technology
BRINKER, J. A., Medicine
BROONER, R. K., Psychiatry
BRUSHART, T. M., Orthopaedic Surgery, Surgery, Plastic Surgery and Neurology
BULKLEY, G. B., Surgery
BURDICK, J. F., Surgery
BURGER, P. C., Pathology, Oncology Center, Neurological Surgery
BURKE, P. J., Oncology Center, Medicine
BURTON, J. R., Medicine
CALKINS, H. G., Medicine and Paediatrics
CAMERON, J. L., Surgery, Oncology
CAMPBELL, J. N., Neurological Surgery
CAMPOCHIARO, P. A., Ophthalmology and Neuroscience
CAPUTE, A. J., Paediatrics
CARSON, B. S., Neurological Surgery, Oncology, Paediatrics and Plastic Surgery
CARTER, H. B., Urology and Oncology
CASELLA, J. F., Paediatrics, Oncology Center
CASERO, R. J., Jr, Oncology
CATALDO, M. F., Psychiatry and Paediatrics
CHAISSON, R. E., Medicine
CHAKRAVARTI, A., Medicine and Paediatrics
CHAN, D. W., Pathology, Oncology, Radiology and Radiological Science, Urology
CHANDRA, N., Medicine

CHANG, A. Y., Oncology
CHAO, E. Y., Orthopaedic Surgery and Biomedical Engineering
CHARACHE, P., Pathology, Oncology, Medicine
CHATTERJEE, S. B., Paediatrics
CIVIN, C. I., Oncology, Paediatrics
CLEMENTS, J. E., Comparative Medicine, Neurology and Pathology
COFFEY, D. S., Urology, Oncology, Pharmacology and Molecular Sciences
COLE, P. A., Pharmacology and Molecular Sciences
COLOMBANI, P. M., Surgery, Paediatric Surgery, Oncology
CORDEN, J. L., Molecular Biology and Genetics
CORNBLATH, D. R., Neurology
COTTER, R. J., Pharmacology and Molecular Sciences, Biophysics and Biophysical Chemistry
CRAIG, N. L., Molecular Biology and Genetics
CRAIG, S. W., Biological Chemistry and Pathology
CUMMINGS, C. W., Otolaryngology—Head and Neck Surgery, Oncology
CUTTING, G. R., Paediatrics and Medicine
DANG, C. V., Medicine, Oncology, Pathology
DANNALS, R. F., Radiology, Radiological Science and Nuclear Medicine
DAVIDSON, N. E., Oncology
DAWSON, T., Neurology and Neuroscience
DE JUAN, E., Jr, Ophthalmology
DELATEUR, B. J., Physical Medicine and Rehabilitation
DENCKLA, M. B., Neurology and Paediatrics
DEPAULO, J. R., Psychiatry
DESIDERIO, S. V., Molecular Biology and Genetics
DEVREOTES, P. N., Biological Chemistry, Cell Biology and Anatomy
DICELLO, J. F., Oncology
DIEHL, A. M., Medicine
DIETZ, H. C., Paediatrics
DONEHOWER, R. C., Oncology and Medicine
DONOWITZ, M., Medicine
DOVER, G. J., Paediatrics and Oncology
DRACHMAN, D. B., Neurology and Neuroscience
EGGLESTON, P. A., Paediatrics
EISELE, D. W., Otolaryngology—Head and Neck Surgery, Anaesthesiology, Critical Care Medicine, Oncology and Urology
ENGLUND, P. T., Biological Chemistry
EPSTEIN, J. I., Pathology, Oncology, Urology
EROZAN, Y. S., Pathology
ETTINGER, D. S., Oncology, Medicine
FAJARDO, L. L., Radiology and Radiological Science, Diagnostic Radiology and Oncology
FEINBERG, A. P., Medicine and Oncology
FINKELSTEIN, D., Ophthalmology
FISHMAN, E. K., Radiology and Radiological Science, Diagnostic Radiology, Oncology
FORASTIERE, A. A., Oncology, Otolaryngology—Head and Neck Surgery
FORTUIN, N. J., Medicine
FOX, H. E., Gynaecology and Obstetrics
FRASSICA, F. J., Orthopaedic Surgery and Oncology
FREEMAN, J. M., Neurology and Paediatrics
FRIED, L. P., Medicine
FROST, J. J., Radiology and Radiological Science, and Nuclear Medicine and Neuroscience
FUCHS, P. A., Otolaryngology—Head and Neck Surgery, Biomedical Engineering and Neuroscience
GARCIA, J. G., Medicine
GEARHART, J. D., Gynaecology and Obstetrics, Comparative Medicine and Physiology
GEARHART, J. P., Urology and Paediatrics

GERSTENBLITH, G., Medicine
GIARDIELLO, F. M., Medicine, Oncology, Pathology
GIBSON, D. W., Pharmacology and Molecular Sciences
GOLDBERG, M. F., Ophthalmology
GOLDSTEIN, G. W., Neurology and Paediatrics
GORDIS, L., Paediatrics
GORDON, B., Neurology
GOTTSCH, J. D., Ophthalmology
GREEN, W. R., Ophthalmology and Pathology
GREENOUGH, W. B., III, Medicine
GREIDER, C. W., Molecular Biology and Genetics, Oncology
GRIFFIN, J. W., Neurology, Neuroscience and Pathology
GRIFFITH, L. S., Medicine
GRIFFITHS, R. R., Psychiatry and Neuroscience
GROSSMAN, S. A., Oncology, Medicine and Neurological Surgery
GUGGINO, W. B., Physiology and Paediatrics
GUYTON, D. L., Ophthalmology
HALPERIN, H. R., Medicine, Biomedical Engineering
HAMILTON, R. G., Medicine
HANDLER, J. S., Medicine
HANLEY, D. F., Neurology, Anaesthesiology and Critical Care Medicine
HAPONIK, E. F., Medicine
HARMON, J. W., Surgery
HARRIS, J. C., Jr, Psychiatry and Paediatrics
HART, G. W., Biological Chemistry
HAWKINS, B. S., Ophthalmology
HAYWARD, G. S., Pharmacology and Molecular Sciences, Oncology and Pathology
HAYWARD, S. D., Pharmacology and Molecular Sciences, Oncology and Pathology
HELLMAN, D. B., Medicine
HENDRY, S. H., Neuroscience
HEPTINSTALL, R. H., Pathology
HESS, A. D., Oncology and Pathology
HOLTZMAN, N. A., Paediatrics
HRUBAN, R. H., Pathology, Oncology
HUBBARD, A. L., Cell Biology, Anatomy and Physiology
HUGANIR, R. L., Neuroscience
HUGGINS, G. R., Gynaecology and Obstetrics
HUNGERFORD, D. S., Orthopaedic Surgery
HUTCHINS, G. M., Pathology
ISAACS, J. T., Oncology and Urology
ISAACS, W. B., Urology, Oncology
JABS, D. A., Ophthalmology and Medicine
JABS, E. W., Paediatrics, Medicine, Surgery and Plastic Surgery
JACKSON, J. B., Pathology
JASINSKI, D. R., Medicine
JOHNS, R. A., Anaesthesiology and Critical Care Medicine
JOHNS, R. J., Medicine
JOHNSON, K. O., Neuroscience and Biomedical Engineering
JOHNSON, R. T., Neurology, Molecular Biology, Genetics and Neuroscience
JOHNSTON, M. V., Neurology and Paediatrics
JONES, B., Radiology and Radiological Sciences, Diagnostic Radiology
JONES, R. J., Oncology
KAN, J. S., Paediatrics
KASHIMA, H. K., Otolaryngology—Head and Neck Surgery, Oncology
KASS, D. A., Medicine and Biomedical Engineering
KAVOUSSI, L. R., Urology
KELEN, G. D., Emergency Medicine
KELLY, T. J., Jr, Molecular Biology and Genetics

ZERHOUNI, E. A., Radiology and Radiological Science, Diagnostic Radiology and Biomedical Engineering
ZIEVE, P. D., Medicine
ZINK, C., Comparative Medicine and Pathology
ZWEIER, J. L., Medicine

Whiting School of Engineering:
ANANDARAJAH, A., Civil Engineering
ANDREOU, A. G., Electrical and Computer Engineering
AWERBUCH, B., Computer Science
BALL, W. P., Geography and Environmental Engineering
BETENBAUGH, M. J., Chemical Engineering
BOLAND, J., Geography and Environmental Engineering
BOUWER, E. J., Geography and Environmental Engineering
BRUSH, G. S., Geography and Environmental Engineering
BUSCH-VISHNIAC, I. J., Mechanical Engineering
CAMMARATA, R., Materials Science and Engineering
CHEN, S., Mechanical Engineering
CHIRIKJIAN, G., Mechanical Engineering
DAVIDSON, F. M., Electrical and Computer Engineering
DONOHUE, M., Chemical Engineering
DOUGLAS, A. S., Mechanical Engineering
ELLIS, J. H., Geography and Environmental Engineering
FILL, J. A., Mathematical Sciences
GERMAN, D., Mathematical Sciences
GOODRICH, M. T., Computer Science
GOUTSIAS, J. I., Electrical and Computer Engineering
GREEN, R. E., Jr, Materials Science and Engineering
HAGER, G. D., Computer Science
HAN, S.-P., Mathematical Sciences
HANKE, S., Geography and Environmental Engineering
HEMKER, K. J., Mechanical Engineering
HOBBS, B. F., Geography and Environmental Engineering
IGUSA, T., Civil Engineering
JELINEK, F., Electrical and Computer Engineering
JONES, N. P., Civil Engineering
JOSEPH, R. I., Electrical and Computer Engineering
KAPLAN, A. E., Electrical and Computer Engineering
KATZ, J., Mechanical Engineering
KATZ, J. L., Chemical Engineering
KHURGIN, J. B., Electrical and Computer Engineering
KNIO, O., Mechanical Engineering
KOSARAJU, S. R., Computer Science
MASSON, G. M., Computer Science
MENEVEAU, C. V., Mechanical Engineering
MEYER, G. G. L., Electrical and Computer Engineering
MILLER, M., Biomedical Engineering
MILLER, M. I., Electrical and Computer Engineering
NAIMAN, D. Q., Mathematical Sciences
O'MELIA, C. R., Geography and Environmental Engineering
PANG, J.-S., Mathematical Sciences
PARLANGE, M. B., Geography and Environmental Engineering
PAULAITIS, M. E., Chemical Engineering
PRIEBE, C. E., Mathematical Sciences
PRINCE, J. L., Electrical and Computer Engineering
PROSPERETTI, A., Mechanical Engineering
RAMESH, K. T., Mechanical Engineering
REVELLE, K., Geography and Environmental Engineering
RUGH, W. J., Electrical and Computer Engineering

SCHEINERMAN, E. R., Mathematical Sciences
SCHOENBERGER, E. J., Geography and Environmental Engineering
SEARSON, P. C., Materials Science and Engineering
SHARPE, W. N., Jr, Mechanical Engineering
SMITH, S. F., Computer Science
STEBE, K., Chemical Engineering
STONE, A. T., Geography and Environmental Engineering
TAYLOR, R. H., Computer Science
WEINERT, H. L., Electrical and Computer Engineering
WIERMAN, J. C., Mathematical Sciences
WILCOCK, P. R., Geography and Environmental Engineering
WOLFF, L. B., Computer Science
WOLMAN, M. G., Geography and Environmental Engineering

School of Advanced International Studies (1730 Massachusetts Ave, Washington, DC 20036):
AJAMI, F., Middle East Studies
BARRET, S., International Relations
BODNAR, G., International Finance
CALLEO, D. P., European Studies
COHEN, E. A., Strategic Studies
CORDEN, W. M., International Economics
DORAN, C. F., Canadian Studies and International Relations
FRANK, I., International Economics
FUKUYAMA, F., Political Economy
GLEIJESES, P., US Foreign Policy and Latin American Studies
GOODELL, G. E., International Development
GRILLI, E., International Economics
JACKSON, K. D., Asian and South East Asia Studies
LAMPTON, D. M., Asian Studies
MANDELBAUM, M., US Foreign Policy
PARROTT, B., Russian and Eurasian Studies
PEARSON, C. S., International Economics
RIEDEL, J. C., International Economics
ROETT, R., Latin American Studies and Western Hemisphere Programmes
THAYER, N. B., Asian Studies
WEDGEWOOD, J. D., International Law and Organization
ZARTMAN, I. W., African Studies

School of Nursing:
ALLEN, J., Preventive Cardiology
BERK, R. A., Psychometrics and Statistics
CAMPBELL, J., Community Health
DONALDSON, S., Physiology and Biophysics
FRALIC, M., Nursing Management
GASTON-JOHANSSON, F., Research Utilization and Pain
HILL, M., Adult Health

Zanvyl Krieger School of Arts and Sciences:
ACHINSTEIN, P., Philosophy
ALEXANDER, K., Sociology
ANDERSON, A., English
ANDERSON, W., Romance Languages and Literatures
ARRIGHI, G., Sociology
BAGGER, J., Physics and Astronomy
BALL, G., Psychology
BALL, L., Economics
BARNETT, B., Physics and Astronomy
BECKWITH, S., Physics and Astronomy
BEEMON, K., Biology
BELL, D., History
BENNETT, C. L., Physics and Astronomy
BERRY, S., History
BESSMAN, M., Biology
BETT, R., Philosophy
BLUMENFELD, B. J., Physics and Astronomy
BOARDMAN, J. M., Mathematics
BOWEN, R., Chemistry
BRAND, L., Biology
BRIEGER, G., History of Science, Medicine and Technology

BROHOLM, C., Physics and Astronomy
BROOKS, J., History
BRYAN, B. M., Near Eastern Studies
BURZIO, L., Cognitive Science
CAMERON, S., English
CAMPE, R., German
CARROLL, C., Economics
CASTRO-KLARÉN, S., Romance Languages and Literatures
CHERLIN, A., Sociology
CHIEN, C.-L., Physics and Astronomy
CHIEN, C.-Y., Physics and Astronomy
CONE, R. A., Biophysics
CONNOLLY, W., Political Science
COOPER, J., Political Science
COOPER, J. S., Near Eastern Studies
CORCES, V., Biology
CRENSON, M., Political Science
CUMMINGS, M., Political Science
DAGDIGIAN, P., Chemistry
DAS, V., Anthropology
DAVID, S., Political Science
DAVIDSEN, A., Physics and Astronomy
DEFAUX, G., Romance Languages and Literatures
DEMPSEY, C., History of Art
DETIENNE, M., Classics
DIETZE, G., Political Science
DITZ, T., History
DIXON, S., Writing Seminars
DOERING, J., Chemistry
DOMOKOS, G., Physics and Astronomy
DRAPER, D., Chemistry
DRAPER, D., Biophysics and Chemistry
EBERT, J. D., Biology
EDIDIN, M., Biology
EGETH, H., Psychology
FALK, A., Physics and Astronomy
FAMBROUGH, D., Biology
FELDMAN, G., Physics and Astronomy
FELDMAN, P., Physics and Astronomy
FERGUSON, F., English
FERRY, J., Earth and Planetary Sciences
FISHER, G. W., Earth and Planetary Sciences
FLATHMAN, R. C., Political Science
FORD, H., Physics and Astronomy
FORNI, P., Romance Languages and Literatures
FORSTER, E., Humanities Center
FREIRE, E., Biology, Biophysics
FRIED, M., Humanities Center, History of Art
GALAMBOS, L. P., History
GALLAGHER, M., Psychology
GARVEN, G., Earth and Planetary Sciences
GERSOVITZ, M., Economics
GINSBERG, B., Political Science
GOLDBERG, J., English
GONZÁLEZ, E., Romance Languages and Literatures
GORDON, R., Sociology
GREENE, J., History
GROSSMAN, A., English
GROSSMAN, J., Political Science
HARDIE, L. A., Earth and Planetary Sciences
HARRINGTON, J., Economics
HECKMAN, T., Physics and Astronomy
HEDGECOCK, E., Biology
HENRY, R., Physics and Astronomy
HERTZ, N., Humanities Center
HOLLAND, P., Psychology
HOYT, M. A., Biology
HUANG, R. C., Biology
IRWIN, J., Writing Seminars
JOHNSON, M., History
JUSCZYK, P., Psychology
KAGAN, R., History
KARGON, R. H., History of Science, Medicine and Technology
KARLIN, K., Chemistry
KARNI, E., Economics
KATZ, R., Political Science
KECK, M., Political Science
KESSLER, H., History of Art

KHAN, M. A., Economics
KINGSLAND, S., History of Science, Medicine and Technology
KNIGHT, F., History
KOHN, M., Sociology
KOLYVAGIN, V., Mathematics
KOVESI-DOMOKOS, S., Physics and Astronomy
KROLIK, J., Physics and Astronomy
LANDAU, B., Cognitive Science
LATTMAN, E., Biophysics
LEE, Y. C., Biology
LEE, Y. K., Physics and Astronomy
LEGENDRE, G., Cognitive Science
LESLIE, S., History of Science, Medicine and Technology
LEYS, R., Humanities Center
LYKKEN, J., Physics and Astronomy
McCARTER, P. K., Jr, Near Eastern Studies
McCARTY, R., Biology
McCLOSKEY, M., Cognitive Science
McGARRY, J., Writing Seminars
MACCINI, L., Economics
MACKSEY, R., Humanities Center
MAGUIRE, H., History of Art
MARSH, B., Earth and Planetary Sciences
MELION, W., History of Art
MEYER, G., Chemistry
MINICOZZI, W. P., Mathematics
MOON, M., English
MOOS, H. W., Physics and Astronomy
MORAVA, J., Mathematics
MORGAN, P., History
MOUDRIANAKIS, E., Biology
NÄGELE, R., German
NEUFELD, D., Physics and Astronomy
NEWMAN, S., Introduction to Policy Analysis (Policy Studies)
NICHOLS, S., Humanities Center
NICHOLS, S., Romance Languages and Literature
NIRENBERG, D., History
NORMAN, C., Physics and Astronomy
OLSON, P. L., Earth and Planetary Sciences
ONO, T., Mathematics
OSBORN, T., Earth and Planetary Sciences
PAGDEN, A., History
PANDEY, G., Anthropology
PAULSON, R., English
PEVSNER, A., Physics and Astronomy
POLAND, D., Chemistry
POSNER, G. H., Chemistry
PRIVALOV, P., Biology
REICH, D., Physics and Astronomy
ROBBINS, M., Physics and Astronomy
ROSEMAN, S., Biology
ROSS, D., History
ROWE, W., History
RUSSELL-WOOD, A. J. R., History
RUSSO, E., Romance Languages and Literature
RYNASIEWICZ, R., Philosophy
SALAMON, L., Political Science
SCHLEIF, R., Biology
SCHROER, T., Biology
SCHWARTZ, G. M., Near Eastern Studies
SHALIKA, J., Mathematics
SHAPIRO, A., Classics
SHEARN, A., Biology
SHIFFMAN, B., Mathematics
SHOKUROV, V. A., Mathematics
SIEBER, H., Romance Languages and Literatures
SILVERSTONE, H. J., Chemistry
SISSA, G., Classics
SMOLENSKY, P., Cognitive Science
SOGGE, C., Mathematics
SPIEGEL, G., History
SPRUCK, J., Mathematics
STANLEY, S., Earth and Planetary Sciences
STEPHENS, W., Romance Languages and Literatures
STROBEL, D., Earth and Planetary Sciences
SVERJENSKY, D., Earth and Planetary Sciences

SWARTZ, M., Physics and Astronomy
SZALAY, A., Physics and Astronomy
TESANOVIC, Z., Physics and Astronomy
TOWNSEND, C., Chemistry
VEBLEN, D., Earth and Planetary Sciences
VISHNIAC, E., Physics and Astronomy
WALKER, J. C., Physics and Astronomy
WALKOWITZ, J., History
WALTERS, R., History
WEISS, D., History of Art
WENTWORTH, R., Mathematics
WESTBROOK, R., Near Eastern Studies
WILLIAMS, M., Philosophy
WILSON, G., Philosophy
WILSON, W. S., Mathematics
WOLF, S., Philosophy
WOODSON, S. A., Biophysics
WYSE, R., Physics and Astronomy
YANTIS, S., Psychology
YARKONY, D., Chemistry
YOUNG, H. P., Economics
ZELDICH, S., Mathematics
ZUCKER, S., Mathematics

LOYOLA UNIVERSITY MARYLAND

4501 N Charles St, Baltimore, MD 21210-2699

Telephone: (410) 617-2000
Internet: www.loyola.edu

Founded 1852 as Loyola College, present name and status 2009
Private control
Academic year: August to May
Pres.: Rev. BRIAN F. LINNANE
Exec. Vice-Pres.: Dr SUSAN DONOVAN
Vice-Pres. for Academic Affairs: Dr AMY R. WOLFSON
Vice-Pres. for Admin.: TERRENCE SAWYER
Vice-Pres. for Advancement: MEGAN GILLICK
Vice-Pres. for Finance and Treas.: RANDALL D. GENTZLER
Vice-Pres. for Enrolment Management and Communications: MARC M. CAMILLE
Vice-Pres. for Student Devt and Dean for Students: Dr SUSAN M. DONOVAN
Library Dir: JOHN McGINTY
Library of 400,000 vols
Number of teachers: 400 (full-time)
Number of students: 6,080 (3,863 undergraduate, 2,217 graduate)

DEANS

Loyola College of Arts and Sciences: Rev. JAMES MIRACKY
School of Education: Dr L. MICKEY FENZEL
Sellinger School of Business and Management: Dr KARYL B. LEGGIO

MARYLAND INSTITUTE COLLEGE OF ART

1300 W Mount Royal Ave, Baltimore, MD 21217

Telephone: (410) 669-9200
E-mail: pr@mica.edu
Internet: www.mica.edu

Founded 1826
Private control
Academic year: August to May
Pres.: FRED LAZARUS, IV
Vice-Pres. for Admission and Financial Aid: THERESA LYNCH BEDOYA
Provost and Vice-Pres. for Academic Affairs: GUNALAN NADARAJAN
Vice-Pres. for Advancement: MICHAEL FRANCO
Vice-Pres. for Fiscal Affairs and Chief Financial Officer: DOUGLAS MANN
Vice-Pres. for Operations: MICHAEL MOLLA
Vice-Pres. for Student Affairs and Dean of Students: J. DAVIDSON PORTER
Vice-Pres for Technology Systems and Services: TOM HYATT

Registrar: CHRISTINE PETERSON
Dir for Library: FLORENCE THORP
Library: 64,000 monographs, 325 current periodical subscriptions, 5,500 full-text journal titles, 35,000 digital images, 215,000 slides and 5,000 DVDs and video cassettes
Number of teachers: 180
Number of students: 2,170 (1,864 undergraduate, 306 graduate)

DEANS

Centre of Art Education: KAREN CARROLL
School for Professional and Continuing Studies: DAVID GRACYALNY

MCDANIEL COLLEGE

Two College Hill, Westminster, MD 21157-4390

Telephone: (410) 848-7000
E-mail: pio@mcdaniel.edu
Internet: www.mcdaniel.edu

Founded 1867 as W Maryland College, current name adopted 2002
Private control
Academic year: August to June
Liberal arts and sciences; teacher certification courses
Pres.: ROGER N. CASEY
Provost and Dean of the Faculty: JEANINE STEWART
Vice-Pres. for Admin. and Finance: ETHAN A. SEIDEL
Vice-Pres. for Enrolment Management and Dean for Admissions: FLORENCE W. HINES
Vice-Pres. for Institutional Advancement: LORI LEWIS
Dean and Vice-Pres. for Student Affairs: BETH R. GERL
Registrar: JAN KIPHART
Library Dir: JESSAME FERGUSON
Library of 200,000 vols
Number of teachers: 135
Number of students: 3,160 (1,600 undergraduate, 1,560 graduate)

MORGAN STATE UNIVERSITY

1700 E Coldspring Lane, Baltimore, MD 21251

Telephone: (443) 885-3333
E-mail: info@morgan.edu
Internet: www.morgan.edu

Founded 1867 as Centenary Biblical Institute, present status 1939
State control
Academic year: August to May
Pres.: Dr DAVID WILSON
Provost and Vice-Pres. for Academic Affairs: Dr T. JOAN ROBINSON
Vice-Pres. for Finance and Management: RAYMOND VOLLMER
Vice-Pres. for Institutional Advancement: CHERYL Y. HITCHCOCK
Vice-Pres. for Planning and Information Technology: Dr JOSEPH POPOVICH
Vice-Pres. for Student Affairs: TANYA RUSH (acting)
Gen. Counsel: JULIE GOODWIN
Dir for Library: Dr RICHARD BRADBERRY
Library of 400,000 vols
Number of teachers: 1,500
Number of students: 8,200

DEANS

College of Liberal Arts: Dr M'BARE N'GOM
School of Architecture and Planning: Dr MARY ANNE AKERS
School of Business and Management: Dr OTIS A. THOMAS
School of Community Health and Policy: Dr ALLAN NOONAN

School of Computer, Mathematical and Natural Sciences: Dr JOSEPH A. WHITTAKER
School of Education and Urban Studies: Dr PATRICIA L. WELCH
School of Engineering: Dr EUGENE M. DELOATCH
School of Graduate Studies: Dr MARK GARRISON
School of Social Work: Dr ANNA MCPHATTER

MOUNT ST MARY'S UNIVERSITY

16300 Old Emmitsburg Rd, Emmitsburg, MD 21727

Telephone: (301) 447-6122
E-mail: admissions@msmary.edu
Internet: www.msmary.edu
Founded 1805
Private control
Academic year: January to December
Pres.: THOMAS H. POWELL
Provost and Vice-Pres. for Academic Affairs: Dr DAVID B. REHM
Exec. Vice-Pres.: DAN S. SOLLER
Vice-Pres. and Seminary Rector: STEVEN P. ROHLFS
Vice-Pres. for Business and Finance: MICHAEL S. MALEWICKI
Vice-Pres. for Enrolment Management: MICHAEL A. POST
Vice-Pres. for Univ. Advancement: ROBERT J. BRENNAN
Vice-Pres. for Univ. Affairs: PAULINE A. ENGELSTÄTTER
Registrar: MARGOT C. RHOADES
Dean for Library: CHARLES L. KUHN
Library of 200,000 vols, 2,000 DVDs and VHS cassettes-documentaries
Number of teachers: 120 (98 full-time, 22 part-time)
Number of students: 2,120
Publication: *Mount Magazine* (2 a year)

DEANS

College of Liberal Arts: JOSHUA P. HOCHSCHILD
Richard J. Bolte Sr School of Business: Dr WILLIAM G. FORGANG
School of Education and Human Services: Dr BARBARA MARTIN PALMER
School of Natural Science and Mathematics: Dr DAVID W. BUSHMAN

NOTRE DAME OF MARYLAND UNIVERSITY

4701 N Charles St, Baltimore, MD 21210
Telephone: (410) 435-0100
E-mail: admiss@ndm.edu
Internet: www.ndm.edu
Founded 1873 as Notre Dame of Maryland Collegiate Institute, current name adopted 2011
Private control
Academic year: August to May
Pres.: Dr JAMES CONNEELY
Vice-Pres. for Academic Affairs: Sis. CHRISTINE DE VINNE
Dir for Admissions: LARRY SHATTUCK
Dir for Library: JOHN MCGINTY
Library of 400,000 vols, 16,000 media items (DVDs, CDs and video cassettes)
Number of teachers: 100 (full-time)
Number of students: 2,930

DEANS

School of Arts and Sciences: Dr DEBRA FRANKLIN
School of Education: SHARON SLEAR
School of Nursing: Dr KATIE COOK
School of Pharmacy: Dr ANNE LIN

SOJOURNER-DOUGLASS COLLEGE

200 N Central Ave, Baltimore, MD 21202
Telephone: (410) 276-0306
Internet: www.sdc.edu
Founded 1972 as Homestead Montebello Center, present status 1980
Private control
Academic year: August to May
6 Campuses: Edgewater, Bahamas, Cambridge, Owings Mills, Lanham and Salisbury
Pres.: Dr CHARLES W. SIMMONS
Provost and Vice-Pres. for Academic Affairs: Dr MARIAN STANTON
Vice-Pres. for Admin. and Fiscal Affairs: DONALD HUTCHINS
Chief Librarian: OMOWALI ALI
Number of teachers: 40
Number of students: 440

ST JOHN'S COLLEGE

60 College Ave, Annapolis, MD 21401
Telephone: (410) 626-2522
E-mail: admissions@sjca.edu
Internet: www.stjohnscollege.edu
Founded 1696 as King William's School, present name and status 1784
Private control
Language of instruction: English
Academic year: August to May
For Santa Fe campus, see under New Mexico
Pres.: CHRISTOPHER B. NELSON
Vice-Pres. for Advancement: BARBARA GOYETTE
Dean: PAMELA KRAUS
Treas.: BRONTE D. JONES
Registrar: JACQUELINE THOMS (acting)
Dir for Admissions: SARAH MORSE
Dir for Alumni Relations: LEO PICKENS
Library Dir: CATHERINE DIXON
Library of 100,000 vols
Number of teachers: 70
Number of students: 450
Publications: *The College* (3 a year), *The St. John's Review*

ST MARY'S COLLEGE OF MARYLAND

18952 E Fisher Rd, St Mary's City, MD 20686-3001
Telephone: (240) 895-2000
E-mail: admissions@smcm.edu
Internet: www.smcm.edu
Founded 1840, current name adopted 1964
State control
Academic year: August to May
Pres.: Dr JOSEPH URGO
Vice-Pres. for Academic Affairs and Dean of Faculty: Dr BETH RUSHING
Vice-Pres. for Advancement: Dr MAUREEN SILVA
Vice-Pres. for Business and Finance: Dr THOMAS J. BOTZMAN
Vice-Pres. and Dean for Admissions and Financial Aid: Dr PATRICIA GOLDSMITH
Dean for Students: Dr LAURA BAYLESS
Dir for Library: Dr CELIA RABINOWITZ
Library of 200,000 vols
Number of teachers: 230 (141 full-time, 89 part-time)
Number of students: 2,020 (1,984 undergraduate, 36 graduate)
Publication: *The Mulberry Tree* (2 a year)

ST MARY'S SEMINARY & UNIVERSITY

5400 Roland Ave, Baltimore, MD 21210-1994
Telephone: (410) 864-4000
E-mail: admissions@stmarys.edu
Internet: www.stmarys.edu
Founded 1791

Private control
Vice-Chancellor, Pres. and Rector: Rev. Dr THOMAS HURST
Vice-Rector: Rev. TIMOTHY KULBICKI
Vice-Pres. for Advancement and Human Resources: ELIZABETH L. VISCONAGE
Vice-Pres. for Finance: RICHARD G. CHILDS
Dean for Students: Rev. EDWARD J. GRISWOLD
Dir for Information Services: ARRYN MILNE
Registrar: PAULA THIGPEN
Library of 22,000 vols, 130,000 monographs, 390 periodical subscriptions
Number of teachers: 45 (21 full-time, 24 part-time)
Number of students: 120 (75 full-time, 45 part-time)

DEANS

Ecumenical Institute of Theology: Dr MICHAEL J. GORMAN
School of Theology: Rev. TIMOTHY KULBICKI

TAI SOPHIA INSTITUTE

7750 Montpelier Rd, Laurel, MD 20723
Telephone: (410) 888-9048
Internet: www.tai.edu
Founded 1974 as College of Chinese Acupuncture, current name adopted 2000
Private control
Courses in acupuncture, Chinese herbs, health coaching, herbal studies, medical herbalism, nutrition and integrative health, therapeutic herbalism, transformative leadership and social change, and wellness coaching
Pres. and CEO: FRANK VITALE
Provost and Exec. Vice-Pres. for Academic Affairs: Dr JUDITH K. BROIDA
Vice-Pres. for Admin. and Gen. Counsel: LOUISE GUSSIN
Vice-Pres. for Business and Financial Services: MARC LEVIN
Vice-Pres. for Marketing and Enrolment Management: LISA CONNELLY-DUGGAN
Number of students: 440

UNIFORMED SERVICES UNIVERSITY OF THE HEALTH SCIENCES

4301 Jones Bridge Rd, Bethesda, MD 20814
Telephone: (301) 295-3101
E-mail: admissions@mxa.usuhs.mil
Internet: www.usuhs.mil
Founded 1972
Pres.: Dr CHARLES S. RICE
Vice-Pres. and Chief Information Officer: TIMOTHY RAPP
Vice-Pres. for Exec. Affairs: WILLIAM BESTER
Vice-Pres. for Finance and Admin.: STEPHEN RICE
Vice-Pres. for Research: Dr STEVEN KAMINSKY
Vice-Pres. for Teaching and Research Support: Dr VERNON D. SCHINSKI
Registrar: GAIL HEWITT-CLARKE
Number of teachers: 430 (on campus)
Number of students: 2,410

DEANS

F. Edward Hébert School of Medicine: Dr LARRY W. LAUGHLIN
Graduate School of Nursing: Dr ADA SUE HINSHAW

UNITED STATES NAVAL ACADEMY

121 Blake Rd, Annapolis, MD 21402-5000
Telephone: (410) 293-1000
E-mail: pao@usna.edu
Internet: www.usna.edu
Founded 1845 as Naval School, current name adopted 1850
State control

Academic year: August to May

Superintendent: Vice Admiral MICHAEL H. MILLER

Commandant of Midshipmen: Capt. ROBERT E. CLARK, II

Academic Dean and Provost: WILLIAM C. MILLER

Dean of Admissions: STEPHEN B LATTA

Registrar: Dr CHRISTOPHER A. DAVIS

Librarian: JAMES RETTIG

Library: see under Libraries and Archives

Number of teachers: 570

Number of students: 4,350 midshipmen

Publications: *Lucky Bag* (1 a year), *Shipmate* (online), *Trident*

UNIVERSITY OF MARYLAND SYSTEM

3300 Metzerott Rd, Adelphi, MD 20783-1690

Telephone: (301) 445-2756

E-mail: webnotes@usmd.edu

Internet: www.usmd.edu

Founded 1988 by merger of 5 Univ. of Maryland instns and 6 mems of the State Univ. and College System of Maryland

State control

12 Instns, 2 regional higher education centres and a system office

Chancellor: Dr WILLIAM ENGLISH KIRWAN

Sr Vice-Chancellor for Academic Affairs: IRWIN GOLDSTEIN

Vice-Chancellor for Admin. and Finance: JOSEPH VIVONA

Vice-Chancellor for Advancement: LEONARD R. RALEY

Vice-Chancellor for Communications: ANNE MOULTRIE

Vice-Chancellor for Govt Relations: PATRICK J. HOGAN

Number of teachers: 13,980 (8,204 full-time, 5,776 part-time)

Number of students: 15,560 ...

CONSTITUENT UNIVERSITIES

Bowie State University

14000 Jericho Park Rd, Bowie, MD 20715-9465

Telephone: (301) 860-4000

E-mail: gradadmissions@bowiestate.edu

Internet: www.bowiestate.edu

Founded 1865 as Baltimore Normal School, present name and status 1988

Academic year: September to May

Pres.: Dr MICKEY L. BURNIM

Provost and Vice-Pres. for Academic Affairs: Dr KAREN JOHNSON SHAHEED

Vice-Pres. and Gen. Counsel: ANTIONETTE MARBRAY

Vice-Pres. for External Relations: MAITLAND DADE

Vice-Pres. for Finance and Admin.: Dr KARL B. BROCKENBROUGH

Vice-Pres. for Institutional Advancement: Dr RICHARD LUCAS

Vice-Pres. for Student Affairs: Dr ARTIE L. TRAVIS

Dean for Library: MARIAN RUCKER-SHAMU

Library of 280,000 vols

Number of teachers: 350 (192 full-time, 158 part-time)

Number of students: 5,620 (4,113 undergraduate, 1,507 graduate)

DEANS

College of Arts and Sciences: Dr GEORGE ACQUAAH,

College of Business: Dr ANTHONY NELSON

College of Education: Dr TRAKI TAYLOR-WEBB

College of Professional Studies: Dr ELLIOTT PARRIS

Graduate School: Dr COSMAS U. NWOKEAFOR

Coppin State University

2500 W North Ave, Baltimore, MD 21216-3698

Telephone: (410) 951-3000

E-mail: admissions@coppin.edu

Internet: www.coppin.edu

Founded 1900 as Colored High School, current name adopted 2004

Academic year: August to May

Pres.: Dr REGINALD S. AVERY

Provost and Vice-Pres. for Academic Affairs: Dr RONNIE L. COLLINS

Vice-Pres. for Admin. and Finance: DICK SIEMER

Vice-Pres. for Enrolment Management: Dr REGINALD G. L. ROSS

Vice-Pres. for IT: Dr AHMED M. EL-HAGGAN (acting)

Vice-Pres. for Institutional Advancement: DOUGLAS DALZELL

Vice-Pres. for Student Affairs: Dr FRANKLIN D. CHAMBERS

Dir of Institutional Research: Dr OYEBANJO LAJUBUTU

Dir of Univ. Relations: URSULA BATTLE

Dir of Library: Dr MARY E. WANZA

Registrar: Dr MARGARET W. TURNER

Library of 81,742 vols, 286,929 microform titles, 705 current periodicals

Number of teachers: 240

Number of students: 3,570 (3,005 undergraduate, 565 graduate)

Publication: *Journal of Minority Affairs* (1 a year)

DEANS

Helene Fuld School of Nursing: Dr MARCELLA A. COPES

Honors College: RON L. COLLINS, SR

School of Arts and Sciences: Dr ALCOTT ARTHUR

School of Education: Dr EDNA SIMMONS

School of Graduate Studies: Dr MARY E. OWENS-SOUTHALL

School of Management Science and Economics: Dr SADIE GREGORY

School of Professional Studies: Dr BEVERLY J. O'BRYANT

Frostburg State University

101 Braddock Rd, Frostburg, MD 21532-2303

Telephone: (301) 687-4000

E-mail: fsuadmissions@frostburg.edu

Internet: www.frostburg.edu

Founded 1898 as State Normal School, current name and status 1987

Pres.: Dr JONATHAN C. GIBRALTER

Provost and Vice-Pres. for Academic Affairs: Dr WILLIAM CHILDS

Vice-Pres. for Admin. and Finance: DAVID ROSE

Vice-Pres. for Economic Devt: STEPHEN SPAHR

Vice-Pres. for Student and Educational Services: Dr THOMAS L. BOWLING

Vice-Pres. for Univ. Advancement: ROSEMARY THOMAS

Registrar: JOHNSTON HEGEMAN

Dir for Admissions: TRISHA GREGORY

Dir for Library: Dr LEA MESSMAN-MANDICOTT

Library of 5,000,000 vols

Number of teachers: 300

Number of students: 5,430 (4,732 undergraduate, 698 graduate)

Publications: *Bittersweet, Joining the Conversation, Nightsun, Profile*

DEANS

College of Business: AHMAD TOOTOONCHI

College of Education: Dr CLARENCE GOLDEN

College of Liberal Arts and Sciences: Dr JOSEPH HOFFMAN

Salisbury University

1101 Camden Ave, Salisbury, MD 21801

Telephone: (410) 543-6000

Internet: www.salisbury.edu

Founded 1922

Academic year: August to May

Pres.: Dr JANET DUDLEY-ESHBACH

Provost and Vice-Pres. for Academic Affairs: Dr DIANE ALLEN

Vice-Pres. for Admin. and Finance: BETTY CROCKETT

Vice-Pres. for Student Affairs: Dr DANE FOUST

Vice-Pres. for Univ. Advancement (vacant)

Registrar: JACQUELINE MORAN MAISEL

Dean for Enrolment Management: JANE DANÉ

Dean for Libraries and Instructional Resources: Dr MARTHA ZIMMERMAN

Library of 254,151 vols, 4,467 audiovisual items

Number of teachers: 580 (389 full-time, 191 part-time)

Number of students: 8,600 (7,889 undergraduate, 711 graduate)

Publications: *Literature/Film Quarterly* (4 a year), *Panorama* (2 a year), *Shoreline, SU Magazine, SU Today* (irregular)

DEANS

Franklin P. Perdue School of Business: Dr BOB G. WOOD

Fulton School: MAARTEN PEREBOOM

Henson School of Science and Technology: Dr KAREN L. OLMSTEAD,

Seidel School of Education and Professional Studies: Dr DENNIS PATANICZEK

Towson University

8000 York Rd, Towson, MD 21252-0001

Telephone: (410) 704-2000

E-mail: admissions@towson.edu

Internet: www.towson.edu

Founded 1866 as State Normal School, present location 1915, current name adopted 1997

Academic year: September to May

Pres.: MARAVENE S. LOESCHKE

Provost and Vice-Pres. for Academic Affairs: MARCIA G. WELSH

Vice-Pres. for Admin. and Finance and Chief Fiscal Officer: MARK BEHM

Vice-Pres. for Economic and Community Outreach: DYAN BRASINGTON

Vice-Pres. for Student Affairs: DEBRA MORIARTY

Vice-Pres. for Univ. Advancement: Dr GARY N. RUBIN

Registrar: DAVID DECKER

Dir for Admissions: LOUISE SHULACK (acting)

Dean for Libraries: DEBORAH NOLAN

Library of 579,824 vols

Number of teachers: 1,640 (839 full-time, 801 part-time)

Number of students: 21,460 (17,515 undergraduate, 3,945 graduate)

Publications: *Grub Street* (1 a year), *iMagazine, Towson Alumni Magazine* (3 a year), *Tower Echoes* (1 a year), *Towson Journal of International Affairs, Transitions* (1 a year)

DEANS

College of Business and Economics: SHOREH KAYNAMA

College of Education: Dr RAYMOND P. LORION

College of Fine Arts and Communication: SUSAN E. PICINICH

College of Health Professions: CHARLOTTE E. EXNER

College of Liberal Arts: TERRY CONNEY

Honors College: JOSEPH MCGINN

Jess and Mildred Fisher College of Science and Mathematics: DAVID A. VANKO

University of Baltimore

1420 N Charles St, Baltimore, MD 21201
Telephone: (410) 837-4200
E-mail: intladms@ubalt.edu
Internet: www.ubalt.edu
Founded 1925
Pres.: ROBERT L. BOGOMOLNY
Provost and Sr Vice-Pres. for Academic Affairs: JOSEPH S. WOOD
Sr Vice-Pres. for Admin. and Finance: HARRY SCHUCKEL
Sr Vice-Pres. for Enrolment Management and Student Affairs: MIRIAM KING
Vice-Pres. for Institutional Advancement: THERESA SILANSKIS
Dir for Library: LUCY HOLMAN

Library of 400,000 vols
Number of teachers: 170
Number of students: 6,440 (3,256 undergraduate, 2,040 graduate, 1,144 law)
Publications: *The Reporter*, *University of Baltimore Magazine* (2 a year)

DEANS

College of Public Affairs: STEPHEN L. PERCY
Robert G. Merrick School of Business: DARLENE BRANNIGAN SMITH
School of Law: F. MICHAEL HIGGINBOTHAM
Yale Gordon College of Arts and Sciences: JEFFREY SAWYER (acting)

University of Maryland, Baltimore

620 W Lexington St, Baltimore, MD 21201
Telephone: (410) 706-3100
Internet: www.umaryland.edu
Founded 1807
Pres.: Dr JAY A. PERMAN
Vice-Pres. for Academic Affairs: ROGER J. WARD
Vice-Pres., Chief Admin. and Finance Officer: KATHLEEN M. BYINGTON
Vice-Pres. and Chief Govt and Community Affairs Officer: T. SUE GLADHILL
Vice-Pres. and Chief Enterprise and Economic Devt Officer: JAMES L. HUGHES
Vice-Pres. for Medical Affairs: Dr E. ALBERT REECE
Vice-Pres. for Planning and Accountability: PETER N. GILBERT
Sr Univ. Counsel: SUSAN GILLETTE

Library of 613,407 vols
Number of teachers: 2,515
Number of students: 6,350 (773 undergraduate, 5,577 graduate)
Publication: *Maryland Magazine* (1 a year)

DEANS

Dental School: CHRISTIAN S. STOHLER
Graduate School: (vacant)
School of Law: PHOEBE A. HADDON
School of Medicine: Dr E. ALBERT REECE
School of Nursing: Dr JANET D. ALLAN
School of Pharmacy: Dr NATALIE D. EDDINGTON
School of Social Work: Dr RICHARD P. BARTH

University of Maryland, Baltimore County

1000 Hilltop Circle, Baltimore, MD 21250
Telephone: (410) 455-1000
E-mail: admissions@umbc.edu
Internet: umbc.edu
Founded 1963
Academic year: September to May
Pres.: FREEMAN A. HRAQBOWSKI, III
Provost and Sr Vice-Pres. for Academic Affairs: PHILIP ROUS
Vice-Pres. for Admin. and Finance: LYNNE SCHAEFER

Vice-Pres. for IT: JOHN SUESS
Vice-Pres. for Institutional Advancement: GREGORY SIMMONS
Vice-Pres. for Research: GEOFFREY P. SUMMERS
Vice-Pres. for Student Affairs: NANCY YOUNG
Gen. Counsel: DAVID GLEASON
Dir of Library: LARRY WILT

Library: 1m.
Number of teachers: 770 (477 full-time, 293 part-time)
Number of students: 13,200 (10,574 undergraduate, 2,626 graduate)

DEANS

College of Arts, Humanities and Social Sciences: JOHN W. JEFFRIES
College of Engineering and Information Technology: WARREN DeVRIES
College of Natural and Mathematical Sciences: WILLIAM LaCOURSE
Erickson School: JUDAH RONCH
Graduate School: JANET RUTLEDGE
School of Social Work: Dr RICHARD BARTH

University of Maryland, College Park

College Park, MD 20742
Telephone: (301) 405-1000
Internet: www.umd.edu
Founded 1856 as Maryland Agricultural College
Academic year: September to May
Pres.: Dr WALLACE D. LOH
Provost and Sr Vice-Pres.: Dr MARY ANN RANKIN
Vice-Pres. for Admin. Affairs: CARLO COLELLA
Vice-Pres. for IT and Chief Information Officer: Dr ANN WYLIE
Vice-Pres. for Research: Dr PATRICK G. O'SHEA
Vice-Pres. for Student Affairs: Dr LINDA M. CLEMENT
Vice-Pres. for Univ. Relations: PETER WEILER
Registrar: ADRIAN R. CORNELIUS
Dean for Libraries: Dr PATRICIA STEELE

Library of 3,768,255 vols
Number of teachers: 4,410
Number of students: 37,270

DEANS

A. James Clark School of Engineering: Dr DARRYLL PINES
College of Agriculture and Natural Resources: Dr CHENG-I WEI
College of Arts and Humanities: Dr BONNIE THORNTON-DILL
College of Behavioural and Social Sciences: Dr JOHN R. TOWNSHEND
College of Computer, Mathematical and Natural Sciences: Dr JAYANTH BANAVAR
College of Education: Dr DONNA L. WISEMAN
College of Information Studies: Dr JENNIFER J. PREECE
Graduate School: Dr CHARLES CARAMELLO
Philip Merrill College of Journalism: Dr LUCY DALGLISH
Robert H. Smith School of Business: Dr ALEXANDER TRIANTIS
School of Architecture, Planning and Preservation: DAVID CRONRATH
School of Public Health: Dr JANE CLARK
School of Public Policy: Dr DONALD KETTL

University of Maryland, Eastern Shore

One Backbone Rd, Princess Anne, MD 21853
Telephone: (410) 651-2200
E-mail: umesadmissions@umes.edu
Internet: www.umes.edu
Founded 1886 as Delaware Conf. Acad., current name adopted 1970, present status 1988
Pres.: Dr MORTIMER H. NEUFVILLE

Vice-Pres. for Academic Affairs: Dr CHARLES WILLIAMS
Vice-Pres. for Admin. Affairs: Dr RONNIE HOLDEN
Vice-Pres. for Institutional Advancement: GAINS HAWKINS
Vice-Pres. for Student Affairs and Enrolment Management: Dr ANTHONY L. JENKINS
Vice-Pres. for Technology and Commercialization: Dr RONALD G. FORSYTHE
Dean for Library Services: Dr ELLIS B. BETECK

Library of 211,000 vols
Number of teachers: 210
Number of students: 3,160

DEANS

School of Agricultural and Natural Sciences: Dr JURGEN SCHWARZ (acting)
School of the Arts and Professions: Dr T. H. BAUGHMAN
School of Business and Technology: Dr AYODELE J. ALADE
School of Graduate Studies: Dr JENNIFER M. KEANE-DAWES
School of Pharmacy and Health Professions: Dr NICHOLAS RONALD BLANCHARD

University of Maryland, University College

3501 University Blvd, E, Adelphi, MD 20783
Telephone: (240) 582-2509
E-mail: umucinfo@info.umuc.edu
Internet: www.umuc.edu
Founded 1947
Academic year: August to May
Pres.: JAVIER MIYARES
Provost: Dr GREG VON LEHMEN (acting)
Vice-Pres. and Chief Financial Officer: EUGENE D. LOCKETT, JR
Vice-Pres. and Chief of Staff: ANDREA Y. HART
Vice-Pres. and Dir: Dr ALLAN J. BERG
Vice-Pres. for Enrolment Management: SEAN CHUNG
Vice-Pres. for the Dept of Defense Relations: JOHN F. JONES, JR
Vice-Pres. for Institutional Advancement: CATHY SWEET-WINDHAM
Vice-Pres. for IT: PETER C. YOUNG
Interim Vice-Pres. and Dir for UMUC Asia: Dr ALLAN J. BERG
Vice-Pres. and Dir for UMUC Europe: Dr ALLEN J. BERG
Vice-Pres. and Gen. Counsel: NANCY WILLIAMSON

Library of 1,337 vols
Number of teachers: 3,100 worldwide
Number of students: 92,210 worldwide

DEANS

Graduate School of Management and Technology: Dr ROBERT GOODWIN
School of Undergraduate Studies: Dr MARIE A. CINI

STEVENSON UNIVERSITY

1525 Greenspring Valley Rd, Stevenson, MD 21153-0641
Telephone: (410) 486-7001
E-mail: admissions@mail.vjc.edu
Internet: www.stevenson.edu
Founded 1947, fmrly Villa Julie College, current name adopted 2008
Private control
Academic year: August to May
campuses in Baltimore, Greenspring and Owings Mills
Pres.: Dr KEVIN J. MANNING
Exec. Vice-Pres. for Academic Affairs and Dean of Staff: Dr PAUL D. LACK
Exec. Vice-Pres. and Chief Financial Officer: TIMOTHY M. CAMPBELL

Vice-Pres. for Univ. Advancement: STEVEN-
SON W. CLOSE, Jr
Registrar: TRACY R. BOLT
Dir for Library Services: MAUREEN A. BECK
Library of 100,000 vols
Number of students: 3,930 (2,986 under-
graduate, 357 graduate)

DEANS

Brown School of Business and Leadership:
NORMAN ENDLICH
School of Design: KEITH D. KUTCH
School of Education: DEBORAH S. KRAFT
School of Humanities and Social Sciences: Dr
JAMES GERARD SALVUCCI
School of the Sciences: Dr SUSAN T. GORMAN

WASHINGTON ADVENTIST UNIVERSITY

7600 Flower Ave, Takoma Park, MD 20912

Telephone: (301) 891-4000
E-mail: info@wau.edu
Internet: www.wau.edu

Founded 1904 as Washington Training Institute, present name and status 2009
Private control

Pres.: Dr WEYMOUTH SPENCE
Provost: SUSAN HORNSHAW
Sr Vice-Pres. for Operations: GERALD ANDER-
SON
Exec. Vice-Pres. for Finance: PATRICK FARLEY
Vice-Pres. for Advancement and Alumni
Relations: BRUCE PEIFER
Vice-Pres. for Min.: BARAKA MUGANDA
Vice-Pres. for Student Life: JEAN WARDEN
Registrar: Dr EMILE JOHN
Librarian: LEE WISEL

Library of 140,000 vols
Number of teachers: 50
Number of students: 1,210

Publications: *The Columbia Journal* (2 a
year), *Golden Memories*, *Montage* (1 a
year), *Reunion* (4 a year)

DEANS

School of Arts and Social Sciences: GASPAR
COLON
School of Graduate and Professional Studies:
Dr JUDE EDWARDS
School of Health Professions, Science and
Wellness: GINA BROWN

WASHINGTON BIBLE COLLEGE/ CAPITAL BIBLE SEMINARY/EQUIP INSTITUTE

6511 Princess Garden Parkway, Lanham,
MD 20706

Telephone: (301) 552-1400
E-mail: iadmissions@bible.edu
Internet: www.bible.edu

Founded 1938 by merger of 3 Bible institutes
Private control
Academic year: July to June
Br in Springfield, Virginia

Pres.: Dr GEORGE M. HARTON
Library Dir: WILLIAM A. BANKS

Library of 93,057 vols
Number of teachers: 50
Number of students: 500

WASHINGTON COLLEGE

300 Washington Ave, Chestertown, MD
21620-1197

Telephone: (410) 778-2800
E-mail: wc_admissions@washcoll.edu
Internet: www.washcoll.edu

Founded 1782
Private control
Academic year: September to July

Offers divs: humanities, natural sciences and
mathematics, and social sciences
Pres.: MITCHELL B. REISS
Provost and Dean of the College: JOHN B.
TAYLOR
Sr Vice-Pres. for Finance and Admin.: JAMES
MANARO
Exec. Vice-Pres.: JOSEPH L. HOLT
Vice-Pres. for Admissions and Enrolment
Management: KEVIN COVENEY
Vice-Pres. for Advancement: GRETCHEN
DWYER
Vice-Pres. for College Relations: MEREDITH
DAVIES HADAWAY
Vice-Pres. and Dean for Student Affairs:
MELA DUTKA
Registrar: JENNIFER BERSHON
College Librarian: RUTH SHOGE

Library of 200,000 vols
Number of teachers: 150
Number of students: 1,400

Publications: *Apeiron* (1 a year), *The Collegian* (12 a year), *The Pegasus* (1 a year),
Treason, *Washington College Review* (1 a
year), *Washington College International
Studies Review*

MASSACHUSETTS

AMERICAN INTERNATIONAL COLLEGE

100 State St, Springfield, MA 01109

Telephone: (413) 737-7000
E-mail: inquiry@aic.edu
Internet: www.aic.edu

Founded 1885
Private control
Academic year: September to May

Pres.: Dr VINCENT M. MANIACI
Exec. Vice-Pres. for Academic Affairs: Dr
GREGORY T. SCHMUTTE
Exec. Vice-Pres. for Admin.: RICHARD BEDARD
Vice-Pres. for Admissions Services: PETER J.
MILLER
Vice-Pres. for Enrolment Management:
LINDA DAGRADI
Vice-Pres. for Finance: Dr THOMAS E. DYBICK
Vice-Pres. for Student Affairs: Dr BLAINE K.
STEVENS
Exec. Dir for Institutional Advancement:
HEATHER CAHILL
Registrar: DIANE FURTEK
Dir of Library Services: ESTELLE SPENCER

Library of 189,000 vols
Number of teachers: 170 (86 full-time, 84
part-time)
Number of students: 3,600 (3,060 undergraduate, 540 graduate)

DEANS

School of Arts and Sciences: Dr VICKIE L.
HESS
School of Business Admin.: Dr LEA A.
JOHNSON
School of Continuing Education: Dr ROLAND
E. HOLSTEAD
School of Health Sciences: Dr CAROL A. JOBE

AMHERST COLLEGE

POB 5000, Amherst, MA 01002-5000

Telephone: (413) 542-2000
E-mail: info@amherst.edu
Internet: www.amherst.edu

Founded 1821
Private control
Academic year: September to May

Depts of American studies, anthropology and
sociology, Asian languages and civilizations,
astronomy, biology, black studies, chemistry,
classics, economics, English, European studies, fine arts, French, geology, German, his-

tory, law, jurisprudence, and social thought,
mathematics and computer science, music,
neuroscience, philosophy, physical education
and athletics, physics, political science,
psychology, religion, Russian, Spanish,
theatre and dance, women's and gender
studies

Pres.: Dr CAROLYN A. MARTIN
Chief Advancement Officer: MEGAN MOREY
Dean of Admission and Financial Aid: THO-
MAS A. PARKER
Dean of Faculty: CATHERINE EPSTEIN
Dean of Students: ALLEN HART
Registrar: KATHLEEN M. GOFF
Librarian: BRYN GEFFERT

Library of 1,023,085 vols, 595,296 media
items
Number of teachers: 200 (full-time)
Number of students: 1,800

Publication: *Amherst Magazine* (4 a year)

ANDOVER NEWTON THEOLOGICAL SCHOOL

210 Herrick Rd, Newton Centre, MA 02459

Telephone: (617) 964-1100
E-mail: admissions@ants.edu
Internet: www.ants.edu

Founded 1807 as Andover Theological Seminary, current name adopted 1965;
attached to Boston Theological Institute
Private control
Academic year: August to May

Offers Masters degree in divinity, ministry,
religious education, theological research,
theological studies

Pres.: Rev. Dr NICK CARTER
Vice-Pres. for Academic Affairs and Dean of
the Faculty: SARAH B. DRUMMOND
Vice-Pres. for Finance and Operations: YI
JUNG
Vice-Pres. for Institutional Advancement:
JENNIFER CRAIG
Vice-Pres. for Strategic Initiatives and Dean
of Students and Community Life: NANCY
NIENHUIS
Registrar: NAYDA AQUILA
Dir of Enrolment: MARGARET L. CARROLL
Dir of Library: JEFFREY L. BRIGHAM

Library of 260,000 vols
Number of teachers: 90
Number of students: 480

ANNA MARIA COLLEGE

50 Sunset Lane Paxton, MA 01612

Telephone: (508) 849-3300
E-mail: admissions@annamaria.edu
Internet: www.annamaria.edu

Founded 1946
Private control
Academic year: August to May (2 semesters)

Divs of business, law and public policy,
environmental, natural and technological
sciences, fine arts, humanities and int. studies, human devt and human services

Pres.: Dr JACK P. CALARESO
Exec. Vice-Pres.: MARY LOU RETELLE
Vice-Pres. for Academic Affairs: BILLYE
AUCLAIR
Vice-Pres. for Student Affairs and Dean of
Retention: ANDREW KLEIN
Dean of Students: Dr JOSEPH FARRAGHER
Dir of Institutional Advancement: BRIDGET
HAVARD
Registrar: BARBARA ZAWALICH
Dir of Library: RUTH PYNE

Library of 95,000 vols
Number of teachers: 220
Number of students: 1,500

ASSUMPTION COLLEGE

500 Salisbury St, Worcester, MA 01609-1296
Telephone: (508) 767-7000
E-mail: admiss@assumption.edu
Internet: www.assumption.edu

Founded 1904
Private control
Language of instruction: English
Academic year: September to May (2 semesters)

Divs of art and music, business studies, economics and global studies, education, English, modern and classical languages and cultures, history, human services and rehabilitation studies, mathematics and computer science, natural sciences, philosophy, political science, psychology, social and rehabilitation services, sociology and anthropology, theology

Pres.: Dr FRANCESCO C. CESAREO
Provost and Academic Vice-Pres.: Dr FRANCIS LAZARUS
Exec. Vice-Pres. for Finance and Admin. and Treas.: CHRISTIAN W. McCARTHY
Vice-Pres. for Enrolment Management: EVAN E. LIPP
Vice-Pres. for Institutional Advancement: TIMOTHY STANTON
Vice-Pres. for Student Affairs: Dr CATHERINE M. WOODBROOKS
Dean for Admissions: KATHLEEN M. MURPHY
Dean for Campus Life: CONWAY CAMPBELL
Dean for Undergraduate Studies: ELOISE KNOWLTON
Assoc. Provost: Dr LOUISE CARROLL KEELEY
Dir for Career and Continuing Education: DENNIS BRAUN
Registrar: DAVID W. AALTO
Dir for Library: DORIS ANN SWEET

Library of 216,668 vols
Number of teachers: 280
Number of students: 2,730

Publication: *Assumption College Magazine* (4 a year)

BABSON COLLEGE

231 Forest St, Babson Park, MA 02457-0310
Telephone: (781) 235-1200
E-mail: ugradadmission@babson.edu
Internet: www.babson.edu

Founded 1919 as Babson Institute, current name adopted 1969
Private control
Academic year: August to August

Pres.: LEONARD A. SCHLESINGER
Provost and Chief Academic Officer: Dr SHAHID ANSARI
Vice-Pres. and Gen. Counsel: JONATHAN MOLL
Vice-Pres. for Admin.: MARY ROSE
Vice-Pres. for Devt: DIANA PRESCOTT ZAIS
Vice-Pres. for Finance and Chief Financial Officer: PHILIP SHAPIRO
Dean of Admissions: GRANT GOSSELIN
Dean of Faculty: CAROLYN HOTCHKISS
Dean of Student Affairs: BETSY NEWMAN
Dir of Libraries: (vacant)

Library of 132,024 vols
Number of teachers: 250
Number of students: 3,340

Publication: *Babson Magazine* (4 a year)

DEANS

Babson Exec. Education: ELAINE EISENMAN
F. W. Olin Graduate School of Business: RAGHU TADEPALLI
Undergraduate School: Dr DENNIS HANNO

BARD COLLEGE AT SIMON'S ROCK

84 Alford Rd, Great Barrington, MA 01230
Telephone: (413) 644-4400
E-mail: admit@simons-rock.edu
Internet: www.simons-rock.edu

Founded 1966
Private control
Academic year: August to May

Divs of arts, languages and literature, mathematics and computing, science, social studies

Pres.: LEON BOTSTEIN
Provost and Vice-Pres.: Dr PETER LAIPSON
Exec. Vice-Pres.: DIMITRI PAPADIMITRIOU
Vice-Pres. for Early College Policies and Programmes: LESLIE DAVIDSON
Dean of Academic Affairs: ANNE O'DWYER
Dean of the College: M. LESLIE DAVIDSON
Dean of Student Affairs: ROBERT GRAVES
Registrar: HEIDI-BETH ROTHBERG
Dir of Library: BRIAN MIKESELL

Library of 90,772 vols
Number of teachers: 40
Number of students: 350

BAY PATH COLLEGE

588 Longmeadow St, Longmeadow, MA 01106
Telephone: (413) 565-1000
E-mail: contact@baypath.edu
Internet: www.baypath.edu

Founded 1897 as Bay Path Institute, current name adopted 1988
Private control
Academic year: August to May

Campus in Burlington andSturbridge

Pres.: Dr CAROL A. LEARY
Provost and Vice-Pres. for Academic Affairs: Dr MELISSA MORRISS-OLSON
Vice-Pres. for Academic and Admin. Technology: Dr DAVID M. DEMERS
Vice-Pres. for Finance and Admin. Services: MICHAEL J. GIAMPIETRO
Vice-Pres. for Institutional Advancement: KATHLEEN M. BOURQUE
Vice-Pres. for Planning and Student Devt: CARON T. HOBIN
Registrar: LAURA K. LANDER
Dir of Library and Information Services: MICHAEL MORAN

Library of 49,713 vols, 84,824 ebooks, 412 periodicals, 4,410 microform units, 2,495 video items, 1,414 DVDs, 6,176 streaming films, 202 audio CDs
Number of teachers: 70
Number of students: 2,190

DEANS

Arts and Sciences: Dr MICHAEL KONIG
Education: Dr LIZ FLEMING
Management and Social Justice: Dr GEOFFREY MILLS

BECKER COLLEGE

Weller Academic Bldg, 61 Sever St, Worcester, MA 01609
Telephone: (508) 791-9241
E-mail: info@becker.edu
Internet: www.becker.edu

Founded 1784 as Leicester Acad., present name 1990
Private control

Academic divs incl. animal studies, business, criminal justice and legal studies, design, education and psychology, nursing and exercise sciences

Pres.: Dr ROBERT E. JOHNSON
Sr Vice-Pres. and Chief Financial Officer: Dr DAVID A. ELLIS
Vice-Pres. for Academic Affairs and Dean of College: Dr ELIZABETH V. FULLER
Vice-Pres. for Devt and Alumni Affairs: DEAN J. HICKEY
Vice-Pres. for Institutional Advancement Dean: J. HICKEY
Vice-Pres. for Student Affairs and Dean of Students: KENNETH S. CAMERON
Dean of Enrolment Management: KAREN SCHEDIN
Registrar: NIKKI ANDREWS
Dir of Libraries: GARRETT EASTMAN

Library of 73,500 vols
Number of students: 1,800

BENJAMIN FRANKLIN INSTITUTE OF TECHNOLOGY

41 Berkeley St, Boston, MA 02116
Telephone: (617) 423-4630
E-mail: admissions@bfit.edu
Internet: www.bfit.edu

Founded 1908
Private control
Academic year: September to May (2 semesters)

Depts of architectural technology, automotive technology, electrical technology, electronics engineering technology, mechanical engineering technology, medical electronics engineering technology, ophthalmic assisting

Pres.: GEORGE C. CHRYSSIS
Academic Dean: ANTHONY BENOIT
Dean of Enrolment Management: MIKE BOSCO
Dean of Students: BRIAN BICKNELL
Chief Financial Officer: KEITH DROPKIN
Dir of Admissions: MARVIN LOISEAU
Dir of Devt: JULIANA FIELD
Registrar: JAMES KLASEN
Dir of Library Services: SHARON BONK

Library of 73,000 vols incl. newspapers, 300 journals
Number of teachers: 170
Number of students: 560

BENTLEY UNIVERSITY

175 Forest St, Waltham, MA 02452
Telephone: (781) 891-2000
E-mail: ugadmission@bentley.edu
Internet: www.bentley.edu

Founded 1917 as school of accounting and finance, present name and status 2008
Private control

Pres.: Dr GLORIA CORDES LARSON
Provost and Vice-Pres. for Academic Affairs: Dr MICHAEL J. PAGE
Vice-Pres. for Business and Finance and Treas.: PAUL CLEMENTE
Vice-Pres. for Devt, Corporate and Alumni Affairs: JOHN W. MOSSER
Vice-Pres. for Enrolment Management: JOANN C. McKENNA
Vice-Pres. for Information Technology: TRACI A. LOGAN
Vice-Pres. for Student Affairs: KATHLEEN L. YORKIS
Vice-Pres. for Univ. Advancement: WILLIAM TORREY
Gen. Counsel: Dr JUDITH A. MALONE
Exec. Dir of Academic Technology, Library and Online Learning: PHIL KNUTEL

Library of 192,566 vols
Number of teachers: 470 (290 full-time, 180 part-time)
Number of students: 5,690 (4291 undergraduate, 1,399 graduate)

Publication: *Business in the Contemporary World* (4 a year)

DEANS

Arts and Sciences: Dr DANIEL L. EVERETT

Business and the McCallum Graduate School: Dr ROY A. WIGGINS

BERKLEE COLLEGE OF MUSIC

1140 Boylston St, Boston, MA 02215-3695

Telephone: (617) 266-1400
E-mail: admissions@berklee.edu
Internet: www.berklee.edu

Founded 1945 as Schillinger House of Music, current name adopted 1970

Private control

Academic year: September to August (3 semesters)

Campus in Valencia

Pres.: ROGER H. BROWN
Sr Vice-Pres. for Academic Affairs and Provost: LAWRENCE J. SIMPSON
Sr Vice-Pres. for Institutional Advancement: CINDY ALBERT LINK
Vice-Pres. for Admin.: JOHN ELDERT
Vice-Pres. for Enrolment: MARK CAMPBELL
Vice-Pres. for External Affairs: THOMAS P. RILEY
Vice-Pres. for Finance: AMELIA KOCH
Vice-Pres. for Student Affairs and Dean of Students: LAWRENCE E. BETHUNE
Dean of Admissions: DAMIEN BRACKEN
Registrar: MICHAEL HAGERTY
Dean of Learning Resources: GARY HAGGERTY
Library of 27,779 vols, 33,430 recordings, 23,302 musical scores, 23,764 lead sheets, 450 periodicals
Number of teachers: 520
Number of students: 4,130

DEANS

Continuing Education: DEBORAH L. CAVALIER
Music Technology Div.: S. JAY KENNEDY
Professional Education Div.: DARLA S. HANLEY,
Professional Performance Div.: MATT MARAVUGLIO
Professional Writing and Music Technology Div.: KARI H. JUUSELA

BLESSED JOHN XXIII NATIONAL SEMINARY

558 South Ave, Weston, MA 02493-2699

Telephone: (781) 899-5500
E-mail: seminary@blessedjohnxxiii.edu
Internet: www.blessedjohnxxiii.edu

Founded 1964
Private control
Academic year: September to May
Areas of study incl. divinity, pre-theology

Rector and Pres.: Rev. WILLIAM B. PALARDY
Academic Dean and Registrar: Dr ANTHONY KEATY
Dean of Seminarians: Rev. THOMAS F. SCHMITT
Dir of Pastoral Ministry Programmes: Rev. MICHAEL A. J. ALFANO
Dir of Pre-Theology Programme: Dr JOHN F. MILLARD
Dir of Spiritual Formation: Rev. PAUL E. MICELI
Library Dir: Sis. JACQUELINE MILLER
Library of 67,000 vols
Number of teachers: 20
Number of students: 70

BOSTON ARCHITECTURAL COLLEGE

320 Newbury St, Boston, MA 02115

Telephone: (617) 262-5000
E-mail: admissions@the-bac.edu
Internet: www.the-bac.edu

Founded 1889 as Boston Architectural Club, current name adopted 1944
Private control

Schools of architecture, design studies, interior design, landscape design

Pres.: Dr THEODORE LANDSMARK
Provost and Academic Vice-Pres.: JULIA HALEVY
Vice-Pres. for External and Govt Relations: JANET OBERTO
Vice-Pres. for Finance and Admin.: KATHY ROOD
Vice-Pres. for Institutional Advancement: EVAN GALLIVAN
Vice-Pres. for Professional and Continuing Education: KAREN MUNCASTER
Dean for Admissions: MIKE RIVAS
Dean for Enrolment and Student Financial Services: JAMES RYAN
Dean for Graduate Studies: DIANA RAMIREZ-JASSO
Dean for Students and Assoc. Provost: RICHARD GRISWOLD
Registrar: ANN ROYALL
Dir for Library: SUSAN LEWIS
Library of 45,700 vols, 45,000 slides, 7,000 images
Number of teachers: 480
Number of students: 1,090 (611 undergraduate, 479 graduate)

BOSTON COLLEGE

140 Commonwealth Ave, Chestnut Hill, MA 02467

Telephone: (617) 552-8000
E-mail: gsasinfo@bc.edu
Internet: www.bc.edu

Founded 1863
Private control
Academic year: September to May

Campuses in Brighton, Newton

Pres.: Rev. WILLIAM P. LEAHY
Provost and Dean of Faculties: DAVID QUIGLEY
Exec. Vice-Pres.: PATRICK J. KEATING
Vice-Pres. for Facilities Management: DANIEL BOURQUE
Vice-Pres. for Finance and Treas.: PETER C. McKENZIE
Vice-Pres. for Student Affairs: Dr PATRICK ROMBALSKI
Dir for Libraries: JEROME YAVARKOVSKY
Library of 2,594,750 vols, 300,000 ebooks
Number of teachers: 1,215 (737 full time, 478 part time)
Number of students: 14,625

Publications: *Boston College Environmental Affairs Law Review* (4 a year), *Boston College International and Comparative Law Review* (2 a year), *Boston College Law Review* (5 a year), *Boston College Third World Law Journal* (2 a year), *Catholic Education: A Journal of Inquiry and Practice*, *Journal of Educational Change*, *Journal of Technology, Learning, and Assessment*, *Learning Disability Quarterly*, *Lonergan Workshop Journal* (1 a year), *Philosophy and Social Criticism* (6 a year), *Religion and the Arts* (4 a year), *The Community, Work and Family Journal*, *The Journal of Corporate Citizenship*, *Uniform Commercial Code Reporter-Digest* (4 a year)

DEANS

Carroll School of Management: ANDREW C. BOYNTON
College and Graduate School of Arts and Sciences: DAVID QUIGLEY
Graduate School of Social Work: Prof. ALBERTO GODENZI
Law School: Prof. Dr VINCENT D. ROUGEAU
Lynch School of Education: Prof. Dr MAUREEN KENNY
School of Theology and Ministry: MARK S. MASSA

William F. Connell School of Nursing: Prof. Dr SUSAN GENNARO
Woods College of Advancing Studies: JAMES A. WOODS

PROFESSORS

Carroll School of Management (140 Commonwealth Ave, Chestnut Hill, MA 02467; tel. (617) 552-3932; e-mail carrollschool.dean@bc.edu):

BARTUNEK, J., Organization Studies
CAMPANELLA, F. B., Finance
CLOTE, P., Computer Science
CRONIN, M., Operations and Strategic Management
FERSON, W. E., Finance
GIPS, J., Computer Science
GRAVES, S., Operations and Strategic Management
HOLDERNESS, C. G., Finance
KANE, E. J., Finance
MARCUS, A., Finance
NIELSEN, R., Organization Studies
O'BRIEN, C., Business Law
PARKER, F. J., Business Law
RAELIN, J., Operations and Strategic Management
RINGUEST, J., Operations and Strategic Management
RITZMAN, L., Operations and Strategic Management
SAFIZADEH, M. H., Operations and Strategic Management
STRAUBING, H., Computer Science
TAGGART, R., Finance
TEHRANIAN, H., Finance
TORBERT, W. R., Organization Studies
TWOMEY, D. P., Business Law
WADDOCK, S., Operations and Strategic Management
WILSON, G. P., Accounting
WOODSIDE, A., Marketing
WRIGHT, A., Accounting

College and Graduate School of Arts and Sciences (140 Commonwealth Ave, Chestnut Hill, MA 02467-3961; tel. (617) 552-2800; e-mail casdean@bc.edu):

ANDERSON, J., Economics
ANNUNZIATO, A., Biology
ARNOTT, R., Economics
ASH, A., Mathematics
BAGLIVO, J., Mathematics
BANUAZIZI, A., Psychology
BARTH, J. R., English
BEDELL, K., Physics
BELSLEY, D., Economics
BERGER, P., Fine Arts
BERNAUER, J. W., Philosophy
BLAKE, R., Fine Arts
BLANCHETTE, O., Philosophy
BODENHEIMER, R., English
BOMBOLAKIS, E. G., Geology and Geophysics
BROIDO, D. A., Physics
BROWN, S., Theology
BROWNELL, H., Psychology
BRUCKNER, M. T., Romance Languages
BRUELL, C., Political Science
BUCKLEY, M., Theology
BUNIE, A., History
BURGESS, D., Biology
BYRNE, P. H., Philosophy
CAHILL, L., Theology
CARPENTER, D. E., Romance Languages
CLARKE, M. J., Chemistry
CLEARY, J. J., Philosophy
CLOONEY, F. X., Theology
CLOTE, P., Biology
COBB-STEVENS, R., Philosophy
COX, D., Economics
CRANE, M., English
CRONIN, J., History
DAVIDOVITS, P., Chemistry
DERBER, C., Sociology
DI BARTOLO, B., Physics

DIETRICH, D., Theology
EASTON, R., Psychology
EBEL, J. E., Geology and Geophysics
EGAN, H., Theology
EYKMAN, C., German Studies
FAULKNER, R. K., Political Science
FLANAGAN, J. F., Philosophy
FLEMING, R., History
FOURKAS, J. T., Chemistry
FRIEDBERG, S., Mathematics
GARCIA, J., Philosophy
GOIZUETA, R., Theology
GOLLOP, F. M., Economics
GOTTSCHALK, P., Economics
GRAY, P., Psychology
GROOME, T. H., Theology
GUILLEMIN, J., Sociology
HACHEY, T. E., History
HAFNER, D. L., Political Science
HASKIN, D., English
HEINEMAN, J., History
HEPBURN, J. C., Geology and Geophysics
HERBECK, D., Communications
HESSE-BIBER, S., Sociology
HIBBS, T., Philosophy
HIMES, M., Theology
HOFFMAN, C., Biology
HOLLENBACH, D., Theology
HOLMSTROM, L. L., Sociology
HOVEYDA, A. H., Chemistry
IRELAND, P., Economics
KANTROWITZ, E. R., Chemistry
KARP, D. A., Sociology
KEARNEY, R., Philosophy
KELLY, C. J., Political Science
KELLY, T. R., Chemistry
KEMPA, K., Physics
KENNEDY, T. F., Music
KENNEY, M., Mathematics
KIRSCHNER, D. A., Biology
KRAUS, M., Economics
KREEFT, P. J., Philosophy
LAMB, M., Theology
LANDY, M., Political Science
LEE, T. O., Music
LEWBEL, A., Economics
LEWIS, P., English
LIEM, R., Psychology
LOWRY, R., Sociology
LYDENBERG, R., English
McFADDEN, D. L., Chemistry
McLAUGHLIN, L. W., Chemistry
MADIGAN, A., Philosophy
MANNING, R., History
MARIANI, P., English
MATELSKI, M., Communications
MATSON, S., English
MEISSNER, W., Theology
MELNICK, R. S., Political Science
MEYERHOFF, G. R., Mathematics
MICHALCZYK, J., Fine Arts
MILLER, S. J., Chemistry
MUNNELL, A. H., Finance
MUSKAVITCH, M., Biology
NAUGHTON, M., Physics
NETZER, N., Fine Arts
NORTHRUP, D., History
NUMAN, M., Psychology
PARIS, J. J., Theology
PERKINS, P., Theology
PFOHL, S. J., Sociology
PHILIPPIDES, D. M. L., Classics
QUINN, J., Economics
RASMUSSEN, D. M., Philosophy
REEDER, M., Mathematics
REINERMAN, A. J., History
RESLER, M., German Studies
RESTUCCIA, F., English
RICHARDSON, A., English
RICHARDSON, W. J., Philosophy
RINTALA, M., Political Science
ROBERTS, M. F., Chemistry
ROSS, R. S., Political Science
ROY, D. C., Geology and Geophysics
RUSSELL, J. A., Psychology
SARDELLA, D. J., Chemistry

SCHERVISH, P. G., Sociology
SCHIANTARELLI, F., Economics
SCHLOZMAN, K. L., Political Science
SCHOR, J., Sociology
SCHRADER, R., English
SCOTT, L. T., Chemistry
SCOTT-JONES, D., Psychology
SEGAL, U., Economics
SEYFRIED, T., Biology
SHELL, S., Political Science
SHOLL, M. J., Psychology
SMITH, J. H., Mathematics
SMYER, M., Psychology
SNAPPER, M. L., Chemistry
TAMINIAUX, J., Philosophy
TAYLOR, D., English
THIE, P. R., Mathematics
VALETTE, R. M., Romance Languages
VAUGHAN, D., Sociology
WEILER, P., History
WILLIAMSON, J. B., Sociology
WILSON, C. P., English
WILT, J., English
WINNER, E., Psychology
WOLFE, A., Political Science
WOLFF, L., History

Graduate School of Social Work (140 Commonwealth Ave, Chestnut Hill, MA 02467; tel. (617) 552-4020; e-mail gssw@bc.edu):

BLYTHE, B.
GODENZI, A.
IATRIDIS, D. S.
KAYSER, K.
MALUCCIO, A. N.

Law School (885 Centre St, Newton Center, MA 02459; tel. (617) 552-8550):

AULT, H. J.
BARON, C. H.
BLOOM, R. M.
BRODIN, M. S.
BROWN, G. D.
COQUILLETTE, D. R.
CUNNINGHAM, L.
FITZGIBBON, S. T.
GOLDFARB, P.
HILLINGER, I. M.
HOWE, R.-A. W.
KATZ, S. N.
KOHLER, T. C.
McMORROW, J. A.
PLATER, Z. J. B.
REPETTI, J. R.
ROGERS, J. S.
SOIFER, A.
SPIEGEL, M.
WELLS, C.
WIRTH, D. A.
YEN, A. C.-C.

Lynch School of Education (140 Commonwealth Ave, Chestnut Hill, MA 02467; tel. (617) 552-4200; e-mail gsoe@bc.edu):

AIRASIAN, P. W.
ALTBACH, P. G.
BLUSTEIN, D.
BRABECK, M. M.
BRISK, M. E.
CASEY, M. B.
COCHRAN-SMITH, M.
DACEY, J. S.
DUDLEY-MARLING, C.
HANEY, W. M.
HARGREAVES, A.
HAUSER-CRAM, P.
HELMS, J. E.
LADD, G. T.
LERNER, J. V.
LYKES, M. B.
MADAUS, G. F.
MULLIS, I. V. S.
PINE, G. J.
PULLIN, D. C.
SHIRLEY, D. L.
STARRATT, R. J.
TWOMEY, E.

WALSH, M. E.
YOUN, E. I. K.
William F. Connell School of Nursing (140 Commonwealth Ave, Chestnut Hill, MA 02467; tel. (617) 552-4250):

BURGESS, A. W.
DUFFY, M. E.
FRY, S. T.
HAWKINS, J. W.
JONES, D. A.
MUNRO, B. H.
ROY, Sr, C.
VESSEY, J. A.
WARDLE, M. G.

BOSTON COLLEGE SCHOOL OF THEOLOGY AND MINISTRY

140 Commonwealth Ave, Chestnut Hill, MA 02467-3800

9 Lake St, Brighton, MA 02135-3841

Telephone: (617) 552-6501

E-mail: stmadmissions@bc.edu

Internet: www.bc.edu/schools/stm

Founded 2008 by merger of Weston Jesuit School of Theology with Institute of Religious Education and Pastoral Ministry

Private control

Academic year: August to DecemberJanuary to August (2 semesters)

Offers bachelors degree in sacred theology; masters degree in pastoral ministry, religious education, theology

Dean: MARK MASSA

Asst Dean and Dir of Admissions: SEAN PORTER

Assoc. Dean of Finance and Admin.: JOHN STACHNIEWICZ

Assoc. Dean of Student Affairs: JACQUELINE REGAN

Librarian: ESTHER GRISWOLD

Library of 2,440,000 vols

BOSTON CONSERVATORY

8 The Fenway, Boston, MA 02215

Telephone: (617) 536-6340

E-mail: admissions@bostonconservatory.edu

Internet: www.bostonconservatory.edu

Founded 1867

Private control

Academic year: September to May

Divs of dance, music, theatre

Pres.: RICHARD ORTNER

Vice-Pres. for Academic Affairs, Dean and Chief Academic Officer: PATRICIA HOY

Vice-Pres. for Admin., Student Affairs and Dean of Students: CARMEN GRIGGS

Vice-Pres. for Finance and Planning: ERIC NORMAN

Dir of Admissions: MEGHAN CADWALLADER

Dir of Devt: EILEEN MENY

Registrar: GREGORY KARAS

Dir of Library: JENNIFER HUNT

Library of 40,000 vols

Number of teachers: 160

Number of students: 730 (522 undergraduate, 208 graduate)

BOSTON GRADUATE SCHOOL OF PSYCHOANALYSIS

1581 Beacon St, Brookline, MA 02446

Telephone: (617) 277-3915

E-mail: bgsp@bgsp.edu

Internet: www.bgsp.edu

Founded 1973

Private control

Academic year: September to June (2 semesters)

Campus in New York; offers MA and doctorate degrees in Psychoanalysis, Psychoanalysis and Culture, Psychoanalytic Counselling

Pres.: Dr JANE SNYDER
Vice-Pres. for Finance and Institutional Relations: Dr CAROL M. PANETTA
Dean of Graduate Studies: Dr LYNN PERLMAN
Dir of Financial Aid, Admissions Coordinator, Int. Student Services: STEPHANIE WOOLBERT
Registrar: ALLISON WILLIAMS
Dir of Library Services: AMY COHEN-ROSE
Library of 5,000 vols incl. journals
Number of teachers: 70
Number of students: 200

BOSTON UNIVERSITY

One Silber Way, Boston, MA 02215
Telephone: (617) 353-2000
E-mail: admissions@bu.edu
Internet: www.bu.edu
Founded 1839 as Newbury Biblical Institute, current name adopted 1869
Private control
Academic year: September to May (2 semesters)

Pres.: Dr ROBERT A. BROWN
Provost: Prof. Dr JEAN MORRISON
Sr Vice-Pres. for External Affairs: Dr STEPHEN P. BURGAY
Sr Vice-Pres., Chief Financial Officer and Treas.: MARTIN J. HOWARD
Sr Vice-Pres., Gen. Counsel and Sec. of Board of Trustees: Dr TODD L. C. KLIPP
Exec. Vice-Pres.: JOSEPH P. MERCURIO
Vice-Pres. for Admin. Services: PETER FIEDLER
Vice-Pres. for Auxiliary Services: PETER P. SMOKOWSKI
Vice-Pres. for Devt and Alumni Relations: SCOTT G. NICHOLS
Vice-Pres. for Enrolment and Student Affairs: Dr LAURIE A. POHL
Vice-Pres. for Govt and Community Affairs: EDWARD KING
Vice-Pres. for Operations: GARY W. NICKSA
Vice-Pres. and Assoc. Provost for Global Operations: WILLIS G. WANG
Vice-Pres. and Assoc. Provost for Research: Dr ANDREI A. RUCKENSTEIN
Dean of Students: KENNETH ELMORE
Registrar: FLORENCE BERGERON
Dir of Library: ROBERT HUDSON
Library: see under Libraries and Archives
Number of teachers: 2,630
Number of students: 31,770

Publications: *Arion*, *Boston University Law Review*, *Journal of Education*, *Journal of Field Archaeology*

DEANS

College and Graduate School of Arts and Sciences: Prof. Dr VIRGINIA SAPIRO
College of Communication: THOMAS E. FIEDLER
College of Engineering: Prof. Dr KENNETH R. LUTCHEN
College of Fine Arts: BENJAMÍN E. JUÁREZ
College of General Studies: Dr LINDA S. WELLS
Henry M. Goldman School of Dental Medicine: Prof. JEFFREY W. HUTTER
Metropolitan College: Dr JAY A. HALFOND
Sargent College of Health and Rehabilitation Sciences: Prof. Dr GLORIA S. WATERS
School of Education: Dr HARDIN L. K. COLEMAN
School of Hospitality Administration: Dr CHRISTOPHER MULLER
School of Law: Prof. MAUREEN O'ROURKE
School of Management: Prof. KENNETH W. FREEMAN
School of Medicine: KAREN H. ANTMAN

School of Public Health: ROBERT F. MEENAN
School of Social Work: Prof. GAIL S. STEKETEE
School of Theology: Prof. MARY ELIZABETH MULLINO MOORE

BRANDEIS UNIVERSITY

415 South St, Waltham, MA 02454-9110
Telephone: (781) 736-2000
E-mail: admissions@brandeis.edu
Internet: www.brandeis.edu
Founded 1948
Private control
Academic year: August to May (2 semesters)

Pres.: Dr FREDERICK M. LAWRENCE
Sr Vice-Pres. and Chief of Staff: Dr DAVID BUNIS
Provost and Chief Academic Officer: Dr STEVE A. N. GOLDSTEIN
Sr Vice-Pres. and Gen. Counsel: Dr JUDITH R. SIZER
Sr Vice-Pres. for Admin.: MARK COLLINS
Sr Vice-Pres. for Finance and Chief Financial Officer: FRANCES A. DROLETTE
Sr Vice-Pres. for Communications and External Affairs: ANDREW GULLY
Sr Vice-Pres. of Institutional Advancement: NANCY K. WINSHIP
Sr Vice-Pres. for Students and Enrolment: ANDREW FLAGEL
Vice-Pres. for Student Affairs and Dean of Student Life: RICK SAWYER
Assoc. Vice-Pres. for Univ. Affairs: JOHN HOSE
Registrar: Dr MARK HEWITT
Provost for Library and Technology Services and Chief Information Officer: Dr JOHN UNSWORTH
Library of 1,202,654 vols, 103,883 current serial subscriptions, 950,712 microforms, 40,021 audiovisual materials, 352,502 ebooks
Number of teachers: 510 (365 full-time, 145 part-time)
Number of students: 5,830 (3,505 undergraduate, 2,325 graduate)
Publications: *Brandeis Magazine* (3 a year), *Catalyst* (2 a year)

DEANS

College of Arts and Sciences: Prof. Dr SUSAN J. BIRREN
Graduate School of Arts and Sciences: Prof. Dr MALCOLM W. WATSON
Heller School for Social Policy and Management: Prof. Dr LISA M. LYNCH
International Business School: Dr BRUCE MAGID

BRIDGEWATER STATE UNIVERSITY

131 Summer St, Bridgewater, MA 02325
Telephone: (508) 531-1000
E-mail: admission@bridgew.edu
Internet: www.bridgew.edu
Founded 1840 as Bridgewater Normal School, current name adopted 2010
State control
Academic year: September to May (2 semesters)

Pres.: Dr DANA MOHLER-FARIA
Provost and Vice-Pres. for Academic Affairs: Dr HOWARD B. LONDON
Vice-Pres. for Admin. and Finance: MIGUEL GOMES, JR (acting)
Vice-Pres. for External Affairs: Dr EDWARD MINNOCK
Vice-Pres. for Student Affairs: Dr D. DAVID OSTROTH
Vice-Pres. for Univ. Advancement and Strategic Planning: BRYAN BALDWIN (acting)
Registrar: IRENE CHECKOVICH
Dir of Libraries: Dr MICHAEL A. SOMMERS
Library of 340,258 vols

Number of teachers: 310 (full-time)
Number of students: 11,200

DEANS

Bartlett College of Science and Mathematics: Dr ARTHUR GOLDSTEIN
College of Education and Allied Studies: Dr ANNA BRADFIELD
College of Graduate Studies: Dr WILLIAM S. SMITH
College of Humanities and Social Sciences: Dr HOWARD B. LONDON (acting)
College of Science and Mathematics: Dr ARTHUR GOLDSTEIN
Ricciardi College of Business: Dr MARIAN M. EXTEJT

CAMBRIDGE COLLEGE

1000 Massachusetts Ave, Cambridge, MA 02138-5304
Telephone: (617) 868-1000
E-mail: registrar@cambridgecollege.edu
Internet: www.cambridgecollege.edu
Founded 1971
Private control
Academic year: September to August

Founder and Chancellor: EILEEN M. BROWN
Pres.: DEBORAH C. JACKSON
Exec. Vice-Pres.: Dr EZAT PARNIA
Provost and Vice-Pres. for Academic Affairs: Dr ELWOOD ROBINSON
Vice-Pres. for College Affairs: Dr JOSEPH DAISY
Vice-Pres. for Finance and Admin.: KIM GAZZOLA
Vice-Pres. for Institutional Advancement: PATRICIA F. DENN
Dean for Enrolment Management: ELAINE LAPOMARDO
Dean for Student Affairs: REGINA ROBINSON
Dir for Admissions: DENISE HAILE
Registrar: L. MARK SLAWSON
Number of teachers: 720
Number of students: 8,300

DEANS

School of Education: Dr N. ALAN SHEPPARD (acting)
School of Management: Dr MARY ANN JOSEPH (acting)
School of Psychology and Counselling: Prof. Dr NITI SETH
School of Undergraduate Studies: Prof. JAMES STEPHEN LEE.

BRANCH CAMPUSES

Cambridge College, California: 8686 Haven Ave, Rancho Cucamonga, CA 91730; tel. (909) 635-0250; Dir GREGORY WHITE.

Cambridge College, Georgia: 753 Broad St, Suite 1000, Augusta, GA 30901; tel. (706) 821-3965; Dir SHARLOTTE EVANS.

Chesapeake Campus: Suite 300, 1403 Greenbrier Parkway, Chesapeake, VA 23320; tel. (757) 424-0333; e-mail chesapeake@cambridgecollege.edu; Dir JIM WALDMAN.

Lawrence Campus: Lawrence Center, 60 Island St, Lawrence, MA 01840-1835; tel. (978) 738-0502; e-mail lawrence@cambridgecollege.edu; Dir DOLORES C. CALAF.

Memphis Campus: Oak Ridge Bldg, Suite 401, 8000 Centerview Parkway, Cordova, TN 38018; tel. (901) 755-9399.

Puerto Rico Center: 268 Ponce de Leon Ave, Suite 1400, Hato Rey, San Juan, PR 00918; tel. (787) 296-1101; e-mail puertorico@cambridgecollege.edu.

Springfield Campus: 570 Cottage St, Springfield, MA 01104; tel. (413) 747-0204; e-mail springfield@cambridgecollege.edu; Dir TERESA FORTE

CLARK UNIVERSITY

950 Main St, Worcester, MA 01610-1477
Telephone: (508) 793-4411
E-mail: admissions@clarku.edu
Internet: www.clarku.edu

Founded 1887
Private control
Academic year: August to May

Areas of study incl. art history, Asian studies, biology, business admin., chemistry and biochemistry, education, engineering, geography, history, physics

Pres.: Prof. Dr DAVID P. ANGEL
Provost and Vice-Pres. for Academic Affairs: Prof. Dr DAVIS BAIRD
Exec. Vice-Pres.: JAMES E. COLLINS
Vice-Pres. for Govt and Community Affairs: JACK FOLEY
Vice-Pres. for Planning and Budget: ANDREA MICHAELS
Vice-Pres. for Univ. Advancement: C. ANDREW MCGADNEY
Dean of Admissions and Financial Aid: DON HONEMAN
Dean of College and Assoc. Provost: Prof. Dr WALTER WRIGHT
Dean of Graduate Studies and Assoc. Provost: PRISCILLA ELSASS
Dean of Research and Assoc. Provost: Dr NANCY BUDWIG
Dean of Students: DENISE DARRIGRAND
Registrar: REBECCA HUNTER
Librarian: GWENDOLYNE ARTHUR

Library of 584,350 vols
Number of teachers: 200 (full-time)
Number of students: 2,200 (undergraduate)

Publications: *Clark University News*, *Economic Geography*, *Idealistic Studies*

COLLEGE OF THE HOLY CROSS

One College St, Worcester, MA 01610-2395
Telephone: (508) 793-2011
Internet: www.holycross.edu

Founded 1843
Private control
Academic year: August to May (2 semesters)

Depts of African studies, American sign language/deaf studies, Asian studies, biochemistry, biological psychology, biology, chemistry, Chinese, classics, economics and accounting, education, engineering, English, environmental studies, French, German, gerontology studies, graduate studies, history, Italian, Latin American and Latino studies, mathematics and computer science, medieval and renaissance studies, modern languages and literatures, music, naval science (NROTC), peace and conflict studies, philosophy, physics, political science, pre-business, pre-law, premedical and pre-dental studies, psychology, religious studies, Russian, Russian and Eastern European studies, science coordinator, sociology and anthropology, Spanish, studies in world literature, theatre, visual arts, women's and gender studies

Pres.: Rev. PHILIP L. BOROUGHS
Sr Vice-Pres.: FRANK VELLACCIO
Vice-Pres. for Academic Affairs and Dean of College: Dr TIMOTHY R. AUSTIN
Vice-Pres. for Admin. and Finance: MICHAEL J. LOCHHEAD
Vice-Pres. for Devt and Alumni Relations: (vacant)
Vice-Pres. for Student Affairs and Dean for Students: JACQUELINE D. PETERSON
Gen. Counsel: Dr TIMOTHY F. MINES
Registrar: PATRICIA RING
Dir for Library Services: KATHLEEN M. CARNEY

Library of 650,000 vols, 4,500 print and ejournals

Number of teachers: 325 (258 full-time, 67 part-time)
Number of students: 2,870

Publications: *Interfaces* (2 a year), *Fosforo*, *Holy Cross Magazine* (4 a year), *The Holy Cross Journal of Law and Public Policy* (1 a year), *The Purple*, *The Purple Patcher* (1 a year)

CONWAY SCHOOL

332 S Deerfield Rd, POB 179, Conway, MA 01341-0179
Telephone: (413) 369-4044
Internet: www.csld.edu

Founded 1972, present status 1989
Private control

Offers MA in landscape planning and design

Dir: PAUL CAWOOD HELLMUND
Assoc. Dir for Admissions and Communication: MOLLIE BABIZE
Assoc. Dir of Finance, Operations and Community Projects: DAVE NORDSTROM

Library of 3,000 vols

CURRY COLLEGE

1071 Blue Hill Ave, Milton, MA 02186
Telephone: (617) 333-0500
E-mail: curryadm@curry.edu
Internet: www.curry.edu

Founded 1879 as School of Elocution and Expression; current name adopted 1943
Private control
Academic year: September to May

Campus in Plymouth; depts of applied technology communication, education, fine and applied arts, humanities, interdisciplinary studies, management, natural sciences and mathematics, nursing, politics and history, psychology, sociology and criminal justice

Pres.: Dr KENNETH K. QUIGLEY, JR
Chief Academic Officer: Dr DAVID POTASH
Chief Devt Officer: CHRISTOPHER LAWSON
Chief Financial Officer: RICHARD F. SULLIVAN
Dean of Admission: JANE P. FIDLER
Dean of Continuing Education and Graduate Studies: Dr RUTH D. SHERMAN
Dean of Faculty: Dr CASSANDRA VOLPE HORII
Dean of Institutional Planning: Dr SUSAN W. PENNINI
Dean of Students: MARYELLEN M. COLLITON KILEY
Registrar: MARIKA HAMILTON
Dir of Library: Prof. EDWARD TALLENT

Number of teachers: 450
Number of students: 3,880

DEAN COLLEGE

99 Main St, Franklin, MA 02038-1994
Telephone: (508) 541-1900
E-mail: admission@dean.edu
Internet: www.dean.edu

Founded 1865, current name adopted 1994
Private control
Academic year: September to May

Pres.: Dr PAULA M. ROONEY
Vice-Pres. for Academic Affairs and Planning: Dr LINDA M. RAGOSTA
Vice-Pres. for Enrolment Services and Marketing: JOHN F. MARCUS
Vice-Pres. for Financial Services and Treas.: DANIEL A. MODELANE
Vice-Pres. for Institutional Advancement: COLEEN P. RESNICK
Chief Human Resources Officer: Dr GARY CONVERTINO
Registrar: DANIEL O'DRISCOLL

Library of 32,000 vols, 105 periodicals
Number of students: 1,600

DEANS

School of Arts: Dr DAVID KRASNER
School of Business: Dr ROBERT CUOMO
School of Continuing Studies: VEATRICE CARABINE
School of Dance: JULIANNE O'BRIEN-PEDERSEN
School of Liberal Arts and Sciences: Dr DAWN POIRIER

EASTERN NAZARENE COLLEGE

23 East Elm Ave, Quincy, MA 02170
Telephone: (617) 745-3000
E-mail: admissions@enc.edu
Internet: www1.enc.edu

Founded 1900
Private control
Academic year: September to May (2 semesters)

Depts incl. biology, business, chemistry, education, history, mathematics, movement arts, music, social work

Pres.: Dr CORLIS MCGEE
Provost and Dean of the College: Dr TIMOTHY WOOSTER
Vice-Pres. for Enrolment: JEFFREY A. WELLS
Vice-Pres. for Finance: JAN WEISEN
Vice-Pres. for Institutional Advancement: Dr SCOTT TURCOTT
Vice-Pres. for Student Devt: VERNON WESLEY
Dir of Admissions: ANDREW WRIGHT
Registrar: MARGARET BALLARD
Dir of Library Services: SUSAN WATKINS

Library of 126,465 vols
Number of teachers: 52
Number of students: 1,075

DEANS

Adult and Graduate Studies: Dr LINDA SCOTT

ELMS COLLEGE

291 Springfield St, Chicopee, MA 01013-2839
Telephone: (413) 594-2761
E-mail: admissions@elms.edu
Internet: www.elms.edu

Founded 1928
Private control
Academic year: September to May

Liberal arts college; divs of business and law, communication sciences and disorders, education, humanities and fine arts, natural sciences, mathematics and technology, nursing, social sciences

Pres.: Dr JAMES H. MULLEN, Jr
Vice-Pres. for Academic Affairs: Dr WALTER C. BREAU
Vice-Pres. for Finance and Admin.: BRIAN E. DOHERTY
Vice-Pres. for Institutional Advancement: KEVIN M. EDWARDS
Vice-Pres. for Student Affairs: JOHN KELLER
Dir of Admission: JOSEPH WAGNER
Registrar: LAURA LANDER
Dir of Library: PATRICIA BOMBARDIES

Library of 103,000 vols, 684 periodicals
Number of teachers: 170 (68 full-time, 11 part-time, 91 adjunct)
Number of students: 1,360

Publication: *Elms College Magazine*

EMERSON COLLEGE

120 Boylston St, Boston, MA 02116-4624
Telephone: (617) 824-8500
E-mail: admission@emerson.edu
Internet: www.emerson.edu

Founded 1880
Private control
Academic year: August to May

Pres.: Dr LEE PELTON (acting)

Vice-Pres. and Gen. Counsel: CHRISTINE HUGHES
Vice-Pres. for Academic Affairs: LINDA MOORE
Vice-Pres. for Admin. and Finance: MAUREEN MURPHY
Vice-Pres. for Devt and Alumni Relations: BARBARA RUTBERG
Vice-Pres. for Enrolment: M. J. KNOLL-FINN
Vice-Pres. for Institutional Advancement: DONALD C. MAIN
Dean of Students: RONALD LUDMAN
Registrar: WILLIAM F. DEWOLF
Dir of Library: ROBERT FLEMING
Library of 125,000 vols
Number of teachers: 470
Number of students: 4,290 (3,453 undergraduate, 837 graduate)
Publications: *Berkeley Beacon* (2 a week), *Emerson Review* (2 a year), *Expression: The Magazine for Alumni and Friends of Emerson College* (3 a year), *Omnivore* (2 a year)

DEANS
Graduate Studies: RICHARD ZAUFT
Liberal Arts: AMY ANSELL
School of Arts: DANIEL TOBIN
School of Communication: JANIS ANDERSEN

EMMANUEL COLLEGE

400 The Fenway, Boston, MA 02115
Telephone: (617) 735-9715
E-mail: enroll@emmanuel.edu
Internet: www.emmanuel.edu
Founded 1919
Private control
Academic year: May to May
Pres.: Sis. JANET EISNER
Exec. Vice-Pres. and Chief Operating Officer: NEIL BUCKLEY
Vice-Pres. for Academic Affairs: JOYCE DE LEO
Vice-Pres. for Devt and Alumni Relations: JOAN CALDWELL (acting)
Vice-Pres. for Finance and Admin.: NEIL BUCKLEY
Vice-Pres. of Student Affairs: Dr PATRICIA A. RISSMEYER
Library Dir: Dr SUSAN VON DAUM THOLL (acting)
Library of 140,000 vols, 2,000 journals
Number of teachers: 80
Number of students: 2,500

DEANS
Arts and Sciences: Dr WILLIAM C. LEONARD

ENDICOTT COLLEGE

376 Hale St, Beverly, MA 01915
Telephone: (978) 927-0585
E-mail: admission@endicott.edu
Internet: www.endicott.edu
Founded 1939
Private control
Academic year: June to August
Pres.: Dr RICHARD E. WYLIE
Exec. Vice-Pres. and Vice-Pres. for Finance: LYNNE B. O'TOOLE
Vice-Pres.: Dr MARY HUEGEL
Vice-Pres. for Admissions and Financial Aid: THOMAS J. REDMAN
Vice-Pres. for Institutional Advancement: DAVID VIGNERON
Vice-Pres. for Student Affairs: Dr BEVERLY DOLINSKY
Registrar: ANITA MCFARLANE
Dir of Library: BRIAN COURTEMANCHE
Library of 116,876 vols, 124,809 e-periodicals
Number of teachers: 370 (114 full-time, 256 part-time)

Number of students: 4,650

DEANS
School of Arts and Sciences: Dr GENE WONG
School of Business: Dr AMY BELL ROSS
School of Communication: Dr LAUREL HELLERSTEIN
School of Education: Dr SARA QUAY
School of Hospitality Management: Dr WILLIAM SAMENFINK
School of Nursing: Dr KELLY FISHER
School of Sport Science and Fitness Studies: Dr DEBORAH SWANTON
School of Visual and Performing Arts: MARK TOWNER
Undergraduate College: Dr LAURA ROSSI-LE
Van Loan School of Graduate and Professional Studies: Dr MARY HUEGEL

EPISCOPAL DIVINITY SCHOOL

99 Brattle St, Cambridge, MA 02138
Telephone: (617) 868-3450
E-mail: admissions@eds.edu
Internet: www.eds.edu
Founded 1974 by merger of Philadelphia Divinity School (f. 1857) with Episcopal Theological School (f. 1867)
Private control
Academic year: September to May
Offers degrees in divinity, ministry, theological studies
Pres. and Dean: Very Rev. Dr KATHERINE HANCOCK RAGSDALE
Academic Dean: Dr ANGELA BAUER-LEVESQUE
Vice-Pres. for Institutional Advancement: HUGO DE LA ROSA
Dean of Student and Community Life: MIRIAM GELFER
Registrar: LISA HOWELL
Library Dir: ESTHER A. GRISWOLD
Library of 232,000 vols
Number of teachers: 22
Number of students: 68 (full-time)

FISHER COLLEGE

118 Beacon St, Boston, MA 02116
Telephone: (617) 236-8800
E-mail: admissions@fisher.edu
Internet: www.fisher.edu
Founded 1903
Private control
Academic year: September to May
Schools of art, business and management, nursing
Pres.: Dr THOMAS M. MCGOVERN
Vice-Pres. for Academic Affairs: JANET KUSER
Vice-Pres. for Admin.: RHONDA PIERONI
Vice-Pres. for Finance: STEVEN RICH
Dean of Admissions: ROBERT MELARAGNI
Dean of Students: SHIELA LALLY
Registrar: ROSA CADENA
College Librarian: JOSHUA MCKAIN
Publication: *Fisher Today* (2 a year)

FITCHBURG STATE UNIVERSITY

160 Pearl St, Fitchburg, MA 01420-2697
Telephone: (978) 665-3000
E-mail: admissions@fitchburgstate.edu
Internet: www.fitchburgstate.edu
Founded 1894 as State Normal School, current name adopted 2010
State control
Academic year: September to June (2 semesters)
Pres.: Dr ROBERT V. ANTONUCCI
Vice-Pres. for Academic Affairs: Dr ROBIN E. BOWEN
Vice-Pres. for Finance and Admin.: JAY BRY
Vice-Pres. for Institutional Advancement: CHRISTOPHER HENDRY

Dean for Enrolment Management and Dir for Financial Aid: PAMELA MCCAFFERTY
Dir for Admissions: KAY REYNOLDS
Registrar: LINDA DUPELL
Dir for Library: ROBERT FOLEY
Library of 210,790 vols, 478,000 microforms, 500 periodicals, 1,000 ebooks, 43,000 ejournals
Number of teachers: 200 (full-time)
Number of students: 6,890 (4,171 undergraduate, 2,791 graduate)
Publication: *Contact* (1 a year)

DEANS
Education: ELAINE E. FRANCIS
Graduate and Continuing Education: CATHERINE CANNEY

FRAMINGHAM STATE COLLEGE

100 State St, POB 9101, Framingham, MA 01701-9101
Telephone: (508) 620-1220
E-mail: admissions@framingham.edu
Internet: www.framingham.edu
Founded 1839
Depts incl. art and music, biology, chemistry and food science, communication arts, computer science, economics and business admin.
State control
Academic year: September to May (2 semesters)
Pres.: Dr TIMOTHY J. FLANAGAN
Sr Vice-Pres. for Admin. and Finance: Dr DALE M. HAMEL
Vice-Pres. for Academic Affairs: Dr LINDA VADEN-GOAD
Vice-Pres. for Enrolment and Student Devt: SUSANNE H. CONLEY
Vice-Pres. for Univ. Advancement: CHRISTOPHER P. HENDRY
Dean of Graduate and Continuing Education: Dr SCOTT GREENBERG
Dean of Students: Dr MELINDA K. STOOPS
Registrar: MARK R. POWERS
Dir of Library Services: BONNIE MITCHELL (acting)
Library of 344,185 vols
Number of teachers: 200
Number of students: 6,415 (4,321 undergraduate, 2,094 graduate)
Publication: *Alumni Magazine* (1 a year)

FRANKLIN W. OLIN COLLEGE OF ENGINEERING

Olin Way, Needham, MA 02492-1200
Telephone: (781) 292-2300
E-mail: info@olin.edu
Internet: www.olin.edu
Founded 1997
Private control
Academic year: August to May
Academic programmes in engineering incl. electrical and computer engineering, mechanical engineering
Pres.: Dr RICHARD K. MILLER
Provost and Dean of Faculty: VINCENT P. MANNO
Exec. Vice-Pres. and Treas.: STEPHEN P. HANNABURY
Vice-Pres. for Admin. and Finance: STEPHEN P. HANNABURY
Exec. Vice-Pres. for Devt, Family and Alumni Relations: J. THOMAS KRIMMEL
Vice-Pres. for External Relations and Dean of Admission: Dr CHARLES S. NOLAN
Vice-Pres. for Innovation and Research: SHERRA E. KERNS
Dean of Student Life: Dr ROGER C. CRAFTS
Registrar: LINDA T. CANAVAN
Dir of Library: DIANNA MAGNONI

Number of teachers: 40
Number of students: 350
Publication: *Journal of Asynchronous Learning Networks* (2–4 a year)

PROFESSORS

BOURNE, J., Electrical and Computer Engineering
DONIS-KELLER, H., Biology and Art
HOLT, S. S., Physics
KERNS, D., Electrical Engineering
KERNS, S., Electrical and Computer Engineering
MILLER, R., Mechanical Engineering
PRATT, G., Electrical and Computer Engineering

GORDON COLLEGE

255 Grapevine Rd, Wenham, MA 01984
Telephone: (978) 927-2300
E-mail: info@gordon.edu
Internet: www.gordon.edu
Founded 1889 as Boston Missionary Training School; current name adopted after merger with Barrington College 1985
Academic year: August to July (2 semesters)
Divs of economics, education, fine arts, humanities, mathematics and computer science, psychology, social work, sociology
Pres.: Dr D. MICHAEL LINDSAY
Provost: Dr MARK L. SARGENT
Sr Vice-Pres. for Finance and Admin.: MICHAEL J. AHEARN
Exec. Vice-Pres. and Chief of Staff: DANIEL B. TYMANN
Vice-Pres. for Marketing and Strategic Communications: RICHARD D. SWEENEY, JR
Vice-Pres. for Development: SANDRA L. BUTTERS
Vice-Pres. for Enrolment: SILVIO VAZQUEZ
Vice-Pres. for Student Devt and Dean of Students: BARRY J. LOY
Dean of College Planning: Dr STEPHEN C. MACLEOD
Registrar: CAROL A. HERRICK
Dir of Library Services: Dr MYRON SCHIRER-SUTER
Library of 190,000 vols, 74,000 ebooks, 51,150 print and online journals
Number of teachers: 170 (97 full-time, 73 part-time)
Number of students: 1,570
Publication: *STILLPOINT* (2 a year)

GORDON-CONWELL THEOLOGICAL SEMINARY

130 Essex St, South Hamilton, MA 01982
Telephone: (978) 468-7111
E-mail: admrep@gcts.edu
Internet: www.gordonconwell.edu
Founded 1969 by merger of Conwell School of Theology (f. 1884) with Gordon Divinity School (f. 1889)
Private control
Academic year: September to May
Br. campuses in Boston, Charlotte, Jacksonville; degree programmes incl. arts, divinity, ministry, theology
Pres.: Prof. Dr DENNIS HOLLINGER
Provost: Prof. Dr FRANK JAMES
Dean of Faculty: CAROL KAMINSKI
Exec. Vice-Pres. and Chief Financial Officer: ROBERT S. LANDREBE
Vice-Pres. for Advancement: KURT DRESCHER
Academic Dean: BARRY H. COREY
Dean of Enrolment Management and Registrar: SCOTT POBLENZ
Dean of Students: LISE SCHLUETER
Head Librarian: FREEMAN BARTON
Library of 250,000 vols
Number of teachers: 50

Number of students: 990

HAMPSHIRE COLLEGE

893 West St, Amherst, MA 01002
Telephone: (413) 549-4600
E-mail: admissions@hampshire.edu
Internet: www.hampshire.edu
Founded 1965
Private control
Academic year: September to June
Pres.: JONATHAN LASH
Sec.: BETH WARD
Vice-Pres. for Academic Affairs and Dean for Faculty: Prof. ALAN GOODMAN
Vice-Pres. for Finance and Admin. and Treas.: MARK K. SPIRO
Chief Advancement Officer: CLAY BALLANTINE
Dean for Students: DAWN ELLINWOOD
Dir for Admissions and Financial Aid: JULIE RICHARDSON
Dir for Library and College Archivist: SUSAN DAYALL (acting)
Library of 121,837 vols, 64,469 ebooks, 9,712 journals, 56,041 ejournals
Number of teachers: 100
Number of students: 1,530

DEANS

School of Cognitive Science: LAURA SIZER
School of Critical Social Inquiry: ANNIE ROGERS
School of Humanities, Arts and Cultural Studies: NORMAN HOLLAND
School of Interdisciplinary Arts: ELLEN DONKIN
School of Natural Science: JASON TOR
School of Social Science: BARBARA YNGVESSON

HARVARD UNIVERSITY

Massachusetts Hall, Cambridge, MA 02138
Telephone: (617) 495-1000
Internet: www.harvard.edu
Founded 1636
Private control
Academic year: September to June
Pres.: Prof. Dr DREW GILPIN FAUST
Provost: Prof. Dr ALAN M. GARBER
Vice-Pres. and Sec.: MARC GOODHEART
Treas.: JAMES ROTHENBERG
Exec. Vice-Pres.: KATHERINE N. LAPP
Vice-Pres. and Gen. Counsel: ROBERT IULIANO (acting)
Vice-Pres. for Alumni Affairs and Devt: TAMARA ROGERS
Vice-Pres. for Campus Services: LISA HOGARTY
Vice-Pres. for Finance and Chief Financial Officer: DAN SHORE
Vice-Pres. for Harvard Information Technology Services and Chief Information Officer: ANNE MARGULIES (acting)
Vice-Pres. for Harvard Library: SARAH E. THOMAS (acting)
Vice-Pres. for Human Resources: MARILYN HAUSAMMANN (acting)
Vice-Pres. for Planning and Project Management: MARK. R. JOHNSON (acting)
Vice-Pres. for Public Affairs and Communications: CHRISTINE HEENAN (acting)
Vice-Pres. for Strategy and Programs: LEAH ROSOVSKY (acting)
Dir of Univ. Library: Prof. Dr ROBERT DARNTON
Library: 17m. vols
Number of teachers: 13,500 (2,500 non-medical, 11,000 medical)
Number of students: 21,000

DEANS

Continuing Education and Univ. Extension: HUNTINGTON D. LAMBERT

Faculty of Arts and Sciences: Prof. Dr MICHAEL D. SMITH
Graduate School of Arts and Sciences: Prof. XIAO-LI MENG
Graduate School of Design: Prof. MOHSEN MOSTAFAVI
Harvard Business School: Prof. NITIN NOHRIA
Harvard College: Prof. DONALD H. PFISTER (acting)
Harvard Divinity School: Prof. DAVID N. HEMPTON
Harvard Graduate School of Education: Prof. JAMES E. RYAN
Harvard Law School: Prof. Dr MARTHA INOW
Harvard Medical School: Prof. Dr JEFFREY S. FLIER
Harvard School of Dental Medicine: Prof. Dr R. BRUCE DONOFF
Harvard School of Public Health: Prof. Dr JULIO FRENK
John F. Kennedy School of Government: Prof. Dr DAVID T. ELLWOOD
Radcliffe Institute for Advanced Study: Prof. Dr LIZABETH COHEN
School of Engineering and Applied Sciences: Prof. Dr CHERRY A. MURRAY

PROFESSORS

Faculty of Arts and Sciences (University Hall, Cambridge, MA 02138; tel. (617) 495-1000; e-mail fascom@fas.harvard.edu; internet www.fas.harvard.edu):

ABBATE, C., Music
ABE, R., Japanese Religions
AGHION, P., Economics
AIZENBERG, J., Materials Science, Chemistry and Chemical Biology
AKYEAMPONG, E. K., History, African and African-American Studies
ALBRIGHT, D., English
ALCOCK, C. R., Astronomy
ALESINA, A., Political Economy
ALT, J. E., Government
ANDERSON, J. G., Atmospheric Chemistry
ANSOLABEHERE, S., Government
ANTRÀS, P., Economics
ARMITAGE, D., History
ASANI, A.S., Indo-Muslim and Islamic Religion and Cultures
ASPURU-GUZIK, A., Chemistry and Chemical Biology
AZIZ, M. J., Materials and Energy Technologies
BANAJI, M., Social Ethics
BARANCZAK, S., Polish Language and Literature
BARRO, R., Economics
BATES, R. H., Science of Government, African and African-American Studies
BECKERT, S., History
BECKFIELD, J., Sociology
BEIZER, J., Romance Languages and Literatures
BELL, D. C., Practice of Electron Microscopy
BERG, H. C., Molecular and Cellular Biology, Physics
BERNSTEIN, R., African and African-American Studies, Women, Gender, and Sexuality
BESTOR, T. C., Social Anthropology
BHABHA, H. K., Humanities
BIEWENER, A. A., Biology
BLACKMORE, J., Language and Literature of Portugal
BLAIR, A., History
BLIER, S. P., Fine Arts, African and African-American Studies
BLITZSTEIN, J. K., Practice in Statistics
BLOXHAM, J., Geophysics
BLYTH, S., Practice in Statistics
BOBO, L. D., Social Sciences, African and African-American Studies
BOL, P. K., East Asian Languages and Civilizations

BOLTON, J. H., Slavic Languages and Literatures
BOSE, S., Oceanic History and Affairs
BOSSERT, W. H., Science
BOYLE, M., Philosophy
BOYM, S., Slavic Languages and Literatures, Comparative Literature
BRANDT, A. M., History of Science, History of Medicine
BRENNER, M. P., Applied Mathematics and Applied Physics, Physics
BRINTON, M. C., Sociology
BRISCOE, J., Practice of Environmental Health
BROCKETT, R. W., Electrical Engineering and Computer Science
BROOKS, D. M., Computer Science
BROWN, V., American History, African and African-American Studies
BROWN-NAGIN, T., Law, History
BRUNO, G., Visual and Environmental Studies
BUCHLOH, B., Modern Art
BUCKLER, J. A., Slavic Languages and Literatures, Comparative Literature
BUCKNER, R., Psychology
BURGARD, P., German
BURIN, K. A., Visual Art
BURT, S., English
CAMPBELL, J. Y., Economics
CAPASSO, F., Applied Physics
CARAMAZZA, A., Psychology
CAREY, S., Psychology
CARPENTER, D., Government
CARPIO, G. R., English, African and African-American Studies
CARRASCO, D., Study of Latin America
CASTAING TAYLOR, L., Visual Arts, Anthropology
CATON, S., Contemporary Arab Studies
CAVANAUGH, C. M., Biology
CHAMBERLAIN, G., Economics
CHAPLIN, J., Early American History
CHARBONNEAU, D., Astronomy
CHETTY, R., Economics
CHIEN, K. R., Stem Cell and Regenerative Biology
CHIERCHIA, G., Linguistics
CLARK, S., Music
CLARKE, D. R., Materials
CLAYBAUGH, A., English
CLUZEL, P., Molecular and Cellular Biology, Applied Physics
COHEN, A. E., Chemistry and Chemical Biology, Physics
COHEN, L., American Studies
COHEN, S. J. D., Hebrew Literature and Philosophy
COLEMAN, K. M., Classics
COLTON, T., Government and Russian Studies
COMAROFF, J., African and African-American Studies, Anthropology
COMAROFF, J., African and African-American Studies, Anthropology
CONLEY, T., Romance Languages and Literatures, Visual and Environmental Studies
CONNORS, J., History of Art and Architecture
COOPER, R., International Economics
COTT, N. F., American History
CRANSTON, E. A., Japanese Literature
CUMMINS, T. B. F., Pre-Columbian and Colonial Art
CUTLER, D. M., Applied Economics
CZERNOWIN, C., Music
DARNTON, R., Cultural History
DAVIS, C. C., Organismic and Evolutionary Biology
DE LA FUENTE, A., Latin American History and Economics, African and African-American Studies, History
DEMLER, E., Physics
DENCH, E., Classics, History
DER MANUELIAN, P., Egyptology

DEVORE, I., Biological Anthropology
DOBBIN, F., Sociology
DOMINGUEZ, J. I., Study of Mexico
DONOGHUE, D., English
DOWLING, J. E., Neurosciences
DOYLE, J. M., Physics
DULAC, C., Molecular and Cellular Biology
ECK, D. L., Comparative Religion and Indian Studies, Law and Psychiatry in Society
ECKERT, C., Korean History
EDWARDS, D. A., Practice of Idea Translation
EDWARDS, S. V., Organismic and Evolutionary Biology
EGGAN, K., Stem Cell and Regenerative Biology
EISENSTEIN, D., Astronomy
EKIERT, G., Government
EL-ROUAYHEB, K., Islamic Intellectual History
ELKIES, N. D., Mathematics
ELKINS, C., History, African and African-American Studies
ELLIOTT, M. C., Chinese and Inner Asian History
ELLISON, P. T., Anthropology
ENGELL, J., English Literature, Comparative Literature
ENGERT, F., Molecular and Cellular Biology
ERIKSON, R. L., Cellular and Developmental Biology
ERSPAMER, F., Romance Languages and Literatures
FARHI, E., Economics
FARMER, P., Global Health and Social Medicine
FARRELL, B. D., Biology
FARRELL, B. F., Meteorology
FASH, W. L., Central American and Mexican Archaeology and Ethnology
FAUST, D. G., American History
FELDMAN, G. J., Science
FELDSTEIN, M. S., Economics
FERGUSON, N., History
FERNÁNDEZ-CIFUENTES, L., Romance Languages and Literatures
FINKBEINER, D., Astronomy, Physics
FISHER, P. J., English
FLAD, R., Anthropological Archaeology
FLIER, M. S., Ukrainian Philology
FOOTE, C., Economics
FRANKLIN, M., Physics
FREDERICK, M. F., African and African-American Studies, Religion
FREEMAN, R. B., Economics
FRIEDEN, J., International Peace
FRIEDMAN, B. M., Political Economy
FRIEDMAN, W., Organismic and Evolutionary Biology
FRIEND, C. M., Chemistry, Materials Science
FRYER, R., Economics
FUDENBERG, D., Economics
GABRIELSE, G., Physics
GAITSGORY, D., Mathematics
GALISON, P. L., History of Science, Physics
GARBER, M., English, Visual and Environmental Studies
GATES, H. L., African and African-American Studies
GAY, C., Government, African and African-American Studies
GAYLORD, M. M., Romance Languages and Literatures
GELBART, W. M., Molecular and Cellular Biology
GEORGI, H. M., Physics
GILBERT, D., Psychology
GIRIBERT, G., Zoology, Organismic and Evolutionary Biology
GIRÓN NEGRÓN, L. M., Comparative Literature, Romance Languages and Literatures
GLAESER, E., Economics

GOLDFARB, W., Modern Mathematics and Mathematical Logic
GOLDIN, C., Economics
GOLOVCHENKO, J. A., Physics, Applied Physics
GOOD, B., Medical Anthropology
GOODMAN, A. A., Astronomy
GOPINATH, G., Economics
GORDON, A., History
GORDON, P. E., History
GORDON, R. G., Chemistry, Materials Science
GORDON-REED, A., Law and History
GORTLER, S. J., Computer Science
GOTTLIEB, R., Practice of Mathematics
GOUGH, M., Modern Art
GRABOWICZ, G. G., Ukrainian Literature
GRAHAM, J., Oratory and Rhetoric
GRAHAM, W. A., Middle Eastern Studies
GRANARA, W. E., Practice of Arabic
GREEN, J. R., Political Economy
GREENBLATT, S., Humanities
GREENE, V., Romance Languages and Literatures
GREENHALGH, S., Chinese Society
GREINER, M., Physics
GRINDLAY, J. E., Practical Astronomy
GROSS, B. H., Mathematics
GROSZ, B. J., Natural Sciences
GUIDOTTI, G., Biochemistry
GUTHKE, K. S., German Art and Culture
GUZZETTI, A. F., Visual Arts
GYATSO, J., Buddhist Studies
HAIG, D., Biology
HALL, E. J., Philosophy
HALL, P. A., European Studies
HALPERIN, B. I., Mathematics and Natural Philosophy
HAM, D., Electrical Engineering and Applied Physics
HAMBURGER, J. F., German Art and Culture
HAMILTON, J., German and Comparative Literature
HAMMOND, E. M., History of Science, African and African-American Studies
HANKEN, J., Biology, Zoology
HANKINS, J., History
HARDACRE, H., Japanese Religions and Society
HARPER, S., Visual Art, Visual and Environmental Studies
HARRINGTON, A., History of Science
HARRINGTON, D. P., Statistics
HARRIS, J. D., Mathematics
HARRIS, J. M., Jewish Studies
HARRISON, S. C., Biological Chemistry and Molecular Pharmacology, Paediatrics
HART, O., Economics
HARTL, D. L., Biology
HASTY, C., Music
HAU, L. V., Physics, Applied Physics
HEINRICHS, W. P., Arabic
HELLER, E. J., Chemistry, Physics
HELPMAN, E., International Trade
HENRICHS, A. M., Greek Literature
HENSCH, T., Molecular and Cellular Biology, Neurology
HERNQUIST, L., Astrophysics
HERZFELD, M., Social Sciences
HERZOG, T., Latin American Affairs
HIGGINBOTHAM, E. B., History, African and African-American Studies
HIGONNET, P. L.-R., French History
HISCOX, M., International Affairs
HOCHSCHILD, J. L., Government, African and African-American Studies
HOEKSTRA, H. E., Zoology, Molecular and Cellular Biology, Organismic and Evolutionary Biology
HOLBROOK, N. M., Forestry
HOOLEY, J., Psychology
HOPKINS, M., Mathematics
HOWE, R. D., Engineering
HOWELL, D., Japanese History

Hu, E., Applied Physics, Electrical Engineering
Huang, C.-T. J., Linguistics
Hunter, C. P., Molecular and Cellular Biology
Hutchinson, J. W., Engineering, Applied Mechanics
Huth, J., Science
Huybers, P., Earth and Planetary Sciences
Hyman, S. E., Stem Cell and Regenerative Biology
Idema, W., Chinese Literature
Ingber, D., Vascular Biology
Ishii, M., Earth and Planetary Sciences
Iversen, T., Political Economy
Iyer, V., Arts
Jacob, D. J., Atmospheric Chemistry and Environmental Engineering
Jacobsen, E., Chemistry
Jacobsen, S. B., Geochemistry
Jacobsen, W., Practice of Japanese Language
Jaffe, A. M., Mathematics and Theoretical Science
Jardine, A., Romance Languages and Literatures, Studies of Women, Gender, and Sexuality
Jasanoff, J., Indo-European Linguistics and Philology
Jasanoff, M., History
Jeyifo, B., African and African-American Studies, Comparative Literature
Johansen, B., Islamic Studies
Johnson, A. F., History
Johnson, J. A., Astronomy
Johnson, W., History, African and African-American Studies
Johnston, A. I., China in World Affairs
Jorgenson, D. W., Economics
Kafadar, C., Turkish Studies
Kahne, D., Chemistry and Chemical Biology, Biological Chemistry and Molecular Pharmacology
Kalavrezou, I., Byzantine Art
Kamm, F., Philosophy and Public Policy, Philosophy
Kane, O., Near Eastern Languages and Civilizations, Contemporary Islamic Religion and Society
Katz, L., Economics
Kaxiras, E., Pure and Applied Physics
Keith, D., Applied Physics, Public Policy
Kelly, S., Philosophy
Kelly, T. F., Music
Kelsey, R., Photography
Khaneja, N., Electrical Engineering
Killip, C., Visual and Environmental Studies
Kim, P., Physics
Kim, S. J., Korean History
Kincaid, J., African and African-American Studies
King, G., Government
Kirby, W. C., China Studies, Business Administration
Kirshner, R. P., Science
Kishlansky, M., History
Kisin, M., Mathematics
Kleckner, N., Molecular Biology
Kleinman, A. M., Medical Anthropology
Kloppenberg, J. T., American History
Knoll, A. H., Natural History, Earth and Planetary Sciences
Koellner, P., Philosophy
Koerner, J., History of Art and Architecture
Korsgaard, C., Philosophy
Kou, S. C. S., Statistics
Kramer, E. M., Organismic and Evolutionary Biologys
Kremer, M. R., Developing Societies
Kronheimer, P., Mathematics
Kuang, Z., Atmospheric and Environmental Science
Kunes, S., Molecular and Cellular Biology

Kung, H. T., Computer Science and Electrical Engineering
Kuriyama, S., Cultural History
Laibson, D., Economics
Lajer-Burcharth, E., Fine Arts
Lamberg-Karlovsky, C. C., Archaeology and Ethnology
Lambert-Beatty, C., History of Art and Architecture, Visual and Environmental Studies
Lamont, M., European Studies, Sociology, African and African-American Studies
Langer, E. J., Psychology
Langmuir, C. H., Geochemistry
Lauder, G. V., Biology, Icthyology
Lee, R. T., Medicine
Lepore, J., American History
Levensen, J. D., Jewish Studies
Levin, R. D., Music
Levine, N., History of Art and Architecture
Levitsky, S., Government
Lewis, H. R., Computer Science
Lewis, J. A., Biologically Inspired Engineering
Lewis, M., History
Li, W.-Y., Chinese Literature
Lichtman, J., Molecular and Cellular Biology, Arts and Sciences
Lieber, C. M., Chemistry
Lieberman, D. E., Biological Sciences
Lippit, Y., History of Art and Architecture
Liu, D. R., Chemistry and Chemical Biology
Liu, J. S., Statistics
Loeb, A., Science
Loncar, M., Electrical Engineering
Losick, R. M., Biology
Losos, J., Study of Latin America
Lue, R. A., Practice of Molecular and Cellular Biology
Lukin, M. D., Physics
Lurie, J., Mathematics
McCann, D., Korean Literature
McCarthy, J. J., Biological Oceanography
McCormick, M., Japanese Art and Culture
McCormick, M., Medieval History
McDonald, C., French Language and Literature, Comparative Literature
McDonough, J., Philosophy
McElroy, M. B., Environmental Studies
McElwee, R., Practice of Filmmaking
McGirr, L., History
Machinist, P., Hebrew and Other Oriental Languages
McKenna, C., Celtic Languages and Literatures
Macklis, J. D., Stem Cell and Regenerative Biology
McMullen, C., Mathematics
McNally, R., Personality Psychology
Mahadevan, L., Applied Mathematics, Organismic and Evolutionary Biology, Physics
Maier, C. S., History
Malmstad, J. E., Slavic Languages and Literatures
Manela, E., History
Mango, S., Molecular and Cellular Biology
Mankiw, N. G., Economics
Manoharan, V. N., Chemical Engineering, Physics
Mansfield, H. C., Government
Marglin, S. A., Economics
Marsden, P. V., Sociology
Martin, P. C., Pure and Applied Physics
Martin, S. T., Environmental Chemistry
Martin, T., Russian Studies
Maskin, E. S., Economics
Mazur, B., Mathematics
Mazur, E., Physics, Applied Physics
Meade, B., Earth and Planetary Sciences
Meister, M., Molecular and Cellular Biology
Melitz, M., Political Economy
Melton, D. A., Molecular and Cellular Biology

Menand, L., English
Meng, X.-L., Statistics
Meselson, M. S., Natural Sciences
Mitchell, J., Psychology
Mitchell, R., Applied Biology
Mitchell, S. A., Scandinavian and Folklore
Mitrovica, J. X., Geophysics
Mitzenmacher, M. D., Computer Science
Monson, I., African-American Music, African and African-American Studies
Mooney, D. J., Bioengineering
Moorcroft, P. R., Organismic and Evolutionary Biology
Moran, J. M., Astrophysics
Moran, R., Philosophy
Morgan, M., African and African-American Studies
Morii, M., Physics
Morris, C. N., Statistics
Morrisett, G., Computer Science
Mottahedeh, R., Islamic History
Mugane, J. M., Practice of African Languages and Cultures
Mullainathan, S., Economics
Murray, A. W., Molecular Genetics, Molecular and Cellular Biology
Murray, C. A., Engineering and Applied Sciences, Physics
Murthy, V. N., Molecular and Cellular Biology
Myers, A., Chemistry and Chemical Biology
Nagpal, R., Computer Science
Nagy, G. J., Classical Greek Literature, Comparative Literature
Najmabadi, A., History, Studies of Women, Gender, and Sexuality
Nakayama, K., Psychology
Narayan, R., Natural Sciences
Narayanamurti, V., Technology and Public Policy, Physics
Necipoğlu, G., Islamic Art
Nelson, D. R., Biophysics, Physics and Applied Physics
Nelson, E., Government
New, E., American Literature
Nickel, B., Philosophy
Nocera, D. G., Energy
Nock, M., Social Sciences
Nowak, M. A., Mathematics and Biology
Nunn, N., Economics
O'Cathasaigh, T., Irish Studies
O'Connell, R. J., Geophysics
O'Shea, E. K., Molecular and Cellular Biology, Chemistry and Chemical Biology
Oja, C. J., Music
Olupona, J., African and African-American Studies, African Religious Traditions
Owen, S., Comparative Literature
Ozment, S. E., Ancient and Modern History
Pager, D., Sociology, Public Policy
Pakes, A., Economics
Park, H., Chemistry and Chemical Biology, Physics
Parker, K., Bioengineering and Applied Physics
Parkes, D. C., Computer Science
Patterson, O., Sociology
Paulus, D., Practice of Theatre
Payne, A., History of Art and Architecture
Pearson, A., Environmental Sciences
Perry, E. J., Government
Pershan, P. S., Science
Pertile, L., Romance Languages and Literatures
Peterson, P. E., Government
Pfister, D. H., Systematic Botany
Pfister, H., Computer Science
Pharr, S. J., Japanese Politics
Pierce, N. E., Biology
Pilbeam, D. R., Human Evolution
Pinker, S., Psychology

PLOKHII, S., Ukrainian History
POLINSKY, M., Linguistics
PRENTISS, M., Physics
PRICE, L., English Literature
PRINA, S., Visual and Environmental Studies
PUCHNER, M., Drama, English and Comparative Literature
PUETT, M., Chinese History
PUTNAM, R. D., Public Policy
RABB, I., Law, History
RABIN, M. O., Computer Science
RAMANATHAN, S., Molecular and Cellular Biology, Applied Physics
RANDALL, L., Science
RAU, J., Linguistics, Classics
REHDING, A., Music
RENTSCHLER, E., Germanic Languages and Literatures
RESKIN, B., Sociology
RICE, J. R., Engineering Sciences and Geophysics
RICHARD, M., Philosophy
RITTER, T., Chemistry and Chemical Biology
ROBERTS, J., Humanities
ROBINSON, J., Government
ROBSON, J., East Asian Languages and Civilizations
ROGOFF, K., Public Policy
ROILOS, P., Modern Greek Studies, Comparative Literature
ROSEN, M. E., Government
ROSEN, S. P., National Security and Military Affairs
ROSENBLUM, N., Ethics in Politics and Government
ROTHSCHILD, E., History
ROXBURGH, D., Islamic Art History
RUBIN, D. B., Statistics
RUBIN, J., Japanese Humanities
RUBIN, L., Stem Cell and Regenerative Biology
RUSSELL, J. R., Armenian Studies
RUVOLO, M., Anthropology
RYAN, J. L., German and Comparative Literature
SACHDEV, S., Physics
SACKS, P., English
SAMUEL, A., Physics
SAMPSON, R. J., Social Sciences
SANDEL, M. J., Government
SANDLER, S., Slavic Languages and Literatures
SANES, J. R., Molecular and Cellular Biology
SASSELOV, D., Astronomy
SATO, V. L., Practice of Molecular and Cellular Biology, Management Practice
SCADDEN, D., Medicine
SCANLAN, R., Practice of Theatre
SCANLON, T. M., Natural Religion, Moral Philosophy, and Civil Policy
SCARRY, E., Aesthetics and the General Theory of Value
SCHACTER, D., Psychology
SCHIEFSKY, M., Classics
SCHIER, A. F., Molecular and Cellular Biology
SCHMID, W., Mathematics
SCHNAPP, J., Romance Languages, Literatures, and Comparative Literature
SCHRAG, D. P., Geology, Environmental Science and Engineering
SCHREFFLER, A., Music
SCHREIBER, S. L., Chemistry and Chemical Biology
SELTZER, M. I., Computer Science
SEN, A., Economics, Philosophy
SEVCENKO, N., Romance Languages and Literatures
SHAIR, M., Chemistry and Chemical Biology
SHAKHNOVICH, E. I., Chemistry and Chemical Biology
SHAPIRO, I. I., Astrophysics

SHAW, J. H., Structural and Economic Geology
SHELBY, T., African and African-American Studies, Philosophy
SHELEMAY, K. K., Music, African and African-American Studies
SHELL, M., Comparative Literature, English
SHEPHARD, N., Economics, Statistics
SHEPSLE, K., Government
SHIEBER, S. M., Computer Science
SHLEIFER, A., Economics
SHREFFLER, A. C., Music
SIDANIUS, J., Psychology, African and African-American Studies
SIEGEL, S., Philosophy
SILVERA, I. F., Natural Sciences
SIMMONS, A., Philosophy
SIMMONS, B., International Affairs
SIMON, E., Germanic Languages and Literatures
SIMPSON, J., English
SIU, Y. T., Mathematics
SKJAERVO, P. O., Iranian
SKOCPOL, T. R., Government and Sociology
SMALL, D. L., History
SMITH, M. D., Engineering and Applied Sciences
SNEDEKER, J., Psychology
SNYDER, J., Government
SOLLORS, W., English Literature, African and African-American Studies
SOMMER, D., Romance Languages and Literatures, African and African-American Studies
SORENSEN, D., Romance Languages and Literatures, Comparative Literature
SPAEPEN, F. A., Applied Physics
SPELKE, E., Psychology
SPIRLING, A., Social Sciences
STAEHLI, A., Classical Archaeology
STAGER, L. E., Archaeology of Israel
STAUFFER, J., English, African and African-American Studies
STEEDLY, M. M., Anthropology
STEIN, J., Economics
STEINKELLER, P., Assyriology
STERNBERG, S. Z., Mathematics
STEWART-MUKHOPADHYAY, S. T., Earth and Planetary Sciences
STILGOE, J. R., History of Landscape
STOCK, J., Political Economy
STROMINGER, A., Physics
STROMINGER, J. L., Biochemistry
STUBBS, C. W., Physics, Astronomy
SUBRAMANIAN, A., Anthropology
SULEIMAN, S. R., Civilization of France, Comparative Literature
SUMMERS, L. H., Economics
SUO, Z., Mechanics and Materials
SWEENEY, L., Government and Technology
SZONYI, M., Chinese History
SZOSTAK, J. W., Chemistry and Chemical Biology, Genetics
TAI, H.-T. H., Sino-Vietnamese History
TAROKH, V., Applied Mathematics
TARRANT, R. J., Latin Language and Literature
TATAR, M. M., Germanic Languages and Literatures, Folklore and Mythology
TAUBES, C. H., Mathematics
TAYLOR, R. L., Mathematics
TCHERKASSOVA, F., Literature, Comparative Literature
TESKEY, G., English
THOMAS, R. F., Greek and Latin
THORNBER, K., Comparative Literature, East Asian Languages and Civilizations
TIAN, X., Chinese Literature
TODD, W. M., Comparative Literature, Literature
TUCK, R., Government
TUROSS, N., Scientific Archaeology
TUTSCHKU, H., Music
TZIPERMAN, E., Oceanography and Applied Physics

UCHIDA, N., Molecular and Cellular Biology
ULRICH, L. T., Early American History
URTON, G., Pre-Columbian Studies
VADHAN, S. P., Computer Science and Applied Mathematics
VAFA, C., Science
VALIANT, L. G., Computer Science and Applied Mathematics
VAN DER KUIJP, L., Tibetan and Himalayan Studies
VAN DER VELDEN, H., History of Art and Architecture
VAN ORDEN, K., Music
VENDLER, H., English
VERDINE, G., Bio- and Organic Chemistry
VLASSAK, J. J., Materials Engineering
WAKELEY, J., Organismic and Evolutionary Biology
WALDO, J. H., Practice of Computer Science
WANG, D., Chinese Literature
WANG, E., Asian Art
WATERS, M. C., Sociology
WATSON, N., English
WEI, G.-Y., Electrical Engineering and Computer Science
WEIR, J. M., Slavic Languages and Literatures, Comparative Literature
WEITZ, D. A., Physics and Applied Physics
WEITZMAN, M., Economics
WESTERN, B., Sociology
WESTERVELT, R. M., Applied Physics, Physics
WHITESIDES, G. M., Chemistry
WHYTE, M. K., International Studies and Sociology
WILLIAMS, D. R., Public Health, African and African-American Studies
WILSON, W. J., African and African-American Studies
WINSHIP, C., Sociology
WISSE, R. R., Yiddish Literature and Comparative Literature
WITZEL, M., Sanskrit
WOFSEY, S. C., Atmospheric and Environmental Science
WOLF, R. K., Music
WOOD, J., Practice of Literary Criticism
WOOD, R. J., Engineering and Applied Sciences
WOODIN, H., Mathematics
WOOLLACOTT, R. M., Biology
WRANGHAM, R. W., Biological Anthropology
WU, T. T., Applied Physics, Physics
XIE, X. S., Chemistry and Chemical Biology
YACOBY, A., Physics, Applied Physics
YANG, W., Electrical Engineering and Computer Science
YAU, H.-T., Mathematics
YAU, S.-T., Mathematics
YODA, T., Japanese Humanities
ZEGHAL, M., Contemporary Islamic Thought and Life
ZERNER, H., History of Art and Architecture
ZHUANG, X., Chemistry and Chemical Biology, Physics
ZIBLATT, D., Government
ZICKLER, T., Electrical Engineering and Computer Science
ZIOLKOWSKI, J., Medieval Latin
ZITTRAIN, J., Computer Science, Law
ZON, L. I., Paediatric Medicine

Graduate School of Design (48 Quincy St, Gund Hall, Cambridge, MA 02138; tel. (617) 495-5453; e-mail admissions@gsd.harvard.edu; internet www.gsd.harvard.edu):

ABALOS, I., Architecture
ALTSHULER, A., Urban Policy and Planning
AZIZ, M., Materials and Energy Technologies
BECHTHOLD, M., Architectural Technology
BERRIZBEITIA, A., Landscape Architecture
BRENNER, N., Urban Theory
BRUNO, G., Visual and Environmental Studies

BUSQUETS, J., Practice of Urban Planning and Design
COHEN, P. S., Architecture
DAVIS, D., Urbanism and Development
FORMAN, R. T. T., Advanced Environmental Studies in the Field of Landscape Ecology
FORSYTH, A., Urban Planning
GOMEZ-IBAÑEZ, J. A., Urban Planning and Public Policy
HAYS, K. M., Architectural History
HILDERBRAND, G., Practice of Landscape Architecture
KARA, H., Practice of Architectural Technology
KAYDEN, J., Urban Planning and Design
KIRKWOOD, N., Landscape Architecture
KOOLHAAS, R., Architecture and Urban Design
KRIEGER, A., Urban Design
KWINTER, S., Architectural Theory and Criticism
LA, G., Architecture
MALKAWI, A., Architectural Technology
MEHROTRA, R., Urban Design and Planning
MONEO, J. R., Architecture
MORI, T., Practice of Architecture
MOSTAFAVI, M., Design
MOUSSAVI, F., Practice of Architecture
NAGINSKI, E., Architectural History
PEISER, R., Real Estate Development
PFISTER, H., Computer Science
PICON, A., History of Architecture and Technology
POLLALIS, S. N., Design Technology and Management
ROWE, P. G., Architecture and Urban Design
SARKIS, H., Landscape Architecture and Urbanism in Muslim Societies
SCHULER, M., Practice of Environmental Technology
SCHWARTZ, M., Practice of Landscape Architecture
SCOGIN, M., Practice of Architecture
SILVETTI, J. S., Architecture
SMITH, C., Architectural History
STILGOE, J. R., History of Landscape Development
THOMPSON, M., Practice of Architecture
VAN VALKENBURGH, M., Practice of Landscape Architecture
WALDHEIM, C., Landscape Architecture
WEITZ, D., Physics, Applied Physics
WODICZKO, K., Art, Design and the Public Domain
WOOD, R., Engineering and Applied Sciences
ZICKLER, T., Electrical Engineering and Computer Science

Graduate School of Education (111 Longfellow Hall, 13 Appian Way, Cambridge, MA 02138; tel. (617) 495-3414; e-mail webeditor@gseharvard.edu; internet www.gse.harvard.edu):

ALONSO, A. A., Practice
BEARDSLEE, W. R., Child Psychiatry
CAREY, S. E., Psychology
DEDE, C., Learning Technologies
ELGIN, C. Z., Education
ELMORE, R. F., Educational Leadership
FISCHER, K. W., Education
FUNG, A., Democracy and Citizenship
GABRIELI, J., Health Sciences and Technology, Cognitive Neuroscience
GARDNER, H. E., Cognition and Education
HARRIS, P. L., Education
HEHIR, T., Practice in Learning Differences
HIGGINS, M. C., Education
HILL, H. C., Education
HILL, N. E., Education
HOCHSCHILD, J. L., Government, African and African-American Studies
JEWELL-SHERMAN, D., Practice
JOHNSON, S. M., Education

KALT, J. P., International Political Economy
KANE, T., Education and Economics
KEGAN, R., Adult Learning and Professional Development
KHANNA, T.
KORETZ, D., Education
LAWRENCE-LIGHTFOOT, S., Education
LESAUX, N. K., Education
LIGHT, R. J., Teaching and Learning
LONG, B. T., Education and Economics
MENAND, L., English
MINOW, M. L., Law
MOORE, M., Education, Management and Organizational Behaviour, Nonprofit Organizations
MURNANE, R. J., Education and Society
MURPHY, J. T., Education
NELSON, C., Paediatrics, Psychology
PERKINS, D., Teaching and Learning
REIMERS, F., International Education
REUBEN, J. A., History of American Education
REVILLE, P., Practice of Educational Policy and Administration
RYAN, J. E., Education
SELMAN, R. L., Education and Human Development, Psychology
SHONKOFF, J. P., Child Health and Development, Paediatrics
SINGER, J. D., Education
SNOW, C. E., Education
SPELKE, E., Psychology
WILLETT, J. B., Education

Harvard Business School (Communications Office, Harvard Business School, Soldiers Field, Boston, MA 02163; tel. (617) 495-6000; e-mail feedback@hbs.edu; internet www.hbs.edu):

ABDELAL, R. E., International Management
ALFARO, L., Business Administration
AMABILE, T. M., Business Administration
ANAND, B. N., Business Administration
APPLEGATE, L. M., Business Administration
BADARACCO, J. L., Business Ethics
BAKER, III, G. P., Business Administration
BAKER, M. P., Business Administration
BALDWIN, C. Y., Business Administration
BAZERMAN, M. H., Business Administration
BELL, D. E., Agriculture and Business
BOWER, J. L., Business Administration
CAMPBELL, D., Business Administration
CASADESUS-MASANELL, R., Business Administration
CHRISTENSEN, C. M., Business Administration
COVAL, J. D., Business Administration
DATAR, S. M., Accounting
DEIGHTON, J. A., Business Administration
DELONG, T. J., Management Practice
DESAI, M. A., Finance
DESHPANDÉ, R., Marketing
DI TELLA, R. M., Business Administration
DOLAN, R. J., Business Administration
ECCLES, R. G., Management Practice
EDMONDSON, A. C., Leadership and Management
EISENMANN, T. R., Business Administration
ELBERSE, A., Business Administration
ELY, R. J., Business Administration
ESTY, B. C., Business Administration
FOLEY, C. F., Business Administration
FREI, F. X., Service Management
GARVIN, D. A., Business Administration
GEORGE, W. W., Management Practice
GILSON, S. C., Business Administration
GOMPERS, P. A., Business Administration
GOURVILLE, J. T., Business Administration
GREEN, J. R., Political Economy
GREENWOOD, R., Finance and Banking
GROYSBERG, B., Business Administration
GULATI, R., Business Administration
GUPTA, S., Business Administration
HALL, B. J., Business Administration
HAMERMESH, R. G., Management Practice

HAMMOND, J. H., Manufacturing
HARDYMON, G. F., Management Practice
HAWKINS, D. F., Business Administration
HEALY, P. M., Business Administration
HENDERSON, R. M., Management
HERZLINGER, R. E., Business Administration
HILL, L. A., Business Administration
HUCKMAN, R. S., Business Administration
IANSITI, M., Business Administration
JONES, G. G., Business History
KANTER, R. M., Business Administration
KESTER, W. C., Business Administration
KHANNA, T., Business Strategy
KHURANA, R., Leadership Development
KIRBY, W. C., Business Administration, China Studies
KOEHN, N. F., Business Administration
KOHLBERG, E., Business Administration
LAL, R., Retailing
LASSITER, J. B., Management Practice in Environmental Management
LEONARD, H. B., Business Administration
LERNER, J., Investment Banking
LORSCH, J. W., Human Relations
McGINN, K. L., Business Administration
MALHOTRA, D., Business Administration
MALLOY, C. J., Business Administration
MARGOLIS, J. D., Business Administration
MONTGOMERY, C. A., Business Administration
MOON, Y., Business Administration
MOSS, D. A., Business Administration
NARAYANAN, V. G., Business Administration
NARAYANDAS, D., Business Administration
NICHOLAS, T., Business Administration
NOHRIA, N., Administration
OBERHOLZER-GEE, F., Business Administration
OFEK, E., Business Administration
PAINE, L. S., Business Administration
PALEPU, K. G., Business Administration
PERLOW, L. A., Leadership
PISANO, G. P., Business Administration
POLZER, J. T., Human Resource Management
PORTER, M. E., Competition and Strategy
QUELCH, J. A., Business Administration
RAMAN, A., Business Logistics
RANGAN, V. K., Marketing
REINHARDT, F. L., Business Administration
RIVKIN, J. W., Business Administration
ROSCINI, D., Management Practice
ROSE, C. S., Management Practice
ROTEMBERG, J. J., Business Administration
RUBACK, R. S., Corporate Finance
SAHLMAN, W. A., Business Administration
SASSER, JR, W. E., Service Management
SATO, V. L., Management Practice
SCHARFSTEIN, D. S., Finance and Banking
SCHLESINGER, L. A., Service Management
SEBENIUS, J. K., Business Administration
SEGEL, A. I., Management Practice
SHIH, W. C., Management Practice in Business Administration
SIMONS, R. L., Business Administration
STAFFORD, E., Business Administration
SUBRAMANIAN, G., Business Law, Law and Business
SUCHER, S. J., Management Practice
TAKEUCHI, H., Management Practice
THOMKE, S. H., Business Administration
TRUMBULL, J. G., Business Administration
TUSHMAN, M. L., Business Administration
VICEIRA, L. M., Finance
VIETOR, R. H. K., Business Administration
WELLS, J. R., Management Practice
YAO, D. A., Business Administration
YOFFIE, D. B., International Business Administration

Harvard Divinity School (45 Francis Ave, Cambridge, MA 02138; tel. (617) 495-5761; e-mail admissions@hds.harvard.edu; internet www.hds.harvard.edu):

AHMED, L., Divinity
ASANI, A. S., Indo-Muslim and Islamic Religion and Cultures
CARRASCO, D. L., Study of Latin America
CLOONEY, F. X., Divinity, Comparative Theology
COX, H. G., Divinity
DER MANUELIAN, P., Egyptology
DYCK, A. J., Ethics
ECK, D. L., Comparative Religion and Indian Studies, Law and Psychiatry in Society
FASH, W., Central American and Mexican Archaeology and Ethnology
FIORENZA, F. S., Roman Catholic Theological Studies
FREDERICK, M., African and African-American Studies, Religion
GIRÓN NEGRÓN, L. M., Romance Languages and Literatures, Comparative Literature
GRAHAM, W. A., Middle Eastern Studies
GYATSO, J., Buddhist Studies
HALL, D. D., New England Church History
HANSON, P. D., Divinity
HARDACRE, H., Japanese Religions and Society
HEHIR, J. B., Practice of Religion and Public Life
HEMPTON, D. N., Evangelical Theological Studies, Divinity
HOLLYWOOD, A., Christian Studies
HOWELL, D. L., Japanese History
JOHANSEN, B., Islamic Religious Studies
KANE, O. O., Contemporary Islamic Religion and Society, Near Eastern Languages and Civilizations
KELLY, T. F., Music
KIENZLE, B. M., Practice in Latin and Romance Languages
KING, K. L., Divinity
KOESTER, H., Divinity, Ecclesiastical History
LAMBERTH, D. C., Philosophy and Theology
LEVENSON, J. D., Jewish Studies
MACHINIST, P., Hebrew and Other Oriental Languages
MADIGAN, K. J., Ecclesiastical History
MONIUS, A. E., South Asian Religions
MOTTAHEDEH, R., Islamic History
NASRALLAH, L. S., New Testament and Early Christianity
OLUPONA, J. K., African Religious Traditions, African and African-American Studies
PATIL, P. G., Religion and Indian Philosophy
PATTON, K. C., Comparative and Historical Study of Religion
PAULSELL, S., Practice of Ministry Studies
ROBSON, J., East Asian Languages and Civilizations
RUSSELL, J. R., Armenian Studies
SCHÜSSLER FIORENZA, E., Divinity
WALTON, J. L., Christian Morals, and Religion and Society
WILLIAMS, P. N., Theology and Contemporary Change
WISSE, R. R., Yiddish Literature, Comparative Literature

Harvard Law School (1563 Massachusetts Ave, Cambridge, MA 02138; tel. (617) 495-3100; e-mail jdadmiss@law.harvard.edu; internet www.law.harvard.edu):

ALFORD, W. P.
ANKER, D. E., Clinical
BARRON, D. J., Public Law
BARTHOLET, E., Public Interest
BEBCHUK, L. A., Law, Economics, and Finance
BENKLER, Y., Entrepreneurial Legal Studies
BLUM, G., Human Rights and Humanitarian Law
BORDONE, R. C., Clinical
BREWER, S.

BROWN-NAGIN, T., Constitutional Law, History
CLARK, R. C.
COATES, J. C., Law and Economics
COHEN, I. G.
DERSHOWITZ, A. M.
DESAI, M. A.
DESAN, C.
DONAHUE, C.
ELHAUGE, E. R.
FALLON, JR, R. H., Constitutional Law
FELDMAN, N., International Law
FERRELL, A., Securities Law
FIELD, M. A.
FISHER, W. W., Intellectual Property Law
FREEMAN, J.
FRIED, C.
FRIED, J. M.
FRUG, G. E.
GASSER, U., Practice
GERSEN, J. E.
GERTNER, N., Practice
GIANNINI, T., Clinical
GLENDON, M. A.
GOLDBERG, J. C. P.
GOLDSMITH, J. L.
GORDON-REED, A., American Legal History, History
GREENWALD, R., Clinical
GREINER, D. J.
GROSSMAN, D. A, Clinical
GUINIER, L.
HALLEY, J.
HALPERIN, D. I.
HANSON, J. D.
HAY, B. L.
HEYMANN, P. B.
JACKSON, H. E.
JACKSON, V. C., Constitutional Law
JACOBS, W. B., Clinical
KAPLOW, L.
KAUFMAN, A. L.
KENNEDY, D. M., General Jurisprudence
KENNEDY, D. W.
KENNEDY, R. L.
KLARMAN, M.
KRAAKMAN, R. H.
LANNI, A.
LAZARUS, R. J.
LESSIG, L.
MACK, K. W.
MANN, B. H.
MANNING, J. F.
MELTZER, D. J.
MINOW, M. L.
MNOOKIN, R. H.
NAGIN, D., Clinical
NANDA, A., Practice
NESSON, C. R.
NEUMAN, G. L., International, Foreign, and Comparative Law
OGLETREE, JR, C. J.
PARKER, R. D., Criminal Justice
PRICE, B. K., Clinical
RABB, I., Clinical
RAKOFF, T. D., Administrative Law
RAMSEYER, J. M., Japanese Legal Studies
ROE, M. J.
ROSENBERG, M. D.
RUBENSTEIN, W. B.
SACHS, B. I.
SARGENTICH, L. D.
SCOTT, H. S., International Financial Systems
SHAVELL, S. M., Law and Economics
SHAY, S. E., Practice
SINGER, J. W.
SITKOFF, R. H.
SMITH, H. E.
SPIER, K. E.
STEIKER, C. S.
STEPHENSON, M. C.
STONE, A. A., Law and Psychiatry
SUBRAMANIAN, G., Law and Business
SUK, J. C., Law and Business
SULLIVAN, R. S., Clinical

SUNSTEIN, C. R.
TRIBE, L. H., Constitutional Law
TUSHNET, M.
UNGER, R. M.
VERMEULE, A.
WARREN, A. C.
WEINREB, L. L.
WESTFAHL, S. A., Practice
WHITE, L. E.
WHITING, A., Practice
WILKINS, D. B.
WOLFMAN, B.
ZITTRAIN, J.

Harvard Medical School (25 Shattuck St, Boston, MA 02115; tel. (617) 432-1000; e-mail admissions_office@hms.harvard.edu; internet hms.harvard.edu):

ABBOTT, W. M., Surgery
ABRAHM, J. L., Medicine
ADELSTEIN, S. J., Medical Biophysics
AFDHAL, N. H., Medicine
AIELLO, L., Ophthalmology
AIRD, W., Medicine
AKINS, C. W., Surgery
ALBERT, M. S., Psychiatry
ALEGRIA, M., Psychiatry
ALEXANDER, M., Neurology
ALI, H. H., Anaesthesia
ALPER, C. A., Paediatrics
ALPER, S., Medicine
ALS, H., Psychology
ALSOP, D., Radiology
ALT, F. W., Genetics
ALPER, C. A., Paediatrics
ALTFELD, M., Medicine
ALTSHULER, D. M., Genetics and Medicine
AMATO, A., Neurology
ANDERSON, E., Comparative Anatomy
ANDERSON, R., Dermatology
ANTIN, J., Medicine
ANTMAN, E., Medicine
APPLEBURY, M. L., Ophthalmology
ARKY, R., Medicine and Medical Education
ARNAOUT, R. L., Medicine
ARNOLD, J. H., Anaesthesia
ARONSON, M., Medicine
ARTAVANIS-TSAKONAS, S., Cell Biology
ASCHERIO, A., Epidemiology and Nutrition
ASHLEY, S. W., Surgery
ASSAD, J., Neurobiology
ASTER, J., Pathology
AUSIELLO, D. A., Clinical Medicine
AUSTEN, K. F., Medicine
AUSTEN, W. G., Surgery
AUSUBEL, F. M., Molecular Biology, Genetics
AVORN, J., Medicine
AVRUCH, J., Medicine
AYANIAN, J., Internal Medicine, General Medicine, Health Management and Policy, Public Policy
BACSKAI, B., Neurology
BAKSHI, R., Neurology
BADEN, H. P., Dermatology
BALDESSARINI, R. J., Psychiatry—Neuroscience
BALK, S., Medicine
BALLEN, K., Medicine
BANGSBERG, D., Medicine
BANKIER, A. A., Radiology
BANKS, P., Medicine
BARBIERI, R. L., Obstetrics, Gynaecology and Reproductive Biology
BARNETT, G. O., Medicine
BARON, R., Medicine
BAROUCHE, D., Medicine
BARSAMIAN, E. M., Surgery
BARSKY, III, A. J., Psychiatry
BATES, D., Medicine
BAUER, K., Medicine
BAUER, M., Psychiatry
BAUER, S., Surgery
BEAN, B. P., Neurobiology
BEARDSLEE, W. R., Psychiatry
BECK, J., Psychiatry

BECKER, A., Global Health and Social Medicine
BECKWITH, J. R., Microbiology and Immunobiology
BELFER, M. L., Psychiatry
BELKIN, M., Surgery
BELLINGER, D., Neurology
BENDER, W. W., Biological Chemistry and Molecular Pharmacology
BENES, F. M., Psychiatry
BENJAMIN, T. L., Microbiology and Immunobiology
BENOIST, C., Microbiology and Immunobiology
BENSON, C. B., Radiology
BENZ, E. J., Genetics
BERESEN, E., Psychiatry
BERKOWITZ, R. S., Obstetrics, Gynaecology and Reproductive Biology
BERLINER, N., Medicine
BERNSTEIN, B., Pathology
BERRY, G., Paediatrics
BERSON, E. L., Ophthalmology
BERTAGNOLI, M., Surgery
BERWICK, D. M., Paediatrics and Health Care Policy
BETENSKY, R., Biostatistics
BHAN, A., Pathology
BHATT, D. L., Medicine
BHATTACHARYYA, N., Otology and Laryngology
BIEDERMAN, J., Psychiatry
BILLER, B., Medicine
BIRRER, M., Medicine
BISCHOFF, J., Surgery
BISTRIAN, B. R., Medicine
BLACK, P. M., Neurosurgery
BLACKBURN, G. L., Nutrition
BLACKER, D., Psychiatry
BLACKLOW, S., Biological Chemistry and Molecular Pharmacology
BLACKWELL, T. K., Genetics
BLENIS, J., Cell Biology
BLOCK, S. D., Psychiatry and Medicine
BLUMBERG, R., Medicine
BLUMENTHAL, D., Medicine, Health Care Policy
BLUTE, M. L., Surgery
BOAS, D., Radiology
BOISELLE, P., Radiology
BOLAND, G, Radiology
BOLMAN, R, Surgery
BOLSHAKOV, V, Psychiatry
BONNER-WEIR, S., Medicine
BONVENTRE, J. V., Medicine
BORN, R., Neurobiology
BORTFELD, T., Radiation Oncology
BORUS, J. F., Psychiatry
BOUMA, B., Dermatology
BOUSSIOTIS, V., Medicine
BRADY, T., Radiology
BRANDT, A. M., History of Medicine, History of Science
BRAUNWALD, E., Theory and Practice of Physic
BREAKEFIELD, X. O., Neurology
BRENNER, B., Medicine
BRENNER, M. B., Medicine
BRETON, S., Medicine
BREWSTER, D. C., Surgery
BRINK, J. A., Radiology
BROCK, D., Legal Medicine
BROCK, D. W., Medical Ethics
BRONSON, R. T., Pathology
BROWN, D., Medicine
BROWN, E. M., Medicine
BROWN, E. N., Anaesthesia
BROWNELL, A.-L., Radiology
BRUGGE, J. S., Cell Biology
BRUGGE, W., Medicine
BRUGNARA, C., Pathology
BUCHANAN, J. R., Medicine
BUCKNER, R., Psychology, Neuroscience
BUENO, R., Surgery
BUNN, H. F., Medicine

BURATOWSKI, S., Biological Chemistry and Molecular Pharmacology
BURING, J., Population Medicine
BURKE, J., Psychiatry
BURROWS, P. E., Radiology
BYRNE, J. G., Surgery
CAMARGO, C., Medicine
CAMPBELL, E. G., Medicine
CANELLOS, G. P., Medicine
CANNISTRA, S., Medicine
CANNON, C. P., Medicine
CANTLEY, L. C., Cell Biology
CANTOR, H. I., Microbiology and Immunobiology
CAPLAN, D. N., Neurology
CAPLAN, L., Neurology
CAREY, M. C., Medicine
CARLEZON, W., Psychiatry
CASSEM, E. H., Psychiatry
CAVINESS, JR, V. S., Child Neurology and Mental Retardation
CELLI, B. R., Medicine
CEPKO, C. L., Genetics
CHABNER, B. A., Medicine
CHANG, G., Psychiatry
CHARNESS, M., Neurology
CHEN, L. B., Pathology
CHENEY, M., Otology and Laryngology
CHERNEW, M. E., Health Care Policy
CHIEN, K., Stem Cell and Regenerative Biology
CHIN, W. W., Translational Medical Science
CHIOCCA, E. A., Surgery
CHODOSH, J., Ophthalmology
CHOI, N., Radiation Oncology
CHOPRA, S., Medicine
CHOU, J. J., Biological Chemistry and Molecular Pharmacology
CHRISTAKIS, N., Social and Natural Science
CHRISTIANI, D. C., Medicine
CHURCH, G. H., Genetics
CHYLACK, JR, L. T., Ophthalmology
CIBAS, E., Pathology
CLAPHAM, D. E., Cardiovascular Research
CLARDY, J., Biological Chemistry and Molecular Pharmacology
CLEARY, P. D., Health Care Policy
CLEVELAND, R. H., Radiology
COEN, D. M., Biological Chemistry and Molecular Pharmacology
COHEN, B. M., Psychiatry
COHEN, D., Medicine and Health Sciences and Technology
COHEN, J. B., Neurobiology
COHN, L. H., Surgery
COLAN, S., Paediatrics
COLE, A., Neurology
COLES, R., Psychiatry and Medical Humanities
COLLIER, R. J., Microbiology and Immunobiology
COLSON, Y., Surgery
COLVIN, R. B., Pathology
COMPTON, C. C., Pathology
CONLIN, P., Medicine
CONNOLLY, J., Pathology
COOK, E., Medicine
COOK, N., Medicine
COREY, D. P., Neurobiology
CORSON, J. M., Pathology
COSIMI, A. B., Surgery
COTE, C., Anaesthesia
COYLE, J. T., Psychiatry and Neuroscience
CRAMER, D., Obstetrics, Gynaecology and Reproductive Biology
CREAGER, M., Medicine
CRONE, E. R., Anaesthesia
CROWLEY, JR, W. F., Medicine
CRUM, C. P., Pathology
CRUMPACKER, C., Medicine
CUNNINGHAM, M., Otology and Laryngology
CURHAN, G., Medicine
CURTIN, H., Radiology
CZEISLER, C. A., Sleep Medicine
DAL CIN, P. S., Pathology

DALEY, G., Biological Chemistry and Molecular Pharmacology
D'AMICO, A., Radiation Oncology
D'AMORE, P. A., Ophthalmology, Pathology
DANA, R., Ophthalmology
DANIELS, G., Medicine
DANUSER, G., Cell Biology
DARRAS, B., Neurology
DARTT, D., Ophthalmology
DAVID, J. R., Medicine
DAVIS, I., Physical Medicine and Rehabilitation
DAVIS, K., Radiology
DAWSON, D. M., Neurology
DE GIROLAMI, U., Pathology
DELBANCO, T., General Medicine and Primary Care
DELGUTTE, B., Otology and Laryngology
DELISI, L., Psychiatry
DEMASO, D., Child Psychiatry
DEMAY, M., Medicine
DEMETRI, G. D., Medicine
DEMLING, R. H., Surgery
DESANCTIS, R. W., Medicine
DESCHLER, D. G., Otology and Laryngology
DESROSIERS, R. C., Microbiology and Immunobiology
DEWOLF, W. C., Surgery
DI CARLI, M., Radiology
DIFIGLIA, M., Neurology
DILLER, L., Paediatrics
DINARDO, J., Anaesthesia
DLUHY, R., Medicine
DOCKERY, D., Environmental Epidemiology
DOGON, I. L., Operative Dentistry
DONAHOE, P. K., Surgery
DONOFF, R. B., Oral and Maxillofacial Surgery
DORF, M. E., Microbiology and Immunobiology
DOUBILET, P., Radiology
DOWLING, J. E., Neuroscience
DRANOFF, G., Medicine
DRAZEN, J. M., Medicine
DRETLER, S. P., Surgery
DRISLANE, F., Neurology
DRYJA, JR, T. P., Ophthalmology
DVORAK, A. M., Pathology
DVORAK, H. F., Pathology
DYMECKI, S. M., Genetics
DYSON, N., Medicine
EARLS, III, F. J., Human Behaviour and Development
EATOCK, R. A., Otology and Laryngology, Neurobiology
ECK, M., Biological Chemistry and Molecular Pharmacology
ECKER, J., Obstetrics, Gynaecology and Reproductive Biology
EDELMAN, E., Medicine
EDLOW, J., Medicine
EGGAN, K. C., Stem Cell and Regenerative Biology
EISENBERG, R., Radiology
EL FAKHRI, G., Radiology
ELION, E., Biological Chemistry and Molecular Pharmacology
ELIOPOULOS, G., Medicine
ELLEDGE, S. J., Genetics, Medicine
EMANS, J. B., Orthopaedic Surgery
EMANS, S., Paediatrics
ENGLE, E., Neurology
EPSTEIN, A., Medicine, Health Care Policy
ERIKSSON, E., Plastic and Reconstructive Surgery
FANTA, C. H., Medicine
FARMER, P., Global Health and Social Medicine
FAVA, M., Psychiatry
FEANY, M., Pathology
FERNANDEZ-DEL CASTILLO, C., Surgery
FERRAN, C., Surgery
FERRARO, M., Pathology
FERRY, J., Pathology
FIFER, M., Medicine
FINKELSTEIN, D., Medicine

FINLEY, D., Cell Biology
FISHL, B., Radiology
FISHMAN, J., Medicine
FISHMAN, S. J., Surgery
FIITZMAURICE, G., Psychiatry
FLANAGAN, J., Cell Biology
FLEISHER, G. R., Paediatrics
FLETCHER, C., Pathology
FLIER, J. S., Medicine
FONTANA, W., Systems Biology
FOSTER, C. S., Ophthalmology
FRANGIONI, J., Medicine
FRANK, R. G., Health Economics
FREEDBERG, K., Medicine
FREEDMAN, S., Medicine
FREEMAN, M. R., Surgery
FREEMAN, R., Neurology
FRICCHIONE, G., Psychiatry
FRIEDMAN, L., Medicine
FRIGOLETTO, JR., F. D., Obstetrics and Gynaecology
FUCHS, C., Medicine
FULTON, A., Ophthalmology
FURIE, B., Medicine
FURIE, B. C., Medicine
GABUZDA, D., Neurology
GALABURDA, A., Neurology and Neuroscience
GARBER, A. M., Health Care Policy, Economics
GARBER, J., Medicine
GARNICK, M. B., Medicine
GAWANDE, A., Surgery
GAZELLE, G., Radiology
GAZIANO, J., Medicine
GEHA, R. S., Paediatrics
GEHRKE, L., Microbiology and Immunobiology
GELBER, R. D., Paediatrics—Biostatistics
GELMAN, S., Anaesthesia
GEORGOPOULOS, K., Dermatology
GERARD, C., Paediatrics
GERARD, N., Medicine
GERSZTEN, R., Medicine
GEVA, T., Paediatrics
GIBSON, C. M., Medicine
GILLICK, M. R., Ambulatory Care and Prevention
GILLMAN, M. W., Population Medicine
GILMORE, M., Ophthalmology
GIMBRONE, M. A., Pathology
GINTY, D., Neurobiology
GIOVANNUCCI, E., Nutrition and Epidemiology
GIPSON, I. K., Ophthalmology
GLADYSHEV, V., Medicine
GLICKMAN, R. M., Medicine
GLIMCHER, L. H., Medicine
GLIMCHER, M. J., Orthopaedic Surgery
GLOWACKI, J., Oral and Maxillofacial Surgery
GLYNN, R., Medicine
GOLAN, D., Biological Chemistry and Molecular Pharmacology
GOLD, D., Medicine
GOLDBERG, A. L., Cell Biology
GOLDBERG, M., Medicine
GOLDBERGER, A., Medicine
GOLDFELD, A. E., Medicine
GOLDFINGER, S., Medicine
GOLDHABER, S., Medicine
GOLDIE, S., Public Health, Global Health and Social Medicine
GOLDMANN, D. A., Paediatrics
GOLDSTEIN, D. P., Obstetrics, Gynaecology and Reproduction
GOLDSTEIN, J., Medicine
GONZALEZ, E., Dermatology
GONZALEZ, R., Radiology
GOOD, B. J., Medical Anthropology
GOOD, M.-J. D., Global Health and Social Medicine
GOODENOUGH, D. A., Anatomy and Cell Biology
GOODMAN, E., Paediatrics
GOROLL, A., Medicine

GOSS, P., Medicine
GOUDSOUZIAN, N., Anaesthesia
GOODMAN, H. M., Genetics
GOYAL, R. K., Medicine
GRABOWSKI, D., Health Care Policy
GRAGOUDAS, E. S., Ophthalmology
GRAND, R. J., Paediatrics
GRAND, S., Paediatrics
GRAY, N., Biological Chemistry and Molecular Pharmacology
GREEN, H., Cell Biology
GREENBERG, M. E., Neurology, Neuroscience
GREENE, M., Obstetrics, Gynaecology and Reproductive Biology
GREENE, R. E., Radiology
GREENFIELD, S., Psychiatry
GRIER, H., Paediatrics
GRIFFIN, J. D., Medicine
GRINSPOON, S. K., Medicine
GRISCOM, N. T., Radiology
GRODSTEIN, F., Medicine
GROOPMAN, J. E., Medicine
GROWDON, J. H., Neurology
GRUNEBAUM, H. U., Psychiatry
GUADAGNOLI, E., Health Care Policy
GUINAN, J.J., Otology and Laryngology
GUNDERSON, J. G., Psychiatry
GUREWICH, V., Medicine
GUSELLA, J. F., Neurogenetics
GUTHEIL, T. G., Psychiatry
GYGI, S., Cell Biology
HAAS, J. S., Medicine
HABENER, J. F., Medicine
HACKNEY, D., Radiology
HALAMKA, J., Medicine
HALES, C. A., Medicine
HALL, F. M., Radiology
HALL, J. E., Orthopaedic Surgery
HANDIN, R. I., Medicine
HARLOW, E. E., Biological Chemistry and Molecular Pharmacology
HARMON, W., Paediatrics
HARPER, J. W., Molecular Pathology
HARRIS, G., Radiology
HARRIS, J. R., Radiation Oncology
HARRIS, M. B., Orthopaedic Surgery
HARRIS, N. L., Pathology
HARRISON, S. C., Basic Biomedical Science
HARTHORNE, J., Medicine
HARTNICK, C. J., Otology and Laryngology
HARTWIG, J., Medicine
HASAN, T., Dermatology
HATABU, H., Radiology
HATEM, C., Medicine
HAUSER, R., Reproductive Physiology
HAYNES, H. A., Dermatology
HE, Z., Neurology
HEALY, G. B., Otology and Laryngology
HECHTMAN, H. B., Surgery
HEDLEY-WHYTE, E. T., Pathology
HEDLEY-WHYTE, J., Anaesthesia and Respiratory Therapy
HEMLER, M. E., Pathology
HENDREN, III, W. H., Surgery
HENSKE, E., Medicine
HERNDON, J. H., Orthopaedic Surgery
HERSCH, S., Neurology
HERZOG, A., Neurology
HERZOG, D. B., Psychiatry
HIATT, H. H., Medicine, Global Health and Social Medicine
HIBBERD, P., Paediatrics
HICKEY, P. R., Anaesthesia
HIGGINS, D. E., Microbiology and Immunobiology
HILLMAN, R. E., Surgery
HIROSE, T., Ophthalmology
HIRSCH, M. S., Medicine
HIRSCHHORN, J., Genetics
HOCHEDLINGER, K., Stem Cell and Regenerative Biology
HOCHSCHILD, A., Microbiology and Immunobiology
HODIN, R., Surgery
HOFFMAN, B., Medicine

HOFFMAN, U., Radiology
HOGLE, J. M., Biological Chemistry and Molecular Pharmacology
HOLLENBERG, A., Medicine
HOLLENBERG, N. K., Medicine
HOLMES, G. L., Neurology
HOLMES, L., Paediatrics
HOLZMAN, R., Anaesthesia
HOOPER, D., Medicine
HORNSTEIN, M., Obstetrics, Gynaecology and Reproductive Biology
HORTON, E. S., Medicine
HOWLEY, P. M., Pathological Anatomy
HU, F., Nutrition and Epidemiology
HUANG, P., Medicine
HUDSON, J., Psychiatry
HUNT, R. D., Comparative Pathology
HUNTER, D., Cancer Prevention
HUNTER, D. G., Ophthalmology
HUSKAMP, H., Health Care Policy
HUSSON, R. N., Paediatrics
HUTTER, A., Medicine
HYMAN, S. E., Stem Cell and Regenerative Biology
IEZZONI, L. I., Medicine
INGELFINGER, J. R., Paediatrics
INOUYE, S., Medicine
INUI, T. S., Ambulatory Care and Prevention
ISACSON, O., Neurology
ISRAEL, E., Medicine
ISSELBACHER, K. J., Medicine
JAFF, M., Medicine
JAIN, R. K., Radiation Oncology
JAMISON, R., Anaesthesia
JANG, I.-K., Medicine
JANUZZI, J., Medicine
JELLINEK, M., Psychiatry
JENIKE, M. A., Psychiatry
JENKINS, K., Paediatrics
JHA, A., Health Policy and Management
JIMERSON, D., Psychiatry
JOHNSON, K., Radiology
JOHNSON, R. P., Medicine
JOLESZ, F. A., Radiology
JOHNSON, B., Medicine
JOHNSON, P., Medicine
JOHNSON, R., Medicine
JONAS, M., Paediatrics
JONES, D., Culture of Medicine
JONES, D. B., Surgery
JOSEPHSON, M. E., Medicine
JUEPPNER, H., Paediatrics
JUNGER, W., Surgery
KABAN, L. B., Oral and Maxillofacial Surgery
KACMAREK, R., Anaesthesia
KAHN, C. R., Medicine
KAHNE, D., Biological Chemistry and Molecular Pharmacology
KAHNE, S., Microbiology and Immunobiology
KAISER, U. B., Medicine
KANE, R., Radiology
KANTOFF, P., Medicine
KAPLAN, J., Neurobiology
KAPTCHUK, T., Medicine
KARCHMER, A. W., Medicine
KASPER, D. L., Microbiology and Immunobiology
KASSER, J. R., Orthopaedic Surgery
KASSIS, A., Radiology
KATZ, J., Medicine
KAUFMANN, W., Neurology
KAWACHI, I., Social Epidemiology
KAZEMI, H., Medicine
KAZLAUSKAS, A., Ophthalmology
KEANE, J., Paediatrics
KELLEY, V., Medicine
KELLY, C., Psychiatry
KELLY, J., Medicine
KENNA, M., Otology and Laryngology
KESSLER, R. C., Health Care Policy
KHANTZIAN, E., Psychiatry
KIBEL, A., Surgery

KIEFF, E. D., Medicine, Microbiology and Molecular Genetics
KIEL, D., Medicine
KIKINIS, R., Radiology
KIM, K.-S., Psychiatry
KIMBALL, A., Dermatology
KINET, J.-P., Pathology
KING, G. L., Medicine
KING, R., Cell Biology
KINGSTON, R. E., Genetics
KINNEY, H. C., Pathology
KIRCHHAUSEN, T., Cell Biology
KIRSCHNER, M. W., Systems Biology
KISHONY, R., Systems Biology
KISSIN, I., Anaesthesia
KISTLER, J., Neurology
KITZ, R. J., Research and Teaching in Anaesthetics and Anaesthesia
KLAGSBRUN, M., Surgery
KLEINMAN, A. M., Medical Anthropology, Anthropology
KLEINMAN, P., Radiology
KLIBANSKI, A., Medicine
KNIPE, D. M., Microbiology and Immunobiology
KOBZIK, L., Pathology
KOCHER, M. S., Orthopaedic Surgery
KOCHEVAR, I., Dermatology
KOHANE, D., Anaesthesia
KOHANE, I., Paediatrics and Health Sciences and Technology
KOLTER, R. G., Microbiology and Immunobiology
KOMAROFF, A. L., Medicine
KOPANS, D., Radiology
KORALNIK, I. J., Neurology
KOTELCHUCK, M., Paediatrics
KRANE, S. M., Clinical Medicine
KRAVITZ, E. A., Neurobiology
KRESSEL, H. Y., Radiology
KRONENBERG, H. M., Medicine
KRUSKAL, J., Radiology
KUCHERLAPATI, R., Genetics, Medicine
KUFE, D. W., Medicine
KULLDORFF, M., Population Medicine
KUNKEL, L. M., Paediatrics and Genetics
KUPPER, T., Dermatology
KURITZKES, D., Medicine
KURODA, M. I., Genetics, Medicine
KUTER, D., Medicine
KWIATKOWSKI, D., Medicine
LAMONT, J. T., Medicine
LANDER, E. S., Systems Biology
LANDON, B., Health Care Policy, Medicine
LANDRUM, M. E., Health Care Policy
LANGE, C., Biostatistics
LANGEVIN, H., Medicine
LANGSTON, D. B., Ophthalmology
LARSEN, P. R., Medicine
LASSER, A., Biological Chemistry and Molecular Pharmacology
LAUFER, M. R., Obstetrics, Gynaecology, and Reproductive Biology
LAUWERS, G., Pathology
LAWLER, J., Pathology
LEANING, J., Practice of Health and Human Rights
LEBOFF, M., Medicine
LEE, I.-M., Medicine
LEE, J. T., Genetics and Pathology
LEE, R. T., Stem Cell and Regenerative Biology
LEE, T., Medicine
LEES, R., Health Sciences and Technology
LENCER, W., Paediatrics
LESSELL, S., Ophthalmology
LEV, M., Radiology
LEVINE, D., Radiology
LEVINE, R., Medicine
LEVITON, A., Neurology
LEVITSKY, S., Surgery
LEVY, J., Paediatrics
LEWANDROWSKI, K., Pathology
LIANG, M., Medicine
LIBBY, P., Medicine
LIBERMAN, M. C., Otology and Laryngology

LIBMAN, H., Medicine
LICHTMAN, A., Pathology
LIEU, T., Population Medicine
LILLY, L., Medicine
LIPSITT, D. R., Clinical Psychiatry
LIPSITT, L., Medicine
LIPSITT, S., Medicine
LIVINGSTON, D. M., Genetics and Medicine
LIVINGSTONE, M. S., Neurobiology
LO, E., Radiology
LODA, M., Pathology
LOEFFLER, J. S., Radiation Oncology
LONGO, D., Medicine
LORING, S., Anaesthesia
LORY, S., Microbiology and Immunobiology
LOUGHLIN, K., Surgery
LOUIS, D. N., Pathology
LOVEJOY, JR, F. H., Paediatrics
LOWELL, B., Medicine
LOWENSTEIN, E., Anaesthetics and Anaesthesia, Global Health and Social Medicine
LU, K. P., Medicine
LUDWIG, D., Paediatrics
LUKAS, S., Psychiatry
LUSCINSKAS, F., Pathology
LUX, IV, S. E., Paediatrics
LYONS-RUTH, K., Psychology
MA, Q., Neurobiology
MAAS, R., Medicine
MCCARLEY, R. W., Psychiatry
MCCARROLL, S., Genetics
MCCLATCHEY, A. I., Pathology
MCCORMICK, M. C., Paediatrics
MCDONALD, M., Neurology
MCDOUGAL, W. S., Urology
MCGILL, T., Otology and Laryngology
MCGUIRE, T., Health Care Economics
MCINTOSH, K., Paediatrics
MCKENNA, M., Otology and Laryngology
MCKEON, F. D., Cell Biology
MCKENNA, M. J., Otology and Laryngology
MACKLIS, J. E., Stem Cell and Regenerative Biology
MCLATCHEY, A., Pathology
MCLOUD, T. C., Radiology
MCMAHON, A., Science
MCNEIL, B. J., Health Care Policy
MADRAS, B., Psychobiology
MADSEN, J., Surgery
MAGUIRE, J., Medicine
MAJZOUB, J. A., Paediatrics, Medicine
MAKRIGIORGOS, G., Radiation Oncology
MALCHAU, H., Orthopaedic Surgery
MANDELL, J., Surgery
MANDL, K. D., Paediatrics
MANNING, W., Medicine
MANSCHRECK, T. C., Psychiatry
MANTZOROS, C., Medicine
MARASCO, W. A., Medicine
MARATOS-FLIER, E., Medicine
MARCANTONIO, E., Medicine
MARGOLIES, M. N., Surgery
MARK, E., Pathology
MARTIN, J. B., Neurobiology
MARTUZA, R., Neuroscience
MARTYN, J. A. J., Anaesthesia
MASLAND, R. H., Ophthalmology
MATHIS, D., Microbiology and Microbiology and Immunobiology
MAUCH, P., Radiation Oncology
MAUNSELL, J., Neurobiology
MAY, J., Surgery
MAYADAS, T., Pathology
MAYER, JR, J. E., Surgery
MAYER, K., Medicine
MAYER, R. J., Medicine
MEHRA, M., Medicine
MEKALANOS, J. J., Microbiology and Microbiology and Immunobiology
MELTON, D. A., Natural Sciences
MENTZER, S., Surgery
MERFELD, D. M., Otology and Laryngology
MEYER, J., Radiology
MICHEL, T., Medicine
MICHELSON, A., Paediatrics

MIHM, JR, M. C., Dermatopathology
MILBERG, W., Psychiatry
MILLER, J. W., Ophthalmology
MILLER, K. W., Pharmacology in Anaesthesia
MILLS, M., Orthopaedic Surgery
MISHLER, E. G., Social Psychology
MITCHELL, R., Pathology and Health Sciences and Technology
MITCHELL, S., Medicine
MITCHISON, T. J., Systems Biology
MOAZED, D., Cell Biology
MODELL, A. H., Psychiatry
MOELLERING, JR, R. C., Medical Research
MOLLICA, R., Psychiatry
MONACO, A. P., Surgery
MONTMINY, M. R., Cell Biology
MOODY, D., Medicine
MOORE, G. T., Population Medicine
MOOTHA, V., Systems Biology
MORRIS, C. N., Health Care Policy, Statistics
MORTON, C. C., Obstetrics, Gynaecology and Reproductive Biology, Pathology
MOSKOWITZ, M. A., Neurology
MUDGE, G., Medicine
MUELLER, P., Radiology
MULLIKEN, J., Surgery
MUNGER, K., Medicine
MURPHY, G., Pathology
MURPHY, J. M., Psychiatry
MURRAY, M., Global Health and Social Medicine
MUTTER, G., Pathology
NÄÄR, A. M., Cell Biology
NABEL, E., Medicine
NADELSON, C. C., Psychiatry
NADLER, L. M., Medicine
NADOL, JR, J. B., Otolaryngology and Laryngology
NAKATANI, Y., Biological Chemistry and Molecular Pharmacology
NATHAN, D., Medicine
NEUTRA, M. R., Paediatrics
NEWBURGER, J. W., Paediatrics
NEWHOUSE, J. P., Health Care Policy, Health Policy and Management
NIBERT, M., Microbiology and Molecular Genetics
NICHOLSON-WELLER, A., Medicine
NIERENBERG, A., Psychiatry
NORMAND, S.-L., Health Care Policy—Biostatistics, Biostatistics
NOTMAN, M. T., Psychiatry
NOVELLINE, R. A., Radiology
O'GARA, P., Medicine
O'LEARY, M., Surgery
O'MALLEY, A. J., Biostatistics
ODZE, R., Pathology
OETTINGER, M., Genetics
OLIVA I ESCRIBA, E., Pathology
OLSEN, B. R., Cell Biology, Oral and Developmental Biology
ONDERDONK, A., Pathology
ORGILL, D., Surgery
ORKIN, S. H., Paediatrics
PAGANETTI, H., Radiation Oncology
PALACIOS, I., Medicine
PALFREY, J. S., Paediatrics, Global Health and Social Medicine
PASCUAL-LEONE, A., Neurology
PAUL, D. L., Neurobiology
PAULS, D., Psychiatry
PELLMAN, D., Cell Biology
PENNEY, JR, J. B., Neurology
PEPPERCORN, M. A., Medicine
PERELMAN, L. T., Obstetrics, Gynaecology and Reproductive Biology
PERRIMON, N., Genetics
PERRIN, J., Paediatrics
PFEFFER, M. A., Medicine
PHILIP, B., Anaesthesia
PHILIP, J. H., Anaesthesia
PHILLIPS, R., Medicine, Global Health and Social Medicine
PICARD, M., Medicine

PIER, G. B., Medicine, Microbiology and Molecular Genetics
PIERCE, E., Ophthalmology
PILLAI, S., Medicine
PINKUS, G. S., Pathology
PITMAN, R., Psychiatry
PIZZO, P., Paediatrics
PLATT, O., Paediatrics
PLATT, R., Population Medicine
POLYAK, K., Medicine
POPE, H., Psychiatry
POPMA, J. J., Medicine
POSS, R., Orthopaedic Surgery
POTTS, JR, J. T., Clinical Medicine
POUSSAINT, A. F., Psychiatry
POUSSAINT, T. Y., Radiology
PRIBAZ, J., Surgery
PRIGERSON, H., Psychiatry
PUIGSERVER, P., Cell Biology
QUAN, S. F., Sleep Medicine
RABKIN, M. T., Medicine
RACOWSKY, C., Obstetrics, Gynaecology and Reproductive Biology
RAO, A., Pharmacology
RAPOPORT, T. A., Cell Biology
RAPTOPOULOS, V., Radiology
RAUCH, S. D., Otology and Laryngology
RECHT, A., Radiation Oncology
REDLINE, S., Sleep Medicine
REED, R., Cell Biology
REGEHR, W., Neurobiology
REICH, D., Genetics
REID, R. C., Neurobiology
REINHERZ, E. L., Medicine
REMOLD, H. G., Medicine
RENNKE, H., Pathology
REPPERT, S. M., Paediatrics
RETIK, A. B., Surgery—Urology
RICHARDSON, C. C., Biological Chemistry and Molecular Pharmacology
RICHARDSON, P. G., Medicine
RICHIE, J. P., Surgery
RIFAI, N., Pathology
RIGOTTI, N., Medicine
RINN, J., Stem Cell and Regenerative Biology
RIORDAN, J. F., Biochemistry
RITZ, J., Medicine
ROBERTS, T. M., Biological Chemistry and Molecular Pharmacology
ROBINSON, D., Medicine
ROCCO, J., Otology and Laryngology
ROCKOFF, M., Anaesthesia
RONTHAL, M., Neurology
ROSAND, J., Neurology
ROSEN, B., Health Sciences and Technology
ROSEN, S. S., Pathology
ROSENBERG, C., History of Science, Social Sciences
ROSENBLATT, M., Molecular Medicine
ROSENTHAL, D. I., Radiology
ROSENTHAL, D. S., Medicine
ROSENZWEIG, A., Medicine
ROSNER, B. A., Medicine—Biostatistics
ROSOW, C., Anaesthesia
ROSOWSKI, J. J., Otology and Laryngology, Health Sciences and Technology
ROSS, D., Medicine
ROTHENBERG, A., Psychiatry
RUBIN, E., Immunology and Infectious Diseases
RUBIN, L. L., Stem Cell and Regenerative Biology
RUBIN, R., Health Sciences and Technology
RUDERMAN, J. V., Anatomy and Cell Biology
RUTKOVE, S., Neurology
RUVKUN, G. B., Genetics
RYAN, E., Medicine
SABATINI, B., Neurobiology
SABIN, J., Population Medicine, Psychiatry
SACHS, D. H., Surgery
SACKS, F., Cardiovascular Disease Prevention
SACKSTEIN, R., Dermatology
SAFREN, S., Psychology

SAINI, S., Radiology
SALLAN, S. E., Paediatrics
SALZMAN, C., Psychiatry
SAMUELS, M. A., Neurology
SANDA, M., Surgery
SAPER, C. B., Neurology and Neuroscience
SAX, P., Medicine
SCADDEN, D., Stem Cell and Regenerative Biology, Medicine
SCAMMELL, T. E., Neurology
SCHACHTER, S., Neurology
SCHIFF, I., Gynaecology
SCHMAHMANN, J., Neurology
SCHNEEBERGER, E. E., Pathology
SCHNEEWEISS, S., Medicine
SCHNIPPER, L. E., Medicine
SCHNITT, S., Pathology
SCHOEN, F. J., Pathology, Health Sciences and Technology
SCHOENFELD, D., Statistics
SCHOMER, D., Neurology
SCHUR, P. H., Medicine
SCHWARTZ, J., Environmental Epidemiology
SCHWARTZSCHILD, M., Neurology
SCHWARTZSTEIN, R., Medical Education
SCHWARZ, T., Neurology and Neurobiology
SCOTT, R. M., Surgery
SECTISH, T., Paediatrics
SEED, B., Genetics
SEELY, E., Medicine
SEGAL, R., Neurobiology
SEIDMAN, C. E., Genetics and Medicine
SEIDMAN, J. G., Genetics
SEIDMAN, L., Psychology
SELKOE, D. J., Neurological Diseases
SELMAN, R. L., Education and Human Development
SELTZER, S. E., Radiology
SELWYN, A. P., Medicine
SERHAN, C. N., Anaesthesia
SEWELL, W. F., Otology and Laryngology
SGROI, D., Pathology
SHAHIAN, D., Surgery
SHANNON, D. C., Paediatrics and Health Sciences and Technology
SHARPE, A. H., Microbiology and Immunobiology
SHEEN, J.-Y., Genetics
SHEFFER, A. L., Medicine
SHEN, J., Neurology
SHENTON, M., Radiology
SHEPARD, J.-A., Radiology
SHERA, C. A., Otology and Laryngology
SHERNAN, S., Anaesthesia
SHI, Y., Cell Biology, Neonatology
SHIELDS, H., Medicine
SHIPLEY, W. U., Radiation Oncology
SHOELSON, S., Medicine
SHONKOFF, J., Child Health and Development
SHORE, M. F., Psychiatry
SICIŃSKI, P., Genetics
SILBERT, J. E., Medicine
SILVER, P. A., Biochemistry, Systems Biology
SILVERMAN, E. K., Medicine
SILVERMAN, S., Radiology
SIMEONE, J. F., Radiology
SIMS, K., Neurology
SINCLAIR, D. A., Genetics
SINGER, D., Medicine
SKLAR, J. L., Pathology
SLACK, W., Medicine
SLAUGHENHAUPT, S., Neurology
SLAVIN, P., Health Care Policy
SMITH, L., Ophthalmology
SMITH, M., Medicine
SMOLLER, J. W., Psychiatry
SOBER, A. J., Dermatology
SODROSKI, J. G., Microbiology and Immunobiology
SOIFFER, R., Medicine
SOLOMON, D., Medicine
SOLOMON, M., Anaesthesia
SOLOMON, S., Medicine

SONIS, S. T., Oral Medicine and Oral Pathology
SORGER, P., Systems Pharmacology
SOUMERAI, S., Population Medicine
SPEALMAN, R. D., Psychobiology
SPECTOR, M., Orthopaedic Surgery—Biomaterials
SPEIZER, F. E., Medicine
SPERLING, R., Neurology
SPIEGELMAN, B. M., Cell Biology
SPITZER, T., Medicine
SPRINGER, T. A., Biological Chemistry and Molecular Pathology
STAHL, G., Anaesthesia
STAMPFER, M., Epidemiology and Nutrition
STARNBACH, M. N., Microbiology and Immunobiology
STEERE, A., Medicine
STEINMAN, T. I., Medicine
STERN, R. S., Dermatology
STEVENS, R., Medicine
STEVENSON, L., Medicine
STEVENSON, W., Medicine
STILES, C. D., Neurobiology
STONE, A. A., Law and Psychiatry
STONE, J. H., Medicine
STONE, P. H., Medicine
STONE, R., Medicine
STONE, V., Medicine
STOSSEL, T. P., Medicine
STREILEIN, J. W., Ophthalmology
STREWLER, G. J., Medicine
STRICHARTZ, G. R., Anaesthesia—Pharmacology
STROM, T. B., Medicine
STROMINGER, J., Biochemistry
STRUHL, K., Biological Chemistry and Molecular Pharmacology
SUIT, H. D., Radiation Oncology
SUKHATME, V. P., Medicine
SWANSON, S., Surgery
SZOSTAK, J. W., Chemistry and Chemical Biology
TABB, K., Medicine
TABIN, C. J., Genetics
TAGHIAN, A., Radiation Oncology
TALMOR, D., Anaesthesia
TANABE, K., Surgery
TARSY, D., Neurology
TASKER, R., Neurology
TAUBMAN, M. A., Oral Biology
TAYLOR, G. A., Radiology—Paediatrics
TEARNEY, G., Pathology
TEMPANY-AFDHAL, C., Radiology
TENEN, D., Medicine
TERHORST, C. P., Medicine—Paediatrics
THADHANI, R., Medicine
THIELE, E., Neurology
THIER, S. O., Medicine and Health Care Policy
THOMPSON, B., Medicine
THRALL, J. H., Radiology
TILLY, J., Obstetrics, Gynaecology and Reproductive Biology
TOKER, A., Pathology
TOLKOFF-RUBIN, N., Medicine
TOMFORD, W., Orthopaedic Surgery
TOMKINS, R. G., Surgery
TONER, M., Health Sciences and Technology
TREVES, S. T., Radiology
TRIEDMAN, J., Paediatrics
TRUOG, R., Anaesthesia—Paediatrics, Medical Ethics
TSOKOS, G., Medicine
TSUANG, M. T., Psychiatry
TULLIUS, S. G., Surgery
VACANTI, J. P., Surgery
VAILLANT, G. E., Psychiatry
VANROOYEN, M., Medicine
VAN VACTOR, D., Cell Biology
VERDINE, G., Chemistry
VEVES, A., Surgery
VIDAL, M., Genetics
VLAHAKES, G., Surgery
VOLPE, J. J., Neurology

VON ANDRIAN-WERBURG, U., Microbiology and Immunobiology
WABER, D. P., Psychiatry
WAGERS, A., Stem Cell and Regenerative Biology
WAGNER, G., Biological Chemistry and Molecular Pharmacology
WALENSKY, R. P., Medicine
WALKER, B., Medicine
WALKER, S., Microbiology and Immunobiology
WALKER, W. A., Nutrition and Paediatrics
WALL, III, C., Otology and Laryngology
WALLS, R., Medicine
WALSH, C. T., Biological Chemistry and Molecular Pharmacology
WALSH, E., Paediatrics
WALTER, J., Biological Chemistry and Molecular Pharmacology
WALZ, T., Cell Biology
WANG, F. C., Medicine
WARFIELD, S., Radiology
WARMAN, M. L., Orthopaedic Surgery, Genetics
WARNER, J., Orthopaedic Surgery
WARSHAW, A. L., Surgery
WEINBERG, A. N., Medicine
WEINBLATT, M. E., Medicine
WEINER, H. L., Neurology
WEINSTEIN, H. J., Paediatrics
WEINSTEIN, M. C., Medicine, Health Policy and Management
WEINTRAUB, R., Surgery
WEIR, G. C., Medicine
WEISS, J. W., Medicine
WEISS, R. D., Psychiatry
WEISS, S. T., Medicine
WEISSLEDER, R., Systems Biology and Radiology
WEISSMAN, B. N., Radiology
WEISZ, J., Psychology
WEITZ, C. J., Neurobiology
WELLER, P. F., Medicine
WEN, P., Neurology
WEYMAN, A. E., Medicine
WHELAN, S. P. J., Microbiology and Immunobiology
WHITE, III, A. A., Medical Education, Orthopaedic Surgery
WHITE, M., Paediatrics
WHITMAN, M., Cell Biology
WHITTEMORE, A., Surgery
WHYTE, R. I., Surgery
WILBUR, D., Pathology
WILHELM, S., Psychology
WILKINS-HAUG, L. E., Obstetrics, Gynaecology and Reproductive Biology
WILLETT, W. C., Epidemiology and Nutrition
WILLIAMS, D., Medicine
WILLIAMS, G. H., Medicine
WILLIAMS, M. A., Public Health
WILMORE, D. W., Surgery
WILSON, R. I., Neurobiology
WINER, E., Medicine
WINKELMAN, J. W., Pathology
WINSTON, F. M., Genetics
WITTENBERG, J., Radiology
WOLF, M., Medicine
WOLFE, J. M., Ophthalmology
WOLFE, N., Neurology
WOLFSDORF, J., Paediatrics
WOODS, E., Paediatrics
WOOLF, A., Paediatrics
WOOLF, C. J., Neurology and Neurobiology
WRAY, S. H., Neurology
WRIGHT, C., Surgery
WU, C.-T., Genetics
WU, H., Biological Chemistry and Molecular Pharmacology
YANKNER, B. A., Pathology and Neurology
YARMUSH, M., Surgery and Bioengineering
YEH, J., Obstetrics, Gynaecology and Reproductive Biology
YELLEN, G., Neurobiology
YOUNG, R. H., Pathology

YUAN, J., Cell Biology
YUNIS, E., Pathology
ZANARINI, M., Psychology
ZAPOL, W. M., Anaesthesia
ZASLAVSKY, A., Health Care Policy—Statistics
ZENATI, M., Surgery
ZERVAS, N. T., Neurosurgery
ZETTER, B. R., Cancer Biology
ZHANG, Y., Genetics and Paediatrics
ZINNER, M. J., Surgery
ZINNER, S. H., Medicine
ZON, L., Stem Cell and Regenerative Biology, Paediatrics
ZOU, L., Pathology

Harvard School of Dental Medicine (Office of Admissions, DMD, 188 Longwood Ave, Boston, MA 02115; tel. (617) 432-1434; e-mail hsdm_dmd_admissions@hsdm.harvard.edu; internet www.hsdm.harvard.edu):

BARON, R., Medicine
DEWHIRST, F., Oral Medicine, Infection, and Immunity
DOGON, I. L., Restorative Dentistry and Biomaterials Sciences
DONOFF, R. B., Oral and Maxillofacial Surgery
GLOWACKI, J., Oral and Maxillofacial Surgery
KABAN, L. B., Oral and Maxillofacial Surgery
OLSEN, B. R., Developmental Biology
PASTER, B. J., Oral Medicine, Infection, and Immunity
SONIS, S. T., Oral Medicine and Diagnostic Sciences
TAUBMAN, M. A., Developmental Biology

Harvard School of Public Health (677 Huntington Ave, Boston, MA 02115; tel. (617) 432-1031; e-mail admissions@hsph.harvard.edu; internet www.hsph.harvard.edu):

ASCHERIO, A., Epidemiology and Nutrition
ATUN, R., Global Health Systems
AYANIAN, J., Health Policy and Management
BAICKER, K., Health Economics
BANGSBERG, D., Global Health and Population
BATES, D., Health Policy and Management
BELLINGER, D., Environmental Health
BERKMAN, L. F., Public Policy, Epidemiology
BERMAN, P., Practice of Global Health Systems and Economics
BETENSKY, R., Biostatistics
BHABHA, J., Practice of Health and Human Rights
BLACKER, D., Epidemiology
BLENDON, R. J., Public Health, Health Policy and Political Analysis
BLOOM, B. R., Public Health
BLOOM, D. E., Economics and Demography
BRAIN, J. D., Environmental Physiology
BURING, J., Epidemiologyt
CAI, T., Biostatistics
CAMARGO, C., Epidemiology
CANNING, D., Population Sciences, Economics and International Health
CHRISTIANI, D. C., Environmental Genetics
CONNOLLY, G. N., Practice of Public Health
COOK, E. F., Epidemiology
COOK, N., Epidemiology
COULL, B., Biostatistics
CRAMER, D., Epidemiology
CURHAN, G., Epidemiology
CUTLER, D., Global Health and Population
D'ANDREA, A. D., Genetics and Complex Diseases
DANIELS, N., Population Ethics, Ethics and Population Health
DE GRUTTOLA, V. G., Biostatistics
DOCKERY, D., Environmental Epidemiology
DOMINICI, F., Biostatistics
DRAZEN, J. M., Environmental Health

EARLS, F. J., Human Behaviour and Development
EPSTEIN, A. M., Health Policy and Management
ESSEX, M. E., Health Sciences
FARMER, P., Global Health and Social Medicine
FAWZI, W., Population Sciences, Nutrition, Epidemiology, and Global Health
FINKELSTEIN, D., Biostatistics
FITZMAURICE, G., Biostatistics
FREDBERG, J. J., Bioengineering and Physiology
FREEDBERG, K., Health Policy and Management
FRENK, J., Public Health and International Development
GARBER, A., Health Policy and Management
GAWANDE, A., Health Policy and Management
GAZELLE, G. S., Health Policy and Management
GELBER, G. S., Biostatistics
GILLMAN, M., Nutrition
GIOVANNUCCI, E., Nutrition and Epidemiology
GLYNN, R., Biostatistics
GOLD, D., Environmental Health
GOLDBERG, M., Immunology and Infectious Diseases
GOLDFIELD, A., Immunology and Infectious Diseases
GOLDIE, S., Public Health
GOLDMANN, D., Immunology and Infectious Diseases
GORTMAKER, S., Practice of Health Sociology
GRAY, R., Biostatistics
GRODSTEIN, F., Epidemiology
GRUSBY, M., Molecular Immunology
HAAS, J., Social and Behavioural Sciences
HAMMITT, J., Economics and Decision Sciences
HARRINGTON, D. P., Biostatistics
HARTL, D., Immunology and Infectious Diseases
HAUSER, R., Reproductive Physiology
HEMENWAY, D., Health Policy
HERNÁN, M., Epidemiology
HIBBERD, P., Global Heath and Population
HILL, A. G., Demography
HIRSCH, M., Immunology and Infectious Diseases
HOTAMISLIGIL, G. S., Genetics and Metabolism
HSIAO, W. C., Economics
HU, F., Nutrition and Epidemiology
HUGHES, M., Biostatistics
HUNTER, D., Cancer Prevention
IRIZARRY, R., Biostatistics
JHA, A., Health Policy and Management
KANE, N., Management
KANKI, P., Immunology and Infectious Diseases
KATZ, J., Epidemiology and Environmental Health
KAWACHI, I., Social Epidemiology
KING, G., Public Health
KOBZIK, L., Environmental Health
KOUTRAKIS, P., Environmental Sciences
KRAFT, P., Epidemiology
KRIEGER, N., Social Epidemiology
KUBZANSKY, L., Social and Behavioural Sciences
LAIRD, N. M., Public Health, Biostatistics
LANGE, C., Biostatistics
LANGER, A., Practice of Public Health
LEANING, J., Practice of Public Health and Human Rights
LEE, I.-M., Epidemiology
LEE, T., Health Policy and Management
LEE, T.-H., Virology
LEVINS, R., Population Sciences
LIANG, M., Health Policy and Management

LIEBERMAN, E., Social and Behavioural Sciences, Epidemiology
LIN, X., Biostatistics
LIPSITCH, M., Epidemiology
LIU, J., Biostatistics
LIU, X., Biostatistics
LUDWIG, D., Nutrition
McCORMICK, M. C., Maternal and Child Health
McDONOUGH, J., Practice of Public Health
MANNING, B. D., Genetics and Complex Diseases
MANSON, J., Epidemiology
MARKS, S. P., Health and Human Rights
MARLINK, R. G., Practice of Public Health
MAYER, K., Global Health and Population
MELLO, M., Law and Public Health
MURRAY, M., Epidemiology
NELSON, C., Social and Behavioural Sciences
NEWHOUSE, J. P., Health Policy and Management
NORMAND, S.-L., Biostatistics
PAGANO, M., Statistical Computing
PALFREY, J., Social and Behavioural Sciences
PARMIGIANI, G., Biostatistics
PAULS, D., Epidemiology
QUACKENBUSH, J., Computational Biology and Bioinformatics
QUELCH, J., Health Policy and Management
REICH, M. R., International Health Policy
RIDKER, P., Epidemiology
ROBINS, J. M., Epidemiology
ROSENTHAL, M. B., Health Economics and Policy
ROSNER, B., Biostatistics
RUBIN, E., Immunology and Infectious Diseases
RYAN, E., Immunology and Infectious Diseases
SACKS, F., Cardiovascular Disease Prevention
SALOMON, J., Global Health
SCHNEEWEISS, S., Epidemiology
SCHOENFELD, D., Biostatistics
SCHWARTZ, G., Environmental Epidemiology
SEAGE, J., Epidemiology
SHONKOFF, J. P., Child Health and Development
SINGER, D., Epidemiology
SMOLLER, J., Epidemiology
SODROSKI, J., Immunology and Infectious Diseases
SORENSON, G., Social and Behavioural Sciences
SPEIZER, F. E., Environmental Science
SPENGLER, J. D., Environmental Health and Human Habitation
SPIEGELMAN, D., Epidemiologic Methods
STAMPFER, M. J., Nutrition and Epidemiology
SUBRAMANIAN, S. V., Population Health and Geography
SWARTZ, K., Health Policy and Economics
TRICHOPOULOS, D. V., Cancer Prevention
VANDERWEELE, T., Epidemiology
VANROOYEN, M., Global Health and Population
WALDOR, M., Immunology and Infectious Diseases
WALKER, B., Immunology and Infectious Diseases
WALKER, W. A., Nutrition
WARE, J. H., Biostatistics
WEI, L. J., Biostatistics
WEINSTEIN, M. C., Health Policy and Management
WEISS, S., Environmental Health
WELLER, P., Immunology and Infectious Diseases
WESSLING-RESNIK, M., Nutritional Biochemistry

WIKLER, D., Population Ethics, Ethics and Population Health
WILLETT, W. C., Epidemiology and Nutrition
WILLIAMS, D. R., Public Health
WILLIAMS, M., Public Health
WIRTH, D. F., Infectious Diseases
YUAN, Z.-M., Radiobiology
ZELEN, M., Statistical Science

John F. Kennedy School of Government—Harvard Kennedy School (79 John F. Kennedy St, Cambridge, MA 02138; tel. (617) 495-1100; e-mail admissions@hks.harvard.edu; internet www.hks.harvard.edu):

ABADIE, A., Public Policy
ALLISON, G. T., Government
ALTSHULER, A., Political Science, Urban Policy and Planning
APPLBAUM, A., Political Leadership and Democratic Values
AVERY, C., Public Policy and Management
BANE, M. J., Public Policy and Management
BAUM, M., Global Communications
BAZERMAN, M., Business Administration
BHABHA, J., Practice of Health and Human Rights
BLENDON, R. J., Health Policy and Political Analysis
BOHNET, I., Public Policy
BOK, D., Law
BORJAS, G. J., Economics and Social Policy
BOWER, J., Business Administration
BUNN, M., Practice
BURNS, R. N., International Relations
CHANDRA, A., Public Policy
CHETTY, R., Economics
CLARK, W. C., International Science, Public Policy and Human Development
CUTLER, D., Applied Economics
EDIN, K., Public Policy and Management
ELLWOOD, D., Political Economy
FELDSTEIN, M. S., Economics
FRANKEL, J. A., Capital Formation and Growth
FUNG, A., Democracy and Citizenship
GARBER, A. M., Public Policy
GERGEN, D., Public Leadership
GLAESER, E., Economics
GOLDSMITH, S., Practice of Government
GOMEZ-IBANEZ, J. A., Urban Planning and Public Policy
GRINDLE, M. S., International Development
HAUSMANN, R., Practice of Economic Development
HEHIR, J. B., Practice of Religion and Public Life
HEYMANN, P. B., Law
HOCHSCHILD, J., Government
HOGAN, W. W., Global Energy Policy
IGNATIEFF, M., Practice
JASANOFF, S., Science and Technology Studies
JENCKS, C., Social Policy
JORGENSON, D., Economics
JUMA, C., Practice of International Development
KAMM, F., Philosophy and Public Policy
KANE, T., Education and Economics
KAYDEN, J., Urban Planning and Design
KEITH, D., Public Policy
KELMAN, S. J., Public Management
KEYSSAR, A., History and Social Policy
KHANNA, T.
KHWAJA, A., Public Policy
KOEHN, N., Business Administration
KREMER, M. R., Developing Societies
LAWRENCE, R. Z., International Trade and Investment
LEONARD, H. B., Public Management
LERNER, J. S., Public Policy and Management
LIEBMAN, J. B., Public Policy
LIGHT, R., Teaching and Learning

MADRIAN, B. C., Public Policy and Corporate Management
MANSBRIDGE, J. J., Political Leadership and Democratic Values
MOORE, M. H., Nonprofit Organizations, Education, Management, and Organizational Behaviour
NARAYANAMURTI, V., Technology and Public Policy
NEWHOUSE, J. P., Health Policy and Management
NYE, J. S., International Affairs and Democratic Governance
O'SULLIVAN, M., Practice of International Affairs
ORREN, G. R., Politics and Leadership
PAGER, D., Public Policy, Sociology
PANDE, R., Public Policy
PATTERSON, T. E., Government and the Press
PERKINS, D. H., Political Economy
PETERSON, P., Government
PORTER, R. B., Business and Government
PRITCHETT, L., Practice of International Development
PUTNAM, R. D., Public Policy
REINHART, C., International Financial System
RISSE, M., Philosophy and Public Policy
RUGGIE, J., Human Rights and International Affairs
SAICH, A., International Affairs
SCHERER, F. M., Public Policy and Corporate Management
SIKKINK, K., Human Rights Policy
SKOCPOL, T., Government and Sociology
SPARROW, M., Practice of Public Management
STAVINS, R. N., Business and Government Environment and Natural Resources Programme
STOCK, J. H., Political Economy
SUNSTEIN, C. R., Law
WALT, S. M., International Affairs
WESTERN, B., Sociology, Criminal Justice
WHEELER, M., Management Practice
WILSON, W. J., Urban Sociology
WINSHIP, C., Sociology
WISE, D., Political Economy
ZASLAVSKY, A., Health Care Policy—Statistics
ZECKHAUSER, R. J., Political Economy
ZITTRAIN, J. L., Law

HEBREW COLLEGE

160 Herrick Rd, Newton Centre, MA 02459
Telephone: (617) 559-8600
E-mail: admissions@hebrewcollege.edu
Internet: www.hebrewcollege.edu
Founded 1921
Private control
Academic year: September to May
Pres.: Rabbi DANIEL L. LEHMANN
Vice-Pres. for Devt: MICHAEL GILBERT
Provost: Dr BARRY MESCH
Dean of Faculty: KAREN REISS MEDWED
Dir of Recruitment and Admissions: DAVID MICLEY
Dir of Student Life: DAVID LIST
Registrar: MARILYN JAYE
Library Dir: HARVEY SUKENIC
Library of 125,000 vols
Number of teachers: 40
Number of students: 200

DEANS

Hebrew College Online: NATHAN EHRLICH
Rabbinical School: Rabbi SHARON COHEN ANISFELD
School of Jewish Music: Dr BRIAN J. MAYER (acting)
Shoolman Graduate School of Jewish Education: MICHAEL SHIRE

HELLENIC COLLEGE–HOLY CROSS GREEK ORTHODOX SCHOOL OF THEOLOGY

50 Goddard Ave, Brookline, MA 02445-7496
Telephone: (617) 731-3500
E-mail: admissions@hchc.edu
Internet: www.hchc.edu
Founded 1937 as Holy Cross Theological School
Private control
Academic year: September to May

Academic programmes incl. classics and Greek studies, elementary education, human devt, literature and history, management and leadership, religious studies
Pres.: Rev. NICHOLAS C. TRIANTAFILOU
Chief Operating Officer: JAMES D. KARLOUTSOS
Dean of Hellenic College: DEMETRIOS KATOS
Dean of Holy Cross: Fr THOMAS FITZGERALD
Registrar: ALBA PAGAN
Library Dir: Very Rev. Dr JOACHIM COTSONIS
Library of 75,000 vols
Number of teachers: 20
Number of students: 210 (78 undergraduate, 132 graduate)

HULT INTERNATIONAL BUSINESS SCHOOL

1 Education St, Cambridge, MA 02141
Telephone: (617) 746-1990
E-mail: admissions@hult.edu
Internet: www.hult.edu
Founded 1964 as Arthur D. Little School of Management, current name adopted 2003
Private control

Campuses in Boston, Dubai, London, San Francisco, Shanghai; offers masters degree in digital marketing, finance, international business, international business management, international marketing, social entrepreneurship
Pres. and Chair.: Dr STEPHEN HODGES
Vice-Pres. for Academic Affairs: Dr RICHARD J. JOSEPH
Chief Academic Officer and Chief Operating Officer: Dr MUKUL KUMAR
Dean of Academic Affairs: Dr RICHARD J. JOSEPH
Registrar: NICOLE GREGOIRE
Librarian: JOHN WALSH
Number of teachers: 40
Number of students: 60

LABOURÉ COLLEGE

2120 Dorchester Ave, Dorchester, MA 02124
Telephone: (617) 296-8300
E-mail: admissions@laboure.edu
Internet: www.laboure.edu
Founded 1892 as Carney Hospital Training School for Nurses, current name adopted 1993
Private control
Academic year: July to August

Academic divs incl. health information technology, neurodiagnostic technology, nursing, radiation therapy, nutrition and food management
Pres.: Dr MAUREEN SMITH (acting)
Vice-Pres. and Dean of Student Affairs: KAREN M. MASTERS
Vice-Pres. and Dir of Institutional Advancement: CATHERIN PHILBIN
Chief Financial Officer: MARK VIRELLO
Dean of Academic Affairs: Dr PAULA VOSBURGH
Registrar: JOHN SACCO
Dir of Library: ANDREW CALO
Number of teachers: 70
Number of students: 620

LASELL COLLEGE

1844 Commonwealth Ave, Newton, MA 02466
Telephone: (617) 243-2000
E-mail: info@lasell.edu
Internet: www.lasell.edu
Founded 1851
Private control
Academic year: September to May
Pres.: MICHAEL B. ALEXANDER
Vice-Pres. for Academic Affairs: Dr JAMES OSTROW
Vice-Pres. for Business and Finance: Dr MICHAEL J. HOYLE
Vice-Pres. for Communications, Community and Govt Relations: RUTH S. SHUMAN
Vice-Pres. for Enrolment Management: Dr KATHLEEN M. O'CONNOR
Vice-Pres. for Student Affairs: DIANE AUSTIN
Registrar: DIANNE POLIZZI
Dir for Library: MARILYN NEGIP
Library of 61,822 vols, 31,140 ejournals
Number of teachers: 330
Number of students: 1,600

LESLEY UNIVERSITY

29 Everett St, Cambridge, MA 02138-2790
Telephone: (617) 349-8300
E-mail: info@lesley.edu
Internet: www.lesley.edu
Founded 1909 as Lesley School, present name and status 2000
Private control
Academic year: September to May
Pres.: Dr JOSEPH B. MOORE
Provost and Vice-Pres. for Academic Affairs: Dr SELASE WILLIAMS
Vice-Pres. and Chief Financial Officer: BERNICE BRADIN
Vice-Pres. for Admin.: MARYLOU BATT
Vice-Pres. for Advancement: RANDY STABILE
Vice-Pres. for Budgeting and Financial Planning: ML DYMSKI
Vice-Pres. for Enrolment Management: JEFFREY HANDLER
Vice-Pres. for Urban Initiatives: WILLIAM DANDRIDGE
Dean of Faculty: LISA FIORE
Dean of Lesley College: Dr MARY COLEMAN
Dean for Student Life and Academic Devt: Dr NATHANIEL MAYS
Registrar: MELISSA JANOT
Dir of Libraries: PATRICIA PAYNE
Library of 100,000 vols
Number of teachers: 190
Number of students: 8,570 (2,331 undergraduate, 6,2379 graduate)
Publication: *Journal of Pedagogy, Pluralism and Practice* (irregular)

DEANS

Art Institute of Boston: STAN TRECKER
Graduate School of Arts and Social Sciences: Dr CATHERINE KOVEROLA
Graduate School of Education: Dr JONATHON H. GILLETTE
Lesley College: Prof. Dr MARY D. COLEMAN

LONGY SCHOOL OF MUSIC

27 Garden St, Cambridge, MA 02138
Telephone: (617) 876-0956
E-mail: music@longy.edu
Internet: www.longy.edu
Founded 1915
Private control
Academic year: August to June (2 semesters)
Offers Masters of music degrees in chamber music, collaborative piano, composition and theory, Dalcroze eurhythmics, early music, experiential education, large ensembles, mind and body studies, modern American music, music history and interdisciplinary studies, opera, organ, percussion, piano, strings, voice and woodwind, brass
Pres.: KAREN L. ZORN
Dean for Conservatory: WAYMAN CHIN
Chief Financial Officer: HOWARD LEVY
Dir for Devt: KIMBERLEE LABONTE
Dir for Library: ROY RUDOLPH
Number of teachers: 160
Number of students: 240

MASSACHUSETTS COLLEGE OF ART AND DESIGN

621 Huntington Ave, Boston, MA 02115
Telephone: (617) 879-7000
E-mail: admissions@massart.edu
Internet: www.massart.edu
Founded 1873
Private control
Academic year: September to May

Academic programmes incl. animation, architectural design, art history, art teacher education, ceramics, community education, community studio education, fashion design, fibres, film/video, glass, graphic design, history of art, illustration, industrial design, jewellery and metalsmithing, museum education, painting, photography, printmaking, sculpture, studio education
Pres.: Dr DAWN BARRETT
Sr Vice-Pres. for Academic Affairs: Dr MAUREEN KELLY
Exec. Vice-Pres.: KURT STEINBERG
Vice-Pres. for Admin. and Finance and Chief Operating Officer: KURT STEINBERG
Vice-Pres. for Institutional Advancement: HUNTER O'HANIAN
Vice-Pres. for Student Devt: MAUREEN KEEFE
Library Dir: PAUL DOBBS
Library of 95,000 vols
Number of teachers: 260
Number of students: 2,430
Publication: *Folio* (2 a year)

MASSACHUSETTS COLLEGE OF LIBERAL ARTS

375 Church St, North Adams, MA 01247
Telephone: (413) 662-5000
E-mail: admissions@mcla.edu
Internet: www.mcla.mass.edu
Founded 1894 as North Adams Normal School, current name adopted 1997
State control
Academic year: September to May

Depts of art, arts management, athletic training, biology, business admin., chemistry, computer science, education, English and communications, fine and performing arts, history, political science and geography, mathematics, modern language, philosophy, physical education, physics, political science and public policy, psychology, sociology, anthropology and social work, women's studies
Pres.: Dr MARY K. GRANT
Vice-Pres. for Academic Affairs: Dr CYNTHIA F. BROWN
Vice-Pres. for Admin. and Finance: Dr JAMES STAKENAS
Vice-Pres. for Enrolment and External Relations: DENISE RICHARDELLO
Chief Advancement Officer: MARIANNE DRAKE
Dean for Academic Affairs: Dr MONICA NESET JOSLIN
Dean for Students: CHARLOTTE F. DEGEN
Registrar: STEVEN P. KING (acting)
Assoc. Dean for Library Services: MAUREEN HORAK (acting)
Library of 172,000 vols, 500 print periodicals, 300,000 microforms, 4,000 online journals

Number of students: 1,890 (1,680 undergraduate, 210 graduate)

MASSACHUSETTS COLLEGE OF PHARMACY AND HEALTH SCIENCES

179 Longwood Ave, Boston, MA 02115-5896
Telephone: (617) 732-2800
E-mail: admissions@mcphs.edu
Internet: www.mcphs.edu

Founded 1823 as Massachusetts College of Pharmacy, current name adopted 1979
Private control
Campuses in Manchester, Worcester
Pres.: CHARLES F. MONAHAN, JR
Provost and Vice-Pres. for Academic Affairs: Dr GEORGE E. HUMPHREY
Exec. Vice-Pres., Chief Operating Officer and Chief Financial Officer: RICHARD J. LESSARD
Vice-Pres. for Devt and Chief of Staff: MARGUERITE C. JOHNSON
Dean of Students and Asst Provost for Student Affairs: JEAN JOYCE-BRAD
Vice-Pres. for Finance and Admin.: RICHARD J. LESSARD
Exec. Dir for Admission: KATHLEEN RYAN
Registrar: MARJORIE MCMAHON
Dean for Library and Learning Resources: RICHARD KAPLAN
Library of 88,065 vols incl. ebooks and journals, 43,616 ejournals, 800 periodicals
Number of teachers: 230
Number of students: 5,330

DEANS

Forsyth School of Dental Hygiene: Dr LINDA D. BOYD
School of Arts and Sciences: Dr DELIA CASTRO ANDERSON
School of Health Sciences: Dr JAMES BLAGG
School of Medical Imaging and Therapeutics: Dr FRANCES KEECH (acting)
School of Nursing: Dr CAROL ELIADI
School of Optometry: LESLEY WALLS
School of Physical Therapy, Worcester: Dr LINDA TSOUMAS
School of Pharmacy, Boston: Dr DOUGLAS J. PISANO
School of Pharmacy, Worcester/Manchester: Dr MICHAEL J. MALLOY
School of Physician Assistant Studies: (vacant)
School of Radiologic Sciences: Dr K. CYRUS WHALEY (acting)

MASSACHUSETTS INSTITUTE OF TECHNOLOGY

Telephone: (617) 253-1000
E-mail: registrar-www@mit.edu
Internet: web.mit.edu

Founded 1861
Private control
Academic year: September to May
Pres.: Prof. Dr L. RAFAEL REIF
Chancellor: Prof. CYNTHIA BARNHART
Provost: Prof. MARTIN A. SCHMIDT
Assoc. Provost: PHILLIP S. KHOURY
Assoc. Provost: KAREN GLEASON
Chancellor for Academic Advancement: Dr W. ERIC L. GRIMSON
Deputy Exec. Vice-Pres. and Interim Vice-Pres. for Human Resources: ANTHONY P. SHARON
Exec. Vice-Pres. and Treas.: ISRAEL RUIZ
Vice-Pres.: Prof. Dr CLAUDE R. CANIZARES
Vice-Pres. and Sec. of the Corp.: Dr KIRK KOLENBRANDER
Vice-Pres. and Gen. Counsel: R. GREGORY MORGAN
Vice-Pres. for Finance: MICHAEL W. HOWARD
Vice-Pres. for Research: Prof. MARIA T. ZUBER

Vice-Pres. for Resource Devt: (vacant)
Vice-Pres. for Information Systems and Technology: JOHN CHARLES
Dean for Graduate Education: Prof. Dr CHRISTINE ORTIZ
Dean for Student Life: CHRIS COLOMBO
Dean for Undergraduate Education: DENNIS FREEMAN
Dir for Libraries: STEVEN GASS
Dir for Digital Learning: SANJAY SARMA
Dir for Lincoln Laboratory: ERIC D. EVANS
Library of 2,839,181 vols
Number of teachers: 1,030
Number of students: 11,300 (4,383 undergraduate, 6,510 graduate)
Publications: *Sloan Management Review* (4 a year), *Technology Review* (24 a year)

DEANS

School of Architecture and Planning: Prof. ADÈLE NAUDÉ SANTOS
School of Engineering: Prof. Dr IAN A. WAITZ
School of Humanities, Arts and Social Sciences: Prof. DEBORAH K. FITZGERALD
School of Science: Prof. MICHAEL SIPSER
Sloan School of Management: Prof. Dr DAVID C. SCHMITTLEIN

PROFESSORS

(Some professors serve in more than one department)

School of Architecture and Planning (77 Massachusetts Ave, Room 7-231, Cambridge, MA 02139-4307; tel. (617) 253-4401; e-mail sap-info@mit.edu; internet sap.mit.edu):

Department of Architecture:

ANDERSON, S., History and Architecture
CHANG, Y., Architecture
DENNIS, M., Architecture
FERNANDEZ, J., Architecture, Building Technology and Engineering Systems
FREELON, P., Architecture
GARCÍA-ABRIL, A., Architecture
GLICKSMAN, L., Building Technology and Mechanical Engineering
GREEN, R., Art, Culture and Technology
JARZOMBEK, M., History and Theory of Architecture
JONES, C., History of Art
KENNEDY, S., Architecture
KNIGHT, T., Design and Computation
NORFORD, L., Building Technology
OCHSENDORF, J., Building Technology and Civil and Environmental Engineering
RABBAT, N., History of Architecture
SANTOS, A., Architecture and Urban Planning
SCOTT, A., Architecture
SPIRN, A., Landscape Architecture and Planning
STINY, G., Design and Computation
TEHRANI, N., Architecture
WAMPLER, J., Architecture
WESCOAT, J., Architecture
YOON, J., Architecture

Department of Urban Studies and Planning:

BEN-JOSEPH, E., Landscape Architecture and Planning
BERGER, A., Urban Design and Landscape Architecture
BRIGGS, X., Community Development and Public Policy
CLAY, P., Urban Studies and Planning
FERREIRA, J., Urban Planning and Operations Research
FOGELSON, R., Urban Studies and History
FRENCHMAN, D., Urban Design
GELTNER, D., Real Estate Finance and Engineering Systems
GLASMEIER, A., Geography and Regional Planning
KLOPFER, E., Education and Engineering Systems
LAYZER, J., Environmental Policy

MCDOWELL, C., Community Development
POLENSKE, K., Regional Political Economy and Planning
SANYAL, B., Urban and Regional Planning
SPIRN, A., Landscape Architecture and Planning
SUSSKIND, L., Urban and Environmental Planning
VALE, L., Urban Design and Planning
WHEATON, W., Economics and Urban Studies

Program in Media Arts and Sciences:

ABELSON, H., Computer Science and Engineering and Media Arts and Sciences
GERSHENFELD, N., Media Arts and Sciences
ISHII, H., Media Arts and Sciences
KLOPFER, E., Education and Engineering Systems
MACHOVER, T., Music and Media
MAES, P., Media Technology
NEGROPONTE, N., Media Technology
PENTLAND, A., Media Arts and Sciences
PICARD, R., Media Arts and Sciences
RESNICK, M., Learning Research

School of Engineering (77 Massachusetts Ave, Room 1-206, Cambridge, MA 02139-4307; tel. (617) 253-3291; e-mail engineering@mit.edu; internet engineering.mit.edu):

Department of Aeronautics and Astronautics:

BINZEL, R., Earth, Atmospheric, and Planetary Sciences and Aeronautics and Astronautics
CRAWLEY, E., Aeronautics and Astronautics and Engineering Systems
DARMOFAL, D., Aeronautics and Astronautics
DE WECK, O., Aeronautics and Astronautics and Engineering Systems
DRELA, M., Aeronautics and Astronautics
DUBOWSKY, S., Mechanical Engineering and Aeronautics and Astronautics
FRAZZOLI, E., Aeronautics and Astronautics
GREITZER, E., Aeronautics and Astronautics
HALL, S., Aeronautics and Astronautics
HANSMAN, R., Aeronautics and Astronautics and Engineering Systems
HARRIS, W., Aeronautics and Astronautics
HASTINGS, D., Aeronautics and Astronautics and Engineering Systems
HOFFMAN, J., Astronautics
HOW, J., Aeronautics and Astronautics
LAGACÉ, P., Aeronautics and Astronautics and Engineering Systems
LEVESON, N., Aeronautics and Astronautics and Engineering Systems
LIEBECK, R., Aerospace Engineering
MILLER, D., Aeronautics and Astronautics
MINDELL, D., History of Engineering and Manufacturing
MODIANO, E., Aeronautics and Astronautics
NEWMAN, D., Aeronautics and Astronautics and Engineering Systems
NIGHTINGALE, D., Aeronautics and Astronautics and Engineering Systems
PERAIRE, J., Aeronautics and Astronautics
RADOVITZKY, R., Aeronautics and Astronautics
SPAKOVSZKY, Z., Aeronautics and Astronautics
WAITZ, I., Aeronautics and Astronautics
WIDNALL, S., Aeronautics and Astronautics and Engineering Systems
WILLCOX, K., Aeronautics and Astronautics
WILLIAMS, B., Aeronautics and Astronautics
WIN, M., Aeronautics and Astronautics

Department of Biological Engineering:

BELCHER, A., Energy, Materials Science and Engineering, and Biological Engineering

BURGE, C., Biology and Biological Engineering

CHAKRABORTY, A., Chemical Engineering

DEDON, P., Toxicology and Biological Engineering

DELONG, E., Civil and Environmental Engineering and Biological Engineering

DEWEY, JR, C., Mechanical and Biological Engineering

ENGELWARD, B., Biological Engineering

ESSIGMANN, J., Chemistry, Toxicology, and Biological Engineering

FOX, J., Biological Engineering

GRIFFITH, L., Teaching Innovation

GRODZINSKY, A., Biological, Electrical, and Mechanical Engineering

HAN, J., Electrical and Biological Engineering

IRVINE, D., Biological Engineering and Materials Science

KAMM, R., Biological and Mechanical Engineering

KLIBANOV, A., Chemistry and Biological Engineering

LANGER, R., Chemical Engineering and Biological Engineering

LAUFFENBURGER, D., Biological Engineering, Chemical Engineering, and Biology

LODISH, H., Biology and Biological Engineering

MANALIS, S., Biological and Mechanical Engineering, and Media Arts and Sciences

SAMSON, L., Toxicology and Biological Engineering

SASISEKHARAN, R., Biological Engineering and Health Sciences and Technology

SO, P., Mechanical and Biological Engineering

TANNENBAUM, S., Biological Engineering, Chemistry, and Toxicology

THILLY, W., Toxicology

TIDOR, B., Biological Engineering and Electrical Engineering and Computer Science

VOIGT, C., Biological Engineering

WEISS, R., Biological Engineering and Computer Science

WHITE, F., Biological Engineering

WITTRUP, K., Chemical Engineering and Biological Engineering

YAFFE, M., Biology and Biological Engineering

YANNAS, I., Mechanical and Biological Engineering

Department of Chemical Engineering:

ARMSTRONG, R., Chemical Engineering

BARTON, P., Chemical Engineering

BAZANT, M., Chemical Engineering and Applied Mathematics

BLANKSCHTEIN, D., Chemical Engineering

BRAATZ, R., Chemical Engineering

CHAKRABORTY, A., Chemical Engineering, Chemistry and Biological Engineering

COHEN, R., Chemical Engineering

COLTON, C., Chemical Engineering

COONEY, O., Chemical and Biochemical Engineering

DEEN, W., Chemical Engineering

DOYLE, P., Chemical Engineering

GLEASON, K., Chemical Engineering

GREEN, W., Chemical Engineering

HAMMOND, P., Engineering

HATTON, T., Chemical Engineering Practice

JENSEN, K., Chemical Engineering and Materials Science and Engineering

LANGER, R., Chemical Engineering and Biological Engineering

LAUFFENBURGER, D., Biological Engineering, Chemical Engineering, and Biology

MYERSON, A., Chemical Engineering

RUTLEDGE, G., Chemical Engineering

STEPHANOPOULOS, G., Chemical Engineering

STEPHANOPOULOS, G., Biotechnology and Chemical Engineering

STRANO, M., Chemical Engineering

TROUT, B., Chemical Engineering

WANG, D., Chemical Engineering

WITTRUP, K., Chemical Engineering and Biological Engineering

Department of Civil and Environmental Engineering:

BARNHART, C., Civil and Environmental Engineering

BEN-AKIVA, M., Civil and Environmental Engineering

BUEHLER, M., Civil and Environmental Engineering

BUYUKOZTURK, O., Civil and Environmental Engineering

CHISHOLM, S., Civil and Environmental Engineering and Biology

CONNOR, J. J., Jr, Civil and Environmental Engineering

DELONG, E., Civil and Environmental Engineering and Biological Engineering

DE NEUFVILLE, R. L., Civil and Environmental Engineering, Engineering Systems

EINSTEIN, H. H., Civil and Environmental Engineering

ELTAHIR, E., Civil and Environmental Engineering

ENTEKHABI, D., Civil and Environmental Engineering

GSCHWEND, P., Civil and Environmental Engineering

HARVEY, C., Civil and Environmental Engineering

HEMOND, H. F., Civil and Environmental Engineering

JAILLET, P., Civil and Environmental Engineering (Head)

KAUSEL, E., Civil and Environmental Engineering

MADSEN, O. S., Civil and Environmental Engineering

MCLAUGHLIN, D. B., Civil and Environmental Engineering

MOAVENZADEH, F., Civil and Environmental Engineering, Engineering Systems

NEPF, H., Civil and Environmental Engineering

OCHSENDORF, J., Building Technology and Civil and Environmental Engineering

ODONI, A. R., Aeronautics and Astronautics and Civil and Environmental Engineering

POLZ, M., Civil and Environmental Engineering

SHEFFI, Y., Civil and Environmental Engineering, Engineering Systems

SIMCHI-LEVI, D., Civil and Environmental Engineering, Engineering Systems

SUSSMAN, J. M., Civil and Environmental Engineering, Engineering Systems

ULM, F.-J., Civil and Environmental Engineering

VENEZIANO, D., Civil and Environmental Engineering

WHITTLE, A. J., Civil and Environmental Engineering

WILLIAMS, J., Civil and Environmental Engineering and Engineering Systems

WILSON, N. H. M., Civil and Environmental Engineering

Department of Electrical Engineering and Computer Science:

ABELSON, H., Computer Science and Engineering and Media Arts and Sciences

AGARWAL, A., Computer Science and Engineering

AKINWANDE, A., Electrical Engineering

AMARASINGHE, S., Computer Science and Engineering

ANTONIADIS, D., Electrical Engineering

BAGGEROER, A., Mechanical, Ocean, and Electrical Engineering

BALAKRISHNAN, H., Computer Science and Engineering

BALDO, M., Electrical Engineering

BARZILAY, R., Computer Science and Engineering

BERGER, B., Applied Mathematics and Computer Science

BERGGREN, K., Electrical Engineering and Computer Science

BERNERS-LEE, T., Engineering

BERS, A., Electrical Engineering

BERTSEKAS, D., Electrical Engineering

BERWICK, R., Computer Science and Engineering and Computational Linguistics

BHATIA, S., Electrical Engineering and Health Sciences and Technology

BONING, D., Electrical Engineering and Computer Science

BRAIDA, L., Electrical Engineering and Health Sciences and Technology

BROOKS, R., Computer Science and Engineering

BULOVIC, V., Emerging Technology and Electrical Engineering

CHAN, V., Electrical Engineering

CHANDRAKASAN, A., Electrical Engineering

CHUANG, I., Electrical Engineering and Physics

DAHLEH, M., Electrical Engineering and Computer Science

DAVIS, R., Computer Science and Engineering

DEL ALAMO, J., Electrical Engineering

DEMAINE, E., Computer Science and Engineering

DEVADAS, S., Electrical Engineering and Computer Science

DRESSELHAUS, M., Electrical Engineering and Physics

DURAND, F., Computer Science and Engineering

EMER, J., Electrical Engineering and Computer Science

FINK, Y., Materials Science and Electrical Engineering and Computer Science

FONSTAD, JR, C., Electrical Engineering

FREEMAN, W., Computer Science and Engineering

FREEMAN, D., Electrical Engineering

FUJIMOTO, J., Electrical Engineering

GALLAGER, R., Electrical Engineering

GIFFORD, D., Computer Science and Engineering

GOLDWASSER, S., Computer Science and Engineering

GRAY, M., Medical and Electrical Engineering

GRIMSON, W., Medical Engineering

GRODZINSKY, A., Biological, Mechanical, and Electrical Engineering

GUTTAG, J., Computer Science and Engineering

HAN, J., Electrical Engineering and Biological Engineering

HENNIE, III, F., Computer Science and Engineering

HORN, B., Computer Science and Engineering

HOYT, J., Electrical Engineering

HU, Q., Electrical Engineering

INDYK, P., Computer Science and Engineering

JAAKKOLA, T., Computer Science and Engineering

JACKSON, D., Computer Science and Engineering

JAILLET, P., Electrical, Civil, and Environmental Engineering

KAASHOEK, M., Computer Science and Engineering

KAELBLING, L., Computer Science and Engineering

KARGER, D., Computer Science and Engineering

KASSAKIAN, J., Electrical Engineering

KATABI, D., Computer Science and Engineering
KELLIS, M., Electrical Engineering and Computer Science
KIRTLEY, JR, J., Electrical Engineering
KOLODZIEJSKI, L., Electrical Engineering
LANG, J., Electrical Engineering
LEE, H., Electrical Engineering
LEEB, S., Electrical and Mechanical Engineering
LEISERSON, C., Computer Science and Engineering
LISKOV, B., Electrical Engineering and Computer Science
LO, A., Finance and Electrical Engineering and Computer Science
LOZANO-PÉREZ, T., Electrical Engineering and Computer Science
LYNCH, N., Software Science and Engineering
MADDEN, S., Computer Science and Engineering
MAGNANTI, T., Operations Research and Electrical Engineering
MARK, R., Health Sciences and Technology and Electrical Engineering and Computer Science
MEDARD, M., Electrical Engineering
MEGRETSKI, A., Electrical Engineering
MEYER, A., Computer Science and Engineering
MICALI, S., Computer Science and Engineering
MILLER, R., Computer Science and Engineering
MITTER, S., Electrical Engineering and Engineering Systems
MORRIS, R., Computer Science and Engineering
MOSES, J., Computer Science and Engineering, and Engineering Systems
OPPENHEIM, A., Engineering
ORLANDO, T., Electrical Engineering
OZDAGLAR, A., Electrical Engineering
PARRILO, P., Electrical Engineering and Computer Science
PEH, L., Electrical Engineering and Computer Science
PENFIELD, JR, P., Electrical Engineering
PERREAULT, D., Power Engineering
RAM, R., Electrical Engineering
REIF, L., Electrical Engineering
RINARD, M., Computer Science and Engineering
RIVEST, R., Computer Science and Engineering
RUBINFELD, R., Computer Science and Engineering
RUS, D., Computer Science and Engineering
SCHINDALL, J., Electrical Engineering & Computer Science
SCHMIDT, M., Electrical Engineering
SHAPIRO, J., Electrical Engineering
SHAVIT, N., Computer Science and Engineering
SMITH, H., Electrical Engineering
SODINI, C., Electrical Engineering
STULTZ, C., Electrical Engineering and Computer Science, and Health Sciences and Technology
SUSSMAN, G., Electrical Engineering
SZOLOVITS, P., Computer Science and Engineering and Health Sciences and Technology
TELLER, S., Computer Science and Engineering
TIDOR, B., Electrical Engineering and Computer Science, and Biological Engineering
TSITSIKLIS, J., Electrical Engineering and Computer Science
VERGHESE, G., Electrical Engineering
VOLDMAN, J., Electrical Engineering
WARD, S., Computer Science and Engineering

WARDE, C., Electrical Engineering
WEISS, R., Biological Engineering and Computer Science
WHITE, J., Electrical Engineering
WILLSKY, A., Electrical Engineering
WINSTON, P., Engineering
WORNELL, G., Electrical Engineering
WYATT, JR, J., Electrical Engineering
ZAHN, M., Electrical Engineering
ZHENG, L., Electrical Engineering
ZUE, V., Electrical Engineering and Computer Science

Department of Materials Science and Engineering:

ALLEN, S., Physical Metallurgy
BALLINGER, R., Materials Science and Engineering and Nuclear Science and Engineering
BELCHER, A., Energy, Materials Science and Engineering and Biological Engineering
CARTER, W., Materials Science and Engineering
CEDER, G., Materials Science and Engineering
CEDER, G., Materials Science and Engineering
CHIANG, Y., Ceramics
CIMA, M., Engineering
CLARK, J., Materials Systems
EAGAR, T., Materials Engineering and Materials Systems
FINK, Y., Materials Science and Electrical Engineering and Computer Science
FITZGERALD, E., Materials Science and Engineering
FLEMINGS, M., Materials Processing without Tenure
GIBSON, L., Materials Science and Engineering, Mechanical Engineering
HOBBS, L., Materials Science and Nuclear Science and Engineering
HOSLER, D., Archaeology and Ancient Technology
IRVINE, D., Biological Engineering and Materials Science and Engineering
JENSEN, K., Chemical Engineering and Materials Science and Engineering
KIMERLING, L., Materials Science and Engineering
LECHTMAN, H., Archaeology and Ancient Technology
ORTIZ, C., Materials Science and Engineering
ROSS, C., Materials Science and Engineering
RUBNER, M., Materials Science and Engineering
SADOWAY, D., Metallurgy
SCHUH, C., Ferrous Metallurgy
SHAO-HORN, Y., Mechanical Engineering and Materials Science and Engineering
THOMPSON, C., Materials Science and Engineering
TULLER, H., Ceramics and Electronic Materials
TULLER, H., Ceramics and Electronic Materials
YIP, S., Nuclear Science and Engineering and Materials Science and Engineering

Department of Mechanical Engineering:

ABEYARATNE, R., Mechanics
AKYLAS, T., Mechanical Engineering
ANAND, L., Mechanical Engineering
ASADA, H., Engineering
BAGGEROER, A., Mechanical, Ocean, and Electrical Engineering
BARBASTATHIS, G., Mechanical Engineering
BATHE, K., Mechanical Engineering
BOYCE, M., Engineering
BRISSON II, J., Mechanical Engineering
CHEN, G., Power Engineering
CHENG, W., Mechanical Engineering

CHRYSSOSTOMIDIS, C., Ocean Science and Engineering, Mechanical and Ocean Engineering
CHUN, J., Mechanical Engineering
CULPEPPER, M., Mechanical Engineering
DEWEY, JR, C., Mechanical and Biological Engineering
DUBOWSKY, S., Mechanical Engineering and Aeronautics and Astronautics
FREY, D., Mechanical Engineering and Engineering Systems
GHONIEM, A., Mechanical Engineering
GIBSON, L., Materials Science and Engineering, Mechanical Engineering
GLICKSMAN, L., Building Technology and Mechanical Engineering
GOSSARD, D., Mechanical Engineering
GRAVES, S., Management Science, Engineering Systems and Mechanical Engineering
GRIFFITH, L., Teaching Innovation, Biological and Mechanical Engineering
GRODZINSKY, A., Biological, Electrical, and Mechanical Engineering
GUTOWSKI, T., Mechanical Engineering
HADJICONSTANTINOU, N., Mechanical Engineering
HARBOUR, J., Naval Construction and Engineering
HARDT, D., Mechanical Engineering
HART, D., Mechanical Engineering
HEYWOOD, J., Mechanical Engineering
HOGAN, N., Mechanical Engineering, Brain and Cognitive Sciences
HOSOI, A., Mechanical Engineering and Applied Mathematics
HUNTER, I., Mechanical Engineering
KAMM, R., Biological and Mechanical Engineering
KAZIMI, M., Nuclear and Mechanical Engineering
KIM, S., Mechanical Engineering
LANGER, R., Chemical Engineering and Biological Engineering
LEEB, S., Electrical and Mechanical Engineering
LEONARD, J., Mechanical and Ocean Engineering
LIENHARD V, J., Mechanical Engineering
LLOYD, S., Mechanical Engineering
MAKRIS, N., Mechanical and Ocean Engineering
MANALIS, S., Biological and Mechanical Engineering and Media Arts and Sciences
McKINLEY, G., Teaching Innovation, Mechanical Engineering
PARKS, D., Mechanical Engineering
PATERA, A., Engineering
PATRIKALAKIS, N., Engineering, Mechanical and Ocean Engineering
ROWELL, D., Mechanical Engineering
SACHS, E., Mechanical Engineering
SARMA, S., Mechanical Engineering
SCHMIDT, H., Mechanical and Ocean Engineering
SCLAVOUNOS, P., Mechanical Engineering and Naval Architecture
SEERING, W., Mechanical Engineering and Engineering Systems
SHAO-HORN, Y., Mechanical Engineering and Materials Science and Engineering
SLOCUM, A., Mechanical Engineering
SLOTINE, J., Mechanical Engineering, Information Sciences, and Brain and Cognitive Sciences
SO, P., Mechanical and Biological Engineering
TRIANTAFYLLOU, M., Marine Technology, Mechanical and Ocean Engineering
TRUMPER, D., Mechanical Engineering
VANDIVER, J., Mechanical and Ocean Engineering
WALLACE, D., Mechanical Engineering and Engineering Systems
WIERZBICKI, T., Applied Mechanics

WIESMAN, R., Mechanical Engineering

WILLIAMS, J., Mechanical Engineering and Writing

YANNAS, I., Mechanical Engineering, Polymer Science, and Biological Engineering

YOUCEF-TOUMI, K., Mechanical Engineering

YUE, D., Engineering, Mechanical and Ocean Engineering

Department of Nuclear Science and Engineering:

BALLINGER, R. G., Nuclear Science and Engineering and Materials Science and Engineering

GOLAY, M. W., Nuclear Science and Engineering

HUTCHINSON, I. H., Nuclear Science and Engineering (Head)

KAZIMI, M. S., Nuclear Engineering and Mechanical Engineering

LESTER, R. K., Nuclear Science and Engineering

LI, J., Nuclear Science and Engineering, Materials Science and Engineering

SMITH, K., Nuclear Science and Engineering

WHYTE, D., Nuclear Science and Engineering

Engineering Systems Division:

BARNHART, C., Engineering, Civil and Environmental Engineering and Engineering Systems

CARROLL, J., Management, Work and Organizational Studies and Engineering Systems

CLARK, J., Materials Systems and Engineering Systems

CRAWLEY, E., Aeronautics and Astronautics and Engineering Systems

CUSUMANO, M., Management, Technological Innovation, Entrepreneurship, Strategic Management, Engineering Systems

DAHLEH, M., Electrical Engineering and Computer Science

DE NEUFVILLE, R., Engineering Systems

DE WECK, O., Aeronautics and Astronautics and Engineering Systems

EAGAR, T., Materials Engineering and Engineering Systems

EPPINGER, S., Management, Operations Management, Management Science and Innovation, Engineering Systems

FERNANDEZ, J., Architecture, Building Technology, and Engineering Systems

FINE, C., Management, Operations Management and Engineering Systems

FREY, D., Mechanical Engineering and Engineering Systems

GELTNER, D., Real Estate Finance and Engineering Systems

GRAVES, S., Management, Operations Management and Leaders for Global Operations, Engineering Systems and Mechanical Engineering

HANSMAN, R., Aeronautics and Astronautics and Engineering Systems

HASTINGS, D., Aeronautics and Astronautics and Engineering Systems

KLOPFER, E., Education and Engineering Systems

KOCHAN, T., Management, Work and Employment Research and Engineering Systems

LAGACÉ, P., Aeronautics and Astronautics and Engineering Systems

LARSON, R., Engineering Systems

LEVESON, N., Aeronautics and Astronautics and Engineering Systems

LLOYD, S., Mechanical Engineering and Engineering Systems

MADNICK, S., Information Technology and Engineering Systems

MAGEE, C., Engineering Systems

MINDELL, D., History of Engineering and Manufacturing, Engineering Systems

MOAVENZADEH, F., Civil and Environmental Engineering and Engineering Systems

MOSES, J., Computer Science and Engineering Systems

NEWMAN, D., Aeronautics and Astronautics and Engineering Systems

NIGHTINGALE, D., Aeronautics and Astronautics Engineering Systems

PENTLAND, A., Media Arts and Sciences and Engineering Systems

SEERING, W., Mechanical Engineering and Engineering Systems

SHEFFI, Y., Engineering Systems, Civil and Environmental Engineering

SIMCHI-LEVI, D., Civil and Environmental Engineering and Engineering Systems

SINSKEY, A., Biology, Health Sciences and Technology, and Engineering Systems

STERMAN, J., System Dynamics, Engineering Systems

SUSSMAN, J., Civil and Environmental Engineering and Engineering Systems

UTTERBACK, J., Management and Innovation, Technological Innovation, and Entrepreneurship, Engineering Systems

VON HIPPEL, E., Management, Management of Innovation and Engineering Systems

WALLACE, D., Mechanical Engineering and Engineering Systems

WELSCH, R., Management, Statistics and Engineering Systems

WIDNALL, S., Aeronautics and Astronautics and Engineering Systems

WILLIAMS, J., Civil and Environmental Engineering and Engineering Systems

School of Humanities, Arts and Social Sciences (77 Massachusetts Ave, Room E51-255, Cambridge, MA 02139-4307; tel. (617) 253-3450; e-mail shass-www@mit.edu; internet shass.mit.edu):

Department of Economics:

ACEMOGLU, K. D., Economics

ANGELETOS, G.-M., Economics

ANGRIST, J., Economics

AUTOR, D., Economics

BANERJEE, A., Economics

CABALLERO, R., Economics (Head)

CHERNOZHUKOV, V., Economics

DUFLO, E., Poverty Alleviation and Development Economics

ELLISON, G., Economics

FINKELSTEIN, A., Economics

GIBBONS, R. S., Management and Economics

GRUBER, J., Economics

HARRIS, J. E., Economics

HAUSMAN, J. A., Economics

HOLMSTRÖM, B. R., Economics (Head)

NEWEY, W. K., Economics

OLKEN, B., Economics

PATHAK, P., Economics

POTERBA, J. M., Economics

PRELEC, D., Management, Marketing, Management Science, Economics, and Brain and Cognitive Sciences

ROSE, N., Economics

ROSS, S., Finance and Economics

TOWNSEND, R., Economics

WERNING, I., Economics

YILDIZ, M., Economics

Department of Linguistics and Philosophy:

BYRNE, A., Philosophy

CHOMSKY, N. A., Linguistics

DEGRAFF, M., Linguistics

FLYNN, S., Second Language Acquisition

FOX, D., Linguistics

HASLANGER, S., Philosophy

HEIM, I., Linguistics

IATRIDOU, S., Linguistics

KENSTOWICZ, M., Linguistics

MCGEE, V., Philosophy

MIYAGAWA, S., Japanese Language and Culture, Linguistics

O'NEIL, W., Linguistics

PESETSKY, D., Linguistics

RAYO, A., Philosophy

RICHARDS, N., Linguistics

SCHWARZSCHILD, R., Linguistics

SETIYA, K., Philosophy

STALNAKER, R., Philosophy

STERIADE, D., Linguistics

VON FINTEL, K., Linguistics

WEXLER, K. N., Psychology and Linguistics

YABLO, S., Philosophy

Department of Political Science:

BERGER, S., Political Science

BERINSKY, A., Political Science

CAMPBELL, A., Political Science

CHOUCRI, N., Political Science

GAVIN, F., Nuclear Security Policy Studies

LIEBERMAN, E., Contemporary Africa

NOBLES, M., Political Science

PETERSEN, R., Political Science

POSEN, B. R., Political Science

SAMUELS, R. J., Political Science

SCHNEIDER, B., Political Science

STEWART, C. III, Political Science (Head)

THELEN, K., Political Science

VAN EVERA, S. W., Political Science

Foreign Languages and Literatures Section:

CONDRY, I., Japanese Cultural Studies (Head)

GARRELS, E., Spanish and Latin American Studies

MIYAGAWA, S., Japanese Language and Culture, Linguistics

TENG, E., Asian Civilizations, Chinese Studies and History

URICCHIO, W., Comparative Media Studies

WANG, J., Chinese Languages and Culture

History Section:

FOGELSON, R. M., History and Urban Studies

KHOURY, P. S., History

MCCANTS, A. E. C., History (Head)

RAVEL, J., History

RITVO, H., History

SMITH, M. R., History of Technology

TENG, E., Asian Civilizations, Chinese Studies and History

WILDER, C., History

WOOD, E. A., History

Literature Section:

BUZARD, J., Literature (Head)

DONALDSON, P. S., Literature

FULLER, M., Literature

HENDERSON, D., Literature

KIBEL, A. C., Literature

PERRY, R., Literature and Women's Studies

RAMAN, S., Literature

TAPSCOTT, S. J., Literature

THORBURN, D., Literature

Music and Theatre Arts Section:

BRODY, A., Theatre Arts

CHILD, P., Music

CUTHBERT, M., Music

HARBISON, J., Music

SCHEIB, J., Theatre Atys

SONENBERG, J., Theatre Arts

THOMPSON, M. A., Music

ZIPORYN, E., Music

Program in Anthropology:

CONDRY, I., Media and Cultural Studies

FISCHER, M., Anthropology and Science and Technology Studies

HELMREICH, S., Anthropology

PAXSON, H., Anthropology

SILBEY, S., Sociology and Anthropology, and Behavioral and Policy Sciences

Program in Comparative Media Studies:

BARTUSIAK, M., Science Writing

CONDRY, I., Japanese Cultural Studies

DIAZ, J., Writing
HENDERSHOT, H., Comparative Media Studies
LEE, H., Fiction Writing
LIGHTMAN, A., Humanities
LEVENSON, T., Science Writing
MANNING, K., Rhetoric and the History of Science
PARADIS, J., Writing
SCHIAPPA, E., Rhetoric and Media
URICCHIO, W., Comparative Media Studies
WANG, J., Chinese Cultural Studies, Chinese Language and Culture
WILLIAMS, R., History of Science and Technology

Program in Science, Technology and Society:

FISCHER, M. M. J., Humanities
FITZGERALD, D. K., History of Technology
KAISER, D., History of Science
LIGHT, J., Science, Technology, and Society
MANNING, K. R., Rhetoric and the History of Science
MINDELL, D. A., History of Engineering and Manufacturing, Engineering Systems (Dir)
POSTOL, T. A., Science, Technology and Nat. Security Policy
SMITH, M. R., History of Technology
TURKLE, S. R., Social Studies of Science and Technology
WILLIAMS, R. H., History of Science and Technology

Program in Writing and Humanistic Studies:

KANIGEL, R., Science Writing
LEVENSON, T., Science Writing
MANNING, K. R., Rhetoric and the History of Science
PARADIS, J., Writing (Programme Head)
WILLIAMS, J. H., Engineering
WILLIAMS, R. H., History of Science and Technology

School of Science (77 Massachusetts Ave, Room 6-123, Cambridge, MA 02139; tel. (617) 253-8900; e-mail scnc@mit.edu; internet web .mit.edu/science):

Department of Biology:

AMON, A., Cancer Research, Biology
BAKER, T., Biology
BARTEL, D., Biology
BELL, S., Biology
BURGE, C., Biology and Biological Engineering
CHEN, J., Biology, Immunology
CHISHOLM, S., Environmental Studies, Civil and Environmental Engineering and Biology
CONSTANTINE-PATON, M., Brain and Cognitive Sciences, Biology
DRENNAN, C., Chemistry and Biology
FINK, G., Genetics
GERTLER, F., Biology
GROSSMAN, A., Biology
GUARENTE, L., Biology
HORVITZ, H., Biology
HOUSMAN, D., Cancer Research
HYNES, R., Cancer Research
IMPERIALI, B., Biology and Chemistry
JACKS, T., Biology, Cancer Research
JAENISCH, R., Biology
KAISER, C., Biology
KING, J., Molecular Biology
KRIEGER, M., Biology, Molecular Genetics
LANDER, E., Biology
LAUFFENBURGER, D., Biological Engineering, Chemical Engineering, and Biology
LEES, J., Cancer Research, Biology
LINDQUIST, S., Biology
LITTLETON, T., Biology
LODISH, H., Biology and Bioengineering
ORR-WEAVER, T., Biology
PAGE, D., Biology
PARDUE, M., Biology
PLOEGH, H., Biology
QUINN, W., Neurobiology

RAJBHANDARY, U., Molecular Biology
RICH, A., Biophysics
SABATINI, D., Biology
SAMSON, L., Toxicology and Biological Engineering
SAUER, R., Biology
SHARP, P., Biology
SINSKEY, A., Microbiology and Health Sciences and Technology
SIVE, H., Biology
SOLOMON, F., Biology
STEINER, L., Immunology
STUBBE, J., Chemistry, Biology
TONEGAWA, S., Biology and Neuroscience
WALKER, G., Biology
WEINBERG, R., Cancer Research
WILSON, M., Biology, Neuroscience
YAFFE, M., Biology and Biological Engineering
YOUNG, R., Biology

Department of Brain and Cognitive Sciences:

ADELSON, E. H., Vision Science
BEAR, M., Neuroscience
BERWICK, R. C., Computational Linguistics
BIZZI, E., Brain Sciences and Human Behaviour
BROWN, E. N., Computational Neuroscience and Health Sciences and Technology
CONSTANTINE-PATON, M., Biology
DESIMONE, R., Neuroscience
DiCARLO, J., Neuroscience
FEE, M., Neuroscience
FENG, G., Neuroscience
GABRIELI, J., Health Sciences and Technology and Cognitive Neuroscience
GIBSON, E., Cognitive Sciences
GRAYBIEL, A. M., Neuroanatomy
HOCKFIELD, S., Neuroscience
HOGAN, N., Mechanical Engineering
KANWISHER, N. G., Cognitive Neuroscience
LITTLETON, J., Biology and Brain and Cognitive Sciences
MILLER, E. K., Visual Neuroscience
NEDIVI, E., Neuroscience
POGGIO, T. A., Brain Sciences and Human Behaviour
POTTER, M. C., Psychology
PRELAC, D., Management
QUINN, W. G., Neurobiology
SCHNEIDER, G. E., Neuroscience
SEUNG, H. S., Computational Neuroscience
SINHA, P., Vision and Computational Neuroscience
SLOTINE, J.-J. E., Mechanical Engineering and Information Sciences
SUR, M., Neuroscience (Head)
TENENBAUM, J., Cognitive Science and Computation
TONEGAWA, S., Biology and Neuroscience
TSAI, L.-H., Neuroscience
WEXLER, K. N., Psychology and Linguistics

Department of Chemistry:

BAWENDI, M. G., Chemistry
BUCHWALD, S. L., Chemistry
CAO, J., Chemistry
CEYER, S. T., Chemistry
CHAKRABORTY, A., Chemical Engineering, Chemistry and Biological Engineering
CUMMINS, C. C., Chemistry
DANHEISER, R. L., Chemistry
DRENNAN, C. L., Chemistry
ESSIGMANN, J. M., Chemistry and Toxicology
FIELD, R. W., Chemistry
GRIFFIN, R. G., Chemistry
HONG, M., Chemistry
IMPERIALI, B., Chemistry and Biology
JAMISON, T., Chemistry
KLIBANOV, A. M., Chemistry and Bioengineering
LIPPARD, S. J., Chemistry
MOVASSAGHI, M., Chemistry
NELSON, K. A., Chemistry
SCHROCK, R. R., Chemistry

SOLOMON, S., Atmospheric Chemistry and Climate Change
STUBBE, J., Chemistry and Biology
SWAGER, T. M., Chemistry (Head)
TANNENBAUM, S. R., Chemistry and Toxicology
TING, A., Chemistry
VAN VOORHIS, T., Chemistry

Department of Earth, Atmospheric and Planetary Sciences:

BINZEL, R. P., Planetary Sciences
BOWRING, S. A., Geology
BOYLE, E. A., Ocean Geochemistry
BURCHFIEL, B. C., Geology
EMANUEL, K. A., Atmospheric Science
ENTEKHABI, D., Civil and Environmental Engineering and Earth, Atmospheric and Planetary Sciences
EVANS, J. B., Geophysics
FERRARI, R., Dynamical Oceanography
FLIERL, G. R., Oceanography
GROVE, T. L., Geology
HAGER, B. H., Earth Sciences
HERRING, T. A., Geophysics
MARSHALL, J., Atmospheric and Oceanic Sciences
MORGAN, F. D., Geophysics
PLUMB, R. A., Meteorology
PRINN, R. G., Atmospheric Chemistry
RIZZOLI, P. M., Physical Oceanography
ROTHMAN, D. H., Geophysics
ROYDEN, L., Geology and Geophysics
SEAGER, S., Physics
SOLOMON, S., Atmospheric Chemistry and Climate Science
SUMMONS, R. E., Geobiology
VAN DER HILST, R., Geophysics
WEISS, B., Planetary Sciences
WISDOM, J., Planetary Sciences
ZUBER, M. T., Planetary Sciences and Geophysics (Head)

Department of Mathematics:

BAZANT, M., Chemical Engineering and Applied Mathematics
BERGER, B., Applied Mathematics
BEZRUKAVNIKOV, R., Mathematics
BORODIN, A., Mathematics
BUSH, J., Applied Mathematics
CHENG, H., Applied Mathematics
COLDING, T. H., Mathematics
DUDLEY, R. M., Mathematics
EDELMAN, A., Applied Mathematics
ETINGOF, P. I., Mathematics
GOEMANS, M., Applied Mathematics
GUILLEMIN, V. W., Mathematics
GUIONNET, A., Mathematics
GUTH, L., Mathematics
HOSOI, S., Mechanical Engineering and Applied Mathematics
JERISON, A., Mathematics
KAC, V., Mathematics
KLEIMAN, S., Mathematics
KIM, J., Mathematics
KLEITMAN, D. J., Applied Mathematics
LEIGHTON, F. T., Applied Mathematics
LUSZTIG, G., Mathematics
MELROSE, R. B., Mathematics
MILLER, H. R., Mathematics
MINICOZZI II, W., Mathematics
MROWKA, T., Mathematics
POONEN, B., Mathematics
ROSALES, R. R., Applied Mathematics
SEIDEL, P., Mathematics
SHEFFIELD, S., Mathematics
SHOR, P., Applied Mathematics
SIPSER, M., Applied Mathematics (Head)
STAFFILANI, G., Mathematics
STANLEY, R. P., Applied Mathematics
STRANG, W. G., Mathematics
VOGAN, D. A., Jr, Mathematics

Department of Physics:

ASHOORI, R., Physics
BELCHER, J., Physics
BERTOZZI, W., Physics

BERTSCHINGER, E., Physics
BUSZA, W., Physics
CANIZARES, C., Physics
CHAKRABARTY, D., Physics
CHEN, M., Physics
CHUANG, I., Electrical Engineering and Physics
CONRAD, J., Physics
COPPI, B., Physics
FARHI, E., Physics
FISHER, P., Physics
FREEDMAN, D., Mathematics and Physics
GUTH, A., Physics
HEWITT, J., Physics
JAFFE, R., Physics, Science
JOANNOPOULOS, J., Physics
JOSS, P., Physics
KARDAR, M., Physics
KASTNER, M., Science
KETTERLE, W., Physics
KOWALSKI, S., Physics
LEE, P., Physics
LEE, Y., Physics
LEVITOV, L., Physics
MAVALVALA, N., Astrophysics
MILNER, R., Physics
NEGELE, J., Physics
PAUS, C., Physics
PORKOLAB, M., Physics
PRITCHARD, D., Physics
RAJAGOPAL, K., Physics
REDWINE, R., Physics
ROLAND, G., Physics
SCHECHTER, P., Astrophysics
SEAGER, S., Earth, Atmospheric, and Planetary Sciences and Physics
SEUNG, H., Computational Neuroscience and Physics
SOLJACIC, M., Physics
STEWART, I., Physics
TAYLOR IV, W., Physics
TEGMARK, M., Physics
TING, S., Physics
TODADRI, S., Physics
VULETIC, V., Physics
WEN, X., Physics
WILCZEK, F., Physics
WYSLOUCH, B., Physics
ZWIEBACH, B., Physics
ZWIERLEIN, M., Physics

Whitaker College of Health Sciences and Technology (77 Massachusetts Ave, Room E25-519, Cambridge, MA 02139; tel. (617) 258-4418; internet hst.mit.edu):

BENEDEK, G. B., Physics and Biological Physics and Health Sciences and Technology
BRAIDA, L. D., Electrical Engineering and Health Sciences and Technology
COHEN, R. J., Biomedical Engineering
CRAVALHO, E. G., Mechanical Engineering and Health Sciences and Technology
EDELMAN, E. R., Health Sciences and Technology
GABRIELI, J., Health Sciences and Technology, Brain and Cognitive Sciences
GEHRKE, L., Health Sciences and Technology
GRAY, M. L., Medical and Electrical Engineering
HOUSMAN, D. E., Biology
LANGER, R. S., Chemical and Biomedical Engineering and Health Sciences and Technology
MARK, R. G., Health Sciences and Technology and Electrical Engineering and Computer Science
SINSKEY, A. J., Biology and Health Sciences and Technology
SZOLOVITS, P., Computer Science and Engineering and Health Sciences and Technology
WURTMAN, R. J., Neuropharmacology and Health Sciences and Technology

YOUNG, L. R., Astronautics and Health Sciences and Technology

Harvard-MIT Division of Health Sciences and Technology

BHATIA, S. N., Health Sciences and Technology, and Electrical Engineering and Computer Science
BRAIDA, L., Electrical Engineering and Health Sciences and Technology
BROWN, E. N., Medical Engineering, Computational Neuroscience and Health Sciences and Technology
CHAKRABORTY, A., Chemical Engineering, Chemistry and Biological Engineering
COHEN, D., Medicine and Health Sciences amd Technology
COHEN, R., Biomedical Engineering
EDELMAN, E., Health Sciences and Technology
FREEMAN, D. M., Electrical Engineering
GABRIELI, J., Health Sciences and Technology and Cognitive Neuroscience
GEHRKE, L., Health Sciences and Technology
GRAY, M., Medical and Electrical Engineering
HOUSMAN, D., Biology
LANGER, R. S., Chemical and Biomedical Engineering, and Health Sciences and Technology
LONDON, I., Biology
MARK, R., Health Sciences and Technology and Electrical Engineering and Computer Science
MITCHELL, R., Pathology and Health Sciences and Technology, HMS
STULTZ, C., Health Sciences and Technology and Electrical Engineering and Computer Science
SZOLOVITS, P., Computer Science and Engineering and Health Sciences and Technology
YOUNG, L., Aeronautics and Astronautics and Health Sciences and Technology

Sloan School of Management (50 Memorial Dr., Cambridge, MA 02142; tel. (617) 253-2659; e-mail communication@sloan.mit.edu; internet mitsloan.mit.edu):

ANCONA, D., Management and Organization Studies
ASQUITH, P., Finance
BARNETT, A., Management Science and Statistics
BERNDT, E., Applied Economics
BERTSIMAS, D., Management and Operations Research
BRYNJOLFSSON, E., Management Science and Information Technology
CARROLL, J., Management, Organization Studies, and Engineering Systems
CORE, J., Accounting
COX, J., Finance
CUSUMANO, M., Management; Technological Innovation, Entrepreneursip, and Strategic Management; and Engineering Systems
DOYLE, JR, J., Management and Applied Economics
EPPINGER, S., Management, Operations Management, Management Science and Innovation, and Engineering Systems
FERNANDEZ, R., Management and Organization Studies
FINE, C., Management, Operations Management, and Engineering Systems
FORBES, K., Management and of Global Economics and Management
FREUND, R., Management Science and Operations Research
GAMARNIK, D., Operations Research
GIBBONS, R., Management and Applied Economics
GRAVES, S., Management, Operations Management, Leaders for Global Operations,

Engineering Systems, and Mechanical Engineering
HANLON, M., Accounting
HAUSER, J., Marketing
HUANG, Y., Chinese Economy and Business of Global Economics and Management
JOHNSON, S., Entrepreneurship and Global Economics and Management
KIRILENKO, A., Practice
KNITTEL, C., Energy Economics and Applied Economics
KOCHAN, T., Management, Work and Employment Research, and Engineering Systems
KOGAN, L., Management and Finance
KOTHARI, S., Management and Accounting
LEVI, R., Management and Operations Management
LITTLE, J., Marketing
LO, A., Finance and of Electrical Engineering and Computer Science
LUCAS, D., Management and Finance
MADNICK, S., Information Technology and Engineering Systems
MAGNANTI, T., Operations Research and Electrical Engineering
MALONE, T., Management and Information Technology
MERTON, R., Finance
MURRAY, F., Entrepreneurship; Technological Innovation, Entrepreneurship, and Strategic Management
MYERS, S., Financial Economics and Finance
ORLIKOWSKI, W., Management, Information Technology, and Organization Studies
ORLIN, J., Management and Operations Research
ORPHANIDES, A., Practice
OSTERMAN, P., Human Resources and Management
PAN, J., Finance
PARKER, J., Management and Finance
PERAKIS, G., Management, Operations Research, and Operations Management
PINDYCK, R., Finance and Economics and Applied Economics
PRELEC, D., Management, Marketing, Management Science, Economics, and Brain and Cognitive Sciences
REAGANS, R., Management and Organization Studies
REPENNING, N., System Dynamics and Organization Studies
RIGOBON, R., Applied Economics
ROBERTS, E., Management of Technology
ROSS, S., Financial Economics and Finance
SCHMITTLEIN, D., Marketing
SCHOAR, A., Entrepreneurship and Finance
SCHULZ, A., Management and Operations Research
SIMESTER, D., Marketing
STERMAN, J., Computer Science and of System Dynamics and Engineering Systems
STERN, S., Management of Technology and Technological Innovation, Entrepreneurship, and Strategic Management
STOKER, T., Management and Economics and of Applied Economics
UTTERBACK, J., Management and Innovation; Technological Innovation, Entrepreneurship, and Strategic Management; and Engineering Systems
VAN MAANEN, J., Management and Organization Studies
VON HIPPEL, E., Management and Management of Innovation and Engineering Systems
WANG, J., Finance
WEBER, J., Management and Accounting
WELSCH, R., Management, Statistics, and Engineering Systems
WERNERFELT, B., Management and Marketing

WHINSTON, M., Management Applied Economics, and Economics

YATES, J., Management; Managerial Communication; and Work and Organization Studies

ZUCKERMAN SIVAN, E., Technological Innovation, Entrepreneurship, and Strategic Management

MASSACHUSETTS MARITIME ACADEMY

101 Academy Dr., Buzzards Bay, MA 02532

Telephone: (508) 830-5000

E-mail: info@maritime.edu

Internet: www.maritime.edu

Founded 1891 as Massachusetts Nautical Training School; current name adopted 1942

State control

Academic year: August to June

Depts of engineering, humanities, int. maritime business, environmental protection, safety and emergency management, marine transportation, science and mathematics, social science

Pres.: RICHARD G. GURNON

Vice-Pres. for Academic Affairs and Dean: BRADLEY K. LIMA

Vice-Pres. for Admin. and Finance: MICHAEL A. JOYCE

Vice-Pres. for Advancement: HOLLY A. KNIGHT

Vice-Pres. for Enrolment Management: ELIZABETH STEVENSON

Vice-Pres. for External Relations and Finance: MICHAEL A. JOYCE

Vice-Pres. for Operations: FRANCIS X. McDONALD

Vice-Pres. for Student Services: EDWARD J. ROZAK

Dir of Admissions: ROY FULGUERAS

Dean of Graduate Studies and Continuing Education: Dr JAMES J. McDONALD

Registrar and Asst Dean: MICHAEL R. CUFF

Dir of Library: SUSAN S. BERTEAUX

Number of teachers: 50

Number of students: 770

MASSACHUSETTS SCHOOL OF LAW AT ANDOVER

500 Federal St, Andover, MA 01810

Telephone: (978) 681-0800

E-mail: mslaw@mslaw.edu

Internet: www.mslaw.edu

Founded 1988

Private control

Academic year: July to July

Academic programmes in business and corporate law, civil litigation, communications sports and entertainment law, criminal law, environmental law, family law, finance and asset management law, intellectual property, media, information law, juvenile law, labour law, land use and planning, litigation, real estate

Dean: Prof. Dr LAWRENCE R. VELVEL

Dir of Admissions: PAULA COLBY-CLEMENTS

Registrar: LOUISE ROSE

Dir of Information Resources: JUDITH WOLFE

Library of 60,000 vols

MASSACHUSETTS SCHOOL OF PROFESSIONAL PSYCHOLOGY

221 Rivermoor St, Boston, MA 02132

Telephone: (617) 327-6777

E-mail: admissions@mspp.edu

Internet: www.mspp.edu

Private control

Academic year: January to December

Pres.: NICHOLAS COVINO

Provost: Dr DAN KING

Vice-Pres. for Finance and Operations: PATRICK CAPOBIANCO

Dean of Students: Dr FRANCES V. MERVYN

Dir of Admissions: MARIO MURGA

Registrar: EILEEN O'DONNELL

Librarian: MATTHEW KRAMER

DEANS

Advanced Graduate Studies: Dr STANLEY BERMAN

Clinical Psychology Dept: Dr ALAN DODGE BECK

MERRIMACK COLLEGE

315 Turnpike St, N Andover, MA 01845

Telephone: (978) 837-5000

E-mail: regoff@merrimack.edu

Internet: www.merrimack.edu

Founded 1947

Private control

Academic year: September to May

Pres.: Dr CHRISTOPHER E. HOPEY

Provost and Sr Vice-Pres. for Academic Affairs: CAROL A. GLOD

Vice-Pres. for Admin. and Gen. Counsel: CHRISTINE ABOWITZ

Vice-Pres. for Enrolment Management, Planning and Strategy: KURT THIEDE

Vice-Pres. for Finance and Chief Financial Officer: MARK VADALA

Vice-Pres. for Mission and Student Affairs: Rev. RAYMOND DLUGOS

Dean for Admissions: MARK BARRETT

Registrar: ELAINE GRELLE

Dir for Library: KATHRYN GEOFFRIONSCANNELL

Library of 125,000 vols, 1,069 current periodicals

Number of teachers: 140

Number of students: 2,000

Publication: *Merrimack Magazine* (4 a year)

DEANS

Francis E. Girard School of Business and International Commerce: MARK CORDANO

School of Education: DAN BUTIN

School of Liberal Arts: MICHAEL ROSSI

School of Science and Engineering: MARY NOONAN

MGH INSTITUTE OF HEALTH PROFESSIONS

36 First Ave, Charleston Navy Yard, Boston, MA 02129-4557

Telephone: (617) 726-2947

E-mail: admissions@mghihp.edu

Internet: www.mghihp.edu

Founded 1980

Private control

Academic year: September to August

Pres.: Prof. Dr JANIS P. BELLACK

Provost and Vice-Pres. for Academic Affairs: Prof. Dr ALEX F. JOHNSON

Vice-Pres. for Finance and Admin.: ATLAS D. EVANS

Chief Devt Officer: HARRIET S. KORNFELD

Academic Dean: KEVIN KEARNS

Dean of Student Affairs: CAROLYN F. LOCKE

Registrar and Asst Dean of Students: JAMES V. VITAGLIANO

Librarian: JESSICA BELL

Library of 50,000 vols

Number of teachers: 80 (65 full-time, 15 part-time)

Number of students: 1,110 (693 full-time, 417 part-time)

DEANS

School of Health and Rehabilitation Sciences: Prof. Dr LESLIE G. PORTNEY

School of Nursing: Dr LAURIE LAUZON CLABO

MONTSERRAT COLLEGE OF ART

23 Essex St, POB 26, Beverly, MA 01915

Telephone: (978) 921-4242

E-mail: admiss@montserrat.edu

Internet: www.montserrat.edu

Founded 1970 as Montserrat School of Visual Arts

Private control

Academic year: September to May (3 semesters)

Areas of study incl. animation and interactive media, art education, graphic design, illustration, interdisciplinary arts, liberal arts, painting and drawing, photography and video, printmaking, sculpture

Pres.: Dr STEPHEN D. IMMERMAN

Dean of Admissions and Enrolment Management: RICK LONGO

Dean of College Relations: JO BRODERICK

Dean of Devt: HOWARD AMIDON

Dean of Faculty and Academic Affairs: LAURA TONELLI

Dean of Students: MAUREEN WARK

Registrar: THERESA SKELLY

Librarian: CHERI COE

Library of 15,000 vols, 90 periodicals

Number of teachers: 60

Number of students: 390 (undergraduate)

MOUNT HOLYOKE COLLEGE

50 College St, S Hadley, MA 01075

Telephone: (413) 538-2000

E-mail: admission@mtholyoke.edu

Internet: www.mtholyoke.edu

Founded 1837 as Mount Holyoke Female Seminary, current name adopted 1893

Private control

Academic year: September to May

Areas of study incl. ancient studies, art studio, chemistry, economics, engineering, geology, music, psychology, sociology, theatre arts, statistics

Pres.: LYNN C. PASQUERELLA

Vice-Pres. for Academic Affairs and Dean of Faculty: CHRISTOPHER BENFEY (acting)

Vice-Pres. for Devt: CHARLES J. HAIGHT

Vice-Pres. for Enrolment and College Relations: DIANE ANCI

Vice-Pres. for Finance and Admin. and Treas.: BEN HAMMOND

Vice-Pres. for Student Affairs and Dean of College: CERRI BANKS

Dean of Students and Assoc. Dean of the College: RENE DAVIS

Dean of Studies: GEOFFREY SUMI

Registrar: ELIZABETH PYLE

Chief Information Officer and Exec. Dir of Library, Information and Technology Services: CHARLOTTE SLOCUM PATRIQUIN

Library of 750,000 vols, 1,300 periodicals

Number of teachers: 280

Number of students: 2,360

Publications: *Vista* (2 a year), *Alumnae Quarterly* (4 a year)

MOUNT IDA COLLEGE

777 Dedham St, Newton, MA 02459

Telephone: (617) 928-4500

E-mail: registrar@mountida.edu

Internet: www.mountida.edu

Founded 1899 as Women's Private High School

Private control

Academic year: August to May

Schools of animal science, arts and sciences, business, design

Pres.: Dr LANCE CARLUCCIO

Vice-Pres. for Academic Affairs: Dr ELLEN BEAULIEU

Vice-Pres. for Devt and Dir of External Relations: Dr DEBORAH HIRSCH
Vice-Pres. for Enrollment Management and Marketing: MAUREEN MORIARTY
Vice-Pres. for Finance and Admin.: CHERYL ST PIERRE-SLEBODA
Vice-Pres. for Student Affairs: Dr ELIZABETH TRUE
Dean of Academic Services: ALYCE CURTIS
Dean of Graduate Studies and Continuing Education: Dr LOIS NUNEZ
Registrar: MAUREEN MORIARTY
Dean of Information Technology and Learning Resources: MARJORIE LIPPINCOTT
Library of 120,000 titles
Number of teachers: 100
Number of students: 1,430

NATIONAL GRADUATE SCHOOL OF QUALITY MANAGEMENT

186 Jones Rd, Falmouth, MA 02540

Telephone: (508) 457-1313
E-mail: info@ngs.edu
Internet: www.ngs.edu
Founded 1993
Private control
Academic year: January to December
Offers degree programmes in business admin. and science
Pres. and Founder: Dr ROBERT GEE
Vice-Pres. for Enrolment Management: VIRGINIA PETISCE
Registrar: VANESSA HOFFMAN
Number of teachers: 250
Number of students: 390 (full-time)

NEW ENGLAND COLLEGE OF BUSINESS AND FINANCE

10 High St, Boston, MA 02110-1605

Telephone: (617) 951-2350
E-mail: info@necb.edu
Internet: www.necb.edu
Founded 1909 as American Banking Institute, present name 2008
Private control
Academic year: January to December
Offers BSc in business administration; MSc in business ethics and compliance, finance
Pres.: Dr HOWARD E. HORTON
Provost: Prof. Dr CHRISTOPHER WEIR
Sr Vice-Pres. for Student Services: PAULA BRAMANTE
Dean of Academic Affairs: Dr CHRISTIAN BROCATO
Dean of Undergraduate Studies: ROGER PAO
Registrar: ROBERT WAGSTAFF
Librarian: Prof. JEFFREY C. CRONIN

NEW ENGLAND COLLEGE OF OPTOMETRY

424 Beacon St, Boston, MA 02115

Telephone: (617) 266-2030
E-mail: admissions@neco.edu
Internet: www.neco.edu
Founded 1894 as Klein School of Optics; current name adopted 1976
Private control
Academic year: September to May
Depts of advanced care, biomedical sciences, primary care and speciality, vision sciences
Pres.: Prof. Dr CLIFFORD SCOTT
Vice-Pres. for Admin.: JOHN CURRAN
Vice-Pres. and Dean of Academic Affairs: Prof. Dr BARRY FISCH
Vice-Pres. and Dean of Students, Admin. and Alumni: Dr TERRANCE B. NEYLON
Vice-Pres. for Devt: LARRY RAFF
Vice-Pres. for Institutional Advancement: NANCY BROUDE

Vice-Pres. for Professional Services: ROGER WILSON
Chief Financial Officer and Treas.: BRUCE BERNIER
Dir of Admissions: Dr TALINE FARRA
Registrar: GLENDA UNDERWOOD
Dir of Library Services: KRISTIN MOTTE
Library of 11,000 vols, 200 journals
Number of teachers: 80
Number of students: 425

NEW ENGLAND CONSERVATORY OF MUSIC

290 Huntington Ave, Boston, MA 02115-5018

Telephone: (617) 585-1100
E-mail: admission@newenglandconservatory.edu
Internet: necmusic.edu
Founded 1867
Private control
Academic year: September to May
Academic programmes in chamber music, composition, historical performance and world music, jazz and contemporary improvisation, music history and theory, music in education, piano, orchestral and wind ensemble conducting, orchestral instruments, orchestras, wind ensembles, voice and opera
Pres.: TONY WOODCOCK
Provost and Dean of College: THOMAS NOVAK
Sr Vice-Pres. for Finance and Operations: EDWARD R. LESSER
Vice-Pres. for Institutional Advancement: DON JONES
Dean of Preparatory and Continuing Education: LESLIE WU FOLEY
Dean of Students: THOMAS HANDEL
Dir of Admissions: CHRIS DALY
Registrar: ROBERT WINKLEY
Dir of Libraries: JEAN MORROW
Library of 150,000 vols
Number of teachers: 400
Number of students: 750
Publications: Journal for Learning through Music (1 a year), Notes (2 a year)

NEW ENGLAND INSTITUTE OF ART

10 Brookline Place W, Brookline, MA 02445-7295

Telephone: (617) 739-1700
E-mail: neiaregistrar@aii.edu
Internet: www.artinstitutes.edu/boston
Founded 1952 as Norm Prescott School of Broadcasting, current name adopted 2003
Private control
Academic year: January to January
BSc degree programmes in advertising, audio and media technology, digital filmmaking and video production, fashion and retail management, graphic design, interior design, media arts and animation, photography, sound and motion picture technical arts, web design and interactive media
Pres.: CHRISTINE MURPHY
Dean for Academic Affairs: RICHARD KETTNER-POLLEY
Dir for Admin. and Financial Services: ROSS SORACI
Dir for Admissions: KIMBERLY ODUSAMI
Registrar: JAMIE CURCIO
Dir for Library: DAMIEN MCCAFFREY
Number of teachers: 160 (51 full-time, 109 part-time)
Number of students: 900

NEW ENGLAND LAW—BOSTON

154 Stuart St, Boston, MA 02116

Telephone: (617) 451-0010
E-mail: admit@nesl.edu
Internet: www.nesl.edu

Founded 1908 as Portia Law School, current name adopted 2008
Private control
Academic year: August to May
Offers degree in advanced legal studies
Dean: JOHN F. O'BRIEN
Dir of Admissions: MICHELLE L'ETOILE
Dir of Student Services: JACQUI PILGRIM
Registrar: DAVID BERTI
Library Dir: Prof. ANNE M. ACTON
Library of 321,000 vols
Number of teachers: 90 (39 full-time, 51 part-time)
Number of students: 1,135 (800 full-time, 335 part-time)
Publications: New England Journal of Comparative and International Law (1 a year), New England Journal on Criminal and Civil Confinement (2 a year), New England Law Review (4 a year)

NEWBURY COLLEGE

129 Fisher Ave, Brookline, MA 02445

Telephone: (617) 730-7000
E-mail: admissions@newbury.edu
Internet: www.newbury.edu
Founded 1962
Private control
Academic year: August to May (2 semesters)
Schools of arts, science and design, business and management, hotel and restaurant management
Pres.: HANNAH M. MCCARTHY
Exec. Vice-Pres.: JOSEPH CHILLO
Exec. Vice-Pres. for Enrolment: JOSEPH CHILLO
Vice-Pres. for Academic Affairs and Dean of the College: Dr HANNAH LEVERTOV
Vice-Pres. for Devt: CLARE MCCULLY
Vice-Pres. for Finance and Chief Financial Officer: JOYCE HANLON
Vice-Pres. for Student Affairs: PAUL MARTIN
Registrar: RACHELLE MAZZA-BORRELLI
Dir of Library Services: PETER G. OBUCHAN
Number of teachers: 1,025

NICHOLS COLLEGE

POB 5000, Dudley, MA 01571
124 Center Rd, Dudley, MA 01571

Telephone: (508) 213-1560
E-mail: admissions@nichols.edu
Internet: www.nichols.edu
Founded 1815 as Nichols Acad., present name and status 1971
Academic year: August to May (2 semesters)
Campuses in Auburn, Devens, Worcester; areas of study incl. accounting, business admin., business communications, business economics, criminal justice management, English, history, mathematics, psychology
Pres.: Dr SUSAN WEST ENGELKEMEYER
Provost and Sr Vice-Pres.: Dr ALAN J. REINHARDT
Vice-Pres. and Dean of Student Services: BRIAN MCCOY
Vice-Pres. for Admin.: MICHAEL J. STANTON
Vice-Pres. for College Advancement: WILLIAM C. PIECZYNSKI
Vice-Pres. for Enrolment and Marketing: THOMAS R. CAFARO
Vice-Pres. for Information Services: KEVIN F. BRASSARD
Vice-Pres. for Student Affairs and Dean of Students: Dr BRIAN T. MCCOY
Registrar: BETIN ROBICHAUD
Dir of Library: JIM DOUGLAS
Library of 67,000 vols
Number of teachers: 50
Number of students: 1,590 (1,342 undergraduate, 248 graduate)

Publication: *Nichols College Magazine*

NORTHEASTERN UNIVERSITY

360 Huntington Ave, Boston, MA 02115
Telephone: (617) 373-2000
E-mail: admissions@neu.edu
Internet: www.northeastern.edu
Founded 1898
Private control
Academic year: August to August
Pres.: Dr JOSEPH E. AOUN
Provost and Sr Vice-Pres. for Academic Affairs: STEPHEN DIRECTOR
Sr Vice-Pres. and Gen. Counsel: RALPH MARTIN
Sr Vice-Pres. and Chief Operating Officer: STEVEN KADISH
Sr Vice-Pres. for Enrolment Management and Student Affairs: PHILOMENA MANTELLA
Sr Vice-Pres. for Exec. Affairs: MARK PUTNAM
Sr Vice-Pres. for External Affairs: MICHAEL ARMINI
Sr Vice-Pres. for Univ. Advancement: DIANE MACGILLIVRAY
Vice-Pres. and Chief Financial Officer: THOMAS NEDELL
Dean for Library: WILLIAM WAKELING
Library of 896,213 vols, 365,520 ebooks, 1,332,128 microforms, 69,468 serial titles, 58,559 ejournals, 18,210 media materials, 110,142 govt documents
Number of teachers: 1,540
Number of students: 24,540

DEANS

Bouvé College of Health Sciences: Dr TERRY FULMER
College of Arts, Media and Design: Dr XAVIER COSTA (acting)
College of Business Administration: Prof. Dr HUGH COURTNEY LANE (acting)
College of Computer and Information Science: LARRY FINKELSTEIN
College of Engineering: NADINE AUBRY (acting)
College of Professional Studies: Dr JOHN G. LABRIE
College of Science: Dr J. MURRAY GIBSON (acting)
College of Social Sciences and Humanities: UTA POIGER
School of Law: Prof. JEREMY PAUL

PINE MANOR COLLEGE

400 Heath St, Chestnut Hill, MA 02467
Telephone: (617) 731-7000
E-mail: admission@pmc.edu
Internet: www.pmc.edu
Founded 1911 as a post-secondary div. of Dana Hall School; present name and status 1977
Private control
Language of instruction: English
Academic year: September to May
Depts of biology, communication, community health, creative writing, English, history, management and organizational change, psychology, social and political systems, visual arts
Pres.: Dr ALANE K. SHANKS
Vice-Pres. for Finance and Business: BETSY ESPE
Vice-Pres. for Institutional Advancement: SUSAN WEBBER
Dean of College: Dr WILLIAM B. VOGELE
Dir of Admissions: ELAINE VINCENT
Dean of Student Services and Community Engagement: WHITNEY RETALLIC
Registrar: JEFF MEI
Library Dir: SARAH WOOLF (acting)
Library of 70,000 vols
Number of teachers: 70

Number of students: 490

REGIS COLLEGE

235 Wellesley St, Weston, MA 02493-1571
Telephone: (781) 768-7000
E-mail: admission@regiscollege.edu
Internet: www.regiscollege.edu
Founded 1927
Private control
Academic year: September to June
Pres.: Dr ANTOINETTE M. HAYS
Vice-Pres. for Academic Affairs: PAULA HARBECKE
Vice-Pres. for Enrolment and Marketing: PAUL VACCARO
Vice-Pres. for Finance and Business: THOMAS G. PISTORINO
Vice-Pres. for Student Affairs: LYNN TRIPP COLEMAN
Chief Devt Officer: MIRIAM FINN SHERMAN
Dean of Students: Dr KARA KOLOMITZ
Dir of Admission: WANDA ESTHER SURIEL
Registrar: ESTHER A. GHAZARIAN
Dir of Library: LYNN TRIPLETT
Library of 133,000 vols
Number of teachers: 110 (73 full-time, 87 part-time)
Number of students: 1,800
Publications: *Hemetera*, *Regis Today* (2 a year)

DEANS

School of Liberal Arts, Education and Social Sciences: Dr ELIZABETH CAWLEY
School of Nursing Sciences and Health Professions: ANTOINETTE HAYS

SALEM STATE UNIVERSITY

352 Lafayette St, Salem, MA 01970
Telephone: (978) 542-6000
E-mail: admissions@salemstate.edu
Internet: www.salemstate.edu
Founded 1854 as Salem Normal School, current name adopted 2010
State control
Academic year: September to May (2 semesters)
Pres.: Dr PATRICIA MAGUIRE MESERVEY
Exec. Vice-Pres.: Dr STANLEY CAHIL
Provost and Vice-Pres. for Academic Affairs: Dr KRISTIN ESTERBERG
Exec. Vice-Pres. for Student Life: Dr STANLEY P. CAHILL
Vice-Pres. for Finance and Facilities: ANDREW SOLL
Vice-Pres. for Institutional Advancement: CYNTHIA MCGURREN
Dean of Students: JAMES G. STOLL
Dean of Library: SUSAN E. CIRILLO
Library of 225,000 vols
Number of teachers: 780 (334 full-time, 446 part-time)
Number of students: 9,650 (6,243 full-time, 3,407 part-time

DEANS

Bertolon School of Business: Dr K. BREWER DORAN
College of Health and Human Services: Dr NEAL DECHILLO
School of Arts and Sciences: Dr JUDE V. NIXON
School of Graduate Studies: Dr CAROL A. GLOD
School of Professional and Continuing Education: Dr ARLENE T. GREENSTEIN

ST JOHN'S SEMINARY

127 Lake St, Brighton, MA 02135
Telephone: (617) 254-2610

E-mail: contact@sjs.edu
Internet: www.sjs.edu
Founded 1884
Private control
Academic year: September to May
Offers degrees in divinity, ministry, philosophy, theology
Rector: Rev. ARTHUR L. KENNEDY
Vice-Rector: Rev. CHRISTOPHER O'CONNOR
Dean of Faculty: Rev. STEPHEN E. SALOCKS
Dean of Students: Rev. CHRISTOPHER K. O'CONNOR
Dir of Communication and Devt: Dr KATHLEEN HECK
Dir of Finance and Operations: RICHARD A. FLAHERTY
Librarian: Rev. Mgr LAURENCE W. MCGRATH
Library of 171,000 vols
Number of teachers: 22
Number of students: 80 (full-time)
Publication: *The Saint John's Seminary Magazine* (2 a year)

SCHOOL OF THE MUSEUM OF FINE ARTS

230 The Fenway, Boston, MA 02115
Telephone: (617) 267-6100
E-mail: admissions@smfa.edu
Internet: www.smfa.edu
Founded 1876
Academic year: September to May
Areas of study incl. film, painting and performance, studio art
Pres.: CHRISTOPHER BRATTON
Provost and Dir of Devt: DAN POTEET
Vice-Pres. and Dean of Enrolment: ERIC THOMPSON
Vice-Pres. for Institutional Advancement and External Relations: ANNE COWIE
Dean of Admissions: ERIC THOMPSON
Dean of Faculty: FRITZ BUEHNER
Dean of School: DEBORAH H. DLUHY
Registrar: DAN JOHNSON
Librarian: DARIN MURPHY
Library of 130,000 vols
Number of teachers: 145 (full-time)
Number of students: 785 (612 undergraduate and diploma, 173 graduate)

SIMMONS COLLEGE

300 The Fenway, Boston, MA 02115
Telephone: (617) 521-2000
E-mail: ugadm@simmons.edu
Internet: www.simmons.edu
Founded 1899
Private control
Academic year: September to May
Pres.: HELEN G. DRINAN
Provost: CHARLENA SEYMOUR
Sr Vice-Pres. for Admin. and Finance and Treas.: STEFANO FALCONI
Vice-Pres. and Gen. Counsel: KATHY ROGERS
Vice-Pres. for Advancement: MARIANNE LORD
Vice-Pres. for Marketing and Admission: CHERYL HOWARD
Dean of Student Life: SARAH NEIL
Registrar: DONNA DOLAN
Dir of Libraries: DAPHNE HARRINGTON
Library of 225,000 vols, 53,000 journals, 8,000 audiovisual items
Number of teachers: 550 (232 full-time, 318 part-time)
Number of students: 5,000
Publications: *Abafazi*, *Essays and Studies*, *Now*, *Sidelines* (2 a year), *Simmons News*, *Simmons Review* (3 a year)

DEANS

College of Arts and Sciences: Prof. Dr RENÉE WHITE

Graduate School of Library and Information Sciences: Dr MICHÈLE V. CLOONAN
School of Management: CATHY MINEHAN
School of Nursing and Health Studies: Dr JUDY BEAL
School of Social Work: Dr STEFAN KRUG

SMITH COLLEGE

Northampton, MA 01063
Telephone: (413) 584-2700
E-mail: admission@smith.edu
Internet: www.smith.edu
Founded 1871
Private control
Academic year: September to May
Areas of study incl. computer science, dance, E Asian languages and cultures, E Asian studies, economics, education and child study, engineering, English language and literature, environmental science and policy, film studies
Pres.: KATHLEEN McCARTNEY
Provost and Dean of Faculty: MARILYN R. SCHUSTER
Vice-Pres. for Advancement: PATRICIA JACKSON
Vice-Pres. for Campus Life and Dean of College: MAUREEN MAHONEY
Vice-Pres. for Devt: PATRICIA JACKSON
Vice-Pres. for Finance and Admin.: RUTH CONSTANTINE
Dean for Admission: DEBRA D. SHAVER
Dean for Students: JULIANNE OHOTNICKY
Registrar: TRICIA O'NEILL
Dir for Libraries: CHRISTOPHER LORING
Library of 1,200,000 vols
Number of teachers: 300 (285 full-time, 15 part-time)
Number of students: 2,780 (2,681 undergraduate, 99 postgraduate)
Publications: *Alumnae Quarterly* (4 a year), *Amazonian Literary Review* (1 a year), *Meridians*

SPRINGFIELD COLLEGE

263 Alden St, Springfield, MA 01109-3797
Telephone: (413) 748-3000
E-mail: admissions@spfldcol.edu
Internet: www.spfldcol.edu
Founded 1885
Private control
Academic year: August to May
Pres.: Dr RICHARD B. FLYNN
Exec. Vice-Pres.: JILL F. RUSSELL
Vice-Pres. for Academic Affairs: Dr JEAN A. WYLD
Vice-Pres. for Devt and Alumni Relations: JOHN WHITE
Vice-Pres. for Finance and Admin.: JOHN MAILHOT
Vice-Pres. for Institutional Advancement: DAVID FRABONI
Vice-Pres. for Student Affairs: Dr DAVID G. BRAVERMAN
Registrar: KEITH INGALLS
Dir of Library: ANDREA TAUPIER
Library of 187,358 vols, 25,586 bound periodicals
Number of teachers: 200 full-time
Number of students: 3,400

DEANS

School of Arts, Science and Professional Studies: Dr ANNE HERZOG
School of Health, Physical Education, and Recreation: Dr CHARLES REDMOND
School of Health Sciences and Rehabilitation Studies: Dr DAVID J. MILLER
School of Human Services: Dr ROBERT J. WILLEY, JR

School of Social Work: Dr FRANCINE J. VECCHIOLLA

STONEHILL COLLEGE

320 Washington St, Easton, MA 02357
Telephone: (508) 565-1000
E-mail: admissions@stonehill.edu
Internet: www.stonehill.edu
Founded 1948
Private control
Academic year: September to May
Areas of study incl. computer science, criminology, history, interdisciplinary studies, mathematics, philosophy
Pres.: Rev. MARK T. CREGAN
Vice-Pres. for Academic Affairs and Provost: KATIE CONBOY
Vice-Pres. for Advancement: FRANCIS X. DILLON
Vice-Pres. for Enrolment Management and Marketing: CHRISTOPHER LYDON
Vice-Pres. for Finance and Treas.: JEANNE FINLAYSON
Vice-Pres. for Mission: Rev. JOHN DENNING
Vice-Pres. for Student Affairs: Rev. JOHN DENNING
Dean of Faculty: KAREN TALENTINO
Registrar: JOHN PESTANA
Dir of Library: SUSAN CONANT
Library of 194,587 vols
Number of teachers: 150 (full-time)
Number of students: 2,620
Publication: *Stonehill Alumni Magazine* (2 a year)

SUFFOLK UNIVERSITY

8 Ashburton Place, Boston, MA 02108-2770
Telephone: (617) 573-8000
E-mail: admission@suffolk.edu
Internet: www.suffolk.edu
Founded 1906 as Suffolk School of Law, current name adopted 1937
Private control
Academic year: September to August
Int. campus in Spain; satellite campus in Lawrence
Pres.: JAMES McCARTHY
Provost and Academic Vice-Pres.: BARRY BROWN (acting)
Vice-Pres. and Treas.: DANIELLE MANNING (acting)
Vice-Pres. for Enrolment Planning and Management: WALTER CAFFEY
Vice-Pres. for Govt Relations and Community Affairs: JOHN A. NUCCI
Dean of College: KENNETH S. GREENBERG
Dean of Student Affairs: NANCY C. STOLL
Dir of Law Library: BETSY McKENZIE
Library of 241,000 vols, 2,070 periodicals, 396,250 microforms
Number of teachers: 400
Number of students: 9,560
Publications: *Journal of Health & Biomedical Law* (2 a year), *Journal of High Technology Law*, *Salamander* (2 a year), *Suffolk Alumni Magazine* (4 a year), *Suffolk Business Magazine* (1 a year), *Suffolk Law School Alumni Magazine* (2 a year), *Suffolk Transnational Law Review* (2 a year), *Suffolk University Law Review* (4 a year), *The Advocate*, *The Suffolk Journal*, *Venture* (1 a year)

DEANS

College of Arts and Sciences: KENNETH S. GREENBERG
Law School: CAMILLE A. NELSON
Sawyer Business School: WILLIAM J. O'NEILL, JR

TUFTS UNIVERSITY

Medford, MA 02155
Telephone: (617) 628-5000
E-mail: admissions.inquiry@ase.tufts.edu
Internet: www.tufts.edu
Founded 1852
Private control
Academic year: September to May
Campuses in Boston, France, Grafton, Somerville, Talloires
Pres.: ANTHONY P. MONACO
Provost and Sr Vice-Pres.: PEGGY NEWELL
Exec. Vice-Pres.: PATRICIA L. CAMPBELL
Vice-Pres. for Finance and Treas.: THOMAS S. McGURTY
Vice-Pres. for Information Technology and Chief Information Officer: DAVID KAHLE
Vice-Pres. for Operations: RICHARD W. REYNOLDS
Vice-Pres. for Univ. Advancement: BRIAN K. LEE
Vice-Pres. for Univ. Relations: MARY R. JEKA
Dean of Student Affairs: BRUCE REITMAN
Dean of Student Services: PAUL STANTON
Dean of Admissions and Financial Aid: LAURIE A. HURLEY
Dir of Library: JEFF KOSOKOFF
Library of 1,214,414 vols, contained in 4 libraries on 3 campuses
Number of teachers: 1,260
Number of students: 9,660
Publications: *International Journal of Middle East Studies*, *Tufts Health and Nutrition Letter*, *Tufts Journal*, *Tufts Medicine*, *Tufts Veterinary Medicine* (2 a year)

DEANS

Cummings School of Medicine: DEBORAH T. KOCHEVAR
Fletcher School of Law and Diplomacy: STEPHEN W. BOSWORTH
Gerald J. and Dorothy Friedman School of Nutrition Science and Policy: ROBIN KANAREK
Graduate School of Arts and Sciences: LYNNE PEPALL
Jonathan M. Tisch College of Citizenship and Public Service: ALAN D. SOLOMONT
Sackler School of Graduate Biomedical Sciences: NAOMI ROSENBERG
School of Arts and Sciences: JOANNE BERGER-SWEENEY
School of Dental Medicine: HUW F. THOMAS
School of Engineering: LINDA M. ABRIOLA
School of Medicine: HARRIS BERMAN

PROFESSORS

ADELMAN, L., Pathology
ADLER, D., Psychiatry
AFSAR, M., Electrical and Computer Engineering
ALEXANDER, S., Paediatric Dentistry
ALONSO, J., Romance Languages
AMATO, R., Paediatrics
AMBADDY, N., Psychology
AMMONS, E., English
AMPOLA, M., Paediatrics
ARIAS, I., Physiology
AUNER, J., Music
AZZOUNI, J., Philosophy
BACHOVCHIN, W., Biochemistry
BACOW, L., Public Health and Family Medicine
BAGHDIANTZ-McCABE, I., History
BANKOFF, M., Radiology
BANKS, H., Orthopaedic Surgery
BARRETT, D., Urology
BAUM, J., Ophthalmology
BEINFELD, M., Pharmacology and Experimental Therapeutics
BELSKY, M., Orthopaedic Surgery
BERESFORD, J., Obstetrics and Gynaecology
BERG, J., Clinical Sciences
BERKMAN, E., Medicine

BERMAN, H., Public Health and Family Medicine
BERNSTEIN, J., Music
BERRY, J., Political Science
BHARUCHA, J., Neuroscience
BIANCHI, D., Paediatrics
BIERBAUM, B., Orthopaedic Surgery
BIRKETT, D., Surgery
BLACHER, R., Psychiatry
BLOOMQUIST, E., Physiology
BLUMENTHAL, S., Psychiatry
BOGHOSIAN, B., Mathematics
BORGERS, C., Mathematics
BOUDREAU, F., Obstetrics and Gynaecology
BOYER, M., Public Health and Family Medicine
BRATT, R., Urban and Environmental Policy and Planning
BRAWERMAN, G., Biochemistry
BRIDGES, R., Biomedical Sciences
BRISS, B., Orthodontics
BRODER, M., Medicine
BRODY, C., Computer Science
BRONSON, R., Biomedical Sciences
BROWN, B., Paediatrics
BROWN, W., Neurology
BROWN, W., Psychiatry
BULLOCK, P., Biochemistry
BURKMAN, R., Obstetrics and Gynaecology
BUSHNELL, E., Psychology
CALLOW, A., Surgery
CAMER, S., Surgery
CAMILLI, A., Molecular Biology and Microbiology
CARPINITO, G., Urology
CARTER, B., Radiology
CASSADY, J., Radiation Oncology
CASTELLOT, J., Anatomy and Cellular Biology
CAVAZOS, L., Public Health and Family Medicine
CEBE, P., Physics and Astronomy
CELLI, B., Medicine
CEPEDA, M., Anaesthesiology
CETRULO, C., Obstetrics and Gynaecology
CHAPMAN, R., Prosthodontics and Operative Dentistry
CHAPRA, S., Civil and Environmental Engineering
CHARM, S., Biochemistry
CHECHILE, R., Psychology
CHELMOW, D., Obstetrics and Gynaecology
CHEN, J., General Dentistry
CHEW, F., Biology
CHOI, I., Radiology
CHONG, F., Pathology
COCHRAN, B., Physiology
COCHRANE, D., Biology
COE, N., Surgery
COFFIN, J., Microbiology—Basic Science
COHEN, L., Psychiatry
CONKLIN, J., Sociology
CONNOLLY, N., Anaesthesiology
COOK, R., Psychology
COOPER, A., Pathology
COSGROVE, G., Neurosurgery
COTTER, S., Clinical Sciences
CRANE, G., Classics
CRAVEN, D., Medicine
CRISCITIELLO, M., Medicine
DAMASSA, D., Anatomy and Cellular Biology
DARLING, D., Radiology
DAVIS, J., Paediatrics
DAWSON-HUGHES, B., Medicine
DENNETT, D., Philosophy
DESFORGES, J., Medicine
DEVIGNE, R., Political Science
DEWALD, R., Chemistry
DICE, J., Physiology
DIGGES, D., English
DODMAN, N., Clinical Sciences
DOGEL, Y., Pathology
DOHERTY, R., Prosthodontics and Operative Dentistry
DRACHMAN, V., History
DRAPKIN, M., Medicine
DUCIBELLA, T., Obstetrics and Gynaecology

DUKER, J., Ophthalmology
DUNLAP, K., Neuroscience
DWYER, J., Medicine
EASTERBROOKS, A., Child Development
EDGERS, L., Civil and Environmental Engineering
ENGELKING, L., Biomedical Sciences
ENGELKING, L., Physiology
ENGELMAN, R., Surgery
EPSTEIN, L., Psychiatry
EPSTEIN, S., Medicine
ERNST, S., Biology
ESTES, N., Medicine
FANBURG, B., Medicine
FEIG, L., Biochemistry
FEINGOLD, D., Dermatology
FELDMAN, D., Child Development
FERNANDEZ-ARMESTO, F., History
FERRONE, J., Orthopaedic Surgery
FIELDING, R., Medicine
FLAX, M., Pathology
FLORES, A., Paediatrics
FLYNN, C., English
FLYTZANI-STEPHANOPOULOS, M., Chemical Engineering
FOLSTEIN, M., Psychiatry
FORD, L., Physics and Astronomy
FORGAC, M., Physiology
FOSTER, E., Pathology
FRANK, E., Physiology
FRANTZ, I., Paediatrics
FREEMAN, R., Surgery
FREIDBERG, S., Neurosurgery
FRIEDBERG, R., Pathology
FRIEDMAN, L., Medicine
FRIEDMANN, P., Surgery
FRISKEN, S., Computer Science
FYLER, J., English
GAASCH, W., Medicine
GALBURT, R., Oral and Maxillofacial Surgery
GALPER, J., Medicine
GANDA, K., General Dentistry
GANG, D., Pathology
GARLICK, J., Cell, Molecular, Developmental Biology
GARVEN, G., Geology
GASARIAN, G., Romance Languages
GELFAND, J., Medicine
GEORGAKIS, C., Chemical Engineering
GERMAIN, M., Medicine
GILL, M., Psychiatry
GITTLEMAN, S., German, Russian, Asian Languages and Literatures
GOLDBERG, E., Microbiology—Basic Science
GOLDBERG, M., Orthopaedic Surgery
GOLDENBERG, D., Medicine
GOLDIN, B., Public Health and Family Medicine
GOLDSTEIN, G., Physics and Astronomy
GONZALEZ, F., Mathematics
GOODMAN, E., Paediatrics
GORBACH, S., Public Health and Family Medicine
GORSON, K., Neurology
GOTTLIEB, A., Dermatology
GRACE, N., Medicine
GRADY, G., Medicine
GREEN, D., Endodontics
GREENBLATT, D., Pharmacology and Experimental Therapeutics
GREIF, R., Mechanical Engineering
GUERTIN, R., Physics and Astronomy
GUNTHER, L., Physics and Astronomy
GUSS, D., Anthropology
GUTIERREZ, M., Mathematics
HAAS, T., Chemistry
HAHN, M., Mathematics
HALL, S., Anaesthesiology
HAMMER, N., Prosthodontics and Operative Dentistry
HAMMER, R., Psychiatry
HAMPF, F., Radiology
HAND, R., Medicine
HANNENBERG, A., Anaesthesiology
HARDER, D., Psychology
HARRINGTON, J., Medicine

HARTMANN, E., Psychiatry
HARTNELL, G., Radiology
HASSELBLATT, B., Mathematics
HAWLEY, C., Periodontology
HAYDON, P., Neuroscience
HAYES, C., Public Health and Community Service
HEIJIN, C., Psychiatry
HENNEMAN, P., Emergency Medicine
HERMAN, I., Physiology
HERN, D., Prosthodontics and Operative Dentistry
HESKETH, P., Medicine
HIBBERD, P., Medicine
HIGBY, D., Medicine
HIGGENS, T., Medicine
HILL, N., Medicine
HINDS, P., Radiation Oncology
HINES, E., Civil and Environmental Engineering
HIRATA, H., German, Russian, Asian Languages and Literatures
HIRAYAMA, H., Prosthodontics and Operative Dentistry
HOLCOMB, P., Psychology
HOMER, M., Radiology
HOPWOOD, J., Electrical and Computer Engineering
HOWE, E., Romance Languages
HSU, L., Psychiatry
HUBER, B., Pathology
HUGHES, W., Physiology
HUVOS, A., Medicine
INOUYE, C., German, Russian, Asian Languages and Literatures
IOANNIDES, Y., Economics
ISBERG, R., Microbiology—Basic Science
ISLAM, S., Civil and Environmental Engineering
JACKENDOFF, R., Philosophy
JACKSON, F., Neuroscience
JACOB, M., Neuroscience
JACOB, R., Computer Science
JACOBSON, S., Anatomy and Cellular Biology
JALAL, A., History
JANKOWSKI, J., Psychiatry
JAY, D., Physiology
JENNINGS, J., Urban and Environmental Policy and Planning
JENSEN, H., Paediatrics
JIANG, L., Medicine
JOHNSON, V., German, Russian, Asian Languages and Literatures
JONES, E., Paediatrics
JOSEPH, P., Sociology
KACHANOV, M., Mechanical Engineering
KAHN, M., Oral Pathology
KANAREK, R., Psychology
KAPLAN, D., Biomedial Engineering
KARAS, R., Medicine
KARMODY, C., Otolaryngology/Head and Neck Surgery
KASSIRER, J., Medicine
KAUER, J., Neuroscience
KEANE, T., Psychiatry
KENLER, K., Obstetrics and Gynaecology
KENNEY, P., Surgery
KENNISON, R., Obstetrics and Gynaecology
KENNY, J., Chemistry
KILARU, P., Anaesthesiology
KILMER, M., Mathematics
KISLIUK, R., Biochemistry
KLAPHOLZ, H., Obstetrics and Gynaecology
KLAUBER, G., Urology
KLINGEMANN, H., Medicine
KONSTAM, M., Medicine
KOPELMAN, R., Medicine
KOPIN, A., Medicine
KOSCH, P., Paediatrics
KOSOWSKY, B., Medicine
KREAM, R., Pharmacology
KRETSCHMAR, C., Paediatrics
KRIMSKY, S., Urban and Environmental Policy and Planning
KRINSKY, N., Biochemistry
KROLL, A., Ophthalmology

KULIG, J., Paediatrics
KUMAMOTO, C., Molecular Biology and Microbiology
KUMAR, K., Chemistry
KUMAR, M., Biomedical Sciences
LANG, K., Physics and Astronomy
LASSER, R., Electrical and Computer Engineering
LAU, J., Medicine
LAURENT, P., History
LAURENZI, G., Medicine
LECHAN, R., Medicine
LEE, M., Medicine
LEIVILLE-WEBSTER, C., Clinical Sciences
LERNER, R., Child Development
LEUPP, G., History
LEVESQUE, P., Anaesthesiology
LEVEY, A., Medicine
LEVINE, H., Medicine
LEVY, S., Molecular Biology and Microbiology
LEWIS, S., Biology
LIBERTINO, J., Urology
LICHTENSTEIN, A., Public Health and Family Medicine
LINSENMAYER, T., Anatomy and Cellular Biology
LIPTZIN, B., Psychiatry
LISCUM, L., Physiology
LITVAK, J., English
LO, T., Radiation Oncology
LOPEZ, M., Surgery
LUNDY, L., Obstetrics and Gynaecology
McCARTHY, H., Surgery
McCARTHY, J., Orthopaedic Surgery
McCAULEY, R., Radiology
MacDONNELL, K., Medicine
MACKEY, W., Surgery
MADIAS, N., Medicine
MADOFF, M., Public Health and Family Medicine
MAHLER, D., Anaesthesiology
MALAMY, M., Microbiology—Basic Science
MALCHOW, H., History
MANN, W., Physics and Astronomy
MANNO, V., Mechanical Engineering
MARCHANT, D., Obstetrics and Gynaecology
MARRONE, S., History
MAZZOTTI, J., Romance Languages
MEHTA, N., General Dentistry
MEIRI, K., Anatomy and Cellular Biology
MEISSNER, H., Paediatrics
MENDELSOHN, M., Medicine
METCALF, G., Economics
MEYDANI, S., Immunology
MICZEK, K., Psychiatry
MICZEK, K., Psychology
MILLER, E., Electrical and Computer Engineering
MILLER, K., Medicine
MILNER, L., Paediatrics
MIRKIN, S., Biology
MIRKIN, S., Genetics
MITCHELL, G., Obstetrics and Gynaecology
MOORE, C., Microbiology—Basic Science
MOREHEAD, J., Anatomy and Cellular Biology
MORGAN, J., Medicine
MULHOLLAND, D., History
MUNSAT, T., Neurology
MURPHY, R., Medicine
MUST, A., Public Health and Family Medicine
NAGINSKI, I., Romance Languages
NAIMI, S., Medicine
NALEBUFF, E., Orthopaedic Surgery
NAPIER, A., Physics and Astronomy
NAPIER, S., German, Russian, Asian Languages and Literatures
NASRAWAY, S., Surgery
NAVAB, F., Medicine
NEUMANN, P., Medicine
NEWBERG, A., Radiology
NIELSEN, H., Paediatrics
NITECKI, Z., Mathematics
NOLLER, K., Obstetrics and Gynaecology
NOONAN, J., Electrical and Computer Engineering

NORMAN, G., Economics
NORTON, R., Medicine
O'DONNELL, K., Surgery
O'DONNELL, T., Surgery
O'GRADY, J., Obstetrics and Gynaecology
OHMAN, J., Medicine
O'LEARY, D., Radiology
OLIVER, W., Physics and Astronomy
ORDOVAS, J., Genetics
OSTRANDER, S., Sociology
OTIS, C., Pathology
OXENKRUG, G., Psychiatry
PAGE, D., Surgery
PAIS, V., Urology
PALMER, C., Public Health and Community Service
PANDIAN, N., Medicine
PANJWANI, N., Ophthalmology
PAPAGEORGE, M., Oral and Maxillofacial Surgery
PAPAS, A., General Dentistry
PATTERSON, J., Medicine
PAUKER, S., Medicine
PAUL, R., Radiology
PAYNE, D., Surgery
PECHENIK, J., Biology
PENNINCK, D., Clinical Sciences
PEPPER, M., Public Health and Family Medicine
PEREIRA, B., Medicine
PERRIN, E., Paediatrics
PERRIN, M., Pathology
PERRONE, R., Medicine
PLAUT, A., Medicine
POLAK, J., Radiology
PORTNEY, K., Political Science
PREIS, D., Electrical and Computer Engineering
QUINTO, E., Mathematics
RABINOVICI, R., Surgery
RABSON, A., Pathology
RANKIN, C., Endodontics
REECE, R., Paediatrics
REED, J., Biology
REICHLIN, S., Medicine
REID, P., Classics
REITER, E., Paediatrics
REUBEN, S., Anaesthesiology
REUTER, K., Radiology
REYNOLDS, R., Anaesthesiology
RICHARD, M., Philosophy
RICHARDS, D., Economics
RICHMOND, J., Orthopaedic Surgery
RIDGE, J., Geology
ROAF, E., Anaesthesiology
ROBBINS, A., Public Health and Family Medicine
ROBERTS, P., Surgery
ROGERS, C., Mechanical Engineering
ROHRER, R., Surgery
ROMERO, C., German, Russian, Asian Languages and Literatures
ROMERO, L., Biology
ROSE, D., Medicine
ROSENBERG, I., Physiology
ROSENBERG, M., Oral and Maxillofacial Surgery
ROSENBERG, N., Pathology
ROSENBLATT, M., Physiology
ROWLAND, T., Paediatrics
RUBENSTEIN, J., Medicine
RUBY, L., Orthopaedic Surgery
RUSH, J., Clinical Sciences
RUSSELL, R., Medicine
SABIN, T., Neurology
SADEGHI-NEJAD, A., Paediatrics
SADOWSKY, N., Radiology
SAFAII, H., Pathology
SAHAGIAN, G., Physiology
SAIGAL, A., Mechanical Engineering
SAMO, R., Radiology
SANAYEI, M., Civil and Environmental Engineering
SAPERSTEIN, G., Environmental and Population Health

SAWKAT, A., Pharmacology and Experimental Therapeutics
SCHAEFER, E., Medicine
SCHALLER, J., Paediatrics
SCHLIEMANN, A., Education
SCHMIDT, K., Anaesthesiology
SCHNEPS, J., Physics and Astronomy
SCHOETZ, D., Surgery
SCHOLZ, F., Radiology
SCHREIBER, J., Paediatrics
SCHULTZ, M., Chemistry
SCHWARTZ, A., Clinical Sciences
SEDDON, J., Ophthalmology
SELKER, H., Medicine
SENELICK, L., Drama and Dance
SHADER, R., Pharmacology
SHAUGHNESSY, A., Public Health and Family Medicine
SHEN, E., Pathology
SHIKORA, S., Surgery
SHOEMAKER, C., Biomedical Sciences
SHUCART, W., Neurosurgery
SIEGEL, E., Biology
SILBERMAN, E., Psychiatry
SILVA, J., Medicine
SINGH, I., Prosthodontics and Operative Dentistry
SKIEST, D., Medicine
SLIWA, K., Physics and Astronomy
SMITH, G., Philosophy
SMITH, L., Obstetrics and Gynaecology
SMITH, T., Political Science
SNYDMAN, D., Medicine
SONENSCHEIN, A., Microbiology—Basic Science
SONNENSCHEIN, C., Anatomy and Cellular Biology
SORBERA, R., Oral and Maxillofacial Surgery
SORGER, K., Pathology
SOTO, A., Anatomy and Cellular Biology
SOUVAINE, D., Computer Science
SPOLAORE, E., Economics
STEARNS, N., Medicine
STECHENBERG, B., Paediatrics
STEER, M., Surgery
STELLER, M., Obstetrics and Gynaecology
STOLOW, R., Chemistry
STRAUSS, G., Medicine
STROM, J., Medicine
SUNG, N., Chemical Engineering
SYLVIA, W., Jr, Prosthodontics and Operative Dentistry
TALAMO, B., Neuroscience
TARLOV, S., Neuroscience
TAYLOR, H., Psychology
TEIXIDOR I BIGAS, M., Mathematics
TERES, D., Medicine
TERRES, G., Physiology
TERRONO, A., Orthopaedic Surgery
THEOHARIDES, T., Pharmacology and Experimental Therapeutics
THORLEY-LAWSON, D., Pathology
TICKLE-DEGNEN, L., Occupational Therapy
TILLMAN, H., General Dentistry
TISCHLER, A., Pathology
TOBIN, R., Physics and Astronomy
TRIMMER, B., Biology
TSICHLIS, P., Medicine
TUERK, I., Urology
TURKSOY-MARCUS, R., Obstetrics and Gynaecology
TURNER, R., Orthopaedic Surgery
TWITCHELL, T., Neurology
TZIPORI, S., Biomedical Sciences
UEDA, R., History
UMLAS, J., Pathology
VALAES, T., Paediatrics
VAN ETTEN, R., Medicine
VILENKIN, A., Physics and Astronomy
VOGEL, R., Civil and Environmental Engineering
WAIT, R., Surgery
WALT, D., Chemistry
WANKE, C., Medicine
WAX, F., Dermatology
WAZER, D., Radiation Oncology

WECHSLER, J., Art and Art History
WEILER, K., Education
WEINER, A., Oral Diagnostics
WEINSTOCK, J., Medicine
WEISS, R., Mathematics
WERTLEIB, D., Child Development
WIDMER, G., Biomedical Sciences
WILL KUO, L., Orthodontics
WILSON, I., Medicine
WILSON, J., English
WINN, P., History
WITTENBERG, S., Medicine
WLEZIEN, R., Mechanical Engineering
WOLF, M., Child Development
WOLFE, L., Paediatrics
WONG, J., Medicine
WORTIS, H., Pathology
WRIGHT, A., Microbiology—Basic Science
WU, J., Neurosurgery
YEE, A., Biochemistry
YUCEL, E., Radiology
ZAMENHOF, R., Radiation Oncology
ZINMAN, L., Urology

UNIVERSITY OF MASSACHUSETTS

225 Franklin St, 33rd Fl., Boston, MA 02110
333 S St, Suite 400, Shrewsbury, MA 01545-4169

Telephone: (617) 287-7100
E-mail: mail@admissions.umass.edu
Internet: www.massachusetts.edu

Founded 1863 as Massachusetts Agricultural College, current name adopted 1947

Pres.: ROBERT L. CARET
Exec. Vice-Pres.: JAMES R. JULIAN
Sr Vice-Pres. for Academic Affairs, Student Affairs and Int. Relations: Dr MARCELLETTE G. WILLIAMS
Vice-Pres. for Admin. and Finance, Treas. and Controller: CHRISTINE M. WILDA
Vice-Pres. for Economic Devt: THOMAS CHMURA
Vice-Pres. for Information Services, Chief Information Officer and CEO for UMassOnline: DAVID GRAY
Vice-Pres. for Management and Fiscal Affairs and Treas.: STEPHEN LENHARDT
Vice-Pres. for Univ. Advancement: KATHERINE V. SMITH
Number of students: 60,000 ...

CONSTITUENT UNIVERSITIES

University of Massachusetts, Amherst

Amherst, MA 01003
Telephone: (413) 545-0111
Internet: www.umass.edu

Founded 1863 as Massachusetts Agricultural College, present name and status 1947
State control
Academic year: September to June

Chancellor: KUMBLE R. SUBBASWAMY
Provost and Sr Vice-Chancellor for Academic Affairs: JAMES V. STAROS
Vice-Chancellor for Admin. and Finance: JAMES SHEEHAN
Vice-Chancellor for Devt and Alumni Relations: MICHAEL A. LETO
Vice Chancellor for Research and Engagement: MICHAEL MALONE
Vice-Chancellor for Student Affairs and Campus Life: JEAN KIM
Vice-Chancellor for Univ. Relations: JOHN KENNEDY
Dean for Students: ENKU GELAYE
Registrar: JOHN LENZI
Dir for Libraries: JAY SCHAFER
Library: 8m. vols
Number of teachers: 1,170 (full-time)
Number of students: 27,570
Publication: *The Massachusetts Review* (4 a year)

DEANS

College of Engineering: Dr THEODORE DJAFERIS
College of Humanities and Fine Arts: JULIA C. HAYES
College of Natural Resources and the Environment: STEVE GOODWIN
College of Natural Sciences and Mathematics: GEORGE M. LANGFORD
College of Social and Behavioral Sciences: ROBERT S. FELDMAN
Commonwealth College: Dr PRISCILLA M. CLARKSON
Graduate School: JOHN MULLIN
Isenberg School of Management: MARK A. FULLER
School of Education: CHRISTINE B. McCORMICK
School of Nursing: Dr STEPHEN J. CAVANAGH
School of Public Health and Health Sciences: C. MARJORIE AELION.

ASSOCIATED INSTITUTE

Stockbridge School of Agriculture: Amherst, MA 01003; tel. (413) 545-2222; e-mail stockbridgeschool@nre.umass.edu; internet www.umass.edu/stockbridge; f. 1918; Dir MARTHA G. BAKER

University of Massachusetts, Boston

100 Morrissey Blvd, Boston, MA 02125-3393
Telephone: (617) 287-6000
E-mail: enrollment.info@umb.edu
Internet: www.umb.edu

Founded 1964 as an urban campus of Univ. of Massachusetts
State control
Language of instruction: English
Academic year: September to December andJanuary to May

Chancellor: J. KEITH MOTLEY
Provost and Sr Vice-Chancellor for Academic Affairs: WINSTON LANGLEY
Vice-Chancellor for Admin. and Finance: ELLEN M. O'CONNOR
Vice-Chancellor for Athletics and Recreation, Special Projects and Programmes: CHARLIE TITUS
Vice-Chancellor for Enrollment Management: LISA JOHNSON
Vice-Chancellor for Govt Relations and Public Affairs: EDWARD LAMBERT
Vice-Chancellor for Univ. Advancement: GINA CAPPELLO
Co-Vice-Chancellor for Student Affairs: LISA BUENAVENTURA
Co-Vice-Chancellor for Student Affairs: JAMES OVERTON
Library of 600,000 vols
Number of teachers: 1,090
Number of students: 16,000

DEANS

College of Advancing and Professional Studies: PHILIP DiSALVIO
College of Education and Human Devt: FELICIA L. WILCZENSKI
College of Liberal Arts: DAVID TERKLA
College of Management: PHILIP L. QUAGLIERI
College of Nursing and Health Sciences: ANAHID KULWICKI
College of Public and Community Service: ANNA MADISON
College of Science and Mathematics: ANDREW GROSOVSKY
Graduate Studies and Intercollegiate Programmes: ZHONG GUO XIA
Honors College: RAJINI SRIKANTH
John W. McCormack Graduate School of Global and Policy Studies: IRA JACKSON
School for the Environment: ROBYN HANNIGAN
School for Global Inclusion and Social Development: WILLIAM E. KIERNAN

University of Massachusetts, Dartmouth

285 Old Westport Rd, N Dartmouth, MA 02747-2300
Telephone: (508) 999-8000
E-mail: admissions@umassd.edu
Internet: www.umassd.edu

Founded 1895
State control
Language of instruction: English
Academic year: September to May

Chancellor: Dr DIVINA GROSSMAN
Provost and Vice-Chancellor for Academic and Student Affairs: Dr MOHAMMAD KARIM
Vice-Chancellor, Chief Operating Officer for Admin. and Fiscal Services: MARK PREBLE
Dir for Undergraduate Admissions: MICHAEL LYNCH
Registrar: CHRISTINE KAYLOR
Dean for Library Services: TERRANCE BURTON
Library of 43,887 vols
Number of teachers: 620 (375 full-time, 245 part-time)
Number of students: 9,050
Publications: *Dart Magazine* (2 a year), *Portuguese Literary and Cultural Studies* (1 a year), *TEMPER* (1 a year)

DEANS

Charlton College of Business: Dr ANGAPPA GUNASEKARAN
College of Arts and Sciences: Dr JEANNETTE RILEY
College of Engineering: Dr ROBERT E. PECK
College of Nursing: Dr JAMES A. FAIN
College of Visual and Performing Arts: Dr ADRIAN TIÓ
Professional and Continuing Education: Dr JOY McGUIRL-HODLEY
School of Law: Dr MARY LU BILEK
School of Marine Science and Technology: Dr STEVEN E. LOHRENZ

University of Massachusetts, Lowell

1 University Ave, Lowell, MA 01854
Telephone: (978) 934-4000
Internet: www.uml.edu

Founded 1894 as Lowell Normal School and Lowell Textile School, merged in 1975 to form Univ. of Lowell, present name and status 1991
s control
Academic year: September to June

Chancellor: MARTY MEEHAN
Exec. Vice-Chancellor: Dr JACQUELINE MOLONEY
Provost and Vice-Chancellor for Academic Affairs: Dr AHMED ABDELAL
Vice-Chancellor for Admin., Finance and Facilities: JOANNE YESTRAMSKI
Vice-Chancellor for Advancement: EDWARD CHIU
Vice-Chancellor for Univ. Relations: PATRICIA McCAFFERTY
Dean for Enrolment and Student Success: THOMAS TAYLOR
Dean for Student Affairs: LARRY SIEGEL
Registrar: PATRICIA A. DUFF
Library of 396,994 vols (incl. books, serials, microforms, audiovisual materials, ebooks)
Number of teachers: 680 (470 full-time, 210 part-time)
Number of students: 15,430 (9,025 undergraduate, 3,702 graduate, 2,703 continuing education)
Publication: *New Solutions* (environmental and occupational health policy, 4 a year)

DEANS

Education: ANITA GREENWOOD
Engineering: JOHN TING
Fine Arts, Humanities and Social Sciences: NINA COPPENS

Health and Environment: SHORTIE MCKIN-
NEY
Marine Sciences: ROBERT GAMACHE
School of Management: KATHRYN CARTER
Sciences: ROBERT TAMARIN

University of Massachusetts Medical School

55 Lake Ave N, Worcester, MA 01655
Telephone: (508) 856-2000
E-mail: ummscommunications@umassmed
.edu
Internet: www.umassmed.edu
Founded 1962
State control
Chancellor: Dr MICHAEL F. COLLINS
Vice-Chancellor: EDWARD J. KEOHANE
Vice-Chancellor for Admin. and Finance:
ROBERT E. JENAL
Vice-Chancellor and Chief Operating Officer:
JOYCE A. MURPHY
Vice-Chancellor for Devt: CHARLIE J. PAGNAM
Vice-Chancellor for Faculty Affairs: Dr
LUANNE THORNDYKE
Vice-Chancellor for Operations: ROBERT E.
JENAL
Vice-Chancellor for Univ. Relations: ALBERT
SHERMAN
Dean and Exec. Deputy Chancellor: TERRY R.
FLOTTE
Registrar: MICHAEL F. BAKER
Dir for Library Services: ELAINE R. MARTIN
Number of teachers: 810
Number of students: 2,680 (full-time)

DEANS

Graduate School of Biomedical Sciences: Dr
ANTHONY CARRUTHERS (acting)
Graduate School of Nursing: Dr PAULETTE
SEYMOUR ROUTE
School of Medicine: Dr TERRY R. FLOTTE

WELLESLEY COLLEGE

106 Central St, Wellesley, MA 02481
Telephone: (781) 283-1000
E-mail: admission@wellesley.edu
Internet: www.wellesley.edu
Founded 1870
Private control
Liberal arts college for women; depts of
Africana studies, anthropology, art, astron-
omy, biological sciences, chemistry, classical
studies, computer science, E Asian languages
and literatures, economics
Pres.: H. KIM BOTTOMLY
Provost and Dean of College: ANDREW SHEN-
NAN
Vice-Pres. for Admin. and Planning: PATRICIA
M. BYRNE
Vice-Pres. for Finance and Treas.: ANDREW B.
EVANS
Dean of Admissions: JENNIFER DESJARLAIS
Dean of Students: DEBRA DEMEIS (acting)
Registrar and Asst Dean of College: CAROL
SHANMUGARATNAM
Chief Information Officer, Library and Tech-
nology Services: GANESAN RAVISHANKER
Library: 1.68m. vols, 32,000 sound and video
recordings, 16,000 maps
Number of teachers: 330 (253 full-time, 77
part-time)
Number of students: 2,340 (2,192 full-time,
152 part-time)

WENTWORTH INSTITUTE OF TECHNOLOGY

550 Huntington Ave, Boston, MA 02115-5998
Telephone: (617) 989-4590
E-mail: admissions@wit.edu
Internet: www.wit.edu
Founded 1904

Private control
Academic year: August to May
Pres.: Dr ZORICA PANTIC
Vice-Pres. of Academic Affairs and Provost:
RUSSELL PINIZZOTTO
Vice-Pres. for Enrolment Management and
Student Affairs: KEIKO BROOMHEAD
Vice-Pres. for Finance: BOB TOTINO
Vice-Pres. for Institutional Advancement:
BRENDA CROSS-SANCHEZ
Registrar: MATTHEW BURKE
Library Dir: WALTER PUNCH
Library of 75,000 vols
Number of teachers: 140 (full-time)
Number of students: 3,890
Publication: *Wentworth Magazine* (2 a year)

DEANS

College of Architecture, Design and Con-
struction Management: GLENN WIGGINS
College of Arts and Sciences: PATRICK HAF-
FORD
College of Engineering and Technology:
FREDERICK DRISCOLL
College of Professional and Continuing Edu-
cation: LARRY CARR

WESTERN NEW ENGLAND UNIVERSITY

1215 Wilbraham Rd, Springfield, MA 01119
Telephone: (413) 782-3111
E-mail: ugradmis@wne.edu
Internet: www.wne.edu
Founded 1919
Private control
Pres.: ANTHONY S. CAPRIO
Provost and Vice-Pres. for Academic Affairs:
JERRY A. HIRSCH
Vice-Pres. for Advancement: BEVERLY
DWIGHT
Vice-Pres. for Enrolment Management:
CHARLES R. POLLOCK
Vice-Pres. for Finance and Admin.: WILLIAM
KELLEHER
Vice-Pres. for Marketing and External
Affairs: BARBARA A. CAMPANELLA
Vice-Pres. for Student Affairs and Dean of
Students: JEANNE HART-STEFFES
Assoc. Dean for Library and Information
Resources: PAT NEWCOMBE
Library of 783,000 vols
Number of teachers: 205 (full-time)
Number of students: 3,700

DEANS

College of Arts and Sciences: SAEED GHAHRA-
MANI
College of Business: JULIE SICILIANO
College of Engineering: CARL RATHMANN
College of Pharmacy: EVAN ROBINSON
School of Law: ARTHUR R. GAUDIO

WESTFIELD STATE UNIVERSITY

POB 1630, Westfield, MA 01086-1630
577 Western Ave, Westfield, MA 01086
Telephone: (413) 572-5300
E-mail: admissions@wsc.ma.edu
Internet: www.wsc.ma.edu
Founded 1838
State control
Majors in art, biology, business management,
computer information systems, computer sci-
ence, criminal justice, economics, education,
English, environmental sciences, French,
general science, history, mass communica-
tion, mathematics, movement science, multi-
cultural and ethnic studies, music,
philosophy, political science, psychology,
regional planning, social work, sociology,
Spanish, theatre arts, women's studies
Pres.: EVAN DOBELLE

Vice-Pres. for Academic Affairs: Dr LIZ
PRESTON
Vice-Pres. for Admin. and Finance: JERRY
HAYES
Vice-Pres. for Advancement and College
Relations: ROBERT ZIOMEK
Vice-Pres. for Enrolment Management:
CAROL PERSSON
Vice-Pres. for Student Affairs: Dr CARLTON
PICKRON
Registrar: JOHN OHOTNICKY
Library Dir: THOMAS RAFFENSPERGER
Library of 136,000 vols
Number of teachers: 170
Number of students: 3,200

WHEATON COLLEGE

26 East Main St, Norton, MA 02766-2322
Telephone: (508) 286-8200
E-mail: info@wheatoncollege.edu
Internet: www.wheatoncollege.edu
Founded 1834 as female seminary
Private control

Depts of African studies, African-American
studies, American studies, ancient studies,
anthropology, art history, studio art, Asian
studies, astronomy, biochemistry, biology,
chemistry, classics, computer science, devt
studies, diaspora studies, economics, education, English, environmental science, environmental studies, family studies, French,
German, Greek, Hispanic studies, history,
int. relations, Italian studies, Latin, Latin
American studies, legal studies, management, mathematics, mathematics and computer science, mathematics and economics,
music, philosophy, physics and astronomy,
political science, psychobiology, psychology,
public policy studies, religion, Russian and
Russian studies, sociology, statistics, theatre
studies and dance, urban studies, women's
studies
Pres.: RONALD A. CRUTCHER
Provost: LINDA EISENMANN
Vice-Pres. for College Advancement: MARY
M. CASEY
Vice-Pres. for Enrolment and Marketing:
GAIL BERSON
Vice-Pres. for Finance and Admin.: (vacant)
Vice-Pres. for Student Affairs and Dean of
Students: LEE BURDETTE WILLIAMS
Registrar and Dean of Academic Systems:
PATRICIA BROWN SANTILLI
Dir of Library Collns and Access: GLORIA L.
BARKER
Library of 352,700 vols
Number of teachers: 150 (full-time)
Number of students: 1,600
Publications: *Quarterly Magazine, Wheaton
Matters*

WHEELOCK COLLEGE

200 The Riverway, Boston, MA 02215
Telephone: (617) 879-2000
E-mail: registrar@wheelock.edu
Internet: www.wheelock.edu
Founded 1888 as Chauncy-Hall School
Private control
Academic year: September to May
Pres.: JACKIE JENKINS-SCOTT
Vice-Pres. and Chief Financial Officer: ANNE
MARIE MARTORANA
Vice-Pres. for Academic Affairs: Dr JULIE E.
WOLLMAN
Vice-Pres. for Campus Life and Information
Services: ROY SCHIFILLITI
Vice-Pres. for Enrolment Management and
Student Success and Chief Diversity Offi-
cer: Dr ADRIAN K. HAUGABROOK
Vice-Pres. for Institutional Advancement
and Devt: LINDA WELTER

Dean of Students: BARBARA MORGAN
Dir of Academic Resources and Library: BRENDA ECSEDY
Library of 85,000 vols
Number of teachers: 65 (full-time)
Number of students: 1,240
Publication: *Magazine*

DEANS

School of Arts and Sciences: Dr SHIRLEY MALONE-FENNER
School of Education, Social Work, Child Life and Family: DONNA MCKIBBENS

WILLIAMS COLLEGE

Hopkins Hall, 880 Main St, Williamstown, MA 01267
Telephone: (413) 597-3131
E-mail: admission@williams.edu
Internet: www.williams.edu
Founded 1793
Private control

Depts of American studies, anthropology, art, Asian studies, astronomy, astrophysics, biology, chemistry, Chinese, classics, comparative literature, computer science, economics, English, French, geosciences, German, history, Japanese, literary studies, mathematics and statistics, music, philosophy, physics, political economy, political science, psychology, religion, Russian, sociology, Spanish, theatre, women's and gender studies

Pres.: ADAM FALK
Provost: WILLIAM DUDLEY
Vice-Pres. for Finance and Admin. and Treas.: FREDERICK W. PUDDESTER
Vice-Pres. for Operations: STEPHEN P. KLASS
Vice-Pres. for Strategic Planning and Institutional Diversity: MIKE REED
Dean of College: Dr SARAH BOLTON
Dean of Faculty: Dr PETER MURPHY
Dir for Admission: DICK NESBITT
Registrar: BARBARA CASEY
Librarian: DAVID M. PILACHOWSKI

Library of 885,000 vols, 61,000 rare books, 30,500 paper and e-periodicals, 480,000 microtexts, 30,000 sound recordings, 11,000 video cassettes, 368,000 govt documents
Number of teachers: 320
Number of students: 2,050

WORCESTER POLYTECHNIC INSTITUTE

100 Institute Rd, Worcester, MA 01609-2280
Telephone: (508) 831-5000
E-mail: president@wpi.edu
Internet: www.wpi.edu
Founded 1865 as Worcester Co Free Institute of Industrial Science
Private control
Academic year: August to May

Pres.: DENNIS D. BERKEY
Exec. Vice-Pres. and Chief Financial Officer: JEFFREY S. SOLOMON
Provost and Vice-Pres. for Academic Affairs: ERIC OVERSTROM
Sr Vice-Pres. for Enrolment and Institutional Strategy: KRISTIN TICHENOR
Vice-Pres. for Student Affairs and Campus Life: JANET RICHARDSON
Chief Information Officer: DEBORAH SCOTT
Registrar: HEATHER L. JACKSON
Dean of Library Services: TRACEY LEGER-HORNBY

Library of 225,000 vols
Number of teachers: 320
Number of students: 5,300 (3,744 undergraduate, 1,556 graduate)

DEANS

Arts and Sciences: Dr KAREN KASHMANIAN OATES
Corporate and Professional Education: STEPHEN P. FLAVIN
Engineering: SELÇUK GÜÇERI
School of Business: Dr MARK RICE

WORCESTER STATE UNIVERSITY

486 Chandler St, Worcester, MA 01602-2597
Telephone: (508) 929-8000
E-mail: admissions@worcester.edu
Internet: www.worcester.edu
Founded 1874 as Worcester Normal School, present name and status 2010

Depts of biology, business admin. and economics, communication, computer science, criminal justice, education, health sciences, history and political science, languages and literature, mathematics, nursing, philosophy, physical and earth sciences, psychology, sociology, visual and performing arts
Private control
Academic year: September to May

Pres.: BARRY M. MALONEY
Vice-Pres. for Academic Affairs: Dr CHARLES CULLUM
Vice-Pres. for Admin. and Finance: KATHY EICHELROTH
Vice-Pres. for Institutional Advancement: THOMAS M. MCNAMARA
Vice-Pres. for Student Affairs: Dr SIBYL BROWNLEE
Registrar: JULIE A. CHAFFEE
Library Dir: JAMES E. HOGAN

Library of 149,662 vols
Number of teachers: 410
Number of students: 5,370

Publications: *Journal of Graduate Research* (1 a year), *Worcester Statement* (2 a year)

MICHIGAN

ADRIAN COLLEGE

110 S Madison St, Adrian, MI 49221-2575
Telephone: (517) 265-5161
E-mail: admissions@adrian.edu
Internet: www.adrian.edu
Founded 1859
Private control
Academic year: September to May

Depts of accounting and business, art and design, biology, chemistry, communication arts and sciences, earth science, economics, English, environmental science/studies, exercise science/physical education, history, interior design, mathematics, modern languages and cultures, music, philosophy/religion, physics, political science, psychology, sociology, social work and criminal justice, teacher education, theatre

Pres.: Dr JEFFREY R. DOCKING
Exec. Vice-Pres.: CYNTHIA BEAUBIEN
Vice-Pres. and Dean for Academic Affairs: Dr AGNES CALDWELL
Vice-Pres. for Devt: RONALD L. REEVES
Vice-Pres. for Enrolment: FRANK J. HRIBAR
Dean for Students: KRISTI HOTTENSTEIN
Registrar: BRIDGETTE WINSLOW
Head Librarian: DAVID CRUSE

Library of 150,000 vols
Number of teachers: 70
Number of students: 1,650

ALBION COLLEGE

611 E Porter St, Albion, MI 49224
Telephone: (517) 629-1000
E-mail: admission@albion.edu
Internet: www.albion.edu

Founded 1835
Private control
Language of instruction: English
Academic year: August to May

Depts of anthropology and sociology, art, art history, athletic training, biology, chemistry, computer science, earth science, economics and management, English, ethnic studies, French, geological sciences, German, history, international studies, mathematics, music, philosophy, physical education, physics, political science, psychology, public policy, religious studies, Spanish, speech communication, theatre, women's and gender studies

Pres.: Dr MICHAEL FRANDSEN
Provost: Dr SUSAN CONNER
Vice-Pres. for Enrolment Management: JOHN HILLE
Vice-Pres. for Finance and Admin.: JAMES GALBALLY
Vice-Pres. for Student Affairs and Dean of Students: Dr SALLY WALKER
Assoc. Vice-Pres. for Communications: SARAH BRIGGS
Dir for Admission: MANDY DUBIEL
Dir for Career Devt: TROY KASE
Dir for Financial Aid: ANN WHITMER
Dir for Residential Life and Residence Hall
Dir for Fraternities: MICHAEL WADSWORTH
Assoc. Dean for Academic Affairs and Registrar: Dr DREW DUNHAM
Co-Dir for Library: MICHAEL VAN HOUTEN
Co-Dir for Library: CLAUDIA DIAZ

Library of 356,176 vols of books, serial backfiles and govt documents, 88,631 current serial subscriptions, 49,107 microforms, 12,851 video cassettes and audiovisual items, 73,942 ebooks
Number of teachers: 140
Number of students: 1,310

Publication: *Io Triumphe!* (print and online, www.albion.edu/alumni/stay-connected/io-triumphe-magazine)

ALMA COLLEGE

614 W Superior St, Alma, MI 48801
Telephone: (989) 463-7111
E-mail: admissions@alma.edu
Internet: www.alma.edu
Founded 1886
Private control

Depts of health sciences, humanities, natural sciences and social sciences

Pres.: Dr JEFF ABERNATHY
Provost and Vice-Pres. for Academic Affairs: Dr MICHAEL L. SELMON
Vice-Pres. for Advancement: CAROL HYBLE
Vice-Pres. for Enrolment: Dr KAREN S. KLUMPP
Vice-Pres. for Student Life: NICHOLAS A. PICCOLO
Dir for Admissions: BOB GARCIA
Registrar: SUSAN M. DEEL
Library Dir: CAROL ZEILE

Library of 246,000 vols, 1,200 periodicals
Number of teachers: 140 (87 full-time, 52 part-time)
Number of students: 1,420

ANDREWS UNIVERSITY

Berrien Springs, MI 49104
Telephone: (269) 471-7771
E-mail: enroll@andrews.edu
Internet: www.andrews.edu
Founded 1874, current name adopted 1960
Private control
Academic year: August to May

Pres.: Dr NIELS-ERIK ANDREASEN
Provost: Dr ANDREA LUXTON

Vice-Pres. for Enrolment Management: STE-PHEN PAYNE
Vice-Pres. for Financial Admin.: LAWRENCE SCHALK
Vice-Pres. for Student Life: FRANCES FAEH-NER
Vice-Pres. for Univ. Advancement: DAVID A. FAEHNER
Gen. Counsel: BRENT G. T. GERATY
Registrar: Dr EMILIO GARCIA-MARENKO
Dean for Libraries: LAWRENCE W. ONSAGER
Library of 743,694 vols, 2,800 periodicals
Number of teachers: 300
Number of students: 3,550

Publications: *Andrews University Seminary Studies* (2 a year), *Christian Leadership Journal*, *Focus* (4 a year), *Journal for Research in Christian Education*, *Missions Journal*

DEANS

College of Arts and Sciences: KEITH E. MAT-TINGLY
College of Technology: VERLYN BENSON
School of Architecture: CAREY CARSCALLEN
School of Business Administration: ALLEN STEMBRIDGE
School of Education: JAMES R. JEFFERY
School of Graduate Studies and Research: CHRISTON ARTHUR
SDA Theological Seminary: DENIS FORTIN

AQUINAS COLLEGE

1607 Robinson Rd, SE, Grand Rapids, MI 49506-1799
Telephone: (616) 632-8900
E-mail: admissions@aquinas.edu
Internet: www.aquinas.edu
Founded 1886
Private control
Academic year: August to May (2 semesters)
College of liberal arts
Pres.: Dr C. JUAN OLIVAREZ
Provost and Dean for Faculty: Dr CHARLES D. GUNNOE, JR
Vice-Pres for Enrolment Management: PAULA T. MEEHAN
Vice-Pres for Institutional Advancement: GREGORY W. MCALEENAN
Registrar: CECELIA MESLER
Dir for Library: FRANCINE PAOLINI
Dir for Library: SHELLIE JEFFRIES
Library of 110,000 vols, 991 periodicals and over 16,000 non-print items
Number of teachers: 190 (89 full-time, 101 part-time)
Number of students: 2,200

Publications: *Aquinas Magazine* (4 a year), *Presidential Perspectives* (2 a year)

BAKER COLLEGE

1050 W Bristol Rd, Flint, MI 48507
Telephone: (810) 766-4250
Internet: www.baker.edu
Founded 1911, present status 1985
Private control
Academic year: September to August
Areas of study: business, education, engineering and technology, health, human service, office administration and computers; 9 campuses, 6 br. locations and online programmes
Pres. and CEO: F. JAMES CUMMINS
Vice-Pres. for Academics: Dr CANDACE A. JOHNSON
Vice-Pres. for Career Services: YVONNE LANG-LEY
Vice-Pres. for Student Services: GERALD MCCARTY, II
Registrar: ROBERT MARTIN
Number of students: 43,000

CALVIN COLLEGE

3201 Burton, SE, Grand Rapids, MI 49546
Telephone: (616) 526-6000
E-mail: info@calvin.edu
Internet: www.calvin.edu
Founded 1876
Private control
Academic year: September to May
Pres.: Dr GAYLEN J. BYKER
Provost: CLAUDIA DeVRIES BEVERSLUIS
Vice-Pres. for Admin., Finance and Information Services: HENRY E. DeVRIES, II
Vice-Pres. for Advancement: KEN ERFFMEYER
Vice-Pres. for Enrolment Management: RUS-SELL BLOEM
Vice-Pres. for Student Life: SHIRLEY VOGEL-ZANG HOOGSTRA
Registrar: THOMAS STEENWYK
Dir for Library: GLENN A. REMELTS
Library of 648,581 vols, 143,072 bound journal vols, 28,017 ejournals, 808,547 microforms, 12,956 DVDs, audio cassettes and CD-ROMs, 1,537 journal subscriptions
Number of teachers: 390
Number of students: 3,970

Publication: *Fides et Historia* (2 a year)

CALVIN THEOLOGICAL SEMINARY

3233 Burton St, SE, Grand Rapids, MI 49546
Telephone: (616) 957-6036
E-mail: admission@calvinseminary.edu
Internet: www.calvinseminary.edu
Founded 1876
Private control
Areas of study: divinity, ministry, theological studies
Pres.: Rev. JULIUS PLANTINGA MEDENBLIK
Vice-Pres. for Academic Affairs: (vacant)
Dean for Academic Programmes: RONALD FEENSTRA
Dir for Admissions: MATTHEW COOKE
Dean for Faculty: LYLE BIERMA
Registrar: JOAN BEELEN
Librarian: PAUL FIELDS
Number of teachers: 30
Number of students: 300 (full-time)

Publications: *Calvin Theological Journal* (2 a year), *Calvin Theological Seminary Forum* (3 a year), *Stromata* (1 a year)

CENTRAL MICHIGAN UNIVERSITY

Mount Pleasant, MI 48859
Telephone: (989) 774-4000
E-mail: cmuline@cmich.edu
Internet: www.cmich.edu
Founded 1892
State control
Academic year: August to May
Offers academic programmes at the undergraduate, specialist and doctoral levels, incl. entrepreneurship, journalism, music, audiology, teacher education and psychology;
Pres.: Dr GEORGE EUGENE ROSS
Provost and Vice-Pres.: E. GARY SHAPIRO
Vice-Pres. for Devt and External Relations: KATHLEEN WILBUR
Vice-Pres. for Enrolment and Student Services: STEVEN JOHNSON
Vice-Pres. for Finance and Admin. Services: DAVID BURDETTE
Registrar: KAREN HUTSLAR
Dean of Students: BRUCE ROSCOE
Dean of Libraries: THOMAS J. MOORE
Number of teachers: 740
Number of students: 28,390

Publication: *Michigan Historical Review* (2 a year)

DEANS

College of Business Administration: CHARLES CRESPY
College of Communication and Fine Arts: SALMA GHANEM
College of Education and Human Services: Dr DALE ELIZABETH PEHRSSON
College of Graduate Studies: ROGER COLES
College of Health Professions: CHRISTOPHER D. INGERSOLL
College of Humanities and Social and Behavioural Sciences: PAMELA GATES
College of Medicine: ERNEST YODER
College of Science and Technology: IAN DAVISON

CLEARY UNIVERSITY

3601 Plymouth Rd, Ann Arbor, MI 48105
Telephone: (734) 332-4477
E-mail: admissions@cleary.edu
Internet: www.cleary.edu
Founded 1883 as Cleary School of Penmanship, present name and status 2002
Private control
Academic year: September to June
Campus at Howell; extension sites at Dearborn Heights and Flint
Pres. and CEO: THOMAS P. SULLIVAN
Provost and Vice-Pres. for Academic Affairs: Dr VINCENT P. LINDER
Dir for Univ. Libraries: JANE ELLEN INNES
Number of teachers: 105
Number of students: 1,000

DEANS

College of Applied Business Science: CLYDE RIVARD
College of Business Innovation and Applied Technology: DAWN MARKELL
College of Graduate Studies: Dr SADHANA ALANGAR
College of Management: DAVID CASTLEGRANT

COLLEGE FOR CREATIVE STUDIES

201 E Kirby, Detroit, MI 48202-4034
Telephone: (313) 664-7400
E-mail: admissions@collegeforcreativestudies.edu
Internet: www.collegeforcreativestudies.edu
Founded 1906 as Detroit Soc. of Arts and Crafts, current name adopted 2001
Private control
Academic year: September to May
Areas of study: advertising design, crafts, fine arts, graphic design, illustration, photography, product design, transportation design, liberal arts
Pres.: RICHARD L. ROGERS
Provost and Vice-Pres. for Academic Affairs: SOOSHIN CHOI
Vice-Pres. for Admin. and Finance: ANNE BECK
Vice-Pres. for Enrolment and Student Services: JULIE HINGELBERG
Vice-Pres. for Institutional Advancement: NINA HOLDEN
Dean for College: IMRE MOLNAR
Registrar: NADINE HAGOORT
Librarian: BETH WALKER
Library of 40,000 vols, 250 periodicals, 120,000 images, 90,000 slides
Number of teachers: 250
Number of students: 1,340

CONCORDIA UNIVERSITY—ANN ARBOR

4090 Geddes Rd, Ann Arbor, MI 48105
Telephone: (734) 995-7300
E-mail: admission@cuaa.edu
Internet: www.cuaa.edu

Founded 1963 as Concordia Lutheran Junior College, present status 1976, current name adopted 2001
Private control
Academic year: September to May
CEO: Dr Russell Nichols
Pres.: Randall W. Luecke (acting)
Vice-Pres. for Academic Affairs: Dr Ross Stueber
Dir for Admissions: Benjamin D. Limback
Registrar: Colleen Cleland
Dir for Library Services: Brenda Burroughs
Number of teachers: 50
Number of students: 770

DEANS

School of Arts and Sciences: Dr Robert McCormick
School of Education: Dr Dennis Genig

CORNERSTONE UNIVERSITY

1001 E Beltline Ave NE, Grand Rapids, MI 49525-5897

Telephone: (616) 949-5300
E-mail: admissions@cornerstone.edu
Internet: www.cornerstone.edu

Founded 1941, present name and status 1999
Private control
Academic year: August to May

Campuses in Kalamazoo and Zeeland; Asia Baptist Theological Seminary in Singapore; Grand Rapids Theological Seminary in Minnesota; divs of Bible, business, communication and media studies, fine arts, history and social science, humanities, kinesiology, religion and minstry, science and mathematics, teacher education
Chancellor: Dr W. Wilbert Welch
Pres.: Dr Joseph M. Stowell, III
Provost: Dr Rick Ostrander
Exec. Vice-Pres.: Marc Fowler
Sr Vice-Pres. for Univ. Advancement: William Knott
Vice-Pres. and Academic Dean for Grand Rapids Theological Seminary: Dr John VerBerkmoes
Registrar: Gail Duhon
Library Dir: Fred Sweet
Number of teachers: 60
Number of students: 2,600 (1,800 undergraduate, 800 graduate)

Publication: Cornerstone Magazine (1 a year)

CRANBROOK ACADEMY OF ART

POB 801, 39221 Woodward Ave, Bloomfield Hills, MI 48303-0801

Telephone: (248) 645-3300
E-mail: caaadmissions@cranbrook.edu
Internet: www.cranbrookart.edu

Founded 1904
Private control
Language of instruction: English
Academic year: September to May

Divs of 2D design, 3D design, architecture, ceramics, fiber, metalsmithing, painting, photography, print media, sculpture
Dir: Reed Kroloff
Registrar and Financial Aid and Admissions Man.: Leslie Tobakas
Library Dir: Judy Dyki
Library of 26,000 vols
Number of teachers: 10
Number of students: 155

DAVENPORT UNIVERSITY

415 East Fulton, Grand Rapids, MI 49503
Telephone: (616) 451-3511
E-mail: info@davenport.edu
Internet: www.davenport.edu

Founded 1866 as Grand Rapids Business College, present name 2000
Private control
Academic year: September to August
30 Campuses throughout Michigan and N Indiana
Pres.: Richard J. Pappas
Exec. Vice-Pres. for Academics and Provost: Linda Rinker
Exec. Vice-Pres. for Advancement: Dennis Washington
Exec. Vice-Pres. for Enrolment and Student Services: Larry Polselli
Exec. Vice-Pres. for Univ. Relations and Communications: Kim Bruyn
Exec. Dir for Library: Sally Page
Number of teachers: 1,200
Number of students: 13,000

DEANS

College of Arts and Sciences: Dr Tom Lonergan
College of Health Professions: Karen Daley
College of Technology: Michael Clancy
Donald W. Maine College of Business: Irene Bembenista

EASTERN MICHIGAN UNIVERSITY

15 Welch, Ypsilanti, MI 48197
Telephone: (734) 487-1849
E-mail: undergraduate.admissions@emich.edu
Internet: www.emich.edu

Founded 1849 as Michigan State Normal School, present name and status 1959
State control
Academic year: September to April
Pres.: Dr Susan W. Martin
Provost and Vice-Pres. for Academic and Student Affairs: Dr Kim Schatzel
Vice-Pres. For Advancement: Tom Stevick
Registrar: Christina Shell
Dean for Library: Tara Lynn Fulton
Library of 2,000,000 vols, 129,847 periodicals
Number of teachers: 700 (full-time)
Number of students: 23,000

DEANS

College of Arts and Science: Thomas Venner
College of Business: Michael Tidwell
College of Education: Jann Joseph
College of Health and Human Services: Murali Nair
College of Technology: Wade Tornquist
Graduate School: James Carroll

FERRIS STATE UNIVERSITY

1201 S State St, CSS 301, Big Rapids, MI 49307
Telephone: (231) 591-2000
E-mail: admissions@ferris.edu
Internet: www.ferris.edu

Founded 1884
State control
Academic year: August to May
Pres.: David L. Eisler
Provost and Vice-Pres. for Academic Affairs: Fritz Erickson
Vice-Pres. for Admin. and Finance: Jerry L. Scoby
Vice-Pres. for Diversity and Inclusion: Dr David Pilgrim
Vice-Pres. for Student Affairs: Jeanine Ward-Roof
Vice-Pres. for Univ. Advancement and Marketing: John Willey
Dean for Library Systems and Operations: Leah Monger
Library of 370,000 vols and periodicals, 45,000 ejournals, newspapers and magazines

Number of teachers: 560 (full-time)
Number of students: 14,380

DEANS

College of Allied Health Sciences: Dr Julie Coon
College of Arts and Sciences: Karen Strasser
College of Business: Dr David M. Nicol
College of Education and Human Services: Dr Michelle A. Johnston
College of Engineering Technology: Dr Ron McKean
College of Pharmacy: Dr Stephen Durst
Michigan College of Optometry: Dr Michael Cron
University College: Dr William Potter

FINLANDIA UNIVERSITY

601 Quincy St, Hancock, MI 49930
Telephone: (906) 482-5300
E-mail: admissions@finlandia.edu
Internet: www.finlandia.edu

Founded 1896
Private control
Academic year: August to July (3 semesters)
Pres.: Dr Philip R. Johnson
Exec. Vice-Pres. for Academic and Student Affairs: TyAnn Lindell
Exec. Vice-Pres. for External Affairs and Chief Advancement Officer: Duane Aho
Univ. Registrar: Evelyn Goke
Head Librarian: Beth Martin
Library of 50,000 vols, 300 periodicals, 500 video cassettes, 13,000 ebooks
Number of students: 500

Publication: the Bridge (3 a year)

DEANS

College of Health Sciences: Dr Fredi de Yampert
International School of Art and Design: Denise Vandeville
International School of Business: Prof. Terry Monson
Suomi College of Arts and Sciences: Dr Christine O'Neil

GRACE BIBLE COLLEGE

POB 910, 1011 Aldon St, SW, Grand Rapids, MI 49509
Telephone: (616) 538-2330
E-mail: info@gbcol.edu
Internet: www.gbcol.edu

Founded 1939 as Milwaukee Bible Institute, current name adopted 1961
Private control
Academic year: August to May
Pres.: Dr Ken B. Kemper
Vice-Pres. for Academics: Paul R. Sweet
Vice-Pres. for Community Life: Brian P. Sherstad
Dir for Enrolment: Kevin Gilliam
Dir for Library: Kathy Molenkamp
Number of teachers: 30
Number of students: 150

Publication: The Journey

GRAND VALLEY STATE UNIVERSITY

1 Campus Dr., Allendale, MI 49401-9403
Telephone: (616) 331-5000
E-mail: admissions@gvsu.edu
Internet: www.gvsu.edu
Founded 1960
State control
Academic year: August to April
Campuses in Muskegon, Holland, Grand Rapids and Traverse City (Michigan)
Pres.: Dr Thomas J. Haas

Provost and Vice-Pres. for Academic Affairs: Dr GAYLE R. DAVIS
Vice-Provost for Student Affairs and Dean for Students: Dr H. BART MERKLE
Vice-Pres. for Devt: MARIBETH G. WARDROP
Vice-Pres. for Finance and Admin.: JIM BACHMEIER
Vice-Pres. for Inclusion and Equity: Dr JEANNE J. ARNOLD
Vice-Pres. for Univ. Relations: MATTHEW E. MCLOGAN
Univ. Counsel: THOMAS A. BUTCHER
Registrar: LYNN BLUE
Dean for Univ. Libraries: LEE VAN ORSDEL
Library of 750,000 vols, 557,000 ejournals and books
Number of teachers: 840
Number of students: 24,660

DEANS

Brooks College of Interdisciplinary Studies: Dr WENDY J. WENNER
College of Community and Public Service: Dr GEORGE GRANT, JR
College of Education: Dr ELAINE COLLINS
College of Health Professions: Dr ROY H. OLSSON, JR
College of Liberal Arts and Sciences: Dr FREDERICK J. ANTCZAK
Graduate Studies: JEFFREY POTTEIGER
Kirkhof College of Nursing: Dr CYNTHIA A. MCCURREN
Padnos College of Engineering and Computing: Dr PAUL D. PLOTKOWSKI
Seidman College of Business: Dr H. JAMES WILLIAMS

GREAT LAKES CHRISTIAN COLLEGE

6211 W Willow Highway, Lansing, MI 48917
Telephone: (517) 321-0242
E-mail: glcc@glcc.edu
Internet: www.glcc.edu
Founded 1949 as Great Lakes Bible College, current name adopted 1992
Private control
Academic year: August to May
Areas of study: Bible/theology, Christian education, Christian ministries, cross-cultural ministry, family life education, history, interpersonal and organizational communication, music, psychology/counselling, youth ministry
Pres.: LAWRENCE L. CARTER
Vice-Pres. for Academic Affairs: DAVID RICHARDS
Vice-Pres. for Enrolment Management: LLOYD SCHARER
Vice-Pres. for Institutional Advancement: PHILIP E. BEAVERS
Dean for Student Affairs: BETSY CARTER
Registrar: BRIAN SLENSKI
Dir for Library Services: JAMES ORME
Library of 52,000 vols, 20,000 ebooks
Number of teachers: 15
Number of students: 190

HILLSDALE COLLEGE

33 E College St, Hillsdale, MI 49242
Telephone: (517) 437-7341
E-mail: admissions@hillsdale.edu
Internet: www.hillsdale.edu
Founded 1844
Private control
Areas of study: accounting, art, biology, chemistry, classical studies, computational mathematics, economics, education (elementary and secondary), English, financial management, French, German, history, marketing management, mathematics, music, philosophy, physical education, physics, political science, psychology, religion, Spanish, speech, theatre

Pres.: LARRY P. ARNN
Provost: DAVID M. WHALEN
Vice-Pres. for Admin.: RICHARD PÉWÉ
Vice-Pres. for External Affairs: DOUGLAS JEFFREY
Vice-Pres. for Institutional Advancement: JOHN CERVINI
Vice-Pres. for Student Affairs: DIANE PHILIPP
Dir for Admissions: JEFFREY S. LANTIS
Registrar: DOUGLAS MCARTHUR
Library Dir: DAN KNOCH
Library of 300,000 vols, 1,000 ebooks, 61,000 microforms, 8,000 audio and visual items, 1,600 journals
Number of teachers: 115
Number of students: 1,400
Publication: *Imprimis* (12 a year)

HOPE COLLEGE

POB 9000, 69 E 10th St, Holland, MI 49422-9000
Telephone: (616) 395-7000
E-mail: admissions@hope.edu
Internet: www.hope.edu
Founded 1866
Private control
Academic year: August to May
Pres.: Dr JOHN KNAPP
Provost: Dr R. RICHARD RAY, JR
Vice-Pres. and Chief Financial Officer: TOM BYLSMA
Vice-Pres. for Admissions: WILLIAM C. VANDERBILT
Vice-Pres. for Student Devt and Dean for Students: Dr RICHARD FROST
Registrar: CAROL DE JONG
Dir for Libraries: KELLY JACOBSMA
Library of 370,000
Number of teachers: 200
Number of students: 3,230
Publication: *Opus* (2 a year)

DEANS

Arts and Humanities: Dr PATRICE RANKINE
Natural and Applied Sciences: Dr JAMES GENTILE
Social Sciences: Dr SCOTT VANDER STOEP

KALAMAZOO COLLEGE

1200 Academy St, Kalamazoo, MI 49006-3295
Telephone: (269) 337-7000
E-mail: admission@kzoo.edu
Internet: www.kzoo.edu
Founded 1833 as Michigan and Huron Institute, current name adopted 1855
Private control
Academic year: September to June
Divs of fine arts, humanities, interdisciplinary studies, natural sciences and mathematics, modern and classical languages and literatures, physical education, social sciences
Pres.: Dr EILEEN WILSON-OYELARAN
Provost: Dr MICHAEL A. MCDONALD
Vice-Pres. for College Advancement: VICTORIA GORRELL
Vice-Pres. for Student Devt and Dean for Students: SARAH WESTFALL
Dean for Enrolment: JOELLEN L. SILBERMAN
Dean for Admission: ERIC STAAB
Registrar: ALYCE BRADY
Dir for Library: STACY A. NOWICKI
Library of 330,000 vols
Number of teachers: 100 (full-time)
Number of students: 1,350

KETTERING UNIVERSITY

1700 W Third Ave, Flint, MI 48504-6214
Telephone: (810) 762-9500

E-mail: admissions@kettering.edu
Internet: www.gmi.edu
Founded 1919, present name and status 1998
Private control
Depts of business, chemistry and biochemistry, computer science, electrical and computer engineering, industrial and manufacturing engineering, liberal arts, mathematics, mechanical engineering, physics
Pres.: Dr ROBERT K. MCMAHAN, JR
Provost and Vice-Pres. for Academic Affairs: Dr JAMES ZHANG
Vice-Pres. for Admin. and Finance: (vacant)
Vice-Pres. for Admissions and Enrolment Services: (vacant)
Vice-Pres. for Univ. Advancement: JACK STOCK (acting)
Vice-Pres. for Student Life and Dean for Students: BETSY HOMSHER
Registrar: SHEILA RUPP
Dir for Library Services: Dr CHARLES D. HANSON
Library of 180,000 vols, 1,900 periodicals
Number of teachers: 135
Number of students: 3,200

KUYPER COLLEGE

3333 E Beltline NE, Grand Rapids, MI 49525
Telephone: (616) 222-3000
E-mail: admissions@kuyper.edu
Internet: www.kuyper.edu
Founded 1939 as Reformed Bible Institute, present name and status 1970
Private control
Academic year: August to April
Areas of study: Bible and theology, cross-cultural studies, educational ministries, general education, liberal arts, physical education, pre-seminary studies, professional education, social work and youth ministry
Pres.: Dr NICHOLAS V. KROEZE
Provost and Vice-Pres. for Academic Admin.: Dr MELVIN J. FLIKKEMA
Vice-Pres. for Enrolment Management: RYAN STRUCK-VANDER HAAK
Vice-Pres. for College Advancement: KEN CAPISCIOLTO
Academic Dean: Dr TAMARA ROSIER
Dir for Library Services: DIANNE ZANDBERGEN
Library of 600,000 vols, 150 periodicals
Number of teachers: 60 (21 full-time, 39 part-time)
Number of students: 340

LAKE SUPERIOR STATE UNIVERSITY

650 W Easterday Ave, Sault Ste Marie, MI 49783
Telephone: (906) 632-6841
E-mail: admissions@lssu.edu
Internet: www.lssu.edu
Founded 1946 as Sault Ste Marie Br. of Michigan College of Mining and Technology, current name adopted 1987
State control
Academic year: September to May
Pres.: Dr TONY MCLAIN
Provost and Vice-Pres. for Academic Affairs: MORRIE WALWORTH
Vice-Pres. for Enrolment Services: WILLIAM EILOLA
Vice-Pres. for Finance: SHERRY BROOKS
Vice-Pres. for Student Affairs: KEN PERESS
Registrar: NANCY NEVE
Dean for Library: (vacant)
Library of 130,000 vols, 850 periodicals, 75,000 microforms
Number of teachers: 125
Number of students: 2,400

DEANS

College of Arts, Letters, Social Sciences and Emergency Services: Dr PAIGE GORDIER
College of Business, Engineering, and Economic Development: Dr DAVID R. FINLEY
College of Natural and Mathematical Sciences: Dr BARBARA KELLER
College of Nursing, Recreation Studies and Exercise Science: (vacant)
School of Nursing: RONALD HUTCHINS
School of Education: DONNA FIEBELKORN

LAWRENCE TECHNOLOGICAL UNIVERSITY

21000 W Ten Mile Rd, Southfield, MI 48075-1058

Telephone: (248) 204-4000
E-mail: admissions@ltu.edu
Internet: www.ltu.edu

Founded 1932
Private control
Academic year: August to May

Pres. and CEO: Dr LEWIS N. WALKER
Provost and Chief Academic Officer: Dr MARIA J. VAZ
Vice-Pres. for Finance and Admin.: LINDA L. HEIGHT
Vice-Pres. for Univ. Advancement: STEPHEN E. BROWN
Dean for Students: KEVIN FINN
Registrar: NOREEN G. FERGUSON
Library Dir: GARY R. COCOZZOLI

Number of teachers: 450
Number of students: 4,500

Publication: *Prism* (1 a year)

DEANS

College of Architecture and Design: GLEN S. LEROY
College of Arts and Sciences: Dr HSIAO-PING MOORE
College of Engineering: Dr NABIL F. GRACE
College of Management: Dr LOUIS A. DeGENNARO

MADONNA UNIVERSITY

36600 Schoolcraft Rd, Livonia, MI 48150-1173

Telephone: (734) 432-5300
E-mail: muinfo@madonna.edu
Internet: www.madonna.edu

Founded 1947
Private control
Academic year: September to July

Pres.: Dr ROSE MARIE KUJAWA
Vice-Pres. for Academic Admin.: Dr ERNEST NOLAN
Vice-Pres. for Student Services: Dr CONNIE TINGSON-GATUZ
Vice-Pres. for Univ. Advancement: ANDREA NODGE
Univ. Registrar: DINA DuBUIS
Dir for Library Services: JOANNE LUMMETTA

Library of 163,678 vols
Number of teachers: 270
Number of students: 4,000

Publications: *Madonna Now, Revelations* (2 a year)

DEANS

College of Arts and Humanities: Dr KATHLEEN MARTIN O'DOWD
College of Education: Dr KAREN OBSNIUK
College of Nursing and Health: Dr TERESA L. C. THOMPSON
College of Science and Mathematics: Dr TED F. BIERMANN
College of Social Sciences: Dr KAREN L. ROSS
Graduate School: Dr EDITH RALEIGH
Outreach and Distance Learning: Dr JAMES NOVACK

School of Business: Dr STUART R. ARENDS

MARYGROVE COLLEGE

8425 W McNichols Rd, Detroit, MI 48221

Telephone: (313) 927-1200
E-mail: info@marygrove.edu
Internet: www.marygrove.edu

Founded 1905
Private control
Academic year: September to April

Pres.: Dr DAVID J. FIKE
Vice-Pres. for Academic Affairs: JANE HAMMANG-BUHL
Vice-Pres. for Finance and Admin.: BILL JOHNSON
Vice-Pres. for Institutional Advancement: KENNETH MALECKE
Vice-Pres. for Student Affairs and Enrolment Management: Dr JULIANA MOSLEY
Dir for Learning Resource Center: DOLORES NOEL

Library of 84,015 vols, 371 periodicals
Number of teachers: 60
Number of students: 1,190 (781 undergraduate, 409 graduate)

Publications: *Contact* (1 a year), *Maxis Review* (1 a year)

DEANS

Arts and Sciences: Dr JUDITH A. HEINEN
Education: CHRISTINE KOENIG SEGUIN
Extended Learning: Dr BRENDA D. BRYANT
Fine Arts: ROSE DE SLOOVER
Professional Studies: JANE HAMMANG-BUHL

MICHIGAN JEWISH INSTITUTE

6890 W Maple, West Bloomfield, MI 48322

Telephone: (248) 414-6900
E-mail: info@mji.edu
Internet: www.mji.edu

Founded 1994
Private control
Academic year: September to August

Areas of study: business and information systems, computer information systems, Judaic studies

Pres. and Chief Financial Officer: KASRIEL SHEMTOV
Sr Vice-Pres. and Dean for Academic Admin.: Dr T. HERSHEL GARDIN
Librarian and Registrar: KAREN ROBERTSON-HENRY

MICHIGAN SCHOOL OF PROFESSIONAL PSYCHOLOGY

26811 Orchard Lake Rd, Farmington Hills, MI 48334-4512

Telephone: (248) 476-1122
Internet: www.mispp.edu

Founded 1980 as Center for Humanistic Studies, current name adopted 2006
Private control
Academic year: August to July (3 semesters)

Pres.: Dr KERRY MOUSTAKAS
Vice-Pres.: DIANE K. ZALAPI
Program Dir: Dr LEE BACH
Registrar: HEATHER N. RIGBY
Academic Librarian: CANDI WILSON

Library of 7,000 vols, 20 journal subscriptions, 270 instructional audiovisual materials
Number of students: 150

MICHIGAN STATE UNIVERSITY

East Lansing, MI 48824

Telephone: (517) 355-6560
E-mail: presmail@msu.edu
Internet: www.msu.edu

Founded 1855 as Agricultural College of the State of Michigan, present status 1955, current name adopted 1964
State control
Academic year: August to May (2 terms)

Pres.: LOU ANN K. SIMON
Provost and Vice-Pres. for Academic Affairs: KIM A. WILCOX
Vice-Pres. for Governmental Affairs: MARK BURNHAM
Vice-Pres. for Legal Affairs and Gen. Counsel: ROBERT A. NOTO
Vice-Pres. for Research and Graduate Studies: J. IAN GRAY
Vice-Pres. for Student Affairs and Services: Dr DENISE B. MAYBANK
Vice-Pres. for Univ. Advancement: ROBERT W. GROVES
Vice-Pres. for Univ. Relations: HEATHER SWAIN
Registrar: NICOLE G. ROVIG (acting)
Dir for Libraries: CLIFFORD H. HAKA

Library: see under Libraries and Archives
Number of teachers: 4,900
Number of students: 47,130

Publications: *Centennial Review* (3 a year), *MSU Alumni Magazine* (4 a year), *The Engaged Scholar Magazine* (1 a year, print and online, engagedscholar.msu.edu)

DEANS

College of Agriculture and Natural Resources: DOUGLAS BUHLER
College of Arts and Letters: KAREN A. WURST
College of Communication Arts and Sciences: PAMELA WHITTEN
College of Education: ROBERT FLODEN
College of Engineering: SATISH UDPA
College of Human Medicine: MARSHA D. RAPPLEY (acting)
College of Law: JOAN HOWARTH
College of Music: JAMES FORGER
College of Natural Science: R. JAMES KIRKPATRICK
College of Nursing: MARY MUNDT
College of Osteopathic Medicine: WILLIAM D. STRAMPEL
College of Social Science: MARIETTA L. BABA
College of Veterinary Medicine: CHRISTOPHER M. BROWN
Eli Broad College of Business and Eli Broad Graduate School of Management: STEFANIE LENWAY
Honors College: Dr CYNTHIA JACKSON-ELMOORE
James Madison College: SHERMAN GARNETT
Lyman Briggs College: ELIZABETH SIMMONS
Residential College in Arts and Humanities: STEPHEN L. ESQUITH (acting)

PROFESSORS

(Departments may be attached to more than one college)

College of Nursing:
ALLEN, G. D.
COLLINS, C.
GIFT, A. G.
GIVEN, B. A.
ROTHERT, M. L.

Department of Accounting:
ARENS, A. A.
BUZBY, S. L.
DILLEY, S. C.
GRAY, J.
HAKA, S.
McCARTHY, W. E.
MEAD, G. C.
O'CONNOR, M. C.
OUTSLAY, E.
SHIELDS, M. D.
SOLLENBERGER, H. M.
WARD, D. D.

Department of Advertising:

PRATT, C.
REECE, B. B.
SALMON, C.
VANDENBERGH, B. G.

Department of Agricultural Economics:

BATIE, S. S.
BERNSTEN, R. H.
BLACK, J. R.
CRAWFORD, E.
HAMM, L. G.
HARSH, S. B.
HARVEY, L. R.
HILKER, J. H.
HOEHN, J.
KELSEY, M. P.
LEHOLM, A. G.
MOSER, C. H.
MYERS, R. J.
NOTT, S. B.
PIERSON, T. R.
RICKS, D. J.
ROBISON, L. J.
SCHMID, A. A.
SCHWAB, G.
STAATZ, J. M.
VAN RAVENSWAAY, E.
WEBER, M.

Department of Agricultural Engineering:

BAKKER-ARKEMA, F. W.
BICKERT, W. G.
BROOK, R.
GERRISH, J.
LOUDON, T. L.
MROZOWSKI, T.
SEGERLIND, L. J.
SRIVASTAVA, A.
STEFFE, J. F.
SURBROOK, T. C.
VAN EE, G. R.
VON BERNUTH, R.

Department of American Thought and Language:

ABRAHAMS, E. C.
BECKWITH, G. M.
BRATZEL, J. N.
BRESNAHAN, R. J.
BUNGE, N. L.
CHAMBERLAIN, W.
COOPER, D. D.
D'ITRI, P. A.
ELLISTON, S. F.
HOPPENSTAND, G. C.
LADENSON, J. R.
LUNDE, E.
MCKINLEY, B. E.
NOVERR, D. A.
ROUT, K.
SOMERS, P. P., Jr
STEINBERG, M.
THOMAS, F. R.
ZIEWACZ, L. E.

Department of Animal Science:

ALLEN, M. S.
AULERICH, R. J.
BEEDE, D. K.
BENSON, M. E.
BUCHOLTZ, H. F.
BURSIAN, S.
DENNIS BANKS, B.
ERICKSON, R. W.
FERRIS, T. A.
FOGWELL, R.
HAWKINS, D. R.
HOGBERG, M. G.
IRELAND, J.
MELLENBERGER, R. W.
RAHN, A. P.
RITCHIE, H. D.
RUST, S. R.
SHELLE, J. E.
VARGHESE, S. K.
YOKOYAMA, M. T.

Department of Anthropology:

CHARTKOFF, J.
CLELAND, C. E.
CLIMO, J.
DERMAN, W.
DWYER, D.
GALLIN, B.
GOLDSTEIN, L. G.
LOVIS, W. A.
POLLARD, H. P.
ROBBINS, L. H.
SAUER, N.
SPIELBERG, J.
WHITEFORD, S.

Department of Art:

BANDES, S. J.
DEUSSEN, P. W.
FAGAN, J. E.
FUNK, R.
GLENDINNING, P.
KILBOURNE, W. G.
KUSZAI, J. J.
LAWTON, J. L.
MACDOWELL
STANFORD, L. O.
TARAN, I. Z.
VANLIERE, E. N.
WOLTER, K. H.

Department of Audiology and Speech Sciences:

CASBY, M.
EULENBERG, J. B.
MOORE, E. J.
PUNCH, J. L.
RAKERD, B. S.
SMITH, L. L.
STOCKMAN, I. G.

Department of Biochemistry and Molecular Biology:

BIEBER, L. L.
FERGUSON-MILLER, S.
FRAKER, P. J.
GREEN, P. G.
HOLLINGSWORTH, R. I.
KAGUNI, J. M.
KAGUNI, L. S.
KINDEL, P. K.
KROOS, L. R.
MCCORMICK, J. J.
MCGROARTY, E. J.
MCINTOSH, L.
MAHER, V. M.
PREISS, J.
RAIKHEL, N. V.
REVZIN, A.
SCHINDLER, M. S.
SMITH, W. L.
TRIEZENBERG, S. J.
WANG, J. L.
WATSON, J. T.
WILSON, J. E.

Department of Botany and Plant Pathology:

DEZOETEN, G. A.
EKERN, F. F.
EWERS, F. W.
FULBRIGHT, D. W.
HAMMERSCHMIDT, R.
HART, L. P.
HOLLENSEN, R.
JONES, A. L.
KEEGSTRA, K. G.
KENDE, H.
KLOMPARENS, K. L.
MURPHY, P. G.
NADLER, K. D.
OHLROGGE, J. B.
POFF, K. L.
SAFIR, G. R.
SEARS, B.
TAGGART, R.
VARGAS, J. M., JR
WALTON, J. D.
WEBBER, P. J.

WOLK, C. P.
ZEEVAART, J. A. D.

Department of Chemical Engineering:

BERGLUND, K.
DALE, B.
DRZAL, L. T.
HAWLEY, M. C.
JAYARAMAN, K.
MILLER, D. J.
NARAYAN, R.
PETTY, C. A.
WORDEN, R. M.

Department of Chemistry:

ALLISON, J.
BABCOCK, G. T.
CHANG, C. K.
CROUCH, S. R.
CUKIER, R. I.
DUNBAR, K.
FROST, J.
HARRISON, J. F.
HUNT, K. C.
HUNT, P. M.
KANATZIDES, M. G.
LEROI, G. E.
MCGUFFIN, V. L.
MCHARRIS, W. C.
MORRISSEY, D. J.
PINNAVAIA, T. J.
RATHKE, M. W.
REUSCH, W. H.
MALECZKA, R.
WAGNER, P. J.
WULFF, W. D.

Department of Civil and Environmental Engineering:

BALADI, G.
DAVIS, M. L.
HARICHANDRAN, R. S.
HATFIELD, F.
LYLES, R. W.
MCKELVEY, F.
SOROUSHIAN, P.
TAYLOR, W. C.
VOICE, T. C.

Department of Communication:

ATKIN, C. K.
BOSTER, F. J.
DONOHUE, W.
SMITH, S. W.

Department of Computer Science and Engineering:

CHUNG, M.-J.
DILLON, L. K.
GREENBERG, L.
HUGHES, H. D.
JAIN, A. K.
MUTKA, M.
NI, L. M.
PRAMANIK, S.
STOCKMAN, G. C.
WEINSHANK, D. J.
WOJCIK, A. S.

Department of Counselling, Educational Psychology and Special Education:

AMES, C.
BECKER, B. J.
CLARK, C. M.
CREWE, N. M.
DICKSON, W. P.
ENGLERT, C. S.
FLODEN, R. E.
HAPKIEWICZ, W. C.
JUNE, L. N.
LEAHY, M. J.
LOPEZ, F. G.
MEHRENS, W. A.
PALAS, A. M.
PERNELL, E.
PHILLIPS, S. E.
PRAWAT, R.
RECKASE, M. D.
SCHMIDT, W. H.

SMITH, G.
SPIRO, R. J.
STEWART, D. A.
YELON, S. L.

Department of Crop and Soil Sciences:

BOYD, S. A.
CHRISTENSON, D. R.
CRUM, J. R.
FOSTER, E. F.
FREED, R. D.
GOODMAN, E.
HARWOOD, R. R.
JACOBS, L. W.
JOHNSTON, T. J.
KELLS, J. D.
KELLY, J. D.
LEEP, R. H.
LEMME, G. D.
LENSKI, R. E.
MOKMA, D. L.
PAUL, E. A.
PENNER, D.
PIERCE, F. J.
RENNER, K. A.
RITCHIE, J. T.
ROBERTSON, G. P.
SMUCKER, A. J. M.
THOMASHOW, M.
TIEDJE, J. M.
WARNCKE, D. D.

Department of Economics:

ALLEN, B. T.
BAILLIE, R. T.
BALLARD, C. L.
BIDDLE, J. E.
BOYER, K. D.
BROWN, B. W.
CHOI, J. P.
DAVIDSON, C.
FISHER, R. C.
GODDEERIS, J. H.
HOLZER, H. J.
KREININ, M. E.
LIEDHOLM, C. E.
LINZ, S. J.
MACKEY, M. C.
MARTIN, L. W.
MATUSZ, S. J.
MENCHIK, P. L.
MEYER, J.
NEUMARK, D. B.
OBST, N. P.
PECCHENINO, R. A.
SCHMIDT, P. J.
SEGERSTROM, P. S.
STRAUSS, J. A.
WILSON, J. D.
WOODBURY, S. A.
WOOLDRIDGE, J.

Department of Educational Administration:

CHURCH, R. L.
CUSICK, P. A.
DAVIS, M.
FAIRWEATHER, J.
GRANDSTAFF, M. E.
IGNATOVICH, F. R.
KAAGAN, S. S.
MOORE, K. M.
PLANK, D. N.
ROMANO, L. G.
SIMON, L. A. K.
SYKES, G.
TURNER, M.
WEILAND, S.

Department of Electrical and Computer Engineering:

ASMUSSEN, J., Jr
DELLER, J.
FISHER, P. D.
FOUKE, J. M.
KHALIL, H.
NYQUIST, D. P.
PIERRE, P. A.
REINHARD, D. K.

ROTHWELL, E. J.
SALAM, F. M.
SCHLUETER, R. A.
SHANBLATT, M.
SIEGEL, M.
TUMMALA, R. L.
WEY, C.-L.

Department of English:

ATHANASON, A. N.
BANKS, J. S.
BRUNNER, D. D.
CRANE, M.
DEWHURST, C. K.
DULAI, S. S.
FISHBURN, K. R.
GASS, S. M.
GOCHBERG, D. S.
GOODSON, A. C.
GROSS, B. E.
HARROW, K.
HILL, J. L.
JOHNSEN, W.
LANDRUM, L. N.
LUDWIG, J. B.
McCLINTOCK, J. I.
McGUIRE, P. C.
MARTIN, R. A.
MATHESON, L. M.
MEINERS, R. K.
O'DONNELL, P. J.
PAANANEN, V. N.
PENN, W. S.
POGEL, N.
ROBINSON, R. F.
ROSENBERG, D. M.
SEATON, J.
SKEEN, A. C.
SMITHERMAN, G.
STALKER, J. C.
STOCK, P. L.
TAVORMINA, M. T.
UPHAUS, R. W.
VINCENT, W. A.
WAKOSKI, D.
WHALLON, W.
WILSON, M.

Department of Entomology:

AYERS, G. S.
BESAW, L. C.
BIRD, G. W.
DELFOSSE, E. S.
GAGE, S.
GRAFIUS, E. J.
HOLLINGWORTH, R. M.
MERRITT, R. W.
MILLER, J. R.
POSTON, F. L.
RAIKHEL, A.
SCRIBER, J. M.
SMITLEY, D. R.
STEHR, F. W.
VanTASSELL, E.
WHALON, M. E.
ZABIK, M. J.

Department of Epidemiology:

PARETH, N.
PATHAK, P. K.

Department of Family and Child Ecology:

AMES, B. D.
BARRATT, M. S.
BOBBITT, N.
BOGER, R.
GRIFFORE, R.
IMIG, D. R.
IMIG, G. L.
JOHNSON, D. J.
KEITH, J. G.
KOSTELNIK, M.
LUSTER, T. J.
McADOO, H. P.
MILLER, J. R.
PHENICE, L.
SCHIAMBERG, L. B.
SODERMAN, A. K.

TAYLOR, C. S.
WALKER, R.
WHIREN, A. P.
YOUATT, J. P.

Department of Family and Community Medicine:

AGUWA, M. I.
BORDINAT, S. M.
CUMMINGS, M.
KURTZ, M.
PAPSIDERO, J.

Department of Family Practice:

ALEXANDER, E.
BRODY, H.
GERARD, R.
GIVEN, C. W.
HICKNER, J.
OGLE, K. S.
PATHAK, D. R.
WHITTIER, H. L.

Department of Finance:

BOOTH, G. G.
GRUNEWALD, A. E.
HENRY, J. B.
KHANNA, N.
LASHBROOKE, E. C., JR
O'DONNELL, J. L.
RAINEY, J. F.
SIMONDS, R. R.
STENZEL, P.

Department of Fisheries and Wildlife:

BATIE, R. E.
D'ITRI, F.
DOBSON, T. A.
GARLING, D. L.
JOHNSON, D. I.
PEYTON, R. B.
PRINCE, H. H.
TAYLOR, W. W.

Department of Food Science and Human Nutrition:

BENNINK, M. R.
BOND, J. T.
BOOREN, A. M.
CASH, J. N.
CHENOWETH, W. L.
GRAY, I. J.
HEGARTY, P. V.
HOERR, S. M.
LINZ, J. E.
PESTKA, J. J.
ROMSOS, D. R.
SMITH, D. M.
SONG, W. O.
UEBERSAX, M. A.
ZABIK, M.
ZILE, M. H.

Department of Forestry:

DICKMANN, D. I.
KEATHLEY, D. E.
KIELBASO, J. J.
KOELLING, M. R.
McDONOUGH, M.
POTTER-WITTER, K. L.

Department of Geography:

CAMPBELL, D. J.
CHUBB, M.
COREY, K. E.
GROOP, R. E.
HAMLIN, R.
HARMAN, J. R.
HINOJOSA, R.
LIM, G.-C.
MANSON, G. A.
MEHRETU, A.
OLSON, J. M.
SCHAETZL, R. J.
SKOLE, D. L.
THOMAS, J.
WILLIAMS, J.
WITTICK, R. I.

Department of Geological Sciences:
ANSTEY, R. L.
CAMBRAY, F. W.
FUJITA, K.
LARSON, G. J.
LONG, D. T.
SIBLEY, D. F.
TROW, J. W.
VELBEL, M. A.
VOGEL, T. A.

Department of History:
ANDERSON, J. R.
EADIE, J. W.
FISHER, A.
GLIOZZO, C. A.
HINE, D. C.
LAURENCE, R. R.
LEVINE, P. D.
MARCUS, H. G.
MOCH, L. P.
RADDING, C. M.
REED, H. A.
ROBINSON, D. W.
SCHOENL, W. J.
SIEGELBAUM, L. H.
SILVERMAN, H.
STEWART, G. T.
SWEENEY, J. M.
THOMAS, R. W.
THOMAS, S. J.
VIETH, J. K.
WILBUR, E.

Department of Horticulture:
BIERNBAUM, J. A.
CAMERON, A. C.
CARLSON, W. H.
DILLEY, D. R.
FLORE, J. A.
HANCOCK, J. F.
HANSON, E. J.
HEINS, R. D.
HERNER, R. C.
HOWELL, G. S.
IEZZONI, A. F.
LOESCHER, W. H.
NAIR, M.
PERRY, R. L.
SINK, K. C.
WIDDERS, I. E.
ZANDSTRA, B. H.

Department of Human Environment and Design:
SONTAG, M. S.
STERNQUIST, B.
STEWART, D. G.

Department of Internal Medicine:
HUGHES, M. J.
OTTEN, R. F.
PYSH, J. J.
RISTOW, G. E.

Department of Kinesiology:
DUMMER, G.
FELTZ, D. L.
HAUBENSTRICKER, J. L.
MALINA, R. M.
PIVARNIK, J. M.

Department of Large Animal Clinical Sciences:
AMES, N. K.
BAKER, J. C.
BARTLETT, P. C.
CARON, J. P.
DERKSEN, F. J.
HERDT, T.
HOLLAND, R. E.
KANEENE, J. B.
KING, L. J.
LLOYD, J. W.
MATHER, E. C.
NACHREINER, R. F.
NICKELS, F. A.
ROBINSON, N. E.

ROOK, J. S.
SEARS, P. M.
SPRECHER, D. J.
STICK, J. A.
STRAW, B. E.

Department of Linguistics and Germanic, Slavic, Asian and African Languages:
ABBOTT, B. K.
BELGARDT, R.
FALK, J. S.
HUDSON, G.
JUNTUNE, T. W.
LIN, Y.-H.
LOCKWOOD, D. G.
MCCONEGHY, P.
PAULSELL, P.
PETERS, G. F.
PRESTON, D.
SENDICH, M.
WILKINS, W. K.
WURST, K. A.

Department of Management:
BARRICK, M.
HOLLENBECK, J. R.
MOCH, M. K.
RUBIN, P. A.
WAGNER, J. A., III

Department of Marketing and Supply Chain Management:
ALLEN, J. W.
BOWERSOX, D. J.
CALANTONE, R. J.
CAVUSGIL, S. T.
CLOSS, D.
DROGE, C. L.
HARRELL, G. D.
MELNYK, S. A.
NARASIMHAN, R.
NASON, R. W.
SONG, X.-X. M.
VICKERY, S. K.
WILSON, R. D.

Department of Materials Science and Mechanics:
ALTIERO, N. J.
CASE, E. D.
CLOUD, G. L.
GRUMMON, D. S.
HUBBARAD, R. P.
LIU, D.
MUKHERJEE, K.
PENCE, T. J.
SOUTAS-LITTLE, R. W.
SUBRAMANIAN, K. N.

Department of Mathematics:
AKBULUT, S.
BAO, P.
BLAIR, D. E.
BROWN, W. C.
CHEN, B.-Y.
DRACHMAN, B.
DUNNINGER, D. R.
FINTUSHEL, R. A.
FRAZIER, M. W.
HALL, J. I.
HESTENES, M.
HILL, R. O.
IVANOV, N.
KUAN, W. E.
KURTZ, J. C.
LAMM, P. K.
LAPPAN, G.
LAPPAN, P. A.
LI, T. Y.
LO, C. Y.
LUDDEN, G. D.
MCCARTHY, J. D.
MACCLUER, C. R.
MASTERSON, J. J.
MEIERFRANKENFELD, U.
MORAN, D. A.
NEWHOUSE, S. E.
OW, W. H.

PALMER, E. M.
PARKER, T. H.
PLOTKIN, J. M.
ROTTHAUS, C.
SAGAN, B. E.
SCHUUR, J. D.
SEEBECK, C. L.
SENK, S. L.
SHAPIRO, J. H.
SLEDD, W. T.
SONNEBORN, L. M.
SREEDHARAN, V. P.
TREIL, S.
ULRICH, B.
VOLBERG, A.
WALD, J. W.
WANG, C.-Y.
WEIL, C. E.
WINTER, D. L.
WINTER, M. J. K.
WOLFSON, J. G.
WONG, P. K.
ZEIDAN, V. M.
ZHOU, Z.

Department of Mechanical Engineering:
FOSS, J. F.
LLOYD, J. R.
MCGRATH, J.
MEDICK, M. A.
RADCLIFFE, C. J.
ROSENBERG, R. C.
SCHOCK, H. J.
SHAW, S. W.
SHIK, T.
THOMPSON, B. S.
WICHMAN, I. S.

Department of Medicine:
ABELA, G. S.
DIMITROV, N. V.
DIPETTE, D. J.
GOSSAIN, V. V.
HASSOUNA, H. I.
HOLMES-ROVNER, M.
HOPPE, R.
JONES, J. W.
MAYLE, J. E.
NEIBERG, A. D.
PENNER, J. A.
ROSENMAN, K. D.
SCHWARTZ, K. A.
SMITH, R. C.
STEIN, G. E.
SWANSON, G. M.
WANG, D. H.

Department of Microbiology and Molecular Genetics:
BAGDASARIAN, M.
BERTRAND, H.
BREZNAK, J. A.
BRUBAKER, R. R.
CONRAD, S. E.
CORNER, T.
DAZZO, F.
DEBRUIJN, F. J.
DODGSON, J. B.
ESSELMAN, W.
FLUCK, M. M.
GARRITY, G. M.
HAUG, A.
HAUSINGER, R. P.
JACKSON, J. H.
KIERSZENBAUM, F.
MAES, R. K.
MULKS, M. H.
ORIEL, P. J.
PATTERSON, M. J.
PATTERSON, R.
REDDY, C. A.
REUSCH, R. N.
SNYDER, L. R.
VELICER, L. F.
WALKER, R. D.

Department of Obstetrics, Gynaecology and Reproductive Biology:

MARSHALL, J. F.
VASILENKO, P.

Department of Osteopathic Manipulative Medicine:

RECHTIEN, J. J.
REYNOLDS, H.
WARD, R. C.

Department of Osteopathic Surgical Specialities:

BECKMEYER, H. E.
HARDING, S. A.
HAUT, R. C.
HOGAN, M. J.
JACOBS, A. W.

Department of Park, Recreation and Tourism Resources:

BRISTOR, J. L.
FRIDGEN, J.
HOLECEK, D. F.
RASMUSSEN, G. A.
STYNES, D. J.
VAN DER SMISSEN, B.

Department of Pathology:

BELL, T. G.
HARKEMA, J. R.
KREHBIEL, J.
LOVELL, K. L.
MACKENZIE, C.
MULLANEY, T. P.
PADGETT, G. A.
REED, W. M.
RHEUBEN, M. B.
TVEDTEN, H.
WILLIAMS, C. S. F.
YAMINI, B.

Department of Paediatrics:

BREITZER, G. M.
MAGEN, M.
SCHNEIDERMAN, D. O.

Department of Paediatrics and Human Development:

CHANG, C. C.
FISHER, R.
GORDON, R.
KALLEN, D. J.
KAUFMAN, D. B.
KULKARNI, R.
KUMAR, A.
MURRAY, D. L.
NETZLOFF, M. L.
SCOTT-EMUAKPOR, A.
SEAGULL, E. A.
SPARROW, A. W.
TROSKO, J. E.

Department of Pharmacology and Toxicology:

ATCHISON, W. D.
BARMAN, S.
BENNETT, J. L.
BRASELTON, W. E., JR
FINK, G. D.
FISCHER, L. J.
GALLIGAN, J. J.
GEBBER, G. L.
GOODMAN, J. I.
KAMINSKI, N. E.
MOORE, K. E.
ROTH, R. A.
THORNBURG, J.

Department of Philosophy:

ANDRE, J. A.
ASQUITH, P. D.
BENJAMIN, M.
ESQUITH, S. L.
FLECK, L. M.
FRYE, M.
GARELICK, H. M.
HALL, R. J.
HANNA, J. F.

KOCH, D. F.
KOTZIN, R. H.
LAWSON, B. E.
MCCRACKEN, C. J.
MILLER, B.
PETERSON, R. T.
TOMLINSON, T.

Department of Physical Medicine and Rehabilitation:

HALLGREN, R.
HINDS, W. C.
KAUFMAN, D.
STANTON, D. F.

Department of Physics and Astronomy:

ABOLINS, M. A.
AUSTIN, S. M.
BALDWIN, J. A.
BASS, J.
BAUER, W. W.
BENENSON, W.
BERZ, M. M.
BORYSOWICZ, J.
BROCK, R. L.
BROMBERG, C. M.
BROWN, B. A.
DANIELEWICZ, P.
DUXBURY, P. M.
DYKMAN, M. I.
GALONSKY, A. I.
GOLDING, B.
HARRISON, M. J.
HARTMANN, W. M.
HUSTON, J. W.
KASHY, E.
LINNEMAN, J. T.
LYNCH, W. G.
MAHANTI, S. D.
POLLACK, G. L.
POPE, B. G.
PRATT, W. P., JR
PUMPLIN, J. C.
REPKO, W. W.
SHERRILL, B. M.
SIGNELL, P. S.
SIMKIN, S. M.
SMITH, H. A.
STEIN, R. F.
THOENNESSEN, M.
THORPE, M. F.
TOMANEK, D.
TUNG, W. K.
WEERTS, H. J.
WESTFALL, G. D.
ZELENVINSKY, V.

Department of Physiology:

ADAMS, T.
HASLAM, S. Z.
HEIDEMANN, S.
HOOTMAN, S. R.
JUMP, D. B.
KREULEN, D. L.
MEYER, R. A.
PETROPOULOS, E. A.
RIEGLE, G. D.
ROOT-BERNSTEIN, R. S.
SPARKS, H.
SPIELMAN, W. S.
TIEN, H. T.
ZIPSER, B.

Department of Political Science:

ABRAMSON, P. R.
ALLEN, W. B.
BRATTON, M.
FINIFTER, A. W.
HALL, M. G.
HAMMOND, T. H.
HULA, R. C.
KNOTT, J. H.
MELZER, A.
OSTROM, C. W., JR
ROHDE, D. W.
SILVER, B. D.
STEIN, B. N.
WAGMAN, J.

WEINBERGER, J. W.

Department of Psychiatry:

BIELSKI, R. J.
COLENDA, C.
OSBORN, G. G.
ROSEN, L. W.
STOFFELMAYR, B.
VAN EGEREN, L. F.
WERNER, A.
WILLIAMS, D. H.

Department of Psychology:

ABELES, N.
BARCLAY, A. M.
BOGAT, G. A.
CALDWELL, R. A.
CARR, T. H.
DAVIDSON, W., II
FERREIRA, M. F.
FITZGERALD, H. E.
FORD, J. K.
HARRIS, L. J.
HENDERSON, J. M.
HUNTER, J. E.
ILGEN, D. R.
JACKSON, L. A.
KARON, B. P.
KERR, N. L.
KOSLOWSKI, S. W.
LEVINE, R. L.
LOMBARDI, V. L.
MESSE, L. A.
NUNEZ, A. A.
PAULUS, G. S.
SCHMITT, N. W.
SISK, C. L.
STOLLAK, G. E.
VON EYE, A. A.
WOOD, G.
ZACKS, J. L.
ZACKS, R. T.

Department of Radiology:

FALLS, W. M.
GOTTSCHALK, A.
HALPERT, R. D.
JOHNSON, J. I.
POTCHEN, E. J.
ROSS, L. M.
WALKER, B. E.

Department of Religious Studies:

GREENE, J. T.
VERSLUIS, A.
WELCH, A. T.

Department of Resource Development:

BARNES-MCCONNELL, P.
BRONSTEIN, D. A.
DERSCH, E.
FEAR, F. A.
KAKELA, P. J.
KAMRIN, M. A.
NICKEL, P. E.
ROWAN, G.
SCHULTINK, G.
WRIGHT, D.

Department of Romance and Classical Languages:

COLMEIRO, J. F.
DONOHOE, J. I.
FIORE, R. L.
FRANCESE, J.
GRAY, E. F.
JOSEPHS, H.
KOPPISCH, M.
MANSOUR, G. P.
MARINO, N. F.
PORTER, L. M.
SNOW, J. T.
TYRRELL, W. B.

Department of Small Animal Clinical Sciences:

ARNOCZKY, S. P.
BRADEN, T. D.
DECAMP, C. E.

EVANS, A. T.
EYSTER, G. E.
FLO, G. L.
HAUPTMAN, J.
JOHNSON, C.
MOSTOSKY, U. V.
PROBST, C. W.
ROSSER, E. J.
SCHALL, W. D.
WALSHAW, R.

Department of Sociology:
BOKEMEIER, J.
BROMAN, C. L.
BUSCH, L. M.
CONNER, T. L.
GALLIN, R. S.
GOLD, S. J.
HAMILTON, R. S.
HILL, R. C.
JOHNSON, N. E.
KAPLOWITZ, S.
MANNING, P. K.
PERLSTADT, H.
RUMBAUT, R. G.
SHLAPENTOKH, V.
VANDERPOOL, C. K.
WILEY, D.
ZINN, M. B.

Department of Statistics and Probability:
ERICKSON, R. V.
FABIAN, V.
FELDMAN, D.
GARDINER, J. C.
GILLILAND, D. C.
HANNAN, J. F.
KOUL, H. L.
LEPAGE, R. D.
MANDREKAR, V.
PAGE, C. F.
RAMAMOORTHI, R. V.
SALEHI, H.
STAPLETON, J.

Department of Surgery:
DEAN, R. E.
HARKEMA, J.
OSUCH, J. R.
TOLEDO, L. H.

Department of Teacher Education:
ALLEMAN, J. E.
ANDERSON, C. W.
ANDERSON, K.
ANDERSON, L. M.
BADER, L. A.
BARNES, H. L.
BOOK, C.
BROPHY, J. E.
CHERRYHOLMES, C.
EDWARDS, P. A.
FEATHERSTONE, J.
FERRINI-MUNDY, J.
FLORIO-RUANE, S.
GALLAGHER, J. J.
JOYCE, W. W.
KENNEDY, M. M.
KOZIOL, S. M.
LABAREE, D. F.
LANIER, J. E.
LANIER, P. E.
LITTLE, T.
NEMSER, S. F.
PEARSON, P. D.
PURCELL-GATES, V.
PUTNAM, J. G.
RIETHMILLER, P. L.
ROEHLER, L. R.
SCHWILLE, J. R.
SEDLAK, M. W.
WEST, B. B.
WHEELER, C.

Department of Telecommunication:
BIOCCA, F. A.
GREENBERG, B. S.
HEETER, C. J.

LA ROSE, R. J.
LEVY, M. R.
LITMAN, B. R.
MODY, B.
MUTH, T. A.
STEINFIELD, C.
WILDMAN, S. S.
WILLIAMS, G. A.

Department of Theatre:
DURR, D. L.
RUTLEDGE, F. C.
RUTLEDGE, G.
SCHUTTLER, G.

Department of Zoology:
AGGARWAL, S. K.
ATKINSON, J. W.
BAND, R. N.
BEAVER, D. L.
BROMLEY, S. C.
BURTON, T. M.
BUSH, G. L.
CATHEY, B.
CLEMENS, L. G.
COOPER, W. E.
DYER, F. C.
EILAND, L. C.
GIESY, J. P.
HALL, D. J.
HILL, R. W.
HOLEKAMP, K. E.
HUGGETT, R. J.
MUZZALL, P. M.
PEEBLES, C.
ROBBINS, L. G.
SNIDER, R. J.
STEVENSON, R. J.
STRANEY, D.
WEBBER, M. M.

Division of Human Pathology:
JONES, M.
KUMAR, K.
SANDER, C. M.
SIEW, S.

James Madison College:
AYOOB, M.
BANKS, R. F.
DORR, R. F.
GARNETT, S. W.
GRAHAM, N. A.
HOEKSTRA, D. J.
RUBNER, M.
SCHECHTER, M.
SEE, K. O.
WALTZER, K.
ZINMAN, M. R.

Lyman Briggs School:
EBERT-MAY, D.
INGRAHAM, E. C.
MERCURO, N.
SAYED, M. M. A.
SIMPSON, W. A.
SPEES, S. T.

National Superconducting Cyclotron Laboratory:
BLOSSER, H. G.
GELBKE, C. K.
HANSEN, P. G.
YORK, R. C.

Office of Medical Education Research and Development:
ABBETT, W. S.
ANDERSON, W. A.
FARQUAR, L. J.
HENRY, R. C.
MOLIDOR, J. B.

School of Criminal Justice:
BONNER, R. W.
BYNUM, T. S.
CARTER, D. L.
HORVATH, F. S.
HUDZIK, J. K.
MASTROFSKI

MORASH, M. A.
NALLA, M. K.
SIEGEL, J.
SMITH, C. E.
STEWART, C. S.

School of Hospitality Business:
CICHY, R.
KASAVANA, M. L.
KNUTSON, B. J.
NINEMEIER, J. D.
SCHMIDGALL, B. H.

School of Journalism:
BOSSEN, H. S.
COTE, W. E.
DAVENPORT, L. D.
DETJEN, J. T.
FICO, F.
LACY, S. R.
MOLLOY, J. D.
SOFFIN, S. I.
SPANIOLO, J. D.

School of Labour and Industrial Relations:
BLOCK, R. N.
CURRY, T. H.
KOSSEK, E. E.
KRUGER, D. H.
MOORE, M. L.
REVITTE, J.
SMITH, P. R.
TOBEY, S. H.
VANDE VORD, N.
WOLKINSON, B. W.

School of Music:
CARMAN, O. W.
CATRON, D. L.
DAN, R. M.
DONAKOWSKI, C.
ELL, F. W.
FORGER, D. M.
FORGER, J. B.
GREGORIAN, L.
HUTCHESON, J. T.
JOHNSON, M. E.
JOHNSON, T. O.
KRATUS, J. K.
LEBLANC, A.
LULLOFF, J. P.
MOON, Y. H.
NEWMAN, R.
OLSON, C.
RUGGIERO, C. H.
SINDER, P. N.
SMITH, C. K.
STOLPER, D.
TIMS, F. C.
VERDEBR, E. L.
VERDEBR, W.
VOTAPEK, R. J.
WARD, B. W.
WHITWELL, J. L.
ZARA, M.

School of Packaging:
BURGESS, C. J.
DOWNES, T. W.
GIACIN, J. R.
HARTE, B.
HUGHES, H. A.
LOCKHART, H. E.
SELKE, S. E. M.

School of Social Work:
ANDERSON, G. R.
DUANE, E. A.
FREDDOLINO, P. P.
HAROLD, R. D.
HERRICK, J. M.
LEVANDE, D. I.
WHITEMAN, V. L.

Centers and Other Administrative Units:
BLINN, L. V.
BOWMAN, H. E.
CARROLL, T. W.
KAUFMAN, G.

LOPUSHINSKY, T.
NERENZ, D. R.
NOVICKI, D. J.
ROSENTHAL, W. H.
SIERRA, L.
VORRO, J.
WILLIAMS, J. G.

Medical Technology Program:
DAVIS, G. L.

Undergraduate University Division:
CURRY, B. P.

Urban Affairs Programs:
DARDEN, J. T.
LANG, M.
SCHWEITZER, J. H.
THORNTON, D.

W. K. Kellogg Biological Station:
GROSS, K. L.
KLUG, M. J.
KNEZEK, B. D.
MITTELBACH, G. G.
TESSIER, A. J.

MICHIGAN TECHNOLOGICAL UNIVERSITY

1400 Townsend Dr., Houghton, MI 49931-1295
Telephone: (906) 487-1885
E-mail: mtu4u@mtu.edu
Internet: www.mtu.edu

Founded 1885 as Michigan Mining School, current name adopted 1964
State control
Academic year: August to April

Pres.: Dr GLENN D. MROZ
Provost and Vice-Pres. for Academic Affairs: Dr MAX SEEL
Vice-Pres. for Admin.: ELLEN HORSCH
Vice-Pres. for Advancement: SHEA MCGREW
Vice-Pres for Governmental Relations: Dr DALE TAHTINEN
Vice-Pres. for Research: Dr DAVID D. REED
Vice-Pres. for Student Affairs: Dr LES COOK
Univ. Librarian and Dir for Library: ELLEN MARKS

Number of teachers: 460
Number of students: 7,150

Publications: *Michigan Tech Magazine* (3 a year), *Michigan Tech Research Magazine* (1 a year)

DEANS

College of Engineering: TIMOTHY J. SCHULZ
College of Sciences and Arts: Dr BRUCE E. SEELY
School of Business and Economics: DARRELL RADSON
School of Forest Resources and Environmental Science: MARGARET GALE
School of Technology: JAMES FRENDEWEY

NORTHERN MICHIGAN UNIVERSITY

1401 Presque Isle Ave, Marquette, MI 49855-5301
Telephone: (906) 227-1000
Internet: www.nmu.edu

Founded 1899 as Northern State Normal School, present name and status 1963
State control
Language of instruction: English
Academic year: August to May

Pres.: Dr FRITZ ERICKSON
Provost and Vice-Pres. for Academic Affairs: Dr PAUL LANG
Vice-Pres. for Advancement: MARTHA HAYNES
Vice-Pres. for Enrolment Management and Student Services: Dr STEVE NEIHEISEL
Vice-Pres. for Finance and Admin.: R. GAVIN LEACH
Dir for Admissions: GERRI DANIELS

Registrar: KIM ROTUNDO
Dean for Academic Information Services: LESLIE WARREN

Library of 478,745 vols, 522,903 govt docs
Number of teachers: 500 (330 full-time)
Number of students: 9,000

DEANS

College of Arts and Sciences: Dr MICHAEL BROADWAY
College of Health Sciences and Professional Studies: Dr KERRI SCHUILLING
Graduate Education and Research: Dr BRIAN CHERRY (Asst Provost)
Walker L. Cisler College of Business: Dr DAVID RAYOME

NORTHWOOD UNIVERSITY

4000 Whiting Dr., Midland, MI 48640-2398
Telephone: (989) 837-4200
E-mail: miadmit@northwood.edu
Internet: www.northwood.edu

Founded 1959, present name and status 2006
Private control
Academic year: September to May

Areas of study: arts, business admin., computer information systems, health care; campuses at West Palm Beach (Florida) and Cedar Hill (Texas)

Pres. and CEO: KEITH A. PRETTY
Exec. Vice-Pres. and Chief Academic Officer: Dr KRISTIN STEHOUWER
Vice-Pres. for Marketing and Enrolment Management: JOHN YOUNG
Vice-Pres. for Univ. Advancement: ARNOLD D'AMBROSIO
Provost for Michigan Campus: WILLIAM BATEMAN
Library Dir: SANDRA POTTS

Library of 60,000 vols, 300 periodicals, 50 DVDs
Number of teachers: 60
Number of students: 3,280

Publication: *Idea* (4 a year, online, www.northwood.edu/idea)

OAKLAND UNIVERSITY

2200 N Squirrel Rd, Rochester, MI 48309-4401
Telephone: (248) 370-2100
Internet: www.oakland.edu

Founded 1957, current name adopted 1963
State control
Academic year: September to August (2 semesters, 2 sessions)

Pres.: Dr GARY D. RUSSI
Provost and Interim Sr Vice-Pres. for Academic Affairs: VIRINDER K. MOUDGIL
Vice-Pres. for Devt, Alumni and Community Engagement: ERIC BARRITT
Vice-Pres. for Finance and Admin.: JOHN W. BEAGHAN
Vice-Pres. for Govt Relations: ROCHELLE A. BLACK
Vice-Pres. for Student Affairs and Enrolment Management: MARY BETH SNYDER
Dean for Library: ADRIENE LIM

Library of 747,000 vols, 1.1m. microfiche
Number of teachers: 530 (full-time)
Number of students: 19,380 (15,839 undergraduate, 3,541 graduate)

DEANS

College of Arts and Sciences: RONALD A. SUDOL
Oakland Univ. William Beaumont School of Medicine: Prof. Dr ROBERT FOLBERG
School of Business Administration: MOHAN TANNIRU
School of Educational and Human Services: MARY L. OTTO

School of Engineering and Computer Science: PIETER FRICK
School of Health Sciences: KENNETH HIGHTOWER
School of Nursing: LINDA THOMPSON-ADAMS

OLIVET COLLEGE

320 S Main St, Olivet, MI 49076
Telephone: (616) 749-7000
Internet: www.olivetcollege.edu

Founded 1844
Private control
Academic year: August to July

Depts of business admin., education, health, physical education, recreation and sport (HPERS), humanities, mathematics and computer science, natural and physical science, social science, visual and performing arts

Pres.: Dr STEVEN M. COREY
Provost and Dean for College: Prof. Dr MARIA G. DAVIS
Vice-Pres. for Admin.: LARRY COLVIN
Vice-Pres. and Dean for Student Life: Dr LINDA LOGAN
Dir for Admissions: MELISSA CASAREZ
Registrar: LESLIE SULLIVAN
Dir for Library: ELAINE HOELTZEL

Library of 90,000 vols, 500 periodicals
Number of teachers: 90
Number of students: 1,140

ROBERT B. MILLER COLLEGE

450 North Ave, Battle Creek, MI 49017-3397
Telephone: (269) 660-8021
E-mail: info@millercollege.edu
Internet: www.millercollege.edu

Founded 2005
Private control

Pres.: DAVE HARRIS
Vice-Pres. for Student Services: CHAD DANIELSON
Registrar: JACKIE WASHBURN

DEANS

Elizabeth H. Binda School of Education: SEAN KOTTKE
School of Arts and Science: HARRY ADAMSON
School of Business: DAVE FISHER
School of Nursing: THERESA DAWSON

ROCHESTER COLLEGE

800 W Avon Rd, Rochester Hills, MI 48307
Telephone: (248) 218-2000
E-mail: admissions@rc.edu
Internet: www.rc.edu

Founded 1959 as North Central Christian College, current name adopted 1997
Private control
Academic year: August to May

Divs of arts and sciences, extended learning and business, nursing, professional studies

Pres.: Prof. RUBEL SHELLY
Provost and Chief Academic Officer: Dr JOHN D. BARTON
Vice-Pres. for Enrolment Services: KLINT PLEASANT
Academic Dean: KATRINA VANDERWOUDE
Dir for Assessment and Institutional Research: MARK MANRY
Dean for Students: BRIAN E. COLE
Registrar: REBEKAH PINCHBACK
Dir for Library Services: ALISON KELLER

Number of teachers: 40
Number of students: 860

Publication: *The Shield*

SACRED HEART MAJOR SEMINARY

2701 Chicago Blvd, Detroit, MI 48206
Telephone: (313) 883-8500
E-mail: information@shms.edu
Internet: www.aodonline.org/shms

Founded 1919 as Sacred Heart Seminary, current name adopted 1988
Private control
Areas of study: arts, pastoral studies and divinity, philosophy, theology
Rector and Pres.: Rev. JEFFREY M. MONFORTON
Vice-Rector and Dean for Seminarians: Rev. GERARD BATTERSBY
Dean for Institute for Min.: JANET DIAZ
Dean for Studies: Rev. TODD LAJINESS
Library Dir: KAREN RAE MEHAFFEY
Library of 115,000 vols, 17,600 bound periodicals, 500 journals
Number of teachers: 70 (34 full-time, 30 part-time)
Number of students: 410 (235 undergraduate, 175 graduate)

SAGINAW VALLEY STATE UNIVERSITY

7400 Bay Rd, University Center, MI 48710
Telephone: (989) 964-4000
E-mail: admissions@svsu.edu
Internet: www.svsu.edu

Founded 1963
State control
Academic year: August to August
Pres.: Dr DONALD J. BACHAND
Provost and Vice-Pres. for Academic Affairs: Dr DEBORAH HUNTLEY
Exec. Vice-Pres. for Admin. and Business Affairs: JIM MULADORE
Vice-Pres. for Enrolment Management: JAMES DWYER
Vice-Pres. for Student Affairs and Dean for Students: MERRY JO BRANDIMORE
Library Dir: ANITA DEY
Library of 233,000 vols, 24,000 journals, 9,000 ebooks, 25,000 audiovisual items, 370,000 microforms
Number of teachers: 300
Number of students: 10,245
Publication: *Reflections*

DEANS

College of Arts and Behavioural Sciences: Dr JONI BOYE-BEAMAN
College of Business and Management: RAMA YELKUR
College of Education: Dr MARY HARMON
College of Science, Engineering and Technology: ANDREW CHUBB
Crystal M. Lange College of Health and Human Services: JUDITH P. RULAND

SIENA HEIGHTS UNIVERSITY

1247 E Siena Heights Dr., Adrian, MI 49221-1796
Telephone: (517) 263-0731
E-mail: admissions@sienaheights.edu
Internet: www.sienaheights.edu

Founded 1919, current name adopted 1998
Private control
Academic year: August to May
Campuses at Battle Creek, Benton Harbor, Jackson, Lansing, Southfield and Monroe in Michigan
Pres.: Dr PEG ALBERT
Vice-Pres. for Academic Affairs: SHARON WEBER
Vice-Pres. for Enrolment Management: C. PATRICK PALMER
Vice-Pres. for Institutional Advancement: MITCHELL P. BLONDE

Dean for Students: MICHAEL ORLANDO
Dir for Admissions: SARA A. JOHNSON
Registrar: BRENDA K. DOREMUS
Dir for Library: ROBERT W. GORDON
Library of 136,082 vols
Number of teachers: 220 (70 full-time, 150 adjunct)
Number of students: 2,410 (2,098 undergraduate, 312 graduate)
Publications: *Reflections* (3 a year), *Spectra* (6 a year)

DEANS

College of Arts and Sciences: Dr MARK SCHERSTEN
College for Professional Studies: DEBORAH CARTER
Graduate College: Dr ANNE HOOGHART

SPRING ARBOR UNIVERSITY

106 E Main St, Spring Arbor, MI 49283
Telephone: (517) 750-1200
E-mail: admissions@arbor.edu
Internet: www.arbor.edu

Founded 1873, current name adopted 2001
Private control
Pres.: Dr CHARLES H. WEBB
Provost and Chief Academic Officer: Dr BETTY J. OVERTON-ADKINS
Vice-Pres. for Enrolment Services: MATT S. OSBORNE
Vice-Pres. for Finance and Admin.: JERRY L. WHITE
Vice-Pres. for Student Devt and Learning: KIM K. HAYWORTH
Vice-Pres. for Technology Services: JEFF EDWARDS
Vice-Pres. for Univ. Advancement: BRENT ELLIS
Registrar: TIM WIEGERT
Library Dir: ROY MEADOR
Library of 120,300 vols
Number of teachers: 90 (full-time)
Number of students: 4,195

DEANS

Gainey School of Business: Dr JAMES COE
School of Arts and Sciences: ROGER VARLAND
School of Education: LINDA SHERRILL
School of Graduate and Professional Studies: NATALIE GIANETTI

THOMAS M. COOLEY LAW SCHOOL

POB 13038, Lansing, MI 48901
300 South Capitol Ave, Lansing, MI 48933
Telephone: (517) 371-5140
E-mail: admissions@cooley.edu
Internet: www.cooley.edu

Founded 1972
Private control
Academic year: September to August
Campuses at Lansing, Grand Rapids, Auburn Hills and Ann Arbor in Michigan
Pres. and Dean: DON LEDUC
Assoc. Dean for Enrolment and Student Services: Dr PAUL ZELENSKI
Assoc. Dean for Devt and Alumni Relations: JAMES ROBB
Assoc. Dean for Faculty: Prof. CHARLES P. CERCONE
Registrar: SHERIDA WYSOCKI
Assoc. Dean for Library and Instructional Support: DUANE STROJNY
Library of 650,000 vols
Number of teachers: 400 (122 full-time, 278 adjunct)
Number of students: 4,000
Publications: *Art and Museum Law Journal*, *Benchmark: The Thomas M. Cooley Law School Magazine*, *Journal of Practical and*

Clinical Law (3 a year), *Thomas M. Cooley Law Review*

UNIVERSITY OF DETROIT MERCY

POB 19900, 4001 W McNichols Rd, Detroit, MI 48221-3038
Telephone: (313) 993-1000
E-mail: admissions@udmercy.edu
Internet: www.udmercy.edu

Founded 1877 as Detroit College, chartered as univ. 1911, merged with Mercy College of Detroit 1990
Private control
Pres.: Dr ANTOINE M. GARIBALDI
Vice-Pres. for Academic Affairs and Provost: PAMELA ZARKOWSKI
Vice-Pres. for Enrolment and Student Affairs: DENISE WILLIAMS MALLETT
Vice-Pres. for Univ. Advancement: GREGORY CASCIONE
Dean for Student Life: MONICA WILLIAMS
Registrar: DIANE M. PRAET
Dean for Univ. Libraries: MARGARET AUER
Library of 830,000 vols, 86,900 journals, 12,000 audiovisual items, 1m. microforms, 91,500 ebooks, 90,000 govt documents
Number of teachers: 340 (full-time)
Number of students: 5,335

DEANS

College of Business Administration: Dr JOSEPH G. EISENHAUER
College of Engineering and Science: LEO HANIFIN
College of Health Professions: Dr CHRISTINE M. PACINI
College of Liberal Arts and Education: Dr ROY FINKENBINE
School of Architecture: WILL WITTIG
School of Dentistry: MERT AKSU
School of Law: PHYLLIS L. CROCKER

UNIVERSITY OF MICHIGAN

Ann Arbor, MI 48109
Telephone: (734) 764-1817
E-mail: info@umich.edu
Internet: www.umich.edu

Founded 1817
State control
Language of instruction: English
Academic year: September to August
Pres.: MARY SUE COLEMAN
Provost and Exec. Vice-Pres. for Academic Affairs: Prof. MARTHA POLLACK
Exec. Vice-Pres. and Chief Financial Officer: TIMOTHY SLOTTOW
Exec. Vice-Pres. for Medical Affairs: Prof. MICHAEL M. E. JOHNS
Vice-Pres. and Gen. Counsel: TIMOTHY LYNCH
Vice-Pres. and Sec.: SALLY CHURCHILL
Vice-Pres. for Devt: JERRY MAY
Vice-Pres. for Global Communications and Strategic Initiatives: LISA RUDGERS
Vice-Pres. for Govt Relations: CYNTHIA WILBANKS
Vice-Pres. for Research: Prof. STEPHEN FORREST
Vice-Pres. for Student Affairs: E. ROYSTER HARPER
Univ. Registrar: PAUL A. ROBINSON
Exec. Dir for Admissions: THEODORE L. SPENCER
Univ. Librarian and Dean for Libraries: PAUL N. COURANT
Library: see under Libraries and Archives
Number of teachers: 6,410
Number of students: 43,430
Publications: *DentalUM* (2 a year), *Dividend* (2 a year), *Emergence* (2 a year, print and online, art-design.umich.edu/news/emergence), *Findings* (2 a year), *Innovator* (1 a year), *Law Quadrangle* (2 a year, print and

online, www.law.umich.edu/quadrangle), *LSA Magazine* (2 a year, online, www.lsa.umich.edu/alumni/magazine), *Medicine at Michigan* (3 a year, online, www.medicineatmichigan.org/magazine), *Michigan Alumnus* (4 a year), *Michigan Engineer* (2 a year, print and online, www.engin.umich.edu/engineer), *Michigan Quarterly Review* (online, www.michiganquarterlyreview.com), *Michigan Today* (11 a year, online, michigantoday.umich.edu), *Montage* (online, www.montage.umich.edu), *Movement* (2 a year, online, www.kines.umich.edu/news-events/movement-magazine), *Muse* (2 a year, online, www.music.umich.edu/muse), *Ongoing* (2 a year, print and online, ssw.umich.edu/ongoing), *Portico* (2 a year, print and online, www.tcaup.umich.edu/publications/portico), *State & Hill* (print and online, www.fordschool.umich.edu/state-and-hill), *Stewards* (online, snre.umich.edu/stewards)

DEANS

College of Engineering: DAVID MUNSON, JR
College of Literature, Science and the Arts: TERRANCE MCDONALD
College of Pharmacy: FRANK ASCIONE
Gerald R. Ford School of Public Policy: SUSAN COLLINS
Graduate Studies: JANET WEISS
Law School: EVAN CAMINKER
Medical School: JAMES WOOLLISCROFT
Penny W. Stamps School of Art and Design: GUNALAN NADARAJAN
School of Dentistry: PETER POLVERINI
School of Education: DEBORAH BALL
School of Information: JEFFREY JACKIE-MASON
School of Kinesiology: RONALD ZERNICKE
School of Music, Theatre and Dance: CHRISTOPHER KENDAL
School of Natural Resources and Environment: MARIE MIRANDA
School of Nursing: KATHLEEN POTEMPA
School of Public Health: MARTIN PHILBERT
School of Social Work: LAURA LEIN
Stephen M. Ross School of Business: ALISON DAVIS-BLAKE
Taubman College of Architecture and Urban Planning: MONICA PONCE DE LEON

PROFESSORS

College of Engineering (1221 Beal Ave, Ann Arbor, MI 48109-2102; tel. (734) 647-7000; internet www.engin.umich.edu):

ACKERMAN, M., Human-Computer Interaction
ADRIAENS, P., Civil and Environmental Engineering
ALLISON, J., Materials Science and Engineering
ANTONUK, L., Biomedical Engineering
ARMSTRONG, T., Industrial and Operations Engineering
ARRUDA, E., Mechanical Engineering
ATKINS, III, D., Computer Science and Engineering
ASHTON-MILLER, J., Mechanical Engineering
ATREYA, A., Atmospheric, Oceanic and Space Science
ATZMON, M., Nuclear Engineering
AUSTIN, T., Computer Science and Engineering
BALTER, J., Biomedical Engineering
BANASZAK-HOLL, M., Biomedical Engineering
BARALD, K., Biomedical Engineering
BARKER, J., Atmospheric, Oceanic and Space Science
BARTEAU, M., Chemical Engineering
BATTERMAN, S., Civil and Environmental Engineering

BAVEJA, S., Computer Science and Engineering
BECK, R., Naval Architecture and Marine Engineering
BERNITSAS, M., Naval Architecture and Marine Engineering
BERNSTEIN, D., Aerospace Engineering
BHATTACHARYA, P., Electrical and Computer Engineering
BIELAJEW, A., Nuclear Engineering
BLAAUW, D., Computer Science and Engineering
BOEHMAN, A., Mechanical Engineering
BOYD, I., Aerospace Engineering
BOZER, Y., Industrial and Operations Engineering
BREI, D., Mechanical Engineering
BURNS, M., Chemical Engineering
CAIN, C., Biomedical Engineering
CAO, Y., Biomedical Engineering
CARROLL, M., Atmospheric, Oceanic and Space Science
CARSON, P., Biomedical Engineering
CECCIO, S., Mechanical Engineering
CEDERNA, P., Biomedical Engineering
CESNIK, C., Aerospace Engineering
CHAO, X., Industrial and Operations Engineering
CHEN, P., Computer Science and Engineering
CHEN, Z., Macromolecular Science and Engineering
CHUPP, T., Biomedical Engineering
DASKIN, M., Industrial and Operations Engineering
DOWLING, D., Mechanical Engineering
DOWNAR, T., Nuclear Engineering
DRAKE, R., Atmospheric, Oceanic and Space Science
DRISCOLL, J., Aerospace Engineering
DUENYAS, I., Industrial and Operations Engineering
DURFEE, E., Computer Science and Engineering
EL-TAWIL, S., Civil and Environmental Engineering
ENGLAND, A., Electrical and Computer Engineering
EWING, R., Materials Science and Engineering
FERRIS, D., Biomedical Engineering
FESSLER, J., Electrical and Computer Engineering
FISK, L., Atmospheric, Oceanic and Space Science
FLYNN, M., Electrical and Computer Engineering
FOGLER, H., Chemical Engineering
FORREST, S., Electrical and Computer Engineering
FOWLKES, J., Biomedical Engineering
FRANCESCHI, R., Biomedical Engineering
FREUDENBERG, J., Electrical and Computer Engineering
FRIEDMANN, P., Aerospace Engineering
GALLIMORE, A., Aerospace Engineering
GALVANAUSKAS, A., Electrical and Computer Engineering
GARIKIPATI, K., Mechanical Engineering
GIANCHANDANI, Y., Electrical and Computer Engineering
GIANNOBILE, W., Biomedical Engineering
GILBERT, A., Electrical and Computer Engineering
GILCHRIST, B., Nuclear Engineering
GILGENBACH, R., Nuclear Engineering
GLOTZER, S., Chemical Engineering
GOLDMAN, R., Materials Science and Engineering
GOMBOSI, T., Atmospheric, Oceanic and Space Science
GOODSITT, M., Nuclear Engineering
GOODSON, III, T., Macromolecular Science and Engineering
GREEN, P., Materials Science and Engineering

GRIZZLE, J., Electrical and Computer Engineering
GROSH, K., Mechanical Engineering
GROTBERG, J., Biomedical Engineering
GULARI, E., Chemical Engineering
HALLORAN, J., Materials Science and Engineering
HANSEN, W., Civil and Environmental Engineering
HAYES, J., Computer Science and Engineering
HE, Z., Nuclear Engineering
HERO, III, A., Electrical and Computer Engineering
HISKENS, I., Electrical and Computer Engineering
HOLLAND, J., Computer Science and Engineering
HOLLISTER, S., Biomedical Engineering
HOLLOWAY, J., Nuclear Engineering
HOPP, W., Industrial and Operations Engineering
HRYCIW, R., Civil and Environmental Engineering
HU, J., Mechanical Engineering
HULBERT, G., Mechanical Engineering
IM, H., Mechanical Engineering
INMAN, D., Aerospace Engineering
IOANNOU, P., Civil and Environmental Engineering
ISLAM, M., Electrical and Computer Engineering
JAGADISH, H., Computer Science and Engineering
JAHANIAN, F., Computer Science and Engineering
JIN, J., Industrial and Operations Engineering
JONES, J., Materials Science and Engineering
KABAMBA, P., Aerospace Engineering
KANICKI, J., Electrical and Computer Engineering
KANNATE-ASIBU, JR, E., Mechanical Engineering
KATOPODES, N., Civil and Environmental Engineering
KAVIANY, M., Mechanical Engineering
KEARFOTT, K., Nuclear Engineering
KEOLEIAN, G., Civil and Environmental Engineering
KEYSERLING, W., Industrial and Operations Engineering
KIEFFER, J., Materials Science and Engineering
KIERAS, D., Computer Science and Engineering
KIKUCHI, N., Mechanical Engineering
KIPKE, D., Biomedical Engineering
KOHN, D., Biomedical Engineering
KOLMANOVSKY, I., Aerospace Engineering
KOPELMAN, R., Chemical Engineering
KOREN, Y., Mechanical Engineering
KOTA, S., Mechanical Engineering
KOTOV, N., Chemical Engineering
KREBSBACH, P., Biomedical Engineering
KRUSHELNICK, K., Nuclear Engineering
KUIPERS, B., Computer Science and Engineering
KUO, A., Mechanical Engineering
KURABAYASHI, K., Mechanical Engineering
KUSHNER, M., Electrical and Computer Engineering
LAFORTUNE, S., Electrical and Computer Engineering
LAHANN, J., Materials Science and Engineering
LAINE, R., Materials Science and Engineering
LAIRD, J., Computer Science and Engineering
LARSEN, E., Nuclear Engineering
LARSON, R., Chemical Engineering
LAU, Y., Nuclear Engineering
LEE, J., Nuclear Engineering

LI, V., Civil and Environmental Engineering
LIKER, J., Industrial and Operations Engineering
LINDERMAN, J., Chemical Engineering
LIU, M., Engineering
LIU, Y., Industrial and Operations Engineering
LOVE, B., Materials Science and Engineering
LOVE, N., Civil and Environmental Engineering
MA, P., Materials Science and Engineering
MAHLKE, S., Computer Science and Engineering
MARKOV, I., Computer Science and Engineering
MARTIN, W., Nuclear Engineering
MATZGER, A., Macromolecular Science and Engineering
MAZUMDER, J., Mechanical Engineering
MAZUMDER, P., Computer Science and Engineering
MEERKOV, S., Electrical and Computer Engineering
MERLIN, R., Electrical and Computer Engineering
MEYHOFER, E., Mechanical Engineering
MICHAILIDIS, G., Electrical and Computer Engineering
MICHALOWSKI, R., Civil and Environmental Engineering
MICHIELSSEN, E., Electrical and Computer Engineering
MILLUNCHICK, J., Materials Science and Engineering
MOLDWIN, M., Atmospheric, Oceanic and Space Science
MORTAZAWI, A., Electrical and Computer Engineering
MUDGE, T., Computer Science and Engineering
MUNSON, JR., D., Electrical and Computer Engineering
MYCEK, M., Biomedical Engineering
NAIR, V., Industrial and Operations Engineering
NAJAFI, K., Electrical and Computer Engineering
NEUHOFF, D., Electrical and Computer Engineering
NI, J., Mechanical Engineering
NOBLE, B., Computer Science and Engineering
NOLL, D., Biomedical Engineering
NOR, J., Biomedical Engineering
NORRIS, T., Electrical and Computer Engineering
OLSEN, L., Technical Communications
PAN, J., Mechanical Engineering
PAN, X., Materials Science and Engineering
PAPAEFTHYMIOU, M., Computer Science and Engineering
PAPALAMBROS, P., Mechanical Engineering
PENG, H., Mechanical Engineering
PENNER, J., Atmospheric, Oceanic and Space Science
PERKINS, N., Mechanical Engineering
PERLIN, M., Naval Architecture and Marine Engineering
POLK, T., Computer Science and Engineering
POLLACK, M., Computer Science and Engineering
POWELL, K., Aerospace Engineering
PRAKASH, A., Computer Science and Engineering
RADEV, D., Computer Science and Engineering
RAND, S., Electrical and Computer Engineering
RASKIN, L., Civil and Environmental Engineering
RENNO, N., Atmospheric, Oceanic and Space Science

ROBERTSON, R., Materials Science and Engineering
ROE, P., Aerospace Engineering
ROMEIJN, E., Industrial and Operations Engineering
ROOD, R., Atmospheric, Oceanic and Space Science
RUF, C., Atmospheric, Oceanic and Space Science
SAIGAL, R., Industrial and Operations Engineering
SAITOU, K., Mechanical Engineering
SAKALLAH, K., Computer Science and Engineering
SAMSON, P., Atmospheric, Oceanic and Space Science
SARABANDI, K., Electrical and Computer Engineering
SARTER, N., Industrial and Operations Engineering
SAVAGE, P., Chemical Engineering
SCAVIA, D., Civil and Environmental Engineering
SCHOTLAND, J., Biomedical Engineering
SCHULTZ, W., Mechanical Engineering
SCHWANK, J., Chemical Engineering
SCOTT, R., Mechanical Engineering
SEIFORD, L., Industrial and Operations Engineering
SEMRAU, J., Civil and Environmental Engineering
SHAW, J., Aerospace Engineering
SHIH, A., Mechanical Engineering
SHIN, K., Mechanical Engineering
SICK, V., Mechanical Engineering
SINGH, J., Electrical and Computer Engineering
SKERLOS, S., Mechanical Engineering
SLAVIN, J., Atmospheric, Oceanic and Space Science
SOLOMON, M., Chemical Engineering
SOLOWAY, E., Computer Science and Engineering
STARK, W., Electrical and Computer Engineering
STEEL, D., Electrical and Computer Engineering
STEFANOPOULOU, A., Mechanical Engineering
STEIN, J., Mechanical Engineering
STOUT, Q., Computer Science and Engineering
STRAUSS, M., Computer Science and Engineering
SUN, J., Naval Architecture and Marine Engineering
SYLVESTER, D., Electrical and Computer Engineering
TAKAYAMA, S., Biomedical Engineering
TAUB, A., Materials Science and Engineering
TENEKETZIS, D., Electrical and Computer Engineering
TERRY, JR., F., Electrical and Computer Engineering
THOMASON, R., Chemical Engineering
THOMPSON, L., Chemical Engineering
THOULESS, M., Mechanical Engineering
TILBURY, D., Mechanical Engineering
TROESCH, A., Naval Architecture and Marine Engineering
ULABY, F., Electrical and Computer Engineering
ULSOY, A., Mechanical Engineering
VLAHOPOULOS, N., Naval Architecture and Marine Engineering
WAAS, A., Aerospace Engineering
WANG, H., Chemical Engineering
WANG, L., Nuclear Engineering
WANG, K., Mechanical Engineering
WAS, G., Nuclear Engineering
WEHE, D., Nuclear Engineering
WELLMAN, M., Computer Science and Engineering
WELSH, M., Electrical and Computer Engineering

WIGHT, J., Civil and Environmental Engineering
WINEMAN, A., Mechanical Engineering
WINFUL, H., Electrical and Computer Engineering
WINICK, K., Electrical and Computer Engineering
WOOLDRIDGE, M., Mechanical Engineering
WRIGHT, S., Civil and Environmental Engineering
YAGLE, A., Electrical and Computer Engineering
YALISOVE, S., Materials Science and Engineering
YANG, R., Chemical Engineering
YOON, E., Electrical and Computer Engineering
ZERNICKE, R., Biomedical Engineering
ZHU, J., Computer Science and Engineering
ZIFF, R., Chemical Engineering
ZURBUCHEN, T., Atmospheric, Oceanic and Space Science

College of Literature, Science and the Arts (500 S State St, Ann Arbor, MI 48109-1382; tel. (734) 764-0322; internet www.lsa.umich.edu):

ABEL, R., Screen Arts and Cultures
ACKERBERG, D., Economics
ADAMS, F., Physics
ADAMS, W., Economics
AHBEL-RAPPE, S., Classical Studies
AKAABOUNE, M., Molecular, Cellular and Development Biology
AKERLOF, C., Physics
AKHOURY, R., Physics
AL-HASHIMI, H., Chemistry
ALDRIDGE, J., Psychology
ALEXANDER, W., English Language and Literature
ALLER, H., Astronomy
AMIDEI, D., Physics
ANDERSON, E., Philosophy
ANDERSON, B., Sociology
ANTONUCCI, T., Psychology
ARENAS, F., Romance Languages and Literature
ASHFORTH, A., Afroamerican and African Studies
AWKWARD, M., English Language and Literature
AXELROD, R., Political Science
BAIK, J., Mathematics
BANASZAK HOLL, M., Chemistry
BAPTISTA, M., Linguistics
BARBER, J., Sociology
BARDAKJIAN, K., Near Eastern Studies
BARRETT, D., Mathematics
BARVINOK, A., Mathematics
BASS, H., Mathematics
BAUMILLER, T., Earth and Environmental Science
BECCHETTI, JR., F., Physics
BECKER, J., Psychology
BECKER, U., Earth and Environmental Science
BECKMAN, G., Near Eastern Studies
BEDDOR, P., Linguistics
BEHAR, R., Anthropology
BELOT, G., Philosophy
BERGIN, E., Astronomy
BERMAN, P., Physics
BERRIDGE, K., Psychology
BERRY, P., Ecology and Evolutionary Biology
BINETTI, V., Romance Languages and Literature
BIRO, M., History of Art
BLAIR, S., English Language and Literature
BLASS, A., Mathematics
BLOCH, A., Mathematics
BLUM, J., Earth and Environmental Science
BOCCACCINI, G., Near Eastern Studies

BOLAND, J., Psychology
BONNER, M., Near Eastern Studies
BORGERS, T., Economics
BOUND, J., Economics
BRANDWEIN, P., Political Science
BRATER, E., English Language and Literature
BREGMAN, J., Astronomy
BRICK, H., History
BRIGHT, C.
BROOKS, III, C., Chemistry
BROWN, C., Economics
BRUSATI, C., History of Art
BURNS, JR, D., Mathematics
BURNS, N., Political Science
CADIGAN, K., Molecular, Cellular and Development Biology
CAIN, A., Psychology
CALVET, N., Astronomy
CANARY, R., Mathematics
CANNING, K., History
CARON, D., Romance Languages and Literature
CASTON, V., Philosophy
CHANG, E., Psychology
CHANG, C., History
CHEN, Z., Chemistry
CHUPP, T., Physics
CLARK, S., Molecular, Cellular and Development Biology
CLARK, W., Political Science
CLARKE, R., Physics
COHEN, C.
COLE, E., Women's Studies
COLE, J., History
CONLON, J., Mathematics
COPPOLA, B., Chemistry
CORNISH, A., Romance Languages and Literature
CRANE, G., English Language and Literature
CRESSMAN, J.
CROWELL, S.
CURZAN, A., English Language and Literature
DAVENPORT, C., Political Science
DAVIES, P., English Language and Literature
DEBACKER, S., Mathematics
DELBANCO, N., English Language and Literature
DELDIN, P., Psychology
DENVER, R., Molecular, Cellular and Development Biology
DERKSEN, H., Mathematics
DESHPANDE, M., Asian Languages and Cultures
DILLARD, A., Afroamerican and African Studies
DISCH, L., Political Science
DOERING, C., Mathematics
DOUGLAS, S., Communication Studies
DOWD, G., American Culture
DUAN, C., Molecular, Cellular and Development Biology
DUAN, L., Physics
DUANMU, S., Linguistics
DUNLAP, P., Ecology and Evolutionary Biology
ECCLES, J., Psychology
EKOTTO, F., Afroamerican and African Studies
ELEY, G., History
ELLIS, N., Psychology
ELLISON, J., American Culture
ELLSWORTH, P., Psychology
EPSTEIN, S., Linguistics
ESEDOGLU, S., Mathematics
EVRARD, A., Physics
EWING, R., Earth and Environmental Science
FALLER, L., English Language and Literature
FEELEY-HARNIK, G., Anthropology
FERNANDES, L., Women's Studies
FIERKE, C., Chemistry

FINE, JR, J., History
FINK, W., Ecology and Evolutionary Biology
FISHER, D., Earth and Environmental Science
FLANNERY, K., Anthropology
FLINN, C., Screen Arts and Cultures
FLORIDA, N., Asian Languages and Cultures
FOMIN, S., Mathematics
FORSDYKE, S., Classical Studies
FRANCIS, A., Chemistry
FRANZESE, JR, R., Political Science
FREEDMAN, J., English Language and Literature
FREESE, K., Physics
FRENCH, K., History
FRICKE, T., Anthropology
FRIER, B., Classical Studies
FULTON, W., Mathematics
GAFNI, A., Biologyphysics
GAINES, K., History
GARBRAH, K., Classical Studies
GARCIA SANTO-TOMAS, E., Romance Languages and Literature
GAZDA, E., History of Art
GEHRING, W., Psychology
GELMAN, S., Psychology
GERDES, D., Physics
GEVA, E., Chemistry
GIBBARD, A., Philosophy
GIDLEY, D., Physics
GILBERT, A., Mathematics
GINGERICH, P., Earth and Environmental Science
GITELMAN, Z., Political Science
GLICK, G., Chemistry
GOCEK, F., Sociology
GOLDBERG, D., Ecology and Evolutionary Biology
GOLDENBERG, E., Political Science
GOLDSTEIN, L., English Language and Literature
GONZALEZ, R., Psychology
GOODISON, L., English Language and Literature
GOODMAN, D., History
GOODSON, III, T., Chemistry
GRAHAM-BERMANN, S., Psychology
GREGERSON, L., English Language and Literature
GRIESS, JR, R., Mathematics
GRZYMALA-BUSSE, A., Political Science
GUNNING, S., Afro-American and African Studies
HALPERIN, D., English Language and Literature
HANCOCK, D., History
HANNOOSH, M., Romance Languages and Literature
HARRISON, K., Communication Studies
HARTMANN, L., Astronomy
HAWES, C., English Language and Literature
HE, X., Statistics
HEATH, J., Linguistics
HECHT, G., History
HELL, J., Germanic Languages and Literature
HERBERT, S., Classical Studies
HERRERO-OLAIZOLA, A., Romance Languages and Literature
HERRMANN, A., English Language and Literature
HERWITZ, D., Comparative Literature
HIGHFILL, J., Romance Languages and Literature
HINES, JR, J., Economics
HOCHSTER, M., Mathematics
HOLLAND, D., Psychology
HOWARD, J., English Language and Literature
HSING, T., Statistics
HUESMANN, L., Communication Studies
HUME, R., Molecular, Cellular and Development Biology

HUNT, N., History
HUNTER, M., Ecology and Evolutionary Biology
HUNTINGTON, C., Mathematics
HUTCHINGS, V., Political Science
IRVINE, J., Anthropology
JACKSON, J., Political Science
JACKSON, T., Mathematics
JACOBSON, D., Philosophy
JAKOB, U., Molecular, Cellular and Development Biology
JANKO, R., Classical Studies
JI, L., Mathematics
JOHNSON, P., History
JONIDES, J., Psychology
JONSSON, M., Mathematics
JORDAN, A., English Language and Literature
JOYCE, J., Philosophy
JUSTER, S., History
KANE, G., Physics
KAPLAN, S., Psychology
KARNI, S., Mathematics
KASISCHKE, L., English Language and Literature
KEANE, W., Anthropology
KEATING, D., Psychology
KEENER, R., Statistics
KELLEY, M., History
KENNEDY, R., Chemistry
KILIAN, L., Economics
KIMBALL, M., Economics
KIMELDORF, H., Sociology
KINDER, D., Political Science
KITAYAMA, S., Psychology
KIVELSON, V., History
KLING, G., Ecology and Evolutionary Biology
KLIONSKY, D., Molecular, Cellular and Development Biology
KNOWLES, L., Ecology and Evolutionary Biology
KNYSH, A., Near Eastern Studies
KOLLMAN, K., Political Science
KONDRASHOV, A., Ecology and Evolutionary Biology
KOPELMAN, R., Chemistry
KOREEDA, M., Chemistry
KRASNY, R., Mathematics
KRISCH, J., Physics
KRIZ, I., Mathematics
KUPPERS, P., English Language and Literature
KURASHIGE, S., American Culture
KURDAK, C., Physics
KUWADA, J., Molecular, Cellular and Development Biology
LAGARIAS, J., Mathematics
LAITNER, J., Economics
LAMBROPOULOS, V., Classical Studies
LANGE, R., Earth and Environmental Science
LARSEN, F., Physics
LARSON, K., English Language and Literature
LAZARSFELD, R., Mathematics
LEE, F., Psychology
LEGASSICK, T., Near Eastern Studies
LEHMAN, J., Ecology and Evolutionary Biology
LEVINSON, M., English Language and Literature
LEWIS, R., Psychology
LI, J., Molecular, Cellular and Development Biology
LIEBERMAN, V., History
LINDNER, R., History
LIU, J., Physics
LOEB, L., Philosophy
LOHMANN, K., Earth and Environmental Science
LOPEZ, JR, D., Asian Languages and Cultures
LORENZON, W., Physics
LUONG, P., Political Science
LUPIA, A., Political Science

MacDonald, M., History
MacLatchy, L., Anthropology
Maddock, J., Molecular, Cellular and Development Biology
Makin, M., Slavic Languages and Literature
Mannheim, B., Anthropology
Mapp, A., Chemistry
Marcus, J., Anthropology
Markovits, A., Germanic Languages and Literature
Markus, G., Political Science
Marsh, E., Chemistry
Martin, K., Sociology
Masuzawa, T., Comparative Literature
Mateo, M., Astronomy
Matzger, A., Chemistry
McCracken, P., Romance Languages and Literature
McKay, T., Physics
McLoyd, V., Psychology
Mebane, Jr, W., Political Science
Megginson, R., Mathematics
Meiners, J., Physics
Merlin, R., Physics
Meyer, D., Psychology
Meyerhoff, M., Chemistry
Michailidis, G., Statistics
Michalowski, P., Near Eastern Studies
Miles, T., American Culture
Miller, P., Mathematics
Mitani, J., Anthropology
Mizruchi, M., Sociology
Montgomery, J., Chemistry
Montgomery, H., Mathematics
Moore, D., History
Morantz-Sanchez, R., History
Moreiras-Menor, C., Romance Languages and Literature
Morenoff, J., Sociology
Morris, M., Chemistry
Morrison, F., Psychology
Morrow, J., Political Science
Moss, T., English Language and Literature
Mrazek, R., History
Mueggler, E., Anthropology
Mustata, M., Mathematics
Myers, P., Ecology and Evolutionary Biology
Nagata, D., Psychology
Nair, V., Statistics
Nakamura, L., Screen Arts and Cultures
Neal, H., Physics
Neuman, W., Communication Studies
Nevett, L., Classical Studies
Newman, M., Physics
Nisbett, R., Psychology
Norich, A., English Language and Literature
Nornes, M., Screen Arts and Cultures
Nussbaum, R., Ecology and Evolutionary Biology
O'Foighil, D., Ecology and Evolutionary Biology
O'Shea, J., Anthropology
OConnor, B., Ecology and Evolutionary Biology
Olsen, L., Molecular, Cellular and Development Biology
Olson, S., Psychology
Orr, B., Physics
Owusu, M., Anthropology
Pachella, R., Psychology
Page, S., Political Science
Paige, J., Sociology
Park, N., Psychology
Paulson, W., Romance Languages and Literature
Pecoraro, V., Chemistry
Pedraza, S., Sociology
Perlmutter, M., Psychology
Pernick, M., History
Peterson, D., History
Pichersky, E., Molecular, Cellular and Development Biology

Pinch, A., English Language and Literature
Pitcher, A., Afroamerican and African Studies
Polk, T., Psychology
Pollack, E., English Language and Literature
Porter, D., English Language and Literature
Porter-Szucs, B., History
Potter, D., Classical Studies
Potts, A., History of Art
Powers, M., History of Art
Prasad, G., Mathematics
Price, R., Psychology
Prins, Y., English Language and Literature
Puff, H., Germanic Languages and Literature
Qian, J., Physics
Rabkin, E., English Language and Literature
Railton, P., Philosophy
Raithel, G., Physics
Ramamoorthy, A., Chemistry
Ramirez-Christensen, E., Asian Languages and Cultures
Rammuny, R., Near Eastern Studies
Ratte, C., Classical Studies
Rauch, J., Mathematics
Raymond, P., Molecular, Cellular and Development Biology
Renne, E., Anthropology
Reuter-Lorenz, P., Psychology
Rhode, P., Economics
Richards, J., Near Eastern Studies
Richstone, D., Astronomy
Riles, K., Physics
Robinson, T., Psychology
Rohani, P., Ecology and Evolutionary Biology
Ronen, O., Slavic Languages and Literature
Root, M., History of Art
Rothman, E., Statistics
Rowley, S., Psychology
Ruan, Y., Mathematics
Rudelson, M., Mathematics
Ruetsche, L., Philosophy
Ruff, L., Earth and Environmental Science
Salant, S., Economics
Sander, L., Physics
Sanford, M., Chemistry
Sanjines, J., Romance Languages and Literature
Sarter, M., Psychology
Savit, R., Physics
Saxonhouse, A., Political Science
Scannell, G., Communication Studies
Schiefelbein, J., Molecular, Cellular and Development Biology
Schmaltz, T., Philosophy
Schoenfeldt, M., English Language and Literature
Schotland, J., Mathematics
Schwarz, N., Psychology
Scodel, R., Classical Studies
Scott, G., Mathematics
Scott, R., History
Sears, E., History of Art
Seifert, C., Psychology
Sekaquaptewa, D., Psychology
Sellers, R., Psychology
Sension, R., Chemistry
Shammas, A., Comparative Literature
Shipan, C., Political Science
Shryock, A., Anthropology
Siebers, T., English Language and Literature
Siegfried, S., History of Art
Silverman, R., History of Art
Simons, P., History of Art
Sinha, M., History
Sklar, L., Philosophy
Slemrod, J., Economics

Smereka, P., Mathematics
Smith, J., Economics
Smith, J., Psychology
Smith, K., Mathematics
Smock, P., Sociology
Smoller, J., Mathematics
Smuts, B., Psychology
Somers, M., Sociology
Spatzier, R., Mathematics
Spector, S., History
Stafford, F., Economics
Stam, A., Political Science
Stein, H., Afroamerican and African Studies
Steinmetz, G., Sociology
Stembridge, J., Mathematics
Stewart, A., Psychology
Stillman, A., American Culture
Strassmann, B., Anthropology
Strauss, M., Mathematics
Suny, R., History
Tang, X., Asian Languages and Cultures
Tarle, G., Physics
Terrenato, N., Classical Studies
Tesar, L., Economics
Thomason, R., Philosophy
Thomason, S., Linguistics
Tinkle, T., English Language and Literature
Toman, J., Slavic Languages and Literature
Tonomura, H., History
Traub, V., English Language and Literature
Traugott, M., Communication Studies
Tsebelis, G., Political Science
Tucker, P., Ecology and Evolutionary Biology
Uher, C., Physics
Uribe-Ahumada, A., Mathematics
Valentino, N., Political Science
van Dam, R., History
van der Meer, J., Ecology and Evolutionary Biology
van der Pluijm, B., Earth and Environmental Science
van der Voo, R., Earth and Environmental Science
van Keken, P., Earth and Environmental Science
Vershynin, R., Mathematics
Vinovskis, M., History
Viswanath, D., Mathematics
von Eschen, P., History
Wald, A., English Language and Literature
Walter, N., Chemistry
Walton, Jr, H., Political Science
Wang, N., Statistics
Ward, L., Psychology
Weatherson, B., Philosophy
Webb, P., Environment
Wellman, H., Psychology
Werner, E., Ecology and Evolutionary Biology
Whallon, Jr, R., Anthropology
Whatley, W., Economics
Williams, G., Romance Languages and Literature
Williams, M., Anthropology
Winter, D., Psychology
Winter, D., Mathematics
Wolfe, J., Chemistry
Wolpoff, M., Anthropology
Wright, H., Anthropology
Wu, S., Mathematics
Xie, Y., Sociology
Yaeger, P., English Language and Literature
Yates, J., Psychology
Ybarra, O., Psychology
Young, Jr, A., Sociology
Young, V., Mathematics
Zaborowska, M., American Culture
Zhang, M., Ecology and Evolutionary Biology

ZHANG, J., Psychology
ZHANG, Y., Earth and Environmental Science
ZHOU, B., Physics
ZHU, J., Statistics
ZIEVE, M., Mathematics

College of Pharmacy (428 Church St, Ann Arbor, MI 48109-1065; tel. (734) 764-7312; internet pharmacy.umich.edu):

AMIDON, G., Pharmaceutical Science
CARLSON, H., Medicinal Chemistry
ELLINGROD, V., Clinical, Social and Administrative Science
FARRIS, K., Clinical, Social and Administrative Science
GARCIA, G., Medicinal Chemistry
LEE, K., Pharmaceutical Science
MOSBERG, H., Medicinal Chemistry
MUELLER, B., Clinical, Social and Administrative Science
SCHWENDEMAN, S., Pharmaceutical Science
SHERMAN, D., Medicinal Chemistry
SHIMP, L., Clinical, Social and Administrative Science
SMITH, D., Pharmaceutical Science
STRINGER, K., Clinical, Social and Administrative Science
WOODARD, R., Medicinal Chemistry
YANG, V., Pharmaceutical Science

Gerald R. Ford School of Public Policy (Joan and Sanford Weill Hall, 735 S State St, Ann Arbor, MI 48109-3091; tel. (734) 764-3490; internet www.fordschool.umich.edu):

AXELROD, R.
CHAMBERLIN, J.
COHEN, D.
COLLINS, S.
CORCORAN, M.
COURANT, P.
DANZIGER, S.
DANZIGER, S.
DEARDORFF, A.
DINARDO, J.
DOMINGUEZ, K.
GERBER, E.
HALL, R.
HOUSE, J.
JACOB, B.
LEVITSKY, M.
RABE, B.
SIMON, C.
SVEJNAR, J.

Law School (625 S State St, Ann Arbor, MI 48109-1215; tel. (734) 764-1358; internet www.law.umich.edu):

AVIYONAH, R.
BAGENSTOS, S.
BARR, M.
BENY, L.
CAMINKER, E.
CLARK, S.
COOPER, E.
CRANE, D.
CROLEY, S.
DAVIS, A.
EISENBERG, R.
ELLSWORTH, P.
FRIEDMAN, R.
FRIER, B.
GROSS, S.
HALBERSTAM, D.
HATHAWAY, J.
HERSHOVITZ, S.
HERZOG, D.
HINES, JR., J.
HOWSON, N.
KAHN, D.
KATZ, E.
KHANNA, V.
KRIER, J.
LITMAN, J.
LOGUE, K.
MACKINNON, C.
MENDELSON, N.

MILLER, W.
NOVAK, W.
PAYTON, S.
POTTOW, J.
PRESCOTT, J.
PRIMUS, R.
PRIMUS, E.
PRITCHARD, A.
RADIN, M.
RATNER, S.
REGAN, D.
REIMANN, M.
SCHLANGER, M.
SCHNEIDER, C.
SCOTT, R.
SEINFELD, G.
WEST, M.
WHITE, J.
WHITMAN, C.

Medical School (1301 Catherine Road, Ann Arbor, MI 48109-5604; tel. (734) 763-9600; internet www.med.umich.edu/medschool):

AARONSON, K., Cardiology
ABELSON, J., Psychiatry
ADAMS, K., Psychiatry
ALBIN, R., Neurology
ALEXANDER, N., Geriatric and Palliative Medicine
ALTSCHULER, R., Otorhinolaryngology
ANDERSON, R., Medical Education
ANDREWS, P., Biological Chemistry
ANNESLEY, T., Pathology
ANTONETTI, D., Ophthalmology and Visual Science
ANTONUK, L., Radiation Oncology
APPELMAN, H., Pathology
ARCHER, S., Ophthalmology and Visual Science
ARMITAGE, R., Psychiatry
ARMSTRONG, W., Cardiology
ARVAN, P., Metabolism, Endocrinology and Diabetes
ATHEY, B., Computational Medicine and Bioinformatics
AUCHUS, R., Metabolism, Endocrinology and Diabetes
BAGHDOYAN, H., Anaesthesiology
BAKER, L., Haematology and Oncology
BAKER, S., Otorhinolaryngology
BALLOU, D., Biological Chemistry
BALTER, J., Radiation Oncology
BANERJEE, R., Biological Chemistry
BARALD, K., Cell and Developmental Biology
BARKAN, A., Metabolism, Endocrinology and Diabetes
BARKS, J., Paediatrics–Neonatal–Perinatal Medicine
BARSAN, W., Emergency Medicine
BATES, E., Cardiology
BEER, D., Thoracic Surgery
BERGUER, R., Vascular Surgery
BIERMANN, J., Orthopaedic Surgery
BISHOP, D., Transplant Surgery
BLOOM, D., Urology
BLOW, F., Psychiatry
BOHNEN, N., Radiology
BOLLING, S., Cardiac Surgery
BOVE, E., Cardiac Surgery
BOXER, L., Paediatrics–Haematology and Oncology
BRADFORD, C., Otorhinolaryngology
BRADLEY, S., Infectious Diseases
BRENNER, D., Haematology and Oncology
BRITTON, S., Anaesthesiology
BROSIUS, III, F., Nephrology
BROWER, K., Psychiatry
BUCHMAN, S., Plastic Surgery
BUDE, R., Radiology
BURANT, C., Metabolism, Endocrinology and Diabetes
BURKE, D., Human Genetics
CAMPER, S., Human Genetics
CAO, Y., Radiation Oncology
CARETHERS, J., Gastroenterology

CAREY, T., Otorhinolaryngology
CARLOS, R., Radiology
CARPENTER, J., Orthopaedic Surgery
CARRUTHERS, V., Microbiology and Immunology
CARSON, P., Radiology
CARTER-SU, C., Molecular and Integrative Physiology
CASTLE, V., Paediatrics–Haematology and Oncology
CASTRO, M., Neurosurgery
CEDERNA, P., Plastic Surgery
CHAN, H., Radiology
CHANDLER, W., Neurosurgery
CHANG, C., Microbiology and Immunology
CHEN, Y., Cardiology
CHENEVERT, T., Radiology
CHENSUE, S., Pathology
CHEPEHA, D., Otorhinolaryngology
CHERVIN, R., Neurology
CHEY, W., Gastroenterology
CHO, K., Radiology
CHO, K., Pathology
CHUNG, K., Plastic Surgery
CLAUW, D., Anaesthesiology
COHAN, R., Radiology
COLLINS, K., Infectious Diseases
COONEY, K., Haematology and Oncology
CORBETT, J., Radiology
CURTIS, J., Pulmonary and Critical Care
CUSTER, J., Paediatrics–Intensive Care
D'ALECY, L., Molecular and Integrative Physiology
DAY, M., Urology
DE VRIES, R., Medical Education
DEEB, G., Cardiac Surgery
DEL VALLE, J., Gastroenterology
DELANCEY, J., Obstetrics and Gynaecology
DELMONTE, M., Ophthalmology and Visual Science
DICK, II, M., Paediatrics–Cardiology
DICKINSON, C., Paediatrics–Gastroenterology
DIPIETRO, M., Radiology
DIRITA, V., Laboratory Animal Medicine
DLUGOSZ, A., Dermatology
DONN, S., Paediatrics–Neonatal–Perinatal Medicine
DRESSLER, G., Pathology
DUCKETT, C., Pathology
DUNNICK, N., Radiology
DUNNICK, W., Microbiology and Immunology
EAGLE, K., Cardiology
EATON, K., Laboratory Animal Medicine
EISBRUCH, A., Radiation Oncology
EITZMAN, D., Cardiology
ELDER, J., Dermatology
ELENITOBA-JOHNSON, K., Pathology
EL-KASHLAN, H., Otorhinolaryngology
ELLIS, C., Dermatology
ELLIS, J., Radiology
ELNER, V., Ophthalmology and Visual Science
ELNER, S., Ophthalmology and Visual Science
ELTA, G., Gastroenterology
ENGEL, J., Cell and Developmental Biology
ENGELKE, D., Biological Chemistry
ENGLEBERG, N., Infectious Diseases
FAERBER, G., Urology
FARLEY, F., Orthopaedic Surgery
FEARON, E., Molecular Medicine and Genetics
FELDMAN, E., Neurology
FENDRICK, A., General Medicine
FENNER, D., Obstetrics and Gynaecology
FERRARA, J., Paediatrics–Haematology and Oncology
FETTERS, M., Family Medicine
FINK, D., Neurology
FINK, J., Neurology
FISHER, G., Dermatology
FITZGERALD, J., Medical Education
FONTANA, R., Gastroenterology
FOWLKES, J., Radiology

Fox, D., Rheumatology
Francis, I., Radiology
Freed, G., Paediatrics
Frey, K., Radiology
Fuller, R., Biological Chemistry
Gardner, T., Ophthalmology and Visual Science
Gebarski, S., Radiology
Geiger, J., Pediatric Surgery
Geisser, M., Physical Medicine and Rehabilitation
Gilman, S., Neurology
Gilsdorf, J., Paediatrics–Infectious Diseases
Giordani, B., Psychiatry
Giordano, T., Pathology
Glover, T., Human Genetics
Gnegy, M., Pharmacology
Goodsitt, M., Radiology
Goold, S., General Medicine
Goulet, J., Orthopaedic Surgery
Greden, J., Psychiatry
Green, C., Anaesthesiology
Greenson, J., Pathology
Grekin, R., Metabolism, Endocrinology and Diabetes
Griggs, J., Haematology and Oncology
Gross, B., Radiology
Grum, C., Pulmonary and Critical Care
Gruppen, L., Medical Education
Guan, J., Molecular Medicine and Genetics
Gumucio, D., Cell and Developmental Biology
Guyer, M., Psychiatry
Haefner, H., Obstetrics and Gynaecology
Haig, A., Physical Medicine and Rehabilitation
Halter, J., Geriatric and Palliative Medicine
Hammer, G., Metabolism, Endocrinology and Diabetes
Hanna, G., Psychiatry
Hanna, P., Microbiology and Immunology
Harrison, R., Medical Education
Hasler, W., Gastroenterology
Hayes, D., Haematology and Oncology
Hayward, R., General Medicine
Heckenlively, J., Ophthalmology and Visual Science
Helvie, M., Radiology
Henke, P., Vascular Surgery
Herman, W., Metabolism, Endocrinology and Diabetes
Hernandez, R., Radiology
Hershenson, M., Paediatrics–Pulmonary Medicine
Hess, J., Pathology
Hirschl, R., Pediatric Surgery
Hofer, T., General Medicine
Hogaboam, C., Pathology
Hogikyan, N., Otorhinolaryngology
Hollenberg, P., Pharmacology
Holoshitz, J., Rheumatology
Holz, R., Pharmacology
Howell, J., General Medicine
Huffnagle, G., Pulmonary and Critical Care
Hughes, B., Ophthalmology and Visual Science
Humes, H., Nephrology
Hussain, M., Haematology and Oncology
Imperiale, M., Microbiology and Immunology
Innis, J., Human Genetics
Isom, L., Pharmacology
Jacobson, J., Radiology
Jalife, J., Cardiology
Jamerson, K., Cardiology
Jepsen, K., Orthopaedic Surgery
Johnson, K., Pathology
Johnson, M., Ophthalmology and Visual Science
Johnson, T., Dermatology
Johnson, T., Obstetrics and Gynaecology
Junck, L., Neurology
Kaminski, M., Haematology and Oncology

Katz, S., General Medicine
Kauffman, C., Infectious Diseases
Kazanjian, P., Infectious Diseases
Kazerooni, E., Radiology
Keep, R., Neurosurgery
Keller, E., Urology
Kerppola, T., Biological Chemistry
Kerr, E., General Medicine
Kilbourn, M., Radiology
Kileny, P., Otorhinolaryngology
King, C., Psychiatry
King, W., Otorhinolaryngology
Kirschner, D., Microbiology and Immunology
Kleer, C., Pathology
Klinkman, M., Family Medicine
Koch, A., Rheumatology
Koenig, R., Metabolism, Endocrinology and Diabetes
Koeppe, R., Radiology
Koopmann, Jr, C., Otorhinolaryngology
Kretzler, M., Nephrology
Kunkel, S., Pathology
Kuzon, Jr, W., Plastic Surgery
Lawrence, D., Cardiology
Lawrence, T., Radiation Oncology
Lee, P., Ophthalmology and Visual Science
Leichtman, A., Nephrology
Lesperance, M., Otorhinolaryngology
Levine, J., Paediatrics–Haematology and Oncology
Liberzon, I., Psychiatry
Lichter, P., Ophthalmology and Visual Science
Lim, M., Pathology
LiPuma, J., Paediatrics–Infectious Diseases
Lloyd, T., Paediatrics–Cardiology
Lok, A., Gastroenterology
Low, M., Molecular and Integrative Physiology
Lowenstein, P., Neurosurgery
Lubman, D., Surgery
Lucchesi, B., Pharmacology
Lukacs, N., Pathology
Lydic, R., Anaesthesiology
McCune, W., Rheumatology
MacDougald, O., Molecular and Integrative Physiology
McGuire, E., Urology
McInnis, M., Psychiatry
McKeever, P., Pathology
McLaughlin, V., Cardiology
McMahon, Jr, L., General Medicine
Macoska, J., Urology
McShan, D., Radiation Oncology
Magee, J., Transplant Surgery
Malviya, S., Anaesthesiology
Marentette, L., Otorhinolaryngology
Margolis, B., Nephrology
Markovitz, D., Infectious Diseases
Martinez, F., Pulmonary and Critical Care
Mata, M., Neurology
Maybaum, J., Pharmacology
Meisler, M., Human Genetics
Menon, K., Obstetrics and Gynaecology
Menon, R., Paediatrics–Endocrinology
Merajver, S., Haematology and Oncology
Merchant, J., Gastroenterology
Merion, R., Transplant Surgery
Messana, J., Nephrology
Meyer, C., Radiology
Miller, J., Otorhinolaryngology
Miller, R., Pathology
Mobley, H., Microbiology and Immunology
Moenter, S., Molecular and Integrative Physiology
Moler, F., Paediatrics–Intensive Care
Montie, J., Urology
Moore, B., Pulmonary and Critical Care
Morady, F., Cardiology
Morgenstern, L., Neurology
Moroi, S., Ophthalmology and Visual Science
Mortensen, R., Molecular and Integrative Physiology

Moseley, R., Gastroenterology
Mukherji, S., Radiology
Mullan, P., Medical Education
Muraszko, K., Neurosurgery
Musch, D., Ophthalmology and Visual Science
Myers, J., Pathology
Myers, M., Metabolism, Endocrinology and Diabetes
Nasr, S., Paediatrics–Pulmonary Medicine
Nelson, C., Ophthalmology and Visual Science
Nesse, R., Psychiatry
Neubig, R., Pharmacology
Neumar, R., Emergency Medicine
Ninfa, A., Biological Chemistry
Nostrant, T., Gastroenterology
Nunez, G., Pathology
Ohl, D., Urology
Ojo, A., Nephrology
Omary, B., Molecular and Integrative Physiology
Omenn, G., Computational Medicine and Bioinformatics
Oral, H., Cardiology
Orringer, M., Thoracic Surgery
Osawa, Y., Pharmacology
O'Shea, S., Cell and Developmental Biology
Owyang, C., Gastroenterology
Padmanabhan, V., Paediatrics–Endocrinology
Pagani, F., Cardiac Surgery
Parent, J., Neurology
Paulson, H., Neurology
Pearlman, M., Obstetrics and Gynaecology
Peters-Golden, M., Pulmonary and Critical Care
Petty, H., Ophthalmology and Visual Science
Pfingst, B., Otorhinolaryngology
Phan, S., Pathology
Pienta, K., Haematology and Oncology
Pierce, L., Radiation Oncology
Pietropaolo, M., Metabolism, Endocrinology and Diabetes
Piette, J., General Medicine
Pinsky, D., Cardiology
Pipe, S., Paediatrics–Haematology and Oncology
Platt, J., Radiology
Platt, J., Transplant Surgery
Punch, J., Transplant Surgery
Puro, D., Ophthalmology and Visual Science
Quint, D., Radiology
Quint, L., Radiology
Raghavan, M., Microbiology and Immunology
Ragsdale, S., Biological Chemistry
Randolph, Jr, J., Obstetrics and Gynaecology
Raphael, Y., Otorhinolaryngology
Reed, B., Family Medicine
Rehemtulla, A., Radiation Oncology
Reynolds, R., Obstetrics and Gynaecology
Richards, J., Ophthalmology and Visual Science
Richardson, B., Rheumatology
Richardson, J., Physical Medicine and Rehabilitation
Robertson, P., Paediatrics–Neurology
Robins, D., Human Genetics
Rocchini, A., Paediatrics–Cardiology
Roessler, B., Rheumatology
Ross, B., Radiology
Roubidoux, M., Radiology
Rubenfire, M., Cardiology
Rubin, J., Radiology
Ruffin, M., Family Medicine
Sagher, O., Neurosurgery
Saint, S., General Medicine
Samaniego, M., Nephrology
Samuelson, L., Molecular and Integrative Physiology
Sandberg, D., Child Behavioural Health

SARAN, R., Nephrology
SATIN, L., Pharmacology
SCHACHT, J., Otorhinolaryngology
SCHEIMAN, J., Gastroenterology
SCHOENFELD, P., Gastroenterology
SCHUMACHER, R., Paediatrics, Neonatal and Perinatal Medicine
SCHWARTZ, J., Molecular and Integrative Physiology
SEGAL, B., Neurology
SERWER, G., Paediatrics–Cardiology
SHANLEY, T., Paediatrics–Intensive Care
SHAYMAN, J., Nephrology
SHEA, M., Cardiology
SHEETS, K., Family Medicine
SHEWACH, D., Pharmacology
SHLAFER, M., Pharmacology
SILK, K., Psychiatry
SILVERSTEIN, F., Paediatrics–Neurology
SIMON, R., Pulmonary and Critical Care
SIMPSON, R., Pharmacology
SING, C., Human Genetics
SITRIN, R., Pulmonary and Critical Care
SMITH, C., Pharmacology
SMITH, D., Haematology and Oncology
SMITH, G., Obstetrics and Gynaecology
SMITH, T., Ophthalmology and Visual Science
SMITH, W., Biological Chemistry
SMITH, Y., Obstetrics and Gynaecology
SOONG, H., Ophthalmology and Visual Science
SPINDLER, K., Microbiology and Immunology
STANDIFORD, T., Pulmonary and Critical Care
STANLEY, J., Vascular Surgery
STERN, A., Obstetrics and Gynaecology
STOOLMAN, L., Pathology
STROUSE, P., Radiology
STUENKEL, E., Molecular and Integrative Physiology
SU, G., Gastroenterology
SUGAR, A., Ophthalmology and Visual Science
SUN, Y., Radiation Oncology
SWANSON, M., Microbiology and Immunology
SWANSON, J., Microbiology and Immunology
TAIT, A., Anaesthesiology
TALPAZ, M., Haematology and Oncology
TATE, D., Physical Medicine and Rehabilitation
TAYLOR, S., Psychiatry
TEITELBAUM, D., Pediatric Surgery
TELESNITSKY, A., Microbiology and Immunology
TELIAN, S., Otorhinolaryngology
TEN HAKEN, R., Radiation Oncology
TERRELL, J., Otorhinolaryngology
THOMPSON, B., Neurosurgery
THOMPSON, D., Ophthalmology and Visual Science
TODISCO, A., Gastroenterology
TRAYNOR, J., Pharmacology
TREMPER, K., Anaesthesiology
TROBE, J., Ophthalmology and Visual Science
TULSKY, D., Physical Medicine and Rehabilitation
URBA, S., Haematology and Oncology
VALDIVIA, H., Cardiology
VALENSTEIN, M., Psychiatry
VAN DYKE, R., Gastroenterology
VARANI, J., Pathology
VAZQUEZ, D., Paediatrics–Endocrinology
VOORHEES, J., Dermatology
WAKEFIELD, T., Vascular Surgery
WANG, S., Haematology and Oncology
WARD, K., Emergency Medicine
WARD, P., Pathology
WARREN, J., Pathology
WARSCHAUSKY, S., Physical Medicine and Rehabilitation
WASKELL, L., Anaesthesiology

WEDER, A., Cardiology
WEI, J., Urology
WEINBERG, J., Nephrology
WELSH, M., Cell and Developmental Biology
WICHA, M., Haematology and Oncology
WIGGINS, R., Nephrology
WILEY, J., Gastroenterology
WILKINS, E., Plastic Surgery
WILLIAMS, D., Anaesthesiology
WILLIAMS, D., Radiology
WILLIAMS, J., Molecular and Integrative Physiology
WOJTYS, E., Orthopaedic Surgery
WOLF, G., Otorhinolaryngology
WOLF, J., Urology
WOODS, J., Pharmacology
XI, G., Neurosurgery
YOUNGER, J., Emergency Medicine
YUNG, R., Geriatric and Palliative Medicine
ZAND, R., Biological Chemistry
ZHENG, P., Surgery
ZIMMERMANN, E., Gastroenterology
ZOU, W., Surgery
ZUBIETA, J., Psychiatry
ZUCKER, R., Psychiatry
ZUIDERWEG, E., Biological Chemistry

Penny W. Stamps School of Art and Design (2000 Bonisteel Blvd, Ann Arbor, MI 48109-2069; tel. (734) 764-0671; internet art-design .umich.edu):

CHUNG, Y.
COGSWELL, JR, J.
HUGHES, H.
INUZUKA, S.
JACKSON, W.
JACOBSEN, C.
MARINARO, L.
NUNOO-QUARCOO, F.
OVERMYER, JR, R.
PAUL, J.
PORTER, M.
POSKOVIC, E.
RODEMER, M.
ROGERS, B.
SMITH, B.
SMITH, S.
VAN GENT, E.
WEST, E.

School of Dentistry (1011 N University, Ann Arbor, MI 48109-1078; tel. (734) 763-6933; e-mail ddsadmissions@umich.edu; internet www.dent.umich.edu):

BAGRAMIAN, R., Community Dentistry
BAYNE, S., Cariology, Restorative Sciences and Endodontics
BRADLEY, R., Biologic and Materials Sciences
CLARKSON, B., Cariology, Restorative Sciences and Endodontics
D'SILVA, N., Oral Medicine, Oncology
FEINBERG, S., Maxillofacial Surgery
FRANCESCHI, R., Periodontics and Oral Medicine
GIANNOBILE, W., Periodontics and Oral Medicine
HEYS, D., Cariology, Restorative Sciences and Endodontics
HOLLAND, G., Cariology, Restorative Sciences and Endodontics
HU, J., Biologic and Materials Sciences
KAPILA, Y., Periodontics and Oral Medicine
KAPILA, S., Orthodontics and Paediatric Dentistry
KOHN, D., Biologic and Materials Sciences
KREBSBACH, P., Biological and Materials Sciences
LANTZ, M., Periodontics and Oral Medicine
MA, P., Biologic and Materials Sciences
MCCAULEY, L., Periodontics and Oral Medicine
MCNAMARA, JR, J., Orthodontics
MISTRETTA, C., Biologic and Materials Sciences

NOR, J., Cariology, Restorative Sciences and Endodontics
PETERS, M., Cariology, Restorative Sciences and Endodontics
RAZZOOG, M., Prosthodontics
SIMMER, J., Prosthodontics
TAICHMAN, R., Periodontics and Oral Medicine
WANG, H., Periodontics

School of Education (610 E University Ave, Ann Arbor, MI 48109-1259; tel. (734) 764-9470; internet www.soe.umich.edu):

BATES, JR, P., Educational Studies
COHEN, D., Educational Studies
CRAIG, H., Educational Studies
DESJARDINS, S., Higher and Postsecondary Education
DUKE, N., Educational Studies
KING, P., Higher and Postsecondary Education
LAMPERT, M., Educational Studies
LARSEN-FREEMAN, D., Educational Studies
LATTUCA, L., Higher and Postsecondary Education
MCCALL, B., Higher and Postsecondary Education
MILLER, K., Educational Studies
MIREL, J., Educational Studies
MOJE, E., Educational Studies
MOSS, P., Educational Studies
NEUMAN, S., Educational Studies
O'CONNOR, C., Educational Studies
PALINCSAR, A., Educational Studies
SCHLEPPEGRELL, M., Educational Studies
SONGER, N., Educational Studies
ST JOHN, E., Higher and Postsecondary Education

School of Information (105 S State St, 4322 N Quad, Ann Arbor, MI 48109-1285; tel. (734) 964-9376; e-mail info@umich.edu; internet www.si.umich.edu):

ACKERMAN, M.
ATKINS, III, D.
CHEN, Y.
EDWARDS, P.
FRIEDMAN, C.
HEDSTROM, M.
KING, J.
MARKEY, K.
MASON, J.
RESNICK, P.
VAN HOUWELING, D.
YAKEL, E.

School of Kinesiology (1402 Washington Heights, Ann Arbor, MI 48109-2013; tel. (734) 764-4472; internet www.kines.umich .edu):

ARMSTRONG, K.
BORER, K.
CARTEE, G.
EDINGTON, D.
FERRIS, D.
FORT, R.
HOROWITZ, J.
KATCH, V.
ROSENTRAUB, M.
SZYMANSKI, S.
ULRICH, D.
ULRICH, B.

School of Music, Theatre and Dance (1100 Baits Dr, Ann Arbor, MI 48109-2085; tel. (734) 764-0583; internet www.music.umich .edu):

AARON, R., Music, Theatre and Dance
BLACKSTONE, J., Music, Theatre and Dance
BORDERS, J., Music, Theatre and Dance
CAMPBELL, W., Music, Theatre and Dance
CHAMBERS, E., Music, Theatre and Dance
DAUGHERTY, M., Music, Theatre and Dance
DEYOUNG, JR, G., Dance
ELLIOTT, A., Music, Theatre and Dance
EVERETT, W., Music, Theatre and Dance
FOGEL, J., Dance
FULCHER, J., Music, Theatre and Dance

GANNETT, D., Music, Theatre and Dance
GENNE, B., Dance
GORDON, O., Theatre
GREENE, A., Music, Theatre and Dance
GUCK, M., Music, Theatre and Dance
HAHN, J., Theatre
HAITHCOCK, M., Music, Theatre and Dance
HALEN, D., Music, Theatre and Dance
HALL, P., Music, Theatre and Dance
HERSETH, F., Music, Theatre and Dance
JENNINGS, A., Music, Theatre and Dance
KAENZIG, F., Music, Theatre and Dance
KANE, A., Dance
KATZ, M., Music, Theatre and Dance
KERR, P., Theatre
KIBBIE, J., Music, Theatre and Dance
KIESLER, K., Music, Theatre and Dance
KING, N., Music, Theatre and Dance
KORSYN, K., Music, Theatre and Dance
LAM, J., Music, Theatre and Dance
MASON, M., Music, Theatre and Dance
MCCARTHY, M., Music, Theatre and Dance
MEAD, A., Music, Theatre and Dance
MOUNTAIN, V., Theatre
NAGEL, L., Music, Theatre and Dance
NEVILLE-ANDREWS, J., Theatre
OLSEN, S., Music, Theatre and Dance
PARMENTIER, E., Music, Theatre and Dance
POGGI, G., Theatre
PORTER, A., Music, Theatre and Dance
RUSH, S., Dance
SARATH, E., Music, Theatre and Dance
SCHOTTEN, Y., Music, Theatre and Dance
SHENG, B., Music, Theatre and Dance
SHIPPS, S., Music, Theatre and Dance
SINTA, D., Music, Theatre and Dance
SKELTON, L., Music, Theatre and Dance
SPARLING, P., Dance
STEIN, L., Music, Theatre and Dance
WASHINGTON, D., Music, Theatre and Dance
WEST, S., Music, Theatre and Dance
WHITING, S., Music, Theatre and Dance
WOODS, L., Theatre

School of Natural Resources and Environment (440 Church St, Ann Arbor, MI 48109-1041; tel. (734) 764-6453; internet www.snre.umich.edu):

AGRAWAL, A.
ALLAN, J.
BIERBAUM, R.
BROWN, D.
BRYANT, JR, B.
BURTON, A.
DIANA, J.
HOFFMAN, A.
KAPLAN, R.
KEOLEIAN, G.
LEMOS, M.
LOW, B.
MOHAI, P.
MOORE, M.
NASSAUER, J.
PERFECTO, I.
TAYLOR, D.
WILEY, M.
YAFFEE, S.
ZAK, D.

School of Nursing (400 N Ingalls, Ann Arbor, MI 48109-5482; tel. (734) 763-5985; e-mail sn-osams@umich.edu; internet www.nursing.umich.edu):

BOYD, C.
DUFFY, S.
HOLDEN, J.
KALISCH, B.
LARSON, J.
NORTHOUSE, L.
PRESSLER, S.
REDMAN, R.
SALES, A.
SAMPSELLE, C.
VILLARRUEL, A.

School of Public Health (1415 Washington Heights, 1700 SPH I, Ann Arbor, MI 48109-2029; tel. (734) 763-5425; e-mail sph.web@umich.edu; internet www.sph.umich.edu):

ABECASIS, G., Biostatistics
BATTERMAN, S., Environmental Health Sciences
BOEHNKE, M., Biostatistics
CHATTERS, L., Health Behaviour and Health Education
CLARK, N., Health Behaviour and Health Education
CONNELL, C., Health Behaviour and Health Education
DIEZ ROUX, A., Epidemiology
ELLIOTT, M., Biostatistics
FOXMAN, B., Epidemiology
FRANZBLAU, A., Environmental Health Sciences
FRIES, B., Health Management and Policy
GRAZIER, K., Health Management and Policy
HARLOW, S., Epidemiology
HARPER, G., Health Behaviour and Health Education
HARRIS, C., Environmental Health Sciences
HIRTH, R., Health Management and Policy
ISRAEL, B., Health Behaviour and Health Education
JACOBSON, P., Health Management and Policy
JOLLIET, O., Environmental Health Sciences
KARDIA, S., Epidemiology
KOOPMAN, J., Epidemiology
KRAUSE, N., Health Behaviour and Health Education
LI, Y., Biostatistics
LIANG, J., Health Management and Policy
LITTLE, R., Biostatistics
LOCH-CARUSO, R., Environmental Health Sciences
MAYNARD, A., Environmental Health Sciences
MCLAUGHLIN, C., Health Management and Policy
MENDES DE LEON, C., Epidemiology
MONTO, A., Epidemiology
MORGENSTERN, H., Epidemiology
NAN, B., Biostatistics
NEIGHBORS, H., Health Behaviour and Health Education
NORTON, E., Health Management and Policy
NRIAGU, J., Environmental Health Sciences
PETERSON, K., Environmental Health Sciences
PEYSER, P., Epidemiology
RAGHUNATHAN, T., Biostatistics
RESNICOW, K., Health Behaviour and Health Education
RICHARDSON, R., Environmental Health Sciences
ROBINS, T., Environmental Health Sciences
SCHAUBEL, D., Biostatistics
SCHULZ, A., Health Behaviour and Health Education
SMITH, D., Health Management and Policy
SONG, P., Biostatistics
STRECHER, V., Health Behaviour and Health Education
TAYLOR, J., Biostatistics
TSODIKOV, A., Biostatistics
WARNER, K., Health Management and Policy
WHEELER, J., Health Management and Policy
WILSON, M., Epidemiology
ZELLERS, E., Environmental Health Sciences
ZIMMERMAN, M., Health Behaviour and Health Education

School of Social Work (1080 S University Ave, Ann Arbor, MI 48109-1106; tel. (734) 764-3309; internet www.ssw.umich.edu):

BURGIO, L.
CHADIHA, L.
CHECKOWAY, B.
DANZIGER, S.
DELVA, J.
FALLER, K.
GANT, L.
GOLDMAN, K.
GUTIERREZ, L.
OYSERMAN, D.
POWELL, T.
ROOT, L.
SAUNDERS, D.
SIEFERT, K.
TAYLOR, R.
TOLMAN, R.
TROPMAN, J.
TUCKER, D.
YOSHIHAMA, M.

Stephen M. Ross School of Business (701 Tappan St, Ann Arbor, MI 48109-1234; tel. (734) 763-5796; internet www.bus.umich.edu):

AHUJA, G.
ANUPINDI, R.
ASHFORD, S.
BAGOZZI, R.
BAKER, W.
BATRA, R.
BUCHMUELLER, T.
CAMERON, K.
CAPOZZA, D.
DAVIS, G.
DUENYAS, I.
DUTTON, J.
FEINBERG, F.
GLADWIN, T.
GORDON, M.
INDJEJIKIAN, R.
KAPUSCINSKI, R.
KAUL, G.
KIM, E.
KINNEAR, T.
KRISHNA, A.
KRISHNAN, M.
LAFONTAINE, F.
LEHAVY, R.
LENK, P.
LIM, L.
LOVEJOY, W.
LYON, T.
MANCHANDA, P.
MASTEN, S.
MUIR, D.
NARAYANAN, M.
OSWALD, L.
QUINN, R.
RAMASWAMY, V.
REILLY, R.
SANDELANDS, L.
SCHIPANI, C.
SCHRIBER, T.
SEYHUN, N.
SHUMWAY, T.
SIEDEL, G.
SPREITZER, G.
SUTCLIFFE, K.
TICHY, N.
ULRICH, D.
WALSH, J.
WESTPHAL, J.
WHITMAN, M.

Taubman College of Architecture and Urban Planning (2000 Bonisteel Blvd, Ann Arbor, MI 48109-2069; tel. (734) 764-1300; internet taubmancollege.umich.edu):

BORUM, C., Architecture
CONSTANT, C., Architecture
DEWAR, M., Urban Planning
FISHMAN, R., Architecture
GROAT, L., Architecture

KELBAUGH, D., Architecture
LEVINE, J., Urban Planning
MURRAY, M., Urban Planning
STRICKLAND, R., Architecture
THOMAS, J., Urban Planning.

REGIONAL CAMPUSES

University of Michigan—Dearborn

4901 Evergreen Rd, Dearborn, MI 48128-1491

Telephone: (313) 593-5000
E-mail: admissions@umd.umich.edu
Internet: www.umd.umich.edu

Founded 1959
State control
Academic year: September to August

Chancellor: Dr DANIEL LITTLE
Provost and Vice-Chancellor for Academic Affairs: Dr CATHERINE A. DAVY
Vice-Chancellor for Enrolment Management and Student Life: STANLEY E. HENDERSON
Vice-Chancellor for Govt Relations: EDWARD J. BAGALE
Vice-Chancellor for Institutional Advancement (vacant)
Registrar: ADRIENNE KELLUM McDAY
Dir for Library: ELAINE LOGAN
Number of teachers: 380 (full-time)
Number of students: 8,600

DEANS

College of Arts, Sciences and Letters: Dr JEROLD L. HALE
College of Business: Dr KIM SCHATZEL
College of Education: Dr EDWARD SILVER
College of Engineering and Computer Science: Dr SUBRATA SENGUPTA

University of Michigan—Flint

302 E Kearsley, Flint, MI 48502-1950
Telephone: (313) 762-3000
E-mail: admissions@umflint.edu
Internet: www.umflint.edu

Founded 1956
State control
Academic year: July to June

Chancellor: Dr RUTH J. PERSON
Provost and Vice-Chancellor for Academic Affairs: Dr GERARD VOLAND
Vice-Chancellor for Admin.: DAVID BARTHELMES
Vice-Chancellor for Student Affairs: MARY-JO SEKELSKY
Registrar: KAREN ARNOULD
Librarian: BOB HOUBECK
Library of 865,795 vols
Number of teachers: 370 (full-time)
Number of students: 8,260 (6,959 undergraduate, 1,303 graduate)

DEANS

College of Arts and Sciences: Dr D. J. TRELA
School of Education and Human Services: Dr BOB BARNETT
School of Health Professions and Studies: DAVID GORDON
School of Management: Dr VAHID LOTFI (acting)

WALSH COLLEGE OF ACCOUNTANCY AND BUSINESS ADMINISTRATION

POB 7006, Troy, MI 48007-7006
3838 Livernois, Troy, MI 48083
Telephone: (248) 689-8282
E-mail: admissions@walshcollege.edu
Internet: www.walshcollege.edu
Founded 1922 as Walsh Institute of Accountancy, current name adopted 1968
Private control
Academic year: September to September

Areas of study: accounting, finance, health care, management; campus at Novi (Michigan); univ. centres at Clinton Township, Harper Woods and Port Huron in Michigan
Pres. and CEO: STEPHANIE W. BERGERON
Exec. Vice-Pres. and Chief Academic Officer: Dr MICHAEL LEVENS
Vice-Pres. for Enrolment Management: JOHN W. LICHTENBERG
Vice-Pres. for Human Resources and Admin.: ELIZABETH A. BARNES
Registrar: KAREN HILLEBRAND
Library Dir: Dr JONATHAN CAMPBELL
Library of 27,000 vols, 250 periodicals
Number of students: 3,150 (1,124 undergraduate, 2,026 graduate)
Publication: *The Walsh Journal*

WAYNE STATE UNIVERSITY

1309 Faculty/Admin. Bldg, Detroit, MI 48202
Telephone: (313) 577-2424
E-mail: emoen@oia.wayne.edu
Internet: www.wayne.edu
Founded 1868, present status 1933
State control
Academic year: August to May

Pres.: ALLAN GILMOUR
Provost and Sr Vice-Pres. for Academic Affairs: RONALD T. BROWN
Vice-Pres. and Gen. Counsel: LOUIS LESSEM
Vice-Pres. for Devt and Alumni Affairs: DAVID RIPPLE
Vice-Pres. for Govt Affairs: HARVEY HOLLINS, III
Vice-Pres. for Research: HILARY RATNER
Dean for Univ. Libraries: SANDRA G. YEE
Library: see under Libraries and Archives
Number of teachers: 1,810 (full-time)
Number of students: 31,505

DEANS

College of Education: CAROLYN M. SHIELDS
College of Engineering: FARSHAD FOTOUHI
College of Fine, Performing and Communication Arts: MATTHEW SEEGER
College of Liberal Arts and Sciences: ROBERT L. THOMAS
College of Nursing: BARBARA K. REDMAN
Eugene Applebaum College of Pharmacy and Health Sciences: LLOYD YOUNG
Graduate School: HILARY RATNER
Irvin D. Reid Honors College: JERRY HERRON
Law School: ROBERT ACKERMAN
School of Business Administration: MARGARET L. WILLIAMS
School of Medicine: VALERIE PARISI
School of Social Work: CHERYL WAITES

PROFESSORS

College of Education
   Admin. and Organizational Studies:
BRANDENBURG, D.
DEMONT, R.
GIPSON, J. H.
MORRISON, G.
RICHEY, R.
   Teacher Education:
BALE, J.
KAPLAN, L.
PETERSON, J. M.
RONEY, R.
SMITH, G.
WHITIN, D.
Theoretical and Behavioural Foundations:
HILLMAN, S.
MARCOTTE, D.
MARKMAN, B. S.
PIETROFESA, J.
SAWILOWSKY, S.

College of Engineering
   Chemical Engineering:
GULARI, E.
HUANG, Y.
NG, K.
PUTATUDNA, S.
ROTHE, E. W.
   Civil Engineering:
AKTAN, H. M.
DATTA, T. K.
FU, G.
MILLER, C.
   Electrical and Computer Engineering:
AUNER, G.
ERLANDSON, R.
HASSOUN, M.
HUANG, C.
LIN, F.
SILVERSMITH, D.
SINGH, H.
SIY, P.
WANG, L.
YING, H.
Industrial and Manufacturing Engineering:
PLONKA, F.
SINGH, N.
   Mechanical Engineering:
BERDICHEVSKY, V.
GIBSON, R.
IBRAHIM, R.
MAI, M.-C.
RIVIN, E.
SINGH, T.
TAN, C.-A.
TARAZA, D.
WHITMAN, A. B.
WU, S.
YANG, K.-H.

College of Fine, Performing and Communication Arts
   Art and Art History:
HEGARTY, J.
JACKSON, M.
MARTIN, R.
NAWARA, J.
ROBARE, D.
ROSAS, M.
WILLIAMS, P.
ZAJAC, J.
   Communication:
SEEGER, M.
   Music:
MARKOU, K.
   Theatre:
CALARCO, J.
KAUSHANSKY, L.
MAGIDSON, D.
PULLIN, N.
SCHRAEDER, T.
THOMAS, J.

College of Liberal Arts
   Africana Studies:
BOYD, M. (H)
HUTCHFUL, E.
   Anthropology:
MONTILUS, G.
SANKAR, A.
   Classics, Greek and Latin:
McNAMEE, K.
   Criminal Justice:
STACK, S.
ZALMAN, M.
   Economics:
BRAID, R.
LEE, L.
ROSSANA, A.
SPURR, S.

English:

BARTON, E.
BRILL, L.
BURGOYNE, R.
COLEMBA, H.
HARRIS, W.
LANDRY, D.
LELAND, C.
LINDBERG, K.
MAROTTI, A.
RAY, R.
SCRIVENER, M.
SKLAR, E.
VLASOPOLOS, A.
WASSERMAN, R.

History:

BUKOWCZYK, J.
FAUE, E.
HYDE, C.
RAUCHER, A.
SMALL, M.

Humanities:

COGAN, M.

Philosophy:

GRANGER, H.
LOMBARD, L.
MCKINSEY, T.
YANAL, R.

Political Science:

ABBOTT, P. R.
BLEDSOE, T.
DOWNING, R. G.
ELDER, C.
FINO, S.
PARRISH, C.

Romance Languages and Literatures:

DITOMMASO, A.
HIGUERO, F.
STIVALE, C.

Sociology:

ESHLEMAN, J. R.
GELFAND, D.
HANKIN, J.
SENGSTOCK, M.
WARSHAY, L.

College of Lifelong Learning

Interdisciplinary Studies Program:

ARONSON, A. R.
BAILS, J. G.
GLABERMAN, M.
KLEIN, J.
MAIER, C. L.
RASPA, R. N.
SCHINDLER, R.
WRIGHT, R. H.

College of Nursing:

AROIAN, K.
HOUGH, E.
NIES, M.
OERMANN, M.
PIPER, B. A.
RICE, V.

College of Science

Biology:

ARKING, R.
FREEMAN, D.
GREENBERG, M.
HEBERLEIN, G.
HOUGH, R.
MIZUKAMI, H.
MOORE, W. S.
SMITH, P. D.
TAYLOR, J.

Chemistry:

BHAGWAT, A.
CHA, J.-K.
LINVELDT, R.
MCCLAIN, W.
MONTGOMERY, J.
POOLE, C.

RABAN, J. P.
ROMANO, L.
RORABCHER, D.
SCHLEGEL, H.

Computer Science:

GOEL, N.
REYNOLDS, R.

Mathematics:

BACHELIS, G. F.
BRENTON, L.
CHOW, P.-L.
COHN, W.
GLUCK, D. H.
HANDEL, D.
KHAN, S.
KHASMINSKII, R.
KLEIN, J.
KOROSTELEV, A.
LIANG, T.
MAGAARD, K.
MAKAR-LIMANOV, L.
MALCOLMSON, P.
MENALDI, J. L.
MORDUKHOVICH, B.
OKOH, F.
RHEE, C.
SCHOCHET, C. L.
SCHREIBER, B. H.
SUN, T.-C.
YIN, G.
ZHANG, Z.

Nutrition and Food Science:

JEN, C.
KLURFELD, D. M.
SHELEF, L.

Physics:

BELLWIED, R.
CHANG, J. J.
CORMIER, T.
DUNIFER, G.
KARCHIN, P.
KAUPPILA, W. E.
KEYES, P. H.
KUO, P. K.
MORGAN, C.
NAIK, R.
SAPERSTEIN, A. M.
STEIN, T. S.

Psychology:

ALEXANDER, S.
COSCINA, D.
FIRESTONE, I. J.
FITZGERALD, J.
KAPLAN, K.
KILBEY, M. M.
LABOUVIE-VIEF, G.
LEVY, S.
URBERG, K.
WEISFELD, G.

College of Urban, Labour and Metropolitan Affairs

Clarence Hillberry Prof. of Urban Affairs:

GALSTER, G.

Coleman A. Young Prof. of Urban Affairs:

YOUNG, A. H.

Geography and Urban Planning:

BOYLE, R. M.
RESSE, L.
SINCLAIR, R.

Urban and Labour Studies:

BATES, T.
BROWN, D. R.
COOKE, W.
MASON, P.
SMOCK, S. M.
WOLMAN, H.
YOUNG, H.

Law School:

BROWN, K.
BURNHAM, W.

CALKINS, S.
DANNIN, E.
FRIEDMAN, J. M.
HENNING, P.
LITMAN, J.
MCINTYRE, M. J.
MOGK, J.
SCHENK, A.

Eugene Applebaum College of Pharmacy and Health Sciences

Anaesthesia:

COOK, K. A.
CRAWFORTH, K. L.
HAGLUND, V. L.
MANGAHAS, P.
WALCZYK, M. L.
WORTH, P. A.

Clinical Laboratory Science:

ALDRIGE, G.
CASTILLO, J. B.
HARAKE, B.
WALLACE, A. M.

Mortuary Science:

BURDA-MASTROGIANIS, L.
FRADE, P.
FRITTS-WILLIAMS, M. L.
HUNTOON, R.

Occupational and Environmental Health Sciences:

BASSETT, D.
BHALLA, D.
KERFOOT, E. J.
TAFFE, B.
WARNER, P. O.

Occupational Therapy:

BROWN, K.
ESDAILE, S.
LUBORSKY, M.
LYSACK, C.
POWELL, N.

Pharmaceutical Sciences:

ABRAMSON, H.
BOLARIN, D.
COMMISSARIS, R.
CORCORAN, G. B.
FULLER, G. C.
GIBBS, R.
HIRATA, F.
LINDBLAD, W.
LOUIS-FERDINAND, R. T.
PITTS, D. K.
SVENSSON, C. K.
WORMSER, H.
WOSTER, P. M.

Pharmacy Practice:

CAPPELLETTY, D.
EDWARDS, D. J.
FAGAN, S.
JABER, L. A.
KALE-PRADHAN, P. B.
KEYS, P.
MILLER, M.
MOSER, L. R.
MUNZENBERGER, P. J.
RHONEY, D.
RYBAK, M. J.
SCHUMANN, W.
SINGH, R.
SLAUGHTER, R. L.
SMITH, G. B.
SMYTHE, M. A.
STEVENSON, J. G.
TISDALE, J. E.
VIVIAN, J. C.
WILSON, J.

Physical Therapy:

AMUNDSEN, L.
CARLSON, C.
DROVIN, J.
DUNLEAVY, K.
MCNEVIN, N.

TALLEY, S.

Physician Assistant Studies:

FRICK, J.
NORMILE, H.
SIDDIQUE, M.
TODD, K.
WORMSER, H.

Radiation Therapy Technology:

CHADWELL, D.
KEMPA, A.

School of Business Administration

Accounting:

BILLINGS, B.
REINSTEIN, A.
SPAULDING, A.
VOLZ, W.

Finance and Business Economics:

HAMILTON, J.
SOMERS, T.
SPENCER, M.

Management:

MARTIN, J. E.
OSBORN, R. N.

Marketing:

BELTRAMINI, R.
CANNON, H.
JACKSON, G.
KELLY, J.
RIORDAN, E.
RYMER, J.
YAPRAK, A.

School of Medicine

Anaesthesiology:

BROWN, E. (H)

Anatomy:

BERNSTEIN, M.
GOODMAN, M.
GOSHGARIAN, H.
HAZLETT, L.
LASKER, G.
MAISEL, H.
MEYER, D.
MITCHELL, J. A.
MIZERES, N. J.
POURCHO, R.
RAFOLS, J.
ROHER, A.
SKOFF, R.

Audiology:

RINTELMANN, W. F. (H)

Biochemistry:

BROOKS, S.
BROWN, R. K.
EDWARDS, B.
EVANS, D.
JOHNSON, R.
LEE, C. P.
ROSEN, B.
ROWND, R.
VINOGRADOV, S.

Cardiology:

KLONER, R.
WYNNE, J.

Community Medicine:

WALLER, J.

Dermatology and Syphilology:

BIRMINGHAM, D.
HASHIMOTO, K.

Family Medicine:

DALLMAN, J.
GALLAGHER, R. E.
WERNER, P.

Immunology and Microbiology:

BERK, R.
BOROS, D. L.
BROWN, W. J.
DEGUISTI, D.
HAZLEH, L.

JEFFRIES, C.
KAPLAN, J.
KONG, Y.-C.
LEFFORD, M.
LEON, M.
LEVIN, S.
LISAK, R.
MONTGOMERY, P. C.
PALCHAUDHURI, S.
SOBEL, J.
SUNDICK, R.
SWANBORG, R. H.
WEINER, L. M.

Internal Medicine:

AL-SARRAF, M.
BAGCHI, N.
BERGSMAN, K. L.
BISHOP, C. R.
BRENNAN, M.
CLAPPER, I.
CORBETT, T.
FERNÁNDEZ-MADRID, F. B.
GRUNBERGER, G.
HEILBRUN, L.
HEPPNER, G.
KESSEL, D.
LERNER, S.
LEWIS, B. M.
LUM, L.
LYNNE-DAVIS, P.
McDONALD, F.
MACK, R.
MAJUMDAR, A.
MARSH, J.
MIGDAL, S.
MILLER, R.
MUTCHNICK, M.
NAKEFF, A.
PRASAD, A. S.
PURI, P.
RESNICK, L.
SAMSON, M.
SANTEN, R.
SENSENBRENNER, L.
SOBEL, J.
SOWERS, J.
SPEARS, J.
TALMERS, F.
TRANCHIDA, L.
VAITKEVICIUS, V.
VALDIVIESO, M.
VALERIOTE, F.
WYNNE, J.

Neurology:

BENJAMINS, J. A.
CHUGANI, H.
DORE-DUFFY, P.
LeWITT, P.
LISAK, R.
NIGRO, M.

Neurosurgery:

DIAZ, F. G.
THOMAS, L. M.

Obstetrics and Gynaecology:

ABEL, E.
AGER, J.
BEHRMAN, S. J.
BERMAN, R.
COTTON, D.
DEPPE, G.
EVANS, M.
FREEDMAN, R.
LANCASTER, W.
MAMMEN, E.
MARIONA, F.
MILLER, O.
MOGHISSI, K.
POLAND, M.
ROMERO, R.
SACCO, A. G.
SHERMAN, A.
SOBEL, J.
SOKOL, R.
STRYKER, J.

SUBRAMANIAN, M.

Ophthalmology:

ESSNER, E.
FRANK, R. N.
JAMPEL, R. S.
PUKLIN, J.
SHICHI, H.
SHIN, D.
SPOOR, T.

Orthopaedic Surgery:

FITZGERALD, R.
MANOLI II, A.
RYAN, J.

Otolaryngology:

COHN, A. M.
DRESCHER, D.
DWORKIN, J.
JACOBS, J.
MATHOG, R. H.

Paediatrics:

BEN-YOSEPH, Y.
BRANS, Y. W.
CASH, R.
CHUGANI, H.
COHEN, S.
COLLINS, J.
DAJANI, A. S.
EPSTEIN, M.
FAROOKI, Z.
FLEISCHMANN, L.
GRUSKIN, A.
GUTAI, J.
KAPLAN, J.
KAUFFMAN, R.
LUM, L.
LUSHER, J.
NIGRO, M.
OSTREA, E.
PINSKY, W. W.
RAUMDRANATH, Y.
ROBIN, A.
SAMAIK, A.
SARNAIK, A.
SENSENBRENNER, L.
SHANKARIAN, G.
SLOVIS, T.

Pathology:

BEDROSSIAN, C.
BROWN, W.
CRISSMAN, J.
DALE, E.
EVANS, M.
GIACOMELLI, F. E.
HONN, K.
KURKINEN, M.
MAMMEN, E.
MILLER, D.
PALUTKE, M.
PERRIN, E. V.
RAZ, A.
SHEAHAN, D.
SPITZ, W. U.
THIBERT, R.
WEINER, L.
WIENER, J.
ZAK, B.

Pharmacology:

ANDERSON, G.
BANNON, M.
CHOPRA, D.
DUTTA, S.
GOLDMAN, H.
HIRATA, F.
HOLLENBERG, P. F.
KESSEL, D.
MARKS, B.
NOVAK, R.
SLOANE, B.
WAKADE, A.

Physiology:

BARRACO, R.
CHURCHILL, P. C.

DUNBAR, J. C.
FOA, P.
GALA, R.
HONG, F. T.
LAWSON, D.
MCCOY, L. E.
MAMMEN, E.
NYBOER, J.
PENNEY, D.
PHILLIS, J. W.
RAM, J.
RILLEMA, J. A.
SEEGERS, W.
WALZ, D. A. (H)

Psychiatry:

BANNON, M.
FISCHHOFF, J.
FREEDMAN, R.
GALLOWAY, M.
KAPATOS, G.
KUHN, D.
LEWITT, P.
LUBY, E.
LYCAKI, H.
POHL, R.
ROSENBAUM, A.
ROSENZWEIG, N.
SARWER-FONER, G.
SCHORER, C.
SITARAM, N.
UHDE, T.

Radiation Oncology:

HERSKOVIC, A. M.
HONN, K. V.
MARUYAMA, Y.
ORTON, C. G.
PORTER, A.

Radiology:

KLING, G.
SOULEN, R.
WOLLSCHLAEGER, G.

Surgery:

BERGUER, R.
FROMM, D.
KLEIN, M.
LEDGERWOOD, A. M.
LUCAS, C.
PHILIPPART, A.
ROSENBERG, J. C.
SILVA, Y. J.
STEPHENSON, L.
SUGAWA, C.
WALT, A. J.
WEAVER, A. W.
WILSON, R. F.

Urology:

JAFFER, D.
MONTIE, J.
PERLMUTTER, A. D.
PONTES, J.

School of Social Work:

BEVERLY, C.
BRANDALL, J.
MOXLEY, D.

University Libraries
  Library and Information Science:

ALBRITTON, R. L.
BAKER, L. M.
BROWN-SYED, C. L.
EZELL, C. L.
FIELD, J. J.
HOLLEY, R.
JOHNSON, N. B.
MIKA, J.
NEAVILL, G. B.
POWELL, R.
SPITERI, L. F.

WESTERN MICHIGAN UNIVERSITY

1903 W Michigan Ave, Kalamazoo, MI 49008-5200

Telephone: (269) 387-1000
E-mail: ask-wmu@wmich.edu
Internet: www.wmich.edu

Founded 1903, present name and status 1957
State control
Academic year: July to June

Pres.: Dr JOHN M. DUNN
Provost and Vice-Pres. for Academic Affairs: Dr TIMOTHY J. GREENE
Assoc. Provost for Enrolment Management: Dr CHRISTOPHER TREMBLAY
Vice-Pres. for Devt and Alumni Relations: JAMES S. THOMAS
Vice Pres. for Diversity and Inclusion: Dr MARTHA B. WARFIELD
Vice-Pres. for Govt Affairs and Univ. Relations: GREGORY J. ROSINE
Vice-Pres. for Research: Dr DANIEL M. LITYNSKI
Vice-Pres. for Student Affairs: Dr DIANE K. ANDERSON
Registrar: CARRIE CUMMING
Dean for Univ. Libraries: Dr JOSEPH G. REISH
Library of 5,032,929 vols, 59,893 periodical titles
Number of teachers: 1,470
Number of students: 24,290

Publications: *Caribe* (2 a year, jtly with Western Michigan Univ. in Kalamazoo, Univ. of Northern Florida in Jacksonville and Marquette Univ. of Milwaukee), *Comparative Drama* (4 a year), *Journal of Sociology and Social Welfare* (4 a year), *Medieval Prosopography* (2 a year), *Mid-American Journal of Business* (4 a year), *Proceedings of the Heraclitean Society* (1 a year), *Reading Horizons Journal* (4 a year), *Studies in Iconography* (1 a year), *Teaching Ethics Journal: The Journal for the Society for Ethics Across the Curriculum* (1 a year), *The Hilltop Review: A Journal of Western Michigan University Graduate Research* (2 a year), *The Open Journal of Occupational Therapy* (online), *Third Coast* (2 a year), *Transference*, *WMU Magazine* (2 a year), *WMU Research Magazine* (2 a year), *Yearbook of Langland Studies* (1 a year)

DEANS

College of Arts and Sciences: Dr ALEXANDER J. ENYEDI
College of Aviation: DAVID M. POWELL
College of Education and Human Development: Dr MING LI
College of Engineering and Applied Sciences: Dr EDMUND TSANG
College of Fine Arts: DANIEL GUYETTE
College of Health and Human Services: Dr EARLIE M. WASHINGTON
Graduate College: Dr SUSAN STAPLETON
Haworth College of Business: Dr KAY M. PALAN
Lee Honors College: Dr CARLA KORETSKY

WESTERN THEOLOGICAL SEMINARY

101 E 13th St, Holland, MI 49423
Telephone: (616) 392-8555
E-mail: admissions@westernsem.edu
Internet: www.westernsem.edu

Founded 1866
Private control
Academic year: September to May
Areas of study: divinity, ministry, theology, social work

Pres.: Dr TIMOTHY L. BROWN
Dean and Vice-Pres. for Academic Affairs: Dr LEANNE VAN DYK

Vice-Pres. for Advancement and Communications: JOHN NORDSTROM
Dir for Admissions: Dr MARK POPPEN
Dean for Students: Dr MATT FLODING
Registrar: PAT DYKHUIS
Library Dir: PAUL M. SMITH

Library of 100,000 vols
Number of teachers: 18
Number of students: 230

MINNESOTA

ADLER GRADUATE SCHOOL

550 E 78th St, Richfield, MN 55423
Telephone: (612) 861-7554
E-mail: info@alfredadler.edu
Internet: www.alfredadler.edu

Founded 1967 as Minnesota Adlerian Soc., present status 1991, present name 2004
Private control
Offers Masters degree in Adlerian counselling and psychotherapy

Pres.: Dr DANIEL A. HAUGEN
Academic Vice-Pres. and Dean: Dr DAVID J. MATHIEU
Vice-Pres. for Finance: LESLIE ROHDE
Dir for Admissions and Student Services: EVELYN HAAS
Registrar: JEANETTE MAYNARD NELSON

AUGSBURG COLLEGE

2211 Riverside Ave S, Minneapolis, MN 55454
Telephone: (612) 330-1000
E-mail: augpres@augsburg.edu
Internet: www.augsburg.edu

Founded 1869
Private control
Areas of study: accounting, American Indian studies, biology, business administration, chemistry, communication studies, computer science, economics, education, engineering, finance, health education, history, international relations, management information systems, marketing, mathematics, medieval studies, metro-urban studies, modern languages, music, philosophy, physical education, physics, political science, psychology, religion, sociology, theatre arts, women's studies

Pres.: PAUL C. PRIBBENOW
Vice-Pres.: CHRISTINE SZAJ
Vice-Pres. for Academic Affairs and Dean for College: BARBARA FARLEY
Vice-Pres. for Enrolment Management: JULIE EDSTROM
Vice-Pres. for Finance and Admin.: TAMMY MCGEE
Vice-Pres. for Institutional Advancement: JEREMY WELLS
Vice-Pres. for Student Affairs: ANN GARVEY
Vice-Pres. and Chief Information Officer: LEIF ANDERSON
Registrar: WAYNE KALLESTAD
Dir for Library Services: JANE ANN NELSON
Library of 190,000 vols
Number of teachers: 300 (122 full-time, 178 part-time)
Number of students: 4,050
Publication: *Augsburg Now* (4 a year)

BETHANY LUTHERAN COLLEGE

700 Luther Dr., Mankato, MN 56001
Telephone: (507) 344-7000
E-mail: admissions@blc.edu
Internet: www.blc.edu

Founded 1911 as Bethany Ladies College
Private control
Liberal arts college

Pres.: Dr DAN R. BRUSS
Vice-Pres. for Student Affairs: STEVE JAEGER
Dean for Academic Affairs: ERIC WOLLER
Dean for Admissions: DON WESTPHAL
Registrar: MARY JO STARKSON
Dir for Library Services: ORRIN AUSEN
Library of 68,000 vols
Number of teachers: 70
Number of students: 610
Publication: *Bethany Report*

BETHEL UNIVERSITY

3900 Bethel Dr., St Paul, MN 55112-6999
Telephone: (651) 638-6400
E-mail: buadmissions-cas@bethel.edu
Internet: www.bethel.edu
Founded 1871, current name adopted 2004
Private control
Academic year: August to June
School of the churches of the Baptist Gen.
Conf.; 3 seminaries in Minnesota, California
and Pennsylvania
Pres.: JAMES H. BARNES, III
Provost and Exec. Vice-Pres.: DAVID CLARK
Sr Vice-Pres. for Finance and Admin.: KATH-
LEEN J. NELSON
Sr Vice-Pres. for Strategic Planning and
Research: JOSEPH D. LALUZERNE
Sr Vice-Pres. for Univ. Relations: PAT
MAZOROL
Vice-Pres. for Devt: BRUCE W. ANDERSON
Vice-Pres. for Student Life: EDEE SCHULZE
Registrar: KATRINA CHAPMAN
Dir for Univ. Libraries: DAVID STEWART
Library of 146,026 vols, 21,027 ebooks,
35,405 journals, 5,000 audio resources,
6,596 video resources
Number of teachers: 240 (209 at colleges and
graduate school, 31 at seminary)
Number of students: 6,400

DEANS

Bethel Seminary: DAVID CLARK (acting)
College of Adult and Professional Studies:
DICK CROMBIE
College of Arts and Sciences: DEB HARLESS
Graduate School: DICK CROMBIE

CAPELLA UNIVERSITY

Capella Tower, 225 S Sixth St, Ninth Fl.,
Minneapolis, MN 55402
Telephone: (612) 339-8650
E-mail: info@capella.edu
Internet: www.capella.edu
Founded 1993 as Graduate School of Amer-
ica, present name and status 1999
Private control
Pres.: Dr DEBORAH BUSHWAY
Provost: Dr CHARLES TIFFIN
Number of teachers: 1,600
Number of students: 35,750

DEANS

Harold Abel School of Social and Behavioural
Sciences: DAVID CHAPMAN
School of Business and Technology: Dr
WILLIAM REED (acting)
School of Education: Dr BARBARA BUTTS
WILLIAMS
School of Public Service Leadership: SUZANNE
HOLMES
School of Undergraduate Studies: FERANDA
WILLIAMSON

CARLETON COLLEGE

1 N College St, Northfield, MN 55057
Telephone: (507) 222-4000
E-mail: admissions@carleton.edu
Internet: www.carleton.edu
Founded 1866

Private control
Academic year: September to June (3 semesters)
Depts of African-American studies; American
studies; Arabic; archaeology; art and art
history; Asian languages and literatures;
Asian studies; biochemistry; biology; chemistry; cinema and media studies; classical
languages; cognitive science; computer science; cross cultural studies; economics; educational studies; English; environmental
studies; European studies; French and
Francophone studies; geology; German; Hebrew; history; international relations; Latin
American studies; linguistics; literary and
cultural studies; mathematics; medieval and
renaissance studies; music; neuroscience;
philosophy; physics and astronomy; political
science; physical education, athletics and
recreation; psychology; religion; Russian;
sociology and anthropology; Spanish; theatre
and dance; women's and gender studies; off-
campus studies, pre-med and summer aca-
demic programmes
Pres.: STEVEN G. POSKANZER
Vice-Pres. and Dean for Admissions and
Financial Aid: PAUL THIBOUTOT
Vice-Pres. and Treas.: FREDERICK ROGERS
Vice-Pres. for External Relations: DON HAS-
SELTINE
Vice-Pres. for Student Devt and Dean for
Students: HUDLIN WAGNER
Dean for College: BEVERLY NAGEL
Registrar: ROGER LASLEY
Librarian: SAM DEMAS
Library of 563,581 vols of books, 446,089
ebooks, 39,060 ejournals, 11,886 spec.
collns, 278,138 vols of govt documents,
12,490 media colln
Number of teachers: 230
Number of students: 1,990
Publication: *Carleton College Voice*

COLLEGE OF SAINT BENEDICT

37 S College Ave, St Joseph, MN 56374-2099
Telephone: (320) 363-5011
E-mail: admission@csbsju.edu
Internet: www.csbsju.edu
Founded 1913
Catholic liberal arts college for women part-
nered with Saint John's Univ. for men; depts
of fine arts, humanities, natural sciences,
social sciences, interdisciplinary and pre-
professional programmes
Private control
Pres.: Dr MARYANN BAENNINGER
Chief of Staff: KATHRYN ENKE
Provost: RITA KNUESEL
Vice-Provost: JOE DES JARDINS
Vice-Pres. for Admission: CAL MOSLEY
Vice-Pres. for Finance and Admin.: SUSAN
PALMER
Vice-Pres. for Institutional Advancement:
KIMBERLY MOTES
Vice-Pres. for Student Devt: MARY GELLER
Academic Dean: Dr RICHARD ICE
Dean for Students: JODY TERHAAR
Dir for Libraries and Media: KATHY PARKER
Library of 640,000 vols
Number of teachers: 200 (171 full-time, 29
part-time)
Number of students: 2,090
Publications: *CSB/SJU Magazine*, *Saint
Benedict's*, *Studio One* (1 a year), *The
Record*

COLLEGE OF ST SCHOLASTICA

1200 Kenwood Ave, Duluth, MN 55811-4199
Telephone: (218) 723-6000
E-mail: admissions@css.edu
Internet: www.css.edu

Founded 1912
Private control
Academic year: September to August
Extended campuses at Brainerd, St Cloud, St
Paul and Rochester in Minnesota
Pres.: Dr LARRY GOODWIN
Vice-Pres. for Academic Affairs: Dr ELIZA-
BETH DOMHOLDT
Vice-Pres. for Enrolment Management: ERIC
BERG
Vice-Pres. for College Advancement: MARGOT
ZELENZ
Vice-Pres. for Student Life and Dean for
Students: STEVE LYONS
Registrar: GEORGE BEATTIE
Library Dir: KEVIN MCGREW
Library of 127,400 vols
Number of teachers: 400 (184 full-time, 12
part-time, 204 adjunct)
Number of students: 4,010

DEANS

School of Arts and Letters: Dr TAMMY
OSTRANDER
School of Business and Technology: Prof. Dr
KURT R. LINBERG
School of Education: JO OLSEN
School of Health Sciences: RONDELL BERKE-
LAND
School of Nursing: Dr MARTHA WITRAK
School of Sciences: GERALD HENKEL-JOHNSON

COLLEGE OF VISUAL ARTS

344 Summit Ave, St Paul, MN 55102
Telephone: (651) 757-4000
E-mail: info@cva.edu
Internet: www.cva.edu
Founded 1924
Private control
Areas of study: fine arts, graphic design,
illustration, photography
Pres. and Chief Academic Officer: ANN LEDY
Vice-Pres. for Admin. and Institutional
Research and Gen. Counsel: Dr SUSAN
SHORT
Dir for Admissions: ELYAN PAZ
Dir for Student Life: ANNE WHITE
Registrar: LOIS CANEDAY
Library Dir: KATHRYN HEUER
Library of 10,200 vols, 31,000 slides, 300
video recordings, 40 journals
Number of teachers: 65
Number of students: 250

CONCORDIA COLLEGE

901 Eighth St S, Moorhead, MN 56562
Telephone: (218) 299-4000
E-mail: admissions@cord.edu
Internet: www.cord.edu
Founded 1891
Private control
Areas of study: education, liberal arts, nurs-
ing
Pres.: Dr WILLIAM J. CRAFT
Provost and Dean for College: Dr MARK
KREJCI
Vice-Pres. for Advancement: TERESA L. HAR-
LAND
Vice-Pres. for Enrolment: STEVEN M.
SCHUETZ
Registrar: NANCY PENNA
Library Dir: SHARON HOVERSON
Library of 300,000 vols, 50 newspapers, 1,200
periodicals
Number of teachers: 190 (full-time)
Number of students: 2,800
Publication: *Concordia Magazine* (2 a year)

CONCORDIA UNIVERSITY, ST PAUL

1282 Concordia Ave, St Paul, MN 55104-5494

Telephone: (651) 641-8278
E-mail: admission@csp.edu
Internet: www.csp.edu

Founded 1893
Private control
Language of instruction: English
Academic year: August to May

Pres.: Rev. THOMAS RIES
Sr Vice-Pres.: Dr ERIC LaMOTT
Exec. Vice-Pres.: Dr CHERYL CHATMAN
Vice-Pres. for Academic Affairs: LONN MALY
Vice-Pres. for Finance: Rev. MICHAEL DORNER
Vice-Pres. for Univ. Advancement: RUSTY SELTZ
Registrar: TONI SQUIRES
Dir for Library Services: Dr CHARLOTTE KNOCHE

Library of 166,000 vols
Number of teachers: 380 (86 full-time, 294 part-time)
Number of students: 3,632

DEANS

College of Arts and Letters: Dr DAVID LUMPP
College of Business and Organizational Leadership: LONN MALY
College of Education and Science: DON HELMSTETTER

CROSSROADS COLLEGE

920 Mayowood Rd SW, Rochester, MN 55902
Telephone: (507) 288-4563
E-mail: academic@crossroadscollege.edu
Internet: www.crossroadscollege.edu

Founded 1913 as Int. Christian Bible College Asscn, current name adopted 2002
Private control
Academic year: August to May

Offers degrees in Biblical thought and literature, business administration, counselling psychology, family, youth and community, general ministry, general studies, intercultural studies, music, pastoral leadership

Pres. and Vice-Pres. for Advancement: MICHAEL KILGALLIN
Vice-Pres. for Academics: Prof. CLAUDIO DIVINO
Vice-Pres. for Admin. and Finance: ROGER LANGSETH
Vice-Pres. for Student Devt: TIM McKINNEY
Dir for Admissions: CHRISTOPHER WILLIAMS
Registrar: ROBERT DAMON
Dir for Library: JIM GODSEY

Library of 35,000 vols, 300 periodicals
Number of teachers: 20
Number of students: 180

CROWN COLLEGE

8700 College View Dr., St Bonifacius, MN 55375
Telephone: (952) 446-4100
E-mail: info@crown.edu
Internet: www.crown.edu

Founded 1916 as St Paul's Bible Institute, current name adopted 1992
Private control
Academic year: August to May

School of arts and sciences and school of online studies; depts of biblical and theological studies, business and sport management, Christian ministry, communication arts, humanities and social sciences, mathematics and science, music, nursing and teacher education

Pres.: Dr D. JOEL WIGGINS
Dean of School of Online Studies and Graduate School: Dr FAWN McCRACKEN

Provost and Vice-Pres. for Academics: Dr SCOTT MOATS
Vice-Pres. for Enrolment and Marketing: MIKE PRICE
Vice-Pres. for Finance and Operations: SUE WILSON
Vice-Pres. for Student Devt: Dr PAUL BLEZIEN
Asst Dean and College Registrar: CHERYL FISK
Dir for Library and Media Services: Dr DENNIS INGOLFSLAND

Library of 168,000 vols, 100,000 catalogued vols (books, CDs and DVDs) and 68,000 ebooks, 70,000 microform vols, articles from 29,000 magazines, journals, access to 1m. Kindle books, Rosetta Stone language programmes
Number of teachers: 90
Number of students: 1,300

DUNWOODY COLLEGE OF TECHNOLOGY

818 Dunwoody Blvd, Minneapolis, MN 55403-1192
Telephone: (612) 374-5800
E-mail: info@dunwoody.edu
Internet: www.dunwoody.edu

Founded 1914
Private control

Offers Bachelors of science in applied management, health informatics, industrial engineering technology, interior design

Pres.: Dr RICH WAGNER
Sr Vice-Pres.: ROBERT DOTY
Vice-Pres. for Devt and Alumni Relations: MARK SKIPPER
Registrar: YUN BOK CHRISTENSON
Librarian: KRISTINA OBERSTAR
Number of students: 1,410

GUSTAVUS ADOLPHUS COLLEGE

800 W College Ave, St Peter, MN 56082
Telephone: (507) 933-8000
E-mail: admission@gustavus.edu
Internet: www.gustavus.edu

Founded 1862
Private control
Academic year: September to June

Divs of education, fine arts, humanities, natural sciences and mathematics, social sciences

Pres.: JACK R. OHLE
Provost and Dean for College: Dr MARK J. BRAUN
Vice-Pres. for Enrolment Management: Dr THOMAS M. CRADY
Vice-Pres. for Institutional Advancement: THOMAS W. YOUNG
Vice-Pres. for Student Life and Dean for Students: Dr JONES VANHECKE
Registrar: KRISTIANNE WESTPHAL
Library Chair.: BARBARA FISTER

Library of 250,000 vols
Number of teachers: 280 (207 full-time, 73 part-time)
Number of students: 2,450 (f. t. e.)

HAMLINE UNIVERSITY

1536 Hewitt Ave, St Paul, MN 55104-1284
Telephone: (612) 523-2800
E-mail: admission@hamline.edu
Internet: www.hamline.edu

Founded 1854
Private control
Campus at Minneapolis (Minnesota)

Pres.: LINDA HANSON
Vice-Pres. for Academic and Student Affairs: DAVID STERN
Dean for Students: ALAN SICKBERT

Dir for Admission: MILYON TRULOVE
Univ. Registrar: TIMOTHY TRAFFIE
Dir for Bush Memorial Library: DIANE CLAYTON
Dir of Bush Memorial Library: JULIE ROCHAT
Dir of Law Library: GRACE M. MILLS

Library of 230,000 vols
Number of teachers: 150
Number of students: 4,900

Publications: *Hamline*, *Hamline Law Review*, *Journal of Law and Religion*, *Journal of Public Law and Policy*

DEANS

College of Liberal Arts: JOHN MATACHEK
School of Business: Dr ANNE M. McCARTHY
School of Education: Dr LARRY HARRIS
School of Law: DONALD LEWIS

LUTHER SEMINARY

2481 Como Ave, St Paul, MN 55108
Telephone: (651) 641-3456
E-mail: infodesk@luthersem.edu
Internet: www.luthersem.edu

Founded 1917
Private control
Academic year: September to May

Offers degrees in arts, divinity, ministry, philosophy, sacred music, social work, theology

Pres.: Rev. Dr RICHARD H. BLIESE
Vice-Pres. for Academic Affairs: DAVID EVERETT
Vice-Pres. for Admin. and Finance: DONALD LEWIS
Vice-Pres. for Seminary Relations: TOM JOLIVETTE
Vice-Pres. for Student Affairs and Enrolment: CARRIE CARROLL
Academic Dean: LESLIE ORTIZ
Dir for Admissions: SARA WILHELM GARBERS
Registrar: DIANE DONCITS
Dir for Library Services: PAUL DANIELS

Library of 250,000 vols
Number of teachers: 50
Number of students: 800

MACALESTER COLLEGE

1600 Grand Ave, St Paul, MN 55105-1899
Telephone: (612) 696-6000
E-mail: admissions@macalester.edu
Internet: www.macalester.edu

Founded 1874
Private control

Areas of study: humanities and fine arts, natural sciences, social sciences

Pres.: BRIAN C. ROSENBERG
Provost and Dean for Faculty: KATHLEEN M. MURRAY
Vice-Pres. for Admin. and Finance: DAVID WHEATON
Vice-Pres. for Advancement: THOMAS P. BONNER
Vice-Pres. for Student Affairs: LAURIE B. HAMRE
Dean for Admissions and Financial Aid: LORNE T. ROBINSON
Dean for Students: JIM HOPPE
Registrar: JAYNE NIEMI
Library Dir: TERESA FISHEL

Library of 400,000 vols
Number of teachers: 170 (full-time)
Number of students: 1,990

Publication: *Macalester Today* (4 a year, print and online, www.macalester.edu/news/macalestertoday)

MARTIN LUTHER COLLEGE

1995 Luther Court, New Ulm, MN 56073-3300
Telephone: (507) 354-8221
E-mail: mlcadmit@mlc-wels.edu
Internet: www.mlc-wels.edu
Founded 1995 by merger of Dr Martin Luther College (f. 1884) with Northwestern College (f. 1865)
Private control
Academic year: August to May
Pres.: Rev. MARK G. ZARLING
Vice-Pres. for Academics: Dr DAVID O. WENDLER
Vice-Pres. for Admin.: Prof. STEVEN R. THIESFELDT
Vice-Pres. for Enrolment Management: Prof. PHILIP M. LEYRER
Vice-Pres. for Student Life: JEFFREY L. SCHONE
Dir for Admissions: MARK STEIN
Registrar: GWEN KRAL
Library Dir: DAVID GOSDECK
Number of teachers: 80
Number of students: 720

DEANS

Educational Ministry: Prof. KURT WITTMER-SHAUS
Pastoral Ministry: Prof. DANIEL BALGE

MAYO MEDICAL SCHOOL, COLLEGE OF MEDICINE

200 First St, SW, Rochester, MN 55905
Telephone: (507) 284-3627
E-mail: medschooladmissions@mayo.edu
Internet: www.mayo.edu/mms
Private control
Dean: KEITH D. LINDOR
Assoc. Dean for Student Affairs: PATRICIA L. BARRIER
Registrar: DELORES BARTZ
Library of 400,003 vols, 4,712 journals, 4,082 ejournals, 92,626 book titles
Number of students: 50
Publications: Mayo Alumni (4 a year), Mayo Clinic Proceedings (12 a year)

MINNEAPOLIS COLLEGE OF ART AND DESIGN

2501 Stevens Ave, Minneapolis, MN 55404
Telephone: (612) 874-3700
E-mail: info@mcad.edu
Internet: www.mcad.edu
Founded 1886 as Minneapolis School of Fine Arts
Private control
Academic year: September to May
Divs of design, fine arts, liberal arts, media arts, science
Pres.: JAY COOGAN
Vice-Pres. for Academic Affairs: Prof. VINCE LEO
Vice-Pres. for Admin.: PAM NEWSOME-PROCHNIAK
Vice-Pres. for Enrolment Management: WILLIAM MULLEN
Vice-Pres. for Institutional Advancement: JOAN GRATHWOL OLSON
Vice-Pres. for Student Affairs: SUSAN CALMENSON
Dir for Continuing Studies: HOWARD ORANSKY
Registrar: JACQUELINE CHESTNUT
Library Dir: SUZANNE DEGLER
Library of 60,000 vols
Number of teachers: 65
Number of students: 700
Publication: MCAD Magazine

MINNESOTA STATE COLLEGES AND UNIVERSITIES

30 E Seventh St, Suite 350, St Paul, MN 55101-7804
Telephone: (612) 296-8012
E-mail: chancellor@so.mnscu.edu
Internet: www.mnscu.edu
Founded 1995
State control
Academic year: August to May
Incorporates 31 colleges and univs, incl. 24 two-year colleges and 7 state univs
Chancellor: STEVEN J. ROSENSTONE
Vice-Chancellor for Academic and Student Affairs: Dr DOUGLAS KNOWLTON
Vice-Chancellor for Advancement: MICHAEL DOUGHERTY
Number of students: 250,000 (system-wide)
Publication: The Minnesota State Colleges & Universities Magazine (2 a year)...

CONSTITUENT UNIVERSITIES

Bemidji State University

1500 Birchmont Ave, NE, Bemidji, MN 56601-2699
Telephone: (218) 755-2001
E-mail: admissions@bemidjistate.edu
Internet: www.bemidjistate.edu
Founded 1919
Pres.: Dr RICHARD HANSON
Provost and Vice-Pres. for Academic Affairs: ROBERT J. GRIGGS
Vice-Pres. for Finance and Admin.: WILLIAM MAKI
Vice-Pres. for Student Devt and Enrolment: Dr MARY WARD
Dir for Admissions: MARYJO CHIRPICH
Registrar: MICHELLE FRENZEL
Dean for Library Services: ROBERT GRIGGS
Library of 400,000 vols, 900 periodicals
Number of teachers: 220 (full-time)
Number of students: 5,000
Publication: Horizons

DEANS

College of Arts and Sciences: Dr P JOAN POOR
College of Business, Technology and Communication: Dr CAROL L. NIELSEN
College of Health Sciences and Human Ecology: Dr PATRICIA L. ROGERS
School of Graduate Studies: Dr PATRICIA L. ROGERS

Metropolitan State University

700 E Seventh St, St Paul, MN 55106-5000
Telephone: (616) 793-1300
Internet: www.metrostate.edu
Founded 1971
Pres.: Dr SUE K. HAMMERSMITH
Provost and Vice-Pres. for Academic Affairs: GARY SEILER
Vice-Pres. for Admin. and Finance: MURTUZA SIDDIQUI
Vice-Pres. for Student Affairs and Enrolment Management: TRENDA BOYUM-BREEN
Vice-Pres. for Univ. Advancement: ROBERT HEUERMANN
Dir for Admissions: JULIO VARGAS-ESSEX
Registrar: DARYL JOHNSON
Dean for Library and Information Services: BRUCE WILLMS (acting)
Number of teachers: 820 (168 full-time, 652 part-time)
Number of students: 9,600

DEANS

College of Arts and Sciences: BECKY L. OMDAHL
College of Management: PAUL HUO

College of Nursing and Health Sciences: ANN LEJA
College of Professional Studies: DANIEL ABEBE
First College: DANIEL ABEBE
School of Law Enforcement and Criminal Justice: VIRGINIA LANE

Minnesota State University, Mankato

309 Wigley Admin. Center, Mankato, MN 56001
Telephone: (507) 389-1111
E-mail: presidentsoffice@mnsu.edu
Internet: www.mnsu.edu
Founded 1868 as Mankato Normal School, current name adopted 1999, present status 2009
Academic year: August to May
Pres.: Dr RICHARD DAVENPORT
Vice-Pres. for Academic Affairs: Dr LINDA BAER (acting)
Vice-Pres. for Finance and Admin.: RICHARD J. STRAKA
Vice-Pres. for Technology: ED CLARK
Vice-Pres. for Univ. Advancement: DOUG MAYO
Vice-Pres. for Student Affairs and Enrolment Management: Dr DAVID P. JONES
Dean for Students: MARY DOWD
Registrar: MARCIUS BROCK
Dean for Library Services: JOAN ROCA
Library of 693,973 vols
Number of teachers: 640
Number of students: 15,000
Publications: Blue Earth Review (online, english.mnsu.edu/blueearth), Today (3 a year)

DEANS

College of Allied Health and Nursing: HARRY KRAMPF
College of Arts and Humanities: WALTER ZAKAHI
College of Business: Dr BRENDA FLANNERY
College of Education: Dr JEAN HAAR
College of Extended Learning: BECKY COPPER-GLENZ
College of Graduate Studies and Research: Dr BARRY RIES
College of Science, Engineering and Technology: Dr VIJENDRA AGARWAL
College of Social and Behavioural Sciences: Dr KIM GREER

Minnesota State University Moorhead

1104 Seventh Ave, S, Moorhead, MN 56563
Telephone: (218) 236-2011
E-mail: admissions@mnstate.edu
Internet: www.mnstate.edu
Founded 1887, present status 1975, current name adopted 2000
Academic year: August to May
Pres.: Dr ANNE BLACKHURST
Provost and Sr Vice-Pres. for Academic Affairs: Dr ANNE E. BLACKHURST
Vice-Pres. for Enrolment Management: DIANE SOLINGER
Vice-Pres. for Finance and Admin. Affairs: JAN MAHONEY
Vice-Pres. for Student Affairs: WARREN K. WIESE
Registrar: RUSSELL CURLEY
Dean for Instructional Resources: BRITTNEY GOODMAN
Library of 595,000 vols
Number of teachers: 550
Number of students: 8,500

DEANS

College of Arts and Humanities: TIM BORCHERS
College of Business and Industry: MARSHA WEBER

College of Education and Human Services: TERI WALSETH
College of Social and Natural Sciences: MICHELLE MALOTT
University College: DENISE GORSLINE

St Cloud State University

720 Fourth Ave, S, St Cloud, MN 56301-4498
Telephone: (320) 308-0121
E-mail: scsu4u@stcloudstate.edu
Internet: www.stcloudstate.edu

Founded 1869, present status 1975
Academic year: August to July

Pres.: EARL H. POTTER, III
Provost and Vice-Pres. for Academic Affairs: DEVINDER MALHOTRA
Vice-Pres. for Admin. Affairs: STEVE LUDWIG
Vice-Pres. for Student Life and Devt: WANDA OVERLAND
Vice-Pres. for Univ. Advancement: CRAIG WRUCK
Dean for Learning Resources Services: RUTH ZIETLOW

Library: 2.767m. vols (incl. 570,000 books, 1.9m. microforms incl. fed. and state documents, 1,000 print periodicals, 15,000 e-periodicals, 1,500 maps, 26,000 media items)
Number of teachers: 650
Number of students: 17,230

Publications: Dimensions (2 a year), Upper Mississippi Harvest (1 a year)

DEANS

College of Liberal Arts: MARK SPRINGER
College of Science and Engineering: DAVID DEGROOTE
Herberger Business School: DIANA LAWSON
School of Education: OSMAN ALAWIYE
School of Health and Human Services: MONICA DEVERS
School of Public Affairs: ORN BODVARSSON

Southwest Minnesota State University

1501 State St, Marshall, MN 56258-1598
Telephone: (507) 537-7021
Internet: www.smsu.edu

Founded 1963
Academic year: August to May

Pres.: Dr RONALD A. WOOD
Provost and Vice-Pres. for Academic and Student Affairs: Dr BETH WETHERBY
Vice-Pres. for Advancement: WILLIAM MULSO
Vice-Pres. for Finance and Admin.: DEBRA KERKAERT
Dean for Students: SCOTT CROWELL
Registrar: PATRICIA CARMODY
Univ. Librarian: KATHLEEN ASHE

Library of 160,000 vols
Number of teachers: 140
Number of students: 6,580

DEANS

College of Arts, Letters and Sciences: Dr JAN LOFT
College of Business, Education, Graduate and Professional Studies: Dr RAPHAEL ONYEAGHALA

Winona State University

POB 5838, 175 W Mark St, Winona, MN 55987
Telephone: (507) 457-5000
E-mail: admissions@winona.edu
Internet: www.winona.edu

Founded 1858
Academic year: August to May

Pres.: Dr JUDITH A. RAMALEY
Provost and Vice-Pres. for Academic Affairs: NANCY O. JANNIK
Vice-Pres. for Finance and Admin. Services: KURT LOHIDE (acting)

Vice-Pres. for Student Life and Devt: CONNIE GORES
Vice-Pres. for Univ. Advancement: JAMES C. SCHMIDT
Dean for Students: KAREN JOHNSON
Dean for Library: THOMAS BREMER

Library of 350,000 vols (incl. 220,000 books, 125,000 bound periodicals, 8,000 video cassettes and DVDs, 1,000 current print periodical subscriptions)
Number of teachers: 350
Number of students: 8,900

Publication: Currents

DEANS

College of Business: JAMES MURPHY
College of Education: HANK RUBIN
College of Liberal Arts: RALPH TOWNSEND
College of Nursing and Health Science: WILLIAM MCBREEN
College of Science and Engineering: HAROLD ORNES (acting)

NORTH CENTRAL UNIVERSITY

910 Elliot Ave, Minneapolis, MN 55404
Telephone: (612) 343-4400
E-mail: info@northcentral.edu
Internet: www.northcentral.edu

Founded 1930 as North Central Bible Institute, current name adopted 1998
Private control
Academic year: August to May

Depts of arts and sciences, Bible and theology, business administration, Carlstrom deaf studies, church leadership, education, English, fine arts, intercultural studies and languages, social and behavioural sciences

Pres.: Dr GORDON ANDERSON
Vice-Pres. for Academic Affairs and Academic Dean: Dr THOMAS BURKMAN
Vice-Pres. for Advancement: PAUL FREITAG
Vice-Pres. for Student Devt: MIKE NOSSER
Vice-Pres. for Univ. Relations and Enrolment: NATE RUCH
Dir for Admissions: JOSHUA MARTIN
Registrar: CODY SCHMITZ
Dir for Library: MELODY REEDY

Library of 70,000 vols
Number of teachers: 90
Number of students: 1,200

NORTHWESTERN COLLEGE

3003 Snelling Ave, N, St Paul, MN 55113-1598
Telephone: (651) 631-5100
E-mail: admissions@nwc.edu
Internet: www.nwc.edu

Founded 1902
Private control
Academic year: August to May

Depts of art and design, Biblical and theological studies, biology and biochemistry, business, Christian ministries, communication, education, English and literature, history and related fields, mathematics and engineering, music, physical education, health and kinesiology, psychology, world languages

Pres.: Dr ALAN S. CURETON
Sr Vice-Pres. for Academic Affairs: Dr JANET SOMMERS
Vice-Pres. for Institutional Advancement: AMY BRAGG CAREY
Vice-Pres. for Student Life: MATT HILL
Dean for Faculty: Dr MARK D. BADEN
Registrar: ANDREW L. SIMPSON
Library Dir: RUTH MCGUIRE

Library of 100,000 vols, 17,000 periodicals
Number of teachers: 120
Number of students: 3,000

NORTHWESTERN HEALTH SCIENCES UNIVERSITY

2501 W 84th St, Bloomington, MN 55431
Telephone: (952) 888-4777
E-mail: info@nwhealth.edu
Internet: www.nwhealth.edu

Founded 1941 as Northwestern College of Chiropractic, present name and status 1999
Private control

Pres.: MARC T. ZIEGLER
Provost and Vice-Pres. for Academic Affairs: MICHAEL R. WELLES
Sr Vice-Pres.: CHARLES E. SAWYER
Exec. Vice-Pres.: JAMES E. MCDONALD
Vice-Pres. for Admin.: ROSS B. DUGAS
Vice-Pres. for Research: Dr GERT BRONFORT
Dean for Student Affairs and Enrolment Management: Dr EMILY J. TWEED
Registrar: RUTH ANN MARKS
Dir for Library Services: DELLA SHUPE

Number of teachers: 140
Number of students: 860

DEANS

College of Acupuncture and Oriental Medicine: MARK MCKENZIE
College of Chiropractic: RENÉE M. DEVRIES
College of Undergraduate Health Sciences: DALE K. HEALEY
School of Massage Therapy: DALE K. HEALEY

OAK HILLS CHRISTIAN COLLEGE

1600 Oak Hills Rd, SW, Bemidji, MN 56601
Telephone: (218) 751-8670
E-mail: oakhills@oakhills.edu
Internet: www.oakhills.edu

Founded 1946 as Oak Hills Christian Training School, present name 1998
Private control

Areas of study: biblical studies, Christian ministries, general education

Pres.: Dr STEVEN HOSTETTER
Vice-Pres. for Advancement: JOAN BERNTSON
Dean for the College: Dr STEVEN WARE
Dir for Admissions: JOHN ENGQUIST
Registrar: MARY HANNAH
Library and Technology Dir: KEITH BUSH

Library of 23,000 vols
Number of teachers: 20
Number of students: 125

RASMUSSEN COLLEGE

8565 Eagle Point Circle, Lake Elmo, MN 55042
Telephone: (651) 259-6600
Internet: www.rasmussen.edu

Founded 1900 as Rasmussen Practical School of Business
Private control

Divs of business, education, health sciences, nursing, technology and design, justice studies; campuses in Minnesota, Illinois, Florida, Wisconsin and N Dakota;

Pres.: KRISTI A. WAITE
Vice-Pres. for Academic Affairs: CARIE ANN POTENZA
Vice-Pres. for Academic Services: GRETA FERKEL
Vice-Pres. for Admissions: SUSAN M. HAMMERSTROM
Vice-Pres. for Student Affairs: TAWNIE L. CORTEZ
Dir for Library and Learning Resources: EMILY O'CONNOR

Number of teachers: 1,000
Number of students: 15,000

ST CATHERINE UNIVERSITY

2004 Randolph Ave, St Paul, MN 55105
Telephone: (651) 690-6000
E-mail: admission@stkate.edu
Internet: www.stkate.edu

Founded 1905, present name and status 2009
Private control
Campus at Minneapolis (Minnesota); liberal arts univ. for women
Pres.: ANDREA J. LEE
Sr Vice-Pres.: COLLEEN HEGRANES
Vice-Pres. for Enrolment Management and Student Affairs: Dr BRIAN BRUESS
Vice-Pres. for External Relations: MARJORIE MATHISON HANCE
Vice-Pres. for Finance and Admin.: THOMAS ROONEY
Registrar: CINDY EGENESS
Dir for Libraries, Media Services and Archives: CAROL JOHNSON

Library of 252,107 vols
Number of teachers: 260
Number of students: 5,330

DEANS

Henrietta Schmoll School of Health: PENELOPE MOYERS
School of Business and Leadership: Dr PAULA KING
School of Humanities, Arts and Sciences: Dr ALAN SILVA
School of Professional Studies: Dr MARYANN JANOSIK

SAINT JOHN'S UNIVERSITY

POB 2000, Collegeville, MN 56321
Telephone: (320) 363-2011
E-mail: admission@csbsju.edu
Internet: www.csbsju.edu

Founded 1857
Academic year: August to May
Private control
Liberal arts college for men partnered with College of Saint Benedict for women; depts of fine arts, humanities, natural science, social science
Pres.: Dr MICHAEL HEMASETH
Provost for Academic Affairs: RITA KNUESEL
Academic Dean: Dr RICHARD ICE
Vice-Pres. for Finance and Admin.: DICK ADAMSON
Vice-Pres. for Institutional Advancement: ROB CULLIGAN
Vice-Pres. for Student Devt: DOUG MULLIN
Dir for Libraries and Media: KATHY PARKER

Library of 640,538 vols, 121,394 microforms, 19,145 govt documents, 33,108 current serial titles, 116,741 ebooks
Number of teachers: 180 (154 full-time, 26 part-time)
Number of students: 2,020

SAINT MARY'S UNIVERSITY OF MINNESOTA

700 Terrace Heights, Winona, MN 55987-1399
Telephone: (507) 457-6987
E-mail: admissions@smumn.edu
Internet: www.smumn.edu

Founded 1912
Private control
Campus at Minneapolis (Minnesota); centres at Apple Valley, Rochester, Minnetonka, Oakdale, Nairobi, Kenya and Jamaica
Chancellor: Dr LOUIS DeTHOMASIS
Pres.: WILLIAM MANN
Sr Vice-Pres. for Univ. Advancement: Dr STEVEN E. TITUS
Exec. Vice-Pres. and Gen. Counsel: ANN E. MERCHLEWITZ

Vice-Pres. for Academic Affairs: Dr DONNA ARONSON
Vice-Pres. for the College: JAMES M. BEDTKE
Registrar: YUNGE DUTTON
Library Dir: LAURA OANES

Library of 180,000 vols, 750 periodicals
Number of teachers: 590
Number of students: 6,060

Publication: *Saint Mary's Magazine*

DEANS

School of Business: THOMAS MARPE
School of Education: SCOTT SORVAAG
School of Humanities and Sciences: Dr ELIZABETH A. THROOP
School of the Arts: MICHAEL CHARRON

ST OLAF COLLEGE

1520 St Olaf Ave, Northfield, MN 55057-1098
Telephone: (507) 786-2222
Internet: www.stolaf.edu

Founded 1874
Private control
Academic year: September to May
Areas of study: fine arts, natural and mathematical sciences, social sciences and humanities
Pres.: DAVID R. ANDERSON
Provost and Dean for College: MARCI SORTOR
Vice-Pres. and Dean for Enrolment: MICHAEL KYLE
Vice-Pres. and Treas.: ALAN NORTON
Vice-Pres. for Advancement and College Relations: MICHAEL STITSWORTH
Vice-Pres. for Student Life and Dean for Students: GREG KNESER
Registrar: MARY CISAR
Dir for the Library Services: ROBERTA LEMBKE

Library of 420,000 vols, 22,000 media items, 5000 periodicals, 18,000 scores
Number of teachers: 260 (f. t. e.)
Number of students: 3,180

Publication: *St Olaf Magazine* (3 a year)

UNITED THEOLOGICAL SEMINARY OF THE TWIN CITIES

3000 Fifth St, NW, New Brighton, MN 55112-2598
Telephone: (651) 633-4311
E-mail: info@unitedseminary.edu
Internet: www.unitedseminary.edu
Private control
Areas of study: divinity, ministry, religious leadership
Pres.: MARY E. McNAMARA
Vice-Pres. for Devt: JIM OLSEN
Vice-Pres. for Finance and Admin.: TOM LOCKHART
Dean for the Seminary: SUSAN K. EBBERS
Dir for Admissions: GLEN N. HERRINGTON-HALL
Registrar: SUSAN HASTINGS
Library Dir: SUSAN K. EBBERS

Library of 83,000 vols
Number of teachers: 30
Number of students: 110 (full-time)

Publication: *ARTS: The Arts in Religious and Theological Studies* (2 a year)

UNIVERSITY OF MINNESOTA

100 Church St, SE, Minneapolis, MN 55455
6 Morrill Hall, 100 Church St, SE, Minneapolis, MN 55455-0110
Telephone: (612) 625-5000
E-mail: feedback@tc.umn.edu
Internet: www1.umn.edu

Founded 1851
State control

Academic year: September to May
Pres.: Dr ERIC W. KALER
Vice-Provost for Student Affairs: GERALD RINEHART
Sr Vice-Pres. for Academic Affairs and Provost: E. THOMAS SULLIVAN
Sr Vice-Pres. for System Academic Admin.: ROBERT J. JONES
Vice-Pres. and Chief Financial Officer: RICHARD PFUTZENREUTER
Vice-Pres. and Chief Information Officer: ANN HILL DUIN
Vice-Pres. for Research: R. TIMOTHY MULCAHY
Vice-Pres. for Univ. Services: KATHLEEN O'BRIEN
Gen. Counsel: MARK ROTENBERG
Librarian: WENDY P. LOUGEE
Library: see under Libraries and Archives
Number of teachers: 4,168 (system-wide)
Number of students: 69,221 system-wide (52,557 Twin Cities campus)

DEANS

Carlson School of Management: SRI ZAHEER
College of Biological Sciences: ROBERT ELDE
College of Continuing Education: MARY NICHOLS
College of Design: THOMAS FISHER
College of Education and Human Devt: JEAN K. QUAM
College of Food, Agricultural and Natural Resource Sciences: ALLEN S. LEVINE
College of Liberal Arts: JAMES A. PARENTE, JR
College of Pharmacy: MARILYN K. SPEEDIE
College of Science and Engineering: STEVEN L. CROUCH
College of Veterinary Medicine: TREVOR R. AMES (acting)
Graduate School: HENNING SCHROEDER
Humphrey School of Public Affairs: ERIC SCHWARTZ
Law School: Prof. DAVID WIPPMAN
Medical School: AARON FRIEDMAN
School of Dentistry: JUDITH BUCHANAN
School of Nursing: Prof. CONNIE W. DELANEY
School of Public Health: JOHN R. FINNEGAN, JR

PROFESSORS

Accounting (Carlson School of Management, 321 19th Ave, S, Suite 3-110, Minneapolis, MN 55455-0438; tel. (612) 624-7511; e-mail macct@umn.edu; internet www.carlsonschool.umn.edu/master-accountancy/index.aspx):
AMERSHI, A.
DICKHAUT, J.
JOYCE, E.
KANODIA, C.
RAYBURN, J.

Aerospace Engineering and Mechanics (107 Akerman Hall, 110 Union St, SE, Minneapolis, MN 55455-0153; tel. (612) 625-8000; e-mail dept@aem.umn.edu; internet www.aem.umn.edu):
BALAS, G.
BEAVERS, G. S.
CANDLER, G. V.
FOSDICK, R. L.
GARRARD, W. L.
LEO, P.
WILSON, T. A.

African-American and African Studies (810 Social Sciences Bldg, 267 19th Ave, S, Minneapolis, MN 55455; tel. (612) 624-9847; e-mail aaas@umn.edu; internet aaas.umn.edu):
FARAH, C.
ISAACMAN, A. F.
McCURDY, R.
NIMTZ, A.
PORTER, P. W.
SCOTT, E.

Agricultural, Food and Environmental Education (320 Vocational and Technical Education Bldg, 1954 Buford Ave, St Paul, MN 55108; tel. (612) 624-2221; internet www .cehd.umn.edu/olpd/grad-programs/afee):

KRUEGER, R.
PETERSON, R.

Agronomy and Plant Genetics (411 Borlang Hall, 1991 Upper Buford Circle, St Paul, MN 55108-6026; tel. (612) 625-7773; e-mail agro@umn.edu; internet agronomy.cfans .umn.edu):

BECKER, R. L.
CARDWELL, V. B.
DURGAN, B. R.
EHLKE, N. J.
GENGENBACH, B. G.
GRONWALD, J. W.
GUNSOLUS, J. L.
HARDMAN, L. L.
HICKS, D. R.
JONES, R. J.
JUNG, H. J.
LUESCHEN, W. E.
ORF, J. H.
PHILLIPS, R. L.
RINES, H. W.
SHEAFFER, C. C.
SIMMONS, S. R.
SOMERS, D. A.
STUTHMAN, D. D.
VANCE, C. P.
WYSE, D. L.

American Studies (104 Scott Hall, 72 Pleasant St, SE, Minneapolis, MN 55455; tel. (612) 624-4190; e-mail amstdy@umn.edu; internet americanstudies.umn.edu):

MAY, E. T.
MAY, L.
NOBLE, D.
PRELL, R. E.
YATES, G. G.

Anaesthesiology (B-515 Mayo Memorial Bldg (MMC 294), 420 Delaware St, SE, Minneapolis, MN 55455; tel. (612) 624-9990; internet www.anesthesiology.umn.edu):

BEEBE, D. S.
BELANI, K. G.
IAIZZO, P. A.
PALAHNIUK, R. J.

Animal Science (305 Haecker Hall, 1364 Eckles Ave, St Paul, MN 55108-6118; tel. (612) 624-2722; internet www.ansci.umn .edu):

CROOKER, B. A.
DAYTON, W. R.
EL HALAWANI, M. E.
FOSTER, D. N.
HANSEN, L. B.
HATHAWAY, M. R.
HAWTON, J. D.
HUNTER, A. G.
JOHNSON, D. G.
JOHNSTON, L. J.
LINN, J. G.
MARX, G. D.
NOLL, S. N.
O'GRADY, S. M.
OSBORN, J. W.
PONCE DE LEÓN, F. A.
RENEAU, J. K.
SEYKORA, A.
SHURSON, G. C.
STERN, M. D.
WHEATON, J. E.
WHITE, M. E.

Anthropology (395 Humphrey Center, 301 19th Ave, S, Minneapolis, MN 55453; tel. (612) 625-3400; e-mail anth@umn.edu; internet www.cla.umn.edu/anthropology):

GIBBON, G.
GUDEMAN, S.
INGHAM, J. M.

MILLER, F. C.
RAHEJA, G. G.
WELLS, P.

Applied Economics (231 Ruttan Hall, 1994 Buford Ave, St Paul, MN 55108; tel. (612) 625-1222; e-mail apecdept@umn.edu; internet www.apec.umn.edu):

APLAND, J. D.
EASTER, K. W.
EIDMAN, V. R.
GARTNER, W. C.
KING, R. P.
KINSEY, J. L.
LEVINS, R. L.
MORSE, G. W.
OLSEN, K. D.
PARLIAMENT, C. D.
PEDERSON, E. D.
POLASKY, S.
ROE, T. L.
RUNGE, C. F.
RUTTEN, V. W.
SCHUH, G. E.
SENAUER, B. H.

Architecture (Rapson Hall, Room 145, 89 Church St, Minneapolis, MN 55455; tel. (612) 624-7866; e-mail archinfo@umn.edu; internet arch.design.umn.edu):

FISHER, T.
LaVINE, L.
ROBINSON, J. W.
ROCKCASTLE, G.
SATKOWSKI, L.

Art (405 21st Ave, Minneapolis, MN 55455; tel. (612) 625-8096; e-mail artdept@umn.edu; internet artdept.umn.edu):

BETHKE, K. E.
HOARD, C. C.
KATSIAFICAS, D.
MORGAN, C.
PHARIS, M.
PORTRATZ, W. E.
ROSE, T. A.

Art History (338 Heller Hall, 271 19th Ave, S, Minneapolis, MN 55455; tel. (612) 624-4500; e-mail arthist@umn.edu; internet www .arthist.umn.edu):

ASHER, F. M.
COOPER, F.
MCNALLY, S.
MARLING, K. A. R.
POOR, R. J.
WEISBERG, G.

Astronomy (356 Tate Lab of Physics, 116 Church St, SE, Minneapolis, MN 53455; tel. (612) 624-0211; internet www.astro.umn .edu):

DAVIDSON, K. D.
DICKEY, J. M.
GEHRZ, R. D.
HUMPHREYS, R. M.
JONES, T.
JONES, T. W.
KUHI, L.
RUDNICK, L.
SKILLMAN, E.
WOODWARD, P. R.

Biochemistry, Molecular Biology and Biophysics (6-155 Jackson Hall, 321 Church St, SE, Minneapolis, MN 55455; tel. (612) 625-6100; e-mail bmbb@umn.edu; internet www.cbs .umn.edu/bmbb):

ALLEWELL, N. M.
ANDERSON, J. S.
ARMITAGE, I. M.
BANASZAK, L. J.
BARRY, B. A.
BERNLOHR, D. A.
BLOOMFIELD, V. A.
CONTI-FINE, B. M.
DAS, A.
DEMPSEY, M. E.
FLICKINGER, M. C.

FUCHS, J. A.
HOGENKAMP, H. P. C.
HOOPER, A. B.
HOWARD, J. B.
KOERNER, J. F.
La PORTE, D. C.
LIPSCOMB, J. D.
LIVINGSTON, D. M.
LOUIS, C. F.
LOVRIEN, R. E.
MAYO, K. H.
NELSESTUEN, G. L.
OEGEMA, T. R.
OHLENDORF, D. H.
SANDERS, M. M.
SCHOTTEL, J. S.
THOMAS, D. D.
TOWLE, H. C.
TSONG, T.
VAN NESS, B. G.
WACKETT, L. P.

Bioethics (N-504 Boynton, 410 Church St, SE, Minneapolis, MN 55455; tel. (612) 624-9440; e-mail bioethx@umn.edu; internet www.ahc.umn.edu/bioethics):

BEBEAU, M.
BURK, D.
CRANFORD, R.
KANE, R.
MAYO, D.

Biomedical Engineering (7–105 Hasselmo Hall, 312 Church St, SE, Minneapolis, MN 55455; tel. (612) 624-4507; e-mail bmedus@ umn.edu; internet bme.umn.edu):

POLLA, D.
SIEGEL, R.
TRANQUILLO, R.

Biostatistics (A-460 Mayo Bldg (MMC 303), 420 Delaware St, SE, Minneapolis, MN 55455; tel. (612) 624-4655; internet www .sph.umn.edu/biostatistics):

CARLIN, B.
CONNETT, J.
DUNSMUIR, W.
GOLDMAN, A.
LE, C.
LOUIS, T.
NEATON, J.
TWEEDIE, R.

Biosystems and Agricultural Engineering (213 Biosystems and Agricultural Engineering, 1390 Eckles Ave, St Paul, MN 55108; tel. (612) 625-7733; e-mail bae@gaia.bae.umn .edu; internet www.bae.umn.edu):

BHATTACHARYA, M.
CLAYTON, C. J.
JACOBSEN, L. D.
JANNI, K. A.
MOREY, R. V.
NIEBER, J. L.
RUAN, R.
WILCKE, W. F.

Biotechnology Institute (240 Gortner Lab, 1479 Gortner Ave, St Paul, MN 55108-6106; tel. (612) 624-6774; e-mail bti@umn.edu; internet www.bti.umn.edu):

BROOKER, R.
FLICKINGER, M.
SADOWSKY, M.
SHERMAN, D.
SRIENC, F.
URRY, D.
WACKETT, L.

Business and Industry Education (425 Vocational and Technical Education Bldg, 1954 Buford Ave, St Paul, MN 55108; tel. (612) 624-3004; internet education.umn.edu/wcfe/ bie):

BROWN, J.
LAMBRECH, J.
LEWIS, T.
MCLEAN, G.
PUCEL, D.

Chemical Engineering and Materials Science (151 Amundson Hall, 421 Washington Ave, SE, Minneapolis, MN 55455-0132; tel. (612) 625-1313; e-mail bates@cems.umn.edu; internet www.cems.umn.edu):

BATES, F.
CARETTA, R.
CARR, R. W.
CARTER, B.
CHELIKOWSKY, J. R.
CUSSLER, E. L.
DAVIS, H. T.
DERBY, J.
EVANS, D. F.
GEANKOPLIS, C. J.
GERBERICH, W. W.
HU, W. S.
KELLER, K. H.
MCCORMICK, A.
MACOSKO, C. W.
PALMSTROM, C.
SCHMIDT, L. D.
SCRIVEN, L. E.
SEIDEL, R.
SHORES, D. A.
SMYRL, W. H.
SRIENC, F.
TRANQUILLO, R.
WARD, M. D.

Chemistry (139 Smith Hall, 207 Pleasant St, SE, Minneapolis, MN 55455; tel. (612) 624-6000; internet www.chem.umn.edu):

BARANY, G.
BLOOMFIELD, V. A.
CARR, P. W.
CRAMER, C. J.
DAVIS, H. T.
ELLIS, J. E.
GENTRY, W. R.
GLADFELTER, W. L.
GRAY, G. R.
HOYE, T.
KASS, S.
LEOPOLD, K.
LIPSKY, S.
LODGE, T.
MANN, K. R.
MILLER, L. L.
NOLAND, W. E.
PIGNOLET, L. H.
QUE, L.
RAFTERY, M.
STANKOVICH, M. T.
TOLMAN, W.
TRUHLAR, D. G.

Child Development (51 E River Parkway, Minneapolis, MN 55455; tel. (612) 624-0526; e-mail icd@umn.edu; internet www.cehd.umn.edu/icd):

BAUER, P.
COLLINS, W. A.
CRICK, N.
EGELAND, B. R.
GUNNAR, M. R.
MARATSOS, M. P.
MASTEN, A. S.
NELSON, C.
PICK, A. D.
PICK, JR, H. L.
SROUFE, L. A.
WEINBERG, R. A.
YONAS, A.

Civil Engineering (122 Civil Engineering Bldg, 500 Pillsbury Dr., SE, Minneapolis, MN 55455-0116; tel. (612) 625-5522; e-mail cive@umn.edu; internet www.ce.umn.edu):

ARNDT, R. E. A.
BREZONIK, P. L.
CROUCH, S. L.
DETOURNAY, E.
DRESCHER, A.
FOUFOULA-GEORGIOU, E.
FRENCH, C. W.
GULLIVER, J. S.

MICHALOPOULOS, P.
PARKER, G. N.
SEMMENS, M. J.
STEFAN, G.
STOLARSKI, H. K.
STRACK, O. D. L.
VOLLER, V. R.

Classical and Near Eastern Studies (245 Nicholson Hall, 216 Pillsbury Dr., SE, Minneapolis, MN 55455; tel. (612) 625-5353; e-mail cnes@umn.edu; internet cnes.cla.umn.edu):

BELFIORE, E.
CLAYTON, T.
COOPER, F.
DOUGLAS, S.
MCNALLY, S.
OLSON, T.
SONKOWSKY, R. P.
STAVROU, T.

Classical Civilization Program (330 Folwell Hall, 9 Pleasant St, SE, Minneapolis, MN 55455; tel. (612) 625-7565):

AKEHURST, F. R.
BELFIORE, E.
CLAYTON, T.
COOPER, F.
LIBERMAN, A.
SONKOWSKY, R.
TRACY, J.
WILSON, L.

Clinical and Population Sciences (225 Veterinary Teaching Hospitals, 1352 Boyd Ave/1365 Gortner Ave, St Paul, MN 55108; tel. (612) 625-7755; e-mail amesx001@tc.umn.edu; internet www.cvm.umn.edu):

AMES, T. R.
BLAHA, T. C.
FAHNING, M. L.
FARNSWORTH, R. J.
FETROW, J. P.
JOO, H. S.
MOLITOR, T. M.
MORRISON, R. B.
PIJOQAN, C. J.
PULLEN, M. M.
SEGUIN, B. E.
TURNER, T. A.

Clinical Pharmacology (6-120 Jackson Hall, 321 Church St, SE, Minneapolis, MN 55455-0217; tel. (612) 626-4460; internet www.pharmacology.med.umn.edu):

HOLZMAN, J. L.
HUNNINGHAKE, D.
PENTEL, P.
YEE, D.

Cognitive Sciences (205 Elliot Hall, 75 East River Rd, Minneapolis, MN 55455; tel. (612) 626-3570; e-mail cogsci@umn.edu; internet www.cogsci.umn.edu/index.shtml):

CHILDERS, T.
GEORGOPOULOS, A.
GINI, M.
GUNDEL, J.
JOHNSON, P.
KERSTEN, D.
LEGGE, G.
MARATSOS, M.
NELSON, C.
OVERMIER, B.
PICK, A.
PICK, H.
SAMUELS, J.
SPEAKS, C.
UGURBIL, K.
VAN DEN BROEK, P.
VIEMEISTER, N.
WADE, M.
YONAS, A.

Communication Disorders (115 Shevlin Hall, 164 Pillsbury Dr., SE, Minneapolis, MN 55455; tel. (612) 624-3322; e-mail cdis@tc.umn.edu; internet www.cdis.umn.edu):

CARNEY, A. E.
REICHLE, J. E.
SPEAKS, C. E.
WINDSOR, J.

Communication Studies (225 Ford Hall, 221 Church St, SE, Minneapolis, MN 55455; tel. (612) 624-5800; internet www.comm.umn.edu):

BROWNE, D. R.
CAMPBELL, K.
HEWES, D.
SCHIAPPA, E.

Community Health Education (300 W Bank Office Bldg, 1300 52nd St, Minneapolis, MN 55455; tel. (612) 624-1878; internet www.sph.umn.edu/programs/che):

FORSTER, J.
GARRAD, J.
JEFFREY, R. W.
LANDO, H. A.
LUEPKER, R. V.
LYTLE, P.
MCGOVERN, P.
PERRY, C. L.
PIRIE, P. L.
VENMGA, R.
WAGENAAR, A. C.

Computer Science and Engineering (4-192 Keller Hall, 200 Union St, SE, Minneapolis, MN 55455; tel. (612) 625-4002; e-mail admissions@cs.umn.edu; internet www.cs.umn.edu):

BOLEY, D. L.
DU, D.
DU, D. Z.
FOX, D.
GINI, M. L.
JANARDAN, R.
KUMAR, V.
NORBERG, A. L.
PAPANIKOLOPOULOUS, W.
PARK, H.
SAAD, Y.
SHEKHAR, S.
SHRAGOWITZ, E.
SRIVASTAVA, J.
TRIPATHI, A. R.
YEW, P.

Counseling and Student Personnel Psychology (250 Education Sciences Bldg, 56 E River Rd, Minneapolis, MN 55455-0364; tel. (612) 624-6827; e-mail cspp@umn.edu; internet www.cehd.umn.edu/edpsych/programs/cspp):

HUMMEL, T.
ROMANO, J.
SKOVHOLT, T.
VEACH, P.

Cultural Studies and Comparative Literature (235 Nicholson Hall, 216 Pillsbury Dr., SE, Minneapolis, MN 55455; tel. (612) 624-8099; internet cscl.umn.edu):

BRENNAN, T.
LEPPERT, R.
MOWITT, J.
SARLES, H. B.
SCHULTE-SASSE, J.

Curriculum and Instruction (125 Peik Hall, 159 Pillsbury Dr., SE, Minneapolis, MN 55455; tel. (612) 625-4006; e-mail ciinfo@umn.edu; internet www.cehd.umn.edu/ci):

AVERY, P.
BEACH, R. W.
COGAN, J.
DILLON, D.
GRAVES, M.
JOHNSON, R.
LAMBRECHT, J.
LAWRENZ, F.
MANNING, J. C.
O'BRIEN, D.
POST, T.
TAYLOR, B.

Dental Research Center for Biomaterials and Biomechanics (16-212 Malcolm Moos Health Sciences Tower, 515 Delaware St, SE, Minneapolis, MN 55455; tel. (612) 625-0950):

COMBE, E.
DOUGLAS, W.

Dermatology (4-240 Phillips-Wangensteen Bldg, 516 Delaware St, SE, Minneapolis, MN 55455; tel. (612) 625-8625; internet www.dermatology.umn.edu):

HORDINSKY, M.
KING, R.

Design, Housing, and Apparel (240 McNeal Hall of Home Economics, 1985 Buford Ave, St Paul, MN 55108; tel. (612) 624-9700; internet dha.che.umn.edu):

ANGELL, W.
DELONG, M.
EICHER, J.
GUERIN, D.
JOHNSON, K.

Ecology, Evolution, and Behaviour (100 Ecology Bldg, 1987 Upper Buford Circle, St Paul, MN 55108; tel. (612) 625-5200; internet www.cbs.umn.edu/eeb):

ALSTAD, D.
BARNWELL, F.
BEATTY, J.
CORBIN, K.
CURTSINGER, J.
CUSHING, E.
LANYON, S.
MEGARD, R.
MORROW, P.
NEUHAUSER, C.
PACKER, C.
PUSEY, A.
REGAL, P.
SHAW, R.
SINIFF, D.
STARFIELD, A.
STERNER, R. W.
TILMAN, G. D.
ZINK, R.

Economics (1035 Walter W Heller Hall, 271 19th Ave, S, Minneapolis, MN 55455; tel. (612) 625-6353; e-mail econdept@econ.umn.edu; internet www.econ.umn.edu):

ALLEN, B.
BOLDRIN, M.
CHARI, V. V.
CHIPMAN, J. S.
ECKSTEIN, Z.
FELDMAN, R. D.
FOSTER, E.
HOLMES, T.
HURWICZ, L.
JONES, L.
KEHOE, T.
KOCHERLAKOTA, N.
MCLENNAN, A.
PRESCOTT, E. C.
RICHTER, M. K.
RUSTICHOTRI, A.
RUTTAN, V.
SCHUH, G. E.
SWAN, C.
WERNER, J.

Education for Work and Community (425 Vocational and Technical Education Bldg, 1954 Buford Ave, St Paul, MN 55108; tel. (612) 624-3004; internet education.umn.edu/wcfe/wcfe):

BROWN, J.
KRUEGER, R.
LEWIS, T.
PETERSON, R.
THOMAS, R.

Educational Policy and Administration (330 Wulling Hall, 86 Pleasant St, SE, Minneapolis, MN 55455; tel. (612) 624-1006; e-mail edpagrad@umn.edu; internet www.education.umn.edu/edpa):

AMMENTORP, W. M.
CHAPMAN, D. W.
COGAN, J. J.
FRY, G. W.
HEARN, J. C.
LEWIS, D. R.
LEWIS, T.
SEASHORE, R.

Educational Psychology (204 Burton Hall, 178 Pillsbury Dr., SE, Minneapolis, MN 55455; tel. (612) 624-1698; e-mail epsy-adm@umn.edu; internet www.education.umn.edu/edpsych):

BART, W. M.
BRUININKS, R.
CHRISTENSON, S.
DAVISON, M. L.
DENO, S.
HARWELL, M.
HUMMEL, T.
HUPP, S.
JOHNSON, D. W.
LAWRENZ, F.
MCCONNELL, S.
MCEVOY, M.
MARUYAMA, G.
PELLEGRINI, A.
ROMANO, J.
SAMUELS, S. J.
SKOVHOLT, T. M.
TENNYSON, R.
VAN DEN BROEK, P.
VEACH, P. M.
YSSELDYKE, J.

Electrical and Computer Engineering (4-178 Electrical Engineering/Computer Science, 200 Union St, SE, Minneapolis, MN 55455; tel. (612) 625-3300; internet www.ece.umn.edu):

COHEN, P. I.
GEORGIOU, T.
GIANNAKIS, G.
GOPINATH, A.
KAVEH, M.
KIEFFER, J. C.
KIEHL, R.
KINNEY, L. L.
KUMAR, K. S. P.
LEE, E. B.
LEGER, J.
LILJA, D.
MAZIAR, C.
MOHAN, N.
MOON, J.
NATHAN, M.
PARHI, K.
PERIA, W. T.
POLLA, D.
ROBBINS, W. P.
RUDEN, P.
TANNENBAUM, A.
TEWFIK, A.
WOLLENBERG, B. F.

Emergency Medicine (A-624 Mayo Memorial Bldg (MMC 911), 420 Delaware St, SE, Minneapolis, MN 55455; tel. (612) 626-6911):

AMSTERDAM, J.
CLINTON, J.
KNOPP, R.
LING, L.
RUIZ, E.

English (207 Lind Hall, 207 Church St, SE, Minneapolis, MN 55455; tel. (612) 625-3363; internet english.cla.umn.edu):

BALES, K.
BRENNAN, T.
BRIDWELL-BOWLES, L.
BROWNE, M. D.
CLAYTON, T.
ELFENBEIN, A.
ESCURE, G.
FIRCHOW, P. E.
GARNER, S.
GRIFFIN, E. M.

HALEY, D.
HAMPL, P. M.
HANCHER, M.
HIRSCH, G.
KENDALL, C.
MINER, V.
MOWITT, J.
RABINOWITZ, P.
REED, P. J.
ROSS, D.
ROTH, M.
SOLOTAROFF, R.
SPRENGNETHER, M.
WEINSHEIMER, J.

English as a Second Language (214 Nolte Center for Continuing Education, 315 Pillsbury Dr., SE, Minneapolis, MN 55455; tel. (612) 624-3331; e-mail eatarone@tc.umn.edu; internet www.iles.umn.edu/esl.htm):

COHEN, A.
TARONE, E.

Entomology (219 Hodson Hall, 1980 Folwell Ave, St Paul, MN 55108; tel. (612) 624-3636; e-mail entodept@tc.umn.edu):

ANDOW, D. A.
ASCERNO, M. E.
HIEMPEL, G. E.
HOLZENTHAL, R. W.
HUTCHINSON, W. G.
KURTTI, T. J.
MESCE, R. D.
MOON, R. D.
OSTLIE, K. R.
RADCLIFFE, E. B.
RAGSDALE, D. W.
WALGENBACH, D. D.

Environmental and Occupational Health (1260 Mayo Memorial Bldg (MMC 807), 420 Delaware St, SE, Minneapolis, MN 55455; tel. (612) 626-0900; internet www.umn.edu/eoh):

GERBERICH, S.
SEXTON, K.
SWACKHAMER, D.
TOSCANO, W.
VESLEY, D.

Epidemiology (300 West Bank Office Bldg, 1300 52nd St, Minneapolis, MN 55455; tel. (612) 624-1878; internet www.epi.umn.edu):

BROWN, J. E.
CROW, R. S.
FINNEGAN, J. R.
FOLSOM, A. R.
FORSTER, J. L.
GARRAD, J.
GLASSER, S. P.
HIMES, J. M.
JACOBS, D. R.
JEFFEREY, R. W.
LANDO, H. A.
LUEPKER, R. V.
MCGOVERN, P.
MENOTTI, A.
PERRY, C. L.
PIRIE, P. L.
SHAHAR, E.
STORY, M. T.
VENINGA, R.
WAGENAAR, A. C.

Experimental and Clinical Pharmacology (7-159 Weaver-Densford Hall, 308 Harvard St, SE, Minneapolis, MN 55455; tel. (612) 626-9937; internet www.pharmacy.umn.edu):

CLOYD, J. C.
FLETCHER, C. V.
GROSS, C.
GUAY, D. R.
HANLON, J. T.
LACKNER, J. E.
MANN, K. J.
ROTSCHAFER, J. C.
ZASKE, D. E.

Family Education (325 Vocational and Technical Education Bldg, 1954 Buford Ave, St Paul, MN 53708; tel. (612) 624-3010; internet education.umn.edu/wcfe/fe):

THOMAS, R.

Family Practice and Community Health (6-240 Phillips-Wangensteen Bldg, 516 Delaware St, SE, Minneapolis, MN 55455; tel. (612) 624-2622; internet www.med.umn.edu/fp):

BLAND, C. J.
COLEMAN, E.
GJEROINGEN, D.
KEENAN, J.
SIMON ROSSER, B. R.

Family Social Science (290 McNeal Hall of Home Economics, 1985 Buford Ave, St Paul, MN 55108; tel. (612) 625-1900; internet fsos.che.umn.edu):

BAUER, J.
BOSS, P.
DANES, S.
DETZNER, D.
DOHERTY, W.
GROTEVANT, H. D.
HOGAN, M. J.
MADDOCK, J.
RETTIG, K.
ROSENBLATT, P.
TURNER, W.

Finance (3-122 Carlson School of Management, 321 19th Ave, S, Minneapolis, MN 55455; tel. (612) 624-2888; internet www.csom.umn.edu):

ALEXANDER, G.
BENVENISTE, L.
BOYD, J.
LEVINE, R.
NANTELL, T.

Fisheries and Wildlife (200 Hodson Hall, 1980 Folwell Ave, St Paul, MN 55455; tel. (612) 624-3600; internet www.fw.umn.edu):

ADELMAN, I.
ANDERSON, D.
COHEN, Y.
COOPER, J.
CUTHBERT, F.
KAPUSCINSKI, A.
PERRY, J.
SMITH, D.
SORENSEN, P.
SPANGLER, G.

Food Science and Nutrition (225 Food Science and Nutrition, 1334 Eckles Ave, St Paul, MN 55108; tel. (612) 624-1290; e-mail fscn@mail.coafes.umn.edu; internet fscn.che.umn.edu):

ADDIS, P. B.
BRADY, L. J.
CSALLANY, A. S.
FULCHER, R. G.
LABUZA, T. P.
MCKAY, L. L.
REINECCIUS, G. A.
SLAVIN, J. L.
SMITH, D. E.
TATINI, S. R.
VICKERS, Z. M.
WARTHESEN, J. J.

Forest Resources (115 Green Hall, 1530 N Cleveland Ave, St Paul, MN 53108; tel. (612) 624-3400; e-mail fr@forestry.umn.edu; internet www.cnr.umn.edu/fr):

ANDERSON, D. H.
BAUER, M. E.
BAUGHMAN, M. J.
BLINN, C. R.
BROOKS, K. N.
BURK, T. E.
EK, A. R.
ELLEFSON, P. B.
PERRY, II, J. A.

REICH, P. B.
ROSE, D. W.

French and Italian (260 Folwell Hall, 9 Pleasant St, SE, Minneapolis, MN 55455; tel. (612) 624-4308; e-mail frit@umn.edu; internet cla.umn.edu/frit):

AKEHURST, F. R. P.
NOAKES, S.
PAGANINI, M.

General College (25 Appleby Hall, 128 Pleasant St, SE, Minneapolis, MN 55455; tel. (612) 625-3339; internet www.gen.umn.edu):

BROTHEN, T. F.
COLLINS, T. G.
GIDMARK, J. B.
HIGHBEE, J. H.
MOORE, R. C.
ROBERTSON, D. F.
YAHNKE, R. E.

Genetics, Cell Biology and Development (6-160 Jackson Hall, 321 Church St, SE, Minneapolis, MN 55455; tel. (612) 624-3110; e-mail gcd@mail.med.umn.edu; internet www.gcd.med.umn.edu):

BAUER, G. E.
BERMAN, J. G.
BERRY, S.
BROOKER, R. J.
ERLANDSEN, S. L.
FAN, D. P.
FARAS, A. H.
GOLDSTEIN, S. F.
HACKETT, P. B.
HAMILTON, D. W.
HERMAN, R. K.
HERMAN, W. S.
JOHNSON, R. G.
KING, R. A.
KURIYAMA, P. A.
LEFEBVRE, P. A.
LINCK, R. W.
MCIVOR, R. S.
MAGEE, P. T.
O'CONNOR, M. B.
ORR, H. T.
SILFLOW, C. D.
SIMMONS, M. J.
SNUSTAD, D. P.
SORENSON, R. L.
VANNESS, B. G.

Geography (414 Social Sciences Bldg, 267 19th Ave, S, Minneapolis, MN 55455; tel. (612) 625-6080; e-mail geog@geog.umn.edu; internet www.geog.umn.edu):

ADAMS, J. S.
BROWN, D. A.
GERSMEHL, P. J.
HART, J. F.
HSU, M. L.
LEITNER, H.
MCMASTER, R. B.
MARTIN, J. A.
SAMATOR, A. I.
SCOTT, E. P.
SHEPPARD, E. S.
SKAGGS, R. H.

Geology and Geophysics (108 Pilsbury Hall, 310 Pilsbury Dr., SE, Minneapolis, MN 55455; tel. (612) 624-1333; e-mail geology@umn.edu; internet www.geo.umn.edu):

ALEXANDER, JR, E. C.
BANERJEE, S. K.
EDWARDS, R. L.
HUDLESTON, P.
ITO, E.
KOHLSTEDT, D.
KOHLSTEDT, S. G.
MOREY, G. B.
MOSHOWITZ, B.
MURTHY, V. R.
PAOLA, C.
PFANNKUCH, H. O.
SEYFRIED, JR, W. E.

SOUTHWICK, D.
STOUT, J.
TEYSSIER, C.
YUEN, D.

German, Scandinavian, and Dutch (205 Folwell Hall, 9 Pleasant St, SE, Minneapolis, MN 55455; tel. (612) 625-2080; internet www.folwell.umn.edu/gsd):

FIRCHOW, E. S.
HASSELMO, N.
HOUE, P.
JOERES, R. B.
LIBERMAN, A.
PARENTE, JR, J.
SCHULTE-SASSE, J.
STOCKENSTRÖM, G.
TERAOKA, A.
ZIPES, J.

Gerontology (D-312 Mayo Memorial Bldg (MMC 197), 420 Delaware St, SE, Minneapolis, MN 55455; tel. (612) 624-3904; e-mail coa@tc.umn.edu; internet www.umn.edu/coa):

AHLBURG, D.
BORN, D.
BOSS, P.
BOULT, C.
CLOYD, J.
CURTSONGER, J.
DETZNER, D.
DIFABIO, R.
DURFEE, W.
DYSKEN, M.
EUSTIS, N.
FELDMAN, B.
GARRARD, J.
GERSHEENSON, C.
GUAY, D.
HANCOCK, P.
HANLON, J.
HELLER, L.
KANE, R.
KANE, R.
KELLER, L.
KIVNICK, H.
LACKNER, T.
LARSON, A.
LE, C.
MCGUE, M.
MEYERS, S.
MILES, S.
PARK, R.
QUAM, J.
SCHONDEMEYER, S.
SEYBOLD, V.
SNYDER, M.
SWIONTKOWSKI, M.
THOMAS, D.
WADE, M.
WYMAN, J.
ZIMMERMAN, S.

Healthcare Management (3-140 Carlson School of Management, 321 19th Ave, S, Minneapolis, MN 55455; tel. (612) 624-8814; internet www.csom.umn.edu/facultydepartments/departments/healthcare-emgmt/healthcaremgmt.cfm):

BEGUN, J.
CHRISTIANSON, J.
WECKWERTH, V.

Health Ecology (15-136 Malcolm Moos Health Sciences Tower, 515 Delaware St, SE, Minneapolis, MN 55455; tel. (612) 625-1191; e-mail tlpash@maroon.tc.umn.edu; internet www.umn.edu/dental/department/prevsei/div_hecology.html):

BEBEAU, M.
BORN, D.
DIANGELIS, A.
MARTENS, L.

Health Informatics (777 Mayo Memorial Bldg (MMC 511), 420 Delaware St, SE, Minneapolis, MN 55455; tel. (612) 625-8440;

e-mail grad@email.labmed.umn.edu;
internet www.hinf.umn.edu):

CONNELLY, D.
FINKELSTEIN, S.
GATEWOOD, L.
SPEEDIE, S.

Health Informatics Graduate Programme
(777 Mayo Memorial Bldg (MMC 511), 420
Delaware St, SE, Minneapolis, MN 55455;
tel. (612) 625-8440; e-mail grad@email
.labmed.umn.edu; internet www.hinf.umn
.edu):

CONNELLY, D.
ELLIS, L.
FAN, D.
FINKELSTEIN, S.
FRICTON, J.
GATEWOOD, L.
HARRIS, I.
JOHNSON, P.
McQUARRIE, D.
PATTERSON, R.
SPEEDIE, S.
WHOLEY, D.
WILCOX, G.

Health Services Research and Policy, Division of (15-200 Phillips-Wangensteen Bldg,
516 Delaware St, SE, Minneapolis, MN
55455; tel. (612) 624-6151; e-mail ihsr@umn
.edu; internet www.hsr.umn.edu):

CHRISTIANSON, J.
DOWD, B.
FELDMAN, R.
GARRARD, J.
HANLON, J.
KANE, R.
KANE, R.
KRALEWSKI, J.
LURIE, N.
McBEAN, M.
MOSCOVICE, I.
NYMAN, J.
SWIONTKOWSKI, M.
VENNIGA, R.

History (614 Social Sciences Bldg, 267 19th
Ave, S, Minneapolis, MN 55455; tel. (612)
624-2800; internet www.hist.umn.edu):

ALTHOLZ, J. L.
BACHRACH, B. S.
BERMAN, H.
EVANS, J.
EVANS, S.
FARMER, E. L.
GOOD, D.
ISAACMAN, A. F.
McCAA, R.
MAYNES, M. J.
MENARD, R. R.
MUNHOLLAND, J. K.
NOONAN, T. S.
PHILLIPS, C.
PHILLIPS, W.
REYERSON, K.
RUGGLES, S.
SAMAHA, J.
STAVROU, T. G.
THAYER, J. A.
TRACY, J. D.
VECOLI, R. J.
WALTNER, A.

History of Medicine (511A Diehl Hall, 505
Essex St, SE, Minneapolis, MN 55455; tel.
(612) 624-4416; internet www.med.umn.edu/
history/home.htm):

EYLER, J. M.

History of Science and Technology (381 Tate
Lab of Physics, 116 Church St, SE, Minneapolis, MN 55455; tel. (612) 624-7069; internet
www.physics.umn.edu):

BEATTY, J.
KOHLSTEDT, S. G.
NORBERG, A. L.
SEIDEL, R. W.

SHAPIRO, A. E.

Hormel Institute (801 16th Ave, NE, Austin,
MN 55912; tel. (507) 433-8804; internet www
.smig.net/hi):

BROCKMAN, H. L.
BROWN, R. E.
DONG, Z.
KISS, Z.
SCHMID, H. H. O.

Horticultural Science (305 Alderman Hall,
1970 Rolwell Ave, St Paul, MN 55108; tel.
(612) 624-5300; internet www.hort.agri.umn
.edu):

BECKER, R. L.
BROWN, D. L.
COHEN, J. D.
GARDNER, G. M.
HOOVER, E. E.
LI, P. H.
LUBY, J. J.
MARKHART, III, A. H.
OLIN, P. J.
PELLETT, H. M.
PRESTON, D.
ROSEN, C. J.
SOWOKINOS, J. R.
WHITE, D. B.
WILDUNG, D. K.

Human Genetics (4-122 Malcolm Moos
Health Sciences Tower, 515 Delaware St,
SE, Minneapolis, MN 55455; tel. (612) 624-
8111; internet www.ihg.med.umn.edu):

BERRY, S.
CONKLIN, K.
HACKETT, P.
KERSEY, J.
KING, R.
McIVOR, R. S.
MOSER, K.
ORR, H.
SOMIA, M.
VanNESS, B.
WHITLEY, C.

Human Resource Development and Adult
Education (425 Vocational and Technical
Education Bldg, 1954 Buford Ave, St Paul,
MN 55108; tel. (612) 624-3004; internet
education.umn.edu/wcfe/hrd/default.html):

BROWN, J.
LEWIS, T.
McLEAN, G.
PUCEL, D.
SWANSON, R.

Human Sexuality (180 West Bank Office
Bldg, 1300 52nd St, Minneapolis, MN
55455; tel. (612) 625-1500):

COLEMAN, E.
ROSSER, S.

Humphrey School of Public Affairs (300
Hubert H. Humphrey Center, 301 19th Ave,
S, Minneapolis, MN 55455; tel. (612) 625-
9505; internet www.hhh.umn.edu):

ADAMS, J.
ARCHIBALD, S.
BRANDL, J.
BRYSON, J.
EUSTIS, N.
FENNELLY, K.
HOENACK, S.
KAPSTEIN, E.
KELLER, K.
KENNEY, S.
KLEINER, M.
KUDRLE, R.
MARKUSEN, A.
MYERS, JR, S. L.
SCHUH, G. E.

Industrial Relations (3-300 Carlson School of
Management, 321 19th Ave, S, Minneapolis,
MN 55455; tel. (612) 624-2500; internet www
.irc.csom.umn.edu):

AHLBURG, D.

ARVEY, R.
BEN-NER, A.
BOGNANNO, M.
FOSSUM, J.
REMINGTON, J.
SCOVILLE, J.
WHITMAN, A.
ZAIDI, M.

Information and Decision Sciences (3-365
Carlson School of Management, 321 19th
Ave, S, Minneapolis, MN 55455; tel. (612)
624-8030; internet www.csom.umn.edu):

ADAMS, C. R.
CHERVANY, N. L.
CURLEY, S.
DAVIS, G. B.
JOHNSON, P. E.
KAUFFMAN, R. J.

Jewish Studies Center (339 Folwell Hall, 9
Pleasant St, SE, Minneapolis, MN 55455; tel.
(612) 624-4914):

BACHRACH, B.
BERMAN, H.
BRUSTEIN, W.
PRELL, R. V.-E.
ZIPES, J.

Journalism and Mass Communication (111
Murphy Hall, 206 Church St, SE, Minneapolis, MN 55455; tel. (612) 625-9824; internet
sjmc.umn.edu):

DICKEN-GARCIA, H.
FABER, R. J.
FANG, I. E.
HANSEN, K. A.
KIRTLEY, J. E.
LEE, C. C.
ROBERTS, N. L.
SULLIVAN, D.
WACKMAN, D. B.

Kinesiology (220 Cooke Hall, 1900 University
Ave, SE, Minneapolis, MN 55455; tel. (612)
625-5300; internet education.umn.edu/kls/
kinesiology/default.html):

KANE, J.
LEON, A.
WADE, M.

Laboratory Medicine and Pathology (D-
242 Mayo Memorial Bldg (MMC 609), 420
Delaware St, SE, Minneapolis, MN 55455;
tel. (612) 625-9171; internet www.borg
.labmed.umn.edu/ateam.html):

AHMED, K.
APPLE, F.
BALFOUR, H. J.
BROWN, D. M.
CLARK, B.
ECKFELDT, J.
ELLIS, L.
FERRIERI, P.
FINKELSTEIN, S.
FURCHT, L. T.
GARRY, V.
GATEWOOD, L. C.
HALBERG, F.
HAUS, E.
HECHT, S.
HORWITZ, C.
JESSURUN, J.
KERSEY, J. H.
LeBIEN, T.
McCARTHY, J.
McCULLOUGH, J. J.
McIVOR, S.
MALEJKA-GIGANTI, D.
MANIVEL, C.
MESCHER, M.
ORR, H.
RAO, G.
ROSE, A.
SHIMIZU, Y.
STANLEY, M.
TSAI, M.
WATTENBERG, L.

WELLS, C.
WHITE, J.
WILSON, M.

Landscape Architecture (1425 University Ave, SE, Minneapolis, MN 55455; tel. (612) 625-6860; internet www.cala.umn.edu/ landscape_architecture/landscape.html):

NECKAR, L.
PITT, D.

Law (285 Mondale Hall, 229 19th Ave, S, Minneapolis, MN 55455; tel. (612) 625-1000; internet www.law.umn.edu):

ADAMS, E.
BEFORT, S.
BURK, P.
BURKHART, A.
CHEN, J.
COOPER, L. J.
DRIPPS, D.
ERICKSON, M.
FARBER, D. A.
FELD, B. C.
FELLOWS, M. L.
FRASE, R. S.
GIFFORD, D. J.
KELLY, B.
KOEPPEN, B.
MARSHALL, D. P.
MATHESON, J.
MORRISON, F. L.
MUNDSTOCK, G.
OKEDIJI, R.
PAULSEN, M.
POWELL, J.
SAMAHA, A.
SCHOETTLE, F.
SHARPE, C.
STEIN, R. A.
TONRY, M. H.
WEISS, F.
WEISSBRODT, D. S.
WOLF, S.
YOUNGER, J.
YUDOF, M.

Life Course Center (1014 Social Sciences Bldg, 267 19th Ave, S, Minneapolis, MN 55455; tel. (612) 624-6333; internet www.soc .umn.edu/research/aboutlcc.htm):

KRUTTSCHNITT, C.
LASLETT, B.
MALMQUIST, C.
MORTIMER, J.
STRYKER, R.

Limnological Research Center (220 Pillsbury Hall, 310 Pillsbury Dr., SE, Minneapolis, MN 55455; tel. (612) 624-7005; internet lrc.geo .umn.edu):

BANERJEE, S. K.
CUSHING, E. J.
EDWARDS, L.
ITO, E.
JOHNSON, T. C.
MEGARD, R. O.

Linguistics (214 Nolte Center for Continuing Education, 315 Pillsbury Dr., SE, Minneapolis, MN 55455; tel. (612) 624-3331; e-mail umling@tc.umn.edu):

GUNDEL, J.

Marketing and Logistics Management (3-150 Carlson School of Managment, 321 19th Ave, S, Minneapolis, MN 55455; tel. (612) 624-5055; internet www.csom.umn.edu/ wwwpages/depts/mktg/mktgdept.htm):

HOUSTON, M.
JOHN, D.
JOHN, G.
LOKEN, B.
MEYERS-LEVY, J.
ROERING, K.
RUEKERT, R.
WALKER, O.

Mathematics (127 Vincent Hall, 206 Church St, SE, Minneapolis, MN 55455; tel. (612) 625-2004; e-mail dpt@math.umn.edu; internet www.math.umn.edu):

ADAMS, S.
AGARD, S.
ANDERSON, G.
ARNOLD, D.
ARONSON, D.
BAXTER, J.
BOBKOV, S.
BRAMSON, M.
CALDERER, M. C.
COCKBURN, B.
FESHBACH, M.
FRISTEDT, B.
GARRETT, P.
GOLDMAN, J.
GRAY, L.
GULLIVER, R.
HARRIS, M.
HEJHAL, D.
JAIN, N.
JODEIT, M.
KAHN, D.
KEYNES, H.
KRYLOV, N.
LITTMAN, W.
LOWENGRUB, J.
LUSKIN, M.
LYUBEZNIK, G.
MCCARTHY, C.
MCGEHEE, R.
MARDEN, A.
MESSING, W.
MEYERS, N.
MILLER, JR, W.
MOECKEL, R.
NI, W.-M.
ODLYZKO, A.
OLVER, P.
OTHMER, H.
POLACIK, P.
PRIKRY, K.
REINER, V.
REITICH, F.
REJTO, P.
ROBERTS, J.
SAFONOV, M.
SANTOSA, F.
SELL, G.
SPERBER, S.
STANTON, D.
STORVICK, D.
WEBB, P.
WHITE, D.

Mechanical Engineering (1100 Mechanical Engineering, 111 Church St, SE, Minneapolis, MN 55455; tel. (612) 625-0705; e-mail mech-eng-info@me.umn.edu; internet www .me.umn.edu):

ARORA, S. R.
BAR-COHEN, A.
DAVIDSON, J.
DONATH, M.
DURFEE, W.
ERDMAN, A. G.
GIRSHICK, S.
HEBERLEIN, J.
KITTLESON, D. B.
KLAMECHI, B.
KUEHN, T. H.
KULACKI, F.
KVALSETH, T. O.
LEWIS, J.
MCMURRY, P. H.
MARPLE, V. A.
PUI, D.
RAMALINGAM, S.
RAMSEY, J. W.
SIMON, T. W.
SPARROW, E. M.
STARR, P.
STELSON, K.
STRYKOWSKI, P.

TAMMA, K.

Medical Biotechnology (7-105 Basic Sciences and Biomedical Engineering, 312 Church St, SE, Minneapolis, MN 55455; tel. (612) 626-2366; internet www.med.umn.edu/imb):

FURCHT, L.
MCCARTHY, J.
MCCULLOUGH, J.
RAO, G.

Medical Technology (15-170 Phillips-Wangensteen Bldg, 516 Delaware St, SE, Minneapolis, MN 55455; tel. (612) 625-9490; e-mail medtech@tc.umn.edu):

TSAI, M.
WELLS, C.

Medicinal Chemistry (8-101 Weaver-Densford Hall, 308 Harvard St, SE, Minneapolis, MN 55455; tel. (612) 624-9919; internet www .pharmacy.umn.edu):

ABUL-HAJJ, Y. J.
HANNA, P. E.
HECHT, S. S.
JOHNSON, R. L.
NAGASAWA, H. T.
PORTOGHESE, P. S.
REMMEL, R. P.
SHIER, W. T.
SPEEDIE, M. K.
VINCE, R.

Medicine (100 Philips-Wangensteen Bldg, 516 Delaware St, SE, Minneapolis, MN 55455; tel. (612) 625-7140):

ANAND, I.
ASINGER, R.
BACHE, R.
BANTLE, J.
BEHRENS, T.
BENDITT, D.
BILLINGTON, C.
BITTERMAN, P.
BLUMENTHAL, M.
BOND, J.
CHESLER, E.
CHRISTIANSON, J.
COHN, J. N.
COLLINS, A.
CROSSLEY, K.
DANIELS, B.
DAVIES, S.
DUANE, W.
FROHNERT, P.
FROM, A.
GEORGOPOULOS, A.
GLASSER, S.
GOLDSMITH, S.
GOODMAN, J.
GRAY, R.
GRIMM, R.
HAASE, A.
HEBBEL, R.
HERTZ, M.
HOLTZMAN, J.
HOSTETTER, T.
HOWE, R.
HUNNINGHAKE, D.
INGBAR, D.
JANOFF, E.
JOHNSON, G.
JOHNSON, J.
KAHN, J.
KASISKE, B.
KEANE, W.
KENNEDY, H.
KING, R.
KUBO, S.
LAKE, J.
LEDERLE, F.
LEVINE, A.
LEVITT, M. D.
LUEPKER, R.
LUIKART, S.
LURIE, N.
MCCLAVE, P.
MAHOWALD, M.

MARIASH, C.
MARINI, J.
MESSNER, R.
MILES, S.
MILLER, J.
MILLER, L.
MILLER, W.
MOLDOW, C.
MUELLER, D.
NICHOL, K.
NIEWOEHNER, D.
NUTTALL, F. O.
PALLER, M.
PENTEL, P.
PETERSON, B.
PETERSON, P. K.
PIERACH, C.
POPKIN, M.
RAIJ, L.
RAO, K.
RAVDIN, J.
ROSENBERG, A.
ROSENBERG, M.
RUBINS, H.
SABATH, L. D.
SIMON, G.
SKUBITZ, K.
STEER, C.
TAYLOR, A.
UGURBIL, K.
VERCELLOTTI, G.
VERFAILLIE, C.
WEIR, E. K.
WEISDORF, D.
WHITE, C.
WILLIAMS, D.
WILSON, R.
WOLF, S.
YEE, D.

Microbial Biochemistry and Biotechnology
(156 Gortner Laboratory, 1479 Gortner Ave,
St Paul, MN 55108; tel. (612) 625-3785;
internet www.cbs.umn.edu/bmbb):

ANDERSON, J. S.
FLICKINGER, M. C.
HOOPER, A. B.
SCHOTTEL, J. L.

Microbiology (1460 Mayo Memorial Bldg
(MMC 196), 420 Delaware St, SE, Minneapolis, MN 55455; tel. (612) 624-6190; e-mail
micro@lenti.med.umn.edu; internet www
.microbiology.med.umn.edu):

BERMAN, J.
CLEARY, P. P.
DUNNY, G.
DWORKIN, M.
FARAS, A. J.
HAASE, A.
HANSON, R.
JENKINS, M.
JOHNSON, R. C.
MAGEE, P. T.
PLAGEMANN, P. G. W.
SCHLIEVERT, P. M.
SHERMAN, D.

Molecular and Cellular Therapy (D-
242 Mayo Memorial Bldg (MMC 609), 420
Delaware St, SE, Minneapolis, MN 55455;
tel. (612) 626-3272; internet www.mbbnet
.umn.edu/institutes/cmct):

MCCULLOUGH, J.
MILLER, J.

Molecular Biology (6-155 Jackson Hall, 321
Church St, SE, Minneapolis, MN 55455; tel.
(612) 625-6100; internet www.cbs.umn.edu/
bmbb):

DAS, A.
FUCHS, J. A.
LAPORTE, D. C.
LIVINGSTON, D. M.
SANDERS, M. M.
TOWLE, H. C.
VANNESS, B. G.

Music (100 Donald N. Ferguson Hall, 2106
4th St, S, Minneapolis, MN 55455; tel. (612)
624-5740; internet www.music.umn.edu):

ANDERSON, J.
ASHWORTH, T.
BALDWIN, D.
BRAGINSKY, A.
CHERLIN, M.
GARRETT, M.
GRAYSON, D.
HAACK, P.
JACKSON, D.
KIRCHHOFF, C.
KONKOLL, K.
LANCASTER, T.
LUBET, A.
MCCURDY, R.
MAURICE, G.
O'REILLY, S.
REMENIKOVA, T.
SHOCKLEY, R.
SUTTON, V.
WARE, D. C.
WELLER, L.
ZAIMONT, J. L.

Naval Science (203 Armory Bldg, 15 Church
St, SE, Minneapolis, MN 55455; tel. (612)
625-6677; e-mail nrotc@umn.edu; internet
www.umn.edu/nrotc):

FREY, W.

Neurology (12-100 Phillips-Wangensteen
Bldg (MMC 295), 516 Delaware St, SE,
Minneapolis, MN 55455; tel. (612) 625-9900;
internet www.neurology.umn.edu):

ANSARI, K.
ASHE, K.
CRANFORD, R.
ETTINGER, M.
GEORGOPOULOS, A.
IADECOLA, C.
KENNEDY, W. R.
KLASSEN, A. C.
KNOPMAN, D.
KRIEL, R.
LOCKMAN, L.
MAHOWALD, M.
MORIARTY, G.
NELSON, C.
PARRY, G.
RAMIREZ-LASSEPAS, M.
ROSS, E. M.
ROTTENBERG, D.
SHAPIRO, E.
TRUWITT, C.
WIRTSCHAFTER, J.

Neuroscience (6-145 Jackson Hall, 321
Church St, SE, Minneapolis, MN 55455; tel.
(612) 626-6800; internet www.neurosci.umn
.edu):

CARROLL, M.
ELDE, R.
EL-FAKAHANY, E.
ENGELAND, W.
FLANDERS, M.
GEORGOPOULOS, A.
GIESLER, JR, G.
IADECOLA, C.
JUHN, S.
LARSON, A.
LETOURNEAU, P.
LEVINE, A.
MCLOON, S.
MANTYH, P.
MILLER, R.
NEWMAN, E.
POPPELE, R.
SANTI, P.
SEYBOLD, V.
SOECHTING, J.
SORENSON, P.
SPARBER, S.
UGURBIL, K.
WILCOX, G.

Neurosurgery (D-429 Mayo Memorial Bldg
(MMC 96), 420 Delaware St, SE, Minneapolis, MN 55455; tel. (612) 624-6666; internet
www.neuro.umn.edu):

EFANGE, S. M. N.
HALL, W. A.
KUCHARCZYK, J.
LOW, W. C.
MAXWELL, R. E.
ROCKSWOLD, G. L.
WIRTSCHAFTER, J. D.

Nuclear Medicine (2-449 Fairview Univ.
Medical Center (MMC 292), 420 Delaware
St, SE, Minneapolis, MN 55455; tel. (612)
273-4092; internet www.med.umn.edu/
radiology):

ANDERSON, Q.
EFRANGE, S.
GOMES, M.

Nursing (6-101 Weaver-Densford Hall, 308
Harvard St, SE, Minneapolis, MN 55455; tel.
(612) 624-9600; internet www.nursing.umn
.edu):

BEARINGER, L.
DISCH, J.
EDWARDSON, S.
GROSS, C.
HODGE, F.
LEONARD, B.
WYMAN, J.

**Obstetrics, Gynaecology and Women's
Health** (12-211 Malcolm Moos Health Sciences Tower, 515 Delaware St, SE, Minneapolis, MN 55455; tel. (612) 626-3111; internet
www.med.umn.edu/obgyn):

CARSON, L.
DE JONGE, C.
GAZIANO, E. P.
KNOX, G. E.
LEUNG, B. S.
MARTENS, M. G.
OKAGAKI, T.
POTISH, R.
RAMAKRISHAN, S.
THOMPSON, T. R.
TROFATTER, K. F.
TWIGGS, L. B.

Operations and Management Science (3-150
Carlson School of Management, 321 19th
Ave, S, Minneapolis, MN 55455; tel. (612)
624-7010; internet carlsonschool.umn.edu/
csom/deptinfo.html):

ANDERSON, J. C.
CHERVANY, N.
HILL, A. V.
NACHTSHEIM, C.
SCHROEDER, R. G.

Ophthalmology (9th Fl., Phillips-Wangensteen Bldg, 516 Delaware St, SE, Minneapolis, MN 55455; tel. (612) 625-4400; internet
www.med.umn.edu/ophthalmology):

DOUGHMAN, D. J.
GREGERSON, D. S.
KRACHMER, J. H.
NELSON, J. D.
SUMMERS, C. G.
WIRTSCHAFTER, J. D.

Oral Sciences (17-252 Malcolm Moos Health
Sciences Tower, 515 Delaware St, SE, Minneapolis, MN 55455; tel. (612) 624-9123;
internet www1.umn.edu/dental/department/
oralsci/dep_oral.html):

ANDERSON, D. L.
COMBE, E.
DELONG, R.
DOUGLAS, W. H.
GERMAINE, G. R.
LILJEMARK, W. F.
ROHRER, M.
SCHACHTELE, C. F.
SHAPIRO, B. L.

Orthodontics (6-320 Malcolm Moos Health Sciences Tower, 515 Delaware St, SE, Minneapolis, MN 55455; tel. (612) 625-5110):

SPEIDEL, T. M.

Orthopaedic Surgery (350 Variety Club Research Center, 401 E River Rd, Minneapolis, MN 55455; tel. (612) 625-1177):

LEWIS, J. L.
OEGEMA, JR, T.
OGILVIE, J.
SWIONTKOWSKI, M.
THOMPSON, JR, R. C.

Otolaryngology (8-240 Phillips-Wangensteen Bldg (MMC 396), 516 Delaware St, SE, Minneapolis, MN 55455; tel. (612) 625-3200):

ADAMS, G.
GIEBINK, G. S.
JUHN, S. K.
MAISEL, R.
MARGOLIS, R.
NELSON, D.
SANTI, P.

Paediatric Dentistry (6-150 Malcolm Moos Health Sciences Tower, 515 Delaware St, SE, Minneapolis, MN 55455; tel. (612) 624-1985; internet www.umn.edu/dental/department/ prevsci/div_pediatric.html):

BEIRAGHI, S.
MOLLER, K.
TILL, M.

Paediatrics (13-118 Phillips-Wangensteen Bldg, 516 Delaware St, SE, Minneapolis, MN 55455; tel. (612) 624-3113):

BALFOUR, H.
BELANI, K.
BERRY, S.
BLAZAR, B.
BLUM, R.
BLUMENTHAL, M.
BROWN, D. M.
CHAVERS, B.
CLAWSON, C. C.
FERRIERI, P.
FISH, A.
GEORGIEFF, M.
GIEBINK, G. S.
HULL, H.
INGBAR, D.
JOHNSON, D.
KAPLAN, E.
KASHTAN, C.
KERSEY, J.
KIM, Y.
KING, R.
KOHEN, D.
KRIEL, R.
LOCKMAN, L.
MAMMEL, M.
MAUER, S. M.
MOLLER, J.
NELSON, C.
NEVINS, T.
OGILVIE, J.
RAMSAY, N.
REMAFEDI, G.
RESNICK, M.
ROBISON, L.
SHAPIRO, E.
SHARP, H.
SINAIKO, A.
STORY, M.
SUMMERS, G.
THOMPSON, T.
TRUWIT, C.
WAGNER, J.
WANGENSTEEN, O. D.
WARWICK, W.
WHITE, J.
WHITLEY, C.

Periodontology (7-368 Malcolm Moos Health Sciences Tower, 515 Delaware St, SE, Minneapolis, MN 55455; tel. (612) 625-5400;

internet www.umn.edu/dental/department/ prevsci/div_perio.html):

BAKDASH, B.
HERZBERG, M. C.
PHILSTROM, B. L.
WOLFF, L. F.

Pharmaceutical Care and Health Systems (7-159 Weaver-Densford Hall, 308 Harvard St, SE, Minneapolis, MN 55455; tel. (612) 626-9938; e-mail tesda001@tc.umn.edu; internet www.pharmacy.umn.edu):

CIPOLLE, R. J.
MORLEY, P. C.
SCHONDELMEYER, S. W.
STRAND, I. M.
WEAVER, L. C.

Pharmaceutics (9-177 Weaver-Densford Hall, 308 Harvard St, SE, Minneapolis, MN 55455; tel. (612) 624-5151; internet www .pharmacy.umn.edu/resgrad/pceutics/pharmaceuticshome.html):

BRAECKMAN, R.
FREY, II, W. H.
GRANT, D. J. W.
RESCIGNO, A.
SAWCHUK, R. J.
SIEGEL, R. A.
SURYANARAYANAN, R. G.

Pharmacology (6-120 Jackson Hall, 321 Church St, SE, Minneapolis, MN 55455; tel. (612) 625-9997; internet www.pharmacology .med.umn.edu):

BEATTIE, C. W.
CONTI-FINE, B.
EL-ZAKAHANY, E.
HANNA, P. E.
HOLTZMAN, J. L.
HUNNINGHAKE, D. B.
LAW, P.
LEE, H. C.
LOH, H. H.
PENTEL, P. R.
SINAIKO, A. R.
SLADEK, N. E.
SPARBER, S. B.
THAYER, A.
WILCOX, G. L.
WOOD, W. G.
YEE, D.
ZIMMERMAN, B. G.

Philosophy (831 Walter W. Heller Hall, 271 19th Ave, S, Minneapolis, MN 55455; tel. (612) 625-6563; internet philosophy.umn .edu):

BOWIE, N.
DAHL, N. O.
EATON, M. M.
GIERE, R.
GUNDERSON, K.
HANSON, W. H.
HELLMAN, G.
HOPKINS, J. S.
KAC, M.
LEWIS, D.
LONGINO, H.
OWENS, J.
PETERSON, S.
SAVAGE, C. W.
SCHEMAN, N.
WALLACE, J. R.

Philosophy of Science (746 Walter W. Heller Hall, 271 19th Ave, S, Minneapolis, MN 55455; tel. (612) 625-6635; internet www .mcps.umn.edu):

GIERE, R.
GUNDERSON, K.
HANSON, W.
HELLMAN, G.
LONGINO, H.
SAVAGE, C. W.
SHAPIRO, A.
STUEWER, R.

Physical Medicine and Rehabilitation (500 Boynton (MMC), Minneapolis, MN 55455; tel. (612) 626-4050; internet www.mcps.umn .edu):

DI FABIO., R.
PATTERSON, R.

Physics and Astronomy (148 Tate Lab of Physics, 116 Church St, SE, Minneapolis, MN 55455; tel. (612) 624-7375; internet www .physics.umn.edu):

BROADHURST, J. H.
CAMPBELL, C. E.
CATTELL, C.
CUSHMAN, P.
DAHLBERG, E. D.
ELLIS, P. J.
GOLDMAN, A. M.
GROSBERG, A.
HALLEY, J. W.
HELLER, K. J.
HUANG, C. C.
KAKALIOS, J.
KAPUSTA, J. I.
LARKIN, A.
LYSAK, R. L.
MARSHAK, M. L.
PEPIN, R. O.
PETERSON, E. A.
POLING, K.
RUDAZ, S.
RUDDICK, K.
RUSACK, R.
SHIFMAN, M.
SHKLOVSKII, B.
VAINSHTEIN, A.
VALLS, O. T.
VOLOSHIN, M.
WALSH, T. F.

Physiology (6-125 Jackson Hall, 321 Church St, SE, Minneapolis, MN 55455; tel. (612) 625-5902; internet physiology.med.umn .edu):

DI SALVO, J.
IAIZZO, P.
LEVITT, D.
LOW, W.
O'GRADY, S.
OSBORN, J.
WANGENSTEEN, O. D.
WEIR, K. E.

Plant Biology (220 Biological Sciences Center, 1445 Gortner Ave, St Paul, MN 55108; tel. (612) 625-1234; e-mail pbio@ux.acs.umn .edu; internet www.cbs.umn.edu/plantbio/ pbio):

BIESBOER, D. D.
BRAMBL, R.
CHARVAT, L.
GLEASON, F. K.
KOUKKARI, W. L.
McLAUGHLIN, D. J.
OLSZEWSKI, N. E.
SNUSTAD, P. D.
VANDENBOSCH, K.
WETMORE, C. M.
WICK, S.

Plant Pathology (495 Borlaug Hall, 1991 Upper Buford Circle, St Paul, MN 55108; tel. (612) 625-8200; internet www.plpa.agri .umn.edu):

BLANCHETTE, R. A.
GROTH, J. V.
JONES, R. K.
KINKEL, L. L.
KRUPA, S. V.
LARSEN, P. O.
LOCKHART, B. E.
MacDONALD, D. H.
NYVALL, R. F.
PERCICH, J. A.
PFLEGER, F. L.
WINDELS, C. E.
YOUNG, N. D.

ZEYEN, R. J.

Political Science (1414 Social Sciences Bldg, 267 19th Ave, S, Minneapolis, MN 55455; tel. (612) 624-4144; internet www.polisci.umn.edu):

DIETZ, M.
DUVALL, R.
FARR, J.
FLANIGAN, W. H.
FOGELMAN, E.
JACOBS, L.
KVAVIK, R.
NIMITZ, A.
ROSENSTONE, S.
SCOTT, T. M.
SHIVELY, W. P.

Psychiatry (F-282/2A W, 2450 Riverside Ave S, Minneapolis, MN 55455; tel. (612) 273-9800; e-mail madso009@umn.edu; internet www.med.umn.edu/psychiatry):

CARROLL, M.
ECKERT, E.
EL-FAKAHANY, E.
HARTMAN, B.
HATSUKAMI, D.
KROLL, J.
MACKENZIE, T.
SCHULTZ, C.

Psychiatry Research (628 Diehl Hall (MMC 392), 505 Essex St, SE, Minneapolis, MN 55455; tel. (612) 626-4034):

CARROLL, M. E.
EL-FAKAHANY, E.
HATSUKAMI, D.

Psychological Foundations of Education (206 Burton Hall, 178 Pillsbury Drive, SE, Minneapolis, MN 55455; tel. (612) 624-6083; internet www.coled.umn.edu/edpsych/default.html):

BART, W.
DAVISON, M.
HARWELL, H.
JOHNSON, D.
LAWRENZ, F.
MARUYAMA, G.
PELLEGRINI, A.
SAMUELS, S. J.
TENNYSON, R.
VAN DEN BROEK, P.

Psychology (N-218 Elliot Hall, 75 East River Rd, Minneapolis, MN 55455; tel. (612) 625-4042; internet www.psych.umn.edu):

BORGIDA, E.
BOUCHARD, T. J.
BURKHARDT, D. A.
BUTCHER, J. N.
CAMPBELL, J. P.
CUDECK, R.
DAVIS, E. R.
DUNETTE, M.
FOX, P.
GARMEZY, N.
HANSEN, J. I.
KERSTEN, D.
LEON, G. R.
LYKKEN, D.
McGUE, M.
MATOWIDLOS, S.
MOTOWIDLO, S.
OVERMIER, J. B.
PATRICK, C.
SACKETT, D.
SNYDER, M.
TELLEGEN, A.
VIEMEISTER, N. F.
WEISS, D. J.

Public Health Administration (D-359 Mayo Memorial Bldg (MMC 97), 420 Delaware St, SE, Minneapolis, MN 55455; tel. (612) 625-9480; internet www.hsr.umn.edu):

McBEAN, M.
VENINGA, R.

Public Health Nutrition (300 W Bank Office Bldg, 1300 52nd St, Minneapolis, MN 55455; tel. (612) 624-1818; internet www.epi.umn.edu):

BROWN, J. E.
HIMES, J. H.
JEFFERY, R. W.
LUEPKER, R. V.
PERRY, C.
STORY, M. T.

Radiology (2-300 Fairview Univ. Medical Center (MMC 292), 420 Delaware St, SE, Minneapolis, MN 55455; tel. (612) 273-6004; internet www.med.umn.edu/radiology):

EFANGE, S.
GARWOOD, M.
HU, X.
HUNTER, D.
JEROSCH-HERALD, M.
KIEFFER, S.
KIM, S.
KUCHARCZYK, J.
REINKE, D.
RITENOUR, E. R.
STEENSON, C.
STILLMAN, A.
TRUWIT, C.
UGURBIL, K.

Recreation and Sports Studies (220 Cooke Hall, 1900 University Ave, SE, Minneapolis, MN 55455; tel. (612) 625-5300; internet www.kls.umn.edu):

KANE, M. J.
McAVOY, L.

Regulatory Biochemistry (374 Gortner Lab, 1479 Gortner Ave, St Paul, MN 55108; tel. (612) 624-3622; internet www.cbs.umn.edu/bmbb):

BERNLOHR, D. A.
CONTI-FINE, B. M.
DEMPSEY, M. E.
KOERNER, J. F.
LOUIS, C. F.
NELSESTUEN, G. L.
OEGEMA, T. G.
RAFTERY, M. A.

Rhetoric (4 Classroom Office Bldg, 1994 Buford Ave, St Paul, MN 55108; tel. (612) 624-3445; internet www.rhetoric.umn.edu):

BECKER, S.
BERKEKOTTER
GROSS, A. G.
LAY, M. M.
McDOWELL, E. E.
MARCHAND, W. M.
MIKELONIS, V. M.
WAHLSTROM, B. J.
WHARTON, W. K.

Rural Sociology and Community Analysis (230 Peters Hall, 1404 Gortner Ave, St Paul, MN 55108; tel. (612) 625-4779; internet ssw.che.umn.edu/centers.htm#crsca):

McTAVISH, D.
MENANTEAU, D.
MEYERS, S. S.

St Anthony Falls Laboratory (2 Third Ave, SE, Minneapolis, MN 55414; tel. (612) 627-4010; internet www.umn.edu/safl):

ARNDT, R.
FARELL, C.
FOUFOULA-GEORGIOU, E.
GULLIVER, J.
PAOLA, C.
PARKER, G.
SONG, C.
STEFAN, H.
VOLLER, V.

School Psychology (344 Elliot Hall, 75 E River Rd, Minneapolis, MN 55455; tel. (612) 624-4156; internet education.umn.edu/edpsych):

CHRISTENSON, S.
McCONNELL, S.
YSSELDYKE, J.

Scientific Computation (Graduate Programme) (7-125 Weaver Densford Hall, 308 Harvard St, SE, Minneapolis, MN 55455; tel. (612) 626-2601):

ANDERSON, R.
BOLEY, D.
CANDLER, G.
CHELIKOWSKY, J.
COCKBURN, B.
CRAMER, C.
DERBY, J.
EBNER, T.
FONTOULA-GEORGIO, E. F.
FRIEDMAN, A.
KERSTEN, D.
KUMAR, V.
LOWENGRUB, J.
LUSKIN, M.
NIEBER, J.
OTHMER, H.
PARK, H.
PATANKAR, S.
SAAD, Y.
SCRIVEN, L. E.
SELL, G.
SONG, C.
SRIVASTAVA, J.
STECH, H.
THOMAS, D.
TIERNEY, L.
TRUHLAR, D.
TWETIK, A. H.
VOLLER, V.
WILCOX, G.
WOODWARD, P.
YUEN, D.

Slavic and Central Asian Languages and Literatures (214 Nolte Center for Continuing Education, 315 Pillsbury Dr., SE, Minneapolis, MN 55455; tel. (612) 624-3331; e-mail iles@umn.edu):

BASHIRI, I.
JAHN, G.

Small Animal Clinical Sciences (C-339 Veterinary Teaching Hospitals, 1352 Boyd Ave and 1365 Gortner Ave, St Paul, MN 55108; tel. (612) 625-7744):

ARMSTRONG, P. J.
BISTNER, S.
FEENEY, D.
HARDY, R.
JESSEN, C.
KLAUSNER, J.
LIPOWITZ, A.
OSBORNE, C.
POLZIN, D.
REDIG, P.
WALLACE, L.

Social Administrative and Clinical Pharmacy (7-155 Weaver-Densford Hall, 308 Harvard St, SE, Minneapolis, MN 55455; tel. (612) 624-2973; internet www.pharmacy.umn.edu):

CIPOLLE, R. J.
GARRARD, J. M.
GATEWOOD, L. C.
LANGLEY, P. C.
MORLEY, P. C.
SCHONDELMEYER, S. W.
SPEEDIE, S. M.
STRAND, L. M.
WEAVER, L. C.
WECKWERTH, V. E.
ZASKE, D. E.

Social Work (105 Peters Hall, 1404 Gortner Ave, St Paul, MN 55108; tel. (612) 625-1220; internet ssw.che.umn.edu):

BAIZERMAN, M.
BEKER, J.
EDLESON, J.

GILGUN, J.
HOLLISTER, D.
KIVNICK, H.
MENANTEAU, D.
MEYERS, S.
QUAM, J.
ROONEY, R.
UMBREIT, M.
WELLS, S.

Sociology (909 Social Sciences Bldg, 267 19th Ave, S, Minneapolis, MN 55455; tel. (612) 624-4300; internet www.soc.umn.edu):

AMINZADE, R.
ANDERSON, J.
ANDERSON, R. E.
GALASKIEWICZ, J.
KNOKE, D.
KRUTTSCHNITT, C.
LASLETT, B.
LEIK, R. K.
MALMQUIST, C.
MARINI, M.
MORTIMER, J.
NELSON, J. I.
STRYKER, R.

Soil, Water, and Climate (439 Borlaug Hall, 1991 Upper Buford Circle, St Paul, MN 55108; tel. (612) 625-1244; internet www.soils.agri.umn.edu):

ALLAN, D. L.
ANDERSON, J. L.
BAKER, J. M.
BLOOM, P. R.
CLAPP, C.
COOPER, T. H.
DOWDY, R. H.
GRAHAM, P. H.
GUPTA, S. C.
HALBACH, T. R.
KOSKINEN, W. C.
LAMB, J. A.
MALZER, G.
MOLINA, J. A.
MONCRIEF, J. F.
MULLA, D. J.
NATER, E. A.
RANDALL, G. W.
REHM, G. W.
REICOSKY, D. C.
ROBERT, P. C.
ROSEN, C. J.
RUSSELLE, M. P.
SADOWSKI, M. J.
SCHMITT, M. A.
SEELEY, M. W.

Spanish and Portuguese (34 Folwell Hall, 9 Pleasant St, SE, Minneapolis, MN 55455; tel. (612) 625-5858; internet spansport.cla.umn.edu):

JARA, R.
SPADACCINI, N.
VIDAL, H.

Special Education Programs (227 Burton Hall, 178 Pillsbury Drive, SE, Minneapolis, MN 55455; tel. (612) 624-2342; internet education.umn.edu/edpsych):

DENO, S.
HUPP, S.
McEVOY, M.

Statistics (313 Ford Hall, 224 Church St, SE, Minneapolis, MN 55455; tel. (612) 625-8046; internet www.stat.umn.edu):

BINGHAM, C.
CHALONER, K.
COOK, R. D.
DICKEY, J.
EATON, M. L.
GEISSER, S.
GEYER, C.
HAWKINS, D.
MEEDEN, G.
OEHLERT, G.
SUDDERTH, W. D.

TIERNEY, L.
WEISBERG, S.

Strategic Management and Organization (3-353 Carlson School of Management, 321 19th Ave, S, Minneapolis, MN 55455; tel. (612) 624-5232; internet www.csom.umn.edu/wwwpages/depts/smo):

BROMILEY, P.
ERICKSON, W. B.
LENWAY, S.
MAITLAND, I.
MARCUS, A.
NICHOLS, M.
SAPIENZA, H.
VAN DE VEN, A.

Structural Biology and Biophysics (140 Gortner Laboratory, 1479 Gortner Ave, St Paul, MN 55108; tel. (612) 625-6100; e-mail bmbb@biosci.cbs.umn.edu; internet www.cbs.umn.edu/bmbb):

ARMITAGE, I. M.
BANASZAK, L. J.
BARRY, B. A.
BLOOMFIELD, V. A.
HOGENKAMP, H. P.
HOWARD, J. B.
LIPSCOMB, J. D.
LOVRIEN, R. E.
MAYO, K. H.
OHLENDORF, D. H.
THOMAS, D. D.
TSONG, T. Y.

Surgery (11-100 Phillips-Wangensteen Bldg (MMC 195), 516 Delaware St, SE, Minneapolis, MN 55455; tel. (612) 625-1400; internet www.surg.umn.edu):

BOLMAN, III, R. M.
BUCHWALD, H.
CERRA, F.
CUNNINGHAM, B.
DALMASSO, A.
DRIES, D.
DUNN, D.
ENGELAND, W.
EYLER, J.
FOKER, J.
GOODALE, R. L.
GRUESSNER, R.
LAKE, J.
LEE, J. T.
LEVINE, A.
LYTE, M.
McQUARRIE, D. G.
MATAS, A.
MILLER, L.
MOLINA, E.
PARK, S.
PAYNE, W.
RODRIGUEZ, J.
ROTHENBERGER, D. A.
SAKO, Y.
SHUMWAY, S.
SUTHERLAND, D.
WARD, H.
WELLS, C.

Surgical Sciences (11-100 Phillips-Wangensteen (MMC 195), 516 Delaware St, SE, Minneapolis, MN 55455; tel. (612) 625-1400):

DALMASSO, A.
ENGELAND, W.
EYLER, J.
WELLS, C.

Theatre Arts and Dance (580 Rarig Center, 330 21st Ave, S, Minneapolis, MN 55455; tel. (612) 625-6699; e-mail theatre@umn.edu; internet cla.umn.edu/theater):

BROCKMAN, C. L.
KOBIALKA, M.
REID, B.

Therapeutic Radiology/Radiation Oncology (M-26 Masonic Cancer Center (MMC 494), 424 Harvard St, SE, Minneapolis, MN 55455;

tel. (612) 626-6146; internet www.ahc.umn.edu):

LEE, C. K.
LEVITT, S. H.
POTISH, R. A.
SONG, C. W.
VALLERA, D.

TMJ/Orofacial Pain (6-320 Malcolm Moos Health Sciences Tower, 515 Delaware St, SE, Minneapolis, MN 55455; tel. (612) 624-3130):

FRICTON, J.

Toxicology Graduate Program (244 Veterinary Diagnostic Lab, 1333 Gortner Ave, St Paul, MN 55108; tel. (612) 625-8787; internet www.mvdl.umn.edu):

ABUL-HAJJ, Y.
BROWN, D.
CARLSON, R.
DiSALVO, J.
DREWES, L.
HANNA, P.
MURPHY, M.
NAGASAWA, H.
NIEMI, G.
PROHASKA, J.
SCHOOK, L.
SPARBER, S.
WALLACE, K.

Urban Studies (348 Social Sciences Bldg, 267 19th Ave, S, Minneapolis, MN 55455; tel. (612) 626-1626; internet urbanstudies.cla.umn.edu):

ADAMS, J. S.
FISHER, T.
GALASKIEWICZ, J.
LEITNER, H.
RUNGE, C. F.
SCOTT, T.
SHEPPARD, E.

Urologic Surgery (A-597 Mayo Memorial Bldg (MMC 394), 420 Delaware St, SE, Minneapolis, MN 55455; tel. (612) 625-9933):

HULBERT, J.

Veterinary Diagnostic Medicine (277 Veterinary Diagnostic Lab, 1333 Gortner Ave, St Paul, MN 55108; tel. (612) 625-8787; internet www.mvdl.umn.edu):

COLLINS, J.
GOYAL, S.
HAYDEN, D.
KURTZ, H.
O'BRIEN, T.
WALSER, M.

Veterinary Pathobiology (205 Veterinary Science, 1971 Commonwealth Ave, St Paul, MN 55108; tel. (612) 625-5255; internet www.cvm.umn.edu):

BEITZ, A. J.
BEY, R. F.
BROWN, D. R.
FLETCHER, T. F.
GALLANT, E. M.
HALVORSON, D. A.
LARSON, A. A.
MAHESWARAN, S. K.
MURTAUGH, M. M.
NAGARAJA, K. V.
SHARMA, J. M.
STROMBERG, B. E.
WEISS, D. J.

Women's Studies (425 Ford Hall, 277 Church St, SE, Minneapolis, MN 55455; tel. (612) 624-6006; internet womenstudy.cla.umn.edu):

KAMINSKY, A.
LONGINO, H.
SCHEMAN, N.

Wood and Paper Science (203 Kaufert Lab of Forest Products and Wood Science, 2004 Folwell Ave, St Paul, MN 55108; tel. (612) 625-5200; internet www.cnr.umn.edu/wps):

BOWYER, J.
MASSEY, J.
SARKANEN, S.
SCHMIDT, E.

Work, Community and Family Education (Adm 210 Vocational and Technical Education Bldg, 1954 Buford Ave, St Paul, MN 55108; tel. (612) 625-3757; e-mail wcfe@umn.edu; internet education.umn.edu/wcfe):

BROWN, J.
LAMBRECHT, J.
LEWIS, T.
MCLEAN, G.
PETERSON, R.
PUCEL, D.
SWANSON, R.
THOMAS, R..

OTHER CAMPUSES

University of Minnesota, Crookston

2900 University Ave, Crookston, MN 56716

Telephone: (218) 281-8020

E-mail: umcinfo@umn.edu

Internet: www1.crk.umn.edu

Founded 1966, current name adopted 1988
State control
Academic year: August to May

Depts of agriculture and natural resources, business and mathematics, liberal arts and education, science and technology

Chancellor: CHARLES H. CASEY
Sr Vice-Chancellor for Academic and Student Affairs: THOMAS BALDWIN
Dir for Admissions and Enrolment Management: AMBER EVANS-DAILY
Registrar: ROBERT NELSON
Dir for Library Services: OWEN WILLIAMS

Number of teachers: 50 (full time)
Number of students: 2,650

PROFESSORS

ALI, ADEL, Computer Software Technology and Information Technology Management
BRORSON, S., Marketing and Management
DEL VECCHIO, R., Agriculture and Natural Resources
GELLER, J., Sociology
KNOWLTON, D., Art and Sciences
MARX, G., Agricultural, Food and Environmental Sciences
NEET, S., Art and Sciences
PETERSON, W. C., Art and Sciences
PETERSON, W., Mathematics
SELZLER, B., Art and Sciences
SVEDARSKY, W. D., Natural Resources
WINDELS, C., Agricultural, Food and Environmental Sciences

University of Minnesota, Duluth

1049 University Dr., Duluth, MN 55812

Telephone: (218) 726-8000

E-mail: sknill@d.umn.edu

Internet: www.d.umn.edu

Founded 1895 as Normal School at Duluth
Academic year: September to May

Chancellor: LENDLEY C. BLACK
Exec. Vice-Chancellor for Academic Affairs: BILIN TSAI
Vice-Chancellor for Advancement: WILLIAM WADE
Vice-Chancellor for Finance and Operations: JOHN KING
Vice-Chancellor for Student Life: LISA ERWIN
Dir for Admissions: BETH ESSELSTROM
Library Dir: BILL SOZANSKY

Library of 261,609 vols, 268,225 ebooks, 27,941 media items, 81,587 ejournals, 109,956 print govt documents, 26,194 electronic govt documents
Number of teachers: 590 (455 full-time, 135 part-time)

Number of students: 11,806

DEANS

College of Education and Human Service Professions: PAUL N. DEPUTY
College of Liberal Arts: SUSAN MAHER
College of Science Engineering: JAMES P. RIEHL
Labovitz School of Business and Economics: KJELL R. KNUDSEN (acting)
Medical School Duluth: GARY DAVIS
School of Fine Arts: WILLIAM E. PAYNE
Swenson College of Science and Engineering: PENNY MORTON

PROFESSORS

ADAMS, S. J., English
ANDERSON, A. C., Music
ANDERSON, C., Economics
ANDREWS, I. T., Biology
BACIG, T., Sociology—Anthropology
BARTLETT, E., Women's Studies
BELOTE, L., Sociology—Anthropology
BRUSH, G., Art
BRUSH, L., Art
BURNS, S. G., Electrical and Computer Engineering
CAPLE, R., Chemistry
CARLSON, H., Education
CARLSON, R. M., Chemistry
CASTLEBERRY, S., Management Studies
CROUCH, D., Computer Science
DAS, A., Psychology
DEPUTY, P. N., Communication Sciences and Disorders
DREWES, L., Biochemistry and Molecular Biology
DUFF, T., Finance and Management Information Sciences
DURGUNOGLA, A. Y., Psychology
EISENBERG, R. M., Pharmacology
ELLIOT, B. A., Behavioural Sciences
ELLIOT, B. A., Family Medicine
EVANS, J., Chemistry
FALK, D., Social Work
FEROZ, E., Accounting
FETZER, J., Philosophy
FIRLING, C., Biology
FLEISCHMAN, W., Sociology—Anthropology
FUGELSO, M., Industrial Engineering
FULKROD, J., Chemistry
GALLIAN, J. A., Mathematics and Statistics
GORDON, R., Psychology
GRANT, J. A., Geological Sciences
GREEN, R., Mathematics and Statistics
HAFFERTY, F., Behavioural Sciences
HARRISS, D. K., Chemistry
HEDIN, T., Art
HEDMAN, S., Biology
HELLER, L. J., Medical and Molecular Physiology
HILLER, J., Physics
HOLST, T., Geological Sciences
JAMES, B., Mathematics and Statistics
JAMES, K. L., Mathematics and Statistics
JANKOFSKY, K. P., English
JESSWEIN, W. A., Economics
JOHNSON, T., Industrial Engineering
JOHNSON, T. C., Geological Sciences
JORDAN, T. F., Physics
KARIM, M. R., Biology
KENDALL, L. A., Industrial Engineering, MSc in Engineering Management
KLEMER, A., Biology
KLUEG, J., Art
KNOPP, JR, L. M., Geography
KRAMER, J., Social Work
KRITZMIRE, J., Music
LAUNDERGAN, J. C., Sociology—Anthropology
LETTENSTROM, D., Art
LEY, E., Health, Physical Education and Recreation
LICHTY, R. W., Economics
LIEVANO, R., Finance and Management Information Sciences
LINDEKE, R., Industrial Engineering

LINN, M. D., Composition
LIU, Z., Mathematics and Statistics
MCCARTHY, D. A., Education
MCCLURE, B., Psychology
MAGNUSON, V. R., Chemistry
MAIOLO, J. C., English
MARCHESE, R., Sociology—Anthropology
MARTIN, K. A., Theatre
MAYO, D., Philosophy
MERRIER, P., Finance and Management Information Sciences
MILLER, K., Psychology
MILLER-CLEARY, L., English
MIZUKO, M. I., Communications Sciences and Disorders
MORTON, R., Geological Sciences
NEWSTROM, J. W., Management Studies
OJAKANGAS, R. W., Geological Sciences
PASTOR, J., Biology
PETERSON, J. M., Economics
PIERCE, J. L., Management Studies
POE, D., Chemistry
PROHASKA, J., Biochemistry and Molecular Biology
RAAB, R. L., Economics
RED HORSE, J. G., American Indian Studies
REGAL, J., Pharmacology
REGAL, R., Mathematics and Statistics
RICHARDS, C., Biology
RIEHL, J. P., Chemistry
RILEY, K., Composition
ROUFS, T. G., Sociology—Anthropology
RUBENFELD, S., Management Studies
SEVERSON, A. R., Anatomy and Cell Biology
SEYBOLT, R., Foreign Languages and Literatures
SHARP, P., Political Science
SHEHADEH, N., Electrical and Computer Engineering
SHEPHARD, M., Social Work
SMITH, D., Sociology—Anthropology
STACHOWITZ, M., Electrical and Computer Engineering
STECH, H., Mathematics and Statistics
STEINNES, D. N., Economics
STORCH, N. T., History
STUECHER, U., Psychology
SUNNAFRANK, M., Communication
SYDOR, M., Physics
THOMPSON, L. C., Chemistry
TRACHTE, G., Pharmacology
TROLANDER, J., Women's Studies
TROLANDER, J. A., History
TSAI, B., Chemistry
WALLACE, K., Biochemistry and Molecular Biology
WARD, P., Pathology and Laboratory Medicine
WEGREN, T., Music
WOLD, S., Music
WONG, S., Finance and Management Information Sciences
ZEITZ, E., Foreign Languages and Literatures
ZHDANKIN, V., Chemistry
ZIEGLER, R., Medical Microbiology and Immunology

University of Minnesota, Morris

600 E Fourth St, Morris, MN 56267

Telephone: (320) 589-6035

E-mail: petersdk@mrs.umn.edu

Internet: www.morris.umn.edu

Founded 1960
Academic year: August to May

Divs of education, humanities, science and mathematics, social sciences

Chancellor: JACQUELINE JOHNSON
Vice-Chancellor for Academic Affairs and Dean: Dr BART D. FINZEL
Vice-Chancellor for Student Affairs: SANDRA OLSON-LOY
Library Dir: LEANN DEAN

Number of teachers: 120
Number of students: 1,700

PROFESSORS

AHERN, W. H., History
CABRERA, V., Modern Languages
CARLSON, J. A., Music
COTTER, J., Geology
DEMOS, V. P., Sociology
FRENIER, M. D., History
GARARASO, P., Philosophy
GOOCH, V., Biology
GUYOTTE, R., History
HINDS, JR, H. E., History
HOPPE, D. M., Biology
INGLE, J. S., Art Studio
KISSOCK, C. M., Education
KLINGER, E., Psychology
LEE, J., Political Science
LEE, M.-L., Modern Languages
LOPEZ, A. A., Computer Science
NELLIS, J. G., Art Studio
O'REILLY, M. F., Mathematics
PAYNE, T. R., Theatre Arts
PETERSON, F. W., Art History
PURDY, D. H., English
SCHUMAN, S., English
SUNGUR, E., Mathematics
TOGEAS, J. B., Chemistry
VAN ALSTINE, J. B., Geology

University of Minnesota, Rochester

111 S Broadway, Suite 300, Rochester, MN 55904

Telephone: (507) 258-8000
E-mail: umrinfo@umn.edu
Internet: www.r.umn.edu

Founded 1959, current status 2000
Academic year: August to May

Chancellor: Dr STEPHEN LEHMKUHLE
Vice-Chancellor for Academic Affairs (vacant)
Dir of Communications and Public Relation: SARAH OSLUND
Dir of Enrolment Management: KAREN REILLY
Librarian: MARY BETH SANCOMB-MORAN
Number of teachers: 50
Number of students: 750

UNIVERSITY OF ST THOMAS

2115 Summit Ave, St Paul, MN 55105
Telephone: (651) 962-5000
E-mail: admissions@stthomas.edu
Internet: www.stthomas.edu

Founded 1885
Private control
Academic year: September to May

Pres.: Rev. DENNIS DEASE
Exec. Vice-Pres and Chief Academic Officer: Dr SUSAN HUBER
Exec. Vice-Pres and Chief Admin. Officer: Dr MARK DIENHART
Vice-Pres. for Information Resources and Technologies: Dr SAMUEL J. LEVY
Vice-Pres. for Mission: JOHN MALONE
Vice-Pres. for Student Affairs: JANE CANNEY
Vice-Pres. for Univ. and Govt Relations: DOUG HENNES
Registrar: PAUL J. SIMMONS
Librarian: DANIEL GJELTEN
Library of 730,000 vols, 95,000 ebooks, 40,000 journals
Number of teachers: 847 (439 full-time, 408 part-time)
Number of students: 10,534 (6,176 under-graduate, 4,358 graduate)
Publications: B. Magazine (2 a year), Logos: A Journal of Catholic Thought and Culture (4 a year), New Hibernia Review (4 a year), Perspectives Magazine (2 a year), St. Thomas Lawyer (2 a year), St. Thomas Magazine (3 a year), Summit Avenue Review

DEANS

College of Applied Professional Studies: Dr BRUCE KRAMER
College of Arts and Sciences: Dr MARISA KELLY
Opus College of Business: Dr CHRISTOPHER PUTO
School of Divinity: Dr CHRISTOPHER THOMPSON
School of Engineering: Dr DONALD WEINKAUF
School of Law: THOMAS MENGLER
School of Social Work: Dr BARBARA SHANK

WALDEN UNIVERSITY

155 Fifth Ave S, Suite 100, Minneapolis, MN 55401

Telephone: (866) 492-5336
E-mail: help@waldenu.edu
Internet: www.waldenu.edu

Founded 1970
Private control
Divs of counselling and social service, education and leadership, health sciences, management, nursing, psychology, public policy and administration

Pres.: JONATHAN A. KAPLAN
Provost: Dr DENISE DEZOLT
Exec. Vice-Pres.: Dr CYNTHIA G. BAUM
Vice-Pres. for Education Policy and Regulation: Dr BONNIE COPELAND
Vice-Pres. for Operations: BRETT LUNDEEN
Chief Academic Officer: Dr ERIC RIEDEL
Dir for Admissions: DEVON LOETZ
Registrar: EVE DAUER
Dir for Library Services: (vacant)
Library of 50,000 vols of journals, 100,000 ebooks and 1.5m. dissertations
Number of teachers: 2,500
Number of students: 46,500

Publications: International Journal of Applied Management and Technology, Journal of Social, Behavioral and Health Sciences, Journal of Social Change, Walden Alumni Magazine

WILLIAM MITCHELL COLLEGE OF LAW

875 Summit Ave, St Paul, MN 55105-3076
Telephone: (651) 227-9171
E-mail: admissions@wmitchell.edu
Internet: www.wmitchell.edu

Founded 1900
Private control
Academic year: August to May

Pres. and Dean: ERIC S. JANUS
Vice-Pres. for Information Technology Services: JAMES VILLARS
Vice-Pres. for Institutional Advancement: LINDA KEILLOR BERG
Vice-Pres. for Student Affairs and Dean for Students: DANIEL THOMPSON
Dir for Admissions: KENDRA DANE
Registrar: JIM STEVENS
Assoc. Dean for Information Resources: SIMON CANICK
Number of teachers: 90 (40 full-time, 50 adjunct)
Number of students: 1,025

Publications: Mitchell on Law, William Mitchell Law Raza Journal (online, web.w-mitchell.edu/lawraza), William Mitchell Law Review (4 a year)

PROFESSORS

BYRNE, A.
COLBERT, B.
DUBE, D.
EASLEY, A.
ERLINDER, P.
HAUGEN, P.
HAYDOCK, R.

HAYNSWORTH, H.
HEIDENREICH, D.
HOGG, J.
IIJIMA, A.
JANUS, E.
JORDAN, M.
JUERGENS, A.
KIRWIN, K.
KLASS, A.
KLEINBERGER, D.
KNAPP, P.
KRISHNAN, J.
KUNZ, C.
LEVINE, R.
LOGAN, W.
MOY, C.
MURPHY, R.
OH, P.
OLIPHANT, R.
PANNIER, R.
PORT, K.
PRINCE, D.
RADSAN, J.
ROBERTS, E.
ROY, D.
SCALLEN, E.
SCHAUMANN, N.
SCHMEDMAN, D.
SONSTENG, J.
STEENSON, M.
VER PLOEG, C.
VER STEEGH, N.
WINER, A.

MISSISSIPPI

ALCORN STATE UNIVERSITY

1000 ASU Dr., Alcorn State, MS 39096-7500

Telephone: (601) 877-6100
E-mail: president@alcorn.edu
Internet: www.alcorn.edu

Founded 1871 as Alcorn Univ., present name and status 1974
State control
Academic year: August to May

Pres.: Dr M. CHRISTOPHER BROWN, II
Provost and Exec. Vice-Pres. for Academic Affairs: Dr SAMUEL L. WHITE
Sr Vice-Pres. for Finance and Administrative Services and Chief Financial Officer: Dr BETTY ROBERTS
Vice-Pres. for Business Affairs: CAROLYN HINTON
Vice-Pres. for Institutional Affairs: MARCUS D. WARD
Vice-Pres. for Student Affairs: E. CHERYL PONDER
Registrar: JIMMY SMITH
Dean for Libraries: Dr BLANCHE SANDERS
Library of 366,116 vols
Number of teachers: 215
Number of students: 4,020

Publications: Alcorn (1 a year), Alcornite (1 a year), ASU Today (2 a year, online)

DEANS

Newtie J. Boyd Academic Support Center: Dr EDWARD VAUGHN
School of Agriculture, Research, Extension and Applied Sciences: Dr BARRY L. BEQUETTE
School of Arts and Sciences: Dr NORRIS EDNEY (acting)
School of Business: Dr VIVEK BHARGAVA
School of Education and Psychology: Dr ROBERT CARR
School of Graduate Studies: Dr DONZEL LEE
School of Nursing: Dr LINDA GODLEY

BELHAVEN UNIVERSITY

1500 Peachtree St, Jackson, MS 39202
Telephone: (601) 968-5940

E-mail: admission@belhaven.edu
Internet: www.belhaven.edu

Founded 1883 as Belhaven College, present name 2010
Private control
Academic year: August to May
Campuses in Atlanta (Georgia), Chattanooga and Memphis (Tennessee), Houston (Texas), Orlando (Florida)
Pres.: Dr ROGER PARROTT
Sr Vice-Pres. and Provost: Dr DANIEL CARL FREDERICKS
Vice-Pres. for Campus Operations: TOM PHILLIPS
Vice-Pres. for Student Affairs and Athletics: SCOTT LITTLE
Vice-Pres. for Univ. Advancement: KEVIN RUSSELL
Chief Financial Officer: VIRGINIA HENDERSON
Dean for Faculty: Dr CURT BECK
Dean for Student Life: GREG HAWKINS
Dir for Admissions: SUZANNE SULLIVAN
Registrar: DONNA WEEKS
Dir for Library: SUSAN SPRINGER
Library of 125,000 vols, 34,000 ebooks
Number of teachers: 195 (51 full-time, 144 adjunct)
Number of students: 3,245 (1,091 undergraduate, 550 graduate)

DEANS

Honors College: Dr MELISSA HAUSE
School of Arts and Sciences: Dr GLENN SUMRALL
School of Business: Dr RALPH A. MASON, III
School of Education: Dr SANDRA L. RASBERRY

BLUE MOUNTAIN COLLEGE

POB 160, Blue Mountain, MS 38610
201 W Main, Blue Mountain, MS 38610
Telephone: (662) 685-4771
Internet: www.bmc.edu

Founded 1873
Private control
Academic year: August to May (2 semesters)
Depts of biblical and associated studies, business, education, fine arts and speech, kinesiology and health studies, language and literature, mathematics and natural science, social and behavioural sciences
Pres.: Dr BETTYE ROGERS COWARD
Vice-Pres. for Academic Affairs: SHARON ENZOR
Vice-Pres. for Planning, Assessment, Graduate Studies and Spec. Programmes: JANICE NICHOLSON
Academic Dean: GARTH E. RUNION
Dean for Enrolment Services and Student Life: JACK MOSER
Dir for Admissions: MARIA TEEL
Registrar: SHEILA FREEMAN
Dir for Library Services: DEREK CASH
Library of 60,500 vols, 36,094 ebooks
Number of teachers: 30
Number of students: 550

DELTA STATE UNIVERSITY

1003 W Sunflower Rd, Cleveland, MS 38733
Telephone: (662) 846-3000
E-mail: admissions@deltastate.edu
Internet: www.deltastate.edu

Founded 1924 as Delta State Teachers College, present name and status 1974
State control
Academic year: August to July (2 semesters)
Pres.: Dr JOHN M. HILPERT
Provost and Vice-Pres. for Academic Affairs: Dr ANN C. LOTVEN
Vice-Pres. for Finance and Admin.: GREG REDLIN

Vice-Pres. for Student Affairs: Dr WAYNE BLANSETT
Vice-Pres. for Univ. Relations: Dr MICHELLE ROBERTS
Dean for Enrolment Management and Dir for Admissions: Dr DEBBIE HESLEP
Dean for Graduate Studies: Dr ALBERT NYLANDER
Registrar: JOHN ELLIOTT
Dir for Library Services: JEFF SLAGELL
Library of 360,000 vols
Number of teachers: 270
Number of students: 4,000

DEANS

College of Arts and Sciences: Dr PAUL HANKINS
College of Business: Dr BILLY MOORE
College of Education: Dr LESLIE GRIFFIN
Graduate and Continuing Studies: Dr ALBERT B. NYLANDER
Robert E. Smith School of Nursing: Dr LIZABETH CARLSON

JACKSON STATE UNIVERSITY

1400 John R. Lynch St, Administration Tower, Jackson, MS 39217-0280
Telephone: (601) 979-2121
E-mail: admappl@jsums.edu
Internet: www.jsums.edu

Founded 1877 as Natchez Seminary, present name and status 1974
State control
Academic year: August to August (2 semesters)
Pres.: Dr CAROLYN MEYERS
Provost and Vice-Pres. for Academic Affairs: Prof. Dr MARK G. HARDY
Vice-Pres. for Business and Finance: MICHAEL THOMAS
Vice-Pres. for Information and Process Management: Dr WILLIE G. BROWN
Vice-Pres. for Research and Fed. Relations: Dr FELIX A. OKOJIE
Vice-Pres. for Student Life: Dr MARCUS A. CHANAY
Registrar: ALFRED JACKSON
Dean for Library and Information Resources: Dr MELISSA DRUCKERY
Library of 376,566 vols
Number of teachers: 505 (385 full-time, 120 part-time)
Number of students: 8,903
Publication: *Blue and White Flash* (4 a year)

DEANS

College of Business: Dr GLENDA GLOVER
College of Education and Human Development: Dr DANIEL WATKINS
College of Liberal Arts: Dr DOLLYE M. E. ROBINSON
College of Public Service: Dr MARIO AZEVEDO
College of Science, Engineering and Technology: Dr PAUL B. TCHOUNWOU
Division of Graduate Studies: Dr DORRIS R. ROBINSON GARDNER
Division of International Studies: ALLY MACK

MILLSAPS COLLEGE

1701 N State St, Jackson, MS 39210-0001
Telephone: (601) 974-1000
E-mail: admissions@millsaps.edu
Internet: www.millsaps.edu

Founded 1890
Private control
Academic year: August to May (2 semesters)
Pres.: Dr ROBERT PEARIGEN
Sr Vice-Pres. for Academic Affairs and Dean of College: Dr S. KEITH DUNN
Vice-Pres. for Finance: LOUISE BURNEY
Vice-Pres. for Institutional Advancement: CHARLES R. LEWIS

Vice-Pres. for Institutional Planning and Assessment: TERRI HUDSON
Vice-Pres. and Dean for Students: Dr BRIT KATZ
Dean for Admissions: MICHAEL THORP
Dean for Faculty: DAVID DAVIS
Librarian: THOMAS HENDERSON
Library of 209,900 vols, 631 print journals, 7,000 ejournals
Number of teachers: 100 (full-time)
Number of students: 1,120 (1,015 undergraduate, 105 graduate)
Publications: *Promenade* (1 a year), *Stylus* (2 a year)

DEANS

Else School of Management: Dr KIMBERLY BURKE

MISSISSIPPI COLLEGE

200 S Capitol St, Clinton, MS 39056
Telephone: (601) 925-3000
E-mail: admissions@mc.edu
Internet: www.mc.edu

Founded 1826 as Hampstead Acad., present name 1830
Private control
Academic year: August to May (2 semesters)
Pres.: Dr LEE G. ROYCE
Vice-Pres. for Academic Affairs: Dr RON HOWARD
Vice-Pres. for Admin. and Govt Relations: Dr STEVE STANFORD
Vice-Pres. for Advancement: Dr BILL TOWNSEND
Vice-Pres. for Enrolment Management and Student Affairs: Dr JIM TURCOTTE
Vice-Pres. for Planning and Assessment and Dean for Graduate Studies: Dr DEBBIE NORRIS
Chief Financial Officer: DONNA LEWIS
Chief Information Officer: BILL CRANFORD
Library Dir: KATHLEEN HUTCHISON
Library of 253,818 vols
Number of teachers: 195 (full-time)
Number of students: 5,270 (3,238 undergraduate, 1,457 graduate, 575 law)

DEANS

School of Business: Prof. Dr MARCELO EDUARDO
School of Christian Studies and the Arts: Prof. WAYNE VANHORN
School of Education: Prof. Dr DON W. LOCKE
School of Humanities and Social Sciences: Prof. Dr GARY K. MAYFIELD
School of Law: Prof. Dr JAMES H. ROSENBLATT
School of Nursing: Prof. Dr MARY JEAN PADGETT
School of Science and Mathematics: Prof. Dr STAN BALDWIN

MISSISSIPPI STATE UNIVERSITY

POB 5325, Mississippi State, MS 39762
Telephone: (662) 325-2323
E-mail: msuinfo@ur.msstate.edu
Internet: www.msstate.edu

Founded 1878 as Agricultural and Mechanical College of State of Mississippi, present name 1958
State control
Academic year: August to May
Pres.: Dr MARK E. KEENUM
Provost and Exec. Vice-Pres. for Academic Affairs: JEROME A. GILBERT
Vice-Pres. for Agriculture, Forestry and Veterinary Medicine: GREGORY BOHACH
Vice-Pres. for Budget and Planning: DON ZANT
Vice-Pres. for Devt and Alumni: JOHN RUSH
Vice-Pres. for Research and Economic Devt: DAVID R. SHAW (acting)

Vice-Pres. for Student Affairs: WILLIAM KIBLER
Chief of Staff and Chief Financial Officer: MICHAEL J. MCGREVEY
Gen. Counsel: JOAN LUCAS
Registrar: BUTCH STOKES
Dean for Graduate School: Dr LOUIS R. D'ABRAMO
Dean for Libraries: FRANCES COLEMAN
Library of 2,124,341 vols, 70,331 journals
Number of teachers: 1,350
Number of students: 20,425

DEANS

College of Agriculture and Life Sciences: Dr GEORGE HOPPER
College of Architecture, Art and Design: JAMES L. WEST
College of Arts and Sciences: Dr GARY L. MYERS
College of Business: SHARON OSWALD
College of Education: Dr RICHARD BLACK-BOURN
College of Forest Resources: GEORGE M. HOPPER
College of Veterinary Medicine: KENT H. HOBLET
James Worth Bagley College of Engineering: SARAH A. RAJALA
Judy and Bobby Shackouls Honors College: CHRISTOPHER A. SNYDER

MISSISSIPPI UNIVERSITY FOR WOMEN

1100 College St, Columbus, MS 39701
Telephone: (662) 329-4750
E-mail: admissions@muw.edu
Internet: www.muw.edu
Founded 1884
State control
Academic year: August to May
Pres.: Dr JIM BORSIG
Provost and Vice-Pres. for Academic Affairs: Dr EVERETT E. CASTON
Vice-Pres. for Finance and Admin.: NORA R. MILLER
Vice-Pres. for Institutional Advancement: KEN KENNEDY
Vice-Pres. for Student Services: JENNIFER MILES
Dean of Library Services: GAIL GUNTER
Library of 426,900 vols
Number of teachers: 130
Number of students: 3,315

DEANS

College of Arts and Sciences: Dr THOMAS C. RICHARDSON
College of Business and Legal Studies: ANNE BALAZS
College of Education and Human Sciences: Dr SUE JOLLY-SMITH
College of Nursing and Speech Language Pathology: Dr SHEILA V. ADAMS
School of Professional Studies: Dr WILLIAM S. STEWART

MISSISSIPPI VALLEY STATE UNIVERSITY

14000 Highway 82, W, Itta Bena, MS 38941-1400
Telephone: (662) 254-9041
E-mail: admsn@mvsu.edu
Internet: www.mvsu.edu
Founded 1946 as Mississippi Vocational College, present name and status 1974
State control
Academic year: August to July (2 semesters)
Pres.: Dr DONNA H. OLIVER
Provost and Exec. Vice-Pres. for Academic Affairs: Dr ANNA M. HAMMOND

Vice-Pres. for Business and Finance: JAMES WASHBURN
Vice-Pres. for Student Affairs, Enrolment Management and Diversity: Dr JERALD ADLEY
Vice-Pres. for Univ. Advancement: ANGELA Y. GETTER
Registrar: MAXCINE B. RUSH
Library Dir: Dr MANTRA HENDERSON
Library of 213,860 vols, 402 periodicals, 2,200 eperiodicals, 42,000 ebooks, 4,026 video titles
Number of teachers: 110
Number of students: 2,450

DEANS

College of Arts and Sciences: Dr TAZINSKI LEE
College of Education: PATRICIA BROOKS
College of Professional Studies: Dr CURRESSIA M. BROWN
Graduate School: RICKEY HILL

REFORMED THEOLOGICAL SEMINARY

5422 Clinton Blvd, Jackson, MS 39209-3099
Telephone: (601) 923-1600
E-mail: rts.jackson@rts.edu
Internet: www.rts.edu
Founded 1966
Private control
Academic year: June to May (2 semesters)
Campuses in Atlanta (Georgia), Charlotte (North Carolina), Jackson (Mississippi), Houston (Texas), Memphis (Tennessee), Oviedo (Florida), McLean (Virginia),
Chancellor and CEO: Dr ROBERT C. CANNADA, JR
Pres. (Atlanta Campus): JOHN SOWELL
Pres. (Jackson Campus): Dr GUY RICHARDSON
Pres. (Orlando Campus): DONALD W. SWEETING
Exec. Vice-Pres.: ROBERT T. BRIDGES
Chief Academic Officer: ROBERT J. CARA
Chief Devt and Communications Officer: LYNWOOD C. PEREZ
Chief Financial Officer: BRADLEY TISDALE
Dir for Admissions and Dean for Students: BRIAN GAULT
Chief Registrar: KIAMA J. LEE
Dir for Libraries: BYRON L. CONLEY
Library of 150,000 vols
Number of teachers: 105
Number of students: 600
Publication: *Ministry & Leadership* (4 a year)

RUST COLLEGE

150 Rust Ave, Holly Springs, MS 38635
Telephone: (662) 252-8000
E-mail: admissions@rustcollege.edu
Internet: www.rustcollege.edu
Founded 1866 as Asbury Methodist Episcopal Church, present name and status 1915
Private control
Academic year: August to April
Divs of business, education, humanities, science and mathematics, social science
Pres.: Dr DAVID L. BECKLEY
Vice-Pres. for Academic Affairs: Dr PAUL C. LAMPLEY
Vice-Pres. for Devt: Dr ISHMELL H. EDWARDS
Vice-Pres. for Finance and Business: DON MANNING-MILLER
Dean for Student Affairs: CAROLYN HYMON
Registrar: CLARENCE E. SMITH
Head Librarian: ANITA W. MOORE
Library of 120,000 vols, 300 periodicals
Number of teachers: 60
Number of students: 1,030

SOUTHEASTERN BAPTIST COLLEGE

4229 Highway 15, N, Laurel, MS 39440
Telephone: (601) 426-6346
E-mail: info@southeasternbaptist.edu
Internet: www.southeasternbaptist.edu
Founded 1948
Private control
Academic year: August to July
Areas of study: business administration and management, Bible studies, general studies
Pres.: Dr MEDRISK SAVELL
Exec. Vice-Pres.: JOSEPH HARRIS
Academic Dean: Dr AARON PARKER
Dean for Students: GREG HILLMAN
Dir for Admissions: RONNIE KITCHENS
Dir for Information Technology: HUBERT DYESS
Librarian: AMY HINTON
Library of 30,000 vols
Number of students: 65

TOUGALOO COLLEGE

500 West County Line Rd, Tougaloo, MS 39174
Telephone: (601) 977-7700
Internet: www.tougaloo.edu
Founded 1869 as teacher training school, present name 1916
Private control
Academic year: August to May (2 semesters)
Pres.: Dr BEVERLEY WADE HOGAN
Provost and Exec. Vice-Pres. for Academic Affairs: Dr BETTYE PARKER-SMITH
Vice-Pres. for Facilities Management: KELLE MENOGAN, SR
Vice-Pres. for Finance and Admin. and Chief Financial Officer: Dr CYNTHIA MELVIN
Vice-Pres. for Information Technology: TERRY JORDAN
Vice-Pres. for Institutional Advancement: SANDRA A.M. BOWIE (acting)
Vice-Pres. for Student Affairs: FRED ALEXANDER
Dir for Admissions: JUNO JACOBS
Registrar: CAROLYN EVANS
Library of 139,600 vols
Number of teachers: 75
Number of students: 920
Publications: *The Harambee* (12 a year), *Tougaloo News* (3 a year)

DEANS

Division of Education, Supervision and Instruction: Dr PAMELA RUSS
Division of Humanities: Dr ANDREA MONTGOMERY
Division of Natural Science: Dr RICHARD MCGINNIS
Division of Social Sciences: Dr KAMAL ABDEL-RAHMAN

UNIVERSITY OF MISSISSIPPI

POB 1848, University, MS 38677-1848
University Ave, University, MS 38677
Telephone: (662) 915-7211
E-mail: admissions@olemiss.edu
Internet: www.olemiss.edu
Founded 1844
State control
Schools of medicine, dentistry, nursing, health related professions are constituents of the Univ. of Mississippi Medical Center, located in Jackson, Mississippi
Chancellor: Dr DANIEL W. JONES
Pres. and Chief Exec. Officer of the Univ. Foundation: WENDELL WEAKLEY
Provost and Vice-Chancellor for Academic Affairs: MORRIS H. STOCKS
Vice-Chancellor for Finance and Admin.: LARRY D. SPARKS

Vice-Chancellor for Research and Sponsored Programmes: ALICE M. CLARK
Vice-Chancellor for Student Affairs: LARRY RIDGEWAY (acting)
Registrar and Dir for Admissions: CHARLOTTE FANT (acting)
Dean for Libraries: JULIA ROLES
Library: 1.9m. vols, 218,625 current periodicals, 184,757 ejournals, 366,145 ebooks
Number of teachers: 780 (full-time)
Number of students: 20,845
Publications: *Law School, Medical Center*

DEANS

College of Liberal Arts: Dr GLENN W. HOPKINS
DeSoto Center: Dr FANNYE LOVE
Graduate School: Dr CHRISTY M. WYANDT
Meek School of Journalism and New Media: Prof. Dr WILL NORTON, JR
Patterson School of Accountancy: Prof. Dr MARK WILDER
Sally McDonnell Barksdale Honors College: Dr DOUGLASS SULLIVAN-GONZÁLEZ
School of Applied Sciences: Prof. Dr CAROL MINOR BOYD
School of Business Administration: Dr KEN B. CYREE
School of Education: Dr DAVID ROCK
School of Engineering: Dr ALEXANDER CHENG
School of Law: Dr RICHARD GERSHON
School of Nursing: Prof. Dr KIM HOOVER
School of Pharmacy: Prof. Dr DAVID D. ALLEN
Tupelo Center: Dr JAMES PATE

UNIVERSITY OF MISSISSIPPI MEDICAL CENTER

2500 N State St, Jackson, MS 39216
Telephone: (601) 984-1080
Internet: www.umc.edu
Founded 1955; attached to Univ. of Mississippi
State control
Academic year: August to May (2 semesters)
Chancellor: Dr DANIEL W. JONES
Vice-Chancellor for Health Affairs: Dr JAMES KEETON
Assoc. Vice-Chancellor for Academic Affairs: Dr HELEN R. TURNER
Assoc. Vice-Chancellor for Research: Dr JOHN E. HALL
Chief Admin. Officer: DAVID POWE
Chief Financial Officer: JAMES L. WENTZ
Chief Information Officer: CHARLES R. ENICKS
Registrar: BARBARA WESTERFIELD
Library Dir: SUSAN CLARK
Library of 252,759 vols, 38,345 microforms, 2,615 audiovisual materials, 348 ebooks, 1,894 journals
Number of teachers: 590
Number of students: 2,500

DEANS

School of Dentistry: Dr GARY REEVES
School of Graduate Studies: Dr JOEY GRANGER
School of Health-Related Professions: Dr BEN L. MITCHELL
School of Medicine: Dr JAMES KEETON,
School of Nursing: Dr KIM HOOVER
School of Pharmacy: Dr DAVID D. ALLEN

UNIVERSITY OF SOUTHERN MISSISSIPPI

POB 5001, 118 College Dr., Hattiesburg, MS 39406-0001
Telephone: (601) 266-1000
E-mail: admissions@usm.edu
Internet: www.usm.edu
Founded 1910 as Mississippi Normal College
State control
Academic year: August to May (2 semesters)

Campus at Long Beach (Mississippi)
Pres.: Dr MARTHA D. SAUNDERS
Provost: Dr DENIS WIESENBURG
Vice-Pres. for Admin. Affairs: CHAD DRISKELL
Vice-Pres. for Advancement: BOB PIERCE
Vice-Pres. for Research: Dr DENIS WIESENBURG
Vice-Pres. for Student Affairs: Dr JOSEPH S. PAUL
Dean for Univ. Admissions: Dr KRISTI MOTTER
Dean for Univ. Libraries: CAROLE KIEHL
Library: 1.3m. vols
Number of teachers: 650
Number of students: 17,250 (14,095 undergraduate, 3,155 graduate)
Publications: *Journal of Mississippi History, Mississippi Review, Southern Quarterly*

DEANS

College of Arts and Letters: Dr STEVEN MOSER
College of Business: Prof. Dr LANCE NAIL
College of Education and Psychology: Prof. Dr ANN P. BLACKWELL
College of Health: Dr MICHAEL FORSTER
College of Science and Technology: Dr JOE B. WHITEHEAD, JR
Graduate School: Dr SUSAN A. SILTANEN
Honors College: Dr DAVID R. DAVIES

WILLIAM CAREY UNIVERSITY

498 Tuscan Ave, Hattiesburg, MS 39401-5499
Telephone: (601) 318-6051
E-mail: admissions@wmcarey.edu
Internet: www.wmcarey.edu
Founded 1892 as Pearl River Boarding School
Private control
Academic year: August to August
Campuses at Biloxi (Mississippi) and New Orleans (Louisiana)
Pres. and CEO: Dr TOMMY KING
Vice-Pres. for Academic Affairs: Dr GARRY M. BRELAND
Vice-Pres. for Advancement and Church Relations: SCOTT HUMMEL
Vice-Pres. for Business Affairs and Chief Financial Officer: GRANT GUTHRIE
Vice-Pres. for Institutional Effectiveness and Planning: Dr BENNIE R. CROCKETT, JR
Vice-Pres. for Medical Education: MICHAEL K. MURPHY
Vice-Pres. for Student Services: BRENDA F. WALDRIP
Graduate Dean: Dr FRANK G. BAUGH
Dean for Enrolment Management and Records: Dr WILLIAM N. CURRY
Registrar: GAYLE KNIGHT
Dir for Libraries and Learning Resources: CHERYL LAUGHLIN
Library of 127,000 resources, 40,000 ebooks, 43,000 ejournals
Number of teachers: 80 (full-time)
Number of students: 2,170

DEANS

College of Osteopathic Medicine: DARRELL E. LOVINS
Cooper School of Missions and Biblical Studies: Dr DANIEL P. CALDWELL
Joseph and Nancy Fail School of Nursing: Dr JANET K. WILLIAMS
Ralph and Naomi Noonkester School of Arts and Letters: Dr MYRON C. NOONKESTER
School of Business: Dr CHERYL D. DALE
School of Education: Dr BARRY MORRIS
School of Natural and Behavioral Sciences: Dr FRANK G. BAUGH
Winters School of Music: Dr DON ODOM

MISSOURI

AQUINAS INSTITUTE OF THEOLOGY

23 S Spring Ave, St Louis, MO 63108-3323
Telephone: (314) 256-8800
E-mail: info@ai.edu
Internet: www.ai.edu
Founded 1925
Private control
Academic year: August to May
Divs of Aquinas ministry formation programme, health care mission, lay spiritual formation, pastoral studies-catechesis of the good shepherd, theology, preaching
Chancellor: BRUNO CADORÉ
Pres.: RICHARD PEDDICORD
Vice-Pres. and Academic Dean: Dr GREGORY HEILLE
Dir for Admissions and Financial Aid: DAVID WERTHMANN
Dir for Finance and Admin.: THOMAS BARBARAK
Dean for Students: GEORGE BOUDREAU
Registrar: JULIE QUINT
Librarian: KATHLEEN TEHAN
Number of teachers: 35
Number of students: 200 (full-time)

ASSEMBLIES OF GOD THEOLOGICAL SEMINARY

1435 N Glenstone Ave, Springfield, MO 65802-2131
Telephone: (417) 268-1000
E-mail: agts@agts.edu
Internet: www.agts.edu
Founded 1972 as Assemblies of God Graduate School, present name 1984
Private control
Academic year: September to July
Depts of Bible and theology, global missions, practical theology
Pres.: Dr BYRON D. KLAUS
Academic Dean: STEPHEN LIM
Dir for Enrolment Management: MARIO GUERREIRO
Registrar: GENEVA M. HEISKELL
Dir for Library Services: JOSEPH F. MARICS, JR
Library of 86,000 vols, 70,000 microforms, 4,000 audiovisual material, 500 current periodical subscriptions
Number of teachers: 15
Number of students: 550

A. T. STILL UNIVERSITY

800 W Jefferson St, Kirksville, MO 63501
Telephone: (660) 626-2121
E-mail: admissions@atsu.edu
Internet: www.atsu.edu
Founded 1892 as Kirksville College of Osteopathic Medicine, present name 1993
Private control
Academic year: August to June
Br. campus at Mesa, Arizona
Pres.: Dr CRAIG PHELPS
Vice-Pres. for Academic Affairs: Dr MICHAEL McMANIS
Vice-Pres. for Research, Grants and Information Systems: Dr JOHN HEARD, JR
Vice-Pres. for Student Affairs: LORI HAXTON
Vice-Pres. for Univ. Advancement: ROBERT L. BASHAM
Registrar: DEANNA HUNSAKER
Univ. Librarian: MIKE KRONENFELD
Library of 80,000 vols, 4,500 audiovisual items
Number of teachers: 100
Number of students: 3,300
Publication: *First Impressions* (2 a year)

DEANS

Arizona School of Dentistry and Oral Health: Dr CHRIS HALLIDAY

Arizona School of Health Sciences: Dr RANDY DANIELSEN

Kirksville College of Osteopathic Medicine: Dr MARGARET WILSON

School of Health Management: Dr DONALD ALTMAN

School of Osteopathic Medicine in Arizona: Dr KAY KALOUSEK

AVILA UNIVERSITY

11901 Wornall Rd, Kansas City, MO 64145

Telephone: (816) 942-8400
E-mail: admission@avila.edu
Internet: www.avila.edu

Founded 1916, present name and status 2001
Private control

Pres.: Dr RONALD A. SLEPITZA
Provost and Vice-Pres. for Academic Affairs: Dr MARIE JOAN HARRIS, SR
Vice-Provost and Vice-Pres. for Information Services: Dr SUE KING
Vice-Pres. for Advancement and External Relations: ANGIE HEER
Vice-Pres. for Finance and Admin. Services: PAUL BOOKMEYER
Dean for Students: DARBY GOUGH
Registrar: DAVE DEITCH
Librarian: KATHLEEN FINEGAN

Library of 74,658 vols, 500 periodicals
Number of teachers: 65
Number of students: 1,820

DEANS

College of Liberal Arts and Social Sciences: Prof. Dr CHARLENE GOULD
School of Business: Dr RICHARD WOODALL
School of Education: Prof. Dr SUE ELLEN MCCALLEY
School of Nursing: Prof. Dr SUSAN H. FETSCH
School of Science and Health: Dr LARRY GARRISON SULLIVAN
School of Visual and Communication Arts: Dr DOTTY HAMILTON

BAPTIST BIBLE COLLEGE AND GRADUATE SCHOOL

628 E Kearney St, Springfield, MO 65803

Telephone: (417) 268-6000
E-mail: info@gobbc.edu
Internet: www.gobbc.edu

Founded 1950
Private control
Academic year: August to May

Chancellor: Dr LELAND KENNEDY
Pres.: JIM EDGE
Vice-Pres. for Academic Affairs: Dr GREGORY T. CHRISTOPHER
Dean for Students: RAY ADAMS
Dir for Institutional Research: LESA CHASTAIN
Dean for Baptist Bible Graduate School: WAYNE SLUSSER
Registrar: TERRY ALLCORN
Dir for Library Services: JON JONES

Library of 82,000 vols, 270 current periodical subscriptions
Number of teachers: 30
Number of students: 805 (746 undergraduate, 59 graduate)

CALVARY BIBLE COLLEGE AND THEOLOGICAL SEMINARY

15800 Calvary Rd, Kansas City, MO 64147-1341

Telephone: (816) 322-0110
E-mail: admissions@calvary.edu
Internet: www.calvary.edu

Founded 1961 by merger of Kansas City Bible College (f. 1932) and Midwest Bible College (f. 1938), Calvary Theological Seminary (f. 1966) as Graduate Div. of Calvary Bible College, present name 1992
Private control
Academic year: August to May

Depts of Bible and theology, biblical counselling, education, general studies, intercultural studies, ministry studies, music, non-traditional studies, theatre arts

Pres.: Dr JAMES L. CLARK
Vice-Pres. and Academic Dean: Dr TEDDY BITNER
Vice-Pres. and Academic Dean for Seminary: Dr THOMAS BAURAIN
Vice-Pres. for Operations: RANDY L. GRIMM
Dean for Students: CORY TROWBRIDGE
Dir for Admissions: BOB CRANK
Registrar: LARRY SPRY
Librarian: HANNAH BITNER

Library of 62,000 vols
Number of teachers: 40
Number of students: 340 (285 undergraduate, 55 graduate)

CENTRAL BIBLE COLLEGE

3000 N Grant Ave, Springfield, MO 65803

Telephone: (417) 833-2551
E-mail: info@cbcag.edu
Internet: www.cbcag.edu

Founded 1922
Private control
Academic year: August to April

Divs of arts and sciences, Biblical education, church ministries, fine arts and communications, missions and evangelism

Pres.: Dr GARY A. DENBOW
Vice-Pres. for Academic Affairs: Dr DAVID ARNETT
Vice-Pres. for Operations: DAVID WILLEMSEN
Vice-Pres. for Student Devt: Rev. Dr JIM P. VIGIL
Librarian: LYNN ANDERSON

Library of 177,512 vols, 11,000 periodical vols, 4,130 journals, 8,000 books and reference sources
Number of teachers: 50 (29 full-time, 18 part-time)
Number of students: 630

CENTRAL CHRISTIAN COLLEGE OF THE BIBLE

911 E Urbandale Dr., Moberly, MO 65270

Telephone: (660) 263-3900
E-mail: admissions@cccb.edu
Internet: www.cccb.edu

Founded 1957
Private control
Language of instruction: English
Academic year: August to May

Areas of study: biblical research, Christian counselling, Christian education, Christian ministries, cross-cultural ministry, preaching, youth and family ministry

Chancellor: LLOYD M. PELFREY
Pres.: Dr RONALD L. OAKES
Vice-Pres. for Academic Affairs: Dr DAVID B. FINCHER
Vice-Pres. for Student Devt and Enrolment: RICHARD REXRODE
Vice-Pres. for Advancement: PHILIP MARLEY
Registrar: FAITH M. AXTON
Library Dir: PATTY AGEE

Number of teachers: 25
Number of students: 315

Publication: *The Sentinel* (2 a year)

CENTRAL METHODIST UNIVERSITY

411 Central Methodist Sq., Fayette, MO 65248

Telephone: (660) 248-3391
E-mail: admissions@centralmethodist.edu
Internet: www.centralmethodist.edu

Founded 1854
Private control
Academic year: August to May

Divs of accounting, business and economics, English, fine and performing arts, foreign languages, health professions, mathematics and computer science, philosophy and religion, professional education, science, social sciences

Pres.: Dr MARIANNE E. INMAN
Vice-Pres. and Dean for the Univ.: Dr RITA GULSTAD
Vice-Pres. for Advancement: DONNA MERRELL
Vice-Pres. for Campus Life: JAMES WEBSTER
Vice-Pres. for Finance and Admin.: JULEE SHERMAN
Vice-Pres. for Information Services: CHAD GAINES
Dir for Information Resources: CYNTHIA DUDENHOFFER

Library of 100,000 vols
Number of teachers: 160
Number of students: 3,420

Publications: *Inscape* (1 a year), *The Talon* (2 a year)

CLEVELAND CHIROPRACTIC COLLEGE

10850 Lowell Ave, Second Fl., Overland Park, Kansas, MO 66210

Telephone: (913) 234-0600
E-mail: kc.admissions@cleveland.edu
Internet: www.cleveland.edu

Founded 1922 as Central Chiropractic College; present name 1924
Private control
Academic year: September to August

Areas of study: biological sciences, health promotion, human biology

Pres.: Dr CARL S. CLEVELAND, III
Provost: ASHLEY E. CLEVELAND
Vice-Pres. for Campus Relations: D. CLARK BECKELY
Dir for Admissions: MELISSA DENTON
Dir for Research: MARK T. PFEFER
Dir for Student Services: JALONNA BOWIE
Library Dir: MARCIA M. THOMAS

Library of 14,800 vols
Number of students: 500

COLLEGE OF THE OZARKS

Point Lookout, MO 65726

Telephone: (417) 334-6411
E-mail: admiss4@cofo.edu
Internet: www.cofo.edu

Founded 1906 as School of the Ozarks, present name 1990
Private control
Academic year: August to May

Depts of accounting, agriculture, art, biology, business administration, chemistry, computer sciences, criminal justice, education, English, family and consumer sciences, foreign languages, graphic arts, history, hotel and restaurant management, mass communications, mathematics-physics, military science, music, nursing, philosophy and religion, physical education, political science, psychology, sociology, speech communication, technology, theatre

Pres.: Dr JERRY C. DAVIS
Exec. Vice-Pres.: M. FRED MULLINAX
Vice-Pres.: Dr HOWELL W. KEETER
Dean for Admin.: Dr MARVIN R. SCHOENECKE

Dean for the College: Dr ERIC W. BOLGER
Dean for Students: NICK SHARP
Registrar: FRANCES L. FOMAN
Library Supervisor: PATTI TURNER
Library of 119,000 vols
Number of teachers: 85 (full-time)
Number of students: 1,345
Publication: *Ozark Visitor* (4 a year)

COLUMBIA COLLEGE

1001 Rogers St, Columbia, MO 65216
Telephone: (573) 875-8700
E-mail: admissions@ccis.edu
Internet: www.ccis.edu
Founded 1851 as Christian Female College,
  present name 1970
Private control
Academic year: August to July
Areas of study: art, business administration,
computer and mathematical sciences, crim-
inal justice administration and human ser-
vices, education, history and social sciences,
humanities, science; 23 extension campuses
throughout the USA
Pres.: Dr GERALD T. BROUDER
Exec. Vice-Pres. and Dean for Academic
  Affairs: Dr TERRY B. SMITH
Vice-Pres. for Adult Higher Education: MIKE
  RANDERSON
Dean for Student Affairs: FAYE BURCHARD
Library Dir: JANET CARUTHERS
Library of 80,000 vols
Number of teachers: 60
Number of students: 25,000

CONCEPTION SEMINARY COLLEGE

POB 501, Conception, MO 64433
Telephone: (660) 944-2821
E-mail: communications@conception.edu
Internet: www.conception.edu
Founded 1886 as College of New Engelberg,
  present name 1972
Private control
Pres. and Rector: SAMUEL RUSSELL
Library Dir: Bro. THOMAS SULLIVAN
Number of teachers: 30
Number of students: 80

CONCORDIA SEMINARY

801 Seminary Pl., St Louis, MO 63105
Telephone: (314) 505-7000
E-mail: admissions@csl.edu
Internet: www.csl.edu
Founded 1839
Private control
Academic year: September to May
Pres.: Rev. Dr DALE A. MEYER
Provost: Prof. ARTHUR D. BACON
Exec. Vice-Pres. for Academic Affairs: Prof.
  Dr ANDREW H. BARTELT
Sr Vice-Pres. for Enrolment Management:
  MICHAEL J. REDEKER
Sr Vice-Pres. for Financial Planning and
  Admin.: MICHAEL A. LOUIS
Registrar: BETH MENNEKE
Dir for Library Services: DAVID O. BERGER
Library of 270,000 vols
Number of teachers: 55
Number of students: 535 (full-time)
Publications: *Around the Tower, Concordia
Journal, Concordia Seminary Magazine*

COTTEY COLLEGE

1000 W Austin, Nevada, MO 64772
Telephone: (417) 667-8181
E-mail: enrollmgt@cottey.edu
Internet: www.cottey.edu
Founded 1884

Private control
Offers BA in English, environmental studies,
international relations and business
Pres.: Dr JUDY ROBINSON ROGERS
Vice-Pres. for Academic Affairs: Dr CATHRYN
  G. PRIDAL
Vice-Pres. for Admin. and Finance: MARY
  HAGGANS
Vice-Pres. for Enrolment Management: RICK
  EBER
Vice-Pres. for Institutional Advancement:
  STUART LANG
Vice-Pres. for Student Life: MARI ANNE
  PHILLIPS
Dir for Admission: JUDI STEEGE
Registrar: MARCIA MORTON
Dir for Library: BECKY KIEL
Library of 50,000 vols
Number of students: 350

COVENANT THEOLOGICAL SEMINARY

12330 Conway Rd, St Louis, MO 63141
Telephone: (314) 434-4044
E-mail: info@covenantseminary.edu
Internet: www.covenantseminary.edu
Founded 1956
Private control
Academic year: September to May
Pres.: Dr BRYAN CHAPELL
Vice-Pres. for Academics and Dean for Fac-
  ulty: Dr MARK DALBEY
Sr Dir for Admissions and Alumni: JEREMY
  KICKLIGHTER
Dean for Students: MIKE HIGGINS
Registrar: BETSY GASOSKE
Library Dir: JAMES C. PAKALA
Library of 68,000 vols
Number of teachers: 40
Number of students: 435 (full-time)
Publication: *Covenant Magazine* (3 a year)

COX COLLEGE

1423 N Jefferson Ave, Springfield, MO 65802
Telephone: (417) 269-3401
E-mail: admissions@coxcollege.edu
Internet: www.coxcollege.edu
Founded 1907 as Burge Deaconess Training
  School for Nurses, present name 2008
Private control
Academic year: August to May
Offers Bachelors and Masters degrees in
nursing
Pres.: Dr ANNE BRETT
Vice-Pres. for Academic Affairs: Dr MARTIN
  SELLERS
Vice-Pres. for Student Services: DAVID
  SCHOOLFIELD
Dir for Admissions: LINDY BIGLIENI
Dean for Information Services: WILMA BUNCH
Number of students: 650

DEANS

Health Science: SONYA HAYTER
Nursing: PATRICIA WAGNER

CULVER-STOCKTON COLLEGE

1 College Hill, Canton, MO 63435
Telephone: (573) 288-6000
E-mail: admission@culver.edu
Internet: www.culver.edu
Founded 1853
Academic year: August to May
Divs of business, education and applied arts,
fine arts, humanities and social sciences,
natural and mathematical sciences
Pres.: RICHARD D. VALENTINE
Vice-Pres. for Academic Affairs: Dr D'ANN
  CAMPBELL

Vice-Pres. for Advancement: ERIC BARKLEY
Dean for the College: Dr DAVID WILSON
Dir for Admission: MISTY MCBEE
Registrar: CHRIS HUEBOTTER
Librarian: SHARON K. UPCHURCH
Library of 164,266 vols
Number of teachers: 50
Number of students: 750
Publication: *Chronicle* (2 a year)

DRURY UNIVERSITY

900 N Benton Ave, Springfield, MO 65802
Telephone: (417) 873-7879
E-mail: drury@drury.edu
Internet: www.drury.edu
Founded 1873
Private control
Liberal arts college; divs of fine arts, human-
ities, mathematics and sciences, social sci-
ences
Pres.: TODD PARNELL
Vice-Pres. for Academic Affairs and Dean for
  College: CHARLES TAYLOR
Vice-Pres. for Admin. Services: BILL SCORSE
Vice-Pres. for Alumni and Devt: Dr KRYSTAL
  MCCULLOCH
Vice-Pres. for Campus Operations and Sus-
  tainability: PETER RADECKI
Vice-Pres. for Enrolment Management:
  DAWN HILES
Vice-Pres. for Student Affairs and Dean for
  Students: TIJUANA JULIAN
Registrar: GALE BOUTWELL
Library Dir: POLLY BORUFF-JONES
Library of 180,000 vols, 550 periodicals
Number of teachers: 120 (f.t.e.)
Number of students: 1,620

EDEN THEOLOGICAL SEMINARY

475 E Lockwood Ave, St Louis, MO 63119-
3192
Telephone: (314) 961-3627
E-mail: dwindler@eden.edu
Internet: www.eden.edu
Founded 1850
Private control
Areas of study: biblical studies, ethics, his-
torical and theological studies, ministry stud-
ies
Pres.: Rev. Dr DAVID M. GREENHAW
Exec. Vice-Pres.: RICK WALTERS
Vice-Pres. for Institutional Advancement:
  BRYCE KRUG
Dir for Admin.: AL SCHON
Dir for Devt: JACQUELINE HAMILTON
Academic Dean: Rev. Dr DEBORAH KRAUSE
Dean for Students: Rev. CARL SCHENCK
Registrar: MICHELLE WOBBE
Library Dir: MICHAEL P. BODDY
Library of 86,000 vols
Number of teachers: 25
Number of students: 130 (full-time)

EVANGEL UNIVERSITY

1111 N Glenstone Ave, Springfield, MO
65802
Telephone: (417) 865-2815
Internet: www.evangel.edu
Founded 1955
Private control
Academic year: September to May
Depts of behavioural sciences, business, com-
munication, education, humanities, music,
kinesiology, science and technology, social
sciences, theology
Chancellor: Dr ROBERT H. SPENCE
Pres.: Dr CAROL TAYLOR
Vice-Pres. for Academic Affairs: Dr GLENN H.
  BERNET, JR

Vice-Pres. for Business and Finance: GEORGE CRAWFORD
Vice-Pres. for Enrolment Management: Dr ANDY DENTON
Vice-Pres. for Institutional Advancement: JIM WILLIAMS
Vice-Pres. for Student Devt: Dr DAVID BUN-DRICK
Registrar: CATHY WILLIAMS
Library Dir: DALE JENSEN
Library of 120,000 vols
Number of teachers: 100
Number of students: 2,170

FONTBONNE UNIVERSITY

6800 Wydown Blvd, St Louis, MO 63105
Telephone: (314) 862-3456
Internet: www.fontbonne.edu
Founded 1923
Private control
Pres.: DENNIS C. GOLDEN
Vice-Pres. for Academic Affairs: GREG TAYLOR
Vice-Pres. for Finance and Admin.: GARY ZACK
Vice-Pres. for Institutional Advancement: RANDY LOECHNER
Vice-Pres. for Student Affairs: RANDI WILSON
Registrar: MAZIE MOORE
Univ. Librarian: SHARON MCCASLIN
Library of 90,020 vols, 510 periodicals
Number of teachers: 280
Number of students: 2,100

GLOBAL UNIVERSITY

211 S Glenstone Ave, Springfield, MO 65804
Telephone: (417) 862-9533
E-mail: info@globaluniversity.edu
Internet: www.globaluniversity.edu
Private control
Languages of instruction: English, French, Spanish
Pres.: Dr GARY L. SEEVERS
Provost: Dr ROBERT A. LOVE
Vice-Provost and Dean for Education: JOHN G. NILL
Vice-Pres. for Center for Evangelism and Discipleship: BART BAGWELL
Vice-Pres. for Global Operations: JOSEPH A. SZABO
Dir for Library Services: RUSS LANGFORD
Library of 25,000 vols

DEANS

Berean School of the Bible: Dr RANDY J. HEDLUN
Graduate School of Theology: Dr CARL W. CHRISNER
Undergraduate School of Bible and Theology: WILLARD D. TEAGUE

HANNIBAL-LAGRANGE UNIVERSITY

2800 Palmyra Rd, Hannibal, MO 63401
Telephone: (573) 221-3675
E-mail: admissions@hlg.edu
Internet: www.hlg.edu
Founded 1858, present name and status 2010
Private control
Divs of business and computer information systems, Christian studies, fine arts, humanities, natural science and mathematics, social science, nursing and allied health
Pres.: Dr WOODROW W. BURT
Vice-Pres. for Academic Affairs: DAVID J. PELLETIER
Vice-Pres. for Enrolment Management: RAYMOND W. CARTY
Vice-Pres. for Institutional Advancement: STEVE MILLER
Registrar: BETH CRUM (acting)
Library Dir: JULIE A. ANDRESEN

Library of 135,000 vols, 300 periodicals
Number of teachers: 50
Number of students: 1,150
Publication: *Reflections*

HARRIS-STOWE STATE UNIVERSITY

3026 Laclede Ave, St Louis, MO 63103
Telephone: (314) 340-3300
E-mail: admissions@hssu.edu
Internet: www.hssu.edu
Founded 1857, present name and status 2005
State control
Pres.: Dr ALBERT WALKER
Vice-Pres. for Academic Affairs: Dr DWYANE SMITH
Exec. Dir for Enrolment Management: LASHANDA BOONE
Dean for Student Affairs: CHARLES GOODEN
Registrar: CHAUVETTE MCELMURRY
Library Dir: BARBARA N. NOBLE
Library of 87,000 vols
Number of teachers: 80
Number of students: 1,980

DEANS

Anheuser-Busch School of Business: Dr FATEMEH ZAKERY
College of Arts and Sciences: Dr LATEEF ADELANI
College of Education: Dr LATISHA SMITH

KANSAS CITY ART INSTITUTE

4415 Warwick Blvd, Kansas City, MO 64111-1820
Telephone: (816) 472-4852
E-mail: info@kcai.edu
Internet: www.kcai.edu
Founded 1885
Private control
Academic year: August to May
Schools of liberal arts, fine arts and design, electronic arts
Pres.: Dr JACQUELINE CHANDA
Exec. Vice-Pres. for Admin.: RONALD CATTELINO
Vice-Pres. and Chief Information Officer: LARRY DICKERSON
Vice-Pres. for Academic Affairs: Dr MARK SALMON
Vice-Pres. for Advancement: PAM SIBERT
Vice-Pres. for Communications: ANNE CANFIELD
Vice-Pres. for Enrolment Management and Student Achievement: Dr BAMBI BURGARD
Registrar: ANDREA KHAN
Library Dir: M. J. POEHLER
Library of 30,000 vols, 111,160 slides
Number of students: 750
Publication: *Sprung Formal* (1 a year)

KANSAS CITY UNIVERSITY OF MEDICINE AND BIOSCIENCES

1750 Independence Ave, Kansas City, MO 64106-1453
Telephone: (816) 654-7000
E-mail: admissions@kcumb.edu
Internet: www.kcumb.edu
Founded 1916 as Kansas City College of Osteopathy and Surgery, present name and structure 2004
Private control
Academic year: August to July
Pres. and CEO: H. DANNY WEAVER
Exec. Vice-Pres. for Academic and Medical Affairs: DARIN HAUG
Vice-Pres. for Advancement: BETH DOLLASE
Vice-Pres. for Enrolment Management and Registrar: HEIDI TERRY

Vice-Pres. for Finance and Admin.: JAMES PARK
Vice-Pres. for Univ. Relations: NATALIE LUTZ
Dir for Admissions: PATTI HARPER
Dir for Library: MARILYN J. DEGEUS
Number of teachers: 50
Number of students: 1,110
Publications: *KCUMB Communicator* (2 a year), *VOICES Magazine*

DEANS

College of Biosciences: DOUG RUSHING
College of Osteopathic Medicine: DARIN HAUG

KENRICK-GLENNON SEMINARY

5200 Glennon Dr., St Louis, MO 63119
Telephone: (314) 792-6100
Internet: www.kenrick.edu
Founded 1898
Private control
Academic year: August to May
Pres. and Rector: JOHN HORN
Vice-Rector: GREGORY MIKESCH
Vice-Rector for Admin. and Finance: Rev. DONALD EDWARD HENKE
Academic Dean: Dr JOHN L. GRESHAM
Dean for Students and Dir for Admissions: Rev. PAUL ROTHSCHILD
Dir for Devt: KATE GUYOL
Registrar: JOE MEIERGERD
Dir for Library: MARY ANN AUBIN
Library of 80,000 vols
Number of students: 110 (30 undergraduate, 80 graduate)

LINCOLN UNIVERSITY

820 Chestnut St, Jefferson City, MO 65101
Telephone: (573) 681-5000
E-mail: enroll@lincolnu.edu
Internet: www.lincolnu.edu
Founded 1866 as Lincoln Institute, present name and status 1921
State control
Academic year: August to July
Pres.: Dr CAROLYN R. MAHONEY
Provost and Vice-Pres. for Academic Affairs: Dr ANN HARRIS
Vice-Pres. for Admin.: CURTIS E. CREAGH
Vice-Pres. for Student Affairs: THERESSA FERGUSON
Vice-Pres. for Univ. Advancement: BENECIA WILLIAMS
Dir for Admissions: ROXANNE SEIDNER
Dean for Library Services and Univ. Archives: JEROME OFFORD, JR
Library of 204,948 vols, 58 periodicals, 190 serial microform titles
Number of teachers: 180
Number of students: 3,390

DEANS

College of Agricultural and Natural Sciences: Dr STEVE MEREDITH
College of Arts and Letters: Dr RUTHI STURDEVANT
College of Behavioral and Technological Sciences: Dr RUTHI STURDEVANT
College of Professional Studies: Dr LINDA S. BICKEL

LINDENWOOD UNIVERSITY

209 S Kingshighway, St Charles, MO 63301
Telephone: (636) 949-2000
E-mail: admissions@lindenwood.edu
Internet: www.lindenwood.edu
Founded 1827
Private control
Academic year: August to May
Pres.: Dr JAMES D. EVANS

Provost and Vice-Pres. for Academic Affairs: Dr JANN R. WEITZEL
Vice-Pres. for Operations: JULIE MUELLER
Vice-Pres. for Institutional Advancement: Dr LUCY MORROS
Vice-Pres. for Student Devt: JOHN OLDANI
Vice-Pres. for Belleville Campus: JERRY BLADDICK
Dean for Students: TERRY RUSSELL
Dean for Library Services: ELIZABETH MAC-DONALD

Library of 93,822 vols, 218 journals, 400 audio books
Number of teachers: 100
Number of students: 7,570

Publications: *Arrow Rock, Connection* (4 a year), *Journal of International and Global Studies, Lindenwood University Academics* (1 a year), *LindenWord* (2 a year), *The Confluence, The Lindenwood Review*

DEANS

School of American Studies: DAVID KNOTTS
School of Business and Entrepreneurship: ROGER ELLIS
School of Communications: MIKE WALL
School of Education: CYNTHIA BICE
School of Fine and Performing Arts: Prof. DONNELL WALSH
School of Humanities: MICHAEL WHALEY
School of Human Services: Assoc. Prof. CARLA MUELLER
School of Sciences: MARILYN ABBOTT

LOGAN COLLEGE OF CHIROPRACTIC/UNIVERSITY PROGRAMS

1851 Schoettler Rd, POB 1065, Chesterfield, MO 63006-1065

Telephone: (636) 227-2100
E-mail: loganadm@logan.edu
Internet: www.logan.edu

Founded 1935
Private control
Academic year: September to April

Pres.: Dr GEORGE A. GOODMAN
Vice-Pres. for Academic Affairs: Dr CARL W. SAUBERT, IV (acting)
Vice-Pres. for Admin. Affairs: SHARON K. KEHRER
Vice-Pres. for Enrolment Management: Dr BOYD A. BRADSHAW
Vice-Pres. for Institutional Advancement: PATRICIA C. JONES
Dir for Admissions: STEVE HELD
Dean for Research and Devt: Dr RODGER TEPE
Dean for Student Services: JAMES PAINE
Registrar: JOHN-HERBERT JAFFRY
Dir for Library: CHABHA HOCINE TEPE

Library of 12,000 vols, 240 journals, 23,050 media items
Number of teachers: 90 (45 full-time, 45 part-time)
Number of students: 1,000

MARYVILLE UNIVERSITY OF SAINT LOUIS

650 Maryville University Dr., St Louis, MO 63141

Telephone: (314) 529-9300
E-mail: admissions@maryville.edu
Internet: www.maryville.edu

Founded 1872
Private control
Academic year: August to May

Pres.: Dr MARK LOMBARDI
Vice-Pres. for Academic Affairs: Dr MARY ELLEN FINCH
Vice-Pres. for Admin. and Finance: Dr LARRY HAYS
Vice-Pres. for Enrolment: JEFF MILLER

Vice-Pres. for Institutional Advancement: TOM ESCHEN
Vice-Pres. for Student Life and Dean for Students: NINA CALDWELL
Registrar: STEPHANIE ELFRINK
Dean of Library: Dr GENIE MCKEE

Library of 252,550 vols, 213,465 books, 62,337 current serials
Number of teachers: 280
Number of students: 3,900
Publication: *Maryville Magazine*

DEANS

College of Arts and Sciences: Dr DANIEL SPARLING
John E. Simon School of Business: Dr PAMELA HORWITZ
School of Education: Dr SAM HAUSFATHER
School of Health Professions: Dr CHARLES J. GULAS

MIDWESTERN BAPTIST THEOLOGICAL SEMINARY AND COLLEGE

5001 N. Oak Trafficway, Kansas City, MO 64118

Telephone: (816) 414-3700
E-mail: admissions@mbts.edu
Internet: www.mbts.edu

Founded 1957
Private control
Academic year: August to July

Pres.: Dr JASON K. ALLEN
Vice-Pres. for Academic Devt: THORVALD B. MADSEN
Vice-Pres. for Institutional Relations: CHARLES W. SMITH
Vice-Pres. for Institutional Effectiveness: RODNEY A. HARRISON
Dean for College: JOHN MARK YEATS
Registrar: MIKE HAWKINS
Dir for Library Services: CRAIG KUBIC

Library of 110,000 vols
Number of teachers: 30
Number of students: 1,500 (full-time)

Publications: *Midwestern Journal of Theology* (2 a year), *The Midwestern* (2 a year)

MISSOURI BAPTIST UNIVERSITY

1 College Park Dr., Saint Louis, MO 63141-8698

Telephone: (314) 434-1115
E-mail: admissions@mobap.edu
Internet: www.mobap.edu

Founded 1957 as campus extension of Hannibal-LaGrange College, present name 1999
Private control
Academic year: August to April

Divs of business, education, fine arts, health and sport sciences, humanities, natural sciences, social and behavioural sciences; graduate programmes; campuses at Franklin Co, Hillsboro and Moscow Mills (Missouri)

Pres.: Dr R. ALTON LACEY
Provost and Sr Vice-Pres. for Academic Affairs: Dr ARLEN R. DYKSTRA
Sr Vice-Pres. for Institutional Advancement: KEITH ROSS
Vice-Pres. for Enrolment Services: TERRY DALE CRUSE
Vice-Pres. for Graduate Studies: Dr CLARK TRIPLETT
Vice-Pres. for Student Devt: Dr ANDY CHAMBERS (acting)
Dir for Admissions: AARON BLACK
Dir for Library Services: NITSA HINDELEH

Number of teachers: 150
Number of students: 5,200 (1,358 graduate, 3,842 undergraduate)
Publication: *MBU Magazine*

MISSOURI SOUTHERN STATE UNIVERSITY

3950 E Newman Rd, Joplin, MO 64801-1595

Telephone: (417) 625-9300
E-mail: info@mssu.edu
Internet: www.mssu.edu

Founded 1937 as Joplin Junior College, present name and status 2003
State control
Academic year: June to May

Pres.: Dr BRUCE W. SPECK (acting)
Vice-Pres. for Academic Affairs: Dr A. J. ANGLIN
Vice-Pres. for Business Affairs: ROB YUST
Vice-Pres. for Devt: Dr MARK PARSONS
Vice-Pres. for Student Affairs: DARREN FULLERTON
Registrar: CHERYL DOBSON
Library Dir: WENDY L. MCGRANE

Library of 274,000 vols, 754,000 microform items
Number of teachers: 290
Number of students: 5,800 (5,750 undergraduate, 50 graduate)

DEANS

Graduate Studies and Lifelong Learning: Dr JO KROLL
Robert W. Plaster School of Business Admin.: Dr BEVERLY BLOCK
School of Arts and Sciences: Dr RICHARD MILLER
School of Education: Dr GLENN COLTHARP
School of Technology: Dr TIA M. STRAIT

MISSOURI STATE UNIVERSITY

901 S National Ave, Springfield, MO 65897

Telephone: (417) 836-5000
E-mail: info@missouristate.edu
Internet: www.missouristate.edu

Founded 1905, current name adopted 2005
public control
Academic year: July to June

Campuses at Mountain Grove and West Plains (Missouri) and in Dalian (People's Republic of China)

Pres.: CLIFTON M. SMART, III
Provost: Dr FRANK EINHELLIG
Vice-Pres. for Admin. and Information Services: KEN MCCLURE
Vice-Pres. for Diversity and Inclusion: Dr KENNETH COOPWOOD
Vice-Pres. for Research and Economic Devt: Dr JIM BAKER
Vice-Pres. for Student Affairs: Dr DEE SISCOE
Vice-Pres. for Univ. Advancement: BRENT DUNN
Dean for Library Services: THOMAS PETERS

Library of 701,592 vols, 971,673 govt docs, 1,054,901 units of microform, 20,050 audiovisual titles, 207,798 maps, 4,206 current periodicals
Number of teachers: 720
Number of students: 22,100

DEANS

College of Arts and Letters: Dr GLORIA GALANES
College of Business Administration: Dr STEPHANIE BRYANT
College of Education: Dr DAVID HOUGH
College of Health and Human Services: Dr HELEN REID
College of Humanities and Public Affairs: Dr VICTOR MATTHEWS
College of Natural and Applied Sciences: Dr TAMERA JAHNKE
Graduate College: (vacant)

MISSOURI VALLEY COLLEGE

500 E College, Marshall, MO 65340
Telephone: (660) 831-4000
Internet: www.moval.edu
Founded 1889
Private control
Academic year: August to July
Pres.: Dr BONNIE L. HUMPHREY
Vice-Pres. for Enrolment Management and Operations: TOM D. FIFER
Vice-Pres. for Institutional Advancement: ERIC SAPPINGTON
Chief Academic Officer: Dr SHARON WEISER
Dir for Admissions: TENNILLE LANGDON
Dean for Student Affairs: HEATH MORGAN
Registrar: MARSHA LASHLEY
Library Dir: PAMELA K. REEDER
Library of 70,000 vols
Number of teachers: 55 (full-time)
Number of students: 1,475

DEANS

Education: Dr EARL WELLBORN
Graduate Studies: Dr JOHN GAULT
Mathematics and Sciences: Dr KATHERINE ADAMS
School of Nursing and Health Sciences: Dr KARLA BRUNTZEL

MISSOURI WESTERN STATE UNIVERSITY

4525 Downs Dr., St Joseph, MO 64507
Telephone: (816) 271-4200
E-mail: admission@missouriwestern.edu
Internet: www.missouriwestern.edu
Founded 1915 as St Joseph Junior College, present name 1969, present name and status 2005
State control
Academic year: August to May
Pres.: Dr ROBERT A. VARTABEDIAN
Provost and Vice-Pres. for Academic Affairs: Dr JEANNE DAFFRON
Vice-Pres. for Financial Planning and Admin.: MELVIN F. KLINKNER
Vice-Pres. for Student Affairs: ESTHER PERÁLEZ
Vice-Pres. for Univ. Advancement: DAN NICOSON
Registrar: SUSAN BRACCIANO
Library Dir: JULIA SCHNEIDER
Library of 226,000 vols, 1,200 journals and state govt documents
Number of teachers: 200
Number of students: 6,300 (6,135 undergraduate, 165 graduate)
Publications: The Saint Joseph Palette, Western Magazine (3 a year)

DEANS

Graduate Studies: Dr BRIAN CRONK
Liberal Arts and Sciences: Dr MURRAY NABORS
Professional Studies: Dr PHILIP S. NITSE
Steven L. Craig School of Business: Dr PHILIP S. NITSE
Western Institute: GORDON MAPLEY

NAZARENE THEOLOGICAL SEMINARY

1700 E Meyer Blvd, Kansas City, MO 64131
Telephone: (816) 268-5400
E-mail: enroll@nts.edu
Internet: www.nts.edu
Founded 1944
Private control
Academic year: August to May
Pres.: Dr DAVID A. BUSIC
Dean for Admin. and Student Services: Dr D. MARTIN BUTLER

Dean for the Faculty: Dr ROGER HAHN
Registrar and Dir for Admissions: PAMELA ASHER
Dir for Library Services: DEBRA L. BRADSHAW
Library of 150,000 vols, 320 periodicals
Number of teachers: 35 (11 full-time, 24 part-time)
Number of students: 250 (full-time)
Publication: Didache

NORTHWEST MISSOURI STATE UNIVERSITY

800 University Dr., Maryville, MO 64468
Telephone: (660) 562-1562
E-mail: admissions@nwmissouri.edu
Internet: www.nwmissouri.edu
Founded 1905
State control
Academic year: August to August
Pres.: Dr JOHN JASINSKI
Provost: Dr DOUGLAS DUNHAM
Vice-Pres. for Student Affairs: Dr MATT BAKER
Vice-Pres. for Univ. Advancement: MICHAEL JOHNSON
Vice-Pres. for Univ. Relations: MITZI LUTZ
Registrar: TERRI VOGEL
Dir for Academic and Library Services: Dr LESLIE GALBREATH
Library of 368,000 vols, 30,000 eperiodicals
Number of teachers: 225
Number of students: 7,225
Publication: Northwest Alumni Magazine (2 a year)

DEANS

College of Arts and Sciences: Dr CHARLES A. MCADAMS
College of Education and Human Services: Dr JOYCE PIVERAL
Graduate School: Dr GREGORY HADDOCK
Melvin D. and Valorie G. Booth College of Business and Professional Studies: Dr GREGORY HADDOCK
Missouri Academy: Dr CLEO SAMUDZI

PARK UNIVERSITY

8700 NW River Park Dr., Parkville, MO 64152
Telephone: (816) 741-2000
E-mail: admissions@park.edu
Internet: www.park.edu
Founded 1875
Private control
Academic year: August to July
40 Campuses in 21 states; online degree programme
Pres.: Dr MICHAEL DROGE
Provost and Vice-Pres. for Academic Affairs: Dr JERRY D. JORGENSEN
Vice-Pres. for Distance Learning: Dr THOMAS W. PETERMAN
Vice-Pres. for Finance and Admin.: DORLA WATKINS
Vice-Pres. for Univ. Advancement: LAURIE D. MCCORMACK
Vice-Pres. and Gen. Counsel: ROGER HERSHEY
Assoc. Vice-Pres. for Student Affairs: CLARINDA H. CREIGHTON
Registrar: (vacant)
Dir for Library Systems: ANN SCHULTIS
Library of 155,000 vols, 1,000 periodicals, 4,000 reels of microfilm
Number of teachers: 100
Number of students: 1,200
Publications: Narva (1 a year), Scholasticus (1 a year), Scribe

DEANS

College of Liberal Arts and Sciences: Dr JANE WOOD

Hauptmann School for Public Affairs: LAURIE DIPADOVA-STOCKS
School for Education: Dr MICHELLE MYERS
School of Business: Prof. Dr BRAD KLEINDL

RANKEN TECHNICAL COLLEGE

4431 Finney Ave, St Louis, MO 63113
Telephone: (314) 286-4809
E-mail: admissions@ranken.edu
Internet: www.ranken.edu
Founded 1907
Private control
Offers BSc in architectural technology and applied management
Pres.: STAN SHOUN
Vice-Pres. for Education: DONALD J. POHL
Vice-Pres. for Finance and Admin.: PETER T. MURTAUGH
Vice-Pres. for Student Success: JOHN E. WOOD
Dean for Academic Affairs: CRYSTAL A. HERRON
Library of 20,000 vols

RESEARCH COLLEGE OF NURSING

2525 E Meyer Blvd, Kansas City, MO 64132
Telephone: (816) 995-2800
Internet: www.researchcollege.edu
Founded 1905 as German Hospital Training School for Nurses
Private control
Academic year: August to May (2 semesters)
Pres. and Dean: Dr NANCY O. DeBASIO
Assoc. Dean of Academic Programmes: (vacant)
Dir for Graduate Programmes: Dr LYNN WARMBRODT
Dir for Student Affairs: LORI VITALE
Dir for Learning Resource Center: TOBEY STOSBERG
Number of students: 400

ROCKHURST UNIVERSITY

1100 Rockhurst Rd, Kansas City, MO 64110
Telephone: (816) 501-4000
E-mail: admission@rockhurst.edu
Internet: www.rockhurst.edu
Founded 1910
Private control
Academic year: August to May
Pres.: Rev. THOMAS B. CURRAN
Vice-Pres. for Academic Affairs: Dr SHARON HOMAN
Vice-Pres. for Advancement: BOB GRANT
Vice-Pres. for Mission and Min.: WILLIAM OULVEY
Vice-Pres. for Student Devt and Athletics: Dr MATT QUICK
Vice-Pres. for Univ. Advancement: Dr JANE LAMPO
Assoc. Vice-Pres. for Admin.: MATT HEINRICH
Assoc. Vice-Pres. for Enrolment Services: LANE RAMEY
Registrar: MINDA THROWER
Dir of Library: LAURIE HATHMAN
Library of 100,000 vols
Number of teachers: 210
Number of students: 3,000
Publication: Rockhurst Magazine

DEANS

College of Arts and Sciences: Dr TIMOTHY MCDONALD
Helzberg School of Management: Dr JAMES M. DALEY
Research College of Nursing: Dr NANCY O. DeBASIO
School of Graduate and Professional Studies: Dr JEFFREY R. BREESE

SAINT LOUIS CHRISTIAN COLLEGE

1360 Grandview Dr., Florissant, MO 63033

Telephone: (314) 837-6777
E-mail: admissions@slcconline.edu
Internet: www.slcconline.edu

Founded 1956
Private control
Academic year: July to June

Areas of study: Christian ministry, educational ministries, intercultural and urban missions, preaching ministry, worship and music ministry

Pres.: Dr GUTHRIE VEECH
Vice-Pres. for Operations: JUDY LINCOLN
Academic Dean: MICHAEL CHAMBERS
Dir for Admissions: CARRIE CHAPMAN
Dean for Students: CHRISTINE CABLE
Registrar: CINDY BINGAMON
Library Man.: MATTHEW DEWITT

Library of 41,000 vols, 150 periodicals, 16,000 microforms, 3,000 audio cassettes, 400 video cassettes
Number of teachers: 10
Number of students: 300

ST LOUIS COLLEGE OF PHARMACY

4588 Parkview Pl., St Louis, MO 63110-1088

Telephone: (314) 367-8700
E-mail: admissions@stlcop.edu
Internet: www.stlcop.edu

Founded 1864
Private control
Academic year: August to July

Pres.: Dr JOHN A. PIEPER
Vice-Pres. for Academic Affairs: Dr WENDY DUNCAN-HEWITT
Vice-Pres. for Advancement: BRETT T. SCHOTT
Vice-Pres. for Enrolment Services: GLORIA J. VERTREES
Vice-Pres. for Finance and Admin.: GARY G. TORRENCE
Vice-Pres. for Student Affairs: Dr KIMBERLY J. KILGORE
Registrar and Dir for Admissions: PENELOPE MYERS BRYANT
Dir for Library: JILL NISSEN

Library of 54,000 vols
Number of teachers: 90 (full-time)
Number of students: 1,260

DEANS

Arts and Sciences: Dr KIMBERLY J. KILGORE
Pharmacy: Dr WENDY DUNCAN-HEWITT

SAINT LOUIS UNIVERSITY

1 N Grand Blvd, St Louis, MO 63103

Telephone: (314) 977-2500
E-mail: admitme@slu.edu
Internet: www.slu.edu

Founded 1818
Private control
Academic year: September to May (2 terms)

Pres.: Rev. LAWRENCE H. BIONDI
Provost: JOE WEIXLMANN
Vice-Pres. for Academic Affairs: Dr MANOJ PATANKAR
Vice-Pres. for Advancement: JEFF FOWLER
Vice-Pres. for Enrolment and Retention Management: JAY GOFF
Vice-Pres. for Facilities Management and Civic Affairs: KATHLEEN T. BRADY
Vice-Pres. for Mission and Min.: PAUL STARK
Vice-Pres. for Research: Dr RAYMOND TAIT
Vice-Pres. for Student Devt: KENT PORTER-FIELD
Vice-Pres. and Gen. Counsel: WILLIAM R. KAUFFMAN
Registrar: JANEL ESKER
Asst Provost for Libraries: GAIL M. STAINES

Library: see Libraries and Archives
Number of teachers: 3,120 (1,300 full-time, 1,820 part-time)
Number of students: 13,200 (8,100 undergraduate, 5,100 graduate)
Publications: *African American Review, Boulevard, Forum for Social Economics, Journal of Gerontology: Social Sciences, Institute of Jesuit Sources, Journal of Health Law and Policy* (2 a year), *Journal of Herpetology, Journal of Policy History, Journal of Urban Affairs, Manuscripta* (2 a year), *Pageoph, Public Law Review* (2 a year), *Review for Religious, Saint Louis University Law Journal, Studies in the Spirituality of Jesuits, The Modern Schoolman* (4 a year), *Theology Digest* (4 a year), *Universitas, Warsaw Trans Atlantic Law Journal*

DEANS

College of Arts and Sciences: MICHAEL D. BARBER
College of Education and Public Service: Dr GERARD FOWLER
College of Philosophy and Letters: MICHAEL BARBER
Doisy College of Health Sciences: Dr CHARLOTTE ROYEEN
John Cook School of Business: Dr ELLEN F. HARSHMAN
Madrid Campus: Dr PAUL VITA
Parks College of Engineering, Aviation and Technology: Dr KRISHNASWAMY RAVINDRA
School for Professional Studies: Dr JENNIFER GIANCOLA
School of Law: ANNETTE CLARK
School of Medicine: PHILIP O. ALDERSON
School of Nursing: Dr TERI A. MURRAY
School of Public Health: EDWIN TREVATHAN
School of Social Work: Dr GERARD FOWLER

PROFESSORS

ABELL, B. F., Meteorology
AL-JUREIDINI, S. B., Paediatrics
ALBERT, S. G., Internal Medicine
ALDRIDGE, R. D., Biology
AMINE, L. S., Marketing
AMON, E., Obstetrics and Gynaecology
ANDERSON, E. L., Internal Medicine
ANDERSON, R. O., Communication
ARMBRECHT, H. J., Internal Medicine
ARTAL, R., Obstetrics and Gynaecology
ASPINWALL, N., Biology
AZZAM, F. J., Anaesthesiology
BACON, B. R., Internal Medicine
BAJAJ, S. P., Internal Medicine
BALDASSARE, J. J., Pharmacological and Physiological Sciences
BALFOUR, I. C., Paediatrics
BANKS, W. A., Internal Medicine
BARBER, M. D., Philosophy
BARENKAMP, S. J., Paediatrics
BARMANN, L. F., American Studies
BARRY, R. C., Paediatrics
BASTANI, B., Internal Medicine
BAUDENDISTEL, L. J., Anaesthesiology
BELLONE, C. J., Molecular Microbiology and Immunology
BELSHE, R. B., Internal Medicine
BENOFY, L. P., Physics
BENOIT, R. P., English
BENTLEY, D. W., Internal Medicine
BERNHARDT, P., Biology
BIONDI, L. H., Modern Languages
BJERREGAARD, P., Internal Medicine
BLASKIEWICZ, R. J., Obstetrics and Gynaecology
BOHMAN, J. P., Philosophy
BOLLA, R. I., Biology
BRENNAN, D. G., Communication Sciences and Disorders
BRENNAN, W. C., Social Work
BRESLIN, R. D., Educational Leadership and Higher Education

BROCKHAUS, R. H., Management
BROWN, W. W., Internal Medicine
BROWNSON, R. C., Community Health
BUCHOLZ, R. D., Surgery
BULLER, R. M., Molecular Microbiology and Immunology
BURDGE, R. E., Orthopaedic Surgery
BURGIN, R. W., Communication
BURKE, W. J., Neurology
BURTON, F. R., Internal Medicine
CANTWELL, J. C., Mathematics and Mathematical Computer Science
CASE, M. E., Pathology
CERVENKA, P. A., Law
CHAITMAN, B. R., Internal Medicine
CHAPNICK, B. M., Pharmacological and Physiological Sciences
CHARRON, W. C., Philosophy
CHEN, S.-C., Paediatrics
CHINNADURAI, G., Molecular Virology
CHOATE, J. W., Obstetrics, Gynaecology and Women's Health
CHU, J.-Y., Paediatrics
CHUNG, H. D., Pathology
COHEN, J. D., Internal Medicine
COOPER, M. H., Anatomy and Neurobiology
COSCIA, C., Biochemistry and Molecular Biology
COUNTE, M. A., Health Administration
CREER, M. H., Pathology
CRITCHLOW, D. T., History
CROSSLEY, D. J., Geophysics
CUMMINGS, S. B., Public Policy Studies
CZYSZ, P. A., Aerospace Engineering
DAHMS, T. E., Anaesthesiology
DAVENPORT, G., Psychology
DELESPESSE, J. B., Aerospace Studies (ROTC)
DEMELLO, D. E., Pathology
DEUEL, R. K., Neurology
DiBISCEGLIE, A., Internal Medicine
DIECK, H. A., Chemistry
DIXIT, V. V., Physics
DORE, I. I., Law
DORSETT, D., Biochemistry and Molecular Biology
DOWDY, J., Mathematics and Mathematical Computer Science
DOYLE, J. P., Philosophy
DOYLE, R. E., Comparative Medicine
DUCKRO, P. N., Community and Family Medicine
DUNSFORD, J. E., Law
ELICEIRI, G. L., Pathology
ELLSWORTH, M. L., Pharmacological and Physiological Sciences
FARRIS, B. E., Jr, Sociology
FEMAN, S. S., Ophthalmology
FERGUSON, D. J., Orthodontics
FERMAN, M. A., Aerospace and Mechanical Engineering
FETE, T. J., Paediatrics
FIORE, A. C., Surgery
FISHER, J. T., Theological Studies
FITCH, C. D., Internal Medicine
FITZGIBBON, S. A., Law
FLETCHER, J. W., Internal Medicine
FLICK, L. H., Community Health
FLIESLER, S. J., Ophthalmology
FORD, C. E., Mathematics and Mathematical Computer Science
FORRESTER, T., Pharmacological and Physiological Science
FRANKOWSKI, S., Law
FREESE, R. W., Mathematics and Mathematical Computer Science
GALE, J. B., Paediatrics
GANNON, P., Psychiatry and Human Behaviour
GARCIA, P., Modern Languages
GARVIN, P. J., Surgery
GIBBONS, J. L., Psychology
GILNER, F. H., Psychology
GILSINAN, J. F., Public Policy Studies
GOLDMAN, R. L., Law
GOLDNER, J. A., Law
GOLDSTEIN, J. K., Law

GORSE, G. J., Internal Medicine
GRADY, M. P., Educational Studies
GRAFF, R. J., Surgery
GRAHAM, M. A., Pathology
GRANDGENETT, D. P., Molecular Virology
GREANEY, T. L., Law
GREEN, M., Molecular Virology
GREEN, M., Molecular Microbiology and Immunology
GRIFFING, G. T., Internal Medicine
GROSSBERG, G. T., Psychiatry and Human Behaviour
GUITHUES, H. J., Finance
HAIRE-JOSHU, D. L., Community Health
HALLETT, G. L., Philosophy
HAMRICK, L. C., Modern Languages
HANDAL, P. J., Psychology
HARRIS, S. G., Mathematics and Mathematical Computer Science
HEANEY, R. M., Internal Medicine
HEBDA, J. J., Mathematics and Mathematical Computer Science
HEIBERG, E., Radiology
HERRMANN, R. B., Geophysics, Earth and Atmospheric Sciences
HITCHCOCK, J. F., History
HOMAN, S. M., Community Health
HOOVER, R. G., Pathology
HORVATH, F. L., Physician Assistant Education
HOWARD, A. J., Law
HRUBETZ, J., Nursing
HUANG, J. S., Biochemistry and Molecular Biology
HUGHES, H. M., Psychology
JANNEY, C. G., Pathology
JENNINGS, J. P., Accounting
JOHNSON, F. E., Surgery
JOHNSON, R. G., Surgery
JOHNSON, S. H., Law
JOHNSON, T. H., Modern Languages
JOIST, J. H., Pathology
JOS, C. J., Psychiatry and Human Behaviour
KALLIONGIS, J. E., Mathematics and Mathematical Computer Science
KAMINSKI, D. L., Surgery
KAO, M. S., Obstetrics and Gynaecology
KARUNAMOORTHY, S. N., Aerospace and Mechanical Engineering
KATZ, B. M., Research Methodology
KATZ, J. A., Management
KAUFMAN, N. H., Law
KAVANAUGH, J. F., Philosophy
KEENAN, W. J., Paediatrics
KEITHLEY, J. P., Accounting
KELLOGG, R. T., Psychology
KENNEDY, D. J., Internal Medicine
KERN, M. J., Internal Medicine
KIM, S. H., Finance
KIM, Y. S., Pharmacological and Physiological Sciences
KIMMEY, J. R., Community Health
KLEIN, C., Biochemistry and Molecular Biology
KNUEPFER, M. M., Pharmacological and Physiological Sciences
KNUTSEN, A. P., Paediatrics
KOLMER, E., American Studies
KORN, J. H., Psychology
KORNBLUTH, J., Pathology
KOWERT, B. A., Chemistry
KRAMER, T. J., Psychology
KURZ, R. S., Health Administration
KWAK, N. K., Decision Sciences and MIS
KWON, I. W., Decision Sciences and MIS
LABOVITZ, A. J., Internal Medicine
LAGUNOFF, D., Pathology
LANE, B. C., Theological Studies
LANG, J. M., Psychiatry and Human Behaviour
LECHNER, A. J., Pharmacological and Physiological Sciences
LEGUEY-FEILLEUX, J. R., Political Science
LEIPPE, M. R., Psychology
LEVARY, R. R., Decision Sciences and MIS
LEWIS, J. E., Law

LIN, Y. J., Meteorology, Earth and Atmospheric Sciences
LIU, M.-S., Pharmacological and Physiological Sciences
LOMPERIS, T. J., Political Science
LONGO, W. E., Surgery
LONIGRO, A. J., Internal Medicine
LUISIRI, A., Radiology
LYNCH, R. E., Paediatrics
McCLURE, H. L., Aviation Science
McGOWAN, J. R., Accounting
McGUIRE, R. A., Communication Sciences and Disorders
McLEOD, F. G., Theological Studies
McSWEENEY, M., Nursing Research
MAGILL, G., Health Care Ethics
MALONE, L. J., Jr, Chemistry
MANCINI, M. J., American Studies
MANOR, D., Aerospace and Mechanical Engineering
MARGOLIS, R. B., Psychiatry and Human Behaviour
MARSKE, C. E., Sociology
MARTIN, D. S., Radiology
MARTIN, K. J., Internal Medicine
MATTFELDT-BEMAN, M., Nutrition and Dietetics
MATUSCHAK, G. M., Internal Medicine
MAYDEN, R. L., Biology
MEDOFF, J., Biology
MENGEL, M. B., Community and Family Medicine
METHENY, N. A., Adult and Gerontological Nursing
MEYER, A. E., Communication
MILLER, D. D., Internal Medicine
MILLER, D. K., Internal Medicine
MILLER, S. W., Marketing
MITCHELL, B. J., Geophysics, Earth and Atmospheric Sciences
MOBERG, T. F., Research Methodology
MODRAS, R. E., Theological Studies
MOISAN, T. E., English
MONTELEONE, J. A., Paediatrics
MONTELEONE, P. L., Paediatrics
MOORADIAN, A. D., Internal Medicine
MOORE, J. T., Meteorology, Earth and Atmospheric Sciences
MOORE, T. L., Internal Medicine
MORLEY, J. E., Internal Medicine
MUNZ, D. C., Psychology
MURDICK, N. L., Educational Studies
MURPHY, D. T., Modern Languages
MURRAY, R. L. E., Mental Health, Family, Community, and Systems Nursing
NAGABHUSHAN, B. L., Aerospace and Mechanical Engineering
NAUNHEIM, K. S., Surgery
NEEDHAM, C. A., Law
NEVINS, F. M., Law
NIKOLAI, R. J., Orthodontics
NOFFSINGER, J. E., Paediatrics
NOGUCHI, A., Paediatrics
O'BRIEN, J. C., Law
O'CONNOR, D. M., Paediatrics
OHAR, J. A., Internal Medicine
OLIVER, J. M., Psychology
ORDOWER, H. M., Law
O'TOOLE, M. L., Obstetrics and Gynaecology
PADBERG, W. H., Social Work
PALETTA, C. E., Surgery
PANNETON, W. M., Anatomy and Neurobiology
PARKER, G. E., Management
PAULY, J. J., Communication
PERMAN, W. H., Radiology
PERRY, E. I., History
PERRY, H. M., Internal Medicine
PERRY, L. C., History
PERRY, S. A., Adult and Gerontological Nursing
PETERSON, G. J., Surgery
PETRUSKA, P. J., Internal Medicine
PIERRON, R. L., Orthopaedic Surgery
POLLARD, C. A., Community and Family Medicine

PUNZO, V. C., Philosophy
PURO, S., Political Science
RAHMAN, H., Electrical Engineering
RANA, W.-U.-Z., Anatomy and Neurobiology
RAO, G. V., Earth and Atmospheric Sciences
RAO, P. S., Paediatrics
RAVINDRA, K., Aerospace and Mechanical Engineering
RAY, R., Internal Medicine
REBORE, R. W., Educational Leadership and Higher Education
REESE, C., Mental Health, Family, Community and Systems Nursing
REIMERS, H. J., Internal Medicine
RENARD, G. J., Jr, Theological Studies
ROHLIK, J., Law
ROMEIS, J. C., Health Services Research
ROSS, M. J., Psychology
ROY, T. S., Radiation Oncology
RUCKDESCHEL, R. A., Social Work
RUDDY, T. M., History
RUH, M. F., Pharmacological and Physiological Sciences
RUH, T. S., Pharmacological and Physiological Sciences
RYERSE, J. S., Pathology
SALIMI, Z., Radiology
SALINAS-MADRIGAL, L., Pathology
SALSICH, P. W., Jr, Law
SAMSON, W. K., Pharmacological and Physiological Sciences
SANCHEZ, J. M., History
SANTHANAM, T. S., Physics
SCALZO, A. J., Paediatrics
SCHLAFLY, D. L., Jr, History
SCHMITZ, H. H., Health Administration
SCHMITZ, P. G., Internal Medicine
SCHULZE, I. T., Molecular Microbiology and Immunology
SCOTT, J. F., English
SEITZ, N. E., Finance
SELHORST, J. B., Neurology
SEVERSON, J. G., Jr, Biology
SHANER, M. C., Management
SHAPIRO, M. J., Surgery
SHEA, W. M., Theological Studies
SHIELDS, J. B., Radiology
SHIPPEY, T. A., English
SILBERSTEIN, M. J., Radiology
SILVERBERG, A. B., Internal Medicine
SLAVIN, R. G., Internal Medicine
SLY, W. S., Biochemistry and Molecular Biology
SMITH, G. S., Surgery
SMITH, K., Jr, Surgery
SOTELO-AVILA, C., Pathology
SPAZIANO, V. T., Chemistry
SPRAGUE, R. S., Internal Medicine
STACEY, L. M., Physics
STANTON, C. M., Educational Leadership and Higher Education
STARK, W., Biology
STEINHARDT, G. F., Urology, Surgery
STEVENS, T. C., Mathematics and Mathematical Computer Science
STOEBERL, P. A., Management
STOLZER, A. J., Aviation Science
STRATMAN, H. G., Internal Medicine
STRETCH, J. J., Social Work
STUMP, D. V., English
STUMP, E. A., Philosophy
SWANSTROM, T., Public Policy Studies
SWIERKOSZ, E. M., Pathology
TAIT, R. C., Psychiatry and Human Behaviour
TAN, Y., Anatomy and Neurobiology
TERRY, N., Law
THACKER, W. D., Physics
THOMAS, C. W., Biomedical Engineering
THOMAS, D. R., Internal Medicine
TOCE, S. S., Paediatrics
TOLBERT, D. L., Anatomy and Neurobiology
TOMAZIC, T. J., Research Methodology
TREADGOLD, W., History
TRUE, W. R., Community Health

TSAU, C. M., Mathematics and Mathematical Computer Science
TUCHLER, D. J., Law
ULTMANN, M. H., Paediatrics
VAGO, S., Sociology
VAN DER BERG, S., English
VIRGO, K. S., Surgery
VOGLER, C. A., Pathology
VOGLER, G. A., Comparative Medicine
WACKER, W. D., Mathematics and Mathematical Computer Science
WALENTIK, C. A., Paediatrics
WARREN, K. F., Political Science
WATSON, S., Law
WEBB, K., Community and Family Medicine
WEBER, T. R., Surgery
WEBSTER, R. O., Internal Medicine
WEINBERGER, A. M., Law
WEIXLMANN, J., English
WELCH, P. J., Economics
WERNET, S. P., Social Work
WESTFALL, T. C., Pharmacological and Physiological Sciences
WHITING, R. B., Internal Medicine
WHITMAN, B., Paediatrics
WILLIAMS, D. R., Law
WILLMORE, L. J., Jr, Neurology
WINN, H. N., Obstetrics and Gynaecology
WOLD, W. S. M., Molecular Microbiology and Immunology
WOLINSKY, F. D., Health Administration
WOLVERSON, M. K., Radiology
WONGSURAWAT, N., Internal Medicine
WOOD, E. G., Paediatrics
WOOD, T. T., Art and Art History
YEAGER, F., Finance
YOUNG, P. A., Anatomy and Neurobiology
ZAHM, D. S., Anatomy and Neurobiology
ZASSENHAUS, H. P., Molecular Microbiology and Immunology
ZENSER, T. V., Internal Medicine

SAINT PAUL SCHOOL OF THEOLOGY

5123 E Truman Rd, Kansas City, MO 64127
Telephone: (816) 483-9600
E-mail: admiss@spst.edu
Internet: www.spst.edu
Private control
Campus at Oklahoma City (Oklahoma)
Pres.: Dr MYRON F. MCCOY
Vice-Pres. for Academic Affairs and Dean: Prof. DON COMPIER
Vice-Pres. for Advancement: JIM OMAN
Dir for Admissions: LEE JOHNSON
Registrar: BRENDA BARROWS
Dir for Library and Information Services: LOGAN S. WRIGHT
Library of 100,000 vols, 500 journals
Number of teachers: 40
Number of students: 280

SCHOOL OF PROFESSIONAL PSYCHOLOGY AT FOREST INSTITUTE

2885 W Battlefield, Springfield, MO 65807-3952
Telephone: (417) 823-3477
Internet: www.forest.edu
Founded 1979
Private control
Pres.: Dr MARK SKRADE
Vice-Pres. for Academic Affairs: BRIAN NEDWEK
Vice-Pres. for Enrolment Services: DAWN MEDLEY
Registrar: CAROLYN SMITH
Library Services Man.: RENEE MCHENRY
Library of 5,500 vols, 208 journals and newspapers, 440 video cassettes
Number of students: 300

SOUTHEAST MISSOURI STATE UNIVERSITY

One University Plaza, Cape Girardeau, MO 63701
Telephone: (314) 651-2000
Internet: www.semo.edu
Founded 1873
State control
Pres.: Dr KENNETH W. DOBBINS
Provost: Dr RONALD ROSATI
Vice-Pres. for Admin. and Enrolment Management: DENNIS HOLT
Vice-Pres. for Univ. Advancement: WAYNE SMITH
Registrar: SANDRA L. HINKLE
Dir of Library: Dr DAVID STARRETT
Library of 430,000 vols, 287,000 govt docs, 2,000 magazines and journals, 1.2m. microforms
Number of teachers: 400
Number of students: 10,100

DEANS

College of Education: Dr TAMELA RANDOLPH
College of Health and Human Services: LORETTA PRATER
College of Liberal Arts: Dr FRANK BARRIOS
College of Science and Mathematics: Dr CHRIS MCGOWAN
Donald L. Harrison College of Business: Dr GERALD MCDOUGALL
School of Extended Learning: GERALD S. MCDOUGALL
School of Graduate Studies: Dr BILL EDDLEMAN
School of Polytechnic Studies: Dr CHRIS MCGOWAN
School of University Studies and Academic Information Services: DAVID STARRETT

SOUTHWEST BAPTIST UNIVERSITY

1600 University Ave, Bolivar, MO 65613
Telephone: (417) 328-5281
E-mail: admitme@sbuniv.edu
Internet: www.sbuniv.edu
Founded 1878 as Southwest Baptist College, present name 1981
Private control
Campuses at Mountain View, Salem, Springfield (Missouri)
Pres.: Dr C. PAT TAYLOR
Provost: Dr WILLIAM BROWN
Vice-Pres. for Admin.: RON MAUPIN
Vice-Pres. for Enrolment Management: Dr STEPHANIE MILLER
Vice-Pres. for Information and Technology Services: Dr BOB MCGLASSON
Vice-Pres. for Univ. Relations: Dr R. STANTON NORMAN
Dean for Students: ROB HARRIS
Registrar: JOHN CREDILLE
Dean for Library Services: EDWARD W. WALTON (acting)
Library of 129,000 vols
Number of teachers: 110
Number of students: 3,600
Publication: SBU Life

DEANS

College of Business and Computer Science: Dr KENNETH E. BANDY
College of Education and Social Science: Dr LINDA WOODERSON
College of Science and Mathematics: Dr PERRY A. TOMPKINS
Courts Redford College of Theology and Min.: Dr RODNEY REEVES
Geneva Casebolt College of Music, Arts and Letters: JEFFERY WATERS
St John's College of Nursing and Health Sciences: Dr MARTHA BAKER

STEPHENS COLLEGE

1200 E Broadway, Columbia, MO 65215
Telephone: (573) 442-2211
E-mail: info@stephens.edu
Internet: www.stephens.edu
Founded 1833
Private control
Academic year: August to May
Pres.: Dr DIANNE LYNCH
Vice-Pres. for Academic Affairs: NANCY CORNWELL
Vice-Pres. for Enrolment Management: CHRIS COLLIER
Vice-Pres. for Finance and Admin.: LINDI OVERTON
Vice-Pres. for Student Services: DEB DUREN
Registrar: LINDA SHARP
Library Dir: CORRIE HUTCHISON
Library of 134,672 vols
Number of teachers: 55 (full-time)
Number of students: 865

DEANS

Liberal Arts: MIMI HEDGES
School of Design and Fashion: MONICA MCMURRY
School of Performing Arts: Prof. BETH LEONARD

TRUMAN STATE UNIVERSITY

100 E Normal, Kirksville, MO 63501
Telephone: (660) 785-4000
E-mail: admissions@truman.edu
Internet: www.truman.edu
Founded 1867 as North Missouri Normal School and Commercial College, present name 1996
State control
Academic year: August to May
Pres.: Dr TROY D. PAINO
Provost and Vice-Pres. for Academic Affairs: RICHARD COUGHLIN
Registrar: MARGARET HERRON
Dean for Libraries: RICHARD COUGHLIN
Library of 335,144 vols, 7,283 spec. collns vol, 2,237 vols of archives, 3,860 rare books
Number of teachers: 360
Number of students: 6,090 (5,600 undergraduate, 250 graduate, 240 int.)
Publications: Detours (2 a year), Truman Review (3 a year, print and online, alumni.truman.edu/trumanreview), Windfall (1 a year)

DEANS

School of Arts and Letters: Dr PRISCILLA RIGGLE
School of Business: Dr DEBRA KERBY
School of Health Sciences and Education: Dr JANET L. GOOCH
School of Science and Mathematics: Dr JONATHAN GERING
School of Social and Cultural Studies: Dr DOUG DAVENPORT

UNIVERSITY OF CENTRAL MISSOURI

POB 800, Warrensburg, MO 64093
Telephone: (660) 543-4111
E-mail: admit@ucmo.edu
Internet: www.ucmo.edu
Founded 1871, present name and status 2006
State control
Academic year: August to May
Pres.: Dr CHARLES M. AMBROSE
Provost: Dr GEORGE WILSON
Vice-Provost for Enrolment Management: Dr RICHARD D. SLUDER
Vice-Pres. for Admin. and Finance: JOHN F. MERRIGAN

Vice-Pres. for Univ. Advancement: Dr JASON S. DRUMMOND
Gen. Counsel: HANK SETSER
Dir for Admissions: ANN E. NORDYKE
Registrar: TERI BOWMAN
Dean for Library Services: MOLLIE DINWIDDIE
Library: 2m. vols, 2,500 newspaper and periodical subscriptions, 829,100 microforms
Number of teachers: 450
Number of students: 11,350 (2,182 graduate, 9,168 undergraduate)

DEANS

College of Arts, Humanities and Social Sciences: Dr GERSHAM NELSON
College of Education: Dr MICHAEL WRIGHT
College of Health and Human Services: Dr RICHARD SLUDER
College of Health, Science and Technology: Dr ALICE GREIFE
Harmon College of Business Administration: Dr ROGER J. BEST
Honors College: JOSEPH D. LEWANDOWSKI
School of Graduate and Extended Studies: Dr JOSEPH VAUGHN

UNIVERSITY OF MISSOURI SYSTEM

Columbia, MO 65211
Telephone: (573) 882-2011
E-mail: mu4u@missouri.edu
Internet: www.umsystem.edu
Founded 1839
State control
Pres.: STEPHEN J. OWENS
Sr Assoc. Vice-Pres. for Academic Affairs: Dr STEVEN W. GRAHAM
Vice-Pres. for Finance and Admin.: NATALIE KRAWITZ
Vice-Pres. for Govt Relations: STEPHEN C. KNORR
Vice-Pres. for Human Resources: ELIZABETH RODRIGUEZ
Vice-Pres. for Information Technology: Dr GARY K. ALLEN
Vice-Pres. for Research and Economic Devt: Dr MICHAEL F. NICHOLS
Library: see Libraries and Archives
Number of teachers: 7,814
Number of students: 71,596 ...

CONSTITUENT CAMPUSES

University of Missouri—Columbia

104 Jesse Hall, Columbia, MO 65211
Telephone: (573) 882-7881
E-mail: mu4u@missouri.edu
Internet: www.missouri.edu
Founded 1839
Academic year: August to May
Chancellor: STEVE OWENS
Provost: BRIAN FOSTER (acting)
Vice-Provost for Enrolment Management: ANN KORSCHGEN
Vice-Chancellor for Admin. Services: JACQUELYN JONES
Vice-Chancellor for Devt and Alumni Relations: THOMAS HILES
Vice-Chancellor for Research: ROBERT DUNCAN
Vice-Chancellor for Student Affairs: CATHY SCROGGS
Registrar: BRENDA SELMAN
Dir for Admissions: BARBARA RUPP
Library of 3,612,144 vols, 7.5m. microforms, 1.7m. govt documents and 53,394 journals
Number of teachers: 2,070
Number of students: 33,805

DEANS

College of Agriculture, Food and Natural Resources: THOMAS PAYNE

College of Arts and Sciences: MICHAEL O'BRIEN
College of Business: JOAN GABEL
College of Education: DANIEL CLAY
College of Engineering: JAMES E. THOMPSON
College of Human Environmental Sciences: STEPHEN JORGENSEN
College of Veterinary Medicine: NEIL OLSON
Graduate School: GEORGE JUSTICE
School of Health Professions: RICHARD OLIVER
School of Journalism: DEAN MILLS (acting)
School of Law: R. LAWRENCE DESSEM
School of Medicine: ROBERT CHURCHILL
School of Nursing: JUDITH FITZGERALD MILLER

University of Missouri—Kansas City

301 Admin. Center, 5100 Rockhill Rd, Kansas City, MO 64110-2499
301 Admin. Center, 5115 Oak St, Kansas City, MO 64112
Telephone: (816) 235-1101
E-mail: umkcchancellor@umkc.edu
Internet: www.umkc.edu
Founded 1929
Academic year: August to July
Chancellor: LEO E. MORTON
Exec. Vice-Chancellor and Provost: Dr GAIL HACKETT
Vice-Chancellor for Finance and Admin. Affairs: SHARON LINDENBAUM
Vice-Chancellor for Student Affairs: MELVIN C. TYLER
Vice-Chancellor for Univ. Advancement: CURT CRESPINO
Dir for Admissions: DORETTA KIDD (acting)
Registrar: DOUG SWINK
Dean for Libraries: Dr SHARON L. BOSTICK
Library of 1,313,266 vols, 1,459,439 microforms, 202,156 ebooks, 129,943 vol govt publs, 7,523 video cassettes and DVDs
Number of teachers: 1,885
Number of students: 15,145

DEANS

College of Arts and Sciences: WAYNE VAUGHT
Conservatory of Music and Dance: PETER WITTE
Henry W. Bloch School of Management: Dr TENG-KEE TAN
School of Biological Sciences: LAWRENCE DREYFUS
School of Computing and Engineering: KEVIN Z. TRUMAN
School of Dentistry: MARSHA A. PYLE
School of Education: Dr WANDA J. BLANCHETT
School of Graduate Studies: Dr DENIS M. MEDEIROS
School of Law: ELLEN SUNI
School of Medicine: BETTY M. DREES
School of Nursing: Dr LORA LACEY-HAUN
School of Pharmacy: Dr RUSSELL B. MELCHERT

Missouri University of Science and Technology

106 Parker Hall, 300 W 13th St, Rolla, MO 65409-1060
Telephone: (573) 341-4114
E-mail: admissions@mst.edu
Internet: www.mst.edu
Founded 1870, fmrly Univ. of Missouri-Rolla, present name and status 2008
Academic year: August to July
Divs of arts and humanities, business and social sciences, engineering, sciences and computing
Chancellor: WARREN K. WRAY
Provost and Exec. Vice-Chancellor for Academic Affairs: ROBERT W. SCHWARTZ
Vice-Provost and Dean for Enrolment Management: LAURA K. STOLL
Vice-Chancellor for Admin. Services: F. STEPHEN MALOTT

Vice-Chancellor for Student Affairs: Dr DEBRA ROBINSON
Vice-Chancellor for Univ. Advancement: JOAN NESBITT
Registrar: DEANNE JACKSON
Library Dir: ANDREW STEWART
Library of 388,000 vols
Number of teachers: 500 (400 full-time, 100 part-time)
Number of students: 7,500 (5,650 undergraduate, 1,850 graduate)
Publication: *Missouri S&T*

University of Missouri—St Louis

1 University Blvd, St Louis, MO 63121-4400
Telephone: (314) 516-5000
E-mail: admissions@umsl.edu
Internet: www.umsl.edu
Founded 1963
Academic year: August to July
Chancellor: Prof. Dr THOMAS F. GEORGE
Provost and Vice-Chancellor for Academic Affairs: Prof. GLEN H. COPE
Vice-Chancellor for Managerial and Technological Services: Prof. Dr JAMES M. KRUEGER
Vice-Chancellor for Univ. Advancement: MARTIN F. LEIFELD
Vice-Provost for Research: Prof. NASSAR ARSHADI
Vice-Provost for Student Affairs: CURTIS C. COONROD
Dean of Enrolment: ALAN BYRD
Dir for Admissions: JERRY HOFFMAN
Registrar: DIANA JOHNSON
Dean for Libraries: CHRISTOPHER R. DAMES
Library: 1.25m. vols, 1.2m. govt documents, 1.3m. microfilm units, 4,030 audiovisual units, 21,945 ebooks
Number of teachers: 1,040
Number of students: 16,440
Publications: *Theory and Society Journal*, *UMSL Magazine* (2 a year)

DEANS

College of Arts and Sciences: RONALD YASBIN
College of Business Administration: CHARLES HOFFMAN
College of Education: Dr CAROL BAISLE
College of Fine Arts and Communication: JEAN MILLER
College of Nursing: Dr SUSAN DEAN-BAAR
College of Optometry: LARRY J. DAVIS
School of Professional and Continuing Studies: WILLIAM T. WALKER
Graduate School: JUDITH WALKER DE FELIX
Pierre Laclede Honours College: Dr ROBERT M. BLISS
UMSL/WU Joint Undergraduate Engineering Program: Dr BERNARD FELDMAN

PROFESSORS

ALTHOF, W., Educational Psychology
ANDERSON, K. C., Art and Art History
BAHAR, S., Physics and Astronomy
BASHKIN, J. K., Chemistry
BEATTY, A. M., Chemistry
BENNETT, E. S., College of Optometry
BERKOWITZ, M. W., Educational Psychology
BOHAN, R. L., Art and Art History
BREAUGH, J., Business Administration
BROWNELL, S. E., Anthropology
BURKHOLDER, M. A., History
BURSIK JR, R. J., Criminology and Criminal Justice
CAMPBELL, J. F., Business Administration
CARROLL, J. C., English
CHAKRABORTY, U. K., Mathematics and Computer Science
CHICKOS, J., Chemistry
CHUI, C., Mathematics and Computer Science
COCHRAN, J. A., Educational Leadership and Policy

COKER, A. A., Theatre and Dance
COOK, R. M., English
COSMOPOULOS, M., Anthropology
COTTONE, R. R., Counselling-College Of Education
DEMCHENKO, A., Chemistry
DIBOOGLU, S., Economics
DING, C. S., Educational Psychology
DUPUREUR, C. M., Chemistry
EBEST, S. B., English
ESBENSEN, F. A., Criminology and Criminal Justice
EVEN, Y., Art and Art History
EYSSELL, T. H., Business Administration
FEIGENBAUM, S. K., Economics
FERNLUND, K., History
FLORES, R. A., Physics and Astronomy
FUNG, H. G., Business Administration
GERTEIS, L. S., History
GILLMAN, M. K., Economics
GOKEL JR, G. W., Chemistry
GRADY, F. W., English
GRANGER, C. R., Biology
GROS, J. G., Political Science
HARBACH, B. C., Music
HARRIS, W. R., Chemistry
HENSON, B. L., Physics and Astronomy
HURLEY, A., History
IYOB, R., Political Science
JIANG, Q., Mathematics and Computer Science
JOSHI, K., Business Administration
KELLOGG, E. A., Biology
KIMBALL, D. C., Political Science
KOPETZ, P. B., Early Childhood, Elementary, TESOL and Special Education
KYLE JR, W. C., Early Childhood, Elementary, TESOL and Special Education
LACITY, M. C., Business Administration
LANKFORD, E. L., Art and Art History
LAURITSEN, J. L., Criminology and Criminal Justice
LAWRENCE, E. C., Business Administration
MACAN, T. H., Psychology
MARQUIS, R. J., Biology
MARTINICH, J. S., Business Administration
MCGINNIS, J. D., Philosophy
MCPHAIL, T. L., Theatre and Dance
MILLER, K. W., Secondary and K-12 Education
MILLER, L. A., Anthropology
MOEHRLE, S. R., Business Administration
MUNDY, R. A., Business Administration
MURRAY, J. Y., Business Administration
MURRAY, M. D., Theatre and Dance
MUSHABEN, J. M., Political Science
NAUSS, R. M., Business Administration
O'BRIEN, J. J., Chemistry
PARKER, P. G., Biology
PAUL, R. H., Psychology
PEDERSON, B. B., Philosophy
POPE, M. L., Counselling-College Of Education
RAO, P. A., Mathematics and Computer Science
RECORDS, K. A., College Of Nursing
RICHARDS JR, J. E., Music
RICHARDSON JR, L. I., Early Childhood, Elementary, TESOL and Special Education
RICKLEFS, R. E., Biology
ROBERTSON, D. B., Political Science
ROCHESTER, J., Political Science
ROGERS, R. L., Early Childhood, Elementary, TESOL and Special Education
RONEN, D., Business Administration
ROSE, D. C., Economics
ROSENFELD, R. B., Criminology and Criminal Justice
ROSS, S. A., Philosophy
ROWAN, S. W., History
SAUL, E. W., Secondary and K-12 Education
SAUTER, V. L., Business Administration
SCHWANTES, C. A., History
SEGAL, U. A., Social Work
SHERRADEN, M. S., Social Work
SHYMANSKY, J. A., Early Chidlhood

SMITH, L. D., Business Administration
SPILLING, C., Chemistry
STEVENS, P. F., Biology
STINE, K., Chemistry
SWANSTROM, T. F., Political Science
TAYLOR, G. T., Psychology
THOMAS, K. P., Political Science
TOULIATOS, D. H., Music
TROY, M., English
TSE, Y., Business Administration
VANDENBERG, B. R., Psychology
VATTEROTT, C., Secondary and K-12 Education
WALL, E. W., English
WANG, X., Biology
WILKING, B. A., Physics and Astronomy
WILLIAMS, L. V., Foreign Languages and Literature
WINKLER, A. E., Economics
WOMER, N. K., Business Administration
WRIGHT, R. T., Criminology and Criminal Justice
YOUNGER, D., Art and Art History
ZARUCCHI, J. M., Art and Art History
ZIMMERMAN, R. S., College of Nursing

WASHINGTON UNIVERSITY IN SAINT LOUIS

Campus Box 1089, One Brookings Dr., Saint Louis, MO 63130-4899

Telephone: (314) 935-6000
E-mail: admissions@wustl.edu
Internet: www.wustl.edu

Founded 1853 as Eliot Seminary, current name adopted 1857

Private control

Academic year: August to May

Chancellor: Prof. Dr MARK S. WRIGHTON
Provost and Exec. Vice-Chancellor for Academic Affairs: HOLDEN H. THORP
Exec. Vice-Chancellor and Gen. Counsel: MICHAEL R. CANNON
Exec. Vice-Chancellor for Admin.: HENRY S. WEBBER
Exec. Vice-Chancellor for Alumni and Devt: DAVID T. BLASINGAME
Exec. Vice-Chancellor for Medical Affairs: LARRY J. SHAPIRO
Vice-Chancellor for Finance: BARBARA A. FEINER
Vice-Chancellor for Govt and Community Relations: PAMELA S. LOKKEN
Vice-Chancellor for Human Resources: LORRAINE A. GOFFE-RUSH
Vice-Chancellor for Public Affairs: JILL D. FRIEDMAN
Vice-Chancellor for Research: EVAN D. KHARASCH
Vice-Chancellor for Students: SHARON STAHL
Number of teachers: 1,220 (888 full-time, 332 part-time)
Number of students: 14,030 (11,149 full-time, 2,881 part-time)

Publication: *Washington Magazine* (6 a year)

DEANS

Faculty of Arts and Sciences: BARBARA A. SCHAAL
George Warren Brown School of Social Work: EDWARD F. LAWLOR
Graduate School of Arts and Sciences: WILLIAM F. TATE
Olin Business School: MAHENDRA R. GUPTA
Sam Fox School of Design and Visual Arts: CARMON COLANGELO
School of Engineering and Applied Science: RALPH S. QUATRANO
School of Law: NANCY C. STAUDT
School of Medicine: LARRY J. SHAPIRO

WEBSTER UNIVERSITY

470 E Lockwood Ave, St Louis, MO 63119-3194

Telephone: (314) 968-6900
E-mail: admissions@webster.edu
Internet: www.webster.edu

Founded 1915, present name and status 1983

Private control

Academic year: August to May

Chancellor: NEIL J. GEORGE
Pres.: Dr ELIZABETH J. STROBLE
Provost and Sr Vice-Pres.: JULIAN Z. SCHUSTER
Vice-Pres. for Enrolment Management and Student Affairs: PAUL CARNEY
Vice-Pres. for Devt and Alumni Programmes: FAITH D. MADDY
Vice-Pres. and Interim Chief Information Officer: KENNETH FREEMAN
Registrar: DON MORRIS
Dean for Univ. Library: EILEEN CONDON

Library of 299,000 vols
Number of teachers: 2,700 (920 full-time, 1,780 part-time)
Number of students: 22,000

DEANS

College of Arts and Sciences: DAVID CARL WILSON
George Herbert Walker School of Business and Technology: Dr BENJAMIN OLA AKANDE
Leigh Gerdine College of Fine Arts: PETER SARGENT
School of Communications: DEBRA CARPENTER
School of Education: BRENDA FYFE

WESTMINSTER COLLEGE

Fulton, MO 65251

Telephone: (573) 592-6241
E-mail: westminster@westminster-mo.edu
Internet: www.westminster-mo.edu

Founded 1851 as Fulton College, present name 1853

Private control

Academic year: August to May

Divs of humanities, natural and mathematical sciences, social sciences

Pres.: Dr GEORGE B. FORSYTHE
Vice-Pres. and Chief Information Officer: SCOTT LOWE
Vice-Pres. and Dean for Enrolment Services: GEORGE WOLF
Vice-Pres. and Dean for Student Life: Dr STEPHANIE KRAUTH
Vice-Pres. and Dir for Churchill Institute: ROB HAVERS
Vice-Pres. for Academic Affairs and Dean for Faculty: Dr CAROLYN PERRY
Vice-Pres. for Institutional Advancement: JOHN COMERFORD
Registrar: PHYLLIS MASEK
Dir for Library Services: ANGELA GERLING
Library of 121,073 vols
Number of teachers: 70
Number of students: 1,100

WILLIAM JEWELL COLLEGE

500 College Hill, Liberty, MO 64068

Telephone: (816) 781-7700
E-mail: admission@william.jewell.edu
Internet: www.jewell.edu

Founded 1849

Private control

Academic year: September to May

Liberal arts college

Pres.: DAVID L. SALLEE
Provost: ANNE C. DEMA
Vice-Pres. for Academic Affairs and Dean: TIMOTHY E. FULOP

Vice-Pres. for Enrolment and Student Affairs: Dr RICHARD P. WINSLOW
Vice-Pres. for Finance and Operations: BRIAN CLEMONS
Vice-Pres. for Institutional Advancement: Dr CHAD J. JOLLY
Registrar: ED LANE
Systems Librarian: STEVEN BAILEY
Library of 260,119 vols
Number of teachers: 130
Number of students: 1,500
Publication: *Achieve Magazine*

WILLIAM WOODS UNIVERSITY

1 University Ave, Fulton, MO 65251
Telephone: (573) 642-2251
E-mail: admissions@williamwoods.edu
Internet: www.williamwoods.edu

Founded 1870 Female Orphan School, current name and status 1993
Private control
Academic year: August to May

Divs of arts and humanities, behavioural and social sciences, business and economics, education, equestrian studies, human performance, mathematics, science; campuses at Blue Springs, Columbia, Jefferson City (Missouri)
Pres.: Prof. Dr JAHNAE H. BARNETT
Vice-Pres.: SCOTT T. GALLAGHER
Vice-Pres. and Dean for Academic Affairs: Prof. Dr SHERRY MCCARTHY
Vice-Pres. and Dean for Graduate College: Prof. MICHAEL WESTERFIELD
Vice-Pres. for Admin.: KATHY GROVES
Dean for Admissions: SARAH MUNNS
Dean for Education: Prof. Dr DOUG EBERSOLE
Dean for Online Education: Prof. Dr ROGER WEN
Dean for Student Life: Dr VENITA MITCHELL
Registrar: TARA EMERSON
Library Dir: ERLENE DUDLEY
Library of 160,000 vols
Number of teachers: 350 (50 full-time, 300 part-time)
Number of students: 3,200

MONTANA

CARROLL COLLEGE

1601 N Benton Ave, Helena, MT 59625
Telephone: (406) 447-4300
Internet: www.carroll.edu
Founded 1909
Private control
Academic year: August to May
Pres.: Dr THOMAS EVANS
Vice-Pres. for Finance and Admin.: LORI PETERSON
Vice-Pres. for Institutional Advancement: TOM MCCARVEL
Vice-Pres. for Student Life: Dr JIM D. HARDWICK
Academic Dean: JOHN SCHARF
Registrar: CATHERINE DAY
Library Dir: CHRISTIAN FRAZZA
Library of 85,000 vols, 2,000 titles, 150 periodicals, 90,000 monographs
Number of teachers: 85
Number of students: 1,500

CHIEF DULL KNIFE COLLEGE

POB 98, Lame Deer, MT 59043
Telephone: (406) 477-6215
Internet: www.cdkc.edu
Founded 1975, fmrly known as Dull Knife Memorial College, present name 2001
Tribal control
Academic year: August to May

Pres.: Dr RICHARD LITTLEBEAR
Vice-Pres.: WILLIAM WERTMAN
Dean for Academic Affairs: MICHELE CURLEE
Dean for Student Affairs: ZANE SPANG
Library of 24,688 vols

MONTANA STATE UNIVERSITY

POB 172000, 100 Culbertson Hall, Bozeman, MT 59717-2000
Telephone: (406) 994-0211
E-mail: president@montana.edu
Internet: www.montana.edu
Founded 1893
Pres.: Dr WADED CRUZADO
Provost and Vice-Pres. for Academic Affairs: Dr MARTHA A. POTVIN
Vice-Pres. for Admin. and Finance: TERRY LEIST
Vice-Pres. for Research, Creativity and Technology Transfer: THOMAS MCCOY
Vice-Pres. for Student Success: Dr ALLEN YARNELL
Dean for Students: MATTHEW CAIRES
Dean for Libraries: TAMARA MILLER
Dir for Admissions: RONDA RUSSELL
Library of 34,000 vols, 1,200 linear ft MSS materials
Number of teachers: 850 (595 full-time, 255 part-time)
Number of students: 14,155

DEANS

College of Agriculture: JEFF JACOBSEN
College of Arts and Architecture: JOSEPH FEDOCK
College of Business: SUSAN DANA
College of Education, Health and Human Development: LARRY BAKER
College of Engineering: BRETT GUNNINK
College of Letters and Science: PAULA LUTZ
College of Nursing: HELEN MELLAND
Gallatin College Programs: ROBERT HIETALA
Graduate School: Dr KARLENE A. HOO

MONTANA STATE UNIVERSITY— BILLINGS

1500 Univ. Dr., Billings, MT 59101
Telephone: (406) 657-2011
E-mail: admissions@msubillings.edu
Internet: www.msubillings.edu
Founded 1927 as Eastern Montana College, current name adopted 1995
State control
Academic year: September to May
Chancellor: Dr SHEILA STEARNS
Provost and Academic Vice-Chancellor: Dr MARK PAGANO
Vice-Chancellor for Admin. Services: TERRIE IVERSON
Vice-Chancellor for Student Affairs: Dr STACY KLIPPENSTEIN
Library Dir: BRENT ROBERTS
Library of 281,258 vols
Number of teachers: 342 (150 full-time, 192 part-time)
Number of students: 4,300

DEANS

College of Allied Health Professions: Dr DIANE DUIN
College of Arts & Sciences: Dr TASNEEM KHALEEL
College of Business: Dr TIMOTHY J. WILKINSON
College of Education: Dr MARY SUSAN FISHBAUGH
College of Technology: Dr MARSHA RILEY

MONTANA STATE UNIVERSITY— GREAT FALLS COLLEGE OF TECHNOLOGY

2100 16th Ave S, Great Falls, MT 59405
Telephone: (406) 771-4300
E-mail: information@msugf.edu
Internet: www.msugf.edu
Founded 1969, present name and status 1994; attached to Montana State Univ.
State control
Pres.: WADED CRUZADO
Dean and CEO: Dr GWENDOLYN G. JOSEPH
Exec. Dir for College Relations: PAM PARSONS
Exec. Dir for Institutional Research and Planning: WENDY DOVE
Exec. Dir for Human Resources: MARY KAY BONILLA
Number of teachers: 115 (42 full-time, 73 part-time)
Number of students: 2,570

MONTANA STATE UNIVERSITY— NORTHERN

POB 7751, 300 W 11th St, Havre, MT 59501
Telephone: (406) 265-3700
E-mail: admissions@msun.edu
Internet: www.msun.edu
Founded 1929
State control
Baccalaureate courses in arts and sciences, business, nursing, teacher education, technology; Masters courses in education; br. educational centres in Great Falls and Lewistown
Chancellor: Dr JAMES LIMBAUGH
Provost and Vice-Chancellor for Academic Affairs: Dr WILLIAM RUGG
Dean for Students and Registrar: LINDSEY BROWN
Library Dir: VICKI GIST
Library of 100,000 vols
Number of teachers: 80
Number of students: 1,215

MONTANA TECH

1300 W Park St, Butte, MT 59701
Telephone: (406) 496-4256
E-mail: enrollment@mtech.edu
Internet: www.mtech.edu
Founded 1893; attached to Univ. of Montana
State control
Academic year: June to May
Chancellor: Dr DONALD M. BLACKKETTER
Provost and Vice-Chancellor for Academic Affairs: Dr DOUG M. ABBOTT
Vice-Chancellor for Admin. and Finance: MAGGIE PETERSON
Vice-Chancellor for Devt and Univ. Relations: JOE MCCLAFFERTY
Assoc. Vice-Chancellor for Student Affairs and Dean for Students: PAUL BEATTY
Dir for Enrolment Management: KATHY WILLIAMS
Registrar: KATHY WILLIAMS
Dir for Library: ANN ST CLAIR
Number of teachers: 215
Number of students: 2,820
Publications: *Catalog*, *MNews*, *The Technocrat*

DEANS

College of Letters, Sciences, and Professional Studies: Dr DOUG COE
College of Technology: Dr JOHN M. GARIC
Graduate School: BEVERLY HARTLINE
School of Mines and Engineering: Dr PETER KNUDSEN

ROCKY MOUNTAIN COLLEGE

1511 Poly Dr., Billings, MT 59102-1796

Telephone: (406) 657-1000

E-mail: president@rocky.edu

Internet: www.rocky.edu

Founded 1947 by merger of Deer Lodge (f. 1878), Wesleyan College and Billings Polytechnic Institute

Private control

Academic year: August to May

Pres.: Dr MICHAEL R. MACE (acting)

Vice-Pres. for Academic Affairs: ANTHONY PILTZ

Vice-Pres. for Admissions: KELLY EDWARDS

Vice-Pres. for Advancement: GREG KOHN

Dir of Library: WILLIAM KEHLER

Library of 86,600 vols

Number of teachers: 85 (45 full-time, 40 part-time)

Number of students: 800

Publication: *Rocky Today*

SALISH KOOTENAI COLLEGE

POB 70, Pablo, MT 59855

58138 US Highway 93, Pablo, MT 59855

Telephone: (406) 275-4800

Internet: www.skc.edu

Founded 1976 as br. campus of Flathead Valley Community College, present name and status 1981

Tribal control

Academic year: September to June

Pres.: Dr LUANA ROSS

Academic Vice-Pres.: CARMEN TAYLOR

Vice-Pres. of Business Affairs: (vacant)

Dir for Library: FRED NOEL

UNIVERSITY OF GREAT FALLS

1301 20th St, S, Great Falls, MT 59405

Telephone: (406) 791-5202

E-mail: enroll@ugf.edu

Internet: www.ugf.edu

Founded 1932 as Great Falls Junior College for Women, present name 1995

Private control

Liberal arts college; 4-year and 2-year degree courses in education, human services and professional counselling

Pres.: Dr EUGENE J. MCALLISTER

Provost and Academic Vice-Pres.: Dr RICHARD MCDOWELL

Vice-Pres. for Enrolment Management: CHARLENE BROWN

Vice-Pres. for Finance and Human Resources: STACEY EVE

Vice-Pres. for Philanthropy: TENIS TENNYSON

Dir for Admissions and Records: R. HENSLEY

Information Services Librarian: SUSAN LEE

Registrar: KERRI KOTESKEY

Library of 97,353 vols

Number of teachers: 80

Number of students: 950

UNIVERSITY OF MONTANA

32 Campus Dr., Missoula, MT 59812

Telephone: (406) 243-0211

Internet: www.umt.edu

Founded 1893

Pres.: Dr ROYCE C. ENGSTROM

Provost and Vice-Pres. for Academic Affairs: Dr PERRY J. BROWN

Exec. Vice-Pres.: JAMES P. FOLEY

Vice-Pres. for Admin. and Finance: ROBERT A. DURINGER

Vice-Pres. for Research and Devt: DAVID FORBES

Vice-Pres. for Student Affairs: Dr TERESA BRANCH

Registrar: EDWIN D. JOHNSON

Dean for Students: Dr CHARLES COUTURE

Dean for Libraries: BONNIE ALLEN

Library of 700,000 vols, 77,600 US govt documents

Number of teachers: 450

Number of students: 13,020

DEANS

College of Arts and Sciences: CHRISTOPHER COMER

College of Forestry and Conservation: Dr JAMES BURCHFIELD

College of Health Professions and Biomedical Sciences: Dr VERNON R. GRUND

College of Technology: BARRY GOOD

College of Visual and Performing Arts: STEPHEN KALM

Div. of Continuing Education: SHARON ALEXANDER

Graduate School: STEPHEN SPRANG

Phyllis J. Washington College of Education and Human Sciences: ROBERTA EVANS

School of Business Administration: Dr LARRY D. GIANCHETTA

School of Extended and Lifelong Learning: Dr ROGER MACLEAN

School of Journalism: PEGGY KUHR (acting)

School of Law: Prof. IRMA S. RUSSELL

UNIVERSITY OF MONTANA WESTERN

710 S Atlantic St, Dillon, MT 59725

Telephone: (406) 683-7331

E-mail: admissions@umwestern.edu

Internet: www.umwestern.edu

Founded 1893

State control

Academic year: September to June

Chancellor: Dr RICHARD STOREY

Provost and Vice-Chancellor for Academic Affairs: Dr KARL ULRICH

Asst Provost: DONNA ROUSE

Vice-Chancellor for Admin. and Finance: SUSAN BRIGGS

Dean for Outreach and Research: ANNELIESE RIPLEY

Dean for Students: C. NICOLE HAZELBAKER

Dir for Admissions: CATHERINE REDHEAD

Dir for Devt and Alumni Relations: AMBERLY PAHUT

Registrar: JASON KARCH

Library Dir: MICHAEL SCHULZ

Number of teachers: 50

Number of students: 1,380 (1,185 full-time, 195 part-time)

NEBRASKA

BELLEVUE UNIVERSITY

1000 Galvin Rd S, Bellevue, NE 68005

Telephone: (402) 293-2000

E-mail: servicedesk@bellevue.edu

Internet: www.bellevue.edu

Founded 1966, present name and status 1994

Private control

Campuses in Midwest-Nebraska, Iowa and S Dakota

Pres.: Dr MARY B. HAWKINS

Vice-Pres. for Academic Affairs: DONNA N. MCDANIEL

Dean for Students: MICHELLE EPPLER

Registrar: PHILLIP E. CHAPMAN

Library Dir: ROBIN BERNSTEIN

Library of 105,000 vols

Number of teachers: 60

Number of students: 9,000

Publication: *The View*

DEANS

College of Arts and Sciences: Dr THERESE MICHELS

College of Business: Dr RODERIC HEWLETT

College of Information Technology: MARY DOBRANSKY

College of Professional Studies: Dr MARTHA MUÑOZ

CHADRON STATE COLLEGE

1000 Main St, Chadron, NE 69337

Telephone: (308) 432-6000

E-mail: inquire@csc.edu

Internet: www.csc.edu

Founded 1911

State control

Academic year: August to May (2 semesters)

Pres.: Dr JANIE C. PARK

Vice-Pres. for Academic and Student Affairs: Dr LOIS VEATH

Vice-Pres. for Admin. and Finance: DALE GRANT

Vice-Pres. for Enrolment Management and Student Services: Dr R. RANDY RHINE

Registrar: DALE WILLIAMSON

Library Dir: MILTON WOLF

Library of 200,000 vols

Number of teachers: 100 (full-time)

Number of students: 2,760

DEANS

School of Business, Entrepreneurship, Applied and Mathematical Sciences and Sciences: Dr JOEL R. HYER

School of Education, Human Performance, Counselling, Psychology and Social Work: Dr MARGARET R. CROUSE

School of Liberal Arts: Dr CHARLES E. SNARE

CLARKSON COLLEGE

101 S 42nd St, Omaha, NE 68131-2739

Telephone: (402) 552-3100

E-mail: admiss@clarksoncollege.edu

Internet: www.clarksoncollege.edu

Founded 1884

Private control

Areas of study: nursing and health care administration

Pres.: Dr LOUIS W. BURGHER

Vice-Pres. for Academic Affairs: Dr JODY WOODWORTH

Vice-Pres. for Operations: TONY DAMEWOOD

Dir for Admissions: DENISE WORK

Registrar: MICHELE STIRTZ

Dir for Library Services: NANCY RALSTON

Number of teachers: 30

Number of students: 980

COLLEGE OF SAINT MARY

7000 Mercy Rd, Omaha, NE 68106-2377

Telephone: (402) 399-2400

E-mail: academicaffairs@csm.edu

Internet: www.csm.edu

Founded 1923

Private control

Academic year: August to August

Divs of arts and sciences, health care professions, professional studies, graduate studies; campus in Lincoln (Nebraska)

Pres.: Dr MARYANNE STEVENS

Vice-Pres. for Academic Affairs: Dr CHRISTINE PHARR

Vice-Pres. for Enrolment Services: JOE SZEJK

Vice-Pres. for Finance and Admin.: SARAH KOTTICH

Vice-Pres. for Institutional Advancement: VERLYN SCHUELER

Vice-Pres. for Student Devt: Dr TARA KNUDSON CARL

Registrar: DEBBIE NUGEN

Library Dir: SARAH WILLIAMS

Number of teachers: 55

Number of students: 1,000
Publication: *College of Saint Mary Magazine* (3 a year)

CONCORDIA UNIVERSITY— NEBRASKA

800 N Columbia Ave, Seward, NE 68434
Telephone: (402) 643-3651
E-mail: info@cune.edu
Internet: www.cune.edu

Founded 1894
Private control
Academic year: August to May
Pres. and CEO: Rev. Dr BRIAN L. FRIEDRICH
Provost: Rev. Dr JENNY MUELLER-ROEBKE
Assoc. Provost: Dr LISA ASHBY
Chief Financial Officer: DAVID KUMM
Vice-Pres. for Enrolment Management, Student Services and Athletics: SCOTT SEEVERS
Vice-Pres. for Institutional Advancement: Rev. RICHARD MADDOX
Registrar: EDWIN SIFFRING
Dir for Library Services: PHILIP HENDRICKSON
Library: see Libraries and Archives
Number of teachers: 65
Number of students: 2,200
Publications: *Broadcaster*, *Issues in Christian Education* (3 a year)

DEANS

College of Arts and Sciences: Dr BRENT ROYUK
College of Education: Dr RON BORK

CREIGHTON UNIVERSITY

2500 California Plaza, Omaha, NE 68178
Telephone: (402) 280-2700
E-mail: info@creighton.edu
Internet: www.creighton.edu

Founded 1878, chartered 1879; attached to Soc. of Jesus
Private control
Academic year: August to May
Pres.: TIMOTHY R. LANNON
Vice-Pres. for Academic Affairs: Prof. PATRICK J. BORCHERS
Vice-Pres. for Admin.: JOHN L. WILHELM
Vice-Pres. for Finance: JAN D MADSEN
Vice-Pres. for Health Sciences: DONALD R. FREY
Vice-Pres. for Information Technology: BRIAN A. YOUNG
Vice-Pres. for Student Services and Dean for Students: Dr JOHN C. CERNECH
Vice-Pres. for Univ. Relations: (vacant)
Gen. Counsel: JAMES S. JANSEN
Registrar: PATRICIA GRAFELMAN HALL
Dir for Alumni Memorial Library: MICHAEL J. LACROIX
Library of 916,571 vols, 1.9m. microforms
Number of teachers: 985 (759 full-time, 226 part-time)
Number of students: 7,730
Publications: *Creighton Law Review* (4 a year), *Creighton University Magazine* (4 a year)

DEANS

Arts and Sciences: Dr ROBERT J. LUEGER
Business Administration: Dr ANTHONY R. HENDRICKSON
Dentistry: MARK A. LATTA
Graduate School: GAIL M. JENSEN
Law: Prof. MARIANNE CULHANE
Medicine: ROWEN K. ZETTERMAN
Nursing: Dr ELEANOR V. HOWELL
Pharmacy and Health Professions: J. CHRISTOPHER BRADBERRY
University College: GAIL M. JENSEN

PROFESSORS

ABEL, P., Pharmacology
AGRAWAL, D., Biomedical Sciences
ALLEN, R., Pathology
ANDERSON, R., Internal Medicine
ANDERSON, T., Law School Instruction
BAECHLE, T., Exercise Sciences
BEISEL, K., Biomedical Sciences
BERTONI, J., Neurology
BEWTRA, C., Pathology
BHATIA, S., Adult and Child Psychiatry
BIRMINGHAM, E., Law School Instruction
BROCK, B., Education
BRUMBACK, R., Pathology
BUCKO, R., Sociology
CARLSON, J., Philosophy
CASALE, T., Internal Medicine
CASEY, M., Obstetrics and Gynaecology
CHENG, S., Mathematics and Computer Sciences
CHERNEY, M., Physics
CHIOU, R., Urological Surgery
CHU, C., Adult Psychiatry
CIPOLLA, S., Physics
CLARK, T., Political Science and International Relations
CULLEN, D., Internal Medicine
DALLON, C., Law School Instruction
DEWAN, N., Internal Medicine
DICKEL, C., Education
DOWD, JR, F., Pharmacology
ECKERSON, J., Exercise Sciences
FEEZELL, R., Philosophy
FENNER, G., Law School Instruction
FILIPI, C., General Surgery
FITZGIBBONS, JR, R., General Surgery
FLECKY, M., Fine and Performing Arts
FLEMING, A., Obstetrics and Gynaecology
FLETCHER, S., Paediatric Cardiology
FORSE, R., General Surgery
FRITZSCH, B., Biomedical Sciences
GAINES, R., General Surgery
GALLAGHER, J., Internal Medicine
GATALICA, Z., Pathology
GOSS, E., MacAllister Chair
GREEN, J., Law School Instruction
GREENSPOON, L., Klutznick Chair
HADDAD, A., Center for Health Policy and Ethics
HALLWORTH, R., Biomedical Sciences
HAMM, M., Graff Chair in Catholic Theology
HARMLESS, J., Theology
HARPER, C., Sociology
HAUSER, R., Theology
HE, Z., Biomedical Sciences
HEANEY, R., University Chair
HOPP, R., Paediatric Allergy
HULCE, M., Chemistry
KELLY, M., Law School Instruction
KROGSTAD, J., Accounting
LANSPA, S., Internal Medicine
LAPPE, J., Internal Medicine
LEAK, G., Psychology
LOGGIE, B., Surgery Oncology
LOVAS, S., Biomedical Sciences
LYNCH, H., Preventive Medicine
McGUIRE, M., Orthopaedic Surgery
McLAUGHLIN WITTEBORT, B., Biomedical Sciences
MACK, R., Law School Instruction
MALIK, D., Mathematics and Computer Sciences
MALINA, B., Theology
MANGRUM, R., Yossem Chair
MATTSON, B., Chemistry
MELILLI, K., Law School Instruction
MOHIUDDIN, S., Internal Medicine
MOOSS, A., Cardiology Education
MORDESON, J., Mathematics and Computer Sciences
MORSE, E., Law School Instruction
MUELLER, J., Theology
MURPHY, R., Biomedical Sciences
MURRAY, J., Philosophy
MURRAY, T., Pharmacology

MURTHY, V., Economics and Finance
NAIR, C., Cardiology Education
NAIR, P., Computer Science
NATH, R., McGraw Chair
NEUMEISTER, K., Law School Instruction
O'BRIEN, J., Internal Medicine
O'KEEFE IV, J., Theology
PEARSON, E., Law School Instruction
PETTY, F., Psychiatry Research
PETZEL, D., Biomedical Sciences
QUINN, T., Biomedical Sciences
RAVAL, V., Accounting
RECKER, R., Internal Medicine
RENDELL, M., Internal Medicine
RENO, R., Theology
RICH, E., Internal Medicine
ROY-HEWITSON, L., Modern Languages and Literatures
SARMA, D., Pathology
SEGER, J., Physics
SIMKINS, R., Theology
SPENCER, B., English
STEPHENS, W., Philosophy
STONE, N., Psychology
SUGIMOTO, J., Cardiac Surgery
SULLIVAN, P., Psychiatry Research
TEPLY, L., Law School Instruction
VOLKMER, R., Law School Instruction
WELIE, J., Center for Health Policy and Ethics
WHITE, M., Law School Instruction
WHITE, R., Philosophy
WHITTEN, R., Law School Instruction
WILLIAMS, M., Cardiology
WILSON, D., Forensic Psychiatry
WINGENDER, J., Economics and Finance
WORKMAN, J., Management and Marketing
WRIGHT, W., Kenefick Chair in Humanities
YEE, J., Biomedical Sciences
ZACH, T., Paediatric Newborn Medicine
ZACHARIAS, G., English
ZEHNDER, J., Environmental and Atmospheric Sciences

DOANE COLLEGE

1014 Boswell, Crete, NE 68333
Telephone: (402) 826-2161
E-mail: admissions@doane.edu
Internet: www.doane.edu

Founded 1872
Private control

Divs of fine arts and humanities, economics and business, science, mathematics, and information science and technology, social sciences and education; campuses at Lincoln and Grand Island (Nebraska)

Pres.: Dr JACQUE CARTER
Vice-Pres. for Academic Affairs and Dean for the Faculty: Dr JOHN M. BURNEY
Vice-Pres. for Admission: JOEL WEYAND
Vice-Pres. for Advancement: JERRY WOOD
Vice-Pres. for Finance and Admin.: JULIE SCHMIDT
Vice-Pres. for Information Services: MIKE CARPENTER
Vice-Pres. for Student Leadership: KIM JACOBS
Registrar: DENISE ELLIS
Library Dir: JAYNE GERMER
Library of 221,435 vols
Number of teachers: 105
Number of students: 2,950

GRACE UNIVERSITY

1311 S Ninth St, Omaha, NE 68108-3629
Telephone: (402) 449-2800
E-mail: admissions@graceuniversity.edu
Internet: www.graceuniversity.edu

Founded 1943 as Grace Bible Institute, present name 1995
Private control
Academic year: August to June

Pres.: Dr JAMES P. ECKMAN
Exec. Vice-Pres.: MICHAEL JAMES
Dir for Admissions: TARA KOTH
Academic Dean: Dr JOHN D. HOLMES
Dean for Enrolment Management: CHRIS PRUITT
Dean for Student Services: DEB OSMANSON
Registrar: KRIS J. UDD
Library Dir: BEN BRICK

Number of teachers: 15
Number of students: 580 (510 undergraduate, 70 graduate)

HASTINGS COLLEGE

710 N Turner Ave, Hastings, NE 68901
Telephone: (402) 463-2402
Internet: www.hastings.edu

Founded 1882
Private control
Academic year: August to May

Depts of art, biology, business and economics, chemistry, computer science, education, history, journalism and media arts, languages and literatures, mathematics, music, nursing, philosophy and religion, physical education, physics, political science, psychology, sociology, teacher education, theatre

Pres.: DON JACKSON
Vice-Pres. for Academic Affairs: Dr GARY JOHNSON
Vice-Pres. for Enrolment Management and Communications: SUSAN MEESKE
Vice-Pres. for Finance and Admin.: GARY FREEMAN
Vice-Pres. for Student Affairs: Dr GILBERT HINGA
Registrar: SHAWN BAKER
Librarian: ROBERT NEDDERMAN

Library of 140,000 vols, 525 print journals
Number of teachers: 70
Number of students: 1,100

MIDLAND UNIVERSITY

900 N Clarkson St, Fremont, NE 68025
Telephone: (402) 941-6250
E-mail: info@midlandu.edu
Internet: www.midlandu.edu

Founded 1883, present name and status 2010
Private control
Academic year: August to May
Liberal arts college

Pres.: Dr BENJAMIN E. SASSE
Vice-Pres.: GREG FRITZ
Vice-Pres. for Academic Affairs: Dr STEVE BULLOCK
Vice-Pres. for Finance and Admin.: JODI BENJAMIN
Dir for Admissions: ELIZA FERZELY
Dir for Library: Dr THOMAS E. BOYLE

Library of 114,000 vols
Number of teachers: 55
Number of students: 950

NEBRASKA CHRISTIAN COLLEGE

12550 S 114th St, Papillion, NE 68046
Telephone: (402) 935-9400
E-mail: info@nechristian.edu
Internet: www.nechristian.edu

Founded 1944
Private control
Academic year: August to May (2 semesters)
Areas of study: biblical studies, Christian education, church music, deaf ministries, family life ministry, general studies, missions, pastoral ministries, youth ministries

Pres. and CEO: RICHARD D. MILLIKEN
Vice-Pres. for Academics and Chief Academic Officer: MARK S. KRAUSE
Dir for Admissions: BRIAN TAYLOR

Dean for Students: DAVID HUSKEY
Registrar: MARK HUDDLESTON
Librarian: LINDA LU LLOYD

Number of teachers: 25
Number of students: 160

NEBRASKA METHODIST COLLEGE OF NURSING AND ALLIED HEALTH

720 N 87th St, Omaha, NE 68114
Telephone: (402) 354-7000
E-mail: admissions@methodistcollege.edu
Internet: www.methodistcollege.edu

Founded 1891 as Diploma School of Nursing, present status 1985
Private control

Divs of arts and sciences, health professions, professional development, nursing

Pres.: Dr DENNIS JOSLIN
Vice-Pres. for Academic Affairs: Dr KENNETH RYALLS
Vice-Pres. for Student Affairs: Dr KRISTINE HESS
Dir for Enrolment Services and Admissions: SARA HANSON
Dean for Students: Dr MELISSA HOFFMAN
Registrar: MELINDA STONER
Library Dir: BEVERLY SEDLACEK

Library of 12,000 vols
Number of teachers: 60
Number of students: 700

NEBRASKA WESLEYAN UNIVERSITY

5000 St Paul Ave, Lincoln, NE 68504-2794
Telephone: (402) 466-2371
E-mail: info@nebrwesleyan.edu
Internet: www.nebrwesleyan.edu

Founded 1887
Private control

Pres.: FREDERIK OHLES
Provost: JUDITH MUYSKENS
Vice-Pres. for Advancement: JOHN GREVING
Vice-Pres. for External Relations: PATTY KARTHAUSER
Vice-Pres. for Finance and Admin.: CLARK CHANDLER
Dir for Admissions: DAVID DUZIK
Dean for Students: PETER ARMSTRONG
Registrar: BETTE OLSON
Univ. Librarian: JOHN MONTAG

Library of 200,000 vols
Number of teachers: 110
Number of students: 2,100

DEANS

College of Liberal Arts and Sciences: Dr KATHY WOLFE
University College: Dr JACK SIEMSEN

PERU STATE COLLEGE

POB 10, 600 Hoyt St, Peru, NE 68421
Telephone: (402) 872-3815
E-mail: admissions@peru.edu
Internet: www.peru.edu

Founded 1867

Pres.: Dr DAN HANSON
Vice-Pres. for Academic Affairs: Dr TODD L. DREW
Vice-Pres. for Admin. and Finance: BRUCE BATTERSON
Vice-Pres. for Enrolment Management and Student Affairs: MICHAELA WILLIS
Library Dir: ROGER BECKER

Library of 600,000 vols
Number of teachers: 50
Number of students: 1,745

DEANS

Graduate Studies: GREG SEAY

School of Arts and Sciences: Dr PATRICK FORTNEY
School of Education: Dr JODI KUPPER
School of Professional Studies: GREG GALARDI

SAINT GREGORY THE GREAT SEMINARY

800 Fletcher Rd, Seward, NE 68434-8145
Telephone: (402) 643-4052
E-mail: sggs@stgregoryseminary.edu
Internet: www.stgregoryseminary.edu

Founded 1997
Private control
Academic year: August to May (2 semesters)

Rector: Rev. JEFFREY R. EICKHOFF
Academic Dean: Rev. LAWRENCE STOLEY
Librarian: Dr TERRENCE D. NOLLEN

Library of 33,000 vols
Number of teachers: 10
Number of students: 50

DEAN

Philosophy: Rev. BRENDAN KELLY

UNION COLLEGE

3800 S 48th St, Lincoln, NE 68506
Telephone: (402) 486-2600
E-mail: ucinfo@ucollege.edu
Internet: www.ucollege.edu

Founded 1891
Private control
Academic year: August to May

Divs of business and computer science, fine arts, health sciences, human development, humanities, religion, science, mathematics

Pres.: Dr JOHN WAGNER
Vice-Pres. for Academic Admin.: MALCOLM RUSSELL
Vice-Pres. for Advancement: LuANN DAVIS
Vice-Pres. for Enrolment and Student Financial Affairs: NADINE NELSON
Vice-Pres. for Student Services: LINDA WYSONG BECKER
Registrar: MICHELLE YOUNKIN
Library Dir: SABRINA RILEY

Library of 176,653 vols
Number of teachers: 75
Number of students: 890

Publication: *CORDmagazine* (2 a year)

UNIVERSITY OF NEBRASKA

Telephone: (402) 472-2111
Internet: www.nebraska.edu

Founded 1869
State control

Pres.: JAMES B. MILLIKEN
Provost and Exec. Vice-Pres.: LINDA R. PRATT
Vice-Pres. and Gen. Counsel: JOEL D. PEDERSEN
Vice-Pres. for Business and Finance: DAVID E. LECHNER
Vice-Pres. for Univ. Affairs: SHARON STEPHAN

Number of teachers: 4,580 (3,460 full-time, 1,122 part-time)
Number of students: 42,800 ...

CONSTITUENT CAMPUSES

University of Nebraska at Kearney

905 W 25th St, Kearney, NE 68849-0601
Telephone: (308) 865-8441
E-mail: intladmin@unk.edu
Internet: www.unk.edu

Founded 1903

Chancellor: DOUGLAS A. KRISTENSEN
Vice-Chancellor for Academic Affairs: CHARLES BICAK

Vice-Chancellor for Business and Finance: BARBARA L. JOHNSON

Vice-Chancellor for Univ. Relations: CURTIS CARLSON

Dean for Student Affairs: Dr JOSEPH A. ORAVECZ

Registrar: KIMRA F. SCHIPPOREIT

Dean for Libraries: JANET WILKE

Library of 250,000 vols, 210,000 print titles, 11,000 ebooks, 114,000 periodical vols, 275,000 USA govt documents, 17,000 state govt documents

Number of teachers: 425 (307 full-time, 118 part-time)

Number of students: 5,700

DEANS

College of Business and Technology: TIM BURKINK

College of Education: ED SCANTLING

College of Fine Arts and Humanities: Dr WILLIAM JURMA

College of Graduate Studies and Research: KENYA TAYLOR

College of Natural and Social Sciences: JOHN C. LA DUKE

University of Nebraska at Lincoln

1400 R St, Lincoln, NE 68588-0419

Telephone: (402) 472-7211

Internet: www.unl.edu

Founded 1869

Chancellor: HARVEY S. PERLMAN

Sr Vice-Chancellor for Academic Affairs: Dr ELLEN WEISSINGER

Vice-Chancellor for Business and Finance: CHRISTINE A. JACKSON

Vice-Chancellor for Research and Economic Devt: Dr PREM PAUL

Vice-Chancellor for Student Affairs: Dr JUAN FRANCO

Vice-Pres. and Vice-Chancellor for Institute of Agriculture and Natural Resources: Dr RONNIE GREEN

Dean for Univ. Libraries: JOAN R. GIESECKE

Library: see Libraries and Archives

Number of teachers: 2,095 (1,698 full-time, 397 part-time)

Number of students: 22,185

Publications: *Nebraska Journal of Economics and Business, Nebraska Law Review, Prairie Schooner* (4 a year), *Quarterly Journal of Finance and Accounting, University of Nebraska Studies*

DEANS

College of Agricultural Sciences and Natural Resources: Dr STEVEN S. WALLER

College of Architecture: Dr JAMES O'HANLON

College of Arts and Sciences: DAVID MANDERSCHEID

College of Business Administration: Dr DONDE PLOWMAN

College of Education and Human Sciences: Dr MARJORIE KOSTELNIK

College of Engineering: TIMOTHY WEI

College of Fine and Performing Arts: CHRISTIN MAMIYA

College of Journalism and Mass Communications: Dr GARY KEBBEL

College of Law: Dr SUSAN POSER

Graduate Studies: PATRICK DUSSAULT

University of Nebraska at Omaha

6001 Dodge St, Omaha, NE 68182

Telephone: (402) 554-2100

E-mail: unoisp@unomaha.edu

Internet: www.unomaha.edu

Founded 1908

Chancellor: Dr JOHN CHRISTIANSEN

Sr Vice-Chancellor for Academic and Student Affairs: Dr B. J. REED

Dir for Univ. Communications: ERIN OWEN

Dean for Univ. Library: STEPHEN SHORB

Library of 700,000 vols, 1.7m. micro-material items, 2,300 print subscriptions, 45,000 e-subscriptions

Number of teachers: 885 (490 full-time, 395 part-time)

Number of students: 11,660

DEANS

College of Arts and Sciences: Dr DAVID BOOCKER

College of Business Administration: Dr LOUIS POL

College of Communication, Fine Arts and Media: GAIL F. BAKER

College of Education: NANCY EDICK

College of Information Science and Technology: HESHAM H. ALI

College of Public Affairs and Community Service: JOHN BARTLE (acting)

Graduate Studies: Dr DEBORAH SMITH-HOWELL

International Studies and Programs: THOMAS E. GOUTTIERRE

University of Nebraska Medical Center

42nd and Emile, Omaha, NE 68198

Telephone: (402) 559-4000

E-mail: unmcgraduatestudies@unmc.edu

Internet: www.unmc.edu

Founded 1880, present status 1902

Chancellor: Dr HAROLD M. MAURER

Vice-Chancellor for Academic Affairs: Dr DAVID CROUSE

Vice-Chancellor for External Affairs: ROBERT D. BARTEE

Vice-Chancellor for Research: Dr JENNIFER LARSEN

Library Dir: Dr NANCY N. WOELFL

Library of 249,000 vols, 67,700 monographs and textbooks, 479 ebooks, 6,700 ejournals

Number of teachers: 1,160 (955 full-time, 205 part-time)

Number of students: 3,255

DEANS

College of Dentistry: Dr JOHN REINHARDT

College of Medicine: BRADLEY BRITIGAN

College of Nursing: Dr JULIANN SEBASTIAN

College of Pharmacy: Dr COURTNEY FLETCHER

College of Public Health: Dr AYMAN EL-MOHANDES

Graduate Studies: Dr DAVID A. CROUSE

School of Allied Health Professions: Dr KYLE P. MEYER

WAYNE STATE COLLEGE

1111 Main St, Wayne, NE 68787

Telephone: (402) 375-7000

E-mail: admissions@wsc.edu

Internet: www.wsc.edu

Founded 1910

State control

Academic year: August to July (2 semesters)

Pres.: CURT FRYE

Vice-Pres. and Dean for Students: Dr JEFF CARSTENS

Vice-Pres. for Academic Affairs: Dr ROBERT McCUE

Vice-Pres. for Admin. and Finance: JEAN DALE

Vice-Pres. for Devt: PHYLLIS CONNER

Library Dir: DAVE GRABER

Library of 350,000 vols

Number of teachers: 125 (full-time)

Number of students: 3,570

DEANS

School of Arts and Humanities: Dr JAMES F. O'DONNELL

School of Business and Technology: Dr VAUGHN BENSON

School of Education and Counseling: Dr NEAL SCHNOOR

School of Natural and Social Sciences: Dr JON DALAGER

YORK COLLEGE

1125 E Eighth St, York, NE 68467

Telephone: (402) 363-5600

E-mail: president@york.edu

Internet: www.york.edu

Founded 1890

Private control

Academic year: August to May

Offers Bachelors in liberal arts and Masters of Arts in education

Chancellor: WAYNE BAKER

Pres.: Dr STEVE W. ECKMAN

Vice-Pres. for Admissions: WILLIE SANCHEZ

Vice-Pres. for Advancement: BRENT MAGNER

Vice-Pres. for Student Devt and Dean for Students: Dr SHANE MOUNTJOY

Academic Dean: Dr TRACEY WYATT

Registrar: TOD J. MARTIN

Dir for Library: KEN GUNSELMAN

Number of teachers: 50

Number of students: 510

NEVADA

MORRISON UNIVERSITY

10315 Professional Circle, Suite 201, Reno, NV 89521

Telephone: (866) 381-6050

E-mail: info@morrisonuniversity.com

Internet: anthem.edu/morrison

Founded 1902 as Nevada Business Institute, present name 1999; attached to Anthem Education

Private control

Academic year: September to September

Offers business-related education and training; Bachelors and Masters degree programmes

Chancellor and CEO: Dr JAMES D. HUTTON

Pres.: MARY MORRISON-LEMBERES

Exec. Vice-Pres.: NORMAN W. SEROSKI

Vice-Pres. for Academics: Dr JOHN BURRUEL

Registrar: GERRE YOUNG

Library Dir: USHA MEHTA

Number of teachers: 20

Number of students: 240

NEVADA SYSTEM OF HIGHER EDUCATION

2601 Enterprise Rd, Reno, NV 89512

Telephone: (775) 784-4901

Internet: system.nevada.edu

Chancellor: DAN KLAICH

Vice-Chancellor for Academic and Student Affairs: CRYSTAL ABBA

Vice-Chancellor for Finance: MARK STEVENS

Vice-Chancellor for Health Sciences: Dr MARCIA TURNER

Vice-Chancellor for Information Technology: STEVEN ZINK...

CONSTITUENT INSTITUTIONS

College of Southern Nevada

W Charleston Campus, 6375 W. Charleston Blvd, Las Vegas, NV 89146

Telephone: (702) 651-5000

Internet: www.csn.edu

Founded 1971

3 Main campuses and multiple academic sites throughout the S Nevada area

Pres.: Dr MICHAEL D. RICHARDS

Sr Vice-Pres. for Finance and Admin.: PATRI-
CIA CHARLTON
Vice-Pres. for Academic Affairs: Dr DARREN
DIVINE
Vice-Pres. for Student Affairs: Dr CHEMENE
CRAWFORD
Number of teachers: 1,470 (494 full-time,
976 part-time)
Number of students: 43,560 (11,741 full-
time, 31,819 part-time)

DEANS

School of Advanced and Applied Technolo-
gies: Dr MICHAEL SPANGLER
School of Arts and Letters: WENDY WEINER
School of Business, Hospitality and Public
Services: HYLA WINTERS
School of Education, Behavioral and Social
Sciences: CHARLES OKEKE
School of Science and Mathematics: SALLY
JOHNSTON
Ralph & Betty Engelstad School of Health
Sciences: PATRICIA CASTRO

Great Basin College

1500 College Parkway, Elko, NV 89801
Telephone: (775) 738-8493
Internet: www.gbcnv.edu
Founded 1967
Career and technical education; community
education; fine arts; health science; human-
ities and social sciences; mathematics, sci-
ence, business, and computing
Pres. and Vice-Pres. for Student Services:
LYNN MAHLBERG
Vice-Pres. for Academic Affairs: Dr MIKE
MCFARLANE
Library of 46,828 vols, 656 microfilms and
113 subscriptions
Number of students: 3,835

Nevada State College

1125 Nevada State Dr., Henderson, NV
89002
Telephone: (702) 992-2130
E-mail: admissions@nsc.nevada.edu
Internet: www.nsc.nevada.edu
Founded 2002
Pres.: Dr BART PATTERSON
Provost and Exec. Vice-Pres.: Dr ERIKA BECK
Sr Vice-Pres. for Finance and Admin.: HARRY
E. NEEL, JR
Library of 14,000 vols
Number of students: 3,000

DEANS

School of Education: Dr JIM LABUDA
School of Liberal Arts and Sciences: Dr ANDY
KUNIYUKI
School of Nursing: Dr SHIRLEE J. SNYDER

University of Nevada, Las Vegas

4505 S Maryland Parkway, Las Vegas, NV
89154
Telephone: (702) 895-3011
E-mail: admissions@unlv.edu
Internet: go.unlv.edu
Founded 1957
Academic year: August to May
Pres.: Dr NEAL SMATRESK
Exec. Vice-Pres. and Provost: Dr MICHAEL
BOWERS
Vice-Pres. for Advancement: Dr WILLIAM G.
BOLDT
Vice-Pres. for Diversity Initiatives and Govt
Affairs: LUIS VALERA
Sr Vice-Pres. for Finance and Business:
GERRY BOMOTTI
Vice-Pres. for Student Affairs: Dr JUANITA
FAIN
Vice-Pres. for Research and Dean of the
Graduate College: Dr RONALD SMITH

Assoc. Vice-Pres. for Community Relations:
SCHYLER RICHARDS
Sr Assoc. Vice-Pres. for Devt: NANCY STROUSE
Registrar: JEFF HALVERSON
Dean of Libraries: PATRICIA A. IANNUZZI
Library: 3m. vols
Number of teachers: 3,100
Number of students: 27,360

DEANS

College of Education: Dr WILLIAM SPEER
College of Fine Arts: Dr JEFFREY P. KOEP
College of Graduate Studies: Dr RON SMITH
College of Health Sciences: Dr CAROLYN SABO
College of Liberal Arts: Dr CHRISTOPHER C.
HUDGINS
College of Sciences: Dr TIMOTHY L. PORTER
Greenspun College of Urban Affairs: Dr LEE
BERNICK
Honors College: Dr PETER L. STARKWEATHER
Howard R. Hughes College of Engineering:
Dr RAMA VENKAT
Lee Business School: PAUL JARLEY
William F. Harrah College of Hotel Admin-
istration: DONALD D. SNYDER
William S. Boyd School of Law: JOHN VALERY
WHITE

University of Nevada, Reno

1664 N Virginia St, Reno, NV 89557-0208
Telephone: (775) 784-1110
E-mail: asknevada@unr.edu
Internet: www.unr.edu
Founded 1874 as State Univ. of Nevada in
Elko, present location 1885
Academic year: August to May
Pres.: Dr MARC JOHNSON
Exec. Vice-Pres. and Provost: Dr HEATHER
HARDY
Vice-Provost for Extended Studies: Dr FRED
HOLMAN
Vice-Provost for Instruction and Under-
graduate Programmes: Dr WILLIAM CATHEY
Vice-Pres. for Admin. and Finance: RONALD
ZUREK
Vice-Pres. for Devt and Alumni Relations:
JOHN K. CARUTHERS
Vice-Pres. for Information Technology and
Dean of Libraries: STEVEN D. ZINK
Vice-Pres. for Marketing and Communica-
tions: CINDY POLLARD
Vice-Pres. for Research: MARSHA READ
Vice-Pres. for Student Services: SHANNON
ELLIS
Registrar: MELISSA N. CHOROSZY
Library: 1.1m. vols
Number of teachers: 940
Number of students: 17,680
Publication: *Electronic Journal of Science
Education* (4 a year)

DEANS

College of Agriculture, Biotechnology, and
Natural Resources: RON PARDINI
College of Business.: GREG MOSIER
College of Education: CHRISTINE CHENEY
College of Engineering: EMMANUEL MARAGA-
KIS
College of Liberal Arts: SCOTT CASPER
College of Science: JEFF THOMPSON
Cooperative Extension: KAREN HINTON
Division of Health Sciences: DENISE MON-
TCALM
Donald W. Reynolds School of Journalism
and Advanced Media Studies: WILLIAM
WINTER
Extended Studies: FRED B. HOLMAN
Graduate School: MARSHA READ
School of Medicine: Dr THOMAS L. SCHWENK

Western Nevada College

2201 W College Parkway, Carson City, NV
89703
Telephone: (775) 445-3000
E-mail: info_desk@wnc.edu
Internet: www.wnc.edu
Founded 1971
State control
3 Campuses: Carson City Campus, Douglas
Campus and Fallon Campus
Academic year: August to May
Pres.: Dr CAROL LUCEY
Vice-Pres. for Finance and Admin. Services:
DANIEL NEVERETT
Dir for Information and Marketing Services:
ANNE HANSEN
Library of 46,000 vols, 185 magazines, 12
newspaper subscriptions, 1,000 maps and
18,000 full-text journals
Number of students: 5,300

SIERRA NEVADA COLLEGE

999 Tahoe Blvd, Incline Village, NV 89451-
9500
Telephone: (775) 831-1314
E-mail: admissions@sierranevada.edu
Internet: www.sierranevada.edu
Founded 1969
Private control
Academic year: August to May
Liberal arts college; interdisciplinary cur-
riculum combining entrepreneurial thinking
and environmental, social, economic and
educational sustainability
Pres.: Dr LYNN. GILLETTE
Provost and Exec. Vice-Pres.: SHANNON BEETS
Dean of Faculty: DAN O'BRYAN
Registrar: ROSEANNA BEENK
Library Dir: Dr BETTS MARKLE
Number of teachers: 130
Number of students: 1,300 (500 undergradu-
ate, 800 graduate)

NEW HAMPSHIRE

COLBY-SAWYER COLLEGE

541 Main St, New London, NH 03257-7835
Telephone: (603) 526-3000
E-mail: colbyweb@colby-sawyer.edu
Internet: www.colby-sawyer.edu
Founded 1837 as New London Acad., present
name 1975
Private control
Academic year: September to May (2 semes-
ters)
Depts of business administration, education,
environmental studies, exercise and sport
sciences, fine and performing arts, health
studies, humanities, natural sciences, nurs-
ing, social sciences
Pres.: THOMAS C. GALLIGAN, JR
Academic Vice-Pres. and Dean for Faculty:
DEBORAH A. TAYLOR
Vice-Pres. for Admin.: DOUGLAS C. ATKINS
Vice-Pres. for Advancement: ELIZABETH A.
CAHILL
Vice-Pres. for Enrolment Management: GRE-
GORY W. MATTHEWS
Vice-Pres. for Finance and Treas.: TODD
EMMONS
Vice-Pres. for Student Devt and Dean for
Students: DAVID A. SAUERWEIN
Academic Dean: BURTON KIRKWOOD
Registrar: CAROLE H. PARSONS
Library Dir: CARRIE THOMAS
Number of teachers: 120
Number of students: 1,250

DANIEL WEBSTER COLLEGE

20 University Dr., Nashua, NH 03063-1300
Telephone: (603) 577-6000
E-mail: registrar@dwc.edu
Internet: www.dwc.edu

Founded 1965 as New England Aeronautical
Institute
Private control
Academic year: August to May (2 semesters)
Pres.: ROBERT E. MYERS
Provost and Vice-Pres. of Academic Affairs:
Dr MICHAEL FISHBEIN
Vice-Pres. for Advancement and Alumni
Affairs: GAIL M. GARCEAU
Vice-Pres. for Business, Finance and Oper-
ations: THOMAS N. DiCONZA
Vice-Pres. for Student Affairs: SUSAN C.
ELSASS
Dean of Students: MICHELLE O'MALLEY
Registrar: MARILYN NIEUWEBOER
Library Dir: SUSAN WAGNER

Library of 34,000 vols
Number of teachers: 60
Number of students: 650

DEANS

School of Arts and Sciences: Dr KATHLEEN M.
HIPP
School of Aviation and Sciences: JONATHAN
PROHASKA
School of Business, Management and Profes-
sional Studies: Dr RONALD E. LIVINGSTON
School of Engineering and Computer Sci-
ences: Dr NICHOLAS BERTOZZI

DARTMOUTH COLLEGE

6016 McNutt Hall, Hanover, NH 03755
Telephone: (603) 646-1110
E-mail: contact@dartmouth.edu
Internet: www.dartmouth.edu

Founded 1769
Private control
Academic year: June to June

Pres.: JIM YONG KIM
Provost: CAROL L. FOLT (acting)
Sr Vice-Pres. for Advancement: CAROLYN A.
PELZEL
Exec. Vice-Pres. and Chief Financial Officer:
STEVEN N. KADISH
Vice-Pres. and Chief Human Resources Offi-
cer: MYRON S. McCOO
Vice-Pres. and Chief Information Officer:
ELLEN WAITE-FRANZEN
Vice-Pres. for Campus Planning and Facil-
ities: LISA HOGARTY
Vice-Pres. for Devt: THOMAS W. HERBERT
Vice-Pres. for Finance: MICHAEL WAGNER
Dean for Admissions and Financial Aid:
MARIA LASKARIS
Registrar: MEREDITH H. BRAZ
Dean for Libraries: JEFFREY L. HORRELL
(acting)

Library of 2,677,605 vols, 368,000 ebooks,
24,000 video items, 192,000 maps, 450,000
photographs, 2,587,446 microforms, 55,382
current, 72,000 digital resources
Number of teachers: 1,000
Number of students: 6,150 (4,248 undergraduate, 1,893 graduate)

Publications: *Dartmouth Engineer* (2 a year),
Dartmouth Medicine (4 a year), *Encruci-
jada* (online), *Linguistic Discovery* (online),
Tuck Today

DEANS

College: CHARLOTTE H. JOHNSON (acting)
Faculty of Arts and Sceinces: MICHAEL MAS-
TANDUNO (acting)
Geisel School of Medicine: WILEY W. SOUBA,
JR (acting)
Graduate Studies: BRIAN POGUE

Thayer School of Engineering: JOSEPH J.
HELBLE (acting)
Tuck School of Business: PAUL DANOS

PROFESSORS

Note: some professors serve in more than one
department

Humanities

Department of African and African-American
Studies:
ALVERSON, H. S., Anthropology
AMADIUMI, I., Religion
COOK, W., English
HALL, R. L., Sociology
KASFIR, N. M., Govt
LANGFORD, G. M., Biology
PEASE, D. L., English
SPITZER, L., History
WALKER, K., French and Italian
WILDER, C., History

Department of Art History:
JORDAN, J., Modern Art
KENSETH, J., Renaissance and Baroque Art

Department of Asian and Middle Eastern
Languages and Literatures:
ALLAN, S., Chinese
GLINERT, L., Hebrew

Department of Classics:
BRADLEY, E. M., Greek and Latin Litera-
ture, Roman and Early Christian Art
and Architecture
RUTTER, J. B., Classical Art and Archae-
ology, Archaeology of the Aegean
SCOTT, W. C., Greek and Latin Literature,
Classical Drama, Homer
TATUM, J., Greek and Latin Literature,
Ancient Fiction, the Classical Tradition,
Roman Comedy

Department of Comparative Literature:
COOK, W., English
CREWE, J., English
GAYLORD, A. T., English
GEMUNDEN, G., German
GLINERT, J. A., Asian, Middle Eastern
Languages and Literature
GREEN, M. J., French and Italian
HEFFERNAN, J. W., English
HIGGINS, L. A., French and Italian
HIRSCH, M., French and Italian
JEWELL, K. J., French and Italian
KOPPER, J. M., Russian
KRITZMAN, L. D., French and Italian
LAWRENCE, A., Film

Department of English:
BOOSE, L., English
COOK, W., English
CREWE, J., English and Comparative Lit-
erature
GAYLORD, A., English
HEBERT, E., English
HEFFERNAN, J. A. W., English
HUNTINGDON, C., English
McKEE, P., English
MATHIS, C., English and Creative Writing
RENZA, L., English
SACCIO, P., English and Shakespearean
Studies
SILVER, B. R., English
SLEIGH, T., English
TRAVIS, P. W., English
WYKES, P., English

Department of Film and Television Studies:
LAWRENCE, A.

Department of French and Italian:
GREEN, M.
HIGGINS, L.
HIRSCH, M.
JEWELL, K.
KRITZMAN, L. D.
RASSIAS, J.
WALKER, K. L.

Department of German:
DUNCAN, B., German Language
GEMUNDEN, G., German, Comparative Lit-
erature
SCHER, S. P., German, Comparative Lit-
erature

Department of Linguistics and Cognitive
Science:
ALVERSON, H. S., Anthropology
DUNBAR, K., Education and Psychology
DUNCAN, B., German
GLINERT, L. H., AMELL
GRENOBLE, L., Russian
HUGHES, H. C., Psychology
JAHNER, E. A., English and Native Ameri-
can Studies
MOOR, J. H., Philosophy
PETTITO, L. A., Education and Psychology
SCHERR, B. P., Russian
SINNOTT-ARMSTRONG, W. P., Philosophy
SORENSEN, R. A., Philosophy
TAUBE, J., Psychology
TRAVIS, P. W., English
WALKER, K. L., French and Italian
WOLFORD, G. L., Psychology

Department of Music:
APPLETON, J. H.
O'NEAL, M.
PINKAS, S.

Department of Philosophy:
DRIVER, J.
GERT, B.
MOOR, J. H.
SINNOTT-ARMSTRONG, W.
SORENSEN, R.

Department of Religion:
ACKERMAN, S.
AMADIUME, I., African Religions
FRANKENBERRY, N., Philosophy of Religion,
Women and Religion, Science and Reli-
gion
GREEN, R. M., Religious Ethics, Business
Ethics
HENRICKS, R. G., Religions of China

Department of Russian:
GRENOBLE, L.
KOPPER, J.
LOSEFF, L.
SCHERR, B.

Department of Spanish and Portuguese:
BUENO-CHAVEZ, R.
PASTOR, B.

Department of Studio Art:
FRANK MOSS, B., IV
RANDALL, C.
THOMPSON, E.

Department of Theatre:
CRICKARD, L.
GAFFNEY, P.
GRENOBLE, L.
SPICER, M.

Women and Gender Studies:
ACKERMAN, S., Religion
AMADIUME, I., Religion
BOOSE, L. E., English
DARROW, M. H., History
DOMOSH, M., Geography
FOWLER, L. L., Govt
FRANKENBERRY, N. K., Religion
GARROD, A. G., Education
GREEN, M. J., French and Italian
HIGGINS, L. A., French and Italian
HIRSCH, M., French and Italian
JEWELL, K. J., French and Italian
LAWRENCE, A., Film
SILVER, B. R., English
SPITZER, L., History

Science

Department of Biological Sciences:

BERGER, E. M., Molecular Genetics, Cell Biology
FOLT, C. L., Aquatic Ecology
GILBERT, J. J., Ecology, Aquatic Biology
GUERINOT, M. L., Molecular Genetics, Microbiology
HOLMES, R. T., Animal Behaviour, Ecology
LANGFORD, G. M., Cell Biology
McCLUNG, C. R., Molecular Genetics
McPEEK, M. A., Community Ecology, Evolution
PEART, D. R., Population and Community Ecology, Forest Ecology
SLOBODA, R. D., Cell Biology, Neurobiology
WITTERS, L. A., Human Biology, Endocrinology/Metabolism

Department of Chemistry:

BELBRUNO, J. J.
BRAUN, C. L.
CANTOR, R. S.
DITCHFIELD, R.
GRIBBLE, G. W.
HUGHES, R. P.
JACOBI, P. A.
LEMAL, D. M.
LIPSON, J. E. G.
SODERBERG, R. H.
SPENCER, T. A.
WILCOX, D. E.
WINN, J. S.

Department of Computer Science:

DONALD, B. R.
DRYSDALE, R. L., III
KOTZ, D. F.
MAKEDON, F. S.
ROCKMORE, D.

Department of Environmental Studies:

FRIEDLAND, A.
HOWARTH, R.
SHEPHERD, J.
VIRGINIA, R.

Department of Mathematics:

ARKOWITZ, M. A.
BAUMGARTNER, J. E.
BICKEL, T. F.
BOGART, K. P.
DOYLE, P.
GORDON, C. S.
GROSZEK, M.
LAHR, C. D.
POMERANCE, C. B.
ROCKMORE, D. N.
SHEMANSKE, T. R.
WALLACE, D. I.
WEBB, D. L.
WILLIAMS, D. P.

Department of Physics and Astronomy:

FESEN, C. G.
FESEN, R. A.
GLEISER, M.
HUDSON, M. K.
LABELLE, J. W.
LAWRENCE, W. E.
MONTGOMERY, D. C.
MOOK, D. E.
THORSTENSEN, J. R.
WEGNER, G. A.
WYBOURNE, M. N.

Social Sciences

Department of Anthropology:

ALVERSON, H.
EICKELMAN, D. F.
ENDICOTT, K.
KAN, S.
NICHOLS, D. L.

Department of Economics:

BLANCHFLOWER, D. G.
FISCHEL, W. A.
GUSTMAN, A. L.

IRWIN, D. A.
KOHN, M.
MARION, N. P.
SAMWICK, A. A.
SCOTT, J. T.
SKINNER, J.
STAIGER, D. O.
VENTI, S. F.

Department of Education:

DUNBAR, K.
GARROD, A.
PETITTO, L. A.

Department of Geography:

DOMOSH, M.
MAGILLIGAN, F. J.
WRIGHT, R. A.

Department of Government:

FOWLER, L. L.
FREEDMAN, J. O.
KASFIR, N. M.
LEBOW, R. N.
MASTANDUNO, M.
SA'ADAH, M. A.
WINTERS, R. F.

Department of History:

CALLOWAY, C.
CROSSLEY, P. K.
DARROW, M.
ERMARTH, H. M.
GARTHWAITE, G. R.
NAVARRO, M.
NELSON, J. B.
SHEWMAKER, K. E.
SPITZER, L.
WHELAN, H. W.
WILDER, C. S.
WRIGHT, J.

Department of Latin American, Latino and Caribbean Studies:

BUENO-CHAVEZ, R., Spanish and Portuguese
NAVARRO, M., History
NICHOLS, D. L., Anthropology
PASTOR, B., Spanish and Portuguese
WALKER, K. L., French and Italian
WRIGHT, R., Geography

Department of Native American Studies:

CALLOWAY, C. G.
KAN, S.
NICHOLS, D. L.

Department of Psychological and Brain Sciences:

DUNBAR, K., Cognitive Psychology
GAZZANIGA, M. S., Cognitive Neuroscience
GRAFTON, S., Functional Brain Imaging
HEATHERTON, T. F., Experimental Social Neuroscience, Personality and Motivation
HUGHES, H. C., Electrophysiological and Psychophysical Studies of Sensory Processing in Humans
HULL, J. G., Structure of Self-knowledge and Function of Self-regulatory Systems
JERNSTEDT, G. C., Learning, Instructional Design Theory, Evaluation Research
KLECK, R. E., Experimental Social Communication Processes
MACRAE, C. N., Social Cognition
MORRIS, W. N., Mood and Emotion
PETITTO, L. A., Cognitive Psychology and Psycholinguistics
TAUBE, J. S.
WOLFORD, G. L.

Department of Sociology:

CAMPBELL, J. L.
HALL, R. L.
PARSA, M.

Dartmouth Medical School (1 Rope Ferry Rd, Hanover, NH 03755-1404; tel. (603) 650-1200; e-mail dms.administration@

dartmouth.edu; internet www.dartmouth.edu/dms):

ADDANTE, R. R., Oral-Maxillofacial Surgery and Anaesthesiology
AHLES, T. A., Psychiatry
ALTO, W. A., Community and Family Medicine
AMBROS, V. R., Genetics
AUBUCHON, J. P., Pathology and Haematology-Oncology
BALDWIN, J. C., Surgery
BANKER, B. Q., Pathology
BARLOWE, C. K., Biochemistry
BARON, J. A., General Internal Medicine and Community and Family Medicine
BARTELS, S. J., Psychiatry
BARTLETT, D., Physiology
BATALDEN, P. B., Paediatrics and Community and Family Medicine
BAUGHMAN, R. D., Dermatology
BEISSWENGER, P. J., Medicine
BERGER, B. J., Psychiatry
BERMAN, S. A., Medicine
BERNAT, J. L., Neurology
BERNINI, P. M., Surgery (Orthopaedics)
BIRD, H. H., Anaesthiology
BLACK, W. C., Radiology
BOYLE, W. E., Paediatrics and Community and Family Medicine
BRINCKERHOFF, C. E., Medicine and Biochemistry
BRINCK-JOHNSER, T., Pathology
BROOKS, J. G., Paediatrics
BROWN, F. E., Plastic Surgery
BURCHARD, K. W., Surgery and Anaesthesiology
BYOCK, I. R., Anaesthiology
BZIK, D. J., Microbiology and Immunology
CAMPBELL, D. G., Surgery (Ophthalmology)
CARPENTER, S. J., Anatomy
CENDRON, M., Surgery
CHAMBERS, W. F., Anatomy
CHANG, T. Y., Biochemistry
CHEUNG, A., Microbiology and Immunology
CLENDENNING, W. E., Medicine
COHEN, J. A., Medicine
COLACCHIO, T. A., Surgery
COLE, C. N., Biochemistry and Genetics
COLE, M. D., Pharmacology and Toxicology
COMPTON, D. A., Biochemistry
CORNELL, C. J., Haematology-Oncology and Paediatrics
CORNELL, G. G., Medicine
CORSON, J. A., Psychiatry
CORWIN, H. L., Medicine and Anaesthesiology
CRAIG, R. W., Pharmacology, Toxicology
CRICHLOW, R. W., Surgery
CROMWELL, L. D., Radiology and Neurosurgery
CRONENWETT, J. L., Surgery
CROW, H. C., Radiology
DARNALL, R. A., Paediatrics and Physiology
DAUBENSPECK, A., Physiology
DELEO, J. A., Anaesthesiology
DIETRICH, A. J., Community and Family Medicine
DMITROVSKY, E., Pharmacology and Toxicology
DONEGAN, J. O., Otolaryngology
DOW, R. W., Surgery
DRAKE, R. E., Psychiatry; Community and Family Medicine
DUHAIME, A.-C., Surgery
DUNLAP, J. C., Genetics and Biochemistry
EASTMAN, A., Pharmacology and Toxicology
EDWARDS, W. H., Paediatrics
EISENBERG, B. L., Surgery
ERNSTOFF, L. T., Haematology-Oncology
ERNSTOFF, M. S., Haematology-Oncology
FANGER, M. W., Microbiology and Immunology
FEJES-TOTH, A. N., Physiology
FEJES-TOTH, G., Physiology
FERM, V. H., Anatomy

FISHER, E. S., Community and Family Medicine
FLOOD, A. B., Community and Family Medicine
FRANK, J. E., Paediatrics
FREY, W. G., Medicine
FRIEDMAN, M. J., Psychiatry, Pharmacology and Toxicology
FROMM, H., Gastroenterology
GALLAGHER, J. D., Anaesthesiology
GALTON, V. A., Physiology
GLASS, D. D., Anaesthesiology
GOODMAN, D. C., Paediatrics
GORMLEY, E. A., Surgery
GOSSELIN, R. E., Pharmacology and Toxicology
GRAFTON, S. T., Medicine
GREEN, A. I., Psychiatry
GREEN, R. L., Psychiatry
GREEN, W. R., Microbiology and Immunology
GREENBERG, R., Community and Family Medicine
GUYRE, P. M., Physiology
HAMILTON, J. W., Pharmacology, Toxicology
HARBAUGH, R. E., Surgery (Neurosurgery) and Radiology
HARBURY, H. A., Biochemistry
HARTMAN, G. S., Anaesthiology
HAZARD, R. G., Orthopaedics
HEAD, J. M., Surgery
HEANEY, J. A., Surgery
HENDERSON, J. V., Community and Family Medicine
HENDERSON, L. P., Physiology
HICKEY, W. F., Pathology
HOFNAGEL, D., Paediatrics
HOLMES, G. L., Medicine
HUG, E. B., Medicine
INSELBURG, J. W., Microbiology
ISRAEL, M. A., Paediatrics and Genetics
JACOBS, N. J., Microbiology
KARAGAS, M., Community and Family Medicine
KARL, R. C., Surgery
KASPER, L. H., Medicine
KELLEY, M. L., Medicine
KERRIGAN, C. L., Surgery
KING, B. H., Psychiatry
KLAUS, S. N., Medicine
KLEIN, R. Z., Paediatrics
KOOP, C. E., Surgery
KORC, M., Medicine
KOVAL, K. J., Orthopaedics
LANE, F. W., Medicine
LAYTON, W. M., Anatomy
LEITER, J. C., Physiology and Medicine
LEVIN, D. L., Paediatrics and Anaesthesiology
LEVINE, G. M., Community and Family Medicine
LEWIS, L. D., Medicine
LIENHARD, G. E., Biochemistry
LITTLE, G. A., Paediatrics; Obstetrics and Gynaecology
LLEWELLYN-THOMAS, H. A., Community and Family Medicine
LONGNECKER, D. S., Pathology
LOROS, J. J., Biochemistry and Genetics
LUBIN, M., Microbiology
McALLISTER, T. W., Psychiatry
McCANN, F. V., Physiology
McCOLLUM, R. W., Community and Family Medicine
McDANIEL, M. D., Anatomy
McINTYRE, D. R., Medicine
MAHLER, D. A., Medicine
MANGANIELLI, P. D., Obstetrics and Gynaecology
MARON-PADILLA, M., Pathology
MARRIN, C. A. S., Surgery
MAUE, R. A., Medicine
MAURER, L. H., Medicine
MAYOR, M. B., Surgery (Orthopaedics)
MEMOLI, V. A., Pathology

MODLIN, J. F., Paediatrics
MOESHLER, J. B., Paediatrics
MOGIELNICKI, R. P., General Internal Medicine
MOHANDAS, T. K., Pathology
MUESER, K. T., Psychiatry; Community and Family Medicine
MUNCK, A. U., Physiology
NAITOVE, A., Surgery
NATTIE, E. E., Physiology
NELSON, E. C., Community and Family Medicine
NELSON, W. H., Psychiatry
NEMIAH, J. C., Psychiatry
NIERENBERG, D. W., Pharmacology and Toxicology
NODA, L. H., Biochemistry
NOELLE, R. J., Microbiology and Immunology
NOLL, W. W., Paediatrics
NORDGREN, R. E., Paediatrics
NORTH, W. G., Physiology
NUGENT, W. C., Surgery
NYE, R. E., Physiology
O'CONNOR, G. T., Community and Family Medicine
O'DONNELL, J. F., Medicine
ONION, D. K., Community and Family Medicine
OXMAN, T. E., Psychiatry; Community and Family Medicine
PAYSON, H. E., Psychiatry
PEARLMAN, J. D., Medicine
PFEFFERKORN, E. R., Microbiology
PLUME, S. K., Surgery
QUILL, T. J., Anaesthesiology
RAVARIS, C. L., Psychiatry
REGAN-SMITH, M. G., Rheumatology; Community and Family Medicine
REEVES, A. G., Medicine
RIGBY, W. F. C., Microbiology and Immunology;
ROBERTS, D. W., Surgery (Neurosurgery)
ROEBUCK, W. D., Pharmacology and Toxicology
ROGERS, C. C., Medicine
ROLETT, E. L., Medicine
ROSENBERG, S. D., Psychiatry
ROTHSTEIN, R. I., Medicine
ROUS, S. N., Surgery
ROZYCKI, A. A., Paediatrics
RUECKERT, F., Surgery
St GERMAIN, D. L., Medicine
St JOHN, W. M., Physiology
SANDERS, J. H., Surgery
SARGENT, J. D., Paediatrics
SATEIA, M. J., Psychiatry
SAUNDERS, R. L., Surgery
SAYKIN, A. J., Psychiatry
SCHNED, A. R., Pathology
SCHWARTZMAN, J. D., Pathology
SCORNIK, O. A., Biochemistry
SILBERFARB, P. M., Psychiatry and Medicine
SIMONS, M., Cardiology; Pharmacology and Toxicology
SKINNER, J. S., Community and Family Medicine
SMITH, B. D., Obstetrics and Gynaecology
SMITH, R. P., Pharmacology and Toxicology
SOBEL, J. M., Psychiatry
SOKOL, H. W., Physiology
SOLOW, C., Psychiatry
SORENSON, G. D., Pathology
SPECK, N. A., Biochemistry
SPENCER, S. K., Dermatology and Surgery (Dermatology)
SPIEGEL, P. K., Radiology
SPIELBERG, S. P., Paediatrics
STANTON, B. A., Physiology
STAUFFER, M. W., Pathology
STOKES, D. C., Paediatrics
STRICKLER, J. C., Medicine
STYS, S. J., Obstetrics and Gynaecology (Maternal-Foetal Medicine)
SUTTON, J. E., Surgery

SWARTZ, H. M., Radiology; Community and Family Medicine; Physiology
TOSTESON, A. N., Community and Family Medicine
TOSTESON, T. D., Community and Family Medicine
TRUMPOWER, B. L., Biochemistry
VALTIN, H., Physiology
VAN LEEUWIN, D. J., Medicine
VARNUM, J. W., Hospital Administration
VIDAVER, R. M., Psychiatry
von REYN, C. F., Medicine
WADE, W. F., Microbiology
WALLACE, A. G., Medicine
WALSH, D. B., Surgery
WASSON, J. H., Community and Family Medicine
WEINSTEIN, J. N., Surgery (Orthopaedics); Community and Family Medicine
WELCH, H. G., Community and Family Medicine
WENNBERG, J. E., Community and Family Medicine
WICKNER, W. T., Biochemistry
WILKINSON, R. H., Radiology
WILLIAMSON, P. D., Medicine
WIRA, C. R., Physiology
YEAGER, M. P., Anaesthesiology
YEO, K.-T. J., Pathology
YOUNG, R. D., Obstetrics and Gynaecology
ZACHARSKI, L. R., Medicine
ZUBKOFF, M., Community and Family Medicine
ZWOLAK, R. M., Surgery

Thayer School of Engineering (14 Engineering Dr., Hanover, NH 03755; tel. (603) 646-2230; e-mail thayer.receptionist@dartmouth.edu; internet engineering.dartmouth.edu):

BAKER, I.
CUSHMAN-ROISIN, B.
CYBENKO, G.
GARMIRE, E.
GRAEVE, R. J.
HUTCHINSON, C. E.
KANTROWITZ, A. R.
KENNEDY, F. E.
LOTKO, W.
LYNCH, D. R.
PAULSEN, K. D.
PETRENKO, V. F.
RICHTER, H. J.
SCHULSON, E. M.
STRATTON, W. D.
TAYLOR, S.
WYMAN, C. E.

Tuck School of Business Administration (100 Tuck Hall, Hanover, NH 03755; tel. (603) 646 8825; e-mail tuck.admissions@tuck.dartmouth.edu; internet www.tuck.dartmouth.edu):

ARGENTI, P. A., Management and Corporate Communication
BAKER, K. R., Management
BERNARD, A., Int. Economics
BLAYDON, C. C., Management
DANOS, P., Business Admin.
DAVENI, R. A., Strategic Management
ECKBO, B. E., Finance
FINKELSTEIN, S., Management
FRENCH, K. R., Finance
GOVINDARAJAN, V., Int. Business
GREENHALGH, L., Management
HANSEN, R. G., Business Admin.
HELFAT, C. E., Strategy and Technology
JOHNSON, M. E., Operations Management
JOYCE, W. F., Strategy and Organizational Theory
KELLER, K. L., Marketing
KELLER, P. A., Management
LaPORTA, R., Finance
MASSEY, J. A., Int. Business
MUNTER, M. M., Management Communication
NESLIN, S. A., Marketing
POWELL, S. G., Business Admin.

PYKE, D. F., Business Admin.
ROGALSKI, R. J., Investments
SHANK, J. K., Managerial Accounting and Management Control
STICKNEY, C. P., Management
ZUBKOFF, M., Health Economics and Management

FRANKLIN PIERCE UNIVERSITY

40 University Dr., Rindge, NH 03461-0060
Telephone: (603) 899-4000
E-mail: admissions@franklinpierce.edu
Internet: www.franklinpierce.edu
Founded 1962 as Franklin Pierce College, present name and status 2007
Private control
Academic year: September to May (2 semesters)
Campuses at Concord, Lebanon, Portsmouth, Manchester in New Hampshire and Goodyear in Arizona
Pres.: Dr JAMES F. BIRGE
Provost and Vice-Pres. for Academic Affairs: Dr KIM MOONEY
Vice-Pres. for College Relations: EVELYN BUCHANAN
Vice-Pres. for Enrolment Management: WILLIAM P. HAWKINS
Vice-Pres. for Finance and Admin. and Chief Financial Officer: RICHARD A. MARSHALL
Vice-Pres. for Institutional Advancement: AHMAD BOURA
Vice-Pres. for Student Affairs: Dr JAMES P. EARLE
Dir for Admissions: LINDA QUIMBY
Dir for Library Services: CARISSA M. CARISSA M. DELIZIO
Registrar: Dr SUSAN R. CHAMBERLIN
Library of 132,015 vols, 13,365 serial subscriptions
Number of teachers: 65
Number of students: 2,300
Publication: *Pierce Radius* (2 a year)

DEANS

College of Graduate and Professional Studies: Dr PATRICIA BROWN

HESSER COLLEGE

3 Sundial Ave, Manchester, NH 03103
Telephone: (603) 668-6660
E-mail: admissions@hesser.edu
Internet: www.hesser.edu
Founded 1900 as Hesser Business College, present status 2006
Private control
Areas of study incl. allied health, arts and sciences, business, criminal justice, early childhood education; 5 regional locations: Concord, Manchester, Nashua, Portsmouth, Salem
Pres.: Dr JACQUELYN ARMITAGE
Vice-Pres. for Academic Affairs: Dr GREGORY FOWLER
Vice-Pres. for Finance and Admin.: JOSEPH A. SERGI
Vice-Pres. for Operations: MAUREEN ZNOJ
Academic Dean: Dr JAN WYATT
Dir for Admissions: KRISTOPHER GOODMAN
Dir for Library Services: ADA KEMP
Registrar: SUSAN PROVENCHER
Library of 25,552 vols, 50,000 ebooks, 1,639 audiovisual items, 170 periodicals

NEW ENGLAND COLLEGE

98 Bridge St, Henniker, NH 03242
Telephone: (603) 428-2000
E-mail: admission@nec.edu
Internet: www.nec.edu
Founded 1946

Private control
Academic year: September to May (2 semesters)
Divs of education, liberal arts and sciences, management
Pres.: Dr MICHELE D. PERKINS
Vice-Pres. for Academic Affairs: Dr HILTON HALLOCK
Vice-Pres. for Enrolment and Marketing: Dr BARBARA LAYNE
Vice-Pres. for Finance and Admin.: PAULA A. AMATO
Vice-Pres. for Strategic Priorities and Institutional Advancement: Dr JAMES GARVEY
Vice-Pres. for Student Devt and Dean for Student Affairs: E. JOSEPH PETRICK
Dean for Admissions: DIANE RAYMOND
Dean for Graduate and Professional Studies: NELLY LEJTER
Dean for Students: LORI RUNKSMEIER
Registrar: FRANK L. HALL
Library Dir: KATHERINE VAN WEELDEN
Library of 100,000 vols, 200 periodicals
Number of teachers: 80 (55 full-time, 25 part-time)
Number of students: 1,000
Publication: *Entelechy International: A Journal of Contemporary Ideas* (1 a year)

RIVIER COLLEGE

420 S Main St, Nashua, NH 03060
Telephone: (603) 888-1311
E-mail: admissions@rivier.edu
Internet: www.rivier.edu
Founded 1933, present status 1935, present location 1941
Private control
Academic year: September to May
Liberal arts college; areas of study: biology, chemistry, communications, criminal justice, human development, mathematics, modern languages, sociology
Pres.: Sis. PAULA MARIE BULEY
Vice-Pres. for Academic Affairs: Sis. THERESE LAROCHELLE
Vice-Pres. for Enrolment Management: DAVID BOISVERT
Vice-Pres. for Finance and Admin.: JOSEPH A. FAGAN
Vice-Pres. for Student Devt: LYNN JANSKY
Academic Dean: Dr ALBERT DECICCIO
Registrar: KEVIN GATELY
Library Dir: DANIEL SPEIDEL
Library of 90,000 vols, 45,000 ebooks
Number of teachers: 75 (full-time)
Number of students: 2,300
Publication: *InSight: Rivier Academic Journal*

SAINT ANSELM COLLEGE

100 St Anselm Dr., Manchester, NH 03102-1310
Telephone: (603) 641-7000
E-mail: admission@anselm.edu
Internet: www.anselm.edu
Founded 1889
Private control
Academic year: August to May (2 semesters)
Liberal arts college; depts of. criminal justice, economics and business, humanities, nursing, philosophy, politics, theology
Pres.: Fr JONATHAN DEFELICE
Exec. Vice-Pres.: Dr SUZANNE K. MELLON
Vice-Pres. for Academic Affairs and Dean for College: AUGUSTINE KELLY
Vice-Pres. for Student Affairs: Dr JOSEPH M. HORTON
Dean for Admission: NANCY DAVIS GRIFFIN
Registrar: MARY ANN ERICSON
Librarian: JOSEPH W. CONSTANCE, JR

Library of 240,000 vols, 1,100 periodical titles, 75,000 microforms
Number of teachers: 170 (136 full-time, 34 part-time)
Number of students: 1,900

SOUTHERN NEW HAMPSHIRE UNIVERSITY

2500 N River Rd, Manchester, NH 03106
Telephone: (603) 626-9100
E-mail: pcmhadmissions@snhu.edu
Internet: www.snhu.edu
Founded 1932 as New Hampshire School of Accounting and Secretarial Science, present name and status 2001
Private control
Academic year: August to May (2 semesters)
Campuses in Maine, Nashua, Portsmouth, Salem
Pres.: Dr PAUL J. LEBLANC
Provost and Sr Vice-Pres. for Academic Affairs: Dr PATRICIA A. LYNOTT
Sr Vice-Pres. for Academics, Student Success and Operations: YVONNE SIMON
Sr Vice-Pres. for Finance and Admin.: WILLIAM MCGARRY
Vice-Pres. for Devt and Human Resources: PAMELA HOGAN
Vice-Pres. for Enrolment Management: BRAD POZNANSKI
Vice-Pres. for Institutional Advancement: DONALD BREZINSKI
Dean for Students: HEATHER LORENZ
Dean for Library: KATHRYN GROWNEY
Registrar: Dr JENNIFER DISTEFANO
Library of 109,000 vols, 53,146 ejournals
Number of teachers: 100
Number of students: 6,400

DEANS

Continuing Education: CAROL BATKER
School of Arts and Sciences: Dr KAREN ERICKSON
School of Business: Dr WILLIAM J. GILLETT
School of Education: Dr MARY S. HEATH

THOMAS MORE COLLEGE OF LIBERAL ARTS

6 Manchester St, Merrimack, NH 03054
Telephone: (603) 880-8308
E-mail: admissions@thomasmorecollege.edu
Internet: www.thomasmorecollege.edu
Founded 1978
Private control
Academic year: September to May (2 semesters)
Areas of study: history, law, literature, philosophy, politics, theology
Pres.: Dr WILLIAM EDMUND FAHEY
Vice-Pres. for Admin.: CLINT HANSON
Vice-Pres. for Institutional Advancement: CHARLIE MCKINNEY
Academic Dean: Prof. Dr CHRISTOPHER OLAF BLUM
Dean for Students: WALTER J. THOMPSON
Dir for Admissions: MARK SCHWERDT
Registrar: CHRISTOPHER BLUM
Librarian: SAMUEL SCHMITT
Library of 40,000 vols, 7,500 periodicals
Number of teachers: 10
Number of students: 80
Publication: *Second Spring: An International Journal of Faith and Culture* (2 a year)

UNIVERSITY SYSTEM OF NEW HAMPSHIRE

Dunlap Center, 25 Concord Rd, Durham, NH 03824-3545
Telephone: (603) 862-1800
E-mail: usnh.chancellor@unh.edu

Internet: www.usnh.edu
Founded 1963
State control
Chancellor: Dr EDWARD R. MACKAY
Vice-Chancellor and Treas.: Dr KEN CODY
Assoc. Vice-Chancellor for Academic and Student Affairs: TOM FRANKE
Assoc. Vice-Chancellor for Govt Affairs: KATHLEEN K. SALISBURY
Gen. Counsel and Sec.: RONALD F. RODGERS
Number of students: 30,998 ...

CONSTITUENT INSTITUTIONS

Granite State College

25 Hall St, Concord, NH 03301
Telephone: (603) 228-3000
E-mail: ask.granite@granite.edu
Internet: www.granite.edu
Founded 1972 as School of Continuing Studies, present name and status 2005
Academic year: July to June (2 semesters)
Regional campuses at Claremount, Conway, Rochester
Pres.: Dr ROXANNE GONZALES
Dean for Academic Affairs: Dr SHEILA TAYLOR-KING
Dean for Enrolment Management: M. B. LUFKIN
Dean for Finance and Admin.: LISA L SHAWNEY
Dean for Students and External Engagement: TESSA H. MCDONNELL
Registrar: KAREN KING
Number of teachers: 320 (adjunct)
Number of students: 33,130

Keene State College

229 Main St, Keene, NH 03435
Telephone: (603) 352-2276
E-mail: admissions@keene.edu
Internet: www.keene.edu
Founded 1909 as Keene Normal School, present name and status 1963
State control
Academic year: September to May (2 semesters)
Pres.: Dr HELEN F. GILES-LEE
Provost and Vice-Pres. for Academic Affairs: Dr EMILE NETZHAMMER
Vice-Pres. for Advancement: MARYANN LACROIX LINDBERG
Vice-Pres. for Finance and Planning: Dr JAY V. KAHN
Vice-Pres. for Student Affairs: Dr ANDREW ROBINSON
Dean of Library: IRENE HEROLD
Registrar: TOM RICHARD
Library of 326,000 vols, 900 periodicals, newspapers and audiovisual materials
Number of teachers: 455 (197 full-time, 258 part-time)
Number of students: 5,740
Publication: *Keene State Today*

DEANS

School of Arts and Humanities: Dr NONA FIENBERG
School of Professional and Graduate Studies: Dr MELINDA TREADWELL
School of Science and Social Sciences: GORDON LEVERSEE

Plymouth State University

17 High St, Plymouth, NH 03264-1595
Telephone: (603) 535-5000
E-mail: plymouthadmit@plymouth.edu
Internet: www.plymouth.edu
Founded 1871 as teacher training school, current name 2003
public control

Academic year: September to May (2 semesters)
Pres.: Dr SARA JAYNE STEEN
Provost and Vice-Pres. for Academic Affairs: Dr JULIE N. BERNIER
Vice-Pres. for Enrolment Management and Student Affairs: JAMES HUNDREISER
Vice-Pres. for Finance and Admin.: STEPHEN J. TASKAR
Vice-Pres. for Univ. Advancement: SALLY C. HOLLAND
Registrar: GEORGE GILMORE
Dean of Library and Academic Support Services: DAVID BERONA
Library of 346,207 vols
Number of teachers: 490
Number of students: 6,690
Publications: *Anthology of Teachers' Writing* (1 a year), *Centripetal* (2 a year), *Plymouth Magazine* (2 a year), *The New Hampshire Journal of Education* (1 a year), *Writing across the Curriculum* (1 a year)

DEANS

College of Arts and Sciences: Dr CYNTHIA W. VASCAK
College of Business Administration: Prof. Dr TRENT E. BOGGESS
College of Education, Health and Human Services: Dr GAIL F. MEARS
Division of Online and Continuing Education: Dr NANCY S. BETCHART

University of New Hampshire

Thompson Hall, 105 Main St, Durham, NH 03824
Telephone: (603) 862-1234
E-mail: admissions@unh.edu
Internet: www.unh.edu
Founded 1866 as New Hampshire College of Agriculture and the Mechanic Arts, current name adopted 1923
State control
Language of instruction: English
Academic year: September to May (2 semesters)
Pres.: Dr MARK W. HUDDLESTON
Provost and Exec. Vice-Pres. for Academic Affairs: Dr LISA MACFARLANE
Vice-Pres. for Advancement: DEBORAH DUTTON
Vice-Pres. for Finance and Admin.: Dr RICHARD K. CANNON
Vice-Pres. for Student and Academic Services: Dr MARK RUBINSTEIN
Dir for Admissions: ROBERT MCGANN
Registrar (vacant)
Dean for Univ. Libraries: Dr ANNIE DONAHUE
Library of 2,223,745 vols, 3,000,100 microforms, 37,529 audiovisual materials, 361,170 ebooks
Number of teachers: 1,000
Number of students: 14,470 (12,290 undergraduate, 2,180 graduate)
Publications: *IDEA: The Intellectual Property Law Review* (4 a year), *Inquiry* (undergraduate research journal), *Main Street Magazine*, *Portuguese Studies Review*, *Seafare* (jtly with Univ. of Maine), *UNH-LAW* (2 a year), *UNH Magazine* (3 a year), *University of New Hampshire Law Review* (1 a year)

DEANS

College of Engineering and Physical Sciences: Dr SAMUEL MUKASA
College of Health and Human Services: Dr MICHAEL FERRARA
College of Liberal Arts: Dr KENNETH FULD
College of Life Sciences and Agriculture: JON M. WRAITH
Graduate School: Dr HARRY J. RICHARDS

Peter T. Paul College of Business and Economics: Dr ARNOLD GARRON
University of New Hampshire at Manchester: Dr J. MICHAEL HICKEY
University of New Hampshire School of Law: JOHN T. BRODERICK, JR

NEW JERSEY

BERKELEY COLLEGE

44 Rifle Camp Rd, Woodland Park, NJ 07424
Telephone: (973) 278-5400
E-mail: info@berkeleycollege.edu
Internet: berkeleycollege.edu
Founded 1931
Private control
Academic year: September to July
Pres.: Dr DARIO A. CORTES
Provost: Dr GLEN ZEITZER
Sr Vice-Pres. and Chief Financial Officer: DONALD DEVINE, II
Sr Vice-Pres. for Enrolment Management: DIANE RECINOS
Sr Vice-Pres. for Govt Relations: TERI DUDA
Vice-Pres. for Operations: MARK WAGENER
Vice-Pres. for Student Accounts: EILEEN LOFTUS-BERLIN
Vice-Pres. for Student Devt and Campus Life: ED HUGHES
Vice-Pres. for Library Services: MARLENE DOTY
Number of students: 8,900
Publication: *Berkley College Viewbook*

DEANS

School of Business: Dr JOHN RAPANOS
School of Liberal Arts: Dr DONALD KIEFFER
School of Professional Studies: Dr JUDITH KORNBERG

BLOOMFIELD COLLEGE

467 Franklin St, Bloomfield, NJ 07003
Telephone: (973) 748-9000
E-mail: admission@bloomfield.edu
Internet: www.bloomfield.edu
Founded 1868 as German Theological Seminary
Private control
Academic year: August to August
Pres.: RICHARD A. LEVAO
Sr Vice-Pres. for Admin. and Finance: JOHN CROSS
Vice-Pres. for Academic Affairs and Dean for Faculty: MARION TERENZIO
Vice-Pres. for Enrolment Management: ADAM CASTRO
Vice-Pres. for Institutional Advancement: KWI BRENNAN
Vice-Pres. for Student Affairs and Dean for Students: PATRICK LAMY
Dir for Admission: NICOLE CIBELLI
Registrar: EILEEN POLAZZI
Library Dir: DAN FIGUEREDO
Library of 70,000 vols
Number of teachers: 180
Number of students: 2,000

CALDWELL COLLEGE

120 Bloomfield Ave, Caldwell, NJ 07006
Telephone: (973) 618-3000
E-mail: admissions@caldwell.edu
Internet: www.caldwell.edu
Founded 1939
Private control
Academic year: August to May
Humanities; physical and biological sciences, and mathematics; and social sciences
Pres.: Dr NANCY H. BLATTNER

Vice-Pres. for Academic Affairs: Dr PATRICK PROGAR
Vice-Pres. for Devt and Alumni Affairs: KEVIN BOYLE
Vice-Pres. for Enrolment Management: JOSEPH L. POSILLICO
Vice-Pres for Finance and Admin.: JACK RAINEY
Vice-Pres. for Institutional Effectiveness: SHEILA N. O'ROURKE
Vice-Pres. and Dean for Student Life: Sis. KATHLEEN TUITE
Librarian: Dr PETER PANOS

Library of 142,356 vols
Number of teachers: 180
Number of students: 2,300 (1,599 full-time)

CENTENARY COLLEGE

400 Jefferson St, Hackettstown, NJ 07840-9930
Telephone: (908) 852-1400
E-mail: admissions@centenarycollege.edu
Internet: www.centenarycollege.edu
Founded 1867
Private control
Academic year: August to June
Campuses in Hackettstown, Parsippany, Edison and Long Valley
Pres.: Dr BARBARA-JAYNE LEWTHWAITE
Provost and Vice-Pres. for Academic Affairs: JAMES PATTERSON
Vice-Pres. for Finance and Chief Financial Officer: ROGER ANDERSON
Sr Vice-Pres. for College Relations and Marketing: DIANE P. FINNAN
Vice-Pres. for Information Systems: NORMAN W. RANKIS
Dean for Students: Rev. DAVID JONES
Registrar: Dr THOMAS BRUNNER
Library Dir: NANCY MADACSI

Library of 100,000 vols
Number of teachers: 150 (full-time, adjunct)
Number of students: 970
Publications: *The Centenarian*, *Viewbooks*

DEANS

School of International Programs: Dr JOSEPH P. LINSKEY
School of Professional Studies: DEIRDRE LETSON

COLLEGE OF NEW JERSEY

POB 7718, 2000 Pennington Rd, Ewing, NJ 08628-0718
Telephone: (609) 771-1855
Internet: www.tcnj.edu
Founded 1855 as New Jersey State Normal School, present name 1996
Academic year: August to May
Pres.: R. BARBARA GITENSTEIN
Provost and Vice-Pres. for Academic Affairs: SUSAN BAKEWELL-SACHS
Vice-Provost: MARK KINSELICA
Vice-Pres. for Admin. and Finance: PETER L. MILLS
Vice-Pres. for College Relations and Advancement: MATHEW GOLDEN
Vice-Pres. for Devt and Alumni Affairs: JOHN MARCY
Vice-Pres. for Student Affairs: JAMES M. NORFLEET
Registrar: FRANK COOPER
Dean of the Library and Information Services: TARAS PAVLOVSKY

Library of 562,000 vols, 13,000 video recordings, 21,000 sound recordings, 30,000 periodical titles, 11,000 reference colln
Number of teachers: 990
Number of students: 7,115 (6460 undergraduate, 655 graduate)
Publication: *TCNJ Magazine*

DEANS

School of Arts and Communication: Dr JOHN C. LAUGHTON
School of Business: Dr WILLIAM KEEP (acting)
School of Education: Dr MARK S. KISELICA
School of Engineering: Dr STEVEN SCHREINER
School of Humanities and Social Sciences: Dr BENJAMIN RIFKIN
School of Nursing, Health, and Exercise Science: Dr MARCIA BLICHARZ
School of Science: Dr JEFFREY M. OSBORN

COLLEGE OF SAINT ELIZABETH

Two Convent Rd, Morristown, NJ 07960-6989
Telephone: (973) 290-4000
E-mail: apply@cse.edu
Internet: www.cse.edu
Founded 1899
Private control
Academic year: August to May
Pres.: Dr HELEN J. STREUBERT
Vice-Pres. and Dean for Academic Affairs: Dr FRANK SARGENT
Vice-Pres. for Finance and Admin. and Treas.: MARIA CAMMARATA
Vice-Pres. for Institutional Advancement: JANICE HILL
Vice-Pres. for Student Life and Dean for Students: KATHERINE M. BUCK
Coordinator of Graduate Programmes: Dr JOSEPH CICCIONE
Asst Dean of Women's College and Undergraduate Studies: Dr JANE OWENS BOURHILL
Library Dir: AMIRA UNVER

Library of 188,000 vols, 450 periodical subscriptions
Number of teachers: 250
Number of students: 2,110

DREW UNIVERSITY

36 Madison Ave, Madison, NJ 07940
Telephone: (973) 408-3000
Internet: www.drew.edu
Founded 1867
Private control
Academic year: September to May
Pres.: VIVIAN BULL
Provost and Academic Vice-Pres.: PAMELA GUNTER-SMITH
Vice-Pres. for Admin. and Univ. Relations: MARGARET E. L. HOWARD
Vice-Pres. for Enrolment Management: RENEE VOLAK
Vice-Pres. for Finance and Business Affairs: HOWARD BUXBAUM
Vice-Pres. for Univ. Advancement: JAY ANGELETTI
Dean for Campus Life and Student Affairs: SARA WALDRON
Dean for Libraries: ANDREW D. SCRIMGEOUR
Registrar: HORACE TATE

Library of 300,000 vols
Number of teachers: 155 (full-time)
Number of students: 2,720
Publication: *Drew Magazine* (3 a year)

DEANS

Caspersen School of Graduate Studies: ROBERT READY
College of Liberal Arts: JONATHAN LEVIN
Theological School: JEFFREY KUAN

FAIRLEIGH DICKINSON UNIVERSITY

1000 River Rd, Teaneck, NJ 07666
Telephone: (201) 692-2000
E-mail: grad@fdu.edu
Internet: www.fdu.edu
Founded 1942, present status 1956

Private control
Academic year: August to May
Campuses at Morris County and Teaneck in New Jersey, Oxfordshire in UK and Vancouver in Canada
Pres.: Dr J. MICHAEL ADAMS
Provost and Sr Vice-Pres. for Academic Affairs: Dr CHRISTOPHER A. CAPUANO
Sr Vice-Pres. for Univ. Advancement: RICHARD REISS
Vice-Pres. and Chief Information Officer: NEAL STURM
Vice-Pres. for Enrolment Management: JONATHAN WEXLER
Vice-Pres. for Finance and Treas.: Dr HANIA FERRARA
Gen. Counsel: JOHN M. CODD
Univ. Librarian: JAMES MARCUM

Library of 650,000 vols
Number of teachers: 840 (265 full-time, 575 part-time)
Number of students: 12,110 (8,585 undergraduate, 3,525 graduate)
Publications: *FDU Magazine*, *Journal of Psychology and the Behavioral Sciences* (1 a year), *The Literary Review* (4 a year)

DEANS

Anthony J. Petrocelli College of Continuing Studies: KENNETH T. VEHRKENS
Maxwell Becton College of Arts and Sciences (Florham-Madison Campus): Dr GEOFFREY WEINMAN
Silberman College of Business: Dr WILLIAM M. MOORE
Univ. College (Teaneck-Hackensack Campus): Dr PATTI A. MILLS
Wroxton College: Dr NICHOLAS D. J. BALDWIN

FELICIAN COLLEGE

262 S Main St, Lodi, NJ 07644-2117
Telephone: (201) 559-6000
E-mail: admissions@inet.felician.edu
Internet: www.felician.edu
Founded 1923 as Immaculate Conception Normal School, present name 1967
Private control
Academic year: August to May
Campuses at Lodi and Rutherford
Pres.: Sis. THERESA MARY MARTIN
Provost and Vice-Pres. for Academic Affairs: Sis. MARY ROSITA BRENNAN
Sr Exec. Vice-Pres.: Dr CHARLES J. ROONEY
Exec. Vice-Pres. for Admin. and Finance: MARC J. CHALFIN
Vice-Pres. for College Services: ROBERT DECKER
Vice-Pres. for Enrolment Management: ARTHUR D. GOON
Vice-Pres. for Student Affairs: MARY TARCILIA JUCHNIEWICZ
Vice-Pres. for Institutional Advancement: CELESTE A. ORANCHAK
Registrar: JUNE FINN
Dir for Library Services: PAUL GLASSMAN

Library of 115,000 vols, 360 print periodicals, 20,000 online journals, 43,000 ebooks, 80,000 microforms
Number of teachers: 30
Number of students: 2,400

DEANS

Div. of Arts and Sciences: Dr EDWARD KUBERSKY
Div. of Business and Management Sciences: Dr BETH CASTIGLIA
Div. of Nursing and Health Management: Dr MURIEL M. SHORE
Div. of Teacher Education: Dr DONNA M. BARRON-BAKER

GEORGIAN COURT UNIVERSITY

900 Lakewood Ave, Lakewood, NJ 08701-2697

Telephone: (732) 364-2700
E-mail: admissions@georgian.edu
Internet: www.georgian.edu

Founded 1908 as Mount Saint Mary College and Acad., present name 1924
Private control
Academic year: September to May

Pres.: Dr ROSEMARY E. JEFFRIES
Provost: EVELYN SAUL QUINN
Chief Financial Officer: RONALD RECK
Dir for Library Services: LAURA GEWISSLER

Library of 157,000 vols, 782 journals
Number of teachers: 270 (105 full-time, 165 adjunct)
Number of students: 2,555 (1,772 undergraduate, 783 graduate)

Publication: *The Fountain Spray*

DEANS

School of Arts and Sciences: Dr RITA SMITH KIPP
School of Business: Dr JANICE WARNER
School of Education: Dr JACQUELINE E. KRESS

KEAN UNIVERSITY

1000 Morris Ave, Union, NJ 07083

Telephone: (908) 737-5326
E-mail: admitme@kean.edu
Internet: www.kean.edu

Founded 1855, present name 1997
Academic year: September to June

Pres.: Dr DAWOOD FARAHI
Exec. Vice-Pres. for Operations: PHILIP CONNELLY
Vice-Pres. for Academic Affairs: Dr JEFFREY TONEY (acting)
Vice-Pres. for Institutional Advancement and Research: Dr KRISTIE REILLY
Vice-Pres. for Student Affairs: JANICE MURRAY-LAURY (acting)
Registrar: KENNETH WOLPIN
Univ. Librarian: LUIS RODRIGUEZ

Library of 275,000 vols
Number of teachers: 340 (full-time)
Number of students: 15,940

Publication: *Kean Magazine*

DEANS

College of Business and Public Management: Dr KATHRYN MARTELL
College of Education: Dr SUSAN POLLIRSTOK
College of Humanities and Social Sciences: Dr KENNETH DOLLARHIDE
College of Natural, Applied and Health Sciences: Dr GEORGE CHANG (acting)
Nathan Weiss Graduate College: Dr STEVEN LORENZET
School of Visual and Performing Arts: HOLLY LOGUE

MONMOUTH UNIVERSITY

400 Cedar Ave, West Long Branch, NJ 07764-1898

Telephone: (732) 571-3400
E-mail: gradadm@monmouth.edu
Internet: www.monmouth.edu

Founded 1933 as Monmouth Jr College, current name and status 1995
Private control

Pres.: PAUL G. GAFFNEY, II
Provost and Vice-Pres. for Academic Affairs: THOMAS PEARSON
Vice-Pres. for Admin. Services: PATRICIA SWANNACK
Vice-Pres. for Enrolment Management: ROBERT D. MCCAIG
Vice-Pres. for Finance: WILLIAM G. CRAIG
Vice-Pres. for Student and Community Services: MARY ANNE NAGY
Vice-Pres. for Univ. Advancement: Dr JEFFERY N. MILLS
Vice-Pres. and Gen. Counsel: GREY J. DIMENNA
Dean for Library: Dr DR. RAVINDRA SHARMA

Library of 252,500 vols, 1,250 periodicals
Number of teachers: 397 (full-time and part-time)
Number of students: 5,311 (4,037 undergraduate, 1,274 graduate)

Publication: *Monmouth University Magazine*

DEANS

Graduate School: Dr DATTA V. NAIK
Honors School: Dr KEVIN L. DOOLEY
Leon Hess Business School: DONALD MOLIVER
Marjorie K. Unterberg School of Nursing and Health Studies: Dr JANET MAHONEY
School of Education: LYNN ROMEO
School of Science: MICHAEL A. PALLADINO
School of Social Work: Dr ROBIN S. MAMA
Wayne D. McMurray School of Humanities and Social Sciences: Dr STANTON GREEN

MONTCLAIR STATE UNIVERSITY

Montclair, NJ 07043

Telephone: (973) 655-4000
E-mail: undergraduate.admissions@montclair.edu
Internet: www.montclair.edu

Founded 1908 as The New Jersey State Normal School, present name 1994
Academic year: September to May

Pres.: Dr SUSAN A. COLE
Provost and Vice-Pres. for Academic Affairs: WILLARD P. GINGERICH
Vice-Pres. for Finance and Treas.: DONALD C. CIPULLO
Vice-Pres. for Human Resources: JUDITH T. HAIN
Vice-Pres. for Student Devt and Campus Life: Dr KAREN PENNINGTON
Vice-Pres. for Univ. Advancement: JACK T. SHANNON
Vice-Pres. for Univ. Facilities: GREGORY W. BRESSLER
Dean for Library Services: JUDITH LIN HUNT

Library of 500,000 vols, 2,000 serials
Number of teachers: 1,275 (509 full-time, 766 part-time)
Number of students: 18,500

DEANS

College of Education and Human Services: ADA BETH CUTLER
College of Humanities and Social Sciences: MARIETTA MORRISSEY
College of Science and Mathematics: Dr ROBERT PREZANT
College of the Arts: Dr GEOFFREY W. NEWMAN
Graduate School: Dr JOAN C. FICKE
School of Business: Dr E. LaBRENT CHRITE

NEW BRUNSWICK THEOLOGICAL SEMINARY

17 Seminary Pl., New Brunswick, NJ 08901-1196

Telephone: (732) 247-5241
E-mail: info@nbts.edu
Internet: www.nbts.edu

Founded 1784
Private control
Academic year: September to May
2 Campuses: New Brunswick, New Jersey, and St John's campus at Queens, New York

Pres.: GREGG ALAN MAST
Academic Dean: RENEE HOUSE
Dean for Students: JESSICA J. DAVIS
Dir for Library: CHRISTOPHER BRENNAN

Library of 150,000 vols, 10,000 periodicals
Number of teachers: 30
Number of students: 200

NEW JERSEY CITY UNIVERSITY

2039 Kennedy Blvd, Jersey City, NJ 07305-1597

Telephone: (201) 200-2000
E-mail: admissions@njcu.edu
Internet: www.njcu.edu

Founded 1927 as New Jersey State Normal School, present name and status 1998
State control
Academic year: September to May

Pres.: Dr CARLOS HERNÁNDEZ
Vice-Pres. for Academic Affairs: Dr JOANNE Z. BRUNO
Vice-Pres. for Admin. and Finance: AARON ASKA
Vice-Pres. for Student Affairs: Dr JOHN MELENDEZ
Vice Pres. for Univ. Advancement: Dr WILLIAM FELLENBERG
Library Dir: GRACE F. BULAONG

Number of teachers: 785 (243 full-time, 5 part-time, 537 adjunct)
Number of students: 8,700 (6,636 undergraduate, 1,689 graduate, 375 continuing)

Publications: *Academic Forum*, *Gothic Magazine* (1 a year), *Journal of the Imagination in Language Learning* (1 a year), *PATHS*, *Transformations* (2 a year)

DEANS

College of Professional Studies: Dr SANDRA BLOOMBERG
Deborah Cannon Partridge Wolfe College of Education: Dr ALLAN A. DE FINA
William J. Maxwell College of Arts and Sciences: Dr BARBARA FELDMAN

NEW JERSEY INSTITUTE OF TECHNOLOGY

University Heights, Newark, NJ 07102-1982

Telephone: (973) 596-3000
E-mail: information@njit.edu
Internet: www.njit.edu

Founded 1881 as Newark Technical School; adopted current name in 1975
State control
Academic year: September to August

Technological university, colleges: Newark College of Engineering, College of Science and Liberal Arts, College of Architecture and Design, School of Management, Albert Dorman Honors College, College of Computing Sciences; has Enterprise Devl. Centers

Pres.: JOEL S. BLOOM
Interim Provost: Dr FADI P. DEEK
Sr Vice-Pres. for Admin. and Treas.: HENRY A. MAUERMEYER
Sr Vice-Pres. for Research and Devt: Dr DONALD H. SEBASTIAN
Vice-Pres. for Academic and Student Services: CHARLES J. FEY
Vice-Pres. for Univ. Advancement: CHARLES R. DEES, Jr
Gen. Counsel: HOLLY STERN
Librarian: RICHARD T. SWEENEY

Library of 181,000 vols
Number of teachers: 490
Number of students: 9,950 (7,125 undergraduate, 2,825 graduate)

Publication: *NJIT Magazine* (3 a year)

DEANS

Albert Dorman Honors College: ATAM DHAWAN
College of Architecture and Design: URS P. GAUCHAT

College of Computing Sciences: JAMES GELLER
College of Engineering: BASIL BALTZIS
College of Science and Liberal Arts: Dr FADI P. DEEK
School of Management: PIUS J. EGBELU
Graduate Studies: RONALD KANE

PRINCETON THEOLOGICAL SEMINARY

POB 821, 64 Mercer St, Princeton, NJ 08542-0803

Telephone: (609) 921-8300
Internet: www.ptsem.edu

Founded 1812
Private control
Academic year: September to May

Pres.: M. CRAIG BARNES
Sr Vice-Pres., Chief Operating Officer and Treas.: JOHN W. GILMORE
Vice-Pres. and Dean for Academic Affairs: JAMES F. KAY
Vice-Pres. for IT: BILL FRENCH
Vice-Pres. for Investment and Chief Investment Officer: ROBERT MANCHEN
Vice-Pres. for Seminary Relations: WILLIAM ROBERT SHARMAN III
Vice-Pres. for Student Relations and Dean for Student Life: JOHN E. WHITE
Registrar: DAVID H. WALL
Librarian: DONALD M. VORP

Library of 1,252,503 books and microforms
Number of teachers: 39
Number of students: 501

Publication: *Theology Today* (4 a year)

PRINCETON UNIVERSITY

Princeton, NJ 08544

Telephone: (609) 258-3000
E-mail: uaoffice@princeton.edu
Internet: www.princeton.edu

Founded 1746 as College of New Jersey, present name and status 1896
Private control
Academic year: September to May

Pres.: SHIRLEY M. TILGHMAN
Provost: CHRISTOPHER L. EISGRUBER
Exec. Vice-Pres.: MARK BURSTEIN
Vice-Pres. and Sec.: ROBERT K. DURKEE
Vice-Pres. for Campus Life: CYNTHIA CHERREY
Vice-Pres. for Devt: ELIZABETH BOLUCH WOOD
Vice-Pres. for Facilities: MICHAEL E. McKAY
Vice-Pres. for Finance and Treas.: CAROLYN N. AINSLIE
Vice-Pres. for Human Resources: LIANNE SULLIVAN-CROWLEY
Vice-Pres. for Information Technology and Chief Information Officer: BETTY LEYDON
Gen. Counsel: PETER G. McDONOUGH
Dean for Admission: JANET LAVIN RAPELYE
Dean for College: VALERIE SMITH
Dean for Faculty: (vacant)
Dean for Religious Life and Chapel: ALISON L. BODEN
Dean for Research: A. J. STEWART SMITH
Dean for Undergraduate Students: KATHLEEN DEIGNAN
Registrar: POLLY WINFREY GRIFFIN
Librarian: KARIN A. TRAINER

Library: see Libraries and Archives
Number of teachers: 1,152 (full-time, part-time, visiting)
Number of students: 7,731 (5,149 undergraduate, 2,582 graduate)

Publications: *American Foreign Policy*, *Annals of Mathematics* (6 a year), *Business Today* (2 a year), *Nassau Literary Review*, *Prism Magazine*, *Princeton Journal of Bioethics*, *Princeton Tory*, *The Princeton Tiger*, *World Politics* (4 a year)

DEANS

Graduate School: SANJEEV KULKARNI
School of Architecture: STANLEY T. ALLEN
School of Engineering and Applied Science: H. VINCENT POOR
Woodrow Wilson School of Public and International Affairs: CHRISTINA H. PAXSON

PROFESSORS

ABBATE, C., Music
ABREU, D. J., Economics
ACTON, F. S., Electrical Engineering and Computer Science
ADELMAN, J. I., Latin American Studies
AGAWU, V. K., African Studies
AIT-SAHALIA, Y., Economics
AIZENMAN, M., Physics
AKSAY, I., Chemical Engineering
ALLEN, L. C., Chemistry
ALTMANN, J., Ecology and Evolutionary Biology
APPIAH, K., Afro-American Studies
ARMSTRONG, C. M., Art and Archaeology
ARNOLD, R. D., Politics and Public Affairs
ASHENFELTER, O. C., Economics
ATKINS, S. D., Classics
AUSTIN, R. H., Physics
AXTMANN, R. C., Chemical Engineering
BABBITT, M. B., Music
BABBY, L. H., Slavic Language and Literature
BAGLEY, R. W., Art and Archaeology
BAHCALL, N., Astrophysical Science
BARTELS, L. M., Public and International Affairs
BAUMOL, W. J., Economics
BELLOS, D. M., Romance Languages and Literatures
BENABOU, R. J.-M., Economics and Public Affairs
BENACERRAF, P., Philosophy
BENDER, M. L., Geosciences
BENTLEY, G. E., English Literature
BENZIGER, J. B., Chemical Engineering
BERMAN, S. L., Comparative Literature
BERNANKE, B., Economics and Public Affairs
BERNASEK, S. L., Chemistry
BERNHEIM, B. D., Economics
BERRY, C. H., Economics and Public Affairs
BHATT, R. N., Electrical Engineering
BILLINGTON, D. P., Civil Engineering
BLINDER, A. S., Economics
BOCARSLY, A. B., Chemistry
BOGDONOFF, S. M., Aeronautical, Mechanical and Aerospace Engineering
BOLTON, P., Finance, Economics
BONINI, W. E., Geophysics and Geological Engineering, Civil Engineering
BOON, J. A., Anthropology
BOYER, M. C., Architecture
BRACCO, F., Mechanical and Aerospace Engineering
BRADFORD, D. F., Economics and Public Affairs
BRANSON, W. H., Economics and International Affairs
BROACH, J. R., Molecular Biology
BROADIE, S. W., Philosophy
BRODSKY LACOUR, C. J., Comparative Literature
BROMBERT, V. H., Romance Languages and Literatures and Comparative Literature
BROWDER, W., Mathematics
BROWN, C. F., Jr, Comparative Literature
BROWN, G. L., Mechanical and Aerospace Engineering
BROWN, P. F., Art and Archaeology
BROWN, P. R., History
BUNNELL, P. C., History of Photography and Modern Art; Art and Archaeology
BURGESS, J. P., Philosophy
CALAPRICE, F. P., Physics
CALLAN, C. G., Jr, Physics
CAMPBELL, B. A., Psychology
CAR, R., Chemistry

CARMONA, R. A., Operations Research and Financial Engineering
CARRASACO, D., Religion
CASE, A. C., Economics and Public Affairs
CATES, G. D., Jr, Physics
CAVA, R. J., Chemistry
CELIA, M. A., Civil and Environmental Engineering
CHAIKIN, P. M., Physics
CHAMPLIN, E. J., Humanities; Classics
CHANCES, E. B., Slavic Languages and Literatures
CHANG, S.-Y. A., Mathematics
CHASE, A. M., Biology
CHAZELLE, B. M., Computer Science
CHENG, S. I., Aeronautical Engineering
CHILDS, W. A. P., Art and Archaeology
CHOU, C.-P., East Asian Studies
CHOU, S. Y., Engineering
CHOW, G. C., Economics, Political Economy
CHRISTODOULOU, D., Mathematics
CINLAR, E., Civil Engineering
CLARK, D., Computer Sciences
CLINTON, J. W., Near Eastern Studies
COALE, A. J., Economics and Public Affairs
COFFIN, D. R., Art and Archaeology
COHEN, M. R., Near Eastern Studies
COLE, M. D., Molecular Biology
COLLCUTT, M. C., East Asian Studies
CONWAY, J. H., Applied and Computational Mathematics
COOPER, J., Psychology
COOPER, J. M., Philosophy
CORNGOLD, S. A., Germanic Languages
ÇOX, E. C., Biology
ÇURČIĆ, S., Art and Archaeology
CURSCHMANN, M. J. H., Germanic Languages
DAHLEN, F. A., Geological and Geophysical Sciences
DANIELSON, M. N., Politics and Public Affairs
DANSON, L. N., English
DARLEY, J. M., Psychology
DARNTON, R. C., History
DAUBECHIES, I. C., Mathematics
DAVIDSON, R. C., Astrophysical Sciences
DAVIES, H. M., Religion
DEATON, A. S., Economics and International Affairs
DEBENEDETTI, P. G., Engineering
DIAMOND, M. L., Religion
DÍAZ-QUIÑONES, A., Romance Languages and Literatures
DI BATTISTA, M. A., English and Comparative Literature
DICKINSON, B. W., Electrical Engineering
DiIULIO, J. J., Politics and Public Affairs
DILLIARD, I., Journalism and Public Relations
DIMAGGIO, P. J., Sociology
DISMUKES, G. C., Chemistry
DIXIT, A. K., Economics and International Affairs
DOBBIN, F. R., Sociology
DOBKIN, D. P., Electrical Engineering and Computer Science
DOIG, J. W., Politics and Public Affairs
DOYLE, M. W., Public and International Affairs
DRAINE, B. T., Astrophysical Sciences
DRYER, F. L., Mechanical and Aerospace Engineering
EBERT, R. P., Germanic Languages and Literatures
EMERSON, C. G., Slavic Languages and Literatures
ENGELSTEIN, L., History
ENQUIST, L. W., Molecular Biology
ERMOLAEV, H., Slavic Languages and Literatures
ESPENSHADE, T. J., Sociology
EVANS, A. G., Engineering
FAGLES, R., Comparative Literature
FALK, R. A., International Law, Politics, and International Affairs
FALTINGS, G., Mathematics
FARBER, H. S., Economics
FEENEY, D. C., Classics

FEFFERMAN, C., Mathematics
FISCH, N. J., Astrophysical Sciences
FISKE, S. T., Psychology
FITCH, V. L., Physics
FLEMING, J. V., English and Comparative Literature
FLINT, S. J., Molecular Biology
FLOUDAS, C. A., Chemical Engineering
FORCIONI, A., Comparative Literature
FORD, A. L., Classics
FORREST, S. R., Electrical Engineering
FOSTER, H. F., Art and Archaeology
FRANKFURT, H. G., Philosophy
FRASSICA, P., Romance Languages and Literatures
FREEDMAN, R. W. B., Comparative Literature
FREIDIN, R. A., Ccl of the Humanities
FRESCO, J. R., Life Sciences
FRIEDBERG, A. L., Politics and International Affairs
GAGER, J. G., Jr, Religion
GANDELSONAS, M. I., Architecture
GARON, S. M., History and East Asian Studies
GARVEY, G., Politics
GEDDES, R. L., Architecture
GEISON, G. L., History and History of Science
GEORGE, R. P., Jurisprudence
GIBBS, N., Journalism and Council of Humanities
GIRGUS, J. S., Psychology
GLASSMAN, I., Mechanical and Aerospace Engineering
GLUCKSBERG, S., Psychology
GOLDMAN, M. P., English
GOLDMAN, N. J., Demography and Public Affairs
GOLDSTON, R. J., Astrophysical Sciences
GOODMAN, J., Astrophysical Sciences
GOSSMAN, J. L., Romance Languages and Literatures
GOTT, J. R., III, Astrophysical Sciences
GOULD, E., Psychology
GOULD, J. L., Biology
GOWA, J., Politics
GOWIN, E. W., Council of the Humanities and Visual Arts
GRAF, F., Classics
GRAFTON, A. T., History
GRANT, P., Biology
GRAVES, M., Architecture
GREENSTEIN, F. I., Politics
GROSS, C. G., Psychology
GROSSMAN, G. M., Economics and Business Policy
GROTH, E. J., III, Physics
GROVES, J. T., Chemistry
GRUNER, S. M., Physics
GUL, F. R., Economics
GUNN, J. E., Astronomy
GUNNING, R. C.
GUTMANN, A., Politics
HAHN, B., Germanic Languages and Literatures
HALDANE, F. D. M., Physics
HAMMOUDI, A., Anthropology and Near East Studies
HAMORI, A. P., Near Eastern Studies
HANIOGLU, M. S., Near Eastern Studies
HAPPER, W., Physics
HARMAN, G. H., Philosophy
HARTOG, H. A., History
HELD, I. M., Geological and Geophysical Sciences, Atmospheric and Oceanic Sciences
HERBST, J. I., Politics and International Affairs
HIMMELFARB, M., Religion
HINDERER, W., Germanic Languages and Literatures
HOCHSCHILD, J. L., Politics and Public Affairs
HOEBEL, B. G., Psychology
HOFFMANN, L.-F., Romance Languages
HOLLANDER, R. B., Jr, European and Comparative Literature

HOLLISTER, L. S., Geological and Geophysical Sciences
HOLMES, P. J., Mechanical and Aerospace Engineering
HONORE, B. E., Economics
HOPFIELD, J. J., Molecular Biology
HORN, H. S., Biology
HOWARTH, W. L., English
HSIANG, W.-C., Mathematics
HUET, M.-H., Romance Languages and Literatures
ISSAWI, C., Near Eastern Studies
ITZKOWITZ, N., Near Eastern Studies
JACOBS, B. L., Psychology
JAFFE, P. R., Civil and Environmental Engineering
JAHN, R. G., Aerospace Sciences
JAMES, H., History
JAMESON, A., Mechanical and Aerospace Engineering
JEFFREY, P., Music
JENNINGS, M. W., Germanic Languages and Literatures
JHA, N. K., Electrical Engineering
JOHNSON, C. L., English
JOHNSON, M., Psychology
JOHNSON-LAIRD, P. N., Psychology
JOHNSTON, M., Philosophy
JONES, M., Chemistry
JORDON, W. C., History
KAHN, A., Electrical Engineering
KAHN, V. A., English and Comparative Literature
KAHNEMAN, D., Psychology
KASTER, R. A., Latin Language and Literature
KATEB, G., Politics
KATZ, N. M., Mathematics
KAUFMANN, T. D., Art and Archaeology
KELLER, G., Geological and Geophysical Sciences
KELLER, S., Sociology
KELLEY, S., Politics
KENEN, P. B., Economics and International Finance
KEVREKIDIS, Y. G., Chemical Engineering
KINCHLA, R. A., Psychology
KING, E. L., Language, Literature, and Civilization of Spain
KLAINERMAN, S., Mathematics
KLEBANOV, I. R., Mathematical Physics
KNAPP, G. R., Astrophysical Sciences
KNOEPFLMACHER, U. C., English
KOBAYASHI, H., Electrical Engineering and Computer Science
KOCHEN, S. B., Mathematics
KOHLI, A., Politics and International Affairs
KOHN, J. J., Mathematics
KOLLAR, J., Mathematics
KOMUNYAKAA, Y., Council of the Humanities and Creative Writing
KORNHAUSER, A. L., Civil Engineering
KOSTIN, M. D., Chemical Engineering
KRIPKE, S., Philosophy
KROMMES, J. A., Astrophysical Sciences
KUNG, S.-Y., Electrical Engineering
LAKE, P. G., History
LAM, S.-H., Mechanical and Aerospace Engineering
LAMB, J., English
LAMONT, M., Sociology
LANGE, V., Modern Languages
LANGLOIS, J. D., Jr, East Asian Studies
LANSKY, P., Music
LA PAUGH, A. S., Computer Science
LAU, N.-C., Geosciences and Atmospheric and Oceanic Sciences
LAW, C. K., Mechanical and Aerospace Engineering
LEE, P. C. Y., Civil Engineering
LEE, R. B.-L., Engineering
LEHMANN, K. K., Chemistry
LEIBLER, S., Physics and Molecular Biology
LERNER, R., Architecture
LEVIN, S. A., Ecology and Evolutionary Biology

LEWIS, D. K., Philosophy
LEWIS, J. P., Economics and International Affairs
LI, K., Computer Science
LIEB, E. H., Mathematical Physics
LINK, E. P., East Asian Studies
LIPTON, R. J., Computer Science
LITTMAN, M. G., Mechanical and Aerospace Engineering
LIU, B., Electrical Engineering
LONGUENESSE, B. M., Philosophy
LOWRY, H. N., Ottoman and Modern Turkish Studies
LYON, S. A., Electrical Engineering
MCDONALD, K. T., Physics
MACEDO, S. J., Politics
MACKEY, S., Music
MCLANAHAN, S. S., Sociology and Public Affairs
MCLENDON, G. L., Chemistry
MCPHERSON, J. M., History
MAHLMAN, J. D., Geological and Geophysical Sciences, and Atmospheric and Oceanic Sciences
MAHONEY, M. S., History and History of Science
MAKINO, S., East Asian Studies
MALIK, S., Electrical Engineering
MALKIEL, B. G., Economics
MALKIEL, N. W., History
MAMAN, A., French, Romance Languages and Literatures
MARLOW, D. R., Physics
MARTIN, E., Anthropology
MARTIN, R. B., English
MATHER, J. N., Mathematics
MEYER, H., Art and Archaeology
MEYERS, P. D., Physics
MILES, R. B., Mechanical and Aerospace Engineering
MILLER, D. T., Psychology
MILLER, G. A., Psychology
MILLER, H. K., English
MITCHELL, L. C., English
MODARRESSI, H., Near Eastern Studies
MOREL, F. M., Geosciences
MORGAN, W. J., Geophysics
MULDOON, P. B., Humanities
MULVEY, J. M., Civil Engineering
MURRIN, J. M., History
NAQUIN, S., History
NASH, S. C., Romance Languages and Literature
NEHAMAS, A., Humanities, Philosophy and Comparative Literature
NELSON, J., Mathematics
NEWTON, A., Molecular Biology
NOLET, A. M., Geological and Geophysical Sciences
NORD, D. E., English
NORD, P. G., History
OBER, J., Classics
ONG, N.-P., Physics
ORLANSKI, I., Geological and Geophysical Sciences, and Atmospheric and Oceanic Sciences
OSTRIKER, J. P., Astrophysical Sciences
PACALA, S., Ecology
PACZYNSKI, B., Astrophysical Sciences
PAGE, L. A., Jr, Physics
PAGELS, E. H., Religion
PAINTER, N. I., History
PANAGIOTOPOULOS, A. Z., Chemical Engineering
PAVEL, T., Comparative Literature, and Romance Languages and Literatures
PAXSON, C. H., Economics and Public Affairs
PEEBLES, P. J. E., Physics
PETERSON, L. I., Computer Science
PETERSON, W. J., East Asian Studies
PHILANDER, S. G. H., Geological and Geophysical Sciences
PHINNEY, R. A., Geological and Geophysical Sciences
PINTO, J. A., Art and Archaeology
PIROUÉ, P. A., Physics

PLAKS, A. H., East Asian Studies
POLYAKOV, A., Physics
POOR, H. V., Electrical Engineering
PORTES, A., Sociology
POWELL, W. B., Civil Engineering
POWERS, H. S., Music
PRAKASH, G., History
PRENTICE, D. A., Psychology
PREVOST, J.-H., Civil Engineering
PRUCNAL, P. R., Electrical Engineering
PRUDHOMME, P. R., Chemical and Electrical Engineering
RABB, T. K., History
RABINBACH, A. G., History
RABITZ, H. A., Chemistry
RABOTEAU, A. J., Religion
REINHARDT, U. E., Economics and Public Affairs, and Political Economy
RICHARDSON, J., English
RIGOLOT, F., Romance Languages and Literatures
ROCHE, T. P., Jr, English
RODGERS, D. T., History
RODRIGUEZ-ITURBE, I., Civil and Environmental Engineering
ROMER, T., Politics and Public Affairs
ROSE, M. D., Molecular Biology
ROSEN, H. S., Economics
ROSEN, L., Anthropology
ROSENTHAL, H., Social Sciences
ROTHSCHILD, M., Economics and Public Affairs
ROYCE, B. S. H., Mechanical and Aerospace Engineering
ROZMAN, G. F., Sociology
RUBENSTEIN, A., Economics
RUBENSTEIN, D. I., Ecology and Evolutionary Biology
RUSSEL, W. B., Chemical Engineering
RYSKAMP, C. A., English
SARMIENTO, J. L., Geological and Geophysical Sciences
SARNAK, P. C., Mathematics
SAVILLE, D. A., Chemical Engineering
SCANLON, R. H., Civil Engineering
SCHAFER, P., Jewish Studies
SCHEDL, P. D., Molecular Biology
SCHEINKMAN, J. A., Economics
SCHERER, G. W., Civil and Environmental Engineering
SCHMIDT, L. E., Religion
SCHOWALTER, W. R., Engineering and Applied Science
SCHUPBACH, G. M., Molecular Biology
SCHUTT, C. E., Chemistry
SCHWARTZ, J., Chemistry
SCHWARTZ, S. C., Electrical Engineering
SCOLES, G., Chemistry
SEAWRIGHT, J. L., Council of Humanities
SEDGEWICK, R., Computer Science
SEMMELHACK, M. F., Chemistry
SEYMOUR, P. D., Mathematics, and Applied and Computational Mathematics
SHAFIR, E. B., Psychology
SHAPIRO, H. T., Economics and Public Affairs
SHAYEGAN, M., Electrical Engineering
SHEAR, T. L., Jr, Classical Archaeology
SHENK, T. E., Molecular Biology
SHIMIZU, Y., Art and Archaeology
SHOWALTER, E., English
SIGMUND, P. E., Politics
SILHAVY, T. J., Molecular Biology
SILVER, L. M., Molecular Biology
SIMS, C. A., Economics
SINAI, Y. G., Mathematics
SINGER, B. H., Public and International Affairs
SINGER, P. A. D., Bioethics
SITNEY, P. A., Council of Humanities
SLABY, S. M., Civil Engineering
SMITH, A. J., Physics
SMITH, J. A., Civil and Environmental Engineering
SMITH, J. C. O., Humanities
SMITH, J. W., Philosophy
SMITH, N., English

SMITS, A., Mechanical and Aerospace Engineering
SMOLUCHOWSKI, R., Solid State Sciences
SOANES, S., Philosophy
SOBOYEJO, W. O., Mechanical and Aerospace Engineering
SOCOLOW, R. H., Mechanical and Aerospace Engineering
SONER, H. M., Engineering and Finance
SOOS, Z. G., Chemistry
SPIRO, T. G., Chemistry
SPITZER, L., Jr, Astronomy
SROLOVITZ, D. J., Mechanical and Aerospace Engineering
STANSELL, M. C., History
STARR, P., Sociology
STEIGLITZ, K., Computer Science
STEIN, E. M., Mathematics
STEIN, S. J., History
STEINBERG, M., Biology
STEINHARDT, P. J., Physics
STENGEL, R. F., Mechanical and Aerospace Engineering
STOCK, J. B., Molecular Biology
STOUT, J. L., Religion
STURM, J. C., Electrical Engineering
SUCKEWER, S., Mechanical and Aerospace Engineering
SULEIMAN, E. N., Politics
SUNDARESAN, S., Chemical Engineering
SUO, Z., Mechanical and Aerospace Engineering
SUPPE, J. E., Geological and Geophysical Sciences
SURTZ, R. E., Romance Languages and Literatures
TARJAN, R. E., Computer Science
TATE, C. C., English
TAYLOR, H. F., Sociology
TAYLOR, J. H., Physics
TEISER, S. F., Buddhist Studies
TEYSSOT, G. M., Architecture
TIENDA, M., Demographic Studies
TIGNOR, R. L., History
TORQUATO, S., Civil Engineering
TOWNSEND, C. E., Slavic Languages and Literatures
TREISMAN, A., Psychology
TREMAINE, S. D., Astrophysical Sciences
TROTTER, H. F., Mathematics
TRUSSELL, T. J., Economics and Public Affairs
TSUI, D. C., Electrical Engineering
TUKEY, J. W., Science, Statistics
TURNER, E. L., Astrophysical Sciences
UDOVITCH, A. L., Near Eastern Studies
UITTI, K. D., Modern Languages, Romance Languages and Literatures
ULLMAN, R., International Affairs
VAN FRAASSEN, B. C., Philosophy
VAN HOUTEN, F. B., Geological and Geophysical Sciences
VANMARCKE, E., Civil Engineering
VERDU, S., Electrical Engineering
VERLINDE, H. L., Physics
VOLKER, P. A., International and Economic Policy
VON GOELER, S. E., Astrophysical Sciences
VON HIPPEL, F. N., Public and International Affairs
WACHTEL, M. A., Slavic Languages and Literatures
WAGNER, S., Electrical Engineering
WALLACE, W. L., Sociology
WARD, B. B., Geosciences
WARREN, S., Chemistry
WATSON, G. S., Statistics
WATSON, M. W., Economics and Public Affairs
WEI, J., Chemical Engineering
WEIGERT, M., Molecular Biology
WEINAN, E., Mathematics
WEISS, T. R., English and Creative Writing
WEITZMANN, K., Art and Archaeology
WEST, C., Afro-American Studies
WEST, C. R., Religion
WESTERGAARD, P. T., Music

WESTERN, B., Sociology
WHITE, L. T., Politics
WHITWELL, J. C., Chemical Engineering
WIESCHAUS, E. F., Biology
WIGHTMAN, A. S., Mathematical Physics
WILENTZ, R. S., History
WILES, A. J., Mathematics
WILKINSON, D. T., Physics
WILLIAMS, E. S., Humanities
WILLIG, R. D., Economics and Public Affairs
WILLIS, J. R., Near Eastern Studies
WILMERDING, J., American Art; Art and Archaeology
WILSON, J. F., Religion
WOLFSON, S. J., English
WOLPERT, J., Geography, Public Affairs and Urban Planning
WOOD, E. F., Civil Engineering
WOOD, M. G., English
WOODFORD, M. D., Economics and Banking
WUTHNOW, R. J., Sociology
YAO, A. L.-L., Computer Science
YU, Y. S., East Asian Studies
ZAKIAN, V. A., Molecular Biology
ZEITLIN, F. I., Classics
ZELIZER, V. A., Sociology
ZIOLKOWSKI, T. J., Germanic Languages and Literatures, and Comparative Literature

RAMAPO COLLEGE OF NEW JERSEY

505 Ramapo Valley Rd, Mahwah, NJ 07430-1680

Telephone: (201) 684-7500
E-mail: admissions@ramapo.edu
Internet: www.ramapo.edu

Founded 1969
State control
Academic year: September to May

Pres.: Dr PETER PHILIP MERCER
Provost and Vice-Pres. for Academic Affairs: Dr BETH E. BARNETT
Vice-Pres. for Institutional Advancement: CATHLEEN DAVEY
Vice-Pres. for Student Affairs: Dr PAMELA M. BISCHOFF
Dean for Students: NANCY MACKIN
Registrar: CYNTHIA BRENNAN
Librarian: ELIZABETH SIECKE

Library of 170,000 vols, 5,000 DVDs
Number of teachers: 190
Number of students: 6,000

Publications: *Eastern Economic Journal* (4 a year), *Ramapo Magazine*, *Viewbook*

DEANS

Anisfield School of Business: Dr LEWIS M. CHAKRIN
School of American and International Studies: Dr HASSAN M. NEJAD
School of Contemporary Arts: STEVEN PERRY
School of Social Science and Human Services: Dr SAMUEL ROSENBERG
School of Theoretical and Applied Science: Dr EDWARD SAIFF

RICHARD STOCKTON COLLEGE OF NEW JERSEY

101 Vera King Farris Dr., Galloway, NJ 08205-9441

Telephone: (609) 652-1776
Internet: www.stockton.edu

Founded 1969 as Richard Stockton State College
Academic year: September to May

Pres.: Dr HERMAN J. SAATKAMP, JR
Provost and Exec. Vice-Pres.: HARVEY KESSELMAN
Vice-Pres. for Admin. and Finance: ROBERT D'AUGUSTINE
Vice-Pres. for Student Affairs: THOMASA GONZALEZ
Gen. Counsel: MELISSA E. HAGER

Registrar: JOSEPH J. LOSASSO
Library Dir: DAVID PINTO
Number of teachers: 280 (full-time)
Number of students: 8,110

DEANS

School of Arts and Humanities: ROBERT GREGG
School of Business: Dr JANET M. WAGNER
School of Education: Dr JOSEPH MARCHETTI
School of General Studies: G. JAN COLIJN
School of Graduate and Continuing Studies: Dr LEWIS LEITNER
School of Health Sciences: Dr Prof. BRENDA STEVENSON MARSHALL
School of Natural Sciences and Mathematics: Dr DENNIS WEISS
School of Social and Behavioral Sciences: Dr CHERYL R. KAUS

RIDER UNIVERSITY

2083 Lawrenceville Rd, Lawrenceville, NJ 08648-3099

Telephone: (609) 896-5000
E-mail: admissions@rider.edu
Internet: www.rider.edu
Founded 1865 as Trenton Business College, present name and status 1994
Private control
Campuses in Lawrenceville and Princeton
Pres.: Dr MORDECHAI ROZANSKI
Provost and Vice-Pres. for Academic Affairs: Dr DONALD A. STEVEN
Vice-Pres. for Enrolment Management: JAMIE O'HARA
Vice-Pres. for Finance and Treas.: JULIE A. KARNS
Assoc. Vice-Pres. for Student Affairs: Dr ANTHONY CAMPBELL
Vice-Pres. for Univ. Advancement: JONATHAN MEER
Dean for Univ. Libraries: F. WILLIAM CHICKERING
Library of 481,000 vols, 650,000 microforms
Number of teachers: 250
Number of students: 5,800 (4,700 undergraduate, 1,100 graduate)
Publication: *Rider University Magazine*

DEANS

College of Business Admin.: Dr LARRY M. NEWMAN
College of Continuing Studies: BORIS VILIC
College of Liberal Arts, Education, and Sciences: Dr PATRICIA MOSTO
Westminster College of the Arts: ROBERT L. ANNIS

ROWAN UNIVERSITY

201 Mullica Hill Rd, Glassboro, NJ 08028
Telephone: (856) 256-4000
E-mail: admissions@rowan.edu
Internet: www.rowan.edu
Founded 1923 as Glassboro Normal School, present name and status 1997
State control
Academic year: July to June
Campuses in Glassboro and Camden
Pres.: Dr ALI HOUSHMAND
Provost: Dr JAMES NEWELL
Vice-Pres. for Facilities and Operations: MICHAEL HARRIS
Vice-Pres. for Finance and Chief Financial Officer: JOSEPH SCULLY
Vice-Pres. for Student Life: RICHARD JONES
Vice-Pres. for Univ. Relations: THOMAS GALLIA
Registrar: MURIEL A. J. FRIERSON
Dean for Camden Campus: Dr TYRONE W. McCOMBS
Dean for Library Services: BRUCE WHITHAM

Library of 350,000 vols
Number of teachers: 1,050
Number of students: 11,820 (10,440 undergraduate, 1,380 graduate)
Publications: *Avant, Image, Rowan Magazine* (3 a year), *The Gallery, Venue*

DEANS

College of Communication: LORIN BASDEN ARNOLD
College of Education: Dr CAROL A. SHARP
College of Engineering: Dr STEVEN CHIN
College of Fine and Performing Arts: JOHN R. PASTIN
College of Graduate and Continuing Education: Dr HORACIO SOSA
College of Liberal Arts and Sciences: Dr PARVIZ ANSARI
Cooper Medical School: Dr PAUL KATZ
Rohrer College of Business: NIRANJAN PATI

RUTGERS, THE STATE UNIVERSITY OF NEW JERSEY

57 US Highway One, New Brunswick, NJ 08901-8554

Telephone: (732) 445-4636
Internet: www.rutgers.edu
Founded 1766 as Queen's College
State control
Academic year: September to May
Pres.: Dr RICHARD L. McCORMICK
Provost for Biomedical and Health Sciences: Dr CHRISTOPHER MOLLOY
Exec. Vice-Pres. for Academic Affairs: Dr RICHARD EDWARDS
Exec. Vice-Pres. for Devt and Alumni Relations: CAROL P. HERRING
Sr Vice-Pres. for Finance and Admin.: BRUCE C. FEHN
Sr Vice-Pres. and Gen. Counsel: JONATHAN R. ALGER
Sr Vice-Pres. for Lifelong Learning: Dr DAVID FEINGOLD
Vice-Pres. for Admin. and Public Safety: JAY KOHL
Vice-Pres. for Alumni Relations: DONNA THORNTON
Vice-Pres. for Continuous Education and Outreach: RAPHAEL J. CAPRIO
Vice-Pres. for Enrolment Management: COURTNEY O. McANUFF
Vice-Pres. for Faculty and Staff Resources: VIVIAN FERNANDEZ
Vice-Pres. for Int. and Global Affairs: Dr JOANNA REGULSKA
Vice-Pres. for Public Affairs: Dr PETER McDONOUGH, JR
Vice-Pres. for Research and and Economic Devt: Dr MICHAEL J. PAZZANI
Vice-Pres. for Student Affairs: Dr GREGORY S. BLIMLING
Vice-Pres. for Undergraduate Education: Dr BARRY QUALLS
Vice-Pres. for Univ. Budgeting: Dr NANCY S. WINTERBAUER
Vice-Pres. for Univ. Relations: KIM MANNING
Sec.: LESLIE A. FEHRENBACH
Camden Campus Chancellor: PHOEBE A. HADDON
Newark Campus Chancellor: Dr PHILIP YEAGLE
Univ. Librarian: MARIANNE GAUNT
Library: see Libraries and Archives
Number of teachers: 7,000 (full-time and part-time)
Number of students: 58,000 (incl. 14,800 postgraduate)
Publications: *Journal of Law and Public Policy, Journal of Regulatory Economics* (4 a year), *Labor Studies Journal, Plant Molecular Biology Reporter, Public Budgeting and Finance, Public Productivity and Management Review, Raritan Review* (4 a year), *Rutgers Business Law Journal, Rutgers Computer and Technology Law Journal* (2 a year), *Rutgers Journal of Law & Religion, Rutgers Law Journal, Rutgers Law Record* (online, www.lawrecord.com), *Rutgers Law Review, Rutgers Race and the Law Review, Signs Journal of Women in Culture and Society* (4 a year), *Society, The American Sociologist, Women's Rights Law Reporter* (4 a year)

DEANS

Camden Campus:

College of Arts and Sciences and the Graduate School: Dr KRISTIE LINDENMEYER
School of Business: Dr JAISHANKAR GANESH
School of Law: RAYMAN SOLOMON
School of Nursing: Dr JOANNE P. ROBINSON

New Brunswick Campus:

College of Nursing (New Brunswick and Newark Campus: Dr WILLIAM L. HOLZEMER
Edward J. Bloustein School of Planning and Public Policy: JAMES W. HUGHES
Ernest Mario School of Pharmacy: Dr JOSEPH A. BARONE (acting)
Graduate School: Dr JEROME J. KUKOR (acting)
Graduate School of Applied and Professional Psychology: STANLEY B. MESSER
Graduate School of Education: RICHARD DE LISI
Mason Gross School of the Arts: GEORGE B. STAUFFER
Rutgers Business School (Newark and New Brunswick): GLENN SHAFER
School of Arts and Sciences: DOUGLAS GREENBERG
School of Communication and Information: JORGE REINA SCHEMENT
School of Engineering: THOMAS N. FARRIS
School of Environmental and Biological Sciences: ROBERT M. GOODMAN
School of Management and Labor Relations: SUSAN J. SCHURMAN (acting)
School of Social Work: KATHLEEN J. POTTICK (acting)

Newark Campus:

College of Arts and Sciences and University College: JAN ELLEN LEWIS (acting)
Graduate School: Dr GARY ROTH
School of Criminal Justice: TODD R. CLEAR
School of Law: Prof. JOHN J. FARMER, JR
School of Public Affairs and Admin.: Dr MARC HOLZER

SAINT PETER'S COLLEGE

2641 John F. Kennedy Blvd, Jersey City, NJ 07306-5997

Telephone: (201) 761-6000
E-mail: gradadmit@spc.edu
Internet: www.spc.edu
Founded 1872
Private control
Academic year: August to May
Pres.: Dr EUGENE J. CORNACCHIA
Provost and Vice-Pres. for Academic Affairs: Dr MARYLOU YAM
Vice-Pres. for Advancement: MICHAEL A. FAZIO
Vice-Pres. for Enrolment Management and Marketing: Dr TERENCE PEAVY
Vice-Pres. for Finance and Business: DENTON STARGEL
Vice-Pres. for Mission and Ministry: Fr MICHAEL L. BRADEN
Academic Dean: Dr VELDA GOLDBERG
Dir for Admissions: DAVID GRIFFEY
Registrar: STEVEN E. SMITH
Library Dir: Dr DAVID ORENSTEIN

Library of 260,000 vols
Number of teachers: 285 (118 full-time, 167 part-time)
Number of students: 3,000 (2,350 undergraduate, 650 graduate)
Publication: *Saint Peter's College Magazine*

DEANS

College of Arts and Sciences and School of Business Administration: Dr VELDA GOLDBERG
School of Professional and Continuing Studies: ELIZABETH KANE

SETON HALL UNIVERSITY

400 S Orange Ave, South Orange, NJ 07079
Telephone: (973) 761-9000
E-mail: thehall@shu.edu
Internet: www.shu.edu
Founded 1856 as Seton Hall College, present status 1950
Private control
Academic year: August to May
Pres.: Dr A. GABRIEL ESTEBAN
Exec. Vice-Pres. and Provost: Dr LARRY A. ROBINSON
Exec. Vice-Pres. for Admin.: Sr PAULA M. BULEY
Vice-Pres. for Enrolment Management: Dr ALYSSA MCCLOUD
Vice-Pres. for Finance and Technology: DENNIS J. GARBINI
Vice-Pres. for Mission and Min.: Mgr ANTHONY ZICCARDI
Vice-Pres. for Student Services: Dr TRACY H. GOTTLIEB
Vice-Pres. for Univ. Advancement: Dr G. GREGORY TOBIN
Vice-Pres. and Gen. Counsel: CATHERINE A. KIERNAN
Dean for Libraries: Dr CHRYSANTHY M. GRIECO
Library of 750,000 vols, 25,000 journals
Number of teachers: 910 (446 full-time, 464 part-time)
Number of students: 9,700 (5,300 undergraduate, 4,400 graduate)
Publications: *Journal of Diplomacy and International Relations* (2 a year), *Mid-Atlantic Journal of Business* (3 a year), *The Chesterton Review* (4 a year), *The Journal of Global Health Governance* (2 a year)

DEANS

College of Arts and Sciences: Dr JOAN F. GUETTI
College of Education and Human Services: Dr JOSEPH DE PIERRO
College of Nursing: Dr PHYLLIS SHANLEY HANSELL
Div. of Continuing Education and Professional Studies: Dr NANCY LOW-HOGAN
Immaculate Conception Seminary School of Theology: Mgr ROBERT COLEMAN
School of Health and Medical Sciences: Dr BRIAN B. SHULMAN
School of Law: PATRICK E. HOBBS
W. Paul Stillman School of Business: Dr JOYCE A. STRAWSER (acting)
Whitehead School of Diplomacy and International Relations: Dr JOHN K. MENZIES

STEVENS INSTITUTE OF TECHNOLOGY

Castle Point on Hudson, Hoboken, NJ 07030-5991
Telephone: (201) 216-5000
Internet: www.stevens-tech.edu
Founded 1870
Private control
Pres.: Dr NARIMAN FARVARDIN

Provost and Univ. Vice-Pres.: GEORGE KORFIATIS
Vice-Pres. and Chief Admin. Officer: MAUREEN P. WEATHERALL
Vice-Pres. for Devt: ED EICHHORN
Vice-Pres. for Facilities and Community Relations: HENRY P. DOBBELAAR
Vice-Pres. for Finance, Chief Financial Officer and Treas.: RANDY L. GREENE
Vice-Pres., Gen. Counsel and Sec.: KATHY L. SCHULZ
Vice-Pres. for Univ. Research and Enterprise Devt: HELENA S. WISNIEWSKI
Dean for Admissions: DANIEL S. GALLAGHER
Dean for Graduate Studies: CHARLES L. SUFFEL
Library Dir: OURIDA OUBRAHAM
Library of 105,000 vols, 48,815 ebooks, 43,887 ejournals
Number of teachers: 440
Number of students: 5,940 (2,240 undergraduate, 3,700 graduate)

DEANS

Charles V. Schaefer, Jr, School of Engineering and Science: Dr MICHAEL BRUNO
College of Arts and Letters: Dr LISA DOLLING
School of Systems and Enterprises: Dr DINESH VERMA
Wesley J. Howe School of Technology Management: Dr GREGORY PRASTACOS

THOMAS EDISON STATE COLLEGE

101 W State St, Trenton, NJ 08608-1176
Telephone: (888) 442-8372
E-mail: info@tesc.edu
Internet: www.tesc.edu
Founded 1972
State control
Pres.: Dr GEORGE A. PRUITT
Vice-Pres. and Provost: WILLIAM J. SEATON
Vice-Pres. and Treas.: MICHAEL J. SCHEIRING
Vice-Pres. for Planning and Research: Dr PENELOPE S. BROUWER
Vice-Pres. for Public Affairs: JOHN P. THURBER
Registrar: SHARON SMITH
Number of students: 20,200

DEANS

Heavin School of Arts and Sciences: Dr SUSAN DAVENPORT
John S. Watson School of Public Service and Continuing Studies: Dr JOSEPH YOUNGBLOOD, II
School of Applied Science and Technology: Dr THOMAS G. DEVINE (acting)
School of Business and Management: Dr SUSAN P. GILBERT
W. Cary Edwards School of Nursing: Dr SUSAN MCMULLEN O'BRIEN

UNIVERSITY OF MEDICINE & DENTISTRY OF NEW JERSEY

POB 1709, 65 Bergen St, Suite 701, Newark, NJ 07107-1709
Telephone: (973) 972-4300
E-mail: uhcontact@umdnj.edu
Internet: www.umdnj.edu
Founded 1970 as College of Medicine and Dentistry of New Jersey, present name and status 1981
Campuses at: Newark, Stratford, Camden, Piscataway/New Brunswick, Scotch Plains
Pres.: Dr DENISE V. RODGERS
Exec. Vice-Pres. for Academic and Clinical Affairs: Dr DENISE V. RODGERS
Sr Vice-Pres. and Gen. Counsel: LESTER ARON
Sr Vice-Pres. for Admin.: Dr CHRISTOPHER KOSSEFF
Sr Vice-Pres. for Finance: DENISE MULKERN

Sr Vice-Pres. for Govt and Community Affairs: JULANE MILLER-ARMBRISTER
Sr Vice-Pres. for Univ. Advancement and Communications: DIANE WEATHERS
Vice-Pres. for Information Services and Technology: DENISE ROMANO
Vice-Pres. for Research: Dr KATHLEEN W. SCOTTO
Univ. Librarian: JUDY COHN
Library of 4,521 vols, 65,600 monographs
Number of teachers: 2,390
Number of students: 5,915
Publications: *UMDNJ*, *UMDNJ Research*

DEANS

Graduate School of Biomedical Sciences: Dr KATHLEEN W. SCOTTO
New Jersey Dental School: Dr CECILE A. FELDMAN
New Jersey Medical School: Dr ROBERT L. JOHNSON
Robert Wood Johnson Medical School: Dr PETER S. AMENTA
School of Health Related Professions: Dr JULIE O'SULLIVAN MAILLET
School of Nursing: Dr SUSAN W. SALMOND
School of Osteopathic Medicine: Dr THOMAS A. CAVALIERI
School of Public Health: Dr GEORGE G. RHOADS

WILLIAM PATERSON UNIVERSITY OF NEW JERSEY

300 Pompton Rd, Wayne, NJ 07470
Telephone: (973) 720-2000
Internet: www.wpunj.edu
Founded 1855 as Paterson City Normal School, present name 1997
State control
Academic year: September to June
Pres.: Dr KATHLEEN WALDRON
Provost and Sr Vice-Pres. for Academic Affairs: Dr EDWARD B. WEIL
Vice-Pres. for Admin. and Finance: STEPHEN BOLYAI
Vice-Pres. for Enrolment Management: KRISTIN E. COHEN
Vice-Pres. for Institutional Advancement: PAMELA L. FERGUSON
Vice-Pres. for Student Devt: JOHN MARTONE
Registrar: MARK EVANGELISTA
Dean for Library Services: Dr ANNE CILIBERTI
Library of 303,545 vols
Number of teachers: 390 (full-time)
Number of students: 11,520 (10,085 undergraduate, 1,435 graduate)

DEANS

College of Arts and Communication: STEPHEN HAHN
College of Education: CANDACE BURNS
College of Humanities and Social Science: KARA RABBITT
College of Science and Health: Dr SANDRA DEYOUNG
Cotsakos College of Business: Dr SAM BASU

NEW MEXICO

EASTERN NEW MEXICO UNIVERSITY

1500 S Ave K, Portales, NM 88130
Telephone: (505) 562-1011
E-mail: enrollment.services@enmu.edu
Internet: www.enmu.edu
Founded 1934
State control
Pres.: Dr STEVEN GAMBLE
Vice-Pres. for Academic Affairs: Dr JAMIE LAURENZ
Vice-Pres. for Student Affairs: Dr JUDITH HAISLETT

Vice-Pres. for Univ. Relations and Enrolment Services: RONNIE BIRDSONG
Registrar: CRYSTAL CREEKMORE
Dir for Library: MELVETA WALKER
Library of 699,847 vols, 300 works of art
Number of teachers: 260
Number of students: 5,080

DEANS

College of Business: Dr D. CHRISTOPHER TAYLOR
College of Education and Technology: Dr JERRY HARMON
College of Fine Arts: Dr JOSEPH KLINE
College of Liberal Arts and Sciences: Dr MARY FANELLI AYALA
Graduate School: Dr LINDA WEEMS

INSTITUTE OF AMERICAN INDIAN AND ALASKA NATIVE CULTURE AND ARTS DEVELOPMENT

83 Avan Nu Po Rd, Santa Fe, NM 87508
Telephone: (505) 424-2300
Internet: www.iaia.edu
Founded 1962
Tribal control
Areas of study: fine arts in creative writing, indigenous liberal studies, museum studies, new media arts, studio arts
Pres.: Dr ROBERT G. MARTIN
Dir for Institutional Advancement: KIRSTEN JASNA
Academic Dean: Dr ANN FILEMYR
Dir for Library Programmes: SARAH KOST-ELECKY

NAVAJO TECHNICAL COLLEGE

POB 849, Crownpoint, NM 87313
Telephone: (505) 786-4100
Internet: www.navajotech.edu
Founded 1979
Tribal control
Academic year: August to May (2 semesters)
Pres.: Dr ELMER J. GUY
Dir for Institutional Devt: JASON ARVISO
Dean for Instruction: TOM DAVIS
Dean for Student Services: Dr LAWRENCE ISAAC, JR
Registrar: DELORIS BECENTI
Librarian: CLYDE HENDERSON
Library of 250,000 vols

NEW MEXICO HIGHLANDS UNIVERSITY

POB 9000, Las Vegas, NM 87701
Telephone: (505) 425-7511
E-mail: admissions@nmhu.edu
Internet: www.nmhu.edu
Founded 1893 as New Mexico Normal School, present name and status 1941
State control
Academic year: August to May (2 semesters)
Pres.: Dr JAMES A. FRIES
Vice-Pres. for Academic Affairs: GILBERT D. RIVERA
Assoc. Vice-Pres. for Finance and Admin. Services: LAWRENCE TRUJILLO
Dean for Student Affairs: Dr FIDEL TRUJILLO
Registrar and Dir for Admissions: JOHN COCA
Dir for Library Services: RUBEN F. ARAGON
Number of teachers: 120
Number of students: 3,810

DEANS

College of Arts and Sciences: Dr ROY LUJAN
School of Business Media and Technology: Dr MARGARET YOUNG
School of Education: Dr MICHAEL ANDERSON
School of Social Work: Dr ALFREDO GARCIA

NEW MEXICO STATE UNIVERSITY

POB 30001, Las Cruces, NM 88003-8001
Telephone: (575) 646-0111
E-mail: president@nmsu.edu
Internet: www.nmsu.edu
Founded 1888 as Las Cruces College, current name and status 1960
State control
Academic year: August to May
Pres.: GARREY CARRUTHERS
Exec. Vice-Pres. and Provost: DANIEL HOWARD
Sr Vice-Pres. for Admin. and Finance: ANGELA THRONEBERRY
Sr Vice-Pres. for External Relations: BENJAMIN WOODS
Vice-Pres. for Economic Devt: KEVIN BOBERG
Vice-Pres. for Research: VIMAL CHAITANYA
Vice-Pres. for Student Success: BERNADETTE MONTOYA
Vice-Pres. for Univ. Advancement: CHERYL HARRELSON
Dean for Library: Dr ELIZABETH TITUS
Library: 1m. vols, 431,225 bound and unbound govt documents, 1.3m. microforms
Number of teachers: 1,020
Number of students: 28,260

DEANS

College of Agriculture, Consumer and Environmental Sciences: LOWELL CATLETT
College of Arts and Sciences: CHRISTA SLATON
College of Business: JAMES HOFFMAN
College of Education: MICHAEL MOREHEAD
College of Engineering: RICARDO JACQUEZ
College of Health and Social Services: TILAHUAN ADERA
Graduate School: LOUI REYES
Honors College: WILLIAM EAMON

NEW MEXICO TECH

801 Leroy Pl., Socorro, NM 87801
Telephone: (575) 835-5434
E-mail: admission@admin.nmt.edu
Internet: www.nmt.edu
Founded 1889 as New Mexico School of Mines, present name 1951
State control
Depts of biology, chemistry, civil and environmental engineering, computer science, electrical engineering, materials engineering, mathematics, mechanical engineering, mineral engineering, physics, psychology
Pres.: Dr DANIEL H. LÓPEZ
Vice-Pres. for Academic Affairs: Dr PETER GERITY
Vice-Pres. for Admin. and Finance: LONNIE G. MARQUEZ
Vice-Pres. for Research and Economic Devt: Dr VAN D. ROMERO
Vice-Pres. for Student and Univ. Relations: MELISSA JARAMILLO-FLEMING
Library Dir: LISA BEINHOFF
Library of 600,000 vols
Number of students: 2,010

NORTHERN NEW MEXICO COLLEGE

POB 160, El Rito, NM 87530
Telephone: (575) 581-4100
Internet: www.nnmc.edu
Founded 1909 as Spanish American Normal School, present name and status 2005
State control
Academic year: August to July
Areas of study: biology, business administration, environmental science, information engineering technology, information technology, integrative healing, integrated studies, mathematics, mechanical engineering (solar

energy), music (jazz studies), nursing, software engineering, teacher education; campus at Española (New Mexico)
Pres.: Dr NANCY BARCELÓ
Provost and Vice-Pres. for Academic Affairs: Dr ANTHONY SENA
Vice-Pres. for Admin.: DAVID SCHUTZ
Vice-Pres. for Student Services and Dir for Admissions: FRANK ORONA
Registrar: JAN C. DAWSON
Dir for Library: ISABEL RODARTE
Number of teachers: 200 (59 full-time, 141 part-time)
Number of students: 2,130

DEANS

College of Arts and Sciences: Dr MELLIS SCHMIDT
College of Community, Workforce and Career Technical Education: Dr CAMILLA BUSTAMANTE
College of Education: Dr CATHERINE BERRY-HILL

ST JOHN'S COLLEGE

1160 Camino Cruz Blanca, Santa Fe, NM 87501-4599
Telephone: (505) 984-6000
E-mail: admissions@sjcsf.edu
Internet: www.sjcsf.edu
Founded 1696 as King William's School, present name 1784, Santa Fe campus 1964
Private control
For Annapolis br. see under Maryland
Pres.: MICHAEL P. PETERS
Dean: J. WALTER STERLING
Dir for Admissions: LARRY CLENDENIN
Registrar: MARLINE MARQUEZ SCALLY
Library Dir: JENNIFER SPRAGUE
Library of 65,000 vols
Number of teachers: 60
Number of students: 450
Publications: *Grout* (1 a year), *The Gadfly*

SANTA FE UNIVERSITY OF ART AND DESIGN

1600 St Michael's Dr., Santa Fe, NM 87505-7634
Telephone: (505) 473-6011
E-mail: admissions@santafeuniversity.edu
Internet: www.santafeuniversity.edu
Founded 1859 as St Michael's College, present name and status 2010
Private control
Academic year: August to August
Depts of art, contemporary music, creative writing and literature, graphic and digital design, liberal arts, moving image arts, performing arts, photography
Pres.: LARRY HINZ
Vice-Pres. for Academic Affairs: GERRY SNYDER
Dir for Admission: CHRISTINE GUEVARA
Dir for Enrolment: RICHARD FERGUSON
Registrar: MARY E. ANGELL
Dir for Library: VALERIE NYE
Library of 170,000 vols in Fogelson Library, also 2 spec. libraries: Chase Art History Library and Beaumont and Nancy Newhall Library
Number of teachers: 80 (full-time)
Number of students: 1,950 (750 full-time, 1,200 part-time)

SOUTHWESTERN COLLEGE

POB 4788, 3960 San Felipe Rd, Santa Fe, NM 87507
Telephone: (877) 471-5756
E-mail: info@swc.edu

Internet: www.swc.edu

Founded 1976 as Quimby College
Private control

Masters programmes in art therapy, counselling; certificate programmes in action methods, art therapy, grief counselling, school counselling

Pres.: Dr JAMES MICHAEL NOLAN
Vice-Pres.: KATHERINE M. NINOS
Academic Dean: Dr WEBB GARRISON
Dir for Admissions: DRU PHOENIX
Registrar: ANDREA PACHECO
Librarian: LESLIE MONSALVE-JONES

UNIVERSITY OF NEW MEXICO

Albuquerque, NM 87131
Telephone: (505) 277-0111
E-mail: unmpres@unm.edu
Internet: www.unm.edu

Founded 1889
State control
Academic year: August to May

Pres.: Dr DAVID J. SCHMIDLY
Exec. Vice-Pres. for Academic Affairs and Provost: Dr SUZANNE TRAGER ORTEGA
Exec. Vice-Pres. for Admin.: DAVID W. HARRIS
Vice-Pres. for Equity and Inclusion: Dr JOSEPHINE DE LEON
Vice-Pres. for Research: Dr JULIA E. FULGHUM
Vice-Pres. for Student Affairs: ELISIO TORRES
Dean for Students: KIMMERLY KLOEPPEL
Registrar: ALEXANDER GONZALEZ
Dean for Univ. Libraries: MARTHA BEDARD
Library: see under Libraries and Archives
Number of teachers: 3,740
Number of students: 28,080 (f. t. e.)

DEANS

Anderson School of Management: DOUGLAS M. BROWN (acting)
College of Arts and Sciences: Dr BRENDA J. CLAIBORNE
College of Education: Dr RICHARD HOWELL
College of Fine Arts: Dr JAMES LINNELL
College of Nursing: Dr NANCY RIDENOUR
Continuing Education: Dr RITA MARTINEZ-PURSON
Graduate Studies: Dr AMY WOHLERT
Pharm. D. College of Pharmacy: Dr DONALD GODWIN
School of Architecture and Planning: GERALDINE FORBES ISAIS (acting)
School of Engineering: Dr CATALIN ROMAN
School of Law: KEVIN WASHBURN
School of Medicine: PAUL B. ROTH
University College: PETER WHITE

PROFESSORS

ABDALLA, R. N., Art and Art History
ABRAMS, J., Medicine
ADAMSON, G. W., Special Education
AHLUWALIA, H. S., Physics and Astronomy
AHMED, N., Electrical and Computer Engineering
ALLEN, F. S., Chemistry
ALTENBACH, J. S., Biology
ALVERSON, D. C., Paediatrics
ANGEL, E. S., Electrical and Computer Engineering
ANGEL, R. M., Music
ANSPACH, J. F., Law
ATENCIO, A. C., Physiology
ATTERBOM, H. A., Health Promotion, Physical Education and Leisure Programmes
AVASTHI, P., Medicine
BACA, O. G., Biology
BAKER, W. E., Mechanical Engineering
BANKHURST, A. D., Medicine
BARBO, D. M., Obstetrics and Gynaecology
BARROW, T. F., Art and Art History
BARTLETT, L. A., English
BARTON, L. M., Biology

BASSALLECK, B., Physics and Astronomy
BASSO, K. H., Anthropology
BAWDEN, G. L., Anthropology
BEAR, D. G., Cell Biology
BEENE, L., English
BENNAHUM, D. A., Medicine
BENNAHUM, J., Theatre and Dance
BENNETT, M. D., Family and Community Medicine
BENZEL, E. C., Surgery
BERGEN, J. J., Spanish and Portuguese
BERGMAN, B. E., Law
BICKNELL, J. M., Neurology
BILLS, G. D., Linguistics
BIRKHOLZ, G. A., Nursing
BLACK, W. C., III, Pathology
BLACKWELL, P. J., Educational Foundations
BORDEN, T. A., Surgery
BORN, J. L., Pharmacy
BOWES, S., Educational Administration
BOYER, C. P., Mathematics and Statistics
BROGAN, J., Civil Engineering
BROOKSHIRE, D. S., Economics
BROWDE, M. B., Law
BROWN, F. L., Jr, Public Administration
BROWN, J., Biology
BRUECK, S. R. J., Electrical and Computer Engineering
BRYANT, H. C., Physics and Astronomy
BUCHNER, M. A., Mathematics and Statistics
BULLERS, W. I., Jr, Management
BURCHIEL, S. W., Pharmacy
BURNESS, H. S., Economics
BURR, S. L., Law
BURRIS, B. H., Sociology
BUSS, W., Pharmacology
BYBEE, J. L., Linguistics
CAHILL, K. E., Physics and Astronomy
CAPUTI, J. E., American Studies
CARDENAS, A. J., Spanish and Portuguese
CARLOW, T. J., Neurology
CAVES, C. M., Physics and Astronomy
CECCHI, J. L., Chemical and Nuclear Engineering
CHAMPOUX, J. E., Management
CHANDLER, C., Physics and Astronomy
CHANG, B. K., Medicine
CHAPDELAINE, M., Music
CHENG, J., Electrical and Computer Engineering
CHRISTENSEN, R. R., Mathematics and Statistics
CIVIKLY-POWELL, J. M., Communications and Journalism
CLARK, J. M., Music
CLOUGH, D. H., Nursing
COES, D. V., Management
COFER, L. F., Psychology
COHEN, E. B., Law Library
COLTON, D. L., Educational Administration
CONDON, J. C., Communication and Journalism
CONNELL-SZASZ, M., History
CORCORAN, G. B., Pharmacy
CORDOVA, I. R., Educational Administration
COUGHLIN, R., Sociology
COUTSIAS, E. A., Mathematics and Statistics
CRAVEN, D. L., Art and Art History
CRAWFORD, M. H., Medicine
CURET, L. B., Obstetrics and Gynaecology
DAIL, W. G., Jr, Anatomy
DAMICO, H., English
DATYE, A. K., Chemical and Nuclear Engineering
DAVIDSON, R., Librarianship
DAVIS, G. L., American Studies
DAVIS, L., Neurology
DAVIS, M., Radiology
DeKEYSER, J., Music
DELANEY, H. D., Psychology
DESIDERIO, R. J., Law
DeVRIES, R. C., Electrical and Computer Engineering
DICKINSON, W. E., Surgery
DIELS, J.-C. M., Physics and Astronomy
DIETERLE, B., Physics and Astronomy

DILLARD, J. F., Management
DINIUS, A., Dental Programme
DODSON, T. A., Music
DORATO, P., Electrical and Computer Engineering
DOUGHER, M. J., Psychology
DRENNAN, J., Orthopaedics
DUBAN, S. L., Paediatrics
DuMARS, C., Law
DUNCAN, M. H., Paediatrics
DURYEA, P. J., Education
DUSZYNSKI, D. W., Biology
EATON, R. P., Medicine
EFROMOVICH, S., Mathematics and Statistics
EL-GENK, M. S., Chemical and Nuclear Engineering
ELIAS, L., Medicine
ELLIOTT, P. C., Management
ELLIS, J. W., Law
ELLISON, J. A., Mathematics and Statistics
ENGELBRECHT, G. A., Counselling and Family Studies
ENKE, C. G., Chemistry
ERIBES, R. A., Architecture and Planning
ESTRIN, J. A., Anaesthesiology
ETULAIN, R., History
EVANS, W., Theatre and Dance
EWING, R. C., Earth Sciences
FEENEY, D., Psychology
FEINBERG, E. A., Art and Art History
FELBERG, L., Music
FIELD, F. R., Training and Learning Technologies
FINLEY, D., Physics and Astronomy
FISCHER, M. R., English
FISHBURN, W. R., Counselling and Family Studies
FLEMING, R. E., English
FLETCHER, M. P., General Library
FLEURY, P. A., Electrical and Computer Engineering
FORMAN, W. B., Medicine
FOUCAR, M. K., Pathology
FRANDSEN, K. D., Communication and Journalism
FRITZ, C. G., Law
FROELICH, J. W., Anthropology
FRONECH, D. K., Electrical and Computer Engineering
FRY, D., Surgery
GAINES, B., English
GALEY, W. R., Jr, Physiology
GALLAGHER, P. J., English
GARCIA, F. C., Political Science
GARRY, P. J., Pathology
GEISSMAN, J. W., Earth Sciences
GELL-MAN, M., Physics and Astronomy
GERDES, D. C., Modern and Classical Languages
GIBSON, A. G., Mathematics and Statistics
GILFEATHER, F., Mathematics and Statistics
GISSER, M., Economics
GLEW, R. H., Biochemistry
GLUCK, J. P., Psychology
GOMEZ-PALACIO, I., Law
GONZALES, R. A., Law
GONZALES-BERRY, E., Modern and Classical Languages
GOODMAN, R., Philosophy
GORDON, W. C., Psychology
GOSZ, J. R., Biology
GRANT, D., Management
GREENBERG, R. E., Paediatrics
GRIFFIN, L. E., Health Promotion, Physical Education and Leisure Programmes
GWIN, M. C., English
HAALAND, K. Y., Psychiatry
HADLEY, W. M., Pharmacy
HAHN, B., Art and Art History
HAIMAN, F. S., General Honours
HALL, G. E., Law
HALL, J., Civil Engineering
HALL, L. B., History
HARJO, J., Engineering
HARRIS, F., Political Science
HARRIS, M., Educational Foundations

HARRIS, R. J., Psychology
HART, F. M., Law
HARTSHORNE, M. F., Radiology
HASHIMOTO, F., Medicine
HAWKINS, C., Electrical and Computer Engineering
HEFFRON, W. A., Family and Community Medicine
HEGGEN, R. J., Civil Engineering
HENNEY, J. E., Medicine
HERMANN, M. S. G., Law
HERZON, F. S., Surgery
HEYWARD, V., Health Promotion, Physical Education and Leisure Programmes
HIGGINS, P. A., Nursing
HINTERBICHLER, K., Music
HOLDER, R. W., Chemistry
HOLLAN, J. D., Computer Science
HUACO, G. A., Sociology
HUMPHRIES, S., Jr, Electrical and Computer Engineering
JAFFE, I. S., Theatre and Dance
JAIN, R., Electrical and Computer Engineering
JAMSHIDI, M., Electrical and Computer Engineering
JEWELL, P. F., Surgery
JOHNSON, D. M., English
JOHNSON, G. V., Biology
JOHNSON, J. D., Paediatrics
JOHNSON, P. J., Psychology
JOHN-STEINER, V. P., Education
JONES, D., English
JOOST-GAUGIER, C., Art and Art History
JORDAN, S. W., Pathology
JUNGLING, K. C., Electrical and Computer Engineering
KARLSTROM, K. E., Earth Sciences
KARNI, S., Electrical and Computer Engineering
KASSICIEH, S. K., Management
KAUFFMAN, D., Chemical and Nuclear Engineering
KAUFMAN, A., Family, Community and Emergency Medicine
KEITH, S. J., Psychiatry
KELLEY, R. O., Anatomy
KELLY, H. W., Pharmacy
KELLY, S. G., Law
KELSEY, C. A., Radiology
KELSEY, C. W., Education
KENDALL, D. L., Electrical and Computer Engineering
KENKRE, V. M., Physics and Astronomy
KERN, R. W., History
KEY, C. R., Pathology
KISIEL, W., Pathology
KLEIN, C., Geology
KLEPPER, D. J., Medicine
KLINE, W., Education
KODRIC-BROWN, A., Biology
KOGOMA, T., Cell Biology
KORNFELD, M., Pathology
KOSTER, F. T., Medicine
KOVNAT, R., Law
KUCHARZ, W., Mathematics and Statistics
KUDO, A. M., Geology
KUES, B. S., Earth Sciences
LaFREE, G., Sociology
LAMPHERE, L., Anthropology
LANCASTER, J. B., Anthropology
LEWIS, S. L., Nursing
LIGON, J. D., Biology
LINDEMAN, R. D., Medicine
LINNELL, J., Theatre and Dance
LIPSCOMB, M. F., Pathology
LIPSKI, J., Modern Languages
LONG, V., Counselling and Family Studies
LOPEZ, A. S., Law
LORENZ, J., Mathematics and Statistics
LOTFIELD, R. B., Biochemistry
LOVE, E. B., Librarianship
LUCKASSON, R. A., Special Education
LUGER, G. F., Computer Science
LUMIA, R., Mechanical Engineering
LUTZ, W., Chemical and Nuclear Engineering

McCARTHY, D. M., Medicine
McCLELLAND, C. E., III, History
McCONNELL, T. S., Pathology
McCULLOUGH-BRABSON, E., Music
McDANIEL, M., Psychology
McFARLANE, D. R., Public Administration
McGRAW, J., Physics and Astronomy
McGUFFEE, L. J., Pharmacology
MACIEL, D. R., History
McIVER, J. K., Physics and Astronomy
McLAUGHLIN, J. C., Pathology
McNAMARA, P. A., Sociology
McNEIL, J., Electrical and Computer Engineering
McPHERSON, D., English
MacPHERSON, W. T., Law
MAKI, G., Electrical and Computer Engineering
MALOLEPSY, J., Theatre and Dance
MANN, B. M., Mathematics and Statistics
MARTINEZ, J. G. R., Special Education
MATHEWSON, A. D., Law
MATTHEWS, J. A. J., Physics and Astronomy
MATTHEWS, O. P., Geography
MATWIYOFF, N. A., Cell Biology
MAY, G. W., Civil Engineering
MAY, P. A., Sociology
MEIZE-GROCHOWSKI, R., Nursing
MELADA, I. P., English
MENNIN, S. P., Anatomy
MERKX, G. W., Sociology
METTLER, F. A., Jr, Radiology
MIGNEAULT, R., Librarianship
MILLER, W. R., Psychology
MILSTEIN, M. M., Educational Administration
MOLD, C., Microbiology
MONEIM, M. S., Orthopaedics
MORAIN, S. A., Geography
MORET, B. M., Computer Science
MORRIS, D. M., Surgery
MORRIS, M. M., Education
MORROW, C., Chemistry
MOSELEY, P. L., Medicine
MURATA, G. H., Medicine
MURPHY, S. J., Paediatrics
NIEMCZYK, T. M., Chemistry
NORDHAUS, R. S., Architecture and Planning
NORWOOD, J. M., Law
NORWOOD, V. L., American Studies
NURNBERG, H. G., Psychiatry
NUTTALL, H. E., Jr, Chemical and Nuclear Engineering
OBENSHAIN, S. S., Paediatrics
OCCHIALINO, M., Law
OGILBY, P. R., Chemistry
OLIVER, J. M., Pathology
OLLER, J. W., Jr, Linguistics
OMDAHL, J. L., Biochemistry
OMER, G., Jr, Orthopaedics
ONDRIAS, M. R., Chemistry
ONNEWEER, C., Mathematics and Statistics
ORRISON, W. W., Radiology
ORTIZ, A. A., Anthropology
ORTIZ, J. V., Chemistry
OVERTURF, G. D., Paediatrics
OWENS, L. D., English
PABISCH, P. K., Foreign Languages and Literature
PADILLA, R. S., Dermatology
PAINE, R. T., Jr, Chemistry
PANITZ, J. A., Physics and Astronomy
PAPADOPOULOS, E. P., Chemistry
PAPIKE, J. J., Geology
PAPILE, L. A., Paediatrics
PARK, S. M., Chemistry
PARKMAN, A. M., Management
PARNALL, T., Law
PARTRIDGE, L. D., Physiology
PATHAK, P. T., Mathematics and Statistics
PEABODY, D. S., Cell Biology
PECK, R. E., English
PEREZ-GOMEZ, J. R., Music
PETERSON, S. L., Pharmacy
PHAM, C., Economics
PIPER, J., Music
PORTER, J., History

PREDOCK-LINNELL, J., Theatre and Dance
PRICE, R. M., Physics and Astronomy
PRINJA, A. K., Chemical and Nuclear Engineering
PRIOLA, D. V., Physiology
PYLE, R. R., Medicine
QUENZER, R. W., Medicine
RABINOWITZ, H., History
RADOSEVICH, R. R., Management
RAIZADA, V., Medicine
RAZANI, A., Mechanical Engineering
REBOLLEDO, T. D., Modern Languages
REED, W. D., Medicine
REES, B. L., Nursing
REEVES, T. Z., Public Administration
REHDER, R. R., Management
REID, R. A., Management
REMMER, K. L., Political Science
REYES, P., Biochemistry
RICHARDS, C. G., Mechanical Engineering
RIENSCHE, L. L., Comm. Disorders
ROBBINS, R. G., History
ROBIN, D. M., Foreign Languages and Literature
RODERICK, N. F., Chemical and Nuclear Engineering
RODRIGUEZ, A., Modern and Classical Languages
ROEBUCK, J., History
ROGERS, E. M., Communication and Journalism
ROLL, S., Psychology
ROMERO, L. M., Law
ROSENBERG, G. A., Neurology
ROSS, H. L., Sociology
ROSS, T. J., Civil Engineering
ROTH, P. B., Emergency Medicine
RUEBUSH, B. K., Psychiatry and Psychology
RUYBAL, S. E., Nursing
SAIERS, J. H., Medicine
SAIKI, J. H., Medicine
SALAND, L. C., Anatomy
SALVAGGIO, R., American Studies
SANTLEY, R. S., Anthropology
SARTO, G. E., Obstetrics and Gynaecology
SAVAGE, D. D., II, Pharmacology
SCALES, A. C., Law
SCALETTI, J. V., Microbiology
SCALLEN, T. J., Biochemistry
SCHADE, D. S., Medicine
SCHARNHORST, G. F., English and American Studies
SCHAU, C. G., Educational Foundations
SCHREYER, H. L., Mechanical Engineering
SCHUELER, G. F., Philosophy
SCHUETZ, J. E., Communication
SCHULTZ, C., Management
SCHUYLER, M. R., Medicine
SCHWARTZ, R. L., Law
SCHWERIN, K. H., Anthropology
SCOTT, P. B., Curriculum and Instruction in Multicultural Teacher Education
SEARLES, R. P., Medicine
SEMO, E., History
SEVERINO, S. K., Psychiatry
SHAHINPOOR, M., Mechanical Engineering
SHAMA, A., Management
SHANE, D. L., Nursing
SHELTON, S. P., Civil Engineering
SHIPMAN, V. C., Counselling and Family Studies
SHOMAKER, D. J., Nursing
SHULTIS, C. L., Music
SIBBITT, W. L., Jr, Medicine
SIEMBIEDA, W. J., Architecture and Planning
SIMONSON, D. G., Management
SKIPPER, B. J., Family, Community and Emergency Medicine
SKLAR, D. P., Emergency Medicine
SKLAR, L. A., Pathology
SMITH, B. T., Computer Science
SMITH, D. D., Special Education
SMITH, D. M., Chemical and Nuclear Engineering
SMITH, H. L., Management

SMITH, M. M., Counselling and Family Studies
SMITH, P. J., Special Education
SMITH, W. S., Jr, Foreign Languages and Literature
SNYDER, R. D., Neurology
SONNENBERG, A., Medicine
SOUTHALL, T. W., Art and Art History
SRUBEK, J., Art Education
STARR, G. P., Mechanical Engineering
STEINBERG, S. L., Mathematics and Statistics
STONE, A. P., Mathematics and Statistics
STRAUS, L. G., Anthropology
STRICKLAND, R. G., Medicine
STURM, F. G., Philosophy
SUMMERS, J. W., Cell Biology
SUTHERLAND, R. J., Psychology
SWINSON, D., Physics and Astronomy
SZASZ, F. M., History
TANDBERG, W. D., Emergency Medicine
TAYLOR, A. P., Architecture and Planning
TAYLOR, S. A., Law
THOMPSON, D. E., Mechanical Engineering
THOMSON, B. M., Civil Engineering
THORNHILL, A. R., Biology
THORSON, J. L., English
TIANO, S. B., Sociology
TOLMAN, J. M., Modern and Classical Languages
TOOLSON, E. C., Biology
TRINKAUS, E., Anthropology
TROTTER, J. A., Anatomy
TROUP, G. M., Pathology
TROUTMAN, W. G., Pharmacy
TUASON, V. B., Psychiatry
TURAN, M., Architecture and Planning
TURNER, P. H., Counseling and Family Studies
TYLER, M., Music
TZAMALOUKAS, A., Medicine
UHLENHUTH, E. H., Psychiatry
USCHER, N. J., Music
USEEM, B., Sociology
UTTON, A. E., Law
VALDES, N., Sociology
VANDERJAGT, D., Biochemistry
VAN DONGEN, R. D., Curriculum and Instruction in Multicultural Teacher Education
VOGEL, K. G., Biology
WALDMAN, J. D., Paediatrics
WALKER, B. R., Physiology
WALTERS, E. A., Chemistry
WANG, M.-L., Civil Engineering
WATERMAN, R. E., Anatomy
WEIGLE, M. M., Anthropology
WEISS, G. K., Physiology
WEISS, J. R., Nursing
WERNLEY, J. A., Surgery
WHEELAND, R. G., Dermatology
WHIDDEN, M. B., English
WHITE, P., English
WIESE, W., Family, Community and Emergency Medicine
WILDIN, M. W., Mechanical Engineering
WILKINS, E. S., Chemical and Nuclear Engineering
WILLIAMS, R. H., Electrical and Computer Engineering
WILLIAMSON, M. R., Radiology
WILLIAMSON, S. L., Radiology
WILLMAN, C. L., Pathology
WINOGRAD, P., Law
WITEMEYER, H., English
WOFSY, C., Mathematics and Statistics
WOLF, S. S., Law
WOLFE, D. M., Physics and Astronomy
WOLFE, J. D., Theatre and Dance
WOOD, C. J., Education Administration
WOOD, J. E., Mechanical Engineering
WOOD, W. F., Music
WOODWARD, L. A., Geology
WORRELL, R. V., Orthopaedics
WRIGHT, J. B., Library
YAGER, J., Psychiatry
YATES, T. L., Biology
ZAGER, P. G., Medicine

ZANNES, E., Communication and Journalism
ZEILIK, M., II, Physics and Astronomy
ZIMMER, W. J., Mathematics and Statistics
ZONGOLOWICZ, H. M.
ZUMWALT, R. E., Pathology

UNIVERSITY OF THE SOUTHWEST

6610 Lovington Highway, Hobbs, NM 88240

Telephone: (575) 392-6561
E-mail: admission@usw.edu
Internet: www.usw.edu

Founded 1956 as Hobbs Baptist College, present name 2008
Private control

Pres.: Dr GARY A. DILL
Vice-Pres. for Academic and Technology Services and Dean for Faculty: Dr JAMES SMITH
Vice-Pres. for Admin. Services: Dr DEE MOONEY
Dean for Enrolment Services and Student Success: JORDAN BODINE
Dean for Students: TOM MULKEY
Dean for Library Services: JOHN MCCANCE

Number of teachers: 50
Number of students: 590

DEANS

School of Business: Dr TOM WILSON
School of Education: Dr MARY HARRIS

WESTERN NEW MEXICO UNIVERSITY

POB 680, 1000 W College St, Silver City, NM 88062

Telephone: (505) 538-6011
E-mail: admissions@wnmu.edu
Internet: www.wnmu.edu

Founded 1893
State control

Pres.: Dr JOHN E. COUNTS
Provost and Vice-Pres. for Academic Affairs: Dr FAYE VOWELL
Vice-Pres. for Institutional Advancement, Economic Devt and Community Affairs: LINDA KAY JONES (acting)
Vice-Pres. for Student Affairs and Enrolment Management: ISAAC BRUNDAGE
Dir for Admissions: DAN TRESSLER
Registrar: BETSY MILLER
Univ. Librarian: Dr GILDA BAEZA-ORTEGO (acting)

Library of 388,193 vols
Number of teachers: 65
Number of students: 3,340

DEANS

School of Applied Technology: ANTONIO MACIAS
School of Business Administration and Economics: Dr LAURIE BARFITT
School of Education: Dr PARTICIA MANZA-NARES-GONZALES
School of Health Sciences and Human Performance: E. WALKER
School of Nursing: PAT MCINTIRE
School of Social Work: BETH WALKER

NEW YORK

ADELPHI UNIVERSITY

POB 701, One S Ave, Garden City, NY 11530-0701

Telephone: (516) 877-3000
E-mail: admissions@adelphi.edu
Internet: www.adelphi.edu

Founded 1863 as Adelphi Aacd., present status 1929
Private control
Academic year: August to May

Off-campus centres: Hauppauge Education and Conf. Center, Hudson Valley Center and Manhattan Center

Pres.: Dr ROBERT A. SCOTT
Provost and Sr Vice-Pres. for Academic Affairs: GAYLE D. INSLER
Sr Vice-Pres. and Treas.: TIMOTHY P. BURTON
Vice-Pres. for Admin. and Student Services: ANGELO B. PROTO
Vice-Pres. for Univ. Advancement: CHRISTIAN P. VAUPEL
Dean for Univ. Libraries: CHARLES W. SIMPSON

Library of 600,000 vols, 806,000 microforms, 33,000 audiovisual materials, 61,000 ejournals
Number of teachers: 990 (330 full-time, 660 part-time)
Number of students: 7,920 (6,100 full-time and 1,820 part-time)
Publications: *Adelphi University Magazine* (2 a year), *Erudition* (1 a year)

DEANS

College of Arts and Sciences: SAM L. GROGG
Gordon F. Derner Institute of Advanced Psychological Studies: JACQUES BARBER
Honors College: RICHARD GARNER
Robert B. Willumstad School of Business: RAKESH GUPTA
Ruth S. Ammon School of Education: JANE ASHDOWN
School of Nursing: PATRICK COONAN
School of Social Work: ANDREW SAFYER

ALBANY COLLEGE OF PHARMACY AND HEALTH SCIENCES

106 New Scotland Ave, Albany, NY 12208-3492

Telephone: (518) 694-7200
E-mail: info@acphs.edu
Internet: www.acphs.edu

Founded 1881
Private control

Campuses in Albany and Vermont

Pres. and Dean: Dr JAMES J. GOZZO
Provost and Vice-Pres. for Academic Affairs: Dr MEHDI BOROUJERDI
Vice-Pres. for Devt: VICKI A. DILORENZO
Vice-Pres. for Enrolment Management: TIFFANY M. GUTIERREZ
Vice-Pres. for Institutional Advancement: VICKI A. DILORENZO
Dean for Student Affairs: Assoc. Prof. JOHN DENIO
Dir for Finance and Business Affairs: WILLIAM M. CRONIN
Dir for Admissions: MATT STEVER
Dir for Library Services: SUE IWANOWICZ
Gen. Counsel: GERALD H. KATZMAN
Registrar: JUDY SCHMONSKY

Number of teachers: 130
Number of students: 1,850
Publications: *Alembic Pharmakon* (1 a year), *Another Creative Perspective* (1 a year), *PostScript, President's Report* (1 a year)

DEANS

School of Arts and Sciences: Dr DAVID W. CLARKE
School of Health Sciences: Prof. Dr HASSAN A. N. EL-FAWAL
School of Pharmacy and Pharmaceutical Sciences: Prof. Dr MEHDI BOROUJERDI

ALBANY LAW SCHOOL

80 New Scotland Ave, Albany, NY 12208-3494

Telephone: (518) 445-2311
E-mail: info@albanylaw.edu
Internet: www.albanylaw.edu

Founded 1851
Private control
Academic year: July to June
Pres. and Dean: CONNIE MAYER
Vice-Pres. for Finance and Business: VICTOR
E. RAUSCHER
Vice-Pres. for Institutional Advancement:
HELEN ADAMS-KEANE
Registrar: JOANN FITZSIMMONS
Assoc. Dean and Dir for Library: HELANE
DAVIS
Library of 700,000 vols
Number of teachers: 110 (55 full-time, 55
part-time)
Number of students: 700
Publications: *Albany Government Law
Review, Albany Law Journal of Science
and Technology, Albany Law Review*

ALBANY MEDICAL COLLEGE

43 New Scotland Ave, Albany, NY 12208
Telephone: (518) 262-5634
E-mail: graduate-studies@mail.amc.edu
Internet: www.amc.edu/academic
Founded 1839; attached to Albany Medical
Center
Private control
Dean and Exec. Vice-Pres. for Health Affairs:
Dr VINCENT P. VERDILE
Dir for Admissions: Dr JOANNE H. NANOS
Librarian: SHERRY HARTMAN
Library of 150,000 vols, 2,700 journals
Number of teachers: 120
Number of students: 750 (566 postgraduate,
184 graduate)

ALFRED UNIVERSITY

1 Saxon Dr., Alfred, NY 14802-1205
Telephone: (607) 871-2115
E-mail: admissions@alfred.edu
Internet: www.alfred.edu
Founded 1836
Private control
Language of instruction: English
Academic year: August to May
Courses in engineering and art and design
Pres.: Dr CHARLES M. EDMONDSON
Provost and Vice-Pres. for Academic Affairs:
Dr WILLIAM HALL
Vice-Pres. for Business and Finance: GIOVINA
M. LLOYD
Vice-Pres. for Enrolment Management: EARL
E. PIERCE
Vice-Pres. for Student Affairs: KATHY
WOUGHTER
Vice-Pres. for Univ. Relations: STANLEY A.
COLLA
Dir for Admissions: CORRY UNIS
Dean for Libraries: STEPHEN S. CRANDALL
Library of 287,000 vols
Number of teachers: 200 (160 full-time, 40
part-time)
Number of students: 2,360
Publications: *Alfred Reporter, Kanakadea* (1
a year)

DEANS
College of Liberal Arts and Sciences: Dr
MARY McGEE
College of Professional Studies: Dr NANCY J.
EVANGELISTA
Inamori School of Engineering: Dr DOREEN
D. EDWARDS
School of Art and Design: LESLIE M. BELLA-
VANCE

BANK STREET COLLEGE OF EDUCATION

610 W 112th St, New York, NY 10025-1898
Telephone: (212) 875-4400
E-mail: gradcourses@bankstreet.edu
Internet: www.bankstreet.edu
Founded 1916
Private control
Academic year: September to July
Pres.: Dr ELIZABETH D. DICKEY
Vice-Pres. for Finance and Admin. and Chief
Operating Officer: FRANK NUARA
Vice-Pres. for Institutional Advancement:
JOHN BORDEN
Dean for College: JON SNYDER
Dean for Continuing Education: FERN KHAN
Dean for Graduate School: VIRGINIA ROACH
Dir for Library: KRISTIN FREDA
Library of 123,215 vols
Number of teachers: 125
Number of students: 1,050

BARD COLLEGE

POB 5000, Annandale-on-Hudson, NY
12504-5000
Telephone: (845) 758-6822
E-mail: admission@bard.edu
Internet: www.bard.edu
Founded 1860 as St Stephen's College, pre-
sent name 1934
Private control
Academic year: August to May
Divs: arts; languages and literature; science,
mathematics, and computing; and social
studies; Bard College Conservatory of Music
Pres.: LEON BOTSTEIN
Exec. Vice-Pres.: DIMITRI B. PAPADIMITRIOU
Vice-Pres. and Dean: MICHÈLE DOMINY
Vice-Pres. and Dean for Graduate Studies:
NORTON BATKIN
Vice-Pres. for Academic Affairs: ROBERT L.
MARTIN
Vice-Pres. for Admin.: JAMES BRUDVIG
Vice-Pres. for Devt and Alumni Affairs:
DEBRA PEMSTEIN
Vice Pres. for Int. Affairs and Academic
Programs and Dean for Int. Studies:
JONATHAN BECKER
Vice-Pres. for Student Affairs: MARY BACK-
LUND
Dean for Studies: DAVID SHEIN
Registrar: PETER GADSBY
Dir for Libraries: JEFFREY KATZ
Library of 280,000 vols (incl. 14,000 journals
in print and online)
Number of teachers: 225
Number of students: 2,000
Publications: *Bard College Catalogue, Bar-
dian* (3 a year), *Bard Music Festival Book
Series, BardPolitik, Conjunctions* (2 a
year), *La Voz* (12 a year, The Voice,
Spanish), *Words without Borders* (12 a
year, online, www.wordswithoutborder-
s.org)

BORICUA COLLEGE

Audubon Terrace Campus: 3755 Broadway,
156th St, New York, NY 10032
Telephone: (212) 694-1000
Internet: www.boricuacollege.edu
Founded 1974
Private control
Academic year: 2 semesters
Campuses in Bronx, Brooklyn and Manhat-
tan
Pres.: Dr VICTOR G. ALICEA
Treas.: SERAFIN MARIEL
Vice-Pres. and Chief Academic Officer: Dr
SHIVAJI SENGUPTA

Vice-Pres. and Dean for Academic Affairs,
Brooklyn Campus: MARIA MONTES MOR-
ALES
Vice-Pres. for Information Technology:
IRVING RAMIREZ
Dir for Finance: ELIAS OYOLA
Library Dir: LIZA RIVERA
Library of 15,778 vols, 9,000 maps
Number of teachers: 40
Number of students: 1,100

BRIARCLIFFE COLLEGE

1055 Stewart Ave, Bethpage, NY 11714
Telephone: (516) 918-3600
Internet: www.briarcliffe.edu
Founded 1966
Private control
Campuses in Bethpage, Patchogue and
Queens; courses in accounting, business
administration, criminal justice, fine arts,
healthcare, networking and computer tech-
nology and paralegal studies
Pres.: Dr GEORGE SANTIAGO, JR
Provost and Chief Academic Officer: Dr
HUBERT BENITEZ
Vice-Pres. for Admissions: GABRIEL CASTANO
Vice-Pres. for Finance and Operations: LOU
COMMISSO
Vice-Pres. for Student Affairs: KATHY GENUA
Dean for College: RACHEL ANDOSCIA
Dean for Students: KATHY GENUA
Registrar: VICTORIA LEVINE
Dir for Library Services: JENNIFER DeVITO
Library of 30,000 vols

BROOKLYN LAW SCHOOL

250 Joralemon St, Brooklyn, NY 11201
Telephone: (718) 625-2200
E-mail: admitq@brooklaw.edu
Internet: www.brooklaw.edu
Founded 1901, present bldg 1969
Private control
Academic year: August to May
Pres.: Prof. JOAN G. WEXLER
Dean: Prof. MICHAEL GERBER
Chief Financial Officer: LAURIE NEWITZ
Chief Information Officer: PHIL ALLRED
Dean for Admissions and Financial Aid:
HENRY W. HAVERSTICK, III
Assoc. Dean for Academic Affairs: MICHAEL
CAHILL
Assoc. Dean for Student Affairs: BERYL R.
JONES-WOODIN
Dir for Alumni Relations: CAITLIN MONCK-
MARCELLINO
Registrar: SUZANNE M. DENNIS
Assoc. Law Librarian: LINDA HOLMES
Number of students: 1,380 (1,205 full-time,
175 part-time)
Publications: *Brooklyn Journal of Corporate,
Financial & Commercial Law, Brooklyn
Journal of International Law, Brooklyn
Law Review, Journal of Law and Policy*

BRYANT & STRATTON COLLEGE

1259 Central Ave, Albany, NY 12205
Telephone: (518) 437-1802
Internet: www.bryantstratton.edu
Founded 1854
Private control
Campuses: Albany, Amherst, Buffalo, Roche-
ster, Orchard Park, Syracuse and Liverpool
in New York; Akron, Cleveland, Eastlake
and Parma in Ohio; Hampton, N Chesterfield
and Virginia Beach in Virginia; Glendale,
Milwaukee and Wauwatosa in Wisconsin
Pres. and CEO: JOHN J. STASCHAK
Exec. Vice-Pres. and Sec.: FRANCIS J. FELSER
Vice-Pres.: DOREEN A. JUSTINGER

Vice-Pres. and Chief Academic Officer: BETH A. TARQUINO
Vice-Pres., Chief Financial Officer and Treas.: DAVID VADEN
Number of students: 14,000

CANISIUS COLLEGE

2001 Main St, Buffalo, NY 14208-1098
Telephone: (716) 883-7000
E-mail: admissions@canisius.edu
Internet: www.canisius.edu
Founded 1870
Private control
Academic year: May to August, August to December, January to May (3 semesters)
Pres.: Rev. JOHN J. HURLEY
Vice-Pres. for Academic Affairs: Dr RICHARD A. WALL
Vice-Pres. for Business and Finance: PATRICK E. RICHEY
Vice-Pres. for Institutional Advancement: CRAIG T. CHINDEMI
Vice-Pres. for Student Affairs: ELLEN CONLEY
Registrar: BLAIR W. FOSTER
Assoc. Vice-Pres for Library and Information Services: Dr JOEL COHEN
Library of 425,000 vols, 24,000 full text e-periodicals
Number of teachers: 505 (230 full-time, 275 part-time)
Number of students: 5,110 (3,368 undergraduate, 1,742 graduate)
Publication: *NetGazette*

DEANS

College of Arts and Sciences: Dr DAVID EWING
Richard J. Wehle School of Business: Dr ANTONE ALBER
School of Education and Human Services: Dr MICHAEL PARDALES

CAZENOVIA COLLEGE

22 Sullivan St, Cazenovia, NY 13035
Telephone: (315) 655-7208
E-mail: admission@cazenovia.edu
Internet: www.cazenovia.edu
Founded 1824 as Seminary of the Genesee Conf., present name 1982
Private control
Academic year: September to May
Areas of study incl.: art and design, business and management, education, humanities, natural sciences, social and behavioural sciences
Pres.: Dr MARK JOHN TIERNO
Exec. Vice-Pres. and Chief Operation Officer: Dr SUSAN A. BERGER
Vice-Pres. for Academic Affairs and Dean for Faculty: Dr DONALD A. McCRIMMON
Vice-Pres for Enrolment Management and Dean for Admissions and Financial Aid: ROBERT A. CROOT
Vice-Pres. for Financial Affairs and Chief Financial Officer: MARK EDWARDS
Vice-Pres. for Institutional Advancement: CAROL M. SATCHWELL
Vice-Pres. for Student Devt and Dean for Student Life: C. JOSEPH BEHAN
Registrar: J. ZACHARY KELLEY
Library Dir: STANLEY J. KOZACZKA
Library of 90,000 vols, 2,200 cassettes and DVDs
Number of teachers: 150 (55 full-time, 95 part-time)
Number of students: 1,000 full-time

CHRIST THE KING SEMINARY

711 Knox Rd, E Aurora, NY 14052-0607
Telephone: (716) 652-8900
E-mail: cksacad@cks.edu

Internet: www.cks.edu
Founded 1857 as St Bonaventure School and Seminary, present name 1974
Private control
Academic year: August to December, January to May (2 semesters)
Pres. and Rector: Rev. PETER J. DRILLING
Vice-Rector: Rev. GREGORY M. FAULHABER
Academic Dean: Dr DENNIS A. CASTILLO
Library Dir: TERESA LUBIENECKI
Library of 160,000 vols
Number of teachers: 25 (18 full-time, 7 adjunct)
Number of students: 95 (full-time)

CITY UNIVERSITY OF NEW YORK

535 E 80th St, New York, NY 10021
Telephone: (212) 794-5555
E-mail: academicaffairs@mail.cuny.edu
Internet: www.cuny.edu
Founded 1847 as Free Acad., current name adopted 1961
State control
24 Colleges and instns in New York city, incl. 11 sr colleges, 7 community colleges
Chancellor: MATTHEW GOLDSTEIN
Exec. Vice-Chancellor and Chief Operating Officer: ALLAN H. DOBRIN
Exec. Vice-Chancellor and Univ. Provost: ALEXANDRA W. LOGUE
Sr Vice-Chancellor for Univ. Relations: JAY HERSHENSON
Sr Vice-Chancellor for Budget, Finance and Fiscal Policy: MARC V. SHAW
Vice-Chancellor for Community Colleges: EDUARDO MARTI
Vice-Chancellor for Research: GILLIAN SMALL
Vice-Chancellor for Student Affairs: FRANK D. SANCHEZ
Dir for Admission: RICHARD P. ALVAREZ
Dean for Advancement: CARLOS FLYNN
Univ. Dean for Education: JOAN M. LUCARIELLO
Univ. Dean for Libraries and Information Resources: CURTIS KENDRICK
Dean for Undergraduate Studies: KARRIN E. WILKS
Library: Combined libraries of 7.6m. vols, 30,000 periodicals
Number of teachers: 6,700 (full-time)
Number of students: 540,000
Publication: *Salute to Scholars* (2 a year)...

CONSTITUENT COLLEGES AND SCHOOLS

Baruch College

One Bernard Baruch Way, 55 Lexington Ave, 24th St, New York, NY 10010
Telephone: (646) 312-1000
E-mail: admissions@baruch.cuny.edu
Internet: www.baruch.cuny.edu
Founded 1919
Pres.: MITCHEL B. WALLERSTEIN
Provost and Sr Vice-Pres. for Academic Affairs: JOHN BRENKMAN
Vice-Pres. for Admin. and Finance: MARY FINNEN
Vice-Pres. for College Advancement: MARK GIBBEL
Vice-Pres. for Student Affairs, Enrolment Management and Dean for Students: BEN CORPUS
Chief Librarian: ARTHUR DOWNING
Library of 450,000 vols, 160,000 ebooks, 2m. units of microform
Number of teachers: 500 (full-time)
Number of students: 17,060 (13,120 undergraduate, 3,940 graduate)

Publications: *Baruch College Alumni Magazine* (2 a year), *Dollars & Sense* (1 a year), *Encounters*

DEANS

School of Public Affairs: DAVID BIRDSELL
Weissman School of Arts and Sciences: JEFFREY M. PECK
Zicklin School of Business: JOHN ELLIOTT

Brooklyn College

2900 Bedford Ave, Brooklyn, NY 11210
Telephone: (718) 951-5000
E-mail: adminqry@brooklyn.cuny.edu
Internet: www.brooklyn.cuny.edu
Founded 1930
Pres.: KAREN L. GOULD
Provost and Vice-Pres. for Academic Affairs: WILLIAM A. TRAMONTANO
Vice-Pres. for Enrolment Management: Dr STEPHEN E. JOYNER
Vice-Pres. for Finance and Admin.: ALAN GILBERT (acting)
Vice-Pres.for Institutional Advancement: Dr ANDREW SILLEN
Vice-Pres. for Student Affairs: Dr MILGA MORALES
Library: 1.5m. vols, 45,000 serials, 43,000 eserials, 40,000 ebooks
Number of teachers: 1,355 (558 full-time, 797 part-time)
Number of students: 16,820 (13,095 undergraduate, 3,725 graduate)
Publication: *Brooklyn College Magazine*

DEANS

School of Business: WILLIE HOPKINS
School of Education: DEBORAH SHANLEY
School of Humanities and Social Sciences: KIMBERLEY L. PHILLIPS
School of Natural and Behavioral Sciences: KLEANTHIS PSARRIS
School of Visual, Media and Performing Arts: MARIA ANN CONELLI

City College of New York

160 Convent Ave, New York, NY 10031
Telephone: (212) 650-7000
E-mail: admissions@ccny.cuny.edu
Internet: www.ccny.cuny.edu
Founded 1847
Pres.: Dr LISA S. COICO
Provost and Vice-Pres. for Academic Affairs: MARTIN MOSKOVITS
Number of teachers: 460 (full-time)
Number of students: 15,000
Publication: *Working Education Magazine*

DEANS

Bernard and Anne Spitzer School of Architecture: GEORGE RANALLI
Division of Humanities and the Arts: GERALDINE MURPHY (acting)
Division of Interdisciplinary Studies at Center for Worker Education: JUAN CARLOS MERCADO
Division of Science: Dr RUTH STARK
Division of Social Sciences: MARILYN HOSKIN
Grove School of Engineering: JOSEPH BARBA
School of Education: DORIS CINTRÓN (acting)
Sophie Davis School of Biomedical Education: Dr MAURIZIO TREVISAN

College of Staten Island

2800 Victory Blvd, Staten Island, NY 10314
Telephone: (718) 982-2000
E-mail: admissions@csi.cuny.edu
Internet: www.csi.cuny.edu
Founded 1976 by merger of Staten Island Community College (f. 1955) with Richmond College (f. 1965)
Academic year: August to May (2 semesters)

Pres.: Dr TOMAS D. MORALES

Provost and Sr Vice-Pres. for Academic Affairs: Dr WILLIAM J. FRITZ

Vice-Pres. for Finance and Admin.: IRA PERSKY (acting)

Vice-Pres. for Institutional Advancement and External Affairs: BARBARA R. ESHOO

Vice-Pres. for Student Affairs: Dr A. RAMONA BROWN

Chief Librarian: Dr WILMA L. JONES

Library of 243,000 vols, 110,400 ebooks, 250 print journals, 42,800 ejournals, 140 e-resources, 3,000 films and video cassettes, 5,000 sound recordings, 400 linear ft of archival materials

Number of teachers: 960 (360 full-time, 600 part-time)

Number of students: 13,860 (10,652 full-time)

Publications: *Caesura* (irregular), *Eye on CSI*, *Operation: Three-Legged Dolphin* (2 a year), *Serpentine*, *Third Rail*

DEANS

Division of Humanities and Social Sciences: Dr CHRISTINE FLYNN SAULNIER

Division of Science and Technology: Dr ALEX CHIGOGIDZE

CUNY Graduate School of Journalism

219 W 40th St, New York, NY 10018

Telephone: (646) 758-7700

E-mail: admissions@journalism.cuny.edu

Internet: www.journalism.cuny.edu

Founded 2006

Academic year: 3 semesters

Dean: Prof. SARAH BARTLETT

Library of 1,500 vols

CUNY School of Law

65–21 Main St, Flushing, NY 11367

Telephone: (718) 340-4200

E-mail: admissions@mail.law.cuny.edu

Internet: www.law.cuny.edu

Founded 1973, present status 1994

Dean: MICHELLE J. ANDERSON

Library of 95,000 vols, 175,000 microforms

Number of teachers: 30 (full-time)

Number of students: 570

Publication: *CUNY Law Magazine*

Graduate Center

365 Fifth Ave, New York, NY 10016-4309

Telephone: (212) 817-7000

E-mail: admissions@gc.cuny.edu

Internet: www.gc.cuny.edu

Founded 1961

Pres.: WILLIAM P. KELLY

Provost and Sr Vice-Pres.: CHASE F. ROBINSON

Library of 305,000 vols, 555,000 microforms, 8,258 electronic and print serials

Number of teachers: 335 (full-time)

Number of students: 4,520

Publication: *Folio Magazine*

DEANS

Humanities and Social Sciences: LOUISE LENNIHAN

Sciences: ANN S. HENDERSON

School of Professional Studies: JOHN MOGULESCU

Hunter College

695 Park Ave, New York, NY 10065

Telephone: (212) 772-4000

E-mail: admissions@hunter.cuny.edu

Internet: www.hunter.cuny.edu

Founded 1870

Pres.: JENNIFER J. RAAB

Provost and Vice-Pres.: VITA RABINOWITZ

Vice-Pres. for Student Affairs: EIJA AYRAVAINEN

Chief Operating Officer: LEONARD ZINNANTI (acting)

Number of teachers: 1,800 (full-time)

Number of students: 22,000

Publications: *Around Hunter*, *At Hunter*, *E Magazine*

DEANS

Hunter-Bellevue School of Nursing: GAIL McCAIN

School of Arts and Sciences: EREC R. KOCH

School of Education: DAVID STEINER

Schools of the Health Professions: Dr KEN OLDEN (acting)

Silberman School of Social Work: Dr JACQUELINE B. MONDROS

John Jay College of Criminal Justice

899 10th Ave, New York, NY 10019

Telephone: (212) 237-8000

E-mail: admissions@jjay.cuny.edu

Internet: www.jjay.cuny.edu

Founded 1964

Pres.: JEREMY TRAVIS

Provost and Sr Vice-Pres. of Academic Affairs: JANE BOWERS

Sr Vice-Pres. for Finance and Admin.: ROBERT PIGNATELLO

Vice-Pres. for Enrolment Management: RICHARD SAULNIER

Library of 300,000 vols

Number of teachers: 260 (full-time)

Number of students: 10,830

Publication: *John Jay Magazine*

Lehman College

250 Bedford Park Blvd, W, Bronx, NY 10468

Telephone: (718) 960-8000

Internet: www.lehman.cuny.edu

Founded 1968

Pres.: Dr RICARDO R. FERNANDEZ

Provost and Sr Vice-Pres. for Academic Affairs: Dr JOSEPH W. RACHLIN

Vice-Pres. for Admin. and Finance: VINCENT W. CLARK

Vice-Pres. for Enrolment Management: Dr ROBERT C. TROY

Vice-Pres. for Institutional Advancement: MARIO DELLAPINA

Vice-Pres. for Student Affairs: JOSE MAGDALENO

Library of 575,160 vols

Number of teachers: 350 (full-time)

Number of students: 12,290 (9,863 undergraduate, 2,427 graduate)

Publication: *Lehman Today* (2 a year)

DEANS

School of Arts and Humanities: Dr TIMOTHY ALBORN

School of Continuing and Professional Studies: Dr MARZIE A. JAFARI

School of Education: Dr HARRIET R. FAYNE

School of Natural and Social Sciences: Dr EDWARD L. JARROLL

Medgar Evers College

1650 Bedford Ave, Brooklyn, NY 11225

Telephone: (718) 951-5000

Internet: www.mec.cuny.edu

Founded 1969

Pres.: Dr WILLIAM L. POLLARD

Provost and Sr Vice-Pres.: Dr HOWARD C. JOHNSON

Sr Vice-Pres. and Chief Operating Officer: Dr LLOYD A. BLANCHARD

Vice-Pres. for Student Support Services and Enrolment Management: Dr VINCENT BANREY

Library of 110,000 vols, 25,000 audiovisual items, 350 journals, magazines and newspapers

Number of teachers: 130 (full-time)

Number of students: 5,060

DEANS

College of Freshman Studies: (vacant)

School of Liberal Arts and Education: Dr CARLYLE VAN THOMPSON (acting)

School of Professional and Community Development: Dr SIMONE RODRIGUEZ-DORESTANT

School of Science, Health and Technology: Dr MOHSIN PATWARY

New York City College of Technology (CUNY)

300 Jay St, Brooklyn, NY 11201

Telephone: (718) 260-5400

Internet: www.citytech.cuny.edu

Founded 1946 as New York State Institute for Applied Arts and Sciences, present status 1964, current name adopted 2002

Academic year: August to June

Pres.: Dr RUSSELL K. HOTZLER

Provost and Vice-Pres. for Academic Affairs: Dr BONNE AUGUST

Vice-Pres. for Admin. and Finance: Dr MIGUEL CAIROL

Vice-Pres. for Enrolment and Student Affairs: Dr MARCELA KATZ ARMOZA

Chief Librarian: DARROW WOOD

Library of 392,317 vols, 86,339 periodical titles

Number of teachers: 1,260 (412 full-time, 848 part-time)

Number of students: 15,960

Publications: *2 Bridges Review* (online), *City Tech Writer* (1 a year), *Journal of Urban Technology*, *Nucleus* (4 a year), *Perspectives*

DEANS

School of Arts and Sciences: Dr PAMELA BROWN

School of Professional Studies: BARBARA GRUMET

School of Technology and Design: KEVIN HOM

Queens College

65–30 Kissena Blvd, Flushing, NY 11367

Telephone: (718) 997-5000

Internet: www.qc.edu

Founded 1937

Pres.: JAMES L. MUYSKENS

Provost and Vice-Pres. for Academic Affairs: JAMES STELLAR

Number of teachers: 640 (full-time)

Number of students: 4,600

Publication: *Queens Magazine*

DEANS

Division of Arts and Humanities: WILLIAM McCLURE (acting)

Division of Education: FRANCINE PETERMAN

Division of Mathematics and Natural Sciences: Dr LARRY LIEBOVITCH

York College

94–20 Guy R. Brewer Blvd, Jamaica, NY 11451

Telephone: (718) 262-2000

Internet: www.york.cuny.edu

Founded 1966, fmrly Alpha College

Pres.: Dr MARCIA C. KEIZS

Provost and Sr Vice-Pres. for Academic Affairs: Dr IVELAW LLOYD GRIFFITH

Chief Operating Officer: RONALD C. THOMAS
Library of 160,000 vols, 55,000 reels of microfilm, 90,000 microfiche cards
Number of teachers: 150 (full-time)
Number of students: 6,030

DEANS

School of Arts and Sciences: Dr PANAYIOTIS MELETIES
School of Business and Information Systems: ALFRED NTOKO
School of Health and Behavioral Sciences: Dr LYNNE W. CLARK

CLARKSON UNIVERSITY

Eight Clarkson Ave, Potsdam, NY 13699-5500

Telephone: (315) 268-6400
E-mail: admission@clarkson.edu
Internet: www.clarkson.edu

Founded 1896 as Thomas S. Clarkson Memorial School of Technology, present name and status 1984
Pres.: Dr ANTHONY G. COLLINS
Provost: Dr THOMAS E. YOUNG
Treas.: JAMES D. FISH
Vice-Pres. for Univ. Outreach and Student Affairs: KATHRYN B. JOHNSON
Dean for Admissions: BRIAN T. GRANT
Registrar: LYNN BROWN
Library Dir: MICHELLE L. YOUNG
Library of 500,000 vols, over 3,700 print and ejournals, 15,000 ebooks
Number of teachers: 245 (221 full-time)
Number of students: 3,540 (3,018 undergraduate, 522 graduate)
Publication: Clarkson

DEANS

School of Arts and Sciences: PETER TURNER
School of Business: TIMOTHY F. SUGRUE
Wallace H. Coulter School of Engineering: GOODARZ AHMADI

COLGATE ROCHESTER CROZER DIVINITY SCHOOL

1100 S Goodman St, Rochester, NY 14620-2589

Telephone: (585) 271-1320
E-mail: admissions@crcds.edu
Internet: www.crds.edu

Founded 1970 by merger of 3 theological seminaries, 1 missionary training school and 1 theological school
Private control
Academic year: September to May
Pres.: Dr MARVIN A. MCMICKLE
Vice-Pres. for Academic Life and Dean of Faculty: Rev. Dr STEPHANIE L. SAUVÉ
Vice-Pres. for Enrolment Services: MELISSA MORRAL
Vice-Pres. for Finance and Chief Financial Officer: GERALD VAN STRYDONCK
Vice-Pres. for Institutional Advancement: PATRICK HANLEY
Registrar: ANDREA MASON
Library Dir: MARGE NEAD
Library: 3m. vols
Number of teachers: 10

COLGATE UNIVERSITY

13 Oak Dr., Hamilton, NY 13346
Telephone: (315) 228-1000
E-mail: admission@colgate.edu
Internet: www.colgate.edu

Founded 1819 as Baptist Education Soc., present name 1890
Private control
Academic year: August to May

4 Academic divs: humanities, natural sciences and mathematics, social sciences and university studies
Pres.: JEFFREY HERBST
Provost and Dean for Faculty: BRUCE SELLECK
Vice-Pres. and Dean for Admission: GARY L. ROSS
Vice-Pres. and Dean for College: SCOTT C. BROWN
Vice-Pres. for Communications: DEBRA K. TOWNSEND
Vice-Pres. for Finance and Admin.: DAVID HALE
Vice-Pres. for Institutional Advancement and Alumni Affairs: MURRAY L. DECOCK
Chief Information Officer: DAVID D. GREGORY
Controller: THOMAS O'NEILL
Registrar: GRETCHEN B. HERRINGER
Librarian: JOANNE A. SCHNEIDER
Library of 766,961 vols, 236,569 ebooks, 551,803 microforms, 461,469 govt documents, 11,317 sound recordings, 869 print journals, 46,711 ejournals
Number of teachers: 290 (full-time)
Number of students: 2,900
Publication: The Colgate Scene (4 a year)

COLLEGE OF MOUNT SAINT VINCENT

6301 Riverdale Ave, Riverdale, NY 10471
Telephone: (718) 405-3267
E-mail: admissions.office@mountsaintvincent.edu
Internet: www.mountsaintvincent.edu

Founded 1847 as Acad. of Mount St Vincent, present name 1911
Private control
Pres.: CHARLES L. FLYNN, JR
Provost and Dean for Faculty: GUY LOMETTI
Exec. Vice-Pres. and Treas.: ABED ELKESHK
Vice-Pres. for Admission and Financial Aid: TIMOTHY NASH
Vice-Pres. for Business: MATTHEW MCDEVITT
Vice-Pres. for Information Technology: W. ADAM WICHERN, III
Vice-Pres. for Institutional Advancement and College Relations: MADELEINE MELKONIAN
Vice-Pres. for Student Affairs and Dean for Students: DIANNA C. DALE
Dir for Library: SEBASTIAN DERRY
Library of 150,000 vols
Number of teachers: 80
Number of students: 1,800
Publication: The Underground

DEANS

School for Professional and Continuing Studies: EDWARD MEYER
Undergraduate College: PAUL DOUILLARD

COLLEGE OF NEW ROCHELLE

29 Castle Pl., New Rochelle, NY 10805
Telephone: (914) 654-5000
E-mail: info@cnr.edu
Internet: www.cnr.edu

Founded 1904 as the College of St Angela
Private control
Academic year: September to May

Campuses at New Rochelle, Brooklyn, Bronx, New York

Pres.: Dr JUDITH HUNTINGTON
Exec. Vice-Pres.: ELLEN CURRY DAMATO
Sr Vice-Pres. for Academic Affairs: Dr DOROTHY ESCRIBANO
Vice-Pres. for College Advancement: BRENNA SHEENAN MAYER
Vice-Pres. for Financial Affairs: KEITH BORGE
Vice-Pres. for Student Affairs: COLETTE GEARY

Dean for Library: ANA M. FONTOURA
Library of 220,000 vols
Number of teachers: 760 (120 full-time, 640 adjunct)
Number of students: 4,500
Publications: Annales (1 a year), Phoenix (4 a year)

DEANS

Graduate School: Dr MARIE RIBARICH
School of Arts and Sciences: Dr RICHARD THOMPSON
School of New Resources: Dr ELZA DINWIDDIE-BOYD
School of Nursing: Dr MARY ALICE DONIUS

COLLEGE OF SAINT ROSE

432 W Ave, Albany, NY 12203-1490
Telephone: (518) 454-5111
E-mail: admit@mail.strose.edu
Internet: www.strose.edu

Founded 1920
Private control
Academic year: September to May
Pres.: Dr R. MARK SULLIVAN
Provost and Vice-Pres. for Academic Affairs: Dr DAVID SZCZERBACKI
Vice-Pres. for Enrolment Management: MARY M. GRONDAHL
Vice-Pres. of Finance and Admin.: MARCUS BUCKLEY
Vice-Pres. of Institutional Advancement: KARIN CARR
Vice-Pres. for Student Affairs: DENNIS MCDONALD
Registrar: JUDITH KELLY
Dir for Library Services: PETER KOONZ
Library of 223,627 vols
Number of teachers: 475
Number of students: 5,000
Publications: Journal of Behavioral and Neuroscience Research, Journal of Undergraduate Research (1 a year)

DEANS

Huether School of Business: SEVERIN CARLSON
School of Arts and Humanities: Dr LORNA SHAW
School of Mathematics and Sciences: RICHARD J. THOMPSON, JR
Thelma P. Lally School of Education: Dr MARGARET KIRWIN

COLLEGE OF WESTCHESTER

325 Central Ave, White Plains, NY 10606
Telephone: (914) 831-0200
E-mail: admissions@cw.edu
Internet: www.cw.edu

Founded 1915
Private control
Academic year: September to August

Schools of allied health, business, digital media, information technology

Pres.: KAREN SMITH
Vice-Pres.: MARY BETH DELBALZO
Vice-Pres. for Academic and Student Affairs: Dr JOANN MULQUEEN
Dir for Admissions: MATTHEW CURTIS
Dean for Faculty: GREG MARCARELLI
Dean for Student Academic Services: JEAN CARLSON
Library Dir: MONECIA SAMUEL

COLUMBIA UNIVERSITY

116th St, Broadway, New York, NY 10027-6902
Telephone: (212) 854-1754
E-mail: askcuit@columbia.edu
Internet: www.columbia.edu

Founded 1754 as King's College, present name and status 1896

Private control

Academic year: September to May

Pres.: LEE C. BOLLINGER

Provost: JOHN H. COATSWORTH

Sr Exec. Vice-Pres.: ROBERT KASDIN

Exec. Vice-Pres. for Arts and Sciences: DAVID MADIGAN

Exec. Vice-Pres. for Communications: DAVID M. STONE

Exec. Vice-Pres. for Devt and Alumni Relations: FRED VAN SICKLE

Exec. Vice-Pres. for Facilities: JOSEPH A. IENUSO

Exec. Vice-Pres. for Finance: ANNE SULLIVAN

Exec. Vice-Pres. for Govt and Community Affairs: MAXINE GRIFFITH

Exec. Vice-Pres. for Research: G. MICHAEL PURDY

Exec. Vice-Pres. for Student and Admin. Services: JEFFREY F. SCOTT

Vice-Pres. for Information Services and Univ. Librarian: JAMES G. NEAL

Gen. Counsel: JANE E. BOOTH

Library: see under Libraries and Archives

Number of teachers: 3,635

Number of students: 28,220

Publications: *Chemical Highlights, Columbia Business Law Review* (3 a year), *Columbia Human Rights Law Review, Columbia Journal of American Studies* (1 a year), *Columbia Journal of Environmental Law, Columbia Journal of Law & the Arts* (4 a year), *Columbia Journal of Transnational Law, Columbia Journalism Review* (6 a year), *Columbia Law Review, Current Musicology* (2 a year), *Germanic Review, Global Political Assessment, Journal of International Affairs* (2 a year), *Journal of the Ancient Near Eastern Society, Journal of Philosophy, Prospects: The Annual for American Cultural Studies, Renaissance Quarterly, Revista Hispánica Moderna* (2 a year), *Romanic Review* (4 a year), *Studies in American Indian Literature, The Astronomical Journal*

DEANS

College of Dental Medicine: Dr IRA LAMSTER

College of Physicians and Surgeons: LEE GOLDMAN

Columbia Business School: Prof. GLENN HUBBARD

Columbia College: Prof. JAMES J. VALENTINI

Columbia Journalism School: NICHOLAS LEMANN

Columbia Law School: DAVID M. SCHIZER

Faculty of Arts and Sciences: NICHOLAS B DIRKS

Fu Foundation School of Engineering and Applied Science: FENIOSKY PEÑA-MORA

Graduate School of Architecture, Planning and Preservation: MARK WIGLEY

Graduate School of Arts and Sciences: CARLOS J. ALONSO

Mailman School of Public Health: LINDA P. FRIED

School of the Arts: CAROL BECKER

School of Continuing Education: KRISTINE A. BILLMYER

School of General Studies: PETER J. AWN

School of International and Public Affairs: JOHN H. COATSWORTH

School of Nursing: BOBBIE BERKOWITZ

School of Social Work: JEANETTE C. TAKAMURA

PROFESSORS

Anaesthesiology:

FINCK, A. D.
FINSTER, M.
HILLEL, Z.
HYMAN, A. I.
MORISHIMA, H. O.

ORNSTEIN, E.
PANG, L.
PANTUCK, E. J.
SMILEY, R. M.
STONE, J. G.
THYS, D. M.
TRINER, L.
WEISSMAN, C.
YOUNG, W. L.

Anatomy and Cell Biology:

AMBRON, R.
APRIL, E. W.
BELLVE, A. R.
BRANDT, P.
BULINSKI, J. C.
GERSHON, M. D.
KESSIN, R. H.
ROLE, L. W.
SILVERMAN, A.-J.
TENNYSON, V. M. S.
TORAN-ALLERAND, C. D.

Anthropology:

ALLAND, A., Jr
COHEN, M. L.
COMBS-SCHILLING, M. E.
D'ALTROY, T.
HOLLOWAY, R. L.
MELNICK, D.
NEWMAN, K.
SKINNER, E. P.
TAUSSIG, M.

Applied Physics:

BOOZER, A. H.
CHU, C. K.
HERMAN, I. P.
MARSHALL, T. C.
MAUEL, M.
NAVRATIL, G.

Architecture, Planning and Preservation:

FRAMPTON, K.
GRAVA, S.
HERDEG, K.
HOLL, S.
McINTYRE, L.
McLEOD, M.
MARCUSE, P.
PLUNZ, R.
POLSHEK, J. S.
SASSEN, S. J.
SCLAR, E.
STERN, R. A. M.
TSCHUMI, B.
WRIGHT, G.

Art History and Archaeology:

BALLON, H. M.
BECK, J. H.
BERGDOLL, B. G.
BRILLIANT, R.
CONNORS, J.
FREEDBERG, D.
KRAUSS, R.
MIDDLETON, R.
MURASE, M. C.
MURRAY, S.
MYCK, A.
PASZTORY, E.
REFF, T.
ROSAND, D.
STALEY, A.

Arts:

FORMAN, M., Film
INSDORF, A., Film
SARRIS, A., Film

Astronomy:

APPLEGATE, J.
BAKER, N.
HALPERN, J. P.
HELFAND, D.
PATTERSON, J.
PRENDERGAST, K. H.
SPIEGEL, E. A.
VAN GORKOM, J.

Biochemistry and Molecular Biophysics:

FEIGELSON, P.
GOFF, S.
GOLD, A. M.
GOLDBERGER, R. F.
GOTTESMAN, M. E.
GREENWALD, I. S.
HENDRICKSON, W. A.
HIRSH, D. I.
HONIG, B.
JESSELL, T.
KRASNA, A. I.
SRINIVASAN, P. R.

Biological Sciences:

BOCK, W. J.
CHALFIE, M.
CHASIN, L. A.
COHEN, D. H.
KELLEY, D. B.
MACAGNO, E. R.
MANCINELLI, A.
MANLEY, J.
POLLACK, R.
POO, M.
PRIVES, C. L.
TZAGOLOFF, A.
ZUBAY, G. L.

Business:

ADLER, M.
ARZAC, E. R.
BARTEL, A.
BROCKNER, J.
BURTON, J. C.
CAPON, N.
DONALDSON, J.
EDWARDS, F.
FEDERGRUEN, A.
GIOVANNINI, A.
GLASSERMAN, P.
GLOSTEN, L. R.
GREEN, L.
GREENWALD, B. C. N.
GUPTA, S.
HARRIGAN, K.
HARRIS, T.
HEAL, G.
HOLBROOK, M.
HORTON, R.
HUBBARD, R. G.
HUBERMAN, G.
HULBERT, J. M.
ICHNIOWSKI, B. E.
KOHLI, R.
KOLESAR, P.
LEFF, N.
LEHMANN, D.
LICHTENBERG, F. R.
MELUMAD, N. D.
MISHKIN, F.
NOAM, E.
OHLSON, J.
PATRICK, H.
SELDEN, L.
SEXTON, D.
STARR, M.
SUNDARESAN, S.
THOMAS, J. K.
TUSHMAN, M.
WARREN, E. K.
WILKINSON, M.
ZIPKIN, P.

Chemical Engineering and Applied Chemistry:

CHEH, H. Y.
DURNING, C.
GRYTE, C.
LEONARD, E. F.
O'SHAUGHNESSY, B.
SPENCER, J.

Chemistry:

BENT, B. E.
BERNE, B. J.
BERSOHN, R.

BRESLOW, R.
DANISHEFSKY, S. J.
EISENTHAL, K. B.
FLYNN, G. W.
FRIESNER, R.
KATZ, T. J.
NAKANISHI, K.
PARKIN, G. F. R.
PECHUKAS, P.
STILL, W. C.
TURRO, N. J.
VALENTINI, J.

Civil Engineering and Engineering Mechanics:

DASGUPTA, G.
DIMAGGIO, F. L.
FRIEDMAN, M. B.
GJELSVIK, A.
GRIFFIS, F. H.
MEYER, C.
STOLL, R. D.
TESTA, R. B.
VAICAITIS, R.

Classics:

BAGNALL, R. S.
CAMERON, A.
COULTER, J. A.
SAID, S.
TARÁN, L.
ZETZEL, J.

Computer Science:

AHO, A. V.
ALLEN, P. K.
FEINER, S. K.
GALIL, Z.
GROSS, J. L.
KAISER, G.
KENDER, J.
MCKEOWN, K.
STOLFO, S.
TRAUB, J. F.
UNGER, S.
WOZNIAKOWSKI, M.
YEMINI, Y.

Dental and Oral Surgery:

CANGIALOSI, T. J.
DAVIS, M. J.
EFSTRATIADIS, S. S.
FORMICOLA, A. J.
HASSELGREN, B. G.
HILLS, H. L.
ISRAEL, H. A.
KAHN, N.
KLYVERT, M.
LAMSTER, I. B.
MOSS-SALENTIJN, L.
MYERS, R.
ODRICH, J.
ROSER, S. M.
TROUTMAN, K. C.
ZEGARELLI, D. J.

Dermatology:

BICKERS, D. R.

East Asian Languages and Cultures:

ANDERER, P.
HYMES, R.
LEDYARD, G. K.
SHIRANE, H.
SMITH, H. D., II
WANG, D. D.-W.
ZELIN, M.

Economics:

BHAGWATI, J.
BLOOM, D.
CHICHILNISKY, G.
CLARIDA, R.
DESAI, P.
DHRYMES, P.
DUTTA, P. K.
ERICSON, R.
FINDLAY, R.
HAYASHI, F.

LANCASTER, K.
MUNDELL, R.
PHELPS, E.
SACHS, J. D.
WATTS, H.
WELLISZ, S. H.

Electrical Engineering:

ACAMPORA, A.
ANASTASSIOU, D.
DIAMENT, P.
HEINZ, T.
LAZAR, A.
MEADOWS, H. E.
OSGOOD, R.
SCHWARTZ, M.
SEN, A. K.
STERN, T. E.
TEICH, M. C.
TSIVIDIS, Y.
WANG, W.
YANG, E. S.
ZUKOWSKI, C. A.

English and Comparative Literature:

BLOUNT, M.
DAMROSCH, D.
DELBANCO, A.
DOUGLAS, A.
EDEN, K.
FERGUSON, R.
FERRANTE, J.
HANNING, R.
HOWARD, J.
KASTAN, D.
KOCH, J. K.
KROEBER, K.
MARCUS, S.
MEISEL, M.
MENDELSON, E.
MILLER, D. A.
MIROLLO, J. V.
MORETTI, F.
O'MEALLY, R. G.
PETERS, J. S.
QUIGLEY, A.
ROSENBERG, J. D.
ROSENTHAL, M.
SEIDEL, M.
SHAPIRO, J.
SPIVAK, G. C.
STADE, G.
TAYLER, E. W.
YERKES, D.

French and Romance Philology:

BLOCH, R. H.
COMPAGNON, A.
CONDE, M.
FORCE, P.
LOTRINGER, S.
MAY, G.
MITTERAND, H.
RIFFATERRE, M.

Genetics and Development:

BESTOR, T.
CARLSON, M.
COSTANTINI, F.
EFSTRATIADIS, A.
GILLIAM, T. C.
OTT, J.
PAPAIOANNOU, V.
ROTHSTEIN, R. J.
SCHON, E. A.
STERN, C. D.
STRUHL, G.
WARBURTON, D.
WOLGEMUTH, D.

Geological Sciences:

BROECKER, W. S.
CHRISTIE-BLICK, N.
FAIRBANKS, R. G.
GORDON, A. L.
HAYES, D. E.
HAYS, J. O.
LANGMUIR, C.

MENKE, W.
MUTTER, J.
OLSEN, P.
RICHARDS, P. G.
SCHLOSSER, P.
SCHOLZ, C.
SIMPSON, H. J.
SYKES, L. R.
WALKER, D.

Germanic Languages:

ANDERSON, M. M.
HUYSSEN, A.
MULLER, H.
VON MUCKE, D. E.

History:

BILLOWS, R.
BLACKMAR, E.
BRINKLEY, A.
BULLIET, R.
BUSHMAN, R.
BYNUM, C.
CANNADINE, D.
DE GRAZIA, V.
DEAK, I.
FIELDS, B.
FONER, E.
GLUCK, C.
GOREN, A. A.
HAIMSON, L.
HARRIS, W. V.
HOWELL, M.
JACKSON, K. T.
KLEIN, H. S.
LYNCH, H. R.
MALEFAKIS, E. E.
MARABLE, M.
PAXTON, R.
ROTHMAN, D.
SCHAMA, S.
SHENTON, J. P.
SMIT, J. W.
STANISLAWSKI, M.
STEPAN, N.
STERN, F.
VON HAGEN, M. L.
WOLOCH, I.
WORTMAN, R.
WRIGHT, M.
YERUSHALMI, Y. H.

Industrial Engineering and Operations Research:

BIENSTOCK, D.
GALLEGO, G.
GOLDFARB, D.
KLEIN, M.
PINEDO, M.
SIGMAN, K.
YAO, D. D.-W.

International and Public Affairs:

MOLZ, R. K.
NELSON, R. R.
RODRIK, D.

Italian:

BAROLINI, T.
REBAY, L.

Journalism:

BELFORD, B.
BENEDICT, H.
CAREY, J. W.
GARLAND, P.
GOLDSTEIN, K. K.
ISAACS, S. D.
KONNER, J.

Krumb School of Mines:

BESHERS, D. N.
DUBY, P. F.
HARRIS, C. C.
SOMASUNDARAN, P.
THEMELIS, N. J.
YEGULALP, T. M.

Law:

BARENBERG, M.

BERGER, C. J.
BERGER, V.
BERMANN, G.
BLACK, B. A.
BLACK, B. S.
BLASI, V.
BRIFFAULT, R.
CHIRELSTEIN, M.
COFFEE, J. C.
CRENSHAW, K. W.
DAMROSCH, L.
EDGAR, H. S. H.
EDWARDS, R.
FARNSWORTH, E. A.
FINEMAN, M.
FLETCHER, G.
GARDNER, R.
GILSON, R. J.
GINSBURG, J. C.
GOLDBERG, V. P.
GOLDSCHMID, H. J.
GORDON, J. N.
GREENAWALT, R. K.
GREENBERG, J.
HOOVER, J.
JONES, W. K.
KORN, H. L.
LEEBRON, D. W.
LIEBMAN, J.
LIEBMAN, L.
LYNCH, G.
MOGLEN, E.
MONAGHAN, H.
NARASIMHAN, S.
NEUMAN, G. L.
PARKER, K. E.
RABB, H. S.
RAPACZYNSKI, A.
ROE, M. J.
SABEL, C. F.
SMIT, H.
SOVERN, M.
STONE, R.
STRAUSS, P. L.
THOMAS, K.
UVILLER, H. R.
WILLIAMS, P. J.
YOUNG, M.
YOUNG, W. F., Jr

Mathematics:
BASS, H.
FRIEDMAN, R.
GALLAGHER, P. X.
GOLDFELD, D.
JACQUET, H. M.
JORGENSEN, T.
KARATZAS, I.
KURANISHI, M.
MORGAN, J.
PHONG, D.
PINKHAM, H. C.

Mechanical Engineering:
CHEVRAY, R.
FREUDENSTEIN, F.
LONGMAN, R. W.
MODI, V.

Medicine:
AL-AWQATI, Q.
APPEL, G. B.
BAER, L. R.
BANK, A.
BIGGER, J. T.
BILEZIKIAN, J. P.
BUTLER, V. P., Jr
CALDWELL, L. P.
CANFIELD, R. E.
CANNON, P. J.
CHESS, L.
CIMINO, J. J.
CLAYTON, P. D.
CORTELL, S.
FIELD, M.
FRANCIS, C. K.
FRANTZ, A. G.

GIARDINA, E.-G.
GINSBURG, H. N.
GOLDBERG, I. J.
GRIECO, M. H.
HOLT, P. R.
JACOBS, T. P.
KEMP, H., Jr
LEGATO, M. J.
LEIFER, E.
LINDENBAUM, J.
LOEB, J.
MELCHER, G.
MORRIS, T. Q.
MORSE, J. E.
NEU, H. C.
PHILLIPS, G. B.
PI-SUNYER, F. X.
ROSNER, W.
SCHWARTZ, M. J.
TABAS, I. A.
TALL, A.
TAPLEY, D. F.
TAUB, R. N.
THOMSON, G. E.
TURINO, G. M.
WARDLAW, S.
WEINSTEIN, I. B.
WEISFELDT, M. L.
WEISS, H. J.

Microbiology:
CALAME, K. L.
FIGURSKI, D.
MITCHELL, A. P.
RACANIELLO, V. R.
SHORE, D. M.
SHUMAN, H. A.
SILVERSTEIN, S. J.
YOUNG, C.

Middle East and Asian Languages and Cultures:
BURRILL, K. R. F.
MADINA, M.
MIRON, D.
PRITCHETT, F.
RICCARDI, T.
SALIBA, G.
VAN DE MIEROOP, M.

Music:
BENT, I.
CHRISTENSEN, D.
EDWARDS, G.
FRISCH, W.
KRAMER, J.
LERDAHL, A. W.
PERKINS, L.
SISMAN, E.
TUCKER, M. T.

Neurological Surgery:
BRISMAN, R.
HOUSEPIAN, E. M.
MCMURTRY, J.
QUEST, D. O.
STEIN, B. M.

Neurology:
BRUST, J. C. M., Jr
COTE, L. J.
DE VIVO, D. C.
DI MAURO, S.
EMERSON, R. G.
FAHN, S.
GHEZ, C.
GOLD, A. P.
HALSEY, J., Jr
HAUSER, W. A.
KARLIN, A.
LATOV, N.
LOVELACE, R. E.
MAYEUX, R.
MOHR, J. P.
PEDLEY, T.
PENN, A. S.
ROWLAND, L. P.
SCHWARTZ, J.

SCIARRA, D.
STERN, Y.
WEXLER, N.

Nursing:
FULMER, T. T.
MUNDINGER, M. O.

Obstetrics and Gynaecology:
BOWE, E. T.
FERIN, M.
HEMBREE, W. C.
JAGIELLO, G.
LOBO, R. A.
NEUWIRTH, R. S.
TIMOR, I. E.
WILLIAMS, S. B.

Ophthalmology:
BEHRENS, M.
BITO, L.
DONN, A.
FARRIS, R. L.
FORBES, M.
GOURAS, P.
L'ESPERANCE, F., Jr
MOORE, S.
SPALTER, H.
SPECTOR, A.
SRINIVASAN, B.
TROKEL, S.
WORGUL, B. V.
YANNUZZI, L. A.

Orthopaedic Surgery:
DICK, H.
EFTEKHAR, N.
FIELDING, J. W.
GRANTHAM, S. A.
LAI, W. M.
MOW, V. C.
RATCLIFFE, A.
SHELTON, M. L.

Otolaryngology:
BLITZER, A.
CLOSE, L. G.
KHANNA, S. M.

Paediatrics:
COOPER, L. Z.
CUNNINGHAM, N.
DECKELBAUM, R. J.
DELL, R. B.
DRISCOLL, J. M.
GERSHON, A. A.
GERSONY, W. M.
HEAGARTY, M.
JACOBS, J.
KRONGRAD, E.
LEBLANC, W.
LEVINE, L.
MELLIN, G. W.
MELLINS, R. B.
NICHOLSON, J. F.
PIOMELLI, S.
SITARZ, A.
STARK, R.
WETHERS, D. L.
WINCHESTER, R. J.

Pathology:
AXEL, R.
DALLA-FAVERA, R.
GELLER, L. M.
GOLDMAN, J. E.
GREENE, L. A.
KAUFMAN, M.
KOHN, D. F.
LEFKOWITCH, J. H.
LIEM, R. K. H.
MASON, C. A.
PERZIN, K. H.
RICHART, R. M.
SHELANSKI, M. L.
SUCIU-FOCA, N.

Pharmacology:
BOYDEN, P.
GOLDBERG, D. J.

GRAZIANO, J. H.
HOFFMAN, B. F.
ROBINSON, R. B.
ROSEN, M. R.
SIEGELBAUM, S. A.
WIT, A. L.

Philosophy:
ALBERT, D.
BEROFSKY, B.
BILGRAMI, A.
GAIFMAN, H.
GOEHR, L. D.
LARMORE, C.
LEVI, I.
POGGE, T.
SIDORSKY, D.

Physical Education and Intercollegiate Athletics:
ROHAN, J. P.

Physics:
APRILE, E.
CHRIST, N. H.
GYULASSY, M.
HAILEY, C. J.
HARTMANN, S.
KAHN, S. M.
LEE, T. D.
LEE, W.
MUELLER, A.
NAGAMIYA, S.
RUDERMAN, M. A.
SCHWARTZ, M.
SCIULLI, F.
SHAEVITZ, M. H.
TUTS, P. M.
UEMURA, Y.
WEINBERG, E.
WILLIS, W. J.
ZAJC, W. A.

Physiology and Cellular Biophysics:
BLANK, M.
DODD, J.
FISCHBARG, J.
KANDEL, E. R.
LOW, M. G.
SCHACHTER, D.
SILVERSTEIN, S. C.
STERN, D.

Political Science:
ANDERSON, L.
BALDWIN, D.
BERNSTEIN, T. P.
BETTS, R. K.
BIALER, S.
CHALMERS, D. A.
COHEN, J. L.
CURTIS, G. L.
ELSTER, J.
FRANKLIN, J. H.
HAMILTON, C. V.
JERVIS, R. L.
JOHNSTON, D. C.
KATZNELSON, I. I.
KESSELMAN, M. J.
LEGVOLD, R.
MILNER, H.
NATHAN, A. N.
ROTHSCHILD, J.
RUGGIE, J.
SCHILLING, W. R.
SHAPIRO, R. Y.
SNYDER, J.
WESTIN, A. F.

Psychiatry:
BENNETT, R.
DEVANAND, D.
DOHRENWEND, B.
DUNTON, H. D.
EHRHARDT, A. A.
ENDICOTT, J.
ERLENMEYER-KIMLING, L.
FIEVE, R. R.
FISCHMAN, M. W.

FOLEY, A. R.
GLASSMAN, A. H.
GORMAN, J. M.
GURLAND, B. J.
HOFER, M.
JAFFE, J.
KLEBER, H. D.
KLEIN, D. F.
KLEIN, R. G.
KUPFERMANN, I.
PARDES, H.
PROHOVNIK, I.
RAINER, J.
RYAN, J.
SACKEIM, H. A.
SHAFFER, D.
SPITZER, R.
TAMIR, H.
WEISSMAN, M. M.

Psychology:
COOPER, L. A.
DWECK, C. S.
GALANTER, E. H.
GIBBON, J.
GRAHAM, N.
HIGGINS, E. T.
HOOD, D. C.
KRANTZ, D.
KRAUSS, R.
MATIN, L.
METCALFE, J.
MISCHEL, W.
TERRACE, H. S.

Public Health:
BAYER, R.
BRANDT-RAUF, P. W.
BROWN, L.
CHALLENOR, B. D.
COLOMBOTOS, J. L.
DAVIDSON, A.
DESPOMMIER, D. D.
FLEISS, J. L.
HASHIM, S. A.
HOWE, G. R.
KANDEL, D.
LEVIN, B.
LINK, B. G.
LO, S.-H.
McCARTHY, J.
OTTMAN, R.
PEARSON, T. A.
PERERA, F. P.
ROSENFIELD, A. G.
SANTELLA, R. P.
SISK, J. E.
STRUENING, E. L.
TSAI, W.-Y.

Radiation Oncology:
AMOLS, H. I.
BRENNER, D. J.
GEARD, C.
HALL, E.
HEI, T. K.
SCHIFF, P. B.

Radiology:
ABLOW, R. C.
ALDERSON, P. O.
BERDON, W.
ESSER, P.
FELDMAN, F.
HILAL, S.
KING, D. L.
NEWHOUSE, J. H.
NICKOLOFF, E. L.
SILVER, A. J.

Rehabilitation Medicine:
DOWNEY, J. A.
EDELSTEIN, J. E.
LIEBERMAN, J. S.
MYERS, S. J.
NEUHAUS, B. E.
THORNHILL, H.

Religion:
AWN, J.
LINDT, G.
PROUDFOOT, W.
RUPP, G.
SOMERVILLE, R.
THURMAN, R.
WEISS-HALIVNI, D.

Slavic Languages:
BELKNAP, R. L.
GASPAROV, B.
MAGUIRE, R. A.
MILLER, F. J.
POPKIN, C.
REYFMAN, I.

Social Work:
AKABAS, S.
BLACK, R. B.
CLOWARD, R. A.
FELDMAN, R.
GARFINKEL, I.
GITTERMAN, A.
HESS, M. M.
IVANOFF, A.
KAMERMAN, S. B.
KIRK, S.
McGOWAN, B.
MEYER, C. H.
MONK, A.
MULLEN, E. J.
POLSKY, H.
SCHILLING, R. F.
SCHINKE, S.
SIMON, B. L.
SOLOMON, R.

Sociology:
COLE, J. R.
GANS, H.
LITWAK, E.
RUGGIE, M.
SILVER, A. A.
SPILERMAN, S.
WHITE, H.

Spanish and Portuguese:
ALAZRAKI, J.
GRIEVE, P. E.
MARTINEZ-BONATI, F.
SILVER, P. W.
SOBEJANO, G.

Statistics:
DE LA PENA, V.
HEYDE, C. C.

Surgery:
ALTMAN, R. P.
CHIU, D. T. W.
FORDE, K.
HARDY, M. A.
HUGO, N.
LO GERFO, P.
MARKOWITZ, A.
NOWYGROD, R.
QUAEGEBEUR, J. M.
REEMTSMA, K.
ROSE, E. A.
SMITH, C. R.
SPOTNITZ, H. M.
STOLAR, C. J. H.
TILSON, M. D.

Urology:
BUTTYAN, R.
HENSLE, T. W.
OLSSON, C. A.
PUCHNER, P. J.
ROMAS, N. S..

AFFILIATED COLLEGES

Barnard College: 3009 Broadway, New York, NY 10027; tel. (212) 854-5262; e-mail admissions@barnard.edu; internet www .barnard.edu; f. 1889; Pres. DEBORA L. SPAR; Dean AVIS E. HINKSON; Provost and Dean for Faculty PAUL HERTZ (acting); Vice-Pres. for

College Relations DOROTHY DENBURG; Vice-Pres. for Devt BRET SILVER; Vice-Pres. for Information Technology CAROL KATZMAN; Gen. Counsel JOMYSHA STEPHEN; Dean for Library and Academic Information Services LISA R. NORBERG; library of 300,000 vols; 375 teachers; 2,390 students.

Teachers' College: 525 W 120th St, New York, NY 10027; tel. (212) 678-3000; e-mail tcinfo@columbia.edu; internet www.tc.columbia.edu; Pres. Dr SUSAN H. FUHRMAN; Provost and Dean Dr THOMAS JAMES; Vice-Pres. for Devt and External Affairs SUZANNE M. MURPHY; Vice-Pres. for Finance and Admin. HARVEY SPECTOR; Gen. Counsel LORI E. FOX; library of 430,432 vols, 237,935 non-print items; 5,370 students; publ. *TC Today*

CONCORDIA COLLEGE

171 White Plains Rd, Bronxville, NY 10708
Telephone: (914) 337-9300
E-mail: admission@concordia-ny.edu
Internet: www.concordia-ny.edu
Founded 1881; attached to Concordia Univ. System
Private control
Academic year: August to May
Pres.: Dr VIJI GEORGE
Chief Financial Officer: DENNIS LONNERGAN
Vice-Pres. for Institutional Advancement: Dr PAUL GRAND PRÉ
Chief Academic Officer: SHERRY J. FRASER
Dean of College: SHERRY FRASER
Dean of Faculty: Dr MANDANA NAKHAI
Dean of Students: JOHN M. BAHR
Registrar: MARK E. BLANCO
Library Dir: WILLIAM PERRENOD
Number of teachers: 30
Number of students: 800 (undergraduate)
Publication: *The Concordia New Yorker* (1 a year)

DEANS

Experiential Learning: JOHN M. BAHR
Nursing: Dr SUSAN APOLD

COOPER UNION FOR THE ADVANCEMENT OF SCIENCE AND ART

30 Cooper Sq., New York, NY 10003-7120
Telephone: (212) 353-4100
E-mail: admissions@cooper.edu
Internet: www.cooper.edu
Founded 1859
Private control
Academic year: September to May
Pres.: Dr JAMSHED BHARUCHA
Chair.: MARK EPSKIN
Vice-Pres. for Finance, Admin. and Treas.: T. C. WESTCOTT
Vice-Pres. for Devt: DEREK A. WITTNER
Vice-Pres. for External Affairs: RONNI DENES
Dean for Student Services: LINDA LEMIESZ
Registrar and Dean for Admissions: MITCH-ELL LIPTON
Library Dir: CAROL SALOMON (acting)
Library of 100,000 vols, 300 periodicals
Number of teachers: 230
Number of students: 1,000
Publication: *At Cooper Union* (2 a year)

DEANS

Albert Nerken School of Engineering: SIMON BEN-AVI (acting)
Faculty of Humanities and Social Sciences: WILLIAM GERMANO
Irwin S. Chanin School of Architecture: ANTHONY VIDLER
School of Art: SASKIA BOS

CORNELL UNIVERSITY

Day Hall Lobby, Ithaca, NY 14853
Telephone: (607) 254-4636
E-mail: info@cornell.edu
Internet: www.cornell.edu
Founded 1865 opened 1868
State and private control
Academic year: September to May
Pres.: DAVID J. SKORTON
Provost: W. KENT FUCHS
Provost for Medical Affairs: LAURIE H. GLIM-CHER
Vice-Pres. for Alumni Affairs and Devt: CHARLES T. PHLEGAR
Vice-Pres. for Facilities Services: KYU-JUNG WHANG
Vice-Pres. for Finance and Chief Financial Officer: JOANNE M. DESTEFANO
Vice-Pres. for Govt and Community Relations: STEPHEN PHILIP JOHNSON
Vice-Pres. for Human Resources: MARY G. OPPERMAN
Vice-Pres. for Planning and Budget: ELMIRA MANGUM
Vice-Pres. for Student and Academic Services: SUSAN H. MURPHY
Vice-Pres. for Univ. Communications: THO-MAS W. BRUCE
Vice-Pres. for Univ. Relations: GLENN C. ALTSCHULER
Dean of Univ. Faculty: WILLIAM FRY
Dean of Students: KENT L. HUBBELL
Univ. Counsel and Sec. of the Corpn: JAMES J. MINGLE
Univ. Librarian: ANNE R. KENNEY
Library: see under Libraries and Archives
Number of teachers: 1,565
Number of students: 22,250
Publications: *Administrative Science Quarterly, Agricultural Finance Review, Andean Past* (academic), *Association, Biological Control of Turfgrass Diseases, Colloqui: Cornell Journal of Planning and Urban Issues, Communique (Ithaca), Cornell Alumni Magazine, Cornell East Asia Series* (academic), *Cornell Engineering Magazine* (2 a year), *Cornell Enterprise, Cornell Field Crops and Soils Handbook, Cornell Hospitality Quarterly, Cornell Hotel School* (magazine), *Cornell International Law Journal* (3 a year), *Cornell Journal of Architecture* (academic), *Cornell Journal of Law and Public Policy, Cornell Law Review* (6 a year), *Cornell Lunatic, Cornell Modern Indonesia Project Publications, Cornell Phonetics Laboratory, Cornell Plantations Magazine, Cornell Recommendations for Commercial Florist Crops, Cornell Recommendations for Field Crops, Cornell Recommendations for Pest Control for Commercial Production and Maintenance of Trees and Shrubs, Cornell Science and Technology Magazine, Cornell Working Papers in Linguistics, Epoch* (3 a year), *Ezra* (4 a year), *Hotelie* (3 a year), *Human Ecology, Indonesia* (2 a year), *Industrial and Labor Relations Review, Industry Perspectives: A White Paper Series from Cornell, Journal of Empirical Legal Studies, LINK* (2 a year), *Living Bird, N K A, Philosophical Review, Traces* (Korean, Chinese, English and Japanese), *Weil Cornell Medicine*

DEANS

College of Agriculture and Life Sciences: KATHRYN J. BOOR
College of Architecture, Art and Planning: KENT KLEINMAN
College of Arts and Sciences: G. PETER LEPAGE
College of Engineering: LANCE R. COLLINS
College of Human Ecology: ALAN D. MATHIOS

College of Veterinary Medicine: MICHAEL I. KOTLIKOFF
Faculty of Computing and Information Science: DANIEL P. HUTTENLOCHER
Graduate School: BARBARA A. KNUTH
Law School: STEWART J. SCHWAB
Samuel Curtis Johnson Graduate School of Management: L. JOSEPH THOMAS
School of Continuing Education and Summer Sessions: GLENN C. ALTSCHULER
School of Hotel Administration: MICHAEL D. JOHNSON
School of Industrial and Labour Relations: HARRY C. KATZ
Weill Graduate School of Medical Sciences: DAVID P. HAJJAR

PROFESSORS

College of Agriculture and Life Sciences (260 Roberts Hall, Ithaca, NY 14853-5905; tel. (607) 255-2241; e-mail cals-studentservices@cornell.edu; internet www.cals.cornell.edu):

Animal Science:

AUSTIC, R.
BAUMAN, D.
BELL, A.
BLAKE, R.
BUTLER, W.
CHASE, L.
CURRIE, W.
EVERETT, R.
FOX, D.
GALTON, D.
GOREWIT, R.
HINTZ, H.
JOHNSON, P.
OLTENACU, P.
PARKS, J.
PELL, A.
POLLAK, E.
QUAAS, R.
THONNEY, M.

Applied Economics and Management:

BARRETT, C.
BILLS, N.
BOISVERT, R.
CHAPMAN, L.
CHRISTY, R.
CONRAD, J.
KAISER, H.
KANBUR, R.
KNOBLAUCH, W.
LADUE, E.
LEE, D.
LESSER, W.
MCLAUGHLIN, E.
MOUNT, T.
NOVAKOVIC, A.
RAJ, S.
SCHULZE, W.
STREEFER, D.
TAUER, L.
WANSINK, B.
WHITE, G.

Biological and Environmental Engineering:

ALBRIGHT, L.
ANESHANSLEY, D.
COOKE, J.
DATTA, A.
GEBREMEDHIN, K.
HAITH, D.
JEWELL, W.
PARLANGE, J.-Y.
SCOTT, N.
SPANSWICK, R.
STEENHUIS, T.
TIMMONS, M.
WALKER, L.
WALTER, M.

Communication:

BOOTH, J.
GAY, G.
OSTMAN, R.
WALTHER, J.

Crop and Soil Sciences:

CHERNEY, J.
COX, W.
DEGLORIA, S.
DUXBURY, J.
FICK, G.
MCBRIDE, M.
OBENDORF, R.
SETTER, T.
VAN ES, H.

Developmental Sociology:

BROWN, D.
EBERTS, P.
FELDMAN, S.
GEISLER, C.
GURAK, D.
HIRSCHL, T.
LYSON, T.
MCMICHAEL, P.
PFEFFER, M.

Earth and Atmospheric Sciences:

COLUCCI, S.
COOK, K.
RIHA, S.
WILKS, D.

Ecology and Evolutionary Biology:

CHABOT, B.
DHONDT, A.
FEENY, P.
FITZPATRICK, J.
HARRISON, R.
HARVELL, C.
HOWARTH, R.
MCCLURE, P.
MARKS, P.
MORIN, J.
ROOT, R.
WINKLER, D.

Education:

CAFFARELLA, R.
CAMP, W.

Entomology:

AGNELLO, A.
HOFFMANN, M.
LIEBHERR, J.
NYROP, J.
PECKARSKY, B.
REISSIG, W.
ROELOFS, W.
RUTZ, D.
SCOTT, J.
SHELTON, A.
SHIELDS, E.
SODERLUND, D.
STRAUB, R.
TINGEY, W.

Food Science:

ACREE, T.
BARBANO, D.
BATT, C.
BRADY, J., Jr
DURST, R.
GRAVANI, R.
HANG, Y.
HOTCHKISS, J.
HRADZINA, G.
LAWLESS, H.
LEE, C.
MILLER, D.
REGENSTEIN, J.
RIZVI, S.
SIEBERT, K.

Horticultural Sciences:

BROWN, S.
HARMAN, G.
LAKSO, A.
POOL, R.
REISCH, B.
TAYLOR, A.

Horticulture:

BASSUK, N.

BELLINDER, R.
BRIDGEN, M.
GOOD, G.
MILLER, W.
PETROVIC, A.
PRITTS, M.
WAKKINS, C.
WEILER, T.
WIEN, H.
WOLFE, D.

International Programs:

UPHOFF, N.

Landscape Architecture:

ADLEMAN, M.
GLEASON, K.
GOTTFRIED, H.
TRANCIK, R.
TROWBRIDGE, P.

Microbiology:

GHIORSE, W.
HELMANN, J.
WINANS, S.
ZINDER, S.

Molecular Biology and Genetics:

CALVO, J.
FOX, T.
GOLDBERG, M.
HANSON, M.
HENRY, S.
KEMPHUES, K.
LIS, J.
MACINTYRE, R.
ROBERTS, J.
SHALLOWAY, D.
TYE, B.
VOGT, V.
WU, R.

Natural Resources:

DECKER, D.
FAHEY, T.
GILLETT, J.
HULLAR, T.
KNUTH, B.
KRASNY, M.
LASSOIE, J.
MILLS, E.

Neurobiology and Behavior:

ADLER, K.
BRADBURY, J.
EISNER, T.
EMLEN, S.
HARRIS-WARRICK, R.
HOPKINS, C.
VEHRENCAMP, S.
WALCOTT, C.

Nutrition:

BENSADOUN, A.
LEVITSKY, D.
NOY, N.
PINSTRUP-ANDERSON, P.

Plant Biology:

BATES, D.
CREPET, W.
DAVIES, P.
DOYLE, J.
NASRALLAH, J.
NASRALLAH, M.
NIKLAS, K.
RODRIGUEZ, E.

Plant Breeding:

COFFMAN, W. R.
EARLE, E.
JOHN, M.
KRESOVICH, S.
MCCOUCH, S.
MUTSCHLER, M.
SORRELLS, M.
TANKSLEY, S.
VIANDS, D.

Plant Pathology:

ABAWI, G.

ALDWINCKLE, H.
BEER, S.
BERGSTROM, G.
BURR, T.
COLLMER, A.
DILLARD, H.
FRY, W.
HOCH, H.
HUDLER, G.
KOELLER, W.
LAZAROWITZ, S.
LORBEER, J.
LORIA, R.
MARTIN, G.
MILGROOM, M.
ROSENBERGER, D.
SEEM, R.
WILCOX, W.
ZITTER, T.

College of Architecture, Art and Planning (129 Sibley Dome, Ithaca, NY 14853; tel. (607) 255-9110; e-mail aapdean@cornell.edu; internet www.aap.cornell.edu):

Architecture:

GOEHNER, W.
GREENBERG, D. P.
HASCUP, G.
HUBBELL, K.
MOSTAFAVI, M.
OTTO, C. F.
RICHARDSON, H.
WELLS, J.

Art:

KORD, V.
LOCEY, J.
SPECTOR, F.
SQUIER, J. L.
WALKINGSTICK, K.

City and Regional Planning:

AZIS, I.
BENERIA, L.
BOOTH, R.
CHRISOPHERSON, S.
CLAVEL, P.
DRENNAN, M.
FORESTER, J.
GOLDSMITH, W.
LEWIS, D.
OLPADWALA, P.
REARDON, K.

College of Arts and Sciences (172 Golden Smith Hall, Ithaca, NY 14853-3201; tel. (607) 255-4833; e-mail as_admissions@cornell.edu; internet www.arts.cornell.edu):

Anthropology:

GREENWOOD, D.
HENDERSON, J.
HOLMBERG, D.
MARCH, K.
SANGREN, P.
SIEGEL, J.
SMALL, M.

Asian Studies:

DE BARY, B.
GOLD, D.
GUNN, E.
MINKOWSKI, C.
SAKAI, N.
TAYLOR, K.

Astronomy:

CAMPBELL, D.
CHERNOFF, D.
CORDES, J.
GIERASCH, P.
GIOVANELLI, R.
GOLDSMITH, P.
HAYNES, M.
HERTER, T.
HOUCK, J.
NICHOLSON, P.
SQUYRES, S.
STACEY, G.

TERZIAN, Y.
VEVERKA, J.
WASSERMAN, I.

Chemistry and Chemical Biology:

ABRUNA, H.
BAIRD, B.
BEGLEY, T.
BURLITCH, J.
CARPENTER, B.
COATES, G.
COLLUM, D.
DAVIS, H.
DISALVO, F.
EALICK, S.
EZRA, G.
FAY, R.
FREED, J.
GANEM, B.
HINES, M.
HOFFMANN, R.
HOUSTON, P.
LEE, S.
LORING, R.
MEINWALD, J.
SOGAH, D.
WIDOM, B.
WOLCZANSKI, P.

Classics:

AHL, F.
CLINTON, K.
COLEMAN, J.
NUSSBAUM, A.
PELLICCIA, H.
PUCCI, P.
RAWLINGS, H., III
RUSTEN, J.

Comparative Literature:

CARMICHAEL, C.
COHEN, W.
KENNEDY, W.
MONROE, J.

Ecology and Systematics:

ELLNER, S.
GREENE, H.
HAIRSTON, N., Jr
KENNEDY, K.
POWER, A.
PROVINE, W.

Economics:

BASU, K.
BLUME, L.
COATE, S.
DAVIS, T.
EASLEY, D.
HONG, Y.
KIEFER, N.
LYONS, T.
MAJUMDAR, M.
MASSON, R.
MITRA, T.
POSSEN, U.
SHELL, K.
VOGELSANG, T.
WAN, H., Jr

English:

BOGEL, F.
BROWN, L.
CHASE, C.
CHEYFITZ, E.
CULLER, J.
FULTON, A.
GILBERT, R.
HERRIN, W.
HILL, T.
HITE, M.
JANOWITZ, P.
JEYIFO, B.
McCALL, D.
McCLANE, K., Jr
McMILLIN, H.
MOHANTY, S.
MORGAN, R.
MURRAY, T.

PARKER, A.
SAMUELS, S.
SAWYER, P.
SCHWARZ, D.
SHAW, H.
SIEGEL, S.
SPILLERS, H.
VAUGHN, S.
WETHERBEE, W., III

German Studies:

ADELSON, L.
GROOS, A., Jr
HOHENDAHL, P.
KITTLER, W.
MARTIN, C.

Government:

BENSEL, R.
BUCK-MORSS, S.
BUNCE, V.
EVANGELISTA, M.
HERRING, R.
KATZENSTEIN, M.
KATZENSTEIN, P.
KRAMNICK, I.
LOWI, T.
MEBANE, W.
PONTUSSON, J.
RABKIN, J.
RUBENSTEIN, D.
SANDERS, M.
SHEFTER, M.
TARROW, S.
VANDEWALLE, N.

History:

ALTSCHULER, G.
BLUMIN, S.
CARON, V.
COCHRAN, S.
DEAR, P.
GREENE, S.
HULL, I.
HYAMS, P.
KAMMEN, M.
KAPLAN, S.
KOSCHMANN, J.
LACAPRA, D.
LOGEVALL, F.
MOORE, R.
NAJEMY, J.
NORTON, M.
PETERSON, C.
POLENBERG, R.
STEINBERG, M.
STRAUSS, B.
WASHINGTON, M.

History of Art:

KUNIHOLM, P.
LAZZARO, C.
RAMAGE, A.

Linguistics:

BOWERS, J.
COLLINS, C.
DIESING, M.
HARBERT, W.
McCONNELL-GINET, S.
ROOTH, M.
ROSEN, C.
WHITMAN, J.
ZEC, D.

Mathematics:

BARBASCH, D.
BILLERA, L.
BROWN, K.
CHASE, S.
CONNELLY, R.
DENNIS, R. K.
DURRETT, R.
DYNKIN, E.
GROSS, L.
GUCKENHEIMER, J.
HATCHER, A.
HENDERSON, D.
HUBBARD, J.

HWANG, J. T.
ILIACHENKO, I.
KAHN, P.
LAWLER, G.
NERODE, A.
NUSSBAUM, M.
SALOFF-COSTE, L.
SCHATZ, A.
SEN, S.
SHORE, R.
SMILLIE, J.
SPEH, B.
STILLMAN, M.
STRICHARTZ, R.
THURSTON, W.
VOGTMANN, K.
WAHLBIN, L.
WEST, J.

Molecular Biology and Genetics:

AGUADRO, C.
BRETSCHER, A.
BROWN, W.
CLARK, A.
FEIGENSON, G.
HESS, G.
HINKLE, P.
HUFFAKER, T.
WILSON, D.
WOLFNER, M.

Music:

BILSON, M.
HARRIS-WARRICLE, R.
HSU, J.
ROSEN, D.
SIERRA, R.
STUCKY, S.
WEBSTER, J., Jr
ZASLAW, N.

Near Eastern Studies:

BRANN, R.
OWEN, D.
POWERS, D.

Neurobiology and Behavior:

BASS, A.
FETCHO, J.
HOWLAND, H.
HOY, R.
SEELEY, T.
SHERMAN, P.

Philosophy:

BOYD, R.
FINE, G.
IRWIN, T.
MACDONALD, S.
MILLER, R.
MOODY-ADAMS, M.
STURGEON, N.

Physics:

ALEXANDER, J.
AMBEGAOKAR, V.
ASHCROFT, N.
BERKELMAN, K.
BODENSCHATZ, E.
CASSEL, D.
DAVIS, J.
DUGAN, G.
ELSER, V.
FITCHEN, D.
GALIK, R.
GINSPARG, P.
GRUNER, S.
HAND, L.
HARTILL, D.
HENLEY, C.
HOFFSTAETTER, G.
LeCLAIR, A.
LEE, D.
LEPAGE, G.
McEUEN, P.
MERMIN, N.
NEUBERT, M.
PARPIA, J.
PATTERSON, J.

RALPH, D.
RICHARDSON, R.
RUBIN, D.
SETHNA, J.
SIEVERS, A., III
STEIN, P.
TALMAN, R.
TEUKOLSKY, S.
THORNE, R.
TYE, S.-H.
YAN, T.-M.
YORK, J.

Plant Biology:

TURGEON, E. G.

Programme on Ethics and Public Life:

SHUE, H.

Psychology:

BEM, D.
BEM, S.
CUTTING, J.
DARLINGTON, R.
DEVOOGD, T.
DUNNING, D.
EDELMAN, S.
FINLAY, B.
GILOVICH, T.
HALPERN, B.
JOHNSTON, R.
KRUMHANSL, C.
MAAS, J.
NEISSER, U.
REGAN, E.

Romance Studies:

BERGER, A.
CASTILLO, D.
GREENBERG, M.
KLEIN, R.
LEWIS, P.
LONG, K.
MIGIEL, M.
RESINA, J.

Russian Literature:

CARDEN, P.
POLLACK, N.
SENDEROVICH, S.
SHAPIRO, G.

Science and Technology Studies:

LYNCH, M.
PINCH, T.
REPPY, J.
ROSSITER, M.

Sociology:

HARRIS, D.
HECKATHORN, D.
MACY, M.
NEE, V.
STRANG, D.
SWEDBERG, R.

Theater, Film and Dance:

BATHRICK, D.
FELDSHUH, D.
GAINOR, J.
GOETZ, K.
LEVITT, B.

College of Engineering (Carpenter Hall, Ithaca, NY 14853-2201; tel. (607) 255-4326; e-mail engr_admissions@cornell.edu; internet www.engineering.cornell.edu):

Applied and Engineering Physics:

BROCK, J.
BUHRMAN, R.
COOL, T.
CRAIGHEAD, H.
GAETA, A.
KUSSE, B.
LINDAU, M.
LOVELACE, R.
SILCOX, J.
WEBB, W.
WISE, F.

Chemical Engineering:

ARCHER, L.
CLANCY, P.
COHEN, C.
KOCH, D.
OLBRICHT, W.
SHULER, M.
STEEN, P.

Civil and Environmental Engineering:

BRUTSAERT, W.
GOSSETT, J.
GRIGORIU, M.
HOVER, K.
INGRAFFEA, A.
KULHAWY, F.
LION, L.
LIU, P.
LOUCKS, D.
MEYBURG, A.
NOZICK, L.
O'ROURKE, T.
PEKOZ, T.
SANSALONE, M.
SCHULER, R.
SHOEMAKER, C.
STEDINGER, J.
TURNQUIST, M.

Computer Sciences:

ARMS, W.
BAILEY, G.
BIRMAN, K.
COLEMAN, T.
CONSTABLE, R.
ELBER, R.
GRIES, D.
HALPERN, J.
HOPCROFT, J.
HUTTENLOCHER, D.
KEDEM, K.
KOZEN, D.
PINGALI, K.
SCHNEIDER, F.
TARDOS, E.
VAN LOAN, C.
VAVASIS, S.

Earth and Atmospheric Sciences:

ALLMENDINGER, R.
BARAZANGI, M.
BROWN, L.
CATHLES, L.
CISNE, J.
GREENE, C.
ISACKS, B.
JORDAN, T.
KAY, R.
KAY, S.
PHIPPS MORGAN, J.
RHODES, F.
WHITE, W.

Electrical Engineering:

BERGER, T.
CHIANG, H.-D.
EASTMAN, L.
FARLEY, D., Jr
FINE, T.
FUCHS, W.
HAAS, Z.
HAMMER, D.
JOHNSON, C., Jr
KELLEY, M.
KINTNER, P., Jr
KLINE, R.
PARKS, T.
POLLOCK, C.
SEYLER, C.
SHEALY, J.
SPENCER, M.
TANG, C.-L.
THOMAS, R.
TIWARI, S.
TONG, L.
WICKER, S.

Materials Science and Engineering:

AST, D.
BLAKELY, J.
DIECKMANN, R.
GIANNELIS, E.
OBER, C.
RUOFF, A.
SASS, S.
VAN DOVER, R.

Mechanical and Aerospace Engineering:

AVEDISIAN, C.
BARTEL, D.
CAUGHEY, D.
COLLINS, L.
DAWSON, P.
GEORGE, A.
GOULDIN, F.
LEIBOVICH, S.
LOUGE, M.
MOON, F.
POPE, S.
TORRANCE, K.
WARHAFT, Z.
WILLIAMSON, C.
ZABARAS, N.

Operations Research and Industrial Engineering:

BLAND, R.
JACKSON, P.
LEWIS, A.
MUCKSTADT, J.
PROTTER, P.
RENEGAR, J.
RESNICK, S.
ROUNDY, R.
RUPPERT, D.
SAMORODNITSKY, G.
SHMOYS, D.
TODD, M.
TROTTER, L., Jr
TURNBULL, B.
WILLIAMSON, D.

Theoretical and Applied Mechanics:

BURNS, J.
CADY, K.
HEALEY, T.
HUI, CH.-Y.
JENKINS, J.
MUKHERJEE, S.
PHOENIX, S.
RAND, R.
RUINA, A.
SACHSE, W.
STROGATZ, S.
ZEHNDER, A.

College of Human Ecology (Martha Van Rensselaer Hall, Ithaca, NY 14853; tel. (607) 255-8774; e-mail humec_admissions@cornell.edu; internet www.human.cornell.edu):

Design and Environmental Analysis:

BECKER, F.
ESHELMAN, P.
EVANS, G.
HEDGE, A.
JENNINGS, J.
LAQUATRA, J., Jr
SIMS, W.

Human Development and Family Studies:

BRUMBERG, J.
CECI, S.
COCHRAN, M.
DEPUE, R.
ECKENRODE, J.
GABARINO, J.
HAMILTON, S.
LUST, B.
PILLEMER, K.
ROBERTSON, S.
SAVIN-WILLIAMS, R.
WILLIAMS, W.

Nutrition:

BISOGNI, C.
BRANNON, P.
BRENNA, J.
GARZA, C.
HAAS, J.
HABICHT, J.-P.
OLSON, C.
PELTO, G.
RASMUSSEN, K.
SAHN, D.
STIPANUK, M.

Policy Analysis and Management:

AVERY, R.
BATTISTELLA, R.
BURKHAUSER, R.
GERNER, J.
KENTEL, D.
MATHIOS, A.
PARROT, A.
PETERS, H.
TROCHIM, W.
WHITE, W.

Textiles and Apparel:

CHU, CH.-CH.
LEMLEY, A.
LOKER, S.
NETRAVALI, A.
OBENDORF, S.

College of Veterinary Medicine (Ithaca, NY 14853-6401; tel. (607) 253-3000; e-mail vet_admissions@cornell.edu; internet www.vet.cornell.edu):

Biomedical Sciences:

BEYENBACH, K.
DELAHUNTA, A.
FARNUM, C.
FORTUNE, J.
GILMOUR, R., Jr
HOUPT, K.
KOTLIKOFF, M.
LOEW, E.
MINOR, R.
NODEN, D.
QUARONI, A.
SCHIMENTI, J.
SCHLAFER, D.
SUAREZ, S.
SUMMERS, B.
YEN, A.

Clinical Sciences:

AINSWORTH, D.
BARR, S.
CENTER, S.
DIVERS, T.
DUCHARME, N.
FUBINI, S.
GILBERT, R.
GLEED, R.
HACKETT, R.
HORNBUCKLE, W.
KALLFELZ, F.
KOLLIAS, G., Jr
LUDDERS, J.
MILLER, W.
MOISE, N.
NIXON, A.
PAGE, R.
RANDOLPH, J.
SCOTT, D.
SMITH, D.
TENNANT, B.

Microbiology, Immunology and Parasitology:

ANTCZAK, D.
APPLETON, J.
BAINES, J.
BLOOM, S.
BOWMAN, D.
BOWSER, P.
DIETERT, R.
LUST, G.
McGREGOR, D.
MARSH, J.

PARRISH, C.
RUSSELL, D.
SCHAT, K.

Molecular Medicine:

CERIONE, R.
GUAN, J.
OSWALD, R.
PAULI, B.
SCHWARK, W.
SHARP, G.
WEILAND, G.

Population Medicine and Diagnostic Services:

CHANG, Y.-F.
ERB, H.
GROHN, Y.
MOHAMMED, H.
SCHUKKEN, Y.
TORRES, A.
WHITE, M.

Law School (Myron Taylor Hall, Ithaca, NY 14853-4901; tel. (607) 255-0565; e-mail lawadmit@law.mail.cornell.edu; internet www.lawschool.cornell.edu):

ALEXANDER, G.
BARCELO, J., III
CLERMONT, K. M.
CLYMER, S.
EISENBERG, T.
FARINA, C.
GARVEY, S.
GERMAIN, C.
GREEN, R.
HAY, G. A.
HEISE, M.
HENDERSON, J., Jr
HILLMAN, R.
HOLDEN-SMITH, B.
JOHNSON, S. L.
LASSER, M.
LEHMAN, J.
MARTIN, P. W.
NDULO, M.
RACHLINSKI, J.
RILES, A.
ROSSI, F. F.
SCHWAB, S.
SHERWIN, E.
SHIFFRIN, S.
SILICIANO, J.
SIMSON, G. J.
SUMMERS, R. S.
TAYLOR, W.
WIPPMAN, D.

New York State College of Industrial and Labour Relations

Collective Bargaining:

DANIEL, C.
GROSS, J.
HURD, R.
KAHN, L.
KATZ, H.
KURUVILLA, S.
LIPSKY, D.
SALVATORE, N.
TURNER, L.

Employment and Disability Institute:

BRUYERE, S.

Human Resource Studies:

BRIGGS, V., Jr
DYER, L.
SNELL, S.
WRIGHT, P.

Labour Economics:

ABOWD, J.
BLAU, F.
BOYER, G.
EHRENBERG, R.
FIELDS, G.
HUTCHENS, R.
SMITH, R.

Organizational Behavior:

BACHARACH, S.
HAMMER, T.
LAWLER, E.
TOLBERT, P.

Social Statistics:

DICICCIO, T.
WELLS, M.

Samuel Curtis Johnson Graduate School of Management (Sage Hall, Ithaca, NY 14853-6201; tel. (607) 255-4526; e-mail mba@cornell.edu; internet www.johnson.cornell.edu):

BENDANIEL, D.
BIERMAN, H., Jr
BLOOMFIELD, R.
DYCKMAN, T.
FRANK, R.
HART, S.
HASS, J.
HILTON, R.
ISEN, A.
JARROW, R.
LEE, C.
LIBBY, R.
McADAMS, A.
McCLAIN, J.
MICHAELY, R.
NELSON, M.
O'HARA, M.
ORMAN, L.
RAO, V.
RUSSO, J.
SMIDT, S.
SWAMINATHAN, B.
SWIERINGA, R.
THOMAS, L.
WALDMAN, M.

School of Hotel Administration (Statler Hall, Ithaca, NY 14853-6902; tel. (607) 255-9393; e-mail hotelschool_admissions@cornell.edu; internet www.hotelschool.cornell.edu):

BROWNELL, J.
CORGEL, J.
DITTMAN, D.
ENZ, C.
GELLER, A.
HINKIN, T.
KIMES, S.
MUTKOSKI, S.
PENNER, R.
REDLIN, M.
SIGUAW, J.
THOMPSON, G.

Weill Cornell Medical College (1300 York Ave, New York, NY 10065; tel. (212) 746-5454; e-mail cumc_admissions@med.cornell.edu; internet www.med.cornell.edu):

Anaesthesiology:

AMAR, D.
DESIDERIO, D.
DINNER, M., Clinical
HALPERN, N. A., Clinical
HARRISON, N., Pharmacology
HEMMINGS, H. C., Jr
KELLY, R. E., Clinical
LIEN, C. A., Clinical
MALHOTRA, V., Clinical
SAVARESE, J.
THOMAS, S. J.
THORNE, A. C., Clinical
WILSON, R. S.
YAO, F.-S. F., Clinical

Biochemistry:

BOSKEY, A. L.
BRESLOW, E. M. G.
COOPER, A. J. L.
McGRAW, T. E.
MAXFIELD, F. R.
MENON, A. K.
NOVOGRODSKY, A.
ROBERTSON, H. D.
RUBIN, A. L.
RYAN, T. A.

STENZEL, K. H.
TATE, S. S.
WU, H.

Cardiothoracic Surgery:

ADKINS, M. S.
ALTORKI, N. K.
ISOM, O. W.
KRIEGER, K. H.
LARAGH, J. H., Medicine
TORTOLANI, A. J.

Cell and Developmental Biology:

BACHVAROVA, R. F.
FISCHMAN, D. A.
HAJJAR, K. A.
MIKAWA, T.
SATO, T. N.

Dermatology:

GRANSTEIN, R. D.
HALPERN, A. C.
VARGHESE, M. C.

Genetic Medicine:

RAFII, S.

Medicine:

ALLISON, J. P., Immunology
AUGUST, P.
BAJORIN, D. F.
BARDES, C. L., Clinical
BASSON, C. T.
BERMAN, E., Clinical
BOCKMAN, R. S.
BORER, J. S.
BOSL, G. J.
BROWN, A. E.
CARMEL, R.
CASPER, E. S.
CHANDRA, P., Clinical
CHARLSON, M. E.
CHEIGH, H., Clinical
CLARKSON, B. D.
CROW, M. K.
CRYSTAL, R. G.
DANNENBERG, A. J.
DEVEREUX, R. B.
DOSIK, H.
ETINGIN, O. R.
FAHEY, T. J., Jr, MClinical
FEIN, O. T., Clinical
FELDMAN, E. J.
FINNS, J. J.
FLOMENBAUM, N. E., Clinical
FUKS, Z. Y., Radiation Oncology
GIBOFSKY, A., Clinical
GOLDE, D. W.
GORDON, B., Clinical
GOTTO, A. M., Jr
GROEGER, J. S., Clinical
HAYES, J. G.
HEMPSTEAD, B. L.
HOUGHTON, A. N.
IMPERATO-MCGINLEY, J. L.
IVANSHKIV, L. B.
JACOBS, J. L., Clinical
JACOBSON, I. M., Clinical
JOHNSON, W. D.
KAGEN, L. J. A.
KELSEN, D. P.
KEMENY, N. E.
KIEHN, T. E., Clinical and Clinical Microbiology
KLEIN, H.
KLIGFIELD, P. D.
KOLESNICK, R. N.
KRIS, M. G.
KROWN, S. E.
KURTZ, R. C., Clinical
LACHS, M. S.
LAURENCE, J. C.
LERMAN, B. B.
LIPKIN, M.
LIVINGSTON, P. O.
LOCKSHIN, M. D.
MCCORMICK, B., Radiation Oncology
MARCUS, A. J.

MARKENSON, J. A., Clinical)
MARKS, P. A.
MAYER, K., Clinical
MESSINEO, F., Clinical
MEYER, B. R., Clinical
MINSKY, B., Radiation Oncology)
MOORE, A., Clinical
MOTZER, R. J.
MURRAY, H. W.
NACHMAN, R. L.
NANUS, D. M., Haematology, Oncology
NIMER, S. D.
NORTON, L.
OETTGEN, H. F.
OFFIT, K.
OKIN, P. M.
PAGET, S. A.
PAMER, E. G.
PAPE, J. W.
PECKER, M. S., Clinical
PFISTER, D. G.
PORTLOCK, C. S., Clinical
POSNETT, D. N.
PRITCHETT, R. A. R., Clinical
RAHAL, J. J.
RIGGIO, R. R., Clinical
RIVLIN, R. S.
ROBBINS, R. J.
ROBERTS, R. B.
ROMAN, M. J.
ROSEN, N.
ROSENFELD, I., Clinical
SAAL, S. D., Clinical
SALMON, J. E.
SALTZ, L. B.
SCHEIDT, S., Clinical
SCHEINBERG, D. A.
SCHER, H. I.
SCHUSTER, M. W., Clinical
SEPKOWITZ, K. A.
SHIKE, M.
SILVER, R. T.
SMITH, K. A.
SPRIGGS, D. R.
STEINBERG, C. R., Clinical
STEINGART, R. M.
STOVER, D. E., Clinical
STRAUS, D. J., Clinical
SUTHANTHIRAN, M.
THOMAS, H. M., III, Clinical
WADLER, S.
WEINSTEIN, A. M.
WEKSLER, B. B.
WEKSLER, M. E.
WHITE, D. A.
WINAWER, S. J.
WITTES, R.
WUEST, D. L., Pathology in Clinical
YAHALOM, J., Radiation Oncology

Microbiology and Immunology:

BARANY, F.
BROT, N.
COICO, R.
DING, A.
FALCK-PEDERSEN, E.
HOLLOMAN, W. K.
MOORE, J. P.
NAQI, S. A.
NATHAN, C.

Neurological Surgery:

GUTIN, P. H.
STEIG, P. E.

Neurology and Neuroscience:

APPEL, S. H., Neurology
BAKER, H., Neuroscience
BEAL, M. F.
BLASBERG, R. G., Neurology
BLASS, J.
BROOKS, D. C., Anatomy
CARONNA, J. J., Neurology (Clinical)
DANNON, M. J., Neurology (Clinical)
DEANGELIS, L. M., Neurology (Clinical)
FOLEY, K. M.
GIBSON, G. E., Neuroscience

IADECOLA, C.
LABAR, D. R.
LATOV, N.
MCDOWELL, F. H.
MILNER, T. A., Neuroscience
PASTERNAK, G. W.
PETITO, F. A., Neurology (Clinical)
PICKEL, V. M., Neuroscience
POLLACK, C. P., Neurology (Clinical)
POSNER, J. B.
RATAN, R. R.
ROSS, M. E.
RUBIN, M., Neurology (Clinical)
VICTOR, J. D.
VOLPE, B. T.
WAGNER, J. A.

Obstetrics and Gynaecology:

CAPUTO, T. A., Clinical
CHERVENAK, F. A.
GOSDEN, R. G.
LIU, H.-C., Reproductive Medicine
POST, R. C., Clinical
ROSENWAKS, Z.
SAXENA, B. B., Endocrinology)
SPITZER, M., Clinical
WITKIN, S. S., Immunology

Ophthalmology:

ABRAMSON, D. H.
COLEMAN, D. J.
RODRIGUEZ-BOULAN, E. J., Cell and Developmental Biology
SILVERMAN, R. H., Computer Science

Orthopaedic Surgery:

BURKE, G. W., Clinical
CORNELL, C. N., Clinical
CRAIG, E. V., Orthopaedic SurgeryClinical
HEALEY, J. H.
HELFET, D. L.
LANE, J. M.
LASKIN, R. S., Clinical
PELLICI, P. M., Clinical
ROOT, L., Clinical
SALVATI, E. A., Clinical
SCULCO, T. P., Clinical
TORZILLI, P. A., Applied Biomechanics
WARREN, R. F.
WEILAND, A. J., Plastic
WICKIEWICZ, T. L., Clinical
WILSON, P. D., Jr
WINDSOR, R. E., Clinical
WOLFE, S. W.
WRIGHT, T. M., Applied Biomechanics

Otorhinolaryngology:

SELESNICK, S. H.

Paediatrics:

BROMBERG, K.
BUSSEL, J. B.
CHUTORIAN, A. B.
COOPER, R. S., Ophthalmology
CUNNINGHAM-RUNDLES, S.
GERMAN, J. L.
GERSONY, W. M.
GIARDINA, P. V., Clinical
GLASS, L.
GREENWALD, B. M., Clinical
HILGARTNER, M. W.
KLEIN, A. A., Clinical
KOSOFSKY, B.
KRAUSS, A. N., Clinical
LEHMAN, T. J. A., Clinical
LOUGHLIN, G. M.
MENDEZ, H. A., Clinical
MOSCONA, A.
O'REILLY, R. J.
PERLMAN, J. M.
RAJEGOWDA, B., Clinical
RUBIN, D. H., Clinical
SOLOMON, G. E., Clinical/Neurology
STEINHERZ, P. G.

Pathology and Laboratory Medicine:

AKHTAR, M.
ALONSO, D. R.
BAERGEN, R., Clinical

BARRIOS, R.
BULLOUGH, P. G.
BURKE, M. D.
CAGLE, P. T.
CHADBURN, A.
CHAGANTI, R. S. K., Genetics
CHEN, Y. T.
CHEN-KIANG, S.
ELLENSON, L. H.
HAJJAR, D. P.
HODA, S. A. F., Clinical
HUVOS, A. G.
JONES, J. G.
KLIMSTRA, D. S.
KNOWLES, D. M.
LAND, G. A., Clinical
LAVI, E.
LEONARD, D. G. B.
LIEBERMAN, M. W.
LIPMAN, N. S., Veterinary Medicine
McNUTT, N. S.
MODY, D. R.
MULLER, W. A.
PEERSCHKE, E. I. B.
PETROVIC, L. M.
REUTER, V. E.
ROSEN, P. P.
ROSENBLUM, M.
SALEEM, A., Pathology and Laboratory Clinical
SESHAN, S. V., Clinical
TRUONG, L. D., Clinical
WOLF, C. F. W., Clinical

Pharmacology:

BUCK, J.
GROSS, S. S.
GUDAS, L. J.
INTURRISI, C.
LEVI, R.
OKAMOTO, M.
REIDENBERG, M. M.
RIFKIND, A. B.
SZETO, H. H.
TOTH, M.

Physiology and Biophysics:

ANDERSEN, O. S.
GARDNER, D.
GRAFSTEIN, B.
HUANG, X.
MAACK, T.
MEHLER, E. L.
PALMER, L. G.
RAMIREZ, F.
ROUX, B.
WEINSTEIN, H.
WINDHAGER, E. E.

Psychiatry:

ADDONIZIO, G. C., Clinical
ALEXOPOULOS, G. S.
AUCHINCLOSS, E. L., Clinical
BARCHAS, J. D.
BREITBART, W.
BRUCE, M. L., Sociology
CAMPBELL, S. S., Psychology
CASEY, B. J., Developmental Psychobiology
CLARKIN, J. F., Clinical Psychology
FERRANDO, S. J., Clinical
FRIEDMAN, R. A., Clinical
GEARY, N. D., Psychology
GIBBS, J. A., Jr
HALMI, K. A.
HERTZIG, M. E.
HOLLAND, J. C. B.
KERNBERG, O. F.
KERNBERG, P. F.
KOCSIS, J. H.
LEDERBERG, M. S., Clinical
LEON, A. C., Biostatistics
MATTSON, M. R. A., Clinical
MEYERS, B. S.
PARDES, H.
PFEFFER, C. R.
POSNER, M. I., Psychology
SACKS, M. H.

SCHULBERG, H. C., Psychology
SHAMOIAN, C. A., Clinical
TARDIFF, K.
WILSON, P. G., Clinical
YOUNG, R. C.

Public Health:

BEGG, C. B., Biostatistics
BOTVIN, G. J., Psychology
DRUSIN, L. M., Clinical
FINKEL, M. L., Clinical
MILLMAN, R. B.
MUSHLIN, A. I.
RUCHLIN, H. S., Economics

Radiology:

ABRAMSON, S. J., Clinical
ADLER, R.
AMOLS, H. I., Physics
ANDERSON, L. L., Physics
AUH, Y. H.
BECKER, D. V.
BRILL, P.
CARAVELLI, J. F., Clinical
COHEN, M. A., Clinical
DECK, M. D. F.
DERSHAW, D. D.
DIVGI, C. R.
FINN, R. D., Physics
GAMSU, G.
GOBIN, Y. P.
GOLDSMITH, S. J.
HANN, L. E.
HEELAN, R. T.
HEIER, L. A., Clinical
HENSCHKE, C. I.
HERZOG, R. J.
HRICAK, H.
KOUTHCER, J. A.
KROL, G., Clinical
LARSON, S.
LI, G. C., Biophysics
LIBERMAN, L.
LING, C. C., Physics
McCAULEY, D., Clinical
NORI, D., Clinical
PANICEK, D. M.
PAVLOV, H.
POTTER, M. R.
PRINCE, M. R.
ROSEN, N. S., Clinical
ROSENBLATT, R., Clinical
SOS, T. A.
SOSTMAN, H. D.
STRAUSS, H. W.
VALLABHAJOSULA, S., Radiopharmacy
WINCHESTER, P.
YANKELEVITZ, D. F.
ZAIDER, M., Physics
ZIMMERMAN, R. D.

Rehabilitation Medicine:

LIEBERMAN, J. S.
O'DELL, M. W., Clinical

Surgery:

BAINS, M. S., Clinical
BARIE, P. S.
BARONE, J. E., Clinical
BESSEY, P. Q.
BLUMGART, L. H.
BRENNAN, M. F.
CHASSIN, J. L., Clinical
CODY, H. S., III, Clinical
CORDEIRO, P. G.
EISENBERG, M. M.
FONG, Y.
GAGNER, M.
HURYN, J. M., Clinical Oral and Maxillofacial Surgery
ISRAEL, H. A., Clinical
KENT, K. C.
LAQUAGLIA, M. P.
MICHELASSI, F.
MILSOM, J. W.
OSBORNE, M. P.
PETREK, J. A.
PIZZI, W. F., Clinical

RUSCH, V. W.
SHAH, J. P., Clinical
SHAHA, A. R.
SMITH, B. H., Clinical
STAIANO-COICO, L., Microbiology
STOLAR, C. J.
STUBENBORD, W. T.
WISE, L.
WONG, G. Y., Statistics
WONG, W. D.
YURT, R. W.

Urology:

BANDER, N. H.
GOLDSTEIN, M.
GUILLONNEAU, B.
HERR, H. W.
SCARDINO, P. T.
SCHLEGEL, P. N.
SHEINFELD, J.
SOGANI, P. C., Clinical
VAUGHAN, E. D.

CULINARY INSTITUTE OF AMERICA

1946 Campus Dr., Hyde Park, NY 12538-1499

Telephone: (845) 452-9600
E-mail: admissions@culinary.edu
Internet: www.ciachef.edu

Founded 1946 as New Haven Restaurant Institute, current name adopted 1951
Private control
Academic year: June to May

Campuses at Hyde Park, New York, San Antonio, Texas, St Helena, California, and Singapore

Pres.: Dr TIM RYAN
Provost: MARK ERICKSON
Sr Vice-Pres. for Finance and Admin.: CHARLES A. O'MARA
Vice-Pres. for Academic Degree Programs: Dr MICHAEL SPERLING
Vice-Pres. for Admin. and Shared Services: RICHARD MIGNAULT
Vice-Pres. for Admissions and Marketing: BRUCE D. HILLENBRAND
Vice-Pres. for Advancement and Business Devt: Dr VICTOR A. L. GIELISSE
Vice-Pres. for Strategic Initiatives and Industry Leadership: GREG DRESCHER
Dir for Library Services and Information: ERIC HINSDALE

Library of 84,000 vols, 4,000 DVDs and video cassettes, 280 current periodical titles
Number of teachers: 150
Number of students: 2,900

Publication: *Food is Life* (online, www.foodislife.org)

DEANS

Baking and Pastry Arts: THOMAS VACCARO
Culinary Arts: BRENDAN WALSH
Liberal Arts and Business Management: Dr KATHLEEN MERGET

DAEMEN COLLEGE

4380 Main St, Amherst, NY 14226
Telephone: (716) 839-8225
E-mail: admissions@daemen.edu
Internet: www.daemen.edu

Founded 1947 as Rosary Hill College, present name 1976
Private control
Academic year: September to May

Pres.: Dr GARY OLSON
Vice-Pres. for Academic Affairs and Dean for College: Dr MICHAEL S. BROGAN
Vice-Pres. for Business Affairs and Treas.: ROBERT C. BEISWANGER, JR
Vice-Pres. for Enrolment Management: PATRICIA RUPPERT BROWN

Vice-Pres. for External Affairs: DAVID A. CRISTANTELLO
Vice-Pres. for Student Affairs and Dean for Students: RICHANNE C. MANKEY
Registrar: PAULETTE A. ANZELONE
Library of 100,000 vols, 24,000 full-text ejournals, over 37,000 ebooks, and 600 print serials titles
Number of teachers: 120
Number of students: 2,880 (2110 under-graduate, 770 graduate)
Publication: *The Loom*

DEANS

Division of Arts and Sciences: KEVIN TELFORD
Division of Health and Human Services: RONALD J. SCHENK

DAVIS COLLEGE

400 Riverside Dr., Johnson City, NY 13790
Telephone: (607) 729-1581
E-mail: info@davisny.edu
Internet: www.davisny.edu
Founded 1900 as Practical Bible Training School, present name 2004
Private control
Academic year: August to May
Offers courses in counselling, Christian ministries, int. ministries, pastoral studies and teaching English as a second language and youth ministries
Pres.: Dr DINO J. PEDRONE
Chief Academic Officer: Dr GILBERT A. PARKER
Chief Enrolment Officer: RICK CRAMER
Student Devt Officer: NICHOLE POST
Registrar: SPENCER KEY
Librarian: SHELLEY R. BYRON
Library of 70,000 vols
Number of teachers: 16
Number of students: 300

DOMINICAN COLLEGE

470 W Highway, Orangeburg, NY 10962
Telephone: (845) 359-7800
E-mail: admissions@dc.edu
Internet: www.dc.edu
Founded 1952
Private control
Academic year: August to May
Offers courses in business, educational media, nursing, occupational therapy, physical therapy, teacher education and teachers of students who are blind or visually impaired
Pres.: Sis. MARY EILEEN O'BRIEN
Vice-Pres. for Academic Affairs and Academic Dean: Dr THOMAS S. NOWAK
Vice-Pres. for Enrolment Management: BRIAN G. FERNANDES
Vice-Pres. for Financial Affairs: CATHLEEN KENNY
Vice-Pres. for Institutional Advancement: DOROTHY CHRISTINE FILORAMO
Vice-Pres. for Student Devt and Dean for Students: DOHN E. HARSHBARGER
Registrar: MARY MCFADDEN
Head Librarian: JOHN BARRIE
Library of 102,000 vols
Number of teachers: 40
Number of students: 1,860

DOWLING COLLEGE

150 Idle Hour Blvd, Oakdale, NY 11769
Telephone: (631) 244-3000
E-mail: admissions@dowling.edu
Internet: www.dowling.edu
Founded 1955, present name 1968
Private control

Campuses in Melville, Oakdale and Shirley
Pres.: JEREMY D. BROWN
Interim Provost and Vice-Pres. for Corporate Programmes: Dr ELANA ZOLFO
Vice-Pres. for College Admin. and Student Affairs: DAVID RING
Vice-Pres. for Enrolment and Student Services: RONNIE MACDONALD
Library of 222,920 vols
Number of teachers: 120 (full-time)
Number of students: 6,300 (undergraduate and postgraduate)

DEANS

School of Arts and Sciences: Dr PAUL ABRAMSON
School of Education: Dr CLYDE PAYNE

D'YOUVILLE COLLEGE

320 Porter Ave, Buffalo, NY 14201-9985
Telephone: (716) 829-8000
E-mail: admissions@dyc.edu
Internet: www.dyc.edu
Founded 1908
Private control
Offers Master's and doctoral programmes in health-related professions; 5-year programmes in education, dietetics, information technology, int. business, nursing, physical therapy and occupational therapy
Pres.: Sis. DENISE A. ROCHE
Sr Vice-Pres.: RICHARD WIESEN
Vice-Pres. for Academic Affairs: Dr ARUP SEN
Vice-Pres. of Admin. Services and External Relations
Vice-Pres. for Financial Affairs and Treas.: EDWARD A. JOHNSON
Vice-Pres. for Institutional Advancement: TIMOTHY G. BRENNAN
Vice-Pres. for Student Affairs and Enrolment Management: ROBERT P. MURPHY
Registrar: DION DALY
Dir for Admissions: RONALD H. DANNECKER
Library Dir: RAND BELLAVIA
Library of 127,000 vols
Number of teachers: 300 (180 full-time, 120 part-time)
Number of students: 3,140
Publication: *D'Mensions*

ELMIRA COLLEGE

One Park Pl., Elmira, NY 14901
Telephone: (607) 735-1800
E-mail: admissions@elmira.edu
Internet: www.elmira.edu
Founded 1855
Private control
Academic year: July to August
Academic divs incl. business and economics, creative arts, humanities, mathematics and natural sciences, professional programmes and social and behavioural sciences
Pres.: Dr THOMAS KEITH MEIER
Vice-Pres. for Academic Affairs: Dr STEPHEN COLEMAN
Vice-Pres. and Dean for Student Life: JULIANNE BAUMANN
Vice-Pres. for Devt and Dean: SHERRY TROCINO
Vice-Pres. for Financial Affairs and Dean for Admin.: Dr ROBERT RUBLE
Dean for Library and Information Technology: ELIZABETH WAVLE-BROWN
Library of 250,000 vols, incl. 25,000 print and ejournals
Number of teachers: 80
Number of students: 1,200 (full-time)
Publications: *Callisophia*, *Sibyl*

EXCELSIOR COLLEGE

Seven Columbia Circle, Albany, NY 12203-5159
Telephone: (518) 464-8500
E-mail: admissions@excelsior.edu
Internet: www.excelsior.edu
Founded 1971 as Regents College, present name 2001
Private control
Centre in Washington DC
Pres.: JOHN F. EBERSOLE
Provost, Chief Academic Officer and Vice-Pres. for Institutional Research: MARY BETH HANNER
Vice-Pres. for Enrolment Management: CRAIG MASLOWSKY
Vice-Pres. for Extended Education and CEO: WAYNE BROWN
Vice-Pres. for Finance and Admin.: JOHN PONTIUS
Vice-Pres. for Human Resources and Admin. Services: EDMUND J. MCTERNAN
Vice-Pres. for Information Technology: SUSAN O'HERN
Vice-Pres. for Institutional Advancement: CATHY KUSHNER
Vice-Pres. for Legal and Govt Affairs and Gen. Counsel: JOSEPH B. PORTER
Number of students: 30,000
Publication: *Live & Learn*

DEANS

School of Business and Technology: Dr JANE LECLAIR
School of Health Sciences: Dr DEBORAH SOPCZYK
School of Liberal Arts: Dr SCOTT DALRYMPLE
School of Nursing: Dr MARY LEE POLLARD

FASHION INSTITUTE OF TECHNOLOGY

227 W 27th St, New York, NY 10001-5992
Telephone: (212) 217-7999
E-mail: fitinfo@fitnyc.edu
Internet: www.fitnyc.edu
Founded 1944; attached to State Univ. of New York
State control
Academic year: August to May
Pres.: Dr JOYCE F. BROWN
Vice-Pres. for Academic Affairs: GIACOMO OLIVA
Vice-Pres. for Communications and External Relations: LORETTA LAWRENCE KEANE
Vice-Pres for Devt and Alumni Relations: DAWN B. DUNCAN
Vice-Pres. for Enrolment Management and Student Success: MARYBETH MURPHY
Vice-Pres for Finance and Admin. and Treas.: SHERRY F. BRABHAM
Vice-Pres. for Human Resources: ARTHUR E. BROWN, JR
Vice-Pres. for Information Technology: GREGG CHOTTINER
Gen. Counsel and Sec.: STEPHEN TUTTLE
Library Dir: Prof. NJ WOLFE
Library of 138,000 vols
Number of teachers: 1,000 (250 full-time, 750 part-time)
Number of students: 10,400 (10,175 undergraduate, 225 graduate)

DEANS

Jay and Patty Baker School of Business and Technology: DEBORAH KLESENSKI (acting)
School of Art and Design: JOANNE ARBUCKLE
School of Continuing and Professional Studies: (vacant)
School of Graduate Studies: JOANNE ARBUCKLE (acting)
School of Liberal Arts: Dr SCOTT STODDART

FIVE TOWNS COLLEGE

305 N Service Rd, Dix Hills, Long Island, NY 11746-5871

Telephone: (631) 656-2110
E-mail: info@ftc.edu
Internet: www.ftc.edu

Founded 1972
Private control
Academic year: August to May

Offers Bachelors, Masters and doctoral degrees in education, fine arts, mass communication, music

Pres.: Dr STANLEY G. COHEN
Provost and Dean for Academic Affairs: Dr ROGER H. SHERMAN
Dean for Admin.: MARTIN L. COHEN
Dean for Enrolment: JERRY L. COHEN
Dean for Students: SUSAN BARR
Registrar: MARA MALTZ
Library Dir: JOHN VANSTEEN

Library of 35,000 vols, 600 scores, 9,000 sound recordings, 2,300 video recordings, 500 periodicals titles
Number of teachers: 115 (37 full-time, 78 adjunct)
Number of students: 1,175 (1,107 undergraduate, 68 graduate)

FORDHAM UNIVERSITY

441 E Fordham Rd, Bronx, NY 10458

Telephone: (718) 817-1000
E-mail: publicaff@fordham.edu
Internet: www.fordham.edu

Founded 1841 as St John's College, present status 1846, present name 1907
Private control
Academic year: July to June

Campuses in Bronx, New York and W Harrison

Pres.: Rev. JOSEPH M. McSHANE
Provost: Dr STEPHEN FREEDMAN
Sr Vice-Pres. and Chief Financial Officer: JOHN J. LORDAN
Vice-Pres. for Academic Affairs: JUDITH MILLS
Vice-Pres. for Admin.: THOMAS A. DUNNE
Vice-Pres. for Devt and Univ. Relations: ROGER MILICI
Vice-Pres. for Enrolment: PETER A. STACE
Vice-Pres. for Finance: FRANK SIMIO
Vice-Pres. for Student Affairs: JEFFREY L. GRAY
Vice-Pres. for Technology: Dr FRANK SIRIANNI
Vice-Pres. for Univ. Mission and Min.: Rev. JOSEPH QUINN
Registrar: KENNETH POKROWSKI
Univ. Librarian: Dr JAMES McCABE

Library: 2m. vols, 15,500 periodicals and 19,000 ejournals
Number of teachers: 1,120 (718 full-time, 402 part-time)
Number of students: 15,200 (8,435 undergraduate, 6,770 graduate)

Publications: Fordham Magazine, International Philosophical Quarterly, Traditio (1 a year)

DEANS

Fordham College at Lincoln Center: Dr ROBERT R. GRIMES
Fordham College at Rose Hill: Dr MICHAEL LATHAM
Gabelli School of Business: Dr DONNA RAPACCIOLI
Graduate School of Arts and Sciences: Dr NANCY BUSCH
Graduate School of Business Administration: Dr DAVID A. GAUTSCHI
Graduate School of Education: Prof. Dr JAMES J. HENNESSY
Graduate School of Religion and Religious Education: Dr JOHN P. HARRINGTON

Graduate School of Social Service: PETER B. VAUGHAN
School of Law: MICHAEL M. MARTIN
School of Professional and Continuing Studies: Dr ISABELLE FRANK

HAMILTON COLLEGE

198 College Hill Rd, Clinton, NY 13323

Telephone: (315) 859-4011
E-mail: admission@hamilton.edu
Internet: www.hamilton.edu

Founded 1793 as Hamilton-Oneida Acad., chartered as Hamilton College 1812
Private control
Academic year: September to May

Areas of study incl. Africana studies; American studies; anthropology; art; art history; Asian studies; astronomy; biochemistry/molecular biology; biology; chemical physics; chemistry; Chinese; cinema and new media studies; classics; communication; comparative literature; computer science; creative writing; dance and movement studies; East Asian languages and literatures; economics; education studies; English and creative writing; environmental studies; foreign languages; French; geoarchaeology; geosciences; German studies; government; Hispanic studies; history; interdisciplinary concentration; Japanese; jurisprudence, law and justice studies; Latin American studies; mathematics; mediaeval and renaissance studies; music; neuroscience; philosophy; physics; psychology; public policy; religious studies; Russian studies; sociology; Spanish; theatre; women's studies; world politics

Pres.: JOAN HINDE STEWART
Vice-Pres. for Academic Affairs and Dean for Faculty: PATRICK REYNOLDS
Vice-Pres. for Admin. and Finance: KAREN LEACH
Vice-Pres. for Admission and Financial Aid: MONICA INZER
Vice-Pres. for Communications and Devt: DICK TANTILLO
Vice-Pres. for Information Technology and Interim Library Dir: DAVE SMALLEN
Vice-Pres. and Dean for Students: NANCY THOMPSON (acting)

Library of 500,000 vols
Number of teachers: 185 (full-time)
Number of students: 1,810

Publication: Alumni Review

HARTWICK COLLEGE

POB 4020, Oneonta, NY 13820-4020

Telephone: (607) 431-4000
E-mail: admissions@hartwick.edu
Internet: www.hartwick.edu

Founded 1797 as Hartwick Seminary
Private control
Academic year: September to May

Pres.: Dr MARGARET L. DRUGOVICH
Provost and Vice-Pres. for Academic Affairs: Dr MICHAEL G. TANNENBAUM
Vice-Pres. for College Advancement: JAMES BROSCHART
Vice-Pres. for Enrolment Management: DAVID B. CONWAY
Vice-Pres. for Finance and Chief Financial Officer: GEORGE ELLSBECK
Vice-Pres. for Institutional Advancement: JIM BROSCHART
Vice-Pres. for Student Affairs: Dr MEG NOWAK
Dean for Academic Affairs: Dr KIM NOLING
Dean for Students: TARA LOEWENGUTH
Dean for Student Success: ROBIN DIANA
Dir for Admissions: LISA STARKEY-WOOD
Dir for Institutional Research: MINGHUI WANG
Dir for IT: DAVIS CONLEY

Dir for Library and Information Resources: PAUL COLEMAN

Library of 300,832 vols
Number of teachers: 200 (112 full-time)
Number of students: 1,615

HEBREW UNION COLLEGE—JEWISH INSTITUTE OF RELIGION

The Brookdale Center, One W Fourth St, New York, NY 10012

Telephone: (212) 674-5300
Internet: huc.edu

Founded 1875, present status 2011
Private control
Languages of instruction: English, Hebrew
Academic year: August to June

Schools of Rabbinical studies, graduate studies, education, Jewish nonprofit management, sacred music, biblical archaeology; campuses: Cincinnati in Ohio, Los Angeles in California, New York in New York, and Jerusalem in Israel

Pres.: Dr DAVID ELLENSON
Vice-Pres. for Academic Affairs: Dr MICHAEL MARMUR
Vice-Pres. for Finance and Admin.: SANDRA M. MILLS
Vice-Pres. for Institutional Advancement: Dr JANE F. KARLIN
Dean for Cincinnati Campus: Dr JONATHAN COHEN
Dean for Los Angeles Campus: JOSHUA HOLO
Dean for New York Campus: SHIRLEY IDELSON
Dean for Jerusalem Campus: NAAMAH KELMAN
Registrar: CLYDE PARRISH
Dir for Admissions: DEBORAH ABELSON
Dir for Libraries: Dr DAVID J. GILNER

Library of 130,000 vols
Number of teachers: 130
Number of students: 780

Publications: American Jewish Archives Journal (online, americanjewisharchives.org/journal), Hebrew Union College Annual

HILBERT COLLEGE

5200 S Park Ave, Hamburg, NY 14075

Telephone: (716) 649-7900
E-mail: info@hilbert.edu
Internet: www.hilbert.edu

Founded 1957
Private control
Academic year: September to August

Divs of arts and science, criminal justice/forensic science, professional studies, social science

Pres.: Dr CYNTHIA ZANE
Provost and Vice-Pres. for Academic Affairs: Dr CHRISTOPHER HOLOMAN
Vice-Pres. for Business and Finance: RICHARD J. PINKOWSKI, JR
Vice-Pres. for Enrolment Management and Dean for Students: PETER S. BURNS
Vice-Pres. for Information Services: MICHAEL A. MURRIN
Vice-Pres. for Institutional Advancement: FRANCES VAUGHAN
Dir for Admissions: TIMOTHY LEE
Registrar: GEORGINA ADAMCHICK
Library Dir: WIL PROUT

Library of 36,500 vols, 50,000 ejournals and 1,300 video cassettes and DVDs
Number of teachers: 125 (49 full-time, 76 part-time)
Number of students: 1,120 (1,090 undergraduate, 30 graduate)

Publications: Hilbert Connections (3 a year), Hilbert Horizons

HOBART AND WILLIAM SMITH COLLEGES

300 Pulteney St, Geneva, NY 14456-3397
Telephone: (315) 781-3000
E-mail: admissions@hws.edu
Internet: www.hws.edu

Founded 1822 (Hobart), 1908 (William Smith)

Academic year: August to May (2 semesters)

Operates under a coordinate college system; men graduate from Hobart College and women from William Smith College

Pres.: MARK D. GEARAN
Provost and Dean for Faculty: PAT McGUIRE
Vice-Pres. for Communications: CATHY WILLIAMS
Vice-Pres. for Enrolment and Admissions: BOB MURPHY
Vice-Pres. for Finance: PETER POLINAK
Vice-Pres. for Human Resources: SANDRA BISSELL
Vice-Pres. for Institutional Advancement: ROBERT O'CONNOR
Vice-Pres. for Student Affairs: ROBB FLOWERS
Chief Information Officer: FRED DAMIANO
Dean for Hobart College: EUGEN BAER
Dean for William Smith College: SUSANNE McNALLY
Treas.: PETER POLINAK
Library Dir: VINCE BOISSELLE

Library of 387,650 vols

Number of teachers: 205 (full-time)

Number of students: 2,225 (2,217 undergraduate, 8 graduate)

Publications: *The Pulteney St Survey* (3 a year), *The Seneca Review* (2 a year)

HOFSTRA UNIVERSITY

144 Hofstra Univ., Hempstead, NY 11549-1000
Telephone: (516) 463-6600
E-mail: admission@hofstra.edu
Internet: www.hofstra.edu

Founded 1935

Private control

Academic year: August to May

Pres.: STUART RABINOWITZ
Provost and Sr Vice-Pres. for Academic Affairs: Dr HERMAN A. BERLINER
Sr Vice-Pres. for Planning and Admin.: Dr M. PATRICIA ADAMSKI
Vice-Pres. for Business Devt: RICHARD V. GUARDINO, JR
Vice-Pres. for Devt and Alumni Affairs: ALAN J. KELLY
Vice-Pres. for Enrolment Management: JESSICA EADS
Vice-Pres. for Facilities and Operations: JOSEPH M. BARKWILL
Vice-Pres. for Financial Affairs and Treas.: CATHERINE HENNESSY
Vice-Pres. for Institutional Research and Assessment: STEPHANIE BUSHEY
Vice-Pres. for IT: ROBERT W. JUCKIEWICZ
Vice-Pres. for Legal Affairs and Gen. Counsel: DOLORES FREDRICH
Vice-Pres. and Dir for Athletics: JEFFREY A. HATHAWAY
Vice-Pres. for Student Affairs: SANDRA S. JOHNSON
Vice-Pres. for Univ. Relations: MELISSA CONNOLLY
Dean for Library and Information Services: Dr DANIEL R. RUBEY (acting)

Library: 1m. vols, 100,000 ebooks, 75,000 full text journals

Number of teachers: 1,123

Number of students: 10,993

Publications: *Hofstra Magazine* (3 a year), *Pulse*

DEANS

Continuing Education: RICHARD V. GUARDINO, JR
Frank G. Zarb School of Business: Dr PATRICK J. SOCCI
Graduate Studies: LIORA P. SCHMELKIN
Hofstra College of Liberal Arts and Sciences: Dr BERNARD J. FIRESTONE
Hofstra North Shore-LIJ School of Medicine: Dr LAWRENCE G. SMITH
Hofstra University Honors College: WARREN G. FRISINA
Lawrence Herbert School of Communication: Dr EVAN W. CORNOG
Maurice A. Deane School of Law: ERIC LANE
School of Education: Dr SEAN A. FANELLI
School of Engineering and Applied Science: Dr SIMON BEN-AVI
School of Health Sciences and Human Services: RONALD BLOOM (acting)
School for University Studies: DIANE HERBERT (Senior Assoc. Dean)

HOUGHTON COLLEGE

One Willard Ave, Houghton, NY 14744
Telephone: (585) 567-9200
E-mail: admission@houghton.edu
Internet: www.houghton.edu

Founded 1883

Private control

Academic year: August to June

Campus in W Seneca

Pres.: Dr SHIRLEY A. MULLEN
Academic Dean: LINDA MILLS WOOLSEY
Vice-Pres. for Advancement: RICK MELSON
Vice-Pres. for Enrolment Management: ERIC CURRIE
Vice-Pres. for Student Life: Dr ROB POOLE
Exec. Dir for Alumni Relations: DANIEL R. NOYES
Dean of the College: LINDA MILLS WOOLSEY
Dir for Library: DAVID STEVICK

Library of 255,000 vols, 10,000 scores, 30,000 journals subscription, 5,000 DVDs and video cassettes

Number of teachers: 135 (81 full-time)

Number of students: 1,100

Publication: *Houghton Magazine*

IONA COLLEGE

715 N Ave, New Rochelle, NY 10801-1890
Telephone: (914) 633-2000
E-mail: admissions@iona.edu
Internet: www.iona.edu

Founded 1940

Private control

Academic year: July to June

Campuses in New Rochelle and Rockland, New York

Pres.: Dr JOSEPH E. NYRE
Provost and Sr Vice-Pres. for Academic Affairs: Dr BRIAN J. NICKERSON
Sr Vice-Pres. for Finance and Admin.: JONATHAN IVEC
Sr Vice-Pres. for Advancement and External Affairs: PAUL J. SUTERA
Vice-Provost for Information Technology: JOANNE LAUGHLIN STEELE
Vice-Provost for Student Devt: CHARLES CARLSON
Dir for Libraries: RICHARD PALLADINO

Library of 266,883 vols (incl. books serial backfiles), 510,186 microforms, 742 serial titles, 4,077 audiovisual materials, 9,581 ebooks

Number of teachers: 360

Number of students: 4,065

Publications: *Journal of Pastoral Counseling* (1 a year), *The Ionian*

DEANS

Hagan School of Business: Dr VINCENT J. CALLUZZO
School of Arts and Science: Dr JEANNE ZAINO

ITHACA COLLEGE

953 Danby Rd, Ithaca, NY 14850
Telephone: (607) 274-3011
E-mail: admission@ithaca.edu
Internet: www.ithaca.edu

Founded 1892 as Ithaca Conservatory of Music

Private control

Academic year: August to May

Pres.: THOMAS R. ROCHON
Provost and Vice-Pres. for Academic Affairs: MARISA KELLY
Vice-Pres. for Enrolment Management: ERIC MAGUIRE
Vice-Pres. for Finance and Admin.: CARL E. SGRECCI
Vice-Pres. for Institutional Advancement: SHELLEY SEMMLER
Vice-Pres. for Student Affairs and Campus Life: BRIAN MCAREE
Vice-Pres. and Gen. Counsel: NANCY PRINGLE
Registrar: BRIAN SCHOLTEN
Librarian: LISABETH CHABOT

Library of 353,000 vols, 70,000 ebooks, 36,000 microforms, 37,250 multimedia, 46,360 full-text serials

Number of teachers: 700 (477 full-time, 223 part-time)

Number of students: 6,760 (6,276 undergraduate, 484 graduate)

Publication: *ICView* (3 a year)

DEANS

Roy H. Park School of Communications: DIANE GAYESKI
School of Business: MARY ELLEN ZUCKERMAN
School of Health Sciences and Human Performance: JOHN SIGG
School of Humanities and Sciences: LESLIE W. LEWIS
School of Music: GREGORY WOODWARD

JEWISH THEOLOGICAL SEMINARY

3080 Broadway, New York, NY 10027
Telephone: (212) 678-8000
E-mail: gsadmissions@jtsa.edu
Internet: www.jtsa.edu

Founded 1886

Private control

Academic year: August to May

Chancellor and Pres. of the Faculties: ARNOLD M. EISEN
Vice-Chancellor and Chief Operating Officer: Rabbi MICHAEL B. GREENBAUM
Vice-Chancellor and Chief Devt Officer: Rabbi MARC WOLF
Vice-Chancellor for Institutional Advancement: Rabbi CAROL DAVIDSON
Provost: Dr ALAN COOPER
Vice-Pres. for Student Affairs: Rabbi JOSEPH A. BRODIE
Chief Financial Officer: FRED SCHNUR
Dean for Academic Affairs: Dr STEPHEN GARFINKEL
Library Dir: NAOMI M. STEINBERGER (acting)

Library of 400,000 vols

Number of teachers: 110 (51 full-time, 59 part-time)

Number of students: 565

Publication: *Quntres: An Online Journal for the History, Culture, and Art of the Jewish Book* (1 a year)

DEANS

Albert A. List College of Jewish Studies: Dr SHULY RUBIN SCHWARTZ

Graduate School: Dr SHULY RUBIN SCHWARTZ
Rabbinical School: Rabbi DANIEL NEVINS
William Davidson Graduate School of Jewish Education: BARRY HOLTZ

JUILLIARD SCHOOL

60 Lincoln Center Plaza, New York, NY 10023-6588

Telephone: (212) 799-5000
E-mail: admissions@juilliard.edu
Internet: www.juilliard.edu

Founded 1905 as Institute of Musical Art, present name and status 1926
Private control
Incl. pre-college div., evening div. and music advancement programme
Pres.: JOSEPH W. POLISI
Provost and Dean: ARA GUZELIMIAN
Vice-Pres. and Dean for Academic Affairs: KAREN WAGNER
Vice-Pres. and Gen. Counsel: LAURIE A. CARTER
Vice-Pres. for Devt and Public Affairs: RICCARDO SALMONA
Vice-Pres. for Enrolment Management: JOAN D. WARREN
Vice-Pres. for Finance and Controller: CHRISTINE TODD
Vice-Pres. for Library and Information Resources: JANE GOTTLIEB
Registrar: KATHERINE GERTSON
Library of 23,000 vols, 7,300 music scores, 25,000 sound recordings, 140 MSS colln
Number of teachers: 310
Number of students: 845 (510 undergraduate)

Publication: *Juilliard Journal*

KEUKA COLLEGE

141 Central Ave, Keuka Park, NY 14478
Telephone: (315) 279-5000
E-mail: admissions@mail.keuka.edu
Internet: www.keuka.edu

Founded 1890
Private control
Academic year: August to May
Courses in dentistry, law, medicine, pharmacy, physical therapy, optometry, veterinary medicine; provides degree programmes in the People's Republic of China at 4 campus locations and at Viet Nam Nat. Univ. in Hanoi
Pres.: Dr JORGE L. DÍAZ-HERRERA
Exec. Vice-Pres.: CAROLANNE MARQUIS
Vice-Pres. for Academic Affairs: Dr ANNE K. WEED
Vice-Pres. for Finance and Admin.: JERRY HILLER
Vice-Pres. for the Center for Professional Studies: Dr GARY SMITH
Vice-Pres. for Student Devt and Dean for Students: Dr JAMES BLACKBURN
Dean for Admissions and Marketing: FRED HOYLE
Dir for Library: LINDA PARK
Library of 88,061 vols, 79,093 titles, 21,194 periodicals, 4,021 microfilm reels, 8,939 ebooks, 2,040 video cassettes, CDs and DVDs
Number of teachers: 90 (79 full-time, 11 part-time)
Number of students: 1,980 (1,645 full-time, 335 part-time)

Publication: *Keuka Magazine*

DEANS

Center for Experiential Learning: Dr ANNE MARIE GUTHRIE

LE MOYNE COLLEGE

1419 Salt Springs Rd, Syracuse, NY 13214-1399

Telephone: (315) 445-4100
Internet: www.lemoyne.edu

Founded 1946
Private control
Academic year: August to May
Pres.: Dr FRED P. PESTELLO
Provost and Vice-Pres. for Academic Affairs: Dr LINDA LeMURA
Vice-Pres. for Enrolment Management: DENNIS DePERRO
Vice-Pres. for Finance and Admin.: ROGER STACKPOOLE
Vice-Pres. for Institutional Advancement: Dr GREGORY STAHL
Vice-Pres. for Student Devt: Dr DEBORAH CADY MELZER
Dean for Admissions: DENNY NICHOLSON
Dir for Library: ROBERT C. JOHNSTON
Library of 242,233 vols
Number of teachers: 360
Number of students: 3,500 (2,800 undergraduate, 700 graduate)

Publication: *Le Moyne College Magazine*

DEANS

Division of Arts and Sciences: Dr J. BARRON BOYD, JR
School of Business: Dr WALLY ELMER

LIM COLLEGE

12 E 53rd St, New York, NY 10022
Telephone: (212) 752-1530
E-mail: admissions@limcollege.edu
Internet: www.limcollege.edu

Founded 1939 as Laboratory Institute of Merchandising (LIM), current name adopted 2009
Private control
Academic year: August to July
Areas of study incl. fashion merchandising, management, marketing, visual merchandising
Pres.: ELIZABETH S. MARCUSE
Exec. Vice-Pres.: LINDA HARRIS PAOLILLO
Sr Vice-Pres. for Academic and Student Affairs: Dr JO-ANN ROLLE
Sr Vice-Pres. for Finance and Operation and Treas.: MICHAEL T. DONOHUE
Vice-Pres. for Student Devt: Dr MICHAEL H. FERRY
Registrar: CAROLYN DISNEW
Dir for Library Services: GEORGE SANCHEZ
Library of 14,000 vols, 900 DVDs, 900 ebooks
Number of teachers: 203
Number of students: 1,647

LONG ISLAND UNIVERSITY

720 N Blvd, Brookville, NY 11548-1327
Telephone: (516) 299-2000
E-mail: attend@liu.edu
Internet: www.liu.edu

Founded 1926
Private control
Campuses in Brooklyn, Brookville (C.W. Post), Brentwood, Riverhead, Rockland and Westchester; Global College: People's Republic of China, Costa Rica and India
Pres.: Dr DAVID J. STEINBERG
Vice-Pres. for Academic Affairs: Dr JEFFREY KANE
Vice-Pres. for Finance and Treas.: ROBERT N. ALTHOLZ
Vice-Pres. for Information Technology: GEORGE BAROUDI
Vice-Pres. for Legal Services and Univ. Counsel: LYNETTE PHILLIPS

Vice-Pres. for Planning and Human Resources: Dr DANIEL J. RODAS
Vice-Pres. for Univ. Relations: RICHARD W. GORMAN
Provost for Brooklyn Campus: Dr GALE STEVENS HAYNES
Provost for C. W. Post Campus: Dr PAUL H. FORESTELL
Library: 2.6.m. vols, incl. 50,000 ebooks
Number of teachers: 1,600 (630 full-time, 970 part-time)
Number of students: 24,300 (9,734 undergraduate, 7,359 graduate)

Publication: *LIU Magazine* (2 a year)

DEANS

Arnold and Marie Schwartz College of Pharmacy and Health Sciences, Brooklyn Campus: Dr DAVID R. TAFT
College of Education and Information Sciences, C. W. Post Campus: Dr ROBERT HANNAFIN
College of Liberal Arts and Sciences, C. W. Post Campus: Dr KATHERINE HILL-MILLER
College of Management, C. W. Post Campus: FRANCIS N. BONSIGNORE
Global College, Brooklyn Campus: Dr ROBERT GLASS
Richard L. Conolly College of Liberal Arts and Sciences, Brooklyn Campus: Dr DAVID COHEN
School of Business, Public Administration and Information Sciences, Brooklyn Campus: MOHAMMED GHRIGA
School of Education, Brooklyn Campus: CECELIA TRAUGH
School of Health Professions, Brooklyn Campus: Dr BARRY S. ECKERT
School of Health Professions and Nursing, C. W. Post Campus: Dr MARYANN CLARK
School of Nursing, Brooklyn Campus: Dr HAZEL M. SANDERSON-MARCOUX (acting)
School of Visual and Performing Arts, C. W. Post Campus: NOEL ZEHLER

MANHATTAN COLLEGE

4513 Manhattan College Parkway, Riverdale, NY 10471

Telephone: (718) 862-8000
E-mail: admit@manhattan.edu
Internet: www.manhattan.edu

Founded 1853, chartered as Manhattan College 1863
Private control
Academic year: August to May
Pres.: Dr BRENNAN O'DONNELL
Provost and Exec. Vice-Pres.: Dr WILLIAM CLYDE
Vice-Pres. for College Advancement: THOMAS MAURIELLO
Vice-Pres. for Enrolment Management: WILLIAM J. BISSET, JR
Vice-Pres. for Facilities: ANDREW RYAN
Vice-Pres. for Finance and Capital Projects: THOMAS J. RYAN
Vice-Pres. for Student Life: Dr RICHARD SATTERLEE
Registrar: LUZ M. TORRES
Dir for Admissions: DANA ROSE
Dir for Library: MAIRE I. DUCHON
Library of 230,000 vols, 3,000 media items, 20,000 periodical titles
Number of teachers: 200 (full-time)
Number of students: 3,500 (2,900 undergraduate, 600 graduate and continuing education)

Publications: *Manhattan Magazine* (2 a year), *Manhattan Monthly* (12 a year)

DEANS

School of Arts: Dr RICHARD K. EMMERSON
School of Business: Dr SALWA AMMAR

School of Education: Dr WILLIAM J. MERRI-MAN
School of Engineering: Dr TIM J. WARD
School of Science: Dr CONSTANTINE E. THEO-DOSIOU

MANHATTAN SCHOOL OF MUSIC

120 Claremont Ave, New York, NY 10027-4689

Telephone: (212) 749-2802
E-mail: administration@msmnyc.edu
Internet: www.msmnyc.edu
Founded 1917
Academic year: July to May
Pres.: Dr ROBERT SIROTA
Vice-Pres. for External Affairs: SUSAN EBER-SOLE
Vice-Pres. for Finance and Admin.: PAUL KELLEHER
Vice-Pres. for Instrumental Performance: DAVID GEBER
Dean for Students: ELSA JEAN DAVIDSON
Registrar: DAVID McDONAGH
Dir for Library Services: PETER CALEB
Library of 95,000 vols, 33,000 sound record-ings, 3,600 DVDs
Number of teachers: 250
Number of students: 925 (402 undergradu-ate, 452 non-doctoral graduate, 71 doc-toral)

MANHATTANVILLE COLLEGE

Purchase, NY 10577
Telephone: (914) 694-2200
E-mail: admissions@mville.edu
Internet: www.manhattanville.edu
Founded 1841 as Acad. of the Sacred Heart
Private control
Academic year: September to May
Pres.: JON CALVERT STRAUSS
Provost and Vice-Pres. for Academic Affairs: GAIL SIMMONS
Vice-Pres. for Admissions and Enrolment Management: KATHY FITZGERALD
Vice-Pres. for Finance: MARINA C. VASARHE-LYI
Vice-Pres. for Institutional Advancement: JOSE R. GONZALEZ
Vice-Pres. for Operations: J. GREGORY PAL-MER
Vice-Pres. for Student Affairs: DOUGLAS GEIGER
Library Dir: JEFF ROSEDALE (acting)
Library of 200,000 vols
Number of teachers: 105 (full-time)
Number of students: 2,700 (1,700 under-graduate, 1,000 graduate)
Publications: Inkwell (1 a year), The Tower Yearbook

MARIST COLLEGE

3399 N Rd, Poughkeepsie, NY 12601
Telephone: (845) 575-3000
E-mail: admissions@marist.edu
Internet: www.marist.edu
Founded 1905 as St. Ann's Hermitage
Private control
Br. campus in Florence, Italy
Pres.: DENNIS J. MURRAY
Exec. Vice-Pres.: Dr GEOFFREY L. BRACKETT
Vice-Pres. for Academic Affairs and Dean for Faculty: Dr THOMAS WERMUTH
Vice-Pres. for Admission and Enrolment Planning: SEAN P KAYLOR
Vice-Pres. for Business Affairs and Chief Financial Officer: JOHN PECCHIA
Vice-Pres. for College Advancement: CHRIS-TOPHER M. DELGIORNO
Vice-Pres. for Information Technology: WIL-LIAM THIRSK

Vice-Pres. and Dean for Student Affairs: DEBORAH DiCAPRIO
Registrar: JUDY IVANKOVIĆ
Librarian: JOHN McGINTY
Library of 207,000 vols, 30,000 journals and newspapers, 5,000 audiovisual items
Number of teachers: 580 (230 full-time, 350 adjunct)
Number of students: 6,300 (4,533 under-graduate, 872 graduate, 569 adult continu-ing education)
Publication: Foxtalk Magazine

DEANS

School of Communication and the Arts: STEVEN RALSTON
School of Computer Science and Mathemat-ics: ROGER NORTON
School of Global and Professional Programs: Dr LAUREN H. MOUNTY
School of Liberal Arts: Dr MARTIN B. SHAFFER
School of Management: ELMORE R. ALEXAN-DER
School of Science: Dr NEIL FITZGERALD
School of Social and Behavioral Science: Prof. MARGARET R. CALISTA

MARYMOUNT MANHATTAN COLLEGE

221 E 71st St, New York, NY 10021
Telephone: (212) 517-0400
Internet: marymount.mmm.edu
Founded 1936 as city campus of Marymount College, present name and status 1961
Private control
Academic year: August to July
Divs of accounting and business manage-ment, fine and performing arts, humanities, sciences, social sciences, interdisciplinary studies
Pres.: Dr JUDSON R. SHAVER
Exec Vice-Pres. for Finance and Admin.: PAUL CIRAULO
Vice-Pres. for Academic Affairs and Dean for the Faculty: DAVID PODELL
Vice-Pres. for Institutional Research and Planning: DEAN PETER H. BAKER
Vice-Pres. for Student Affairs and Dean for Students: CAROL JACKSON
Dean for Admissions: JIM ROGERS
Library Dir: DONNA HURWITZ
Library of 85,000 vols
Number of teachers: 140
Number of students: 2,000 (undergraduate)

MEDAILLE COLLEGE

18 Agassiz Circle, Buffalo, NY 14214
Telephone: (716) 880-2000
E-mail: admissionsug@medaille.edu
Internet: www.medaille.edu
Founded 1875, current name and status 1968
Private control
Academic year: September to May
Campuses in Buffalo, Williamsville and Rochester in New York
Pres.: Dr RICHARD T. JURASEK
Vice-Pres. for Academic Affairs: Dr NORMAN MUIR
Vice-Pres. for Business and Finance: MAT-THEW CARVER
Vice-Pres. for College Relations: JOHN P. CRAWFORD
Vice-Pres. for Enrolment Management: KAREN McGRATH
Chief Information Officer: BOB CHYKA
Dean for Students: AMY DEKAY
Registrar: KATHLEEN LAZAR
Library Dir: PAMELA JONES
Library of 54,000 vols
Number of teachers: 155
Number of students: 3,030 (2,172 under-graduate, 858 graduate)

Publication: Medaille College Magazine

DEANS

School of Adult and Graduate Education: Dr JENIFER BAVIFARD
School of Education: Dr ILLANA LANE
Undergraduate College: Dr JOSEPH SAVARESE

MERCY COLLEGE

555 Broadway, Dobbs Ferry, NY 10522
Telephone: (914) 674-7307
E-mail: admissions@mercy.edu
Internet: www.mercy.edu
Founded 1950
Private control
Academic year: September to May
Campuses in Dobbs Ferry, Bronx, Manhat-tan, White Plains, Yorktown Heights
Pres.: Dr KIMBERLY R. CLINE
Provost and Vice-Pres. for Academic Affairs: Dr MICHAEL B. SPERLING
Vice-Pres. for Enrolment Management: DEIRDRE WHITMAN
Vice-Pres. for Finance: JEANNE T. PLECENIK
Vice-Pres. for Institutional Advancement: DEBORAH SONTUPE
Dir for Admissions: MARCELLE HICKS
Dean for Library: Dr BRADLEE
Library of 215,000 vols
Number of teachers: 195 (full-time)
Number of students: 9,675 (4,105 full-time undergraduate)
Publication: Engage

DEANS

School of Business: LUCRETIA S. MANN (act-ing)
School of Education: Dr ALFRED S. POSAMEN-TIER
School of Health and Natural Sciences: Dr TOM OLSON
School of Liberal Arts: Dr MIRIAM SAHATDJIAN GOGOL
School of Social and Behavioral Sciences: Dr LOIS A. WIMS

METROPOLITAN COLLEGE OF NEW YORK

431 Canal St, New York, NY 10013
Telephone: (212) 343-1234
E-mail: admissions@metropolitan.edu
Internet: www.metropolitan.edu
Founded 1964 as Women's Talent Corps, present name 2002
Private control
Academic year: January to AprilMay to AugustSeptember to December (3 semes-ters)
Pres.: VINTON THOMPSON
Sr Vice-Pres. and Chief Financial Officer: VINCENT MASSARO
Vice-Pres. for Enrolment Management: COLL-ETTE GARRITY
Dean for Students: DONA SOSA
Registrar: NOREEN SMITH
Dir for Library Services: JAY DATEMA
Library of 145,196 vols
Number of teachers: 180 (26 full-time, 154 part-time)
Number of students: 1,100

DEANS

Audrey Cohen School for Human Services and Education: Dr RUTH LUGO
School of Management: Dr HUMPHREY CROO-KENDALE

MOLLOY COLLEGE

1000 Hempstead Ave, Kellenberg Hall, Rockville Centre, NY 11571-5002

Telephone: (516) 678-5000
E-mail: info@molloy.edu
Internet: www.molloy.edu

Founded 1955 as Molloy Catholic College for Women
Private control
Academic year: September to May
Pres.: Dr DREW BOGNER
Vice-Pres. for Academic Affairs and Dean for Faculty: Dr VALERIE COLLINS
Vice-Pres. for Advancement: EDWARD J. THOMPSON
Vice-Pres. for Enrolment Management: LINDA ALBANESE
Vice-Pres. for Finance and Treas.: MICHAEL A. MCGOVERN
Vice-Pres. for Mission: Sr DOROTHY FITZGIBBONS
Vice-Pres. for Information Technology, Planning and Research: Dr ROBERT PATERSON
Vice-Pres. for Student Affairs: ROBERT HOULIHAN
Registrar: SUE FORTMAN
Library Dir: JUDITH BRINK-DRESCHER
Library of 80,000 vols, 400 periodicals
Number of teachers: 210
Number of students: 4,435 (3,415 undergraduate, 1,020 graduate)
Publications: *Lions Land*, *Molloy Magazine*, *Molloy Matters*

DEANS

Division of Business: Dr EDWARD WEIS
Division of Education: Dr MAUREEN WALSH
Division of Humanities: Dr A. NICHOLAS FARGNOLI
Division of Natural Sciences, Mathematics and Computer Science, Allied Heath Sciences and Speech Language-Pathology: Dr ANTHONY TOLVO
Division of Nursing: Dr JEANNINE D. MULDOON
Division of Social Sciences: Dr KATHLEEN MAURER SMITH

MONROE COLLEGE

2501 Jerome Ave, Bronx, NY 10468

Telephone: (718) 933-6700
Internet: www.monroecollege.edu

Founded 1933 as Monroe School of Business
Private control
Academic year: September to August
Campuses in Bronx, New Rochelle and St Lucia
Pres.: STEPHEN J. JEROME
Sr Vice-Pres. and Chief Financial Officer: ANTHONY ALLEN
Exec. Vice-Pres.: ALEX EPHREM
Vice-Pres.: MARC JEROME
Vice-Pres. for Academic Affairs: KARENANN CARTY
Vice-Pres. for Admissions: W. JEFF WALLIS
Vice-Pres. for Student Financial Services: ROBERTA GREENBERG
Vice-Pres. for Student Affairs: EVAN JEROME
Library of 50,000 vols

DEANS

King Graduate School: ROBERTA HARRIS
School of Allied Health Professions: JERRY KOSTROFF
School of Business and Accounting: MICHAEL MARINACCIO
School of Criminal Justice: MICHELE S. RODNEY
School of Education: Dr JOSEPHINE MOFFETT
School of Hospitality Management and the Culinary Arts: Dr FRANK C. COSTANTINO

School of Information Technology: Dr JANICE GIRARDI

MOUNT SAINT MARY COLLEGE

330 Powell Ave, Newburgh, NY 12550

Telephone: (845) 569-3100
E-mail: admissions@msmc.edu
Internet: www.msmc.edu

Founded 1959
Private control
Academic year: May to May
Pres.: Fr KEVIN MACKIN
Vice-Pres. for Academic Affairs: IRIS J. TURKENKOPF
Vice-Pres. for College Advancement: JOSEPH VALENTI
Vice-Pres. for Enrolment Management: ART CRISS
Vice-Pres. for Finance and Admin. and Treas.: CATHLEEN KENNY
Vice-Pres. for Facilities and Operations: JAMES M. RAIMO
Vice-Pres. for Planning and Assessment: MARY HINTON
Chief Information Officer: DENNIS RUSH
Vice-Pres. for Student Affairs: HARRY STEINWAY
Registrar: DEBRA MILLER (acting)
Dir for Library: BARBARA WHITNEY PETRUZZELLI
Library of 90,247 vols, 28,743 online subscriptions
Number of teachers: 75 full-time, 140 part-time, 130 f.t.e.
Number of students: 2,700 (1,800 undergraduate)
Publication: *Mount Saint Mary College Magazine*

NAZARETH COLLEGE

4245 E Ave, Rochester, NY 14618-3790

Telephone: (585) 389-2525
E-mail: admissions@naz.edu
Internet: www.naz.edu

Founded 1924
Private control
Academic year: August to August
Pres.: DAAN BRAVEMAN
Vice-Pres. for Academic Affairs: SARA VARHUS
Vice-Pres. for Enrolment Management: THOMAS K. DARIN
Vice-Pres. for Finance and Treas.: MARGARET CASS FERBER
Vice-Pres. for Student Devt: KEVIN D. WORTHEN
Vice-Pres. for Institutional Advancement: KELLY E. GAGAN
Registrar: ANDREW H. MORRIS
Library Dir: CATHERINE DOYLE (acting)
Library of 266,000 vols, 2,004 serials
Number of teachers: 495 (158 full-time, 339 part-time)
Number of students: 3,100 (2,170 undergraduate, 930 graduate)
Publications: *Connections* (3 a year), *Elbowroom* (1 a year)

DEANS

College of Arts and Sciences: Dr DEBORAH DOOLEY
School of Education: Dr CRAIG HILL
School of Health and Human Services: Dr SHIRLEY SZEKERES
School of Management: GERARD F. ZAPPIA

NEW SCHOOL

66 W 12th St, New York, NY 10011

Telephone: (212) 229-5600
E-mail: communications@newschool.edu
Internet: www.newschool.edu

Founded 1919
Private control
Academic year: August to May
Pres.: DAVID E. VAN ZANDT
Provost and Chief Academic Officer: TIM MARSHALL
Sr Vice-Pres. for Academic Affairs: BRYNA SANGER
Sr Vice-Pres. for Finance and Business: FRANK BARLETTA
Sr Vice-Pres. for Information Technology: SHELLEY E. REED
Sr Vice-Pres. for Student Services: LINDA ABRAMS REIMER
Vice-Pres. and Treas.: CRAIG BECKER
Vice-Pres. for Communications and External Affairs: PETER TABACK (acting)
Vice-Pres. for Devt and Alumni Relations: PAMELA BESNARD
Vice-Pres. for Enrolment Management: BOB GAY
Vice-Pres. for Legal Affairs and Gen. Counsel: ROY P. MOSKOWITZ
Library: 4.1m. vols
Number of teachers: 2,100 (415 full-time, 1,685 part-time)
Number of students: 11,700 (6,810 undergraduate, 1,175 full-time freshman, 3,715 graduate)
Publications: *Constellations* (4 a year), *Graduate Faculty Philosophy Journal* (2 a year), *International Journal of Politics, Culture and Society* (4 a year), *Social Research* (4 a year)

DEANS

Eugene Lang College the New School for Liberal Arts: STEPHANIE BROWNER
Mannes College the New School for Music: Dr RICHARD KESSLER
New School for Social Research: MICHAEL SCHOBER
Parsons the New School for Design: JOEL TOWERS
The New School for Public Engagement: DAVID SCOBEY

NEW YORK CHIROPRACTIC COLLEGE

2360 State Route 89, Seneca Falls, NY 13148

Telephone: (315) 568-3052
E-mail: camsonline@nycc.edu
Internet: www.nycc.edu

Founded 1919 as Columbia Institute of Chiropractic
Private control
Academic year: May to June
Pres.: Dr FRANK J. NICCHI
Exec. Vice-Pres. and Provost: Dr MICHAEL A. MESTAN
Vice-Pres. for Enrolment Management: DIANE C. DIXON
Vice-Pres. for Finance and Admin. Services: SEAN J. ANGLIM
Vice-Pres. for Institutional Advancement: PETER VAN TYLE
Vice-Pres. for Institutional Quality and Assessment: DAVID R. ODIORNE
Dir for Admissions: MICHAEL LYNCH
Dean for Chiropractic Education: KAREN A. BOBAK
Dean for Research: Dr JEANMARIE R. BURKE
Dir for Library: BETHYN A. BONI
Library of 32,000 vols, more than 3,500 media titles, 200 journal titles
Number of students: 720
Publication: *Transitions Magazine*

DEANS

Chiropractic Clinical Education: WENDY L. MANERI
Finger Lakes School of Acupuncture and Oriental Medicine: JASON A. WRIGHT

Postgraduate aand Continuing Education: THOMAS A. VENTIMIGLIA

NEW YORK COLLEGE OF PODIATRIC MEDICINE

53 E 124th St, New York, NY 10035
Telephone: (212) 410-8147
E-mail: enrollment@nycpm.edu
Internet: www.nycpm.edu
Founded 1911 as New York School of Chiropody, present name 1972
Private control
Academic year: July/August to May
Pres. and CEO: LOUIS L. LEVINE
Dean and Vice-Pres. for Academic Affairs: Dr MICHAEL J. TREPAL
Vice-Pres. for Admin.: JOEL A. STURM
Vice-Pres. for Information Technology and Operations: WILLIAM H. GRAHAM
Chief Financial Officer: GREG ONAIFO
Dean for Student Services: LAURENCE J. LOWY
Registrar: VERNESE PANNELL
Dir for Library Services: THOMAS P. WALKER
Library of 13,000 vols
Number of teachers: 120
Number of students: 285

DEANS

Division of Clinical Studies: Dr ROBERT ECKLES
Division of Pre-Clinical Sciences: Dr EILEEN DALY CHUSID
Graduate Medical Education: Dr ROBERT A. ECKLES
Medical Education: Dr MARK H. SWARTZ

NEW YORK INSTITUTE OF TECHNOLOGY

POB 8000, N Blvd, Old Westbury, NY 11568-0800
Telephone: (516) 686-1000
E-mail: asknyit@nyit.edu
Internet: www.nyit.edu
Founded 1955
Private control
Academic year: September to May
Campuses in Old Westbury and Manhattan in NY; int. campuses in UAE, Jordan, Bahrain and People's Republic of China
Pres.: Dr EDWARD GUILIANO
Provost and Vice-Pres. for Academic Affairs: Dr RAHMAT SHOURESHI
Chief Financial Officer and Treas.: LEONARD AUBREY
Vice-Pres. for Academic Affairs and Dean for Faculty: ALEXANDRA W. LOGUE
Vice-Pres. for Devt: JOHN ELIZANDRO
Vice-Pres. for Enrolment, Communications and Marketing: Dr JACQUELYN NEALON
Vice-Pres. for Financial Affairs, Chief Financial Officer and Treas.: LEONARD AUBREY
Vice-Pres. for Health Sciences and Medical Affairs: Dr BARBARA ROSS-LEE
Vice-Pres. for Information Technology and Infrastructure: Dr NIYAZI BODUR
Vice-Pres. for Planning and Assessment: HARRIET ARNONE
Vice-Pres. for Student Affairs: JOE FORD
Gen. Counsel: CATHERINE R. FLICKINGER
Library of 100,000 vols, 13,000 ebooks and video cassettes
Number of teachers: 845 (282 full-time, 563 part-time)
Number of students: 14,000
Publication: *NYIT Magazine* (3 a year)

DEANS

College of Arts and Sciences: Dr ROGER YU
New York College of Osteopathic Medicine (NYCOM): Dr THOMAS SCANDALIS

School of Architecture and Design: JUDITH DIMAIO
School of Education: MICHAEL UTTENDORFER
School of Engineering and Computing Sciences: Dr NADA ANID
School of Health Professions: Dr PATRICIA M. CHUTE
School of Management: Dr JESS BORONICO

NEW YORK LAW SCHOOL

185 W Broadway, New York, NY 10013-2921
Telephone: (212) 431-2100
E-mail: admissions@nyls.edu
Internet: www.nyls.edu
Founded 1891
Private control
Academic year: August to May
Dean: Prof. ANTHONY CROWELL
Vice-Pres. for Finance and Admin.: FRED DEJOHN
Vice-Pres. and Assoc. Dean for Devt and Alumni Relations: SUZANNE J. S. DAVIDSON
Assoc. Dean for Academic Affairs: JETHRO K. LIEBERMAN
Assoc. Dean for Faculty Devt: Dr STEPHEN J. ELLMANN
Assoc. Dean for Professional Devt: Dr MARI-ANA HOGAN
Registrar: ORAL C. HOPE
Library Dir: CAMILLE BROUSSARD
Library of 500,000 vols
Number of teachers: 275 (94 full-time, 181 adjunct)
Number of students: 1,750
Publications: *Media Law & Policy* (3 a year), *New York Law School Law Review*, *New York Law School Magazine*

NEW YORK MEDICAL COLLEGE

40 Sunshine Cottage Rd, Valhalla, NY 10595
Telephone: (914) 594-4000
Internet: www.nymc.edu
Founded 1860 as New York Homeopathic Medical College, present name 1938
Private control
Pres.: Dr ALAN KADISH
Provost: Dr RALPH A. O'CONNELL
Vice-Provost for Admin. and Finance and Sr Vice-Pres. for Finance: STEPHEN PICCOLO, JR
Vice-Pres. and Gen. Counsel: WALDEMAR A. COMAS
Vice-Pres. for Devt and Alumni Relations: JULIE A. KUBASKA
Vice-Pres. for Strategic Planning: WILLIAM A. STEADMAN, II
Registrar: Dr JUDITH A. EHREN
Assoc. Dean and Dir for Library: DIANA CUNNINGHAM
Library of 140,000 vols, 46,332 unique titles, 16,543 journal titles, 14,814 ebooks
Number of teachers: 3,000
Number of students: 1,400

DEANS

Graduate School of Basic Medical Sciences: Dr FRANCIS L. BELLONI
School of Health Sciences and Practice: Dr ROBERT W. AMLER
School of Medicine: Dr WILLIAM A. STEADMAN, II

NEW YORK SCHOOL OF INTERIOR DESIGN

170 E 70th St, New York, NY 10021
Telephone: (212) 472-1500
E-mail: info@nysid.edu
Internet: www.nysid.edu
Founded 1916, chartered in 1924
Private control

Academic year: September to July
Acting Pres. and Exec. Vice-Pres.: DAVID SPROULS
Vice-Pres. for Academic Affairs and Dean: ELLEN FISHER
Vice-Pres. for Enrolment Management: DAVID SPROULS
Vice-Pres. for Finance and Admin.: JANE CHEN
Dir for Library: SARAH FALLS
Library of 15,000 vols
Number of teachers: 90
Number of students: 730 (290 full-time, 440 part-time)

NEW YORK THEOLOGICAL SEMINARY

475 Riverside Dr., Suite 500, New York, NY 10115-0083
Telephone: (212) 870-1211
E-mail: online@nyts.edu
Internet: www.nyts.edu
Founded 1900 as Bible Teachers' College, present name 1966
Private control
Academic year: August to May
Pres.: Prof. DALE T. IRVIN
Vice-Pres. for Academic Affairs and Academic Dean: Rev. Dr ELEANOR MOODY-SHEPHERD
Vice-Pres.: Dr LAURA PIRES-HESTER
Registrar: LYDIA RODRIGUEZ-BUMGARDNER
Dir for Library Services: Dr JERRY REISIG
Number of teachers: 35
Number of students: 650

NEW YORK UNIVERSITY

70 Washington Sq. S, New York, NY 10012
Telephone: (212) 998-1212
Internet: www.nyu.edu
Founded 1831
Private control
Academic year: September to May
Pres.: Dr JOHN SEXTON
Provost: Dr DAVID W. MCLAUGHLIN
Exec. Vice-Pres.: Dr MICHAEL ALFANO
Exec. Vice-Pres. for Finance and Information Technology: Dr MARTIN S. DORPH
Exec. Vice-Pres. for Operations: ALISON LEARY
Sr Vice-Pres., Gen. Counsel and Sec. for the Univ.: Dr BONNIE BRIER
Sr Vice-Pres. for Univ. Relations and Public Affairs: Dr LYNNE P. BROWN
Sr Vice-Pres. for Devt and Alumni Relations: Dr DEBRA A. LAMORTE
Vice-Pres. for Budget and Planning: ANTHONY P. JIGA
Vice-Pres. for Enrolment Management: RANDALL DEIKE
Vice-Pres. for Information Technology: MARILYN MCMILLAN
Vice-Pres. for Public Affairs: JOHN BECKMAN
Vice-Pres. for Public Resource Admin.: RICHARD N. BING
Vice-Pres. for Student Affairs: MARC L. WAIS
Sr Vice-Provost and Vice-Chancellor: Dr KATHERINE E. FLEMING
Sr Vice-Provost for Academic Policies: PIERRE HOHENBERG
Sr Vice-Provost for Planning: Dr RON ROBIN
Sr Vice-Provost for Research: Dr PAUL HORN
Sr Vice-Provost for Undergraduate Education and Univ. Life: LINDA G. MILLS
Sr Vice-Provost for Undergraduate Academic Affairs: Dr MATTHEW SANTIROCCO
Vice-Provost for Globalization and Multicultural Affairs: ULRICH BAER
Vice-Provost for Int. Education and Outreach: CAROL BRANDT
Vice-Provost for Science and Engineering Devt: GERARD BEN-AROUS

Registrar: ROGER PRINTUP
Dean for Libraries: CAROL A. MANDEL
Library: see Libraries and Archives
Number of teachers: 8,320
Number of students: 43,797 (22,097 undergraduate, 18,243 graduate, 3,457 first professionals)
Publications: *Clinical Law Review* (2 a year), *Environmental Law Journal* (3 a year), *I•CON, The International Journal of Constitutional Law* (4 a year), *Inquiry* (1 a year), *Journal of Accounting, Auditing and Finance* (4 a year), *Journal of International Financial Management and Accounting* (3 a year), *Journal of International Law and Politics* (4 a year), *Journal of Legislation and Public Policy* (2 a year), *Moot Court Casebook* (1 a year), *New York University Annual Survey of American Law* (4 a year), *New York University Law Review* (6 a year), *NYU Journal of Law & Business, Review of Law & Social Change* (6 a year), *Tax Law Review* (4 a year), *TDR: A Journal of Performance Studies* (4 a year), *The Journal of Law & Liberty, Victorian Literature and Culture* (2 a year), *Washington Square* (2 a year), *Women and Performance: a Journal of Feminist Theory* (2 a year), *Wordsworth Circle* (4 a year)

DEANS

College of Arts and Science: G. GABRIELLE STARR (acting)
College of Dentistry: Dr CHARLES N. BERTOLAMI
Gallatin School of Individualized Study: SUSANNE L. WOFFORD
Graduate School of Arts and Science: THOMAS J. CAREW
Leonard N. Stern School of Business: PETER BLAIR HENRY
NYU College of Nursing: Dr JUDITH HABER
NYU School of Medicine: ROBERT I. GROSSMAN
Robert F. Wagner Graduate School of Public Service: ELLEN SCHALL
School of Continuing and Professional Studies: ROBERT S. LAPINER
School of Law: RICHARD L. REVESZ
Silver School of Social Work: Dr LYNN VIDEKA
Steinhardt School of Culture, Education and Human Development: MARY M. BRABECK
Tisch School of the Arts: MARY SCHMIDT CAMPBELL

PROFESSORS

College of Arts and Science (100 Washington Square E, Room 910 New York, NY 10003-6688; internet www.nyu.edu/cas):

AARONSON, D., Psychology
AFFRON, C., French
ALEXANDER, J. J. G., Fine Arts
ALLEN, L. R., Psychology
AMENTA, E., Sociology
ANDERSEN, S. M., Psychology
ANDERSON, H. M., Spanish and Portuguese Languages and Literatures
AVELLANEDA, M., Mathematics
AVERILL, G., Music
AZMITIA, E. C., Biology, Neural Science
BACIC, Z., Chemistry
BAER, N. S., Conservation, Fine Arts
BAILEY, R., Music
BAKER, P. R., History
BALTIN, M. R., Linguistics
BARGH, J. A., Psychology
BAUMOL, W. J., Economics
BEAUJOUR, M., French
BEIDELMAN, T. O., Anthropology
BENDER, T., History
BENHABIB, J., Political Economy, Economics
BERENSON, E., History, French Studies
BERGER, M., Computer Science

BERMAN, S. M., Mathematics
BISHOP, T., French Literature, Comparative Literature
BLOCK, N., Philosophy, Psychology
BLOOM, H., English and American Literature, English
BOGHOSSIAN, P., Philosophy
BOGOMOLOV, F. A., Mathematics
BONFANTE, L., Classics
BOORMAN, S. H., Music
BRAMS, S. J., Politics
BRANDT, K. W.-G., Fine Arts
BRANDT, R. A., Physics
BRATHWAITE, K., Comparative Literature
BROWN, H. H., Jr, Physics
BROWN, J., Fine Arts
BROYDE, S., Biology
BRUNER, J., Psychology
BUDICK, B., Physics
BUENO DE MESQUITA, B., Politics
BURNS, F. J., Environmental Science
BURROWS, D. L., Music
BURROWS, W. E., Journalism and Mass Communication
CALHOUN, C. J., Sociology
CANARY, J. W., Chemistry
CANTOR, N. F., History, Comparative Literature, Sociology
CAPLIN, A., Economics
CAPPELL, S., Mathematics
CARNEVALE, P., Psychology
CARRASCO, M., Psychology and Neuroscience
CARRUTHERS, M. J., Literature
CHAIKEN, S., Psychology
CHAUDHURI, U., English
CHAZAN, R., Modern Jewish History
CHEEGER, J., Mathematics
CHELKOWSKI, P. J., Middle Eastern Studies
CHILDRESS, W. S., Mathematics
CHIOLES, J., Comparative Literature
CHUSID, M., Music
CLASTER, J. N., History
COHEN, B. S., Environmental Medicine
COHEN, J.-L., History of Architecture
COHEN, S. F., Russian Studies and History
COLE, R., Computer Science
COLLINS, C., English
COONS, E. E., Psychology, Neural Science
CORRADI, J. E., Sociology
CORUZZI, G. M., Biology
COSTA, M., Environmental Science
COSTELLO, J. R., Linguistics
DASH, J. M., French
DEIFT, P., Mathematics
DESPLAN, C., Biology
DEWAR, R. B. K., Computer Science
DIAWARA, M., Comparative Literature
DINER, H. R., American Jewish History, Hebrew and Judaic Studies, History
DINSHAW, C., English
DJEBAR, A., French
DOCTOROW, E. L., American Letters, English
DONOGHUE, D., English and American Letters
DOUBROVSKY, S., French
DOWNS, G. W., Jr, Politics
DUSTER, T., Sociology
DWORKIN, R., Law, Philosophy
EISLER, C., Fine Arts
ELBOURNE, P. D., Linguistics
ELLIS, M. H., Fine Arts
ENGEL, D., Holocaust Studies, Hebrew and Judaic Studies, and History
EVANS, H. L., Environmental Science
FAIRCHILD, S., Conservation
FARRAR, G., Physics
FELDMAN, S. M., Neural Science, Psychology
FELDMAN, Y. S., Hebrew Culture and Education
FERNANDEZ, R., Economics
FIELD, H. H., Philosophy
FINE, K., Philosophy
FLINN, C. J., Economics

FRECCERO, J., Italian, Comparative Literature
FRYDMAN, R., Economics
FURMANSKI, P., Biology
GALE, D., Economics
GANS, P. J., Chemistry
GARABEDIAN, P. R., Mathematics
GARLAND, D., Sociology
GATELY, D., Economics
GEACINTOV, N. E., Chemistry
GERSON, K., Sociology
GERSON, S., French
GERTLER, M., Economics
GILMAN, E. B., English
GILSENAN, M., Humanities, Middle Eastern Studies, Anthropology
GINSBURG, F., Anthropology
GITLIN, T., Journalism and Mass Communication, Education, Sociology
GOLDSTEIN, G. R., Dental Materials Science
GOLLWITZER, P. M., Psychology
GOODMAN, J., Mathematics
GOTTLIEB, A., Computer Science
GREENBERG, D. F., Sociology
GREENGARD, L., Mathematics
GREENLEAF, F. P., Mathematics
GRIFFIN, D., English
GRISHMAN, R., Computer Science
GROMOV, M., Mathematics
GROSS, J. T., Politics
GUILLORY, J., English
GURLAND, R. H., Philosophy
GUY, G. R., Linguistics
HAMEIRI, E., Mathematics
HANSEN, D., Ancient Middle Eastern Art and Archaeology
HARDIN, R., Politics
HARLEY, N. H., Environmental Science
HAROOTUNIAN, H., History
HARPER, P. B., English, American Studies
HARRINGTON, C., Politics
HARRISON, T., Anthropology
HAUSNER, M., Mathematics
HAVERKAMP, A., English
HAWKEN, M. J., Neural Science, Psychology
HEEGER, D. J., Psychology and Neural Science
HEILMAN, M., Psychology
HENDIN, J. G., English
HEYDEBRAND, W., Sociology
HEYNS, B., Sociology
HOFER, H., Mathematics
HOFFERT, M. I., Physics
HOFFMAN, M., Psychology
HOLLIER, D., French
HOROWITZ, R., Sociology
HOY, P. C., English
HSIUNG, J. C., Politics
HUGGINS, P., Physics
HULL, R. W., History
HÜPPAUF, B. R., German
HYMAN, I., Fine Arts
IVRY, A. L., Modern Jewish Thought, Hebrew and Judaic Studies, Middle Eastern Studies
JACOBY, L., Psychology
JAEGER, R. J., Environmental Science
JASSO, G., Sociology
JAVITCH, D., Comparative Literature, Italian
JOHNSON, P., History
JOLLY, C. J., Anthropology
JOVANOVIĆ, B., Economics
JUDT, A., European Studies, History
KALLENBACH, N. R., Chemistry
KAMM, F. M., Philosophy, Law
KAPLAN, F. E. S., Museum Studies
KAPLAN, M. A., Hebrew and Judaic Studies
KARCHIN, L., Music
KAYNE, R. S., Linguistics
KAZEMI, F., Politics, Middle Eastern Studies
KEDEM, Z. M., Computer Science
KELLEY, R. D. G., History
KINNELL, G., Creative Writing, English

KIRSHENBLATT-GIMBLETT, B., Performance Studies, Hebrew and Judaic Studies
KOHN, R. V., Mathematics
KOPCKE, G., Humanities
KRABBENHOFT, K., Spanish and Portuguese Languages and Literatures
KRAUSKOPF, J., Neural Science, Psychology
KRINSKY, C., Fine Arts
KRISER, D. B., Anthropology
KULICK, D., Anthropology
KUPPERMAN, K., History
LANDAU, S., Fine Arts
LANDY, M. S., Psychology, Neural Science
LAX, P. D., Mathematics
LeDOUX, J. E., Neural Science and Psychology
LeGEROS, R. Z., Dental Materials Science
LEHMAN, E. W., Sociology
LENNIE, P., Neural Science
LEVINE, B. A., Bible and Ancient Near Eastern Studies, Hebrew and Judaic Studies
LEVY, P. M., Physics
LIN, F.-H., Mathematics
LIPPMANN, M., Environmental Science
LOCKMAN, Z., Middle Eastern Studies, History
LOCKRIDGE, L. S., English
LOW, A., English
LOWENSTEIN, J. H., Physics
LUKES, S. M., Sociology
LYNCH, O. M., Urban Anthropology
McCHESNEY, R. D., Middle Eastern Studies
McKEAN, H. P., Mathematics
McLAUGHLIN, D. W., Mathematics
McNELIS, E. J., Chemistry
MAGNUSON, P. A., English
MAJDA, A. J., Mathematics
MANIN, B., Politics
MANOFF, R. K., Journalism and Mass Communication
MARINCOLA, M. D., Conservation
MARMOR, M., Environmental Medicine
MARSHALL, P., English
MARTIN, E., Anthropology
MARTÍNEZ, H. S., Spanish and Portuguese Languages and Literatures
MATHEWS, T. F., History of Art
MATTHEWS, T. J., Psychology, Neural Science
MATTINGLY, P., History
MAYNARD, J., English
MEAD, L. M., Politics
MEISEL, P., English
MICHELSON, A., Cinema Studies
MINCER, A., Physics
MISHRA, B., Computer Science
MITCHELL, C., Politics
MITCHELL, T., Politics, Middle Eastern Studies
MITSIS, P., Hellenic Culture and Civilization, Classics
MOLLOY, S., Spanish and Portuguese Languages and Literatures, Comparative Literature
MORTON, R. B., Politics
MOVSHON, J. A., Neural Science, Psychology
MURPHY, G. L., Psychology
MURPHY, L. B., Law, Philosophy
MYERS, F. R., Anthropology
NADIRI, M. I., Economics
NAGEL, T., Philosophy
NELKIN, D., Sociology
NEMETHY, P., Physics
NEWMAN, C. M., Mathematics
NICOLE, E., French
NIRENBERG, L., Mathematics
NOCHLIN, L., Modern Art
NOLAN, M., History
NYARKO, Y., Economics
O'CONNOR, D., Ancient Egyptian Art
OLDS, S., English
OLIVA, L. J., European Studies, History
OLLMAN, B., Politics
ORDOVER, J. A., Economics

OVERTON, M., Computer Science
PEACHIN, M., Classics
PEACOCKE, C., Philosophy
PELLI, D. G., Psychology, Neural Science
PERCUS, J. K., Mathematics, Physics
PERSELL, C. H., Sociology
PESKIN, C. S., Mathematics
PETERS, F. E., Middle Eastern Studies, Religious Studies, History
PINES, M. S., Dental Materials Science
PNUELI, A., Computer Science
POLLACK, R., Mathematics
POOVEY, M., English
PORRATI, M., Physics
POSNER, D., Fine Arts
POSNOCK, R., English
POSTAL, P. M., Linguistics
PRATT, M. L., Spanish and Portuguese
PRZEWORSKI, A., Politics
RAMSEY, J. B., Economics
RANDALL, R. S., Politics
RAPP, R., Anthropology
RAY, D., Economics
REGALADO, N. F., French
REIMERS, D. E., History
REISS, C. S., Biology
REISS, T. J., Comparative Literature
RICHARDSON, J., Philosophy
RICHARDSON, R. W., Physics
RINZEL, J., Neural Science, Mathematics
ROBINSON, E. J., Physics
ROELOFS, H. M., Politics
ROESNER, E. H., Music
RONELL, A., Germanic Languages and Literatures, Comparative Literature
ROSENBERG, L., Physics
ROSENBLUM, R., Modern European Art
ROSS, A., Comparative Literature
ROSS, K., Comparative Literature
ROSSMAN, T. G., Environmental Science
RUBLE, D. N., Psychology
RUDDICK, W., Philosophy
SAMMONS, J. T., History
SANDLER, L., Art History
SANTIROCCO, M. S., Classics
SARNAK, P., Mathematics
SCALLY, R. J., History, Classics
SCHAIN, M., Politics, French Studies
SCHECHNER, R., Performance Studies
SCHIEFFELIN, B. B., Anthropology
SCHIFFER, S., Philosophy
SCHIFFMAN, L. H., Hebrew and Judaic Studies
SCHLESINGER, R. B., Environmental Science
SCHLICK, T., Chemistry, Mathematics
SCHONBERG, E., Computer Science
SCHOTTER, A., Economics
SCHUCKING, E. L., Physics
SCHULMAN, A., Dental Materials Science
SCHUSTER, D. I., Chemistry
SCHWARTZ, J. T., Computer Science
SCHWEITZER, A., Humanities, Spanish and Portuguese Languages and Literatures, Comparative Literature
SCOTT, W., Biology
SCULLI, J., Physics
SEEMAN, N. C., Chemistry
SEIDMAN, E., Psychology
SEIGEL, J., History
SENNETT, R., Sociology, History
SHAPLEY, R. M., Sciences, Neural Science, Biology, Psychology
SHASHA, D., Computer Science
SHATAH, J., Mathematics
SHELLEY, P., Mathematics
SHINN, M., Psychology
SHOHAT, E., Art and Public Policy, Middle Eastern Studies
SHORE, R. E., Environmental Science
SHROUT, P., Psychology
SIDER, D., Classics
SIEBURTH, R., Comparative Literature, French
SIFAKIS, G. M., Hellenic Culture and Civilization, Classics
SILVER, K., Fine Arts, French Studies

SINGLER, J. V., Linguistics
SIRLIN, A., Physics
SKLAR, R., Cinema Studies
SMITH, M. S., Hebrew and Judaic Studies
SNODGRASS, J. G., Psychology
SOKAL, A. D., Physics
SOLOMON, S. D., Journalism and Mass Communication
SORENSEN, R. A., Philosophy
SOUCEK, P., Islamic Art
SPENCER, J. H., Computer Science, Mathematics
STAM, R., Cinema Studies
STEHLIN, S. A., History
STEPHENS, M., Journalism and Mass Communication
STIMPSON, C. R., Arts and Science
STOTZKY, G., Biology
STROKE, H. H., Physics
SUBIRATS, E., Spanish and Portuguese Languages and Literatures
SULLIVAN, E., Fine Arts
SZABOLCSI, A., Linguistics
TAYLOR, D., Performance Studies, Spanish
TING, L., Mathematics
TRACHTENBERG, M., History of Fine Arts
TROPE, Y., Psychology
TURNER, R., Art and Humanities
TYLER, T. R., Psychology
ULEMAN, J. S., Psychology
UNGER, I., History
UNGER, P., Philosophy
VARADHAN, S. R. S., Science, Mathematics
VITZ, E. B., French
VITZ, P. C., Psychology
VOLOGODSKII, A. V., Chemistry
WALEY-COHEN, J., History
WALKOWITZ, D., History
WEINEN, E., Mathematics
WEITZNER, H., Mathematics
WELKOWITZ, J., Psychology
WHITE, R., Anthropology
WIDLUND, O. B., Computer Science
WILSON, C. A., Economics
WILSON, S. R., Chemistry
WOLFF, E. N., Economics
WOLFSON, E., Hebrew Studies, Religious Studies
WRIGHT, M. H., Computer Science
XIN, Z., Mathematics
YAP, C. K., Computer Science
YAU, H.-T., Mathematics
YELLIN, V. F., Music
YOUNG, M. B., History
YÚDICE, G., Spanish and Portuguese and American Studies
ZASLAVSKY, G. M., Physics, Mathematics
ZHANG, J. Z. H., Chemistry
ZWANZIGER, D., Physics, Mathematics

College of Dentistry (345 E 24th St, New York, NY 10010; tel. (212) 998-9800; internet www.nyu.edu/dental):

BAHN, S., Biological Sciences, Medicine and Surgery
BRAL, M., Periodontics
CALAMIA, J., Restorative and Prosthodontics
CAUFIELD, P. W., Cariology and Operative Dentistry
GLICKMAN, R., Oral Maxillofacial Surgery
GOLDSTEIN, G., Prosthodontics
GUTTENPLAN, J., Basic Sciences (Biochemistry)
KATZ, R., Epidemiology and Health Promotion
KINNALLY, K., Basic Sciences
KIREMIDJIAN-SCHUMACHER, L., Basic Sciences
KUFTINEC, M., Orthodontics
LeGEROS, R., Implant Dentistry and Restorative and Prosthodontic Sciences
PINES, M., Biomaterials
REKOW, D., Basic Sciences and Craniofacial Biology and Orthodontics
ROSENBERG, P., Endodontics

ROY, M., Basic Sciences
SCHERER, W., Reconstructive and Comprehensive Care
SHIP, J. A., Oral Medicine
SINGH, I., Basic Sciences
SPIELMAN, A., Basic Science and Craniofacial Biology
TARNOW, D., Implant Dentistry
TERRACIO, L., Basic Sciences and Craniofacial Biology
VERNILLO, A., Oral Pathology

Institute of Fine Arts (One E 78th St, New York, NY 10075; tel. (212) 992-5800; e-mail ifa.program@nyu.edu; internet www.nyu.edu/gsas/dept/fineart):

ALEXANDER, J. J. G., Fine Arts
BAER, N. S., Conservation
BROWN, J., Fine Arts
COHEN, J.-L., History of Architecture
EISLER, C., Fine Arts
ELLIS, M. H., Conservation
FAIRCHILD, S., Fine Arts
HANSEN, D. P., Fine Arts
KOPCKE, G. H., Humanities
MARINCOLA, M., Conservation
MATHEWS, T. F., History of Art
NOCHLIN, L., Modern Art
O'CONNOR, D., Ancient Egyptian Art
POSNER, D., Fine Arts
ROSENBLUM, R., Modern European Art, Fine Arts
SANDLER, L. F., Fine Arts
SOUCEK, P. P., Islamic Art
STORR, R., Modern Art
SULLIVAN, E. J., Fine Arts
TRACHTENBERG, M., History of Fine Arts
VARNEDOE, J. K. T., History of Art
WALLACE, L. A., Ancient Egyptian Art
WEIL-GARRIS BRANDT, K., Fine Arts
WESTERMANN, M., Fine Arts

Leonard N. Stern School of Business (Henry Kaufman Management Center, 44 W Fourth St, New York, NY 10012; tel. (212) 998-0100; internet www.stern.nyu.edu):

BALACHANDRAN, K. R., Accounting and Operations Management
BARDES, P., Accounting and Finance
BARTOV, E., Accounting, Business Ethics
BILDERSEE, J. S., Accounting
BRIEF, R., Statistics and Accounting
HIPSCHER, A., Accounting, Taxation and Business Law
JONES, S., Accounting, Taxation and Business Law
LIVNAT, J., Accounting
MORAN, M. J., Accounting
NICHOLS, C. W., Business Ethics
RONEN, J., Accounting
SORTER, G. H., Accounting and Law
WIESEN, J., Accounting, Taxation and Business Law
ZICKLIN, L., Accounting

Robert F. Wagner Graduate School of Public Service (The Puck Bldg, 295 Lafayette St, Second Fl., New York, NY 10012-9604; tel. (212) 998-7400; internet www.nyu.edu/wagner):

BERNE, R., Public Policy and Financial Management
BOISE, W. B., Public Administration
BOUFFORD, J. I., Health Policy and Public Service
BRECHER, C. M., Public and Health Administration
CHERKASKY, M., Health Policy and Management
FINKLER, S. A., Public and Health Administration, Accounting, and Financial Management
KOVNER, A., Public and Health Management
KROPF, R., Health Management
LEW, J. J., Public Administration
LIGHT, P., Public Service

MOSS, M., Urban Policy and Planning
RODWIN, V. G., Health Policy and Management
SCHALL, E., Health Policy and Management
SCHILL, M. H., Law and Urban Planning
SPARROW, R. L., Public Management
STAFFORD, W. W., Public Policy and Planning
STIEFEL, L., Economics
ZIMMERMAN, R., Planning and Public Administration

School of Law (40 Washington Sq. S, New York, NY 10012; tel. (212) 998-6100; internet www.law.nyu.edu):

ADLER, A. M., Law
ADLER, B. E., Law
ALLEN, W. T., Law and Business
ALSTON, P., Law
AMSTERDAM, A. G., Law
ANGELOS, C., Law
ARLEN, J., Law
BEEN, V. L., Law
BENKLER, Y., Law
BILLMAN, B. D., Law
BURNS, S. E., Clinical Law
CALDWELL, P. M., Law
CHASE, O. G., Law
CHEVIGNY, P. G., Law
COHEN, J. A., Law
CUNNINGHAM, N. B., Law
DAINES, R. M., Law
DALE, H. P., Philanthropy and the Law
DAVIS, P. C., Lawyering and Ethics
DORSEN, N., Law
DREYFUSS, R. C., Law
DWORKIN, R. M., Law
ESTREICHER, S., Law
EUSTICE, J. S., Taxation
FIRST, H., Law
FOX, E. M., Trade Regulation
FRIEDMAN, B., Law
GALOWITZ, P., Law
GARLAND, D. W., Law
GEISTFELD, M., Law
GILLERS, S., Law
GILLETTE, C. P., Contract Law
GOLOVE, D. M., Law
GUGGENHEIM, M. F., Clinical Law
HERSHKOFF, H., Law
HERTZ, R. A., Clinical Law
HOLMES, S. T., Law
JACOBS, J. B., Constitutional Law and the Courts
KAHAN, M., Law
KINGSBURY, B., Law
KORNHAUSER, L. A., Law
LAW, S. A., Law
LEVINSON, D., Law
LÓPEZ, G., Clinical Law
LOWENFELD, A. F., International Law
MAGUIGAN, H., Clinical Law
MALMAN, L. L., Law
MARTELL, L. A., Law
MERON, T., Law
MILLER, G. P., Law
MORAWETZ, N., Clinical Law
MURPHY, L., Law
NAGEL, T., Law
NELSON, W. E., Law
NEUBORNE, B., Law
NOBLE, R. K., Law
PILDES, R. H., Law
PRICE, M. K., Law
REID, J. P., Law
REVESZ, R. L., Law
RICHARDS, D. A. J., Law
SAGER, L., Law
SCHENK, D. H., Taxation
SCHILL, M. H., Law and Urban Planning
SCHMOLKA, L. L., Law
SCHULHOFER, S. J., Law
SCOTT, H. S., Law
SEXTON, J., Law
SHAVIRO, D. N., Law

SIEGEL, S., Law
SILBERMAN, L. J., Law
SORTER, G. H., Law
STEINES, J. P., Jr, Law
STEWART, R. B., Law
TAYLOR-THOMPSON, K. A., Clinical Law
THOMPSON, A. C., Law
UPHAM, F. K., Law
WEILER, J. H. H., Law
ZIMMERMAN, D. L., Law

School of Medicine (550 First Ave, New York, NY 10016; tel. (212) 263-7300; internet www.med.nyu.edu):

ABADIR, A. R., Anaesthesiology
ABELE, M. G., Radiology
ABRAMS, S., Psychiatry
ABRAMSON, S. B., Medicine, Rheumatology, Pathology
ADESNIK, M. B., Cell Biology
AIGES, H. W., Paediatrics
AL-ASKARI, S., Urology
ALBANO, A. M., Psychiatry
ALBOM, M. J., Dermatology
AMELAR, R. D., Urology
ANGRIST, B. M., Psychiatry
ARGYROS, T. G., Medicine
ARKEL, Y. S., Obstetrics and Gynaecology
ARLOW, J. A., Psychiatry
ARONOFF, M. S., Psychiatry
ARTMAN, M., Paediatric Surgery, Pharmacology
ASTON, S. J., Surgery
AUERBACH, R., Dermatology
AXEL, L., Radiology
AXELROD, F. B., Dysautonomia Treatment, Neurology
AYVAZIAN, L. F., Medicine
BAKER, R. G., Physiology, Neuroscience
BALDWIN, D. S., Medicine, Nephrology
BALLARD, H. S., Medicine
BARKIN, L., Psychiatry
BARRON, B. A., Obstetrics and Gynaecology
BASCH, R. S., Pathology
BASILICO, C., Microbiology
BAUMANN, F. G., Surgery
BEASLEY, R. W., Surgery, Plastic and Reconstructive Surgery
BEATTIE, C. N., Anaesthesiology
BECKER, J. A., Radiology
BELASCO, J. G., Microbiology
BELMAN, S., Environmental Medicine
BEN-YISHAY, Y., Rehabilitation Medicine
BENJAMIN, V., Neurosurgery
BERANBAUM, S. L., Radiology
BERCZELLER, P. H., Medicine
BERG, P., Medicine
BERGER, M. M., Psychiatry
BERKELEY, A. S., Obstetrics and Gynaecology
BERNSTEIN, R. L., Anaesthesiology
BHANOT, O. S., Environmental Medicine
BHARDWAJ, N., Medicine Physiology, Neuroscience Pharmacology
BIRNBAUM, B. A., Radiology
BLANCK, T. J. J., Anaesthesiology, Physiology, Neuroscience
BLASER, M., Internal Medicine, Microbiology
BLAUGRUND, S. M., Otolaryngology
BLOCK, J. M., Neurology
BLUM, H. P., Psychiatry
BLUM, M., Medicine, Endocrinology, Radiology
BODIAN, E. L., Dermatology
BOGART, B. I., Cell Biology
BORKOWSKY, W., Paediatrics
BOSLAND, M. C., Environmental Medicine, Urology
BOUFFORD, J. I., Paediatrics
BOXER, R. A., Paediatrics
BOYD, A. D., Surgery, Cardiothoracic Surgery
BRANCACCIO, R. R., Dermatology
BRODIE, J. D., Psychiatry
BROOME, J. D., Pathology

BROTMAN, A. W., Psychiatry
BROWN, E. R., Neurosurgery
BROWN, J. W., Neurology
BRUNO, M. S., Clinical Medicine
BUDMAN, D. R., Medicine, Oncology
BURAKOFF, S. J., Medicine, Oncology
BURDEN, S. J., Pharmacology
BURDOCK, E. I., Psychiatry
BURNS, F. J., Environmental Medicine
BUYON, J. P., Medicine, Rheumatology
BYSTRYN, J.-C., Dermatology
CAHILL, K. M., Medicine
CALANOG, A. M., Obstetrics and Gynaecology
CANCRO, R., Psychiatry
CAPAN, L., Anaesthesiology
CARR, R. E., Ophthalmology
CASTELLANOS, F. X., Child and Adolescent Psychiatry, Clinical Radiology
CHALFIN, L. S., Psychiatry
CHANDRA, M. M., Paediatrics
CHANDRA, R., Radiology
CHAO, M. V., Cell Biology
CHARAP, M. H., Medicine, General Medicine
CHARLES, N. C., Ophthalmology
CHARNEY, A. N., Medicine, Nephrology
CHASSIN, J. L., Surgery
CHESLER, M., Neurosurgery, Physiology and Neuroscience
CHESS, S., Psychiatry
CHIORAZZI, N., Medicine, Infectious Diseases and Immunology, Pathology
CHIU, D. T., Surgery, Plastic and Reconstructive Surgery
CITROME, L. L., Psychiatry
CLAPS, A. A., Paediatrics
COBRINIK, R., Paediatrics
COHEN, B. S., Environmental Medicine
COHEN, I. J., Ophthalmology
COHEN, N. L., Otolaryngology
COHEN, T., Medicine
COLLINS, A. H., Psychiatry
COLOMBO, A., Medicine
COLTRERA, J. T., Psychiatry
COOPER, J. S., Radiation Oncology
COOPER, N. S., Pathology
COOPER, P. R., Neurosurgery, Orthopaedic Surgery
COPLAN, N. L., Medicine
COSTA, M., Environmental Medicine, Pharmacology
COSTA E SILVA, J. A., Psychiatry
COWAN, N. J., Biochemistry
CRONSTEIN, B. N., Medicine, Rheumatology, Pathology, Pharmacology
CULLIFORD, A. T., Surgery, Cardiothoracic Surgery
CURTIN, J. P., Obstetrics and Gynaecology
D'AMICO, R. A., Ophthalmology
DANCIS, J., Paediatrics
DANILOWICZ, D. A., Paediatrics
DANTUONO, L. M., Obstetrics and Gynaecology
DAUM, F., Paediatrics
DAVID, R., Paediatrics
DAVIES, E. A., Paediatrics
DAVIS, J. E., Urology
DE LEON, M. J., Psychiatry
DEBROVNER, C. H., Obstetrics and Gynaecology
DEFENDI, V., Oncology, Pathology
DEGNAN, T. J., Medicine, Oncology
DELISI, L. E., Psychiatry
DELPHIN, E. S., Anaesthesiology
DEMOPOULOS, R. I., Pathology
DEPASQUALE, N. P., Medicine
DEUTSCH, B. G., Psychiatry
DEVINSKY, O., Neurology
DEWEY, S. L., Psychiatry
DHAWAN, V., Neurology
DILLER, L., Rehabilitation Medicine
DODICK, J. M., Ophthalmology
DOLGIN, M., Medicine, Cardiology
DRLICA, K. A., Microbiology
DUBIN, L., Urology

DUBNAU, D., Microbiology
DUBOIS, M. Y., Anaesthesiology
DUSTIN, M. L., Pathology
EBERSTEIN, A., Rehabilitation Medicine
EIDELBERG, D., Neurology, Neurosurgery
ELSBACH, P., Medicine
ENG, K., Surgery
EVANS, H. L., Environmental Medicine
FANTL, J. A., Obstetrics and Gynaecology
FARBER, S. J., Medicine, Nephrology
FARCON, E. M., Urology
FARCY, J.-P. C., Orthopaedic Surgery
FEINBERG, A. W., Medicine, Geriatrics
FEINER, H. D., Pathology
FERRIS, S. H., Psychiatry
FINGER, P. T., Ophthalmology
FINLAY, J. L., Paediatrics, Neurosurgery
FINLAY, J. R., Ophthalmology
FIRESTEIN, S. K., Psychiatry
FISCHEL, R. E., Psychiatry
FISHER, A. A., Dermatology
FISHER, M. M., Paediatrics
FISHER, Y. L., Ophthalmology
FISHMAN, G. I., Medicine, Cardiology, Physiology and Neuroscience, Pharmacology
FLOWER, R. W., Ophthalmology
FORMENTI, S. C., Medical Oncology
FOSTER, J. R., Psychiatry
FOX, A. C., Medicine, Cardiology
FRANCES, R. J., Psychiatry
FRANGIONE, B., Pathology, Psychiatry
FRANK, J., Cell Biology
FRANKEL, V. H., Orthopaedic Surgery
FRANKS, A. G., Jr, Dermatology
FREEDBERG, I. M., Dermatology, Cell Biology
FREEDMAN, M. L., Medicine, Geriatrics
FRENKEL, K., Environmental Medicine, Pathology
FRIEDMAN, H. S., Medicine
FRIEDMAN-KIEN, A. E., Dermatology
FROST, J. O., Otolaryngology
FURMANSKI, P., Pathology
GABRIEL, H. P., Psychiatry
GALANTER, M., Psychiatry
GALLOWAY, A. C., Surgery, Cardiothoracic Surgery
GARAY, S. M., Medicine, Pulmonary and Critical Care
GARDNER, E. P., Physiology and Neuroscience
GENIESER, N. B., Radiology
GEORGE, A. E., Radiology
GERONEMUS, R. G., Dermatology
GITTELMAN, M. I., Psychiatry
GLENN, J., Psychiatry
GLICKMAN, R. M., Medicine
GODSON, G. N., Biochemistry
GOLDBERG, E., Neurology
GOLDBERG, J. D., Environmental Medicine
GOLDBERGER, M., Psychiatry
GOLDFRANK, L. R., Medicine, Emergency Medicine, Surgery
GOLDRING, R. M., Medicine, Pulmonary and Critical Care
GOLDSTEIN, N., Psychiatry
GOLDSTEIN, S. R., Obstetrics and Gynaecology
GOLIMBU, C. N., Radiology
GOLIMBU, M. N., Urology
GOLOMB, F. M., Surgery, Surgical Oncology
GONEN, O., Radiology
GOODGOLD, A. L., Neurology, Radiology
GOPINATHAN, G., Neurology
GOUGE, T. H., Surgery
GRANT, A. D., Orthopaedic Surgery
GREBB, J. A., Psychiatry
GRECO, J., Ophthalmology
GREEN, M. R., Psychiatry
GREENE, J. B., Medicine
GREENSTEIN, V. C., Ophthalmology
GREGERSEN, P. K., Medicine, Rheumatology, Pathology
GRIECO, A. J., Medicine, General Medicine
GRIFO, J. A., Obstetrics and Gynaecology

GROSSI, E. A., Surgery, Cardiothoracic Surgery
GROSSMAN, R. I., Radiology, Neurosurgery, Neurology, and Physiology and Neuroscience
GROSSMAN, S., Psychiatry
GRUEN, P. H., Psychiatry
GUYER, D. R., Ophthalmology
HAGIN, R. A., Psychiatry
HAJDU, S. I., Pathology
HALPERIN, J. J., Neurology
HALPERT, E., Psychiatry
HARIN, A., Paediatrics
HARLAP, S., Obstetrics and Gynaecology
HARLEY, N. H., Environmental Medicine
HARPER, R. G., Paediatrics, Obstetrics and Gynaecology
HARRIS, H. W., Medicine, Pulmonary and Critical Care
HARRIS, M. N., Surgery, Surgical Oncology
HARRISON, R. M., Ophthalmology
HAZZI, C. G., Medicine
HEITLER, M. S., Paediatrics
HELPERN, J. A., Radiology, Psychiatry, Physiology and Neuroscience
HILLER, J. M., Psychiatry
HILLMAN, D. E., Physiology and Biophysics
HILZ, M. J., Neurology, Medicine
HIRSCH, C. S., Forensic Medicine, Pathology
HIRSCHHORN, R., Medicine, Genetics, Cell Biology, Paediatrics
HOFFMAN, I. R., Medicine
HOLZMAN, R. S., Medicine, Infectious Diseases and Immunology, Environmental Medicine
HOOD, R. M., Surgery
HORNBLASS, A., Ophthalmology
HOROWITZ, L., Medicine
HOROWITZ, M. H., Psychiatry
HORWITZ, S. T., Obstetrics and Gynaecology
HSU, L. Y.-F., Paediatrics, Obstetrics and Gynaecology
IOACHIM, H. L., Pathology
ISRAEL, J. S., Anaesthesiology
ITIL, T., Psychiatry
ITOH, M., Rehabilitation Medicine
JACOBS, A. J., Obstetrics and Gynaecology
JACOBS, D. R., Medicine
JACOBS, J. B., Otolaryngology
JACOBS, T. J., Psychiatry
JAFAR, J. J., Neurosurgery
JAFFE, W. L., Orthopaedic Surgery
JAHSS, M. H., Orthopaedic Surgery
JAVITT, D. C., Psychiatry
JAVITT, N. B., Medicine, Gastroenterology, Paediatrics
JELINEK, J. E., Dermatology
JELINEK, W. R., Biochemistry
JIMENEZ, A. C., Rehabilitation Medicine
JOHANSON, K.-E., Urology
JOHN, E. R., Psychiatry
JONAS, S., Neurology
JONG, A. Y., Psychiatry
JOYNER, A. L., Cell Biology, Physiology and Neuroscience
KAHN, E. I., Surgical Pathology, Clinical Paediatrics
KAHN, M. L., Cardiology
KALOGERAKIS, M. G., Psychiatry
KAMHOLZ, S. L., Medicine
KAMM, F. M., Medicine
KANOF, N. B., Dermatology
KANTOR, T. G., Medicine
KAPLAN, L. A., Pathology
KAPLAN, M. H., Medicine, Infectious Diseases and Immunology
KAPLAN, S. J., Clinical Psychiatry
KARPATKIN, M. H., Paediatrics
KARPATKIN, S., Medicine, Haematology
KATZ, J. L., Clinical Psychiatry
KATZ, R. L., Medicine, Nephrology
KATZ, S., Medicine
KATZ, S. E., Psychiatry
KEEGAN, A. F., Radiology

KEILL, S. L., Psychiatry
KELLY, P. J., Neurosurgery
KENAN, S., Orthopaedic Surgery
KENNEDY, J. T., Medicine
KERMANI, E. J., Psychiatry
KESSLER, R. E., Surgery
KHATAMEE, M. A., Obstetrics and Gynaecology
KING, S. A., Psychiatry
KITTREDGE, R. D., Radiology
KLEIN, H. L., Biochemistry, Medicine
KLEIN, I. L., Medicine, Endocrinology, Cell Biology
KLEIN, R. G., Psychiatry
KLEINBERG, D. L., Medicine, Endocrinology
KOCHEN, J. A., Paediatrics
KOHAN, S. L., Obstetrics and Gynaecology
KOLODNY, E. H., Neurology
KOMISAR, A., Otolaryngology
KOPF, A. W., Dermatology
KOPLEWICZ, H. S., Child and Adolescent Psychiatry, Clinical Paediatrics
KORELITZ, B. I., Medicine
KOVAL, K. J., Orthopaedic Surgery
KOZ, G., Psychiatry
KRAMER, E. L., Radiology
KRAMER, F. R., Microbiology
KRAMER, M., Psychiatry
KRASINSKI, K. M., Paediatrics, Environmental Medicine
KRASNER, R. C. J., Medicine
KREIBICH, G., Cell Biology
KREIS, W., Medicine, Oncology
KREY, L. C., Obstetrics and Gynaecology, Cell Biology
KRONZON, I., Medicine, Cardiology
KUHNS, T. R., Ophthalmology
KUMMER, F., Orthopaedic Surgery
KUPERSMITH, M. J., Neurology, Ophthalmology
KUSCHNER, M., Pathology, Environmental Medicine
LAJTHA, A. L., Psychiatry
LANE, M. E., Rehabilitation Medicine
LANYI, V. F., Rehabilitation Medicine
LASKA, E. M., Psychiatry
LASKIN, M., Psychiatry
LAVKER, R. M., Dermatology
LEE, M. H. M., Rehabilitation Medicine
LEE-HUANG, S., Biochemistry
LEGGIADRO, R. J., Paediatrics
LEHMAN, W. B., Orthopaedic Surgery
LEHMANN, R., Cell Biology
LEHNEIS, H. R., Rehabilitation Medicine
LEITMAN, B. S., Radiology
LEPOR, H., Urology, Pharmacology
LESSER, G. T., Medicine
LEVIN, R. I., Medicine, Cardiology
LEVINE, B. B., Medicine, Infectious Diseases and Immunology
LEVINE, D. N., Neurology
LEVINE, I. S., Psychiatry
LEVITZ, M., Obstetrics and Gynaecology
LEVY, D. E., Molecular Pathology
LEW, A., Psychiatry
LEWIS, D. O., Psychiatry
LIFSHITZ, K., Psychiatry
LIFSHITZ, M. S., Pathology
LILLESKOV, R. K., Psychiatry
LINDENMAYER, J.-P., Psychiatry
LIPKIN, G., Dermatology
LIPKIN, M., Jr, Medicine, Primary Care
LIPPMANN, M., Environmental Medicine
LISMAN, R., Ophthalmology
LITTMAN, D. R., Molecular Immunology, Pathology and Microbiology
LLINAS, R., Physiology and Neuroscience
LOCKWOOD, C. J., Obstetrics and Gynaecology
LOFTUS, T. A., Psychiatry
LOVECCHIO, J. L., Obstetrics and Gynaecology
LOWENSTEIN, J., Medicine, Nephrology
LUNTZ, M. H., Ophthalmology
LUSSKIN, R., Orthopaedic Surgery
LYNFIELD, J., Paediatrics

MA, D. M., Rehabilitation Medicine
McCARTHY, J. G., Plastic Surgery
MAGRAMM, I., Ophthalmology
MAHONEY, C. J., Forensic Medicine
MALACH, M., Medicine
MANGER, W. M., Medicine
MANGIARDI, J. R., Neurosurgery
MANHEIMER, E. D., Medicine
MANNUZZA, S., Psychiatry
MARCOS, L. R., Psychiatry
MARGOLIS, R. U., Pharmacology
MARGOULEFF, D., Medicine, Nuclear Medicine
MARKOWITZ, J. F., Paediatrics
MARMOR, M., Environmental Medicine, Medicine, Pulmonary and Critical Care
MARSHALL, C. H., Radiology
MAS, F. G., Psychiatry
MASDEU, J. C., Neurology
MATTSSON, A., Psychiatry
MEGIBOW, A. J., Radiology
MEHL, S. J., Medicine
MEISELAS, L. E., Medicine, General Medicine
MEISLIN, A. G., Paediatrics
MERLINO, J. P., Psychiatry
MERUELO, D., Pathology
MESSITE, J., Environmental Medicine
MEYERSON, A. T., Psychiatry
MICHELIS, M. F., Medicine
MILANO, A. M., Medicine
MINDICH, L., Microbiology
MINUCHIN, P. P., Psychiatry
MINUCHIN, S., Psychiatry
MITNICK, H. J., Medicine
MONTEAGUDO, A., Obstetrics and Gynaecology
MORALES, P. A., Urology
MOSCATELLI, D. A., Cell Biology
MOSES, J. W., Medicine
MOSKOWITZ, P. K., Internal Medicine
MUGGIA, F. M., Oncology
NACHTIGALL, L. E., Obstetrics and Gynaecology
NACHTIGALL, R. H., Medicine
NAFTCHI, N. E., Rehabilitation Medicine
NAIDICH, D. P., Radiology
NAIDICH, J. B., Radiology
NARINS, R. S., Dermatology
NASS, R. D., Neurology
NEOPHYTIDES, A. N., Neurology
NEUBAUER, P. B., Psychiatry
NEWMAN, D., Psychiatry
NEZIROGLU, F. A., Psychiatry
NICHOLSON, C., Physiology and Neuroscience
NIXON, R. A., Psychiatry, Cell Biology
NORDIN, M., Orthopaedic Surgery, Environmental Medicine
NOVICK, R. P., Microbiology, Medicine, Pulmonary and Critical Care
NOZ, M. E., Radiology
NUSSENZWEIG, R. S., Medical and Molecular Parasitology
NUSSENZWEIG, V., Pathology
OBSTBAUM, S. A., Ophthalmology
O'HARE, D. B., Paediatrics
OLIVA-LOPEZ, E., Environmental Medicine
OPLER, L. A., Psychiatry
ORENTREICH, N., Dermatology
ORGEL, S., Psychiatry
ORLOW, S. J., Paediatric Dermatology
ORRIS, L., Environmental Medicine
ORT, P. J., Orthopaedic Surgery
OSTRER, H., Paediatrics, Pathology, Medicine
OVARY, Z., Pathology
PACHTER, H. L., Surgery
PACKER, S., Ophthalmology
PAHWA, S., Paediatrics
PANKOVICH, A. M., Orthopaedic Surgery
PAPERNIK, D. S., Psychiatry
PARISIEN, J. S., Orthopaedic Surgery
PARKS, W. P., Paediatrics, Microbiology
PASTERNACK, B. S., Environmental Medicine

PEARSON, J., Pathology
PELCOVITZ, D., Psychiatry
PELLICER, A. G., Pathology
PEPPER, B., Psychiatry
PERRY, R. I., Psychiatry
PESELOW, E. D., Psychiatry
PHILLIPS, R. A., Medicine
PHILLIPS-QUAGLIATA, J. M., Pathology
PINE, D. S., Psychiatry
PINTER, A., Microbiology
PLAINE, L., Urology
POMARA, N., Psychiatry
PORGES, R. F., Obstetrics and Gynaecology
PORTNOW, S. L., Psychiatry
POSNER, M. A., Orthopaedic Surgery
POST, R. C., Obstetrics and Gynaecology
POTMESIL, M., Radiology
POTTASH, A. C., Psychiatry
PRINCE, A. M., Pathology
QUARTERMAIN, D., Neurology, Physiology and Neuroscience
RACKOW, E., Medicine, Cardiology
RAFII, M., Radiology
RAICHT, R. F., Medicine, Gastroenterology
RAMSAY, D. L., Clinical Dermatology
RAUSEN, A. R., Paediatrics
RAYNOR, R. B., Neurosurgery
REEM, G. H., Pharmacology
REES, T. D., Surgery, Plastic and Reconstructive Surgery
REICH, T., Experimental Surgery
REISBERG, B., Psychiatry
RICHARDSON, M. A., Psychiatry
RIFKIN, D. B., Medicine and Cell Biology
RIGEL, D. S., Dermatology
RILES, T. S., Surgery
ROBBINS, E. S., Psychiatry
ROBBINS, H., Orthopaedic Surgery
ROBINS, P., Dermatology
ROGERS, B. O., Surgery
ROM, W. N., Jr, Medicine and Environmental Medicine
RON, D., Medicine, Endocrinology
ROSENBERG, Z. S., Radiology
ROSENBLUTH, J., Physiology and Neuroscience
ROSENFELD, D. L., Obstetrics and Gynaecology
ROSES, D. F., Surgery
ROSNER, R., Psychiatry
ROSSMAN, T. G., Environmental Medicine
ROTHSTEIN, A. A., Psychiatry
ROTROSEN, J. P., Psychiatry
ROUBIN, G. S., Medicine
ROVIT, R. L., Neurosurgery
ROWAN, R. L., Urology
ROY, A., Psychiatry
RUBERMAN, W., Environmental Medicine
RUBIN, S. E., Ophthalmology
RUDY, B., Physiology and Neuroscience, Biochemistry
RUOFF, M., Medicine
SABATINI, D. D., Cell Biology
SADOCK, B. J., Psychiatry
SADOCK, V. A., Psychiatry
SALZER, J. L., Neurology, Cell Biology
SAMUELS, H. H., Pharmacology and Medicine
SARNO, J. E., Jr, Rehabilitation Medicine
SARNO, M. T., Rehabilitation Medicine
SAXE, D. H., Surgery
SCHACHNE, L., Ophthalmology
SCHACHT, R. G., Paediatrics
SCHARFMAN, M. A., Psychiatry
SCHERR, L., Medicine, General Medicine
SCHLOSSMAN, A., Ophthalmology
SCHMIDT-SAROSI, C. L., Obstetrics and Gynaecology
SCHNEIDER, R. J., Microbiology
SCHOENFELD, M., Psychiatry
SCHREIBER, S. S., Clinical Medicine
SCHWARTZ, S., Medicine
SEDLIS, E., Paediatrics
SEIPLE, W. H., Ophthalmology
SHAPIRO, E., Urology
SHAW, L. N., Psychiatry

SHENGOLD, L. L., Psychiatry
SHORE, R. E., Environmental Medicine
SHUPACK, J. L., Dermatology
SIDTIS, J. J., Psychiatry
SIEGEL, C., Psychiatry
SIEGEL, I. M., Experimental Ophthalmology
SILBER, A., Psychiatry
SILVER, J., Medicine, Molecular Medicine, Pathology
SILVER, J. M., Psychiatry
SILVERBERG, M., Paediatrics
SILVERMAN, M. A., Psychiatry
SIMMS, H. H., Surgery
SIMON, E. J., Psychiatry, Pharmacology
SIMPSON, J. I., Physiology and Neuroscience
SINGER, M. H., Psychiatry
SKOLNICK, P., Psychiatry
SLABY, A. E., Psychiatry
SLAKTER, J. S., Ophthalmology
SLIPP, S., Psychiatry
SMALL, A. M., Psychiatry
SMITH, B. F., Ophthalmology
SMITH, I., Microbiology
SMITH, R. C., Psychiatry
SNYDER, C. A., Environmental Medicine
SOBERMAN, R. J., Medicine, Nephrology
SOLOMON, J. J., Environmental Medicine
SOLOWEY, A. C., Surgery
SOTER, N. A., Dermatology
SPATZ, M., Urology
SPEISER, P. W., Clinical Paediatrics
SPENCER, F. C., Surgery
SPEYER, J. L., Medicine, Oncology
SPITZER, M., Clinical Obstetrics and Gynaecology
SPRITZ, N., Medicine, Endocrinology
STEIGBIGEL, N. H., Medicine
STEINETZ, B. G., Environmental Medicine
STENSON, S. M., Ophthalmology
STERN, A., Pharmacology
STONE, E. A., Psychiatry
STONE, S. M., Paediatrics
SUGIMORI, M., Physiology and Neuroscience
SUN, T.-T., Dermatology
SUNSHINE, A., Medicine
SUSSMAN, N., Psychiatry
SVERDLIK, S. S., Rehabilitation Medicine
TAINTOR, Z. C., Psychiatry
TANCREDI, L. R., Psychiatry
TANG, M.-S., Environmental Medicine, Pathology Medicine
TAPPER, M. L., Medicine
TEEBOR, G. W., Pathology, Environmental Medicine
TESSLER, A. N., Urology
TESTA, N. N., Orthopaedic Surgery
THOMAS, A., Psychiatry
TICE, D. A., Surgery
TIMOR, I. E., Obstetrics and Gynaecology
TOBIAS, H., Medicine
TOLK, C. S., Psychiatry
TOMATIS, L., Environmental Medicine
TONIOLO, P. G., Environmental Medicine, Obstetrics and Gynaecology
TRUJILLO, M., Psychiatry
TUCHMAN, M., Medicine
TUNICK, P. A., Medicine, Cardiology
TZIMAS, N. A., Orthopaedic Surgery
VADASZ, C., Psychiatry
VALENTINE, F. T., Medicine, Infectious Diseases and Immunology
VANDERBERG, J. P., Medical and Molecular Parasitology
VAZQUEZ, C. I., Psychiatry
VILCEK, J. T., Microbiology
VINCIGUERRA, V. P., Medicine, Oncology
VOGEL, S. A., Psychiatry
VOLAVKA, J., Psychiatry
VORONTSOV, M. A., Physiology and Neuroscience
WAISMAN, J., Pathology
WALKER, P. S., Orthopaedic Surgery

WALLACH, R. C., Obstetrics and Gynaecology
WALLACH, S., Medicine
WALTZMAN, S. B., Otolaryngology
WAN, L. S., Obstetrics and Gynaecology
WANG, B. C., Anaesthesiology
WAPNIR, R. A., Paediatrics, Biochemistry
WARNER, R. S., Urology
WARSHAW, L. J., Environmental Medicine
WEINBERG, H. J., Neurology
WEINBERG, S., Dermatology
WEINSTEIN, H. C., Psychiatry
WEISSMANN, G., Medicine, Rheumatology
WELSH, H. K., Psychiatry
WEST, A. B., Pathology
WIKLER, N. S., Clinical Medicine
WILKES, B. M., Medicine, Nephrology
WISHNICK, M. M., Paediatrics
WITKOVSKY, P., Experimental Ophthalmology, Physiology and Neuroscience
WOLFF, B. B., Psychiatry
YANNUZZI, L. A., Ophthalmology
YARYURA-TOBIAS, J. A., Psychiatry
YOUNG, B. K., Obstetrics and Gynaecology
YOUNG, L. Y., Environmental Medicine
YUVIENCO, F. P., Urology
ZAVALA, F., Medical and Molecular Parasitology
ZELIKOVSKY, G., Urology
ZIDE, B. M., Surgery, Plastic and Reconstructive Surgery
ZIFF, E. B., Biochemistry
ZIMMON, D. S., Medicine, Gastroenterology
ZOLLA-PAZNER, S. B., Pathology
ZUCKER-FRANKLIN, D., Medicine, Haematology
ZUCKERMAN, J. D., Orthopaedic Surgery

Silver School of Social Work (One Washington Sq. N, New York, NY 10003-6654; tel. (212) 998-5910; e-mail ssw.admissions@nyu.edu; internet www.nyu.edu/socialwork):

ANASTAS, J. W.
DANE, B.
ENGLAND, S.
FESTINGER, T. B.
GOLDSTEIN, E. G.
HOLDEN, G.
LANDSBERG, G.
MEENAGHAN, T. M.
MILLS, L. G.
MISHNE, J.
PADGETT, D.
SEINFELD, J.
STRAUSSNER, S. L.

Steinhardt School of Culture, Education and Human Development (82 Washington Sq. E, New York, NY 10003; tel. (212) 998-5030; internet www.nyu.edu/education):

CAROTHERS, S. C., Teaching and Learning
KOVNER, C., Nursing
MCCLOWRY, S., Nursing
MAYHER, J. S., English Education
MILLER, M. C., Culture and Communication
NORMAN, E., Nursing
RICHARDSON, R., Higher Education
STAGE, F., Higher Education

Tisch School of the Arts (721 Broadway, 12th Fl., New York, NY 10003; tel. (212) 998-1800; internet www.nyu.edu/tisch):

CAMPBELL, M. S., Art and Public Policy
CANEMAKER, J., Film and Television
COOPER, P., Film and Television
DANCYGER, K., Film and Television
FROST, E. C., Film, Television and Radio
JENKIN, L., Dramatic Writing
KIMBRELL, M. A., Acting and Directing Studies
KIRSHENBLATT-GIMBLETT, B., Performance Studies
MARTIN, R., Art and Public Policy
MICHELSON, A., Cinema Studies
MILLER, T., Cinema Studies
NEIPRIS, J., Dramatic Writing

SCHECHNER, R., Performance Studies
SHOHAT, E., Art and Public Policy
SKLAR, R., Cinema Studies
SMITH, A. D., Performance Studies
STAM, R., Cinema Studies
STONEY, G. C., Film
TAYLOR, D., Performance Studies
WILLIS, D., Photography and Imaging

NIAGARA UNIVERSITY

NY 14109

Telephone: (716) 285-1212

Internet: www.niagara.edu

Founded 1856 as College and Seminary of Our Lady of Angels

Private control

Academic year: September to May

Pres.: Rev. JOSEPH L. LEVESQUE

Exec. Vice-Pres.: Dr BONNIE ROSE

Vice-Pres. for Academic Affairs: Dr TIMOTHY M. DOWNS

Vice-Pres. for Admin. Affairs: MICHAEL S. JASZKA

Vice-Pres. for Institutional Advancement: MARY BORGOGNONI

Vice-Pres. for Student Life: Dr KEVIN HEARN

Dir for Admissions: MARK WOJNOWSKI

Dir for Libraries: DAVID SCHOEN

Library of 198,622 vols

Number of teachers: 385 (158 full-time)

Number of students: 4,045 (3,175 undergraduate, 870 graduate)

Publications: *Aquila Literary Journal*, *Eagle* (4 a year, online, www.eagleonline.niagara.edu), *Niagaran* (1 a year)

DEANS

College of Arts and Sciences: Dr NANCY E. MCGLEN

College of Business Administration: Dr SHAWN DALY

College of Education: Dr DEBRA COLLEY

College of Hospitality and Tourism Management: Dr GARY D. PRATZEL

NYACK COLLEGE

One S Blvd, Nyack, NY 10960-3698

Telephone: (845) 358-1710

E-mail: admissions@nyack.edu

Internet: www.nyack.edu

Founded 1882, fmrly Missionary Training Institute, present name 1972

Private control

Academic year: September to May

Campuses in New York city, New York, Washington, DC, and in Puerto Rico

Pres.: Dr MICHAEL G. SCALES

Provost and Vice-Pres. for Academic Affairs: Dr DAVID F. TURK

Exec. Vice-Pres. and Treas.: Dr DAVID C. JENNINGS

Vice-Pres. for Advancement: JEFFREY G. CORY

Vice-Pres. for Enrolment and Marketing: Dr ANDREA M. HENNESSY

Registrar: SUE HO

Dean for Library Services: LINDA POSTON

Library of 133,000 vols

Number of teachers: 305 (109 full-time, 196 adjunct)

Number of students: 3,265 (2042 undergraduate, 492 graduate, 731 Alliance Theological Seminary)

DEANS

Alliance Theological Seminary: Dr RONALD WALBORN

College of Arts and Sciences: Dr FERNANDO ARZOLA, JR

School of Business and Leadership: Dr ANITA UNDERWOOD

School of Education: Dr JoANN LOONEY
School of Music: Dr GLENN KOPONEN

PACE UNIVERSITY

One Pace Plaza, New York, NY 10038
Telephone: (866) 722-3338
E-mail: infoctr@pace.edu
Internet: www.pace.edu
Founded 1906
Private control
3 Campuses in New York City, Westchester and White Plains
Pres.: STEPHEN J. FRIEDMAN
Provost and Exec. Vice-Pres. for Academic Affairs: Dr HARRIET FELDMAN
Exec. Vice-Pres., Chief Financial Officer and Treas.: TOBY WINER
Vice-Pres. for Devt and Alumni Relations: JENNIFER BERNSTEIN
Vice-Pres. for Enrolment and Placement: ROBINA C. SCHEPP
Vice-Pres. for IT: THOMAS A. HULL
Vice-Pres. for Univ. Relations: MARIE J. TOULANTIS
Univ. Counsel: STEPHEN BRODSKY
Univ. Registrar: STEVEN L. JOHNSON
Univ. Librarian: WILLIAM J. MURDOCK (acting)
Library of 938,158 vols, 5,100 periodicals
Number of teachers: 1,200
Number of students: 12,704 (7,807 undergraduate, 4,042 graduate, 855 law graduate)

DEANS

College of Health Professions: Dr GERALDINE COLOMBRARO
Dyson College of Arts and Sciences: Dr NIRA HERRMANN
Lubin School of Business: NEIL S. BRAUN
School of Education: Dr ANDREA SPENCER
School of Law: DAVID YASSKY
Seidenberg School of Computer Science and Information Systems: Dr CONSTANCE A. KNAPP

PAUL SMITH'S COLLEGE

POB 265, Route 86 and 30, Paul Smiths, NY 12970-0265
Telephone: (518) 327-6227
E-mail: admissions@paulsmiths.edu
Internet: www.paulsmiths.edu
Private control
Academic year: May to June
Pres.: Dr JOHN W. MILLS
Provost: Dr RICHARD NELSON
Vice-Pres. for Business and Finance: ANN MARIE SOMMA
Vice-Pres. for Enrolment Management: ERIC FELVER
Vice-Pres. for Information Systems: JAMES BUYEA
Vice-Pres. for Institutional Advancement: F. RAYMOND AGNEW
Registrar: Dr LORALYN TAYLOR
Dir for Educational Resources: NEIL SURPRENANT

DEANS

Division of Forestry, Natural Resources and Recreation: Dr JEFFREY T. WALTON
Division of Hospitality Resort and Culinary Management: ERNIE WILSON
Division of Science, Liberal Arts and Business: Dr PHILIP TAYLOR

PLAZA COLLEGE

74–09 37th Ave, Jackson Heights, NY 11372
Telephone: (718) 779-1430
E-mail: info@plazacollege.edu
Internet: www.plazacollege.edu

Founded 1916
Private control
Bachelors in management and patient information management
Pres. and Provost: CHARLES E. CALLAHAN
Vice-Pres. for Financial Services: ELIZABETH K. CALLAHAN
Dean for Academic Affairs: MARIE DOLLA
Dean for Admin.: ROSE ANN BLACK
Dir for Library and Learning Resource Center: KATHLEEN D'APRIX

POLYTECHNIC INSTITUTE OF NEW YORK UNIVERSITY

Six MetroTech Center, Brooklyn, NY 11201
Telephone: (718) 260-3600
E-mail: uadmit@poly.edu
Internet: www.poly.edu
Founded 1854 as Brooklyn Collegiate and Polytechnic Institute, fmrly Polytechnic Univ., present name and status 2008
Academic year: September to May
Campuses at Long Island, Manhattan and Westchester
Pres.: JERRY MacARTHUR HULTIN
Provost: Dr KATEPALLI SREENIVASAN
Vice-Pres.: BARBARA NOSEWORTHY
Vice-Pres. for Academic Affairs: Dr RICHARD S. THORSEN
Vice-Pres. for Finance and Business Affairs: DENNIS D. DINTINO
Vice-Pres. for Strategic Initiatives and Chief of Staff: ELIZABETH LUSSKIN
Dean for Admissions: JOY COLELLI
Dean for Student Affairs: ANITA FARRINGTON
Dir for Library Services: JANA STEVENS-RICHMAN
Number of teachers: 140 (full-time)
Number of students: 4,000
Publication: *Cable*

PRATT INSTITUTE

200 Willoughby Ave, Brooklyn, NY 11205
Telephone: (718) 636-3600
E-mail: info@pratt.edu
Internet: www.pratt.edu
Founded 1887
Academic year: August to May
Campuses in Brooklyn and Manhattan
Pres.: Dr THOMAS F. SCHUTTE
Provost: PETER BARNA
Vice-Pres. for Finance and Admin.: EDMUND RUTKOWSKI
Vice-Pres. for Institutional Advancement: TODD GALITZ
Vice-Pres. for Student Life: Dr HELEN MATUSOUR-AYRES
Registrar: LISLE HENDERSON
Dir for Libraries: RUSS ABELL
Library of 200,000 vols, incl. 600 periodicals, rare books and the college archives
Number of teachers: 1,000
Number of students: 4,730 (3,005 undergraduate, 1,725 graduate)
Publication: *Prattfolio* (2 a year)

DEANS

School of Architecture: TOM HANRAHAN
School of Art and Design: Dr CONCETTA M. STEWART
School of Information and Library Science: Dr TULA GIANNINI
School of Liberal Arts and Sciences: Dr ANDREW W. BARNES

RENSSELAER POLYTECHNIC INSTITUTE

110 Eighth St, Troy, NY 12180-3590
Telephone: (518) 276-6000

E-mail: admissions@rpi.edu
Internet: www.rpi.edu
Founded 1824
Pres.: Dr SHIRLEY ANN JACKSON
Provost: PRABHAT HAJELA
Vice-Pres.: JOHN MINASIAN
Vice-Pres. for Admin.: CLAUDE ROUNDS
Vice-Pres. for Enrolment and Dean for Undergraduate and Graduate Admissions: PAUL MARTHERS
Vice-Pres. for Finance and Chief Financial Officer: VIRGINIA GREGG
Vice-Pres. for Human Resources: CURTIS POWELL
Vice-Pres. for Information Services and Technology and Chief Information Officer: JOHN KOLB
Vice-Pres. for Institute Advancement: BRENDA WILSON-HALE
Vice-Pres. for Student Life: TIMOTHY E. SAMS
Vice-Pres. for Strategic Communications and External Relations: WILLIAM WALKER
Registrar: SHARON KUNKEL
Dir for Libraries: BOB MAYO
Library of 475,000 vols, 3,117 periodicals, 100,000 slides
Number of teachers: 480 (375 full-time, 105 part-time)
Number of students: 6,910 (5,240 undergraduate, 1,180 graduate)

DEANS

Lally School of Management and Technologyt: THOMAS BEGLEY
School of Architecture: EVAN DOUGLIS
School of Engineering: DAVID ROSOWSKY (acting)
School of Humanities, Arts and Social Sciences: MARY SIMONI
School of Science: LAURIE LESHIN

ROBERTS WESLEYAN COLLEGE

2301 Westside Dr., Rochester, NY 14624-1997
Telephone: (585) 594-6000
E-mail: admissions2@roberts.edu
Internet: www.roberts.edu
Founded 1866
Private control
Academic year: September to May
Liberal arts college; incl. Northeastern Seminary
Pres.: JOHN A. MARTIN
Provost and Sr Vice-Pres.: ROBERT ZWIER
Sr Vice-Pres. for Advancement and External Relations: JACK CONNELL
Sr Vice-Pres. and Treas.: JAMES E. CUTHBERT
Vice-Pres. for Academic and Student Support: NELSON W. HILL
Vice-Pres. for Admin.: RUTH LOGAN
Vice-Pres. for Admissions and Marketing: LINDA KURTZ
Registrar: LESA KOHR
Dir for Student Financial Services: STEPHEN FIELD
Dir for Library Services: AL KROBER
Library of 137,679 vols, 111,232 titles, 3,500 journals, 124,240 books
Number of teachers: 75
Number of students: 1,930
Publication: *Roberts Today* (4 a year)

DEANS

School of Liberal Arts and Sciences: JULIA GRIMM
School of Professional Studies: DAVID BASINGER

ROCHESTER INSTITUTE OF TECHNOLOGY

One Lomb Memorial Dr., Rochester, NY 14623-5603

Telephone: (585) 475-2411
E-mail: admissions@rit.edu
Internet: www.rit.edu

Founded 1829 as the Rochester Athenaeum
Private control

Pres.: Dr WILLIAM W. DESTLER
Provost and Sr Vice-Pres. for Academic Affairs: Dr JEREMY HAEFNER
Sr Vice-Pres. for Enrolment Management and Career Services: JAMES MILLER
Sr Vice-Pres. for Finance and Admin.: Dr JAMES H. WATTERS
Sr Vice-Pres. for Student Affairs: Dr MARY-BETH COOPER
Vice-Pres. for Devt and Alumni Relations: LISA CAUDA
Vice-Pres. for Govt and Community Relations: DEBORAH STENDARDI
Vice-Pres. for Research and Assoc. Provost: Dr RYNE RAFFAELLE
Vice-Pres. for Strategic Planning and Spec. Initiatives: KIT MAYBERRY
Dir for RIT Libraries: SHIRLEY BOWER

Library of 498,000 vols, 45,000 ebooks, 30,000 ejournals, and 11,000 audio, film and video titles
Number of teachers: 1,530 (1,020 full-time, 15 part-time, 495 adjunct)
Number of students: 17,650 (14,751 undergraduate, 2,899 graduate)

Publication: *The University Magazine* (3 a year)

DEANS

B. Thomas Golisano College of Computing and Information Sciences: Dr ANDREW L. SEARS
College of Applied Science and Technology: Dr H. FRED WALKER
College of Health Sciences and Technology: Dr DANIEL B. ORNT
College of Imaging Arts and Sciences: LORRAINE JUSTICE
College of Liberal Arts: JAMES J. WINEBRAKE
College of Science: Dr SOPHIA MAGGELAKIS
E. Philip Saunders College of Business: Dr ASHOK RAO
Kate Gleason College of Engineering: Dr HARVEY PALMER
National Technical Institute for the Deaf: Dr GERAD BUCKLEY

ROCKEFELLER UNIVERSITY

1230 York Ave, New York, NY 10065

Telephone: (212) 327-8000
E-mail: pubinfo@rockefeller.edu
Internet: www.rockefeller.edu

Founded 1901 as Rockefeller Institute for Medical Research, present status 1954, present name 1965

Centre for research and graduate education in biomedical sciences, chemistry, bioinformatics and physics; 73 laboratories

Pres.: MARC TESSIER-LAVIGNE
Vice-Pres. for Academic Affairs: MICHAEL W. YOUNG
Vice-Pres. for Devt: MAREN E. IMHOFF
Vice-Pres. for Educational Affairs and Dean: SIDNEY STRICKLAND
Vice-Pres. for Finance and Treas.: JAMES H. LAPPLE
Vice-Pres. for Human Resources: VIRGINIA HUFFMAN
Vice-Pres. for Medical Affairs: BARRY S. COLLER
Vice-Pres. for Scientific and Facility Operations: JOHN TOOZE

Vice-Pres. and Chief Investment Officer: AMY C. FALLS
Vice-Pres. and Gen. Counsel: HARRIET RABB
Corporate Sec.: JANE RENDALL (acting)
Librarian: CAROL A. FELTES

Library of 230,000 vols
Number of teachers: 250
Number of students: 545 (350 post-doctoral research, 170 doctoral, 25 MD–PhD)

Publications: *Journal of Cell Biology* (12 a year), *Journal of Clinical Investigation* (12 a year), *Journal of Experimental Medicine* (12 a year), *Journal of General Physiology* (12 a year)

SAGE COLLEGES

65 First St, Troy, NY 12180

Telephone: (518) 244-2000
E-mail: vpmem@sage.edu
Internet: www.sage.edu

Founded 1916
Private control
Academic year: May to May

Pres.: Dr SUSAN C. SCRIMSHAW
Vice-Pres. for Academic Affairs: Dr SALLY A. LAWRENCE
Vice-Pres. for Finance and Admin.: WILLIAM BECKMAN
Vice-Pres. for Marketing and Enrolment Management: (vacant)
Dir for Libraries: LISA BRAINARD

Library of 200,000 vols, 60,000 vols of bound periodicals, 30,000 media items
Number of teachers: 160 (full-time)
Number of students: 3,000 (full-time)

Publications: *Connections, Crossroads*

DEANS

Russell Sage College: Dr SHARON P. ROBINSON
Sage College of Albany: Dr SAROLTA TAKACS
Esteves School of Education: Dr LORI QUIGLEY
Sage Graduate School of Health Sciences: ESTHER HASKVITZ
Sage Graduate School of Management: Dr DAN ROBESON

ST BONAVENTURE UNIVERSITY

3261 W State Rd, St Bonaventure, NY 14778

Telephone: (716) 375-2000
E-mail: admissions@sbu.edu
Internet: www.sbu.edu

Founded 1855 as St Bonaventure's College, present name 1950
Academic year: August to June

Pres.: Sr MARGARET CARNEY
Provost and Vice-Pres. for Academic Affairs: Dr MICHAEL J. FISCHER
Vice-Provost for Student Life: RICHARD TRIETLEY, JR
Sr Vice-Pres. for Finance and Admin.: BRENDA L. MCGEE
Vice-Pres. for Univ. Advancement: MARY DRISCOLL
Vice-Pres. for Univ. Relations: Dr EMILY F. SINSABAUGH
Registrar: HEATHER L. JACKSON
Dir for Library: PAUL J. SPAETH

Library of 325,000 vols, 11,500 reference titles, over 35,000 e-serials
Number of teachers: 160
Number of students: 2,020 (1,970 undergraduate)

Publications: *Bonadieu* (1 a year), *Bonaventure, Cithara* (2 a year), *Cord* (4 a year), *Laurel* (2 a year), *The Works of William of Ockham*

DEANS

School of Arts and Sciences: Dr WOLFGANG NATTER

School of Business: Dr CAROL M. FISCHER
School of Education: Dr JOSEPH E. ZIMMER
School of Franciscan Studies: Bro. F. EDWARD COUGHLIN
School of Graduate Studies: Dr PEGGY YEHL BURKE
School of Journalism and Mass Communication: Dr PAULINE HOFFMANN

ST FRANCIS COLLEGE

180 Remsen St, Brooklyn Heights, NY 11201

Telephone: (718) 522-2300
E-mail: admissions@sfc.edu
Internet: www.sfc.edu

Founded 1859 as St Francis Acad., present name and status 1884
Private control
Academic year: September to August

Graduate programmes in accounting and project management

Pres.: BRENDAN J. DUGAN
Exec. Vice-Pres.: JUNE MCGRISKEN
Provost and Vice-Pres. for Academic Affairs: Dr TIMOTHY HOULIHAN
Vice-Pres. for Devt: THOMAS FLOOD
Dean for Students: Dr CHERYL HOWELL
Dir for Library Services: JAMES P. SMITH
Registrar: ROXANNE PERSAUD

Library of 177,000 vols
Number of teachers: 155
Number of students: 2,500

Publications: *Arthur Miller Journal* (2 a year), *ASEBL Journal, Assisi* (online)

ST JOHN FISHER COLLEGE

3690 E Ave, Rochester, NY 14618

Telephone: (585) 385-8000
E-mail: admissions@sjfc.edu
Internet: www.sjfc.edu

Founded 1948
Private control
Academic year: September to June

Pres.: Dr DONALD E. BAIN
Provost and Dean: Dr RONALD J. AMBROSETTI
Sr Vice-Pres. for Enrolment Management and Planning: Dr GERARD J. ROONEY
Vice-Pres. for Finance and Business: Dr THOMAS E. O'NEIL
Vice-Pres. for Institutional Advancement: Dr WILLIAM J. O'CONNOR
Vice-Pres. for Student Affairs and Diversity Initiatives: Dr RICHARD DeJESÚS-RUEFF
Registrar: JULIE THOMAS
Dir for Library: MELISSA JADLOS

Library of 160,000 vols
Number of students: 3,100

DEANS

Bittner School of Business: Dr DAVID MARTIN
Ralph C. Wilson, Jr. School of Education: Dr WENDY PATERSON
School of Arts and Sciences: Dr DAVID PATE
Wegmans School of Nursing: Dr DIANNE COONEY MINER
Wegmans School of Pharmacy: Dr SCOTT A. SWIGART

ST JOHN'S UNIVERSITY

8000 Utopia Parkway, Queens, NY 11439

Telephone: (718) 990-2000
E-mail: admhelp@stjohns.edu
Internet: www.stjohns.edu

Founded 1870, chartered 1871, re-chartered by Regents of the Univ. of the State of New York 1906
Private control
Academic year: September to May

Campuses at Queens, Staten Island, Manhattan and Oakdale in New York; global campuses at Rome in Italy and Paris in France

Pres.: Rev. DONALD J. HARRINGTON
Provost: Dr JULIA A. UPTON
Exec. Vice-Pres. for Mission and Student Services: Rev. JAMES J. MAHER
Sr Vice-Pres. and Chief of Staff: ROBERT D. WILE
Sr Vice-Pres. for Finance and Operations and Treas.: MARTHA HIRST
Sr Vice-Pres. for Human Resources and Strategic Planning: MARY T. HARPER HAGAN
Vice-Pres. and Sec. to the Univ.: Dr DOROTHY E. HABBEN
Vice-Pres. for Academic Support Services: Dr ANDRÉ MCKENZIE
Vice-Pres. for Community Relations: JOSEPH SCIAME
Vice-Pres. for Enrolment Management: BETH M. EVANS
Vice-Pres. for Institutional Research and Academic Planning: CLOVER HALL
Vice-Pres. for Int. Relations: Dr CECILIA CHANG
Vice-Pres. for Planning and Information Technology: Dr FRANK SIRIANNI
Vice-Pres. for Student Affairs: KATHRYN T. HUTCHINSON
Vice-Pres. for Univ. Min.: PAMELA SHEA-BYRNES
Gen. Counsel: JOSEPH E. OLIVA
Dean forf Libraries: Dr JAMES BENSON
Academic year: August to May
Library: 1.75m. vols
Number of teachers: 1,440
Number of students: 21,350 (15,720 undergraduate, 5,630 graduate)
Publications: *American Bankruptcy Institute Law Review* (2 a year), *Journal of Civil Rights and Economic Development* (4 a year), *St. John's Law Review* (4 a year), *New York International Law Review* (2 a year), *N.Y. Real Property Law Journal* (4 a year), *NY Litigator Law Journal* (irregular), *Professional Studies Review, Recipe, Res Gestae, St John's Today, St. John's Journal of International and Comparative Law* (online), *Sequoya Art and Literary Magazine, The Journal of Catholic Legal Studies, The Spectator, The Stormfront, The Torch, Vincentian Yearbook*

DEANS

College of Pharmacy and Allied Health Professions: ROBERT A. MANGIONE
College of Professional Studies: KATHLEEN VOUTÉ MACDONALD
Peter J. Tobin College of Business: Dr VICTORIA L. SHOAF
St John's College of Liberal Arts and Sciences: Dr JEFFERY FAGEN (acting)
School of Education: Dr JERROLD ROSS
School of Law: Prof. MICHAEL A. SIMONS

ST JOSEPH'S COLLEGE

245 Clinton Ave, Brooklyn, NY 11205
Telephone: (718) 940-5300
Internet: www.sjcny.edu
Founded 1916 as St Joseph's College for Women, present name 1970
Private control
Campuses in Brooklyn and Long Island
Pres.: Sis. ELIZABETH A. HILL
Provost: Sis. LORETTA MCGRANN
Vice-Pres. for Enrolment Management: THERESA LaROCCA-MEYER
Vice-Pres. for Institutional Advancement: NANCY CONNORS
Vice-Pres. for Planning: Dr THOMAS G TRAVIS
Chief Financial Officer: JOHN ROTH
Dean for Students: Dr SUSAN HUDEC
Dir for Library, Brooklyn: Dr WILLIAM MENG

Dir for Library, Long Island: TERRI CORBIN-HUTCHINSON
Library of 156,600 vols, 50,000 ebooks and ejournals
Number of teachers: 640
Number of students: 5,835 (5,035 undergraduate, 800 graduate)

DEANS

School of Arts and Sciences (Brooklyn Campus): Dr RICHARD GREENWALD
School of Arts and Sciences (Long Island Campus): Dr CHRISTOPHER FROST
School of Professional and Graduate Studies: Dr THOMAS G. TRAVIS

SAINT JOSEPH'S SEMINARY, DUNWOODIE

201 Seminary Ave, Yonkers, NY 10704-1896
Telephone: (914) 968-6200
E-mail: sjs@dunwoodie.edu
Internet: www.dunwoodie.edu
Founded 1896
Private control
Rector: Most Rev. GERALD T. WALSH
Academic Dean: Rev. KEVIN P. O'REILLY
Dean for Students and Admissions: Rev. ANDREW R. KING
Registrar: Sis. MARY FRANCES MILLS
Dir for Library Services: Sis. MONICA WOOD
Library of 103,000 vols, incl. 2,500 bound periodicals
Number of teachers: 22 (12 full-time, 10 part-time)

ST LAWRENCE UNIVERSITY

23 Romoda Dr., Canton, NY 13617
Telephone: (315) 229-5011
E-mail: admissions@stlawu.edu
Internet: www.stlawu.edu
Founded 1856
Private control
Academic year: August to May
Pres.: WILLIAM L. FOX
Vice-Pres. and Dean for Academic Affairs: VALERIE D. LEHR
Vice-Pres. and Dean for Admissions and Financial Aid: JEFFREY RICKEY
Vice-Pres. for Admin. Operations: THOMAS COAKLEY
Vice-Pres. for Communications: TOM EVELYN
Vice-Pres. for Finance and Treas.: JOSEPH P. MANORY
Vice-Pres. for Student Life: JOSEPH A. TOLLIVER
Vice-Pres. for Univ. Advancement: LAURA ELLIS
Sec.: ANGELA M. JOHNSTON
Registrar: CAROLYN FILIPPI
Librarian: MICHAEL ALZO BART HARLOE (acting)
Library: 1.5m. vols, incl. 417,000 govt documents, 1,900 print subscriptions, 597,000 microform units, over 6,100 video cassettes
Number of teachers: 190 (170 full-time, 20 part-time)
Number of students: 2,450 (2,355 undergraduate, 95 graduate)
Publications: *Gridiron* (1 a year), *Laurentian* (1 a year), *St Lawrence Magazine* (4 a year)

ST THOMAS AQUINAS COLLEGE

125 Route 340, Sparkill, NY 10976
Telephone: (845) 398-4000
E-mail: admissions@stac.edu
Internet: www.stac.edu
Founded 1952
Private control
Academic year: August to May

Schools of arts and sciences, business, education
Pres.: Dr MARGARET MARY FITZPATRICK
Provost and Vice-Pres. for Academic Affairs: Dr L. JOHN DURNEY
Vice-Pres. for Admin. and Finance and Treas.: JOSEPH DONINI
Vice-Pres. for Enrolment Management and Campus Communications: VIN CRAPANZANO
Vice-Pres. for Institutional Advancement: KEVIN P. DUIGNAN
Vice-Pres. and Dean for Student Devt: Dr KIRK MANNING
Registrar: MILLIE ALEXIOU
Library Dir: (vacant)
Library of 95,000 vols, 420 magazines, newspapers, journals; 2,000 video cassettes and DVDs
Number of students: 2,700

ST VLADIMIR'S ORTHODOX THEOLOGICAL SEMINARY

575 Scarsdale Rd, Yonkers, NY 10707-1699
Telephone: (914) 961-8313
E-mail: info@svots.edu
Internet: www.svots.edu
Founded 1938
Private control
Academic year: August to May
Chancellor: Rev. Dr CHAD HATFIELD
Dean: Rev. Dr JOHN BEHR
Assoc. Dean for Academic Affairs: Dr JOHN BARNET
Assoc. Dean for Student Affairs: Rev. DAVID MEZYNSKI
Assoc. Chancellor for Finance: MELANIE RINGA
Dir for Admissions and Financial Aid: Dr DAVID WAGSCHAL
Librarian: ELEANA S. SILK
Library of 142,000 vols, 350 periodical subscriptions
Number of teachers: 14
Number of students: 55
Publication: *The St. Vladimir's Theological Quarterly*

SARAH LAWRENCE COLLEGE

One Mead Way, Bronxville, NY 10708-5999
Telephone: (914) 395-2510
E-mail: slcadmit@sarahlawrence.edu
Internet: www.slc.edu
Founded 1926
Private control
Academic year: August to May
Pres.: KAREN R. LAWRENCE
Vice-Pres. for Admin.: THOMAS BLUM
Vice-Pres. for Advancement: CHARLES J. RASBERRY
Vice-Pres. for Communications and Marketing: Dr GERALD A. SCHORIN
Vice-Pres. for Finance and Operations: VINCENT MASSARO
Dean for College: Dr JERRILYNN D. DODDS
Dean for Enrolment: KEVIN MCKENNA
Dean for Graduate Studies: SUSAN GUMA
Dean for Student Affairs: Dr PAIGE CRANDALL
Dean for Studies and Student Life: Dr ALLEN GREEN (acting)
Registrar: DANIEL LICHT
Dir for Library: BOBBIE SMOLOW
Library of 200,000 vols
Number of teachers: 238
Number of students: 1,670 (1,328 undergraduate, 342 graduate)
Publications: *Sarah Lawrence Magazine* (online, www.slc.edu/magazine/starting-from-scratch), *SLC Vanguard, The Phoenix, The SLC Visual Arts Review, The Sarah Lawrence Literary Review*

SCHOOL OF VISUAL ARTS

209 E 23 St, New York, NY 10010-3994
Telephone: (212) 592-2000
E-mail: admissions@sva.edu
Internet: www.schoolofvisualarts.edu
Founded 1947 as Cartoonists and Illustrators
School, present name 1956
Private control
Academic year: September to May
Pres.: DAVID RHODES
Exec. Vice-Pres.: ANTHONY P. RHODES
Provost: JEFFREY NESIN
Chief Financial Officer: GARY SHILLET
Exec. Dir for Student Affairs: JAVIER VEGA
Dir for Institutional Research: JEROLD L.
DAVIS
Registrar: JON TODD
Library Dir: ROBERT LOBE
Library of 72,000 vols, 450 magazines and
journals subscription
Number of teachers: 1,000
Number of students: 3,980 (3,416 under-
graduate, 564 graduate)
Publication: *Visual Arts Journal*

SEMINARY OF THE IMMACULATE CONCEPTION

440 W Neck Rd, Huntington, NY 11743
Telephone: (631) 423-0483
E-mail: info@icseminary.edu
Internet: www.icseminary.edu
Founded 1930
Private control
Rector: Rev. Mgr PETER I. VACCARI
Vice-Rector: Rev. Mgr RICHARD HENNING
Academic Dean: Dr Sis. MARY LOUISE BRINK
Dean for Seminarians: Rev. NICHOLAS ZIEN-
TARSKI
Dir for Library and Information Services:
ELYSE HAYES
Library of 50,000 vols, 250 journals subscrip-
tion, 600 audiovisual items, 4,000 old and
rare books
Number of teachers: 14
Publication: *Seat of Wisdom* (online,
www.seatofwisdomjournal.org)

SIENA COLLEGE

515 Loudon Rd, Loudonville, NY 12211-1462
Telephone: (518) 783-2300
E-mail: website@siena.edu
Internet: www.siena.edu
Founded 1937
Private control
Academic year: September to May
Pres.: Fr Dr KEVIN MULLEN
Vice-Pres. for Academic Affairs: Dr LINDA
RICHARDSON
Vice-Pres. for Devt and External Affairs:
DAVID SMITH
Vice-Pres. for Enrolment Management: NED
JONES
Vice-Pres. for Finance and Admin.: PAUL
STEC
Vice-Pres. for Student Affairs: Dr MARYELLEN
GILROY
Chief of Staff: KEN PAULLI
Library Dir: GARY B. THOMPSON
Library of 3,604,698 vols
Number of teachers: 355 (210 full-time, 145
part-time)
Number of students: 3,270
Publications: *Pendragon* (1 a year), *The Saga*
(1 a year)

DEANS

School of Business: Dr JEFFREY A. MELLO
School of Liberal Arts: Dr JANET SHIDELER
School of Science: Dr ALLAN WEATHERWAX

SKIDMORE COLLEGE

815 N Broadway, Saratoga Springs, NY
12866
Telephone: (518) 580-5000
E-mail: info@skidmore.edu
Internet: www.skidmore.edu
Founded 1903 as Young Women's Industrial
Club of Saratoga, present name and status
1922
Private control
Academic year: September to May
Liberal arts college
Pres.: PHILIP A. GLOTZBACH
Vice-Pres. for Academic Affairs: Dr SUSAN A.
KRESS
Vice-Pres. for Advancement: MICHAEL CASEY
Vice-Pres. for Finance and Admin., Treas.:
MICHAEL D. WEST
Dean for Faculty: BEAU BRESLIN
Dean for Spec. Programmes: Prof. PAUL
CALHOUN
Dean for Student Affairs: W. ROCHELLE
CALHOUN
Dean for Admissions and Student Aid: MARY
LOU BATES
Dir for Alumni Affairs: MIKE SPOSILI
Librarian: RUTH S. COPANS
Registrar: DAVE DeCONNO
Library of 400,000 vols
Number of teachers: 250 (full-time)
Number of students: 2,400
Publications: *Salmagundi* (4 a year), *Scope* (3
a year)

STATE UNIVERSITY OF NEW YORK

State Univ. Plaza, 353 Broadway, Albany,
NY 12246
Telephone: (518) 320-1100
E-mail: asksuny@suny.edu
Internet: www.suny.edu
Founded 1816
Chancellor: NANCY L. ZIMPHER
Provost and Exec. Vice-Chancellor: DAVID K.
LAVALLEE
Sr Vice-Chancellor, Sec. and Gen. Counsel:
WILLIAM F. HOWARD
Sr Vice-Chancellor for Community Colleges:
JOHANNA DUNCAN-POITIER
Vice-Chancellor for Academic Programmes
and Planning and Vice-Provost: ELIZABETH
L. BRINGSJORD
Vice-Chancellor for Financial Services and
Chief Financial Officer: BRIAN HUTZLEY
Vice-Chancellor for Global Affairs: MITCH
LEVENTHAL
Vice-Chancellor for Human Resources: CUR-
TIS L. LLOYD
Library: 18m. vols
Number of teachers: 33,500 (full-time)
Number of students: 468,000 (426,400
undergraduate, 41,600 graduate)
Publication: *SUNYergy* (4 a year, online)...

CAMPUSES

University at Albany

1400 Washington Ave, Albany, NY 12222
Telephone: (518) 442-3305
E-mail: geninfo@uamail.albany.edu
Internet: www.albany.edu
Founded 1844, present status 1962
Academic year: August to May
Pres.: GEORGE M. PHILIP
Provost and Vice-Pres. for Academic Affairs:
SUSAN D. PHILLIPS
Vice-Provost for Enrolment Management:
WAYNE A. LOCUST
Vice-Pres. for Communications and Market-
ing: CATHERINE HERMAN
Vice-Pres. for Finance and Business: STE-
PHEN J. BEDITZ

Vice-Pres. for Research: JAMES A. DIAS
Vice-Pres. for Student Success: CHRISTINE A.
BOUCHARD
Vice-Pres. for Univ. Devt: FARDIN SANAI
Sr Counsel: JOHN H. REILLY
Chief Information Officer: CHRISTINE HAILE
Library of 1,613,524 vols
Number of teachers: 1,000
Number of students: 17,600 (12,950 under-
graduate, 4,650 graduate)
Publication: *UAlbany*

DEANS

College of Arts and Sciences: Dr EDELGARD
WULFERT
College of Computing and Information:
PETER A. BLONIARZ
Rockefeller College of Public Affairs and
Policy: DAVID L. ROUSSEAU
School of Business: Prof. DONALD SIEGEL
School of Criminal Justice: Prof. Dr ALAN
LIZOTTE
School of Education: ROBERT L. BANGERT-
DROWNS
School of Public Health: Dr PHILIP C. NASCA
School of Social Welfare: Prof. Dr KATHARINE
BRIAR-LAWSON

Binghamton University

POB 6000, Binghamton, NY 13902-6000
4400 Vestal Parkway E, Binghamton, NY
13902
Telephone: (607) 777-2000
E-mail: info@binghamton.edu
Internet: www.binghamton.edu
Founded 1946
Academic year: August to May
Pres.: Dr HARVEY G. STENGER
Provost and Vice-Pres. for Academic Affairs:
DONALD G. NIEMAN
Vice-Pres. for Admin.: JAMES VAN VOORST
Vice-Pres. for External Affairs: MARCIA CRA-
NER
Vice-Pres. for Research: BAHGAT SAMMAKIA
Vice-Pres. for Student Affairs: BRIAN ROSE
Library of 2,380,358 vols, 1,869,980 micro-
forms, 81,959 journal holdings, 2,671 CD-
ROMs, 118,937 sound recordings, 120,955
maps, 3,518 video cassettes and DVDs and
212 e-databases
Number of teachers: 845
Number of students: 14,750 (11,865 under-
graduate and 2,885 graduate)
Publication: *Binghamton Magazine*

DEANS

College of Community and Public Affairs:
LAURA BRONSTEIN
Decker School of Nursing: Prof. Dr JOYCE
FERRARIO
Graduate School: NANCY E. STAMP
Harpur College of Arts and Sciences: (vacant)
School of Management: Dr UPINDER DHILLON
S. G. Grant Graduate School of Education:
Dr S. G. GRANT
Thomas J. Watson School of Engineering and
Applied Science: Dr KRISHNASWAMI SRIHARI

University at Buffalo

12 Capen Hall, Buffalo, NY 14260-1660
Telephone: (716) 645-2400
E-mail: ubinfo@buffalo.edu
Internet: www.buffalo.edu
Founded 1846
Academic year: August to May
Pres.: SATISH K. TRIPATHI
Provost and Exec. Vice-Pres. for Academic
Affairs: BRUCE D. McCOMBE
Senior Vice-Pres.: ROBERT J. WAGNER
Vice-Pres. for Devt and Alumni Relations:
NANCY L. WELLS
Vice-Pres. for Finance and Admin.: LAURA E.
HUBBARD

Vice-Pres. for Health Sciences: MICHAEL E. CAIN
Vice-Pres. for Research and Economic Devt: ALEXANDER N. CARTWRIGHT
Vice-Pres. for Univ. Life and Services: DENNIS R. BLACK
Library: 3.6m. vols, 30,000 journals
Number of teachers: 2,260 (1,577 full-time, 683 part-time)
Number of students: 28,600 (19,057 undergraduate, 9,543 graduate and professional)
Publications: *buffaloBOOKS*, *Intersight*

DEANS

College of Arts and Sciences: E. BRUCE PITMAN
Graduate School of Education: Dr MARY H. GRESHAM
Law School: MAKAU W. MUTUA
School of Architecture and Planning: ROBERT G. SHIBLEY
School of Dental Medicine: Dr MICHAEL L. GLICK
School of Engineering and Applied Sciences: RAJAN BATTA (acting)
School of Management: ARJANG A. ASSAD
School of Medicine and Biomedical Sciences: Dr MICHAEL E. CAIN
School of Nursing: Dr MARSHA L. LEWIS
School of Pharmacy and Pharmaceutical Sciences: Dr WAYNE K. ANDERSON
School of Public Health and Health Professions: Dr LYNN T. KOZLOWSKI
School of Social Work: Prof. NANCY J. SMYTH

Stony Brook University

Stony Brook, NY 11794
Telephone: (631) 632-6000
E-mail: enroll@stonybrook.edu
Internet: www.stonybrook.edu
Founded 1957
Academic year: August to May
Pres.: SAMUEL L. STANLEY, JR
Provost and Sr Vice-Pres. for Academic Affairs: DENNIS N. ASSANIS
Vice-Pres. for Economic Devt: YACOV SHAMASH
Vice-Pres. for Facilities and Services: BARBARA CHERNOW
Vice-Pres. for Finance and Admin.: KAROL KAIN GRAY
Vice-Pres. for Research: Dr JOHN HARMEN MARBURGER, III
Library: 2.1 m. vols, incl. 130,000 maps, 11,000 books and 8,000 DVDs
Number of teachers: 2,200
Number of students: 24,100

DEANS

College of Arts and Sciences: Dr NANCY SQUIRES
College of Business: Dr MANUEL LONDON
College of Engineering and Applied Sciences: YACOV SHAMASH
Graduate School: LAWRENCE MARTIN
School of Dental Medicine: Dr RAY C. WILLIAMS
School of Health Technology and Management: Dr CRAIG LEHMANN
School of Journalism: HOWARD SCHNEIDER
School of Marine and Atmospheric Sciences: MINGHUA ZHANG
School of Medicine: Dr KENNETH KAUSHANSKY
School of Nursing: Dr LEE ANNE XIPPOLITOS
School of Professional Devt: Dr PAUL JAY EDELSON
School of Social Welfare: Dr FRANCES L. BRISBANE
Undergraduate Colleges: CHARLES ROBBINS..

UNIVERSITY COLLEGES

State University College at Buffalo: 1300 Elmwood Ave, Buffalo, NY 14222; tel. (716) 878-4000; e-mail admissions@buffalostate .edu; internet www.buffalostate.edu; f. 1871; Pres. Dr AARON PODOLEFSKY; Provost Dr DENNIS K PONTON; Vice-Pres. for Finance and Management Dr STANLEY KARDONSKY; Vice-Pres. for Student Affairs HAL D. PAYNE; Assoc. Vice-Pres. Vice-Pres. MARYRUTH F. GLOGOWSKI; library of 675,000 vols; 1,792 teachers (1,221 full-time, 571 part-time); 11,695 students (9,788 undergraduate, 1,907 graduate).

State University College at Cortland: POB 2000, Cortland, NY 13045-0900; tel. (607) 753-2011; e-mail registrar@cortland .edu; internet www2.cortland.edu/home; f. 1868; Pres. Dr ERIK J. BITTERBAUM; Provost Vice-Pres. for Student Affairs C. GREGORY SHARER; Vice-Pres. for Finance and Management WILLIAM E. SHAUT; Vice-Pres. for Institutional Advancement RAYMOND D. FRANCO; Dir for Libraries GAIL WOOD; 578 teachers (301 full-time, 277 part-time); 7,358 students (6,310 undergraduate, 1,048 graduate).

State University College at Fredonia: 280 Central Ave., Fredonia, NY 14063; tel. (716) 673-3111; e-mail admissions@fredonia .edu; internet www.fredonia.edu; f. 1826; Pres. DENNIS L. HEFNER; Vice-Pres. Dr VIRGINIA SCHAEFER HORVATH; Vice-Pres. for Univ. Advancement DAVID TIFFANY; Assoc. Vice-Pres. for Admin. JUDY LANGWORTHY; Dir for Admissions CHRISTOPHER DEARTH; Librarian RANDY GADIKIAN; 474 teachers (251 full-time; 223 part-time); 5,730 students (5,398 undergraduate, 332 graduate).

State University College at Geneseo: One College Circle, Geneseo, NY 14454; tel. (585) 245-5000; e-mail admissions@geneseo .edu; internet www.geneseo.edu; f. 1871; Pres. CHRISTOPHER C. DAHL; Provost Dr CAROL LONG; Vice-Pres. for Admin. and Finance Dr JAMES B. MILROY; Registrar DELBERT BROWN; Dir for Libraries CYRIL OBERLANDER; library of 516,700 vols; 265 (full-time) teachers; 5,038 students (4,950 undergraduate, 88 graduate).

State University College at New Paltz: One Hawk Dr., New Paltz, NY 12561; tel. (845) 257-2121; e-mail admissions@newpaltz .edu; internet www.newpaltz.edu; f. 1828 as New Paltz Classic Acad.; Pres. Dr DONALD P. CHRISTIAN; Provost and Vice-Pres. for Academic Affairs CHERYL B. TORSNEY; Vice-Pres. for Enrolment Management L. DAVID EATON; Dean for Library CHUI-CHUN LEE; library of 500,000 vols; 325 (full-time) teachers; 7,885 students (6,582 undergraduate, 1,303 graduate).

State University College at Old Westbury: POB 210, Old Westbury, NY 11568-0210; tel. (516) 876-3000; e-mail enroll@ oldwestbury.edu; internet www.oldwestbury .edu; f. 1965; Pres. Dr CALVIN O. BUTTS, III; Provost and Vice-Pres. for Academic Affairs PATRICK O'SULLIVAN; Vice-Pres. for Enrolment Services MARYBOOK MARQUEZ BELL; Vice-Pres. for Student Affairs Dr ML LANGLIE; Registrar PATRICIA A. SMITH; Library Dir STEPHEN KIRKPATRICK; 122 (full-time) teachers; 3,300 students.

State University College at Oneonta: 108 Ravine Parkway, Oneonta, NY 13820; tel. (607) 436-3500; e-mail admissions@oneonta .edu; internet www.oneonta.edu; f. 1889; academic year August to DecemberJanuary to May (2 semesters); Pres. Dr NANCY KLENIEWSKI; Vice-Pres. for Finance and Admin. TODD FOREMAN; Vice-Pres. for Student Devt STEVEN R. PERRY; Registrar MAUREEN P. ARTALE; Dir for Admissions KAREN BROWN; Dir for Library MARY LYNN BENSEN; library of 500,000 vols; 503 teachers (258 full-time, 245 part-time); 6,000 students.

State University College at Oswego: 7060 Route 104, Oswego, NY 13126-3599; tel. (315) 312-2500; e-mail admiss@oswego .edu; internet www.oswego.edu; f. 1861 as Oswego Primary Teachers' Training School; Pres. DEBORAH F. STANLEY; Vice-Pres. for Academic Affairs and Provost LORRIE CLEMO; Vice-Pres. for Admin. and Finance NICHOLAS LYONS; Vice-Pres. for Student Affairs and Enrolment JOSEPH F. GRANT, JR; library of 450,000 vols; 8,212 students (7,212 undergraduate, 928 graduate).

State University College at Plattsburgh: 101 Broad St, Plattsburgh, NY 12901; tel. (518) 564-2000; e-mail admissions@ plattsburgh.edu; internet www.plattsburgh .edu; Pres. Dr JOHN ETTLING; Provost and Vice-Pres. for Academic Affairs Dr JAMES LISZKA; Vice-Pres. for Admin. JOHN R. HOMBURGER; Vice-Pres. for Institutional Advancement ANNE HANSEN; Vice-Pres. for Student Affairs WILLIAM D. LAUNDRY; Dean for Library and Information Services CERISE G. OBERMAN; 6,496 students (5,906 undergraduate, 547 graduate).

State University College at Purchase: 735 Anderson Hill Rd, Purchase, NY 10577; tel. (914) 251-6000; e-mail admissions@ purchase.edu; internet www.purchase.edu; f. 1967; Pres. THOMAS J. SCHWARZ; Provost and Exec. Vice-Pres. for Academic Affairs BARBARA B. DIXON; Vice-Pres. for Enrolment Management DENNIS CRAIG; Vice-Pres. for Student Affairs ROBIN KAUFMAN; Dir for Library PATRICK CALLAHAN; 4,200 students.

State University Empire State College: Two Union Ave, Saratoga Springs, NY 12866; tel. (518) 587-2100; e-mail admissions@esc.edu; internet www.esc.edu; f. 1971; Pres. ALAN R. DAVIS; Provost and Vice-Pres. for Academic Affairs MEG BENKE; Vice-Pres. for Admin. PAUL TUCCI; Vice-Pres. for Enrolment Management and Student Services HUGH B. HAMMETT; 1,400 teachers (250 full-time, 1,150 part-time).

State University of New York at Potsdam: 44 Pierrepont Ave, Potsdam, NY 13676; tel. (315) 267-2000; e-mail admissions@potsdam.edu; internet www .potsdam.edu; f. 1816 as St Lawrence Acad., present status 1948; academic year August to May; Pres. JOHN F. SCHWALLER; Provost MARGARET MADDEN; Vice-Pres. for Institutional Effectiveness and Enrolment Management RICK A. MILLER; Dir for Libraries JENICA ROGERS; 4,423 students (3,988 undergraduate, 435 graduate).

State University of New York—College at Brockport: 350 New Campus Dr., Brockport, NY 14420; tel. (585) 395-2119; e-mail iss@brockport.edu; internet www.brockport .edu; f. 1835; Pres. Dr JOHN R. HALSTEAD; Provost and Vice-Pres. for Academic Affairs Dr MARY ELLEN ZUCKERMAN; Vice-Pres. for Admin. and Finance LOUIS SPIRO; Vice-Pres. for Advancement ROXANNE JOHNSTON; Vice-Pres. for Enrolment Management and Student Affairs KATHRYN WILSON; Chief Communications Officer DAVID MIHALYOV; library of 511,605 vols, 11,880 video cassettes and DVDs, 107,000 periodicals; 594 teachers; 8,413 students (7,166 undergraduate, 1,247 graduate); publ. *Kaleidoscope.*.

COLLEGES OF TECHNOLOGY

State University of New York—Alfred State: 10 Upper College Dr., Alfred, NY 14802; tel. (607) 587-4215; e-mail admissions@alfredstate.edu; internet www .alfredstate.edu; f. 1908; Pres. Dr SKIP SULLIVAN; Vice-Pres. for Academic Affairs CRAIG CLARK; Vice-Pres. for Admin. and Enrolment VALERIE NIXON; Vice-Pres. for Student Affairs Dr STEVE TYRELL; Dir for Libraries DAVID HAGGSTROM; library of 59,000 vols, 141 journal titles and 96,854 full-text periodicals; 203 (full-time) teachers; 3,500 students.

State University of New York College of Technology at Canton: 34 Cornell Dr., Canton, NY 13617; tel. (315) 386-7011; e-mail admissions@canton.edu; internet www.canton.edu; Pres. JOSEPH L. KENNEDY; Provost and Vice-Pres. for Academic Affairs Dr CARLI SCHIFFNER; Vice-Pres. for Student Affairs Dr MOLLY MOTT; Dir for Library Services MICHELLE CURRIER; 3,800 students.

State University of New York College of Agriculture and Technology at Cobleskill: State Route 7, Cobleskill, NY 12043; tel. (518) 255-5700; internet www.cobleskill .edu; e-mail admissions@cobleskill.edu; f. 1916; Officer-in-Charge CANDACE S. VANCKO; Provost and Vice-Pres. for Academic Affairs DEBRA H. THATCHER; Vice-Pres. for Student Devt STEVEN M. ACKERKNECHT; Vice-Pres. for Institutional Advancement REGINA M. LaGATTA; Dean for Library ELIZABETH D. ORGERON; library of 77,000 vols, 5,400 audiovisual materials; 200 teachers.

State University of New York College of Technology at Delhi: Two Main St, Delhi, NY 13753-1190; e-mail enroll@delhi.edu; internet www.delhi.edu; f. 1913; Pres. Dr CANDACE VANCKO; Provost Dr JOHN NADER; Vice-Pres. for Finance and Admin. CAROL BISHOP; Vice-Pres. for Student Life BARBARA JONES; Dir for Library PAM PETERS; library of 50,000 vols, 30,000 online magazines and journals; 3,100 students.

State University of New York College of Technology at Farmingdale: 2350 Broadhollow Rd, Farmingdale, NY 11735-1021; tel. (631) 420-2000; e-mail admissions@ farmingdale.edu; internet www.farmingdale .edu; f. 1912; Pres. Dr W. HUBERT KEEN; Provost and Vice-Pres. for Academic Affairs Dr LUCIA CEPRIANO (acting); Sr Vice-Pres. and CFO GEORGE P. LaROSA; Vice-Pres. for Institutional Advancement PATRICK CALABRIA; Vice-Pres. for Student Affairs Dr TOM CORTI; Dir for Information Resources MICHAEL KNAUTH; 512 teachers; 6,988 students.

State University of New York College of Agriculture and Technology at Morrisville: POB 901, 80 Eaton St, Morrisville, NY 13408-0636; tel. (315) 684-6000; e-mail admissions@morrisville.edu; internet www .morrisville.edu; Pres. RICHARD J. CARRENO; Vice-Pres. for Academic Affairs DAVID E. ROGERS; Dir for Libraries CHRISTINE RUDECOFF; library of 95,000 vols, 250 print magazine and newspaper subscriptions, 1,600 audio and video recordings..

SPECIALIZED COLLEGES

State University Institute of Technology at Utica/Rome: 100 Seymour Rd, Utica, NY 13502; tel. (315) 792-7500; e-mail admissions@sunyit.edu; internet www .sunyit.edu; f. 1966; academic year August to May; Pres. Prof. BJONG WOLF YEIGH; Provost WILLIAM W. DURGIN; Vice-Pres. for Admin. BRUCE REICHEL; Registrar JOHN LASHER.

State University of New York College of Environmental Science and Forestry: One Forestry Dr., Syracuse, NY 13210; tel. (315) 470-6500; e-mail esfinfo@esf.edu; internet www.esf.edu; f. 1911 as New York State College of Forestry at Syracuse Univ.; Pres. Dr CORNELIUS B. MURPHY, JR; Provost and Vice-Pres. for Academic Affairs BRUCE C. BONGARTEN; Vice-Pres. for Admin. JOSEPH L. RUFO; Vice-Pres. for Enrolment Management and Marketing ROBERT C. FRENCH; 174 teachers (127 full-time, 47 part-time); 2,718 students (543 graduate, 1,586 full-time and 587 part-time undergraduate).

State University of New York College of Optometry at New York City: 33 W 42nd St, New York, NY 10036; tel. (212) 938-4000; e-mail admissions@sunyopt.edu; internet www.sunyopt.edu; f. 1971; Chancellor Dr NANCY L. ZIMPHER; Pres. DAVID A. HEATH; Vice-Pres. and Dean for Academic Affairs Dr DAVID TROILO; Vice-Pres. for Admin. and Finance DAVID BOWERS; Vice-Pres. for Clinical Affairs Dr RICHARD SODEN; Vice-Pres. for Institutional Advancement ANN WARWICK; Vice-Pres. for Student Affairs Dr JEFFREY PHILPOTT; Dir for Library Services ELAINE WELLS; library of 40,000 vols; 126 teachers (60 full-time, 60 part-time); 315 students.

SUNY Downstate Medical Center: 450 Clarkson Ave, Brooklyn, NY 11203; tel. (718) 270-1000; e-mail admissions@downstate.edu; internet www.downstate.edu; f. 1962; Pres. Dr JOHN C. LaROSA; Vice-Pres. and Chief Financial Officer ALAN DZIJA; Dir for Admissions Dr SHUSHAWNA DeOLIVEIRA; library of 67,078 vols, 388,320 journals, 4,000 ejournals and 356 ebooks.

State University of New York Maritime College: 6 Pennyfield Ave, Throggs Neck, NY 10465; tel. (718) 409-7200; e-mail admissions@sunymaritime.edu; internet www.sunymaritime.edu; Pres. Rear-Admiral WENDI B. CARPENTER; Provost and Vice-Pres. for Academic Affairs Dr JOSEPH C. HOFFMAN, JR; 1,850 students.

Upstate Medical University: 750 E Adams St, Syracuse, NY 13210-2375; tel. (315) 464-5540; e-mail admiss@upstate.edu; internet www.upstate.edu; f. 1834; Pres. Dr DAVID R. SMITH; Sr Vice-Pres. for Admin. and Finance STEVEN C. BRADY; Sr Vice-Pres. for Hospital Affairs Dr JOHN McCABE; Sr Vice-Pres. for Operations Dr WANDA M. THOMPSON; library of 220,160 vols, 730 ebooks, 146,482 journals, 4,331 audiovisual items; 669 teachers (488 full-time, 181 part-time); 1,542 students

SYRACUSE UNIVERSITY

Syracuse, NY 13244-5040

Telephone: (315) 443-1870

E-mail: gradinfo@syr.edu

Internet: www.syr.edu

Founded 1870

Private control

Academic year: August to July

Campuses in Los Angeles, Washington DC, New York city; 8 overseas centres: Beijing, People's Republic of China; Florence, Italy; Hong Kong; Istanbul, Turkey; London, United Kingdom; Madrid, Spain; Santiago, Chile; Strasbourg, France

Chancellor and Pres.: NANCY CANTOR

Vice-Chancellor and Provost: ERIC F. SPINA

Sr Vice-Pres. and Dean for Student Affairs: THOMAS V. WOLFE

Sr Vice-Pres. and Gen. Counsel: THOMAS EVANS

Sr Vice-Pres. for Public Affairs: KEVIN C. QUINN

Exec. Vice-Pres. for Advancement and External Affairs: THOMAS J. WALSH

Exec. Vice-Pres. and Chief Financial Officer: LOUIS G. MARCOCCIA

Vice-Pres. for Business Operations: JENA PRIDEAUX McWHA

Vice-Pres. for Community Engagement and Economic Devt: MARILYN HIGGINS

Vice-Pres. for Enrolment Management: DONALD A. SALEH

Vice-Pres. for Information Technology and Chief Information Officer: CHRISTOPHER M. SEDORE

Vice-Pres. for Research: GINA LEE-GLAUSER

Registrar: JERRY P. ROSS

Dean for Library: SUZANNE THORIN

Library: see under Libraries and Archives

Number of teachers: 1,513 (981 full-time, 86 part-time, 446 adjunct)

Number of students: 20,407 (13,504 full-time undergraduate, 697 part-time undergraduate, 4,381 full-time graduate and law school, 1,825 part-time graduate and law school)

Publications: *Syracuse Law Review* (4 a year), *Syracuse University Magazine* (3 a year)

DEANS

College of Arts and Sciences: GEORGE M. LANGFORD

College of Law: HANNAH R. ARTERIAN

College of Visual and Performing Arts: ANN CLARKE

David B. Falk College of Sport and Human Dynamics: DIANE LYDEN MURPHY

Graduate School: BEN WARE

L. C. Smith College of Engineering and Computer Science: LAURA J. STEINBERG

Martin J. Whitman School of Management: MELVIN T. STITH

Maxwell School of Citizenship and Public Affairs: JAMES B. STEINBERG

School of Architecture: MARK ROBBINS

School of Education: DOUGLAS BIKLEN

School of Information Studies: ELIZABETH D. LIDDY

S. I. Newhouse School of Public Communications: LORRAINE BRANHAM

University College: BETHAIDA GONZÁLEZ

TOURO COLLEGE

27–33 W 23 St, New York, NY 10010

Telephone: (212) 463-0400

Internet: www.touro.edu

Founded 1970

Private control

Campuses in: Manhattan, Brooklyn, Queens, Long Island, California, Florida, Nevada, Israel, Italy and Germany; incl. New York Medical College

Chancellor: DONIEL LANDER

Pres.: Dr ALAN KADISH

Sr Vice-Pres. and Chief Admin. Officer: ALAN P. SCHOOR

Sr Vice-Pres. and Chief Financial Officer: MELVIN NESS

Sr Vice-Pres. for College Affairs: MOSHE KRUPKA

Sr Vice-Pres. for Graduate and Professional Education: SHALOM Z. HIRSCHMAN

Vice-Pres. for Academic Affairs: Dr JAY SEXTER

Vice-Pres. for Institutional Advancement: ERIC LEVINE

Vice-Pres. for Int. Affairs: Dr ISRAEL SINGER

Vice-Pres. for Planning and Assessment and Dean of Students: ROBERT GOLDSCHMIDT

Vice-Pres. for Undergraduate Education and Dean of Faculties: Dr STANLEY L. BOYLAN

Dir for Libraries: BASHE SIMON

Library of 183,700 vols, incl. 550 print journals

Number of teachers: 4,930 (2,091 full-time, 1,317 part-time, 1,522 clinical)

Number of students: 19,000

Publication: *Touro Lawyer*

DEANS

Graduate School of Business: MICHAEL WILLIAMS

Graduate School of Education: Dr LaMAR P. MILLER

Graduate School of Jewish Studies: Dr MICHAEL SHMIDMAN

Graduate School of Psychology: Dr RICHARD WAXMAN

Graduate School of Social Work: Dr STEVEN HUBERMAN

Graduate School of Technology: Dr ISSAC HERSKOWITZ
School of Health Sciences: Dr LOUIS H. PRIMAVERA
Touro College of Osteopathic Medicine: Dr ROBERT B. GOLDBERG
Touro College Jacob D. Fuchsberg Law Center: LAWRENCE RAFUL
Touro College of Pharmacy: Dr STUART FELDMAN

UNIFICATION THEOLOGICAL SEMINARY

30 Seminary Dr., Barrytown, NY 12507

Telephone: (845) 752-3000
E-mail: registrar@uts.edu
Internet: www.uts.edu

Founded 1975
Private control
Language of instruction: English
Academic year: August to May

Pres.: Dr RICHARD A. PANZER
Vice-Pres. for Academic Affairs: Dr KATHY WININGS
Dir for Admissions: (vacant)
Dir for Student Life: RACHEL CURRY
Dean for the Undergraduate Program: Dr STEPHEN MURRAY
Registrar: UTE DELANEY
Library Dir: Dr KEISUKE NODA

Library of 50,000 vols
Number of teachers: 20
Number of students: 100

Publication: *Journal of Unification Studies* (1 a year)

UNION COLLEGE

807 Union St, Schenectady, NY 12308

Telephone: (518) 388-6000
E-mail: admissions@union.edu
Internet: www.union.edu

Founded 1795
Private control
Academic year: September to June

Courses in humanities, social sciences, sciences and engineering

Pres.: STEPHEN C. AINLAY
Vice-Pres. for Academic Affairs and Dean for Faculty: THERESE McCARTY
Vice-Pres. for Admissions, Financial Aid and Enrolment: MATTHEW MALATESTA
Vice-Pres. for College Relations: STEPHEN DARE
Vice-Pres. for Finance and Admin.: DIANE BLAKE
Vice-Pres. for Student Affairs and Dean for Students: STEPHEN LEAVITT
Dir for Admissions: ANN FLEMING BROWN
Registrar: PENELOPE ADEY
College Librarian: FRANCES MALOY

Library of 617,945 vols
Number of teachers: 200 (full-time)
Number of students: 2,185 (full-time)

Publications: *President's Report* (1 a year), *Union College Magazine* (4 a year)

UNION GRADUATE COLLEGE

80 Nott Terrace, Schenectady, NY 12308

Telephone: (518) 631-9900
E-mail: info@uniongraduatecollege.edu
Internet: www.uniongraduatecollege.edu; attached to Union College

Private control
Academic year: May to June

Pres.: Dr LAURA SCHWEITZER
Vice-Pres. for Enrolment: JOANNE FITZGERALD
Vice-Pres. for Finance and Operations: JOSEPH M. McDONALD
Vice-Pres. for Institutional Advancement: DAN CHRISTOPHER

Registrar and Dir for Admissions: RHONDA SHEEHAN
Dir for Library Services: MARY ANNE WALTZ

DEANS

School of Education: Dr PATRICK F. ALLEN
School of Engineering and Computer Science: ROBERT KOZIK
School of Management: BELA MUSITS

UNION THEOLOGICAL SEMINARY

3041 Broadway, 121st St, New York, NY 10027

Telephone: (212) 662-7100
E-mail: contactus@uts.columbia.edu
Internet: www.uts.columbia.edu

Founded 1836
Private control
Academic year: September to May

Pres.: Rev. Dr SERENE JONES
Exec. Vice-Pres.: FREDERICK DAVIE
Vice-Pres. for Finance and Operations: RICHARD A. MADONNA, JR
Vice-Pres. for Institutional Advancement: BOB BOMERSBACH
Academic Dean: ROSEMARY SKINNER KELLER
Dean for Academic Affairs: DAISY MACHADO
Dir for Admissions and Financial Aid: NICHELLE JENKINS
Registrar: EDITH T. HUNTER
Library Dir: SARA J. MYERS

Library of 700,000 vols
Number of teachers: 45
Number of students: 285

Publications: *The Union Seminary Quarterly Review*, *Union Now* (2 a year)

UNITED STATES MILITARY ACADEMY

606 Thayer Rd, West Point, NY 10996-1797

Telephone: (845) 938-4041
E-mail: admissions@usma.edu
Internet: www.usma.edu

Founded 1802

Superintendent: Lt-Gen. DAVID HUNTOON
Commandant of Cadets: Brig. Gen. THEODORE D. MARTIN
Dean for Academic Board: Brig. Gen. TIMOTHY TRAINOR
Vice-Dean of Education: Dr JEAN BLAIR
Dir for Academic Affairs: Dr BRUCE KEITH
Dir for Admissions: Col DEBORAH McDONALD
Librarian and Assoc. Dean: Dr CHRISTOPHER BARTH

Library of 460,000 vols, 60,000 journals
Number of teachers: 560
Number of students: 4,400

UNIVERSITY OF ROCHESTER

500 Joseph C. Wilson Blvd, Rochester, NY 14627

Telephone: (585) 275-2121
E-mail: admit@rochester.edu
Internet: www.rochester.edu

Founded 1850
Private control
Academic year: September to May (two terms)

Pres.: JOEL SELIGMAN
Provost and Exec. Vice-Pres.: RALPH KUNCL
Sr Vice-Pres. and Robert L. and Mary L. Sproull Dean of the Faculty of Arts, Sciences and Engineering: PETER LENNIE
Sr Vice-Pres. and Chief Advancement Officer: JAMES D. THOMPSON
Sr Vice-Pres. and Gen. Counsel: SUE S. STEWART
Sr Vice-Pres. for Admin. and Finance, Chief Financial Officer and Treas.: RONALD J. PAPROCKI

Sr Vice-Pres. for Health Sciences: BRADFORD C. BERK
Sr Vice-Pres. for Institutional Resources: DOUGLAS W. PHILLIPS
Sr Vice-Pres. and Gen. Sec.: SUE S. STEWART
Vice-Pres. for Communications: BILL MURPHY
Univ. Dean: PAUL J. BURGETT
Dean for Research: PAUL SLATTERY
Registrar: NANCY SPECK
Dean for River Campus Libraries: SUSAN GIBBONS

Library: see under Libraries and Archives
Number of teachers: 2,000
Number of students: 8,570 (5,360 undergraduate, 3,210 graduate)

DEANS

Eastman School of Music: DOUGLAS LOWRY
Graduate Studies: WENDI HEINZELMAN
Hajim School of Engineering and Applied Sciences: ROBERT CLARK
Margaret Warner Graduate School of Education and Human Devt: RAFFAELLA BORASI
School of Arts and Sciences: JOANNA B. OLMSTED
School of Medicine and Dentistry: Dr MARK B. TAUBMAN
School of Nursing: KATHY H. RIDEOUT
Simon School of Business: MARK ZUPAN

US MERCHANT MARINE ACADEMY

300 Steamboat Rd, Kings Point, NY 11024-1699

Telephone: (516) 726-5800
E-mail: admissions@usmma.edu
Internet: www.usmma.edu

Founded 1943
State control
Academic year: July to June

Superintendent and Academic Dean: Dr SHASHI KUMAR
Chief of Staff: Capt. ERIC YORK WALLISCHECK
Dir for Admissions: Capt. ROBERT JOHNSON
Librarian: GEORGE BILLY

Library of 180,000 vols
Number of teachers: 80
Number of students: 950 midshipmen

UTICA COLLEGE

1600 Burrstone Rd, Utica, NY 13502

Telephone: (315) 792-3006
E-mail: admiss@utica.edu
Internet: www.utica.edu

Founded 1946
Private control
Academic year: August to August

Pres.: Dr TODD S. HUTTON
Provost and Vice-Pres. for Academic Affairs: Dr JUDITH A. KIRKPATRICK
Sr Vice-Pres. and Chief Advancement Officer: LAURA CASAMENTO
Vice-Pres. for Enrolment Management: PATRICK QUINN
Vice-Pres. for Financial Affairs and Treas.: R. BARRY WHITE
Vice-Pres. for Legal Affairs and Gen. Counsel: WALTER DeSOCIO
Vice-Pres. for Planning and Analysis: CAROL MACKINTOSH
Vice-Pres. for Strategic Initiatives: JAMES BROWN
Vice-Pres. for Student Affairs: STEVE PATTARINI
Asst Vice-Pres. for Library and Information Technology Services: BEVERLY MARCOLINE

Library of 192,500 vols, 40,000 microform units, 1,250 serial subscriptions, 1,000 online journals
Number of teachers: 130 (full-time)
Number of students: 3,100 (2,540 undergraduate, and 740 graduate)

VASSAR COLLEGE

124 Raymond Ave, Poughkeepsie, NY 12604
Telephone: (845) 437-7000
E-mail: admissions@vassar.edu
Internet: www.vassar.edu
Founded 1861
Academic year: September to May
Pres.: CATHERINE BOND HILL
Vice-Pres. for Alumni Affairs and Devt: CATHERINE BAER
Vice-Pres. for Finance and Treas.: ELIZABETH EISMEIER
Dir for College Relations: SUSAN DEKREY
Dean for College: CHRISTOPHER F. ROELLKE
Dean for Faculty: JONATHAN L. CHENETTE
Dean for Students: DAVID BROWN
Dean for Studies: JOANNE LONG
Registrar: COLLEEN R. MALLET
Dir for Libraries: SABRINA PAPE
Library: see under Libraries and Archives
Number of teachers: 290
Number of students: 2,400

VAUGHN COLLEGE OF AERONAUTICS AND TECHNOLOGY

86-01 23rd Ave, Flushing, NY 11369
Telephone: (718) 429-6600
E-mail: admissions@vaughn.edu
Internet: www.vaughn.edu
Founded 1932 as Casey Jones School of Aeronautics, present name 1986
Private control
Academic year: 2 semesters
Pres.: Dr JOHN C. FITZPATRICK
Vice-Pres. for Enrolment Services and Public Affairs: ERNIE SHEPELSKY
Vice-Pres. for Finance and Business Services: ROBERT WALDMANN
Vice-Pres. for Student Affairs: JOHN F. AGNELLI
Librarian: JO ANN JAYNE
Number of teachers: 120
Number of students: 1,700 (1,310 full-time, 390 part-time)
Publication: *Vaughn College Magazine* (2 a year)

VILLA MARIA COLLEGE

240 Pine Ridge Rd, Buffalo, NY 14225
Telephone: (716) 896-0700
E-mail: admissions@villa.edu
Internet: www.villa.edu
Founded 1961
Private control
Specializes in arts and music
Pres.: Sis. MARCELLA MARIE GARUS
Vice-Pres. for Academic Affairs: Dr JANET R. REOHR
Vice-Pres. for Business Affairs: VINCENT GRIZANTI
Vice-Pres. for Devt: Sis. MARY MARCINE BOROWIAK
Vice-Pres. of Enrolment Management: RANDYLL BOWEN
Vice-Pres. for Student Affairs: Sis. MARY LOUIS RUSTOWICZ
Registrar: MELANY SHIELDS
Dir for Library Services: Sis. MARY ANNA FALBO
Number of students: 500

WAGNER COLLEGE

One Campus Rd, Staten Island, NY 10301
Telephone: (718) 390-3100
E-mail: admissions@wagner.edu
Internet: www.wagner.edu
Founded 1883
Private control
Pres.: Dr RICHARD GUARASCI

Provost and Vice-Pres. for Academic Affairs: Dr LILY MCNAIR
Dean for Admissions and Financial Aid: BOB HERR
Dean for Integrated Learning: PATRICIA TOOKER
Dean for Libraries: DOROTHY DAVISON
Library of 150,000 vols
Number of teachers: 100 (full-time)
Number of students: 2,150 (1,850 undergraduate, 300 graduate)

WEBB INSTITUTE

298 Crescent Beach Rd, Glen Cove, NY 11542-1398
Telephone: (516) 671-2213
E-mail: inquiry@webb-institute.edu
Internet: www.webb-institute.edu
Founded 1889
Academic year: August to June
Courses in naval architecture and marine engineering
Pres.: Admiral ROBERT C. OLSEN, JR
Dir for Enrolment Management: WILLIAM MURRAY
Dir for Financial Affairs: ANDREW BERKO
Registrar: JOCELYN WILSON
Library Dir: PATRICIA PRESCOTT
Library of 50,000 vols
Number of teachers: 10 (full-time)
Number of students: 80

WELLS COLLEGE

170 Main St, Aurora, NY 13026
Telephone: (315) 364-3266
E-mail: admissions@wells.edu
Internet: www.wells.edu
Founded 1868
Private control
Academic year: August to May
Women's liberal arts college
Pres.: LISA MARSH RYERSON
Provost and Dean for College: Dr CINDY J. SPEAKER
Vice-Pres. for Advancement: MICHAEL MCGREEVEY
Vice-Pres. for Communications and Marketing: ANN S. ROLLO
Dean for Students: JOEL ANDREW MCCARTHY
Dir for Admissions and Financial Aid: SUSAN RAITH SLOAN
Registrar: Dr ANDRE SIAMUNDELE
Treas.: JOHN DENTES
Dir for Library: MURIEL GODBOUT
Library of 218,000 vols
Number of teachers: 55
Number of students: 560
Publication: *Wells College Express* (4 a year)

YESHIVA UNIVERSITY

500 W 185th St, New York, NY 10033
Telephone: (212) 960-5400
E-mail: yuadmit@yu.edu
Internet: www.yu.edu
Founded 1886
Private control
Languages of instruction: English, Hebrew
3 Campuses in Manhattan and 1 in Bronx
Pres.: Dr RICHARD M. JOEL
Chancellor: Dr NORMAN LAMM
Provost and Sr Vice-Pres. for Academic Affairs: Dr MORTON LOWENGRUB
Vice-Pres. and Chief of Staff: JOSH JOSEPH
Vice-Pres. for Admin.: JEFFREY ROSENGARTEN
Vice-Pres. for Business Affairs: J. MICHAEL GOWER
Vice-Pres. for Information Technology: MARC MILSTEIN

Vice-Pres. for Institutional Advancement: DANIEL T. FORMAN
Vice-Pres. for Legal Affairs, Sec. and Gen. Counsel: ANDREW J. LAUER
Vice-Pres. for Medical Affairs: Dr ALLEN M. SPIEGEL
Vice-Pres. for Univ. Affairs: HERBERT DOBRINSKY
Dean for Univ. Libraries: PEARL BERGER
Library: Hedi Steinberg Library: 170,000 vols; Mendel Gottesman Library of Hebraica: 300,000 vols; Pollack Library: 317,000 vols; all libraries access 50,000 ejournals, and 428,000 ebook titles
Number of teachers: 1,100
Number of students: 7,250 (2,865 undergraduate, 3,550 graduate, 291 seminary)
Publications: *Yeshiva University Review*, *Yeshiva University Today*

DEANS

Albert Einstein College of Medicine: Dr ALLEN M. SPIEGEL
Azrieli Graduate School of Jewish Education and Administration: Dr DAVID J. SCHNALL
Benjamin N. Cardozo School of Law: Dr MATTHEW DILLER
Bernard Revel Graduate School of Jewish Studies: Dr DAVID BERGER
Ferkauf Graduate School of Psychology: Dr LAWRENCE J. SIEGEL
Stern College for Women: Dr KAREN BACON
Syms School of Business: MOSES PAVA
Wurzweiler School of Social Work: Dr CARMEN ORTIZ HENDRICKS
Yeshiva College: Dr BARRY L. EICHLER
Yeshiva Programme and Mazer School of Talmudic Studies: YONA REISS

NORTH CAROLINA

BARTON COLLEGE

POB 5000, Wilson, NC 27893-7000
Telephone: (252) 399-6300
Internet: www.barton.edu
Founded 1902 as Atlantic Christian College, present name 1990
Private control
Academic year: September to May (2 semesters)
Pres.: Dr NORVAL C. KNETEN
Provost and Vice-Pres. for Academic Affairs: Dr JOHN P. MARSDEN
Vice-Pres. for Admin. and Finance: Dr KRIS LYNCH
Vice-Pres. for External Relations: Dr KELLY THOMPSON
Vice-Pres. for Student Affairs: GEORGE SOLAN
Dir of Admissions: AMANDA METTS
Registrar: SHEILA MILNE
Dir of Library: JASON FLEMING
Library of 169,000 vols, 22,000 ebooks, 390 periodicals and newspapers, 13,000 eperiodicals
Number of teachers: 70 (full-time)
Number of students: 1,200
Publication: *Scope*

DEANS

School of Arts and Sciences: Dr TERRENCE L. GRIMES
School of Business: Dr JOHN J. BETHUNE
School of Education: Dr JACKIE ENNIS
School of Nursing: Dr SHARON I. SARVEY
School of Social Work: Dr BARBARA CONKLIN

BELMONT ABBEY COLLEGE

100 Belmont-Mt Holly Rd, Belmont, NC 28012-1802
Telephone: (704) 461-6700
E-mail: admissions@bac.edu

Internet: www.belmontabbeycollege.edu

Founded 1876 as St. Mary's College, present name 1913, present status 1952

Private control

Academic year: August to May (2 semesters)

Academic programmes incl. applied psychology, biology, history, liberal studies, sports management, theology

Chancellor: Rev. PLACID SOLARI

Pres.: Dr WILLIAM K. THIERFELDER

Vice-Pres. for Academic Affairs and Dean of Faculty: Dr ANNE CARSON DALY

Vice-Pres. for Admin. and Finance: WAYNE SCROGGINS

Vice-Pres. for College Relations: KENNETH DAVISON, JR

Vice-Pres. for Enrolment Management and Student Affairs: Dr LUCAS LAMADRID

Dir of Admissions: ROGER JONES

Registrar: Fr DAVID BROWN

Dir of Library Services: DONALD BEAGLE

Library of 130,000 vols, 57,000 ebooks, 13,000 old and rare books, 650 periodical titles

Number of teachers: 50

Number of students: 1,000

Publications: *Agora*, *Crossroads*

BENNETT COLLEGE

Greensboro, NC 27401-3239

Telephone: (336) 517-2100

E-mail: admiss@bennett.edu

Internet: www.bennett.edu

Founded 1873

Private control

Academic year: August to May (2 semesters)

Offers Bachelors degree in arts, fine arts, science, social work

Pres.: Dr JULIANNE MALVEAUX

Provost and Vice-Pres. for Academic Affairs: ESTHER TERRY

Vice-Pres. for Admin. Services: ANDRENA COLEMAN

Vice-Pres. for Business and Finance: LATONYA FLAMER

Vice-Pres. for Enrolment Management: LES FERRIER, JR

Vice-Pres. for Institutional Advancement: IRIS RAMEY

Registrar: KAREN GREEN

Library Dir: JOAN WILLIAMS

Library of 100,000 vols, 90,000 monographs, 36,000 ebooks, 2,400 audiovisual items, 23,000 periodicals

Number of teachers: 60 (full-time)

Number of students: 735 (671 full-time, 64 part-time)

BREVARD COLLEGE

One Brevard College Dr., Brevard, NC 28712

Telephone: (828) 883-8292

E-mail: admissions@brevard.edu

Internet: www.brevard.edu

Founded 1934 by merger of Rutherford College with Weaver Methodist College

Private control

Academic year: August to May (2 semesters)

Major programmes incl. art, biology, business and organizational leadership, criminal justice, English, environmental science, environmental studies, exercise science, general science, health science studies, history, integrated studies, mathematics, music, music education, psychology, religious studies, theatre studies, wilderness leadership and experiential education

Pres.: Dr DAVID JOYCE

Vice-Pres. for Academic Affairs and Dean of Faculty: JOHN S. HARDT

Vice-Pres. for Admissions and Financial Aid: MATHEW COX

Vice-Pres. for Business and Finance: DEBORAH P. HALL

Vice-Pres. for Institutional Advancement: SUSAN L. COTHERN

Dean for Students: CHRISTOPHER J. HOLLAND

Registrar: AMY HERTZ

Dir for Library: MICHAEL M. MCCABE

Library of 58,000 vols, 120,000 ebooks, 4,490 audiovisual materials, 200 periodicals, 22,000 ejournals

Number of teachers: 55 (full-time)

Number of students: 660

CABARRUS COLLEGE OF HEALTH SCIENCES

401 Medical Park Dr., Concord, NC 28025-2405

Telephone: (704) 403-1555

E-mail: admissions@cabarruscollege.edu

Internet: www.cabarruscollege.edu

Founded 1942 as Cabarrus Co Hospital School of Nursing, present name 1996, present status 2000

Private control

Academic year: August to May (2 semesters)

Degree offered in health services leadership and management, medical imaging, nursing

Chancellor: Dr DIANNE O. SNYDER

Provost: Prof. Dr MEG PATCHETT

Dean of Admin. and Financial Services: MARK E. COLEMAN

Dean of Student Services and Enrolment Management: CHRISTINE L. CORSELLO

Registrar: MICHAEL SMITH

Librarian: EMILY PATRIDGE

Library of 6,000 vols, 1,000 video cassettes and journals

Number of students: 475

CAMPBELL UNIVERSITY

POB 567, Buie's Creek, NC 27506

Telephone: (910) 893-1200

E-mail: buildyourfuture@campbell.edu

Internet: www.campbell.edu

Founded 1887 as Buies Creek Acad., present name 1979

Private control

Academic year: August to May (2 semesters)

Chancellor: Dr NORMAN ADRIAN WIGGINS

Pres.: Prof. Dr JEREMY M. WALLACE

Provost and Vice-Pres. for Academic Affairs: Dr M. DWAINE GREENE

Sr Vice-Pres. for Institutional Advancement: Dr JACK BRITT

Vice-Pres. for Business and Treas.: JIM ROBERTS

Vice-Pres. for Enrolment Management: Dr JOHN ROBERSON

Vice-Pres. for Institutional Advancement: BRITT DAVIS

Vice-Pres. for Student Life: Dr DENNIS BAZEMORE

Registrar: J. DAVID MCGIRT

Dean of Library: Dr BORRÉE P. KWOK

Library of 225,000 vols, 129,000 ebooks, 284 periodicals, 50,000 eperiodicals, 500,000 microforms

Number of teachers: 430 (175 full-time, 255 part-time)

Number of students: 9,400

Publications: *Accolades* (1 a year), *Campbell Magazine* (2 a year), *Pine Burr* (year book)

DEANS

College of Arts and Sciences: Prof. Dr MARK L. HAMMOND

College of Pharmacy and Health Sciences: Prof. Dr RONALD W. MADDOX

Divinity School: Prof. Dr ANDREW H. WAKEFIELD

Lundy-Fetterman School of Business: Dr BENJAMIN M. HAWKINS

Norman Adrian Wiggins School of Law: Prof. MELISSA ESSARY

School of Education: Dr KAREN P. NERY

School of Osteopathic Medicine: Dr JOHN M. KAUFFMAN

CATAWBA COLLEGE

2300 W Innes St, Salisbury, NC 28144

Telephone: (704) 637-4111

E-mail: admission@catawba.edu

Internet: www.catawba.edu

Founded 1851

Private control

Academic year: (2 semesters)

Pres.: BRIEN LEWIS

Provost: Dr W. RICHARD STEPHENS, JR

Sr Vice-Pres. for Devt: THOMAS C. CHILDRESS

Vice-Pres. for Enrolment Management: LOIS H. WILLIAMS

Dean of Students: G. BEN SMITH

Registrar: P. CAROL GAMBLE

Library Dir: STEVEN MCKINZIE

Library of 200,000 vols

Number of teachers: 115 (72 full-time, 43 part-time)

Number of students: 1,300

DEANS

Adrian L., Jr and Dorothy L. Shuford School of Performing Arts: Dr BARRY SANG

Enoch A. and Dorothy H. Goodman School of Education: Dr JAMES STRINGFIELD

James F. and Gerry T. Hurley School of Arts and Sciences: Dr STEVEN COGGIN

Ralph W. Ketner School of Business: Dr PAMELA THOMPSON

School of Evening and Graduate Studies: Dr EDITH BOLICK

CHOWAN UNIVERSITY

1 University Pl., Murfreesboro, NC 27855

Telephone: (252) 398-6500

E-mail: admissions@chowan.edu

Internet: www.chowan.edu

Founded 1848 as Chowan Baptist Female Institute, present name and four year co-ed status since 2006

Private control

Academic year: August to May (2 semesters)

Pres.: Dr M. CHRISTOPHER WHITE

Provost and Vice-Pres. for Academic Affairs: Dr DANNY B. MOORE

Vice-Pres. of Business Affairs: DONNIE O. CLARY

Vice-Pres. of Devt: JOHN TAYLOE

Vice-Pres. for Enrolment Management and Dean of Admissions: CRAIG JANNEY

Vice-Pres. for Student Affairs: RANDY HARRELL

Dir of Univ. Relations: JOSH BARKER

Registrar: DONNA WOODARD

Exec. Dir of Library Services: GEORGIA E. WILLIAMS

Library of 230,000 vols, 29,000 periodicals

Number of teachers: 65 (full-time)

Number of students: 1,300

Publication: *CU Today Magazine*

DEANS

School of Arts and Sciences: Dr ROMEY PEAVLER

School of Business: Dr LINDA L. MILES

School of Education: Dr BRENDA S. TINKHAM

School of Liberal Arts: Dr JOHN DILUSTRO

DAVIDSON COLLEGE

POB 7171, Davidson, NC 28035-7171
209 Ridge Rd, Davidson, NC 28035
Telephone: (704) 894-2000
E-mail: admission@davidson.edu
Internet: www.davidson.edu

Founded 1837
Private control
Academic year: August to May (2 semesters)
Br. campus in Lake; depts of anthropology, art biology, interdisciplinary studies, chemistry, art, classics, economics, English, environmental studies, French and Francophone studies, German studies, Hispanic studies, history, Latin American studies, mathematics, music, philosophy, physics, political science, psychology, religion, sociology, theatre

Pres.: Dr CAROL QUILLEN
Vice-Pres. for Academic Affairs and Dean of Faculty: CLARK G. ROSS
Vice-Pres. for College Relations: EILEEN KEELEY
Vice-Pres. for Finance and Admin.: EDWARD A. KANIA
Vice-Pres. for Student Life and Dean of Students: THOMAS C. SHANDLEY
Vice-Pres. and Dean of Admissions and Financial Aid: CHRISTOPHER J. GRUBER
Registrar: Dr HANSFORD M. EPES
Dir for Library: JILL GREMMELS

Library of 600,000 vols, 500,000 ebooks, 200,000 fed. govt documents
Number of teachers: 160 (full-time)
Number of students: 1,750

Publications: *Davidson Journal* (4 a year), *Hobart Park* (literary, 1 a year), *Oak Row Report* (12 a year)

DUKE UNIVERSITY

Durham, NC 27708
Telephone: (919) 684-8111
E-mail: registrar@duke.edu
Internet: www.duke.edu

Founded 1838 as Union Institute Soc. in Randolph Co, present name and status 1924
Private control
Academic year: September to August

Pres.: Prof. Dr RICHARD H. BRODHEAD
Chancellor for Health Affairs and CEO: Dr VICTOR J. DZAU
Provost: SALLY KORNBLUTH
Exec. Vice-Pres. and Treas.: Dr TALLMAN TRASK, III
Vice-Pres. and Gen. Counsel: Dr PAMELA J. BERNARD
Vice-Pres. and Univ. Sec.: RICHARD RIDDELL
Vice-Pres. for Admin.: KYLE CAVANAUGH
Vice-Pres. for Alumni Affairs and Devt: ROBERT SHEPARD
Vice-Pres. for Durham and Regional Affairs: PHAIL WYNN, JR
Vice-Pres. for Information Technology and Chief Information Officer: TRACY FUTHEY
Vice-Pres. for Student Affairs: Dr LARRY MONETA
Registrar: BRUCE CUNNINGHAM
Univ. Librarian and Vice-Provost for Library Affairs: Dr DEBORAH JAKUBS

Library of 6,340,456 vols
Number of teachers: 1,800
Number of students: 14,800 (6,550 undergraduate, 8,250 graduate and professional)

Publications: *American Literary Scholarship* (1 a year), *American Literature* (4 a year), *American Speech* (4 a year), *boundary 2* (3 a year), *Camera Obscura* (3 a year), *Common Knowledge* (2 a year), *Comparative Studies of South Asia, Africa and the Middle East* (2 a year), *Duke Gifted Letter* (4 a year), *Duke Mathematical Journal* (15 a year), *Eighteenth-Century Life* (3 a year),

Environmental History (4 a year), *Ethnohistory* (4 a year), *French Historical Studies* (4 a year), *GLQ: A Journal of Lesbian and Gay Studies* (4 a year), *Hispanic American Historical Review* (4 a year), *History of Political Economy* (4 a year), *Journal of Health Politics, Policy and Law* (6 a year), *Journal of Medieval and Early Modern Studies* (3 a year), *Lesbian and Gay Studies Newsletter* (3 a year), *Mediterranean Quarterly* (4 a year), *Modern Language Quarterly* (4 a year), *Nepantla: Views from the South* (3 a year), *Pedagogy* (3 a year), *Poetics Today* (4 a year), *Positions* (3 a year), *Public Culture* (3 a year), *Radical History Review* (3 a year), *Social Science History* (4 a year), *Social Text* (4 a year), *South Atlantic Quarterly* (4 a year), *Theater* (3 a year), *Transition* (4 a year)

DEANS

Divinity School: Prof. Dr RICHARD HAYS
Fuqua School of Business: Dr WILLIAM BOULDING
Graduate School: Prof. Dr DAVID BELL
Nicholas School of the Environment: WILLIAM L. CHAMEIDES
Pratt School of Engineering: Prof. Dr THOMAS C. KATSOULEAS
Sanford School of Public Policy: Prof. Dr BRUCE R. KUNIHOLM
School of Law: Dr DAVID F. LEVI
School of Medicine: Prof. Dr NANCY C. ANDREWS
School of Nursing: Prof. Dr CATHERINE L. GILLISS
Trinity College of Arts and Sciences: LAURIE L. PATTON

PROFESSORS

ABOU-DONIA, M. B., Pharmacology and Cancer Biology
ADDISON, W. A., Obstetrics and Gynaecology
AERS, D., English
AGARWAL, P. K., Computer Science
AKWARI, O. E., Surgery
ALBALA, D. M., Surgery
ALDRICH, J., Political Science
ALLARD, W. K., Mathematics
ALLEN, N. B., Medicine
ANDERSON, E. E., Surgery
ANDERSON, P. A. W., Paediatrics
ANDERSON, R. W., Surgery
ANDERSON, W. B., Ophthalmology
ANDREWS, E., Slavic Languages and Literature
ANLYAN, W. G., Surgery
ANSCHER, M. S., Radiation Oncology
APPLEWHITE, J. W., English
ASHER, S. R., Psychology, Social and Health Sciences
ASHTON, R. H., Business Administration
AUGUSTINE, JR, G. J., Neurobiology
AVISSAR, R., Civil and Environmental Engineering
BAILLIE, J., Medicine
BAKER, H. A., English
BAKER, P. A., Earth and Ocean Sciences
BALDWIN, S. W., Chemistry
BARANGER, H. U., Physics
BARBER, R. T., Marine Sciences
BARR, R. C., Biomedical Engineering
BARTLETT, J. A., Medicine
BARTLETT, K., Law
BASHORE, T. M., Medicine
BASSETT, III, F. H., Surgery
BEALE, J. T., Mathematics
BEALE, S. S., Law
BECKWITH, S., English
BEEN, M. D., Biochemistry
BEHAR, V. S., Medicine
BEHRINGER, R. P., Physics
BEJAN, A., Mechanical Engineering
BELL, D. F., Romance Studies
BENFEY, P. N., Biology

BENNETT, G. V., Cell Biology
BENNETT, P. B., Anaesthesiology
BERATAN, D. N., Chemistry
BERCHUCK, A., Obstetrics and Gynaecology
BERGER, J. O., Statistics
BERTOZZI, A. L., Mathematics
BETTMAN, J. R., Business Administration
BIERMANN, A. W., Computer Science
BIGNER, D. D., Pathology
BISSET, III, G. S., Radiology
BLAND, K. P., Religion
BLAZER, D. G., Psychiatry and Behavioural Sciences
BLUMENTHAL, J. A., Psychiatry and Behavioural Sciences
BOATWRIGHT, M. T., Classical Studies
BOLLERSLEV, T., Economics
BOLLINGER, R. R., Surgery
BOLOGNESI, D. P., Surgery
BONAVENTURA, C. J., Marine Sciences
BONAVENTURA, J., Marine Sciences
BONK, J. F., Chemistry
BORCHARDT, F. L., Germanic Languages
BOSSEN, E. H., Pathology
BOULDING, W. F., Business Administration
BOWIE, J. D., Radiology
BOYLE, J. D. A., Law
BRADFORD, W. D., Pathology
BRADLEY, M., Business Administration
BRADY, D. J., Electrical and Computer Engineering
BRANDON, R. N., Philosophy
BREEDEN, D. T., Business Administration
BRIZEL, D. M., Radiation Oncology
BRODIE, H. K. H., Psychiatry and Behavioural Sciences
BROWN, A. S., Electrical and Computer Engineering
BROWN, H. L., Obstetrics and Gynaecology
BRUZELIUS, C., Art and Art History
BRYANT, R., Mathematics
BUCKLEY, E. G., Ophthalmology
BUCKLEY, P. J., Pathology
BUCKLEY, R. H., Paediatrics
BUEHLER, A., Health, Physical Education and Recreation
BURCH, JR, W. M., Medicine
BURIAN, P. H., Classical Studies
BURNS, B. J., Psychiatry and Behavioural Sciences
BURTON, R. M., Business Administration
BUTTERS, R. R., English
CALIFF, R. M., Medicine
CARIN, L., Electrical and Computer Engineering
CARON, M. G., Cell Biology
CARRINGTON, P. D., Law
CARROLL, B. A., Radiology
CARTER, J. H., Psychiatry and Behavioural Sciences
CARTMILL, M., Biological Anthropology and Anatomy
CASEY, P. J., Pharmacology and Cancer Biology
CHAFE, W. H., History
CHAO, N. J., Medicine
CHEN, Y., Paediatrics
CHIKARAISHI, D. M., Neurobiology
CHRISTENSEN, N. L., Earth and Environmental Sciences
CHRISTIE, G. C., Law
CLARK, E. A., Religion
CLARK, J. S., Biology
CLARK, R. L., Mechanical Engineering
CLARKE-PEARSON, D. L., Obstetrics and Gynaecology
CLAY, D., Classical Studies
CLEMENTS, III, D. A., Paediatrics
CLIPP, E. C., Nursing
CLOTFELTER, C., Public Policy Studies
CLUM, J. M., Theatre Studies
COBB, F. R., Medicine
COCKS, F. H., Mechanical Engineering
COFFMAN, T. M., Medicine
COHEN, H. J., Medicine
COHEN, W. M., Business Administration

COHN, J. A., Medicine
COIE, J. D., Psychology, Social and Health Sciences
COLEMAN, R. E., Radiology
COLEMAN, W. J., Business Administration
COLVIN, O. M., Medicine
COOK, D. R., Anaesthesiology
COOK, P. J., Public Policy Studies
COOKE, M., Asian and African Language and Literature
COREY, G. R., Medicine
CORLISS, B., Earth and Ocean Sciences
COSTANZO, P. R., Psychology, Social and Health Sciences
COSTELLO, E. J., Psychiatry and Behavioural Sciences
COX, J. D., Law
CRAWFORD, J., Medicine
CRENSHAW, J. L., Divinity
CROVITZ, H. F., Psychiatry and Behavioural Sciences
CROWDER, L. B., Marine Sciences
CROWLEY, T. J., Earth and Ocean Sciences
CRUMBLISS, A. L., Chemistry
CULLEN, B. R., Molecular Genetics and Microbiology
CULP, J. M., Law
DAVIDSON, C. N., English
DAVIDSON, J. R., Psychiatry and Behavioural Sciences
DAVIS, N. G., Classical Studies
DAWSON, J. R., Immunology
DE BELLIS, M. D., Psychiatry and Behavioural Sciences
DELLINGER, W. E., Law
DELONG, G. R., Paediatrics
DE MARCHI, N., Economics
DEMOTT, D., Law
DENEEF, A. L., English
DESANCTIS, G., Business Administration
DEWHIRST, M. W., Radiation Oncology
DI GIULIO, R. T., Earth and Environmental Sciences
DIPRETE, T. A., Sociology
DODGE, K. A., Public Policy Studies
DOWELL, E. H., Mechanical Engineering
ECKERMAN, C. O., Psychological and Brain Sciences
EDELSBRUNNER, H., Computer Science
EDWARDS, G. S., Physics
EFIRD, J. M., Divinity
ELLINWOOD, JR, E. H., Psychiatry and Behavioural Sciences
ELLIS, C. S., Computer Science
ENDOW, S. A., Cell Biology
ENGLISH, P. C., History
EPSTEIN, D. L., Ophthalmology
ERICKSON, C. J., Psychological and Brain Sciences
ERICKSON, H. P., Cell Biology
EVERETT, R. O., Law
FAIR, R. B., Electrical and Computer Engineering
FALLETTA, J. M., Paediatrics
FARMER, J. C., Surgery
FEINGLOS, M. N., Medicine
FISCHER, G. W., Business Administration
FISH, P. G., Political Science
FISHER, S. R., Surgery
FITZPATRICK, D., Neurobiology
FLANAGAN, O., Philosophy
FLEISHMAN, J., Law
FLOYD, JR, C. E., Radiology
FOREMAN, J. W., Paediatrics
FORWARD, R. B., Marine Sciences
FRANCES, A. J., Psychiatry and Behavioural Sciences
FRANCIS, J., Business Administration
FRANK, M. M., Paediatrics
FREEMARK, M. S., Paediatrics
FRIEDMAN, A. H., Surgery
FRIEDMAN, H. S., Paediatrics
FRIEDMAN, M., Biomedical Engineering
FULKERSON, JR, W. J., Medicine
GAINES, J. M., Literature

GARCIA-BLANCO, M. A., Molecular Genetics and Microbiology
GARCI-GOMEZ, M., Romance Studies
GARG, D. P., Mechanical Engineering
GASPAR, B., History
GAVINS, R., History
GELFAND, A., Statistics
GEORGE, L. K., Sociology
GEORGE, S. L., Biostatistics and Bioinformatics
GEORGIADE, G. S., Surgery
GEREFFI, G., Sociology
GILBOA, E., Surgery
GILLESPIE, M. A., Political Science
GILLIAM, B., Music
GLANDER, K. E., Biological Anthropology and Anatomy
GLOWER, JR, D. D., Surgery
GOCKERMAN, J. P., Medicine
GOLDBERG, R. N., Paediatrics
GOLDING, M. P., Philosophy
GOLDSCHMIDT, P. J., Medicine
GOLDSTEIN, L. B., Medicine
GOODMAN, P. C., Radiology
GOODWIN, C. D., Economics
GOODWYN, L. C., History
GOSHAW, A. T., Physics
GRABOWSKI, H. G., Economics
GRAHAM, D. A., Economics
GRANT, A. O., Medicine
GRANT, J. P., Surgery
GRANT, R. W., Political Science
GREENBERG, C. S., Medicine
GREENFIELD, JR, J. C., Medicine
GREENLEAF, A. L., Biochemistry
GREENSIDE, H., Physics
GREER, M. R., Romance Studies
GRIECO, J., Political Science
GRIFFITHS, P. A., Mathematics
HAAGEN, P. H., Law
HAFF, P. K., Earth and Ocean Sciences
HAIN, R., Mathematics
HALL, K. C., Mechanical Engineering
HALL, III, R. P., Medicine
HALL, W. C., Neurobiology
HALL, W. G., Psychological and Brain Sciences
HALPERIN, E. C., Radiation Oncology
HAMILTON, J. A., Psychology, Social and Health Sciences
HAMILTON, J. D., Medicine
HAMMES, G. G., Biochemistry
HAMMOND, C. B., Obstetrics and Gynaecology
HAN, M. Y., Physics
HANEY, A. F., Obstetrics and Gynaecology
HARER, J., Mathematics
HARMAN, C. M., Mechanical Engineering
HARRELSON, J. M., Surgery
HARVEY, C. R., Business Administration
HAUERWAS, S. M., Divinity
HAVIGHURST, C. C., Law
HAYNES, B. F., Medicine
HAYS, R. B., Divinity
HEALY, R. G., Earth and Environmental Sciences
HEINZ, E. R., Radiology
HEITMAN, J. B., Molecular Genetics and Microbiology
HEITZENRATER, R. P., Divinity
HELMS, C. A., Radiology
HERRUP, C. B., History
HERSHFIELD, M. S., Medicine
HERTZBERG, B. S., Radiology
HILL, G. B., Obstetrics and Gynaecology
HILL, R. L., Biochemistry
HILLERBRAND, H. J., Religion
HINTON, D. E., Earth and Environmental Sciences
HOCHMUTH, R. M., Mechanical Engineering
HOFFMAN, M. R., Pathology
HOLLOWAY, K., English
HOROWITZ, D. L., Law
HOUGH, J. F., Political Science
HOWELL, C. R., Physics
HSIEH, D. A., Business Administration
HSIEH, T., Biochemistry

HUANG, A. T., Medicine
HUBER, J. C., Business Administration
HYLANDER, W. L., Biological Anthropology and Anatomy
JAFFE, G. J., Ophthalmology
JAFFE, S., Music
JAMESON, F., Literature
JASZCZAK, R. J., Radiology
JENNINGS, R. B., Pathology
JENTLESON, B. W., Public Policy Studies
JIRTLE, R. L., Radiation Oncology
JOHNSON, G. A., Radiology
JOHNSON, K. M., Engineering
JOHNSON, V. E., Statistics
JOINES, W. T., Electrical and Computer Engineering
JONES, L. G., Divinity
JONES, R. H., Surgery
JONES, T., Law
KAMAKURA, W. A., Business Administration
KANE, W. H., Medicine
KAPLAN, A., Romance Studies
KARSON, J. A., Earth and Ocean Sciences
KATUL, G. G., Earth and Environmental Sciences
KATZ, D. F., Biomedical Engineering
KATZ, L. C., Neurobiology
KAY, R. F., Biological Anthropology and Anatomy
KEEFE, F. J., Psychiatry and Behavioural Sciences
KEENE, J. D., Molecular Genetics and Microbiology
KELLER, T. F., Business Administration
KELLEY, A. C., Economics
KELSOE, G. H., Immunology
KEOHANE, N. O., Political Science
KEOHANE, R., Political Science
KERN, F. H., Anaesthesiology
KIEHART, D. P., Biology
KILLENBERG, P. G., Medicine
KIMBROUGH, K. P., Economics
KINNEY, T. R., Paediatrics
KIRBY, M. L., Paediatrics
KISSLO, J. A., Medicine
KITSCHELT, H. P., Political Science
KLINTWORTH, G. K., Pathology
KOCH, W. J., Surgery
KOONZ, C., History
KORNBERG, A., Political Science
KORT, W. A., Religion
KRAMER, R. A., Earth and Environmental Sciences
KREDICH, N. M., Medicine
KREUZER, K. N., Biochemistry
KRISHNAN, K. R. R., Psychiatry and Behavioural Sciences
KROLIK, J. L., Electrical and Computer Engineering
KUHN, C. M., Pharmacology and Cancer Biology
KUNIHOLM, B. R., Public Policy Studies
KUO, P. C., Surgery
KURTZBERG, J., Paediatrics
KYLE, A. S., Business Administration
LADD, H., Public Policy Studies
LAHUSEN, T., Literature
LAND, K. C., Sociology
LANGE, D. L., Law
LANGE, P., Political Science
LAUGHHUNN, D. J., Business Administration
LAVINE, M. L., Statistics
LAWLER, G. F., Mathematics
LAWRENCE, B. B., Religion
LAYTON, H., Mathematics
LEE, P. P., Ophthalmology
LEFKOWITZ, R. J., Medicine
LEIGHT, G. S., Surgery
LEIGHTEN, P., Art and Art History
LENTRICCHIA, F., Literature
LEVIN, L. S., Surgery
LEWIN, A. Y., Business Administration
LEWIS, D. V., Paediatrics
LIDDLE, R. A., Medicine
LIN, N., Sociology
LIND, E. A., Business Administration

LINNEY, E. A., Molecular Genetics and Microbiology
LISCHER, R., Divinity
LIVINGSTONE, D. A., Biology
LOCHMULLER, C. H., Chemistry
LOCKHEAD, G. R., Psychological and Brain Sciences
LOGUE, P. E., Psychiatry and Behavioural Sciences
LONGINO, M., Romance Studies
LOONEY, J. G., Psychiatry and Behavioural Sciences
LOWE, J. E., Surgery
LYERLY, H. K., Surgery
LYLES, K. W., Medicine
LYNCH, J. G., Business Administration
MCCANN, R. L., Surgery
MCCARTHY, G., Radiology
MCCLAIN, P. D., Political Science
MCCLAY, D. R., Biology
MCCUEN, B. W., Ophthalmology
MCDONNELL, D. P., Pharmacology and Cancer Biology
MCELROY, M. B., Economics
MCGOVERN, F. E., Law
MCGOWN, L., Chemistry
MCINTOSH, T. J., Cell Biology
MACINTYRE, N. R., Medicine
MCLENDON, R. E., Pathology
MCNAMARA, J. O., Sr, Neurobiology
MCPHAIL, A. T., Chemistry
MADDEN, D. J., Psychiatry and Behavioural Sciences
MAHONEY, E. P., Philosophy
MALIN, P. E., Earth and Environmental Sciences
MARCH, J. S., Psychiatry and Behavioural Sciences
MARCUS, J., Divinity
MARINOS, P. N., Electrical and Computer Engineering
MARK, D. B., Medicine
MARK, J. B., Anaesthesiology
MARKS, L. B., Radiation Oncology
MARTINEZ, S., Radiology
MASON, R. M., Surgery
MASSEY, J. M., Medicine
MASSOUD, H. Z., Electrical and Computer Engineering
MATCHAR, D. B., Medicine
MAUSKOPF, S., History
MEANS, A. R., Pharmacology and Cancer Biology
MECK, W. H., Psychological and Brain Sciences
MEDINA, M. A., Civil and Environmental Engineering
METZLOFF, T. B., Law
MEYERS, C. L., Religion
MEYERS, E. M., Religion
MICKIEWICZ, E., Public Policy Studies
MIGNOLO, W., Literature
MILLER, M. A., History
MILLS, E., Pharmacology and Cancer Biology
MITCHELL, W. G., Business Administration
MODRICH, P. L., Biochemistry
MOI, T., Literature
MOON, R. E., Anaesthesiology
MOORE, J. O., Medicine
MOORMAN, C., Business Administration
MOREIRAS, A., Romance Studies
MORGAN, S. P., Sociology
MORRIS, J. J., Medicine
MORRIS, M., Law
MORRISON, D. R., Mathematics
MOSTELLER, R. P., Law
MUDIMBE, V., Literature
MUELLER, B., Physics
MUNGER, M. C., Political Science
NADLER, J. V., Pharmacology and Cancer Biology
NEEDHAM, D., Mechanical Engineering
NELSON, R. C., Radiology
NEVINS, J. R., Molecular Genetics and Microbiology

NEWGARD, C. B., Pharmacology and Cancer Biology
NEWMAN, M. F., Anaesthesiology
NICKLAS, R. B., Biology
NICOLELIS, M. A., Neurobiology
NIJHOUT, H. F., Biology
NIOU, E. S., Political Science
NOLTE, L. W., Electrical and Computer Engineering
NOWICKI, S., Biology
NUNLEY, II, J. A., Surgery
O'BARR, W. M., Cultural Anthropology
OH, S., Physics
OLSEN, E. A., Medicine
O'RAND, A. M., Sociology
OREN, R., Earth and Environmental Sciences
ORR, L., Romance Studies
OSTBYE, T., Community and Family Medicine
PALETZ, D. L., Political Science
PALMER, R. A., Chemistry
PALMER, R. G., Physics
PAPPAS, T. N., Surgery
PARDON, W. L., Mathematics
PARKERSON, G. R., Community and Family Medicine
PATZ, E. F., Radiology
PAULSON, D. F., Surgery
PAULSON, E. K., Radiology
PAYNE, C. M., History
PAYNE, J. W., Business Administration
PERFECT, J. R., Medicine
PERICAK-VANCE, M. A., Medicine
PETER, R. H., Medicine
PETROSKI, H., Civil and Environmental Engineering
PHILLIPS, III, H. R., Medicine
PIANTADOSI, C. A., Medicine
PIMM, S. L., Earth and Environmental Sciences
PIRRUNG, M. C., Chemistry
PISETSKY, D. S., Medicine
PIZZO, S. V., Pathology
POPE, D., English
PORTER, J. A., English
POWELL, H. J., Law
POWELL, R. J., Art and Art History
PREMINGER, G. M., Surgery
PRICE, D. E., Political Science
PRICE, E. R., English
PROSNITZ, L. R., Radiation Oncology
PROVENZALE, J. M., Radiology
PUROHIT, D., Business Administration
PURVES, D., Neurobiology
PUTALLAZ, M., Psychology, Social and Health Sciences
QUARLES, L. D., Medicine
QUILLIGAN, M., English
QUINN, N., Cultural Anthropology
RADTKE, R. A., Medicine
RADWAY, J. A., Literature
RAETZ, C. R. H., Biochemistry
RAJAGOPALAN, K. V., Biochemistry
RAMUS, J. S., Marine Sciences
RAUSHER, M. D., Biology
RAVIN, C. E., Radiology
RECKHOW, K. H., Earth and Environmental Sciences
REDDY, W. M., History
REED, M. C., Mathematics
REEDY, M. K., Cell Biology
REICHERT, W. M., Biomedical Engineering
REICHMAN, J. H., Law
REIF, J. H., Computer Science
REINSMOEN, N. L., Pathology
RELLER, L. B., Pathology
REMMER, K. L., Political Science
REPPY, W. A., Law
REYNOLDS, J. F., Biology
RICHARDS, J. F., History
RICHARDSON, C. J., Earth and Environmental Sciences
RICHARDSON, D. C., Biochemistry
RICHARDSON, J. S., Biochemistry
RICHTER, D. D., Earth and Environmental Sciences
RIGSBY, K. J., Classical Studies

ROBBOY, S. J., Pathology
ROCKEY, D. C., Medicine
ROCKMAN, H. A., Medicine
ROGGLI, V. L., Pathology
ROLAND, A., History
ROLLESTON, J. L., Germanic Languages
ROSE, D., Computer Science
ROSENBERG, A., Philosophy
ROTH, S., Psychology, Social and Health Sciences
ROWE, T. D., Law
RUBIN, D. C., Psychological and Brain Sciences
RYAN, T. J., Medicine
SABISTON, D. C., Surgery
SACKS, J., Statistics
ST CLAIR, E. W., Medicine
SAMULSKI, T. V., Radiation Oncology
SANDERS, D. B., Medicine
SANDERS, E. P., Religion
SANDERS, S. P., Paediatrics
SANFORD, D. H., Philosophy
SCHAEFFER, D. G., Mathematics
SCHANBERG, S. M., Pharmacology and Cancer Biology
SCHIFFMAN, S. S., Psychiatry and Behavioural Sciences
SCHLESINGER, W. H., Biology
SCHMALBECK, R. L., Law
SCHMECHEL, D. E., Medicine
SCHOEN, C. L., Mathematics
SCHOMBERG, D. W., Obstetrics and Gynaecology
SCHROEDER, C., Law
SCHULMAN, K. A., Medicine
SCHWAB, S. J., Medicine
SCHWARCZ, S. L., Law
SCHWARTZ, D. A., Medicine
SCHWARTZ-BLOOM, R. D., Pharmacology and Cancer Biology
SCHWINN, D. A., Anaesthesiology
SEIGLER, H. F., Surgery
SEXTON, D. J., Medicine
SHATZMILLER, J., History
SHAUGHNESSY, E. J., Mechanical Engineering
SHAW, A. J., Biology
SHAW, B. R., Chemistry
SHELBURNE, J. D., Pathology
SHENOLIKAR, S., Pharmacology and Cancer Biology
SHEPPARD, B. H., Business Administration
SHERWOOD, A., Psychiatry and Behavioural Sciences
SIEDOW, J. N., Biology
SIEGEL, L. M., Biochemistry
SIEGLER, I. C., Psychiatry and Behavioural Sciences
SIMEL, D. L., Medicine
SIMON, J. D., Chemistry
SIMON, S. A., Neurobiology
SIMONS, E. L., Biological Anthropology and Anatomy
SIMPSON, I. H., Sociology
SLOAN, F. A., Economics
SLOTKIN, T. A., Pharmacology and Cancer Biology
SMITH, B. C., Philosophy
SMITH, B. H., Literature
SMITH, K. K., Biology
SMITH, P. K., Surgery
SMITH, S. W., Biomedical Engineering
SMITH, T. P., Radiology
SNYDERMAN, R., Medicine
SOPER, J. T., Obstetrics and Gynaecology
SPENNER, K. I., Sociology
SPICER, L. D., Radiology
SPRAGENS, T. A., Political Science
SPRITZER, C. E., Radiology
STADDON, J. E. R., Psychological and Brain Sciences
STAELIN, R., Business Administration
STAMLER, J. S., Medicine
STANLEY, D. K., Classical Studies
STEEGE, D. A., Biochemistry
STEINMETZ, D. C., Divinity
STERN, M. A., Mathematics

STEWART, P., Romance Studies
STILES, G. L., Medicine
STRANDBERG, V. H., English
STRAUMAN, T. J., Psychology, Social and Health Sciences
STRITTMATTER, W. J., Medicine
STROHBEHN, J. W., Biomedical Engineering
SUGARMAN, J., Medicine
SULLENGER, B. A., Surgery
SULLIVAN, K. M., Medicine
SURIN, K. J., Literature
SURWIT, R. S., Psychiatry and Behavioural Sciences
SVETKEY, L. P., Medicine
SWARTZ, M. S., Psychiatry and Behavioural Sciences
TAN, T. Y., Mechanical Engineering
TAUCHEN, G. E., Economics
TAYLOR, C. R., Economics
TEDDER, T. F., Immunology
TELEN, M. J., Medicine
TERBORGH, J. W., Earth and Environmental Sciences
THOMAS, J., Romance Studies
THOMAS, J. E., Physics
THOMPSON, J. H., History
THOMPSON, R. J., Psychology, Social and Health Sciences
THOMPSON, W. M., Radiology
TIRYAKIAN, E. A., Sociology
TODD, R. L., Music
TOONE, E. J., Chemistry
TORGOVNICK, M., English
TORNOW, W., Physics
TOWER, E., Economics
TRAHEY, G. E., Biomedical Engineering
TRANGENSTEIN, J. A., Mathematics
TREEM, W. R., Paediatrics
TRIVEDI, K. S., Electrical and Computer Engineering
TRUSKEY, G. A., Biomedical Engineering
TURNER, B. S., Nursing
TURNER, D. A., Surgery
TYREY, E. L., Obstetrics and Gynaecology
ULSHEN, M. H., Paediatrics
UNDERKUFFLER, L. S., Law
URBANIAK, J. R., Surgery
UYENOYAMA, M. K., Biology
VAN ALSTYNE, W. W., Law
VANCE, J. M., Medicine
VAN ROMPAY, L., Religion
VAN SCHAIK, C., Biological Anthropology and Anatomy
VENAKIDES, S., Mathematics
VERNON, J. M., Economics
VIDMAR, N. J., Law
VILGALYS, R. J., Biology
VISWANATHAN, S., Business Administration
VOGEL, S., Biology
VON RAMM, O. T., Biomedical Engineering
WACKER, G. A., Divinity
WAINWRIGHT, G., Divinity
WALLACH, M. A., Psychological and Brain Sciences
WALTER, R. L., Physics
WALTHER, P. J., Surgery
WANG, P. P., Electrical and Computer Engineering
WARE, R. E., Paediatrics
WARNER, D. S., Anaesthesiology
WEBSTER, G. D., Surgery
WEBSTER, R. E., Biochemistry
WEINBERG, J. B., Medicine
WEINER, R. D., Psychiatry and Behavioural Sciences
WEINERTH, J. L., Surgery
WEINHOLD, K. J., Surgery
WEINTRAUB, E. R., Economics
WEISTART, J. C., Law
WELLER, H. R., Physics
WELLS, S. A., Surgery
WEST, M., Statistics
WHALEY, R. E., Business Administration
WHARTON, A. W., Art and Art History
WHITE, R. A., Biology
WIENER, J. B., Law

WILBUR, R. L., Biology
WILKINS, R. H., Surgery
WILKINSON, W. E., Biostatistics and Bioinformatics
WILLIAMS, C. L., Psychological and Brain Sciences
WILLIAMS, K. J., English
WILLIAMS, R. B., Psychiatry and Behavioural Sciences
WILLIAMS, R. S., Medicine
WILLIMON, W. H., Divinity
WILSON, J., Sociology
WILSON, J. A. P., Medicine
WILSON, K. H., Medicine
WILSON, R. L., Nursing
WINKLER, R. L., Business Administration
WITT, R. G., History
WOLBARSHT, M. L., Psychological and Brain Sciences
WOLFE, W. G., Surgery
WOLPERT, R. L., Statistics
WONG, D. B., Philosophy
WOOD, P. H., History
WRIGHT, J. R., Cell Biology
YANG, W., Chemistry
YARGER, W. E., Medicine
YOUNG, S. L., Medicine
ZALUTSKY, M. R., Radiology
ZHOU, X., Mathematics
ZHOU, X., Sociology
ZIPKIN, P. H., Business Administration

ELON UNIVERSITY

100 Campus Dr., Elon, NC 27244

Telephone: (336) 278-2000
E-mail: admissions@elon.edu
Internet: www.elon.edu

Founded 1889 as Elon College, present name and status 2001
Private control
Academic year: September to May (2 semesters)

Pres.: Dr LEO M. LAMBERT
Exec. Vice-Pres.: GERALD L. FRANCIS
Provost and Vice-Pres. for Academic Affairs: STEVEN D. HOUSE
Sr Vice-Pres. for Business, Finance and Technology: GERALD O. WHITTINGTON
Vice-Pres. for Admissions and Financial Planning: SUSAN C. KLOPMAN
Vice-Pres. for Student Life and Dean for Students: G. SMITH JACKSON
Vice-Pres. for Univ. Advancement: JIM PIATT
Vice-Pres. for Univ. Communications: DANIEL J. ANDERSON
Dean and Univ. Librarian: KATE D. HICKEY

Library of 300,000 vols, 40,000 ejournals, 20,000 audiovisual items
Number of teachers: 365 (full-time)
Number of students: 5,900 (5,215 undergraduate, 685 graduate)

DEANS

Elon College, College of Arts and Sciences: Dr ALISON MORRISON-SHETLAR
Martha and Spencer Love School of Business: Dr SCOTT BUECHLER
School of Communications: Prof. Dr PAUL PARSONS
School of Education: Prof. Dr DAVID COOPER
School of Health Sciences: Dr ELIZABETH A. ROGERS
School of Law: Prof. Dr GEORGE R. JOHNSON, JR

GARDNER-WEBB UNIVERSITY

POB 997, Boiling Springs, NC 28017
110 S Main St, Boiling Springs, NC 28017

Telephone: (704) 406-4000
E-mail: admissions@gardner-webb.edu
Internet: www.gardner-webb.edu

Founded 1905 as Boiling Springs High School; present name and status 1993
Private control
Academic year: August to May

Pres.: Prof. Dr ARNOLD FRANK BONNER
Provost and Sr Vice-Pres.: Dr BEN C. LESLIE
Vice-Pres. and Dean of Student Devt: BRUCE MOORE
Vice-Pres. for Advancement: RALPH DIXON, JR
Vice-Pres. for Business and Finance: MIKE W. HARDIN
Vice-Pres. for Enrolment Management: JACK BUCHANAN
Registrar: STEPHEN SAIN
Dean of Libraries: MARY ROBY

Library of 200,000 vols, 27,000 ebooks
Number of teachers: 145 (full-time)
Number of students: 4,300

GREENSBORO COLLEGE

815 W Market St, Greensboro, NC 27401-1875

Telephone: (336) 272-7102
E-mail: admissions@gborocollege.edu
Internet: www.greensboro.edu

Founded 1838
Private control
Academic year: August to May (2 semesters)

Depts of accounting, art, business administration and economics, education, English and communication studies, history, kinesiology, mathematics and computer science, music, natural sciences, political science and legal administration, psychology, religion, sociology, theatre

Pres.: Prof. Dr LAWRENCE D. CZARDA
Vice-Pres. for Academic Affairs and Dean of Faculty: Prof. Dr PAUL L. LESLIE
Vice-Pres. for Enrolment Management and Marketing: (vacant)
Vice-Pres. for Institutional Advancement: JOAN GLYNN
Vice-Pres. for Operations: ROBIN L. DANIEL
Dean of Students: ILONA T. OWENS
Dir of Admissions: JULIANNE SCHATZ
Registrar: PHYLLIS CHAMBERS
Library Dir: CHRISTINE A. WHITTINGTON

Library of 500,000 vols
Number of teachers: 115 (65 full-time, 50 part-time)
Number of students: 1,250

Publication: *Points Of Pride* (1 a year)

GUILFORD COLLEGE

5800 W Friendly Ave, Greensboro, NC 27410

Telephone: (336) 316-2000
E-mail: admission@guilford.edu
Internet: www.guilford.edu

Founded 1837 as New Garden Boarding School, present name and status 1888
Private control
Academic year: August to May (2 semesters)

Liberal arts college; areas of study incl. accounting, art, English, geology, integrative studies, int. political economy, peace and conflict studies, philosophy, physics, political science, psychology, sociology and anthropology, sport admin., theatre studies, visual arts

Pres.: Prof. Dr KENT JOHN CHABOTAR
Vice-Pres. for Academic Affairs and Academic Dean: ADRIENNE ISRAEL
Vice-Pres. for Admin.: JON VARNELL
Vice-Pres. for Advancement: MIKE POSTON
Vice-Pres. for Enrolment Services: RANDY DOSS
Vice-Pres. for Finance: GREG BURSAVICH
Vice-Pres. for Student Affairs and Dean of Students: AARON FETROW
Library Dir: LEAH MCGINNIS DUNN

Library of 240,000 vols incl. periodicals
Number of teachers: 130 (full-time)

Number of students: 2,740

Publications: *Journal of Undergraduate Mathematics* (2 a year), *Journal of Undergraduate Research in Physics* (2 a year), *The Greenleaf Review* (1 a year), *The Southern Friend* (2 a year)

HIGH POINT UNIVERSITY

833 Montlieu Ave, High Point, NC 27262-3598

Telephone: (336) 841-9000
Internet: www.highpoint.edu
Founded 1924 as High Point College, present name 1991
Private control
Academic year: August to May (2 semesters)
Pres.: Dr NIDO R. QUBEIN
Provost and Vice-Pres. for Academic Affairs: Dr DENNIS G. CARROLL
Vice-Pres. and Chief of Staff: CHRISTOPHER DUDLEY
Vice-Pres. for Business Affairs: Dr DENNY G. BOLTON
Vice-Pres. for Enrolment: ANDY BILLS
Vice-Pres. for Institutional Advancement: BETH BRAXTON
Vice-Pres. for Student Life: GAIL C. TUTTLE
Dean of Students: Dr KEVIN SNYDER
Registrar: DIANA LEE ESTEY
Dir of Library Services: DAVID L. BRYDEN
Library of 310,000 vols
Number of teachers: 165 (full-time)
Number of students: 3,690 (undergraduate)
Publication: *HPU Magazine*

DEANS

College of Arts and Science: Dr CAROLE B. STONEKING
Earl N. Phillips School of Business: Dr JAMES B. WEHRLEY
Nido R. Qubein School of Communication: WILFRED TREMBLAY
Norcross Graduate School: Dr ALBERTA HERRON
School of Art and Design: TURPIN JOINS
School of Education: Dr MARIANN TILLERY

JOHNSON C. SMITH UNIVERSITY

100 Beatties Ford Rd, Charlotte, NC 28216
Telephone: (704) 378-1000
E-mail: admissions@jcsu.edu
Internet: www.jcsu.edu
Founded 1867 as Biddle Memorial Institute, present name 1923
Private control
Academic year: August to May (2 semesters)
Pres.: Dr RONALD CARTER
Exec. Vice-Pres. and Chief Operating Officer: Dr ELFRED PINKARD
Vice-Pres. for Business and Finance: GERALD HECTOR
Vice-Pres. for Institutional Advancement: JOY PAIGE
Vice-Pres. for Student Affairs: JEFFREY SMITH
Dean of Enrolment Services: CATHERINE HURD
Dean of Students: CATHY JONES
Dir of Admissions: DWIGHT SANCHEZ
Registrar: KEISHA WILSON
Dir of Library Services: MONIKA RHUE
Library of 113,000 vols
Number of teachers: 95 (full-time)
Number of students: 1,550 (1,500 full-time, 50 part-time)
Publications: *The Treewell, Undergraduate Research Journal* (1 a year)

DEANS

College of Arts and Letters: JOSEPH TURNER
College of Professional Studies: Dr HELEN CALDWELL

College of Science, Technology, Engineering and Mathematics: Dr MAGDY ATTIA
Metropolitan College: Dr ZENOBIA EDWARDS

LAUREL UNIVERSITY

1215 Eastchester Dr., High Point, NC 27265
Telephone: (336) 887-3000
E-mail: admissions@laureluniversity.edu
Internet: www.laureluniversity.edu
Founded 1903 as Greensboro Bible and Training School; present name 2011
Private control
Academic year: August to July (3 semesters)
Pres.: Dr LARRY McCULLOUGH
Exec. Vice-Pres.: Dr OWEN ALLEN
Academic Dean of Undergraduate Studies: Dr JOHN LINDSEY
Dean of Graduate Studies: Prof. Dr ROBERT BRUMLEY
Registrar: GREG WORKMAN
Dir of Library Services: APRIL LINDSEY
Library of 40,000 vols
Number of teachers: 18 (6 full-time, 12 part-time)
Number of students: 145

DEANS

Adult, Professional and Graduate Studies: GARY LOUNSBERRY
School of Management: Dr OWEN ALLEN

LEES-MCRAE COLLEGE

191 Main St, POB 128, Banner Elk, NC 28604
Telephone: (828) 898-5241
E-mail: admissions@lmc.edu
Internet: www.lmc.edu
Founded 1900 as a girls' school; present name 1931
Private control
Academic year: August to May (2 semesters)
Academic programmes incl. Appalachian studies, art and design, athletic training, biology, business admin., communication arts, criminal justice, English, history, humanities, interdisciplinary studies, international studies, mathematics, musical theatre, outdoor adventure studies, performing arts studies, philosophy, psychology, religious studies, sport management, sport science
Pres.: Dr BARRY M. BUXTON
Vice-Pres. for Academic Affairs: Dr KACY E. CRABTREE
Vice-Pres. for Advancement: CAROLINE O. HART
Vice-Pres. for Enrolment Management: GINGER HANSEN
Vice-Pres. for Finance and Business Affairs: KEN BUCHANAN
Dean of Students: ALLISON NORRIS
Registrar: LYNN HINSHAW
Dir of Libraries: RUSSELL TAYLOR
Library of 100,000 vols, periodicals, microforms, audiovisual materials
Number of teachers: 50 (full-time)
Number of students: 900

LENOIR-RHYNE UNIVERSITY

625 Seventh Ave NE, Hickory, NC 28601-3984
Telephone: (828) 328-7300
E-mail: admissions@lr.edu
Internet: www.lr.edu
Founded 1891 as Highland College, present name 2008
Private control
Academic year: August to May (2 semesters)
Pres.: Dr WAYNE POWELL
Provost: Dr LARRY HALL

Vice-Pres. for Admin. and Finance: PETER J. KENDALL
Vice-Pres. of Enrolment Management: RACHEL A. NICHOLS
Vice-Pres. for Institutional Advancement: Dr W. SCOTT SHRODE
Dean of Students: Dr KATIE PATTILLO FISHER
Dir of Admissions: KAREN B. FEEZOR
Registrar: KATHY HAHN
Dir of Library Services: RITA JOHNSON
Library of 160,000 vols
Number of teachers: 100 full-time
Number of students: 1,850

DEANS

College of Arts and Sciences: Prof. Dr DANIEL W. KISER
College of Education and Human Services: Dr HANK WEDDINGTON
College of Health Sciences: Prof. Dr KATHERINE PASOUR
College of Professional and Mathematical Studies: Prof. Dr WILLIAM M. MAUNEY
Graduate and Lifelong Learning Programmes: Dr AMY WOOD

LIVINGSTONE COLLEGE

701 W Monroe St, Salisbury, NC 28144-5213
Telephone: (704) 216-6000
E-mail: admissions@livingstone.edu
Internet: www.livingstone.edu
Founded 1879 as Zion Wesley Institute, current name adopted 1887
Private control
Academic year: August to May (2 semesters)
Divs of business, education, social work and psychology, liberal arts, mathematics and sciences
Pres.: Dr JIMMY R. JENKINS, SR (acting)
Vice-Pres. for Academic Affairs: Dr LEROY SIMMONS
Vice-Pres. for Business and Finance: WILLIAM JAMES
Vice-Pres. for Institutional Advancement: HERMAN J. FELTON, JR
Vice-Pres. for Student Affairs: Dr STANLEY J. ELLIOTT
Registrar: WENDY R. JACKSON
Dir for Library Services: GWENDOLYN PEART
Library of 80,000 vols
Number of teachers: 81 (59 full-time, 22 part-time)
Number of students: 1,156 (1,146 full-time, 10 part-time)
Publications: *Bears' Tale* (1 a year), *The Livingstonian* (1 a year)

MARS HILL COLLEGE

POB 6663, Mars Hill, NC 28754
100 Athletic St, Mars Hill, NC 28754
Telephone: (828) 689-1201
E-mail: admissions@mhc.edu
Internet: www.mhc.edu
Founded 1856 as French Broad Baptist Institute, present name 1859
Private control
Academic year: August to May (2 semesters)
Academic divs incl. humanities and social science, mathematics and natural sciences, professional programmes and interdisciplinary majors and minors
Pres.: Dr DAN G. LUNSFORD
Exec. Vice-Pres. and Vice-Pres. for Academic and Student Affairs: Dr JOHN W. WELLS
Vice-Pres. for Enrolment Management: CRAIG GOFORTH
Vice-Pres. for Finance: NEIL TILLEY
Vice-Pres. for Institutional Advancement: BUD CHRISTMAN
Registrar: EDITH L. WHITT
Library Dir: BEV ROBERTSON

Library of 90,000 vols
Number of teachers: 85
Number of students: 1,200

MEREDITH COLLEGE

3800 Hillsborough St, Raleigh, NC 27607-5298

Telephone: (919) 760-8600
E-mail: admissions@meredith.edu
Internet: www.meredith.edu

Founded 1891 as Baptist Female Univ., present name 1909
Private control
Academic year: August to May (2 semesters)
Pres.: Dr Jo Allen
Sr Vice-Pres. for Academic Admin.: Denise Rotondo
Vice-Pres. for Academic Planning and Programmes: Elizabeth Wolfinger
Vice-Pres. for Business and Finance: Craig Barfield
Vice-Pres. for College Programmes: Dr Jean Jackson
Vice-Pres. for Institutional Advancement: Lennie Barton
Dir of Admissions: Jen Miller-Hogg
Registrar: Amanda Steele-Middleton
Dean of Library Information Services: Laura Davidson

Library of 190,000 vols, 16,000 microforms, 3000 newspaper and journals
Number of teachers: 140 (full-time)
Number of students: 2,130 (1,825 undergraduate, 305 graduate)

DEANS

School of Business: Prof. Dr Denise M. Rotondo
School of Education: Prof. Marie Chamblee
School of Humanities and Social Science: Prof. Dr Garry Walton
School of the Arts: Prof. Dr Rebecca Bailey

METHODIST UNIVERSITY

5400 Ramsey St, Fayetteville, NC 28311-1420

Telephone: (910) 630-7000
E-mail: pmcevoy@methodist.edu
Internet: www.methodist.edu

Founded 1956 as Methodist College, present name and status 2006
Private control
Academic year: August to May
Pres.: Dr Ben E. Hancock, Jr
Exec. Vice-Pres. and Academic Dean: Dr Delmas S. Crisp, Jr
Vice-Pres. for Business Affairs: Gene T. Clayton
Vice-Pres. for Enrolment Services: Rick Lowe
Vice-Pres. for Institutional Advancement: Robin Davenport
Vice-Pres. for Planning and Evaluation: Dr Donald Lassiter
Vice-Pres. for Student Devt and Services: William Walker
Dean of Admissions: Jamie Legg
Registrar: Jasmin Brown
Dir of Library Services: Tracey Pearson

Library of 111,224 vols, 45,000 non-book holdings
Number of teachers: 210
Number of students: 2,400

DEANS

Reeves School of Business: Joseph F. Doll
School of Arts and Humanities: Dr Lori Brookman
School of Graduate Studies: Dr Lori Brookman
School of Public Affairs: Dr Bonita Belcastro

School of Science and Human Development: Dr Tat W. Chan

MID-ATLANTIC CHRISTIAN UNIVERSITY

715 N Poindexter St, Elizabeth City, NC 27909

Telephone: (252) 334-2000
E-mail: admissions@macuniversity.edu
Internet: www.macuniversity.edu

Founded 1948 as Roanoke Bible College, present name 2009
Private control

Depts of arts and sciences, biblical studies, Christian ministry, marketplace ministry; schools of professional studies, undergraduate studies
Pres.: Dr D. Clay Perkins
Vice-Pres. for Academic Affairs: Dr Kevin W. Larsen
Vice-Pres. for Devt: W. Keith Wood
Vice-Pres. for Enrolment Services: Dr Kendall S. Greene
Vice-Pres. for Finance: Kurtis L. Kight
Vice-Pres. for Student Life: Dr Kendall S. Greene
Registrar: Joan U. Sawyer
Library Dir: Trish Griffin

Number of teachers: 17
Number of students: 195

MONTREAT COLLEGE

310 Gaither Circle, POB 1267, Montreat, NC 28757

Telephone: (828) 669-8011
E-mail: admissions@montreat.edu
Internet: www.montreat.edu

Founded 1916 as Montreat Normal School, present name 1934
Private control
Academic year: August to May (2 Semesters)
Br. campuses in Asheville, Black Mountain, Charlotte, Morganton, Raleigh, Rocky Mount; schools of arts and sciences, professional and adult studies; graduate programmes in arts, sciences
Pres.: Dr Dan Struble
Provost and Sr Vice-Pres.: Dr Marshall E. Flowers, Jr
Vice-Pres. and Dean of Academics: Dr Abby Fapetu
Vice-Pres. for Advancement: Joe B. Kirkland
Vice-Pres. for Enrolment and Marketing: Jonathan E. Shores
Vice-Pres. for Finance and Admin.: Geoff Bremer
Vice-Pres. for Institutional Advancement: Joe Kirkland
Vice-Pres. for Student Services and Dean of Students: Charles A. Lance
Dean of Admissions and Financial Aid: Lisa Lankford
Registrar: Merrill Nix McCarthy
Library Dir: Elizabeth Pearson

Number of teachers: 90
Number of students: 1,040
Publication: Reflection

MOUNT OLIVE COLLEGE

634 Henderson St, Mount Olive, NC 28365
Telephone: (919) 658-2502
E-mail: admissions@moc.edu
Internet: www.moc.edu

Founded 1951 as Mount Allen Jr College, present name 1970, present status 1980
Private control
Academic year: August to July (2 semesters)

Br. campuses in Goldsboro, Jacksonville, New Bern, Research Triangle Park, Washington, Wilmington
Pres.: Dr Philip Paul Kerstetter
Exec. Vice-Pres.: Dr Carol G. Carrere
Vice-Pres. for Academic Affairs: Prof. Dr Ellen S. Jordan
Vice-Pres. for Enrolment: Dr Barbara R. Kornegay
Vice-Pres. for Finance: Debra Smith
Vice-Pres. for Institutional Advancement: Dr Kevin Jean
Vice-Pres. for Student Affairs: Dan Sullivan
Registrar: David Bourgeois
Dir of Library Services: Pamela R. Wood

Library of 100,000 vols, 7,500 journals and periodicals, 30,000 ebooks
Number of teachers: 315 (88 full-time, 227 part-time)
Number of students: 5,000

DEANS

School of Arts and Sciences: Prof. Dr David Hines
Tillman School of Business: Dr Ronald Pressley

NORTH CAROLINA WESLEYAN COLLEGE

3400 N Wesleyan Blvd, Rocky Mount, NC 27804–8630

Telephone: (252) 985-5100
E-mail: registrar@ncwc.edu
Internet: www.ncwc.edu

Founded 1956
Private control
Academic year: January to May

Liberal arts college; academic divs incl. business, education, mathematics and sciences, social sciences and humanities
Pres.: James A. Gray, III
Provost and Sr Vice-Pres. for Academic Affairs: Dr Robert Jay Stubblefield
Vice-Pres. for Enrolment Management: Bill Allen
Vice-Pres. for Finance: Loren Loomis Hubbell
Vice-Pres. for Student Affairs and Dean of Students: Randy Williams
Dir of Library: Kathy Winslow

Library of 100,000 vols, 30,000 ebooks
Number of teachers: 70
Number of students: 1,700

PFEIFFER UNIVERSITY

48380 US Highway 52, Misenheimer, NC 28109

Telephone: (704) 463-1360
E-mail: admis@pfeiffer.edu
Internet: www.pfeiffer.edu

Founded 1885 as Oberlin Home and School, present name and status 1996
Private control
Academic year: August to May (2 semesters)
Br. campuses in Charlotte, Triangle
Pres.: Dr Michael C. Miller
Chief Operating Officer and Exec. Vice-Pres.: David Olive
Provost and Vice-Pres. for Academic Affairs: Dr Tracy Espy
Vice-Pres. for Advancement and Chief Operating Officer: Bobby Stewart
Vice-Pres. for Enrolment Management and Marketing: Michael Poll
Vice-Pres. for Finance and Chief Financial Officer: Robin Leslie
Vice-Pres. for Student Devt and Dean for Students: Dr Russ Sharples
Registrar: Lourdes Silva
Library Dir: Lara Little

Library of 132,471 vols, 29,735 microform units, 3,766 audiovisual materials, 22,115 ejournals
Number of teachers: 95 (full-time)
Number of students: 2,020 (1,018 undergraduate, 1,002 graduate)
Publication: *Pfeiffer Phoenix* (1 a year)

DEANS

Continuing Education and Adult Professional Studies: PAULITA BROOKER
School of Humanities: Prof. Dr DAVID HECKEL
School of Natural and Health Sciences: Dr MARK MCCALLUM
School of Religion: Dr DOUG HUME
School of Social and Behavioural Sciences: Prof. Dr DONALD POE, JR

QUEENS UNIVERSITY OF CHARLOTTE

1900 Selwyn Ave, Charlotte, NC 28274
Telephone: (704) 337-2200
E-mail: admissions@queens.edu
Internet: www.queens.edu
Founded 1857 as Charlotte Female Institute, present name and status 2002
Private control
Academic year: August to May
Pres.: Dr PAMELA L. DAVIES
Provost and Vice-Pres. for Academic Affairs: Dr ABIODUN GOKE-PARIOLA
Vice-Pres. for Admin. and Chief Financial Officer: MATT PACKEY
Vice-Pres. for Enrolment Management: Dr BRIAN RALPH (acting)
Vice-Pres. for Univ. Advancement: JAMES BULLOCK
Registrar: EDWARD ADAMS
Univ. Librarian: Dr CAROL WALKER JORDAN
Library of 150,000 vols
Number of teachers: 110 (full-time)
Number of students: 2,600
Publication: *Odyssey* (4 a year)

DEANS

Blair College of Health and Presbyterian School of Nursing: Dr TAMA L. MORRIS
College of Arts and Sciences: Dr LYNN MORTON
Hayworth College for Adult Studies: KRISTA TILLMAN
James L. Knight School of Communication: VAN KING
McColl School of Business: Dr TERRY BRODERICK
Wayland H. Cato, Jr School of Education: Dr DARREL MILLER

SAINT AUGUSTINE'S COLLEGE

1315 Oakwood Ave, Raleigh, NC 27610-2298
Telephone: (919) 516-4000
E-mail: admissions@st-aug.com
Internet: www.st-aug.edu
Founded 1867
Private control
Academic year: August to May
Pres.: Dr DIANNE BOARDLEY SUBER
Exec. Vice-Pres.: LEON SCOTT
Vice-Pres. of Institutional Advancement and Devt: MARC A. NEWMAN
Dean of Students: DORIS BULLOCK
Registrar: CRYSTAL WILLIAMS
Dean of the Library Services: CLEVELL S. ROSEBORO, II
Library of 100,000 vols, 300 periodicals
Number of teachers: 100
Number of students: 1,600

DEANS

Div. of Allied Health: Dr HENGAMEH G. ALLEN
Div. of Business: KENT LUSK

Div. of Extended Studies: ROLAND BULLARD
Div. of Liberal Arts and Education: Dr M. IYAILU MOSES
Div. of Natural Sciences and Mathematics: MARK MELTON

SALEM COLLEGE

601 S Church St, Winston-Salem, NC 27101
Telephone: (336) 721-2600
Internet: www.salem.edu
Founded 1772
Private control
Academic year: August to August
Areas of study incl. business administration, interior design, mathematics, philosophy and religion, sociology
Pres.: Dr SUSAN E. PAULY
Vice-Pres. for Academic Affairs and Student Affairs and Dean of College: Dr SUSAN CALOVINI
Vice-Pres. for Institutional Advancement: VICKI WILLIAMS SHEPPARD
Dean of Admissions and Financial Aid: KATHERINE KNAPP WATTS
Dean of Students: KRISPIN W. BARR
Dir for Admin.: ANNA BECK GALLIMORE
Registrar: MARK ASHLEY
Dir for Libraries: Dr ROSE A. SIMON
Library of 159,000 vols, 57,000 ebooks, 24,000 eperiodicals
Number of teachers: 105 (full-time)
Number of students: 1,100

DEANS

Martha H. Fleer Center for Adult Education: SUZANNE WILLIAMS

SHAW UNIVERSITY

118 E South St, Raleigh, NC 27601
Telephone: (919) 546-8200
E-mail: admissions@shawu.edu
Internet: www.shawu.edu
Founded 1865, present name and status 1875
Private control
Academic year: August to May (2 semesters)
Pres.: Dr DOROTHY COWSER YANCY
Exec. Vice-Pres.: MARTEL PERRY
Vice-Pres. for Academic Affairs: Dr MARILYN SUTTON-HAYWOOD
Vice-Pres. for Fiscal Affairs: DEBRA LATIMORE
Vice-Pres. for Institutional Advancement: ANITA BROWER
Vice-Pres. for Student Affairs and Admin.: Dr JEFFREY A. SMITH
Dean of Enrolment Management: ROCHELLE KING
Dean of Students: DORIS BULLOCK
Registrar: JODY HAMILTON-DAVIS
Dir of Library Services: CAROLYN PETERSON
Library of 130,000 vols, 127,000 microfiche units
Number of teachers: 240
Number of students: 2,720

DEANS

College of Arts and Sciences: Dr RENATA DUSENBURY
College of Graduate and Professional Studies: Dr GADDIS FAULCON
Divinity School: Dr BRUCE GRADY

SOUTHEASTERN BAPTIST THEOLOGICAL SEMINARY

POB 1889, Wake Forest, NC 27588
120 S Wingate St, Wake Forest, NC 27587
Telephone: (919) 761-2100
E-mail: admissions@sebts.edu
Internet: www.sebts.edu
Founded 1950
Private control

Academic year: August to May
Degrees offered incl. BA in Christian studies, master of church music, divinity
Pres.: Dr DANIEL L. AKIN
Sr Vice-Pres. for Academic Admin. and Dean of Faculty: Dr KENNETH KEATHLEY
Sr Vice-Pres. for Business Admin.: RYAN R. HUTCHINSON
Vice-Pres. for Institutional Advancement: DENNIS DARVILLE
Vice-Pres. for Student Services and Dean of Students: Dr MARK LIEDERBACH
Dean of College: BRUCE R. ASHFORD
Registrar: SHELDON H. ALEXANDER
Dir for Library: SHAWN C. MADDEN
Library of 300,000 vols
Number of teachers: 80
Number of students: 1,500

ST ANDREWS UNIVERSITY

1700 Dogwood Mile, Laurinburg, NC 28352
Telephone: (910) 277-5555
E-mail: admissions@sapc.edu
Internet: www.sapc.edu
Founded 1958 as St. Andrews Presbyterian College by merger of Flora Macdonald College (f. 1896) with Presbyterian Jr College (f. 1928), present name 2011; attached to Webber International Univ., Florida
Private control
Academic year: August to May
Academic programmes incl. biology, business admin., elementary education, English and creative writing, forensic science, sport and recreation studies
Pres.: PAUL BALDASARE
Vice-Pres. for Academic Affairs and Dean of College: Dr ROBERT J. HOPKINS
Vice-Pres. for Admin. and Dean of Students: GLENN BATTEN
Vice-Pres. for Business and Finance: TERRY LAUGHTER
Vice-Pres. for Enrolment Management: JEFF BENNETT
Registrar: DEBORAH A. SMITH
Library Dir: MARY MCDONALD
Library of 170,000 vols incl. ebooks, 200 current periodicals
Number of teachers: 65 (30 full-time, 35 part-time)
Number of students: 740
Publication: *Cairn* (1 a year)

UNIVERSITY OF NORTH CAROLINA

910 Raleigh Rd, POB 2688, Chapel Hill, NC 27514
Telephone: (919) 962-1000
Internet: www.northcarolina.edu
Founded 1789
Pres.: THOMAS W. ROSS
Sr Vice-Pres. for Academic Affairs: SUZANNE ORTEGA
Vice-Pres. and Gen. Counsel: LAURA LUGER
Vice-Pres. for Academic Planning: (vacant)
Vice-Pres. for Finance: CHARLIE PERUSSE
Vice-Pres. for Govt Relations: ANITA WATKINS
Vice-Pres. for Information Resources and Chief Information Officer: JOHN LEYDON
Vice-Pres. for Research: Dr STEVEN LEATH
Sec. of Univ.: BART CORGNATI
Number of students: 221,727 ...

CONSTITUENT UNIVERSITIES

Appalachian State University
Boone, NC 28608
Telephone: (828) 262-2000
E-mail: admissions@appstate.edu
Internet: www.appstate.edu

Founded 1899 as Watauga Acad., current name adopted 1967

Academic year: August to May (2 semesters)

Chancellor: Dr KENNETH E. PEACOCK

Provost and Exec. Vice-Chancellor: Dr LORI GONZALEZ

Vice-Chancellor for Business Affairs: GREGORY M. LOVINS

Vice-Chancellor for Student Devt: CINDY WALLACE

Vice-Chancellor for Univ. Advancement: SUSAN PETTYJOHN

Registrar: ANDREA WAWRZUSIN

Univ. Librarian: MARY REICHEL

Library of 925,290 vols, 1,542,256 microforms

Number of teachers: 870 (full-time)

Number of students: 17,350 (15,460 undergraduate, 1,890 graduate)

Publication: *Appalachian Today* (2 a year)

DEANS

College of Arts and Sciences: Dr ANTHONY G. CALAMAI

College of Business: Dr RANDAL K. EDWARDS

College of Education: Dr CHARLES DUKE

College of Fine and Applied Arts: Dr GLENDA TREADAWAY

College of Health Sciences: Dr FRED WHITT

Hayes School of Music: Dr WILLIAM PELTO

Research and Graduate Studies: Dr EDELMA D. HUNTLEY

East Carolina University

East Fifth St, Greenville, NC 27858-4353

Telephone: (252) 328-6131

E-mail: admis@ecu.edu

Internet: www.ecu.edu

Founded 1907

Academic year: August to May (2 semesters)

Chancellor: Dr STEVE BALLARD

Provost and Sr Vice-Chancellor for Academic Affairs: Dr MARILYN SHEERER

Vice-Chancellor for Admin. and Finance: Dr RICK NISWANDER

Vice-Chancellor for Research and Graduate Studies: Dr DEIRDRE MAGEEAN

Vice-Chancellor for Student Affairs: Dr VIRGINIA HARDY

Vice-Chancellor for Univ. Advancement: CHRISTOPHER DYBA

Registrar: ANGELA R. ANDERSON

Dir of Admissions: DONALD C. JOYNER

Dean of Academic Library and Learning Resources: LARRY BOYER

Library: 1.3m. vols

Number of teachers: 2,050

Number of students: 27,800

Publications: *The Children's Folklore Review* (2 a year), *Tar River Poetry* (2 a year), *Technical Communication* (4 a year), *The North Carolina Folklore Journal* (2 a year), *The North Carolina Literary Review* (1 a year)

DEANS

Brody School of Medicine: Dr PAUL R. G. CUNNINGHAM

College of Allied Health Sciences: Prof. Dr STEPHEN THOMAS

College of Business: Dr STANLEY G. EAKINS

College of Education: Prof. Dr LINDA ANN PATRIARCA

College of Fine Arts and Communication: Dr MICHAEL DORSEY

College of Health and Human Performance: Dr GLEN GILBERT

College of Human Ecology: Dr JUDY SIGUAW

College of Nursing: Dr SYLVIA T. BROWN

College of Technology and Computer Science: Dr DAVID WHITE

Graduate School: Dr PAUL GEMPERLINE

Honors College: Dr RICHARD R. EAKIN

School of Dental Medicine: Dr D. GREGORY CHADWICK

Thomas Harriot College of Arts and Sciences: Dr ALAN WHITE

Elizabeth City State University

1704 Weeksville Rd, Elizabeth City, NC 27909

Telephone: (252) 335-3400

E-mail: infoline@mail.ecsu.edu

Internet: www.ecsu.edu

Founded 1891 as a normal school; current name adopted 1969

Academic year: August to May (2 semesters)

Chancellor: Dr WILLIE J. GILCHRIST

Provost and Vice-Chancellor for Academic Affairs: Dr ALI A. KHAN

Vice-Chancellor for Business and Finance and Chief Financial Officer: BENJAMIN DURANT

Vice-Chancellor for Institutional Advancement: WILLIAM G. SMITH

Vice-Chancellor for Student Affairs: Dr ANTHONY BROWN

Registrar: VINCENT L. BEAMON

Dir of Library Services: JUANITA MIDGETTE SPENCE

Number of teachers: 175 (full-time)

Number of students: 3,300 (2,910 full-time, 390 part-time)

Publication: *ECSU Magazine* (2 a year)

DEANS

School of Arts and Humanities: Dr MUREL JONES

School of Education and Psychology: Prof. Dr CHARLES CHERRY

School of Mathematics, Science and Technology: Dr HARRY BASS

Walter R. Davis School of Business and Economics: DAVID BEJOU

Fayetteville State University

1200 Murchison Rd, Fayetteville, NC 28301-4298

Telephone: (910) 672-1111

E-mail: admissions@uncfsu.edu

Internet: www.uncfsu.edu

Founded 1867 as Howard School, present name and status 1969

Chancellor: Dr JAMES A. ANDERSON

Provost and Vice-Chancellor for Academic Affairs: Dr JON YOUNG

Vice-Chancellor and Chief of Staff: Dr THOMAS E. H. CONWAY, JR

Vice-Chancellor for Business and Finance: ROBERT L. BOTLEY

Vice-Chancellor for Institutional Advancement: ARTHUR G. AFFLECK

Vice-Chancellor for Student Affairs: Dr JANICE HAYNIE

Registrar: SARAH BAKER

Dir of Library Services: BOBBY C. WYNN

Library of 317,412 vols, 64,000 ebooks, 1,005,010 microforms, 2,769 periodicals, 56 newspapers, 19,751 audiovisual items

Number of teachers: 250 (full-time)

Number of students: 5,780

DEANS

College of Arts and Sciences: Dr DAVID BARLOW

Graduate Studies: Dr LADELLE OLION

School of Business and Economics: Dr ASSAD TAVAKOLI

School of Education: Dr LEONTYE LEWIS

University College: Dr JOHN BROOKS

North Carolina Agricultural and Technical State University

1601 E Market St, Greensboro, NC 27411

Telephone: (336) 334-7500

E-mail: uadmit@ncat.edu

Internet: www.ncat.edu

Founded 1891 as Agricultural and Mechanical College, present name and status 1967

Chancellor: Dr HAROLD L. MARTIN, SR

Provost and Vice-Chancellor for Academic Affairs: Dr WINSER ALEXANDER

Vice-Chancellor for Business and Finance: ROBERT POMPEY, JR

Vice-Chancellor for Research and Economic Devt: Dr CELESTINE NTUEN

Vice-Chancellor for Student Affairs: Dr MELODY C. PIERCE

Vice-Chancellor for Univ. Advancement: ROBERT POMPEY, JR

Dean of Students: Dr JUDY RASHID

Registrar: LESTER LUGO

Dean of Library Services: VICKI COLEMAN

Library of 416,000 vols

Number of teachers: 550 (full-time)

Number of students: 10,900 (9,220 undergraduate, 1,680 graduate)

Publication: *A&T Today* (3 a year)

DEANS

College of Arts and Sciences: Prof. Dr NATHAN F. SIMMS

College of Engineering: Dr ROBIN N. COGER

Joint School of Nanoscience and Nanoengineering: Prof. Dr JAMES G. RYAN

School of Agriculture and Environmental Sciences: Dr WILLIAM RANDLE

School of Business and Economics: Dr QUIESTER CRAIG

School of Education: Dr WILLIAM B. HARVEY

School of Graduate Studies: Dr SANJIV SARIN

School of Nursing: Dr INEZ TUCK

School of Technology: Dr BENJAMIN UWAKWEH

North Carolina Central University

1801 Fayetteville St, Durham, NC 27707

Telephone: (919) 530-6100

Internet: www.nccu.edu

Founded 1910 as Nat. Religious Training School and Chautauqua for the Colored Race, current name adopted 1969

Academic year: August to May

Chancellor: Dr CHARLIE NELMS

Provost and Vice-Chancellor for Academic Affairs: Dr DEBBIE THOMAS

Vice-Chancellor and Chief of Staff: SUSAN HESTER

Vice-Chancellor for Admin. and Finance: WENDELL M. DAVIS

Vice-Chancellor for Institutional Advancement: LOIS D DELOATCH

Vice-Chancellor for Research and Economic Devt: Dr HAZELL REED

Vice-Chancellor for Student Affairs and Enrolment Management: Dr KEVIN D. ROME

Registrar: Dr JEROME GOODWIN

Dir of Library Services: Dr THEODOSIA SHIELDS

Library of 850,000 vols, 6,165 periodicals

Number of teachers: 390

Number of students: 8,650

Publication: *Campus Echo*

DEANS

College of Behavioural and Social Sciences: Dr ELWOOD L. ROBINSON

College of Liberal Arts: Dr CARLTON WILSON

College of Science and Technology: Dr ABDUL K. MOHAMMED

School of Business: Dr D. KEITH PIGUES

School of Education: Dr CECELIA STEPPE-JONES

School of Graduate Studies: Dr CHANTA HAYWOOD

School of Law: RAYMOND C. PIERCE

School of Library and Information Science: Dr IRENE OWENS

University College: Dr ONTARIO WOODEN

North Carolina State University

Raleigh, NC 27695

Telephone: (919) 515-2011
E-mail: undergrad_admissions@ncsu.edu
Internet: www.ncsu.edu

Founded 1887 as North Carolina College of Agriculture and Mechanic Arts, current name adopted 1965
Academic year: August to May
Chancellor: Dr WILLIAM RANDOLPH. WOODSON
Provost and Exec. Vice-Chancellor: Dr WARWICK ARDEN
Vice-Chancellor and Gen. Counsel: EILEEN S. GOLDGEIER
Vice-Chancellor for Finance and Business: CHARLES D. LEFFLER
Vice-Chancellor for Research and Graduate Studies: Dr TERRI L. LOMAX
Vice-Chancellor for Student Affairs: THOMAS H. STAFFORD, JR
Vice-Chancellor for Univ. Advancement: NEVIN E. KESSELER
Registrar: Dr LOUIS D. HUNT
Vice-Provost and Dir of Libraries: SUSAN K. NUTTER

Library: 4.4m. vols, 400,000 ebooks, 63,271 periodicals, 69,223 serials
Number of teachers: 2,080
Number of students: 34,400

DEANS

College of Agriculture and Life Sciences: Dr JOHNNY C. WYNNE
College of Design: MARVIN J. MALECHA
College of Education: Dr M. JAYNE FLEENER
College of Engineering: LOUIS MARTIN-VEGA
College of Humanities and Social Sciences: JEFFERY P. BRADEN
College of Management: Dr IRA R. WEISS
College of Natural Resources: Dr ROBERT BROWN
College of Physical and Mathematical Sciences: Dr DANIEL L. SOLOMON
College of Textiles: Dr A. BLANTON GODFREY
College of Veterinary Medicine: DAVID G. BRISTOL
Graduate School: DUANE K. LARICK
Undergraduate Academic Programmes: JOHN T. AMBROSE

University of North Carolina at Asheville

One University Heights, Asheville, NC 28804-3299

Telephone: (828) 251-6600
E-mail: admissions@unca.edu
Internet: www.unca.edu

Founded 1927 as Buncombe County Jr College, present status 1969
Academic year: August to August (2 semesters)

Chancellor: Prof. Dr ANNE PONDER
Provost and Vice-Chancellor for Academic Affairs: Dr JANE K. FERNANDES
Vice-Chancellor for Finance and Campus Operations: JOHN G. PIERCE
Vice-Chancellor for Student Affairs: Dr BILL HAGGARD
Dean of Admissions: PATRICE MITCHELL
Registrar: DEBBIE RACE
Univ. Librarian (vacant)

Library of 275,323 vols, 9,185 audiovisual materials
Number of teachers: 210 (full-time)
Number of students: 3,700

Publication: *UNC Asheville Magazine*

DEANS

Humanities: Dr GWEN M. ASHBURN
Natural Sciences: Dr KEITH E. KRUMPE
Social Sciences: Dr JEFF KONZ

University of North Carolina at Chapel Hill

103 South Bldg, POB 9100, Chapel Hill, NC 27599-9100

Telephone: (919) 962-2211
E-mail: unchelp@admissions.unc.edu
Internet: www.unc.edu

Founded 1795, present status 1931
Academic year: August to May
Chancellor: CAROL L. FOLT
Exec. Vice-Chancellor and Provost: JAMES DEAN
Vice-Chancellor and Gen. Counsel: LESLIE STROHM
Vice-Chancellor for Finance and Admin.: KAROL KAIN GRAY
Vice-Chancellor for Research and Economic Devt: BARBARA ENTWISLE
Vice-Chancellor for Student Affairs: Dr WINSTON B. CRISP
Vice-Chancellor for Univ. Advancement: JULIA GRUMBLES
Vice-Chancellor for Workforce Strategy, Equity and Engagement: FELICIA A. WASHINGTON
Univ. Registrar and Asst Provost: CHRISTOPHER DERICKSON
Assoc. Provost for Univ. Libraries and Dir for Academic Affairs: SARAH C. MICHALAK

Library: see under Libraries and Archives
Number of teachers: 3,518
Number of students: 29,137

Publications: *Baseline* (3 a year), *Centerpieces* (12 a year), *Current Contents* (4 a year), *Endeavors* (3 a year), *Southern Economic Journal* (4 a year), *The High School Journal* (4 a year)

DEANS

College of Arts and Sciences: Dr KAREN GIL
Eshelman School of Pharmacy: Dr ROBERT BLOUIN
General College: Dr CAROLYN CANNON
Gillings School of Global Public Health: Dr BARBARA K. RIMER
Graduate School: Dr STEVE MATSON
Kenan-Flagler Business School: Dr DOUGLAS A. SHACKELFORD
School of Dentistry: Dr JANE WEINTRAUB
School of Education: Prof. Dr BILL MCDIARMID
School of Government: Dr MICHAEL R. SMITH
School of Information and Library Science: Dr GARY MARCHIONINI
School of Journalism and Mass Communication: Dr DULCIE STAUGHAN
School of Law: JOHN BOGER
School of Medicine: Dr WILLIAM L. ROPER
School of Nursing: Dr KRISTEN SWANSON
School of Social Work: Dr JACK M. RICHMAN
Summer School: Dr JAN YOPP

PROFESSORS

Allied Medical Programmes:
  MITCHELL, M. M.
  MITCHELL, R. U.
  PETERS, R. W.
  SAKATA, R.
  YODER, D. E.

American Studies Curriculum:
  ALLEN, R. C.
  KASSON, J. S.

Anaesthesiology:
  BOYSEN, P. G.
  GHIA, J. N.
  KAFER, E. R.
  MUELLER, R. A.
  NORFLEET, E. A.
  SPIELMAN, F. J.
  SPRAGUE, D. H.
  VAUGHAN, R. W.

Anthropology:
  CRUMLEY, C. L.
  EVENS, T. M.
  FINKLER, K.
  HOLLAND, D. C.
  JOHNSON, N. B.
  LARSEN, C. S.
  LUTZ, C. A.
  PEACOCK, III, J. L.
  STEPONAITIS, V. P.
  WINTERHALDER, B.

Art:
  FOLDA, III, J. T.
  GRABOWSKI, S. E.
  KINNAIRD, R. W.
  MARKS, A. S.
  NOE, J. L.
  SHERIFF, M. D.
  STURGEON, C.
  ZABOROWSKI, D. J.

Biochemistry:
  CAPLOW, M.
  CARTER, JR, C. W.
  CHANEY, S. G.
  ERREDE, B. J.
  HERMANS, J.
  LEE, D. C.
  LENTZ, B. R.
  MARZLUFF, W. F.
  MEISSNER, G. W.
  MORELL, P.
  NAYFEH, S. N.
  SANCAR, A.
  SWANSTROM, R. I.
  TIDWELL, P. F.
  TRAUT, T. W.
  VAN DYKE, T. A.
  WOLFENDEN, R. V.

Biology:
  BLOOM, K. S.
  BOLLENBACHER, W. E.
  DICKISON, W. C.
  FEDUCCIA, J. A.
  GENSEL, P. G.
  GILBERT, L. I.
  HARRIS, JR, A. K.
  MATSON, S. W.
  MATTHYSSE, A. G.
  PARKS, C. R.
  PEET, R. K.
  PETES, T. D.
  PRINGLE, J. R.
  QUATRANO, R. S.
  SALMON, E. D.
  SCOTT, T. K.
  STAFFORD, D. W.
  STIVEN, A. E.
  WHITE, P. S.
  WILEY, JR, R. H.

Biomedical Engineering Programme:
  LUCAS, C. N.
  TSUI, B. M.

Biostatistics:
  DAVIS, C. E.
  HELMS, R. W.
  KALSBEEK, W. D.
  KOCH, G. G.
  KUPPER, L. L.
  MARGOLIN, B. H.
  QUADE, D. E.
  SEN, P. K.
  SUCHINDRAN, C. M.
  SYMONS, M. J.

Business Administration:
  ALDER, R. S.
  ANDERSON, C. R.
  ARMSTRONG, G. M.
  BATEMAN, T. S.
  BAYUS, B. L.
  BETTIS, R. A.
  BLOCHER, E. J.
  BLOOM, P. N.

COLLINS, J. H.
CONRAD, J. S.
EDWARDS, J. R.
ELVERS, D. A.
EVANS, J. P.
FISCHER, W. A.
HARTZELL, D. J.
KASARDA, J. D.
KLOMPMAKER, J. E.
LANDSMAN, W. R.
MCENALLY, R. W.
MANN, R. A.
MARUCHECK, A. E.
NEEBE, A. W.
PEIRCE, E. R.
PERREAULT, JR, W. D.
PRINGLE, J. J.
RAVENSCRAFT, D. J.
RENDLEMAN, R. J.
ROBERTS, B. S.
RONDINELLI, D. A.
ROSEN, B.
RUBIN, D. S.
SHAPIRO, D. L.
SULLIVAN, R. S.
TILLMAN, R.
WAGNER, H. M.
WHYBARK, D. C.

Cell Biology and Anatomy:
BURRIDGE, K. W. T.
GRANGER, N. A.
HACKENBROCK, C. R.
HENSON, JR, O. W.
HERMAN, B.
JACOBSON, K. A.
KOCH, W. E.
LAUDER, J. M.
LEMASTERS, J. J.
MONTGOMERY, R. L.
O'RAND, M. G.
PENG, H. B.
PETRUSZ, P.
RUSTIONI, A.
SADLER, T. W.
SULIK, K. K.

Chemistry:
BAER, T.
BROOKHART, M. S.
BUCK, R. P.
COKE, J. L.
CRIMMINS, M. T.
DESIMONE, J. M.
ERICKSON, B. W.
EVANS, JR, S. A.
IRENE, E. A.
JICHA, D. C.
JOHNSON, JR, C. S.
JORGENSON, J. W.
KROPP, P. J.
MEYER, T. J.
MILLER, R. E.
MURRAY, R. W.
PEDERSEN, L. G.
SAMULSKI, E. T.
SORRELL, T. N.
SPREMULLI, L. L.
TEMPLETON, J. L.
THOMPSON, N. L.
WIGHTMAN, R. M.

City and Regional Planning:
GODSCHALK, D. R.
GOLDSTEIN, H. A.
KAISER, E. J.
LACEY, L.
LUGER, M. I.
MALIZIA, E. E.
MOREAU, D. H.
ROHE, W. M.

Classics:
BROWN, E. L.
HOUSTON, G. W.
LINDERSKI, J.
MACK, S.
RACE, W. H.

RECKFORD, K. J.
SAMS, G. K.
STADTER, P. A.
WEST, III, W. C.
WOOTEN, C. W.

Communication Studies:
BALTHROP, V. W.
COX, JR, J. R.
DYSON, M. E.
GROSSBERG, L.
HORNE, G. C.
KINDEM, G. A.
LONG, B. W.
ROSENFELD, L. B.
WOOD, J. T.

Comparative Literature:
FURST, L. R.

Computer Science:
BROOKS, JR, F. P.
FUCHS, H.
HALTON, J. H.
MAGO, G. A.
PIZER, S. M.
PLAISTED, D. A.
SMITH, J. B.
WEISS, S. F.

Curriculum, African and Afro-American Studies:
NYANG'ORO, J. E.
SELASSIE, B. H.

Curriculum, Asian Studies:
SEATON, J. P.

Curriculum, Linguistics and Non-West Languages:
HENDRICK, R. J.
MELCHERT, H. C.
TSIAPERA, M.

Curriculum, Public Policy Analysis:
DILL, D. D.
STEGMAN, M. A.

Dentistry:
ARNOLD, R. R.
AUKHIL, I.
BAWDEN, J. W.
BAYNE, S. C.
BECK, J. D.
BURKES, E. J.
CRENSHAW, M. A.
HANKER, J. S.
HERSHEY, H. G.
HEYMANN, H. O.
HUNT, R. J.
HUTCHENS, JR, L. H.
JENZANO, J. W.
KUSY, R. P.
MCIVER, F. T.
MURRAH, V. A.
OFFENBACHER, S.
OLDENBURG, T. R.
PROFFIT, W. R.
ROBERSON, T. M.
SHUGARS, D. A.
SIMPSON, D. M.
STAMM, J. W.
STRAUSS, R. P.
TROPE, M.
TULLOCH, J. F. C.
TURVEY, T. A.
VANN, JR, W. F.
WARREN, D. W.
WHITE, R. P.
WHITE, JR, R. P.
WILLIAMS, R. C.
WRIGHT, J. T.
YAMAUCHI, M.
WOOD, M. T.

Dermatology:
BRIGGAMAN, R. A.
FINE, J. D.
O'KEEFE, E. J.

Developmental Disabilities Training Institute:
BAROFF, G. S.

Dramatic Art:
BARRANGER, M. S.
HAMMOND, D. A.
OWEN, R. A.
RAPHAEL, B. N.
TURNER, C. W.

Economics:
AKIN, J. S.
BENAVIE, A.
BLACK, III, S. W.
BLAU, D. M.
CONWAY, P. J.
DARITY, JR, W. A.
FIELD, JR, A. J.
FRIEDMAN, J. W.
FROYEN, R. T.
GALLANT, A. R.
GALLMAN, R. E.
GUILKEY, D. K.
MROZ, T. A.
MURPHY, J. L.
ROSEFIELDE, S. S.
SALEMI, M. K.
STEWART, J. F.
TARASCIO, V. J.
TAUCHEN, H. V.

Education:
BALLEW, J. H.
BRANTLEY, J. C.
BROWN, D.
BROWN, F.
BURKE, W. I.
COOP, R. H.
CUNNINGHAM, J.
DAY, B. D.
FITZGERALD, W. J.
FRIERSON, H. T.
GALASSI, J. P.
GALLAGHER, J. J.
HENNIS, R. S.
HUNTER, R. C.
LILLIE, D. L.
MARSHALL, C.
MORRISON, J. L.
NOBLIT, G. W.
ODOM, JR, S. L.
PALMER, W.
PRYZWANSKY, W. B.
SIMEONSON, R. J.
SPIEGEL, D. L.
STEDMAN, D. J.
STUCK, G. B.
TOM, A. R.
UNKS, G.
WARE, W. B.
WASIK, B. H.
WHITE, K. P.

Emergency Medicine:
TINTINALLI, J. E.

English:
ANDREWS, W. L.
AVERY, L. G.
BETTS, D. W.
DESSEN, A. C.
EBLE, C. C.
FLORA, J. M.
GLESS, D. J.
GREENE, J. L.
GURA, P. F.
HARMON, W. R.
HARRIS, T.
HENDERSON, M. G.
HOBSON, JR, F. C.
KENNEDY, E. D.
KING, J. K.
LENSING, JR, G. S.
LINDEMANN, E.
LUDINGTON, JR, C. T.
MCGOWAN, J. P.
MOSKAL, J.

O'NEILL, P. P.
PATTERSON, D. W.
RAPER, J. R.
RUST, R. D.
SHAPIRO, A. R.
TAYLOR, B. W.
THOMPSON, J. P.
THORNTON, W.
WAGNER-MARTIN, L. C.
WHISNANT, D. E.
WITTING, J. S.
ZUG, III, C. G.

Environmental Science and Engineering:
ANDREWS, R. N.
CHRISTAKOS, G.
CHRISTMAN, R. F.
CRAWFORD-BROWN, D. J.
DIGIANO, F. A.
FOX, D. L.
GLAZE, W. H.
GOLD, A.
JEFFRIES, H.
KAMENS, R. M.
LAURIA, D. T.
LEITH, D.
MILLER, C. T.
PFAENDER, F.
RAPAPORT, S. M.
REIST, P. C.
SINGER, P. C.
SOBSEY, M. D.
SWENBERG, J. A.
WATSON, JR, J. E.
WHITTINGTON, D.

Epidemiology:
HEISS, G.
HULKA, B.
IBRAHIM, M. A.
SAVITZ, D. A.
SEED, J. R.

Family Medicine:
CURTIS, P.
FIELDS, K. B.
GWYTHER, R. E.
LEA, J. W.
OLSON, P. R.
REEB, K. G.
SLOANE, P. D.

Geography:
BAND, L. E.
BIRDSALL, S. S.
FLORIN, J. W.
GESLER, W. M.
GREENLAND, D. E.
JOHNSON, JR, J. H.
MEADE, M.
MORIARTY, B. M.
PALM, R. I.
ROBINSON, P. J.
WALSH, S. J.
ZONN, L. E.

Geology:
BENNINGER, L. K.
CARTER, J. G.
DENNISON, J. M.
FULLAGAR, P. D.
POWELL, C. A.
TEXTORIS, D. A.

German:
KOELB, C. T.
MEWS, S. E.
PIKE, D. C.
ROBERGE, P. T.

History:
BARNEY, W. L.
BULLARD, M. M.
CHOJNACKI, S. J.
FILENE, P. G.
FINK, L. R.
FLETCHER, W. M.
GRIFFITHS, D. M.
HALL, J. D.

HARRIS, B. J.
HEADLEY, J. M.
HIGGINBOTHAM, R. D.
HUNT, M. H.
JARAUSCH, K. H.
KASSON, J. F.
KESSLER, L. D.
KOHN, R. H.
KRAMER, L. S.
LOTCHIN, R. W.
MCNEIL, G. R.
MCVAUGH, M. R.
MATHEWS, D. G.
NELSON, J. K.
PEREZ, L. A.
PFAFF, R. W.
SEMONCHE, J. E.
SOLOWAY, R. A.
TALBERT, R. J.
WATSON, H. L.
WILLIAMSON, J. R.

Information and Library Science:
CHATMAN, E. A.
DANIEL, E. H.
MORAN, B. B.
SHAW, JR, W. M.

Institute of Government:
ALLRED, S.
BELL, II, A. F.
BRANNON, J. G.
CAMPBELL, W. A.
CLARKE, S. H.
DELLINGER, A. M.
DRENNAN, J. C.
FARB, R. L.
FERRELL, J. S.
JOYCE, R. P.
LAWRENCE, D. M.
LINER, C. D.
LOEB, JR, B. F.
MASON, J.
MESIBOV, L. L.
OWENS, D. W.
SMITH, M. R.
VOGT, A. J.
WHITAKER, G. P.

Journalism:
BLANCHARD, M. A.
BOWERS, T. A.
BROWN, J. D.
COLE, R. R.
ELAM, A. R.
LAUTERBORN, R. F.
LINDEN, T. R.
MEYER, P. E.
SHAVER, M. A.
SHAW, D. L.
SIMPSON, R. H.
STEVENSON, R. L.
STONE, JR, C. S.
WALDEN, R. C.

Law:
BILIONIS, L. D.
BLAKEY, W.
BOGER, J. C.
BROOME, L. L.
BROUN, K. S.
BROWN, C. N.
BRYAN, P. L.
BYRD, R. G.
CALMORE, J. O.
CLIFFORD, JR, D. F.
CONLEY, J. M.
CORRADO, M. L.
CRAIN, M. G.
DAYE, C. E.
GIBSON, S. E.
HASKELL, P. G.
HAZEN, T. L.
HORNSTEIN, D. T.
KALO, J. J.
LINK, R. C.
LOEWY, A. H.
MARKHAM, J. W.

MCUSIC, M. S.
ORTH, J. V.
ROSEN, R. A.
SHARP, S. B.
TURNIER, W. J.
WEGNER, J. W.
WEISBURD, A. M.
YARBROUGH, M. V.
ZELENAK, L. A.

Law Library:
GASAWAY, L. N.

Leisure Studies and Recreation Administration:
HENDERSON, K. A.

Marine Sciences:
BANE, JR, J. M.
FRANKENBERG, D.
HAY, M. E.
KOHLMEYER, J. J.
MARTENS, C. S.
NEUMANN, A. C.
PAERL, H. W.
PETERSON, C. H.
SCHWARTZ, F. J.
WELLS, J. T.
WERNER, P. E.

Maternal and Child Health Care:
BUEXENS, P.
KOTCH, J. B.
KOTELCHUCK, M.
TSUI, A. O.
UDRY, J. R.

Mathematics:
ASSANI, I.
BRYLAWSKI, T. H.
CIMA, J. A.
DAMON, J. N.
EBERLEIN, P. B.
FOREST, M. G.
GEISSINGER, L. D.
GOODMAN, S. E.
GRAVES, W. H.
HAWKINS, J. M.
KERZMAN, N.
KUMAR, S.
PETERSEN, K. E.
PFALTZGRAFF, J. A.
PLANTE, J. F.
PROCTOR, R. A.
SCHLESSINGER, M.
SMITH, W. W.
STASHEFF, J.
TAYLOR, M. E.
VARCHENKO, A.
WAHL, J. M.
WILLIAMS, M.
WOGEN, W. R.

Medical Allied Health Prof.:
BAILEY, D.
LEGRYS, V. A.
SAKATA, R.
YODER, D. E.

Medicine:
BERKOWITZ, L. R.
BERNARD, S. A.
BONDURANT, S.
BOUCHER, JR, R. C.
BOZYMSKI, E. M.
BRENNER, D. A.
BROMBERG, P. A.
CAREY, T. S.
CLEMMONS, D. R.
COHEN, M. S.
COHEN, P. L.
COLINDRES, R. E.
DEHMER, G. J.
DONOHUE, J. F.
DROSSMAN, D. A.
EARP, III, H. S.
FALK, R. J.
FINN, W. F.
GABRIEL, D. A.

GETTES, L. S.
GONZALEZ, J. J.
GREGANTI, M. A.
GRIGGS, T. R.
HEIZER, W. D.
HOOLE, A. J.
HUANG, E. S.
KIZER, J. S.
KNOWLES, M. R.
LANE, T. W.
LIU, E. T.
MATTERN, W. D.
MITCHELL, B. S.
NUZUM, C. T.
ONTJES, D. A.
ORRINGER, E. P.
PAGANO, J. S.
RANSOHOFF, D. F.
ROBERTS, H.
ROGERS, C. S.
RUTALA, W. A.
SANDLER, R. S.
SARTOR, R. B.
SHEA, T. C.
SIMPSON, JR, R. J.
SMITH, S. C.
SPARLING, P. F.
UNGARO, P. C.
WHITE, II, G. C.
WILLIAMS, M. E.
WILLIS, P. W.
WINFIELD, J. B.
YOUNT, W. J.

Microbiology and Immunology:
BACHENHEIMER, S. L.
BOTT, K. F.
CANNON, J. G.
CLARKE, S. H.
EDGELL, M. H.
FRELINGER, J. A.
GILLIGAN, P. H.
GRIFFITH, J.
HAUGHTON, G.
HUTCHISON, C. A.
JOHNSTON, R. E.
KLAPPER, D. G.
NEWBOLD, J. E.
RAAB-TRAUB, N.
TING, J. P.
WYRICK, P. B.

Microelectronics—Chemistry:
IRENE, E. A.

Music:
BONDS, M. E.
FINSON, J. W.
KETCH, J. E.
MCKINNON, J. W.
NADAS, J. L.
NEFF, S.
OEHLER, D. L.
SMITH, B.
WARBURTON, T. A.
ZENGE, M. W.

Neurology:
GREENWOOD, R. S.
HALL, C. D.
HOWARD, J. N.
MANN, J. D.
SUZUKI, K.

Nursing:
DALTON, J. B.
DAVIS, D. H.
DOUGHERTY, M. C.
FOGEL, C. I.
FREUND, C. M.
FUNK, S. G.
GOEPPINGER, J.
HARRELL, J. S.
KJERVIK, D. K.
MILES, M. S.
MILIO, N.
MISHEL, M. H.
SANDELOWSKI, M. J.

Obstetrics and Gynaecology:
DROEGEMUELLER, W.
FOWLER, JR, W. C.
FRITZ, M. A.
GRANADOS
HASKILL, J. S.
PARISI, Y. M.
STEEGE, J. F.
WALTON, L. A.

Operations Research:
FISHMAN, G.
PROVAN, J. S.
STIDHAM, JR, S.
TOLLE, J. W.

Ophthalmology:
COHEN, K. L.
EIFRIG, D. E.
GRIMSON, B. S.
PEIFFER, JR, R. L.

Paediatrics:
AYLSWORTH, A. S.
BOSE, C. L.
CARSON, J. L.
COLLIER, A. M.
COOPER, H. A.
D'ERCOLE, A. J.
FERNALD, G. W.
FRENCH, F. S.
HAMRICK, H.
HENDERSON, F. W.
HENRY, G. W.
INGRAM, D. L.
KRAYBILL, E. N.
LAWSON, E. E.
LEIGH, M. W.
LEVINE, M. D.
LODA, F. A.
LOHR, J. A.
ROBERTS, K. B.
SCHALL, S. A.
SIMMONS, M. A.
STILES, A. D.
UNDERWOOD, L. E.
WILLIAMS, R. G.
WILSON, E. M.
WOOD, R. E.

Pathology and Laboratory Medicine:
ANDERSON, N. N.
BELLINGER, D. A.
BENTLEY, S. A.
BOULDIN, T. W.
CHAPMAN, J. F.
CROSS, R. E.
FARBER, R. A.
FOLDS, J. D.
FORMAN, D. T.
GRISHAM, J. W.
HAMMOND, J. E.
JENNETTE, J. C.
KAUFMAN, D. G.
LORD, S. T.
MAEDA, N.
REISNER, H. M.
SILVERMAN, L. M.
SMITH, C. G.
SMITHIES, O.
SUZUKI, K. I.
TIDWELL, R. R.
TOPAL, M. D.
WEISSMAN, B. E.

Pharmacology:
CREWS, F. T.
DER, C. J.
DUDLEY, K. H.
GATZY, JR, J. T.
GOZ, B.
HARDEN, T. K.
JULIANO, R. L.
KOLE, R.
MCCARTHY, K. D.
SCARBOROUGH, G. A.
THURMAN, R. G.

Pharmacy:
BROUWER, K. R.
CAMPBELL, W. H.
COCOLAS, G. H.
ECKEL, F. M.
HADZIJA, B. W.
HALL, I. H.
HARTZEMA, A. G.
LEE, K. H.
PIEPER, J. A.
THAKKER, D. R.

Philosophy:
ANTONY, L. M.
BLACKBURN, S. W.
BOXILL, B. R.
HILL, JR, T. E.
HOOKER, M.
LONG, D. C.
LYCAN, W. G.
MUNSAT, S. M.
POSTEMA, G. J.
RESNIK, M. D.
ROSENBERG, J. F.
SAYRE-MCCORD, G. D.
SCHLESINGER, G.
SMYTH, R. A.

Physical Education, Exercise and Sport Science:
BILLING, J. E.
HYATT, R. W.
MCMURRAY, R. G.
MUELLER, F. O.
PRENTICE, JR, W. E.
SILVA, J. M.

Physics/Astronomy:
CARNEY, B. W.
CHRISTIANSEN, W. A.
CLEGG, T. B.
DOLAN, L. A.
DY, K. S.
FRAMPTON, P. H.
HERNANDEZ, J.
KARWOWSKI, H. J.
LUDWIG, E. J.
MCNEIL, L. E.
NG, Y. J.
ROSE, J. A.
ROWAN, L. G.
SCHROEER, D.
THOMPSON, W. J.
VAN DAM, H.
YORK, JR, J. W.

Physiology:
ARENDSHORST, W. J.
FABER, J. E.
FAREL, P. B.
FAUST, R. G.
FROEHNER, S. C.
LIGHT, A. R.
LUND, P. K.
MCILWAIN, D. L.
OXFORD, G. S.
PERL, E. R.
REID, L. M.
SEALOCK, R. W.
STUART, A. E.
WHITSEL, B. L.

Political Science:
BEYLE, T. L.
CONOVER, P. J.
HARTLYN, J.
HUBER, E. H.
LOWERY, D. L.
MARKS, G. W.
PHAY, R. E.
RABINOWITZ, G.
RICHARDSON, R. J.
SCHOULTZ, L. G.
SCHWARTZ, J.
SEARING, D. D.
STEINER, J.
STEPHENS, J. D.
STIMSON, J. A.

WHITE, J. W.
WRIGHT, D. S.

Psychiatry:

BREESE, JR, G. R.
GOLDEN, R. N.
HOUPT, J. L.
JANOWSKY, D. S.
LIEBERMAN, J. A.
LIGHT, K. C.
MCCARTNEY, C. F.
MAILMAN, R. B.
MARCUS, L. M.
MESIBOV, G. B.
STABLER, B.
VAN BOURGONDIE, M. E.
WHITT, J. K.

Psychology:

BAUCOM, D. H.
CAIRNS, R. B.
CHAMBLESS, D. L.
DYKSTRA-HYLAND, L. A.
ECKERMAN, D. A.
FILLENBAUM, S.
GRAY-LITTLE, B.
HOLLINS, M.
INSKO, C. A.
JOHNSON, E. S.
ORNSTEIN, P.
SCHOPLER, J. H.
SHINKMAN, P. G.
THISSEN, D. M.
THOMPSON, V. D.
WALLSTEN, T. S.
YOUNG, F. W.

Public Health:

ROPER, W. L.

Health Behaviour and Health Education:

BAUMAN, K. E.
DEVELLIS, B. M.
EARP, J. L.
MUTRAN, E.
SORENSON, J.
STECKLER, A. B.

Health Policy and Administration:

JAIN, S.
KALUZNY, A. D.
KILPATRICK, K. E.
ROZIER, R. G.
VENEY, J. E.
ZELMAN, W. N.

Nutrition:

ANDERSON, J. J.
COLEMAN, R. A.
KOHLMEIER, L.
POPKIN, B. M.
ZEISEL, S. H.

Public Health Nursing:

ATWOOD, J. R.
SALMON, M. E.

Radiation Oncology:

CHANEY, E. L.
LEADON, S. A.
RALEIGH, J. A.
ROSENMAN, J. G.
TEPPER, J. E.
VARIA, M. A.

Radiology:

JAQUES, P. F.
JOHNSTON, R. E.
KWOCK, L.
LEE, J. K.
MCCARTNEY, W. H.
MITTELSTAEDT, C. A.
MAURO, M. A.

Religious Studies:

ERNST, C. W.
HALPERIN, D. J.
KAUFMAN, P. I.
SASSON, J. M.
TYSON, JR, R. W.
VAN SETERS, J.

Romance Languages:

BANDERA, C.
CASADO, P. G.
CERVIGNI, D. S.
CILVETI, A. L.
CLARK, F. M.
DOMINGUEZ, F. A.
HAIG, II, I. R. S.
ILLIANO, A.
KING, L. D.
MALEY, C. A.
MASTERS, G. M.
RECTOR, M. P.
SALGADO, M. A.
SHERMAN, C. L.
VOGLER, F. W.

Slavic Languages:

DEBRECZENY, P.
JANDA, L. A.
LEVINE, M. G.

Social Medicine:

CHURCHILL, L. R.
CROSS, A. W.
DE FRIESE, G. H.
ESTROFF, S. E.
MADISON, D. L.
MORRISSEY, J. P.
RUNYAN, D. K.

Social Work:

BOWEN, G. L.
COOKE, P. W.
DOBELSTEIN, A. W.
EDWARDS, R. L.
FRASER, M. W.
GALINSKY, M. J.
HENLEY, H. C.
NELSON, G. M.
ORTHNER, D. K.
USHER, C. L.
WEIL, M. O.

Sociology:

ALDRICH, H. E.
BEARMAN, P. S.
BLAU, J. R.
ELDER, G. H.
ENTWISLE, B.
KALLEBERG, A. L.
KLEINMAN, S.
NEILSEN, F. D.
OBERSCHALL, A. R.
REED, JR, J. S.
RINDFUSS, R. R.
SIMPSON, R. L.
UHLENBERG, P.

Statistics:

ADLER, R.
CARLSTEIN, E.
CHAKRAVARTI, I. M.
KALLIANPUR, G.
KARR, A. F.
KELLY, D. G.
LEADBETTER, M. R.
MARRON, J. S.
SIMONS, G.
SMITH, R. L.

Surgery:

BAKER, C. C.
BLIGHT, A. R.
BUNZENDAHL, H.
BURNHAM, S. J.
CARSON, III, C. C.
HALL, III, J. W.
KEAGY, B. A.
MANDEL, S. R.
MAXWELL, J. G.
MEYER, A. A.
NAKAYAMA, D. K.
OLLER, D. W.
PECK, M. D.
PILLSBURY, III, H. C
PRAZMA, J.
SHELDON, G. F.

SHOCKLEY, W. M.
SLOAN, G. M.
STAREK, P. J.
WEISSLER, M. C.
WILCOX, B. R.

Women's Studies Programme:

BURNS, E. J.
HOFFERT, S. D.

University of North Carolina at Charlotte

9021 University City Blvd, Charlotte, NC 28223-0001

Telephone: (704) 687-8622
E-mail: admissions@uncc.edu
Internet: www.uncc.edu

Founded 1946 as an extension centre of Univ. of North Carolina, present status 1965
Language of instruction: English
Academic year: August to May (2 semesters)

Chancellor: Dr PHILIP L. DUBOIS
Vice-Chancellor for Academic Affairs and Provost: Dr JOAN F. LORDEN
Vice-Chancellor for Business Affairs: ELIZABETH A. HARDIN
Vice-Chancellor for Research and Economic Devt: ROBERT G. WILHELM
Vice-Chancellor for Student Affairs: Dr ARTHUR JACKSON
Vice-Chancellor for Univ. Advancement: NILES SORENSEN
Univ. Registrar: CHRISTOPHER B. KNAUER
Univ. Librarian: STANLEY J. WILDER

Library of 1,098,590 vols, 514,147 ebooks, 57,471 serial subscriptions, 2,196,277 microforms, 15,876 video and audio material

Number of teachers: 1,474
Number of students: 26,571 (21,503 undergraduate, 5,068 graduate)

DEANS

Belk College of Business: Dr STEVE H. OTT
College of Arts and Architecture: KENNETH A. LAMBLA
College of Computing and Informatics: Dr YI DENG
College of Education: Dr ELLEN MCINTYRE
College of Health and Human Services: Dr NANCY FEY-YENSAN
College of Liberal Arts and Sciences: Dr NANCY A. GUTIERREZ
Graduate School: THOMAS L. REYNOLDS
William States Lee College of Engineering: Dr ROBERT E. JOHNSON

University of North Carolina at Greensboro

1400 Spring Garden St, Greensboro, NC 27402

Telephone: (336) 334-5000
E-mail: registrar@uncg.edu
Internet: www.uncg.edu

Founded 1891 as a normal college, present status 1931, current name adopted 1963
Academic year: August to May (2 semesters)

Chancellor: Dr LINDA P. BRADY
Provost and Vice-Chancellor for Academic Affairs: Dr DAVID H. PERRIN
Vice-Chancellor for Business Affairs: READE TAYLOR
Vice-Chancellor for Research and Economic Devt: Dr TERRI SHELTON
Vice-Chancellor for Student Affairs: Dr CHERYL M. CALLAHAN
Vice-Chancellor for Univ. Advancement: Dr PATRICIA W. STEWART
Dean of Students: Dr BRETT A. CARTER
Registrar: Dr KELLY ROWETT-JAMES
Dean of Univ. Libraries: ROSANN V. BAZIRJIAN

Library: 2.5m. vols, 60,000 journals, 300,000 ebooks

Number of teachers: 1,070 (840 full-time, 230 part-time)
Number of students: 18,800
Publication: *UNCG Magazine*

DEANS

Bryan School of Business and Economics: Prof. Dr McRae C. Banks
College of Arts and Sciences: Dr Timothy D. Johnston
Division of Continual Learning: Dr Robert M. Brown
Graduate School: Dr William Wiener
Joint School of Nanoscience and Nanoengineering: Prof. Dr James G. Ryan
Joseph M. Bryan School of Business and Economics: Dr MacRae Banks
Lloyd International Honors College: Dr Jerry Pubantz
School of Education: Dr Karen Wixson
School of Health and Human Sciences: Dr Celia R. Hooper
School of Music, Theatre and Dance: Dr John J. Deal
School of Nursing: Prof. Dr Lynne G. Pearcey

University of North Carolina at Pembroke

POB 1510, Pembroke, NC 28372-1510
Telephone: (910) 521-6000
E-mail: registrar@uncp.edu
Internet: www.uncp.edu
Founded 1887 as Croatan Normal School, present status 1969
Academic year: August to May (2 semesters)
Chancellor: Prof. Dr Kyle R. Carter
Provost and Vice-Chancellor for Academic Affairs: Dr Kenneth D. Kitts
Vice-Chancellor for Advancement: Wendy Lowery
Vice-Chancellor for Business Affairs and Chief Financial Officer: R. Neil Hawk
Vice-Chancellor for Enrolment Management: Jacqueline H. Clark
Vice-Chancellor for Student Affairs: Dr Diane Jones
Registrar: Sharon Kissick
Dean of Library Services: Dr Elinor Foster
Library of 385,294 vols, 67,298 ebooks, 700,185 microforms, 11,030 audiovisual material, 40,475 current serial titles
Number of teachers: 550
Number of students: 6,950
Publication: *UNCP Today* (alumni magazine)

DEANS

Graduate Studies: Dr Sara Simmons (acting)
College of Arts and Sciences: Dr Mark Canada
School of Business: Dr Ramin Maysami (acting)
School of Education: Dr Leah Fioretino

University of North Carolina at Wilmington

601 S College Road, Wilmington, NC 28403-5931
Telephone: (910) 962-3000
E-mail: admissions@uncw.edu
Internet: www.uncw.edu
Founded 1947 as Wilmington College, present name and status 1969
Academic year: August to May
Chancellor: Gary L. Miller
Provost and Vice-Chancellor for Academic Affairs: Dr Cathy L. Barlow
Vice-Chancellor for Business Affairs: Charles A. Maimone
Vice-Chancellor for Student Affairs: Patricia Leonard
Vice-Chancellor for Univ. Advancement: Mary Gornto

Dean of Students: Michael A. Walker
Registrar: Gilbert C. Bowen
Librarian: Sarah Watstein
Library of 1,071,435 vols, 30,715 ebooks, 34,825 video items, 105,047 bound periodicals
Number of teachers: 964
Number of students: 13,145
Publications: *Arts and Sciences* (1 a year), *Connections* (1 a year), *Re:search* (1 a year), *UNCW Magazine* (3 a year)

DEANS

Cameron School of Business: Dr Lawrence S. Clark
College of Arts and Sciences: Aswani Volety
College of Health and Applied Human Sciences: Dr Charles J. Hardy
Graduate School: Dr Robert D. Roer
School of Nursing: Dr James McCann
Watson School of Education: Dr Kenneth Teitelbaum

University of North Carolina School of the Arts

POB 12189 Winston-Salem, NC 27117-2189
1533 S Main St, Winston-Salem, NC 27127-2738
Telephone: (336) 770-3399
E-mail: admissions@uncsa.edu
Internet: www.uncsa.edu
Founded 1963
Academic year: August to May
Chancellor: John F. Mauceri
Provost: David Nelson
Dean of Students: Ward Caldwell
Chief Academic Officer: David Nelson
Chief Advancement Officer (vacant)
Univ. Sec.: Amanda Balwah
Registrar: Erin Morin
Dir of Library: Vicki L. Weavil
Library of 122,441 vols, 24,957 microforms, 75,945 audiovisual materials, 422 current serial
Number of teachers: 170 (126 full-time, 44 part-time)
Number of students: 1,180

DEANS

High School Academic Programmes: Jill Lane
School of Dance: Brenda Daniels
School of Design and Production: Joseph Tilford
School of Drama: Gerald Freedman
School of Film-Making: Jordan Kerner
School of Music: Wade Weast
University Programmes: Dean Wilcox

Western Carolina University

Cullowhee, NC 28723
Telephone: (828) 227-7211
E-mail: admiss@wcu.edu
Internet: www.wcu.edu
Founded 1889, current name adopted 1953, present status 1972
Academic year: August to May (2 semesters)
Chancellor: David O. Belcher
Provost: Angela Brenton
Sr Vice-Chancellor for Academic Affairs: Fred Hinson
Vice-Chancellor for Admin. and Finance: Robert T. Edwards
Vice-Chancellor for Advancement and External Affairs: Clifton B. Metcalf
Vice-Chancellor for Student Affairs: Sam Miller
Dir of Admissions: Phil Cauley
Registrar: Larry Hammer (acting)
Dean of Library Service: Dana Sally
Library of 702,000 vols incl. bound periodicals, 1,513,000 microfilm, 23,000 ebooks, 3,330 current serials

Number of teachers: 457 (full-time)
Number of students: 9,429

DEANS

College of Arts and Sciences: Dr H. Gibbs Knotts
College of Business: Prof. Darrell Franklin Parker
College of Education and Allied Professions: Dr Perry Schoon
College of Fine and Performing Arts: Dr Robert Kehrberg
College of Health and Human Sciences: Dr Linda Seestedt-Stanford
Educational Outreach: Regis Gilman
Honors College: Dr Brian Railsback
Kimmel School of Construction Management and Technology: (vacant)
Research and Graduate Studies: Dr Scott Higgins

Winston-Salem State University

601 S Martin Luther King, Jr Dr., Winston-Salem, NC 27110
Telephone: (336) 750-2000
E-mail: admissions@wssu.edu
Internet: www.wssu.edu
Founded 1892 as Slater Industrial Acad., current name adopted 1963, present status 1972
Academic year: August to May
Chancellor: Dr Donald J. Reaves
Provost and Vice-Chancellor for Academic Affairs: Brenda A. Allen
Vice-Chancellor for Finance and Admin.: Gerald E. Hunter
Vice-Chancellor for Student Affairs: Dr Trae T. Cotton
Vice-Chancellor for Univ. Advancement: Michelle M. Cook
Registrar: Sharon Hush
Dir of Library Services: Dr Mae L. Rodney
Library of 158,858 vols
Number of teachers: 400 (full-time)
Number of students: 6,450
Publication: *Archway* (3 a year)

DEANS

College of Arts and Sciences: Dr Charles W. Ford, Jr
School of Business and Economics: Dr Jessica Bailey
School of Graduate Studies and Research: Dr Fidelis M. Ikem
School of Health Science: Dr Peggy Valentine
University College: Dr Michelle B. Releford

WAKE FOREST UNIVERSITY

1834 Wake Forest Rd, Winston-Salem, NC 27106
Telephone: (336) 758-5000
E-mail: wfuadmis@wfu.edu
Internet: www.wfu.edu
Founded 1834, present name 1839
Private control
Academic year: August to May
Pres.: Prof. Dr Nathan O. Hatch
Provost: Dr Mark Welker
Sr Vice-Pres. of Finance and Admin. and Chief Financial Officer: Hof Milam
Vice-Pres. and Gen. Counsel: Dr J. Reid Morgan
Vice-Pres. for Student Life: Kenneth A. Zick
Vice-Pres. for Univ. Advancement: Mark A. Petersen
Dean of Admissions: Martha Blevins Allman
Univ. Registrar: Dr Harold Pace
Dean of Library: Dr Lynn Sutton

Library: 1.7m. vols, 4,500 journals, 50,000 ejournals
Number of teachers: 1,740 (1,158 full-time, 582 part-time)
Number of students: 7,350 (4,780 undergraduate, 2,570 graduate and professional)

DEANS

Divinity School: Prof. Dr GAIL R. O'DAY
Graduate School of Arts and Sciences: Dr LORNA GRINDLAY MOORE
School of Business: (vacant)
School of Law: Dr BLAKE D. MORANT
School of Medicine: Dr EDWARD ABRAHAM
Wake Forest College: Prof. Dr JACQUELYN S. FETROW

PROFESSORS

Graduate School of Arts and Sciences:

ABRAMSON, J. S., Paediatrics
ADAMS, M. R., Comparative Medicine
AKMAN, S. A., Cancer Biology, Internal Medicine
ALTMAN, D. G., Public Health Sciences
ANDERSON, J. P., Education
ASCHNER, M., Physiology and Pharmacology
BAREFIELD, J. P., History
BASS, D. A., Medicine
BAXLEY, J. V., Mathematics
BECK, R. C., Psychology
BERRY, M. J., Health and Exercise Science
BEST, D. L., Psychology
BO, W. J., Neurobiology and Anatomy
BOND, M. G., Neurobiology and Anatomy
BORWICK, S. H., Music
BOWDEN, D. W., Biochemistry
BOYD, S. B., Religion
BROSNIHAN, K. B., Physiology and Pharmacology
BROWN, D. G., Economics
BROWNE, C. L., Biology
BROWNE, R. A., Biology
BRUNSO-BECHTOLD, J. K., Neurobiology and Anatomy
BUCKALEW, JR, V. M., Medicine (Nephrology)
BURKE, G. L., Public Health Sciences
BUSIJA, D. W., Physiology and Pharmacology
BYINGTON, R. P., Public Health Sciences
CARMICHAEL, R. D., Mathematics
CHILDERS, S. R., Physiology and Pharmacology
CHILTON, F. H., Internal Medicine
CLAIBORNE, JR, H. A., Biochemistry
CLARKSON, JR, T. B., Comparative Medicine
COLLINS, J. E., Religion
CONNER, W. E., Biology
COTTON, N., English
CRAMER, S. D., Cancer Biology, Internal Medicine
CROUSE, III, J. R., Medicine (Endocrinology and Metabolism)
CUNNINGHAM, C. C., Biochemistry
CUNNINGHAM, P. M., Education
CURRAN, J. F., Biology
DANIEL, L. W., Biochemistry
DEADWYLER, S. A., Physiology
DESHAZER, M. K., English
DIMOCK, JR, R. V., Biology
DURANT, R. H., Paediatrics and Public Health Sciences
EISENACH, J. C., Anaesthesia
ESCH, G. W., Biology
ESCOTT, P. D., History
ESPELAND, M. A., Public Health Sciences (Biostatistics)
ETTIN, A. V., English
EURE, H. E., Biology
FELDMAN, S. R., Dermatology, Pathology
FERRARIO, C. M., Surgical Sciences
FRANKEL, A. E., Medicine and Cancer Biology
FREY, D. E., Economics

FURBERG, C. D., Medicine and Public Health Sciences
GLADDING, S. T., Education
GRANT, K. A., Physiology and Pharmacology, Comparative Medicine
HALL, M. A., Law and Public Health Sciences
HAMILTON, W. S., Russian
HANS, J. S., English
HAYASHI, E. K., Mathematics and Computer Science
HAZEN, M. D., Communication
HEARN, JR, T. K., Philosophy
HENDRICKS, JR, J. E., History
HINZE, W. L., Chemistry
HOLZWARTH, G. M., Physics
HOLZWARTH, N. A. W., Physics
HOWARD, F. T., Mathematics
HUGHES, M. L., History
HUTSON, S. M., Biochemistry
HYDE, M. J., Communication Ethics
JARRETT, D. B., Physiology and Pharmacology
JOHNSTON, W. D., English
KAMMER, G. M., Internal Medicine
KAPLAN, J. R., Comparative Medicine, Anthropology
KERR, W. C., Physics
KIMBALL, C. A., Religion
KIRKMAN, E. E., Mathematics
KOMAN, L. A., Orthopaedics
KONDEPUDI, D. K., Chemistry
KUBERSKI, P., English
KUCERA, L. S., Microbiology
KUHN, R. E., Biology
KUZMANOVICH, J., Mathematics
LANE, H. C., Biology
LEARY, M. R., Psychology
LEONARD, W. J., Divinity School
LITCHER, J. H., Education
LIVELY, M. O., Biochemistry
LONGINO, C. F., Sociology, Public Health Sciences
LORENTZ, JR, W. B., Paediatrics
LYLES, D. S., Microbiology and Immunology
McCALL, C. E., Medicine (Infectious Disease), Microbiology and Immunology
McMILLAN, J. J., Communication
McPHAIL, L. C., Biochemistry
MAINE, B. G., English
MARGITIC, M. R., Romance Languages
MARTIN, D. R., Accountancy
MARTIN, JR, J. A., Religion
MATTHEWS, G. E., Physics
MAY, J. G., Mathematics
MEIS, P. J., Obstetrics and Gynaecology
MELSON, G. A., Chemistry
MESSIER, S. P., Health and Exercise Science
MILLER, H. S., Medicine
MILNER, J. O., Education
MIZEL, S. B., Microbiology and Immunology
MORAN, P. R., Radiology
MORGAN, T. M., Public Health Sciences
MOSS, W. M., English
NADER, M. A., Physiology and Pharmacology
NIELSEN, L. N., Education
NOFTLE, R. E., Chemistry
O'FLAHERTY, J. T., Medicine
OPPENHEIM, R. W., Anatomy
OVERING, G. R., English
OWEN, J., Medicine
PARKS, J. S., Pathology
PLEMMONS, R. J., Mathematics and Computer Science
PORRINO, L. J., Physiology and Pharmacology
PRINEAS, R., Public Health Sciences
REIFLER, B. V., Psychiatry
REJESKI, W. J., Health and Exercise Science
RIBISL, P. M., Health and Exercise Science
RICH, S. S., Public Health Sciences

RICHMAN, C. L., Psychology
ROBERTS, D. C. S., Physiology and Pharmacology
ROSE, J. C., Physiology, Obstetrics and Gynaecology
RUBIN, B. K., Paediatrics, Physiology, and Pharmacology
RUDEL, L. L., Comparative Medicine, Biochemistry
ST CLAIR, R. W., Pathology (Physiology)
SAMSON, III, H. H., Physiology and Pharmacology, Comparative Medicine
SHAPERE, D., Philosophy and History of Science
SHERERTZ, R. J., Medicine
SHIHABI, Z. K., Pathology (Clinical Chemistry)
SHIVELY, C. A., Comparative Medicine, Psychology
SHUMAKER, S. A., Public Health Sciences
SIGAL, G., English
SILVER, W. L., Biology
SIMONELLI, J. M., Anthropology
SINCLAIR, M. L., History
SMITH, E., Sociology, American Ethnic Studies
SMITH, J. E., Physiology and Pharmacology
SMITH, J. H., History
SMITH, M. S., Art
SMITH, P. B., Biochemistry
SONNTAG, W. E., Physiology
SORCI-THOMAS, M., Comparative Medicine
STEIN, B. E., Neurobiology and Anatomy
STRANDHOY, J. W., Pharmacology
SWOFFORD, R. L., Chemistry
TAYLOR, T. C., Accountancy
THOMAS, M. J., Biochemistry
TOOLE, J. F., Neurology
TORTI, F. M., Cancer Biology, Internal Medicine
TOWER, JR, R. B., Taxation
TRIBLE, P., Religion
VALBUENA, O., English
VAN DE RIJN, I., Microbiology and Immunology
VELEZ, R., Internal Medicine
WAGNER, W. D., Comparative Medicine
WASILAUSKAS, B. L., Pathology (Clinical Microbiology)
WEAVER, D. S., Anthropology
WEBBER, R. L., Dentistry, Medical Engineering
WEIGL, P. D., Biology
WEINBERG, R. B., Internal Medicine
WELKER, M. E., Chemistry
WELLS, B. R., Romance Languages
WHEELER, JR, K. T., Radiology
WILKERSON, JR, J. E., Accounting
WILLIAMS, A. J., History
WILLIAMS, J. K., Comparative Medicine
WILLIAMS, R. T., Physics
WILLINGHAM, M. C., Pathology
WILSON, E. G., English
WOODALL, J. N., Anthropology
WOODWARD, D. J., Physiology and Pharmacology
WYKLE, R. L., Biochemistry

Graduate School of Management:

BALIGA, B. R., Management
FLYNN, B. B., Operations Management
HARRIS, F. H. DE B., Managerial Economics and Finance
MEREDITH, J. R., Management
NARUS, J. A., Business Marketing
PATEL, A., Finance
RESNICK, B. G., Banking and Finance
SHOESMITH, G. L., Economics
SMUNT, T. L., Management

School of Business and Accountancy:

AKINC, U., Production and Operations Management
EWING, S., Management and Statistics
HARRISON, K., Management
JURAS, P., Academic Excellence
KNIGHT, L., Accounting

MARTIN, D., Financial Accounting
ROBIN, D., Business Ethics
TAYLOR, T., Accounting
TOWER, R., Taxation
WILKERSON, J., Accounting

School of Law:
ANDERSON, C. B.
BILLINGS, R. B.
CASTLEMAN, D. R.
CORBETT, JR, L. H.
COVINGTON, III, I. B.
CURTIS, M. K.
DAVIS, T.
FOY, III, H. M.
GREBELDINGER, S. K.
HALL, M. A.
HERRING, B. O. H.
LOGAN, D. A.
MEWHINNEY, K.
MONTAQUILA, S. R.
NEWMAN, J. S.
PALMITER, A. R.
PARKER, D. L.
PARKER, J. W.
PARKER, M. F.
PEEPLES, R. A.
REYNOLDS, S.
ROBERTS, P. J.
ROBERTS, T. E.
ROSE, JR, C. P.
ROSE, S.
SCHNEIDER, JR, R. C.
SHORES, D. F.
STEELE, T. M.
TAYLOR, M. H.
WALKER, G. K.
WALSH, R. K.
WRIGHT, JR, R. F.
ZICK, II, K. A.

School of Medicine:
ABRAMSON, J. S., Paediatrics
ADAMS, M. R., Comparative Medicine
ADAMS, P. L., Internal Medicine (Nephrology)
ADCOCK, III, E. W., Paediatrics
AKMAN, S. A., Cancer Biology, Internal Medicine (Haematology/Oncology)
ALTMANN, D. G., Public Health Sciences (Social Sciences and Health Policy)
APPLEGATE, R. J., Internal Medicine (Cardiology)
APPLEGATE, W. B., Internal Medicine
ARGENTA, L. C., Surgical Sciences (Plastic/Reconstructive)
ASCHNER, M., Physiology and Pharmacology
ASSIMOS, D. G., Surgical Sciences (Urology)
BASS, D. A., Internal Medicine (Pulmonary Critical Care Medicine)
BECHTOLD, R. E., Radiological Sciences (Radiology)
BLEECKER, E. R., Internal Medicine (Pulmonary Critical Care Medicine)
BO, W. J., Neurobiology and Anatomy
BOND, M. G., Neurobiology and Anatomy
BOWDEN, D. W., Biochemistry
BOWTON, D. L., Anaesthesiology, Internal Medicine (Pulmonary Critical Care Medicine)
BROSNIHAN, K. B., Surgical Sciences (General)
BRUNSO-BECHTOLD, J. K., Neurobiology and Anatomy
BUCKALEW, JR, V. M., Internal Medicine (Nephrology)
BURKART, J. M., Internal Medicine (Nephrology)
BURKE, G. L., Public Health Sciences
BUSIJA, D. W., Physiology and Pharmacology
BUSS, D. H., Pathology
BUTTERWORTH, J. F., IV, Anaesthesiology
BYINGTON, R., Public Health Sciences (Epidemiology)
CHALLA, V. R., Pathology

CHENG, C.-P., Internal Medicine (Cardiology)
CHEW, F. S., Radiological Sciences (Radiology)
CHILDERS, S. R., Physiology and Pharmacology
CHILES, C., Radiological Sciences (Radiology)
CHILTON, F. L., Internal Medicine (Pulmonary Critical Care Medicine)
CLAIBORNE, A., Biochemistry
CLARKSON, T. B., Comparative Medicine
COATES, M. L., Family and Community Medicine
COOPER, M. R., Internal Medicine (Haematology/Oncology)
COVITZ, W., Paediatrics
CROUSE, III, J. R., Internal Medicine (Endocrinology/Metabolism)
CUNNINGHAM, C. C., Biochemistry
CURL, W. W., Surgical Sciences (Orthopaedics)
DANIEL, L. W., Biochemistry
DEAN, R. H., Surgical Sciences (General)
DENTON, W. H., Psychiatry and Behavioural Medicine
DEWAN, D. M., Obstetric Anaesthesiology
DILLARD, R. G., Paediatrics
DIXON, R. L., Radiological Sciences (Radiology)
DIZ, D. I., Surgical Sciences (General), Physiology and Pharmacology
DONOFRIO, P. D., Neurology (Neuromuscular Diseases)
DURANT, R. H., Paediatrics, Public Health Sciences
DYER, R. B., Radiological Sciences (Radiology)
EISENACH, J. E., Obstetric Anaesthesiology
ELSTER, A. D., Radiological Sciences (Radiology)
ERNEST, III, J. M., Obstetrics and Gynaecology (Maternal/Fetal Medicine)
ESPELAND, M. A., Public Health Sciences (Biostatistics)
FELDMAN, S. R., Pathology
FERRARIO, C. M., Surgical Sciences (General)
FERREE, C. R., Radiation Oncology
FLEISCHER, JR, A. B., Dermatology
FRANKEL, A. E., Cancer Biology, Internal Medicine (Haematology/Oncology)
FURBERG, C. D., Public Health Sciences
GARRISON, R. S., Dentistry
GARVIN, A. J., Pathology
GEISINGER, K. R., Pathology
GELFAND, D. W., Radiological Sciences (Radiology)
GIVNER, L. G., Paediatrics
GMEINER, W. H., Biochemistry
GOOD, D. C., Neurology
GREVEN, C. M., Surgical Sciences (Orthopaedics)
GREVEN, K. M., Radiation Oncology
HALL, M., Public Health Sciences (Social Sciences and Health Policy)
HAMMON, JR, J. W., Surgical Sciences (Cardiothoracic)
HANSEN, K. J., Surgical Sciences (General)
HARLE, T. S., Radiological Sciences (Radiology)
HARRIS, M. B., Surgical Sciences (Orthopaedics)
HENKEL, C. K., Neurobiology and Anatomy
HERRINGTON, D. M., Internal Medicine (Cardiology)
HILL, I. D., Paediatrics
HUDSPETH, A. S., Surgical Sciences (Cardiothoracic)
HURD, D. D., Internal Medicine (Haematology/Oncology)
HUTSON, S. M., Biochemistry
JANEWAY, R., Neurology
JOHNSON, C. A., Paediatrics
JORIZZO, J. L., Dermatology

KAMMER, G. M., Internal Medicine (Rheumatology)
KAPLAN, J. R., Comparative Medicine, Anthropology
KELLEY, A. E., Psychiatry and Behavioural Medicine (Child/Adolescent Psychiatry)
KELLY, JR, D. L., Surgical Sciences (Ophthalmology)
KOMAN, L. A., Surgical Sciences (Orthopaedics)
KON, N., Surgical Sciences (Cardiothoracic)
KOUFMAN, J. A., Surgical Sciences (Otolaryngology)
KREMKAU, F. W., Medical Ultrasound
KROWCHUK, D. P., Paediatrics, Dermatology
KUCERA, L. S., Microbiology and Immunology
LAWLESS, M. R., Paediatrics
LICHSTEIN, P. R., Internal Medicine
LINK, K. M., Radiological Sciences (Radiology)
LITTLE, W. C., Internal Medicine (Cardiology)
LIVELY, III, M. O., Biochemistry
LONGINO, JR, C. F., Public Health Sciences (Epidemiology)
LORENTZ, W. B., Paediatrics
LYLES, D. S., Microbiology and Immunology
McCALL, C. E., Microbiology and Immunology, Internal Medicine (Infectious Diseases)
McCALL, W. V., Psychiatry and Behavioural Medicine
McCULLOUGH, D. L., Surgical Sciences (Urology)
McGUIRT, SR, W. F., Surgical Sciences (Otolaryngology)
MACH, R. H., Radiological Sciences (Radiology), Physiology and Pharmacology
McPHAIL, L. C., Biochemistry
MARKS, M. W., Surgical Sciences (Plastic/Reconstructive)
MAYNARD, C. D., Radiological Sciences (Radiology)
MEIS, P. J., Obstetrics and Gynaecology (Maternal/Fetal Medicine), Family and Community Medicine
MEREDITH, J. Q., Surgical Sciences (General)
MEYERS, D. A., Paediatrics
MICHIELUTTE, R. L., Family and Community Medicine
MILLER, A. A., Internal Medicine (Haematology/Oncology)
MILLER, M. E., Public Health Sciences (Biostatistics)
MIZEL, S. B., Microbiology and Immunology
MOODY, D. M., Radiological Sciences (Radiology)
MORGAN, T. M., Public Health Sciences (Biostatistics)
MORTON, K. A., Radiological Sciences (Radiology)
MOSKOVITZ, J., Public Health Sciences
MUELLER-HEUBACH, E., Obstetrics and Gynaecology
NELSON, III, L. H., Obstetrics and Gynaecology (Maternal/Foetal Medicine)
NELSON, T. E., Anaesthesiology
OBER, K. P., Internal Medicine (Endocrinology/Metabolism)
O'FLAHERTY, J. T., Internal Medicine (Haematology/Oncology)
OPPENHEIM, R., Neurobiology and Anatomy
O'SHEA, T. M. D., Paediatrics
OTT, D. J., Radiological Sciences (Radiology)
OWEN, J., Internal Medicine (Haematology/Oncology)
PARKS, J. S., Comparative Medicine
PAUCA, A. L., Anaesthesiology
PEACOCK, JR, J. E., Internal Medicine (Haematology/Oncology)

PEGRAM, P. S., Internal Medicine (Haematology/Oncology)

PENNELL, T. C., Surgical Sciences (General)

PETROZZA, P. H., Anaesthesiology

POEHLING, G. G., Surgical Sciences (Orthopaedics)

PONS, T., Surgical Sciences (Neurosurgery), Physiology and Pharmacology

POWELL, B. L., Internal Medicine (Haematology/Oncology)

PRIELIPP, R. C., Anaesthesiology

PRINEAS, R. J., Public Health Sciences (Epidemiology)

QUANDT, S. A., Public Health Sciences (Epidemiology)

RAPP, S. R., Psychiatry and Behavioural Medicine (Geriatric Medicine)

RAUTAHARJU, P. M., Public Health Sciences

REIFLER, B. V., Psychiatry and Behavioural Medicine

RICH, S. S., Public Health Sciences

RILEY, W. A., Neurology

ROGERS, L. F., Radiological Sciences (Radiology)

ROHR, M. S., Surgical Sciences (General)

ROSE, J. C., Obstetrics and Gynaecology (Maternal/Fetal Medicine)

ROUFAIL, W. M., Internal Medicine (Gastroenterology)

ROY, R. C., Anaesthesiology

ROYSTER, R. L., Anaesthesiology

RUBIN, B. K., Paediatrics, Physiology and Pharmacology

RUDEL, L. L., Comparative Medicine, Biochemistry

ST CLAIR, R. W., Pathology

SANGÜEZA, O. P., Pathology

SARTIANO, G. P., Internal Medicine (Haematology/Oncology)

SCUDERI, P. E., Anaesthesiology

SHAW, E. G., Radiation Oncology

SHERERTZ, R. J., Internal Medicine (Infectious Diseases), Microbiology and Immunology

SHIHABI, Z. K., Pathology

SHIVELY, C. A., Comparative Medicine

SHUMAKER, S. A., Public Health Sciences (Social Sciences and Health Policy)

SIMON, J. L., Paediatrics

SINAL, S. H., Paediatrics, Family and Community Medicine

SLUSHER, M. M., Surgical Sciences (Ophthalmology)

SMITH, J. E., Physiology and Pharmacology

SMITH, P. B., Biochemistry

STEIN, B. E., Neurobiology and Anatomy

STRANDHOY, J. W., Physiology and Pharmacology

SUMNER, T. E., Radiological Sciences (Radiology)

TEGELER, C. H., IV, Neurology

THOMAS, M. J., Biochemistry

THOMPSON, J. N., Surgical Sciences (Otolaryngology)

TOOLE, J. F., Neurology

TORTI, F. M., Cancer Biology, Internal Medicine (Haematology/Oncology)

TROOST, B. T., Neurology

TYTELL, M., Neurobiology and Anatomy

VAN DE RIJN, I., Microbiology and Immunology

VEILLE, J.-C., Obstetrics and Gynaecology (Maternal/Fetal Medicine)

VELEZ, R., Internal Medicine

WAGNER, W. D., Comparative Medicine

WALKER, F. O., Neurology (Neuromuscular Diseases)

WARD, W. G., Surgical Sciences (Orthopaedics)

WASILAUSKAS, B. L., Pathology

WEBB, L. X., Surgical Sciences (Otolaryngology)

WEBBER, R. L., Radiological Sciences (Medical Engineering), Dentistry

WEINBERG, R. B., Internal Medicine (Gastroenterology)

WHEELER, JR, K. T., Radiological Sciences (Radiology)

WILLIAMS, J. K., Comparative Medicine

WILLINGHAM, M. C., Pathology

WOOD, F. B., Neurology (Neuropsychology)

WOODWARD, D. J., Physiology and Pharmacology

WYKLE, R. L., Biochemistry

ZAGORIA, R. J., Radiological Sciences (Radiology)

ZAMKOFF, K. W., Internal Medicine (Haematology/Oncology)

Divinity School:

KIMBALL, C. A., Religion

LEONARD, W. J., Church History

TRIBLE, P., Religion

TUPPER, E. F., Theology

WARREN WILSON COLLEGE

POB 9000, Asheville, NC 28815-9000

701 Warren Wilson Rd, Swannanoa, NC 28778

Telephone: (828) 298-3325

E-mail: admit@warren-wilson.edu

Internet: www.warren-wilson.edu

Founded 1894 as Asheville Farm School

Private control

Academic year: August to May

Areas of study incl. art, Appalachian studies, biology, business, chemistry, creative writing, English, environmental studies, global studies, history and political science, integrative studies, mathematics, modern languages, music and archaeology, philosophy, psychology, religious studies, social work, sociology and anthropology, sustainable business, theatre

Pres.: Dr WILLIAM SANBORN PFEIFFER

Vice-Pres. for Academic Affairs and Dean of College: Dr PAULA GARRETT

Vice-Pres. for Admin. and Finance: JONATHAN EHRLICH

Vice-Pres. for Advancement, Admission and Marketing: RICHARD BLOMGREN

Dean of Students: DEBORAH MYERS

Registrar: CHRISTA BRIDGMAN

Library Dir: CHRISTINE RICHERT NUGENT

Library of 100,000 vols

Number of teachers: 70

Number of students: 1,000

WILLIAM PEACE UNIVERSITY

15 E Peace St., Raleigh, NC 27604-1194

Telephone: (919) 508-2000

E-mail: admissions@peace.edu

Internet: www.peace.edu

Founded 1857 as Peace Institute, current name and status 2011

Private control

Academic year: August to May

Academic programmes in biology, business administration, communication, criminal justice, education, English, liberal studies, musical theatre, political science, pre-law and psychology, simulation and game design, theatre

Pres.: Dr DEBRA M. TOWNSLEY

Vice-Pres. for Academic Affairs: Dr CINDY GNADINGER

Vice-Pres. for Admin. and Chief Financial Officer: ROCKY YEARWOOD

Vice-Pres. for Engagement: JULIE RICCIARDI

Vice-Pres. for Enrolment Management: JUSTIN G. ROY

Vice-Pres. for School of Professional Studies: LAURIE ALBERT

Vice-Pres. for Student Services: FRANK RIZZO

Library of 47,000 vols, 38,000 ebooks

Number of students: 827

WINGATE UNIVERSITY

POB 159, Wingate, NC 28174-9905

Telephone: (704) 233-8000

E-mail: admit@wingate.edu

Internet: www.wingate.edu

Founded 1896, present status 1995

Private control

Academic year: August to May

Pres.: Dr JERRY E. MCGEE

Sr Vice-Pres. for Academic Affairs: Dr MARTHA S. ASTI

Vice-Pres. for Business and Chief Financial Officer: WILLIAM H. DURHAM

Vice-Pres. for Graduate and Professional Programmes: Dr ROBERT B. SUPERNAW

Vice-Pres. for Resource Devt: VINT TILSON

Vice-Pres. for Student Life and Enrolment Services: T. RHETT BROWN

Dir of Admissions: LINDSAY KREIS

Registrar: NICCI C. BROWN

Library Dir: AMEE ODOM

Library of 102,000 vols

Number of teachers: 105

Number of students: 2,530

DEANS

Charles A. Cannon College of Arts and Sciences: Prof. Dr H. DONALD MERRILL

Lloyd and Georgia Thayer School of Education: Dr SARAH HARRISON-BURNS

Porter B. Byrum School of Business: Prof. JOSEPH M. GRAHAM

School of Pharmacy: Prof. Dr ROBERT B. SUPERNAW

School of Sport Sciences: Dr MICHAEL R. JUDD

NORTH DAKOTA

FORT BERTHOLD COMMUNITY COLLEGE

POB 490, 220 Eighth Ave N, New Town, ND 58763

Telephone: (701) 627-4738

Internet: www.fortbertholdcc.bia.edu

Founded 1973

Tribal control

Academic year: August to May

Offers BSc in education and environmental science; BA in Native American studies

Pres.: RUSSELL D. MASON, JR

Vice-Pres. for Academics: Dr CLARICE BAKER-BIG BACK

Vice-Pres. for Native Studies: ALYCE SPOTTED BEAR

Dean for Students: ROZ ST CLAIRE

Library Dir: QUINCEE BAKER

Library of 19,000 vols, 200 periodicals

JAMESTOWN COLLEGE

6000 College Lane, Jamestown, ND 58405

Telephone: (701) 252-3467

E-mail: admissions@jc.edu

Internet: www.jc.edu

Founded 1883

Private control

Academic year: August to May

Depts of biology, business, accounting and economics, chemistry, communication, computer science and technology, criminal justice, English, fine arts, foreign language, health and physical education, history, mathematics, music, nursing, psychology, religion and philosophy, teacher education, theatre

Pres.: Dr ROBERT S. BADAL

Vice-Pres. and Dean for Academic Services: Dr GARY WATTS

Vice-Pres. for Institutional Advancement: POLLY PETERSON

Dean for Enrolment Management: TENA LAWRENCE
Dean for Students: GARY VAN ZINDEREN
Registrar: MICHAEL WOODLEY
Dir for Library: PHYLLIS BRATTON
Library of 150,000 vols
Number of teachers: 60
Number of students: 1,000

MEDCENTER ONE COLLEGE OF NURSING

512 N Seventh St, Bismarck, ND 58501
Telephone: (701) 323-6271
Internet: medcenterone.com/collegeofnursing
Founded 1988
Private control
Academic year: August to May (2 semesters)
Provost and Dean: Dr KAREN LATHAM
Library Dir: TRAVIS SCHULZ

NORTH DAKOTA UNIVERSITY SYSTEM

Dept 215, 10th Fl., State Capitol, 600 E Boulevard Ave, Bismarck, ND 58505-0230
Telephone: (701) 328-2960
E-mail: ndus.office@ndus.edu
Internet: www.ndus.edu
Founded 1990
State control
Chancellor: Dr LARRY SKOGEN (acting)
Vice-Chancellor for Academic and Student Affairs: MICHEL HILLMAN
Vice-Chancellor for Admin. Affairs: LAURA GLATT
Vice-Chancellor for Strategic Planning: MARSHA KROTSENG
Dean for Libraries: JAMES COUNCIL
Number of teachers: 4,000
Number of students: 36,000 (f.t.e.)...

CONSTITUENT UNIVERSITIES

Dickinson State University

291 Campus Dr., Dickinson, ND 58601-4896
Telephone: (701) 483-2507
E-mail: dsu.hawk@dickinsonstate.edu
Internet: www.dickinsonstate.edu
Founded 1918
Pres.: Dr D. C. COSTON (acting)
Vice-Pres. for Academic Affairs: Dr CYNTHIA PEMBERTON
Vice-Pres. for Finance and Admin.: TAD TORGERSON
Vice-Pres. for Student Devt: PATTIE CARR
Registrar: KATHLEEN MEYER
Dir for Library Services: RITA ENNEN
Library of 164,000 vols, 21,000 periodicals, 10,000 ebooks
Number of teachers: 235 (142 part-time, 93 full-time)
Number of students: 2,650

DEANS

College of Arts and Sciences: Dr KENNETH HAUGHT
College of Education, Business and Applied Sciences: Dr DAWN OLSON

Mayville State University

330 Third St, NE, Mayville, ND 58257-1299
Telephone: (701) 786-2301
E-mail: askmsu@mayvillestate.edu
Internet: www.mayvillestate.edu
Founded 1889, present name 1987
Academic year: August to May
Divs of business and computer information systems, education and psychology, health, liberal arts, physical education and recreation, science and mathematics

Pres.: GARY HAGEN
Vice-Pres. for Academic Affairs: Dr KEITH STENEHJEM
Vice-Pres. for Student Affairs and Institutional Research: Dr RAYMOND GERSZEWSKI
Registrar: PAM BRAATEN
Dir for Library Services: KELLY KORNKVEN
Library of 83,964 vols
Number of teachers: 75
Number of students: 930
Publication: *MSU Today* (1 a year)

Minot State University

500 University Ave, W, Minot, ND 58707-0001
Telephone: (701) 858-3000
E-mail: msu@minotstateu.edu
Internet: www.minotstateu.edu
Founded 1913
Pres.: Dr DAVID FULLER
Vice-Pres. for Academic Affairs: Dr LENORE M. KOCZON
Vice-Pres. for Admin. and Finance: BRIAN FOISY
Vice-Pres. for Advancement: MARV SEMRAU
Vice-Pres. for Student Affairs: Dr RICHARD R. JENKINS
Registrar: REBECCA PORTER
Library Dir: SARAH HENDERSON
Library of 500,000 vols
Number of teachers: 220
Number of students: 3,870

DEANS

Center for Extended Learning: Dr KRIS WARMOTH
College of Arts and Sciences: Dr CONRAD DAVIDSON
College of Business: Dr JOANN LINRUD
College of Education and Health Sciences: Dr NEIL NORDQUIST
Graduate School: Dr LINDA CRESAP

North Dakota State University

POB 6050, Fargo, ND 58108-6050
1340 Administration Ave, Fargo, ND 58102
Telephone: (701) 231-8011
E-mail: ndsu.admission@ndsu.edu
Internet: www.ndsu.edu
Founded 1890
Pres.: Dr DEAN L. BRESCIANI
Provost: Dr J. BRUCE RAFERT
Vice-Pres. for Finance and Admin.: BRUCE BOLLINGER
Vice-Pres. for Information Technology: BONNIE NEAS
Vice-Pres. for Research, Creative Activities and Technology Transfer: PHILIP BOUDJOUK
Vice-Pres. for Student Affairs: PRAKASH C. MATHEW
Asst Vice-Pres. for Univ. Relations: LAURA McDANIEL
Registrar: KRISTI WOLD-McCORMICK
Dean for Libraries: MICHELE M. REID
Library: see under Libraries and Archives
Number of teachers: 685
Number of students: 14,400

DEANS

College of Agriculture, Food Systems and Natural Resources: KEN GRAFTON
College of Arts, Humanities and Social Sciences: Dr KENT SANDSTROM
College of Business: RONALD D. JOHNSON
College of Engineering and Architecture: GARY R. SMITH
College of Human Development and Education: VIRGINIA CLARK JOHNSON
College of Pharmacy, Nursing and Allied Sciences: CHARLES D. PETERSON
College of Science and Mathematics: Dr KEVIN McCAUL

University of North Dakota

University Station, Grand Forks, ND 58202
Telephone: (701) 777-3000
E-mail: und.info@email.und.edu
Internet: www.und.edu
Founded 1883
Academic year: August to May
Pres.: Dr ROBERT O. KELLEY
Provost and Vice-Pres. for Academic Affairs: PAUL LeBEL
Vice-Pres. for Finance and Operations: ALICE BREKKE
Vice-Pres. for Research and Economic Devt: PHYLLIS E. JOHNSON
Vice-Pres. for Student Affairs: LORI REESOR
Dir for Libraries: WILBUR STOLT
Library: see under Libraries and Archives
Number of teachers: 610
Number of students: 14,700

DEANS

College of Arts and Sciences: KATHLEEN TIEMANN
College of Business and Public Administration: DENNIS J. ELBERT
College of Education and Human Devt: DAN RICE
College of Nursing: DENISE KORNIEWICZ
Graduate School: WAYNE SWISHER
John D. Odegard School of Aerospace Sciences: BRUCE A. SMITH
School of Engineering and Mines: HESHAM EL-REWINI
School of Law: KATHRYN RAND
School of Medicine and Health Sciences: JOSHUA WYNNE

Valley City State University

101 College St, SW, Valley City, ND 58072
Telephone: (701) 845-7990
Internet: www.vcsu.edu
Founded 1890
Divs of business and information technology, communication arts and social science, education and graduate studies, fine arts, mathematics, physical education, science and health
Pres.: Dr STEVEN W. SHIRLEY
Vice-Pres. for Academic Affairs: Dr MARGARET DAHLBERG
Vice-Pres. for Student Affairs: VITALIANO FIGUEROA
Registrar: JODY KLIER
Library Dir: DONNA JAMES
Library of 80,000 vols
Number of teachers: 55
Number of students: 1,385

DEANS

School of Education and Graduate Studies: GARY THOMPSON

There are five two-year colleges offering assoc. and trade/technical degrees

SITTING BULL COLLEGE

9299 Highway 24, Fort Yates, ND 58538
Telephone: (701) 854-8000
E-mail: info@sbci.edu
Internet: www.sittingbull.edu
Founded 1973 as Standing Rock Community College, present name 1996
Tribal control
Offers BSc in business administration, education, early childhood education, elementary education, environmental science, general studies, secondary science education; campuses at McLaughlin and Mobridge (South Dakota)
Pres.: Dr LAUREL VERMILLION

Vice-Pres. for Academics: Dr KOREEN RESSLER
Vice-Pres. for Finance: LEONICA ALKIRE
Librarian: MARK HOLMAN
Library of 20,000 vols
Number of teachers: 20
Number of students: 315

TRINITY BIBLE COLLEGE

50 Sixth Ave, S, Ellendale, ND 58436
Telephone: (701) 349-3621
E-mail: president@trinitybiblecollege.edu
Internet: www.trinitybiblecollege.edu
Founded 1948 as Lakewood Park Bible School, present name 1983
Private control
Academic year: August to May
Areas of study: biblical studies, Christian leadership, elementary education, general studies, intercultural studies, physical education
Pres.: JACK STROM
Sr Vice-Pres. and Dean for the College: Dr MICHAEL L. DUSING
Vice-Pres. for Academic Affairs: Dr DAYTON KINGSRITER
Dir for Enrolment: JAN DRESSANDER
Registrar: RACHELLE SPRINGER
Dir for Library: DIANE OLSON
Library of 90,000 vols, 11,700 ebooks
Number of teachers: 25
Number of students: 280

TURTLE MOUNTAIN COMMUNITY COLLEGE

POB 340, Belcourt, ND 58316
10145 BIA Rd 7, Belcourt, ND 58316
Telephone: (701) 477-7862
Internet: www.tm.edu
Founded 1972
Tribal control
Academic year: August to July
Offers BSc degrees in elementary education and secondary science
Pres.: Dr JIM DAVIS
Academic Dean: LARRY HENRY
Dean for Student Services: WANDA LADUCER
Registrar: ANGEL GLADUE
Library Dir: KATHE JO ZASTE-PELTIER
Library of 26,278 vols

UNITED TRIBES TECHNICAL COLLEGE

3315 University Dr., Bismarck, ND 58504
Telephone: (701) 255-3285
Internet: www.uttc.edu
Founded 1969 as United Tribes of North Dakota Devt Corpn, present name 1987
tribal control
Areas of study: business administration, criminal justice, elementary education
Pres.: Dr DAVID M. GIPP
Vice-Pres. for Academic, Career and Technical Education: PHIL BAIRD
Vice-Pres. for Student and Campus Services: RUSSELL SWAGGER
Assoc. Vice-Pres. for Enrolment Management: NATHAN STRATTON
Registrar: JOETTA MCLEOD
Librarian: CHARLENE WEIS
Library of 7,500 vols, 100 magazines and journals, 40 newspapers
Number of students: 650

UNIVERSITY OF MARY

7500 University Dr., Bismarck, ND 58504
Telephone: (701) 255-7500
E-mail: admissions@umary.edu

Internet: www.umary.edu
Founded 1955 as Mary College, present name and status 1986
Private control
Academic year: August to May
Pres.: JAMES P. SHEA
Exec. Vice-Pres.: GREG VETTER
Vice-Pres. for Academic Affairs: Dr DIANE FLADELAND
Vice-Pres. for Public Affairs: NEAL KALBERER
Vice-Pres. for Student Devt: Dr TIM SEAWORTH
Library Dir: CHERYL BAILEY
Library of 70,000 vols, 600 periodicals, 5,000 audiovisual items
Number of teachers: 100
Number of students: 3,000

DEANS

Gary Tharaldson School of Business: JOHN WARFORD
School of Arts and Sciences: Dr DAVID FLEISCHACKER
School of Education and Behavioral Sciences: Dr ROD A. JONAS
School of Health Sciences: Dr JODI ROLLER

OHIO

AIR FORCE INSTITUTE OF TECHNOLOGY

2950 Hobson Way, Wright-Patterson Air Force Base, OH 45433-7765
Telephone: (937) 255-3636
E-mail: pa@afit.edu
Internet: www.afit.edu
Founded 1919 as Air School of Application, present name and status 1947
State control
Commandant: Col Dr TIMOTHY J. LAWRENCE
Vice-Commandant: TIMOTHY J. DUENING
Dir forAdmissions: EDWARD HART
Library Dir: JAMES T. HELLING
Library of 120,000 vols
Number of teachers: 280

DEANS

Civil Engineering School: Col RODGER G. SCHULD
Graduate School of Engineering and Management: Dr MARLIN U. THOMAS
School of Systems and Logistics: Col TIMOTHY J. FENNELL

ANTIOCH UNIVERSITY

900 Dayton St, Yellow Springs, OH 45387
Telephone: (937) 769-1340
Internet: www.antioch.edu
Founded 1852
Private control
Academic year: July to June
Areas of study: arts, education, environmental studies and sustainability, health and human development, humanities, liberal studies, management and leadership, psychology; campuses in Los Angeles and Santa Barbara (California), Midwest (Ohio), New England (New Hampshire), and Seattle (Washington)
Chancellor: Dr TONI A. MURDOCH
Vice-Chancellor for Univ. Academic Affairs: Dr LAURIEN ALEXANDRE
Vice-Chancellor for Univ. Advancement: GRADY JONES
Registrar: VICKIE NIGHSWANDER
Number of teachers: 270
Number of students: 5,000

ART ACADEMY OF CINCINNATI

1212 Jackson St, Cincinnati, OH 45202
Telephone: (513) 562-6262
E-mail: admissions@artacademy.edu
Internet: www.artacademy.edu
Founded 1869 as McMicken School of Design, present name 1887
Private control
Academic year: August to May
Offers BA in art history, communication arts, fine arts; MA in education
Pres. and Academic Dean: DIANE K. SMITH
Vice-Pres. for Enrolment Management: Dr GREGORY STEWART
Dir for Admissions: JOHN WADDELL
Dir for Student Life: LIZ NEAL
Registrar: SUE HUTCHENS
Number of teachers: 38 (14 full-time, 24 adjunct)
Number of students: 220 (200 undergraduate, 20 graduate)

ASHLAND UNIVERSITY

401 College Ave, Ashland, OH 44805
Telephone: (419) 289-4142
E-mail: enrollme@ashland.edu
Internet: www.ashland.edu
Founded 1878 as Ashland College, present name 1989
Private control
Academic year: August to May
Pres.: Dr FREDERICK J. FINKS
Provost: Prof. Dr FRANK E. PETTIGREW
Vice-Pres. and Pres. for the Seminary: Dr JOHN C. SHULTZ
Vice-Pres. for Devt and Institutional Advancement: RON HUIATT
Vice-Pres. for Enrolment Management and Marketing: SCOTT VAN LOO
Vice-Pres. for Student Affairs and Dean for Students: B. SUE HEIMANN
Registrar: KATHLEEN HALL
Dir for Libraries: ED KRAKORA
Library of 280,000 vols
Number of teachers: 205
Number of students: 6,460
Publications: Accent Magazine, American Secondary Education (3 a year), Executive Eagle, River Teeth (2 a year)

DEANS

College of Arts and Sciences: Dr DAWN WEBER
Dwight Schar College of Education: Dr JAMES P. VAN KEUREN
Dwight Schar College of Nursing: FAYE GRUND
Founders School of Continuing Education: Dr DWIGHT L. MCELFRESH
Graduate School: Dr W. GREGORY GERRICK
Richard E and Sandra J. Dauch School of Business and Economics: Dr JEFFREY E. RUSSELL

ATHENAEUM OF OHIO

6616 Beechmont Ave, Cincinnati, OH 45230
Telephone: (513) 231-2223
E-mail: ath@mtsm.org
Internet: www.mtsm.org
Founded 1829, present name and status 1928
Private control
Language of instruction: English
Academic year: September to June
Offers Master's degrees in biblical studies, divinity, pastoral counselling, theology
Pres. and Rector: Rev. BENEDICT O'CINNSEALAIGH
Vice-Pres. for Finance and Admin.: DENNIS K. EAGAN
Dean: Rev. EARL FERNANDES

Dean of Spec. Studies: Dr TERRANCE D. CALLAN

Registrar: MICHAEL E. SWEENEY

Dir for Library: CONNIE SONG

Library of 111,000 vols; spec. colln of 9,000 books, incl. 35 MSS and 22 incunabula

Number of teachers: 60

Number of students: 215

Publication: *Athenaeum Magazine*

BALDWIN-WALLACE COLLEGE

275 Eastland Rd, Berea, OH 44017-2005

Telephone: (440) 826-2900

E-mail: info@bw.edu

Internet: www.bw.edu

Founded 1845

Private control

Divs of business administration, education, health and physical education, humanities, conservatory, science and mathematics, social sciences

Pres.: RICHARD W. DURST

Sr Vice-Pres.: RICHARD L. FLETCHER

Vice-Pres. for Academic Affairs and Dean for College: Dr MARY LOU HIGGERSON

Vice-Pres. for Enrolment Management: SUSAN DILENO

Vice-Pres. for Finance and Admin.: WILLIAM M. RENIFF

Vice-Pres. for Student Affairs: Dr TRINA DOBBERSTEIN

Vice-Pres. for Univ. Advancement: WILLIAM J. SPIKER

Dir for Libraries: Dr PATRICK SCANLAN

Library of 210,000 vols

Number of teachers: 165 (full-time)

Number of students: 4,080

BLUFFTON UNIVERSITY

1 University Dr., Bluffton, OH 45817-2104

Telephone: (419) 358-3000

E-mail: admissions@bluffton.edu

Internet: www.bluffton.edu

Founded 1899 as Bluffton College, present name and status 2004

Private control

Academic year: August to May

Divs of business studies, communication and fine arts, education and sport science, humanities, natural sciences, social and behavioural sciences

Pres.: JAMES M. HARDER

Vice-Pres. and Academic Dean: SALLY WEAVER SOMMER

Vice-Pres. for Enrolment Management and Student Life: ERIC FULCOMER

Vice-Pres. for Institutional Advancement: HANS HOUSHOWER

Dir for Admissions: CHRIS JEBSEN

Registrar: IRIS NEUFELD

Dir for Libraries: MARY JEAN JOHNSON

Library of 160,000 vols

Number of teachers: 110 (62 full-time, 48 part-time)

Number of students: 1,230 (1,115 undergraduate, 115 graduate)

BOWLING GREEN STATE UNIVERSITY

Bowling Green, OH 43403-0001

Telephone: (419) 372-2531

Internet: www.bgsu.edu

Founded 1910, present status 1935

State control

Academic year: August to May

Pres.: Dr MARY ELLEN MAZEY

Provost and Sr Vice-Pres. for Academic Affairs: Dr RODNEY ROGERS

Vice-Pres. for Enrolment Management: ALBERT COLOM

Vice-Pres. for Finance and Admin.: SHERIDEEN S. STOLL

Vice-Pres. for Research and Economic Devt: Dr MICHAEL OGAWA

Vice-Pres. for Univ. Advancement: THOMAS HILES

Dean for Students: JILL CARR

Registrar: CHRISTOPHER PHILIP COX

Dean for Univ. Libraries: SARA BUSHONG

Library of 2,884,569 vols, 74,411 ebooks, 57,592 ejournals, 2,373,898 microform units, 2,437 periodicals

Number of teachers: 800 (full-time)

Number of students: 21,000

Publications: *BGSU Magazine*, *Dimensions Magazine*, *Journal of Popular Culture* (4 a year, online, www.msu.edu/~tjpc), *Mid-American Review*, *Philosopher's Index* (4 a year)

DEANS

College of Arts and Sciences: Dr SIMON MORGAN-RUSSELL

College of Business Administration: Dr B. MADHU RAO

College of Education and Human Development: Dr BRAD COLWELL

College of Health and Human Services: Dr LINDA PETROSINO

College of Musical Arts: Dr JEFFREY SHOWELL

College of Technology: Dr FARIS MALHAS

Firelands College: Dr WILLIAM K. BALZER

Graduate College: Dr MICHAEL OGAWA

CAPITAL UNIVERSITY

1 College and Main, Columbus, OH 43209-2394

Telephone: (614) 236-6011

Internet: www.capital.edu

Founded 1830

Private control

Academic year: August to May (2 terms)

Schools of communications, conservatory of music, humanities, law, management and leadership, natural sciences, nursing and health, social sciences and education

Pres.: Dr DENVY A. BOWMAN

Provost and Vice-Pres. for Academic and Student Affairs: Dr RICHARD M. ASHBROOK

Vice-Pres. for Business and Finance: SUSAN TATE

Exec. Vice-Pres. for Planning and Strategy: Dr KEVIN W. SAYERS

Dir for Admission: AMANDA L. STEINER

Dean for the College: Dr CEDRIC ADDERLEY

Registrar: BRENT A. KOERBER

Number of teachers: 400 (200 full-time, 200 part-time)

Number of students: 3,550

CASE WESTERN RESERVE UNIVERSITY

10900 Euclid Ave, Cleveland, OH 44106

Telephone: (216) 368-2000

Internet: www.case.edu

Founded 1967 by merger of Western Reserve Univ. (f. 1826 as College) with Case Institute of Technology (f. 1880 as Case School of Applied Science)

Private control

Academic year: August to May

Pres.: BARBARA R. SNYDER

Provost and Exec. Vice-Pres.: WILLIAM A. BAESLACK, III

Sr Vice-Pres. for Admin.: JOHN WHEELER

Sr Vice-Pres. for Univ. Relations and Devt: BRUCE LOESSIN

Vice-Pres. for Enrolment: RICK BISCHOFF

Vice-Pres. for Govt Relations: DAVID BELL

Vice-Pres. for Inclusion, Diversity and Equal Opportunity: MARILYN SANDERS MOBLEY

Vice-Pres. for IT Services and Chief Information Officer: LEV S. GONICK

Vice-Pres. for Student Affairs: GLENN NICHOLLS

Vice-Pres. for Univ. Planning: CHRISTINE ASH

Gen. Counsel: COLLEEN TREML

Registrar: AMY S. HAMMETT

Univ. Librarian: ARNOLD HIRSHON

Library: see under Libraries and Archives

Number of teachers: 2,745 (full-time)

Number of students: 9,837 (4,227 undergraduate, 5,610 graduate and professional)

Publication: *Think* (2 a year, online, www.case.edu/magazine)

DEANS

Case School of Engineering: NORMAN TIEN

College of Arts and Sciences: CYRUS TAYLOR

Frances Payne Bolton School of Nursing: MARY E. KERR

Mandel School of Applied Social Sciences: GROVER GILMORE

School of Dental Medicine: JEROLD GOLDBERG

School of Graduate Studies: CHARLES ROZEK

School of Law: LAWRENCE MITCHELL

School of Medicine: PAMELA BOWES DAVIS

Weatherhead School of Management: MOHAN REDDY

Undergraduate Studies: JEFFREY WOLCOWITZ

PROFESSORS

ABDEL-WAHAB, M., Medicine

ABDUL-KARIM, F., Pathology

ABU-ELMAGD, K., Surgery

ACHESON, L., Family Medicine and Community Health

ADAMS, H., Art History and Art

ADAMS, M., Mechanical and Aerospace Engineering

ADELSTEIN, D., Medicine

ADLER, J., Law

ADVINCULA, R., Macromolecular Science

AGARWAL, A., Surgery

AGLE, D., Psychiatry

AKE, D., Music

AKKUS, O., Mechanical and Aerospace Engineering

ALMASAN, A., Molecular Medicine

ALTOSE, M., Medicine

ANAND, A., Medicine

ANDERSON, A., Chemistry

ANDERSON, J., Pathology

ARAFAH, B., Medicine

ARMITAGE, K., Medicine

ARON, D., Medicine

ASKARI, A., Medicine

ATAYA, K., Reproductive Biology

ATTALA, M., Anaesthesiology

AULISIO, M., Bioethics

AVRIL, N., Radiology

BAER, E., Macromolecular Science

BAESLACK, W., Materials Science and Engineering

BAHLER, R., Medicine

BAKER, M., Radiology

BALDWIN, W., Molecular Medicine

BALEY, J., Paediatrics

BALLOCK, R., Surgery

BANERJEE, A., Biochemistry

BARBER, M., Surgery

BARDENSTEIN, D., Ophthamology and Visual Sciences

BARKLEY, M., Chemistry

BARKSDALE, E., Surgery

BARNETT, G., Surgery

BARTHOLOMEW, J., Medicine

BASILION, J., Radiology

BEAL, T., Religious Studies

BEALL, C., Anthropology

BECKWITH, K., Political Science

BENETZ, B., Ophthamology and Visual Sciences

BENNINGER, M., Surgery

BENZEL, E., Surgery
BERG, J., Law
BERGER, N., Medicine
BERGMANN, C., Molecular Medicine
BIEGEL, D., Applied Social Sciences
BILIMORIA, D., Organizational Behavior
BINGAMAN, W., Surgery
BIRNKRANT, D., Paediatrics
BISSADA, N., Dental Medicine
BLACKSTONE, E., Surgery
BLANTON, R., General Medical Sciences
BLAZEY, L., Accountancy
BODNER, D., Urology
BOLAND, R., Design and Innovation
BOLWELL, B., Medicine
BONOMO, R., Medicine
BOOM, W., Medicine
BORAWSKI, E., Epidemiology and Biostatistics
BORDEN, E., Molecular Medicine
BORON, W., Physiology and Biophysics
BOYATZIS, R., Organizational Behaviour
BOYLE, A., Medicine
BRADLEY, L., Surgery
BRADY-KALNAY, S., Molecular Biology and Microbiology
BRANDT, C., Surgery
BRENNER, B., Emergency Medicine
BRONSON, D., Medicine
BROWN, D., Anaesthesiology
BROWN, R., Physics
BRUNENGRABER, H., Nutrition
BRUNKEN, R., Radiology
BUCHANAN, G., Design and Innovation
BUDD, G., Medicine
BURDA, C., Chemistry
BURNEY, E., Ophthamology and Visual Sciences
CALABRESE, L., Medicine
CALABRESE, J., Psychiatry
CALLES-ESCANDON, J., Medicine
CALVETTI, D., Mathematics
CAMPBELL, J., Family Medicine
CAMPBELL, S., Surgery
CAPLAN, A., Biology
CAREY, P., Biochemistry
CAREY, W., Medicine
CARLIN, C., Molecular Biology and Microbiology
CARNEY, D., Law
CASCORBI, H., Anaesthesiology and Perioperative Medicine
CATALANO, P., Reproductive Biology
CATHCART, M., Molecular Medicine
CAVUSOGLU, M., Electrical Engineering and Computer Science
CEBUL, R., Medicine
CERQUEIRA, M., Radiology
CHAE, J., Physical Medicine and Rehabilitation
CHAK, A., Medicine
CHANCE, M., General Medical Sciences
CHAO, J., Family Medicine and Community Health
CHATTERJEE, S., Design and Innovation
CHENG, J., Anaesthesiology
CHIEL, H., Biology
CHISOLM, G., Molecular Medicine
CHOTTINER, G., Physics
CHUMAKOV, P., Molecular Medicine
CHUNG, M., Medicine
CLAIR, D., Surgery
CLARK, G., Physical Medicine and Rehabilitation
COBANOGLU, A., Surgery
COHEN, J., Medicine
COHEN, S., Medicine
COHEN, H., Organizational Behavior
COHEN, M., Pathology
COLARES, J., Law
COLE-KELLY, K., Family Medicine and Community Health
COLLOPY, F., Design and Innovation
COMINELLI, F., Medicine
CONNORS, A., Medicine
COOPER, K., Dermatology
COOPER, G., Medicine

COOPER, B., Medicine
COOPERRIDER, D., Organizational Behavior
COPELAN, E., Medicine
CORRADI, R., Psychiatry
COSTA, M., Medicine
COUCE, M., Pathology
COULTON, C., Applied Social Sciences
COVAULT, C., Physics
COWART, G., Music
CRABB, J., Ophthalmology
CRAGO, P., Biomedical Engineering
CROMER, B., Paediatrics
CROWE, J., Surgery
CULLIS, C., Biology
CUMMINGS, J., Medicine
CUPAR, J., Law
CYDULKA, R., Emergency Medicine
DAI, L., Macromolecular Science
DALY, B., Nursing
DANESHGARI, F., Urology
DANIELPOUR, D., GMS-Comprehensive Cancer Centre
DANNEFER, W., Sociology
DAROFF, R., Neurology
DAVIS, B., Dermatology
DAVIS, M., Medicine
DAVIS, P., Paediatrics
DAWSON, N., Medicine
DEAL, W., Religious Studies
DEARBORN, D., Environmental Health Sciences
DEBANNE, S., Epidemiology and Biostatistics
DE BOER, P., Molecular Biology and Microbiology
DE GEORGIA, M., Neurology
DE GOLIA, P., Family Medicine and Community Health
DE HASETH, P., GMS-RNA Centre
DEIMLING, G., Sociology
DELANEY, C., Surgery
DE LIMA, M., Medicine
DEMAREE, H., Psychological Sciences
DENERIS, E., Neurosciences
DENT, G., Law
DEVEREAUX, M., Neurology
DICK, T., Medicine
DI CORLETO, P., Molecular Medicine
DIMARCO, A., Physical Medicine and Rehabilitation
DISTELHORST, C., Medicine
DONLEY, B., Surgery
DOWLATI, A., Medicine
DRAKE, R., Surgery
DREICER, R., Medicine
DRISCOLL, D., Molecular Medicine
DRUMM, M., Paediatrics
DUBIN, R., Economics
DUBYAK, G., Physiology and Biophysics
DUERK, J., Radiology
DUFFIN, R., Music
DUMOT, J., Medicine
DUNLAP, M., Medicine
DURAND, D., Biomedical Engineering
DWEIK, R., Medicine
EGELHOFF, T., Molecular Medicine
EINSTADTER, D., Medicine
ELLIS, S., Medicine
ELSTON, R., Epidemiology and Biostatistics
EMANCIPATOR, S., Pathology
EMERMAN, C., Emergency Medicine
ENG, C., Genetics and Genome Sciences
ENGEL, A., Pharmacology
ENTIN, J., Law
ERNST, F., Materials Science and Engineering
ERZURUM, S., Medicine
EXLINE, J., Psychological Sciences
FADDOUL, F., Dental Medicine
FAIRCHILD, R., Molecular Medicine
FALCONE, T., Surgery
FARAH, M., Medicine
FASS, R., Medicine
FASTENAU, P., Neurology
FAULHABER, P., Radiology
FAZIO, V., Surgery
FEENY, N., Psychological Sciences

FEKE, D., Chemical Engineering
FELDMAN, S., Design and Innovation
FERGUSON, R., Radiology
FERNANDEZ, H., Medicine
FERRETTI, G., Dental Medicine
FINE, S., Banking and Finance
FINKE, J., Molecular Medicine
FIOCCHI, C., Molecular Medicine
FITZPATRICK, J., Nursing
FLAMM, S., Radiology
FLANNERY, D., Applied Social Sciences
FLECHNER, S., Surgery
FOGARTY, T., Accountancy
FOLDVARY-SCHAEFER, N., Medicine
FOX, P., Molecular Medicine
FOX, J., Physiology and Biophysics
FRANCO-BRONSON, K., Medicine
FRENCH, R., Materials Science and Engineering
FRIEDMAN, L., Psychiatry
FRY, R., Organizational Behavior
FUKAMACHI, K., Molecular Medicine
FUNG, J., Surgery
FURLAN, A., Neurology
GABINET, L., Law
GAINES, A., Anthropology
GALBRAITH, G., Dance
GAMBETTI, P., Pathology
GARCIA-SANZ, M., Electrical Engineering and Computer Science
GARVIN, J., Physiology and Biophysics
GARY, F., Nursing
GASPARINI, D., Civil Engineering
GASTMAN, B., Surgery
GASTON, B., Paediatrics
GENUTH, S., Medicine
GERHART, P., Law
GERKEN, T., Paediatrics
GERSON, S., Medicine
GHANNOUM, M., Dermatology
GIANNELLI, P., Law
GILKESON, R., Radiology
GILMORE, G., Psychological Sciences
GLADSON, C., Molecular Medicine
GOLDBERG, J., Dental Medicine
GOLDBERG, V., Orthopaedics
GOLDBERG, J., Surgery
GOLDBLUM, J., Pathology
GOLDFARB, J., Paediatrics
GOLDFARB, D., Surgery
GOLDING, L., Molecular Medicine
GOLDSTEIN, M., Anthropology
GORDON, J., Law
GORDON, R., Law
GRAHAM, L., Surgery
GRASS, J., Anaesthesiology and Perioperative Medicine
GRAVENSTEIN, S., Medicine
GREENE, R., Psychological Sciences
GREENFIELD, E., Orthopaedics
GREENFIELD, M., Reproductive Biology
GREENSPAN, N., Pathology
GREKSA, L., Anthropology
GRISWOLD, M., Radiology
GROH-WARGO, H., Paediatrics
GROZA, V., Applied Social Sciences
GUPTA, A., Banking and Finance
GUPTA, M., Pathology
GUPTA, S., Urology
GURARIE, D., Mathematics
GUYURON, B., Plastic Surgery
HAAGA, J., Radiology
HAAS, P., Religious Studies
HAINES, J., Epidemiology and Biostatistics
HALL, G., Pathology
HALL, H., Paediatrics
HALLIBURTON, S., Radiology
HAMILTON, T., Molecular Medicine
HAMMACK, D., History
HANS, M., Dental Medicine
HAQQI, T., Medicine
HARDING, C., Pathology
HARRIS, L., Medicine
HARTE, P., Genetics and Genome Sciences
HASCALL, V., Molecular Medicine
HATZOGLOU, M., Nutrition

HAUGUEL-DE MOUZON, S., Reproductive Biology
HAYEK, S., Anaesthesiology and Perioperative Medicine
HAZEN, S., Molecular Medicine
HEFLING, S., Music
HEINBERG, L., Medicine
HELPER, S., Economics
HENDERSON, J., Surgery
HERTS, B., Radiology
HESTON, W., Molecular Medicine
HEUER, A., Materials Science and Engineering
HICKNER, J., Family Medicine
HILL, B., Law
HODGSON, J., Medicine
HOFFMAN, S., Law
HOFFMAN, G., Medicine
HOIT, B., Medicine
HOKENSTAD, M., Applied Social Sciences
HOLLYFIELD, J., Ophthalmology
HOPPEL, C., Pharmacology
HORWATH, W., Psychiatry
HOSTETTER, T., Medicine
HOUGHTON, J., Molecular Medicine
HRICIK, D., Medicine
HSI, E., Pathology
HUANG, S., Ophthamology and Visual Sciences
HULL, T., Surgery
HURLEY, M., Mathematics
IANNOTTI, J., Surgery
IMREY, P., Medicine
ISHIDA, H., Macromolecular Science
ISMAIL-BEIGI, F., Medicine
IYENGAR, S., Epidemiology and Biostatistics
IZEN, S., Mathematics
JACOBBERGER, J., GMS-Comprehensive Cancer Center
JACOBS, M., Pathology
JACOBSEN, D., Molecular Medicine
JAFFE, D., Law
JAIN, M., Medicine
JAMIESON, A., Macromolecular Science
JANIGRO, D., Molecular Medicine
JANKOWSKY, E., GMS-RNA Center
JASKIW, G., Psychiatry
JAWORSKY, C., Dermatology
JENNINGS, A., Civil Engineering
JENSEN, E., Law
JOHNSON, J., Medicine
JONES, K., Nursing
JONES, S., Physiology and Biophysics
JONES, J., Surgery
JOSEPHSON, R., Medicine
KADAMBI, J., Mechanical and Aerospace Engineering
KAHANA, E., Sociology
KAISER, P., Ophthalmology
KAISERMAN-ABRAMOF, I., Anatomy
KALAYCIO, M., Medicine
KALHAN, S., Molecular Medicine
KALTENBACH, J., Molecular Medicine
KAMOTANI, Y., Mechanical and Aerospace Engineering
KAO, H., Biochemistry
KAOUK, J., Surgery
KAPADIA, S., Medicine
KAPLAN, D., Pathology
KARN, J., Molecular Biology and Microbiology
KARNIK, S., Molecular Medicine
KASH, K., Physics
KASHYAP, V., Surgery
KASS, L., Pathology
KATIRJI, M., Neurology
KATTAN, M., Medicine
KATZ, L., Law
KATZ, J., Medicine
KATZ, D., Neurosciences
KAUFMAN, E., Medicine
KAZURA, J., GMS-Global Health and Disease
KEITH, M., Orthopaedics
KENNEY, M., Chemistry
KENNY, M., Law
KERI, R., Pharmacology
KERN, T., Medicine

KERR, M., Nursing
KIKANO, G., Family Medicine and Community Health
KIM, C., Philosophy
KIM, J., Surgery
KING, C., GMS-Global Health and Disease
KING, C., GMS-Global Health and Disease
KINGSBERG, S., Reproductive Biology
KIRBY, D., Medicine
KIRSCH, R., Biomedical Engineering
KIRWAN, J., Molecular Medicine
KLEIN, A., Medicine
KLEIN, E., Surgery
KOCH, C., Anaesthesiology
KODISH, E., Paediatrics
KONSTAN, M., Paediatrics
KORBIN, J., Anthropology
KORMAN, N., Dermatology
KOSTRITSKY, J., Law
KOTAGAL, P., Medicine
KOTTKE-MARCHANT, K., Pathology
KOTZ, M., Psychiatry
KOWALSKI, K., Physics
KRAAY, M., Orthopaedics
KRISHNAN, C., Banking and Finance
KRUEGER, R., Ophthalmology
KU, R., Law
KUBU, C., Medicine
KURZ, A., Anaesthesiology
LABHASETWAR, V., Molecular Medicine
LACKS, D., Chemical Engineering
LALUMANDIER, J., Dental Medicine
LAM, M., Medicine
LaMANNA, J., Physiology and Biophysics
LAMBRECHT, W., Physics
LANDAU, U., Chemical Engineering
LANDMESSER, L., Neurosciences
LANDRETH, G., Neurosciences
LANG, D., Medicine
LANGER, J., Mathematics
LANZIERI, C., Radiology
LASHNER, B., Medicine
LASS, J., Ophthamology and Visual Sciences
LATHERS, M., Modern Languages and Literature
LAVELLE, K., Political Science
LAVERTU, P., Otolaryngology
LAZARUS, H., Medicine
LAZEBNIK, R., Paediatrics
LAZEBNIK, N., Reproductive Biology
LEDERMAN, R., Medicine
LEDERMAN, M., Medicine
LEE, I., Chemistry
LEE, J., Surgery
LEITMAN, M., Mathematics
LERNER, A., Neurology
LETTERIO, J., Paediatrics
LEVIN, M., History
LEVIN, K., Medicine
LEVINE, A., Medicine
LEVITAN, N., Medicine
LEWANDOWSKI, J., Materials Science and Engineering
LEWIS, W., Medicine
LEWIS, S., Paediatrics
LEWIS, B., Psychological Sciences
LHATOO, S., Neurology
LI, L., Family Medicine and Community Health
LI, X., Molecular Medicine
LICINA, M., Anaesthesiology
LIEDTKE, C., Paediatrics
LIN, W., Electrical Engineering and Computer Science
LIN, V., Medicine
LINCOFF, S., Medicine
LIPTON, J., Law
LIU, C., Chemical Engineering
LIU, J., Reproductive Biology
LOPARO, K., Electrical Engineering and Computer Science
LOUE, S., Bioethics
LOVE, T., Medicine
LU, Z., Biomedical Engineering
LUCK, R., Astronomy
LUDERS, H., Neurology

LUDINGTON, S., Nursing
LUSE, D., Molecular Medicine
LYTLE, B., Surgery
LYYTINEN, K., Design and Innovation
MACE, S., Medicine
MACHTAY, M., Radiation Oncology
MACIEJEWSKI, J., Medicine
MACKLIS, R., Medicine
MACKNIN, M., Paediatrics
MacLENNAN, G., Pathology
MADIGAN, E., Nursing
MAHONEY, G., Applied Social Sciences
MALAKOOTI, B., Electrical Engineering and Computer Science
MALANGONI, M., Surgery
MALEMUD, C., Medicine
MANAS-ZLOCZOWER, I., Macromolecular Science
MANDELL, B., Medicine
MANSOUR, J., Mechanical and Aerospace Engineering
MANSOUR, E., Surgery
MARCUS, R., Orthopaedics
MARGOLIS, K., Law
MARKOWITZ, S., Medicine
MARKS, J., Surgery
MARLING, W., English
MARSHALL, P., Bioethics
MARTIN, D., Ophthalmology
MARTIN, R., Paediatrics
MASARYK, T., Radiology
MATHUR, K., Operations
MATISOFF, G., Earth, Environment, and Planetary Sciences
MATLOUB, Y., Paediatrics
MATTHEWS, A., Genetics and Genome Sciences
MAVISSAKALIAN, M., Psychiatry
McCALL, P., Earth, Environment, and Planetary Sciences
McCLARY, S., Music
McCOMSEY, G., Paediatrics
McCRAE, K., Molecular Medicine
McCULLOUGH, A., Medicine
McDAVID, L., Paediatrics
McFARLANE, M., Medicine
McGAUGH, S., Astronomy
McGUFFIN-CAWLEY, J., Materials Science and Engineering
McHENRY, C., Surgery
McINTYRE, T., Molecular Medicine
McLAIN, R., Surgery
McLARTY, C., Philosophy
McLENNAN, G., Radiology
McMUNIGAL, K., Law
McNALLY, L., Law
MEDOF, M., Pathology
MEGERIAN, C., Otolaryngology
MEHLMAN, M., Law
MEHREGANY, M., Electrical Engineering and Computer Science
MEHTA, A., Medicine
MEKHAIL, N., Anaesthesiology
MERCER, K., Law
MERCER, B., Reproductive Biology
MEROPOL, N., Medicine
MERRICK, W., Biochemistry
MICHAEL, C., Pathology
MIEYAL, J., Pharmacology
MIHALJEVIC, T., Surgery
MIHOS, J., Astronomy
MILAS, K., Surgery
MILLER, R., Medicine
MILLER, R., Neurosciences
MILLER, C., Surgery
MINIACI, A., Surgery
MOBLEY, M., English
MODIC, M., Radiology
MONGA, Y., Surgery
MONNIER, V., Pathology
MONTAGUE, D., Surgery
MONTENEGRO, H., Medicine
MOORE, S., Nursing
MOORE, J., Paediatrics
MORRISON, H., Astronomy
MULLEN, K., Medicine

MURRAY, P., Anaesthesiology
MUSCHLER, G., Surgery
MUSIL, C., Nursing
NAGARAJ, R., Ophthamology and Visual Sciences
NAGY, L., Molecular Medicine
NAIR, R., Medicine
NANCE, D., Law
NARD, C., Law
NATOWICZ, M., Pathology
NEARMAN, H., Anaesthesiology and Perioperative Medicine
NEDOROST, S., Dermatology
NEDRUD, J., Pathology
NEEDLMAN, R., Paediatrics
NEILS, J., Art History and Art
NELSON, S., Dental Medicine
NEMUNAITIS, G., Physical Medicine and Rehabilitation
NEWMAN, W., Electrical Engineering and Computer Science
NEWMAN, C., Surgery
NILSEN, T., GMS-RNA Center
NISSEN, S., Medicine
NOSEK, T., Physiology and Biophysics
NOY, N., Pharmacology
OAKLEY, T., Cognitive Science
OBRIEN, R., Epidemiology and Biostatistics
OBUCHOWSKI, N., Medicine
OCCHIONERO, R., Dental Medicine
ODONNELL, J., Radiology
OHARA, P., Surgery
OLEINICK, N., Radiation Oncology
OLNESS, K., Paediatrics
ONDERS, R., Surgery
ORLOCK, J., English
OSBORNE, R., Design and Innovation
OTOOLE, E., Medicine
OVERHOLSER, J., Psychological Sciences
OZSOYOGLU, Z., Electrical Engineering and Computer Science
OZSOYOGLU, G., Electrical Engineering and Computer Science
PADGETT, R., Molecular Medicine
PALCZEWSKI, K., Pharmacology
PAPACHRISTOU, C., Electrical Engineering and Computer Science
PAPAY, F., Surgery
PARAISO, M., Surgery
PARK, M., Pathology
PARK, S., Surgery
PARKER, L., Accountancy
PARKER, R., Surgery
PATTERSON, B., Orthopaedics
PEACHEY, N., Ophthalmology
PEARLMAN, E., Ophthamology and Visual Sciences
PEARSON, A., Chemistry
PECKHAM, P., Biomedical Engineering
PEEREBOOM, D., Medicine
PETRULIS, A., Medicine
PETSCHEK, R., Physics
PIKULEVA, I., Ophthamology and Visual Sciences
PIROUZ, P., Materials Science and Engineering
PLAUTZ, G., Paediatrics
PLOW, E., Molecular Medicine
PODGURSKI, H., Electrical Engineering and Computer Science
PONSKY, J., Surgery
PRAHL, J., Mechanical and Aerospace Engineering
PRAKASH, V., Mechanical and Aerospace Engineering
PRAYSON, R., Pathology
PRESTON, D., Neurology
PREVITS, G., Accountancy
PROCOP, G., Pathology
PROTASIEWICZ, J., Chemistry
QIN, J., Molecular Medicine
QUINN, R., Mechanical and Aerospace Engineering
QUTUBUDDIN, S., Chemical Engineering
RABINOVICH, M., Electrical Engineering and Computer Science

RACKLEY, R., Surgery
RANSOHOFF, R., Molecular Medicine
RAO, S., Medicine
REDDY, N., Design and Innovation
REDLINE, R., Pathology
REMER, E., Radiology
REMZI, F., Surgery
RESNICK, P., Psychiatry
RICE, T., Surgery
RICH, J., Molecular Medicine
RILEY, D., Neurology
RIMM, A., Epidemiology and Biostatistics
RIMNAC, C., Mechanical and Aerospace Engineering
RINI, B., Medicine
RITCHKEN, P., Banking and Finance
RITZMANN, R., Biology
ROBERTSON, C., Law
ROCKE, A., History
RODRIGUEZ, E., Pathology
ROGERS, L., Neurology
ROIZEN, M., Anaesthesiology
ROIZEN, N., Paediatrics
ROLLINS, A., Biomedical Engineering
ROME, E., Paediatrics
RONIS, R., Psychiatry
ROS, P., Radiology
ROSE, P., Reproductive Biology
ROSEN, C., Paediatrics
ROSEN, M., Surgery
ROSENBLATT, C., Physics
ROSS, J., Urology
ROSSMAN, M., Law
ROTE, N., Reproductive Biology
ROTHBERG, M., Medicine
ROTTA, A., Paediatrics
ROWAN, S., Macromolecular Science
RUBIN, B., Pathology
RUDICK, R., Medicine
RUEDRICH, S., Psychiatry
RUFF, R., Neurology
RUGGIERI, P., Radiology
RUHL, J., Physics
RUSS, S., Psychological Sciences
RZESZOTARSKI, M., Radiology
SAADA, A., Civil Engineering
SABANEGH, E., Surgery
SABIK, J., Surgery
SAHGAL, V., Anaesthesiology and Perioperative Medicine
SAIDEL, G., Biomedical Engineering
SAJATOVIC, M., Psychiatry
SALATA, R., Medicine
SALOMON, R., Chemistry
SALZ, H., Genetics and Genome Sciences
SAMOLS, D., Biochemistry
SANTIAGO, A., Applied Social Sciences
SARMA, D., Religious Studies
SAUNTHARARAJAH, Y., Medicine
SAVINELL, R., Chemical Engineering
SCHACHAT, A., Ophthalmology
SCHARF, M., Law
SCHAUER, P., Surgery
SCHELLING, J., Medicine
SCHER, M., Paediatrics
SCHERSON, D., Chemistry
SCHILLING, W., Physiology and Biophysics
SCHIRALDI, D., Macromolecular Science
SCHLUCHTER, M., Epidemiology and Biostatistics
SCHMAIER, A., Medicine
SCHULTE, E., Paediatrics
SCOTT, J., Theatre
SEDOR, J., Medicine
SEDWICK, W., Medicine
SEHGAL, A., Medicine
SEITZ, W., Surgery
SEKERES, M., Medicine
SELMAN, W., Neurological Surgery
SEN, G., Molecular Medicine
SESSLER, D., Anaesthesiology
SEYMOUR, C., Law
SHAFFER, J., Orthopaedics
SHANE, S., Economics
SHEELER, J., English
SHEN, B., Medicine

SHORT, E., Psychological Sciences
SHOSKES, D., Surgery
SIEBENSCHUH, W., English
SIEG, S., Medicine
SIEGEL, R., Pharmacology
SIEMIONOW, M., Surgery
SILA, C., Neurology
SILVER, J., Neurosciences
SILVERMAN, R., Molecular Medicine
SILVERS, J., Banking and Finance
SIMON, D., Medicine
SIMPSON, S., Anatomy
SINGER, M., Applied Social Sciences
SINGER, L., Environmental Health Sciences
SINGER, D., Mathematics
SINGER, N., Medicine
SINGER, K., Physics
SINGH, J., Design and Innovation
SINGH, A., Ophthalmology
SINGH, N., Pathology
SIPERSTEIN, A., Surgery
SIVAK, E., Medicine
SIVIT, C., Radiology
SKOWRONSKI, J., Molecular Biology and Microbiology
SMEDIRA, N., Surgery
SMITH, C., Anaesthesiology
SMITH, C., Family Medicine and Community Health
SMITH, J., Molecular Medicine
SNYDER, C., Family Medicine and Community Health
SNYDER, B., Law
SOBEL, M., Operations
SOLOW, D., Operations
SOMERSALO, E., Mathematics
SPIRNAK, J., Surgery
SREENATH, N., Electrical Engineering and Computer Science
STACEY, D., Molecular Medicine
STAHL, J., Neurology
STAMLER, J., Medicine
STANCIN, T., Paediatrics
STANGE, K., Family Medicineand Community Health
STANTON-HICKS, M., Anaesthesiology
STARKMAN, G., Physics
STARLING, R., Medicine
STARR, N., Anaesthesiology
STEIGER, E., Surgery
STEINBERG, T., History
STEINEMANN, T., Surgery
STERN, R., Paediatrics
STEWART, P., Pharmacology
STOHLMAN, S., Medicine
STOLLER, J., Medicine
STORK, E., Paediatrics
STRANGI, G., Physics
STRASSFELD, R., Law
STRAUSS, M., Otolaryngology
STROHL, K., Medicine
STROWBRIDGE, B., Neurosciences
STULBERG, B., Surgery
SUH, J., Medicine
SUN, J., Epidemiology and Biostatistics
SUNDARAM, M., Radiology
SUNSHINE, J., Radiology
SUPER, D., Paediatrics
SUREWICZ, W., Physiology and Biophysics
SVENSSON, L., Surgery
SY, M., Pathology
SZAREK, S., Mathematics
SZCZOTKA-FLYNN, L., Ophthamology and Visual Sciences
TANG, W., Medicine
TARR, R., Radiology
TARTAKOFF, A., Pathology
TAYLOR, M., Accountancy
TAYLOR, D., Medicine
TAYLOR, H., Paediatrics
TAYLOR, C., Physics
TAYLOR, P., Physics
TEPPER, S., Medicine
TETZLAFF, J., Anaesthesiology
THACKER, H., Medicine
THOMAS, S., Banking and Finance

THOMAS, J., Medicine
THOMAS, A., Surgery
THOMPSON, G., Orthopaedics
THOMPSON, L., Psychological Sciences
TIEN, J., Mechanical and Aerospace Engineering
TOLTZIS, P., Paediatrics
TOMASHEFSKI, J., Pathology
TOOSSI, Z., Medicine
TOWNSEND, A., Applied Social Sciences
TRABOULSI, E., Ophthalmology
TRACY, E., Applied Social Sciences
TRAPP, B., Neurosciences
TRIOLO, R., Orthopaedics
TUBBS, R., Pathology
TUCKER, H., Otolaryngology
TUOHY, V., Molecular Medicine
TURNER, M., Cognitive Science
TUXHORN, I., Paediatrics
TUZCU, E., Medicine
UMRIGAR, T., English
VAIRAKTARAKIS, G., Operations
VALLIER, H., Orthopaedics
VANLUNTEREN, E., Medicine
VANORMAN, J., Earth, Environment, and Planetary Sciences
VIDIMOS, A., Medicine
VINCE, D., Molecular Medicine
VOGELBAUM, M., Surgery
WALDO, A., Medicine
WALSER, R., Music
WALSH, R., Medicine
WALSH, M., Paediatrics
WALSH, R., Surgery
WALTERS, M., Surgery
WANG, B., Medicine
WANG, Q., Molecular Medicine
WATANABE, M., Paediatrics
WEINBERG, A., Dental Medicine
WEISS, M., Biochemistry
WELSCH, G., Materials Science and Engineering
WERNER, E., Mathematics
WESSELS, B., Radiation Oncology
WHITE, J., Political Science
WHITEHOUSE, P., Neurology
WHITING, P., Earth, Environment, and Planetary Sciences
WIDING, R., Design and Innovation
WILBER, J., Orthopaedics
WILKOFF, B., Medicine
WILSON, D., Biomedical Engineering
WILSON, S., Ophthalmology
WILSON, R., Theatre
WILSON-COSTELLO, D., Paediatrics
WISE, J., GMS-RNA Center
WISNIESKI, J., Medicine
WIZNITZER, M., Paediatrics
WNEK, G., Macromolecular Science
WOLANSKY, L., Radiology
WOLFE, M., Medicine
WOLFE, H., Reproductive Biology
WONG, R., Medicine
WOODMANSEE, M., English
WOYCZYNSKI, W., Mathematics
WRIGHT, J., Medicine
WRIGHT, M., Paediatrics
WU, Q., Molecular Medicine
WYLLIE, E., Paediatrics
WYLLIE, R., Paediatrics
WYNSHAW-BORIS, A., Genetics and Genome Sciences
XIA, P., Molecular Medicine
YAN, R., Molecular Medicine
YANG, Y., Biochemistry
YEARBY, R., Law
YEN-LIEBERMAN, B., Pathology
YI, Q., Molecular Medicine
YOUNG, J., Medicine
YOUNGNER, S., Bioethics
YOWLER, C., Surgery
YU, X., Biomedical Engineering
ZAGORSKI, M., Chemistry
ZAHKA, K., Paediatrics
ZAUSZNIEWSKI, J., Nursing
ZENG, X., Civil Engineering

ZHANG, G., Electrical Engineering and Computer Science
ZHU, X., Epidemiology and Biostatistics
ZHU, L., Macromolecular Science
ZIGMOND, R., Neurosciences
ZIMMERMAN, P., GMS-Global Health and Disease
ZINS, J., Surgery
ZOU, W., Pathology

CEDARVILLE UNIVERSITY

251 N Main St, Cedarville, OH 45314
Telephone: (937) 766-7700
E-mail: admissions@cedarville.edu
Internet: www.cedarville.edu
Founded 1887 as Cedarville College, present name and status 2000
Private control
Academic year: August to May
Pres.: Dr THOMAS WHITE
Chancellor: Dr WILLIAM E. BROWN
Chancellor: Dr PAUL H. DIXON
Provost: Dr JOHN S. GREDY
Academic Vice-Pres. and Chief Academic Officer: Dr THOMAS CORNMAN
Vice-Pres. for Advancement: WILLIAM L. BIGHAM
Vice-Pres. for Business and Chief Financial Officer: CHRISTOPHER SOHN
Vice-Pres. for Christian Ministries: ROBERT K. ROHM
Vice-Pres. for Enrolment Management: JANICE L. SUPPLEE
Vice-Pres. for Operations: RODNEY S. JOHNSON
Vice-Pres. for Student Life: KIRSTEN GIBBS (acting)
Registrar: FRAN CAMPBELL
Dean for Library Services: LYNN A. BROCK
Library of 285,000 vols, 9,000 ejournal subscriptions, 47,000 ebooks
Number of teachers: 225 (215 full-time, 10 part-time)
Number of students: 3,465
Publications: *Cedarville Magazine*, *Inspire* (3 a year), *Journal of Biblical Integration in Business* (1 a year), *Torch* (2 a year)

DEANS

College of Arts and Sciences: Dr STEVEN WINTEREGG
College of Extended Learning: Dr ANDREW RUNYAN
College of Health Professions: Dr PAMELA DIEHL JOHNSON
College of Professions: Dr MARK MCCLAIN
Graduate Studies: Dr ANDY RUNYAN
School of Business Administration: LOREN RENO
School of Nursing: Dr JANET CONWAY
School of Pharmacy: Prof. Dr MARC SWEENEY

CENTRAL STATE UNIVERSITY

1400 Brush Row Rd, Wilberforce, OH 45384
Telephone: (937) 376-6011
E-mail: info@centralstate.edu
Internet: www.centralstate.edu
Founded 1887 as Combined Normal and Industrial Dept at Wilberforce Univ., present name and status 1965
State control
Pres.: JOHN W. GARLAND
Provost and Vice-Pres. for Academic Affairs: Dr JULIETTE B. BELL
Vice-Pres. for Admin.: COLETTE PIERCE BURNETTE
Vice-Pres. for Information Technology: Dr DONALD STEWARD
Vice-Pres. for Institutional Advancement: ANTHONY FAIRBANKS
Vice-Pres. for Student Affairs: Dr JERRYL BRIGGS

Registrar: LATONYA BRANHAM
Library Dir: JOHNNY W. JACKSON
Library of 223,745 vols, 846,190 units of microfiche and microfilm, 383 periodicals, 28,400 vols of periodicals, 21,000 ebooks, 41,000 ejournals
Number of teachers: 80
Number of students: 2,170

DEANS

College of Business: Dr CHARLES H. SHOWELL
College of Education: Dr REGINALD NNAZOR
College of Humanities, Arts and Social Sciences: Dr LOVETTE CHINWAH-ADEGBOLA
College of Science and Engineering: Dr SUBRAMANIA I. SRITHARAN

CINCINNATI CHRISTIAN UNIVERSITY

2700 Glenway Ave, Cincinnati, OH 45204
Telephone: (513) 244-8100
E-mail: info@ccuniversity.edu
Internet: www.ccuniversity.edu
Founded 1924 as Cincinnati Bible Seminary by merger of McGarvey Bible College (f. 1923) with Cincinnati Bible Institute (f. 1923), present name and status 2004
Private control
Language of instruction: English, Greek, Hebrew
Academic year: August to May
3 Colleges: Bible college, college of adult learning, Bible seminary
Pres.: Dr DAVID FAUST
Vice-Pres. for Advancement: BARBARA RENDEL
Vice-Pres. Finance and Operations: Dr CHARLES ABBOTT
Academic Dean for Seminary: JOHNNY G. PRESSLEY
Dean for Students: KRIS MERRILL
Exec. Dir of Admissions: JEFFREY DERICO
Registrar: DON THOMASON
Dir for Libraries: JAMES H. LLOYD
Library of 150,000 vols
Number of teachers: 90 (35 full-time, 55 adjunct)
Number of students: 1,000

DEANS

College of Adult Learning: JUDY PRATT
College of Business: AARON BURGESS
College of Education and Behavioral Sciences: JODIE EDWARDS
Cincinnati Bible Seminary: DAVID RAY
Foster School of Biblical Studies: PAUL FRISKNEY
Russell School of Ministry: MIKE SHANNON

CINCINNATI COLLEGE OF MORTUARY SCIENCE

645 W North Bend Rd, Cincinnati, OH 45224-1462
Telephone: (513) 761-2020
E-mail: info@ccms.edu
Internet: www.ccms.edu
Founded 1882 as Cincinnati School of Embalming, present name 1966
Private control
Pres.: KAREN GILES
Academic Dean: Dr JULIE GILL
Exec. Dir for Enrolment Management and Registrar: PATRICIA SULLIVAN
Dir for Library and Information Technology: MICHAEL WELLS
Library of 2,000 vols
Number of teachers: 6
Number of students: 120

CLEVELAND INSTITUTE OF ART

11141 East Blvd, Cleveland, OH 44106-1710

Telephone: (216) 421-7000
E-mail: admissions@cia.edu
Internet: www.cia.edu

Founded 1882, present name and status 1949
Private control
Academic year: August to May

Areas of study: craft and material culture, design, foundation art, integrated media, liberal arts, visual arts and technologies

Pres. and CEO: GRAFTON J. NUNES
Sr Vice-Pres. for Institutional Advancement: R. MICHAEL COLE
Vice-Pres. for Academic and Faculty Affairs: CHRIS WHITTEY
Vice-Pres. for Business Affairs: ALMUT ZVO-SEC
Exec. Dir for Enrolment and Financial Aid: ROBERT BORDEN
Dean for Student Affairs: NANCY NEVILLE
Registrar: KAREN HUDY
Library Dir: CRISTINE C. ROM

Library of 45,000 vols, 145 periodical subscriptions, 125,000 art and architecture slides, 1,600 sound recordings, 600 video cassettes, DVDs and films
Number of teachers: 90 (50 full-time, 40 adjunct)
Number of students: 500

CLEVELAND INSTITUTE OF MUSIC

11021 East Blvd, Cleveland, OH 44106

Telephone: (216) 791-5000
E-mail: info@cim.edu
Internet: www.cim.edu

Founded 1920
Private control
Academic year: August to May

Pres.: JOEL SMIRNOFF
Dean: ADRIAN DALY
Dir for Admissions: WILLIAM FAY
Dir for Devt: CHRIS DUNWORTH
Registrar: HALLIE MOORE
Library Dir: JEAN TOOMBS

Library of 52,000 vols, 23,000 audiovisual materials
Number of teachers: 100
Number of students: 400

CLEVELAND STATE UNIVERSITY

2121 Euclid Ave, Cleveland, OH 44115-2214

Telephone: (216) 687-2000
E-mail: admissions@csuohio.edu
Internet: www.csuohio.edu

Founded 1964
State control

Pres.: Dr RONALD M. BERKMAN
Provost and Sr Vice-Pres. for Academic Affairs: GEOFFREY S. MEARNS
Vice-Pres. for Enrolment Services and Student Affairs: CARMEN A. BROWN
Vice-Pres. for Institutional Diversity: Dr NJERI NURU-HOLM
Vice-Pres. for Research and Graduate Studies: Dr GEORGE E. WALKER
Vice-Pres. for Univ. Advancement: BERINTHIA LEVINE
Dir for Libraries: GLENDA THORNTON

Library of 856,978 vols, 4,005 periodicals, 625,191 microforms
Number of teachers: 575 (full-time)
Number of students: 16,000

Publications: *Perspective*, *Whiskey Island*

DEANS

College of Education and Human Sciences: Dr SAJIT ZACHARIAH
College of Graduate Studies: Dr CRYSTAL M. WEYMAN

College of Liberal Arts and Social Sciences: Dr GREGORY M. SADLEK
College of Sciences and Health Professions: Dr MEREDITH BOND
Cleveland-Marshall College of Law: CRAIG M. BOISE
Fenn College of Engineering: Dr CHIN Y. KUO
Maxine Goodman Levin College of Urban Affairs: Dr EDWARD HILL
Monte Ahuja College of Business: Dr ROBERT F. SCHERER

COLLEGE OF MOUNT ST JOSEPH

5701 Delhi Rd, Cincinnati, OH 45233-1670

Telephone: (513) 244-4200
E-mail: info@mail.msj.edu
Internet: www.msj.edu

Founded 1920
Private control

Pres.: Dr ANTHONY ARETZ
Vice-Pres. for Institutional Advancement: (vacant)
Chief Academic Officer and Dean for the Faculty: Dr ALAN DeCOURCY
Chief Information Officer: KEITH WEBER
Dir for Admissions: PEGGY MINNICH
Dean for Students: Dr DOUGLAS K. FRIZZELL
Registrar: PATSY J. KENNER
Dir for Library Services: PAUL JENKINS

Library of 96,000 vols
Number of teachers: 123 (full-time)
Number of students: 2,324

DEANS

Division of Arts and Humanities: Dr MARGE KLOOS
Division of Behavioural and Natural Sciences: Dr DIANA DAVIS
Division of Business: Dr CHARLES KRONCKE
Division of Education: Dr MARY WEST
Division of Health Sciences: Dr SUSAN JOHNSON

COLLEGE OF WOOSTER

1189 Beall Ave, Wooster, OH 44691

Telephone: (330) 263-2000
E-mail: admissions@wooster.edu
Internet: www.wooster.edu

Founded 1866
Private control
Academic year: August to May

Liberal arts college

Pres.: GRANT H. CORNWELL
Provost: CAROLYN NEWTON
Vice-Pres. for Devt: LAURIE K. HOUCK
Vice-Pres. for Enrolment and College Relations: SCOTT FRIEDHOFF
Dean for Admissions: JENNIFER D. WINGE
Dean for Students: KURT C. HOLMES
Registrar: SUZANNE BATES
Dir for Libraries: MARK CHRISTEL

Library of 1,269,829 vols
Number of teachers: 177 (full-time)
Number of students: 2,060

COLUMBUS COLLEGE OF ART AND DESIGN

60 Cleveland Ave, Columbus, OH 43215

Telephone: (614) 224-9101
E-mail: admissions@ccad.edu
Internet: www.ccad.edu

Founded 1879 as Columbus Art School, present name 1959
Private control
Academic year: August to August

Pres.: DENNISON W. GRIFFITH
Vice-Pres. for Academic Affairs: KEVIN J. CONLON
Vice-Pres. for Enrolment Management: JONATHAN W. LINDSAY

Vice-Pres. for Institutional Advancement: LAURIE BETH SWEENEY
Vice-Pres. for Student Affairs and Dean for Students: DWAYNE TODD
Dean for Faculty: CHAR NORMAN
Registrar: MICHELE KIBLER
Dir for Library: GAIL STORER

Library of 50,000 vols, 275 periodicals
Number of teachers: 195
Number of students: 1,300

Publication: *IMAGE Magazine* (2 a year)

DEANS

Fine Arts: Prof. JULIE TAGGART
Industrial and Interior Design: Prof. CARL GARANT
Liberal Arts: Prof. Dr EDWARD LATHY
Media Studies: Prof. RON SAKS
Visual Communications: Prof. RICHARD ASCHENBRAND

DEFIANCE COLLEGE

701 N Clinton St, Defiance, OH 43512

Telephone: (419) 784-4010
E-mail: admissions@defiance.edu
Internet: www.defiance.edu

Founded 1850 as Defiance Female Seminary, present name 1903
Private control

Divs of arts and humanities, behavioural and applied social sciences, business and allied health, education, science and mathematics

Pres.: MARK C. GORDON
Provost and Vice-Pres. for Academic Affairs: Dr BARBARA R. SCHIRMER
Vice-Pres. for Enrolment Management: MIKE SUZO
Vice-Pres. for Institutional Advancement: RICH PEJEAU
Vice-Pres. for Student Engagement and Dean for Students: Dr KENNETH WETSTEIN
Dir for Admissions: BRAD HARSHA
Registrar: MARIAH ORZOLEK
Dir for Library and Informational Resources: ANDREW WHITIS

Library of 90,000 vols
Number of teachers: 85
Number of students: 1,100

Publication: *The Magazine*

DENISON UNIVERSITY

100 W College St, Granville, OH 43023-0603

Telephone: (740) 587-0810
E-mail: admissions@denison.edu
Internet: www.denison.edu

Founded 1831
Private control
Academic year: September to May

Liberal arts

Pres.: DALE T. KNOBEL
Provost: BRADLEY W. BATEMAN
Vice-Pres. and Dir for Admissions: PERRY ROBINSON
Vice-Pres. for Student Devt: LAUREL KENNEDY
Vice-Pres. for Institutional Advancement: JULIA HOUPT
Dean for Students: LAURA NEFF
Registrar: YADIGAR COLLINS
Library Dir: MARY PROPHET

Library of 462,409 vols, 360,324 documents, 963 periodicals, 35,147 audiovisual material, 127,645 microforms, 762 linear ft archives
Number of teachers: 210 (full-time)
Number of students: 2,160

Publications: *Collage: A Magazine for Language & the Arts*, *Denison Journal of Biological Science* (1 a year), *Denison Journal of Geosciences* (1 a year), *Denison*

Journal of Religion (1 a year), *Denison Magazine* (4 a year), *Ephemeris* (1 a year), *Episteme*, *Prologue* (1 a year)

FRANCISCAN UNIVERSITY OF STEUBENVILLE

1235 University Blvd, Steubenville, OH 43952

Telephone: (740) 283-3771
E-mail: admissions@franciscan.edu
Internet: www.franciscan.edu

Founded 1946
Private control
Academic year: August to May

Pres.: Rev. TERENCE HENRY
Chancellor: Rev. MICHAEL SCANLAN
Exec. Vice-Pres.: Dr ROBERT FILBY
Vice-Pres. for Academic Affairs: THOMAS WILSON
Vice-Pres. for Advancement: MICHAEL HERNON
Vice-Pres. for Enrolment: JOEL RECZNIK
Vice-Pres. for Student Life: DAVID SCHMIESING
Dir for Admissions: MARGARET WEBER
Library Dir: WILLIAM JAKUB

Library of 232,156 vols, 250,968 microfiche, 5,400 ejournals
Number of teachers: 225 (115 full-time, 107 part-time)
Number of students: 2,550 (2,125 undergraduate, 425 graduate)
Publications: *Fides Quaerens Intellectum* (4 a year), *Franciscan Way Magazine*

FRANKLIN UNIVERSITY

201 S Grant Ave, Columbus, OH 43215

Telephone: (614) 797-4700
E-mail: info@franklin.edu
Internet: www.franklin.edu

Founded 1902 as YMCA School of Commerce, present name 1933
Private control

Campuses at Delaware, Dublin, Westerville (Ohio) and Indianapolis (Indiana); online degree programmes

Pres.: Dr DAVID R. DECKER
Provost and Sr Vice-Pres. for Academic Affairs: Dr CHRISTOPHER WASHINGTON
Sr Vice-Pres. for Admin.: JANE ROBINSON
Sr Vice-Pres. for Univ. Advancement and Strategic Relations: BONNIE SMITH QUIST
Exec. Dir for Enrolment Management: SCOTT BOOTH
Dean for Students: Dr WILLIAM MOLASSO
Dir for Library Services: JOHN CANTER
Number of students: 11,000
Publication: *CLOCKTOWER*

DEANS

College of Arts, Sciences and Technology: Dr KEITH GROFF
College of Business: Dr ROSS WIRTH
College of Health and Public Administration: ROBERT CURTIS

HEIDELBERG UNIVERSITY

310 E Market St, Tiffin, OH 44883-2462

Telephone: (419) 448-2000
E-mail: adminfo@heidelberg.edu
Internet: www.heidelberg.edu

Founded 1850, present name and status 2009
Private control
Academic year: August to May

Pres.: Dr ROBERT H. HUNTINGTON
Provost and Vice-Pres. for Academic Affairs: Dr DAVID A. WEININGER
Vice-Pres. for Enrolment Management: LINDSAY SOOY

Vice-Pres. for Institutional Advancement and Univ. Relations: Dr JAMES A. TROHA
Dean for Students: DUSTIN BRENTLINGER
Registrar: CYNTHIA SUTER
Dir for Library Services: NANCY RUBENSTEIN

Library of 432,509 vols, 119,517 books, 8,556 audiovisual materials, 162,336 govt documents, 68,000 ebooks
Number of teachers: 150 (63 full-time, 87 part-time)
Number of students: 1,200
Publication: *Morpheus*

DEANS

School of Business: Dr HASEEB AHMED
Undergraduate Faculty: Dr VICKI B. OHL

HIRAM COLLEGE

POB 67, Hiram, OH 44234
11715 Garfield Rd, Hiram, OH 44234

Telephone: (330) 569-5169
E-mail: interal@hiram.edu
Internet: www.hiram.edu

Founded 1850 as Western Reserve Eclectic Institute, current name and status 1867
Private control
Academic year: August to May

Liberal arts college

Pres.: THOMAS V. CHEMA
Vice-Pres. and Dean for Students: ERIC R. RIEDEL
Dean for the College: BOB HAAK
Registrar: VIRGINIA TAYLOR
Dir for Admission: SHERMAN DEAN
Dir for Int. Admission: FRANK BOWMAN
Library Dir: DAVID EVERETT

Library of 200,000 vols, 425 periodicals, 10,000 CDs, 2,500 video cassettes, 65,000 ebooks, 50,000 periodicals
Number of teachers: 85 (full-time)
Number of students: 1,316 (1,296 undergraduate, 20 graduate)
Publications: *Hiram Poetry Review* (2 a year), *Hiram Magazine* (4 a year)

JOHN CARROLL UNIVERSITY

1 John Carroll Blvd, University Heights, OH 44118

Telephone: (216) 397-1886
Internet: www.jcu.edu

Founded 1886, present name 1923
Private control
Academic year: September to May

Pres.: Rev. ROBERT L. NIEHOFF
Provost and Academic Vice-Pres.: Dr JOHN T. DAY
Vice-Pres. for Enrolment: BRIAN G. WILLIAMS
Vice-Pres. for Finance and Admin. Services: RICHARD F. MAUSSER
Vice-Pres. for Student Affairs: Dr MARK D. MCCARTHY
Vice-Pres. for Univ. Advancement: DOREEN KNAPP RILEY
Registrar: KATHLEEN DI FRANCO
Dir for Library: Dr JEANNE SOMERS

Library of 778,287 vols, 850 periodical subscriptions, 701,253 microforms, 9,985 audiovisual materials, 11,159 ejournals, 76,346 ebooks
Number of teachers: 375 (205 full-time, 170 part-time)
Number of students: 3,700 (3,000 undergraduate, 700 graduate)
Publication: *John Carroll magazine* (online, sites.jcu.edu/magazine)

DEANS

Boler School of Business: Dr KAREN SCHUELE
College of Arts and Sciences: Dr JEANNE COLLERAN

KENT STATE UNIVERSITY

Kent, OH 44242

Telephone: (330) 672-3000
Internet: www.kent.edu

Founded 1910
State control
Academic year: July to June

7 Regional campuses in Ashtabula, East Liverpool, Geauga, Salem, Stark, Trumbull, Tuscarawas (Ohio)

Pres.: Dr LESTER A. LEFTON
Provost and Sr Vice-Pres. for Academic Affairs: ROBERT G. FRANK
Vice-Pres. for Diversity, Equity and Inclusion: ALFREDA BROWN
Vice-Pres. for Enrolment Management and Student Affairs: GREG JARVIE
Vice-Pres. for Finance and Admin.: GREGG S. FLOYD
Vice-Pres. for Information Services: EDWARD G. MAHON
Vice-Pres. for Institutional Advancement: EUGENE J. FINN
Vice-Pres. for Research: W. GRANT MCGIMPSEY
Vice-Pres. for Univ. Relations: IRIS HARVEY
Registrar: GLENN DAVIS
Dean for Univ. Libraries: JAMES BRACKEN

Library: 2.3m. vols
Number of teachers: 2,520
Number of students: 42,200

DEANS

College of Architecture and Environmental Design: DOUGLAS STEIDL
College of Arts: JOHN CRAWFORD
College of Arts and Sciences: TIMOTHY MOERLAND
College of Business Administration: Dr KATHRYN WILSON
College of Communication and Information: STANLEY WEARDEN
College of Education, Health and Human Services: DAN MAHONY
College of Nursing: Dr LAURA COX DZUREC
College of Public Health: SONIA ALEMAGNO
College of Technology: JACK GRAHAM
Graduate Studies: MARY ANN STEPHENS
Honors College: DON WILLIAMS
Undergraduate Studies: (vacant)

KENYON COLLEGE

Gambier, OH 43022-9623

Telephone: (740) 427-5000
E-mail: admissions@kenyon.edu
Internet: www.kenyon.edu

Founded 1824
Private control
Academic year: August to May

Depts of fine arts, humanities, natural sciences, social sciences

Pres.: S. GEORGIA NUGENT
Provost: NAYEF SAMHAT
Vice-Pres. for College Relations: SARAH H. KAHRL
Vice-Pres. for Finance: JOSEPH G. NELSON
Dir for Admissions: C. DARRYL UY
Dean for Admissions and Financial Aid: JENNIFER DELAHUNTY BRITZ
Dean for Students: HENRY P. TOUTAIN
Registrar: ELLEN K. HARBOURT
Vice-Pres. for Library and Information Services: RONALD K. GRIGGS

Library: 1m. vols, 1,000 periodical subscriptions, 330,000 ebooks, 7,300 ejournals
Number of teachers: 200
Number of students: 1,600
Publication: *Kenyon College Alumni Bulletin* (online, bulletin.kenyon.edu)

KETTERING COLLEGE OF MEDICAL ARTS

3737 Southern Blvd, Kettering, OH 45429
Telephone: (937) 395-8601
E-mail: information@kc.edu
Internet: www.kc.edu

Founded 1967
Private control

Divs of allied health, arts and sciences, graduate studies, nursing

Pres.: Dr CHARLES SCRIVEN
Dean for Academic Affairs: Dr WILLIAM NELSON
Dean for Enrolment Management: VICTOR BROWN
Dir for Admissions: BECKY MCDONALD
Registrar: ROBIN VANDERBILT
Dir for Library: BEV COBB (acting)

Library of 25,000 vols, 250 journal subscriptions, 1,500 audiovisual items

LAKE ERIE COLLEGE

391 W Washington St, Painesville, OH 44077
Telephone: (440) 296-1856
E-mail: admissions@lec.edu
Internet: www.lec.edu

Founded 1856
Private control
Academic year: August to May

Pres.: MICHAEL T. VICTOR
Vice-Pres. for Academic Affairs and Chief Academic Officer: Dr JANA HOLWICK
Vice-Pres. for Admin. and Finance: RICK EPLAWY
Vice-Pres. for Enrolment Management and Student Affairs: ROBIN MCDERMOTT
Vice-Pres. for Institutional Advancement: SCOTT EVANS
Dean for Admissions and Financial Aid: CHRISTOPHER HARRIS
Registrar: BARBARA ARILSON
Library Dir: CHRISTOPHER BENNETT

Library of 100,000 vols
Number of teachers: 45 (full-time)
Number of students: 1,200

DEANS

School of Arts, Humanities and Social Science: Dr MIMI PIPINO
School of Business: Prof. ROBERT TREBAR
School of Equine Studies: Prof. ELISABETH GIEDT
School of Natural Science and Mathematics: Dr STEVEN REYNOLDS, JR
School of Professional and Continuing Education: JOHN MEEHL

LAURA AND ALVIN SIEGAL COLLEGE OF JUDAIC STUDIES

26500 Shaker Blvd, Cleveland, OH 44122
Telephone: (216) 464-4050
E-mail: info@siegalcollege.edu
Internet: www.siegalcollege.edu

Founded 1947 as Cleveland Institute of Jewish Studies, present name 2002
Private control
Languages of instruction: English, Hebrew

Pres.: Dr SEYMOUR KOPELOWITZ
Provost: Dr BRIAN AMKRAUT
Library Dir: JEAN LETTOFSKY

Library of 40,000 vols, 160 periodicals
Number of teachers: 20
Number of students: 30

LOURDES UNIVERSITY

6832 Convent Blvd, Sylvania, OH 43560
Telephone: (419) 885-5291
E-mail: admissionslcadmits@lourdes.edu
Internet: www.lourdes.edu

Founded 1958 as Lourdes Junior College, present name and status 2011
Private control

Pres.: Dr ROBERT HELMER
Provost: Dr JANET ROBINSON
Vice-Pres. for Finance and Admin.: MICHAEL KILLIAN
Vice-Pres. for Institutional Advancement: MARY ARQUETTE
Vice-Pres. for Student Services: ROSANNE GILL-JACOBSON
Dean for Enrolment: AMY L. MERGEN
Dir for Admissions: AMY MERGEN
Registrar: MICHELLE RABLE
Dir for Library: SANDRA RUTKOWSKI

Library of 60,000 vols, 200 periodicals
Number of students: 2,660

DEANS

College of Arts and Sciences: Dr GEOFFREY J. GRUBB
College of Business and Leadership: Dr DEAN C. LUDWIG
College of Education and Human Services: Dr MICHAEL J. SMITH
College of Nursing: Dr JUDY DIDION

MALONE UNIVERSITY

2600 Cleveland Ave, NW, Canton, OH 44709
Telephone: (330) 471-8100
E-mail: admissions@malone.edu
Internet: www.malone.edu

Founded 1892, present name and status 2008
Private control

Pres.: Dr DAVID A. KING
Provost: Dr DONALD L. TUCKER
Vice-Pres. for Advancement: HOWARD E. TAYLOR
Vice-Pres. for Enrolment Management: Dr BROCK C. SCHROEDER
Vice-Pres. for Student Devt: Dr CHRISTOPHER T. ABRAMS
Dir for Admissions: DAVID L. KLEFFMAN
Registrar: GARY L. PHELPS
Dir for Library Services: STANFORD TERHUNE

Library of 969,436 vols
Number of teachers: 90 (full-time)
Number of students: 2,200 (f.t.e.)

Publications: *Malone Magazine*, *Sightlines* (online, www.sightlinesmag.org)

DEANS

College of Theology, Arts and Sciences: Dr D. NATHAN PHINNEY
School of Business and Leadership: MARJORIE F. CARLSON HURST
School of Education and Human Development: Dr RHODA C. SOMMERS
School of Nursing and Health Sciences: DEBRA LEE

MARIETTA COLLEGE

215 Fifth St, Marietta, OH 45750
Telephone: (740) 376-4643
E-mail: admit@marietta.edu
Internet: www.marietta.edu

Founded 1797 as Muskingum Acad., present name and status 1835
Private control
Academic year: August to May

Areas of study: Asian and international studies, computer science, economics, environmental science, fine arts, international business, liberal arts and sciences, management and accounting, petroleum engineering, sports medicine

Pres.: Dr JEAN A. SCOTT
Provost and Dean for Faculty: Prof. GAMA PERRUCI
Vice-Pres. for Admin. and Finance: DAN BRYANT

Vice-Pres. for Advancement: LORI LEWIS
Vice-Pres. for Enrolment Management: DAVID RHODES
Vice-Pres. for Student Life and Dean for Students: Dr ROBERT PASTOOR
Dir for Admission: JASON TURLEY
Dir for Library: DOUGLAS ANDERSON

Library of 250,000 vols, 450 print, 4,000 online periodicals
Number of teachers: 100
Number of students: 1,400

MERCY COLLEGE OF OHIO

2221 Madison Ave, Toledo, OH 43604
Telephone: (419) 251-1313
Internet: www.mercycollege.edu

Founded 1918, present name 2011
Private control

Offers BSc in health care administration and nursing

Pres.: JOHN F. HAYWARD
Vice-Pres. for Academic Affairs and Dean for Faculty: Dr ANNE LOOCHTAN
Vice-Pres. for Admin. Services and Dean for Students: JAMES L. HARTER
Dir for Admissions: AIMEE BISHOP-STUART
Registrar: HEATHER HOPPE
Library Man.: DEBORAH L. JOHNSON

Library of 10,000 vols

METHODIST THEOLOGICAL SCHOOL IN OHIO

3081 Columbus Pike, Delaware, OH 43015
Telephone: (740) 363-1146
E-mail: admit@mtso.edu
Internet: www.mtso.edu

Founded 1958
Private control
Academic year: August to May

Pres.: JAY RUNDELL
Vice-Pres. for Admin. Services: JON JUMP
Academic Dean: RANDY LITCHFIELD
Dir for Admissions: APRIL CASPERSON
Dir for Student Life: LESLIE TAYLOR
Registrar: SUSAN LAMPHERE
Library Dir: PAUL BURNAM

Library of 130,000 vols
Number of teachers: 32 (17 full-time, 15 part-time)
Number of students: 225

Publication: *The Story*

MIAMI UNIVERSITY

501 E High St, Oxford, OH 45056
Telephone: (513) 529-1809
E-mail: admission@miamioh.edu
Internet: www.miamioh.edu

Founded 1809
public control
Academic year: August to May (2 semesters)

Pres.: Dr DAVID C. HODGE
Provost and Exec. Vice-Pres. for Academic Affairs: CONRADO M. GEMPESAW
Vice-Pres. for IT: DEBRA ALLISON
Vice-Pres. for Student Affairs: BARBARA JONES
Vice-Pres. for Univ. Advancement: JAYNE E. WHITEHEAD
Dean for Students: Dr SUSAN MOSLEY-HOWARD
Registrar: DAVE SAUTER
Dean and Univ. Librarian: JUDITH SESSIONS

Library of 4,111,957 vols, 23,060 video cassettes, 572,506 ebooks
Number of teachers: 849 (full-time)
Number of students: 23,239

DEANS

College of Arts and Science: Dr PHYLLIS CALLAHAN
Farmer School of Business: RAY GORMAN
Graduate School: JIM ORIS
School of Education, Health and Society: CARINE M. FEYTEN
School of Engineering and Applied Science: Prof. MAREK DOLLÁR
School of Fine Arts: Dr JAMES LENTINI

MOUNT CARMEL COLLEGE OF NURSING

127 S Davis Ave, Columbus, OH 43222

Telephone: (614) 234-5800
E-mail: admissions@mccn.edu
Internet: www.mccn.edu

Founded 1903 as Mount Carmel School of Nursing, present name and status 1990
Private control
Academic year: August to May (2 semesters)
Campus in Lancaster

Pres. and Dean: Dr ANN SCHIELE
Library Dir: STEVO ROKSANDIC
Number of students: 910

MOUNT VERNON NAZARENE UNIVERSITY

800 Martinsburg Rd, Mount Vernon, OH 43050

Telephone: (740) 392-6868
Internet: www.mvnu.edu

Founded 1968
Private control

Pres.: Dr DANIEL J. MARTIN
Provost and Chief Academic Officer: Dr HENRY SPAULDING, II
Vice-Pres. for Enrolment Devt and Marketing: DOUG BANBURY
Vice-Pres. for Student Life: Dr LANETTE SESSINK
Dir for Admissions and Student Recruitment: JAMES W. SMITH
Registrar: R. MERRILL SEVERNS
Dir for Library: DAVID E. TIPTON
Number of teachers: 240 (full-time)
Number of students: 2,575

DEANS

Jetter School of Business: Dr ROBERT ROLLER
School of Arts and Humanities: Dr BARNEY COCHRAN
School of Education and Professional Studies: Dr SONJA SMITH
School of Natural and Social Sciences: Dr RICHARD L. SUTHERLAND
School of Nursing and Health Sciences: Dr TERESA L. WOOD
School of Theology and Philosophy: Dr C. JEANNE SERRÃO

MUSKINGUM UNIVERSITY

163 Stormont St, New Concord, OH 43762
Telephone: (740) 826-8211
Internet: www.muskingum.edu

Founded 1837
Private control

Pres.: ANNE C. STEELE
Vice-Pres. for Academic Affairs: JAMES CALLAGHAN
Vice-Pres. for Enrolment: JEFF ZELLERS
Vice-Pres. for Institutional Advancement: KATHLEEN FITZGERALD
Vice-Pres. for Student Affairs and Dean of Students: JANET HEETER-BASS
Registrar: DANIEL WILSON
Librarian: SHEILA ELLENBERGER
Library of 215,000 vols, 600 periodicals, 140,000 microforms
Number of teachers: 80

Number of students: 1,700

NORTHEAST OHIO MEDICAL UNIVERSITY

4209 State Route 44, Rootstown, OH 44272-0095

Telephone: (330) 325-6600
E-mail: admission@neomed.edu
Internet: www.neomed.edu

Founded 1973, current name adopted 2011
State control
Academic year: July to June

Pres.: Dr JAY A. GERSHEN
Vice-Pres. for Admin. and Finance: JOHN WRAY
Vice-Pres. for External Affairs: KATHLEEN RUFF
Vice-Pres. for Research: Dr WALTER E. HORTON, JR
Chief Student Affairs Officer: Dr SANDRA M. EMERICK
Gen. Counsel: MARIA SCHIMER
Registrar: MICHELLE C. COLLINS
Dir for Library: BETH A. LAYTON
Library of 100,588 vols
Number of teachers: 75
Number of students: 750
Publication: *Ignite*

DEANS

College of Graduate Studies: Dr WALTER E. HORTON, JR
College of Medicine: JEFFREY L. SUSMAN
College of Pharmacy: Dr RICHARD J. KASMER

NOTRE DAME COLLEGE

4545 College Rd, S Euclid, OH 44121-4293

Telephone: (216) 381-1680
E-mail: admissions@ndc.edu
Internet: www.notredamecollege.edu

Founded 1922
Private control
Academic year: September to May

Divs of arts and humanities, business administration, education, nursing, science and mathematics

Pres.: THOMAS KRUCZEK
Provost: Dr MARY B. BRECKENRIDGE
Sr Vice-Pres. for Finance and Admin.: JOHN PHILLIPS
Vice-Pres. for Devt: DAVID ARMSTRONG
Dean for Admissions and Financial Aid: BETH FORD
Dean for Student Affairs: BRIAN J. EMERSON
Registrar: JAMEKA WINDHAM
Dir for Library: KAREN ZOLLER
Library of 877,773 vols
Number of teachers: 60 (full-time)
Number of students: 2,160

OBERLIN COLLEGE

101 N Professor St, Oberlin, OH 44074
Telephone: (440) 775-8121
Internet: www.oberlin.edu

Founded 1833 as Oberlin Collegiate Institute, present name 1850
Private control
Academic year: September to May

Pres.: MARVIN KRISLOV
Vice-Pres. for Devt and Alumni Affairs: WILLIAM BARLOW
Dean for Admissions and Financial Aid: DEBRA CHERMONTE
Dean for Students: ERIC ESTES
Dean for Studies: KATHRYN STUART
Registrar: ELIZABETH CLERKIN
Dir for Libraries: RAY ENGLISH
Library: 1.3m. vols
Number of teachers: 250

Number of students: 2,800

DEANS

College of Arts and Sciences: Prof. SEAN DECATUR
Conservatory of Music: Prof. DAVID STULL

OHIO CHRISTIAN UNIVERSITY

1476 Lancaster Pike, Circleville, OH 43113

Telephone: (740) 474-8669
E-mail: enroll@ohiochristian.edu
Internet: www.ohiochristian.edu

Founded 1948 as Circleville Bible College
Private control
Academic year: September to May

Pres.: Dr MARK A. SMITH
Provost: Dr HANK KELLY
Exec. Vice-Pres.: HENRY F. KELLY
Vice-Pres. for Academic Affairs: Dr JOE C. BROWN
Vice-Pres. for Enrolment: MIKE EGENREIDER
Vice-Pres. for Student Devt and Athletics: RICK CHRISTMAN
Vice-Pres. for Univ. Advancement: MARK TAYLOR
Registrar: RODNEY SONES
Library Dir: BARBARA MEISTER
Library of 62,000 vols
Number of teachers: 25
Number of students: 2,400

OHIO COLLEGE OF PODIATRIC MEDICINE

6000 Rockside Woods Blvd, Independence, OH 44131

Telephone: (216) 231-3300
Internet: www.ocpm.edu

Founded 1916 as Ohio College of Chiropody, present name 1974
Private control
Academic year: August to May

Depts of basic sciences, general medicine, podiatric biomechanics and orthopedics, podiatric medicine, podiatric surgery

Pres.: THOMAS V. MELILLO
Exec. Vice-Pres.: Dr DAVID R. NICOLANTI
Vice-Pres. and Dean of Academic Affairs: Dr VINCENT J. HETHERINGTON
Dean for Student Affairs and Admissions: LOIS LOTT
Registrar: DAVID PUTMAN
Dir for Library Services: DONNA PERZESKI
Library of 15,000 vols
Number of students: 375
Publication: *Footsteps*

OHIO DOMINICAN UNIVERSITY

1216 Sunbury Rd, Columbus, OH 43219

Telephone: (614) 251-4500
E-mail: admissions@ohiodominican.edu
Internet: www.ohiodominican.edu

Founded 1911 as College of St Mary of the Springs, current name adopted 1968, present status 2002
Private control
Academic year: September to May (2 terms and a summer session)

Divs of arts and letters, business, education, mathematics, computer and natural sciences, social and behavioural sciences

Pres.: Dr PETER CIMBOLIC
Vice-Pres. for Academic Affairs and Dean for the Faculty: Dr ALISON MEARNS BENDERS
Vice-Pres. for Advancement: MURLEY MILLER
Vice-Pres. for Finance and Admin.: DAVID KOSANOVIĆ
Vice-Pres. for Student Devt: Dr JAMES CARIDI
Dir for Admission: NICOLE EVANS
Registrar: SHIRLEY McBRAYER

Dir for Library Services: JIM LAYDEN
Library of 133,412 vols
Number of teachers: 165
Number of students: 2,900
Publication: *ODU Magazine* (2 a year)

OHIO NORTHERN UNIVERSITY

525 S Main St, Ada, OH 45810
Telephone: (419) 772-2000
E-mail: admissions-ug@onu.edu
Internet: www.onu.edu

Founded 1871 as Northwestern Ohio Normal School, current name adopted 1885
Private control
Academic year: September to May
Pres.: Dr DANIEL A. DIBIASIO
Vice-Pres. for Academic Affairs: Dr DAVID C. CRAGO
Vice-Pres. for Enrolment Management: LAWRENCE LESICK
Vice-Pres. for Financial Affairs: Dr ROGER YOUTH
Vice-Pres. and Dean for Student Affairs: ADRIANE THOMPSON-BRADSHAW
Vice-Pres. for Univ. Advancement: KENNETH BLOCK
Registrar: TAMELA BASH
Dir for Library: PAUL LOGSDON
Library of 500,000 vols
Number of teachers: 225
Number of students: 3,350

DEANS

College of Arts and Sciences: Dr CATHERINE ALBRECHT
College of Business: Dr JAMES W. FENTON, JR
College of Engineering: Dr ERIC T. BAUMGARTNER
College of Law: Dr DAVID C. CRAGO
College of Pharmacy: Dr JON E. SPRAGUE

OHIO STATE UNIVERSITY

Enarson Hall, 154 W 12th Ave, Columbus, OH 43210
Telephone: (614) 292-4373
Internet: www.osu.edu
Founded 1870
State control
Campuses at Lima, Mansfield, Marion and Newark in Ohio
Pres.: Dr E. GORDON GEE
Provost and Exec. Vice-Pres.: Dr JOSEPH A. ALUTTO
Sr Vice-Pres. for Admin. and Planning: JAY KASEY
Sr Vice-Pres. for Devt: JEFF KAPLAN
Sr Vice-Pres. for Outreach and Engagement: JOYCE BEATTY
Sr Vice-Pres. for Univ. Communications: TOM KATZENMEYER
Sr Vice-Pres. and Gen. Counsel: CHRISTOPHER M. CULLEY
Vice-Pres. for Research: CAROLINE WHITACRE
Vice-Pres. for Student Life: Dr JAVAUNE ADAMS-GASTON
Chief Information Officer: KATHLEEN STARKOFF
Registrar: BRAD A. MYERS
Dir for Univ. Libraries: CAROL DIEDRICHS
Library: see under Libraries and Archives
Number of teachers: 5,300 (f.t.e.)
Number of students: 64,400

Publications: *American Periodicals: A Journal of History, Criticism and Bibliography* (2 a year, online, www.amperiodicals.org), *EHE Inspire* (1 a year), *Journal of Higher Education* (6 a year, online, ohiostatepress.org/index.htm?journals/jhe/jhe-main.htm), *Journal of Money, Credit and Banking* (6 a year, online, jmcb.osu.edu), *Narrative* (3 a year), *Ohio State Alumni*

Magazine, Ohio State Engineer (4 a year, online, osemagazine.org.ohio-state.edu), *Ohio State Journal of Criminal Law* (2 a year, online, moritzlaw.osu.edu/osjcl), *Ohio State Journal on Dispute Resolution* (4 a year, online, moritzlaw.osu.edu/jdr), *Ohio State Law Journal* (6 a year, online, moritzlaw.osu.edu/lawjournal), *The Leibniz Review* (Mansfield Campus, 1 a year), *Theory into Practice* (4 a year, online, ehe.osu.edu/publications/tip)

DEANS

College of Arts and Sciences: JOSEPH E. STEINMETZ (Exec. Dean)
College of Dentistry: PATRICK M. LLOYD
College of Education and Human Ecology: CHERYL L. ACHTERBERG
College of Engineering: DAVID B. WILLIAMS
College of Food, Agricultural and Environmental Sciences: BOBBY D. MOSER
College of Medicine: CHARLES J. CHARLES J. LOCKWOOD
College of Nursing: BERNADETTE MELNYK
College of Optometry: MELVIN D. SHIPP
College of Pharmacy: ROBERT W. BRUEGGEMEIER
College of Public Health: STANLEY A. LEMESHOW
College of Social Work: TOM GREGOIRE
College of Veterinary Medicine: LONNIE KING
Graduate School: PATRICK S. OSMER
Max M. Fisher College of Business: CHRISTINE A. POON (acting)
Moritz College of Law: ALAN C. MICHAELS

OHIO UNIVERSITY

Athens, OH 45701
Telephone: (740) 593-1000
Internet: www.ohio.edu
Founded 1804
State control
Academic year: September to June
Regional campuses at Chillicothe, Ironton, Lancaster, St Clairsville, Zanesville
Pres.: Dr RODERICK J. MCDAVIS
Provost and Exec. Vice-Pres.: Dr PAMELA J. BENOIT
Vice-Provost for Enrolment Management: CRAIG CORNELL
Vice-Pres. for Finance and Admin.: STEPHEN T. GOLDING
Vice-Pres. for Research and Creative Activity: Dr JOSEPH SHIELDS
Vice-Pres. for Student Affairs: Dr KENT J. SMITH, JR
Vice-Pres. for Univ. Advancement: J. BRYAN BENCHOFF
Registrar: DEBRA M. BENTON
Dean for Univ. Libraries: SCOTT SEAMAN
Library of 2,979,370 vols
Number of teachers: 1,900 (1,110 full-time, 790 part-time)
Number of students: 35,300

Publications: *New Ohio Review* (online, www.ohio.edu/nor), *Ohio Research and Clinical Review, Perspective* (2 a year), *Quarter After Eight* (1 a year, online, www.quarteraftereight.org), *Sphere*

DEANS

College of Arts and Sciences: Dr HOWARD DEWALD
College of Business: Dr HUGH SHERMAN
College of Fine Arts: CHARLES MCWEENY
College of Health Sciences and Professions: Dr RANDY LEITE
Graduate College: Dr JOSEPH SHIELDS
Heritage College of Osteopathic Medicine: JOHN BROSE
Honors Tutorial College: Dr JEREMY WEBSTER
Patton College of Education and Human Services: Dr RENÉE MIDDLETON

Russ College of Engineering and Technology: Dr DENNIS IRWIN
Scripps College of Communications: Dr SCOTT TITSWORTH
University College: Dr DAVID DESCUTNER

OHIO WESLEYAN UNIVERSITY

61 S Sandusky St, Delaware, OH 43015
Telephone: (740) 368-2000
E-mail: owupr@owu.edu
Internet: www.owu.edu
Founded 1842
Private control
Academic year: August to May

Depts of ancient, medieval, and renaissance studies, Black World studies, botany-microbiology, chemistry, E Asian studies, economics, education, English, environmental studies, fine arts, geology and geography, health professions advising, history, humanities-classics, international studies, journalism, Latin American studies, mathematics and computer science, modern foreign languages, music, neuroscience, philosophy, physical education, physics and astronomy, politics and government, psychology, religion, sociology-anthropology, theatre and dance, urban studies, women's and gender studies, zoology

Pres.: ROCK JONES
Provost: DAVID O. ROBBINS
Vice-Pres. for Finance and Admin.: ERIC ALGOE
Vice-Pres. for Student Affairs: CRAIG ULLOM
Vice-Pres. for Univ. Enrolment and Strategic Communication: REBECCA ECKSTEIN
Vice-Pres. for Univ. Relations: COLLEEN GARLAND
Registrar: SHELLY A. MCMAHON
Dir for Libraries: CATHERINE CARDWELL
Library of 550,000 vols
Number of teachers: 135 (full-time)
Number of students: 1,850

Publications: *Civic Arts Review* (4 a year, online, car.owu.edu), *Ohio Wesleyan Magazine* (online, magazine.owu.edu), *Zumari: a Journal of Black World Studies* (2 a year)

OTTERBEIN UNIVERSITY

1 S Grove St, Westerville, OH 43081-2006
Telephone: (614) 890-3000
E-mail: uotterb@otterbein.edu
Internet: www.otterbein.edu
Founded 1847
Private control
Academic year: September to August
Pres.: Dr KATHY KRENDL
Provost and Vice-Pres. for Academic Affairs: Dr VICTORIA MCGILLIN
Vice-Pres. for Enrolment Management: JEFFERSON BLACKBURN-SMITH
Vice-Pres. for Institutional Advancement: HEIDI TRACY
Vice-Pres. for Student Affairs and Dean for Students: ROBERT M. GATTI
Registrar: DONALD W. FOSTER
Library Dir: LOIS SZUDY
Library of 200,000 vols
Number of teachers: 140
Number of students: 3,000

Publications: *Aegis: The Otterbein Humanities Journal* (1 a year), *Journal of Teacher Initiated Research* (1 a year), *Towers Magazine*

DEANS

Graduate School and Research: Dr BARBARA H. SCHAFFNER
School of Arts and Sciences: Prof. Dr PAUL EISENSTEIN

School of Professional Studies: Dr BARBARA H. SCHAFFNER

PONTIFICAL COLLEGE JOSEPHINUM

7625 N High St, Columbus, OH 43235
Telephone: (614) 885-5585
Internet: www.pcj.edu
Founded 1888, present status 1892
Private control
College of liberal arts and school of theology
Rector and Pres.: Prof. Rev. JAMES A. WEHNER
Exec. Vice-Pres.: Prof. Dr CHRISTOPHER J. SCHRECK
Academic Dean: Dr MICHAEL D. ROSS
Registrar: BARBARA COUTS
Dir for Library: PETER G. VERACKA
Publication: *Josephinum Journal of Theology* (2 a year, online, www.pcj.edu/journal)

SAINT MARY SEMINARY AND GRADUATE SCHOOL OF THEOLOGY

28700 Euclid Ave, Wickliffe, OH 44092-2585
Telephone: (440) 943-7600
E-mail: mal@dioceseofcleveland.org
Internet: www.stmarysem.edu
Founded 1848 as a diocesan seminary, present name 1968
Private control
Academic year: August to May
Pres.-Rector: Rev. Dr MARK LATCOVICH
Dean for Academic Formation: MARY McCORMICK
Dean for Students: MICHAEL WOOST
Registrar: Dr BRENDON ZAJAC
Librarian: ALAN K. ROME
Library of 60,000 vols, 340 periodicals, 1,000 audio and video cassettes
Number of teachers: 20
Number of students: 130

SHAWNEE STATE UNIVERSITY

940 Second St, Portsmouth, OH 45662-4344
Telephone: (740) 351-4778
E-mail: info@shawnee.edu
Internet: www.shawnee.edu
Founded 1986
State control
Academic year: September to June
Pres.: Dr RITA RICE MORRIS
Provost and Vice-Pres. for Academic Affairs: Dr DAVID TODT
Vice-Pres. for Finance and Admin.: Dr ELINDA C. BOYLES
Vice-Pres. for Student Affairs: Dr MARY OLING-SISAY
Dir for Admissions: BOB TRUSZ
Registrar: MARK MOORE
Library Dir: CONNIE SALYERS STONER
Library of 160,000 vols
Number of teachers: 300
Number of students: 4,200

DEANS

College of Arts and Sciences: Dr TIMOTHY E. SCHEURER
College of Professional Studies: Dr JAMES R. KADEL

TIFFIN UNIVERSITY

155 Miami St, Tiffin, OH 44883
Telephone: (419) 447-6443
E-mail: info@tiffin.edu
Internet: www.tiffin.edu
Founded 1888
Private control
Academic year: August to May
12 Regional campuses

Pres.: Dr PAUL MARION
Vice-Pres. for Academic Affairs: Dr CHARLES CHRISTENSEN
Vice-Pres. for Devt: Dr MICHAEL GRANDILLO
Vice-Pres. for Enrolment Management: RON SCHUMACHER
Vice-Pres. for Finance and Admin.: JAMES WHITE
Dean for Students: LISA KIRCHNER
Registrar: ALICE NICHOLS
Library Dir: FRANCES A. FLEET
Number of teachers: 130
Number of students: 4,900
Publications: *Challenge Magazine* (2 a year), *TU Review* (online, www.tiffin.edu/tureview)

DEANS

Graduate Studies: Dr BONNIE TIELL
School of Arts and Sciences: Dr GENE CRUTSINGER
School of Business: Dr LILLIAN SCHUMACHER
School of Criminal Justice and Social Sciences: ROBERT JAMES ORR, III

TRINITY LUTHERAN SEMINARY

2199 E Main St, Columbus, OH 43209-2334
Telephone: (614) 235-4136
E-mail: communications@tlsohio.edu
Internet: www.tlsohio.edu
Founded 1830 as Evangelical Lutheran Theological Seminary, present name 1978
Private control
Academic year: September to May
Pres.: MARK R. RAMSETH
Academic Dean: Dr BRAD A. BINAU
Dir for Admissions: SHARI L. AYERS
Registrar: CAROL M. DIXON
Dir for Library: RAY A. OLSON
Library of 140,000 vols, 6,000 audiovisual items
Number of teachers: 20
Number of students: 250
Publications: *Te Deum*, *Trinity Seminary Review* (2 a year)

UNION INSTITUTE & UNIVERSITY

440 E McMillan St, Cincinnati, OH 45206-1925
Telephone: (513) 861-6400
E-mail: admissions@myunion.edu
Internet: www.myunion.edu
Founded 1964
Private control
Offers doctoral degrees in interdisciplinary studies, psychology and education; academic centres in Cincinnati (Ohio), N Miami Beach (Florida), Los Angeles (California), Sacramento (California), Brattleboro (Vermont), Montpelier (Vermont)
Pres.: Dr ROGER H. SUBLETT
Provost: Dr RICHARD HANSEN
Vice-Pres. for Devt and Univ. Relations: KRISTINE HOWLAND
Vice-Pres. for Enrolment Management: JON MAYS
Registrar: LEW RITA MOORE
Library Dir: MATTHEW PAPPATHAN
Library of 50,000 vols, 2,000 periodicals, 60,000 online monographs
Number of teachers: 400
Number of students: 2,000
Publication: *InsideUnion* (4 a year, online, magazine.myunion.edu)

UNITED THEOLOGICAL SEMINARY

4501 Denlinger Rd, Trotwood, OH 45426
Telephone: (937) 529-2201
E-mail: utscom@united.edu

Internet: www.united.edu
Founded 1954 by merger of Bonebrake Theological Seminary with Evangelical School of Theology
Private control
Offers doctoral degrees in ministry and missiology; campuses at Dayton and Buffalo (New York)
Pres.: Dr WENDY J. DEICHMANN
Vice-Pres. for Academic Affairs and Academic Dean: Dr DAVID F. WATSON
Vice-Pres. for Enrolment: Dr HAROLD HUDSON
Registrar: MARTHA M. ANDERSON
Dir for Library and Information Services: SARAH D. BROOKS BLAIR
Library of 150,000 vols
Number of teachers: 12
Number of students: 170 (full-time)

UNIVERSITY OF AKRON

302 Buchtel Common, Akron, OH 44325-3101
Telephone: (330) 972-7111
E-mail: international@uakron.edu
Internet: www.uakron.edu
Founded 1870 as Buchtel College, present status 1967
State control
Academic year: August to May
Pres.: Dr LUIS M. PROENZA
Sr Vice-Pres. and Provost and Chief Operating Officer: Dr WILLIAM M. SHERMAN
Vice-Pres. and Chief of Staff: CANDACE CAMPBELL-JACKSON
Vice-Pres. and Gen. Counsel: TED A. MALLO
Vice-Pres. for Finance and Admin.: DAVID J. CUMMINS
Vice-Pres. for Information Technology: JIM SAGE
Vice-Pres. for Research: Dr GEORGE R. NEWKOME
Vice-Pres. for Student Engagement and Success: Dr CHARLES J. FEY
Dean for Univ. Libraries: CHERYL KERN-SIMIRENKO
Library: 2.9m. vols
Number of teachers: 2,550
Number of students: 29,000
Publications: *Akron Magazine* (3 a year, online, www.uakron.edu/alumni-friends/akron-magazine.dot), *International Journal of Strategic Cost Management* (4 a year), *The Akron Intellectual Property Journal* (2 a year), *The Akron Tax Journal* (1 a year)

DEANS

Buchtel College of Arts and Sciences: Prof. CHAND K. MIDHA
College of Business Administration: Prof. RAVI KROVI
College of Creative and Professional Arts: Dr CHAND K. MIDHA
College of Education: MARK D. SHERMIS
College of Engineering: Prof. Dr GEORGE K. HARITOS
College of Health Sciences and Human Services: Dr ROBERTA DePOMPEI
College of Nursing: Dr ROBERTA DePOMPEI
College of Polymer Science and Polymer Engineering: Prof. Dr STEPHEN Z. CHENG
Graduate School: Dr GEORGE R. NEWKOME
Honors College: Dr DALE H. MUGLER
School of Law: Prof. MARTIN H. BELSKY
Summit College: STANLEY B. SILVERMAN
University College: STANLEY B. SILVERMAN
Wayne College: NEIL SAPIENZA

UNIVERSITY OF CINCINNATI

2624 Clifton Ave, Cincinnati, OH 45221
Telephone: (513) 556-6000
Internet: www.uc.edu

Founded 1819 as Cincinnati College, present status 1977
State control
Academic year: September to June
Pres.: Prof. Dr SANTA JEREMY ONO
Provost and Sr Vice-Pres. for Academic Affairs: Prof. Dr LAWRENCE J. JOHNSON
Sr Vice-Pres. for Admin. and Finance: ROBERT F. AMBACH
Exec. Vice-Pres.: KAREN K. FAABORG
Vice-Pres. for Devt and Alumni Relations: STEVE WILSON
Vice-Pres. for Finance: JAMES D. PLUMMER
Vice-Pres. for Governmental Relations and Univ. Communications: GREGORY J. VEHR
Vice-Pres. for Information Technology and Chief Information Officer: MIKE LIEBERMAN
Vice-Pres. for Research: WILLIAM BALL
Vice-Pres. for Student Affairs and Services: Dr MITCHEL D. LIVINGSTON
Registrar: Dr DOUGLAS K. BURGESS
Dean and Univ. Librarian: Dr VICTORIA MONTAVON
Library: see under Libraries and Archives
Number of teachers: 4,370 (2,270 full-time, 2,100 part-time)
Number of students: 42,420 (31,985 undergraduate, 9,375 postgraduate, 1,060 professional)
Publications: *Freedom Center Journal* (1 a year), *Journal of Crime and Justice* (2 a year), *The Cincinnati Review* (online, www.cincinnatireview.com), *UC Magazine* (3 a year, print and online, magazine.uc.edu)

DEANS

Blue Ash College: Dr CADY SHORT-THOMPSON
Carl H. Lindner College of Business: DAVID M. SZYMANSKI
Clermont College: Dr GREGORY S. SOJKA
College-Conservatory of Music: PETER LANDGREN
College of Allied Health Sciences: Dr ELIZABETH C. KING
College of Design, Architecture, Art and Planning: ROBERT PROBST
College of Education, Criminal Justice and Human Services: Dr LAWRENCE J. JOHNSON
College of Engineering and Applied Science: Dr CARLO D. MONTEMAGNO
College of Law: LOUIS D. BILLIONIS
College of Medicine: THOMAS F. BOAT
College of Nursing: Dr GREER GLAZER
Graduate School: Dr ROBERT ZIEROLF
James L. Winkle College of Pharmacy: Dr WILLIAM K. FANT
Lindner College of Business: DAVID SZYMANSKI
McMicken College of Arts and Sciences: VALERIE GRAY HARDCASTLE

UNIVERSITY OF DAYTON

300 College Park, Dayton, OH 45469
Telephone: (937) 229-1000
E-mail: info@udayton.edu
Internet: www.udayton.edu

Founded 1850 as St. Mary's School for Boys, present name and status 1920
Private control
Academic year: August to May
Pres.: Dr DANIEL J. CURRAN
Provost: Dr JOSEPH E. SALIBA
Vice-Pres. for Enrolment Management: SUNDAR KUMARASAMY
Vice-Pres. for Finance and Admin. Services: THOMAS E. BURKHARDT
Vice-Pres. for Research: Dr MICKEY MCCABE

Vice-Pres. for Student Devt: WILLIAM FISCHER
Vice-Pres. for Univ. Advancement: DAVID HARPER
Registrar: THOMAS J. WESTENDORF
Dean for Libraries: KATHLEEN M. WEBB
Library: 1m. vols, 295,000 vols of printed legal materials and microfilms
Number of teachers: 860 (540 full-time, 320 part-time)
Number of students: 11,060
Publications: *Law Review* (3 a year), *Orpheus* (2 a year), *UD Magazine* (online, udquickly.udayton.edu/category/udmagazine)

DEANS

College of Arts and Sciences: Dr PAUL H. BENSON
Graduate, Professional and Continuing Education: Dr PAUL VANDERBURGH
School of Business Administration: Dr JOSEPH CASTELLANO
School of Education and Allied Professions: Dr KEVIN R. KELLY
School of Engineering: (vacant)
School of Law: PAUL E. MCGREAL

UNIVERSITY OF FINDLAY

1000 N Main St, Findlay, OH 45840
Telephone: (419) 422-8313
Internet: www.findlay.edu

Founded 1882, present name 1989
Private control
Pres.: Dr KATHERINE ROWE FELL
Vice-Pres. for Academic Affairs: Dr DANIEL J. MAY
Vice-Pres. for Devt: DAVID P. FERGUSON
Vice-Pres. for Student Services: DAVID W. EMSWELLER
Vice-Pres. for Univ. Advancement: Dr JOHN W. MOSSER
Registrar: TONY G. GOEDDE
Dir for Library: MARGARET HIRSCHY
Library of 127,000 vols
Number of teachers: 340
Number of students: 3,700
Publication: *Findlay Magazine* (2 a year)

DEANS

College of Business: Dr PAUL SEARS
College of Education: Dr JULIE MCINTOSH
College of Health Professions: Dr ANDREA W. KOEPKE
College of Liberal Arts: Dr GARY JOHNSON
College of Pharmacy: Dr DONALD STANSLOSKI
College of Sciences: Prof. Dr TERRY D. SCHWANER

UNIVERSITY OF MOUNT UNION

1972 Clark Ave, Alliance, OH 44601
Telephone: (330) 821-5320
E-mail: info@mountunion.edu
Internet: www.mountunion.edu

Founded 1846, present name and status 2010
Private control
Pres.: Dr RICHARD F. GIESE
Vice-Pres. for Academic Affairs and Dean for Univ.: Dr PATRICIA DRAVES
Vice-Pres. for Enrolment Services: AMY A. TOMKO
Vice-Pres. for Student Affairs and Dean for Students: JOHN FRAZIER
Vice-Pres. for Univ. Advancement: GREGORY KING
Dir for Admission: GRACE CHALKER
Registrar: KAREN MORIARTY
Library Dir: ROBERT R. GARLAND
Number of teachers: 90 (full-time)
Number of students: 2,260 (2,200 undergraduate, 60 graduate)

DEANS

Arts and Humanities: Dr ANDREW PRICE
Mathematics and Sciences: Dr JONATHAN SCOTT
Professional Studies: Dr PATRICIA MATTHEWS
Social Sciences: Dr RICHARD DUTSON

UNIVERSITY OF NORTHWESTERN OHIO

1441 N Cable Rd, Lima, OH 45805
Telephone: (419) 998-3120
E-mail: info@unoh.edu
Internet: www.unoh.edu

Founded 1920
Private control
Pres.: Dr JEFFREY A. JARVIS
Provost and Vice-Pres. for Academic Affairs: Dr CHERYL MUELLER
Vice-Pres. for Devt: STEVE FARMER
Vice-Pres. for Enrolment Management: RICK MORRISON
Vice-Pres. for Student Life: ROBERT FRICKE
Registrar: STACIA BURGOON
Dir for Library: GEORGENA NANSON

DEANS

College of Applied Technologies: THOMAS GROTHOUS
College of Business: DEAN HOBLER

UNIVERSITY OF RIO GRANDE

218 N College Ave, Rio Grande, OH 45674-3131
Telephone: (740) 245-5353
E-mail: info@rio.edu
Internet: www.rio.edu

Founded 1876
Private control
Academic year: August to May
Pres.: Dr BARBARA GELLMAN-DANLEY
Provost and Vice-Pres. for Academic Affairs: Dr KENNETH J. PORADA
Vice-Pres. for Admin. Services and Student Services: PAUL HARRISON
Dean for Enrolment Management: MARK F. ABELL
Dean for Student Services: AARON QUINN
Library Dir: J. DAVID MAUER
Library of 94,197 vols, 230 periodicals, 446,409 microforms, 2,412 audiovisual materials, 30,000 govt documents
Number of teachers: 85
Number of students: 2,400

DEANS

College of Liberal Arts and Sciences: Dr KENNETH PORADA
College of Professional Studies: Prof. DAVID LAWRENCE

UNIVERSITY OF TOLEDO

2801 W Bancroft, Toledo, OH 43606-3390
Telephone: (419) 530-4636
Internet: www.utoledo.edu

Founded 1872 as Toledo Univ. of Arts and Trades, present status 1967
State control
Pres.: Dr LLOYD A. JACOBS
Chancellor: Dr JEFFREY P. GOLD
Provost and Exec. Vice-Pres. for Academic Affairs: Dr WILLIAM MCMILLEN
Vice-Pres. for Admin.: CHARLES LEHNERT
Vice-Pres. for Govt Relations: Dr WILLIAM MCMILLEN
Vice-Pres. for Institutional Advancement: C. VERNON SNYDER
Vice-Pres. for Research and Economic Devt: Dr FRANK J. CALZONETTI
Vice-Pres. for Student Affairs: KAYE PATTEN WALLACE

Registrar: SHERRI ARMSTRONG
Dean for Libraries: JOHN GABOURY
Library: 1m. vols
Number of teachers: 1,700
Number of students: 22,600
Publication: *UT Alumni Magazine*

DEANS

College of Adult and Lifelong Learning: Dr DENNIS LETTMAN
College of Business and Innovation: Dr THOMAS GUTTERIDGE
College of Engineering: Prof. Dr NAGI G. NAGANATHAN
College of Graduate Studies: Dr PATRICIA KOMUNIECKI
College of Languages, Literature and Social Sciences: Dr JAMIE BARLOWE
College of Law: Prof. DANIEL J. STEINBOCK
College of Medicine: JEFFREY P. GOLD
College of Natural Sciences and Mathematics: Dr KAREN BJORKMAN
College of Nursing: Prof. Dr TIMONTHY GASPAR
College of Pharmacy and Pharmaceutical Sciences: Prof. Dr JOHNNIE EARLY, II
College of Visual and Performing Arts: DEBRA A. DAVIS
Judith Herb College of Education, Health Science and Human Service: Dr BEVERLY J. SCHMOLL

URBANA UNIVERSITY

579 College Way, Urbana, OH 43078
Telephone: (937) 484-1400
E-mail: admissions@urbana.edu
Internet: www.urbana.edu
Founded 1850 as Urbana Seminary, present name and status 1985
Private control
Pres.: Dr STEPHEN JONES
Sr Vice-Pres. for Academic Affairs and Dean for the Faculty: Dr KIRK PETERSON
Vice-Pres. for Admin. Services: BARBARA STEWART
Vice-Pres. for Institutional Advancement: JAMES THORNTON
Vice-Pres. for Student and Enrolment Services and Dean for Students: Dr JAMES WEISGERBER
Dir for Admissions: MARY ANNE BARR
Registrar: KATHY YODER
Library Dir: BARBARA MACKE
Library of 71,000 vols, 800 periodicals
Number of teachers: 50 (full-time)
Number of students: 1,500 (1,330 undergraduate, 170 graduate)

DEANS

College of Arts and Sciences: Prof. Dr CHERYL FENNO
College of Business: Dr HERSCHEL PURDUE
College of Education and Sports Studies: LUCINDA LEUGERS
College of Nursing and Allied Health: Prof. Dr NANCY SWEENEY
College of Social and Behavioral Sciences: Prof. Dr ALICE E. SIDDLE
School of Adult and Continuing Education: WILLIAM D. BLIZZARD

URSULINE COLLEGE

2550 Lander Rd, Pepper Pike, Cleveland, OH 44124
Telephone: (440) 449-4200
E-mail: info@ursuline.edu
Internet: www.ursuline.edu
Founded 1871
Private control
Academic year: August to May
Pres.: Dr DIANA STANO

Vice-Pres. for Academic Affairs: Dr JoANNE PODIS
Vice-Pres. for Institutional Advancement: KEVIN GLADSTONE
Vice-Pres. for Student Affairs: DEANNE HURLEY
Registrar: LEAH SULLIVAN
Library Dir: BETSEY BELKIN
Library of 120,000 vols
Number of teachers: 150
Number of students: 1,500
Publication: *Voices*

DEANS

Breen School of Nursing: Dr CHRISTINE WYND
Graduate and Professional Studies: DEBRA L. FLEMING
School of Arts and Sciences: BETH KAVRAN

WALSH UNIVERSITY

2020 E Maple St, NW, N Canton, OH 44720
Telephone: (330) 490-7090
Internet: www.walsh.edu
Founded 1960 as Walsh College
Private control
Campuses at N Canton, Akron, Medina (Ohio)
Pres.: RICHARD JUSSEAUME
Provost and Vice-Pres. for Academic Affairs: Dr LAURENCE F. BOVE
Vice-Pres. for Academic Projects: NANCY BLACKFORD
Vice-Pres. for Advancement and Univ. Relations: BRIDGETTE NEISEL
Vice-Pres. for Business and Finance: PHILIP DANIELS
Vice-Pres. for Enrolment Management: BRETT FRESHOUR
Dean for Students: AMY K. MALASKA
Registrar: EDNA MCCULLOH
Library Dir: DANIEL SUVAK
Library of 141,000 vols, 90,000 ebooks, 3,000 audiovisual items
Number of teachers: 125 (full-time)
Number of students: 3,000
Publication: *Walsh Times* (3 a year)

DEANS

DeVille School of Business: Dr CAROLE C. MOUNT
School of Nursing: Dr LINDA LINC

WILBERFORCE UNIVERSITY

POB 1001, 1055 N Bickett Rd, Wilberforce, OH 45384-1001
Telephone: (937) 376-2911
E-mail: admission@wilberforce.edu
Internet: www.wilberforce.edu
Founded 1856
Private control
Academic year: August to May
Pres.: Dr PATRICIA LOFTON HARDAWAY
Vice-Pres. for Academic Affairs: Dr MURIEL WRIGHT-BRAILEY
Vice-Pres. for Admin. and Financial Affairs: TIJUANA HUDSON
Dir for Admissions: JUAN ALEXANDER
Dean for Students: PARRIS CARTER
Registrar: GAIL D. LASH
Dir for Library: Dr WILLETTE STINSON
Library of 62,000 vols, 500 journal and magazine subscriptions
Number of teachers: 75 (55 full-time, 20 part-time)
Number of students: 850
Publications: *The Wilberforcean, The Yard*

DEANS

Arts and Sciences: Dr EUGENIA SHITTU
Engineering and Computing: Dr EDWARD ASIKELE

WILMINGTON COLLEGE

1870 Quaker Way, Wilmington, OH 45177
Telephone: (937) 382-6661
E-mail: admission@wilmington.edu
Internet: www.wilmington.edu
Founded 1870
Private control
Academic year: August to May

Programmes in accounting, agriculture, art, athletic training, biology, business administration, chemistry and physics, communication arts, criminal justice, education, English, environmental science, equine studies, history, mathematics, music, psychology, religion and philosophy, social and political studies, social work, Spanish, sports management and health/PE, theatre; campus at Blue Ash and on-site programmes at Cincinnati State Technical and Community College

Pres.: JIM REYNOLDS
Vice-Pres. for Academic Affairs and Dean for Faculty: Dr ERIKA GOODWIN
Vice-Pres. for College Advancement: ROBERT C. HARROD
Vice-Pres. for Enrolment Management: MARK DENNISTON
Vice-Pres. for External Programmes: IRIS KELSON
Vice-Pres. for Student Affairs and Dean for Students: SIGRID B. SOLOMON
Registrar: KAREN M. GARMAN
Dir for Library: JEAN MULHERN
Library of 110,000 vols
Number of teachers: 65 (full-time)
Number of students: 1,500

WINEBRENNER THEOLOGICAL SEMINARY

950 N Main St, Findlay, OH 45840
Telephone: (419) 434-4200
E-mail: admissions@winebrenner.edu
Internet: www.winebrenner.edu
Founded 1942, present name and status 1961
Private control
Academic year: August to May
Pres.: Dr DAVID E. DRAPER
Vice-Pres. for Academic Advancement: Prof. JOEL W. COCKLIN
Vice-Pres. for Institutional Advancement: JIM SMARKEL
Registrar: SHARI BRANDEBERRY
Dir for Library Services: MARGARET HIRSCHY
Library of 38,000 vols, 145 periodicals
Number of teachers: 17
Number of students: 120

WITTENBERG UNIVERSITY

POB 720, 200 W Ward St, Springfield, OH 45501-0720
Telephone: (937) 327-6231
E-mail: admission@wittenberg.edu
Internet: www.wittenberg.edu
Founded 1845
Private control
Academic year: August to May

Programmes in Africana studies, American studies, art, biochemistry and molecular biology, biology, chemistry, communication, community education, computer science, dance, East Asian studies, economics, education, engineering, English, environmental studies, forestry, geography, geology, global studies, health/fitness/sport, history, languages, management, marine biology, mathematics, music, nursing, occupational therapy, philosophy, physics, political science, pre-law, pre-medicine, psychology, religion, Russian area studies, sociology, theatre and dance, urban studies, women's studies

Pres.: Dr MARK H. ERICKSON

Provost: Prof. CHRISTOPHER M. DUNCAN
Vice-Pres. for Enrolment Management and Dean for Students: SARAH M. KELLY
Vice-Pres. for Univ. Advancement: JIM GEIGER
Dir for Admissions: KAREN HUNT
Registrar: JACK CAMPBELL
Dir for Library: DOUGLAS LEHMAN

Library of 367,000 vols, 1,500 periodicals
Number of teachers: 180 (full-time)
Number of students: 1,900

Publications: *East Asian Studies Journal* (1 a year), *History Journal* (1 a year), *Journal of Political Science* (1 a year), *Pholeos* (2 a year), *Spectrum* (1 a year), *Wittenberg Review of Literature and Art*

WRIGHT STATE UNIVERSITY

3640 Colonel Glenn Highway, Dayton, OH 45435

Telephone: (937) 775-3333
E-mail: registrar@wright.edu
Internet: www.wright.edu

Founded 1967
State control

Campus at Celina (Ohio)

Pres.: Dr DAVID R. HOPKINS
Provost: Dr STEVEN R. ANGLE
Vice-Pres. for Advancement: REBECCA COLE
Vice-Pres. for Enrolment Management: Dr JACQUELINE MCMILLAN
Vice-Pres. for Research and Graduate Studies: Dr ROBERT E. W. FYFFE
Vice-Pres. for Student Affairs: Dr DAN ABRAHAMOWICZ
Registrar: MARIAN BRAINERD
Dean for Libraries: Dr STEPHEN FOSTER

Library of 696,000 vols
Number of teachers: 860 (full-time)
Number of students: 19,700

Publications: *The Grand Lake Review* (online, www.wright.edu/~martin.kich/glr/glrIndex.htm), *Wright State University Magazine* (2 a year)

DEANS

Boonshoft School of Medicine: HOWARD M. PART
College of Education and Human Services: Dr CHARLOTTE HARRIS
College of Engineering and Computer Science: Dr S. NARAYANAN
College of Liberal Arts: Dr CHARLES S. TAYLOR
College of Nursing and Health: Dr ROSALIE O'DELL MAINOUS
College of Science and Mathematics: Dr YI LI
Graduate School: Dr ANDREW T. HSU
Raj Soin College of Business: Dr BERKWOOD M. FARMER
School of Professional Psychology: Dr LARRY C. JAMES

XAVIER UNIVERSITY

3800 Victory Parkway, Cincinnati, OH 45207
Telephone: (513) 745-3000
Internet: www.xavier.edu

Founded 1831
Private control
Academic year: August to May

Pres.: Rev. MICHAEL J. GRAHAM
Provost and Chief Academic Officer: Dr SCOTT A. CHADWICK
Sr Vice-Pres. and Chief Financial Officer: MARIBETH AMYOT
Vice-Pres. for Admin.: Dr JOHN F. KUCIA
Vice-Pres. for Enrolment Management: TERRY RICHARDS
Vice-Pres. for Univ. Relations: GARY R. MASSA

Assoc. Vice-Pres. for Academic Affairs and Dean of the Graduate School: Dr STEVEN HERBERT
Assoc. Provost and Chief Information Officer: ANNETTE MARKSBERRY

Library of 479,256 vols, 752,229 microfilm items, 13,936 audiovisual items, 58,509 periodicals (incl. electronic)
Number of teachers: 356 (full-time)
Number of students: 6,650

Publication: *Xavier Magazine* (online, www.xavier.edu/magazine)

DEANS

College of Arts and Sciences: Dr JANICE B. WALKER
College of Social Science, Health and Education: Dr MARK MEYERS
Williams College of Business: Dr BRIAN TILL

YOUNGSTOWN STATE UNIVERSITY

1 University Plaza, Youngstown, OH 44555
Telephone: (330) 941-3000
Internet: web.ysu.edu

Founded 1908
State control
Academic year: September to August (4 terms)

Pres.: Dr CYNTHIA E. ANDERSON
Provost and Vice-Pres. for Academic Affairs: Dr IKRAM KHAWAJA
Vice-Pres. for Finance and Admin.: EUGENE P. GRILLI
Vice-Pres. for Student Affairs: JACK P. FAHEY
Vice-Pres. for Univ. Advancement: (vacant)
Registrar: JEANNE HERMAN
Exec. Dir for Library: PAUL J. KOBULNICKY

Library of 700,000 vols, 300,000 govt documents, 800,000 microforms
Number of teachers: 460 (full-time)
Number of students: 15,200

Publication: *YSU Magazine*

DEANS

Beeghly College of Education: Dr MARY LOU DIPILLO
Bitonte College of Health and Human Services: Dr JOSEPH L. MOSCA
College of Fine and Performing Arts: Dr BRYAN DEPOY
College of Liberal Arts and Social Sciences: Dr SHEARLE FURNISH
College of Science, Technology, Engineering and Mathematics: Dr MARTIN ABRAHAM
School of Graduate Studies and Research: Dr PETER J. KASVINSKY
Williamson College of Business Administration: Dr BETTY JO LICATA

OKLAHOMA

BACONE COLLEGE

2299 Old Bacone Rd, Muskogee, OK 74403
Telephone: (918) 683-4581
E-mail: admissionsoffice@bacone.edu
Internet: www.bacone.edu

Founded 1880, present name 1910
Private control

Divs of adult education, arts and sciences, business, education, general studies, health sciences

Pres.: Rev. Dr ROBERT J. DUNCAN, JR
Exec. Vice-Pres. and Dean for Faculty: ROBERT BROWN
Asst Vice-Pres. for Institutional Advancement: EUGENE G. BLANKENSHIP
Asst Vice-Pres. for Student Life: SHELLI HOPKINS
Dir for Admissions: MIKE JACKSON

Dir for Enrolment Management: KATHYE WATSON
Registrar: VIRGINIA THOMPSON

CAMERON UNIVERSITY

2800 W Gore Blvd, Lawton, OK 73505-6377
Telephone: (580) 581-2200
E-mail: admissions@cameron.edu
Internet: www.cameron.edu

Founded 1909
State control
Academic year: June to August

Pres.: CINDY ROSS
Provost: Dr JOHN M. MCARTHUR
Vice-Pres. for Student Services: JENNIFER HOLLAND
Vice-Pres. for Univ. Advancement: ALBERT JOHNSON, JR
Assoc. Vice-Pres. for Enrolment Management: JAMIE GLOVER
Dir for Library: SHERRY YOUNG

Number of teachers: 75
Number of students: 6,000

Publications: *The Oklahoma Review* (2 a year, online, www.cameron.edu/okreview), *The Southwest Business & Economics Journal*

DEANS

School of Business: Dr ORIS L. ODOM, II
School of Education and Behavioural Sciences: Prof. RONNA VANDERSLICE
School of Liberal Arts: VON UNDERWOOD
School of Science and Technology: Dr REZA KAMALI

EAST CENTRAL UNIVERSITY

1100 E 14th St, Ada, OK 74820
Telephone: (580) 332-8000
E-mail: parmstro@ecok.edu
Internet: www.ecok.edu

Founded 1909, current name adopted 1985
State control

Pres.: Dr JOHN R. HARGRAVE
Provost and Vice-Pres. for Academic Affairs: Dr DUANE C. ANDERSON
Vice-Pres. for Admin. and Finance: STEVE TURNER
Vice-Pres. for Student Devt: JERRY FORBES
Dir for Enrolment Management: BONITA BLACKBURN
Dean for Student Affairs: BRONSON WARREN
Registrar: PAMLA ARMSTRONG
Dir for Library: ADRIANNA LANCASTER

Library of 275,000 vols
Number of teachers: 265 (165 full-time, 100 part-time)
Number of students: 5,725

DEANS

College of Education and Psychology: BRENDA WALLING
College of Health and Sciences: Dr BRUCE WEEMS
College of Liberal Arts and Social Sciences: Prof. Dr MARK HOLLINGSWORTH (acting)
School of Business: WENDELL GODWIN
School of Graduate Studies: Dr RICK WETHERILL

LANGSTON UNIVERSITY

POB 1500, Langston, OK 73050
Telephone: (405) 466-3428
E-mail: admissions@lunet.edu
Internet: www.lunet.edu

Founded 1897
State control
Academic year: August to May

Campuses at Tulsa and Oklahoma City in Oklahoma

Pres.: Dr HENRY PONDER
Vice-Pres. for Academic Affairs: Dr CLYDE MONTGOMERY, JR
Vice-Pres. for Fiscal and Admin. Affairs: ANGELA R. WATSON
Vice-Pres. for Institutional Advancement and Devt: MISTY WAKEFIELD
Vice-Pres. for Student Affairs and Enrolment Management: Dr ANGELIA YOUNG JONES
Registrar: KATHY SIMMONS
Dir for Univ. Libraries: BETTYE BLACK (acting)
Number of teachers: 145
Number of students: 3,500
Publication: *Greatness Magazine*

DEANS

Physical Therapy: Dr MILAGROS JORGE
School of Agriculture and Applied Sciences: Dr MARVIN BURNS
School of Arts and Sciences: Dr CLARENCE A. HEDGE (acting)
School of Business: Dr SOLOMON S. SMITH
School of Education and Behavioural Sciences: Dr JOE HORNBEAK
School of Nursing and Health Professions: Dr CAROLYN T. KORNEGAY

MID-AMERICA CHRISTIAN UNIVERSITY

3500 SW 119th St, Oklahoma City, OK 73170
Telephone: (405) 691-3800
E-mail: info@macu.edu
Internet: www.macu.edu
Founded 1953 as South Texas Bible Institute, current name adopted 2003
Private control
Academic year: August to May
Schools of business, behavioural science, general education, mathematics and science, ministry, music, teacher education
Pres. and CEO: Dr JOHN D. FOZARD
Vice-Pres. for Academic Affairs: Dr KATHALEEN REID-MARTINEZ
Vice-Pres. for Enrolment Management: MAURICE SHOE
Vice-Pres. for Strategic Initiatives: Dr ERIC ANTHONY JOSEPH
Chief Admin. Officer: SEVIER OWEN
Dir for Admissions: DUSTIN ROWTON
Dir for Student Services: DIANE CLEARY
Dean for College of Adult and Graduate Studies: Dr SHIRLEY RODDY
Univ. Registrar: BOBBIE SPURGEON-HARRIS
Library Dir: MICHAEL FOOTE
Library Dir: ELISSA PATADAL
Number of teachers: 60
Number of students: 1,500

NORTHEASTERN STATE UNIVERSITY

600 N Grand Ave, Tahlequah, OK 74464-2399
Telephone: (918) 456-5511
E-mail: nsuinfo@nsuok.edu
Internet: www.nsuok.edu
Founded 1846 as Cherokee Nat. Female Seminary, current name adopted 1985
State control
Academic year: August to July
Campuses at Broken Arrow and Muskogee in Oklahoma
Pres.: Dr DON BETZ
Provost and Vice-Pres. for Academic Affairs: Dr MARTIN TADLOCK
Vice-Pres. for Admin. and Finance: DAVID KOEHN
Vice-Pres. for Operations: TIM FOUTCH
Vice-Pres. for Teaching and Learning: Dr CHARLES ZIEHR
Vice-Pres. for Univ. Relations: MARK KINDERS

Exec. Dir for Enrolment Management: JERRETT PHILLIPS
Dean for Graduate Studies and Research: Dr THOMAS JACKSON
Dean for Broken Arrow Campus: Dr CHRISTEE JENLINK
Dean for Muskogee Campus: Dr TIM McELROY
Registrar: JULIE SAWYER
Exec. Dir for Libraries: PAULA SETTOON
Library of 424,278 vols, 5,749 current serial titles, 758,474 microforms, 71,985 audiovisual materials, 43,030 ebooks
Number of teachers: 500 (350 full-time, 150 part-time)
Number of students: 9,260

DEANS

College of Business and Technology: Dr ROGER COLLIER
College of Education: Dr KAY GRANT
College of Extended Learning: Dr CHRISTEE JENLINK
College of Liberal Arts: Dr PAUL WESTBROOK
College of Optometry: Dr DOUGLAS K. PENISTEN
College of Science and Health Professions: Dr MARTIN VENNEMAN
Graduate College: Dr THOMAS JACKSON

NORTHWESTERN OKLAHOMA STATE UNIVERSITY

709 Oklahoma Blvd, Alva, OK 73717-2799
Telephone: (580) 327-1700
E-mail: recruit@nwosu.edu
Internet: www.nwosu.edu
Founded 1897, current name adopted 1974
State control
Academic year: August to May
Campuses at Enid and Woodward in Oklahoma
Pres.: Dr JANET CUNNINGHAM
Exec. Vice-Pres.: Dr STEVE LOHMANN
Vice-Pres. for Admin.: DAVID PECHA
Vice-Pres. for Student Affairs and Enrolment Management: BRAD FRANZ
Dean for Enid Campus: Dr CHERYL EVANS
Dean for Woodward Campus: Dr DEENA FISHER
Registrar: SHERI LAHR
Dir for Libraries: SUSAN K. JEFFRIES
Library of 500,000 vols (incl. microforms)
Number of teachers: 170
Number of students: 2,230

DEANS

School of Arts and Sciences: Dr MIKE KNEDLER
School of Professional Studies: Dr JAMES BROWN

OKLAHOMA BAPTIST UNIVERSITY

500 W University, Shawnee, OK 74804
Telephone: (405) 275-2850
E-mail: info@okbu.edu
Internet: www.okbu.edu
Founded 1910
Private control
Academic year: August to May
Pres.: Dr DAVID W. WHITLOCK
Provost and Exec. Vice-Pres. for Campus Life: Dr R. STANTON NORMAN
Sr Vice-Pres. for Academic Services: Dr DEBBIE BLUE
Exec. Vice-Pres. for Business and Admin. Services: RANDY L. SMITH
Vice-Pres. for Univ. Advancement: WILL SMALLWOOD
Dean for Enrolment Management: BRUCE PERKINS
Dean for Students: BRANDON SKAGGS
Dir for Graduate Studies: Dr SCOTT HARRIS

Dean for Library Services: Dr RICHARD CHEEK
Library of 220,000 vols, 310,000 microforms
Number of teachers: 115
Number of students: 1,870
Publication: *OBU Magazine*

DEANS

College of Arts and Humanities: Dr PAM ROBINSON
College of Business: Dr DAVID C. HOUGHTON
College of Fine Arts: Dr KEN GABRIELSE
College of Humanities and Social Sciences: Dr PAM ROBINSON
College of Nursing: Dr LANA BOLHOUSE
College of Science and Mathematics: Dr DEBORAH BLUE
College of Theology and Ministry: Dr MARK McCLELLAN

OKLAHOMA CHRISTIAN UNIVERSITY

POB 11000, Oklahoma City, OK 73136
2501E Memorial Rd, Edmond, OK 73013
Telephone: (405) 425-5000
E-mail: info@oc.edu
Internet: www.oc.edu
Founded 1950 as Central Christian College, current name adopted 1997
Private control
Academic year: August to April
Pres.: Dr MIKE E. O'NEAL
Exec. Vice-Pres.: BILL GOAD
Sr Vice-Pres. for Academic Affairs: Dr ALLISON D. GARRETT
Sr Vice-Pres. for Advancement: Dr JOHN deSTEIGUER
Vice-Pres. and Dean for Students: NEIL ARTER
Vice-Pres. for Enrolment Management: RISA FORRESTER
Vice-Pres. for Finance: JEFF BINGHAM
Vice-Pres. for Univ. and Marketing Communications: RON FROST
Dir for Admissions: DARCI THOMPSON
Registrar: MICKEY D. BANISTER
Library Dir: TAMIE WILLIS
Library of 110,000 vols and media, 30,000 ebooks, access to 8,000 periodicals in electronic or print format
Number of teachers: 105
Number of students: 2,160
Publication: *View magazine*

DEANS

College of Arts and Sciences: Dr DAVID LOWRY
College of Biblical Studies: Dr ALAN MARTIN
College of Professional Studies: Dr PHIL LEWIS

OKLAHOMA CITY UNIVERSITY

2501 N Blackwelder, Oklahoma City, OK 73106-1493
Telephone: (405) 208-5000
Internet: www.okcu.edu
Founded 1904 as Epworth Univ., current name adopted 1924
Private control
Language of instruction: English
Academic year: August to July
Pres. and CEO: Dr ROBERT HENRY
Provost and Vice-Pres. for Academic Affairs: Dr SUSAN C. BARBER
Asst. Provost: Dr KENT BUCHANAN
Vice-Pres. for Church Relations: Rev. MARGARET A. BALL
Vice-Pres. for Enrolment Management: KEVIN WINDHOLZ
Vice-Pres. for Student Affairs: Dr RICHARD E. HALL

Vice-Pres. for Univ. Advancement and External Relations: MARTY O'GWYNN
Assoc. Vice-Pres. for Student Affairs and Dean for Students: LIZ DONNELLY
Registrar: CHARLES L. MONNOT
Dir for Library: Dr VICTORIA SWINNEY

Library of 327,986 vols, 238,620 microfilms, 16,599 video and audio items, 200,379 monographs, 16,763 periodicals, 89,000 ebooks
Number of teachers: 386
Number of students: 3,212
Publications: *Oklahoma City University Law Review* (3 a year), *Scarab* (1 a year), *Stellar* (1 a year)

DEANS

Ann Lacy School of American Dance and Arts Management: JOHN BEDFORD
Kramer School of Nursing: Dr MARVEL L. WILLIAMSON
Meinders School of Business: Dr STEVE C. AGEE
Petree College of Arts and Sciences: Dr MARK Y. A. DAVIES
School of Adult and Continuing Education: (vacant)
School of Law: VALERIE COUCH
School of Religion: Dr SHARON BETSWORTH
School of Theatre: BRIAN PARSONS
Wanda L. Bass School of Music: MARK E. PARKER

OKLAHOMA PANHANDLE STATE UNIVERSITY

POB 430, Goodwell, OK 73939
Telephone: (580) 349-2611
E-mail: opsu@opsu.edu
Internet: www.opsu.edu

Founded 1909 as Pan-Handle Agricultural Institute, current name adopted 1974
State control
Academic year: August to May (2 semesters)
Pres.: DAVID A. BRYANT
Vice-Pres. for Academic Affairs and Outreach: WAYNE E. MANNING
Vice-Pres. for Fiscal Affairs: LARRY PETERS
Dir for Student Services and Activities: JESSICA LOFLAND
Dir for Univ. College: CAROLYN MCCARGISH
Registrar and Dir for Admissions: BOBBY JENKINS
Dir for Library: TONY HARDMAN

Library of 91,000 vols, 33,000 ebooks
Number of teachers: 70
Number of students: 1,400

DEANS

Agriculture: Prof. Dr PETER CAMFIELD
Business and Technology: Prof. DIANE MURPHEY
Development Studies: CAROLYN MCCARGISH
Education: Prof. R. WAYNE STEWART
Liberal Arts: Prof. Dr SARAH JANE RICHTER
Science, Mathematics and Nursing: Prof. Dr JUSTIN K. COLLINS

PROFESSORS

CAMFIELD, P., Animal Science
COLLINS, J. K., Biology
MURPHEY, D. M., Computer Information Systems
RICHTER, S. J., English
SHAFER, L., Education
STEWART, R. W., Education
THATCHER, R. M., Education
TOWNSEND, J., Agriculture

OKLAHOMA STATE UNIVERSITY

Stillwater, OK 74078
Telephone: (405) 744-5000
E-mail: admit@okstate.edu

Internet: osu.okstate.edu

Founded 1890
State control
Academic year: August to May
Pres.: BURNS HARGIS
Provost, Sr Vice-Pres. and Vice-Pres. for Academic Affairs: Dr ROBERT J. STERNBERG
Vice-Pres. for Admin. and Finance: JOE WEAVER
Vice-Pres. for Enrolment Management: KYLE WRAY
Vice-Pres. for Research and Technology Transfer: Dr STEPHEN W. MCKEEVER
Vice-Pres. for Student Affairs: Dr LEE E. BIRD
Vice-Pres. for Univ. Relations: GARY C. CLARK
Assoc. Vice-Pres. for Institutional Diversity: Dr JASON KIRKSEY
Registrar: Dr K. CELESTE CAMPBELL
Dean for Libraries: SHEILA G. JOHNSON
Library: see Libraries and Archives
Number of teachers: 1,060
Number of students: 30,500
Publications: *International Fire Service Journal of Leadership and Management* (4 a year), *Journal of Computer Information Systems* (4 a year), *The Review of Regional Studies* (3 a year)

DEANS

Center for Veterinary Health Sciences: JEAN E. SANDER
College of Agricultural Sciences and Natural Resources: Dr ROBERT E. WHITSON
College of Arts and Sciences: Dr PETER M. A. SHERWOOD
College of Education: Dr C. ROBERT DAVIS
College of Engineering, Architecture and Technology: Dr KHALED A. M. GASEM
College of Human Sciences: Dr STEPHAN M. WILSON
Graduate College: Dr SHERYL TUCKER
Spears School of Business: Dr LAWRENCE A. CROSBY

OKLAHOMA STATE UNIVERSITY INSTITUTE OF TECHNOLOGY— OKMULGEE

1801 E Fourth St, Okmulgee, OK 74447
Telephone: (918) 293-4680
E-mail: information@okstate.edu
Internet: www.osuit.edu
State control
Academic year: May to February

Divs of allied health science, arts and sciences, automotive service technologies, construction technology, culinary arts, engineering technologies, heavy equipment and vehicle institute, information technologies

Pres. and Provost: Dr DAVID BOSSERMAN
Exec. Vice-Pres. for Academic Affairs: Dr LINDA AVANT
Vice-Pres. for Enrolment Management: INA AGNEW
Vice-Pres. for Univ. and External Relations: ANITA GORDY-WATKINS
Dir for Library: JENNY DUNCAN
Number of students: 3,000 (2,100 full-time, 900 part-time)

OKLAHOMA WESLEYAN UNIVERSITY

2201 Silver Lake Rd, Bartlesville, OK 74006
Telephone: (918) 335-6200
E-mail: info@okwu.edu
Internet: www.okwu.edu
Founded 1910 as Colorado Springs Bible College, present name 2001
Private control
Academic year: August to July

Pres.: Dr EVERETT PIPER
Exec. Vice-Pres. and Academic Dean: Dr ROBERT M. MEYERS
Vice-Pres. for Academic Programme Devt: Dr BRETT ANDREWS
Vice-Pres. for Adult and Graduate Studies: Dr PAULITA BROOKER
Vice-Pres. for Devt: Dr RANDY THOMPSON
Vice-Pres. for Enrolment: JOHN MEANS
Vice-Pres. for Student Life: KYLE WHITE
Registrar: CINDY RIFFE
Library Dir: WENDELL THOMPSON

Library of 80,000 vols
Number of teachers: 70
Number of students: 960

DEANS

School of Arts and Sciences: GAIL RICHARDSON
School of Business: Prof. Dr BRETT ANDREWS
School of Education: Dr SHELDON BUXTON
School of Nursing: BECKY LE
School of Religion and Philosophy: Prof. Dr MARK WEETER

ORAL ROBERTS UNIVERSITY

7777 S Lewis Ave, Tulsa, OK 74171
Telephone: (918) 495-6161
E-mail: admissions@oru.edu
Internet: www.oru.edu

Founded 1965
Private control
Academic year: August to May
Pres.: Dr MARK RUTLAND
Provost: Dr RALPH FAGIN
Exec. Vice-Pres.: TIM PHILLEY
Exec. Vice-Pres. and Chief Financial Officer: MICHELLE FINLEY
Vice-Pres. and Gen. Counsel: TERRY KOLLMORGEN
Vice-Pres. for Academic Affairs: Dr DEBBIE SOWELL
Vice-Pres. for Enrolment Management: Dr NANCY BRAINARD
Vice-Pres. for Sponsored Programmes and Admin. Affairs: KELLY BAILEY
Registrar: DAVID FULMER
Dean for Learning Resources: Dr WILLIAM JERNIGAN

Library: 1m. vols
Number of teachers: 275
Number of students: 3,260

DEANS

College of Arts and Cultural Sciences: Dr WENDY SHIRK
College of Business: Dr STEVE GREENE
College of Education: Dr KIM BOYD
College of Nursing: Dr KENDA JEZEK
College of Science and Engineering: Dr DOMINIC HALSMER
College of Theology and Ministry: Dr THOMSON MATHEW

PHILLIPS THEOLOGICAL SEMINARY

901 N Mingo Rd, Tulsa, OK 74116
Telephone: (918) 610-8303
Internet: www.ptstulsa.edu

Founded 1906 as College of the Bible, present name 1995
Private control
Pres.: GARY PELUSO-VERDEND
Vice-Pres. for Academic Affairs and Dean: Dr DON A. PITTMAN
Vice-Pres. for Admin.: LORA CONGER
Registrar: TONI WINE IMBLER
Library Dir: SANDY SHAPOVAL

Library of 90,000 vols, 80,000 monographs, 750 journals
Number of teachers: 15
Number of students: 200

ROGERS STATE UNIVERSITY

1701 W Will Rogers Blvd, Claremore, OK 74017

Telephone: (918) 343-7777
Internet: www.rsu.edu

Founded 1909 as Eastern Univ. Preparatory School, present name 1999

State control

Campuses at Bartlesville and Pryor

Pres.: Dr LARRY RICE
Provost: BILL R. BEIERSCHMITT
Exec. Vice-Pres. for Admin. and Finance: THOMAS VOLTURO
Vice-Pres. for Academic Affairs: Dr RICHARD A. BECK
Vice-Pres. for Student Affairs: Dr TOBIE TITSWORTH
Dir for Library: ALAN LAWLESS

Library of 76,000 vols, 46,000 ebooks, 40,000 ejournals, 225 periodical subscriptions, 1,200 DVDs, 1,200 CDs
Number of students: 4,300

Publication: *Cooweescoowee* (1 a year)

DEANS

School of Business and Technology: Prof. Dr BRUCE GARRISON
School of Liberal Arts: Dr FRANK ELWELL
School of Mathematics, Science and Health Sciences: Prof. Dr KEITH W. MARTIN

SAINT GREGORY'S UNIVERSITY

1900 W MacArthur St, Shawnee, OK 74804

Telephone: (405) 878-5100
E-mail: info@stgregorys.edu
Internet: www.stgregorys.edu

Founded 1875
Private control
Academic year: August to June
Divs of business, humanities, natural science, social science, theology

Chancellor: Rt Rev. LAWRENCE STASYSZEN
Pres.: D. GREGORY MAIN
Provost: Dr RON FAULK
Exec. Vice-Pres.: TERRY McCULLAR
Assoc. Vice-Pres. for Enrolment: RONALD G. BROWN
Dean for Students: JOSHUA CLARY
Registrar and Assoc. Dean for Academic Services: KAY K. STITH
Library Dir: ANITA M. SEMTNER
Number of students: 740

DEANS

College for Working Adults: Dr JEAN THORNBRUGH
College of Arts and Sciences: DANY DOUGHAN

SOUTHEASTERN OKLAHOMA STATE UNIVERSITY

1405 N Fourth St, Durant, OK 74701

Telephone: (580) 745-2000
Internet: www.se.edu

Founded 1909 as Southeastern State Normal School, current name adopted 1974
State control
Academic year: August to May (and summer session)

Pres.: Dr LARRY MINKS
Vice-Pres. for Academic Affairs, Educational Outreach and Project Devt: Dr DOUGLAS N. McMILLAN
Vice-Pres. for Student Affairs: SHARON ROBINSON
Dean for Enrolment Management: ELIZABETH McCRAW
Registrar: KRISTIE LUKE
Library Dir: Dr SHARON MORRISON

Library of 191,240 vols, 513,852 microforms, 981 current periodicals, 231,527 govt documents, 14,381 Oklahoma documents, 9,400 ebooks
Number of students: 4,100

DEANS

John Massey School of Business: Dr WALTER GASTER
School of Arts and Sciences: Dr LUCRETIA SCOUFOS
School of Education and Behavioral Sciences: Dr WILLIAM T. MAWER
School of Graduate and University Studies: Dr BRYON CLARK

SOUTHERN NAZARENE UNIVERSITY

6729 NW 39th Expressway, Bethany, OK 73008-2605

Telephone: (405) 789-6400
E-mail: admissions@snu.edu
Internet: www.snu.edu

Founded 1899
Private control
Academic year: August to June (2 summer sessions and 2 terms)

Pres.: Dr LOREN P. GRESHAM
Provost: Dr MARY JONES
Vice-Pres. for Business and Financial Affairs: Dr DONNA NANCE
Vice-Pres. for Enrolment Management: Dr MIKE REDWINE
Vice-Pres. for Student Devt: SCOTT STRAWN
Vice-Pres. for Univ. Advancement and Church Relations: Dr TERRY N. TOLER
Dir for Admissions: Dr LINDA CANTWELL
Registrar: CHARLES S. CHITWOOD
Library Dir: Dr ARLITA HARRIS

Library of 105,000 vols, 13,000 periodicals, 339,000 microform items
Number of teachers: 120
Number of students: 2,100

DEANS

College of Business, Education and Kinesiology: Dr MARY JONES (acting)
College of Humanities: Dr MELANY KYZER
College of Natural, Social and Health Sciences: Dr DENNIS WILLIAMS
College of Professional and Graduate Studies: Dr W. DAVIS BERRYMAN
College of Teaching and Learning: Dr DENNIS WILLIAMS

SOUTHWESTERN CHRISTIAN UNIVERSITY

7210 NW 39th Expressway, Bethany, OK 73008

Telephone: (405) 789-7661
E-mail: admissions@swcu.edu
Internet: www.swcu.edu

Founded 1946 as Southwestern Bible College, current name adopted 2001
Private control

Pres.: Dr ED HUCKEBY
Provost and Vice-Pres. for Academic Affairs: Dr REGGIES WENYIKA
Vice-Pres. for Institutional Advancement: JON R. CHASTEEN
Vice-Pres. for Student Affairs and Dean for Students: DAVID CHISSOE
Vice-Pres. for Student Devt: JEFF KEENEY
Dir for Admissions and Enrolment Management: CHAD PUGH
Registrar: JEAN PERDUE
Library Dir: MARILYN A. HUDSON

Library of 25,000 vols
Number of teachers: 25
Number of students: 150

DEANS

School of Adult and Graduate Studies: Dr TERRY TRAMEL

School of Arts and Sciences: Dr DONNA McCOY
School of Professional Studies: ADRIAN HINKLE

SOUTHWESTERN OKLAHOMA STATE UNIVERSITY

100 Campus Dr., Weatherford, OK 73096

Telephone: (580) 774-3782
E-mail: admissions@swosu.edu
Internet: www.swosu.edu

Founded 1901 as Southwestern Normal School, current name adopted 1974
public control
Academic year: July to June

Pres.: Dr RANDY BEUTLER
Exec. Vice-Pres.: TOM FAGAN
Vice-Pres. for Academic Affairs and Provost: Dr JAMES SOUTH
Vice-Pres. for Student Affairs: Dr CINDY FOUST
Dean for Students and Dir for Student Activities: CINDY DOUGHERTY
Registrar: BOB KLAASSEN
Dir for Libraries: JASON DUPREE

Library of 242,406 vols
Number of teachers: 210
Number of students: 4,571 (f.t.e.)

DEANS

College of Arts and Sciences: Dr PETER GRANT
College of Pharmacy: Dr DENNIS THOMPSON
College of Professional and Graduate Studies: Dr KEN ROSE

UNIVERSITY OF CENTRAL OKLAHOMA

100 N University Dr., Edmond, OK 73034

Telephone: (405) 974-2000
Internet: www.uco.edu

Founded 1890, present name 1990
State control

Pres.: Dr DON BETZ
Provost and Vice-Pres. for Academic Affairs: Dr WILLIAM J. RADKE
Exec. Vice-Pres. for Admin.: STEVE KREIDLER
Vice-Pres. for Devt: ANNE HOLZBERLEIN
Vice-Pres. for Enrolment Management: Dr MYRON L. POPE
Vice-Pres. for Student Affairs: Dr KATHRYN GAGE
Exec. Dir for Univ. Library: Dr BONNIE McNEELY

Library of 706,000 vols
Number of teachers: 450 (full-time)
Number of students: 17,000

DEANS

College of Business Administration: Dr MICKEY HEPNER (acting)
College of Education and Professional Studies: Dr JAMES MACHELL
College of Fine Arts and Design: Dr JOHN CLINTON
College of Liberal Arts: Dr PAMELA WASHINGTON
College of Mathematics and Science: Dr JOHN BARTHELL
Dr Joe C. Jackson College of Graduate Studies: Dr RICHARD BERNARD

UNIVERSITY OF OKLAHOMA

660 Parrington Oval, Norman, OK 73019-0390

Telephone: (405) 325-0311
E-mail: publicaffairs@ou.edu
Internet: www.ou.edu

Founded 1890
State control

Academic year: August to May (summer session June and July)

Campuses at Norman, Oklahoma City and Tulsa in Oklahoma

Pres.: DAVID L. BOREN

Sr Vice-Pres. and Provost: Dr NANCY L. MERGLER

Sr Vice-Pres. and Provost: DEWAYNE ANDREWS

Exec. Vice-Pres. and Vice-Pres. for Admin. and Finance: NICHOLAS S. HATHAWAY

Vice-Pres.: ANIL GOLLAHALLI

Vice-Pres. for Enrolment and Student Financial Services and Registrar: MATTHEW HAMILTON

Vice-Pres. for Information Technology and Chief Information Officer: LORETTA EARLY

Vice-Pres. for Research: Dr KELVIN DROEGEMEIER

Vice-Pres. for Student Affairs and Dean for Students: CLARKE STROUD

Vice-Pres. for Univ. Devt: TRIPP HALL (acting)

Vice-Pres. for Univ. Governance: Dr CHRIS A. PURCELL

Dean for Univ. Libraries: SUL H. LEE

Library: see under Libraries and Archives

Number of teachers: 1,700 (1,430 full-time, 270 part-time)

Number of students: 30,600

Publications: *American Indian Law Review* (2 a year), *Genre: Forms of Discourse and Culture* (4 a year), *Oklahoma Law Review* (4 a year), *Papers on Anthropology* (2 a year), *World Literature Today* (4 a year)

DEANS

College of Architecture: Dr CHARLES GRAHAM

College of Arts and Sciences: Dr PAUL B. BELL

College of Atmospheric and Geographic Sciences: Dr BERRIEN MOORE

College of Engineering: THOMAS L. LANDERS

College of Law: JOSEPH HARROZ

College of Liberal Studies: JAMES P. PAPPAS

Gaylord College of Journalism and Mass Communication: Prof. JOE FOOTE

Graduate College: Dr T. H. LEE WILLIAMS

Jeannine Rainbolt College of Education: Dr GREGG A. GARN

Joe C. and Carole Kerr McClendon Honors College: Dr DAVID RAY

Mewbourne College of Earth and Energy: Dr LARRY GRILLOT

Michael F. Price College of Business: Dr KENNETH R. EVANS

Tulsa Graduate College: Dr WILLIAMS RAY

University College: Dr DOUGLAS GAFFIN

Weitzenhoffer Family College of Fine Arts: RICHARD C TAYLOR.

CAMPUSES

University of Oklahoma Health Sciences Center

POB 26901, Oklahoma City, OK 73126-0901

1000 Stanton L. Young Blvd, Oklahoma City, OK 73117-1208

Telephone: (405) 271-4000

E-mail: student-affairs@ouhsc.edu

Internet: www.ouhsc.edu

Founded 1900

Academic year: June to May

Sr Vice-Pres. and Provost: M. DEWAYNE ANDREWS

Vice-Provost for Academic Affairs and Faculty Devt: Dr VALERIE N. WILLIAMS

Vice-Pres. for Admin. and Finance: KENNETH D. ROWE

Vice-Pres. for Research: Dr JOHN J. IANDOLO

Number of teachers: 1,320 (1,055 full-time, 265 part-time)

Number of students: 4,230 (f.t.e.)

DEANS

College of Allied Health: KEVIN RUDEEN

College of Dentistry: STEPHEN K. YOUNG

College of Medicine: DEWAYNE ANDREWS

College of Nursing: Dr LAZELLE BENEFIELD

College of Pharmacy: Dr JOLAINE REIERSON DRAUGALIS

College of Public Health: GARY RASKOB

Graduate College: JAMES J. TOMASEK

University of Oklahoma—Tulsa Schusterman Center

4502 E 41st St, Tulsa, OK 74135-2515

Telephone: (918) 660-3000

Internet: www.ou.edu/tulsa

Pres.: GERARD P. CLANCY

Library Dir: STEWART M. BROWER

Library of 18,000 vols, 500 print journals

DEANS

Graduate College: WILLIAM O. RAY

School of Community Medicine: F. DANIEL DUFFY

UNIVERSITY OF SCIENCE AND ARTS OF OKLAHOMA

1727 W Alabama, Chickasha, OK 73018-5322

Telephone: (405) 224-3140

Internet: www.usao.edu

Founded 1908, present name 1973

State control

Academic year: May to April

Divs of arts and humanities, business and social sciences, education and speech language pathology, mathematics, science and physical education; teacher education programme

Pres.: JOHN FEAVER

Vice-Pres. for Academic Affairs: Dr JOHN D. MARBLE

Vice-Pres. for Business and Finance: MICHAEL COPONITI

Vice-Pres. for Enrolment Management and Student Affairs: MONICA TREVINO

Vice-Pres. for Information Services and Technology: J. LYNN BOYCE

Vice-Pres. for Univ. Advancement: Dr MICHAEL NEALEIGH

Dir for Admissions: MONICA TREVINO

Dean for Students: NANCY HUGHES

Registrar: JOE EVANS

Librarian: KELLY BROWN

Library of 97,000 vols

Number of teachers: 55

Number of students: 1,050

Publications: *Crosstimbers* (literary journal, 2 a year), *USAO Magazine* (1 a year)

UNIVERSITY OF TULSA

800 S Tucker Dr., Tulsa, OK 74104-9700

Telephone: (918) 631-2000

E-mail: admission@utulsa.edu

Internet: www.utulsa.edu

Founded 1894 as Henry Kendall College, reorganized and current name adopted 1920

Private control

Academic year: August to May

Pres.: Dr STEADMAN UPHAM

Provost and Vice-Pres. for Academic Affairs: Dr ROGER N. BLAIS

Exec. Vice-Pres.: KEVAN C. BUCK

Vice-Pres. for Enrolment and Student Services: EARL JOHNSON

Vice-Pres. for Public Affairs and Research: SUSAN NEAL

Dean for Students: YOLANDA D. TAYLOR

Registrar: GINNA LANGSTON

Dean for Libraries: ADRIAN W. ALEXANDER

Library: 3m. vols (incl. 29,000 ejournals, 2,000 print journals, 30,000 ebooks), 128,000 rare books, 3,500 linear ft of literary and historical MSS

Number of teachers: 334

Number of students: 4,597

Publications: *James Joyce Quarterly*, *Nimrod International Journal*, *Tulsa Studies in Women's Literature*

DEANS

College of Engineering and Natural Sciences: JAMES SOREM

College of Law: JANET LEVIT

Collins College of Business: GALE SULLENBERGER

Graduate School: Dr JANET HAGGERTY

Henry Kendall College of Arts and Sciences: Dr KALPANA MISRA

PROFESSORS

ADAMS, C. W., Law

ALLISON, G. D., Law

ANDERSON, C. L., Languages

ARNOLD, M. T., Law

ASHENAYI, K., Electrical Engineering

BAILEY, G. A., Anthropology

BAJAJ, A., Accounting

BAKER, W. L., Art

BASSO, M. R., Psychology

BENEDIKTSON, D. T., Languages

BERRY, J. O., Psychology

BLAIR, D. M., Law

BRADLEY, J. C., History

BROWN, C. R., Biological Science

BUCHHEIM, M. A., Biological Science

BUCHOLTZ, B. K., Law

BURGESS, R. C., Finance

BUTKIN, R. A., Law

CARUSO, J. F., Athletic Training

CHASE, S. E., Sociology

CHIANG, W. C., Finance

CHRISTOPHER, R. L., Law

COBURN, T. C., Finance

COLLIER, G. E., Biological Science

COLLINS, J. M., Finance

CONSTANDA, C., Mathematics

CRAVENS, K. S., Accounting

DIAZ, J. C., Computer Science

DOTY, D. R., Mathematics

DUGGER, W. M., Economics

ENGLE, L. D., English

ENTZEROTH, L. S., Law

FULLER, R. J., English

GAMBLE, R. F., Computer Science

HALE, J. C., Computer Science

HENRY, D. O., Anthropology

HENSHAW, J. M., Mechanical Engineering

HILL, P. S. M., Biological Science

HITTINGER, F. R., Philosophy and Religion

HORNE, T. A., Political Science

HOWARD, R. E., Chemistry

HOWLAND, J. A., Philosophy and Religion

JENSEN, J. K., Communication

KANE, G. R., Electrical Engineering

KELKAR, B. G., Petroleum Engineering

KESTNER, J. A., English

LAIRD, H. A., English

LATHAM, S. P., English

LEONARD, L. N. K., Accounting

LEVETIN AVERY, E., Biological Science

LIMAS, V. J., Law

LINDSTROM, L. C., Anthropology

LOPRESTI, P. G., Electrical Engineering

MANNING, F. S., Chemical Engineering

MANSFIELD, M. E., Law

MCLAURY, B. S., Mechanical Engineering

MICHAEL, P. J., Geosciences

MILLER, G. P., Physics

MISKA, S. Z., Petroleum Engineering

MOHAN, R. S., Mechanical Engineering

MOSHER, M. A., Political Science

NEWMAN, E., Psychology

O'NEIL, K. A., Mathematics

PARKER, J. C., Law

PIETY, T. R., Law
POTTER, W. T., Chemistry
POWELL, J. S., Music
PRICE, G. L., Chemical Engineering
PRICE, W. R., Music
PURSER, G. H., Chemistry
REDNER, R. A., Mathematics
REED, T. L., Music
REEDER, R. L., Biological Science
REYNOLDS, A. C., Petroleum Engineering
RIPPLE, R. D., Finance
RIVERS, J. L., Music
ROYSTER, J. V., Law
RUSSELL, R. A., Finance
SAMIEE, S., Management and Marketing
SARICA, C., Petroleum Engineering
SCHOENEFELD, D. A., Computer Science
SEN, S., Computer Science
SETTLE, C. E., Economics
SHENOI, S., Computer Science
SHIRAZI, S. A., Mechanical Engineering
SHOHAM, O., Petroleum Engineering
SINGH, S., Electrical Engineering
SPOO, R. E., Law
STEIB, S., Economics
STROMBERG, P. G., Anthropology
SUBLETTE, K. L., Chemical Engineering
TAI, H. M., Electrical Engineering
TAKACH, N. E., Chemistry
TEETERS, D. C., Chemistry
TIPTON, S. M., Mechanical Engineering
TOMLINS, C. B., Art
URBAN, T. L., Finance
WAINWRIGHT, R. L., Computer Science
WEBER, R. F., Law
WELLS, H., Biological Science
WHALEN, M. E., Anthropology
WILSON, L. C., Theatre
WISECARVER, K. D., Chemical Engineering
WOFFORD, L. E., Bovaird Chair
WOOD, A. G., History
YASSER, R. L., Law
YEVTUSHENKO, Y. A., English
ZEDALIS, R. J., Law

OREGON

ART INSTITUTE OF PORTLAND

1122 NW Davis St, Portland, OR 97209-2911

Telephone: (503) 228-6528
E-mail: aipdadm@aii.edu
Internet: www.artinstitutes.edu

Founded 1963, fmrly Bassist College
Private control
Academic year: October to September

Liberal education and professional education

Pres.: TIMOTHY MOSCATO
Dean for Student Affairs: JASON CLARY
Dir for Admin.: ANGELA BOSTOCK
Dir for Learning Resources: NANCY THURSTON
Library Dir: TRICIA JUETTEMEYER
Registrar: ROBERT TUFTS

Number of teachers: 35 full-time, 60 adjunct per quarter
Number of students: 1,540

CONCORDIA UNIVERSITY

2811 NE Holman St, Portland, OR 97211

Telephone: (503) 288-9371
E-mail: registrar@cu-portland.edu
Internet: www.cu-portland.edu

Founded 1905 as a 4-year acad., present name and status 1995
Private control
Academic year: August to May

Pres.: Dr CHARLES E. SCHLIMPERT
Provost and Chief Operating Officer: Dr MARK WAHLERS
Dean for Admission: BOBI SWAN
Dean for Students: Dr STEVE DEKLOTZ
Dir of Enrolment Services: JIM CULLEN

Registrar: PAUL RÉVER
Librarian: BRENT MAI

Number of teachers: 60
Number of students: 2,500

DEANS

College of Education: Dr JOSEPH MANNION
College of Health and Human Services: Dr MARK D. JAGER
College of Theology, Arts and Sciences: Dr CHARLES J. KUNERT
School of Law: Dr CATHY R. SILAK

CORBAN UNIVERSITY

5000 Deer Park Dr., SE, Salem, OR 97317-9392

Telephone: (503) 581-8600
E-mail: president@corban.edu
Internet: www.corban.edu

Founded 1935 as Bible Institute, Western Baptist College 1946, present name 2005
Private control
Academic year: August to April

Pres.: Dr RENO R. HOFF
Provost and Exec. Vice-Pres.: MATT LUCAS
Vice-Pres. for Advancement: MICHAEL BATES
Vice-Pres. for Business: KEVIN BRUBAKER
Vice-Pres. for Marketing: J. STEVEN HUNT
Vice-Pres. for Student Life: NANCY HEDBERG
Vice-Pres. for Enrolment Management: MARTIN ZIESEMER
Dean of Students: JANINE ALLEN
Registrar: CHRIS VETTER

Library of 115,000 vols, 600 periodicals
Number of teachers: 60
Number of students: 1,175

DEANS

Education Programme: Dr JANINE ALLEN
Human Performance Programme: Dr DAVID B. BALE
School of Ministry: Dr GREG TRULL

EASTERN OREGON UNIVERSITY

One Univ. Blvd, La Grande, OR 97850-2807

Telephone: (541) 962-3672
E-mail: admissions@eou.edu
Internet: www.eou.edu

Founded 1929
Academic year: July to June

Pres.: JAY KENTON
Provost and Vice-Pres. for Academic Affairs: STEVE ADKISON
Vice-Pres. for Finance and Admin.: LON WHITAKER
Vice-Pres. for Student Affairs: Dr CAMILLE CONSOLVO
Dir for Libraries: KAREN CLAY

Library of 153,000 vols, 1,300 periodicals
Number of teachers: 120 full-time, 25 part-time
Number of students: 4,135

Publication: Eastern Oregon Science Journal

DEANS

College of Arts and Sciences: SARAH WITTE (acting)
College of Business: DAN MIELKE
College of Education: DAN MIELKE

GEORGE FOX UNIVERSITY

414 N Meridian St, Newberg, OR 97132-2697

Telephone: (503) 538-8383
E-mail: president@georgefox.edu
Internet: www.georgefox.edu

Founded 1891 as Pacific College, current name 1996
Private control
Academic year: September to April

Pres.: Dr ROBIN E. BAKER

Provost: LINDA SAMEK
Exec. Vice-Pres. for Enrolment and Marketing: ROB WESTERVELT
Vice-Pres. for Advancement Strategy and Donor Relations: BRIAN GARDNER
Vice-Pres. for Student Life: BRAD LAU
Univ. Librarian: MERRILL JOHNSON

Library of 200,000 vols
Number of teachers: 220
Number of students: 3,712

Publication: George Fox Journal (3 a year)

DEANS

College of Arts and Sciences: LAURA HARTLEY
College of Behavioural and Health Sciences: JIM FOSTER
College of Business: DIRK BARRAM
College of Education: SCOT HEADLEY
College of Engineering: BOB HARDER
George Fox Evangelical Seminary and College of Christian Studies: CHUCK CONNIRY

LEWIS AND CLARK COLLEGE

0615 SW Palatine Hill Rd, Portland, OR 97219

Telephone: (503) 768-7000
E-mail: wwwadmin@lclark.edu
Internet: www.lclark.edu

Founded 1867 as Albany Collegiate Institute, present status 1966
Private control

Pres.: BARRY GLASSNER
Provost and Vice-Pres.: JANE MONNIG ATKINSON
Vice-Pres., Sec. and Gen. Counsel: DAVID ELLIS
Vice-Pres. for Business and Finance: CARL B. VANCE
Vice-Pres. for Institutional Advancement: HAL ABRAMS
Dean for Students: ANNA GONZALEZ
Dean for Admissions: LISA MEYER
Registrar: JUDY C. FINCH
Dir of Library: MARK DAHL

Library of 477,010 vols
Number of teachers: 190
Number of students: 3,500

Publication: Journal

DEANS

College of Arts and Sciences: TUAJUANDA JORDAN
Graduate School of Education and Counseling: SCOTT FLETCHER
Law School: ROBERT KLONOFF

MARYLHURST UNIVERSITY

POB 261, 17600 Pacific Highway, Marylhurst, OR 97036-0261

Telephone: (503) 636-8141
E-mail: admissions@marylhurst.edu
Internet: www.marylhurst.edu

Founded 1893 as St. Mary's Acad. and College, current name adopted 1998
Private control

Pres.: Dr JUDITH JOHANSEN
Provost: Dr DAVID PLOTKIN
Exec. Vice-Pres. and Chief Financial Officer: MICHAEL LAMMERS
Vice-Pres. for Enrolment Management: BETH WOODWARD
Vice-Pres. for Human Resources and Org. Excellence: CELINA RATLIFF
Vice-Pres. for Information Technology: ETHAN BENATAN
Vice-Pres. for Univ. Advancement: LYNN MAWE

Library of 100,000 vols, 2,500 video cassettes, 1,700 CDs, 200 print periodical subscriptions

Number of teachers: 510 (55 full-time, 455 part-time)
Number of students: 1,920 (985 graduate, 935 undergraduate)

MULTNOMAH UNIVERSITY

8435 NE Glisan St, Portland, OR 97220
Telephone: (503) 255-0332
E-mail: admiss@multnomah.edu
Internet: www.multnomah.edu
Founded 1936 as Multnomah School of the Bible, current name adopted 2008
Private control
Academic year: August to May
Multnomah Bible College and Multnomah Biblical Seminary
Pres.: Dr DANIEL R. LOCKWOOD
Academic Dean and Vice-Pres.: Dr WAYNE STRICKLAND
Vice-Pres. and Dir of Information Systems: Dr JOE WONG
Dean of Student Services: MATTHEW RYGG
Registrar: Prof. AMY STEPHENS
Dir of Library: Dr PHILIP JOHNSON
Library of 500,000 vols
Number of teachers: 105 (incl. full-time and part-time)
Number of students: 930

NEW HOPE CHRISTIAN COLLEGE

2155 Bailey Hill Rd, Eugene, OR 97405
Telephone: (541) 485-1780
E-mail: admissions@newhope.edu
Internet: www.newhope.edu
Founded 1925
Private control
Academic year: August to May (3 semesters)
Works towards devt of Christian leaders with a focus on theology, ministry skills and character
Chancellor and Pres.: Dr WAYNE CORDEIRO
Vice-Pres.: GUY HIGASHI
Academic Dean: Dr LARRY R. BURKE
Dir for Student Ministry: LONNY R. BURKE
Registrar: Dr JAMES WICK
Librarian: JANET L. KELLEY
Number of teachers: 15
Number of students: 200

NORTHWEST CHRISTIAN UNIVERSITY

828 E 11th Ave, Eugene, OR 97401
Telephone: (541) 343-1641
Internet: www.nwcu.edu
Founded 1895 as Eugene Divinity School, current name adopted 2008
Academic year: September to June
Pres.: Dr JOSEPH WOMACK
Vice-Pres. for Academic Affairs: Prof. Dr DENNIS LINDSAY
Vice-Pres. for Advancement: GREG STRAUSBAUGH
Vice-Pres. for Enrolment and Student Devt: MICHAEL FULLER
Vice-Pres. for Finance and Admin.: LISA CASTLEBURY
Library Dir: STEVE SILVER
Registrar: AARON PRUITT
Library of 74,000 vols
Number of teachers: 30
Number of students: 625

OREGON HEALTH & SCIENCE UNIVERSITY

3181 SW Sam Jackson Park Rd, Portland, OR 97239-3098
Telephone: (503) 494-8311
Internet: www.ohsu.edu

Founded 1887 as Univ. of Oregon Dept of Medicine, present name 1981
Pres.: Dr PETER O. KOHLER
Provost: Dr JEANETTE MLADENOVIĆ
Vice-Provost for Academic and Student Affairs: ROBERT L. VIEIRA
Chief Financial Officer: LAWRENCE J. FURNSTAHL
Exec. Vice-Pres.: STEVEN D. STADUM
Library of 90,809 vols, 16,267 ebooks, 2,008 journals, 12,634 ejournals with electronic access
Number of students: 3,400

DEANS

College of Pharmacy: MARK ZABRISKIE
School of Dentistry: Dr GARY CHIODO
School of Medicine: Dr MARK A. RICHARDSON
School of Nursing: MICHAEL BLEICH

OREGON STATE UNIVERSITY

Corvallis, OR 97331
Telephone: (541) 737-1000
E-mail: osuadmit@oregonstate.edu
Internet: oregonstate.edu
Founded 1868 as Corvallis College
State control
Academic year: September to June
Pres.: Dr EDWARD J. RAY
Provost and Exec. Vice-Pres.: SABAH U. RANDHAWA
Vice-Provost for Academic Affairs: LARRY ROPER
Vice-Provost for Student Affairs: REBECCA L. WARNER
Vice-Pres. for Finance and Admin.: MARK E. McCAMBRIDGE
Vice-Pres. for Research: RICK SPINRAD
Vice-Pres. for Univ. Relations and Marketing: STEVE CLARK
Registrar: BARBARA S. BALZ
Univ. Librarian: FAYE CHADWELL
Library: 2m. vols, 1,905,093 microfilms
Number of teachers: 3,480
Number of students: 25,000
Publications: *Beaver* (1 a year), *Oregon Agricultural Progress* (3 a year), *Oregon Stater* (3 a year), *Prism* (literary magazine, 1 a year), *Research OSU* (1 a year)

DEANS

College of Agricultural Sciences: SONNY RAMASWAMY
College of Business: Dr ILLENE K. KLEINSORGE
College of Education: LARRY FLICK
College of Engineering: SCOTT ASHFORD
College of Forestry: HAL SALWASSER
College of Liberal Arts: LARRY RODGERS
College of Oceanic and Atmospheric Sciences: Prof. Dr MARK R. ABBOTT
College of Pharmacy: Prof. Dr MARK ZABRISKIE
College of Public Health and Human Sciences: TAMMY M. BRAY
College of Science: Prof. SHERMAN H. BLOOMER
College of Veterinary Medicine: CYRIL R. CLARKE
Graduate School: BRENDA McCOMB
Univ. Honors College: DAN ARP

PACIFIC NORTHWEST COLLEGE OF ART

1241 NW Johnson St, Portland, OR 97209
Telephone: (503) 226-4391
E-mail: admissions@pnca.edu
Internet: www.pnca.edu
Founded 1909
Private control
Academic year: September to May

Offers Bachelors and Masters in fine arts, applied craft and design, collaborative design and visual studies
Pres.: Dr THOMAS MANLEY
Vice-Pres. for Academic Affairs: GREG WARE
Vice-Pres. for Finance and Admin.: NANCY BARROWS
Dir for Advancement: SUZANNE HASHIM
Registrar: JENNIFER DeKALB
Library Dir: RACHEL MENDEZ
Number of teachers: 100 (30 full-time, 70 part-time)
Number of students: 620

PACIFIC UNIVERSITY

1411 SW Morrison St, Suite 201, Portland, OR 97205
Telephone: (503) 352-6151
Internet: www.pacificu.edu
Founded 1849
Pres.: Dr LESLEY M. HALLICK
Provost and Vice-Pres. for Academic Affairs: Dr JOHN MILLER
Vice-Pres. for Finance and Admin.: MIKE MALLERY
Vice-Pres. for Student Affairs and Dean of Students: EVA C. KREBS
Co-Vice-Pres. for Univ. Advancement: JAN STRICKLIN
Co-Vice-Pres. for Univ. Advancement: TAMMY SPENCER
Assoc. Dir for Admissions: TANIA M. HAND
Library Management Team Coordinator: ALEX TOTH
Library of 100,000 vols, 2,500 newspapers, magazines and journals and 4,000 reference resources
Number of teachers: 80 (full-time)
Number of students: 1,750 (full-time)
Publication: *Pacific Magazine*

DEANS

College of Arts and Sciences: Dr JOHN HAYES
College of Education: Dr MARK E. ANKENY
College of Health Professions: Dr ANN BARR
College of Optometry: Dr JENNIFER SMYTHE
School of Pharmacy: Dr SUSAN STEIN
School of Professional Psychology: Dr JAMES LANE

PORTLAND STATE UNIVERSITY

POB 751, Portland, OR 97207-0751
1825 SW Broadway, Portland, OR 97201
Telephone: (503) 725-3000
E-mail: admissions@pdx.edu
Internet: www.pdx.edu
Founded 1946
Academic year: September to June
Pres.: Prof. MICHAEL REARDON
Provost and Vice-Pres. for Academic Affairs: ROY KOCH
Vice-Provost and Dean of Extended Studies: MICHAEL BURTON
Vice-Provost for Graduate Studies and Research: WILLIAM FEYERHERM
Vice-Provost for Student Affairs: DAN FORTMILLER
Vice-Pres. for Enrolment Management and Student Affairs: JACKIE BALZE
Vice-Pres. for Finance and Admin.: LINDSAY DESROCHERS
Assoc. Vice-Pres. for Information Technology: MARK GREGORY
Dean for Student Life: MICHELE TOPPE
Dir for Financial Aid: PHILLIP RODGERS
Dir for Institutional Research and Planning: KATHI KETCHESON
Univ. Dir for Library: LYNN K. CHMELIR
Library of 1,805,336 vols
Number of teachers: 1,260
Number of students: 29,700

Publication: *Portland State Magazine*

DEANS

College of Liberal Arts and Sciences: SUSAN
BEATTY
College of Urban and Public Affairs: LAWR-
ENCE WALLACK
Graduate School of Education: Dr RANDY
HITZ
Maseeh College of Engineering and Com-
puter Science: Dr RENJENG SU
School of Business Administration: Dr SCOTT
DAWSON
School of Extended Studies: MICHAEL BURTON
School of Fine and Performing Arts: BARBARA
SESTAK
School of Social Work: Prof. Dr NANCY
KOROLOFF

REED COLLEGE

3203 SE Woodstock Blvd, Portland, OR
97202-8199
Telephone: (503) 771-1112
Internet: www.reed.edu
Founded 1908
Private control
Academic year: August to May
Pres.: COLIN S. DIVER
Vice-Pres. and Treas.: EDWIN O. MCFARLANE
Vice-Pres. and Dean of Student Services:
MICHAEL BRODY
Vice-Pres. for College Relations: HUGH POR-
TER
Registrar: NORA MCLAUGHLIN
Dean of Admissions: KEITH TODD
Dean for the Faculty: PATRICK G. MCDOUGAL
(acting)
Dean for Institutional Diversity: CRYSTAL
ANN WILLIAMS
Dir for Devt: JAN KURTZ
Dir for Institutional Research: MICHAEL
TAMADA
Librarian: DENA HUTTO
Library of 490,000 vols, 10,000 journals
Number of teachers: 135
Number of students: 1,400
Publication: *Reed Magazine* (4 a year)

SOUTHERN OREGON UNIVERSITY

1250 Siskiyou Blvd, Ashland, OR 97520
Telephone: (541) 552-7672
Internet: www.sou.edu
Founded 1926
State control
Academic year: September to June
3 Campuses: Ashland and the Rogue Valley
campus, Ashland campus and Medford cam-
pus
Pres.: MARY CULLINAN
Provost and Vice-Pres. for Academic Affairs:
JAMES M. KLEIN
Registrar: MATT STILLMAN
Dean for Library: PAUL ADALIAN
Library of 335,371 vols, 302,340 govt docu-
ments, 803,548, microfilms, 3,571 period-
ical subscriptions, 10,492 audiovisual
holdings, 43,829 ebooks
Number of teachers: 290
Number of students: 6,750

DEANS

College of Arts and Sciences: ALISSA ARP
School of Business: RAJ PARIKH
School of Education: GEOFF MILLS

UNIVERSITY OF OREGON

POB 3237 Eugene, OR 97403-0237
Telephone: (541) 346-1000
E-mail: pres@uoregon.edu
Internet: www.uoregon.edu

Founded 1872
State control
Academic year: September to June
Pres.: ROBERT M. BERDAHL
Sr Vice-Pres. and Provost: LORRAINE DAVIS
(acting)
Vice-Pres. for Academic Affairs: RUSSELL S.
TOMLIN
Vice-Pres. for Devt: MICHAEL ANDREASEN
Vice-Pres. for Finance and Admin.: FRANCES
DYKE
Vice-Pres. for Public and Govt Affairs:
MICHAEL REDDING
Vice-Pres. for Research and Innovation:
KIMBERLY ANDREWS ESPY
Vice-Pres. for Student Affairs: ROBIN HOLMES
Vice-Pres. for Univ. Relations: MICHAEL RED-
DING
Registrar: HERBERT R. CHERECK
Dean of Libraries: DEBORAH A. CARVER
Library: see under Libraries and Archives
Number of teachers: 1,170
Number of students: 24,400

Publications: *Bulletin of the Museum of Natural History*, *Comparative Literature*, *Governmental Research Bulletins*, *Imprint
Oregon*, *Northwest Review*, *Oregon Business Review* (4 a year), *Oregon Law Review*

DEANS

College of Arts and Sciences: Dr SCOTT
COLTRANE
College of Education: MICHAEL BULLIS
Graduate School: KIMBERLY ANDREWS ESPY
Lundquist College of Business: CORNELIS A.
DE KLUYVER
Robert D. Clark Honors College: DAVID A.
FRANK
School of Architecture and Allied Arts:
FRANCES BRONET
School of Journalism and Communication:
TIMOTHY GLEASON
School of Law: MICHAEL MOFFITT
School of Music and Dance: BRAD FOLEY

PROFESSORS

ACRES, A. J., Art History
AGUIRRE, C. A., History
AIKENS, C. M., Anthropology
ALBAUM, G. S., Business
ALBERTGALTIER, A., Romance Languages
ALLEY, H. M., Honours College
ALPERT, L. J., Fine Arts
ALTMANN, B., Romance Languages
ANDERSON, F. W., Mathematics
ANDERSON, M. C., Psychology
ANDERSON, S. C., German
ANDERSON-INMAN, L., Education Policy and
Management
AOKI, K., Law
ARIOLA, Z., Computer and Information Sci-
ence
ASH, A. D., Political Science
AXLINE, M. D., Law
AYRES, W. S., Anthropology
BALDWIN, D. A., Psychology
BALDWIN, J. H., Planning Public Policy Man-
agement
BAMBURY, J. E., Architecture
BARACCHI, C., Philsophy
BARKAN, A., Biology
BARNES, B. A., Mathematics
BARNHARD, R. J., Chemistry
BARR, S. A., Dance
BARTLEIN, P., Geography
BARTON, R. F., Theatre Arts
BAUGH, W. H., Political Science
BAUMGOLD, D. J., Political Science
BAYLESS, M. J., English
BELITZ, D., Physics
BENDER, S. W., Law
BENGSTON, M. C., Fine Arts
BENNETT, R. W., Music
BENZ, M. R., Education Policy and Manage-
ment

BERK, G. P., Political Science
BEST, R. J., Business
BEUDERT, M. C., Music
BIERSACK, A., Anthropology
BIRN, R. F., History
BIVINS, T. H., Journalism
BJERRE, C., Law
BLANDY, D. E., Arts and Administration
BLONIGEN, B. A., Economics
BOGEL, C. J., Art History
BOLTON, C. R., Recreation and Tourist Man-
agement
BONDS, A. B., Theatre Arts
BONINE, J. E., Law
BOREN, J. L., English
BOROVSKY, Z. P., German
BOSS, J. F., III, Music
BOTHUN, G. D., Physics
BOTVINNIK, B., Mathematics
BOUSH, D. M., Business
BOWDITCH, P. L., Classics
BOWERMAN, B. A., Biology
BOYNTON, S. L., Music
BRADSHAW, W. E., Biology
BRANCHAUD, B. P., Chemistry
BRAU, J. E., Physics
BRICK, H., History
BRICKER, D. D., Special Education
BRODIE, D. W., Law
BROKAW, C. J., History
BROWN, G. Z., Architecture
BROWN, S. T., East Asian Languages
BROWN, W. B., Business
BROX, R. M., Romance Languages
BULLIS, M. D., Education Policy and Man-
agement
BURRIS, V. L., Sociology
BUSTAMANTE, C. J., Chemistry
BYBEE, C. R., Journalism
BYRD, B. K., Labour Education Center
CALHOON, K. S., German
CALIN, F. G., Romance Languages
CAMPBELL, E. A., Music
CAPALDI, R. A., Biology
CARMICHAEL, H. J., Physics
CARNINE, D. W., Education Policy and Man-
agement
CARPENTER, G. M., Recreation and Tourism
Management
CARPENTER, K. L., Linguistics
CARROLL, G. C., Biology
CARTER, L. R., Sociology
CARTIER, C. L., Geography
CARTWRIGHT, V., Architecture
CASHMAN, K. V., Geological Sciences
CASTENHOLZ, R. W., Biology
CASTILLO, D., Romance Languages
CHALMERS, J. M., Business
CHANDLER, V. L., Biology
CHANEY, R. P., Anthropology
CHATFIELD, S. J., Dance
CHENG, N. YEN-WEN, Architecture
CINA, J., Chemistry
CLARK, R., Music
CLARK, S., English
COGAN, F. B., Honours College
COHEN, J. D., Physics
COHEN, S. E., Geography
COLEMAN, E. L., II, English
COLLIN, R. M., Law
COLLINS, P. F., Psychology
CONERY, J. S., Computer and Information
Science
CONLEY, D. T., Education Policy and Man-
agement
CORNER, D. B., Architecture
CRAIG, J. P., Dance
CROSSWHITE, J. R., English
CRUMB, D. R., Music
CRUZ, J., Romance Languages
CSONKA, P. L., Physics
CUNY, J., Computer and Information Science
DAHLQUIST, F. W., Chemistry
DANN, L. Y., Business
DARST, R. G., Political Science
DAVIE, W. E., Philosophy

DAVIES, P. H., Creative Writing
DAVIS, H., Architecture
DAVIS, R. L., Romance Languages
DAWSON, J. I., Political Science
DEGGE, R. M., Arts and Administration
DELANCEY, S. C., Linguistics
DELGUERCIO, D. G., Business
DENNIS, M., History
DESCUTNER, J. W., Dance
DESHPANDE, N. G., Physics
DEVRIES, P. J., Biology
DIAMOND, I., Political Science
DICKMAN, A. W., Biology
DIETHELM, J. K., Landscape Architecture
DISHION, T. J., Special Education
DOERKSEN, D. P., Music
DOERKSEN, P. F., Music
DOLEZAL, M.-L., Art History
DORSEY, R. J., Geological Science
DOUGLAS, S. A., Computer and Information Science
DOWD, C. R., Music
DOWNES, B. T., Planning Public Policy Management
DOXSEE, K. M., Chemistry
DREILING, M. C., Sociology
DUFEK, J. S., Exercise and Movement Sciences
DUFF, S. F., Architecture
DUGAW, D. M., English
DUNCAN, I. H., English
DURRANT, S., East Asian Languages
DYER, M. N., Mathematics
DYKE, T. R., Chemistry
EARL, J. W., English
EDSON, C. H., Education Policy and Management
EISEN, J. S., Biology
ELLIS, C. J., Economics
EMLET, R. B., Biology
ENGELKING, P. C., Chemistry
EPPLE, J. A., Romance Languages
EPPS, G., Law
EPSTEIN, M., East Asian Languages
ERLANDSON, J. M., Anthropology
ETTINGER, L. F., Arts and Administration
EVANS, G. W., Economics
EXTON, D., Chemistry
FAGOT, B. I., Psychology
FAIR, L. J., History
FANG, Y., Business
FARLEY, A. M., Computer and Information Science
FARWELL, M. R., English
FICKAS, S. F., Computer and Information Science
FIGLIO, D. N., Economics
FISHLEN, M. B., East Asian Languages
FLYNN, G. C., Chemistry
FORD, K. J., English
FORELL, C. A., Law
FOSTER, J. B., Sociology
FRACCHIA, J. G., Honours College
FRANK, D. A., Honours College
FRANKLIN, J. D., Journalism
FRAZIER, G. V., Business
FREINKEL, L. A., English
FREY, R. E., Physics
FREYD, J. J., Psychology
FRIESTAD, M. S., Business
FRISHKOFF, P., Business
FRY, G., International Studies
FUJII, N., East Asian Languages
FULLER, L. O., Sociology
GAGE, J. T., English
GALE, M. K., Planning Public Policy Management
GALL, M. D., Education Policy and Management
GARCIA-PABON, L., Romance Languages
GARY, S. N., Law
GASSAMA, I. J., Law
GAST, W. G., Architecture
GENASCI, D. B., Architecture
GEORGE, K. M., Anthropology
GEORGE, O., English

GERBER, T. P., Sociology
GERNON, H., Business
GERSTEN, R. M., Special Education
GILKEY, P. B., Mathematics
GILLAND, W. G., Architecture
GIRLING, C. L., Landscape Architecture
GIVON, T., Linguistics
GLADHART, A., Romance Languages
GLASER, S. R., Business
GLEASON-RICKER, M. M., Education Policy and Management
GLOVER, E., Special Education
GOBLE, A. E., History
GOLDMAN, M. S., Sociology
GOLDMAN, P., Education Policy and Management
GOLDRICH, D., Political Science
GOLDSCHMIDT, S. M., Education Policy and Management
GOLES, G. G., Geological Sciences
GOOD, R. H., III, Special Education
GOODMAN, B., History
GORDON-LICKEY, B., Psychology
GORDON-LICKEY, M., Psychology
GOULD, E., Romance Languages
GRAFF, R. J., Fine Arts
GRAY, J., Biology
GRAY, J. A., Economics
GREENE, F. D., Law
GREENE, R. A., Comparative Literature
GREENLAND, D. E., Geography
GREGORY, S., Physics
GRIFFITH, O. H., Chemistry
GROSENICK, J. K., Education Policy and Management
GRUDIN, R., English
GWARTNEY, P., Sociology
HACKMAN, R. M., Academic Affairs
HALEY, M. M., Chemistry
HANES, J. E., History
HARBAUGH, W. T., Economics
HARFORD, W. T., Business
HARRIS, L. J., Law
HARVEY, S. M., Anthropology
HASKETT, R. S., History
HATON, D. S., Music
HAUSHALTER, G. D., Business
HAWKINS, D. I., Business
HAWLEY, D. K., Chemistry
HAWN, A. W., Architecture
HAYDOCK, R., Physics
HAYNES, S. E., Economics
HECKER, S. F., Labour Education Center
HELPHAND, K. I., Landscape Architecture
HERRICK, D. R., Chemistry
HESSLER, J. M., History
HIBBARD, J., Planning Public Policy Management
HIBBARD, M. J., Planning Public Policy Management
HICKMAN, R. C., Fine Arts
HILDRETH, R. G., Law
HINTZMAN, D. L., Psychology
HO, S., Architecture
HODGES, S. D., Psychology
HOKANSON, K. E., Comparative Literature
HOLCOMB, J. M., Fine Arts
HOLLAND, M. J., Law
HOLLANDER, J. A., Sociology
HONGO, G. K., Creative Writing
HORNER, R. H., Center on Human Devt
HOSAGRAHAR, J., Architecture
HOUSWORTH, E. A., Mathematics
HOWARD, D. R., Business
HUDSON, B. S., Chemistry
HUHNDORF, S. M., English
HULSE, D. W., Landscape Architecture
HUMMER, T. R., Creative Writing
HUMPHREYS, E. D., Geological Sciences
HURWIT, J. M., Art History
HURWITZ, R., Music
HUTCHINSON, J., Chemistry
HYMAN, R., Psychology
IMAMURA, J. N., Physics
ISENBERG, J., Mathematics
JACOBS, D., Political Science

JACOBSON, J. L., Law
JACOBSON-TEPFER, E., Art History
JAEGER, M. K., Classics
JEWETT, W. J., Architecture
JOHNSON, B. R., Landscape Architecture
JOHNSON, D. C., Chemistry
JOHNSON, L. B., Fine Arts
JOHNSON, L. T., Architecture
JOHNSON, M. L., Philosophy
JOHNSTON, A. D., Geological Sciences
JONES, B. J. K., Arts and Administration
JONES, S. I., Landscape Architecture
KAHLE, L. R., Business
KAMEENUI, E. J., Education Policy and Management
KANAGY, R., East Asian Languages
KANTOR, W. M., Mathematics
KARLYN, K., English
KATAOKA, H. C., East Asian Languages
KAYS, M. A., Geological Sciences
KEANA, J. F. W., Chemistry
KELLETT, R. W., Architecture
KELLMAN, M. E., Chemistry
KELSKY, K. L., Anthropology
KEMPNER, K. M., Education Policy and Management
KESSLER, L. J., Journalism
KEVAN, S. D., Physics
KEYES, P. A., Architecture
KIMBALL, R. A., History
KIMBLE, D. P., Psychology
KIMMEL, C. B., Biology
KING, R. D., Business
KINTZ, L. C., English
KIRKPATRICK, L. C., Law
KLESHCHEV, A., Mathematics
KLOPPENBERG, L. A., Law
KLUG, G. A., Exercise and Movement Sciences
KOCH, R. M., Mathematics
KOHL, S. W., East Asian Languages
KOKIS, G., Fine Arts
KOLPIN, V. W., Economics
KOREISHA, S. G., Business
KRAMER, D. F., Music
KRAUS, R. C., Political Science
KRUSOE, S., Fine Arts
KYR, R. H., Music
LAFER, G. C., Labour Education
LANDE, R., Biology
LARSON, S., Music
LARSON, S. J., English
LARSON, W. A., East Asian Languages
LASKAYA, C. A., English
LAUX, D. L., Creative Writing
LAVERY, R. M., Journalism
LAWRENCE, M. S., Law
LEAHY, J. V., Mathematics
LEE, C.-R., Creative Writing
LEES, C. A., English
LEFEVRE, H. W., Physics
LEONG, A., Russian
LESAGE, J. L., English
LEVI, D. S., Philosophy
LIBERMAN, K. B., Sociology
LIBESKIND, S., Mathematics
LIN, H., Mathematics
LIVELYBROOKS, D. W., Physics
LO, V. M., Computer and Information Science
LOCKERY, S. R., Biology
LONERGAN, M., Chemistry
LONG, J. W., Chemistry
LOVINGER, R. J., Landscape Architecture
LOWENSTAM, S. D., Classics
LUCKTENBERG, K., Music
LUEBKE, D. M., History
LUKACS, J. R., Anthropology
LUKS, E. M., Computer and Information Science
LYNCH, M. R., Biology
LYONS, R. M., Creative Writing
LYSAKER, J. T., Philosophy
McCOLE, J. J., History
McDOWELL, P. F., Geography
McGOWEN, R. E., History

McKERNIE, G., Theatre Arts
McLAUCHLAN, G., Sociology
McWHIRTER, B. T., Behaviour and Communication Sciences
McWHIRTER, E. H., Behaviour and Communication Sciences
MADDEX, J. P., Jr, History
MADRIGAL, R., Business
MAITLAND-GHOLSON, J. C., Arts and Administration
MALLE, B. F., Psychology
MALLINCKRODT, B. S., Counselling Psychology
MALONY, A., Computer and Information Science
MALSCH, D. L., Linguistics
MANCE, A. M., English
MANGA, M., Geological Sciences
MARCUS, A. H., Chemistry
MARROCCO, R. T., Psychology
MARTIN, G. M., Music
MARTINS, E., Biology
MATE, M., History
MATHAS, A., German
MATSUNAGA, S. R., Business
MATTHEWS, B. W., Physics
MATTHEWS, K. M., Architecture
MAURO, R., Psychology
MAVES, L. C., Jr, Music
MAXWELL, A., Journalism
MAY, B. D., Romance Languages
MAY, G. A., History
MEDLER, J. F., Political Science
MEEKS-WAGNER, D. R., Biology
MELONE, N. P., Business
MERSKIN, D. L., Journalism
MEYER, A. D., Business
MEYER, G. W., Computer and Information Science
MIKKELSON, W. H., Business
MILLS, P. K., Business
MITCHELL, R. B., Political Science
MOHR, J. C., History
MONROE, S. M., Psychology
MOONEY, R. J., Law
MOORE, J. R., Music
MOORE, R. S., Music
MORENO-BLACK, G., Anthropology
MORGEN, S. L., Sociology
MORROGH, A., Art History
MORSE, D. C., Business
MOSES, L., Psychology
MOSS, M. L., Anthropology
MOSSBERG, T. W., Physics
MOURSUND, D. G., Education Policy and Management
MOURSUND, J. P., Counselling Psychology
MOWDAY, R. T., Business
MOYE, G. W., Architecture
MURPHY, A. B., Geography
MYAGKOV, M. G., Political Science
NATELLA, D. C., Fine Arts
NEAL, L. L., Recreation and Tourism Management
NEVILLE, H., Psychology
NICHOLSON, K., Art History
NICOLS, J., History
NIPPOLD, M. A., Special Education
NOVKOV, J. L., Political Science
O'BRIEN, R. M., Sociology
O'CONNELL, K. R., Fine Arts
O'FALLON, J. M., Law
O'KEEFE, T., Business
ORBELL, J. M., Political Science
OSTERNIG, L. R., Exercise and Movement Sciences
OSTLER, J., History
OVERLEY, J. C., Physics
OWEN, H. J., Music
OWEN, S. W., Music
PAGE, C. J., Chemistry
PAINTER, R. W., Law
PALMER, T. W., Mathematics
PAN, Y., Business
PARIS, M. L., Law
PARK, K., Physics
PARTCH, M. M., Business

PASCOE, P. A., History
PAUL, K. H., Fine Arts
PAYNE, D. L., Linguistics
PENA, R. B., Architecture
PEPPIS, P. W., English
PETING, D. L., Architecture
PETTINARI, J. A., Architecture
PHILLIPS, N. C., Mathematics
PICKETT, B. S., Fine Arts
PIELE, P. K., Education Policy and Management
POLOGE, S., Music
PONDER, S. E., Journalism
PONTO, R. D., Music
POPE, B. C., Women's Studies
POPE, D. A., History
POSNER, M. I., Psychology
POSTLETHWAIT, J. H., Biology
POVEY, D. C., Planning Public Policy Management
POWELL, D. T., Fine Arts
PRATT, S. L., Philosophy
PRENTICE, M. H., Fine Arts
PROSKUROWSKI, A., Computer and Information Science
PROUDFOOT, R. C., International Studies
PSAKI, F. R., Romance Languages
PYLE, F. B., III, English
RACETTE, G. A., Business
RAISKIN, J. L., Women's Studies
RAMIREZ, E. C., Theatre Arts
RAMSING, K. D., Business
RAVITS, M. A., Women's Studies
RAYFIELD, G. W., Physics
RAYMER, M. G., Physics
RECKER, G. W., Music
REED, M. H., Geological Sciences
REMINGTON, S. J., Physics
RETALLACK, G. J., Geological Sciences
REYNOLDS, J. S., Architecture
RIBE, R. G., Landscape Architecture
RICE, J. L., Russian
RICE, J. M., Geological Sciences
RICE, K. S., Physical Education and Recreation Services
RICHARDS, L. E., Business
RICHMOND, G. L., Chemistry
ROBERTS, W. M., Biology
ROBINSON, D. M., Journalism
ROCHA, E., Planning Public Policy Management
ROCKETT, G. W., English
RONDEAU, J. F., History
ROSE, J., Theatre Arts
ROSS, K. A., Mathematics
ROSSI, W. J., English
ROTH, L. M., Art History
ROTHBART, M., Psychology
ROTHBART, M. K., Psychology
ROWE, G. E., English
ROWELL, J., Architecture
RUSH, K. L., Behaviour and Communication Sciences
RUSSIAL, J. T., Journalism
RUSSO, M. V., Business
RYAN, C. C., Philosophy
RYAN, W. E., II, Journalism
SABRY, A., Computer and Information Science
SADOFSKY, H., Mathematics
SANG, T., East Asian Languages
SARANPA, K., German
SAUCIER, G. T., Psychology
SAYRE, G. M., English
SCHACHTER, J., Linguistics
SCHOMBERT, J. M., Physics
SCHULTZ, K. L., German
SCHUMAN, D., Law
SCHWARZ, I. E., Special Education
SEGALL, Z., Computer and Information Science
SEITZ, G. M., Mathematics
SELKER, E. U., Biology
SERCEL, P. C., Physics
SHANKMAN, S., English
SHANKS, A. L., Institute of Marine Biology

SHAO, Q. M., Mathematics
SHAPIRO, L., Biology
SHELTON, B. S., Mathematics
SHERER, P. D., Business
SHERIDAN, G. J., Jr, History
SHERMAN, S. R., English
SHINN, M. R., Special Education
SHURTZ, N. E., Law
SIERADSKI, A. J., Mathematics
SILVA, E. C., Economics
SILVERMAN, C. T., Anthropology
SIMMONS, D. C., Education Policy and Management
SIMMONS, W. S., Art History
SIMONDS, P. E., Anthropology
SIMONS, A. D., Psychology
SIMONSEN, W. S., Planning Public Policy Management
SINGELL, L. D., Jr, Economics
SISLEY, B. L., Physical Education and Recreation Services
SKALNES, L., Political Science
SLOVIC, P., Psychology
SMITH, J. R., Business
SMITH, M. E., Music
SOHLBERG, M. M., Behavioural and Communication Sciences
SOHLICH, W. F., Romance Languages
SOKOLOFF, D. R., Physics
SOPER, D. E., Physics
SOUTHWELL, P., Political Science
SPALTENSTEIN, J. N., Mathematics
SPRAGUE, G. F., Jr, Biology
SPRAGUE, K. U., Biology
STAHL, F. W., Biology
STAVITSKY, A. G., Journalism
STEEVES, H. L., Journalism
STEIN, A. J., Sociology
STEIN, R. L., English
STEINHARDT, V., Music
STEVENS, K. A., Computer and Information Science
STEVENS, T. H., Chemistry
STEVENSON, R. C., English
STOCKARD, A. J., Sociology
STOLET, J., Dance
STONE, J. A., Economics
STORMSHAK, E. A., Behaviour and Communication Sciences
STRAKA, L. M., Music
STROM, D. M., Physics
SUGAI, G. M., Education Policy and Management
SUNDT, R. A., Art History
SUTTMEIER, R. P., Political Science
SWAN, P. N., Law
SZURMUK, M., Romance Languages
TAKAHASHI, T. T., Biology
TAN, Y., Fine Arts
TAYLOR, M. E., Psychology
TAYLOR, Q., Jr, History
TEDARDS, A. B., Music
TEICH, N., English
TERBORG, J. R., Business
TERWILLIGER, N. B., Biology
THALLON, R., Architecture
THEODOROPOULOS, C., Architecture
THOMA, M. A., Economics
THOMAS, S., Mathematics
THOMPSON, A. C., Religious Studies
TICE, J. T., Architecture
TINDAL, G., Education Policy and Management
TIRAS, S. L., Business
TOKUNO, K., Religious Studies
TOMLIN, R., Linguistics
TONER, J., Physics
TOOMEY, D. R., Geological Sciences
TROMBLEY, R., Music
TUAN, M. H. C., Sociology
TUANA, N., Philosophy
TUBLITZ, N. J., Biology
TUCKER, D. M., Psychology
TYLER, D. R., Chemistry
UDOVIC, J. D., Biology
UNGSON, G. R., Business

UPSHAW, J. R., Journalism
UTSEY, G. F., Architecture
UTSEY, M. D., Architecture
VAKARELIYSKA, C., Russian
VANDENNOUWELAND, A., Economics
VANHEECKEREN, J., Business
VAN HOUTEN, D. R., Sociology
VAN SCHEEUWIJCK, M., Music
VARGAS, M., Music
VERSACE, G. T., Music
VETRI, D. R., Law
VITULLI, M. A., Mathematics
VLATTEN, A., German
VONHIPPEL, P. H., Chemistry
WACHTER, C. L., Music
WAFF, H. S., Geological Sciences
WAGLE, K. E., Fine Arts
WALKER, H. M., Center on Human Devt
WALKER, P. A., Geography
WANG, H., Physics
WANTA, W. M., Journalism
WARPINSKI, T. L., Fine Arts
WASKO, J., Journalism
WATSON, J. C., Theatre Arts
WEEKS, E. C., Planning Public Policy Management
WEEKS, J. C., Biology
WEINSTEIN, M. G., Business
WEISS, A. M., International Studies
WEISS, J., Romance Languages
WEISS, M. R., Exercise and Movement Sciences
WEISS, R. L., Psychology
WELCH, M. C., Architecture
WELDON, R. J., Geological Sciences
WELKE, B. Y., History
WESTERFIELD, M., Biology
WESTLING, L. H., English
WESTLING, W. T., Law
WESTON, J. A., Biology
WHEELER, T. H., Journalism
WHITELAW, W. E., Economics
WHITLOCK, C. L., Geography
WIDENOR, M. R., Labour Education Center
WILLIAMS, J. P., Music
WILLIAMS, J. R., Theatre Arts
WILLIS, J. H., III, Biology
WILSON, C. B., Computer and Information Science
WILSON, M. C., Classics
WILSON, W. W., Economics
WIXMAN, R., Geography
WOJCIK, D. N., English
WOLFE, A. S., East Asian Languages
WOLFE, J. M., Mathematics
WONHAM, H. B., English
WOOD, A. M., Biology
WOOD, M. C., Law
WOOD, M. E., English
WOOLLACOTT, M. H., Exercise and Movement Sciences
WRIGHT, C. R. B., Mathematics
WRIGHT, P. L., Business
WYBOURNE, M. N., Physics
XU, D., Mathematics
XU, Y., Mathematics
YOUNG, J. E., Architecture
YOUNG, M. T., Computer Science
YOUNG, P. D., Anthropology
YUZVINSKY, S., Mathematics
ZILIAK, J. P., Economics
ZIMMER, L. K., Architecture
ZIMMERMAN, R. L., Physics
ZINBARG, R., Psychology
ZUCK, O. V., German

UNIVERSITY OF PORTLAND

5000 N Willamette Blvd, Portland, OR 97203-5798

Telephone: (503) 943-8000
E-mail: intl-adm@up.edu
Internet: www.up.edu

Founded 1901 as Columbia Univ., current name adopted 1930

Private control
Language of instruction: English
Academic year: August to May
Pres.: Rev. MARK L. POORMAN
Provost: Dr DONALD J. STABROWSKI
Exec. Vice-Pres.: Rev. MARK POORMAN
Vice-Pres. for Financial Affairs: ALAN P. TIMMINS
Vice-Pres. for Student Affairs: Rev. GERRY OLINGER
Vice-Pres. for Univ. Operations: JIM RAVELLI
Vice-Pres. for Univ. Relations: JAMES LYONS
Registrar: BOBBI LINDAHL
Dean of the Library: DREW HARRINGTON
Library of 248,000 vols, 17,000 audiovisual resources, over 1,200 journals
Number of teachers: 320 (full-time and part-time)
Number of students: 3,800

DEANS

College of Arts and Sciences: Rev. Dr STEPHEN C. ROWAN
Graduate School: Dr THOMAS GREENE
Pamplin School of Business: ROBIN D. ANDERSON
School of Education: Prof. JOHN L. WATZKE
School of Nursing: Prof. JOANNE WARNER
Shiley School of Engineering: Dr SHARON A. JONES

PROFESSORS

ADRANGI, B., Business Administration
ALBRIGHT, R. J., Engineering
ARWOOD, E., Education
ASARNOW, H., English and Foreign Languages
ASKAY, R., Philosophy
BAILLIE, J., Philosophy
BOWEN, E., Drama
DOYLE, R. O., Music
DRAKE, B. H., Business Administration
DUFF, R., Psychology and Social Science
FALLER, T., Philosophy
FAVERO, T., Biology
FREED, E., Business Administration
GAYLE, B., Communication Studies
GRITTA, P. R., Business Administration
HODDICK, J. P., Theatre
HOSINSKI, T., Theology
HOUCK, B., Biology
INAN, A., Engineering
KHAN, K. H., Engineering
KLESYNSKI, K., Music
KOLMES, S., Biology
LINCOLN, S., Chemistry
LUM, L., Mathematics and Computer Science
MALE, J., Engineering
MASSON, L., English
MONTO, M., Sociology
MURTY, D., Engineering
RUTHERFORD, H. R., Theology
SHANK, T., Business
SHERRER, C., English and Foreign Languages
SNOW, M., Physics
UTLAUT, M., Physics
WYNNE, A., Nursing

UNIVERSITY OF WESTERN STATES

2900 NE 132nd Ave, Portland, OR 97230-3099

Telephone: (503) 256-3180
E-mail: info@uws.edu
Internet: www.uws.edu

Founded 1904 as Marshes' School and Cure, present name and status 2010
Private control
Academic year: September to June
Pres.: Dr JOSEPH E. BRIMHALL
Vice-Pres. for Academic Affairs:: GARY SCHULTZ
Vice-Pres. for Clinics: JOSEPH PFEIFER

Vice-Pres. for Enrolment and Student Services: Dr PATRICK BROWNE
Vice-Pres. for Finance and Admin.: ERIC BLUMENTHAL
Univ. Librarian: JANET TAPPER
Number of teachers: 35
Number of students: 400

WARNER PACIFIC COLLEGE

2219 SE 68th Ave, Portland, OR 97215

Telephone: (503) 517-1020
E-mail: admiss@warnerpacific.edu
Internet: www.warnerpacific.edu

Founded 1937 as Pacific Bible College, present name 1959
Private control
Academic year: August to May
Pres.: Dr ANDREA P. COOK
Vice-Pres. for Academic Affairs and Dean of Faculty: Dr COLE P. DAWSON
Vice-Pres. for Institutional Advancement and External Relations: KEVIN BRYANT
Vice-Pres. for Operations: STEVE STENBERG
Dir for Institutional Research: GALE ROID
Dean for the Adult Degree Programme: TONI PAULS
Registrar: TORI CUMMINGS
Gen. Library Admin.: ALICE KIENBERGER
Library of 53,000 vols
Number of teachers: 35 (incl. 29 full time)
Number of students: 1,680

WESTERN OREGON UNIVERSITY

345 N Monmouth Ave, Monmouth, OR 97361

Telephone: (503) 838-8000
E-mail: president@wou.edu
Internet: www.wou.edu

Founded 1856 as Monmouth Univ., present name 1997
Academic year: September to June
Pres.: MARK D. WEISS
Provost and Vice-Pres. for Academic Affairs: Dr KENT NEELY
Vice-Pres. for Student Affairs: Dr GARY L. DUKES
Dean for the Library: Dr ALLEN W. MCKIEL
Registrar: MARIA L. MARTINEZ
Number of teachers: 150
Number of students: 6,600 (undergraduates and graduates)
Publication: *The WOU Magazine*

DEANS

College of Education: Dr HILDA ROSSELLI
College of Liberal Arts and Sciences: Dr STEPHEN H. SCHECK

WESTERN SEMINARY

5511 SE Hawthorne Blvd, Portland, OR 97215

Telephone: (503) 517-1800
E-mail: western@westernseminary.edu
Internet: www.westernseminary.edu

Founded 1927 as Western Baptist Theological Seminary
Private control
Academic year: September to April
Campuses at Portland (Oregon), San Jose and Sacramento (California)
Pres.: Dr RANDY. ROBERTS
Academic Dean and Provost: Dr RANDAL R. ROBERTS
Vice-Pres. for Advancement: DUANE STOREY
Dean for Student Devt and Registrar: Dr ROBERT W. WIGGINS
Library Dir: Dr ROBERT A. KRUPP
Number of teachers: 40
Number of students: 890
Publication: *Western Magazine* (2 a year)

WILLAMETTE UNIVERSITY

900 State St, Salem, OR 97301

Telephone: (503) 370-6300
E-mail: communications@willamette.edu
Internet: www.willamette.edu

Founded 1842
Private control

Pres.: STEPHEN E. THORSETT
Vice-Pres.: KRISTEN GRAINGER
Vice-Pres. for Admin. Services: JAMES R. BAUER
Vice-Pres. for Admissions and Financial Aid: MADELEINE E. RHYNEER
Vice-Pres. for Devt and Alumni Relations: DENISE CALLAHAN
Vice-Pres. for Enrolment Management: MADELEINE E. RHYNEER
Vice-Pres. for Financial Affairs: WILLIAM A. YASINSKI
Dean for Campus Life: DAVID A. DOUGLASS
Registrar: THOMAS H. HIBBARD
Dir for Library: RICHARD BREEN

Library of 285,000 vols, 1,355 periodicals
Number of teachers: 375
Number of students: 2,825

Publications: *Willamette College of Law Journal*, *Willamette Scene*

DEANS

College of Law: PETER V. LETSOU
College of Liberal Arts: MARLENE MOORE
George H. Atkinson Graduate School of Management: DEBRA J. RINGOLD
Graduate School of Education: JULIE GESS-NEWSOME

PENNSYLVANIA

ALBRIGHT COLLEGE

POB 15234, 13th and Bern Sts, Reading, PA 19612-5234

1621 N, 13th St, Reading, PA 19604

Telephone: (610) 921-2381
E-mail: transcripts@alb.edu
Internet: www.albright.edu

Founded 1856 as Union Seminary, current name adopted 1898
Private control
Academic year: May to May

Liberal arts college

Pres.: Dr LEX O. MCMILLAN, III
Provost and Vice-Pres. for Academic Affairs: Dr ANDREA CHAPDELAINE
Vice-Pres. for Advancement: Dr TIMOTHY A. MCELWEE
Vice-Pres. for Admin. and Financial Services: WILLIAM W. WOOD
Vice-Pres. for Enrolment Management and Dean for Admission: GREGORY E. EICHHORN
Vice-Pres. for Student Affairs and Dean for Students: Dr GINA-LYN CRANCE
Library Dir: ROSEMARY DEEGAN

Library of 240,000 vols
Number of teachers: 120 (full-time)
Number of students: 1,660

Publications: *Albright Reporter*, *The Lowdown*

ALLEGHENY COLLEGE

520 N Main St, Meadville, PA 16335

Telephone: (814) 332-3100
E-mail: admissions@allegheny.edu
Internet: www.allegheny.edu

Founded 1815
Private control
Academic year: September to May

Pres.: JAMES H. MULLEN, JR
Provost and Dean for College: LINDA C. DEMERITT

Exec. Vice-Pres. and Treas.: DAVID MCINALLY
Vice-Pres. for Devt and Alumni Affairs: MARJORIE KLEIN
Vice-Pres. for Enrolment and Communications: BRIAN DALTON
Chief Information Officer: RICHARD HOLMGREN
Registrar: ANN SHEFFIELD
Dean for Students: JOSEPH J. DICHRISTINA
Dir for Library: LINDA BILLS

Library of 956,133 vols, 35,000 journals, 5,000 video cassettes and DVDs
Number of teachers: 165 (full-time)
Number of students: 2,125 (undergraduates on campus)

Publications: *Allegheny Magazine* (3 a year), *Allegheny Review* (1 a year), *Film Criticism* (3 a year), *Kaldron* (1 a year), *The Soapbox* (1 a year)

PROFESSORS

BARRY, M. J., Mathematics
BENSEL, T., Environment Science
BOWDEN, R. D., Environmental Science
BUCK, S., Art
BULMAN, J. C., English
BYWATER, JR, W. G., Philosophy and Religious Studies
CASLER, S. D., Economics
CHIEN, A. F.-L., Music
CROSS, J. D., Psychology
CUPPER, R. D., Computer Science
D'AMICO, D., English
DELAMARTER, W. A., Psychology
DODGE, C. B., Modern and Classical Languages
ENSBERG, P., Modern and Classical Languages
GEFFEN, A. B., Art
GOLDSTEIN, D., Economics
HEPLER, L. E., Music
HEUCHERT, J. W. P., Psychology
HOLLAND, G. S., Philosophy and Religious Studies
JAMISON, W. M., Music
KEELEY, M. N., Communication Arts/Theatre
LO BELLO, A. J., Mathematics
LYONS, S. M., History
MANIATES, M. F., Political Science
MICHAELS, L., English
MILLER, D. C., English
MUMME, R. L., Biology
NESSET, K., English
OLSON, C., Philosophy and Religious Studies
OSTROFSKY, M. L., Biology
OZORAK, E. W., Psychology
PALLANT, E. T., Environmental Science
QUINN, L., English
RAHMAN, S. M., Physics
RANKIN, S. M., Biology
RICHTER, J. H., Modern and Classical Languages
ROLAND, G. S., Art
SCHWARTZ, R. K., Geology
SEDDIG, R. G., Political Science
SERRA, M. J., Chemistry
SHAPIRO, B. M., History
SHEA, D. M., Political Science
SHEFFIELD, A. E., Chemistry
SMITH, B. J., Political Science
STATMAN, D., Physics
TAMASHIRO, H., Political Science
TRECKEL, P. A., History
WILLEY, D. R., Physics
WISSINGER, S. A., Biology
WOLFE, P. J., Modern and Classical Languages

ALVERNIA UNIVERSITY

400 St Bernardine St, Reading, PA 19607-1799

Telephone: (610) 796-8228
E-mail: admissions@alvernia.edu
Internet: www.alvernia.edu

Founded 1926 as Teacher's Seminarium, current name and status 2008
Private control
Academic year: August to May

Pres.: Dr THOMAS F. FLYNN
Provost: Dr SHIRLEY J. WILLIAMS
Vice-Pres. for Enrolment Management: JOHN MCCLOSKEY, JR
Vice-Pres. for Finance and Admin.: DOUGLAS F. SMITH
Vice-Pres. for Marketing and Communications: BRAD DREXLER
Vice-Pres. for Mission: Sis. ROSEMARY STETS
Vice-Pres. for Univ. Life and Dean for Students: Dr JOSEPH J. CICALA
Registrar: BEKI STEIN
Library Dir: SHARON A. NEAL

Library of 92,464 vols, 900 periodicals
Number of teachers: 85
Number of students: 2,170

DEANS

College of Arts and Sciences: Dr BETH ARACENA
College of Professional Programmes: Dr KAREN THACKER

AMERICAN COLLEGE

270 S Bryn Mawr Ave, Bryn Mawr, PA 19010

Telephone: (610) 526-1000
E-mail: graduate.school@theamericancollege.edu
Internet: www.theamericancollege.edu

Founded 1927
Private control

Distance-education instn; professional diplomas and designations; graduate degrees in the financial sciences and management

Pres. and CEO: Dr LAURENCE BARTON
Sr Vice-Pres.: STEPHEN D. TARR
Sr Vice-Pres. for Advancement: CHARLES CRONIN, III
Vice-Pres. for Academics and Dean: Dr WALT J. WOERHEIDE
Vice-Pres. for Information Technology: EDWARD M. MCEVOY
Chief Operating Officer: NEAL R. FEGELY
Exec. Dir for Online Learning: BILLY L. WILLIAMS
Librarian: JUDITH L. HILL

Library of 8,000 vols, 500 journals
Number of teachers: 20
Number of students: 35,000

ARCADIA UNIVERSITY

450 S Easton Rd, Glenside, PA 19038-3295

Telephone: (215) 572-2900
E-mail: admiss@arcadia.edu
Internet: www.arcadia.edu

Founded 1853, present name and status 2000
Academic year: September to May

Pres.: Dr CARL OXHOLM, III
Provost and Vice-Pres. for Academic Affairs: Dr STEVE O. MICHAEL
Vice-Pres. for Enrolment Management: MARK LAPREZIOSA
Vice-Pres. for Finance and Treas.: MICHAEL COVENEY
Vice-Pres. for Technology and Chief Information Officer, Library and Technology: STEVE ALTER
Vice-Pres. for Univ. Advancement: NICK COSTA
Gen. Counsel: MICHAEL J. KOROLISHIN
Dir for Library Services: JEANNE BUCKLEY
Registrar: BILL ELNICK

Library of 140,000 vols, 97,000 titles, 56,940 microforms
Number of teachers: 125 (full-time)
Number of students: 4,078 (2,228 undergraduate, 1,850 graduate)

Publication: *Arcadia Magazine*

DEANS

College of Arts and Sciences: Dr BARBARA NODINE

College of Global Studies: Dr DENNIS DUTSCHKE

College of Health Sciences: Dr ARCHIE J. VOMACHKA

School of Business: Dr N. J. DELENER

School of Continuing Studies: Dr ERIK NELSON

School of Education: Dr GRACIELA SLESARANSKY-POE

ART INSTITUTE OF PITTSBURGH

420 Blvd of the Allies, Pittsburgh, PA 15219-1301

Telephone: (412) 263-6600

E-mail: admissions-aip@aii.edu

Internet: www.artinstitutes.edu/pittsburgh

Founded 1921, present location 2001

Private control

Academic year: July to June

Courses in advertising, culinary management, entertainment design, fashion and retail management, fashion design, hotel and restaurant management, industrial design and interior design

Pres.: GEORGE W. SEBOLT

Vice-Pres. for Academic Affairs: Dr DANIEL J. GARLAND

Vice-Pres. for Admissions: LEE COLKER

Vice-Pres. and Dir for Admin. and Financial Services: JANICE M. VUCIĆ

Vice-Pres. and Dir for Human Resources: MALINDA A. HALLET

Vice-Pres. and Dean for Student Affairs: NADINE W. JOSEPHS

Dir for Library Services: KATHLEEN S. OBER

Number of teachers: 160

Number of students: 2,200

BAPTIST BIBLE COLLEGE AND SEMINARY

538 Venard Rd, Clarks Summit, PA 18411

Telephone: (570) 586-2400

E-mail: admissions@bbc.edu

Internet: www.bbc.edu

Founded 1932

Private control

Academic year: August to May

Pres.: JAMES JEFFERY

Provost and Vice-Pres.: Dr JAMES LYTLE

Seminary Dean and Vice-Pres. for Seminary Academics: Dr MICHAEL D. STALLARD

Vice-Pres. for Alumni Services and Church Relations: MEL WALKER

Vice-Pres. for Business and Finance: HAL CROSS

Vice-Pres. for College Academics: Dr BARRY PHILLIPS

Vice-Pres. for Enrolment Management and Marketing Services: KENNETH M. SHEPARD

Vice-Pres. for Institutional Advancement: DONALD PATTEN

Dean for Students: MATT POLLOCK

Registrar: ALLEN DREYER

Library Dir: JOSHUA MICHAEL

Library of 100,000 vols

Number of teachers: 45

Number of students: 1,050 (671 college, 173 graduates, 206 seminary)

Publications: *Journal of Ministry & Theology*, *Paraklesis* (3 a year), *Summit Magazine*

BIBLICAL SEMINARY

200 N Main St, Hatfield, PA 19440

Telephone: (215) 368-5000

E-mail: admissions@biblical.edu

Internet: www.biblical.edu

Founded 1971 as Biblical School of Theology

Private control

Campus in Philadelphia

Pres.: Dr DAVID G. DUNBAR

Vice-Pres. for Student Advancement: PAM SMITH

Dean for Faculty and Academic Advancement: R. TODD MANGUM

Dir for Library Services: DANIEL LaVALLA

Library of 52,000 vols, 400 periodicals

Number of teachers: 30 (14 full-time, 16 adjunct)

Number of students: 320

Publication: *Missional Journal* (irregular)

BRYN ATHYN COLLEGE

POB 462, 2945 College Dr., Bryn Athyn, PA 19009-0717

Telephone: (267) 502-2400

E-mail: admissions@brynathyn.edu

Internet: www.brynathyn.edu

Founded 1877

Private control

Academic year: August to May

Pres.: Dr KRISTIN KING

Chief Financial Officer: DANIEL T. ALLEN

Dean for Academics and Faculty: Dr ALLEN J. BEDFORD

Dean for Students: KIRI K. ROGERS

Library Dir: CARROLL C. ODHNER

Library of 118,000 vols

Number of teachers: 40

Number of students: 230

Publications: *The Academy Journal*, *The Lion's Pride*

DEANS

Theological School: The Rev. Dr ANDREW M. T. DIBB

BRYN MAWR COLLEGE

101 N Merion Ave, Bryn Mawr, PA 19010-2899

Telephone: (610) 526-5000

E-mail: info@brynmawr.edu

Internet: www.brynmawr.edu

Founded 1885

Private control

Academic year: September to May

Pres.: JANE DAMMEN MCAULIFFE

Provost: KIMBERLY E. CASSIDY

Chief Admin. Officer: JERRY BERENSON

Chief Enrolment and Communications Officer: JENNIFER RICKARD

Chief Financial Officer and Treas.: JOHN GRIFFITH

Dean for Undergraduate College: MICHELE RASMUSSEN

Dir for Libraries: ELLIOTT SHORE

Library: 1m. vols

Number of teachers: 155 (full-time)

Number of students: 1,300 (undergraduate)

Publications: *Bryn Mawr Classical Review* (online), *Bryn Mawr Review of Comparative Literature* (1 a year)

DEANS

Graduate School of Arts and Sciences: MARY OSIRIM

Graduate School of Social Work and Social Research: DARLYNE BAILEY

BUCKNELL UNIVERSITY

1 Dent Dr., Lewisburg, PA 17837

Telephone: (570) 577-2000

E-mail: admisssions@bucknell.edu

Internet: www.bucknell.edu

Founded 1846 as Univ. at Lewisburg, current name adopted 1886

Private control

Academic year: August to May

Pres.: Dr JOHN C. BRAVMAN

Provost: MICHAEL SMYER

Vice-Pres. for Devt: SCOTT ROSEVEAR

Vice-Pres. for Finance and Admin.: DAVID SURGALA

Vice-Pres. for Enrolment Management: WILLIAM CONLEY

Dean for Graduate Studies: JAMES RICE

Dean for Students: SUSAN LANTZ

Dir for Information Services and Resources: PARAM BEDI

Gen. Counsel: AMY FOERSTER

Library of 890,318 vols

Number of teachers: 384 (370 full-time, 14 part-time)

Number of students: 3,609 (3,504 full-time undergraduates, 28 part-time; 52 full-time graduate students, 25 part-time)

Publication: *Aperçus*

DEANS

College of Arts and Sciences: Dr GEORGE C. SHIELDS

College of Engineering: Dr KEITH BUFFINTON

CABRINI COLLEGE

610 King of Prussia Rd, Radnor, PA 19087-3698

Telephone: (610) 902-8100

E-mail: admit@cabrini.edu

Internet: www.cabrini.edu

Founded 1957

Private control

Academic year: August to May

Pres.: DONALD B. TAYLOR

Provost and Vice-Pres. for Academic Affairs: Dr ANNE A. SKLEDER

Vice-Pres. for Enrolment Management: DENNIS KELLY

Vice-Pres. for Finance and Admin.: STEVEN FELD

Vice-Pres. for Marketing and Communications and Interim Vice-Pres. for Institutional Advancement: GENE CASTELLANO

Vice-Pres. for Student Devt: Dr CHRISTINE LYSIONEK

Dean for Graduate and Professional Studies: Dr DENNIS DOUGHTERY

Dir for Admissions: CHARLES SPENCER

Library Dir: Dr ROBERTA JACQUET

Library of 112,500 vols, 7,215 periodicals

Number of teachers: 195 (56 full-time, 137 part-time)

Number of students: 3,225 (1,300 undergraduate, 1,925 graduate)

CARLOW UNIVERSITY

3333 Fifth Ave, Pittsburgh, PA 15213

Telephone: (412) 578-6000

E-mail: admissions@carlow.edu

Internet: www.carlow.edu

Founded 1929 as Mount Mercy College, present name and status 2004

Private control

Academic year: August to May

Pres.: Dr MARY HINES

Provost and Vice-Pres. for Academic Affairs: Dr MARGARET MCLAUGHLIN

Vice-Pres. for Finance and Operations: TYLER KELSCH

Vice-Pres. for Institutional Relations: ANN RAGO

Vice-Pres. for Student Affairs: Dr CAROL A. GRUBER

Vice-Pres. for Univ. Advancement: Dr KAREN GALENTINE

Vice-Pres. for Univ. Communications and External Relations: LOUISE CAVANAUGH SCIANNAMEO
Dir for Admissions: SUSAN WINSTEL
Dir for Graduate and Adult Admissions: SUSAN SHUTTER
Registrar: JASON KRALL
Librarian: ELAINE MISKO
Library of 109,600 vols, 15,000 print and ejournals, 820 video cassettes and DVDs
Number of teachers: 280 (92 full-time, 188 part-time)
Number of students: 2,345 (1,445 undergraduate, 900 graduate)
Publications: *Accent on Progress*, *The Carlow Journal*, *The Carlow Sun* (24 a year)

DEANS

College of Arts and Science: Dr KARYN Z. SPROLES
College of Professional Studies and Graduate School: Dr M. CYNTHIA ROTHENBERGER

CARNEGIE MELLON UNIVERSITY

5000 Forbes Ave, Pittsburgh, PA 15213
Telephone: (412) 268-2000
Internet: www.cmu.edu
Founded 1900 as Carnegie Technical Schools, present name and status 1967
Private control
Academic year: August to May
Pres.: JARED L. COHON
Provost: Dr MARK S. KAMLET
Vice-Pres. for Campus Affairs: MICHAEL MURPHY
Vice-Pres. for Finance and Chief Financial Officer: DEBORAH MOON
Vice-Pres. for Research: RICHARD McCULLOUGH
Vice-Pres. for Univ. Advancement: ROBBEE BAKER KOSAK
Dean for Univ. Libraries: GLORIANA ST CLAIR
Library of 961,507 vols
Number of teachers: 1,315
Number of students: 11,530 (6,020 undergraduate, 5,510 graduate)
Publications: *Carnegie Mellon Today*, *Gigapan Magazine* (online, www.gigapanmagazine.org), *Huntia*, *Journal of Field Robotics*

DEANS

Carnegie Institute of Technology: PRADEEP KHOSLA
College of Fine Arts: DAN MARTIN
Dietrich College of Humanities and Social Sciences: JOHN LEHOCZKY
H. John Heinz III College: RAMAYYA KRISHNAN
Mellon College of Science: FRED GILMAN
School of Computer Science: RANDAL BRYANT
Tepper School of Business: Dr ROBERT M. DAMMON

PROFESSORS

Carnegie Institute of Technology (tel. (412) 268-2481; internet www.cit.cmu.edu):
AKAY, A., Mechanical Engineering
AMON, C., Mechanical Engineering
ANDERSON, J., Chemical Engineering
BAUMANN, D. M. B., Mechanical Engineering
BHAGAVATULA, V., Electrical and Computer Engineering
BIEGLER, L. T., Chemical Engineering
BIELAK, J., Civil Engineering
CAGAN, J., Mechanical Engineering
CARLEY, L. R., Electrical and Computer Engineering
CASASENT, D., Electrical and Computer Engineering
CHIGIER, N. A., Mechanical Engineering
CRAMB, A., Materials Science Engineering

DAVIDSON, C., Civil Engineering
DOMACH, M., Chemical Engineering
DZOMBAK, D. A., Civil Engineering
FRUEHAN, R. J., Materials Science Engineering
GABRIEL, K. S., Electrical and Computer Engineering
GARRETT, J. H., Civil Engineering
GARRISON, JR, W. M., Materials Science Engineering
GELLMAN, A., Chemical Engineering
GREVE, D. W., Electrical and Computer Engineering
GRIFFIN, J. H., Mechanical Engineering
GROSSMANN, I. E., Chemical Engineering
HENDRICKSON, C. T., Civil Engineering
HOBURG, J. F., Electrical and Computer Engineering
JHON, M. S., Chemical Engineering
KHOSLA, P., Electrical and Computer Engineering
KIM, H. S., Electrical and Computer Engineering
KROGH, B., Electrical and Computer Engineering
KRYDER, M. H., Electrical and Computer Engineering
KUMTA, P., Materials Science Engineering
LAMBETH, D. N., Electrical and Computer Engineering
LAUGHLIN, D. E., Materials Science Engineering
McHENRY, M., Materials Science Engineering
McMICHAEL, F. C., Civil Engineering
MALY, W., Electrical and Computer Engineering
MORGAN, M. G., Engineering and Public Policy
MOURA, J. M., Electrical and Computer Engineering
NEUMAN, C. P., Electrical and Computer Engineering
OPPENHEIM, I. J., Civil Engineering
PIEHLER, H. R., Materials Science Engineering
PILEGGI, L., Electrical and Computer Engineering
POWERS, G., Chemical Engineering
PRIEVE, D. G., Chemical Engineering
REHAK, D. R., Civil Engineering
ROHRER, G., Materials Science Engineering
ROLLETT, T., Materials Science Engineering
RUBIN, E. S., Engineering and Public Policy
RUTENBAR, R., Electrical and Computer Engineering
SAIGAL, S., Civil Engineering
SCHLESINGER, E., Electrical and Computer Engineering
SHEN, J., Electrical and Computer Engineering
SIDES, P. J., Chemical Engineering
SINCLAIR, G. B., Mechanical Engineering
SIRBU, M. A., Engineering and Public Policy
SKOWRONSKI, M., Materials Science Engineering
SMALL, M. J., Civil Engineering
STANCIL, D. D., Electrical and Computer Engineering
STEIF, P. S., Mechanical Engineering
STERN, R., Electrical and Computer Engineering
STROJWAS, A., Electrical and Computer Engineering
TALUKDAR, S., Electrical and Computer Engineering
THOMAS, JR, D. E., Electrical and Computer Engineering
WESTERBERG, A. W., Chemical Engineering
WHITE, L. R., Chemical Engineering
WHITE, R., Electrical and Computer Engineering
WICKERT, J., Mechanical Engineering

WYNBLATT, P., Materials Science Engineering
YAO, S.-C., Mechanical Engineering
YDSTIE, B. E., Chemical Engineering
ZHU, J., Electrical and Computer Engineering

College of Fine Arts (tel. (412) 268-2349; internet www.cmu.edu/cfa):
AKIN, O., Architecture
ANDERSON, B. J. B., Drama
ANDERSON, C. R., Drama
BALADA, L. I., Music
BALLAY, J. M., Design
BAXTRESSER, J., Music
BECKLEY, J., Art
BELLAN-GILLEN, P., Art
BENNETT, R., Art
BOYARSKI, D., Design
BUCHANAN, R., Design
BURGESS, L., Art
CARDENES, A., Music
COOPER, W. D., Architecture
FLEMMING, U., Architecture
FRISCH, P., Drama
HARTKOPF, V., Architecture
IZQUIERDO, J.-P., Music
JOHNSTON, B., Drama
JOSEPH, A., Music
KEELING, SR, K., Music
KING, E., Art
KRISHNAMURTI, R., Architecture
KUMATA, C., Art
LEE, S., Architecture
LEHANE, G., Drama
LOFTNESS, V., Architecture
MAHDAVI, A., Architecture
MAIER, J., Art
MARINELLI, D., Drama
MENTZER, M., Design
MIDANI, A., Drama
OLDS, H. T., Art
PREKOP, M., Art
SLAVICK, S., Art
STITT, M., Drama
SWINEHART, R. O., Design
THOMAS, M., Music
VOGEL, C. M., Design
WADSWORTH, D. H., Drama
WEIDNER, M., Art

Dietrich College of Humanities and Social Sciences (tel. (412) 268-2830; internet hss.cmu.edu):
ANDERSON, J. R., Psychology
BALAS, E., History
BICCHIERI, C., Philosophy
CARLEY, K. M., Social and Decision Sciences
CARPENTER, J., Psychology
CARRIER, D. S., Philosophy
CLARK, M., Psychology
COHEN, S. A., Psychology
COHEN, W., Social and Decision Sciences
COSTANZO, G., English
DANIELS, J., English
DAVIS, O. A., Social and Decision Sciences
DAWES, R., Social and Decision Sciences
EDDY, W. F., Statistics
FEINBERG, S. E., Statistics
FISCHHOFF, B., Social and Decision Sciences
FLOWER, L. S., English
FREED, B. F., Modern Languages
GLYMOUR, C., Philosophy
GREENHOUSE, J., Statistics
HAYES, A. L., English
HAYES, J. R., Psychology
HOPPER, P., English
HOUNSHELL, D. A., History and Social and Decision Sciences
JOHNSTONE, B., English
JUST, M. A., Psychology
KADANE, J. B., Statistics
KASS, R. E., Statistics
KAUFER, D., English
KEECH, W., Social and Decision Sciences

KELLY, K. T., Philosophy
KENNEDY, A., English
KLAHR, D., Psychology
KLATZKY, R., Psychology
KLEPPER, S., Social and Decision Sciences
KNAPP, P., English
KOTOVSKY, K., Psychology
LEHOCZKY, J. P., Statistics
LINDEMANN, M., History
LOEWENSTEIN, G., Social and Decision Sciences
LYNCH, K., History
McCLELLAND, J., Psychology
MacWHINNEY, B., Psychology
MASTERS, H., English
MILLER, D. W., History
MILLER, J. H., Social and Decision Sciences
MODELL, J., History
REDER, L., Psychology
RESNICK, D. P., History
ROEDER, K., Statistics
SCHEIER, M. F., Psychology
SCHERVISH, M., Statistics
SCHLOSSMAN, B. F., Modern Languages
SCHLOSSMAN, S., History
SEIDENFELD, T., Philosophy
SHUMWAY, D., English
SIEG, W., Philosophy
SIEGLER, R. S., Psychology
SPIRTES, P. L., Philosophy
STEINBERG, E. R., English
SUTTON, D., History
TARR, J. A., History
TROTTER, J., History
TUCKER, G. R., Modern Languages
WASSERMAN, L., Statistics

H. John Heinz III College (tel. (412) 268-2159; e-mail hnzadmit@andrew.cmu.edu; internet www.heinz.cmu.edu):

BABCOCK, L. C., Economics
BLUMSTEIN, A., Urban Systems and Operations Research
CAULKINS, J. P., Operations Research
DUNCAN, G., Statistics
FLORIDA, R., Public Policy and Management
GAYNOR, M. S., Economics and Health Policy
GORR, W., Public Policy and Management Information Systems
KRACKHARDT, D. M., Organizations and Public Policy
KRISHNAN, R., Management Science and Information Systems
LARKEY, P. D., Public Policy and Decision-making
NAGIN, D., Management
ROUSSEAU, D., Organization Behaviour
STEWMAN, S., Sociology and Demography
STRAUSS, R. P., Economics and Public Policy
TAYLOR, L., Economics and Public Policy

Mellon College of Science (tel. (412) 268-7699; e-mail mcsdean@andrew.cmu.edu; internet www.cmu.edu/mcs):

ANDREWS, P. B., Mathematical Sciences
BERRY, G. C., Chemistry
BROWN, W. E., Biology
COLLINS, T., Chemistry
FEENSTRA, R., Physics
FERGUSON, T., Physics
FONSECA, I., Mathematical Sciences
FRANKLIN, G. B., Physics
FRIEZE, A., Physics
GAROFF, S., Physics
GILMAN, F., Physics
GREENBERG, J., Mathematical Sciences
GRIFFITHS, R. B., Physics
GRIFFITHS, R. E., Physics
GURTIN, M. E., Mathematical Sciences
HACKNEY, D., Biology
HEATH, D. C., Mathematical Sciences
HO, C., Biology
HOLLINGER, J. O., Biology
HOLMAN, R. F., Physics

HRUSA, W. J., Mathematical Sciences
JONES, E. W., Biology
KAPLAN, M., Chemistry
KAROL, P., Chemistry
KINDERLEHRER, D., Mathematical Sciences
KISSLINGER, L. S., Physics
KRAEMER, R. W., Physics
LEVINE, M. J., Physics
LI, L.-F., Physics
LLINÁS, M., Chemistry
McCLURE, W. R., Biology
McCULLOUGH, R., Chemistry
MAJETICH, S., Physics
MATYJASZEWSKI, K., Chemistry
MIZEL, V. J., Mathematical Sciences
MÜNCK, E., Chemistry
NAGLE, J. F., Physics
NICOLAIDES, R. A., Mathematical Sciences
OWEN, D. R., Mathematical Sciences
PATTERSON, G. D., Chemistry
RUSS, J. S., Physics
SCHÄFFER, J. W., Mathematical Sciences
SCHUMACHER, R. A., Physics
SEKERKA, R. F., Physics
SHREVE, S. E., Mathematical Sciences
STALEY, S. W., Chemistry
STATMAN, R., Mathematical Sciences
STEWART, R. F., Chemistry
SUTER, R., Physics
SWENDSEN, R. H., Physics
TA'ASAN, S., Mathematical Sciences
TARTAR, L., Mathematical Sciences
VOGEL, H., Physics
WAGGONER, A., Biology
WALKINGTON, N. J., Mathematical Sciences
WIDOM, M., Physics
WILLIAMS, J. F., Biology
WILLIAMS, W. O., Mathematical Sciences
WOOLFORD, J., Biology
YOUNG, H., Physics

School of Computer Science (tel. (412) 268-8525; e-mail www-team@cs.cmu.edu; internet www.cs.cmu.edu):

BLELLOCH, G. E., Computer Science
BRYANT, R. E., Computer Science
CARBONELL, J. G., Computer Science
CLARK, JR, E. M., Computer Science
FALOUTSOS, C. N., Computer Science
HARPER, R. W., Computer Science
HERBERT, M., Robotics
KANADE, T., Robotics
KIESLER, S., Human–Computer Interaction
KRAUT, R. E., Human–Computer Interaction
LEE, P., Computer Science
MASON, M. T., Computer Science
MILLER, G. L., Computer Science
MITCHELL, T. M., Computer Science
MORRIS, J., Computer Science
PAUSCH, R. F., Human–Computer Interaction
REDDY, R., Computer Science
REYNOLDS, J. C., Computer Science
SATYANARAYANEN, M., Computer Science
SCOTT, D. F., Computer Science, Mathematics and Philosophy
SHAW, M., Computer Science
SIEWIOREK, D., Human–Computer Interaction
SLEATOR, D. D., Computer Science
WAIBEL, A., Language Technologies
WING, J., Computer Science

Tepper School of Business (tel. 412-268-2268; internet www.gsia.cmu.edu):

ARGOTE, L., Organizational Behaviour
BALAS, E., Industrial Administration and Mathematics
BAYBARS, I., Industrial Administration
CORNUEJOLS, G. P., Operations Research and Mathematics
DUNN, D., Industrial Administration and Statistics
EPPLE, D., Economics
GOODMAN, P. S., Industrial Administration and Psychology

GREEN, R. C., Financial Economics
HOOKER, JR, J., Industrial Administration
IJIRI, Y., Industrial Administration
KEKRE, S., Industrial Administration
KYDLAND, F. E., Economics
LAVE, L. B., Economics
McCALLUM, B. T., Economics
MELTZER, A. H., Economics, Industrial Administration and Public Policy
MILLER, R., Economics
MUKHOPADHYAY, T., Information Systems
SHAW, K., Economics
SPATT, C. S., Economics and Finance
SPEAR, S., Economics
SRINIVASAN, K., Industrial Administration
SRIVASTAVA, S., Economics and Finance
TAYUR, S.
THOMPSON, G. L., Industrial Administration and Mathematics
WILLIAMS, J., Industrial Administration
ZIN, S., Economics and Finance

CEDAR CREST COLLEGE

100 College Dr., Allentown, PA 18104

Telephone: (610) 437-4471
E-mail: admissions@cedarcrest.edu
Internet: www.cedarcrest.edu

Founded 1867
Private control
Academic year: August to May

Liberal arts college for women; courses in art, business and management, education and nursing; certificate course in child welfare

Pres.: CARMEN TWILLIE AMBAR
Provost: Dr ELIZABETH M. MEADE (acting)
Sr Exec. Vice-Pres. for Enrolment Management and Student Affairs: KIMBERLY OWENS
Vice-Pres. for Institutional Advancement: PATRICIA MORAN
Chief Financial Officer and Treas.: AUDRA J. KAHR
Library Dir: KYLE CRIMI

Library of 144,037 vols, 1,705 ebooks, 15,053 current serials titles, 14,637 microform units, 19,329 audiovisual material
Number of teachers: 90 (full-time)
Number of students: 1,400

Publications: *Alumnae Magazine*, *Exchange* (4 a year), *Pitch*

CENTRAL PENN COLLEGE

POB 309, 600 Valley Rd, Summerdale, PA 17093-0309

Telephone: (717) 732-0702
E-mail: admissions@centralpenn.edu
Internet: www.centralpenn.edu

Founded 1881 as Pennsylvania Business College, current name adopted 2000
Private control
Academic year: July to September, October to December, January to March, April to June (4 terms)

Campuses in Summerdale, Lancaster and Lehigh Valley

Pres.: Dr KAREN SCOLFORO
Provost: JANICE MOORE
Vice-Pres. for Enrolment Management: STACEY OBI
Dean for Academic Affairs: KATHY ANDERSEN
Dean for Student Services: ED LIESCH
Chief Financial Officer: RICHARD VARMECKY
Registrar: JEN CORRELL
Library Dir: DIANE PORTERFIELD

Library of 137,000 vols
Number of teachers: 150
Number of students: 1,265

Publication: *PennDulum*

CHATHAM UNIVERSITY

Woodland Rd, Pittsburgh, PA 15232

Telephone: (412) 365-1100
E-mail: admissions@chatham.edu
Internet: www.chatham.edu

Founded 1869 as Pennsylvania Female College, present name and status 2007
Private control
Academic year: August to May
Campuses: Eden Hall campus, Eastside campus and Shadyside campus

Pres.: Dr ESTHER L. BARAZZONE
Vice-Pres. for Academic Affairs: Dr LAURA ARMESTO
Vice-Pres. for Enrolment Management: WENDY BECKEMEYER
Vice-Pres. for Finance and Admin.: WALT FOWLER
Vice-Pres for Student Affairs and Dean for Students: Dr ZAUYAH WAITE
Vice-Pres. for Univ. Advancement: RICHARD DONOVAN
Library Dir: JILL AUSEL

Library of 117,078 vols, 970 CDs, 526 DVDs
Number of teachers: 295 (101 full-time)
Number of students: 2,220 (903 undergraduate, 1,317 graduate)

DEANS

Chatham College for Women: Dr KAROL E. DEAN
College for Graduate Studies: Dr DAVID DONNELLY
School of Sustainability and Environment: Dr DAVID HASSENZAHL

CHESTNUT HILL COLLEGE

9601 Germantown Ave, Philadelphia, PA 19118

Telephone: (215) 248-7000
E-mail: admissions@chc.edu
Internet: www.chc.edu

Founded 1924
Private control

Pres.: Dr CAROL JEAN VALE
Provost: Dr JOHN FLYNN
Sr Vice-Pres. and Vice-Pres. for Academic Affairs: KENNETH J. SOPRANO
Vice-Pres. for Academic Affairs: Dr KENNETH J. SOPRANO
Vice-Pres. for Enrolment Management: JODIE K. SMITH
Vice-Pres. for Financial Affairs: LAURI STRIMKOVSKY
Vice-Pres. for Information Technology: Dr GEORGE P. MCKENNA
Vice-Pres. for Institutional Advancement: KENNETH M. HICKS
Vice-Pres. for Student Life: Dr LYNN ORTALE
Registrar: DEBORAH EBBERT
Dean for Library: MARY JOSEPHINE LARKIN

Library of 135,554 vols
Number of teachers: 120
Number of students: 1,545
Publication: *Chestnut Hill Magazine*

DEANS

School of Continuing and Professional Studies: Dr ELAINE R. GREEN
School of Graduate Studies: Dr STEVEN GUERRIERO
School of Undergraduate Studies: Dr CECELIA J. CAVANAUGH

MISERICORDIA UNIVERSITY

301 Lake St, Dallas, PA 18612
Telephone: (570) 674-6400
E-mail: admiss@misericordia.edu
Internet: www.misericordia.edu

Founded 1924 as College Misericordia, present name and status 2007
Private control
Academic year: August to May

Pres.: Dr MICHAEL A. MACDOWELL
Vice-Pres. for Academic Affairs: MARI P. KING
Vice-Pres. for Finance and Admin.: JOHN RISBOSKIN
Vice-Pres. for Planning, Assessment and Research: Dr BARBARA SAMUEL LOFTUS
Vice-Pres. for Student Affairs: JEAN MESSAROS
Vice-Pres. for Univ. Advancement: SUSAN M. HELWIG
Dean for Students: KIT FOLEY
Registrar: JOSEPH REDINGTON
Library Dir: MARTHA STEVENSON

Library of 71,546 vols, 2,832 video cassettes
Number of teachers: 110 (full-time)
Number of students: 2,830 (1,719 full-time, 707 part-time, 404 graduate)

DEANS

College of Arts and Sciences: Dr RUSS POTTLE
College of Health Sciences: Dr JEAN A. DYER
College of Professional Studies and Social Sciences: FRED J. CROOP

CURTIS INSTITUTE OF MUSIC

1726 Locust St, Philadelphia, PA 19103

Telephone: (215) 893-5252
E-mail: info@curtis.edu
Internet: www.curtis.edu

Founded 1924
Private control
Academic year: September to May

Areas of study: composition; conducting; keyboard instruments (piano, organ, harpsichord); orchestral instruments (strings, harp, woodwinds, brass, timpani, percussion); vocal studies (voice, opera); guitar

Pres. and CEO: ROBERTO DÍAZ
Exec. Vice-Pres. and Chief Operating Officer: ELIZABETH WARSHAWER
Dean: PAUL BRYAN
Dir of Music Library and Information Resources: MICHELLE OSWELL

Library of 65,000 vols, incl. musical scores and books, 33,000 recordings
Number of teachers: 110
Number of students: 165
Publication: *Overtones* (2 a year)

DELAWARE VALLEY COLLEGE

Doylestown, PA 18901
Telephone: (215) 345-1500
E-mail: info@delval.edu
Internet: www.delval.edu

Founded 1896 as Nat. Farm School, current name adopted 1989
Private control
Academic year: August to May

Pres.: Dr JOSEPH S. BROSNAN
Vice-Pres for Academic Affairs and Dean for Faculty: Dr BASHAR W. HANNA
Vice-Pres. for Institutional Advancement: JASON KETTER
Vice-Pres. for Student Affairs: JOHN BROWN
Registrar: ROBERT P. MORAN
Library Dir: PETER KUPERSMITH

Library of 73,600 vols
Number of teachers: 80
Number of students: 2,000 (1,600 undergraduate)

DEANS

Agriculture and Environmental Sciences: RUSSELL REDDING
Business, Education, Arts and Sciences: Dr BENJAMIN E. RUSILOSKI

DESALES UNIVERSITY

2755 Station Ave, Center Valley, PA 18034

Telephone: (610) 282-1100
E-mail: admiss@desales.edu
Internet: www.desales.edu

Founded 1964 as Allentown College of St Francis de Sales, current name and status 2001
Private control
Academic year: August to May
Campuses in Bethlehem, Center Valley and Lansdale

Pres.: Fr BERNARD F. O'CONNOR
Provost and Vice-Pres. for Academic Affairs: Dr KAREN DOYLE WALTON
Vice-Pres. for Admin. and Finance: ROBERT SNYDER
Vice-Pres. for Institutional Advancement: THOMAS L. CAMPBELL
Vice-Pres. for Student Life: Dr GERARD JOYCE
Dean for Enrolment Management: MARY BIRKHEAD
Dean for Graduate Education: PETER LEONARD
Dean for Students: LINDA ZERBE
Dean for Undergraduate Education: Dr ROBERT BLUMENSTEIN
Registrar: THOMAS MANTONI
Library Dir: DEBORAH MALONE

Library of 163,935 vols, 447,834 microform items, 7,901 audiovisual items, 12,355 print and electronic periodicals
Number of teachers: 315 (108 full-time, 207 part-time)
Number of students: 3,265 (2,481 undergraduate, 784 graduate)
Publication: *DeSales University Magazine* (2 a year)

DICKINSON COLLEGE

POB 1773, Carlisle, PA 17013-2896

Telephone: (717) 243-5121
Internet: www.dickinson.edu

Founded 1783
Private control
Academic year: August to May

Global campuses: Australia, Cameroon, China, England, France, Germany, Italy, Japan, Republic of Korea, Mexico, Russia and Spain

Pres.: WILLIAM G. DURDEN
Provost: NEIL WEISSMAN
Vice-Pres. for College Advancement: CAROLYN YEAGER
Vice-Pres. for Enrolment, Marketing and Communications and Dean for Admissions: STEPHANIE BALMER
Vice-Pres. for Finance and Admin. and Treas.: THOMAS A. K. QUEENAN
Vice-Pres. for Student Devt: APRIL VARI
Gen. Counsel: DANA SCADUTO
Dean for Students: LEONARD BROWN, JR
Registrar: KAREN WEIKEL
Dir for Library: ELEANOR MITCHELL

Library of 510,000 vols, 1,600 periodical subscriptions
Number of teachers: 210
Number of students: 2,365

Publications: *Dickinson Magazine*, *The Dickinson Review* (1 a year), *Frontiers* (1 a year)

DREXEL UNIVERSITY

3141 Chestnut St, Philadelphia, PA 19104

Telephone: (215) 895-2000
E-mail: univrel@drexel.edu
Internet: www.drexel.edu

Founded 1891 as Drexel Institute of Art, Science and Industry, present name and status 1970

Private control
Academic year: September to August
Pres.: JOHN A. FRY
Provost and Sr Vice-Pres. for Academic Affairs: Dr MARK GREENBERG
Vice-Provost for Institutional Research: Dr CRAIG N. BACH
Sr Vice-Pres. for Enrolment Management: JOAN T. McDONALD
Sr Vice-Pres. for Finance and Treas.: HELEN Y. BOWMAN
Sr Vice-Pres. for Institutional Advancement: Dr ELIZABETH A. DALE
Sr Vice-Pres. for Student Life and Admin. Services: JAMES R. TUCKER
Sr Vice-Pres. for Univ. Communications: LORI N. DOYLE
Sr Vice-Pres. and Exec. Dir: BRIAN T. KEECH
Sr Vice-Pres. and General Counsel: MICHAEL J. EXLER
Vice-Pres. for Govt and Community Relations: DAVID E. WILSON
Vice-Pres. for Information Resources and Technology: Dr JOHN A. BIELEC
Vice-Pres. for Univ. Facilities: ROBERT FRANCIS
Vice-Pres. and Comptroller: SUSAN WILMER
Dean for Students: Dr DAVID A. RUTH
Dean for Libraries: Dr DANUTA NITECKI
Library of 611,143 vols
Number of teachers: 1,760 (1,044 full-time, 716 part-time)
Number of students: 23,500
Publications: *BMa: The Sonia Sanchez Literary Review*, *Drexel Law Review*, *Drexel Med Journal*, *Journal of Culture and Retail* (irregular), *Maya Literary Magazine*, *The Smart Set*

DEANS

Antoinette Westphal College of Media Arts and Design: ALLEN SABINSON
Bennett S. LeBow College of Business: Dr GEORGE P. TSETSEKOS
College of Arts and Sciences: Dr DONNA MURASKO
College of Engineering: Dr JOSEPH HUGHES
College of Information Science and Technology: Dr DAVID E. FENSKE
College of Nursing and Health Professions: Dr GLORIA F. DONNELLY
Drexel Univ. College of Medicine: Dr DANIEL V. SCHIDLOW
Earle Mack School of Law: Dr ROGER J. DENNIS
Goodwin College—School of Technology and Professional Studies: Dr WILLIAM F. LYNCH
Pennoni Honors College: Dr D. B. JONES
School of Public Health: Dr MARLA J. GOLD

DUQUESNE UNIVERSITY

600 Forbes Ave, Pittsburgh, PA 15282
Telephone: (412) 396-6000
E-mail: admissions@duq.edu
Internet: www.duq.edu
Founded 1878 as Pittsburgh Catholic College
Private control
Academic year: August to May
Pres.: Dr CHARLES J. DOUGHERTY
Provost and Academic Vice-Pres.: Dr RALPH L. PEARSON
Exec. Vice-Pres. for Student Life: Rev. SEAN M. HOGAN
Vice-Pres. for Legal Affairs, Gen. Counsel and Univ. Sec.: Dr LINDA DRAGO
Vice-Pres. for Management and Business: STEPHEN A. SCHILLO
Vice-Pres. for Univ. Advancement: JOHN PLANTE
Registrar: PATRICIA JAKUB
Librarian: Dr LAVERNA SAUNDERS
Library of 723,919 vols, 328,312 microforms

Number of teachers: 990 (480 full-time, 510 part-time)
Number of students: 10,000 (5,750 undergraduate, 3,615 graduate, 635 law)
Publications: *Classical World* (4 a year), *Duquesne Business Law Journal*, *Duquesne Criminal Law Journal* (2 a year), *Duquesne Law Review* (4 a year), *Duquesne University Magazine*

DEANS

Bayer School of Natural and Environmental Sciences: Dr DAVID W. SEYBERT
Mary Pappert School of Music: Dr EDWARD KOCHER
McAnulty College and Graduate School of Liberal Arts: Dr JAMES C. SWINDAL (acting)
Mylan School of Pharmacy: Dr J. DOUGLAS BRICKER
Palumbo Donahue School of Business: Dr ALAN R. MICIAK
Rangos School of Health Sciences: Dr GREGORY H. FRAZER
School of Education: Dr OLGA M. WELCH
School of Law: Dr KEN GORMLEY
School of Leadership and Professional Advancement: Dr DOROTHY BASSETT
School of Nursing: Dr EILEEN ZUNGOLO

EASTERN UNIVERSITY

1300 Eagle Rd, St Davids, PA 19087-3696
Telephone: (610) 341-5800
Internet: www.eastern.edu
Founded 1932 as dept of Eastern Baptist Theological Seminary, present name and status 2001
Private control
Academic year: August to May
Pres.: Dr ROBERT DUFFETT
Provost and Chief Academic Officer: Dr R. KEITH IDDINGS
Exec. Vice-Pres. for Marketing, Innovation and New Ventures: Dr M. THOMAS RIDINGTON
Vice-Pres. for Admin. and Univ. Registrar: DIANA BACCI
Vice-Pres. for Devt: JAMES ROGERS
Vice-Pres. for Enrolment Management: Dr KENTON SPARKS
Vice-Pres. for Finance and Operations: J. PERNELL JONES
Vice-Pres. for Institutional Planning, Research and Assessment: CHRISTINE MAHAN
Vice-Pres. for Student Devt: Dr BETTIE ANN BRIGHAM
Dir for Library: JAMES L. SAUER
Library of 500,000 vols (incl. ebooks), 65,429 online periodicals
Number of teachers: 496 (147 full-time, 349 part-time)
Number of students: 4,004
Publication: *Spirit Magazine*

DEANS

Campolo College of Graduate and Professional Studies: Dr DEBRA HEATH-THORNTON
College of Arts and Sciences: Dr JOHN PAULEY
Esperanza College: Dr ELIZABETH CONDE-FRAZIER
Palmer Theological Seminary: Dr DIANE CHEN
Templeton Honors College: Dr JONATHAN YONAN

ELIZABETHTOWN COLLEGE

One Alpha Dr., Elizabethtown, PA 17022-2290
Telephone: (717) 361-1000
E-mail: admissions@etown.edu
Internet: www.etown.edu
Founded 1899

Private control
Academic year: August to May
Pres.: CARL J. STRIKWERDA
Provost and Sr Vice-Pres.: Dr SUSAN TRAVERSO
Vice-Pres. for Admin.: DAVID DENTLER
Vice-Pres. for Enrolment: PAUL CRAMER
Vice-Pres. for Financial Services and Treas.: RICHARD L. BAILEY
Vice-Pres. for Institutional Advancement and Community Relations: DAVID C. BEIDLEMAN
Dean for Faculty: FLETCHER McCLELLAN
Dean for Students: MARIANNE CALENDA
Dir for Library: BETH ANN ZAMBELLA
Library of 256,000 vols
Number of teachers: 125 (full-time)
Number of students: 1,900
Publications: *The Business & Economics Digest*, *The Oyster* (2 a year)

EVANGELICAL SEMINARY

121 S College St, Myerstown, PA 17067-1299
Telephone: (717) 866-5775
E-mail: info@evangelical.edu
Internet: www.evangelical.edu
Founded 1953 as Evangelical Congregational School of Theology, present name 2011
Private control
Academic year: 2 semesters
Pres.: Dr ANTHONY L. BLAIR
Vice-Pres. for Finance and Operations: KEVIN C. HENRY
Vice-Pres. for Institutional Advancement: ANN E. STEEL
Dean for Academic Programmes: LAURIE A. MELLINGER
Dean for Admissions: TOM M. MAIELLO
Registrar: ELLIS I. KIRK
Head Librarian: TERRY M. HEISEY
Library of 75,000 vols; 550 periodical titles
Number of teachers: 15
Number of students: 200
Publication: *The Evangelical Journal* (2 a year)

FRANKLIN & MARSHALL COLLEGE

POB 3003, Lancaster, PA 17604-3003
415 Harrisburg Ave, Lancaster, PA 17603
Telephone: (717) 291-3911
Internet: www.fandm.edu
Founded 1787, present name and status 1853
Private control
Academic year: August to May
Pres.: DAN POTERFIELD
Provost: Dr ANN STEINER
Vice-Pres. for College Advancement: LEWIS E. THAYNE
Dean: Dr KENT TRACHTE
Registrar: CHRISTINE D. ALEXANDER
Librarian: PAMELA SNELSON
Library of 523,323 vols, 29,096 periodicals
Number of teachers: 215
Number of students: 2,230
Publication: *The Liberal Arts Review*

GANNON UNIVERSITY

109 University Sq., Erie, PA 16541-0001
Telephone: (814) 871-7000
Internet: www.gannon.edu
Founded 1925
Private control
Academic year: 2 semesters
Pres.: Dr KEITH TAYLOR
Provost and Vice-Pres. for Academic Affairs: Dr LINDA FLEMING
Vice-Pres. for Enrolment: WILLIAM R. EDMONDSON

Vice-Pres. for Finance and Admin.: LINDA WAGNER
Vice-Pres. for Mission: Rev. GEORGE STROHMEYER
Vice-Pres. for Univ. Advancement: JACK H. SIMS
Dean for Students: WARD MCCRACKEN
Registrar: MARILYN MOORE
Library Dir: KEN BRUNDAGE
Library of 265,000 vols, 4000 audiovisual items
Number of teachers: 290 (196 full-time, 144 adjunct)
Number of students: 4,075 (2,925 undergraduate, 1,150 graduate)

DEANS

College of Engineering and Business: Dr MELANIE L. HATCH
College of Humanities, Education and Social Sciences: Prof. JOHN YOUNG
Morosky College of Health Professions and Sciences: Dr CAROLYNN B. MASTERS

GENEVA COLLEGE

3200 College Ave, Beaver Falls, PA 15010
Telephone: (724) 846-5100
E-mail: admissions@geneva.edu
Internet: www.geneva.edu
Founded 1848
Private control
Academic year: August to May
Depts: Bible, Christian ministries and philosophy; biology; business; chemistry; communication; computer science, mathematics and physics; education; engineering; English; history, political science and sociology; languages and cultures; music; psychology, counselling and human services; physical education
Pres.: Dr KENNETH A. SMITH
Provost: KEN CARSON
Exec. Vice-Pres.: LARRY GRIFFITH
Vice-Pres. for Advancement: JEFF JONES
Chief Financial Officer: MIKE FOX
Dean for Academic Programmes: Dr MELINDA STEPHENS
Dean for Faculty and Admin.: Dr TERRI WILLIAMS
Registrar: ANDREA KORCAN-BUZZA
College Librarian: JOHN DONCEVIĆ
Library of 167,206 vols, 879 periodicals, 198,624 units of micro texts and instructional media
Number of teachers: 95 (full-time)
Number of students: 1,880

GETTYSBURG COLLEGE

300 N Washington St, Gettysburg, PA 17325
Telephone: (717) 337-6300
E-mail: admiss@gettysburg.edu
Internet: www.gettysburg.edu
Founded 1832 as Pennsylvania College, current name adopted 1921
Private control
Academic year: August to May
Pres.: JANET MORGAN RIGGS
Provost: CHRISTOPHER ZAPPE
Exec. Vice-Pres.: JANE NORTH
Vice-Pres. for College Life and Dean for Students: JULIE L. RAMSEY
Dir for Admissions: GAIL SWEEZEY
Library Dir: ROBIN WAGNER
Library of 425,000 vols, 11,000 sound recordings, 19,000 DVDs and video cassettes, 3,400 linear ft of MSS and archives, 9,000 music scores, 70,800 microforms
Number of teachers: 175
Number of students: 2,600
Publication: Gettysburg Review

GRATZ COLLEGE

7605 Old York Rd, Melrose Park, PA 19027
Telephone: (215) 635-7300
E-mail: enroll@gratz.edu
Internet: www.gratzcollege.edu
Founded 1856 as Hebrew Teacher's College
Private control
Academic year: September to May
Courses in Jewish communal service, Jewish early childhood education, Jewish education, Jewish music, Jewish non-profit management, Jewish studies
Pres. and Chief Operating Officer: Dr JOY W. GOLDSTEIN
Dean for Academic Affairs: Dr JERRY M. KUTNICK
Library Dir: ELIEZER M. WISE
Library of 125,000 vols
Number of teachers: 15
Number of students: 150

GROVE CITY COLLEGE

100 Campus Dr., Grove City, PA 16127
Telephone: (724) 458-2000
E-mail: admissions@gcc.edu
Internet: www.gcc.edu
Founded 1876
Private control
Academic year: August to May
Pres.: Dr RICHARD G. JEWELL
Provost and Vice-Pres. for Academic Affairs: Dr WILLIAM P. ANDERSON
Vice-Pres. for Financial Affairs: ROGER K. TOWLE
Vice-Pres. for Institutional Advancement: JEFFREY PROKOVICH
Vice-Pres. for Operations: THOMAS W. GREGG
Vice-Pres. for Student Life and Learning: LARRY HARDESTY
Dean for Int. Studies, Graduate Advancement and Faculty Devt: Dr CHARLES W. DUNN
Registrar: JOHN G. INMAN
Library Dir: DIANE H. GRUNDY
Number of teachers: 115
Number of students: 2,530

DEANS

Hopeman School of Science, Engineering and Mathematics: Dr STACY BIRMINGHAM,
Calderwood School of Arts and Letters: Dr JOHN A. SPARKS

GWYNEDD-MERCY COLLEGE

POB 901, 1325 Sumneytown Pike, Gwynedd Valley, PA 19437-0901
Telephone: (215) 646-7300
E-mail: admissions@gmc.edu
Internet: www.gmc.edu
Founded 1948 as Gwynedd-Mercy Junior College, current name adopted 1963
Private control
Academic year: August to December
Campuses at Bensalem, Gwynedd Valley and East Norriton
Pres.: Dr KATHLEEN OWENS
Vice-Pres. for Academic Affairs: Dr ROBERT N. FUNK
Vice-Pres. for Enrolment Management: JAMES ABBUHL
Vice-Pres. for Finance and Admin.: KEVIN O'FLAHERTY
Vice-Pres. for Institutional Advancement: GERALD MCLAUGHLIN
Vice-Pres. for Student Services: Dr CHERYL LYNN HORSEY
Registrar: THERESA ANDERSON
Library Dir: DANIEL SCHABERT
Number of teachers: 80 (full-time)

Number of students: 2,700 (1,260 undergraduate)
Publications: The Griffin, Today

DEANS

School of Allied Health Professions: LINDA REILLY
School of Arts and Sciences: LISA MCGARRY
School of Business and Center for Lifelong Learning: Dr MUHAMMAD LATIB
School of Education: Dr SANDRA D. MANGANO
School of Nursing: ANDREA HOLLINGSWORTH

HAVERFORD COLLEGE

370 Lancaster Ave, Haverford, PA 19041-1392
Telephone: (610) 896-1000
E-mail: admission@haverford.edu
Internet: www.haverford.edu
Founded 1833 as Haverford School
Private control
Academic year: September to May
Liberal arts college
Pres.: Dr JOANNE V. CREIGHTON
Provost: LINDA BELL
Vice-Pres. for Admin. and Finance and Treas.: G. RICHARD WYNN
Vice-Pres. for Institutional Advancement: MICHAEL KIEFER
Dean for Admissions and Financial Aid: JESS H. LORD
Dean for College: MARTHA DENNEY
Registrar: LEE WATKINS
Librarian: TERRY SNYDER
Library of 595,522 vols
Number of teachers: 140 (120 full-time, 20 part-time)
Number of students: 1,175
Publication: Haverford Magazine (3 a year)

HOLY FAMILY UNIVERSITY

9801 Frankford Ave, Philadelphia, PA 19114
Telephone: (215) 637-7700
E-mail: admissions@holyfamily.edu
Internet: www.holyfamily.edu
Founded 1954
Private control
Academic year: October to May (two semesters)
Campuses in Northeast Philadelphia, Newtown and Bensalem
Pres.: Sis. Dr FRANCESCA ONLEY
Vice-Pres. for Academic Affairs: Sis. Dr MAUREEN MCGARRITY
Vice-Pres. for Finance and Admin.: JOHN JASZCZAK
Vice-Pres. for Institutional Advancement: MARGARET S. KELLY
Vice-Pres. for Student Services: Sis. Dr MARCELLA BINKOWSKI
Exec. Dir for Admissions: LAUREN CAMPBELL
Dir for Library Services: LORI A. SCHWABENBAUER
Library of 106,000 vols
Number of teachers: 255
Number of students: 3,185 (1,972 undergraduate, 910 graduate, 22 doctoral, 281 accelerated)
Publications: Familogue (1 a year), Folio, Mosaic, The Family Tree

DEANS

School of Arts and Sciences: Dr MICHAEL MARKOWITZ
School of Business Administration: Dr JACK V. KIRNAN
School of Education: Dr LEONARD G. SOROKA
School of Nursing and Allied Health Professions: Dr CHRISTINE ROSNER

IMMACULATA UNIVERSITY

1145 King Rd, Immaculata, PA 19345

Telephone: (610) 647-4400

Internet: www.immaculata.edu

Founded 1920 as Villa Maria College, present name and status 2002

Private control

Pres.: Sis. Dr R. PATRICIA FADDEN

Vice-Pres.for Academic Affairs: Sis. Dr ANN M. HEATH

Vice-Pres. for Finance and Admin.: JENNIFER M. SAUER

Vice-Pres. for Student Devt and Engagement: Dr BARBARA W. WILLIAMS

Vice-Pres. for Univ. Advancement: Dr STEPHEN J. PUGLIESE

Vice-Pres. for Univ. Communications: ROBERT D. COLE

Registrar: JANICE BATES

Dir for Admissions: NICOLA DiFRONZO-HEITZER

Library Dir: JEFFREY ROLLISON

Library of 115,000 vols

Number of teachers: 165

Number of students: 4,400 (3,200 undergraduate, 1,200 graduate and doctoral)

DEANS

College of Graduate Studies: Dr JANET KANE

College of Lifelong Learning: Dr SAMUEL WRIGHTSON

College of Undergraduate Studies: Sis. Dr ELAINE GLANZ

JUNIATA COLLEGE

1700 Moore St, Huntingdon, PA 16652

Telephone: (814) 641-3000

E-mail: info@juniata.edu

Internet: www.juniata.edu

Founded 1876

Private control

Academic year: August to May

Depts: accounting, business, and economics; art; biology; chemistry; communication; environmental sciences; education; English; geology; health professions; history; information technology, computer science, and digital media; international education; international studies; mathematics; music; peace and conflict studies; philosophy; physics and engineering physics; politics; psychology; religious studies; sociology, anthropology, and social work; theatre; world languages and cultures

Pres.: Dr THOMAS R. KEPPLE, JR

Provost and Exec. Vice-Pres. for Student Devt: JAMES LAKSO

Exec. Vice-Pres. for Enrolment and Retention: JOHN HILLE

Vice-Pres. for Advancement and Marketing: GABE WELSCH

Vice-Pres. for Finance and Operations: ROB YELNOSKY

Assoc. Vice-Pres. and Chief Information Officer: DAVE FUSCO

Dean for Students: KRIS CLARKSON

Registrar: ATHENA FREDERICK

Library Dir: JOHN MUMFORD

Number of teachers: 145

Number of students: 1,620 (full-time)

KEYSTONE COLLEGE

POB 50, One College Green, La Plume, PA 18440-0200

Telephone: (570) 945-8000

E-mail: admissions@keystone.edu

Internet: www.keystone.edu

Founded 1868 as Keystone Acad., current name adopted 1995

Private control

Divs: business, management and technology; communication arts and humanities; education; fine arts; natural sciences and mathematics; social and behavioural sciences

Pres.: Dr EDWARD G. BOEHM, JR

Vice-Pres. for Academic Affairs and Dean for College: THEA A. HARRINGTON

Vice-Pres. for Enrolment: SARAH KEATING

Vice-Pres. for Finance and Admin.: KEVIN WILSON

Vice-Pres. for Student Affairs and Dean for Students: Dr ROBERT J. PERKINS

Registrar: KATE OWENS

Dir for Admissions: KATHRYN REILLY

Library Dir: MARI FLYNN

Number of students: 1,775

KING'S COLLEGE

133 N River St, Wilkes-Barre, PA 18711

Telephone: (570) 208-5900

E-mail: admissions@kings.edu

Internet: www.kings.edu

Founded 1946

Private control

Academic year: August to May

Pres.: Rev. JOHN J. RYAN

Vice-Pres for Academic Affairs: Dr JOSEPH EVAN

Vice-Pres for Business Affairs and Treas.: JOHN LOYACK

Vice-Pres. for Enrolment Management: CORRY UNIS

Vice-Pres for Institutional Advancement: FREDERICK A. PETTIT

Vice-Pres for Student Affairs: JANET E. MERCINCAVAGE

Assoc. Vice-Pres. for Student Success and Retention: TERESA PECK

Dean for Students: ROBERT B. McGONIGLE

Registrar: DANIEL CEBRICK

Library Dir: Dr TERRENCE MECH

Library of 185,081 vols

Number of teachers: 231 (135 full-time, 96 part-time)

Number of students: 2,144

LA ROCHE COLLEGE

9000 Babcock Blvd, Pittsburgh, PA 15237-5898

Telephone: (412) 367-9300

E-mail: admsns@laroche.edu

Internet: www.laroche.edu

Founded 1963

Private control

Pres.: Sis. Dr CANDACE INTROCASO

Vice-Pres. for Academic Affairs and Academic Dean: Dr HOWARD J. ISHIYAMA

Vice-Pres. for Admin. Services: GEORGE ZAFFUTO

Vice-Pres. for Finance and Chief Financial Officer: ROBERT VOGEL

Vice-Pres. for Enrolment Management and Marketing: WILLIAM H. FIRMAN, JR

Vice-Pres. for Institutional Advancement: MICHAEL ANDREOLA

Vice-Pres. for Student Life and Dean of Students: COLLEEN RUEFLE

Dir for Admissions: STEPHEN STEPPE

Gen. Counsel: Dr MARY BETH FETCHKO

Registrar: JOAN CUTONE

Library Dir: LaVERNE P. COLLINS

Number of teachers: 155

Number of students: 1,355 (984 undergraduate)

LA SALLE UNIVERSITY

1900 W Olney Ave, Philadelphia, PA 19141

Telephone: (215) 951-1000

Internet: www.lasalle.edu

Founded 1863

Private control

Academic year: August to May

Pres.: Bro. MICHAEL J. McGINNISS

Provost: Dr JOSEPH R. MARBACH

Vice-Pres. for Finance and Admin.: MATTHEW S. McMANNESS

Vice-Pres. for Student Affairs and Dean for Students: JAMES E. MOORE

Vice-Pres. for Univ. Advancement: BRIAN ELDERTON

Exec. Dir for Admissions: JIM PLUNKETT

Library Dir: JOHN BAKY

Library of 375,000 vols

Number of teachers: 210 (full-time)

Number of students: 7,330 (3,358 full-time undergraduate, 1,314 part-time undergraduate and 2,658 graduate)

Publications: *Four Quarters* (4 a year), *La Salle Bulletin* (4 a year), *La Salle Magazine* (4 a year)

DEANS

College of Professional and Continuing Studies: JOSEPH Y. UGRAS

School of Arts and Sciences: Dr THOMAS A. KEAGY

School of Business: PAUL R. BRAZINA

School of Nursing and Health Sciences: Dr ZANE ROBINSON WOLF

LAFAYETTE COLLEGE

Quad Dr., Easton, PA 18042

Telephone: (610) 330-5100

E-mail: admissions@lafayette.edu

Internet: www.lafayette.edu

Founded 1826

Private control

Academic year: August to May

Pres.: DANIEL H. WEISS

Provost and Dean for Faculty: WENDY L. HILL

Registrar: FRANCIS A. BENGINIA

Dean for College: HANNAH W. STEWART-GAMBINO

Dean for Libraries: NEIL J. McELROY

Library of 502,603 vols

Number of teachers: 215 (full-time)

Number of students: 2,360

LAKE ERIE COLLEGE OF OSTEOPATHIC MEDICINE

1858 W Grandview Blvd, Erie, PA 16509-1025

Telephone: (814) 866-6641

Internet: www.lecom.edu

Founded 1993

Private control

Academic year: August to May

Campuses: Greensburg and Seton Hill, Pennsylvania; Bradenton, Florida

Pres. and CEO: Dr JOHN M. FERRETT

Provost, Sr Vice-Pres. and Dean for Academic Affairs: SILVIA M. FERRETTI

Vice-Pres. for Academic Affairs: Dr HERSHEY BELL

Vice-Pres. for Fiscal Affairs and Chief Financial Officer: RICHARD P. OLINGER

Dir for Student Affairs: RONALD SHIVELY

DEANS

School of Pharmacy: Dr HERSHEY BELL

LANCASTER BIBLE COLLEGE

901 Eden Rd, Lancaster, PA 17601

Telephone: (717) 569-7071

E-mail: admissions@lbc.edu

Internet: www.lbc.edu

Founded 1933

Private control

Depts: arts and sciences, Bible and theology, Church and min. leadership, counselling and social work, education, health and physical education, worship and performing arts

Pres.: Dr PETER W. TEAGUE

Exec. Vice-Pres.: RICHARD A. WILSON

Vice-Pres. for Academic Affairs: Dr PHILIP E. DEARBORN

Vice-Pres. for Enrolment Management: JOSHUA BEERS

Dean for Undergraduate Education: G. GORDON GREGORY, JR

Library Dir: GERALD E. LINCOLN

Library of 201,051 vols

Number of teachers: 105 (55 full-time, 50 part-time)

Number of students: 1,115 (955 undergraduate, 160 graduate)

LANCASTER GENERAL COLLEGE OF NURSING & HEALTH SCIENCES

410 N Lime St, Lancaster, PA 17602

Telephone: (717) 544-4912

E-mail: lgc_admissions@lancastergeneral.org

Internet: www.lancastergeneralcollege.edu

Founded 1903 as Lancaster Gen. Hospital School of Nursing, present name and status 2001

Private control

Academic year: August to May

Pres.: SIMCOX MARY GRACE

Vice-Pres. for Academic Affairs: PENNI ATEN LONGENECKER

Vice-Pres. for Finance and Admin.: THOMAS HULSTINE

Vice-Pres. for Learning Devt: DONNA WILLIAMSON

Dean for Enrolment Management: SANDRA ZERBY

Dir of Admissions: LYN LONGENECKER

Registrar: GERALDINE MAY

Library Dir: CYNTHIA McCLELLAN

Library of 8,000 vols, incl. 400 print journals

Publication: *Destiny* (3 a year)

DEANS

Division of General Education: Dr PEGGY ROSARIO

Division of Health Sciences: CONSTANCE CORRIGAN

Division of Nursing: CHERYL GRAB

LANCASTER THEOLOGICAL SEMINARY

555 W James St, Lancaster, PA 17603

Telephone: (717) 393-0654

E-mail: seminary@lancasterseminary.edu

Internet: www.lts.org

Founded 1825 as Seminary of the Reformed Church

Private control

Pres.: Dr CAROL E. LYTCH

Vice-Pres. for Academic Affairs and Acting Dean: Dr DAVID M. MELLOTT

Vice-Pres. for Business and Finance: VALERIE A. CALHOUN

Vice-Pres. for Advancement and Communications: CRYSTAL MILLS

Library Dir: RICHARD BERG

Library of 150,000 vols

Number of teachers: 12

Number of students: 150

LEBANON VALLEY COLLEGE

101 N College Ave, Annville, PA 17003-1400

Telephone: (717) 867-6100

E-mail: admission@lvc.edu

Internet: www.lvc.edu

Founded 1866

Private control

Academic year: August to May

Courses in physical therapy, business administration, music education and science education

Pres.: STEPHEN C. MACDONALD

Vice-Pres. for Academic Affairs and Dean for Faculty: MICHAEL R. GREEN (acting)

Vice-Pres. for Admin. and Information Technology: ROBERT A. RILEY

Vice-Pres. for Advancement: ANNE M. BERRY

Vice-Pres. for Enrolment: WILLIAM J. BROWN

Vice-Pres. for Finance: DEBORAH R. FULLAM

Vice-Pres. for Student Affairs: GREGORY H. KRIKORIAN

Registrar: JEREMY A. MAISTO

Dir for Library: FRANK MOLS

Library of 225,000 vols, 3,000 print and ejournal subscriptions

Number of teachers: 100 (full-time)

Number of students: 2,100 (1,630 full-time undergraduate, 155 part-time undergraduate, 315 graduate)

Publication: *The Valley Magazine*

LEHIGH UNIVERSITY

27 Memorial Dr., W, Bethlehem, PA 18015-3089

Telephone: (610) 758-3000

Internet: www.lehigh.edu

Founded 1865

Private control

Academic year: August to May

Pres.: ALICE P. GAST

Provost and Vice-Pres. for Academic Affairs: PATRICK V. FARRELL

Vice-Provost for Institutional Research: J. GARY LUTZ

Vice-Provost for Library and Technology Services: BRUCE M. TAGGART

Vice-Provost for Student Affairs: JOHN W. SMEATON

Vice-Pres. for Advancement: JOSEPH KENDER

Vice-Pres. for Communications and Public Affairs: FREDERICK J. McGRAIL

Vice-Pres. for Finance and Admin.: MARGARET F. PLYMPTON

Vice-Pres. for Int. Affairs: MOHAMED EL-AASSER

Gen. Counsel: FRANK ROTH

Registrar: EMIL GNASSO

Library of 1,324,500 vols, 25,000 periodicals, 100,000 ebooks

Number of teachers: 665 (463 full-time)

Number of students: 7,035 (4,765 undergraduate, 2,270 graduate)

DEANS

College of Arts and Sciences: Dr DONALD E. HALL

College of Business and Economics: PAUL R. BROWN

College of Education: SASSO GARY

P. C. Rossin College of Engineering and Applied Science: S. DAVID WU

PROFESSORS

College of Arts and Sciences (tel. (610) 758-3300):

ABEL, J. H., Biological Sciences
ALHADEFF, J., Chemistry
BARKEY, H., Int. Relations
BAYLOR, M., History
BEARN, G., Philosophy
BEHE, M., Biological Sciences
BEIDLER, P., English
BICKHARD, M., Psychology
BORSE, G., Physics
BROSS, A., English
CARRELL-SMITH, K., History
CARSON, R., Earth and Environmental Sciences

CHABUT, M.-H., Modern Languages and Literature
COLON, F., Political Science
CUNDALL, D., Biological Sciences
DAVIS, D., Mathematics
DeLEO, G., Physics
DOBRIC, V., Mathematics
DOTY, A., English
DUFFY, I., History
EISENBERG, B., Mathematics
EVENSON, E., Earth and Environmental Sciences
FERGUS, J., English
FIFER, E., English
FOLK, R., Physics
FRIEDMAN, S., Journalism
GALLAGHER, E., English
GANS, L., Art and Architecture
GATEWOOD, J., Sociology and Anthropology
GHOSH, B. K., Mathematics
GIRARDOT, N., Religion
GOLDMAN, S., Philosophy
GORNEY, C., Journalism
GUNTON, J., Physics
HEINDEL, N. D., Chemistry
HERRENKOHL, R., Sociology and Anthropology
HICKMAN, P., Physics
HUANG, W.-M., Mathematics
HUENNEKENS, J., Physics
HYLAND, D., Psychology
ITZKOWITZ, M., Biological Sciences
KANOFSKY, A., Physics
KHABBAZ, S., Mathematics
KIM, Y., Physics
KING, J. P., Mathematics
KLIER, K., Chemistry
KODAMA, K., Earth and Environmental Sciences
KRAFT, K., Religion
KRAWIEC, S., Biological Sciences
KRITZ, A., Physics
KROLL, B., English
LARSEN, J., Chemistry
LASKER, J., Sociology and Anthropology
LULE, J. F., Journalism
McCLUSKEY, G. E., Mathematics
McINTOSH, J., Sociology and Anthropology
MALT, B., Psychology
MARKLEY, N. G., Mathematics
MASON, D., Art and Architecture
MATTHEWS, R., Political Science
MELTZER, A. S., Earth and Environmental Sciences
MENON, M. R., International Relations
MILET, J., Theatre
MOON, B., International Relations
MORGAN, E., Political Science
MUNDHENK, R., English
MYERS, P. B., Earth and Environmental Sciences
NYBY, J. G., Biological Sciences
OLSON, L., Political Science
OU-YANG, D., Physics
PANKENIER, D., Modern Languages and Literature
PETERS, T., Art and Architecture
PHILLIPS, C. R., History
RAPOSA, M., Religion
REGEN, S. L., Chemistry
RICHTER, M., Psychology
RIPA, A., Theatre
ROSENWEIN, R., Sociology and Anthropology
SAEGER, J. S., History
SALATHE, E., Mathematics
SALERNI, P., Music
SAMETZ, S., Music
SANDS, J., Biological Sciences
SCHRAY, K., Chemistry
SCOTT, W. R., History
SILBERSTEIN, L., Religion
SIMMONS, G. W., Chemistry
SIMON, N., Biological Sciences
SIMON, R., History
SINE, N., Music

SMALL, D., Sociology and Anthropology
SMOLANSKY, O., International Relations
SODERLUND, J., History
STANLEY, L., Mathematics
STAVOLA, M., Physics
STEFFEN, L., Religion
STENGLE, G. A., Mathematics
STEWART-GAMBINO, H., Political Science
TANNENBAUM, N., Sociology and Anthropology
TOULOUSE, J., Physics
TRAISTER, B., English
USSLER, C., Art and Architecture
VIERA, R., Art and Architecture
WEINTRAUB, S. H., Mathematics
WEISS, R., Philosophy
WEISSLER, L. E. C., Religion
WILLIAMSON, C., Earth and Environmental Sciences
WOLFGANG, L., Modern Languages and Literature
WRIGHT, B., Religion
WYLIE, R., International Relations
YUKICH, J., Mathematics
ZAKNIC, I., Art and Architecture
ZEITLER, P., Earth and Environmental Sciences
ZEROKA, D., Chemistry

College of Business and Economics (tel. (610) 758-3400):

ARONSON, J. R., Business and Economics
BARSNESS, R. W., Management
BUELL, S. G., Finance
DEARDEN, J. A., Economics
DURAND, R. M., Management and Marketing
FALCINELLI, D. F., Marketing and Management
HYCLAK, T. J., Economics
KING, A. E., Economics
KISH, R. J., Finance
KOLCHIN, M. G., Management
KUCHTA, R., Management and Marketing
LARGAY, J. A., III, Accounting
MUNLEY, V. G., Economics
NATION, G. A., III, Law and Business
NAYAR, N., Finance
O'BRIEN, A. P., Economics
PAUL, J. W., Accounting
SHERER, S. A., Management and Technology
SINCLAIR, K. P., Accounting
SIVAKUMAR, K., International Marketing and Logistics
SMACKEY, B. M., Marketing and Manufacturing Systems Engineering
STEVENS, J. E., Management
TAYLOR, L. W., Economics
THORNTON, R. J., Economics
ZIRKEL, P. A., Education and Law

College of Education (tel. (610) 758-3225):

BAMBARA, L. M., Special Education
CATES, W. M., Instructional Design and Devt
COLE, C., Psychology
DUPAUL, G., Psychology
JITENDRA, A., Special Education
MILLER, D. N., Psychology
SHAPIRO, E., Psychology
ZIRKEL, P., Education and Law

P. C. Rossin College of Engineering and Applied Science (tel. (610) 758-4025):

BLYTHE, P. A., Chemical Engineering, Mechanical Engineering and Mechanics
BOULT, T. E., Computer Science and Engineering
BROWN, F. T., Mechanical Engineering and Mechanics
CARAM, H. S., Chemical Engineering
CARGILL, G. S., III, Materials Science and Engineering
CHAN, H. M., Materials Science and Engineering
CHARLES, M., Chemical Engineering

CHAUDHURY, M. K., Chemical Engineering
CHEN, J. C., Chemical Engineering
CHRISTODOULIDES, D., Electrical and Computer Engineering
COULTER, J. P., Mechanical Engineering and Mechanics
DECKER, D. R., Electrical and Computer Engineering
DELPH, T. J., Mechanical Engineering and Mechanics
EADES, J. A., Materials Science and Engineering
EL-AASSER, M. S., Chemical Engineering
FARRINGTON, G. C., Chemical Engineering
FISHER, J. W., Civil and Environmental Engineering
FREY, D. R., Electrical and Computer Engineering
FRITCHMAN, B. D., Electrical and Computer Engineering
GARDINER, K. M., Industrial and Systems Engineering
GROOVER, M. P., Industrial and Systems Engineering
GULDEN, S. L., Computer Science and Engineering
HARLOW, D. G., Mechanical Engineering and Mechanics
HARMER, M. P., Materials Science and Engineering
HARTRANFT, R. J., Mechanical Engineering and Mechanics
HATALIS, M., Electrical and Computer Engineering
HEINDEL, N. D., Chemistry
HERTZBERG, R. W., Materials Science and Engineering
HILLMAN, D. J., Computer Science and Engineering
HSU, J. T., Chemical Engineering
HWANG, J. C. M., Electrical and Computer Engineering
JAIN, H., Materials Science and Engineering
JOHNSON, S. H., Mechanical Engineering and Mechanics
KALNINS, A., Mechanical Engineering and Mechanics
KAY, E. J., Computer Science and Engineering
KAZAKIA, J. Y., Mechanical Engineering and Mechanics
KLEIN, A., Chemical Engineering
KORTH, H., Computer Science and Engineering
KOSTEM, C. N., Civil and Environmental Engineering
LARSEN, J. W., Chemistry
LENNON, G. P., Civil and Environmental Engineering
LEVY, E. K., Mechanical Engineering and Mechanics
LU, L.-W., Civil and Environmental Engineering
LUCAS, R. A., Mechanical Engineering and Mechanics
LUYBEN, W. L., Chemical Engineering
MCAULAY, A. D., Electrical and Computer Engineering
MCHUGH, A., Chemical Engineering
MACPHERSON, A. K., Mechanical Engineering and Mechanics
MARDER, A. R., Materials Science and Engineering
NAGEL, R. N., Computer Science and Engineering
NETI, S., Mechanical Engineering and Mechanics
NIED, H. F., Mechanical Engineering and Mechanics
NOTIS, M. R., Materials Science and Engineering
OCHS, J. B., Mechanical Engineering and Mechanics
ODREY, N. G., Industrial and Systems Engineering

OU-YANG, H. D., Physics
REGEN, S. L., Chemistry
ROBERTS, R., Mechanical Engineering and Mechanics
ROCKWELL, D. O., Mechanical Engineering and Mechanics
SAWYERS, K. N., Mechanical Engineering and Mechanics
SCHIESSER, W. E., Chemical Engineering
SCHRAY, K. J., Chemistry
SENGUPTA, A. K., Chemical Engineering, Civil and Environmental Engineering
SILEBI, C. A., Chemical Engineering
SIMMONS, G. W., Chemistry
SMITH, C. R., Mechanical Engineering and Mechanics
SORENSEN, R. M., Civil and Environmental Engineering
SPERLING, L. H., Chemical Engineering, Materials Science and Engineering
STENGER, H. G., Jr, Chemical Engineering
TARBY, S. K., Materials Science and Engineering
TZENG, K. K., Electrical and Computer Engineering
VARLEY, E., Mechanical Engineering and Mechanics
VOLOSHIN, A. S., Mechanical Engineering and Mechanics
WACHS, I. E., Chemical Engineering
WALKER, J. D. A., Mechanical Engineering and Mechanics
WEI, R. P., Mechanical Engineering and Mechanics
WEISMAN, R. N., Civil and Environmental Engineering
WHITE, M. H., Electrical and Computer Engineering
WILLIAMS, D. B., Materials Science and Engineering
WILSON, J. L., Civil and Environmental Engineering
WU, S. D., Industrial and Systems Engineering
ZIMMERS, E. W., Jr, Industrial and Systems Engineering

LINCOLN UNIVERSITY OF THE COMMONWEALTH OF PENNSYLVANIA

POB 179, 1570 Baltimore Pike, PA, 19352

Telephone: (484) 365-8000
E-mail: admiss@lu.lincoln.edu
Internet: www.lincoln.edu

Founded 1854 as Ashmun Institute
Academic year: August to April

Pres.: Dr ROBERT R. JENNINGS
Provost and Sr Vice-Pres. for Academic Affairs: Dr GRANT VENERABLE, II
Exec. Vice-Pres.: MICHAEL B. HILL
Exec. Vice-Pres. for Devt, Relations and Services: MICHAEL HILL
Vice-Pres. for External Affairs: REGAN FARLEY
Vice-Pres. for Fiscal Affairs and Admin.: JAMES T. LEWIS
Vice-Pres. for Institutional Advancement: ANDRE DIXON
Vice-Pres. for Student Affairs: F. CARL WALTON
Dean for Enrolment Services: THELMA ROSS
Dean for Students: JERRYL BRIGGS
Registrar: CATHERINE RUTLEDGE
Library Dir: NEAL CARSON

Library of 159,007 vols
Number of teachers: 110 (full-time)
Number of students: 2,240

DEANS

School of Humanities and Graduate Studies: (vacant)
School of Natural Sciences and Mathematics: JOHN O. CHIKWEM

School of Social Sciences and Behavioural Studies: Dr PATRICIA A. JOSEPH

LUTHERAN THEOLOGICAL SEMINARY AT GETTYSBURG

61 Seminary Ridge, Gettysburg, PA 17325-1795

Telephone: (717) 334-6286
E-mail: info@ltsg.edu
Internet: www.ltsg.edu
Founded 1826, present location 1832
Private control
Academic year: September to May
Pres.: Rev. MICHAEL L. COOPER-WHITE
Dean: Rev. Dr ROBIN J. STEINKE
Registrar: Rev. Dr MARTY STEVENS
Treas.: LARRY WEBBER
Library Dir: BRIANT BOHLEKE
Library of 190,000 vols
Number of teachers: 20
Number of students: 230

Publication: *Seminary Ridge Review* (2 a year)

LUTHERAN THEOLOGICAL SEMINARY AT PHILADELPHIA

7301 Germantown Ave, Philadelphia, PA 19119-1794

Telephone: (215) 248-4616
E-mail: admissions@ltsp.edu
Internet: www.ltsp.edu
Founded 1864
Private control
Pres.: Rev. Dr PHILIP D. W. KREY
Vice-Pres. for Advancement: Rev. JOHN V. PUOTINEN
Dean: PAUL RAJASHEKAR
Dir for Admissions: Rev. LOUISE N. JOHNSON
Registrar: RENÉ DIEMER
Library Dir: KARL KRUEGER
Library of 200,000 vols
Number of teachers: 35
Number of students: 220 (full-time)

Publication: *PS Magazine*

LYCOMING COLLEGE

700 College Pl., Williamsport, PA 17701

Telephone: (717) 321-4000
E-mail: admissions@lycoming.edu
Internet: www.lycoming.edu
Founded 1812 as Williamsport Acad. for the Education of Youth in the English and other Languages, in the Useful Arts, Science and Literature, current name adopted 1948
Private control
Language of instruction: English
Areas of study: liberal arts and sciences, health care administration, actuarial mathematics and environmental sustainability
Pres.: Dr KENT TRACHTE
Provost and Dean: Dr PHILIP SPRUNGER
Vice-Pres. for Admissions and Financial Aid: JAMES D. SPENCER
Vice-Pres. for College Advancement: CHIP EDMONDS
Vice-Pres. for Finance and Admin.: JEFF BENNETT
Dean for Student Affairs: Dr DANIEL P. MILLER
Registrar: WHITNEY MERINAR
Dir for Library Services: JANET MCNEIL HURLBERT
Library of 187,722 vols, 1,200 periodicals
Number of teachers: 90 (full-time)
Number of students: 1,400

Publication: *Lycoming Magazine*

MARYWOOD UNIVERSITY

2300 Adams Ave, Scranton, PA 18509-1598

Telephone: (570) 348-6211
E-mail: yourfuture@marywood.edu
Internet: www.marywood.edu
Founded 1915 as Marywood College
Private control
Pres.: Sis. Dr ANNE MUNLEY
Vice-Pres. for Academic Affairs: Dr ALAN M. LEVINE
Vice-Pres. for Business Affairs and Treas.: JOSEPH X. GARVEY
Vice-Pres. for Student Life: Dr RAYMOND P. HEATH
Vice-Pres. for Univ. Advancement: CLAYTON N. PHEASANT
Dir for Library: CATHY SCHAPPERT
Library of 216,191 vols
Number of teachers: 400 (150 full-time)
Number of students: 3,400

DEANS

College of Health and Human Services: Dr MARK E. RODGERS
College of Liberal Arts and Sciences: Dr MICHAEL A. FOLEY
Insalaco College of Creative and Performing Arts: COLLIER A. PARKER
Reap College of Education and Human Development: Dr MARY ANNE FEDRICK
School of Architecture: GREGORY K. HUNT

MERCYHURST COLLEGE

501 E 38th St, Erie, PA 16546-0001

Telephone: (814) 824-2000
Internet: www.mercyhurst.edu
Founded 1926
Private control
Academic year: September to May
Pres.: Dr THOMAS J. GAMBLE
Provost: Dr JAMES M. ADOVASIO
Exec. Vice-Pres.: Dr GARY M. BROWN
Vice-Pres. for Academic Affairs: Dr PHILLIP J. BELFIORE
Vice-Pres. for Enrolment Management: Dr GERAD TOBIN
Vice-Pres. for Finance and Treas.: JANE M. KELSEY
Vice-Pres. for Advancement: Dr DAVID LIVINGSTON
Registrar: Sis. PATRICIA WHALEN
Dir for Libraries: DARCI JONES
Number of teachers: 150 (full-time)
Number of students: 3,075

MESSIAH COLLEGE

1 College Ave, Mechanicsburg, PA 17055

Telephone: (717) 766-2511
E-mail: admiss@messiah.edu
Internet: www.messiah.edu
Founded 1909
Private control
Satellite campus: Harrisburg
Academic year: September to May
Pres.: Dr KIM S. PHIPPS
Provost: Dr RANDALL G. BASINGER
Vice-Pres. for Advancement: BARRY G. GOODLING
Vice-Pres. for Finance and Planning: Dr DAVID WALKER
Vice-Pres. for Operations: KATHIE SHAFER
Vice-Pres. of Enrolment Management: JOHN CHOPKA
Vice-Pres. for Human Resources: AMANDA COFFEY
Vice-Pres. for IT and Assoc. Provost: Dr WILLIAM STRAUSBAUGH
Vice-Provost and Dean for Students: Dr KRIS HANSEN-KIEFFER
Registrar: JAMES J. SOTHERDEN

Dir for Library: JONATHAN D. LAUER
Library of 282,906 vols, 620 microforms and 20,546 audiovisual materials
Number of teachers: 312 (175 full-time, 137 part-time)
Number of students: 3,017 (2,798 undergraduate, 219 graduate)

Publication: *The Bridge*

DEANS

School of Arts: Dr RICHARD E. ROBERSON
School of Business, Education and Social Sciences: Dr CAROLINE MAURER
School of Humanities: Dr PETER K. POWERS
School of Science, Engineering and Health: Dr W. RAY NORMAN

MOORE COLLEGE OF ART AND DESIGN

20th Sst and The Parkway, Philadelphia, PA 19103-1179

Telephone: (215) 568-4000
E-mail: info@moore.edu
Internet: www.moore.edu
Founded 1848 as the Philadelphia School of Design for Women, current name adopted 1989
Private control
Academic year: August to May
Pres.: Dr HAPPY CRAVEN FERNANDEZ
Vice-Pres. for Finance and Admin.: WILLIAM L. HILL, II
Academic Dean: DONA LANTZ
Dean for Students: RUTH ROBBINS
Registrar: DIANNE SARIDAKIS
Library Dir: SHARON WATSON-MAURO
Number of teachers: 135
Number of students: 580 (525 undergraduate, 55 graduate and postgraduate)

MORAVIAN COLLEGE

1200 Main St, Bethlehem, PA 18018

Telephone: (610) 861-1300
E-mail: admissions@moravian.edu
Internet: www.moravian.edu
Founded 1742, present name and status 1954
Private control
Academic year: August to May
Pres.: Dr CHRISTOPHER M. THOMFORDE
Vice-Pres. for Academic Affairs and Dean for Faculty: GORDON WEIL
Vice-Pres. for Admin.: MARK REED
Vice-Pres. for Enrolment Management: KEN HUUS
Vice-Pres. for Institutional Advancement: GARY CARNEY
Vice-Pres. for Student Affairs: BEVERLY J. KOCHARD
Dean for Student Life: NICOLE LOYD
Registrar: MARY MARGARET GROS
Library Dir: DAVID SCHAPPERT
Library of 256,000 vols
Number of teachers: 120 (full-time)
Number of students: 1,565

Publication: *Moravian College Magazine*

MOUNT ALOYSIUS COLLEGE

7373 Admiral Peary Highway, Cresson, PA 16630-1999

Telephone: (814) 886-4131
E-mail: admissions@mtaloy.edu
Internet: www.mtaloy.edu
Founded 1853
Private control
Academic year: August to May
Offers courses in arts and sciences, business administration, community counselling, criminal justice management, health care, psychology

Pres.: Dr THOMAS P. FOLEY
Sr Vice-Pres. for Academic Affairs and Dean for Faculty: Dr TIMOTHY FULOP
Vice-Pres. for Enrolment Management and Dean for Undergraduate and Graduate Admissions: FRANCIS C. CROUSE, JR
Vice-Pres. for Student Affairs: Dr JANE M. GRASSADONIA
Registrar: Dr CHRISTOPHER LOVETT
Dir for Library: ROBERT STERE

Library of 100,000 vols, 15,000 current print and electronic journals
Number of teachers: 175
Number of students: 2,500 (1,300 full-time undergraduate, 1,200 part-time undergraduate, graduate and continuing education)

MUHLENBERG COLLEGE

2400 W Chew St, Allentown, PA 18104-5586
Telephone: (484) 664-3100
E-mail: admissions@muhlenberg.edu
Internet: www.muhlenberg.edu

Founded 1848, present name 1867
Private control

Liberal arts and pre-professional studies

Pres.: PEYTON RANDOLPH HELM
Provost: Dr JOHN RAMSAY
Vice-Pres. for Devt and Alumni Relations: REBEKKAH L. BROWN
Dean for Academic Life: Dr SHINER WILSON
Dean for Admissions and Financial Aid: CHRIS HOOKER-HARING
Dean for Students: KAREN GREEN
Library Dir: TINA HERTEL

Library of 310,000 vols, 360,000 microforms, 29,000 print and ejournals
Number of teachers: 285 (170 full-time, 115 part-time)
Number of students: 2,225

NEUMANN UNIVERSITY

One Neumann Dr., Aston, PA 19014-1298
Telephone: (610) 459-0905
E-mail: neumann@neumann.edu
Internet: www.neumann.edu

Founded 1965 as Our Lady of Angels College, present name and status 2009
Private control
Academic year: August to May

Pres.: Dr ROSALIE M. MIRENDA
Vice-Pres. and Gen. Counsel: JONATHAN PERI
Vice-Pres. for Academic Affairs: Dr GERALD P. O'SULLIVAN
Vice-Pres. for Enrolment Management and Student Affairs: DENNIS MURPHY
Vice-Pres. for Finance and Admin.: JOSEPH GORMAN
Vice-Pres. for Institutional Advancement and College Relations: HENRY A. SUMNER
Vice-Pres. for Mission and Min. Affairs: Sr MARGUERITE O'BEIRNE
Dean of Students: Sr Dr PEGGY EGAN
Registrar: LARRY S. FRIEDMAN
Library Dir: TIFFANY McGREGOR

Number of teachers: 320 (97 full-time, 223 part-time)
Number of students: 3,085 (2,615 undergraduate, 470 graduate)
Publications: Accent Magazine (2 a year), Journal of Neumann's First-Year Knight Writers, The Neumann Business Review (1 a year), Viewbook

DEANS

Division of Arts and Sciences: Dr MAC GIVEN
Division of Business and Information Management: JANET MASSEY
Division of Continuing Adult and Professional Studies: Dr TISH SZYMURSKI

Division of Education and Human Services: Dr JOSEPH E. GILLESPIE
Division of Nursing and Health Sciences: Dr KATHLEEN GEIGER HOOVER

PEIRCE COLLEGE

1420 Pine St, Philadelphia, PA 19102
Telephone: (215) 545-6400
E-mail: info@peirce.edu
Internet: www.peirce.edu

Founded 1865
Private control
Academic year: September to May

Areas of study incl. business, healthcare, information technology and paralegal studies
Pres. and CEO: JAMES J. MERGIOTTI
Provost and Sr Vice-Pres. for Academic Advancement and: Dr PATRICIA A. RUCKER
Sr Vice-Pres. for Finance and Admin.: JAMES M. VITALE
Vice-Pres. for Institutional Advancement: CHARLES A. WRIGHT, III
Dean for Enrolment Management: NADINE M. MAHER
Dean for Students: Dr RITA J. TOLIVER-ROBERTS

PENNSYLVANIA COLLEGE OF ART & DESIGN

POB 59, 204 N Prince St, Lancaster, PA 17608-0059
Telephone: (717) 396-7833
E-mail: bwitmer@pcad.edu
Internet: www.pcad.edu

Founded 1982 as Pennsylvania School of the Arts, present name 2003
Private control
Academic year: August to May

Pres.: MARY COLLEEN HEIL
Vice-Pres. for Finance and Operations: PATRICIA ERNST
Dean for Academic Affairs: MARC TORICK
Dean for Students: PAMELA RICHARDSON
Registrar: FAITH GADDIE
Dir for Admissions: NATALIE A. LASCEK-SPEAKMAN
Library Dir: KAREN HUTCHISON

PENNSYLVANIA STATE SYSTEM OF HIGHER EDUCATION

Office of the Chancellor, Dixon Univ. Center, 2986 N Second St, Harrisburg, PA 17110
Telephone: (717) 720-4000
E-mail: feedback@passhe.edu
Internet: www.passhe.edu

Chancellor: Dr JOHN C. CAVANAUGH
Exec. Vice-Chancellor: Dr PETER GARLAND
Vice-Chancellor for Admin. and Finance: JAMES DILLON
Chief Counsel: LEONIDAS PANDELADIS
Number of students: 120,000 ...

CONSTITUENT INSTITUTIONS

Bloomsburg University of Pennsylvania
400 E Second St, Bloomsburg, PA 17815-1301
Telephone: (570) 389-4000
E-mail: buadmiss@bloomu.edu.edu
Internet: www.bloomu.edu

Founded 1839, present name and status 1983
Pres.: Dr DAVID L. SOLTZ
Provost and Sr Vice-Pres.: Dr IRA BLAKE
Vice-Pres. for Admin. and Finance: RICHARD RUGEN
Registrar: JOSEPH KISSELL

Library of 493,467 vols, 2,136,712 micro-text, 13,558 non-print holdings
Number of teachers: 520

Number of students: 9,510
Publication: Bloomsburg: The University Magazine

DEANS

College of Business: MICHAEL TIDWELL
College of Education: ELIZABETH K. MAUCH
College of Liberal Arts: JAMES BROWN
College of Science and Technology: ROBERT MARANDE

California University of Pennsylvania
250 University Ave, California, PA 15419-1394
Telephone: (724) 938-4000
Internet: www.calu.edu

Founded 1852
Pres.: GERALDINE M. JONES (acting)
Vice-Pres. for Admin. and Finance: ROBERT THORN
Vice-Pres. for Marketing and Univ. Relations: CRAIG BUTZINE
Vice-Pres. for Student Affairs: Dr LENORA ANGELONE
Vice-Pres. for Univ. Devt and Alumni Relations: SHARON NAVONEY
Dean for Admissions: WILLIAM A. EDMONDS
Dean for Library Services: DOUGLAS A. HOOVER

Library of 260,485 vols, 901,363 microforms
Number of teachers: 255
Number of students: 8,800
Publication: Inkwell

DEANS

College of Education and Human Services: Dr KEVIN KOURY
College of Liberal Arts: Dr MUHAMMAD YAMBA
Eberly College of Science and Technology: Dr LEONARD COLELL
School of Graduate Studies and Research: Dr JOHN R. CENCICH

Cheyney University of Pennsylvania
POB 200, 1837 University Circle, Cheyney, PA 19319-0200
Telephone: (610) 399-2275
E-mail: admissions@cheyney.edu
Internet: www.cheyney.edu

Founded 1837 as Institute for Colored Youth, present name and status 1983
Academic year: August to May

Pres.: Dr MICHELLE R. HOWARD-VITAL
Provost and Vice-Pres. for Academic Affairs: Dr IVAN BANKS
Vice-Pres. for Finance and Admin.: GERALD COLEMAN
Vice-Pres. for Institutional Devt: LAWRENCE GREEN
Vice-Pres. for Student Affairs and Student Life: Dr SUZANNE D. PHILLIPS
Dir of Enrolment Management: MICHAEL TAYLOR
Librarian: LUT NERO

Library of 238,699 vols
Number of teachers: 100
Number of students: 2,000
Publication: Cheyney Magazine

DEANS

School of Arts and Sciences: Dr BERNADETTE CARTER
School of Education and Professional Studies: Dr LARNELL FLANNAGAN

Clarion University
840 Wood St, Clarion, PA 16214-1232
Telephone: (814) 393-2000
E-mail: info@clarion.edu
Internet: www.clarion.edu

Founded 1867
Academic year: August to May

Pres.: Dr Karen M. Whitney
Provost and Vice-Pres. for Academic Affairs:
Dr Ronald Nowaczyk
Vice-Pres. for Finance and Admin.: W. Paul
Bylaska
Vice-Pres. for Student and Univ. Affairs:
Harry E. Tripp
Dir for Admissions: William D. Bailey
Dean for Libraries: Terry Latour
Library of 454,580 vols
Number of teachers: 390
Number of students: 7,315 (6,225 under-
graduate, 1,090 graduate)

DEANS

College of Arts and Sciences: Dr Rachelle C.
Prioleau
College of Business Administration: Dr
James G. Pesek
College of Education and Human Services:
Dr John Groves

East Stroudsburg University

200 Prospect St, East Stroudsburg, PA
183301-2999
Telephone: (570) 422-3532
E-mail: undergrads@po-box.esu.edu
Internet: www.esu.edu
Founded 1893 as East Stroudsburg Normal
School, current name adopted 1983
Academic year: August to May
Pres.: Dr Robert J. Dillman
Provost and Vice-Pres. for Academic Affairs:
Dr Van A. Reidhead
Vice-Pres. for Economic Devt and Research
Support: Mary Frances Postupack
Vice-Pres. for Enrolment Management: Dr
Victoria L. Sanders
Vice-Pres. for Finance and Admin.: Richard
A. Staneski
Vice-Pres. for Student Affairs: Doreen Tobin
Registrar: Kizzy Morris
Dean for Library and Univ. Collns: Edward
Owusu-Ansah
Library of 361,410 vols, 28,600 print and e-
periodicals, 91,600 govt documents, 1.4m.
microform items
Number of teachers: 325
Number of students: 7,385 (6,370 under-
graduate, 1,015 graduate)

DEANS

College of Arts and Sciences: Dr Peter
Hawkes
College of Business and Management: Dr
Alla L. Wilson
College of Education: Dr Pamela Kramer
Ertel
College of Health Sciences: Dr Mark J.
Kilker
Graduate College: Dr Marilyn J. Wells

Edinboro University

219 Meadville St, Edinboro, PA 16444
Telephone: (814) 732-2000
E-mail: eup_admissions@edinboro.edu
Internet: www.edinboro.edu
Founded 1857
state Control
Academic year: August to May
Pres.: Dr Julie Wollman
Provost and Vice-Pres. for Academic Affairs:
Dr Michael Hannan
Vice-Pres. for Finance and Admin.: Gordon
J. Herbst
Vice-Pres. for Student Affairs and Student
Success: Dr Kahan Sablo
Vice-Pres. for Univ. Advancement: Tina
Mengine
Registrar: Tim Pilewski
Dir for Admissions: Craig Grooms
Assoc. Vice-Pres. for Univ. Libraries: Dr
Donald Dilmore

Library of 485,338 vols
Number of teachers: 430
Number of students: 7,460

DEANS

School of Arts and Sciences: Dr Terry L.
Smith
School of Business: Dr Scott Miller
School of Education: Dr Nomsa Geleta
School of Graduate Studies and Research: Dr
Alan Biel

Indiana University of Pennsylvania

1011 S Dr., Indiana, PA 15705
Telephone: (724) 357-2100
E-mail: graduate-admissions@iup.edu
Internet: www.iup.edu
Founded 1875 as Indiana State Normal
School
Academic year: September to May (2 ses-
sions)
Pres.: Dr David Werner
Provost and Vice-Pres. for Academic Affairs:
Dr Gerald W. Intemann
Vice-Pres. for Admin. and Finance: Dr Cor-
nelius Wooten
Vice-Pres. for Enrolment Management and
Communications: James Begany
Vice-Pres. for Student Affairs: Dr Rhonda
Luckey
Vice-Pres. for Univ. Relations: Robert O.
Davies
Dean for Graduate Studies and Research: Dr
Timothy Mack
Dean for Libraries: Dr Luis J. Gonzalez
Library of 800,000 vols, 50,000 audiovisual
items, 16,000 journals
Number of teachers: 755
Number of students: 15,125
Publication: IUP Magazine (4 a year)

DEANS

College of Education and Educational Tech-
nology: Dr A. Keith Dils
College of Fine Arts: Dr Michael Hood
College of Health and Human Services: Dr
Mary Swinker
College of Humanities and Social Sciences:
Dr Yaw A. Asamoah
College of Natural Sciences and Mathemat-
ics: Dr Deanne L. Snavely
Eberly College of Business and Information
Technology: Dr Robert C. Camp
School of Continuing Education: Dr Nicho-
las E. Kolb
School of Graduate Studies and Research: Dr
Timothy P. Mack

Kutztown University

POB 730, 15200 Kutztown Rd, Kutztown, PA
19530
Telephone: (610) 683-4000
E-mail: admission@kutztown.edu
Internet: www.kutztown.edu
Founded 1866 as Keystone State Normal
School, present name and status 1983
Academic year: September to May
Pres.: Dr Francisco Javier Cevallos
Provost and Vice-Pres. for Academic and
Student Affairs: Dr Carlos Vargas-
Aburto
Vice-Pres. for Admin. and Finance: Gerald
L. Silberman
Dir for Admissions: Dr Valerie Reidout
Registrar: Michelle Hughes
Dean for Library Services: Dr Barbara
Darden
Library of 555,000 vols, 56,000 print and e-
periodical subscriptions
Number of teachers: 365
Number of students: 10,285

DEANS

College of Business: Dr William Dempsey
College of Education: Dr Darrell Garber
(acting)
College of Liberal Arts and Sciences: Dr
Anne Zayaitz (acting)
College of Visual and Performing Arts: Dr
William Mowder

Lock Haven University

401 N Fairview St, Lock Haven, PA 17745
Telephone: (570) 484-2011
E-mail: admissions@lhup.edu
Internet: www.lhup.edu
Founded 1870 as the Central State Normal
School, present status 1983
Academic year: August to May
Pres.: Dr Michael Fiorentino, Jr
Provost and Vice-Pres. for Academic Affairs:
Dr David White
Vice-Pres. for Finance and Admin.: William
Hanelly
Vice-Pres. for Student Affairs: Dr Linda D.
Koch
Registrar: Jill R. Mitchley
Dir for Admissions: Robin Rockey
Dir of Library Services: Brenda Corman
Library of 352,369 vols
Number of teachers: 270
Number of students: 5,040
Publications: Lock Haven International
Review (1 a year), The Haven magazine

DEANS

College of Arts and Sciences: Dr Zakir
Hossain
College of Education and Human Services:
Mary L. Rose-Colley

Mansfield University

Mansfield, PA 16933
Telephone: (570) 662-4000
E-mail: admissions@mansfield.edu
Internet: www.mansfield.edu
Founded 1857 as Mansfield Classical Semin-
ary
Academic year: September to May
Pres.: Dr Allan Golden
Provost and Vice-Pres. for Academic Affairs:
Dr Peter Keller
Vice-Pres. for Finance and Admin.: Dr
Daniel DoBell
Vice-Pres. for Student Affairs: Bill Malloy
Registrar: Lori Cass
Dir for Admissions: Christine Bell
Dir for Library Information Resources: Scott
DiMarco
Library of 222,650 vols
Number of teachers: 215 (150 full-time)
Number of students: 3,400

Millersville University

POB 1002, 1 S George St, Millersville, PA
17551-0302
Telephone: (717) 872-3011
E-mail: admissions@millersville.edu
Internet: www.millersville.edu
Founded 1855 as Lancaster Co Normal
School, present name and status 1983
public control
Academic year: September to August
Pres.: Dr John M. Anderson
Provost and Vice-Pres. for Academic Affairs:
Dr Vilas A. Prabhu
Vice-Pres. for Enrollment Management:
Brian Hazlett
Vice-Pres. for Finance and Admin.: Roger V.
Bruszewski
Vice-Pres. for Student Affairs: Dr Aminta H.
Breaux
Registrar: Alison M. Hutchinson

Dir of Library Operations: ANDREW G. WELA-ISH
Library of 364,190 vols
Number of teachers: 456 (full-time)
Number of students: 8,279 (7,388 under-graduate, 891 graduate)

DEANS

College of Graduate and Professional Stud-ies: Dr VICTOR S. DESANTIS
School of Education: Dr HELENA TULEYA-PAYNE
School of Humanities and Social Sciences: Dr DIANE M. UMBLE
School of Science and Mathematics: Dr ROBERT T. SMITH

Shippensburg University of Pennsylvania

1871 Old Main Dr., Shippensburg, PA 17257-2299
Telephone: (717) 477-7447
E-mail: admiss@ship.edu
Internet: www.ship.edu
Founded 1871 as Cumberland Valley State Normal School, present name and status 1983
Academic year: August to May
Pres.: Dr WILLIAM N. RUUD
Provost and Sr Vice-Pres. for Academic Affairs: Dr BARBARA G. LYMAN
Vice-Pres. for Admin. and Finance: DENNY E. TERRELL
Vice-Pres. for Student Affairs: Dr ROGER L. SERR
Dean for Admissions: JOSEPH CRETELLA
Dean for Library and Media Services: Dr MARIAN B. SCHULTZ
Registrar: CATHY SPRENGER
Library: 2m. vols
Number of teachers: 325 (full-time)
Number of students: 8,300 (7,200 under-graduate and 1,200 graduate)
Publication: Proteus: A Journal of Ideas (2 a year)

DEANS

College of Arts and Sciences: Dr JAMES H. MIKE
College of Education and Human Services: Dr JAMES R. JOHNSON
John L. Grove College of Business: Dr JOHN G. KOOTI
School of Extended Studies: Dr CHRISTINA M. SAX
School of Graduate Studies: Dr TRACY SCHOOLCRAFT

Slippery Rock University

One Morrow Way, Slippery Rock, PA 16057
Telephone: (724) 738-9000
E-mail: asktherock@sru.edu
Internet: www.sru.edu
Founded 1889 as Slippery Rock State Normal School, present name and status 1983
Academic year: June to May
Pres.: Dr CHARLES CURRY (acting)
Provost and Vice-Pres. for Academic Affairs: Dr WILLIAM F. WILLIAMS
Vice-Pres. for Student Life: Dr CONSTANCE FOLEY
Vice-Pres. for Univ. Advancement: BARBARA ENDER
Dir for Admissions: W. C. VANCE
Dir for Library Services: PHILIP TRAMDACK
Library of 500,000 vols, 10,000 online full text journals, magazines and newspapers
Number of teachers: 440 (380 full-time, 60 part-time)
Number of students: 8,850
Publications: Ginger Hill (1 a year), Saxigena (1 a year), The Rock (4 a year)

DEANS

College of Business, Information and Social Sciences: Dr KURT E. SCHIMMEL
College of Education: Dr KATHLEEN STRICK-LAND
College of Health, Environment and Sci-ences: Dr SUSAN HANNAM
College of Humanities, Fine and Performing Arts: Dr EVA TSUQUIASHI-DADDESIO

West Chester University of Pennsylvania

700 S High St, West Chester, PA 19383
Telephone: (610) 436-1000
E-mail: ugadmiss@wcupa.edu
Internet: www.wcupa.edu
Founded 1871
Pres.: Dr GREG R. WEISENSTEIN
Provost and Vice-Pres. for Academic Affairs: Dr LINDA L. LAMWERS
Vice-Pres. for Finance and Admin.: MARK P. MIXNER
Vice-Pres. for Information Services: ADEL BARIMANI
Vice-Pres. for Student Affairs: Dr MATTHEW BRICKETTO
Dir for Admissions: Ms MARSHA HAUG
Dir for Library Services: RICHARD SWAIN
Registrar: JOSEPH SANTIVASCI
Library: 4.8m. vols
Number of teachers: 840 (571 full-time, 269 part-time)
Number of students: 15,100
Publications: College Literature: A Journal of Critical Literary Studies, West Chester University Magazine (3 a year)

DEANS

College of Arts and Sciences: LORI A. VER-MEULEN
College of Business and Public Affairs: Dr CHRISTOPHER M. FIORENTINO
College of Education: Dr KENNETH D. WIT-MER, JR
College of Health Sciences: Dr DONALD E. BARR
College of Visual and Performing Arts: Dr TIMOTHY V. BLAIR

PENNSYLVANIA STATE UNIVERSITY

University Park, PA 16802
Telephone: (814) 865-4700
E-mail: admissions@psu.edu
Internet: www.psu.edu
Founded 1855 as Agricultural College of Pennsylvania, current name adopted 1953
Academic year: August to May
Campuses: Abington, Altoona, Beaver, Berks, Brandywine, DuBois, Erie (Behrend College), Fayette, Greater Allegheny, Harris-burg, Hazleton, Lehigh Valley, Mont Alto, New Kensington, Schuylkill, Shenango, Uni-versity Park, Wilkes-Barre, Worthington Scranton and York
Pres.: Dr ERIC J. BARRON
Exec. Vice-Pres. and Provost: NICHOLAS P. JONES
Sr Vice-Pres. for Devt and Alumni Relations: RODNEY P. KIRSCH
Sr Vice-Pres. for Finance and Business and Treas.: DAVID J. GRAY
Sr Vice-Pres. for Health Affairs: HAROLD L. PAZ
Vice-Pres. and Dean for Undergraduate Edu-cation: ROBERT N. PANGBORN
Vice-Provost for Academic Affairs: BLANNIE BOWEN
Vice-Pres. for Admin.: THOMAS G. POOLE
Vice-Pres. for Commonwealth Campuses: MADLYN L. HANES
Vice-Pres. for Educational Equity: W. TER-RELL JONES

Vice-Pres. for Outreach: CRAIG D. WEIDE-MANN
Vice-Pres. for Research: NEIL SHARKEY
Vice-Pres. for Strategic Communications: M. FREDERIC VOLKMANN
Vice-Pres. for Student Affairs: DAMON SIMS
Vice-Pres. and Gen. Counsel: STEPHEN S. DUNHAM
Dean for Libraries and Scholarly Communi-cations: BARBARA I. DEWEY
Library: see under Libraries and Archives
Number of teachers: 8,700 (6,000 full-time, 2,700 part-time)
Number of students: 96,600
Publications: iConnect, Research Penn State, Science Journal, Smeal Report

DEANS

College of Agriculture: BARBARA CHRIST
College of Arts and Architecture: BARBARA O. KORNER
College of Communications: DOUGLAS A. ANDERSON
College of Earth and Mineral Sciences: WILLIAM E. EASTERLING
College of Education: DAVID H. MONK
College of Engineering: AMR S. ELNASHAI
College of Health and Human Development: ANN C. CROUTER
College of Information Sciences and Technol-ogy: DAVID HALL
College of Medicine: Dr HAROLD L. PAZ
College of the Liberal Arts: SUSAN WELCH
Dickinson School of Law: JAMES HOUCK
Eberly College of Science: DANIEL J. LARSON
Graduate School: Dr REGINA VASSILATOS-YOUNKEN
School of Nursing: Dr PAULA MILONE-NUZZO
Schreyer Honors College: CHRISTIAN BRADY
Smeal College of Business: CHARLES H. WHITEMAN

PROFESSORS

ABDALLA, C., Agricultural and Environmen-tal Economics
ABLER, D., Agricultural, Environmental/Regional Economics and Demography
ACHARYA, R., Computer Systems and Engin-eering
ADAIR, J., Materials Science and Bioengineer-ing
AIRHIHENBUWA, C., Biobehavioural Health
ALBERT, R., Physics and Biology
ALLCOCK, H., Chemistry
ALMEIDA, D., Human Development and Fam-ily Studies
ALTER, T., Agricultural Environment and Regional Economics
AMMON, C., Geosciences
ANANDAKRISHNAN, S., Geosciences
ANANTHESWARAN, R., Food Science
ANESKO, M., English
ARMSTRONG, D., Music
ARNETT, P., Psychology
ARNOLD, S., Statistics
ARTECA, R., Horticultural Physiology
ARTHUR, M., Geosciences
ASHOK, S., Engineering Sciences
AWADELKARIM, O., Engineering Science and Mechanics
AZAR, S., Psychology
AZZARA, C., Agricultural Economics, Soci-ology and Education
BABITZKE, P., Biochemistry and Molecular Biology
BABU, G., Statistics/Astrology and Astrophys-ics
BACKER, L., Law
BACKMAN, P., Plant Pathology
BADDING, J., Chemistry
BAGBY, J., Information Sciences and Tech-nology
BAHNFLETH, W., Architectural Engineeruing
BAHRY, D., Political Science
BAKER, D., Education/Sociology

BANASZAK, L., Political Science
BANNON, P., Atmospheric Science
BANYAGA, A., Mathematics
BARBERCHECK, M., Entomology
BARBIERI, A., Communications
BARLOW, J., Computer Science and Engineering
BARRON, O., Accounting
BEIERLEIN, J., Agricultural Economics
BELCHER, N., Architecture
BELEGUNDU, A., Mechanical Engineering
BERENBAUM, S., Psychology and Paediatrics
BERLYAND, L., Mathematics
BEVILACQUA, P., Chemistry
BEYER, D., Plant Pathology
BICE, D., Geosciences
BIESCHKE, K., Counselling and Psychology
BJORNSTAD, O., Entomology
BLANDFORD, D., Agricultural and Environmental Economics
BLOOD, G., Communication Disorders
BLOOD, I., Communication Sciences and Disorders
BLUE, W., Spanish
BLUME, G., Education
BOJOWALD, M., Physics
BOLLINGER, J., Chemistry
BONTRAGER, L., Music
BOOTHBY, T., Architectural Engineering
BORHAN, A., Chemical Engineering
BOWEN, C., Agricultural and Extension Education
BRAITHWAITE-READ, V., Fisheries and Biology
BRALOWER, T., Geosciences
BRASSEUR, J., Mechanical Engineering, Mathematics, Bioengineering
BREAKALL, J., Electrical Engineering
BRENTNER, K., Aerospace Engineering
BREWER, C., Geography
BRITTINGHAM-BRANT, M., Wildlife Research
BROOKS, R., Geography
BROWN, K., Post-Harvest Psychology
BROWN, P., Ethics and Religious Affairs
BROWN, V., Music
BROWNE, S., Communication Arts and Science
BRUNE, W., Meteorology
BUCKLEY, W., Exercise/Health Education
BUNDY, O., Music
BURAGO, D., Mathematics
BURGOS, W., Civil and Environmental Engineering
BURROWS, D., Astronomy and Astrophysics
CAMCI, C., Aerospace Engineering
CANNON, F., Civil and Environmental Engineering
CANTORNA, M., Molecular Immunology
CAO, G., Computer Science and Engineering
CAO, W., Mathematics and Materials Research
CARBONNEAU, T., Law
CARLETON, A., Geography
CARLSEN, W., Education
CARLSON, R., Psychology
CARPENTER, B., Art Education
CARROLL, J., Information Sciences and Technology
CASERIO, R., English
CASTONGUAY, L., Psychology
CATCHEN, G., Nuclear Engineering
CHALLIS, J., Kinesiology
CHANDRA, M., Industrial Engineering
CHANG, L., Mechanical Engineering
CHARLTON, J., Astrology and Astrophysics
CHEN, L., Materials Science and Engineering
CHEUNG, F., Mechanical and Nuclear Engineering
CHIAROMONTE, F., Statistics
CHOPRA, S., Maize Genetics
CHUNG, T., Polymer Science
CIARDULLO, R., Astrophysics and Astronomy
CIMBALA, J., Mechanical Engineering
CLARIANA, R., Education
CLOTHIAUX, E., Meteorology
COATSWORTH, J., Human Development and Family Studies

COBB, W., English
COLBURN, J., Law
COLBY, R., Materials Science
COLLINS, L., Human Development and Family Studies
CONROY, D., Kinesiology
COOK, K., Music
COOPER, R., Economics
CORWIN, R., Nutritional Neuroscience
COSGROVE, D., Biology
COSTANZO, F., Mathematics
COULSON, D., Economics
COUPLAND, J., Food Science
COUTU, S., Physics and Astronomy
COWEN, D., Physics and Astronomy
COX-FOSTER, D., Entomology
CRASSWELLER, R., Horticulture
CUI, L., Entomology
CURRAN, W., Weed Science
CURTIS, W., Chemical Engineering
CUSUMANO, J., Engineering Science and Mechanics
DANNIN, E., Law
DATTA, S., Electrical Engineering
DATTILO, J., Recreation and Tourism Management
DAVIS, D., Plant Pathology
DAVIS, K., Meteorology
DEBROY, T., Materials Science and Engineering
DECASTRO, W., Theatre
DECOTEAU, D., Horticulture
DEIGHTON, T., Music
DEMETER, E., Industrial Engineering
DEMIRCI, A., Agricultural and Bioengineering
DE MORAES, C., Entomology
DENKER, M., Mathematics
DEPAMPHILIS, C., Biology
DERICKSON, A., Labour and Employment Relations
DE SOUZA, M., Kinesiology
DEVON, R., Engineering Design
DIEHL, R., Physics
DING, M., Marketing
DIRSMITH, M., Accounting
DOAN, W., Theatre and Women's Studies
DOHERTY, J., Electrical Engineering
DORN, L., Nursing
DOWNS, R., Geography
DRAFALL, L., Outreach and Marketing
DUFFY, C., Civil Engineering
DUMAS, C., Theatre
DUNN, J., Agricultural Economics
DURRAN, D., Music
DYRESON, M., Kinesiology
ECKHARDT, R., Developmental Genetics
EISSENSTAT, D., Woody Plant Physics
ELKIN, R., Poultry Science
ELLIOTT, H., Agricultural Engineering
ELSWORTH, D., Environmental Engineering
ENGELDER, J., Geosciences
ERACLEOUS, M., Astrophysics
ESER, S., Energy and Geoenvironment
EVANS, J., Meteorology
FAGAN, G., History
FARMER, S., Law
FARR, J., Psychology
FEDDERKE, J., International Affairs
FEDOROFF, N., Science
FEIGELSON, E., Astronomy and Astrophysics and Statistics
FELDMAN, K., Chemistry
FELMLEE, D., Sociology
FELTON, G., Entomology
FICHTHORN, K., Chemistry, English and Physics
FINKE, R., Sociology and Religious Studies
FINLEY, J., Forest Research
FINN, L., Physics and Astronomy and Astrophysics
FISHER, D., Geosciences
FISHER, C., Biology
FITZGERALD, L., Trumpet
FLEISCHER, S., Entomology
FOOLAD, M., Plant Genetics
FOTI, V., Philosophy

FRAZIER, J., Entomology
FREEMAN, K., Geosciences
FREIHAUT, J., Architectural Engineering
FREIVALDS, A., Industrial Engineering
FRIESZ, T., Industrial Engineering
FRISQUE, R., Biochemistry/Molecular Biology
FUENTES, J., Meteorology
FUNK, R., Chemistry
FURER, M., Computer Science and Engineering
FURLONG, K., Geosciences
GAROIAN, C., Art Education
GARRETT, S., Acoustics
GARTNER, S., International Affairs
GEISER, D., Plant Pathology
GERIN, W., Biobehavioural Health
GHOSH, D., Statistics
GIBBLE, K., Physics
GILES, C., Information Systems and Technology
GILMOUR, D., Molecular and Cell Biology
GINZBERG, L., History and Women's Studies
GLOCKE, D., Music
GOLBECK, J., Biochemistry and Biophysics
GOPALAN, V., Materials Sciences
GRACE, J., Education
GRAEFE, A., Leisure Studies
GRAHAM, J., Human Development and Family Studies
GRAY, B., Organizational Behaviour
GRAYSON, R., Energy and Mineral Sciences
GREEN, E., Economics and Mathematics
GREEN, M., Nutritional Sciences
GREEN, P., Education
GREWAL, R., Marketing
GRIEL, L., Veterinary Science
GRIFFIN, P., Industrial Engineering
GROSSMAN, K., French
GUIDE, V., Operations
GUILTINAN, M., Plant Molecular Biology
GUNAYDIN, M., Physics
HAGEN, D., Animal Science
HAIDER, J., Architecture
HALE, R., Education and Psychology
HALL, R., Agricultural Management
HAMPTON, G., Meteorology
HANCOCK, W., Bioengineering
HANKEY, P., Veterinary Science
HAQUE, M., Mechanical Engineering
HARPER, J., Agricultural Economics
HARTMAN, W., Education
HARVILL, E., Microbiology and Infectious Diseases
HAUG, S., Music
HAWHEE, D., English
HAWORTH, D., Mechanical Engineering
HAYES, J., Education
HAZLER, R., Education
HEDGES, S., Biology
HEINEMANN, P., Agricultural and Bioengineering
HEINRICHS, A., Dairy and Animal Science
HENDERSON, D., Mathematics
HENDRICKSON, R., Education
HEPPELMANN, S., Physics
HERBERT, J., Education
HIRTH, K., Anthropology
HOLDSWORTH, D., Geography
HOOVER, K., Entomology
HORN, M., Engineering Science and Mechanics
HORNEY, J., Crime, Law and Justice
HOUSE, C., Geosciences
HOUSER, K., Architectural Engineering
HUDSON, B., History/Medieval Studies
HUFF, D., Turfgrass
HUGHES, C., Education
HUNT, B., Rehabilitation
HYDE, J., Agricultural Economics
ISARD, S., Aerobiology
IVANITS, L., Russian
JACOBS, R., Psychology
JACOBSON, M., Forest Resource
JANOWIAK, J., Wood Products Engineering
JAYARAO, B., Veterinary Science
JENKINS, W., Electrical Engineering

JENSSEN, H., Mathematics
JETT, D., International Affairs
JOHNS, R., Petroleum and Natural Gas Engineering
JOHNSON, A., Avian Biology
JOHNSON, D., Sociology and Human Development and Family Studies
JOHNSON, J., Early Childhood Education
JOHNSON, K., Language Learning and Applied Linguistics
JONES, B., Biobehavioral Health/Pharmacology
JOSHI, S., Industrial Engineering
JOVANIS, P., Civil Engineering
KALISPERIS, L., Architecture
KANDEMIR, M., Computer Science and Engineering
KANE, T., Electrical Engineering and Meteorology
KANG, S., Plant Pathology
KAPLAN, M., Agricultural and Extension Education
KAPUR, V., Veterinary and Biomedical Sciences
KASDORF, J., English
KATOK, S., Mathematics
KAYE, D., Law
KEATING, C., Chemistry
KEIFER-BOYD, K., Art Education and Women's Studies
KELLY HALL, J., Applied Linguistics
KELMELIS, J., International Affairs
KELSEY, T., Agricultural Economics
KENNEDY, R., Music
KENNETT, D., Anthropology
KENNEY, W., Physiology
KEPHART, K., Animal Science
KERSTETTER, D., Recreation Park and Tourism Management
KESIDIS, G., Electrical Engineering
KING, G., Biobehavioural Health
KING, V., Sociology/Demography/Human Development and Family Studies
KINPORTS, K., Law
KLEIT, A., Meteorology and Atmospheric Science
KNABEL, S., Food Science
KNIGHT, S., Education
KOCH, P., Biobehavioural Health/Health Education
KOLANOWSKI, A., Nursing/Psychiatry
KRAMER, J., Sociology
KREBS, C., Chemistry
KRETCHMAR, R., Exercise Sport Sciences
KUBICKI, J., Geosciences
KUBINA, R., Education
KULIKOWICH, J., Education
KULKARNI, A., Mechanical Engineering
KUMAR, A., Information Systems
KUR, B., Theatre
LAI, Z., Biology
LAMAN, J., Civil and Environmental Engineering
LAMANCUSA, J., Mechanical Engineering
LAMONT, W., Vegetable Crop
LANAGAN, M., Engineering Science and Mechanics
LANDSCHOOT, P., Turfgrass Management
LEACH, A., Music
LEE, B., Sociology and Demography
LEE, S., Meteorology
LESK, A., Biochemistry/Molecular Biology
LEVI, M., Mathematics
LEVIN, D., Aerospace Engineering
LI, B., Statistics
LI, L., Mathematics
LI, P., Psychology/Linguistics
LI, Q., Physics
LIBKIN, C., Theatre
LIECHTY, J., Marketing
LIN, H., Soil Hydrology
LINDBERG, D., Architecture
LINDSAY, B., Education
LINN, S., Political Science
LINZELL, D., Civil Engineering
LIPOWSKY, H., Bioengineering

LISSENDEN, C., Engineering Science and Mechanics
LIU, C., Mathematics
LIU, P., Information Systems Technology
LIU, Y., Physics
LIU, Z., Materials Science and Engineering
LLOYD, G., Education
LOPATKA, J., Law
LOUGY, R., English
LOUIS, H., Accounting
LOWRY, M., Finance
LULOFF, A., Agricultural Economics
LUSCHER, B., Biology
LUSK, M., Music
LUTHE, D., Plant Stress Biology
LVOV, S., Energy and Mineral Sciences
LYNCH, J., Nutrition and Agriculture
LYON, J., Music
MACEACHREN, A., Geography
MACKENZIE, D., Crime, Law and Justice
MADDOX, J., Art
MAGGS, J., Human Development and Family Studies
MAKOVA, K., Biology
MANIAS, E., Polymers
MANN, M., Meteorology
MARANAS, C., Chemical Engineering
MARDEN, J., Biology
MARKLE, R., Science
MARONCELLI, M., Chemistry
MASTRO, A., Microbiology and Cell Biology
MATHEWS, J., Electrical Engineering
MATSOUKAS, T., Chemical Engineering
MATTILA, A., Hospitality Management
MAUGHMER, M., Aerospace Engineering
MAYER, T., Electrical Engineering
MC BRIDE, D., African History
MC HALE, S., Human Development and Family Studies
MC NITT, A., Soil Science
MCALLISTER, M., Communication and Communication Arts/Science
MCCARTER, R., Biobehavioural Health
MCLAUGHLIN, D., Aerospace Engineering
MCLAUGHLIN, D., Rural Sociology/Demography
MCMURRY, S., American History
MELTON, R., Aerospace Engineering
MENGISTEAB, K., African Study
MESSNER, J., Architectural Engineering
METZNER, J., Computer Science and Engineering
MICCI, M., Aerospace Engineering
MICHAEL, J., Wood Products
MILES, J., Finance
MILLER, D., Electrical Engineering
MILLER, W., Biology
MILNER, S., Chemical Engineering and Materials Science and Engineering
MINCEMOYER, C., Agricultural and Extension Education
MITCHELL, J., Electrical Engineering
MITTRA, R., Electrical Engineering
MOHNEY, S., Materials Science and Engineering
MOORMAN, G., Plant Pathology
MORRISSON, M., English
MORTENSEN, D., Weed Ecology
MOTTA, A., Nuclear Engineering
MUELLER, K., Chemistry
MULLEN, G., Mathematics
MULLIN, C., Entomology
MUNN, M., Greek History and Greek Archaeology
MURPHY, P., Education
MUSCARELLA, C., Finance
MYERS, J., Education
NAIRN, R., Music
NAJJAR, R., Meteorology
NARAYANAN, R., Electrical Engineering
NARAYANAN, V., Computer Science and Engineering and Electrical Engineering
NELSON, K., Psychology
NEMBHARD, H., Industrial Engineering
NEWMAN, M., Psychology/Psychiatry
NG, O., History

NICKOLS-RICHARDSON, S., Nutritional Sciences
NISTOR, V., Mathematics
NIXON, B., Biochemistry/Molecular Biology
NOUSEK, J., Astronomy and Astrophysics
NUSSBAUM, J., Human Development and Family Studies
OCNEANU, A., Mathematics
OHMOTO, H., Geochemistry
O'LEARY, H., Art
OLIVA, R., Marketing
OMIECINSKI, C.
ORDWAY, R., Biology
OROPESA, R., Sociology and Demography
OSGOOD, D., Sociology
OSTHOFF, S., Art
OTT, T., Reproductive Physiology
PALMER, G., Political Science
PANTANO, C., Materials Research
PARIZEK, R., Geosciences
PASKO, V., Electrical Engineering
PASSMORE, D., Education
PATTERSON, P., Poultry Science
PAULSON, R., Veterinary Science
PENNYPACKER, E., Landscape Architecture
PENROD, J., Nursing
PEREZ-BLANCO, H., Engineering
PERKINS, D., Human Development and Family Studies
PETRUNIN, A., Mathematics
PEUQUET, D., Geography
PINCUS, A., Psychology
PINKSE, C., Economics
PLUTZER, E., Political Science and Sociology
POLLOCK, T., Management
PONG, S., Education
POST, D., Science
POST, E., Biology
POSTLE, K., Biochemistry/Molecular Biology
PRABHU, V., Industrial Engineering
PRESTINE, N., Education
PROCTOR, D., Kinesiology
PROSEK, R., Communication Disorders
PURAO, S., Information Systems and Technology
PURDY, D., German
QUACKENBUSH, E., Art
RADHAKRISHNA, R., Agricultural and Extension Education
RADOVIC, L., Energy and Mineral Engineering
RAHN, C., Mechanical Engineering
RAJOTTE, E., Entomology
RANGASWAMY, A., Marketing
RAVINDRAN, A., Industrial Engineering
RAY, W., Psychology
READY, R., Agricultural and Environmental Economics
REDFORD, D., History
REDWING, J., Materials Science Engineering
REED, C., English
REESE, J., Biochemistry
RICHARDS, D., Statistics
RICHARDS, M., Astrophysics
RICHTSMEIER, J., Anthropology
RIDLEY, J., Theatre Arts
RISLEY, J., Journalism
ROBERTS, B., Economics
ROBERTS, M., Economics
ROBINETT, R., Physics
RODRIGUEZ HERTZ, F., Mathematics
ROEBER, A., History and Religious Studies
ROGERS, C., Law
ROIBAN, R., Physics
ROLLS, B., Nutrition and Biobehavioural Health
ROMERO, V., Law
ROOSSINCK, M., Plant Pathology and Biology
ROSE, P., History
ROSENBERGER, J., Statistics
ROSS, A., Nutrition
ROTH, G., Agronomy
ROTHWELL, W., Education
ROVINE, M., Human Development and Family Studies
RUBACK, R., Sociology

RUHL, K., Education
RUNT, J., Polymer Science
RUSCH, F., Education
RUSSELL, D., Acoustics
RUTKOWSKI, J., Music Education
SAFFER, D., Geosciences
SAINBURG, R., Kinesiology and Neurology
SANTAVICCA, D., Mechanical Engineering
SAUNDERS, M., Entomology
SAUNDERS-BARTON, M., Music
SCANLON, A., Civil Engineering
SCHAAK, R., Chemistry
SCHAEFFER, S., Biology
SCHRODT, P., Political Science
SCHULMAN, S., Theatre Arts
SCHUSTER, S., Biochemistry and Molecular Biology
SCOTT, G., Law
SEGALL, A., Engineering Science and Mechanics
SELLECK, S., Biochemistry and Molecular Biology
SELLMER, J., Ornamental Horticulture
SEN, A., Chemistry
SHAFER, T., Music
SHALER, R., Forensic Science
SHANNON, P., Education
SHAPIRO, D., Economics, Demography and Women's Studies
SHAW, B., Engineering Science and Mechanics
SHEA, K., Biology
SHIELDS, S., Psychology
SHORT, P., Health Policy and Administration
SHRIVER, M., Anthropology
SICA, A., Sociology
SIGURDSSON, S., Astrophysics
SILVER, E., Sociology
SILVERMAN, W., French and Jewish Studies
SIMPSON, T., Industrial Engineering and Mechanical Engineering
SINHA, A., Mechanical Engineering
SIVASUBRAMANIAM, A., Computer Science and Engineering
SLINGERLAND, R., Geology
SLIWINSKI, M., Human Development and Family Studies
SLOBOUNOV, S., Kinesiology/Neurosurgery
SMITH, E., Aerospace Engineering
SMITH, E., Human Development and Family Studies
SMITH, P., Forest Resource
SMITH, S., Music
SMYTH, J., Biobehavioural Health and Medicine
SNOW, D., Anthropology
SOMMER, H., Mechanical Engineering
SOMMERS, P., Physics and Astronomy and Astrophysics
SOMMESE, K., Graphic Design
SPANIER, S., English
SPARROW, V., Acoustics
SPENCER, D., Aerospace Engineering
SPIVEY, F., Music
SREBRIC, J., Architectural Engineering
STALEY, C., Art
STANKIEWICZ, M., Art Education
STEFANOU, S., Agricultural Economics
STEFFENSMEIER, D., Sociology
STEHOUWER, R., Environmental Soil Science
STEINER, K., Forest Biology
STEPHENSON, A., Biology
STEVENS, R., Education
STIFTER, C., Human Development and Psychology
SULLIVAN, G., English
SULLIVAN, G., Art Education
SUSMAN, E., Biobehavioural Health and Nursing
SWIM, J., Psychology
TACCONI, M., Musicology
TADIGADAPA, S., Electrical Engineering and Biological Engineering
TALMGE, G., Mechanical Engineering
TAMMINGA, K., Landscape Architecture
TAN, S., Biochemistry

TAYLOR, A., Geography
TEMPELMAN, A., Statistics/Mathematics
TERRONES MALDONADO, M., Physics and Materials Science Engineering
THOMPSON, C., Art Education
THOMPSON, S., Law
THYNELL, S., Mechanical Engineering
TIEN, M., Biochemistry
TORRES CACOULLOS, R., Spanish and Linguistics
TRAUTH, E., Information Systems and Technology
TRIDIMAS, P., Law
TRUSTY, J., Education
TSAI, W., Business Administration
TU, C., Biochemistry
TURNS, S., Mechanical Engineering
TURRISI, R., Biobehavioural Health
TYBOUT, J., Economics
UCHINO, K., Actuators and Transducers
UDDIN, W., Plant Pathology
UHL, C., Biology
ULMER, J., Sociology
VANDEN HEUVEL, J., Veterinary Science
VANSAUN, R., Veterinary Science
VASERSTEIN, L., Mathematics
VAUGHAN, R., Mathematics
VENTURA, J., Industrial Engineering
VICERE, A., Business Administration
VOGLER, E., Materials Science Engineering
VUILLEMIN, J., French
WANG, J., Information Systems and Technology
WANG, Q., Polymers
WANNER, A., Slavic Literature
WANNER, C., History and Religious Studies
WATSON, J., Crop and Soil Science
WEAVER, R., Agricultural Economics
WEBSTER, D., Anthropology
WEINER, B., Physics
WEISS, D., Physics
WHEELER, E., Agricultural Engineering
WILKINSON, K., Communication Science Disorders
WILLIS, R., Physics
WILLIS, D., Architecture
WINES, J., Architecture
WINOGRAD, N., Chemistry
WISE, J., Theatre Arts
WOOD, J., Anthropology and Demography
WOOD, T., Chemistry
WOODRUFF, N., Modern US History
WOOLRIDGE, J., Finance
WRIGHT, M., Geography
WYSOCKI, K., Mathematics
XU, H., Management Science
YAARI, M., French
YAPA, L., Geography
YARNAL, B., Geography/Statistics
YAVUZKURT, S., Mechanical Engineering
YENER, A., Electrical Engineering
YETTER, R., Mechanical Engineering
YIN, S., Electrical Engineering
YODER, E., Extension Education
YODER, M., Music
YOUNG, G., Meteorology
YU, H., Applied Linguistics
ZARKHIN, Y., Mathematics
ZATSIORSKY, V., Kinesiology
ZBIEK, R., Education
ZHANG, F., Meteorology
ZIEGLER, G., Food Science
ZIKATANOV, L., Mathematics
ZIMMERER, K., Geography

PHILADELPHIA BIBLICAL UNIVERSITY

200 Manor Ave, Langhorne, PA 19047
Telephone: (215) 752-5800
E-mail: admissions@pbu.edu
Internet: www.pbu.edu

Founded 1913 as Bible Institute of Pennsylvania, present name and status 2000
Private control

Academic year: August to May
Pres.: Dr TODD J. WILLIAMS
Sr Vice-Pres. for Finance and Admin.: JAN M. HAAS
Provost: Dr BRIAN TOEWS
Sr Vice-Pres. for Univ. Advancement: SCOTT A. KEATING
Vice-Pres. for Research and Planning: MAE E. STEWART
Vice-Pres. and Dir for Learning Resources: TIMOTHY HUI
Library of 132,778 vols
Number of teachers: 135
Number of students: 1,225

DEANS

School of Arts and Sciences: Dr JEAN MINTO
School of Bible and Ministry: Dr HERB HIRT
School of Business and Leadership: RON FERNER
School of Education: Dr DEB MacCULLOUGH
School of Music and Performing Arts: PAUL ISENSEE

PHILADELPHIA COLLEGE OF OSTEOPATHIC MEDICINE

4170 City Ave, Philadelphia, PA 19131
Telephone: (215) 871-6100
E-mail: admissions@pcom.edu
Internet: www.pcom.edu

Founded 1899, present name 1921
Private control

2 Campuses: Philadelphia and Georgia
Pres. and CEO: Dr MATTHEW SCHURE
Provost and Sr Vice-Pres. for Academic Affairs and Dean: Dr KENNETH J. VEIT
Vice-Pres. for Alumni Relations and Devt: FLORENCE D. ZELLER
Vice-Pres. for Finance and Chief Financial Officer: PETER DOULIS
Vice-Pres. for Graduate Programmes and Academic Planning: Dr ROBERT G. CUZZOLINO
Registrar: DEBORAH A. CASTELLANO
Number of students: 1,410

Publication: *Digest*

PHILADELPHIA UNIVERSITY

4201 Henry Ave, Philadelphia, PA 19144-5497
Telephone: (215) 951-2700
E-mail: pr@philau.edu
Internet: www.philau.edu

Founded 1884 as Philadelphia Textile School, present name and status 1999
Private control
Academic year: September to August
Pres.: Dr STEPHEN SPINELLI, JR
Provost and Dean for Faculty: RANDY SWEARER
Vice-Pres. for Academic Affairs: CAROL S. FIXMAN
Vice-Pres. for Devt and Alumni Relations: JESSE R. SHAFER
Vice-Pres. for Finance and Admin.: RANDALL D. GENTZLER
Vice-Pres. for Enrolment and Student Affairs: JANE H. ANTHEIL
Dean for Students: MARK GOVONI
Registrar: JULIA AGGREH
Library Dir: KAREN ALBERT
Library of 88,000 vols, 16,000 periodicals, 5,500 microforms
Number of teachers: 400
Number of students: 3,200

Publication: *Innovator Magazine*

DEANS

College of Architecture and the Built Environment: L. PADULO

College of Design, Engineering and Commerce: (vacant)
College of Science, Health and the Liberal Arts: MATT DANE BAKER

PITTSBURGH THEOLOGICAL SEMINARY

616 N Highland Ave, Pittsburgh, PA 15206-2525
Telephone: (412) 362-5610
Internet: www.pts.edu
Founded 1794
Private control
Academic year: September to May
Pres.: Rev. Dr WILLIAM CARL, III
Vice-Pres. for Academic Affairs and Dean for Faculty: BYRON JACKSON
Vice-Pres. for Business and Admin.: ANN GETKIN
Vice-Pres. for Planning and Institutional Effectiveness: JIM DOWNEY
Vice-Pres. for Strategic Advancement: THOMAS PAPPALARDO
Vice-Pres. for Student Services and Dean for Students: JOHN WELCH
Registrar: ANNE MALONE
Library Dir: SHARON TAYLOR
Library of 400,000 vols, incl. 296,000 books
Number of teachers: 25
Number of students: 305 (250 full-time, 55 part-time)

POINT PARK UNIVERSITY

201 Wood St, Pittsburgh, PA 15222
Telephone: (412) 391-4100
E-mail: ptenroll@pointpark.edu
Internet: www.pointpark.edu
Founded 1933, present name and status 2003
Private control
Academic year: August to May
Pres.: Dr PAUL HENNIGAN
Sr Vice-Pres. for Academic and Student Affairs and Dean for Faculty: Dr KAREN S. McINTYRE
Sr Vice-Pres. for Finance and Operations: BRIDGET MANCOSH
Vice-Pres. for Devt and Alumni Affairs: RICK HASKINS
Vice-Pres. for External Affairs: MARIANN K. GEYER
Registrar: JENNIFER FEDELE
Library Dir: LIZ EVANS
Number of teachers: 1,500
Number of students: 3,920

DEANS

Conservatory of Performing Arts: FRED JOHNSON
School of Arts and Sciences: Dr ROBERT K. FESSLER (acting)
School of Business: Dr ANGELA ISAAC
School of Communication: RONALD ALLAN-LINDBLOM (acting)

RECONSTRUCTIONIST RABBINICAL COLLEGE

1299 Church Rd, Wyncote, PA 19095
Telephone: (215) 576-0800
E-mail: info@rrc.edu
Internet: www.rrc.edu
Founded 1968, present location 1982
Private control
Pres.: DAN EHRENKRANTZ
Vice-Pres. for Admin.: JENNIFER ABRAHAM
Vice-Pres. for Academic Affairs: Dr S. TAMAR KAMIONKOWSKI
Vice-Pres. for Governance: Dr DEBORAH WAXMAN
Asst Vice-Pres. for Devt: BARBARA G. LISSY
Library Dir: DEBORAH STERN

Number of teachers: 40 (full-time, adjunct)
Number of students: 80

ROBERT MORRIS UNIVERSITY

6001 University Blvd, Moon Township, PA 15108
Telephone: (412) 397-5200
E-mail: admissionsoffice@rmu.edu
Internet: www.rmu.edu
Founded 1921 as Pittsburgh School of Accountancy, present name and status 2002
Private control
Language of instruction: English
Academic year: August to May
Pres.: Dr GREGORY G. DELL'OMO
Provost and Sr Vice-Pres. for Academic Affairs: DAVID L. JAMISON
Sr Vice-Pres. for Business Affairs: DAN KIENER
Sr Vice-Pres. for Institutional Advancement: JAY T. CARSON
Vice-Pres. and Gen. Counsel: SIDNEY ZONN
Vice-Pres. for Enrolment: WENDY BECKEMEYER
Vice-Pres. for Financial Operations: JEFFREY A. LISTWAK
Registrar: FRANCIS E. PERRY
Library of 115,350 vols
Number of teachers: 470 (195 full-time)
Number of students: 5,180
Publications: *Foundations Magazine*, *Sentry*

DEANS

School of Business: Dr JOHN BEEHLER
School of Communications and Information Systems: Dr BARBARA J. LEVINE
School of Education and Social Sciences: Dr MARY ANN RAFOTH
School of Engineering, Mathematics and Science: Dr MARIA V. KALEVITCH
School of Nursing and Health Sciences: Dr LYNDA J. DAVIDSON

ROSEMONT COLLEGE

1400 Montgomery Ave, Rosemont, PA 19010
Telephone: (610) 527-0200
E-mail: admissions@rosemont.edu
Internet: www.rosemont.edu
Founded 1921
Private control
Academic year: August to May
Pres.: Dr SHARON LATCHAW HIRSH
Provost and Vice-Pres. for Academic and Student Affairs: Dr B. CHRISTOPHER DOUGHERTY
Vice-Pres. for College Relations: CHRISTYN MORAN
Vice-Pres. for Enrolment Management: DENNIS MURPHY
Vice-Pres. for Finance and Admin.: RANDY ELDRIDGE
Registrar: JOSEPH T. ROGERS
Exec. Dir for Library Services: CATHERINE M. FENNELL
Library of 166,220 vols, 1,960 serials, 22,908 microforms, 3,413 audiovisual units, 4,175 ebooks
Number of teachers: 148
Number of students: 960

DEANS

Schools of Graduate and Professional Studies: DENNIS DOUGHERTY
Undergraduate College: PAULETTE HUTCHINSON

SAINT CHARLES BORROMEO SEMINARY

100 E Wynnewood Rd, Wynnewood, PA 19096
Telephone: (610) 667-3394
E-mail: developmentscs@adphila.org
Internet: www.scs.edu
Founded 1838
Private control
Academic year: September to May
Rector: Rev. SHAUN L. MAHONEY
Vice-Rector: Rev. JOSEPH BONGARD
Vice-Pres. for Finance and Operations: ELAINE K. RICE
Registrar: LAWRENCE A. HEYMAN
Library Dir: CAIT KOKOLUS
Library of 148,000 vols, 500 periodicals
Number of teachers: 30
Number of students: 140 (full-time)
Publications: *The Brook*, *The Fact Book*

DEANS

Graduate School of Theology and Program of Catholic Studies: Dr KELLY BOWRING

SAINT FRANCIS UNIVERSITY

POB 600, 117 Evergreen Dr., Loretto, PA 15940
Telephone: (814) 472-3000
E-mail: admissions@francis.edu
Internet: www.francis.edu
Founded 1847
Academic year: August to May
Pres.: Rev. Fr MALACHI VAN TASSELL
Provost: Dr WAYNE POWEL
Vice-Pres. for Academic Affairs: Rev. ANTHONY DE CONCILIIS
Vice-Pres. for Advancement: ROBERT CRUSCIEL
Vice-Pres. for Enrolment Management: ERIN McCLOSKEY
Vice-Pres. for Finance: ROBERT DATSKO
Vice-Pres. for Student Devt: Dr FRANK MONTECALVO
Dir for Devt: RAYMOND PONCHIONE
Dir for Library: SANDRA A. BALOUGH
Library of 120,800 vols, 6,200 microforms, 30,000 journals
Number of teachers: 113 (full-time)
Number of students: 2,449 (1,832 undergraduate, 617 graduate)

DEANS

School of Arts and Letters: Dr TIMOTHY WHISLER
School of Business: Dr RANDY L. FRYE
School of Health Sciences: Dr DOUGLAS R. SOUTHARD
School of Sciences: Dr CHARLES MacVEAN

SAINT JOSEPH'S UNIVERSITY

5600 City Ave, Philadelphia, PA 19131-1395
Telephone: (610) 660-1000
E-mail: admit@sju.edu
Internet: www.sju.edu
Founded 1851
Private control
Pres.: JOHN SMITHSON
Provost: Dr BRICE WACHTERHAUSER
Vice-Pres. for Financial Affairs: LOUIS J. MAYER
Vice-Pres. for Planning: Dr KATHLEEN D. GAVAL
Gen. Counsel: MARIANNE SCHIMELFENIG
Registrar: GERARD DONAHUE
Librarian: EVELYN MINICK
Library of 354,850 vols, 57,000 ejournals, 4,700 ebooks, 863,500 microforms, 4,850 audiovisual materials
Number of teachers: 300 (full-time)

Number of students: 8,950
Publication: *SJU Magazine*

DEANS

College of Arts and Sciences: Dr WILLIAM MADGES
College of Professional and Liberal Studies: Dr PAUL L. DEVITO
Erivan K. Haub School of Business: Dr JOSEPH A. DIANGELO

SAINT VINCENT COLLEGE

300 Fraser Purchase Rd, Latrobe, PA 15650-2690
Telephone: (724) 532-6600
E-mail: admission@stvincent.edu
Internet: www.stvincent.edu

Founded 1846 as St Vincent Archabbey and College
Pres.: Bro. NORMAN HIPPS
Vice-Pres. for Academic Affairs and Academic Dean: Dr JOHN SMETANKA
Vice-Pres. for Finance and Admin.: DENNIS BRANSON (acting)
Vice-Pres. for Institutional Advancement: TRACY H. TAYLOR
Vice-Pres. for Student Affairs: MARY COLLINS
Registrar: CELINE R. HAAS
Librarian: Rev. CHRYSOSTOM V. SCHLIMM
Library of 340,000 vols
Number of teachers: 100
Number of students: 1,940 (1,695 undergraduate, 245 graduate)
Publication: *Saint Vincent Magazine* (4 a year)

DEANS

Alex G. McKenna School of Business, Economics and Government: Dr GARY M. QUINLIVAN
Herbert W. Boyer School of Natural Sciences, Mathematics and Computing: STEPHEN M. JODIS
School of Humanities and Fine Arts: Fr RENE M. KOLLAR
School of Social Sciences, Communication and Education: Dr MARY BETH SPORE

SALUS UNIVERSITY

8360 Old York Rd, Elkins Park, PA 19027-1516
Telephone: (215) 780-1400
E-mail: admissions@salus.edu
Internet: www.salus.edu

Founded 1919
Academic year: August to May
Pres.: Dr THOMAS L. LEWIS
Vice-Pres. for Academic Affairs: ANTHONY F. DI STEFANO
Vice-Pres. and Dean for Student Affairs: ROBERT E. HORNE
Assoc. Vice-Pres. for Finance: DONALD C. KATES
Dir for Devt: LYNNE C. CORBOY
Dir for Library: KEITH LAMMERS
Library of 21,000 vols, 160 video cassettes, 9,650 audio cassettes and 100 slide sets
Number of teachers: 70 (46 full-time, 24 part-time)
Number of students: 1,800

DEANS

College of Education and Rehabilitation: Dr AUDREY J. SMITH
College of Health Sciences: Dr ANTHONY F. DI STEFANO
George S. Osborne College of Audiology: Dr VICTOR H. BRAY
Pennsylvania College of Optometry: Dr LINDA CASSER

SETON HILL UNIVERSITY

One Seton Hill Dr., Greensburg, PA 15601
Telephone: (724) 834-2200
E-mail: admit@setonhill.edu
Internet: www.setonhill.edu

Founded 1885, present name and status 2002
Private control
Academic year: August to May
5 Academic divs: education, humanities, natural and health sciences, social sciences, visual and performing arts
Pres.: Dr JOANNE W. BOYLE
Provost and Dean for Faculty: Dr MARY ANN GAWELEK
Vice-Pres. for Advancement: CHRISTINE M. MUESELER
Vice-Pres. for Finance and Admin.: PAUL T. ROMAN
Vice-Pres. for Enrolment Services: BARBARA HINKLE
Vice-Pres. for Mission and Student Life: Sis. Dr LOIS SCULCO
Dir for Library: DAVID STANLEY
Library of 119,000 vols
Number of teachers: 115 (59 full-time, 56 part-time)
Number of students: 2,145

SUSQUEHANNA UNIVERSITY

51 University Ave, Selinsgrove, PA 17870
Telephone: (574) 374-0101
E-mail: suadmiss@susqu.edu
Internet: www.susqu.edu

Founded 1858
Pres.: Dr L. JAY LEMONS
Provost and Dean for Faculty: Dr CARL O. MOSES
Exec. Vice-Pres. for Admin. and Planning: SARA G. KIRKLAND
Vice-Pres. for Enrolment Management: DEBORAH C. STIEFFEL
Vice-Pres. for Finance and Treas.: MICHAEL A. COYNE
Vice-Pres. for Student Life and Dean for Students: Dr PHILIP E. WINGER
Vice-Pres. for Univ. Relations: RONALD A. COHEN
Registrar: MIMI ARCURI
Dir for Library: KATHLEEN GUNNING
Library of 341,000 vols, 67,000 ebooks, 50,000 journals, 8,680 DVDs, video cassettes and audio CDs, 4,750 printed scores, 8,300 pieces of sheet music
Number of teachers: 125
Number of students: 2,300
Publications: *Susquehanna Currents* (3 a year), *Ventures* (2 a year)

DEANS

School of Arts, Humanities and Communications: VALERIE G. MARTIN
School of Natural and Social Sciences: Dr LUCIEN T. WINEGAR
Sigmund Weis School of Business: Dr ALICIA J. JACKSON

SWARTHMORE COLLEGE

500 College Ave, Swarthmore, PA 19081-1397
Telephone: (610) 328-8000
E-mail: admissions@swarthmore.edu
Internet: www.swarthmore.edu

Founded 1864
Private control
Academic year: September to May
Pres.: REBECCA CHOPP
Provost: THOMAS STEPHENSON
Vice-Pres. and Dean for Admissions: JAMES L. BOCK

Vice-Pres. for College and Community Relations: MAURICE G. ELDRIDGE
Vice-Pres. for Devt and Alumni Relations: KARL CLAUSS
Vice-Pres. for Facilities and Services: C. STUART HAIN
Vice-Pres. for Finance and Treas.: SUZANNE P. WELSH
Registrar: MARTIN O. WARNER
Dean for Admissions and Financial Aid: JAMES L. BOCK
Dean for Students: H. ELIZABETH BRAUN
Librarian: PEGGY SEIDEN
Library of 900,000 vols, 15,164 ejournals, 501,811 ebooks
Number of teachers: 165
Number of students: 1,545
Publication: *Swarthmore College Bulletin*

TEMPLE UNIVERSITY

1801 N Broad St, Philadelphia, PA 19122
Telephone: (215) 204-7000
E-mail: askanowl@temple.edu
Internet: www.temple.edu

Founded 1884 as Temple College, current name adopted 1907
State control
Language of instruction: English
4 Regional campuses; int. campuses in Rome, Italy and Tokyo, Japan
Pres.: Dr NEIL THEOBALD
Provost: Dr HAI-LUNG DAI
Vice-Provost for Faculty Affairs: Dr DIANE C. MALESON (acting)
Sr Vice-Pres. for Govt, Community and Public Affairs: KENNETH LAWRENCE
Sr Vice-Pres. for Institutional Advancement: TILGHMAN MOYER
Sr Vice-Pres. for Research: Dr MICHELE MASUCCI
Vice-Pres. for Financial Affairs, Chief Financial Officer and Treas.: KEN KAISER
Vice-Pres. for Univ. College: Dr VICKI LEWIS McGARVEY
Deputy Univ. Counsel: MICHAEL GEBHARDT
Dean for Libraries: JOE LUCIA
Library of 4,060,061 vols, 80,484 current serials, 10m. photographs and other graphic images
Number of teachers: 2,600
Number of students: 37,700
Publications: *HSR: Health Services Research* (6 a year), *Journal of Economics and Business* (6 a year), *Journal of Information Technology & Tourism, Journal of International Management, Journal of Management, Spirituality and Religion, Journal of Product Innovation Management, Journal of Risk Finance, Law Quarterly, Risk Management and Insurance Review, Temple Review, The American Journal of Legal History, The Asia-Pacific Journal of Risk and Insurance*

DEANS

Beasley School of Law: JOANNE EPPS
Boyer College of Music and Dance: ROBERT STROKER
College of Education: GREGORY M. ANDERSON
College of Engineering: KEYA SADEGHIPOUR
College of Health Professions and Social Work: LAURA SIMINOFF
College of Liberal Arts: TERESA SOUFAS
College of Science and Technology: MICHAEL KLEIN
Fox School of Business and Management: MOSHE PORAT
Maurice H. Kornberg School of Dentistry: AMID ISMAIL
School of Environmental Design: TERESA SOUFAS
School of Media and Communication: DAVID BOARDMAN

School of Medicine: LARRY KAISER
School of Pharmacy: PETER DOUKAS
School of Podiatric Medicine: JOHN A. MATTIACCI
School of Tourism and Hospitality Management: MOSHE PORAT
Temple University Japan: BRUCE STRONACH
Temple University Rome: KIM STROMMEN
Tyler School of Art: ROBERT STROKER

THIEL COLLEGE

75 College Ave, Greenville, PA 16125
Telephone: (724) 589-2345
E-mail: admissions@thiel.edu
Internet: www.thiel.edu
Founded 1866
Private control
Academic year: August to May

Pres.: Dr TROY D. VANAKEN
Vice-Pres. for Academic Affairs and Dean for College: Dr LYNN FRANKEN
Vice-Pres. for Enrolment Management: DAVID RHODES
Vice-Pres. for Finance and Management: ROBERT SCHMOLL
Vice-Pres. for Student Life: MICHAEL McKINNEY
Dir for Int. Student Affairs: SHANNON REESH
Dir for Library: ALLEN S. MORRILL

Library of 135,000 vols
Number of teachers: 108
Number of students: 1,100

Publications: *Endymion*, *The Bell*

THOMAS JEFFERSON UNIVERSITY

1020 Walnut St, Philadelphia, PA 19107
Telephone: (215) 955-6000
E-mail: jcgs-info@jefferson.edu
Internet: www.jefferson.edu
Founded 1824 as Jefferson Medical College, present name and status 1969

Pres.: Dr ROBERT L. BARCHI
Sr Vice-Pres. for Strategic Initiatives: JUDITH L. BACHMAN
Vice-Pres. and Univ. Counsel: CRISTINA G. CAVALLERI
Vice-Pres. for Finance: RICHARD SCHMLD
Vice-Pres. for Research: Dr STEVEN E. McKENZIE
Librarian: EDWARD N. TAWYEA

Library of 167,504 vols
Number of teachers: 760
Number of students: 2,600

Publications: *American Journal of Medical Quality—Official Journal of the American College of Medical Quality*, *Biotechology Healthcare—Official Journal of the Biologic Finance and Access Council*, *P&T (Pharmacy and Therapeutics)*, *Population Health Management*

DEANS

Jefferson College of Graduate Studies: GERALD B. GRUNWALD
Jefferson Medical College: Dr MARK L. TYKOCINSKI
Jefferson School of Health Professions: Dr JANICE P. BURKE
Jefferson School of Pharmacy: Dr REBECCA S. FINLEY
Jefferson School of Population Health: Dr DAVID B. NASH

TRINITY SCHOOL FOR MINISTRY

311 11th St, Ambridge, PA 15003
Telephone: (724) 266-3838
E-mail: info@tsm.edu
Internet: www.tsm.edu
Founded 1975
Private control

Pres. and Dean: Rev. Dr JUSTYN TERRY
Academic Dean: Dr MARK STEVENSON
Dean for Students and Dir for Admissions: Rev. TINA LOCKETT
Registrar: Rev. BILL STARKE
Library Dir: SUSANAH HANSON

Library of 80,000 vols, 400 periodicals
Number of teachers: 40
Number of students: 110 (full-time)

Publication: *Trinity Journal for Theology & Ministry* (2 a year)

UNIVERSITY OF PENNSYLVANIA

3451 Walnut St, Philadelphia, PA 19104
Telephone: (215) 898-5000
E-mail: info@admissions.upenn.edu
Internet: www.upenn.edu
Founded 1740 as Acad. and Charitable School in the Province of Pennsylvania
Private control
Academic year: September to May, and two six-week summer terms

Pres.: Dr AMY GUTMANN
Provost: VINCENT PRICE
Vice-Provost and Dir for Libraries: CARTON ROGERS, III
Exec. Vice-Pres.: CRAIG CARNAROLI
Exec. Vice-Pres. for Univ. of Pennsylvania Health System: J. LARRY JAMESON
Sr Vice-Pres. and Gen. Counsel: WENDY WHITE
Vice-Pres. and Chief of Staff: GREGORY S. ROST
Vice-Pres. and Sec.: LESLIE LAIRD KRUHLY
Vice-Pres. for Business Services: MARIE WITT
Vice-Pres. for Devt and Alumni Relations: JOHN H. ZELLER
Vice-Pres. for Finance and Treas.: STEPHEN D. GOLDING
Vice-Pres. for Govt and Community Affairs: JEFFREY COOPER
Vice-Pres. for Human Resources: JOHN J. HEUER
Vice-Pres. for Information Systems and Computing: ROBIN BECK
Vice-Pres. for Institutional Affairs: JOANN MITCHELL
Vice-Pres. for Univ. Communications: STEPHEN J. MacCARTHY
CEO for Univ. of Pennsylvania Health System: RALPH W. MULLER
Registrar: MICHELLE H. BROWN-NEVERS
Dean for Admissions: ERIC J. FURDA

Library: see under Libraries and Archives
Number of teachers: 4,250
Number of students: 24,850 (21,340 full-time, 3,510 part-time)

Publications: *Arts at Penn*, *Red and Blue*, *Research at PENN* (online)

DEANS

Annenberg School for Communication: Dr MICHAEL X. DELLI CARPINI
Graduate School of Education: Dr ANDREW C. PORTER
Raymond and Ruth Perelman School of Medicine: Dr J. LARRY JAMESON
School of Arts and Sciences: Dr REBECCA BUSHNELL
School of Dental Medicine: DENIS F. KINANE
School of Design: MARILYN JORDAN TAYLOR
School of Engineering and Applied Science: Dr EDUARDO GLANDT
School of Law: MICHALE A. FITTS
School of Nursing: AFAF I. MELEIS
School of Social Policy and Practice: Dr RICHARD GELLES
School of Veterinary Medicine: Dr JOAN C. HENDRICKS
Wharton School: Dr THOMAS S. ROBERTSON

PROFESSORS

Annenberg School for Communication
Communications:

CAPPELLA, J.
DELLI CARPINI, M.
FISHBEIN, M.
GANDY, O. H.
GROSS, L.
HORNIK, R.
JAMIESON, K. H.
JEMMOTT, J.
KATZ, E.
KRIPPENDORFF, K.
LINEBARGER, D.
MARVIN, C.
MESSARIS, P.
PRICE, V.
TUROW, J.
ZELIZER, B.

Wharton School
Accounting:

BAIMAN, S.
GONEDES, N.
HOLTHAUSEN, R.
ITTNER, C.
LAMBERT, R. A.
LARCKER, D.
VERRECCHIA, R.

Business and Public Policy:

ALLEN, W. B.
BAILEY, E.
FAULHABER, G.
PACK, H.
PACK, J.
WALDFOGEL, J.

Finance:

ABEL, A.
ALLEN, H. F.
BLUME, M.
GIBBONS, M.
GORTON, G.
HERRING, R.
INMAN, R.
KEIM, D.
KIHLSTROM, R.
LEWIS, K. K.
MACKINLAY, A. C.
MARSTON, R.
RAMASWAMY, K.
SIEGEL, J.
STAMBAUGH, R.

Health Care Systems:

BURNS, L.
DANZON, P.
HARRINGTON, S.
PAULY, M.

Insurance and Risk Management:

BABBEL, D.
CUMMINS, J. D.
DOHERTY, N.
LEMAIRE, J.
MITCHELL, O.
ROSENBLOOM, J.

Legal Studies:

BELLACE, J.
DONALDSON, T.
DUNFEE, T.
ORTS, E.
ROSOFF, A.
SHELL, G. R.
SHROPSHIRE, K.

Management:

AMIT, R.
CAPPELI, P.
GERRITY, T.
GULLEN, M.
HAMILTON, W. F.
HOUSE, R.
KIMBERLY, J.
KLEIN, K.
KOBRIN, S.

LEVINTHAL, D.
MACMILLAN, I.
MEYER, M.
PENNINGS, J.
SINGH, H.
SINGH, J.
USEEM, M.
WEIGELT, K.
WINTER, S.

Marketing:

ARMSTRONG, J. S.
DAY, G.
ELIASHBERG, J.
FADER, P.
HOCH, S.
HUTCHISON, J.
IANOBUCCI, D.
KAHN, B.
LODISH, L.
MEYER, R.
RAJU, J. S.
REIBSTEIN, D.
SCHMITTLEIN, D.
WARD, S.
WIND, Y.

Operations and Information Management:

CLEMONS, E.
COHEN, M.
FISHER, M.
GUIGNARD-SPIELBERG, M.
HARKER, P.
HERSHEY, J.
KIMBROUGH, S.
KLEINDORFER, P.
KUNREUTHER, H.
ULRICH, K.
ZHENG, Y.

Real Estate:

GYOURKO, J.
LINNEMAN, P.
POINDEXTER, G.
WACHTER, S.

Statistics:

BROWN, L.
BUJA, A.
GEORGE, E.
KRIEGER, A.
LOW, M.
ROSENBAUM, P.
SHAMAN, P.
STEELE, J. M.
STINE, R.

Raymond and Ruth Perelman School of Medicine (295 John Morgan, Philadelphia, PA 19104-6055; internet www.med.upenn.edu):

Anaesthesia:

DEUTSCHMANN, C.
ECKENDOFF, R.
FLEISHER, L.
LONGNECKER, D.

Biochemistry and Biophysics:

DEGRADO, W.
DREYFUSS, G.
DUTTON, P. L.
ENGLANDER, S. W.
KALLEN, R.
LEMMON, M.
LEWIS, M.
LIEBMAN, P.
MATSCHINSKY, F.
OHNISHI, T.
VAN DUYNE, G.
VANDERKOOI, J.
WAND, A. J.
WILSON, D.
YONETANI, T.

Biostatistics and Epidemiology:

HEITJAN, D.
KUMANYIKA, S.
LANDIS, J. R.
LEE, H.

REBBECK, T.
STROM, B.
TEN HAVE, T.

Cancer Biology:

ALWINE, J.

Cell and Developmental Biology:

DINARDO, S.
FRANZINI-ARMSTRONG, C.
SANGER, J.
SIMON, M.
WEISEL, J.

Dermatology:

ROOK, A.
STANLEY, J.

Emergency Medicine:

BAXT, W. G.
THORN, S.

Family Practice and Community Medicine:

BOWMAN, M.

Genetics:

BUCAN, M.
GASSER, D.
KADESCH, T.
KAZAZIAN, H.
LIEBHABER, S.
SPIELMAN, R.

Medical Ethics:

CAPLAN, A.

Medicine:

ALBELDA, S.
ASCH, D.
BENNETT, J.
BIRNBAUM, M.
BLUMBERG, B.
BRASS, L.
COHEN, P.
COLLMAN, R.
COOKE, N.
DANIELE, R.
EISENBERG, R.
EMERSON, S. G.
EPSTEIN, J.
FELDMAN, H.
FITZGERALD, G.
FRIEDMAN, H. M.
GEWIRTZ, A.
GLICK, J.
HILLMAN, A.
HOXIE, J.
KELLEY, W.
LAZAR, M.
LEVINSON, A.
MACGREGOR, R. R.
MADAIO, M.
PACK, A.
PANETTIERI, R.
PARMACEK, M.
PHILLIPS, S.
PYERITZ, R.
RUBENSTEIN, A.
RUBIN, H.
RUSTGI, A.
SCHAFER, A.
SCHREIBER, A.
SCHUMACHER, H.
SCHWARTZ, J.
SNYDER, P.
TANNEN, R.
THOMPSON, C.
TURKA, L.
TURNER, B.
WEBER, B.
WILSON, J.
ZIYADEH, F.

Microbiology:

BOETTIGER, D.
BUSHMAN, F.
DAVIES, H. C.
FRANKEL, F.
FRASER, N.
GOLDFINE, H.

KAJI, A.
PATERSON, Y.
ROSS, S.
WEISS, S.

Neurology:

BARCHI, R.
BERMAN, P.
BROWN, M.
COSLETT, H. B.
DICHTER, M.
GONZALEZ-SCARANO, F.
PLEASURE, D.
SCHERER, S.
SELZER, M.
TENNEKOON, G. I.

Neuroscience:

HAYDON, P.
LEVITAN, I.
LINDSTROM, J.
NUSBAUM, M.
PALMER, L.
RAPER, J.
ROSENQUIST, A.
SALZBERG, B.
SEHGAL FIELD, A.
STERLING, P.

Neurosurgery:

GRADY, M. S.
WELSH, F.

Obstetrics and Gynaecology:

HECHT, N.
MASTROIANNI, L.
MENNUTI, M.
RUBIN, S.
STRAUSS, J.

Ophthalmology:

BENNETT, J.
FINE, S.
JACOBSON, S.
LATIES, A.
PUGH, E.
STONE, R.

Orthopaedic Surgery:

FITZGERALD, R.
HEPPENSTALL, R.
KAPLAN, F.
SOSLOWSKY, L.

Otorhinolaryngology:

DOTY, R.
KENNEDY, D.
O'MALLEY, B.
SAUNDERS, J.

Paediatrics:

ASAKURA, T.
BALLARD, P. L.
BRODEUR, G.
DOUGLAS, S.
EMANUEL, B.
FOX, W.
GRUNSTEIN, M.
HIGH, K.
HONIG, P.
HOYER, J.
JOHNSON, P.
LEVY, R.
OFFIT, P.
PONCZ, M.
SEGAL, S.
SILBER, J.
YUDKOFF, M.

Pathology and Laboratory Medicine:

ARGON, Y.
CANCRO, M.
CHOI, Y.
CINES, D.
DAVIES, P.
DOMS, R.
GAULTON, G.
GONATAS, N.
GREENE, M.
HANCOCK, W.

JARETT, L.
JUNE, C. H.
KAMOUN, M.
KORETZKY, G. A.
LAMBRIS, J.
LEE, V. M.-Y.
LIVOLSI, V.
MONROE, J.
MUSCHEL, R.
NOWELL, P.
SCHLAEPFER, W.
SHAW, L.
TROJANOWSKI, J.
TYKOCINSKI, M.
WOLF, B.
YOUNG, D.

Pharmacology:

ASSOIAN, R.
BLAIR, I.
EBERWINE, J.
MANNING, D.
PENNING, T.
PITTMAN, R.
WHITEHEAD, A. S.

Physiology:

BAYLOR, S. M.
CIVAN, M.
COBURN, R.
DE WEER, P.
DEUTSCH, C.
FISHER, A.
FOSKETT, J. K.
GOLDMAN, Y.
HOLZBAUR-HOWARD, E.
JAMMEY, P.
LAHIRI, S.
LU, Z.
SWEENEY, H. L.
WINEGRAD, S.

Psychiatry:

ASTON-JONES, G.
BERRETTINI, W.
COYNE, J.
CRITS-CHRISTOPH, P.
DINGES, D. F.
EVANS, D.
FOA, E.
GUR, R.
KATZ, I.
LERMAN, C.
LUCKI, I.
NICHOLLS, R.
O'BRIEN, C.
PRICE, R.
RICKELS, K.
WADDEN, T.
WELLER, E.

Radiation Oncology:

BIAGLOW, J.
BLOCH, P.
GLATSTEIN, E.
KENNEDY, A.
KOCH, C.
MCKENNA, W.

Radiology:

BAUM, S.
BRYAN, R. N.
JOSEPH, P.
KARP, J.
KUNG, H.
LEIGH, J.
SCHNALL, M.
UDUPA, J.
WEHRLI, F.

Surgery:

ADZICK, N. S.
BARKER, C. F.
DREBIN, J.
EDMUNDS, L.
FLAKE, A.
KAISER, L.
NAJI, A.
NUSBAUM, M.

ROMBEAU, J.
ROSATO, E.
SHAKED, A.
SPRAY, T.
WEIN, A.
WHITAKER, L.

School of Arts and Sciences

Anthropology:

DIBBLE, H. L.
KOPYTOFF, I.
LEVENTHAL, R.
POSSEHL, G.
SABLOFF, J.
SANDAY, P.
SHARER, R.
SILVERSTEIN, M.
SPOONER, B.
URBAN, G.

Biology:

BINNS, A.
CASHMORE, A.
CASPER, B.
CEBRA, J.
CHENEY, D.
DALDAL, M. F.
DUNHAM, A. E.
EWENS, W.
GUILD, G.
JANZEN, D.
KIM, J.
PETRAITIS, P.
POETHIG, R. S.
REA, P. A.
ROME, L.
ROOS, D. S.
SCHULTZ, R.
WALDRON, I.
WEINBERG, E.
ZIGMOND, S.

Chemistry:

BERRY, D.
BLASIE, J. K.
CHRISTIANSON, D.
COOPERMAN, B.
DAI, H.-L.
FITTS, D.
HOCHSTRASSER, R.
JOULLIE, M.
KLEIN, M.
LESTER, M. I.
LU, P.
MACDIARMID, A.
MOLANDER, G.
PERCEC, V.
SMITH, A. B.
SNEDDON, L.
THERIEN, M.
THORNTON, E.
TOPP, M. R.
WAYLAND, B.
WINKLER, J.

Classical Studies:

COPELAND, R.
FARRELL, J., Jr
MURNAGHAN, S.
ROSEN, R.

Criminology:

SHERMAN, L.

Earth and Environmental Science:

GIEGENGACK, R.
JOHNSON, A.
PFEFFERKORN, H.
SCATENA, F.

East Asian Languages and Civilizations:

HURST, G.
LAFLEUR, W.
MAIR, V.
STEINHARDT, N.

Economics:

BEHRMAN, J. R.
BURDETT, K.

CASS, D.
DIEBOLD, F.
ETHIER, W.
LEVINE, H.
MAILATH, G.
MATTHEWS, S.
MERLO, A.
POSTLEWAITE, A.
RIOS-RULL, J.-V.
ROB, R.
WOLPIN, K.
WRIGHT, R.

English:

AUERBACH, N.
BERNSTEIN, C.
BUSHNELL, R.
CONN, P.
CORRIGAN, T.
CURRAN, S.
DAVIS, T.
DE GRAZIA, M.
ENGLISH, J.
FILREIS, A.
KAPLAN, A.
KAUL, S.
LOOMBA, A.
MAHAFFEY, V.
PERELMAN, R.
QUILLIGAN, M.
RABATE, J.
RICHETTI, J.
STALLYBRASS, P.
STEINER, W.
STEWART, S.
WALLACE, D.

Germanic Languages and Literatures:

TROMMLER, F.
WEISSBERG, L.

History:

BEEMAN, R.
BERRY, M. F.
CHILDERS, T.
ENGS, R. F.
FARRISS, N.
HACKNEY, S.
HAHN, S.
KATZ, M.
KORS, A.
KUKLICK, B.
LEES, L. H.
LICHT, W.
LUDDEN, D.
MCDOUGALL, W.
PEISS, K.
PETERS, E.
RICHTER, D.
RUDERMAN, D.
SAVAGE, B.
STEINBERG, J.
SUGRUE, T. J.
TODD, M.
WALDRON, A.
ZUCKERMAN, M.

History and Sociology of Science:

COWAN, R.
FEIERMAN, S.
KOHLER, R.
KUKLICK, H.
LINDEE, M.
SIVIN, N.

History of Art:

BROWNLEE, D.
HOLOD, R.
MEISTER, M.
PITTMAN, H.
SILVER, L.

Linguistics:

CARDONA, G.
KROCH, A.
LABOV, W.
LIBERMAN, M
PRINCE, E.
RINGE, D.

SANKOFF, G.

Mathematics:

CHAI, C.
CHINBURG, T.
CROKE, C.
DeTURCK, D.
DONAGI, R.
EPSTEIN, C.
FREYD, P.
GERSTENHABER, M.
GLUCK, H.
HARBATER, D.
KADISON, R. V.
KAZDAN, J.
KIRILLOV, A.
MINSKY, Y.
PEMANTLE, R.
PIMSNER, M.
POP, F.
PORTER, G.
POWERS, R.
SCEDROV, A.
SHANESON, J.
SHATZ, S.
WILF, H.
ZILLER, W.

Music:

BERNSTEIN, L.
KALLBERG, J.
NARMOUR, E.
PRIMOSCH, J.
REISE, J.
TOMLINSON, G.

Near Eastern Languages and Civilizations:

ALLEN, R.
BEN-AMOS, D.
SILVERMAN, D.
STERN, D.
TIGAY, J. H.

Philosophy:

BICCHIERI, C.
DOMOTOR, Z.
FREEMAN, S.
GUYER, P.
HATFIELD, G.
KAHN, C.
ROSS, J.
WEINSTEIN, S.

Physics and Astronomy:

BALAMUTH, D.
BEIER, E.
CVETIC, M.
DURIAN, D.
FORTUNE, H.
HEINEY, P.
HOLLEBEEK, R.
KAMIEN, R.
LANDE, K.
LANGACKER, P. G.
LIU, A.
LOCKYER, N.
LUBENSKY, T.
MELE, E.
NELSON, P.
OVRUT, B.
SEGRE, G.
SOVEN, P.
WILLIAMS, H.
YODH, A.

Political Science:

CALLAGHY, T.
DIIULIO, J.
FRANKEL, F.
GOLDSTEIN, A.
GUMANN, A.
KENNEDY, E.
KETTI, D.
LUSTICK, I. S.
MANSFIELD, E.
MUTZ, D.
NAGEL, J.
NORTON, A.
O'LEARY, B.

REED, A.
SMITH, R.
TEUNE, H.

Psychology:

BARON, J.
BRAINARD, D.
CHAMBLESS, D.
DeRUBEIS, R.
FARAH, M.
GRILL, H.
KAHANA, M.
NORMAN, M. F.
RESCORLA, R.
RICHARDS, V.
RODIN, J.
ROZIN, P.
SABINI, J. P.
SELIGMAN, M.
SEYFARTH, R.

Religious Studies:

DUNNING, S.
DYSON, M.
MATTER, E. A.

Romance Languages:

ALONSO, C.
BROWNLEE, K.
DeJEAN, J.
DONALDSON-EVANS, L.
KIRKHAM, V.
LOPEZ, I.
MARCUS, M.
PRINCE, G.

Slavic Languages:

STEINER, P.

Sociology:

ALLISON, P.
ANDERSON, E.
BERG, I.
BIELBY, W.
BOSK, C.
COLLINS, R.
ENGLAND, P.
FURSTENBERG, F.
JACOBS, J.
MADDEN, J. F.
PRESTON, S.
SMITH, H.
WATKINS, S.
ZUBERI, T.

South Asian Regional Studies:

ROCHER, R.
SCHIFFMAN, H.

School of Dental Medicine

Anatomy/Cell Biology:

MACARAK, E.
GIBSON, C.

Biochemistry:

ADAMS, S.
GOLUB, E. E.
LeBOY, P.
MALAMUD, D.

Endodontics:

KIM, S.

Microbiology:

COHEN, G.
DiRIENZO, J.
RICCIARDI, R.

Oral Medicine:

GREENBERG, M.

Oral Surgery:

FONSECA, R.
HERSH, E.
QUINN, P.

Orthodontics:

KATZ, S.
VANARSDALL, R.

Pathology:

LALLY, E.

SHENKER, B.

Periodontics:

EVIANS, C.
JEFFCOAT, M.
POLSON, A.

School of Education:

BOE, E.
BORUCH, R.
FANTUZZO, J.
FUHRMAN, S.
GOERTZ, M.
GOODMAN, J.
HORNBERGER, N.
INGERSOLL, R.
KURILOFF, P.
LAZERSON, M.
McDERMOTT, P.
MAYNARD, R.
PICA, T.
SLAUGHTER-DEFOE, D.
SPENCER, M. B.
WAGNER, D.
WORTHAM, S.
ZEMSKY, R. M.

School of Engineering and Applied Science:

ALUR, R.
AYYASWAMY, P.
BADLER, N.
BASSANI, J.
BAU, H.
BONNELL, D.
BORDOGNA, J.
BUCHSBAUM, G.
CASSEL, T.
CHEN, I.-W.
COHEN, I.
DAVIDSON, S.
DAVIES, P.
DIAMOND, S.
DUCHEYNE, P.
EGAMI, T.
ENGHETA, N.
FARHAT, N.
FINKEL, L.
FISCHER, J.
FOSTER, K.
GALLIER, J. H.
GIRIFALCO, L.
GLANDT, E.
GORTE, R.
GRAHAM, W.
GUERIN, R.
HAMMER, D.
JAGGARD, D.
JOSHI, A.
KANNAN, S.
KASSAM, S.
KEARNS, M.
KEENAN, J.
KUMAR, V.
LAIRD, C.
LAKER, K.
LEE, I.
LIOR, N.
LUZZI, D.
MACARAK, E.
MARCUS, M. P.
MARGULIES, S.
MEANEY, D.
MINTZ, M.
PEREIRA, F.
PIERCE, B.
PONTE-CASTANEDA, P.
POPE, D.
RABII, S.
SCHERER, P.
SEIDER, W.
SHIEH, W.
SILVERMAN, B.
SMITH, J. M.
SMITH, T.
SOSLOWSKY, L.
TANNEN, V. B.
ULRICH, K.

VAN DER SPEIGEL, J.
VITEK, V.
VOHS, J.
VUCHIC, V.

School of Law:
ADLER, M.
ALLEN-CASTELLITO, A.
AUSTIN, R.
BAKER, C. E.
BURBANK, S.
CHANG, H.
deLISLE, J.
EWALD, W.
FINKELSTEIN, C.
FITTS, M.
GOODMAN, F.
GORDON, S.
JOHNSTON, J.
KATZ, L.
KNOLL, M.
KREIMER, S.
KUBLER, F.
LESNICK, H.
MANN, B.
MOONEY, C.
MORSE, S.
PARCHOMOVSKY, G.
PERRY, S.
REITZ, C.
ROBINSON, P.
ROCK, E.
RUBIN, E.
SANCHIRICO, C.
SCHEPPLE, K. L.
SHULDINER, R.
SKEEL, D.
WACHTER, M.
WAX, A.

School of Nursing:
AIKEN, L.
BARNSTEINER, J.
BROWN, L. P.
BUHLER-WILKERSON, K.
EVANS, L.
GENNARO, S.
JEMMOTT, L.
LANG, N.
MCCAULEY, L.
MEDOFF-COOPER, B.
MELEIS, A.
NAYLOR, M.
O'SULLIVAN, A.
STRUMPF, N.

School of Social Work
Social Work:
CNAAN, R.
ESTES, R.
SANDS, R.
SELTZER, V.
SOLOMON, P.
SPIGNER, C.
STERN, M.

School of Veterinary Medicine:
AQUIRRE, G.
ATCHISON, M.
AVADHANI, N.
BEECH, J.
BELLO, L.
BENSON, C.
BOSTON, R.
BRINSTER, R.
CHACKO, S.
CHALUPA, W.
DAVIES, R.
DODSON, P.
DROBATZ, K.
EISENBERG, R.
FARRELL, J.
FERGUSON, J.
FERRER, J.
FLUHARTY, S.
GIGER, U.
GOLDSCHMIDT, M. H.

HARVEY, C.
HASKINS, M.
HENDRICKS, J. C.
KELLY, A.
KING, L.
KLIDE, A.
LASTER, L.
MISELIS, R.
NEWTON, C.
NUNAMAKER, D.
RAMBERG, C.
REEF, V.
RICHARDSON, D.
ROSS, M.
ROZMIAREK, H.
SCHAD, G.
SCOTT, P.
SERPELL, J.
SHAPIRO, B.
SMITH, G.
SOMA, L.
SPEAR, J.
SWEENEY, C.
WEBER, W.
WEISS, L.
WOLFE, J. H.

PennDesign:
GYOURKO, J.
LINNEMAN, P.
POINDEXTER, G.
RYBCZYNSKI, W.
SAGALYN, L.

UNIVERSITY OF PITTSBURGH

Pittsburgh, PA 15260

Telephone: (412) 624-4141

Internet: www.pitt.edu

Founded 1787 as Pittsburgh Acad., current name adopted 1908, current status 1966

State control

Academic year: August to April (2 semesters)

Chancellor: MARK A. NORDENBERG

Provost and Sr Vice-Chancellor: PATRICIA E. BEESON

Assoc. Chancellor: VIJAI SINGH

Exec. Vice-Chancellor and Gen. Counsel: JEROME COCHRAN

Sr Vice-Chancellor for Health Sciences: Dr ARTHUR S. LEVINE

Chief Financial Officer: ARTHUR G. RAMICONE

Vice-Chancellor for Communications: KENNETH P. SERVICE

Vice-Chancellor for Community Initiatives and Govt Relations: PAUL SUPOWITZ

Vice-Chancellor for External Relations and Chief of Staff: G. REYNOLDS CLARK

Vice-Chancellor for Health Sciences Devt: CLYDE B. JONES, III

Vice-Chancellor for Institutional Advancement: ALBERT J. NOVAK, JR

Vice-Chancellor for Research Conduct and Compliance: RANDY JUHL

Vice-Provost and Dean for Students: KATHY W. HUMPHREY

Univ. Registrar: PATTI J. MATHAY

Gen. Counsel: P. JEROME RICHEY

Dir for Univ. Library System: RUSH G. MILLER

Library: see under Libraries and Archives

Number of teachers: 4,874

Number of students: 28,649

Publications: *Pitt Magazine* (4 a year), *Pitt Med* (4 a year), *Pittsburgh Economic Quarterly*, *The Original* (2 a year)

DEANS

College of General Studies: N. JOHN COOPER

Dietrich School of Arts and Sciences: N. JOHN COOPER

Graduate School of Public and International Affairs: JOHN T. S. KEELER

Graduate School of Public Health: Dr DONALD S. BURKE

Joseph M. Katz Graduate School of Business and College of Business Administration: JOHN T. DELANEY

School of Dental Medicine: THOMAS W. BRAUN

School of Education: ALAN M. LESGOLD

School of Health and Rehabilitation Sciences: CLIFFORD E. BRUBAKER

School of Information Sciences: RONALD L. LARSEN

School of Law: WILLIAM M. CARTER

School of Medicine: Dr ARTHUR S. LEVINE

School of Nursing: Dr JACQUELINE DUNBAR-JACOB

School of Pharmacy: PATRICIA D. KROBOTH

School of Social Work: LARRY E. DAVIS

Swanson School of Engineering: GERALD D. HOLDER

University Honors College: EDWARD M. STRICKER.

REGIONAL CAMPUSES

University of Pittsburgh at Bradford: 300 Campus Dr., Bradford, PA 16701; tel. (814) 362-7500; internet www.upb.pitt.edu; f. 1963; academic year August to April; 5 academic divs: behavioural and social sciences, biological and health sciences, communication and the arts, management and education, physical and computational sciences; Pres. Dr LIVINGSTON ALEXANDER; Vice-Pres. and Dean for Academic Affairs Dr STEVE HARDIN; Registrar JAMES L. BALDWIN; library of 95,000 vols, 3,782 audiovisual materials, 1,055 microform items, 50,000 ejournals, 300,000 ebooks; 98 (76 full-time, 22 part-time) teachers; 1,481 students.

University of Pittsburgh at Greensburg: 150 Finoli Dr., Greensburg, PA 15601; tel. (724) 837-7040; e-mail upgadmit@pitt.edu; internet www.greensburg.pitt.edu; f. 1963; academic year August to April; Pres. SHARON P. SMITH; Vice-Pres. for Academic Affairs Dr J. WESLEY JAMISON; Registrar LINDA SMITH; library of 78,000 vols; 100 teachers; 1,677 students.

University of Pittsburgh at Johnstown: 450 Schoolhouse Rd, Johnstown, PA 15904; tel. (814) 269-7050; e-mail upjadmit@pitt .edu; internet www.upj.pitt.edu; f. 1927; academic year August to April; divs: education; engineering technology; humanities; natural science; nursing and health sciences; social science; Pres. Dr JEM M. SPECTAR; Vice-Pres. for Academic Affairs Dr JANET L. GRADY; Vice-Pres. for Enrolment Services and Planning Dr JAMES F. GYURE; Vice-Pres. for Finance and Admin. Dr AMY BUXBAUM; Vice-Pres. for Student Affairs SHAWN E. BROOKS; library of 230,000 vols; 147 (134 full-time, 13 part-time) teachers; 2,840 students.

University of Pittsburgh at Titusville: 504 E Main St, Titusville, PA 16354; tel. (888) 878-0462; internet www.upt.pitt.edu; f. 1963; academic year August to April; Vice-Pres. for Academic Affairs Dr DAVID E. FITZ; Exec. Dir for Student Affairs PARRIS CARTER; Registrar CHRISTOPHER COAT; library of 40,000 vols; 44 teachers; 367 students; publ. *Panther Print*

UNIVERSITY OF SCRANTON

800 Linden St, Scranton, PA 18510-4699

Telephone: (570) 941-7400

E-mail: info@scranton.edu

Internet: www.scranton.edu

Founded 1888 as St Thomas College, present status 1938

Private control

Academic year: August to May

Pres.: Rev. Dr KEVIN QUINN

Provost and Vice-Pres. for Academic Affairs: Dr HAROLD W. BAILLIE

Exec. Vice-Pres.: PATRICK LEAHY
Vice-Pres. for Alumni and Public Relations: GERALD C. ZABOSKI
Vice-Pres. for Finance and Treas.: EDWARD J. STEINMETZ
Vice-Pres. for Student Affairs: Dr VINCENT CARILLI
Registrar: HELEN H. STAGER
Gen. Counsel: ROBERT B. FARRELL
Dean for Library: CHARLES E. KRATZ
Library of 514,915 vols, 17,498 non-print item, 48,201 journals print and online
Number of teachers: 285 (full-time)
Number of students: 6,000
Publications: *Diakonia*, *The Scranton Journal* (4 a year), *Windhover* (1 a year)

DEANS

Arthur J. Kania School of Management: Dr MICHAEL O. MENSAH
College of Arts and Sciences: Dr BRIAN P. CONIFF
College of Graduate and Continuing Education: Dr WILLIAM JEFFREY WELSH
Panuska College of Professional Studies: Dr DEBRA A. PELLIGRINO

UNIVERSITY OF THE ARTS

320 S Broad St, Philadelphia, PA 19102
Telephone: (215) 717-6030
E-mail: admissions@uarts.edu
Internet: www.uarts.edu
Founded 1985 by merger of Philadelphia College of Art (f. 1876) with Philadelphia College of the Performing Arts (f. 1870), present name and status 1984
Private control
Academic year: September to May
Pres.: SEAN T. BUFFINGTON
Provost: Dr KIRK E. PILLOW
Vice-Pres. for Advancement: LUCIE HUGHES
Vice-Pres. for Enrolment, Retention and Student Affairs: R. ALAN LEFFERS
Vice-Pres. for Facilities Management and Operations: PHILLIP VAN CLEAVE
Vice-Pres. for Finance and Admin.: STEPHEN J. LIGHTCAP
Vice-Pres. for Technology and Information Services: THOMAS H. CARNWATH
Vice-Pres. for Univ. Communications: PAUL F. HEALY
Dean for Admissions: SUSAN GANDY
Dean for Students: ALLEN LEFFERS
Dir for Libraries: CAROL GRANEY
Number of teachers: 545 (125 full-time, 420 part-time)
Number of students: 2,200

DEANS

College of Art, Media and Design: CHRISTOPHER SHARROCK
Division of Continuing Studies: ERIN ELMAN
Division of Liberal Arts: PETER STAMBLER

UNIVERSITY OF THE SCIENCES

600 S 43rd St, Philadelphia, PA 19104-4495
Telephone: (215) 596-8800
E-mail: admit@usciences.edu
Internet: www.usciences.edu
Founded 1821 as Philadelphia College of Pharmacy
Private control
Academic year: August to May
Pres.: Dr MARVIN SAMSON
Provost and Sr Vice-Pres. for Academic Affairs: Dr RUSSELL J. DiGATE
Sr Vice-Pres. for Finance and Treas.: JOSEPH G. TRAINOR
Sr Vice-Pres. for Operations and Chief Operations Officer: SARA M. CAMPBELL
Vice-Pres. for External Affairs: WILLIAM L. ASHTON

Vice-Pres. for Institutional Effectiveness: Dr PETER MILLER
Dean for Students: Dr WILLIAM CUNNINGHAM
Registrar: M. THERESE SCANLON
Dir for Library and Information Services: CHARLES J. MYERS
Library of 76,000 vols
Number of teachers: 160 (full-time)
Number of students: 2,970 (2,600 undergraduate, 370 graduate)
Publication: *The Bulletin*

DEANS

College of Graduate Studies: Dr RODNEY J. WIGENT
Mayes College of Healthcare Business and Policy: ANDREW PETERSON
Misher College of Arts and Sciences: Dr SUZANNE MURPHY
Philadelphia College of Pharmacy: Dr LISA LAWSON
Samson College of Health Sciences: Dr LAURIE SHERWEN

URSINUS COLLEGE

POB 1000, 601 E Main St, Collegeville, PA 19426-1000
Telephone: (610) 409-3000
E-mail: admissions@ursinus.edu
Internet: www.ursinus.edu
Founded 1869
Private control
Pres.: Dr BOBBY FONG
Sr Vice-Pres. for Advancement: JILL MARSTELLER
Vice-Pres. for Academic Affairs: JUDITH T. LEVY
Vice-Pres. for Enrolment: RICK DiFELICIANTONIO
Vice-Pres. for Finance and Admin.: WINFIELD GUILMETTE
Dean for Student Affairs: DEBORAH NOLAN
Registrar: BARBARA BORIS
Library Dir: CHARLIE JAMISON
Library of 420,000 vols
Number of teachers: 165
Number of students: 1,750
Publication: *The Lantern* (2 a year)

VALLEY FORGE CHRISTIAN COLLEGE

1401 Charlestown Rd, Phoenixville, PA 19460
Telephone: (610) 935-0450
E-mail: admissions@vfcc.edu
Internet: www.vfcc.edu
Founded 1931 as Maranatha Summer Bible School, current name adopted 1977
Private control
Academic year: August to May
Pres.: Dr DONALD G. MEYER
Provost and Vice-Pres. for Academic Affairs: Dr PHILIP McLEOD
Vice-Pres. for Finance: RICK DUNHAM
Vice-Pres. for Institutional Advancement: CHARLES COLES
Vice-Pres. for Student Life: JENNIFER GALE
Registrar: RUSSELL CAMBRIA
Dir for Library: PAUL MATHIAS
Number of teachers: 75
Number of students: 860

VILLANOVA UNIVERSITY

800 E Lancaster Ave, Villanova, PA 19085-1603
Telephone: (610) 519-4500
E-mail: gotovu@villanova.edu
Internet: www.villanova.edu
Founded 1842
Academic year: August to May

Private control
Pres.: Rev. Dr PETER M. DONOHUE
Vice-Pres. and Gen. Counsel: DOROTHY MALLOY
Vice-Pres. for Academic Affairs: Rev. Dr KAIL C. ELLIS
Vice-Pres. for Admin. and Finance: Rev. KENNETH G. VALOSKY
Vice-Pres. for Institutional Advancement: JOHN M. ELIZANDRO
Vice-Pres. for Student Life: Rev. JOHN P. STACK
Registrar: PAMELA J. BRAXTON
Librarian: JOSEPH LUCIA
Library of 1,010,421 vols, 2,998 periodicals, 1,789,816 microforms
Number of teachers: 820 (511 full-time, 309 part-time)
Number of students: 10,500
Publication: *Villanova Magazine*

DEANS

College of Engineering: Dr GARY A. GABRIELE
College of Liberal Arts and Science: Dr JEAN ANN LINNEY
College of Nursing: Dr M. LOUISE FITZPATRICK
School of Law: JOHN Y. GOTANDA
Villanova School of Business: Dr KEVIN D. CLARK

WASHINGTON & JEFFERSON COLLEGE

60 S Lincoln St, Washington, PA 15301
Telephone: (724) 503-1001
E-mail: info@washjeff.edu
Internet: www.washjeff.edu
Founded 1781
Private control
Academic year: September to May
Pres.: Dr TORI HARING-SMITH
Vice-Pres. for Academic Affairs and Dean for Faculty: JOHN ZIMMERMAN
Vice-Pres. for Business and Finance and Chief Financial Officer: DENNIS McMASTER
Vice-Pres. for Devt and Alumni Relations: MICHAEL GRZESIAK
Vice-Pres. for Enrolment: ALTON E. NEWELL
Vice-Pres. and Dean for Student Life: Dr EVA CHATTERJEE-SUTTON
Dir for Admissions: ROBERT ADKINS
Dir for Financial Aid: MICHELLE ANDERSON
Registrar: LESLIE MAXIN
Dir for Library Services: ALEXIS RITTENBERGER
Library of 188,195 vols, 15,610 microforms, 10,089 audiovisual materials, 4,264 ebooks, 43,897 current serial subscriptions and periodicals
Number of teachers: 154 (114 full-time, 40 part-time)
Number of students: 1,328 (1,318 full-time, 10 part-time)
Publications: *Washington & Jefferson College Review* (1 a year), *Wooden Tooth Review* (1 a year)

PROFESSORS

BENNETT, E., Psychology
BENZE, JR, J., Political Science
BRLETIC, P., Chemistry
CAMERON, W., Theatre and Communication
CANNON, J., Physics
CARPENTER, R., Education
CAVOTI, N., Psychology
CRABTREE, M., Psychology
DiSARRO, J., Political Science
DREW-BEAR, A., English
FRANK, T. S., Theatre and Communication
GAI, Z., Political Science
GORMLY, J., History
GREGOR, J., Economics and Business
HANNON, C., Computing and Information Studies

KUHN, S., Economics and Business
KYLER, C., English
LAMBERTSON, J., Art
LEE, A., Biology
LIST, V., History
LONGO, J., Education
MAINWARING, T., History
MALONEY, P., Art
MILLER, S., Sociology
MISAWA, B., Political Science
PETTERSEN, M., Physics
REMBERT, G. A., Philosophy
ROBISON, W., Economics and Business
SHEERS, W., Physics
TROOST, L., English
WILSON, L., Psychology
WOLTERMANN, M., Mathematics
WONG, R., Mathematics
WOODARD, S., Music

WAYNESBURG UNIVERSITY

51 W College St, Waynesburg, PA 15370
Telephone: (724) 627-8191
E-mail: admissions@waynesburg.edu
Internet: www.waynesburg.edu
Founded 1849 as Waynesburg College
Private control
Academic year: August to May
Pres.: TIMOTHY R. THYREEN
Provost: Dr ROBERT GRAHAM
Sr Vice-Pres. for Enrolment and Marketing: ROBIN L. KING
Sr Vice-Pres. for Institutional Planning, Research and Educational Services: RICHARD L. NOFTZGER, Jr
Exec. Vice-Pres. for Institutional Advancement: DOUG LEE
Vice-Pres. for Business and Finance: ROY R. BARNHART
Vice-Pres. of Student Devt: GERALD WOOD
Dir for Admissions: SARAH E. ZWINGER
Dir for Univ. Relations: BETHANY DOYLE
Registrar: VICKI WILSON
Library Dir: REA REDD
Library of 100,000 vols
Number of teachers: 130
Number of students: 2,500 (1,500 undergraduate, 900 graduate and professional adults)
Publication: *The Lamp*

WESTMINSTER COLLEGE

319 S Market St, New Wilmington, PA 16172-0001
Telephone: (724) 946-8761
Internet: www.westminster.edu
Founded 1852
Private control
Academic year: August to May
Pres.: Dr RICHARD H. DORMAN
Vice-Pres. for Academic Affairs and Dean for College: JESSE T. MANN
Vice-Pres. for Enrolment: BRADLEY P. TOKAR
Vice-Pres. for Finance and Management Services: KENNETH J. ROMIG
Vice-Pres. for Institutional Advancement: GLORIA C. CAGIGAS
Vice-Pres. for Student Affairs and Dean of Students: NEAL A. EDMAN
Registrar: JUNE G. PIERCE
Head Librarian: MOLLY P. SPINNEY
Library of 224,000 vols
Number of teachers: 100
Number of students: 1,550
Publications: *Scrawl, Westminster Magazine* (4 a year)

WESTMINSTER THEOLOGICAL SEMINARY

POB 27009, Philadelphia, PA 19118
2960 W Church Rd, Glenside, PA 19038
Telephone: (215) 887-5511
E-mail: admissions@wts.edu
Internet: www.wts.edu
Founded 1929
Private control
Academic year: June to May
4 Campuses: Philadelphia, Dallas, New York and London, United Kingdom
Pres.: Dr PETER A. LILLBACK
Provost: Dr CARL TRUEMAN
Chief Administrative Officer: STEVEN CARTER
Chief Financial Officer: MARK WILSON
Chief Operating Officer: A. D. DABNEY
Vice-Pres. for Academic Affairs: Dr CARL R. TRUEMAN
Vice-Pres. and Dean of Texas Campus: STEVEN T. VANDERHILL
Vice-Pres. for Devt: WILLIAM BROWN VINCENT, JR
Vice-Pres. for Institutional Partnerships: Dr DAVID B. GARNER
Dean for Students: GREG HOBAUGH
Registrar and Dir for Financial Aid: MELINDA E. G. DUGAN
Library Dir: ALEXANDER FINLAYSON
Library of 140,000 vols, 700 current periodical titles
Number of teachers: 50
Number of students: 450 (full-time)

WIDENER UNIVERSITY

One University Pl., Chester, PA 19013-5792
Telephone: (610) 499-4000
E-mail: presoffc@widener.edu
Internet: www.widener.edu
Founded 1821, fmrly Widener College, present name and status 1979
Private control
Campuses in Delaware, Exton and Harrisburg
Pres.: Dr JAMES T. HARRIS, III
Provost and Sr Vice-Pres. for Academic Affairs: Dr STEPHEN C. WILHITE
Sr Vice-Pres. for Admin. and Finance: JOSEPH J. BAKER
Sr Vice-Pres. for Univ. Advancement: LINDA S. DURANT
Dean for Student Services: DENISE GIFFORD
Library Dir: ROBERT DANFORD
Library of 845,762 vols
Number of teachers: 720 (326 full-time, 394 part-time)
Number of students: 7,400 (3,850 full-time, 3,550 part-time)
Publications: *Corporate Law Journal, Law Review, Widener Law Symposium Journal*

DEANS

College of Arts and Sciences: Dr MATTHEW POSLUSNY
School of Business Administration: Dr SAVAS ÖZATALAY
School of Engineering: Dr FRED A. AKL
School of Hospitality Management: NICHOLAS J. HADGIS
School of Human Service Professions: Dr PAULA T. SILVER (acting)
School of Nursing: Dr DEBORAH R. GARRISON
University College: Dr DON DEVILBISS

WILKES UNIVERSITY

84 W S St, Wilkes-Barre, PA 18766
Telephone: (570) 408-5000
E-mail: info@wilkes.edu
Internet: www.wilkes.edu

Founded 1933 as Bucknell Univ. Jr College, present name and status 1990
Private control
Academic year: August to May
Pres.: PATRICK F. LEAHY
Provost: REYNOLD VERRET
Vice-Pres. for Advancement: MICHAEL WOOD
Vice-Pres. for Devt: MARTY WILLIAMS
Vice-Pres. for Enrolment: MELANIE MICKELSON
Vice-Pres. for Finance and Gen. Counsel: LOREN D. PRESCOTT, JR
Vice-Pres. for Human Resources: MAGGIE LUND
Vice-Pres. for Student Affairs: PAUL S. ADAMS
Registrar: SUSAN A. HRITZAK
Dean for Library: JOHN STACHACZ
Library of 200,000 vols, 800,000 microforms, 400 current journals
Number of teachers: 120 (full-time)
Number of students: 2,000 (full-time)

DEANS

College of Arts, Humanities and Social Sciences: Dr LINDA A. WINKLER
College of Graduate and Professional Studies: MICHAEL SPEZIALE
College of Science and Engineering: Dr DALE A. BURNS
Jay S. Sidhu School of Business and Leadership: Dr JEFFREY R. ALVES
Nesbit College of Pharmacy of Nursing: Dr BERNARD W. GRAHAM
School of Education: MICHAEL SPEZIALE

WILSON COLLEGE

1015 Philadelphia Ave, Chambersburg, PA 17201-1285
Telephone: (717) 264-4141
E-mail: admissions@wilson.edu
Internet: www.wilson.edu
Founded 1869
Private control
Academic year: August to May
Liberal arts college for women
Pres.: Dr BARBARA K. MISTICK
Vice-Pres. for Academic Affairs and Dean for Faculty: MARY HENDRICKSON
Vice-Pres. for Enrolment: MARY ANN NASO
Vice-Pres. for Finance and Admin.: LORI TOSTEN
Vice-Pres. for College Advancement: JEFF ZUFELT
Registrar: JEAN HOOVER
Library Dir: KATHLEEN MURPHY
Library of 177,491 vols, 450 periodicals
Number of teachers: 75 (37 full-time, 38 part-time)
Number of students: 800

WON INSTITUTE OF GRADUATE STUDIES

137 S Easton Rd, Glenside, PA 19038
Telephone: (215) 884-8942
E-mail: administration@woninstitute.edu
Internet: www.woninstitute.edu
Courses in acupuncture studies, applied meditation studies and Won Buddhist studies
Private control
Pres.: Dr BOKIN KIM
Chief Academic Officer: COLLEEN O'CONNELL
Chief Finance Officer: MARIA PERRY
Academic Dean: Dr LINDA LELII

YORK COLLEGE OF PENNSYLVANIA

441 Country Club Rd, York, PA 17403-3651
Telephone: (717) 846-7788
E-mail: admissions@ycp.edu
Internet: www.ycp.edu

Founded 1787 as York County Acad., current name adopted 1968

Private control

Academic year: August to May

Courses in behavioural sciences; biological sciences; business; education; English and humanities; history and political science; hospitality, recreation and sport management; music, art and communication; nursing; physical sciences

Pres.: Dr PAMELA GUNTER-SMITH

Dean for Academic Services: Dr DEBORAH RICKER (acting)

Dean for College Advancement: DANIEL HELWIG

Dean for Student Affairs: JOSEPH F. MERKLE

Registrar: REBECCA LINK

Library Dir: SUSAN M. CAMPBELL

Number of teachers: 160 (full-time)

Number of students: 4,900 (4,600 full-time undergraduate, 300 graduate)

Publication: *Past and Present*

RHODE ISLAND

BROWN UNIVERSITY

Providence, RI 02912

Telephone: (401) 863-1000

E-mail: president@brown.edu

Internet: www.brown.edu

Founded 1764 as College of Rhode Island

Private control

Academic year: September to May

Chancellor: THOMAS J. TISCH

Pres. and CEO: RUTH J. SIMMONS

Provost: MARK S. SCHLISSEL

Sr Vice-Pres. for Corporation Affairs and Governance: RUSSELL CAREY

Sr Vice-Pres. for Univ. Advancement: STEVEN KING

Exec. Vice-Pres. for Finance and Admin.: ELIZABETH HUIDEKOPER

Exec. Vice-Pres. for Planning: RICHARD R. SPIES

Vice-Pres. and Chief Investment Officer: CYNTHIA E. FROST

Vice-Pres. and Gen. Counsel: BEVERLY E. LEDBETTER

Vice-Pres. for Campus Life and Student Services: MARGARET KLAWUNN

Vice-Pres. for Computing and Information Services: MICHAEL PICKETT (acting)

Vice-Pres. for Devt: (vacant)

Vice-Pres. for Facilities Management: STEPHEN MAIORISI

Vice-Pres. for Int. Affairs: MATTHEW GUTMANN

Vice-Pres. for Public Affairs and Univ. Relations: MARISA QUINN

Vice-Pres. for Research: CLYDE BRIANT

Vice-Pres. and Chief Information Officer: MICHAEL PICKETT

Dean for College: (vacant)

Dean for Admission: JAMES MILLER

Dean for Faculty: KEVIN MCLAUGHLIN

Univ. Registrar: ROBERT F. FITZGERALD

Univ. Librarian: EDWARD WIDMER

Library: 6.8m. vols

Number of teachers: 688

Number of students: 8,454 (6,118 undergraduate, 1,919 graduate, 417 medical)

Publications: *Brown Alumni Magazine* (2 a year), *Somos* (2 a year), *Visions* (1 a year)

DEANS

Continuing Education: KAREN SIBLEY

Division of Biology and Medicine: Dr EDWARD J. WING

Graduate School: Prof. PETER M. WEBER

School of Engineering: LAWRENCE LARSON

BRYANT UNIVERSITY

1150 Douglas Pike, Smithfield, RI 02917-1284

Telephone: (401) 232-6000

E-mail: admission@bryant.edu

Internet: www.bryant.edu

Founded 1863 as Bryant and Stratton Nat. Business College, current name adopted 2004

Private control

Academic year: September to August

Pres.: RONALD K. MACHTLEY

Vice-Pres. for Academic Affairs: Dr JOSÉ-MARIE GRIFFITHS

Vice-Pres. for Business Affairs: BARRY MORRISON

Vice-Pres. for Enrolment Management: LORNA J. HUNTER

Vice-Pres. for Information Services: CHUCK LoCURTO

Vice-Pres. for Student Affairs: J. THOMAS EAKIN

Vice-Pres. for Univ. Advancement: JAMES DAMRON

Dir for Library Services: MARY F. MORONEY

Library: over 150,000 vols, 25,000 journals

Number of students: 3,615 (3,370 undergraduate, 245 graduate)

Publication: *Bryant magazine* (3 a year)

DEANS

College of Arts and Sciences: DAVID LUX

College of Business: MICHAEL COOPER

JOHNSON & WALES UNIVERSITY

8 Abbott Park Pl., Providence, RI 02903

Telephone: (401) 598-1000

E-mail: admissions@jwu.edu

Internet: www.jwu.edu

Founded 1914 as business school, present name 1988, present status 1992

Private control

Academic year: September to August

Campuses in Charleston (South Carolina), Denver (Colorado), N Miami (Florida)

Chancellor: Dr JOHN J. BOWEN

Vice-Chancellor: THOMAS L. G. DWYER

Provost: Dr VEERA S. GAUL

Chief Financial Officer and Treas.: WILLIAM F. MCARDLE

Sr Vice-Pres. and Gen. Counsel: Dr WAYNE M. KEZIRIAN

Sr Vice-Pres. for Enrolment Management: KENNETH F. DiSAIA

Sr Vice-Pres. for Student Services: MARIE BERNARDO-SOUSA

Vice-Pres. for Academic Affairs: Dr JEFFREY SENESE

Vice-Pres. for Finance: JOSEPH J. GREENE

Vice-Pres. for Student Affairs: Dr RONALD L. MARTEL

Registrar: TAMMY HARRIGAN

Dean for Libraries: Dr HELENA RODRIGUES

Number of students: 17,230

Publication: *JWU Magazine* (4 a year)

DEANS

Alan Shawn Feinstein Graduate School: Dr FRANK PONTARELLI

College of Business: Dr DAVID M. MITCHELL

College of Culinary Arts: KARL J. GUGGENMOS

Hospitality College: RICHARD L. BRUSH

John Hazen White School of Arts and Sciences: Dr ANGELA R. RENAUD

School of Technology: FRANCIS X. TWEEDIE

NEW ENGLAND INSTITUTE OF TECHNOLOGY

1 New England Tech Blvd, East Greenwich, RI 02818-1205

Telephone: (401) 467-7744

E-mail: info@neit.edu

Internet: www.neit.edu

Founded 1940 as New England Technical Institute, present name 1977, present status 1984

Private control

Areas of study: criminal justice technology, interior design, software engineering technology

Pres.: RICHARD I. GOUSE

Provost and Sr Vice-Pres.: Dr THOMAS F. WYLIE

Sr Vice-Pres. for Financial Affairs: CHERYL C. CONNORS

Exec. Vice-Pres.: SETH A. KURN

Vice-Pres. and Gen. Counsel: PHILIP G. PARSONS

Vice-Pres. for Devt and Alumni Relations: ALLAN A. LANGER

Vice-Pres. for Student Support Services: CATHERINE KENNEDY

Dir for Admissions: MARK BLONDIN

Registrar: DOREEN LASIEWSKI

Library Dir: SHARON J. CHARETTE

Number of students: 3,200

PROVIDENCE COLLEGE

1 Cunningham Sq., Harkins 103, Providence, RI 02918

Telephone: (401) 865-2535

E-mail: pcadmiss@providence.edu

Internet: www.providence.edu

Founded 1917

Private control

Academic year: September to May

Pres.: Rev. BRIAN J. SHANLEY

Provost and Sr Vice-Pres. for Academic Affairs: Dr HUGH LENA

Sr Vice-Pres. and Chief Financial Officer: JOHN SWEENEY

Sr Vice-Pres. for Institutional Advancement: DAVID WEGRZYN

Exec. Vice-Pres. and Treas.: Rev. KENNETH SICARD

Vice-Pres. and Gen. Counsel: MARIFRANCES McGINN

Vice-Pres. for Academic Affairs: Dr HUGH LENA

Vice-Pres. for College Relations and Planning: STEVEN J. MAURANO BAILEY

Vice-Pres. for Student Affairs: KRISTINE GOODWIN

Dean for Admission and Financial Aid: RAÚL A. FONTS

Librarian: Dr D. RUSSELL BAILEY

Library of 375,000 vols, 240,000 ebooks, 38,000 ejournals

Number of teachers: 310 (276 full-time, 34 part-time)

Number of students: 4,500

DEANS

International Studies: ADRIAN G. BEAULIEU

Multicultural Affairs: RAFAEL A. ZAPATA

School of Arts and Sciences: Dr SHEILA ADAMUS LIOTTA

School of Business: Dr SYLVIA MAXWELL

School of Continuing Education: JANET L. CASTLEMAN

School of Professional Studies: Dr BRIAN M. McCADDEN

RHODE ISLAND COLLEGE

600 Mount Pleasant Ave, Providence, RI 02908-1991

Telephone: (401) 456-8000

E-mail: graduatestudies@ric.edu

Internet: www.ric.edu

Founded 1854 as Rhode Island State Normal School, current name adopted 1959

State control

Academic year: August to August (2 semesters)
Pres.: NANCY CARRIUOLO
Vice-Pres. for Academic Affairs: RONALD E. PITT
Vice-Pres. for Admin. and Finance: WILLIAM H. GEARHART
Vice-Pres. for College Advancement: JAMES SALMO
Vice-Pres. for Student Affairs: GARY M. PENFIELD
Dir for Admissions: LUCILLE RIOS SAUNDERS
Library Dir: HEDI BENAICHA
Library of 654,000 vols, 2,600 print and eperiodicals, 1m. microforms
Number of teachers: 375
Number of students: 9,050

DEANS

Faculty of Arts and Sciences: EARL SIMSON
Feinstein School of Education and Human Development: ALEXANDER SIDORKIN
School of Management: DAVID BLANCHETTE
School of Nursing: JANE WILLIAMS
School of Social Work: SUE PEARLMUTTER

RHODE ISLAND SCHOOL OF DESIGN

2 College St, Providence, RI 02903-2784
Telephone: (401) 454-6100
E-mail: admissions@risd.edu
Internet: www.risd.edu
Founded 1877
Private control
Academic year: September to May
Pres.: ROSANNE SOMERSON
Provost: PRADEEP SHARMA
Vice-Pres. for Institutional Engagement: ERIC GRAAGE
Chief Operating Officer: JEAN C. EDDY
Dir for Library Services: CAROL TERRY
Library of 150,782 vols, 400 periodicals
Number of teachers: 546
Number of students: 2,420

DEANS

Architecture and Design: Prof. NANCY SKOLOS
Fine Arts: Prof. ANAIS A. MISSAKIAN
Foundation Studies: Prof. JOANNE STRYKER
Graduate Studies + Research: Prof. PATRICIA PHILLIPS
Liberal Arts: Dr DANIEL CAVICCHI

ROGER WILLIAMS UNIVERSITY

1 Old Ferry Rd, Bristol, RI 02809
Telephone: (401) 253-1040
E-mail: admit@rwu.edu
Internet: www.rwu.edu
Founded 1919 as br. of Northeastern Univ., present name and status 1992
Private control
Academic year: September to May
Pres.: Dr DONALD J. FARISH
Provost: Dr ROBERT A. POTTER
Sr Vice-Pres. for Enrolment Management: LYNN M. FAWTHROP
Sr Vice-Pres. for Legal Affairs and Gen. Counsel: ROBERT H. AVERY
Vice-Pres. and Chief Information Officer: JOSEPH PANGBORN
Exec. Vice-Pres. for Finance and Admin.: JEROME F. WILLIAMS
Vice-Pres. for Student Affairs: Dr JOHN J. KING
Vice-Pres. for Univ. Advancement: ROBERT L. WEST
Registrar: ANNIE RUSSELL (acting)
Dean for Libraries: PETER DEEKLE
Number of teachers: 315

Number of students: 5,170 (3,840 full-time undergraduate, 824 postgraduate and professional, 506 continuing studies)
Publications: *RWU Law*, *RWU: The Magazine of Roger Williams University* (2 a year)

DEANS

Feinstein College of Arts and Sciences: Dr ROBERT A. COLE
Mario J. Gabelli School of Business: JERRY DAUTERIVE
School of Architecture, Art and Historic Preservation: STEPHEN WHITE
School of Education: Dr ROBERT A. COLE
School of Engineering, Computing and Construction Management: Dr ROBERT A. POTTER
School of Graduate and Continuing Studies: Dr ROBERT W. ROBERTSON
School of Justice Studies: Dr STEPHANIE PICOLO MANZI
School of Law: Prof. DAVID A. LOGAN

SALVE REGINA UNIVERSITY

100 Ochre Point Ave, Newport, RI 02840-4192
Telephone: (401) 847-6650
E-mail: sruadmis@salve.edu
Internet: www.salve.edu
Founded 1947
Private control
Language of instruction: English
Academic year: September to May (2 semesters)
Pres.: Dr JANE GERETY
Chancellor: Dr M. THERESE ANTONE
Provost and Dean for Faculty: Dr DEAN DE LA MOTTE
Vice-Pres. for Admin. and Chief Financial Officer: WILLIAM B. HALL
Vice-Pres. for Student Affairs: Dr MARGARET HIGGINS
Vice-Pres. for Univ. Relations and Advancement: MICHAEL SEMENZA
Dean for Students: MALCOLM SMITH
Registrar: LOUISE MONAST
Dir for Library Services: KATHLEEN BOYD
Library of 125,000 vols
Number of teachers: 118 (full-time)
Number of students: 2,603 (2,026 undergraduate, 577 graduate)

DEANS

Arts and Sciences: Dr LAURA O'TOOLE
Professional Studies: Dr TRACI WARRINGTON

US NAVAL WAR COLLEGE

686 Cushing Rd, Newport, RI 02841-1207
Telephone: (401) 841-3089
Internet: www.usnwc.edu
Founded 1884
State control
Pres.: JOHN N. CHRISTENSON
Provost: MARY ANN PETERS
Dean for Academic Affairs: Prof. Dr JOHN GAROFANO
Dean for Students: RAY KELEDEI
Library Dir: Prof. TERRY METZ
Library of 290,000 vols, 450,000 microfiches, 1,000 MSS, 1,700 periodical titles
Number of teachers: 165

DEANS

College of Naval Warfare: Prof. ROBERT RUBEL
College of Operational and Strategic Leadership: JAMIE KELLY
International Programmes: Prof. THOMAS MANGOLD

UNIVERSITY OF RHODE ISLAND

Kingston, RI 02881
Telephone: (401) 874-1000
E-mail: admissions@uri.edu
Internet: www.uri.edu
Founded 1888 as State Agricultural School, current name adopted 1951
State control
Academic year: September to May (2 semesters)
Campuses in Providence, Narragansett Bay, West Greenwich
Pres.: Dr DAVID M. DOOLEY
Provost and Vice-Pres. for Academic Affairs: Dr DONALD H. DEHAYES
Vice-Pres. for Admin. and Finance: ROBERT A. WEYGAND
Vice-Pres. for Research and Economic Devt: Dr PETER ALFONSO
Vice-Pres. for Student Affairs: Dr THOMAS R. DOUGAN
Vice-Pres. for Univ. Advancement: ROBERT L. BEAGLE
Chief Information Officer: GARRY BOZYLINSKY
Dean for Graduate School: Dr NASSER H. ZAWIA
Registrar: ROBERT STROBEL
Dean for Univ. Libraries: DAVID MASLYN
Library: 1.5m. vols, 27,000 periodical subscriptions, 2.3m. items of govt documents, audiovisual materials, computer files, MSS, archives, maps, nautical charts, microforms
Number of teachers: 720
Number of students: 16,000 (13,000 undergraduate, 3,000 graduate)
Publication: *Maritimes* (4 a year)

DEANS

College of Arts and Sciences: WINIFRED E. BROWNELL
College of Business Administration: Prof. Dr MARK HIGGINS
College of Engineering: Dr RAYMOND M. WRIGHT
College of Environment and Life Sciences: Dr JOHN KIRBY
College of Human Science and Services: Dr W. LYNN MCKINNEY
College of Nursing: Dr DAYLE H. JOSEPH
College of Pharmacy: Dr RONALD P. JORDAN
Graduate School of Oceanography: STEVEN L. D'HONDT
University College: Dr JAYNE RICHMOND

SOUTH CAROLINA

ALLEN UNIVERSITY

1530 Harden St, Columbia, SC 29204
Telephone: (803) 376-5700
E-mail: admissions@allenuniversity.edu
Internet: www.allenuniversity.edu
Founded 1870
Private control
Academic year: August to May (2 semesters)
Divs of business administration, humanities, mathematics and natural sciences, religion
Pres.: Dr PAMELA M. WILSON
Exec. Vice-Pres.: Dr WILLIE L. PARSON
Vice-Pres. for Academic Affairs: Dr JUNE HUBBARD-COLE
Vice-Pres. for Fiscal Affairs: THOMAS POITIER
Vice-Pres. for Planning, Research and Sponsored Programmes: MARCUS V. BELL
Vice-Pres. for Student Affairs: Dr ORLANDO W. LEWIS
Gen. Counsel: RENARDO L. HICKS
Library of 50,000 vols
Number of teachers: 35
Number of students: 800

ANDERSON UNIVERSITY

316 Blvd, Anderson, SC 29621-40350
Telephone: (864) 231-2000
E-mail: admissions@andersonuniversity.edu
Internet: www.andersonuniversity.edu
Founded 1911 as Anderson College, present name and status 2006
Private control
Academic year: August to May
Pres.: Dr Evans P. Whitaker
Provost: Dr Danny M. Parker
Vice-Pres. for Enrolment Management: Omar Rashed
Vice-Pres. for Finance and Operations: James A. Wright, Jr
Vice-Pres. for Institutional Advancement: R. Dean Woods
Vice-Pres. for Student Devt: Dr Bob L. Hanley
Registrar: Kendra B. Woodson
Library Dir: Kent Millwood

Library of 100,000 vols, 41,000 ebooks
Number of teachers: 150
Number of students: 2,280

DEANS

College of Adult and Professional Studies: Dr W. David Shirley
College of Arts and Sciences: (vacant)
College of Business: Prof. Dr Carol L. Karnes
College of Education: Dr Raymond S. Locy
College of Visual and Performing Arts: Prof. Dr David W. Larson
Graduate, Online and Non-Traditional Programmes: Prof. Dr Sandra M. Mancuso
School of Interior Design: E. Anne Martin
School of Nursing: Dr Pamela Binns-Turner

BENEDICT COLLEGE

1600 Harden St, Columbia, SC 29204
Telephone: (803) 253-5000
Internet: www.benedict.edu
Founded 1870 as Benedict Institute, current name adopted 1894
Private control
Academic year: August to May
Pres.: Dr David Holmes Swinton
Exec. Vice-Pres.: Dr Ruby W. Watts
Vice-Pres. for Academic Affairs: Dr Janeen P. Witty
Vice-Pres. for Business and Finance: Brenda Walker
Vice-Pres. for Community Devt: Jabari Simama
Vice-Pres. for Institutional Advancement: Barbara C. Moore (acting)
Vice-Pres. for Institutional Effectiveness: Dr Gayla B. Thomas
Vice-Pres. for Student Affairs: Gary E. Knight
Registrar: Wanda Scott-Kinney
Library Dir: Darlene Zinnerman-Bethea

Library of 100,000 vols, 300 journals, 1,600 govt publs
Number of teachers: 160 (127 full-time, 33 part-time)
Number of students: 3,135

DEANS

School of Business and Economics: Gerald H. Smalls
School of Continuing Education: Dr Burnett Joiner
School of Education: Dr Allen J. Coles
School of Honors: Dr Warren Robinson
School of Humanities, Arts and Social Sciences: Dr Charles P. Austin, Sr
School of Science, Technology, Engineering and Mathematics: Dr Samir S. Raychoudhury

CHARLESTON SOUTHERN UNIVERSITY

9200 University Blvd, Charleston, SC 29406
Telephone: (843) 863-7000
Internet: www.csuniv.edu
Founded 1964
Private control
Academic year: August to April
Pres.: Dr Jairy C. Hunter, Jr
Provost: Dr A. Kennerley Bonnette
Vice-Pres. for Advancement: Dave Baggs
Vice-Pres. for Business Affairs: Luke Blackmon
Vice-Pres. for Enrolment Management: Debra B. Williamson
Vice-Pres. for Student Affairs: Dr Rick Brewer
Registrar: Amanda Sisson
Library Dir: Sandra H. Hughes

Library of 250,000 vols
Number of teachers: 140 (full-time)
Number of students: 3,300 (2,920 undergraduate, 380 graduate)
Publication: *CSU Magazine* (3 a year)

DEANS

College of Distance and Continuing Education: Dr James H. Jones
College of Humanities and Social Sciences: Dr Donald L. Martin, Jr
College of Science and Mathematics: Prof. Dr Jeryl W. Johnson
School of Business: Prof. Dr John B. Duncan
School of Education: Dr Norma Harper
School of Nursing: Prof. Dr Tara Hulsey

CITADEL

171 Moultrie St, Charleston, SC 29409
Telephone: (843) 225-3294
E-mail: admissions@citadel.edu
Internet: www.citadel.edu
Founded 1842
State control
Academic year: August to May
Pres.: Lt-Gen. John W. Rosa
Provost and Dean for College: Dr Samuel M. Hines, Jr
Exec. Vice-Pres. for Finance, Admin. and Operations: Brig. Gen. Thomas J. Elzey
Vice-Pres. for External Affairs: Dr Jeff Perez
Commandant of Cadets: Col Leo A. Mercado
Registrar: Sylvia L. Nesmith (acting)
Dir for Library Services: Elizabeth Connor

Library of 1,128,798 vols, 449,390 microfilms
Number of teachers: 245 (164 full-time, 53 part-time, 28 ROTC)
Number of students: 3,250 (2,160 undergraduate, 1,090 graduate)
Publications: *Citadel Review*, *Le Gaulois Litteraire* (1 a year), *The Art of Good Taste*, *The Brigadier*, *The Citadel* (1 a year), *The Gold Star Journal* (1 a year), *The Guidon*, *The Shako* (1 a year), *The Sphinx*

DEANS

Graduate College: Steve A. Nida
School of Business Administration: Dr Ronald F. Green
School of Education: Dr Tony W. Johnson
School of Engineering: Dr Ronald W. Welch
School of Humanities and Social Sciences: Dr Winfred B. Moore, Jr
School of Science and Mathematics: Dr Isaac S. Metts, Jr

CLAFLIN UNIVERSITY

400 Magnolia St, Orangeburg, SC 29115
Telephone: (803) 535-5000
E-mail: admissions@claflin.edu
Internet: www.claflin.edu

Founded 1869
Private control
Academic year: August to May (2 semesters)
Pres.: Dr Henry N. Tisdale
Exec. Vice-Pres.: Drexel B. Ball
Vice-Pres. for Academic Affairs: Dr Howard D. Hill
Vice-Pres. for Devt and Alumni Affaris: Rev. Whittaker V. Middleton
Vice-Pres. for Planning, Assessment and Information Services: Dr Zia Hasan
Vice-Pres. for Student Devt and Services: Dr Leroy A. Durant
Dir for Admissions: Dr Michael Zeigler
Registrar: Roe B. Hunt
Library Dir: Marilyn Pringle

Library of 162,000 vols, 445 periodicals, 17,000 e-periodicals, 47,000 ebooks, 1,200 audiovisual materials
Number of teachers: 50
Number of students: 965

DEANS

School of Business: Dr Harpal S. Grewal
School of Education: Dr Valerie E. Harrison
School of Humanities and Social Science: Dr Peggy Stevenson Ratliff
School of Natural Science and Mathematics: Prof. Dr Verlie A. Tisdale

CLEMSON UNIVERSITY

Clemson, SC 29634
Telephone: (864) 656-3311
E-mail: graduate_school@clemson.edu
Internet: www.clemson.edu
Founded 1889 as Clemson Agricultural College, current name adopted 1964
State control
Academic year: August to May (2 semesters)
Pres.: James F. Barker
Provost and Vice-Pres. for Academic Affairs: Doris R. Helms
Vice-Pres. for Advancement: A. Neill Cameron, Jr
Vice-Pres. for Agriculture, Public Service and Economic Devt: John W. Kelly, Jr
Vice-Pres. for Finance and Operations: Brett A. Dalton
Vice-Pres. for Research: Gerald Sonnenfeld
Vice-Pres. for Student Affairs: Dr Gail A. DiSabatino
Gen. Counsel: Chip Hood
Registrar: Stan Smith
Dean for Libraries: Kay Wall

Library: 1.8m. vols
Number of teachers: 1,200 (1,055 full-time, 145 part-time)
Number of students: 19,450

DEANS

College of Agriculture, Forestry and Life Sciences: Dr Thomas R. Scott
College of Architecture, Arts and Humanities: Dr Richard E. Goodstein
College of Business and Behavioral Science: Dr Claude C. Lilly
College of Engineering and Science: Dr R. Larry Dooley
College of Health, Education and Human Development: Dr Lawrence R. Allen
Graduate School: Dr Karen Burg

COASTAL CAROLINA UNIVERSITY

POB 261954, Conway, SC 29528-6054
Telephone: (843) 347-3161
E-mail: admissions@coastal.edu
Internet: www.coastal.edu
Founded 1954 as Coastal Carolina Jr College, present name and status 1993
State control
Academic year: August to May (2 semesters)
Pres.: Dr David A. DeCenzo

Provost and Sr Vice-Pres. for Academic and Student Affairs: Dr ROBERT SHEEHAN
Exec. Vice-Pres. and Chief Operating Officer: EDGAR DYER
Vice-Pres. for Enrolment Services: Dr GREG THORNBURG
Vice-Pres. for Finance and Admin.: STACIE BOWIE
Vice-Pres. for Student Affairs: Dr DEBBIE CONNER
Registrar: DANIEL LAWLESS
Dean for Students: TRAVIS OVERTON
Dean for Library Services: BARBARA BURD
Number of teachers: 345 (full-time)
Number of students: 9,100
Publications: *Archarios* (1 a year), *Coastal Carolina* (1 a year), *Tempo* (1 a year)

DEANS

College of Business Administration: Dr J. RALPH BYINGTON
College of Education: EDWARD JADALLAH
College of Science: Dr MICHAEL H. ROBERTS
Thomas W. and Robin W. Edwards College of Humanities and Fine Art: Prof. Dr DANIEL ENNIS
University College: Dr NELLJEAN M. RICE

COKER COLLEGE

300 E College Ave, Hartsville, SC 29550
Telephone: (843) 383-8000
E-mail: admissions@coker.edu
Internet: www.coker.edu
Founded 1894 as Welsh Neck High School, current name adopted 1969
Private control
Academic year: September to May (2 semesters)
Areas of study: art, behavioural and social science, business administration, communication, language and literature, dance, music and theatre, education, history, philosophy and religion, physical education and sport studies, science and mathematics, social work
Pres.: Dr ROBERT L. WYATT
Provost: Dr TRACY PARKINSON
Vice-Pres. for Business Operations: GERALD O. SILVER
Vice-Pres. for Institutional Advancement: THOMAS W. GIFFIN
Vice-Pres. for Student and Enrolment Services: Dr STEPHEN B. TERRY
Registrar: STACY ATKINSON
Dir for Library: ALEXA E. BARTEL
Library of 170,000 vols, 105,000 ebooks
Number of teachers: 70 (full-time)
Number of students: 1,100

COLLEGE OF CHARLESTON

66 George St, Charleston, SC 29424
Telephone: (843) 805-5507
E-mail: admissions@cofc.edu
Internet: www.cofc.edu
Founded 1770
State control
Academic year: August to July (2 semesters)
Pres.: Dr P. GEORGE BENSON
Provost and Sr Vice-Pres. for Academic Affairs: GEORGE W. HYND
Exec. Vice-Pres. for Business Affairs: STEPHEN C. OSBORNE
Exec. Vice-Pres. for External Relations: MICHAEL R. HASKINS
Exec. Vice-Pres. for Student Affairs: VICTOR K. WILSON
Exec. Vice-Pres. for Institutional Advancement: GEORGE P. WATT, JR
Vice-Pres. for Legal Affairs and Gen. Counsel: TOM TRIMBOLI
Registrar: CATHERINE C. BOYD

Dean for Libraries: DAVID J. COHEN
Library of 817,658 vols
Number of teachers: 540 (full-time)
Number of students: 11,650 (10,460 undergraduate, 1,190 graduate)
Publications: *Chrestomathy* (1 a year), *College of Charleston Magazine* (3 a year), *Crazyhorse* (2 a year), *Illuminations* (1 a year), *Polyphony* (1 a year)

DEANS

Graduate School: Dr AMY T. MCCANDLESS
School of Arts: VALERIE B. MORRIS
School of Business: Prof. Dr ALAN T. SHAO
School of Education, Health and Human Performance: Dr FRANCES C. WELCH
School of Humanities and Social Sciences: Dr CYNTHIA J. LOWENTHAL
School of Languages, Cultures and World Affairs: Dr DAVID J. COHEN
School of Sciences and Mathematics: Dr MICHAEL AUERBACH

COLUMBIA COLLEGE

1301 Columbia College Dr., Columbia, SC 29203
Telephone: (803) 786-3871
E-mail: admissions@columbiasc.edu
Internet: www.columbiasc.edu
Founded 1854
Private control
Academic year: August to May (2 semesters)
Divs of arts and communication studies, behavioural studies and human inquiry, business, mathematics and sciences, education, languages and literatures
Pres.: Dr CAROLINE WHITSON
Provost and Vice-Pres. for Academic Affairs: Dr LAURIE B. HOPKINS
Vice-Pres. for Advancement: BARBARA PARKS
Vice-Pres. for Enrolment Management: Dr RONALD G. WHITE
Vice-Pres. for Finance: JOHN D. JONES
Dean of Students: Dr LaNaé BRIGGS BUDDEN
Registrar: Dr SCOTT A. SMITH
Dir for Library and Information Technology Services: DAN MURPHY
Library of 177,000 vols, 400 journals and magazines, 30,000 media items
Number of teachers: 163 (81 full-time, 82 part-time)
Number of students: 1,300

COLUMBIA INTERNATIONAL UNIVERSITY

7435 Monticello Rd, Columbia, SC 29203
Telephone: (803) 754-4100
E-mail: yesciu@ciu.edu
Internet: www.ciu.edu
Founded 1923 as Columbia Bible School, present name 1994
Private control
Academic year: August to May (2 semesters)
Pres.: Dr WILLIAM H. JONES
Chancellor: Dr GEORGE W. MURRAY
Provost and Sr Vice-Pres. for Academic and Student Affairs: Dr JAMES LANPHER
Vice-Pres. for Devt and Operations: KEITH MARION
Vice-Pres. for Enrolment Management and Corporate Communications: MIKE BLACKWELL
Vice-Pres. for Institutional Assessment: BOB KALLGREN
Registrar: KATHY KROLL
Dean for Student Life: RICK SWIFT
Library Dir: JO ANN RHODES
Library of 122,551 vols
Number of teachers: 75
Number of students: 980

Publications: *Connection* (2 a year), *President's Letter* (3 a year), *Upward* (3 a year)

DEANS

College of Arts and Sciences: Dr BRYAN E. BEYER
College of Counseling: HARVEY PAYNE
College of Education: Dr CONNIE MITCHELL
College of Intercultural Studies: Dr MIKE BARNETT
Seminary and School of Ministry: JOHN D. HARVEY

CONVERSE COLLEGE

580 E Main St, Spartanburg, SC 29302
Telephone: (864) 596-9000
E-mail: admission@converse.edu
Internet: www.converse.edu
Founded 1889
Private control
Academic year: September to May
Pres.: Dr ELIZABETH A. FLEMING
Sr Vice-Pres.: THOMAS McDANIEL
Vice-Pres. for Academic Affairs: JEFFREY BARKER
Vice-Pres. for Enrolment and Marketing: SALLY HAMMOND
Vice-Pres. for Finance and Admin.: SUSAN STEVENSON
Vice-Pres. for Institutional Advancement: BOBBY STEWART
Vice-Pres. for Student Life and Dean for Students: MOLLY DUESTERHAUS
Dir for Admissions: APRIL LEWIS
Registrar: MARY BROWN
Librarian: WADE WOODWARD
Library of 155,000 vols, 87,000 microforms, 500 periodicals
Number of teachers: 85
Number of students: 1,200

DEANS

School of Education and Graduate Studies: Dr KATHY GOOD
School of Humanities and Sciences: Prof. Dr JEFFREY BARKER
School of the Arts: RICHARD HIGGS

ERSKINE COLLEGE

POB 338, Due West, SC 29639
2 Washington St, Due West, SC 29639
Telephone: (864) 379-2131
E-mail: admissions@erskine.edu
Internet: www.erskine.edu
Founded 1839
Academic year: August to May (2 semesters)
Depts of art, athletic training, bible, biology, business administration, chemistry, education, English, health and human performance, history and politics, mathematics, modern languages, music, physics, psychology, religion and philosophy
Pres.: Dr DAVID A. NORMAN
Vice-Pres. and Dean for College: BRAD CHRISTIE
Vice-Pres. for Advancement: DAVID EARLE
Vice-Pres. for Erskine Theological Seminary: STEVE LOWE
Vice-Pres. for Finance and Operations: GREG HASELDEN
Vice-Pres. for Student Services: ROBYN AGNEW
Dir for Admissions: TOBE R. FRIERSON
Registrar: TRACY SPIRES
Library Dir: JOHN F. KENNERLY, JR
Library of 155,000 vols, 20,000 periodical, 57,000 microforms, 1,500 audiovisual, media and multimedia items, 15,000 archives and spec, colln items, 7,000 ejournals
Number of teachers: 60
Number of students: 600

Publication: *Inside Erskine* (2 a year)

FRANCIS MARION UNIVERSITY

POB 100547, Florence, SC 29502-0547
Telephone: (843) 661-1231
E-mail: admissions@fmarion.edu
Internet: www.fmarion.edu

Founded 1970, present name and status 1992
State control
Academic year: August to May (2 semesters)
Pres.: Dr LUTHER F. CARTER
Provost and Dean for College: Dr RICHARD N. CHAPMAN
Vice-Pres. for Admin.: Dr CHARLENE WAGES
Vice-Pres. for Business Affairs: JOHN J. KISPERT
Vice-Pres. for Devt: JOHN P. DOWD, III
Vice-Pres. for Student Affairs and Dean for Students: TERESA JOHNSON RAMEY
Dir for Admissions: PERRY T. WILSON
Registrar: DOLLIE J. NEWHOUSE
Dean for Library: JOYCE M. DURANT
Library of 410,000 vols, 1,100 journals, 21,000 ejournals, 27,500 ebooks
Number of teachers: 260
Number of students: 4,200 (3,880 undergraduate, 320 graduate)
Publication: *View Magazine* (2 a year)

DEANS

College of Liberal Arts: Dr RICHARD N. CHAPMAN
School of Business: Dr M. BARRY O'BRIEN
School of Education: Dr JAMES RON FAULKENBERRY

FURMAN UNIVERSITY

3300 Poinsett Highway, Greenville, SC 29613
Telephone: (864) 294-2000
E-mail: admission@furman.edu
Internet: www.furman.edu

Founded 1826, present name and status 1850
Private control
Academic year: August to May (2 semesters)
Depts of arts, Asian studies, business, education, humanities, military science, neuroscience, sciences and mathematics, social sciences, sustainability science
Pres.: Dr RODNEY ALAN SMOLLA
Vice-Pres. for Academic Affairs and Dean: JOHN STEPHEN BECKFORD
Vice-Pres. for Admin. and Finance: MARY LOU MERKT
Vice-Pres. for Devt: MICHAEL D. GATCHELL
Vice-Pres. for Student Life: CONNIE L. CARSON
Registrar: BRAD E. BARRON
Dir for Library: JANIS BANDELIN
Library: 1.3m. items incl. 450,000 vols, 15,000 print and online journals, 140,000 govt documents and maps, 800,000 microforms
Number of teachers: 240
Number of students: 2,900 (2,700 undergraduate, 200 graduate)
Publications: *ConBrio*, *Engage*, *Furman Magazine* (4 a year), *Humanities Review* (1 a year), *The Echo* (2 a year)

LANDER UNIVERSITY

320 Stanley Ave, Greenwood, SC 29649-2099
Telephone: (864) 388-8000
E-mail: admissions@lander.edu
Internet: www.lander.edu

Founded 1872 as Williamston Female College, current name adopted 1992
State control
Academic year: August to April (2 semesters)

Pres.: Dr DANIEL W. BALL
Provost and Vice-Pres. for Academic Affairs: DANNY L. MCKENZIE
Vice-Pres. for Business and Admin.: GLENDA E. RIDGELY
Vice-Pres. for Student Affairs: HUEY RANDALL BOUKNIGHT
Vice-Pres. for Univ. Advancement: RALPH E. PATTERSON
Dir for Admissions: JENNIFER M. MATHIS
Registrar: MAC KIRKPATRICK
Dean for Library Services: SAMUEL D. MASH
Library of 275,000 vols
Number of teachers: 135 (full-time)
Number of students: 3,000

DEANS

College of Arts and Humanities: Prof. ALICE TAYLOR-COLBERT
College of Business and Public Affairs: DOUG GRIDER
College of Education: JUDITH A. NEUFELD
College of Science and Mathematics: Prof. DAVID A. SLIMMER

LIMESTONE COLLEGE

1115 College Dr., Gaffney, SC 29340-3799
Telephone: (864) 489-7151
E-mail: admiss@limestone.edu
Internet: www.limestone.edu

Founded 1845
Private control
Academic year: August to May (2 semesters)
Campuses in Aiken, Charleston, Columbia, Florence, Greer, Kingstree and Yemassee; depts of arts and letters, natural science, professional studies, social and behavioural science, interdisciplinary studies
Pres.: Dr WALT GRIFFIN
Vice-Pres. for Academic Affairs: Dr KAREN W. GAINEY
Vice-Pres. for Enrolment Services: CHRISTOPHER N. PHENICIE
Vice-Pres. for Financial Affairs: DAVID S. RILLING
Vice-Pres. for Institutional Advancement: Dr WILLIAM H. BAKER
Vice-Pres. for Student Services: ROBERT OVERTON
Registrar: BRENDA WATKINS
Dir for Library: LORI HETRICK
Library of 151,677 vols, 2,873 microforms, 2,900 audio and video cassettes, 91,000 ebooks
Number of teachers: 80 (full-time)
Number of students: 3,625
Publication: *Limestone Today* (2 a year)

LUTHERAN THEOLOGICAL SOUTHERN SEMINARY

4201 Main St, Columbia, SC 29203-5898
Telephone: (803) 786-5150
E-mail: admissions@ltss.edu
Internet: www.ltss.edu

Founded 1830
Private control
Academic year: August to May
Pres.: Rev. Dr MARCUS J. MILLER
Vice-Pres. for Academic Affairs: Rev. Dr VIRGINIA BARFIELD
Vice-Pres. for Devt and Seminary Relations: RON WALRATH
Dir for Admin. and Finance: ANDY SMITH
Library Dir: Dr LYNN A. FEIDER
Library of 100,000 vols, 400 journal subscriptions
Number of teachers: 15
Number of students: 150
Publication: *Taproot*

MEDICAL UNIVERSITY OF SOUTH CAROLINA

171 Ashley Ave, Charleston, SC 29425
Telephone: (843) 792-1414
E-mail: oes-web@musc.edu
Internet: www.musc.edu

Founded 1824
State control
Academic year: August to August
Pres.: Dr RAYMOND S. GREENBERG
Provost and Vice-Pres. for Academic Affairs and: Dr MARK SOTHMANN
Vice-Pres. for Devt: JIM FISHER
Vice-Pres. for Finance and Admin.: LISA MONTGOMERY
Vice-Pres. for Information Technology: Dr FRANK C. CLARK
Vice-Pres. for Medical Affairs: Dr ETTA PISANO
Dir for Libraries: Prof. THOMAS G. BASLER
Number of teachers: 1,280
Number of students: 2,340
Publication: *Humanitas* (1 a year)

DEANS

College of Dental Medicine: Prof. Dr JOHN J. SANDERS
College of Graduate Studies: Dr PERRY V. HALUSHKA
College of Health Professions: Prof. Dr LISA S. SALADIN
College of Medicine: Dr ETTA D. PISANO
College of Nursing: Prof. Dr GAIL W. STUART

MORRIS COLLEGE

100 W College St, Sumter, SC 29150-3599
Telephone: (803) 934-3200
Internet: www.morris.edu

Founded 1908
Private control
Academic year: August to May (2 semesters)
Divs of business administration, education, general studies, natural sciences and mathematics, religion and humanities, social sciences
Pres.: LUNS C. RICHARDSON
Academic Dean: Prof. LEROY STAGGERS
Dean for Student Affairs: ELIZA E. BLACK
Dir for Admissions and Records: DEBORAH C. CALHOUN
Dir for Institutional Advancement: MELVIN MACK
Number of teachers: 70
Number of students: 880

NEWBERRY COLLEGE

2100 College St, Newberry, SC 29108
Telephone: (803) 276-5010
E-mail: admissions@newberry.edu
Internet: www.newberry.edu

Founded 1856, present location 1911
Private control
Academic year: August to May
Areas of study: arts and communications, business, behavioural and social sciences, education, humanities, music, nursing, sciences and mathematics, military science
Pres.: JOHN H. HUDGENS, II (acting)
Exec. Vice-Pres. for Academic Affairs and Dean for College: TIMOTHY ELSTON
Vice-Pres. for Admin. Affairs and Chief Financial Officer: RON MATTHIAS
Dean for Enrolment Management: SHEILA M. WENDELN
Dean for Students: KAY BANKS
Registrar: CAROL BICKLEY
Dir for Library Services: LAWRENCE ELLIS
Library of 80,000 vols, 146 magazines, scholarly journals, newspapers
Number of teachers: 60 (full-time)

Number of students: 1,155

Publication: *Dimensions* (2 a year)

NORTH GREENVILLE UNIVERSITY

POB 1892, Tigerville, SC 29688

7801 N Tigerville Rd, Tigerville, SC 29688

Telephone: (864) 977-7000

E-mail: admissions@ngu.edu

Internet: www.ngu.edu

Founded 1892 as North Greenville High School

Private control

Academic year: August to May (2 semesters)

Pres.: Dr JAMES B. EPTING

Vice-Pres. and Dean for Graduate Studies: J. SAMUEL ISGETT, JR

Vice-Pres. for Academic Affairs: Dr RANDALL J. PANNELL

Vice-Pres. for Admissions and Financial Planning: KELI SEWELL

Vice-Pres. for Business Affairs: MICHELLE SABOU

Vice-Pres. for Campus Ministries: STEPHEN G. CROUSE

Vice-Pres. for Student Services: TONY BEAM

Vice-Pres. for Univ. Advancement: ALEXANDER A. MILLER

Registrar: PAMELA FARMER

Dir for Library: CARLA C. McMAHAN

Library of 60,000 vols, 536 periodicals, 1,168 video materials, 1,600 audio items

Number of teachers: 35

Number of students: 1,300

DEANS

College of Business and Sport Professions: Dr RALPH JOHNSON

College of Christian Studies: Dr WALTER JOHNSON

College of Education: Dr ROBIN JOHNSON

College of Fine Arts: Dr JACQUELYN H. GRIFFIN

College of Humanities: Dr CATHERINE SEPKO

College of Science and Mathematics: Dr THOMAS C. ALLEN

Graduate School of Business: Dr TRACY R. KRAMER

Graduate School of Christian Ministry: LARRY S. McDONALD

Graduate School of Education: Dr VIVIAN R. DUGLE

PRESBYTERIAN COLLEGE

503 S Broad St, Clinton, SC 29325

Telephone: (864) 833-2820

E-mail: admissions@presby.edu

Internet: www.presby.edu

Founded 1880 as Clinton College

Private control

Academic year: August to May (2 semesters)

Pres.: Dr JOHN VINCENT GRIFFITH

Provost: Dr ANITA OLSON GUSTAFSON

Exec. Vice-Pres. for Finance and Admin.: MORRIS M. GALLOWAY, JR

Vice-Pres. for Advancement: RAYMOND E. CARNLEY

Vice-Pres. for Enrolment Management: DEBORAH J. THOMPSON

Dean for Students: LINDA C. JAMEISON

Dir for Admissions: BRIAN J. FORTMAN

Registrar: KEITH KARRIKER

Dir for Library: DAVID W. CHATHAM

Library of 166,110 vols

Number of teachers: 85 (full-time)

Number of students: 1,200

DEANS

School of Pharmacy: Dr RICHARD E. STULL

SHERMAN COLLEGE OF CHIROPRACTIC

POB 1452, Spartanburg, SC 29304

2020 Springfield Rd, Boiling Springs, SC 29316

Telephone: (864) 578-8770

E-mail: admissions@sherman.edu

Internet: www.sherman.edu

Founded 1973

Private control

Academic year: January to December

Pres.: Dr JON SCHWARTZBAUER

Vice-Pres. for Academic Affairs: Dr ROBERT IRWIN

Vice-Pres. for Business and Finance: TIMOTHY D. REVELS

Vice-Pres. for Enrolment Services: KELLEY JONES ASHCRAFT

Dean for Student Affairs: LaSHANDA HUTTO-HARRIS

Registrar: MELODY SABIN

Dir for Learning Resources: CRISSY LEWIS

Publication: *Sherman*

DEANS

Basic Sciences: Dr PENGJU LUO

Clinical Sciences: Dr JOSEPH J. DONOFRIO

Clinics: KEITH HENRY

SOUTH CAROLINA COLLEGE OF PHARMACY

Medical University of South Carolina Campus: 274 Calhoun St, MSC 141, Charleston, SC 29425-1410

Telephone: (843) 792-3740

University of South Carolina: Coker Life Science Bldg, 715 Sumter St, Columbia, SC 29208

Telephone: (803) 777-4151

E-mail: office@sccp.sc.edu

Internet: www.sccp.sc.edu

Founded 2004; attached to Medical Univ. of South Carolina and Univ. of South Carolina

State control

Depts of clinical pharmacy and outcome sciences, pharmaceutical and biomedical sciences

Exec. Dean: Dr JOSEPH T. DiPIRO

Medical Univ. of South Carolina Campus Dean: Dr PHILIP D. HALL

Univ. of South Carolina Campus Dean: Dr RANDALL C. ROWEN

Number of teachers: 75 (full-time)

Number of students: 190

Publication: *PharmSC* (4 a year)

SOUTH CAROLINA STATE UNIVERSITY

300 College St, NE, Orangeburg, SC 29117

Telephone: (803) 536-7000

E-mail: registrar@scsu.edu

Internet: www.scsu.edu

Founded 1896 as Normal, Industrial, Agricultural and Mechanical College, current name adopted 1992

State control

Academic year: August to May

Pres.: Dr RITA JACKSON TEAL (acting)

Vice-Pres. for Finance and Facilities: JOSEPH M. PEARMAN

Vice-Pres. for Institutional Advancement: Dr ANTHONY L. HOLLOMAN

Vice-Pres. for Research and Economic Devt and Public Service: Dr G. DALE WESSON

Vice-Pres. for Student Affairs: Dr VALERIE FIELDS

Registrar: ANNIE BELTON

Dean for Library and Information Services: ADRIENNE C. WEBBER

Library of 302,768 vols, 1,028,132 microforms, 974 journal and magazine subscriptions

Number of teachers: 310

Number of students: 5,000

DEANS

College of Business and Applied Professional Sciences: Dr ORA SPANN

College of Education, Humanities and Social Sciences: Dr RONALD E. SPEIGHT

College of Science, Mathematics and Engineering Technology: Dr KENNETH D. LEWIS

Honors College: Dr HARRIET A. ROLAND

School of Graduate Studies: Dr FREDERICK M. G. EVANS

SOUTHERN WESLEYAN UNIVERSITY

POB 1020, 907 Wesleyan Dr., Central, SC 29630-1020

Telephone: (864) 644-5557

E-mail: president@swu.edu

Internet: www.swu.edu

Founded 1906 as Wesleyan Methodist Bible Institute, current name adopted 1995

Private control

Academic year: August to May

Pres.: Dr TODD S. VOSS

Provost and Academic Vice-Pres.: Dr KEITH IDDINGS

Sr Vice-Pres. for Finance: MARTY ATCHESON

Vice-Pres. for Admin. and Programme Operations: GARY CARR

Vice-Pres. for Devt: Rev. JAMES WIGGINS

Vice-Pres. for Student Life: Dr JOE BROCKINTON

Dir for Admissions and Enrolment Management: AMANDA YOUNG

Registrar: ROCK McCASKILL

Dir for Library Services: ROBERT E. SEARS

Library of 115,000 vols

Number of teachers: 130

Number of students: 2,415 (1,695 undergraduate, 720 graduate)

DEANS

College of Arts and Sciences: Dr WALT SINNAMON

School of Business: Prof. Dr ROYCE CAINES

School of Education: Dr PAUL SHOTSBERGER

UNIVERSITY OF SOUTH CAROLINA

Columbia, SC 29208

Telephone: (803) 777-7000

E-mail: info@sc.edu

Internet: www.sc.edu

Founded 1801 as South Carolina College, current name adopted 1866

State control

Academic year: August to May (2 semesters)

Campuses in Aiken, Allendale, Beaufort, Lancaster, Spartanburg, Sumter, Union

Pres.: Dr HARRIS PASTIDES

Provost and Exec. Vice-Pres. for Academic Affairs: Dr MICHAEL D. AMIRIDIS

Vice-Provost for Academic Affairs and Dean for Undergraduate Studies: Dr HELEN I. DOERPINGHAUS

Vice-Provost for System Affairs and Exec. Dean for Extended Univ.: Dr CHRIS P. PLYLER

Vice-Pres. for Research: Dr PRAKASH NAGARKATTI

Vice-Pres. for Student Affairs: Dr DENNIS A. PRUITT

Registrar: Dr AARON MARTERER

Chancellor of USC Aiken: Dr THOMAS L. HALLMAN

Chancellor of USC Beaufort: Dr JANE T. UPSHAW

Chancellor of USC Upstate: THOMAS F. MOORE

Dean for Libraries: Dr TOM MCNALLY
Library: 9m. vols
Number of teachers: 2,185 (full-time; all campuses)
Number of students: 45,775 (all campuses)
Publications: *Journal of Law & Education* (4 a year), *Real Property, Trust & Estate Law Journal* (4 a year), *South Carolina Journal of International Law and Business* (2 a year), *South Carolina Law Review* (1 a year), *Southeastern Environmental Law Journal* (2 a year)

DEANS

Arnold School of Public Health: Dr G. THOMAS CHANDLER
College of Arts and Sciences: Dr MARY ANNE FITZPATRICK
College of Education: Dr LEMUEL WATSON (acting)
College of Engineering and Computing: Dr ANTHONY AMBLER
College of Hospitality, Retail and Sport Management: Dr BRIAN J. MIHALIK (acting)
College of Mass Communications and Information Studies: CHARLES BIERBAUER
College of Nursing: Dr PEGGY HEWLETT
College of Social Work: Prof. Dr ANNA SCHEYETT
Graduate School: Dr LACY FORD
Moore School of Business: Dr HILDY J. TEEGEN
School of Law: ROBERT M. WILCOX
School of Medicine: Dr RICHARD A. HOPPMANN
School of Music: Dr TAYLOE HARDING
South Carolina Honors College: Dr STEVEN LYNN

VOORHEES COLLEGE

POB 678, Denmark, SC 29042
Telephone: (803) 780-1234
E-mail: info@voorhees.edu
Internet: www.voorhees.edu
Founded 1897 as Denmark Industrial School, present name and status 1962
Private control
Academic year: August to May
Pres. and CEO: Dr CLEVELAND L. SELLERS, JR
Exec. Vice-Pres. for Academic Affairs: Dr PAUL BAKER
Vice-Pres. for Fiscal and Admin. Affairs and Chief Financial Officer: V. DIANE O'BERRY
Vice-Pres. for Institutional Advancement: COURTNEY L. DAVENPORT
Vice-Pres. for Planning, Information Management and Technology: SAMUEL BLACKWELL
Vice-Pres. for Student Affairs: WILLIE JEFFERSON
Registrar: MELIKA JACKSON
Library Dir: Dr MARIE MARTIN
Number of teachers: 40 (full-time)
Number of students: 640 (undergraduate)

DEANS

Division of Arts and Sciences: Dr DORIS J. WARD
Division of Business and Professional Studies: Dr BERNARD MOSES
Division of General Studies: LUGENIA ROCHELLE

WINTHROP UNIVERSITY

701 Oakland Ave, Rock Hill, SC 29733
Telephone: (803) 323-2191
E-mail: admissions@winthrop.edu
Internet: www.winthrop.edu
Founded 1886, present name and status 1992
State control
Academic year: August to May (2 semesters)
Pres.: Dr ANTHONY J. DiGIORGIO

Vice-Pres. for Academic Affairs and Dean of Faculty: Dr DEBRA C. BOYD
Vice-Pres. for Finance and Business: J. P. MCKEE
Vice-Pres. for Student Life: Dr FRANK P. ARDAIOLO
Vice-Pres. for Univ. Advancement: Dr KATHRYN HOLTEN
Registrar: GINA G. JONES
Dir for Admissions: DEBI BARBER
Dean for Library Services: Dr MARK Y. HERRING
Library of 357,110 vols
Number of teachers: 400
Number of students: 5,900 (4,850 undergraduate, 1,050 graduate)
Publications: *The Johnsonian* (52 a year), *The Tatler*, *The Winthrop Anthology* (1 a year)

DEANS

College of Arts and Sciences: Dr PETER JUDGE
College of Business Administration: ROGER D. WEIKLE
College of Visual and Performing Arts: DAVID WOHL
Graduate School: Dr DEBRA BOYD
Richard W. Riley College of Education: JENNIE RAKESTRAW
University College: GLORIA G. JONES

WOFFORD COLLEGE

429 N Church St, Spartanburg, SC 29303-3663
Telephone: (864) 597-4000
E-mail: admission@wofford.edu
Internet: www.wofford.edu
Founded 1854
Private control
Academic year: September to May (2 semesters)
Liberal arts college
Pres.: Dr BENJAMIN BERNARD DUNLAP
Sr Vice-Pres. for Academic Affairs and Dean for College: DAVID SHIEL WOOD
Sr Vice-Pres. for Devt and College Relations: MARION B. PEAVEY
Sr Vice-Pres. for Operations and Finance: ROBERT L. KEASLER
Vice-Pres.: B. G. STEPHENS
Vice-Pres.: LARRY MCGEHEE
Vice-Pres. for Academic Admin. and Planning: BOYCE M. LAWTON, III
Vice-Pres. for Admin.: DAVID M. BEACHAM
Vice Pres. for Enrolment: BRAND R. STILLE
Vice-Pres. for Student Affairs and Dean for Students: ROBERTA HURLEY BIGGER
Dean for Int. Programmes: Dr ANA MARÍA WISEMAN
Registrar: JENNIFER R. ALLISON
Dean for Library: OAKLEY HERMAN COBURN
Library of 250,000 vols, 135,000 ebooks, 39,000 ejournals
Number of teachers: 126 (full-time)
Number of students: 1,536

SOUTH DAKOTA

AUGUSTANA COLLEGE

2001 S Summit Ave, Sioux Falls, SD 57197
Telephone: (605) 274-0770
E-mail: admission@augie.edu
Internet: www.augie.edu
Founded 1860
Private control
Depts of art/anthropology, biology, business administration, chemistry, communication, computer science, economics, education, English, government and international affairs, health, history, international studies, mathematics, modern foreign languages, music,

nursing, philosophy and classics, physical education and recreation, physics, psychology, religion, sociology, theatre
Pres.: ROBERT C. OLIVER
Vice-Pres. for Academic Affairs and Dean for the College: Dr SUSAN HASSELER
Vice-Pres. for Devt: JON HENKES
Vice-Pres. for Enrolment: NANCY DAVIDSON
Vice-Pres. for Finance and Admin.: THOMAS M. MEYER
Vice-Pres. for Marketing and Communications: ROBERT PRELOGER
Vice-Pres. for Student Services and Dean for Students: Dr JAMES BIES
Registrar: JONI KRUEGER
Dir for Mikkelsen Library: RONELLE THOMPSON
Library of 228,000 vols
Number of teachers: 140
Number of students: 1,790

BLACK HILLS STATE UNIVERSITY

1200 University St, Spearfish, SD 57799-9502
Telephone: (605) 642-6088
E-mail: admissions@bhsu.edu
Internet: www.bhsu.edu
Founded 1883 as Dakota Territorial Normal School
State control
Academic year: August to May
Pres.: Dr KAY SCHALLENKAMP
Provost and Vice-Pres. for Academic Affairs: Dr RODNEY CUSTER
Vice-Pres. for Finance and Admin.: KATHY JOHNSON
Vice-Pres. for Institutional Advancement: STEVE MEEKER
Vice-Pres. for Student Life: LOIS FLAGSTAD
Chief Information Officer: WARREN WILSON
Dir for Admissions: BETH AZEVEDO
Dean for Libraries: RAJEEV BUKRALIA
Library of 235,000 vols, 70,000 govt documents, 635,000 vols of additional resource materials, 2,225 vols of state, co and local histories, 7,000 vols on history of English literature
Number of teachers: 180
Number of students: 4,420
Publication: *BHSU Alumni Magazine*

DEANS

College of Business and Natural Sciences: Dr PRISCILLA ROMKEMA
College of Education and Behavioral Sciences: PATRICIA SIMPSON
College of Liberal Arts: Dr CURTIS CARD

DAKOTA STATE UNIVERSITY

Madison, SD 57042
820 N Washington Ave, Madison, SD 57042-1799
Telephone: (605) 256-5111
E-mail: dsuinfo@pluto.dsu.edu
Internet: www.dsu.edu
Founded 1881
State control
Academic year: September to May
Pres.: Dr DAVID BOROFSKY
Vice-Pres. and Dean for Student Affairs: MARCUS GARSTECKI
Vice-Pres. for Academic Affairs: Dr JUDY DITTMAN
Vice-Pres. for Business and Admin. Services: STACY KRUSEMARK
Vice-Pres. for Univ. Advancement: KATHY LARSON
Registrar: KATHRYN CALLIES
Dean for Graduate Studies and Research: OMAR EL-GAYAR
Dir for Admissions: AMY CRISSINGER

Dir for Library: ETHELLE BEAN
Library of 158,662 vols
Number of teachers: 125
Number of students: 3,130
Publication: *Dakota State Magazine* (1 a year)

DEANS

College of Arts and Sciences: Dr BENJAMIN JONES
College of Business and Information Systems: Dr TOM HALVERSON
College of Education: Dr GALE WIEDOW

DAKOTA WESLEYAN UNIVERSITY

1200 W University Ave, Mitchell, SD 57301
Telephone: (605) 995-2600
E-mail: admissions@dwu.edu
Internet: www.dwu.edu
Founded 1885
Private control
Pres.: Dr ROBERT G. DUFFETT
Provost and Exec. Vice-Pres.: AMY C. NOVAK
Vice-Pres. for Business and Institutional Advancement: THERESA KRIESE
Vice-Pres. for Univ. Relations: LORI ESSIG
Registrar: KAREN KNOELL
Dir for Learning Resources: KEVIN KENKEL
Library of 65,000 vols, 400 current magazine subscriptions
Number of teachers: 50
Number of students: 780

DEANS

College of Arts and Humanities: Dr VINCE REDDER
College of Healthcare, Fitness and Sciences: Dr ROCHELLE VON EYE
College of Leadership and Public Service: Dr DONALD C. SIMMONS

PROFESSORS

ALMJELD, P., Music
CATALANO, M., Mathematics
DITTA, J., English
FARNEY, M. N., Mathematics
McGREEVY, M. J., Criminal Justice
MILLER, M. H., Religion and Philosophy
MITCHELL, D. B., Business Administration and Economics
MULLICAN, T. R., Biology
NIELSON, G. E., Sociology
TATINA, R. E., Biology

MOUNT MARTY COLLEGE

1105 W Eighth St, Yankton, SD 57078-3725
Telephone: (605) 668-1545
E-mail: mmcadmit@mtmc.edu
Internet: www.mtmc.edu
Founded 1936
Private control (Benedictine)
Academic year: August to May (2 semesters)
Areas of study: business and social sciences, humanities, natural sciences, nursing, teacher education; campuses at Sioux Falls, Watertown and Yankton in South Dakota
Pres.: Dr JOSEPH N. BENOIT
Vice-Pres. and Dean for Academic Affairs: ROBERT TERESHINSKI
Vice-Pres. and Dean for Student Affairs: SARAH CARDA
Vice-Pres. for Enrolment Management: BRANDI DeFRIES
Vice-Pres. for Finance and Admin.: DAISY HALVORSON
Vice-Pres. for Institutional Advancement: DEREK WESLEY
Registrar: JONNA SUPURGECI
Dir for Library: SANDRA BROWN
Library of 75,000 vols
Number of teachers: 65

Number of students: 1,100

NATIONAL AMERICAN UNIVERSITY

5301 S Highway 16, Suite 200, Rapid City, SD 57701
Telephone: (605) 721-5200
E-mail: info@national.edu
Internet: www.national.edu
Founded 1941 as Nat. School of Business
Private control
Academic year: September to August
Areas of study: communications, humanities, information technology, mathematics, science, social and behavioural sciences; campuses in Centennial, Denver and Colorado Springs (Colorado), Albuquerque and Rio Rancho (New Mexico), Lee's Summit, Independence and Kansas City (Missouri), Bloomington, Brooklyn Center, Minnetonka, and Minneapolis (Minnesota), Allen and Austin (Texas), Overland Park and Wichita (Kansas) and Sioux Falls (S Dakota)
Univ. Pres.: JERRY L. GALLENTINE
CEO: RONALD SHAPE
Provost and Gen. Counsel: SAMUEL D. KERR
Assoc. Provost and System Vice-Pres. for Curriculum and Instruction: MARILYN HOLMGREN
System Vice-Pres. for Graduate Studies and Dean for the Graduate School: PHYLLIS OKREPKIE
System Vice-Pres. for Academic Operations and Learner Services: JASON WARR
Chief Information Officer: JOHN BUXTON
Registrar: TOM MAHON
System Librarian: PAT HAMILTON

NORTHERN STATE UNIVERSITY

1200 S Jay St, Aberdeen, SD 57401
Telephone: (605) 626-3011
E-mail: info@northern.edu
Internet: www.northern.edu
Founded 1901 as Northern Normal and Industrial School, present name and status 1989
State control
Pres.: Dr JAMES SMITH
Provost and Vice-Pres. for Academic Affairs: Dr TOM HAWLEY
Vice-Pres. for Finance and Admin.: DON ERLENBUSCH
Vice-Pres. for Student Affairs: RHODA SMITH
Dir for Univ. College: STEVE RASMUSSEN
Dir for Univ. Relations: BRENDA DREYER
Registrar: PEGGY HALLSTROM
Dir for Libraries: ROBERT RUSSELL
Library of 250,000 vols
Number of teachers: 150
Number of students: 2,700

DEANS

College of Arts and Sciences: Dr CELESTINO MENDEZ
School of Business: Dr WILLARD BROUCEK
School of Education: CONSTANCE GEIER
School of Fine Arts: Dr ALAN D. LaFAVE

OGLALA LAKOTA COLLEGE

3 Mile Creek Rd, POB 490, Kyle, SD 57752-0490
Telephone: (605) 455-6000
Internet: www.olc.edu
Founded 1971, present name 1983
Tribal control
Academic year: August to May
Areas of study: liberal arts and information technology; centres at Allen (Pass Creek College Center), Batesland (East Wakpamni College Center), Eagle Butte (OLC Cheyenne River College Center), Kyle (Pejuta Haka

College Center), Manderson (Wounded Knee College Center), Martin (LaCreek College Center), Oglala (White Clay College Center), Pine Ridge (Pine Ridge College Center), Porcupine (Pahin Sinte College Center), Rapid City (He Sapa Center) and Wanblee (Eagle Nest College Center)
Pres.: THOMAS SHORTBULL
Vice-Pres. for Business: ARLENE QUIST
Vice-Pres. for Instruction: Dr GERALD GIRAUD
Registrar: LESLIE MESTETH
Library Dir: LaVERA ROSE
Library of 20,000 vols
Number of teachers: 15
Number of students: 1,400 (full-time)

PRESENTATION COLLEGE

1500 N Main St, Aberdeen, SD 57401
Telephone: (605) 229-8505
E-mail: admit@presentation.edu
Internet: www.presentation.edu
Founded 1922 as Notre Dame Junior College; present name 1965
Private control
Academic year: August to May (2 semesters)
Depts of allied health, arts and sciences, business, education, nursing, social work; campuses at Aberdeen and Eagle Butte (S Dakota), and Fairmont (Minnesota)
Pres.: VIRGINIA TOBIN
Vice-Pres. for Advancement: LORI HARMEL
Vice-Pres. for Enrolment: JoELLEN LINDNER
Vice-Pres. for Finance: CATHY HALL
Vice-Pres. for Student Services: BOB SCHUCHARDT
Registrar: MAUREEN SCHUCHARDT
Dir for Libraries: LEA BRIGGS
Number of teachers: 50
Number of students: 650

SINTE GLESKA UNIVERSITY

POB 105, Mission, SD 57555
Telephone: (605) 856-8100
E-mail: admin@sinte.edu
Internet: www.sintegleska.edu
Founded 1970 as Sinte Gleska College, present name 1992
Tribal control
Academic year: August to May
Depts of art and sciences, business administration and management, education, human services
Pres.: LIONEL R. BORDEAUX
Vice-Pres. for Academic Affairs: CHERYL MEDEARIS
Vice-Pres. for Education: MIKE BENGE
Vice-Pres. for Institutional Relations and Resource Devt: GEORGIA HACKETT
Vice-Pres. for Student Services: MIKE BENGE
Registrar: JACK HERMAN
Library Dir: RACHEL LINDVALL
Number of teachers: 40
Number of students: 1,080 (960 undergraduate, 120 postgraduate)

SIOUX FALLS SEMINARY

2100 S Summit Ave, Sioux Falls, SD 57105
Telephone: (605) 336-6588
E-mail: info@sfseminary.edu
Internet: www.sfseminary.edu
Founded 1949
Private control
Academic year: September to May
Areas of study: Christian leadership, counselling, marriage and family therapy, ministry, theological studies
Pres.: Dr G. MICHAEL HAGAN
Academic Vice-Pres. and Dean: Dr RONALD D. SISK

Dir for Enrolment: NATE HELLING
Registrar: BRENDA MEDALEN
Library of 72,500 vols, 300 periodicals
Number of teachers: 10
Number of students: 250

SOUTH DAKOTA SCHOOL OF MINES AND TECHNOLOGY

501 E St Joseph St, Rapid City, SD 57701
Telephone: (605) 394-2511
E-mail: info@sdsmt.edu
Internet: www.sdsmt.edu

Founded 1885
State control
Academic year: September to May

Depts of atmospheric sciences, chemical and biological engineering, chemistry, civil and environmental engineering, electrical and computer engineering, geology and geological engineering, humanities, industrial engineering, materials and metallurgical engineering, mathematics and computer science, mechanical engineering, military science, mining engineering, physical education, physics, social sciences
Pres.: ROBERT A. WHARTON
Provost and Vice-Pres. for Academic Affairs: DUANE HRNCIR
Vice-Pres. for Finance and Admin.: TIMOTHY G. HENDERSON
Vice-Pres. for Research: RONALD WHITE
Vice-Pres. for Student Affairs and Dean for Students: PATRICIA G. MAHON
Vice-Pres. for Univ. Relations: CHRISTY A. HORN
Dir for Library: PATRICIA M. ANDERSEN
Library of 220,224 vols
Number of teachers: 130 (full-time)
Number of students: 2,300
Publication: *Hardrock Magazine*

SOUTH DAKOTA STATE UNIVERSITY

POB 2201, Brookings, SD 57007
Telephone: (605) 688-4121
E-mail: sdsu.admissions@sdstate.edu
Internet: www.sdstate.edu

Founded 1881 as Dakota Agricultural College, univ. status in 1964
State control
Academic year: August to May
Pres.: Dr DAVID L. CHICOINE
Provost and Vice-Pres. for Academic Affairs: Dr LAURIE NICHOLS
Vice-Pres. for Admin.: Dr MICHAEL REGER
Vice-Pres. for Information Technology: Dr MICHAEL F. ADELAINE
Vice-Pres. for Research: Dr KEVIN D. KEPHART
Vice-Pres. for Student Affairs: Dr MARYSZ RAMES
Dean for Libraries: DAVID GLEIM
Library: see Libraries and Archives
Number of teachers: 650 (510 full-time, 140 part-time)
Number of students: 12,800

DEANS

College of Agriculture and Biological Sciences: Dr BARRY DUNN
College of Arts and Sciences: (vacant)
College of Education and Human Sciences: JILL THORNGREN
College of Engineering: Dr LEWIS F. BROWN
College of Nursing: Dr ROBERTA K. OLSON
College of Pharmacy: DENNIS D. HEDGE
Graduate School: (vacant)
University College: Dr KEITH CORBETT

UNIVERSITY OF SIOUX FALLS

1101 W 22nd St, Sioux Falls, SD 57105
Telephone: (605) 331-5000
E-mail: admissions@usiouxfalls.edu
Internet: www.usiouxfalls.edu

Founded 1883 as Dakota Collegiate Institute, present name 1995
Private control
Academic year: September to August
Areas of study: information sciences, liberal arts, music, philosophy, social work, theology
Pres.: MARK BENEDETTO
Provost and Vice-Pres. for Academic Affairs: BRETT BRADFIELD
Vice-Pres. for Business and Finance: Dr MARSHA DENNISTON
Vice-Pres. for Institutional Advancement: JON HIATT
Vice-Pres. for Student Devt and Enrolment Management: AIMEE VANDERFEEN
Assoc. Vice-Pres. for Student Devt and Dean for Students: KAREN SUMNER
Registrar: ANNA HECKENLAIBLE
Dir for Library Services: RACHEL CROWLEY
Library of 84,354 vols
Number of teachers: 185 (64 full-time; 121 part-time)
Number of students: 1,500 (1,170 undergraduate, 330 graduate)

UNIVERSITY OF SOUTH DAKOTA

414 E Clark St, Vermillion, SD 57069
Telephone: (605) 677-5011
E-mail: admissions@usd.edu
Internet: www.usd.edu

Founded 1862
State control
Academic year: August to May
Pres.: JAMES W. ABBOTT
Provost and Vice-Pres. for Academic Affairs: KURT HACKEMER (acting)
Vice-Pres. for Admin. and Technology: ROBERTA AMBUR
Vice-Pres. for Finance: SHEILA GESTRING
Vice-Pres. for Research: LAURA JENSKI
Vice-Pres. for Student Services and Dean for Students: KIMBERLY GRIEVE
Registrar: JENNIFER THOMPSON
Dean for Univ. Libraries: DAN DAILY
Library: see under Libraries and Archives
Number of teachers: 443
Number of students: 10,235
Publications: *Business Connections* (1 a year), *South Dakotan Lawyer* (1 a year), *South Dakotan MD* (2 a year), *The South Dakotan* (2 a year), *USD Nursing* (1 a year)

DEANS

Beacom School of Business: MICHAEL J. KELLER
College of Arts and Sciences: Dr MATTHEW C. MOEN
College of Fine Arts: Dr LARRY SCHOU
Graduate School: Dr LAURIE BECVAR
School of Education: Dr RICK MELMER
School of Law: Prof. THOMAS E. GEU

TENNESSEE

AMERICAN BAPTIST COLLEGE

1800 Baptist World Centre Dr., Nashville, TN 37207-4952
Telephone: (615) 256-1463
E-mail: mspring@abcnash.edu
Internet: www.abcnash.edu

Founded 1924 as American Baptist Theological Seminary
Private control
Academic year: August to May (2 semesters)

Degree programmes in arts, pastoral studies, theology
Pres. and CEO: Dr FORREST ELLIOTT HARRIS, SR
Vice-Pres. for Academic Affairs: Dr RENITA WEEMS
Chief Financial Officer: CLARA A. WILLIAMS
Chief of Campus Operations: JOYCE ACKLEN
Dir for Enrolment Management: Dr RENITA WEEMS
Admissions and Registrar Administrator: PAM TABOR
Dir of Library Services: Dr CHERISNA JEAN-MARIE
Library of 20,000 vols, 170 periodicals

AQUINAS COLLEGE

4210 Harding Pike, Nashville, TN 37205
Telephone: (615) 297-7545
E-mail: admissions@aquinascollege.edu
Internet: www.aquinascollege.edu

Founded 1928 as St Cecilia Normal School, present name and status 1994
Private control
Academic year: August to May (2 semesters)
Areas of study incl. business, liberal arts, nursing, teacher education
Pres.: Sis. MARY SARAH
Vice-Pres. for Academic Affairs: Sis. ELIZABETH ANNE
Vice-Pres. for Admin. Affairs: Sis. MARY CECILIA
Vice-Pres. for Institutional Advancement: TIM STRANSKY
Chief Financial Officer: ROGER MUEHE
Dir of Admissions: CONNIE HANSOM
Dir of Student Affairs: SUZETTE TELLI
Registrar: ETTA MASON
Head Librarian: J. MARK HALL
Library of 70,000 vols
Publication: *Aquinas College Magazine* (2 a year)

DEANS

Nursing: Bro. IGNATIUS

AUSTIN PEAY STATE UNIVERSITY

601 College St, Clarksville, TN 37044
Telephone: (931) 221-7011
E-mail: gov@apsu.edu
Internet: www.apsu.edu

Founded 1927 as Austin Peay Normal School, present status 1967, present name 1943
State control
Academic year: August to May
Campuses in Dickson, Fort Campbell in KY, Springfield in TN
Pres.: Dr TIMOTHY L. HALL
Provost and Vice-Pres. for Academic Affairs: Dr TRISTAN DENLEY
Vice-Pres. for Admin. and Finance: MITCH ROBINSON
Vice-Pres. for Student Affairs: Dr SHERYL A. BYRD
Dean of Students: GREGORY R. SINGLETON
Exec. Dir for Univ. Advancement: ROY GREGORY
Dir for Admissions: AMY DEATON
Registrar: TELAINA WRIGLEY
Dir for Library: JOSEPH E. WEBER
Library of 222,219 vols, 55,135 ebooks, 52,950 bound periodicals, 695 journals, 34,204 e-journal titles, 674,316, microforms, 6,685 audiovisual items, 91,786 govt publs, 2,040 maps
Number of teachers: 625
Number of students: 10,900

DEANS

College of Arts and Letters: Dr DIXIE WEBB

College of Behavioral and Health Sciences: Dr DAVID DENTON
College of Business: Dr WILLIAM RUPP
College of Education: Dr CARLETTE HARDIN
College of Graduate Studies: Dr DIXIE DENNIS
College of Science and Mathematics: Dr JAIME R. TAYLOR
Extended and Distance Education: DANA WILLETT

BAPTIST COLLEGE OF HEALTH SCIENCES

1003 Monroe Ave, Memphis, TN 38104
Telephone: (901) 575-2247
E-mail: admissions@bchs.edu
Internet: www.bchs.edu
Founded 1912 as Baptist Memorial Hospital, present name 1994
Private control
Pres.: BETTY SUE MCGARVEY
Provost: Dr WILLIAM J. SOBOTOR
Vice-Pres. for Business and Financial Services: LEANNE SMITH
Dean of Student Services: NANCY REED
Dir of Admissions: LISSA MORGAN
Registrar: JANA D. TURNER
Number of students: 975

DEANS

Div. of Allied Health: Dr LINDA REED
Div. of General and Health Studies: Dr BARRY SCHULTZ
Div. of Nursing: Dr ANNE PLUMB

BELMONT UNIVERSITY

1900 Belmont Blvd, Nashville, TN 37212-3757
Telephone: (615) 460-6000
E-mail: admissions@belmont.edu
Internet: www.belmont.edu
Founded 1890 as Belmont College, present name 1991
Private control
Academic year: August to May (2 semesters)
Pres.: Dr ROBERT C. FISHER
Chancellor: Dr HERBERT GABHART
Provost: Dr THOMAS BURNS
Vice-Pres.: Dr SUSAN H. WEST
Vice-Pres. for Admin. and Univ. Counsel: Dr JASON B. ROGERS
Vice-Pres. for Finance and Operations: STEVEN T. LASLEY
Vice-Pres. for Univ. Advancement: Dr BETHEL E. THOMAS, JR
Dean for Enrolment Services: DAVID MEE
Dean for Students and Assoc. Provost: Dr ANDREW J. JOHNSTON
Registrar: STEVEN REED
Library Dir: Dr ERNEST WILLIAM HEARD, JR
Library of 335,000 vols, 1,000 periodicals
Number of teachers: 660 (318 full-time, 342 part-time)
Number of students: 6,365 (4,974 undergraduate, 1,391 graduate)
Publications: Belmont Circle (4 a year), Explore (1 a year), The Tower (1 a year)

DEANS

College of Arts and Sciences: Dr BRYCE F. SULLIVAN
College of Business Admin.: Dr J. PATRICK RAINES
College of Law: ALBERTO GONZALES
College of Visual and Performing Arts: Dr CYNTHIA R. CURTIS
Gordon E. Inman College of Health Sciences and Nursing: Dr CATHY R. TAYLOR
Mike Curb College of Entertainment and Music Business: Dr WESLEY A. BULLA
School of Pharmacy: Dr PHIL JOHNSTON
School of Religion: Dr DARRELL GWALTNEY
Univ. College: Dr JIMMY T. DAVIS

BETHEL UNIVERSITY

325 Cherry Ave, McKenzie, TN 38201
Telephone: (731) 352-4000
E-mail: admissions@bethelu.edu
Internet: www.bethelu.edu
Founded 1842 as Bethel Seminary, present name and status 2009
Private control
Academic year: August to May (2 semesters)
Pres.: Dr ROBERT PROSSER
Vice-Pres. for Univ. Devt: MIKE PARKER
Chief Financial Officer: SANDY ASHLEY
Dean of Enrolment Services: TINA HODGES
Registrar: BECKY HAMES
Dir of Library: JILL WHITFILL
Library of 43,000 vols, 48 periodicals, 100,000 e-periodicals
Number of teachers: 36
Number of students: 4,673
Publications: Bethel Beacon (52 a year), Bethel Captions (4 a year), Log Cabin (1 a year)

DEANS

College of Graduate Studies: Dr DOROTHY BLACK
College of Liberal Arts: CINDY MALLARD
College of Professional Studies: LISA VAUGHN

BRYAN COLLEGE

POB 7000, Dayton, TN 37321-7000
721 Bryan Dr., Dayton, TN 37321-7000
Telephone: (423) 775-2041
E-mail: info@bryan.edu
Internet: www.bryan.edu
Founded 1930 as William Jennings Bryan Univ., present name 1993
Private control
Academic year: August to May
Areas of study incl. Biblical studies, biology, business administration, Christian ministry, Christian leadership, Christian thought, communication studies, creative writing, criminal justice, education, English, environmental science, exercise and health science, history, liberal arts, mathematics, music, politics and government, nursing, psychology, Spanish, theatre
Pres.: Dr STEPHEN LIVESAY
Academic Vice-Pres.: Dr BRADFORD SAMPLE
Vice-Pres. for Advancement: BLAKE HUDSON
Vice-Pres. for Enrolment Management: MICHAEL SAPIENZA
Vice-Pres. for Finance: VANCE BERGER
Vice-Pres. for Operations: TIM HOSTETLER
Registrar: JANET M. PIATT
Library Dir: Dr GARY FITSIMMONS
Library of 181,220 vols, 30,299 periodicals, 71 microforms
Number of teachers: 45 (full-time)
Number of students: 1,400
Publications: Bryan Life (4 a year), Illumine

DEANS

School of Adult and Graduate Studies: Dr MICHAEL CHASE

CARSON-NEWMAN COLLEGE

2130 Branner Ave, Jefferson City, TN 37760
Telephone: (865) 471-2000
E-mail: admitme@cn.edu
Internet: www.cn.edu
Founded 1851 as Mossy Creek Missionary Baptist Seminary, present name 1889
Private control
Academic year: August to May (2 semesters)
Pres.: Prof. Dr J. RANDALL O'BRIEN
Provost: Dr KINA MALLARD
Vice-Pres. for Advancement: Dr WILLIAM DANNY NICHOLSON

Vice-Pres. for Student Affairs: Dr ROSS BRUMMETT
Chief Financial Officer: MARTHA H. CHAMBERS
Dean of Enrolment Services and Registrar: SHERYL M. GRAY
Dean of Library Service: BRUCE G. KOCOUR
Library of 200,000 vols, 166,000 ebooks, 8,000 periodicals
Number of teachers: 125 (full-time)
Number of students: 2,065
Publications: Baptist History and Heritage, CN Studies, JOURNEY Magazine, Mossy Creek Reader, NUA—Studies in Contemporary Irish Writing

DEANS

School of Business: Prof. Dr CLYDE E. HERRING
School of Education: Prof. Dr SHARON TEETS
School of Family and Consumer Sciences: Prof. Dr KITTY ROBERTS COFFEY
School of Fine Arts: Dr MARK HUSSUNG
School of Humanities: Dr MARY E. BALDRIDGE
School of Natural Sciences and Mathematics: Prof. Dr CAREY R. HERRING
School of Nursing and Behavioral Health: Dr GREGORY CASALENUOVO
School of Religion: Prof. Dr DAVID E. CRUTCHLEY
School of Social Sciences: Prof. Dr LAURA R. WADLINGTON

CHRISTIAN BROTHERS UNIVERSITY

650 E Parkway, S, Memphis, TN 38104
Telephone: (901) 321-3000
E-mail: admissions@cbu.edu
Internet: www.cbu.edu
Founded 1871 as Christian Brothers College, present name 1990; attached to De La Salle Christian Brothers (Brothers of the Christian Schools)
Private control
Academic year: August to May
Pres.: Dr JOHN SMARRELLI, JR
Vice-Pres. for Academic Affairs: Dr FRANK BUSCHER
Vice-Pres. for Advancement: ANDREW PRISLOVSKY
Vice-Pres. for Enrolment Management: JAMES SCHLIMMER
Vice-Pres. for Finance and Admin.: C. DANIEL WORTHAM
Vice-Pres. for Student Life: Bro. DOMINIC EHRMANTRAUT
Dean of Admissions: Dr ANNE KENWORTHY
Registrar: MELODY NABORS
Librarian: KAY CUNNINGHAM
Library of 97,000 vols, 300 print periodicals, 60,000 ebooks, 1,800 DVDs, CDs and video cassettes
Number of teachers: 105 (full-time)
Number of students: 1,675

DEANS

Adult Professional Studies: Dr TONI ROSS
School of Arts: Dr PAUL HAUGHT
School of Business: Dr JOHN HARGETT
School of Engineering: Dr ERIC B. WELCH
School of Sciences: Dr JOHNNY B. HOLMES

CUMBERLAND UNIVERSITY

1 Cumberland Sq., Lebanon, TN 37087-3408
Telephone: (615) 444-2562
E-mail: admissions@cumberland.edu
Internet: www.cumberland.edu
Founded 1842
Private control
Academic year: August to May (2 semesters)
Pres.: Dr HARVILL C. EATON
Exec. Vice-Pres.: EDDIE PAWLAWSKI

Vice-Pres. for Academic Affairs and Registrar: Dr WILBUR PETERSON

Vice-Pres. for Admin.: JOE GRAY

Vice-Pres. for Advancement: RUSTY RICHARDSON

Vice-Pres. for Business and Finance: JUDY JORDAN

Dir for Enrolment Services: BEATRICE LA CHANCE

Dir for Library: ELOISE HITCHCOCK

Library of 35,000 vols, 40,000 ebooks, 300 periodicals, 1,300 audio–video materials

Number of teachers: 125

Number of students: 1,500 (1,140 full-time, 360 part-time)

DEANS

Jeanette C. Rudy School of Nursing: Dr CAROLE ANN BACH

Labry School of Business and Technology: Dr PAUL STUMB

School of Education and Public Service: Dr K. CHARLES COLLIER

School of Liberal Arts and Sciences: Dr LAURIE P. DISHMAN

School of Music and the Arts: TED CHARLES ROSE

EAST TENNESSEE STATE UNIVERSITY

807 University Pkwy, POB 70267, Johnson City, TN 37614-1700

Telephone: (423) 439-1000

E-mail: pittsm@etsu.edu

Internet: www.etsu.edu

Founded 1911 as East Tennessee State Normal School, current name and status 1963

State control

Academic year: August to May (2 semesters)

Pres.: Dr BRIAN NOLAND

Provost and Vice-Pres. for Academic Affairs: Dr BERT C. BACH

Vice-Pres. for Admin. and Finance: Dr DAVID D. COLLINS

Vice-Pres. for Univ. Advancement: Dr RICHARD A. MANAHAN

Vice-Provost and Dean for Students: Dr JOE H. SHERLIN, JR

Registrar: SHERYL BURNETTE

Dean for Univ. Libraries: Dr JEAN FLANIGAN

Library of 467,613 vols, 80,000 ebooks, 272 journals, 22,755 audiovisual materials, 19,685 ejournals

Number of teachers: 650

Number of students: 15,000

Publications: *Aethlon: Journal of Sport Literature* (2 a year), *ETSU Today Magazine* (2 a year), *Science Educator* (2 a year), *Storytelling World* (2 a year), *The Tennessee Reading Educator* (2 a year)

DEANS

Claudius G. Clemmer College of Education: Dr W. HAL KNIGHT

College of Arts and Sciences: Dr GORDON ANDERSON

College of Business and Technology: Dr LINDA R. GARCEAU

College of Clinical and Rehabilitative Health Sciences: Dr NANCY J. SCHERER

College of Nursing: Dr WENDY NEHRING

College of Public Health: Dr RANDY WYKOFF

Gatton College of Pharmacy: Prof. Dr LARRY D. CALHOUN

Honors College: Dr REBECCA A. PYLES

Quillen College of Medicine: Dr ROBERT T. MEANS

School of Continuing Studies and Academic Outreach: Dr RICK OSBORN

School of Graduate Studies: Dr CECILIA MCINTOSH

EMMANUEL CHRISTIAN SEMINARY

One Walker Dr., Johnson City, TN 37601

Telephone: (423) 926-1186

E-mail: admissions@ecs.edu

Internet: www.ecs.edu

Founded 1965

Private control

Academic year: August to May (2 semesters)

Offers Masters degree in arts, divinity, religion

Pres.: MICHAEL L. SWEENEY

Chancellor: C. ROBERT WETZEL

Exec. Dir of Devt: DAN R. LAWSON

Dir of Admissions and Recruitment: ERIN LAYTON

Dir of Finance: DAVID MARSHALL

Dean and Registrar: JACK HOLLAND

Librarian: JOHN MARK WADE

Library of 171,000 vols

FISK UNIVERSITY

1000 17th Ave, N, Nashville, TN 37208-3051

Telephone: (615) 329-8500

E-mail: admit@fisk.edu

Internet: www.fisk.edu

Founded 1866 as Fisk School, present name and status 1867

Private control

Academic year: August to May

Pres.: Dr H. JAMES WILLIAMS

Provost and Exec. Vice-Pres.: Dr PRINCILLA EVANS MORRIS

Vice-Pres. for Finance and Chief Financial Officer: GARY MOORE

Vice-Pres. for Institutional Assessment: Dr MICHAEL SELF

Dir of Admissions: ANTHONY JONES

Dean of Student Engagement: LAMETRIUS DANIELS

Vice-Pres. of Student Engagement and Enrollment Management: JASON MERIWETHER

Dean of Library: JESSIE CARNEY SMITH

Library of 210,000 vols

Number of teachers: 50 (full-time)

Number of students: 480

Publications: *Fisk Focus* (6 a year), *Fisk News* (1 a year)

DEANS

School of Humanities and Social Sciences: Prof. Dr REAVIS L. MITCHELL, JR

School of Natural Sciences, Mathematics and Business: Prof. Dr LEE E. LIMBIRD

FREE WILL BAPTIST BIBLE COLLEGE

3606 West End Ave, Nashville, TN 37205

Telephone: (615) 844-5000

Internet: www.fwbbc.edu

Founded 1942

Private control

Academic year: August to May (2 semesters)

Areas of study incl. accounting, biblical and ministry studies, business administration, child development and learning, history, languages, music, pastoral studies, psychology, science

Pres.: Dr J. MATHEW PINSON

Chancellor: Dr TOM MALONE

Provost: Dr GREG KETTEMAN

Vice-Pres. for Financial Affairs: CRAIG MAHLER

Vice-Pres. for Institutional Advancement: DAVID WILLIFORD

Vice-Pres. for Institutional Planning: Dr MILTON FIELDS

Vice-Pres. for Student Services and Dean of Students: Dr JON FORLINES

Dir of Enrolment Services: RUSTY CAMPBELL

Librarian: CAROL REID (acting)

Library of 60,000 vols

Number of students: 350

FREED-HARDEMAN UNIVERSITY

158 E Main St, Henderson, TN 38340-2399

Telephone: (731) 989-6648

Internet: www.fhu.edu

Founded 1869 as Private High School and College, present name 1919, present status 1990

Private control

Academic year: August to May (2 semesters)

Pres.: Dr JOE A. WILEY

Exec. Vice-Pres. and Chief Financial Officer: Dr DWAYNE H. WILSON

Vice-Pres. for Academics and Enrolment Management: Dr CHARLES J. VIRES

Vice-Pres. for Student Services and Dean of Students: Dr E. WAYNE SCOTT

Vice-Pres. for Univ. Advancement: DAVID A. CLOUSE

Registrar: LARRY OLDHAM

Library Dir: HOPE SHULL

Library of 153,276 vols, 126,310 ebooks, 34,696 periodicals, 48,500 audiovisual items

Number of students: 2,000

DEANS

Honors College: Dr JENNIFER S. JOHNSON

School of Arts and Humanities: Dr W. STEPHEN JOHNSON

School of Biblical Studies: Dr WILLIAM R. SMITH

School of Business: Prof. Dr KEITH W. SMITH

School of Education: Dr SHAREN L. CYPRESS

School of Sciences and Mathematics: Dr LEANN SELF-DAVIS

HARDING SCHOOL OF THEOLOGY

1000 Cherry Rd, Memphis, TN 38117-5499

Telephone: (901) 761-1350

E-mail: hstadmissions@hst.edu

Internet: hst.edu

Founded 1952 as Harding Univ. Graduate School of Religion, current name adopted 2011; attached to Harding Univ. in Searcy, Ark

Private control

Pres.: Dr DAVID B. BURKS

Vice-Pres.: Dr JIM MARTIN

Vice-Pres. and Dean: Dr EVERTT W. HUFFARD

Dir for Admissions: MATT CARTER

Dir for Advancement: LARRY ARICK

Librarian: DON L. MEREDITH

Library of 140,000 vols, 590 periodicals

HIWASSEE COLLEGE

225 Hiwassee College Dr., Madisonville, TN 37354

Telephone: (423) 442-2001

E-mail: enroll@hiwassee.edu

Internet: www.hiwassee.edu

Founded 1826 as Tullagalla Acad., present name 1849, present status 1980

Private control

Academic year: August to May (2 semesters)

Bachelors degree in arts, science

Pres.: Dr ROBIN J. TRICOLI

Vice-Pres. for Academic and Student Affairs and Academic Dean: Dr BETH R. SCRUGGS

Vice-Pres. for Admissions and Financial Aid: J. RON HEMPHILL

Vice-Pres. for Business Affairs and Treas.: WALTON LIPSCOMB

Vice-Pres. for Financial Aid: RON HEMPHILL

Vice-Pres. for Institutional Advancement: D. MARK ELAM

Dean of Students: MARK JOHNSON

Registrar: JANE DYE
Dir of Library Services: Dr CURTIS CHAPMAN
Library of 30,000 vols, 300 periodicals, 110 magazines and newspapers

JOHNSON UNIVERSITY

7900 Johnson Dr., Knoxville, TN 37998
Telephone: (865) 573-4517
E-mail: johnsonu@johnsonu.edu
Internet: www.johnsonu.edu
Founded 1893 as School of the Evangelists, present name and status 2011
Private control
Academic year: August to May (2 semesters)
Academic programmes incl. arts, biblical studies, intercultural studies, music, science
Pres.: Dr GARY E. WEEDMAN
Vice-Pres. for Academics and Academic Dean: Dr RICHARD K. BEAM
Vice-Pres. for Advancement: PHILIP A. EUBANKS
Vice-Pres. for Business and Finance: CHRISTOPHER R. ROLPH
Vice-Pres. for Student Services and Dean of Students: DAVID A. LEGG
Vice-Provost for Research and Planning: Dr MARK PIERCE
Dean for the Chapel: BILL WOLF
Dean for Enrollment: TIM WINGFIELD
Chief Information Officer: CLIFF MCCARTNEY
Registrar: SANDRA BLEVINS
Library Dir: CARRIE BETH LOWE
Library of 111,000 vols, 80,000 ebooks
Number of teachers: 55
Number of students: 845 (725 undergraduate, 120 graduate)
Publication: *Johnson* (3 a year)

DEANS

Center for Global Studies: ALICIA CRUMPTON
School of Arts and Science: TOMMY SMITH
School of Bible and Theology: CARL BRIDGES
School of Congregational Ministry: DANIEL OVERDORF
School of Creative Arts: MATTHEW BROADDUS
School of Education: JEFF BOND
School of Intercultural Studies: LINDA WHITMER

KING COLLEGE

1350 King College Rd, Bristol, TN 37620
Telephone: (423) 652-4861
E-mail: admissions@king.edu
Internet: www.king.edu
Founded 1867
Private control
Academic year: August to May (2 semesters)
Pres.: Dr GREGORY D. JORDAN
Provost and Vice-Pres. for Academic Affairs: Dr PAUL M. PERCY
Vice-Pres. for Business Operations and Chief Financial Officer: JAMES P. DONAHUE
Vice-Pres. for Institutional Advancement: WILLIAM M. MCELROY
Vice-Pres. for Student Affairs: Dr ROBERT A. LITTLETON
Registrar: SARAH L. DILLOW
Dean of Library Services: ERIKA BRAMMER
Library of 140,000 vols incl. books, periodicals, microforms, audiovisual items, govt documents
Number of teachers: 70
Number of students: 1,515
Publications: *The Descant, Tornado*

DEANS

Peeke School of Mission: FRED FOY STRANG
School of Arts and Sciences: Prof. Dr KATHERINE VANDE BRAKE
School of Business: Prof. Dr TODD H. ERICKSON

School of Education: Prof. Dr CARA E. ANDERSON
School of Nursing: Dr JOHANNE A. QUINN

LANE COLLEGE

545 Lane Ave, Jackson, TN 38301-4598
Telephone: (731) 426-7500
E-mail: admissions@lanecollege.edu
Internet: www.lanecollege.edu
Founded 1882 as C. M. E. High School, current name adopted 1896
Private control
Academic year: August to June
Pres.: GLENN MILLER VAULXS
Exec. Vice-Pres.: Dr JERRY WOODS
Vice-Pres. for Academic Affairs: Dr DEBORAH BUCHANAN
Vice-Pres. for Business and Finance: MELVIN ROSS HAMLETT
Vice-Pres. for Institutional Advancement: RICHARD HULON DONNELL
Vice-Pres. for Student Affairs: SHERRILL BERRY SCOTT
Registrar: TERRY BLACKMON
Head Librarian: LAN WANG
Library of 154,000 vols
Number of teachers: 100
Number of students: 2,200

LEE UNIVERSITY

1120 N Ocoee St, Cleveland, TN 37320-3450
Telephone: (423) 614-8000
E-mail: admissions@leeuniversity.edu
Internet: www.leeuniversity.edu
Founded 1918 as Bible Institute, present status 1997
Private control
Pres.: Dr CHARLES PAUL CONN
Vice-Pres. for Academic Affairs: Dr CAROLYN DIRKSEN
Vice-Pres. for Admin.: WALTER C. MAULDIN
Vice-Pres. for Business and Finance: CHRIS CONINE
Vice-Pres. for Enrolment Management: PHIL COOK
Vice-Pres. for Information Services: Dr JAYSON VAN HOOK
Vice-Pres. for Student Devt: Dr MIKE HAYES
Vice-Pres. for Univ. Relations: Dr JEROME HAMMOND
Dir of Library Services: BARBARA MCCULLOUGH
Library of 150,000 vols, 400 periodicals, 32,000 ejournals, 110,000 ebooks
Number of students: 4,400

DEANS

College of Arts and Sciences: Dr J. MATTHEW MELTON
Helen DeVos College of Education: Dr DEBORAH MURRAY
School of Music: WILLIAM GREEN
School of Religion: Prof. Dr TERRY L. CROSS

LEMOYNE—OWEN COLLEGE

807 Walker Ave, Memphis, TN 38126
Telephone: (901) 435-1000
E-mail: contact@nile.loc.edu
Internet: www.loc.edu
Founded 1968 by merger of LeMoyne College (f. 1862) with Owen College (f. 1947)
Private control
Academic year: July to May
Divs of business and economic development, education, liberal arts and humanities, natural and mathematical sciences, social and behavioural sciences
Pres.: JOHNNIE B. WATSON
Vice-Pres. for Academic Affairs and Chief Academic Officer: Dr BARBARA FRANKLE

Vice-Pres. for Finance and Chief Financial Officer: JIM DUGGER
Dean of Students: EDYTHE COBB
Dir of Admin. Services: JESSE CHATMAN
Registrar: ADDIE HARVEY
Dir of Library: ANNETTE HUNT
Library of 117,000 vols, 375 periodicals
Number of teachers: 40
Number of students: 1,200

LINCOLN MEMORIAL UNIVERSITY

6965 Cumberland Gap Parkway, Harrogate, TN 37752
Telephone: (423) 869-3611
E-mail: admissions@lmunet.edu
Internet: www.lmunet.edu
Founded 1897
Private control
Academic year: August to May (2 semesters)
Pres.: Dr B. JAMES DAWSON
Vice-Pres.: Dr RAY E. STOWERS
Vice-Pres. for Academic Affairs: Dr CLAYTON HESS
Vice-Pres. for Finance: RANDY ELDRIDGE
Vice-Pres. for Univ. Advancement: CYNTHIA WHITT
Dean for Admin.: LISA BLAIR-COX
Dean for Enrolment Management: SHERRY MCCREARY
Dean for Students: FRANK SMITH
Dir for Admissions: SHERRY MCCREARY
Registrar: HELEN BAILEY
Dir for Library Services: GABRIEL MORLEY
Library of 326,800 vols ebooks, ejournals, periodicals, microfilm, audiovisual materials
Number of teachers: 275 (169 full-time, 84 part-time)
Number of students: 4,550 (1,753 graduate, 1,858 undergraduate, 939 professional)
Publication: *The Lincoln Herald* (4 a year)

DEANS

Carter and Moyers School of Education: Dr MICHAEL CLYBURN
Caylor School of Nursing: Prof. Dr MARY ANNE MODRCIN
DeBusk College of Osteopathic Medicine: Dr RAY E. STOWERS
Duncan School of Law: SYDNEY BECKMAN
Paul V. Hamilton School of Arts and Sciences: Dr AMIEL JARSTFER
School of Allied Health: Prof. RANDALL K. EVANS
School of Business: Dr JACK T. MCCANN

LIPSCOMB UNIVERSITY

One University Park Dr., Nashville, TN 37204-3951
3901 Granny White Pike, Nashville, TN 37204-3951
Telephone: (615) 269-1000
E-mail: registrar@lipscomb.edu
Internet: www.lipscomb.edu
Founded 1891 as Nashville Bible School, present name 1994
Private control
Academic year: August to May (2 semesters)
Pres.: Prof. Dr L. RANDOLPH LOWRY, III
Provost: Dr W. CRAIG BLEDSOE
Sr Vice-Pres. for Finance and Admin.: DANNY H. TAYLOR
Vice-Pres.: Dr MIKE HAMMOND
Vice-Pres. and Chief Information Officer: MIKE GREEN
Vice-Pres. for Devt and Alumni Relations: Dr BENNIE HARRIS
Vice-Pres. for Student Devt and Dean of Campus Life: Dr SCOTT MCDOWELL
Vice-Pres. for Univ. Relations: WALT LEAVER
Registrar: JANET CATES
Library Dir: CAROLYN T. WILSON

Library of 400,000 vols incl. books, periodicals, microforms
Number of teachers: 300
Number of students: 4,200
Publication: *Lipscomb Now*

DEANS

College of Arts and Sciences: Dr NORMA BURGESS
College of Bible and Ministry: Dr TERRY BRILEY
College of Business: TURNEY STEVENS
College of Education: Prof. Dr CANDICE MCQUEEN
College of Pharmacy and Health Sciences: Dr ROGER L. DAVIS
Raymond B. Jones College of Engineering: GREG G. NORDSTROM

MARTIN METHODIST COLLEGE

433 W Madison St, Pulaski, TN 38478-2799
Telephone: (931) 363-9800
E-mail: info@martinmethodist.edu
Internet: www.martinmethodist.edu

Founded 1870 as Martin Female College, present name 1986
Private control
Academic year: July to May (2 semesters)
Liberal arts college; academic divs incl. business, education, humanities, mathematics and science, nursing, social science
Pres.: Dr TED BROWN
Vice-Pres. for Academic Affairs: JAMES T. MURRELL
Vice-Pres. for Enrolment and Campus Life: ROBBY SHELTON
Vice-Pres. for Finance and Admin.: DAVID STEPHENS
Vice-Pres. for Planning and Effectiveness: Dr DENNIS HASKINS
Registrar: ANDREW B. BROWN
Library Dir: RICHARD MADDEN
Library of 100,000 vols incl. print and ebooks, 2,000 print and ejournals

MARYVILLE COLLEGE

502 E Lamar Alexander Parkway, Maryville, TN 37804
Telephone: (865) 981-8000
E-mail: campusvisit@maryvillecollege.edu
Internet: www.maryvillecollege.edu

Founded 1819 as Southern and Western Theological Seminary, present name 1842
Private control
Academic year: August to May (2 semesters)
Academic divs incl. behavioural sciences, education, fine arts, humanities, languages and literature, mathematics and computer science, natural sciences, social sciences
Pres.: Dr WILLIAM TOM BOGART
Vice-Pres. and Dean for College: Dr BARBARA WELLS
Vice-Pres. and Dean for Students: VANDY KEMP
Vice-Pres. and Treas.: DANA SMITH
Vice-Pres. for Advancement and Community Relations: HOLLY JACKSON-SULLIVAN
Vice-Pres. for Enrolment: Dr DOLPHUS HENRY
Registrar: KATHI WILSON
Library Dir: ANGELA QUICK
Library of 132,000 vols, 144,000 ebooks, 20,000 journal titles
Number of teachers: 110 (70 full-time, 40 part-time)
Number of students: 1,100
Publications: *Impressions* (2 a year), *Laurels* (2 a year)

MEHARRY MEDICAL COLLEGE

1005 Dr D. B. Todd, Jr Blvd, Nashville, TN 37208
Telephone: (615) 327-6000
E-mail: recordsdepartment@mmc.edu
Internet: www.mmc.edu

Founded 1876 as medical dept of Central Tennessee College, present status 1915
Private control
Academic year: August to July
Pres.: Prof. Dr WAYNE J. RILEY
Provost and Exec. Vice-Pres.: Dr ANGELA L. FRANKLIN
Sr Vice-Pres., Gen. Counsel and Corporate Sec.: BENJAMIN RAWLINS
Sr Vice-Pres. for Finance: LAMEL BANDY-NEAL
Sr Vice-Pres. for Institutional Advancement: ROBERT POOLE
Vice-Pres. for Research: Dr RUSSELL POLAND
Vice-Pres. for Student and Academic Affairs: PAMELA WILLIAMS
Registrar: SHANITA BROWN
Library Dir: FATIMA MNCUBE-BARNES
Library of 66,104 vols, 4,165 ejournals, 1,264 ebooks
Number of teachers: 220 (full-time)
Number of students: 780

DEANS

School of Dentistry: Dr JANET H. SOUTHERLAND (acting)
School of Graduate Studies and Research: Dr MARIA DE FATIMA LIMA
School of Medicine: Dr CHARLES P. MOUTON

MEMPHIS COLLEGE OF ART

Overton Park, 1930 Poplar Ave, Memphis, TN 38104-2764
Telephone: (901) 272-5100
E-mail: info@mca.edu
Internet: www.mca.edu

Founded 1936
Private control
Academic year: August to May (2 semesters)
Areas of study incl. animation, liberal studies, digital media, drawing, graphic design, illustration, painting, photography, printmaking, sculpture
Pres.: Dr RON JONES
Dean: REMY MILLER
Vice-Pres. for Academic Affairs: KEN STRICKLAND
Vice-Pres. for College Advancement: KIM WILLIAMS
Vice-Pres. for Finance and Admin.: SHERRY YELVINGTON
Vice-Pres. for Student Affairs: SUSAN MILLER
Dean for Admissions: ANNETTE JAMES MOORE
Director for Student Life: CARLA RUFFER
Registrar: ELESHA NEWBERRY
Librarian: LESLIE HOLLAND
Library of 19,000 vols
Number of teachers: 60
Number of students: 300

MEMPHIS THEOLOGICAL SEMINARY

168 East Parkway, S, Memphis, TN 38104
Telephone: (901) 458-8232
E-mail: admissions@memphisseminary.edu
Internet: www.memphisseminary.edu

Founded 1908 as Theological Seminary by merger of Cumberland Presbyterians with Presbyterian Church, present name 1964
Private control
Academic year: August to May (2 semesters)
Pres.: Prof. Dr DANIEL J. EARHEART-BROWN
Vice-Pres. for Academic Affairs and Dean: Dr ROBERT S. WOOD
Vice-Pres. for Advancement: CATHI JOHNSON

Vice-Pres. for Operations and Chief Financial Officer: CASSANDRA PRICE-PERRY
Registrar: GAIL D. ROBINSON
Library Dir: STEVEN R. EDSCORN
Library of 87,000 vols, 382 periodicals, microfilm, microfiche, audiovideo items
Number of students: 310

MID-AMERICA BAPTIST THEOLOGICAL SEMINARY

2095 Appling Rd, Cordova, TN 38016
Telephone: (901) 751-8453
E-mail: info@mabts.edu
Internet: www.mabts.edu

Founded 1971 as School of the Prophets, current name adopted 1972
Private control
Academic year: August to May (2 semesters)
Campus in Albany, NY
Pres.: Dr MICHAEL R. SPRADLIN
Exec. Vice-Pres.: Dr BRADLEY C. THOMPSON
Academic Vice-Pres.: Dr TIMOTHY SEAL
Vice-Pres. for Finance and Operations: RANDY REDD
Vice-Pres. for Institutional Advancement: DUFFY GUYTON
Dir for Institutional Assessment: Dr JULIA BICKLEY
Registrar: ROSE MINK
Dir for Library Services: TERRENCE NEAL BROWN
Library of 163,000 vols
Publications: *The Journal of Evangelism and Missions*, *The Messenger* (3 a year)

MIDDLE TENNESSEE SCHOOL OF ANESTHESIA

POB 417, Madison, TN 37116
315 Hospital Dr., Madison, TN 37115
Telephone: (615) 732-7662
E-mail: info@mtsa.edu
Internet: www.mtsa.edu

Founded 1950 as Madison Hospital School of Anesthesia, present name 1980
Private control
Areas of study incl. nurse anaesthesia
Pres.: Dr KENNETH L. SCHWAB
Vice-Pres. and Dean: Dr MARY E. DEVASHER
Vice-Pres. for Advancement and Alumni: JAMES B. CLOSSER
Dir of Learning Resource Centre and Dir of Information Systems Support: Dr AMY C. GIDEON
Library of 400 vols

MIDDLE TENNESSEE STATE UNIVERSITY

1301 East Main St, Murfreesboro, TN 37132-0001
Telephone: (615) 898-2300
E-mail: admissions@mtsu.edu
Internet: www.mtsu.edu

Founded 1911 as Middle Tennessee State Normal School, present name and status 1965
State control
Academic year: August to May (2 semesters)
Pres.: Prof. Dr SIDNEY A. MCPHEE
Provost and Exec. Vice-Pres.: Prof. Dr BRAD BARTEL
Sr Vice-Pres. for Business and Finance: Dr JOHN W. COTHERN
Vice-Pres. for Devt and Univ. Relations: WILLIAM J. BALES
Vice-Pres. for Finance and Admin.: DUANE STUCKY
Vice-Pres. for Student Affairs and Vice-Provost for Enrolment and Academic Services: Dr DEBRA SELLS

Registrar: CATHY KIRCHNER
Dean of Library: DON OMACHONU (acting)
Library of 1,000,000 vols
Number of teachers: 900
Number of students: 26,000

DEANS

College of Basic and Applied Sciences: Dr
TOM CHEATHAM
College of Behavioral and Health Sciences:
Dr HAROLD D. WHITESIDE
College of Education: Dr LANA C. SEIVERS
College of Liberal Arts: Dr MARK BYRNES
College of Mass Communication: Prof. Dr
ROY L. MOORE
Graduate Studies: Dr MICHAEL D. ALLEN
Honors College: Prof. Dr JOHN R. VILE
Jennings A. Jones College of Business: Prof.
Dr E. JAMES BURTON
Univ. College: Dr MIKE BOYLE

MILLIGAN COLLEGE

POB 500, Milligan College, TN 37682
Telephone: (423) 461-8700
E-mail: admissions@milligan.edu
Internet: www.milligan.edu
Founded 1866 as Buffalo Male and Female
Institute, present name 1881
Private control
Academic year: August to May (2 semesters)
Academic programmes incl. accounting,
allied health, art, Bible, biology, business
administration, chemistry, communications,
economics, education history, legal studies,
management, nursing, pharmacy, Psych-
ology, Spanish, sports management, theatre
Pres.: Dr WILLIAM B. GREER
Vice-Pres. for Academic Affairs and Dean: Dr
GARLAND YOUNG
Vice-Pres. for Business and Finance: JACQUI
STEADMAN
Vice-Pres. for Enrolment Management and
Marketing: Dr LEE FIERBAUGH
Vice-Pres. for Institutional Advancement:
JACK SIMPSON
Vice-Pres. for Student Devt and Dean of
Students: MARK FOX
Registrar: SUE SKIDMORE
Dir of Library Service: GARY F. DAUGHT
Library of 108,500 vols
Number of teachers: 75 (full-time)
Number of students: 1,200

O'MORE COLLEGE OF DESIGN

423 S Margin St, Franklin, TN 37064
Telephone: (615) 794-4254
E-mail: admissions@omorecollege.edu
Internet: www.omorecollege.edu
Founded 1970
Private control
Academic year: August to May (2 semesters)
Areas of study incl. fashion design, fine art,
interior design, liberal arts, visual communi-
cations
Pres.: Dr K. MARK HILLIARD
Vice-Pres. for Academic Affairs: SHARI FOX
Vice-Pres. for Student Affairs: AMY SHELTON
Dir of Admissions: MELINDA DABBS
Librarian: ALLISON CRAWFORD

PENTECOSTAL THEOLOGICAL SEMINARY

POB 3330, Cleveland, TN 37320-3330
Telephone: (423) 478-1131
E-mail: president@ptseminary.edu
Internet: www.ptseminary.edu
Founded 1975
Private control
Academic year: July to August

Areas of study incl. Christian formation,
Church ministries, counselling and disciple-
ship, divinity
Pres.: Prof. Dr STEVEN JACK LAND
Vice-Pres. for Academics: Prof. Dr SANG-EHIL
HAN
Vice-Pres. for Finance: ROBERT BUXTON
Vice-Pres. for Institutional Advancement: Dr
KENNETH R. DAVIS
Dir of Admin. Services: ALANNA HENRY
Registrar and Dir of Admissions: ANITA
BLEVINS
Library Dir: BARBARA McCULLOUGH
Library of 150,000 vols, 400 periodicals,
70,000 ebooks

RHODES COLLEGE

2000 N Parkway, Memphis, TN 38112-1690
Telephone: (901) 843-3000
E-mail: adminfo@rhodes.edu
Internet: www.rhodes.edu
Founded 1848
Private control
Academic year: August to May
Liberal arts college; academic depts incl.
anthropology and sociology, art, biology,
chemistry, commerce and business, econom-
ics, education, English, Greek and Roman
studies, history, int. studies
Pres.: WILLIAM E. TROUTT
Provost: CHARLOTTE G. BORST
Vice-Pres. for Academic Affairs and Dean of
Faculty: Dr MICHAEL R. DROMPP
Vice-Pres. for College Relations: RUSSELL T.
WIGGINTON
Vice-Pres. for Devt: JENNA GOODLOE WADE
Vice-Pres. for Enrolment and Communica-
tions and Dean of Admissions: CAREY
THOMPSON
Vice-Pres. for Finance and Business Affairs:
JAMES ALLEN BOONE, JR
Vice-Pres. for Information Services: ROBERT
M. JOHNSON, JR
Dean of Students: CAROL E. CASEY
Registrar: DEANNA ADAMS
Dir of Library: DARLENE BROOKS
Library of 338,950 vols incl. 287,950 print
publs, 51,000 ebooks
Number of teachers: 165 full-time
Number of students: 1,710
Publication: *Rhodes Magazine* (3 a year)

SOUTH COLLEGE

3904 Lonas Dr., Knoxville, TN 37909
Telephone: (865) 251-1800
Internet: www.southcollegetn.edu
Founded 1882 as br. of Nashville Business
College, present name 2001
Private control
Academic year: September to June
Masters degree in health science; Bachelors
degree in business administration, science
Pres.: STEPHEN A. SOUTH
Exec. Vice-Pres.: Dr KIMBERELY B. HALL
Vice-Pres. for Admin. and Regulatory Com-
pliance: STEVE WOODFORD
Vice-Pres. for Business Operations: KEVIN
SPARKS
Vice-Pres. for Enrolment Management: WAL-
TER HOSEA
Vice-Pres. for Institutional Effectiveness and
Student Services: BARBARA BRIMI
Dean for Student Services: CAROLYN HILLE-
GAS
Dir for Admissions: CARRIE MAJOR
Registrar: KIM WOOD
Head Librarian: MEL McHUGH

SOUTHERN ADVENTIST UNIVERSITY

POB 370, Collegedale, TN 37315-0370
5010 University Dr., Collegedale, TN 37315
Telephone: (423) 238-2111
E-mail: postmaster@southern.edu
Internet: www.southern.edu
Founded 1892 as Graysville Acad., present
name and status 1996
Private control
Academic year: August to May
Pres.: GORDON BIETZ
Sr Vice-Pres. for Academic Admin.: ROBERT
YOUNG
Sr Vice-Pres. for Financial Admin.: TOM
VERRILL
Vice-Pres. for Advancement: CHRIS CAREY
Vice-Pres. for Enrolment Services: MARC
GRUNDY
Vice-Pres. for Student Services: BILL WOH-
LERS
Registrar: JONI ZIER
Dir of Libraries: Dr JOSIP MOCNIK
Library of 175,000 vols, 11,163 periodical
subscriptions, 587,809 microforms
Number of teachers: 110 (107 full-time, 3
part-time)
Number of students: 3,000
Publication: *Columns*

DEANS

Graduate Studies: CARL SWAFFORD
School of Business and Management: Dr DON
VAN ORNAM
School of Nursing: Prof. BARBARA JAMES
School of Religion: Prof. Dr GREG A. KING
School of Social Work: Dr RENÉ DRUMM
School of Visual Art and Design: RANDY
CRAVEN

SOUTHERN COLLEGE OF OPTOMETRY

1245 Madison Ave, Memphis, TN 38104-2222
Telephone: (901) 722-3200
E-mail: informationservices@sco.edu
Internet: www.sco.edu
Founded 1932
Private control
Academic year: August to May (2 semesters)
Offers doctorate degree in optometry
Pres.: Dr RICHARD W. PHILLIPS
Vice-Pres. for Academic Affairs: Dr LEWIS N.
REICH
Vice-Pres. for Clinical Programmes: JAMES E.
VENABLE
Vice-Pres. for Finance and Admin.: DAVID
WEST
Vice-Pres. for Institutional Advancement:
KRISTIN K. ANDERSON
Vice-Pres. for Student Services: JOSEPH H.
HAUSER
Dir of Admissions and Enrolment Services:
MICHAEL N. ROBERTSON
Dir of Library Services: Dr SHARON E.
TABACHNICK
Number of teachers: 60

TENNESSEE STATE UNIVERSITY

POB 9609, Nashville, TN 37209
3500 John A. Merritt Blvd, Nashville, TN
37209-1561
Telephone: (615) 963-5000
E-mail: admissions@tnstate.edu
Internet: www.tnstate.edu
Founded 1912, present name 1968, merger of
former Univ. of Tennessee at Nashville
with Tennessee State Univ. 1979
State control
Academic year: August to May (2 semesters)

Pres.: Dr PORTIA HOLMES SHIELDS
Provost and Exec. Vice-Pres. for Academic Affairs: Dr MILLICENT LOWNES-JACKSON
Vice-Pres. for Academic Affairs for Research and Sponsored Programmes: Dr MICHAEL BUSBY
Vice-Pres. for Business and Finance: CYNTHIA BROOKS
Vice-Pres. for Student Affairs: Dr ADRIAN DEXTER SAMUELS
Vice-Pres. for Univ. Relations and Devt: WILLIAM NELSEN
Dean of Students: PEGGY EARNEST
Registrar: THELRIA HARDAWAY
Dean of Libraries and Media Centres: Dr YILDIZ BINKLEY
Library of 442,802 vols, 1,386 periodicals subscriptions, 93,597 bound periodicals, 15,202 microfilms, 888,562 microfiche
Number of teachers: 450
Number of students: 9,165 (7,105 undergraduate, 2,060 graduate)
Publication: *Alumni Life Magazine* (1 a year)

DEANS

College of Agriculture, Human and Natural Sciences: Prof. Dr CHANDRA REDDY
College of Business: Dr TILDEN CURRY
College of Education: Dr PETER E. MILLET
College of Engineering, Technology and Computer Science: Prof. Dr S. KEITH HARGROVE
College of Health Sciences: KATHLEEN McENERNEY
College of Liberal Arts: Dr GLORIA C. JOHNSON
College of Public Service and Urban Affairs: Dr BRUCE ROGERS
School of Graduate Studies and Research: Dr ALEX SEKWAT
School of Nursing: Prof. Dr KATHY MARTIN

TENNESSEE TECH UNIVERSITY

1 William L. Jones Dr., Cookeville, TN 38505
Telephone: (931) 372-3888
E-mail: admissions@tntech.edu
Internet: www.tntech.edu
Founded 1912 as Dixie College
State control
Academic year: August to May
Pres. and CEO: Dr ROBERT R. BELL
Provost and Vice-Pres. for Academic Affairs: Dr MARK STEPHENS
Vice-Pres. for Business and Fiscal Affairs: Dr CLAIRE STINSON
Vice-Pres. for Extended Programmes and Regional Devt: Dr SUSAN ELKINS
Vice-Pres. for Student Affairs: MARC BURNETT
Vice-Pres. for Univ. Advancement: MARK HUTCHINS
Registrar: ELIZABETH ROGERS
Dean of Library and Learning Assistance: Dr DOUGLAS BATES
Library of 353,000 vols, 27,000 ebooks, 1.5m. microforms, 3,050 magazines, journals and newspapers
Number of teachers: 400
Number of students: 11,800 (9,940 undergraduate, 1,860 graduate)

DEANS

College of Agricultural and Human Sciences: Prof. PAT BAGLEY
College of Arts and Sciences: Dr PAUL SEMMES
College of Business: JAMES JORDAN-WAGNER
College of Education: MATTHEW R. SMITH
College of Engineering: Prof. Dr JOSEPH J. RENCIS
School of Interdisciplinary Studies: Dr SUSAN ELKINS

TENNESSEE TEMPLE UNIVERSITY

1815 Union Ave, Chattanooga, TN 37404-3587
Telephone: (423) 493-4100
E-mail: ttuinfo@tntemple.edu
Internet: www.tntemple.edu
Founded 1946 as Tennessee Temple College, present name and status 1979
Private control
Academic year: August to May
Dept of Bible and Christian ministries, business administration; divs of arts and sciences, education
Chancellor: Dr DAVID E. BOULER
Pres.: Dr D. JAMES O'NEILL
Vice-Pres. for Academic Services: Dr SUSAN LOVETT
Chief Operating Officer: Dr JEFF RECTOR
Dir of Student Services Centre and Admissions: Dr PAM FREJOSKI
Registrar: RICHARD D. VAUPEL
Dir of Library Services: KEVIN WOODRUFF
Library of 154,000 vols, 9,000 periodicals

TENNESSEE WESLEYAN COLLEGE

204 E College St, Athens, TN 37303
Telephone: (423) 745-7504
E-mail: admissions@twcnet.edu
Internet: www.twcnet.edu
Founded 1857 as Athens Female College, present name 1954
Private control
Academic year: August to May (2 semesters)
Programmes of study incl. arts, applied science, chemistry, Church vocations, criminal justice, English, exercise and sports sciences, general science, history, music education, science, science in nursing
Pres.: Dr HARLEY KNOWLES
Sr Vice-Pres.: LARRY WALLACE
Vice-Pres. for Academic Affairs: Dr SUZANNE HINE
Vice-Pres. for Enrolment Services: STAN HARRISON
Vice-Pres. for Financial Affairs: GAIL HARRIS
Vice-Pres. for Student Life: Dr SCOTT MASHBURN
Chief Advancement Officer: RANDY NELSON
Registrar: JULIE McCASLIN
Assoc. Dir of Library: JULIE E. ADAMS
Library of 57,251 vols, 1,173 periodicals, 8,260 microforms, 146,129 ebooks
Number of teachers: 100 (52 full-time, 48 part-time)
Number of students: 1,100
Publication: *ARCHES Magazine* (2 a year)

TREVECCA NAZARENE UNIVERSITY

333 Murfreesboro Rd, Nashville, TN 37210
Telephone: (615) 248-1200
E-mail: admissions@trevecca.edu
Internet: www.trevecca.edu
Founded 1901 as Literary and Bible Training School for Christian Workers, present name 1995
Private control
Academic year: August to May (2 semesters)
Pres.: Prof. Dr DAN BOONE
Provost: Prof. Dr STEPHEN M. PUSEY
Exec. Vice-Pres. for Finance and Admin.: DAVID CALDWELL
Vice-Pres. for External Relations: PEGGY COONING
Dean of Academic Affairs and Assoc. Provost: CAROL MAXSON
Dean of Enrolment Management and Assoc. Provost: KATHRYN BAUGHER
Dean of Student Devt and Assoc. Provost: STEPHEN HARRIS
Registrar: BECKY NIECE

Dir of Library Services: RUTH KINNERSLEY
Library of 103,571 vols, 507 print periodicals, 3,632 audiovisual items, 295,265 microforms, e-periodicals
Number of teachers: 100 (full-time)
Number of students: 2,480 (2,050 full-time, 430 part-time)

DEANS

College of Lifelong Learning: DAVID PHILLIPS
Millard Reed School of Religion: Dr TIMOTHY GREEN
School of Arts and Sciences: Dr LENA HEGI WELCH
School of Business and Technology: Dr JAMES HIATT
School of Education: Dr ESTHER SWINK

TUSCULUM COLLEGE

POB 5093, Greeneville, TN 37743
60 Shiloh Rd, Greeneville, TN 37743
Telephone: (423) 636-7300
E-mail: admissions@tusculum.edu
Internet: www.tusculum.edu
Founded 1794
Private control
Academic year: August to May (2 semesters)
Centres in Knoxville, Morristown, Tri-Cities; areas of study incl. computer information systems, film and broadcasting, history, museum studies, religious studies
Pres.: Dr NANCY B. MOODY
Provost and Vice-Pres. for Academic Affairs: Prof. Dr MELINDA DUKES
Vice-Pres. and Chief Financial Officer: STEPHEN GEHRET
Vice-Pres. for Admin.: MARK A. STOKES
Vice-Pres. for Enrolment Management: Dr THOMAS STEIN
Vice-Pres. for Institutional Advancement: HEATHER PATCHETT
Dean of Students: Dr DAVID McMAHAN
Registrar: BOBBIE CLARKSTON
Library Dir: MYRON J. SMITH, JR
Library of 192,000 vols
Number of teachers: 130
Number of students: 2,200

UNION UNIVERSITY

1050 Union University Dr., Jackson, TN 38305
Telephone: (731) 668-1818
E-mail: info@uu.edu
Internet: www.uu.edu
Founded 1823 as Jackson Male Acad., present name 1907
Private control
Academic year: September to May
Campuses in Germantown, Hendersonville
Pres.: Prof. Dr SAMUEL W. DUB
Provost and Exec. Vice-Pres.: Prof. Dr CARLA D. SANDERSON
Sr Vice-Pres. for Business and Financial Services: GARY L. CARTER
Sr Vice-Pres. for Enrolment Services: RICH GRIMM
Sr Vice-Pres. for Univ. Relations: Dr JERRY N. TIDWELL
Vice-Pres. for Academic Admin.: GENE FANT
Vice-Pres. for Regional Campuses: JIMMY DAVIS
Vice-Pres. for Student Services and Dean of Students: Dr KIMBERLY C. THORNBURY
Registrar: BARBARA McMILLIN (acting)
Dir of Library and Assoc. Vice-Pres. for Academic Resources: ANNA BETH MORGAN
Library of 225,319 vols, 76,918 ebooks
Number of teachers: 197
Number of students: 4,050

DEANS

College of Arts and Sciences: Prof. Dr GENE FANT
College of Education and Human Studies: Prof. Dr THOMAS R. ROSEBROUGH
McAfee School of Business Administration: Prof. Dr R. KEITH ABSHER
School of Nursing: Prof. Dr TIMOTHY L. SMITH
School of Pharmacy: Dr SHEILA L. MITCHELL
School of Theology and Missions: Prof. Dr GREGORY A. THORNBURY

UNIVERSITY OF MEMPHIS

Memphis, TN 38152

Telephone: (901) 678-2000
E-mail: admissions@memphis.edu
Internet: www.memphis.edu

Founded 1912 as West Tennessee State Normal School, present status 1957, present name 1994
State control
Academic year: August to May

Pres.: Dr SHIRLEY C. RAINES
Provost: Dr RALPH J. FAUDREE
Vice-Pres. for Advancement: JULIE A. JOHNSON
Vice-Pres. for Business and Finance: DAVID ZETTERGREN
Vice-Pres. for Information Systems and Chief Information Officer: Dr DOUGLAS E. HURLEY
Vice-Pres. for Student Affairs: Dr ROSIE PHILLIPS BINGHAM
Registrar: DONNA VAN CANNEYT
Dean of Univ. Libraries: Dr SYLVERNA V. FORD

Library of 1,200,795 vols, 64,339 ebooks, 592,140 govt documents, 9,728,360 MSS, 60,728 maps, 760,582 photographs, 3,512,244 microfiche
Number of teachers: 930 (full-time)
Number of students: 22,725

Publications: *Law Review*, *Mid-South Business Journal*, *Memphis Economy*, *The Southern Journal of Philosophy* (4 a year), *The University of Memphis Magazine* (4 a year)

DEANS

Cecil C. Humphreys School of Law: Prof. Dr KEVIN H. SMITH
College of Arts and Sciences: Dr HENRY A. KURTZ
College of Communication and Fine Arts: Dr RICHARD R. RANTA
College of Education, Health and Human Sciences: Dr DONALD I. WAGNER
Fogelman College of Business And Economics: Prof. Dr RAJIV GROVER
Herff College of Engineering: Dr RICHARD C. WARDER, JR
Loewenberg School of Nursing: Prof. Dr LIN ZHAN
School of Audiology And Speech Language Pathology: Dr MAURICE I. MENDEL
School of Public Health: Dr LISA M. KLESGES
Univ. College: Dr DAN L. LATTIMORE

UNIVERSITY OF TENNESSEE SYSTEM

Knoxville, TN 37996

Telephone: (615) 974-1000
Internet: www.tennessee.edu

Founded 1968 as Blount College, present name and status 1968
State control
Academic year: September to August

Pres.: Dr JOSEPH A. DIPIETRO
Exec. Vice-Pres. and Vice-Pres. for Research and Economic Devt: Dr DAVID MILLHORN
Sr Vice-Pres. and Chief Financial Officer: Dr GARY W. ROGERS

Vice-Pres. for Academic Affairs and Student Success: Dr KATIE HIGH
Vice-Pres. for Agriculture: Dr JOSEPH A. DIPIETRO
Vice-Pres. for Devt and Alumni Affairs: JOHNNIE RAY
Vice-Pres for Public and Govt Relations: HANK DYE, HANK DYE
Gen. Counsel and Sec.: CATHERINE S. MIZELL
Library: see under Libraries and Archives
Number of teachers: 3,030
Number of students: 49,600

Publications: *Extension Series* (4–6 a year), *Horizons* (4 a year), *Tennessee Alumnus* (4 a year), *The University Record*...

MAJOR CAMPUSES

University of Tennessee at Chattanooga

615 McCallie Ave, Chattanooga, TN 37403-2598

Telephone: (423) 425-4111
E-mail: utcmocs@utc.edu
Internet: www.utc.edu

Founded 1886 as Chattanooga Univ., present name and status 1969
Academic year: August to May

Chancellor: Dr ROGER G. BROWN
Provost and Vice-Chancellor for Academic Affairs: Dr PHILIP B. OLDHAM
Sr Vice-Chancellor for Advancement: BOB LYON
Sr Vice-Chancellor for Finance, Operations and Information Technology and Chief Financial Officer: Dr RICHARD BROWN
Vice-Chancellor for Student Devt: Dr JOHN DELANEY
Registrar: LINDA ORTH
Dean of Libraries: THERESA LIEDTKA

Library of 510,890 vols, 20,982 audiovisual materials, 344 microforms, 1,991 e-journal
Number of students: 11,400 (9,860 undergraduate, 1,530 graduate)
Number of teachers: 760 (453 full-time, 307 part-time)

DEANS

College of Arts and Sciences: Dr HERBERT BURHENN
College of Business: Dr ROBERT S. DOOLEY
College of Engineering and Computer Science: Dr WILLIAM SUTTON
College of Health, Education and Professional Studies: Dr MARY TANNER (acting)

University of Tennessee Health Science Center

920 Madison Ave, Memphis, TN 38163

Telephone: (902) 448-5500
E-mail: uthscadmit@thsc.edu
Internet: www.uthsc.edu

Founded 1911

Campuses in Chattanooga, Knoxville
Academic year: August to July (3 semesters)

Chancellor: Dr STEVE J. SCHWAB
Exec. Vice-Chancellor and Chief Operations Officer: Dr KENNARD D. BROWN
Vice-Chancellor for Academic, Faculty and Student Affairs: Dr CHERYL R. SCHEID
Vice-Chancellor for Finance and Operations: ANTHONY A. FERRARA
Vice-Chancellor for Devt and Alumni Affairs: BETHANY GOOLSBY
Vice-Pres. and Gen. Counsel: CATHERINE MIZELL
Registrar and Dir of Academic Records: Dr GLENDA K. ALEXANDER

Library of 260,000 vols, 150 current periodical titles, 2,800 e-journal titles
Number of students: 2,815

DEANS

College of Allied Health Sciences: Prof. Dr NOMA BENNETT ANDERSON
College of Dentistry: TIMOTHY L. HOTTEL
College of Graduate Health Sciences: Dr CHERYL R. SCHEID
College of Medicine: DAVID M. STERN
College of Nursing: NAURA TALBOT
College of Pharmacy: MARIE CHISHOLM-BURNS

University of Tennessee at Knoxville

Knoxville, TN 37996

Telephone: (615) 974-1000
E-mail: chancellor@utk.edu
Internet: www.utk.edu

Founded 1794 as Blount College, present name 1879
Academic year: August to August (3 semesters)

Chancellor: Dr JIMMY G. CHEEK
Provost and Sr Vice-Chancellor for Academic Affairs: Dr SUSAN MARTIN
Vice-Chancellor for Devt and Alumni Affairs: SCOTT RABENOLD
Vice-Chancellor for Finance and Admin.: CHRIS CIMINO
Vice-Chancellor for Research and Engagement: LEE RIEDINGER
Vice-Chancellor for Student Life: W. TIMOTHY ROGERS
Registrar and Assoc. Dean of Enrolment: MONIQUE ANDERSON
Dean of Libraries: Dr STEVEN SMITH

Library: 2.3m. vols
Number of teachers: 1,300
Number of students: 27,500 (21,300 undergraduate, 6,200 graduate)

DEANS

College of Agricultural Sciences and Natural Resources: Dr CAULA BEYL
College of Architecture and Design: SCOTT POOLE
College of Arts and Sciences: Dr THERESA M. LEE
College of Business Administration: Dr JAN WILLIAMS
College of Communications and Information: Dr MICHAEL WIRTH
College of Education, Health and Human Sciences: Dr ROBERT RIDER
College of Engineering: Dr WAYNE T. DAVIS
College of Law: DOUGLAS A. BLAZE
College of Nursing: Dr VICTORIA NIEDERHAUSER
College of Social Work: Dr KAREN SOWERS
College of Veterinary Medicine: Dr JAMES THOMPSON
Graduate School: Dr CAROLYN R. HODGES
Graduate School of Medicine: Dr JAMES J. NEUTENS
Tennessee Agricultural Experiment Station: Dr WILLIAM F. BROWN
UT Extension, Univ. Outreach and Continuing Education: Dr TIM CROSS

PROFESSORS

Center for Assessment Research:
McGLASSON, N.

College of Agriculture:
ALLEN, F. L., Plant and Soil Science
ASHBURN, E. L., Plant and Soil Science
BERNARD, E. C., Entomology and Plant Pathology
BLEDSOE, B. L., Agricultural Engineering
BOST, S. C., Entomology and Plant Pathology
BREKKE, C. J., Food Science and Technology
BROOKER, J. R., Agricultural Economics
BUCKNER, E. R., Forestry
BURGESS, E. E., Entomology and Plant Pathology

CALLAHAN, L. M., Ornamental Horticulture and Landscape Design
CARTER, C. E., Jr, Agricultural Extension Education
CHAMBERS, A. Y., Entomology and Plant Pathology
CLELAND, C. L., Agricultural Economics
COFFEY, D. L., Plant and Soil Science
COLLINS, J. L., Food Technology and Science
CONATSER, G. E., Animal Science
CONGER, B. V., Plant and Soil Science
COOK, O. F., Four-H Club
CRATER, G. D., Ornamental Horticulture and Landscape Design
DALY, R. T., Home Economics
DEARDEN, B. L., Forestry
DIMMICK, R. W., Forestry
DRAUGHON, F. A., Food Science and Technology
EASTWOOD, D. B., Agricultural Economics
ENGLISH, B. C., Agricultural Economics
FARMER, C. M., Agricultural Economics
FLINCHUM, W. T., Plant and Soil Science
FOSS, J. E., Plant and Soil Science
FRIBOURG, H. A., Plant and Soil Science
GARLAND, C. D., Agricultural Economics
GERHARDT, R. R., Entomology and Plant Pathology
GILL, W. W., Animal Science
GOAN, H. C., Animal Science
GODKIN, J. D., Animal Science
GRAHAM, E. T., Ornamental Horticulture and Landscape Design
GRAVES, C. R., Plant and Soil Science
GRESSHOFF, P. M., Ornamental Horticulture, Center of Excellence
HADDEN, C. H., Entomology and Plant Pathology
HALL, R. F., Extension Veterinary Medicine
HAYES, R. M., Plant and Soil Science
HENRY, Z. A., Agricultural Engineering
HILL, T. K., Forestry
HOPPER, G. M., Forestry
HOWARD, D. D., Plant and Soil Science
HUNTER, D. L., Agricultural Economics
JENKINS, R. P., Agricultural Economics
KIRKPATRICK, F. D., Animal Science
LAMBDIN, P. L., Entomology and Plant Pathology
LANE, JR, C. D., Animal Science
LESSLY, R. R., Agricultural Extension Education
LEUTHOLD, F. O., Agricultural Economics
LITTLE, R. L., Forestry
LOCKWOOD, D. W., Plant and Soil Science
McDANIEL, G. L., Ornamental Horticulture and Landscape Design
McLEMORE, D. L., Agricultural Economics
MAYS, G. C., Communication
MEADOWS, D. G., Animal Science (Beef)
MELTON, C. C., Food Technology
MELTON, S. L., Food Technology and Science
MILLER, J. K., Animal Science
MILLER, R. D., Plant and Soil Science
MONTGOMERY, M. J., Animal Science
MORRIS, W. C., Food Science and Technology
MOTE, C. R., Agricultural Engineering
MULLINS, C. A., Plant and Soil Science
MUNDY, S. D., Agricultural Economics
NEEL, J. B., Animal Science
NEWMAN, M. A., Entomology and Plant Pathology
OLIVER, S. P., Animal Science
OSTERMEIER, D. M., Forestry
PARK, W. M., Agricultural Economics
PATRICK, C. R., Entomology and Plant Pathology
PELTON, M. R., Forestry
PENFIELD, M. P., Food Technology and Science
PLESS, C. D., Entomology and Plant Pathology

POWELL, B. T., Four-H
RAWLS, E. L., Agricultural Economics
RAY, D. E., Agricultural Economics
REINHARDT, C. A., Communication
RENNIE, J. C., Forestry
REYNOLDS, J. H., Plant and Soil Science
ROBBINS, K. R., Animal Science
ROBERTS, R. K., Agricultural Economics
RUTLEDGE, A. D., Plant and Soil
SAMS, C. E., Plant and Soil Science
SAMS, D. W., Plant and Soil Science
SANDERS, W. L., Statistics
SAXTON, A. M., Statistics
SIMMS, R. H., Animal Science
SMITH, G. F., Agricultural Economics
SOUTHARDS, C. J., Entomology and Plant Pathology
STRANGE, R. J., Forestry
TODD, J. D., Agricultural Extension and Education
TYLER, D. D., Plant and Soil Science
WEST, D. R., Plant and Soil Science
WESTBROOK, E. M., Home Economics and Family Economy
WILHELM, L. R., Agricultural Engineering
WILLIAMS, D. B., Ornamental Horticulture and Landscape Design
WILLIAMSON, H., Agricultural Economics
WILLS, J. B., Agricultural Engineering
WILSON, J. L., Forestry

College of Business Administration:
BARNABY, D. J., Marketing and Transportation
BLACK, H. A., Finance
BOEHM, T. P., Finance
BOHM, R. A., Economics
BOWLBY, R. L., Economics
CADOTTE, E. R., Marketing and Transportation
CARROLL, S. L., Economics
CHANG, H., Economics
CLARK, D. P., Economics
COLE, W. E., Economics
DAVIDSON, P., Economics
DAVIS, F. W., Jr, Marketing and Transportation
DEWHIRST, H. D., Management
DICER, G. N., Marketing and Transportation
FISHER, B. D., Accounting
FOX, W. F., Economics
GARRISON, C. B., Economics
HERRING, H. C., Accounting
HERZOG, H. W., Economics
JAMES, L. R., Management
KIGER, J. E., Accounting
LANGLEY, JR, C. J., Marketing and Transportation
LEE, F.-Y., Economics
MAYHEW, A., Economics
MAYO, J. W., Economics
MENTZER, J. T., Marketing Logistics and Transportation
MUNDY, R. A., Marketing and Transportation
PARR, W. C., Statistics
PATTON, E. P., Marketing and Transportation
PHILIPPATOS, G. C., Finance
PHILPOT, J. W., Statistics
REEVE, J. M., Accounting
ROTH, H. P., Accounting
RUSH, M. C., Management
SANDERS, R. D., Statistics
SCHLOTTMANN, A., Economics
SHRIEVES, R. E., Finance
STAHL, M. J., Business Admin.
STANGA, K. G., Accounting
SYLWESTER, D. L., Statistics
WACHOWICZ, J. M., Finance
WANSLEY, J. W., Finance
WILLIAMS, J. R., Accounting
WOODRUFF, R. B., Marketing Logistics and Transportation

College of Communications:
ASHDOWN, P. G., Journalism
BOWLES, D. A., Journalism
CROOK, J. A., Journalism
EVERETT, G. A., Journalism
HOWARD, H. H., Broadcasting
LITTMANN, M. E., Journalism
MILLER, M. M., Journalism
MOORE, B. A., Broadcasting
SINGLETARY, M. W., Journalism
SMYSER, R. D., Journalism
STANKEY, M. J., Advertising
SWAN, N. R., Jr, Broadcasting
TAYLOR, R. E., Advertising

College of Education:
ALEXANDER, J. E., Holistic Teaching and Learning
ALLISON, C. B., Cultural Studies in Education
BENNER, S. M., Inclusive Early Childhood Education
BLANK, K. J., Inclusive Early Childhood Education
BOGUE, E. G., Leadership Studies
BUTEFISH, W. L., Education in Science and Mathematics
CAMERON, W., Psychoeducational Studies
COLEMAN, L. J., Inclusive Early Childhood Education
DAVIS, A. R., Holistic Teaching and Learning
DAVIS, K. L., Counsellor Education and Counseling Psychology
DESSART, D. J., Curriculum and Instruction
DICKINSON, D. J., Education in Science and Mathematics
DOAK, E. D., Education in Science and Mathematics
FRENCH, R. L., Education in Science and Mathematics
GEORGE, T. W., Educational Administration
HARGIS, C. H., Holistic Teaching and Learning
HARRIS, G., Leadership Studies
HECTOR, M. A., Counsellor Education and Counseling Psychology
HIPPLE, T. W., Holistic Teaching and Learning
HOWLEY, E. T., Exercise Science
HUCK, S. W., Counsellor Education and Counseling Psychology
HUFF, P. E., Holistic Teaching and Learning
HULL, H. N., Language Communication and Humanities Education
JOST, K. J., Holistic Teaching and Learning
KASWORM, C. E., Bureau of Educational Research and Services
KNIGHT, L. N., Holistic Teaching and Learning
KOZAR, A. J., Exercise Science
KRONICK, R. F., Holistic Teaching and Learning
LIEMOHN, W. P., Exercise Science
McCALLUM, R. S., Psychoeducational Studies
McINTYRE, L. D., Education in Science and Mathematics
MALIK, A., Cultural Studies in Education
MEAD, B. J., Cultural Studies in Education
MERTZ, N. T., Leadership Studies
MILLER, J. H., Rehabilitation and Deafness Programs
MORGAN, W. J., Cultural Studies in Education
MYER, JR, M. E., Education in Science and Mathematics
PAUL, M. J., Cultural Studies in Education
PETERS, J. M., Psychoeducational Studies
PETERSON, M. P., Counsellor Education and Counseling Psychology
POPPEN, W. A., Counsellor Education and Counseling Psychology

RAY, J. R., Education in Science and Mathematics
ROCKETT, I. R. H., Exercise Science
ROESKE, C. E., Education in Science and Mathematics
ROWELL, C. G., Educational Administration
SCHINDLER, W. J., Holistic Teaching and Learning
THOMPSON, C. L., Counsellor Education and Counseling Psychology
TURNER, T. N., Holistic Teaching and Learning
UBBEN, G. C., Leadership Studies
WELCH, O. M., Rehabilitation and Deafness Programs
WILEY, P. D., Language Communication and Humanities Education
WILLIAMS, R. L., Psychoeducational Studies
WOODRICK, W. E., Rehabilitation and Deafness Programmes
WRISBERG, C. A., Cultural Studies in Education

College of Engineering:

ALEXEFF, I., Electrical Engineering
ARIMILLI, R. V., Mechanical and Aerospace Engineering
BAILEY, J. M., Electrical Engineering
BAKER, A. J., Engineering Science and Mechanics
BENNETT, R. M., Civil and Environmental Engineering
BIENKOWSKI, P. R., Chemical Engineering
BIRDWELL, J. D., Electrical Engineering
BISHOP, A. O., Jr, Electrical Engineering
BLALOCK, T. V., Electrical Engineering
BODENHEIMER, R. E., Electrical Engineering
BOGUE, D. C., Chemical Engineering
BONTADELLI, J. A., Industrial Engineering
BOSE, B. K., Electrical Engineering
BOULDIN, D. W., Electrical Engineering
BROOKS, JR, C. R., Materials Science and Engineering
BUCHANAN, R. A., Materials Science and Engineering
BURDETTE, E. G., Civil and Environmental Engineering
CARLEY, T. G., Engineering Science and Mechanics
CHATTERJEE, A., Civil and Environmental Engineering
CLARK, E. S., Materials Science and Engineering
CLAYCOMBE, W. W., Industrial Engineering
COUNCE, R. M., Chemical Engineering
CUMMINGS, P. T., Chemical Engineering
DAVIS, W. T., Civil and Environmental Engineering
DEPORTER, E. L., Industrial Engineering
DODDS, H. L., Nuclear Engineering
DRUMM, E. C., Civil and Environmental Engineering
EDMONDSON, A. J., Mechanical and Aerospace Engineering
FELLERS, J. F., Materials Science and Engineering
FORRESTER, J. H., Engineering Science and Mechanics
FRAZIER, G. C., Chemical Engineering
GHOSH, M. M., Civil and Environmental Engineering
GONZALEZ, R. C., Electrical Engineering
GOODPASTURE, D. W., Civil and Environmental Engineering
GREEN, W. L., Electrical Engineering
HANSEN, M. G., Chemical Engineering
HODGSON, J. W., Mechanical and Aerospace Engineering
HOFFMAN, G. W., Electrical Engineering
HUNG, J. C., Electrical Engineering
JENDRUCKO, R. J., Engineering Science and Mechanics
JOHNSON, W. S., Mechanical and Aerospace Engineering
KENNEDY, E. J., Electrical Engineering

KERLIN, T. W., Jr, Nuclear Engineering
KIM, K. H., Engineering Science and Mechanics
KRANE, R. J., Mechanical and Aerospace Engineering
KRIEG, R. D., Engineering Science and Mechanics
LANDES, J. D., Engineering Science and Mechanics
LAWLER, J. S., Electrical Engineering
LIAW, P. K., Materials Science and Engineering
LUNDIN, C. D., Materials Science and Engineering
MILLER, L. F., Nuclear Engineering
MILLER, W. A., Civil and Environmental Engineering
MILLIGAN, M. W., Mechanical and Aerospace Engineering
MOORE, C. F., Chemical Engineering
NEFF, JR, H. P., Electrical Engineering
OLIVER, B. F., Materials Science and Engineering
PACE, M. O., Electrical Engineering
PARANG, M., Mechanical and Aerospace Engineering
PARSONS, J. R., Mechanical and Aerospace Engineering
PEDRAZA, A. J., Materials Science and Engineering
PERONA, J. J., Chemical Engineering
PHILLIPS, P. J., Materials Science and Engineering
PITTS, D. R., Engineering—Admin.
PRADOS, J. W., Chemical Engineering
REED, G. D., Civil and Environmental Engineering
ROBERTS, M. J., Electrical Engineering
ROBINSON, R. B., Civil and Environmental Engineering
ROTH, J. R., Electrical Engineering
SCHMITT, H. W., Industrial Engineering
SCOTT, W. E., Engineering Science and Mechanics
SHANNON, T. E., Nuclear Engineering
SMITH, G. V., Mechanical and Aerospace Engineering
SNIDER, J. N., Industrial Engineering
SOLIMAN, O., Engineering Science and Mechanics
SPECKHART, F. H., Mechanical and Aerospace Engineering
SPRUIELL, J. E., Materials Science and Engineering
SYMONDS, F. W., Electrical Engineering
TOMPKINS, F. D., Engineering Academic
TRIVEDI, M. M., Electrical Engineering
TSCHANTZ, B. A., Civil and Environmental Engineering
UHRIG, R. E., Nuclear Engineering
UPADHYAYA, B. R., Nuclear Engineering
WASSERMAN, J. F., Engineering Science and Mechanics
WEGMANN, F. J., Civil and Environmental Engineering
WEITSMAN, Y. J., Center of Excellence
WILKERSON, H. J., Mechanical and Aerospace Engineering
WILSON, C. C., Mechanical and Aerospace Engineering

College of Human Ecology:

BLANTON, P. W., Child and Family Studies
CAMPBELL, C. P., Human Resources Devt
CARRUTH, B. R., Nutrition
CHEEK, G. D., Human Resources Devt
COAXLEY, C. B., Human Resources Devt
CRAIG, D. G., Human Resources Devt
CUNNINGHAM, J. L., Child and Family Studies
DELONG, A. J., Textiles, Retailing and Interior Design
DRAKE, M. F., Textiles, Retailing and Interior Design
DUCKETT, K. E., Textiles, Retailing and Interior Design

FOX, G. L., Child and Family Studies
GORSKI, J. D., Health, Leisure and Safety Sciences
HAMILTON, C. B., Health, Leisure and Safety Sciences
HANSON, R. R., Human Resources Devt
HASKELL, R. W., Human Resources Devt
HAYES, G. A., Health, Leisure and Safety Sciences
KIRK, R. H., Health, Leisure and Safety Sciences
MORAN, J. D., Admin.
NORDQUIST, V. M., Child and Family Studies
SACHAN, D. S., Nutrition
SKINNER, J. D., Nutrition
STEELE, C., Child and Family Studies
TWARDOSZ, S. L., Child and Family Studies
WADSWORTH, L. C., Textiles, Retailing and Interior Design
WALLACE, B. C., Health, Leisure and Safety Sciences
ZEMEL, M. B., Nutrition

College of Law:

BLAZE, D. A.
COHEN, N. P.
COOK, J. G.
DESSEM, R. L.
HARDIN, P.
HESS, A. M.
KING, JR, J. H.
LECLERQ, F. S.
LLOYD, R. M.
PHILLIPS, J. J.
RIVKIN, D. H.
SOBIESKI, JR, J. L.

College of Liberal Arts:

ADCOCK, J. L., Chemistry
AIKEN, C. S., Geography
ALEXANDRATOS, S. D., Chemistry
ALEXIADES, V., Mathematics
ALIKAKOS, N., Mathematics
ANDERSON, D. F., Mathematics
AQUILA, R. E., Philosophy
ASP, C. W., Audiology and Speech Pathology
BAGBY, R. M., Zoology
BAKER, D. C., Chemistry
BAKER, G. A., Mathematics
BALL, C. H., Music
BARRETTE, P., Romance and Asian Languages
BARTMESS, J. E., Chemistry
BECKER, J. M., Microbiology
BELL, T. L., Geography
BERGERON, P. H., History
BETZ, M., Sociology
BINGHAM, C. R., Physics
BITZAS, G. C., Music
BLACK, J. A., Sociology
BLAIN, S. J., Arts
BLASS, W. E., Physics
BRADY, P. S., Romance and Asian Languages
BRAKKE, P. M., Arts
BRATTON, E. W., English
BREINIG, M., Physics
BRENKERT, G. G., Philosophy
BROADHEAD, T., Geological Sciences
BROCK, JR, J. P., Music
BUGG, W. M., Physics
BUHITE, R. D., History
BULL, W. E., Chemistry
BUNTING, D. L., II, Ecology
BURGDOERFER, J. E., Physics
BURGHARDT, G. M., Psychology
BURSTEIN, A. G., Psychology
CALHOUN, W. H., Psychology
CALLCOTT, T. A., Physics
CAPONETTI, J. D., Botany
CARNEY, P. J., Audiology and Speech Pathology
CARROLL, D. A., English
CARRUTH, J. H., Mathematics
CEBIK, L. B., Philosophy

CHAMBERS, J. Q., Chemistry
CHEN, T. T., Zoology
CHILDERS, R. W., Physics
CHMIELEWSKI, E. V., History
CHURCHICH, J. E., Biochemistry
CLARK, C. E., Mathematics
COBB, C. W., Romance and Asian Languages
COBB, J. C., History
COHEN, C. P., Psychology
COHN, H. O., Physics
COKER, J., Music
COMBS, F. M., Music
CONDO, G. T., Physics
CONWAY, J. B., Mathematics
COOK, K. D., Chemistry
COOKE, T. P., Theatre
COTHRAN, JR, R. M., Theatre
COX, D. R., English
CUNNINGHAM, R. B., Political Science
CUSTER, M., Theatre
CUTLER, E. W., History
DAEHNERT, R. H., Arts
DAVERMAN, R. J., Mathematics
DOBBS, D. E., Mathematics
DONGARRA, J., Computer Science
DRAKE, JR, R. Y., English
DUNGAN, D. L., Religious Studies
DYDAK, J., Mathematics
ECHTERNACHT, A. C., Zoology
EDWARDS, R. B., Philosophy
EGUILUZ, A. G., Physics
ELSTON, S. B., Physics
ENSOR, A. R., English
ETNIER, D. A., Zoology
FALSETTI, J. S., Arts
FARRIS, W. W., History
FAULKNER, C. H., Anthropology
FIELD, R. C., Theatre
FINGER, J. R., History
FINNERAN, R. J., English
FITZGERALD, M. R., Political Science
FORESTA, R., Geography
FOX, K., Physics
FRANDSEN, H., Mathematics
GANT, M. M., Political Science
GEORGHIOU, S., Physics
GESELL, G. C., Classics
GOLDENSTEIN, M. B., Arts
GORMAN, R., Political Science
GOSLEE, N. M., English
GRABER, G. C., Philosophy
GRIMM, F. A., Chemistry
GROSS, L. J., Mathematics
GUIDRY, M. W., Physics
GUIOCHON, G. A., Chemistry
HAAS, A. G., History
HALLAM, T. G., Mathematics
HANDEL, M. A., Zoology
HANDEL, S. J., Psychology
HANDELSMAN, M. H., Romance and Asian Languages
HANDLER, L., Psychology
HANDLER, T., Physics
HAO, YEN-PING, History
HARRIS, W. F., Biology
HART, E. L., Physics
HASTINGS, D. W., Sociology
HATCHER, R. D., Zoology
HEFFERNAN, T. J., English
HEFLIN, W. H., Romance and Asian Languages
HICKOK, L. G., Botany
HINTON, D. B., Mathematics
HOLTON, R. W., Botany
HOOD, T. C., Sociology
HUGHES, K. W., Botany
HUSCH, L. S., Mathematics
JACKSON, C. O., Admin.
JACOBS, K. A., Music
JACOBSON, H. C., Admin.
JANTZ, R. L., Anthropology
JEON, K. W., Zoology
JOHANNSON, K., Mathematics
JONES, W. H., Psychology
JORDAN, G. S., Mathematics

JOSHI, J. G., Biochemistry
JOY, D. C., Zoology
JUMPER, S. R., Geography
KABALKA, G. W., Chemistry
KALLET, M., English
KAMYCHKOV, I. A., Physics
KARAKASHIAN, O., Mathematics
KEELING, K. A., Music
KEENE, M. L., English
KELLY, R. M., English
KENNEDY, J. R., Zoology
KENNEDY, W. C., Arts
KLEINFELTER, D. C., Chemistry
KLIPPEL, W. E., Anthropology
KOPP, O. C., Geology
KOVAC, J. D., Chemistry
LABOTKA, T. C., Geological Sciences
LANGSTON, M. A., Computer Science
LAWLER, J. E., Psychology
LAWLER, K., Psychology
LEE, B. S., Arts
LEGGETT, B. J., English
LEKI, I., English
LELAND, W. E., Arts
LENHART, S. M., Mathematics
LESTER, L. W., Admin.
LEVY, K. D., Romance and Asian Languages
LINGE, D. E., Religious Studies
LIVINGSTON, P. R., Arts
LOFARO, M. A., English
LUBAR, J., Psychology
LYONS, W., Political Science
MACCABE, J. A., Zoology
MCCLELLAND, D. K., Music
MCCONNEL, R. M., Mathematics
MCCORMICK, J. F., Ecology
MCCRACKEN, G. F., Zoology
MACEK, J. H., Physics
MCSWEEN, H. Y., Geological Sciences
MAGDEN, N. E., Arts
MAGID, L. J., Chemistry
MAGID, R. M., Chemistry
MAHAN, G. D., Physics
MALAND, C., English
MALONE, JR, J. C., Psychology
MARSH, F. H., Arts
MARTINSON, F. H., Arts
MASHBURN, R. R., Speech and Theatre
MATHEWS, H. T., Mathematics
MISRA, K. C., Geology
MONTIE, T. C., Microbiology
MONTY, K. J., Biochemistry
MOORE, M. C., Music
MOORE, R. N., Microbiology
MOSER, H. D., History
MULLIN, B. C., Botany
NABELEK, A. K., Audiology and Speech Pathology
NAZAREWICZ, W., Physics
NORMAN, R. V., Religious Studies
NORTHINGTON, D. B., Music
PAGNI, R. M., Chemistry
PAINTER, L. R., Physics
PEACOCK, D., Arts
PEDERSON, D. M., Music
PEGG, D. J., Physics
PENNER, A. R., English
PETERSEN, R. H., Botany
PETERSON, H. A., Audiology and Speech Pathology
PETERSON, J. R., Chemistry
PIMM, S. L., Zoology
PLAAS, H., Political Science
PLOCH, D. R., Sociology
PLUMMER, E. W., Physics
POLLIO, H. R., Psychology
POORE, J. H., Computer Science
POSTOW, C. B., Philosophy
PULSIPHER, L. M., Geography
QUINN, J. J., Physics
RAJPUT, B. S., Mathematics
RALSTON, B. A., Geography
REESE, J. E., English
REYNOLDS, C. H., Religious Studies
RIECHERT, S. E., Zoology

RIESING, T. J., Arts
RIGGSBY, W. S., Microbiology
RIVERA-RODAS, O., Romance and Asian Languages
ROMEISER, J. B., Romance and Asian Languages
ROSINSKI, J., Mathematics
ROTH, L. E., Zoology
RUTLEDGE, H. C., Classics
SAMEJIMA, F., Psychology
SANDERS, N. J., English
SAUDARGAS, R. S., Psychology
SAVAGE, D. C., Psychology
SAYLER, G. S., Microbiology
SCHAEFER, P. W., Mathematics
SCHEB, J. M., Political Science
SCHILLING, E., Botany
SCHMUDDE, T. H., Geography
SCHWEITZER, G. K., Chemistry
SCURA, D. M., English
SELLIN, I. A., Physics
SEPANIAK, M. J., Chemistry
SERBIN, S. M., Mathematics
SHIH, C. C., Physics
SHIVERS, C. A., Zoology
SHOVER, N. E., Sociology
SHURR, W. H., English
SILVERSTEIN, B., Audiology and Speech Pathology
SIMPSON, H. C., Mathematics
SMITH, T. A., Political Science
SMITH, W. O., Botany
SONI, K., Mathematics
SONI, R. P., Mathematics
SORENSEN, S. P., Physics
STACEY, G., Microbiology
STEPHENS, JR, O. H., Political Science
STEPHENSON, K., Mathematics
STEWART, F. C., Arts
STUTZENBERGER, D. R., Music
SUNDBERG, C., Mathematics
SUNDELL, S. E., Physics
SUNDSTROM, E. D., Psychology
TAYLOR, L. A., Geology
THISTLETHWAITE, M. B., Mathematics
THOMAS, J. C., English
THOMASON, M. G., Computer Science
THOMPSON, JR, J. R., Physics
THONNARD, N., Science Alliance
TIPPS, A. W., Music
TRAHERN, J. B., English
TRAVIS, C. B., Psychology
UNGS, T. D., Political Science
VAN DE VATE, JR, D., Philosophy
VANHOOK, A., Chemistry
VAUGHN, G. L., Zoology
WADE, W. R., II, Mathematics
WAGNER, C. G., Mathematics
WAHLER, R. G., Psychology
WALKER, K. R., Geology
WALLACE, S. E., Sociology
WALNE, P. L., Botany
WARD, B. F. L., Physics
WARD, R. C., Computer Science
WASHBURN, Y. M., Romance and Asian Languages
WEHRY, E. L., Chemistry
WEIR, A., English
WELBORN, D. M., Political Science
WHEELER, T. V., English
WHEELER, W. B., History
WHITE, D. C., Microbiology
WHITSON, G. L., Zoology
WICKS, W. D., Biochemistry
WILLIAMS, T. F., Chemistry
WOODS, C., Chemistry
WUNDERLICH, B., Chemistry
YATES, S. A., Arts
ZAK, T., Mathematics
ZHANG, J. Y., Physics

College of Veterinary Medicine:

BRACE, J. J., Administration
BRIAN, D. A., Microbiology and Veterinary Medicine

BRIGHT, R. M., Small Animal Clinical Sciences
DORN, A. S., Small Animal Clinical Sciences
EDWARDS, D. F., Pathology
FARKAS, W. R., Comparative Medicine
GREEN, E. M., Large Animal Clinical Sciences
HENRY, R. W., Animal Science
HOPKINS, F. M., Large Animal Clinical Sciences
KRAHWINKEL, D. J., Jr, Small Animal Clinical Sciences
LEGENDRE, A. M., Small Animal Clinical Sciences
McCORD, S. P., Comparative Medicine
McDONALD, T. P., Animal Science and Veterinary Medicine
McGAVIN, M. D., Pathology
OLIVER, J. W., Comparative Medicine
PATTON, C. S., Pathology
POTGIETER, L. N. D., Comparative Medicine
ROUSE, B. T., Microbiology and Veterinary Medicine
SCHULLER, H. M., Pathology
SHULL, R. M., Pathology
SHULTZ, T. W., Animal Science and Veterinary Medicine
SIMS, M. H., Animal Science and Veterinary Medicine
SLAUSON, D. O., Pathology

Energy, Environment and Resources Center:
COLGLAZIER, E. M.

Graduate School of Biomedical Sciences:
OLINS, A. L.
OLINS, D. E.
POPP, R. A.

Graduate School of Library and Information Science:
ESTES, G. E.
TENOPIR, C.

Graduate School of Planning:
JOHNSON, D. A.
PROCHASKA, J. M.
SPENCER, J. A.

Graduate School of Social Work:
CETINGOK, M.
FAVER, C. A.
GLISSON, C. A.
HIRAYAMA, H.
NOOE, R. M.
RUBINSTEIN, H.

Learning Research Center:
HUMPHREYS, WALTER L.

Library:
BAYNE, P. S.
BEST, R. A., Law
CRAWFORD, M. F.
FELDER-HOEHNE, F. H.
GRADY, A. M.
LECLERCQ, A. W.
PHILLIPS, L. L.
PIQUET, D. C., Law
RADER, J. C.

School of Architecture:
ANDERSON, G.
GRIEGER, F.
KELSO, R. M.
KERSAVAGE, J. A.
KINZY, S. A.
LAUER, W. J.
LESTER, A. J.
LIZON, P.
ROBINSON, M. A.
RUDD, J. W.
SHELL, W. S.
WATSON, J. S.
WODEHOUSE, L. M.

School of Nursing:
ALLIGOOD, M. R.
GOODFELLOW, D. H.

MOZINGO, J.
THOMAS, S. P.

Space Institute:
ANTAR, B. N.
COLLINS, F. G.
CRATER, H. W.
CRAWFORD, L. W.
CRAWFORD, R. A.
FLANDRO, G. A.
GARRISON, G. W.
KEEFER, D. R.
KUPERSCHMIDT, B. A.
LEWIS, J. W.
LO, C.
McCAY, M. H.
PALUDAN, C. T. N.
PETERS, C. E.
PUJOL, A.
SCHULZ, R. J.
SHAHROKHI, F.
SHETH, A. C.
WU, J. M.

University of Tennessee at Martin

Martin, TN 38328
Telephone: (731) 881-7000
E-mail: chancellor@utm.edu
Internet: www.utm.edu
Founded 1900 as Hall-Moody Institute, current name adopted 1967
State control
Academic year: August to May
Chancellor: Dr THOMAS A. RAKES
Provost and Vice-Chancellor for Academic Affairs: Dr E. JERALD OGG, JR
Vice-Chancellor for Finance and Admin.: NANCY YARBROUGH
Vice-Chancellor for Student Affairs: Dr MARGARET Y. TOSTON
Vice-Chancellor for Univ. Advancement: ANDREW WILSON
Registrar: BRANDY D. CARTMELL
Library Dir: CHARLES JULIAN
Library of 500,000 vols, incl. ebooks, 8,000 print and online journals
Number of students: 7,423

DEANS

College of Agriculture and Applied Sciences: Dr TODD WINTERS
College of Business and Global Affairs: Dr ROSS DICKENS
College of Education, Health and Behavioural Sciences: Dr GAIL STEPHENS
College of Engineering and Natural Sciences: Dr RICHARD J. HELGESON
College of Humanities and Fine Arts: Prof. Dr LYNN M. ALEXANDER
Dept of Agriculture, Geosciences and Natural Resources: Dr JOEY MEHLHORN
Graduate Studies: Prof. Dr VICTORIA S. SENG

UNIVERSITY OF THE SOUTH

735 University Ave, Sewanee, TN 37383-1000
Telephone: (931) 598-1000
E-mail: admiss@sewanee.edu
Internet: www.sewanee.edu
Founded 1858
Private control
Academic year: August to May
Pres. and Vice-Chancellor: Dr JOHN M. McCARDELL, JR
Provost: Dr JOHN R. SWALLOW
Vice-Pres. for Univ. Relations: JAY FISHER
Treas.: JERRY FORSTER
Dean of College: JOHN J. GATTA, JR
Dean of Students: ERIC HARTMAN
Dean of Admission and Financial Aid: LEE ANN M. AFTON-BACKLUND
Registrar: PAUL G. WILEY, II

Univ. Librarian and Assoc. Provost for Information Technology Services: Dr VICKI SELLS
Library of 749,105 vols
Number of teachers: 170 (135 full-time, 35 part-time)
Number of students: 1,550 (1,470 undergraduate, 80 graduate)
Publications: *Sewanee Review*, *Sewanee Theological Review*

DEANS

College of Arts and Sciences: Dr JOHN J. GATTA
School of Theology: Rev. Dr WILLIAM S. STAFFORD

VANDERBILT UNIVERSITY

211 Kirkland Hall, Nashville, TN 37240
Telephone: (615) 322-7311
E-mail: admissions@vanderbilt.edu
Internet: www.vanderbilt.edu
Founded 1873
Private control
Academic year: August to April
Chancellor: Prof. NICHOLAS ZEPPOS
Provost and Vice-Chancellor for Academic Affairs: (vacant)
Vice-Chancellor for Admin.: JERRY FIFE
Vice-Chancellor for Devt and Alumni Relations: SUSIE STALCUP
Vice-Chancellor for Finance and Chief Financial Officer: BRETT SWEET
Vice-Chancellor for Health Affairs: JEFFREY BALSER
Vice-Chancellor for Univ. Affairs and Athletics, Gen. Counsel and Sec. of the Univ.: DAVID WILLIAMS, II
Vice-Provost for Enrolment and Dean of Admissions: DOUGLAS L. CHRISTIANSEN
Dean of Libraries: CONNIE VINITA DOWELL
Library of 2,607,058 vols (incl. books and serial backfiles), 78,041 serial subscriptions, 69,255 audiovisual items
Number of teachers: 4,000 (3,556 full-time, 445 part-time)
Number of students: 12,900 (6,840 undergraduate, 6,060 graduate and professional)
Publications: *Acorn Chronicle* (online — www.vanderbilt.edu/magazines/acorn-chronicle), *Alumniexclusive* (online — www.vanderbilt.edu/alumni/alumni-exclusive), *Arts and Science* (online —www.vanderbilt.edu/magazines/arts-and-science), *Peabody Reflector* (2 a year, online — www.vanderbilt.edu/magazines/peabody-reflector), *The Spire* (online —www.vanderbilt.edu/alumni/magazines/spire), *Vanderbilt Business* (online — www.vanderbilt.edu/magazines/vanderbilt-business), *Vanderbilt Engineering* (online —www.vanderbilt.edu/magazines/vanderbilt-engineering), *Vanderbilt Lawyer* (online —law.vanderbilt.edu/alumni/alumni-publications/index.aspx), *Vanderbilt Magazine*, *Vanderbilt Medicine* (online (www.mc.vanderbilt.edu/vanderbiltmedicine)), *Vanderbilt Nurse* (online (www.vanderbilt.edu/vanderbiltnurse))

DEANS

Blair School of Music: Prof. Dr MARK WAIT
College of Arts and Science: Dr CAROLYN DENVER
Divinity School: Prof. Dr JAMES HUDNUT-BEUMLER
George Peabody College: Dr CAMILLA P. BENBOW
Graduate School: DENNIS G. HALL
Ingram Commons: FRANK WCISLO
Law School: Prof. Dr CHRIS GUTHRIE
Owen Graduate School of Management: Prof. Dr JAMES BRADFORD

School of Engineering: Prof. Dr KENNETH F. GALLOWAY
School of Medicine: Dr JEFFREY R. BALSER
School of Nursing: Prof. Dr COLLEEN CONWAY-WELCH

PROFESSORS

ABKOWITZ, M. D., Civil and Environmental Engineering
ABUMRAD, N. N., Surgery
AHNER, J., Mathematics
ALBRIDGE, R. G., Physics and Astronomy
ALDROUBI, A., Mathematics
ALLEN, G. S., Neurological Surgery
ARMSTRONG, R. N., Biochemistry
ARTEAGA, C. L., Medicine
ATACK, J., Economics
ATKINSON, III, J. B., Pathology
AURBACH, M. L., Art and Art History
AVISON, M. J., Radiology and Radiological Sciences
BADER, D. M., Medicine
BALDWIN, H. S., Paediatrics
BALDWIN, L. V., Religious Studies
BALL, C. A., Management
BALLARD, D. W., Microbiology and Immunology
BALSER, J. R., Anaesthesiology
BARRY, B., Management
BARSKY, R. F., French and Italian
BASU, P. K., Civil and Environmental Engineering
BEAUCHAMP, R. D., Surgery
BELL, V. M., English
BELTON, R., Law
BENBOW, C. P., Psychology and Human Development
BERNARD, G. R., Medicine
BESS, F. H., Hearing and Speech Sciences
BETH, A. H., Molecular Physiology and Biophysics
BIAGGIONI, I. O., Medicine
BICKMAN, L., Psychology and Human Development
BISCH, D., Mathematics
BLACKBURN, J. O., Management
BLACKETT, R., History
BLAKE, R., Psychology
BLAKELY, R. D., Pharmacology
BLANNING, R. W., Management
BLOCH, F. S., Law
BOEHM, F. H., Obstetrics and Gynaecology
BÖER, G. B., Management
BOLTON, R., Management
BOND, E., Economics
BONDS, III, A. B., Electrical Engineering and Computer Science
BOOTH, W. J., Political Science
BORNHOP, D. J., Chemistry
BOYD, S. B., Oral and Maxillofacial Surgery
BRANDON, M. E., Law
BRANDT, S. J., Medicine
BRASH, A. R., Pharmacology
BRAU, C. A., Physics and Astronomy
BRAXTON, J., Leadership, Policy and Organizations
BRESSMAN, L. S., Law
BREYER, M. D., Medicine
BROADIE, K., Biological Sciences
BROWN, R. L., Law
BRUCE, J. W., Law
BUERHAUS, P. I., Nursing
BURK, R. F., Medicine
BURNETT, L. S., Obstetrics and Gynaecology
BURNS, J. P., Divinity
BURR, I. M., Paediatrics
BYRD, III, B. F., Medicine
CADZOW, J. A., Electrical Engineering and Computer Science
CAMARATA, S. M., Hearing and Speech Sciences
CAPDEVILA, J. H., Medicine
CAPRIOLI, R. M., Biochemistry
CARBONE, D. P., Medicine
CARPENTER, G. F., Biochemistry

CARROLL, JR, F. E., Radiology and Radiological Sciences
CARTER, C. E., Biological Sciences
CASAGRANDE, V. A., Cell Biology
CHALKLEY, G. R., Molecular Physiology and Biophysics
CHANEY, P. K., Management
CHAZIN, W. J., Biochemistry
CHERRINGTON, A. D., Molecular Physiology and Biophysics
CHRISTIE, W. G., Management
CHRISTMAN, J. W., Medicine
CHURCHILL, L. R., Medicine
CLAYTON, E., Paediatrics
CLAYTON, J. B., English
COBB, P. A., Teaching and Learning
COFFEY, R. J., Jr, Medicine
COLE, D. A., Psychology and Human Development
COLLINS, R. D., Pathology
COMPAS, B., Psychology and Human Development
CONLEY, J., Economics
CONN, P. J., Pharmacology
CONTURE, E. G., Hearing and Speech Sciences
CONWAY-WELCH, C. M., Nursing
COOK, G. E., Electrical Engineering and Computer Science
CORBIN, J. D., Molecular Physiology and Biophysics
CORDRAY, D. S., Psychology and Human Development
CORN, A. L., Special Education
CORNFIELD, D. B., Sociology
COTTON, R. B., Paediatrics
COVINGTON, R. N., Law
CROOKE, III, P. S., Mathematics
CROWSON, R., Leadership, Policy and Organizations
CUMMINGS, P., Chemical Engineering
D'AQUILA, R. T., Medicine
DAFT, R. L., Management
DALLEY, A. F., Cell Biology
DAMON, W. W., Economics
DANZO, B. J., Obstetrics and Gynaecology
DAUGHETY, A. F., Economics
DAVIDSON, J. L., Electrical Engineering and Computer Science
DAVIDSON, J. M., Pathology
DAVIS, S. N., Medicine
DAVIS, T. M., English
DEFELICE, L. J., Pharmacology
DELBEKE, D., Radiology and Radiation Sciences
DEMAREST, A. A., Anthropology
DERMODY, T. S., Paediatrics
DESHPANDE, J. K., Paediatrics
DESPREZ, R. M., Nursing
DEUTCH, A. Y., Psychiatry
DEY, S. K., Paediatrics
DIBENEDETTO, E., Mathematics
DICKERSON, D. C., History
DILLEHAY, T. D., Anthropology
DILTS, D., Electrical Engineering and Computer Science
DITTUS, R. S., Medicine
DOKECKI, P. R., Human and Organizational Development
DOWDY, L. W., Electrical Engineering and Computer Science
DOWNING, J. W., Anaesthesiology
DOYLE, D. H., History
DREWS, R., Classical Studies
DRINKWATER, JR, D. C., Cardiac and Thoracic Surgery
DRISKILL, R. A., Economics
DuBOIS, JR, R. N., Medicine
DUNCAVAGE, J. A., Otolaryngology
DUPONT, W. D., Preventative Medicine
DYKENS, E. A., Psychology and Human Development
EAKIN, M. C., History
EBNER, F. F., Psychology
EDELMAN, P. H., Mathematics
EDEN, B., Economics

EDWARDS, K. M., Paediatrics
ELLEDGE, W. P., English
ELLIOTT, S. N., Special Education
ELY, J. W., History
ELY, J. W., Law
ENTERLINE, L., English
ENTMAN, S. S., Obstetrics and Gynaecology
EPSTEIN, J. A., History
ERNST, D. J., Physics and Astronomy
EXTON, J. H., Molecular Physiology and Biophysics
FAN, Y., Economics
FANNING, E. H., Biological Sciences
FARRAN, D., Teaching and Learning
FAZIO, S., Medicine
FELZMAN, L. C., Physics and Astronomy
FENICHEL, G. M., Neurology
FITZ, E. E., Spanish and Portuguese
FITZPATRICK, J. M., Electrical Engineering and Computer Science
FLEETWOOD, D. M., Electrical Engineering and Computer Science
FLEISCHER, A. C., Radiology and Radiological Sciences
FLEXNER, J. M., Medicine
FOGO, A. B., Pathology
FOLGARAIT, L., Art and Art History
FOSTER, J. E., Economics
FOX, R., Psychology
FRANKS, J. J., Psychology
FREEMAN, M. L., Radiation Oncology
FREEMON, F. R., Neurology
FRIEDMAN, E. H., Spanish and Portuguese
FRIEDMAN, R. A., Management
FROMENT-MEURICE, M., French and Italian
FRYD, V. G., Art and Art History
FUCHS, D. H., Special Education
FUCHS, L. S., Special Education
FURBISH, D. J., Geology
GABBE, S. G., Obstetrics and Gynaecology
GAFFNEY, F. A., Medical Admin.
GALLOWAY, K. F., Electrical Engineering and Computer Science
GALLOWAY, JR, R. L., Biomedical Engineering
GARBER, J., Psychology and Human Development
GAY, V. P., Religious Studies
GEE, E. G., Law
GEER, J., Political Science
GEORGE, JR, A. L., Medicine
GIRGUS, S. B., English
GIUSE, N. B., Biomedical Informatics
GOLDBERG, J. C., Law
GOLDENRING, J. R., Surgery
GOLDRING, E., Leadership, Policy and Organizations
GOODMAN, L. E., Philosophy
GORDON, J., Nursing
GORE, J. C., Radiology and Radiological Sciences
GOTTFRIED, R. K., English
GOULD, K. L., Cell and Developmental Biology
GOULD, M. I., Mathematics
GRAHAM, JR, G. J., Political Science
GRAHAM, JR, T. P., Paediatrics
GRANNER, D. K., Molecular Physiology and Biophysics
GRANTHAM, D. W., Hearing and Speech Sciences
GREEN, N. E., Orthopaedics and Rehabilitation
GREENE, J. W., Paediatrics
GREER, J. P., Medicine
GREGOR, T. A., Anthropology
GRIFFIN, L. J., Sociology and Political Science
GRIFFIN, M. R., Preventive Medicine
GUENGERICH, F. P., Biochemistry
GUTHRIE, C. P., Law
GUTHRIE, J. W., Leadership, Policy and Organizations
HAGLUND, R. F., Physics and Astronomy
HAHN, B., German and Slavic Language
HAINES, J. L., Molecular Physiology and Biophysics
HALL, D., Physics and Astronomy

SANDERS-BUSH, E., Pharmacology
SANDLER, H. M., Psychology and Human Development
SANDLER, M. P., Radiology and Radiological Sciences
SAPIR, M., Mathematics
SASSON, J., Divinity
SCHAFFNER, W., Preventative Medicine
SCHALL, J. D., Psychology
SCHAUBLE, L., Teaching and Learning
SCHERRER, R. J., Physics and Astronomy
SCHLUNK, H. J., Law
SCHMIDT, D., Electrical Engineering and Computer Science
SCHNELLE, K. B., Chemical Engineering
SCHOENBLUM, J. A., Law
SCHRIMPF, R., Electrical Engineering and Computer Science
SCHUENING, F. G., Medicine
SCHULMAN, G., Medicine
SCHUMAKER, L. L., Mathematics
SCHWARTZ, H. S., Orthopaedics and Rehabilitation
SCHWARTZ, T. A., History
SCUDDER, G. D., Management
SEGOVIA, F. F., Divinity
SELIGSON, M. A., Political Science
SERGENT, J. S., Medicine
SEVIN, D. H. O., German and Slavic Languages
SHACK, R. B., Plastic Surgery
SHELTON, R. C., Psychiatry
SHENAI, J., Paediatrics
SHEPHERD, V. L., Pathology
SHERRY, S., Law
SHIAVI, R. G., Biomedical Engineering
SHU, X. O., Medicine
SHYR, Y., Preventative Medicine
SIAMI, G., Medicine
SIEGFRIED, J. J., Economics
SINGLETON, C. K., Biological Sciences
SLOVIS, C. M., Emergency Medicine
SMITH, H. W., History
SMITH, JR, J. A., Urologic Surgery
SMITH, W. P., Psychology
SNELL, JR, J. D., Medicine
SODERQUIST, L. D., Law
SOSMAN, J. A., Medicine
SPENGLER, D. M., Orthopaedics and Rehabilitation
SPICKARD, JR, W. A., Medicine
SPINDLER, K. P., Orthopaedics and Rehabilitation
SRIRAM, S., Neurology
STAHLMAN, M. T., Paediatrics
STEAD, W. W., Medicine
STEIGER, J. H., Psychology and Human Development
STEIN, R. W., Molecular Physiology and Biophysics
STEINBERG, R., Sociology
STERNBERG, P., Ophthalmology and Visual Sciences
STOLL, H. R., Management
STONE, M. P., Chemistry
STONE, W. J., Medicine
STONE, W. L., Paediatrics
STRANGE, K., Anaesthesiology
STRAUSS, A. M., Mechanical Engineering
STRAUSS, A. W., Paediatrics
STRICKLIN, G. P., Medicine
STUBBS, G. J., Biological Sciences
STUHR, J. J., Philosophy
SUNDELL, H. W., Paediatrics
SWAIN, C. M., Law
SWIFT, L. L., Pathology
SYVERUD, J., Electrical Engineering and Computer Science
SZTIPANOVITS, J., Electrical and Computer Engineering
TAM, J. P., Microbiology and Immunology
TANNER, R. D., Chemical Engineering
TATE, C. N., Political Science
TELLINGHUISEN, J., Chemistry
TELOH, H. A., Philosophy
THOITS, P. A., Sociology

THOMAS, J. W., II, Medicine
THOMAS, R. S., Law
THOMPSON, P. W., Teaching and Learning
THOMPSON, R. B., Law
TICHI, C., English
TOLK, N. H., Physics and Astronomy
TRANGENSTEIN, P., Nursing
TULIPAN, N. B., Neurological Surgery
UMAR, S. A., Physics and Astronomy
USNER, D. H., History
VAN KAER, L., Microbiology and Immunology
VAUGHAN, D. E., Medicine
VICTOR, B., Management
WAGNER, C., Biochemistry
WALDEN, T. A., Psychology and Human Development
WALKER, L. S., Paediatrics
WALLER, N., Psychology and Human Development
WALLSTON, K. A., Nursing
WANG, P., Economics
WANG, T. G., Mechanical Engineering
WARD, P. A., French and Italian
WASHINGTON, M. K., Pathology
WASSERMAN, D. H., Molecular Physiology and Biophysics
WASSERSTEIN, D. J., History
WATERMAN, M. R., Biochemistry
WEBB, G. F., Mathematics
WEBSTER, M. S., Physics and Astronomy
WEIL, P. A., Molecular Physiology and Biophysics
WEILER, T. J., Physics and Astronomy
WEINER, E. E., Nursing
WELLER, R. A., Electrical Engineering and Computer Science
WENTE, S. R., Cell and Development Biology
WEYMARK, J. A., Economics
WIKSWO, J. P., Physics and Astronomy, Molecular Physiology and Biophysics
WILEY, R. G., Neurology
WILKINSON, G. R., Pharmacology
WILSON, J. R., Medicine
WILTSHIRE, S. F., Classical Studies
WOLERY, M., Special Education
WONG, K. K., Leadership, Policy and Organizations
WOOD, A. J., Medicine
WOOD, D. C., Philosophy
WRENN, K. D., Emergency Medicine
WRIGHT, C. V., Cell and Developmental Biology
WRIGHT, P. F., Paediatrics
XIA, D., Mathematics
YODER, P. J., Special Education
YU, G., Mathematics
ZEPPOS, N. S., Jr, Law
ZHENG, W., Medicine
ZUTTER, M. M., Pathology

VICTORY UNIVERSITY

255 N Highland St, Memphis, TN 38111

Telephone: (901) 320-9777
E-mail: admissions@victory.edu
Internet: www.victory.edu

Founded 1944 as Mid-South Bible Center, present status 1958, present name 2010
Private control
Academic year: August to August

Depts of arts and sciences, behavioural sciences, bible and theology, business, education

Pres.: Dr SHIRLEY ROBINSON PIPPINS
Provost: Dr SHERYL WEEMS
Vice-Pres. for Academic and Student Affairs: BILL ALEXANDER
Vice-Pres. for Financial Affairs: TROY R. GRAHAM
Vice-Pres. for Student Enrolment: DARREL HANBURY
Dir of Student Devt: BRIAN DUFFY
Registrar: SEAN SCOTT
Library Dir: PAM B. WALKER

Library of 56,000 vols (incl. books, bound journals, video cassettes, DVDs, tapes, CDs, microfiche), 64 periodicals
Number of teachers: 65 (35 full-time, 30 adjunct)
Number of students: 1,110

TEXAS

ABILENE CHRISTIAN UNIVERSITY

ACU Box 29100, Abilene, TX 79699-9100

Telephone: (325) 674-2000
E-mail: info@admissions.acu.edu
Internet: www.acu.edu

Founded 1906 as Childers Classical Institute, current name adopted 1976
Private control
Academic year: August to May

Pres.: Dr PHIL SCHUBERT
Chancellor: Dr ROYCE MONEY
Provost: Dr ROBERT RHODES
Vice-Pres.: Dr MAC McCALEB
Exec. Vice-Pres.: Dr ALLISON GARRETT
Vice-Pres. for Advancement: JIM ORR
Registrar and Dir for Academic Records: Dr ERIC GUMM
Dean for Library and Information Resources: Dr JOHN WEAVER

Library of 557,006 vols, 221,531 ebooks
Number of teachers: 291
Number of students: 4,241
Publication: *ACU Today Magazine*

DEANS

College of Arts and Sciences: Dr GREG STRAUGHN
College of Biblical Studies: Dr KEN CUKROWSKI
College of Business Administration: Dr RICK LYTLE
College of Education and Human Services: Dr LLOYD GOLDSMITH
Graduate School: Dr STEPHEN JOHNSON
Honors College: Dr JASON MORRIS
School of Nursing: Dr BECKY HAMMACK

ARLINGTON BAPTIST COLLEGE

3001 W Division St, Arlington, TX 76012

Telephone: (817) 461-8741
E-mail: info@abconline.org
Internet: www.abconline.org

Founded 1927 as Fundamental Bible Institute, present name and location 1955
Private control
Academic year: August to May

Divs incl. biblical/theological studies, general studies, professional studies

Pres.: Dr D. L. MOODY
Academic Dean: Dr HELEN SULLIVAN
Dean for Students: EMIL BALLIET
Registrar: JANIE TAYLOR

Library of 30,000 vols

ART INSTITUTE OF HOUSTON

4140 Southwest Freeway, Houston, TX 77027

Telephone: (713) 623-2040
E-mail: aihadm@aii.edu
Internet: www.artinstitutes.edu/houston

Founded 1965 as Houston School of Commercial Art, present name 1978
Private control
Academic year: October to September

Part of art institutes system of schools; areas of study: culinary, design, fashion, general education, media arts

Pres.: LARRY HORN
Dean for Academic Affairs: KENNETH PASCAL
Dean for Student Affairs: JOHN WILLIS

Sr Dir for Admissions: BOBBI RABINE
Dir for Admin. and Student Financial Services: THOMAS KUPER
Dir for Institutional Effectiveness and Research: CHARLES LARTEY
Registrar: KIMBERLY JOYNER
Dir for Library: ELENE GEDEVANISHVILI
Library of 30,916 vols, 160 periodicals
Number of students: 2,000

AUSTIN COLLEGE

900 N Grand Ave, Sherman, TX 75090-4400
Telephone: (903) 813-2000
E-mail: admission@austincollege.edu
Internet: www.austincollege.edu

Founded 1849
Private control
Academic year: September to June

Pres.: Dr MARJORIE HASS
Vice-Pres. for Academic Affairs and Dean for the Faculty: MICHAEL A. IMHOFF
Vice-Pres. for Business Affairs: HEIDI ELLIS
Vice-Pres. for Institutional Advancement: BROOKS HULL
Vice-Pres. for Institutional Enrolment: NAN DAVIS
Vice-Pres. for Student Affairs and Athletics: TIMOTHY P. MILLERICK
Dean for Student Services: Dr ROSE ROTHMEIER
Registrar: TEX RUEGG
Library Dir: JOHN WEST
Library of 200,000 vols, 4,000 media items
Number of teachers: 120 (90 full-time, 30 part-time)
Number of students: 1,300

DEANS

Humanities Division: Prof. Dr PATRICK DUFFEY
Sciences Division: Dr STEVE GOLDSMITH
Social Sciences Division: Prof. Dr JERRY JOHNSON

AUSTIN GRADUATE SCHOOL OF THEOLOGY

7640 Guadalupe St, Austin, TX 78752-1333
Telephone: (512) 476-2772
E-mail: info@austingrad.edu
Internet: www.austingrad.edu

Founded 1917 as Bible Chair at Univ. of Texas, present name 2001
Private control
Academic year: August to August

Chancellor: DAVID WORLEY
Vice-Chancellor: JACK WRIGHT
Pres.: STANLEY G. REID
Vice-Pres.: DAVE ARTHUR
Dir for Devt: NEIL HANEY
Dean for Students: R. MARK SHIPP
Registrar: CELESTE SCARBOROUGH
Dir for Library: M. TODD HALL
Library of 30,000 vols, 135 journal subscriptions
Number of students: 100
Publication: *Christian Studies*

AUSTIN PRESBYTERIAN THEOLOGICAL SEMINARY

100 E 27th St, Austin, TX 78705-5711
Telephone: (512) 404-4800

Internet: www.austinseminary.edu

Founded 1902
Private control
Academic year: January to May

Pres.: Rev. THEODORE J. WARDLAW
Vice-Pres. for Admissions: JOHN H. BARDEN
Vice-Pres. for Business Affairs: KURT A. GABBARD
Vice-Pres. for Institutional Advancement: DONNA G. SCOTT
Vice-Pres. for Student Affairs and Vocation: JACQULINE L. SAXON
Academic Dean: ALLAN HUGH COLE, JR
Registrar: JACQUELINE D. HEFLEY
Dir for Library: TIMOTHY D. LINCOLN
Library of 160,000 vols

Publications: *Communitas* (1 a year), *Horizons in Biblical Theology* (2 a year), *Insights* (2 a year), *Windows*

BAPTIST MISSIONARY ASSOCIATION THEOLOGICAL SEMINARY

POB 670, 1530 E Pine St, Jacksonville, TX 75766-5407

Telephone: (903) 586-2501
E-mail: bmatsem@bmats.edu
Internet: www.bmats.edu

Founded 1957
Private control
Academic year: August to May

Pres.: Dr CHARLEY HOLMES
Dean and Registrar: Dr PHILIP ATTEBERY
Dir for Student Services: RONIE JEFF JOHNSON
Dir for Library: Dr JAMES C. BLAYLOCK
Library of 128,000 vols

BAYLOR COLLEGE OF MEDICINE

1 Baylor Plaza, Houston, TX 77030
Telephone: (713) 798-4951
E-mail: admissions@bcm.edu
Internet: www.bcm.edu

Founded 1900 as Univ. of Dallas Medical Dept, present name and status 1969
Private control
Academic year: July to June

Pres. and CEO: Dr PAUL KLOTMAN
Vice-Pres. and Chief Technology Officer, Information Technology: ALEXANDER IZAGUIRRE
Vice-Pres., Gen. Counsel and Corporate Sec.: ROBERT F. CORRIGAN, JR
Vice-Pres. for Communications and Marketing: CLAIRE M. BASSETT
Vice-Pres. for Devt: KRISTI SHERWOOD COOPER
Vice-Pres. for Facilities: ROCK MORILLE
Vice-Pres. for Research: Dr ADAM KUSPA
Chief Academic Officer: LORIE TABAK
Registrar and Sr Dir for Student Affairs: JOHN RAPP

Number of teachers: 2,200 (1,780 full-time, 420 part-time)
Number of students: 330

Publication: *Solutions*

DEANS

Graduate School of Biomedical Sciences: Dr HIRAM F. GILBERT
Medical School: Dr STEPHEN B. GREENBERG

National School of Tropical Medicine: Dr PETER J. HOTEZ
School of Allied Health Sciences: Dr J. DAVID HOLCOMB

BAYLOR UNIVERSITY

1 Bear Place, Waco, TX 76798
Telephone: (254) 710-1011
E-mail: registrar@baylor.edu
Internet: www.baylor.edu

Founded 1845
Private control
Academic year: August to May

Pres.: Dr KENNETH WINSTON STARR
Provost and Exec. Vice-Pres.: ELIZABETH DAVIS
Vice-Pres. for Finance and Admin.: REAGAN RAMSOWER
Vice-Pres. for Student Life: KEVIN JACKSON
Vice-Pres. for Univ. Devt: JERRY HAAG
Dean for Univ. Libraries and Vice-Pres. for Information Technology: Dr PATTIE ORR

Library of 2,521,216 vols, 73,204 serials, 394,559 ebooks, 68,607 ejournals, 2,213,631 microforms, 128,845 audiovisual items
Number of teachers: 775
Number of students: 15,000 (12,560 undergraduate, 2,440 graduate/professional)

Publications: *Baylor Business Review*, *Baylor Geological Studies*, *Baylor Line*, *Baylor Magazine* (6 a year), *Baylor News*, *Journal of Church and State*, *Law Review*, *The Lariat*

DEANS

College of Arts and Sciences: Dr LEE NORDT
George W. Truett Theological Seminary: Dr DAVID E. GARLAND
Graduate School: Dr LARRY LYON
Hankamer School of Business: Dr TERRY S. MANESS
Honors College: Prof. Dr THOMAS S. HIBBS
Law School: BRAD TOBEN
Louise Herrington School of Nursing: Prof. Dr SHELLEY F. CONROY
School of Education: Dr JON M. ENGELHARDT
School of Engineering and Computer Science: Dr BENJAMIN S. KELLEY
School of Music: WILLIAM V. MAY
School of Social Work: DIANA R. GARLAND

BRAZOSPORT COLLEGE

500 College Dr., Lake Jackson, TX 77566
Telephone: (979) 230-3000
Internet: www.brazosport.edu

Founded 1968 as Brazosport Jr College, present name 1970
State control
Academic year: August to May (2 semesters)

Pres.: Dr MILLICENT M. VALEK
Provost and Dean for Academic and Student Affairs: KEN TASA
Exec. Dir for Institutional Advancement: SERENA ANDREWS
Dean for Admin. Services and Chief Financial Officer: FRED SCOTT
Dean for Students: PAMELA DAVENPORT
Dir for College Services: GARY DICKS
Dir for Information Technology: RON PARKER
Librarian: JO ANNE ALCORN

Library of 70,000 vols, 43,000 ebooks
Number of teachers: 90
Number of students: 15,400

CONCORDIA UNIVERSITY TEXAS

11400 Concordia Univ. Dr., Austin, TX 78726

Telephone: (512) 313-3000
E-mail: admissions@concordia.edu
Internet: www.concordia.edu

Founded 1926, present name and status 1995
Private control
Academic year: July to June

Pres.: Dr THOMAS CEDEL
Provost: ALAN RUNGE
Vice-Pres. for Academic Services: JOEL HECK
Vice-Pres. for Advancement: JOHN SCHOEDEL
Vice-Pres. for Business Services: PAMELA LEE
Vice-Pres. for External Relations: DON ADAM
Vice-Pres. for Student Services: WILLIAM DRISKILL
Vice-Pres. for Univ. Services: Dr DAVID L. KLUTH
Dir for Library Services: MIKAIL MCINTOSH-DOTY
Registrar: CONNIE BERAN
Number of students: 2,500

Publication: *Concordia University Texas Magazine* (4 a year)

DEANS

College of Business: Dr DONALD CHRISTIAN
College of Education: Dr JIM MCCONNELL
College of Liberal Arts: Dr KEN SCHMIDT
College of Science: Dr MICHAEL MOYER

CRISWELL COLLEGE

4010 Gaston Ave, Dallas, TX 75246

Telephone: (214) 821-5433
E-mail: admission@criswell.edu
Internet: www.criswell.edu

Founded 1970
Private control
Academic year: August to July

Areas of study: biblical languages, Christian leadership, counselling ministry, education ministry, evangelism/missions, humanities, Jewish studies, pastoral ministry, philosophy, preaching, student ministry

Pres.: Dr JERRY A. JOHNSON
Provost and Exec. Vice-Pres.: LAMAR E. COOPER, SR
Vice-Pres. for Business and Chief Financial Officer: MICHAEL W. RODGERS
Vice-Pres. for Devt: KATE FINLEY
Dean for Students: JOE THOMAS
Dir for Admissions: JOSEPH F. THOMAS
Registrar: RON LOWERY
Dir for Library Services: PHILLIP NOTT

Library of 75,000 vols, 500 periodical titles
Number of teachers: 17 (full-time)
Number of students: 460

Publication: *Criswell Theological Review* (2 a year)

DALLAS BAPTIST UNIVERSITY

3000 Mountain Creek Parkway, Dallas, TX 75211-9299

Telephone: (214) 333-7100
E-mail: admiss@dbu.edu
Internet: www.dbu.edu

Founded 1898, fmrly Decatur Baptist College, present name 1985
Private control

Pres.: Dr GARY COOK
Provost: Dr GAIL LINAM
Exec. Vice-Pres.: Dr J. BLAIR BLACKBURN
Vice-Pres. for Advancement: Dr ADAM WRIGHT
Vice-Pres. for External Affairs: Dr CORY HINES
Vice-Pres. for Financial Affairs: ERIC BRUNTMYER

Vice-Pres. for Graduate and Corporate Affairs and Sr Assoc. Provost: Dr DENNIS DOWD
Vice-Pres. for Technology: MATT MURRAH
Library Dir: DEBRA Y. COLLINS

Library of 810,447 vols, 1,119 periodicals
Number of teachers: 125 (full-time)
Number of students: 5,550

DEANS

College of Business: Dr CHARLENE CONNER
College of Fine Arts: RONALD BOWLES
College of Humanities and Social Sciences: Dr JACK GOODYEAR
College of Natural Sciences and Mathematics: Dr BEVERLY GILTNER
College of Professional Studies: Dr DONOVAN FREDRICKSEN
Dorothy M. Bush College of Education: Dr CHARLES CARONA
Gary Cook Graduate School of Leadership: Dr DENNIS DOWD (acting)
Mary C. Crowley College of Christian Faith: Dr STEVE MULLEN
Online Education: Dr JEKABS BIKIS

DALLAS CHRISTIAN COLLEGE

2700 Christian Parkway, Dallas, TX 75234-7299

Telephone: (972) 241-3371
E-mail: admissions@dallas.edu
Internet: www.dallas.edu

Founded 1950
Private control
Academic year: August to May

Depts of arts and sciences, Bible, business administration, education, psychology

Pres.: DUSTIN D. RUBECK
Vice-Pres. for Academic Affairs: Dr PAUL KISSLING
Vice-Pres. for Institutional Effectiveness: Dr RON RIFE
Dir for Student Life: ERIC HINTON
Registrar: CRYSTAL LAIDACKER
Dir for Library: JANE REYNOLDS

Library of 35,000 vols, 17,000 ebooks, 250 periodicals, 3,000 ejournals

DALLAS THEOLOGICAL SEMINARY

3909 Swiss Ave, Dallas, TX 75204

Telephone: (214) 824-3094
E-mail: registrar@dts.edu
Internet: www.dts.edu

Founded 1924 as Evangelical Theological College, present name 1969
Private control

Campuses in Atlanta, Austin, Guatemala, Houston, Knoxville, Philadelphia, San Antonio, Tampa, Washington; depts of biblical counselling, biblical exposition, Christian education, ministry, New Testament studies, Old Testament studies, pastoral ministries, philosophy, spiritual formation and leadership, theological studies, world missions, and intercultural studies

Pres.: Dr MARK L. BAILEY
Vice-Pres. for Academic Affairs and Academic Dean: Dr JOHN GRASSMICK
Vice-Pres. for Advancement: KIMBERLY TILL
Vice-Pres. for Business and Finance: DALE LARSON
Vice-Pres. for Operations: ROBERT RIGGS
Vice-Pres. for Student Services and Dean for Students: Dr ROBERT GARIPPA
Dir for Admissions: JOSHUA BLEEKER
Dir for Library: MARVIN HUNN

Library of 303,000 vols (incl. 215,000 print vols, 59,000 microforms, 29,000 audiovisual items)
Number of students: 2,000

Publications: *Bibliotheca Sacra*, *Kindred Spirit* (3 a year), *Veritas* (5 a year)

EAST TEXAS BAPTIST UNIVERSITY

1 Tiger Dr., Marshall, TX 75670-1498

Telephone: (903) 935-7963
E-mail: admissions@etbu.edu
Internet: www.etbu.edu

Founded 1912 as College of Marshall, present name and status 1984
Private control
Academic year: August to May

Pres.: Dr SAMUEL W. OLIVER
Provost and Vice-Pres. for Academic Affairs: Dr SHERILYN EMBERTON
Vice-Pres. for Admin. and Finance: NED CALVERT
Vice-Pres. for Enrolment Management and Marketing: VINCE BLANKENSHIP
Vice-Pres. for Student Affairs: Dr DENNIS ROBERTSON
Vice-Pres. for Univ. Advancement: CATHERINE A. CRAWFORD
Registrar: CHRIS WOOD
Librarian: Dr CYNTHIA L. PETERSON

Library of 96,393 vols, 97,806 ebooks, 15,175 serials, 22,458 ejournals, 41,458 audiovisual items
Number of teachers: 55
Number of students: 1,200

DEANS

School of Business: Dr SCOTT RAY
School of Christian Studies: Dr JOHN L. HARRIS
School of Education: Dr DONNA HARRELL LUBCKER
School of Fine Arts: Dr THOMAS R. WEBSTER
School of Humanities: Dr JERRY L. SUMMERS
School of Natural and Social Science: Dr LYNN NEW
School of Nursing: Dr ELLEN FINEOUT-OVERHOLT

FISHER MORE COLLEGE

3020 Lubbock Ave, Fort Worth, TX 76109

Telephone: (817) 923-8459
E-mail: admissions@fishermore.edu
Internet: www.fishermore.edu

Founded 1981 as Saint Thomas More Institute, present name 2012
Private control
Language of instruction: English
Academic year: September to May

Liberal arts college

Pres.: Dr MICHAEL G. KING
Dean for College: Dr RYAN DOUGLAS MADISON
Dir for Communications: SHANTI GUY
Dir for Enrolment Management: PETER CAPANI
Dir for Operations: Dr MATT GRAHEK
Dir for Student Affairs: LINDSAY JENNINGS
Registrar: JOHN HEITZENRATER
Chancellor: Dr TAYLOR REED MARSHALL
Head Librarian: MARILYN ANKENBAUER

Library of 14,451 vol, 543 audiovisual items

GRADUATE INSTITUTE OF APPLIED LINGUISTICS (GIAL)

7500 W Camp, Wisdom Rd, Dallas, TX 75236

Telephone: (972) 708-7415
E-mail: info@gial.edu
Internet: www.gial.edu

Founded 1998
Private control
Academic year: July to June

Pres.: Dr DAVID A. ROSS
Vice-Pres. for Finance: L. RODNEY JENKINS
Dean for Academic Affairs: Dr DOUGLAS R. TIFFIN

Dean for Students: RUTH E. SCHILBERG
Dir for Admissions: MAGGIE JOHNSON
Dir for Devt: JUDY POLLACK
Chief Financial Officer: ROD JENKINS
Registrar: LYNNE M. LAMIMAN
Dir for Library: FERNE WEIMER
Library of 55,000 vols
Number of teachers: 22
Number of students: 108
Publication: *GIALens: Electronic Notes Series* (3 a year)

HARDIN-SIMMONS UNIVERSITY

2200 Hickory, Abilene, TX 79698
Telephone: (325) 670-1000
Internet: www.hsutx.edu
Founded 1891 as Simmons College, present name 1934
Private control
Academic year: August to May (2 semesters)
Pres.: LANNY HALL
Provost and Chief Academic Officer: Dr THOMAS BRISCO
Sr Vice-Pres. for Finance and Management: HAROLD R. PRESTON
Sr Vice-Pres. for Student Devt: Dr MIKE WHITEHORN
Vice-Pres. for Enrolment Management and Marketing Management: Dr SHANE DAVIDSON
Vice-Pres. for Institutional Advancement: MIKE HAMMACK
Registrar: KACEY HIGGINS
Dean for Univ. Libraries: ALICE W. SPECHT
Library of 337,596 vols
Number of teachers: 200 (137 full-time, 63 part-time)
Number of students: 2,350 (1,890 undergraduate, 460 graduate)
Publications: *Range Rider* (2 a year), *The Bronco* (1 a year)

DEANS

Cynthia Ann Parker College of Liberal Arts: Prof. Dr ALAN STAFFORD
Holland School of Sciences and Mathematics: Prof. Dr CHRISTOPHER L. MCNAIR
Irvin School of Education: Dr PAMELA K. WILLIFORD
Kelley College of Business: Dr MICHAEL L. MONHOLLON
Logsdon School of Theology: Dr DON WILLIFORD
Logsdon Seminary: Dr DONALD D. WILLIFORD
School of Music and Fine Arts: Dr ROBERT BROOKS

HOUSTON BAPTIST UNIVERSITY

7502 Fondren Rd, Houston, TX 77074-3298
Telephone: (281) 649-3000
E-mail: admissions@hbu.edu
Internet: www.hbu.edu
Founded 1960 as Houston Baptist College, present name 1973
Private control
Academic year: August to May
Pres.: Dr ROBERT B. SLOAN, JR
Provost: Dr ROBERT STACEY
Vice-Pres. for Advancement: CHARLES BACARISSE
Vice-Pres. for Enrolment Management: JAMES STEEN
Vice-Pres. for Financial Operations: SANDY MOONEY
Vice-Pres. for Univ. Communications: R. KIMBERLY GAYNOR
Vice-Pres. for Univ. Relations: SHARON SAUNDERS
Dir for Student Life: WHITTINGTON GOODWIN
Registrar: ERINN HUGHES
Dean for Library: ANN NOBLE

Library of 300,000 vols, 100,000 ebooks, 60,000 ejournals
Number of teachers: 225
Number of students: 2,600

DEANS

College of Arts and Humanities: Dr CHRISTOPHER HAMMONS
College of Science and Mathematics: Dr DORIS WARREN
Graduate School: Dr MOHAN KURUVILLA
Honors College: Dr ROBERT STACEY
School of Business: Dr MOHAN KURUVILLA
School of Education: Dr D. R. WILSON (acting)
School of Nursing and Allied Health: Dr MARGARET UGALDE

HOWARD PAYNE UNIVERSITY

1000 Fisk St, Brownwood, TX 76801
Telephone: (325) 649-8020
E-mail: enroll@hputx.edu
Internet: www.hputx.edu
Founded 1889 as Howard Payne College, present name 1974
Private control
Academic year: August to May
Pres.: Dr WILLIAM N. ELLIS
Provost and Chief Academic Officer: Dr WILLIAM MARK TEW
Sr Vice-Pres. for Finance and Admin.: BRENDA J. MCLENDON
Sr Vice-Pres. for Institutional Advancement: Dr BRAD JOHNSON
Vice-Pres. for Devt: PAUL A. DUNNE
Vice-Pres. for Student Life and Dean for Students: Dr BRENT A. MARSH
Registrar: LANA WAGNER
Dean for Libraries: NANCY ANDERSON
Library of 116,667 vols
Number of teachers: 125
Number of students: 1,400

DEANS

Advising and General Education: Dr WENDY MCNEELEY
School of Business: Dr LESLIE PLAGENS
School of Christian Studies: Dr DONNIE AUVENSHINE
School of Education: Dr MICHAEL ROSATO
School of Humanities: Dr JUSTIN MURPHY
School of Music and Fine Arts and Extended Education: Dr ROBERT TUCKER
School of Science and Mathematics: Dr LYNN LITTLE

HUSTON-TILLOTSON UNIVERSITY

900 Chicon St, Austin, TX 78702-2795
Telephone: (512) 505-3000
E-mail: admission@htu.edu
Internet: www.htu.edu
Founded 1952 by merger of Samuel Huston College (f. 1876) with Tillotson College (f. 1875), present name 2005
Private control
Academic year: July to June
Pres.: Dr LARRY L. EARVIN
Provost and Vice-Pres. for Academic and Student Affairs: Dr VICKI VERNON LOTT
Vice-Pres. for Admin. and Finance: VALERIE D. HILL
Vice-Pres. for Institutional Advancement: Dr RODERICK L. SMOTHERS
Dean for Enrolment Management: Dr B. SHERRANCE RUSSELL
Dean for Student Affairs: EDMUND GRAHAM
Registrar: EARNESTINE STRICKLAND
Dir for Library and Media Services: PATRICIA WILKINS

Library of 97,000 vols
Number of teachers: 80
Number of students: 950

DEANS

College of Arts and Sciences: Dr MICHAEL HIRSCH
School of Business and Technology: Dr STEVEN EDMOND

JARVIS CHRISTIAN COLLEGE

POB 1470, Highway 80E, Private Rd 7631, Hawkins, TX 75765-1470
Telephone: (903) 730-4890
Internet: www.jarvis.edu
Founded 1912 as Jarvis Christian Institute, present name 1950
Private control
Academic year: August to May
Areas of study: art, biology, business administration, chemistry, computer information systems, criminal justice, English, environmental science, history, kinesiology, mathematics, music, professional education/teacher certification, psychology, religion, social work, sociology, Spanish, speech
Pres.: Dr LESTER C. NEWMAN
Vice-Pres. for Academic Affairs: Dr MARTIN YALE
Vice-Pres. for Admin. and Finance: REGINALD DICKENS
Dir for Library: RODNEY ATKINS
Registrar: AUTRY ACREY

LETOURNEAU UNIVERSITY

POB 7001, Longview, TX 75607
2100 S Mobberly Ave, Longview, TX 75602
Telephone: (903) 233-4300
E-mail: admissions@letu.edu
Internet: www.letu.edu
Founded 1946 as LeTourneau Technical Institute, present name and status 1989
Private control
Academic year: August to May
Campuses in Austin, Bedford, Dallas, Houston, Tyler
Pres.: Dr DALE A. LUNSFORD
Provost and Exec. Vice-Pres.: Dr PHILIP A. COYLE
Exec. Vice-Pres. for External Relations: (vacant)
Vice-Pres. for Devt: BEN Y. MARCH
Vice-Pres. for Enrolment Services: Dr STEPHEN M. CONDON
Vice-Pres. for Finance and Admin.: MIKE S. HOOD
Vice-Pres. for the School of Graduate and Professional Studies: Dr CAROL C. GREEN
Dean for Faculty and Assoc. Provost: Dr STEVEN D. MASON
Dean for Students: COREY R. ROSS
Registrar: GINGER MOORE
Dir for Library: LINDA PRICE
Library of 76,495 vols, 52,058 ebooks, 13,017 e-periodical titles, 688 microform titles, 181 serial subscriptions
Number of teachers: 75 (full-time)
Number of students: 2,950

DEANS

School of Aeronautical Science: Prof. Dr FRED RITCHEY, JR
School of Arts and Sciences: Dr LARRY J. FRAZIER
School of Business: Prof. Dr BOB WHARTON
School of Education: Dr WAYNE J. JACOBS
School of Engineering and Engineering Technology: Dr RONALD A. DELAP

LUBBOCK CHRISTIAN UNIVERSITY

5601 19th St, Lubbock, TX 79407
Telephone: (806) 720-7151
E-mail: admissions@lcu.edu
Internet: www.lcu.edu

Founded 1957 as Lubbock Christian College, present name and status 1987
Private control
Academic year: August to May
Pres.: L. TIMOTHY PERRIN
Chancellor: Dr L. KEN JONES
Provost and Chief Academic Officer: Dr ROD BLACKWOOD
Exec. Vice-Pres.: Dr BRIAN STARR
Vice-Pres. for Facilities: MIKE SELLECK
Vice-Pres. for Financial Affairs: TIA CLARY
Vice-Pres. for Univ. Advancement: JOHN KING
Chief Financial Officer: TIA CLARY
Dir for Admissions: CHARLIE WEBB
Registrar: JANICE STONE
Dir for Library: PAULA GANNAWAY
Library of 121,889 vols, 50,575 ebooks

DEANS

B. Ward Lane College of Professional Studies: Dr TOBY ROGERS
College of Biblical Studies and Behavioral Sciences: Dr JESSE LONG
J. E. and Eileen Hancock College of Liberal Arts and Education: Dr SUSAN BLASSINGAME

McMURRY UNIVERSITY

POB 278, 1 McMurry Station, Abilene, TX 79697
Telephone: (325) 793-3800
E-mail: admissions@mcm.edu
Internet: www.mcm.edu
Founded 1923 as McMurry College, present name 1990
Private control
Academic year: August to May
Pres.: Dr JOHN H. RUSSELL
Vice-Pres. for Academic Affairs: Dr PAUL FABRIZIO
Vice-Pres. for Devt: DEBRA HULSE
Vice-Pres. for Financial Affairs: LISA WILLIAMS
Vice-Pres. for Information and Support Services: BRAD POORMAN
Vice-Pres. for Institutional Advancement: STEVE CRISMAN
Dean for Students: VANESSA ROBERTS
Registrar: CAROLYN CALVERT
Dir for Library: TERRY YOUNG
Library of 150,000 vols, 240 journals, magazines and newspapers
Number of teachers: 120
Number of students: 1,400

DEANS

School of Arts and Letters: Dr CHRISTINA H. WILSON
School of Business: Dr K. O. LONG
School of Education: Dr PERRY KAY HALEY BROWN
School of Natural and Computational Sciences: Dr ALICIA WYATT
School of Social Sciences and Religion: Dr PHILIP LeMASTERS

MIDLAND COLLEGE

3600 N Garfield, Midland, TX 79705
Telephone: (432) 685-4500
E-mail: president@midland.edu
Internet: www.midland.edu
Founded 1969
State control
Academic year: August to May (2 semesters)
Pres.: Dr STEVE THOMAS
Exec. Vice-Pres.: RICHARD JOLLY
Vice-Pres. for Administrative Services: RICK BENDER
Vice-Pres. for Information Technology and Facilities: DENNIS SEVER
Vice-Pres. for Instruction: REX PEEBLES

Vice-Pres. for Student Services: RITA NELL DIFFIE
Dean for Enrolment Management: MICHAEL CHAVEZ
Registrar: ANGELA BALCH
Library of 62,000 vols, 300 magazine, journal and newspaper subscriptions
Number of teachers: 155 (full-time)
Number of students: 7,425
Publication: *Chaparral* (1 a year)

DEANS

Adult and Developmental Education: LYNDA WEBB
Business Studies: GAVIN FRANTZ
Distance Learning and Continuing Education: DALE BEIKIRCH
Fine Arts and Communications: WILLIAM FEELER
Health Sciences: BECKY HAMMACK
Mathematics and Sciences: MARGARET WADE
Social and Behavioral Sciences and Education Studies: WILLIAM MORRIS
Technical Studies: CURT PERVIER

MIDWESTERN STATE UNIVERSITY

3410 Taft Blvd, Wichita Falls, TX 76308
Telephone: (940) 397-4000
E-mail: admissions@mwsu.edu
Internet: www.mwsu.edu
Founded 1922 as Wichita Falls Jr College, present name 1975
State control
Academic year: August to May (2 semesters)
Pres.: Dr JESSE W. ROGERS
Provost: ALISA R. WHITE
Vice-Pres. for Admin. and Finance: JUAN SANDOVAL
Vice-Pres. for Admin. and Institutional Effectiveness: Dr ROBERT E. CLARK
Vice-Pres. for Business Affairs and Finance: JUAN SANDOVAL
Vice-Pres. for Student Affairs and Enrolment Management: Dr KEITH LAMB
Vice-Pres. for Univ. Advancement and Public Affairs: Dr HOWARD FARRELL
Dean for Students: DAIL NEELY
Dir for Admissions: BARBARA MERKLE
Registrar: DARLA INGLISH
Librarian: CLARA LATHAM
Library of 900,000 vols
Number of teachers: 230 (full-time)
Number of students: 6,200 (5,475 undergraduate, 725 graduate)
Publications: *Faculty Forum Papers* (1 a year), *The Wai-Kun* (1 a year), *The Wichitan* (52 a year), *Voices* (1 a year)

DEANS

College of Health Sciences and Human Services: Dr PATTI HAMILTON
College of Science and Mathematics: Dr LYNN LITTLE
Dillard College of Business Administration: Dr BARBARA NEMECEK
Gordon T. and Ellen West College of Education: MATTHEW CAPPS
Graduate School: DEVAH SCHOLL
Lamar D. Fain College of Fine Arts: Prof. RON FISCHLI
Prothro-Yeager College of Humanities and Social Sciences: SAMUEL WATSON, III

OBLATE SCHOOL OF THEOLOGY

285 Oblate Dr., San Antonio, TX 78216-6693
Telephone: (210) 341-1366
E-mail: info@ost.edu
Internet: www.ost.edu
Founded 1903 as San Antonio Philosophical and Theological Seminary
Private control

Pres.: Fr RONALD ROLHEISER
Academic Dean: Dr R. SCOTT WOODWARD
Exec. Vice-Pres.: Rev. WARREN BROWN
Vice-Pres. for Admin. Affairs: Rev. DAVID KALERT
Vice-Pres. for Finance: RENE ESPINOSA
Vice-Pres. for Institutional Advancement: LEA KOCHANEK
Registrar and Dir for Admissions: JAMES OBERHAUSEN
Dir for Library: MARIA M. GARCIA

OUR LADY OF THE LAKE UNIVERSITY

411 SW 24th St, San Antonio, TX 78207
Telephone: (210) 434-6711
E-mail: registrar@lake.ollusa.edu
Internet: www.ollusa.edu
Founded 1895
Private control
Academic year: August to May
Campuses in Harlingen, Houston
Pres.: Dr TESSA MARTINEZ POLLACK
Exec. Vice-Pres.: Dr DAVID C. ESTES
Vice-Pres. for Academic Affairs: Dr HELEN J. STREUBERT
Vice-Pres. for Enrolment Management: MICHAEL ACOSTA
Vice-Pres. for Finance and Facilities: ALLEN KLAUS
Vice-Pres. for Institutional Advancement: DAN YOXALL
Vice-Pres. for Student Life: JACK HANK
Dean for Library: JUDY LARSON
Library of 254,419 vols
Number of teachers: 114 (full-time)
Number of students: 2,660 (1,595 undergraduate, 1,065 graduate)

DEANS

College of Arts and Sciences: Dr ROGER V. BENNETT
School of Business and Leadership: Dr ROBERT BISKING
School of Professional Studies: Dr ROBERT BISKING

PARKER UNIVERSITY

2540 Walnut Hill Lane, Dallas, TX 75229
Telephone: (972) 438-6932
E-mail: future@parker.edu
Internet: www.parker.edu
Founded 1982 as Parker College of Chiropractic, present name 2011
Private control
Academic year: January to December
Areas of study: anatomy, chiropractic, health and wellness
Pres.: Dr FABRIZIO MANCINI
Provost: Dr GERY HOCHANADEL
Vice-Pres. for Academics: Dr KENNETH C. THOMAS
Vice-Pres. for Business Affairs: DAVID GARAFOLA
Vice-Pres. for Devt: JoLYNNE JENSEN
Vice-Pres. for Finance: DAVID GARAFOLA
Vice-Pres. for Research, Wellness Centres, Seminars and Continuing Education: Dr GILLES LAMARCHE
Dean for Enrolment Services: LYNN NASATO
Dean for Student Affairs: VICTOR BALLESTEROS
Registrar: JUDITH VERGARA
Library of 16,000 vols, 33,000 ebooks
Number of students: 847

PATTY HANKS SHELTON SCHOOL OF NURSING

2149 Hickory St, Abilene, TX 79601
Telephone: (325) 671-2399

Internet: www.phssn.edu; attached to Abilene Christian Univ., Hardin-Simmons Univ. and McMurry Univ.

Private control

Offers BSc and MSc in family nurse practitioner, nursing

Dean: Dr NINA OUIMETTE
Graduate Dir: Prof. Dr AMY TOONE
Undergraduate Dir: Dr INDIRA D. TYLER

PAUL QUINN COLLEGE

3837 Simpson-Stuart Rd, Dallas, TX 75241
Telephone: (214) 376-1000
E-mail: admissions@pqc.edu
Internet: www.pqc.edu

Founded 1872
Private control
Academic year: August to May

Depts of business and legal studies, education, general education, science and technology

Pres.: MICHAEL J. SORRELL
Exec. Vice-Pres.: Dr HOMERO LOPEZ
Vice-Pres. for Academic Affairs: Dr KIZUWANDA GRANT
Chief Operating Officer: ANTWANE OWENS
Dean for Students: KELSEL THOMPSON
Dir for Enrolment Management: EDDIE FRANCIS
Registrar: BEVERLY SMITH
Dir for Library: CLARICE P. MEDLEY-WEEKS

Library of 51,000 vols
Number of teachers: 50
Number of students: 780

Publication: *Paul Quinn Gazette*

RICE UNIVERSITY

POB 1892, Houston, TX 77251-1892
6100 Main St, Houston, TX 77005-1827
Telephone: (713) 348-0000
E-mail: info@rice.edu
Internet: www.rice.edu

Founded 1891 as The Rice Institute
Private control

Pres.: DAVID W. LEEBRON
Provost: GEORGE L. MCLENDON
Vice-Pres. and Gen. Counsel: RICHARD A. ZANSITIS
Vice-Pres. for Admin.: KEVIN E. KIRBY
Vice-Pres. for Enrolment: CHRIS MUÑOZ
Vice-Pres. for Finance: KATHY COLLINS
Vice-Pres. for Public Affairs: LINDA L. THRANE
Vice-Pres. for Resource Devt: DARROW ZEIDENSTEIN
Registrar: DAVID TENNEY
Vice-Provost and Univ. Librarian: SARA LOWMAN

Library of 2,570,000 vols, 68,000 ebooks, 72,000 journal subscriptions, 3,276,000 units of microform
Number of teachers: 1,110 (670 full-time, 107 part-time, 333 adjunct)
Number of students: 6,080 (3,707 undergraduate, 2,373 graduate)

Publications: *Close Up, Baker Institute Report, Environmental Toxicology and Chemistry, Feminist Economics, Houston Area Survey* (1 a year), *Jones Journal* (2 a year), *Journal of Southern History* (4 a year), *Macrocosm, Rice Magazine, Rice University Studies, Studies in English Literature 1500–1900* (4 a year), *The Sarmatian Review* (3 a year)

DEANS

George R. Brown School of Engineering: NED THOMAS
Graduate and Postdoctoral Studies: Dr PAULA SANDERS

Jesse H. Jones Graduate School of Management: WILLIAM GLICK
School of Architecture: SARAH WHITING
School of Humanities: NICOLAS SHUMWAY
School of Social Sciences: LYN RAGSDALE
Shepherd School of Music: ROBERT YEKOVICH
Susanne M. Glasscock School of Continuing Studies: Dr MARY B. MCINTIRE
Undergraduate Education: Dr JOHN S. HUTCHINSON
Wiess School of Natural Sciences: DANIEL D. CARSON

PROFESSORS

AAZHANG, B., Electrical and Computer Engineering
AKIN, J. E., Mechanical Engineering
ALCOVER, M., French
ALFORD, J. R., Political Science
AMBLER, J. S., Political Science
ANDERSON, J. B., Earth Science
ANTOULAS, A. C., Electrical and Computer Engineering
ARESU, B., French Studies
ARMENIADES, C. D., Chemical Engineering
ATHANASIOU, A., Bioengineering
AVE-LALLEMANT, H. G., Earth Science
BAGOZZI, R., Management
BAKER, S. D., Physics and Astronomy
BARRON, A., Chemistry
BAYAZITOGLU, Y., Mechanical Engineering and Materials Science
BECKINGHAM, K., Biochemistry and Cell Biology
BEDIENT, P. B., Civil and Environmental Engineering
BENNETT, G., Biochemistry and Cell Biology
BILLUPS, W. E., Chemistry
BLACK, E., Political Science
BOLES, J. B., History
BONNER, B. E., Physics and Astronomy
BOSHERNITZAN, M., Mathematics
BRACE, P., Political Science
BRITO, D. L., Economics
BRODY, B. A., Philosophy
BROKER, K. L., Art and Art History
BROOKS, P. R., Chemistry
BROWN, B. W., Economics and Statistics
BROWN, J. N., Economics
BRYANT, J., Economics
BURRUS, C. S., Electrical and Computer Engineering
BUYSE, L., Music
CAMFIELD, W. A., Art and Art History
CANNADY, W. T., Architecture
CARROLL, M. M., Computational and Applied Mathematics
CARTWRIGHT, R. S., Computer Science
CASBARIAN, J. J., Architecture
CASTAÑEDA, J. A., Hispanic and Classical Studies
CHANCE, J., English
CHAPMAN, W. G., Chemical Engineering
CITRON, M., Music
CLARK, J. W., Jr, Electrical and Computer Engineering
CLOUTIER, P. A., Physics and Astronomy
COCHRAN, T., Mathematics
COOPER, K. D., Computer Science
CORCORAN, M., Physics and Astronomy
COX, D., Statistics
COX, S. G., Philosophy
COX, S. J., Computational and Applied Mathematics
CROWELL, S. G., Philosophy
CURL, R. F., Jr, Chemistry
CUTHBERTSON, G. M., Political Science
DAVIDSON, C., Sociology
DAVIS, P. W., Linguistics
DHARAN, B. G., Management
DIPBOYE, R., Psychology
DOODY, T., English
DRISKILL, L., English
DUCK, I., Physics and Astronomy
DUFOUR, R. J., Physics and Astronomy
DUNHAM, J. F., Music

DUNNING, F. B., Physics and Astronomy
DURRANI, A. J., Civil and Environmental Engineering
EIFLER, M., German and Slavic Studies
EL-GAMAL, M., Economics
ELLISON, P., Music
ENGEL, P. S., Chemistry
ENGELHARDT, T., Philosophy
ENSOR, K. B., Statistics
FARWELL, J., Music
FELLEISEN, M., Computer Science
FEW, A., Physics and Astronomy
FISCHER, N., Music
FISHER, F. M., Jr, Ecology and Evolutionary Biology
FORMAN, R., Mathematics
GEORGE, J., Management
GLANTZ, R. M., Biochemistry and Cell Biology
GLASS, G. P., Chemistry
GOLDMAN, R. N., Computer Science
GOLDSMITH, K., Music
GOMER, R. H., Biochemistry and Cell Biology
GONZÁLEZ-STEPHEN, B., Hispanic and Classical Studies
GORDON, R., Earth Science
GORRY, G. A., Management
GOTTSCHALK, A. W., Music
GOUX, J., French
GRANDY, R. E., Philosophy
GROB, A., English
GRUBER, I. D., History
HALAS, N., Electrical and Computer Engineering
HAMM, K. E., Political Science
HANNON, J. P., Physics and Astronomy
HARCOMBE, P., Ecology and Environmental Biology
HARDT, R. M., Mathematics
HARTLEY, P. R., Economics
HARVEY, F. R., Mathematics
HASKELL, T., History
HEMPEL, J., Mathematics
HIGHTOWER, J. W., Chemical Engineering
HILL, T. W., Physics and Astronomy
HIRASAKI, G., Chemical Engineering
HOLLOWAY, C., Music
HUANG, H. W., Physics and Astronomy
HUFFER, L., French Studies
HUGHES, J. B., Civil and Environmental Engineering
HULET, R., Physics and Astronomy
HUSTON, J. D., English
HUTCHINSON, J. S., Chemistry
IAMMARINO, N., Kinesiology
ISLE, W., English
JOHNSON, D. H., Electrical and Computer Engineering
JONES, B. F., Mathematics
JUMP, J. R., Electrical and Computer Engineering
KANATAS, G., Administrative Science
KAUN, K., Music
KELBER, W. H., Religious Studies
KENNEDY, K. W., Jr, Computer Science
KIMMEL, M., Statistics
KINSEY, J. L., Chemistry
KLEIN, A., Religious Studies
KLINEBERG, S. L., Sociology
KONISKY, J., Biochemistry and Cell Biology
KULSTAD, M., Philosophy
LANE, N., Physics and Astronomy
LEE, B., Anthropology
LEEMAN, W. P., Earth Science
LEVANDA, R. A., Music
LEVANDER, A. R., Earth Science
LIANG, E., Physics and Astronomy
LUCA, S., Music
MCINTIRE, L. V., Chemical Engineering
MCINTOSH, R. J., Anthropology
MCINTOSH, S. K., Anthropology
MCLELLAN, R. B., Materials Science
MANCA, J., Art and Art History
MARCUS, G. E., Anthropology
MARGRAVE, J. L., Chemistry
MARTIN, R. C., Psychology
MARTIN, W. C., Sociology

MATUSOW, A., History
MICHIE, H., English
MIESZKOWSKI, P., Economics
MIETTINEN, H. E., Physics and Astronomy
MIKOS, A., Bioengineering
MILLER, C. A., Chemical Engineering
MORGAN, T. C., Political Science
MORRIS, W. A., English
MORRISON, D. R., Philosophy
MOULIN, H. M., Economics
MUTCHLER, G. S., Physics and Astronomy
NAPIER, H. A., Management
NELSON, D., French Studies
NORDLANDER, P., Physics and Astronomy
ODHIAMBO, A., History
OLSON, J. S., Biochemistry
ORCHARD, M. T., Electrical and Computer Engineering
OSHERSON, D., Psychology
PARKER, J. K., Music
PARRY, R. J., Chemistry
PATTEN, R. L., English
POLKING, J. C., Mathematics
POULOS, B., Art and Art History
QUELLER, D. C., Ecology and Evolutionary Biology
RACHLEFF, L., Music
RAU, C., Physics and Astronomy
REIFF, P., Physics and Astronomy
ROBERT, M., Chemical Engineering
ROBERTS, J. B., Physics and Astronomy
ROJO, J., Statistics
ROUX, R., Music
RUDOLPH, F. B., Biochemistry and Cell Biology
SAN, K. Y., Bioengineering
SASS, R. L., Ecology and Evolutionary Biology
SAWYER, D., Earth Science
SCHNEIDER, D. J., Psychology
SCHNOEBELEN, A. M., Music
SCOTT, D. W., Statistics
SCUSERIA, G., Chemistry
SEED, P., History
SEMMES, S. W., Mathematics
SHER, G., Philosophy
SHIBATANI, M., Linguistics
SICKLES, R., Economics
SKURA, M., English
SMALLEY, R. E., Chemistry
SMITH, G., Art and Art History
SMITH, G. W., Economics
SMITH, R. J., History
SNOW, E. A., English
SOLIGO, R., Economics
SORENSEN, D. C., Computational and Applied Mathematics
SPANOS, P. D., Mechanical Engineering and Materials Science
SPENCE, D. W., Kinesiology
STEIN, R., Political Science
STEVENSON, P. M., Physics and Astronomy
STEWART, C. R., Biochemistry and Cell Biology
STOKES, G., History
STOLL, R. J., Political Science
STRASSMAN, J., Ecology and Evolutionary Biology
STRONG, R., Mathematics
STROUP, J. M., Religious Studies
SYMES, W. W., Computational and Applied Mathematics
TALWANI, M., Earth Science
TAPIA, R. A., Computational and Applied Mathematics
TAYLOR, J., Anthropology
TAYLOR, R. N., Management
TEZDUYAR, T. E., Mechanical Engineering and Materials Science
THOMPSON, E. M., German and Slavic Studies
THOMPSON, J. R., Statistics
TITTEL, F., Electrical and Computer Engineering
TOMSON, M. B., Civil and Environmental Engineering
TOUR, J., Chemistry
TYLER, S. A., Anthropology

UECKER, W. C., Management
VARDI, M. Y., Computer Science
VEECH, W. A., Mathematics
VELETSOS, A. S., Civil and Environmental Engineering
WARD, C. H., Civil and Environmental Engineering
WARREN, J. D., Computer Science
WATKINS, M. J., Psychology
WEISMAN, R. B., Chemistry
WEISSENBERGER, K. H., German and Slavic Studies
WESTBROOK, R. A., Management
WHITAKER, G., Management
WHITMIRE, K. H., Chemistry
WIENER, M. J., History
WIESNER, M., Civil and Environmental Engineering
WILLIAMS, E. E., Management
WILSON, L. J., Chemistry
WILSON, R. K., Political Science
WILSON, W. L., Electrical and Computer Engineering
WINDSOR, D., Management
WINKLER, K., Music
WINNINGHAM, G. L., Art and Art History
WITTENBERG, G., Architecture
WOLF, M., Mathematics
WOLF, R. A., Physics and Astronomy
WOOD, S., English
WYSCHOGROD, E., Religious Studies
YOUNG, J. F., Electrical and Computer Engineering
YUNIS, H., Hispanic and Classical Studies
ZAMMITO, J. H., History
ZEFF, S. A., Management
ZODROW, G., Economics
ZWAENEPOEL, W., Computer Science
ZYGOURAKIS, K., Chemical Engineering

SCHREINER UNIVERSITY

2100 Memorial Blvd, Kerrville, TX 78028

Telephone: (830) 896-5411

E-mail: admissions@schreiner.edu

Internet: www.schreiner.edu

Founded 1923 as Schreiner College, present name 2001

Private control

Academic year: August to May

Pres.: Dr TIM SUMMERLIN

Provost and Vice-Pres. for Academic Affairs: Dr CHARLIE MCCORMICK

Vice-Pres. for Admin. and Finance: BILL MUSE

Vice-Pres. for Advancement and Public Affairs: MARK TUSCHAK

Vice-Pres. for Enrolment and Student Services: PEG LAYTON

Dean for Admissions and Financial Aid: SANDY SPEED

Registrar: DARLENE BANNISTER

Dir for Library: Dr CANDICE SCOTT

Library of 83,000 vols, 200 periodical subscriptions, 10,000 ejournals, 30,000 ebooks

Number of teachers: 120

Number of students: 1,120

Publication: *Scene* (2 a year)

DEANS

Cailloux School of Professional Studies: Dr DAVID SMITH

School of Liberal Arts: Dr WILLIAM WOODS

Trull School of Sciences and Math: Dr DIANA COMUZZIE

SEMINARY OF THE SOUTHWEST

POB 2247, Austin, TX 78768

501 East 32nd, Austin, TX 78705

Telephone: (512) 472-4133

E-mail: seminary@ssw.edu

Internet: www.ssw.edu

Founded 1951 as Episcopal Theological Seminary, present name 2008

Private control

Academic year: August to May

Pres. and Dean: Very Rev. Dr DOUGLAS TRAVIS

Exec. Vice-Pres. of Admin. and Finance: JOHN BENNET WATERS

Vice-Pres. for Advancement: TARA HOLLEY (acting)

Vice-Pres. of Devt: NANCY SPRINGER-BALDWIN

Academic Dean: CYNTHIA BRIGGS KITTREDGE

Exec. Dir for Enrolment: JENNIELLE STROTHER

Registrar: MADELYN SNODGRASS

Dir for Library: Dr DONALD E. KEENEY

Library of 100,000 vols, 1,000 periodicals, 10,000 e-serial titles

Number of students: 115

SOUTH TEXAS COLLEGE

POB 9701, McAllen, TX 78502-9701

3201 W Pecan, McAllen, TX 78501

Telephone: (956) 872-8311

Internet: www.southtexascollege.edu

Founded 1993

State control

Academic year: August to May

Campuses in Weslaco and Rio Grande City

Pres.: Dr SHIRLEY A. REED

Vice-Pres. for Academic Affairs: JUAN E. MEJIA

Vice-Pres. for Finance and Admin. Services: DIANA A. PENA

Vice-Pres. for Student Affairs and Enrollment Management: Dr WILLIAM SERRATA

Dir for Admissions and Registrar: MATTHEW HEBBARD

Dean for Library Services and Instructional Technologies: NOEMI GARZA

Library of 140,000 vols

Number of students: 28,000

DEANS

Division of Business and Technology: MARIO REYNA

Division of Liberal Arts and Social Sciences: Dr MARGARETHA E. BISCHOFF

Division of Math and Science: Dr ALI ESMAEILI

Division of Nursing Allied Health: Dr MELBA TREVINO

SOUTH TEXAS COLLEGE OF LAW

1303 San Jacinto St, Houston, TX 77002-7000

Telephone: (713) 659-8040

E-mail: admissions@stcl.edu

Internet: www.stcl.edu

Founded 1923 as South Texas School of Law, present name 1945

Private control

Academic year: August to May

Pres. and Dean: DONALD J. GUTER

Exec. Vice-Pres.: Prof. HELEN BISHOP JENKINS

Sr Vice-Pres. and Chief Financial Officer: GREGORY A. BROTHERS

Vice-Pres. and Assoc. Dean for Academic Admin.: Prof. BRUCE A. MCGOVERN

Vice-Pres. and Assoc. Dean for Academic Affairs: Prof. JOHN J. WORLEY

Vice-Pres. for Devt and Alumni Relations: KIM PARKER

Vice-Pres. for Strategic Planning and Institutional Research: Prof. JEFFREY L. RENSBERGER

Dir for Library Services and Vice-Pres.: Prof. DAVID G. COWAN

Library of 500,000 vols

Number of teachers: 55 (full-time)

Number of students: 1,305

Publications: *Construction Law Journal, Currents International Trade Law Journal, Law Review, Texas Journal of Business Law*

SOUTHERN METHODIST UNIVERSITY

6425 Boaz, Dallas, TX 75205

Telephone: (214) 768-2000
E-mail: enrol_serv@mail.smu.edu
Internet: www.smu.edu

Founded 1911
Private control
Academic year: August to May

Campuses in Plano (Texas) and Ranchos de Taos (New Mexico)

Pres.: Dr R. GERALD TURNER
Provost and Vice-Pres. for Academic Affairs: Dr PAUL W. LUDDEN
Vice-Pres. for Business and Finance: CHRISTINE C. REGIS
Vice-Pres. for Devt and External Affairs: BRAD E. CHEVES
Vice-Pres. for Exec. Affairs: Dr THOMAS E. BARRY
Vice-Pres. for Legal Affairs and Govt Relations, Gen. Counsel and Univ. Sec.: PAUL WARD
Vice-Pres. for Student Affairs: LORI S. WHITE
Assoc. Vice-Pres. and Dean for Student Life: JOANNE VOGEL
Registrar and Exec. Dir for Enrolment Services: JOHN HALL
Dean for Central Univ. Libraries: GILLIAN M. McCOMBS

Library: 3m. vols
Number of teachers: 668 (full-time)
Number of students: 10,938 (6,192 undergraduate, 3,372 graduate)

Publications: *Journal of Air Law and Commerce* (4 a year), *Law and Business Review of the Americas* (4 a year), *SMU Law Review* (4 a year), *SMU Magazine* (2 a year), *SMU Science and Technology Law Review* (3 a year), *Southwest Review* (4 a year), *The International Lawyer* (4 a year)

DEANS

Annette Caldwell Simmons School of Education and Human Development: DAVID J. CHARD
Dedman College of Humanities and Sciences: Dr WILLIAM M. TSUTSUI
Dedman School of Law: JOHN B. ATTANASIO
Edwin L. Cox School of Business: Dr ALBERT W. NIEMI, JR
Lyle School of Engineering: Dr GEOFFREY C. ORSAK
Meadows School of the Arts: Dr JOSÉ ANTONIO BOWEN
Perkins School of Theology: Dr WILLIAM B. LAWRENCE
Research and Graduate Studies: JAMES E. QUICK

SOUTHWESTERN ADVENTIST UNIVERSITY

POB 567, Keene, TX 76059-0567
100 W Hillcrest, Keene, TX 76059

Telephone: (817) 202-6794
E-mail: enroll@swau.edu
Internet: www.swau.edu

Founded 1893 as Keene Industrial Acad., present name 1996
Private control

Areas of study: biology and geology, business administration, communication, computer science, education, English, history and social sciences, kinesiology, mathematics and physical science, modern languages, music, nursing, psychology, religion

Pres.: ERIC ANDERSON
Vice-Pres. for Academic Admin.: BENJAMIN McARTHUR
Vice-Pres. for Enrolment: ENGA ALMEIDA
Vice-Pres. for Financial Admin.: LARRY GARRETT
Vice-Pres. for Student Services: JAMES
Vice-Pres. for Univ. Advancement: GARY TEMPLE
Registrar: BOB GARDNER
Univ. Librarian: CRISTINA THOMSEN

Library of 100,000 vols, 450 journals and magazines, 27,000 ebooks
Number of students: 790

SOUTHWESTERN ASSEMBLIES OF GOD UNIVERSITY (SAGU)

1200 Sycamore St, Waxahachie, TX 75165

Telephone: (972) 937-4010
E-mail: info@sagu.edu
Internet: www.sagu.edu

Founded 1941 by merger of Southwestern Bible School (f. 1927), Shield of Faith Bible Institute (f. 1931) and Southern Bible College (f. 1931), fmrly as Southwestern Bible Institute, present name 1994
Private control

Pres.: Dr KERMIT S. BRIDGES
Vice-Pres. for Academics: PAUL BROOKS
Vice-Pres. for Advancement: IRBY McKNIGHT
Vice-Pres. for Business and Finance: JAY TREWERN
Vice-Pres. for Enrolment and Retention: EDDIE DAVIS
Vice-Pres. for Student Services: TERRY PHIPPS
Registrar: HEATHER FRANCIS
Dir for Library: EUGENE HOLDER

Library of 110,000 vols
Number of students: 2,060

DEANS

College of Arts and Professions: LARRY GOODRICH
College of Bible and Church Ministries: LeROY BARTEL

SOUTHWESTERN BAPTIST THEOLOGICAL SEMINARY

POB 22000, Fort Worth, TX 76122
2001 W Seminary Dr., Fort Worth, TX 76115

Telephone: (817) 923-1921
E-mail: presidentsoffice@swbts.edu
Internet: www.swbts.edu

Founded 1901 as part of theological dept at Baylor Univ., present name 1907
Private control
Academic year: August to August (4 semesters)

Pres.: Dr PAIGE PATTERSON
Provost and Exec. Vice-Pres.: CRAIG BLAISING
Vice-Pres. for Business Admin.: KEVIN ENSLEY
Vice-Pres. for Institutional Advancement: MIKE HUGHES
Vice-Pres. for Student Services and Communications: THOMAS WHITE
Dean for Libraries: BERRY DRIVER

Library of 1,068,877 vols, 35,000 audiovisual items, 2,200 periodical subscriptions
Number of teachers: 115 (full-time)
Number of students: 3,250

Publications: *Southwestern Journal of Theology* (4 a year), *Southwestern News* (4 a year)

DEANS

College at Southwestern: Dr STEVEN SMITH
Jack D. Terry, Jr, School of Church and Family Ministries: Dr WAYLAN OWENS
J. Dalton Havard School for Theological Studies: Prof. Dr DENNY AUTREY

Roy Fish School of Evangelism and Missions: Prof. Dr KEITH EITEL
School of Church Music: Dr STEPHEN JOHNSON
School of Theology: Prof. Dr DAVID L. ALLEN
Southwestern Centre for Extension Education: DERON BILES
William R. Marshall Centre for Theological Studies: RUDY GONZÁLEZ

SOUTHWESTERN CHRISTIAN COLLEGE

POB 10, Terrell, TX 75160

Telephone: (972) 524-3341
Internet: www.swcc.edu

Founded 1948 as Southern Bible Institute, present name 1949
Private control
Academic year: August to May (2 semesters)

Offers BSc degrees

Pres.: Dr JACK EVANS, SR
Vice-Pres. for Academic Affairs: ZoaAnn TURNER
Vice-Pres. for Fiscal Affairs: DOUGLAS HOWIE
Vice-Pres. for Institutional Expansion: Dr JAMES MAXWELL
Vice-Pres. for Student Affairs: Dr BEN FOSTER
Dir for Admissions: WALTER PRICE
Librarian: DORIS JOHNSON

Library of 26,000 vols, 190 magazines, journals and newspapers
Number of teachers: 20
Number of students: 220

SOUTHWESTERN UNIVERSITY

1001 E University Ave, Georgetown, TX 78626

Telephone: (512) 863-6511
E-mail: admission@southwestern.edu
Internet: www.southwestern.edu

Founded 1840
Private control
Academic year: August to May

Pres.: JAKE B. SCHRUM
Provost and Dean for the Faculty: Dr JAMES W. HUNT
Vice-Pres. for Enrolment Services: DAVID J. VOSKUIL
Vice-Pres. for Fiscal Affairs: RICHARD L. ANDERSON
Vice-Pres. for Institutional Advancement and Univ. Relations: C. RICHARD McKELVEY
Vice-Pres. for Student Life: Dr GERALD D. BRODY
Registrar: DAVID STONES
Dean for Library Services: LYNNE BRODY

Library of 300,000 vols
Number of teachers: 115
Number of students: 1,370

Publications: *The Megaphone* (52 a year), *Southwestern Magazine* (4 a year), *The Sou' Wester* (1 a year)

DEANS

Brown College of Arts and Sciences: Dr G. BENJAMIN OLIVER
Sarofin School of Fine Arts: Dr PAUL J. GAFFNEY

ST EDWARD'S UNIVERSITY

3001 South Congress Ave, Austin, TX 78704-6489

Telephone: (512) 448-8400
E-mail: seu.admit@stedwards.edu
Internet: www.stedwards.edu

Founded 1885, present name 1925
Private control
Academic year: August to May

Campus in Angers (France)

Pres.: Dr GEORGE E. MARTIN

Provost and Exec. Vice-Pres.: DONNA M. JURICK

Vice-Pres. for Academic Affairs: Dr BRENDA VALLANCE

Vice-Pres. for Financial Affairs: RHONDA CARTWRIGHT

Vice-Pres. for Information Technology: DAVID WALDRON

Vice-Pres. for Marketing and Enrolment Management: PAIGE BOOTH

Vice-Pres. for Student Affairs: Dr SANDRA PACHECO

Vice-Pres. for Univ. Advancement: MICHAEL F. LARKIN

Assoc. Vice-Pres. for Academic Affairs: Dr MOLLY E. MINUS

Assoc. Vice-Pres. and Dean for Admissions: TRACY MANIER

Dean for Graduate and Adult Services: Dr WILLIAM CLABBY

Dean for Univ. Programmes: Dr CORY LOCK

Dir for Campus Min.: Fr PETER WALSH

Registrar: Dr LANCE R. HAYES

Dir for Library: PONGRACZ SENNYEY

Library of 215,912 vols
Number of teachers: 530
Number of students: 5,100

Publications: *Directions*, *St. Edward's University Magazine*

DEANS

New College: Dr HELENE CAUDILL

School of Behavioural and Social Sciences: RUSSELL FROHARDT

School of Education: Dr GRANT W. SIMPSON, JR

School of Humanities: SHARON NELL

School of Management and Business: Dr MARSHA C. KELLIHER

School of Natural Sciences: Dr THOMAS MITZEL

ST MARY'S UNIVERSITY

1 Camino Santa Maria, San Antonio, TX 78228-8572

Telephone: (210) 436-3011
E-mail: uadm@stmarytx.edu
Internet: www.stmarytx.edu

Founded 1852
Private control
Academic year: August to May

Pres.: Dr CHARLES L. COTRELL

Provost and Vice-Pres. for Academic Affairs: Dr ANDRÉ HAMPTON (acting)

Vice-Pres. for Admin. and Finance: REBECKAH J. DAY

Vice-Pres. for Enrolment Management: SUZANNE M. PETRUSCH

Vice-Pres. for Student Devt: KATHERINE M. SISOIAN

Vice-Pres. for Univ. Advancement: Dr PAUL T. KETTERING, III

Dean for Students: Dr TIM BESSLER

Registrar: CHRISTINA F. VILLANUEVA

Librarian: H. PALMER HALL

Library of 500,000 vols
Number of teachers: 190 (full-time)
Number of students: 4,100

Publications: *St. Mary's Journal on Legal Malpractice and Ethics*, *St. Mary's Law Journal* (4 a year)

DEANS

Bill Greehey School of Business: Dr TANUJA SINGH (acting)

Graduate School: Dr HENRY FLORES

School of Humanities and Social Sciences: Dr JANET B. DIZINNO

School of Law: Dr CHARLES E. CANTÚ

School of Science, Engineering and Technology: Prof. Dr WINSTON EREVELLES

STEPHEN F. AUSTIN STATE UNIVERSITY

1936 North St, Nacogdoches, TX 75962

Telephone: (936) 468-3401
E-mail: admissions@sfasu.edu
Internet: www.sfasu.edu

Founded 1923 as Stephen F. Austin State Teachers College, present name and status 1969

State control
Academic year: August to May

Pres.: Dr BAKER PATTILLO

Provost and Vice-Pres. for Academic Affairs: Dr RICHARD BERRY

Vice-Pres. for Devt: Dr SID WALKER

Vice-Pres. for Finance and Admin.: DANNY R. GALLANT

Vice-Pres. for Univ. Affairs: Dr STEVE WESTBROOK

Dir of Library: SHIRLEY DICKERSON

Library of 1,465,322 vols
Number of teachers: 745
Number of students: 12,900

DEANS

James I. Perkins College of Education: Dr JUDY A. ABBOTT

College of Fine Arts: Dr A. C. HIMES

Arthur Temple College of Forestry and Agriculture: Dr STEVEN H. BULLARD

College of Liberal and Applied Arts: Dr BRIAN MURPHY (acting)

College of Sciences and Mathematics: Dr KIMBERLY CHILDS

Graduate School: JAMES STANDLEY

Nelson Rusche College of Business: Dr DANNY R. ARNOLD

TEXAS A&M UNIVERSITY SYSTEM

301 Tarrow St, College Station, TX 77840

Telephone: (979) 458-7700
E-mail: syscomm@tamu.edu
Internet: www.tamus.edu

Founded 1948
Academic year: September to August

Chancellor: Dr JOHN SHARP

Deputy Chancellor for Academic Institutions and Agencies: Dr LEO SAYAVEDRA

Chief Financial Officer and Treas.: GREGORY R. ANDERSON

Vice-Chancellor for Academic Affairs: JAMES HALLMARK

Vice-Chancellor for Agriculture: Dr EDWARD HILER

Vice-Chancellor for Business Services: TOM KALE

Vice-Chancellor for Engineering: Dr C. ROLAND HADEN

Vice-Chancellor for Facilities Planning and Construction: Gen. WESLEY PEEL

Vice-Chancellor for Fed. and State Relations: Dr GUY DIEDRICH

Vice-Chancellor for Research, Planning and Continuing Education: Dr J. CHARLES LEE

Number of students: 120,400 ...

CONSTITUENT UNIVERSITIES

Prairie View A&M University

POB 519, Prairie View, TX 77446-0519
FM 1098 Rd and University Dr., Prairie View, TX 77446

Telephone: (936) 261-3311
E-mail: ire@pvamu.edu
Internet: www.pvamu.edu

Founded 1876 as Alta Vista Agriculture and Mechanical College of Texas for Colored Youths, present name and status 1973

Academic year: August to May

Pres.: GEORGE C. WRIGHT

Provost and Sr Vice-Pres. for Academic Affairs: E. JOAHANNE THOMAS-SMITH

Sr Vice-Pres. for Business Affairs: COREY S. BRADFORD

Vice-Pres. for Admin. and Auxiliary Services: FRED E. WASHINGTON

Vice-Pres. for Research: WILLIE F. TROTTY

Vice-Pres. for Student Affairs and Institutional Advancement: LAURETTA F. BYARS

Dir for Devt: NELSON BOWMAN

Registrar: DEBORAH DUNGEY

Dir for Library: Dr ROSIE L. ALBRITTON

Library of 370,000 vols, 700 periodicals, 42,000 eperiodicals, over 30,000 ebooks
Number of teachers: 500
Number of students: 8,800

DEANS

College of Agriculture and Human Sciences: Dr FREDDIE L. RICHARDS, SR

College of Business: Dr MUNIR QUDDUS

College of Juvenile Justice and Psychology: Dr DENNIS E. DANIELS

College of Nursing: Dr BETTY N. ADAMS

Graduate School: Dr WILLIE F. TROTTY

Marvin D. and June Samuel Brailsford College of Arts and Sciences: Dr DANNY R. KELLEY

Roy G. Perry College of Engineering and Architecture: Dr KENDALL T. HARRIS

Northwest Houston Center: Dr MICHAEL MCFRAZIER

School of Architecture: Dr IKHLAS SABOUNI

Whitlowe R. Green College of Education: Prof. Dr LUCIAN YATES, III

Tarleton State University

POB T-0001, Stephenville, TX 76402
333 W Washington, Stephenville, TX 76402

Telephone: (254) 968-9000
E-mail: uadm@tarleton.edu
Internet: www.tarleton.edu

Founded 1899 as John Tarleton College, present status 1917, present name 1973

Academic year: September to August

Pres.: Dr F. DOMINIC DOTTAVIO

Provost and Exec. Vice-Pres. for Academic Affairs: Dr KAREN MURRAY

Vice-Pres. for Finance and Admin.: JERRY GRAHAM

Vice-Pres. for Enrolment and Information Management: Dr BRAD CHILTON

Vice-Pres. for Institutional Advancement: Dr RICK RICHARDSON

Vice-Pres. for Student Life and Dean for Students: RUSTY JERGINS

Registrar: DENISE GROVES

Librarian: DONNA SAVAGE

Library: 1m. items
Number of teachers: 940
Number of students: 9,470

DEANS

College of Agricultural and Environmental Sciences: Dr DON CAWTHON

College of Business Administration: Dr ADOLFO BENEVIDAS

College of Education: Dr JILL BURK

College of Graduate Studies: Dr LINDA JONES

College of Liberal and Fine Arts: Dr KELLI STYRON

College of Science and Technology: Dr JAMES PIERCE

Texas A&M Health Science Center (TAMHSC)

8441 State Highway 47, 1 Clinical Bldg, Suite 3100, Bryan, TX 77807

Telephone: (979) 436-9100
E-mail: registrar@tamhsc.edu
Internet: www.tamhsc.edu

Founded 1999
Academic year: August to May (2 semesters)

Pres.: Dr NANCY W. DICKEY

Exec. Vice-Pres.: Dr ELVIN E. SMITH

Vice-Pres. for Academic Affairs: Dr RODERICK E. McCALLUM
Vice-Pres. for Finance and Admin.: Dr BARRY C. NELSON
Vice-Pres. for Governmental Affairs: Dr JENNY E. JONES
Vice-Pres. for Institutional Advancement and Communications: Dr RUSS GIBBS
Vice-Pres. for Research: Dr DAVID S. CARLSON
Registrar: DANA PENCE
Dir for Medical Sciences Library: GUADALUPE REYES

Library of 32,000 vols, 6,000 ejournals
Number of students: 1,300

DEANS

Baylor College of Dentistry: Dr LAWRENCE WOLINSKY
College of Medicine: Dr THOMAS SHOMAKER
College of Nursing: Dr SHARON WILKERSON
Irma Lerma Rangel College of Pharmacy: Dr INDRA K. REDDY
School of Graduate Studies: Dr CHRISTOPHER COLENDA
School of Rural Public Health: Dr CRAIG H. BLAKELY

Texas A&M International University

5201 University Blvd, Laredo, TX 78041-1900
Telephone: (956) 326-2001
Internet: www.tamiu.edu
Founded 1970, current status 1989, current name 1993
public control
Languages of instruction: English, Spanish
Academic year: August to August (3 semesters)
Pres.: Dr RAY M. KECK, III
Provost and Vice-Pres. for Academic Affairs: Dr PABLO ARENAZ
Vice-Pres. for Finance and Admin.: JUAN J. CASTILLO, JR
Vice-Pres. for Institutional Advancement: CANDY HEIN
Vice-Pres. for Student Success: Dr MINITA RAMIREZ
Dean of Graduate Studies and Research: JEFFREY M. BROWN
Dir for Admissions: ROSIE A. DICKINSON
Registrar: JUAN G. GARCIA, JR
Dir of Library: DOUGLAS M. FERRIER

Library of 259,086 vols, 1,079,218 microfiche and microfilm, over 51,298 state and fed. documents, 1,464 print subscriptions, approx. 28,895 ejournals, 46,000 ebooks
Number of teachers: 307
Number of students: 7,431

Publications: International Trade Journal, Journal of Border Education Research, Journal of Social and Ecological Boundaries, Western Hemispheric Trade Digest

DEANS

A. R. Sanchez, Jr School of Business Administration: Dr R. STEPHEN SEARS
College of Arts and Sciences: Dr THOMAS R. MITCHELL
College of Education: Dr CATHERYN J. WEITMAN
College of Nursing and Health Sciences: Dr GLENDA C. WALKER

Texas A&M University

College Station, TX 77843-1246
Telephone: (979) 845-3211
E-mail: admissions@tamu.edu
Internet: www.tamu.edu
Founded 1876 as a college, present name and status 1963
Academic year: August to August (2 semesters)
Br. campuses in Galveston, Qatar

Pres.: Dr R. BOWEN LOFTIN
Provost and Exec. Vice-Pres. for Academic Affairs: Dr KARAN L. WATSON
Vice-Pres. and Assoc. Provost for Diversity: Dr CHRISTINE A. STANLEY
Vice-Pres. for Admin.: Dr RODNEY P. McCLENDON
Vice-Pres. for Finance and Chief Financial Officer: B. J. CRAIN
Vice-Pres. for Research: Dr JEFFREY R. SEEMANN
Vice-Pres. for Student Affairs: Lt-Gen. JOSEPH F. WEBER
Registrar: VENESA A. HEIDICK
Dean for Univ. Libraries: Dr CHARLES GILREATH

Library of 4,577,598 vols, 936,270 ebooks, 108,064 serials, 5,714,052 microforms
Number of teachers: 2,900
Number of students: 50,000

DEANS

Bush School of Government and Public Service: ANDREW H. CARD, JR (acting)
College of Agriculture and Life Sciences: Dr MARK A. HUSSEY
College of Architecture: Prof. JORGE VANEGAS
College of Education and Human Development: Dr DOUGLAS J. PALMER
College of Geosciences: Dr KATE C. MILLER
College of Liberal Arts: Dr JOSÉ LUIS BERMÚDEZ
College of Medicine: Dr T. SAM SHOMAKER
College of Science: Dr H. JOSEPH NEWTON
College of Veterinary Medicine and Biomedical Sciences: Dr ELEANOR M. GREEN
Dwight Look College of Engineering: Dr M. KATHERINE BANKS
Mays Business School: Dr JERRY R. STRAWSER

Texas A&M University—Central Texas

1001 Leadership Pl., Killeen, TX 76549
Telephone: (254) 519-5400
E-mail: info@ct.tamus.edu
Internet: www.ct.tamus.edu
Founded 1999 as Tarleton-Central Texas, present name and status 2009
Academic year: August to May
Schools of arts and sciences, business administration, education; div. of graduate studies
Pres.: Dr MARC A. NIGLIAZZO
Provost and Vice-Pres. for Academic and Student Affairs: Dr PEG GRAY-VICKREY
Vice-Pres. for Finance and Admin.: GAYLENE NUNN
Registrar: DAWN KHOURY
Dir for Library Services: MARK HARRIS

Library of 120,000 vols, 25,800 periodicals and govt documents
Number of teachers: 60
Number of students: 2,550

Texas A&M University—Commerce

POB 3011, Commerce, TX 75429
2600 S Neal St, Commerce, TX 75428
Telephone: (903) 886-5014
E-mail: admissions@tamu-commerce.edu
Internet: www.tamu-commerce.edu
Founded 1889, present status 1996
Academic year: August to May
Pres. and CEO: Dr DAN JONES
Provost and Vice-Pres. for Academic Affairs: Dr LARRY F. LEMANSKI
Vice-Pres. for Business and Admin.: BOB BROWN
Vice-Pres. for Institutional Advancement: RANDY VAN DEVEN
Registrar: PAIGE BUSSELL
Dir for Libraries: GREG MITCHELL

Library: 1m. vols
Number of teachers: 450 (full-time)
Number of students: 8,900

Publication: PRIDE

DEANS

College of Business and Entrepreneurship: Dr HAL LANGFORD
College of Education and Human Services: Prof. Dr BRENT MANGUS
College of Humanities, Social Sciences and Arts: Prof. Dr SALVATORE ATTARDO
College of Science, Engineering and Agriculture: Prof. Dr GRADY PRICE BLOUNT

Texas A&M University—Corpus Christi

6300 Ocean Dr., Unit 5756, Corpus Christi, TX 78412-5756
Telephone: (361) 825-5700
E-mail: admiss@tamucc.edu
Internet: www.tamucc.edu
Founded 1947 as Univ. of Corpus Christi, present status 1989, present name 1993
Academic year: August to August
Pres. and CEO: Dr FLAVIUS C. KILLEBREW
Provost and Vice-Pres. for Academic Affairs: Dr CHRIS MARKWOOD
Exec. Vice-Pres. for Finance and Admin.: KATHRYN FUNK-BAXTER
Vice-Pres. for Institutional Advancement: Dr S. TRENT HILL
Vice-Pres. for Research, Commercialization and Outreach: Dr LUIS CIFUENTES
Vice-Pres. for Student Engagement and Success: Dr DON ALBRECHT
Registrar: MICHAEL RENDON
Library Dir and Asst Vice-Pres.: CHRISTINE SHUPALA

Library: 1.1m. vols
Number of teachers: 335
Number of students: 10,000

DEANS

College of Business: Dr MOUSTAFA H. ABDELSAMAD
College of Education: Dr ARTHUR HERNANDEZ
College of Liberal Arts: Dr KELLY QUINTANILLA
College of Nursing and Health Sciences: Dr MARY JANE HAMILTON
College of Science and Engineering: Dr FRANK L. PEZOLD, III
Community Outreach: Dr JAMES NEEDHAM
Graduate Studies: Dr JOANN CANALES
Teacher Education: ART HERNANDEZ

Texas A&M University—Kingsville

700 University Blvd, MSC 101, Kingsville, TX 78363-8202
Telephone: (361) 593-2111
E-mail: registrar@tamuk.edu
Internet: www.tamuk.edu
Founded 1917 as South Texas Normal School, present status 1989, present name 1993
Academic year: August to May (2 semesters)
Pres.: STEVEN H. TALLANT
Provost and Vice-Pres. for Academic Affairs: REX GANDY
Sr Vice-Pres. for Fiscal and Student Affairs: TERISA RILEY
Vice-Pres. for Enrolment Management: MANUEL LUJAN
Vice-Pres. for Finance and Admin.: MARILYN FOWLÉ
Vice-Pres. for Institutional Advancement: D. SCOTT GINES
Dean for Students: KIRSTEN COMPARY
Registrar: GEORGE WEIR
Library Dir: BRUCE R. SCHUENEMAN

Library of 2,742,941 vols, 2,122 periodicals, 853 journals, 40,501 ebooks, 654,007 microforms, 9,722 audiovisual items
Number of teachers: 385
Number of students: 6,200

DEANS

College of Arts and Sciences: Dr MICHAEL S. HOUF

College of Business Administration: Dr V. THOMAS DOCK

College of Education and Human Performance: Dr ALBERTO RUIZ

Dick and Mary Lewis Kleberg College of Agriculture, Natural Resources and Human Sciences: Dr G. ALLEN RASMUSSEN

Frank H. Dotterweich Engineering: Dr STEPHAN NIX

College of Graduate Studies: Dr MOHAMED ABDELRAHMAN

Honors College: Dr DOLORES GUERRERO

Texas A&M University—San Antonio

1 University Way, San Antonio, TX 78224

Telephone: (210) 784-1000

E-mail: ir@tamusa.tamus.edu

Internet: www.tamusa.tamus.edu

Founded 2000

State control

Language of instruction: English

Academic year: August to May

Schools of arts and sciences, business, education and kinesiology, graduate studies

Pres.: Dr MARIA HERNANDEZ FERRIER

Provost and Vice-Pres. for Academic Affairs: Dr BRENT MARRIOTT SNOW

Vice-Pres. for Finance and Admin. and Chief Financial Officer: KEN MITTS

Vice-Pres. for Strategic Initiatives, Institutional Advancement and Military Affairs: Dr CHARLES RODRIGUEZ

Univ. Librarian: STEFANIE WITTENBACH

Number of teachers: 185

Number of students: 4,100 (2,975 undergraduate, 1,125 graduate)

Texas A&M University—Texarkana

7101 University Ave, Texarkana, TX 75503

Telephone: (903) 223-3000

E-mail: admissions@tamut.edu

Internet: tamut.edu

Founded 1971 as E Texas State Univ. at Texarkana, present status 1996

Academic year: August to May

Pres.: Dr CARLISLE B. RATHBURN, III

Provost and Vice-Pres. for Academic Affairs: ROSANNE STRIPLING

Vice-Pres. for Finance and Admin. and Chief Financial Officer: RANDY RIKEL

Vice-Pres. for Student Engagement and Success: DANIEL KENT KELSO

Number of teachers: 50 (full-time)

Number of students: 1,740

DEANS

College of Business: Dr LARRY DAVIS

College of Education and Liberal Arts: Dr GLENDA BALLARD

College of Science, Technology, Engineering and Mathematics: Dr ARTHUR E. LINKINS

West Texas A&M University

2501 Fourth Ave, Canyon, TX 79016-0001

2403 Russell Long Blvd, Canyon, TX 79015

Telephone: (806) 651-0000

E-mail: cbarnes@wtamu.edu

Internet: wtamu.edu

Founded 1910 as West Texas State Normal College, present name 1993

Academic year: August to May

Pres. and CEO: Dr J. PATRICK O'BRIEN

Provost and Vice-Pres. for Academic Affairs: Dr WADE SCHAEFFER

Vice-Pres. for Business and Finance: GARY BARNES

Vice-Pres. for Enrolment Management: DAN D. GARCIA

Vice-Pres. for Institutional Advancement: Dr NEAL R. WEAVER

Vice-Pres. for Student Affairs: Dr DON D. ALBRECHT

Chief Information Officer: JAMES D. WEBB

Dir of Information and Library Resources: SHAWNA KENNEDY-WITTHAR

Library of 350,000 vols, 650,000 govt documents

Number of teachers: 250 (full-time)

Number of students: 7,900 (6,618 undergraduate, 1,282 graduate)

DEANS

College of Agriculture, Science and Engineering: Dr DON R. TOPLIFF

College of Business: Dr NEIL TERRY

College of Education and Social Sciences: Dr EDDIE HENDERSON

College of Nursing and Health Sciences: Dr J. DIRK NELSON

Graduate School and Research: ANGELA SPAULDING

Sybil B. Harrington College of Fine Arts and Humanities: Dr JESSICA MALLARD

TEXAS CHIROPRACTIC COLLEGE

5912 Spencer Highway, Pasadena, TX 77505-1699

Telephone: (281) 487-1170

E-mail: admissions@txchiro.edu

Internet: www.txchiro.edu

Founded 1908

Private control

Academic year: September to August

Pres.: Dr RICHARD G. BRASSARD

Provost and Sr Vice-Pres.: Dr CLAY McDONALD

Vice-Pres. for Academic and Program Devt: AL ADAMS

Vice-Pres. for Administrative Affairs: Dr STEPHEN L. HASLUND

Vice-Pres. for Enrolment Management: Dr FRED ZUKER

Vice-Pres. for Student Affairs: Dr STEPHEN HASLUND

Chief Fiscal Officer: WILLIAM S. QUINN

Dean for Academic Affairs: JOHN MROZEK

Library of 18,135 vols, 1,148 audiovisual items, 182 journals

Number of teachers: 25

Number of students: 400

TEXAS CHRISTIAN UNIVERSITY

2800 S University Dr., Fort Worth, TX 76129

Telephone: (817) 257-7000

E-mail: frogmail@tcu.edu

Internet: www.tcu.edu

Founded 1873 as Addran Male and Female College, present name 1902

Private control

Academic year: August to May

Chancellor: VICTOR J. BOSCHINI, JR

Provost and Vice-Chancellor for Academic Affairs: R. NOWELL DONOVAN

Vice-Chancellor for Finance and Admin.: BRIAN G. GUTIERREZ

Vice-Chancellor for Govt Affairs: LARRY D. LAUER

Vice-Chancellor for Student Affairs: KATHY CAVINS-TULL

Vice-Chancellor for Univ. Advancement: DONALD J. WHELAN, JR

Registrar: PATRICK MILLER

Dean for Library: Dr JUNE KOELKER

Library of 2,020,927 vols incl. 75,302 periodicals titles

Number of teachers: 665

Number of students: 9,725

Publications: *Image Magazine*, *Neeley Magazine*, *TCU Magazine* (4 a year)

DEANS

Addran College of Liberal Arts: Dr ANDREW SCHOOLMASTER

College of Communication: Dr DAVID WHILLOCK

College of Education: Dr MARY M. PATTON

College of Fine Arts: Dr SCOTT A. SULLIVAN

College of Science and Engineering: PHIL HARTMAN

Harris College of Nursing and Health Sciences: Dr PAULETTE BURNS

John V. Roach Honors College: Dr PEGGY W. WATSON

Neeley School of Business: Dr O. HOMER EREKSON

TEXAS COLLEGE

2404 N Grand Ave, Tyler, TX 75702

Telephone: (903) 593-8311

Internet: www.texascollege.edu

Founded 1894

Private control

Academic year: August to May (2 semesters)

Divs of business and social sciences, education, general studies and humanities, natural and computational sciences

Pres.: Dr DWIGHT J. FENNELL

Vice-Pres. for Academic Affairs: CYNTHIA MARSHALL-BIGGINS

Vice-Pres. for Business and Finance: JAMES HARRIS

Vice-Pres. for Institutional Advancement: JOHNNYE JONES

Vice-Pres. for Student Affairs: CALVIN GREEN

Dean for Student Affairs: ANTHONY MEYERS

Registrar: JOHN ROBERTS

Dir for Library Services: JOYCE ARPS

Number of teachers: 65

Number of students: 740

TEXAS LUTHERAN UNIVERSITY

1000 W Court St, Seguin, TX 78155

Telephone: (830) 372-8000

E-mail: admissions@tlu.edu

Internet: www.tlu.edu

Founded 1891

Private control

Language of instruction: English

Academic year: August to May

Offers courses in accountancy, arts, business administration, computer science, history, mathematics, music, politcal science, psychology, science, sociology

Pres.: Dr STUART DORSEY

Vice-Pres. and Dean of Student Life and Learning: KRISTI QUIROS

Vice-Pres. for Academic Affairs: Dr DEBBIE COTTRELL

Vice-Pres. for Devt and Alumni Relations: RICK ROBERTS

Vice-Pres. for Enrolment Services: TOM OLIVER

Vice-Pres. for Finance and Admin.: ANDREW NELSON

Registrar: GLENN YOCKEY

Univ. Librarian: Prof. MARTHA RINN

Library of 135,000 vols, 37,161 ebooks

Number of teachers: 75 (full-time)

Number of students: 1,320

TEXAS SOUTHERN UNIVERSITY

3100 Cleburne Ave, Houston, TX 77004

Telephone: (713) 313-7011

E-mail: admissions@tsu.edu

Internet: www.tsu.edu

Founded 1947 as Texas State Univ. for Negroes, present name 1951

State control

Academic year: September to August

Pres.: Dr JOHN M. RUDLEY
Provost and Vice-Pres. for Academic Affairs and Research: Dr SUNNY E. OHIA
Sr Vice-Pres. for Admin.: BRUCE WILSON
Vice-Pres. for Academic Services and Dean for Students: WILLIE MARSHALL
Vice-Pres. for Finance and Chief Financial Officer: JIM C. MCSHAN
Vice-Pres. for Univ. Advancement: WENDY H. ADAIR
Registrar: MARILYNN SQUARE
Dir for Libraries: Dr NORMA BEAN
Library of 261,506 vols, 504,149 microforms, 1,462 govt documents, 1,774 periodicals
Number of teachers: 590
Number of students: 9,500
Publications: *Ex-Press* (4 a year), *Inside TSU* (12 a year), *Urban Notebook* (4 a year)

DEANS

Barbara Jordan-Mickey Leland School of Public Affairs: Dr ROBERT D. BULLARD
College of Continuing Education: Dr IRVINE EPPS
College of Education: Dr LILLIAN B. POATS
College of Liberal Arts and Behavioral Sciences: Dr DANILLE K. TAYLOR
College of Pharmacy and Health Sciences: Dr SHIRLETTE G. MILTON
College of Science and Technology: Prof. Dr LEI YU
Graduate School: Dr GREGORY H. MADDOX
Jesse H. Jones School of Business: Dr RONALD A. JOHNSON
School of Communication: Dr JAMES W. WARD
Thomas F. Freeman Honors College: Dr HUMPHREY A. REGIS
Thurgood Marshall School of Law: Prof. DANNYE HOLLEY

TEXAS STATE UNIVERSITY SYSTEM

Thomas J. Rusk Bldg, 208 E 10th St, Suite 600, Austin, TX 78701-2407
Telephone: (512) 463-1808
E-mail: chancellor@tsus.edu
Internet: www.tsus.edu
Founded 1911 as State Normal School Board of Regents, current name adopted 1975
Chancellor: Dr BRIAN McCALL
Vice-Chancellor and Gen. Counsel: Dr FERNANDO GOMEZ
Vice-Chancellor for Academic Affairs: Dr PERRY MOORE
Vice-Chancellor for Contract Administration: Dr PETER GRAVES
Vice-Chancellor for Finance: Dr ROLAND SMITH
Vice-Chancellor for Governmental Relations: Dr SEAN CUNNINGHAM
Number of students: 70,000 (at 9 univs and colleges)...

CONSTITUENT UNIVERSITIES

Lamar University

4400 MLK Blvd, POB 10009, Beaumont, TX 77710
Telephone: (409) 880-7011
E-mail: records@lamar.edu
Internet: www.lamar.edu
Founded 1923 as South Park Jr College, current name adopted 1971
Academic year: August to May
Pres.: Dr JAMES M. SIMMONS
Provost and Vice-Pres.: Dr STEPHEN DOBLIN
Vice-Pres. for Finance and Operations: Dr GREGG LASSEN
Vice-Pres. for Student Affairs: NORMAN BELLARD
Vice-Pres. for Univ. Advancement: CAMILLE MOUTON
Registrar: DAVID SHORT

Dir of Library Services: DAVID CARROLL
Library: 1m. vols, 1,000 periodicals
Number of teachers: 510
Number of students: 14,400

DEANS

College of Arts and Sciences: Dr BRENDA NICHOLS
College of Business: Dr ENRIQUE R. VENTA
College of Education and Human Devt: Dr HOLLIS LOWERY-MOORE
College of Engineering: Dr JACK R. HOPPER
College of Fine Arts and Communications: Dr RUSS A. SCHULTZ
College of Graduate Studies: Dr VICTOR A. ZALOOM

Sam Houston State University

POB 2026, Huntsville, TX 77341
Telephone: (409) 294-1013
E-mail: adm_smm@shsu.edu
Internet: www.shsu.edu
Founded 1879 as Sam Houston Normal Institute, current name adopted 1969
Academic year: August to May
Pres.: Dr DANA L. GIBSON
Provost and Vice-Pres. for Academic Affairs: Dr JAIMIE HEBERT
Vice-Pres. for Enrolment Management: Dr HEATHER THIELEMANN
Vice-Pres. for Finance and Operations: ALVIN G. HOOTEN
Vice-Pres. for Student Services: FRANK PARKER
Vice-Pres. for Univ. Advancement: FRANK R. HOLMES
Dean of Students: JOHN YARABECK
Registrar: JOELLEN TIPTON
Dir for Libraries: ANN HOLDER
Library of 1,379,682 vols, 3,556 periodicals, 1,379,682 microforms, 629,489 records and tapes
Number of teachers: 820
Number of students: 17,600
Publications: *Advancing Women in Leadership*, *Crime and Justice International*, *Ed Leadership Review*, *Heritage Magazine* (2 a year), *Journal of Business Strategies*, *Texas Review* (2 a year), *The Texas Crime Pole*

DEANS

College of Business Administration: Dr MITCHELL J. MUEHSAM
College of Criminal Justice: Dr VINCENT J. WEBB
College of Education: Prof. Dr GENEVIEVE BROWN
College of Fine Arts and Mass Communication: Dr MARY ROBBINS
College of Humanities and Social Sciences: Dr JOHN DE CASTRO
College of Sciences: Dr JERRY COOK
Graduate Studies: Dr KANDI TAYEBI

Sul Ross State University

POB C-114, Alpine, TX 79832
Telephone: (432) 837-8011
E-mail: president@sulross.edu
Internet: www.sulross.edu
Founded 1917 as Sul Ross State Normal College, current name and status 1969
Academic year: September to August
Pres.: Dr RICARDO MAESTAS
Provost and Vice-Pres. for Academic and Student Affairs: Dr JIM CASE
Vice-Pres. for Enrolment Management: DENISE GROVES
Vice-Pres. for Finance and Operations: CESARIO VALENZUELA
Registrar: ROBERT CULLINS
Dean of Library: DON DOWDEY
Library of 760,700 vols

Number of teachers: 115
Number of students: 5,200

DEANS

School of Agricultural and Natural Resource Sciences: Dr ROBERT KINUCAN
School of Arts and Sciences: Dr CHRISTOPHER RITZI
School of Professional Studies: Dr MELANIE A. CROY.

ATTACHED COLLEGE

Rio Grande College: 205 Wildcat Dr., Del Rio, TX 78840; tel. (830) 703-4808; internet rgc.sulross.edu; f. 1985 as Sul Ross State Univ. Study Center, current name adopted 1995; campuses at Eagle Pass, Uvalde; offers Bachelors degree in biology, chemistry, criminal justice, English, general business, history, interdisciplinary studies, mathematics, psychology, social science, Spanish; offers Masters degree in business administration, education; 1,100 students; Dean and Assoc. Provost Dr J. PAUL SORRELS; Dir of Admissions and Records CLAUDIA R. WRIGHT

Texas State University

601 University Dr., JCK 883, San Marcos, TX 78666
Telephone: (512) 245-2111
E-mail: registrar@txstate.edu
Internet: www.txstate.edu
Founded 1899 as Southwest Texas State Normal School, current name and status 2003
Academic year: August to May
Pres.: Dr DENISE M. TRAUTH
Provost and Vice-Pres. for Academic Affairs: Dr EUGENE J. BOURGEOIS
Vice-Pres. for Finance and Support Services: WILLIAM A. NANCE
Vice-Pres. for IT: Dr C. VAN WYATT
Vice-Pres. for Student Affairs: Dr JOANNE SMITH
Vice-Pres. for Univ. Advancement: Dr BARBARA BREIER
Registrar: LOUIS JIMENEZ
Assoc. Vice-Pres. for Univ. Library: JOAN HEATH
Library of 1,461,532 vols, 1,987,802 microforms, 116,439 audiovisual items, 546,707 ebooks
Number of teachers: 1,711
Number of students: 35,546
Publications: *Electronic Journal of Differential Equations*, *Persona* (1 a year), *Southwestern American Literature* (2 a year), *Texas Books in Review* (4 a year), *The Journal of Texas Music History* (2 a year)

DEANS

College of Applied Arts: Dr T. JAIME CHAHIN
College of Education: Dr STAN CARPENTER
College of Fine Arts and Communication: Dr TIMOTHY MOTTET
College of Health Professions: Dr RUTH B. WELBORN
College of Liberal Arts: Dr MICHAEL HENNESSY
College of Science and Engineering: Dr STEPHEN SEIDMAN
Emmett and Miriam McCoy College of Business Administration: Dr DENISE SMART
Graduate College: Dr ANDREA GOLATO
Honors College: Dr HEATHER GALLOWAY
University College: Dr DANIEL BROWN

PROFESSORS

ADAMS, J., Military Science
ALI, M., Computer Science
ALLEN, J., Family/Consumer Sciences
ALLISON, E., English
ANGIRASA, A., Agriculture
ARAGON, S., Curriculum/Instruction

ARCHER, R., Psychology
ARON, G., Biology
ASH, G., Curriculum/Instruction
BALANOFF, H., Political Science
BANDY, C., Mathematics
BEALL, G., Chemistry
BECK, J., Education
BEEBE, S., Communication Studies
BELL, J., Management
BELL-METEREAU, R., English
BERNO, T., Art and Design
BIBLE, J., Finance and Economics
BLAIR, J., English
BLANCHARD-BOEHM, D., Geography
BLANDA, M., Chemistry
BLANKMEYER, E., Finance and Economics
BOEHM, R., Geography
BONNER, T., Biology
BOONE, M., Educational Leadership
BOURGEOIS, E., History
BOUSMAN, C., Anthropology
BRENNAN, M., History
BRINCKMEYER, L., Music
BRITTAIN, V., Political Science
BRITTAIN, W., Chemistry
BROOKS, A., Adult Education
BROWN, B., Geography
BROWN, R., History
BUSBY, M., English
BUTLER, D., Geography
CADE, T., Agriculture
CARPENTER, D., Education
CASSELLS, C., English
CAVERLY, D., Curriculum/Instruction
CAVITT, M., Music
CHAHIN, T., Social Work
CHAMLIN, M., Criminal Justice
CHAVKIN, A., English
CHAVKIN, N., Social Work
CHEATHAM, T., Communication Studies
CHIODO, B., Management
CLARK, T., Music
COHEN, P., English
COLOMBIK, R., Art and Design
CONROY, M., Art and Design
COSTELLO, J., Theatre
COVINGTON, B., Physics
CRIXELL, S., Family/Consumer Sciences
CUEVAS, G., Mathematics
CURTIN, E., Mathematics
CZYZEWSKA, M., Psychology
DAVIDSON, I., Music
DAVIS, B., Agriculture
DAVIS, B., Curriculum/Instruction
DAVIS, J., Psychology
DAVIS, J., Art and Design
DAVIS, R., CIS and Quant Methods
DAY, F., Geography
DAY, S., Sociology
DE LA TEJA, J., History
DEAN, N., Mathematics
DELL, J., Art and Design
DIX, J., Mathematics
DIXON, R., Geography
DOLEZAL, C., Curriculum/Instruction
DONNELLY, D., Physics
DROOPAD, R., Engineering
DUNN, D., History
EARL, R., Geography
EASTER, D., Chemistry
ECHEVERRIA, M., Modern Languages
EDGELL, J., Mathematics
ERBIN-ROESEMANN, M., Spanish American
  Literature
ESTAVILLE, L., Geography
FALL, K., Professional Counseling
FEAKES, D., Chemistry
FELSON, M., Criminal Justice
FISCHER, R., Modern Languages
FISK, R., Marketing
FITE, K., Curriculum/Instruction
FLEMING, J., Theatre
FORREST, J., Modern Languages
FORSTNER, M., Biology
FRIEDMAN, B., Family/Consumer Sciences
FULMER, G., Philosophy

FURNEY, S., Health/Human Performance
GABOR, C., Biology
GALLOWAY, H., Physics
GARBER, J., Anthropology
GARCIA, C., English
GARCIA, D., Biology
GAROFALO, C., Political Science
GEURAS, D., Philosophy
GINSBURG, H., Psychology
GIORDANO, A., Geography
GIUFFRE, P., Sociology
GLAJAR, V., Modern Languages
GOLATO, A., Modern Languages
GONZALEZ, G., Music
GORDON, J., Philosophy
GORDON, S., Educational Leadership
GORMAN, R., Political Science
GOWENS, P., Finance and Economics
GRASSO, K., Political Science
GRATZ, R., Communication Studies
GRAYSON, N., English
GREATHOUSE, D., Physical Therapy
GRIMES, T., English
GRIMES, T., Journalism and Mass Communi-
  cation
GU, W., Mathematics
HABINGREITHER, R., Engineering Technology
HAGER, H., Music
HAHN, D., Biology
HANKS, C., Philosophy
HARGETT, S., Theatre
HARNEY, L., Modern Languages
HARTER, R., Health/Human Performance
HARTMAN, G., History
HAWKINS, C., Social Work
HEABERLIN, D., English
HENNESSY, M., British Literature
HOLT, E., English
HOLTZ, M., Physics
HOMEYER, L., Professional Counseling
HORNE, F., Biology
HUFFMAN, D., Biology
HULING, L., Secondary Education
HULL, R., Philosophy
HURT, C., Music
HUSTON, M., Biology
HUTCHESON, P., Philosophy
HWANG, C., Computer Science
JAFFE, C., Modern Languages
JAMIESON, J., Criminal Justice
JIA, X., Mathematics
JIANG, Z., Mathematics
JOHANNESSEN, B., Curriculum/Instruction
JONES, J., Music
JONES, R., English
JOY, G., Philosophy
KEELEY-VASSBERG, M., Communication Stud-
  ies
KELEMEN, W., Psychology
KELLER, T., Mathematics
KENS, P., Political Science
KIRBY, E., Management
KISHAN, R., Finance and Economics
KNOX, K., Social Work
KNUDSON, D., Health/Human Performance
KOTARBA, J., Sociology
LAIRD, J., English
LAMAN, J., Family/Consumer Sciences
LARSEN, R., Geography
LASSER, J., School Psychology
LAUMER, J., Music
LEDBETTER, K., English
LEDBETTER, L., Music
LEDER, P., English
LEMKE, D., Biology
LESAGE, J., Finance and Economics
LOCHMAN, D., English
LONGLEY, G., Aquatic Resources
LONGORIA, T., Political Science
LOPES, V., Biology
LU, Y., Geography
LUIZZI, V., Philosophy
MACEY, S., Geography
MAKOWSKI, E., History
MANDZIUK, R., Communication Studies
MARGERISON, K., History

MARTIN, C., Modern Languages
MARTIN, G., Curriculum/Instruction
MARTIN, J., Music
McBRIDE, M., Journalism and Mass Commu-
  nication
McCLELLAN, S., Engineering
McGEE, J., Finance and Economics
McGEE, R., Anthropology
McLEAN, R., Biology
McWILLIAMS, J., History
MEANEY, K., Health/Human Performance
MEEK, W., Art and Design
MEHTA, M., CIS and Quant Methods
MENDEZ, R., Psychology
MIDDLEBROOK, B., Management
MIJARES, T., Criminal Justice
MINIFIE, J., Management
MIRELES, S., Mathematics
MOGAB, J., Finance and Economics
MONROE, D., English
MONTONDON, L., Accounting
MOREY, S., Mathematics
MORRIS, R., Accounting
MORRISON, E., Health Administration
MORRISON, S., English
MOTTET, T., Communication Studies
MULLINS, W., Criminal Justice
MUNIZ SOLARI, O., Geography
MURRAY, T., Health/Human Performance
MYERS, T., Physics
NELSON, D., Mass Communication
NEY, C., Theatre
NEY, M., Theatre
NGU, H., Computer Science
NIBLETT, M., Art and Design
NICE, C., Biology
NIELSEN, E., Art and Design
NOBLE, D., Social Work
NOWICKI, M., Health Administration
O'BRIEN, W., English
OGLETREE, S., Psychology
OLES, C., Business Administration
OLSON, D., Physics
OLSON, M., English
OPHEIM, C., Political Science
OSBORNE, R., Psychology
OSKAM, J., Journalism and Mass Communi-
  cation
PANDEY, R., Engineering
PANKEY, R., Health/Human Performance
PASSTY, G., Mathematics
PATTISON, P., Finance and Economics
PAULSON, E., Curriculum/Instruction
PEELER, W., Theatre
PEIRCE, K., English
PEIRCE, K., Journalism and Mass Communi-
  cation
PENG, W., Computer Science
PENN, B., Art and Design
PERKINS, D., Criminal Justice
PETERSEN, J., Geography
PETROFF, P., Respiratory Therapy
PINER, E., Physics
PINO, N., Sociology
PLOTTS, C., School Psychology
POLLOCK, J., Criminal Justice
PRICE, L., Education Assessment
RAHE, C., Agriculture
RAHM, D., Political Science
RAIBORN, C., Accounting
RANSONE, J., Health/Human Performance
RAO, S., Journalism and Mass Communica-
  tion
RAST, W., Aquatic Resources
RECHNER, P., Management
REID, R., Art and Design
REILLY, F., Anthropology
RENFRO, P., Journalism and Mass Communi-
  cation
RENICK, C., Health Administration
RICHARDSON, C., Agriculture
ROHDE, R., Clinical Lab Science
ROSS-GORDON, J., Adult Education
ROSSMO, K., Criminal Justice
ROW, B., Art and Design
RUDZINSKI, W., Chemistry

RUNYAN, R., Family/Consumer Sciences
RUTLEDGE, R., Accounting
SALEM, P., Communication Studies
SANDERS, B., Physical Therapy
SANDERS, D., Finance and Economics
SCHEUERMANN, B., Curriculum/Instruction
SCHMIDT, E., Professional Counselling
SCHMIDT, J., Music
SCHULER, N., Music
SEIDMAN, S., Mathematics
SELBER, K., Social Work
SELLERS, C., Criminal Justice
SHAH, V., CIS and Quant Methods
SHANMUGAM, R., Health Administration
SHEN, J., Mathematics
SHI, H., Computer Science
SHIELDS, P., Political Science
SKERPAN-WHEELER, E., English
SMART, D., Business Administration
SMITH, B., Journalism and Mass Communication
SMITH, K., Marketing
SMITH, L., Theatre
SODDERS, R., Theatre
SRIRAMAN, V., Engineering Technology
STAFFORD, M., Criminal Justice
STEPHAN, K., Engineering
STERN, H., Engineering
STIMMEL, D., Psychology
STONE, W., Criminal Justice
STOUFFER, W., Political Science
STUTTS, M., Marketing
SUCKLING, P., Geography
TAYLOR, R., Marketing
TEMPONI, C., Management
THICKSTUN, T., Mathematics
THOMAS, N., Music
THOMPSON, S., Accounting
THORNE, D., Busniess Administration
TIEFENBACHER, J., Geography
TODD, M., Art and Design
TOEWS, M., Family/Consumer Sciences
TOMASSO, J., Biology
TORREJON, R., Mathematics
TRAUTH, D., Mass Communication
UGALDE, S., Modern Languages
VATTEM, D., Family/Consumer Sciences
VILLAGRAN, M., Communication Studies
VISWANATHAN, V., Engineering
WAITE, D., Educational Leadership
WALKER, J., Health/Human Performance
WALTER, R., Chemistry
WARD, K., Political Science
WARMS, R., Anthropology
WARSHAUER, M., Mathematics
WATKINS, A., Accounting
WATT, T., Sociology
WECKERLY, F., Biology
WELBORN, R., Nursing and Healthcare Delivery
WELSH, S., Mathematics
WHEELER, L., Curriculum/Instruction
WILEY, D., Health/Human Performance
WILLIAMS, M., Communication Studies
WILLIAMS, S., Family/Consumer Sciences
WILLIAMSON, P., Biology
WILSON, M., English
WILSON, S., English
WINEK, G., Engineering Technology
WINKING, K., Music
WITHROW, B., Criminal Justice
YICK, J., History
ZHAN, F., Geography

Other constituent institutions awarding Assoc.-level degrees include: Lamar Institute of Technology, Lamar State College-Orange and Lamar State College-Port Arthur

TEXAS TECH UNIVERSITY SYSTEM

Lubbock, TX 79409-2005
Telephone: (806) 742-0012
E-mail: chancellor@ttu.edu
Internet: www.texastech.edu

Founded 1996
State control
Academic year: August to May
Chancellor: Dr KENT R. HANCE
Vice-Chancellor: Dr TIM HUDSON
Vice-Chancellor and Chief Financial Officer: JIM BRUNJES
Vice-Chancellor and Gen. Counsel: JOHN T. HUFFAKER
Vice-Chancellor for Academic Affairs: Dr JOSEPH C. RALLO
Vice-Chancellor for Facilities Planning and Construction: MICHAEL MOLINA
Vice-Chancellor for Governmental Relations: MIKE SANDERS
Vice-Chancellor for Institutional Advancement: Dr KELLY OVERLEY
Vice-Chancellor for Policy and Planning: Dr JOHN OPPERMAN
Vice-Chancellor for Research and Commercialization: JODEY ARRINGTON...

CONSTITUENT UNIVERSITIES

Angelo State University

c/o Office of Admissions, ASU Station 11014, San Angelo, TX 76909-1014
2601 West Ave N, San Angelo, TX 76909
Telephone: (325) 942-2041
E-mail: admissions@angelo.edu
Internet: www.angelo.edu
Founded 1928 as San Angelo Jr College, present name 1965
Academic year: September to August
Pres.: Dr JOSEPH C. RALLO
Provost and Vice-Pres. for Academic Affairs: Dr BRIAN J. MAY
Vice-Pres. for Devt and Public Relations: Dr JASON C. PENRY
Vice-Pres. for Finance and Admin.: MICHAEL REID
Vice-Pres. for Student Affairs and Enrolment Management: Dr JAVIER FLORES
Dir of Admissions and Recruitment Services: MICHAEL LOEHRING
Registrar: CYNTHIA D. WEEAKS
Library Exec. Dir: Dr MAURICE G. FORTIN
Library of 1,705,900 items
Number of teachers: 330
Number of students: 7,100

DEANS

College of Arts and Sciences: Dr PAUL K. SWETS
College of Business: Dr CORBETT F. GAULDEN, JR
College of Education: Dr JOHN J. MIAZGA, JR
College of Graduate Studies: Dr BRIAN J. MAY
College of Health and Human Services: Prof. Dr LESLIE M. MAYRAND

Texas Tech University

2500 Broadway, Lubbock, TX 79409-2005
Telephone: (806) 742-2011
E-mail: admissions@ttu.edu
Internet: www.ttu.edu
Founded 1923 as Texas Technological College, present name 1969
Academic year: August to May
Pres.: Dr GUY BAILEY
Provost and Sr Vice-Pres.: Dr BOB SMITH
Sr Vice-Pres. for Research: TAYLOR EIGHMY
Vice-Pres. for Admin. and Finance and Chief Financial Officer: KYLE CLARK
Vice-Pres. for Research: TAYLOR EIGHMY
Registrar: BOBBIE BROWN
Dean of Libraries: DON DYAL
Library of 1,700,000 vols
Number of teachers: 1,575
Number of students: 31,600
Publications: *Engineering Our Future* (2 a year), *Envision* (1 a year), *Estate Planning and Community Property Law Journal* (2 a year), *Texas Tech Administrative Law Journal* (2 a year), *Texas Tech Law Review* (4 a year)

DEANS

College of Agricultural Sciences and Natural Resources: Dr MICHAEL GALYEAN
College of Architecture: Prof. ANDREW VERNOOY
College of Arts and Sciences: Dr LAWRENCE SCHOVANEC
College of Education: Dr SCOTT RIDLEY
College of Human Sciences: Dr LINDA C. HOOVER
College of Mass Communication: JERRY HUDSON
College of Visual and Performing Arts: Dr CAROL EDWARDS
Edward E. Whitacre College of Engineering: Dr AL SACCO, JR
Graduate School: Dr PEGGY GORDON MILLER
Honors College: Dr STEPHEN E. FRITZ
Rawls College of Business Admin.: Dr ALLEN T. MCINNES
School of Law: Prof. Dr DARBY DICKERSON
Univ. College: Dr VALERIE PATON

Texas Tech University Health Sciences Center

3601 Fourth St, Lubbock, TX 79430
Telephone: (806) 743-1000
Internet: www.ttuhsc.edu
Founded 1969 as Texas Tech University School of Medicine, present name and status 1979
Campuses in Abilene, Amarillo, Dallas Fort Worth, El Paso, Permian Basin
Pres.: Dr TEDD MITCHELL
Exec. Vice-Pres. and Provost and Vice-Pres. for Medical Affairs: Dr STEVEN L. BERK
Exec. Vice-Pres. for Finance and Admin.: ELMO CAVIN
Exec. Vice-Pres. for Research: Dr DOUGLAS M. STOCCO
Sr Vice-Pres. for Academic Affairs: Dr RIAL ROLFE
Library of 54,500 vols, 23,000 ejournals, 50,000 ebooks
Number of teachers: 860 (full-time)
Number of students: 4,100

DEANS

Anita Perry School of Nursing: Dr MICHAEL EVANS
Gayle Greve Hunt School of Nursing: Dr JOSEFINA LUJAN
Graduate School of Biomedical Sciences: Dr DOUGLAS M. STOCCO
Paul L. Foster School of Medicine: Dr JOSE MANUEL DE LA ROSA
School of Allied Health Sciences: Dr PAUL P. BROOKE, JR
School of Medicine: Dr STEVEN LEE BERK
School of Nursing: Dr MICHAEL EVANS
School of Pharmacy: Dr ARTHUR A. NELSON, JR

TEXAS WESLEYAN UNIVERSITY

1201 Wesleyan St, Fort Worth, TX 76105-1536
Telephone: (817) 531-4444
E-mail: info@txwesleyan.edu
Internet: www.txwes.edu
Founded 1890 as Polytechnic College, present name 1989
Private control
Academic year: September to May
Pres.: Prof. FREDERICK G. SLABACH
Provost and Sr Vice-Pres.: Dr ALLEN H. HENDERSON
Vice-Pres. for Advancement: JOAN CANTY

Vice-Pres. for Enrolment and Student Services: PATI ALEXANDER
Vice-Pres. for Finance and Admin.: KAREN MONTGOMERY
Registrar: KAHLA VAN TOORN
Univ. Librarian: CINDY SWIGGER
Library of 219,053 vols
Number of teachers: 170 (full-time)
Number of students: 3,180
Publication: *Wesleyan Magazine* (2 a year)

DEANS

School of Arts and Letters: Dr STEVEN DANIELL
School of Business Administration: Dr HECTOR QUINTANILLA
School of Education: Dr CARLOS MARTINEZ
School of Natural and Social Sciences: Dr TREVOR MORRIS
Texas Wesleyan School of Law: FREDERIC WHITE

TEXAS WOMAN'S UNIVERSITY

POB 425589, 304 Administration Dr., Denton, TX 76204
Telephone: (940) 898-2000
E-mail: admissions@twu.edu
Internet: www.twu.edu
Founded 1901 as Girls Industrial College, present name 1957
State control
Academic year: August to May
Chancellor and Pres.: Dr ANN STUART
Provost and Vice-Pres. for Academic Affairs: Dr ROBERT NEELY
Vice-Pres. for Finance and Admin.: Dr BRENDA FLOYD
Vice-Pres. for Information Services: BILL PALMERTREE
Vice-Pres. for Institutional Advancement: (vacant)
Vice-Pres. for Student Life: Dr RICHARD NICHOLAS
Dean for Libraries: SHERILYN BIRD
Library of 788,271 vols
Number of teachers: 990
Number of students: 14,200

DEANS

College of Arts and Sciences: Dr ANN Q. STATON
College of Health Sciences: Dr JIMMY H. ISHEE
College of Nursing: PATRICIA HOLDEN-HUCHTON
College of Professional Education: Dr L. NAN RESTINE
Graduate School: Dr JENNIFER MARTIN

TRINITY UNIVERSITY

1 Trinity Pl., San Antonio, TX 78212-7200
Telephone: (210) 999-8401
E-mail: admissions@trinity.edu
Internet: www.trinity.edu
Founded 1869
Private control
Academic year: August to May
Liberal arts and sciences
Pres.: Dr DENNIS A. AHLBURG
Vice-Pres. for Faculty and Student Affairs: Dr MICHAEL FISCHER
Vice-Pres. for Finance and Admin.: MARK A. DETTERICK
Vice-Pres. for Information Resources: CHARLES B. WHITE
Dean for Admissions: CHRISTOPHER ELLERTSON
Dean for Students and Assoc. Vice-Pres. for Student Affairs: DAVID M. TUTTLE
Registrar: ALFRED RODRIGUEZ
Librarian: DIANE GRAVES

Library: 1m. vols
Number of teachers: 245 (full-time)
Number of students: 2,400

UNIVERSITY OF DALLAS

1845 E Northgate Dr., Irving, TX 75062-4736
Telephone: (972) 721-5000
Internet: www.udallas.edu
Founded 1956
Private control
Academic year: June to May
Pres.: THOMAS W. KEEFE
Provost and Exec. Vice-Pres.: Dr J. WILLIAM BERRY
Exec. Vice-Pres.: ROBERT M. GALECKE
Vice-Pres. and Dean for Enrolment: Dr JOHN G. PLOTTS
Vice-Pres. for Univ. Advancement: Dr AMANDA RAINEY
Exec. Dir for Devt and Alumni Relations: BENJAMIN HART
Dean for Student Life: DENISE PHILLIPS
Registrar: JANET BURK
Dir for Library and Univ. Research: Dr ROBERT S. DUPREE
Library of 372,071 vols, incl. books, serials, ebooks, microforms and audiovisual materials
Number of teachers: 130 (full-time)
Number of students: 2,840 (1,335 undergraduates and 1,505 graduates)

DEANS

Braniff Graduate School of Liberal Arts: Dr DAVID R. SWEET
College of Business: Dr ROBERT SCHERER
Constantin College of Liberal Arts: Dr CHARLES W. EAKER
School of Ministry: Dr MARK GOODWIN

UNIVERSITY OF HOUSTON SYSTEM

4800 Calhoun, Houston, TX 77004-2018
Telephone: (713) 743-8189
Internet: www.uhsa.uh.edu
Chancellor: Dr RENU KHATOR
Number of students: 65,000 ...

CONSTITUENT INSTITUTIONS

University of Houston

4800 Calhoun Rd, Houston, TX 77004
Telephone: (713) 743-1000
E-mail: president@uh.edu
Internet: www.uh.edu
Founded 1927, present status 1977
Academic year: September to August
Pres.: Dr RENU KHATOR
Provost and Sr Vice-Pres. for Academic Affairs: Dr JOHN J. ANTEL
Exec. Vice-Pres. for Admin. and Finance: Dr CARL CARLUCCI
Vice-Pres. for Community Relations and Institutional Access: Dr ELWYN C. LEE
Vice-Pres. for Govt Relations: GROVER CAMPBELL
Vice-Pres. for Legal Affairs and Gen. Counsel: Dr DONA HAMILTON CORNELL
Vice-Pres. for Research and Technology Transfer: Dr RATHINDRA N. BOSE
Vice-Pres. for Student Affairs: Dr J. RICHARD WALKER
Vice-Pres. for Univ. Advancement: ELOISE DUNN STUHR
Dean for Students: Dr WILLIAM F. MUNSON
Dean for Libraries: DANA C. ROOKS
Library: 2.7m. vols, 76,000 journals
Number of teachers: 3,450
Number of students: 39,800
Publications: *Experts Directory, UHouston*

DEANS

College of Education: Dr ROBERT McPHERSON
College of Liberal Arts and Social Sciences: JOHN W. ROBERTS
College of Natural Sciences and Mathematics: Dr MARK A. SMITH
College of Optometry: Prof. Dr EARL L. SMITH, III
College of Pharmacy: F. LAMAR PRITCHARD
College of Technology: Dr WILLIAM E. FITZGIBBON, III
Conrad N. Hilton College of Hotel and Restaurant Management: Dr JOHN T. BOWEN
C. T. Bauer College of Business Administration: Prof. Dr LATHA RAMCHAND
Cullen College of Engineering: Prof. Dr JOSEPH W. TEDESCO
Gerald D. Hines College of Architecture: PATRICIA BELTON OLIVER
Graduate College of Social Work: Prof. Dr IRA C. COLBY
Honors College: Prof. Dr WILLIAM MONROE
Law Center: Prof. RAYMOND T. NIMMER

University of Houston–Clear Lake

2700 Bay Area Blvd, Houston, TX 77058-1098
Telephone: (281) 283-7600
E-mail: president@cl.uh.edu
Internet: www.uhcl.edu
Founded 1974
Academic year: September to August
Pres.: Prof. Dr WILLIAM A. STAPLES
Sr Vice-Pres. for Academic Affairs and Provost: CARL A. STOCKTON
Vice-Pres. for Admin. and Finance: MICHELLE DOTTER
Dean for Students: DAVID RACHITA
Registrar (vacant)
Exec. Dir: KAREN WEILHORSKI
Library of 2,222,020 vols
Number of teachers: 745
Number of students: 8,100

DEANS

School of Business: Dr WILLIAM THEODORE CUMMINGS
School of Education: Dr DENNIS W. SPUCK
School of Human Sciences and Humanities: Dr RICK SHORT
School of Science and Computer Engineering: Dr ZBIGNIEW CZAJKIEWICZ

University of Houston—Downtown

1 Main St, Houston, TX 77002
Telephone: (713) 221-8000
E-mail: uhdinfo@uhd.edu
Internet: www.uhd.edu
Founded 1974
State control
Academic year: August to July
Pres.: Dr WILLIAM V. FLORES
Provost and Sr Vice-Pres. for Academic Affairs: ED HUGETZ
Vice-Pres. for Admin. and Finance: DAVID BRADLEY
Vice-Pres. for Advancement and External Relations: JOHANNA WOLFE
Vice-Pres. for Operations and Employment Services: IVONNE MONTALBANO
Assoc. Vice-Pres. for Information Technology: HOSSEIN SHAHROKHI
Asst Vice-Pres. for Facilities Management: CHRIS McCALL
Dir for Admissions: SPENCER LIGHTSY
Dir for Student Activities: PATRICK EDWARDS
Dean for Students: Dr SARA JAHANSOUZ
Dean for Enrolment Management: TOMIKIA LeGRANDE
Exec. Dir for Information Technology: ERIN MAYER
Exec. Dir for Univ. Relations: DIANE SUMMERS

Dir for Presidential Affairs: GILDA PARKER
Exec. Dir for W. I. Dykes Library: PAT ENSOR
Library of 208,180 vols, incl. 208,180 books, serial back files and govt documents; 9,731 electronic and print periodicals, 315,743 ebooks, 3,785 audiovisual materials, 5,690 microforms
Number of teachers: 662
Number of students: 13,757

DEANS

College of Business: Dr D. MICHAEL FIELDS
College of Humanities and Social Sciences: Dr DoVEANNA FULTON
College of Public Service: Dr BETH PELZ
College of Sciences and Technology: Dr AKIF UZMAN
Univ. College: Dr CHRIS BIRCHAK

University of Houston—Victoria

3007 N Ben Wilson, Victoria, TX 77901
Telephone: (361) 570-4848
E-mail: webmaster@uhv.edu
Internet: www.uhv.edu
Founded 1973 as Univ. of Houston Victoria Center, present name and status 1983
Academic year: August to May (2 semesters)
Pres.: Dr PHIL CASTILLE
Provost and Vice-Pres. for Academic Affairs: Dr DON SMITH
Vice-Pres. for Admin. and Finance: WAYNE B. BERAN
Registrar: TRUDY WORTHAM
Sr Dir for Libraries: Dr JOE DAHLSTROM
Library of 250,000 vols, 45,000 ebooks, 23,293 microforms, 23,293 audiovisual materials
Number of teachers: 210
Number of students: 4,330
Publications: *American Book Review* (6 a year), *Symplokē*

DEANS

School of Arts and Sciences: Prof. Dr JEFFREY R. DiLEO
School of Business Administration: Dr FARHANG NIROOMAND
School of Education and Human Devt: Dr DIANE PRINCE
School of Nursing: Dr KATHRYN TART

UNIVERSITY OF MARY HARDIN-BAYLOR

900 College St, Belton, TX 76513
Telephone: (254) 295-8642
E-mail: registrar@umhb.edu
Internet: www.umhb.edu
Founded 1845, present name 1978
Private control
Academic year: August to May (2 semesters)
Pres.: Dr RANDY G. O'REAR
Provost and Sr Vice-Pres. for Academic Affairs: Dr STEVE L. OLDHAM
Dir for Admissions: BRENT BURKS
Registrar: AMY McGILVRAY
Dir for Learning Resources and Librarian: DENISE KARIMKHANI
Library of 202,229 vols, 26,760 ebooks, 878 journals, 74,000 ejournals, 6,869 audiovisual items, 1,944 CDs, 13,712 microforms
Number of teachers: 320 (full-time)
Number of students: 3,140

DEANS

College of Business: Dr JAMES R. KING, JR
College of Christian Studies: Prof. Dr TIMOTHY G. CRAWFORD
College of Education: Dr MARLENE ZIPPERLEN
College of Humanities: Dr DANIEL S. MYNATT
College of Nursing: Dr SHARON SOUTER
College of Sciences: Dr DARRELL G. WATSON

College of Visual and Performing Arts: Prof. TED BARNES
Graduate School: Dr COLIN WILBORN

UNIVERSITY OF NORTH TEXAS SYSTEM

UNT System Bldg, 1901 Main St, Dallas, TX 75201
Telephone: (214) 752-8585
E-mail: untsystem@untsystem.edu
Internet: untsystem.edu
State control
Chancellor: LEE F. JACKSON
Vice-Chancellor for Academic Affairs and Student Success: ROSEMARY R. HAGGETT
Vice-Chancellor for Administrative Services: RAYNARD O. KEARBEY
Vice-Chancellor for Finance: TERRY PANKRATZ
Vice-Chancellor for Government Relations: JACK MORTON
Vice-Chancellor for Strategic Partnerships: WILLIAM H. LIVELY...

CONSTITUENT UNIVERSITIES

University of North Texas at Dallas

7300 University Hills Blvd, Dallas, TX 75241
Telephone: (972) 780-3600
E-mail: untdallas@unt.edu
Founded 1999
Pres.: Dr JOHN ELLIS PRICE
Provost and Vice-Pres.: Dr JOHN BEEHLER
Vice-Pres. for Finance and Admin: WAYNE USRY
Vice-Pres. for Univ. Advancement: J. DOUGLAS SMITH
Head Librarian: BRENDA ROBERTSON

DEANS

Division of Education and Human Services: Dr SHERYL SANTOS-HATCHETT
Division of Liberal Arts and Life Sciences: Dr GERARD RAMBALLY
Division of Urban and Professional Studies: Dr JEHAD YASIN

University of North Texas at Denton

1155 Union Circle 311277, Denton, TX 76203-5017
Telephone: (940) 565-2000
E-mail: undergrad@unt.edu
Internet: www.unt.edu
Founded 1890 as Texas Normal College and Teacher Training Institute, present name 1988
State control
Academic year: August to May
Pres.: NEAL SMATRESK
Provost and Vice-Pres. for Academic Affairs: Dr WARREN BURGGREN
Vice-Pres. and Gen. Counsel: Dr RICHARD RAFES
Vice-Pres. for Admin. and Finance: ANDREW M. HARRIS
Vice-Pres. for Advancement: LISA BIRLEY BARONIO
Vice-Pres. for External Affairs: WALTER E. PARKER
Vice-Pres. for Institutional Equity and Diversity: Dr GILDA GARCIA
Vice-Pres. for Research and Economic Devt: Dr GEOFF GAMBLE
Vice-Pres. for Student Affairs: Dr ELIZABETH WITH
Vice-Pres. for Univ. and Community Affairs: Dr HERMAN TOTTEN
Vice-Pres. for Univ. Relations, Communications and Marketing: DEBORAH LELIAERT
Dir for Admissions: MARCILLA COLLINSWORTH
Registrar: JONEEL J. HARRIS
Dean for Libraries: Dr MARTIN HALBERT
Library: 6m. vols

Number of teachers: 1,044 (full-time)
Number of students: 33,431 (26,305 undergraduate, 7,126 graduate)

University of North Texas Health Science Center at Fort Worth

3500 Camp Bowie Blvd, Fort Worth, TX 76107
Telephone: (817) 735-2000
Internet: www.hsc.unt.edu
Founded 1970 as Texas College of Osteopathic Medicine, present status 1999
Pres.: Dr SCOTT B. RANSOM
Provost and Exec. Vice-Pres. for Academic Affairs: Dr THOMAS YORIO
Exec. Vice-Pres.: Dr KATHLEEN FORBES
Vice-Pres. and Chief Financial Officer: JOHN A. HARMAN
Vice-Pres. and Chief Medical Officer: ROBERT C. ADAMS
Vice-Pres. for Admin. and Chief of Staff: JENNIFER M TREVIÑO
Vice-Pres. for Devt and Institutional Advancement: GARY GRANT
Vice-Pres. for Financial Services: MICHAEL MUELLER
Vice-Pres. for Governmental Affairs: DANIEL M. JENSEN
Vice-Pres. for Research: Dr GLENN DILLON
Vice-Pres. for Student Affairs: Dr THOMAS MOORMAN
Library of 27,000 vols, 16,000 ejournals
Number of teachers: 400
Number of students: 1,760

DEANS

College of Pharmacy: Dr MYRON K. JACOBSON
Graduate School of Biomedical Sciences: Dr JAMBOOR VISHWANATHA
School of Health Professions: Dr J. WARREN ANDERSON
School of Public Health: Dr RICHARD KURZ
Texas College of Osteopathic Medicine: Dr DON PESKA

UNIVERSITY OF ST THOMAS

3800 Montrose, Houston, TX 77006-4626
Telephone: (713) 522-7911
E-mail: admissions@stthom.edu
Internet: www.stthom.edu
Founded 1947
Private control
Academic year: August to May
Pres.: Dr ROBERT R. IVANY
Vice-Pres. for Academic Affairs: Dr DOMINIC A. AQUILA
Vice-Pres. for Finance: JAMES M. BOOTH
Vice-Pres. for Institutional Advancement: CYNTHIA COLBERT RILEY
Vice-Pres. for Marketing Communications and Enrolment Management: VICKIE ALLEMAN
Vice-Pres. for Planning and Technology: GARY McCORMACK
Vice-Pres. for Student Affairs: PATRICIA MCKINLEY
Registrar: KIMBERLY SANDERS
Dean for Univ. Libraries: JAMES PICCININNI
Library of 250,263 vols, 58,041 periodicals
Number of teachers: 335
Number of students: 3,700
Publications: *Star View Newsletter* (18 a year), *St Thomas Magazine* (3 a year), *The Summa* (8 a year), *UST Insider* (3 a year)

DEANS

Cameron School of Business: Dr BARRY WILBRATTE
Extended Programs: Dr RAVI SRINIVAS
School of Arts and Sciences: Rev. JOSEPH PILSNER

School of Education: Dr NORA HUTTO
School of Nursing: Dr POLDI TSCHIRCH
School of Theology: Dr SANDRA MAGIE

UNIVERSITY OF TEXAS SYSTEM

601 Colorado St, Austin, TX 78701-2982

Telephone: (512) 499-4200

E-mail: chancellor@utsystem.edu

Internet: www.utsystem.edu

Founded 1883

Chancellor: Dr FRANCISCO GONZALEZ CIGAR-ROA

Exec. Vice-Chancellor for Academic Affairs: Dr PEDRO REYES

Exec. Vice-Chancellor for Business Affairs: SCOTT C. KELLEY

Vice-Chancellor for Admin.: TONYA MOTEN BROWN

Vice-Chancellor for Community and Business Relations: JOHN DE LA GARZA, JR

Vice-Chancellor for External Relations: RANDA S. SAFADY

Vice-Chancellor for Fed. Relations: WILLIAM H. SHUTE

Vice-Chancellor for Governmental Relations: BARRY R. MCBEE

Vice-Chancellor and Gen. Counsel: BARRY D. BURGDORF

Number of teachers: 18,893
Number of students: 211,213 ...

CONSTITUENT INSTITUTIONS

University of Texas at Austin

1 University Station, Austin, TX 78712

Telephone: (512) 471-3434

E-mail: president@po.utexas.edu

Internet: www.utexas.edu

Founded 1883 as Univ. of Texas, current name adopted 1967

Academic year: September to May (2 terms)

Pres.: WILLIAM POWERS, JR

Provost and Exec. Vice-Pres.: GREGORY L. FENVES

Vice-Pres. and Chief Financial Officer: KEVIN P. HEGARTY

Vice-Pres. for Research: JUAN M. SANCHEZ

Vice-Pres. for Student Affairs: JUAN C. GONZÁLEZ

Vice-Pres. for Univ. Operations: PATRICIA L. CLUBB

Chief Information Officer and Assoc. Vice-Pres.: BRAD ENGLERT

Dean for Students and Sr Assoc. Vice-Pres. for Student Affairs: Dr SONCIA REAGINS-LILLY

Vice-Provost and Registrar: SHELBY STANFIELD

Vice-Provost and Dir for Libraries: FRED M. HEATH

Library: see under Libraries and Archives

Number of teachers: 3,271

Number of students: 51,195

DEANS

Cockrell College of Engineering: Dr GREGORY L. FENVES

College of Communication: RODERICK P. HART

College of Education: Prof. Dr MANUEL J. JUSTIZ

College of Fine Arts: DOUGLAS DEMPSTER

College of Liberal Arts: Dr RANDY L. DIEHL

College of Natural Sciences: Prof. Dr LINDA HICKE

College of Pharmacy: Dr M. LYNN CRISMON

Dell Medical School: CLAY JOHNSTON

Graduate School: Dr JUDITH H. LANGLOIS

Jackson School of Geosciences: Dr SHARON MOSHER

LBJ School of Public Affairs: Dr ROBERT HUTCHINGS

McCombs School of Business: Dr THOMAS W. GILLIGAN

School of Architecture: Dr FREDERICK R. STEINER

School of Information: Prof. Dr ANDREW P. DILLON

School of Law: WARD FARNSWORTH

School of Nursing: Prof. Dr ALEXA K. STUIF-BERGEN

School of Social Work: Prof. Dr LUIS H. ZAYAS

School of Undergraduate Studies: Prof. PAUL WOODRUFF

PROFESSORS

School of Architecture:

ALOFSIN, A.
ARUMI, F. N.
ATKINSON, S. D.
BENEDIKT, M. L.
BLACK, J. S.
GARRISON, M. L.
KAHN, T. D.
KWALLEK, N. P.
LEIDING, G.
SPECK, L. W.
SWALLOW, R. P.
WILSON, P. A.

School of Information:

DAVIS, D. G., JR
GRACY, II, D. B.
HALLMARK, J.
HARMON, E. G.
IMMROTH, B. F.
LUKENBILL, W. B.
MIKSA, F. L.
ROY, L.

School of Law:

ANDERSON, D. A.
ASCHER, M. L.
BAKER, L. A.
BERMAN, M. N.
BLACK, B. S.
BLAIS, L. E.
BOBBITT, P. C.
CARSON, II, L. C.
CHURGIN, M. J.
CLEVELAND, S. H.
COHEN, J. M.
DAWSON, R. O.
DIX, G. E.
DZIENKOWSKI, J. S.
ENGLE, K. L.
FORBATH, W. E.
GERGEN, M. P.
GETMAN, J. G.
GOODE, S. J.
GRAGLIA, L. A.
HANSEN, P. I.
HU, H. T. C.
JOHANSON, S. M.
JOHNSON, C. H.
KLEIN, S. R.
LAYCOCK, H. D.
LEITER, B. R.
LEVINSON, S. V.
MCGARITY, T. O.
MANN, R. J.
MARKESINIS, B. S.
MARKOVITS, I.
MARKOVITS, R. S.
MULLENIX, L. S.
PERONI, R. J.
POWE, L. A., JR
RABBAN, D. M.
RAU, A. S.
REESE, R. A.
ROBERTSON, D. W.
ROBERTSON, J. A.
SAGER, L.
SAMPSON, J. J.
SHARLOT, M. M.
SILVER, C. M.
SMITH, E. E.
STEIKER, J. M.

STURLEY, M. F.
TORRES, G.
WAGNER, W. E.
WEINBERG, L.
WELLBORN, O. G.
WESTBROOK, J. L.
WOOLLEY, P.
YOUNG, E. A.

School of Nursing:

GROBE, S. J.
HOUSTON, L. S.
PENTICUFF, J. H.
REW, D. L.
STUIFBERGEN, A. M.
WALKER, L. O.

School of Social Work:

CHOI, N.
DINITTO, D. M.
FONG, R.
FRANKLIN, C. G. S.
GREENE, R. R.
LAUDERDALE, M. L.
LEIN, L.
MCROY, R. G.
POOLE, D. L.
RUBIN, A.
SCHWAB, A. J., JR
SHORKEY, C. T.
STREETER, C. L.

LBJ School of Public Affairs:

APFEL, K. S.
AUERBACH, R. D.
BOSKE, L. B.
EATON, D. J.
FLAMM, K.
GALBRAITH, J. K.
HAMILTON, D. S.
INMAN, B. R.
RHODES, L.
SCHOTT, R. L.
SPELMAN, W. G.
WARNER, D. C.
WILSON, R. H.

McCombs School of Business:

ALLISON, J. R., Management Science and Information Systems
ALPERT, M. I., Marketing Admin.
ANDERSON, U. L., Accounting
ATIASE, R., Accounting
BAGCHI, U., Management
BALAKRISHNAN, A., Management Science and Information Systems
BARUA, A., Management Science and Information Systems
BROCKETT, P. L., Management Science and Information Systems
BRONIARCZYK, S. M., Marketing Admin.
BROWN, K. C., Finance
BUTLER, J. S., Management
COX III, E. P., Marketing Admin.
CROSS, F. B., Management Science and Information Systems
CUNNINGHAM, W. H., Marketing Admin.
DAMIEN, P., Management Science and Information Systems
DAVIS-BLAKE, A., Management
DEITRICK, J. W., Accounting
DUKERICH, J. M., Management
DYER, J. S., Management Science and Information Systems
FITZSIMMONS, J. A., Management
FREDRICKSON, J. W., Management
FREEMAN, R. N., Accounting
GOLDEN, L. L., Marketing Admin.
GRANOF, M. H., Accounting
HENION, II, K. E., Marketing Admin.
HIRST, D. E., Accounting
HOYER, W. D., Marketing Admin.
HUBER, G. P., Management
HUFF, D. L., Marketing Admin.
JARVENPAA, S. L., Management Science and Information Systems
JEMISON, D. B., Management
JENNINGS, R. G., Accounting

KACHELMEIER, S. J., Accounting
KINNEY, W. R., Jr, Accounting
KOEHLER, J. J., Management Science and Information Systems
KOONCE, L. L., Accounting
LASDON, L. S., Management Science and Information Systems
LIMBERG, S. T., Accounting
MCALISTER, L. M., Marketing Admin.
MCDANIEL, R. R., JR, Management Science and Information Systems
MAGEE, S. P., Finance
MAHAJAN, V., Marketing Admin.
MAY, R. G., Accounting
METTLEN, R. D., Finance
MORRICE, D. J., Management
MURRAY, P. C., Management Science and Information Systems
NEWMAN, D. P., Accounting
PETERSON, R. A., Marketing Admin.
PRENTICE, R. A., Management Science and Information Systems
RAO, R. K. S., Finance
ROBINSON, J. R., Accounting
RONN, E. I., Finance
RUEFLI, T. W., Management Science and Information Systems
SAGER, T. W., Management Science and Information Systems
SALBU, S. R., Management Science and Information Systems
SHAW, B. M., Management Science and Information Systems
SHIVELY, T. S., Management Science and Information Systems
SPELLMAN, L. J., Finance
STARKS, L. T., Finance
TITMAN, S., Finance
WESTPHAL, J. D., Management
WHINSTON, A. B., Management Science and Information Systems
YU, G., Management Science and Information Systems

College of Communication:
ALVES, R. C., Journalism
BERG, C. E., Radio, Television, Film
BRANHAM, L. E., Journalism
BROWNING, L. D., Communication Studies
BRUMMETT, B., Communication Studies
BURNS, N. M., Advertising
CHAMPLIN, C. A., Communication Sciences and Disorders
CHERWITZ, R. A., Communication Studies
CUNNINGHAM, I. C., Advertising
DALY, J. A., Communication Studies
DARLING, D. C., Journalism
DAVIS, B. L., Communication Sciences and Disorders
GILLAM, R. B., Communication Sciences and Disorders
KNAPP, M. L., Communication Studies
LECKENBY, J. D., Advertising
MCCOMBS, M. E., Journalism
MARQUARDT, T. P., Communication Sciences and Disorders
MARTIN, F. N., Communication Sciences and Disorders
MAXWELL, M. M., Communication Studies
MORRISON, D. K., Advertising
MURPHY, J. H., Advertising
OLASKY, M. N., Journalism
REESE, S. D., Journalism
RICHARDS, J. I., Advertising
SCHATZ, T. G., Radio-Television-Film
STAIGER, J., Radio-Television-Film
STEKLER, P. J., Radio-Television-Film
STOUT, P. A., Advertising
STRAUBHAAR, J., Radio-Television-Film
STROVER, S. L., Radio-Television-Film
TODD, R. G., Journalism
VANGELISTI, A. L., Communication Studies
WILCOX, G. B., Advertising
WILLIAMS, J. D., Advertising

College of Education:
ABRAHAM, L. D., Curriculum and Instruction
AINSLIE, R. C., Educational Psychology
BARUFALDI, J. P., Curriculum and Instruction
BETHEL, L. J., Curriculum and Instruction
BORICH, G. D., Educational Psychology
BRYANT, D. P., Special Education
CANTU, N. V., Educational Admin.
CARLSON, C. I., Educational Psychology
CHALIP, L. H., Kinesiology and Health Education
COYLE, E. F., Kinesiology and Health Education
DAVIS, O. L., JR, Curriculum and Instruction
DODD, B. G., Educational Psychology
DUNCAN, J. P., Educational Adminstration
EMMER, E. T., Educational Psychology
FALBO, T. L., Educational Psychology
FARRAR, R. P., Kinesiology and Health Education
FIELD, S. L., Curriculum and Instruction
FOLEY, D. E., Curriculum and Instruction
GOTTLIEB, N. H., Kinesiology and Health Education
GUSZAK, F. J., Curriculum and Instruction
HOFFMAN, J. V., Curriculum and Instruction
HOLAHAN, C. K., Kinesiology and Health Education
HORWITZ, E. K., Curriculum and Instruction
IVY, J. L., Kinesiology and Health Education
KAMEEN, M. C., Educational Admin.
KEITH, T. Z., Educational Psychology
KOCH, W. R., Educational Psychology
LASHER, W. F., Educational Adminstration
MANASTER, G. J., Educational Psychology
MOORE, W., Educational Admin.
ORTIZ, A. A., Special Education
OVANDO, M. N., Educational Admin.
PARKER, R. M., Special Education
REIFEL, S., Curriculum and Instruction
RESTA, P. E., Curriculum and Instruction
RICHARDSON, F. C., Educational Psychology
RIETH, H. J., Special Education
ROSER, N. L., Curriculum and Instruction
ROUECHE, J. E., JR, Educational Admin.
SCHALLERT, D. L., Educational Psychology
SCRIBNER, J. D., Educational Admin.
SEMRUD-CLIKEMAN, M., Educational Psychology
SIGAFOOS, J., Special Education
SPIRDUSO, W. W., Kinesiology and Health Education
STARK, K. D., Educational Psychology
STARNES, J. W., Kinesiology and Health Education
STEINHARDT, M. A., Kinesiology and Health Education
THOMAS, M. P., JR, Educational Admin.
VALENCIA, R., Educational Psychology
VAUGHN, S., Special Education
WEINSTEIN, C. E., Educational Psychology
WICKER, F. W., Educational Psychology
YATES, J. R., Educational Admin.

College of Engineering:
ABRAHAM, J. A., Electrical and Computer Engineering
AGGARWAL, J. K., Electrical and Computer Engineering
ALLEN, D. T., Chemical Engineering
AMBLER, A. P., Electrical and Computer Engineering
ARAPOSTATHIS, A., Electrical and Computer Engineering
BABUSKA, I. M., Aerospace Engineering
BALDICK, R., Electrical and Computer Engineering
BANERJEE, S. K., Electrical and Computer Engineering

BARBER, K. S., Electrical and Computer Engineering
BARD, J. F., Mechanical Engineering
BARNES, J. W., Mechanical Engineering
BARR, R. E., Mechanical Engineering
BEAMAN, J. J., JR, Mechanical Engineering
BECKER, E. B., Aerospace Engineering
BECKER, M. F., Electrical and Computer Engineering
BENNIGHOF, J. K., Aerospace Engineering
BISHOP, R. H., Aerospace Engineering
BOGARD, D. G., Mechanical Engineering
BONNECAZE, R. T., Chemical Engineering
BOSTICK, F. X., JR, Electrical and Computer Engineering
BOURELL, D. L., Mechanical Engineering
BOVIK, A. C., Electrical and Computer Engineering
BREEN, J. E., Civil Engineering
BRYANT, M. D., Mechanical Engineering
BUCKMAN, A. B., Electrical and Computer Engineering
CAMPBELL, J. C., Electrical and Computer Engineering
CAREY, G. F., Aerospace Engineering
CHARBENEAU, R. J., Civil Engineering
CHEN, R. T., Electrical and Computer Engineering
COGDELL, J. R., Electrical and Computer Engineering
CORSI, R. L., Civil Engineering
CRAWFORD, M. E., Mechanical Engineering
CRAWFORD, M. M., Mechanical Engineering
CRAWFORD, R. H., Mechanical Engineering
DAWSON, C. N., Aerospace Engineering
DE VECIANA, G. A., Electrical and Computer Engineering
DEMKOWICZ, L. F., Aerospace Engineering
DEPPE, D. G., Electrical and Computer Engineering
DILLER, K. R., Biomedical Engineering
DODABALAPUR, A., Electrical and Computer Engineering
DOLLING, D. S., Aerospace Engineering
DRIGA, M. D., Electrical and Computer Engineering
EDGAR, T. F., Chemical Engineering
EKERDT, J. G., Chemical Engineering
ELLZEY, J. L., Mechanical Engineering
ENGELHARDT, M. D., Civil Engineering
FAHRENTHOLD, E. P., Mechanical Engineering
FLAKE, R. H., Electrical and Computer Engineering
FOWLER, D. W., Civil Engineering
FOWLER, W. T., Aerospace Engineering
FRANK, K. H., Civil Engineering
FREEMAN, B. D., Chemical Engineering
GARG, V. K., Electrical and Computer Engineering
GEORGIOU, G., Chemical Engineering
GHOSH, J., Electrical and Computer Engineering
GIBSON, G. E., Jr, Civil Engineering
GOODENOUGH, J. B., Mechanical Engineering
GRADY, W. M., Electrical and Computer Engineering
GRAY, K. E., Petroleum and Geosystems Engineering
GREEN, P. F., Chemical Engineering
HAAS, C. T., Civil Engineering
HALL, M. J., Mechanical Engineering
HALLOCK, G. A., Electrical and Computer Engineering
HAMILTON, M. F., Mechanical Engineering
HAYES, L. J., Aerospace Engineering
HO, P. S., Mechanical Engineering
HOWELL, J. R., Mechanical Engineering
HUGHES, T. J., Aerospace Engineering
HULL, D. G., Aerospace Engineering
JIRSA, J. O., Civil Engineering
JOHNSTON, K. P., Chemical Engineering
JOSE-YACAMAN, M., Chemical Engineering
KINNAS, S. A., Civil Engineering
KLINGNER, R. E., Civil Engineering

KOEN, B. V., Mechanical Engineering
KWONG, D.-L., Electrical and Computer Engineering
KYRIAKIDES, S., Aerospace Engineering
LAKE, L. W., Petroleum and Geosystems Engineering
LANDSBERGER, S., Mechanical Engineering
LAWLER, D. F., Civil Engineering
LEE, J. C., Electrical and Computer Engineering
LIECHTI, K. M., Aerospace Engineering
LILJESTRAND, H. M., Civil Engineering
LING, H., Electrical and Computer Engineering
LIPOVSKI, G. J., Electrical and Computer Engineering
LLOYD, D. R., Chemical Engineering
MACHEMEHL, R. B., Civil Engineering
MCKINNEY, D. C., Civil Engineering
MAIDMENT, D. R., Civil Engineering
MALINA, J. F., JR, Civil Engineering
MANTHIRAM, A., Mechanical Engineering
MARK, H. M., Aerospace Engineering
MASADA, G. Y., Mechanical Engineering
MATTHEWS, R. D., Mechanical Engineering
MEAR, M. E., Aerospace Engineering
MOON, T. J., Mechanical Engineering
MULLINS, C. B., Chemical Engineering
NEIKIRK, D. P., Electrical and Computer Engineering
NICHOLS, S. P., Mechanical Engineering
O'CONNOR, J. T., Civil Engineering
ODEN, J. T., Aerospace Engineering
PANDY, M. G., Biomedical Engineering
PANTON, R. L., Mechanical Engineering
PATT, Y. N., Electrical and Computer Engineering
PAUL, D. R., Chemical Engineering
PEARCE, J. A., Electrical and Computer Engineering
PEPPAS, N. A., Biomedical Engineering
PERRY, D. E., Electrical and Computer Engineering
PETERS, E. J., Petroleum and Geosystems Engineering
POPE, G. A., Petroleum and Geosystems Engineering
POWERS, E. J., JR, Electrical and Computer Engineering
QIN, S. Z. J., Chemical Engineering
RALLS, K. M., Mechanical Engineering
RAPPAPORT, T. S., Electrical and Computer Engineering
RAVI-CHANDAR, K. A., Aerospace Engineering
REIBLE, D. D., Civil Engineering
RICHARDS KORTUM, R. R., Biomedical Engineering
ROCHELLE, G. T., Chemical Engineering
RODIN, G. J., Aerospace Engineering
ROSSEN, W. R., Petroleum and Geosystems Engineering
RYLANDER III, H. G., Biomedical Engineering
SANCHEZ, I. C., Chemical Engineering
SANDBERG, I. W., Electrical and Computer Engineering
SCHMIDT, P. S., Mechanical Engineering
SCHUTZ, B. E., Aerospace Engineering
SEPEHRNOORI, K., Petroleum and Geosystems Engineering
SHARMA, M. M., Petroleum and Geosystems Engineering
SORBER, C. A., Civil Engineering
SPEITEL, G. E., JR, Civil Engineering
STEARMAN, R. O., Aerospace Engineering
STOKOE, II, K. H., Civil Engineering
SWARTZLANDER, E. E., JR, Electrical and Computer Engineering
TAPLEY, B. D., Aerospace Engineering
TASSOULAS, J. L., Civil Engineering
TESAR, D., Mechanical Engineering
VALVANO, J. W., Electrical and Computer Engineering
VANRENSBURG, W. C. J., Petroleum and Geosystems Engineering
VARGHESE, P. L., Aerospace Engineering

VLIET, G. C., Mechanical Engineering
WAGNER, T. J., Electrical and Computer Engineering
WALSER, R. M., Electrical and Computer Engineering
WALTON, C. M., Civil Engineering
WELCH, A. J., Biomedical Engineering
WHEELER, M. F., Aerospace Engineering
WILLSON, C. G., Chemical Engineering
WOMACK, B. F., Electrical and Computer Engineering
WOOD, K. L., Mechanical Engineering
WOOD, S. L., Civil Engineering
WRIGHT, S. G., Civil Engineering
YURA, J. A., Civil Engineering

College of Fine Arts:

ALLEN, G. D., Music
ANTOKELETZ, E. M., Music
BALTZER, R. A., Music
BARNITZ, J. E., Art and Art History
BEHAGUE, G. H., Music
BLOOM, M., Theatre and Dance
BOLIN, P. E., Art and Art History
BRICKENS, N. O., Music
BROCKETT, O. G., Theatre and Dance
BROOKS, R. L., Art and Art History
CHANDLER, B. G., Music
CLARKE, J. R., Art and Art History
COLES, T. R., Art and Art History
DALY, S. J., Art and Art History
DEMPSTER, D. J., Theatre and Dance
DESIMONE, R. A., Music
DOLAN, J. S., Theatre and Dance
DORN, F., Theatre and Dance
DUKE, R. A., Music
ERLMANN, V. F., Music
GARRETT, N. B., Music
GLAVAN, J. J., Theatre and Dance
GOODMAN, M. K., Art and Art History
GRANTHAM, D. J., Music
GUERRA, L. A., Music
HALE, K. J., Art and Art History
HELLMER, J. L., Music
HENDERSON, L. D., Art and Art History
HILLEY, M. F., Music
HOLLADAY, J. A., Art and Art History
HOLZMAN, A., Music
ISACKES, R. M., Theatre and Dance
JELLISON, J. A., Music
JENNINGS, C. A., Theatre and Dance
JUNKIN, J. F., Music
LEWIS, W. L., Music
LUCERO, A. L., Theatre and Dance
LUNDBERG, W. A., Art and Art History
MCFARLAND, L. D., Art and Art History
MARCH, H. C., Music
MARIANI, V. A., Art and Art History
MILLER, L. C., Theatre and Dance
MILLIKEN, G., Art and Art History
NEL, A., Music
NEUBERT, B. D., Music
NEUMEYER, D. P., Music
PINKSTON, R. F., Music
PITTEL, H. C., Music
RICHTER, G. A., Music
SASAKI, R. K., Music
SAWYER, M. L., Art and Art History
SCHMIDT, R. N., Theatre and Dance
SHIFF, R. A., Art and Art History
SLAWEK, S. M., Music
SMITH, J. C., Art and Art History
STUART, D. S., Art and Art History
TAYLOR, R. A., Music
TUSA, M. C., Music
ULBRICHT, J. W., Art and Art History
WELCHER, D. E., Music
WILEY, D. C., Music
WIMAN, L. R., Art and Art History
YOUNG, P. C., Music
ZEDER, S. L., Theatre and Dance

College of Liberal Arts:

ABBOUD, P. F., Middle Eastern Studies
ABZUG, R. H., History
ALBRECHT, D. G., Psychology
ALLAIRE, E. B., Philosophy

ANGEL, R. J., Sociology
ANGELELLI, I. A., Philosophy
ARENS, K. M., Germanic Studies
ARMSTRONG, D., Classics
ASHER, N. M., Philosophy
AYRES, J. B., English
BAKER, M.-F. J., French and Italian
BAR-ADON, A., Middle Eastern Studies
BARANY, Z. D., Government
BARNOUW, J., English
BEALER, G., Philosophy
BERNUCCI, L. M., Spanish and Portuguese
BERTELSEN, L., English
BINI, D., French and Italian
BIOW, D. G., French and Italian
BIRDSONG, D. P., French and Italian
BLOCKLEY, M. E., English
BONEVAC, D. A., Philosophy
BRAYBROOKE, D., Government
BRONARS, S. G., Economics
BROW, J. B., Anthropology
BROWN, J. C., History
BROWN, N. D., History
BUCHANAN, II, B., Government
BUDZISZEWSKI, J., Government
BUMP, J. F., English
BUSS, A. H., Psychology
BUSS, D. M., Psychology
BUTZER, K. W., Geography
CABLE, T. M., English
CARLSON, C. L., Psychology
CARTER, J. C., Classics
CARTON, E. B., English
CARVER, L. D., English
CAUSEY, R. L., Philosophy
CAUVIN, J.-P. B., French and Italian
CHANG, S.-S., Asian Studies
CHARNEY, D. H., Rhetoric and Composition
COHEN, L. B., Psychology
COOPER, R. W., Economics
CORBAE, P. D., Economics
CREW, D. F., History
CULLINGFORD, E., English
CVETKOVICH, A., English
DACY, D. C., Economics
DAVIES, C. S., Geography
DAWSON, R. L., French and Italian
DEIGH, J., Philosophy
DIEHL, R. L., Psychology
DIETZ, H. A., Government
DOMJAN, M. P., Psychology
DONAHUE, F. E., Germanic Studies
DONALD, S., Economics
DOOLITTLE, W., Geography
DOUGHTY, R. W., Geography
DULLES, J. W. F., American Studies
DUSANSKY, R., Economics
EDLUND-BERRY, I. M., Classics
EDWARDS, D. V., Government
ELLISON, C. G., Sociology
ENELOW, J. M., Government
ENGLAND, N. C., Linguistics
FAIGLEY, L. L., English
FALOLA, O. O., History
FARRELL, J. P., English
FLORES, R. R., Anthropology
FREEMAN, G. P., Government
FRIEDMAN, A. W., English
FRISBIE, W. P., Sociology
FULLERTON, D., Economics
FURMAN, L. J., English
GAGARIN, M., Classics
GALINSKY, G. K., Classics
GALLE, O. R., Sociology
GARRISON, J. D., English
GEISLER, III, W. S., Psychology
GERACI, V. J., Economics
GHANOONPARVAR, M., Middle Eastern Studies
GHOSE, Z. A., English
GILDEN, D. L., Psychology
GLADE, W. P., Economics
GLENN, N. D., Sociology
GOETZMANN, W. H., History
GONZALEZ-GERTH, M., Spanish and Portuguese

GONZALEZ-LIMA, F., Psychology
GRAHAM, D. B., English
HAKE, S., Germanic Studies
HAMERMESH, D. S., Economics
HANCOCK, I. F., Linguistics
HANKINSON, R. J., Philosophy
HANSEN, K. G., Asian Studies
HARLOW, B. J., English
HARMS, R. T., Linguistics
HEINZELMAN, K. O., English
HELMREICH, R. L., Psychology
HENDRICKS, K., Economics
HENRY, C. M., Government
HENSEY, F. G., Spanish and Portuguese
HIGGINS, K. M., Philosophy
HIGLEY, J. C., Government
HILFER, A. C., English
HILLMANN, M. C., Middle Eastern Studies
HINICH, M. J., Government
HINOJOSASMITH, R., English
HOBERMAN, J. M., Germanic Studies
HOCHBERG, H. I., Philosophy
HOLAHAN, C. J., Psychology
HOLDEN, G. W., Psychology
HOPKINS, A. G., History
HORN, J. M., Psychology
HUBBARD, T. K., Classics
HUMMER, R. A., Sociology
JACOBSOHN, G. J., Government
KALLET, L., Classics
KANE, R. H., Philosophy
KAPPELMAN, J. W., Jr, Anthropology
KAULBACH, E. N., English
KELLY, W. R., Sociology
KENDRICK, D. A., Economics
KING, R. D., Linguistics
KOLSTI, J. S., Slavic Languages and Literatures
KOONS, R. C., Philosophy
KROLL, J. H., Classics
KRONZ, F. M., Philosophy
KRUPPA, J. E., English
KURTZ, L. R., Sociology
LAMBRECHT, K. P., French and Italian
LAMPHEAR, J. E., History
LANGLOIS, J. H., Psychology
LASALLE, P. N., English
LEVACK, B. P., History
LIEBOWITZ, H. A., Middle Eastern Studies
LIMON, J. E., English
LINDSTROM, N. E., Spanish and Portuguese
LIPPMANN, J. N., French and Italian
LITVAK, L., Spanish and Portuguese
LOUIS, W. R., History
LUJAN, M. E., Spanish and Portuguese
McFADDEN, D., Psychology
MACKAY, C. H., English
MACNEILAGE, P. F., Psychology
MAGNUSON, J. L., English
MANNERS, I. R., Geography
MARKMAN, A. B., Psychology
MARSHALL, S. E., Sociology
MARTINICH, A. P., Philosophy
MEIER, R. P., Linguistics
MEIKLE, J. L., American Studies
MENCHACA, M., Anthropology
MINAULT, G., History
MIROWSKY, J., Sociology
MONTREUIL, J.-P., French and Italian
MORGAN, M. G., Classics
MOURELATOS, A., Philosophy
MULLIN, J. A., Rhetoric and Composition
NAPIER, S. J., Asian Studies
NETHERCUT, W. R., Classics
NEWTON, A. Z., English
NORMAN, A. L., Economics
OLIVELLE, J. P., Asian Studies
OSHINSKY, D. A., History
PALAIMA, T. G., Classics
PANGLE, T. L., Government
PARKER, D. S., Classics
PELLS, R. H., History
PENNEBAKER, J. W., Psychology
PEREZ, F. L., Geography
PHILLIPS, S. H., Philosophy
POTTER, J. E., Sociology

PRINDLE, D. F., Government
PULLUM, T. W., Sociology
RAMIREZ III, M., Psychology
RAPPAPORT, G. C., Slavic Languages and Literature
REBHORN, W. A., JR, English
RENWICK, R. D., English
ROBERTS, B. E., Government
ROBERTS, B. R., Sociology
ROSS, C. E., Sociology
ROSSMAN, C. R., English
RUMRICH, J. P., English
RUSZKIEWICZ, J. J., Rhetoric and Composition
SAINSBURY, R. M., Philosophy
SARKAR, S., Philosophy
SCHALLERT, T. J., Psychology
SCHEICK, W. J., English
SEUNG, T. K., Philosophy
SHELMERDINE, C. W., Classics
SHERZER, D. M., French and Italian
SHERZER, J. F., Anthropology
SHUMWAY, N., Spanish and Portuguese
SINGH, D., Psychology
SJOBERG, G. A., Sociology
SLESNICK, D. T., Economics
SMITH, C. S., Linguistics
SOLE, C. A., Spanish and Portuguese
SOLOMON, R. C., Philosophy
STAFFORD, M. C., Sociology
STAHL, II, D. O., Economics
STINCHCOMBE, M. B., Economics
STROSS, B. M., Anthropology
SUSSMAN, H. M., Linguistics
SWAFFAR, J. K., Germanic Studies
SWANN, W. B., Jr, Psychology
TELCH, M. J., Psychology
TRIMBLE, J. R., English
TULLY, W. A., History
TWINAM, A., History
TYE, M., Philosophy
TYLER, R. C., History
UMBERSON, D. J., Sociology
VAN OLPHEN, H. H., Asian Studies
WAGNER, R. H., Government
WALKER, J., Rhetoric and Composition
WALKER, J. E., History
WALKER, S. S., Anthropology
WALTERS, S. K., Linguistics
WARD, P., Sociology
WARR, E. M., Sociology
WEINSTOCK, J. M., Germanic Studies
WEVILL, D. A., English
WEYLAND, K. G., Government
WHIGHAM, F. F., JR, English
WHITBREAD, T. B., English
WHITE, L. M., Classics
WILCZYNSKI, W., Psychology
WILLIAMS, C. L., Sociology
WILSON, P. W., Economics
WILSON, S. M., Anthropology
WINSHIP, M. B., English
WOLITZ, S. L., French and Italian
WOODBURY, A. C., Linguistics
WOODRUFF, P. B., Philosophy
ZIMIC, S., Spanish and Portuguese
ZONN, L. E., Geography

College of Natural Sciences:

ANSLYN, E. V., Chemistry and Biochemistry
ANTONIEWICZ, P. R., Physics
APPLING, D. R., Chemistry and Biochemistry
ARBOGAST, T. J., Mathematics
ARMENDARIZ, E. P., Mathematics
ARTZT, K. J., Molecular Genetics and Microbiology
BAJAJ, C. L., Computer Sciences
BANNER, J. L., Geological Sciences
BARBARA, P. F., Chemistry and Biochemistry
BARD, A. J., Chemistry and Biochemistry
BASH, F. N., Astronomy
BATORY, D. S., Computer Sciences
BAULD, N. L., Chemistry and Biochemistry

BECKNER, W., Mathematics
BENGTSON, R. D., Physics
BENNETT, P. C., Geological Sciences
BERK, H. L., Physics
BICHTELER, K. R., Mathematics
BITTNER, G. D., Neurobiology
BOHM, A. R., Physics
BOSE, H. R., Molecular Genetics and Microbiology
BOYER, R. S., Computer Sciences
BRAND, J. J., Molecular Cell and Development Biology
BRILEY, M. E., Human Ecology
BRODBELT, J. S., Chemistry and Biochemistry
BRONSON, F. H., Integrative Biology
BROWN, R. M., JR, Molecular Genetics and Microbiology
BROWNE, J. C., Computer Sciences
BULL, J. J., Integrative Biology
BUSKEY, E. J., Marine Science
CAFFARELLI, L. A., Mathematics
CAMPION, A., Chemistry and Biochemistry
CARLSON, W. D., Geological Sciences
CHENEY, E. W., Mathematics
CHIU, C. B., Physics
CLINE, A. K., Computer Sciences
CLOOS, M. P., Geological Sciences
COKER, W. R., Physics
COWLEY, A. H., Chemistry and Biochemistry
CREWS, D. P., Integrative Biology
DANIEL, J. W., Mathematics
DAVIS, R. E., Chemistry and Biochemistry
DE LA LLAVE, R., Mathematics
DE LOZANNE, A. L., Physics
DICUS, D. A., Physics
DINERSTEIN, H. L., Astronomy
DISTLER, J., Physics
DOWNER, M. W., Physics
DRUMMOND, W. E., Physics
DUDLEY, J. P., Molecular Genetics and Microbiology
DUNTON, K. H., Marine Science
DURBIN, J. R., Mathematics
EARHART, C. F., Molecular Genetics and Microbiology
ELLINGTON, A., Chemistry and Biochemistry
EMERSON, II, E. A., Computer Sciences
ENGQUIST, B., Mathematics
ERSKINE, J. L., Physics
EVANS, II, N. J., Astronomy
FINK, M., Physics
FISCHLER, W., Physics
FISHER, W. L., Geological Sciences
FOWLER, N. L., Integrative Biology
FREED, D. S., Mathematics
FREELAND, J. H., Human Ecology
FREEMAN, G. L., Integrative Biology
FROMMHOLD, L. W., Physics
FUSSELL, D. S., Computer Sciences
GAMBA, I. M., Mathematics
GARDNER, W. S., Marine Science
GENTLE, K. W., Physics
GERTH III, F. E., Mathematics
GILBERT, J. C., Chemistry and Biochemistry
GILBERT, J. E., Mathematics
GILBERT, L. E., Integrative Biology
GLEESON, A. M., Physics
GOMPF, R. E., Mathematics
GORDON, C. M., Mathematics
GOUDA, M. G., Computer Sciences
GRAND, S. P., Geological Sciences
GUY, W. T., JR, Mathematics
HACKERT, M. L., Chemistry and Biochemistry
HAMRICK, G. C., Mathematics
HARRIS, R. A., Neurobiology
HARSHEY, R. M., Molecular Genetics and Microbiology
HARVEY, P. M., Astronomy
HAZELTINE, R. D., Physics
HEINZEN, D. J., Physics
HEITMANN, R. C., Mathematics

HERRIN, D. L., Molecular Cell and Development Biology
HILLIS, D. M., Integrative Biology
HOFFMANN, G. W., Physics
HOLCOMBE, J. A., Chemistry and Biochemistry
HORTON, C. W., Jr, Physics
HUNT, W. A., JR, Computer Sciences
HUSTON, A. C., Human Ecology
HUSTON, T. L., Human Ecology
IVERSON, B. L., Chemistry and Biochemistry
JACOBVITZ, D. B., Human Ecology
JAFFE, D. T., Astronomy
JANSEN, R. K., Integrative Biology
JAYARAM, M., Molecular Genetics and Microbiology
JOHNSON, K., Chemistry and Biochemistry
JOHNSTON, D., Neurobiology
JONES, R. A., Chemistry and Biochemistry
KALTHOFF, K. O., Molecular Cell and Development Biology
KAPLUNOVSKY, V., Physics
KEEL, S. M., Mathematics
KETO, J. W., Physics
KIRKPATRICK, M. A., Integrative Biology
KITTO, G. B., Chemistry and Biochemistry
KLEINMAN, L., Physics
KLINE, K., Human Ecology
KOCH, H. A., Mathematics
KOCUREK, G. A., Geological Sciences
KORMENDY, J., Astronomy
KRISCHE, M. J., Chemistry and Biochemistry
KRUG, R. M., Molecular Genetics and Microbiology
KUIPERS, B. J., Computer Sciences
KUMAR, P., Astronomy
KYLE, J. R., Geological Sciences
LA CLAIRE, II, J. W., Molecular Cell and Development Biology
LACY, J. H., Astronomy
LAGOW, R. J., Chemistry and Biochemistry
LAGOWSKI, J. J., Chemistry and Biochemistry
LAGOWSKI, J. M., Neurobiology
LAM, S. S., Computer Sciences
LAMBOWITZ, A., Molecular Genetics and Microbiology
LANG, K., Physics
LARIMER, J. L., Neurobiology
LAUDE, D. A., Chemistry and Biochemistry
LEVIN, D. A., Integrative Biology
LIFSCHITZ, V., Computer Sciences
LONG, L. E., Geological Sciences
LOOP, R., Human Ecology
LUECKE, J. E., Mathematics
MABRY, T. J., Molecular Cell and Development Biology
MCADAM, S. J., Mathematics
MCBRIDE, E. F., Geological Sciences
MCDEVITT, J. T., Chemistry and Biochemistry
MACDONALD, A. H., Physics
MACDONALD, P. M., Molecular Cell and Development Biology
MAGNUS, P. D., Chemistry and Biochemistry
MARDER, M. P., Physics
MARKERT, J. T., Physics
MARTIN, S. F., Chemistry and Biochemistry
MATZNER, R. A., Physics
MAUSETH, J. D., Integrative Biology
MEYER, R. J., Molecular Genetics and Microbiology
MIIKKULAINEN, R. P., Computer Sciences
MISRA, J., Computer Sciences
MOK, A. K., Computer Sciences
MOLINEUX, I. J., Molecular Genetics and Microbiology
MONTAGNA, P. A., Marine Science
MOONEY, R. J., Computer Sciences
MOORE, C. F., Physics
MOORE, II, J. S., Computer Sciences
MORRISON, P. J., Physics
MOSHER, S., Geological Sciences

NAKAMURA, Y., Geological Sciences
NIU, Q., Physics
NOVAK, G. S., JR, Computer Sciences
OAKES, M. E. L., Physics
ODELL, E. W., Mathematics
PALKA, B. P., Mathematics
PAYNE, S. M., Molecular Genetics and Microbiology
PIANKA, E. R., Integrative Biology
PLAXTON, C. G., Computer Sciences
POLLAK, G. D., Neurobiology
PORTER, B. W., Computer Sciences
RADIN, C. L., Mathematics
RAIZEN, M. G., Physics
RAMACHANDRAN, V., Computer Sciences
REICHL, L. E., Physics
REID, A. W., Mathematics
RICHARDSON, R. H., Integrative Biology
RIGGS, II, A. F., Neurobiology
RILEY, P. J., Physics
RITCHIE, J. L., Physics
ROBERTUS, J. D., Chemistry and Biochemistry
ROBINSON, E. L., Astronomy
ROSENTHAL, H. P., Mathematics
ROSSKY, P. J., Chemistry and Biochemistry
ROUX, S. J., JR, Molecular Cell and Development Biology
ROWE, T. B., Geological Sciences
RYAN, M. J., Integrative Biology
SADUN, L. A., Mathematics
SALTMAN, D. J., Mathematics
SANDERS, B. G., Molecular Genetics and Microbiology
SCALO, J. M., Astronomy
SCHIEVE, W. C., Physics
SCHWITTERS, R. F., Physics
SEN, M. K., Geological Sciences
SESSLER, J. L., Chemistry and Biochemistry
SHANKLAND, S. M., Molecular, Cellular and Developmental Biology
SHAPIRO, P. R., Astronomy
SHARP, J. M., JR, Geological Sciences
SHIELDS, G. A., Astronomy
SHIH, C.-K., Physics
SIMPSON, B. B., Integrative Biology
SINGER, M. C., Integrative Biology
SITZ, G. O., Physics
SMITH, M. K., Mathematics
SNEDEN, C. A., Astronomy
SOUGDANIDIS, P. E., Mathematics
SPRINKLE, J. T., Geological Sciences
STANTON, J. F., Chemistry and Biochemistry
STARBIRD, M. P., Mathematics
STEEL, R. J., Geological Sciences
SUDARSHAN, G., Physics
SURRA, C. A., Human Ecology
SWIFT, J. B., Physics
SWINNEY, H. L., Physics
SZANISZLO, P. J., Molecular Genetics and Microbiology
TATE, J. T., Mathematics
TATHAM, R. H., Geological Sciences
THOMAS, P., Marine Science
THOMPSON, W. J., Neurobiology
TREISMAN, P. U., Mathematics
TUCKER, P. W., Molecular Genetics and Microbiology
UDAGAWA, T., Physics
UHLENBECK, K., Mathematics
VAALER, J. D., Mathematics
VAN DE GEIJN, R. A., Computer Sciences
VIN, H. M., Computer Sciences
VISHIK, M. M., Mathematics
VOLOCH, J. F., Mathematics
WALKER, J. R., Molecular Genetics and Microbiology
WARNOW, T., Computer Sciences
WEBBER, S. E., Chemistry and Biochemistry
WEINBERG, S., Physics
WHEELER, J. C., Astronomy
WHITE, J. M., Chemistry and Biochemistry
WILLIS, R. A., Human Ecology

WILLS, D., Astronomy
WILSON, C. R., Geological Sciences
WINGET, D. E., Astronomy
WYATT, R. E., Chemistry and Biochemistry
XIN, J., Mathematics
XU, B., Human Ecology
ZAKON, H. H., Neurobiology
ZARIPHOPOULOU, T., Mathematics
ZUCKERMAN, D. I., Computer Sciences

College of Pharmacy:
ABELL, C. W.
BUSSEY, H. I.
COMBS, A. B.
CRISMON, M. L.
DAVIS, P. J.
ERICKSON, C. K.
GONZALES, R. A.
KEHRER, J. P.
KOELLER, J. M.
KUHN, J. G.
LITTLEFIELD, L. C.
LIU, H.-W.
MCGINITY, J. W.
PEARLMAN, R.
RASCATI, K. L.
SHEPHERD, M. D.
STAVCHANSKY, S. A.
TALBERT, R. L., JR
WHITMAN, C. P.
WILCOX, R. E.

University of Texas at Arlington

701 S Nedderman Dr., Arlington, TX 76019

Telephone: (817) 272-2011

Internet: www.uta.edu

Founded 1895 as Arlington College, present name 1965

Academic year: August to May

Pres.: Dr JAMES D. SPANIOLO

Provost and Vice-Pres. for Academic Affairs: Dr RONALD L. ELSENBAUMER

Sr Vice-Pres. for Finance and Admin.: M. DAN WILLIAMS

Vice-Pres. for Admin. and Campus Operations: JOHN D. HALL

Vice-Pres. for Devt: JIM LEWIS

Vice-Pres. for Research: Dr CAROLYN L. CASON

Vice-Pres. for Student Affairs: Dr FRANK LAMAS

Dean for Library: JULIE ALEXANDER

Library of 1,204,064 vols, 275,606 ebooks, 34,160 print eserial titles, 38,231 eserial titles, 1,486,429 microforms, 9,033 video items, 3,141 audio items, 34,722 maps

Number of teachers: 1,000

Number of students: 33,400 (25,419 undergraduate, 8,020 graduate)

Publication: *Research* (1 a year)

DEANS

College of Business: Prof. Dr DAVID A. GRAY
College of Education and Health Professions: Dr JEANNE MARCUM GERLACH
College of Engineering: Dr JEAN-PIERRE BARDET
College of Liberal Arts: Dr BETH WRIGHT (acting)
College of Nursing: Prof. Dr ELIZABETH C. POSTER
College of Science: Dr PAMELA JANSMA
Graduate School: Dr PHILIP COHEN
School of Architecture: Prof. DONALD F. GATZKE
School of Social Work: Dr SCOTT D. RYAN
School of Urban and Public Affairs: Dr BARBARA BECKER

University of Texas at Brownsville and Texas Southmost College

80 Fort Brown, Brownsville, TX 78520

Telephone: (956) 8828200

E-mail: admissions@utb.edu

Internet: www.utb.edu

Founded 1991

Languages of instruction: English, Spanish

Academic year: August to December

Pres.: Dr JULIET V. GARCÍA

Provost: Dr ALAN F. J. ARTIBISE

Vice-Pres. for Business Affairs: ROSEMARY MARTÍNEZ

Vice-Pres. for Economic Devt and Community Services: IRVINE DOWNING

Vice-Pres. for External Affairs: Dr TONY ZAVALETA

Vice-Pres. for Institutional Advancement: Dr MELONEY LINDER

Vice-Pres. for Partnership Affairs: Dr DAVID PEARSON

Vice-Pres. for Research: Dr LUIS COLOM

Vice-Pres. for Student Affairs: Dr HILDA SILVA

Registrar: AL BARREDA

Univ. Librarian: ANNABEL TREVINO

Library of 300,000 vols

Number of teachers: 600

Number of students: 13,840

DEANS

College of Biomedical Sciences and Health Professions: Dr ELDON NELSON

College of Education: Dr MIGUEL ANGEL ESCOTET

College of Liberal Arts: Dr DANIEL HEIMMERMANN

College of Nursing: Dr EDNA GARZA-ESCOBEDO

College of Science, Mathematics and Technology: Dr MIKHAIL BOUNIAEV

Graduate Studies: Dr CHARLES LACKEY

School of Business: Dr MARK KROLL

School of Health Sciences: Dr ELDON NELSON

Univ. College: Dr TERRY OVERTON

University of Texas at Dallas

800 W Campbell Rd, Richardson, TX 75080-3021

Telephone: (972) 883-2111

E-mail: utdallas@utdallas.edu

Internet: www.utdallas.edu

Founded 1961 as Graduate Research Center of the Southwest, current name 1969

Academic year: September to August

Pres.: Dr DAVID E. DANIEL

Provost and Exec. Vice-Pres.: Dr B. HOBSON WILDENTHAL

Vice-Pres. for Admin.: Dr CALVIN JAMISON

Vice-Pres. for Budget and Finance: TERRY PANKRATZ

Vice-Pres. for Devt and Alumni Relations: Dr AARON CONLEY

Vice-Pres. for Research: Dr BRUCE GNADE

Vice-Pres. for Student Affairs: Dr DARRELENE RACHAVONG

Dir for Enrolment Management: MATTHEW SANCHEZ

Registrar: JENNIFER MCDOWELL

Dir for Libraries: Dr ELLEN SAFLEY

Library of 2,651,814 vols, 1,897,937 titles, 2,394,056 microform units, 14,950 audiovisual items, 28,843 maps, 1,147,698 ebooks, 67,950 ejournals, 185,284 govt documents

Number of teachers: 706 full-time

Number of students: 21,193

Publications: *The Exley*, *Issues in Science and Technology* (4 a year), *Political Research Quarterly*, *Public Administration Review* (6 a year), *Translation Review* (3 a year)

DEANS

Erik Jonsson School of Engineering and Computer Science: Dr MARK W. SPONG

Graduate Studies: Dr AUSTIN J. CUNNINGHAM

Naveen Jindal School of Management: Dr HASAN PIRKUL

School of Arts and Humanities: Dr DENNIS M. KRATZ

School of Behavioral and Brain Sciences: Dr BERT S. MOORE

School of Economic, Political and Policy Sciences: Dr DENIS DEAN

School of Interdisciplinary Studies: Dr GEORGE W. FAIR

School of Natural Sciences and Mathematics: Dr BRUCE NOVAK

Undergraduate Education: Dr ANDREW BLANCHARD

PROFESSORS

ABDI, H., Cognition, Neuroscience
AIKEN, C., Geosciences
AL-DHAHIR, N., Electrical Engineering
ALEXANDER, B., Sociology
ALI, A., Accounting
AMMANN, L., Mathematics
ANDERSON, P., Physics
ARCE, D., Economics
ASSMANN, P., Cognition, Speech Science
AUCIELLO, O., Material Science Engineering
BALKUS, K., Chemistry
BALSARA, P., Electrical Engineering
BAMBACH, C., Humanities
BARDHAN, I., Information Systems
BARON, M., Mathematics
BARTLETT, J., Cognition, Neuroscience
BASTANI, F., Computer Science
BAUGHMAN, R., Chemistry
BENSOUSSAN, A., Operations Management
BERON, K., Economics, Public Policy
BERRY, B., Geospatial Sciences
BHATIA, D., Electrical Engineering
BOLTON, G., Finance
BRETTELL, R., Humanities
BRUNELL, T., Political Science
BULLA, L., Biology
CAKANYILDIRIM, M., Operations Management
CAMPBELL, T., Speech Science
CHABAL, Y., Material Science Engineering
CHAMPAGNE, A., Political Science
CHAN, J., Chemistry
CHANDRASEKARAN, R., Computer Science
CHANNELL, D., Humanities
CHAPMAN, S., Cognition, Neuroscience
CHO, K., Material Science Engineering
CLARKE, H., Political Science
COHEN, D., Accounting
COHEN, M., Humanities
COLEMAN, A., Electrical Engineering
COLEMAN, J., Electrical Engineering
CREADY, W., Accounting
CURCHACK, F., Arts
DAESCU, O., Computer Science
DAWANDE, M., Operations Management
DAY, T., Finance
DESMEDT, Y., Computer Science
DESS, G., International Management
D'MELLO-KA, S., Biology
DOLLAGHAN, C., Speech Science
DOWLING, W., Cognition, Neuroscience
DRAGOVIC, V., Mathematics
DRAPER, R., Biology
DU, D., Computer Science
DUMAS, L., Political Economy, Public Policy
EDMUNDS, R., Humanities
EFROMOVICH, S., Mathematics
ELLIOTT, E., Political Economy, Public Policy
EVANS, J., Speech Science
FAHIMI, B., Electrical Engineering
FARAGO, A., Computer Science
FERGUSON, J., Geosciences
FERRARIS, J., Chemistry
FISCHETTI, M., Material Science Engineering
FISHWICK, P., Arts
FONSEKA, J., Electrical Engineering
FORD, D., International Management
FRENSLEY, W., Electrical Engineering
FUMAGALLI, A., Electrical Engineering
GAO, X., Mechanical Engineering
GEISSMAN, J., Geosciences

GLOSSER, R., Physics
GOECKNER, M., Mathematics
GOLDEN, R., Cognition, Neuroscience
GONZALEZ, J., Biology
GOSSIN, P., Humanities
GRIFFITH, D., Geospatial Sciences
GU, M., Humanities
GUPTA, G., Computer Science
HAAS, Z., Computer Science
HANSEN, J., Electrical Engineering
HARPHAM, E., Political Science
HART, J., Cognition, Neuroscience
HEELIS, R., Physics
HELMS, R., Electrical Engineering
HICKS, D., Economics, Public Policy
HOFFMAN, J., Physics
HOOSHYAR, M., Mathematics
HSU, J., Material Science Engineering
HULSE, R., Science Education
HUYNH, D., Computer Science
IZEN, J., Physics
JACOB, V., Information Systems
JACOBS, B., Criminology
JANAKIRAMAN, G., Operations Management
JERGER, S., Psychology
JUE, J., Computer Science
KATOK, E., Operations Management
KATZ, W., Speech Science
KEHTARNAVAZ, N., Electrical Engineering
KHAN, L., Computer Science
KIASALEH, K., Electrical Engineering
KIEL, L., Public Administration
KIM, J., Material Science Engineering
KIM, M., Material Science Engineering
KRAWCEWICZ, W., Mathematics
KUKSOV, D., Marketing
LEAF, M., Political Economy
LEE, G., Electrical Engineering
LEE, J., Electrical Engineering
LEE, M., Physics
LEEPER PIQ, N., Criminology
LEVENE, S., Biology
LIEBOWITZ, S., Finance
LIN, Z., International Management
LINEHAN, T., Arts
LIU, J., Electrical Engineering
LOU, X., Physics
LOWRY, R., Political Science
LU, H., Mechanical Engineering
MACFARLANE, D., Electrical Engineering
MADRIGUERA, E., Arts
MAJUMDAR, S., Information Systems
MALINA, R., Arts
MANTON, W., Geosciences
MARQUART, J., Criminology
MCLEAN, A., Arts
MCMECHAN, G., Geosciences
MINKOFF, S., Mathematics
MOLDOVAN, D., Computer Science
MOLLER, A., Audiology, Neuroscience
MOOKERJEE, V., Information Systems
MURDOCH, J., Economics, Public Policy
MURTHI, B., Marketing
MUSSELMAN, I., Chemistry
NADIN, M., Arts
NAMGOONG, W., Electrical Engineering
NIU, S., Operations Management
NOSRATINIA, A., Electrical Engineering
NTAFOS, S., Computer Science
O, K., Electrical Engineering
OBER, R., Electrical Engineering
OLDOW, J., Geosciences
O'TOOLE, A., Cognition, Neuroscience
OVERZET, L., Electrical Engineering
OWEN, M., Psychology
OZER, A., Operations Management
OZSVATH, Z., Humanities
PAGE, I., Computer Science
PARK, D., Cognition, Neuroscience
PATTERSON, D., Humanities
PENG, M., International Management
PIQUERO, A., Criminology
POMARA, J., Arts
PRABHAKARAN, B., Computer Science
PRAGER, K., Psychology, Interdisciplinary Studies

PRAKASH, R., Computer Science
PRIETO, R., Humanities
RABE, S., Humanities
RACHINSKIY, D., Mathematics
RADHAKRISHNAN, S., Accounting
RAGHAVACHARI, B., Computer Science
RAGHUNATHAN, S., Information Systems
RAJASHEKARAN, P., Electrical Engineering
RAMAKRISHNA, V., Mathematics
RAO, R., Marketing
RATCHFORD, B., Marketing
REBELLO, M., Finance
REDLINGER, L., Sociology
REDMAN, T., Humanities
REITZER, L., Biology
REYNOLDS, C., Humanities
RICCIO, T., Arts
RINDLER, W., Physics
RODRIGUEZ, R., Arts
ROEMER, N., Humanities
ROESER, R., Audiology
ROTEA, M., Mechanical Engineering
RUGG, M., Cognition, Neuroscience
SALAMON, M., Physics
SANDLER, T., Economics, Political Economy
SANTROCK, J., Psychology
SAQUIB, M., Electrical Engineering
SARKAR, S., Information Systems
SCHULTE, R., Humanities
SCOTCH, R., Sociology, Political Economy
SECHEN, C., Electrical Engineering
SERFLING, R., Mathematics
SETHI, S., Operations Management
SHA, H., Computer Science
SHERRY, A., Chemistry
SMITH, D., Chemistry
SPENCE, M., Psychology
STECKE, K., Operations Management
STERN, R., Geosciences
STEWART, M., Political Science
STILLMAN, R., Speech Science
SUDBOROUGH, I., Computer Science
SUL, D., Economics
TAMIL, L., Electrical Engineering
TAYLOR, R., Criminology
THIBODEAU, L., Audiology
THURAISINGHAM, B., Computer Science
TINSLEY, B., Physics
TOBEY, E., Audiology, Speech Science
TOWNER, T., Humanities
TURI, J., Mathematics
TURNER, F., Humanities
ULATOWSKA, H., Speech Science
UNDERWOOD, M., Psychology
VAN KLEECK, A., Speech Science
VENKATESAN, S., Computer Science
VIDYASAGAR, M., Biomedical Engineering
WALIGORE, M., Arts
WALLACE, R., Material Science Engineering
WIORKOWSKI, J., Mathematics
WONG, W., Computer Science
WORRALL, J., Criminology
WU, W., Computer Science
YEN, I., Computer Science
YOU, S., Biomedical Engineering
YURKOVICH, S., Systems Engineering
ZAKHIDOV, A., Chemistry
ZHANG, M., Biology
ZHANG, L., Biology
ZHANG, K., Computer Science
ZHANG, H., Finance
ZHENG, S., Computer Science
ZHOU, D., Electrical Engineering
ZWECK, J., Mathematics

University of Texas at El Paso

500 W University Ave, El Paso, TX 79968-0500
Telephone: (915) 747-5000
E-mail: uc@utep.edu
Internet: www.utep.edu
Founded 1914 as Texas School of Mines and Metallurgy, present name 1967
Academic year: August to August
Pres.: Prof. Dr DIANA NATALICIO

Sr Exec. Vice-Pres.: HAWARD C. DAUDISTEL
Exec. Vice-Pres.: RICARDO ADAUTO, III
Provost and Vice-Pres. for Academic Affairs: Dr JUNIUS GONZALES
Vice-Pres. for Business Affairs: CYNTHIA VIZCAINO VILLA
Vice-Pres. for Information Resources and Planning: STEPHEN RITER
Vice-Pres. for Research: Dr ROBERTO A. OSEGUEDA
Vice-Pres. for Student Affairs: GARY EDENS
Dean for Students: Dr WILLIAM SCHAFER
Exec. Dir for Admissions: LUISA M. HAVENS
Library Dir and Assoc. Vice-Pres.: ROBERT L. STAKES
Library: see under Libraries and Archives
Number of teachers: 1,240
Number of students: 22,640

Publications: *Nova* (9 a year), *Minero* (2 a year), *Rio Grande Review*, *Shangri-La*, *Southwestern Studies* (irregular), *Southwest Journal of Business and Economics* (irregular), *The Prospector*

DEANS

College of Business Administration: Dr ROBERT NACHTMANN
College of Education: Dr JOSEFINA V. TINAJERO
College of Engineering: Dr RICHARD SCHOEPHOERSTER
College of Health Sciences: Dr KATHLEEN A. CURTIS
College of Liberal Arts: Dr PATRICIA WITHERSPOON
College of Sciences: Dr ANNY MORROBEL-SOSA
Graduate School: Dr BENJAMIN FLORES
School of Nursing: Dr PROVENCIO-VASQUEZ

University of Texas at San Antonio

1 UTSA Circle, San Antonio, TX 78249
Telephone: (210) 4584011
E-mail: registrar@utsa.edu
Internet: www.utsa.edu
Founded 1969
Pres.: Prof. Dr RICARDO ROMO
Provost and Vice-Pres. for Academic Affairs and Interim Vice-Pres. for Research: Dr JOHN FREDERICK
Vice-Pres. for Business Affairs: KERRY L. KENNEDY
Vice-Pres. for Extended Services: Dr JUDE VALDEZ
Vice-Pres. for Research: ROBERT GRACY
Vice-Pres. for Student Affairs: GAGE PAINE
Vice-Pres. for Univ. Advancement: MARJIE FRENCH
Asst Vice-Pres. and Univ. Registrar: JOE DECRISTOFORO
Dean for Libraries: Dr KRISELLEN MALONEY
Library of 1,747,099 vols, 3,215,276 microforms, 422,000 ebooks, 34,500 ejournals, 3,556,960 audiovisual items
Number of teachers: 620
Number of students: 30,300

DEANS

College of Architecture: Dr JOHN D. MURPHY, JR
College of Business: Dr LYNDA Y. DE LA VIÑA
College of Education and Human Devt: Dr BETTY MERCHANT
College of Engineering: Prof. Dr C. MAULI AGRAWAL
College of Liberal and Fine Arts: Dr DANIEL J. GELO
College of Public Policy: Dr ROGELIO SAENZ
College of Sciences: Dr GEORGE PERRY
Graduate School: Dr DOROTHY FLANAGAN
Honors College: Dr RICHARD A. DIEM

University of Texas at Tyler

3900 University Blvd, Tyler, TX 75799
Telephone: (903) 5667203
E-mail: enroll@uttyler.edu
Internet: www.uttyler.edu
Founded 1971 as Tyler State College, present name 1979
Academic year: August to May
Br. campuses in Longview, Palestine
Pres.: Dr RODNEY H. MABRY
Provost and Vice-Pres. for Academic Affairs: Dr DONNA DICKERSON
Vice-Pres. for Business Affairs: Dr RANDALL POWELL
Vice-Pres. for Univ. Advancement: JERRE IVERSEN
Registrar: SONJA MORALE
Library Dir: JEANNE STANDLEY
Library of 215,000 vols
Number of teachers: 390
Number of students: 6,700 (5,118 undergraduate, 1,582 graduate)
Publication: *UT Tyler Magazine* (2 a year)

DEANS

College of Arts and Sciences: Prof. Dr MARTIN SLANN
College of Business and Technology: Prof. Dr D. HAROLD DOTY
College of Education and Psychology: Prof. Dr WILLIAM L. GEIGER
College of Engineering and Computer Science: Prof. Dr JAMES K. NELSON, JR
College of Nursing and Health Sciences: Dr LINDA KLOTZ

University of Texas of the Permian Basin

4901 E Univ., Odessa, TX 79762
Telephone: (915) 552-2020
E-mail: president@utpb.edu
Internet: www.utpb.edu
Founded 1969
Pres.: W. DAVID WATTS
Provost and Vice-Pres. for Academic Affairs: Dr DANIEL HEIMMERMANN
Vice-Pres. for Business Affairs: CHRISTOPHER R. FORREST
Vice-Pres. for Student Services: Dr SUSAN LARA
Dir for Institutional Research, Planning and Effectiveness: DENISE WATTS
Univ. Registrar: HECTOR A. GOVEA
Dir for Library (vacant)
Library of 763,000 vols
Number of teachers: 185
Number of students: 2,400

DEANS

College of Arts and Sciences: Dr MYLAN REDFERN
School of Business: Dr JACK D. LADD
School of Education: Dr RACHEL JUAREZ-TORRES

University of Texas—Pan American

1201 W University Dr., Edinburg, TX 78539-2999
Telephone: (956) 665-8872
E-mail: info@panam.edu
Internet: www.utpa.edu
Founded 1927 as Edinburg College, present name and status 1989
Academic year: September to August
Pres.: Dr ROBERT S. NELSEN
Provost and Vice-Pres. for Academic Affairs: Dr HAVIDÁN RODRÍGUEZ
Vice-Pres. for Business Affairs: MARTIN V. BAYLOR
Vice-Pres. for Student Affairs: Dr MARTHA A. CANTU (acting)
Vice-Pres. for Univ. Advancement (vacant)

Dean for Admissions and Enrolment Services and Assoc. Vice-Pres.: Dr MAGDALENA HINOJOSA

Dean for Univ. Libraries: FARZANEH RAZZAGHI

Library of 655,000 vols, 159,000 govt documents, 30,000 print and ejournals

Number of teachers: 800

Number of students: 19,000 (16,600 undergraduate, 2,400 graduate)

DEANS

College of Arts and Humanities: Dr DAHLIA GUERRA

College of Business Admin.: Dr TEOFILO OZUNA, JR

College of Education: Dr SALVADOR HECTOR OCHOA

College of Engineering and Computer Science: Dr DAVID H. ALLEN

College of Health Sciences and Human Services: Dr JOHN RONNAU

College of Science and Mathematics: Dr JOHN M. TRANT

College of Social and Behavioral Sciences: Dr WALTER DÍAZ

University of Texas Southwestern Medical Center

5323 Harry Hines Blvd, Dallas, TX 75390

Telephone: (214) 648-3111

E-mail: admissions@utsouthwestern.edu

Internet: www.utsouthwestern.edu

Founded 1943 as Southwestern Medical School, present name 1987

Academic year: July to June

Pres.: Dr DANIEL K. PODOLSKY

Provost and Exec. Vice-Pres. for Academic Affairs: Prof. Dr J. GREGORY FITZ

Exec. Vice-Pres. for Business Affairs: ARNIM E. DONTES

Exec. Vice-Pres. for Clinical Operations: Dr JOHN DOUGLAS RUTHERFORD

Vice-Pres. and Chief of Staff: Dr ROBIN M. JACOBY

Vice-Pres. for External Relations: CYNTHIA BASSEL

Vice-Pres. for Financial Affairs: MICHAEL SERBER

Vice-Pres. for Devt: Dr RANDY L. FARMER

Vice-Pres. for Student and Alumni Affairs: Prof. WES NORRED

Asst Vice-Pres. for Library Services: LAURIE THOMPSON

Library of 259,000 vols, 62,685 ejournals

Number of teachers: 4,050

Number of students: 4,600

DEANS

Southwestern Graduate School of Biomedical Sciences: Prof. Dr MICHAEL ROTH

Southwestern Medical School: Prof. Dr J. GREGORY FITZ

Southwestern School of Health Professions: Dr RAUL CAETANO

University of Texas Medical Branch at Galveston

301 University Blvd, Galveston, TX 77555-0144

Suite 6, 100 Admin, Bldg, Galveston, TX 77555-0144

Telephone: (409) 772-1011

E-mail: public.affairs@utmb.edu

Internet: www.utmb.edu

Founded 1891 as Univ. of Texas Medical Dept, present name 1919

Pres.: Dr DAVID L. CALLENDER

Exec. Vice-Pres. and Provost: Dr CARY W. COOPER

Exec. Vice-Pres. and CEO: DONNA K. SOLLENBERGER

Exec. Vice-Pres. and Chief Business and Finance Officer: WILLIAM R. ELGER

Sr Vice-Pres. and Gen. Counsel: Dr CAROLEE KING

Vice-Pres.: Dr ELIZABETH J. PROTAS

Vice-Pres. and Chief of Staff: Dr KATRINA M. LAMBRECHT

Vice-Pres. for Education: PAMELA G. WATSON

Assoc. Vice-Pres. for Academic Resources and Dir for Library: Dr BRETT A. KIRKPATRICK

Number of teachers: 1,200

Number of students: 2,800 (2,534 f.t.e.)

DEANS

Graduate School of Biomedical Sciences: Dr CARY W. COOPER

School of Health Professions: Dr ELIZABETH J. PROTAS

School of Medicine: Dr DONALD S. PROUGH

School of Nursing: Dr PAMELA G. WATSON

University of Texas Health Science Center at Houston

7000 Fannin, Suite 1200, Houston, TX 77030

Telephone: (713) 500-4472

E-mail: info@uth.tmc.edu

Internet: www.uthouston.edu

Founded 1972

Academic year: August to August (3 semesters)

Pres.: Dr GIUSEPPE N. COLASURDO

Sr Exec. Vice-Pres., Chief Operating and Financial Officer: KEVIN DILLON

Exec. Vice-Pres. for Academic and Research Affairs: Dr GEORGE M. STANCEL

Sr Vice-Pres. for Finance and Business Services: MICHAEL TRAMONTE

Vice-Pres. for Advancement (vacant)

Vice-Pres. and Chief Human Resources Officer: ERIC FERNETTE

Registrar: ROBERT JENKINS

Number of teachers: 1,540 (1,273 full-time, 267 part-time)

Number of students: 4,600

DEANS

Graduate School of Biomedical Sciences: Prof. Dr GEORGE M. STANCEL

Medical School: Prof. Dr GIUSEPPE N. COLASURDO

School of Biomedical Informatics: Prof. Dr JIAJIE ZHANG

School of Dentistry: Prof. Dr JOHN A. VALENZA

School of Nursing: Prof. Dr PATRICIA LEE STARCK

School of Public Health: Dr ROBERTA B. NESS

University of Texas Health Science Center at San Antonio

7703 Floyd Curl Dr., San Antonio, TX 78229

Telephone: (210) 567-7000

E-mail: registrars@uthscsa.edu

Internet: www.uthscsa.edu

Founded 1959 as South Texas Medical School, present name 1972

Academic year: July to August

Pres.: Dr WILLIAM L. HENRICH

Sr Exec. Vice-Pres. and Chief Operating Officer: MICHAEL E. BLACK

Vice-Pres. and Chief Communications Officer: A. JEROME YORK

Vice-Pres. for Academic, Faculty and Student Affairs: Dr DENISE WILBUR

Vice-Pres. for Business Affairs and Chief Financial Officer: ANDREA MARKS

Vice-Pres. for Devt and Chief Devt Officer: DEBORAH H. MORRILL

Vice-Pres. for Governmental Relations: ARMANDO DIAZ

Vice-Pres. for Institutional Advancement and Chief Devt Officer: DEBORAH H. MORRILL

Vice-Pres. for Research: Dr DAVID S. WEISS

Vice-Pres. for South Texas Programmes: Dr JOSEPH B. McCORMICK

Registrar: BLANCA GUERRA

Exec. Dir for Libraries: RAJIA TOBIA

Library of 192,576 vols

Number of students: 3,270

DEANS

Dental School: Dr KENNETH L. KALKWARF

Graduate School of Biomedical Sciences: Dr DAVID S. WEISS

School of Health Professions: Dr JUANITA S. WALLACE

School of Medicine: Dr FRANCISCO GONZÁLEZ-SCARANO

School of Nursing: Prof. Dr EILEEN T. BRESLIN

University of Texas Health Science Center at Tyler

11937 US Highway 271, Tyler, TX 75708-3154

Telephone: (903) 877-7777

E-mail: library@uthct.edu

Internet: www.uthct.edu

Founded 1948 as East Texas Tuberculosis Sanatorium; present status 1977

Schools of medical biological sciences, community health and health professions

Pres.: Dr KIRK A. CALHOUN

Exec. Vice-Pres. and Chief of Staff: Dr JOSEPH WOELKERS

Vice-Pres. for Clinical and Academic Affairs: Dr DAVID COULTAS

Vice-Pres. for Research and Post-Graduate Education: Dr STEVEN IDELL

Library of 3,000 vols, 5,000 periodicals

University of Texas MD Anderson Cancer Center

1515 Holcombe Blvd, Houston, TX 77030

Telephone: (713) 7922121

E-mail: andersonnetwork@mdanderson.org

Internet: www.mdanderson.org

Founded 1941

Academic year: August to July

Pres.: Dr RONALD DePINHO

Provost and Exec. Vice-Pres.: Dr RAYMOND DuBOIS

Exec. Vice-Pres. and Chief Business Officer: Dr LEON J. LEACH

Exec. Vice-Pres. and Physician-in-Chief: Dr THOMAS BURKE

Sr Vice-Pres. for Academic Affairs: Dr OLIVER BOGLER

Exec. Vice-Pres. for Operations: ADRIENNE LANG

Exec. Dir for Library: STEPHANIE FULTON

Library of 27,197 bound journal vols, 7,439 ebooks, 844 audiovisual items, 25,248 microform units

Number of teachers: 1,500

Number of students: 6,900

DEANS

Graduate School of Biomedical Sciences: Dr GEORGE STANCEL

School of Health Professions: Dr MICHAEL AHEARN

UNIVERSITY OF THE INCARNATE WORD

4301 Broadway, San Antonio, TX 78209-6397

Telephone: (210) 829-6000

E-mail: admis@uiwtx.edu

Internet: www.uiw.edu

Founded 1881 as Acad. of the Incarnate Word, current status 1996

Private control

Academic year: August to May

Chancellor: Dr DENISE DOYLE

Pres.: Dr Louis J. Agnese, Jr
Provost: Dr Kathi Light
Vice-Pres. for Business and Finance: Dr Douglas B. Endlsey
Vice-Pres. for Enrolment Management and Student Services: Dr David Jurenovich
Vice-Pres. for Extended Academic Programmes: Dr Cyndi Wilson-Porter
Vice-Pres. for Information Resources: Dr Marshall Eidson
Vice-Pres. for Institutional Advancement: Sis. Kathleen Coughlin
Vice-Pres. for Int. Affairs: Dr Marcos Fragoso
Vice-Pres. for Mission and Ministry: Sis. Walter Maher
Gen. Counsel: Cynthia Escamilla
Registrar: Dr Bobbye G. Fry
Dean for Library Services: Dr Cheryl Anderson

Library of 273,468 vols, 70,017 current serial subscriptions, 301,272 microforms, 11,350 audiovisual items
Number of teachers: 533
Number of students: 9,188

Publications: *Illuminatus, Journal of the Life and Culture of San Antonio, Quirk—Student Journal of Collegiate Inquiry and Debate, Verbum Incarnatum*

DEANS

College of Humanities, Arts and Social Sciences: Dr Jack Healy
Dreeben School of Education: Dr Denise Staudt
Feik School of Pharmacy: Dr Arcelia Johnson-Fannin
H. E. B. School of Business and Administration: Dr Jeannie Scott
Ila Faye Miller School of Nursing and Health Professions: Dr Mary Hoke
Rosenberg School of Optometry: Dr Andrew Buzzelli
School of Graduate Studies and Research: Dr Kevin B. Vichcales
School of Mathematics, Science and Engineering: Dr Carlos Garcia
School of Media and Design: Dr Sharon Welkey
School of Physical Therapy: Dr Caroline Goulet

WADE COLLEGE

1950 N Stemmons Freeway, Suite 4080, LB 562, Dallas, TX 75207
Telephone: (214) 637-3530
Internet: www.wadecollege.edu
Founded 1962
Academic year: October to September
Private control
Areas of study: art, design, business, computers, liberal arts
Pres.: Harry Davros
Vice-Pres. for Education: John Conte
Exec. Dir: Sue Wade
Dir for Academic and Student Affairs: Mitzi Morris
Dir for Admissions and Marketing: Julia Andalman
Dir for Financial Services: Lisa Hoover
Dir for Student Services: Rusty Bell
Registrar and Dir for Institutional Support: Kimberly Parker
Dir for Library: Bobbie Baumgarten
Library of 5,100 vols, 131 periodicals, 400 audiovisual items
Publication: *D&M Magazine*

WAYLAND BAPTIST UNIVERSITY

1900 W Seventh St, Plainview, TX 79072
Telephone: (806) 291-1000
E-mail: admityou@wbu.edu

Internet: www.wbu.edu
Founded 1908 as Wayland Literary and Technical Institute, chartered 1908, present name and status 1981
Private control
Academic year: June to May
Campuses in Albuquerque (NM), Altus (OK), Amarillo (TX), Anchorage (AK), Clovis (NM), Fairbanks (AK), Lubbock (TX), Mililani (HI), Phoenix (AZ), San Antonio (TX), Sierra Vista (AZ), Tucson (AZ), Wichita Falls (TX), Vance AFB, Kenya (Africa)
Pres.: Dr Paul Armes
Provost and Exec. Vice-Pres.: Dr Bobby Hall
Vice-Pres. for Enrolment Management: Dr Claude Lusk
Vice-Pres. for External Campuses and Graduate Services: Dr Elane Seebo
Chief Financial Officer: James Smith
Dean for Students: Tom Hall
Registrar: Julie Bowen
Dir for Libraries: Dr Polly Lackey
Library of 129,646 vols
Number of teachers: 100
Number of students: 1,725
Publication: *Footprints* (24 a year)

DEANS

Don Williams School of Education and Exercise and Sport Science: Dr James Todd
School of Behavioral and Social Sciences: Dr Estelle Owens
School of Business: Dr Otto B. Schacht
School of Fine Arts: Dr Marti Runnels
School of Languages and Literature: Dr Cindy McClenagan
School of Math and Sciences: Dr Herbert Grover
School of Music: Dr Ann B. Stutes
School of Nursing: Dr Diane Frazor
School of Religion and Philosophy: Dr Paul Sadler

WILEY COLLEGE

711 Wiley Ave, Marshall, TX 75670
Telephone: (903) 927-3300
Internet: www.wileyc.edu
Founded 1873
Private control
Academic year: August to May
Pres. and CEO: Dr Haywood L. Strickland
Provost and Exec. Vice-Pres.: Dr Glenda F. Carter
Vice-Pres. for Academic Affairs: Dr Ernest Plata
Vice-Pres. for Business and Finance: Willie Hughey
Vice-Pres. for Student Affairs and Enrolment Services: Dr Joseph L. Morale
Dir for Admissions and Recruitment: Ashley L. Bennett
Dir for Devt: Dr Prince Brown
Registrar: Vanessa Valentine
Dir for Library: Alma Ravenell
Library of 98,000 vols (incl. 27,000 ebooks and 350 periodicals)
Number of teachers: 70
Number of students: 1,350

DEANS

Division of Business and Technology: Prof. Dr Abdalla F. Hagen
Division of Sciences: Dr Walter Shumate
Division of Social Sciences and Humanities: Dr Sherlynn H. Byrd

UTAH

BRIGHAM YOUNG UNIVERSITY

A-41 ASB, Provo, UT 84602
Telephone: (801) 378-4636

E-mail: admissions@byu.edu
Internet: home.byu.edu/home
Founded 1875 as Brigham Young Acad., present name 1903
Private control
Academic year: August to April
Pres.: Kevin J. Worthen
Chief Financial Officer and Vice-Pres. for Admin.: Brian K. Evans
Vice-Pres. for Academic Affairs: Brent W. Webb
Vice-Pres. for Advancement: Kevin J. Worthen
Vice-Pres. for Student Life: Janet S. Scharman
Gen. Counsel and Asst to the Pres.: Michael R. Orme
Dean for Admissions and Records: Erlend D. Peterson
Dean for Students: Vernon L. Heperi
Univ. Librarian: H. Julene Butler
Library: 8m. vols (incl. 3.3m. books, 27,000 journals, 250,000 maps, 1m. photographs and a colln of video cassettes)
Number of teachers: 1,500
Number of students: 39,577

DEANS

College of Family, Home and Social Sciences: Benjamin M. Ogles
College of Fine Arts and Communications: Stephen M. Jones
College of Humanities: John R. Rosenberg
College of Life Sciences: Rodney T. Brown
College of Nursing: Beth V. Cole
College of Physical and Mathematical Sciences: Scott D. Summerfeldt
College of Religious Education: Terry Ball
Continuing Education: Wayne J. Lott
David McKay School of Education: K. Richard Young
Ira A. Fulton College of Engineering and Technology: Alan R. Parkinson
J. Reuben Clark Law School: James R. Rasband
Marriott School of Management: Gary C. Cornia
Religious Education: Terry B. Ball

DIXIE STATE COLLEGE OF UTAH

225 S 700E, St. George, UT 84770
Telephone: (435) 652-7500
E-mail: jointhestorm@dixie.edu
Internet: www.dixie.edu
Founded 1935
State control
Academic year: August to May (2 semesters)
Pres.: Dr Stephen D. Nadauld
Vice-Pres. for Admin. Services: Stan Plew
Exec. Dir Campus Services: Sherry Ruesch
Exec. Dir Business Services: Scott Talbot
Dean and Dir for the Library: Daphne Selbert
Number of teachers: 175
Number of students: 10,000

DEANS

School of Arts and Letters: Donald R. Hinton
School of Education: Dr Brenda Sabey
School of Nursing and Allied Health: Dr Carole Grady
School of Science and Technology: Dr Victor Hasfurther
Udvar-Hazy School of Business: Dr William J. Christensen

ITT TECHNICAL INSTITUTE

920 W LeVoy Dr., Murray, UT 84123
Telephone: (801) 263-3313
Internet: www.itt-tech.edu
Founded 1969

Private control

Breckinridge School of Nursing; School of Business; School of Criminal Justice; School of Drafting and Design; School of Electronics Technology; School of Health Sciences; School of Information Technology

Exec. Sec.: NORMA JEAN SEGER

Number of students: 80,000

UNIVERSITY OF UTAH

201 President's Circle, Room 201, Salt Lake City, UT 84112-9009

Telephone: (801) 581-7200

Internet: www.utah.edu

Founded 1850 as Univ. of Deseret, present name 1892

Academic year: August to May

Pres.: Dr A. LORRIS BETZ

Sr Vice-Pres. for Academic Affairs: DAVID W. PERSHING

Sr Vice-Pres. for Health Sciences: A. LORRIS BETZ

Vice-Pres. for Admin. Services: ARNOLD B. COMBE

Vice-Pres. for Human Resources: LORETTA F. HARPER

Vice-Pres. for Institutional Advancement: FRED C. ESPLIN

Vice-Pres. for Research: THOMAS N. PARKS

Vice-Pres. for Student Affairs: BARBARA H. SNYDER

Exec. Asst to the Pres.: LIZ McCOY

Gen. Counsel: JOHN K. MORRIS

Registrar: TIM EBNER

Dir for Library: JOYCE L. OGBURN

Number of teachers: 3,275

Number of students: 31,000

Publications: *Hinckley Journal of Politics*, *Journal of Land Resources and Environmental Law*, *Journal of Law and Family Studies*, *Political Research Quarterly*, *Quarterly West* (creative writing journal), *Tanner Lectures on Human Values* (cumulative volume of transcripts), *Undergraduate Research Abstracts*, *Utah Foreign Language Abstracts*, *Utah Law Review* (4 a year), *Western Humanities* (4 a year)

DEANS

College of Architecture and Planning: BRENDA CASE SCHEER

College of Education: MICHAEL L. HARDMAN

College of Engineering: RICHARD B. BROWN

College of Fine Arts: RAYMOND TYMAS-JONES

College of Health: Dr JAMES E. GRAVES

College of Humanities: ROBERT NEWMAN

College of Mines and Earth Sciences: FRANCIS H. BROWN

College of Nursing: Dr MAUREEN R. KEEFE

College of Pharmacy: Dr CHRIS M. IRELAND

College of Science: Dr PIERRE V. SOKOLSKY

College of Social and Behavioral Science: M. DAVID RUDD

College of Social Work: JANNAH MATHER

Continuing Education: CHUCK WIGHT

David Eccles School of Business: TAYLOR RANDALL

Graduate School: Dr CHARLES A. WIGHT

Honors College: Dr SYLVIA TORTI

School of Medicine: Dr VIVIAN S. LEE

S. J. Quinney College of Law: HIRAM E. CHODOSH

UTAH STATE UNIVERSITY

Office of the Pres., 1400 Old Main Hill, Logan, UT 84322-1400

Telephone: (435) 797-1000

E-mail: prm@usu.edu

Internet: www.usu.edu

Founded 1888 as Agricultural College of Utah, present name 1957

Academic year: January to December

Pres.: STAN L. ALBRECHT

Exec. Vice-Pres. and Provost: NOELLE COCKETT

Exec. Sr Vice-Provost: LAURENS H. SMITH

Vice-Pres. for Business and Finance: DAVE COWLEY

Vice-Pres. for Extension and Agriculture: KEN WHITE

Vice-Pres. for Research and Dean of Graduate Studies: MARK R. McLELLAN

Vice-Pres. for Student Services: JAMES D. MORALES

Chief Information Officer: ERIC HAWLEY

Chief Operating Officer for Univ. Advancement: ANNETTE HARDNER

Library of 1,505,000 vols (incl. 620,800 books, 300,370 govt documents, over 100,000 maps, 12,760 current serial subscriptions)

Number of teachers: 880

Number of students: 28,400

Publications: *Outlook* (6 a year), *Outreach* (12 a year), *Utah Science* (4 a year), *Western American Literary Journal* (4 a year), *Western Historical Quarterly*

DEANS

Caine College of the Arts: CRAIG JESSOP

College of Agriculture: KEN WHITE

College of Engineering: H. SCOTT HINTON

College of Humanities and Social Sciences: JOHN C. ALLEN

College of Natural Resources: Dr CHRIS LUECKE

College of Science: JIM MacMAHON

Emma Eccles Jones College of Education and Human Services: BETH FOLEY

Jon M. Huntsman School of Business: DOUGLAS D. ANDERSON

School of Graduate Studies: MARK R. McLELLAN

UTAH VALLEY UNIVERSITY

800 W Univ. Parkway, Orem, UT 84058

Telephone: (801) 863-8000

E-mail: instantinfo@uvu.edu

Internet: www.uvu.edu

Founded 1941 as Central Utah Vocational School, present name 2008

State control

Academic year: January to December

Pres.: Dr MATTHEW S. HOLLAND

Vice-Pres. for Academic Affairs: IAN WILSON

Vice-Pres. for Admin. and Legislative Affairs: VAL L. PETERSON

Vice-Pres. for Advancement: MARC ARCHAMBAULT

Vice-Pres. for Devt and Alumni: MARC ARCHAMBAULT

Vice-Pres. for Student Affairs: CORY DUCKWORTH

Vice-Pres. for Univ. Relations: VAL HALE

Library of 61,000 vols, 184,106 books, 12,222 ebooks, 2,742 maps, 19,364 video cassettes, 5,132 audio CDs, 1,571 archival materials

Number of students: 28,800

DEANS

College of Humanities and Social Sciences: DAVID P. YELLS

College of Science and Health: SAM RUSHFORTH

College of Technology and Computing: ERNEST CAREY

School of the Arts: PATRICK M. JONES

School of Education: BRIANT J. FARNSWORTH

University College: K. D. TAYLOR

Woodbury School of Business: NORMAN S. WRIGHT

WEBER STATE UNIVERSITY

3848 Harrison Blvd, Ogden, UT 84408

Telephone: (801) 626-6000

E-mail: mediarelations@weber.edu

Internet: www.weber.edu

Founded 1889 as Weber Stake Acad., present name 1991

State control

Academic year: August to August

Pres.: F. ANN MILLNER

Provost: MICHAEL B. VAUGHAN

Vice-Pres. for Admin. Services: NORMAN TARBOX

Vice-Pres. for Information Technology: BRET R. ELLIS

Vice-Pres. for Student Affairs: Dr JAN WINNIFORD

Vice-Pres. for Univ. Advancement: BRAD MORTENSEN

Registrar: Dr WINSLOW L. HURST

Dir for Library: JOAN G. HUBBARD

Library of 458,115 vols, 90,628 electronic resources

Number of teachers: 440

Number of students: 25,000

Publications: *Metaphor* (1 a year), *WSU Viewbook*, *Weber State University Magazine* (2 a year, online), *Weber Studies* (4 a year)

DEANS

College of Applied Science and Technology: DAVID FERRO

College of Science: DAVID MATTY

College of Social and Behavioral Sciences: FRANCIS B. HARROLD

Dr Ezekiel R. Dumke College of Health Professions: Dr YASMEN SIMONIAN

Jerry and Vickie Moyes College of Education: Dr JACK RASMUSSEN

John B. Goddard School of Business and Economics: JEFF STEAGALL

Telitha E. Lindquist College of Arts and Humanities: MADONNE MINER

WESTMINSTER COLLEGE

1840 S 1300 E St, Salt Lake City, UT 84105

Telephone: (801) 484-7651

Internet: www.wcslc.edu

Founded 1875 as Salt Lake Collegiate Institute, present name 1902

Private control

Pres.: Dr MICHAEL S. BASSIS

Provost and Vice-Pres. for Academic Affairs: JAMES E. SEIDELMAN

Exec. Vice-Pres. and Treas.: STEPHEN MORGAN

Dean of the Faculty: Dr STEPHEN R. BAAR

Vice-Pres. for Advancement and Alumni Relations: NANCY MICHAEKO

Vice-Pres. for Enrolment Services: JOEL BAUMAN

Vice-Pres. for Finance and Admin.: CURTIS R. RYAN

Vice-Pres. for Information Technology: Dr SHERYL PHILLIPS

Dean for Students: MARK FERNE

Library Dir: DIANE VANDERPOL

Library of 84,000 vols

Number of teachers: 325 (135 full-time, 190 part-time)

Number of students: 3,000 (graduate and undergraduate)

DEANS

Bill and Vieve Gore School of Business: Dr JIN WANG

Division of New Learning: ARIC KRAUSE

School of Arts and Sciences: Dr MARY JANE CHASE

School of Education: Dr ROBERT SHAW

School of Nursing and Health Sciences: SHERYL STEADMAN

VERMONT

BENNINGTON COLLEGE

1 College Dr., Bennington, VT 05201-6003
Telephone: (802) 442-5401
E-mail: admissions@bennington.edu
Internet: www.bennington.edu
Founded 1932
Private control
Academic year: September to June

Areas of study: acting, animation, anthropology, architecture, art history, astronomy, biology, ceramics, chemistry, Chinese, computer science, conflict resolution, dance, design, digital arts, directing, drama, drawing, economics, education, environmental science, film and video, French, history, int. relations, Italian, Japanese, literature, mathematics, music, painting, philosophy, photography, physics, playwriting, political science, printmaking, psychology, religion, sculpture, Spanish, teaching, theatre, visual arts, writing

Pres.: ELIZABETH COLEMAN
Vice-Pres. and Chief Financial Officer: LAURA KRAUSE
Vice-Pres. for External Relations: PAIGE BARTELS
Vice-Pres. for Planning and Admin.: DAVID REES
Vice-Pres. for Planning and Spec. Projects: JOAN GOODRICH
Dean for Admissions and Financial Aid: KEN HIMMELMAN
Dean for College: ISABEL ROCHE
Dean for Students: EVA CHATTERJEE-SUTTON
Registrar: KATHY POSEY
Dir for Library and Information Services: OCEANA WILSON

Library of 108,000 vols
Number of teachers: 70
Number of students: 820 (685 undergraduate, 135 graduate)

BURLINGTON COLLEGE

351 N Ave, Burlington, VT 05401
Telephone: (802) 862-9616
E-mail: admissions@burlington.edu
Internet: www.burlington.edu
Founded 1972 as Vermont Institute of Community Involvement, present name 1979
Private control

Areas of study: expressive arts, graphic design, humanities, hospitality and event management, photography, social sciences, woodworking, writing, literature

Pres.: (vacant)
Vice-Pres. for Academic and Student Affairs: ARTHUR HESSLER
Vice-Pres. for Admin. and Finance: CHRISTINE PLUNKETT
Vice-Pres. for Institutional Advancement: MICHAEL LUCK
Dir for Admissions: GILLIAN HOMSTED
Dir for Devt: SARAH JUDD
Dir for Library and Information Services: JESSICA ALLARD
Registrar: MELISSA HOWANITZ

Library of 13,000 vols, 1,000 video cassettes, 500 sound recordings
Number of teachers: 75
Number of students: 195

CASTLETON STATE COLLEGE

86 Seminary St, Castleton, VT 05735
Telephone: (802) 468-5611
E-mail: info@castleton.edu
Internet: www.csc.vsc.edu
Founded 1787 as Rutland County Grammar School, present status 1962

State control
Academic year: August to May

Depts of art, business administration, communication, criminal justice, economics and politics, education, English, geography, geology, health science, history, mathematics, music, natural science, nursing, physical education, psychology, sociology, social work, sports administration, Spanish, theatre arts

Pres.: DAVID S. WOLK
Dean for Academics: Dr JOSEPH T. MARK
Dean for Admin.: SCOTT DIKEMAN
Dean for Education: HONORÉE FLEMING
Dean for Enrolment: MAURICE OUIMET
Dean for Students: DENNIS PROULX
Dir for Communications: ENNIS DULING
Dir for Devt: GEORGE MCGURL
Registrar: LORI ARNER
Dir for Library: SANDRA DULING

Library of 208,454 vols, 49,974 print and e-journal subscriptions
Number of teachers: 95 (full-time)
Number of students: 2,200

CHAMPLAIN COLLEGE

246 S Willard St, Burlington, VT 05401
Telephone: (802) 860-2700
E-mail: admission@champlain.edu
Internet: www.champlain.edu
Founded 1878 as Burlington Business School, present name 1958
Private control
Academic year: August to May

Pres.: Dr DAVID F. FINNY
Provost and Chief Academic Officer: Dr ROBIN ABRAMSON
Sr Vice-Pres. for Finance and Admin.: DAVID PROVOST
Vice-Pres. for Advancement: SHELLEY RICHARDSON
Vice-Pres. for Devt and Alumni Affairs: SHELLEY RICHARDSON
Vice-Pres. Enrolment Management: IAN MORTIMER
Registrar: BECKY PETERSON
Library Dir: JANET COTTRELL

Number of teachers: 110
Number of students: 2,000

DEANS

Core Division: Dr ELIZABETH BEAULIEU
Division of Business: Prof. DAVID STRUBLER
Division of Communication and Creative Media: Prof. JEFF RUTENBECK
Division of Continuing Professional Studies: CHUCK MANISCALCO
Division of Education and Human Studies: Prof. SUE ROWLEY
Division of Information Technology and Sciences: Dr ALI RAFIEYMEHR

COLLEGE OF ST. JOSEPH

71 Clement Rd, Rutland, VT 05701
Telephone: (802) 773-5900
E-mail: admissions@csj.edu
Internet: www.csj.edu
Founded 1956 as St Joseph's Teacher's College, present name 1983
Language of instruction: English
Private control
Academic year: September to May

Divs of arts and sciences, business, criminal justice, education, psychology and human services

Pres.: FRANK G. MIGLORIE
Vice-Pres. for External Affairs: SUSAN ENGLESE
Academic Dean: NANCY J. KLINE
Dean for Admissions: JOEL WINCOWSKI
Dean for Students: ROBERT LUKASKIEWICZ

Registrar: PATRICIA C. MIGLORIE
Librarian: DOREEN J. MCCULLOUGH
Library of 140,000 vols, 3,000 periodicals
Number of students: 425

GODDARD COLLEGE

123 Pitkin Rd, Plainfield, VT 05667
Telephone: (802) 454-8311
E-mail: admissions@goddard.edu
Internet: www.goddard.edu
Founded 1863 as Green Mountain Central Institute, present location 1938
Private control

Areas of study: creative writing, education and licensure, health arts and sciences, psychology and counselling

Pres.: BARBARA VACARR
Vice-Pres. for Academic Affairs: MARIANNE REIFF
Chief Finance and Admin. Officer: FAITH BROWN
Dean for Enrolment Management: PETER BURNS
Registrar: JOSH CASTLE
Dir for Information Access: CLARA BRUNS

Library of 72,000 vols, 39,000 ebooks
Number of teachers: 105
Number of students: 500

GREEN MOUNTAIN COLLEGE

1 Brennan Circle, Poultney, VT 05764
Telephone: (802) 287-8000
E-mail: admiss@greenmtn.edu
Internet: www.greenmtn.edu
Founded 1834 as Troy Conf. Acad., present name 1957
Private control
Academic year: August to May (2 semesters)

Depts of business and economics, education, English and communications, environmental liberal arts, environmental studies, liberal studies, natural and mathematical sciences, natural resource management, philosophy, recreation and outdoor studies, resort and hospitality management, social and behavioural science, visual and performing arts

Pres.: Dr PAUL J. FONTEYN
Provost and Vice-Pres. for Academic Affairs: Prof. Dr WILLIAM THROPP
Vice-Pres. for Finance and Admin.: JOSEPH MANNING, III
Vice-Pres. for Student Life: E. JOSEPH PETRICK
Dir for Admissions: MAIA HANRON-SANFORD
Dir for Devt: MARY LOU WILLITS
Dean for Faculty: THOMAS J. MAUHS-PUGH
Registrar: SHARON L. HOFFMAN
Dir for Library, IT Services and Learning Support: PAUL MILLETTE

Library of 72,000 vols, 46,000 ebooks, 27,250 ejournals, 300 journals
Number of teachers: 45 (full-time)
Number of students: 750

JOHNSON STATE COLLEGE

337 College Hill, Johnson, VT 05656-9464
Telephone: (802) 635-2356
E-mail: jscadmissions@jsc.edu
Internet: www.jsc.edu
Founded 1828, present name 1962
State control
Academic year: August to May

Depts of behavioural sciences, business and economics, education, environmental and health sciences, fine and performing arts, humanities, mathematics, writing and literature

Pres.: BARBARA E. MURPHY
Academic Dean: DANIEL REGAN

Dean for Admin.: SHARRON SCOTT
Dean for Students: DAVID BERGH
Registrar: DOUGLAS EASTMAN
Faculty Librarian: JOSEPH FARARA

Library of 111,000 vols, 6,500 ebooks, 36,000 ejournals, 384 journals

Number of teachers: 145 (55 full-time, 90 part-time)

Number of students: 2,000

LYNDON STATE COLLEGE

POB 919, Lyndonville, VT 05851

Telephone: (802) 626-6413
E-mail: admissions@lyndonstate.edu
Internet: www.lyndonstate.edu

Founded 1911, present name and status 1961
State control

Academic year: August to May

College of liberal arts and professional programmes; depts of arts, atmospheric sciences, business administration, education, electronic journalism arts, English, exercise science, film studies, general studies, liberal studies, music and performing arts, mountain recreation management, mathematics and computer science, natural sciences, philosophy, psychology, social sciences, visual arts

Pres.: Dr STEVE GOLD
Dean for Academic and Student Affairs: DONNA DALTON
Dean for Admin.: WAYNE T. HAMILTON
Dean for Institutional Advancement: ROBERT E. WHITTAKER
Library Dir: GARET NELSON

Library of 113,000 vols

Number of teachers: 150 (58 full-time, 92 part-time)

Number of students: 1,430

MARLBORO COLLEGE

POB A, Marlboro, VT 05344-0300
2582 South Rd, Marlboro, VT 05344

Telephone: (802) 257-4333
E-mail: admissions@marlboro.edu
Internet: www.marlboro.edu

Founded 1946
Private control

Academic year: August to May

Areas of study: arts, humanities, liberal studies, natural sciences, social sciences, world studies

Pres.: ELLEN MCCULLOCH-LOVELL
Chief Advancement Officer: LISA CHRISTENSEN
Dean for Admissions: NICOLE CURVIN
Dean for Faculty and Graduate Education: RICHARD GLEJZER
Dean for Students: KEN SCHNECK
Registrar: TOBIAS GELSTON
Library Dir: EMILY ALLING

Library of 75,000 vols, 17,000 periodicals
Number of teachers: 40 (full-time)
Number of students: 330

MIDDLEBURY COLLEGE

Middlebury, VT 05753

Telephone: (802) 443-5000
E-mail: presoff@middlebury.edu
Internet: www.middlebury.edu

Founded 1800
Private control

Academic year: September to May (2 semesters)

Depts of history of art and architecture, international politics and economics, literary studies, molecular biology and biochemistry, political science, studio art, writing programmes

Pres.: Prof. RONALD D. LIEBOWITZ
Provost and Exec. Vice-Pres.: ALISON BYERLY
Sr Vice-Pres.: MICHAEL D. SCHOENFELD
Vice-Pres. for Academic Affairs: Prof. TIM SPEARS
Vice-Pres. for Admin.: TIMOTHY SPEARS
Vice-Pres. for College Advancement: JAMES R. KEYES
Vice-Pres. for Finance and Treas.: PATRICK NORTON
Vice-Pres. for Language Schools, Schools Abroad and Graduate Programmes: MICHAEL GEISLER
Vice-Pres. for Planning and Assessment: Prof. SUSAN CAMPBELL BALDRIDGE
Dean for Admissions: GREGORY B. BUCKLES
Dean for College and Chief Diversity Officer: SHIRLEY M. COLLADO
Dean for Faculty: JAMES RALPH
Dean for Library and Information Services: MARY BACKUS

Library of 1,000,000 vols
Number of teachers: 280
Number of students: 2,450 (undergraduate)

Publications: *Middlebury Magazine* (4 a year), *New England Review* (4 a year)

NORWICH UNIVERSITY

158 Harmon Dr., Northfield, VT 05663

Telephone: (802) 485-2000
E-mail: nuadm@norwich.edu
Internet: www.norwich.edu

Founded 1819 as private military college
Private control

Academic year: August to May

Pres.: Dr RICHARD W. SCHNEIDER
Sr Vice-Pres. for Academic Affairs and Dean for Faculty: Dr GUIYOU HUANG
Vice-Pres. for Devt and Alumni Relations: DAVID J. WHALEY
Vice-Pres. for Enrolment and Communication: KAREN P. MCGRATH
Vice-Pres. for Student Affairs and Commandant of Corps of Cadets: MICHAEL B. KELLEY
Chief Admin. Officer: DAVID MAGIDA
Chief Financial Officer and Treas.: LAUREN D. WOBBY
Library Dir: ELLEN HALL

Library of 240,000 vols and microfilms; military history colln

Number of teachers: 110 (full-time)
Number of students: 2,300

Publication: *The Record* (4 a year)

DEANS

David Crawford School of Engineering: Dr SAEED MOAVENI
School of Architecture and Art: ARON P. TEMKIN
School of Business and Management: Dr FRANK THOMAS VANECEK
School of Graduate and Continuing Studies: Dr WILLIAM CLEMENTS
School of Humanities: ANDREW KNAUF
School of Mathematics and Science: Prof. CATHY M. FREY
School of Social Sciences: Dr THOMAS FRANK TAYLOR

SAINT MICHAEL'S COLLEGE

POB 7, 1 Winooski Park, Colchester, VT 05439

Telephone: (802) 654-3000
E-mail: admission@smcvt.edu
Internet: www.smcvt.edu

Founded 1904 as St Michael's Institute
Private control

Majors in accounting, American studies, art, biochemistry, biology, business, chemistry, classics, computer science, East Asian studies, economics, education, engineering, English, environmental science, environmental studies, finance, fine arts, French, gender/women's studies, geography, global studies, history, information systems, int. business, Italian, journalism and mass communication, language and linguistics, management, marketing, mathematics, medieval studies, modern languages and literature, music, peace and justice, philosophy, physical science, physics, political science, psychology, religious studies, sociology/anthropology, Spanish, theatre

Academic year: August to May

Pres.: Dr JACK J. NEUHAUSER
Provost and Vice-Pres. of Academic Affairs: Dr KAREN A. TALENTINO
Vice-Pres. for Enrolment: JERRY E. FLANAGAN
Vice-Pres. for Finance and Treas.: NEAL E. ROBINSON
Vice-Pres. for Instn Advancement: PATRICK J. GALLIVAN
Vice-Pres. for Student Life: MICHAEL D. SAMARA
Dean for College: Dr JEFFREY A. TRUMBOWER
Registrar: JOHN D. SHEEHEY
Dir for Library and Information Services: JOHN K. PAYNE

Library of 270,000 vols, 60,000 ejournals, 7,000 video cassettes
Number of teachers: 150 (full-time)
Number of students: 2,800 (1,900 undergraduate, 650 graduate, 250 int.)

SIT GRADUATE INSTITUTE

POB 676, 1 Kipling Rd, Brattleboro, VT 05302-0676

Telephone: (802) 257-7751
E-mail: info@sit.edu
Internet: www.sit.edu

Founded as School for International Training, present name 2007
Private control

Academic year: August to June

Areas of study: conflict transformation, international education, intercultural service, leadership and management, sustainable development

Pres. and CEO: Dr ADAM S WEINBERG
Sr Vice-Pres. for Academic Programmes: JOHN LUCAS
Dean for Academic Admin. and Assessment: ELLEN HOLMES
Dean for External Relations and Strategic Enrolment Management: LAURIE BLACK
Dean: Dr PREETI SHROFF-MEHTA
Dean for Student Affairs: MICHAEL SMALLIS
Registrar: GINNY NELLIS
Dir for Libraries and Academic Resources: PAMELA CONTAKOS

SOUTHERN VERMONT COLLEGE

982 Mansion Dr., Bennington, VT 05201-6002

Telephone: (802) 442-4000
E-mail: registrar@svc.edu
Internet: www.svc.edu

Founded 1926 as St Joseph College, present name 1974
Private control

Academic year: August to May

Divs of business, humanities, nursing, science and technology, social sciences

Pres.: KAREN GROSS
Provost: ALBERT DECICCIO
Chief Financial Officer: JAMES BECKWITH
Dean for Academics: REBECCA M. DILIDDO
Dean for Advancement: KAREN TRUBRITT
Dean for Enrolment: JOEL WINCOWSKI
Dean for Students: ANNE HOPKINS GROSS
Registrar: JAMES FREDERICK
Dir for Library: SARAH K. SANFILIPPO

Number of teachers: 40
Number of students: 550

STERLING COLLEGE

POB 72, Craftsbury Common, VT 05827
16 Sterling Dr., Craftsbury Common, VT 05827
Telephone: (802) 586-7711
E-mail: admissions@sterlingcollege.edu
Internet: www.sterlingcollege.edu
Founded 1958
Academic year: September to August (3 semesters)
Areas of study: conservation ecology, environmental humanities, natural history, northern studies, outdoor education, sustainable agriculture
Pres.: WILLIAM R. WOOTTON
Exec. Vice-Pres.: NED HOUSTON
Dean for Academics: PAVEL CENKL
Dir for Advancement: TIM PATTERSON
Dean for Students: JILL FINEIS
Dir for Admissions: LYNNE A. BIRDSALL
Registrar: LAURIE LAGGNER
Librarian: PETRA VOGEL
Library of 3,000 vols, 100 journal titles
Number of students: 125

Publication: *Common Voice* (2 a year)

UNIVERSITY OF VERMONT

Burlington, VT 05405
Telephone: (802) 656-3131
E-mail: admissions@uvm.edu
Internet: www.uvm.edu
Founded 1791, current status 1862
State control
Academic year: September to May
Pres.: E. THOMAS SULLIVAN
Sr Vice-Pres. and Provost: Dr DAVID ROSOWSKY
Vice-Provost for Student Affairs: Dr ANNIE STEVENS
Vice-Pres. for Enrolment Management: Dr JOHN F. RYAN
Vice-Pres. for Finance and Treas.: RICHARD CATE
Vice-Pres. for Human Resources, Diversity and Multicultural Affairs: Dr WANDA HEADING-GRANT
Vice-Pres. for Legal Affairs and Gen. Counsel: FRANCINE T. BAZLUKE
Vice-Pres. for Research: Dr JOHN EVANS
Vice-Pres. for Univ. Relations and Admin.: Dr THOMAS J. GUSTAFSON
Registrar: KEITH P. WILLIAMS
Chief Information Officer, Dean for Libraries and Learning Resources: MARA R. SAULE
Library of 3,064,472 vols
Number of teachers: 1,491 (1,191 full-time, 300 part-time)
Number of students: 12,723 (10,912 undergraduate, 1,811 graduate)

DEANS

College of Agriculture and Life Sciences: Dr THOMAS C. VOGELMANN
College of Arts and Sciences: Dr ANTONIO CEPEDA-BENITO
College of Education and Social Services: Dr FAYNEESE MILLER
College of Engineering and Mathematical Sciences: Dr LUIS GARCIA
College of Medicine: Dr FREDERICK C. MORIN, III
College of Nursing and Health Sciences: Dr PATRICIA A. PRELOCK
Continuing and Distance Education: CYNTHIA L. BELLIVEAU
Graduate College: Dr CYNTHIA FOREHAND
Honors College: Dr LISA SCHNELL

Rubenstein School of Environment and Natural Resources: Dr NANCY E. MATHEWS
School of Business Administration: SANJAY SHARMA

VERMONT LAW SCHOOL

POB 96, 164 Chelsea St, S Royalton, VT 05068
Telephone: (802) 831-1000
E-mail: admiss@vermontlaw.edu
Internet: www.vermontlaw.edu
Founded 1972
Private control
Academic year: August to May (2 semesters)
Pres. and Dean: Prof. GEOFFREY B. SHIELDS
Vice-Dean for Academic Affairs: Prof. GIL KUJOVICH
Vice-Pres. for Finance and Admin.: LORRAINE ATWOOD
Vice-Pres. for Operations: DENNIS STERN
Exec. Dir for Institutional Advancement: MATTHEW RIZZO
Registrar: KATHY MAIELI
Dir for Library: CARL A. YIRKA
Library of 349,000 vols, 149,000 titles
Number of teachers: 105 (54 full-time, 9 visiting, 42 adjunct)
Number of students: 205

Publications: *Vermont Journal of Environmental Law* (online), *Vermont Law Review* (4 a year)

VERMONT TECHNICAL COLLEGE

POB 500, Randolph Center, VT 05061-0500
Telephone: (802) 728-1000
E-mail: admissions@vtc.edu
Internet: www.vtc.edu
Founded 1866 as Randolph State Normal School, present name 1962
State control
Academic year: August to May
Areas of study: architectural engineering technology, aviation, business technology and management, computer engineering technology, computer information technology, computer software engineering, construction practice and management, dental hygiene, diversified agriculture, electrical engineering technology, electromechanical engineering technology, equine studies, sustainable design and technology
Pres.: Dr PHILIP A. CONROY, JR
Dean for Academic Affairs: PATRICIA MENCHINI
Dean for Admin.: G. GEOFFREY LINDEMER
Dean for College: MICHAEL VAN DYKE
Registrar: MICHAEL DEMPSEY
Library Dir: DAVID STURGES
Number of students: 1,450

VIRGINIA

AVERETT UNIVERSITY

420 W Main St, Danville, VA 24541
Telephone: (434) 791-5600
E-mail: admit@averett.edu
Internet: www.averett.edu
Founded 1859 as Union Female College, present name 2001
Private control
Academic year: July to June
Pres.: Dr TIFFANY McKILLIP FRANKS
Exec. Vice-Pres.: CHARLES HARRIS
Vice-Pres. and Chief Financial Officer: THOM DAVIS
Vice-Pres. for Academic Affairs: Dr JANET LAUGHLIN
Vice-Pres. for Admin. and Finance: PEGGY C. WRIGHT

Vice-Pres. for Enrolment Management: Dr STUART JONES
Vice-Pres. for Institutional Advancement: BUDDY RAWLEY
Vice-Pres. for Student Services: CHARLES HARRIS
Dean for Students: WILLIAM WOODWARD
Dir for Admissions: JOEL NESTER
Registrar: JANET ROBERSON
Dir for Library: ELAINE L. DAY
Library of 162,878 vols, 36,957 current serial subscriptions, 101,773 microforms, 749 sheets or reels, 688 audiovisual materials
Number of teachers: 125 (60 full-time, 65 part-time)
Number of students: 925

Publications: *Averett Journal* (1 a year), *Averett TODAY Magazine* (1 a year)

DEANS

Graduate and Professional Studies: A. KENDALL CARTER

BAPTIST THEOLOGICAL SEMINARY AT RICHMOND

3400 Brook Rd, Richmond, VA 23227
Telephone: (804) 355-8135
E-mail: admissions@btsr.edu
Internet: www.btsr.edu
Founded 1991
Private control
Academic year: September to May
Pres.: RONALD CRAWFORD
Vice-Pres. for Institutional Advancement: TIMOTHY BRUCE HEILMAN
Academic Dean: Prof. ISRAEL GALINDO
Dir for Admissions and Recruitment: TIFFANY KELLOGG PITTMAN
Dir for Business Affairs: JAMES F. PEAK, JR
Registrar and Dir for Financial Aid: IDA MAE HAYS
Dir for Library: MILTON COALTER
Library of 300,000 vols, 1,300 periodical subscriptions, 6,000 ejournals
Number of teachers: 10
Number of students: 135

BLUEFIELD COLLEGE

3000 College Dr., Bluefield, VA 24605
Telephone: (276) 326-3682
E-mail: bluefield@bluefield.edu
Internet: www.bluefield.edu
Founded 1922
Private control
Academic year: August to August
Divs of business, Christian studies, education, exercise sports science, fine arts, language, literature and communications, science and mathematics, social science
Pres.: DAVID W. OLIVE
Vice-Pres. for Academic Affairs: ROBERT SHIPPEY
Vice-Pres. for Advancement: RUTH BLANKENSHIP
Vice-Pres. for Enrolment Management: TRENT ARGO
Vice-Pres. for Finance and Admin.: SARAH BEAMER
Vice-Pres. for Institutional Advancement: RUTH BLANKENSHIP
Vice-Pres. for Student Devt and Exec. Dir for Faith Formation and Church Relations: DAVID TAYLOR
Dir for Admissions: MARK HIPES
Dir for Library Services: NORA LOCKETT
Registrar: AMANDA PARKS
Library of 40,000 vols, 63,000 ebooks, 16,000 magazines and journals

BRIDGEWATER COLLEGE

402 E College St, Bridgewater, VA 22812
Telephone: (540) 828-8000
E-mail: admissions@bridgewater.edu
Internet: www.bridgewater.edu
Founded 1880
Private control
Academic year: August to May

Depts of art, biology, chemistry, communication studies and theatre, economics and business administration, education, English, family and consumer sciences, foreign languages, health and exercise science, history and political science, mathematics and computer science, music, philosophy and religion, physics, psychology, sociology
Pres.: Dr ROY W. FERGUSON, JR
Exec. Vice-Pres.: ROY W. FERGUSON, JR
Vice-Pres. and Dean of Academic Affairs: Dr CAROL A. SCHEPPARD
Vice-Pres. for Enrolment Management: REGGIE A. WEBB
Vice-Pres. for Finance: ANNE B. KEELER
Vice-Pres. for Institutional Advancement: BRUCE D. SMITH
Dean for the College: ART HESSLER
Dean for Students: Dr WILLIAM D. MIRACLE
Registrar: CYNTHIA K. HOWDYSHELL
Dir for Library: ANDREW PEARSON
Library of 174,000 vols, 35,000 ejournals
Number of teachers: 140 (105 full-time, 35 part-time)
Number of students: 1,650
Publication: *The Philomathean* (1 a year)

CHRISTENDOM COLLEGE

134 Christendom Dr., Front Royal, VA 22630-6534
Telephone: (540) 636-2900
E-mail: info@christendom.edu
Internet: www.christendom.edu
Founded 1977
Private control
Academic year: August to May
Liberal arts college
Pres.: Dr TIMOTHY T. O'DONNELL
Vice-Pres. for Academic Affairs: Dr STEVEN C. SNYDER
Vice-Pres. for Advancement: JOHN F. CISKANIK
Academic Dean: Dr PATRICK KEATS
Dean for Student Life: JESSE DORMAN
Dir for Admissions: TOM MCFADDEN
Registrar: WALTER JANARO
Dir for Library: ANDREW ARMSTONG
Library of 90,000 vols, 5,000 audiovisual items, 30,000 periodicals
Number of students: 405

CHRISTOPHER NEWPORT UNIVERSITY

1 University Place, Newport News, VA 23606-3072
Telephone: (757) 594-7000
E-mail: admit@cnu.edu
Internet: www.cnu.edu
Founded 1960 as 2-year br. of College of William and Mary, present name and status 1992
State control
Academic year: August to May (2 semesters)
Pres.: PAUL S. TRIBLE, JR
Provost: Dr MARK W. PADILLA
Vice-Provost: Dr LAURA DEIULIO
Dean for Enrolment Services and Univ. Registrar: LISA DUNCAN RAINES
Dean for Students: Dr KEVIN HUGHES
Univ. Librarian: MARY SELLEN
Library of 207,932 vols, 46,400 periodicals (print and electronic)

Number of students: 4,800
Publication: *Currents* (1 a year)

DEANS

College of Arts and Humanities: STEVEN BREESE
College of Natural and Behavioral Sciences: Dr DAVID DOUGHTY
College of Social Sciences: Dr ROBERT E. COLVIN

COLLEGE OF WILLIAM & MARY

POB 8795, Williamsburg, VA 23187-8795
Telephone: (757) 221-4000
E-mail: admiss@wm.edu
Internet: www.wm.edu
Founded 1693
State control
Academic year: September to May
Campuses in Gloucester Point (Virginia) and Dupont Circle (Washington, DC)
Pres.: W. TAYLOR REVELEY, III
Provost and Chief Academic Officer: MICHAEL R. HALLERAN
Vice-Pres. for Admin.: ANNA MARTIN
Vice-Pres. for Devt: SEAN PIERI
Vice-Pres. for Finance: SAMUEL E. JONES
Vice-Pres. for Strategic Initiatives: JAMES GOLDEN
Vice-Pres. for Student Affairs: VIRGINIA AMBLER
Registrar: SARA L. MARCHELLO
Dean for Libraries: CARRIE L. COOPER
Library: 2m. vols
Number of teachers: 590 (full-time)
Number of students: 8,200 (6,071 undergraduate, 2,129 graduate)
Publications: *Business Review* (1 a year), *James Blair Historical Review* (1 a year), *William & Mary Magazine*, *William and Mary Environmental Law and Policy Review*, *William and Mary Law Review*, *The Monitor*, *The William and Mary Quarterly*

DEANS

Arts and Sciences: EUGENE R. TRACY
Law School: DAVISON M. DOUGLAS
Mason School of Business: LAWRENCE B. PULLEY
School of Education: Dr VIRGINIA L. MCLAUGHLIN
School of Marine Science: Dr JOHN T. WELLS

EASTERN MENNONITE UNIVERSITY

1200 Park Rd, Harrisonburg, VA 22802-2462
Telephone: (540) 432-4000
E-mail: admiss@emu.edu
Internet: www.emu.edu
Founded 1917 as Eastern Mennonite School, present name 1994
Private control
Academic year: August to May (2 semesters)
Liberal arts college, with emphasis on international education; campus at Lancaster (Pennsylvania)
Pres.: LOREN SWARTZENDRUBER
Provost: Dr FRED KNISS
Vice-Pres. and Seminary Dean: MICHAEL A. KING
Vice-Pres. and Undergraduate Academic Dean: NANCY HEISEY
Vice-Pres. for Advancement: KIRK L. SHISLER
Vice-Pres. for Enrolment: LUKE HARTMAN
Vice-Pres. for Finance: DARYL W. BERT
Vice-Pres. for Student Life: KEN L. NAFZIGER
Graduate Dean: P. DAVID GLANZER
Dir for Admissions: DON YODER
Registrar: DAVE DETROW
Dir for Library: BERYL BRUBAKER
Library of 149,000 vols

Number of teachers: 90
Number of students: 1,500
Publications: *Crossroads Magazine* (3 a year), *Peacebuilder* (2 a year)

EASTERN VIRGINIA MEDICAL SCHOOL

POB 1980, Norfolk, VA 23501-1980
714 Woodis Ave, Norfolk, VA 23501
Telephone: (757) 446-5600
Internet: www.evms.edu
Founded 1973
Private control
Pres.: HARRY T. LESTER
Provost and Dean: Dr RICHARD V. HOMAN
Vice-Pres. for Admin. and Finance: MARK BABASHANIAN
Asst Dean for Admissions and Enrolment: Dr DONALD MEYER
Asst Dean for Student Affairs: Dr ANN E. CAMPBELL
Registrar: JENNIFER GRAY
Assoc. Dean for Library and Learning: JUDITH ROBINSON MERCER
Number of teachers: 1,600
Publication: *EVMS Magazine* (3 a year)

DEANS

School of Health Professions: Dr C. DONALD COMBS

ECPI UNIVERSITY

5555 Greenwich Rd, Virginia Beach, VA 23462
Telephone: (757) 490-9090
Internet: www.ecpi.edu
Private control
Schools of business and criminal justice, culinary arts, health science, technology; campuses at Newport News and Richmond (Virginia), Raleigh and Charlotte (North Carolina)

EMORY & HENRY COLLEGE

POB 947, Emory, VA 24327
Telephone: (276) 944-4121
E-mail: ehadmiss@ehc.edu
Internet: www.ehc.edu
Founded 1836
Private control
Academic year: August to May (2 semesters)
Areas of study: art, biology, business administration, chemistry, economics, English, geography, history, languages, mass communications, mathematics, music, philosophy, physical education, physics, political science, psychology, religion, sociology, theatre
Pres.: Dr ROSALIND REICHARD
Vice-Pres. for Academic Affairs and Dean for Faculty: LINDA HARRIS DOBKINS
Vice-Pres. for Business and Finance: DIRK WILMOTH
Vice-Pres. for Enrolment Management: DAVID HAWSEY
Vice-Pres. for Institutional Advancement: JOSEPH TAYLOR
Vice-Pres. for Student Life and Dean for Students: PAMELA GOURLEY
Dir for Institutional Research and Institutional Effectiveness: KEVORK HORRISSIAN
Registrar: TAMMY SHEETS (acting)
Dir for Library and Information Services: LORRAINE N. ABRAHAM
Library of 350,000 vols, 400 journal subscriptions
Number of teachers: 70 (full-time)
Number of students: 980 (940 undergraduate, 40 graduate)

FERRUM COLLEGE

POB 1000, Ferrum, VA 24088
Telephone: (540) 365-2121
E-mail: admissions@ferrum.edu
Internet: www.ferrum.edu
Founded 1913
Private control
Academic year: August to May (2 semesters)
Pres.: Dr JENNIFER L. BRAATEN
Provost and Exec. Vice-Pres.: Dr LESLIE LAMBERT
Assoc. Provost and Chief Information Officer: CHRISTINE H. STINSON
Dir for Int. Programmes: SASHA A. SAARI
Dir for Professional Studies: DAVID R. SULZEN
Dean for Academic Planning and Programmes: GAIL L. SUMMER
Registrar: YVONNE S. WALKER
Dir for Library: GEORGE LOVELAND
Library of 210,000 vols
Number of students: 1,500

DEANS

School of Arts and Humanities: Dr JOHN W. BRUTON
School of Natural Science and Mathematics: Dr JASON POWELL
School of Social Sciences and Professional Studies: Dr KEVIN REILLY

GEORGE MASON UNIVERSITY

4400 University Dr., Fairfax, VA 22030-4444
Telephone: (703) 993-1000
E-mail: registrar@gmu.edu
Internet: www.gmu.edu
Founded 1957 as N Virginia br. of Univ. of Virginia, present name and status 1972
State control
Academic year: August to May (2 semesters)
Campuses at Arlington, Manassas and Sterling
Pres.: Dr ALAN G. MERTEN
Provost: Dr PETER N. STEARNS
Sr Vice-Pres. for Finance and Planning: Dr MAURICE W. SCHERRENS
Vice-Pres. for Enrolment Services and Vice-Provost for Academic Affairs: LINDA A. SCHWARTZSTEIN
Vice-Pres. for Global Strategies: ANNE SCHILLER
Vice-Pres. for Research and Economic Devt: ROGER STOUGH
Vice-Pres. for Univ. Devt and Alumni Affairs: MARC BRODERICK
Vice-Pres. for Univ. Life: Dr SANDRA SCHERRENS
Vice-Pres. for Univ. Relations: PAUL LIBERTY
Univ. Registrar: SUSAN H. JONES
Univ. Librarian: JOHN ZENELIS
Library of 2,846,733 vols
Number of teachers: 1,658 (965 full-time, 693 part-time)
Number of students: 33,300
Publications: *Faculty Bibliography* (1 a year), *Mason Research* (1 a year)

DEANS

College of Education and Human Development: MARK GINSBERG
College of Humanities and Social Sciences: JACK CENSER
College of Health and Human Services: SHIRLEY S. TRAVIS
College of Science: VIKAS CHANDHOKE
College of Visual and Performing Arts: WILLIAM REEDER
Honors College: ZOFIA BURR
School of Law: DANIEL POLSBY
School of Management: JORGE HADDOCK
School of Public Policy: EDWARD RHODES
Volgeneau School of Engineering: LLOYD GRIFFITHS

HAMPDEN-SYDNEY COLLEGE

POB 859 Hampden-Sydney, VA 23943
Telephone: (434) 223-6000
E-mail: info@hsc.edu
Internet: www.hsc.edu
Founded 1775
Private control
Academic year: August to May
Men's college of liberal arts and sciences
Pres.: Dr CHRISTOPHER B. HOWARD
Vice-Pres. for Admin., Strategy and Board Affairs: Dr DALE JONES
Vice-Pres. for Business Affairs and Finance and Treas.: W. GLENN CULLEY, JR
Vice-Pres. for Institutional Advancement: Dr LEE KING
Dean for Admissions: ANITA H. GARLAND
Dean for the Faculty: ROBERT T. HERDEGEN, III
Dean for Students: DAVID A. KLEIN
Registrar: DAWN L. CONGLETON
Dir for Library and Academic Information Services: CYRUS I. DILLON, III
Library of 250,000 vols
Number of teachers: 100 (full-time)
Number of students: 1,100

HAMPTON UNIVERSITY

100 E Queen St, Hampton, VA 23668
Telephone: (757) 727-5000
Internet: www.hamptonu.edu
Founded 1868 Hampton Normal and Agricultural Institute, present name 1984
Private control
Academic year: August to May (2 semesters)
Pres.: Dr WILLIAM R. HARVEY
Provost: Dr PAMELA V. HAMMOND
Exec. Vice-Pres.: Dr JOANN W. HAYSBERT
Vice-Pres. and Gen. Counsel: FAYE HARDY-LUCAS
Vice-Pres. for Admin. Services: Dr RODNEY D. SMITH
Vice-Pres. for Business Affairs and Treas.: DORETHA J. SPELLS
Vice-Pres. for Devt: LARON J. CLARK
Vice-Pres. for Student Affairs: Dr BARBARA INMAN
Dir for Admissions: ANGELA BOYD
Registrar: JORSENE S. COOPER
Library of 331,727 vols
Number of teachers: 465 (330 full-time, 134 part-time)
Number of students: 5,400 (4,600 undergraduate, 800 graduate)

DEANS

College of Education and Continuing Studies: Dr CASSANDRA HERRING
Graduate College: Dr WILLIAM I. YOUNG, JR
School of Business: Dr SID HOWARD CREDLE
School of Engineering and Technology: Dr ERIC JAMES SHEPPARD
School of Liberal Arts: Dr MAMIE E. LOCKE
School of Nursing: Dr DEBORAH E. JONES
School of Pharmacy: Dr WAYNE T. HARRIS
School of Science: Dr ROBERT DIXON
Scripps Howard School of Journalism and Communication: Prof. ROSALYNNE WHITAKER-HECK

HOLLINS UNIVERSITY

POB 9707, Roanoke, VA 24020-1707
Telephone: (540) 362-6000
E-mail: huadm@hollins.edu
Internet: www.hollins.edu
Founded 1842 as Valley Union Seminary, present name 1998
Private control
Academic year: August to August
Liberal arts college; undergraduate programme for women, selected graduate programmes or both men and women
Pres.: NANCY OLIVER GRAY (acting)
Provost: L. WAYNE MARKERT
Vice-Pres. for Academic Affairs: JEANINE STEWART
Vice-Pres. for Enrolment: STEFANIE NILES
Vice-Pres. for External Relations: MARK JONES
Vice-Pres. for Finance and Admin.: KERRY EDMONDS
Dean for Students: PATRICIA O'TOOLE
Dir for Admissions: NICOLE L. WILLIAMS
Dir for Scholarships and Financial Assistance: MARY JEAN CORRISS
Univ. Registrar and Exec. Dir for Institutional Research: ANNA K. GOODWIN
Univ. Librarian: JOAN D. RUELLE
Library of 212,000 vols
Number of teachers: 99 (71 full-time, 28 part-time)
Number of students: 1,008 (759 undergraduate, 249 graduate)
Publications: *Hollins Magazine* (3 a year), *The Hollins Critic* (4 a year)

INSTITUTE FOR THE PSYCHOLOGICAL SCIENCES

2001 Jefferson Davis Highway, Suite 511, Arlington, VA 22202
Telephone: (703) 416-1441
E-mail: admissions@ipsciences.edu
Internet: ipsciences.edu
Founded 1997 as Institute for Faith and Psychological Sciences, present name 1999
Private control
Academic year: August to August
Pres.: Rev. Dr CHARLES SIKORSKY
Academic Dean: Dr GLADYS M. SWEENEY
Vice-Pres. of Finance and Admin.: ROBERTO PARTARRIEU
Vice-Pres. for Institutional Effectiveness, Research and Planning: Dr MARY ANN LAFLEUR
Dean for Students: Dr G. ALEXANDER ROSS
Dir for Admissions and Marketing: ANNE-MARIE D. MINNIS
Dir for Enrolment Services and Registrar: JENNIFER KARNS
Dir for Library: JEFFREY ELLIOTT
Library of 10,000 vols

JAMES MADISON UNIVERSITY

800 S Main St, Harrisonburg, VA 22807-0001
Telephone: (540) 568-6211
E-mail: admissions@jmu.edu
Internet: www.jmu.edu
Founded 1908 as State Normal and Industrial School for Women, present name 1977
State control
Academic year: August to May (2 semesters)
Pres.: Dr LINWOOD H. ROSE
Exec. Vice-Pres.: (vacant)
Interim Provost and Sr Vice-Pres. for Academic Affairs: Dr A. JERRY BENSON
Sr Vice-Pres. for Admin. and Finance: CHARLES KING
Sr Vice-Pres. for Student Affairs and Univ. Planning: Dr MARK WARNER
Vice-Pres. for Univ. Advancement: Dr NICK LANGRIDGE (acting)
Univ. Registrar: MICHELE WHITE
Dean for Libraries and Educational Technologies: RALPH ALBERICO
Library of 700,000 vols, 13,000 journals
Number of teachers: 1,265 (905 full-time, 360 part-time)
Number of students: 19,725 (17,900 undergraduate, 1,825 graduate)

DEANS

College of Arts and Letters: DAVID K. JEFFREY
College of Business: Dr IRVINE CLARKE, III
College of Education: Dr PHIL WISHON
College of Integrated Science and Technology: Dr SHARON LOVELL
College of Science and Mathematics: Dr DAVID BRAKKE
College of Visual and Performing Arts: Dr GEORGE E. SPARKS
The Graduate School: Dr REID LINN
University Studies: LINDA CABE HALPERN

JEFFERSON COLLEGE OF HEALTH SCIENCES

101 Elm Ave, SE, Roanoke, VA 24013

Telephone: (540) 985-8483
E-mail: admissions@jchs.edu
Internet: www.jchs.edu

Founded 1914 as Jefferson Hospital School of Nursing, present name 2003
Private control
Academic year: August to August (3 semesters)

Areas of study: health psychology, humanities and social sciences, nursing, occupational therapy

Pres.: Dr NATHANIEL L. BISHOP
Dean for Academic Affairs: Prof. Dr LISA ALLISON-JONES
Dean for Admin. Services: ANNA MILLIRONS
Dir for Admissions: JUDITH MCKEON
Dean for Student Affairs: SCOTT HILL
Registrar: LINDA WILLIAMS
Dir for Library Services: MONA THISS

Library of 5,140 vols, 424 audiovisual items
Number of teachers: 70 (full-time)
Number of students: 1,030

Publication: *Jefferson Chronicle* (2 a year)

LIBERTY UNIVERSITY

1971 University Blvd, Lynchburg, VA 24502

Telephone: (434) 582-2000
E-mail: admissions@liberty.edu
Internet: www.liberty.edu

Founded 1971
Private control
Academic year: August to May (2 semesters)

Chancellor and Pres.: JERRY FALWELL, JR
Provost and Sr Vice-Pres. for Academic Affairs: RONALD S. GODWIN
Vice-Provost: Dr RONALD E. HAWKINS
Exec. Vice-Pres.: NEAL A. ASKEW
Sr Vice-Pres. for Enrolment Management: CHRIS E. JOHNSON
Sr Vice-Pres. for Student Affairs: MARK HINE
Vice-Pres. for Admin.: SHARON J. HARTLESS
Vice-Pres. for Devt: TOM ARNOLD
Vice-Pres. for Investment Management and Chief Financial Officer: DON MOON
Vice-Pres. for Outreach and Strategic Partnerships: BARRY N. MOORE
Vice-Pres. for Student Leadership: Dr TODD CAMPO
Registrar and Vice-Pres. for Admin. Information Management: LAWRENCE SHACKLETON
Dean for Integrated Learning Resource Center: CARL MERAT

Library of 315,000 vols, 1,31,000 ebooks, 67,000 ejournals
Number of teachers: 2,000
Number of students: 82,500 (12,500 residential, 70,000 online)

DEANS

Center for Academic Support and Advising Services: Dr BRIAN C. YATES
College of Arts and Sciences: Dr ROGER SCHULTZ
College of General Studies: Dr EMILY HEADY

Graduate School: Dr KEVIN CORSINI
Helms School of Government: SHAWN D. AKERS
Liberty Baptist Theological Seminary: ELMER L. TOWNS
School of Aeronautics: DAVID L. YOUNG
School of Business: SCOTT HICKS
School of Communication: Dr CECIL V. KRAMER
School of Education: Dr KAREN L. PARKER
School of Engineering and Computational Sciences: Prof. Dr RON SONES
School of Law: MATHEW D. STAVER
School of Religion: ELMER TOWNS

LONGWOOD UNIVERSITY

201 High St, Farmville, VA 23909

Telephone: (434) 395-2000
E-mail: admit@longwood.edu
Internet: www.longwood.edu

Founded 1839 as Farmville Female Seminary, present name 2002
State control
Academic year: August to May (2 semesters)

Pres.: Dr PATRICK FINNEGAN
Vice-Pres. for Academic Affairs: KENNETH B. PERKINS
Vice-Pres. for Admin. and Finance: KATHY S. WORSTER
Vice-Pres. for Facilities Management: RICHARD W. BRATCHER
Vice-Pres. for Student Affairs: Dr TIM J. PIERSON
Vice-Pres. for Univ. Advancement: Dr BRYAN K. ROWLAND
Dir for Financial Aid: KAREN SCHINABECK
Registrar: CYNTHIA ERICKSON
Dean for Library: SUZY SZASZ PALMER

Library of 288,175 vols
Number of teachers: 215 (full-time)
Number of students: 4,800

DEANS

College of Business and Economics: Dr PAUL T. BARRETT
College of Education and Human Services: Dr DENEESE L. JONES
College of Graduate and Professional Studies: Dr JEANNINE R. PERRY
Cook-Cole College of Arts and Sciences: Dr CHARLES D. ROSS
Cormier Honors College: Dr ALIX FINK

LYNCHBURG COLLEGE

1501 Lakeside Dr., Lynchburg, VA 24501-3113

Telephone: (434) 544-8100
E-mail: president@lynchburg.edu
Internet: www.lynchburg.edu

Founded 1903
Private control
Academic year: August to May (2 semesters)

Pres.: Dr KENNETH R. GARREN
Vice-Pres. and Dean for Academic Affairs: Dr JULIUS SIGLER
Vice-Pres. and Dean for Student Devt: JOHN ECCLES
Vice-Pres. for Advancement: DENISE MCDONALD
Vice-Pres. for Business and Finance: STEPHEN E. BRIGHT
Vice-Pres. for Enrolment Management: RITA DETWILER
Dean for the College: Dr RICHARD C. BURKE
Dir for Admissions: SHARON WALTERS-BOWER
Registrar: JAY K. WEBB
Dir for Library: CHRISTOPHER MILLSON-MARTULA

Library of 243,300 vols
Number of teachers: 170 (full-time)
Number of students: 2,830 (2,280 undergraduate, 550 graduate)

Publication: *Lynchburg College Magazine* (2 a year)

DEANS

School of Business and Economics: Dr JOSEPH H. TUREK
School of Communication and the Arts: Dr OEIDA M. HATCHER
School of Education and Human Development: Dr JAN S. STENNETTE
School of Health Sciences and Human Performance: Dr LINDA ANDREWS
School of Humanities and Social Sciences: Dr KIMBERLY MCCABE
School of Sciences: Dr BARRY LOBB

MARINE CORPS UNIVERSITY

2076 South St, Quantico, VA 22134-5068

Telephone: (703) 784-6837
E-mail: mcu_web_inquiries@usmc.mil
Internet: www.mcu.usmc.mil

Founded 1989
State control
Academic year: July to June

Comprises College of Distance Education and Training, Command and Staff College, Enlisted Professional Military Education, Expeditionary Warfare School, Lejeune Leadership Institute, Marine Corps War College, School of Advanced War Fighting

Pres.: Major Gen THOMAS M. MURRAY
Vice-Pres. for Academic Affairs: Dr Col JERRE WILSON
Vice-Pres. for Instructional and Research Support: Col Dr KURT A. SANFTLEBEN
Vice-Pres. for Student Affairs and Business Operations: DARRELL BROWNING
Registrar: STEFAN ROHAL
Dir for Library: CAROL E. RAMKEY

Library of 150,000 vols, 400 periodicals, 120,000 microforms
Number of students: 7,650

Publication: *Marine Corps University Journal* (2 a year)

MARY BALDWIN COLLEGE

POB 1500, Staunton, VA 24402
318 Prospect St, Staunton, VA 24401

Telephone: (540) 887-7019
E-mail: info@mbc.edu
Internet: www.mbc.edu

Founded 1842 as Augusta Female Seminary, current name adopted 1923
Private control
Language of instruction: English
Academic year: August to May

Schools of arts, humanities and renaissance studies; education, health and social work; science; social sciences, business and global studies

Pres.: PAMELA FOX
Sr Vice-Pres. for Business and Finance: DAVID MOWEN
Vice-Pres. for Academic Affairs and Dean for the College: CATHARINE O'CONNELL
Vice-Pres. for Institutional Advancement: SHERRI MYLOTT
Registrar, Assoc. Dean for the College and Dir for Institutional Research: LEWIS D. ASKEGAARD
Assoc. Dean for the College: LALLON POND
Dir for Library: CAROL CREAGER

Library of 137,425 vols, 57,900 current serials, 62,200 microforms, 3,820 audiovisual items, 26,200 ebooks
Number of teachers: 128
Number of students: 1,797

MARYMOUNT UNIVERSITY

2807 N Glebe Rd, Arlington, VA 22207-4299
Telephone: (703) 284-1500
E-mail: admissions@marymount.edu
Internet: www.marymount.edu
Founded 1950 as Marymount College, present name 1986
Private control
Academic year: August to May (2 semesters)
Pres.: Dr MATTHEW D. SHANK
Provost and Vice-Pres. for Academic Affairs: SHERRI HUGHES
Vice-Pres. for Enrolment and Student Services: CHRIS DOMES
Vice-Pres. for Financial Affairs and Treas.: RALPH KIDDER
Vice-Pres. for Univ. Devt: EMILY MAHONY
Dir for Student Services: ALISON MALLOY
Univ. Registrar: SCOTT SPENCER
Dean for Library: ZARY MOSTASHARI
Library of 236,000 vols, 37,000 journals (print and electronic)
Number of teachers: 345 (145 full-time, 200 part-time)
Number of students: 3,570

DEANS

Malek School of Health Professions: Dr THERESA CAPPELLO
School of Arts and Sciences: Dr GEORGE CHEATHAM
School of Business Administration: JAMES RYERSON
School of Education and Human Services: Dr WAYNE LESKO

NORFOLK STATE UNIVERSITY

700 Park Ave, Norfolk, VA 23504
Telephone: (757) 823-8600
E-mail: president@nsu.edu
Internet: www.nsu.edu
Founded 1935 as Norfolk unit of Virginia Union Univ., present name and status 1979
State control
Academic year: August to May (2 semesters)
Pres.: Dr TONY ATWATER
Provost and Vice-Pres. for Academic Affairs: Dr SANDRA J. DELOATCH
Vice-Pres. for Finance and Admin.: REGINA V. K. WILLIAMS
Vice-Pres. for Research and Economic Devt: Dr JOSEPH C. HALL
Vice-Pres. for Student Affairs: SHARON B. LOWE
Vice-Pres. for Univ. Advancement: PHILLIP ADAMS
Exec. Dir for Enrolment Management: TERRICITA SASS
Registrar: REGINA BYNUM
Dir for Library: Dr TOMMY L. BOGGER
Library of 348,953 vols, 59,542 periodicals, 25,633 microforms, 18,294 ejournals, 48,601 ebooks
Number of teachers: 270
Number of students: 7,090 (6,264 undergraduate, 826 graduate)

DEANS

College of Liberal Arts: Dr BELINDA C. ANDERSON
College of Science, Engineering and Technology: Dr SANDRA DELOATCH (acting)
Graduate School: Dr MILDRED K. FULLER
Honors College: Dr PAGE LAWS
School of Business: Dr STEVEN PAPAMARCOS
School of Education: Dr JEAN BRAXTON
School of Extended Learning: Dr MARGARET MASSEY
School of Social Work: Dr DOROTHY C. BROWNE

OLD DOMINION UNIVERSITY

5155 Hampton Blvd, Norfolk, VA 23529
Telephone: (757) 683-3000
E-mail: admissions@odu.edu
Internet: www.odu.edu
Founded 1930 as Norfolk Div. of The College of William and Mary, present name and status 1969
State control
Pres.: Dr JOHN R. BRODERICK
Provost and Vice-Pres. for Academic Affairs: CAROL SIMPSON
Vice-Provost for Planning and Institutional Effectiveness: MARTHA SMITH SHARPE
Vice-Pres. for Admin. and Finance: ROBERT L. FENNING
Vice-Pres. for Research: MOHAMMAD A. KARIM
Vice-Pres. for Student Engagement and Enrolment Services: ELLEN NEUFELDT
Vice-Pres. for Univ. Advancement: ALONZO C. BRANDON
Registrar: MARY SWARTZ
Librarian: VIRGINIA S. O'HERRON (acting)
Library: 3.2m. items (incl. 20,000 journals, 2m. microforms, 68,000 maps and audiovisual items)
Number of teachers: 1,225 (725 full-time, 502 part-time)
Number of students: 24,500 (19,000 undergraduate, 5,500 graduate)
Publication: *Monarch*

DEANS

College of Arts and Letters: Dr CHARLES E. WILSON, JR
College of Business and Public Administration: GILBERT YOCHUM
College of Health Sciences: Dr SHELLEY MISHOE
College of Sciences: Dr CHRIS D. PLATSOUCAS
Darden College of Education: Dr LINDA IRWIN-DEVITIS
Frank Batten College of Engineering and Technology: Dr OKTAY BAYSAL
Honors College: Dr DAVID METZGER

RADFORD UNIVERSITY

East Main St, Radford, VA 24142
Telephone: (540) 831-5000
E-mail: admissions@radford.edu
Internet: www.radford.edu
Founded 1910 as State Normal and Industrial School for Women, present name and status 1979
State control
Academic year: August to May (2 semesters)
Pres.: Dr PENELOPE W. KYLE
Provost and Vice-Pres. for Academic Affairs: Dr SAM MINNER
Vice-Provost for Enrolment Planning and Management: JAMES PENNIX
Vice-Pres. for Finance and Admin. and Chief Financial Officer: RICHARD ALVAREZ
Vice-Pres. for Information Technology: DANNY M. KEMP
Vice-Pres. for Student Affairs: Dr MARK SHANLEY
Vice-Pres. for Univ. Advancement: Dr DEBORAH J. ROBINSON
Dean for Students: DON APPIARIUS
Registrar: MATTHEW BRUNNER
Dean for the Library: STEVEN HELM
Library of 552,687 vols
Number of teachers: 625 (407 full-time, 218 part-time)
Number of students: 9,370
Publications: *Gaelic*, *The Beehive* (1 a year)

DEANS

College of Business and Economics: Dr FAYE W. GILBERT
College of Education and Human Development: Dr PATRICIA SHOEMAKER
College of Graduate and Professional Studies: Dr DENNIS GRADY
College of Humanities and Behavioral Sciences: Dr KATHERINE HAWKINS
College of Science and Technology: Dr J. ORION ROGERS
College of Visual and Performing Arts: Dr JOSEPH SCARTELLI
Waldron College of Health and Human Services: RAYMOND LINVILLE

RANDOLPH-MACON COLLEGE

POB 5005, Ashland, VA 23005-5505
Telephone: (804) 752-7200
E-mail: admissions@rmc.edu
Internet: www.rmc.edu
Founded 1830
Private control
Academic year: September to May
Liberal arts college
Pres.: Dr ROBERT R. LINDGREN
Treas.: JOHN A. AHLADAS
Provost and Vice-Pres. for Academic Affairs: Dr WILLIAM T. FRANZ
Vice-Pres. for Advancement: DIANE M. LOWDER
Dean for Admissions and Financial Aid: DAVID L. LESESNE
Dean for Students: Dr GRANT L. AZDELL
Dir for Institutional Research: Dr TIM MERRILL
Registrar: ALANA R. DAVIS
Dir for Library: Dr GINGER YOUNG
Library of 182,368 vols
Number of teachers: 90 (full-time)
Number of students: 1,240

RANDOLPH COLLEGE

2500 Rivermont Ave, Lynchburg, VA 24503-1526
Telephone: (434) 947-8000
E-mail: admissions@randolphcollege.edu
Internet: www.randolphcollege.edu
Founded 1891 as Randolph-Macon Woman's College, present name 2007
Private control
Academic year: August to May
Liberal arts college
Pres.: JOHN E. KLEIN
Vice-Pres. for Academic Affairs and Dean for the College: DENNIS STEVENS
Vice-Pres. for Enrolment Management: Dr SANDRA C. BARTHOLOMEW
Vice-Pres. for Finance and Admin.: CHRISTOPHER L. BURNLEY
Vice-Pres. for Institutional Advancement: JAN Y. MERIWETHER
Vice-Pres. for Student Affairs and Dean for Students: Dr SARAH L. SWAGER
Dir for Devt: LEE MAYHALL
Dean for Students and Dir for Residence Life: TERRY BODINE
Registrar: BARBARA THRASHER
Librarian: THEODORE JON HOSTETLER
Library of 200,000 vols, 300 print periodical subscriptions and 70,000 e-periodical subscriptions
Number of teachers: 100
Number of students: 760
Publications: *Hail, Muse!* (1 a year), *Randolph* (3 a year)

REGENT UNIVERSITY

1000 Regent University Dr., Virginia Beach, VA 23464
Telephone: (757) 352-4127
E-mail: admissions@regent.edu
Internet: www.regent.edu

Founded 1978

Private control

Academic year: August to July

Chancellor and Founder: Dr PAT ROBERTSON

Pres.: Dr CARLOS CAMPO

Exec. Vice-Pres.: PAUL BONICELLI

Vice-Pres. and Gen. Counsel: LOUIS ISAKOFF

Vice-Pres. for Academic Affairs: Dr FRED ROVAI

Vice-Pres. for Advancement: ANN LeBLANC

Vice-Pres. for Devt and Communications: MAUREEN McDONNELL

Vice-Pres. for Enrolment Management and Information Technology: TRACY STEWART

Vice-Pres. for Finance: DEAN WOOTEN

Vice-Pres. for Student Services: Dr JEFF PITTMAN

Registrar: ALTHEA KIMES

Dean for Library: Dr SARA BARON

Library of 304,000 vols, 593,000 microforms, 14,000 audiovisual items, 156,000 ebooks, 98,900 journal titles

Number of teachers: 510

Number of students: 5,915

Publications: *Christian Leader, Emerging Leadership Journeys* (2 a year), *Faith and Therapy* (12 a year), *Inner Resources for Leaders* (3 a year), *International Journal of Leadership Studies, Journal of Biblical Perspectives in Leadership* (2 a year), *Journal of Practical Consulting, Journal of Strategic Leadership, Journal of Virtues & Leadership, Law Review* (2 a year), *Leadership Advance Online, Regent Global Business Review* (6 a year), *Regent Journal of International Law* (2 a year), *Regent Journal of Law & Public Policy, Regent University Law Review, The Journal of Virtues & Leadership*

DEANS

Robertson School of Government: Dr GARY ROBERTS

School of Education: Dr ALAN ARROYO

School of Communication and the Arts: Dr MITCH LAND

School of Divinity: Dr MICHAEL PALMER

School of Global Leadership and Entrepreneurship: Dr BRUCE WINSTON

School of Law: Dr JEFF BRAUCH

School of Psychology and Counseling: Dr WILLIAM HATHAWAY

School of Undergraduate Studies: Dr GERSON MORENO-RIANO

ROANOKE COLLEGE

221 College Lane, Salem, VA 24153

Telephone: (540) 375-2500

E-mail: admissions@roanoke.edu

Internet: roanoke.edu

Founded 1842 as Virginia Institute, present name 1853

Private control

Academic year: August to May

Liberal arts college

Pres.: MICHAEL CREED MAXEY

Vice-Pres. and Dean for the College: Prof. Dr RICHARD A. SMITH

Vice-Pres. for Business Affairs: MARK P. NOFTSINGER

Vice-Pres. for Enrolment and Dean for Admissions and Financial Aid: BRENDA PORTER POGGENDORF

Vice-Pres. for Resource Devt: CONNIE CARMACK

Vice-Pres. For Student Affairs and Dean for Students: EUGENE L. ZDZIARSKI, II

Assoc. Dean and Registrar: LEAH L. RUSSELL

Dir for Library: STANLEY F. UMBERGER

Library of 400,000 vols, 1,000 DVDs

Number of teachers: 125

Number of students: 2,060

Publications: *Roanoke* (3 a year), *Teacher-Scholar* (1 a year)

SAINT PAUL'S COLLEGE

115 College Dr., Lawrenceville, VA 23868

Telephone: (434) 848-3111

Internet: saintpaulsnet.com

Founded 1888 as St Paul Normal and Industrial School, present name 1957

Private control

Liberal arts college

Pres. and CEO: Dr EDDIE N. MOORE, JR

Provost and Vice-Pres. for Academic and Student Affairs: Dr RAYMOND HOLMES

Vice-Pres. for Financial Affairs and Comptroller: GERALDINE JONES

Vice-Pres. for Institutional Advancement: KIMBERLY TETLOW

Registrar: HELEN JACKSON

Dir for Library Services: MARC L. FINNEY

SHENANDOAH UNIVERSITY

1460 University Dr., Winchester, VA 22601

Telephone: (540) 665-4500

E-mail: admit@su.edu

Internet: www.su.edu

Founded 1875 as Shenandoah Seminary, present name and status 1991

Private control

Academic year: August to May (2 semesters)

Pres.: Dr TRACY FITZSIMMONS

Sr Vice-Pres. and Vice-Pres. for Academic Affairs: Dr BRYON L. GRIGSBY

Vice-Pres. for Admin. and Finance: RICHARD C. SHICKLE

Vice-Pres. for Advancement: MITCHELL L. MOORE

Vice-Pres. for Enrolment Management and Student Success: CLARRESA MOORE MORTON

Vice-Pres. for Student Life: Rev. Dr RHONDA VanDYKE

Registrar: MELANIE WINTER

Dir for Univ. Libraries: CHRISTOPHER BEAN

Library of 275,000 vols (incl. 131,000 books and journals), 13,000 audio items, 16,000 scores, 1,500 video cassettes, 32,000 print and ejournals, 115,000 ERIC documents

Number of teachers: 440

Number of students: 4,050

DEANS

Bernard J. Dunn School of Pharmacy: Dr ALAN B. McKAY

College of Arts and Sciences: Dr CALVIN H. ALLEN, JR

Conservatory: MICHAEL J. STEPNIAK

Harry F. Byrd, Jr, School of Business: W. RANDY BOXX

School of Health Professions: (vacant)

STRATFORD UNIVERSITY

7777 Leesburg Pike, Falls Church, VA 22043

Telephone: (703) 821-8570

E-mail: registrar@stratford.edu

Internet: www.stratford.edu

Founded 1976

Private control

Academic year: January to December

Campuses in Baltimore (Maryland); Newport News, Richmond and Woodbridge (Virginia); int. campus in New Delhi (India)

Pres. and CEO: Dr RICHARD R. SHURTZ, II

Exec. Vice-Pres.: MARY ANN SHURTZ

Vice-Pres. for Human Resources: SHIRLEY DIAZ

Vice-Pres. for Int. Programmes: FEROZE KHAN

Chief Financial Officer: JOHN DOVI

Dir for Admissions: CARL SIEBECKER

Registrar: HEATHER RICHARDS

DEANS

School of Computer Information Systems: (vacant)

School of Culinary Arts and Hospitality Management: JORDAN LICHMAN

School of Health Sciences: Dr BENNETT SOLBERG

School of Nursing: Dr SHARRON GUILLETT

STRAYER UNIVERSITY

Suite 300, 1133 15th St, NW, Washington, DC 20005

Telephone: (202) 408-2400

E-mail: washington@strayer.edu

Internet: www.strayer.edu

Founded 1892 as Strayer Business College, present name 1998

Private control

Academic year: September to September

Pres. and CEO: ROBERT S. SILBERMAN

Provost and Academic Dean: Dr J. CHRIS TOE

Campus Man.: ED DOBSON

Library of 32,000 vols

Number of teachers: 575 (125 full-time, 450 adjunct)

Number of students: 16,500

DEANS

Jack Welch Management Institute: Dr DANNY SZPIRO

School of Arts and Sciences: Dr MARILYN BROADUS-GAY

School of Business: Dr WENDY HOWARD

School of Education: Dr VANESSA P. ESLINGER-BROWN

School of Information Systems and Technology: Dr BILL DAFNIS

SWEET BRIAR COLLEGE

134 Chapel Rd, Sweet Briar, VA 24595

Telephone: (804) 381-6100

E-mail: info@sbc.edu

Internet: www.sbc.edu

Founded 1901

Private control

Academic year: August to May

Areas of study: arts management, biochemistry and molecular biology, biology, business, chemistry, classics, creative writing, dance, economics, education, science

Pres.: Dr JO ELLEN PARKER

Vice-Pres. and Chief of Staff: LOUISE SWIECKI ZINGARO

Vice-Pres. for Academic Affairs and Dean for the Faculty: Dr AMY JESSEN-MARSHALL

Vice-Pres. for Alumni and Devt: HEIDI HANSEN McCRORY

Vice-Pres. for Finance and Admin.: SCOTT C. SHANK

Vice-Pres. for Student Affairs and Dean for Co-Curricular Life: Dr CHERYL L. STEELE

Dean for Admissions: GRETCHEN GRAVLEY-TUCKER

Registrar: DEBORAH L. POWELL

Dir for Libraries and Integrated Learning Resources: JOHN G. JAFFE

Library of 250,000 vols, 375,000 microforms, 1,000 periodicals, 6,500 audiovisual items

Number of teachers: 125 (75 full-time, 50 part-time)

Number of students: 760

Publication: *Alumnae Magazine* (3 a year)

UNION PRESBYTERIAN SEMINARY

3401 Brook Rd, Richmond, VA 23227

Telephone: (804) 355-0671

E-mail: admissions@upsem.edu

Internet: www.upsem.edu

Founded 1812 as Union Theological Seminary, current name adopted 2010

Private control

Academic year: September to June

Campus at Charlotte (NC)

Pres.: Dr BRIAN K. BLOUNT

Vice-Pres. for Enrollment Management and Student Services: MICHELLE WALKER

Vice-Pres. for Finance and Admin.: MICHAEL B. CASHWELL

Vice-Pres. for Institutional Advancement: RICHARD WONG

Dean for Union Presbyterian Seminary (Richmond Campus): STANLEY H. SKRESLET

Dean for Union Presbyterian Seminary (Charlotte Campus): THOMAS W. CURRIE

Assoc. Dean for Academic Programmes: E. CARSON BRISSON

Dir for Admissions: KATE FIEDLER BOSWELL

Dir for Student Services: MIMI SIFF

Registrar: J. STANLEY HARGRAVES

Dir for Library and Institutional Effectiveness: MILTON J. COALTER

Library of 317,000 vols, 500 print periodical subscriptions, 6,000 e-journal subcsriptions

Number of teachers: 25

Number of students: 200

UNIVERSITY OF MARY WASHINGTON

1301 College Ave, Fredericksburg, VA 22401-5300

Telephone: (540) 654-1000

E-mail: admit@umw.edu

Internet: www.umw.edu

Founded 1908 as Fredericksburg's State Normal and Industrial School for Women, current name adopted 2004

State control

Academic year: August to July

Pres.: RICHARD V. HURLEY

Provost: Dr IAN D. C. NEWBOULD

Vice-Pres. for Admin. and Finance: RICHARD R. PEARCE

Vice-Pres. for Advancement and Univ. Relations: SALVATORE M. MERINGOLO

Vice-Pres. for Student Affairs: DOUGLAS N. SEARCY

Registrar: RITA F. DUNSTON

Univ. Librarian: ROSEMARY HUFF ARNESON

Library of 367,000 vols

Number of teachers: 175

Number of students: 5,000 (4,000 undergraduate, 1,000 graduate)

DEANS

College of Arts and Sciences: Dr RICHARD FINKLESTEIN

College of Business: Dr LYNNE D. RICHARDSON

College of Education: Dr MARY GENDERNALIK-COOPER

UNIVERSITY OF RICHMOND

28 Westhampton Way, University of Richmond, VA 23173

Telephone: (804) 289-8000

E-mail: admissions@richmond.edu

Internet: www.richmond.edu

Founded 1830 as Richmond College, current name adopted 1920

Private control

Academic year: August to May

Pres.: Dr EDWARD L. AYERS

Chancellor: Dr E. BRUCE HEILMAN

Chancellor: Dr RICHARD L. MORRILL

Provost and Vice-Pres.: Dr STEPHEN ALLRED

Vice-Pres. for Advancement: THOMAS C. GUTENBERGER

Vice-Pres. for Business and Finance and Treas.: Dr HOSSEIN SADID

Vice-Pres. for Student Devt: Dr STEPHEN DAMIAN BISESE

Asst Vice-Pres. and Dean for Admission: GIL VILLANUEVA

Registrar: SUSAN DENMAN BREEDEN

Univ. Librarian: KEVIN BUTTERFIELD

Library of 500,000 vols, 100,000 bound periodicals and e-resources, 10,000 video titles, 1,500 audiobooks, 500 audio cassettes, 16,000 scores, 9,100 CDs

Number of teachers: 560 (380 full-time, 180 part-time)

Number of students: 4,400

Publications: *Richmond Alumni Magazine* (4 a year), *Richmond International* (1 a year)

DEANS

International Education: Dr ULIANA GABARA

Jepson School of Leadership Studies: Dr SANDRA J. PEART

Richmond College: Dr JOSEPH R. BOEHMAN

Robins School of Business: Dr NANCY A. BAGRANOFF

School of Arts and Sciences: Dr KATHLEEN ROBERTS SKERRETT

School of Law: WENDY COLLINS PERDUE

School of Professional and Continuing Studies: Prof. Dr JAMES L. NARDUZZI

Westhampton College: Dr JULIETTE L. LANDPHAIR

UNIVERSITY OF VIRGINIA

POB 400229, Charlottesville, VA 22904-4229

Telephone: (434) 924-0311

E-mail: undergradadmission@virginia.edu

Internet: www.virginia.edu

Founded 1819

public control

Academic year: August to May

Pres.: TERESA A. SULLIVAN

Provost and Exec. Vice-Pres.: JOHN D. SIMON

Sr Vice-Pres. for Devt and Public Affairs: ROBERT D. SWEENEY

Exec. Vice-Pres. and Chief Operating Officer: PATRICK D. HOGAN

Vice-Pres.: Dr NANCY E. DUNLAP

Vice-Pres. and CEO for Health System: R. EDWARD HOWELL

Vice-Pres. and Chief Financial Officer: (vacant)

Vice-Pres. and Chief Human Resources Officer: SUSAN A. CARKEEK

Vice-Pres. and Chief Information Officer: JAMES L. HILTON

Vice-Pres. and Chief Student Affairs Officer: PATRICIA M. LAMPKIN

Vice-Pres. for Management and Budget: COLETTE SHEEHY

Vice-Pres. for Research: THOMAS C. SKALAK

Dean for Admissions (Undergraduate): GREGORY W. ROBERTS

Dean for Students: ALLEN GROVES

Univ. Librarian and Dean for Libraries: KARIN WITTENBORG

Library: see under Libraries and Archives

Number of teachers: 1,264

Number of students: 23,464

Publications: *Virginia Law Review*, *Virginia Law Weekly*, *Virginia Quarterly Review*

DEANS

College and Graduate School of Arts and Sciences: Dr MEREDITH JUNG-EN WOO

Curry School of Education: ROBERT C. PIANTA

Darden School of Business: ROBERT F. BRUNER

Frank Batten School of Leadership and Public Policy: HARRY HARDING

McIntire School of Commerce: CARL P. ZEITHAML

School of Architecture: KIM TANZER

School of Continuing and Professional Studies: BILLY CANNADAY, JR

School of Engineering and Applied Science: Prof. JAMES H. AYLOR

School of Law: PAUL G. MAHONEY

School of Medicine: Dr STEVEN T. DEKOSKY

School of Nursing: Dr DORRIE FONTAINE

PROFESSORS

Curry School of Education (POB 400260, Charlottesville, VA 22904-4260; tel. (434) 924-3334; e-mail curry@virginia.edu; internet curry.edschool.virginia.edu):

BREDO, E., Leadership, Foundations and Policy Studies

BRENEMAN, D., Education

BULL, G., Leadership, Foundations and Policy Studies

BURBACH, H., Leadership, Foundations and Policy Studies

BUTLER, A., Leadership, Foundations and Policy Studies

CALLAHAN, C., Leadership, Foundations and Policy Studies

COHEN, S., Curriculum, Instruction and Special Education

CORNELL, D., Human Services

DUKE, D., Leadership, Foundations and Policy Studies

FAN, X., Leadership, Foundations and Policy Studies

GAESSER, G., Human Services

GANSNEDER, B., Leadership, Foundations and Policy Studies

HALLAHAN, D., Curriculum, Instruction and Special Education

HANSEN, J., Education

INGERSOLL, C., Human Services

INVERNIZZI, M., Curriculum, Instruction and Special Education

KELLY, L., Human Services

KNEEDLER, R., Education

LAWRENCE, E., Human Services

LLOYD, J., Education

LOPER, A., Human Services

MCKENNA, M., Curriculum, Instruction and Special Education

MCNERGNEY, J., Education

MCNERGNEY, R., Leadership, Foundations and Policy Studies

MILLER, M., Leadership, Foundations and Policy Studies

PATE, R., Education

REEVE, R., Human Services

RICHARDS, H., Leadership, Foundations and Policy Studies

SHERAS, P., Human Services

SHORT, J., Leadership, Foundations and Policy Studies

SMOLKIN, L., Curriculum, Instruction and Special Education

SNELL, M., Curriculum, Instruction and Special Education

STRANG, H., Leadership, Foundations and Policy Studies

TOMLINSON, C., Leadership, Foundations and Policy Studies

WELTMAN, A., Human Services

Darden School (Graduate School of Business Administration) (POB 400321, Charlottesville, VA 22904-4321; tel. (434) 924-3900; internet www.darden.edu):

ALLEN, B.

BECKENSTEIN, A.

BODILY, S.

BOURGEOIS, L.

BROWNLEE, E.

CHAPLINSKY, S.

CHEN, M.

CLAWSON, J.

COLLEY, J.

DAVIS, E.

DOYLE, J.

EADES, K.

EAKER, M.

FARRIS, P.

FREEMAN, R.

FREY, S.

GLYNN, J.

HARRIS, R.
HASKINS, M.
HESS, E.
HORNIMAN, A.
LANDEL, R.
LIEDTKA, J.
MOORE, M.
PFEIFER, P.
SIHLER, W.
SNELL, S.
SPEKMAN, R.
VENKATARAMAN, S.
WEISS, E.
WERHANE, P.

McIntire School of Commerce (POB 400173, Charlottesville, VA 22904-4173; tel. (434) 924-3257; internet www.commerce.virginia.edu):

ATCHISON, M.
BATEMAN, T.
BROOME, O.
DE MONG, R.
KEHOE, W.
KEMP, R.
LINDGREN, J.
MALONEY, D.
MARSTON, F.
MICK, D.
NELSON, R.
NETEMEYER, R.
OVERSTREET, G.
SMITH, D.
WEBB, R.
WILHELM, W.
WILLIAMS, S.

School of Architecture (POB 400122, Charlottesville, VA 22904-4122; tel. (434) 924-3715; internet www.virginia.edu/arch):

BEATLEY, T., Planning
BEDNAR, M., Architecture
BOESCHENSTEIN, W., Architecture
CLARK, W., Architecture
DRIPPS, R., Architecture
FORD, E., Architecture
LUCY, W., Planning
MORRISH, W., Architecture
SCHWARTZ, K., Architecture
SPAIN, D., Planning
WALDMAN, P., Architecture
WILSON, R., Architectural History

School of Arts and Sciences (POB 400772, Charlottesville, VA 22904-4772; tel. (434) 924-3389; e-mail grad-a-s@virginia.edu; internet artsandsciences.virginia.edu):

ADLER, P., Biology
ALLEN, J., Psychology
ALLEN, R., Chemistry
ANDERSON, A., Spanish, Italian and Portuguese
ANDERSON, S., Economics
ANDREWS, L., Chemistry
ANTONOVICS, J., Biology
ARNOLD, A., French Literature and General Linguistics
ARNOLD, K., Music
ARNOLD, P., Physics
ARON, M., History
ARRAS, J., Philosophy
BAKER, P., English
BAROLSKY, P., Art
BEATTIE, A., Creative Writing
BELANGER, T., Book Arts Press
BELL, M., Art
BENNETT, B., German Literature
BERLANSTEIN, L., History
BEST, T., German Literature
BLACK, D., Sociology
BLOOM, G., Biology
BLOOMFIELD, L., Physics
BLUMBERG, R., Sociology
BOND, H., History
BOOTH, A., English
BRADEN, G., English
BRODIE, E., Biology

BRUNJES, P., Psychology
BRYANT, R., Chemistry
BURNETT, R., Chemistry
BURTON, E., Economics
CAFISO, D., Chemistry
CANTOR, P., English
CARGILE, J., Philosophy
CASEY, J., Creative Writing
CATES, G., Physics
CEASER, J., Government and Foreign Affairs
CHANG, T., Statistics
CHAPEL, R., Drama Operations
CHASE LEVENSON, K., English
CHEN, J., History
CHEVALIER, R., Astronomy
CHILDRESS, J., Religious Studies
CLAY, J., Classics
CLORE, G., Psychology
COLOMB, G., English
CONETTI, S., Physics
CONFINO, A., History
CONNOLLY, J., Slavic Languages and Literature
CONTINI-MORAVA, E., Anthropology
COX, B., Physics
CRABB, D., Nuclear and Particle Physics
CRACKEL, T., Editing Wash Papers
CRAWFORD, J., Classics
CRONMILLER, C., Biology
CROSBY, E., History
CROZIER, R., Art
CUSHMAN, S., English
DAMON, F., Anthropology
DASS, D., Art
DAVIS, R., Environmental Sciences
DAY, D., Nuclear and Particle Physics
DEAVER, B., Physics
DELLA COLETTA, C., Spanish, Italian and Portuguese
DELOACHE, J., Psychology
DEMAS, J., Chemistry
DEVEREUX, D., Philosophy
DOBBINS, J., Art
DOLAN, R., Environmental Sciences
DOVE, R., Creative Writing
DRUCKER, J., Media Studies
DUKES, E., Physics
EDMUNDSON, M., English
EISENBERG, D., Creative Writing
ELSON, M., Slavic Languages and Literature
ELZINGA, K., Economics
EMERY, R., Psychology
ENGERS, M., Economics
FATTON, R., Government and Foreign Affairs
FELDMAN, J., English
FELSKI, R., English
FENDLEY, P., Physics
FERREIRA, M., Religious Studies
FISHBANE, P., Physics
FOGARTY, G., Religious Studies
FOWLER, M., Physics
FRAIMAN, S., English
FRASER, C., Chemistry
FREEMAN, J., Psychology
FRICK, J., Drama Operations
FRIESEN, W., Biology
FUCHS, S., Sociology
FUENTES, J., Environmental Sciences
GALLAGHER, G., History
GALLAGHER, T., Physics
GALLOWAY, J., Environmental Sciences
GAMBLE, H., Religious Studies
GARRETT, R., Biology
GEIGER, P., Art
GERLI, E., Spanish, Italian and Portuguese
GERRANS, G., Chemistry
GEYSEN, H., Chemistry
GIES, D., Spanish, Italian and Portuguese
GOEDDE, L., Art
GRAINGER, R., Biology
GREEN, C., Biology
GRISHAM, C., Chemistry
GRONER, P., Religious Studies

GUTERBOCK, T., Sociology
HABERLY, D., Spanish, Italian and Portuguese
HANDLER, R., Anthropology
HARMAN, W., Chemistry
HARRISON, A., Chemistry
HART, K., Religious Studies
HAWLEY, J., Astronomy
HAYDEN, B., Environmental Sciences
HECHT, S., Chemistry
HERBST, I., Mathematics
HERMAN, J., Environmental Sciences
HESS, G., Physics
HILL, D., Psychology
HILL, R., Spanish, Italian and Portuguese
HIRSH, J., Biology
HOH, L., Drama Operations
HOLSINGER, B., Music
HOLT, C., Economics
HOLT, M., History
HORNBERGER, G., Environmental Sciences
HOWARD, A., Environmental Sciences
HUECKSTEDT, R., Middle Eastern and South Asian Languages and Culture
HUMPHREYS, P., Philosophy
HUNT, D., Chemistry
HUNTER, J., English
HUNTER, J., Sociology
IMBRIE, J., Mathematics
JAMES, J., Economics
JOHNSON, W., Economics
JONES, R., Physics
JORDAN, D., Government and Foreign Affairs
JOST, W., English
KAWASAKI, M., Biology
KEEN, R., Psychology
KEENAN, D., Statistics
KEENE, W., Environmental Sciences
KELLER, R., Biology
KETT, J., History
KHARE, R., Anthropology
KINGSTON, P., Sociology
KINNEY, A., East Asian Languages, Literature and Cultures
KINNEY, J., English
KLOSKO, G., Government and Foreign Affairs
KOVACS, P., Classics
KRETSINGER, R., Biology
KRIETE, T., Mathematics
KUBOVY, M., Psychology
KUHN, N., Mathematics
KUMAR, J., Sociology
LAGOS, M., Spanish, Italian and Portuguese
LANDERS, J., Chemistry
LANE, A., History
LANG, K., Religious Studies
LASIECKA, I., Mathematics
LEFFLER, M., History
LEFFLER, P., History
LEGRO, J., Government and Foreign Affairs
LEHMANN, K., Chemistry
LENDON, J., History
LERDAU, M., Environmental Sciences
LEVENSON, M., English
LILLARD, A., Psychology
LINDGREN, R., Nuclear and Particle Physics
LLEWELLYN, P., Psychology
LOMASKY, L., Philosophy
LOTT, E., English
LYNCH, A., Government and Foreign Affairs
LYONS, J., French Literature and General Linguistics
MacCLUER, B., Mathematics
McCRIMMON, K., Mathematics
McCURDY, C., History
MACDONALD, T., Chemistry
McDONALD, W., German Literature
McDOWELL, D., English
McGANN, J., English
McKINLEY, M., French Literature and General Linguistics
McKINNON, S., Anthropology

McLaren, J., Economics
Macko, S., Environmental Sciences
Majewski, S., Astronomy
Marlatt, M., Art
Marsh, C., Religious Studies
Marshall, J., Chemistry
Martens, L., German Literature
Mattern, D., Editing Madison Papers
Maus, K., English
Megill, A., History
Mellon, D., Biology
Menaker, M., Biology
Merricks, T., Philosophy
Metcalf, P., Anthropology
Michaels, P., Environmental Sciences
Midelfort, H., History
Mikalson, J., Classics
Milani, F., Middle Eastern and South Asian Languages and Culture
Milkis, S., Government and Foreign Affairs
Miller, J., Classics
Miller, J., History
Mills, A., Environmental Sciences
Mills, D., Economics
Mirman, L., Economics
Most, R., Undergraduate College Operations
Nelson, R., English
Nesselroade, J., Psychology
Nima, T., Religious Studies
Nock, S., Sociology
Nohrnberg, J., English
Nolan, B., English
Norum, B., Physics
O'Brien, D., Government and Foreign Affairs
O'Connell, R., Astronomy
Ochs, P., Religious Studies
Olick, J., Sociology
Olsen, E., Economics
Onuf, P., History
Opere, F., Spanish, Italian and Portuguese
Orr, G., Creative Writing
Osheim, D., History
Papovich, J., Undergraduate College Operations
Parker, D., Spanish, Italian and Portuguese
Parshall, B., Mathematics
Parshall, K., Mathematics
Pate, B., Chemistry
Patterson, C., Psychology
Periasamy, A., Biology
Perkowski, J., Slavic Languages and Literature
Pham, H., Physics
Plog, S., Anthropology
Pocanic, D., Physics
Poon, J., Physics
Pope, R., Spanish, Italian and Portuguese
Press, A., Sociology
Proffitt, D., Psychology
Pu, L., Chemistry
Quandt, W., Government and Foreign Affairs
Railton, S., English
Ramazani, R., English
Ramirez, D., Mathematics
Rapinchuk, A., Mathematics
Ray, B., Religious Studies
Reppucci, N., Psychology
Reynolds, B., Economics
Rhoads, S., Government and Foreign Affairs
Rini, J., Spanish, Italian and Portuguese
Roberts, M., Art
Roger, P., French Literature and General Linguistics
Rood, R., Astronomy
Ross, M., English
Sachedina, A., Religious Studies
Salthouse, T., Psychology
Sarazin, C., Astronomy
Saslaw, W., Astronomy

Savage, J., Government and Foreign Affairs
Sawaie, M., Middle Eastern and South Asian Language and Culture
Schoppa, L., Government and Foreign Affairs
Schuker, S., History
Schwartz, H., Government and Foreign Affairs
Scott, D., Philosophy
Scott, L., Mathematics
Seneviratne, H., Anthropology
Shatin, J., Music
Shaw, D., Spanish, Italian and Portuguese
Shugart, H., Environmental Sciences
Simmons, A., Philosophy
Skrutskie, M., Astronomy
Smith, D., Environmental Sciences
Spearing, A., English
Spellman, B., Psychology
Stagg, J., Editing Madison Papers
Stern, S., Economics
Stewart, G., Undergraduate College Options
Summers, J., Art
Sundberg, R., Chemistry
Taylor, D., Biology
Thacker, H., Physics
Thomas, L., Mathematics
Thomas, M., History
Thompson, A., Religious Studies
Thornton, S., Physics
Thuan, T., Astronomy
Tilghman, C., Creative Writing
Timko, M., Biology
Tolbert, C., Astronomy
Triggiani, R., Mathematics
Trindle, C., Chemistry
Tucker, H., English
Turkheimer, E., Psychology
Turner, E., Art
Upton, D., Art
Van Wincoop, E., Economics
Vander Meulen, D., English
Voris, R., German Literature
Wagner, R., Anthropology
Walker, K., Psychology
Wall, C., English
Wang, W., Mathematics
Warner, R., Drama Operations
Weber, A., Spanish, Italian and Portuguese
West, G., Drama Operations
White, S., Government and Foreign Affairs
Whittle, D., Astronomy
Wiberg, P., Environmental Sciences
Wicke, J., English
Wilbur, H., Biology
Wilken, R., Religious Studies
Williams, B., Sociology
Willingham, D., Psychology
Wilson, M., East Asian Languages, Literature and Cultures
Wilson, M., Psychology
Wilson, T., Psychology
Womack, B., Government and Foreign Affairs
Woodman, A., Classics
Wright, C., Creative Writing
Zelikow, P., History
Zieman, J., Environmental Sciences
Zunz, O., History

School of Continuing and Professional Studies:

Abouzeid, M.
Harrison, E.
Roberson, S.

School of Engineering and Applied Science (POB 400246, Charlottesville, VA 22904-4246; tel. (434) 924-3072; internet www.seas.virginia.edu):

Acton, S., Electrical and Computer Engineering

Allaire, P., Mechanical and Aerospace Engineering
Bailey, M., Computer Science
Baragiola, R., Materials Science and Engineering
Barrett, L., Mechanical and Aerospace Engineering
Bean, J., Electrical and Computer Engineering
Berger, T., Electrical and Computer Engineering
Brown, D., Systems and Information Engineering
Cahen, G., Materials Science and Engineering
Campbell, J., Electrical and Computer Engineering
Carlson, W., Science, Technology and Society
Carta, G., Chemical Engineering
Crandall, J., Mechanical and Aerospace Engineering
Davidson, J., Computer Science
Davis, R., Chemical Engineering
Demetsky, M., Civil and Environmental Engineering
Dorning, J., Materials Science and Engineering
Dugan, J., Electrical and Computer Engineering
Fernandez, E., Chemical Engineering
Ford, R., Chemical Engineering
Gangloff, R., Materials Science and Engineering
Garber, N., Civil and Environmental Engineering
Gillies, G., Mechanical and Aerospace Engineering
Gorman, M., Science, Technology and Society
Grimshaw, A., Computer Science
Gupta, M., Electrical and Computer Engineering
Haimes, Y., Systems and Information Engineering
Haj-Hariri, H., Mechanical and Aerospace Engineering
Harriott, L., Electrical and Computer Engineering
Hoel, L., Civil and Environmental Engineering
Holmes, A., Electrical and Computer Engineering
Horgan, C., Civil and Environmental Engineering
Horowitz, B., Systems and Information Engineering
Howe, J., Materials Science and Engineering
Hudson, J., Chemical Engineering
Hull, R., Materials Science and Engineering
Humphrey, J., Mechanical and Aerospace Engineering
Humphrey, M., Computer Science
Iwasaki, T., Mechanical and Aerospace Engineering
Jesser, W., Materials Science and Engineering
Johnson, B., Electrical and Computer Engineering
Johnson, D., Science, Technology and Society
Johnson, R., Materials Science and Engineering
Johnson, W., Materials Science and Engineering
Jones, A., Computer Science
Kelly, R., Materials Science and Engineering
Kent, R., Mechanical and Aerospace Engineering
King, M., Chemical Engineering
Kirwan, D., Chemical Engineering
Knight, J., Computer Science

KRZYSZTOFOWICZ, R., Systems and Information Engineering

LIN, Z., Electrical and Computer Engineering

LUNG, W., Civil and Environmental Engineering

MCDANIEL, J., Mechanical and Aerospace Engineering

MARSHALL, P., Electrical and Computer Engineering

MASLEN, E., Mechanical and Aerospace Engineering

MIKSAD, R., Civil and Environmental Engineering

NEUROCK, M., Chemical Engineering

NORRIS, P., Mechanical and Aerospace Engineering

O'CONNELL, J., Chemical Engineering

PINDERA, M., Civil and Environmental Engineering

REED, M., Electrical and Computer Engineering

REYNOLDS, P., Computer Science

RICHARDS, L., Mechanical and Aerospace Engineering

ROBERTS, W., Mechanical and Aerospace Engineering

ROBINS, G., Computer Science

SCHERER, W., Systems and Information Engineering

SCULLY, J., Materials Science and Engineering

SHIFLET, G., Materials Science and Engineering

SKALAK, T., Biomedical Engineering Department

SMITH, J., Civil and Environmental Engineering

SOFFA, M., Computer Science

SOFFA, W., Materials Science and Engineering

SON, S., Computer Science

STANKOVIC, J., Computer Science

STARKE, E., Materials Science and Engineering

TAO, G., Electrical and Computer Engineering

THACKER, J., Mechanical and Aerospace Engineering

THORNTON, K., Science, Technology and Society

TOWNSEND, I., Science, Technology and Society

VEERARAGHAVAN, M., Electrical and Computer Engineering

WADLEY, H., Materials Science and Engineering

WEAVER, A., Computer Science

WEIKLE, R., Electrical and Computer Engineering

WHITE, K., Systems and Information Engineering

WILSON, S., Electrical and Computer Engineering

WOLF, S., Materials Science and Engineering

WOOD, H., Mechanical and Aerospace Engineering

WULF, W., Computer Science

School of Law (POB 400405, Charlottesville, VA 22904-4405; tel. (434) 924-7354; internet www.law.virginia.edu):

ABRAHAM, K.
ARMACOST, B.
BAGLEY, M.
BALNAVE, R.
BEVIER, L.
BLASI, V.
BONNIE, R.
BROWN, D.
BROWN-NAGIN, T.
BUCK, D.
CANNON, J.
COHEN, G.
COLLINS, M.

COUGHLIN, A.
CUSHMAN, B.
DOOLEY, M.
DUDLEY, E.
FORDE-MAZRUI, K.
GOLUBOFF, R.
HARRISON, J.
HOWARD, A.
HYNES, R.
IBBEKEN, D.
JOHNSON, A.
KITCH, E.
KLARMAN, M.
KORDANA, K.
KRAUS, J.
LESLIE, D.
LOW, P.
MAGILL, M.
MAHONEY, J.
MAHONEY, P.
MARTIN, D.
MITCHELL, P.
MONAHAN, J.
MOORE, J.
NACHBAR, T.
NELSON, C.
O'CONNELL, J.
ORTIZ, D.
RILEY, M.
ROBINSON, G.
ROBINSON, M.
RUTHERGLEN, G.
RYAN, J.
SAYLER, R.
SCHRAGGER, R.
SETEAR, J.
SINCLAIR, K.
SMITH, S.
STEPHAN, P.
TURNER, R.
VERKERKE, J.
WALKER, W.
WALT, S.
WHITE, G.
WHITE, T.
WOOLHANDLER, N.
YIN, G.

School of Medicine (POB 800793, Charlottesville, VA 22908-0793; tel. (434) 924-5118; internet www.healthsystem.virginia.edu/internet/som/home.cfm):

ABEL, M., Paediatric Orthotics
ALFORD, B., Musculoskeletal Medicine
APPREY, M., Psychiatry
ARLET, V., Orthopaedics (Spine)
AYERS, C., Cardiovascular Medicine
BALIAN, G., Orthopedic Research
BARRETT, E., Endocrinology
BARRETT, P., Pharmacology
BARTH, J., Psychiatry
BAUM, V., Anaesthesiology
BAYLISS, D., Pharmacology
BECKER, D., Medicine
BELLER, G., Cardiovascular Medicine
BENDER, T., Microbiology
BENNETT, J., Neurology
BERGIN, J., Cardiovascular Medicine
BERTRAM, E., Neurology
BEYER, A., Microbiology
BLOODGOOD, R., Cell Biology
BOLTON, W., Nephrology
BORISH, L., Allergy
BOUTON, A., Microbiology
BRADDOCK, S., Genetics
BRADY, W., Emergency Medicine
BRANT, W., Thoracoabdominal Radiology
BRAUTIGAN, D., Cell Signalling
BROOKEMAN, J., Radiological Research
BROWN, J., Microbiology
BURKE, D., Biochemistry and Molecular Genetics
BUSHWELLER, J., Molecular Physics and Biophysics
CANTERBURY, R., Psychiatry
CAREY, R., Endocrinology

CASANOVA, J., Cell Biology
CASTLE, J., Cell Biology
CHIRGWIN, J., Endocrinology
CLAYTON, A., Psychiatry
COHEN, M., Breast Imaging
COMINELLI, F., Gastroenterology
CONCANNON, P., Biochemistry and Molecular Genetics
CONNELLY, J., Medicine
CONWAY, B., Ophthalmology
CORBETT, E., Medicine
CORWIN, J., Neuroscience
COUSAR, J., Clinical Pathology
COX, D., Psychiatry
CREUTZ, C., Pharmacology
DALKIN, A., Endocrinology
DEREWENDA, Z., Molecular Physics and Biophysics
DESIMONE, D., Cell Biology
DIDUCH, D., Sports Medicine
DIMARCO, J., Cardiovascular Medicine
DONOWITZ, G., Infectious Diseases
DULING, B., Molecular Physics and Biophysics
DURBIN, C., Anaesthesiology
DURIEUX, M., Anaesthesiology
DUTTA, A., Biochemistry and Molecular Genetics
EGELMAN, E., Biochemistry and Molecular Genetics
ENGELHARD, V., Microbiology
ERNST, P., Gastroenterology
EVANS, W., Endocrinology
FOX, J., Microbiology
FRACASSO, P., Haematology and Oncology
FRYSINGER, R., Multiple Neuralgia
FU, S., Rheumatology
GAL, T., Anaesthesiology
GALAZKA, S., Family Medicine
GARRISON, J., Pharmacology
GASKIN, F., Psychiatry
GEAR, A., Biochemistry and Molecular Genetics
GIBSON, R., Cardiovascular Medicine
GIMPLE, L., Cardiovascular Medicine
GOLDBERG, J., Microbiology
GREER, K., Dermatology
GREYSON, C., Psychiatry
GUERRANT, R., Infectious Diseases
GUISE, T., Endocrinology
GUMBINER, B., Cell Biology
GUYENET, P., Pharmacology
HACKETT, J., Molecular Physics and Biophysics
HAGSPIEL, K., Radiology
HALEY, E., Neurology
HAMLIN, J., Biochemistry and Molecular Genetics
HAMMARSKJOLD, M., Microbiology
HARRISON, M., Neurology
HARVEY, J., Breast Imaging
HAYDEN, F., Epidemiology
HERR, J., Cell Biology
HESS, C., Haematology and Oncology
HEWLETT, E., Clinical Pharmacy
HINTON, B., Cell Biology
HOFFMAN, P., Infectious Diseases
HOLROYD, S., Psychiatry
HORWITZ, A., Cell Biology
HOWARDS, S., Urology
JAGGER, J., Infectious Diseases
JEVTOVIĆ-TODOROVIĆ, V., Anaesthesiology
JOHNSON, B., Psychiatry
JOHNSON, M., Pharmacology
JOHNSTON, K., Neurology
JU, S., Rheumatology
KAPUR, J., Neurology
KASSELL, N., Cardiovascular Disease
KERRIGAN, D., Physical Medicine and Rehabilitation
KIM, Y., Biomedical Engineering
KOENIG, S., Pulmonary Medicine
KRAMER, C., Radiological Research
KUTCHAI, H., Molecular Physics and Biophysics
LARNER, J., Radiation Oncology

LAURENCIN, C., Sports Medicine
LEE, K., Neuroscience
LEY, K., Biomedical Engineering
LI, M., Psychiatry
LIN, K., Plastic Surgery
LINDEN, J., Cardiovascular Medicine
LOGIN, K., Neurology
LYNCH, C., Anaesthesiology
LYNCH, K., Pharmacology
McCALL, A., Endocrinology
McDUFFIE, M., Microbiology
McNAMARA, C., Cardiovascular Medicine
MACARA, I., Cell Signalling
MARSHALL, J., Endocrinology
MARTIN, M., Emergency Medicine
MILLER, M., Sports Medicine
MINOR, W., Molecular Physics and Biophysics
MOENTER, S., Endocrinology
MOORMAN, J., Cardiovascular Medicine
MORGAN, R., Plastic Surgery
MUGLER, J., Radiological Research
NADLER, J., Endocrinology
NAKAMOTO, R., Molecular Physics and Biophysics
NEWMAN, S., Ophthalmology
OBRIG, T., Nephrology
O'CONNOR, R., Emergency Medicine
OKUSA, M., Nephrology
OLDFIELD, E., Neuroendocrinology
OWENS, G., Molecular Physics and Biophysics
PARKER, W., Neurology
PARSONS, J., Microbiology
PARSONS, S., Microbiology
PEARSON, R., Geographic Medicine
PEARSON, W., Biochemistry and Molecular Genetics
PEREZ-REYES, E., Pharmacology
PETERS, C., Urology
PETRI, W., Infectious Diseases
PEURA, D., Gastroenterology
PHILBRICK, J., Medicine
PHILLIPS, L., Neurology
PLATTS-MILLS, T., Allergy
PORTERFIELD, P., Psychiatry
POWERS, R., Medicine
RAVICHANDRAN, K., Microbiology
REIN, M., Infectious Diseases
REKOSH, D., Microbiology
REMBOLD, C., Cardiovascular Medicine
REYNOLDS, P., Medicine
RICH, G., Anaesthesiology
RICH, T., Radiation Oncology
RISSMAN, E., Biochemistry and Molecular Genetics
RODEHEAVER, G., Plastic Surgery
ROSE, C., Pulmonary Medicine
ROWLINGSON, J., Anaesthesiology
RUST, R., Neurology
SALEH, K., Adult Reconstruction
SALLER, D., Maternal Foetal Medicine
SANDO, J., Anaesthesiology
SANTEN, R., Endocrinology
SCHELD, W., Infectious Diseases
SCHIFF, D., Neurology
SCHLAGER, T., Emergency Medicine
SCHORLING, J., Medicine
SCHWARTZ, M., Microbiology
SHAFFREY, C., Neuro-Oncology
SHAFFREY, M., Neuro-Oncology
SHAO, Z., Molecular Physics and Biophysics
SHUPNIK, M., Endocrinology
SILVERMAN, L., Clinical Pathology
SINKIN, R., Neonatology
SIRAGY, H., Endocrinology
SLAWSON, D., Family Medicine
SMITH, M., Microbiology
SOMLYO, A., Molecular Physics and Biophysics
STEERS, W., Urology
STEINER, L., Gamma Knife Radiosurgery
STOLER, M., Surgical Pathology
STOVALL, D., Reproductive Endocrinology and Infertility

STURGILL, T., Pharmacology
SURATT, P., Pulmonary Medicine
SUTHERLAND, W., Cell Biology
SYVERUD, S., Emergency Medicine
SZABO, G., Molecular Physics and Biophysics
TAMM, L., Molecular Physics and Biophysics
TAYLOR, R., Biochemistry and Molecular Genetics
THEODORESCU, D., Urology
THISSE, B., Cell Biology
THISSE, C., Cell Biology
THORNER, M., Endocrinology
TIEDEMAN, J., Ophthalmology
TRUWIT, J., Pulmonary Medicine
TURNER, T., Urology
TUTTLE, J., Neuroscience
VANCE, M., Endocrinology
WARREN, J., Psychiatry
WATERS, D., Family Medicine
WATSON, D., Radiological Research
WEBER, M., Microbiology
WEISS, G., Haematology and Oncology
WHITE, J., Cell Biology
WHITEHILL, R., Orthopaedics (Spine)
WILLIAMS, M., Haematology and Oncology
WILLIAMS, M., Medicine
WILLIAMSON, B., Nuclear Medicine
WISPELWEY, B., Infectious Diseases
WOOTEN, G., Neurology
YEAGER, M., Molecular Physics and Biophysics

School of Nursing (POB 800782, Charlottesville, VA 22908-0782; tel. (434) 924-0141; e-mail nur-osa@virginia.edu; internet www.nursing.virginia.edu):

BRASHERS, V.
HAUENSTEIN, E.
HOLLEN, P.
KEELING, A.
LYDER, C.
MERWIN, E.
PARKER, B.
STEEVES, R.
TAYLOR, A..

AFFILIATED COLLEGE

University of Virginia's College at Wise: 1 College Ave, Wise, VA 24293; tel. (276) 328-0100; e-mail info@uvawise.edu; f. 1954; liberal arts college; 140 teachers; 2,067 students; Chancellor DAVID J. PRIOR; Provost SANDERS HUGUENIN; Vice-Chancellor for Devt and College Relations TAMI ELY; Vice-Chancellor for Enrolment Management RUSSELL D. NECESSARY; Vice-Chancellor for Finance and Admin. SIMEON E. EWING; Vice-Chancellor for Information Technology and Chief Information Officer J. KEITH FOWLKES; Dean for Students JEWELL WORLEY; Registrar NARDA PORTER; Dir for Library Services ROBIN BENKE

VIRGINIA COMMONWEALTH UNIVERSITY

910 W Franklin St, Richmond, VA 23284
Telephone: (804) 828-0100
E-mail: ugrad@vcu.edu
Internet: www.vcu.edu
Founded 1838 as Hampden-Sydney College, present status 1968
State control
Academic year: August to May
Campuses at Northern Virginia, Doha (Qatar), Charles City County (Virginia)
Pres.: Dr MICHAEL RAO
Provost and Vice-Pres. for Academic Affairs: Dr BEVERLY J. WARREN
Vice-Provost for Student Affairs and Enrolment Services: HENRY G. RHONE
Vice-Pres. for Devt and Alumni Relations: JOHN I. BLOHM

Vice-Pres. for Finance and Admin.: DAVID HANSON
Vice-Pres. for Health Sciences and CEO of the VCU Health System: Dr SHELDON M. RETCHIN
Vice-Pres. for Research: Dr FRANCIS L. MACRINA
Vice-Pres. for Univ. Outreach: SUE A. MESSMER
Asst. Vice-Pres. for Advancement Services: LAUREN L. SHIVER
Exec. Dir for Govt Relations: MARK E. RUBIN
Registrar: NATASHA WILLIAMS
Univ. Librarian: JOHN E. ULMSCHNEIDER
Library of 1,680,393 vols, 3,007,035 microforms, 9,188 printed journals, 17,441 ejournals
Number of teachers: 1,660 (full-time)
Number of students: 31,900

DEANS

College of the Humanities and Sciences: JAMES S. COLEMAN
Graduate School: F. DOUGLAS BOUDINOT
Honors College: Dr TIMOTHY L. HULSEY
School of Allied Health Professions: Dr CECIL B. DRAIN
School of the Arts: JOSEPH H. SEIPEL
School of Business: ED GRIER
School of Dentistry: Dr DAVID C. SARRETT
School of Education: Dr MICHAEL D. DAVIS
School of Engineering: Dr J. CHARLES JENNETT
School of Medicine: JEROME F. STRAUSS, III
School of Nursing: Dr NANCY F. LANGSTON
School of Pharmacy: Dr VICTOR A. YANCHICK
School of Social Work: Dr JAMES E. HINTERLONG
University College: JOSEPH A. MAROLLA

VIRGINIA INTERMONT COLLEGE

1013 Moore St, Bristol, VA 24201
Telephone: (276) 466-7867
E-mail: viadmit@vic.edu
Internet: vic.edu
Founded 1884 as Southwest Virginia Institute, current name adopted 1891
Private control
Academic year: August to May
Divs of arts and sciences, fine arts, professional studies
Pres.: Dr E. CLORISA PHILLIPS
Provost: Dr MARK A. ROBERTS
Vice-Pres. for Admin.: CONNY W. SAULS
Vice-Pres. for Business and Finance: LINDA C. MORGAN
Vice-Pres. for Institutional Advancement: MARY ANNE HOLBROOK
Dean for Student Devt: RONDA K. COLE
Dir for Admission: ROBIN BROOKS
Registrar: PAM HAMMOND
Library Dir: JONATHAN TALLMAN
Library of 160,000 vols, 97,000 ebooks
Number of teachers: 75
Number of students: 585

VIRGINIA MILITARY INSTITUTE

Lexington, VA 24450
Telephone: (540) 464-7207
E-mail: registrar@vmi.edu
Internet: www.vmi.edu
Founded 1839
public control
Academic year: August to May
Divs of arts and humanities, engineering, leadership, natural science and mathematics, social science
Superintendent: Gen. J. H. BINFORD PEAY, III
Deputy Superintendent for Academics and Dean for the Faculty: Brig. Gen. R. WANE SCHNEITER

Deputy Superintendent for Finance, Admin. and Support: Brig. Gen. ROBERT L. GREEN
Business Exec.: Brig. Gen. ROBERT GREEN
Commandant: Col THOMAS H. TRUMPS
Treas.: Col GARY R. KNICK
Registrar: Col JANET M. BATTAGLIA
Head Librarian: Col DONALD H. SAMDAHL, JR
Library of 300,000 vols, 200,000 govt documents, 60,000 ejournals, 300 periodicals
Number of teachers: 206 (119 full-time, 61 part-time, 26 military)
Number of students: 1,500

VIRGINIA POLYTECHNIC INSTITUTE AND STATE UNIVERSITY

Blacksburg, VA 24061-0002
Telephone: (540) 231-6000
E-mail: vtadmiss@vt.edu
Internet: www.vt.edu
Founded 1872 as Virginia Agricultural and Mechanical College, current name adopted 1896
State control
Academic year: August to May
Pres.: Dr CHARLES W. STEGER
Provost and Sr Vice-Pres.: MARK G. McNAMEE
Vice-Provost for Academic Affairs: DAVID FORD
Exec. Vice-Pres. and Chief Operating Officer: JAMES HYATT
Vice-Pres. for Admin. Services: SHERWOOD G. WILSON
Vice-Pres. for Devt and Univ. Relations: ELIZABETH A. FLANAGAN
Vice-Pres. for Finance and Chief Financial Officer: M. DWIGHT SHELTON, JR
Vice-Pres. for Information Technology: EARVING L. BLYTHE
Vice-Pres. for Research: ROBERT WALTERS
Vice-Pres. for Student Affairs: EDWARD F. D. SPENCER
Univ. Treas. and Chief Operating Officer for Virginia Tech Foundation: RAYMOND D. SMOOT, JR
Dir for Admissions: NORRINE BAILEY SPENCER
Registrar: WANDA HANKINS DEAN
Dean for Univ. Libraries: TYLER WALTERS
Library of 2,686,659 vols, 6,330,610 microforms, 148,411 maps, 399,525 govt documents, 13528 audio items, 40,922 journals
Number of teachers: 1,300 (full-time)
Number of students: 30,950
Publications: *Research Magazine*, *Virginia Tech Magazine*

DEANS

College of Agriculture and Life Sciences: ALAN GRANT
College of Architecture and Urban Studies: A. JACK DAVIS
College of Engineering: RICHARD BENSON
College of Liberal Arts and Human Sciences: SUE OTT ROWLANDS
College of Natural Resources and Environment: PAUL M. WINISTORFER
College of Science: LAY NAM CHANG
Graduate School: KAREN P. DePAUW
Pamplin College of Business: RICHARD E. SORENSEN
Virginia-Maryland Regional College of Veterinary Medicine: GERHARDT SCHURIG
Virginia Tech Carilion School of Medicine: CYNDA A. JOHNSON

VIRGINIA STATE UNIVERSITY

1 Hayden Dr., Petersburg, VA 23806
Telephone: (804) 524-5000
E-mail: admiss@vsu.edu
Internet: www.vsu.edu

Founded 1882 as Virginia Normal and Collegiate Institute, current name adopted 1979
State control
Academic year: August to May
Pres.: Dr KEITH T. MILLER
Provost and Vice-Pres. for Academic Affairs: Dr W. WELDON HILL
Vice-Provost and Graduate Dean: Dr JAMES E. HUNTER
Vice-Pres. for Admin. and Finance: DAVID J. MEADOWS
Vice-Pres. for Devt and Univ. Relations: ROBERT L. TURNER, JR
Vice-Pres. for Student Affairs: Dr MICHAEL SHACKLEFORD
Registrar: DEBERA S. BONNER
Dean for Library: Dr ELSIE WEATHERINGTON
Library of 245,731 vols
Number of teachers: 190
Number of students: 5,900

DEANS

Reginald F. Lewis School of Business: Dr MIRTA M. MARTIN
School of Agriculture: JEWEL HAIRSTON
School of Engineering, Science and Technology: Dr KEITH M. WILLIAMSON
School of Graduate Studies, Research and Outreach: Dr JAMES E. HUNTER
School of Liberal Arts and Education: Dr ANDREW KANU

VIRGINIA THEOLOGICAL SEMINARY

3737 Seminary Rd, Alexandria, VA 22304
Telephone: (703) 370-6600
E-mail: admissions@vts.edu
Internet: www.vts.edu
Founded 1823
Private control
Academic year: September to May
Dean and Pres.: Very Rev. Dr IAN S. MARKHAM
Vice-Pres. and Assoc. Dean for Academic Affairs: Dr TIMOTHY F. SEDGWICK
Vice-Pres. for Admin. and Finance: HEATHER ZDANCEWICZ
Vice-Pres. for Institutional Advancement: Rev. Dr J. BARNEY HAWKINS, IV
Registrar: TAMI SHEPHERD
Head Librarian: Prof. Dr MITZI JARRETT BUDDE
Library of 185,000 vols, 6,800 microforms, 1,050 journals, periodicals and newspaper subscriptions, 600 music CDs
Number of students: 230
Publications: *Episcopal Teacher* (4 a year), *The Journal of Episcopal Church Canon Law* (2 a year), *The Virginia Seminary Journal* (2 a year)

VIRGINIA UNION UNIVERSITY

1500 N Lombardy St, Richmond, VA 23220
Telephone: (804) 257-5600
E-mail: visitus@vuu.edu
Internet: www.vuu.edu
Founded 1865
Private control
Academic year: August to July (3 semesters)
Pres. and CEO: Dr CLAUDE G. PERKINS
Sr Vice-Pres.: Dr JOSEPH F. JOHNSON
Vice-Pres. for Academic Affairs: Dr W. FRANKLIN EVANS
Vice-Pres. for Enrolment Management and Student Affairs: (vacant)
Vice-Pres. for Financial Affairs: GREGORY LEWIS
Vice-Pres. for Institutional Advancement: Dr ANTHONY THOMPSON
Vice-Pres. for Research, Planning and Special Programmes: Dr JOY GOODRICH

Vice-Pres. for Student Affairs: Dr JOSEPH JOHNSON
Dir for Univ. Services: GILBERT L. CARTER
Registrar: MARILYN A. BROOKS
Dir for Library: Dr DELORES PRETLOW
Library of 562,000 vols
Number of teachers: 105 (85 full-time, 20 part-time)
Number of students: 1,500

DEANS

Evelyn Reid Syphax School of Education, Psychology and Interdisciplinary Studies: Dr MARSHA TAYLOR HORTON
Samuel DeWitt Proctor School of Theology: Dr JOHN W. KINNEY
School of Humanities and Social Sciences: Dr LINDA SCHLICHTING
School of Mathematics, Science and Technology: Dr PHILLIP W. ARCHER
Sydney Lewis School of Business: Dr ADELAJA O. ODUTOLA

VIRGINIA WESLEYAN COLLEGE

1584 Wesleyan Dr., Norfolk, VA 23502-5599
Telephone: (757) 455-3200
E-mail: admissions@vwc.edu
Internet: www.vwc.edu
Founded 1961
Private control
Academic year: August to May (2 semesters)
Divs of humanities, natural sciences and mathematics, social sciences
Pres.: WILLIAM T. GREER, JR
Vice-Pres. for Academic Affairs and Kenneth R. Perry Dean for the College: Dr TIMOTHY G. O'ROURKE
Vice-Pres. for College Advancement: MARGUERITE K. VAIL
Vice-Pres. for Finance: CARY A. SAWYER
Vice-Pres. for Operations: BRUCE VAUGHAN
Vice-Pres. for Student Affairs and Dean for Enrolment Services: DAVID E. BUCKINGHAM
Assoc. Vice-Pres. for Institutional Research and Effectiveness and Dir for Strategic Planning: R. BRYAN PRICE
Dean for Admissions: PATTY PATTEN
Registrar: BOBBIS S. ADAMS
Dir for Library: JAN PACE
Library of 132,514 vols, 59,354 ebooks, 231 journals, 37,416 ejournals, 15,953 microfilms, 3,599 audiovisual items
Number of teachers: 135 (85 full-time, 45 part-time)
Number of students: 1,400

WASHINGTON AND LEE UNIVERSITY

204 W Washington St, Lexington, VA 24450-2116
Telephone: (540) 458-8400
E-mail: admissions@wlu.edu
Internet: www.wlu.edu
Founded 1749 as Augusta Acad., current name adopted 1870
Private control
Academic year: September to June
Pres.: Dr KENNETH P. RUSCIO
Provost: Dr ROBERT A. STRONG
Vice-Pres. for Finance and Treas.: STEVEN G. McALLISTER
Vice-Pres. for Student Affairs and Dean for Students: SIDNEY SPRINGFIELD EVANS
Vice-Pres. for Univ. Advancement: DENNIS W. CROSS
Dean for Student Life: DAVID M. LEONARD
Registrar: D. SCOTT DITTMAN
Univ. Librarian: TERRANCE J. METZ
Library of 956,354 vols, 10,362 paper, microforms and e-periodical subscriptions, 17,300 audiovisual items; law library incl. 428,517 vols

Number of teachers: 230 (205 full-time, 25 adjunct)

Number of students: 2,150

Publications: *Journal of Science, Political Review, Shenandoah* (4 a year), *Washington and Lee Law Review*

DEANS

Ernest Williams II School of Commerce, Economics and Politics: Dr LARRY C. PEPPERS

School of Law: Dr MARK H. GRUNEWALD

The College: Dr HOWARD DOBIN

WASHINGTON

ART INSTITUTE OF SEATTLE

2323 Elliott Ave, Seattle, WA 98121-1642

Telephone: (206) 448-6600

E-mail: aisadm@aii.edu

Internet: www.artinstitutes.edu/seattle

Founded 1946 as the Burnley School for Professional Art, present name and status 1982

Private control

Culinary, design, fashion, liberal arts, media arts

Pres.: ELDEN MONDAY

Dir for Admin. and Financial Services: GREG WOODARD

Sr Dir for Admissions: LIANE SOOHOO

Dean for Academic Affairs: SCOTT CARNZ

Dean for Student Affairs: MEGAN KIJEWSKI

Dir for Human Resources: NATASHA OILAR

Dir for Library Services: ANDREW HARBISON

Number of students: 2,300

BASTYR UNIVERSITY

14500 Juanita Dr., NE, Kenmore, WA 98028-4966

Telephone: (425) 823-1300

E-mail: admissions@bastyr.edu

Internet: www.bastyr.edu

Founded 1978 as John Bastyr College of Naturopathic Medicine

Natural health, arts and sciences

Pres.: Dr DANIEL K. CHURCH

Library of 19,000 vols

Number of teachers: 170 (52 full-time, 118 part-time)

Number of students: 1,000

DEAN

School of Naturopathic Medicine: Dr JANE GUILTINAN

CENTRAL WASHINGTON UNIVERSITY

400 E Univ. Way, Ellensburg, WA 98926

Telephone: (509) 963-2111

Internet: www.cwu.edu

Founded 1891 as Washington State Normal School, present name 1977

Pres.: JAMES L. GAUDINO

Provost and Vice-Pres. for Academic Affairs: Dr MARILYN LEVINE

Vice-Pres. for Business and Financial Affairs: GEORGE CLARK

Vice-Pres. for Student Affairs and Enrollment Management: CHARLOTTE TULLOS

Vice-Pres. for Univ. Advancement: (vacant)

Registrar: TRACY

Dean for Library Services: PATRICIA CUTRIGHT

Library of 485,417 vols

Number of teachers: 370

Number of students: 10,750

DEANS

College of Arts and Humanities: MARJI MORGAN

College of Business: Dr ROY SAVOIAN

College of Education and Professional Studies: Dr CONNIE LAMBERT

College of the Sciences: KIRK A. JOHNSON

Graduate Studies: WAYNE QUIRK

CITY UNIVERSITY OF SEATTLE

11900 NE First St, Bellevue, WA 98005

150–120th Ave, NE, Bellevue, WA 98005

Telephone: (425) 637-1010

E-mail: info@cityu.edu

Internet: www.cityu.edu

Founded 1973 as City College, current name adopted 1982

Private control

Sites in states of Washington and California, and in Australia, Bulgaria, Canada, China, Czech Republic, Greece, Mexico, Romania, Slovakia and Switzerland

Pres.: LEE GORSUCH

Provost: Dr STEVEN OLSWANG

Exec. Vice-Pres. for Academic Affairs: Dr FERNANDO LEON GARCIA

Exec. Vice-Pres. for Finance and Admin. and Chief Financial Officer: BRUCE BRYANT

Vice-Pres. for Academic and Institutional Assessment: CHRIS J. RIGOS

Vice-Pres. for Admissions and Student Services and Registrar: Dr MELISSA MECHAM

Vice-Pres. for the Business Office and Controller: MARIETA C. JOHNSON

Vice-Pres. for European Operations: Ing. JAN REBRO

Vice-Pres. for External Relations: Dr WINSTON C. ADDIS

Vice-Pres. for Univ. Advancement: CHRISTOPHER ROSS

Dir for Human Resources: TIMOTHY SPRAKE

Dir for Library Affairs: MARY MARA

Number of teachers: 1,300

Number of students: 6,850 worldwide

DEANS

Gordon Albright School of Education: Dr CRAIG SCHEIBER

School of Management: Dr KURT KIRSTEIN

CLARK COLLEGE

1933 Fort, Vancouver Way, Vancouver, WA 98663

Telephone: (360) 699-6398

E-mail: admissions@clark.edu

Internet: www.clark.edu

Founded 1933

State control

Dental hygiene, social work and technology

Pres.: ROBERT K. KNIGHT

Vice-Pres. for Instruction: Dr TIM COOK

Vice-Pres. for Admin. Services: BOB WILLIAMSON

Vice-Pres. for Student Affairs: WILLIAM BELDEN

Dean for Libraries: MICHELLE BAGLEY

Number of students: 16,000

Publications: *Clark 24/7* (24 a year), *Clark College Connections* (4 a year), *The Clark Journal* (12 a year)

CORNISH COLLEGE OF THE ARTS

1000 Lenora St, Seattle, WA 98121

Telephone: (206) 726-5016

E-mail: provostoffice@cornish.edu

Internet: www.cornish.edu

Founded 1914

Offers Baccalaureate studies in the performing and visual arts; major fields of study: art, dance, design, music, performance production and theatre

Pres.: Dr NANCY J. USCHER

Provost and Vice-Pres. for Academic Affairs: Dr LOIS HARRIS

Vice-Pres. for Finance and Admin.: JEFF RIDDELL

Vice-Pres. for Institutional Advancement: JANE EWING

Dean for Enrolment Management: GARY CRAIG

Dir for Library Services: HOLLIS NEAR

Registrar: ADRIENNE M. BOLYARD

Number of teachers: 145

Number of students: 800

EASTERN WASHINGTON UNIVERSITY

Office of Academic Affairs, 220 Showalter Hall, Cheney, WA 99004

Telephone: (509) 359-7900

E-mail: universityre@ewu.edu

Internet: www.ewu.edu

Founded 1882, present name and status 1978

State control

Language of instruction: English

Academic year: September to June

Pres.: Dr RODOLFO ARÉVALO

Provost and Vice-Pres. for Academic Affairs: Dr REX FULLER

Vice-Pres. for Student Affairs: Dr STACEY MORGAN FOSTER

Registrar: ERIN MORGAN

Assoc. Vice-Pres. for Enrolment Management: Dr LAWRENCE BRIGGS

Dean for Libraries: Dr RICHARD WILSON

Library of 1,113,167 vols, 750,000 books, 3,100 ebooks, 903 current periodicals, 43 periodical microforms

Number of teachers: 365

Number of students: 10,750

DEANS

College of Arts, Letters and Education: Dr LYNN BRIGGS

College of Business and Public Administration: Dr ELIZABETH TIPTON

College of Science, Health and Engineering: Dr JUDD A. CASE

College of Social and Behavioural Sciences and Social Work: Dr VICKIE RUTLEDGE SHIELDS

EVERGREEN STATE COLLEGE

2700 Evergreen Parkway, NW, Olympia, WA 98505

Telephone: (360) 867-6000

E-mail: admissions@evergreen.edu

Internet: www.evergreen.edu

Founded 1971

State control

Liberal arts college; 3 campuses: Grays Harbor, Olympia and Tacoma

Pres.: Dr THOMAS LES PURCE

Provost and Vice-Pres. for Academic Affairs: KEN TABBUTT

Vice-Pres. for College Advancement: D. LEE HOEMANN

Vice-Pres. for Finance and Admin.: JOHN HURLEY

Vice-Pres. for Student Affairs: ART COSTANTINO

Exec. Dir for Tacoma Campus: Dr ARTEE F. YOUNG

Dean for the Library and Media Service: BILL BRUNER

Library of 35,000 journals, spec. collns, rare books, archival material and govt documents

Number of teachers: 250

Number of students: 4,900

Publication: *Evergreen Magazine*

GONZAGA UNIVERSITY

502 E. Boone Ave, Spokane, WA 99258-0102

Telephone: (509) 328-4220

Internet: www.gonzaga.edu

Founded 1881 as Gonzaga College

Private control

Academic year: August to May, and summer session

Chancellor: BERNARD J. COUGHLIN
Pres.: Dr THAYNE M. MCCULLOH
Exec. Vice-Pres.: EARL F. MARTIN
Vice-Pres. for Academic Affairs: Dr PATRICIA O'CONNELL KILLEN
Vice-Pres. for Admin. and Planning: HARRY H. SLADICH
Vice-Pres. for Finance: CHARLES J. MURPHY
Vice-Pres. for Student Life: Dr SUE WEITZ
Vice-Pres. for Univ. Relations: MARGOT J. STANFIELD (acting)
Dean for Admissions: PHILLIP BALLINGER
Librarian: EILEEN BELL-GARRISON

Library of 425,000 vols

Number of teachers: 365

Number of students: 7,840

Publications: *Charter* (1 a year), *Gonzaga Magazine* (12 a year), *Reflections* (1 a year), *Report of the President* (1 a year), *Spires Yearbook* (1 a year)

DEANS

College of Arts and Sciences: MARC MANGA-NARO
College of Business Administration: Dr CLAR-ENCE H. BARNES
School of Education: Dr JON D. SUNDERLAND
School of Engineering and Applied Science: DENNIS R. HORN
School of Law: JANE KORN
School of Professional Studies: Dr MICHAEL R. L. CAREY

HERITAGE UNIVERSITY

3240 Fort Rd, Toppenish, WA 98948

Telephone: (888) 272-6190

E-mail: admissions@heritage.edu

Internet: www.heritage.edu

Founded 1907 as Spokane's Fort Wright College, univ. status 2004

Private control

Academic year: August to June

Liberal arts univ.; 3 regional sites in Moses Lake, Tri-Cities and S Seattle

Pres.: Dr JOHN BASSETT
Provost and Vice-Pres. for Academic Affairs: Dr SNEH B. VEENA
Vice-Pres. for Advancement: MICHAEL P. MOORE
Vice-Pres. for Support Services and Chief Financial Officer: RICK R. GAGNIER
Dir for Admissions and Recruitment: MIGUEL PUENTE
Dean for Students: MELISSA FILKOWSKI
Dean for Enrolment Management Services: NORBERTO T. ESPINDOLA
Library Dir: BILL MCCAY

Library of 70,000 vols (in print), 45,000 vols (electronic)

Number of teachers: 170 (45 full-time, 125 part-time)

Number of students: 1,355

DEANS

Arts and Sciences: KAZUHIRO SONODA
Education and Psychology: Dr ROBERT LYNN SMART

NORTHWEST UNIVERSITY

POB 579, Kirkland, WA 98083-0579

5520 108th Ave, NE, Kirkland, WA 98033

Telephone: (425) 822-8266

E-mail: recpt@northwestu.edu

Internet: www.northwestu.edu

Founded 1934 as Northwest Bible Institute, current name adopted 2005

Private control

Language of instruction: English

Academic year: August to May

Pres.: Dr JOSEPH CASTLEBERRY
Chancellor: Dr DON ARGUE
Exec. Vice-Pres.: DAN NEARY
Provost: JIM HEUGEL
Sr Vice-Pres. for Finance: DAN SCHIMELPFE-NIG
Vice-Pres. for Advancement: JASON MILES
Vice-Pres. for Campus Ministries: PHIL RAS-MUSSEN
Vice-Pres. for Student Devt: PAUL BANAS
Assoc. Vice-Pres. for Marketing: MERLIN QUIGGLE
Asst Vice-Pres. for Devt: JEFF LOCKHART
Asst Vice-Pres. for Enrolment: ROSE-MARY SMITH
Dir for Library: ADAM EPP

Library of 88,794 vols, 12,458 periodicals

Number of teachers: 55

Number of students: 11,750

DEANS

College of Arts and Sciences: Prof. DARREL HOBSON
College of Ministry: Prof. WAYDE GOODALL
College of Social and Behavioral Sciences: Dr MATT NELSON
School of Business and Management: TERESA GILLESPIE
School of Education: GARY NEWBILL
School of Nursing: Dr CARL CHRISTENSEN

PROFESSORS

CHARETTE, BLAINE, Bible, Greek
HARRIS, MOSES, Education, Modern Languages
JOHNSON, LEROY, History, Interdisciplinary Studies, Political Science
JUNGJIN, DOO, Chemistry
LEACH, KEVIN, Psychology
KOWALSKI, WALDEMAR, Bible, Theology
KRESS, PAUL, Education
MESTRE, MICHEL, Business
STALLMAN, ROBERT, Bible, Hebrew
THOMPSON, MICHAEL, Christian Education, Youth Ministries

PACIFIC LUTHERAN UNIVERSITY

12180 Park St S, Tacoma, WA 98447-0003

Telephone: (206) 531-6900

E-mail: admission@plu.edu

Internet: www.plu.edu

Founded 1890

Private control

Pres.: Dr LOREN J. ANDERSON
Provost: Dr STEVEN P. STARKOVICH
Vice-Pres. for Admission and Enrolment Services: KARL STUMO
Vice-Pres. for Devt and Univ. Relations: STEPHEN J. OLSON
Vice-Pres. for Finance and Operations: Dr SHERI TONN
Vice-Pres. for Student Life: Dr LAURA F. MAJOVSKI
Dean for Information Resources: CHRIS D. FERGUSON

Library of 363,580 vols

Number of teachers: 285 (247 full-time, 38 part-time)

Number of students: 3,450

SAINT MARTIN'S COLLEGE

5000 Abbey Way, SE, Lacey, WA 98503-7500

Telephone: (206) 491-4700

E-mail: information@stmartin.edu

Internet: www.stmartin.edu

Founded 1895 as Saint Martin's College, current name adopted 2005

Academic year: September to May

Chancellor: ABBOT NEAL ROTH
Pres.: Dr ROY F. HEYNDERICKX
Provost and Vice-Pres. for Academic Affairs: Dr JOSEPH D. BESSIE
Vice-Pres. for Finance: SUSAN HELTSLEY
Vice-Pres. for Institutional Advancement: ROSANNE A. NICHOLS
Vice-Pres. Int. Programmes and Devt: JOSE-PHINE YUNG
Dean for Students: MELANIE RICHARDSON
Registrar: MARY LAW
Librarian: DALIA HAGAN

Library of 85,000 vols

Number of teachers: 70

Number of students: 980

DEANS

College of Arts and Sciences: Dr ERIC APFELSTADT
College of Education and Professional Psychology: Dr JOYCE V. S. WESTGARD
School of Business: Dr RICHARD BEER
School of Engineering: Dr ZELLA L. KAHN-JETTER

SEATTLE PACIFIC UNIVERSITY

3307 Third Ave W, Seattle, WA 98119-1997

Telephone: (206) 281-2000

Internet: www.spu.edu

Founded 1891

Private control

Academic year: September to June

Pres.: PHILIP W. EATON
Sr Vice-Pres. for Admin. and Univ. Relations: MARJORIE R. JOHNSON
Sr Vice-Pres. for Business and Planning: DONALD W. MORTENSON
Vice-Pres. for Academic Affairs: BRUCE CON-GDON
Vice-Pres. and Dean for Student Life: JEF-FREY C. JORDAN
Vice-Pres. for Univ. Advancement: THOMAS W. BOX
Assoc. Vice-Pres. for Information and Data Management: JANET L. WARD
Dir for Student Academic Services and Univ. Registrar: RUTH L. RUTH L. ADAMS
Univ. Librarian: MICHAEL PAULUS

Library of 200,000 vols, 1,300 journals and database

Number of teachers: 360

Number of students: 4,170

DEANS

College of Arts and Sciences: Prof. BRUCE D. CONGDON
School of Business and Economics: Dr JEF-FREY VAN DUZER
School of Education: Dr RICK EIGENBROOD
School of Health Sciences: Dr LUCILLE M. KELLEY
School of Psychology, Family and Community: Dr MÍCHEÁL D. ROE
School of Theology: Dr DOUG STRONG

SEATTLE UNIVERSITY

POB 222000, 901 12th Ave, Seattle, WA 98122-1090

Telephone: (206) 296-6000

E-mail: admissions@seattleu.edu

Internet: www.seattleu.edu

Founded 1891 as Seattle College, present name 1948

Private control

Academic year: October to July

Pres.: STEPHEN V. SUNDBORG
Provost: ISIAAH CRAWFORD
Exec. Vice-Pres.: TIMOTHY P. LEARY

Vice-Pres. for Enrolment Management: MARILYN CRONE
Vice-Pres. for Finance: JAMES ADOLPHSON
Vice-Pres. for Human Resources and Univ. Services: JERRY HUFFMAN
Vice-Pres. for Mission and Ministry: PETER ELY
Vice-Pres. for Student Devt: JACOB DIAZ
Vice-Pres. for Univ. Advancement: MARY KAY MCFADDEN
Vice-Pres. for Univ. Planning and Vice-Provost: ROBERT J. DULLEA
Dean for Admissions: MICHAEL MCKEON
Univ. Librarian: JOHN POPKO

Library of 234,978 vols
Number of teachers: 440
Number of students: 7,900

DEANS

Albers School of Business and Economics: Dr JOSEPH M. PHILLIPS
College of Arts and Sciences: DAVID V. POWERS
College of Education: SUE SCHMITT
College of Nursing: Dr AZITA EMAMI
College of Science and Engineering: Dr MICHAEL J. QUINN
Matteo Ricci College: Dr JODI KELLY
School of Law: Dr MARK NILES
School of Theology and Ministry: Dr MARK S. MARKULY

TRINITY LUTHERAN COLLEGE

2802 Wetmore Ave, Everett, WA 98201

Telephone: (425) 249-4800
E-mail: info@tlc.edu
Internet: tlc.edu

Founded 1944 as Lutheran Bible Institute of Seattle, present name 1998
Private control

Pres.: JOHN REED
Academic Dean: Dr JEFF MALLINSON
Registrar: CHUCK NELSON

UNIVERSITY OF PUGET SOUND

1500 N Warner, Tacoma, WA 98416

Telephone: (253) 879-3419
E-mail: mediarelations@pugetsound.edu
Internet: www.pugetsound.edu

Founded 1888
Private control

Pres.: RONALD R. THOMAS
Vice-Pres. for Academics and Dean for the Univ.: KRISTINE M. BARTANEN
Vice-Pres. for Enrolment: GEORGE H. MILLS
Vice-Pres. for Finance and Admin.: SHERRY MONDOU
Vice-Pres. for Student Affairs and Dean for Students: MICHAEL SEGAWA
Vice-Pres. for Univ. Relations: DAVID R. BEERS
Registrar: JOHN FINNEY
Library Dir: JANE A. CARLIN

Library of 580,000 vols
Number of teachers: 220
Number of students: 2,600 full-time

UNIVERSITY OF WASHINGTON

POB 351270, Seattle, WA 98195-1270

Telephone: (206) 543-2100
E-mail: uwvic@u.washington.edu
Internet: www.washington.edu

Founded 1861
State control

Pres.: MICHAEL YOUNG
Provost: Dr ANA MARI CAUCE
Sr Vice-Pres. for Finance and Facilities: V'ELLA WARREN
Vice-Pres. for External Affairs: RANDY HODGINS
Vice-Pres. for Human Resources: MINDY KORNBERG
Vice-Pres. for Minority Affairs and Diversity: SHEILA EDWARDS LANGE (acting)
Vice-Pres. for Student Life: ERIC GODFREY
Vice-Pres. for Univ. Advancement: CONNIE KRAVAS
Exec. Vice-Provost: DOUG WADDEN (acting)
Vice-Provost for Academic Personnel: CHERYL A. CAMERON (acting)
Vice-Provost for Educational Outreach: DAVID SZATMARY
Vice-Provost for Global Affairs: STEPHEN E. HANSON
Vice-Provost for the Graduate School: GERALD BALDASTY
Vice-Provost for Minority Affairs and Diversity: SHEILA EDWARDS LANGE
Vice-Provost for Planning and Budgeting: PAUL JENNY
Vice-Provost for Research: MARY LIDSTROM
Vice-Provost for Special Programs: GUS K. J. KRAVAS
Vice-Provost for Undergraduate Academic Affairs: ED TAYLOR
Dir of Fed. Relations: CHRISTY GUILLION
Dir of State Relations: MARGARET SHEPHERD
Dir of Libraries: LIZABETH WILSON

Library: see under Libraries and Archives
Number of teachers: 4,000
Number of students: 48,000

Publications: *American Journal of Human Genetics, Biochemistry, Journal of Financial and Quantitative Analysis, Journal of Limnology and Oceanography, Modern Language Quarterly, Pacific Northwest Quarterly, Papers of Regional Science Association, Poetry Northwest, Trends in Engineering, Washington Law Review*

DEANS

College of Arts and Sciences: ROBERT STACEY
College of Built Environments: Dr DANIEL S. FRIEDMAN
College of Education: TOM STRITIKUS
College of Engineering: MATTHEW O'DONNELL (acting)
College of the Environment: LISA GRAUMLICH (acting)
College of Ocean and Fishery Sciences: ARTHUR NOWELL
Evans School of Public Affairs: SANDRA O. ARCHIBALD
Graduate School: GERALD BALDASTY (acting)
Information School: HARRY BRUCE
Michael G. Foster School of Business: JAMES JIAMBALVO (acting)
School of Dentistry: (vacant)
School of Law: KELLYE TESTY
School of Medicine: PAUL G. RAMSEY
School of Nursing: MARLA E. SALMON
School of Pharmacy: THOMAS A. BAILLIE
School of Public Health: Dr HOWARD FRUMKIN
School of Social Work: Dr EDWINA UEHARA (acting)

PROFESSORS

College of Architecture and Urban Planning (Box 355726, Seattle, WA 98195; tel. (206) 543-7679; internet www.caup.washington.edu):

BADANES, S. P., Architecture
BLANCO, H. J., Urban Design and Planning
CHING, F. D. K., Architecture
DANIALI, S., Construction Management
FINROW, J. V., Architecture
MILLER, D. E., Architecture
MILLER, D. H., Urban Design and Planning
MUGERAUER, R., Architecture
OCHSNER, J. K., Architecture
PYATOK, M., Architecture
STREATFIELD, D. C., Landscape Architecture
SUTTON, S. E., Architecture

VERNEZ-MOUDON, A., Urban Design and Planning

College of Arts and Sciences (50 Communications #353765, Univ. of Washington, Seattle, WA 98195-3765; tel. (206) 543-5340; internet www.artsci.washington.edu):

ADELBERGER, E. G., Physics
ALEXANDER, E., English
ALLEN, C., English
AMMERLAHN, H., German
AMMIRATI, J. F., Biology
ANDERSEN, N. H., Chemistry
ANDERSON, S., Astronomy
BACHMAN, D. M., International Studies
BALDASTY, G. J., Communication
BALICK, B., Astronomy
BARASH, D. P., Psychology
BARDEEN, J. M., Physics
BARLOW, T. E., Women Studies
BARRACK, C. M., German
BARZEL, Y., Economics
BATTISTI, D. S., Atmospheric Science
BEECHER, M. D., Psychology
BEHLER, D. I., German
BEHLMER, G. K., History
BENDICH, A. K., Biology
BENNETT, W. L., Political Science
BERGANTZ, G. W., Earth and Space Sciences
BERGER, P. E., Art
BERNARD, J. W., Music
BERNSTEIN, I. L., Psychology
BERTSCH, G. F., Physics
BESAG, J. E., Statistics
BEYERS, W. B., Geography
BIERDS, L. L., English
BLAKE, K., English
BLAU, H., English
BLIQUEZ, L. J., Classics
BLONDELL, R., Classics
BOARCH-JACOBSEN, M., Comparative Literature
BOERSMA, P. D., Biology
BOLTZ, W., Asian Languages and Literatures
BONJOUR, L. A., Philosophy
BOOKER, J. R., Earth and Space Sciences
BORDEN, W. T., Chemistry
BOULWARE, D. G., Physics
BOURGEOIS, J., Earth and Space Sciences
BOYNTON, P., Physics
BOZARTH, G. S., Music
BRADSHAW, H. D., Biology
BRAME, M. K., Linguistics
BRAVMANN, R. A., Art
BRENOWITZ, E. A., Psychology
BRETHERTON, C. S., Atmospheric Science
BROWN, J. K., German
BROWN, J. M., Earth and Space Sciences
BROWN, M. J., English
BROWNLEE, D. E., Astronomy
BRUCE, N., Economics
BUBE, K. P., Mathematics
BUCK, S. L., Psychology
BULGAC, A., Physics
BURDZY, K., Mathematics
BURKE, J. V., Mathematics
BURNETT, T. H., Physics
BURSTEIN, P., Sociology
BUTLER, J. E., American Ethnic Studies
CALLIS, J. B., Chemistry
CAMPBELL, C. T., Chemistry
CAMPBELL, P. S., Music
CAPORASO, J. A., Political Science
CASTERAS, S. P., Art
CATTOLICO, R. A., Biology
CAUCE, A. M., Psychology
CHALOUPKA, V., Physics
CHAN, K. W., Geography
CHEN, Z., Mathematics
CHENEY, E. S., Earth and Space Sciences
CHIROT, D., International Studies
CIRTAUTAS, I. D., Near Eastern Languages and Literatures
CLATTERBAUGH, K. C., Philosophy

CLAUSEN, M. L., Art
CLAUSS, J. J., Classics
CLOSE, A. E., Anthropology
COBURN, R. C., Philosophy
COHEN, S. M., Philosophy
COLDEWEY, J. C., English
COLLINGWOOD, D., Mathematics
COMAI, L., Biology
COVEY, E., Psychology
COWAN, D. S., Earth and Space Sciences
COX, C. D., Asian Languages and Literatures
CRAMER, J. G., Jr, Physics
CREAGER, K. C., Earth and Space Sciences
CRIMINALE, W. O., Jr, Applied Mathematics
CRUTCHFIELD, R. D., Sociology
CURTIS, E. B., Mathematics
DAHLSTROM, R. A., Drama
DALTON, L. R., Chemistry
DANIEL, T. L., Sociology
DAWSON, G., Psychology
DEL MORAL, R., Biology
DEN NIJS, M. P., Physics
DIAZ, F. L., Psychology
DILLON, G. L., English
DOVICHI, N. J., Chemistry
DROBNY, G. P., Chemistry
DUCHAMP, T. E., Mathematics
DUNN, R. J., English
DURAND, J., Music
DURRAN, D. R., Atmospheric Science
EBREY, P. B., History
ELLINGSON, T. J., Music
ELLIS, J. M., Geography
ELLIS, S. D., Physics
ENGEL, T., Chemistry
EPIOTIS, N., Chemistry
ERICKSON, K. B., Mathematics
EROS, P. S., Music
FAILING, P. A., Art
FAIN, S. C., Physics
FINDLEY, J. M., History
FINE, A. I., Philosophy
FLORES, L. H., American Ethnic Studies
FOLLAND, G. B., Mathematics
FOLSOM, R. C., Speech and Hearing Sciences
FORTSON, E. N., II, Physics
FREY, C. H., English
GAMMON, R. H., Chemistry
GARCIA, A., Physics
GATES, S. N., Drama
GEIST, A. L., Romance Languages and Literatures
GELB, M. H., Chemistry
GHOSE, S., Earth and Space Sciences
GIFFARD, C. A., Communications
GOLDE, H., Computer Science
GOLDSTEIN, A. A., Mathematics
GORE, W. J., Political Science
GOTTMAN, J. M., Psychology
GOUTERMAN, M. P., Chemistry
GRAYSON, D. K., Anthropology
GREENBERG, R., Mathematics
GREENWALD, A. G., Psychology
GREGORY, N. W., Chemistry
GROSSMAN, A. J., Music
GRUNBAUM, B., Mathematics
GUARRERA, F. P., Music
GUEST, A. M., Sociology
GURALNIK, M. J., Psychology and Paediatrics
HALL, B. D., Genetics
HALLET, B., Geological Sciences
HALPERIN, C. S., Botany
HALPERN, I., Physics
HALSEY, G. D., Jr, Chemistry
HALVORSEN, R., Economics
HANEY, J. V., Slavic Languages and Literatures and International Studies
HANKINS, T. L., History
HANLEY, S. B., International Studies
HARMON, D. P., Classics and Comparative Literature
HARRELL, C. S., Anthropology and International Studies

HARTMANN, D., Atmospheric Sciences
HARTWELL, L. H., Genetics
HASKINS, E. F., Botany
HEER, N. L., Near Eastern Languages and Literature
HELLER, E. J., Chemistry and Physics
HELLMANN, D. C., Political Science and School of International Studies
HENLEY, E. M., Physics
HERTLING, G. H., Germanics
HILDEBRAND, G., Art History and Architecture
HIRSCHMAN, C., Sociology
HIXSON, W. J., Art
HOBBS, P. V., Atmospheric Sciences
HODGE, P. W., Astronomy
HOLTON, J. R., Atmospheric Sciences
HOSTETLER, P. S., Drama
HOUZE, R. A., Atmospheric Physics
HU, M., Art
HUEY, R. B., Zoology
HUNN, E. S., Anthropology
HUNT, E. B., Psychology
HUTTON, R. S., Psychology
INGALLS, R. L., Physics
IRVING, R., Mathematics
JACKSON, W. A. D., Geography and School of International Studies
JACOBSON, N., Psychology
JAEGER, C. S., German
JANS, J. P., Mathematics
JOHNSON, C. R., English
JONES, R. C., Art
KAPETANIC, D., Slavic Languages and Literature, and International Studies
KAPLAN, A., Music
KARTIGANER, D. M., English
KENAGY, G. J., Zoology
KEYES, C. F., Anthropology
KEYT, D., Philosophy
KINGSBURY, M., Art History
KLAUSENBURGER, J., Romance Languages and Literature
KLEE, V. M., Jr, Mathematics
KNAPP, J. S., Dance
KNECHTGES, D. R., Asian Languages and Literature
KOBLITZ, N., Mathematics
KOHN, A. J., Zoology
KORG, J., English
KOTTLER, H. W., Art
KOTTWITZ, R., Mathematics
KOWALSKI, B. R., Chemistry
KRUMME, G., Geography
KUHL, P. K., Speech and Hearing
KWIRAM, A. L., Chemistry
LADNER, R. E., Computer Science
LAIRD, C. D., Zoology
LANG, G. E., Communications, Political Science and Sociology
LANG, K., Communications
LARDY, N., International Studies
LAZOWSKA, E., Computer Science
LEGTERS, L. H., School of International Studies
LEOPOLD, E. B., Botany and Forest Resources
LEOVY, C. B., Atmospheric Sciences and Geophysics
LEV, D. S., Political Science
LEVI, M. A., Political Science
LEVY, F. J., History
LEWIS, B., Geophysics and Oceanography
LIND, D. A., Mathematics
LISTER, C. R. B., Geophysics and Oceanography
LOCKARD, J. S., Psychology and Neurosurgery
LOCKWOOD, T. F., English
LOFTUS, E. J., Psychology
LOFTUS, G. R., Psychology
LOPER, R. B., Drama
LORD, J. J., Physics
LUBATTI, H. J., Physics
LUJAN, H. D., Political Science
LUNDIN, N. K., Art

LUNDQUIST, B. R., Music
LUNNEBORG, C., Psychology and Statistics
MCCALLUM, I. S., Geological Sciences
MCCOLL, W. D., Music
MCCRACKEN, J. D., English
MCCRONE, D. J., Political Science
MCDERMOTT, L. C., Physics
MCDERMOTT, M. N., Physics
MCELROY, C. W., English
MCGEE, J. S., Economics
MCHUGH, H., English
MACKAY, P. A., Classics, Comparative Literature, Near Eastern Language and Civilization
MARGON, B., Astronomy
MARKS, C. E., Philosophy
MARLATT, G. A., Psychology
MARSHALL, D., Mathematics
MARSHALL, J. C., Art
MARTIN, R. D., Statistics
MATTHEWS, D. R., Political Science
MAYER, J., Geography
MELTZOFF, A., Psychology
MERRILL, R. T., Geophysics and Geological Sciences
MICHAEL, E. A., Mathematics
MICKLESEN, L. R., Slavic Languages and Literature, Linguistics and International Studies
MIGDAL, J. S., International Studies
MILLER, G., Physics
MILLER, R. A., Asian Languages and Literature
MINIFIE, F. D., Speech and Hearing Sciences
MITCHELL, T. R., Management and Organization and Psychology
MODELSKI, G., Political Science
MODIANO, R., English and Comparative Literature
MORRILL, R. L., Geography and Environmental Studies
MORROW, J. A., Mathematics
MOSELEY, S., Art
NAMIOKA, I., Mathematics
NASON, J. D., Anthropology
NELSON, C. R., Economics
NELSON, T. O., Psychology
NEUMAN, D. M., Art
NEWELL, L. L., Anthropology
NEWMEYER, F. J., Linguistics
NOE, J. D., Computer Science
NORMAN, J. G., Chemistry
NORMAN, J. L., Asian Languages and Literatures
NUNKE, R. J., Mathematics
NUTE, P. E., Anthropology
ODELL, G. M., Zoology
O'DOAN, N. D., Music
OLSON, D. J., Political Science
OPPERMAN, H. N., Art
ORIANS, G. H., Zoology and Environmental Studies
OSBORNE, M. S., Mathematics
OTTENBERG, S., Anthropology
PAINE, R. T., Jr, Zoology
PALAIS, J. B., International Studies and History
PALKA, J. M., Zoology
PALMER, J. M., Prosthodontics and Speech and Hearing Sciences
PARKS, G. K., Geophysics
PARKS, R. W., Economics
PASCAL, P., Classics
PEASE, O. A., History
PEMBER, D. R., Communication
PERLMAN, M. D., Statistics
PERRY, E., International Studies
PETERS, P. C., Physics
PHELPS, R. R., Mathematics
PIZZUTO, E., Art
POCKER, Y., Chemistry
PORTER, S. C., Geological Sciences
POTTER, K. H., International Studies and Philosophy
PRINS, D., Speech and Hearing Sciences

PUFF, R. D., Physics
PUNDT, G. H., Art and Architecture
PYKE, R., Mathematics
PYLE, K. B., International Studies and History
RAGOZIN, D., Mathematics
RAHN, J., Music
RAYMOND, C. F., Geophysics
REED, R., Atmospheric Sciences
REHR, J. J., Physics
REID, B. R., Chemistry
REINERT, O., English and Comparative Literature
RENSBERGER, J. M., Geological Sciences
RESHETAR, J. S., Jr, Political Science
RICHMAN, R. J., Philosophy
RIDDIFORD, L. M., Zoology
RIEDEL, E. K., Physics
ROCKAFELLAR, R. T., Mathematics
ROHWER, S. A., Zoology
RORABAUGH, W. J., History
ROSE, N. J., Chemistry
ROSSEL, S. H., Scandinavian Languages and Literatures
ROTHBERG, J. E., Physics
RUBIN, J., Asian Languages and Literatures
RUSS, J., English
RUTHERFOORD, J. P., Physics
RUZICKA, J., Chemistry
SACKETT, G. P., Psychology
SALE, R. H., English
SAPORTA, S., Linguistics and Romance Languages
SARASON, I. G., Psychology
SARASON, L., Mathematics
SAUM, L. O., History
SAX, G., Education
SCHEIDEL, T. M., Speech
SCHEINGOLD, S. A., Political Science
SCHICK, M., Physics
SCHIFFMAN, H. F., Asian Languages and Literatures
SCHMITT, D. R., Sociology
SCHOMAKER, V., Chemistry
SCHUBERT, W. M., Chemistry
SCHUBIGER, G. A., Zoology
SCHURR, J. M., Chemistry
SCHWARTZ, P., Sociology
SCOTT, J. W., American Ethnic Studies, Sociology
SEGAL, J., Mathematics
SHAW, A. C., Computer Science
SHORACK, G. R., Statistics
SHULMAN, R., English
SIKI, B., Music
SILBERBERG, E., Economics
SILBERGELD, J. L., Art
SIMONSON, H. P., English
SIMPSON, J. B., Psychology
SKOWRONEK, F. E., Music
SLUTSKY, L. J., Chemistry
SMITH, C. W., Art
SMITH, J. D., Oceanography, Geophysics and Geological Sciences
SMITH, R. E., Psychology
SMITH, S. W., Geophysics
SMITH, W. O., Music
SNYDER, L., Computer Science
SNYDER, R., Zoology
SPAFFORD, M. C., Art
STADLER, D. R., Genetics
STAMM, R. K., Communications
STARK, R., Sociology
STARYK, S. S., Music
STEELE, C. M., Psychology
STEENE, B., Scandinavian Languages and Literature and Comparative Literature
STERN, E. A., Physics
STEVICK, R. D., English
STORCH, L., Music
STOUT, E. L., Mathematics
STRATHMANN, R. R., Zoology
STREITBERGER, W., English
STUIVER, M., Geological Sciences

SUGAR, P. F., History and International Studies
SULLIVAN, J. B., Mathematics
SULLIVAN, W., Astronomy
SWINDLER, D. R., Anthropology
TANIMOTO, S. L., Computer Science
TAYLOR, M. J., Political Science
TELLER, D. Y., Psychology and Physiology
THOMAS, C. S., History
THOMAS, M. D., Geography
THOMPSON, E. A., Statistics
THOMPSON, G., Speech and Hearing Sciences
THORNTON, J., Economics
THOULESS, D. J., Physics
TOWNSEND, J. R., International Studies and Political Science
TREADGOLD, D. W., International Studies and History
TRUMAN, J. W., Zoology
TSUKADA, M., Botany
TUFTS, P. D., Music
UHLMANN, G. A., Mathematics
ULLMAN, J. C., History
UNTERSTEINER, N., Atmospheric Sciences and Geophysics
VAN DEN BERGHE, P. L., Sociology
VANDENBOSCH, R., Chemistry
VANDYCK, R. S., Physics
VELIKONJA, J., Geography
VILCHES, O. E., Physics
VOYLES, J. B., Germanics
WAALAND, J. R., Botany
WADDEN, D. J., Art
WAGER, L. W., Sociology
WAGONER, D. R., English
WALLACE, J. M., Atmospheric Sciences
WALLERSTEIN, G., Astronomy
WAN, F. Y., Applied Mathematics
WANG, C. H., Asian Languages and Literature and Comparative Literature
WARASHINA, P. B., Art
WARD, P., Geological Sciences
WARFIELD, R. B., Mathematics
WARNER, G. W., Jr, Mathematics
WATTS, R. O., Chemistry
WEBB, E., International Studies and Comparative Literature
WEIS, J. G., Sociology
WELLNER, J. A., Statistics
WESTWATER, M. J., Mathematics
WHISLER, H. C., Botany
WHITEHILL-WARD, J., Art
WILETS, L., Physics
WILEY, H., Dance
WILLEFORD, W., English and Comparative Literature
WILLIAMS, R. W., Physics
WILLOWS, A. O. D., Zoology
WILSON, W. R., Speech and Hearing Sciences
WINANS, E. V., Anthropology
WINGFIELD, J., Zoology
WITHERSPOON, G., Anthropology
WOODS, S. C., Psychology
YAMAMURA, K., International Studies
YANTIS, P. A., Speech and Hearing Sciences
YOUNG, K. K., Physics
YOUNG, P. R., Computer Science
ZOLLER, W. H., Chemistry

College of Education (POB 353600, Seattle, WA 98195-3600; e-mail coe@u.washington.edu; internet education.washington.edu):
ABBOTT, R. D.
AFFLECK, J. Q.
ANDERSON, R.
ANDREWS, R. L.
BANKS, J. A.
BILLINGSLEY, F. F.
BOLTON, D. L.
BRAMMER, L. M.
BURGESS, C. O.
BUTTERFIELD, E. C.
DOI, J. I.
EDGAR, E. B.

EVANS, E. D.
GOODLAD, J. I.
HARING, N. G.
HUNKINS, F. P.
JENKINS, J. R.
KALTSOUNIS, T.
KERR, D. H.
KERR, S. T.
KLOCKARS, A. J.
LIEBERMAN, A.
LOVITT, T. C.
LOWENBRAUN, S.
MCCARTIN, R. E.
MADSEN, D. L.
MORISHIMA, J. K.
NEEL, R. S.
OLSTAD, R. G.
PECKHAM, P. D.
RYCKMAN, D. B.
SAX, G.
SCHILL, W. J.
SEBESTA, S. L.
THOMPSON, M. D.
TOSTBERG, R. E.
WHITE, O.
WINN, W. D.

College of Engineering (371 Loew Hall, Box 352180, Seattle, WA 98195-2180; tel. (206) 543-0340; e-mail coeinfo@u.washington.edu; internet www.engr.washington.edu):
AKSAY, I. A., Materials Science Engineering
ALBRECHT, R. W., Electrical and Nuclear Engineering
ALEXANDER, D. E., Mechanical Engineering
ALEXANDRO, F., Electrical Engineering
ALLAN, G. G., Forest Resources and Chemical Engineering
ANDERSEN, J., Electrical Engineering
ARCHBOLD, T. F., Mining, Metallurgical and Ceramic Engineering
BABB, A. L., Chemical and Nuclear Engineering
BALISE, P. L., Mechanical Engineering
BEREANO, P., Interdepartmental Curricular Programme
BERG, J. C., Chemical Engineering
BOGAN, R. H., Civil Engineering
BOLLARD, R. J. H., Aeronautics and Astronautics
BOWEN, J. R., Chemical Engineering
BRADT, R. C., Mining, Metallurgical and Ceramic Engineering
BROWN, C. B., Civil Engineering
BURGES, S. J., Civil Engineering
CHALUPNIK, J. D., Mechanical Engineering
CHEUNG, P. W., Electrical Engineering and Bioengineering
CHRISTIANSEN, W. H., Aeronautics and Astronautics
CLARK, R. N., Electrical Engineering
COLCORD, J. E., Civil Engineering
CORLETT, R. C., Mechanical Engineering
DALY, N., Mechanical Engineering
DAVIS, E. J., Chemical Engineering
DECHER, R., Aeronautics and Astronautics
DEPEW, C. A., Mechanical Engineering
DOW, D. G., Electrical Engineering
ELIAS, Z. M., Civil Engineering
EMERY, A. F., Mechanical Engineering
EVANS, R. J., Civil Engineering
FERGUSON, J. F., Civil Engineering
FINLAYSON, B. A., Chemical Engineering
FISCHBACH, D. B., Materials Science and Engineering
FYFE, I. M., Aeronautics and Astronautics
GARLID, K. L., Chemical and Nuclear Engineering
GESSNER, F., Mechanical Engineering
HARALICK, R. M., Electrical Engineering
HAWKINS, N. M., Civil Engineering
HEIDEGER, W. J., Chemical Engineering
HERTZBERG, A., Aeronautics and Astronautics

HOFFMAN, A. S., Chemical Engineering and Bioengineering
HOLDEN, A., Electrical Engineering
HOLSAPPLE, K. A., Aeronautics and Astronautics
HSU, C.-C., Electrical Engineering
ISHIMARU, A., Electrical Engineering
JOHNSON, D. E., Bioengineering
JOHNSON, D. L., Electrical Engineering
JOPPA, R. G., Aeronautics and Astronautics
JORGENSEN, J. E., Mechanical Engineering
KEVORKIAN, J. K., Aeronautics and Astronautics
KIPPENHAM, C. J., Mechanical Engineering
KOBAYASHI, A. S., Mechanical Engineering
KOSALY, G., Nuclear and Mechanical Engineering
KUROSAKA, M., Aeronautics and Astronautics
LAURITZEN, P. O., Electrical Engineering
LYTLE, D. W., Electrical Engineering
McCORMICK, N. J., Nuclear Engineering
McKEAN, W. T., Chemical Engineering and Forest Resources
MALTE, P. C., Mechanical Engineering
MAR, B. W., Civil Engineering
MARKS, R. J., Electrical Engineering
MATTOCK, A. H., Civil Engineering
MEDITCH, J. S., Electrical Engineering
MONTGOMERY, D. C., Industrial Engineering
MORITZ, W. E., Electrical Engineering
NECE, R. E., Civil Engineering
NIHAN, N. L., Civil Engineering
NOGES, E., Electrical Engineering
PARMETER, R. R., Aeronautics and Astronautics
PEARSON, C. E., Aeronautics and Astronautics, Applied Mathematics
PEDEN, I., Electrical Engineering
PILAT, M. J., Civil Engineering
PINTER, R. E., Electrical Engineering
POLONIS, D. H., Mining, Metallurgical and Ceramic Engineering
PORTER, R. P., Electrical Engineering
PRATT, D. T., Mechanical Engineering
RAO, Y. K., Mining, Metallurgical and Ceramics Engineering
RATNER, B., Bioengineering and Chemical Engineering
RIBE, F. L., Nuclear Engineering
RILEY, J., Mechanical Engineering
ROBKIN, M. A., Nuclear Engineering
ROEDER, C. W., Civil Engineering
RUSSELL, D. A., Aeronautics and Astronautics
SCHNEIDER, J. B., Urban Planning and Civil Engineering
SCOTT, W. D., Mining, Metallurgical and Ceramic Engineering
SEFERIS, J. C., Chemical Engineering
SIGELMANN, R. A., Electrical Engineering
SLEICHER, C. A., Jr, Chemical Engineering
SPINDEL, R. C., Electrical Engineering
STEAR, E. B., Electrical Engineering
STENSEL, H. D., Civil Engineering
STOEBE, T. G., Mining, Metallurgical and Ceramic Engineering
TAGGART, R., Mechanical Engineering
TSANG, L., Electrical Engineering
VAGNERS, J., Aeronautics and Astronautics
VENKATA, S. S., Electrical Engineering
VERESS, S. A., Civil Engineering
VESPER, K. H., Mechanical Engineering and Management and Organization, Marine Studies
VLASES, G. C., Nuclear Engineering
WELCH, E. B., Civil Engineering
WOLAK, J., Mechanical Engineering
WOODRUFF, G. L., Nuclear Engineering
YEE, S. S., Electrical Engineering
ZICK, G. L., Electrical Engineering

College of Forest Resources:
ADAMS, D. M.
AGEE, J. K.

ALLAN, G. G., Forest Resources and Chemical Engineering
BARE, B. B.
BETHEL, J. S.
BRUBAKER, L. B.
COLE, D. W.
DOWDLE, B.
EDMONDS, R. L.
FIELD, D. R.
FRITSCHEN, L. J.
GARA, R. I.
HATHEWAY, W. H.
HINCKLEY, T. M.
HRUTFIORD, B. F.
LEE, R. G.
MANUWAL, D. A.
OLIVER, C.
PICKFORD, S. G.
SARKENEN, K., Forest Resources and Chemical Engineering
SCHREUDER, G. F.
SHARPE, G. W.
STETTLER, R. F.
THORUD, D. B.
TUKEY, H. B.
UGOLINI, F. C.
WAGGENER, T. R.
WOTT, J. A.

College of Ocean and Fishery Science
School of Oceanography:
BANSE, K.
CARPENTER, R.
COACHMAN, L.
CREAGER, H. S.
DELANEY, J.
EMERSON, S.
ERIKSEN, C.
FROST, B. W.
HEATH, G. R.
HEDGES, J.
HERSHMAN, M. J.
JUMARS, P. A.
LEWIS, B.
LISTER, C. R. B.
McMANUS, D. A.
MERRILL, R. T.
MILES, E. L.
MURPHY, S. R.
MURRAY, J.
NOWELL, A. R. M.
RHINES, P. B.
RICHARDS, F. A.
SMITH, J. D.
STERNBERG, R. W.
WELANDER, P.
WINTER, D. R.
WOOSTER, W. S.

School of Fisheries:
BRANNON, E. L.
BROWN, G. W.
CHEW, K. K.
FORD, E. D.
FRANCIS, R. C.
GALLUCCI, V. F.
HALVER, J. D.
HILBORN, R. W.
LANDOLT, M.
LISTON, J.
MATCHES, J. R.
MATHEWS, S. B.
MILLER, B. S.
PIETSCH, T. W.
PIGOTT, G. M.
SCHELL, W. R.
SMITH, L. S.
STICKNEY, R. R.
TAUB, F.
WHITNEY, R. R.

Graduate School of Library and Information Science:
CHISHOLM, M. E.

Graduate School of Public Affairs:
DENNY, B. C.

KROLL, M., Public Affairs and Political Science
LOCKE, H. G.
LYDEN, F. J.
WILLIAMS, W.
ZERBE, R. O.

School of Business:
ALBERTS, W. W., Finance, Business Economics and Quantitative Methods
BOURQUE, P. J., Finance, Business Economics and Quantitative Methods
CHIU, J. S. Y., Management Science
D'AMBROSIO, C. A., Finance, Business Economics
DUKES, R. E., Accounting
ETCHESON, W. W., Marketing
FAALAND, B. H., Finance, Business Economics and Quantitative Methods
FROST, P. A., Finance, Business Economics and Quantitative Methods
HALEY, C. W., Finance, Business Economics and Quantitative Methods
HEATH, L. C., Accounting
HENNING, D. A., Management and Organization
HESS, A. C., Finance, Business Economics and Quantitative Methods
HIGGINS, R. C., Finance, Business Economics and Quantitative Methods
INGENE, C., Marketing and International Business
JACOB, N. L., Finance, Business Economics and Quantitative Methods
JIAMBALVO, J., Accounting
JOHANSSON, J. K., Marketing, Transportation, and International Business
JOHNSON, D. W., Finance, Business Economics and Quantitative Methods
KLASTORIN, T., Management Science
KNUDSON, H. R., Management and Organization
LATHAM, G., Management and Organization
MacLACHLAN, D. L., Marketing
MITCHELL, T. R., Management and Organization
MOINPOUR, R., Marketing, Transportation and International Business
MUELLER, G. G., Accounting
NARVER, J. C., Marketing, Transportation and International Business
NEWELL, W. T., Management and Organization, Management Science
NOREEN, E. W., Accounting
PAGE, A. N., Finance, Business Economics and Quantitative Methods
PETERSON, R. B., Finance, Business Economics and Quantitative Methods
RAMANATHAN, K. V., Accounting
ROLEY, V. V., Finance and Business Economics
SAXBERG, B. O., Management and Organization
SCHALL, L. D., Finance, Business Economics and Quantitative Methods
SCOTT, W. G., Management and Organization
SPRATLEN, T. H., Marketing, Transportation and International Business
SUMMER, C. E., Management and Organization
SUNDEM, G. L., Accounting
WHEATLEY, J. J., Marketing, Transportation and International Business
YALCH, R., Marketing

School of Dentistry (D322 Health Sciences Bldg, Box 356365, Seattle, WA 98195-6365; internet www.dental.washington.edu):
AMMONS, W. F., Periodontics
BOLENDER, C. L., Prosthodontics
BRUDVIK, J. S., Prosthodontics
CANFIELD, R. C., Restorative Dentistry
CLAGETT, J. A., Periodontics and Microbiology

CONRAD, D. A., Dental Public Health Sciences and Health Services
DERONEN, T. A., Dental Public Health Services, Biostatistics
DWORKIN, S. F., Oral Surgery
ENGEL, D., Periodontics
FRANK, R. P., Prosthodontics
GEHRIG, J. D., Oral Surgery
HARRINGTON, G. W., Endodontics
JOHNSON, R. H., Periodontics
KOKICH, V., Orthodontics
LEWIS, T. M., Restorative Dentistry
LITTLE, R. M., Orthodontics
MILGROM, P. M., Dental Public Health Services
MOFFETT, B. C., Orthodontics
MYALL, R. W., Oral Surgery
NATKIN, E., Endodontics
NICHOLLS, J. I., Restorative Dentistry
OMNELL, K.-A., Oral Medicine
PAGE, R. C., Pathology and Periodontics
PALMER, J. M., Speech and Hearing Sciences and Prosthodontics
ROBINOVITCH, M. R., Oral Biology
SHAPIRO, P., Orthodontics
SMITH, D. E., Prosthodontics
TAMARIN, A., Oral Biology
WARNICK, M. E., Restorative Dentistry
WORTHINGTON, P., Oral and Maxillofacial Surgery
YUODELIS, R. A., Restorative Dentistry

School of Law (William H. Gates Hall, Box 353020, Seattle, WA 98195-3020; tel. (206) 543-2100; e-mail lawadm@uw.edu; internet www.law.washington.edu):

ANDERSON, W. R.
ARONSON, R. H.
BURKE, W. T.
CHISUM, D. S.
FITZPATRICK, J. F.
FLETCHER, R. L.
HALEY, J. O.
HARDISTY, J. H.
HAZELTON, P. A.
HENDERSON, D. F.
HJORTH, R. L.
HUME, L. S.
HUSTON, J. C.
JAY, S. M.
JOHNSON, R. W.
JUNKER, J. M.
KUMMERT, R. O.
LOH, W. D.
MORRIS, A.
PECK, C. J.
PRICE, J. R.
PROSTERMAN, R. L.
RODDIS, R. S.
RODGERS, W. H.
ROMBAUER, M.
SMITH, F. W., Jr
STOEBUCK, W. B.
TRAUTMAN, P. A.

School of Medicine (325 Ninth Ave, Seattle, WA 98104-2499; tel. (206) 744-3000; internet uwmedicine.washington.edu):

ABELSON, H. T., Paediatrics
ABRASS, I., Medicine
ADAMSON, J. W., Medicine
ALBERT, R., Medicine
ALMERS, W., Physiology and Biophysics
ALVORD, E. C., Pathology
ANDERSON, M. E., Rehabilitation Medicine and Physiology
ANSELL, J. S., Urology
APPELBAUM, F., Medicine
BARNES, G. W., Urology
BASSINGTHWAIGHTE, J. B., Bioengineering
BEAVO, J., Pharmacology
BECKER, J., Psychiatry, Psychology
BELKNAP, B. H., Medicine
BENEDETTI, T. J., Obstetrics and Gynaecology
BEN-MENACHEM, Y., Radiology
BERGER, A. J., Physiology and Biophysics

BERGMAN, A. B., Paediatrics
BERNSTEIN, I. D., Paediatrics
BIERMAN, E. L., Medicine
BINDER, M., Physiology and Biophysics
BIRD, T., Medicine
BLACKMON, J. R., Medicine
BLAGG, C. R., Medicine
BLEYER, W. A., Paediatrics
BORNSTEIN, P., Medicine and Biochemistry
BOWDEN, D. M., Psychiatry
BREMNER, W. J., Medicine
BRENGELMANN, G., Physiology and Biophysics
BROWN, B. G., Medicine
BRUNZELL, J. D., Medicine
BUCHANAN, T. M., Medicine and Pathobiology
BUCKNER, C. D., Medicine
BUNT-MILAM, A. H., Ophthalmology
BUTLER, J., Medicine
BYERS, P., Medicine and Pathology
CARR, J. E., Psychiatry and Psychology
CARRICO, C. J., Surgery
CATTERALL, W. A., Pharmacology
CHAIT, A., Medicine
CHAMPOUX, J. J., Microbiology
CHAPMAN, C. R., Anaesthesiology and Psychiatry
CHAPMAN, W. H., Urology
CHATRIAN, G. E., Laboratory Medicine and Neurological Surgery
CHEEVER, M. A., Medicine
CHENEY, F. W., Anaesthesiology
CHESNUT, C. H., Radiology and Medicine
CLARREN, S., Paediatrics
COBB, L. A., Medicine
COPASS, M. K., Medicine
COREY, L., Laboratory Medicine and Microbiology
COUNTS, G. W., Medicine
COUSER, W. G., Medicine
CRILL, W. E., Medicine, Physiology and Biophysics
CROAKE, J. S., Psychiatry
CULLEN, B. F., Anaesthesiology
CUMMINGS, C. W., Otolaryngology
DALE, D. C., Medicine
DAVIE, E. W., Biochemistry
DEISHER, R. W., Paediatrics
DELATEUR, B. J., Rehabilitation Medicine
DETTER, J. C., Laboratory Medicine
DETWILER, P., Physiology and Biophysics
DILLARD, D. H., Surgery
DOBIE, R. A., Otolaryngology
DODGE, H. T., Medicine
DODRILL, C. B., Neurological Surgery
DOERR, H. O., Psychiatry and Psychology
DOHNER, C. W., Medicine and Education
DONALDSON, J. A., Otolaryngology
DUNNER, D. L., Psychiatry
EISENBERG, M., Medicine
EMANUEL, I., Epidemiology and International Health and Paediatrics
ENSINCK, J. W., Medicine
ESCHENBACH, D., Obstetrics and Gynaecology
EYRE, D. R., Orthopaedics
FARRELL, D. F., Medicine
FEFER, A., Medicine
FEIGL, E., Physiology and Biophysics
FETZ, E. E., Physiology and Biophysics
FIALKOW, P. J., Medicine and Genetics
FIGGE, D. C., Obstetrics and Gynaecology
FIGLEY, M. M., Radiology
FISCHER, E. H., Biochemistry
FRENCH, J. W., Paediatrics
FUCHS, A., Physiology and Biophysics
FUJIMOTO, W. Y., Medicine
GARTLER, S. M., Medicine and Genetics
GEYMAN, J. P., Family Medicine
GILLILAND, B., Laboratory Medicine and Medicine
GLOMSET, J. A., Medicine and Biochemistry
GODWIN, J. D., Radiology
GOLDMAN, M. L., Radiology
GOODNER, C. J., Medicine

GORDON, A. M., Physiology and Biophysics
GORDON, M., Biochemistry
GRAHAM, C. B., Radiology and Paediatrics
GREENBERG, P., Medicine
GREENE, H. L., Medicine
GREER, B. E., Obstetrics and Gynaecology
GRIFFIN, T. W., Radiation Oncology
GROMAN, N. B., Microbiology
GROUDINE, M., Radiation Oncology
GUNTHEROTH, W. G., Paediatrics
GUY, A., Rehabilitation Medicine and Bioengineering
HAGGITT, R. C., Pathology
HAKOMORI, S., Pathobiology and Microbiology
HALAR, E. M., Rehabilitation Medicine
HANDSFIELD, H. H., Medicine
HANSEN, J. A., Medicine
HANSEN, S., Orthopaedics
HARLEY, J. D., Radiology
HARRIS, A. B., Neurological Surgery
HAUSCHKA, S. D., Biochemistry
HAYDEN, P., Paediatrics
HEIMAN, J., Psychiatry and Behavioural Sciences
HEIMBACH, D. M., Surgery
HELLSTROM, I. E., Microbiology
HELLSTROM, K. E., Pathology
HENDERSON, M., Medicine and Epidemiology
HENDRICKSON, A. E., Ophthalmology and Biological Structure
HERMAN, C. M., Surgery
HILDEBRANDT, J., Physiology and Medicine
HILLE, B., Physiology and Biophysics
HLASTALA, M. P., Physiology and Biophysics and Medicine
HODSON, W. A., Paediatrics
HOLBROOK, K. A., Biological Structure
HOLMES, K. K., Medicine
HORITA, A., Pharmacology
HORNBEIN, T. F., Anaesthesiology, Physiology and Biophysics
HUDSON, L. D., Medicine
HUNTSMAN, L. L., Bioengineering
INUI, T. S., Medicine and Health Services
IVEY, T. D., Surgery
JOHANSEN, K. H., Surgery
JOHNSON, R. H., Psychiatry
JONES, R. F., Surgery
JONSEN, A. R., Medical History and Ethics
JUCHAU, M. R., Pharmacology
KALINA, R. E., Ophthalmology
KEHL, T. H., Physiology, Biophysics and Computer Science
KELLY, W. A., Neurological Surgery
KENNEDY, J. W., Medicine
KENNY, M. A., Laboratory Medicine
KLEBANOFF, S. J., Medicine
KNOPP, R. H., Medicine
KOEHLER, J. K., Biological Structure
KOERKER, D. J., Physiology and Biophysics and Medicine
KRAFT, G. H., Rehabilitation Medicine
KREBS, E. G., Pharmacology and Biochemistry
KROHN, K., Radiology
LABBE, R. F., Laboratory Medicine
LAKSHMINARAYAN, S., Medicine
LANDESMAN, S., Psychiatry
LARAMORE, G., Radiation Oncology
LARSON, E., Medicine
LEHMANN, J. F., Rehabilitation Medicine
LEIN, J. N., Obstetrics and Gynaecology
LEMIRE, R. J., Paediatrics
LIVINGSTON, R. B., Medicine
LOCKARD, J. S., Neurological Surgery
LOEB, L. A., Pathology
LOESER, J. B., Neurological Surgery
LOGERFO, J. P., Medicine and Health Services
LOOP, J. W., Radiology
LUFT, J. H., Biological Structure
McARTHUR, J. R., Medicine
McDONALD, G. B., Medicine
MACK, L. A., Radiology

MACKLER, B., Paediatrics
MANNIK, M., Medicine
MARAVILLA, K. R., Radiology and Neurological Surgery
MARCHIORO, T. L., Surgery
MARTIN, G. M., Pathology
MARTIN, J. C., Psychiatry
MATSEN, F. A., Orthopaedics
MAYO, M. E., Urology
MEYERS, J., Medicine
MILLS, R. P., Ophthalmology
MONSEN, E. R., Medicine
MORRIS, D. R., Biochemistry
MOSS, A. A., Radiology
MOTTET, N. K., Pathology and Environmental Health
MOTULSKY, A., Genetics and Medicine
MURPHY, T. M., Anaesthesiology
NEFF, J. M., Paediatrics
NEIMAN, P. E., Medicine
NELP, W. B., Medicine and Radiology
NELSON, J. A., Radiology
NESTER, E. W., Microbiology
NORWOOD, T., Pathology
NOVACK, A. H., Paediatrics
OCHS, H. D., Paediatrics
ODLAND, G. F., Medicine, Biological Structure
OJEMANN, G. A., Neurological Surgery
OMENN, G. S., Medicine and Environmental Health
PAGE, R. C., Pathology and Periodontics
PALMER, J., Medicine
PALMITER, R. D., Biochemistry
PAPAYANNOPOULOU, T., Medicine
PARSON, W. W., Biochemistry
PAULSEN, C. A., Medicine
PETRA, P. H., Obstetrics and Gynaecology and Biochemistry
PHILLIPS, T. J., Family Medicine
PIERSON, D., Medicine
PIOUS, D. A., Paediatrics
PLORDE, J. J., Laboratory Medicine
POLLACK, G. H., Bioengineering
POPE, C. E., Medicine
PORTE, D., Medicine
PRESTON, T. A., Medicine
PRINZ, P., Psychiatry
RAISYS, V., Laboratory Medicine
RASEY, J. S., Radiation Oncology
RASKIND, M. A., Psychiatry
RAUSCH, R. L., Animal Medicine and Pathobiology
REICHENBACH, D. D., Pathology
REICHLER, R. J., Psychiatry
REID, B. R., Biochemistry and Chemistry
RICE, C. L., Surgery
RITCHIE, J. L., Medicine
ROBERTS, T. S., Neurological Surgery
ROBERTSON, W. O., Paediatrics
ROBINSON, N. L., Psychiatry
RODIECK, R. W., Ophthalmology
ROHRMAN, C. A., Radiology
ROOS, B. A., Medicine
ROSENBLATT, R. A., Family Medicine
ROSS, R., Pathology
ROSSE, C., Biological Structure
ROWELL, L. B., Physiology and Biophysics
RUBELL, E. W., Otolaryngology
RUBIN, C. E., Medicine
RUVALCABA, R., Paediatrics
SAARI, J. C., Ophthalmology and Biochemistry
SALE, G., Pathology
SAUNDERS, D. R., Medicine
SCHER, A. M., Physiology and Biophysics
SCHMER, G., Laboratory Medicine
SCHOENKNECHT, F. D., Laboratory Medicine and Microbiology
SCHUFFLER, M., Medicine
SCHWARTZ, S. M., Pathology
SCHWARTZKROIN, P., Neurological Surgery and Physiology, Biophysics
SCHWINDT, P. C., Physiology and Biophysics
SCOTT, C. R., Paediatrics

SCRIBNER, B. H., Medicine
SELLS, C. J., Paediatrics
SHAPIRO, B. M., Biochemistry
SHAW, C., Pathology
SHEPARD, T. H., Paediatrics
SHERRARD, D. J., Medicine
SHERRIS, J. C., Microbiology
SHURTLEFF, D. B., Paediatrics
SILVERSTEIN, F., Medicine
SIMKIN, P. A., Medicine
SINGER, J., Medicine
SLICHTER, S., Medicine
SMITH, A. L., Paediatrics
SMITH, O. A., Jr, Physiology and Biophysics
SNYDER, J. M., Otolaryngology
SOULES, M. R., Obstetrics and Gynaecology
SPADONI, L. R., Obstetrics and Gynaecology
SPENCE, A. M., Medicine
STAHELI, L. T., Orthopaedics
STAHL, W., Medicine, Physiology and Biophysics
STALEY, J. T., Microbiology
STAMATOYANNOPOULOS, G., Medicine
STAMM, W., Medicine
STEINER, R., Obstetrics and Gynaecology, Physiology and Biophysics
STENCHEVER, M. A., Obstetrics and Gynaecology
STEVENSON, J. G., Paediatrics
STIRLING, C. E., Physiology and Biophysics
STOLOV, W. C., Rehabilitation Medicine
STORM, D. R., Pharmacology
STRANDJORD, P. E., Laboratory Medicine
STRANDNESS, D. E., Surgery
STREISSGUTH, A. P., Psychiatry
SUMI, S. M., Medicine and Pathology
SWANSON, P. D., Medicine
TAPPER, D., Surgery
TELLER, D. C., Biochemistry
TELLER, D. Y., Physiology and Psychology
THOMAS, E. D., Medicine
THOMPSON, A. R., Medicine
TOWE, A. L., Physiology and Biophysics
TOWNES, B. D., Psychiatry
TRIER, W. C., Surgery
TRUOG, W. E., Paediatrics
TUCKER, G. J., Psychiatry
TURCK, M., Medicine
VANARSDEL, P. P., Medicine
VAN CITTERS, R. L., Physiology and Biophysics, Medicine
VANHOOSIER, G. L., Animal Medicine
VESTAL, R., Medicine
VINCENZI, F. F., Pharmacology
VONTVER, L., Obstetrics and Gynaecology
VRACKO, R., Pathology
WALKER, R. D., Psychiatry and Behavioural Science
WALLACE, J. F., Medicine
WALSH, K. A., Biochemistry
WARD, R. J., Anaesthesiology
WEDGWOOD, R. J., Paediatrics
WESTRUM, L. E., Neurological Surgery and Biological Structure
WEYMULLER, E. A., Otolaryngology
WHITELEY, H. R., Microbiology
WHORTON, J. C., Biomedical History
WIGHT, T., Pathology
WINN, H. R., Neurological Surgery
WINTERSCHEID, L. C., Surgery
WOODRUM, D. E., Paediatrics
WOOTON, P., Radiation Oncology
YOUNG, E. T., Biochemistry
ZAGER, R., Medicine

School of Nursing (Box 357260, Seattle, WA 98195; tel. (206) 543-8736; internet nursing .uw.edu):

BARNARD, K. E., Parent and Child Nursing
BATEY, M. V., Community Health Care Systems
BENOLIEL, J. Q., Community Health Care Systems
CHRISMAN, N. J., Community Health Care Systems

DE TORNYAY, R., Community Health Care Systems
EYRES, S. J., Parent and Child Nursing
GALLUCCI, B. J., Physiological Nursing
GOERTZEN, I. E., Community Health Care Systems
HORN, B. J., Community Health Care Systems
HEGYVARY, S. T., Community Health Care Systems
KOGAN, H., Psychosocial Nursing
KURAMOTO, A., Physiological Nursing
LEWIS, F. M., Community Health Care Systems
MITCHELL, P. H., Physiological Nursing
OSBORNE, O. H., Psychosocial Nursing
PATRICK, M. I., Physiological Nursing
ROSE, M. H., Parent and Child Nursing
WOLF-WILETS, V. C., Psychosocial Nursing
WOODS, N. A., Physiological Nursing

School of Pharmacy (Box 357631, H362 Health Sciences Bldg, Seattle, WA 98195-7631; tel. (206) 543-6100; e-mail pharminf@ uw.edu; internet sop.washington.edu):

BAILLIE, T., Medicinal Chemistry
BRADY, L. R., Medicinal Chemistry
CAMPBELL, W. H., Pharmacy Practice
GIBALDI, M., Pharmaceutics
KRADJAN, W., Pharmacy Practice
LEVY, R. H., Pharmaceutics
NELSON, S. D., Medicinal Chemistry
NELSON, W. L., Medicinal Chemistry
PLEIN, J. B., Pharmacy Practice
TRAGER, W. F., Medicinal Chemistry

School of Public Health and Community Medicine (Box 357230, Seattle, WA 98195; tel. (206) 543-1144; e-mail publichealth@uw .edu; internet sph.washington.edu):

BRESLOW, N. E., Biostatistics
BUCHANAN, T. L., Pathobiology and Medicine
CROWLEY, J. J., Biostatistics
DALING, J. R., Epidemiology
DAVIS, K. A., Biostatistics
DAY, R. W., Health Services
DE ROUEN, T., Biostatistics
DIEHR, P. K., Biostatistics
EMANUEL, I., Epidemiology and Paediatrics
FEIGL, P., Biostatistics
FISHER, L. D., Biostatistics
FLEMING, T. R., Biostatistics
FOY, H. M., Epidemiology
GALE, J. I., Epidemiology
GRAYSTON, J. T., Epidemiology
HAKOMORI, S., Pathobiology and Microbiology
HENDERSON, M. M., Epidemiology and Medicine
INUI, T. S., Health Services and Medicine
JACKSON, K. L., Environmental Health
KENNY, G. E., Pathobiology
KOEPSELL, T., Health Services, Epidemiology
KRONMAL, R. A., Biostatistics
KUO, C.-C., Pathobiology
LEE, J. A., Environmental Health
LOGERFO, J. P., Health Services and Medicine
MARTIN, D. C., Biostatistics
MOOLGAVKAR, S. H., Epidemiology
MOTTET, N. K., Environmental Health and Pathology
MURPHY, S. D., Environmental Health
OMENN, G. S., Environmental Health and Medicine
PATRICK, D. L., Health Services
PERINE, P. L., Epidemiology
PERRIN, E. B., Health Services
PETERSON, A. V., Biostatistics
PRENTICE, R. L., Biostatistics
RAUSCH, R. L., Pathobiology
ROBKIN, M. A., Environmental Health and Nuclear Engineering
THOMAS, D. B., Epidemiology
VAN BELLE, G., Biostatistics

WAGNER, E. H., Health Services
WAHL, P. W., Biostatistics
WANG, S., Pathobiology
WEISS, N. S., Epidemiology
WILSON, J. T., Environmental Health
WORTHINGTON-ROBERTS, B., Epidemiology

School of Social Work (Box 354900, Seattle, WA 98195-4900; tel. (206) 543-5640; internet socialwork.uw.edu):

BRIAR, S.
GOTTLIEB, N. R.
HAWKINS, J. D.
JAFFEE, B.
LEVY, R. L.
PATTI, R. J.
RESNICK, H.
TAKAGI, C. Y.
WHITTAKER, J. K.

WALLA WALLA UNIVERSITY

204 S College Ave, College Place, WA 99324
Telephone: (509) 527-2615
E-mail: info@wallawalla.edu
Internet: www.wallawalla.edu
Founded 1892 as Walla Walla College, current name adopted 2007
Private control
Academic year: September to June
Campuses at Anacortes (WA), Billings, Missoula (MT), Portland (OR)
Pres.: JOHN K. MCVAY
Vice-Pres. for Academic Admin.: GINGER KETTING-WELLER
Vice-Pres. for Financial Admin.: STEVE ROSE
Vice-Pres. for Marketing and Enrolment Services: JODI WAGNER
Vice-Pres. for Student Life and Mission: KEN ROGERS
Vice-Pres. for Univ. Advancement: PATSY WAGNER
Registrar: CAROLYN DENNEY
Dir for Libraries: CAROLYN GASKELL
Library of 190,000 vols, 3,000 current periodicals
Number of teachers: 210 (115 full-time, 95 part-time)
Number of students: 1,865

WASHINGTON STATE UNIVERSITY

POB 641227, Pullman, WA 99164-5910
Telephone: (509) 335-3564
E-mail: presidentsoffice@wsu.edu
Internet: www.wsu.edu
Founded 1890 as Washington Agricultural College and School of Science, univ. status 1959
State control
Academic year: August to May
Pres.: Dr ELSON S. FLOYD
Provost and Exec. Vice-Pres.: WARWICK M. BAYLY
Vice-Pres. for Business and Finance: ROGER PATTERSON
Vice-Pres. for Information Services and Chief Information Officer: VIJI MURALI
Vice-Pres. for Student Affairs and Enrolment Management: JOHN FRAIRE
Chancellor for Spokane Campus: BRIAN PITCHER
Chancellor for Tri-Cities Campus: VICKY CARWEIN
Chancellor for Vancouver Campus: HAROLD DENGERINK
Registrar: JULIA POMERENK
Dean for Libraries: JAY STARRATT
Library of 2,178,040 vols
Number of teachers: 1,650
Number of students: 27,327
Publications: *ESQ: A Journal of the American Renaissance* (3 a year), *LandEscapes, Western Journal of Black Studies* (4 a year)

DEANS

College of Agriculture, Human and Natural Resource Sciences: DANIEL I. BERNARDO
College of Business: Dr ERIC SPANGENBERG
College of Education: A. G. RUD
College of Engineering and Architecture: CANDIS CLAIBORN
College of Liberal Arts: DOUGLAS EPPERSON
College of Nursing: PATRICIA BUTTERFIELD
College of Pharmacy: GARY M. POLLACK
College of Sciences: Dr DARYLL B. DEWALD
College of Veterinary Medicine: BRYAN K. SLINKER
Edward R. Murrow College of Communication: LAWRENCE PINTAK
Graduate School: HOWARD D. GRIMES
Honors College: Dr LIBBY WALKER

WESTERN WASHINGTON UNIVERSITY

516 High St, Bellingham, WA 98225
Telephone: (360) 650-3000
E-mail: admit@cc.wwu.edu
Internet: www.wwu.edu
Founded 1893 as Bellingham Normal School, current name adopted 1977
Academic year: September to June
Pres.: BRUCE SHEPARD
Provost and Vice-Pres. for Academic Affairs: Dr BRENT CARBAJAL
Vice-Pres. for Business and Financial Affairs: Dr RICHARD VAN DEN HUL
Vice-Pres. for Enrolment and Student Services: Dr EILEEN V. COUGHLIN
Vice-Pres. for External Affairs: ROBERT EDIE
Vice-Pres. for Univ. Advancement: STEPHANIE BOWERS
Dean for Libraries: CHRISTOPHER COX
Library: 1.4m. vols
Number of teachers: 615
Number of students: 15,000
Publications: *Bellingham Review* (literary, 2 a year), *Journal of Cross-Cultural Psychology* (int., 1 a year), *Journal of Rural Sociology* (1 a year), *Northwest Journal of Business and Economics* (1 a year), *Studies in American Indian Literature* (4 a year)

DEANS

College of Business and Economics: CRAIG DUNN
College of Fine and Performing Arts: DAN GUYETTE
College of Humanities and Social Sciences: Dr BRENT CARBAJAL
College of Sciences and Technology: JEFF WRIGHT
Fairhaven College of Interdisciplinary Studies: Prof. ROGER GILMAN
Huxley College of the Environment: Dr BRADLEY F. SMITH
Woodring College of Education: Dr FRANCISCO RIOS

WHITMAN COLLEGE

345 Boyer Ave, Walla Walla, WA 99362
Telephone: (509) 527-5111
E-mail: communication@whitman.edu
Internet: www.whitman.edu
Founded 1882
Private control
Academic year: August to May (2 semesters)
Pres.: Dr GEORGE BRIDGES
Provost and Dean for Faculty: PAT SPENCER
Vice-Pres. for Devt and College Relations: JOHN W. BOGLEY
Dean for Admission and Financial Aid: TONY CABASCO
Dean for Students: CHARLES E. CLEVELAND
Registrar: RONALD F. URBAN
College Librarian: DALIA CORKRUM

Library of 400,000 vols (incl. 3,500 linear ft archival and MSS and over 5,000 rare books), 21,000 journals
Number of teachers: 100 full-time
Number of students: 1,600

WHITWORTH UNIVERSITY

300 W Hawthorne Rd, Spokane, WA 99251
Telephone: (509) 777-1000
Internet: www.whitworth.edu
Founded 1890
Private control
Pres.: Dr BECK A. TAYLOR
Vice-Pres. for Academic Affairs: Dr MICHAEL K. LEROY
Dir for Admissions: MARIANNE HANSEN
Library Dir: Dr HANS BYNAGLE
Library of 176,000 vols
Number of teachers: 155 full-time
Number of students: 3,000

WEST VIRGINIA

ALDERSON-BROADDUS COLLEGE

101 College Hill Dr., Philippi, WV 26416
Telephone: (304) 457-1700
Internet: www.ab.edu
Founded 1932 by merger of Broaddus College (f. 1871) with Alderson Acad. and Junior College (f. 1901)
Private control
Academic year: August to May
Divs of education and special programmes, health sciences, humanities, natural sciences and social sciences
Pres.: RICK CREEHAN
Provost and Exec. Vice-Pres. for Academic Affairs: Dr JOAN PROPST
Vice-Pres. for Business and Finance: BRUCE BLANKENSHIP
Vice-Pres. for Enrolment Management: TANYA SHELTON
Vice-Pres. for Institutional Advancement: J. NIKKY LUNA
Dir for Devt: ANNETTE FETTY
Dir for Financial Aid: AMY KING
Dir for Marketing and Communications: ASHLEY MITTELMEIER
Dean for Student Affairs: SARAH WARD
Registrar: SAUNDRA HOXIE
Librarian: DAVID E. HOXIE
Library of 40,000 books, serial back files and govt documents, 11,000 current serial titles, 1,500 audiovisual items, 140,000 ebooks
Number of teachers: 80 (65 full-time, 15 part-time)
Number of students: 870

AMERICAN PUBLIC UNIVERSITY SYSTEM

111 W Congress St, Charles Town, WV 25414
Telephone: (877) 777-9081
E-mail: info@apus.edu
Internet: www.apus.edu
Founded 1991 as American Military Univ., present name and students 2002
Private control
2 Online univs: American Public Univ. and American Military Univ.
Pres. and CEO: Dr WALLACE E. BOSTON
Provost and Exec. Vice-Pres.: Dr KARAN POWELL
Exec. Vice-Pres. and Chief Financial Officer: HARRY T. WILKINS
Exec. Vice-Pres. and Chief Operations Officer: Dr SHARON VAN WYK
Sr Vice-Pres. and Chief Admin. Officer: PETER W. GIBBONS

Sr Vice-Pres. and Chief Information Officer: W. DALE YOUNG
Vice-Pres. and Dean for Libraries and Course Materials: Dr FRED STIELOW
Vice-Pres. for Enrolment Management: TERRY GRANT
Vice-Pres. for Research and Devt: Dr PHIL ICE
Vice-Pres. for Student Services: LYN GEER
Vice-Pres. for Student Services: Dr RONALD KOVACH

Library of 100,000 vols, 30,000 scholarly journals
Number of teachers: 1,600
Number of students: 100,000

DEANS

School of Arts and Humanities: Dr LINDA MOYNIHAN
School of Business: Dr CHAD PATRIZI
School of Education: Dr HENRY G. BRZYCKI
School of Management: Dr SHAWN BLACK
School of Public Safety and Health: Dr MICHAEL JACKSON
School of Science and Technology: DAN BENJAMIN
School of Security and Global Studies: Dr ELENA MASTORS

APPALACHIAN BIBLE COLLEGE

161 College Dr., Mount Hope, WV 25880
Telephone: (304) 877-6428
E-mail: abc@abc.edu
Internet: www.abc.edu

Founded 1950, present name 1978
Private control

Areas of study: Bible and theology, elementary education, music, ministries

Pres.: Dr DANIEL L. ANDERSON
Vice-Pres. for Academics: DANIEL HANSHEW
Vice-Pres. for Business: KEN LILLY
Vice-Pres. for Devt: Dr JONATHAN RINKER
Vice-Pres. for Student Services: DAVID CHILDS

Library of 52,000 vols
Number of students: 300

BETHANY COLLEGE

Main St, Bethany, WV 26032
Telephone: (304) 829-7000
E-mail: admission@bethanywv.edu
Internet: www.bethanywv.edu

Founded 1840
Private control
Academic year: August to May (2 semesters)

Pres.: Dr SCOTT D. MILLER
Assoc. Provost: Dr WALLACE B. NEEL
Exec. Vice-Pres. and Gen. Counsel: WILLIAM R. KIEFER
Vice-Pres. for Academic Affairs and Dean for Faculty: Dr DARIN E. FIELDS
Vice-Pres. for Institutional Advancement: SVEN DE JONG
Dean for Students: GERALD STEBBINS
Registrar: JOANN SUSAN DOTY
Dir for Libraries: HEATHER MAY-RICCIUTI

Library of 200,000 vols, 50,000 ebooks, 2,000 periodical subscriptions, 100,000 microforms
Number of teachers: 65 (56 full-time, 9 part-time)
Number of students: 1,030
Publication: *Bethany Today* (2 a year)

PROFESSORS

BURNS, J., Biology
CSAPLAR, Jr, W., Economics
FARWELL, J., Religious Studies and Philosophy
HULL, E., English
HULL, J., Psychology

LOVANO, J., World Languages and Cultures
MAFFETT, C., Political Science
MCGOWAN, J., Physical Education and Sports Studies
MENZ, H., World Languages and Cultures
MORGAN, K., Fine Arts
PAYSEN, A., Chemistry
RAMJEE, A., Business
RICCIUTI, H., Learning Resources
SAWTARIE, F., Computer Science
SHELEK-FURBEE, K., Social Work
SUTHERLAND, P., Communications
WEAVER, H., Fine Arts

BLUEFIELD STATE COLLEGE

219 Rock St, Bluefield, WV 24701-2198
Telephone: (304) 327-4000
E-mail: bscadmit@bluefieldstate.edu
Internet: www.bluefieldstate.edu

Founded 1895 as Bluefield Colored Institute, present name 1943
State control
Academic year: August to May

Pres.: Dr THOMAS E. BLEVINS
Provost, Vice-Pres. for Academic Affairs and Dean for Academic Affairs: Dr LEWIS L. JONES
Vice-Pres. for Financial and Admin. Affairs: SHELIA D. JOHNSON
Vice-Pres. for Student Affairs and Enrolment Management: JOHN C. CARDWELL
Dir for Admissions: KENNY MANDEVILLE
Dir for Library Services: JOANNA THOMPSON

Library of 75,700 vols
Number of teachers: 90
Number of students: 3,600

DEANS

School of Arts and Sciences: Dr DAVID HAUS
School of Education: Dr ELISABETH M. STEENKEN
School of Engineering Technology and Computer Science: E. FRANK HART
School of Nursing and Allied Health: ANGELA M. LAMBERT
W. Paul Core, Jr, School of Business: Dr GLEN STEVE BOURNE

CONCORD UNIVERSITY

POB 1000, Vermillion St, Athens, WV 24712-1000
Telephone: (304) 384-5249
E-mail: info@concord.edu
Internet: www.concord.edu

Founded 1872 as Concord State Normal School, current name adopted 2004
State control
Academic year: September to May

Areas of study: arts, history, language and literature, mathematics and sciences, philosophy

Pres.: Dr GREGORY F. ALOIA
Vice-Pres. and Academic Dean: Dr KENDRA BOGGESS
Vice-Pres. for Admin.: RICK DILLON
Vice-Pres. for Advancement: ALICIA BESENYEI
Vice-Pres. for Business and Finance: Dr CHUCK BECKER
Vice-Pres. for Student Affairs, Dean for Students and Dir for Retention: Dr MARJIE FLANIGAN
Dir for Enrolment: KENT J. GAMBLE
Dir for Library: Dr STEPHEN D. ROWE

Library of 200,000 vols, 5,000 periodicals
Number of teachers: 110
Number of students: 2,800

DAVIS AND ELKINS COLLEGE

100 Campus Dr., Elkins, WV 26241
Telephone: (304) 637-1900

Internet: www.dewv.edu

Founded 1904
Private control
Academic year: August to May

Depts of biology and environmental science, business administration. and economics, chemistry, communications and foreign languages, computer science and physics, education, English, fine and performing arts, health, history and political science, mathematics, nursing, psychology and human services, religion and philosophy, sociology and criminology, sport and movement sciences

Pres.: Dr G. T. BUCK SMITH
Provost: MICHAEL P. MIHALYO, Jr
Exec. Vice-Pres.: KEVIN WILSON
Vice-Pres. for Academic Affairs and Dean for the Faculty: Dr LAURENCE B. MCARTHUR
Vice-Pres. for College Advancement: PATRICIA J. SCHUMANN
Vice-Pres. for Student Affairs: SCOTT D. GODDARD
Registrar: Prof. Dr STEPHANIE E. HAYNES
Dir for the Library: JACKIE SCHNEIDER

Library of 116,000 vols
Number of teachers: 45 (full-time)
Number of students: 750

FAIRMONT STATE UNIVERSITY

1201 Locust Ave, Fairmont, WV 26554
Telephone: (304) 367-4892
E-mail: admit@fairmontstate.edu
Internet: www.fairmontstate.edu

Founded 1865 as West Virginia Normal School, present name 2004
State control

Pres.: Dr MARIA C. BENNETT ROSE
Provost and Vice-Pres. for Academic Affairs: CHRISTINA LAVORATA
Sr Vice-Pres. for Enrolment and Student Services: MICHAEL BELMEAR
Vice-Pres. for Admin. and Fiscal Affairs: ENRICO PORTO
Vice-Pres. and Chief Information Officer: DAVID TAMM
Vice-Pres. for Institutional Advancement: DEVANNA CORLEY
Dean for Graduate Studies: Dr VAN DEMPSEY
Dir for Communications: SARAH HENSLEY
Dir for Library Services: THELMA HUTCHINS

Library of 265,000 vols, 50,000 ebooks
Number of teachers: 190
Number of students: 7,450

DEANS

College of Liberal Arts: Prof. Dr DEANNA SHIELDS
College of Science and Technology: Prof. Dr ANTHONY F. GILBERTI
School of Business: Dr RICHARD HARVEY
School of Education, Health and Human Performance: Prof. Dr VAN DEMPSEY
School of Fine Arts: PETER LACH
School of Human Services: Prof. Dr BETH NEWCOME

GLENVILLE STATE COLLEGE

200 High St, Glenville, WV 26351
Telephone: (304) 462-7361
E-mail: admissions@glenville.edu
Internet: www.glenville.edu

Founded 1872
State control
Academic year: August to May

Depts of business, criminal justice, English, fine arts, land resources, mathematics, social science, teacher education

Pres.: Dr PETER B. BARR
Provost and Sr Vice-Pres.: M. KATHERINE BUTLER

Exec. Vice-Pres.: ROBERT O. HARDMAN
Sr Vice-Pres. for External Relations: Dr WILLIAM D. NICHOLSON
Vice-Pres. for College Advancement: DENNIS J. POUNDS
Vice-Pres. for Enrolment Management: D. DUANE CHAPMAN
Dean for Student Affairs: JERRY L. BURKHAMMER
Library Dir: GAIL WESTBROOK

Library of 110,000 vols, 483,000 microforms, 625 hard-copy periodical titles, 18 newspaper titles
Number of teachers: 85 (58 full-time, 27 part-time)
Number of students: 1,445

MARSHALL UNIVERSITY

1 John Marshall Dr., Huntington, WV 25755
Telephone: (304) 696-3646
E-mail: admissions@marshall.edu
Internet: www.marshall.edu
Founded 1837 as Marshall Acad.
State control
Academic year: August to May
Extended campus sites: S Charleston, Point Pleasant, Beckley, Logan and Gilbert
Pres.: Dr STEPHEN J. KOPP
Chief of Staff: MATTHEW TURNER
Provost and Sr Vice-Pres. for Academic Affairs: Dr GAYLE L. ORMISTON
Gen. Counsel and Sr Vice-Pres. for Exec. Affairs: LAYTON COTTRILL
Sr Vice-Pres. for Finance and Admin.: Dr KAREN KIRTLEY
Vice-Pres. for Multicultural Affairs: Dr SHARI CLARKE
Vice-Pres. for Research: Dr JOHN MAHER
Dir for Admissions: Dr TAMMY R. JOHNSON
Univ. Librarian and Dir for Libraries Operations: JINGPING ZHANG

Library of 1,411,480 vols
Number of teachers: 665 (full-time)
Number of students: 14,200

DEANS

College of Education: Dr ROBERT BOOKWALTER
College of Fine Arts: DONALD VAN HORN
College of Health Professions: Dr MICHAEL PREWITT
College of Information Technology and Engineering: Dr WAEL ZATAR
College of Liberal Arts: Dr DAVID PITTENGER
College of Science: CHARLES SOMERVILLE
Graduate College: Dr DONNA J. SPINDEL
Graduate School of Education and Professional Devt: TERESA EAGLE
Honors College: Dr MARY TODD
Joan C. Edwards School of Medicine: ROBERT C. NERHOOD, Jr
Lewis College of Business: Dr CHONG W. KIM
W. Page Pitt School of Journalism and Mass Communications: Dr CORLEY DENNISON

OHIO VALLEY UNIVERSITY

1 Campus View Dr., Vienna, WV 26105-8000
Telephone: (304) 865-6000
E-mail: admissions@ovu.edu
Internet: www.ovu.edu
Founded 1958
Private control
Chancellor: Dr E. KEITH STOTTS
Pres.: Dr HAROLD SHANK
Exec. Vice-Pres.: DENVER LUCKY
Vice-Pres. for Academic Affairs: Dr JAMES BULLOCK
Vice-Pres. for Advancement: Dr SUSIE BULLOCK
Vice-Pres. for Enrolment: LARRY LYONS
Vice-Pres. for Marketing and Financial Aid: DENNIS COX

Dean for Student Services: KATHY MULLER
Dir for Admissions: AMY BORTELL
Library Dir: RODNEY WOOTEN

Library of 34,000 vols, 142 print periodical subscriptions, 60,203 microforms, 6,779 audiovisual materials, 30 electronic databases for periodicals, reference sources and 93,763 ebook titles
Number of students: 500

DEANS

College of Arts and Sciences: Prof. Dr STEVEN HARDY
College of Biblical Studies and Behavioural Sciences: Dr MICHAEL MOSS
College of Business: Dr JOY JONES
College of Education: JO PENNINGTON

SALEM INTERNATIONAL UNIVERSITY

223 W Main St, Salem, WV 26426
Telephone: (304) 326-1109
E-mail: admissions@salemu.edu
Internet: www.salemu.edu
Founded 1888 as Salem College, present name 2000
Private control
Areas of study: arts and sciences, business, criminal justice, education, information technology, nursing
Chancellor and CEO: J. WILLIAM BROOKS
Pres.: JOHN A. LUOTTO
Provost and Chief Academic Officer: Dr DEBRA HARRISON
Exec. Vice-Pres.: C. ERIC KIRKLAND
Vice-Pres. for Admissions and Enrolment Management: ANDREW ANDERSON
Vice-Pres. for Business Affairs and Chief Financial Officer: DAN NELANT
Vice-Pres. for Information Technology and Chief Information Officer: PIETER BRESLER
Registrar: REBECCA HALL
Dean for Library Services: Dr PHYLLIS D. FREEDMAN

Library of 74,000 vols, 84 periodicals, 5 newspapers, 2,765 ejournals, 300,000 microfiche
Number of teachers: 55
Number of students: 810

SHEPHERD UNIVERSITY

POB 3210, Shepherdstown, WV 25443-3210
Telephone: (304) 876-5000
Internet: www.shepherd.edu
Founded 1871, present name and status 2004
State control
Academic year: August to May
Areas of study: business administration, liberal arts, natural sciences, social sciences, teacher education
Pres.: Dr SUZANNE SHIPLEY
Vice-Pres. for Academic Affairs: Dr RICHARD J. HELLDOBLER
Vice-Pres. for Admin. and Finance: RICK STAISLOFF (acting)
Vice-Pres. for Advancement: Dr DIANE MELBY
Vice-Pres. for Enrolment Management: KIMBERLY SCRANAGE
Vice-Pres. for Student Affairs: Dr THOMAS C. SEGAR
Dean for Graduate and Continuing Education: Dr SCOTT BEARD
Dean for the Library: ANN WATSON
Library of 500,000 vols, 6,000 periodicals
Number of teachers: 325 (118 full-time, 207 part-time)
Number of students: 4,185
Publication: *Shepherd University Magazine* (3 a year)

DEANS

School of Arts and Humanities: DOW BENEDICT, IV
School of Business and Social Sciences: Dr ANN LEGREID
School of Education and Professional Studies: Dr VIRGINIA HICKS
School of Natural Sciences and Mathematics: Dr COLLEEN NOLAN

UNIVERSITY OF CHARLESTON

2300 MacCorkle Ave, SE, Charleston, WV 25304
Telephone: (304) 357-4800
E-mail: admissions@ucwv.edu
Internet: www.ucwv.edu
Founded 1888 as Barboursville Seminary, current name adopted 1978
Private control
Academic year: August to April
Areas of study: business administration, forensic accounting, nursing, pharmacy
Pres.: Dr EDWIN H. WELCH
Vice-Pres. for Academic Affairs and Dean for the Faculty: Dr LETHA ZOOK
Vice-Pres. for Admin. and Finance: CLETA M. HARLESS
Vice-Pres. for Communications: JENNIE O. FERRETTI
Vice-Pres. for Devt: BEN BEAKES
Dir for Library Services: JOHN ADKINS
Library of 120,000 vols, 250 print journals and magazines
Number of teachers: 65 (full-time)
Number of students: 1,400

DEANS

School of Business: Dr CHARLES F. STEBBINS
School of Pharmacy: Dr MICHELLE EASTON

WEST LIBERTY UNIVERSITY

POB 295, 208 University Dr., West Liberty, WV 26074
101 Faculty Dr., West Liberty, WV 26074-0295
Telephone: (304) 336-5000
E-mail: admissions@westliberty.edu
Internet: westliberty.edu
Founded 1837 as West Liberty Acad.
State control
Academic year: August to May (2 semesters)
Pres.: Prof. ROBIN C. CAPEHART
Provost: Dr ANTHONY KOYZIS
Exec. Vice-Pres. and Chief Financial Officer: JOHN WRIGHT, III
Exec. Vice-Pres. and Gen. Counsel: JOHN L. DAVIS
Vice-Pres. for Institutional Advancement: JASON KOEGLER
Dir for Admissions and Recruitment: BRENDA KING
Dir for Institutional Research and Assessment: PAULA TOMASIK
Dean for Students and Registrar: SCOTT A. COOK
Library Dir: CHERYL R. HARSHMAN
Library of 200,000 vols
Number of teachers: 200 (120 full-time, 80 part-time)
Number of students: 2,600 (f.t.e.)

DEANS

College of Arts and Communication: Dr WILLIAM BARONAK
College of Education: Dr KEELY CAMDEN
College of Liberal Arts: BRIAN CRAWFORD
College of Sciences: Dr ROBERT KREISBERG
Gary E. West College of Business: Dr LOREN A. WENZEL
School of Professional Studies: Dr THOMAS MICHAUD

WEST VIRGINIA SCHOOL OF OSTEOPATHIC MEDICINE

400 N Lee St, Lewisburg, WV 24901

Telephone: (304) 647-6238
E-mail: dgetson@osteo.wvsom.edu
Internet: www.wvsom.edu

Founded 1972
State control
Academic year: August to May

Areas of study: biomedical sciences, clinical sciences, osteopathic medical education

Pres.: Dr MICHAEL ADELMAN
Vice-Pres. for Academic Affairs and Dean: LORENZO L. PENCE
Vice-Pres. for Admin. and External Relations: Dr JAMES W. NEMITZ
Vice-Pres. for Finance and Facilities: LARRY WARE
Dir for Admissions: DONNA VARNEY
Registrar: JENNIFER D. SEAMS
Dir for Library: ANNIE MCMILLION

Library of 17,000 vols (incl. 450 print journals), 2,000 multimedia titles, 8,000 full-text ejournals, 23,000 osteopathic articles
Number of teachers: 55 (full-time)
Number of students: 800

Publication: *WVSOM Magazine* (4 a year)

WEST VIRGINIA STATE UNIVERSITY

POB 1000, Institute, WV 25112-1000

Telephone: (304) 766-3000
E-mail: admissions@wvstateu.edu
Internet: www.wvstateu.edu

Founded 1891 as West Virginia Collegiate Institute, current name and status 2004
State control

Pres.: Dr HAZO W. CARTER, Jr
Provost and Vice-Pres. for Academic Affairs: Dr R. CHARLES BYERS
Vice-Pres. for Admin. Services: Dr CASSANDRA B. WHYTE
Vice-Pres. for Business and Finance: MELVIN JONES
Vice-Pres. for Planning and Advancement: Dr JOHN M. BERRY
Vice-Pres. for Student Affairs: S. BRYCE CASTO
Dir for Library: DAVID CLENDINNING

Library of 200,000 vols, 300 periodical subscriptions, 9,000 bound periodical vols, 200,000 items in microfilm and microfiche
Number of teachers: 253 (137 full-time, 116 part-time)
Number of students: 3,750

DEANS

College of Arts and Humanities: Dr BARBARA LADNER
College of Business and Social Sciences: Dr ABAINESH MITIKU
College of Natural Science and Mathematics: Dr KATHERINE HARPER
College of Professional Studies: Dr ROBERT L. HARRISON, Jr

WEST VIRGINIA UNIVERSITY

POB 6201, Morgantown, WV 26506-6201

Telephone: (304) 293-0111
E-mail: internationaladmissions@mail.wvu.edu
Internet: www.wvu.edu

Founded 1867
State control
Academic year: August to May

Brs in Potomac State College in Keyser and WVU Institute of Technology in Montgomery

Pres.: Dr E. GORDON GEE
Provost: Dr MICHELE G. WHEATLY
Chancellor for Robert C. Byrd Health Sciences Center: CHRISTOPHER COLENDA

Vice-Pres. for Admin. and Finance: NARVEL G. WEESE, Jr
Vice-Pres. for Human Resources: MARGARET R. PHILLIPS
Vice-Pres. for Legal Affairs: WILLIAM H. HUTCHENS, III
Vice-Pres. for Research and Economic Devt: Dr CURT M. PETERSON
Vice-Pres. for Student Affairs: KENNETH D. GRAY
Vice-Pres. for Univ. Relations: SHARON MARTIN
Dean for Libraries: JON E. CAWTHORNE

Library: 1.9m. vols, 229 electronic databases, approx. 45,000 online full-text journals, access to 36m. vols through a book-sharing consortium; 5 library facilities: Downtown Library Complex, Evansdale Library, Health Sciences Library, Law Library, Libraries Depository see under Libraries and Archives
Number of teachers: 1,532 (1,042 full-time and 590 part-time)
Number of students: 29,466 (22,757 undergraduate, 5,077 graduate, and 1,632 professional)

DEANS

College of Business and Economics: Dr JOSE V. SARTARELLI
College of Creative Arts: Dr PAUL KREIDER, College of Education and Human Services: Dr LYNNE SCHRUM
College of Engineering and Mineral Resources: Dr GENE V. CILENTO
College of Law: JOYCE E. MCCONNELL
Davis College of Agriculture, Natural Resources and Design: DAN ROBISON
Eberly College of Arts and Sciences: Dr ROBERT JONES
Perley Isaac Reed School of Journalism: MARYANNE REED
Potomac State College: Dr LEONARD A. COLELLI
School of Dentistry: Dr DAVID A. FELTON
School of Medicine: Dr ARTHUR J. ROSS, III
School of Nursing: ELISABETH SHELTON
School of Pharmacy: Dr PATRICIA A. CHASE
School of Physical Activity and Sports Science: Dr DANA D. BROOKS

WEST VIRGINIA UNIVERSITY AT PARKERSBURG

300 Campus Dr., Parkersburg, WV 26104-8647

Telephone: (304) 424-8000
E-mail: wvupinfo@mail.wvu.edu
Internet: www.wvup.edu

Founded 1961 as Parkersburg Br. of West Virginia Univ., present name and status 1989
State control

Areas of study: business, economics, education and humanities, health sciences, languages, mathematics, science and technology, social sciences; technical college affiliated with West Virginia Univ.

Pres.: Dr MARIE FOSTER GNAGE
Sr Vice-Pres. for Academic Affairs: Dr RHONDA TRACY
Vice-Pres. for Student Services: ANTHONY UNDERWOOD
Vice-Pres. for Workforce and Community Education: MARY BETH BUSCH
Registrar: LESLIE SIMS
Library Dir: STEPHEN HUPP
Number of students: 4,300

WEST VIRGINIA WESLEYAN COLLEGE

59 College Ave, Buckhannon, WV 26201

Telephone: (304) 473-8000

Internet: www.wvwc.edu

Founded 1890
Private control

Offers degrees in arts, athletic training, business administration, education, fine arts—creative writing, music education, science, science in nursing

Pres.: PAMELA BALCH
Vice-Pres. for Academic Affairs and Dean for the College: Dr LARRY R. PARSONS
Vice-Pres. for Admin. and Finance: Dr BARRY R. PRITTS
Vice-Pres. for Information Technology: R. DUWANE SQUIRES
Vice-Pres. for Institutional Advancement: BRENT A. BUSH
Vice-Pres. for Student Affairs and Enrolment Management: JULIA A. KEEHNER
Dir for Admin. Services: KEITH NICHOLS
Dir for Marketing and Communication: ROBERT N. SKINNER, II
Dir for Admission: JOHN R. WALTZ
Dean for Graduate Studies and Extended Learning: Dr KATHLEEN M. LONG
Dir for Library Services: PAULA L. MCGREW

Library of 149,085 vols
Number of teachers: 170 (77 full-time, 93 part-time)
Number of students: 1,400 (undergraduate)

WHEELING JESUIT UNIVERSITY

316 Washington Ave, Wheeling, WV 26003-6295

Telephone: (304) 243-2000
E-mail: news@wju.edu
Internet: www.wju.edu

Founded 1954 as Wheeling College
Private control
Academic year: August to May

Areas of study: biology, business chemistry, communications and fine arts, computer science, English, history, mathematics, modern languages, nuclear medicine, nursing, philosophy, physical therapy, physics, professional education, psychology, respiratory therapy, social science, theology

Pres.: RICHARD ALLEN BEYER
Univ. Vice-Pres. and Chief of Staff: Fr JAMES FLEMING
Vice-Pres. for Academic Affairs and Dean for the Faculty: Dr STEPHEN STAHL
Vice-Pres. for Enrolment Management: LARRY VALLAR
Vice-Pres. for Institutional Advancement: JAMES HOLT
Dean for Student Devt: Dr CHRISTINE OHL-GIGLIOTTI
Dir for Admissions: JAY DEFRUSCIO (acting)
Registrar: MARK ULSETH
Dir for Library: KELLY MUMMERT (acting)

Library of 139,000 vols
Number of teachers: 95
Number of students: 1,500

WISCONSIN

ALVERNO COLLEGE

POB 343922, 3400 S 43rd St, Milwaukee, WI 53234-3922

Telephone: (414) 382-6000
E-mail: admissions@alverno.edu
Internet: www.alverno.edu

Founded 1887
Private control
Academic year: August to May

BA, music, science, science in nursing; MA, business administration, science in nursing; Master of science in community psychology

Chair.: MAURICE J. MCSWEENEY
Pres.: Dr MARY J. MEEHAN

Sr Vice-Pres. for Academic Affairs: Dr KATH-
LEEN O'BRIEN
Sr Vice-Pres. for Finance and Management
Services: JAMES K. OPPERMANN
Vice-Pres. for Marketing and Enrolment
Management: SUSAN M. SMITH
Registrar: PATRICIA HARTMAN
Dir for Library: CAROL BRILL
Library of 82,416 vols, 1,382 periodicals,
287,726 microforms, 15,728 audiovisual
items
Number of teachers: 120 (full-time)
Number of students: 2,760
Publication: *Alverno Magazine*

BELLIN COLLEGE

3201 Eaton Rd, Green Bay, WI 54311
Telephone: (920) 433-6699
E-mail: info@bellincollege.edu
Internet: www.bellincollege.edu
Founded 1909 as Deaconess Sanitarium
Training School, current name adopted
2009
Private control
Offers BSc in nursing and radiologic sci-
ences; MSc in nursing
Pres. and CEO: Dr CONNIE J. BOERST
Vice-Pres. for Academic Affairs: Dr CONNIE J.
BOERST
Vice-Pres. for Business and Finance: JOSEPH
KEEBAUGH
Vice-Pres. for Devt and Public Relations:
MATT RENTMEESTER
Vice-Pres. for Student Services: JOANN WOEL-
FEL
Dir for Admissions: KATIE KLAUS
Registrar: VICKY SCHAULAND
Librarian: CINDY REINL
Number of teachers: 20
Number of students: 290

BELOIT COLLEGE

700 College St, Beloit, WI 53511
Telephone: (608) 363-2000
E-mail: admiss@beloit.edu
Internet: www.beloit.edu
Founded 1846
Private control
Academic year: August to May
Pres.: SCOTT BIERMAN
Provost and Dean for the College: ANN
DAVIES
Vice-Pres. for Admin. and Treas.: JOHN M.
NICHOLAS
Vice-Pres. for Enrolment Services: NANCY
MONNICH
Dean for Students: CHRISTINA KLAWITTER
Dir for Admissions: JIM ZIELINSKI
Registrar: MARY BOROS-KAZAI
Dir for Library and Archives: LISA VIEZBICKE
Library of 268,000 vols, 31,726 periodical and
newspaper titles
Number of teachers: 125
Number of students: 1,275
Publications: *Avatar* (1 a year), *Beloit Maga-
zine* (3 a year), *The Round Table* (36 a
year)

CARDINAL STRITCH UNIVERSITY

6801 N Yates Rd, Milwaukee, WI 53217
Telephone: (414) 410-4000
Internet: www.stritch.edu
Founded 1937, present name and status 1997
Private control
Academic year: April to August
Chancellor: Dr M. CAMILLE KLIEBHAN
Pres.: Dr JAMES P. LOFTUS
Exec. Vice-Pres. and Chief Operating Officer:
DAVID WEINBERG-KINSEY

Exec. Vice-Pres. for Academic Affairs: Dr TIA
BOJAR
Exec. Vice-Pres. for Admin. and Chief Finan-
cial Officer: THOMAS W. VANHIMBERGEN
Vice-Pres. and Chief Information Officer:
THOMAS J. RAINS
Vice-Pres. for Enrolment Services: JOHN
MUELLER
Vice-Pres. for Student Devt and Dean for
Students: CHRISTINE ROBINSON
Vice-Pres. for Univ. Advancement: MICHAEL
J. BRAUER
Registrar: CHRISTINE L. GLYNN
Dir for Library and Learning Services: DAVID
WEINBERG-KINSEY
Library of 139,000 vols
Number of teachers: 100
Number of students: 6,100
Publication: *Stritch Magazine* (2 a year,
online, www.stritch.edu/magazine)

DEANS

College of Arts and Sciences: Dr DANIEL
SCHOLZ
College of Business and Management: Dr
PETER J. HOLBROOK
College of Education and Leadership: Dr
FREDA RUSSELL
Ruth S. Coleman College of Nursing: Dr
RUTH M. WAITE

CARROLL UNIVERSITY

100 N East Ave, Waukesha, WI 53186
Telephone: (414) 547-1211
E-mail: info@carrollu.edu
Internet: www.carrollu.edu
Founded 1846 as Carroll College, current
name and status 2008
Academic year: August to July (2 semesters)
Pres.: Dr DOUGLAS N. HASTAD
Provost and Vice-Pres. for Academic Affairs:
Dr JOANNE PASSARO
Dean for Students: Dr THERESA BARRY
Library Dir: LELAN E. MCLEMORE
Library of 196,000 vols, 140,000 journals
Number of teachers: 125 full-time
Number of students: 3,535 full-time

DEANS

College of Humanities and Social Sciences:
CHARLES A. BYLER
College of Natural Sciences, Health Sciences
and Business: JANE F. HOPP

CARTHAGE COLLEGE

2001 Alford Park Dr., Kenosha, WI 53140
Telephone: (262) 551-8500
E-mail: admissions@carthage.edu
Internet: www.carthage.edu
Founded 1847, current name adopted 1870
Private control
Academic divs: education, fine arts, human-
ities, interdisciplinary studies, natural sci-
ence, social science
Pres.: Dr F. GREGORY CAMPBELL
Provost: Prof. JULIO RIVERA
Assoc. Provost: DAVID STEEGE
Sr Vice-Pres. for Academic Resources: BRAD
ANDREWS
Sr Vice-Pres. for Admin. and Business:
WILLIAM ABT
Vice-Pres. for Library and Information Ser-
vices: TODD KELLEY
Assoc. Vice-Pres. for Communications:
ROBERT ROSEN
Dean for Students: LOUISE PASKEY
Number of teachers: 150
Number of students: 3,400

COLLEGE OF MENOMINEE NATION

N 172 Hwy 47/55, POB 1179, Keshena, WI
54135
Telephone: (715) 799-5600
E-mail: admissions@menominee.edu
Internet: www.menominee.edu
tribal control
Academic year: August to July
Areas of study: arts and sciences, applied
science, nursing, science, technical; campus
at Green Bay
Pres.: Dr S. VERNA FOWLER
Vice-Pres. for Academic Affairs: DONNA POW-
LESS
Vice-Pres. for Finance: LAURIE REITER
Vice-Pres. for Student Services: GARY BESAW
Vice-Pres. for Oneida Campus: NORBERT
HILL, JR
Vice-Pres. for Planning and Operations:
RONALD JURGENS
Library of 154,336 vols
Number of teachers: 50 (28 full-time, 22
part-time)
Number of students: 635 (357 full-time, 278
part-time)

COLUMBIA COLLEGE OF NURSING, INC.

4425 N Port Washington Rd, Glendale, WI
53212
Telephone: (414) 326-2330
E-mail: cconinformation@ccon.edu
Internet: www.ccon.edu
Founded 1901, current name adopted 1909
Private control
Academic year: August to May (2 semesters)
Areas of study: medical sonography and
radiologic technology
Dean and CEO: Prof. Dr JILL WINTERS
Registrar: HALEY JO GEIGER
Man. for Library Services: SHARON WOCHOS

CONCORDIA UNIVERSITY WISCONSIN

12800 N Lake Shore Dr., Mequon, WI 53097-
2418
Telephone: (262) 243-5700
E-mail: admissions@cuw.edu
Internet: www.cuw.edu
Founded 1881 as Concordia College, present
name and status 1989
Pres.: Rev. Dr PATRICK T. FERRY
Exec. Vice-Pres. and Chief Operating Officer:
ALLEN J. PROCHNOW
Vice-Pres. for Academic Operations: Dr
MICHAEL BESCH
Vice-Pres. for Student Affairs: Dr ANDREW
LUPTAK
Dir for Library Services: CHRISTIAN R. HIMSEL
Library of 114,000 vols, 600 print periodical
subscriptions, 20,000 e-periodicals
Number of teachers: 275 (128 full-time, 149
part-time)
Number of students: 7,485 (3,610 full-time,
3,875 part-time)

DEANS

School of Arts and Sciences: Dr GAYLUND K.
STONE
School of Business and Legal Studies: Dr
DAVID BORST
School of Education: Dr MICHAEL UDEN
School of Human Services: Dr RUTH GRESLEY
School of Pharmacy: Dr DEAN L. ARNESON

EDGEWOOD COLLEGE

1000 Edgewood College Dr., Madison, WI
53711-1997
Telephone: (608) 663-4861

E-mail: admissions@edgewood.edu
Internet: www.edgewood.edu
Founded 1927
Private control
Academic year: September to May
Pres.: Dr DANIEL J. CAREY
Vice-Pres. for Academic Affairs and Academic Dean: MARY KELLY-POWELL
Vice-Pres. for Student Devt and Dean for Students: Dr MAGGIE BALISTRERI-CLARKE
Registrar: ELLEN FEHRING
Dir for Library: SYLVIA CONTRERAS
Library of 125,000 vols
Number of teachers: 160 (73 full-time, 87 part-time)
Number of students: 2,650

DEANS

School of Arts and Sciences: Dr BRANDON CLAYCOMB
School of Business: Prof. MARTIN A. PREIZLER
School of Education: Dr JANE BELMORE
School of Integrative Studies: DEAN A. PRIBBENOW
School of Nursing: Dr MARGARET C. NOREUIL

HERZING UNIVERSITY

5218 E Terrace Dr., Madison, WI 53718
Telephone: (608) 249-6611
E-mail: info@msn.herzing.edu
Internet: www.herzing.edu
Founded 1965, present name and status 2009
Private control
Academic year: January to December (3 semesters)
11 Campuses in 8 states: Birmingham (Alabama), Winter Park (Florida), Atlanta (Georgia), Kenner (Los Angeles), Crystal (Minnesota), Omaha (Nebraska), Akron (Ohio), Toledo (Ohio); areas of study: business management, electronics, graphic design and public safety, health care
Pres.: RENÉE HERZING
Vice-Pres. for Finance and Chief Financial Officer: RYAN O'DESKY
Vice-Pres. for Information Technology: CHRISTY CRUTE
Chief Academic Officer: Dr BILL GETTER

LAKELAND COLLEGE

POB 359, Sheboygan, WI 53082-0359
Telephone: (414) 565-2166
Internet: www.lakeland.edu
Founded 1862 as Missionshaus, current name adopted 1956
Areas of study: business administration, creative arts, education, general. studies, humanities, natural sciences, social sciences; 7 campuses in Wisconsin and 1 campus in Tokyo; distance education programmes
Private control
Pres.: Dr STEPHEN A. GOULD
Sr Vice-Pres. for Admin.: DANIEL W. ECK
Vice-Pres. for Academic Affairs and Dean for the College: Dr MARGARET ALBRINCK
Vice-Pres. for Advancement: KEN D. STRMISKA
Vice-Pres. for Finance: JOSEPH D. BOTANA, II
Vice-Pres. for Int. Programmes and Gen. Counsel: E. ANTHONY FESSLER
Vice-Pres. for Student Devt: NATHAN D. DEHNE
Dean for Students: SANDRA GIBBONS-VOLLBRECHT
Dir for Library Services: ANN PENKE
Library of 65,000 vols, 300 periodicals
Number of teachers: 40
Number of students: 4,000
Publication: *Lakeland* (3 a year)

LAWRENCE UNIVERSITY

711 E Boldt Way, SPC 29 Appleton, WI 54911
115 S Drew St, Appleton, WI 54911
Telephone: (920) 832-7000
E-mail: excel@lawrence.edu
Internet: www.lawrence.edu
Founded 1847, present name and status 1964
Private control
Academic year: September to June
Languages of instruction: English, French, German, Japanese, Russian, Spanish
College of liberal arts and sciences with conservatory of music
Pres.: Dr JILL BECK
Provost and Dean for the Faculty: DAVID BURROWS
Vice-Pres. for Alumni, Devt and Communications: CALVIN HUSMANN
Vice-Pres. for Student Affairs and Dean for Students: NANCY D. TRUESDELL
Dean for Admissions and Financial Aid: KEN ANSELMENT
Registrar: ANNE S. NORMAN
Library Dir: PETER GILBERT
Library of 394,383 vols, 344,118 govt documents, 2,478 current periodical subscriptions, 17,786 music scores, and 143,083 video cassettes, recordings and microform items, 3,400 rare book colln
Number of teachers: 155 (full-time)
Number of students: 1,565
Publication: *Lawrence Today* (4 a year)

MARANATHA BAPTIST BIBLE COLLEGE

745 West Main St, Watertown, WI 53094
Telephone: (920) 261-9300
E-mail: admissions@mbbc.edu
Internet: www.mbbc.edu
Founded 1968
Private control
Academic year: September to May
Areas of study: applied science, Bible and church ministries, business, humanities, music, nursing, teacher education
Pres.: Dr S. MARTIN MARRIOTT
Vice-Pres. for Academic Affairs: WILL LICHT
Vice-Pres. for Business Affairs: MARK STEVENS
Vice-Pres. for Institutional Advancement: Dr JIM HARRISON
Dean for Students: Rev. JOHN DAVIS
Registrar: STEVE CARLSON
Library of 124,000 vols
Number of teachers: 60
Number of students: 1,050

MARIAN UNIVERSITY

45 S National Ave, Fond du Lac, WI 54935-4699
Telephone: (920) 923-7600
Internet: www.marianuniversity.edu
Founded 1936 as Marian College, current name and status 2008
Private control
Academic year: August to May
Campuses at Appleton, West Allis, Green Bay, Kenosha, Madison, Watertown, Wausau and West Bend
Pres.: ROBERT FALE
Exec. Vice-Pres. for Academic Affairs: Dr EDWARD H. OGLE
Vice-Pres. for Enrolment Management: STACEY AKEY
Vice-Pres. for Mission and Student Engagement: KATE CANDEE
Dean for Student Engagement: PAUL KRIKAU
Registrar: CHERYL TEICHMILLER
Dir for Libraries: MARY ELLEN GORMICAN

Library of 92,000 vols
Number of teachers: 105 (100 full-time, 5 part-time)
Number of students: 2,615 (full-time)
Publication: *Marian University Magazine* (2 a year)

DEANS

School of Arts and Sciences: Dr JAMES VAN DYKE
School of Business and Public Safety: Dr JEFFREY G. REED
School of Education: Dr SUE STODDART
School of Nursing and Health Professions: Dr JULIE LUETSCHWAGER

MARQUETTE UNIVERSITY

POB 1881, Milwaukee, WI 53201-1881
1250 W Wisconsin Ave, Milwaukee, WI 53233
Telephone: (414) 288-7250
E-mail: admissions@marquette.edu
Internet: www.marquette.edu
Founded 1881 as Marquette College, chartered as univ. in 1907
Private control
Pres.: Rev. SCOTT R. PILARZ
Provost: Dr JOHN J. PAULY
Provost: Dr GARY MEYER
Vice-Provost for Research and Dean for the Graduate School: Dr JEANNE HOSSENLOPP
Assoc. Sr Vice-Pres.: Dr THOMAS J. PETERS
Assoc. Sr Vice-Pres.: ANNE O'BRIEN
Vice-Pres. and Gen. Counsel: CYNTHIA M. BAUER
Vice-Pres. for Admin.: ARTHUR F. SCHEUBER
Vice-Pres. for Finance: JOHN C. LAMB
Vice-Pres. for Marketing and Communication: TRICIA GERAGHTY
Vice-Pres. for Mission and Ministry: STEPHANIE RUSSELL
Vice-Pres. for Public Affairs: RANA H. ALTENBURG
Vice-Pres. for Student Affairs: Dr L. CHRISTOPHER MILLER
Vice-Pres. for Univ. Advancement: JULIE TOLAN
Dean for Undergraduate Admissions and Enrollment Planning: ROBY BLUST
Dean for Univ. Libraries: JANICE SIMMONS-WELBURN
Library of 4,000,000 vols
Number of teachers: 1,100
Number of students: 12,000 (8,385 undergraduate, 3,615 professional)

DEANS

College of Business Administration and Graduate School of Management: Dr LINDA M. SALCHENBERGER
College of Education: WILLIAM A. HENK
College of Engineering: Dr ROBERT H. BISHOP
College of Health Sciences: Dr WILLIAM E. CULLINAN
College of Nursing: Dr MARGARET FAUT-CALLAHAN
College of Professional Studies: Dr ROBERT J. DEAHL
Helen Way Klingler College of Arts and Sciences: PHILIP J. ROSSI
J. William and Mary Diederich College of Communication: Dr LORI BERGEN
Law School: JOSEPH D. KEARNEY
School of Dentistry: Dr WILLIAM K. LOBB
The Graduate School: Dr JEANNE HOSSENLOPP

MEDICAL COLLEGE OF WISCONSIN

8701 Watertown Plank Rd, Milwaukee, WI 53226
Telephone: (414) 955-8296
E-mail: officeofthepresident@mcw.edu

Internet: www.mcw.edu

Founded 1893 as Wisconsin College of Physicians and Surgeons, present name 1970

Private control

Offers degrees in basic and translational research, biochemistry, biophysics, biostatistics, cell biology, neurobiology and anatomy, micro biology and molecular genetics, pharmacology and toxicology, physiology, public and community health and functional imaging

Pres. and CEO: JOHN R. RAYMOND, Sr

Exec. Vice-Pres. and Dean for Medical School: Dr JOSEPH E. KERSCHNER

Sr Vice-Pres. for Finance and Admin.: GLENN ALLEN BOLTON, Jr

Assoc. Dean for Student Affairs: Dr RICHARD HOLLOWAY

Library of 252,000 vols, 6,000 online journals, 3,400 ebooks

Number of teachers: 1,590

Number of students: 1,265

MILWAUKEE INSTITUTE OF ART AND DESIGN

273 E Erie St, Milwaukee, WI 53202

Telephone: (414) 847-3200

E-mail: miadadm@miad.edu

Internet: www.miad.edu

Founded 1920, present name and status 1974

Private control

Areas of study: advertising, animation, art history, business, communication design, drawing, illustration, industrial design, integrated studio arts, interior architecture and design, multidisciplinary fine arts, painting, photography, printmaking, sculpture, time-based media, video, writing

Pres.: NEIL HOFFMAN

Provost and Vice-Pres. for Academic Affairs: DAVID MARTIN (acting)

Vice-Pres. for Enrolment Management: MARY SCHOPP

Assoc. Vice-Pres. for Academic Planning and Assessment: CYNTHIA LYNCH

Dean for Students: TONY NOWAK

Registrar: JEAN WEIMER

Library of 500,000 vols, 2,000 video cassettes

Number of students: 700

Number of teachers: 200

MILWAUKEE SCHOOL OF ENGINEERING

1025 N Broadway, Milwaukee, WI 53202-3109

Telephone: (414) 277-6763

E-mail: explore@msoe.edu

Internet: www.msoe.edu

Founded 1903

Private control

Academic year: September to May

Int. programmes in Lübeck, Germany, Prague, Czech Republic, India

Pres.: Dr HERMANN VIETS

Vice-Pres. for Academics: Dr FREDERICK BERRY

Vice-Pres. for Devt: FRANK HABIB

Vice-Pres. for Enrolment Management: TIM VALLEY

Vice-Pres. for Finance and Chief Financial Officer: ARMUND JANTO

Vice-Pres. for Student Life and Dean for Students: PATRICK J. COFFEY

Library Dir: GARY SHIMEK

Library of 45,000 vols, 300 print journals, 100,000 ebooks and 90,000 ejournals

Number of teachers: 135 (full-time)

Number of students: 2,500

Publication: *Dimensions* (3 a year)

MOUNT MARY COLLEGE

2900 N Menomonee River Parkway, Milwaukee, WI 53222-4597

Telephone: (414) 258-4810

E-mail: mccrediw@mtmary.edu

Internet: www.mtmary.edu

Founded as St. Mary's Institute, present name and status 1913

Private control

Areas of study: art and design, business administration., education and mathematics, health and sciences, language, literature and communication, philosophy and theology, social sciences

Pres.: Dr EILEEN SCHWALBACH

Vice-Pres. for Academic and Student Affairs: Dr DAVID NIXON

Vice-Pres. for Enrolment Services: DAVE WEGENER

Vice-Pres. for External Relations: DONNA GASTEVICH

Vice-Pres. for Finance and Admin.: REYES GONZALEZ

Vice-Pres. for Mission and Identity: Dr JOAN PENZENSTADLER

Library Dir: JULIE KAMIKAWA

Library of 111,000 vols

Number of teachers: 145

Number of students: 1,965

NASHOTAH HOUSE

2777 Mission Rd, Nashotah, WI 53058

Telephone: (262) 646-6500

E-mail: nashotah@nashotah.edu

Internet: www.nashotah.edu

Founded 1842, chartered in 1847

Private control

Academic year: July to June

Seminary of the Episcopal Church in the Anglican Communion of Churches; areas of study: Anglican studies, arts, divinity and ministry, theological studies

Pres. and Dean: Rt Rev. EDWARD L. SALMON, Jr

Provost: Rev. Dr RICHARD LONGABAUGH

Assoc. Dean for Academic Affairs: Rev. Dr STEVEN PEAY

Dir for Admissions: Dr CAROL KLUKAS

Dir for Library: DAVID SHERWOOD

Library of 100,000 vols, 280 current periodicals

Number of teachers: 10

Number of students: 125

Publication: *The Missioner*

NORTHLAND COLLEGE

1411 Ellis Ave, Ashland, WI 54806-3999

Telephone: (715) 682-1699

E-mail: admit@northland.edu

Internet: www.northland.edu

Founded 1892, present name and status 1906

Private control

Academic year: September to May

Language of instruction: English

Pres.: MICHAEL A. MILLER

Vice-Pres. for Academic Affairs and Academic Dean: ALAN BREW

Vice-Pres. for Enrolment Management: RICK J. SMITH

Vice-Pres. for Finance and Admin.: ROBERT JACKSON

Vice-Pres. for Institutional Advancement: KRISTY LIPHART

Vice-Pres. for Marketing: DAVID WAHLBERG

Dean for Student Life: MICHELE MEYER

Dir for Sigurd Olson Environmental Institute: MARK LEACH

Registrar: KATHY TRAYNOR

Library Dir: JULIA WAGGONER

Library of 76,640 vols, 250 print periodical subscriptions

Number of teachers: 45 (full-time)

Number of students: 700

Publications: *Eco-Vision* (1 a year), *Northland College Magazine* (2 a year), *The Drifts* (student paper, print and online)

PROFESSORS

ALLDRITT, L., Religion

DAMRELL, J., Sociology and Anthropology

DILLENSCHNEIDER, C., Outdoor Education

GLICKMAN, J., Music

GOETZ, B., Geoscience

GORMAN, W., Biology

GOYKE, A., Biology

JOYAL, R., Business Administration and Economics

KIM, Y., Mathematics and Computer Information Systems

SMALL, M., English and Modern Languages

RIPON COLLEGE

POB 248, Ripon, WI 54971

Telephone: (920) 748-8115

E-mail: adminfo@ripon.edu

Internet: www.ripon.edu

Founded 1851, present status 1863

Private control

Academic year: August to June (2 semesters)

Liberal arts and sciences college

Pres.: Rev. Dr DAVID C. JOYCE

Vice-Pres. and Dean for Faculty: GERALD SEAMAN

Vice-Pres. and Dean for Students: CHRISTOPHER M. OGLE

Vice-Pres. for Advancement: WAYNE WEBSTER

Vice-Pres. for Finance: MARY deREGNIER

Dean for Admissions: LEIGH MLODZIK

Dean for Faculty and Registrar: MICHELE WITTLER

Chair. for Library Dept: ANDREW PRELLWITZ

Library of 150,000 vols

Number of teachers: 75

Number of students: 1,060

SACRED HEART SCHOOL OF THEOLOGY

POB 429, 7335 S Highway 100, Hales Corners, WI 53130-0429

Telephone: (414) 425-8300

Internet: www.shst.edu

Founded 1932, current name adopted 1972

Private control

Academic year: August to June

Language of instruction: English

Pres. and Rector: Very Rev. ROSS A. SHECTERLE

Vice-Rector and Vice-Pres. for External Affairs: Rev. THOMAS L. KNOEBEL

Vice-Pres. for Academic Affairs and Academic Dean: Dr PATRICK RUSSELL

Vice-Pres. for Finance: SALLY A. SMITS

Vice-Pres. for Human and Spiritual Formation: Rev. STEPHEN MALKIEWICZ

Academic Dean: Dr PATRICK RUSSELL

Dir for Pastoral Education: Rev. ROBERT SCHIAVONE

Registrar: ROSE KOPENEC

Dir for Library: SUSANNA PATHAK

Library of 100,000 vols, 450 periodicals

Number of teachers: 40

Number of students: 175

ST NORBERT COLLEGE

100 Grant St, De Pere, WI 54115-2099

Telephone: (920) 403-3005

E-mail: admit@snc.edu

Internet: www.snc.edu

Founded 1898

Private control
Languages of instruction: English, French, German, Japanese, Spanish
Academic year: August to May
Areas of study: humanities and fine arts, natural sciences, social sciences
Pres.: THOMAS KUNKEL
Vice-Pres. for Business and Finance: EILEEN M. JAHNKE
Vice-Pres. for College Advancement: PHIL OSWALD
Vice-Pres. for Mission and Student Affairs: Rev. Dr JAY FOSTNER
Assoc. Vice-Pres. for Enrolment: EDWARD LAMM
Dean for the College and Academic Vice-Pres.: Dr JEFFREY FRICK
Registrar: RICHARD GUILD
Chief Information Officer: RAECHELLE CLEMMONS
Dir for Library: SALLY L. HANSEN
Library of 300,000 vols
Number of teachers: 200 (138 full-time, 62 part-time)
Number of students: 2,300 (2,240 undergraduate, 60 graduate)
Publications: *Graphos* (literary journal), *St. Norbert College Magazine* (3 a year, print and online, www.snc.edu/magazine), *The Rectangle* (1 a year), *The Sigma Tau Delta Review* (1 a year)

SILVER LAKE COLLEGE OF THE HOLY FAMILY

2406 S Alverno Rd, Manitowoc, WI 54220-9319
Telephone: (920) 684-6691
E-mail: admslc@sl.edu
Internet: www.sl.edu
Founded 1935, current name adopted 1972
Private control
Academic year: May to August
Depts of art, English and world languages, history, mathematics and computer sciences, music, natural science, nursing, psychology, religious studies and philosophy, social science, studio art
Pres.: Dr GEORGE ARNOLD
Vice-Pres. for Advancement and External Relations: JAKE CZARNIK-NEIMEYER
Academic Dean: Dr JULIE MAYROSE
Dean for Students: Dr GEORGE GRINDE
Registrar: JANICE STINGLE
Dir for Library Services: RITA ROSE STAHL
Library of 60,000 vols, 250 current print periodicals and newspapers
Number of teachers: 120 (40 full-time, 80 part-time)
Number of students: 1,000
Publications: *Silver Reflections* (1 a year), *SLC Update* (52 a year)

UNIVERSITY OF WISCONSIN SYSTEM

1720 Van Hise Hall, 1220 Linden Dr., Madison, WI 53706-1559
Telephone: (608) 262-2321
Internet: www.wisconsin.edu
Founded 1848 as Univ. of Wisconsin, merged with the Wisconsin State Univs system 1971
State control
13 Instns offering 4-year courses (constituent univs), and 2 other instns offering 2-year courses (other constituent instns)
Pres.: KEVIN P. REILLY
Sr Vice-Pres. for Admin. and Fiscal Affairs: MICHAEL MORGAN
Sr Vice-Pres. for Academic Affairs: MARK NOOK
Vice-Pres. for Finance: DEBORAH A. DURCAN

Assoc. Vice-Pres. for Academic and Faculty Programs: STEPHEN KOLISON
Assoc. Vice-Pres. for Budget and Planning: FREDA HARRIS
Assoc. Vice-Pres. for Equity, Diversity and Inclusion: VICKI WASHINGTON
Assoc. Vice-Pres. for Human Resources: ALAN CRIST
Gen. Counsel: TOMAS STAFFORD
Number of teachers: 32,000
Number of students: 182,000 (26 campuses)...

CONSTITUENT UNIVERSITIES

University of Wisconsin—Eau Claire

POB 4004, 105 Garfield Ave, Eau Claire, WI 54702-4004
Telephone: (715) 836-2637
Internet: www.uwec.edu
Founded 1916 as Eau Claire State Normal School, present status 1971
Academic year: September to May
Chancellor: Dr JAMES C. SCHMIDT
Provost and Vice-Chancellor for Academic Affairs: PATRICIA A. KLEINE
Vice-Chancellor for Student Affairs: BETH A. HELLWIG
Dean for Students: BRIAN CARLISLE
Registrar: JIM BARRETT
Dir for Libraries: JOHN POLITZ
Library of 1,680,588 vols, 162,756 govt documents, 27,085 Wisconsin documents, 1,066,446 microfilms and microfiches, 36,768 periodical and newspaper subscriptions, 12,152 audiovisual materials, 61,087 maps
Number of teachers: 795
Number of students: 11,230

DEANS

College of Arts and Sciences: MARTY WOOD
College of Business: DIANE HOADLEY
College of Education and Human Sciences: GAIL SCUKANEC
College of Nursing and Health Sciences: Prof. Dr LINDA K. YOUNG

University of Wisconsin—Green Bay

2420 Nicolet Dr., Green Bay, WI 54311-7001
Telephone: (920) 465-2000
E-mail: uwgb@uwgb.edu
Internet: www.uwgb.edu
Founded 1965
Academic year: September to May
Chancellor: Dr THOMAS HARDEN
Provost and Vice-Chancellor for Academic Affairs: Dr JULIA E. WALLACE
Vice-Chancellor for Business and Finance (vacant)
Vice-Chancellor for Planning and Budget: Dr DEAN RODEHEAVER
Dean for Students: BRENDA AMENSON-HILL
Registrar: AMANDA HRUSKA
Library Dir: PAULA GANYARD
Library of 285,000 vols, 1m. bibliographic items, 50,000 maps, 2,000 music scores
Number of teachers: 355
Number of students: 6,635

DEANS

College of Liberal Arts and Sciences: SCOTT R. FURLONG
College of Professional Studies: Dr SUE J. MATTISON

University of Wisconsin—La Crosse

1725 State St, La Crosse, WI 54601
Telephone: (608) 785-8000
Internet: www.uwlax.edu
Founded 1909 as La Crosse Normal School
Chancellor: JOE GOW

Provost and Vice-Chancellor for Academic Affairs: KATHLEEN ENZ FINKEN
Vice-Chancellor for Admin. and Finance: BOB HETZEL
Asst Chancellor and Dean for Students: Dr PAULA M. KNUDSON
Dean for Student Devt and Academic Services: Dr PAULA M. KNUDSON
Dir for Library: ANITA EVANS
Library of 500,370 vols, 209,745 ebooks, 10,697 current serial titles, 581,624 microforms, 14,372 audiovisual material, 120,0331 govt documents
Number of teachers: 610
Number of students: 10,135

DEANS

College of Business Administration: Dr BILL COLCLOUGH
College of Liberal Studies: RUTHANN E. BENSON
College of Science and Health: BRUCE RILEY

University of Wisconsin—Madison

Madison, WI 53706
Telephone: (608) 263-2400
Internet: www.wisc.edu
Founded 1848, present status 1904
Academic year: September to May
Chancellor: DAVID WARD
Provost and Vice-Chancellor for Academic Affairs: PAUL M. DELUCA, Jr
Vice-Chancellor for Admin. and Budget: DARRELL BAZZELL
Vice-Chancellor for Medical Affairs: ROBERT N. GOLDEN
Vice-Chancellor for Research and Dean for Graduate School: MARTIN T. CADWALLADER
Vice-Chancellor for Univ. Relations: VINCE SWEENEY
Dean for Students: LORI BERQUAM
Registrar: SCOTT OWCZAREK
Dir for Admissions: ADELE C. BRUMIELD
Dir-Gen. for Library System: KENNETH FRAZIER
Library: see under Libraries and Archives
Number of teachers: 2,175
Number of students: 42,600

DEANS

College of Agricultural and Life Sciences: KATHRYN VANDENBOSCH
College of Engineering: PAUL S. PEERCY
College of Letters and Science: GARY SANDEFUR
Division of Continuing Studies: JEFFREY RUSSELL
Division of Int. Studies: GILLES BOUSQUET
Law School: MARGARET RAYMOND
School of Education: JULIE UNDERWOOD
School of Human Ecology: ROBIN A. DOUTHITT
School of Medicine and Public Health: Dr ROBERT N. GOLDEN
School of Nursing: Prof. KATHARYN A. MAY
School of Pharmacy: JEANETTE ROBERTS
School of Veterinary Medicine: Dr DARYL D. BUSS
Wisconsin School of Business: FRANÇOIS ORTALO-MAGNÉ

PROFESSORS

Some professors serve in more than one college or school

College of Agriculture and Life Sciences (116 Agricultural Hall, 1450 Linden Dr., Madison, WI 53706; tel. (608) 262-3003; e-mail info@cals.wisc.edu; internet www.cals.wisc.edu):

ALANEN, A. R., Landscape Architecture
ALBRECHT, K. A., Agronomy
ALBRECHT, R. M., Animal Science
AMASINO, R. M., Biochemistry
ANDERSON, P., Genetics
ANDREWS, J. H., Plant Pathology
ARMENTANO, L. E., Dairy Science

ATKINSON, R. L., Nutritional Sciences, Medicine
ATTIE, A. D., Biochemistry
BALKE, N. E., Agronomy
BARHAM, B. L., Programme on Agricultural Technology Studies
BISHOP, J. R., Food Science
BISHOP, R. C., Agricultural and Applied Economics
BLAND, W. L., Soil Science
BLATTNER, F. R., Genetics
BLEAM, W. F., Soil Science
BOCKHEIM, J. G., Soil Science
BOERBOOM, C. M., Agronomy
BOHNHOFF, D. R., Biological Systems Engineering
BROMLEY, D. W., Agricultural and Applied Economics
BROWN, M. R., Life Sciences Communication
BUEGE, D. R., Animal Science
BUNDY, L. G., Soil Science
BUONGIORNO, J., Forest Ecology and Management
BUTTEL, F. H., Rural Sociology
CAMPBELL, G. R., Agricultural and Applied Economics
CARROLL, S. B., Genetics
CARTER, M. R., Agricultural and Applied Economics
CHAMBLISS, G. H., Bacteriology
CHENOWETH, R. E., Urban and Regional Planning
CLAGETT-DAME, M., Biochemistry
CLAYTON, M. K., Statistics
CLELAND, W. W., Biochemistry
COLLINS, J. L., Rural Sociology, Women's Studies Programme
COMBS, D. K., Dairy Science
CONVERSE, J. C., Biological Systems Engineering
COOK, M. E., Animal Science
COORS, J. G., Agronomy
COX, M. M., Biochemistry
COX, T. L., Agricultural and Applied Economics
COXHEAD, I. A., Agricultural and Applied Economics
CRAIG, E. A., Biochemistry
CRAVEN, S. R., Wildlife Ecology
CRENSHAW, T. D., Animal Science
DAMODARAN, S., Food Science
DELLER, S. C., Agricultural and Applied Economics
DELUCA, H. F., Biochemistry
DOEBLEY, J., Genetics
DOLL, J. D., Agronomy
DONOHUE, T. J., Bacteriology
DOWNS, D. M., Bacteriology
DUKE, S. H., Agronomy
EIDE, D. J., Nutritional Sciences
ENGELS, W. R., Genetics
ESCALANTE, J. C., Bacteriology
ETZEL, M. R., Food Science
FIELD, D. R., Forest Ecology and Management
FILUTOWICZ, M. S., Bacteriology
FIRST, N. L., Animal Science
FOX, B. G., Biochemistry, Enzyme Institute
FREY, P. A., Biochemistry
FRIESEN, P. D., Biochemistry, Institute for Molecular Virology
GANETZKY, B. S., Genetics
GERMAN, T. L., Entomology
GIANOLA, D., Animal Science
GILBERT, J. C., Rural Sociology
GOLDMAN, I. L., Horticulture
GOODMAN, R. M., Plant Pathology
GOODMAN, W. G., Entomology
GOURSE, R. L., Bacteriology
GOWER, S. T., Forest Ecology and Management
GRAU, C. R., Plant Pathology
GREASER, M. L., Animal Science
GREEN, G. P., Rural Sociology
GRUMMER, R. R., Dairy Science

GUNASEKARAN, S., Biological Systems Engineering
GUNTHER, A. C., Life Sciences Communication
GURIES, R. P., Forest Ecology and Management
HANDELSMAN, J., Plant Pathology
HARRINGTON, J. A., Landscape Architecture
HARRIS, P. E., Agricultural and Applied Economics
HARTEL, R. W., Food Science
HAYES, C. E., Biochemistry
HELMKE, P. A., Soil Science
HICKEY, W. J., Soil Science
HITCHON, J. C., Life Sciences Communication
HOLDEN, H. M., Biochemistry
HOLMES, B. J., Biological Systems Engineering
HOWELL, E. A., Landscape Architecture
INGHAM, S. C., Food Science
INMAN, R. B., Biochemistry
INMAN, R. B., Institute for Molecular Virology
JEANNE, R. L., Entomology
JESSE, E. V., Agricultural and Applied Economics
JIANG, J., Horticulture
JOHNSON, E. A., Food Microbiology and Toxicology
JOHNSON, M. B., Agricultural and Applied Economics
JONES, B. L., Agricultural Database for Decision Support
KAEPPLER, S. M., Agronomy
KAMMEL, D. W., Biological Systems Engineering
KARASOV, W. H., Wildlife Ecology
KASPAR, C. W., Food Microbiology and Toxicology
KELLER, N. P., Food Microbiology and Toxicology, Plant Pathology
KIMBLE, J. E., Biochemistry
KIRKPATRICK, B. W., Animal Science
KLOPPENBURG, J. R., Rural Sociology
KRUGER, E. L., Forest Ecology and Management
KUNG, C., Genetics, Molecular Biology
KUNG, K.-J. S., Soil Science
KUSSOW, W. R., Soil Science
LAGRO, J. A., Jr, Urban and Regional Planning
LANDICK, R. C., Bacteriology
LAUER, J. G., Agronomy
LAUGHON, A. S., Genetics
LINDROTH, R. L., Entomology
LINDSAY, R. C., Food Science
LORIMER, C. G., Forest Ecology and Management
LOWERY, B., Soil Science
MCCLAIN, W. H., Bacteriology
MCCOWN, B. H., Horticulture
MACGUIDWIN, A. E., Plant Pathology
MADISON, F. W., Soil Science
MAHR, D. L., Entomology
MANSFIELD, J. M., Bacteriology
MARKLEY, J. L., Biochemistry
MARTIN, T. F. J., Biochemistry
MASSON, P. H., Genetics
MENON, A. K., Biochemistry
MLADENOFF, D. J., Forest Ecology and Management, Statistics
NELSON, D. L., Biochemistry
NEY, D. M., Nutritional Sciences
NIENHUIS, J., Horticulture
NITZKE, S. A., Nutritional Sciences
NORBACK, J. P., Food Science
NORDHEIM, E. V., Statistics
NORMAN, J. M., Soil Science
NOWAK, P., Soil and Water Conservation
NTAMBI, J. M., Biochemistry, Nutritional Sciences
OSBORN, T. C., Agronomy
PALMENBERG, A. C., Biochemistry
PALTA, J. P., Horticulture

PARIZA, M. W., Food Microbiology and Toxicology
PARKIN, K. L., Food Science
PARRISH, J. J., Animal Science
PASKEWITZ, S. M., Entomology
PETERSON, J. O., Environmental Resources Center
PHILLIPS, G. N., Jr, Biochemistry
PIKE, J. W., Biochemistry
PINGREE, S., Life Sciences Communication
POSNER, J. L., Agronomy
RAFFA, K. F., Entomology
RAINES, R. T., Biochemistry
RAYMENT, I., Biochemistry, Enzyme Institute
REED, G. H., Biochemistry
REINEMANN, D. J., Biological Systems Engineering
REZNIKOFF, W. S., Biochemistry
ROBERTS, G. P., Bacteriology
ROPER, T. R., Horticulture
ROUSE, D. I., Plant Pathology
RUTLEDGE, J. J., Animal Science
SCHAEFER, D. M., Animal Science
SCHOELLER, D. A., Nutritional Sciences
SCHULER, R. T., Biological Systems Engineering
SHAVER, R. D., Dairy Science
SHEFFIELD, L. G., Dairy Science
SHINNERS, K. J., Biological Systems Engineering
SHOOK, G. E., Dairy Science
SMITH, S. M., Nutritional Sciences
STANOSZ, G. R., Plant Pathology
STEELE, J. L., Food Science
STEVENSON, W. R., Plant Pathology
STIER, J. C., Forest Ecology and Management
STIMART, D. P., Horticulture
STOLTENBERG, D. E., Agronomy
SUNDE, R. A., Nutritional Sciences
SUSSMAN, M. R., Biochemistry
TEMPLE, S. A., Wildlife Ecology
THOMAS, D. L., Animal Science
TIGGES, L. M., Rural Sociology
TRACY, W. F., Agronomy
TYLER, E. J., Small-scale Waste, Soil Science
UNDERSANDER, D. J., Agronomy
VIERSTRA, R. D., Genetics
VOSS, P. R., Rural Sociology
WALSH, P. W., Biological Systems Engineering
WENDORFF, W. J., Food Science
WENTWORTH, B. C., Animal Science
WICKENS, M. P., Biochemistry
WILTBANK, M. C., Dairy Science
WONG, A. C., Food Microbiology and Toxicology
WYMAN, J. A., Entomology
YOUNG, D. K., Entomology

College of Engineering (2640 Engineering Hall, 1415 Engineering Dr., Madison, WI 53706; tel. (608) 262-3484; e-mail contact-us@engr.wisc.edu; internet www.engr.wisc.edu):

ABBOTT, N. L., Chemical Engineering
ADAMS, T. M., Civil and Environmental Engineering
ANDERSON, D. T., Electrical and Computer Engineering
ANDERSON, M. A., Civil and Environmental Engineering
ARMSTRONG, D. E., Civil and Environmental Engineering
BABCOCK, S. E., Materials Science and Engineering
BANK, L., Civil and Environmental Engineering
BARMISH, B. R., Electrical and Computer Engineering
BENSON, C. H., Civil and Environmental Engineering
BIER, V. M., Industrial Engineering

BISOGNANO, J. J., Synchrotron Radiation Center

BLANCHARD, J. P., Engineering Physics

BOOSKE, J. H., Electrical and Computer Engineering

BOSSCHER, P. J., Civil and Environmental Engineering

BOTEZ, D., Electrical and Computer Engineering

BUCKLEW, J. A., Electrical and Computer Engineering

CARAYON, P., Industrial Engineering

CERRINA, F., Electrical and Computer Engineering

CHANG, Y. A., Materials Science and Engineering

CORRADINI, M. L., Engineering Physics

CRAMER, S. M., Civil and Environmental Engineering

DAVIS, J. L., Engineering Outreach Technical Japanese, Technical Communications

DEMARCO, C., Electrical and Computer Engineering

DEPABLO, J. J., Chemical Engineering

DEVRIES, M. F., Mechanical Engineering

DOBSON, I., Electrical and Computer Engineering

DRUGAN, W. J., Engineering Physics

DUFFIE, N. A., Mechanical Engineering

DUMESIC, J. A., Chemical Engineering

EDIL, T. B., Civil and Environmental Engineering

ENGELSTAD, R. L., Mechanical Engineering

EOM, C.-B., Materials Science and Engineering

FARRELL, P. V., Mechanical Engineering

FONCK, R. J., Engineering Physics

FOSTER, D. E., Mechanical Engineering

FRONCZAK, F. J., Mechanical Engineering

GIACOMIN, A. J., Mechanical Engineering

GRAHAM, M. D., Chemical Engineering

HAIMSON, B. C., Materials Science and Engineering

HANNA, A. S., Civil and Environmental Engineering

HELLSTROM, E. E., Materials Science and Engineering

HENDERSON, D. L., Engineering Physics

HERSHKOWITZ, N., Engineering Physics

HILL, C. G., Jr, Chemical Engineering

HITCHON, W. N., Electrical and Computer Engineering

HOOPES, J. A., Civil and Environmental Engineering

HU, Y. H., Electrical and Computer Engineering

JAHNS, T., Electrical and Computer Engineering

KAMMER, D. C., Engineering Physics

KLEIN, S. A., Mechanical Engineering

KOU, S., Materials Science and Engineering

KUECH, T. F., Chemical Engineering

LAGALLY, M. G., Materials Science and Engineering

LAKES, R. C., Engineering Physics

LARBALESTIER, D. C., Materials Science and Engineering

LIPO, T. A., Electrical and Computer Engineering

LORENZ, R. D., Mechanical Engineering

LOVELL, E. G., Mechanical Engineering

LUMELSKY, V. J., Mechanical Engineering

MCCAUGHAN, L., Electrical and Computer Engineering

MARTIN, J. K., Mechanical Engineering

MOSES, G. A., Engineering Physics

MOSKWA, J. J., Mechanical Engineering

MURPHY, R. M., Chemical Engineering

OLEARY, P. R., Engineering Professional Devt

OSSWALD, T. A., Mechanical Engineering

PARK, J. K., Civil and Environmental Engineering

PEREPEZKO, J. H., Materials Science and Engineering

PLESHA, M. E., Engineering Physics

POTTER, K. W., Civil and Environmental Engineering

RADWIN, R. G., Biomedical Engineering

RAMANATHAN, P., Electrical and Computer Engineering

RAWLINGS, J. B., Chemical Engineering

REITZ, R. D., Mechanical Engineering

ROBINSON, S. M., Industrial Engineering

ROWLANDS, R. E., Mechanical Engineering

RUSSELL, J. S., Civil and Environmental Engineering

RUTLAND, C. J., Mechanical Engineering

SALUJA, K. K., Electrical and Computer Engineering

SCHARER, J. E., Electrical and Computer Engineering

SETHARES, W. A., Electrical and Computer Engineering

SHAPIRO, V., Mechanical Engineering

SHI, L., Industrial Engineering

SHOHET, J. L., Electrical and Computer Engineering

SMITH, J. E., Electrical and Computer Engineering

SMITH, M. J., Industrial Engineering

STEUDEL, H. J., Industrial Engineering

SURI, R., Industrial Engineering, Manufacturing Systems Engineering

TOMPKINS, W. J., Biomedical Engineering

UICKER, J. J., Jr, Mechanical Engineering

VANDERHEIDEN, G. C., Industrial Engineering

VANDERWEIDE, D. W., Electrical and Computer Engineering

VAN VEEN, B. D., Electrical and Computer Engineering

VEERAMANI, D., Industrial Engineering

VONDEROHE, A. P., Civil and Environmental Engineering

WENDT, A. E., Electrical and Computer Engineering

YIN, J., Chemical Engineering

ZIMMERMANN, D. R., Industrial Engineering

College of Letters and Science (5Suite 155, 1305 Linden Dr., Madison, WI 53706-1523; tel. (608) 262-5858; internet www.ls.wisc .edu):

ABRAMSON, L. Y., Psychology

ACKERMAN, S. A., Space Science and Engineering Center

ADELL, S. A., Afro-American Studies

ADEM, A., Mathematics

ADLER, H., German

AHERN, P. R., Mathematics

ALBUQUERQUE, S. J., Spanish and Portuguese

ALEY, J. E., School of Music

ALIBALI, M. W., Psychology

ALLEN, T. F., Botany

ANDERSON, L. A., School of Music

ANDERSON, M. P., Geology and Geophysics

ANDREONI, J., Economics

ANGENENT, S. B., Mathematics

ARCHDEACON, T. J., History

ASSADI, A. H., Mathematics

ATIS, S. G., Languages and Cultures of Asia

BACH, C. E., Computer Sciences

BAHR, J. M., Geology and Geophysics

BAKER, T. B., Gen. Internal Medicine

BALANTEKIN, A. B., Physics

BARGER, V. D., Physics

BARTLEY, L. L., School of Music

BATES, D. M., Statistics

BAUGHMAN, J. L., Journalism and Mass Communication

BAUM, D. A., Botany

BECK, A., Mathematics

BECKER, D. E., School of Music

BEISSINGER, M., Political Science

BENDER, T. K., English

BENKART, G. M., Mathematics

BERG, W. J., French and Italian

BERGHAHN, K. L., German

BERNARD-DONALS, M. F., English

BERNAULT, F., History

BERNSTEIN, S. D., English

BERRIDGE, C. W., Psychology

BERRY, P. E., Botany

BETHEA, D. M., Slavic Languages

BICKNER, R. J., Languages and Cultures of Asia

BILBIJA, K., Spanish and Portuguese

BLAIR, S. S., Zoology

BLANCO, A., Spanish and Portuguese

BLEECKER, A. B., Botany

BLESS, D. M., Communicative Disorders

BLUM, D. L., Journalism and Mass Communication

BOLOTIN, S. V., Mathematics

BORN, S. M., Urban and Regional Planning

BOSTON, N., Mathematics

BOWIE, K. A., Anthropology

BOYDSTON, J., History

BOYETTE, P. J., Theatre and Drama

BRANDT, D. L., English

BRANTLY, S. C., Scandinavian Studies

BRENNER, R. F., Hebrew and Semitic Studies

BRIGHOUSE, M. H., Philosophy

BROCK, W. A., Economics

BROWER, A. M., Social Work

BROWN, P. E., Geology and Geophysics

BRUALDI, R. A., Mathematics

BRUCH, L. W., Physics

BUCCINI, S., French and Italian

BUENGER, B. C., Art History

BÜHNEMANN, G., Languages and Cultures of Asia

BUNKER, S. G., Sociology

BUNN, H. T., Anthropology

BURKE, S. D., Chemistry

BURSTYN, J. N., Chemistry

BURT, J. E., Geography

BUSBY, K. R., French and Italian

BYERS, C. W., Geology and Geophysics

CAI, J.-Y., Computer Sciences

CALDERON, J. F., School of Music

CAMIC, C., Sociology

CANCIAN, M., Institute for Research on Poverty

CANON, D. T., Political Science

CARD, C. F., Philosophy

CARLSMITH, D. L., Physics

CARPENTER, S. R., Zoology

CARROLL, A. R., Geology and Geophysics

CARROLL, N., Philosophy

CASEY, C. P., Chemistry

CASPI, A., Psychology

CASSINELLI, J. P., Astronomy

CASTRONOVO, R., English

CAULKINS, J. H., French and Italian

CHAPPELL, R. J., Biostatistics and Medical Informatics

CHAVEZ, M. M. T., German

CHE, Y.-K., Economics

CHENG, T. F., East Asian Languages and Literature

CHIAL, M. R., Communicative Disorders

CHINN, M. D., Economics

CHISHOLM, S. L., School of Music

CHUBUKOV, A. V., Physics

CHURCHWELL, E. B., Astronomy

COE, C. L., Psychology

COHEN, C. L., History

COHEN, L. K., Comparative Literature

COLEMAN, J. J., Political Science

COOK, S. C., School of Music

COOPER, J. M., Jr, History

COPPERSMITH, S. N., Physics

CORFIS, I. A., Spanish and Portuguese

CORN, R. M., Chemistry

CORTEZ, E. M., Library and Information Studies

COURTENAY, W. J., History

COWELL, D. C., African Languages and Literature

Cox, D. P., Physics
Cravens, T. D., French and Italian
Crim, F. F., Jr, Chemistry
Cronon, W., History
Crook, D., School of Music
Curtin, M. J., Communication Arts
Cutter, R. J., East Asian Languages and Literature
D'Acci, J., Communication Arts
Dahl, L. F., Chemistry
Dannemiller, J. L., Psychology
Davidson, R. J., Psychology
Davis, R., School of Music
De Stasio, G., Physics
Debaisieux, M. M., French and Italian
DeLamater, J. D., Sociology
Dembski, S., School of Music
Demets, D. C., Geology and Geophysics
Deneckere, R. J., Economics
Desan, S. M., History
Desautels, E. J., Computer Sciences
Devine, P. G., Psychology
DeWitt, D. J., Computer Sciences
Dickey, L. W., History
Dickey, R. W., Mathematics
Dill, C. W., School of Music
Doane, A. N., English
Dodson, S. I., Zoology
Doksum, K. A., Statistics
Dolinin, A. A., Slavic Languages
Donnelly, J. S., Jr, History
Dorn, D. L., Theatre and Drama
Downs, D. A., Political Science
Draine, B., English
Drechsel, R. E., Journalism and Mass Communication
Dresang, D. L., Political Science
Drewal, H. J., Art History
DuBois, T. A., Scandinavian Studies
Dubrow, H., English
Dunlavy, C. A., History
Dunwoody, S. L., Journalism and Mass Communication
Durand, B., Physics
Durlauf, S. N., Economics
Dyer, C. R., Computer Sciences
Earp, L. M., School of Music
Ediger, M. D., Chemistry
Eells, E. T., Philosophy
Elder, J. W., Languages and Cultures of Asia
Ellis, A. B., Chemistry
Ellis Weismer, S., Communicative Disorders
Enc, M., Linguistics
Engel, C. M., Economics
Erwin, A. R., Physics
Essig, L., Theatre and Drama
Fair, J. E., Journalism and Mass Communication
Fernandez, D. E., Botany
Ferree, M. M., Sociology
Ferris, M. C., Computer Sciences
Filipowicz, H., Slavic Languages
Fink, M. D., School of Music
Fischer, C. N., Computer Sciences
Fitzpatrick, M. A., Communication Arts
Foley, J. A., Sustainability and Global Environment
Ford, C. E., English
Forster, M. R., Philosophy
Fowler, C. G., Communicative Disorders
Fox, M. V., Hebrew and Semitic Studies
Franklin, C. H., Political Science
Friedland, L. A., Journalism and Mass Communication
Friedman, E., Political Science
Friedman, S. S., English
Fujimura, J., Sociology
Fulmer, M. K., School of Music
Gallagher, J. S., III, Astronomy
Gamoran, A., Center for Education Research
Geary, D. H., Geology and Geophysics
Geiger, G. L., Art History
Gellman, S. H., Chemistry

George, K. M., Anthropology
Gernsbacher, M. A., Psychology
Givnish, T. J., Botany
Glenberg, A. M., Psychology
Goldsmith, H. H., Psychology
Goldstein, K. M., Political Science
Goodkin, R. E., French and Italian
Goodman, J. R., Computer Sciences
Gorski, P. S., Sociology
Gottlieb, P. L., Philosophy
Graham, L. K., Botany
Greenberg, J. S., Social Work
Greive, T. D., School of Music
Griffeath, D. S., Mathematics
Gross, S. D., German
Guerin Gonzales, C., Chicano Studies
Haeberli, W., Physics
Halzen, F. L., Physics
Hamers, R. J., Chemistry
Han, T., Physics
Hansen, B. E., Economics
Harackiewicz, J. M., Psychology
Hardin, J. D., Zoology
Harris, R. A., Spanish and Portuguese
Hauser, R. M., Sociology
Hausman, D., Philosophy
Hawkins, R. P., Journalism and Mass Communication
Hendel, I. E., Economics
Hildner, D. J., Spanish and Portuguese
Hill, D. D., School of Music
Hill, M. D., Computer Sciences
Hill, R. J., English
Hilmes, M., Communication Arts
Hilts, V. L, History of Science
Himpsel, F. J., Physics
Hinden, M. C., English
Hitchman, M. H., Atmospheric and Oceanic Sciences
Hoessel, J. G., Astronomy
Horwitz, S. B., Computer Sciences
Howell, R. B., German
Huber, D. L., Physics
Huddleston, J. R., Urban and Regional Planning
Hunt, L. H., Philosophy
Hunter, L., African Languages and Literature
Hutchinson, S. E., Anthropology
Hutchison, J. C., Art History
Hutchinson, S., Spanish and Portuguese
Hyde, J. S., Women's Studies Research Center
Hyer, B., School of Music
Ionel, E.-N., Mathematics
Isaacs, I. M., Mathematics
Ives, A. R., Zoology
Jacobs, H. M., Urban and Regional Planning
Jacobs, L., Communication Arts
James, C. J., German
James, S. M., Afro-American Studies
Jenison, R. L., Psychology
Jensen, J. L., School of Music
Jin, S., Mathematics
Johnson, A. A., Mathematics
Johnson, C. M., Geology and Geophysics
Johnson, R. A., Statistics
Joynt, R. J., Physics
Kaiser, N. A., German
Kaiser, N. A., Women's Studies Programme
Kaiser, R. J., Geography
Karp, P. D., School of Music
Kautsky, C. C., School of Music
Keene, N., Communication Arts
Keller, L., English
Kelley, T. M., English
Kennan, J. F., Economics
Kenoyer, J. M., Anthropology
Kent, R. D., Waisman Center for Mentally Retarded People and Human Devt
Kepley, V. I., Communication Arts
Kercheval, J. L., English
Khazanov, A., Anthropology
Kiessling, L. L., Biochemistry

Kirsch, J. A. W., Zoology
Kitchell, J. F., Zoology
Kleinhenz, C., French and Italian
Kluender, K. R., Psychology
Kluge, C. L., German
Knowles, R. A. J., English
Knox, J. C., Geography
Knutson, L. D., Physics
Koshar, R. J., History
Kosorok, M. R., Biostatistics and Medical Informatics
Kravetz, D., Social Work
Kritzer, H. M., Political Science
Kuelbs, J. D., Mathematics
Kunen, K., Mathematics
Kurtz, T. G., Mathematics
Kurtz, T. G., Statistics
Landis, C. R., Chemistry
Langer, U. G., French and Italian
Lawler, J. E., Physics
Layoun, M. N., Comparative Literature
Leary, J. P., Folklore
Leckrone, M. E., School of Music
Lee, J. B., History
Lempp, S., Mathematics
Lepowsky, M. A., Anthropology
Lezra, J., English
Li, Y., Linguistics
Lin, C. C., Physics
Lindstrom, D. L., History
Liu, Z.-U., Atmospheric and Oceanic Sciences
Livny, M., Computer Sciences
Loewenstein, D. A., English
Loh, W.-Y., Statistics
Longinovic, T., Slavic Languages
Louden, M. L., German
Lucas, S. E., Communication Arts
Lundin, A. H., Library and Information Studies
Lutfi, R. A., Communicative Disorders
Macaulay, M. A., Linguistics
McCammon, D., Physics
McClintock, A. P., English
McClure, L. K., Integrated Liberal Studies
McCoy, A. W., History
McDonald, D. M., History
Macdonald, M. C., Psychology
McGloin, N. H., East Asian Languages and Literature
McKay, N. Y., Afro-American Studies
McKay, N. Y., English
McKeown, J. C., Classics
McLeod, D. M., Journalism and Mass Communication
McMahon, R. J., Chemistry
Macken, M. A., Linguistics
Magnan, S. S., French and Italian
Mallon, F. E., History
Manion, M., Political Science
Manoogian, V. I., School of Music
Manuelli, R. E., Economics
Marcouiller, D. W., Urban and Regional Planning
Marler, C. A., Psychology
Marquez, B., Political Science
Martin, J. E., Atmospheric and Oceanic Sciences
Mathieu, R. D., Astronomy
Mayer, K. R., Political Science
Maynard, D. W., Sociology
Mazzaoui, M. F., History
Memon, M. U., Languages and Cultures of Asia
Menocal, N. G., Art History
Meyer, D. R., Social Work
Meyer, R. R., Computer Sciences
Mickelson, D. M., Geology and Geophysics
Miernowski, J., French and Italian
Milewski, P. A., Mathematics
Miller, A. W., Mathematics
Miller, B. P., Computer Sciences
Miller, J. F., Communicative Disorders
Mitman, G. A., History of Science
Moffitt, T. E., Psychology

MOORE, C. F., Psychology
MOORE, J. W., Chemistry
MOORE, M. L., English
MORAHG, G., Hebrew and Semitic Studies
MORGAN, D. O., Institute for Humanities Research
MORSE, R. M., Physics
MORTENSEN, C. D., Communication Arts
MURPHY, J. J., Communication Arts
MURRAY, J. K., Art History
NADLER, S. M., Philosophy
NARAYAN, K., Anthropology
NATHANSON, G. M., Chemistry
NAUGHTON, J. F., Computer Sciences
NELSEN, S. F., Chemistry
NEWLANDS, C., Classics
NEWMAN, J. P., Psychology
NICHOLS, D. A., Lafollette School of Public Affairs
NIENHAUSER, W. H., East Asian Languages and Literature
NILES, J. D., English, Institute for Humanities Research
NIXON, R. D., English
NORDSIECK, K. H., Astronomy
NYSTRAND, P. M., English
OGELMAN, H. B., Physics
OH, Y.-G., Mathematics
OHNUKI-TIERNEY, E., Anthropology
OLANIYAN, T., African Languages and Literature
OLIVER, P. E., Sociology
OLSSON, M. G., Physics
ONELLION, M. F., Physics
ONO, K., Mathematics
ORLIK, P. P., Mathematics
OSTERGREN, R. C., Geography
PALLONI, A., Sociology
PAN, Z., Communication Arts
PASSMAN, D. S., Mathematics
PAWLEY, J. B., Zoology
PAYNE, L. A., Political Science
PAYNE, S. G., History
PECK, J. A., Geography
PERRY, D., School of Music
PETTY, G. W., Atmospheric and Oceanic Sciences
PHILLIPS, Q. E., Art History
PILIAVIN, J. A., Sociology
PLUMMER, B. G., Afro-American Studies
PODESTA, G. A., Spanish and Portuguese
PONDROM, C. N., English
PONDROM, L. G., Physics
PORTER, W. P., Zoology
POWELL, B. B., Classics
PRAGER, S. C., Physics
PREPOST, R., Physics
PRICE, T. D., Anthropology
RABINOWITZ, P. H., Mathematics
RADANO, R. M., School of Music
RAFFERTY, E. M., Languages and Cultures of Asia
RAM, A., Mathematics
RAMAKRISHNAN, R., Computer Sciences
RAND, N. T., French and Italian
RAO, V. N., Languages and Cultures of Asia
REAMES, S. L., English
RECORD, M. T., Jr, Biochemistry
REEDER, D. D., Physics
REICH, H. J., Chemistry
REPS, T. W., Computer Sciences
RESCHOVSKY, A. M., Lafollette School of Public Affairs
REYNOLDS, A. J., Waisman Center for Mentally Retarded People and Human Devt
REYNOLDS, R. J., Astronomy
RICHARDSON, N. R., Political Science
RICHARDSON, W. W., Music
RIFKIN, B., Slavic Languages
RILEY, P. T., Political Science
RISLEY, W. R., Spanish and Portuguese
ROBBIN, J. W., Mathematics
ROBBINS, L. S., Library and Information Studies

ROBERTS, M. L., History
ROESLER, F. L., Physics
RON, A., Computer Sciences
ROSAY, J.-P., Mathematics
ROSENMEYER, P., Classics
ROTHSTEIN, E., English
RUAN, Y., Mathematics
RZCHOWSKI, M. S., Physics
SACK, R. D., Geography
SAIZ, P., Comparative Literature
SALMONS, J. C., German
SALOMON, F. L., Anthropology
SAMUELSON, L. W., Economics
SAPIRO, V., Academic Affairs
SAVAGE, B. D., Astronomy
SCARANO, F. A., History
SCHAEFFER, N. C., Sociology
SCHAFER, B. E., Political Science
SCHAFER-LANDAU, R. S., Philosophy
SCHAFFER, J. W., School of Music
SCHAMILOGLU, U., Languages and Cultures of Asia
SCHAPIRO, L. A., Philosophy
SCHATZBERG, M. G., Political Science
SCHAUB, T. H., English
SCHEUB, H. E., African Languages and Literature
SCHEUFELE, D. A., Journalism and Mass Communication
SCHLEICHER, A. Y., African Languages and Literature
SCHOLZ, J. K., Economics
SCHULTZ, S. K., History
SCHWARTZ, D. C., Chemistry
SEEGER, A., Mathematics
SEIDENBERG, M. S., Psychology
SEIDMAN, G. W., Sociology
SHAH, D. V., Journalism and Mass Communication
SHAH, H. G., Journalism and Mass Communication
SHAKHASHIRI, B. Z., Chemistry
SHANK, M. H., History of Science
SHAO, J., Statistics
SHARKEY, T. D., Botany
SHARPLESS, J. B., History
SHAVLIK, J. W., Computer Sciences
SHCHEGLOV, Y. K., Slavic Languages
SIBERT, E. L., Chemistry
SIDELLE, A. G., Philosophy
SILBERMAN, M. D., German
SIMO, J. A., Geology and Geophysics
SKINNER, J. L., Chemistry
SKLOOT, R., Theatre and Drama
SLEMROD, M., Mathematics
SMITH, J. R., School of Music
SMITH, LESLIE M., Mathematics
SMITH, LLOYD M., Chemistry
SMITH, W. H., Physics
SNOWDON, C. T., Psychology
SOBER, E. R., Philosophy
SOHI, G. S., Computer Sciences
SOLL, A. I., Philosophy
SOLOMON, M. H., Computer Sciences
SOMMERVILLE, J. P., History
SORKIN, D. J., Institute for Humanities Research
SPALDING, E. P., Botany
SPARKE, L. S., Astronomy
SPROTT, J. C., Physics
STAIGER, R. W., Economics
STAMPE, D. W., Philosophy
STEAKLEY, J. D., German
STEELE, J. A., English
STERN, S. J., History
STEUDEL, K. L., Zoology
STEVENS, J. D., School of Music
STOWE, J. C., School of Music
STRETTON, A. O., Zoology
STRIER, K. B., Anthropology
STRIKWERDA, J. C., Computer Sciences
SUCHMAN, M. C., Sociology
SUTTON, R. A., School of Music
SWACK, J. R., School of Music
SWEENEY, S. R., Theatre and Drama
SYTSMA, K. J., Botany

TAYLOR, M. S., Economics
TEMPRANO, J. C., Spanish and Portuguese
TERRY, P. W., Physics
TERWILLIGER, P. M., Mathematics
TESFAGIORGIS, F. H. W., Afro-American Studies
THIMMIG, L. L., School of Music
THOMSON, E. J., Sociology
THORNTON, M. C., Afro-American Studies
THURBER, C. H., Geology and Geophysics
TIMBIE, P. T., Physics
TREICHEL, P. M., Chemistry
TRIPOLI, A., Political Science
TRIPP, G. J., Atmospheric and Oceanic Sciences
TSUI, K.-W., Statistics
TURNER, M. G., Zoology
TZAVARAS, A., Mathematics
UHLENBROCK, D., Mathematics
VALLEY, J. W., Geology and Geophysics
VAN DEBURG, W. L., Afro-American Studies
VANDENHEUVEL, M. J., Theatre and Drama
VARDI, U., School of Music
VAUGHN, S. L., Journalism and Mass Communication
VERNON, M. K., Computer Sciences
WAHBA, G. G., Statistics
WAINGER, S., Mathematics
WALEFFE, F., Mathematics
WALKER, J. R., Economics
WALKER, T. G., Physics
WALLACE, R. W., English
WALLER, D. M., Botany
WANDEL, L. P., History
WANDEL, L. P., Institute for Humanities Research
WANG, P.-K., Atmospheric and Oceanic Sciences
WARDROP, R. L., Statistics
WEIMER, D., Political Science
WEINBROT, H. D., English
WEINHOLD, F. A., Chemistry
WEISMER, G. G., Communicative Disorders
WEISSHAAR, J. C., Chemistry
WELBOURNE, T. G., School of Music
WERNER, C., Afro-American Studies
WEST, K. D., Economics
WHITEHEAD, N. L., Anthropology
WHITLOCK, H. W., Jr, Chemistry
WILSON, F. D., Sociology
WILSON, G. K., Political Science
WILSON, R. L., Mathematics
WINICHAKUL, T., History
WINK, A., History
WINOKUR, M. J., Physics
WINSPUR, S., French and Italian
WITTE, J. F., Political Science
WOFFORD, S., English
WOLF, K., Scandinavian Studies
WOOD, D. A., Computer Sciences
WOODS, R. C., Chemistry
WORCESTER, N. A., Women's Studies Programme
WRIGHT, E. O., Sociology
WRIGHT, J. C., Chemistry
WRIGHT, S. J., Computer Science
WU, S. L. Y., Physics
YANDELL, K. E., Philosophy
YETHIRAJ, A., Chemistry
YOUNG, J. A., Atmospheric and Oceanic Sciences
YOUNG, R. F., English
ZAMORA, M. M., Spanish and Portuguese
ZEDLER, J. B., Arboretum: Tours
ZEDLER, J. B., Botany
ZEITLIN, J., Sociology
ZEPPENFELD, D., Physics
ZIMMERER, K. S., Geography
ZIMMERMAN, H. E., Chemistry
ZUENGLER, J., English
ZWEIBEL, E. G., Physics

Law School (975 Bascom Hall, Madison, WI 53706; tel. (608) 262-2240; e-mail deansoffice@law.wisc.edu; internet www.law.wisc.edu):

ALTHOUSE, A.
BRITO, T. L.
CARSTENSEN, P. C.
CHARO, R. A.
CHURCH, W. L.
CLAUSS, C. A.
DICKEY, W. J.
ERLANGER, H. S.
GREENE, L. S.
IRISH, C. R.
KAPLAN, L. V.
KIDWELL, J. A.
KLUG, H. J.
KOMESAR, N. K.
LARSON, J. E.
MACAULAY, S.
McEVOY, A. F.
MERTZ, E. E.
MORAN, B. I.
NOURSE, V. F.
PALAY, T. M.
SCHACTER, J. S.
SCHULTZ, D. E.
SHAFFER, G. C.
SMITH, D. G.
SMITH, M. E.
THOMPSON, C. F.
TRUBEK, D. M.

School of Education (Dean's Office, 377 Education Bldg, 1000 Bascom Hall, Madison, WI 53706; tel. (608) 262-1763; e-mail easinfo@education.wisc.edu; internet www.education.wisc.edu):

ABBEDUTO, L. J., Educational Psychology
APPLE, M. W., Curriculum and Instruction
BECKER, D. H., Art
BERVEN, N. L., Rehabilitation Psychology and Spec. Education
BLOCH, M., Curriculum and Instruction
BRECKENRIDGE, B. M., Art
BREDESON, P. V., Gen. Education
BROWN, B. B., Educational Psychology
CABRERA, A. F., Gen. Education
CAPPER, C. A., Gen. Education
CHAN, F., Rehabilitation Psychology and Spec. Education
COLEMAN, H. L. K., Counselling Psychology
CONRAD, C. F., Gen. Education
DAMER, J. F., Art
DERRY, S. J., Educational Psychology
ENRIGHT, R. D., Educational Psychology
ESCALANTE, J. A., Art
FENNELL, P., Art
FENSTER, F., Art
FEREN, S. F., Art
FULTZ, M., Educational Policy Studies
GEE, J. P., Curriculum and Instruction
GETTINGER, M., Educational Psychology
GLORIA, A. M., Counselling Psychology
GOMEZ, M. L., Curriculum and Instruction
GRANT, C. A., Curriculum and Instruction
GRAUE, M. E., Center for Education Research
HANLEY-MAXWELL, C. D., Rehabilitation Psychology and Spec. Education
HAYES, E. R., Curriculum and Instruction
HEWSON, P. W., Curriculum and Instruction
JI, L.-L., Kinesiology
KALISH, C. W., Educational Psychology
KAZAMIAS, A. M., Educational Policy Studies
KETCHUM, C. G., Art
KNOX, A. B., Gen. Education
KOYKKAR, J. N., Dance
KOZA, J. E., Curriculum and Instruction
KRATOCHWILL, T. R., Center for Education Research, Educational Psychology
LADSON-BILLINGS, G. J., Curriculum and Instruction
LEE, S. J., Educational Policy Studies
LI, C.-P., Dance
LOCKWOOD, A. L., Curriculum and Instruction
LOESER, T., Art

LONG, R. L., Art
LOWE, T. T., Art
LYNCH, R. T., Rehabilitation Psychology and Spec. Education
MARSCHALEK, D. G., Art
MELROSE, C. A., Dance
METZ, M. H., Educational Policy Studies
MORGAN, W. P., Kinesiology
MYERS, F. J., Art
ODDEN, A. R., Center for Education Research
OLNECK, M. R., Educational Policy Studies
PEKARSKY, D. N., Educational Policy Studies
PETERSON, K. D., Gen. Education
PHELPS, L. A., Center on Education and Work
POPKEWITZ, T. S., Curriculum and Instruction
PRICE, G. G., Curriculum and Instruction
PYLANT, C. S., Art
QUINTANA, S. M., Counselling Psychology
REESE, W. J., Educational Policy Studies
RIEBEN, J. R., Art
SCHEER, J. M., Art
SCHNEIDER, M. L., Kinesiology
SCHRAG, F. K., Educational Policy Studies
SERLIN, R. C., Educational Psychology
STEWART, J. H., Curriculum and Instruction
STREIBEL, M. J., Curriculum and Instruction
SUBKOVIAK, M. J., Educational Psychology
TARVER, S. G., Rehabilitation Psychology and Spec. Education
TOCHON, F. V., Curriculum and Instruction
VANDELL, D. L., Educational Psychology
WAMPOLD, B. E., Counselling Psychology
ZEICHNER, K. M., Curriculum and Instruction

School of Human Ecology (Third Fl., 1305 Linden Dr., Madison, WI 53706; tel. (608) 262-2608; e-mail csdept@mail.sohe.wisc.edu; internet www.sohe.wisc.edu):

APPLE, R. D., Consumer Science
AQUILINO, W. S., Human Devt and Family Studies
BOGENSCHNEIDER, K. P., Human Devt and Family Studies
BOYD, V. T., Environment, Textiles and Design
DOHR, J. H., Environment, Textiles and Design
DONG, W., Environment, Textiles and Design
GOEBEL, K. P., Consumer Science
GORDON, B., Environment, Textiles and Design
HOLDEN, K. C., Lafollette School of Public Affairs
HOYT, A. A., Consumer Science
HUNT, M. E., Environment, Textiles and Design
JASPER, C. R., Consumer Science
MARKS, N. F., Human Devt and Family Studies
RILEY, D. A., Human Devt and Family Studies
ROSSING, B. E., Interdisciplinary Studies
SARMADI, M., Environment, Textiles and Design
SHEEHAN, D., Environment, Textiles and Design
SMALL, S. A., Human Devt and Family Studies
WAY, W. L., Gen. Science
ZEPEDA, L., Consumer Science

School of Medicine and Public Health (750 University Ave, Madison, WI 53705; tel. (608) 263-8668; internet www.med.wisc.edu):

ABBOTT, D. H., Primate Research Center
ABBS, J. H., Neurology
ALBANESE, M. A., Population Health Sciences

ALBERT, D. M., Ophthalmology and Visual Sciences
ALLEN-HOFFMANN, B. L., Anatomic Pathology
ANDERSON, R. A., Pharmacology
ANDERSON, W. H., History of Medicine
BACH-Y-RITA, P., Rehabilitation Medicine
BANGS, J. D., Medical Microbiology
BENCA, R. M., Psychiatry
BENTZ, M. L., Dental and Plastic Surgery
BERSU, E. T., Anatomy
BERTICS, P. J., Biomolecular Chemistry
BIANCO, J. A., Nuclear Medicine
BIRD, I. M., Obstetrics and Gynaecology
BRADFIELD, C. A., Oncology
BRANDT, C. R., Ophthalmology and Visual Sciences
BRESNICK, E. H., Pharmacology
BROOKS, B. R., Neurology
BROW, D. A., Biomolecular Chemistry
BRUSKEWITZ, R. C., Urology
BURGESS, R. R., Oncology
CARNES, M. L., Geriatrics and Adult Devt
CHIU, S.-Y., Physiology
COMPTON, T., Oncology
CORONADO, R., Physiology
CRAIG, W. A., Infectious Disease
CRUICKSHANKS, K. J., Ophthalmology and Visual Sciences
DAHL, J. L., Pharmacology
DAHLBERG, J. E., Biomolecular Chemistry
DALESSANDRO, A., Transplant Research and Devt
DEJESUS, O. T., Medical Physics
DELUCA, P. M., Jr, Medical Physics
DEMETS, D. L., Biostatistics and Medical Informatics
DEMPSEY, J. A., Population Health Sciences
DEMPSEY, R. J., Neurological Surgery
DENNISTON, C., Genetics
DESMET, A. A., Diagnostic
DIAMOND, R. J., Psychiatry
DOVE, W. F., Sr, Oncology
DREZNER, M. K., Endocrinology
DRINKWATER, N. R., Oncology
EHRMEYER, S. L., Clinical Laboratory Science Programme
EPSTEIN, M. L., Anatomy
ERVASTI, J. M., Physiology
FAHL, W. E., Oncology
FALLON, J. F., Anatomy
FETTIPLACE, R., Physiology
FILLINGAME, R. H., Biomolecular Chemistry
FIORE, M. C., Gen. Internal Medicine
FLEMING, J. O., Neurology
FLEMING, M. F., Research Grants
FOLTS, J. D., Cardiology
FORD, C. N., Otolaryngology
FOST, N. C., Paediatrics
FREY, J. J., Family Medicine
FRYBACK, D. G., Population Health Sciences
GENTRY, L. R., Diagnostic
GERN, J. E., Paediatrics
GJERDE, C. L., Education Research and Devt
GLASSROTH, J. L., Medicine
GOLOS, T. G., Obstetrics and Gynaecology
GOULD, M. N., Oncology
GRAZIANO, F. M., Rheumatology
GREENSPAN, D. S., Anatomic Pathology
GREER, F. R., Paediatrics
GRIEP, A. E., Anatomy
GRIST, T. M., Diagnostic
GURMAN, A. S., Psychiatry
GUSTAFSON, J. P., Psychiatry
HABERLY, L. B., Anatomy
HACKNEY, C. M., Anatomy
HALL, T. J., Medical Physics
HARMS, B. A., Gen. Surgery
HART, M. N., Anatomic Pathology
HARTING, J. K., Anatomy
HAUGHTON, V. M., Diagnostic
HERMANN, B. P., Neurology
HOFFMANN, F. M., Oncology

HOLDEN, J. E., Medical Physics
JACKSON, M. B., Physiology
JANUARY, C. T., Cardiology
JARJOUR, N. N., Pulmonary Medicine
JEFCOATE, C. R., Pharmacology
KAHAN, L., Biomolecular Chemistry
KALAYOGLU, M., Transplant Research and Devt
KALIL, K., Anatomy
KALIL, R. E., Center for Neuroscience
KALIN, N. H., Psychiatry
KANAREK, M. S., Population Health Sciences
KAUFMAN, P. L., Ophthalmology and Visual Sciences
KEENE, J. S., Orthopedics
KELLEY, A. E., Psychiatry
KILEY, P. J., Biomolecular Medicine
KIM, K.-M., Biostatistics and Medical Informatics
KLEIN, B. E. K., Ophthalmology and Visual Sciences
KLEIN, B. S., Paediatrics
KLEIN, M. H., Psychiatry
KLEIN, R., Ophthalmology and Visual Sciences
KLIEWER, M. A., Diagnostic
KNECHTLE, M. J., Transplant Research and Devt
KUDSK, K. A., Gen. Surgery
KUHLMAN, J. E., Diagnostic
LALLEY, P. M., Physiology
LAMBERT, P. F., Oncology
LAUBE, D. W., Obstetrics and Gynaecology
LEAVITT, J. W., History of Medicine
LEAVITT, L. A., Paediatrics
LEMANSKE, R. F., Paediatrics
LINZER, M., Gen. Internal Medicine
LIPTON, P., Physiology
LOEB, D. D., Oncology
LONGLEY, B. J., Dept of Dermatology
LOVE, R. R., Clinical Oncology
LUCEY, M. R., Gastroenterology
MCBRIDE, P. E., Cardiology
MACDONALD, M. J., Paediatrics
MACK, E. A., Gen. Surgery
MACKIE, T. R., Medical Physics
MAGNESS, R. R., Obstetrics and Gynaecology
MAKI, D. G., Infectious Disease
MAKIELSKI, J. C., Cardiology
MALKOVSKY, M., Medical Microbiology
MALTER, J. S., Anatomic Pathology
MARES, J. A., Ophthalmology and Visual Sciences
MARSHALL, J. R., Psychiatry
MEHTA, M. P., Human Oncology
MEISNER, L. F., Population Health Sciences
MERTZ, J. E., Oncology
MEYER, K. C., Pulmonary Medicine
MISTRETTA, C. A., Medical Physics
MONTERO, V. M., Physiology
MOSHER, D. F., Hematology
MOSS, R. L., Physiology
MUKHTAR, H., Dept of Dermatology
MULLAHY, J., Population Health Sciences
NICKLES, R. J., Medical Physics
NIEDERHUBER, J. E., Comprehensive Cancer Center
NIETO, F. J., Population Health Sciences
NUMBERS, R. L., History of Medicine
OBERLEY, T. D., Anatomic Pathology, Medicine
OERTEL, D., Physiology
OLIVE, D. L., Obstetrics and Gynaecology
PALIWAL, B. R., Human Oncology
PALTA, M., Population Health Sciences
PAULI, R. M., Genetics
PAULNOCK, D. M., Medical Microbiology
PEARCE, R. A., Anaesthesiology
PROCTOR, R. A., Infectious Disease, Medical Microbiology
RAPRAEGER, A. C., Anatomic Pathology
REMINGTON, P. L., Population Health Sciences
RHODE, W. S., Physiology

RIKKERS, L., Dept of Surgery
ROBBINS, J., Gastroenterology
ROBINS, H. I., Clinical Oncology
ROSS, J., Oncology
RUOHO, A. E., Pharmacology
RUTECKI, P. A., Neurology
SANDOR, M., Anatomic Pathology
SCHILLER, J. H., Clinical Oncology
SCHULTZ, E., Anatomy
SKATRUD, J. B., Pulmonary Medicine
SKOCHELAK, S. E., Family Medicine
SOBKOWICZ, H. M., Neurology
SOLLINGER, H. W., Transplant Research and Devt
SONDEL, P. M., Paediatrics
SONZOGNI, W. C., Environmental Health Admin.
STAFSTROM, C. E., Neurology
STARLING, J. R., Gen. Surgery
STEELE, T. H., Nephrology
SUGDEN, W. M., Oncology
SUTULA, T. P., Neurology
SVENDSEN, C. N., Anatomy
TERASAWA-GRILLEY, E. I., Primate Research Center
THOMSON, J. A., Anatomy
TONONI, G., Psychiatry
TURNIPSEED, W. D., Gen. Surgery
TURSKI, P. A., Diagnostic
UEHLING, D. T., Urology
VALDIVIA, H. H., Physiology
VANDERBY, R., Jr, Orthopedics
VERMA, A. K., Human Oncology
WAKAI, R. T., Medical Physics
WALKER, J. W., Physiology
WATKINS, D. I., Anatomic Pathology
WEIDANZ, W. P., Medical Microbiology
WEINDRUCH, R. H., Geriatrics and Adult Devt
WEISBLUM, B., Pharmacology
WELCH, R. A., Medical Microbiology
WESTGARD, J. O., Anatomic Pathology
WHITE, J. G., Molecular Biology
WOLFE, B. L., Population Health Sciences
WOLFF, J. A., Paediatrics
WOOD, G. S., Dept of Dermatology
YIN, T. C. T., Physiology
YOUNG, J. A. T., Oncology
YOUNG, T. B., Population Health Sciences
ZAGZEBSKI, J. A., Medical Physics
ZDEBLICK, T. A., Orthopedics
ZISKIND-CONHAIM, L., Physiology

School of Nursing (K6/287 Clinical Science Center, 600 Highland Ave, Madison, WI 53792-2455; tel. (608) 263-5200; e-mail clangsdo@facstaff.wisc.edu; internet www .son.wisc.edu):

BAUMANN, L. J.
BOWERS, B. J.
BRENNAN, P.
BROWN, R. L.
DIEKELMANN, N. L.
DIEMER, G. A.
ESSER-ANDERSON, J. J.
GALAROWICZ, L. R. B.
KIRCHHOFF, K.
LASKY, P. A.
LITTLEFIELD, V. M.
MCCARTHY, D. O.
MCCUBBIN, M. A.
MAY, K. A.
OWEN, B. D.
RATHER, M. L.
RIESCH, S.
WARD, S. E.
WELLS, T.

School of Pharmacy (Renn and Bohm Hall, 777 Highland Ave, Madison, WI 53705-2222; tel. (608) 262-6234; internet www.pharmacy .wisc.edu):

DEMUTH, J. E., Pharmacy Outreach
HANSON, A. L., Pharmacy Outreach
HEIDEMAN, W.
HORNEMANN, U.
KRELING, D. H.

MELLON, W. S.
NORTHROP, D. B.
PETERSON, R. E.
RICH, D. H.
ROBINSON, J. R.
RUDY, T. A.
SCARBOROUGH, J.
SHEN, B.
THORSON, J. S.

School of Veterinary Medicine (2015 Linden Dr., Madison, WI 53706-1102; tel. (608) 263-2525; e-mail oaa@vetmed.wisc.edu; internet www.vetmed.wisc.edu):

AIKEN, J. M.
BEHAN, M., Comparative Biosciences
BJORLING, D. E., Surgical Sciences
BOSU, W. T., Medical Sciences
CAREY, H. V., Comparative Biosciences
CHRISTENSEN, B. M.
COLLINS, M.
CZUPRYNSKI, C. J
DUBIELZIG, R. R.
DUNCAN, I. D., Medical Sciences
ELFARRA, A. A., Comparative Biosciences
GINTHER, O. J.
HELLEKANT, G.
KAWAOKA, Y.
McGUIRK, S. M., Medical Sciences
MACWILLIAMS, P. S.
MANLEY, P. A., Surgical Sciences
MARKEL, M. D., Medical Sciences
MESSING, A.
MILETIC, V., Comparative Biosciences
MITCHELL, G. S., Comparative Biosciences
MURPHY, C. J., Surgical Sciences
OAKS, J. A., Comparative Biosciences
OLSEN, C. W.
SCHULER, L. A., Comparative Biosciences
SCHULTZ, R. D.
SPLITTER, G. A.
WILSMAN, N. J., Comparative Biosciences
YOSHINO, T. P.

Division of Continuing Studies (tel. (608) 262-1156; e-mail info@dcs.wisc.edu; internet www.dcs.wisc.edu):

AUERBACH, E. K., Liberal Studies and the Arts
CAMPBELL, J. A., Professional Devt and Applied Studies
COOK, M. J., Liberal Studies and the Arts
KESSEL, R., Professional Devt and Applied Studies
NELSON, L. J., Liberal Studies and the Arts
ORTON, B. M., Professional Devt and Applied Studies
PADDOCK, S. C., Professional Devt and Applied Studies
SCHULENBURG, J. A., Liberal Studies and the Arts
WILLIAMS, R. T., Professional Devt and Applied Studies

Nelson Institute for Environmental Studies, The (122 Science Hall, 550 N Park St, Madison, WI 53706-1491; tel. (608) 265-5296; internet www.ies.wisc.edu):

ADAMS, M. S., Botany
ALANEN, A. R., Landscape Architecture
ALBRECHT, K. A., Agronomy
ALLEN, T. F., Botany, Integrated Liberal Studies
ALVARADO, F. L., Electrical and Computer Engineering
ANDERSON, D. R., Business
ANDERSON, M. P., Geology and Geophysics
ANDREN, A. W., Civil and Environmental Engineering
ANDREWS, J. H., Plant Pathology
ARMSTRONG, D. E., Civil and Environmental Engineering
BAHR, J. M., Geology and Geophysics, Geological Engineering
BARROWS, R. L., Agricultural and Applied Economics
BAYLIS, J. R., Zoology

BERRY, P. E., Botany
BISHOP, R. C., Agricultural and Applied Economics
BLEAM, W. F., Soil Science
BOCKHEIM, J. G., Soil Science
BORN, S. M., Urban and Regional Planning
BRETHERTON, F. P., Atmospheric and Oceanic Sciences
BRINKMANN, W. A. R., Geography
BROWN, M. R., Agricultural Journalism
BUBENZER, G. D., Biological Systems Engineering
BUONGIORNO, J., Forest Ecology and Management
BUTTEL, F. H., Rural Sociology
CAMPBELL, G. R., Agricultural and Applied Economics
CARD, C. F., Philosophy, Women's Studies
CARPENTER, S. R., Zoology
CHENOWETH, R. E., Urban and Regional Planning
COLLINS, J. L., Sociology, Women's Studies
COMPTON, J. L., Forest Ecology and Management
CONVERSE, J. C., Biological Systems Engineering
CORRADINI, M. L., Engineering Physics, Mechanical Engineering
CRONON, W., History, Geography
DEWITT, C. B., Environmental Studies
DODSON, S., Zoology
DUNWOODY, S. L., Journalism and Mass Communication
ELDER, J. W., Sociology, Languages and Cultures of Asia
FELSTEHAUSEN, H. H., Urban and Regional Planning
FELTSKOG, E. N., English
FIELD, D. R., Forest Ecology and Management, Rural Sociology
FREUDENBURG, W. R., Rural Sociology
FRIEDMAN, E., Political Science
GIVNISH, T. J., Botany
GOODMAN, R. M., Plant Pathology
GRAHAM, L. K., Botany
GURIES, R. P., Forest Ecology and Management
HAMERS, R. J., Chemistry
HARRINGTON, J. A., Landscape Architecture
HAVEMAN, R. H., Economics
HEBERLEIN, T. A., Rural Sociology
HILL, R. J., English, American Indian Studies
HOOPES, J. A., Civil and Environmental Engineering
HOWELL, E. A., Landscape Architecture
HUDDLESTON, J. R., Urban and Regional Planning
IRISH, C. R., Law
JACOBS, H. M., Urban and Regional Planning
JEANNE, R. L., Entomology
JEFFRIES, T. W., Bacteriology
JOERES, E. F., Civil and Environmental Engineering
KANAREK, M. S., Preventive Medicine
KARASOV, W. H., Wildlife Ecology, Zoology
KITCHELL, J. F., Zoology
KNOX, J. C., Geography
KOEGEL, R. C., Biological Systems Engineering, Mechanical Engineering
KULCINSKI, G. L., Engineering Physics
KUTZBACH, J. E., Atmospheric and Oceanic Sciences
LEPOWSKY, M., Anthropology, Women's Studies
LILLESAND, T. M., Forest Ecology and Management, Civil and Environmental Engineering
LINDROTH, R. L., Entomology
LONG, W. F., Electrical and Computer Engineering
LOWERY, B., Soil Science
McCOWN, B. H., Horticulture
McEVOY, A. F., Law, History
McSWEENEY, K., Soil Science

MADISON, F. W., Soil Science
MARIEN, E. J., Business
MICKELSON, D. M., Geology and Geophysics
MITCHELL, J. W., Mechanical Engineering
MOERMOND, T. C., Zoology
NIEMANN, B. J., Jr, Urban and Regional Planning
NORMAN, J. M., Soil Science, Atmospheric and Oceanic Sciences
NOWAK, P., Rural Sociology
O'KEEFE, G. J., Life Sciences Communication
O'LEARY, P. R., Biological Systems Engineering
PALLONI, A., Sociology
PINGREE, S., Life Sciences Communication, Human Ecology
PORTER, W. P., Zoology
POSNER, J. L., Agronomy
POTTER, K. W., Civil and Environmental Engineering
RAY, R. O., Forest Ecology and Management
REED, J. D., Animal Sciences, Dairy Science
RICHARDSON, N. R., Political Science
RUTLEDGE, J. J., Animal Sciences, Genetics
SCARPACE, F. L., Civil and Environmental Engineering
SCHMIT, J. T., Business
SCHULER, R. T., Biological Systems Engineering
SNOWDON, C. T., Psychology, Zoology
SONZOGNI, W. C., Civil and Environmental Engineering
STEVENSON, R. E., Business
STEVENSON, W. R., Plant Pathology
STEWART, J. H., Curriculum and Instruction
STIER, J. C., Forest Ecology and Management
STRAUB, R. J., Biological Systems Engineering
STRIER, K. B., Anthropology, Zoology
TAYLOR, M. S., Economics
TEMPLE, S. A., Wildlife Ecology
TISHLER, W. H., Landscape Architecture
TRIPLETT, E. W., Agronomy
VALE, T. R., Geography
VANDELL, K. D., Business
VENTURA, S. J., Soil Science
VONDEROHE, A. P., Civil and Environmental Engineering
WALLER, D. M., Botany
WANG, P. K., Atmospheric and Oceanic Sciences
YANDELL, B. S., Statistics, Horticulture
YUILL, T. M., Animal Health and Biomedical Sciences, Pathobiological Sciences, Wildlife Ecology
ZEDLER, J. B., Botany, Arboretum
ZEDLER, P. H., Arboretum
ZIMMERER, K. S., Geography

Wisconsin School of Business (2265 Grainger Hall, 975 University Ave, Madison, WI 53706; tel. (608) 262-1550; e-mail busundergrads@bus.wisc.edu; internet www.bus.wisc.edu):

ALDAG, R. J.
ANDERSON, D. R.
ANTONIONI, D. T.
BROWN, D. P.
BROWNE, M. J.
COVALESKI, M. A.
DAVIS, J. S.
DUNHAM, R. B.
EICHENSEHER, J. W.
FREES, E. W.
GERHART, B. A.
HARMATUCK, D. J.
HAUSCH, D. B.
HEIDE, J. B.
HODDER, J. E.
JOHANNES, J. M.
KRAINER, R. E.

MALPEZZI, S.
MARIEN, E. J.
MILLER, R. B.
MINER, A. S.
MORRIS, J. G.
NAIR, R. D.
NEVIN, J. R.
PETER, J. P.
RIDDIOUGH, T. J.
RITTENBERG, L. E.
SCHMIT, J. T.
SHILLING, J. D., Real Estate
STEVENSON, R. E.
THOMPSON, J. C., Marketing
VANDELL, K. D.
WEMMERLÖV, U.
WEYGANDT, J. J.
WILD, J. J.

University of Wisconsin—Milwaukee

2200 E Kenwood Blvd, POB 413, Milwaukee, WI 53201-0413

Telephone: (414) 229-1122

Internet: www4.uwm.edu

Founded 1885

Academic year: September to May

Chancellor: MARK MONE

Provost and Vice-Chancellor for Academic Affairs: JOHANNES J. BRITZ

Vice-Chancellor for Devt and Alumni Relations: PAT BORGER

Vice-Chancellor for Finance and Admin. Affairs: CHRISTY L. BROWN

Vice-Chancellor for Student Affairs: MICHAEL R. LALIBERTE

Vice-Chancellor for Univ. Relations: TOM LULJAK

Dir for Libraries: EWA BARCZYK

Library: 5.2m. vols, 450,000 photographs

Number of teachers: 1,007

Number of students: 30,502

DEANS

College of Engineering and Applied Science: Prof. TIEN-CHIEN JEN

College of Health Sciences: CHUKUKA S. ENWEMEKA

College of Letters and Science: RODNEY A. SWAIN

College of Nursing: Dr SALLY P. LUNDEEN

Graduate School: DAVID YU

Helen Bader School of Social Welfare: Dr STAN STOJKOVIĆ

Peck School of the Arts: WADE HOBGOOD

School of Architecture and Urban Planning: SHARADHA NATRAJ

School of Continuing Education: Dr PATRICIA ARREDONDO

School of Education: CAROL COLBECK

School of Information Studies: DIETMAR WOLFRAM

Sheldon B. Lubar School of Business: TIMOTHY L. SMUNT

CHAIRS OF DEPARTMENT

College of Engineering and Applied Science (POB 784, Milwaukee, WI 53201-0784 3200 N Cramer St, Milwaukee, WI 53211; tel. (414) 229-4768; e-mail ceas-adv@uwm.edu; internet www.uwm.edu/ceas):

Civil Engineering and Mechanics: HECTOR BRAVO
Computer Science: HOSSEIN HOSSEINI
Electrical Engineering: GEORGE HANSON
Industrial and Manufacturing Engineering: ARUN GARG
Materials Engineering: NIDAL ABU-ZAHRA
Mechanical Engineering: ANOOP DHINGRA

College of Health Sciences (POB 413, Milwaukee, WI 53201-0413; tel. (414) 229-2758; e-mail chs-info@uwm.edu; internet www4.uwm.edu/chs):

Communication Sciences and Disorders: Dr MARYLOU GELFER

Health Informatics and Admin.: Dr TIMOTHY PATRICK
Health Sciences: Dr JERI-ANNE LYONS
Human Movement Sciences: Dr BARBARA MEYER
Occupational Science and Technology: Dr GINNY STOFFEL

College of Letters and Science (142 Holton Hall, 2442 E Hartford Ave, POB 413, Milwaukee, WI 53201; tel. (414) 229-4654; e-mail let-sci@uwm.edu; internet www.uwm.edu/letsci):

Africology: JOYCE KIRK
Anthropology: THOMAS MALABY
Art History: KENNETH BENDINER
Biological Sciences: DAAD SAFFARINI
Chemistry and Biochemistry: PETER GEISSINGER
Communication: WILLIAM KEITH
Economics: MOHSEN BAHMANI
English: LIAM CALLANAN
Foreign Languages and Literature: KEVIN MUSE
French, Italian and Comparative Literature: PETER PAIK
Geography: MARK SCHWARTZ
Geosciences: JOHN ISBELL
History: MERRY WIESNER-HANKS
Journalism, Advertising and Media Studies: DAVID ALLEN
Linguistics: HAMID OUALI
Mathematical Sciences: RICHARD STOCKBRIDGE
Philosophy: RICHARD TIERNEY
Physics: ALAN WISEMAN
Political Science: THOMAS HOLBROOK
Psychology: JAMES MOYER
Sociology: KENT REDDING
Spanish and Portuguese: R. JOHN MCCAW

College of Nursing (1921 E Hartford Ave, POB 413, Milwaukee, WI 53201; tel. (414) 229-4801; e-mail asknursing@uwm.edu; internet www.umw.edu/dept/nursing):

Foundations of Nursing: BETH ROGERS
Health Maintenance: EILEN SHEIL
Health Restoration: MARY WIERENGA

School of Architecture and Urban Planning (POB 413, Milwaukee, WI 53201; tel. (414) 229-4014; e-mail sarup-advising@uwm.edu; internet www.uwm.edu/sarup):

Architecture: LISA DISALVO
Urban Planning: LINDA SCUNCIO

School of Education (POB 413, Milwaukee, WI 53201-0413
Enderis Hall, 2400 E Hartford Ave, Milwaukee, WI 53211; tel. (414) 229-4721; e-mail soedean@uwm.edu; internet www.uwm.edu/soe):

Admin. Leadership: BARB DALEY
Curriculum and Instruction: Dr HOPE LONGWELL-GRICE
Educational Policy and Community Studies: AARON SCHUTZ
Educational Psychology: NADYA FOUAD
Exceptional Education: AMY OTIS-WILBORN

Peck School of the Arts (POB 413, Milwaukee, WI 53201; tel. (414) 229-4762; internet www.uwm.edu/soa):

Art and Design: LEE ANN GARRISON
Dance: Assoc. Prof. SIMONE FERRO
Film: ROB YEO
Music: Dr JON WELSTEAD
Theatre: LEROY STONER

University of Wisconsin—Oshkosh

800 Algoma Blvd, Oshkosh, WI 54901

Telephone: (920) 424-1234
Internet: www.uwosh.edu

Founded 1871, present name and status 1971

Chancellor: RICHARD H. WELLS
Provost and Vice-Chancellor for Academic Affairs: Dr LANE EARNS

Vice-Chancellor for Student Affairs: PETRA ROTA
Vice-Chancellor for Admin. Services: TOM SONNLEITNER
Dean for Students: SHARON KIPETZ
Dir for Library: PATRICK WILKINSON

Library of 448,751 vols, 12,812 ebooks, 96,046 bound periodical vols, 1,183 current periodical subscriptions, 133,282 vols of govt documents, 1.4m. microforms, 34,000 maps and 2,400 linear ft of archival material
Number of teachers: 280
Number of students: 13,000

DEANS

College of Business: Dr WILLIAM TALLON
College of Education and Human Services: Dr FREDERICK YEO
College of Letters and Science: Dr JOHN KOKER
College of Nursing: Dr ROSEMARY SMITH

University of Wisconsin—Parkside

900 Wood Rd, POB 2000, Kenosha, WI 53141-2000

Telephone: (262) 595-2345
Internet: www.uwp.edu

Founded 1968

Academic year: September to May

Chancellor: Dr DEBORAH FORD
Provost and Vice-Chancellor: Dr TERRY BROWN
Assoc. Provost for Academic Affairs: DENNIS ROME
Vice-Chancellor and Dean for Students: STEVE MCLAUGHLIN
Vice-Chancellor for Admin. and Fiscal Affairs: WILLIAM STREETER
Vice-Chancellor for Institutional Effectiveness: ANN ZANZIG
Vice-Chancellor for Univ. Relations and Advancement: KAREN COY-ROMANO
Registrar: RHONDA KIMMEL
Library Dir: VANAJA MENON

Library of 400,000 vols
Number of teachers: 125 full-time
Number of students: 5,300

DEANS

College of Arts and Sciences: Prof. Dr DEAN YOHNK
School of Business and Technology: Prof. Dr FRED EBEID

University of Wisconsin—Platteville

1 University Plaza, Platteville, WI 53818

Telephone: (608) 342-1491
E-mail: pr@uwplatt.edu
Internet: www.uwplatt.edu

Founded 1866 as Platteville Normal School, present name 1966, present status 1971

Chancellor: DENNIS J. SHIELDS
Provost and Vice-Chancellor for Academic Affairs: MITTIE NIMOCKS
Assoc. Vice-Chancellor: DAVID VAN BUREN
Asst Chancellor for Admission and Enrolment Services: ANGELA UDELHOFEN
Asst Chancellor for Admin. Services: ROBERT CRAMER
Asst Chancellor for Student Affairs: JOANNE WILSON
Asst Chancellor for Univ. Advancement: DENNIS COOLEY
Library Dir: ZORA SAMPSON

Library of 195,000 vols
Number of teachers: 265
Number of students: 7,930

DEANS

College of Business, Industry, Life Science and Agriculture: WAYNE WEBER

College of Engineering, Mathematics and Science: BILL HUDSON
College of Liberal Arts and Education: LAURA ANDERSON

University of Wisconsin—River Falls

410 S Third St, River Falls, WI 54022

Telephone: (715) 425-3911
Internet: www.uwrf.edu

Founded 1874 as State Normal School, present name and status 1971

Academic year: August to May

Chancellor: Dr DEAN VAN GALEN
Provost and Vice-Chancellor for Academic Affairs: Dr FERNANDO P. DELGADO
Vice-Chancellor for Admin. and Finance: JOSEPH HARBOUK
Assoc. Vice-Chancellor for Student Affairs: GREGG HEINSELMAN
Library Dir: VALERIE MALZACHER

Library of 220,500 vols
Number of teachers: 220
Number of students: 6,600

DEANS

College of Agriculture, Food and Environmental Sciences: DALE GALLENBERG
College of Arts and Sciences: BRAD CASKEY
College of Business and Economics: GLENN POTTS
College of Education and Professional Studies: LARRY SOLBERG
Outreach and Graduate Studies: Dr DOUG JOHNSON

University of Wisconsin—Stevens Point

2100 Main St, Stevens Point, WI 54481-3897

Telephone: (715) 346-0123
Internet: www.uwsp.edu

Founded 1894

Academic year: September to May

Chancellor: Dr BERNIE L. PATTERSON
Provost and Vice-Chancellor for Academic Affairs: GREGORY SUMMERS
Vice-Chancellor for Business Affairs: GREGORY M. DIEMER
Vice-Chancellor for Student Affairs: ALFRED THOMPSON
Library Dir: KATHY DAVIS

Library of 1,925,000 vol items
Number of teachers: 400
Number of students: 9,500

Publication: *Issues in Writing* (2 a year)

DEANS

College of Fine Arts and Communication: JEFFREY W. MORIN
College of Letters and Science: CHRISTOPHER CIRMO
College of Natural Resources: CHRISTINE THOMAS
College of Professional Studies: Dr MARTIN J. LOY

University of Wisconsin—Stout

Menomonie, WI 54751

Telephone: (715) 232-1122
Internet: www.uwstout.edu

Founded 1891, present name and status 1971

Academic year: September to May

Chancellor: Dr ROBERT MEYER
Provost and Vice-Chancellor for Academic and Student Affairs: Dr JOSEPH BESSIE
Vice-Chancellor for Admin. and Student Life Services: PHIL LYONS
Vice-Chancellor for Univ. Advancement and Marketing: MARK PARSONS
Dean for Students: JOAN THOMAS
Assoc. Vice-Chancellor: JACKIE WEISSENBURGER
Dir for Univ. Library (vacant)

Library of 264,332 vols

Number of teachers: 472
Number of students: 9,247
Publication: *Stoutonia* (14 a year)

DEANS

College of Arts, Humanities and Social Sciences: MARIA ALM
College of Education, Health and Human Sciences: Dr MARY HOPKINS-BEST
College of Management: ABEL ADEKOLA
College of Science, Technology, Engineering and Mathematics: JEFFREY ANDERSON

University of Wisconsin—Superior

Belknap and Catlin, POB 2000, Superior, WI 54880-4500

Telephone: (715) 394-8101
E-mail: relations@uwsuper.edu
Internet: www.uwsuper.edu

Founded 1893, present name and status 1971

Chancellor: Dr RENÉE WACHTER
Provost, Interim Vice-Chancellor for Academic Affairs and Dean for Faculties: Dr FAITH HENSRUD
Vice-Chancellor for Admin. and Finance: JANET HANSON
Vice-Chancellor for Univ. Advancement: JEANNE THOMPSON
Registrar: DIANE DOUGLAS
Dir for Library Services: DEBRA NORDGREN
Library of 240,000 vols
Number of teachers: 268 (112 full time, 56 part time)
Number of students: 2,867

University of Wisconsin—Whitewater

800 W Main St, Whitewater, WI 53190-1790

Telephone: (262) 472-1234
Internet: www.uww.edu

Founded 1868
Academic year: August to May

Chancellor: RICHARD J. TELFER
Provost and Vice-Chancellor for Academic Affairs: BEVERLY KOPPER
Vice-Chancellor for Admin. Affairs: JEFF ARNOLD
Vice-Chancellor for Student Affairs: THOMAS RIOS
Vice-Chancellor for Univ. Advancement: JON ENSLIN
Library Dir: MYRNA MCCALLISTER
Library of 601,533 vols (incl. books, serial backfiles and govt documents), 438,658 microforms and 19,137 audiovisual items, 6,822 current serial subscriptions, 75,922 ebooks, 15,000 print and ejournals
Number of teachers: 565
Number of students: 11,643

DEANS

College of Arts and Communication: MARK MCPHAIL
College of Business and Economics: Dr CHRISTINE CLEMENTS
College of Education and Professional Studies: KATY HEYNING
College of Letters and Sciences: MARY PINKERTON
School of Graduate Studies and Continuing Education: JOHN STONE..

OTHER CONSTITUENT INSTITUTIONS

University of Wisconsin Colleges

Central Administrative Offices, 780 Regent St, Suite 130, Madison, WI 53715-2635

Telephone: (608) 262-1783
Internet: www.uwc.edu

Colleges at Barron Co, Baraboo/Sauk Co, Fox Valley, Fond du Lac, Manitowoc, Marathon Co, Marshfield/Wood Co, Marinette, Richland, Rock Co, Sheboygan, Washington Co, Waukesha; 2-year courses at all colleges
Chancellor: RAY CROSS
Provost and Vice Chancellor: GREG HUTCHINS
Provost and Vice-Chancellor for Academic Affairs: GREG LAMPE
Vice-Chancellor for Admin. Services: STEVEN WILDECK
Registrar: LARRY GRAVES
Number of students: 14,385 at 13 campuses

University of Wisconsin Extension

432 N Lake St, Madison, WI 53706

Telephone: (608) 262-3786
Internet: www.uwex.edu

Works in partnership with 26 Univ. of Wisconsin System campuses, 72 Wisconsin counties, 3 tribal govts and public and private orgs; provides online distance programmes, spec. programmes and distance learning programmes

Chancellor: RAY CROSS
Provost and Vice-Chancellor: GREGORY HUTCHINS
Vice-Chancellor for Admin. and Financial Services: STEVE WILDECK

VITERBO UNIVERSITY

900 Viterbo Dr., La Crosse, WI 54601

Telephone: (608) 796-3000
E-mail: communication@viterbo.edu
Internet: www.viterbo.edu

Founded 1890, present name and status 2000
Private control
Academic year: August to May

Pres.: Dr RICHARD B. ARTMAN
Vice-Pres. for Academic Affairs: BARBARA GAYLE
Vice-Pres. for Admin. and Finance: TODD ERICSON
Vice-Pres. for Admission: ROLAND NELSON
Vice-Pres. for Communications and Marketing: PATRICK KERRIGAN
Vice-Pres. for Institutional Advancement: GARY KLEIN
Vice-Pres. for Mission and Ministry: Fr TOM O'NEILL
Vice-Pres. for Student Devt: DIANE BRIMMER
Dean for Admission: ROBERT FORGET
Registrar: AMY GLEASON
Library Dir: GRETEL STOCK-KUPPERMAN
Library of 90,000 vols
Number of teachers: 175 (92 full-time, 83 part-time)
Number of students: 3,200

DEANS

Dahl School of Business: THOMAS E. KNOTHE
School of Education: SUE BATELL
School of Fine Arts: TIMOTHY SCHORR
School of Letters and Sciences: GLENA G. TEMPLE
School of Nursing: Dr SILVANA F. RICHARDSON

WISCONSIN LUTHERAN COLLEGE

8800 W Bluemound Rd, Milwaukee, WI 53226

Telephone: (414) 443-8800
E-mail: admissions@wlc.edu
Internet: www.wlc.edu

Founded 1973
Private control

Pres.: Dr DANIEL W. JOHNSON
Provost: Dr JOHN KOLANDER
Vice-Pres. for Adult and Graduate Studies: JIM BRANDT
Vice-Pres. for Devt: CRAIG RUSSOW

Vice-Pres. for Finance: GARY SCHMID
Vice-Pres. for Student Affairs: Dr DENNIS MILLER
Assoc. Vice-Pres. for Marketing and Communication: VICKI HARTIG
Registrar: CAROL KOELPIN
Dir for Library Services: STARLA SIEGMANN
Number of students: 1,000

DEANS

College of Adult and Graduate Studies: JOYCE S. NATZKE
College of Arts and Sciences: JARROD ERBE
College of Professional Studies: DAVID BRIGHTSMAN

WISCONSIN SCHOOL OF PROFESSIONAL PSYCHOLOGY

9120 W Hampton Ave 212, Milwaukee, WI 53225-4960

Telephone: (414) 464-9777
E-mail: admissions@wspp.edu
Internet: www.wspp.edu

Founded 1978
Private control

Pres.: Dr KATHLEEN M. RUSCH
Dean: Dr DALE BASPALEC

Library of 100 vols

WYOMING

UNIVERSITY OF WYOMING

POB 3314, Laramie, WY 82071
1000 E University Ave, Laramie, WY 82071

Telephone: (307) 766-1121
E-mail: uwpres@uwyo.edu
Internet: www.uwyo.edu

Founded 1886
State control
Language of instruction: English
Academic year: September to May

Pres.: Dr THOMAS BUCHANAN
Provost: MYRON ALLEN
Assoc. Provost: NICOLE BALLENGER
Assoc. Provost: ANDREW HANSEN
Assoc. Provost and Dean for the Outreach School: MAGGI MURDOCK
Vice-Pres. for Academic Affairs: MAGGI MURDOCK
Vice-Pres. for Admin.: DOUGLAS H. VINZANT
Vice-Pres. for Information Technology: ROBERT AYLWARD
Vice-Pres. for Institutional Advancement: BEN BLALOCK
Vice-Pres. for Research and Economic Devt: WILLIAM GERN
Vice-Pres. for Student Affairs: SARA AXELSON
Dean for Univ. Libraries: MAGGIE FARREL
Library: see under Libraries and Archives
Number of teachers: 685
Number of students: 13,476

Publication: *UWYO Magazine* (3 a year)

DEANS

College of Agriculture and Natural Resources: FRANK GALEY
College of Arts and Sciences: Prof. Dr PAULA M. LUTZ
College of Business: BRENT HATHAWAY
College of Education: KAY PERSICHITTE
College of Engineering and Applied Science: ROB ETTEMA
College of Health Sciences: JOE STEINER
College of Law: STEVE EASTON
Graduate School: DON ROTH
Outreach School: Dr MAGGI MURDOCK

GUAM

The Higher Education System

Higher education in the unincorporated US territory of Guam is principally provided by the University of Guam (founded in 1952; present name and status adopted 1968 and 1984, respectively) and Guam Community College (founded in 1977), the latter of which provides vocational training programmes, which grant direct access to employment or transfer to a four-year college or university degree elsewhere. Enrolment at both institutions, which are accredited by the USA's Western Association of Schools and Colleges, has expanded in recent years, with 10,268 students enrolled at the Guam Community College in 2005/06, rising to 17,138 in 2011/12, and 3,387 students enrolled at the University of Guam in 2008/09, rising to 3,721 in 2011/12. Mangilao is home to the main campus of the Pacific Islands University (founded in 1976 as the Micronesian Institute of Biblical Studies on the island of Tol in Chuuk; present name and status adopted 2009); the Christian liberal arts institution is accredited by the USA's Transnational Association of Christian Colleges and Schools, and had a total enrolment of 100 students in 2011/12.

Regulatory Body

GOVERNMENT

Department of Chamorro Affairs: POB 2950, GU 96932; Terlaje Professional Bldg, First Fl., 194 Hernan Cortez Ave, Hagatna, GU 96910; tel. (671) 475-4278; internet www .dca.guam.gov; Chair. JOHN MAFNAS; Pres. JOSEPH ARTERO-CAMERON.

Guam Department of Education: POB DE, Hagåtña, GU 96932; Manuel F. Leon Guerrero Admin. Bldg, 312 Aspinall Ave, Hagåtña, GU 96910; tel. (671) 475-0462; e-mail geis@teleguam.net; internet www .gdoe.net; Superintendent JON FERNANDEZ.

Department of Youth Affairs/Depåttamenton Asunton Manhoben: POB 23672, GMF, GU 96921; 169 San Isidro St, Mangilao, GU 96923; tel. (671) 735-5010; internet dya.guam.gov; Dir ADONIS J. MENDIOLA.

Guam Historic Resources Division: 490 Chalan Palasyo, Agana Heights, GU 96910; tel. (671) 475-6294; internet historicguam .org; attached to Dept of Parks and Recreation; also known as the State Historic Preservation Office (SHPO); implements projects and activities that help engage in comprehensive historic preservation programmes that promote the use, conservation, preservation and presentation of historic properties; Guam State Historic Preservation Officer LYNDA BORDALLO-AGUON.

FUNDING

Guam Council on the Arts and Humanities/Kahan I Kutturan Guahan: POB 2950, GU 96932; Terlaje Professional Bldg, First Fl., 194 Hernan Cortez Ave, Hagatna, GU; tel. (671) 475-3661; e-mail info@caha .guam.gov; internet www.guamcaha.org; f. 1967 as Insular Arts Council; assures issuance of grants to individuals and orgs for the perpetuation of arts and culture of Guam; Dir. JOSEPH ARTERO-CAMERON.

Learned Societies

BIBLIOGRAPHY, LIBRARY SCIENCE AND MUSEOLOGY

Guam Library Association: POB 210, Hagatna, GU 96932; tel. (671) 475-4753; e-mail guam.library.association@gmail.com; internet sites.google.com/site/ guamlibraryassociation/home; promotes knowledge; develops and improves library services, resources on the island; provides continuing library-related education; Pres. CYNTHIA PRUSKI; Vice-Pres. for Membership

PATRIA SABLAN; Vice-Pres. for Programmes (vacant); Sec. OMAIRA BRUNAL-PERRY; Treas. MARIA OVALLES.

Guam Museum Foundation, Inc: POB 518, GU 96932; tel. (671) 475-4634; internet www.guammuseum.com; promotes cultural and historical activities; helps organize non-profit foundations under the laws of Guam; works closely with all govt entities, educational and religious instns, public and private orgs to maximize public benefits and opportunities.

ECONOMICS, LAW AND POLITICS

Guam Chamber of Commerce: 173 Aspinall Ave, Suite 101, Ada Plaza Center, Hagåtña, GU 96910; tel. (671) 472-6311; internet www.guamchamber.com.gu; develops, encourages, promotes and protects commercial, professional, financial, and gen. business interests of the Territory of Guam; extends and promotes trade and commerce, and fosters, develops and protects the industry of the Territory; procures laws and regulations desirable for the benefit of business in gen.; Chair. MARK J. SABLAN; Pres. DAVID P. LEDDY; Sec. and Treas. JOE ARNETT.

FINE AND PERFORMING ARTS

Guam Preservation Trust/Inangokkon Inadahi Guahan: POB 3036, Hagåtña, GU 96932; Historic Lujan House, 167, Padre Palomo St, Hagåtña, GU 96910; tel. (671) 472-9439; e-mail jqpreservation@guam.net; internet www.guampreservationtrust.com; f. 1990; acquires titles for preservation threatened historical sites; supports activities related to public appreciation of historic places; awards grants for property documentation, protection through stabilization, rehabilitation, reconstruction and restoration; archival and archaeological research; Chief Programme Officer JOSEPH E. QUINATA; Programme Officer ROSANNA BARCINAS.

Guam Symphony Society: POB 4069, Hagåtña, GU 96932; tel. (671) 477-1959; e-mail guamsymphonysociety@gmail.com; internet www.guamsymphony.com; f. 1967; promotes classical music; develops local musical talent; conducts spec. orchestral performances; 50 volunteer musicians; 44 mems; Dir for Music and Conductor STEPHEN C. BEDNARZYK; Pres. CLIFFORD A. GUZMAN; Vice-Pres. JOHN ROBERTSON; Sec. APRIL BRIGGS; Treas. MONICA PIDO.

MEDICINE

Guam Medical Association: tel. (671) 483-6600; e-mail guammedicalassociation@gmail .com; internet www.gma-assn.org; promotes art and science of medicine; advocates for community and public health issues; Pres. Dr PATRICK SANTOS; Pres.-Elect Dr THOMAS SHIEH; Exec. Dir PRAM SULLIVAN; Sec. Dr BEVAN GESLANI; publ. GMA Medical Journal.

Research Institutes

HISTORY, GEOGRAPHY AND ARCHAEOLOGY

WERI–Water and Environmental Research Institute of the Western Pacific: UOG Station, Mangilao, GU 96923; tel. (671) 735-2690; internet www.weriguam .org; f. 1975, fmrly the Water and Energy Research Institute of the Western Pacific, current name adopted 1998; attached to Univ. of Guam; research on water problems and water-related phenomena, incl. engineering, environmental chemistry, environmental toxicology, geology, geohydrology, hydrology, mapping and modelling, meteorology; production, distribution and management of freshwater resources; teaching and outreach programmes; Dir Prof. Dr GARY DENTON; Sec. NORMA C. BLAS.

LANGUAGE AND LITERATURE

Richard F. Taitano Micronesia Area Research Center (MARC): UOG Station, Mangilao, GU 96923; tel. (671) 735-2150; internet www.uog.edu/marc; attached to Univ. of Guam; preserves and provides access to collns of archival maps, photographs, texts and cultural materials related to the Micronesian geographical region; offers a programme in archaeological studies; instns: Micronesian Language Institute, Chamorro Language and Culture Center; 200 titles in separate series; library of 40,000 vols on Guam, Micronesia and the Pacific; 800 dissertations and theses, news clippings and brochures; Dir Dr JOHN A. PETERSON; Dir for Chamorro Language and Culture Center Dr MARILYN SALAS (acting).

MEDICINE

Cancer Research Center: UOG Station, Mangilao, GU 96923; tel. (671) 735-3036; e-mail u54@uguam.uog.edu; internet www .guamcancerresearch.org; f. 2004; attached to Univ. of Guam; promotes improvement in cancer research capabilities; undergraduate and postgraduate education and training; Prin. Investigator Dr HELEN WHIPPY.

NATURAL SCIENCES

Western Pacific Tropical Research Center: UOG Station, Mangilao, GU 96923; tel.

(671) 735-2684; internet www.wptrc.org; attached to Univ. of Guam; research in agricultural profitability, economic devt using natural resources, improvement in quality and safety of food products, protection of environment; offers Masters programmes in biology and environmental science; field stations in Ija, Inarajan and Yigo; soil testing laboratory; Dean and Dir Dr LEE S. YUDIN; Assoc. Dir Dr GREG WIECKO; Assoc. Dean Dr HENRY TAIJERON; publ. *WPTRC Impact Report* (1 a year).

Libraries and Archives

Hagåtña

Guam Law Library: 141 San Ramon St, Hagåtña, GU 96910-4333; tel. (671) 477-7623; e-mail gll@teleguam.net; internet www.guamlawlibrary.org; f. 1978; maintains the Judicial Center br. libraries serving judges and law clerks of the Guam Supreme and Superior courts; serves as depository for all public laws, exec. orders, legislative materials and decisions of the courts; 55,623 vols; Pres. VERNON PEREZ; Vice-Pres. BRIDGET ANN KEITH; Sec. JUDITH HATTORI; Treas. MITCHELL THOMPSON; Exec. Dir and Librarian GERALDINE A. CEPEDA.

Guam Public Library System: 254 Martyr St, Hagåtña, GU 96910-5141; tel. (671) 475-4751; e-mail gpls@gpls.guam.gov; internet gpls.guam.gov; f. 1949; promotes literacy and lifelong learning; maintains materials of cultural significance on the island; cooperates with libraries on other islands; local govt document depository; br. libraries in Barrigada, Dededo, Yona; 1 bookmobile; Dir and Acting Territorial Librarian TERESITA KENNIMER; Sec. BERTHA GUERRERO.

Branch Libraries:

Barrigada Public Library: 177 San Roque Dr., Barrigada; tel. (671) 734-5007.

Dededo Public Library: 283 W Santa Barbara Ave, Dededo; tel. (671) 632-5503.

Yona Public Library: 265 Sister Mary Eucharita Dr., Yona; tel. (671) 789-5010.

Mangilao

University of Guam, Robert F. Kennedy Memorial Library: Tan Siu Lin Bldg, UOG Station, Mangilao, GU 96923; tel. (671) 735-2331; e-mail csctsmth@uguam.uog.edu; internet www.uog.edu/library; f. 1963; central library facility at the Univ. of Guam; 126,987 vols, 99,502 print titles, 925,693 microfilm and microfiche units, 1,527 serial titles, 8,023 audiovisual items, 28,845 ejournals; Dir CHRISTINE K. SCOTT-SMITH.

Museums and Art Galleries

Agana

Marianas Military Museum: POB 455, 152 FPO AP, GU 96540-1000; tel. (617) 339-3319; e-mail milmuseum@kuentos.guam.net; internet www.guam.net/pub/milmuseum; f. 1999; helps explore the history of the relationship between the United States military, the Japanese military and island people of the W Pacific during the years of the Second World War; collns consist of American liberator and Japanese defender history and artefacts.

Jeff's Seaside Museum: 111 S Chalan Antigo, Ipan Talofofo, Agana, GU 96915-3708; tel. (671) 789-2683; e-mail info@jeffspiratescove.com; internet www .jeffspiratescove.com/museum.htm; f. 2000; displays unique artefacts, glass fish floats, stone tools, ifit wood sculptures, rare seashells, pottery, fine oil paintings, black coral and floating rock, actual wheel from the USS Battleship Oregon of 1893; CEO and Gen. Man. JEFFREY E. PLEADWELL.

Hagåtña

Guam Gallery of Arts: POB 362, Chamorro Village, Hagåtña, GU 96932; tel. (671) 472-9659; e-mail guamarts@ite.net; f. 1994; displays and sells original artwork and reproductions by local artists; seasonal exhibits and art events; Dir FILAMORE PALOMO ALCON.

Guam Museum of Culture, Art and History: POB 518, Hagåtña, GU 96932; 238 Archbishop Felixberto Flores St, DNA Bldg, 4th Fl., Suite 405, A, Hagåtña, GU 96910; tel. (671) 475-4634; e-mail leona@guammuseum .com; internet www.guammuseum.com; attached to Guam Museum Foundation Inc.; represents Guam and Chamorro cultures; holds artefacts and remnants destroyed during the Second World War; Dir ANTHONY RAMIREZ (acting).

Kahan i Kutturan Guahan—The Gallery: c/o Guam Ccl on Arts and Humanities Agency, POB 2950, Hagåtña GU 96932; Dos Amantes Complex, Two Lovers' Leap, Tamuning; tel. (671) 475-2781; e-mail info@ caha.guam.gov; internet www.guamcaha .org; f. 1972 as the Insular Arts Ccl Gallery; attached to Guam Ccl on the Arts and Humanities Agency; local art exhibits; fellowship programmes; grants and services to local artists; Chair. MONICA GUZMAN; Dir PATRICK BAMBA.

National Museum of the Dulce Nombre de Maria Cathedral Basilica: Cathedral-Basilica Pastoral Center, 207 Archbishop Felixberto C. Flores St, Hagåtña, GU 96910; tel. (671) 472-6201; e-mail info@ aganacathedral.org; internet aganacathedral .org; f. 2006; attached to Dulce Nombre de Maria Cathedral Basilica; displays frame views of the *Plaza de España*; inspirational art by local artists; Rector Mgr JAMES LEON GUERRERO BENAVENTE.

Pacific War Museum: POB 2037, Hagåtña, GU 96932; tel. (671) 477-8355; internet www .guammuseum.com/pacific-war.htm; f. 2008; Chair. JOHN GERBER; Admin. Dir MELA L. GOMEZ.

War in the Pacific National Historical Park: 135 Murray Blvd, Suite 100, Hagåtña, GU 96910; tel. (671) 477-7278; internet www .nps.gov/wapa; attached to Nat. Park Service (USA); battlefields, gun emplacements, trenches and historic structures recreate life in Guam during the Second World War; Memorial Wall: displays 16,142 names of Chamorro and US casualties; Liberator's Memorial: honours the armed forces of the 1944 landing on Guam; tropical resources incl. 3,500 marine species and 200 coral species.

Mangilao

Isla Center for the Arts: House 15, Dean's Circle, Univ. of Guam, Mangilao, GU 96923; tel. (671) 735-2965; e-mail islacenter@gmail .com; internet www.uog.edu/isla; f. 1980; attached to Univ. of Guam; conducts exhibitions, workshops, lectures; promotes appreciation and awareness of cultures of the W Pacific; permanent colln: indigenous arts and crafts from Micronesia, Europe and Philippines, items of contemporary W fine art, sculpture and Pre-Columbian art; Isla colln: 492 2-D and 3-D objects of folk art (produced for decorative purposes), ceremonial art (used by specific cultures in ceremonies and rituals), utilitarian crafts; other 2-D and 3-D works produced in Asian or Western cultures; Dir Dr VELMA YAMASHITA.

Universities

PACIFIC ISLANDS UNIVERSITY

POB 22619 GMF, Mangilao, GU 96921-2619
172 Kinney's Rd, Mangilao, GU 96913

Telephone: (671) 734-1812
E-mail: guamcampus@piu.edu
Internet: www.piu.edu

Founded 1976 as Micronesian Institute of Biblical Studies, present name and status 2009
Private control
Academic year: July to June
Christian liberal arts education; comprises Pacific Islands Bible College, Pacific Islands Evangelical Seminary, Pacific Islands Christian College
Chair.: HOWARD MERRELL
Sec.: SISKA HUTAPEA
Pres.: Dr DAVID L. OWEN
Provost and Academic Vice-Pres.: CHRISTEL WOOK (acting)
Vice-Pres. for Advancement: LISA COLLINS
Dir for Finance: CELIA ATOIGUE
Dir for Operations: CELIA ATOIGUE
Vice-Pres. for Student Life: ROBERT WATT
Registrar and Dir for Enrolment Management: URTE SCHERER
Dir for Libraries: LISA COLLINS
Library of 13,500 vols
Number of teachers: 30
Number of students: 165 (160 undergraduate, 5 graduate)

UNIVERSITY OF GUAM/ UNIBETSEDÅT GUAHAN

UOG Station, Mangilao, GU 96923

Telephone: (671) 735-2990
E-mail: admitme@uguam.uog.edu
Internet: www.uog.edu

Founded 1952 as the Territorial College of Guam, present campus 1960, accredited 1963 and 1965, current name adopted 1968, present status 1984
State control
Language of instruction: English
Academic year: August to May
Pres.: Dr ROBERT A. UNDERWOOD
Sr Vice-Pres. for Academic and Student Affairs: Dr HELEN J. D. WHIPPY
Vice-Pres. for Admin. and Finance: DAVID M. O'BRIEN
Dean for Enrolment Management and Student Services: Dr JULIE ULLOA-HEATH
Registrar: REMY B. CRISTOBAL
Library: see under Libraries and Archives
Number of teachers: 260
Number of students: 3,640

Publications: *Impact* (1 a year), *Isla* (2 a year), *Micronesian Educator* (1 a year), *Micronesica* (2 a year), *Storyboard: A Journal of Pacific Imagery*, *University Magazine* (1 a year)

DEANS

College of Liberal Arts and Social Sciences: Dr JAMES D. SELLMANN
College of Natural and Applied Sciences: Dr LEE S. YUDIN
School of Business and Public Administration: Dr ANITA BORJA-ENRIQUEZ
School of Education: Dr ELIZABETH HAWTHORNE
School of Nursing and Health Sciences: Dr MARIA SALOMON

PUERTO RICO

The Higher Education System

The Universidad de Puerto Rico (founded in 1903) is the oldest institution of higher education in the Commonwealth of Puerto Rico and currently has eleven branch campuses with 61,967 students enrolled. The US unincorporated territory has a further three public higher education institutions, and 33 private higher education institutions, some of which are sizeable, with a number of branch campuses dispersed throughout the island. In 2011/12 there were 250,011 students enrolled at institutions of higher education, with 62,257 in public institutions and 187,754 in private institutions; of these, 29,631 were pursuing postgraduate qualifications. A strong US influence is evident within the Puerto Rican education system as a whole, and the higher education sector is no different.

Since 2010, responsibility for the provision of higher education within Puerto Rico lies with the Consejo de Educación de Puerto Rico (Puerto Rico Council on Education). Quality assurance and accreditation is the responsibility of the Council's División de Licenciamiento y Acreditación (Division of Licensing and Accreditation). A number of institutions are concurrently accredited by the USA's Middle States Association of Colleges and Schools.

Admission to degree-level education requires students to hold the High School Graduation Diploma and to sit an entrance examination. Some programmes at certain institutions may have additional entrance requirements. The Grado Asociado (Associate degree), which allows specialization in either the arts or the sciences, requires at least two years' study and can lead to further study or grant direct access to employment. The Grado de Bachillerato (Bachelors degree) can last between three and six years, depending on the course and grant access to postgraduate programmes of study. The main postgraduate qualification is the Grado de Maestría (Masters degree), which requires an additional one to three years of study following the Grado de Bachillerato. Certificado Profesional Post Bachillerato (Professional Postgraduate Certificate) and Certificado Post Maestría (Post-Masters Certificate) programmes are also available, and require one or two semesters of study following the Grado de Bachillerato or the Grado de Maestría, respectively. The Doctorado (Doctorate) is the highest academic qualification and requires a further five years of study following the Grado de Bachillerato or four years following the Grado de Maestría.

Technical and vocational education is offered by technical colleges, which offer two-year Certificate courses and two-year Associate degrees, as well as university bridging courses. A number of vocational courses are also provided by the Department of Education, some of which lead to specific careers and others of which are more general in nature.

Regulatory and Representative Bodies

GOVERNMENT

Consejo de Educación de Puerto Rico (Board of Education of Puerto Rico): POB 19900, San Juan, PR 00910-1900; Ave Ponce de León 268, Edif. Hato Rey Center, 15°, Hato Rey, San Juan, PR 00918; tel. (787) 641-7100; e-mail info@cge.gobierno.pr; internet www.ce.pr.gov; f. 2010, by merger of Consejo de Educación Superior de Puerto Rico (CESPR) with Consejo General de Educación (CGE); 9 mems; Pres. Dr RICARDO APONTE PARSI; Dir Dr CARMEN LUZ BERRIOS RIVERA.

Department of Education: POB 190759, San Juan, PR 00919-0759; Calle Federico Costa No 150 Hato Rey, San Juan, PR 00919-0759; tel. (787) 773-5800; internet www.de.gobierno.pr; Sec. RAFAEL ROMÁN MELÉNDEZ.

Learned Societies

GENERAL

Ateneo de Ponce (Athenaeum of Ponce): POB 32144, Ponce, PR 00732-2144; e-mail ateneodeponce@yahoo.com; internet www.ateneodeponce.com; f. 1956; lectures, competitions, confs and concerts; publs 5 divs of fine arts, history, literature, moral and political sciences, physics, natural science and mathematics; Pres. Prof. JOSÉ R. CEPEDA; Vice-Pres. Prof. ADA HILDA MARTÍNEZ DE ALICEA; Sec. Prof. MARÍA ISABEL CHAPARRO DE ESCABÍ; publ. *Primera Antología de Poesía.*

Ateneo Puertorriqueño (Puerto Rican Athenaeum): Apdo 9021180, San Juan, PR 00902-1180; Parada 1, Ave Constitución, Puerta de Tierra, San Juan, PR 00902; tel. (787) 721-3877; e-mail info@ateneopr.org; internet www.ateneopr.org; f. 1876; promotes science, literature and fine arts; art gallery: holds 450 works of art; 600 mems; library of 30,000 vols, periodicals, old newspapers and microfiche; Pres. Lic. EDUARDO MORALES COLL; Vice-Pres. Dr EDGAR QUILES FERRER; Sec. Dr RIGOBERTO FIGUEROA; publ. *Revista* (2 a year).

Fundación Puertorriqueña de las Humanidades (Puerto Rican Foundation for the Humanities): POB 9023920, San Juan, PR 00902-3920; 109 Calle San José Esq. Luna 3°, San Juan, PR; tel. (787) 721-2087; e-mail contacto@fphpr.org; internet www.fphpr.org; f. 1977; attached to Nat. Endowment for the Humanities; promotes appreciation of Puerto Rican culture; stimulates exchange of ideas and diffusion of humanistic knowledge in soc.; sponsors humanities projects; develops educational programmes, educational instns, public and private entities, cultural centres around Puerto Rico; Pres. RAFAEL MARTÍNEZ MARGARIDA; Exec. Dir Dr JUAN M. GONZÁLEZ LAMELA.

BIBLIOGRAPHY, LIBRARY SCIENCE AND MUSEOLOGY

Sociedad de Bibliotecarios de Puerto Rico (Society of Librarians of Puerto Rico): Apdo 22898, San Juan, PR 00931-2898; tel. (787) 764-0000; e-mail sbpr1961@gmail.com; internet www.sociedadbibliotecarios.org; f. 1961; attached to Dept of State of Puerto Rico; protects, nurtures and educates its mems in information services; mems incl. academic librarians, scholars, specialists, archivists, librarians, booksellers, publishers and other professionals in the field of information; organizes confs, continuing education activities; promotes Library Week; 280 mems; Pres. Dr SNEJANKA PENKOVA; Vice-Pres. JUAN VARGAS; Sec. NYDIA HERNÁNDEZ REVERÓN; publ. *Acceso: Revista Puertorriqueña de Bibliotecología y Documentación* (1 a year).

FINE AND PERFORMING ARTS

Fundación Nacional para la Cultura Popular (National Foundation for Popular Culture): Apdo 9023971, San Juan, PR 00902-3971; Calle Fortaleza No 56, Viejo San Juan, PR 00901; tel. (787) 724-7165; e-mail info@prpop.org; internet www.prpop.org; f. 1996; attached to Dept of State of Puerto Rico; promotes popular culture, classical and folk music of Puerto Rico; Dir JAVIER SANTIAGO.

Instituto de Cultura Puertorriqueña (Institute of Puerto Rican Culture): Apdo 9024184, San Juan, PR 00902-4184; Antiguo Asilo de Beneficencia, Barrio Ballajá Viejo, San Juan, PR; tel. (787) 724-0700; e-mail webicp@icp.gobierno.pr; internet www.icp.gobierno.pr; f. 1955; studies and preserves Puerto Rican historical and cultural patrimony; Pres. ANGEL DARÍO CARRERO; Exec. Dir LILLIANA RAMOS COLLADO; publ. *Revista del Instituto de Cultura Puertorriqueña.*

HISTORY, GEOGRAPHY AND ARCHAEOLOGY

Academia Puertorriqueña de la Historia (Puerto Rican Academy of History): Apdo 1447, San Juan; Del Cristo 52, San Juan, PR 00901-1308; tel. (787) 721-5200; f. 1932; 40 mems; Pres. LUIS E. GONZÁLEZ VALES.

LANGUAGE AND LITERATURE

Academia Puertorriqueña de la Lengua Española (Puerto Rican Academy of the Spanish Language): Apdo 36-4008, San Juan, PR 00936-4008; Cuartel de Ballajá, 3°, Viejo San Juan, PR 00906; tel. (787) 721-6070; e-mail info@academiapr.org; internet www.academiapr.org; f. 1955; attached to Asociación de Academias de la Lengua Española; represents Puerto Rico internationally; conducts research and ensures representation of Spanish in all academic publs; 28 mems; Dir Dr JOSÉ LUIS VEGA;

Deputy Dir LUCE LÓPEZ BARALT; Sec. EDUARDO FORASTIERI (acting); publ. *DILO* (2 a year).

PEN Club de Puerto Rico Internacional (International PEN Club of Puerto Rico): POB 362765, San Juan, PR 00936-2765; 6 Mariano Ramírez Bages, Apartment 4B, San Juan, PR 00907; tel. (787) 421-5080; e-mail penclubpr@gmail.com; internet www .pen-international.org/centres/puerto-rican-centre; f. 1966; promotes literature and defends freedom of expression; 40 mems; Pres. ELSA TIÓ FERNÁNDEZ; Vice-Pres. YOLANDA LÓPEZ LÓPEZ.

MEDICINE

Sociedad Puertorriqueña de Endocrinología y Diabetología (Puerto Rican Society of Endocrinology and Diabetology): POB 364208, San Juan, PR 00936-4208; tel. (787) 309-3707; e-mail sped.endos@gmail.com; internet www.spedpr.org; f. 1977; Pres. Dr HARRY JIMÉNEZ; Sec. Dra MYRNA LYZETTE LÓPEZ; publ. *Revista Diabetes*.

NATURAL SCIENCES

General

Sociedad de Historia Natural de Puerto Rico (Natural History Society of Puerto Rico): POB 361036, San Juan, PR 00936-1036; internet www.shnpr.org; f. 1960; promotes, studies, conserves environment and natural resources; incl. monthly confs and field trips; Pres. GLORIA MEDINA; Sec. CARMEN MEDINA.

Biological Sciences

Heliconia Society of Puerto Rico, Inc.: Urb. Atlantic View, 44 Calle Venus, Carolina, PR 00979-4806; tel. (787) 396-6544; internet www.heliconiasocietypr.org; f. 1996; promotes understanding of Heliconia and related plants of the order of Zingiberales through education, research and communication; interacts with Heliconia Soc. Int; 60 mems; Pres. HÉCTOR MÉNDEZ CARATINI; Sec. YVETTE RIVERA.

Research Institutes

AGRICULTURE, FISHERIES AND VETERINARY SCIENCE

International Institute of Tropical Forestry: USDA Forest Service IITF, Jardín Botánico Sur, 1201 Calle Ceiba, San Juan, PR 00926-1119; tel. (787) 766-5335; internet www.fs.fed.us/global/iitf; f. 1939; attached to US Dept of Agriculture, Forest Service; research on issues affecting tropical forests and grasslands; cooperative assistance to state and private forest landowners, timber processors; cooperative research with univs and US and foreign governmental agencies; trains foreign forestry students in cooperation with FAO and USAID; library of 15,000 vols; Dir Dr ARIEL E. LUGO.

Tropical Agriculture Research Station: 2200 Pedro Albizu Campos Ave, Suite 201, Mayagüez, PR 00680-5470; tel. (787) 831-3435; internet www.ars.usda.gov/main/site_main.htm?modecode=66-35-05-00; f. 1901; attached to Agricultural Research Service, US Dept of Agriculture; conducts research to develop solutions to agricultural problems of high nat. priority; protects human health and environment; Coordinator Dr RICARDO GOENAGA; Sec. MARIBEL ROLDÁN.

MEDICINE

Puerto Rico Health Services Research Institute: POB 365067, San Juan, PR 00936; Graduate School of Public Health, Puerto Rico Health Services Research Institute, Univ. of Puerto Rico, Medical Sciences Campus, San Juan, PR 00936; tel. (787) 758-2525; internet prhsri.rcm.upr.edu; f. 2003; attached to Univ. of Puerto Rico, Medical Sciences Campus; develops research-based knowledge to help decision-makers in evaluating health policy options; Dir Prof. Dr ROBERTO E. TORRES ZENO.

NATURAL SCIENCES

Biological Sciences

Institute for Tropical Ecosystem Studies: POB 70377, San Juan, PR 00936-8377; 207 Anexo Facundo Bueso, Ponce de León Ave, Univ. of Puerto Rico, Río Piedras campus, San Juan, PR 00931; tel. (787) 764-0000; e-mail ecortescoss@gmail.com; internet www .ites.upr.edu; f. 1957 as PR Nuclear Center; attached to Faculty of Natural Sciences, Univ. of Puerto Rico; research and devt of tropical terrestrial ecological studies; graduate-level research and training centre in basic ecological principles, primarily for minorities; increases public awareness on the importance of natural ecosystems to human welfare; field station in Rio Grande; Dir Dr NICHOLAS BROKAW; Sec. EVA CORTES.

Puerto Rico Water Resources and Environmental Research Institute: POB 9000, Mayagüez, PR 00681-9000; tel. (787) 833-0300; e-mail prwreri@uprm.edu; internet prwreri.uprm.edu; f. 1964; attached to Univ. of Puerto Rico, Mayagüez Campus; conducts basic and applied research to solve water and environmental problems of Puerto Rico, the Caribbean and Latin America; trains scientists and engineers through hands-on participation in research; Dir Dr JORGE RIVERA SANTOS; Assoc. Dir Dr WALTER SILVA ARAYA.

Physical Sciences

Arecibo Observatory: HC-3, POB 53995, Arecibo, PR 00612; Route 625 Barrio Esperanza, Arecibo, PR 00612; tel. (787) 878-2612; e-mail prcz@naic.edu; internet www.naic .edu; f. 1960; attached to Nat. Astronomy and Ionosphere Center; provides observing time, electronics, computer, travel and logistic support to scientists from all over the world; research in radio astronomy, planetary radar, terrestrial aeronomy; library of 2,300 vols, 845 periodicals; Dir Dr ROBERT KERR.

RELIGION, SOCIOLOGY AND ANTHROPOLOGY

Instituto de Estudios del Caribe (Institute of Caribbean Studies): POB 23345, San Juan, PR 00931-3345; tel. (787) 764-0000; e-mail iec.ics@upr.edu; internet iec-ics.uprrp .edu; f. 1958; attached to Faculty of Social Sciences, Univ. of Puerto Rico; research and outreach programmes on topics of the Greater Caribbean; Dir Dr HUMBERTO GARCÍA MUÑIZ; Admin. Officer EDUARDO RODRÍGUEZ LEON; Sec. MILDRED SANTIAGO; publ. *Caribbean Studies*.

Libraries and Archives

Bayamón

Biblioteca Municipal de Bayamón Dra Pilar Barbosa (Dr Pilar Barbosa Bayamón Municipal Library): POB 1588, Bayamón, PR 00960; Paseo del Parque, Esq. Calle Betances, Bayamón, PR 00960; tel. (787) 787-5161; f. 2000; attached to Dept of Municipal Education; provides information services for digital print, process devt research and education; Dir GLADYS GALLARDO JANER.

Mayagüez

Biblioteca General Recinto Universitario de Mayagüez (General Library University Campus of Mayagüez): POB 9000, Mayagüez, PR 00681; Univ. of Puerto Rico, Mayagüez Campus, Mayagüez, PR 00681; tel. (787) 265-3810; e-mail library@uprm.edu; internet www.uprm.edu/library; f. 1911; attached to Univ. de Puerto Rico; main library and 1 spec. departmental colln; subject areas incl. agriculture, animal industries, energy, engineering, marine and environmental sciences, natural and applied sciences, technology; 164,068 vols, 5,259 journals, 263,982 microfiches, 12,719 microcards, 19,486 microfilms, 561,641 govt documents, 949 films, 8,149 maps, 8,458 sound recordings, 606 musical scores, 917 sound magnetic tapes, 24,810 slides, 4,550 video cassettes, 687 film strips, 3,585 theses and dissertations, 7m. US patents and 3m. US issues trademarks; Dir Prof. NORMA I. SOJO (acting); publs *Bibliorum* (4 a year), *Conoce Tu Biblioteca* (1 a year).

Ponce

Biblioteca Encarnación Valdés (Encarnación Valdés Library): 2250 Boulevard Luis A. Ferré Aguayo, Suite 509, Ponce, PR 00717-9997; tel. (787) 841-2000; f. 1969; attached to Pontifical Catholic Univ. of Puerto Rico; spec. collns: Puerto Rican materials, Murga Colln; 269,000 vols, 46,000 periodicals, 4,600 microfilms, 5,000 records, 358 classical music CDs and 363 cassettes of classical and popular music; spec. colln incl. 6,000 vols of Puerto Rican journals; Dir MAGDA I. VARGAS RODRÍGUEZ; Exec. Sec. CECILIA LUGO CASIANO.

Biblioteca Publica de Ponce/Biblioteca Municipal Mariana Suárez de Longo or Biblioteca Municipal de Ponce (Ponce Public Library): Apdo 331709, Ponce, PR 00733-1709; Marginal Conchita Dapena Blvd Miguel Pou Ponce, Ponce, PR 00731; tel. (787) 812-3004; e-mail biblioteca .municipal.msl@ponce.pr.gov; f. 1937; library system in Ponce; incl. 5 satellite libraries, 2 digital education centres; 20,000 vols; Administrator JO ARLEEN TORRES; Librarian M. MADERA.

Biblioteca Mons. Fremiot Torres Oliver (Mons. Fremiot Torres Oliver Library): 2250 Blvd Luis A. Ferré Aguayo, Suite 544, Ponce, PR 00717-9997; tel. (787) 841-2000; e-mail bib-derecho@pucpr.edu; internet www .spserver2008.pucpr.edu/lawlibrary/; f. 1961; attached to School of Law, Pontifical Catholic Univ. of Puerto Rico; spec. collns: UN and US fed. documents; 207,095 vols; Dir NOELIA PADUA; Sec. PEREZ SOLMARIE; publ. *Revista de Derecho Puertorriqueño* (4 a year).

San Juan

Archivo General de Puerto Rico (General Archive of Puerto Rico): Instituto de Cultura Puertorriqueña, Apdo 9024184, San Juan, PR 00902-4184; Ave Constitución 500, Puerta de Tierra, San Juan, PR 00902-4184; tel. (787) 725-1060; e-mail archivogeneral@icp.gobierno.pr; f. 1955; attached to Instituto de Cultura Puertorriqueña; 80,000 cu ft of documents, incl. text, graphics (drawings, maps), print (newspapers, journals), films and recordings in various formats; Dir and Archivist JOSÉ A. FLORES.

Biblioteca de Derecho de la Universidad de Puerto Rico (Law Library of the University of Puerto Rico): Univ. of Puerto Rico, POB 23310, San Juan, PR 00931-3310; tel. (787) 999-9684; internet www.law.upr.edu/biblioteca; f. 1913; attached to Univ. de Puerto Rico; incl. Caribbean, European Union, Puerto Rican, Spanish legal colln; foreign law, international law colln; rare books, special colln of the Supreme Court of Puerto Rico; 400,000 vols, 4,000 serials; Dir Dr MARÍA M. OTERO DE LEÓN; Archivist JOSEPH H. MORALES CARDONA; Sec. ARLENE I. AGOSTO GARCÍA.

Biblioteca del Departamento de Justicia (Library of the Department of Justice): GPOB 9020192, San Juan, PR 00902-0192; Calle Olimpo, Esq. Axtmayer, Parada 11, No 601, Miramar, San Juan, PR; tel. (787) 724-6869; e-mail webmail@justicia.gobierno.pr; internet www.justicia.gobierno.pr/ rs_template/v2/secauxase/secauxase_biblo .html; f. 1950; attached to Dept of Justice of Puerto Rico; provides and manages bibliographic and reference services required by the Office of the Atty Gen.; allocates library resources to lawyers and specialized divs of the Dept of Justice; incl. dictionaries, encyclopedias, treatises, Puerto Rican colln files, legislative histories, fed. and state collns, texts by subject, colln of Spanish jurisprudence, magazines and annual reports of public agencies; 75,000 vols; Dir for the Law Library Licda KARLA RIVERA AVILÉS; publs *Anuario Estadístico*, *Informe Anual del Secretario de Justicia de Puerto Rico*, *Opiniones del Secretario de Justicia de Puerto Rico*.

Biblioteca del Tribunal Supremo (Library of the Supreme Court): Apdo 9022392, San Juan, PR 00902-2392; Ave Muñoz Rivera, Parada 8 ½ Puerta de Tierra (Parque Muñoz Rivera), San Juan, PR; tel. (787) 723-3550; internet www.ramajudicial .pr/sistema/supremo/biblioteca.htm; f. 1953; attached to Dept of Justice of Puerto Rico; non-lending library for general public; spec. collns: law reviews, US statutes and cases, rare 19th-century law books, Puerto Rican law, common and Spanish civil law; 80,000 vols; Head Librarian IVETTE TORRES ALVAREZ; Sec. CECILIA SANTANA GONZALEZ; publ. *Nuevas Adquisiciones* (12 a year).

Biblioteca Madre María Teresa Guevara (Madre María Teresa Guevara Library): Apdo 12383, San Juan, PR 00914-8505; tel. (787) 728-1515; internet biblioteca.sagrado .edu; f. 1935; attached to Univ. del Sagrado Corazón; incl. historical archives of reports, catalogues, directories, maps, correspondence, photographs, posters and magazines of the univ.; Puerto Rican colln of journals and brochures published by govt agencies; 130,000 vols, 1,297 periodicals, 17,000 reference materials incl. dictionaries, encyclopedias, handbooks; Dir SONIA DÍAZ LATORRE.

Biblioteca Nacional de Puerto Rico (National Library of Puerto Rico): Instituto de Cultura Puertorriqueña, Apdo 9024184, San Juan, PR 00902-4184; Ave de la Constitución (antes Ponce de León) 500, Puerta de Tierra, San Juan, PR 00902-4184; tel. (787) 725-1060; e-mail biblioteca@icp .gobierno.pr; internet www.icp.gobierno.pr/ programas/biblioteca-nacional-de-puerto-rico; f. 2003; attached to Instituto de Cultura Puertorriqueña; acquires, preserves and disseminates the literature written and published in Puerto Rico; incl. rare and general books on Puerto Rico, Van Deussen library of Puerto Rico, house library of Concha Meléndez; 70,000 vols incl. Puerto Rican colln, colln of Eugenio Maria de Hostos; Dir JOSEFINA GÓMEZ DE HILLYER.

Biblioteca Regional del Caribe y de Estudios Latinoamericanos (Regional Library of Caribbean and Latin American Studies): Edif. José M. Lázaro, 1°, Ala Oeste, San Juan, PR 00931-1927; tel. (787) 764-0000; e-mail afigueroa@uprrp.edu; internet biblioteca.uprrp.edu/caribe.htm; f. 1946 in Trinidad, current location 1975; attached to Univ. of Puerto Rico, Río Piedras campus; research library, specializes in all topics related to Latin America and Caribbean; resources available in Dutch, English, French, Spanish; 50,000 vols; spec. colln of Caribbean Comm. documents; Librarian Prof. ALMALUCES FIGUEROA ORTIZ.

Carnegie Public Library: 7 Ave Ponce de León, Puerta de Tierra, San Juan, PR 00901-2010; tel. (787) 722-4753; f. 1903 as Island Library, current name and bldg 1918; attached to Dept of Education of Puerto Rico; 50,000 vols; Dir MARY JEAN HAVER.

Museums and Art Galleries

Ponce

Museo de Arte de Ponce (Ponce Museum of Art): 2325 Blvd Luis A. Ferré, Ponce, PR 00717-0776; tel. (787) 840-1510; e-mail info@ museoarteponce.org; internet www .museoarteponce.org; f. 1959; European, American and Hispanic American paintings and sculptures; western art from Renaissance to 19th century; permanent colln consists of 4,500 paintings, sculptures, decorative arts, ceramics, 3D objects, photographs, prints, drawings, cassettes and sound art installations; library of 7,000 vols; Exec. Dir ALEJANDRA PEÑA; Assoc. Curator MARÍA A. DE LA SERNA; publ. *ARTEPONCE*.

Museo de la Historia de Ponce (Museum of the History of Ponce): Calle 53 Isabel, Ponce, PR 00730; tel. (787) 844-7071; e-mail museodelahistoriadeponce@yahoo.com; f. 1992; promotes research and preservation of Ponce's heritage for the devt of the Puerto Rican culture; 10 galleries display colln of 3,000 Ponce historical relics, photos and documents.

Museo de la Música Puertorriqueña (Museum of Puerto Rican Music): Calle Isabel, Esq. Salud, Ponce, PR; tel. (787) 848-7016; e-mail museosyparques@icp .gobierno.pr; f. 1990; attached to Museos y Parques, Instituto de Cultura Puertorriqueña; neoclassical residence that displays the history of indigenous Puerto Rican music from pre-Columbian times to the present; Dir NICOLE PIETRI.

San Germán

Museo de Arte Religioso Santo Domingo de Porta Coeli (Museum of Religious Art Santo Domingo de Porta Coeli): Apdo 1160, San Germán, PR 00683; Frente a la Plaza Santo Domingo, San Germán, PR; tel. (787) 892-5845; e-mail museosyparques@icp .gobierno.pr; attached to Museos y Parques, Instituto de Cultura Puertorriqueña; 17th-century church of Porta Coeli; restored and converted into museum of religious art (paintings, pictures, sculptures, ornaments and ritual objects) in 1960; Admin. GUIDO BARLETTA.

San Juan

Museo de Arte Contemporáneo de Puerto Rico (Puerto Rico Museum of Contemporary Art): POB 362377, San Juan, PR 00936-2377; Edif. Histórico Rafael M. de Labra, Ave Juan Ponce de León, Esq. Ave Roberto H. Todd, Parada 18, Santurce, San Juan, PR; tel. (787) 977-4030; e-mail adm1@ museocontemporaneopr.org; internet www .museocontemporaneopr.org; f. 1984; collects, preserves, documents and disseminates art produced in Puerto Rico, the Caribbean and Latin America from the 1940s to present; library of 32,000 vols; Pres. SALVADOR ALEMAÑY; Sec. HÉCTOR SALDAÑA EGOZCUE; publs *25 Años del Museo de Arte Contemporáneo de Puerto Rico, Arnaldo Roche Rabell: Azul, David LaChapelle. NosOtros: La Humanidad al Borde*.

Museo de Arte de Puerto Rico (Museum of Art of Puerto Rico): Ave de Diego 299, Santurce, San Juan, PR 00910; tel. (787) 977-6277; e-mail info@mapr.org; internet www .mapr.org; f. 2000; colln of Puerto Rican fine art from 17th century to present; 1,100 works of art incl. drawings, prints, photography, sculpture and new media; Pres. ARTURO GARCIA-SOLA (acting); Exec. Dir Dr LOURDES RAMOS; Sec. DIEGO R. FIGUEROA (acting).

Museo de Arte e Historia de San Juan (Museum of Art and History in San Juan): Calle Norzagaray 150, San Juan, PR; tel. (787) 724-1875; f. 1979; museum bldg reflects Spanish colonial architecture; showcases history of San Juan from 1521 to the present; displays artworks by local artists; Dir for Education Program ZIGRY IGNACIO.

Museo de Historia Militar (Museum of Military History): c/o Instituto de Cultura Puertorriqueña, POB 9024184, San Juan, PR 00902-4184; tel. (787) 723-7837; e-mail webicp@icp.gobierno.pr; small Spanish fort from 16th century.

Museo La Casa del Libro (The House of the Book Museum): Calle del Cristo 255, POB 9023544, San Juan, PR 00902-3544; 199 Callejón de la Capilla, San Juan, PR; tel. (787) 723-0354; e-mail lcdl@prw.net; internet www.lacasadellibro.org; f. 1955; devoted to the art and history of book; library of 7,000 vols (incl. MSS, incunabula and works on book arts and the history of book); Curator MARIAN TOLEDO; Adminstrator TAYRA WALLÉ.

Universities

AMERICAN UNIVERSITY OF PUERTO RICO

POB 2037, Bayamón, PR 00960
Carretera 2 km, 14 Hato Tejas, Bayamón, PR 00960-2037

Telephone: (787) 620-2040
Internet: www.aupr.edu

Founded 1963 as American Business College, present status 1982
Private control
Language of instruction: Spanish
Academic year: August to December

Depts of arts and sciences, business administration, education and technology

Pres.: JUAN C. NAZARIO-TORRES
Chancellor: Dr JOSE RAMIREZ-FIGUEROA
Vice-Pres. for Academic and Student Affairs: Dr CONSUELO CASTRO-MELÉNDEZ
Vice-Pres. for Admin. and Finance: MAGDA CANCEL
Vice-Pres. for Enrolment Management: JAIME GONZÁLEZ RIVERA
Dir for Admissions: KEREN LLANOS-FIGUEROA
Registrar: MARÍA A. RODRÍGUEZ-PAZ
Dir for Library: DIRZA ALMESTICA
Number of teachers: 120
Number of students: 1,500

Publication: *Punto EDU_M.A*

CARIBBEAN UNIVERSITY

POB 493, Bayamón, PR 00960-0493
Telephone: (787) 780-0070
E-mail: registraduria@caribbean.edu
Internet: www.caribbean.edu

Founded 1969 as Caribbean Jr College, current name adopted 1978
Private control
Languages of instruction: English, Spanish
Academic year: August to May

Campuses in Bayamòn, Carolina, Ponce, Vega Baja

Pres.: Dr ANA E. CUCURELLA-ADORNO
Registrar: KENDRA M. ORTIZ RIVERA

CARLOS ALBIZU UNIVERSITY

POB 9023711, San Juan, PR 00902-3711
Telephone: (787) 725-6500
Internet: www.albizu.edu

Founded 1966
Private control
Languages of instruction: Spanish, English
Academic year: August to May
Campus in Miami
Pres.: Dr ILEANA RODRIGUEZ-GARCÍA
Chancellor: Dr JOSE CABIYA
Vice-Chancellor for Academic Affairs: Dr JAIME VERAY
Registrar: VICTOR BONILLA
Dean of Students: CARMEN RIVERA
Librarian: YOLANDA ROSARIO
Publication: *Ciencias de la Conducta* (1 a year, print and online, www.albizu.edu/Ciencias-de-la-Conducta)

COLUMBIA CENTRO UNIVERSITARIO (Columbia University Centre)

POB 8517, Caguas, PR 00726
Carretera 183, km 1.7, Salida hacia San Lorenzo, Caguas, PR
Telephone: (787) 743-4041
E-mail: info@columbiaco.edu
Internet: www.columbiaco.edu
Founded 1966
Private control
Languages of instruction: Spanish, English
Academic year: September to August
Campus in Yauco; divs of administration, arts, health, technology
Pres.: ALEX R. DE JORGE
Vice-Pres. for Academic Affairs: CARMEN J. LÓPEZ
Vice-Pres. of Admin.: DARITZA MULERO
Vice-Pres. for Operations: CARMEN M. RIVERA
Vice-Pres. for Student Affairs: BRENDALIZ ZAYAS
Dean of Academic Affairs: MYRNA TORRES
Registar: WILMARIE TORRES
Librarian: LUZ Z. NEGRÓN
Library of 17,665 vols

DEWEY UNIVERSITY

POB 19538, San Juan, PR 00910-9538
427 Ave Barbosa San Juan, San Juan, PR 00923
Telephone: (787) 753-0039
Internet: www.dewey.edu
Founded 1992
Private control
Languages of instruction: Spanish, English
Academic year: August to May
Centres in Arroyo, Bayamón, Carolina, Fajarado, Hatillo, Hato Rey, Juana Díaz, Manatí, Mayagüez, Naranjito
Pres.: Dr CARLOS A. QUIÑONES ALFONSO
Vice-Pres.: CARMELO RODRÍGUEZ
Vice-Pres.: WILSON RUIZ
Sec.: MAYRA VILANOVA
Dean for Admin.: MARÍA DE LOURDES SOTO SIMONETTI
Registrar: VIRGEN DEL S. COLÓN GONZÁLEZ
Publication: *Dewey Today*

EDP UNIVERSITY OF PUERTO RICO, INC.

POB 192303, San Juan, PR 00919-2303
560 Ave Ponce de León, Hato Rey, San Juan, PR 00918
Telephone: (787) 765-3560
E-mail: info@edpuniversity.edu
Internet: www.edpuniversity.edu
Founded 1968 as EDP College of Puerto Rico, Inc., current name and status 2013
Private control
Languages of instruction: Spanish, English
Academic year: August to May
Campus in San Sebastian, extension centres in Manatí, Humacao
Pres.: Ing. GLADYS NIEVES
Publication: *Revista Academia* (2 a year)

PONTIFICIA UNIVERSIDAD CATÓLICA DE PUERTO RICO (Pontifical Catholic University of Puerto Rico)

2250 Blvd Luis A. Ferré Aguayo, Ponce, PR 00717-9997
Telephone: (787) 841-2000
E-mail: info@pucpr.edu
Internet: www.pucpr.edu
Founded 1948 as Santa María Univ., current name adopted 1991
Private control
Languages of instruction: Spanish, English
Academic year: August to May (2 semesters and 2 summer sessions)
Campuses at Arecibo, Mayagüez
Grand Chancellor: FÉLIX LÁZARO MARTÍNEZ
Pres.: Dr JORGE IVÁN VÉLEZ AROCHO (acting)
Vice-Pres. for Academic Affairs: Dr LEANDRO A. COLÓN ALICEA
Vice-Pres. for Finance and Admin.: Prof. IRMA RODRÍGUEZ
Vice-Pres. for Student Affairs: Prof. FREDDIE MARTINEZ SOTOMAYOR
Rector for Arecibo Campus: Dr EDWIN HERNÁNDEZ VERA
Rector for Mayagüez Campus: Dra OLGA N. HERNÁNDEZ DE PATIÑO
Dir of Admissions: Dr ANA O. BONILLA DE SÁNCHEZ
Registrar: Prof. IVÁN E. DÁVILA
Dir for Libraries: MAGDA I. VARGAS RODRÍGUEZ
Library: 1m. vols
Number of teachers: 710
Number of students: 8,300
Publications: *Horizontes*, *Revista Collage* (2 a year), *Revista de Derecho Puertorriqueño*

DEANS

College of Arts and Humanities: Prof. ALFONSO SANTIAGO CRUZ
College of Business Administration: Dr JAIME L. SANTIAGO CANET
College of Education: Dr MYRIAM ZAYAS ZENGOTITA
College of Graduate Studies in Behavioural Sciences and Community Affairs: Dr HERNÁN A. VERA RODRÍGUEZ
College of Science: Dr ALMA L. SANTIAGO CORTÉS
School of Architecture: JAVIER DE JESÚS MARTÍNEZ
School of Law: JOSÉ A. FRONTERA AGENJO

SISTEMA UNIVERSITARIO ANA G. MENDEZ (Ana G. Mendez University System)

POB 21345, San Juan, PR 00928-1345
Ave Ana G. Méndez (Carretera 176) km 0.3 Cupey Bajo, San Juan, PR
Telephone: (787) 751-0178
Internet: www.suagm.edu
Founded 1941 as Puerto Rico High School of Commerce, current name adopted 1993
Private control
Languages of instruction: Spanish, English
Academic year: August to May
Pres.: JOSÉ F. MÉNDEZ
Vice-Pres. for Admin. Affairs: JESÚS A. DÍAZ
Vice-Pres. for Financial Affairs: ALFONSO L. DÁVILA SILVA
Vice-Pres. for Human Resources: VICTORIA DE JESÚS
Vice-Pres. for Planning, Academic Affairs and Research: JORGE L. CRESPO ARMÁIZ
Vice-Pres. for Marketing and Student Affairs: MAYRA CRUZ RIVERA
Number of students: 35,000

DEANS

School of Continuing Education: YANAIRA VÁZQUEZ
School of Professional Studies: MILDRED Y. RIVERA
School of Technical Studies: JOSÉ R. DEL VALLE.

CAMPUSES

Universidad del Este (University of the East)

POB 2010, Carolina, PR 00984-2010
Rd 190, km 1.8 Barrio Sabana Abajo, Carolina, PR 00983
Telephone: (787) 257-7373
Internet: www.suagm.edu/une
Founded 1949 current status 2001
Private control
Languages of instruction: English, Spanish'
Academic year: August to May
Univ. centres in Arecibo, Barceloneta, Cabo Rojo, Santa Isabel, Yauco
Chancellor: ALBERTO MALDONADO RUIZ
Vice-Chancellor: MILDRED HUERTAS SOLÁ
Vice-Rector for Information Resources and Telecommunications: CARMEN ORTEGA
Vice-Rector for Student Affairs: NAHOMY CURET
Registrar: ELISA QUILES
Dir for Library: ELSA MARIANI
Library of 224,979 vols
Number of teachers: 845 (145 full-time, 700 part-time)
Number of students: 12,700
Publication: *Ámbito de Encuentros*

DEANS

IEN Business School: Dr MARITZA I. ESPINA
José A. (Tony) Santana International School of Hospitality and Culinary Arts: TERESTELLA GONZÁLEZ-DENTON
School of Continuing Education: LITZA RIVERA
School of Education: MARÍA DEL CARMEN ARRIBAS
School of Health Sciences: Dr HAYDEE ENCARNACIÓN
School of Sciences and Technology: Dr WILFREDO COLÓN GUASP
School of Social and Human Sciences: Dr LUIS M. MAYO-SANTANA
School of Technical Studies: NYDIA FELICIANO

Universidad del Turabo (University of Turabo)

POB 3030, Estación Universidad Gurabo, Gurabo, PR 00778-3030
Carretera 189, km 3.3, Gurabo, PR 00778
Telephone: (787) 743-7979
Internet: www.suagm.edu/turabo
Founded 1972
Centres in Barceloneta, Cayey, Isabela, Naguabo, Ponce and Yabucoa
Rector: Dr DENNIS ALICEA RODRÍGUEZ
Vice-Rector: Dr ROBERTO LORÁN SANTOS
Vice-Rector for Admin. Affairs: Dr GLADYS L. BETANCOURT GÓMEZ
Vice-Rector for Information Resources: SARAI LASTRA DE LEÓN
Vice-Rector for Int. Affairs: Dr DAVID MÉNDEZ
Vice-Rector for Student Affairs: BRUNILDA APONTE
Registrar: ZORAIDA ORTIZ
Dir for Library: LUISA TORRES
Number of teachers: 1,256 (211 full-time, 1045 part-time)
Number of students: 17,040

DEANS

International School of Design: AURORISA MATEO

School of Business and Entrepreneurship: Dr MARCELINO RIVERA LÓPEZ
School of Education: ANGELA CANDELARIO
School of Engineering: Dr JACK T. ALLISON
School of Health Sciences: ANGEL L. RIVERA ORTIZ
School of Professional Studies: MILDRED Y. RIVERA
School of Science and Technology: Dr TERESA LIPSETT-RUIZ (acting)
School of Social Sciences: MARCO A. GIL DE LAMADRID

Universidad Metropolitana
(Metropolitan University)

POB 21150, San Juan, PR 00928-1150
1399 Ave Ana G Méndez, San Juan, PR 00926-2602
Telephone: (787) 766-1717
Internet: www.suagm.edu/umet
Founded 1967 as Cupey campus of Puerto Rico Jr College, current name and status 1985
Private control
Univ. centers in Aguadilla, Bayamón, Jayuya
Rector: Dr CARLOS M. PADÍN BIBILONI
Vice-Rector: ZAIDA VEGA LUGO
Vice-Rector for Admin. Affairs: MARÍA DE P. CHARNECO
Vice-Rector for External Resources: GLADYS CORA IZQUIERDO
Vice-Rector for Information Resources: CARLOS M. FUENTES (acting)
Vice-Rector for Student Affairs: CARMEN ROSADO LEÓN
Dir for Admissions: YADIRA RIVERA LUGO
Dir for Library: MARÍA DE LOS ÁNGELES LUGO
Number of teachers: 1,069 (129 full time, 940 part-time)
Number of students: 13,616
Publications: *Panorama*, *Perspectivas* (1 a year), *Revista Cupey*

DEANS

School of Business Administration: JUAN OTERO SERRANO
School of Education: Dra JUAN CANALES
School of Environmental Affairs: Dra MARÍA CALIXTA ORTÍZ RIVERA
School of Health Sciences: Dra LOURDES MALDONADO
School of Science and Technology: KAREN GONZÁLEZ PARRILLA
School of Social Sciences, Humanities and Communications: Dra ELOISA GORDON

UNIVERSIDAD ADVENTISTA DE LAS ANTILLAS
(Adventist University of the Antilles)

POB 118, Mayagüez, PR 00681-0118
Carretera 106 km 2.2 Interior, Mayagüez, PR 00680
Telephone: (787) 834-9595
E-mail: admissions@uaa.edu
Internet: www.uaa.edu
Founded 1957 as Mayagüez Puerto Rican Adventist College, current name adopted 1989
Private control
Languages of instruction: Spanish, English
Academic year: August to May
Depts of business studies, science and technology, theology and music; schools of education, humanities and psychology, nursing and health sciences
Pres.: Dr OBED JIMÉNEZ
Vice-Pres. for Academic Affairs: MYRNA COLÓN
Vice-Pres. for Financial Affairs: MISAEL JIMÉNEZ
Vice-Pres. for Institutional Advancement: Dr ÁUREA ARAÚJO

Vice-Pres. for Student Affairs: JAVIER DÍAZ
Dir for Admissions: YOLANDA FERRER
Registrar: ANA D. TORRES
Dir for Library: AIXA VEGA
Library of 85,000 vols, 6,000 journals, 7,000 ebooks
Number of teachers: 100
Number of students: 1,200
Publications: *Adventist Today* (4 a year), *College and University Dialogue* (3 a year, in English, French, Portuguese, Spanish), *Ministry* (12 a year), *Spectrum* (4 a year), *The Journal of Adventist Education* (22 a year)

UNIVERSIDAD CENTRAL DE BAYAMÓN
(Central University of Bayamón)

POB 1725, Bayamón, PR 00960-1725
Urb. La Milagrosa, Avda Zaya Verde, Bayamón, PR 00960
Telephone: (787) 786-3030
E-mail: information@ucb.edu.pr
Internet: www.ucb.edu.pr
Founded 1961 as an extension of Catholic Univ. of Puerto Rico, present name and status 1970
Private control
Languages of instruction: Spanish, English
Academic year: August to May
Colleges of business and technology development, education and professional conduct, graduate studies, liberal arts and humanities, sciences and health professions
Pres.: Dr LILLIAN NEGRÓN COLÓN
Dean for Academic Affairs: Dra PURA ECHANDI
Dean for Finance and Admin.: ROSIMAR FERRER
Dean for Student Affairs: Prof. NIZA ZAYAS
Dir for Admissions: CHRISTINE HERNANDEZ CORTIELLA
Registrar: VICTOR COLÓN-RODRÍGUEZ
Dir of Library: ANNETTE VALENTÍN
Library of 52,000 vols
Number of teachers: 60 (full-time)
Number of students: 3,300
Publications: *Cruz Ansata* (1 a year), *Familia y Escuela* (12 a year), *Revista Halcón*, *President's Letter* (4 a year)

UNIVERSIDAD CENTRAL DEL CARIBE
(Central University of the Caribbean)

POB 60327, Bayamón, PR 00960-6032
Ave Laurel 100, Santa Juanita, Bayamón, PR 00956
Telephone: (787) 798-3001
E-mail: ucc@uccaribe.edu
Internet: www.uccaribe.edu
Founded 1976 as Cayey School of Medicine, current name adopted 1978
Private control
Languages of instruction: Spanish, English
Academic year: August to May
School of medicine incl. depts of anatomy and cell biology, biochemistry, emergency medicine, family medicine, internal medicine, microbiology and immunology, neuroscience, obstetrics and gynaecology, pathology, paediatrics, pharmacology, physical medicine and rehabilitation, physiology, psychiatry, radiology, surgery
Pres.: Dr JOSE GINEL RODRIGUEZ
Dean for Academic Affairs: Dra NEREDIA DÍAZ
Dean for Admin. Affairs: EMILIA SOTO
Dean for Admissions and Student Affairs: Dr OMAR PÉREZ
Registrar: NILDA MONTAÑEZ
Dir for Library: MILDRED I. RIVERA VAZQUEZ
Number of teachers: 40 (full-time)

Number of students: 500

UNIVERSIDAD DE PUERTO RICO
(University of Puerto Rico)

POB 364984, San Juan, PR 00936-4984
Telephone: (787) 250-0000
Internet: www.upr.edu
Founded 1903, present status 1998
public control
Languages of instruction: Spanish, English
Academic year: August to May
Pres.: Dr URAYOAN WALKER
Vice-Pres. for Academic Affairs: Dr DELIA CAMACHO
Vice-Pres. for Research and Technology: Dr JOSÉ A. LASALDE DOMINICCI
Library of 1,663,564 vols
Number of teachers: 4,766
Number of students: 57,772
Publications: *Diálogo* (12 a year), *La Torre*, *RIE* (4 a year)..

ATTACHED CAMPUSES

Recinto de Ciencias Médicas (Campus of Medical Sciences): Apdo 365067, San Juan, PR 00936-5067; tel. (787) 758-2525; internet www.rcm.upr.edu; f. 1926; library of 125,000 vols; 830 teachers; 2,500 students; Rector RAFAEL RODRÍGUEZ-MERCADO (acting); Dean for Academic Affairs Dr RICARDO R. GONZÁLEZ MÉNDEZ; Dean for Admin. IRVING A. JIMÉNEZ (acting); Dean for Student Affairs Dra NITZA HEBÉ RIVERA PACHECO; Registrar REINALDO POMALES; Dir for Library Dra IRMA QUIÑONES-MAURÁS; publ. *Buhití*, *Puerto Rico Health Science Journal*

DEANS

School of Dental Medicine: NOEL J. AYMAT
School of Health Professions: Dra ESTELA S. ESTAPÉ GARRASTAZÚ
School of Medicine: Dr INES GARCIA GARCIA
School of Nursing: Dra NANCY DÁVILA
School of Pharmacy: Dra WANDA T. MALDONADO
School of Public Health: Dr JOSÉ F. CORDERO CORDERO

Universidad de Puerto Rico en Aguadilla (University of Puerto Rico in Aguadilla): POB 6150, Aguadilla, PR 00604-6150;Calle Belt, Edif. 252, Antigua Base Ramey, Aguadilla, PR 00603; tel. (787) 890-2681; e-mail aguadilla@upr.edu; internet www.uprag.edu; f. 1972 as Colegio Regional de Aguadilla, present status 1997; 160 teachers; 3,000 students; Rector JOSÉ M. PLANAS RIVERA; Dean for Academic Affairs Dra SANDRA PÉREZ; Dean for Admin. EDNA E. HERNÁNDEZ BONILLA (acting); Dir for Library SHARON J. RIVERA.

Universidad de Puerto Rico en Arecibo (University of Puerto Rico in Arecibo): POB 4010, Arecibo, PR 00614-4010; tel. (787) 815-0000; e-mail expresate.arecibo@upr.edu; internet www.upra.edu; f. 1967 as Arecibo Regional College, present status 1998; depts of biology, business administration, chemical physics, computer science, counselling and guidance, education, English, humanities, mathematics, nursing, social sciences, Spanish, tele-radio communication; 280 teachers; 4,000 students; Rector Prof. JUAN RAMÍREZ-SILVA; Dean for Academic Affairs Dra MAIELLA L. RAMOS FONTÁN; Dean for Admin. Affairs Prof. JUAN PÉREZ GONZÁLEZ; Dean for Student Affairs Prof. DIÓMEDES PAGÁN NAVARETTE; Dir for Admissions MAGALY MÉNDEZ CARDONA; Registrar MILAGROS PITRE NIEVES; Dir for Library VICTOR MALDONADO MALDONADO (acting); publ. *Cuarto Propio: Revista Literaria* (Spanish, online, cuartopropio.upra.edu).

Universidad de Puerto Rico en Bayamón (University of Puerto Rico in Bayamón): 170 Industrial Minillas Carretera 174, Bayamón, PR 00959-1919; tel. (787) 993-0000; e-mail admisiones.bayamon@upr.edu; internet www.uprb.edu; f. 1971, present status 1998; depts of early childhood education, electronics, materials engineering, natural science, physical education; 270 teachers; 5,000 students; Rector ORLANDO GONZÁLEZ GONZÁLEZ; Dean for Academic Affairs Dr JORGE ROVIRA ÁLVAREZ; Dean for Admin. Affairs BRENDALIS SÁNCHEZ NEGRÓN; Dean for Student Affairs ELSA FLORES ORTIZ; Dir for Admissions CARMEN I. MONTES BURGOS; Registrar CARMEN M. CINTRÓN OTERO; publ. *Milenio, Tapiz*.

Universidad de Puerto Rico en Carolina (University of Puerto Rico in Carolina): Apdo 4800, Carolina, PR 00984-4800; tel. (787) 257-0000; e-mail prensa.carolina@upr.edu; internet www.uprc.edu; f. 1974; depts of business administration, design, education, engineering and technology, English, humanities, natural sciences, social science and criminal justice, Spanish; 220 teachers; 4,100 students; Rector LUIS D. TORRES TORRES; Dean for Academic Affairs Dr JUAN BONILLA GONZÁLEZ; Dean for Admin. Affairs Dr JOSÉ MEZA PEREIRA; Dean for Student Affairs Dr JAMIE CABRERA PINTOR; Registrar ABELARDO MARTÍNEZ; Dir for Library STANLEY PORTELA VALENTÍN.

Universidad de Puerto Rico en Cayey (University of Puerto Rico in Cayey): POB 372230, Cayey, PR 00736;205 Ave Antonio R. Barceló, Cayey, PR 00736; tel. (787) 738-2161; e-mail osi.cayey@upr.edu; internet www.cayey.upr.edu; f. 1967; depts of biology, business administration, chemistry, Hispanic studies, humanities, mathematics and physics, natural sciences, social sciences, pedagogy; 230 teachers; 3,700 students; Rector JOSÉ N. CARABALLO; Dean for Academic Affairs Dra GLORIVEE ROSARIO PÉREZ; Dean for Admin. Affairs SAMUEL GONZÁLEZ GONZÁLEZ; Dean for Student Affairs Dra SARAH MALAVÉ LEBRÓN; Registrar DAISY RAMOS; Dir for Library SONIA DÁVILA COSME; publ. *Revista Cayey, Revista Identidades, Revista Taurus*.

Universidad de Puerto Rico en Humacao (University of Puerto Rico in Humacao): POB 860, Humacao, PR 00792;Ave José E. Aguiar Aramburu, Carretera 908 km 1.2, Humacao, PR; tel. (787) 850-0000; e-mail rectoria.uprh@upr.edu; internet www.uprh .edu; f. 1962, present status 1973; depts of biology, business administration, chemistry, communication education, English, humanities, mathematics, nursing sciences, occupational therapy, physics and electronics, physical therapy, social sciences, social work, Spanish; 290 teachers; 4,400 students; Rector Dra CARMEN J. HERNÁNDEZ CRUZ (acting); Dean for Academic Affairs Dra IVELISSE RIVERA BONILLA (acting); Dean for Admin. MARIOLGA ROTGER GONZÁLEZ; Dean for Students WANDA L. RODRÍGUEZ TORO; Dir for Admissions ELIZABETH GERENA; Registrar JORGE L. ACEVEDO GÓMEZ; Dir for Library FELIX NERIS BAEZ; publ. *ADEM Investiga, Cuaderno Internacional de Estudios Humanísticos y Literatura, Exégesis*.

Universidad de Puerto Rico en Ponce (University of Puerto Rico in Ponce): POB 7186, Ponce, PR 00732-7186;Ave Santiago de Los Caballeros, Ponce, PR 00734; tel. (787) 844-8181; internet www.uprp.edu; f. 1970 as Regional College of Ponce, present name and status 2000; depts of allied health studies, biology, business administration, chemistry and physics, computer science, education, engineering, English, humanities, mathematics, social sciences, Spanish; 200 teach-ers; 3,100 students; Rector MARGARITA E. VILLAMIL TORRES (acting); Dean for Academic Affairs Dr LEONARDO MORALES TOMASSINI; Dean for Admin. Affairs Dr DRIANFEL E. VÁZQUEZ TORRES (acting); Dean for Student Affairs ACMIN VELÁZQUEZ RIVERA; Registrar MARYA SANTIAGO CANCEL; Dir for Library BRETT DÍAZ SIMMONS; publ. *Ceiba* (1 a year).

Universidad de Puerto Rico en Río Piedras (University of Puerto Rico in Rio Piedras): POB 23301, San Juan, PR 00931-3301; tel. (787) 764-0000; internet www .uprrp.edu; f. 1903; colleges and schools of architecture, business administration, communication, education, general studies, humanities, law, natural sciences, planning, sciences and information technology, social sciences; system of 29 libraries; 1,240 teach-ers; 18,000 students; Rector Dra ETHEL RÍOS ORLANDI; Dean for Academic Affairs ASTRID CUBANO IGUINA; Dean for Admin. RAQUEL L. RODRÍGUEZ RIVERA; Dean for Graduate Studies and Research Dra HAYDEE SEIJO MALDONADO; Dean for Students Dra MAYRA CHARRIEZ; Dir for Library Dra ADA MYRIAM FELICIÉ; publ. *Análisis, Carribeana, Caribbean Studies, Centro de Investigaciones Comerciales e Iniciativas Académicas* (online, cicia.uprrp.edu/forum.html), *Contornos Caribeños, Inventio* (2 a year, English and Spanish), *Paideia* (print and online, paideia.uprrp.edu), *Psychiko, Revista de Administración Pública, Revista de Ciencias Sociales, Revista Griot, Revista Pedagogia* (online, revistapedagogia.uprrp.edu), *Sargasso, Teknokultura* (online, teknokultura.uprrp.edu), *Tonguas* (1 a year).

Universidad de Puerto Rico en Utuado (University of Puerto Rico in Utuado): POB 2500, Utuado, PR 00641-2500;Barrio Salto Arriba, Carretera 123, km 52 hm. 7, Utuado, PR; tel. (787) 894-2828; internet www .uprutuado.edu; f. 1978; depts of agricultural technology, business administration and office systems, education and social sciences, language and humanities, natural sciences; Rector RAÚL M. NÚÑEZ ACEVEDO; Dean for Academic Affairs CELIA R. QUIÑONES SEIGLIE; Dean for Admin. Affairs Dr SAMUEL QUIÑONES GARCÍA; Dean for Student Affairs CAROLYN MERCADO ROSADO; Registrar MARILIA SANTIAGO VILLAFAÑE; 80 teachers; 1,600 students.

Universidad de Puerto Rico Recinto de Mayagüez (University of Puerto Rico Campus of Mayagüez): Apdo 9000, Mayagüez, PR 00681-9000; tel. (787) 832-4040; e-mail rectoria@uprm.edu; internet www.uprm.edu; f. 1911 as College of Agriculture at Mayagüez, present status 1966; library of 706,021 vols; 890 teachers; 14,000 students; Pres. ANDRÉS CALDERÓN COLÓN (acting); Dean for Academic Affairs JAIME SEGUEL (acting); Dean for Admin. LUCAS N. AVILÉS (acting); Dean for Student Affairs MARTA I. COLÓN PEREA (acting); Dir for Library Prof. CYNDIA CARABALLO; publ. *Atenea* (2 a year, English and Spanish), *Ceteris Paribus: The Puerto Rico Economic Review* (2 a year), *Journal of Agriculture of the University of Puerto Rico* (2 a year), *LACJEE* (2 a year), *Revista Internacional de Desastres Naturales, Accidentes e Infraestructura Civil* (2 a year), *The Caribbean Journal of Science* (2 a year)

DEANS

Faculty of Arts and Sciences: MANUEL VALDÉS PIZINI
Faculty of Agricultural Sciences: GLADYS M. GONZÁLEZ SOTO
Faculty of Business Administration: ANA E. MARTÍN QUIÑONES
Faculty of Engineering: AGUSTÍN RULLÁN

UNIVERSIDAD DEL SAGRADO CORAZÓN
(Sacred Heart University)

POB 12383, San Juan, PR 00914-8505

Telephone: (787) 728-1515
E-mail: admision@sagrado.edu
Internet: www.sagrado.edu

Founded 1880, current name adopted 1976
Private control
Languages of instruction: Spanish, English
Academic year: August to May

Depts of business administration, communication, education, humanities and social sciences, natural sciences

Pres.: Dr JOSÉ JAIME RIVERA RODRÍGUEZ
Dean for Academic and Student Affairs: Dra LYDIA E. ESPINET DE JESÚS
Dean for Admin.: JOSÉ L. RICCI ASENCIO
Dean for Devt Affairs: ADLÍN RÍOS RIGAU
Dir for Library: SONIA DÍAZ LATORRE

Number of teachers: 400
Number of students: 6,335 (5,498 undergraduate, 837 graduate)

Publication: *Revista Sagrado*

UNIVERSIDAD INTERAMERICANA DE PUERTO RICO
(Inter American University of Puerto Rico)

POB 363255, San Juan, PR 00936-3255

Telephone: (787) 766-1912
E-mail: webmaster@inter.edu
Internet: www.inter.edu

Founded 1912 as Polytechnic Institute of Puerto Rico
Private control
Languages of instruction: English, Spanish
Academic year: August to May (2 semesters)

Pres.: MANUEL J. FERNÓS
Vice-Pres. for Academic and Student Affairs and Systemic Planning: AGUSTÍN ECHEVARRÍA SANTIAGO
Vice-Pres. for Admin., Finance and Systematic Services: LUIS R. ESQUILÍN HERNÁNDEZ
Vice-Pres. for Religious Affairs: Rev. Fr NORBERTO DOMÍNGUEZ

Number of teachers: 2,600
Number of students: 43,000

Publications: *Homines, Revista Interamericana...*

ATTACHED CAMPUSES

Recinto de Aguadilla
(Aguadilla Campus)

POB 20000, Aguadilla, PR 00605
Carretera 459, Interior 463 Barrio Corrales, Sector Calero, Aguadilla, PR
Telephone: (787) 891-0925
Internet: www.aguadilla.inter.edu

Founded 1957 current status 1991; attached to Univ. Interamericana de Puerto Rico

Rector: Dr ELIE AGÉSILAS
Dean for Admin.: ISRAEL AYALA
Dean for Students: ANA C. MELÓN
Dean for Studies: LYMARI NEGRÓN VELÁZQUEZ
Dir for Admissions: DORIS PÉREZ
Dir for Library: MONSERRATE YULFO
Registrar: MARÍA PÉREZ

Library of 75,203 vols incl. 62,645 gen. colln, 11,219 audiovisual materials, 406 microforms and 933 CDs and DVDs
Number of teachers: 280
Number of students: 5,000

Publication: *Revista Inter Tigre*

Recinto de Arecibo
(Arecibo Campus)

POB 4050, Arecibo, PR 00614-4050

Carretera No 2, km 80.4 Barrio San Daniel, Sector Las Canelas, Arecibo, PR

Telephone: (787) 878-5475

Internet: www.arecibo.inter.edu

Founded 1957; attached to Univ. Interamericana de Puerto Rico

Rector: Dr RAFAEL RAMIREZ RIVERA
Dean for Academic Affairs: Dr ANNETTE VEGA
Dean for Admin.: WANDA I. PÉREZ RAMÍREZ
Dean for Student Affairs: ILVIS AGUIRRE FRANCO
Dean for Studies: VÍCTOR CONCEPCIÓN SANTIAGO
Dir of Admissions: PROVI MONTALVO BONILLA
Dir for Library: SARA E. ABREU
Registrar: CARMEN L. RODRÍGUEZ MARTÍNEZ

Number of teachers: 310
Number of students: 4,700

Publication: *Prism*

Recinto de Barranquitas
(Barranquitas Campus)

POB 517, Barranquitas, PR 00794

Barrio Helechal Carretera 156 Intersección 719, Barranquitas, PR 00794

Telephone: (787) 857-3600

Internet: www.br.inter.edu

Founded 1957; attached to Univ. Interamericana de Puerto Rico

Rector: Dra IRENE FERNÁNDEZ
Dean for Admin.: JOSÉ E. ORTIZ ZAYAS
Dean for Students: ARAMILDA CARTAGENA SANTIAGO
Dean for Studies: Dra PATRICIA ÁLVAREZ SWIHART
Dir for Admission: EDGARDO CINTRÓN VEGA
Registrar: SANDRA MORALES RODRÍGUEZ

Number of teachers: 200
Number of students: 2,500

Publication: *Revista CECIA*

Recinto de Bayamón
(Bayamón Campus)

500 Carretera Dr John Will Harris, Bayamón, PR 00957-6257

Telephone: (787) 279-1912

E-mail: interbcinfo@bc.inter.edu

Internet: bc.inter.edu

Founded 1956, current name adopted 1991; attached to Univ. Interamericana de Puerto Rico

Schools of aeronautics, engineering; depts of business administration, communication, computer science, health sciences, humanistic studies, natural science and mathematics

Rector: JUAN MARTÍNEZ RODRÍGUEZ
Dean for Admin.: LUIS M. CRUZ
Dean for Research: Dr ARMANDO RODRÍGUEZ
Dean for Students: GEMA C. TORRES
Dean for Studies: Dr CARLOS OLIVARES
Registrar: EDDIE AYALA MÉNDEZ

Number of teachers: 340
Number of students: 5,200

Publication: *Interesante*

Recinto de Fajardo
(Fajardo Campus)

POB 70003, Fajardo, PR 00738-7003

Parque Batey Central Carretera 195, Fajardo, PR 00738

Telephone: (787) 863-2390

Internet: www.fajardo.inter.edu

Founded 1960; attached to Univ. Interamericana de Puerto Rico

Depts of business administration, education and social sciences, humanities, sciences and technology

Rector: ISMAEL SUÁREZ
Dean for Academic Affairs: Dra PAULA SAGARDÍA
Dean for Admin.: LYDIA E. SANTIAGO
Dean for Students: JAVIER MARTÍNEZ
Dir for Admissions: ADA CARABALLO CARMONA
Registrar: ARLENE PARRILLA

Number of teachers: 150
Number of students: 2,400

Recinto de Guayama
(Guayama Campus)

POB 10004, Guayama, PR 00785-0004

Barrio Machete, Carretera 744, km 1.2, Guayama, PR

Telephone: (787) 864-2222

E-mail: jlima@inter.edu

Internet: www.guayama.inter.edu

Founded 1956 current status 1993; attached to Univ. Interamericana de Puerto Rico

Depts of business administration, education and social sciences, health sciences, humanities, natural science and technology

Rector: CARLOS E. COLÓN RAMOS
Dean for Admin.: NESTOR LEBRÓN TIRADO
Dean for Students: ROSA J. MARTÍNEZ RAMOS
Dir for Admissions: LAURA E. FERRER
Registrar: LUIS A. SOTO

Number of teachers: 190
Number of students: 2,400

Publication: *Revista Sapiencia*

Recinto de Ponce
(Ponce Campus)

104 Turpeaux Ind Park, Ponce, PR 00715-1602

Telephone: (787) 284-1912

E-mail: admisiones@ponce.inter.edu

Internet: www.ponce.inter.edu

Founded 1962, current status in 1992; attached to Univ. Interamericana de Puerto Rico

Rector: Dra VILMA E. COLÓN ACOSTA
Dean for Admin.: VÍCTOR A. FELIBERTY-RUBERTÉ
Dean for Students: EDDA COSTAS VÁZQUEZ
Dean for Studies: Dr JACQUELINE ÁLVAREZ PEÑA
Dir for Admissions: FRANCO L. DÍAZ VEGA
Registrar: MARÍA DEL CARMEN PÉREZ RODRÍGUEZ

Number of teachers: 350
Number of students: 6,500

Publication: *Revista 360°*

Recinto de San Germán
(San Germán Campus)

POB 5100, San Germán, PR 00683

Telephone: (787) 264-1912

E-mail: webmaster@sg.inter.edu

Internet: www.sg.inter.edu

Founded 1912 as Puerto Rico Polytechnic Institute; attached to Univ. Interamericana de Puerto Rico

Depts of biology, chemistry and environmental sciences, business and management sciences, education and physical education, fine arts, health sciences, languages and literature, mathematics and applied sciences, social sciences and liberal arts

Rector: AGNES MOJICA
Dean for Admin.: FRANCES CARABALLO
Dean for Student Affairs: EFRAÍN ANGLERÓ
Dean for Studies: NYVIA ALVARADO
Dir for Admissions: MILDRED CAMACHO
Registrar: ARLEEN SANTANA

Library of 160,000 vols
Number of teachers: 350
Number of students: 5,500

Publication: *Revista Poly Relays*

Recinto Metro
(Metro Campus)

Apdo 191293, San Juan, PR 00919-1293

Carretera No 1, Calle Francisco Sein, Rio Piedras, PR 00919

Telephone: (787) 250-1912

Internet: www.metro.inter.edu

Founded 1912; attached to Univ. Interamericana de Puerto Rico

Faculties of economics and administrative sciences, education and professional conduct, humanistic studies, science and technology

Rector: MARILINA LUCCA WAYLAND
Dean for Admin.: JIMMY CANCEL
Dean for Students: CARMEN A. OQUENDO
Dean for Studies: MIGDALIA TEXIDOR
Registrar: LISETTE RIVERA ORTIZ

Number of teachers: 630
Number of students: 10,700

Publications: *Cuarto Piso, Huellas de Tigre, Kálathos: Revista Transdisciplinaria Metro-Inter* (2 a year, online, www.kalathos.metro.inter.edu/index.asp), *La revista de la Asociación de Estudiantes Graduados en Historia de la Universidad Interamericana de Puerto Rico, Revista Empresarial Inter Metro* (2 a year, online, www.ceajournal.metro.inter.edu)

UNIVERSIDAD INTERNACIONAL IBEROAMERICANA
(Iberoamericana International University)

POB 3385, Arecibo, PR 00613-3385

Carretera 658 km 1.3, Barrio Arenalejos, Sector Palaches, Arecibo, PR 00613

Telephone: (787) 878-2126

E-mail: admisiones@unini.org

Internet: www.unini.org

Founded 2010

Private control

Languages of instruction: Spanish, English
Academic year: August to May

Depts of education and communications, environment and sustainability, health sciences, innovation, business and new technologies, language sciences, technology

Rector: Dra CARMEN RITA ROMÁN
Gen. Sec.: Dr HÉCTOR A. SOLANO LAMPHAR
Dean for Academic Affairs and Strategic Management: Dr LUIS ALONSO DZUL LÓPEZ
Dean for Admin., Finance and Student Services: Dr FERNANDO AMAGO
Librarian: GERINALDO CAMACHO

Publication: *Hereditas*

UNIVERSIDAD POLITÉCNICA DE PUERTO RICO
(Polytechnic University of Puerto Rico)

POB 192017, San Juan, PR 00919-2017

377 Ponce de León Ave, Hato Rey, PR 00918

Telephone: (787) 622-8000

E-mail: admisiones@pupr.edu

Internet: www.pupr.edu

Founded 1966

Private control

Languages of instruction: Spanish, English
Academic year: August to May

Campuses in Miami and Orlando in the US; depts of chemical engineering, civil engineering, electrical and computer engineering, environmental engineering, geomatic sciences, industrial engineering, mechanical engineering

Pres.: ERNESTO VÁZQUEZ-BARQUET
Vice-Pres. for Academic Affairs: Dr MIGUEL RIESTRA
Vice-Pres. for Admin. and Finance: Ing. ERNESTO VÁZQUEZ-MARTINEZ

Vice-Pres. for Enrolment Management and Student Services: CARLOS PÉREZ
Dir for Admission: TERESA CARDONA
Registrar: MAYRA LÓPEZ
Dir for Library: MIRTA COLÓN
Library of 140,000 vols
Number of teachers: 310
Number of students: 6,000
Publication: *Polimorfo*

DEANS

School of Architecture: CARLOS E. BETANCOURT-LLAMBÍAS
School of Graduate Studies: MIRIAM PABÓN
School of Management and Entrepreneurship: JOSÉ O. RIVERA-RIVERA

UNIVERSITY OF PHOENIX

B7 Calle Tabonuco, Santander Tower at San Patricio, Guaynabo, PR 00968

Telephone: (787) 731-5400
Internet: www.phoenix.edu

Founded 1980, founded in 1976 in Arizona, USA
Private control
Languages of instruction: Spanish, English
Academic year: August to May
Pres.: Dr WILLIAM J. PEPICELLO
Publication: *Journal of Leadership Studies* (4 a year)

Colleges

Atlantic University College: POB 3918, Guaynabo, PR 00970; 9 Calle Colton, Frente a la Plaza de Recreo de Guaynabo, Guaynabo, PR; tel. (787) 720-1022; e-mail contacto@atlanticu.edu; internet www.atlanticu.edu; f. 1983; Pres. TERESA DE DIOS UNANUE; Exec. Vice-Pres. HERI MARTÍNEZ DE DIOS.

Cambridge College: The Hato Rey Center Bldg, Suite 1400, 268 Ponce de León Ave, Hato Rey, PR; tel. (787) 296-1101; internet puertorico.cambridgecollege.edu; f. 1971; main campus in Massachusetts, USA; school of education; Dir Dr JOSÉ R. IRIZARRY.

Centro de Estudios Avanzados de Puerto Rico y El Caribe (Centre for Advanced Studies of Puerto Rico and the Caribbean): Apdo 9023970, San Juan, PR 00902-3970; Calle Cristo 52, Viejo San Juan, PR; tel. (787) 723-4481; e-mail centro@ceaprc.org; internet www.ceaprc.edu; f. 1832; library: 17,000 vols, 400 theses, colln on Hispanic literature, literature of Central and South America, philosophical issues, films and documentaries on Puerto-Rican culture and history; Rector MIGUEL RODRÍGUEZ LÓPEZ; Dir for Library Prof. FRANCIS JAVIER MOJICA GARCÍA; Registrar MAYRA RAMÍREZ VALDEJULLI.

Colegio Universitario de San Juan (University College of San Juan): Apdo 70179, San Juan, PR 00936; tel. (787) 480-2400; internet www.cunisanjuan.edu; f. 1972; Rector Dra HAYDÉE M. ZAYAS HERNÁNDEZ.

Conservatorio de Música de Puerto Rico (Conservatory of Music of Puerto Rico): 951 Avda Ponce de León, Miramar, Santurce, San Juan, PR 00907-3373; tel. (787) 751-0160; e-mail info@cmpr.edu; internet www.cmpr.edu; f. 1959; library: 50,000 vols; 140 teachers; 1,600 students; Pres. MARIA CRISTINA FIRPI; Vice-Pres. RAFAEL IRIZARRY CUEBAS; Rector LUIS HERNÁNDEZ MERGAL.

Escuela de Artes Plásticas de Puerto Rico (School of Visual Arts of Puerto Rico): POB 9021112, San Juan, PR 00902-1112; Campo del Morro, Barrio Ballajá, Viejo San Juan, PR; tel. (787) 725-8120; e-mail info@eap.edu; internet www.eap.edu; f. 1966; library: 30,000 vols; Rector Arq. IVONNE MARÍA MARCIAL VEGA.

Escuela de Optometría (School of Optometry): 500 John Will Harris Ave, Rd 830, Bayamón, PR 00957-6257; tel. (787) 765-1915; e-mail admissions@inter.edu; internet www.optonet.inter.edu; f. 1981, current status 1992; attached to Univ. Interamericana de Puerto Rico; languages of instruction: English, Spanish; 40 teachers; 220 students; Dean Dr ANDRÉS PAGÁN; Dir for Library WILMA MARRERO ORTIZ.

Facultad de Derecho (Faculty of Law): POB 70351, San Juan, PR 00936-8351; Calle Federico Costa 170, Hato Rey, San Juan, PR; tel. (787) 751-1912; e-mail admisiones@juris.inter.edu; internet www.derecho.inter.edu; f. 1961; attached to Univ. Interamericana de Puerto Rico; language of instruction: Spanish; library: 200,000 vols; 80 teachers; 900 students; Dean JULIO FONTANET MALDONADO; Dir for Admissions ANGELA R. TORRES; Registrar MARÍA DE LOURDES RIVERA NIEVES; Dir for Library HECTOR R. SÁNCHEZ FERNÁNDEZ; publs *Law Review* (3 a year), *Revista Clave*.

Facultad de Derecho Eugenio María de Hostos (Eugenio Maria de Hostos Faculty of Law): Apdo 1900, Mayagüez, PR 00681-1900; Calle Peral No 57 Sur, Esq. Calle Muñoz Rivera, Mayagüez, PR; tel. (787) 265-2900; internet www.hostos.edu; f. 1995; Dean CARLOS RODRÍGUEZ SIERRA; publ. *Revista Barco de Papel*.

Humacao Community College: POB 9139, Calle Georgetti No 69, Humacao, PR 00792; tel. (787) 852-1430; internet www.hccpr.edu; f. 1978; Pres. Lic. JORGE E. MOJICA; Vice-Pres. Prof. AIDA E. RODRÍGUEZ; Registrar VIVIAN E. TORRES MILLÁN.

Ponce School of Medicine and Health Sciences: POB 7004, Ponce, PR 00732-7004; 388 Zona Ind Reparada 2, Ponce, PR 00716-2347; tel. (787) 840-2575; e-mail info@psm.edu; internet www.psm.edu; f. 1980, present status 1980; 500 teachers; 700 students; Pres. and Dean Dr OLGA RODRÍGUEZ DE ARZOLA; Dir for Admissions Dr WANDA VELEZ; Dir for Library CARMEN MALAVET.

San Juan Bautista School of Medicine: POB 4968, Caguas, PR 00726-4968; Luis A. Ferré Highway, Rd 172, Caguas to Cidra, Turabo Gardens, Caguas, PR 00725; tel. (787) 743-3038; e-mail admissions@sanjuanbautista.edu; internet www.sanjuanbautista.edu; f. 1978; 70 teachers; 300 students; Pres. and Dean Prof. Dra YOCASTA BRUGAL-MENA; Dean for Admin. and Human Resources CARLOS F. ABREU.

Seminario Evangélico de Puerto Rico (Evangelical Seminary of Puerto Rico): 776 Ponce de León, San Juan, PR 00925; tel. (787) 763-6700; e-mail registro@se-pr.edu; internet www.se-pr.edu; f. 1919 by merger of Seminario Teológico Portorricense (Presbyterian) in Mayagüez, Grace Conaway Institute (Baptist) in Río Piedras, Instituto Robinson (Methodist) in Hatillo, Instituto Discípulos de Cristo in Bayamón; library: 70,000 vols, 365 journals; Pres. Dr SERGIO OJEDA-CÁRCAMO; Dean for Academic Affairs Dr JOSÉ R. IRIZARRY MERCADO; publ. *PRESENCIA*.

UNITED STATES VIRGIN ISLANDS

The Higher Education System

The Virgin Islands' Department of Education is responsible for the provision of higher education in the US unincorporated territory, serving as both a local education agency and a state-level agency. The University of the Virgin Islands (founded in 1962 as the College of the Virgin Islands; present name and status adopted 1986) has two campuses—one on St Croix and the other on St Thomas—at which it offers Associate, Bachelors and Masters degree programmes. The University also offers Certificate and training courses through its Community Engagement and Lifelong Learning Center. In 2012 there were a total of 2,513 students enrolled at the University, which is accredited by the USA's Middle States Association of Colleges and Schools.

Regulatory Body

GOVERNMENT

Department of Education: 1834 Kongens Gade, St Thomas, VI 00802; tel. (340) 774-0100; e-mail ideas@doe.vi; internet www.vide.vi; Commr Dr LaVerne Terry.

Department of Planning & Natural Resources: Cyril E. King Airport, Terminal Bldg, Second Fl., Suite 6, 8100 Lindberg Bay, St Thomas, VI 00802; tel. (340) 774-3320; e-mail robertmathes@dpnr.gov.vi; internet www.dpnr.gov.vi; Commr Alicia Barnes.

Department of Sports, Parks & Recreation: Property and Procurement Bldg 1, Sub Base, Second Fl., Room 206, Charlotte Amalie, St Thomas, VI 00802; tel. (340) 774-0255; e-mail info@dspr.vi; internet www.dspr.vi; f. 1954; Commr Claire N. Williams.

Learned Societies

GENERAL

Virgin Islands Humanities Council: 1829 Kongens Gade, St Thomas, VI 00802; tel. (340) 776-4044; e-mail info@vihumanities.org; internet www.vihumanities.org; f. 1984; non-profit org.; supports research, education and promotion of public projects in humanities; Exec. Dir Ayesha Morris; Chair Opal Palmer Adisa; Sec. Charlene A. Matthew; Treas. Celestina Nkechi Lapenna.

BIBLIOGRAPHY, LIBRARY SCIENCE AND MUSEOLOGY

Virgin Islands Library Association: POB 446, Kingshill, VI 00851-0446; tel. (340) 692-4132.

HISTORY, GEOGRAPHY AND ARCHAEOLOGY

St Croix Landmarks Society: 52 Estate Whim, Frederiksted, St Croix, VI 00840; tel. (340) 772-0598; e-mail info@stcroixlandmarks.org; internet www.stcroixlandmarks.org; f. 1948; advances understanding and appreciation of historical and cultural legacy of St Croix through preservation, research and education; attached museums: Apothecary Hall Museum, Estate Whim Museum and Lawaetz Family Museum; library of 6,000 vols; holdings incl. traditional research resources such as artwork, collns of photographs, maps and MSS, drawings of the Virgin Islands by Henry Morton (1843–44) and Dr Allen Voorhees Lesley (1856), extensive photographic colln from Axel Ovesen (1902–72), street scenes from Christiansted and Frederiksted and images of bldgs from both the towns and country estates in the 19th and 20th centuries; Exec. Dir Sonia Jacobs Dow.

St John Historical Society: POB 1256, St John, VI 00831; e-mail contactus@stjohnhistoricalsociety.org; internet www.stjohnhistoricalsociety.org; f. 1974; promotes appreciation and deeper understanding of history and cultural heritage of the island of St John; Pres. David W. Knight; Sec. Mary Andrews; Treas. Margie Labrenz.

St Thomas Historical Trust: POB 6707, Charlotte Amalie, St Thomas, VI 00804; tel. (340) 774-5541; e-mail execdirector@stthomashistoricaltrust.org; internet www.stthomashistoricaltrust.org; f. 1965; advocacy and education; identifies, protects and preserves historical sites, structures and cultural heritage of St Thomas; Pres. Ronald S. Lockhart; Vice-Pres. Bernice Turnbull; Sec. Lisa Chamley-Aqui; Treas. Frank McConnell.

MEDICINE

US Virgin Islands Medical Society (VIMS): POB 5986, Sunny Isle, St Croix, VI; tel. (340) 712-2402; e-mail vimedicalsociety@hotmail.com; internet www.viqio.org/links/vims.html; f. 1955; represents physicians of the Virgin Islands; elevates and makes effective the opinions of the profession in all scientific, legislative, public health, material and social affairs, to the end that medical science may be advanced and the profession receives respect and support within its own ranks and from the community; affiliated to American Medical Asscn and Nat. Medical Asscn; Pres. Dr Ronald C. Nimmo; Pres.-Elect Dr Raymond Cintron; Exec. Sec. and Treas. Dr Cora L. E. Christian; Sec. Dr Gilbert Commissiong; Treas. Dr Alfred O. Heath.

NATURAL SCIENCES

Biological Sciences

Island Resources Foundation: 6292 Estate Nazareth 100, Red Hook, St Thomas, VI 00802; tel. (340) 775-6225; e-mail irf@irf.org; internet www.irf.org; f. 1972; not-for-profit org.; assists small islands to meet the challenges of social, economic and institutional growth while protecting and enhancing their environments; library of 10,000 vols; Pres. Bruce Potter; Vice-Pres. Dr Barbara J. Lausche; Sec. and Treas. Judith A. Towle.

St Croix Environmental Association: 5032 Anchor Way, Suite 3, Christiansted, St Croix, VI 00820; tel. (340) 773-1989; e-mail info.atsea@gmail.com; internet www.stxenvironmental.org; f. 1986; advocacy, research and programmes in conservation and education for a sustainable environment; 500 mems; Chair. Dr Ken Haines; Vice-Chair. Michael Baron; Sec. Melanie Feltmate; Treas. Theo T. Broodie; Exec. Dir Paul Chakroff; Programme Dir Carol Cramer-Burke.

Research Institutes

GENERAL

Virgin Islands Experimental Program to Stimulate Competitive Research (VI-EPSCoR): Univ. of the Virgin Islands, 2 John Brewer's Bay, St Thomas, VI 00802-9990; tel. (340) 693-1428; e-mail viepscor@uvi.edu; internet epscor.uvi.edu; attached to Univ. of the Virgin Islands; conducts research on areas of scientific inquiry linked to the Territory's economic devt; improves research infrastructure to strengthen competitiveness; increases participation of students in science and technology in order to build a skilled workforce; builds partnerships between govt, NGOs, and private sector to create a foundation of research and devt for economic growth; Asst Dir Nick Drayton.

AGRICULTURE, FISHERIES AND VETERINARY SCIENCE

Agricultural Experiment Station: RR 1, POB 10,000, Kingshill, St Croix, VI 00850; tel. (340) 692-4020; internet www.uvi.edu; attached to Univ. of the Virgin Islands; conducts basic and applied research to meet the needs of the local agricultural community in increasing production, improving efficiency, developing new enterprises, preserving and propagating germplasm unique to the Virgin Islands, and protecting the natural resource base; Dir Robert W. Godfrey.

Cooperative Extension Service: Univ. of the Virgin Islands, 2 John Brewer's Bay, St Thomas, VI 00802-9990; tel. (340) 693-2083; internet www.uvi.edu; attached to Univ. of the Virgin Islands; delivers programmes in areas of agriculture and natural resources, 4-H, family and consumer science, and communications, technology and distance education; State Dir Kwame Garcia.

Virgin Islands Sustainable Farm Institute (VISFI): POB 2903, Frederiksted, St Croix, VI 00841; tel. (340) 220-0466; internet www.visfi.org; f. 2003; community education in environmental sustainability; promotes agroecology and creation of sustainable life systems; Co-Founder Ben Jones; Dir Nate Olive.

ECONOMICS, LAW AND POLITICS

Eastern Caribbean Center: Univ. of the Virgin Islands, St Thomas Campus, 2 John Brewer's Bay, St Thomas, VI 00802-9990; tel.

(340) 693-102; internet www.uvi.edu; attached to Univ. of the Virgin Islands; compiles and analyzes demographic, social and economic data, and disseminates this data into various forums and formats; conducts scientific surveys to measure the Territory's population and housing characteristics; provides training in geographic information systems; Dir FRANK MILLS.

MEDICINE

Caribbean Exploratory NIMHD Research Center: Univ. of the Virgin Islands, St Thomas Campus, 2 John Brewer's Bay, St Thomas,VI 00802-9990; tel. (340) 693-1178; internet cercuvi.com; attached to School of Nursing, Univ. of the Virgin Islands; research in diabetes, cancer, obesity and HIV/AIDS; Dir Dr GLORIA B. CALLWOOD.

Virgin Islands Medical Institute, Inc.: POB 5989, 1AD Diamond Ruby, Sunny Isle, Christiansted, VI 00823-5989; tel. (340) 712-2400; e-mail askvimi@viqio.sdps.org; internet www.viqio.org; f. 1977; researches and documents areas of devt and improvement in healthcare; monitors the quality of the healthcare system on the Islands; non-profit org.; Pres. Dr ALFRED O. HEATH; Vice-Pres. Dr EMMANUEL GRAHAM; Sec. LEONARD W. BONELLI, SR; Treas. JOYCE L. CHRISTIAN; Medical Dir Dr CORA L. E. CHRISTIAN; publ. *Medicare Watch* (1 a year).

NATURAL SCIENCES
General

Caribbean Green Technology Center: Univ. of the Virgin Islands, St Thomas Campus, 2 John Brewer's Bay, St Thomas,VI 00802-9990; tel. (340) 693-1158; internet cgtc.uvi.edu; attached to College of Science and Mathematics, Univ. of the Virgin Islands; fosters research, education and public service on sustainability; advances interdisciplinary investigations and learning; collaborates with governmental agencies and industry partners; researches, develops, demonstrates and monitors green technology; Dir Dr WAYNE ARCHIBALD.

Biological Sciences

Center for Marine and Environmental Studies: Univ. of the Virgin Islands, RR1 10,000, Kingshill, St Croix, VI 00850-9781; tel. (340) 693-1380; internet www.uvi.edu; f. 1999; attached to Univ. of the Virgin Islands; research areas incl. evolutionary and ecological patterns and processes, ocean and coastal processes and environmental analysis and management; Dir Dr KONSTANTINOS T. ALEXANDRIDIS (acting).

Water Resources Research Institute: 2 John Brewers Bay, St Thomas, VI 00802-9990; tel. (340) 693-1062; internet www.uvi.edu/sites/uvi/pages/wrri-home.aspx; f. 1973; attached to Univ. of the Virgin Islands; research, information dissemination and training on water resources and related areas; Dir Dr HENRY H. SMITH.

Libraries and Archives
St Croix

St George Village Botanical Library: 127 Estate St George, Frederiksted, St Croix, VI 00840; tel. (340) 692-2874; e-mail infoatthegarden@gmail.com; internet www.sgvbg.org/library; historical, horticultural and botanical information; 500 vols; Exec. Dir DAVID HAMADA.

Virgin Islands Public Library System: Div. of Libraries, Archives and Museums, 1122 King St, Christiansted, St Croix, VI 00820; tel. (340) 773-5715 23 Dronningens Gade, St Thomas, VI 00802; tel. (340) 774-3407; e-mail dlmdir@vipowernet.net; internet www.virginislandspubliclibraries.org; attached to Div. of Libraries, Archives and Museums, Dept of Planning and Natural Resources; depository of govt records; preserves historical and public records; spec. collns: Von Scholten Colln, Caribbean Colln; houses books, MSS, pamphlets; newspapers on microfilm; church records incl. birth and death certificates, other archival materials; Territorial Dir Dr INGRID A. BOUGH; Asst Dir DONALD G. COLE.

Public Libraries:

Athalie McFarlane Petersen Public Library: Strand St, Frederiksted, St Croix,VI 00840; tel. (340) 772-0315.

Elaine I. Sprauve Public Library: POB 30, Enighed Estate, St John, VI 00831; tel. (340) 776-6359; internet www.virginislandspubliclibraries.org; f. 1980; Librarian IV CAROL McGUINNESS.

Enid M. Baa Public Library: 20 Dronningens Gade, St. Thomas, VI 00802; tel. (340) 774-0630; f. 1920 fmrly St Thomas library, present name 1978.

Florence Williams Public Library: 1122 King St, Christiansted, St Croix, VI 00820; tel. (340) 773-5715; f. 1920; 30,000 vols.

VI Regional Library for the Blind & Physically Handicapped (Talking Books Library): 3012 Golden Rock, Christiansted, St Croix, VI 00820; tel. (340) 718-2250; e-mail reglib@vipowernet.net; Head Librarian LETITIA GITTENS.

Museums and Art Galleries
St Croix

Fort Frederik–Frederiksfort: Waterfront, Frederiksted, St Croix, VI 00840; tel. (340) 772-2021; named after Frederik V of Denmark; deep red rubble and masonry fort represents classic Danish military architecture of the period; indoor exhibits display colonial military life; listed in the Nat. Register for Historic Places in 1996 and Nat. Historic Landmark in 1997.

St George Village Museum: 127 Estate St George, Frederiksted, St Croix, VI 00840; tel. (340) 692-2874; e-mail infoatthegarden@gmail.com; internet www.sgvbg.org/museum; attached to St George Village Botanical Gdn; display of artefacts of early Amerindian settlers; Exec. Dir DAVID HAMADA; Sec. CAROLYN FORNO; Treas. SANDRA J. RADCZENKO.

St John

Bajo el Sol Gallery: Mongoose Junction, Cruz Bay, St John, VI; tel. (340) 693-7070; e-mail bajoelsol@pennswoods.net; internet www.bajoelsolgallery.com; f. 1993; ceramics, jewellery, painting, sculpture and works by local artists.

Galeria del Mar: Wharfside Village, Cruz Bay, St John, VI; tel. (340) 693-9399; Caribbean fine arts and crafts gallery; original works and ltd edn prints by local artists, glasswork, pottery and wood sculptures.

Ivan Jadan Museum: 251 Contant, POB 84, Cruz Bay, St John, VI 00831; tel. (340) 776-6423; e-mail ijadan@islands.vi; internet www.ijadan.vi; 5,000 artefacts relating to the life of Russian tenor Ivan Jadan; collns incl. books, historical documents, photographs, CDs and video cassettes; Curator DORIS JADAN.

St Thomas

American Caribbean Historical Museum: 32 Raadets Gade, Charlotte Amalie, St Thomas, VI; tel. (340) 714-5150; history of the Virgin Islands since 15th century; exhibits incl. artefacts, documents, historic costumes and photographs.

Fort Christian and Virgin Islands Museum: Waterfront, Charlotte Amalie, St Thomas, VI; tel. (340) 776-8605; historic museum housed within Fort Christian, the oldest standing structure in St Thomas (built in 1672); exhibits incl. antique maps, handmade W Indian furnishings, military hardware, natural history colln, period furniture; attached art gallery; added to Nat. Register of Historic Places in 1977.

University
UNIVERSITY OF THE VIRGIN ISLANDS

St Croix Campus: RR1 POB 10,000, Kingshill, St Croix, VI 00850-9781

Telephone: (340) 692-4158

St Thomas Campus: 2 John Brewer's Bay, St Thomas, VI 00802-9990

Telephone: (340) 693-1160 (St Thomas)
E-mail: admissions@uvi.edu
Internet: www.uvi.edu

Founded 1962 as College of the Virgin Islands, present name 1986
State control
Academic year: August to DecemberJanuary to May (2 semesters)
Pres.: Dr DAVID HALL
Provost: Dr KARL S. WRIGHT
Vice-Pres. for Admin. and Finance: SHIRLEY LAKE-KING
Vice-Pres. for Institutional Advancement: Dr DIONNE V. JACKSON
Vice-Provost for Access and Enrolment: Dr JUDITH EDWIN
Vice-Provost for Research and Public Service: Dr HENRY H. SMITH
Chief Information Officer: TINA M. KOOPMANS
Library: St Croix Campus: 53,000 vols, 167 periodicals; spec. colln incl. VI govt documents and ERIC documents; St Thomas campus: 80,500 vols, 690 periodicals, 590,000 microforms, 15,000 US govt documents, 20,000 other items; spec. collns: Virgin Islands Digital colln, Ralph D. DeChabert spec. colln, Caspar Holstein Colln, Charles William Taussig Memorial colln and Caribbean colln
Number of teachers: 615 (390 full-time, 225 part-time)
Number of students: 2,610
Publications: *The Caribbean Writer* (1 a year), *UVI Magazine* (1 a year)

DEANS

College of Liberal Arts and Social Sciences: Dr GEORGE LORD
College of Science and Mathematics: Dr CAMILLE McKAYLE
School of Business: Dr CHARLES WILLIAMS
School of Education: Dr LINDA V. THOMAS
School of Nursing: Dr CHERYL FRANKLIN

URUGUAY

The Higher Education System

Institutions of higher education date from after Uruguay's independence from Spain in 1825, the oldest being the Universidad de la República, which was founded in 1849 and is the sole public university. Education at this establishment is state-funded and, therefore, free of charge. At all other institutions (other than the public non-university institutions) tuition fees apply. The country's first private university, the Universidad Católica del Uruguay Dámaso A Larrañaga, was not founded until 1984. Higher education is provided by universidades (universities both public and private), institutos universitarios (university institutes, all of which are private) and institutos terciarios no universitario (non-university higher institutions both public and private). In 2011, according to statistics published by the Ministerio de Educación y Cultura, some 112,891 students were enrolled at the Universidad de la República, a total of 20,427 were enrolled at the country's four private universities and 2,236 were attending 10 university institutes.

The main requirement for admission to higher education is the Bachillerato Diversificado, the main secondary school award, with specialization during the final two years, depending on the degree applied for. Carreras intermedios (intermediate degrees) last two-and-a-half to three years, contain about one-half of the content of a full degree and often culminate with the award of a professional title; students may then graduate to full undergraduate degrees. Carreras de grado (undergraduate degrees) last a minimum of four years and lead to the award of Título de Licenciado (Bachelor's degree) in the subject studied. Some professional degrees, such as Licenciado en Enfermería (nursing), Licenciado en Nutrición (nutrition) and Licenciado en Psicología (psychology) last four-and-a-half years. Until 2006 medical degrees were available only at the Universidad de la República and lasted eight years, with students receiving the title Doctor en Medicina. Since 2006 a six-year medicine programme accredited by El Mecanismo Experimental de Acreditación de Carreras del Mercosur (see below) has also been available at Centro Latinoamericano de Economía Humana (CLAEH). The first postgraduate degree is the especialización (specialist course), which lasts for a minimum of one year and leads to award of the Título de Especialista or Título de Diplomado. The Título de Maestría or Magister (Master's degree) lasts a minimum of two years, with students required to submit a thesis in the second year. For business studies the title Máster is often used. Finally, the highest level of postgraduate study is at doctoral level, where students work for a minimum of three years, following completion of the Master's degree, to achieve the Doctorado (Doctorate).

The Consejo de Educación Técnico y Professional—Universidad del Trabajo del Uruguay (UTUthe country's second oldest higher education institution, founded in 1878) is responsible for providing post-secondary technical and vocational education (although, despite what its name might suggest, it does not offer degree-level qualifications). The primary qualification awarded at this level is the Título Técnico or the Título Tecnólogo in the subject studied. This qualification is necessary for admission to undergraduate courses in certain subjects, such as engineering.

Guidelines aimed at maintaining uniformity of teaching standards across private tertiary education institutions were set out in 1995 by Law 308/995, although individual institutions have considerable autonomy regarding the academic content of their programmes. The Ley General de Educación (Law 18.437) of December 2008 established the Instituto Universitario de Educación (IUDE), which aimed to train technical specialists, social educators and general teachers. Uruguay is a member of Mercado Común del Sur (Mercosur—Southern Common Market) and therefore participates in El Mecanismo Experimental de Acreditación de Carreras del Mercosur, which has so far accredited programmes in agronomy, medicine and engineering. However, Uruguay remains the only member of Mercosur that has yet to establish a national accreditation or quality assurance agency for its higher education sector.

Regulatory Body

GOVERNMENT

Ministry of Education and Culture: Reconquista 535, 11000 Montevideo; tel. 2915 0103; e-mail centrodeinformacion@mec.gub.uy; internet www.mec.gub.uy; Minister Dr RICARDO EHRLICH.

Learned Societies

AGRICULTURE, FISHERIES AND VETERINARY SCIENCE

Asociación Rural del Uruguay (Rural Association of Uruguay): Avda Uruguay 864, 11100 Montevideo; tel. 2902 0484; e-mail aruinforme@aru.org.uy; internet www.aru.com.uy; f. 1871; promotes agriculture and related industries; 3,000 mems; library of 3,000 vols; Pres. RUBÉN ECHEVERRÍA NÚÑEZ; Sec. GONZALO GAMBETTA; Sec. RICHARD REILLY ARRARTE; publ. *Revista Asociación Rural* (12 a year, Spanish, print and online, www.duplex.com.uy/aru.html).

ARCHITECTURE AND TOWN PLANNING

Sociedad de Arquitectos del Uruguay (Architects' Association of Uruguay): Gonzalo Ramírez 2030, 11200 Montevideo; tel. 2411 9556; e-mail sau@sau.org.uy; internet www.sau.org.uy; f. 1914, received legal status 1921; 2,300 mems; library of 1,500 vols, 1,000 pamphlets and 165 journal titles; Pres. Arq. ENEIDA DE LEÓN; Sec.-Gen. Arq. ANAHÍ RICCA; publ. *Boletín de Arquitectura* (6 a year).

BIBLIOGRAPHY, LIBRARY SCIENCE AND MUSEOLOGY

Agrupación Bibliotecológica del Uruguay (Library Association of Uruguay): Cerro Largo 1666, 11200 Montevideo; tel. 2400 5740; f. 1960; activities incl. library science, archives, documentation, bibliography, history and numismatics; 238 mems; Pres. LUIS ALBERTO MUSSO; publs *Anales del Senado del Uruguay-Cronología*, *Aportes para la Historia de la Bibliotecología en el Uruguay*, *Bibliografía Básica de la Historia de la República Oriental del Uruguay*, *Bibliografía Bibliográfica y BiblioTecología*, *Bibliografía de Bibliografías Uruguayas*, *Bibliografía del Poder Legislativo desde sus Comienzos hasta el Año 1965*, *Bibliografía Uruguaya sobre Brasil*, *Bibliografía Uruguaya sobre Historia Argentina*, *Bibliografía y Documentación en el Uruguay*, *Documentalistas Uruguayos*, *El Río de la Plata en el Archivo de Indias, Historiografía y Bibliografía sobre los Canarios en el Uruguay*.

Asociación de Bibliotecólogos del Uruguay (Uruguayan Librarians' Association): Eduardo V. Haedo 2255, 11200 Montevideo; tel. 2409 9989; e-mail abu@adinet.com.uy; internet www.abu.net.uy; f. 1945 as Asociación de Bibliotecarios Diplomados del Uruguay; adopted current name 1990; represents and promotes professional interests of the librarians; assists in devt and improvement of information units; 300 mems; Pres. Lic. CARINA PATTERN; Sec. Lic. MANUELA COLLAZO; publ. *Panel de Noticias*.

HISTORY, GEOGRAPHY AND ARCHAEOLOGY

Instituto Histórico y Geográfico del Uruguay (Historical and Geographical Institute of Uruguay): Río Negro 1495/a 202, 11100 Montevideo; e-mail histogeo@adinet.com.uy; f. 1843; 40 academicians; Pres. Prof. EDMUNDO M. NARANCIO; publ. *Revista*.

LANGUAGE AND LITERATURE

Academia Nacional de Letras (National Academy of Literature): Ituzaingó 1255, 11000 Montevideo; tel. 2915 2374; e-mail academiauruguayaletras@gmail.com; internet www.mec.gub.uy/academiadeletras; f.

1943; researches in Spanish language, mainly lexicography, especially Uruguayan spoken Spanish; also Uruguayan literature; organizes lectures, readings of Uruguayan literature, workshops; contributes to comprehensive works elaborated within the ASALE (Asociación de Academias de la Lengua Española) such as the Nueva Gramática de la lengua española, Diccionario de Americanismos, Ortografía de la lengua española, etc.; 19 mems, 33 corresp. mems; Pres. Dr WILFREDO PENCO; Sec. MABEL LÓPEZ VALÍN; publ. *Revista de la Academia* (irregular).

Alliance Française: Blvr Artigas 1271, 11200 Montevideo; tel. 2400 0505; e-mail accueil@alliancefrancaise.edu.uy; internet www.alliancefrancaise.edu.uy; f. 1923; offers courses and examinations in French language and culture, promotes cultural exchange with France; attached teaching centres in Florida, Maldonado, Melo, Mercedes, Montevideo, Paysandú, Rocha, Salto, San José, and Tacuarembó; Pres. PEDRO NICOLÁS BARIDON; Dir-Gen. PAUL LALLOZ.

Goethe-Institut: Santiago de Chile 874, 11200 Montevideo; tel. 2908 0234; e-mail info@montevideo.goethe.org; internet www.goethe.de/montevideo; offers courses and examinations in German language and culture; promotes cultural exchange with Germany; library of 8,000 vols, 23 periodicals; Dir Dr ELISABETH LATTARO.

MEDICINE

Academia Nacional de Medicina del Uruguay (National Academy of Medicine of Uruguay): 18 de Julio 2175, 5°, Montevideo; tel. 2408 4103; e-mail academiamed@adinet.com.uy; internet www.anm.org.uy; f. 1976; 26 mems; Pres. Acad. HERNÁN ARTUCIO; Sec.-Gen. Acad. EDUARDO WILSON; publ. *Boletín* (1 a year).

Asociación de Uruguay Psicoterapia Psicoanalítica (AUDEPP) (Association of Uruguay Psychoanalytic Psychotherapy): Canelones 2208, 11200 Montevideo; tel. 2408 4985; e-mail contacto@audepp.org; internet www.audepp.org; f. 1981; focuses on professional training of psychoanalytic psychotherapy and psychoanalysis; 300 mems; Pres. Dr ROSARIO ALLEGUE; Sec. Dr ROSARIO OYENARD.

Asociación Odontológica Uruguaya (Odontological Association of Uruguay): Avda Durazno 937–39, 11100 Montevideo; tel. 2900 1572; e-mail contactoaou@aou.org.uy; internet www.aou.org.uy; f. 1946; comprises 8 depts and 6 sections; museum; 3,000 mems; library of 6,000 vols; Pres. Dr ALVARO RODA; Sec. Dr RAFAEL PÉREZ VERDEROSA; publ. *Odontología Uruguaya* (2 a year).

Sociedad de Cirugía del Uruguay (Surgical Society of Uruguay): Canelones 2280, 11200 Montevideo; tel. 2402 6820; e-mail secretaria@scu.org.uy; internet www.scu.org.uy; f. 1920; scientific sessions, meetings, annual Uruguayan congress of surgery; 443 mems; library of 2,800 vols; Pres. Dr RUBEN DANIEL VARELA; Sec. Dr RUBENS NEIROTTI; publ. *Cirugía del Uruguay* (3 a year).

Sociedad de Radiología e Imagenología del Uruguay (Radiology and Imaging Society of Uruguay): Julio César 1460 bis, 11600 Montevideo; tel. 2481 1714; e-mail sriu@adinet.com.uy; internet www.sriuy.org.uy; f. 1923; scientific activity linked to the Médicos Imagenólogos; holds confs and seminars; 190 mems; Pres. Dr CARLOS GALEANO; Sec. Dra LILIANA SERVENTE; publ. *Revista de Imagenología del Uruguay.*

Attached Institutes:

Gremial Uruguaya de Médicos Radiólogos: Montevideo; f. 1972; 70 mems; Pres. Dr ERNESTO H. CIBILS.

Sociedad Uruguaya de Historia de la Medicina (SUHM) (Uruguayan Society of History of Medicine): Avda Gral. Flores 2125, Montevideo; tel. 2924 3414; e-mail histmed@fmed.edu.uy; f. 1970; research on history of medicine and allied sciences; 80 mems; Pres. Prof. Dr RICARDO POU FERRARI; Sec. Dr SANDRA BURGUES ROCA; publ. *Sesiones de la Sociedad Uruguaya de Historia de la Medicina* (1 a year).

Sociedad Uruguaya de Pediatría (Paediatrics Society of Uruguay): Centro Hospitalario Pereira Rossell, Blvr Artigas 1550, 11600 Montevideo; tel. 2709 1801; e-mail secretaria@sup.org.uy; internet www.sup.org.uy; f. 1915; 500 mems, affiliated to the Asociación Latino Americana de Pediatría; library of 3,500 vols, 6,500 periodicals; Pres. Dr WALTER PÉREZ; Sec. Dr GABRIEL PELUFFO; publ. *Archivos de Pediatría del Uruguay* (4 a year).

NATURAL SCIENCES

Biological Sciences

Sociedad Malacológica del Uruguay (Malacological Society of Uruguay): Casilla 1401, 11000 Montevideo; e-mail smu@adinet.com.uy; f. 1957; 210 mems; Pres. JORGE BROGGI; Sec. JUAN CARLOS ZAFFARONI; publ. *Comunicaciones* (1 a year, print and online, www.smdu.org.uy).

Sociedad Zoológica del Uruguay (Zoological Society of Uruguay): Iguá 4225, 11400 Montevideo; tel. 2525 8618; e-mail info@szu.org.uy; internet www.szu.org.uy; f. 1961; 200 mems; Pres. ANITA AISENBERG; Sec. JOSÉ CARLOS GUERRERO; publ. *Boletín* (irregular, online).

TECHNOLOGY

Academia Nacional de Ingeniería (National Academy of Engineering of Uruguay): Cuareim 1492, 11100 Montevideo; tel. 2901 1762; e-mail cutinella@redfacil.com.uy; internet www.aniu.org.uy; f. 1965; 37 full mems, 3 honorary and 6 corresp. mems; Pres. Ing. ANDRÉS TIERNO ABREU; Sec. Ing. ADRIANA GAMBOGI.

Asociación de Ingenieros del Uruguay (Association of Uruguayan Engineers): Cuareim 1492, 11100 Montevideo; tel. 2901 1762; e-mail aiu@adinet.com.uy; internet www.aiu.org.uy; f. 1905; affiliated to the Unión Panamericana de Asociaciones de Ingenieros; 1,400 mems, also hon. and corresp. mems abroad; library of 2,000 vols; Pres. Ing. LUCAS BLASINA; Sec. Ing. MARIANA BERNASCONI; publ. *Revista de Ingeniería* (3 a year).

Research Institutes

GENERAL

Dirección Nacional de Ciencia, Tecnología y Innovación (DINACYT) (National Directorate for Science, Technology and Innovation): Paraguay 1470, 2°, 11100 Montevideo; tel. 2901 4285; e-mail webmaster@dicyt.gub.uy; internet www.dicyt.gub.uy; f. 1961 as Consejo Nacional de Investigaciones Científicas y Técnicas (CONICYT), adopted current name 2001; coordinates, manages and executes development projects in science, technology and innovation; 22 mems; library of 7,000 vols, 275 periodicals; Dir GABRIEL AINTABLIAN; publs *Claro Que Se Puede* (irregular), *El Proceso de Innovación en la Industria Uruguaya* (every 2 years),

Indicadores de Ciencia y Tecnología (irregular), *Informe a la Sociedad*.

UNESCO Office Montevideo: Casilla de correo 859, Montevideo; Edificio del MERCOSUR, Calle Dr Luis Piera 1992 (2°), 11200 Montevideo; tel. 2413 2075; e-mail montevideo@unesco.org.uy; internet www.unesco.org.uy; f. 1949; designated Cluster Office for Argentina, Brazil, Paraguay, Uruguay; coordinates UNESCO's programmes in the region, particularly: basic sciences, environmental and water sciences, science, technology and society, earth sciences and natural hazards, marine sciences, information and communication, education, culture and world heritage; Dir JORGE GRANDI.

AGRICULTURE, FISHERIES AND VETERINARY SCIENCE

Centro de Investigaciones Pesqueras y Piscicultura (Fisheries and Pisciculture Research Institute): c/o DINARA, Villa Constitución Salto; tel. 4764 2014; internet www.dinara.gub.uy; attached to State Office for Aquatic Resources; Nat. Dir for Aquatic Resources Dr DANIEL GILARDONI.

Instituto Nacional de Investigación Agropecuaria (National Agricultural Research Institute): Andes 1365, Piso 12, 11100 Montevideo; tel. 2902 0550; e-mail iniadn@inia.org.uy; internet www.inia.org.uy; f. 1914; library of 12,000 vols, 1,000 periodicals; Dir MARIO ALLEGRI; publs *Boletín de Divulgación*, *Hojas de Divulgación*, *Serie Actividades de Difusión*, *Serie Técnica*.

ECONOMICS, LAW AND POLITICS

Centro de Estadísticas Nacionales y Comercio Internacional del Uruguay (CENCI Uruguay) (National Centre for Statistics and International Trade Uruguay): Juncal 1327D, 16, Oficina 1603, 11000 Montevideo; tel. 2915 2930; e-mail cenci@cenci.com.uy; internet www.cenci.com.uy; f. 1955; provides economic and statistical information on all American countries; operates computer programs handling import tariffs on commodities; library of 900 vols; Dir KENNETH BRUNNER; publs *Anuario Estadístico Sobre el Intercambio Comercial* (1 a year), *Dictámenes de Clasificación Arancelaria—MERCOSUR*, *Estudios del Mercado*, *Industrias por Sectores de Actividad*, *Manual Práctico* (Practical manuals for importers, exporters, customs and tax payers, 12 a year), *Régimen de Origen—ALADI y MERCOSUR*.

Instituto Nacional de Estadística (National Institute of Statistics): Río Negro 1520, 11100 Montevideo; tel. 2902 7303; e-mail difusion@ine.gub.uy; internet www.ine.gub.uy; f. 1852; library of 4,000 vols; Technical Dir LAURA NALBARTE; Sec. MARINA CASTILLO; publs *Anuario Estadístico* (1 a year), *Encuesta Continua de Hogares* (1 a year), *Indicadores de Actividad y Precios del Sector Inmobiliario Añp* (1 a year), *Síntesis Estadística*, *Uruguay en Cifras* (1 a year).

HISTORY, GEOGRAPHY AND ARCHAEOLOGY

Servicio Geográfico Militar del Uruguay (Military Geographical Service): Avda 8 de Octubre 3255, 11600 Montevideo; tel. 2487 1810; e-mail sgm@iau.gub.uy; internet www.sgm.edu.uy; f. 1913; cartography, geodesy and surveying, geophysics, mapping and GIS, photogrammetry; library of 3,500 vols, 4,000 cartographic and 400 historical documents; Dir Col CÉSAR F. RODRÍGUEZ; publ. scale aeronautic and aerial maps.

MEDICINE

Instituto Nacional del Cáncer (National Cancer Institute): Joanicó 3265, Montevideo; tel. 2487 5098; e-mail direccion.inca@asse.com.uy; internet www.asse.com.uy/uc_5222_1.html; f. 1960; Dir Dr Álvaro Luongo.

Liga Uruguaya contra la Tuberculosis (Anti-Tuberculosis League): Magallanes 1320, 11200 Montevideo; tel. 2408 3570; e-mail ligatub@adinet.com.uy; f. 1902; specializes in combating tuberculosis in children and the elderly; library of 3,000 vols; Pres. Máximo A. Saavedra; Sec. Dr Lorenzo Píriz Lostao.

NATURAL SCIENCES

Biological Sciences

Instituto de Investigaciones Biológicas Clemente Estable (Institute for Biological Research Clemente Stable): Avda Italia 3318, 11600 Montevideo; tel. 2487 1616; e-mail asistentes@iibce.edu.uy; internet www.iibce.edu.uy; f. 1927; 3 divs, 10 depts, 6 laboratories; biological research; library of 12,000 vols; Pres. Dr Pablo Zunino.

Physical Sciences

Dirección Nacional de Meteorología del Uruguay (National Meteorological Directorate): Javier Barrios Amorín 1488, 11200 Montevideo; tel. 2400 5516; e-mail dnm25255@adinet.com.uy; internet www.meteorologia.com.uy; f. 1895, adopted current name 1979; library of 6,000 vols, 13,800 documents; Nat. Dir Beatriz Cuello; publs Anuario Climatológico, Boletín Agrometeorológico, Boletín Pluviométrico, Notas Técnicas.

Observatorio Astronómico de Montevideo (Montevideo Astronomical Observatory): Liceo No. 35 IAVA, J. E. Rodó y E. Acevedo, Montevideo; tel. 2408 5825; e-mail observatoriodemontevideo@gmail.com; internet iava.edu.uy/astronomia.htm; f. 1927; library of 5,000 vols.

RELIGION, SOCIOLOGY AND ANTHROPOLOGY

Instituto Interamericano del Niño (Inter-American Children's Institute): Avda 8 de Octubre 2904, 11600 Montevideo; tel. 2487 2150; e-mail iin@iinoea.org; internet www.iin.oea.org; f. 1927; specialized institute of the Organization of American States (OAS); library: specialized library of 42,500 vols and 12,700 full text scanned documents, open to the public; computerized information centre; Pres. Carmen Bergés de Amaro; Dir-Gen. Prof. Maria de los Dolores Aguilar Marmolejo.

TECHNOLOGY

Dirección Nacional de Minería y Geología (National Directorate of Mining and Geology): Calle Hervidero 2861, 11800, Montevideo; tel. 2200 1951; e-mail secretaria@dinamige.miem.gub.uy; internet www.dinamige.gub.uy; f. 1912; library of 4,800 vols, 150 journal titles, 500 technical reports; Nat. Dir Prof. Pier Rossi; publ. Industria Extractiva del Uruguay (1 a year).

Dirección Nacional de Tecnología Nuclear (National Directorate of Nuclear Technology of Uruguay): Mercedes 1041, P2, 11100 Montevideo; tel. 2908 6330; e-mail dntncoop@adinet.com.uy; f. 1955 as Comisión Nacional de Energía Atómica; controls activities involving the use of radioactive materials or equipment producing ionizing radiation; prepares technical and safety rules for activities involving nuclear technology; liaises with nat. and int. institutions on procedural aspects of nuclear technology; library of 3,500 vols; colln of microfiches; Dir Rosario Odino; publs Memoria (1 a year), Revista (1 a year).

Instituto Uruguayo de Normas Técnicas (Uruguayan Standards Institution): Plaza Independencia 812, 2°, Montevideo; tel. 2901 2048; e-mail unit-iso@unit.org.uy; internet www.unit.org.uy; f. 1939; standardization, certification, information on standards, training in high-level management; library of 250,000 vols; Dir Ing. Pablo J. Benia Salvadores; publ. UNIT Standards.

Libraries and Archives

Florida

Biblioteca Municipal (Municipal Library): C/Barreiro 420, 94000 Florida; tel. 352 2102; f. 1889; 42,000 vols; Dir Fernando Gabriel Giordano Foligno.

Montevideo

Archivo General de la Nación (National Archives): Calle Convención 1474, 11100 Montevideo; tel. 2900 7232; e-mail direccion@agn.gub.uy; internet www.agn.gub.uy; f. 1926; 14,000 vols; Dir Lic. Alicia Casas de Barrán; publ. Revista.

Biblioteca Central de Educación Secundaria (Central Library of Secondary Education): Eduardo Acevedo 1427, 11200 Montevideo; tel. 2408 4273; e-mail biblos@adinet.com.uy; internet www.ces.edu.uy; f. 1885; books for higher education; collns incl. ancient and rare books section (dating from 16th century); 80,000 vols; Librarian Marianela Falero.

Biblioteca del Palacio Legislativo (Library of The Legislative Palace): Avda Libertador Brigadier Gral Lavalleja y Avda Gral Flores, Montevideo; f. 1929; legal deposit library in conjunction with National Library; 322,000 vols; specializes in jurisprudence; Dir Luis H. Boions Pombo; publs Bibliografía Uruguaya, Boletín Bibliográfico (12 a year).

Biblioteca Municipal 'Dr Francisco Albero Schinca' (Municipal Library 'Dr Francisco Albero Schinca'): Avda 8 de Octubre 4210, Montevideo; tel. 2508 8152; f. 1929; 14,000 vols; Dir Graciela Navarro.

Biblioteca Municipal 'Joaquín de Salterain' (Municipal Library 'Joaquín de Salterain'): Solis 1456 e/ 25 de Mayo y Cerrito, Montevideo; tel. 2915 6282; 36,000 vols; incl. a slide library; Librarian Rosario Cruz.

Biblioteca Nacional del Uruguay (National Library of Uruguay): Avda 18 de Julio 1790, 11200 Montevideo; tel. 2400 5385; e-mail bibliotecanacional@bibna.gub.uy; internet www.bibna.gub.uy; f. 1816; comprises reference service, copyright office, legal deposit, Uruguayan and special materials, restoration of printed works, Nat. Information System project, cultural extension; 900,000 vols, 20,000 periodicals; Dir Carlos Liscano; publ. Revista de la Biblioteca Nacional.

Attached Institute:

Centro Nacional de Documentación Científica, Técnica y Económica: Avda 18 de Julio 1790, Montevideo; tel. 2408 4172; f. 1953; part of Nat. Library; Dir Elena Castro.

Biblioteca Pedagógica Central 'Mtro. Sebastián Morey Otero' (Central Pedagogical Library 'Mtro. Sebastián Morey Otero'): Plaza Cagancha 1175, Montevideo; tel. 2902 0915; e-mail bibliotecapedagogica@gmail.com; f. 1889; 20,000 vols of biblio-graphic books and journals; Dir Anair Martinol; publs Bibliografía Uruguaya sobre Educación, Información Bibliográfica (2 a year), Temas, Traducciones.

Museums and Art Galleries

Montevideo

Museo de Descubrimiento (Discovery Museum): Zabala 1583 y Piedras, 11000 Montevideo; tel. 2915 9951; evokes the journeys of Cristóbal Colón, the meeting of the two worlds; maps, dioramas and photographs.

Museo Del Fútbol (Football Museum): Estadio Centenario, Av Ricaldoni Olympic podium, Guayabos 1531, 11000 Montevideo; tel. 2480 1259; e-mail auf@auf.org.uy; internet www.auf.org.uy/portal/football_museum; f. 1975; colln of football mementos, historical objects and images of Uruguayan teams.

Museo Histórico Nacional (National Historical Museum): Casa Rivera, Calle Rincón 437, 11000 Montevideo; tel. 2915 1051; e-mail museohistorico@mhn.gub.uy; internet www.mhn.gub.uy; f. 1900; sectional collns of local Indian cultures (prehistoric, colonial epoch, development and political history of the country); portraits, relics, arms, documents, coins, medals, etc., relating to the Wars of Independence, British invasion, early revolutions, etc.; Dir Prof. Enrique Mena Sagarra; publ. Revista Histórica.

Museo Municipal de Bellas Artes 'Juan Manuel Blanes' (Museum of Fine Arts 'Juan Manuel Blanes'): Avda Millán 4015, 11700 Montevideo; tel. 2336 2248; e-mail blanes@internet.com.uy; internet www.blanes.montevideo.gub.uy; f. 1930; paintings, drawings, wood-carvings, sculptures; Coordinator Arq. Gabriel Peluffo.

Museo Nacional de Antropología (National Anthropology Museum): Avda de las Instrucciones 948, 12900 Montevideo; tel. 2355 1480; e-mail anthropos@adinet.com.uy; internet www.mna.gub.uy; f. 1981; colln incl. archaeology, botany, ethnography, folklore, geology, palaeontology and zoology; library of 2,500 vols; Dir Arturo Toscano.

Museo Nacional de Artes Visuales (National Museum of Visual Arts): Tomás Giribaldi 2283 esq. Julio Herrera y Reissig, Parque Rodó, 11300 Montevideo; tel. 2711 6124; e-mail informatica@mnav.gub.uy; internet www.mnav.gub.uy; f. 1911; 6,200 paintings, engravings, drawings, sculptures, ceramics; library of 11,000 vols of books on sociology, psychology, aesthetics, philosophy and art, etc.; Dir Enrique Aguerre.

Museo Nacional de Historia Natural (National Museum of Natural History): 25 de Mayo 582-CC. 399, 11000 Montevideo; tel. 2916 0908; e-mail info@mnhn.gub.uy; internet www.mnhn.gub.uy; f. 1837 as Nat. Museum; colln incl. botany, paloaeontology and zoology; library of 250,000 vols; Dir Javier González; publ. 4 journals on anthropology, botany, paloeontology and zoology; publs Anales del Museo (irregular), Publicación Extra (irregular).

Museo Pedagógico 'José Pedro Varela' (Pedagogical Museum 'José Pedro Varela'): Plaza Cagancha 1175, 11100 Montevideo; tel. 2900 4744; e-mail museopedagogico@gmail.com; internet www.cep.edu.uy/index.php/msspg-museo; f. 1889; contains 5,000 exhibits, 2,000 photographs; library of 6,500 vols and periodicals; Dir Susana Luzardo Briano.

Museo Torres García (Museum of Torres Garcia): Peatonal Sarandí 683, 11000 Montevideo; tel. 2916 2663; e-mail coordinacionmtg@gmail.com; internet www.torresgarcia.org.uy; f. 1953; portraits of historical icons and Cubist paintings by Joaquín Torres García; Dir ALEJANDRO DIAZ.

Museo y Archivo Histórico Municipal (Municipal Museum and Historical Archive): Palacio del Cabildo, Calle Juan Carlos Gómez 1362, 11100 Montevideo; tel. 2915 9685; e-mail cabildodemontevideo@gmail.com; internet cabildo.montevideo.gub.uy; f. 1915; permanent exhibition of the history of Montevideo from 1726; furniture, icons, paintings, jewellery and maps; library of 9,000 vols; Hon. Dir JORGE R. DELUCCHI; publ. *Anales*.

Museo y Jardin Botánico de Montevideo 'Prof. Atilio Lombardo' (Museum and Botanical Garden of Montevideo 'Prof. Atilio Lombardo'): Avda 19 de Abril 1181, 11700 Montevideo; tel. 2336 4005; e-mail botanico@adinet.com.uy; internet jardinbotanico.montevideo.gub.uy; f. 1902; displays the flora of different geographical areas of the world, aquatic plants and shade plants; teaching of botany; promotes research of local flora and vegetation; Dir Ing. PABLO B. ROSS.

Museo Zoológico 'Dámaso Antonio Larrañaga' (Zoological Museum 'Dámaso Antonio Larrañaga'): Rambla República de Chile 4215, Montevideo; tel. 2622 0258; e-mail museodal@correo.imm.gub.uy; f. 1956; instruction on nat. and exotic fauna, taxidermy; library: 2,000 specialized vols; 2,000 species of fauna and molluscs, etc.; Dir Prof. BEATRIZ MARTINEZ MORANTE.

San José de Mayo

Museo de Bellas Artes Departamental de San José (Departmental Museum of Fine Arts of San Jose): Calle Dr Julián Becerro de Bengoa 493, 80000 San José de Mayo; tel. 4342 3672; e-mail museosanjose@adinet.com.uy; internet www.museo.ensanjose.com; f. 1947; school of art; paintings, drawings, sculptures, ceramics and wood carvings; library of 6,000 vols of books; 3,000 slides; Pres. NORMA AGARLA; Dir CÉSAR BERNESCONI; publ. *Notimuseo* (12 a year).

Tacuarembó

Museo del Indio y del Gaucho (Museum of the Indians and the Gauchos): General Artigas 256, 11300 Tacuarembó; tel. 4632 4671; affiliated to the Museo Histórico Nacional; large colln representing ancient native crafts, weapons and other implements of aboriginal Indians and Gauchos; Founder and Dir WASHINGTON ESCOBAR.

Universities

UNIVERSIDAD CATÓLICA DEL URUGUAY
(Catholic University of Uruguay)

Avda 8 de Octubre 2738, 11600 Montevideo
Telephone: 2487 2717
E-mail: infoweb@ucu.edu.uy
Internet: www.ucu.edu.uy
Founded 1882, reopened by Society of Jesus 1985
Private control
Language of instruction: Spanish
Academic year: March to November
Grand Chancellor: Mgr Dr NICOLÁS COTUGNO FANIZZI
Vice-Grand Chancellor: Fr ALEJANDRO TILVE
Rector: Fr Dr EDUARDO CASAROTTI
Vice-Pres. for Academics: Dr ARIEL TABLE

Vice-Pres. for Devt and Economic Management: Ing. OMAR PAGANINI
Rector. for Middle College: Fr ÁLVARO PACHECO
Librarian: Dr. PABLO LANDONI COUTURE
Library of 115,000 vols of books, 265 periodical titles and 30 databases; 6 sites
Number of teachers: 607
Number of students: 5,000

Publications: *Actas Odontológicas* (2 a year), *Cuadernos de Negocios Internacionales e Integración*, *Ciencias Psicológicas* (2 a year), *Cuaderno de Economía* (1 a year, print and online, cuadernodeeconomia.ucu.edu.uy), *Dixit* (2 a year, print and online, revistadixit.ucu.edu.uy), *Enfermería: Cuidados Humanizados* (2 a year), *Medialógos* (1 a year), *Páginas de Educación* (Education Pages, 1 a year), *Relaciones Laborales en el Uruguay*, *Anuario de Actividades de Investigación* (1 a year), *Revista Ciencias Sociales* (1 a year), *Revista de Derecho* (1 a year), *Revista FCE (Facultad de Ciencias Empresariales)*, *Revista Lazos*, *Revista Págines del Área Educación*

DEANS

Faculty of Business Administration: Dr JOHN MILES
Faculty of Dentistry: Dr JORGE LIEBER
Faculty of Engineering and Technology: Dr ÁLVARO PARDO
Faculty of Humanities: Mag. ARZUAGA MONICA
Faculty of Law: Dr CARLOS DELPIAZZO
Faculty of Psychology: Dr MARIA LUISA BLANCO
Postgraduate Centre: Dr CARONLINA GREISING (Dir)
School of Nursing and Health Technologies: Lic. ISABEL CAL

UNIVERSIDAD DE LA EMPRESA–UDE
(Business University)

Soriano 959, 11100 Montevideo
Telephone: 2900 2442
E-mail: info@ude.edu.uy
Internet: www.ude.edu.uy
Founded 1992 as UDE Business School, univ. status 1998
Private control
Language of instruction: Spanish
Academic year: March to November

Faculties of agricultural sciences, business, design and communication, educational sciences, engineering sciences, health sciences and law; School of Business Development and Teacher Training Institute

Rector: CR. ROBERTO BREZZO
Dir for Academics: CR. RAÚL CORREA
Dir-Gen.: GUILLERMO JASIDAKIS
Dir for Admin.: NILO PEILE
Dir for Commercial: CAROLINA ABUCHALJA

DEANS

Faculty of Agricultural Sciences: Ing. JAVIER DURAN

UNIVERSIDAD DE LA REPÚBLICA
(University of the Republic)

Avda 18 de Julio 1968 (2° piso), 11200 Montevideo
Telephone: 2400 9201
E-mail: comentarios@universidad.edu.uy
Internet: www.universidad.edu.uy
Founded 1849
State control
Language of instruction: Spanish
Academic year: March to December
Rector: Dr RODRIGO AROCENA
Vice-Rector: Dr EDUARDO MANTA

Pro-Rector for Academic Affairs: Dr LUIS CALEGARI
Pro-Rector for Admin. Management: Dr RICARDO ROCA
Pro-Rector for Extension: Dr HUMBERTO TOMMASINO
Pro-Rector for Research: Dr GREGORY RANDALL
Sec.: VERÓNICA PÉREZ MANUKIÁN

Library: 1m. vols
Number of teachers: 6,130
Number of students: 81,774

DEANS

Faculty of Agronomy: Ing. FERNANDO GARCÍA PRÉCHAC
Faculty of Architecture: Arq. GUSTAVO SCHEPS
Faculty of Chemistry: Dr EDUARDO MANTA
Faculty of Dentistry: Dr HUGO CALABRIA
Faculty of Economics and Management Sciences: RODRIGO ARIM
Faculty of Engineering: Ing. HÉCTOR CANCELA
Faculty of Humanities and Education Sciences: Dr ÁLVARO RICO
Faculty of Law: DORA BAGDASSARIAN
Faculty of Medicine: Dr FERNANDO TOMASINA
Faculty of Nursing: Prof. MERCEDES PÉREZ
Faculty of Psychology: Prof. Lic. LUIS LEOPOLD
Faculty of Science: Dr JUAN CRISTINA
Faculty of Social Sciences: Dr SUSANA MALLO
Faculty of Veterinary Medicine: Dr DANIEL CAVESTANY

UNIVERSIDAD DE MONTEVIDEO
(University of Montevideo)

Prudencio de Pena 2440, 11600 Montevideo
Telephone: 2707 4461
Internet: www.um.edu.uy
Founded 1986 as Montevideo Institute of Business Studies (IEEM), granted univ. status 1997
Private control
Language of instruction: Spanish
Academic year: March to November
Univ. of Christian identity, offers undergraduate and postgraduate studies
Rector: Prof. Dr SANTIAGO PÉREZ DEL CASTILLO
Academic Sec.: JUAN MANUEL GUTIÉRREZ CARRAU
Gen. Man.: MARCELO GUILLERMO SCORZA
Counsellor: MERCEDES ROVIRA
Gen. Sec.: MARIA CELIA AMATO
Dir. for Library: ESTHER PAILOS

Publications: *Memoria de Trabajos de Difusión Científica y Técnica* (1 a year, print and online, www2.um.edu.uy/ingenieria/revista/index.htm), *Revista Biomedicina* (3 a year, print and online, ccb.um.edu.uy/publicaciones/revista-biomedicina), *Revista de Derecho* (2 a year, print and online, revistaderecho.um.edu.uy), *Revista de Negocios* (6 a year, print and online, socrates.ieem.edu.uy/revista)

DEANS

Centre for Biomedical Sciences: MARTHA RAGO
College of Engineering: CLAUDIO RUIBAL
Faculty of Business Admin. and Economics: JOSÉ LUIS OLIVERA
Faculty of Communication: ENRIQUE ETCHEVARREN
Faculty of Humanities: FERNANDO AGUERRE
Faculty of Law: NICOLÁS ETCHEVERRY ESTRÁZULAS
IEEM Business School: PABLO REGENT

UNIVERSIDAD ORT URUGUAY
(University ORT Uruguay)

Cuareim 1451, 11100 Montevideo

Telephone: 2902 1505

E-mail: info@ort.edu.uy

Internet: www.ort.edu.uy

Founded 1942 as ORT Uruguay; univ. status 1996

Private control

Language of instruction: Spanish

Academic year: March to November

Rector: Dr JORGE A. GRÜNBERG

Man. Dir: CHARLOTTE DE GRÜNBERG

Dir for Student Services: CARLOS PODESTA

Dean of Academic Devt and Student Affairs Dir: Ing. JULIO FERNÁNDEZ

Sec. for Communication: A. P. MYRIAM BRODER

Sec. for Academic Management: T. E. PABLO SAN NICOLÁS

Sec. for Student Services: ENRIQUE REMUÑÁN

Sec. for Systems: A. S. TERESA HERMIDA

Sec. for Logistics and Services: ALBERTO BOLATTO

Library Coordinator for Library Centre: ROSANA IZQUIERD

Library Coordinator for Pocitos Library: VERÓNICA RODRÍGUEZ

Library of 90,000 printed vols, 135 periodical titles, spec. library of 3,000 titles

Number of teachers: 1,000

Number of students: 11,500

Publications: *Anales de Investigación en Arquitectura* (irregular), *Cuadernos de Investigación Educativa* (Journal of Educational Research, 1 a year, in Spanish and English)

DEANS

Faculty of Administration and Social Sciences: Dr GASTON J. LABADIE

Faculty of Architecture: Arq. GASTÓN BOERO FALCINI

Faculty of Communication and Design: Ing. EDUARDO HIPOGROSSO

Faculty of Engineering: Ing. MARIO FERNÁNDEZ CÍTERA

Institute of Education: Ing. ANA OLMEDO (Sec.)

University Institutes

Escuela Universitaria de Bibliotecología y Ciencias Afines 'Ing. Federico E. Capurro'/Instituto de Información (University School of Library and Related Sciences 'Ing. Federico E. Capurro'): Emilio Frugoni 1427, 11200 Montevideo; tel. 2401 0788; e-mail direccion@eubca.edu.uy; internet www.eubca.edu.uy; f. 1945; attached to Univ. de la República; 4-year courses in library and information science, and archive studies; library: 13,465 books and monographs, 350 periodicals; 55 teachers; 500 students; Dir Prof. MARÍO BARITÉ; publ. *Informatio*.

Facultad de Teología del Uruguay 'Monseñor Mariano Soler' (Uruguayan Faculty of Theology 'Monsignor Mariano Soler'): 1019 San Fructuoso, 11800 Montevideo; tel. 2208 5808; e-mail contactenos@facteologia.edu.uy; internet www.facteologia.edu.uy; f. 1966 as Instituto Teológico del Uruguay Monseñor Mariano Soler, present name and status 2000; offers Bachelors and Masters degrees in theology; library: 60,000 vols, 150 periodicals; Sec. SILVANA DEL NEGRO; Librarian MA DEL PILAR POMI BARRIOLA.

Instituto Metodista Universitario Crandon (Methodist University Institute Crandon): Juan Ramón Gómez 2706, 11600 Montevideo; tel. 2487 3375; e-mail secretaria@universitariocrandon.edu.uy; internet www.universitariocrandon.edu.uy; f. 1949; offers exec. training programmes, specialization and training courses; Dir ANÍBAL MARINONI; Pres. Dr RICHARD MILLÁN.

Instituto Universitario Asociación Cristiana de Jóvenes (IUACJ) (University Institute Young Christian Association): Colonia 1870 piso 6 y 7, 11200 Montevideo; tel. 2408 9922; e-mail web@iuacj.edu.uy; internet www.iuacj.edu.uy; f. 2000; degrees in physical education, recreation and sports; library: 2,959 vols; Pres. JORGE SANGIOVANNI; Vice-Pres. Dr CÉSAR HERRERA; publ. *Revista Universitaria de la Educación Física y el Deporte* (1 a year).

Instituto Universitario Centro de Docencia, Investigación e Información en Aprendizaje (CEDIIAP) (University Institute Centre for Teaching, Research and Information in Learning): Bvar. España 2433, Montevideo; tel. 2707 3169; e-mail bedelia@cediiap.edu.uy; internet www.cediiap.edu.uy; f. 1995, current name adopted 2001; Bachelors degrees in psychology and psychomotor skills; Rector Prof. MARIA ANTONIETA REBOLLO.

Instituto Universitario Centro de Estudio y Diagnóstico de las Disgnacias del Uruguay (IUCEDDU) (Central University Institute for the Study and Diagnosis of Malocclusions): Juan M. Blanes 1060, 11200 Montevideo; tel. 2410 3274; e-mail info@iuceddu.com.uy; internet www.iuceddu.com.uy; f. 1988, recognized 2005; courses in orthodontics and orthopaedics.

Instituto Universitario Centro Latinoamericano de Economía Humana (CLAEH) (University Institute Latin American Centre for Human Economy): Zelmar Michelini 1220, 11100 Montevideo; tel. 2900 7194; e-mail info@claeh.org.uy; internet www.claeh.edu.uy; f. 1957, recognized 1997; courses in cultural management, law and medicine; Rector ANDRÉS LALANNE; Dir-Gen. LEOPOLDO FONT.

Instituto Universitario de Postgrado en Psicoanálisis (Graduate Institute of Psychoanalysis): 1571 Canelones, 11200 Montevideo; tel. 2410 7418; internet www.apuruguay.org/node/91; f. 1955, recognized 2003; offers Masters degree in psychoanalytic training; conducts seminars and provides supervised practice; library: 3,200 vols; Dean Dr MARIA CRISTINA FULCO; Librarian MARTHA GOMEZ DE SPRECHMANN; publ. *Revista Uruguaya de Psicoanálisis (RUP)*.

Instituto 'Universitario Francisco de Asis' (University Institute 'Francisco of Asis'): 25 de Mayo esq. Román Guerra, 20000 Maldonado; tel. 4223 3897; e-mail secretaria@unifa.edu.uy; internet www.unifa.edu.uy; f. 1988, recognized 2001; offers Bachelors degrees in business administration, psychology, public accountancy, tourism; 12 short term courses; Rector CR. ALFREDO OLIVEROS.

Other Higher Education Institutions

Centro de Formación y Estudios (CENFORES) (Centre for Training and Studies of the Institute for Children and Adolescents in Uruguay): Piedras 482, 11000 Montevideo; tel. 2915 7317; e-mail web@inau.gub.uy; internet www.inau.gub.uy; f. 1934, recognized 2005; attached to Instituto del Niño y Adolescente del Uruguay (INAU); offers courses in Lifelong Learning Programme, Programme of Studies and Academic Support.

Centro de Navegación (Centre of Navigation): Circunvalación Durango 1445, 11000 Montevideo; tel. 2916 0995; e-mail cennave@cennave.com.uy; internet www.cennave.com.uy; f. 1916 as Transatlantic Sailing Center, current name adopted 1994, recognized 2002; provides training in customs, foreign trade, international transportation, logistics and port management; Gen. Man. LETICIA CRA GALLARRETA.

Escuela Multidisciplinaria de Arte Dramático 'Margarita Xirgú' (EMAD) (Multidisciplinary School of Dramatic Arts 'Margarita Xirgú'): Mercedes 1838 esq. Tristan Narvaja, 11200 Montevideo; tel. 2408 6897; e-mail comunicacion@emad.edu.uy; internet www.emad.edu.uy; f. 1947, adopted current name 2011; provides Bachelors degrees in acting and theatre design; 40 teachers; Artistic Dir MARIANA PERCOVICH; Sec.-Gen. RICARDO PRATO.

Escuela de Guerra Naval (Naval War College of Uruguay): Rambla 25 de Agosto de 1825 S/N y Maciel, 11300 Montevideo; tel. 2915 5500; e-mail repar@armada.mil.uy; internet www.esgue.edu.uy; f. 1941; attached to Armada Nacional República Oriental del Uruguay; provides training to senior staff of the navy; Dir Capt. RODOLFO CUÑARRO PINTOS.

Escuela de Sanidad 'Dr José Scosería' (School of Health 'Dr José Scosería'): Sarandi 122, 11000 Montevideo; tel. 2915 1817; internet www.fenf.edu.uy/index.php/scoseria; f. 1968; attached to Faculty of Nursing Univ. of Republic; Dir Prof. MABEL MIRABALLES.

Escuela Militar de Aeronáutica (Military Aviation School): Ruta 101, 31,500 km, 11100 Pando Canelones; tel. 2288 5670; e-mail bedeliaema@adinet.com.uy; internet www.ema.edu.uy; f. 1913; provides training in military aviation; Dir Col HUGO E. MARENCO.

Escuela Nacional de Arte Lírico (National School of Lyric Art): Citadel 1471, 11000 Montevideo; tel. 2901 9138; e-mail enalsodre@gmail.com; internet www.sodre.gub.uy/sodre/sodre/servicios/escuelas/tabid/167/default.aspx; f. 1986; provides training in vocal techniques, music reading, chamber singing; Dir RAQUEL PIEROTTI.

Escuela Nacional de Danza (National School of Dance): Juilo Herrera y Obes 1489, 11000 Montevideo; tel. 2901 6750; e-mail escuelaballetsodre@adinet.com.uy; internet www.sodre.gub.uy/sodre/sodre/servicios/escuelas/tabid/167/default.aspx; f. 1975; 2 divs: ballet and folklore; 140 students; Dir HORTENSIA CAMPANELLA COMESAÑA.

Escuela Nacional de Policía (National Police School): Camino Maldonado 5952, 12100 Montevideo; tel. 2513 1610; e-mail escuela@minterior.gub.uy; internet enp.minterior.gub.uy; f. 1829; provides education and training of police officers; Dir MARÍA CRISTINA DOMÍNGUEZ MARTÍNEZ.

Escuela Naval (Naval Academy): Miramar 1643 entre Av. Rivera y Rambla Tomás Berreta, 11500 Montevideo; tel. 2600 5222; internet www.escuelanaval.edu.uy; f. 1907; offers Bachelors degrees in naval activities; Dir GABRIEL VACCAREZZA.

Escuela Universitaria Centro de Diseño Industrial (University School Centre for Industrial Design): Br. Artigas 1031, 11200 Montevideo; tel. 2400 1106; e-mail contacto@farq.edu.uy; internet www.cdi.edu.uy; f. 1988; attached to Facultad de Arquitectura, Universidad de la República; offers courses in fashion, product and textile design.

Instituto Militar de Estudios Superiores (Military Institute of Advanced Studies): Blvr General Artigas 2425, 11800 Montevideo; tel. 2209 4505; e-mail ees@imes.edu.uy; internet www.imes.edu.uy; f. 1928, adopted current name 1941; provides training in military sciences; defence research and testing centre; Dir-Gen. Gen. LUIS A. PEREZ;

publ. *Revista del IMES* (irregular, print and online, www.imes.edu.uy/revista).

Instituto Superior de Educación Física (Higher Institute of Physical Education): Casa de los Deportes, Campus de Maldonado, 20000 Maldonado; tel. 4223 6595; e-mail comunicacion@isef.edu.uy; internet www.isef

.edu.uy; f. 1939; attached to Junta Central de la Univ. de la República; campuses in Maldonado, Montevideo and Paysandu; library: 3,000 vols of monographs, dictionaries and encyclopaedias, 30 national titles and foreign periodicals, full text documents, videos and DVDs; Dir MA CECILIA RUEGGER.

UZBEKISTAN

The Higher Education System

Institutions of higher education pre-date the independence of Uzbekistan (formerly the Uzbek SSR) from the USSR in 1991, the oldest being the National University of Uzbekistan named after Mirzo Ulugbek, Tashkent State Medical Institute and Tashkent Institute of Irrigation and Melioration. In 1997 major reforms of the education system at all levels commenced under the National Programme for Personnel Training (NPPT). Reforms specific to the higher education sector include the remodelling of the degree system, particularly the abolition of the old-style Soviet-era degrees and introduction of two-tier Bachelors and Masters degrees; institutional restructuring; strengthening of links between universities and industries; and improvements to part-time and distance education programmes. In 2004 higher education was provided in 63 institutes, which had a combined enrolment of 263,600 students. There are also several foreign universities operating in Uzbekistan, including the Tashkent branches of the Westminster International University, the Russian Economic University named after G. V. Plekhanov and the Singapore Institute of Management. In 2011 there were some 277,437 students enrolled in higher education.

The main laws governing education in Uzbekistan are the Law on Education (1990) and the Law on Education (1997). Higher education is mostly the responsibility of the Ministry of Higher and Specialized Secondary Education, although other ministries administer the relevant specialist schools; for example the Ministry of Public Education has five pedagogical institutes. The Monitoring Department of the Ministry of Higher and Specialized Secondary Education is responsible for accreditation and quality assurance at the tertiary level, standards for which are defined by the Ministry.

The main requirements for admission to higher education are the O'rta Ma'lumot To'g'risida Shahodatnoma (Diploma of Specialized Secondary Education) and results achieved in a national university entrance examination, the Kirish Imtakhoni, which is administered by the Devlet Test Markazi (State Testing Centre). The old-style Soviet degree system consisted primarily of a single five-year Specialist Diploma followed by doctoral-level studies. Since the implementation of the NPPT, students are required to gain both the Bakalavr Diplomi and Magistr Diplomi (Bachelors and Masters degrees) before pursuing doctoral studies. The Bakalavr Diplomi typically lasts four years divided into two phases of two years each, although programmes in some (usually professional) fields of study last longer—for example, dentistry, medicine and veterinary medicine (which last five or six years). In the first phase, students undertake a general programme of study before, in the second phase, focusing on a 'major' subject. Graduates who have been awarded the Bakalavr Diplomi are eligible for the Magistr Diplomi, which is a two-year course, often in the same subject as the undergraduate degree. At the doctoral level, the Soviet distinction between the titles of Candidate of Science and Doctor of Science has been retained, albeit under their Uzbek names of, respectively, Fanlari Nomzodi and Fanlari Doctori. The Fanlari Nomzodi is a three-year period of study consisting of independent research leading to the submission of a thesis. Students intending to pursue a career in research or academia then work towards the Fanlari Doctori, which is awarded after an unspecified period of study and research and is the highest academic award available in Uzbekistan.

Post-secondary technical and vocational education takes the form of two- to four-year courses in 260 areas of specialization, resulting in the award of the O'rta Maxsus Ta'lim To'g'risidagi Diplom (Diploma of Post-Secondary Vocational Education).

Regulatory Bodies

GOVERNMENT

Ministry of Culture and Sport Affairs: Mustakillik Sq. 5, Tashkent 100159; tel. (71) 239-83-31; e-mail minister@mcs.uz; internet www.mcs.uz; Minister MINXAJIDIN XODJIMATOV.

Ministry of Higher and Specialized Secondary Education: Apt 96, 2-Chimbay str., Tashkent 100095; tel. (71) 246-01-95; e-mail mhsse@edu.uz; internet www.edu.uz; Minister BAXODIR Y. XODIYEV.

Ministry of Public Education: 5 Mustakillik Sq., Tashkent 100078; tel. (71) 239-17-35; e-mail press@xtv.uz; internet www.uzedu.uz; Minister ULUG'BEK SInoyatov.

Learned Societies

GENERAL

UNESCO Office in Tashkent: 9 Ergashev St, Tashkent 100084; tel. (71) 120-71-16; e-mail tashkent@unesco.org; internet www.tashkent.unesco.org; f. 1996; contributes to bldg of peace, alleviation of poverty, sustainable devt and intercultural dialogue through education, sciences, culture, communication and information; Head JORGE IVAN ESPINAL.

Uzbekistan Academy of Sciences: Ya Gulomov Str. 70, Tashkent 100047; tel. (71) 233-68-47; e-mail academy@academy.uznet.net; internet www.academy.uz; f. 1943; divs of natural sciences, physical-mathematical and technical sciences, social and humanitarian sciences; 2 regional brs and 33 attached research institutes: see under Research Institutes; library: see under Libraries and Archives; 156 mems (71 ordinary, 85 corresp.); Pres. Acad. SHAVKAT SALIKHOV; Sec.-Gen. Prof. Dr BAKHTIER IBRAGIMOV; publs Chemistry of Natural Compounds, Doklady (Reports), Geliotechnica, Obshchestvennye Nauki v Uzbekistane (Social Sciences in Uzbekistan), Science and Life, Uzbek Geological Journal, Uzbekskii Fizicheskii Zhurnal (Uzbek Journal of Physics), Uzbekskii Khimicheskii Zhurnal (Uzbek Chemical Journal), Uzbekskii Matematicheskii Zhurnal (Uzbek Journal of Mathematics), Uzbekskii Zhurnal—Problemy Informatiki i Energetiki (Uzbek Journal—Problems in Informatics and Energetics), Uzbekskii Zhurnal—Problemy Mekhaniki (Uzbek Journal—Problems in Mechanics), Uzbeksky Biologichesky Zhurnal (Uzbek Biological Journal), Uzbeksky Yazik i Literatura (Uzbek Language and Literature).

LANGUAGE AND LITERATURE

British Council: 13th Fl., Block A, Int. Business Centre, 107A Amir Temur St, Tashkent 100084; tel. (71) 140-06-60; e-mail bc-tashkent@britishcouncil.uz; internet www.britishcouncil.org/uzbekistan; f. 1996; offers courses and examinations in English language and British culture; promotes cultural exchange with the UK; library of 5,000 vols; Dir STEVE McNULTY.

Goethe-Institut: Amir Timur ko'chasi 42, Tashkent 100000; tel. (71) 140-14-70; e-mail info@taschkent.goethe.org; internet www.goethe.de/taschkent; offers courses and examinations in German language and culture; promotes cultural exchange with Germany; Dir Dr JOHANNES DAHL.

Research Institutes

GENERAL

Buxoro Scientific Centre: Naqshbandi 153, Buxoro 200109; tel. (65) 225-02-41; e-mail alexz@uzpak.uz; attached to Uzbekistan Acad. of Sciences; Dir I. SAFAROV.

Karakalpak Branch of the Uzbek Academy of Sciences: Berdakh gazari 41, Nukus, Qoraqalpog'iston 230100; tel. (61) 222-17-44; e-mail nukus@aknuk.uzsci.net; internet www.aknuk.uzsci.net; Pres. AIMBETOV NAGMET KALLIEVICH.

Khorezm Mamun Academy: Markaz-1, Khiva 220900; tel. (62) 375-70-01; e-mail mamun1000@mail.ru; internet www.mamun.uz; f. 1997; attached to Uzbekistan Acad. of Sciences; promotes historical sciences, protection of architectural monuments, ecological and agricultural problems of Khorezm; library of 16,400 vols; Dir Dr RUZUMBOY ESHCHANOV.

Research Institute of Regional Problems: Temur Malik 3, Samarqand 140100; tel. (662) 33-19-94; e-mail samacdem@online.ru; attached to Uzbekistan Acad. of Sciences; Dir B. KHUJAYOROV.

Samarqand Branch of the Uzbek Academy of Sciences: Temur Malik 3, Samarqand 703000; tel. (662) 33-19-94; e-mail samacdem@online.ru; internet www .academy.uz; Chair. T. SHIRINOV.

AGRICULTURE, FISHERIES AND VETERINARY SCIENCE

Research Institute of Karakul Sheep Breeding and Ecology of Deserts: Mirzo Ulugbek ko'chasi 47, Samarqand 140100; tel. (662) 33-32-79; e-mail ecokar@rol.uz; f. 1930; library of 56,000 vols; Dir Dr SURATBEK YUNUSOVICH YUSUPOV; publ. *Collection of Contributions Concerning Karakul Sheep Breeding and Arid Fodder Production* (every 2 years).

State Research Institute of Soil Science and Agrochemistry: Kamarniso ko'chasi 3, Tashkent 100179; tel. (71) 246-09-50; e-mail gosniipa@rambler.ru; Dir D. S. SATTAROV.

ECONOMICS, LAW AND POLITICS

Abu Rayhan Biruni Institute of Oriental Studies: Mirzo Ulugbek str. 81, Tashkent 100170; tel. (71) 262-54-61; f. 1943; attached to Uzbekistan Acad. of Sciences; research activity in the sphere of medieval oriental MSS and in the field of medieval and modern history of Central Asia; library of 39,300 vols, 25,261 MSS; Dir B. A. ABDUKHALIMOV; publ. *Sharqshunoslik* (1 a year).

Institute of Economics: Borovskogo ko'chasi 5, Tashkent 100060; tel. (71) 133-14-78; e-mail econ@uzsci.net; f. 1943; attached to Uzbekistan Acad. of Sciences; Dir O. KHIKMATOV.

Muminov, I., Institute of Philosophy and Law: Muminov ko'chasi 9, Tashkent 100170; tel. (71) 262-38-87; e-mail ifpanuz@yahoo .com; attached to Uzbekistan Acad. of Sciences; Dir Prof. R. D. RUZIEV.

EDUCATION

Scientific-Training Centre 'Fanum': Muminov ko'chasi 9, Tashkent 100170; tel. (71) 289-13-78; e-mail fanum@uznet.net; attached to Uzbekistan Acad. of. Sciences; conducts lessons for postgraduate students and research workers with scientific degrees on programmes est. by VAK (Higher Appraisal Commission) under the Cabinet of the Ministries of the Republic of Uzbekistan; organizes translation activities; promotes public education; Dir Prof. N. Y. TURAEV; publ. *Uzbek Physics Journal*.

HISTORY, GEOGRAPHY AND ARCHAEOLOGY

Institute of Archaeology: Abdullayev ko'chasi 3, Samarqand 140151; tel. (662) 232-15-13; e-mail uzarchae@inbox.uz; internet www.archaeology.uz; f. 1970; attached to Uzbekistan Acad. of Sciences; Dir T. SHIRINOV.

Institute of History: Muminov ko'chasi 9, Tashkent 100170; tel. (71) 262-38-73; e-mail tarih@uzsci.net; internet www.tarix.uzsci .net; f. 1943; attached to Uzbekistan Acad. of Sciences; Dir ABDOOLLAYEV RAVSHAN MAJIDOVICH; Scientific Sec. PAYZIYEVA MOOKADDAS HABIBOOLLAYEVNA; publ. *Uzbekiston Tarihi* (4 a year).

Institute of History, Archaeology and Ethnography: Amir Temur 179A, Nukus, Qoraqalpog'iston 230100; tel. (61) 224-05-98; e-mail vyagodin@online.ru; attached to Uzbekistan Acad. of Sciences; Dir V. YAGODIN.

LANGUAGE AND LITERATURE

Institute of Language and Literature named after Alisher Navoi: I. Moominova,

9, Tashkent 100170; tel. (71) 262-42-64; e-mail uzlit@uzsci.net; internet www .til-adabiyot.fan.uz; f. 1934; attached to Uzbekistan Acad. of Sciences; Dir MAHMOODOV NIZOMIDDIN; Scientific Sec. BARAKAYEV RAHMATOOLLA.

Institute of Language and Literature named after Alisher Navoi: Muminov ko'chasi 9, Tashkent 100170; tel. (71) 262-42-64; e-mail uzlit@uzsci.net; internet www .til-adabiyot.fan.uz; f. 1934; attached to Uzbekistan Acad. of Sciences; Dir Prof. NIZAMIDDIN MAMADALIYEVICH MAKHMUDOV; publ. *O'zbek tili va adabiyoti* (6 a year).

MEDICINE

Institute for Dermatology and Venereology: Farabi 3, Tashkent 100109; tel. (71) 246-08-07; f. 1932; attached to Min. of Health; library of 14,000 vols; Dir Prof. V. A. AKOVBAYAN; publ. *Pathogenesis and Therapy for Skin and Venereal Diseases* (1 a year).

Institute of Haematology and Blood Transfusion: Druzhba Narodov 42, Tashkent 100059; tel. (71) 279-79-35.

Institute of Immunology: Ya. Gulamov 74, Tashkent 100060; tel. (71) 233-08-05; e-mail humangenomics.immunology-uzas@yandex .ru; internet www.immunology.uz; attached to Uzbekistan Acad. of Sciences; research and investigation into the genetic peculiarity of human pathogens; Dir Prof. TAMARA ARIPOVA.

Institute of Vaccines and Sera: Abdurashidov 37, Tashkent 100084; tel. (71) 243-79-53; Dir B. A. SHEVCHENKO.

L. M. Isaev Research Institute of Medical Parasitology: Isaeva 38, Samarqand 140105; tel. (662) 37-42-42; f. 1923; library of 45,000 vols; Dir FARKHAD ABDIEV; publ. *Current Problems in Medical Parasitology* (1 a year).

Republic Specialized Centre of Cardiology: Osio 4, Tashkent 100052; tel. (71) 236-08-16; e-mail cardio@sarkor.com; f. 1976; library of 30,000 vols; Dir Prof. RAVSHANBEK DAVLETOVICH KURBANOV.

Research Institute of Clinical and Experimental Medicine: M. Gorkogo ko'chasi 185, Nukus, Qoraqalpog'istan 230100; tel. (612) 24-50-41.

Research Institute of Epidemiology, Microbiology and Infectious Diseases: Reshetova 2, Tashkent 100133; tel. (71) 243-36-05; e-mail info.niiemiz@minzdrav.uz; f. 1961; Dir FARUKH SAIPOV (acting).

Uzbek Institute of Rehabilitation and Physiotherapy (Semashko Institute): Khurshida 4, Tashkent 100084; tel. (71) 234-55-00; f. 1919; physiotherapy in cardiology, arthropology, neurology and pulmonology, oriental medicine, phytotherapy; library of 16,210 vols; Dir Prof. KARIM U. ULDASHEV; publ. *Collection of Scientific Works* (1 a year).

Uzbek Research Institute of Traumatology and Orthopaedics: Pakhlavon Makhmud str. 78, Tashkent 100047; tel. (371) 233-10-30; f. 1932; library of 30,000 vols; Dir Prof. M. AZIMOV.

NATURAL SCIENCES

General

Institute for Natural Sciences: Berdakh gazari 41, Nukus, Qoraqalpog'istan 230100; tel. (612) 22-17-45; f. 1996; attached to Uzbekistan Acad. of Sciences; Dir BAKHYT NARYMBETOV.

Biological Sciences

Acad. A. Sadikov Institute of Bio-organic Chemistry: Abdullayev ko'chasi 83, Tashkent 100143; tel. (71) 262-35-40; e-mail ibchem@uzsci.net; f. 1977; attached to Uzbekistan Acad. of Sciences; bio-organic chemistry, chemistry of natural physiologic active compounds; Dir Prof. ABBOSKHON S. TURAEV.

Institute of Biochemistry: Abdullayev ko'chasi 56, Tashkent 100143; tel. (71) 162-25-66; attached to Uzbekistan Acad. of Sciences; Dir T. S. SAATOV.

Institute of Bioecology: Berdakh gazari 1, Nukus, Qoraqalpog'istan 230100; tel. (612) 17-17-13; e-mail ecol@online.ru; attached to Uzbekistan Acad. of Sciences; Dir A. BAKHIYEV.

Institute of Botany: Khodzhayev ko'chasi 32, Tashkent 100143; tel. (71) 162-70-65; e-mail botany@uzsci.net; attached to Uzbekistan Acad. of Sciences; Dir Prof. Dr OZODBEK A. ASHURMETOV.

Institute of the Chemistry of Plant Substances: Mirzo Ulugbek St 77, Tashkent 100170; tel. (71) 262-70-00; e-mail shakhidoyatov@yahoo.com; attached to Uzbekistan Acad. of Sciences; organic synthesis, nature chemistry, physical chemistry; Dir Prof. Dr KHUSNUTDIN SHAKHIDOYATOV; publ. *Chemistry of Natural Compounds*.

Institute of Genetics and Plant Experimental Biology: Kibrai Dist., Yukori-Yuz, Tashkent 702151; tel. (71) 112-32-71; e-mail inst@gen.org.uz; internet genetics.uzsci.net; attached to Uzbekistan Acad. of Sciences; Dir A. ABDUKARIMOV.

Institute of Microbiology: Abdulla Kadiri gazari 7B, Tashkent 100128; tel. (71) 144-25-19; e-mail imbasru@uzsci.net; f. 1965; attached to Uzbekistan Acad. of Sciences; Dir K. DAVRANOV; publ. *Uzbeksky Biologichesky Zhurnal*.

Institute of Physiology and Biophysics: A. Niyazov str. 1, Tashkent 100095; tel. (71) 246-95-17; f. 1975; attached to Uzbekistan Acad. of Sciences; Dir Prof. PULAT B. USMANOV.

Institute of Zoology: A. Niyazov St 1, Tashkent 100095; tel. (71) 246-07-18; e-mail zool-uz@uzsci.net; f. 1950; attached to Uzbekistan Acad. of Sciences; Dir DJALOLIDDIN AZIMOV.

Mathematical Sciences

Institute of Mathematics: Akademgorodok, Dormon Yoli 29, Tashkent 100125; tel. (71) 262-56-94; e-mail mathinst@umail.uz; internet www.mathinst.uz; f. 1943, fmrly Institute of Mathematics and Information Technologies, present name and status 2012; attached to Nat. Univ. of Uzbekistan; research in pure and applied mathematics, mathematical modelling, informatics; library of 112,000 vols; Dir Prof. Dr Acad. SHAVKAT AYUPOV; publ. *Uzbek Mathematical Journal* (4 a year).

Physical Sciences

G. Mavlynov Institute of Seismology: Zulfiyakhonim str. 3, Tashkent 700128; tel. (712) 135-75-34; e-mail tashkent@seismo.org .uz; internet www.seismos.uz; f. 1966, current name adopted 1990; attached to Uzbekistan Acad. of Sciences; research into problems of seismic zoning, earthquakes risk management, earthquakes prediction, physics of earthquake sources; library of 43,000 vols; Dir Prof. KAKHARBAY NASIRBEKOVICH ABDULLABEKOV; publ. *Uzbek Geological Journal* (6 a year).

Heat Physics Department of the Uzbek Academy of Sciences: Katartal St 28,

Tashkent 100135; tel. (71) 276-44-57; e-mail hpd@uzsci.net; f. 1977; Dir PULAT KHABIBUL-LAYEV.

Institute of General and Inorganic Chemistry: Amir Temur ko'chasi 77A, Tashkent 100170; tel. (71) 162-56-60; e-mail ionxanruz@mail.ru; internet www.igic.uzsci.net; f. 1933; attached to Uzbekistan Acad. of Sciences; researches colloidal, inorganic and petroleum chemistry, involved in localization of new fertilizers, defoliants for agriculture, materials of construction, flocculating agents, surfactants, oil additives, depressors, corrosion inhibitors for domestic industry; library of 50,000 vols; Dir Prof. BAHTYER ZAKIROV; Deputy Dir Dr AKHMED REYMOV; publs *Reports of Uzbekistan Academy of Sciences—Joint Academic Institutes Journal* (6 a year), *Uzbekistan Journal of Chemistry* (6 a year).

Institute of Mineral Resources: T. Shevchenko St 11A, Tashkent 100060; tel. (71) 256-13-49; e-mail gpniimr@evo.uz; internet www.gpniimr.uz; f. 1957; Dir M. U. ISOKOV; publ. *Geology and Mineral Resources* (6 a year).

Institute of Nuclear Physics: Ulugbek, Tashkent 100214; tel. (71) 150-30-70; e-mail info@inp.uz; internet www.inp.uz; f. 1956; attached to Uzbekistan Acad. of Sciences; research areas incl. activation analysis, nuclear physics, radiochemistry and radioisotope production, research works automation, solid-state radiation physics, radiation material science and instrumentation devt; library of 221,215 vols; Dir Prof. UMAR SAGITOVICH SALIKHBAEV.

Institute of Polymer Chemistry and Physics: A. Kadyri str. 7B, Tashkent 700128; tel. (71) 142-85-94; e-mail carbon@uzsci.net; f. 1979; attached to Uzbekistan Acad. of Sciences; research fields incl. chemistry, native polymers, physics and technology of synthetics; Dir SAYERA RASHIDOVA.

Kh. M. Abdullaev Institute of Geology and Geophysics: Khodjibaeva str. 49, Tashkent 100041; tel. (71) 262-65-16; e-mail ingeo@ingeo.uz; internet www.ingeo.uz; f. 1939; attached to Uzbekistan Acad. of Sciences; study of the structure, composition and evolution of the lithosphere; devt of the fundamentals of expansion of mineral raw materials in Uzbekistan and effective exploitation of mineral deposits; research areas incl. geology, petrology, mineralogy, geochemistry, ecology, geophysics, mathematical geology, oil geology and history of geology; Dir Dr BAKHTIAR NURTAEV; publ. *Geology and Mineral Resources* (6 a year).

Physical–Technical Institute: . Mavlyanova 2B, Tashkent 700084; tel. (71) 233-12-71; e-mail lutp@physic.uzsci.net; internet fti.fan.uz; f. 1943; attached to Uzbekistan Acad. of Sciences; research and devt of high-technology products; Dir S. LUTPULLAYEV; publ. *Applied Solar Engineering*.

Ulugh Beg Astronomical Institute: Astronomiya 33, Tashkent 100052; tel. (71) 235-81-02; e-mail admin@astrin.uz; internet www.astrin.uz; f. 1873 as Tashkent Astronomical Observatory, present name and status 1966; attached to Uzbekistan Acad. of Sciences; research divs incl. extraterrestrial astronomy, galactic astronomy and cosmology, solar-terrestrial physics, stellar astrophysics, theoretical astrophysics; Dir Prof. SHUHRAT A. EHGAMBERDIEV.

RELIGION, SOCIOLOGY AND ANTHROPOLOGY

Institute for Socio-Economic Problems of the Aral Sea Region: Amir Temur St 179A, Nukus, Qoraqalpog'istan 742000; tel.

(61) 224-22-09; e-mail nagmet@aknuk.uzsci.net; internet www.aknuk.uzsci.net; attached to Uzbekistan Acad. of Sciences; Dir NAGMET AIMBETOV.

TECHNOLOGY

Institute of Cybernetics: F. Khodjaev St 34, Tashkent 700125; tel. (71) 262-72-47; e-mail uzkiber@cyber.ccc.uz; f. 1966; attached to Uzbekistan Acad. of Sciences; library of 100,000 vols; Dir FAZILOV SHAVKAT; publs *Algoritmy* (3 a year), *Problemy Informatiki i Energetiki* (6 a year), *Voprosy Kibernetiki* (3 a year), *Voprosy Modelirovaniya i Informatizatsii Ekonomiki* (3 a year), *Voprosy Vychislitelnoi i Prikladnoi Matematiki* (3 a year).

Institute of Electronics named after U. A. Arifov: F. Khodjaev str. 33, Tashkent 100125; tel. (71) 262-79-40; e-mail aie@aie.uz; internet www.aie.uz; f. 1967; attached to Uzbekistan Acad. of Sciences; Dir KHATAM R. ASHUROV.

Institute of Hydrogeology and Engineering Geology: Olimlar St 64, Tashkent 100041; tel. (71) 262-75-90; e-mail hydrouz@rambler.ru; f. 1960; attached to Int. Consortium of Landslides, Int. Union of Geological Sciences; research into hydrogeology, petroleum, geoecology, landslides and remote-sensing; library of 18,000 vols; Dir ASLON A. MAVLONOV; publs *Geology and Mineral Resources* (6 a year), *Hydrogeology and Engineering Geology Problems in Uzbekistan* (1 a year).

Institute of Materials Science: Bodomzor yoli 2B, Tashkent 100084; tel. (71) 235-75-06; e-mail mirzasul@yahoo.com; attached to Uzbekistan Acad. of Sciences; Dir Dr ABDU-JABBAR ABDURAKHMANOV.

Institute of Mechanics and Seismic Stability of Structures: Akademia Shaharchasi, Dormon yoli 31, Tashkent 100125; tel. (71) 162-72-97; e-mail seismo@uzsci.net; internet www.seismos.uz; f. 1959; attached to Uzbekistan Acad. of Sciences; Dir Prof. ANVAR ABDULLAEVICH RIZAEV; publ. *Problems in Mechanics* (6 a year).

Institute of Power Engineering and Automation: Akademgorodok, Tashkent 100143; tel. (71) 262-05-22; e-mail ipea@uzsci.net; f. 1941; attached to Uzbekistan Acad. of Sciences; Dir TIMUR SALIKHOV.

Institute of Water Problems: Khodjayev St 25A, Tashkent 100187; tel. (71) 269-12-70; e-mail root@pwater.tashkent.su; f. 1992; attached to Uzbekistan Acad. of Sciences; Dir ERNAZAR J. MAKHMUDOV.

Scientific and Production Association 'Akadempribor': Akademia Shaharchasi, Tashkent 100125; tel. (71) 262-72-73; e-mail bahramov@mail.ru; f. 1962; attached to Uzbekistan Acad. of Sciences; research, design and production of the instruments and equipment for scientific orgs, agriculture, medicine and industry; Dir-Gen. Prof. SAGDILLA A. BAKHRAMOV.

Scientific Production Centre 'Modern Information Technologies': F. Hodjaev St 34, Tashkent 700143; tel. (71) 262-72-47; e-mail shavkat@cyber.ccc.uz; attached to Uzbekistan Acad. of Sciences; Dir OZOD NABIEV.

Uzbek Research Institute of Sericulture: Jar-Arik, Zangyata, Tashkent 111812; f. 1927; attached to Min. of Agriculture and Water Resource; Dir SH. YULDASHEV; publ. *Silk*.

UzLITIneftgaz/Uzbekistan Research and Design Institute of the Gas and Oil Industry: T. Shevchenko ko'chasi 2, Tashkent 100029; tel. (71) 256-74-17; Dir U. S.

NAZAROV; publ. *Uzbek Journal of Oil and Gas* (4 a year).

Libraries and Archives

Samarqand

Samarqand State University Central Library: Pl. Navoi 15, Samarqand 140100; tel. (662) 35-19-38; e-mail soleev@samuni.silk.org; 1,632,000 vols; spec. collns incl. ancient oriental literature; Dir R. KHOLMURODOV.

Tashkent

Central State Archive: Chilonzar ko'chasi 2, Tashkent 700043; tel. (71) 277-04-80; e-mail csa@archive.uz; internet central.archive.uz; Dir SHUHRATBAY KHODJIBAEV.

Foundation Library of the Uzbekistan Academy of Sciences: Muminov str. 13, Tashkent 100170; tel. (71) 262-74-56; e-mail acadlib@acadlib.uzsci.net; internet www.acadlib.uzsci.net; f. 1934; Uzbekistan Acad. of Sciences, library system incl. 24 other research institute libraries; 5m. vols; Dir ZUHRA SH. BERDIEVA.

Library of the National University of Uzbekistan named after Mirzo Ulugbek: Vozgorodok, Universitet ko'chasi 95, Tashkent 100095; tel. (371) 2466771; e-mail info@nuu.uz; 18 brs; 350,000 vols, 45,000 journals, 2,600 govt documents, 4,000 maps; Dir IRINA LVOVNA KISLITSINA.

National Library of Uzbekistan named after Alisher Navoi: Milliy kutubxonasi, Xorazm ko'chasi 51, Tashkent 100047; tel. (71) 2392-83-92; e-mail navoi@natlib.uz; internet natlib.webmaster.uz; f. 1870, has incorporated Republican Library for Science and Technology since 2002; 10,720,000 vols; Dir KHODJAYEV ASAD AZADBEKOVICH.

Museums and Art Galleries

Nukus

Botanical Garden: Chimbay St, Nukus, Qoraqalpog'istan 142004; tel. (61) 222-30-47; attached to Uzbekistan Acad. of Sciences; Dir TULEGEN OTENOV.

Karakalpak Historical Museum: Rakhmatov ko'chasi 3, Nukus, Qoraqalpog'istan 230100; e-mail museum_savitsky@intal.uz; illustrates the part played by the Uzbek people in the October Socialist Revolution, the Civil War and the Second World War.

Karakalpak State Museum of Art named after I. V. Savitsky: K. Rzaev St, w/n, Nukus, Qoraqalpog'istan 230100; tel. (61) 222-25-56; e-mail museum_savitsky@mail.ru; internet museum.kr.uz; f. 1966; archaeology of ancient Khorezym, Karakalpak folk art, Russian and Central Asian avant-garde art 1910–1935, contemporary art of Karakalpakstan; library of 10,500 vols; Dir MARINIKA BABANAZAROVA; Chief Curator VALENTINA SYCHEVA.

Samarqand

Samarqand State United Historical–Architectural and Art Museum Preserve: Ozgarish St 18, Tashkent 700027; tel. (1) 44-38-94; f. 1982; comprises 9 museums in Samarqand city and Viloyat, containing more than 182,000 exhibits in total.

Tashkent

Alisher Navoi State Museum of Literature: Navoi str. 69, Tashkent 100011; tel. (71) 241-02-75; e-mail a_navoi@uzsci.net; internet www.navoimuseum.uz; f. 1936; attached to Uzbekistan Acad. of Sciences;

collects, investigates, maintains and displays the history of Uzbek literature, incl. MSS, documents, pictures, archives and photographic materials; Dir Prof. SAIDBEK KHASANOV; publ. *Adabiyot kozgusi* (12 a year).

Museum of Applied Art: Rakatboshi St 15, Tashkent 100031; tel. (71) 256-40-42; e-mail artmuzey@mail.ru; internet www .artmuseum.uz; f. 1927, fmrly Permanent Exhibition of Applied Art of Uzbekistan, present name and status 1997; displays 7,000 rare works of applied art.

Museum of Uzbek History: Sharaf Rashidov ko'chasi 3, Tashkent 100000; tel. (71) 139-10-83; f. 1992 by merger of the Museum of the History of the People of Uzbekistan and the Lenin Central Museums; more than 300,000 exhibits; Dir G. R. RASHIDOV.

Oibek, M. T., Historical Museum of Uzbekistan: Sh. Rashidov ko'chasi 3, Tashkent 100047; tel. (71) 139-10-83; attached to Uzbekistan Acad. of Sciences; Dir K. INOYATOV.

State Museum of Arts: Amir Temur pr 16, Tashkent 100060; tel. (71) 236-74-36; e-mail info@fineartmuzeum.uz; internet fineartmuzeum.uz; f. 1918; attached to Min. of Culture and Sports; colln incl. works of arts of Uzbekistan, East, Russian and Western Europe; library of 22,700 vols; Dir D. S. RUSIBAYEV.

State Museum of Timurid History: Amir Temur 1, Tashkent 700000; tel. (71) 232-02-12; e-mail temurid@temurid.uz; internet www.temurid.uz; f. 1996; attached to Uzbekistan Acad. of Sciences; Dir N. KHABIBULLAYEV.

Universities

ACADEMY OF STATE AND SOCIAL CONSTRUCTION

Uzbekistan St 45, Tashkent 100029

Telephone: (71) 232-60-60

E-mail: info@assc.uz

Founded 1995

State control

Languages of instruction: Uzbek, Russian

Courses incl. bases and principles of market economy, interstate relations and foreign economic relations, retraining and professional devt, state and social construction

Rector: NAZAROV KIYOM NORMIRZAEVICH

ANDIJAN STATE UNIVERSITY

Bldg 129, 170020 Andijon

Telephone: (74) 225-05-09

E-mail: adu@andijon.uz

Founded 1939

State control

Languages of instruction: Russian, Uzbek

Academic year: September to June

Rector: Prof. Dr T. A. MADUMAROV

Library of 320,314 vols

Number of teachers: 430

Number of students: 5,000

DEANS

Faculty of Biology: ALIJON DADAMIRZAYEV
Faculty of Chemistry: MIRAHMAD KHOJIMATOV
Faculty of History: ZOKIR KUTIBOYEV
Faculty of Mathematics: ABDUVAHOB MILADJONOV
Faculty of Philology: DILMUROD QURONOV
Faculty of Physical Education: DEHQONBOY MAMATISAQOV
Faculty of Physical Training: NOIB YULDASHEV
Faculty of Physics: ABDULQAHOR ORTIQOV
Faculty of Teacher Training: MUHTOR VOHIDOV

BRANCH OF THE RUSSIAN ECONOMIC UNIVERSITY AFTER G. V. PLEKHANOV IN TASHKENT

Uzbekistan St 49, Seventh Bldg, Third Fl., Tashkent 100003

Telephone: (71) 232-60-23

E-mail: rea@rea.uz

Internet: rea.uz

State control; attached to Russian Economic Univ. after G. V. Plekhanov

Economy of firm and br. markets; finance and credit; financial economy; labour economy

Dir: K. KH. ABDURAKHMANOV

BUXORO DAVLAT UNIVERSITETI (Bukhara State University)

Muhammad Ikbol str. 11, Bukhara 200100

Telephone: (65) 223-23-14

E-mail: bsu_info@edu.uz

Internet: www.buxdu.uz

Founded 1930

State control

Languages of instruction: English, Russian, Uzbek

Academic year: September to June

Rector: Prof. Dr ZOKIRKHODJA TADJIKHODJAEV
Vice-Rector for Educational Affairs: Dr DURDIMUROD DURDIEV
Vice-Rector for Scientific Affairs: Prof. Dr SIDDIK KAHHAROV

Library of 700,000 vols

Number of teachers: 470

Number of students: 6,400

Publications: *Buxoro Universiteti* (12 a year), *Pedagogical Competence* (4 a year), *Psychology* (4 a year), *University Review* (12 a year)

DEANS

Faculty of Chemistry and Biology: Dr HAFIZA ORTIKOVA
Faculty of History: Dr SOHIB RAUPOV
Faculty of Pedagogics: Prof. Dr SHARIF BAROTOV
Faculty of Philology: Dr ANVAR HAYDAROV
Faculty of Physics and Mathematics: Prof. Dr SHAVKAT MIRZAEV
Military Faculty: Dr ERGASH SULAYMONOV
Social-Economical Faculty: Dr ABROR JURAEV
Sports Faculty: Dr BAHODIR MAMUROV

FARG'ONA DALVAT UNIVERSITETI (Ferghana State University)

Murabbiylar str. 19, Ferghana 150100

Telephone: (73) 224-28-71

E-mail: frsu_info@edu.uz

Founded 1991

State control

Languages of instruction: Uzbek, Russian, English

Rector: MADAMINBEK KHOTAMOVICH AKHMEDOV

Library of 757,461 vols

Number of teachers: 460

Number of students: 5,600

GULISTAN DAVLAT UNIVERSITETI (Gulistan State University)

Microraion 4, Gulistan 120100

Telephone: (672) 25-02-75

E-mail: gdu@intal.uz

Internet: www.guldu.uz

Founded 1992

State control

Languages of instruction: Russian, Uzbek

Faculties of economics and engineering, education, foreign languages, history and Uzbek

philology, Kazakh philology, natural sciences, physics and mathematics

Rector: EMINOV ASHRAP MAMUROVICH
Pro-Rector for Science and Informational Technologies: KUSHIEV KHABIB HOJIBOBOEVICH
Pro-Rector for Scientific Works: KARSHIBAEV KHAZRATKUL KILICHOVICH
Pro-Rector for Spiritual and Moral Education: MAKHMUDOV RAVSHANBEK JALILOVICH

Library of 195,000 vols

Number of teachers: 400

Number of students: 4,200

KARAKALPAK STATE UNIVERSITY

Ch. Abidov 1, Nukus, Qoraqalpog'istan 742000

Telephone: (61) 223-60-47

E-mail: karsu@karsu.uz

Internet: www.karsu.uz

Founded 1979

State control

Faculties of agriculture, chemistry, construction, engineering, economics, law and history, natural sciences, philology, physics and mathematics

Rector: Prof. Dr MATCHANOV AZAT TAUBALDIEVICH

Number of students: 7,000

KARSHI STATE UNIVERSITY

Kuchabog 17, Karshi 140103

Telephone: (752) 25-34-13

E-mail: kardu@mail.ru

Internet: www.kasu.uz

Founded 1956

State control

Languages of instruction: Uzbek, Russian

Academic year: September to June

Rector: Prof. MURADULLA NORMURADOV

Library of 10,000 vols

NAMANGAN STATE UNIVERSITY

Uychi 316, Namangan 116019

Telephone: (692) 27-01-44

E-mail: uzb2001@gmail.com

Internet: www.namdu.uz

Founded 1942

State control

Languages of instruction: Uzbek, Russian, English

Academic year: September to June

Rector: Prof. Dr ABDUSALAM UMAROV

Library: 1m. vols

Number of teachers: 450

Number of students: 6,000

Publication: *Periodical of Namangan State University*

DEANS

Faculty of Art and Drawing: BOTIRSHER JABBOROV
Faculty of Biology and Chemistry: YOLDOSHALI TOSHMATOV
Faculty of Education: MUNOJATHON MIRABDULLAYEVA
Faculty of Geography and Economics: MUHAMMADSOLI MUMINOV
Faculty of Graduate Studies: SHAVKAT ABDULLAYEV
Faculty of History: RUZIMAT JURAYEV
Faculty of Law: YULDOSHALI RHIMOV
Faculty of Mathematics: SOBIRJON ALIHANOV
Faculty of Physical Education and Sport: SOBITHON AZIZOV
Faculty of Physics and Labour Education: TOSHKINBOY UMARALIYEV
Faculty of Uzbek Philology: TOHIRJON RAHMONOV

Faculty of World Languages: SAIDUMOR SAI-DALIYEV

NATIONAL UNIVERSITY OF UZBEKISTAN NAMED AFTER MIRZO ULUGBEK

Vozgorodok, Tashkent 100174

Telephone: (71) 227-12-24
E-mail: rector@nuu.uz
Internet: www.nuu.uz

Founded 1918 as Muslim People's Univ., present name and status 2000
State control
Languages of instruction: Russian, Uzbek
Academic year: September to June

Faculties of biology and soil science, chemistry, economics, foreign philology, geography, geology, history, journalism, law, mechanics and mathematics, philosophy, physics, Uzbek philology

Rector: Prof. Dr GAFURDJAN ISRAILOVICH MUXAMEDOV
Pro-Rector: Q. Q. KURANBOEV
Library Dir: I. L. KISLITSINA

Library: 3m. vols
Number of teachers: 990
Number of students: 8,500

Publication: ACTA NUUz

NIZOMIY NOMIDAGI TOSHKENT DAVLAT PEDAGOGIKA UNIVERSITETI
(Tashkent State Pedagogical University named after Nizami)

Yu. X. Xadijb 103, 700100 Tashkent

Telephone: (71) 254-92-02
E-mail: tdpu@yandex.ru
Internet: www.tdpu.uz

Founded 1935
State control
Languages of instruction: Uzbek, Russian, Kazakh, Korean, German, English
Academic year: September to June

Rector: INOYATOV ULUG'BEK ILYOSOVICH
Pro-Rector: DILSHOD ERGASHEVICH UNAROV

Number of teachers: 930
Number of students: 10,400

DEANS

Faculty of Applied Physiologists Training: FAZLIDDIN KHAYDAROV
Faculty of Arts: S. ABDURASULOV
Faculty of Drawing and Applied Art: BOTOR BOYMETOV
Faculty of Elementary Education: D. H. SHODMONKULOVA
Faculty of Foreign Languages: A. KURBONOV
Faculty of Handicrafts Education: NARZULLA MUSLIMOV
Faculty of History: O. MANSUROV
Faculty of Military Physical Training: ILHOM IKROMOV
Faculty of Music: HAMIDULLA NURMATOV
Faculty of Natural Sciences: FARIDA MIRXA-MIDOVA
Faculty of Pedagogics and Psychology: N. S. SAFAYEV
Faculty of Physics and Mathematics: K. JUMANIYAZOV
Faculty of Professional Training: O. AVAZ-BOYEV
Faculty of Russian and Korean Philology: RUSTAM KOBILOV
Faculty of Teaching Skills Enhancement: NURIDDIN DOSANOV
Faculty of Uzbek Language and Literature: I. AZIMOV

SAMARQAND DAVLAT UNIVERSITETI
(Samarqand State University)

Universitet ko'chasi 15, Samarqand 140104
Telephone: (66) 235-16-02

E-mail: support@samdu.uz
Internet: www.samdu.uz

Founded 1927
State control
Languages of instruction: Russian, Tajik, Uzbek
Academic year: September to June

Faculties of applied mathematics, biology, chemistry, economics, foreign languages, geography, history, law, management, mathematics, musical education, physical training, physics, pre-school and primary education, sociology, Uzbek, Tajik and Russian philology

Rector: Dr U. N. TASHKENBAEV
Vice-Rector: Prof. M. K. KODIROV

Number of teachers: 800
Number of students: 13,000

Publication: Samarqand Davlat Universiteti (52 a year)

TOSHKENT DAVLAT IQTISODIYOT UNIVERSITETI
(Tashkent State University of Economics)

Uzbekistanskaya 49, Tashkent 100003

Telephone: (71) 132-64-21
E-mail: info@tdiu.uz
Internet: www.tdiu.uz

Founded 1931

Faculties of accounting, agricultural economics, economic cybernetics, economic planning, financial economics, trade economics; campus in Andijon

Rector: Prof. NODIR JUMAEV

Library of 300,000 vols
Number of teachers: 600
Number of students: 11,000

TOSHKENT ISLOM UNIVERSITETI
(Tashkent Islamic University)

Abdulla Kadiri 11, Tashkent 100011

Telephone: (71) 244-00-56
E-mail: info@tiu.uz
Internet: www.tiu.uz

Founded 1999
State control
Languages of instruction: Arabic, English, Persian, Uzbek
Academic year: September to June

Faculties of advanced training, Islamic history and philosophy, Islamic law, economy and natural sciences

Rector: Prof. RAVSHAN ABDULLAEV

Library of 40,000 vols
Number of teachers: 80
Number of students: 500

TERMIZ DAVLAT UNIVERSITETI
(Termez State University)

F. Hodjaev 43, Termiz 190111

Telephone: (762) 300000
Internet: www.terdu.uz

Founded 1992
State control
Languages of instruction: Russian, Uzbek
Academic year: September to June

Faculties of economics, history, natural sciences and geography, pedagogy, philology, physical education, physics and mathematics, professional education, technics and chemistry

Rector: Prof. KHAYDAROV MAMAT
Pro-Rector: IMANOV BAKHTIYOR
Pro-Rector: RUZIEV OYBEK

Library of 300,000 vols
Number of teachers: 516
Number of students: 7,000

URGANCH DAVLAT UNIVERSITETI
(Urgench State University named after Al-Khorezmi)

H. Olimjon St, Urgench 220100

Telephone: (62) 226-61-66
E-mail: xabursu@mail.ru
Internet: www.urgenchsu.narod.ru

Founded 1992
State control
Languages of instruction: Russian, Uzbek
Academic year: September to June

Rector: Prof. Dr RUZUMBOY ESHCHANOV

Library of 360,000 vols
Number of teachers: 500
Number of students: 7,000

Publication: Ilm sarchashmasi

DEANS

Faculty of Natural Science and Geography: Dr IKRAM ABDULLAEV

WESTMINSTER INTERNATIONAL UNIVERSITY IN TASHKENT

Istiqbol St 12, Tashkent 100047

Telephone: (71) 238-74-17
E-mail: info@wiut.uz
Internet: www.wiut.uz

Founded 2002; attached to Univ. of Westminster, UK

Faculties of business development, human resources and management, economics, English, finance and accounting, information technology and computing, law, marketing and quantitative analysis

Rector: Dr ABDUMALIK DJUMANOV
Deputy Rector for Academic Affairs: ALAN FRANCE

Other Higher Educational Institutes

Academy of Arts of Uzbekistan: Sharif Rashidov gazari 40, Tashkent 100029; tel. (71) 256-50-47; e-mail acart@umid.uz; internet www.arts-academy.uz; f. 1997 by merger of existing instns; 190 teachers; 900 students; Rector TURSUNALI KUZIYEV.

Ajiniyaz Nomidagi Nukus Davlat Pedagogika Instituti (Nukus State Teacher-Training Institute named after Ajiniyaz): A. Dosnazarov St 104, Nukus, Qoraqalpog'iston 230100; tel. (61) 222-65-10; e-mail nkspi_info@edu.uz; internet www.ndpi.uz; f. 1934, present name and status 1992; attached to Min. of Public Education; faculties of history, Karakalpak language and literature, natural sciences, pedagogy, primary education, philology, physical training, physics and mathematics; Rector MURAT KARLIBAEVICH BERDIMURATOV; Vice-Rector for Academic Affairs MAMAN KTAYBEKOVICH SARIBAEV; publ. Science and Society.

Andijon Cotton Institute: Selo Kuigan-Yar, Andijon 170600; tel. (74) 224-54-34.

Andijon Davlat Tibbiyot Instituti (Andijan State Medical Institute): Atabekova 1, Andijon 170100; tel. (74) 237-93-53; e-mail rector@andmi.uz; internet www.andmi.uz; f. 1955; faculties of curative science, medical pedagogies, nurses training, paediatrics; library: 286,000 vols; Rector Prof. Dr SHODMONOV ALISHER KAYUMOVICH; Pro-Rector for Academic Affairs Prof. Dr MADAZIMOV MADAMIN MUMINOVICH; Pro-Rector for Scientific Affairs Prof. Dr KHAJIMATOV GULOMJON MINHODJIEVICH.

Andijon State Pedagogical Institute of Languages: Babur ko'chasi 5, Andijon 170111; tel. (74) 224-75-15; e-mail adtpi@online.ru; f. 1966; faculties of Russian language and literature, foreign languages (English, German, French); Rector RAHMONOV TOJIDDIN YAKUBOVICH; publ. *Scientific Proceedings*.

Buxoro State Medical Institute: Navoi ko'chasi 1, Buxoro 200118; tel. (65) 223-00-50; e-mail buhme@rambler.ru; internet www .buhmi.uz; f. 1990; library: 90,000 vols; 240 teachers; 1,728 students; Rector Prof. RAKHMAT M. AKHMEDOV.

Buxoro Technological Institute of Food and Light Industry: K. Murtazoyev 15, Buxoro 200117; tel. (65) 223-61-97; e-mail javlonbek@intal.uz; f. 1976; faculties of business and management, food technology, light industry, mechanical engineering, oil and gas, professional education; 320 teachers; 4,800 students; Rector Prof. INOBAT HIKMATOVA.

Farg'ona Polytechnic Institute: Ferganskaya ko'chasi 86, Farg'ona 150100; tel. (732) 22-13-50; e-mail monitoring@farpi.uz; internet www.farpi.uz; f. 1967; faculties of chemical technology, construction, economics, mechanics, power; device building centre; library: 290,000 vols; 234 teachers; 3,239 students; Rector RASUL J. TOJIYEV; publ. *Scientific-Technical Journal* (4 a year).

Samarqand Agricultural Institute: M. Ulugbek 77, Samarqand 140103; tel. (662) 34-33-20; e-mail samsi@uzpak.uz; f. 1929; faculties of agro-engineering, agronomics, animal husbandry, economics and accounting, karakul (sheep-breeding), veterinary science, zootechnics; library: 533,777 vols; 274 teachers; 3,500 students (2,000 full-time, 1,500 correspondence); Rector Prof. ABDIKADIR ERGASHEV.

Samarqand Cooperative Institute: A. Temur 9, Samarqand 140100; tel. (662) 33-38-72; e-mail samki@intal.uz; f. 1931; faculties of accounting, engineering technology, trade, trade economics; library: 205,718 vols; 210 teachers; 7,000 students; Rector AKBARALI N. JABRIYEV.

Samarqand Davlat Chet Tillar Instituti (Samarqand State Institute of Foreign Languages): Akhunbabayev str. 93, Samarqand 140104; tel. (66) 233-78-43; e-mail ssifl_info@ mail.ru; internet samdchti.uz; f. 1994; faculties of English philology, Roman and German philology, translation; library: 91,000 vols; 225 teachers; 2,165 students (1,387 undergraduate, 778 postgraduate); Rector Prof. SHAHRIYOR SAFAROV.

Samarqand State Architectural and Civil Engineering Institute: Lolazor 70, Samarqand 140147; tel. (662) 37-15-93; e-mail unesco_aliance@rambler.uz; f. 1966; depts of architecture, building, building engineering and ecology, building technology, economics, engineering, machine construction and land cadastre, professional education; library: 400,000 vols; 266 teachers; 2,000 students; Rector SOBIR M. BOBOEV.

Samarqand State Medical Institute: Amir Temur 18, Samarqand 140100; tel. (662) 33-54-21; e-mail info@sammi.samuni .silk.org; f. 1930; faculties of general practice and paediatrics; library: 330,000 vols; Rector B. U. SOBIROV.

State Conservatory of Uzbekistan: B. Zakirova St 1, Tashkent 700027; tel. (71) 144-53-20; e-mail uzkonservatory@mail.ru; internet www.konservatoriya.uz; f. 1936; choral conducting, composition, orchestral, musicology, piano, singing, sound production, Uzbek folk instruments; library: 243,000 vols; 188 teachers; 1,000 students; Rector Prof. DILORA MURADOVA.

Tashkent Abu Reihan Beruni State Technical University: Universitetskaya 2, Tashkent 100095; tel. (71) 246-46-00; e-mail intdep@online.ru; internet www.tstu.re.uz; f. 1929; faculties of automation and computer hardware, electronics, humanities, mechanical engineering and machine building, mining and geology, oil and gas, power engineering; 2,000 teachers; 20,000 students; Rector KAKHRAMON R. ALLAYEV.

Tashkent Institute of Architecture and Construction: Navoi 13, Tashkent 100011; tel. (71) 241-10-84; e-mail otvtasi@uzsci.net; internet www.tasi.uzsci.net; faculties of architecture, construction of buildings, construction management, engineering and construction; 200 teachers; 2,400 students; Rector MIRAKHMEROV MAKHAMADJON MIRAKHMEDOVICH.

Tashkent Institute of Irrigation and Melioration: 39 Qori-Niyoziy St, Tashkent 100000; tel. (71) 237-38-79; e-mail admin@ tiim.uz; internet www.tiim.uz; f. 1934 as Tashkent Institute of Irrigation and Agricultural Mechanization Engineers, present name 2004; faculties of agricultural mechanization, economics, education science, electrical energetic of agriculture and water management, hydromelioration, irrigation and land improvement of hydromeliorative works, land management, magistracy, management and marketing, natural resources management; library: 864,000 vols; 484 teachers; 5,371 students; Rector Prof. UKTAM PARDAYEVICH UMURZAKOV (acting).

Tashkent Institute of Railway Transport Engineers: Adilkhodjayeva 1, Tashkent 100167; tel. (71) 191-14-40; f. 1931; faculties of automation, engineering, construction, economics, industrial and civil construction, telemechanics and communication, traffic management; library: 500,000 vols; 400 teachers; 12,000 students; Rector FERUZA FUZAILOVNA KARIMOVA (acting); Pro-Rector BATIR ZAKIROV.

Tashkent Institute of Textile and Light Industry: Shohjahon St 5, Yakkasaroy Dist., Tashkent 100100; tel. (71) 253-06-06; e-mail rector@titli.uz; internet titli.uz; f. 1932; faculties of chemical technology, cotton technology, engineering economics, mechanical technology, technology for light industry; library: 644,000 vols; 242 teachers; 2,214 students; Rector Prof. Dr JUMANIYAZOV KADAM JUMANIYAZOVICH; Vice-Rector for Academic Affairs Prof. Dr KAMILOVA XOLIDA XAFIZOVNA; Vice-Rector for Science BAZAROV ORIFJAN SHADIEVICH.

Tashkent Paediatric Medical Institute: Obidova 223, Tashkent 100140; tel. (71) 262-34-22; e-mail tpmiim@gmail.com; internet tashpmi.uz; f. 1972, fmrly Middle Asian Paediatric Medical Institute; offers education in emergency, health economics, management and marketing in medicine, medical law, preventive medicine; 3,453 students; Rector Prof. B. T. DAMINOV.

Tashkent Pharmaceutical Institute: Oybek str. 45, Tashkent 100015; tel. (71) 256-37-38; e-mail pharmi@bcc.com.uz; internet www.pharmi.uz; f. 1937; faculties of improvement in industrial pharmacy, pharmacists' skills, pharmacy; library: 423,420 vols; 212 teachers; 1,323 students; Rector Prof. Dr AKHMADKHODJA NIGMANOVICH YUNUSKHOJAYEV; Pro-Rector ZOKIRJON ABIDOVICH YULDASHEV (acting); publ. *Pharmaceutical Journal*.

Tashkent State Agrarian University: Universitetskaya 5, Kibray Dist., Tashkent 100140; tel. (71) 260-48-00; e-mail tuag-info@ edu.uz; internet www.agrar.uz; f. 1930; depts of accounting, agrochemistry and soil science, agronomy, economy, finance and planning, forestry, fruit and vegetable growing, horticulture and viticulture, information technology, initial control and monitoring, marketing, plant protection, silkworm breeding; library: 196,000 vols; 320 teachers; 7,200 students; Rector H. C. H. BURIYEV.

Toshkent Avtomobil-yo'llar Instituti (Tashkent Automobile and Road Construction Institute): Mavoraunnakhr 20A, Tashkent 100060; tel. (71) 232-14-39; e-mail tadi_info@edu.uz; internet www.tayi.uz; f. 1972; faculties of automobile mechanics, management of transport and transport communications, road construction, road transport; br. in Termez; 142 teachers; 4,000 students; Rector IKRAMOV MURAT AKRAMOVICH.

Toshkent Davlat Yuridik Instituti (Tashkent Law Institute): Sayilgokh 3, Tashkent 100047; tel. (71) 133-41-09; e-mail rektor@tsil.uz; internet www.tsil.uz; 3 faculties of law; 221 teachers; 2,182 students; Rector Prof. Dr MIRZAYUSUF HAKIMOVICH RUSTAMBAYEV; Pro-Rector for Academic Work RUSTAM AKHMEDOVICH ZUFAROV.

Toshkent Moliya Instituti (Tashkent Financial Institute): Asomova 7, Tashkent 100084; tel. (71) 234-53-34; e-mail rektor@tfi .uz; internet www.tfi.uz; f. 1991; offers courses in areas of auditing and accounting, banking, finance, insurance, projects financing, securities, stock exchange, taxation; 350 teachers; 4,200 students; Rector Prof. Dr ALISHER V. VAKHABOV; publ. *Moliya*.

Tashkent State Institute of Culture named after Abdulla Qadiri: Yalangach St 127A, Tashkent 100164; tel. (71) 262-03-23; e-mail tdmi@uzsci.net; f. 1974; librarianship, educational and cultural work; br. in Namangan; 170 teachers; 1,500 students; Rector Prof. AZIZ APPAKOVICH TURAEV; First Pro-Rector Prof. Dr ABDUKHALIL ABDULKHAEVICH MAVRULOV; Pro-Rector for Educational Work and Information Technologies ANVAR SHOMURADOVICH NORBEKOV.

Tashkent State Medical Institute: Musahanov St 103, Tashkent 700048; tel. (71) 267-63-05; e-mail tashmi@mail.ru; f. 1920; trains general practitioners and stomatologists; library: 600,000 vols; 450 teachers; 3,000 students; Rector Prof. T. A. DAMINOV.

Tashkent University of Information Technology: Amir Temur 108, Tashkent 100084; tel. (71) 138-64-20; e-mail teic@ uzpak.uz; f. 1955 as Tashkent Electrotechnical Institute of Communication, present name and status 2002; faculties of economics, radio communication, special communication, telecommunication networks and switching systems, telecommunication transmission systems, television and broadcasting; library: 500,000 vols; 400 teachers; 8,500 students; Rector Prof. Dr MADJID KARIMOV.

University of World Economics and Diplomacy: Buyuk Ipak yuli 54, Tashkent 100045; tel. (71) 267-67-69; e-mail uwed@ list.ru; internet www.uwed.uz; f. 1992; 350 teachers; 1,200 students; Rector ABDUJABBAR ABDUVAKHITOV.

Uzbek State World Languages University: Kichik halqa yuli str. 21A, Uchtepa Dist., Tashkent 100138; tel. (71) 275-97-95; e-mail usuw_info@edu.uz; internet www .uzswlu.uz; f. 1992 by merger of Tashkent State Pedagogical Institute of Foreign Languages and Republican Russian Language and Literature Pedagogic Institute; faculties of English, German, French, Spanish, Chinese and Russian philology, int. journalism, theory and practice of translation; 587 teachers; 7,073 students; Rector A. ISMAILOV; Vice-Rector for Academic Affairs N. ARTIKOV; Vice-Rector for Scientific Affairs G. BAKIYEVA.

VANUATU

The Higher Education System

Higher education in Vanuatu is limited, the only institution being a campus of the University of the South Pacific, which opened in 1989 and which offers courses leading to certificates, diplomas, degrees and postgraduate qualifications. The campus in Port Vila, known as the Emalus Campus, houses the University's law school. Students from Vanuatu may also receive higher education at the University's principal faculties (in Suva, Fiji), or at higher education institutions in Papua New Guinea, Australia or New Zealand, while those from Vanuatu's French schools may attend institutions in New Caledonia or French Polynesia. In 2002 there were 2,124 students enrolled in tertiary education. According to UNESCO estimates, this number had fallen to only 955 in 2004. Gross enrolment at tertiary level was just 5% in 2005.

Admission to the University of the South Pacific is primarily via the Pacific Senior Secondary Certificate and completion of preparatory Preliminary and/or Foundation Programmes, which are designed to bridge the gap between secondary and tertiary education. The Bachelors degree typically lasts three years, although some courses may last longer—for example, medicine, which is a four-year programme of study. The Masters degree lasts between one and two years upon completion of the Bachelors. The Doctorate, which is the highest academic award available, requires a minimum of two additional years of study and research following award of the Masters.

Technical and vocational education training (TVET) is an area currently undergoing reform in order to standardize, harmonize and improve access. The Vanuatu Institute of Technology is the largest provider of TVET and has its main campus in Port Vila and two provincial training centres, in Sanma and Tafea provinces. It provides Certificate-level courses in accounting, building and computing, among other fields of study. Two-year teacher training courses are also offered at the Vanuatu Institute of Teacher Training, which has an annual intake of 100 students.

Regulatory Body

GOVERNMENT

Ministry of Education: PMB 9028, Port Vila; tel. 22309; internet www .governmentofvanuatu.gov.vu/index.php/ government/education; Minister CHARLOT SALWAI.

Learned Societies

BIBLIOGRAPHY, LIBRARY SCIENCE AND MUSEOLOGY

Pacific Islands Museums Association (PIMA): Vanuatu Cultural Centre, Port Vila; tel. 28063; e-mail pimasg@gmail.com; f. 1994; preserves, celebrates and nurtures the heritage of the peoples of the Pacific Islands; Sec.-Gen. TARISI VUNIDILO.

Vanuatu Library Association/Vanuatu Laebri Asosiesen/Association des Bibliothèques Vanuatuanes: Port Vila; tel. 22888; internet www.vanuatu.usp.ac.fj/ library/vla; develops and improves library services; supports and encourages devt of libraries, archives and associated professions; Pres. SYLVIE TAPASEI; Sec. PAULINE KALO; Treas. KYM FRERICKS.

Research Institute

NATURAL SCIENCES

Biological Sciences

Environment Unit: Pompidou Complex, Port Vila; e-mail environ@vanuatu.com.vu; internet www.biodiversity.com.vu; provides technical advice and organizes programmes for devt, conservation and management of natural resources; Head ERNEST BANI.

Libraries and Archives

Port Vila

National Library: Nat. Museum Bldg, Port Vila; tel. 22129; e-mail nasonal.laebri@ vanuatuculture.org; internet www .vanuatuculture.org/site-bm2/library; 2 spec. collns, Pacific and Vanuatu, in English, French and Bislama; linguistics section on the 113 vernacular languages; anthropological and archaeological materials, art and arts references, autobiographical records and biographies, large section of works on the languages of Vanuatu, mission histories, oral traditions, cultural, historical and political records; Chief Librarian ANNE NAUPA; Librarian JUNE NORMAN.

National Photo, Film and Sound Archive: POB 184, Port Vila; tel. 23197; e-mail filmandaudio@vanuatuculture.org; internet www.vanuatuculture.org/site-bm2/film-sound; preserves information about customs, culture and tradition; 3,000 hours of footage (8mm films, Video 8 and VHS $\frac{1}{2}$-inch video) and photographs of oral traditions and rituals.

Port Vila Public Library: Cultural Centre Bldg, Port Vila; tel. (678) 23837; e-mail pablik.laebri@vanuatu.com.vu; internet www.vanuatuculture.org/site-bm2/library/ 050517_publiclibrary.shtml; f. 1960; only public library in Vanuatu; Librarian NAOMI ANIEL.

Museum

Port Vila

Vanuatu Cultural Centre and National Museum/Vanuatu Kaljoral Senta: POB 184, Port Vila; tel. 23197; e-mail vks@ vanuatu.com.vu; internet www .vanuatuculture.org; f. 1960 as Port Vila Library, Museum opened in 1995; incl. Malakula Cultural Centre in Lakatoro; houses Vanuatu Cultural and Historic Sites Survey (VCHSS), Young People's Project, Women's Cultural Project; supports and encourages preservation, protection and devt of cultural heritage; collns of canoe paraphernalia, photographs, informational text, identification labels and DVDs on story of canoes; archaeological items; traditional artefacts (masks, slit gongs, outrigger canoes); historical and contemporary art; Dir of Vanuatu Cultural Centre MARCELLIN ABONG.

University

UNIVERSITY OF THE SOUTH PACIFIC, EMALUS CAMPUS

PMB 9072, Port Vila

Telephone: 22748

Internet: www.vanuatu.usp.ac.fj

Founded 1989

Pacific Languages Unit, School of Early Childhood Education, School of Law

Dir: JEAN PIERRE NIRUA

Librarian: MARGARET AUSTRAI-KAILO

Library of 15,596 vols (incl. Emalus Campus, Santo Centre and Tanna Centre)

Number of students: 930

VATICAN CITY

The Higher Education System

The State of the Vatican City is situated entirely within the Italian capital, Rome. In 1929 the Lateran Treaty was concluded between the Italian Government and the Holy See (a term designating the papacy, i.e. the office of the Pope, and thus the central governing body of the Roman Catholic Church). Higher education principally consists of Pontifical universities, colleges and institutes offering training for the priesthood and conducting research relating to the Roman Catholic Church, the oldest being the Pontificia Universitas Gregoriana, which was founded in 1553. The majority of institutions are located in Rome outside the boundaries of the Vatican City itself. Many of the institutions award graduate degrees, including doctorates.

The Holy See has adhered to the Bologna Process since 2003. The Congregazione per l'Educazione Cattolica (Congregation for Catholic Education) has authority over all universities, faculties, institutes and higher schools of study—either ecclesial or civil but dependent on ecclesial persons—that belong to the Holy See's higher education system throughout the world. L'Agenzia della Santa Sede per la Valutazione e la Promozione della Qualità delle Università e Facoltà Ecclesiastiche (AVEPRO—Holy See's Agency for the Evaluation and Promotion of Quality in Ecclesiastical Universities and Faculties) was established in 2007 as the agency responsible for promoting, developing and evaluating quality in higher education institutions.

Regulatory and Representative Bodies

GOVERNMENT

Congregation for Catholic Education: see under International Organizations.

Pontifical Council for Culture: Vatican City, 00120 Rome; tel. (6) 69893811; e-mail cultura@cultura.va; internet www.cultura.va; Pres. HE Cardinal GIANFRANCO RAVASI.

ACCREDITATION

ENIC/NARIC Holy See: Congregation for Catholic Education, 00120 Vatican City; tel. (6) 69884167; e-mail educatt@ccatheduc.va; internet www.vatican.va; Contact Rev. PASCALE IDE.

Learned Societies

GENERAL

Pontificia Academia Sancti Thomae Aquinatis (Pontifical Academy of St Thomas Aquinas): 00120 Vatican City; tel. (6) 69881441; e-mail past@past.va; internet www.past.va; f. 1879; theological, philosophical and juridico-economic sections; 54 mems; Pres. Prof. LLUÍS CLAVELL; Sec. Prof. HE MARCELO SÁNCHEZ SORONDO; publ. *Doctor Communis* (irregular).

ECONOMICS, LAW AND POLITICS

Pontificia Accademia delle Scienze Sociali (Pontifical Academy of Social Sciences): Casina Pio IV, 00120 Vatican City; tel. (6) 69881441; e-mail pass@pass.va; internet www.pass.va; f. 1994; social, economic, political and juridical sciences; 37 mems; Pres. Prof. MARY ANN GLENDON; Chancellor Prof. HE MARCELO SÁNCHEZ SORONDO; publs *Acta*, *Miscellanea*.

FINE AND PERFORMING ARTS

Pontificia Insigne Accademia di Belle Arti e Lettere dei Virtuosi al Pantheon: Via della Conciliazione 5, 00193 Rome, Italy; tel. (6) 69882232; f. 1542; 90 mems; Pres. Dott. VITALIANO TIBERIA; Sec. Prof. GIOVANNI CARBONARA; publ. *Annali* (1 a year).

HISTORY, GEOGRAPHY AND ARCHAEOLOGY

Pontificia Accademia Romana di Archeologia (Pontifical Roman Academy of Archaeology): Via della Conciliazione 5, 00193 Rome, Italy; e-mail segreteria@pont-ara.org; f. 1810; 109 mems; Pres. MARCO BUONOCORE; Sec. PAOLO LIVERANI; publs *Memorie*, *Rendiconti*.

NATURAL SCIENCES

General

Pontificia Academia Scientiarum (Pontifical Academy of Sciences): Casina Pio IV, 00120 Vatican City; tel. (6) 69883451; e-mail pas@pas.va; internet www.pas.va; f. 1603; promotes the mathematical, physical and natural sciences and the study of related epistemological problems; 80 mems; Pres. Prof. WERNER ARBER; Chancellor Prof. HE MARCELO SÁNCHEZ SORONDO; publs *Acta*, *Commentari*, *Documenta*, *Scripta Varia*.

RELIGION, SOCIOLOGY AND ANTHROPOLOGY

Collegium Cultorum Martyrum: Via Napoleone III 1, 00185 Rome, Italy; tel. 4455833; e-mail cultorum.martyrum@org.va; f. 1879; 750 mems; Master Mgr EMANUELE CLARIZIO; Sec. LUIGI CIOTTI.

Pontificia Academia Mariana Internationalis (Pontifical International Marian Academy): Via Merulana 124, 00185 Rome, Italy; premises in Vatican City; tel. (6) 70373235; e-mail pami@pami.info; internet www.pami.info; f. 1946, Pontifical since 1959; studies on Our Lady; 80 mems, 155 corresp. mems, 134 hon. mems; Pres. VINCENZO BATTAGLIA; Sec. STEFANO CECCHIN; publ. *Scientific collections*.

Pontificia Accademia dell'Immacolata (Academy of the Immaculate Conception): Via del Serafico 1, 00142 Rome, Italy; f. 1835; 15 mems; promotes Marian studies and culture, especially the doctrine of the Immaculate Conception in the fields of theology, literature and art; Pres. Cardinal ANDREA M. DESKUR; Sec. and Archivist Fr ZDZISLAW J. KIJAS.

Pontificia Accademia di Teologia: Piazza St Giovanni in Laterano 4, 00120 Vatican City; tel. (6) 69895513; e-mail path@pul.it; f. 1718; 7 emeritus mems; 39 ordinary mems: 25 normally resident in Rome, 6 in the rest of Italy and 8 in other countries; 16 corresp. mems; Pres. MARCELLO BORDONI; Sec. Prof. PIERO CODA; publ. *PATH*.

Research Institute

NATURAL SCIENCES

Physical Sciences

Vatican Observatory: 00120 Vatican City; tel. (6) 69885266; f. 1889; carries out research into dark matter and energy in the cosmos, the acceleration of the universe, quasars, globular clusters; library of 33,000 vols; Dir Fr JOSÉ GABRIEL FUNES..

Attached Centre:

Vatican Observatory Research Group (VORG): see entry for Mount Graham International Observatory in USA chapter.

Libraries and Archives

Vatican City

Archivio Segreto Vaticano (Papal Archives): 00120 Vatican City; internet www.archiviosegretovaticano.va; f. 1611; attached school: see under Schools; Prefect HE SERGIO PAGANO; publs *Collectanea Archivi Vaticani*, *Varia*.

Biblioteca Apostolica Vaticana (Vatican Library): 00120 Vatican City; tel. (6) 69879400; e-mail bav@vatlib.it; internet www.vaticanlibrary.va; f. 1451 as a public library by Pope Nicholas V, and provided with staff and a structure by Sixtus IV in 1475; 75,000 MSS, 80,000 archival files, 1.6m. engravings, 8,000 incunabula, and 1m. other vols; collns incl. those of the Dukes of Urbino (1657), of Queen Christina of Sweden (1690), of the Florentine Marquis Capponi (1745), of Barberini (1902), of Chigi (1923), and the Borghese colln, which incl. many items housed in the Papal Library at Avignon; the Sistine Chapel colln is of importance to historians of music; holds a 4th-century Greek Bible, Vergils from the 4th–6th centuries, a 4th–5th century palimpsest of Cicero's *Republic*, autographs of St Thomas Aquinas, Tasso, Petrarch, Boccaccio, Poliziano, Michelangelo, and Luther; numismatic colln; attached museums: see under Museums and Art Galleries; attached school:

see under Schools; Protector Cardinal JEAN-LOUIS BRUGUÈS; Prefect Mons. CESARE PASINI; Vice-Prefect Dr AMBROGIO M. PIAZZONI.

Museums and Art Galleries
Vatican City

Museo Sacro (o Cristiano): Vatican City; e-mail info@museosacro.es; f. 1756 by Pope Benedict XIV; contains objects of liturgical art, historical relics and curios from the Lateran; objects of palaeolithic, medieval and Renaissance minor arts, paintings of the Roman era; Curator Dr GUIDO CORNINI.

Vatican Museums: 00120 Vatican City; tel. (6) 69883333; internet www.museivaticani .va; Dir-Gen. Prof. ANTONIO PAOLUCCI; Admin. PAOLO NICOLINI; Sec. Dr ARNOLD NESSELRATH; publs *Bollettino dei Monumenti, Musei e Gallerie Pontificie*.

Constituent Museums:

Collezione d'Arte Religiosa Moderna (Collection of Modern Religious Art): 00120 Vatican City; f. 1973 by Pope Paul VI; paintings, sculptures and drawings offered to the Pope by over 200 artists and donors; Curator Dott. MICOL FORTI.

Museo Chiaramonti e Braccio Nuovo (Chiaramonti Museum and 'New Side'): 00120 Vatican City; f. by Pope Pius VII at the beginning of the 19th century; houses the many new findings excavated in the 19th century; exhibits incl. the statues of the Nile, of Demosthenes and of the Augustus 'of Prima Porta'; Curator Dott. GIANDOMENICO SPINOLA.

Museo Gregoriano Egizio (Gregorian Egyptian Museum): 00120 Vatican City; internet mv.vatican.va/3_en/pages/mez/ mez_main.html; f. 1839 by Pope Gregory XVI; contains artefacts from Ancient Egypt; 9 exhibition rooms dating from 2600BC to 8th century AD incl. hieroglyphic stelae and statues, finds from Ancient Mesopotamia and Syria–Palestine, Hellenistic and Roman Egypt; Curator Dott. ALESSIA AMENTA.

Museo Gregoriano Etrusco (Gregorian Etruscan Museum): 00120 Vatican City; tel. (6) 69883041; e-mail aei.musei@scv.va; internet mv.vatican.va/3_en/pages/mge/ mge_main.html; f. 1837 by Pope Gregory XVI; artefacts from the early Iron Age to the end of the Roman Empire; jewellery, bronzes, terracottas, glassware, Etruscan sculptures and reliefs; figured vases (Greek, Etruscan and Italiote) from Etruria and Magna Graecia; grave goods from the Tomba Regolini Galassi of Cerveteri, the Mars of Todi, the amphora by Exekias; Curator Dott. MAURIZIO SANNIBALE.

Museo Gregoriano Profano (Gregorian Museum of Profane Art): 00120 Vatican City; f. by Gregory XVI in 1844 and housed in the Lateran Palace; transferred from fmr site in the Vatican and opened to the public in 1970; Roman sculptures from the Pontifical States; portrait-statue of Sophocles, the Marsyas of the Myronian group of Athena and Marsyas, the Flavian reliefs from the Palace of the Apostolic Chancery; Curator Dott. GIANDOMENICO SPINOLA.

Museo Missionario Etnologico (Ethnological Missionary Museum): 00120 Vatican City; internet mv.vatican.va/3_en/ pages/met/met_main.html; f. by Pius XI in 1926 and housed in the Lateran Palace; transferred from that site in the Vatican and opened to the public in 1973; ethno-graphical collns from all over the world; Curator Rev. NICOLA MAPELLI.

Museo Pio Clementino (Museum of Popes Clement XIV and Pius VI): 00120 Vatican City; f. by Pope Clement XIV (1769–74), and enlarged by his successor, Pius VI (1775–1799); exhibits include the Apollo of Belvedere, Roman copies of the Apoxyomenos by Lysippus, of the Meleager by Skopas and of the Apollo Sauroktonous by Praxiteles; the original Vatican Colln was begun with the Apollo—already in possession of Pope Julius II when he was still a Cardinal, at the end of the 15th century—and the Laocoon Group, found in 1506; Curator Dott. GIANDOMENICO SPINOLA.

Museo Pio Cristiano Lapidario Cristiano Lapidario Ebraico (Early Christian Art Museum—Christian and Jewish Lapidaries): 00120 Vatican City; tel. (6) 69881349; e-mail ap.musei@scv.va; f. 1854 by Pius IX, housed in the Lateran Palace; transferred from fmr site in the Vatican and opened to the public in 1970; largest colln in the world of early Christian sarcophagi; the Good Shepherd; Latin and Greek inscriptions from Christian cemeteries and Roman basilicas; inscriptions from Jewish catacombs of Monteverde; Curator Prof. Dr UMBERTO UTRO.

Padiglione delle Carrozze (Carriage Pavilion): 00120 Vatican City; f. 1973 by Pope Paul VI; located in the Vatican gardens, containing carriages, berlins and the first cars used by the Popes; Dir Asst Mons. PIETRO AMATO.

Pinacoteca Vaticana (Vatican Picture Gallery): 00120 Vatican City; internet mv .vatican.va/3_en/pages/pin/pin_main.html; inaugurated by Pope Pius XI in 1932; incl. paintings by Giotto, Fra Angelico, Raphael, Leonardo da Vinci, Titian and Caravaggio, and the Raphael Tapestries; Curator Dott. ARNOLD NESSELRATH.

Vatican Palaces: 00120 Vatican City; Nicoline Chapel decorated by Beato Angelico (1448–50); Sistine Chapel restructured by Sixtus IV (1477–83): frescoes by Perugino, Botticelli, Cosimo Rosselli, Ghirlandaio, Luca Signorelli, Michelangelo; Borgia Apartment: decorated by Pinturicchio and his workshop; Chapel of Urban VIII (1631–35); Raphael Stanze and loggias decorated by Raphael and his assistants; Gallery of Maps (1580–83), Gallery of Tapestries, etc.; Curator Dott. ARNOLD NESSELRATH.

Universities

PONTIFICIA UNIVERSITÀ DELLA SANTA CROCE
(Pontifical University of the Holy Cross)

Piazza di Sant'Apollinare 49, 00186 Rome

Telephone: (6) 681641

E-mail: santacroce@pusc.it

Internet: www.pusc.it

Founded 1984; univ. status 1998

Private control (erected by the Holy See)

Chancellor: Rev. Bishop JAVIER ECHEVARRÍA
Vice-Chancellor: Mgr Prof. FERNANDO OCÁRIZ
Rector: Mgr Prof. LUIS ROMERA
Vice-Rector: Rev. Prof. HÉCTOR FRANCESCHI
Gen. Sec.: Rev. MANUEL MIEDES
Dir of Academic Affairs: Rev. Prof. FRANCISCO FERNÁNDEZ
Dir of Communications: Prof. NORBERTO GONZÁLEZ GAITANO
Dir of Devt: Dr JOAQUÍN GÓMEZ-BLANES
Librarian: Dott. JUAN DIEGO RAMÍREZ

Number of teachers: 208 (incl. 126 permanent profs and 28 visiting profs in 4 faculties; 46 permanent profs and 8 visiting profs in the Higher Institute for Religious Studies)

Number of students: 1,470 (1,003 students in the 4 faculties; 467 students in the Higher Institute for Religious Studies)

Publications: *International Canon Law journal: 'IUS Ecclesiae', International Philosophy journal: 'Acta Philosophica', International Theology journal: 'Annales Theologici'.*

AFFILIATED INSTITUTE

Institut de Formation Théologique de Montréal: 2065 rue Sherbrooke Ouest, Montréal, QC H3H 1G6, Canada; tel. (514) 935-1169; e-mail info@iftm.ca; internet www.iftm .ca; library of 140,000 monographs, 175 periodicals; Rector Prof. CHARLES LANGLOIS; Dean of Studies Prof. PETER KRASUSKI; publ. *L'entre deux tours* (online, www.iftm.ca/iftm_bulletin.php)

DEANS

Department of Canon Law: Prof. ERNEST CAPARROS
Department of Pastoral Theology: Prof. GUY GUINDON
Department of Philosophy: Prof. TÉLESPHORE GAGNON
Department of Theology: Prof. JAROSLAW KAUFMANN

PROFESSORS

Faculty of Church Communications:

ARASA, D.
BAILLY-BAILLIÉRE, A.
BARILLARI, A.
BÜHREN, R. V.
CALOGERO, F.
CANTONI, L.
CARROGGIO, M.
CONTRERAS, D.
DE LA CIERVA, Y.
DOLZ, M.
ESPOZ, C.
FUSTER, E.
GAGLIARDI, F.
GARCÍA-NOBLEJAS, J. J.
GONZÁLEZ GAITANO, N.
GRAZIANI, N.
GRONOWSKI, D.
JIMÉNEZ, A.
JIMÉNEZ CATAÑO, R.
LA PORTE, J. M.
MACCARINI, A.
MASTROIANNI, B.
MILÁN, J.
MORA, J. M.
PILAVAKIS, M.
POLENGHI, G.
ROMOLO, R.
RUIZ LUCIO, A.
RUSSO, M.
SHAW, R.
TAPIA, S.
TRIDENTE, G.
WAUCK, J.

Faculty of Theology:

AGULLES, P.
AREITIO, J. R.
ARROYO, J. M.
BELDA, M.
BOSCH, V.
CHACÓN, A.
COLOM, E.
DE SALIS AMARAL, M.
DE VIRGILIO, G.
DÍAZ DORRONSORO, R.
DIÉGUEZ, J.
DUCAY, A.
ESTRADA, B.
FABBRI, M. V.

GALVÁN, J. M.
GARCÍA IBÁÑEZ, A.
GONZÁLEZ, E.
GOYRET, P.
GRANADOS, A.
GROHE, J.
JÓDAR, C.
LAMERI, A.
LEAL, J.
LIMBURG, K.
LÓPEZ DÍAZ, J.
MARTÍNEZ-FERRER, L.
MASPERO, G.
MIRA, M.
MIRALLES, A.
NIN, M.
O'CALLAGHAN, P.
OSSANDÓN, J. C.
PIOPPI, C.
PORRAS, A.
REALE, V.
REQUENA, F.
REQUENA, P.
RIESTRA, J. A.
RIO GARCÍA, M.
RODRÍGUEZ LUÑO, A.
ROSSI ESPAGNET, C.
SANZ, S.
SCHLAG, M.
SILVESTRE, J. J.
TÁBET, M.
TANZELLA-NITTI, G.
TORRES, E.
TOUZE, L.
VIAL, W.
WIELOCKX, R.

School of Canon Law:

ÁLVAREZ DE LAS ASTURIAS, N.
ARAÑA, J. A.
ARRIETA, J. I.
BACCARI, M. P.
BAURA, E.
CANOSA, J.
CITO, D.
DEL POZZO, M.
EISENRING, G.
ERRÁZURIZ M., C. J.
FRANCESCHI, H.
GEFAELL, P.
GÓMEZ-IGLESIAS, V.
GUTIÉRREZ, J. L.
LLOBELL, J.
MARTÍN DE AGAR, J. T.
MIÑAMBRES, J.
NAVARRO, L.
ORTIZ, M. A.
PUIG, F.
SÁNCHEZ-GIL, A. S.
SCHOUPPE, J.-P.

School of Philosophy:

ACERBI, A.
AIELLO, A.
BERGAMINO, F.
BROCK, S. L.
CHIRINOS, M. A.
CLAVELL, L.
DALLEUR, P.
D'AVENIA, M.
FARO, G.
FERNÁNDEZ LABASTIDA, F.
FERRARI, M. A.
GAHL, R. A.
IPPOLITO, B.
ITURBE, M.
LOMBO, J. A.
MALO, A.
MARTÍNEZ, R.
MERCADO, J. A.
PÉREZ DE LABORDA, M.
PORTA, M.
QUINTILIANI, M.
REYES, C.
RHONHEIMER, M.
ROMERA, L.
RUSSO, F.

SANGUINETI, J. J.
VITORIA, M. A.
YARZA, I.

PONTIFICIA UNIVERSITÀ SAN TOMMASO D'AQUINO
(St Thomas Aquinas Pontifical University)

Largo Angelicum 1, 00184 Rome, Italy

Telephone: (6) 67021
E-mail: segreteria@pust.it
Internet: www.pust.it

Founded 1580 as college, became Univ. 1909; present title conferred 1963
Languages of instruction: Italian, English
Academic year: October to June

Grand Chancellor: Rev. BRUNO CADORÉ
Rector Magnificus: Rev. MIROSLAV KONSTANC ADAM
Administrator: Rev. VIRGILIO AMBROSINI
Sec.-Gen.: Rev. GLENN MORRIS
Librarian: Rev. BERNHARD BLANKENHORN

Library of 200,000 vols
Number of teachers: 150
Number of students: 1,100

Publications: *Angelicum, Istituto S. Tommaso: Studi, Oikonomia* (ethics and social sciences, 3 a year), *Rassegna di Letteratura Tomistica, Studia Univ. S. Thomae In Urbe*

DEANS

Faculty of Canon Law: Rev. MICHAEL CARRAGHER
Faculty of Philosophy: Rev. PHILIPPE-ANDRE HOLZER
Faculty of Social Sciences: Rev. Sr HELEN ALFORD
Faculty of Theology: JOSEPH AGIUS

PONTIFICIA UNIVERSITAS GREGORIANA
(Pontifical Gregorian University)

Piazza della Pilotta 4, 00187 Rome, Italy

Telephone: (6) 67011
E-mail: segreteria@unigre.it
Internet: www.unigre.it

Founded by St Ignatius Loyola and St Francis Borgia, and constituted by Pope Julius III in 1553; confirmed and established by Pope Gregory XIII in 1582
The central university for ecclesiastical studies is under the direction of the Jesuit Order; Pontificium Institutum Biblicum and Pontificio Istituto Orientale are autonomous colleges associated with the Univ.
Languages of instruction: English, French, German, Italian, Portuguese, Spanish
Academic year: October to June (2 terms)

Grand Chancellor: HE Cardinal ZENON GROCHOLEWSKI
Vice-Grand Chancellor: Rev. PETER-HANS KOLVENBACH
Rector Magnificus: Rev. GIANFRANCO GHIRLANDA
Vice-Rector: Rev. FRANCISCO J. EGAÑA
Academic Vice-Rector: Rev. SERGIO BASTIANEL
Admin. Vice-Rector: Rev. VITALE SAVIO
Sec.-Gen.: LUIGI ALLENA
Librarian: Dr MARTA GIORGI DEBANNE

Library of 900,000 vols
Number of teachers: 423
Number of students: 2,949

Publications: *Acta Nuntiaturae Gallicae, Analecta Gregoriana, Archivum Historiae Pontificiae, Documenta Missionalia, Gregorianum, Inculturation, Miscellanea Historiae Pontificiae, Periodica de re morali*

canonica liturgica, Saggi ISR, Studia Missionalia, Studia Socialia, Tesi Gregoriana

DEANS AND DIRECTORS

Cultural Heritage of the Church: J. JANSSENS
Faculty of Canon Law: M. HILBERT
Faculty of Ecclesiastical History: M. INGLOT
Faculty of Missionary Work: A. WOLANIN
Faculty of Philosophy: K. FLANNERY
Faculty of Social Sciences: J. JELENIC
Faculty of Theology: L. LADÁRIA
Institute of Psychology: T. HEALY
Institute of Religious Sciences: S. BARLONE
Institute of Spirituality: M. SZENTMÁRTONI
Interdisciplinary Centre of Social Communication: J. SRAMPICKAL

PROFESSORS

Cultural Heritage of the Church (tel. (6) 67015114; e-mail segrbcc@unigre.it):

JANSSENS, J., Church History
PFEIFFER, H., Art History

Faculty of Canon Law (tel. (6) 67015123; e-mail hilbert@unigre.it):

ASTIGUETA, D., Text of Canon Law
CONN, J., Text of Canon Law
GHIRLANDA, G., Canon Law and Theology of Church Law
HILBERT, M., Text of Canon Law
KOWAL, J., Canon Law and Sacraments
SUGAWARA, Y., Text of Canon Law

Faculty of Ecclesiastical History (tel. (6) 67015410; e-mail inglot@unigre.it):

BENITEZ, J. M., Modern Church History
DE LASALA CLAVER, F., History of the Roman Curia
GUTIERREZ, A., Church History of Latin America
INGLOT, M., History of the Roman Curia
JANSSENS, J., Christian Archaeology—Historical Methodology
MEZZADRI, L., Modern Church History
PFEIFFER, H., Christian Art

Faculty of Missionary Work (tel. (6) 67015240; e-mail wolanin@unigre.it):

FARAHIAN, E., Missionary Biblical Theology
FUSS, M., Buddhism
SHELKE, C., Comparative Study of Religions
WOLANIN, A., Mission Dogmatics

Faculty of Philosophy (tel. (6) 67015441; e-mail filosofia@unigre.it):

BABOLIN, S., Aesthetics and Philosophy of Human Culture
CARUANA, L., Philosophy of Science and Nature
DI MAIO, A., Medieval Philosophy
FLANNERY, K., Greek Philosophy
GILBERT, P., Metaphysics
GORCZYCA, J., Ethics
LECLERC, M., History of Modern Philosophy
LUCAS, R., Philosophical Anthropology
NKERAMIHIGO, T., Philosophy of Theology
PANGALLO, M., History of Medieval Philosophy

Faculty of Social Sciences (tel. (6) 67015316; e-mail scienzesoc@unigre.it):

BAUGH, L., Film and Television Language
JELENIC, J., Social Sciences
SCARVAGLIERI, G., General Religious Sociology

Faculty of Theology (tel. (6) 67015262; e-mail teologia@unigre.it):

ATTARD, M., Moral Theology
BASTIANEL, S., Moral Theology
CALDUCH BENAGES, N., Old Testament Exegesis
CHAPPIN, M., Church History
CONROY, C., Old Testament Exegesis
COSTACURTA, B., Exegesis
FARRUGIA, M., Dogmatic Theology
GALLAGHER, M. P., Fundamental Theology

GRILLI, M., New Testament Exegesis
HENN, W., Dogmatic Theology
LADÁRIA, L., Dogmatic Theology
MEYNET, R., New Testament Exegesis
MILLÁS, J. M., Dogmatic Theology
PASTOR, F., Dogmatic Theology
PECKLERS, K., Liturgy
SCHMITZ, P., Moral Theology
TANNER, N., Patristic Theology
VITALI, D., Dogmatic Theology

Institute of Psychology (tel. (6) 67015299;
e-mail psicologia@unigre.it):

HEALY, T., Psychology and Statistics
IMODA, F., Psychology
KIELY, B., Psychopathology
VERSALDI, G., Psychology and Psychotherapy

Institute of Religious Sciences (tel. (6)
67015405; e-mail segrsr@unigre.it):

BARLONE, S., Fundamental Theology
FINAMORE, R., Education
SALATIELLO, G., Anthropology

Institute of Spirituality (tel. (6) 67015532;
e-mail szentmartoni@unigre.it):

COSTA, M., Spiritual Theology
GARCÍA MATEO, R., Spiritual Theology
SECONDIN, B., Pastoral Theology
SZENTMÁRTONI, M., Pastoral Psychology

Interdisciplinary Centre of Social Communication (tel. (6) 67015393; e-mail
comunicazione@unigre.it):

BABOLIN, S., Symbology
BAUGH, L., Film and Television Language

AFFILIATED INSTITUTES

Filozofsko-Teološki Institut Družbe Isusove: Jordanovac 110, 41001 Zagreb, Croatia; e-mail ftidi@ftidi.hr; internet www.ftidi.hr; Dir M. STEINER.

Institut de Philosophie St Pierre Canisius: Kimwenza, BP 3724, Kinshasa-Gombe, Democratic Republic of the Congo; e-mail philocanisius@gmail.com; internet www.fpsp-canisius.com; library of 100,000 vols; Rector Dr BERNARD MUHIGIRWA; Dean Dr C. BWANGILA; Academic Sec. Dr ADRIEN LENTIAMPA; Academic Sec. BENOÎT MBUYI; publ. *Actes des Journées Philosophiques de Canisius*, *Raison Ardente* (for students), *Revue Philosophique de Kimwenza*.

Instituto Superior de Direito Canônico do Brasil: Rua Benjamin Constant 23, 20241 Rio de Janeiro, Brazil; internet pisdc.com.br; Dir L. MADERO LOPEZ.

Istituto Superiore per i Formatori: Seminario Vescovile, c/o Almo Collegio Capranica 98, 00186 Rome, Italy; e-mail segreteria@isfo.it; Dir A. RAVAGLIOLI.

Istituto Superiore di Scienze Religiose 'Giuseppe Toniolo': Via S. Benedetto da Norcia 2, 65127 Pescara, Italy; e-mail toniolo@diocesipescara.it; internet www.marien.it/toniolo; Pres. G. CILLI.

Istituto di Filosofia 'Aloisianum': Via Donatello 24, 35123 Padua, Italy; Dir S. BONGIOVANNI.

Jesuit School of Philosophy and Theology 'Arrupe College': POB MP320, Mount Pleasant, Harare, Zimbabwe; Pres. A. L. SHIRIMA.

Pontificio Istituto 'Regina Mundi': Lungotevere Tor di Nona 7, 00186 Rome, Italy; Rector C. MCGOVERN.

Priesterseminar Redemptoris Mater des Erzbistum Berlin: Fortunaallee 29, 12683 Berlin, Germany; Rector S. LATINI

PONTIFICIA UNIVERSITAS LATERANENSIS
(Pontifical Lateran University)

Piazza S. Giovanni in Laterano, 400120 Vatican City

Telephone: (6) 69895599
E-mail: segreteria.generale@pul.it
Internet: www.pul.it

Founded 1773
Language of instruction: Italian
Academic year: October to June

Grand Chancellor: HE Cardinal AGOSTINO VALLINI
Rector: HE Bishop ENRICO DAL COVOLO
Vice-Rector: Rev. Mgr PATRICK VALDRINI
Gen. Sec. and Registrar: Dr ULDERICO CONTI
Chief Bursar: Ing. FLAMINIA SACERDOTI
Library of 600,000 vols
Number of teachers: 142
Number of students: 3,903

Publications: *Apollinaris* (questions in canon and comparative law, 2 a year), *Aquinas* (philosophy, 4 a year), *Lateranum* (theology, 4 a year), *Studia et Documenta Historiae et Iuris* (Roman law, 1 a year)

DEANS

Faculty of Canon Law: Rev. Prof. LUIS BOMBIN BOMBIN
Faculty of Civil Law: Prof. VINCENZO BUONOMO
Faculty of Philosophy: Rev. Prof. GIANFRANCO BASTI
Faculty of Theology: Rev. Prof. RENZO GERARDI

INCORPORATED INSTITUTES

Istituto di Teologia della Vita Consacrata 'Claretianum': Largo Lorenzo Mossa 4, 00165 Rome, Italy; Pres. Fr JOSU MIRENA ALDAY.

Istituto Patristico 'Augustinianum': Via Paolo VI 25, 00193 Rome, Italy; Pres. Rev. Fr ROBERT J. DODARO.

Istituto Superiore di Teologia Morale 'Accademia Alfonsiana': Via Merulana 31, 00185 Rome, Italy; Pres. Rev. Fr MARTIN MCKEEVER.

AGGREGATED INSTITUTES

Institut de Formation Théologique de Montréal Département de Philosophie: 2065 rue Sherbrooke Ouest, Montréal, QC H3H 1G6, Canada; tel. (514) 935-1169; e-mail info@iftm.ca; internet www.iftm.ca; academic year September to May; Rector Prof. CHARLES LANGLOIS; Dean of Studies Prof. PETER KRASUSKI; library: 14,000 monographs, 175 periodicals; publ. *L'etre deux tours* (online, www.iftm.ca/iftm_bulletin.php)

DEAN

Department of Philosophy: Prof. TÉLESPHORE GAGNON

Instituto di Direito Canônico 'Pe. Dr Giuseppe Beinto Pegoraro': Av. Nazaré 993, Ipiranga, 04263-100 São Paulo, Brazil; e-mail dir_canonico@yahoo.com.br; Dir Mgr MARTIN SEGÚ GIRONA.

Instituto Diocesano de Estudios Canónicos: Calle Corona 34, 46003 Valencia, Spain; Pres. Rev. ANTONIO CORBÍ COPOVÍ.

Istituto Superiore per l'Insegnamento del Diritto 'Université St Paul la Sagesse' de Beyrouth: POB 50–501, Furn El Chebbak, Baada 1011 2050, Lebanon; teaching of law; Pres. Mgr JOSEPH MERHEJ.

Istituto Teologico di Assisi: Piazza S. Francesco 2, 06081 Assisi Santuario, Italy; Pres. Mgr GIOVANNI CAPPELLI.

Istituto Teologico Marchigiano: Via Monte Dago 87, 60131 Ancona, Italy; Pres. Mgr MARIO FLORIO.

AFFILIATED INSTITUTES

Istituto Filosofico della Facoltá di Teologia di Lugano: Via Buffi 13, CP 4663, 69004 Lugano, Switzerland; Rector Prof. LIBERO GEROSA.

Istituto Teologico Abruzzese-Molisano di Chieti: Via Nicoletto Vernia 1, 66100 Chieti, Italy; Prefect of Studies Rev. GIOVANNI GIORGIO.

Istituto Teologico-Cattolico per l'Oceania 'Blessed Diego Luis de San Vitores' di Guam: Catholic Theological Institute for Oceania, 130 Chalan Seminariu, Yona, 96915 Guam, USA; Prefect of Studies Mgr DAVID C. QUITUGUA.

Istituto Teologico della Comunità 'Saint Martin': BP 34, 41120 Candé sur Beuvron, France; Prefect of Studies Rev. Fr FRANÇOIS-REGIS MOREAU.

Istituto Teologico del Seminario di Alba Iulia: Str. Bibliotecii 3, 510009 Alba Iulia, Romania; Prefect of Studies Fr ZSOLT F. KOVACS.

Istituto Teologico del Seminario di Denver: St John Vianney Theological Seminary, 1300 S Steele St, Denver, CO 80210-2599, USA; Prefect of Studies Dr ANTHONY LILLES.

Istituto Teologico del Seminario di Guadalajara: Seminario Mayor, Santo Domingo 1120, Col. Chapalita, 45040 Guadalajara, Jal., Mexico; Prefect of Studies Rev. FRANCISCO GARCÍA VELARDE.

Istituto Teologico del Seminario di Györ: R. K. Hittudományi Főiskola, Káptalandomb 7, 9021 Györ, Hungary; Prefect of Studies Rev. GÁBOR NÉMETH.

Istituto Teologico del Seminario di Iași: Str. Vâscâuteanu 6, 700462 Iași, Romania; Prefect of Studies Rev. MIHAI PATRASCU.

Istituto Teologico del Seminario di Kamyanets-Podilskyi 'Seminarium Maius S. Spiritus': Provulok O. Wanagsa 14, 32000 Gorodok, Khmelnystka obl., Ukraine; Prefect of Studies Rev. JERZY KURCEK.

Istituto Teologico del Seminario di Rīga: Rigas Teologijas Instituts, Katolu iela 16, 1003 Rīga, Latvia; Pro-Prefect of Studies Rev. EDGAR CAKULS.

Istituto Teologico del Seminario Maggiore Rolduc: Heyendallaan 82, 6464 EP Kerkrade, Netherlands; tel. (45) 5466888; e-mail info@rolduc.nl; internet www.rolduc.nl/seminarie; Rector Dr JAN VRIES; Prefect of Studies Dr LAMBERT HENDRIKS.

Istituto Teologico del Seminario San Giuseppe di Vilnius: Juozapo Kunigu Seminarija, Kalvariju 325, 2021 Vilnius, Latvia; Prefect of Studies Rev. HANS FRIEDRICH FISCHER.

Istituto Teologico 'Josephinum' di Columbus: Pontifical College Josephinum, 7625 N High St, Columbus, OH 80210-2599, USA; Prefect of Studies Rev. Fr MICHAEL ROSS.

Istituto Teologico 'St Giovanni Crisostomo' del Seminario di St Pietroburgo: Vysshaya Dukhovnaya Seminariya 'Maria-Tsaritsa Apostolov', Ul. 1-aya Krasnoarmeiskaya 11, 198005 St Petersburg, Russia; Prefect of Studies Rev. JAKUB BLASZCZYSZYN.

Istituto Teologico 'Willibrordhuis' della Diocesi di Haarlem: Willibrordhuis, Zilkerduinweg 375, 2114 Vogelenzang, Netherlands; Prefect of Studies Fr J. MANUEL TERCERO SIMÓN.

Studio Filosofico dell' 'Oratorio di San Filippo Neri': 1372 King St, W, Toronto, ON MGK 1H3, Canada.

Studio Filosofico del Seminario Patriarcale Latino di Gerusalemme: Séminaire Patriarchal Latin, POB 14152, Jerusalem, Israel; tel. (2) 2742612; e-mail adibz@latinseminary.org; Rector Fr ADIB ZOOMOT.

Studio Teologico del Seminario di Gerusalemme: Séminaire Patriarcal Latin, POB 14152, Jerusalem, Israel; tel. (2) 2742612; e-mail adibz@latinseminary.org; Rector Fr ADIB ZOOMOT; Prefect of Studies JAMAL KHADER.

Studio Teologico 'Studium Theologicum': CP 153, 80001-970 Curitiba, PR, Brazil;Ave Presidente Getúlio Vargas 1193, 80250-180 Curitiba, PR, Brazil; Dir Rev. Fr JAIME SANCHEZ BOSCH.

INSTITUTES WITHIN THE PREMISES

Pontifical John Paul II Institute for Studies on Marriage and Family: Pres. HE Bishop RINO FISICHELLA.

Pontifical Pastoral Institute 'Redemptor Hominis': Piazza St Giovanni in Laterano 4, 00120 Rome, Italy; Pres. Mgr DARIO E. VIGANÒ

PONTIFICIA UNIVERSITAS URBANIANA
(Pontifical Urbanian University)

Via Urbano VIII 16, 00165 Rome, Italy

Telephone: (6) 69889611
E-mail: segreteria@urbaniana.edu
Internet: www.urbaniana.edu

Founded 1627 by Pope Urban VIII
Language of instruction: Italian
Academic year: October to June

Chancellor: Cardinal FERNANDO FILONI
Vice-Chancellor: Mgr SAVIO HON TAI-FAI
Rector Magnificus: Rev. ALBERTO TREVISIOL
Vice-Rector: Rev. L. GODFREY ONAH
Sec.-Gen.: Rev. DON ROBERTO CHERUBINI
Librarian: Rev. Fr MAREK ROSTKOWSKI

Library of 400,000 vols
Number of teachers: 160 (incl. 50 full-time)
Number of students: 1,450

Publications: *Annales*, *Bibliografia Missionaria*, *Euntes Docete*, *IUS Missionale*, *Urbaniana*

DEANS

Faculty of Canon Law: Rev. Prof. ANDREA D'AURIA
Faculty of Missiology: Rev. Prof. BENEDICT KANAKAPALLY
Faculty of Philosophy: Rev. Prof. GUIDO MAZZOTTA
Faculty of Theology: Rev. Prof. FRANCESCO CICCIMARRA

PROFESSORS

Faculty of Canon Law:
D'AURIA, A., General Norms
MOSCA, V., Matrimony and Canon Law
PAPALE, C., Oriental Canon Law
SABBARESE, L., Matrimony and Canon Law

Faculty of Missiology:
BARREDA, J., Ecumenism
COLZANI, G., Missionary Systematic Theology
DOTOLO, C., History and Phenomenology of Religions
MAZZOLINI, S., Ecclesiology
SCAIOLA, D., Scriptures
TREVISIOL, A., History of Missions

Faculty of Philosophy:
CONGIUNTI, L., Hermeneutics
MAZZOTTA, G., Metaphysics

NORECA, A., Logic, Philosophy of Knowledge
ONAH, I. G., Methodology, Anthropology
VENDEMIATI, A., General Ethics

Faculty of Theology:
BIGUZZI, G., New Testament Exegesis
CICCIMARRA, F., Canon Law
DEIANA, G., Biblical Languages and Scriptures
GONZALEZ FERNANDEZ, F., Church History
PIRC, J., Ecclesiology
RIZZI, G., Old Testament Exegesis
ZUCCARO, C., Moral Theology

UNIVERSITÀ PONTIFICIA SALESIANA
(Salesian Pontifical University)

Piazza Ateneo Salesiano 1, 00139 Rome, Italy

Telephone: (6) 872901
E-mail: segreteria@unisal.it
Internet: www.unisal.it

Founded 1940, univ. status granted by Pope Paul VI 1973
Private control
Language of instruction: Italian
Academic year: October to June (2 semesters)
Chancellor: Very Rev. ÁNGEL FERNÁNDEZ ARTIME
Rector: Very Rev. CARLO NANNI
Vice-Rector: Very Rev. GIANFRANCO COFFELE
Vice-Rector: Very Rev. MAURO MANTOVANI
Vice-Rector: Very Rev. VITO ORLANDO
Admin.: Very Rev. STANISLAW RAFALKO
Sec.-Gen.: Very Rev. JAROSŁAW ROCHOWIAK
Librarian: Very Rev. PAOLO ZUCCATO

Library of 750,000 vols
Number of teachers: 278
Number of students: 4,602

Publications: *Orientamenti Pedagogici* (6 a year), *Salesianum* (4 a year)

DEANS

Department of Youth, Pastoral Theology and Catechetics: Very Rev. UBALDO MONTISCI
Faculty of Canon Law: Very Rev. SABINO ARDITO
Faculty of Education: Very Rev. PAOLO GAMBINI
Faculty of Letters (Christian and Classics): Very Rev. MANLIO SODI
Faculty of Philosophy: Very Rev. LUIS ROSON GALACHE
Faculty of Social Communication Sciences: Very Rev. MAURO MANTOVANI
Faculty of Theology: Very Rev. DAMASIO MEDEIROS
Postgraduate School of Clinical Psychology: Prof. CARLA DE NITTO

PROFESSORS

Faculty of Canon Law (tel. (6) 87290639; e-mail diritto@unisal.it):
ARDITO, S., Text of Canon Law
GRAULICH, M., Foundation and History of Canon Law
PUDUMAI DOSS, M. J., Canon Law
URÍA, J., Text of Canon Law

Faculty of Education (tel. (6) 87290426; e-mail fse@unisal.it):
BAY, M., Methodology of Research
CANGIÀ, C., Pedagogy of Communication
CASELLA, F., History of Pedagogy
COLASANTI, A., Psychology
COMOGLIO, M., Didactics
CURSI, G., Sociology of Deviance
DE LUCA, M., Psychopathology
DE NITTO, C., Psychology
DE SOUZA, C., Anthropology and Catechesis
DELLAGIULIA, A., Developmental Psychology
DESBOUTS, C., Didactics
FORMELLA, Z., Psychology of Education

GAHUNGU, M., Pedagogic Methodology
GAMBINI, P., General Psychology
GRZADZIEL, D., General Pedagogy
LLANOS, M., Pedagogic Methodology
MASTROMARINO, R., Psychology
MESSANA, C., Psychology
MONTISCI, U., Theology of Education
MORAL DE LA PARTE, J., Religious Pedagogy
NANNI, C., Philosophy of Education
ORLANDO, V., Social Pedagogy
PASTORE, C., Bible and Catechesis
QUINZI, G., Pedagogical Methodology
ROGGIA, G., Pedagogical Methodology
SCHIETROMA, S., Psychology
TOGNACCI, S., Psychobiology and Physiological Psychology
VALLABARAJ, J., Catechesis
VETTORATO, G., Sociology of Deviance
WIERZBICKI, M., Religious Pedagogy
ZANNI, N., Didactics

Faculty of Letters (Christian and Classics) (tel. (6) 87290304; e-mail lettere@ups.urbe.it):
BOLOGNA, O., Ancient Greek Literature
BRACCHI, R., History of the Greek and Latin Languages
FILACCHIONE, P., Archaeology
SAJOVIC, M., Ancient Christian Latin Literature
SODI, M., Medieval Latin Literature
SPATARO, R., Ancient Christian Greek Literature

Faculty of Philosophy (tel. (6) 87290625; e-mail filosofia@unisal.it):
ABBÀ, G., Ethics
ALESSI, A., Metaphysics
FRENI, C., Linguistics and Rhetoric
KUREETHADAM, J., Philosophy of Science
KURUVACHIRA, J., Philosophical Anthropology
MANTOVANI, M., Metaphysics
MARIN, M., History of Ancient Philosophy
ROSON GALACHE, L., Philosophical Anthropology
THURUTHIYIL, S., History of Modern Philosophy

Faculty of Social Communication Sciences (tel. (6) 87290331; e-mail fsc@unisal.it; internet fscs.ups.urbe.it):
ALVATI, C., Theory and Technics of Media
CASSANELLI, E., Theory and Technics of Media
CEPEDA, E., Theory and Research of Social Communication
DEVADOSS, J., Theory of Social Communication
GONSALVES, P., Theory and History of Social Communication
LEVER, F., Theory and Technics of Television
LEWICKI, T., Theory and Technics of Theatre
PASQUALETTI, F., Theory and Technics of Radio
PRESERN, V., Theory and Research of Social Communication

Faculty of Theology (tel. (6) 87290297; e-mail teologia@unisal.it):
ANTHONY, F., Pastoral Theology
ARNAULD, D., History of the Church
BALDACCI, A., Liturgy
BESSO, C., Patrology
BIANCARDI, G., Catechesis
BOZZOLO, A., Dogmatics
CABANAS, V., Old Testament
CAPUTA, G., Fundamental Theology
CARELLI, R., Dogmatics
CARLOTTI, P., Moral Theology
CASTELLANO, A., Dogmatics
CHUNKAPURA, J., Missiology
COFFELE, G., Fundamental Theology
ESCUDERO CABELLO, A., Dogmatics
FERNANDO, R., Canon Law
FERNANDO, S., Moral Theology

FISSORE, M., Spiritual Theology
FRIGATO, S., Moral Theology
GARCÍA, J., Spiritual Theology
GIANAZZA, P., Dogmatics
GIRAUDO, A., Spiritual Theology
GRACH, P., Dogmatics
KRASON, F., Liturgy
MARCHIS, M., Canon Law
MARITANO, M., Ancient Church History and Patristics
MEDEIROS DE SANTOS, D., Liturgy
MERLO, P., Moral Theology
MULE STAGNO, A., Liturgy
MUSONI, A., Ecclesiology and Ecumenism
ONI, S., History of the Church
PALOMBELLA, M., Dogmatics
PLASCENCIA, J., Dogmatics
PULIANMACKAL, B., Moral Theology
ROSSETTI, M., New Testament
RUSSELL POLLOCK, W., Dogmatics
SARBINOWSKI, M., Fundamental Theology
VICENT, R., Old Testament
WYCKOFF, E., New Testament

SALESIAN HOUSE THEOLOGICAL STUDIES

Centre Saint-Augustin: Villa Contiguë au Village S.O.S., BP 15222, Dakar-Fann, Senegal; e-mail diraugus@orange.sn; Dean Very Rev. JOSEPH NDONG.

Département de Philosophie de l'Institut Catholique de l'Afrique Centrale: BP 11628, Yaoundé, Cameroon; Dean Rev. KIZITO FORBI.

Departamento de Filosofía del Instituto de Teología para Religiosos: 3A Avda con 6A Transversal (H. B. Pinto), Apdo 68865 Altamira, Caracas 1062-A, Venezuela; Dean Rev. CARLOS LUIS SUÁREZ CODORNIÚ.

Institut de Philosophie 'Saint-Joseph-Mukasa': Nkol-Bisson, BP 185, Yaoundé, Cameroon; Dean Rev. KRZYSZTOF ZIELENDA.

Institut de Theologie Saint François de Sales Lubumbashi: Democratic Republic of Congo; tel. (243) 970-176-94; e-mail theosdb_lubum@yahoo.com; Pres. Prof. JEAN-LUC VANDE KERKHOVE.

Institut 'Santo Tomás de Aquino': Rua Itutinga 300-B, Minas Brasil, 30535-640 Belo Horizonte, MG, Brazil; Dean Very Rev. PAULO ROBERTO GOMES.

Institut Superior de Ciencias Religioses 'Don Bosco': Avda Cardenal Vidal i Barraquer 15, 08035 Barcelona, Spain; tel. 934291803; internet www.marti-codolar.org; f. 1999; Catholic theology and religious sciences; library of 58,472 vols; 24 teachers; 114 students; Dean Very Rev. Dr JORDI LATORRE I CASTILLO; Chief Sec. and Librarian Rev. Dr JOAN JOSEP MORÉ I RAMIRO.

Instituto Superior de Estudios Teologicos 'Cristo Buen Pastor' (ISET): Hipólito Yrigoyen 3951, 1208 Buenos Aires, Argentina; Dir Very Rev. JUAN PICCA.

Instituto de Teología para Religiosos– ITER: 3A Avda con 6A Transversal (H. B. Pinto), Apdo 68865 Altamira, Caracas 1062-A, Venezuela; Dean Rev. CARLOS LUIS SUÁREZ CODORNIÚ.

Instituto Teológico Pio XI: Rua Pio XI, 1100–Alto da Lapa, 05060-001 São Paulo, Brazil; tel. (11) 364-902-00; e-mail secretaria@institutoteologico.org.br; Pres. Prof. RONALDO ZACHARIAS.

Instituto Teológico Salesiano 'Cristo Resucitado' Tlaquepaque: Apdo POB 66, 45500, San Pedro Tlaquepaque, Mexico; tel. (3) 657-45-55; e-mail teologia_its@yahoo.com .mx; Pres. SERGIO DE LA CRUZ LOERA.

Instituto Universitario Salesiano 'Padre Ojeda': Avda El Liceo, Apdo 43, Los Teques, 1201-A Venezuela; Dean Very Rev. JULIÁN RODRÍGUEZ V.

Philosophische-Theologische Hochschule der Salesianer: Don Bosco-Str. 1, 83671 Benediktbeuern, Germany; Rector Very Rev. LOTHAR BILY.

Salesian House for Theological Studies 'S. Tommaso d'Aquino', Messina: Via del Pozzo 43-CP 28, 98121 Messina, Italy; Dean Very Rev. GIOVANNI RUSSO.

Salesian House Philosophical Studies, Nave: Centro di Studi 'Paolo VI', Via S. Giovanni Bosco 1, 25075 Nave, Italy; Dean Very Rev. PAOLO ZINI.

Salesian House Philosophical Studies, Santiago: Avda Lo Cañas 3636, Casilla 53, La Florida, Santiago, Chile; Dean Very Rev. NILO DAMIÁN ZÁRATE LÓPEZ.

Salesian House Theological Studies, Bangalore: Kristu Jyoti College, Bosco Nagar, Krishnarajapuram, Bangalore 560036, India; Dean Very Rev. ANTON PAUL PADINJARATHALA.

Salesian House Theological Studies 'Don Bosco', Manila: POB 8206, CPO 1700, Parañaque City, Metro Manila, Philippines; Dean Very Rev. RAFAEL DELA CRUZ.

Salesian House Theological Studies, Guatemala: 20 Avda 13–45, Zona 11, Guatemala City, Guatemala 01011; Dean Very Rev. FÉLIX VALLEJOS.

Salesian House Theological Studies, Meghalaya: Sacred Heart Theological College, Mawlai, Shillong 793008, Meghalaya, India; Dean Very Rev. JOSEPH PUYKUNNEL.

Salesian Institute of Philosophy: Divya Daan, Don Bosco Marg, College Rd, Nasik 422005, India; Dean Very Rev. ROBERT PEN.

Studium Theologicum Salesianum, Faculty of Theology, Jerusalem: 26 Rehov Shmuel Hanagid St, POB 7336, 91072 Jerusalem, Israel; tel. (2) 6259171; e-mail president.ratisbonne@gmail.com; internet ratisbonnesdb.net; library of 40,000 vols; 15 teachers; 50 students; Prin. Rev. Dr BIJU MICHAEL.

Colleges

ATHENAEUM PONTIFICIUM REGINA APOSTOLORUM

Via degli Aldobrandeschi 190, 00163 Rome, Italy

Telephone: (6) 66527800
E-mail: segreteria@upra.org
Internet: www.upra.org

Founded 1993

Rector: Fr PAOLO SCARAFONI
Sec.-Gen.: Fr LUCA MARIA GALLIZIA

DEANS

Faculty of Bioethics: Fr GONZALO MIRANDA
Faculty of Philosophy: Fr MICHAEL RYAN
Faculty of Theology: Fr THOMAS WILLIAMS

PONTIFICIA FACOLTÀ DI SCIENZE DELL'EDUCAZIONE 'AUXILIUM'

Via Cremolino 141, 00166 Rome, Italy

Telephone: (6) 6157201
E-mail: segreteria@pfse-auxilium.org
Internet: www.pfse-auxilium.org

Founded 1954
Language of instruction: Italian
Academic year: October to July

Grand Chancellor: Prof. ANGEL FERNANDEZ ARTIME
Vice-Grand Chancellor: Prof. YVONNE REUNGOAT
Dean: Prof. GIUSEPPINA DEL CORE
Vice-Dean: Prof. ANTONELLA MENEGHETTI
Sec.-Gen.: Prof. M. GIOVANNA CERUTI

Librarian: Dr MARIA ANTONIETTA VALENTINO

Library of 130,000 vols, 1,000 periodicals of which 570 are currently active
Number of teachers: 59
Number of students: 550

Publication: *Rivista di Scienze dell'Educazione* (3 a year)

PROFESSORS

CAVAGLIÁ, P., Special Educational Methodology
CHANG, H., Teaching Methodology
DEL CORE, G., Developmental Psychology
DOSIO, M., Catechetical Methodology
FARINA, M., Fundamental Theology
KO, H., Scripture
LANFRANCHI, R., History of Education
LOPARCO, G., History of the Church
MAZZARELLO, M., Catechetical Methodology
MENEGHETTI, A., Fundamental Theology
RUFFINATTO, P., Methodology of Education
SEIDE, M., Theology of Education
SMERILLI, A., Political Economy
SPÓLNIK, M., Philosophy of Education
STEVANI, M., Dynamic Psychology
TORAZZA, B., Psychodiagnostics Methodology
TRICARICO, M., Visual Communication

PONTIFICIA FACOLTÀ TEOLOGICA SAN BONAVENTURA

Via del Serafico 1, 00142 Rome, Italy

Telephone: (6) 5192007
E-mail: segreteria@seraphicum.org
Internet: www.seraphicum.org

Founded 1587, re-founded 1905
Language of instruction: Italian
Academic year: October to June

Grand Chancellor: Most Rev. MARCO TASCA
Pres.: Rev. Fr DOMENICO PAOLETTI
Vice-Pres.: Rev. Fr DINH ANH NHUE NGUYEN
Sec.: Rev. Fr JUAN MIGUEL VICENTE
Librarian: Rev. Fr EMIL KUMKA

Library of 250,000 vols
Number of teachers: 51
Number of students: 289

Publication: *Miscellanea Francescana* (2 a year)

PONTIFICIA FACOLTÀ TEOLOGICA 'MARIANUM'

Viale Trenta Aprile 6, 00153 Rome, Italy

Telephone: (6) 58391601
E-mail: marianum@marianum.it
Internet: www.marianum.it

Founded 1950
Academic year: October to July

Grand Chancellor: Rev. Fr ÁNGEL M. RUIZ GARNICA
Pres.: Rev. Fr SALVATORE M. PERRELLA
Sec.: Sis. ORNELLA DI ANGELO

Library of 110,000 vols on Mariological studies
Number of teachers: 45
Number of students: 205

Publication: *Marianum* (2 a year)

PONTIFICIA FACOLTÀ TEOLOGICA TERESIANUM

Piazza San Pancrazio 5A, 00152 Rome, Italy

Telephone: (6) 58540248
E-mail: segreteria@teresianum.org
Internet: www.teresianum.org

Founded 1935
Academic year: October to June

Grand Chancellor: Most Rev. Fr LUIS AROSTEGUI GAMBOA
Pres.: Fr VIRGILIO PASQUETTO
Sec.-Gen.: Fr ADRIAN ATTARD
Librarian: Fr ARTURO BELTRAN

Library of 500,000 vols (open to the public)
Number of teachers: 51
Number of students: 450

Publications: *Bibliographia Internationalis Spiritualitatis, Studia Theologica, Teresianum* (2 a year).

ATTACHED INSTITUTE
Pontificio Istituto di Spiritualità: f. 1957; 30 teachers; 300 students; centre for bibliographical research in field of spiritual theology; Moderator Fr BENITO GOYA

PONTIFICIO ATENEO ANTONIA

Via Merulana 124, 00185 Rome, Italy
Telephone: (6) 70373502
E-mail: segreteriapaa@ofm.org
Internet: www.antonianum.ofm.org
Founded 1933
Franciscan Int. Univ.
Grand Chancellor: Most Rev. J. RODRÍGUEZ CARBALLO
Rector Magnificus: Rev. Fr JOHANNES B. FREYER
Vice-Rector: Rev. P. MANUEL BLANCO
Sec.-Gen.: Rev. Fr JORGE HORTA
Librarian: Rev. Fr MARCELLO SARDELLI
Library of 500,000 vols
Number of professors: 145
Publication: *Antonianum*

DEANS
Faculty of Biblical Science and Archaeology: Rev. Fr GIOVANNI C. BOTTINI
Faculty of Canon Law: Rev. Fr PRIAMO ETZI
Faculty of Philosophy: Rev. Fr STÉPHANE OPPES
Faculty of Theology: Rev. Fr VINCENZO BATTAGLIA

DIRECTORS
Higher Institute of Religious Studies: Sr M. MELONE
Higher School of Medieval and Franciscan Studies: Rev. Fr A. CACCIOTTI
Institute of Ecumenical Studies: Rev. Fr R. GIRALDO
Institute of Spirituality: Rev. Fr P. MARTINELLI

PONTIFICIO ATENEO ST ANSELMO

Piazza Cavalieri di Malta 5, 00153 Rome, Italy
Telephone: (6) 5791401
E-mail: segreteria@santanselmo.org
Internet: www.santanselmo.org
Founded 1687
Language of instruction: Italian
Academic year: October to June
Grand Chancellor: Most Rev. Fr NOTKER WOLF
Rector Magnificus: Rev. Fr MARK SHERIDAN
Registrar: Rev. Fr STEFANO VISINTIN
Librarian: Rev. Fr JAMES LEACHMAN
Treas.: Rev. Fr GERARDO GAREGNANI
Library of 131,000 vols
Number of teachers: 78
Number of students: 423

Publications: *Corpus Consuetudinum Monasticarum, Ecclesia Orans* (Liturgical Inst. Review), *Rerum Ecclesiasticarum Documenta* (Critical Editions of Liturgical Texts), *Studia Anselmiana*

DEANS
Faculty of Philosophy: Rev. Mons. ANICETO MOLINARO
Faculty of Theology: Rev. Fr DANIEL HOMBERGEN
Pontifical Liturgical Institute: Rev. Fr JUAN JAVIER FLORES ARCAS

PONTIFICIO ISTITUTO DI ARCHEOLOGIA CRISTIANA

Via Napoleone III 1, 00185 Rome, Italy
Telephone: (6) 4465574
E-mail: piac@piac.it
Internet: www.piac.it
Founded 1925 by Pope Pius XI
Academic year: November to May
Grand Chancellor: Bishop ZENON GROCHOLEWSKI
Rector: Prof. VINCENZO FIOCCHI NICOLAI
Sec.: Dr OLOF BRANDT
Librarian and Prefect of Collns: Dr GIORGIO NESTORI
Library of 60,000 vols
Number of teachers: 8
Number of students: 80

Publications: *Inscriptiones Christianae Urbis Romae, Monumenti di Antichità Cristiana, Rivista di Archeologia Cristiana, Roma Sotterranea Cristiana, Studi di Antichità Cristiana, Sussidi allo Studio delle Antichità Cristiane*

PROFESSORS
BISCONTI, F., Christian Iconography
DATTRINO, L., Patristics
FIOCCHI NICOLAI, V., Christian Cemeteries and Topography of Ancient Rome
GUIDOBALDI, F., Ancient Sacred Architecture
HEID, S., Hagiography and Liturgy of the Early Church
MAZZOLENI, D., Classical and Christian Epigraphy
PERGOLA, PH., 'Orbis Christianus' and Classical Topography
RAMIERI, A. M., Art History
SPERA, L., Christian Topography of Rome

PONTIFICIO ISTITUTO DI MUSICA SACRA

Via di Torre Rossa 21, 00165 Rome, Italy
Telephone: (6) 6638792
E-mail: pims@musica-sacra.va
Internet: www.vatican.va
Founded 1911 by Pope Pius X
Language of instruction: Italian
Academic year: October to June
Grand Chancellor: HE Rev. Mgr ZENON GROCHOLEWSKI
Pres.: Mgr VALENTINO MISERACHS GRAU
Sec.: Dott. GIUSEPPE MORETTI
Librarian: Dott. ANTONIO ADDAMIANO
Library of 40,000 vols
Number of teachers: 18
Number of students: 141
Publication: *Calendar* (1 a year)

PONTIFICIO ISTITUTO ORIENTALE
(Pontifical Oriental Institute)

Piazza Santa Maria Maggiore 7, 00185 Rome, Italy
Telephone: (6) 4474170
E-mail: segreteria@pontificio-orientale.it
Internet: www.unipio.org
Founded 1917 by Pope Benedict XV for the benefit of Eastern and Western scholars both Catholic and non-Catholic, interested in Oriental ecclesiastical questions
Associated with the Pontifical Gregorian University (see above)
Rector: Rev. Prof. JAMES M. MCCANN
Gen. Sec.: MAURIZIO DOMENICUCCI
Librarian: Rev. FRANÇOIS GICK
Library of 200,000 vols
Number of teachers: 77
Number of students: 380

Publications: *Anaphorae Orientales, Kanonika, Orientalia Christiana Analecta, Orientalia Christiana Periodica*

DEANS
Faculty of Oriental Canon Law: Rev. Prof. MICHAEL J. KUCHERA
Faculty of Oriental Ecclesiastical Studies: Rev. Prof. PHILIPPE LUISIER

PROFESSORS
CECCARELLI MOROLLI, D., Oriental Canon Law
ČEMUS, R., Oriental Spirituality
FARRUGIA, E., Dogmatic Theology and Oriental Patrology
GIRAUDO, C., Liturgy and Dogmatic Theology
KOKKARAVALAYIL, S., Oriental Canon Law
KUCHERA, M., Oriental Canon Law
KULIČ, J., Church History and Balkan History
LUISIER, P., Coptic Patrology and Language
MARANI, G., Oriental Theology
MCCANN, J., Slavic and Russian History
PAMPALONI, M., Oriental Patrology
RUGGIERI, V., Byzantine History and Archaeology
RUYSSEN, G., Oriental Canon Law
SENKO, E., Slavic and Russian History
SIMON, C., Slavic History
VASIL, C., Oriental Canon Law
YOUSSIF, P., Syriac Patrology
ZARZECZNY, R., Oriental Patrology

PONTIFICIO ISTITUTO DI STUDI ARABI E D'ISLAMISTICA

Viale di Trastevere 89, 00153 Rome, Italy
Telephone: (6) 58392611
E-mail: info@pisai.it
Founded 1949
Academic year: October to June
Dir: Fr MIGUEL ÁNGEL AYUSO GUIXOT
Librarian: Fr PIET HORSTEN
Library of 32,500 vols
Number of teachers: 10
Number of students: 52

Publications: *Encounter* (Documents for Christian-Muslim Understanding, 10 a year), *Etudes Arabes* (1 a year), *Islamochristiana* (1 a year)

PONTIFICIUM INSTITUTUM BIBLICUM

Via della Pilotta 25, 00187 Rome
Telephone: (6) 695261
E-mail: pibsegr@biblico.it
Internet: www.biblico.it
Founded 1909 by Pope Pius X for scriptural studies, Faculty of Ancient Oriental Studies added 1932, Pontifical Biblical Institute of Jerusalem (f. 1927), br. of Roman Institute
Languages of instruction: English, Italian
Academic year: October to June
Associated with the Pontifical Gregorian University (see above)
Rector: Rev. JOSÉ MARIA ABREGO DE LACY
Sec.: CARLO VALENTINO
Librarian: Rev. J. JANSSENS
Number of teachers: 40
Number of students: 300
Library of 165,000 vols

Publications: *Acta Pont. Inst. Biblici* (1 a year), *Analecta Biblica, Analecta Orientalia, Bible in Dialogue, Biblica* (4 a year), *Biblica et Orientalia, Elenchus of Biblica* (1 a year), *Orientalia* (4 a year), *Studia Pohl, Subsidia Biblica*

DEANS

Faculty of Ancient Oriental Studies: Rev. A. GIANTO

Faculty of Biblical Studies: Rev. P. DUBOVSKY

PROFESSORS

Faculty of Ancient Oriental Studies:

ALTHANN, R., Languages and Literature of Ancient Israel

GIANTO, A., Semitic Philology and Linguistics

MAYER, W., Accadian Language and Literature

MORRISON, C., Syriac and Targumic-Aramaic Languages

Faculty of Biblical Studies:

ALETTI, J.-N., New Testament Exegesis

BARBIERO, G., Old Testament Exegesis

BECHARD, D., New Testament Exegesis

BOVATI, P., Old Testament Exegesis

LUZARRAGA, J., New Testament Exegesis

NEUDECKER, R., Rabbinic Literature

PISANO, S., Textual Criticism

SIEVERS, J., History and Literature of the Intertestamental Period

SKA, J. L., Old Testament Exegesis

Schools

Scuola Vaticana di Biblioteconomia (Vatican School of Library Services): 00120 Vatican City; tel. (6) 69879526; e-mail scuola@vatlib.it; internet www-urbs.vatlib.it/scuola; f. 1934; attached to Vatican Apostolic Library; 6 teachers; 48 students a year; Dir Prof. Don RAFFAELE FARINA.

Scuola Vaticana di Paleografia, Diplomatica e Archivistica (Vatican School of Palaeography, Diplomacy and Archive Science): Cortile del Belvedere, 00120 Vatican City; tel. (6) 69883595; e-mail scuolavaticana@asv.va; internet www.scuolavaticanapaleografia.va; f. 1884; Dir SERGIO PAGANO; publ. *Littera Antiqua*.

VENEZUELA

The Higher Education System

Institutions of higher education pre-date Venezuela's independence from Spain in 1830, the oldest being Universidad Central de Venezuela, which was founded in 1721. The next oldest institution is Universidad de los Andes, which was founded in 1785 (current status 1810). One of the more recent universities is the Universidad Bolivariana de Venezuela, which was founded in 2003 by President Hugo Chávez as part of Misión Sucre, a government scholarship programme aimed at supporting free access to higher education as part of a socially inclusive system. The university has branches in nine regions and about 200 satellite classrooms throughout the country. Total enrolment at the institution was estimated at some 87,000 students in 2012.

The Ministry of University Education has supreme authority over higher education, which consisted in 2012 of six universidades nacionales autónomas (state autonomous universities—the country's oldest and most prestigious higher education institutions), 28 universidades nacionales experimentales (state experimental universities) and 29 universidades privadas (private universities). In addition, there were 81 university institutes (53 of which specialized in technology), 15 university colleges, two ecclesiastical and nine military university institutes, as well as 11 public and two private non-university institutes. A total of 13 new universities were created under the administration of Hugo Chávez, with nine established in 2010 alone. In that year, according to government statistics, there were 2,293,914 students enrolled in higher education. Enrolment rates in the sector were estimated at 83% of the relevant age group in 2012, which represented the second highest rate in Latin America (after Cuba), and the fifth highest in the world. Legislation approved in December 2010 that would have increased government control over several key areas of the public and private university systems was rescinded in January 2011 following widespread popular criticism over the perceived challenge to universities' autonomy and the proposed concentration of power in the Ministry of Education.

The main requirement for admission to higher education is the Bachillerato, the secondary school certificate. In addition, the Oficina de Planificación del Sector Universitario (OPSU), a national agency within the Ministry of Education, sets an aptitude test in verbal reasoning and numeracy, the Prueba de Aptitud Académica. The resultant Indice Académico de Ingreso (Academic Admissions Index) gives a score, derived 60% from the Bachillerato and 40% from the test, which is used for university admission. There are two levels of undergraduate qualifications: carreras cortas (short-cycle degrees) and carreras largas (long-cycle degrees). The former last between two and three years and lead to award of the Título de Técnico Superior Universitario (Title of Higher University Technician). Long-cycle degrees typically last five years, although a few programmes, including medicine, last upwards of six years, and lead to award of the Licenciatura or a professional title. Following this, graduates may study for a further year for the Título de Especialista, which indicates specialization in a particular area or subject. Alternatively, graduates may study for the Maestría (Masters degree), a two-year course of study including the submission of a thesis. Finally, the highest university degree is the Doctorado (Doctorate), a research-based degree usually lasting three years following the award of either the Maestría or Especialización.

The Instituto Nacional de Cooperación Educativa, an autonomous agency under the Ministry of Education, is the national agency responsible for the provision of technical and vocational education. Post-secondary technical and vocational education is offered by a range of higher education institutions (see above), although the qualifications they offer are regarded as sub-degree level. The main qualification is the Técnico Superior, a three-year course comprising mostly practical study.

There is currently no external agency that accredits undergraduate programmes, although the Consejo Nacional de Universidades (National Council of Universities) maintains a register of authorized degree programmes. All postgraduate programmes are subject to accreditation by the Consejo Consultivo Nacional de Postgrado (National Graduate Advisory Council), an independent accreditation body established by the Ministry of Education.

Regulatory and Representative Bodies

GOVERNMENT

Ministry of Popular Power for Culture: Avda Panteón Foro Libertador, Edif. Archivo General de la Nación, Caracas; tel. (212) 509-5681; e-mail mppc@mincultura.gob.ve; internet www.mincultura.gob.ve; Minister FIDEL BARBARITO.

Ministry of Popular Power for Education: Esq. de Salas a Caja de Agua, Edif. Sede del MPPE, Parroquia Altagracia, Caracas 1010; tel. (212) 596-4111; e-mail atencionsocial@me.gob.ve; internet www.me.gob.ve; Minister MARYANN HANSON FLORES.

Ministry of Popular Power for Science, Technology and Innovation: Avda Universidad, Esq. El Chorro, Torre Ministerial, La Hoyada, Caracas; tel. (212) 555-7401; e-mail mcti@mcti.gob.ve; internet www.mcti.gob.ve; Minister MANUEL FERNÁNDEZ MELÉNDEZ.

Ministry of Popular Power for University Education: 1–7 Pisos, Avda Universidad, esq. el Chorro, Caracas 1010; tel. (212) 596-5177; e-mail webmaster@mppeu.gob.ve; internet www.mppeu.gob.ve; Minister PEDRO CALZADILLA.

NATIONAL BODIES

Asociación Venezolana de Rectores Universitarios (AVERU) (Venezuelan Association of University Rectors): Avda Santa Fe Sur, Edif. 'Araucaria', 4°–43°, Urb. Santa Fe, Caracas; tel. (212) 975-1462; e-mail averu.venezuela@gmail.com; Pres. CECILIA GARCÍA AROCHA.

Consejo Nacional de Universidades (National Council of Universities): Avda La Salle, Centro Capriles Planta Baja, Caracas; tel. (212) 709-1200; e-mail webmaster@cnu.gov.ve; internet www.opsu.gob.ve/?ir=cnu; f. 1946; coordinates academic relations within the higher education system and fosters links between univs and the rest of the nat. educational system; establishes and develops academic, cultural and scientific policies in the higher education sector; suggests regulations on the recognition of studies and qualifications to the Nat. Exec.; proposes annual univ. budget and distributes funding to nat. univs; library of 2,000 vols; Pres. PÉDRO CALZADILLA; Permanent Sec. ASALIA VENEGAS SIMANCAS; publ. Boletín Informativo (4 a year).

Learned Societies

GENERAL

Academia Venezolana de la Lengua (Venezuelan Academy of Language): Apdo 1421, Caracas; Palacio de las Academias, Bolsa a San Francisco, Caracas 1010; tel. (212) 481-2890; e-mail acadlengv@cantv.net; internet www.avelengua.org.ve; f. 1883; corresp. of the Real Academia Española (Madrid, Spain); 139 mems (50 foreign corresp., 10 hon., 29 individual and 50 nat. corresp. mems); library: see under Libraries and Archives; Pres. FRANCISCO JAVIER PÉREZ; Sec. HORACIO BIORD CASTILLO; publ. Clásicos Venezolanos.

ARCHITECTURE AND TOWN PLANNING

Colegio de Arquitectos de Venezuela (College of Architects of Venezuela): Avda Río de Oro con calle Girasol, Edif. Stagio, primer Piso, Urb. Prados del Este, Caracas; tel. (212) 977-5672; internet cav.org.ve; f.

1945 as Sociedad Venezolana de Arquitectos; represents architecture professionals at public and private instns; 3,600 mems; Pres. MARIANELLA GENATIOS; Sec.-Gen. CAROLINA HERNANDEZ; publ. *Revista CAV* (2 a year).

BIBLIOGRAPHY, LIBRARY SCIENCE AND MUSEOLOGY

Colegio de Bibliotecólogos y Archivólogos de Venezuela (Venezuelan Librarians' and Archivists' Association): Avda Urdaneta, Esq. de Urapal, Centro Urapal 16–04 16°, Caracas 1011; tel. (212) 572-7871; e-mail cbiarchiv@hotmail.com; f. 1987; 440 mems; Pres. Lic. ELSI JIMENEZ DE DÍAZ; Vice-Pres. Lic. FLOR MARINA LUNA; publs *AB Te Informa* (4 a year), *CBActualidad* (irregular).

ECONOMICS, LAW AND POLITICS

Academia de Ciencias Políticas y Sociales (Academy of Political and Social Sciences): Palacio de las Academias, Avda Universidad, Bolsa a San Francisco, Caracas 1010; tel. (212) 482-8845; e-mail acienpol@cantv.net; internet www.acienpol.org.ve; f. 1915; 35 mems; Pres. Dr LUÍS COVA ARRIA; Sec. Dr HUMBERTO ROMERO-MUCI.

Colegio de Abogados del Distrito Capital (Lawyers' Association of Capital District): Apdo Postal 1060, Caracas; Avda Veracruz, Edif. Keope, 1°, Of. 15-B, Las Mercedes, Caracas; tel. (212) 991-9845; e-mail secretaria@justicia.net; internet www.justicia.net; f. 1788; 2,000 mems; Pres. Abog. RAFAEL VELOZ GARCIA; Sec. Abog. ROSAURA SÁNCHEZ.

EDUCATION

Grupo Universitario Latinoamericano de Estudio para la Reforma y el Perfeccionamiento de la Educación (GULERPE) (Latin American University Group for Reform and Improvement in Education): Residencias Araucaria, Apdo 43, Santa Fe Sur, Caracas 1080-150; 4°, Avda Santa Fe Sur, Santa Fe, Caracas 1080-150; tel. (212) 979-9263; e-mail eliza_caldera@hotmail.com; internet www.escotet.org/gulerpe/index.htm; f. 1965; discusses measures for improvement of Latin American post-secondary educational instns; 150 mems; Pres. Dra ELIZABETH Y. DE CALDERA; Exec. Sec. Prof. FELIPE BEZARA FACURE; publ. *Universitas 2000* (4 a year).

FINE AND PERFORMING ARTS

Asociación Venezolana Amigos del Arte Colonial (AVAAC) (Venezuelan Association of Friends of Colonial Art): Museo de Arte Colonial, Quinta de 'Anauco', Avda Panteón, San Bernardino, Caracas 1011; tel. (212) 551-8517; e-mail artecolonialanauco@cantv.net; internet www.quintadeanauco.org.ve/avaac.htm; f. 1942; collects and preserves arts and crafts from the Spanish period; Pres. JUAN CARLOS SOSA AZPÚRUA; Sec. GONZALO RODRÍGUEZ MATOS; publ. *Revista*.

HISTORY, GEOGRAPHY AND ARCHAEOLOGY

Academia de Historia del Táchira (Academy of History of Táchira): Casa Bolivariana, Calle 4 entre carreras 3 y 4, San Cristóbal, Estado Táchira; f. 1942; Pres. Dr LUIS GILBERTO SANTANDER RAMÍREZ; Sec. Dr INÉS CECILIA FERRERO KELLERHOFF.

Academia de Historia del Zulia (Academy of History of Zulia): Calle 95 Esq. con Avda 5, Sector Plaza Bolívar, al lado del Palacio de Gobierno del Zulia, Maracaibo, Estado Zulia; tel. (261) 725-1194; e-mail academiadehistoriadelzulia@gmail.com; f.

1940; 25 mems; Pres. ALFREDO RINCÓN RINCÓN; Sec. ANTONIO MÁRQUEZ MORALES.

Academia Nacional de la Historia (National Academy of History): Palacio de las Academias, Bolsa a San Francisco, Caracas 1010; tel. (212) 482-6720; e-mail anhistoria@cantv.net; internet www.acadnachistoria.org; f. 1888; library: see under Libraries and Archives; Dir RAFAEL FERNÁNDEZ HERES; Sec. MARIANELA PONCE; publ. *Memorias*.

Centro de Historia Larense (Larense Historical Centre): Carrera 17 frente a la Plaza Lara, Barquisimeto, Estado Lara; f. 1941; 12 mems; library of 1,000 vols; Pres. CARLOS EDUARDO LÓPEZ; publ. *Boletín*.

Junta Nacional Protectora y Conservadora del Patrimonio Histórico y Artístico de la Nación (Commission for the Protection and Preservation of the Historical and Artistic Heritage of the Nation): Palacio de Miraflores, Avda Urdaneta, Caracas; 1 subsidiary office in each state; authorizes exploration and excavation of sites.

Sociedad Bolivariana de Venezuela (Bolivarian Society of Venezuela): San Jacinto a Traposos, Urb. Catedral, Caracas; tel. (212) 545-7271; internet www.sociedadbolivariana.org; f. 1842 as Gran Sociedad de Caracas, current name adopted 1938; promotes knowledge of Simón Bolívar's life, works and ideas; publishes about 15,000 vols of historical works per year; 300 mems; library of 6,000 vols; Pres. Gen. CORONEL ARTURO CASTILLO; publ. *Revista*.

LANGUAGE AND LITERATURE

Alliance Française: Avda Mohedano entre 1A y 2A Transversal, Quinta Wilmarú, Urb. La Castellana, Caracas; tel. (212) 264-4611; e-mail info@afvenezuela.org; internet www.afvenezuela.org; offers courses and exams in French language and culture and promotes cultural exchange with France; 9 teaching centres in Barinas, Barquisimeto, Caracas, Maracaibo, Maracay, Mérida, Nueva Esparta, Puerto La Cruz and Valencia; Del. Gen. ALAIN VILLECHALANE.

British Council: Torre Credicard, 3°, Avda Principal de El Bosque, Chacaíto, Caracas 1050; tel. (212) 952-9965; e-mail information@britishcouncil.org.ve; internet www.britishcouncil.org/es/venezuela; teaching centre; offers courses and exams in English language and British culture and promotes cultural exchange with the UK.

Goethe-Institut: Torre AltAvila, Planta Baja, Avda Luis Roche entre 3 y 4 Transversal, Urb. Altamira Apdo 60508, Caracas 1060-A; tel. (212) 814-3030; e-mail info@caracas.goethe.org; internet www.goethe.de/venezuela; offers courses and exams in German language and culture and promotes cultural exchange with Germany; library of 4,000 vols; Dir Dr ULRICH GMÜNDER.

MEDICINE

Academia de Medicina del Zulia (Academy of Medicine of Zulia): Apdo 4005, Maracaibo 4001, Estado Zulia; tel. (414) 613-1780; e-mail academia_de_medicina_del_zulia@hotmail.com; f. 1967; 150 mems; library of 950 vols; Pres. Dr GILBERTO OLIVARES; Sec. Dr JOSÉ A. COLINA-CHOURIO; publ. *Revista*.

Academia Nacional de Medicina (National Academy of Medicine): Bolsa a San Francisco, Apdo 804, Caracas 1010; tel. (212) 421-8683; internet www.anm.org.ve; f. 1904; represents nation's physicians; 134 mems (37 individual, 50 nat. corresp., 21 foreign corresp. and 26 guest mems); library:

see under Libraries and Archives; Pres. Dr RAFAEL MUCI-MENDOZA; Sec. Dr LEOPOLDO BRICEÑO-IRAGORRY; publ. *Gaceta Médica de Caracas* (4 a year).

Colegio de Farmacéuticos del Distrito Federal y Estado Miranda (Pharmaceutical College of Federal District and Miranda State): Urb. Las Mercedes, Caracas 1060; deals with all aspects of the pharmaceutical industry; 1,200 mems; library of 600 vols; Pres. Dr PEDRO RODRÍGUEZ MURILLO; Sec. Dra ESTHER VALERA DE PÉREZ B.; publ. *Revista 'Colfar'*.

Colegio de Médicos del Distrito Metropolitano de Caracas (Medical College of the Metropolitan District of Caracas): Avda Principal de Santa Fe, Torre Colegio de Médicos No 5, Caracas; tel. (212) 979-9846; e-mail info@cmdmc.com.ve; internet www.cmdmc.com.ve; f. 1942; 32,800 mems; Pres. Dr FERNANDO JOSE BIANCO COLMENARES; Sec. Gen. Dra TAHIRI MARIÑEZ; publ. *El Colega*.

Colegio de Médicos del Estado Miranda (Doctors' Association of Miranda State): Avda El Golf, Quinta La Setentiseis, Urb. El Bosque, Caracas 1041; tel. (212) 731-2024; f. 1944; 3,100 mems; Pres. Dr HERNÁN VÁSQUEZ RIGUAL; Gen. Sec. Dr RUBEN HERNÁNDEZ SERRANO; publ. *Cuadernos Medicos*.

Sociedad de Obstetricia y Ginecología de Venezuela (Society of Obstetrics and Gynaecology): Maternidad Concepción Palacios, Avda San Martín, Apdo 20081, Caracas 1020; tel. (212) 461-6442; e-mail sogvzla01@gmail.com; internet www.sogvzla.org; f. 1940; 3,000 mems; library of 5,900 vols, incl. 74 books on obstetrics and gynaecology, 132 research spec. works, 210 titles and 4,914 magazines; Pres. Dr RODRIGO ALFONSO ARIAS; Sec. Dra LUISA OBREGÓN YÁNEZ; publ. *Revista de Obstetricia y Ginecología de Venezuela* (4 a year).

Sociedad Venezolana de Anestesiología (Venezuelan Society of Anaesthesiologists): Final Avda Guaicaipuro, Edif. Edicentro, 4°, Of. 4-B, diagonal a la entrada principal del Centro Médico de Caracas, Urb. San Bernardino, Caracas; tel. (212) 552-8780; e-mail svanestesiologia@cantv.net; internet www.sva.org.ve; f. 1954; 1,260 mems; Pres. Dr NERIO BRACHO UZCATEGUI; Sec. JOSE VERA PEREIRA.

Sociedad Venezolana de Cardiología (Venezuelan Society of Cardiology): Of. B-1, 2°, Torre Colegio de Médicos, Avda José María Vargas, Urb. Santa Fe Norte, Caracas 1080; tel. (212) 263-5787; e-mail editorweb@svcardiologia.org; internet www.svcardiologia.org; f. 1954; 879 mems; Pres. GABRIEL D'EMPAIRE YANEZ; Sec. Gen. JOSE MIGUEL TORRES VIERA; publs *Revista Venezolana de Cardiología*, *Revista de Salud Cardiovascular*.

Sociedad Venezolana de Cirugía (Venezuelan Society of Surgery): Avda Sucre, Los Dos Caminos, Edif. Centro, Parque Boyacá, Torre Centro, 17°, Of. 173, Caracas; tel. (212) 286-8106; e-mail cirugia.secretario@gmail.com; internet www.sociedadvenezolanadecirugia.org; f. 1944; Pres. Dr JESÚS VELÁZQUEZ GUITIÉRREZ; Sec.-Gen. Dr JESÚS TATÁ AMOLDONI.

Sociedad Venezolana de Cirugía Ortopédica y Traumatología (Venezuelan Society of Orthopaedics and Traumatological Surgery): Avda La Estancia, Centro Ciudad Comercial Tamanaco (CCCT), Torre Pirámide Invertida, 2°, Of. 226, Urb. Chuao, Caracas; tel. (212) 959-3572; e-mail svcot@svcot.org.ve; internet www.svcot.org.ve; f. 1949; 2,654 mems; Pres. Dr ALBERTO JOSÉ SERRANO FERMÍN; Sec. Dra RITA MORENO GALÍNDEZ; publ. *Revista Venezolana de Ciru-*

gía Ortopédica y Traumatología (2 a year, in Spanish).

Sociedad Venezolana de Dermatología y Cirugía Dermatología (Venezuelan Society of Dermatology and Dermatological Surgery): Avda Francisco de Miranda, Edif. Menegrande, 6°, Of. 6–4, Urb. Los Palos Grandes, Caracas 1080; tel. (212) 285-5284; e-mail info@svderma.org; internet www .svderma.org/ve; f. 1946; Pres. Dr NAHIR HELENA LOYO ZAMBRANO; Gen. Sec. Dr JORGE LUIS VERA TOLEDO; publ. *Dermatología Venezolana* (2 a year).

Sociedad Venezolana de Gastroenterología (Venezuelan Society of Gastroenterology): Paseo Enrique Eraso, Torre La Noria, 5°, Of. 5-B3, Urb. Las Mercedes, Caracas 1061; tel. (212) 991-2660; e-mail sovegastro1945@gmail.com; internet www .sovegastro.org; f. 1945; promotes study of endoscopy, gastroenterology, hepatology, imagery, paediatric gastroenterology and neuro-gastroenterology; 606 mems; Pres. Dr LEONARDO SOSA VALENCIA; Sec. Dr GUILLERMO VEITIA; publ. *GEN* (4 a year, print and online, www.revistagen.org/index.php).

Sociedad Venezolana de Hematología (Venezuelan Society of Haematology): Avda Primera Transversal, C.C. Plaza, Nivel Torre C, Of. 14E, Urb. Los Palos Grandes, Caracas 1080; tel. (212) 286-4118; e-mail informacion@svh-web.org.ve; internet www .svh-web.org.ve; f. 1959; library of 527 vols, 14 periodicals; Pres. Dra CLEMENTINA LANDOLFI; Sec. Dr JAIME BRACHO.

Sociedad Venezolana de Historia de la Medicina (Venezuelan Society of the History of Medicine): Avda Universidad, Palacio de las Academias, Bolsa a San Francisco, Caracas 1010; tel. (212) 483-4361; e-mail info@svhm.org.ve; internet www.svhm.org .ve; f. 1944; promotes study and research of medicine; 75 mems; Pres. Dr FRANCISCO PLAZA RIVAS; Sec. for Corresp. Dr ANDRÉS SOYANO; publ. *Revista de la Sociedad Venezolana de Historia de la Medicina* (2 a year, print and online, revista.svhm.org.ve).

Sociedad Venezolana de Medicina Interna (Venezuelan Society of Internal Medicine): Avda Francisco de Miranda, Edif. Mene Grande, 6°, Of. 6–4, Los Palos Grandes, Caracas 1010; tel. (212) 285-0237; e-mail socvmi@cantv.net; internet www .web.ve; f. 1956; Pres. Dra MARÍA INÉS MARULANDA; Gen. Sec. Dra VIRGINIA SALAZAR; publ. *Medicina Interna* (3 a year).

Sociedad Venezolana de Oftalmología (Venezuelan Society of Ophthalmology): Avda Principal de Los Ruices, Centro Empresarial Los Ruices 5°, Of. 507, Caracas; tel. (212) 239-8127; internet www.svo.org.ve; e-mail jlrincon@iumo.com; f. 1953; encourages creation of eye institutes; 600 mems; Pres. Dra MORAYMA ACEVEDO S; Sec.-Gen. Dr JOSÉ LUIS RINCÓN; publ. *Revista Oftalmológica Venezolana* (4 a year).

Sociedad Venezolana de Otorrinolaringología (Venezuelan Society of Otorhinolaryngology): Avda Principal de Santa Fe (Avda José María Vargas), Edif. Colegio de Médicos del Distrito Capital, 2°, Of. 10, Santa Fe Norte, Caracas; tel. (212) 978-3311; internet www.svorl.org.ve; e-mail svorl@hotmail.com; Pres. Dra NORA HERNANDEZ; Sec. Dra SAJIDXA MARIÑO; publ. *Acta Otorrinolaringologica* (1 a year).

Sociedad Venezolana de Psiquiatría (Venezuelan Society of Psychiatry): Colegio de Médicos del Estado Miranda, Ubz. El Bosque, Avda El Golf, Quinta 76, Caracas 1010; tel. (212) 731-2024; e-mail amobilli@gmail.com; internet www.svp.org.ve; f. 1942; 600 mems; library of 1,650 vols; Pres. Dra YOLANDA ALVARADO P.; Sec.-Gen. Dr ADELE

MOBILLI R.; publ. *Archivos Venezolanos de Psiquiatría y Neurología* (2 a year).

Sociedad Venezolana de Puericultura y Pediatría (Society of Childcare and Paediatrics): Apdo 3122, Caracas 1010A; Urb. La Castellana, Avda San Felipe, entre 2da Transversal y Calle José Angel Lamas, Centro Coinasa, Mezzanina 6, Caracas; tel. (212) 263-7378; e-mail svpediatria@gmail .com; internet www.svpediatria.org; f. 1939; Pres. Dra ARMANDO ARIAS GÓMEZ; Exec. Sec. Dr MAGDALENA SÁNCHEZ AGUILAR; publ. *Archivos Venezolanos de Puericultura y Pediatría* (4 a year).

Sociedad Venezolana de Radiología y Diagnóstico por Imágenes (Society of Radiology and Diagnostic Imaging): Urb. Campo Claro, Transversal F entre Principal La Carlota y Avda 4 Quinta Costiera, Caracas; tel. (212) 830-9887; e-mail soveradi .ofc@gmail.com; internet www.soveradi.org .ve; 104 mems; Pres. Dr ESTEBAN BRICEÑO VOIRIN; Sec.-Gen. Dr RAFAEL PEROZO RIVAS; Treas. Dr JOSE BRICEÑO POLACRE.

NATURAL SCIENCES

General

Academia de Ciencias Físicas, Matemáticas y Naturales (Academy of Physical, Mathematical and Natural Sciences): Bolsa a San Francisco, Avda Universidad, Apdo 1421, Caracas 1010; tel. (212) 482-2954; e-mail info@acfiman.org.ve; internet www .acfiman.org.ve; f. 1917; 80 mems (30 ordinary, 20 Venezuelan corresp., 30 foreign corresp.); Pres. CLAUDIO BIFANO; Sec. JOSÉ M. CARRILLO.

Asociación Venezolana para el Avance de la Ciencia (ASOVAC) (Venezuelan Association for the Advancement of Science): Edif. Fundavac–AsoVAC, Avda Neverí, Colinas de Bello Monte, Caracas; tel. (212) 753-5802; e-mail asovac.caracas@gmail.com; internet www.asovac.org; f. 1950; 3,000 mems; Pres. MARISOL AGUILERA MENESES; Sec.-Gen. YAJAIRA FREITES; publ. *Acta Científica Venezolana* (6 a year).

Fundación La Salle de Ciencias Naturales (La Salle Foundation of Natural Sciences): Edif. Fundación La Salle, Avda Boyacá, (Cota Mil) con Maripérez, Caracas 1010; tel. (212) 709-5803; internet www .fundacionlasalle.org.ve; f. 1957; agronomy, anthropology, aquaculture, limnology, mining and forestry, oceanography; runs stations for marine, agricultural and hydrobiological research; 6 educational and research institutes; 1,300 mems; library: see under Libraries and Archives; Pres. FRANCER ALBERTO GOENAGA; publs *Antropológica* (4 a year), *Memoria* (2 a year), *Natura* (4 a year).

Biological Sciences

Sociedad de Ciencias Naturales 'La Salle' ('La Salle' Society of Natural Sciences): Edif. Fundación La Salle, Avda Boyacá, Apdo 1930, Caracas 1010; tel. (212) 709-5803; f. 1940; comprises 3 depts: botany, publs, zoology; the museum contains more than 100,000 exhibits; 589 mems (17 hon., 42 nat. and 30 foreign corresps, 500 associates); Dir Lic. FERNANDO MORALES; Pres. Dr LUIS RIVAS L.; Sec. Dr CARLOS ACEVEDO; publs *Memoria* (2 a year), *Natura* (4 a year).

Sociedad Venezolana de Ciencias Naturales (Venezuelan Society of Natural Sciences): Ubicación Avda Sanz, Edif. Sociedad Venezolana de Ciencias Naturales, El Marqués, Caracas 1071; tel. (212) 271-7653; e-mail info@svcn.com.ve; internet www.svcn .org.ve; f. 1929; annual exhibitions, lectures, films on nature conservation; dept of speleology for study of caves; biological station; dept for education on environmental protec-

tion; depts for the study of tropical orchids, bromeliads and astronomy; environmental pollution studies; 1,100 mems; library of 32,000 vols of scientific publs; Pres. MARIO GABALDON LÓPEZ; Gen. Sec. Dr RICARDO MUÑOZ TÉBAR; publ. *Boletín de la SVCN*.

Physical Sciences

Sociedad Venezolana de Geólogos (Venezuelan Geological Society): Apdo 17493, Parque Central, Caracas 1015; Avda A, Quinta Mercedes 13-10, Urb., La Carlota, Caracas; tel. (212) 234-4085; e-mail svg@mailser.reacciun.ve; internet www.socvengeo .org; f. 1955; 1,050 mems; Pres. DANIEL LOUREIRO; Sec. FRANCISCO BARRIOS; publs *Boletín* (3 a year), *Geologia de Venezuela*.

TECHNOLOGY

Asociación Venezolana de Ingeniería Sanitaria y Ambiental (Venezuelan Association of Sanitary and Environmental Engineering): El Trigal Centro, Calle Pocaterra 88–20, Quinta los Corales, Valencia 2002, Estado Carabobo; tel. (241) 842-1435; e-mail avisa@eldish.net; Pres. Ing. RAFAEL DAUTANT.

Colegio de Ingenieros de Venezuela (Engineers' Association of Venezuela): Avda Principal de Quebrada Honda, Los Caobos, Caracas 1050; tel. (212) 575-3532; internet www.civ.net.ve; f. 1861; 7,000 mems; library of 4,000 vols; Pres. DARÍO BRILLEMBOURG; Sec. JULIO URBINA; publ. *Boletín* (12 a year).

Sociedad Venezolana de Geotecnia (Venezuelan Society of Geotechnics): Avda Principal de Quebrada Honda, Los Caobos, Caracas 1050; e-mail civ.svdg@gmail.com; internet www.svdg.org.ve; f. 1958 as Sociedad Venezolana de Mecánica del Suelo e Ingeniería de Fundaciones, current name adopted 1992; Pres. Ing. GUSTAVO IRIBARREN RENDÓN; Sec. Ing. MARÍA EUGENIA CHACÍN.

Sociedad Venezolana de Ingeniería Hidráulica (Venezuelan Society of Hydraulic Engineering): c/o Colegio de Ingenieros de Venezuela, Los Caobos, Caracas; tel. (414) 868-2570; internet www .svihvenezuela.org.ve; f. 1960; Pres. ARTURO MARCANO.

Sociedad Venezolana de Ingenieros Agrónomos (Venezuelan Society of Agricultural Engineers): c/o Colegio de Ingenieros de Venezuela, Avda Principal de Quebrada Honda, Los Caobos, Caracas 1050; tel. (212) 576-7738; f. 1944; Pres. Ing. Agr. HUMBERTO FONTANA.

Sociedad Venezolana de Ingenieros Civiles (Venezuelan Society of Civil Engineers): c/o Colegio de Ingenieros de Venezuela, Avda Principal de Quebrada Honda, Los Caobos, Caracas 1050; tel. (212) 368-6077; e-mail sovinciv@sovinciv.com; internet www .sovinciv.com; f. 1995; Pres. MANUEL FERNANDO MEJÍAS.

Sociedad Venezolana de Ingenieros de Petróleo (Venezuelan Society of Petroleum Engineers): Calle Negrín con calle Las Flores, Torre Negrín, 5°, Of. 5A, Sabana Grande, Caracas 1050; tel. (212) 761-4497; e-mail soveip@cantv.net; internet www.svip .org; f. 1958; promotes exploration of oil resources; Pres. LINFOLFO LEÓN; Sec. AMINTA CARRASQUEL.

Sociedad Venezolana de Ingenieros Forestales (Venezuelan Society of Forestry Engineers): Edif. B, 1°, Sede del Convenio ULA SVIF, Seccional Mérida, Mérida 5101; tel. (274) 240-1509; e-mail svif@ula.ve; internet www.forest.ula.ve/svif; f. 1958; 1,122 mems; library of 8,000 vols; Pres. GERMAN DUQUE; Sec. RAFAEL RODRÍGUEZ; publ. *Revista Forestal* (4 a year).

Sociedad Venezolana de Ingenieros Químicos (Venezuelan Society of Chemical Engineers): c/o Colegio de Ingenieros de Venezuela; Avda Principal de Quebrada Honda, Los Caobos, Caracas 1050; f. 1958; 1,000 mems; Exec. Dir YOLANDA DE OSORIO; publ. *Boletín* (4 a year).

Research Institutes

GENERAL

Instituto Venezolano de Investigaciones Científicas (IVIC) (Venezuelan Scientific Research Institute): Carretera Panamericana, km 11, Altos de Pipe, Caracas 1020, Estado Miranda; tel. (212) 504-1111; e-mail oac@ivic.ve; internet www.ivic.gob.ve; f. 1959; library: see under Libraries and Archives; Dir Dr ELOY SIRA.

AGRICULTURE, FISHERIES AND VETERINARY SCIENCE

Estación Experimental Táchira (Experimental Station of Táchira): Bramón, Rubio 6070, Estado Táchira; tel. (76) 66783; f. 1953; agricultural research; library of 1,100 vols; Dir JOSÉ ROSARIO MANRIQUE.

Instituto de Investigaciones Veterinarias (Veterinary Research Institute): Apdo 70, Maracay, Estado Aragua; Avda Las Delicias, Maracay, Estado Aragua; tel. (243) 414-365; f. 1940; small specialized library; 55 mems; Dir Dr CLAUDIO FUENMAYOR F.

Instituto Nacional de Investigaciones Agrícolas de Venezuela (National Institute for Agricultural Research of Venezuela): Via El Limon, Maracay, Estado Aragua; e-mail prensainia@gmail.com; internet www.inia.gov.ve; f. 1961 as Fondo Nacional de Investigaciones Agropecuarias, current name adopted 2000; centres and experimental stations: Amazonas, Anzoátegui, Apure, Barinas, CENIAP, Delta Amacuro, Falcón, Guárico, Lara, Mérida, Miranda, Monagas, Portuguesa, Sucre, Táchira, Trujillo, Yaracuy, Zulia; Dir TATIANA PUGH; publs *Agronomía Tropical* (1 a year, print and online, sian.inia.gob.ve/repositorio/revistas_ci/Agronomia%20Tropical/atindex.htm), *Caña de Azúcar* (2 a year, print and online, sian.inia.gob.ve/repositorio/revistas_ci/canadeazucar/ca_index.htm), *Veterinaria Tropical* (2 a year, print and online, sian.inia.gob.ve/repositorio/revistas_ci/VeterinariaTropical/vt_index.htm), *Zootecnia Tropical* (4 a year, print and online, sian.inia.gob.ve/repositorio/revistas_ci/ZootecniaTropical/info.htm).

Instituto Nacional de Tierras (National Land Institute): Calle San Carlos, Urb. Vista Alegre, Quinta La Barranca, Caracas; tel. (212) 471-0222; internet www.inti.gob.ve; f. 1949; performs agrarian reform activities; Chair. WILLIAM GUDINO; publ. *Memoria y Cuenta*.

ARCHITECTURE AND TOWN PLANNING

Dirección General de Ordenación del Territorio Urbanístico del Ministerio del Poder Popular para Vivienda y Habitat (Directorate General of Urban Development of the Ministry for Housing and Habitat): Avda Francisco de Miranda, Torre Minfra, 10°, Chacao, Caracas; f. 1946; 350 mems; library of 20,000 vols; Dir MARIBEL CHELLINI AROCHA.

ECONOMICS, LAW AND POLITICS

Centro de Estudios del Desarrollo—Universidad Central de Venezuela (Centre for Development Studies—Central University of Venezuela): Avda Neverí, Edif. Fundavac, Colinas de Bello Monte, POB 47604, Caracas 1040; tel. (212) 753-3475; e-mail contacto@cendes-ucv.edu.ve; internet www.ucv.ve; f. 1961; centre for research and graduate studies on problems relating to economic, social, educational, regional, political, ecological, environmental and scientific-technological devt of Venezuela and Latin America; library of 12,000 vols, 35,100 documents, 900 periodicals and 600 theses; Dir Dr CARLOS WALTER; publs *Cuadernos del CENDES* (3 a year), *Revista Cuadernos del CENDES* (3 a year).

Instituto Iberoamericano de Derecho Agrario, Reforma Agraria y Cooperativismo (IIDARA) (Iberoamerican Institute of Agricultural Law, Land Reform and Cooperatives): Facultad de Ciencias Jurídicas y Políticas, Universidad de los Andes, Mérida, Estado Mérida; tel. (274) 240-2065; e-mail iidara@ula.ve; internet www.saber.ula.ve/handle/123456789/14269; f. 1973; 12 mem. countries; training and research in agrarian law, agricultural economics, rural sociology; postgraduate courses; library of 4,000 vols; Pres. Dr ALBERTO GARCÍA MÜLLER; publ. *Revista de Derecho Agrario y Reforma Agraria*.

Oficina Central de Estadística e Informática (Central Office of Statistics and Informatics): Apdo 4593, Caracas 1010; tel. (212) 782-1133; e-mail ocei@platino.gov.ve; internet www.ocei.gov.ve; f. 1978; Dir Dr GUSTAVO MÉNDEZ; publs *Anuario del Comercio Exterior de Venezuela*, *Anuario Estadístico de Venezuela*.

HISTORY, GEOGRAPHY AND ARCHAEOLOGY

Instituto de Geografía y Conservación de Recursos Naturales (Institute of Geography and Conservation of Natural Resources): Vía Chorros de Milla, Mérida 5101; tel. (274) 240-1604; e-mail intgeogr@ula.ve; internet www.forest.ula.ve/geografiayconservacion; f. 1959; attached to Universidad de Los Andes; research in theoretical geography, applied geography and geographical techniques; committees for research and teaching technical coordination; documentation and information; library of 20,200 vols and 44,500 periodicals; Dir Prof. JUAN CARLOS RIVERO; publs *Cuadernos Geográficos* (irregular), *Revista Geográfica Venezolana* (2 a year).

MEDICINE

Instituto de Medicina Experimental (Institute of Experimental Medicine): Apdo 50587, Sabana Grande, Ciudad Universitaria, Caracas 1051; tel. (212) 693-1862; internet www.med.ucv.ve/escuelas_institutos/ime/index.html; f. 1940; attached to Universidad Central de Venezuela; research in biochemistry, general and applied pathology, neurology, pharmacology, physiology; library of 30,200 vols, 4,100 periodicals; Dir Prof. MARCELO ALFONZO; Librarian Lic. TRINA YANES DE RAMÍREZ.

Instituto Nacional de Nutrición (National Institute of Nutrition): Avda Baralt, Esq. El Carmen, Edif. INN, Quinta Crespo, Municipio Libertador, Caracas; tel. (212) 483-3378; e-mail inn.prensa@gmail.com; internet www.inn.gob.ve; f. 1949; library of 10,000 vols; Dir Dr MARILYN DI LUCA; publ. *Archivos Latinoamericanos de Nutrición*.

NATURAL SCIENCES

General

Estación de Investigaciones Marinas (EDIMAR) (Marine Research Station): Apdo 144, Punta de Piedras, Isla de Margarita, Porlamar, Estado Nueva Esparta; tel. (295) 239-8051; e-mail marllano@edimar.org; internet www.edimar.org; f. 1958; affiliated to Fundación La Salle de Ciencias Naturales (see under Learned Societies); aquaculture, fisheries, marine biology, marine geology, marine food processing, oceanography; library of 18,000 vols, 1,200 periodicals; Dir CARMEN GUTIERREZ; publ. *Memoria de la Sociedad La Salle de Ciencias Naturales*.

Biological Sciences

Estación Biológica de los Llanos (Biological Station of Los Llanos): Calabozo, Estado Guárico; f. 1960; library of 3,200 vols; Dirs F. TAMAYO, R. A. HOSTOS, L. ARISTEGUIETA.

Fundación Instituto Botánico de Venezuela 'Dr Tobías Lasser' (Botanical Foundation Institute of Venezuela 'Dr Tobias Lasser'): Apdo 2156, Jardín Botánico de Caracas, Avda Salvador Allende, Caracas 1010; tel. (212) 605-3989; e-mail unidad.educacion.fibv@gmail.com; internet www.ucv.ve; f. 1991; library of 14,000 vols, 1,300 periodicals; Pres. Dr ANÍBAL CASTILLO SUÁREZ; publs *Acta Botanica Venezuelica* (2 a year), *Flora de Venezuela*.

Physical Sciences

Dirección de Geología del Ministerio del Poder Popular de Petróleo y Minería (Department of Geology of the Ministry for Popular Power of Petroleum and Mining): Torre Oeste, 4°, Parque Central, Caracas 1010; f. 1936; conducts nat. geological surveys; research in geotechnics, marine geology and mineralogy; library of 120,000 vols; Dir SIMÓN E. RODRIGUEZ; publs *Boletín de Geología* (2 a year), *Boletín Informativo del Centro de Análisis de Información Geológica-Minera (CAIGEOMIN)* (2 a year), *Cuadernos Geológicos* (3 a year), research bulletins, statistics and other data.

Observatorio Naval Cagigal (Cagigal Naval Observatory): Apdo 6745, La Planicie, 23 Enero, Caracas; tel. (212) 481-2266; e-mail dhn@truevision.net; f. 1888; astronomy, hydrography, meteorology, oceanography, planetarium; Dir GREGORIO PÉREZ MORENO; publs *Almanaque Astronómico Venezolano*, *Boletín Avisos a los Navegantes*, *Boletín Climatológico Anual*, *Boletín Meteorologico* (1 a year).

RELIGION, SOCIOLOGY AND ANTHROPOLOGY

Instituto Caribe de Antropología y Sociología (Caribbean Institute of Anthropology and Sociology): Avda Boyacá (Cota Mil) con Maripérez, al lado de la Estación del Teleférico 'Avila Mágica', Caracas; tel. (212) 709-5861; e-mail pedro.rivas@fundacionlasalle.org.ve; internet www.fundacionlasalle.org.ve; f. 1961; anthropological research and devt programmes among Indian populations of Venezuela; dept of the Fundación La Salle de Ciencias Naturales (see under Learned Societies); library of 40,000 vols; Pres. FRANCER ALBERTO GOENAGA; Dir PEDRO RIVAS; publ. *Antropológica* (2 a year).

TECHNOLOGY

INTEVEP—Centro de Investigación y Apoyo Tecnológico (INTEVEP—Centre for Research and Technology Support): Apdo 76343, Caracas 1070A; Urb. Santa Rosa, Sector El Tambor, Los Teques, Caracas 1070A; tel. (212) 330-6011; internet www.pdvsa.com; f. 1974; attached to Petróleos de Venezuela, SA (PDVSA); research and devt br. of Petróleos de Venezuela, concerned with hydrocarbons and petrochemicals; connected to int. online systems; library of 1,600 vols of periodicals, information centre of 30,000 publs; Pres. FRANCISCO PRADAS; publ. *Visión Tecnológica* (2 a year).

Libraries and Archives

Barquisimeto

Biblioteca Pública 'Pio Tamayo' (Public Library 'Pio Tamayo'): Calle 26, entre Carreras 20 y 21, Barquisimeto, Estado Lara; f. 1911; 21,943 vols; Librarian GERMÁN HURTADO REYES.

Caracas

Archivo General de la Nación (General Archives of the Nation): Avda Panteón, Foro Libertador, Edif. Archivo General de la Nación, Caracas 1010; tel. (212) 509-5879; e-mail mppc@ministeriodelacultura.gob.ve; internet www.agn.gob.ve; f. 1910; sections: La Colonia (1498–1810), La Revolución (1810–21), La Gran Colombia (1821–30), La República (1830 to present day); comprises Seminario de Investigación Archivística; courses on palaeography; Dir CARMEN ALIDA SOTO; publs *Biblioteca Venezolana de Historia* (2 a year), *Boletín* (2 a year).

Biblioteca Ayacucho (Ayacucho Library): Centro Financiero Latino, 12°, Of. 1, 2 y 3, Avda Urdaneta, Ánimas a Plaza España, Caracas 1010; tel. (212) 561-6691; e-mail atencionalciudadano@bibliotecayacucho.gob.ve; internet www.bibliotecayacucho.gob.ve; f. 1974; spec. collns: Clásica, Claves Políticas de América, Expresión Americana, Prólogos; Pres. HUMBERTO MATA.

Biblioteca Central de la Universidad Católica 'Andrés Bello' (Central Library of the Catholic University 'Andrés Bello'): Edif. de Biblioteca, 1°, Urb. Montalbán, La Vega, Caracas; tel. (212) 407-4172; e-mail nimartin@ucab.edu.ve; internet www.ucab.edu.ve/inicio.947.html; f. 1953; 343,883 vols; Librarian RAFAEL ÁNGEL RIVAS DUGARTE; publ. *Montalbán*.

Biblioteca Central de la Universidad Central de Venezuela (Central Library of the Central University of Venezuela): Apdo 1050, Caracas; Edif. Biblioteca Central, Ciudad Universitaria, Los Chaguaramos, Caracas; tel. (212) 605-4190; e-mail bibcentral@sicht.ucv.ve; internet www.sicht.ucv.ve:8080/bc; f. 1850; sections on social science, humanities, pure science and technology; official publs; reference section; 280,000 vols, 3,500 periodicals; Dir MARIANELA HERMOSO.

Biblioteca Central del Ministerio del Poder Popular para Relaciones Exteriores (Central Library of the Ministry of Popular Power for Foreign Affairs): Esq. de Conde a Principal, Casa Amarilla, Planta Baja, Patio Central, Caracas; tel. (212) 806-4887; e-mail dgab.divisionbiblioteca@mre.gob.ve; internet www.mre.gov.ve; f. 1906; specializes in int. law; attached archive with documents of the Min. of Foreign Affairs from 1747–1994; 7,450 titles; Librarian Lic. TERESA I. PINTO GONZÁLEZ.

Biblioteca Central del Ministerio del Trabajo y Seguridad Social (Central Library of the Ministry of Labour and Social Security): Centro Simón Bolívar, Edif. Sur, 5°, Caracas; f. 1988; 3,200 vols; Librarian MARCELA GARCÍA JORDAN.

Biblioteca de la Academia Nacional de la Historia (Library of the National Academy of History): Palacio de las Academias, Avda Universidad, Bolsa a San Francisco, Caracas; tel. (212) 482-3849; e-mail webmaster@anhvenezuela.org; internet www.anhvenezuela.org/biblioteca.php; f. 1888; 120,000 vols, spec. collns incl. books, pamphlets and reference works from the 19th and 20th centuries: Carlos Felice Cardot, Gerardo Santiago Suarez, Hector Parra Marquez, Jose Antonio Calcaño; Dir ILDEFONSO LEAL; Vice-Dir. of Library and Archives MARIANELA PONCE, SR; publ. *Boletín de la Academia Nacional de la Historia*.

Biblioteca de la Academia Nacional de Medicina (Library of the National Academy of Medicine): Apdo 1121-A, Caracas; Palacio de las Academias, Avda Universidad, Bolsa a San Francisco, Caracas; tel. (212) 481-8939; e-mail bibliotanm@yahoo.es; internet www.msinfo.info/default/anm; f. 1893; 4,000 vols, spec. collns incl. nat. and int. periodicals, theses, incorporation papers, old publs: Revista Clínica de los Niños Pobres, La Gaceta Medica; Librarian and Archivist Dr GUILLERMO COLMENARES ARREAZA; publ. *Gaceta Médica de Caracas*.

Biblioteca de la Academia Venezolana de la Lengua (Library of the Venezuelan Academy of Language): Apdo 1421, Caracas; Palacio de las Academias, Bolsa a San Francisco, Caracas 1010-A; e-mail acadlengv@cantv.net; internet avelengua.org.ve/la-academia/biblioteca; f. 1883; 25,000 vols, spec. collns: Venezuelan classics, dictionaries, Ayacucho collection, 'El Coyo Ilustrado'; Librarian RAFAEL ÁNGEL RIVAS DUGARTE.

Biblioteca del Ministerio de Relaciones Interiores, Justicia y Paz (Library of the Ministry of the Interior, Justice and Peace): Esq. de Carmelitas, 2°, Caracas; e-mail bibliodoc@mir.es; 3,585 vols; Librarian Dr RUIZ LANDER.

Biblioteca Virtual en Salud Venezuela (Virtual Health Library in Venezuela): Parque Central, Torre Oeste 30°–41°, Caracas; e-mail redbvsvenezuela@gmail.com; internet www.bvs.org.ve; f. 2004; attached to Min. of Popular Power for Health; 9,400 vols; Librarian ESPERANZA REYES BAENA; publs *Memorias del MSAS*, *Revista Venezolana de Sanidad y Asistencia Social*.

Biblioteca del Tribunal Supremo de Justicia (Library of the Supreme Tribunal of Justice): Edif. del Tribunal Supremo de Justicia, Mezanina, final de la Avda Baralt, esq. dos pilitas, Caracas; tel. (212) 801-9051; e-mail biblioteca@tsj.gov.ve; internet www.tsj.gov.ve/index.shtml; f. 1942; literature on legal matters; online access to Supreme Court decisions; 4,500 vols; Dir Br FERNANDO ARAUJO M.

Biblioteca 'Dr Manuel Antonio Sánchez Carvajal' ('Dr Manuel Antonio Sánchez Carvajal' Library): Apdo 20081, Caracas 1020; Edif. de la Sociedad de Obstetricia y Ginecología de Venezuela, Maternidad Concepción Palacios, Avda San Martín, Caracas 1020; tel. (212) 451-0895; e-mail sogvzla.biblioteca@gmail.com; internet sogv.msinfo.info; f. 1940; attached to Sociedad de Obstetricia y Ginecología de Venezuela; 8,500 vols, 4,914 magazines series publs 'Oscar Aguero', 74 old books on obstetrics and gynaecology, 113 periodicals, 132 research special works (TEI), 210 titles, also MSS and medical history colln; Librarian Dr FREDDY GONZÁLEZ.

Biblioteca Ernesto Peltzer del Banco Central de Venezuela (Ernesto Peltzer Library of Central Bank of Venezuela): Apdo 2017, Caracas 1010; Esq. de Mijares, Plaza Juan Pedro López, Mezzanina 2, Altagracia, Caracas 1010; tel. (212) 801-8617; e-mail biblio@bcv.org.ve; internet www.bcv.org.ve/biblioteca/biblioep.htm; f. 1940; provides material for study, research and training in economics and finance; 100,000 vols, 862 periodicals and 1,767 books from the 16th–19th centuries; Dir SILVIO CASTELLANOS.

Biblioteca Juan Pablo Pérez Alfonzo (Juan Pablo Pérez Alfonzo Library): Avda Lecuna, Parque Central, Torre Oeste, 2°, Caracas; tel. (212) 507-5206; e-mail carolineb30b@cantv.net; internet www.menpet.gob.ve; f. 1950; attached to Ministry of Popular Power for Energy and Oil; specializes in gas, geology, mines, petroleum, petrochemicals, refinement; 28,000 vols, 11,000 monographs and 370 videos; Librarian Lic. SILVIA PERNIA C.; publs *Boletín de Geología*, *Carta Semanal*, *Compendia Estadística del Sector Eléctrico*, *Memoria y Cuenta del Ministerio de Energía y Minas*, *Petróleo y otros Datos Estadísticos*.

Biblioteca Luís Beltrán Prieto Figueroa (Luís Beltrán Prieto Figueroa Library): Monjas a San Francisco, Palacio Federal Legislativo, El Silencio, Caracas; internet www.bibliotecalbpf.an.gob.ve; f. 1915; 9,000 vols; Librarian Lic. LUÍS PÉREZ PESCADOR.

Biblioteca Nacional de Venezuela (National Library of Venezuela): Distrito Capital, Parroquia Altagracia, Final Avda Panteón, Municipio Libertador, Caracas 1010; tel. (212) 505-9120; e-mail desarrollo.colecciones@bnv.gob.ve; internet www.bnv.gob.ve; f. 1833; consists of 727 library services organized in 24 public authority networks of which 4 are autonomous libraries; 6.5m. books, newspapers, MSS and audiovisual items, 2.5m. records on database; spec. collns: Antigua Documentary, Febres Cordero, Hemerographic; Exec. Dir LUIS EDGAR PÁEZ PÉREZ; publ. *Revista Bibliotecas Públicas* (4 a year).

Biblioteca Pública Mariano Picón Salas (Public Library Mariano Picón Salas): Avda Andrés Bello, cruce con Avda Principal de Maripérez, Parque Arístides Rojas, Maripérez, Caracas; tel. (212) 781-4378; f. 1965; 23,700 vols; Dir Lic. ROMULO NAVEA SOTO.

Centro de Documentación y Archivo/Fundación La Salle de Ciencias Naturales (Documentation and Archive Centre, 'La Salle' Foundation for Natural Sciences): Apdo 1930, Caracas 1050; Avda Boyacá, Cota Mil, Edif. Fundación La Salle, Caracas 1010; tel. (212) 709-5818; e-mail mireya.viloria@fundacionlasalle.org.ve; internet www.fundacionlasalle.org.ve/cont; f. 1942; 410,000 vols; spec. collns: botany, cultural anthropology, local languages, natural resources contamination, zoology, Venezuelan Indians; Librarian MIREYA VILORIA DE INSAUSTI.

Cumaná

Biblioteca General de la Universidad de Oriente (General Library of University of the East): Avda Universidad, Cerro Colorado, Cumaná 6101, Estado Sucre; tel. (293) 400-8158; e-mail bashiru@udo.edu.ve; internet bibliotecadigital.udo.edu.ve; f. 1958; 500,000 vols; Librarian Lic. ROSA GONZÁLEZ DE LÓPEZ; publs *Boletin del Instituto Oceanografico* (2 a year), *Saber* (2 a year).

Maracaibo

Biblioteca Central 'General Rafael Urdaneta' (Central Library 'General Rafael Urdaneta'): Apdo Postal 526, Maracaibo 4001-A, Estado Zulia; tel. (261) 759-6700; e-mail bibcentral.serbi@luz.edu.ve; internet www1.serbi.luz.edu.ve; f. 1946; attached to Universidad del Zulia; 19,000 vols; Librarian ANA JUDITH PAREDES.

Biblioteca Pública María Calcaño (María Calcaño Public Library): Avda 2 (El Milagro), Maracaibo, Estado Zulia; tel. (261) 793-7333; e-mail prensabibliotecadelzulia@gmail.com;

internet www.bibliotecapublicadelzulia.org
.ve; f. 1873 as Biblioteca Zuliana; adopted
current name 1995; administered by the
Instituto Zuliano de la Cultura (q.v.); Dir
FERNANDO GUERRERO MATHEUS.

Maracay

**Biblioteca Central del Centro Nacional
de Investigaciones Agropecuarias**
(Library of the National Agricultural
Research Centre): Avda Casanova Godoy,
Zona Universitaria, Maracay 2103, Estado
Aragua; tel. (243) 245-2491; internet sian
.inia.gob.ve/index.php; f. 1937; 200,000 vols,
116 monographic titles; Library Asst NANCY
GARCÉS DE HERNÁNDEZ.

Mérida

**Servicios Bibliotecarios Universidad de
los Andes** (Los Andes University Library
Services): Avda Tulio Febres Cordero, Edif.
Administrativo de la Universidad de los
Andes, 5°, Mérida 5101, Estado Mérida; tel.
(274) 240-2731; e-mail bdigital@ula.ve;
internet www.serbi.ula.ve/serbiula; f. 1889;
reference books for all subjects taught in the
univ.; small colln of 16th- and 17th-century
books; 250,000 vols, 7,800 periodical titles;
Dir of Digital Library NILDA FABIOLA
ROSALES.

Valencia

**Biblioteca Central de la Universidad de
Carabobo** (Central Library of the University of Carabobo): Urb. Prebo, Avda Andrés
Eloy Blanco c/o 137-20, Edif. Centro Escor-
pio, 2° y 3°, Valencia 2001, Estado Carabobo;
tel. (241) 822-2606; e-mail bc@uc.edu.ve;
internet www.bc.uc.edu.ve; f. 2008; manages
academic information system, publishes
newsletters, organizes seminars and work-
shops, spec. collns incl. archives of Albert
Einstein, Francisco de Miranda, Libertador,
Royal Historical Society; musical collns incl.
Chamber Orchestra, Latin American Popular
Music Group, Voices Claras UC, Witches and
Ragwort, etc.; 11,000 vols; Dir-Gen. Prof.
THAIRY BRICEÑO; Librarian JOSÉ GOMÉZ.

Museums and Art Galleries

Barinas

Museo de los Llanos (Museum of the
Plains): Avda 23 de Enero, al lado del Parque
La Federación, Barinas, Estado Barinas; tel.
(426) 474-4113; e-mail
relacionesinstitucionalesfmn@gmail.com;
internet www.fmn.gob.ve/fmn_losllanos.htm;
f. 2011; attached to Fundación Museos
Nacionales; crafts, painting, photography
and sculpture of the Plains region; Dir
LEONARDO RUIZ.

Calabozo

Museo de la Ciudad de Calabozo
(Museum of the City of Calabozo): Calle 5
entre carreras 9 y 10, frente a la Plaza Páez,
Calabozo, Estado Guárico; tel. (246) 415-
9699; e-mail museodelaciudadcalabozo@
yahoo.com; internet www.fmn.gob.ve/
fmn_calabozo.htm; f. 2004; attached to Fundación Museo Nacionales; architecture,
crafts, and visual arts of the city.

Caracas

**Casa Natal del Libertador Simón
Bolívar** (Simón Bolívar's Birthplace): San
Jacinto a Traposos, Caracas; tel. (212) 541-
2563; murals by Tito Salas depicting the life
of Bolívar and events of the Independence
Movement; Curator JOSEFINA DE SANDOVAL.

Centro de Arte La Estancia (La Estancia
Art Centre): Avda Francisco de Miranda,
Urb. La Floresta, Altamira, Caracas; tel.
(212) 208-6274; e-mail laestancia@pdvsa
.com; internet www.pdvsa.com; f. 1988;
attached to Petróleos de Venezuela S. A.;
traditional and modern arts in natural space;
Man. Dir Dr BEATRICE SANSÓ DE RAMÍREZ.

Colección Ornitológica Phelps (Phelps
Ornithological Collection): Blvd Sabana
Grande, Edif. Gran Sabana, 3°, Apdo 2009,
Caracas, 1050; tel. (212) 761-5631; internet
www.fundacionwhphelps.org; f. 1938; spec.
colln of 1,399 species collected from 933
locations in Venezuela; library of 10,000
vols, incl. 3,000 books, 170 journal titles
and 6,000 reprints; Pres. JOHN P. PHELPS
TOVAR; Curator MARGARITA MARTINEZ.

Galería de Arte Nacional (National Art
Gallery): Plaza de los Museos, Los Caobos,
Apdo 6729, Caracas 1010; tel. (212) 576-8707;
e-mail eventosgan1@gmail.com; internet
www.fmn.gob.ve/fmn_gan.htm; f. 1974;
attached to Fundación Museos Nacionales;
Venezuelan visual art from pre-Hispanic
times to the present; library of 13,000 vols,
6,050 records, 260,000 news articles, 212
titles, 96,000 photographs, 816 audio cassettes and 380 videos; Pres. CLEMENTINA
VAAMONDE B.; Exec. Dir RAFAEL SANTANA.

Museo Alejandro Otero (Alejandro Otero
Museum): Complejo Cultural La Rinconada,
Caracas; tel. (212) 682-0941; e-mail
prensa_mao@cantv.net; internet www.fmn
.gob.ve/fmn_mao.htm; f. 1990; attached to
Fundación Museos Nacionales; preserves
modern art, particularly of Alejandro Otero;
Dir MORELLA JURADO.

Museo Arturo Michelena (Arturo Michelena Museum): Esq. de Urapal, No 82, La
Pastora, Caracas; tel. (212) 860-4802; e-mail
prensafmn.mam@gmail.com; internet www
.fmn.gob.ve/fmn_mam.htm; f. 1963; attached
to Fundación Museos Nacionales; consists of
works by Arturo Michelena; drawings,
watercolours, smoked dishes, palettes; Dir
ROSIRIS TORO.

Museo Bolivariano (Bolívar Museum):
Esq. San Jacinto a Traposos, Urb. San
Jacinto, Caracas; tel. (212) 545-9828; f.
1911; contains 1,546 exhibits; mementos,
portraits, personal relics and historical
paintings of Simón Bolívar and his fellow-
workers in the Independence Movement;
library of 1,200 vols; Dir ANITA TAPIAS.

Museo de Arte Colonial (Museum of Colonial Art): Quinta de Anauco, Avda Panteón,
San Bernardino, Caracas 1011; tel. (212) 551-
8650; e-mail artecolonialanauco@cantv.net;
internet www.quintadeanauco.org.ve; f.
1942; painting, sculpture, decorative arts;
library; under the supervision of the Asociación Venezolana de Amigos del Arte Colonial
(q.v.); Pres. JUAN CARLOS SOSA AZPÚRUA;
Admin. Dir CARLOS F. DUARTE G.

**Museo de Arte Contemporáneo de Car-
acas Sofía Imber** (Sofía Imber Museum of
Contemporary Art in Caracas): Zona Cultural, Parque Central, Apdo 17093, Caracas
1010; tel. (212) 573-8289; e-mail educación
.delmac@gmail.com; internet www.fmn.gob
.ve/fmn_mac.htm; f. 1973; attached to Fundación Museos Nacionales; incl. works by
Picasso, Braque, Chagall, Bacon, Matisse,
Kandinsky and Miró; Dir RITA SALVESTRINI.

Museo de Bellas Artes de Caracas
(Museum of Fine Arts in Caracas): Plaza de
los Morelos, Parque los Caobos, Caracas; tel.
(212) 578-0653; e-mail educacionmba@gmail
.com; internet www.fmn.gob.ve/fmn_mba
.htm; f. 1917; attached to Fundación Museos
Nacionales; paintings and sculptures by nat.
and foreign artists; library of 12,500 vols,

10,000 exhibition catalogues and 200 titles;
Dir MARÍA ELENA RAMOS.

Museo de Ciencias Naturales (Museum of
Natural Sciences): Avda Mexico, Plaza de los
Museos, Parque Los Caobos, Apdo Postal
5883, Caracas 1010; tel. (212) 577-5094;
e-mail prensafmn1@gmail.com; internet
www.fmn.gob.ve/fmn_mc.htm; f. 1875 as
Museo Nacional; attached to Fundación
Museos Nacionales; spec. colln of 1m. pieces
and samples of anthropology, archaeology,
entomology, ethnology, geology, palaeontology, zoology; library of 2,100 vols; Pres.
Ing. SERGIO ANTILLANO ARMAS.

**Museo de la Estampa y el Diseño Carlos
Cruz-Diez** (Museum of Prints and Carlos
Cruz-Diez Design): Avda Bolívar, Calle Sur
11 con Calle 8, Parque Vargas, Caracas; tel.
(212) 571-2401; e-mail educacionmccd@gmail
.com; internet www.museocruzdiez.com; f.
1989; attached to Fundación Museos Nacionales; displays work of nat. and int. designers and graphic artists.

Museo del Oeste 'Jacobo Borges'
(Museum of the West 'Jacobo Borges'): Avda
Sucre Parque del Oeste 'Alí Primera', Catia,
Caracas; tel. (212) 862-0427; e-mail
prensafmn1@gmail.com; internet www.fmn
.gob.ve/fmn_mujabo.htm; f. 1995; attached to
Fundación Museos Nacionales; drawings,
graphic arts, installations, mosaics, painting,
photography, sculptures and visual arts by
Venezuelan artists; Dir ADRIANA MENESES.

Museo del Teclado (Keyboard Museum):
Parque Central, Edif. Tacagua, Caracas; tel.
(212) 577-4611; internet www.fundarte.gob
.ve/museo-del-teclado/; f. 1972; musical
instruments, esp. piano; Dir ALMA MANJAR-
REZ.

**Museo Nacional de Arquitectura (MUS-
RAQ)** (National Museum of Architecture):
Avda Bolívar, Sur 9 y Este 8, Paseo Vargas,
Caracas; tel. (212) 573-6009; e-mail
museodearquitectura@gmail.com; internet
www.fmn.gob.ve/fmn_musarq.htm; f. 2006;
attached to Fundación Museos Nacionales;
displays architectural styles during the colonial, contemporary, modern and republican
periods; Dir JUAN PEDRO POSANI.

Museo Nacional de Arte Popular
(National Museum of Popular Art): Sede
Museo de Arte Contemporáneo, Parque Central, Sótano 2, Caracas; tel. (212) 576-1745;
e-mail museonacionaldeartepopular@gmail
.com; internet www.fmn.gob.ve/fmn_popular
.htm; attached to Fundación Museos Nacionales; contains objects and documents
related to Venezuelan soc. and culture.

Museo Nacional de la Fotografía
(National Museum of Photography): Sede
del Museo Alejandro Otero, Complejo Cultural La Rinconada, Caracas; tel. (212) 682-
0941; e-mail relacionesinstitucionalesfmn@
gmail.com; internet www.fmn.gob.ve/
fmn_munafoto.htm; f. 2010; attached to
Fundación Museos Nacionales; documents,
photographic collns provided by various cultural instns, museums and personalities.

Ciudad Bolívar

Museo 'Talavera' (Talavera Museum):
Quinta San Isidro, Ciudad Bolívar 8001,
Estado Bolívar; f. 1940; pre-Columbian and
colonial period exhibits, religious art, natural
science, numismatics; Dir Dr J. GABRIEL
MACHADO; publ. Museo Talavera.

Coro

Museo de Arte Coro (Coro Art Museum):
Balcón Bolívar, paseo Talavera con Calle
Hernández, Coro, Estado Falcón; tel. (268)
652-5152; e-mail museodeartecoro@gmail
.com; internet www.fmn.gob.ve/fmn_coro
.htm; f. 1988; attached to Fundación Museos

Nacionales; paintings, sculptures and ceramics by Venezuelan artists; Dir ARMANDO GALLIARDI.

Maracaibo

Museo Histórico 'General Rafael Urdaneta' (Historical Museum 'General Rafael Urdaneta'): Calle 91A No. 7A-70, Sector Veritas, Maracaibo, Estado Zulia; tel. (261) 721-3414; f. 1936; collns of art, arms, sculpture, numismatic and philatelic items, photographs; Dir LIGIA BERBESI.

Trujillo

Museo 'Cristóbal Mendoza' (Museum 'Cristóbal Mendoza'): Trujillo, Estado Trujillo; f. 1930; nat. and regional historic objects, pre-Hispanic pieces, picture gallery of Trujillo in colonial times.

Universities

UNIVERSIDAD 'ALEJANDRO DE HUMBOLDT'
(University 'Alejandro de Humboldt')

Avda Rómulo Gallegos, Con 1ra. Transversal de Montecristo, Edif. Universidad Alejandro de Humboldt, Caracas

Telephone: (212) 239-1026
E-mail: info@unihumboldt.edu.ve
Internet: www.unihumboldt.edu.ve
Founded 1997
Private control
Language of instruction: Spanish
Campuses in Caracas (Dos Caminos, Andres Bello, Plaza Venezuela and El Bosque) and Valencia

UNIVERSIDAD 'ALONSO DE OJEDA'
(University 'Alonso de Ojeda')

Calle Vargas, entre Avda 51 y 54 a dos cuadras del Santuario del Divino Niño, Ciudad Ojeda, Estado Zulia
Avda 34, entre Calle 'N' y 'O', Ciudad Ojeda, Estado Zulia

Telephone: (265) 631-1741
E-mail: info@uniojeda.edu.ve
Internet: www.uniojeda.edu.ve
Founded 1997, univ. status 2002
Private control
Language of instruction: Spanish
Academic year: September to July
Rector: Dr JUAN MENDOZA ARAUJO
Vice-Rector for Academics: Dr JOSÉ A. CHIRINOS
Vice-Rector for Admin.: Dr LUIS JIMÉNEZ BESSIL
Vice-Rector for Distance Education: Dr JOSÉ MENA DUARTE
Sec.: Dr HELIMENES DOMINGUEZ

DEANS

Faculty of Engineering: Dra ASNEIDA LEAL
Faculty of Humanities and Education: Dr ZULLY ZABALA
Faculty of Management: Dr HENIO MELENDEZ
Research and Graduate Studies: Dr HENRY DE JESÚS VÁZQUEZ

UNIVERSIDAD 'ARTURO MICHELENA'
(Arturo Michelena University)

Avda Giovanni Nani (A 1 km del Distribuidor La Cumaca), Sector El Polvero, Campus UAM, San Diego, Valencia, Estado Carabobo

Telephone: (241) 891-0092
E-mail: grados@uam.edu.ve
Internet: www.uam.edu.ve

Founded 1999
Private control
Language of instruction: Spanish
Academic year: September to July
Rector: Prof. CARLOS HERRERA
Vice-Rector for Academics: Dr ÁNGEL SALOMÓN
Vice-Rector for Admin.: Ing. JAVIER HIGA
Sec.: ANA CHIQUITO

DEANS

Faculty of Economics and Social Sciences: Lic. CARLOS HERRERA
Faculty of Engineering: JOSÉ LORENZO TORRES
Faculty of Health Sciences: Dr DARIO DE JESUS SANCHEZ
Faculty of Humanities and Arts: Lic. OLGA OLIVEROS
Faculty of Political Science and Law: Dra HERVIZ GONZÁLEZ

UNIVERSIDAD BICENTENARIA DE ARAGUA
(Bicentennial University of Aragua)

Avda Intercomunal Santiago Mariño c/c Avda Universidad, Sector la Providencia, Turmero, Estado Aragua

Telephone: (243) 265-0103
E-mail: ubaweb@uba.edu.ve
Internet: www.uba.edu.ve
Founded 1986
Private control
Language of instruction: Spanish
Academic year: September to July

UNIVERSIDAD BOLIVARIANA DE LOS TRABAJADORES 'JESÚS RIVERO'
(Bolivarian Workers University 'Jesus Rivero')

Esq. de Reducto a Municipal, Caracas
E-mail: ubtjr.dc@gmail.com
Founded 2008
State control
Language of instruction: Spanish
Rector: ARCHIMEDES MUNDARAÍN
Dir: Prof. OMAR GUARARIMA

UNIVERSIDAD BOLIVARIANA DE VENEZUELA
(Bolivarian University of Venezuela)

Los Chaguaramos, Caracas
Telephone: (212) 606-3714
E-mail: cnielg2012@gmail.com
Internet: www.ubv.edu.ve
Founded 2003
State control
Language of instruction: Spanish
Campuses in Aragua, Barinas, Bolívar, Carabobo, Cojedes, Falcon, Guarico, Merida, Monagas, Táchira, Trujillo, Valles del Tuy and Zulia
Rector: Dr PRUDENCIO CHACÓN
Vice-Rector: Dr LUIS BIGOTT
Vice-Rector for Territorial: SERGIO GARCÍA
Gen. Sec.: JOSÉ BERRIOS
Nat. Coordinator for Library Services: EDGAR LEÓN

UNIVERSIDAD CATÓLICA 'ANDRÉS BELLO'
(Catholic University 'Andrés Bello')

Urb. Montalbán, Parroquia La Vega, Caracas 1020
Telephone: (212) 407-4268
E-mail: webmaster@ucab.edu.ve
Internet: www.ucab.edu.ve
Founded 1953
Private control

Academic year: September to July
Campuses in Los Teques, Coro and Guayana
Chancellor: Mgr JORGE UROSA SAVINO
Vice-Chancellor: ARTURO PERAZA
Rector: JOSÉ VIRTUOSO
Vice-Rector for Academics: Prof. SILVANA CAMPAGNARO
Vice-Rector for Admin.: RAFAEL HERNÁNDEZ
Sec.-Gen.: MARÍA ISABEL MARTÍNEZ
Librarian: Lic. EMILIO PÍRIZ PÉREZ
Library: see Libraries and Archives
Number of teachers: 1,200
Number of students: 14,100
Publications: *Analogías del Comportamiento, Cuadernos Venezolanos de Filosofía, Encuentro EAC y Cuadernos UCAB-Educación, Espacios, Pensamiento Agustiniano, Revista de Fiolosofía* (1 a year), *Revista de la Facultad de Derecho, Revista Montalbán, Revista de Relaciones Industriales y Laborales, Revista Tekhné de la Facultad de Ingeniería, Tekhné* (1 a year), *Temas de Comunicación Social* (2 a year), *Temas de Coyuntura*

DEANS

Faculty of Engineering: JOSÉ OCHOA ITURBE
Faculty of Humanities and Education: MIGUEL DEL VALLE HUERGA
Faculty of Law: JUAN LUIS MODOLELL
Faculty of Social and Economic Sciences: MARITZA IZAGUIRRE
Faculty of Theology: Dr JUAN PABLO PERÓN

UNIVERSIDAD CATÓLICA 'CECILIO ACOSTA'
(Catholic University 'Cecilio Acosta')

96 J Calle 97, Maracaibo, Estado Zulia
Telephone: (261) 300-6830
E-mail: prensayrrpp@unica.edu.ve
Internet: www.unica.edu.ve
Founded 1983
Private control
Language of instruction: Spanish
Chancellor: Mgr UBALDO SANTANA
Rector: Dr ANGEL LOMBARDI
Vice-Rector for Academics: MARÍA MERCEDES RODRÍGUEZ
Vice-Rector for Admin.: CARMELO CHAPERO
Sec.: JESÚS ALBERTO FUENMAYOR

DEANS

Faculty of Arts and Music: JESÚS CONTRERAS
Faculty of Educational Sciences: VALMORE MUÑOZ
Faculty of Philosophy and Theology: ONEIDA CHIRINO
Faculty of Social Communication: GINETTE GUTIÉRREZ
Research and Graduate Studies: Dra LILIA BOSCÁN DE LOMBARDI

UNIVERSIDAD CATÓLICA DEL TÁCHIRA
(Catholic University of Táchira)

Barrio Obrero, Calle 14 con Carrera 14, San Cristóbal, Estado Táchira
Telephone: (276) 344-2289
E-mail: asosa@ucat.edu.ve
Internet: www.ucat.edu.ve
Founded 1982
Language of instruction: Spanish
Academic year: September to July
Chancellor: Mgr MARIO DEL VALLE MORONTA RODRÍGUEZ
Rector: Dr ARTURO SOSA ABASCAL
Vice-Rector for Academics: Dr JAVIER YONEKURA SHIMIZU
Vice-Rector for Admin.: Dra FÉLIDA ROA DE ROA
Gen. Sec.: Dr SAMIR SÁNCHEZ ESCALANTE

Librarian: Dra ALIDA PAOLINI

Number of teachers: 400

Number of students: 7,000

Publications: *Derecho y Tecnología* (1 a year), *Paramillo* (1 a year), *Revista Derecho y Tecnología* (1 a year), *Revista Tachirense de Derecho* (1 a year), *Tributum* (1 a year)

DEANS

Faculty of Economics and Social Sciences: MIREYA CASTILLO DE MÉNDEZ

Faculty of Humanities and Education: EDITA MAGAY SALAS DE MALDONADO

Faculty of Law and Political Science: GABRIEL DE SANTIS TEBALDINI

Faculty of Religious Sciences: FELIX MARÍA CAICEDO LOPEZ

UNIVERSIDAD CATÓLICA SANTA ROSA
(Catholic University Santa Rosa)

Calle El Seminario, Sabana del Blanco, final Avda Boyacá (Cota Mil) con Avda Baralt (detrás de la Estación de Servicio PDV), La Pastora, Caracas

Telephone: (276) 344-2289

E-mail: jmachmud@ucsar.edu.ve

Internet: www.ucsar.com.ve

Founded 1999

Private control

Language of instruction: Spanish

Rector: Dr ALI RAMÓN ROJAS O.

Vice-Rector for Academics: Prof. MARIO CORRO W.

Vice-Rector for Graduate Studies: Prof. DAYANA LÓPEZ

Vice Rector for Admin.: Prof. JOSÉ HERNÁNDEZ

Sec.: Prof. RICARDO ALDAZORO M.

Publication: *Revista UCSAR* (2 a year)

DEANS

Faculty of Education: Prof. CANDELARIA MARTÍN P.

Faculty of Humanities and Social Sciences: Dr PEDRO BALZA

Faculty of Theology: Prof. JULIO CÉSAR HENRÍQUEZ

UNIVERSIDAD CENTRAL DE VENEZUELA
(Central University of Venezuela)

Apdo Postal 1050, Ciudad Universitaria, Los Chaguaramos, Caracas 1051

Telephone: (212) 605-4050

Internet: www.ucv.ve

Founded 1721

State control

Language of instruction: Spanish

Academic year: January to December

Rector: CECILIA GARCÍA-AROCHA

Vice-Rector for Academics: NICOLÁS BIANCO COLMENARES

Vice-Rector for Admin.: MENDEZ BERNARDO ACOSTA

Registrar: Dr ANTONIO DEL NOGAL

Gen. Coordinator: JEANETTE BLANCO DE MÉNDEZ

Sec.: AMALIO BELMONTE GUZMÁN

Librarian: Dr EUDIS BORRA

Number of teachers: 6,987

Number of students: 45,000

Publications: *Acta Odontologica*, *Acta Biologica Venezuelica* (1 a year, print and online, saber.ucv.ve/ojs/index.php/revista_abv/index), *Acta Botánica Venezuelica* (2 a year, print and online, saber.ucv.ve/ojs/index.php/rev_abv/about/index), *Akademos* (2 a year, print and online, saber.ucv.ve/ojs/index.php/rev_ak/about/index), *Anuario ININCO/ Investigaciones de la Comunicación* (2 a year, print and online, saber.ucv.ve/ojs/index.php/rev_ai/about/index), *Apuntes Filosóficos* (Philosophical Notes, 2 a year, print and online, saber.ucv.ve/ojs/index.php/rev_af/index), *Aula Magna*, *Boletín del Archivo Histórico*, *Boletín de Lingüística*, *Correo Ucevista*, *Cuadernos de la Escuela de Salud Pública* (1 a year, print and online, saber.ucv.ve/ojs/index.php/rev_edsp/index), *Ernstia* (2 a year, print and online, saber.ucv.ve/ojs/index.php/rev_erns/index), *Gaceta Universitaria*, *Investigaciones Literarias* (1 a year, print and online, saber.ucv.ve/ojs/index.php/rev_il/index), *Revista Alcance 57* (organic soil science, 2 a year), *Revista del Centro de Información y Documentación* (6 a year), *Revista Escuela de Metalurgia*, *Revista de la Facultad de Agronomía* (3 a year, saber.ucv.ve/ojs/index.php/rev_agro/index), *Revista de la Facultad de Ciencias Jurídicas y Políticas* (4 a year), *Revista de la Facultad de Ciencias Veterinarias* (2 a year, print and online, saber.ucv.ve/ojs/index.php/revisfcv/index), *Revista de la Facultad de Farmacia* (4 a year, in Spanish and English, print and online, saber.ucv.ve/ojs/index.php/rev_ff*), *Revista de la Facultad de Ingeniería* (4 a year, print and online, saber.ucv.ve/ojs/index.php/rev_fiucv/index), *Revista de la Facultad de Medicina* (2 a year, print and online, saber.ucv.ve/ojs/index.php/rev_fmed/index), *Revista de la Sociedad Venezolana de Ciencias Morfológicas* (1 a year, print and online, saber.ucv.ve/ojs/index.php/rev_svcm/index), *Revista de Pedagogía* (2 a year, print and online, saber.ucv.ve/ojs/index.php/rev_ped/index), *Revista Digital de Postgrado* (2 a year, print and online, saber.ucv.ve/ojs/index.php/rev_dp/index), *Revista Latinoamericana de Estudios Avanzados*, *Revista Tharsis*, *Revista Urbana* (town planning, 2 a year), *Revista Venezolana de Economía y Ciencias Sociales* (Venezuelan Journal of Economics and Social Sciences, 4 a year, print and online, saber.ucv.ve/ojs/index.php/rev_rvec/index), *Revista Venezolana del Análisis de Coyuntura (IIES-FaCES-UCV)* (Revista Venezolana Situation Analysis, 2 a year, print and online, saber.ucv.ve/ojs/index.php/rev_ac/index), *Revista Venezolana de Estudios de la Mujer* (1 a year, print and online, saber.ucv.ve/ojs/index.php/rev_vem/index), *Revista Venezolana de Estudios Internacionales*, *Serendipia Revista Electrónica del PCI* (1 a year, online, saber.ucv.ve/ojs/index.php/rev_s/index), *Tecnología y Construcción* (3 a year, online, saber.ucv.ve/ojs/index.php/rev_tc/index), *Revista de la Sociedad Venezolana de Microbiología* (2 a year, print and online, saber.ucv.ve/ojs/index.php/rev_vm/index), *Urbana*

DEANS

Faculty of Agronomy: Dr LEONARDO TAYLHARDAT

Faculty of Architecture and Urbanism: GUILLERMO BARRIOS

Faculty of Dentistry: Prof. AURA YOLANDA OSORIO

Faculty of Economic and Social Sciences: Dr ADELAIDA STRUCK

Faculty of Engineering: Prof. MARÍA ESCULPI

Faculty of Humanities and Education: Prof. PIERO LO MÓNACO

Faculty of Law and Political Science: Prof. IRMA BEHRENS DE BUNIMOV.

Faculty of Medicine: Prof. EMIGDIO BALDA

Faculty of Pharmacy: MARGARITA SALAZAR-BOOKAMAN

Faculty of Science: VENTURA ECHANDÍA

Faculty of Veterinary Science: Prof. RAFAEL INFANTES

UNIVERSIDAD CENTRO-OCCIDENTAL 'LISANDRO ALVARADO'
(Central-Western University 'Lisandro Alvarado')

Apdo 400, Barquisimeto, Estado Lara

Carrera 19 (entre calles 8 y 9) Edif. Antiguo Hotel Nueva Segovia, 2°, Barquisimeto, Estado Lara

Telephone: (251) 259-1061

E-mail: postgrado@ucla.edu.ve

Internet: www.ucla.edu.ve

Founded 1963 as Experimental Centre of Higher Education; univ. status 1968

State control

Language of instruction: Spanish

Academic year: January to December

Rector: Dr FRANCESCO LEONE DURANTE

Vice-Rector for Academics: Prof. NELLY VELÁSQUEZ

Vice-Rector for Admin.: EDGAR ALVARADO

Sec.-Gen.: Prof. FRANCISCO UGEL

Librarian: Lic. MORELLA BARRANCOS

Number of teachers: 1,000

Number of students: 10,000

Publications: *El Veterinario* (12 a year), *Escuela de Administración*, *Escuela de Agronomía*, *Memoria y Cuenta* (1 a year), *Publicaciones en Ciencias y Tecnología* (2 a year, print and online, revistapcyt.blogspot.in/p/la-revista.html), *Revista Gestión y Gerencia* (3 a year, print and online, www.ucla.edu.ve/dac/gestionygerencia.htm), *Revista de Investigación Científica COMPENDIUM* (2 a year, print and online, www.ucla.edu.ve/dac/compendium), *Tarea Común* (4 a year)

DEANS

Faculty of Administration and Accountancy: Dr FERNANDO ALBERTO SOSA GÓMEZ

Faculty of Agronomy: VIRGINIA ALMAO

Faculty of Civil Engineering: Ing. HERMES ESPINOZA

Faculty of Health Sciences: AURIS DE FINIZOLA

Faculty of Humanities and Arts: FREDDY RENÉ PÉREZ

Faculty of Science and Technology: Prof. YENNY SALAZAR

Faculty of Veterinary Medicine: SHEILA MÁRQUEZ

ATTACHED INSTITUTES

Consejo Asesor de Investigación y Servicios (Advisory Council on Research and Services): assessment and consultation on the planning of research; Pres. Dr FRANCISCO MONTES DE OCA.

Instituto de la Uva (Institute for Research on Grapes): research on grape cultivation and advisory service to wine growers; Dir MARIA LUISA DE PIRE

UNIVERSIDAD DE CARABOBO
(University of Carabobo)

Avda Bolívar Norte, Sede del Rectorado U.C., Valencia, Estado Carabobo

Telephone: (241) 600-5000

E-mail: di@uc.edu.ve

Internet: www.uc.edu.ve

Founded 1852

State control

Academic year: September to February;-March to July

Rector: Prof. JESSY DIVO DE ROMERO

Vice-Rector for Academics: Prof. ULISES ROJAS

Vice-Rector for Admin.: Prof. JOSÉ ANGEL FERREIRA

Sec.: Prof. PABLO AURE

Dir-Gen. for Library: Prof. THAIRY BRICEÑO

Library: see under Libraries and Archives

Number of teachers: 2,585

Number of students: 44,700

Publications: *Boletín Universitario, Revista ARJÉ, Salus* (irregular, print and online, salus-online.fcs.uc.edu.ve/index.html), *Utopia y Praxis*

DEANS

Faculty of Dentistry: YNGRID J. ACOSTA M.
Faculty of Economics and Social Sciences: Dr BENITO HAMIDIAN
Faculty of Education: Lic. BRIDGET GINOID FRANCO SANCHEZ
Faculty of Engineering: Prof. JOSÉ LUÍS NAZAR
Faculty of Health Sciences: Prof. JOSÉ CORADO
Faculty of Law: MIRIAM GUTIÉRREZ
Faculty of Sciences and Technology: Prof. JOS MARCANO
Postgraduate Studies: WILLIN ÁLVAREZ

UNIVERSIDAD DE LOS ANDES
(University of Los Andes)

Avda 3, Independencia, Edif. Rectorado, Mérida 5101, Estado Mérida

Telephone: (275) 240-1111
E-mail: dsia@ula.ve
Internet: www.ula.ve

Founded 1785 as the Real Colegio Seminario de San Buenaventura de Mérida; univ. status 1810
State control
Language of instruction: Spanish
Academic year: January to December

Rector: MARIO BONUCCI R.
Vice-Rector for Academics: PATRICIA ROSENZWEIG
Vice-Rector for Admin.: MANUEL ARANGUREN R.
Sec.: JOSÉ MARÍA ANDÉREZ
Librarian: NILZA GONZÁLEZ DE GUTIÉRREZ

Library: see under Libraries and Archives
Number of teachers: 3,000
Number of students: 34,000

Publication: *Revista Investigación*

DEANS

Faculty of Architecture and Design: Arq. INÉS BENAVIDES
Faculty of Dentistry: Dr JUSTO BONOMIE
Faculty of Economic and Social Sciences: RAÙL HUIZZIL
Faculty of Engineering: Prof. JOSÉ DAVID SILVA
Faculty of Forestry and Environment: Prof. DARÍO A. GARAY JEREZ
Faculty of Humanities and Education: Prof. LUIS ALFREDO ANGULO RIVAS
Faculty of Law and Political Science: Prof. ANDREY GROMIKO URDANETA
Faculty of Medicine: Dr GERARDO J. TOVITTO PAREDES
Faculty of Odontology: Dr PATRICIO JARPA
Faculty of Pharmacy and Bioanalysis: Dr JOSÉ RAFAEL LUNA
Faculty of Sciences: NELSON VILORIA
Rafael Rangel Campus: Dr CONRADO DABOÍN VÁSQUEZ
Táchira Campus: Dr RAMÓN GONZÁLEZ E.

UNIVERSIDAD DE FALCÓN
(University of Falcon)

Avda Ollarvides, Sector Doña Emilia, Frente a la Urb. Los Caciques, Edif. UDEFA, Punto Fijo, Estado Falcón

Telephone: (269) 246-6349
Internet: www.udefa.edu.ve
Founded 2004
Private control
Language of instruction: Spanish

Rector: Dr SOLANO CALLES
Vice-Rector for Academics: MARIA DE PALM

Dir. for Admin.: RAÚL AMOR
Gen. Sec.: ADOLFO PRIMERA
Publication: *Digiciencia UDEFA* (1 a year, online, www.udefa.edu.ve/digiciencia.php?id=4)

DEANS

Faculty of Engineering: Ing. JUAN NICOLAIDIS
Faculty of Legal and Political Sciences: Dra GUELCY GONZÁLEZ
Faculty of Social Sciences: Dr ADALBERTO CHACÓN

UNIVERSIDAD DE MARGARITA
(University of Margarita)

Avda Concepción Mariño, Sector El Toporo, El Valle del Espíritu Santo, Isla de Margarita, Estado Nueva Esparta

Telephone: (295) 287-1722
E-mail: info@unimar.edu.ve
Internet: www.unimar.edu.ve
Founded 2000
Private control
Language of instruction: Spanish
Academic year: September to July

Pres.: PEDRO CABELLO POLEO
Rector: PEDRO A. BEAUPERTHUY U.
Vice-Rector for Academics: JOSÉ M. CAMINO AGUILERA
Vice-Rector for Extension: GRACIELA RODRÍGUEZ DE TINEO
Dir.-Gen. for Admin.: ALESSANDRA D'ALTORIO
Gen. Sec.: ANTONIETA ROSALES DE OXFORD

DEANS

Faculty of Engineering and Related: ORLANDA DE TOCHÓN
Faculty of General Studies: DAMELIS VÁSQUEZ DE VILLEGAS
Faculty of Humanities, Arts and Education: ESTHER IZAGUIRRE
Faculty of Law and Political Sciences: ANA LUISA GANDICA SILVA
Faculty of Social and Economic Sciences: JOSÉ MARTÍN CARABALLO

UNIVERSIDAD DE ORIENTE
(University of the East)

Edif. Rectorado, Apdo 094, Cumaná, Estado Sucre

Telephone: (293) 400-8300
E-mail: rectora@udo.edu.ve
Internet: www.udo.edu.ve
Founded 1958
State control
Academic year: February to December

Campuses in Anzoátegui, Bolívar, Monagas, Nueva Esparta and Sucre

Rector: Dra MILENA BRAVO ROMERO
Vice-Rector for Academics: JESÚS MARTÍNEZ YÉPEZ
Vice-Rector for Admin.: Dra TAHÍS PICO DE OLIVERO
Sec.-Gen.: JUAN BOLAÑOS CURVELO

Library: see under Libraries and Archives
Number of teachers: 1,400
Number of students: 94,000

Publications: *Boletín del Instituto Oceanográfico, Catálogo de la UDO* (1 a year), *Lagena, La UDO Investiga, Oriente Agropecuario*..

CONSTITUENT CAMPUSES

Universidad de Oriente, Nucleo Anzoátegui
(University of the East, Core Anzoátegui)

Apdo Postal 4327, Puerto La Cruz, Estado Anzoátegui

Telephone: (281) 420-3400

E-mail: rectora@udo.edu.ve
Internet: www.anz.udo.edu.ve
Founded 1965
Dean: Prof. MANUEL LÓPEZ FARÍAS
Number of teachers: 418
Number of students: 9,000

Universidad de Oriente, Nucleo Bolívar
(University of the East, Core Bolívar)

La Sabanita, Ciudad Bolívar, Estado Bolívar

Telephone: (285) 632-3738
E-mail: rectora@udo.edu.ve
Internet: www.bolivar.udo.edu.ve
Founded 1960
Dean: Prof. MARIA COROMOTO CASADO
Number of teachers: 1,000
Number of students: 20,000

Universidad de Oriente, Nucleo de Monagas
(University of the East, Core Monagas)

Avda Universidad Los Guaritos, Maturín, Estado Monagas

Telephone: (291) 641-7755
E-mail: rectora@udo.edu.ve
Internet: www.monagas.udo.edu.ve
Founded 1961
Dean: Dr ERNESTO HURTADO
Publication: *Oriente Agropecuario* (2 a year)

Universidad de Oriente, Nucleo Nueva Esparta
(University of the East, Core Nueva Esparta)

Apdo Postal 147, Guatamare, Estado Nueva Esparta

Telephone: (295) 400-6403
E-mail: rectora@udo.edu.ve
Internet: www.ne.udo.edu.ve
Founded 1958
Dean: MILENA BRAVO DE ROMERO

Universidad de Oriente, Nucleo de Sucre
(university of the East, Core Sucre)

Avda Universidad, Cumaná, Estado Sucre
E-mail: rectora@udo.edu.ve
Internet: www.sucre.udo.edu.ve

Dean: Prof. NORYS JORDAN

UNIVERSIDAD DEL ZULIA
(University of Zulia)

Avda 16 con Calle 67B, Edif. Nueva Sede Rectoral, Maracaibo, Estado Zulia

Telephone: (261) 412-4125
E-mail: web@dgc.luz.edu.ve
Internet: www.luz.edu.ve
Founded 1891, closed 1904, reopened 1946
State control
Academic year: September to July

Rector: JORGE PALENCIA
Vice-Rector for Academics: JUDITH AULAR DE DURÁN
Vice-Rector for Admin.: MARÍA GUADALUPE NÚÑEZ
Sec.: Dra MARLENE PRIMERA GALUÉ
Librarian: Dr ANA JUDITH PAREDES CHACÍN

Library: see under Libraries and Archives
Number of teachers: 3,700
Number of students: 48,000

Publication: 24 journals in each discipline; can be accessed in print and online format at revistas.luz.edu.ve/index.php

DEANS

Faculty of Agronomy: Dr ELVIS PORTILLO
Faculty of Architecture and Design: Prof. SUSANA GÓMEZ ARVELO

Faculty of Dentistry: Dra MARY CARMEN RINCÓN F.
Faculty of Economic and Social Sciences: IVÁN CAÑIZALES CAMACHO
Faculty of Engineering: Prof. MARIO HERRERA BOSCÁN
Faculty of Experimental Sciences: Prof. MERLIN ROSALES
Faculty of Humanities and Education: Prof. DORIS SALAS DE MOLINA
Faculty of Law and Political Science: Dra DIANA ROMERO LA ROCHE
Faculty of Medicine: Dr SERGIO OSORIO MORALES
Faculty of Veterinary Sciences: JOSÉ MANUEL RODRÍGUEZ

UNIVERSIDAD 'DR JOSÉ GREGORIO HERNÁNDEZ'
(University 'Dr José Gregorio Hernández')

Calle 88 A con Avda Las Delicias, Maracaibo, Estado Zulia

Telephone: (261) 783-5597
E-mail: info@ujgh.edu.ve
Internet: www.ujgh.edu.ve

Founded 1997 as Instituto Universitario de Tecnología; univ. status 2003
Private control
Language of instruction: Spanish

Rector: OSCAR NAVEDA
Vice-Rector for Academics: ADLYZ AIMEL DE CHAVES
Vice-Rector for Admin.: AIVEL ANAMAR CALIMÁN RINCÓN
Sec.: GISELA DEL VALLE QUIJADA OQUENDO

UNIVERSIDAD 'DR RAFAEL BELLOSO CHACÍN'
(University 'Dr Rafael Belloso Chacín')

3109 POB 25233 Miami FL 33102-5233, Maracaibo, Estado Zulia
Prolongación Circunvalación No 2 con Avda 16 Guajira, al lado de la Plaza de Toros, Maracaibo, Estado Zulia

Telephone: (261) 200-8723
E-mail: info@urbe.edu
Internet: www.urbe.edu

Founded 1989
Private control
Language of instruction: Spanish
Academic year: September to July

Rector: OSCAR ENRIQUE BELLOSO MEDINA
Vice-Rector for Academics: Dr RENÉ AGUIRRE BRACHO
Vice-Rector for Admin.: MARCOS ALBARRÁN BRICEÑO
Sec.: Dr HUMBERTO PEROZO REYES

Library of 11,040 vols of book titles, 349 int. videos, 12,473 journals, 19,900 nat. technical articles, 322 periodical titles, 14,887 theses

Publication: Telos (3 a year, print and online, www.publicaciones.urbe.edu/index.php/telos)

DEANS

Dean of Extension: Dra ADINORA OQUENDO
Faculty of Administrative Sciences: Dra JANETH HERNÁNDEZ CORONA
Faculty of Computer Science: LUIS SUÁREZ
Faculty of Engineering: Dr PLACIDO MARTINEZ PAZ
Faculty of Humanities and Education: Dr MIKE GONZÁLEZ BERMÚDEZ
Faculty of Law and Political Sciences: Dr CARLOS D'ABREU
Faculty of Research and Graduate Studies: Dr MIGUEL ANGEL ROBLES

UNIVERSIDAD 'FERMÍN TORO'
(University 'Fermín Toro')

Urb. Chucho Briceño, Cabudare, Estado Lara
Telephone: (251) 710-0170
E-mail: decanato_postg@uft.edu.ve
Internet: www.uft.edu.ve
Private control
Language of instruction: Spanish

UNIVERSIDAD IBEROAMERICANA DEL DEPORTE
(Iberoamerican University of Sports)

Vía Manrique, Avda Universidad, km 2 (Villa Deportiva), San Carlos, Estado Cojedes
Telephone: (258) 433-0349
Internet: www.uideporte.edu.ve
Founded 2006
State control
Language of instruction: Spanish

Rector: ALBERTO MARTÍN PHILLYS ROBERTS
Vice-Rector: DAYSE YAMILA MACHADO PALACIOS
Gen. Sec.: MIRIAM JOSEFINA RODRÍGUEZ QUIRÓZ

Publications: Gacetas (4 a year), Revista Científica 'Dimensión Deportiva' (2 a year)

UNIVERSIDAD 'JOSÉ ANTONIO PÁEZ'
(University 'José Antonio Páez')

Municipio San Diego, Calle No 3, Urb. Yuma II, Valencia, Estado Carabobo
Telephone: (241) 872-0269
E-mail: web@ujap.edu.ve
Internet: web.ujap.info
Founded 1997
Private control
Language of instruction: Spanish
Academic year: January to December
Offices in Barquisimeto, Caracas, Guanare, Maracay, Porlamar, San Carlos, San Felipe and Los Teques

Pres.: Ing. FRANCA RIBALDI LANGELLA
Vice-Pres.: Ing. PEDRO VIVAS GONZÁLEZ
Rector: Prof. INÉS GONZÁLEZ DE SALAMA
Vice-Rector for Academics: Dr JOSÉ GÓMEZ ZAMUDIO
Vice-Rector for Admin.: Lic. JULIÁN GUTIÉRREZ MORA
Sec.: MARÍA BEATRIZ SERRANO

DEANS

Faculty of Education: Dra ELYDA MARITZA SEGURA
Faculty of Engineering: OCTAVIO CRIOLLO
Faculty of Health Sciences: Dra NORA DE FRAÍNO
Faculty of Law and Political Sciences: Dra MARLENE ROBLES DE RODRÍGUEZ
Faculty of Social Sciences: TARZYS VIZCARRONDO

UNIVERSIDAD 'JOSÉ MARÍA VARGAS'
('José María Vargas' University)

HQ: Avda Sucre, Urb. Los Dos Caminos, Caracas
Telephone: (212) 284-6401
Chacao HQ: Avda Andrés Galarraga, Edif. Pier Sanz, Caracas
Telephone: (212) 265-6023
E-mail: ude@ujmv.edu
Internet: www.ujmv.edu
Founded 1983
Private control
Language of instruction: Spanish
Academic year: January to December

Rector: Dr RAMÓN GONZÁLEZ PAREDES
Vice-Rector for Academics: ISABEL BEATRIZ PIÑATE FRANCO
Vice-Rector for Admin.: VARVARA CANCEL

Sec.: LUISA CRISTINA GARCÍA JÁUREGUI

DEANS

Faculty of Administration, Management and Accounting: ERASMO DE JESÚS TUDARES TRÓCOLI
Faculty of Architecture and History of Museology Plastic Arts: MARLA HORTENSIA PÉREZ MACHADO
Faculty of Education: AURA MARINA FORSYTH DE MARCHENA
Faculty of Engineering: JUAN RODRÍGUEZ CARRASCO
Faculty of Legal and Political Sciences and School of Law: JOSÉ GUILLERMO ANDUEZA ACUTLA

UNIVERSIDAD METROPOLITANA
(Metropolitan University)

Apdo 76819, Caracas 1070
Caracas Campus: Distribuidor Universidad Autopista Petare-Guarenas, Urb. Terrazas del Avila, Caracas
Telephone: (212) 240-3200
Puerto La Cruz Campus: Avda Municipal Cruce, con Calle Carabobo Centro Seguros La Previsora, Puerto La Cruz, Estado Anzoátegui
Telephone: (281) 268-7046
E-mail: cvicentini@unimet.edu.ve
Internet: www.unimet.edu.ve
Founded 1970
Private control
Language of instruction: Spanish
Academic year: January to December

Pres.: Ing. HERNAN ANZOLA
Rector: BENJAMÍN SCHARIFKER
Vice-Rector for Academics: Dra MERCEDES DE LA OLIVA FERNÁNDEZ
Vice-Rector for Admin.: MARÍA ELENA CEDEÑO
Registrar: Prof. MARÍA DE LOURDES ACEDO DE SUCRE
Sec.: Dra MARY CARMEN LOMBAO
Librarian: Dr ELEIDA GARCÍA
Number of teachers: 438
Number of students: 4,670

Publications: Anales de la Universidad Metropolitana (2 a year), Revista Almanaque (2 a year), Revista UNIMET (12 a year)

DEANS

Academic Research and Development: ROBERTO RÉQUIZ CORDERO
Faculty of Arts and Sciences: Prof. JAVIER RÍOS
Faculty of Economics and Social Sciences: Prof. JOSÉ ANGEL VELÁZQUEZ
Faculty of Engineering: Ing. SUSANA ROMAGNI
Faculty of Legal and Political Studies: HUMBERTO NJAIM

UNIVERSIDAD MONTEÁVILA
(Monteávila University)

Final Avda El Buen Pastor, Urb. Boleíta Norte, Caracas
Telephone: (212) 232-5255
E-mail: info@uma.edu.ve
Internet: www.uma.edu.ve
Founded 1998
Private control
Language of instruction: Spanish
Academic year: January to December

Pres.: FERNANDO VERA
Rector: Dr JOAQUÍN RODRÍGUEZ AONSO
Vice-Rector for Academics: Dr FRANCISCO FEBRES-CORDERO
Vice-Rector for Admin.: CAROLINA ARCAY DE LÓPEZ
Gen. Sec.: ANA BEATRIZ MONTEVERDE BARALT
Dir for Library: CAROLINA AMAYA DE ESCOBAR

Publication: Revista Derecho y Sociedad

DEANS

Faculty of Communication and Information: CAROLINA AMAYA DE ESCOBAR

Faculty of Economics and Administrative Sciences: RAFAEL ÁVILA DOS RAMOS

Faculty of Education: MERCEDES GONZÁLEZ DE AGUELLO

Faculty of Law and Political Science: Dr EUGENIO HERNÁNDEZ-BRETÓN

UNIVERSIDAD NACIONAL ABIERTA
(National Open University)

Apdo 2096, Caracas 1010

Avda Los Calvani No 18, San Bernardino, Caracas 1010

Telephone: (212) 555-2111

E-mail: cservest@una.edu.ve

Internet: www.una.edu.ve

Founded 1977

State control

Language of instruction: Spanish

Academic year: October to July

One nat. centre in Caracas, 22 regional centres in state capitals and 12 support units

Rector: Dr MANUEL CASTRO PEREIRA

Vice-Rector for Academics: Dr NÉSTOR LEAL ORTIZ

Vice-Rector for Admin.: Prof. ARNALDO ANTONIO ESCALONA PEÑUELA

Sec.: Prof. ARELIS COROMOTO SAAVEDRA

Librarian: MILDRED HENRIQUEZ

Number of teachers: 800

Number of students: 62,000

Publications: *Informe de Investigaciones Educativas* (2 a year, print and online, biblo.una.edu.ve/ojs/index.php/IIE/index), *Una Documenta*, *UNA Investig@ción* (2 a year, print and online, biblo.una.edu.ve/ojs/index.php/UNAINV/index)

UNIVERSIDAD NACIONAL EXPERIMENTAL DE GUAYANA
(National Experimental University of Guayana)

Avda Las Américas, Edif. General de Seguros, Puerto Ordaz, Estado Bolívar

Telephone: (286) 922-5673

E-mail: secretaria@uneg.edu.ve

Internet: www.uneg.edu.ve

Founded 1982

State control

Depts of education, humanities and arts, man and the environment, management, science and technology

Rector: Dra MARÍA ELENA LATUFF

Vice-Rector for Academic Affairs: Dr ARTURO FRANCESCHI

Vice-Rector for Admin.: Dr WILFREDO GUAITA

Sec.-Gen.: Dra LEONARDA CASANOVA

Publications: *Copérnico* (2 a year, print and online, copernico.uneg.edu.ve), *Kaleidoscopio* (2 a year, print and online, kaleidoscopio.uneg.edu.ve), *Strategos* (2 a year, print and online, fondoeditorial.uneg.edu.ve/strategos)

UNIVERSIDAD NACIONAL EXPERIMENTAL DE LAS ARTES
(National Experimental University of the Arts)

Avda México, Calle Tito Salas, Edif. Santa María, Mezzanina, Sartenejas, Caracas, 1080

Telephone: (212) 962-0866

E-mail: secretariageneral@unearte.edu.ve

Internet: www.unearte.edu.ve

Founded 2008

State control

Language of instruction: Spanish

UNIVERSIDAD NACIONAL EXPERIMENTAL DE LOS LLANOS CENTRALES 'ROMULO GALLEGOS'
(National Experimental University of the Central Plains 'Romulo Gallegos')

Ciudad Universitaria, Avda Universitaria, vía El Castrero, San Juan de los Morros, Estado Guárico

Telephone: (246) 431-0584

E-mail: webmaster@unerg.edu.ve

Internet: www.unerg.edu.ve

Founded 1977

State control

Language of instruction: Spanish

Academic year: March to December (2 semesters)

Rector: Dra MARÍA ARISELA MEDINA

Vice-Rector for Academics: Dra EVELÍN FERNANDEZ

Vice-Rector for Admin.: Dr OMAR E. OJEDA

Coordinator for Library: Lic. CARLOS SIERRA

Dean for Postgraduate Studies: Dr DEYANIRA CARRIOLA

Dean for Research and Extension: Dr GIUSEPPE SCHEMBARI VALERO

Number of teachers: 367

Number of students: 5,306

Publications: *Horizontes Universitarios*, *NEXOS* (3 a year, print and online, investigacion.unerg.edu.ve/nexos)

DEANS

Continuing Education: Prof. MARÍA FLORANGEL RAMÍREZ

Faculty of Economics: Dr MERCEDES FLORES

Faculty of Education: Lic. MAURELLA ALVARADO

Faculty of Engineering, Architecture and Technology: Dr PABLO QUIROZ

Faculty of Health: Dra MARTHA CANTAVELLA

Faculty of Odontology: Dr BARBARA MORENO

Faculty of Systems Engineering: Ing. JENNY PADILLA

Faculty of Veterinary Medicine: SALVADOR DE J. PÉREZ ALEMÁ

ATTACHED INSTITUTE

Centre for Legal Studies: Dir Abog. GLADYS BOYER

UNIVERSIDAD NACIONAL EXPERIMENTAL DE LOS LLANOS OCCIDENTALES 'EZEQUIEL ZAMORA'
(National Experimental University of the Western Plains 'Ezequiel Zamora')

Avda 23 de Enero, Redoma de Punto Fresco, Barinas, Estado Barinas

Telephone: (73) 41201

Internet: www.unellez.edu.ve

Founded 1975

Language of instruction: Spanish

Academic year: January to December (2 semesters)

Experimental govt-sponsored institute of higher education, serving the Los Llanos Occidentales region, and the states of Apure, Barinas, Cojedes and Portuguesa

Rector: WILLIAM PÁEZ

Vice-Rector for Infrastructure and Industrial Processes: EDITH JULIETA MORENO GARCÍA

Vice-Rector for Agricultural Production: Prof. ADOLFO PAREDES

Vice-Rector for Planning and Regional Devt: Prof. RAFAEL DELGADO

Vice-Rector for Planning and Social Devt: PEDRO GONZÁLEZ REQUENA

Vice-Rector for Services: BEXTALIA LOVERA

Gen. Sec.: YOVANY BENAVENTA

Librarian: ZULAY ACOSTA

Number of teachers: 600

Number of students: 8,000

Publications: *Biollania*, *Revista UNELLEZ de Ciencia y Tecnología*

UNIVERSIDAD NACIONAL EXPERIMENTAL DEL TÁCHIRA
(National Experimental University of Táchira)

Apdo 436, Avda Universidad, Paramillo, San Cristóbal, Estado Táchira

Telephone: (276) 353-0422

E-mail: rectorad@unet.edu.ve

Internet: www.unet.edu.ve

Founded 1974

State control

Language of instruction: Spanish

Academic year: February to December

Rector: Dr JOSÉ VICENTE SÁNCHEZ FRANK

Vice-Rector for Academics: Ing. CARLOS CHACÓN LABRADOR

Vice-Rector for Admin.: Dra DORIS AVENDAÑO

Sec.: Arq. ÓSCAR ALÍ MEDINA HERNÁNDEZ

Dean for Extension: Ing. JOSÉ LUIS RODRÍGUEZ

Dean for Graduate Studies: Dr EDGAR PERNIA

Dean for Research: BENITO MARCANO

Dean for Teaching: ALEXANDER CONTRERAS

Dean for Student Devt: Prof. LUIS VERGARA

Librarian: Ing. ERLAND MARTÍNEZ

Number of teachers: 530

Number of students: 10,500 (6,000 undergraduate, 1,500 propaedeutic, 3,000 graduate)

Publications: *Aleph sub cero*, *Boletín*, *Gaceta*, *Revista Científica UNET*, *Vocero Universitario*

UNIVERSIDAD NACIONAL EXPERIMENTAL DEL YARACUY
(National Experimental University of Yaracuy)

Zona Industrial Agustín Rivero, Edif. Fundación CIEPE, San Felipe, Estado Yaracuy

Telephone: (254) 232-2441

E-mail: rectorado@uney.edu.ve

Internet: www.uney.edu.ve

Founded 1999

State control

Courses in food science and sport

Rector: YANIRA LÓPEZ ZORRILLA

Vice-Rector: MANUEL MILLA PINO

Sec.-Gen.: LYLE RODRÍGUEZ

UNIVERSIDAD NACIONAL EXPERIMENTAL FRANCISCO DE MIRANDA
(National Experimental University Francisco de Miranda)

Edif. Rectorado, Calle Norte, Santa Ana de Coro, Estado Falcón

Telephone: (293) 250-2406

E-mail: webmaster@unefm.edu.ve

Internet: www.unefm.edu.ve

Founded 1977

Academic year: January to December (two semesters)

Chancellor: SIMON ALBERTO CONSALVI

Rector: Dr JOSÉ YANCARLOS YEPEZ HURTADO

Vice-Rector for Academics: Dr OLVIS SUBERO

Vice-Rector for Admin.: Prof. RUBÉN PEROZO

Sec.: Dra MARÍA AUXILIADORA FERRER

Librarian: Lic. NIDYA PETIT DE MOTTA

Number of teachers: 400

Number of students: 3,000

Publications: *Cultura Falconiana* (4 a year), *De la Crítica* (2 a year, print and online, www.unefm.edu.ve/web/revistaliteraria), *Gaceta Universitaria* (4 a year)

DEANS

Faculty of Civil and Industrial Engineering: Ing. ORANGEL NUÑEZ
Faculty of Medicine: Dr ROBERTO GRAND L.
Faculty of Veterinary Medicine and Agriculture: Dr DIOGENES RODRÍGUEZ

UNIVERSIDAD NACIONAL EXPERIMENTAL MARÍTIMA DEL CARIBE
(National Experimental Maritime University of the Caribbean)

Calle El Ejército, Catia La Mar, Vargas, Caracas

Telephone: (212) 351-0834
Internet: www.umc.edu.ve

Founded 2000
State control
Language of instruction: Spanish

Rector: Prof. JOSÉ CARLOS GAITÁN SÁNCHEZ
Vice-Rector for Academic Affairs: Prof. MIGUEL DARÍO PIÑANGO
Vice-Rector for Admin.: ORLANDO QUINTERO
Sec.: Dr ALEXI MARCANO

UNIVERSIDAD NACIONAL EXPERIMENTAL POLITÉCNICA 'ANTONIO JOSÉ DE SUCRE'
(National Experimental Polytechnic University 'Antonio José De Sucre')

Apdo Postal 539, Barquisimeto, Estado Lara
Avda Corpahuaico entre Avdas, Rotaria y La Salle, Parroquia Juan de Villegas, Municipio Iribarren, Barquisimeto, Estado Lara

Telephone: (251) 441-2348
E-mail: vracad@unexpo.edu.ve
Internet: www.unexpo.edu.ve/principal

Founded 1962
Private control

Campuses in Barquisimeto, Caballero Mejías and Puerto Ordaz; faculties of chemistry and industrial engineering, electrical engineering, electronic engineering, mechanical engineering, metallurgy, systems

Rector: Lic. RITA AÑEZ
Vice-Rector for Academics: Dra FRAISA CODECIDO
Vice-Rector for Admin.: Ing. MAZRA MORALES
Sec.: Ing. MAGLY MELÉNDEZ DE PERAZA
Dir for Research and Postgraduate Studies: Ing. WILLIAM OSAL

Library of 19,200 vols, 9,000 periodicals
Number of teachers: 900
Number of students: 10,000

Publications: *Avance Universitario* (2 a year), *Boletín Bibliográfico de Publicaciones Recibidas* (2 a year), *Información General de la Universidad* (1 a year), *REDIP—Revista Digital de Investigación y Postgrado* (4 a year, print and online, redip.bqto.unexpo.edu.ve/index.php/redip)

UNIVERSIDAD NACIONAL EXPERIMENTAL POLITÉCNICA DE LA FUERZA ARMADA NACIONAL
(National Experimental University of the Armed Forces)

Avda La Estancia con Calle Holanda Chuao, 16°, Caracas

Telephone: (212) 908-2212
E-mail: decano@cip.unefa.edu.ve
Internet: www.unefa.edu.ve

Founded 1974
State control
Language of instruction: Spanish

Campuses in Barinas, Barquisimeto, Betijoque, Caracas, Guanare, Guatire, Maracaibo, Mérida, Miranda, San Fernando de Apure, San Tome, Sucre, Táchira, Tucupita, and Vargas

Rector: JESÚS GREGORIA GONZÁLEZ
Vice-Rector for Academics: PEDRO PABLO PAREDES GÓMEZ
Vice-Rector for Admin.: VIVIAM DURÁN GARCÍA
Vice-Rector for Social Affairs and Citizenship: Prof. RONALD BLANCO LA CRUZ
Gen. Sec.: Dra MARÍA JOSÉ TORRES

UNIVERSIDAD NACIONAL EXPERIMENTAL 'RAFAEL MARÍA BARALT'
(National Experimental University 'Rafael María Baralt')

Avda El Rosario, Parroquia Carmen Herrera, Cabimas, Estado Zulia

Telephone: (264) 241-5306
E-mail: rectorado@unermb.edu.ve
Internet: www.unermb.edu.ve

Founded 1982
State control
Language of instruction: Spanish

Campuses in Aldea Coro, Bachaquero, Ciudad Ojeda, La H, Los Laureles, Los Puertos, Medicina, Mene Grande, Miraflores, R 10, San Francisco, Santa Rita and Quinta Yoli

Rector: Dra MAYELA VÍLCHEZ MARTÍNEZ
Vice-Rector for Academic Affairs: Dr MIGUEL SÁNCHEZ PIÑA
Vice-Rector for Admin.: Dr YOGRY CASTILLO VERA
Sec.-Gen.: Dra ODA GONZÁLEZ RINCÓN

UNIVERSIDAD NACIONAL EXPERIMENTAL SIMÓN RODRÍGUEZ
(National Experimental University Simón Rodríguez)

Calle 1, Zona Industrial Urb. Palo Verde, Caracas

Telephone: (212) 251-3684
Internet: www.unesr.edu.ve

Founded 1974

Faculties of administration, education and food technology

Pres.: Dr GUSTAVO GONZÁLEZ ERASO
Rector: Dra MIRIAN BALESTRINI
Vice-Rector for Academics: Dra MIGDALIA PARRA
Vice-Rector for Admin.: MOISÉS GAMERO VÉLIZ
Sec.: OSCAR RODRÍGUEZ

Number of teachers: 400
Number of students: 13,000

Publications: *Gaceta Universitaria* (4 a year), *Gaudeamus* (1 a year), *Revista de Cultura* (4 a year), *Revista de Filosofía y Sociopolítica de la Educación* (2 a year)

UNIVERSIDAD NORORIENTAL PRIVADA 'GRAN MARISCAL DE AYACUCHO'
(Northeastern Private University 'Gran Mariscal de Ayacucho')

Avda José Antonio Anzoátegui, Edif. UGMA, Anaco, Estado Anzoátegui

Telephone: (282) 424-9455
E-mail: zaudi.marcano@ugma.edu.ve
Internet: www.ugma.edu.ve

Founded 1987 as Northeastern University; current name adopted 1993
Private control
Language of instruction: Spanish

Campuses in Anaco, Barcelona, Ciudad Bolívar, Ciudad Guayana, Cumaná, El Tigre and Maturín

Rector: EDGAR ORTIZ ORDAZ
Vice-Rector for Academics: ARELLY TOUSAINT
Vice-Rector for Admin.: Ing. LUÍS EDUARDO MARTÍNEZ H.

Vice-Rector for Student Affairs: ARÍSTIDES MAZA DUERTO
Sec.: Dr FRANCISCO ASTUDILLO

DEANS

Faculty of Dentistry: Dr ARÍSTIDES MAZA ANDUZE
Faculty of Economics and Social Sciences: Dra DELIA UGAS
Faculty of Engineering: ARMANDO MARIÑO
Faculty of Law: Dra MERY REQUENA

UNIVERSIDAD NUEVA ESPARTA
(University Nueva Esparta)

Avda Sur 7, Los Naranjos, Municipio El Hatillo, Edif. 2, 2°, Caracas

Telephone: (212) 985-2536
E-mail: informacion@une.edu.ve
Internet: www.une.edu.ve

Founded 1954
Private control
Language of instruction: Spanish
Academic year: January to December

Rector: GLADYS CARMONA DE MARCANO
Vice-Rector for Academics: ROSE MARY DIAZ DEL VALLE
Vice-Rector for Admin.: MAGALY GONZÁLEZ
Sec.: EFREN SCOTT NÚÑEZ
Dir of Library: ANABEL WEAPONS

DEANS

Faculty of Administration: LUISA ELENA GUERRERO
Faculty of Computer Science: WILPIA FLORES
Faculty of Engineering: INGMAR RAMÍREZ
Graduate Studies: MIGUEL SOTO

UNIVERSIDAD PANAMERICANA DEL PUERTO
(Panamerican University of Puerto)

Calle Anzoátegui, Casco Histórico de Puerto Cabello, Edif. Universidad, Puerto Cabello, Estado Carabobo

Telephone: (242) 361-9353
E-mail: secretaria@unipap.edu.ve
Internet: www.unipap.edu.ve

Founded 2009
Private control
Language of instruction: Spanish

Rector: Dr JESUS LEAL GUTIERREZ
Vice-Rector for Academics: Prof. CIRA BRACHO DE LOPEZ
Sec.: Dr VICENTE COLMENARES
Number of students: 1,200

DEANS

Faculty of Economics and Social Sciences: Prof. ROSARIO MONTERO RAMIREZ
Faculty of Education and Humanities: Prof. ADRIANA DE OLIVEIRA
Faculty of Engineering: Prof. DOMINGO OSORIO

UNIVERSIDAD PEDAGÓGICA EXPERIMENTAL LIBERTADOR
(Pedagogical Experimental University Libertador)

Avda Sucre, Parque del Oeste, Catia, Caracas 1030

Telephone: (212) 864-7511
Internet: www.upel.edu.ve

Founded 1983
State control
Language of instruction: Spanish
Academic year: September to July

Rector: Dr RAÚL LÓPEZ SAYAGO
Vice-Rector for Extension: Prof. MARÍA TERESA CENTENO DE ALGOMEDA
Vice-Rector for Research and Postgraduate Studies: Dra MORAIMA ESTÉVES GONZÁLEZ
Vice-Rector for Teaching: Dra DORIS PÉREZ

Sec.: Dra NILVA LIUVAL MORENO DE TOVAR..

CONSTITUENT INSTITUTES

Instituto de Mejoramiento Profesional del Magisterio

Avda Rómulo Gallegos, Segunda Transversal de Montecristo, Caracas 1071, Estado Miranda

Telephone: (212) 234-6640
E-mail: pontivero@impm.upel.edu.ve
Internet: www.impm.upel.edu.ve

Instituto Pedagógico de Barquisimeto

Avda Los Horcones con Calle 64, Barquisimeto, Estado Lara

Telephone: (251) 442-5333
E-mail: nsilva@ipb.upel.edu.ve
Internet: www.ipb.upel.edu.ve

Dir: NELSON SILVA

Instituto Pedagógico de Caracas

Avda Páez, El Paraíso, Caracas 1020

Telephone: (212) 461-6121
E-mail: webmaster@ipc.upel.edu.ve
Internet: www.ipc.upel.edu.ve

Founded 1936 as Instituto Pedagógico Nacional; present status 1987
Academic year: May to February (2 semesters)

Dean and Dir: Prof. PABLO OJEDA
Sub-Dir for Extension: Prof. HERNÁN HERNÁNDEZ
Sub-Dir for Research and Postgraduate Studies: Prof. ELIZABETH SOSA
Sub-Dir for Teaching: Prof. ALIX AGUDELO
Sec.: JUAN ACOSTA

Publications: *Candidus Infantil* (4 a year), *Lingvo & Internacia Komunikado*, *Revista de Investigación*, *Tiempo y Espacio*

Instituto Pedagógico de Maturín

Carretera Sur, Avda Raúl Leoní, Frente a Sigo la Proveduria, Maturín 6263, Estado Monagas

Telephone: (291) 640-0116
E-mail: azaragoza@ipm.upel.edu.ve
Internet: www.ipm.upel.edu.ve

Dir: ALCIDES ZARAGOZA

Instituto Pedagógico de Miranda

Calle 6, Edif. Papeca Modulo 2, Urbanización La Urbina, Caracas 1070

Telephone: (212) 461-6472
Internet: www.ipmjmsm.upel.edu.ve

Founded 1976 as Instituto Pedagógico del Este, current name adopted 1978

Campuses in Sede la Urbina, Extensión Río Chico and Extensión Nueva Cúa

Dir: NANCY BARRETO

Instituto Pedagógico Rural 'El Mácaro'

Avda las Delicias, Antiguo Parque de Ferias, Maracay 2115, Estado Aragua

Telephone: (243) 241-6367
E-mail: aperales@iprm.upel.edu.ve
Internet: www.iprm.upel.edu.ve

Dir: ANDREA HERNÁNDEZ

Instituto Pedagógico Rural 'Gervasio Rubio'

Final Avda Dr 'Manuel Pulido Méndez', Vía Bramón, Rubio, Estado Táchira

Telephone: (276) 762-1746
E-mail: oquintero@iprgr.upel.edu.ve
Internet: www.iprgr.upel.edu.ve

Dir: OSCAR ORLANDO QUINTERO

UNIVERSIDAD 'RAFAEL URDANETA' (University 'Rafael Urdaneta')

Avda El Milagro con Calle 86, Maracaibo, Estado Zulia

Telephone: (261) 200-0879
E-mail: comunicaciones@uru.edu
Internet: www.uru.edu

Founded 1974
Private control
Language of instruction: Spanish

Rector: Dr JESÚS ESPARZA BRACHO
Vice-Rector for Academics: Ing. MAULIO RODRÍGUEZ
Librarian: NANCY VILLARROEL
Sec.: Ing. SALVADOR CONDE

Publications: *Cuestiones Jurídicas* (2 a year), *La Revista Tecnocientífica* (2 a year), *Nueva Política* (2 a year)

DEANS

Faculty of Agricultural Sciences: Dr HUGO HERNÁNDEZ
Faculty of Engineering: OSCAR URDANETA
Faculty of Political, Administrative and Social Sciences: ALFREDO LEÓN

UNIVERSIDAD 'SANTA MARÍA' (University 'Santa María')

km. 4 de la Carretera Petare, Santa Lucia, en el Municipio Sucre, Caracas, Estado Miranda

Telephone: (212) 918-0800
Internet: www.usm.edu.ve

Founded 1953
Private control
Language of instruction: Spanish
Academic year: September to July

Campuses in Caracas (2 brs), Puerto La Cruz, Barinas and Puerto Ayacucho

Rector: Dr JOSÉ CEBALLOS G.
Vice-Rector for Academics: Dr RAMÓN DE TORRES C.
Vice-Rector for Admin.: Dr CARLOS ENRIQUE PEÑA
Sec.-Gen.: Dr LUIS BELISARIO ESPINAL VÁSQUEZ

DEANS

Dean of the Graduate Studies: Dr LEOPOLDO ALFREDO MARRERO RODRÍGUEZ
Faculty of Dentistry: Dra ANTONIETA COTIS OLIVARES
Faculty of Economics and Social Sciences: AMABLE A. INFANTE M.
Faculty of Engineering and Architecture: Ing. FERNANDO RAMÓN MIRALLES GOUVERNEUR
Faculty of Law: Dr INOCENCIO FIGUEROA
Faculty of Pharmacy: Dr CARLOS VIDAL BRITO BRITO

UNIVERSIDAD SIMÓN BOLÍVAR (Simón Bolívar University)

Apdo 89000, Sartenejas, Baruta, Estado Miranda

Telephone: (212) 906-3111
E-mail: vr-acad@usb.ve
Internet: www.usb.ve

Founded 1970
State control
Language of instruction: Spanish
Academic year: September to July

Rector: Prof. ENRIQUE PLANCHART
Vice-Rector for Academics: Prof. RAFAEL ESCALONA
Vice-Rector for Admin.: Prof. WILLIAM COLMENARES
Gen. Sec.: Prof. CRISTIAN PUIG
Dean for General Studies: RUBÉN DARÍO JAIMES

Dean for Postgraduate Studies: Prof. SIMÓN E. LOPEZ
Dean for Professional Studies: Prof. MARÍA GABRIELA GÓMEZ
Dean for Research and Devt: ELIA GARCÍA
Dean for Technology Studies: ARMANDO JIMÉNEZ
Dean for Extension: OSCAR GONZÁLEZ
Librarian: Dra ROSARIO GASSOL DE HOROWITZ

Library of 300,000 vols, 9,000 serial titles, 5,000 theses, 300 standards and patents on microfilm
Number of teachers: 850
Number of students: 10,000

Publications: *Argos*, *Atlántida*, *Perfiles*

UNIVERSIDAD TECNOLÓGICA DEL CENTRO (Central University of Technology)

Guacara Campus: Edif. Carabobo, Vía Aragüita (2 km de la Carretera Nacional), Guacara 2016, Estado Carabobo

Telephone: (245) 564-7092

Valencia Campus: Urb. Prebo, Fundación Cipriano Jiménez Macías, Calle 130, N° 107–211, Valencia, Estado Carabobo

Telephone: (241) 822-7908
E-mail: unitecl@telcel.net.ve
Internet: www.unitec.edu.ve

Founded 1979
Private control
Language of instruction: Spanish

Courses in information science, mechanical engineering, administration, business studies, electrical engineering, productivity and knowledge management

Rector: LUIS EDUARDO MARTÍNEZ HIDALGO
Vice-Rector for Academics: NILDA SANABRIA
Vice-Rector for Admin.: Ing. REINALDO PLAZ
Administrator: Lic. IDERMA JIMÉNEZ
Librarian: Ing. OSVALDO CRUZ

Number of teachers: 100
Number of students: 1,500

Publication: *El Innovador*

UNIVERSIDAD VALLE DEL MOMBOY (University of Valle del Momboy)

Avda Principal de Carvajal, Sector La Llanada Frente a Residencias 'Los Manguitos', Estovacuy Carvajal, Estado Trujillo

Telephone: (271) 414-7019
E-mail: linaresar@uvm.edu.ve
Internet: www.uvm.edu.ve

Founded 1997
Private control
Language of instruction: Spanish

Rector: FRANCISCO GONZÁLEZ CRUZ
Vice-Rector: MARIA TERESA BRAVO
Sec. for Academics: JOSÉ LUIS BRICEÑO VILORIA
Dir for Admin.: ESMIRNA RIVAS
Dir for Library: DOMITILA PEÑA BASTIDAS

Publication: *Revista Arbitrada Momboy* (1 a year)

DEANS

Faculty of Economics, Administrative and Managerial Studies: CRISTINA VIERAS SALCEDO
Faculty of Engineering: BETZABETH LEÓN
Faculty of Legal, Political and Social Studies: ANA LINARES DE MÉNDEZ
Research and Graduate Studies: ALBA HERNÁNDEZ

UNIVERSIDAD YACAMBÚ
(Yacambú University)

Campus Mora I: Parque Residencial La Mora, Calle 1 A entre Avdas 3 y 4, Final Avda Intercomunal de Cabudare, Barquisimeto, Estado Lara

Telephone: (251) 710-2000*Campus Mora II*: Parque Residencial La Mora, Avda 2 esq. Calle 2, Final Avda Intercomunal de Cabudare, Barquisimeto, Estado Lara

Telephone: (251) 710-2133
E-mail: invepuny@uny.edu.ve
Internet: www.uny.edu.ve

Founded 1989
Private control
Language of instruction: Spanish
Academic year: January to December

Campuses in Barquisimeto and Acarigua

Rector: Dr JUAN PEDRO PEREIRA MEDINA
Vice-Rector for Academics: Dr JESÚS RUIZ
Vice-Rector for Admin.: Ing. LUÍS EDUARDO MARTÍNEZ H.
Vice-Rector for Graduate Studies: Dra RUTH DE PEREIRA
Vice-Rector for Portuguese Centre: Ing. MARISABEL PEREIRA
Sec.: Dra LISBETH PÉREZ

Publication: *Revista Honoris Causa* (2 a year)

DEANS

Faculty of Engineering: Dra MARIA ALONSO
Faculty of Humanities: Dra DULCE REINOSO
Faculty of Law and Political Science: Dr ALEXIS PELUFFO
Faculty of Management Sciences: Dr TARQUINO BARRETO

University Institutes

Academia Militar de Venezuela (Military Academy of Venezuela): Fort Tiuna, 5101, Caracas; internet www.academiamilitar.edu .ve; f. 1810; Rector ALEXIS JOSÉ RODRÍGUEZ CABELLO.

Escuela de Aviación Militar (Military Aviation School): Carretera Nacional Maracay, Mariara, Base Aérea Mariscal Sucre, Maracay, Estado Aragua; tel. (243) 554-0176; internet www.aviacion.mil.ve; f. 1920.

Instituto Universitario Adventista de Venezuela (Adventist University Institute of Venezuela): Apdo 3205, Salom diversion Panamerican Highway, Las Lagunas, Nirgua, Estado Yaracuy; tel. (254) 803-1326; e-mail contactoiunav@gmail.com; internet www.iunav.com; f. 1999; Gen. Dir Dr EDGAR BRITO LA ROSA.

Instituto Universitario de Administración y Gerencia (University Institute of Administration and Management): Avda Universidad, entre las esq. de Sociedad a San Francisco, Edif. IUDAG, Caracas; tel. (212) 543-3332; e-mail info@iudag.com; internet www.iudag.com; f. 1996.

Instituto Universitario de Ciencias Administrativas y Fiscales (University Institute of Administrative and Fiscal Sciences): Calle Boyaca entre Avda Ayacucho y Calle Pichincha No 115, Edif. Prezziuso, Maracay, Estado Aragua; tel. (243) 246-8489; internet www.iucaf.tec.ve; f. 2002; 47 teachers; 2,000 students.

Instituto Universitario de Diseño 'Las Mercedes' (University Institute of Design 'Las Mercedes'): Avda Rio de Janeiro cruce con Calle Roraima, Quinta Los Abuelos, Chuao, Caracas; tel. (212) 993-9139; e-mail info@iud.edu.ve; internet www.iud.edu.ve; f. 1999.

Instituto Universitario de Educación Especializada (University Institute of Special Education): Calle 77 (Avda 5 de Julio) con Calle 15 Delicias, Maracaibo, Estado Zulia; tel. (261) 759-3019; e-mail info@iune .edu.ve; internet www.iune.edu.ve.

Instituto Universitario de Gerencia y Tecnología (University Institute of Management and Technology): Avda Francisco Solano López, Torre Solano, Sabana Grande, Caracas; tel. (212) 762-8882; e-mail informacion@iugtvirtual.tec.ve; internet www.iugtvirtual.tec.ve; f. 2000; 47 teachers.

Instituto Universitario de la Audición y el Lenguaje (University Institute of Hearing and Language): Edif. IVAL Calle Cuchivero, Caracas 1071; tel. (212) 242-0343; internet www.funda-ival.com.ve; f. 1956.

Instituto Universitario de la Frontera (University Institute of the Frontier): La Potrera, San Cristóbal, Estado Táchira; tel. (276) 516-5404; e-mail webmaster@iufront .edu.ve; internet www.iufront.net; f. 1988; campuses in San Antonio, San Cristóbal, Mérida and La Grita; Founding Dir FREDDY MOLINA.

Instituto Universitario de Mercadotecnia (University Institute of Marketing): Avda Casanova, C. C. Cediáz, Sabana Grande, Al lado del Meliá, Caracas; tel. (212) 762-6769; internet www.isum.com.ve.

Instituto Universitario de Nuevas Profesiones (University Institute for New Professions): Avda Rómulo Gallegos, Edif. IUNP Los Dos Caminos, Caracas; tel. (212) 234-1639; internet www.iunp.edu.ve; f. 1978.

Instituto Universitario de Profesiones Gerenciales (University Institute of Management Professions): Avda Universidad estación de Metro La Hoyada, Edif. Instituto Universitario de Profesiones Gerenciales, Caracas; tel. (212) 541-2432; internet www .iupg.net.ve; f. 1996; campuses in La Hoyada and Sabana Grande; Dir Dr JOSÉ JACINTO VIVAS.

Instituto Universitario de Relaciones Públicas (University Institute of Public Relations): Avda Sur 3, Esquinas de Pinto a Miseria, Edif. IUDERP, Parroquia Santa Rosalía, Caracas 1010; tel. (212) 542-3128; e-mail iuderp_1972@hotmail.com; internet www.iuderp.edu.ve; f. 1964, recognized 2004; Dir Dr JULIO CORREDOR; Sub-Dir for Academics Dra LUISA CÁCERES.

Instituto Universitario de Seguros (University Institute of Insurance): Urb. La Florida, Avda Los Jabillos, Quinta Doña Kata, Vertical a la Funeraria Vallés, Caracas; tel. (212) 730-9333; e-mail docentes .ius@gmail.com; internet www .institutouniversitariodeseguros.com.ve; f. 1970.

Instituto Universitario de Tecnología Agroindustrial (University Institute of Agroindustrial Technology): Avda Teotimo D'Pablos Antiguo Parque Exposicion 'Teotimo D'Pablos'-La Concordia, San Cristóbal, Estado Táchira; tel. (276) 346-5260; e-mail sistemas@mail.iutai.tec.ve; internet www .iutai.tec.ve; f. 1971; Coordinator RICHARD ALEXANDER PÉREZ; Deputy Dir for Academics DOUGLAS GUERRERO.

Instituto Universitario de Tecnología Alberto Adriani (University institute of Technology Alberto Adriani): Calle Baruta, cruce con la Avda los Cerritos, Urb. Bello Monte, Edif. IUAA, Parroquia El Recreo, Municipio Libertador, Caracas; tel. (212) 951-5274; e-mail informacion@iuaa.com.ve; internet www.iuaa.com.ve.

Instituto Universitario de Tecnología 'Alonso Gamero' (Institute of Technology 'Alonso Gamero'): Avda Libertador con Calle Alí Primera Parq, Los Orumos Coro, Estado Falcón; e-mail webinfoiutag@gmail.com; internet www.iutag.org; f. 1980; Coordinator Ing. RAFAEL PINEDA PIÑA; Sub Dir for Academics PEDRO SIERRA GRATEROL.

Instituto Universitario de Tecnología 'Américo Vespucio' (University Institute of Technology 'Américo Vespucio'): Avda Principal de los Chorros, a 200 m de la Estación del Metro Los Dos Caminos, Caracas; tel. (212) 285-7066; e-mail direccionadjunta.iutav@gmail.com; internet www.gav.edu.ve; f. 1988; Academic Dir Dr LORENA DI PAOLO.

Instituto Universitario de Tecnología 'Antonio José de Sucre' (University Institute of Technology 'Antonio José de Sucre'): Edif. ALSA, ubicado en la Calle 9 de la Urbina, Caracas; tel. (212) 242-7016; e-mail caracas@uts.edu.ve; internet www.uts.edu .ve; f. 1972; campuses in Anaco, Aragua de Barcelona, Barcelona, Barquisimeto, Bolívar, Caracas, Charallave, Guarenas, Maracaibo, Maracay, Mérida, Porlamar, Guiana, Punto Fijo, San Cristobal, San Felipe, Socopo and Valencia.

Instituto Universitario de Tecnología Bomberil (Bomberil University Institute of Technology): Avda Ezio Valeri Moreno, Mérida 5101, Estado Mérida; tel. (274) 658-6838; e-mail iutb_direccion@hotmail.com; internet www.iutb.edu.ve; f. 1989; library: 1,200 vols; Dir Prof. OMAR VELÁSQUEZ.

Instituto Universitario de Tecnología 'Cristóbal Mendoza' (University Institute of Technology 'Cristóbal Mendoza'): Avda Bolívar, No 19-A (Sector Coco Frío), El Vigía, Estado Mérida; tel. (275) 881-0431; e-mail carreras@iutcm.edu.ve; internet www.iutcm .edu.ve; campuses in El Vigía and Mérida.

Instituto Universitario de Tecnología 'Coronel Agustín Codazzi' (University Institute of Technology 'Colonel Agustín Codazzi'): Avda Adonay Parra, Frente al Aeropuerto Nacional de Barinas, Parroquia El Carmen, Municipio Barinas, Barinas, Estado Barinas; tel. (273) 532-4295; e-mail info@tac.edu.ve; internet www.tac.edu.ve; f. 1998.

Instituto Universitario de Tecnología de Administración Industrial (University Institute of Industrial Management Technology): Edif. Tequendama, Mezzanina, Avda México, diagonal al Liceo Andrés Bello, entre las estaciones de Bellas Artes y Parque Carabobo, Caracas; tel. (212) 572-8590; internet www.iutarc.edu.ve; f. 1990; campuses in Baralt, Jesuitas, Guarenas, Paraiso and Mirandinos.

Instituto Universitario de Tecnología de Cabimas (University Institute of Technology of Cabimas): Urb. el Amparo, Calle la Estrella, No 117, Cabimas, Estado Zulia; tel. (264) 241-3125; e-mail atencionusuario@ iutcabimas.tec.ve; internet www.iutcabimas .tec.ve; f. 1974 as Colegio Universitario de Cabimas.

Instituto Universitario de Tecnología de Cumaná (University Institute of Technology of Cumaná): Carretera Cumaná-Cumanacoa km 4, Cumaná, Estado Sucre; tel. (293) 467-2138; e-mail webiutcumana@gmail.com; internet iutcumana-edu-ve.blogspot.in.

Instituto Universitario de Tecnología de Maracaibo (University Institute of Technology of Maracaibo): Avda 85, Urb. La Floresta, Maracaibo, Estado Zulia; tel. (261) 754-9996; e-mail academiaiutm@hotmail.com; internet www.iutm.edu.ve.

Instituto Universitario de Tecnología de Valencia (University Institute of Technology of Valencia): Avda Paseo Cuatricentenario, Complejo Educacional 'La Manguita',

Vía Guataparo, Valencia, Estado Carabobo; tel. (241) 820-5111; e-mail iutvenlinea@iutvalencia.edu.ve; internet www.iutvalencia.edu.ve; f. 1977; Pres. WLADIMIR LABRADOR; Sec. MARIO EVÍES.

Instituto Universitario de Tecnología de Yaracuy (University Institute of Technology of Yaracuy): Apdo 83, San Felipe 3201, Estado Yaracuy; Avda Alberto Ravell con Avda José Antonio Páez, San Felipe 3201, Estado Yaracuy; tel. (254) 31-3168; internet www.iuty.edu.ve/iuty; f. 1974.

Instituto Universitario de Tecnología del Estado Bolívar (University Institute of Technology of Bolívar State): Calle Igualdad, entre Calle Progreso y Rosario, No 28, Edif. IUTEB, Ciudad Bolívar, Estado Bolívar; tel. (285) 634-0339; e-mail iuteb.rrpp@gmail.com; internet iutebprincipal.no-ip.org/portal; f. 2001; Sub-Dir of Academics MARIA LUISA GONZÁLEZ.

Instituto Universitario de Tecnología del Estado Portuguesa 'Juan de Jesús Montilla' (University Institute of Technology of the Portuguese State 'Juan de Jesús Montilla'): Avda Circunvalacion Sur, Sector Bellas Artes, Acarigua, Estado Portuguesa; tel. (255) 623-7538; e-mail posgrado@iutep.tec.ve; internet www.iutep.tec.ve; f. 1978; offices in Guanare and Turen; experimental stations in Mijaguito, Chabasquén and the Majaguas; Rector Ing. WILLIAMS RAFAEL ROMERO PEÑA; Academic Head CLAUDIA MARCELA INOSTROZA REYES.

Instituto Universitario de Tecnología del Oeste 'Mariscal Sucre' (University Institute of Technology of the West 'Mariscal Sucre'): Calle Este 2, entre Esq. Dr Paúl y Salvador de León, Torre sede del CNU, (antigua torre del Banco Caribe) Pquia Catedral, Municipio Libertador, Caracas; tel. (212) 506-0506; e-mail ingreso@opsu.gob.ve; internet loeu.opsu.gob.ve.

Instituto Universitario de Tecnología 'Dr Delfín Mendoza' (University Institute of Technology 'Dr Delfín Mendoza'): Avda Orinoco antiguas instalaciones de Lagoven, Tucupita, Estado Delta Amacuro; tel. (287) 721-1810; internet www.iutdelta.edu.ve; Dir MARIA DE LOURDES PÉREZ BARRETO.

Instituto Universitario de Tecnología 'Dr Federico Rivero Palacio' (University Institute of Technology 'Dr Federico Rivero Palacio'): Carretera Panamericana km 8, Los Teques, Estado Miranda; tel. (212) 352-3232; e-mail cestudios@iutfrp.edu.ve; internet www.iutfrp.edu.ve; f. 1971; nat. training programmes in the following disciplines: engineering, dentistry, administration, computer, science, etc.

Instituto Universitario de Tecnología 'Dr José Gregorio Hernández' (University Institute of Technology 'Dr José Gregorio Hernández'): Avda 6 con Calle 6, Edif. UNIHER, Parroquia Juan Ignasio Montilla, Valera, Estado Trujillo; tel. (271) 221-0245; e-mail uniher@email.com.ve; nat. training programmes in architecture, engineering, sports science and technology.

Instituto Universitario de Tecnología 'Elías Calixto Pompa' (University Institute of Technology 'Elías Calixto Pompa'): Avda Principal, Urb. Valle Arriba, C. C. Daymar, Acceso Lateral, Guatire, Estado Miranda; tel. (212) 342-1801; e-mail brachoa@cantv.net; internet www.iutecp.com.

Instituto Universitario de Tecnología Industrial 'Rodolfo Loero Arismendi' (University Institute of Industrial Technology 'Rodolfo Loero Arismendi'): Final Avda Caurimare, Caracas; tel. (212) 751-1842; internet www.iutirla.web.ve; f. 1978; campuses in Barcelona, Barquisimeto, Caracas,

Ciudad Bolívar, Ciudad Guayana, Cumana, Maturin, Porlamar, Punto Fijo, Valera and Vargas; Dir Dr RICHARD TUCKER LOERO.

Instituto Universitario de Tecnología 'José María Carreño' (University Institute of Technology 'José María Carreño'): Prolongación Avda Monseñor Pellín, entrada Urb. Las Brisas, Cúa, Municipio Urdaneta, Estado Miranda; tel. (239) 511-2160; internet www.iutjmc.com.

Instituto Universitario de Tecnología 'Juan Pablo Perez Alfonzo' (University Institute of Technology 'Juan Pablo Perez Alfonzo'): Avda Kerdell (Prolongacion Miranda), No 121–64, a 30 m del Palacio de Los Iturriza, Valencia; tel. (241) 821-2195; e-mail viperbutt@hotmail.com; internet www.iutepal.net; f. 1989; brs in Puerto Cabello, Maracay, San Cristóbal, Maracaibo, San Francisco, Cabimas, Puerto la Cruz and Puerto Piritu.

Instituto Universitario de Tecnología 'Laura Evangelista Alvarado Cardozo' (University Institute of Technology 'Laura Evangelista Alvarado Cardozo'): Edif. Martins, Parish Mother Mary of St. Joseph, Municipio Girardot, Maracay; tel. (243) 245-1099; e-mail info@iutleac.net; internet www.iutleac.net; f. 1998, recognized 2002; Dir SOJO NUBIA PARRA.

Instituto Universitario de Tecnología para la Informática (University Institute for Computer Technology): C.C. Save, Avda Industrial, Zona Industrial y Comercial La Isabelica, Valencia, Estado Carabobo; tel. (241) 833-9564; internet www.iutepi.edu; f. 1988, recognized in 1992; campuses in Acarigua, Guanare and Valencia; Pres. Ing. ANÍBAL GÓMEZ; Nat. Dir Dr RAFAEL ADRIÁN CASTILLO QUINTERO.

Instituto Universitario de Tecnología 'Pascal' (University Institute of Technology 'Pascal'): Calle Mariño, C/C Páez Edif. 102-02-10, 1°, Sector El Barrancón, Cagua, Municipio Sucre, Estado Aragua; tel. (244) 395-7121; internet www.iutepascal.com.ve; f. 1996.

Instituto Universitario de Tecnología 'Pedro Emilio Coll' (University Institute of Technology 'Pedro Emilio Coll'): Avda 17 (Rafael María Baralt) No 72.18, Maracaibo, Estado Zulia; tel. (261) 751-3447; e-mail iutpec@iutpec.com; internet www.iutpec.com; f. 1983; campuses in Maracaibo and Puerto Ordaz; Nat. Dir CARLOS ACOSTA KENNY; Sub-Dir for Academics Dr EUDY GONZÁLEZ URDANETA.

Instituto Universitario de Tecnología 'POLYCOM' (University Institute of Technology 'POLYCOM'): Avda Bolívar Este CC Pacifico Planta Baja Locales 14–15 a 50 m del CC Parque Aragua, Maracay, Estado Aragua; tel. (243) 233-4425; e-mail administracion@polycomiut.edu.ve; internet polycomiut.tec.ve; f. 2002; Dir for Academics ROBERT SIERRA GARCÍA.

Instituto Universitario de Tecnología 'Tomás Lander' (University Institute of Technology 'Tomás Lander'): Estamos ubicados en la Avda Ribas, Edif. Universitario, Ocumare del Tuy, Estado Miranda; tel. (239) 225-9474; e-mail informatica@iuttol.edu.ve; internet iuttol.edu.ve; f. 1998.

Instituto Universitario de Tecnología Venezuela (Venezuela University Institute of Technology): Edif. Seguros La Metropolitana, Avda Universidad Perico a Monroy, Caracas; tel. (212) 577-5575; internet www.iutv.com.ve.

Instituto Universitario Experimental de Tecnología 'Andrés Eloy Blanco' (Experimental University Institute of Technology 'Andrés Eloy Blanco'): Avda Los Horcones

con Avda La Salle, Sector Pueblo Nuevo, Barquisimeto, Estado Lara; tel. (251) 266-5244; e-mail direccion@iuetaeb.tec.ve; internet www.iuetaeb.tec.ve; Rector Dra BERTHA PULIDO LEÓN.

Instituto Universitario Gran Colombia (Grand Colombia University Institute): Edif. Libertador, Calle 7, No 12–45, Diagonal al Parque Maltín Polar, La Concordia, San Cristóbal, Estado Táchira; tel. (276) 347-8422; f. 1998.

Instituto Universitario 'Jesús Enrique Lossada' (University Institute 'Jesús Enrique Lossada'): Calle 78, No 17–129, Edif. IUJEL, Parroquia Chiquinquirá, Maracaibo, Estado Zulia; tel. (261) 752-5006; f. 1980, recognised 2002.

Instituto Universitario Salesiano 'Padre Ojeda' (Salesian University Institute 'Father Ojeda'): Avda El Liceo Jorge Losch (al lado del Liceo San José), Los Teques, Estado Miranda; tel. (212) 322-9812; e-mail iusposal@cantv.net; internet www.iuspo.edu.ve; f. 1996.

Instituto Universitario YMCA 'Lope Mendoza' (YMCA University Institute 'Lope Mendoza'): Avda Guaicaipuro Edif. YMCA, 5°, San Bernardino, (Diagonal Centro Médico), Caracas; tel. (212) 552-0891; e-mail iuymcalm@gmail.com; internet ymcacaracas.org.ve; f. 1983.

University Colleges

Colegio Universitario de Administración y Mercadeo (University College of Management and Marketing): Urb. La Campiña II, Calle 197 con la Avda 3, Edif. CUAM, Naguanagua, Estado Carabobo; tel. (241) 600-1101; e-mail webmaster@cuam.tec.ve; internet www.cuam.tec.ve; f. 1990; campuses in Cagua, Calabozo, Caracas, Guacara, Industrial (Valencia), Puerto Cabello, Naguanagua and San Felipe; Dir Ing. JOSE BOTELLO; publ. *Revista Talento*.

Colegio Universitario de Caracas (University College of Caracas): Avda Principal de la Floresta cruce con Avda Francisco de Miranda, Urb. La Floresta, Edif. Sucre, Chacao, Estado Miranda; tel. (212) 278-7545; e-mail atencion-cuc@hotmail.com; internet www.cuc.edu.ve; f. 1971; 33,250 students; Dir Dr ARMANDO ALVAREZ LUGO.

Colegio Universitario de Enfermería Centro Médico de Caracas (University Nursing College Medical Centre of Caracas): Avda Mariscal Sucre, Quinta 12, San Bernardino, Caracas; tel. (212) 552-5991; e-mail info@cuecmc.edu.ve; internet www.cuecmc.edu.ve; f. 1987; Dir Dr JOSÉ MARÍA RODRÍGUEZ ARAÚZ.

Colegio Universitario de Enfermería de la Alcaldía Metropolitana de Caracas (University College of Nursing of the Metropolitan Mayoralty of Caracas): Avda San Martín, Puente 9 de Diciembre, 2°, Ala Oeste, Parroquia San Juan, Municipio Libertador, Caracas; tel. (212) 636-6168; e-mail direccion_cue@hotmail.com.

Colegio Universitario de Enfermería de la Cruz Roja de Venezuela (University College of Nursing of the Red Cross of Venezuela): Avda Andrés Bello, Edif. Cruz Roja Venezolana, 2°, No 4, Municipio Libertador, Parroquia Candelaria, Caracas, Distrito Capital; tel. (212) 577-1345; f. 1988; Dir Dr JESÚS R. ROMERO GUZMÁN.

Colegio Universitario de Psicopedagogía (University College of Psychopedagogy): Avda San Gabriel, No 45, Urb. El Ávila, entre Alta Florida y Country Club, Caracas; tel.

(212) 730-1994; e-mail cup-ve@cantv.net; internet www.cup.edu.ve; f. 1971; Pres. JORGE LUIS BOLÍVAR.

Colegio Universitario de Rehabilitación 'May Hamilton' (University College of Rehabilitation 'May Hamilton'): Calle la Guayanita, Bella Vista, Centro Nacional de Rehabilitación 'Dr. Alejandro Rhode', Planta Baja, Caracas; tel. (212) 472-4767; e-mail curmayhamilton@ivss.gob.ve; internet www.ivss.gov.ve/rehabilitacion-may-hamilton; f. 1975; attached to Instituto Venezolano de los Seguros Sociales.

Colegio Universitario 'Dr Rafael Belloso Chacín' (University College 'Dr Rafael Belloso Chacín'): Calle 77 (Blvd 5 de Julio) Esq. Avda 3H, Edif. CUNIBE, Maracaibo, Estado Zulia; tel. (261) 791-1252; e-mail obelloso@cunibe.org; internet www.cunibe.org; Pres. Dr OSCAR BELLOSO MEDINA.

Colegio Universitario 'Fermín Toro' (University College 'Fermín Toro'): Carrera 29, entre Calles 20 y 21, No 20–27, Parroquia Catedral, Municipio Iribarren, Barquisimeto, Estado Lara; tel. (251) 231-5331; e-mail cuft.informacion@gmail.com; internet www.cuft.tec.ve; f. 1975; campuses in Acarigua, Barquisimeto, and Caracas.

Colegio Universitario 'Francisco de Miranda' (University College 'Francisco de Miranda'): Esq. de Mijares, Parroquia Altagracia, diagonal al Banco Central de Venezuela, Caracas; tel. (212) 862-1179; internet www.cufm.tec.ve; f. 1974; Dir JUDITH SALGADO.

Colegio Universitario 'Monseñor de Talavera' (University College 'Monseñor de Talavera'): Avda Principal de La Castellana, cruce con Calle Los Granados, Urb. La Castellana, Caracas; tel. (212) 266-9966; internet www.cumt.edu; f. 1975; campuses in Acarigua, Cabimas, Caracas, Cristóbal, Maracaibo, Puerto Ordaz, San Cristóbal and Valencia; Dir ELIA DE AGUAR.

Colegio Universitario 'Profesor José Lorenzo Pérez' (University College 'Profesor José Lorenzo Pérez'): Edif. Mercurio, 3°, Calle 8 de la Urbina, Sucre, Estado Miranda; tel. (212) 241-1118; e-mail educacioncupjppr@cantv.net; f. 1991; Dir FRANKLIN GONZÁLEZ.

Other Higher Education Institutions

Centro de Investigaciones Psiquiatricas, Psicológicas y Sexológicas de Venezuela (Psychiatric Research Centre, Psychology and Sexology in Venezuela): Avda Paramaconi, Torre Bianco, Urb. San Bernardino, Caracas; tel. (212) 551-3055; e-mail info@cippsv.com; internet www.cippsv.com; f. 1975; Pres. Dr FERNANDO BIANCO; Dir Dr JUAN JOSÉ MOLES; publ. *Sexología* (2 a year).

Conservatorio de Música José Luis Paz (Conservatory of Music José Luis Paz): Avda 2 El Milagro, Edif. Secretaría de Cultura, 2°, Maracaibo, Estado Zulia; tel. (261) 808-6231; internet conservatoriojlp.com.ve; f. 1943; Dir JEAN WILLIAMS FUENMAYOR.

Escuela Superior de Arte 'Neptali Rincón' (School of Art 'Neptali Rincón'): Centro Vocacional Dr O. Hernández, Avda El Milagro diagonal al Hospital Central, Maracaibo, Estado Zulia; tel. (261) 223-8683; f. 1957; 12 teachers; 300 students; Dir CONSUELO BUSTOS.

Fundación Teresa Carreño (Teresa Carreño Foundation): Teatro Teresa Carreño, Final Paseo Colón, Caracas; tel. (212) 574-9122; e-mail webmaster@teatroteresacarreno.com; internet www.teatroteresacarreno.com; f. 1983; concerts, opera, ballet, master classes and courses for opera singers; Dir-Gen. BEATRICE RANGEL MANTILLA.

Instituto de Altos Estudios de la Defensa Nacional (Higher Institute of National Defence Studies): Avda Los Próceres, e/ IPSFA y Círculo Militar, El Valle, Caracas; tel. (212) 693-8716; e-mail iaeden@iaeden.edu.ve; internet www.iaeden.edu.ve; f. 1970; Dir PASCUALINO ANGIOLILLO FERNÁNDEZ.

Instituto de Altos Estudios Diplomáticos 'Pedro Gual' (Higher Institute of Diplomatic Studies 'Pedro Gual'): Esq. Santa Capilla a Principal, Caracas; tel. (212) 806-4734; e-mail director.pedrogual@mre.gov.ve; internet www.institutopedrogual.edu.ve; f. 1977 as Instituto de Asuntos Internacionales; current name adopted 1998; Dir-Gen. ENRIQUE ACUÑA.

Instituto de Altos Estudios en Salud Publica 'Dr Arnoldo Gabaldon' (Higher Institute of Public Health Studies 'Dr

Arnoldo Gabaldon'): Apdo 2171–2113, Maracay 2101, Estado Aragua; Avda Bermúdez, Maracay 2101, Estado Aragua; tel. (243) 232-5633; e-mail iaes.comunicaciones@gmail.com; internet www.iaesp.edu.ve; f. 1936 as Escuela de Expertos Malariólogos, current name adopted 2002; Exec.-Dir Dra TULIA HERNÁNDEZ; publs *Boletín de Malariología y Salud Ambiental* (2 a year, print and online, www.iaesp.edu.ve/index.php/centro-de-descargas/viewcategory/15), *Revista Salud de los Trabajadores* (2 a year, print and online, www.iaesp.edu.ve/index.php/centro-de-descargas/viewcategory/5).

Instituto de Estudios Superiores de Administración (Institute for Advanced Studies of Management): Barrio Los Erasos, Caracas; tel. (212) 555-4201; e-mail comunicacionesiesa@iesa.edu.ve; internet www.iesa.edu.ve; f. 1965; Pres. GUSTAVO ROOSEN; Academic Dir Prof. ROSA AMELIA GONZÁLEZ; publ. *Ediciones IESA*.

Instituto Nacional de Higiene 'Rafael Rangel' (National Hygiene Institute 'Rafael Rangel'): Ciudad Universitaria, detrás del Hospital Clínico Universitario, Caracas; tel. (212) 219-1600; internet www.inhrr.gob.ve; f. 1938 as Instituto Nacional de Higiene, current name adopted 1977; Chair. Dra ESPERANZA BRICEÑO.

Instituto Venezolano de Planificación Nacional (Venezuelan Institute of National Planning): Avda Intercomunal Valle-Coche, Edif. Escuela Venezolana de Planificación, Urb. la Rinconada, Caracas 1090; tel. (212) 682-1219; e-mail evpcontroldeestudios@gmail.com; internet www.fevp.gob.ve; f. 2006.

La Escuela Nacional de Administración y Hacienda Pública–Instituto Universitario de Tecnología (ENAHP-IUT) (National School of Public Administration and Finance—University Institute of Technology): Edif. ENAHP-IUT, Avda Francisco de Miranda entre Avda Diego Cisneros y Calle Los Laboratorios, Los Ruíces, Caracas; tel. (212) 232-8918; e-mail postgrado.enahp@gmail.com; internet www.enahp.edu.ve; f. 1937 as Instituto de Administración Comercial y de Hacienda; current name 1977; attached to Ministerio del Poder Popular de Finanzas; Dir-Gen. ZULEIMA AGUILARTE.

VIET NAM

The Higher Education System

Institutions of higher education pre-date Viet Nam's partition in 1954 (it was reunified as the Socialist Republic of Viet Nam in 1976), the oldest being Hanoi Medical University, which was founded in 1902 when Viet Nam was under French colonial rule. Over 30 institutions were founded during the period of partition (1954–76), including major universities in Hanoi and Ho Chi Minh City (formerly Saigon). In 1989 Viet Nam's first private college since 1954 was opened in Hanoi; Thang Long College was to cater for university students. The presence of foreign universities is increasing with universities such as the Royal Melbourne Institute of Technology and the University of Hawaii offering degrees in fields such as business, English as a second language and information technology. According to preliminary estimates, in 2010/11 there were 414 universities and colleges of higher education, with a total enrolment of 2.5m. students; of these, 86 were private institutions (46 universities and 40 colleges).

The Ministry of Education and Training is responsible for higher education, with the exception of technical and vocational education, which is the responsibility of the Ministry of Labour, Invalids and Social Affairs, and institutions of health education and military or security training, which come under the appropriate ministries. The National Council for Education Accreditation, which was established in October 2008, is responsible for accreditation and quality assurance in the higher education sector.

Since the 2002/03 academic year, a national university entrance examination has been the determining factor in university admissions; students sit examinations in one of four subject streams, depending on the course of study for which the student has applied. A credit-based degree system is being introduced and was expected to have been fully implemented by 2012/13. The Tot Nghiep Dai Hoc (College Diploma or Associate degree) is a three-year course that can be upgraded to a Bang tot nghiep dai hoc (Bachelors degree) after one year. The Bachelors is the main undergraduate qualification and often lasts four years, although degrees in veterinary medicine (five years) and medicine (six years) are longer in duration. Graduates who have been awarded the Bachelors degree are eligible to sit the entrance examination for admission to the Thac si (Masters degree), a two-year taught or research-based course. The Tien si (Doctorate) is open to students who hold either the Bachelors or the Masters degree and admission is again based on competitive examination. However, students with Bachelors degrees must study for four to five years to gain the Doctorate (and usually earn a Masters 'in passing'), while students with the Masters are awarded the Doctorate after two or three years. Technical and vocational education at the post-secondary level is offered by colleges, universities, training centres, agencies, social organizations and private companies and leads to award of the Vocational Education Graduation Diploma, which requires one to two years of study following completion of secondary school education, or the Junior College Graduation Diploma, which has a practical focus and typically lasts three years.

In 2009 the World Bank approved a US $50m. loan for its higher education development policy programme in Viet Nam; in return, the bank is expecting a 40% increase in student enrolments by 2020. Meanwhile, the Vietnamese Government initiated the Higher Education Reform Agenda for the period 2006–20 with a view to improving the quality, efficiency and governance of the higher education system, increasing the enrolment rate at universities, and strengthening the quality of teaching and research at universities and other higher education institutions.

Regulatory Bodies

GOVERNMENT

Ministry of Culture, Sports and Tourism: No 51–53 Ngo Quyen St, Hoan Kiem Dist., Hanoi; tel. (4) 39439915; e-mail bovanhoathethaodulich@chinhphu.vn; internet www.cinet.gov.vn; Minister HOÀNG TUẤN ANH.

Ministry of Education and Training: 49 Dai Co Viet St, Hai Ba Trung Dist., Hanoi; tel. (4) 38697215; e-mail bogddt@moet.edu.vn; internet www.moet.gov.vn; Minister Prof. Dr PHAM VŨ LUAN.

Ministry of Science and Technology: 113 Tran Duy Hung St, Trung Hoa Ward, Cau Giay Dist., Hanoi; tel. (4) 39437056; e-mail ttth@most.gov.vn; internet www.most.gov.vn; Minister NGUYEN QUÂN.

Learned Societies

GENERAL

UNESCO Office Hanoi: 23 Cao Ba Quat St, Hanoi; tel. (4) 7470275; e-mail registry@unesco.org.vn; internet www.unesco.org.vn; gender equality, HIV/AIDS prevention, youth devt and poverty reduction; Dir DUNG DOAN THI.

Viet Nam Union of Literary and Arts Associations: 51 Tran Hung Dao St, Hanoi; tel. (4) 8682608; f. 1957; 10 mem. orgs (assocs of writers, cinematographers, fine arts, composers and musicologists, theatre artists, photographers, folklorists, dancers, architects, and minority writers and artists), with a total of 10,000 mems; Pres. NGUYEN DINH THI; Sec.-Gen. THANH TO NGOC; publ. *Dien dan van nghe Viet Nam* (Forum of Vietnamese Literature and Arts, 4 a year).

Viet Nam Union of Science and Technology Associations: 53 Nguyen Du St, Hanoi; tel. (4) 9432206; e-mail thongtin@vusta.vn; internet www.vusta.org.vn; f. 1983; 114 mem. socs; Chair. Prof. Dr HO UY LIEM (acting).

AGRICULTURE, FISHERIES AND VETERINARY SCIENCE

National Association of Vietnamese Gardeners: 15 Thanh Cong St, Hanoi; tel. (4) 8345216; f. 1985; Pres NGUYEN NGOC TRIU.

Viet Nam Forestry Association: 114 Hoang Quoc Viet St, Cau Giay District, Hanoi; tel. (4) 7541311; Pres. NGUYEN NGOC LUNG; Sec.-Gen. NGO DUC MINH.

ECONOMICS, LAW AND POLITICS

Economics Association: 1B Cam Hoi St, Hai Ba Trung Dist., Hanoi; tel. (4) 9712899; e-mail vie-lam@fpt.vn; f. 1974, recognized by Govt. 1975; attached to ASEAN Fed. of Economics Asscns, Int. Economics Asscn, Viet Nam Union of Science and Technology Asscns (VUSTA); 2,000 mems.

Viet Nam Lawyers Association: A2-261 Thuy Khue St, Tay Ho District, Hanoi; tel. (4) 8474826; e-mail vla@fpt.vn; internet www.hoiluatgiavn.org.vn; attached to ASEAN Law Asscn; Sec.-Gen. (vacant).

HISTORY, GEOGRAPHY AND ARCHAEOLOGY

Vietnamese Association of Historians: 25 Tong Dan St, Hanoi; tel. (4) 8256588; Pres. PHAN HUY LE; Sec.-Gen. DUONG TRUNG QUOC.

LANGUAGE AND LITERATURE

British Council: 40 Cat Linh St, Dong Da District, Hanoi; tel. (4) 8436780; e-mail bchanoi@britishcouncil.org.vn; internet www.britishcouncil.org/vietnam; f. 1993; offers courses and exams in English language and British culture, and promotes cultural exchange with the UK; attached teaching centre in Ho Chi Minh City; Dir KEITH DAVIES; Training Centre Man. TIM HOOD.

Goethe-Institut: Nguyen Thai Hoc St 56–58, Ba Dinh Dist., Hanoi; tel. (4) 37342251; e-mail info@hanoi.goethe.org; internet www.goethe.de/so/han/deindex.htm; offers courses and exams in German language and culture, and promotes cultural exchange with Germany; Dir Dr ALMUTH MEYER-ZOLLITSCH.

MEDICINE

Traditional Medicine Association of Viet Nam: 19 Tong Dan St, Hanoi; tel. (4) 8253006; Pres. NGUYEN XUAN HUONG.

Viet Nam General Association: 68A Ba Trieu St, Hanoi; tel. (4) 39439323; e-mail vgamp@hn.vnn.vn; internet tonghoiyhoc.org.vn; f. 1955; 21 mem. socs; Pres. Prof. PHAM SONG; Sec.-Gen. TRAN HUU THANG; publ. *Y hoc Viet Nam* (magazine).

NATURAL SCIENCES
Biological Sciences

Viet Nam Association of Biological Science Societies: Biological Experiment Centre, Ha Noi Pedagogical Institute, Hanoi; tel. (4) 8347654; Pres. VU TUYEN HOANG; Sec.-Gen. NGUYEN LAN HUNG.

Mathematical Sciences

Viet Nam Mathematical Society: 46 Lieu Giai St, Hanoi; tel. (4) 8682414; e-mail vms@vms.org.vn; Pres. DO LONG VAN; Sec.-Gen. TONG DINH QUY.

Physical Sciences

Geological Society of Viet Nam: 6 Pham Ngu Lao St, Hanoi; tel. (4) 8260752; e-mail gsv@hn.vnn.vn; f. 1983; 5,000 mems; Sec.-Gen. NGUYEN TIEN THANH.

Viet Nam Physical Society: P104-46 Nguyen Van Ngoc St, Hanoi; tel. (4) 8349209; Pres. PHAN HONG KHOI.

TECHNOLOGY

Mining Association: 54 Hai Ba Trung St, Hanoi; tel. (4) 9342723; Pres. NGUYEN VAN LONG; Sec.-Gen. DINH NGOC DANG.

Viet Nam Foundry and Metallurgical Association: 54 Hai Ba Trung St, Hanoi; tel. (4) 8262052; Pres. PHAN TU PHUNG.

Vietnamese Association of Mechanics: 264 Doi Can, Badinh, Hanoi; tel. (4) 7625804; e-mail phong@mail.hut.edu.vn; internet www.cohocvietnam.org.vn; Pres. NGUYEN HOA THINH; Sec.-Gen. DINH VAN PHONG.

Research Institutes
GENERAL

Viet Nam Institute of Culture and Arts: 32 Pho Hao Nam, La Thanh, Phuong O Cho Dua, Quan Dong Da, Hanoi; tel. (4) 8569160; e-mail vncvhnt@fpt.vn; f. 1971; attached to Min. of Culture, Sports and Tourism; 50 staff; study of Vietnamese culture in all its aspects and relations with other countries; library of 5,000 vols; Dir-Gen. Prof. NGUYEN CHI BEN; publ. *Culture Research Information*.

AGRICULTURE, FISHERIES AND VETERINARY SCIENCE

Food Crops Research Institute: Lien Hong, Gia Loc, Hai Duong Province; tel. (320) 3716463; e-mail vcltctp@fpt.vn; f. 1968; research on varietal and technological improvement of rice, root and tuber crops, legumes, vegetables and fruit-tree crops; library of 1,950 vols, 170 journals; Dir Prof. Dr HOAN NGUEN TRI (acting); publ. *Research Bulletin of Field Crops* (every 2–3 years).

Forest Science Institute of Viet Nam (FSIV): Chem, Tu Liem Dist., Hanoi; tel. (4) 8389031; e-mail info@fsiv.org.vn; internet www.fsiv.org.vn; f. 1988; Dir-Gen. Prof. Dr TRIEU VAN HUNG; publ. *Vietnam Forestry Review* (4 a year).

Fruits and Vegetables Research Institute: Thi Tran Trau Quy, Huyen Gia Lam, Thanh Pho, Hanoi; tel. (4) 8276254; e-mail vrqhnvn@hn.vnn.vn; f. 1969; attached to Viet Nam Acad. of Agricultural Sciences; responsible for scientific research and technology transfer on vegetables, fruits, flowers, landscape plants, mulberry silk.

Institute of Agricultural Science of South Viet Nam: 121 Nguyen Binh Khiem St, 1st District, Ho Chi Minh City; tel. (8) 38291746; fax (8) 38297650; e-mail iasvn@vnn.vn; internet iasvn.org; f. 1925; research on pedology, crop sciences and animal sciences, agricultural systems, agricultural and development economics; library of 10,000 vols; collection of insects; Dir Prof. BUI CHI BUU.

Institute of Soil and Fertilizer Research: East Ngac, Tu Liem Dist., Hanoi; tel. (4) 8362379; e-mail khkh_tnnh@hn.vnn.vn; f. 1968; attached to Viet Nam Acad. of Agricultural Sciences; Dir Dr BUI HUY HIEN.

National Institute of Animal Husbandry: Chem Thuy Phuong, Hanoi; tel. (4) 385022; e-mail vccuong@netnam.vn; f. 1969; research on domestic animals; extension service; Dir Dr LE VIET LY; publ. *Scientific and Technical Journal on Animal Husbandry*.

National Institute of Veterinary Research: 86 Truong Chinh Rd, Dong Da Precinct, Hanoi; tel. (4) 8686817; e-mail longlinh5@yahoo.com; f. 1968.

Plant Protection Research Institute: Dongngac, Tu Liem District, Hanoi; tel. (4) 38389724; e-mail nipp-tonghop@hn.vnn.vn; internet www.vaas.org.vn; f. 1968; attached to Viet Nam Acad. of Agricultural Sciences; plant protection research and development with emphasis on biological and genetic control, integrated pest management of food and vegetable and specific tropical crops; library of 700 vols; Dir Dr NGO VINH VIEN; publ. *Plant Protection Bulletin* (6 a year).

Research Institute for Aquaculture: Dinh Bang, Tu Son, Bac Ninh; tel. (4) 271368; e-mail vanphong@ria1.org; internet www.ria1.org; f. 1975.

Research Institute of Marine Fisheries: 170 Le Lai St, Haiphong; tel. (31) 3836656; e-mail vhs@rimf.org.vn; f. 1961; study, training and research in fisheries biology, stock assessment, brackish water aquaculture, mariculture, oceanography, technology of fishing and processing; library of 12,000 vols; Dir Prof. Dr DO VAN KHUONG; publs *Aquaculture, Aquaculture Asia, Aquaculture International, Aquaculture Research, Infofish International, Journal of Fish Disease, World Fishing*.

Rubber Research Institute of Viet Nam: 177 Hai Ba Trung St, Ho Chi Minh City; tel. (8) 8294139; e-mail rriv@rriv.org.vn; f. 1975; library of 3,000 vols; Gen. Dir MAI VAN SON.

Viet Nam Institute of Agricultural Engineering: A2 Phuong Mai, Dong Da, Hanoi; tel. (4) 8523187; f. 1968; research machinery for agricultural production and food processing; library of 3,000 vols; Dir Prof. Dr PHAM VAN LANG; publ. *Agricultural and Food Industries* (12 a year, in Vietnamese with a summary in English).

Viet Nam Academy of Agricultural Sciences: Vinhquynh, Thanh Tri District, Hanoi; tel. (4) 3861548; internet www.vaas.vn; f. 1952 as the Institute of Crop Production; current name adopted 2005; Pres. Prof. Dr NGUYEN VAN BO.

ECONOMICS, LAW AND POLITICS

Central Institute of Economic Management: 68 Phan Dinh Phung, Ba Dinh, Hanoi; tel. (4) 7338930; e-mail info@ciem.org.vn; internet www.ciem.org.vn; f. 1978.

Institute of Economics: 27 Tran Xuan Soan St, Hanoi; tel. (4) 8261633; f. 1960; library of 16,000 vols; attached to Viet Nam National Centre for Social Sciences and Humanities; Dir DO HOAI NAM; publs *Nghien Cuu Kinh Te* (Economic Studies Review, 12 a

year in Vietnamese), *Viet Nam's Socio-Economic Development* (4 a year).

Institute of Finance: 7 Ly Thuong Kiet St, Hoan Kiem District, Hanoi; tel. (4) 9331872; fax (4) 9331865; e-mail hvtc@hn.vnn.vn; f. 1961.

Institute for International Relations: 69 Chua Lang St, Dong Da District, Hanoi; tel. (4) 8344540; e-mail bbtwebsite_dav@mofa.gov.vn; internet www.dav.edu.vn; f. 1959; library of 25,000 vols; publ. *International Studies* (6 a year in Vietnamese, 2 a year in English).

Institute of Labour Science and Social Affairs: 2 Dinh Le St, Hanoi; tel. (4) 8258801; f. 1978; labour relations, working conditions, wages and living standards, levels of skill, social security; Dir Dr DO MINH CUONG.

Institute of Social Sciences: 49 Nguyen Thi Minh Khai St, District 1, Ho Chi Minh City; tel. (8) 8223995; f. 1978; Dir Dr NGUYEN THE NGHIA; publ. *Journal of Social Sciences* (6 a year).

Institute of State and Law: 27 Tran Xuan Soan St, Hai Ba Trung, Hanoi; tel. (4) 39784637; f. 1960; attached to Viet Nam Acad. of Social Sciences; Dep. Dir NGUYEN NHU THE.

Institute of Statistical Science: 48A Lang Trung, Dong Da, Hanoi; tel. (4) 8244234; f. 1976; library of 3,700 vols (2,600 foreign books, 1,100 Vietnamese); spec. collns in field of statistics; Dir NGUYEN VIET CUONG; publs *Bulletin of Statistical Science*, selection of information dissemination periodicals.

Research Institute of Trade: 46 Ngo Quyen St, Hoan Kiem District, Hanoi; tel. (4) 8262720; f. 1995 following merger of Research Institute for Foreign Economic Relations and Institute of Economic and Technological Research on Trade.

EDUCATION

Centre for Information and Library Educational Science: 101 Tran Hung Dao St, Hanoi; tel. (4) 8220911; fax (4) 8223213; e-mail dinhphuong@bdvn.vnmail.vnd.net; f. 1961 as National Institute for Educational Science; library of 5,000 vols and 1,500 periodicals; Dir Assoc. Prof. Dr DANG THANH HUNG; publ. *Information on Educational Sciences* (6 a year).

Research Centre for Vocational and Higher Education: 101 Tran Hung Dao St, Hanoi; tel. (4) 9423108; e-mail vkhgd.qhqt@bdvn.vnd.net; f. 1977; attached to National Institute for Education Strategy and Curriculum Development; Dir Assoc. Prof. Dr NGUYEN HUU CHAU.

Viet Nam Sports Science Institute: 141 Nguyen Thai Hoc St, Ba Dinh, Hanoi; tel. (4) 7330286; e-mail vkh-tt@fpt.vn; f. 1979; 5,000 mems; library of 10,000 vols on sports science; publ. *Bulletin* (16 a year).

FINE AND PERFORMING ARTS

Ha Noi Institute of Stage and Cinematography: Tu Liem, Hanoi; tel. (4) 8243397; f. 1978.

Vietnamese Institute for Musicology: 32 Nguyen Thai Hoc St, Ba Dinh District, Hanoi; tel. (4) 8457368; e-mail musicology@hn.vnn.vn; f. 1976; research in the national heritage of music, song, dance; Dir Prof. NGUYEN PHUC LINH; publ. *Bulletin* (in English and Vietnamese, 3 a year).

HISTORY, GEOGRAPHY AND ARCHAEOLOGY

Institute of Archaeology: 61 Phan Chu Trinh, Quan Hoan Kiem, Hanoi; tel. (4)

8255449; f. 1968; Dir and Editor-in-Chief HA VAN TAN; Dep. Dirs HA VAN PHUNG, TONG TRUNG TIN.

Institute of History: 38 Hang Chuoi, Quan Hai Ba Trung, Hanoi; tel. (4) 9711682; f. 1960; attached to Viet Nam Acad. of Social Sciences; library of 70,000 vols from fmr library of École Français d'Extrême-Orient; Dir NGUYEN VAN NHAT; publ. *Nghien cuu Lich su (Historical Studies) Review*.

Viet Nam Research Institute of Land Administration: Hoang Quoc Viet St, Cau Giay, Hanoi; tel. (4) 7561154; e-mail vgcr@hn .vnn.vn; internet www.virila.ac.vn; f. 1994; attached to Min. of Natural Resources and the Environment; scientific research and technological devt in geodesy, cartography and land administration; dependent centres: GIS and databases, geodynamics, spatial images and aerial photography; 240 staff; Dir Dr NGUYEN DUNG TIEN.

LANGUAGE AND LITERATURE

Institute of Linguistics: 36 Hang Chuoi St, Hanoi; tel. (4) 9710968; e-mail lytoanthang@ yahoo.com; f. 1968; library of 12,000 vols; Dir Dr LY TOAN CHANG; publ. *Ngon Ngu* (4 a year).

(Viet Nam) Institute of Literature: 20 Ly Thai To St, Hanoi; tel. (4) 8253548; e-mail vienvanhoc@hn.vnn.vn; internet vienvanhoc .vass.gov.vn; f. 1953; library of 180,000 vols; Dir Prof. Dr NGUYEN DANG DIEP; publ. *Tap chi Nghien cuu Van hoc* (Literary Studies Review, 12 a year).

MEDICINE

Ho Chi Minh City Institute of Hygiene and Public Health: 159 Hung Phu St, District 8, Ho Chi Minh City; tel. (8) 8559503; e-mail vienvsytcc@hcm.vnn.vn; f. 1977; Dir Prof. LE THE THU.

Institute of Malariology, Parasitology and Entomology: Luong The Vinh St, Hanoi; tel. (4) 8543035; e-mail moh@vnn.vn; f. 1957.

Institute for the Protection of the Mother and Newborn Child: 43 Trang Thi St, 08-4 Hanoi; tel. (4) 8252161; e-mail ipmn@hn.vnn.vn; f. 1966; obstetrics, gynae- cology, care of the newborn child and family planning, in vitro fertilization; library of 5,000 vols; Dir Dr NGUYEN DUC VY; publs *Nôi san San Phu Khoa* (internal journal of obstetrics and gynaecology, 1 a year), *Tông kêt công trinh nghiên cúu khoa hoc* (review of scientific studies, 1 a year).

Institute of Traditional Medicine in Ho Chi Minh City: 273 Nam Ky Khoi Nghia St, Phu Nhuan Dist., Ho Chi Minh City; tel. (8) 38443047; e-mail v.ydhdt@tphcm.gov.vn; internet www.vienydhdt.com.vn; f. 1975; short-term courses in health: acupuncture, acupressure, massage (foot and body), yoga.

Institute of Vaccines and Medical Biolo- gicals: 9 Pasteur St, Nha Trang, Khanh Hoa; e-mail ivac@dng.vnn.vn; f. 1979.

National Hospital of Odonto—Stomatol- ogy/Benh Vien Rang Ham Mat Trung uong Hanoi: 40B Trang Thi St, Hoan Kiem Dist., Hanoi; tel. (4) 8269723; e-mail ranghammat@hotmail.com; internet www .ranghammat.vn; f. 2002 by merger of Odonto-Maxillo-Facial dept of Hanoi Medical University and Hanoi Odonto-Maxillo-Facial Institute; attached to Min. of Health; treats patients with dental and facial diseases; researches and trains the provinces' hospital staff; provides a practical centre for Hanoi Medical Univ.; Dir Assoc. Prof. Dr TRINH DINH HAI.

National Institute of Drug Quality Con- trol: 48 Hai Ba Trung St, Hoan Kiem Dist.,

Hanoi; tel. (4) 38255742; e-mail dc_son@ yahoo.com; f. 1957 as Drug Quality Control Laboratory; drug quality control analysis and specification evaluation, devt of standards and reference substances, scientific research and training, participating in devt of Vietna- mese pharmacopoeia; library of 1,450 vols; Dir Prof. Dr THAO NGUYEN THI PHUONG; publ. *Journal of Drug Quality Control* (4 a year).

National Institute of Hygiene and Epi- demiology: 1 Yersin St, 10000 Hanoi; tel. (4) 8212416; e-mail nihe@netnam.org.vn; f. 1924; epidemiology of communicable dis- eases, vaccine devt; library of 12,000 vols; Dir Prof. NGUYEN TRAN HIEN; publ. *Tap Chi Ve Sinh Phong Dich* (journal, in Vietnamese with abstract in English, 4 a year).

National Institute of Medicinal Mater- ials: 3B Quang Trung St, Hoan Kiem Dis- trict, Hanoi; tel. (4) 8252644; e-mail tttv-nimm@vienduoclieu.org.vn; internet www.nimm.org.vn; f. 1961; multidisciplinary research on pharmaceutical materials, mainly medicinal plants; postgraduate train- ing; library of 6,000 vols; Dir Prof. NGUYEN GIA CHAN; publ. *Materia Medica Bulletin* (4 a year).

National Institute of Nutrition: 48B Tang Bat Ho St, Hanoi; tel. (4) 39717090; e-mail ninvietnam@viendinhduong.vn; internet www.viendinhduong.vn; f. 1980; depts of basic nutrition, community nutrition, applied nutrition, clinical nutrition, food science, food safety, dietetics, experiment workshop, library, food and nutrition behaviour research; Dir Prof. LE THI HOP; publs *Jour- nal of Food and Nutrition Sciences*, *Nutri- tion, Health and Life*.

National Institute of Occupational and Environmental Health Research: c/o Ministry of Health, Ib pho Yersin, Hanoi; tel. (4) 9713649; e-mail byt@moh.gov.vn; Dir Prof. Dr LE VAN TRUNG.

National Institute of Otolaryngology: Bachmai Hospital Centre, 78 Giai Phong St, Phuong Mai, Hanoi; tel. (4) 8693731; f. 1969; 200 staff; library of 1,000 vols; Dir Prof. LUONG SY CAN; publs *Noi San Tai Mui Hong* (1 a year), *Thong Tin Tai Mui Hong* (1 a year).

National Institute of Paediatrics: 18/ 8779 La Thanh, Dong Da, Hanoi; tel. (4) 8343700; e-mail nip_vn@hn.vnn.vn; internet www.benhviennhitu.org.vn; f. 1969 as the Institute of Child Care, renamed Viet Nam— Sweden Children's Hospital and the Olof Palme Paediatric Institute, present name since 1997; Dir Assoc. Prof NGUYEN THANH LIEM.

National Institute of Traditional Medi- cine: The National Hospital of Traditional Medicine, 29 Nguyen Binh Khiem, Hanoi; tel. (4) 9432442; e-mail yhcotruyen@hn.vnn .vn; internet www.natiotradimedhos.org.vn; f. 1957; traditional medicine; library of 19,343 vols, spec. colln of books on Chinese medicine and medicine in Viet Nam since 15th century; Dir Prof. Dr CHU QUOC TRUONG; publ. *Journal of Research in Viet- namese Traditional Medicine and Pharmacy* (4 a year).

National Institute of Tuberculosis and Respiratory Diseases: 120 Hoang Hoa Tham St, Hanoi; tel. (4) 8326249; f. 1957; research on asthma, chronic bronchitis, lung cancer, occupational lung diseases, tubercu- losis; operates two national programmes: Acute Respiratory Infections in Children, National Tuberculosis Control Programme; library of 10,000 vols; Dir Prof. N. V. Co; publ. *Lao và bênh phôi* (4 a year).

Nha Trang Institute of Hygiene and Epidemiology: 10 Tran Phu St, Nha Trang, Phu Khanh Province; f. 1976.

Tay Nguyen Institute of Hygiene and Epidemiology: Buon Ma Thuoc, Dak Lak Province; f. 1976; Man. for Planning and Science HAU VAN PHAM; Vice-Man. HAU PHAM VAN.

Vietnam National Institute of Ophthal- mology: 85 Ba Trieu St, Hanoi; tel. (4) 9438004; e-mail bvmtw@vnio.vn; internet www.vnio.vn; f. 1957.

NATURAL SCIENCES

General

National Centre for Scientific Research of Viet Nam, Ho Chi Minh City Branch: 1 Mac Dinh Chi St, Dist. 1, Ho Chi Minh City; tel. (8) 222246; f. 1975; chemistry, funda- mental and applied research in biology, geoscience, mathematics, physics; Pres. Prof. Dr HO SI THOANG; Sec. Prof. Dr NGUYEN VAN TRONG.

Biological Sciences

Dalat Institute of Biology: 116 Xo Viet Nghe Tinh, Dalat, Lam Dong; tel. (63) 822078; e-mail sdhl@vnn.vn; internet www .vast.ac.vn; f. 1975; attached to Viet Nam Acad. of Science and Technology; biochemis- try and molecular biology of nitrogen fix- ation; plant genetics; Dir Prof. LE XUAN TU; publ. *Journal of Biology*.

Mathematical Sciences

Institute of Mathematics: Vietnamese Acad. of Science and Technology, 18 Hoang Quoc Viet, 10307 Hanoi; tel. (4) 7563474; e-mail vientoan@math.ac.vn; internet www .math.ac.vn; f. 1969; attached to Vietnamese Acad. of Science and Technology; algebra, dynamic systems, discrete mathematics, functional analysis, geometry and topology, methods of mathematical physics, numerical analysis, operations research, optimal con- trol theory, partial differential equations, probability and mathematical statistics; library of 12,000 vols, 350 periodicals; Dir Prof. HA HUY KHOAI, Prof. Dr NGO VIET TRUNG; publ. *Acta Mathematica Vietnamica* (3 a year).

Physical Sciences

Institute of Chemistry: 18 Hoang Quoc Viet Rd, Cau Giay District, Hanoi; tel. (4) 7564312; e-mail info@vienhoahoc.ac.vn; internet www.vienhoahoc.ac.vn; f. 1978; attached to Vietnamese Acad. of Science and Technology; basic and applied research and engineering in organic, inorganic, phy- sicochemical and analytical chemistry; chem- istry of natural products and polymers; library of 6,000 vols; Dir Prof. Dr TRAN VAN SUNG; publs *Collection of Selected Scientific Works* (1 a year), *Tap chí Hóa hoc* (Journal of Chemistry, 6 a year).

Institute of Geological Sciences: 84 Chua Lang St, Dong Da, Hanoi; tel. (4) 37754798; e-mail info@igsvn.ac.vn; internet www.igsvn .ac.vn; f. 1967; Dir Dr TRONG-HUE TRAN.

Institute of Meteorology and Hydrology: Gate 62/5, Nguyen Chi Thanh, Dong Da, Hanoi; tel. (4) 7733090; e-mail mandt@vkttv .edu.vn; internet www.imh.ac.vn; f. 1977; Dir Dr TRAN THUC.

Institute of Oceanography: 01 Cau Da, Nha Trang, Khanh Hoa Province; tel. (58) 590036; e-mail haiduong@dng.vnn.vn; internet www.vnio.org.vn; f. 1923; library of 60,000 vols; incorporates National Oceano- graphic Museum and Aquarium; Dir Dr NGUYEN TAC AN; publs *Collection of Marine Research Works* (1 a year), *Journal of Marine Science and Technology* (4 a year).

Institute of Physics: 10 Dao Tan, Thu Le, Ba Dinh, Hanoi; tel. (4) 22123631; e-mail office@iop.vast.ac.vn; internet iop.vast.ac.vn; f. 1969; attached to Viet Nam Acad. of Science and Technology; Deputy Dir Assoc. Prof. Dr NGUYEN HONG QUANG.

Viet Nam Institute of Geosciences and Mineral Resources: Min. of Natural Resources and Environment, Thanh Xuan, Hanoi; tel. (4) 8547335; e-mail van@vigmr .vn; f. 1976; Dir Assoc. Prof. NGUYEN XUAN KHIEN; publ. *Geology and Mineral Resources* (irregular).

PHILOSOPHY AND PSYCHOLOGY

Institute of Philosophy: 59 Lang Ha St, Ba Dinh Dist., Hanoi; tel. (4) 5143338; e-mail ducphilosophy@yahoo.com; internet www .vientriethoc.com.vn; f. 1962; research into theoretical and practical issues of the devt of Viet Nam; scientific foundation for the planning of the Party and Govt's policies and guidelines in Viet Nam; research on philosophical issues and practice of devt of philosophy in Viet Nam, devts and achievements of philosophical research both in Viet Nam and abroad; other research and teaching activities incl. training MA and PhD students, organizing nat. and int. seminars and confs; library of 50,000 vols; Dir Prof. PHAM VAN DUC; publ. *Philosophy* (12 a year, in Vietnamese; English edn 4 a year).

RELIGION, SOCIOLOGY AND ANTHROPOLOGY

Institute of Ethnology: 27 Tran Xuan Soan, Quan Hai Ba Trung, Hanoi; tel. (4) 9784867; e-mail khongdienvdt@hn.vnn.vn; f. 1968; research in cultural history and social structure of the nationalities in Viet Nam and SE Asia; 62 staff; library of 10,000 vols; attached to Viet Nam Acad. of Social Sciences; Dir PHAM QUANG HOAN; publ. *Ethnographical Studies* (4 a year).

TECHNOLOGY

Food Industry Research Institute: Km. 8 Nguyen Trai Rd, Thanh Xuan, Hanoi; tel. (4) 8584318; e-mail vu@fii.ac.vn; f. 1967; carries out research into biotechnology, food processing technology using local raw materials, and other areas connected with food; Dir Prof. Dr LE DUC MANH.

Hydraulic Engineering Consultants Corporation No. 1: 95/2 Chùa Bôc, Dong Da, Hanoi; tel. (4) 8534162; e-mail hec1@hn .vnn.vn; f. 1956; library of 9,000 vols; Dir-Gen. HOANG MINH DZUNG; publ. *Hydraulic Engineering* (1 a year).

Institute for Building Science and Technology: Tran Cung St, Nghia Tan Ward, Cau Giay District, Hanoi; tel. (4) 7544196; e-mail ibst_vn@fpt.vn; internet www.ibst.vn; f. 1963; concrete and concrete technology, construction chemistry, corrosive research and structural protection, construction technology, environmental engineering, fire safety for houses and engineering works, geotechnical and foundation engineering, geodesy and engineering surveying, structural engineering, structural testing, water supply and drainage technology; 370 mems; library of 22,000 vols; Dir Assoc. Prof. Dr CAO DUY TIEN; publ. *Building Science and Technology Journal* (4 a year).

Institute for Tropical Technology: 18 Hoang Quoc Viet, Cau Giay, Hanoi; tel. (4) 8360376; e-mail hien-vktnd@hn.vnn.vn; f. 1980; corrosion testing and metal protection, concrete protection, testing of non-metallic materials, their resistance to tropical climates and lifetime prediction, development of new materials, new coatings (organic and inorganic), tropic-proofing of electrical and electronic equipment; small library; Dir Dr LE XUAN HIEN.

Institute of Information Technology: 18 Hoang Quoc Viet Rd, Cau Giay Dist., Hanoi; tel. (4) 37564405; e-mail vanthu@ioit.ac.vn; internet www.ioit.ac.vn; f. 1976 as Institute of Computer Science and Cybernetics (ICSC), current name adopted 1993; Dir Prof. Dr THAI QUANG VINH.

Institute of Electronics, Informatics and Automation: 156A, Quan Thanh St, Hanoi; tel. (4) 37164855; e-mail vielina@hn.vnn.vn; internet www.vielina.com.vn; f. 1985 as Viet Nam Institute of Research and Development in Electronics; informatics and automation, research and application of new technologies, techniques and products concerned with electronics; centeres and laboratories: Automatic Control Centre, High-Tech Centre, Hydrodynamics and Automation, Information Technology Centre, Information Technology Support Centre, Quality Measurement Centre, Robotics Laboratory, High Quality Printed Circuit Laboratory, Special Laboratory of PLC; 81 researchers and employees; Dir Prof. Dr NGUYEN XUAN QUYNH..

Branch Office:

> **Branch Institute of Electronics, Informatics and Automation:** 138 To Thien Thanh St, 10th District, Ho Chi Minh City; tel. (8) 8652126; juridical basics.

Institute of Energy: Ton That Tung St, Khuong Thuong, Dong Da, Hanoi; tel. (4) 8523741; e-mail bbt@ievn.com.vn; f. 1988; research, programmes and projects concerning energy devt in Viet Nam; depts: science and technology; nuclear, thermal power and the environment; electrical design; computers; electrical power systems devt; energy demand forecasting and management; energy economics; high voltage electrical techniques; Gia Sang Research Station for the Protection of Electrical Lines from Lightning; hydropower; electrical network planning; biogas energy; rural energy planning and fuel; solar and wind energy; basic construction projects; production; Dir Dr TRAN QUOC CUONG.

Institute of Industrial Chemistry: 2 Pham Ngu Lao St, Hoan Kiem District, Hanoi; tel. (4) 8253930; e-mail vienhoacn@ hn.vnn.vn; internet www.vinachem.com.vn/ english/companydetail.asp?comid=43; f. 1959; Dir Prof. Dr MAI NGOC CHUC.

Institute of Machinery and Industrial Instruments: 34 Lang Ha St, Dong Da Dist., Hanoi; tel. (4) 8344372; f. 1973; library of 10,000 vols; Dir Dr TRAN VIET HUNG.

Institute of Mechanics: 264 Doi Can St, Ba Dinh, Hanoi; tel. (4) 8325541; f. 1979; basic and applied research in the fields of fluids, deformable solids and vibration mechanics; library of 14,182 vols; Dir Prof. NGUYEN TIEN KHIEM; publ. *Journal of Mechanics* (4 a year).

Institute of Mining Science and Technology: Phuong Lien St, Dong Da Dist., Hanoi; tel. (4) 8642024; e-mail ttthan@hn .vnn.vn; f. 1979; research into underground and opencast mining, mine development and construction, excavating and tunnelling, environmental mine safety, ventilation, electro-mechanization, transport, coal preparation and processing; library of 9,000 vols; Dir Dr PHUNG MANH DAC; publs *Mining Management* (12 a year), *Mining Technology Information* (6 a year), *Works Collection* (every 5 years).

Institute of Paper and Cellulose Research: Thanh Xuan District, Hanoi, Vinh Phu Province; tel. (4) 8581072; f. 1970.

Institute of Transport Science and Technology: 80 Tran Hung Dao St, Hoan Kiem, Hanoi; tel. (4) 38224464; e-mail itc-mot@mt.gov.vn; f. 1978; attached to Ministry of Transport.

National Institute for Urban and Rural Planning: 37 Le Dai Hanh St, Hanoi; tel. (4) 9760691; f. 1956, current name 1990; research and establishment of construction planning projects, and environmental and landscape organization in the territorial regions, urban and rural settlements; 8 research, design and planning divisions, 4 administrative divisions; centres: Centre for Research on Urban and Rural Environmental Planning, Centre for Rural Planning and Development, Centre for Urban and Rural Planning in the Middle Regions; 290 staff; Dir Prof. Dr LE HONG KE.

National Research Institute for Mechanical Engineering: Thang Long St, Caugiay, Hanoi; tel. (4) 8344225; f. 1962 as the Institute of Mechanical Design and Manufacture; 4 professional depts: administration and personnel, economic planning, finance, scientific management; research depts: 'cold' welding, dynamics, hydromechanical and hydroelectrical heavy mechanics, mechanical design, technology; 265 staff; Dir Prof. Dr HAN DUC KIM.

National Research Institute of Mining and Metallurgy: 30B Doan Thi Diem St, Hanoi; tel. (4) 8233775; e-mail vimluki@ netnam.org.vn; f. 1967; library of 10,000 vols; Dir Dr NGUYEN ANH.

Research Institute for Agricultural Machinery: Km 9 Nguyen Trai St, Thanh Xuan, Dong Da, Hanoi; tel. (4) 8544429; f. 1970; research, machinery design; library of 5,500 vols; Dir NGUYEN VAN HOI.

Research Institute of Posts and Telecommunications: 122 Hoang Quoc Viet Rd, Nghia Tan, Cau Giay Dist., Hanoi; tel. (4) 7562037; e-mail vkhktbdld@hn.vnn.vn; internet www.ptit.edu.vn/ptit_english.asp; Dir Prof. Dr NGUYEN CANH TUAN; publ. *Ket Qua Nghien Cuu Khoa Hoc* (1 a year).

Scientific and Technological Institute for Communications and Transport: 80 Tran Hung Dao St, Hoan Kiem, Hanoi; tel. (4) 38224464; e-mail vukhcn@mt.gov.vn; internet khcn.mt.gov.vn; f. 1956.

Shipbuilding Science and Technology Institute—SHIPSCITECH: 80B Tran Hung Dao St, Hanoi; tel. (4) 8257070; f. 1983; devt and application of new technologies in shipbuilding, design, building and modernization of marine facilities, consultancy services, training of staff and devt of standards; units and facilities: professional design dept, Centre for Research and Testing of Models, pilot production workshops, testing tank; Dir Dr NGO CAN (acting).

Textile Research Institute: 478 Minhkhai St, Hanoi; tel. (4) 8624025; e-mail viendetmay@hn.vnn.vn; f. 1969; research in material technology, machinery for spinning, weaving and finishing; inspection of quality of material and finished products, fashion design; library of 3,500 vols; Dir Dr NGUYEN VAN THONG; publs *Textiles Magazine* (6 a year), *Textile Research Journal* (1 a year).

Viet Nam Atomic Energy Commission: 59 Ly Thuong Kiet St, Hanoi; tel. (4) 9423479; e-mail hg.vaec@hn.vn.vnn; internet www.vaec.gov.vn; f. 1979; nuclear science and technology; Chair. TRAN HUU PHAT; publ. *Nuclear Science and Technology*.

Viet Nam Institute for Building Materials: 235 Nguyen Trai St, Thanh Xuan, Hanoi; tel. (4) 8581111; e-mail vienvlxd@hn .vnn.vn; internet www.vibm.vn; f. 1975; Pres. THAI DUY SAM.

Viet Nam Institute of Water Conservation: 299 Tayson St, Dong Da District, Hanoi; tel. (4) 8522086; f. 1959; units: Centre for Termite Prevention, Centre for Irrigation, Centre for Water Treatment and Environmental Research, Centre for Research in River and Marine Dynamics, Centre for Hydraulic Research, Centre for Structures and Materials, Centre for Small-Scale Hydroelectric Research, Geotechnics Division, Hydraulic Research Division, Irrigation Systems Management Division, Pump Research Division; 236 staff; Dir Dr NGUYEN TUAN ANH.

Libraries and Archives

Hanoi

Central Health Information and Technology Institute: 15 Le Thanh Tong, Hoan Kiem and valley 135 Nui Truc, Ba Dinh, Hanoi; tel. (4) 37368315; e-mail cimsi@cimsi.org.vn; internet www.cimsi.org.vn; f. 1979 by merger of Central Library for Medical Sciences (2001) and Central Institute for Medical Sciences Information (1979); attached to Min. of Health; specializes in medical information and technology services to all orgs of health sector in Viet Nam; 7,000 vols; Gen. Dir Dr LUONG CHI THANH; publs *Health Newsweek from Internet* (48 a year), *Medical and Pharmaceutical Information Journal* (12 a year).

Central Library for Science and Technology: 24 Lý Thuòng Kiêt, Hanoi; tel. (4) 9349111; e-mail thutt@vista.gov.vn; internet www.clst.ac.vn; f. 1960; attached to the National Centre for Scientific and Technological Information and Documentation; 230,000 vols, 4,500 periodicals; Dir VU VAN SON.

Institute of Social Sciences Information—National Social Sciences Library: 26 Ly Thuong Kiet, Hanoi; tel. (4) 8253074; f. 1975 by amalgamation of Dept. of Social Sciences Information and Central Social Sciences Library; attached to Viet Nam Academy of Social Sciences; 1m. vols; Dir Prof. HO SI QUY; publs *Bibliography of Social Sciences* (1 a year), *Review of Social Sciences Information* (12 a year).

National Centre for Scientific and Technical Information: 24 Ly Thuong Kiet St, Hanoi; tel. (4) 9342945; e-mail techmart@vista.gov.vn; internet vista.gov.vn; f. 1990 by merger of the Central Institute for Scientific and Technical Information and the Central Library; formulation and implementation of Science and Technology programmes; national databank, documentation sources and publications; publs *Information and Documentation* (4 a year), *KCM—S&T Information* (12 a year), *Vietnam S&T Abstracts* (6 a year).

National Library of Viet Nam: 31 Trang Thi, 10000 Hanoi; tel. (4) 8253040; e-mail ptkhang@nlv.gov.vn; f. 1917; attached to Min. of Culture, Sports and Tourism; 1.2m. vols, 8,000 periodical titles; Dir PHAM THE KHANG; publs *Information on Culture and Arts*, *Library and Bibliographical Work* (4 a year), *Library Magazine* (4 a year), *National Bibliography* (12 a year and 1 a year).

Ho Chi Minh City

General Sciences Library of Ho Chi Minh City: 69 Ly Tu Trong, Dist. 1, Ho Chi Minh City; tel. (8) 8225055; e-mail gsl.hcmc@hcm.vnn.vn; internet www.gslhcm.org.vn; f. 1976; attached to Service of Culture, Sports and Tourism of Ho Chi Minh City; 700,000 vols, 4,500 periodical titles, databases; Dir BUI XUAN DUC.

Social Sciences Library: 49 Nguyen Thi Minh Khai, Dist. 3, Ho Chi Minh City; tel. (8) 8228934; e-mail siss@hcm.vnn.vn; f. 1975; attached to Institute of Social Sciences; the collections of the fmr Archaeological Research Institute have been added to the library; provides facilities for research in archaeology, economics, ethnology, history, law, literature, linguistics, philosophy, sociology; 145,000 vols; Dir TRAN MINH DUC.

Museums and Art Galleries

Haiphong

Haiphong Museum: c/o Dept. of Tourism, 44 Lach Tray, Haiphong; 65 Dien Bien Phu St, Haiphong; tel. (31) 852720; f. 1919; local history.

Hanoi

Bao tàng Cách mang Viêt Nam (National Museum of Vietnamese Revolution): 25 Tong Dan St, 216 Tran Quang Khai, Hoan Kiem District, Hanoi; tel. (4) 8254323; e-mail baotangcmvn@hn.vnn.vn; internet www.baotangcm.gov.vn; f. 1959; study of revolutionary history of Viet Nam; library of 21,000 vols and historical documents, 17,900 documentary photographs; Dir Prof. Dr TRIEU VAN HIEN.

Ho Chi Minh Museum: 19 Ngoc Ha St, Ba Dinh Dist., Hanoi; tel. (4) 8463572; f. 1990 1977; study of Ho Chi Minh's life and work; Dir HA HUY GIAP.

Viet Nam Fine Arts Museum: 66 Nguyên Thai Hoduc St, Ba Dinh Dist., Hanoi; tel. (4) 38233084; e-mail binhtruong451@hn.vnn.vn; f. 1966; preservation and presentation of nat. cultural heritage; research into ancient and modern fine arts, ceramics, handicrafts, folk arts; exhibitions of foreign art; library of 1,100 vols; Dir TRUONG QUOC BINH.

Viet Nam History Museum: 1 Trang Tien, Hanoi; tel. (4) 8253518; f. 1958; research and conservation, history of Viet Nam from palaeolithic period to 1945; Dir Dr PHAM QUOC QUÂN; publ. *Bulletin* (1 a year).

Viet Nam Military History Museum: 28A Dien Bien Phu St, Ba Dinh, Hanoi; tel. (4) 7334682; e-mail btqsvn@bt.vnn.vn; internet www.btlsqsvn.org.vn; f. 1959; fmrly People's Army Museum; exhibits Viet Nam's military history since the founding of the country to the Ho Chi Minh era; 4,000 of 160,000 objects on display; Dir LE CHIEU.

Ho Chi Minh City

Ho Chi Minh City Museum: 65 Ly Tu Trong, Ward Dist. 1 Ho Chi Minh City; tel. (8) 8299741; e-mail bttphcm@hcm.vnn.vn; internet www.hcmc-museum.edu.vn; f. 1977; 2 sections: 1 devoted to the revolution, the other to ancient arts.

Hue

Hue Royal Antiquities Museum: 3 Le Truc St, Hue; tel. (54) 3524429; e-mail hueroyalmuseum@yahoo.com.vn; f. 1923; history of the old capital; administered by the Hue Monuments Conservation Centre; library of 1,345 vols; Man. NGUYEN PHUOC HAI TRUNG; Head of Exhibition Dept HOANG NGOC SON; publ. *Hue Royal Antiquities Museum*.

Thai Nguyen

Museum of the Cultures of Ethnic Groups in Viet Nam: Doi Can Rd, Thai Nguyen 84, Thai Nguyen Province; tel. (280) 855781; e-mail baotangvh@hn.vnn.vn; f. 1960; conserves and publicizes the cultural heritage of Viet Nam's ethnic groups; Dir HA THI NU.

Vinh

Nghe-Tinh Museum: 10 Dao Tan, Khoi 3, Cong Vien Thanh Co, Phuong Cua Nam, Thanh Pho Vinh, Nghe Tinh Province; tel. (38) 841890; f. 1960; study of the Nghe-Tinh 'Soviet' Uprising, 1930–31; artefacts on view incl. photographs and documents related to the uprising, weapons and equipment used, including the personal possessions of leading revolutionaries Nguyen Phong Sac, Nguyen Tiem and Nguyen Chau; Man. PHAN XUAN THANH.

Universities

CAN THO UNIVERSITY

3/2 St, Cantho City, Cantho Province

Telephone: (710) 3838237
E-mail: ductri@ctu.edu.vn
Internet: www.ctu.edu.vn

Founded 1966
State control
Academic year: September to July

Rector: TRAN THUONG TUAN
Vice-Rector: CHAU VAN LUC
Vice-Rector: Dr LE QUANG MINH

Library of 30,000 vols
Number of teachers: 750
Number of students: 14,000

DEANS

College of Information Technology: VO VAN CHIN
School of Agriculture: Prof. TRAN THUONG TUAN
School of Economics and Business Administration: NGUYEN TAN NHAN
School of Education: Dr LE PHUOC LOC
School of Law: Dr NGUYEN NGOC DIEN
School of Medicine, Dentistry and Pharmacy: PHAM HUNG LUC
School of Sciences: NGUYEN XUAN TRANH
School of Technology: LE QUANG MINH

DA NANG UNIVERSITY OF TECHNOLOGY

54 Nguyen Luong Bang Hoa Khanh, Lien Chieu, Da Nang City

Telephone: (511) 842308
E-mail: dhbk@ud.edu.vn
Internet: www.dut.edu.vn

Founded 1975, fmrly Univ. Polytechnic Da Nang

DUY TAN UNIVERSITY

184 Nguyen Van Linh St, Thank Khe Dist., Da Nang City

Telephone: (511) 3650403
E-mail: webmaster@dtu.edu.vn
Internet: www.dtu.edu.vn

Founded 1994

Faculties of accountancy and finance, business, engineering, languages, technology

Pres.: LE CONG CO

FOREIGN TRADE UNIVERSITY

91 Chua Lang, Lang Thuong, Dong Da, Hanoi

Telephone: (4) 32595168
E-mail: qhqt@ftu.edu.vn
Internet: www.ftu.edu.vn

Founded 1960

Chair. of Board of Trustees: Prof. Dr VU CHI LOC
Pres: Prof. Dr HOANG VAN CHAU

Vice-Pres.: Prof. Dr BUI NGOC SON
Vice-Pres.: Assoc. Prof. Dr DAO THI THU GIANG
Vice-Pres.: Assoc. Prof. Dr NGUYEN DINH THO
Vice-Pres.: Prof. Dr NGUYEN VAN HONG
Rector: Prof. Dr NGUYEN THI MO
Vice-Rector: Prof. Dr HOANG NGOC THIET
Vice-Rector: Prof. Dr HOANG VAN CHAU
Vice-Rector: Prof. Dr NGUYEN PHUC KHANH

Number of teachers: 190
Number of students: 10,720

Publication: *External Economics Review* (4 a year)

DEANS

Faculty of Basic and Fundamental Studies: Prof. Dr LE THANH CUONG
Faculty of Business Administration: Dr BU NGOC SON
Faculty of Business English: Dr NGUYEN DUC HOAT
Faculty of Foreign Trade Economics: Dr VU SY TUAN
Faculty of In-Service Training: NGUYEN THI MO
Faculty of Marxism and Leninism Studies: Dr DOAN VAN KHAI
Faculty of Postgraduate Studies: Prof. Dr VU CHI LOC

HAIPHONG UNIVERSITY OF MEDICINE

213 Tran Quoc Toan (Lach Tray), Ngo Quyen, Haiphong
Telephone: (31) 731907
E-mail: dhyhp@hn.vnn.vn

Rector: HUU CHINH NGUYEN

HANOI AGRICULTURAL UNIVERSITY

Trau Quy, Gia Lam, Hanoi
Telephone: (4) 62617586
E-mail: raico@hua.edu.vn
Internet: www.hau.edu.vn/en

Founded 1956
State control
Languages of instruction: English, Vietnamese
Academic year: August to June

Faculties of agronomy and agricultural resources environment management, animal husbandry and veterinary medicine, economics and rural development, farm engineering and rural electricity, land resources and environment, post-harvest technology and food processing, postgraduate studies and technical teachers training; Institute of Agricultural Biology; Experimental and Demonstration Station, Viet Nam Agricultural College Training, Research and Devt Centre, Centre for Sustainable Agriculture Research and Devt, Professional Dogs Research Centre, Botanical Garden and Germplasm Conservation, Centre for Agricultural Research and Environmental Studies, Cadastral Centre

Rector: DUC VIEN TRAN

Number of teachers: 850
Number of students: 12,900

Publication: *Journal of Scientific Development*

HANOI ARCHITECTURAL UNIVERSITY

Km 10, Nguyen Trai Rd, Thanh Xuan, Hanoi
Telephone: (4) 8544346
Internet: www.hau.edu.vn

Founded 1969

Rector: Prof. Dr Arch. TRONG HAN TRAN
Vice-Rector: Prof. Dr Arch. CHE DINH HOANG
Vice-Rector: Dr DO DINH DUC

Vice-Rector: Prof. Dr Arch. DO HAU
Dir for Centre of Information and Library: PHAM VAN THRNH

DEANS

Dept of Political Theory: PHAM KHOAN
Faculty of Architecture: Dr Arch. LE QUAN
Faculty of Civil Engineering: Asst Prof. Dr NGUYEN TAI TRUNG
Faculty of Infrastructure Techniques and Urban Environment: Asst Prof. HOANG VAN HUE
Faculty of Rural and Urban Planning: Asst Prof. Dr Arch. LE DUC THANG
Faculty of Urban Management: Asst Prof. Dr Arch. NGUYEN TO LANG
In-Service Faculty: Asst Prof. Dr VUONG VAN THANH
Postgraduate Faculty: Asst Prof. Dr Arch. DANG DUC QUANG

HANOI LAW UNIVERSITY

87 Nguyen Chi Thanh, Duong Lang, Hanoi
Telephone: (4) 8352630
Internet: www.hlu.edu.vn

Founded 1979

Faculties of administrative and state law, economic law, international law, justice, part-time learning, postgraduate training

Rector: LE MINH TAM

HANOI MEDICAL UNIVERSITY

1 Ton That Tung St, Dong Da, Hanoi
Telephone: (4) 38523798
E-mail: daihocyhn@hmu.edu.vn
Internet: www.hmu.edu.vn

Founded 1902
Academic year: September to June

Dir: Prof. NGUYEN LAN VIET
Rector: Prof. NGUYEN DUC HINH
Vice-Rector: Dr LUU NGOC HOAT
Vice-Rector for Finance: DOAN NGOC XUAN
Vice-Rector for Postgraduate Training: TA THANH VAN
Vice-Rector for Scientific Research: TA THANH VAN
Vice-Rector for Undergraduate Training: NGUYEN HUU TU

Number of teachers: 510
Number of students: 6,000

Publication: *Journal of Medical Research* (1 a year)

HANOI NATIONAL ECONOMICS UNIVERSITY

207 Duong Giai Phong, Quan Hai Ba Trung, Hanoi
Telephone: (4) 36280280
E-mail: nghind@neu.edu.vn
Internet: www.neu.edu.vn

Founded 1956
Languages of instruction: English, French

Faculties of accountancy and auditing, agricultural economics, banking and finance, industrial economics, labour economics, planning and statistics

Number of teachers: 1,000
Number of students: 32,000

Publication: *Economics and Development Review* (12 a year)

HANOI NATIONAL UNIVERSITY OF EDUCATION

136 Duong Xuan Thuy, Quan Hoa Cau Giay, Tu Liem, Hanoi
Telephone: (4) 7547823
E-mail: p.qhqt@hnue.edu.vn
Internet: www.hnue.edu.vn

Founded 1951
Faculties of foreign languages education, teacher training

HANOI OPEN UNIVERSITY

Nha B-101 Phuong Bach Khoa, Quan Hai Ba Trung, Hanoi
Telephone: (4) 8694821
E-mail: dhm-hou@hn.vnn.vn
Internet: www.hou.edu.vn

Founded 1990, univ. status since 1993
Language of instruction: Vietnamese
Academic year: August to June

Faculties of biological technology, education and training, foreign languages, industrial design, information systems, law, management training, telecommunication technology; multimedia centre; research centre of distance education

Number of teachers: 470
Number of students: 19,000

HANOI UNIVERSITY OF CIVIL ENGINEERING

5 Giai Phong Rd, Hanoi
Telephone: (4) 8691302
E-mail: dngoaidhxd@hn.vnn.vn
Internet: www.dhxd.edu.vn

Founded 1956, univ. status since 1966
Language of instruction: Vietnamese
Academic year: August to June

Faculties of architecture, civil and industrial engineering, construction engineering, environmental engineering, highway and bridge construction, hydraulic engineering, industrial economics, information technology, mechanical engineering, postgraduate studies; institute of offshore engineering; centre for continuing education

Number of teachers: 700
Number of students: 14,000

Publication: *Science-Technology*

Rector: LE NINH NGUYEN

HANOI UNIVERSITY OF CULTURE

418 De La Thanh, Dong Da Dist., Hanoi
Telephone: (4) 8511971
E-mail: daihocvanhoahanoi@gmail.com
Internet: www.huc.edu.vn

Founded 1977

Faculty of cultural studies, library and information, tourism, postgraduate training

Number of teachers: 130
Number of students: 2,500

Rector: Prof. Dr TRAN DUC NGON

HANOI UNIVERSITY OF FINE ARTS

42 Yet Kieu, Quan Hoan Kiem, Hanoi
Telephone: (4) 8224013
E-mail: dhmythuathn@hn.vnn.vn

Founded 1957 as the Hanoi College of Fine Art, univ. status 1981

Offers 5-year Bachelors of fine arts programmes, 2- and 3-year full and part-time MA programmes in painting, graphic art, sculpture

Dir: NGUYEN LUONG TIEU BACH
Dept Dir: LE ANH VAN

HANOI UNIVERSITY OF FOREIGN STUDIES

Km 9, Nguyen Trai St, Thanh Xuan, Hanoi
Telephone: (4) 38544338
E-mail: hanu@hanu.vn
Internet: www.hunu.edu.vn

Founded 1959

Depts of accountancy, business, commerce, economics, human resource management, international studies, languages and tourism
Pres.: NGUYEN DINH LUAN

HANOI UNIVERSITY OF FOREIGN TRADE

91 Chua Lang St, Dong Da Dist., Hanoi
Telephone: (4) 8356800
E-mail: qhqt@ftu.edu.vn
Internet: www.ftu.edu.vn

Founded 1965
Faculties of int. business, business admin., commercial English
Pres: Prof. Dr HOANG VAN CHAU
Rector: Prof Dr THI MO NGUYEN
Vice-Rector: Prof. Dr NGUYEN HONG DAM
Vice-Rector: HOANG NGOC THIET

HANOI UNIVERSITY OF INDUSTRIAL FINE ARTS

360 La Thanh, O Cho Dua, Dong Da, Hanoi
Telephone: (4) 8517364
E-mail: pkhmtcn@fpt.vn

Founded 1965
Dept of industrial art
Rector: LE HUYEN

HANOI UNIVERSITY OF MINING AND GEOLOGY

Dong Ngac, Tu Liem, Hanoi
Telephone: (4) 37520835
E-mail: ichumg@humg.edu.vn
Internet: www.humg.edu.vn

Founded 1966
State control
Academic year: September to June
Rector: Assoc. Prof. Dr TRAN DINH KIEN
Vice-Rector: LE AN
Vice-Rector: NGUYEN TRUONG XUAN
Dir for Library: TRAN THANH HAI

Library of 100,000 vols, 900 periodicals
Number of students: 23,500

DEANS

Faculty of Civil Engineering: VO TRONG HUNG
Faculty of Economics and Business Management: NGUYEN DUY LAC
Faculty of Electro-Mechanics: NGUYEN CHI TINH
Faculty of Environmental Technology: NGUYEN PHUONG
Faculty of General Education: TRAN DINH SON
Faculty of Geology: NGUYEN VAN LAM
Faculty of Information Technology: NGUYEN TRUONG XUAN
Faculty of Mining: Assoc. Prof. Dr BUI XUAN NAM
Faculty of Oil and Gas: NGUYEN THE VINH
Faculty of Surveying and Mapping: TRAN THUY DUONG

HANOI UNIVERSITY OF TECHNOLOGY

1 Dai Co Viet Rd, Hanoi
Telephone: (4) 8693796
E-mail: qhqt@mail.hut.edu.vn
Internet: www.hut.edu.vn

Founded 1956
Language of instruction: Vietnamese
Academic year: August to July
Rector: QUOC THANG TRAN
Vice-Rector: Prof. Dr CONG HOA LE
Chief Admin. Officer: DUONG VAN NGHI
Librarian: GIAN HUU CAN

Library of 700,000 vols

Number of teachers: 1,500
Number of students: 35,650
Publication: *Sciences et Techniques* (4 a year)

DEANS

Applied Mathematics: Dr NGUYEN CANH LUONG
Chemical Technology: Dr VU DAO THANG
Economics and Management: Dr TRAN VAN BINH
Electronics and Telecommunications: Dr PHAM MINH VIET
Engineering Education: Prof. NGUYEN HOA TOAN
Foreign Languages: DO VAN MOC
General Chemistry: LE CONG HOA
Hydraulic Machinery and Automation: NGUYEN PHU VINH
Industrial Management: NGUYEN MINH DUE
Information Technology: Prof. NGUYEN THUC HAI
Mechanical Engineering: Prof. TANG HUY
Metallurgy and Materials Technology: Prof. DO MINH NGHIEP
Physical Education: LE VAN LINH
Social Sciences: Prof. NGO MINH KHANG
Textile Engineering: Dr TRAN MINH NAM

HANOI WATER RESOURCES UNIVERSITY

175 Tay Son St, Dong Da, Hanoi
Telephone: (4) 8522201
E-mail: wru@wru.edu.vn
Internet: www.wru.edu.vn

Founded 1959
Rector: Assoc. Prof. Dr DO VAN HUA
Rector: Prof. Dr LE KIM TRUYEN
Vice-Rector: Prof. Dr DAO XUAN HOC
Vice-Rector: Assoc. Prof. Dr PHAM NGOC QUY
Chief Librarian: Dr NGUYEN HUU THAI

Number of teachers: 520
Number of students: 6,930

DEANS

Department of Foreign Languages: LE VAN KHANG (Head)
Department of Marxist-Leninist Philosophy and Sociology: Dr NGUYEN QUOC LUAT (Head)
Department of Military and Physical Education: Sr Lt-Col NGUYEN SY HOI (Head)
Faculty of Hydraulic Construction: Assoc. Dr NGUYEN VAN MAO
Faculty of Hydraulic Machinery and Equipment: Dr NGUYEN DANG CUONG
Faculty of Hydrology and Environment: Assoc. Prof. Dr DO TAT TUC
Faculty of Hydrology Power: Assoc. Prof. Dr HO SY DU
Faculty of Information Technology: Prof. Dr NGUYEN VAN LE
Faculty of In-Service Training: TRAN NGU PHUC
Faculty of Planning and Management of Water Resources Systems: Dr PHAM NGOC HAI
Faculty of Postgraduate Studies: Assoc. Prof. Dr DUONG VAN TIEN
Faculty of Water Resources Economics: Dr NGUYEN XUAN PHU

HO CHI MINH CITY OPEN UNIVERSITY

97 Vo Van Tan, Ward 6, Dist. 3, Ho Chi Minh City
Telephone: (8) 9300210
E-mail: international@ou.edu.vn
Internet: www.ou.edu.vn

Founded 1990, univ. status since 1993
Language of instruction: Vietnamese
Academic year: September to July

Faculties of biotechnology, computer science, economics and business admin., engineering and technology, foreign languages, South-East Asian studies and sociology; centres of applied computer science, distance training, foreign languages and overseas studies, professional accounting
Rector: Assoc. Prof. Dr LE BAO DONG
Vice-Rector: Dr NGUYEN THUAN

Library of 12,000
Number of teachers: 530
Number of students: 14,000

HO CHI MINH CITY UNIVERSITY OF ARCHITECTURE

196 rue Pasteur, Quan 3, Ho Chi Minh City
Telephone: (83) 8222748
E-mail: vuvietanh@hcmuarc.edu.vn
Internet: www.hcmuarc.edu.vn

Founded 1976
State control
Languages of instruction: English, Vietnamese
Rector: Dr PHAM TU
Vice-Rector: Dr LE QUANG QUY
Vice-Rector: Dr LE VAN THUONG
Vice-Rector: TRUONG NGOC AN
Librarian: NGUYEN THI THANH THUY

Number of teachers: 450
Number of students: 8,000

DEANS

Architecture: Dr TRINH DUY ANH
Civil Engineering: Dr CHUNG BAC AI
Industrial Art: Dr NGO THI THU TRANG
Interior Architecture: Dr LE THANH SON
Interior Design: (vacant)
Urban Infrastructure: Dr PHAM ANH DUNG
Urban Planning: Dr NGUYEN THANH HA

HO CHI MINH CITY UNIVERSITY OF FINE ARTS

5 Phan Dang Luu, Ho Chi Minh City
Telephone: (8) 84126010
E-mail: dhmt@hcm.vnn.vn

Founded 1913
Courses taught incl. graphic arts and graphic design, painting, sculpture; depts of applied arts, basic knowledge, fine arts pedagogy, fine arts critique, fine arts higher education
Dir: Prof. NGUYEN HUY LONG

Number of teachers: 60
Number of students: 700

Publication: *Fine Arts Information*

HO CHI MINH CITY UNIVERSITY OF FOREIGN LANGUAGES AND INFORMATION TECHNOLOGY

155 Su Van Hanh St (Extension), Ward 13, Dist. 10, Ho Chi Minh City
Telephone: (8) 8632052
E-mail: daotaohuflit@hcm.vnn.vn
Internet: www.huflit.vnn.vn

Founded 1994
Schools of computer sciences and eastern cultures and languages, foreign languages
Chair.: HUYNH THE CUOC

Number of teachers: 100
Number of students: 1,200

HO CHI MINH CITY UNIVERSITY OF LAW

2 Nguyen Tat Thanh, Phuong 12, Quan 4, Ho Chi Minh City
Telephone: (8) 9400989
E-mail: quantrimang@hcmulaw.edu.vn
Internet: www.hcmulaw.edu.vn

Founded 1996

Faculties of administrative and state law, business law, civil law, criminal law, international law, part-time training, postgraduate training

Rector: VAN LUYEN NGUYEN

HO CHI MINH CITY UNIVERSITY OF MEDICINE AND PHARMACY

217 Hong Bang, Quan 5, Ho Chi Minh City

Telephone: (8) 38558411

E-mail: nphau@yds.edu.vn

Internet: www.yds.edu.vn

Founded 1947 as Saigon Univ. of Medicine and Pharmacy, current name adopted 1976

Faculties of basic sciences, dentistry, pharmacy, public health, nursing-medical engineering, traditional medicine

Rector: DINH HOI NGUYEN

Number of teachers: 1,000

Number of students: 8,000

Library of 30,000 vols, 700 periodicals

Publication: *Journal of Medicine of Ho Chi Minh City* (4 a year)

HO CHI MINH CITY UNIVERSITY OF PEDAGOGY

280 An Duong Vuong, Quan 5, Ho Chi Minh City

Telephone: (8) 8352020

E-mail: nttrac@vol.vnn.vn

Internet: www.hcmupeda.edu.vn

Founded 1976

Faculties of education, teacher training

Rector: MANH NHI BUI

HO CHI MINH CITY UNIVERSITY OF TRANSPORT

2 D3 St, Binh Thanh Dist. M, Ho Chi Minh City

Telephone: (8) 8992862

E-mail: ird@hcmutrans.edu.vn

Internet: www.hcmutrans.edu.vn

Founded 1962 as part of Viet Nam Maritime Univ., ind. status since 2001

Faculties of construction, information technology, marine electrical, marine engineering and electronic engineering, mechanics and transport economics, naval architecture and floating construction, navigation; departments of basic education, foreign languages, in-service training, political reasoning education, postgraduate studies; Centre of Foreign Languages and Information Technology; Merchant Marine Training Centre; Training Centre of Transport Vocation

Rector: CANH VINH TRAN

Vice-Rector: VAN THU NGUYEN

Vice-Rector: VAN THU NGUYEN

Number of teachers: 300

Number of students: 8,100

HO CHI MINH UNIVERSITY OF TECHNICAL EDUCATION

1 Vo Van Ngan St, Thu Duc, Ho Chi Minh City

Telephone: (8) 37221223

E-mail: webmaster@hcmute.edu.vn

Internet: www.hcmute.edu.vn

Founded 1962 as Ho Chi Minh City Pedagogical Univ. of Technology; became College of Technical Teacher Training 1996; present name and status 2002

State control

Languages of instruction: English, Vietnamese

Academic year: September to May

Pres.: Assoc. Prof. Dr THAI BA CAN

Vice-Pres.: Assoc. Prof. Dr DO VAN DUNG

Vice-Pres.: Dr LAM MAI LONG

Vice-Pres.: NGUYEN VAN MINH

Librarian: VU TRONG LUAT

Library of 298,332 vols, 227 articles and journals

Number of teachers: 700

Number of students: 26,340

Publication: *Tap san Su Pham Ky Thuat* (4 a year)

DEANS

Faculty of Automotive Engineering: NGUYEN TAN QUOC

Faculty of Chemical and Food Technology: Assoc. Prof. Dr NGUYEN VAN SUC

Faculty of Civil Engineering and Applied Mechanics: Assoc. Prof. Dr NGUYEN HOAI SON

Faculty of Economics: Dr TRAN DANG THINH

Faculty of Electrical and Electronic Engineering: Assoc. Prof. Dr QUYEN HUY ANN

Faculty of Foreign Languages: Dr NGUYEN DINH THU

Faculty of Foundation Sciences: Dr VO THANH TAN

Faculty of Garment Technology and Fashion Design: VU MINH HANH

Faculty of Graphic Arts and Media: Dr NGO ANH TUAN

Faculty of Information Technology: Dr DANG TRUONG SON

Faculty of Marxism-Leninism and Ho Chi Minh's Ideology: Assoc. Prof. DOAN DUC HIEU

Faculty of Mechanical Engineering: Dr NGUYEN NGOC PHUONG

Faculty of Technical Education: Dr NGUYEN VAN TUAN

HONG DUC UNIVERSITY

307 Duong Le Lai Rd, Phuong Dong Son, Thanh Hoa City

Telephone: (37) 910222

E-mail: info@hdu.edu.vn

Internet: www.hdu.edu.vn

Founded 1977 by amalgamation of 3 colleges

DEANS

Department of Foreign Languages: PHAM VAN CHU

Faculty of Agriculture and Forestry: Dr LE HUU CAN

Faculty of Economics and Business Administration: Dr NGUYEN HUU DIEN

Faculty of Medicine: NGUYEN THI TRUONG

Faculty of Natural Science: Dr DUONG DINH HOAN

Faculty of Nursery Teacher Training: NGUYEN THI TRUONG

Faculty of Primary Teacher Training: Dr NGUYEN DINH MAI

Faculty of Social Science: Dr NGUYEN VAN TRUONG

Faculty of Technology: Dr NGUYEN MANH AN

HUE UNIVERSITY

3 Le Loi, Hue City, Thua Thien Hue

Telephone: (54) 845658

E-mail: bantin_dhh@hueuni.edu.vn

Internet: www.hueuni.edu.vn

Founded 1957

Language of instruction: Vietnamese

Academic year: November to July

Colleges of agriculture and forestry, economics, medicine, pedagogy, sciences

Rector: VIEN THO NGUYEN

Library of 30,000

Number of teachers: 1,320

Number of students: 35,570 (16180 full-time, 19,390 part-time)

HUE UNIVERSITY OF AGRICULTURE AND FORESTRY

102 Phung Hung, Hue

Telephone: (54) 3522535

E-mail: admin@huaf.edu.vn

Internet: www.huaf.edu.vn

Founded 1967

State control

Languages of instruction: English, Vietnamese

Academic year: September to July

Rector: Prof. Dr NGUYEN MINH HIEU

Vice-Rector: Assoc. Prof. Dr LE DUC NGOAN

Vice-Rector: Assoc. Prof. Dr LE THANH BON

Vice-Rector: Assoc. Prof. Dr LE VAN AN

Library of 200,000

Number of teachers: 400

Number of students: 6,800

DEANS

Central Research and Development in Agro-Forestry Technology: Dr HOANG MANH QUAN (Dir)

Centre for Rural Development: Assoc. Prof. Dr LE VAN AN (Dir)

Department of Sciences and International Relations: PHUNG THANG LONG (Dir)

Faculty of Agricultural Engineering and Post-Harvest Technology: LE THANH LONG

Faculty of Agronomy: Dr TRAN DANG HOA

Faculty of Animal Sciences: Dr DAM VAN TIEN

Faculty of Forestry: DANG THAI DUONG

NHA TRANG UNIVERSITY

2 Nguyen Dinh Chieu, Nha Trang City, Khan Hoa Province

Telephone: (58) 831149

E-mail: censtrad@ntu.edu.vn

Internet: www.ntu.edu.vn

Founded 1959

Faculties of aquaculture, basic sciences, fishery economics, marine mechanics, marine products processing, navigation and marine exploitation

Rector: Assoc. Prof. Dr QUAC DINH LIEN

Vice-Rector: Dr THAI VAN NGAN

Vice-Rector: Assoc. Prof. Dr TRAN THI LUYEN

Vice-Rector: VU VAN THUNG

Library of 18,000 vols, 500 periodicals

Number of teachers: 300

Number of students: 7,000

Publications: *Fisheries Journal* (4 a year), *Journal of Science and Technology* (4 a year)

NONG LAM UNIVERSITY

Khu Pho 6, Linh Trung Ward, Thu Duc Dist., Ho Chi Minh City

Telephone: (8) 8960711

E-mail: vp@hcmuaf.edu.vn

Internet: www.hcmuaf.edu.vn

Founded 1955, as Univ. of Forestry and Agriculture

Language of instruction: Vietnamese

Academic year: September to July

Faculties of agricultural energy and machinery research centre; agronomy, animal science and veterinary medicine, biotechnological research centre; fruit and vegetable processing research centre; centre for research and application of cadastral science and technology; chemical and biological analysis and experiment centre; computer centre; continuing education and placement service economics, engineering, fishery, environmental technology and management centre; environmental technology, experimental research and technology transfer centre; food science and technology, foreign language centre; foreign languages, forestry, industrial crops centre; information technology; science, technology research centre and veterinary clinic; wood science

Rector: Dr BUI CACH TUYEN

Library of 60,000
Number of teachers: 400
Number of students: 11,000
Publication: *University Journal of Agricultural Sciences and Technology* (4 a year)

RMIT INTERNATIONAL UNIVERSITY VIET NAM

702 Nguyen Van Linh Blvd, Tan Phong Ward, Dist. 7, Ho Chi Minh City
Telephone: (8) 37761300
E-mail: enquiries@rmit.edu.vn
Internet: www.rmit.edu.vn
Founded 2001
Private control
Language of instruction: English
Academic year: February to January
Undergraduate programmes: univ. preparation, BSc (applied science in software engineering, commerce, information technology for business, information technology and multimedia); postgraduate programmes: Certificate in Teaching English to Speakers of Other Languages (CELTA) courses, English programmes; Graduate Diploma in Tertiary Teaching and Learning, MBA and Management, Master of Education in Leadership
Pres.: Prof. MERILYN LIDDELL
Vice-Pres. for Academic Affairs: Prof. RON EDWARDS
Exec. Dir for Operations and Planning: MATTHEW SUKUMARAN
Exec. Dir for Students: STEVE PARIS
Head of Hanoi Campus: JOHN CROOK
Number of teachers: 350
Number of students: 6,000

THAI BINH MEDICAL UNIVERSITY

373 Ly Bon St, Thai Binh
Telephone: (36) 838545
E-mail: dhytb@hn.vnn.vn
Internet: www.tbmc.edu.vn
Founded 1968
State control
Rector: Assoc. Prof. LUONG XUAN HIEN
Vice-Rector: NGUYEN VAN SAI
Vice-Rector: Assoc. Prof. TRAN QUOC KHAM

Library of 30,000
Number of teachers: 305
Number of students: 2,500

DEANS

Faculty of Biology: LUONG XUAN HIEN
Faculty of Public Health: PHAM VAM TRONG
Faculty of Traditional Medicine: BUI THI NGUYET

THAI NGUYEN UNIVERSITY

Luong Ngoc Quyen St, Tan Thinh Ward, Thai Nguyen
Telephone: (280) 751681
E-mail: bancntt@tnu.edu.vn
Internet: www.tnu.edu.vn
Founded 1994
State control
Academic year: September to June
Pres.: LE CAO THANG
Number of teachers: 1,400
Number of students: 39,000 (incl. 23,000 full-time)

DEANS

Faculty of Foreign Languages: (vacant)

Faculty of Information Technology: PHAM VIET BINH
Faculty of Natural and Social Sciences: (vacant)
Vocational School of Economics and Techniques: (vacant)

ATTACHED CENTRE

Learning Resource Centre: Tan Thinh Ward, Thai Nguyen; tel. (280) 3656600; e-mail vyhong@lrc-tnu.edu.vn; internet www.lrc-tnu.edu.vn; Librarian VU THI YEN HONG.

UNIVERSITY COLLEGES

College of Agriculture and Forestry

Quyet Thang Commune, Thai Nguyen
Telephone: (280) 855564
E-mail: aitc@tuaf.edu.vn
Internet: www.tuaf.edu.vn
Rector: Assoc. Prof. DANG KIM VUI
Vice-Rector: Assoc. Prof. NGUYEN QUANG TUYEN
Vice-Rector: Assoc. Prof. NGUYEN THI KIM LAN
Vice-Rector: Assoc. Prof. TRAN NGOC NGOAN

DEANS

Faculty of Agricultural Extension and Rural Development: Assoc. Prof. Dr NGUYEN DUY HOAN
Faculty of Agricultural Pedagogy: Dr NGUYEN THI LIEN
Faculty of Agricultural Sciences: Assoc. Prof. Dr LUAN THI DEP
Faculty of Animal Husbandry: Dr NGUYEN VAN QUANG
Faculty of Forestry: Dr LE SY TRUNG
Faculty of Natural Resources and Environment Agriculture: Assoc. Prof. Dr NGUYEN NGOC NONG

College of Economics and Business Administration

Km 9, Duong 3/2 Tich Luong, Thai Nguyen
Telephone: (280) 647685
E-mail: tueba@tueba.edu.vn
Internet: www.tueba.edu.vn
Rector: Assoc. Prof. Dr TRAN CHI THIEN

DEANS

Faculty of Accounting: Dr NGUYEN THI MINH THO
Faculty of Basic Science: Assoc. Prof. NGUYEN THI THU HUONG
Faculty of Business Administration: Assoc. Prof TRAN QUANG HUY
Faculty of Economics: Dr DO QUANG QUY
Postgraduate Studies: Dr TRAN DINH TUAN

Thai Nguyen University of Education

Luong Ngoc Quyen St, Thai Nguyen
Telephone: (280) 859431
Internet: www.dhsptn.edu.vn
State control
Languages of instruction: English, Vietnamese
Academic year: August to June
Rector: NGUYEN VAN LOC
Vice-Rector: DUONG DUY HUNG
Vice-Rector: PHAM HIEN BANG
Vice-Rector: PHAM HONG QUANG
Vice-Rector: PHAM VIET DUC
Number of teachers: 419
Number of students: 11,500

DEANS

Faculty of Chemistry: LE HUU THIENG
Faculty of Foreign Languages: NGUYEN VINH QUANG
Faculty of History: DAM THI UYEN
Faculty of Languages: NGUYEN HANG PHUONG

Faculty of Marxist-Leninist Political Theory: DONG VAN QUAN
Faculty of Mathematics: PHAM VIET DUC
Faculty of Physical Education: NGUYEN VAN LUC
Faculty of Physics: PHAM THAI CUONG
Faculty of Psychology: NGUYEN THI TINH

College of Industrial Technology

3–2 St, Thai Nguyen
Telephone: (2) 80847145
E-mail: phonghcth.dtk@moet.edu.vn
Internet: www.tnut.edu.vn
Rector: Assoc. Prof. Dr PHAN QUANG THE
Vice-Rector: Assoc. Prof Dr. NGUYEN NHU HIEN
Vice-Rector: Assoc. Prof. Dr VU NGOC PI
Vice-Rector: Dr TRAN MINH DUC
Vice-Rector: Dr TRAN XUAN MINH

DEANS

Faculty of Civil and Environmental Engineering: Dr DUONG THE HUNG
Faculty of Electrical Engineering: DO TRUNG HAI
Faculty of Electronics Engineering: NGUYEN DUY CUONG
Faculty of Fundamental Sciences: DINH CANH NHAC
Faculty of Industrial Economics: DOAN QUANG THIEU
Faculty of Mechanical Engineering: HOANG VI
Faculty of Technical Teacher Training: TRUONG THU HUONG

College of Medicine and Pharmacy

284 Duong Luong Ngoc, Quyen Thanh, Thai Nguyen
Telephone: (280) 852671
E-mail: dhyktn@hn.vnn.vn
Internet: www.tnmc.edu.vn
Founded 1968
Rector: Assoc. Prof. Dr NGUYEN THANH TRUNG

THAI NGUYEN UNIVERSITY OF AGRICULTURE AND FORESTRY

Quyet Thinhdan Commune, Thai Nguyen City, Thai Nguyen
Telephone: (280) 3855564
E-mail: tuaf@hn.vnn.vn
Internet: www.tuaf.edu.vn
Founded 1970
Faculties of agricultural economics, agricultural technology, agronomy, animal husbandry and veterinary science, forestry, graduate studies, land management, pedagogy; agro-forestry research and devt centre for northern mountainous regions of Viet Nam; centre for mountainous natural resources and environment; experimental farm; life science research institute; centre for agricultural experiment and practices; centre for foreign language studies; centre for applied information technologies; centre for international training cooperation and consultancy
Rector: Prof. Dr DANG KIM VUI
Number of teachers: 300
Number of students: 10,000

UNIVERSITY OF ECONOMICS HO CHI MINH CITY (UEH)

59C, Nguyen Dinh Chieu, Dist. 3, Ho Chi Minh City
Telephone: (8) 8295299
E-mail: tchc@ueh.edu.vn
Internet: www.ueh.edu.vn
Founded 1976
State control

Languages of instruction: Vietnamese, English, French

Academic year: January to December

Rector: DONG PHONG NGUYEN

Vice-Rector: Assoc. Prof. Dr HOANG NGAN TRAN

Vice-Rector: Assoc. Prof. Dr NGOC DINH NGUYEN

Vice-Rector: Assoc. Prof. Dr THI BICH NGUYET PHAN

Vice-Rector: Prof. Dr. TRONG HOAI NGUYEN

Head of Int. Relations Office: Assoc. Prof. Dr. VIET TIEN HO

Dir of Univ. Library: THUY DOAN THI

Library of 100,000 vols

Number of teachers: 700

Number of students: 50,000

Publication: *Journal of Economic Development* (12 a year in Vietnamese, 4 a year in English)

DEANS

Dept of Foreign Languages: DINH PHUOC VO

Dept of Political Studies: Dr MINH TUAN NGUYEN

Faculty of Accounting and Auditing: Assoc. Prof. Dr VAN NHI VO

Faculty of Business Administration: Assoc. Prof. Dr TIEN DUNG HO

Faculty of Commerce, Tourism and Marketing: Dr TAN BUU LE

Faculty of Corporate Finance: Prof. Dr NGOC THO TRAN

Faculty of Development Economics: Assoc. Prof. Dr HOANG BAO NGUYEN

Faculty of Economical Mathematics and Statistics: Dr THANH VAN NGUYEN

Faculty of Economics Law: Assoc. Prof. Dr DUY NGHIA PHAM

Faculty of Management Information System: Dr MINH THUYET TRAN

Faculty of Public Finance: Assoc. Prof. Dr DINH THANH SU

ATTACHED INSTITUTES

Centre for Economic Studies and Application (CESAIS): 59C Nguyen Dinh Chieu, Dist. 3, Ho Chi Minh City; tel. (8) 8223408.

Centre for Excellence in Management Development: 196 Tran Quang Khai St, Dist. 1, Ho Chi Minh City; tel. (8) 38483107; e-mail cemd@ueh.edu.vn; internet www.cemd.ueh.edu.vn.

Institute of Development Economics Research: 279 Nguyen Tri Phuong, Dist. 10, Ho Chi Minh City; tel. (8) 8561250; e-mail vnckt@idr.edu.vn; internet www.idr.edu.vn; Dir HO DUC HUNG.

International Centre for Informatics Training (KOVIT): 279 Nguyen Tri Phuong, Dist. 10, Ho Chi Minh City; tel. (8) 8549352.

International Commerce Training Centre: 54 Nguyen Van Thu, Dist 1, Ho Chi Minh City; tel. (8) 8297233; e-mail ict@ueh.edu.vn; internet www.ueh.edu.vn/ict/default.htm; Dir DONG NGUYEN PHONG

UNIVERSITY OF DALAT

1 Phu Dong Thien, Vuong, Dalat, Lamdong

Telephone: (63) 3822246

E-mail: irdept@dlu.edu.vn

Internet: www.dlu.edu.vn

Founded 1958

State control

Languages of instruction: Vietnamese, English

Academic year: September to June

Faculties of agronomy, biology, business administration, chemistry, environmental studies, foreign languages, graduate studies history, information technology, law, mathematics, oriental philology, physics, social work and community development, studies, teacher training, tourism

Rector: Assoc. Prof. Dr LE BA DUNG

Vice-Rector: Dr NGUYEN DUC HOA

Vice-Rector: Dr MAI XUAN TRUNG

Vice-Rector: Dr NGUYEN DINH HAO

Number of teachers: 500

Number of students: 13,000

Publication: *Scientific Journal* (1 a year)

UNIVERSITY OF DANANG— LEARNING AND INFORMATION RESOURCE CENTER

91A Nguyen Thi Minh Khai St, Da Nang

Telephone: (511) 3837570

E-mail: pttnga@lirc.udn.vn

Internet: www.lirc.udn.vn

Founded 2000

State control

Library of 150,000 vols, 130 periodicals

Number of teachers: 2,100

Number of students: 90,000

Dir: PHAN THI THU NGA

Vice-Pres.: Prof. Dr BUI VAN GA

Vice-Pres.: Dr LE THE GIOI

VAN LANG UNIVERSITY

45 Nguyen Khac Nhu, Quan 1, Ho Chi Minh City

Telephone: (8) 38367933

E-mail: tuyensinh@vanlangunni.edu.vn

Internet: www.vanlanguni.edu.vn

Faculty of foreign languages

Rector: DUNG NGUYEN

VIET NAM FORESTRY UNIVERSITY

Main Campus, Xuan Mai, Chuong My, Hanoi

Second Campus, Trang Bom, Trang Bom, Dong Na

Telephone: (4) 33840441

E-mail: lienhe@vfu.edu.vn

Internet: www.vfu.edu.vn

Founded 1964

Academic year: August to June

Research and production units: centre for experimental research and forest industry technology transfer, consulting company for forestry investment and development, institute for forest ecology and environment

Rector: TRAN HUU VIEN

Library of 29,302 books, 15,696 periodicals

Number of teachers: 320

Number of students: 11,760

Publications: *Forest Science and Technology Newsletter* (4 a year), *Scientific Research Periodical* (4 a year)

DEANS

Faculty of Economics and Business Administration: TRAN HUU DAO

Faculty of Engineering: LE TAN QUYNH

Faculty of Forest Products Technology: VU HUY DAI

Faculty of Forest Resources and Environmental Management: NGUYEN THE NHA

Faculty of Marx-Lenin: DOAN VAN HANH

Faculty of Postgraduate Training: NGUYEN PHAN THIET

Faculty of Silviculture: NGUYEN TRONG BINH

High School for Ethnic Students: NGUYEN QUANG CHUNG

PROFESSORS

HINH, V.

HUU VIEN, T.

PHAN THIET, N.

VAN CHU, T.

VAN CHUONG, P.

VAN TUAN, N.

XUAN HOAN, P.

VIET NAM MARITIME UNIVERSITY

19B/260, Thuy Khue, Tay Ho, Hanoi

Telephone: (4) 8470279

E-mail: duyluat@bigwall.com

Internet: www.vimaru.edu.vn

Founded 1956

Academic year: August to May

Rector: Dr DANG VAN UY

Vice-Rector: Dr LUONG CONG NHO

Vice-Rector: Prof. Dr PHAM TIEN TINH

Vice-Rector: Prof. Dr PHAM VAN CUONG

Librarian: TRAN THI YEN

Number of teachers: 800

Number of students: 15,000

DEANS

Department of Postgraduate Studies: LE VIET LUONG

Faculty of Information Technology: LE QUOC DINH

Faculty of Marine Electrical and Electronic Engineering: PHAM NGOC TIEP

Faculty of Marine Engineering: NGUYEN DAI AN

Faculty of Navigation: DINH XUAN MANH

Faculty of Sea-Transport Economics: PHAM VAN CUONG

Faculty of Shipbuilding: NGUYEN VINH PHAT

Faculty of Waterway Construction: NGUYEN VAN NGOC

VIET NAM NATIONAL UNIVERSITY, HANOI

144 Xuan Thuy Rd, Cau Giay, Hanoi

Telephone: (4) 8332015

E-mail: vandao@vnu.ac.vn

Internet: www.vnu.edu.vn

Founded 1993 by amalgamation of Univ. of Hanoi and other instns of higher education in Hanoi

State control

Academic year: September to July

Faculties of general education, foreign languages, science, social sciences and humanities, teacher training; colleges of foreign languages, science, social sciences, humanities; school of business; institute of information technology training; centres of biotechnology, cooperation in mechanics training, education quality assurance and research development, natural resources management and environmental studies, systems development, teachers of political theory, Vietnamese and intercultural studies and women's studies; research centres in applied microbiology and Asian studies

Rector: Prof. Dr DAO TRONG THI

Vice-Rector: Prof. NGUYEN DUC CHINH

Librarian: NGUYEN HUY CHUONG

Library of 800,000 vols, 3,000 periodicals

Number of teachers: 1,320

Number of students: 22,761

Publication: *Tap Chi Khoa Hoc* (Journal of Science, print and online (tapchi.vnu.edu.vn))

VIET NAM NATIONAL UNIVERSITY, HO CHI MINH CITY

KP6, Linh-Trung, Thu Duc Dist., Ho Chi Minh City

Telephone: (84) 87242160

E-mail: hopthu_tuyensinh@vnuhcm.edu.vn

Internet: www.vnuhcm.edu.vn

Founded 1954, present structure since 1995

Dir: Dr PHAN THANH BINH..

CONSTITUENT UNIVERSITIES

University of Natural Sciences

227 Nguyen Van Cu, Dist. 5, Ho Chi Minh City

Telephone: (8) 8353193

Internet: www.hcmuns.edu.vn

Founded as a div. of the Indochina College of Sciences, Hanoi 1942, became Faculty of Sciences of Univ. of Saigon 1956; part of Ho Chi Minh Univ. 1977; current status since 1996

Rector: Assoc. Prof. Dr DUONG AI PHUONG

Vice-Rector: Assoc. Prof. Dr DONG THI BICH THUY

Vice-Rector: NGUYEN THANH HUONG

Vice-Rector: Assoc. Prof. Dr PHAM DINH HUNG

Library Dir: NGUYEN MINH HIEP

Library of 50,000 vols, 392 periodicals

DEANS

Department of Foreign Languages: NGUYEN HOANG TUAN (Head)

Department of Material Science: Prof. Dr LE KHAC BINH (Head)

Department of Physical Education: NGUYEN VAN HUNG

Faculty of Biology: Assoc. Prof. Dr TRAN LINH THUOC

Faculty of Chemistry: Assoc. Prof. Dr HA THUC HUY

Faculty of Environmental Science: Assoc. Prof. Dr LE MANH TAN

Faculty of Geology: TRAN PHU HUNG

Faculty of Information Technology: Dr DUONG ANH DUC

Faculty of Mathematics and Informatics: Dr TO ANH DUNG

Faculty of Physics: Dr DAV VAN LIET

University of Social Sciences and Humanities

10–12 Dinh Tien Hoang St, Ho Chi Minh City

E-mail: ussh@hcmussh.edu.vn

Internet: www.hcmussh.edu.vn

Founded 1996

Language of instruction: Vietnamese

Academic year: October to June

Faculties of Chinese linguistics and literature, English linguistics and literature, French linguistics and literature, geography, German linguistics and literature, history, linguistics and journalism, literature, oriental studies, philosophy, Russian linguistics and literature, sociology, Viet Nam studies and Vietnamese for foreigners; sections of anthropology, culture studies and physical education; centre for foreign languages; centre for informatics technology; centre for overseas studies; centre for research in social development and poverty reduction; Vietnamese and SE Asian research centre

Rector: VAN LE NGO

Librarian: Dr BUI LOAN THUY

Library of 87,784 vols, 375 periodicals

Ho Chi Minh City University of Technology

268 Ly Thuong Kiet St, Dist. 10, Ho Chi Minh City

Telephone: (8) 38652442

E-mail: inter@hcmut.edu.vn

Internet: www.hcmut.edu.vn

State control

Academic year: September to July

Training and research; 11 faculties of applied sciences, chemical technology, civil engineering, computer science and engineering, electrical and electronic engineering, environment, geology and petroleum, industrial management, information technology, material technology, mechanical engineering, transportation engineering; school of industrial management

Rector: Assoc. Prof. Dr THANH VU DINH

VIET NAM UNIVERSITY OF COMMERCE

Mai Dich, Cau Giay, Hanoi

Telephone: (4) 37643219

E-mail: dhtm@vcu.edu.vn

Internet: www.vcu.edu.vn

Founded 1965

Rector: Prof. Dr PHAM VU LUAN

Vice-Rector: NGUYEN THIEN DAT

Vice-Rector: Assoc. Prof. Dr TRAN THI DUNG

Vice-Rector: Assoc. Prof. Dr NGUYEN BACH KHOA

Library Dir: VU THI HUE

Library of 100,000 vols

Number of teachers: 270

Number of students: 7,600

DEANS

Faculty of Business Administration: VU THUY DUONG

Faculty of Economics: Dr THAN DANH PHUC

Faculty of Finance and Accounting: Dr DO MINH THANH

Faculty of Hospitality and Tourism: Dr BUI XUAN NHAN

Faculty of International Trade: Dr NGUYEN VAN THANH

Faculty of Part-Time Training: Assoc. Prof. Dr NGUYEN THI MINH NGUYET

Faculty of Postgraduate Training: Dr NGUYEN VAN MINH

Faculty of Trading Business: Dr DO THI NGOC

Section of Environment Economics: NGUYEN QUOC TIEN (Head)

Section of Foreign Languages: NGUYEN DUC CHAU (Head)

Section of the History of Viet Nam's Communist Party and Socialism: NGO XUAN DAU (Head)

Section of Mathematics: Dr HOANG VAN LAM (Head)

Section of Philosophy: Dr PHUONG KY SON (Head)

Section of Physical and Military Training: NGUYEN VAN KHANH (Head)

Section of Political Economy: Dr DINH THI THUY (Head)

VINH UNIVERSITY

182 Le Duan St, Vinh

Telephone: (38) 3855452

E-mail: lprvvinh@hn.vnn.vn

Rector: NGUYEN DINH HUAN

Vice-Rector: NGUYEN NGOC HOI

Vice-Rector: TRAN NGOC GIAO

Number of students: 10,000

Colleges

ART AND SOCIAL ARTS AND CONSERVATOIRES

College of Law: Thuong Tin, Lang Ha Hanoi, Son Binh Province; tel. (4) 8343251.

Dong Nai College of Decorative Arts: 368 Quoc Lo 1, Thanh Pho Bien Hoa, Tinh Dong Nai; tel. (61) 822042; e-mail mythuat.tung@gmail.com; internet dongnaiart.edu.vn; f. 1965; administered directly by the Min. of Culture, Sports and Tourism; specializes in art, ceramics, bronze-casting and natural and artificial stone sculpturing.

Hanoi College of Fine Arts: 42 Yet Kieu St, Hanoi; 3 faculties.

Hanoi Cultural College: 103 De La Thanh St, Hanoi; tel. (4) 8512606; 4 faculties.

Hanoi National Conservatory of Music: 77 Hao Nam, O Cho Dua, Dong Da Hanoi; e-mail nhacvienhn@netnam.vn; internet www.nhacvienhanoi.vn; Dir NGO THANH VAN.

Hanoi University of Drama and Cinematography: Mai Dich, Cau Giay, Hanoi; tel. (4) 7643397; e-mail skda@fpt.vn; f. 1980; undergraduate and postgraduate degrees in cinematography, screenwriting and theatre direction; Dir Prof. Dr NGUYEN MANH LAN.

Ho Chi Minh City College of Performing Arts and Cinema: 125 Cong Quynh St, Ho Chi Minh City; tel. (8) 8393658; f. 1995; costume design, film and cinematography, pantomime and mime, radio and television, theatre.

Ho Chi Minh City Conservatory: 112 Nguyen Du St, Dist. 1, Thanh Po Ho Chi Minh City; tel. (8) 8225841; e-mail nhacvienhcm@hcm.vnn.vn; f. 1956; composition, conducting, electric instruments, singing, national and orchestral instruments, theory; 136 teachers; 758 students; Dir Prof. HOANG CUONG.

ECONOMICS AND PLANNING

Academy of Finance: 7 Ly Thuong Kiet St, Hoan Kiem Dist., Hanoi; tel. (4) 9331853; e-mail hvtc@hn.vnn.vn; internet www.hvtc.edu.vn; f. 2001; faculties of accounting, banking and insurance, business administration, continuing education, corporate finance, customs taxation, economic information systems, foundation studies, international finance, Marx-Lenin-Ho Chi Minh ideology, postgraduate training, public finance; institutes of financial science, and for market and price research; library: 157,000 vols (16,500 titles), 162 current periodicals, 2,100 other publications; 350 teachers; 13,274 students; Dir-Gen. CHI NGO THE; publs *Finance and Accounting Research* (12 a year), *Financial Bulletin* (2 a month), *International Economics and Finance News* (52 a year), *Market and Price Bulletin* (in English, 52 a year), *Market Bulletin* (online, 365 a year), *Monography* (5 a year), *News for Leaders* (24 a year), *Scientific Research* (10 a year).

College of Commerce: Mai Dich, Tu Liem Dist., Hanoi; tel. (4) 8343207; 5 faculties.

College of Economics: 144 Xuan Thuy St, Hanoi; tel. (4) 7547506; e-mail kinhte@vnu.edu.vn; internet www.economics.vnu.edu.vn; attached to Viet Nam National Univ.; 12 faculties.

Ho Chi Minh City College of Finance and Accountancy: College Library, 279 Nguyen Tri Phuong St, Dist. 10, Ho Chi Minh City; tel. (8) 8550783; 3 faculties.

MEDICINE, PHYSICAL EDUCATION AND SPORTS

College of Physical Training and Sports: Tu Son Dist., Bac Ninh Province; tel. (241) 831609; f. 1959; 6 faculties; 215 teachers; 2,500 students; Dir Prof. Dr TRAN DUC DUNG.

Hanoi College of Pharmacy: 13–15 Le Thanh Tong St, Hanoi; tel. (4) 8254539; e-mail dhduochn@netnam.org.vn; f. 1961; 160 teachers; 780 students; library: 20,000 vols; Dean Prof. Dr NGUYEN THANH DO.

TECHNICAL AND INDUSTRIAL

Posts and Telecommunications Training Centre No. 1: 10 Km, Nguyen Trai Rd, Hadong, Hatay, Hanoi; tel. (4) 8547795; e-mail pttci@hn.vnn.vn; internet www.ptit.edu.vn; f. 1953; library: 7,000 vols; Dir Dr CHU QUANG TOAN.

YEMEN

The Higher Education System

Institutions of higher education pre-date Yemen's formation from a merger of the Yemen Arab Republic and the People's Democratic Republic of Yemen in 1990, the oldest being San'a University, which was founded in 1970. In 1975 the University of Aden was founded and these two universities remained the principal institutions of higher education until the 1990s. In 2008/09 there were 256,125 students enrolled at institutions of higher education, which numbered 16 in 2004/05. In 2010 the World Bank signed a US $13m. credit agreement intended to assist with the enactment of university reforms, curriculum development and the introduction of new academic programmes, together with the development of a higher education committee to oversee academic curricula and standards. A further six agreements, collectively worth $5.8m., were signed between the Yemeni Government and the World Bank in February 2011, which were intended to upgrade facilities and launch science-based programmes at the public universities in Taiz, Aden, Ibb, Dhamar and Amran.

The most recent legislation pertaining to higher education is the Law on Private Universities (No. 13, 2005) and the Universities, Colleges and Institutions of Higher Education Law (No. 14, 2005). The Ministry of Higher Education and Scientific Research is split into two main departments. The first is the University Affairs division, which is responsible for qualifications and certificates, equivalency, approval and recognition, with responsibility for both public and private universities. The second department is the National Accreditation Committee (NAC), which in 2012 was not yet fully established; however, it was implementing partial accreditation procedures and processes with regards to the monitoring of public and private universities, and as such its work was largely limited to determining whether or not institutions should have the legal right to operate; this function is reflected in the Law on Private Universities, which gives the Ministry the power to shut down deficient programmes and courses. The Council for Quality Assurance and Accreditation in Higher Education was created by presidential decree (No. 210) in 2009.

The Ministry of Technical Education and Vocational Training, which was established in 2001, is the national body responsible for technical and vocational education in Yemen.

The Thanawiya (General Secondary Education Certificate) is the principal requirement for admission to both public and private higher education. In 2001 the pass mark in the Thanawiya for entry to all undergraduate degrees was set at 70%; additionally, applicants to popular programmes such as engineering or medicine may have to sit a university entrance examination and attend a personal interview. Universities offer two-year, sub-degree Diplomas in professional and technical fields from which students can progress onto advanced degree programmes. Bachelors degrees must last at least four years, and students are required to accumulate a minimum of 132 'credits' for graduation. (The Bachelors of Medicine is a six-year programme of study and Engineering five.) Traditionally, Yemeni graduate students travelled abroad to study for postgraduate degrees; however, in recent years Yemeni institutions have begun awarding postgraduate degrees (although the range is still quite limited). The first postgraduate qualification is the postgraduate Diploma (referred to variously as the Higher Diploma, the Specialist Diploma, the Graduate Diploma or the Preparatory Diploma), which is a one-year course that is also regarded as a preparatory course for the Masters degree, which lasts two years and is now available at both public and private universities. Finally, although Doctorates are now being offered by universities on an 'in-house' basis, there is no uniform system for their award.

Post-secondary technical and vocational education is offered by a range of different professional and vocational institutes and is divided into Regular (or General), Parallel and Further (or Continuing) Education and Training. The Certificate in Technical Education is awarded after a two-year course at technical institutes and is open to students with either the Thanawiya or the Certificate of Vocational Training. US-style 'community' colleges have been established and they specialize in three-year Diploma courses, admission to which requires the Thanawiya.

Regulatory Bodies

GOVERNMENT

Ministry of Culture: POB 129, San'a; tel. (1) 235461; e-mail moc@y.net.ye; Minister Dr ABDULLAH AUBAL MANDHOUQ.

Ministry of Education: Marib St, San'a; tel. (1) 252732; e-mail moe@yemen.net.ye; internet www.yemenmoe.net; Minister ABD AL-RAZZAQ YAHYA AL-ASHWAL.

Ministry of Higher Education and Scientific Research: San'a; Minister YAHYA MUHAMMAD AL-SHU'AIBI.

Ministry of Technical Education and Vocational Training: POB 25235, San'a; tel. (1) 469279; e-mail mtevt@yemen.net.ye; internet www.mtevt.info; Minister Dr ABD AL-HAFEZ NOMU'AN.

Learned Society

LANGUAGE AND LITERATURE

British Council: 3rd Fl., Administrative Tower, San'a Trade Centre, Algiers St, POB 2157, San'a; tel. (1) 448356; e-mail information@ye.britishcouncil.org; internet www.britishcouncil.org/me-yemen.htm;

offers courses and exams in English language and British culture, and promotes cultural exchange with the UK; Asst Dir, Resources AZIZ AL-BAAR.

Libraries and Archives

San'a

British Council Library: Al-Sanabani Roundabout, Al Jame'a St, San'a; tel. (1) 373248; e-mail h.jailan@ust.edu.ye; internet www.britishcouncil.org/me-yemen-learning-centre-membership-details.htm; 10,000 vols, 36 periodicals; Dir RAJA'A BAZARA.

Library of the Great Mosque of San'a: San'a; f. 1925; the colln of 10,000 MSS and printed vols is not at present accessible to the public; Librarian ZAID BIN ALI ENAN.

Universities

UNIVERSITY OF ADEN

POB 6312, Khormaksar, Aden
Telephone: (2) 234428
E-mail: rector@adenuniversity.edu.ye
Internet: www.adenuniversity.edu.ye
Founded 1975
State control
Languages of instruction: Arabic, English
Academic year: September to June

Rector: Prof. Dr ABDUL WAHAB RAWEH
Vice-Rector for Academic Affairs: Assoc. Prof. Dr SAEED ABDO GABALI
Vice-Rector for Scientific Research and Postgraduate Studies: Assoc. Prof. Dr AHMED ALI AL-HAMDANI
Vice-Rector for Students' Affairs: Asst Prof. Dr NASSER A. NASSER
Sec.-Gen.: Assoc. Prof. Dr AHMED SALEH MUNASSER

Number of teachers: 1,480
Number of students: 22,760

Publications: *Al-Tawassul* (2 a year), *Al-Yemen* (2 a year), *Journal of Natural and Applied Sciences* (2 a year), *Journal of Social Sciences and Humanities* (2 a year), *Saba* (2 a year), *Yemen Engineer* (3 a year), *Yemeni Journal for Agricultural Research* (2 a year)

DEANS

Faculty of Administration: Assoc. Prof. FUAD RASHED ABDO

Faculty of Agricultural Sciences: Assoc. Prof. Dr ABBAS BAWAZIR

Faculty of Arts: Assoc. Prof. Dr SULAIMAN FARAJ BIN AZOON

Faculty of Economics: Prof. Dr MUHAMMAD A. WARET

Faculty of Education (Aden): Asst Prof. Dr YACOOB A. KASSEM

Faculty of Education (Dalea): Asst Prof. Dr MOHD S. OBADI

Faculty of Education (Loder): Asst Prof. Dr SALEH A. AL BORKANI

Faculty of Education (Radfan): Asst Prof. Dr ABDULLA MUHAMMAD

Faculty of Education (Sabr): Assoc. Prof. Dr ALI QASEM AKLAN

Faculty of Education (Shabwa): Assoc. Prof. Dr NASER SALEH. HABTOOR

Faculty of Education (Tur Al-Baha): Asst Prof. Dr HAMID ABDUL MAGEED QUBATI

Faculty of Education (Yafai): Assoc. Prof. Dr ABDUL RAHMAN AL-WALI

Faculty of Education (Zingibar): Assoc. Prof. Dr MUHAMMAD A. HOSEEN

Faculty of Engineering: Assoc. Prof. Dr ABDUL WALI HADI

Faculty of Law: Assoc. Prof. Dr SAAD M. SAAD

Faculty of Medicine: Assoc. Prof. Dr ABDULLA SAEED HATAB

Faculty of Oil and Minerals: Asst Prof. Dr KHALED ALI. AL SHAMSI

THAMAR UNIVERSITY

POB 87246, Dhamar

Telephone: (6) 509592

E-mail: info@thuniv.net

Internet: www.thuniv.net

Founded 1996

Faculties of admin. sciences, art, dentistry, education, engineering, law, medicine, nursing, physical sciences, tourism, veterinary medicine

Rector: AHMED AL-HADHRANI

HADHRAMOUT UNIVERSITY OF SCIENCE AND TECHNOLOGY

POB 50512–50511, Mukalla-Hadhramout Governate

Telephone: (5) 360865

E-mail: hadhramoutuniv@y.net.ye

Internet: www.hust.edu.ye

Founded 1993

State control

Faculties of admin. sciences, applied science, arts, engineering and technology, environment science and marine biology, nursing; College for Women, College of Education

Vice-Rector: SALEM AWAD RAMODHA

HODEIDAH UNIVERSITY

POB 3114, Hodeidah

Telephone: (3) 250490

E-mail: hoduniv@hoduniv.net.ye

Internet: www.hoduniv.net.ye

Founded 1996

State control

Faculties of education, management systems, marine sciences

Rector: Dr HUSSEIN OMAR ABU BAKR

IBB UNIVERSITY

POB 70270, Ibb

Telephone: (4) 408069

E-mail: icd@ibb-univ.net

Internet: www.ibb-univ.net

Founded 1996

State control

Languages of instruction: Arabic, English

Academic year: September to July

Rector: Prof. Dr ABDUL-AZIZ AL-SHUAIBI

Vice-Rector: Prof. Dr AHMED AL-JAUFI

Dean for Academic Affairs: Assoc. Prof. Dr. MUHAMMAD AL-JAUFI

Dean for Int. Cooperation and Relations: Assoc. Prof. Dr. ABDULLAH ALQUDAMI

Dean for Postgraduate and Research: Prof. Dr. ABDULLAH AL-FALAHI

Dean for Quality Assurance: Assoc. Prof. Dr. TARIQ AL-MANSOOB

Dean for Students Affairs: Dr. ABDU-SALAM AL-ERIANI

Library of 50,000 vols

Number of teachers: 650

Number of students: 12,000

DEANS

Faculty of Administrative Sciences: Assoc. Prof. Dr LUTF AL-JUHAIFI

Faculty of Agriculture: Assoc. Prof. Dr ABDO AL-HADDI

Faculty of Arts: Assoc. Prof. Dr MUNEER AL-ARIQI

Faculty of Dentistry: Asst Prof. Dr ABDUL-HAQ AL-HASANI

Faculty of Education—Annaderah Branch: Assoc. Prof. Dr FAIEZ AL-GHARAZI

Faculty of Education—Ibb Branch: Prof. Dr MUHAMMAD AL-MEKHLAFI

Faculty of Engineering: Asst Prof. Dr AHMED EMAAD

Faculty of Science: Assoc. Prof. Dr MUHAMMAD AL-ZUHAIRI

QUEEN ARWA UNIVERSITY

Asteen St-Fajj Attan, Sana'a

Telephone: (1) 445991

E-mail: arwauniversity@y.net.ye

Internet: www.arwauniversity.org

Founded 1996

Private control

Languages of instruction: Arabic, English

Academic year: September to June

Colleges of arts and human science, economics and admin., engineering and computer science, law, medicine and pharmacy

Vice-Rector: MUHAMMAD A. ALKHAYYAT

Dean of Student Affairs: Dr HAZZA ABDO SALEM AL-HOMAIDI

Library of 30,000 vols

Number of teachers: 150

Number of students: 3,000

Publication: *Queen Arwa University Magazine* (2 a year)

SAN'A UNIVERSITY

POB 1247, San'a

Telephone: (1) 464483

E-mail: info@suye.ac

Internet: www.new.suye.ac/en

Founded 1970

State control; financial support from Kuwait

Languages of instruction: Arabic, English

Academic year: October to June

Pres.: Dr KHALID ABDULLAH TAMEM

Number of teachers: 332

Number of students: 10,715

DEANS

Faculty of Agriculture: Dr NASSER AULAQI (acting)

Faculty of Arts: Dr AHMED AL SAYDI

Faculty of Commerce and Economics: Dr NASSER AULAQI

Faculty of Education: Dr MUHAMMAD AL KHADER

Faculty of Engineering: Dr AWAD SALEH

Faculty of Law and Shari'a: Dr ABDUL MUNIM AL BADRAWI

Faculty of Medicine and Health Sciences: Dr ABDALLAH AL-HURAYBI

Faculty of Science: Dr ALI AL SHUKAI

TAIZ UNIVERSITY

POB 6803, Taiz

Telephone: (4) 221378

E-mail: prof.malshaiby@gmail.com

Internet: www.taizuniversity.net

Founded 1995

State control

Languages of instruction: Arabic, English

Pres.: Prof. MOHAMED SAEED ALSHAIBY

Dean for Libraries: Dr MUHAMMAD FADHEL

Library of 101,630 vols, 3,400 periodicals

Number of teachers: 980

Number of students: 27,000

Publications: *Journal of Educational and Academic Development Centre* (1 a year), *Journal of Educational Sciences and Psychology* (1 a year), *Journal of the Faculty of Arts* (1 a year), *Taiz University Journal* (1 a year), *Taiz University Research Journal* (1 a year)

DEANS

Faculty of Administrative Science: Dr YAHYIA ABDULGHAFAR

Faculty of Applied Sciences: Dr KHALID AHMAD SAAD ALOSABI

Faculty of Arts: Prof. Dr ABDUL HAKIM NASIR ALI

Faculty of Education: Prof. Dr ANISA ABDU MUGAHED

Faculty of Education in Turba: Dr HESHAM ABDULGHANI HAMEED

Faculty of Engineering and IT: Dr ABDUL GHANY AHMAD

Faculty of Languages and Translation: Prof. DR WAHBIYA ABDULKARIM MOHARRAM

Faculty of Law: Dr MOHAMED SAEED ALMAAMRY

Faculty of Medicine: ABDUL GHAFOR QASSIM

PROFESSORS

ABDULKARIM MOHARRAM, W., English Language Teaching

ABDULRAHMAN ALBANA, F., Islamic Studies

ABDU MOGAHED, A., Mental Health

AHMAD ALTHAIFANY, A., Foundation of Education

ALBUHAIRY, M., Physics

AL HAKIMY, A. H., Science Education

ALI ALAMEERY, A., Psychology

ALI KAHTAN, M., Planning Management of National Economy

ALMEKHLAFY, S., Educational Management

AL SAYAGHI, K., Psychology (Special Education)

AL SHAMIRY, A., Microbiology

ALZOBIRI, A., Microbiology

HADI ALI, M., Social Studies

HASSAN KAID, A., Educational Research

MALIK ANAM, A., Morphology and Syntax (Arabic Language)

MUHAMMAD ALHAKIMY, A., Plant Physiology

MUHAMMAD ALHUSAINI, A., Arabic Literature

MUHAMMAD TARBUSH, K., General Law

NASIR ALI, A., Geography

RAHMAN SABRI, A., Agricultural Economy

SAEED ALSHAIBY, M., General International Law

SALEH ALUG, A., Geology

SALEH SUFIAN, N., Psychology

SHARAF GHALEB, A., Geology (Minerals)

SOSWAH, A., Linguistics (Arabic Language)

TARESH, M., Educational Planning

TALIB, A., Science Education

College

High College of Koran Kareem: POB 11229, Riyadh Ave, San'a; tel. (1) 216865; e-mail high-kuraan@y.net; Shari'a and Islamic studies.

ZAMBIA

The Higher Education System

Institutions of higher education pre-date the independence of the Republic of Zambia (formerly Northern Rhodesia) from the United Kingdom in 1964, the oldest being Zambia College of Agriculture, which was founded in 1947. In 1965 the University of Zambia was founded and it remained the only university-level institution until the foundation of Copperbelt University in 1987, which offers degrees in professional fields only; in 2010 a total of 16,655 students were enrolled at these two universities. In 2008 the National College of Management and Development Studies was converted into Mulungushi University by the Government in a public-private partnership with Konkola Copper Mines. Under the University Act of 1999, which allowed for the establishment and regulation of both public and private universities, some 12 new private universities were operating by 2010. There are also a number of technical, vocational and teacher-training colleges. In 1999/2000 there were an estimated 24,553 students enrolled in tertiary education, which is administered by the Ministry of Education, Science, Vocational Training and Early Education. Affirmative action programmes, including the creation of bursaries for academically gifted female students who could otherwise not afford to pay for tertiary education, have significantly reduced gender disparities within higher education in recent years. The Government's Sixth National Development Plan for the period 2011–15, which was launched in February 2011, had a strong focus on higher education, particularly on improving access to and participation in university education and on expanding research activities; the plan included proposals to establish a quality assurance mechanism by which to regulate university-level education and to establish a student loan scheme. In October 2011 the newly elected President, Michael Sata, announced plans to reform the higher education sector, including the establishment of three new universities, the opening of new technical colleges in each of Zambia's nine provinces, and the upgrading and updating of the country's existing institutions.

The standard administrative structure consists of the Chancellor, Vice-Chancellor, Registrar, Bursar, University Council, Senate, Boards of Studies, Deans and Heads of Department. The Chancellor is appointed by the Head of State while the Vice-Chancellors are appointed by the Minister of Education, Science, Vocational Training and Early Education, who also appoints the University Council; the University Council in turn appoints the Registrar and Bursar. Other than the state budget, the main source of university funding is students' tuition fees.

Students are required to obtain five credit-level passes on the Zambian School Certificate (Grade 12) for admission to university. The Bachelors is the main undergraduate degree and is generally four years in duration, although degrees in professional fields may last longer, including agriculture, architecture, engineering (five years), veterinary science (six years) and medicine (seven years). Postgraduate Certificate and Diploma programmes, which typically last between one and two years, are offered in a wide range of subjects. The Masters degree is open to students who have been awarded the Bachelors and is a two- to four-year programme of study. The PhD is the highest university degree in Zambia but is available only in a limited number of specialized subjects; it requires up to four years of study.

The Ministry of Education, Science, Vocational Training and Early Education is responsible for providing post-secondary vocational and technical education and oversees 23 training institutions, the National Institute for Scientific and Industrial Research and the National Technology Business Centre. The principal qualifications are (in ascending order) the Craft Certificate, Certificate, Advanced Certificate and Diploma. In 2004 a total of 26,642 students were admitted to technical and vocational courses.

Regulatory Bodies

GOVERNMENT

Ministry of Education, Science, Vocational Training and Early Education: Civic Center Area, Plot 89, cnr Mogadishu and Chimanga Rds, POB 50093, Lusaka 10101; tel. (21) 1250855; Minister Dr JOHN T. N. PHIRI.

Learned Societies

BIBLIOGRAPHY, LIBRARY SCIENCE AND MUSEOLOGY

Zambia Library Association: POB 38636, Lusaka 10101; internet www.zla.co.zm; Chair. BENSON NJOBVU; Hon. Sec. MUTINTA NABUYANDA; publ. *Journal* (4 a year).

LANGUAGE AND LITERATURE

Alliance Française: Plot 22725, Alick Nkhata Ave, Longacres, POB 30948, 10101 Lusaka; tel. (21) 1253467; e-mail directionaflusaka@gmail.com; internet www.aflusaka.org; offers courses and exams in French language and culture; promotes cultural exchange with France; attached teaching centres in Kabwe, Kitwe, Livingstone and Ndola; Dir PASCAL TOMASINI; Sec. LAURA KERESIA.

British Council: Aquarius House, Katima Mulilo Rd, POB 34571, Lusaka; tel. (21) 1376700; e-mail info@britishcouncil.org.zm; internet www.britishcouncil.org.zm; offers courses and exams in English language and British culture; promotes cultural exchange with the UK; Dir JOHN MITCHELL.

MEDICINE

Zambia Medical Association: POB RW 148, Lusaka; e-mail zma@zambiamedicalassociation.org; internet www.zambiamedicalassociation.org; Pres. Dr AARON MUJAJATI; Sec.-Gen. Dr JOYCE BANDA; publ. *Medical Journal of Zambia* (4 a year, print and online, www.mjz.co.zm).

NATURAL SCIENCES

Biological Sciences

Wildlife and Environmental Conservation Society of Zambia: POB 30255, Lusaka; tel. (1) 251630; e-mail wecsz@zamnet.zm; internet www.conservationzambia.org; f. 1953; dedicated to promoting wildlife and natural resource conservation, environmental education; 2,000 mems; Pres. ADAM JONATHAN POPE; Programme Coordinator PATRICK SHAWA; publs *Black Lechwe* (4 a month), *Chongololo Magazine and Guide* (24 a year), *Chipembele Magazine and Guide* (24 a year).

TECHNOLOGY

Engineering Institution of Zambia: CL/7 New Brentwood Dr., Longacres, POB 51084, Lusaka; tel. (21) 1255161; e-mail eiz@eiz.org.zm; internet www.eiz.org.zm; f. 1955; 2,600 mems; Pres. G. K. CHIBUYE; Vice-Pres. Dr K. AKAPELWA; publ. *Journal* (4 a year).

Research Institutes

GENERAL

National Institute for Scientific and Industrial Research: POB 310158, International Airport Rd, Lusaka 15302; tel. (1) 281082; e-mail directorate@nisir.org.zm; internet www.nisir.org.zm; f. 1967; statutory body to conduct scientific and industrial research and to collect and disseminate scientific information; incorporates Building and Industrial Minerals Research Unit, Food Technology Research Unit, Information Services Unit, Livestock and Pest Research Centre, Material Testing Unit, Radioisotopes Research Unit, Tree Improvement Research Centre, Technical Services Unit, Water Resources Research Unit; library of 9,200 vols, 100 periodicals; Exec. Dir Dr MWANA-NYANDA MBIKUSITA LEWANIKA; publs *Sci-Tech Newsletter* (4 a year), *Zambia Journal of*

Science and Technology (irregular), *Zambia Science Abstracts* (1 a year).

AGRICULTURE, FISHERIES AND VETERINARY SCIENCE

Central Fisheries Research Institute: POB 350100, Chilanga; tel. (1) 278597; e-mail piscator@zamnet.zm; f. 1965; hydrobiological research directed towards increasing fish production, co-management research directed towards sustainable fisheries management, fish-stock assessment, social and economic studies in fishing regions; library of 4,700 vols; Deputy Dir C. K. KAPASA; Chief Fisheries Research Officer P. NGALANDE; publs *Fisheries Statistics*, *Project Reports* (irregular).

Central Veterinary Research Station: POB 33980, Lusaka; tel. (1) 233444; e-mail cvri@zamnet.zm; f. 1926; directed by the Ministry of Agriculture and Livestock; general veterinary diagnosis and research; Prin. Veterinary Research Officer Dr S. H. KABILIKA.

Division of Forest Products Research: POB 20388, Kitwe; tel. (2) 227088; f. 1963; controls research into wood utilization, timber properties preservation, engineering, forest products and wood composite studies; Chief Officer S. M. MUTEMWA; publ. *Records* (irregular).

Division of Forest Research: POB 22099, Kitwe; tel. (2) 220456; f. 1956; ecological and botanical studies; soil and site assessment investigations; silvicultural research, exotic plantations and indigenous forests and woodlands; mensurational studies of plantation growth; tree breeding and selection; agroforestry and fuelwood projects; forest pathology and entomology; seed colln, processing, testing and low-temperature storage; library of 7,800 vols, 150 periodicals and 100 serials; Chief Forest Research Officer F. M. MALAYA.

International Red Locust Control Organization for Central and Southern Africa: POB 240252, Ndola; tel. (2) 651251; e-mail locust@zamnet.zm; f. 1970; prevents plague of red locust by controlling outbreaks, assists mem. countries in the management of army worm and grain-eating birds; carries out research and training; mem. countries: Kenya, Malawi, Mozambique, Tanzania, Zambia, Zimbabwe; library of 3,000 vols, 35 periodicals; Dir MOSES M. OKHOBA; publ. *Scientific Papers*.

Mount Makulu Agricultural Research Station: Zambia Agriculture Research Institute, Private Bag 7, Chilanga; tel. (1) 278130; internet www.zari.gov.zm/makuluresearchtest.php; f. 1952; Headquarters of Department of Research and Specialist Services, Ministry of Agriculture and Livestock and 11 regional and specialist research stations; research on soils, soil classification, vegetation types and land classification; agronomy; chemistry; ecology; entomology; pasture research; phytosanitary services; plant breeding; plant pathology; Seeds Control and Certification Institute; stored products entomology; cotton entomology; main crops under investigation: beans, cotton, groundnuts, maize, pastures and pasture legumes, sorghum, soyabeans, tobacco, wheat; library of 30,000 vols, 20,000 reports, 15,000 reprints; Prin. Agricultural Research Officer BERNADETTE LUBOZUYA; publs *Accessions List* (6 a year), *Production Farming in Zambia* (12 a year), *Reprints of Articles by Staff Members*, *Research Branch Memoranda* (irregular).

ECONOMICS, LAW AND POLITICS

Pan-African Institute for Development, East and Southern Africa: POB 80448, Kabwe; tel. (21) 5223651; e-mail paidesa@zamnet.zm; f. 1979; training, research, surveys, follow-up action; library of 8,000 vols; Dir Dr LUTHER BANGA; publ. *Current Contents: Development Studies* (4 a year).

MEDICINE

National Food and Nutrition Commission: POB 32669, Lusaka 10101; tel. (1) 227803; e-mail nfnc@zamnet.zm; f. 1967; statutory body to improve the nutritional status of the people of Zambia; 98 mems; Chair. CRESTA KALUBA; Exec. Dir PRISCILLA N. LIKWASI.

Occupational Health Safety and Research Bureau: Independence Ave, POB 20205, Kitwe; tel. (2) 228977; e-mail ohmb@zamnet.zm; internet www.geocities.com/ohsrb; f. 1950; research on pneumoconiosis and related chest diseases, assessment and advice on control of hazardous conditions in industrial workplaces; library of 300 vols; Dir Dr DANSTER CHOMBA MWILA (acting).

Tropical Diseases Research Centre: POB 71769, Ndola; tel. (2) 620737; e-mail info@tdrc.org.zm; internet www.tdrc.org.zm; f. 1976; research in communicable diseases, support for disease control and primary health-care programmes; trains Zambian scientists in the field of biomedical research, serves as int. research and training centre; epidemiological research, clinical trials, research in malaria, schistosomiasis, trypanosomiasis, diarrhoeal diseases, etc.; 28 researchers, 76 support staff; library of 3,300 vols, 219 periodicals; Dir Dr EMMANUEL KAFWEMBE.

NATURAL SCIENCES

Physical Sciences

Department of Geological Survey: POB 50135, Lusaka; tel. (21) 1250174; e-mail gsd@zamnet.zm; f. 1951; attached to Min. of Mines, Energy and Water Devt; statutory depository for all mining and prospecting records and reports; assists the public on mineral matters and advises Ministry on mineral and geological matters, economic mineral investigations, geological mapping; library of 89,346 vols; Dir D. MULELA; publs *Economic Reports*, *Memoirs*, *Occasional Papers*, *Records*, *Reports*, and maps.

Libraries and Archives

Kitwe

Hammarskjöld Memorial Library: POB 21493, Kitwe; tel. (2) 211488; e-mail daglib@zamnet.zm; internet www.mindolo.org/dml; f. 1963; 26,000 vols; colln of films, filmstrips, slides, microfiche, video cassettes, tape-recordings on local history; rare book colln on the history of central Africa; specializes in social sciences; research library and archives of the Mindolo Ecumenical Foundation; colln on American society and culture; Librarian DUNSTAN CHIKONKA.

Kitwe Public Library: POB 2007, Kaunda Sq., Kitwe; tel. (21) 2213685; f. 1954; 33,000 vols.

Lusaka

Lusaka City Libraries: POB 31304, Katondo Rd, Lusaka; tel. (1) 227282; f. 1943; 3 br. libraries and a mobile library; 145,000 vols, 200 periodicals, 320 maps; Librarian J. C. NKOLE; publ. *Library Bulletin* (4 a year).

National Archives of Zambia: POB 50010, Lusaka; tel. (21) 1254081; e-mail naz@zamnet.zm; f. 1947; covers national literature from 1890 to the present day in the form of national archives, historical MSS, microfilms, cartographic, philatelic, currency, pictorial and printed publication collns; 18,000 linear m of records; depository and reference library of 17,000 vols and 11,000 periodicals; Dir CRISPIN HAMOOYA; Senior Archivist T. M. SUUYA; Senior Librarian H. K. NYENDWA.

Zambia Library Service: c/o Ministry of Education, Science, Vocational Training and Early Education, POB 50093, Civic Center Area Plot 82, cnr Mogadishu and Chimanga Rd, Lusaka 10101; tel. (1) 250855; internet www.moe.gov.zm; f. 1962; aims to provide a countrywide free public library service; 6 regional libraries, 18 br. libraries; 500,000 vols; Chief Librarian ETHEL N. TEMBO; publ. *Zambia Library Service Newsletter* (irregular).

Museums and Art Galleries

Livingstone

Livingstone Museum: Mosi-oa-Tunya Rd, POB 60498, Livingstone; tel. (3) 321204; e-mail livmus@zamnet.zm; f. 1934; ethnology of the peoples of Zambia; prehistory, history and natural history of Zambia; autograph, letters and relics of David Livingstone; library of 20,000 vols, 200 periodicals, including spec. colln of 2,000 vols on prehistory, history, ethnography and Africana; supporting depts of taxidermy, conservation and education; Dir V. K. KATANEKWA; publs *The Livingstone Museum Newsletter*, *Zambia Museum Journal*.

Mbala

Moto Moto Museum: POB 420230, Mbala; tel. (4) 450243; e-mail motomoto@zamtel.zm; f. 1974; research in ethnography, prehistory and history; educational and exhibition programmes; library of 5,000 vols; Dir NKOLE E. SOSALA; publ. *Zambia Museums Journal* (irregular).

Ndola

Copperbelt Museum: 911 Buteko Ave, POB 71444, Ndola; tel. (2) 613591; e-mail cbmus@zamnet.zm; f. 1962; colln, conservation, preservation, documentation and exhibit of geological and historical items, ethnography and natural history; Dir STANFORD MUDENDA SIACHOONO.

Universities

COPPERBELT UNIVERSITY

POB 21692, Kitwe

Telephone: (2) 225155

E-mail: registrar@cbu.ac.zm

Internet: www.cbu.edu.zm

Founded 1979 as Ndola Campus of Univ. of Zambia, present status 1987

State control

Language of instruction: English

Academic year: March to December (3 terms)

Chancellor: Prof. MUYUNDA MWANALUSHI

Vice-Chancellor: Prof. NAISON NGOMA (acting)

Deputy Vice-Chancellor: Dr SHADRECK CHAMA (acting)

Registrar: ALLAN M. ILLUNGA

Librarian: CHARLES B. M. LUNGU

Number of teachers: 770

Number of students: 10,300

Publication: *Journal of Business* (4 a year)

DEANS

Academic Development Centre: Prof. ADELE PATRICK PHIRI

School of Built Environment: Dr ROY CHILESHE

School of Business: Dr SUMBYE KAPENA

School of Engineering: CHARLES MHANGO (acting)

School of Graduate Studies: Dr THOMAS K. TAYLOR

School of Mathematics and Natural Sciences: Prof. FRANK TAILOKA

School of Medicine: Prof. KASONDE BOWA

School of Mines and Mineral Sciences: Prof. GLASWELL NKONDE

School of Natural Resources: Dr EXHILDAH CHISHA-KASUMU

School of Technology: Dr I. S. SINGH

PROFESSORS

KASONDE, B., School of Medicine

LUNGU, J., School of Business

MASEKA, K., School of Mathematics and Natural Sciences

NKONDE, G., School of Mines and Mineral Sciences

PHIRI, A., Academic Development Centre

SHUMBA, O., School of Mathematics and Natural Sciences

SIULAPWA, J., School of Medicine

SIZIYA, P., School of Medicine

TAILOKA, F., School of Mathematics and Natural Sciences

TEMBO, J., School of Business

CONSTITUENT SCHOOLS

School of Built Environment: tel. (2) 225086; e-mail deansbe@cbu.ac.zm.

School of Business: tel. (2) 227946; e-mail deansb@cbu.ac.zm.

School of Natural Resources: tel. (2) 227946; e-mail forestry@cbu.ac.zm.

School of Technology: tel. (2) 228212; e-mail deanst@cbu.ac.zm.

ATTACHED INSTITUTES

Centre for Lifelong Education: Dir Col (rtd) LLOYD MWILA.

Institute of Environmental Management: Dir M. NABUYANDA

UNIVERSITY OF ZAMBIA

POB 32379, Lusaka

Telephone: (1) 291777

E-mail: registrar@unza.zm

Internet: www.unza.zm

Founded 1965

State control

Language of instruction: English

Academic year: July to May

Chancellor: Dr JACOB M. MWANZA

Vice-Chancellor: Prof. STEPHEN SIMUKANGA

Deputy Vice-Chancellor: Dr WILSON MWENYA

Registrar: Dr ALVERT N'GANDU

Librarian: Dr V. CHIFWEPA

Number of teachers: 535

Number of students: 13,500

Publications: *African Social Research, Journal of Humanities, Journal of Medicine, Journal of Sciences and Technology, Zambia Law Journal, Zambian Papers, Zango*

DEANS

Agricultural Sciences: Dr MIKE MWALA

Distance Education: ZANZINI NDHLOVU (Dir)

Education: OSWELL CHAKULIMBA

Engineering: Dr MUNDIA MUYA

Humanities and Social Sciences: Dr SIAMWIZA BENARD

Law: Dr M. MUNALULA

Medicine: Dr F. GOMA

Mines: Dr O. SIKAZWE

Natural Sciences: Dr HENRY M. SICHINGABULA

Research and Graduate Studies: Prof. S. NYAMBE (Dir)

Veterinary Medicine: Dr AARON MWEENE

PROFESSORS

BANDA, G. P. A., Geography

BANDA, S. F., Chemistry

BANDA, S. S., Medical Education

BHAT, G. J., Paediatrics and Child Health

CHAKANIKA, W., Adult Education and Extension Studies

CHISHIMBA, C. P., In-Service Education and Advisory Science Education

CHITAMBO, H., Paraclinical Studies

DILLON-MALONE, C., Philosophy

ERZINGATSIAN, K., Surgery

HAMBOKOMA, C., Mathematics and Science Education

HAWORTH, A., Psychiatry

KAELA, L. C. W., Political and Administrative Studies

KAFUMUKACHE, E. B., Anatomy

KAILE, T., Pathology and Microbiology

KALINDA, T., Agricultural Economics and Extension Education

KAMBANI, S., Mining Engineering

KASEBA, C., Obstetrics and Gynaecology

KWENDAKWEMA, N. J., Agricultural Engineering

LAMBWE, E., Post-Basic Nursing

LEMBA, M., Social Development Studies

LIPALITE, M., Development Studies

LUNGU, I. O., Soil Science

LUSWILI, J., Mathematics and Statistics

MANAKOV, A. K., Physiological Sciences

MATONDO, P., Internal Medicine

MILIMO, M. C., Gender Studies

MSANGO, H. J., Educational Administration and Policy Studies

MULENGA, F. E., History

MULENGA, M. N., Civil Engineering

MWALA, M. S., Crop Science

MWEENE, H. V., Physics

MWIKISA, C. N., Economics

NAMBOTA, A., Disease Control

NG'ANDU, A. N., Mechanical Engineering

NGANDU, S. K., Educational Psychology, Sociology and Special Education

NKHUWA, C. W., Geology

NSOMBO, P., Surveying

NYIRENDA, L. D., Electrical and Electronic Engineering

PHIRI, I. K., Clinical Studies

SIAKALIMA, D. (acting), Psychology

SIKULUMBA, J. K., Literature and Languages

SIULAPWA, J. N., Biomedical Sciences

SIZIYA, S., Community Medicine

TAMBULUKANI, G. (acting), Language and Social Sciences Education

WACHINGA, D. M., Biological Sciences

WITIKA, L. K., Metallurgy and Mineral Processing

YAMBAYAMBA, E. S. K., Animal Sciences

ZULU, S., Library and Information Studies

Colleges

Evelyn Hone College of Applied Arts and Commerce: POB 30029, Lusaka; tel. (1) 235344; e-mail ehcbs@zamnet.zm; f. 1963; library: 14,000 vols; 145 teachers; 3,000 students (1,600 full-time, 1,400 part-time); Prin. MICHAEL TANDEO; Librarian SEBASTIAN NGWIRA.

National Institute of Public Administration: POB 31990, 10101 Lusaka; tel. (1) 228802; e-mail nipa@zamnet.zm; f. 1963; trains govt administrators and accounting personnel for central and local govt; offers training and consultancy in the private sector in management, secretarial work, purchasing and supplies, and law and information technology; library: 28,000 vols; 50 teachers; 1,316 students; Exec. Dir Dr M. C. BWALYA; Registrar PAUL SIMUKOKO; Librarian N. MTANGA.

Natural Resources Development College: POB 310099, Lusaka; No 7132 Off Great East Rd, Chelstone, Lusaka; tel. (1) 283698; e-mail info@nrdc.biz; internet www.nrdc.biz; f. 1965; depts of agribusiness, agricultural engineering, animal science, crop science, education, fisheries, horticulture, nutrition, water engineering; library: 32,000 vols; 50 teachers; 430 students; Prin. T. F. F. MALUZA; Librarian M. M. MISENGO.

Northern Technical College: POB 250093, Ndola; tel. (2) 680141; e-mail nortec@zamnet.zm; f. 1960; automotive, electrical, heavy duty and mechanical engineering, business studies and communication skills, refrigeration and air-conditioning; library: 20,000 vols; 96 teachers (68 full-time, 28 part-time); 1,300 students (800 full-time, 500 part-time); Prin. (vacant); Librarian NABOMBE PUMULO.

Zambia College of Agriculture: POB 660053, Monze; f. 1947; library: 3,000 vols; 40 teachers; 240 students; Prin. D. H. MCCLEERY.

ZIMBABWE

The Higher Education System

Institutions of higher education pre-date the independence of Zimbabwe (formerly Southern Rhodesia) from the United Kingdom in 1980, the oldest being Esigodini Agricultural Institute, which was founded in 1921. The oldest university-level institution is the University of Zimbabwe (formerly the University College of Rhodesia), which was founded in 1955 (present status since 1970 and present name since 1980). There has been a steady increase in the number of state-run universities in recent years, largely as a result of a deliberate government policy to create regional universities in each of the states. There are now 10 universities (including the Zimbabwe Open University), compared with two at the turn of the millennium. There are also several private universities including Africa University, Solusi University and the Women's University in Africa. The latter was founded in 2002 to address gender disparity in university education; enrolment figures have grown steadily from 145 students in 2002 to an estimated 2,300 in 2012. There is also an Open University for those who cannot attend residential university programmes. In 2008/09 a total of 49,645 students were enrolled at institutions of higher education. A national higher education plan for the period 2011–15 was launched in July 2011, the stated objective of which was to reverse an alarming decline in higher education standards precipitated by political and economic instability during the post-independence era, particularly from the early 2000s, and to transform Zimbabwe into a regional leader for higher education.

The Ministry of Higher and Tertiary Education, Science and Technology Development is the national agency responsible for the provision of higher education in Zimbabwe. In 2006 the Zimbabwe Council for Higher Education Act was introduced to develop policy on higher education, accredit all higher education institutions and design a quality assurance system.

The minimum requirement for admission to undergraduate studies is two grade 'E' passes at GCE A-level; however, the strength of competition has effectively raised the bar for admission to grade 'C' in at least three subjects. Admission is also granted to applicants who hold the National Diploma. The principal undergraduate degree is the Bachelors, which may be classified either 'General' or 'Honours' (the distinction lies in the content rather than the length of the course). On average, the Bachelors lasts three to four years, but in some subjects the period of study is longer, such as the Bachelors of Medicine and Bachelors of Surgery (both five years). Masters degrees are the first postgraduate-level qualifications, and vary in length from one to three years; they are usually a composite of coursework and research for a dissertation, but the MPhil, which lasts two to three years, is usually a purely research-based degree. The main doctoral-level degree is the DPhil, which is three to four years in duration.

A priority for the Government has been to improve the quality of teacher training. The Zimbabwe Integrated Teacher Education Course (ZINTEC) had operated previously to provide training for unqualified primary school teachers. ZINTEC colleges are now affiliated to the Department of Teaching at the University of Zimbabwe, as are all other teacher colleges. Entry qualifications to the three-year teaching courses were raised to a minimum of five O-levels, with English as a compulsory subject. Teachers at upper secondary level are generally expected to have a Bachelors of Education or Bachelors of Science/Arts in Education. In 2011 there were 14 teacher training colleges.

In 1990 the Government initiated wide-ranging reforms of technical and vocational education owing to the failure of the secondary and higher education sectors to match the expectations of both students and employers. Vocational training centres were first established in 1998 to provide for a government initiative known as the Skills Training programme. The principal post-secondary technical and vocational awards are as follows: National Certificate, National Diploma and Higher National Diploma. Apprenticeships are also available, and are offered in about 80 trade areas. Apprenticeships typically last between three and four years, and comprise a mixture of practical and theoretical work, with 'on the job' training constituting around 80% of the programme. In 2002 all Technical Colleges were upgraded to Polytechnics and since then the Harare Polytechnic has become a degree-awarding Institute of Technology. The Zimbabwe Occupational Standards Services was established in 1999 as part of the new reform of technical and vocational education and training, and in 2004 plans were put into place for a National Steering Committee to develop a Zimbabwe Qualifications Framework.

Regulatory and Representative Bodies

GOVERNMENT

Ministry of Higher and Tertiary Education, Science and Technology Development: Bag CY 7732, Causeway, Harare; Govt Composite Bldg, Block F, 5th Fl., cnr Fourth St and Samora Machel Ave, Harare; tel. (4) 796440; e-mail chitonhom@mhet.gov.zw; internet www.mhtestd.gov.zw; Minister OLIVIA MUCHENA.

Ministry of Sports, Arts and Culture: Ambassador House, Union Ave, POB CY 121, Causeway, Harare; tel. (4) 734071; Minister ANDREW LANGA.

NATIONAL BODIES

Zimbabwe Universities' Vice-Chancellors' Association: PB 9055, Gweru, Midlands; tel. (54) 60753; e-mail msuvcoffice@yahoo.com.

Learned Societies

GENERAL

UNESCO Office Harare: POB HG 435, Highlands, Harare; 8 Kenilworth Rd, Newlands, Harare; tel. (4) 776775; e-mail harare@unesco.org; designated Cluster Office for Botswana, Malawi, Mozambique, Zambia and Zimbabwe; Dir Prof. LUC RUKINGAMA.

AGRICULTURE, FISHERIES AND VETERINARY SCIENCE

Zimbabwe Agricultural Society: POB 442, Harare; Exhibition Park, Samora Machel Ave, Harare; tel. (4) 780966; f. 1895; 3,500 mems; Gen. Man. (vacant).

Zimbabwe Veterinary Association: POB CY 168, Causeway, Harare; tel. (4) 303574; f. 1920; 175 mems; Pres. Dr G. GELDART; publ. *Zimbabwe Veterinary Journal* (2 a year).

BIBLIOGRAPHY, LIBRARY SCIENCE AND MUSEOLOGY

Zimbabwe Library Association: POB 3133, Harare; tel. (4) 792641; e-mail membership@zimla.co.zw; internet www.zimbabwereads.org/zimla; f. 1959; 254 mems; Chair. T. G. BHOWA; publ. *Zimbabwe Librarian*.

HISTORY, GEOGRAPHY AND ARCHAEOLOGY

Prehistory Society of Zimbabwe: POB A 723, Avondale, Harare; tel. (4) 744651; e-mail adele@zol.co.zw; f. 1958; promotion of the study of early history, prehistory and archaeology in Africa, with particular reference to Zimbabwe; 100 mems; library of 400 vols; Chair. (vacant); publ. *Journal of Zimbabwe Prehistory* (1 a year).

LANGUAGE AND LITERATURE

Alliance Française: 328 Herbert Chitepo Ave, POB 2515, Harare; tel. (4) 704801; e-mail info@afharare.co.zw; internet www

.afzim.org/afharare/hre.html; offers courses and exams in French language and culture, and promotes cultural exchange with France; attached teaching centre in Bulawayo; Pres. LILLIAN NYATHI-MOYO.

British Council: 16 Cork Rd, Belgravia, POB 664, Harare; tel. (4) 701658; e-mail general.enquiries@britishcouncil.org.zw; internet www.britishcouncil.org/africa-zw-contact-us.htm; offers courses and exams in English language and British culture, and promotes cultural exchange with the UK; attached office in Bulawayo; Regional Dir, Central Africa DAVID MARTIN; Dir Operations, Zimbabwe RAJIV BENDRE.

Zimbabwe Writers Union: 18 Gilford Crescent, Southerto, Harare.

MEDICINE

Pharmaceutical Society of Zimbabwe: 12 Divine Rd, Milton Park, POB 1476, Harare; tel. (4) 741829; e-mail psz@zol.co.zw; internet www.psz.co.zw; f. 1898; promotes training of pharmacists; advocates the profession of pharmacy; 320 mems; Pres. DOTHAN MOYO; Sec. VIMBAIASHE MUKUDU.

Zimbabwe Dental Association: 1 Thorton Ave, POB 1268, Bulawayo; tel. (9) 62402; e-mail musiyaw@netconnect.co.zw; f. 1939; affiliated to World Dental Fed.; 130 mems; Pres. Dr WEBSTER MUSIYA.

Zimbabwe Medical Association: POB 3671, Harare; 172 Baines Ave., Avenues, Harare; tel. (4) 7915612; Pres. B. G. MAUCHAZA; Sec. E. VUSHE.

NATURAL SCIENCES

General

Zimbabwe Scientific Association: POB CY 124, Causeway, Harare; tel. (4) 335143; f. 1899; 380 mems; Pres. Dr L. MHLANGA; Sec. Dr J. HUSSEIN; publs *Transactions* (1 a year), *Zimbabwe Science News* (2 a year).

Biological Sciences

BirdLife Zimbabwe: POB RVL 100, Runiville, Harare; tel. (4) 481496; e-mail birds@zol.co.zw; internet www.birdlifezimbabwe.co.zw; f. 1951; 480 mems; Dir CHIPANGURA CHIRARA; publs *Babbler* (6 a year), *Honeyguide* (2 a year).

Wildlife and Environment Zimbabwe: POB HG 996, Highlands, Harare; tel. (4) 747500; e-mail zimwild@mweb.co.zw; internet www.zimwild.co.zw; f. 1927; all aspects of wildlife conservation and environmental awareness; 2,500 mems; Pres. ISAIAH NYAKUSENDWA; Dir Dr WILLIE K. NDUKU; publ. *Zimbabwe Wildlife* (4 a year, online).

Physical Sciences

Geological Society of Zimbabwe: Central Ave, Harare; tel. (4) 700196; f. 1981; 320 mems; Chair. M. L. VINYU; Sec. H. A. JELSMA.

TECHNOLOGY

Zimbabwe Institution of Engineers: POB 660, 256 Samora Machel Ave, Eastlea, Harare; tel. (4) 746821; e-mail zie@zarnet.ac.zw; internet www.zie.org.zw; f. 1944; 2,568 mems; CEO Dr SANZAN DIARRA; publs *Proceedings* (2 a year), *Zimbabwe Engineer* (12 a year).

Research Institutes

GENERAL

Research Council of Zimbabwe: Block A, Delken Complex, Mount Pleasant, Harare; tel. (4) 369407; e-mail technical@rcz.ac.zw; internet www.rcz.ac.zw; f. 1964, reconstituted 1984; advisory body to the Govt on general scientific policy and official channel for exchange of nat. and int. scientific and technical information; Chair. EBEN MABIBI MAKONESE; Exec. Dir S. MUZITE; publs *Directory of Organizations concerned with Scientific Research and Services in Zimbabwe* (every 2 years), *Symposium Proceedings* (every 2 years), *Zimbabwe Research Index* (1 a year).

AGRICULTURE, FISHERIES AND VETERINARY SCIENCE

Agricultural Research Trust: POB MP 84, Mount Pleasant, Harare; tel. (4) 2930359; e-mail artfarm@mweb.co.zw; internet www.artfarm.co.zw; f. 1980; research into cereals, grains, oilseed and horticultural crops and the provision of research field sites for crop breeders, agronomists and the crop chemical industry; Dir NICK BROOKE; Research Man. LANGTON T. MUTEMERI; Financial Man. GORDON A. LIND.

Department of Research and Specialist Services: POB CY 594, Causeway, Harare; tel. (4) 704531; internet www.drss.gov.zw; f. 1967; advises on agricultural research policy and programmes in Zimbabwe; administers regional research institutes and stations listed below; Prin. Dir DANISILE HIKWA; publs *Kirkia—Journal of Botany of Zimbabwe* (1 a year), *Zimbabwe Agricultural Journal* (6 a year), *Zimbabwe Journal of Agricultural Research* (2 a year).

Research Institutes and Stations:

Chemistry and Soil Research Institute: POB CY 550, Causeway, Harare; tel. (4) 704531; e-mail csri.rsd@drss.gov.zw; f. 1905; research and advisory work on soils and agricultural chemistry; registration and regulation of fertilizers and foodstuffs; crop nutrition, chemistry, pedology, soil physics and soil productivity research sections; Head C. F. MUSHAMBI.

Coffee Research Institute: POB CY 594, Causeway, Harare; tel. (4) 704531; e-mail rscoffee@mango.zw; f. 1964; research into all aspects of coffee management, growth, pest and disease control; tea research projects; Officer-in-Charge D. KUTYWAYO.

Cotton Research Institute: POB CY 594, Causeway, Harare; tel. (4) 704531; e-mail zimcott@africaonline.co.zw; f. 1925; all aspects of cotton agronomy, breeding, pest and disease research; Head L. T. GONO (acting).

Crop Breeding Institute: POB CY 550, Causeway, Harare; tel. (4) 704531; f. 1948; research into plant breeding agronomy, crop ecology and crop production; Head BUSISO MAVANKENI (acting).

Fertilizer, Farm Feeds and Remedies Institute: POB CY 594, Causeway, Harare; tel. (4) 704531; registration of pesticides—import and export, regulation and distribution; registration of and facilitation of fertilizer import; registration of and facilitation of farm feeds import; advisory services on pesticide and fertilizer use.

Genetic Resources Institute: POB CY 594, Causeway, Harare; tel. (4) 704531; e-mail ngbz@iwayafriza.co.zw; maintains and enhances the diversity of crop genetic diversity, incl. indigenous crops; holds the Nat. Genebank of Zimbabwe.

Grasslands Research Institute: PMB 3701, Marondera; tel. (79) 22243; f. 1930; research on pasture, animal and crop production for the high-rainfall sandveld area; selection and testing of Rhizobium strains and commercial production of legume inoculants; Head G. MANYAN.

Henderson Research Institute: PMB 2004, Mazowe; tel. (71) 1279408; f. 1948; pasture work on the introduction and screening of grasses and legumes for suitability as fertilized pastures; research in ruminant nutrition; herbicide and weed control research; Head Mr SCHAKEREDZA (acting).

Horticultural Research Institute: POB CY 594, Causeway, Harare; tel. (4) 704531; f. 1975; research into planting materials and technologies for vegetables, tropical and sub-tropical fruit and nut trees, flowers, herbs and spices, root and tuber crops; Head V. CHINGWARA.

Lowveld Research Institute: POB 97, Chiredzi; tel. (31) 2397; f. 1967; research in irrigation agronomy in SE Lowveld; sub-tropical horticulture and vegetable crops; Head Dr P. NYAMUDEZA.

Makoholi Experiment Institute: PMB 9182, Masvingo; f. 1962; research into problems of animal and crop production for sandveld and medium rainfall districts of Zimbabwe; crop agronomy, cattle production (indigenous breeds) and natural grazing management; Head I. CHIGAMBA.

Matopos Research Institute: PMB K 5137, Bulawayo; tel. (9) 8383327; f. 1903; research in veld management, ecology of regional soil types, bush encroachment, cattle breeding, and beef production; Head Dr S. MAYO.

Nyanga Experimental Station: POB 2061, Nyanga; f. 1911; pome fruit research; Officer-in-Charge N. NAUBE.

Plant Protection Research Institute: POB CY 554, Causeway, Harare; tel. (4) 704531; e-mail plantpro@ecoweb.co.zw; f. 1964; research and advisory work on plant pests and diseases; biological control, entomology, pathology and nematology sections; Head Dr S. Z. SITHOLE.

Plant Quarantine Services Institute: POB CY 554, Causeway, Harare; tel. (4) 704531.

Seed Services Institute: POB CY 554, Causeway, Harare; tel. (4) 704531; e-mail seedserve@mweb.co.zw; f. 1971; research into the production of high quality seed, contains an official seed testing laboratory accredited to the Int. Seed Testing Asscn.

Department of Veterinary Services; Tsetse Control Branch: POB CY 52, Causeway, Harare; tel. (4) 707381; f. 1909; attached to Ministry of Agriculture, Mechanisation and Irrigation Devt; for the control of the tsetse fly population and the investigation of methods of control; laboratory at Harare and research station in the Zambezi Valley; Chief Research Officer W. SHERENI..

Attached Laboratory:

Central Veterinary Laboratory: POB CY 551, Causeway, Harare; tel. (4) 705885; e-mail vetlabs@africaonline.co.zw; f. 1906; diagnostic centre and research institute for animal diseases; 35 mems; library of 1,500 vols; Head of Veterinary Diagnostics and Research Branch Dr P. V. HAKAYA.

Forestry Commission: POB HG 139, Highlands, Harare; tel. (4) 498439; f. 1954; state forest authority, responsible for formulating forest policy in Zimbabwe; engaged in large-scale plantation operations; research and advisory services, forestry extension and wildlife utilization..

Attached Centre:

Forest Research Centre: POB HG 595, Highlands, Harare; tel. (4) 498816; conducts research into many aspects of forestry, principally high-yielding plantations, with special emphasis on tree genetics and the production of progressively improved pine and eucalypt seed, wood quality, general plantation management and fertilizer research; screening of multi-purpose tree species for use in fuel-wood plantations and social forestry; Deputy Gen. Man. C. M. GUMBIE; publ. *Format* (4 a year).

Tobacco Research Board: POB 1909, Harare; tel. (4) 575289; e-mail tobres@kutsaga.co.zw; f. 1950; conducts research into all types of tobacco, agronomy, breeding, engineering and pest control; operates 3 research stations; board mems, appointed by the Minister of Agriculture, represent growers, buyers and Min. of Agriculture, Mechanisation and Irrigation Devt; library of 12,000 vols, 250 periodicals; Chair. Dr R. M. MUPAWOSE; Dir A. J. MASUKA.

ECONOMICS, LAW AND POLITICS

Institute of Development Studies: University of Zimbabwe, POB MP 167, Harare; tel. (4) 333341; e-mail mnyoni@cso.zarnet.ac.zw; f. 1982; undertakes policy-oriented research, consultancy and training; 3 research depts: Agrarian and Labour Studies, Economics and Technology Studies, and Int. Relations and Social Devt Studies; Poverty Reduction Forum; library of 17,500 vols, 24,000 documents; Dir Dr DONALD P. CHIMANIKIRE.

Zimbabwe National Statistics Agency (ZIMSTAT): 20th Fl. Kaguvi Bldg, Cnr Fourth St./Central Ave, POB CY 342, Causeway, Harare; tel. (4) 706681; e-mail denmab@mweb.co.zw; internet www.zimstat.co.zw; f. 1927; Dir L. MACHIROVI.

MEDICINE

Public Health Laboratory: POB CY 430, Causeway, Harare; tel. (4) 720746; e-mail maxhove@yahoo.com; f. 1909; Dir Dr M. G. M. HOVE; Pathologist Dr D. MADZIWA; Chief Medical Technologist L. ZAWAIRA; Chief Medical Technologist Dr O. MAYO.

NATURAL SCIENCES
Physical Sciences

Geological Survey of Zimbabwe: POB CY 210, Causeway, Harare; tel. (4) 726342; internet www.geosurvey.co.zw; f. 1910; geological mapping and survey of mineral resources; library of 1,400 vols, 800 symposia, 11,900 periodicals, 2,600 technical files; museum displaying Zimbabwean geology and economic minerals; Dir W. MAGALELA; publs *Bulletins*, *Mineral Resources Series* (irregular), short reports and maps.

Meteorological Service: POB BE 150, Belvedere, Harare; tel. (4) 778173; e-mail director@weather.utande.co.zw; internet www.weather.co.zw; f. 1897; part of the Min. of Transport, Communication and Infrastructural Devt; Dir RUNGANO P. KARIMANZIRA; publs *Agromet Bulletin* (October–March), *Climate Handbook Supplements*, *Monthly Meteorological Summaries*, *Rainfall Handbook Supplements*, daily weather reports and forecasts, weekly rainfall maps during rainy season November–March.

Affiliated Institute:

Goetz Observatory: POB AC 65, Ascot, Bulawayo; tel. (9) 66197; also seismology; publs *Agricultural Meteorological Bulletin* (12 a year), *Seismological Bulletin*.

TECHNOLOGY

Department of Metallurgy: Ministry of Mines and Mining Devt, Stand No 694 Rekai Tangwena St, POB CY 1375, Causeway, Harare; tel. (4) 726629; e-mail metallurgy@technopark.com; f. 1962; conducts investigations on methods of economic extraction from precious, base-metal and non-metallic ores, and industrial minerals evaluation, also on physical metallurgy; library of 280 vols; Dir T. I. NYATSANGA; publ. *Testwork Reports*.

Standards Association of Zimbabwe: POB 2259, Harare; tel. (4) 885511; e-mail info@saz.org.zw; internet www.saz.org.zw; f. 1957; laboratory facilities for testing raw materials and manufactured goods and operates certification mark schemes; prepares and publishes Zimbabwean nat. standards; provides information service on standards and a WTO/Technical Barriers to Trade enquiry point on standards and conformity assessment; provides training on standards; Chair. TRUST CHIKOHORA; Dir-Gen. EVE CHRISTINE GADZIKWA; publs *Catalogue of Zimbabwe Standards*, *Fulcrum* (official bulletin).

Libraries and Archives
Bulawayo

Bulawayo Public Library: 100 Fort St, Bulawayo; tel. (9) 60965; e-mail bpl@gatorzw.com; internet www.angelfire.com/ky/bpl/; f. 1896; reference, lending, junior library; mobile library; postal service to rural readers; braille colln; African and Zimbabwe collns; Zimbabwe map colln; legal deposit library for Zimbabwe; video and audio cassette collns; 100,000 vols; Librarian and Sec. ROBIN WILLIAM DOUST.

National Library and Documentation Service, National Free Library of Zimbabwe: POB 1773, Bulawayo; 12th Ave, South Park, Bulawayo; tel. 9232359; f. 1943 as nat. lending library for educational, scientific and technical books; nat. centre for inter-library loans; maintains Nat. Union Catalogue; 100,000 vols; Librarian H. R. NCUBE.

Harare

Harare City Library: POB 1087, Harare; tel. (4) 751834; e-mail hararecitylibrary@yahoo.com; f. 1902; 150,000 vols; Public Subscription Library; Librarian and Sec. TRYMORE SIMANGO.

National Archives of Zimbabwe: PMB 7729, Causeway, Harare; tel. (4) 792741; f. 1935 as the Govt Archives of Southern Rhodesia; inc. archives of Northern Rhodesia and Nyasaland and designated the Central African Archives 1947; became Nat. Archives of Rhodesia and Nyasaland 1958–63; reverted January 1964 to Rhodesian Govt and responsibility for Northern Rhodesia archives ceased; also serves Zimbabwean municipalities and some parastatal bodies and holds archives of Federation of Rhodesia and Nyasaland; comprises sections of Records Management, Research (Public Archives, Historical Manuscripts), Library (nat. historical reference colln, incl. photographic and map collns; legal deposit, depository for UNESCO publs) and Technical (Reprographic Unit, Conservation Unit, Oral History, Automation, Audiovisual Archives Unit); exhibition gallery; 4 provincial records centres; Dir. I. MURAMBIWA; publs *Bibliographical Series*, *Current Periodicals*, *Directory of Libraries*, *Guide to the Historical Manuscripts in the National Archives*, *Guide to the Public Archives of Rhodesia, Vol. 1, 1890–1923*, *Oppenheimer Series*, *Report of the Director* (1 a year), *Zimbabwe National Bibliography* (1 a year).

Parliament of Zimbabwe Library: POB CY 298, Causeway, Harare; tel. (4) 252936 ext. 2187; e-mail munatsir@parliament.gov.zw; internet www.parlzim.gov.zw; f. 1923; parliamentary and govt documents from Zimbabwe Parliament and from several Commonwealth countries; gen. colln specializing in political science, history, political biography, economics, sociology, public admin. and management, education, foreign relations; separate law colln, separate archival and reference colln and Zimbabwean publs; 116,000 vols; Prin. Librarian RONALD MUNATSI.

University of Zimbabwe Library: POB MP 45, Mount Pleasant, Harare; tel. (4) 303211; e-mail librarian@uzlib.uz.ac.zw; internet www.uz.ac.zw/library; f. 1956; c. 700,000 vols; more than 10,000 periodicals; Africana (Zimbabweana) colln; education library; colln of African languages; Institute of Devt Studies library; Lake Kariba Research Station library; law library; map library; medical library; Mpilo Hospital library; veterinary library; U. Z. Theses Colln; Librarian A. CHIKONZO; publ. *Newsletter* (12 a year).

Mutare

City of Mutare Public Libraries: POB 48, Mutare; tel. (20) 63412; f. 1902; incorporates Sakubva Public Library (f. 1972, 27,000 vols), Dangamvura Public Library (f. 1988, 18,000 vols), Turner Memorial Library (f. 1902, 40,000 vols), Chikanga Public Library (f. 2004, 5,000 vols); Head of Library Services D. MANDOWO.

Museums and Art Galleries
Bulawayo

Natural History Museum of Zimbabwe: Leopold Takawira Ave and Park Rd, POB 240, Bulawayo; tel. (9) 230046; e-mail natmuse@netconnect.co.zw; internet www.naturalhistorymuseumzimbabwe.com; f. 1901; entomological, geological, palaeontological, zoological; study collns and exhibits covering Ethiopian region, with spec. reference to southern Africa; historic, ethnographic and prehistoric exhibits pertaining to Zimbabwe and adjacent regions; Dir MOIRA FITZPATRICK; Curator of Arachnology M. J. FITZPATRICK; Curator of Archaeology T. MAKWENDE; Curator of Entomology D. MADAMBA; Curator of Herpetology D. BROADLEY; Curator of Ichthyology N. SEBATA; Curator of Mammals T. MAPONGA; Curator of Ornithology V. MAKAVAZA; Sr Librarian P. TSHABANGU; publs *Arnoldia Zimbabwe*, *Syntarsus*.

Gweru

Military Museum of Zimbabwe: Lobengula Ave, POB 1300, Gweru; tel. (54) 22816; f. 1972; history of Zimbabwe Midlands and military history of Zimbabwe; Dir T. TSOMONDO.

Harare

National Gallery of Zimbabwe: POB CY 848, Causeway, Harare; 20 Julius Nyerere Way, Harare; tel. (4) 704666; e-mail info@nationalgallery.co.zw; internet www.nationalgallery.co.zw; f. 1957; nat. colln of sculpture, paintings, drawings, prints, ceramics and artefacts by Zimbabwean and other Southern African artists; incl. European works of art dating from 16th century, and traditional and contemporary African art; regular exhibition programme; education programme; Visual Art Studios for emerging young artists; library of 6,500 vols; Exec. Dir DOREEN J. SIBANDA; Chief Curator and Deputy Dir RAPHAEL CHIKUKWA; publ. *ArtLife*.

ZIMBABWE

WORLD OF LEARNING

National Herbarium and Botanic Garden: POB A 889, Avondale, Harare; tel. (4) 744170; e-mail srgh@mweb.co.zw; internet www.nationalherbarium.co.zw; f. 1909; attached to Dept of Agricultural Research and Extension (AREX); maintains a comprehensive colln of 500,000 specimens, provides an identification service for workers in agriculture and related fields, and contributes to knowledge of the flora of South-Central Africa; taxonomic and ecological research, and research on medicinal and poisonous plants; library of 544 vols; Head NOZIPO NOBANDA; publ. *Kirkia* (1 a year).

Zimbabwe Museum of Human Sciences: Civic Centre, POB CY 33, Causeway, Harare; tel. (4) 751797; e-mail nmmz@mweb.co.zw; internet www.nmmz.co.zw/northern_intro.php; f. 1902; zoological, ethnographical, archaeological and historical exhibits, study collns of archaeological and ethnographical material, and rock art pertaining to Zimbabwe and adjacent areas; Dir T. MASONA; publs *Cookeia*, *Zimbabwea*.

Masvingo

Great Zimbabwe National Monument: PB 1060, Masvingo; tel. (39) 62080; e-mail nmmz@mweb.co.zw; internet www.nmmz.co.zw; ruins of mediaeval dry-stone bldgs representing the Zimbabwe culture; history and devt of Great Zimbabwe shown in site museum; world heritage site; Dir E. MATENGA.

Mutare

Mutare Museum: Aerodrome Rd, POB 920, Mutare; tel. (20) 63672; e-mail mutarmus@comone.co.zw; internet www.zimheritage.co.zw; f. 1959; archaeological, zoological and historical exhibits, pertaining to the Eastern Districts in particular; nat. colln of road transport and firearms; aviary with 200 birds of 24 species; Dir Dr PAUL MUPIRA; publs *Cookeia*, *Syntarsus*, *Zimbabwea*.

Universities

AFRICA UNIVERSITY

POB 1320, Mutare
E-mail: info@africau.ac.zw
Internet: www.africau.edu
Founded 1992
Private control
Chancellor: Rev. DAVID KEKUMBA YEMBA
Vice-Chancellor: FANUEL TAGWIRA

DEANS

Agriculture and Natural Resources: Dr Z. CHITEKA
Education: Dr V. I. OYEDELE
Health Sciences: Dr P. O. FASAN
Humanities and Social Sciences: Dr T. A. CHITEPO
Institute of Peace Leadership and Governance: Dr P. MACHAKANJA SHANKANGA
Theology: Dr B. MAENZANISE

BINDURA UNIVERSITY OF SCIENCE EDUCATION

Private Bag 1020, Bindura, Mashonaland Central
Telephone: (271) 7621
E-mail: info@buse.ac.zw
Internet: www.buse.ac.zw
Founded 1996 as part of Univ. of Zimbabwe, present status 2000
State control
Language of instruction: English
Academic year: August to July
Vice-Chancellor: Prof. EDIAS MWENJE

Registrar: TARIRO F. RUMHUMA
Deputy Registrar for Academics: STAENNLY CHITERA
Deputy Registrar for Human Resources: EUNIAH MANHANDO
Librarian: AUDREY MHALANGA
Library of 31,087 vols, 175,000 ebooks and ejournals
Number of teachers: 342
Number of students: 6,405
Publication: *Southern Africa Journal of Science and Technology* (2 a year)

DEANS

Faculty of Agriculture and Environmental Science: INNOCENT W NYAKUDYA
Faculty of Commerce: LANGTON RUNYOWA
Faculty of Science: Dr WILSON PARAWIRA
Faculty of Science Education: MARONI R. NYIKAHADZOYI
Faculty of Social Science and Humanities: Prof. CHARLES PFUKWA

PROFESSORS

BERDUIT, I. R., Education
DE LA CRUZ, G. J. M., Sports Science
FEREIRA, A. A. H., Maths and Physics
LAMAGNE, P. J., Maths and Physics
LLERA, D. C. D., Biology
MWENJE, E., Biology
PARAWIRA, W., Biology
PFUKWA, C., Education
VERDICIA, E. Y., Computer Science

CATHOLIC UNIVERSITY IN ZIMBABWE

POB 1366, Causeway, Harare
Telephone: (4) 570570
E-mail: catholicuni@gmail.com
Private control
Faculties of business management, humanities, information and technology
Chancellor: The Rev. Archbishop of Harare ROBERT CHRISTOPHER NDLOVU
Rector: SIMON JULIUS NONDO

CHINHOYI UNIVERSITY OF TECHNOLOGY

PMB 7724, Chinhoyi
Telephone: (67) 22203
Internet: www.cut.ac.zw
Founded 1991 as Chinhoyi Technical Teacher's College, present status 2001
State control
Vice-Chancellor: Prof. DAVID JAMBGWA SIMBI
Pro-Vice-Chancellor: Dr P. K. KUIPA
Registrar: T. B. BHEBHE
Bursar: O. SIFILE
Librarian: GLORIA KADAMATIMBA

DEANS

Agricultural Sciences and Technology: Prof. S. MAKUZA
Art and Design: P. PASHAPA
Business Science and Management: D. M. CHAVUNDUKA
Engineering Sciences and Technology: E. MANYUMBA
School of Hospitality and Tourism: SEBASTIAN VENGESAYI
Institute of Lifelong Learning: JOSEPH ZANO ZVAPERA MATOWANYIKA

HARARE INSTITUTE OF TECHNOLOGY

POB BE 277, Belvedere, Harare
Telephone: (4) 741422
E-mail: communications@hit.ac.zw
Internet: www.hit.ac.zw
Founded 1988, present name and status 2005

State control
Faculties of business and management sciences, engineering and technology, information science and technology, technology
Vice-Chancellor: QUINTON C. KANHUKAMWE (acting)
Registrar: MARY E. SAMUPINDI
Finance Dir: MAXWELL RUTIZIRIRA (acting)
Librarian: JASPER LEE MAENZANISE

LUPANE STATE UNIVERSITY

10th Floor, Pioneer House, POB AC 255, Ascot, Bulawayo
Telephone: (9) 73770
E-mail: admissions@lsu.ac.zw
Internet: www.lsu.ac.zw
Founded 2004
State control
Faculties of agricultural sciences, commerce, humanities and social sciences
Vice-Chancellor: Dr MACLEAN J. BHALA (acting)
Registrar: C. S. MAKONI (acting)
Bursar: S. C. SIBANDA (acting)

MIDLANDS STATE UNIVERSITY

PMB 9055, Gweru
Telephone: (54) 260409
E-mail: registrar@msu.ac.zw
Internet: www.msu.ac.zw
Founded 1999
State control
Academic year: March to December
Vice-Chancellor: Prof. NGWABI BHEBE
Pro-Vice-Chancellor: Prof. KADMIEL H. WEKWETE
Pro-Vice-Chancellor: Prof. VICTOR N. MUZVIDZIWA
Registrar: ERASMUS MUPFIGA
Librarian: NYARAI MACHEKA
Library of 50,850 vols
Number of teachers: 229
Number of students: 8,979
Publications: *Southern African Journal of Science and Agriculture and Technology* (4 a year), *The Dyke* (4 a year)

DEANS

Faculty of Arts: A. VIRIRI
Faculty of Commerce: R. DUVE
Faculty of Education: Prof. A. S. CHIROMO
Faculty of Law: G. MANYATERA
Faculty of Natural Resources Management and Agriculture: A. KAPENZI
Faculty of Science and Technology: Prof. A. CHAWANDA
Faculty of Social Sciences: C. N. GWATIDZO

NATIONAL UNIVERSITY OF SCIENCE AND TECHNOLOGY

POB AC 939, Ascot, Bulawayo
Telephone: (9) 282842
Internet: www.nust.ac.zw
Founded 1990
State control
Language of instruction: English
Academic year: August to May
Chancellor: Pres. of Zimbabwe R. G. MUGABE
Vice-Chancellor: Prof. L. R. NDLOVU
Registrar: F. MHULANGA
Number of teachers: 150 full-time
Number of students: 2,800

DEANS

Faculty of Applied Sciences: Dr D. J. HLATYWAYO
Faculty of Built Environment: V. MADIRO
Faculty of Commerce: R. TADU

Faculty of Communication and Information Science: Dr L. Hikwa
Faculty of Industrial Technology: Dr Z. B. Dlodlo
Faculty of Medicine: Dr Ndiweni

SOLUSI UNIVERSITY

Post Office Solusi, Bulawayo
Telephone: (9) 887124
E-mail: admissions@solusi.ac.zw
Internet: www.solusi.ac.zw
Private control
Faculties of arts, business, education, science and technology
Vice-Chancellor: Dr J. Musvosvi
Registrar: Wilmore Ncube
Librarian: Rosemary Maturure

UNIVERSITY OF ZIMBABWE

POB MP 167, Mount Pleasant, Harare
Telephone: (4) 303212
Internet: www.uz.ac.zw
Founded 1955 as Univ. College of Rhodesia; became Univ. of Rhodesia in 1970, present name 1980
Language of instruction: English
Academic year: August to June
Chancellor: Pres. of Zimbabwe R. G. Mugabe
Vice-Chancellor: Prof. Levi Nyagura
Pro-Vice-Chancellor: Dr T. Munyanyiwa
Registrar: Sergeant Chevo
Librarian: A. C. Chikonzo
Number of teachers: 830
Number of students: 12,500
Publications: *Central African Journal of Medicine* (12 a year), *Journal of Applied Science in Southern Africa* (2 a year), *Zambezia* (2 a year)

DEANS

College of Health Science: Prof. M. M. Chidzonga
Faculty of Agriculture: Dr C. Mutisi
Faculty of Arts: Prof. P. Mashiri
Faculty of Commerce: Dr I. Chaneta
Faculty of Education: Prof. R. Moyana
Faculty of Engineering: W. Nyemba
Faculty of Law: E. Magade
Faculty of Science: Dr M. Muchuweti
Faculty of Social Studies: Prof. R. Gaidzanwa
Faculty of Veterinary Science: Prof. T. Hove

WOMEN'S UNIVERSITY IN AFRICA

POB MP 1222, Mount Pleasant, Harare
Telephone: (4) 33139
Internet: www.wua.ac.zw
Founded 2002
Private control
Vice-Chancellor: Prof. Hope Sadza

Dean for Studies: Elizabeth Chikwiri

DEANS

Agriculture: Handsen Tibugari
Management and Entrepreneurial Studies: Ennety Ruzario
Social Sciences and Gender Development: Magumise Johnson

ZIMBABWE OPEN UNIVERSITY

POB MP 1119, Mt Pleasant, Harare
Telephone: (4) 793002
E-mail: information@zou.ac.zw
Internet: www.zou.ac.zw
Founded 1999
State control
Language of instruction: English
Faculties of applied social science, arts and education, commerce and law, science and technology
Chancellor: The President of the Republic of Zimbabwe
Vice-Chancellor: Prof. K. P. Dzvimbo
Registrar: R. E. Mhasvi
Librarian: L. Maenzanise
Library of 16,214 vols of books, 16 periodicals
Number of teachers: 80 full-time
Number of students: 13,900 (13,450 under-graduate, 450 postgraduate)

Polytechnics and Colleges

Bulawayo Polytechnic: Park Rd, 12th Ave, POB 1392, Bulawayo; tel. (9) 233181; e-mail bulawayopoly@mhet.ac.zw; depts of applied sciences, art and design, automative engineering, civil engineering, commerce, electrical engineering, information and technology, mechanical engineering; Prin. A. Mwadiwa.

Chibero College of Agriculture: PMB 901, Norton; tel. (62) 2238; f. 1960; 2-year nat. diploma in agriculture; library: 6,000 vols; 15 teachers; 120 students; Prin. M. E. Nyamangara; publ. *Agricultural Education*.

Esigodini Agricultural Institute: PMB 5808, Esigodini; tel. (88) 297; f. 1921; 18 teachers; 120 students; Prin. David Themba Mguni.

Gwebi College of Agriculture: PMB 376B, Harare; tel. (4) 304515; e-mail gwebiagric@gta.gov.zw; f. 1950; 3-year Diploma in agriculture, 15-month Higher Nat. Diploma in horticulture; library: 2,300 vols; 15 teachers; 120 students; Prin. W. Matizha.

Gweru Polytechnic: POB 137, Gweru; tel. (54) 23117; depts of applied sciences, commerce, engineering, education; 35 teachers; 1,365 students; Prin. O. Mavengere.

Harare Polytechnic: POB CY 407, Causeway, Harare; tel. (4) 752311; f. 1927; full-time and sandwich courses for technicians and craftsmen; courses in printing and adult education; full-time and part-time courses in automotive engineering, business studies, civil construction, computer studies, library and information science, mass communication, mechanical engineering, science and technology, secretarial studies; library: 68,000 vols; 500 teachers (incl. part-time); 9,000 students; Prin. S. Raza.

Joshua Mqabuko Nkomo Polytechnic: PMB 5832, Gwanda; tel. (84) 2390; e-mail joshuamnkomo1@mhet.ac.zw; f. 1981; 45 teachers; Prin. M. Dube.

Kushinga-Phikelela National Farmer Training Centre: PMB 3705, Marondera; tel. (79) 24329; e-mail kushinga@africaonline.co.zw; f. 1982; 3-year Certificate courses in commercial farming; short courses in animal production, crop production, farm machinery, and farm and agri-business; library: 3,100 vols; 13 teachers; 120 students; Prin. B. Nleya.

Kushinga Phikelela Polytechnic: POB 3705, Marondera; tel. (79) 24462; courses offered in accountancy, public sector accounting, business studies, marketing management, micro-enterprise cooperative management; Prin. S. J. Makoni.

Kwekwe Polytechnic: POB 399, Kwekwe; tel. (55) 22991; e-mail kwekwepoly@mhet.ac.zw; courses offered in accountancy, business studies, automotive engineering, computer studies, education, electrical power engineering, machine-shop engineering, motor vehicle mechanics, production engineering, secretarial studies, staff development; Prin. J. Mbudzi.

Masvingo Polytechnic: POB 800, Masvingo; tel. (39) 52269; e-mail masvingopoly@mhet.ac.zw; 67 teachers; Prin. B. Taderera.

Mlezu Institute of Agriculture: POB 8062, Kwekwe; f. 1982; 2-year course; Prin. J. K. D. Maripfonde (acting).

Mutare Polytechnic: POB 640, Mutare; tel. (20) 63141.

School of Social Work: PMB 66022, Kopje, Harare; tel. (4) 752965; e-mail sswprinc@samara.co.zw; f. 1964; first degrees, Certificate, Masters degree and Diploma courses; library: 19,870 vols; 13 teachers; 250 students; Dir Prof. E. Kaseke.

Zimbabwe College of Music: POB 66352, Kopje, Harare; tel. (4) 749077; e-mail zcmlib@zol.co.zw; f. 1948; library: 3,000 vols; 35 teachers; 500 students; Chair. Ben Zulu; Dir Christopher Timbe; Registrar Friday Mbirimi; Librarian Priscilla Chidohwe.

INDEX OF INSTITUTIONS

Accademia Toscana di Scienze e Lettere 'La Colombaria', 1188
Accident Research Centre, Dhaka, 222
Accounting Machine Building Research Institute, Moscow, 1899
Accra Central Library, 963
Accra Polytechnic, 966
Accra Technical Training Centre, 966
Accreditation Agency for Degree Programmes in Engineering, Informatics, Natural Sciences and Mathematics, 844
Accreditation Agency in Health and Social Sciences, 844
Accreditation and Quality Assurance Commission, 1698
Accreditation Board, Basseterre, 1956
Accreditation, Certification and Quality Assurance Institute, Bayreuth, 844
Accreditation Commission, 2000
Accreditation Commission on Colleges of Medicine (ACCM), 1156
Accreditation Commission, Prague, 651
Accreditation Committee of Cambodia, Phnom-Penh, 377
Accreditation Council, Bonn, 844
Accreditation Council for Business Schools and Programs, 2442
Accreditation Council of Trinidad and Tobago (ACTT), Port-of-Spain, 2203
Accreditation Organisation of the Netherlands and Flanders, 1559
Accreditation Service for International Colleges (ASIC), Stockton-on-Tees, 2276
Accrediting Agency of Chartered Colleges and Universities in the Philippines, Inc. (AACCUP), Quezon City, 1732
Accrediting Commission of Career Schools and Colleges (ACCSC), 2442
Accrediting Council for Independent Colleges and Schools (ACICS), 2443
Accrington and Rossendale College, 2410
ACE Education, London, 2282
Acelin Institute of Business, Adelaide, 180
Acharya N. G. Ranga Agricultural University, 1051
Acharya Nagarjuna University, 1051
Acharya Narendra Dev Library, 1049
Acharya Narendra Dev Pustakalaya, 1049
Ackland Art Museum, 2535
Aconcagua University, 477
Acoustical Society of America, 2460
Acoustical Society of China, 482
Acoustical Society of Finland, 745
Acoustics Research Institute, Vienna, 191
Acropolis Museum, 973
Acton Public Library, 2480
Actuarial Society of Finland, 741
Acuario Nacional de Cuba, 637
ACUM (Society of Authors, Composers and Music Publishers in Israel), 1167
Ada Community Library, 2485
Adair County Public Library, 2494
Adam Mickiewicz Museum of Literature, 1774
Adam Mickiewicz University in Poznań, 1778
Adams County Library, 2500
Adams County Library System, Gettysburg, 2502
Adams National Historical Park, 2526
Adams State College, 2596
Adamson University, 1736
Adamson University Library, 1734
Adams-Pratt Oakland County Law Library, 2492
Adana Bölge Müzesi, 2213
Addis Ababa University, 736
Addis Ababa University Libraries, 736
Addison Gallery of American Art, 2526
Adelaide Central School of Art, 180
Adelaide College of Divinity, 180
Adelaide College of Ministries, 180
Adelhausermuseum, Freiburg im Breisgau, 876
Adelphi University, 2818
Adhesion Institute, Delft, 1564

Adler Graduate School, 2766
Adler Museum of Medicine, Johannesburg, 2033
Adler Planetarium, Chicago, 2520
Adler School of Professional Psychology, 2650
Administración Nacional de Laboratorios e Institutos de Salud 'Dr Carlos G. Malbran', Buenos Aires, 121
Administration of State Castles and Gardens, 874
Administrative Bibliotek, Copenhagen, 678
Administrative Library, 678
Administrative Staff College of India, 1106
Admiral Makarov State Maritime Academy, St Petersburg, 1951
Admiral Makarov State University for Maritime and Inland Shipping, 1936
Adnan Malki Museum, Damascus, 2169
Adnan Menderes Üniversitesi, Aydin, 2215
Adolfo Ibáñez University, 476
Adolfo Lutz Institute, 310
Adrian College, 2743
Adriatic Institute, Zagreb, 625
Adriatic Society of Sciences, 1192
Adult Education Association of Guyana Inc. M.S., 991
Adult Educational Centre, Copenhagen, 686
Adult Learning Australia Inc, 142
Advance Material and Process Research Institute, Bhopal, 1039
Advanced Centre for Technical Development of Punjabi Language, Literature and Culture, 1043
Advanced Centre for Treatment, Research and Education in Cancer (ACTREC), Mumbai, 1044
Advanced School for Computing and Imaging, 1574
Advanced Science and Technology Institute, Manila, 1733
Advanced Virtual Reality Research Centre, Loughborough, 2310
Adventist Theological College, Pécel, 1025
Adventist University Institute of Venezuela, 3058
Adventist University of Africa, Nairobi, 1377
Adventist University of Central Africa, 1955
Adventist University of Central America, 614
Adventist University of Nicaragua, 1616
Adventist University of Paraguay, 1710
Adventist University of the Antilles, 3018
Adventista Teológiai Főiskola, 1025
Advisory Council on Research and Services, 3052
Advokatska Komora FBiH, 297
Advokatska-Odvjetnicka Komora Federacije Bosne i Hercegovine, 297
Adyar Library and Research Centre, 1049
Adygea Agricultural Research Institute, 1883
Adyghe State University, Maykop, 1916
AECL Research, Chalk River Laboratories, 392
AECL Research, Whiteshell Laboratories, 392
Aegean University, 2220
AEI-NOOSR, Canberra, 141
Aeronautical Institute, 135
Aeronautical Society of India, 1038
Aeronautical Society of South Africa (AeSSA), 2029
Aeroseum, Gothenburg, 2116
Aerospace Medical Association, Alexandria, 2454
Aerospace Museum, Rio de Janeiro, 315
Afanasev, V. A., Research Institute of Fur-Bearing Animals and Rabbits, Moscow, 1883
Afet İşleri Genel Müdürlüğü Deprem Araştırma Dairesi, Ankara, 2212
Afghan Cultural House, 92

Afghan Institute of Archaeology, 92
Afghan National Public Health Institute, 92
Afghan Rectors' Conference, 91
Afghanistan Geological Survey, 92
Afghanistan Institute in Switzerland, 2145
Afghanistan Research and Evaluation Unit (AREU), 92
Afghanistan Technical Vocational Institute, 94
Afonso Chaves Society, 1820
Africa Centre, 932
Africa Institute of South Africa, 2029
Africa Nazarene University, Nairobi, 1377
Africa Rice Centre, 50
Africa University, 3080
African Academy of Sciences, 81
African American Heritage Center, Inc, 2523
African and Asian Studies Centre, Lisbon, 1817
African and Malagasy Council for Higher Education, 60
African Art Museum, Tenafly, 2532
African Association for the Advancement of Science and Technology, 81
African Centre for Applied Research and Training in Social Development (ACARTSOD), Tripoli, 1443
African Medical and Research Foundation (AMREF), 75
African Network of Scientific and Technological Institutions (ANSTI), Nairobi, 1375
African Organization for Cartography and Remote Sensing, 81
African Regional Centre for Technology, Dakar, 1969
African Studies Association of the United Kingdom, 2294
African Studies Association, Piscataway, 2462
African Training and Research Centre in Administration for Development, 57
African Virtual University, Nairobi, 1377
Africana Museum, Monrovia, 1439
Africana Studies and Research Center, Ithaca, 2474
Afrikaans Language Museum, 2034
Afrikaanse Taalmuseum, 2034
AFRO Health Sciences Library and Documentation Centre, 611
Afro-Antillian Museum, 1703
AFW Wirtschaftsakademie Bad Harzburg GmbH, 846
Afyon Kocatepe Üniversitesi, 2215
Aga Khan University, 1680
Agence de la Francophonie, Paris, 766
Agence de l'OCDE pour l'Energie Nucléaire, 87
Agence Nationale de Développement et de la Recherche Universitaire, Algiers, 100
Agence Nationale de Valorisation des Résultats de la Recherche et du Développement Technologique, Algiers, 100
Agence Nationale pour le Développement de la Recherche en Santé, Algiers, 101
Agence pour l'Evaluation de la Qualité de l'Enseignement Supérieur, 258
Agence Universitaire de la Francophonie, 60
Agencia Española de Cooperación Internacional para el Desarrollo (AECID), 2051
Agencia Estatal de Meteorología, Madrid, 2061
Agencia Nacional de Evaluación de la Calidad y Acreditación, 2050
Agencia Nacional de Evaluación y Acreditación de la Educación Superior (ANEAES), Asunción, 1709
Agencija za Statistiku Bosne i Hercegovine, 298
Agencija za znanost i visoko obrazovanje, 623

Agency for Higher Education Quality Assurance and Career Development (AQA), Moscow, 1879
Agency for Quality Assurance and Accreditation Austria, 183
Agency for Quality Assurance and Accreditation of Canonical Programmes of Studies in Germany, 843
Agency for Science and Higher Education, Zagreb, 623
Agency for Science, Innovation and Technology, Vilnius, 1447
Agency for Statistics of Bosnia and Herzegovina, 298
Agenţia Română de Asigurare a Calităţii în Învăţământul Superior, 1835
Agentur für Qualitätssicherung durch Akkreditierung von Studiengängen, 844
Agentur für Qualitätssicherung und Akkreditierung kanonischer Studiengänge in Deutschland eV, 843
Agenzia Nazionale per le Nuove Tecnologie, l'Energia e lo Sviluppo Economico Sostenibile (ENEA), Rome, 1200
AGH University of Science and Technology, 1809
Agjencia e Akreditimit te Kosovës, 1410
Agnes Scott College, 2636
Ago Medical Educational Center-Bicol Christian College of Medicine, Legazpi City, 1750
Agostinho Neto University, 114
Agraren Universitet Plovdiv, 364
Agrarian Economists Association of Romania, 1836
Agrarian Institute, Moscow, 1883
Agrarian Law Society, Utrecht, 1561
Agrarian Society, Valletta, 1484
Agrarsoziale Gesellschaft eV (ASG), Göttingen, 845
AgResearch, 1605
Agricultural Association of China, Taipei, 2171
Agricultural Biotechnology Research Institute of Iran (ABRII), Karaj, 1134
Agricultural Chemical Research Institute, Pyongyang, 1383
Agricultural Cooperative College, 1409
Agricultural Economics Institute, São Paulo, 309
Agricultural Economics Research Centre, 1091
Agricultural Economics Research Institute, Giza, 712
Agricultural Economics Research Institute, Ulan Bator, 1530
Agricultural Economics Society, Uckfield, 2278
Agricultural Engineering Research Institute, Giza, 712
Agricultural Experiment Station, 3022
Agricultural Extension and Rural Development Research Institute, Giza, 712
Agricultural Genetic Engineering Research Institute, 712
Agricultural History Society, Washington, 2447
Agricultural Information Centre, Pretoria, 2031
Agricultural Information Centre, Ras Al Khaimah, 2270
Agricultural Institute, Barcelona, 2052
Agricultural Institute, Centre for Agricultural Research, Hungarian Academy of Sciences, 1002
Agricultural Institute of Canada, 387
Agricultural Institute of Slovenia, 2018
Agricultural Institute, Shumen, 356
Agricultural Irrigation Research Institute, Onchon County, 1383
Agricultural Mechanization Research Institute, Pyongyang, 1384
Agricultural Museum, 1254
Agricultural Museum, Cairo, 714
Agricultural Museum, Damascus, 2169
Agricultural Polytechnic School of Manabi, 709

Agricultural Research and Extension Trust, Lilongwe, 1468

Agricultural Research Centre Library, Tripoli, 1442

Agricultural Research Centre, Ministry of Agriculture, Giza, 712

Agricultural Research Corporation, Central Library, Wad Medani, 2100

Agricultural Research Corporation, Wad Medani, 2099

Agricultural Research Council, Pretoria, 2029

Agricultural Research Council, Rome, 1197

Agricultural Research Institute, Baku, 212

Agricultural Research Institute for South-East Region (ARISER), Saratov, 1883

Agricultural Research Institute for the Central Areas of the Non-Black Soil (Nechernozem) Zone, 1883

Agricultural Research Institute, Khovd, 1530

Agricultural Research Institute (Mlingano), 2182

Agricultural Research Institute of Panama, 1702

Agricultural Research Institute of Rwanda–Ruhande Station, 1954

Agricultural Research Institute, Reykjavík, 1030

Agricultural Research Organization, Bet-Dagan, 1169

Agricultural Research Trust, Harare, 3078

Agricultural Science Information Centre, Taipei, 2174

Agricultural Society of Kenya, 1376

Agricultural Society of Trinidad and Tobago, 2203

Agricultural Technology and Production Studies Centre, Lisbon, 1817

Agricultural Technology Science, Technology and Production Corporation, Ulan Bator, 1531

Agricultural University of Athens, 976

Agricultural University of Ecuador, 703

Agricultural University of Habana, 640

Agricultural University of Iceland, 1031

Agricultural University of Tiranë, 98

Agricultural University Plovdiv, 364

Agriculture and Food Development Authority, 1158

Agriculture Technologies Transfer Centre (ATTC), Shkodër, 96

Agri-Food and Biosciences Institute, Belfast, 2298

AgriFood Economics Centre, Lund, 2111

Agri-Horticultural Society of India, 1034

Agri-Horticultural Society of Madras, 1034

Agro-Economic Research Centre, Santiniketan, 1041

Agronomic Institute, Campinas, 309

Agronomic Research Institute, Huambo, 113

Agronomical Society of Chile, 465

Agronomists Society, Bucharest, 1836

Agronomy Society of New Zealand, 1603

AgroParisTech, 816

Agrophysical Research Institute, St Petersburg, 1883

Agroscope, 2143

Agrupación Bibliotecológica del Uruguay, 3024

Aguadilla Campus, 3019

Agualva-Cacém Municipal Library, 1821

Agung Rai Museum of Art, 1114

Agustín Codazzi Geographic Institute, 593

Agustín P. Justo National Military Library, 122

Ägyptisches Museum und Papyrussammlung, Berlin, 873

Ahlia University, Manama, 219

Ahmadu Bello University, Zaria, 1628

Ahmed Al-Farsi Library (College of Health Sciences), Manama, 219

Ahmedabad Textile Industry's Research Association, 1047

Ahsan Manzil Museum, Dhaka, 225

Ahsanullah University of Science and Technology, 225

Ahwaz Jondishapour University of Medical Sciences, 1136

AIB College of Business, 2678

Aichi Gakuin University, 1332

Aichi Prefectural University, Aichi, 1256

Aichi University, 1332

Aif—German Federation of Industrial Research Associations, 862

Aigantighe Art Gallery, 1608

Ain Shams University, Cairo, 715

Air Force Academy, Trondhiem, 1666

Air Force Institute of Technology, Wright-Patterson Air Force Base, 2874

Air Museum Foundation of Honduras, 996

Air Museum, Pêro Pinheiro, 1825

Air University, Islamabad, 1680

Air University, Montgomery, 2547

Aircraft Building Society, Moscow, 1882

Aisthesis, 263

AIUB Library, 224

Aiud Museum of History, 1847

Aiud Natural Sciences Museum, 1847

Ajiniyaz Nomidagi Nukus Davlat Pedagogika Instituti, 3034

Ajman University of Science and Technology (AUST), 2271

Ajou University, 1396

Ajtte Svenskt Fjäll- och Samemuseum, 2117

Ajtte Swedish Mountain and Sami Museum, 2117

Ajuda Library, 1822

AK Bibliothek Wien für Sozialwissenschaften, Vienna, 194

Akademi Seni Karawitan Indonesia Padang Panjang, 1132

Akademi Teknologi Kulit, 1112

Akademia di Músika 'Edgar Palm', 1600

Akademia e Shkencave dhe e Arteve e Kosovës, 1410

Akademia Górniczo-Hutnicza Im. Stanisława Staszica w Krakowie, 1809

Akademia im. Jana Długosza w Częstochowie, 1810

Akademia Inżynierska w Polsce, 1759

Akademia Morska w Gdyni, 1810

Akademia Morska w Szczecinie, 1810

Akademia Muzyczna im. Feliksa Nowowiejskiego w Bydgoszczy, 1812

Akademia Muzyczna im. Grażyny i Kiejstuta Bacewiczów w Łodzi, 1812

Akademia Muzyczna im. Ignacego Jana Paderewskiego w Poznaniu, 1812

Akademia Muzyczna im. Karola Lipińskiego we Wrocławiu, 1812

Akademia Muzyczna im. Karola Szymanowskiego w Katowicach, 1813

Akademia Muzyczna im. Stanisława Moniuszki w Gdańsku, 1813

Akademia Muzyczna w Krakowie, 1813

Akademia Sztuk Pięknych im. Eugeniusza Gepperta we Wrocławiu, 1813

Akademia Sztuk Pięknych im. Jana Matejki w Krakowie, 1813

Akademia Sztuk Pięknych im. Władysława Strzemińskiego w Łodzi, 1813

Akademia Sztuk Pięknych w Gdańsku, 1813

Akademia Sztuk Pięknych w Warszawie, 1813

Akademia Teatralna im. Al. Zelwerowicza w Warszawie, 1813

Akademia Techniczno-Humanistyczna w Bielsku-Białej, 1810

Akadémia umení v Banskej Bystrici, 2016

Akademie der Bildenden Künste in Nürnberg, 957

Akademie der Bildenden Künste, Munich, 957

Akademie der Bildenden Künste Wien, 197

Akademie der Künste, Berlin, 844

Akademie der Wissenschaften und der Literatur Mainz, 845

Akademie der Wissenschaften zu Göttingen, 844

Akademie für Fremdsprachen Gmbh—Private Fachschule, Berlin, 958

Akademie für Raumforschung und Landesplanung, Hanover, 856

Akademie múzických umění v Praze, 669

Akademie věd České republiky AV ČR, 651

Akademie výtvarných umění v Praze, 669

Akademiebibliothek der Berlin-Brandenburgischen Akademie der Wissenschaften, Berlin, 863

Akademiet for de Tekniske Videnskaber, Lyngby, 675

Akademija Nauka i Umjetnosti BiH, 296

Akademija umetnosti, Belgrade, 1972

Akademin för Tekniska Vetenskaper ry, Espoo, 746

Akademisk Arkitektforening, 672

Akadēmiskās Informācijas Centrs, Rīga, 1426

Akadimia Athinon, 968

Akaki Tsereteli State University, 840

Akanu Ibiam Federal Polytechnic, Unwana, 1644

Akdeniz Üniversitesi, 2215

Akhmet Baitursynov Kostanay State University, 1366

Akita Prefectural Library, 1252

Akkreditierungs-, Certifizierungs- und Qualitätssicherungs-Instituts (ACQUIN), 844

Akkreditierungsagentur für Studiengänge der Ingenieurwissenschaften, der Informatik, der Naturwissenschaften und der Mathematik—ASIIN eV, Duesseldorf, 844

Akkreditierungsagentur im Bereich Gesundheit und Soziale (AHPGS), Freiburg, 844

Akkreditierungsrat, Bonn, 844

Aklan State University, 1736

Akmola Agricultural Research Institute, 1363

Akred\itačni komise, 651

Akreditačná Komisia, Bratislava, 2000

Akron Art Museum, 2537

Akron Law Library, 2500

Akron-Summit County Public Library, 2500

Aktobe Regional History and Local Lore Museum, 1365

Aktobe State Medical Institute, 1373

Aktobe State Pedagogical Institute, 1366

Aktobe State University named after K. Zhubanov, 1367

Aktogay Archaeological and Ethnographic Museum, 1366

Akustinen Seura ry, 745

AKV – St Joost Breda, 1596

Al al-Bayt University, Mafraq, 1358

Al Buraimi University College, 1670

Al Maktabah Al Wataniah, Aleppo, 2169

Al Mustansiriya University, Baghdad, 1151

Al Nahrain University, 1151

Al. Philippide Institute of Romanian Philology, 1841

Al Zahiriah, Damascus, 2169

Alabama Agricultural and Mechanical University, 2547

Alabama Department of Archives and History, 2476

Alabama Museum of Natural History, 2509

Alabama State University, 2547

Alagappa University, 1052

Al-Ahliyya Amman University, 1358

Al-Ain Museum, 2271

Al-Ain University of Science and Technology, 2271

Alamance County Public Libraries, 2499

Alameda County Law Library, 2479

Alameda Laboratory of Arts, 1498

Åland Art Museum, 763

Åland Board of Antiquities, 764

Åland Cultural Foundation, 763

Åland Hunting and Fishing Museum, 763

Åland Islands' Emigrant Institute, 763

Åland Islands Peace Institute, 763

Åland Maritime Museum, 763

Åland's Camera Museum, 763

Åland University of Applied Sciences, 764

Ålands Cancer Association, 763

Ålands Cancerförening, 763

Ålands Emigrantinstitut, 763

Ålands Fotografiska Museum, 763

Ålands Fredsinstitut, 763

Ålands Hälso–och Sjukvård, 763

Ålands Health, 763

Ålands Jakt och Fiskemuseum, 763

Ålands Konstmuseum, 763

Ålands Kulturstiftelse r.s., 763

Ålands Landskapsarkiv, 763

Ålands Museum, 763

Ålands Sjöfartsmuseum, 763

Alapítvány Érc- és Ásványbányászati Múzeum, Rudabánya, 1011

Al-Aqsa University, Gaza, 1699

Al-Arab Medical University, 1442

Alaska Bible College, 2552

Alaska Museum of Science and Nature, 2509

Alaska Native Heritage Center Museum, 2509

Alaska Pacific University, 2552

Alaska Resources Library and Information Services, 2477

Alaska State Library, 2477

Alaska State Museum, 2509

Al-Awqaf Central Library, Baghdad, 1150

Al-Azhar University, Cairo, 715

Al-Azhar University, Gaza, 1699

Al-Azhar University Library, 714

Alba 'Lucian Blaga' District Library, 1844

Al-Baath University, Homs, 2169

Al-Baha Museum, 1963

Al-Balqa' Applied University, 1359

Albanian Institute for International Studies, 96

Albanian National Culture Museum, Tiranë, 98

Albanian Rectors' Conference, 95

Albany College of Pharmacy and Health Sciences, 2818

Albany County Public Library, 2508

Albany Law School, 2818

Albany Medical College, 2819

Albany Museum, Grahamstown, 2033

Albany Museum of Art, 2518

Albany Regional Museum, 2538

Albany State University, 2636

Alberoni University, 93

Albert Einstein University, 721

Albert Schweitzer Institute, 2465

Alberta College of Art and Design, 458

Alberta Innovates—Technology Futures, 390

Albertina, 196

Albert-Ludwigs-Universität Freiburg, 882

Albert-Ludwigs-Universität Universitätsbibliothek, Freiburg, 867

Alberto Hurtado University, 476

'Alberto Masferrer' Salvadorean University, 724

Alberto Sampaio Museum, 1824

Albertus Magnus College, 2600

Albertus-Magnus-Institut, 851

Albion College, 2743

Albrecht-Dürer-Haus, Nuremberg, 880

Albrecht-Kemper Museum of Art, 2529

Albright College, 2899

Albright-Knox Art Gallery, Buffalo, 2534

Albuquerque Museum of Art and History, 2533

Albuquerque/Bernalillo County Library System, 2497

Alcázar de Colón, 695

Alcona County Library, 2492

Alcorn State University, 2783

Alderney Maritime Trust, 2438

Alderney Society, 2438

Alderney Society Museum, 2438

Alderson-Broaddus College, 2995

All-Russia Research Institute for Floriculture and Subtropical Crops, 1883

All-Russia Research Institute for Horse Breeding, 1883

All-Russia Research Institute for Irrigated Arable Farming, 1883

All-Russia Research Institute for Irrigated Horticulture and Vegetable Crops Production, 1883

All-Russia Research Institute for Mechanization in Agriculture, 1883

All-Russia Research Institute for Nature Conservation, 1893

All-Russia Research Institute for Nuclear Power Plant Operation, 1899

All-Russia Research Institute for Oil Refining JSC, 1899

All-Russia Research Institute for Sheep and Goat Breeding, 1883

All-Russia Research Institute for the Agricultural Use of Reclaimed and Improved Land, 1883

All-Russia Research Institute for the Biosynthesis of Protein Substances, 1883

All-Russia Research Institute for the Canned and Vegetable Dry Products Industry, 1899

All-Russia Research Institute for the Dairy Industry, 1899

All-Russia Research Institute for the Geology and Mineral Resources of the World's Oceans, St Petersburg, 1895

All-Russia Research Institute for the Protection of Metals from Corrosion, 1899

All-Russia Research Institute for the Refrigeration Industry, 1899

All-Russia Research Institute for Vegetable Breeding and Seed Production, 1883

All-Russia Research Institute for Veterinary Sanitation, Hygiene and Ecology, 1883

All-Russia Research Institute of Agricultural Microbiology, 1884

All-Russia Research Institute of Animal Husbandry, 1884

All-Russia Research Institute of Applied Microbiology, 1893

All-Russia Research Institute of Arable Farming and Soil Erosion Control, 1884

All-Russia Research Institute of Chemical Technology, 1895

All-Russia Research Institute of Economic Problems in Development of Science and Technology, 1886

All-Russia Research Institute of Economics in Agriculture, 1884

All-Russia Research Institute of Electrical Insulating Materials and Foiled Dielectrics, 1899

All-Russia Research Institute of Electromechanics (VNIIEM), 1899

All-Russia Research Institute of Exploration Geophysics, 1899

All-Russia Research Institute of Fibre-Optic Systems of Communication and Data Processing, 1899

All-Russia Research Institute of Food Biotechnology, 1899

All-Russia Research Institute of Fuel and Energy Problems (VNIIKTEP), 1899

All-Russia Research Institute of Helium Technology, 1899

All-Russia Research Institute of Hydrolysis, 1895

All-Russia Research Institute of Information, Technological and Economic Research on the Agro-Industrial Complex, 1884

All-Russia Research Institute of Marine Fisheries and Oceanography, 1884

All-Russia Research Institute of Medicinal and Aromatic Plants, 1884

All-Russia Research Institute of Mineral Resources and the Use of the Subsurface, 1899

All-Russia Research Institute of Natural Gases and Gas Technology, 1895

All-Russia Research Institute of Optical and Physical Measurements, 1895

All-Russia Research Institute of Organic Fertilizers and Peat, 1884

All-Russia Research Institute of Organic Synthesis (VNIIOS), 1900

All-Russia Research Institute of Pharmaceutical Plants, 1888

All-Russia Research Institute of Physical-Technical and Radiotechnical Measurements—VNIIFTRI, 1895

All-Russia Research Institute of Phytopathology, 1884

All-Russia Research Institute of Pond Fishery, 1884

All-Russia Research Institute of Problems of Computer Technology and Information Science, 1900

All-Russia Research Institute of Radiotechnology, 1900

All-Russia Research Institute of Refractory Metals and Hard Alloys, 1900

All-Russia Research Institute of Restoration, 1886

All-Russia Research Institute of Starch Products, 1900

All-Russia Research Institute of Television and Radio Broadcasting JSC, 1900

All-Russia Research Institute of the Cable Industry, 1900

All-Russia Research Institute of the Technology of Blood Substitutes and Hormonal Preparations, 1888

All-Russia Research Institute of Tobacco, Makhorka and Tobacco Products, 1884

All-Russia Research Institute of Trunk Pipeline Construction, 1900

All-Russia Rice Research Institute, 1884

All-Russia Scientific and Research Institute of Patent Information (VNIIPI), 1905

All-Russia Scientific Research Institute for Exploration Methods and Engineering, St Petersburg, 1900

All-Russia Scientific Research Institute of Fats, 1900

All-Russia Scientific Research Institute of Mineral Resources, 1895

All-Russia Scientific Research Institute of Natural and Synthetic Diamonds and Tools, 1900

All-Russia Vegetable Production Research Institute, 1884

All-Russia Veterinary Research Institute for Poultry Diseases, 1884

All-Russia 'Znanie' Society, Moscow, 1880

All-Russian Distance Institute of Finance and Economics, 1951

All-Russian Extra-Mural Agricultural Institute, 1951

All-Russian Geological Library, St Petersburg, 1907

All-Russian Plant Quarantine Centre, 1884

All-Russian Rapeseed Research Institute, 1884

All-Russian Research Institute of Geological, Geophysical and Geochemical Systems (VNIIgeosystem), 1895

All-Russian Research Institute of Horticultural Breeding, Zhilina, 1883

All-Russian Scientific Research Institute of Agroforest Reclamation, Volgograd, 1884

All-Russian Scientific Research Institute of Aviation Materials (VIAM), Moscow, 1900

All-Russian Scientific Research Institute of Technical Physics and Automation, Moscow, 1900

All-Russian Williams Fodder Research Institute, 1884

Alma College, 2743

Al-Maktoum Institute for Arabic and Islamic Studies, 2429

Al-Math'af, 1699

Almaty Academy of Economics and Statistics, 1374

Almaty History and Local Lore Museum, 1365

Almaty State Theatrical and Cinema Institute, 1374

Almaty Technological University, 1367

Almaty University of Power Engineering and Telecommunication, 1367

Almedals Library, 2116

Almedalsbiblioteket, 2116

Al-Mustansiriya University Library, Baghdad, 1150

Al-Neelain University, Khartoum, 2100

Alpen-Adria-Universität Klagenfurt, 198

Alpha Meridian College, 2410

Alphacrucis College, 179

Alpiarça Museum, 1823

Al-Quds Human Rights Clinic, 1700

Al-Quds Nutrition and Health Research Institute, 1700

Al-Quds Open University, East Jerusalem, 1699

Al-Quds University, Jerusalem, 1699

Alšova jihočeská galerie, 658

Altai Experimental Farm, 1884

Altai State Agrarian University, 1914

Altai State Institute of Culture, 1953

Altai State Medical University, 1934

Altai State University, 1916

Altai State University Library, 1905

Általános Vállalkozási Főiskola, 1025

Alte Nationalgalerie, Berlin, 873

Altemberger House: Museum of History, 1851

Alterra, 1566

Altes Schloss, Giessen, 876

Altona Museum in Hamburg/North German Regional Museum, 877

Altonaer Museum für Kunst und Kulturgeschichte, 877

Alupka State Palace and Park Preserve, 2254

Alushta Literary Memorial Museum of S. M. Sergeev-Tsensky, 2254

Alutiiq Museum Archaeological Repository, 2510

Alvar Aalto Museo, 750

Alvar Aalto Museum, 750

Alvar and Carmen T. de Carrillo Gil Museum of Art, 1498

Alvernia University, 2899

Alverno College, 2998

Alvesta Bibliotek, 2113

Alvesta Library, 2113

Al-Yamamah University, 1964

Alytaus Kolegija, 1454

Alytus College, 1454

Al-Zahra University, Tehran, 1136

Al-Zaiem Al-Azhari University, 2100

Al-Zaytoonah University, 1359

Amadora Municipal Libraries, 1821

Amalienborg Museum, 680

Amalienborgmuseet, 680

Amapá Historical Museum, 315

Amar Telidji of Laghouat University, 103

Amarillo Museum of Art, 2542

Amarillo Public Library, 2505

Amasya Müzesi, 2213

Amathole Museum, 2033

Amatller Institute of Hispanic Art, 2053

Amazon Centre of Anthropology and Practical Application, 1715

Amazon Museum, 1717

Amazon National University of Madre de Dios, 1722

Amazonian University of Pando, 292

Amazonica State University, 705

Amber World Museum, 695

Ambrose Alli University, 1640

AMDEL, Melbourne, 149

American Academy in Rome, 1198

American Academy of Allergy, Asthma & Immunology, 2454

American Academy of Arts & Sciences, 2445

American Academy of Arts and Letters, 2445

American Academy of Family Physicians, 2454

American Academy of Ophthalmology, 2454

American Academy of Otolaryngology—Head and Neck Surgery, 2455

American Academy of Pediatrics, 2455

American Academy of Periodontology, 2455

American Academy of Political and Social Science, 2449

American Academy of Religion, 2462

American Accounting Association, 2449

American Anthropological Association, 2462

American Antiquarian Society, 2452

American Arbitration Association, 2449

American Association for Cancer Research, Philadelphia, 2468

American Association for State and Local History, 2452

American Association for the Advancement of Science, 2458

American Association of Anatomists, 2455

American Association of Colleges of Nursing, 2443

American Association of Collegiate Registrars and Admissions Officers (AACRAO), Washington, 2444

American Association of Immunologists, 2455

American Association of Law Libraries, 2448

American Association of Museums, 2448

American Association of Petroleum Geologists, 2460

American Association of State Colleges and Universities (AASCU), 2444

American Association of University Professors, Washington, 2444

American Astronomical Society, 2460

American Baptist College, 2933

American Baptist Seminary of the West, 2564

American Bar Association, 2449

American Cancer Society, 2455

American Caribbean Historical Museum, St Thomas, 3023

American Catholic Historical Association, 2452

American Center of PEN, 2454

American Ceramic Society, 2463

American Chemical Society, 2460

American Classical League, 2454

American College, Bryn Mawr, 2899

American College Dublin, 1164

American College of Chest Physicians, 74

American College of Dubai, 2273

American College of Education, 2669

American College of Greece, Athens, 982

American College of Management and Technology, Zagreb, 631

American College of Obstetricians and Gynecologists, 2455

American College of Physicians, 2455

American College of Rheumatology, 2455

American College of Surgeons, 2455

American College University, 1616

American Comparative Literature Association, 2454

American Conservatory Theater, 2564

American Council of Engineering Companies, 2463

American Council of Learned Societies, 2445

American Council on Education, Washington, 2444

American Counseling Association, 2462

American Crystallographic Association, Inc., 2460

American Dairy Science Association, 2447

American Dental Association, 2455

American Dialect Society, 2454

American Dietetic Association, 2455

American Economic Association, 2450

American Educational Research Association, 2467

American Federation for Medical Research, 2468

Argentine Association of American Studies, 120
Argentine Association of Astronomy, 119
Argentine Association of Biology and Nuclear Medicine, 118
Argentine Association of Electrotechnology, 120
Argentine Association of Geophysicists and Geodesists, 119
Argentine Association of Mycology, 119
Argentine Association of Natural Sciences, 119
Argentine Association of Orthopaedia and Traumatology, 118
Argentine Association of Palaeontology, 119
Argentine Association of Pharmacy and Industrial Biochemistry, 118
Argentine Association of Soil Science, 117
Argentine Association of Surgery, 118
Argentine Biochemical Association, 119
Argentine Centre of Engineers, 120
Argentine Centre of Scientific and Technological Information, 122
Argentine Centre of Speleology, 119
Argentine Chemical Association, 119
Argentine Colour Group, 119
Argentine Dental Association, 118
Argentine Entomological Society, 119
Argentine Federal Police Museum, 123
Argentine Federation of Associations of Anaesthesia, Analgesia and Resuscitation, 118
Argentine Geological and Mining Service, 121
Argentine Geological Association, 119
Argentine Institute of Oceanography, 121
Argentine League Against Tuberculosis, 118
Argentine Library for the Blind, 122
Argentine Mathematical Union, 119
Argentine Medical Association, 118
Argentine Ophthalmological Society, 119
Argentine Scientific Society, 119
Argentine Society of Anthropology, 120
Argentine Society of Authors, 118
Argentine Society of Authors and Music Composers, 118
Argentine Society of Biology, 119
Argentine Society of Clinical Research, 119
Argentine Society of Dermatology, 118
Argentine Society of Endocrinology and Metabolism, 118
Argentine Society of Gastroenterology, 118
Argentine Society of Gerontology and Geriatrics, 118
Argentine Society of Haematology, 118
Argentine Society of Paediatrics, 119
Argentine Society of Pathology, 119
Argentine Society of Pharmacology and Therapeutics, 118
Argentine Society of Physiology, 118
Argentine Society of Plant Physiology, 119
Argentine Society of Sociology, 120
Argentine Standards and Certification Institute, 122
Argentine University for Lawyers, 134
Argentine University of Administration Sciences, 125
Argentine Wool Federation, 120
Argeş County Museum, 1850
Argeş District Library 'Dinicu Golescu', 1846
Argonne National Laboratory, 2472
Argosy University, 2564
Arheološki Institut, 1973
Arheološki muzej u Splitu, 626
Arheološki muzej u Zagrebu, 627
Arhiv Bosne i Hercegovine, 299
Arhiv Federacije Bosne i Hercegovine, 299
Arhiv Hercegovine Mostar, 299
Arhiv Jugoslavije, 1973
Arhiv Republike Slovenije, 2019
Arhiv Republike Srpske, 299
Arhiv Srbije, 1973
Arhiv Tuzlanskog kantona, 299

Arhiv Unsko-Sanskog Kantona Bihać, 299
Arhiv Vojvodine, 1974
Arhivele Naţionale ale României, 1844
Århus Art Museum, 679
Århus Kommunes Biblioteker, 677
Århus Kunstakademi, 687
Århus Public Libraries, 677
Århus School of Architecture, 687
Århus School of Business Library, Business and Social Sciences, 678
Aristoteleio Panepistimio Thessalonikis, 974
Aristotelian Society, London, 2293
Aristotle University of Thessaloniki, 974
Aristotle University of Thessaloniki Library, 973
Arizona Archaeological and Historical Society, 2452
Arizona Christian University, Phoenix, 2553
Arizona Historical Society Library and Archives, 2478
Arizona Radio Observatory (ARO), 2473
Arizona State Library, Archives and Public Records, 2478
Arizona State Museum, 2510
Arizona State University, 2553
Arizona State University Art Museum, 2510
Arizona State University Libraries, 2478
Arizona-Sonora Desert Museum, 2510
Arkalyk State Pedagogical Institute named after I. Altynsarin, 1374
Arkansas Air Museum, 2511
Arkansas Arts Center, Little Rock, 2511
Arkansas Baptist College, 2560
Arkansas City Public Library, 2487
Arkansas History Commission Library, Little Rock, 2478
Arkansas Inland Maritime Museum, 2511
Arkansas State Library, Little Rock, 2478
Arkansas State University, 2560
Arkansas State University Museum, 2511
Arkansas Supreme Court Library, 2478
Arkansas Tech University, 2561
Arken Museum for Moderne Kunst, 681
Arken Museum of Modern Art, 681
Arkeologisk Museum i Stavanger, 1653
Arkhangelsk State Museum, 1908
Arkhangelsk State Museum of Fine Arts, 1908
Arkhangelsk State Technical University, 1936
Arkib Negara Malaysia, 1472
Arkitektskolen i Århus, 687
Arkitektur- och designcentrum, 2118
Arkitektur- og Designhøgskolen i Oslo, 1666
Arkitekturbiblioteket, 2113
Arkkitehtuurimuseo, 749
Arkítektafélag Íslands, 1029
Arktisk Institut, Copenhagen, 673
Arlington Baptist College, 2947
Arlis UK and Ireland, 2280
Armádní muzeum Žižkov, Prague, 659
Armagh County Museum, 2329
Armagh Observatory, 2307
Armagh Public Library, 2312
Armed Forces Medical College, Dhaka, 243
Armed Forces Medical College, Pune, 1108
Armed Forces Museum, Oslo, 1652
Armenian Agricultural Academy, 139
Armenian Artistic Union, Cairo, 711
Armenian Centre for National and International Studies, 137
Armenian Genocide Museum–Institute, 137
Armenian Institute of Spa Treatment and Physiotherapy, 137
Armenian Museum of All Saviour's Cathedral, Isfahan, 1135
Armenian Research Centre of Maternal and Child Health Care, 137
Armenian State Historical Museum, 138

Armenian State Institute of Physical Education, 139
Armenian State Pedagogical University, 138
Armenian–Russian (Slavonic) State University, Yerevan, 138
Armeria Albicini, 1208
Armeria Reale, Turin, 1213
Armley Mills (Leeds Industrial Museum), 2332
Armoury, 875
Armoury, Moscow, 1910
Armstrong Atlantic State University, 2637
Army Academy, Oslo, 1666
Army Library, 313
Army Library, Lisbon, 1822
Army Museum, 659
Army Museum, Delft, 1581
Army Museum of Peru, 1717
Army Polytechnic School, 709
Army War College, Madrid, 2090
Arnhem Historical Museum, 1580
Arnhem Public and Learned Library, 1577
Árni Magnússon Institute for Icelandic Studies, 1029
Arnold Bergstraesser Institut für Kulturwissenschaftliche Forschung (ABI), Freiburg im Breslau, 858
ARoS Århus Kunstmuseum, 679
Arquivo da Universidade de Coimbra, 1821
Arquivo Distrital de Braga, 1821
Arquivo Distrital de Bragança, 1821
Arquivo Distrital de Leiria, 1822
Arquivo Distrital de Setúbal, 1823
Arquivo Distrital de Vila Real, 1823
Arquivo Distrital de Viseu, 1823
Arquivo Distrital do Porto, 1822
Arquivo do Arco do Cego, Lisbon, 1822
Arquivo do Estado de São Paulo, 314
Arquivo do Reino de Galicia, 2063
Arquivo Fotográfico, Lisbon, 1822
Arquivo Histórico de Macau, 588
Arquivo Histórico de Moçambique, 1543
Arquivo Histórico de São Tomé e Príncipe, 1961
Arquivo Histórico, Lisbon, 1822
Arquivo Histórico Militar, 1822
Arquivo Histórico Municipal do Porto, 1822
Arquivo Histórico Nacional, Luanda, 113
Arquivo Histórico Parlamentar, 1822
Arquivo Intermédio, Lisbon, 1822
Arquivo Municipal de Lisboa, 1822
Arquivo Municipal de Sintra/Arquivo Histórico, 1823
Arquivo Nacional, Rio de Janeiro, 313
Arquivo Público do Estado do Pará, 312
Arquivo Público Estadual do Espírito Santo, Vitória, 314
Arquivo Regional da Madeira, 1821
ARRB Group Ltd, 149
ARRS: American Roentgen Ray Society, Reston, 2457
Ars Aevi—Museum of Contemporary Art Sarajevo, 300
Arsip Nasional Republik Indonesia, 1113
Art Academy of Cincinnati, 2874
Art Academy of Latvia, 1430
Art and Museum Library of the City of Cologne, 865
Art Center College of Design, Pasadena, 2565
Art Centre Silkeborg Bad, 682
Art Complex Museum, Duxbury, 2526
Art Gallery of Alberta, 395
Art Gallery of Bosnia and Herzegovina, 300
Art Gallery of Hamilton, 396
Art Gallery of Matica Srpska, 1974
Art Gallery of New South Wales, 152
Art Gallery of Nova Scotia, 396
Art Gallery of Ontario, 396
Art Gallery of South Australia, 152
Art Gallery of Western Australia, 153
Art Gallery, Skopje, 1461
Art Gallery 'Stanislav Dospevsky', 363
Art Historians Association, 1754
Art History Institute in Florence—Max Planck Institute, 853

Art History Society, Vienna, 184
Art Institute of Atlanta, 2637
Art Institute of Chicago, 2520
Art Institute of Houston, 2947
Art Institute of Pittsburgh, 2900
Art Institute of Portland, 2893
Art Institute of Seattle, 2987
Art Libraries Society of North America (ARLIS/NA), 2448
Art Libraries Society of United Kingdom and Ireland, 2280
Art Library of Calouste Gulbenkian Foundation, 1822
Art Museum at the University of Kentucky, 2523
Art Museum Brasov, 1848
Art Museum, Constanţa, 1849
Art Museum, DeKalb, 2520
Art Museum, New Territories, 579
Art Museum of Bayreuth, 872
Art Museum of Estonia, 731
Art Museum of Greater Lafayette, 2521
Art Museum of Ploiesti City, 1850
Art Museum of Rio Grande do Sul, 315
Art Museum of Southeast Texas, 2543
Art Museum of the Americas, Washington, 2515
Art Museum of University of Memphis (AMUM), 2542
Art museum Winterthur, 2150
Art Museums of Colonial Williamsburg, 2544
Art Palace Museum (incorporating the Art Academy Collection and Hentrich Glass Museum), 876
Art School of Porto, 1832
Art Society of India, 1035
Arte Music Academy, Nicosia, 650
Artesis Hogeschool Antwerpen, 278
Arteveldehogeschool, 278
ArtEZ Academie voor Art & Design, Enschede, 1596
ArtEZ Academy of Art & Design, 1596
ArtEZ Hogeschool voor de Kunsten, 1596
ArtEZ Institute of the Arts, 1596
Arthritis Research UK, 2303
Arthur M. Sackler Gallery, Washington, 2515
Arthur M. Sackler Museum of Art and Archaeology, Beijing, 489
Arti et Amicitiae, Amsterdam, 1561
Artificial Intelligence Research Institute, Barcelona, 2058
Artistic Training School 'Gudelia Alarco de Vargas', 1731
Artists Association of Bucharest, 1836
Artists' Association of Finland, 743
Artists' Association of the 18th November, Copenhagen, 673
Artists' Society, Nuuk, 690
Arts & Science Center, Pine Bluff, 2511
Arts and Crafts Centre, Aiwo, 1555
Arts and Humanities Research Council (AHRC), Swindon, 2276
Arts and Humanities Research Council, Bristol, 2303
Arts and Industries Building, Washington, 2516
Arts and Letters Circle, Escaldes-Engordany, 111
Arts Centre Dusseldorf, 876
Arts Centre, Helsingborg, 2116
Arts Centre Mannheim, 879
Arts Council, Dublin, 1157
Arts Council Norway, 1648
Arts Council of England, 2282
Arts Council of Northern Ireland, 2282
Arts Council of Pakistan, 1673
Arts Council of Sri Lanka, 2092
Arts Council of Wales, 2282
Arts Educational Schools London, 2413
Arts University College at Bournemouth, 2409
Arturo Michelena Museum, 3050
Arturo Michelena University, 3051
Arturo Prat University, 471
Aruba Numismatic Museum, 1598
Aruban Historical Museum, 1598
Aruban Model Trains Museum, 1598
Aruban School of Music, 1599
Arusha Declaration Museum, 2183
Arusha Natural History Museum, 2183

Austrian State Archives, Vienna, 195
Austrian Statistical Society, 184
Austrian Theatre Museum, 197
Austrian Zoological-Botanical Society, 187
Auswärtiges Amt, Referat 116, Bibliothek und Informationsvermittlung, Bonn, 864
Autauga-Prattville Public Library, 2476
Author School, Copenhagen, 687
Authority for Nature Conservation, Institute for Ornithology, Budapest, 1004
Authority for the Protection and Management of Angkor and the Region of Siem Reap (APSARA), 377
Automotive Industry Institute, Warsaw, 1769
Automotive Research Association of India, 1047
Automotive Safety Centre, Birmingham, 2297
Autonomous Indigenous University of México, 1517
Autonomous National Institute of Agricultural Research, Quito, 701
Autonomous National School of Fine Arts, Lima, 1730
Autonomous Regional University of the Andes, 706
Autonomous School of Fine Arts of Cusco 'Diego Quispe Tito', 1730
Autonomous University of Aguascalientes, 1500
Autonomous University of Asunción, 1710
Autonomous University of Baja California, 1500
Autonomous University of Baja California Sur, 1501
Autonomous University of Beni 'José Ballivián', 292
Autonomous University of Bucaramanga, 595
Autonomous University of Campeche, 1501
Autonomous University of Carmen, 1501
Autonomous University of Central America, 615
Autonomous University of Chiapas, 1501
Autonomous University of Chihuahua, 1502
Autonomous University of Chinandega, 1617
Autonomous University of Chiriquí, 1704
Autonomous University of Ciudad Juárez, 1502
Autonomous University of Coahuila, 1503
Autonomous University of Encarnación, 1711
Autonomous University of Entre Ríos, 125
Autonomous University of Estado de Hidalgo, 1510
Autonomous University of Guadalajara, 1511
Autonomous University of Guerrero, 1510
Autonomous University of la Laguna, 1503
Autonomous University of Lisbon, 1827
Autonomous University of Mexico State, 1508
Autonomous University of Monterrey, 615
Autonomous University of Nayarit, 1513
Autonomous University of Nuevo León, 1513
Autonomous University of Paraguay, 1711
Autonomous University of Piedras Negras, 1503
Autonomous Academy of Querétaro, 1516
Autonomous University of San Luis Potosí, 1517
Autonomous University of Santa Ana, 721
Autonomous University of Sinaloa, 1517

Autonomous University of Tamaulipas, 1519
Autonomous University of the City of México, 1504
Autonomous University of the Northeast, Saltillo, 1503
Autonomous University of the State of Morelos, 1512
Autonomous University of Tlaxcala, 1520
Autonomous University of Yucatán, 1521
Autonomous University of Zacatecas, 1521
Autorinnen und Autoren der Schweiz AdS, Zürich, 2140
Autry, 2511
Avalon University School of Medicine (AUSOM), 1600
Avans Hogeschool, 1596
Avans University of Applied Sciences, 1596
Ave Maria School of Law, 2625
Ave Maria University, 2625
Avele College, 1959
Avele College Library, Apia, 1959
Averett University, 2975
Avery Research Center for African American History and Culture, 2541
Aviation Museum, Kbely, 659
Avicenna Tajik State Medical University, 2179
Avila University, Kansas City, 2787
Avinashilingam Deemed University for Women, 1100
Avon Free Public Library, 2481
Avondale College, Cooranbong, 178
Awadhesh Pratap Singh University, 1053
Awasa Agriculture Research Centre, Awasa, 736
Ayacucho Library, 3049
Ayala Museum, Makati City, 1735
Ayasofya (Hagia Sophia—Saint Sophia) Museum, Istanbul, 2214
Aydın Müzesi, 2214
Ayesha Abed Library, 224
Aylesbury College, 2410
Azabu University, 1333
Azarbaycan Milli Kitabxanası, 213
Azerbaijan Institute of Traumatology and Orthopaedics, 212
Azerbaijan Institute of Tuberculosis and Pulmonology, 212
Azerbaijan Medical Association, 212
Azerbaijan Medical University, 213
Azerbaijan National Academy of Sciences, 211
Azerbaijan National Aerospace Agency, 212
Azerbaijan National Library, 213
Azerbaijan Petroleum Machinery Research and Design Institute (Azinmash), 213
Azerbaijan Research Institute of Haematology and Blood Transfusion, 212
Azerbaijan Research Institute of Ophthalmology, 212
Azerbaijan Scientific Gas Research and Projects Institute, 213
Azerbaijan Scientific-Research and Design-Prospecting Power Engineering Institute, 213
Azerbaijan State Academy for Physical Training and Sports, 216
Azerbaijan State Marine Academy, 216
Azerbaijan State Museum of Art, 213
Azerbaijan State Oil Academy, 216
Azerbaijan State Pedagogical University 'Nasreddin Tusi', 213
Azerbaijan State University of Culture and Art, 213
Azerbaijan State University of Economics, 214
Azerbaijan Technical University, 214
Azerbaijan Technological University, 214
Azerbaijan University, 215
Azerbaijan University of Architecture and Construction, 215
Azerbaijan University of Languages, 215

Azeredo da Silveira Library, 312
Aziya Seikei Gakkai, 1242
Azorean Institute of Culture, 1815
Azov-Black Sea Institute of Agricultural Mechanization, 1951
Azusa Pacific University, 2565

B

B & O Railroad Museum, 2525
B. B. Comer Memorial Library, 2476
B. M. Institute of Mental Health, 1044
B. P. Koirala Institute of Health Science, 1558
B. Verkin Institute of Low Temperature Physics and Engineering, Kharkiv, 2252
Baba Farid University of Health Sciences, 1053
Babasaheb Bhimrao Ambedkar University, 1053
Babcock University, Ikeja, 1643
Babraham Institute, Cambridge, 2299
Babson College, 2710
Babylon, Centre for the Study of Superdiversity, 1573
Bacalod City Library, 1734
Bacău 'Costache Sturdza' District Library, 1844
Bacău 'Iulian Antonescu' Museum Complex, 1847
Bacone College, 2888
Bács-Kiskun Megyei Múzeumi Szervezet Kiskun Múzeum, 1010
Badakhshan Institute of Higher Education, 94
Badakhshan Provincial Library, 92
Badan Akreditasi Nasional Perguruan Tinggi, 1110
Badan Meteorologi Klimatologi dan Geofisika, 1112
Badan Penelitian dan Pengembangan Kehutanan, 1111
Badan Pengawas Obat dan Makanan, 1112
Badan Perpustakaan dan Arsip Daerah Yogyakarta, 1113
Badan Pusat Statistik, 1112
Badan Tenaga Nuklir Nasional, 1112
Baden-Württemberg Film Academy, 958
Badge Museum, 112
Badghis Provincial Library, 92
Badische Landesbibliothek, Karlsruhe, 868
Badisches Landesmuseum Karlsruhe, 877
Bagan Archaeological Museum, 1546
Baghdad Museum, 1150
Baghlan Provincial Library, 92
Baghlan University, 93
Bagian Fotogrametri, Dittopad, 1112
Bahamas Historical Society, 217
Bahamas National Trust, 217
Bahauddin Zakariya University, 1681
Bahauddin Zakariya University Library, 1679
Bahçeşehir Üniversitesi, 2217
Bahia Medical Association, 307
Bahia State Public Library, 314
Bahia University Centre, 318
Bahir Dar University, 737
Bahrain AMA International University, Salmabad, 219
Bahrain Arts Society, 218
Bahrain Bar Society, 218
Bahrain Centre for Studies and Research, 219
Bahrain Contemporary Art Association, 218
Bahrain Historical and Archaeological Society, 218
Bahrain Information Technology Society, 219
Bahrain Medical Society, 219
Bahrain National Museum, 219
Bahrain Society of Engineers, 219
Bahrain Society of Sociologists, 219
Bahrain Writers and Literature Association, 218
Bahria University, 1681
Baia Mare Mineralogical Museum, 1848

Baikov, A. A., Institute of Metallurgy, Moscow, 1895
Bailey House Museum, 2519
Bainbridge Island Historical Museum, 2545
Bait al-Hikmah Library, 1678
Baituna al-Talhami Museum, 1699
Bajo el Sol Gallery, St John, 3023
Baka Agricultural Research Station, 1468
Baker College, 2744
Baker IDI Heart and Diabetes Institute, 147
Baker University, 2683
Bakerville Library, 2481
Bakh, A. N., Institute of Biochemistry, Moscow, 1893
Bakhchisarai Historical and Cultural State Preserve, 2254
Bakhet El-Rudda University, Khartoum, 2100
Bakhtar Institute of Higher Education, 93
Bakhtar University, 93
Bakony Mountains Natural History Museum, 1012
Bakonyi Természettudományi Múzeum, 1012
Baku Business University, 215
Baku Islamic University, 215
Baku Museum of Education, 213
Baku Slavic University, 215
Baku State University, 215
Bakulev Scientific and Research Centre for Cardiovascular Surgery, 1888
Balai Besar Industri Agro, Bogor, 1111
Balai Besar Kerajinan dan Batik, 1113
Balai Besar Kulit, Karet dan Plastik (BBKKP), 1113
Balai Besar Penelitian Veteriner Bogor, 1111
Balai Penelitian Bioteknologi Perkebunan Indonesia, 1111
Balai Penelitian Bioteknologi Tanaman Pangan, Bogor, 1111
Balai Penelitian dan Pengembangan Botani, Bogor, 1112
Balai Penelitian dan Pengembangan Mikrobiologi, Indonesia, 1112
Balai Penelitian dan Pengembangan Zoologi, Bogor, 1112
Balai Penelitian Tanah, 1111
Balai Penelitian Tanaman Buah Tropika, 1111
Balai Penelitian Tanaman Jagung dan Serealia Lain, Maros, 1111
Balai Penelitian Tanaman Kacang-Kacangan dan Umbi-Umbian Malang, 1111
Balai Penelitian Tanaman Padi, Cikampek Subang, 1111
Balai Penelitian Tanaman Pangan Lahan Rawa, Banjarbaru, 1111
Balai Pengkajian Teknologi Pertanian Jawa Barat, 1131
Balanghai Shrine, 1735
Balassa Bálint Múzeum, 1009
Balaton Limnological Institute, Centre for Ecological Research, Hungarian Academy of Sciences, 1004
Balatoni Múzeum, 1009
Balda Museum, Dhaka, 225
Baldwin-Wallace College, 2875
Balfour and Newton Libraries, Cambridge, 2314
Balikesir Üniversitesi, 2217
Balkanmedia Association, Sofia, 355
Balkh Provincial Mowlana Khasta Library, 92
Balkh University, 93
Balkh University Library, 92
Balkhash History Museum, 1366
Ball State University, 2669
Balliol College Library, Oxford, 2325
Balliol College, Oxford, 2399
Balmes Library, 2063
Balneologické Múzeum, Piešťany, 2007
Balochi Academy, 1673
Balochistan University of Engineering and Technology, 1681
Balochistan University of Information Technology, Engineering and Management Sciences (BUITEMS), 1681

Belarus Research Institute for Soil Science and Agrochemistry, 248
Belarus Research Institute of Power Engineering for Agro-Industrial Complex, 248
Belarus State Academy of Arts, 255
Belarus State Agricultural Academy, 255
Belarus State Economic University, 251
Belarus State Technological University, 251
Belarusian Institute of System Analysis and Information Support for Scientific and Technical Sphere (BELISA), Minsk, 250
Belarusian Medical Academy of Postgraduate Education, 255
Belarusian National Technical University, Minsk, 251
Belarusian State Academy of Music, Minsk, 256
Belarusian State Agrarian Technical University, 252
Belarusian State Pedagogical University 'M. Tank', 252
Belarusian State University, 252
Belarusian State University Library, 250
Belarusian State University of Informatics and Radioelectronics, 252
Belarusian State University of Physical Culture, 253
Belarusian State University of Transport, 253
Belarusian Trade and Economic University of Consumer Cooperatives, 253
Belarusian-Russian University, 251
Belau National Museum, 1697
Belfast Bible College, 2418
Belfast Education and Library Board, 2312
Belfast Metropolitan College, 2418
Belgian Academy in Rome, 1198
Belgian Association for Cancer Research, 260
Belgian Association of Photography and Cinematography, 259
Belgian Association of Public Health, 260
Belgian Institute for Space Aeronomy, 264
Belgian Institute of Advanced Chinese Studies, 261
Belgian International Exchange Service, 259
Belgian Mathematical Society, 261
Belgian National Centre for Research in Logic, 265
Belgian Nuclear Research Centre, 264
Belgian Political Science Association, 259
Belgian Royal Academy of Medicine, 260
Belgian Society for Byzantine Studies, 259
Belgian Society for Clinical Biology, 261
Belgian Society for Geographical Studies, 259
Belgian Society for Microbiology, 261
Belgian Society of Authors, Composers and Publishers, 260
Belgian Society of Biochemistry and Molecular Biology, 261
Belgian Society of Human Genetics, 261
Belgian Society of Ophthalmology, French-Speaking section, 260
Belgisch Instituut voor Hogere Chinese Studiën, Brussels, 261
Belgisch Instituut voor Ruimte-Aëronomie, 264
Belgisch Instituut voor Wetenschap der Politiek, 259
Belgische Dienst Internationale Ruil, 259
Belgische Vereniging voor Biochemie en Moleculaire Biologie (BVBMB), 261
Belgische Vereniging voor Klinische Biologie, 261
Belgische Vereniging voor Microbiologie, 261
Belgische Vereniging voor Tropische Geneeskunde, 260

Belgium Campus, 2046
Belgorod State Agricultural Academy, 1948
Belgorod State Technological University 'V. G. Shukov', 1937
Belgorod State University, 1917
Belgorod University of Consumer Co-operatives, 1917
Belgrade Business School, 1990
Belgrade City Library, 1973
Belgrade City Museum, 1974
Belgrade Community Library, 2495
Belgrade Meteorological Observatory, 1973
Belhaven University, 2783
Belinsky, V. G., State Museum, 1908
Belize Archives Department, 283
Belize Audubon Society, 283
Bellairs Research Institute, St James, 245
Bellapart Museum, 695
Bellarmine University, 2688
Belleville Public Library and Information Center, 2496
Bellevue Arts Museum, 2545
Bellevue University, Nebraska, 2798
Bellin College, 2999
Belmont Abbey College, 2854
Belmont Public Library, 2491
Belmont University, 2934
Beloit College, 2999
'Belovezhskaya Pushcha' National Park Museum, 251
Belskie Museum of Art & Science, 2532
Beltei International Institute, 380
Belvedere-Tiburon Library, 2479
Bélyegmúzeum, 1008
Belz Museum of Asian & Judaic Art, 2542
Ben Gurion University of the Negev, 1176
Ben Gurion University of the Negev Aranne Library, 1173
Benaki Museum, 973
Benaki Museum Library, 972
Benaki Phytopathological Institute, 969
Benedict College, 2927
Benedictine Abbey Library, Pannonhalma, 1007
Benedictine College, Atchison, 2684
Benedictine University, 2650
Benedito Leite Public Library, 314
Benemérita Universidad Autónoma de Puebla, 1515
Beneski Museum of Natural History, 2526
Bengal Engineering and Science University, 1054
Benghazi Museum, 1442
Benguet State University, 1737
Ben-Gurion House, 1175
Benh Vien Rang Ham Mat Trung uong Hanoi, 3063
Benha Higher Institute of Technology, 719
Benito Juárez Autonomous University of Oaxaca, 1514
Benjamin Constant Institute, 310
Benjamin Franklin Institute of Technology, 2710
Benjamin Franklin Public Library, San Pedro Sula, 995
Benjamin Triwaks Bee Research Centre, Rehovot, 1171
Bennett College, 2855
Bennett Methodist University Centre, 333
Bennington College, 2973
Bennington Free Library, 2506
Bennington Museum, 2544
Benson Idahosa University, Benin City, 1644
Bensusan Museum of Photography and Library, Johannesburg, 2033
Bentley University, 2710
Benue State Polytechnic, Ugbokolo, 1644
Benue State University, 1641
Ben-Zvi Institute for the Study of Jewish Communities in the East, 1172
Ben-Zvi Institute for the Study of Jewish Communities in the East, Jerusalem, 1172

Berea College, 2688
Beredskapsmuseet, 2120
Bergen Academy of Art and Design, 1668
Bergen Arkitekthøgskole, 1666
Bergen County Cooperative Library System, Hackensack, 2496
Bergen Fortress Museum, 1652
Bergen offentlige Bibliotek, 1651
Bergen School of Architecture, 1666
Bergen University College, 1665
Bergenhus Festningsmuseum, 1652
Bergianska stiftelsen, 2112
Bergische Universität Wuppertal, 884
Bergius Foundation, Stockholm, 2112
Bergtheil Museum, Durban, 2033
Berhampur University, 1054
Beritashvili Institute of Physiology, Tbilisi, 838
Berkeley College, Woodland Park, 2807
Berkeley County Library System, 2504
Berkeley Heights Public Library, 2496
Berklee College of Music, 2711
Berkshire Museum, 2526
Berlin Central and Provincial Library, 864
Berlin Gallery, 872
Berlin Mathematical Society, 850
Berlin Regional Library, 864
Berlin Society for Anthropology, Ethnology and Prehistory, 851
Berlin University of the Arts, 935
Berlin Weissensee School of Art, 957
Berlin-Brandenburg Academy of Sciences and Humanities, 845
Berlin-Brandenburgische Akademie der Wissenschaften, 845
Berliner Gesellschaft für Anthropologie, Ethnologie und Urgeschichte, 851
Berliner Mathematische Gesellschaft eV, 850
Berlinische Galerie, 872
Berman Museum of Art, 2539
Bermuda Aquarium, Museum & Zoo, 2435
Bermuda Archives, 2434
Bermuda Arts Centre at Dockyard, 2435
Bermuda Audubon Society, 2434
Bermuda College, 2435
Bermuda Dental Association, 2434
Bermuda Historical Society, 2434
Bermuda Institute of Ocean Sciences, 2434
Bermuda Maritime Museum, 2435
Bermuda Medical Society, 2434
Bermuda National Gallery, 2435
Bermuda National Library, 2435
Bermuda National Trust, 2434
Bermuda National Trust Museum at the Globe Hotel, 2435
Bermuda Pharmaceutical Association, 2434
Bermuda Professional Photographic Association, 2434
Bermuda Society of Arts, 2434
Bern University of Applied Sciences, 2166
Bernadsville Public Library, Bernardsville, 2496
Bernardino Rivadavia Argentine Museum of Natural Sciences, 123
Bernberg Fashion Museum, Johannesburg, 2033
Bernese Botanical Society, 2141
Bernhard-Nocht-Institut für Tropenmedizin, Hamburg, 859
Bernhard-Nocht-Institute for Tropical Medicine, 859
Bernheim Library, 830
Bernische Botanische Gesellschaft, 2141
Bernisches Historisches Museum, 2147
Bernoulli Interfaculty Centre of Mathematics, 2144
Berry College, Mount Berry, 2637
Berthoud Community Library District, 2480
Berufsverband Information Bibliothek eV, Reutlingen, 846
Bessarabia and Bucovina Cultural Association, 1836
Bessemer Public Library, 2476
Beta Research School for Operations Management and Logistics, 1574

Betanien Diaconal University College, 1664
Betanien Diakonale Høgskole, 1664
Beth Hatefutsoth (Nahum Goldmann Museum of the Jewish Diaspora), Tel-Aviv, 1175
Bethany College, Bethany, 2996
Bethany College, Lindsborg, 2684
Bethany Lutheran College, 2766
Bethany Theological Seminary, Richmond, 2669
Bethel College, Mishawaka, 2669
Bethel College, North Newton, 2684
Bethel University, 2767
Bethel University, McKenzie, 2934
Bethlehem Bible College, 1701
Bethlehem Folklore Museum, 1699
Bethlehem Public Library, 2481
Bethlehem University, 1700
Bethune—Cookman College, 2626
Beulah Heights University, 2637
Bexley Libraries, 2319
Beyazıt Devlet Kütüphanesi, 2213
Beykent Üniversitesi, 2217
Bezalel Academy of Arts and Design, 1186
BFI National Archive, London, 2319
BFI Southbank, 2282
BGC Trust Medical College, 243
BGC Trust University Bangladesh, 229
Bhabha Atomic Research Centre, 1045
Bhaktivedanta College for Religious Science, Budapest, 1025
Bhaktivedanta Hittudományi Főiskola, 1025
Bhandarkar Oriental Research Institute, 1043
Bharat Kala Bhavan, 1051
Bharata Ganita Parisad, Lucknow, 1038
Bharata Itihasa Samshodhaka Mandala, 1036
Bharath University, 1100
Bharathiar University, 1054
Bharathidasan University, 1055
Bharati Vidyapeeth Deemed University, Pune, 1100
Bharatiya Vidya Bhavan, Mumbai, 1108
Bhatkhande Music Institute Deemed University, 1100
Bhavnagar University, 1055
BHF National Centre for Physical Activity and Health, 2303
Bhupendra Narayan Mandal University, 1055
BI Norwegian Business School, 1666
Białystok University of Technology, 1798
Bible College SA, 180
Bible Lands Museum Jerusalem, 1174
Bible Society's Library, 2313
Biblical and Missionary Institute of the Romanian Orthodox Church, 1838
Biblical Seminary, Hatfield, 2900
Bibliographical Institute of the Ministry of Education of the Province of Buenos Aires, 120
Bibliographical Society, London, 2280
Bibliographical Society of America, 2449
Bibliographical Society of Australia and New Zealand, 142
Bibliographical Society of Canada, 387
Bibliographical Society of the University of Virginia, 2449
Bibliomedia Schweiz Suisse Svizzera, Solothurn, 2147
Biblioteca Acadêmico Luiz Viana Filho, Brasília, 312
Biblioteca Academiei Române, 1845
Biblioteca Agropecuaria de Colombia, 593
Biblioteca Alfonso Borrero Cabal, S. J., 593
Biblioteca Americana, Asunción, 1710
Biblioteca 'Ana Maria Poppovic', 314
Biblioteca 'Angel Andrés García' de la Universidad 'Vicente Rocafuerte', 701
Biblioteca Angelica, Rome, 1204
Biblioteca Apostolica Vaticana, 3037
Biblioteca Archeologica e Numismatica, Milan, 1202
Biblioteca Argentina 'Dr Juan Alvarez' de la Municipalidad de Rosario, 123

British Council Library, Bengaluru, 1049

British Council Library, Chandigarh, 1048

British Council Library, Hyderabad, 1048

British Council Library, Mombasa, 1377

British Council Library, San'a, 3072

British Council, Lilongwe, 1467

British Council, Lisbon, 1816

British Council, Ljubljana, 2018

British Council, London, 2278

British Council, Lusaka, 3074

British Council, Madrid, 2054

British Council, Manama, 218

British Council, Manila, 1733

British Council, Maputo, 1543

British Council, Mauritius, 1490

British Council, Mexico City, 1493

British Council, Moscow, 1881

British Council, Muscat, 1669

British Council, Nairobi, 1376

British Council, New Delhi, 1036

British Council, Nicosia, 644

British Council, Oslo, 1648

British Council, Ottawa, 388

British Council, Paris, 769

British Council, Podgorica, 1535

British Council, Port-of-Spain, 2203

British Council, Prague, 652

British Council, Pretoria, 2028

British Council, Rabat, 1539

British Council, Riga, 1427

British Council, Riyadh, 1962

British Council, Rome, 1191

British Council, Sana'a, 3072

British Council, Santiago, 465

British Council, Sarajevo, 297

British Council, Seoul, 1387

British Council, Seychelles, 1991

British Council, Singapore, 1994

British Council, Skopje, 1459

British Council, Sofia, 355

British Council, Stockholm, 2109

British Council, Taipei, 2172

British Council, Tajikistan, 2178

British Council, Tallinn, 729

British Council, Tashkent, 3030

British Council, Tblisi, 837

British Council, Tehran, 1134

British Council, Tel Aviv, 1167

British Council, Tiranë, 96

British Council, Tokyo, 1243

British Council, Tripoli, 1441

British Council, Tunis, 2206

British Council, Valletta, 1484

British Council, Vienna, 185

British Council, Vilnius, 1447

British Council, Warsaw, 1754

British Council, Washington, DC, 2454

British Council, Windhoek, 1553

British Council, Yangon, 1545

British Council, Yaoundé, 383

British Council, Yerevan, 137

British Council, Zagreb, 624

British Cryogenics Council, 2292

British Dental Association, 2288

British Dietetic Association, 2288

British Ecological Society, 2291

British Educational Leadership Management and Administration Society, 2282

British Geological Survey, 2306

British Geological Survey Library, 2317

British Geological Survey, London Information Office, 2319

British Geriatrics Society, 2288

British Horological Society, 2292

British Institute at Ankara, 2212

British Institute for the Study of Iraq, 1150

British Institute in Eastern Africa, Nairobi, 1376

British Institute of Florence, 1198

British Institute of International and Comparative Law, 2281

British Institute of Persian Studies, Tehran, 1133

British Institute of Professional Photography, Ware, 2282

British Institute of Radiology, 2288

British Institute of Technology and E-Commerce, 2414

British Interplanetary Society, 2292

British Library, 2319

British Library of Political and Economic Science, 2319

British Medical Association, 2288

British Medical Association Library, 2319

British Museum, 2333

British Mycological Society, 2291

British Numismatic Society, 2284

British Nutrition Foundation, 2288

British Ornithologists' Union, 2291

British Orthodontic Society, 2288

British Orthopaedic Association, 2288

British Pharmacological Society, 2288

British Postal Museum & Archive, London, 2333

British Psychoanalytical Society, 2288

British Psychological Society, 2293

British Records Association, 2284

British School at Athens, 981

British School at Rome, 1198

British Science Association, 2290

British Society for Middle Eastern Studies, 2294

British Society for Plant Pathology, 2291

British Society for Research on Ageing, 2288

British Society for Rheumatology, 2288

British Society for the History of Mathematics, 2292

British Society for the History of Science, 2290

British Society of Aesthetics, 2293

British Society of Animal Science, 2278

British Society of Gastroenterology, 2288

British Society of Painters, Ilkley, 2282

British Society of Rheology, 2294

British Society of Soil Science, 2278

British Sociological Association, 2294

British Trust for Ornithology, 2291

British University in Dubai, 2271

British Veterinary Association, 2278

British Watercolour Society, 2283

Brlić House (Ivana Brlić-Mažuranić Memorial), 626

Brno Municipal Museum, 658

Brno University of Technology, 668

Brock University, St Catharines, Ontario, 398

Brockway Library, 2483

Bromley College of Further and Higher Education, 2410

Bromley Libraries, 2319

Bronisław Markiewicz State School of Higher Vocational Education in Jarosław, 1811

Brontë Society, Haworth, 2286

Bronx Museum, 2534

Brookhaven National Laboratory, Long Island, 2475

Brookings Public Library, 2504

Brookings, Washington, 2466

Brooklands Museum, Weybridge, 2337

Brooklyn Botanic Garden, 2534

Brooklyn College, New York, 2820

Brooklyn Historical Society, 2452

Brooklyn Law School, 2819

Brooklyn Museum, 2534

Brooklyn Public Library, 2497

Brooks Institute, Santa Barbara, 2565

Brooksby Melton College, 2411

Broward College, 2626

Broward County Division of Libraries, 2483

Brown University, 2925

Brown University Library, Providence, 2503

Brownsville Public Library System, 2505

Bruce Museum, 2514

Brücke-Museum, Berlin, 872

Brüder Grimm-Museum Kassel Brüder Grimm-Gesellschaft eV, 878

Bruges Public Library, 266

Bruggemuseum, 269

Brukenthal National Museum, 1851

Brunei Agricultural Research Centre, Department of Agriculture, Brunei, 352

Brunei Darussalam National Accreditation Council, Berakas, 352

Brunei History Centre, 352

Brunei Museum, 352

Brunel University, 2339

Bruning Regional Archaeological Museum of Lambayeque, 1717

Brussels Royal Academy of Fine Arts, 282

Brussels Society for Latin Studies, 260

Bryan College, 2934

Bryansk State Agricultural Academy, 1948

Bryansk State Museum of Soviet Fine Arts, 1908

Bryansk State Technical University, 1937

Bryansk State University, 1918

Bryansk Technological Institute, 1952

Bryant & Stratton College, 2819

Bryant University, 2925

Bryn Athyn College, 2900

Bryn Mawr College, 2900

BSI Group (British Standards Institution), 2294

Bu-Ali Sina University, Hamadan, 1136

Bucerius Law School, 957

Bucharest Metropolitan Library, 1845

Bucharest Municipality Museum, 1848

Bucharest University of Economic Studies, 1878

Bucheon Museum of Bow, 1389

Büchereien Wien, 195

Buckinghamshire County Libraries, 2312

Buckinghamshire New University, 2340

Bucknell University, 2900

Bucovina National Museum, 1851

Budapest Business School, 1025

Budapest City Archives, 1005

Budapest College of Communication and Business, 1025

Budapest College of Management, 1025

Budapest Contemporary Dance Academy, 1027

Budapest Főváros Levéltára, 1005

Budapest History Museum, 1008

Budapest University of Technology and Economics, 1013

Budapest University of Technology and Economics National Technical Information Centre and Library, 1005

Budapesti Corvinus Egyetem, 1012

Budapesti Corvinus Egyetem Entz Ferenc Könyvtár és Levéltár, 1005

Budapesti Corvinus Egyetem Központi Könyvtár, 1005

Budapesti Gazdasági Főiskola, 1025

Budapesti Kommunikációs és Üzleti Főiskola, 1025

Budapesti Kortárstánc Főiskola, 1027

Budapesti Műszaki és Gazdaságtudományi Egyetem, 1013

Budapesti Műszaki és Gazdaságtudományi Egyetem Országos Műszaki Információs Központ és Könyvtár (BME OMIKK), 1005

Budapesti Történeti Múzeum, 1008

Budavári Mátyás-Templom Egyházművészeti Gyüjteménye, 1008

Buddhist Academy of Ceylon, 2092

Buddhist Association Khmer Republic, Phnom-Penh, 377

Buddhist Institute, Phnom Penh, 378

Buddhist Research Centre, Bangkok, 2188

Budnikov, P. P., All-Russia Research Institute of Construction Materials and Structures, Moscow, 1900

Buena Vista University, 2678

Buenos Aires City Bar Association, 117

Buenos Aires Institute of Numismatics and Antiquities, 118

Buenos Aires Institute of Technology, 135

Buenos Aires Psychological Society, 119

Buffalo and Erie County Public Library System, 2497

Buffalo Bill Historical Center, 2546

Buffalo Museum of Science, 2534

Buffalo Nations Museum, Banff, 395

Buffalo Society of Natural Sciences, 2458

Bugema University, 2243

Build Bright University, 380

Building and Road Research Institute, Kumasi, 962

Building Centre, Middelfart, 675

Building Institute, Ulan Bator, 1530

Building Research Establishment (BRE), Watford, 2310

Building Research Institute, 1761

Building Research Institute, Tsukuba, 1251

Built Environment Research Institute, 2300

Bukbu Library, 1388

Bukhara State University, 3033

Bukkyo University, 1333

Bukovinian State Medical University, Chernivtsi, 2262

Bulacan State University, Malolos, 1738

Bulawayo Polytechnic, 3081

Bulawayo Public Library, 3079

Bülent Ecevit Üniversitesi, 2217

Bulgarian Academy of Sciences, 354

Bulgarian Association of Criminology, 355

Bulgarian Association of International Law, 355

Bulgarian Astronautical Society, 356

Bulgarian Botanical Society, 355

Bulgarian Comparative Education Society, 354

Bulgarian Geographical Society, 355

Bulgarian Geological Society, 355

Bulgarian Pedagogical Society, 355

Bulgarian Philologists' Society, 355

Bulgarian Philosophical Association, 355

Bulgarian Psychological Society, 356

Bulgarian Rectors' Conference, 354

Bulgarian Society for Parasitology, 355

Bulgarian Society of Natural History, Sofia, 355

Bulgarian Society of Neurology, 355

Bulgarian Society of Sports Medicine and Kinesitherapy, 355

Bulgarian Sociological Association, 356

Bulgarian–Romanian Interuniversity Europe Center, 371

Bulgaria–Romania Interuniversity Europe Center, Giurgiu, 1878

Bund Schweizer Architekten, 2137

Bunda College of Agriculture, 1468

Bundelkhand University, 1055

Bundesamt für Landwirtschaft, Bern, 2143

Bundesamt für Meteorologie und Klimatologie (MeteoSchweiz), Zürich, 2141

Bundesamt für Seeschiffahrt und Hydrographie, Hamburg, 860

Bundesamt und Forschungszentrum für Landwirtschaft, Wien, 188

Bundesamt und Forschungszentrum für Wald, 188

Bundesamts für Bauwesen und Raumordnung, Wissenschaftliche Bibliothek, Bad Godesberg, 864

Bundesanstalt für Agrarwirtschaft, 188

Bundesanstalt für Alpenländische Landwirtschaft, Gumpenstein, 188

Bundesanstalt für Geowissenschaften und Rohstoffe (BGR), 861

Bundesanstalt für Materialforschung und -Prüfung, Berlin, 862

Bundesarchiv, Koblenz, 868

Bundesdenkmalamt, Vienna, 184

Bundesforschungsinstitut für Kulturpflanzen Informationszentrum und Bibliothek, Brunswick, 865

Bundesinstitut für Bevölkerungsforschung, Wiesbaden, 862

Bundesstaatliche Paedagogische Bibliothek beim Landesschulrat für Niederösterreich, 194

Bundeswehr Museum of Military History, 875

Bündner Kunstmuseum, Chur, 2148

Bunge Foundation, 306

Buniatian, H. Institute of Biochemistry NAS RA, 137

Bunin Museum, Orel, 1911

Bunkyo University, Tokyo, 1257

Canadian Information Centre for International Credentials (CICIC), 386

Canadian Institute of Chartered Accountants, 388

Canadian Institute of International Affairs, 388

Canadian Institute of Mining, Metallurgy and Petroleum, 390

Canadian Institutes of Health Research, 391

Canadian Library Association, 387

Canadian Linguistic Association, 388

Canadian Lung Association, 389

Canadian Mathematical Society, 390

Canadian Medical Association, 389

Canadian Meteorological and Oceanographic Society, 390

Canadian Museum of History, 397

Canadian Museum of Nature, 396

Canadian Museums Association, 387

Canadian Music Centre, 388

Canadian Network for Innovation in Education (CNIE), 387

Canadian Paediatric Society, 389

Canadian Pharmacists Association, 389

Canadian Philosophical Association, 390

Canadian Physiological Society, 389

Canadian Phytopathological Society, 389

Canadian Political Science Association, 388

Canadian Psychiatric Association, 389

Canadian Psychological Association, 390

Canadian Public Health Association, 389

Canadian Sculpture Centre, 388

Canadian Society for Analytical Sciences and Spectroscopy, 390

Canadian Society for Cellular and Molecular Biology, 389

Canadian Society for Immunology, 389

Canadian Society for Molecular Biosciences, 390

Canadian Society for Nutritional Sciences, 389

Canadian Society for the Study of Education, 388

Canadian Society of Animal Science, 387

Canadian Society of Biblical Studies, 390

Canadian Society of Landscape Architects, 387

Canadian Society of Microbiologists, 389

Canadian Society of Petroleum Geologists, 390

Canadian University of Dubai, 2271

Canadian Veterinary Medical Association, 387

Çanakkale Onsekiz Mart Üniversitesi, 2218

Canarian Museum, 2066

Canberra Campus, 154

Canberra Institute of Technology, 177

Cancer Care Ontario, 391

Cancer Institute and Hospital, Beijing, 484

Cancer Institute, Japanese Foundation for Cancer Research, 1250

Cancer Research Center, Mangilao, 3012

Cancer Research Institute, Karachi, 1676

Cancer Research Institute of Slovak Academy of Sciences, 2004

Cancer Research Institute, Tomsk, 1892

Cancer Research UK, 2304

Cancer Research UK Beatson Institute, 2304

Cancer Research UK Jersey, 2440

Cancer Research UK Manchester Institute, 2304

Cancer Society of Finland, 744

Canillo Community Library, 112

Canisius College, 2820

Çankaya Üniversitesi, 2218

Canning House Library, 2319

Canolfan Ymchwil Cymru, 2298

Cantacuzino Institute, 1841

Canterbury and York Society, 2284

Canterbury Cathedral Archives and Library, 2315

Canterbury Christ Church University, 2340

Canterbury Medical Research Foundation, 1605

Canterbury Museum, 1607

Canton Museum of Art, 2537

Cantonal and County Archive, Travnik, 299

CAP Art Centre and President Osmeña Memorabilia, Cebu City, 1735

CAPC Musée d'Art Contemporain de Bordeaux, 782

Cape Breton University, Sydney, 398

Cape Coast Castle Museum, 963

Cape Fear Museum of History and Science, 2536

Cape Peninsula University of Technology, 2034

Cape Town Baptist Seminary, 2046

Cape Verde National Statistical Institute, 459

Capella University, 2767

Capital City Public Library, Brussels, 267

Capital Library, Beijing, 488

Capital Medical University, Beijing, 497

Capital Normal University, Beijing, 499

Capital University, Columbus, 2875

Capitan Public Library, 2497

Capitol College, Laurel, 2700

Cappella Brancacci, 1207

Cappella degli Scrovegni, Padua, 1210

Captain General Gerardo Barrios University, 721

Caracal Museum of the Romanaţiului, 1849

Carbon County Library System, 2508

Carbon County Museum, 2547

Cardiff and Vale College, 2433

Cardiff Libraries, 2315

Cardiff University, Cardiff, 2430

Cardiff University Libraries, 2315

Cardinal Stafford Library, 2480

Cardinal Stefan Wyszyński Institute of Cardiology, 1764

Cardinal Stefan Wyszyński University in Warsaw, 1783

Cardinal Stritch University, 2999

Care Society, Malé, 1480

Career Guidance and Counselling Institute, Lisboa, 1818

Carey Hall and Carey Theological College, Vancouver, 429

Caribbean Agricultural Research and Development Institute (CARDI), 2204

Caribbean Area Network for Quality Assurance in Tertiary Education (CANQATE), 67

Caribbean Conservation Association, St Michael, 245

Caribbean Exploratory NIMHD Research Center, 3023

Caribbean Food and Nutrition Institute (CFNI), Kingston, 1238

Caribbean Green Technology Center, 3023

Caribbean Institute of Anthropology and Sociology, Caracas, 3048

Caribbean International University, Piscadera Bay, 1600

Caribbean Law Institute Centre, 246

Caribbean Network of Educational Innovation for Development (CARNEID), 62

Caribbean Regional Centre, 616

Caribbean Regional Council for Adult Education, 62

Caribbean University, Bayamon, 3016

Carinthian Association of Natural Sciences, 187

Carinthian Botanic Centre, 196

Carinthian Conservatory of Music, 210

Carinthian Provincial Archives, 193

Carl Nielsen Museet, 681

Carl Nielsen Museum, 681

Carl von Ossietzky Universität Oldenburg, 884

Carleton College, 2767

Carleton University, 399

Carleton University Library, 393

Carlos Albizu University, 2626

Carlos Albizu University, San Juan, 3016

Carlos Chagas Foundation, 307

Carlos Chávez National Centre for Research and Music Documentation, 1498

'Carlos I' Institute of Theoretical and Computational Physics, 2061

Carlos Reis Municipal Museum, 1825

'Carlos Spegazzini' Botanical Institute, 121

Carlow College, 1164

Carlow University, 2900

Carlsberg Laboratory, 675

Carlyle's House, London, 2333

CARMABI Foundation, 1599

Carmarthenshire College, 2433

Carmarthenshire County Libraries, 2315

Carmarthenshire County Museum, 2330

Carnegie Corporation of New York, 2451

Carnegie Endowment for International Peace, Washington, 2450

Carnegie Institution for Science, Washington, 2470

Carnegie Library, Curepipe, 1490

Carnegie Library of Pittsburgh, 2502

Carnegie Mellon Qatar, 1834

Carnegie Mellon University, 2901

Carnegie Mellon University, Heinz College—Australia, 180

Carnegie Museum of Art, Pittsburgh, 2539

Carnegie Museum of Natural History, Pittsburgh, 2539

Carnegie Public Library, San Juan, 3016

Carnegie Science Center, Pittsburgh, 2539

Carnegie-Stout Public Library, 2487

Carnuntinum Archaeological Museum, Bad Deutsch-Altenburg, 195

Caro and Cuervo Institute, 591

Carolinas Aviation Museum, 2536

Caroline County Public Library, Denton, 2490

Carpet Museum, 2240

Carré d'Art Bibliothèques, Nîmes, 779

Carré d'Art-Musée d'Art Contemporain, Nîmes, 784

Carriage Pavilion, Vatican City, 3038

Carrick Higher Education, Sydney, 178

Carrie Bow Marine Field Station— Caribbean Coral Reef Ecosystems (CCRE), 283

Carroll College, Helena, 2797

Carroll University, Waukesha, 2999

Carson-Newman College, 2934

Carter Observatory, Wellington, 1606

Carthage College, 2999

Cartographic Society of Finland, 743

Cartography Centre, Lisbon, 1817

Cary Library, 2489

Casa de la Cultura Ecuatoriana 'Benjamín Carrión', Quito, 700

Casa de la Gastronomía Peruana, 1717

Casa de la Independencia, Asunción, 1710

Casa de La Libertad, Sucre, 292

Casa de la Vall, 112

Casa de las Américas, Havana, 634

Casa de Velázquez, 2051

Casa del Manzoni, 1209

Casa di Carlo Goldoni, Venice, 1214

Casa dos Patudos—Museu de Alpiarça, 1823

Casa Gorordo Museum, Cebu City, 1735

Casa Memoriala Anton Pann, 1850

Casa Museo 'Jorge Eliécer Gaitán', 594

Casa Museo Quinta de Bolívar, 594

Casa Museu Fernando de Castro, Porto, 1825

Casa Museu Teixeira Lopes, 1825

Casa Museu Verdaguer, 2065

Casa Natal del Libertador Simón Bolívar, Caracas, 3050

Casa Pairal, Musée Catalan des Arts et Traditions Populaires, Perpignan, 786

Casa Rull de Sispony, 112

Casa Taller José Clemente Orozco, 1498

Casa-Fuerte de Ponce de León, 695

Casa-Museu Dr Anastácio Gonçalves, 1824

Case Western Reserve University, 2875

Case Western Reserve University Astronomy, Cleveland, 2472

Case Western Reserve University Libraries, 2500

Casimir Onderzoekschool, 1572

Casimir Research School, 1572

Caspian Research Institute for Arid Arable Farming, Astrakhan, 1884

Caspian State University of Technology and Engineering named after Sh. Yesenov, 1367

'Cassiano Ricardo' Public Library, 314

Castello D'Albertis Museo delle Culture del Mondo, Genoa, 1208

Castello del Buonconsiglio–Monumenti e Collezioni Provinciali, Trento, 1213

Castello di San Giusto e Civico Museo del Castello, Lapidario Tergestino, Trieste, 1213

Castillo de la Real Fuerza de la Havana, 637

Castle Museum, Gotha, 877

Castle Museum Nagytétény, 1008

Castle of the Royal Garrison of Havana, 637

Castle Seeburg Private University, 201

Castleton State College, 2973

Castletown Library, 2439

Castro Carazo Metropolitan University, 618

Catalan Foundation for Research and Innovation, 2059

Catalysis Society of Japan, 1247

Catalyst—Science Discovery Centre and Museum, Widnes, 2337

Catawba College, 2855

Catholic Academic Foreigner Service, 844

Catholic Agricultural University of the Dry Tropics 'Presbyter Francisco Luis Espinoza Pineda', 1616

Catholic Auxilium Salesian University Centre, 350

Catholic Educational Association of the Philippines (CEAP), 1732

Catholic Institute of Kabyagi, 1955

Catholic Library Association, Pittsfield, 2449

Catholic Record Society, London, 2284

Catholic Theological Union, Chicago, 2651

Catholic University 'Andrés Bello', 3051

Catholic University Cardinal Raùl Silva Henriquez, 476

Catholic University 'Cecilio Acosta', 3051

Catholic University College VIVES— Campus Bruges, 281

Catholic University in Ružomberok, 2007

Catholic University in Zimbabwe, 3080

Catholic University Los Ángeles of Chimbote, 1719

Catholic University of America, Washington, 2616

Catholic University of Angola, 114

Catholic University of Brasília, 319

Catholic University of Córdoba, 125

Catholic University of Costa Rica, 615

Catholic University of Cuenca, 703

Catholic University of Cuyo, 126

Catholic University of Daegu, 1396

Catholic University of Eastern Africa, 1377

Catholic University of El Salvador, 721

Catholic University of Honduras 'Our Lady Queen of Peace', 996

Catholic University of Korea, 1396

Catholic University of La Plata, 126

Catholic University of Leuven, 272

Catholic University of Louvain, 272

Catholic University of Manizales, 595

Catholic University of Maule, 471

Catholic University of 'Our Lady of the Assumption', 1711

Catholic University of Pelotas, 334

Catholic University of Pereira, 595

Catholic University of Pernambuco, 329

Catholic University of Petrópolis, 330

Catholic University of Portugal, 1827

Central Laboratory of Applied Physics, Plovdiv, 361

Central Laboratory of Geodesy, Sofia, 359

Central Laboratory of Mechatronics and Instrumentation, Sofia, 361

Central Laboratory of Physico-Chemical Mechanics, Sofia, 361

Central Laboratory of Seismic Mechanics and Earthquake Engineering, Sofia, 361

Central Laboratory of Socio-Economic Measurements, Moscow, 1886

Central Laboratory of Solar Energy & New Energy Sources, Sofia, 359

Central Leather Research Institute, Chennai, 1040

Central Leprosy Teaching and Research Institute, Chengalpattu, 1044

Central Library, 2147

Central Library and Archive of the Leibniz Institute for Regional Geography, 868

Central Library and Archives of the University of West Hungary, 1007

Central Library and Documentation Centre of Shahid Beheshti University, 1135

Central Library and Documentation Centre of University of Tehran, 1135

Central Library and Information Centre of the University of Veterinary and Pharmaceutical Sciences, 656

Central Library, Bahawalpur, 1677

Central Library, Bandung Institute of Technology, 1113

Central Library for Science and Technology, Hanoi, 3065

Central Library for the County of North Jutland, 677

Central Library 'General Rafael Urdaneta', 3049

Central Library, Institute of Agricultural Research, Santiago, 468

Central Library of Cantabria, 2065

Central Library of Higher University of San Andrés, 291

Central Library of Ignacy Łukasiewicz Rzeszow University of Technology, 1771

Central Library of Labour and Social Security, Warsaw, 1771

Central Library of Petroleum-Gas University of Ploieşti, 1846

Central Library of Physical Training, 658

Central Library of Politehnica University of Bucharest, 1845

Central Library of Prof Dr. Clodoaldo Beckmann federal University of Pará, 312

Central Library of St Lucia, 1957

Central Library of Secondary Education, Montevideo, 3026

Central Library of Semmelweis University, 1006

Central Library of Silesian University of Technology, 1770

Central Library of Świętokrzyska Technical University, 1770

Central Library of the Academy of Economic Studies, Bucharest, 1845

Central Library of the Bulgarian Academy of Sciences, Sofia, 361

Central Library of the Catholic University 'Andrés Bello', Caracas, 3049

Central Library of the Central University of Venezuela, Caracas, 3049

Central Library of the Diocese of Regensburg, 870

Central Library of the European Commission, 267

Central Library of the Federal University of Pernambuco, 313

Central Library of the Georgian Academy of Sciences, 839

Central Library of the Gheorghe Ionescu-Şişeşti Academy of Agricultural and Forestry Sciences, 1845

Central Library of the 'Gr. T. Popa' University of Medicine and Pharmacy in Iaşi, 1846

Central Library of the Higher University of St Francis Xavier, 292

Central Library of the Hungarian National Museum, 1006

Central Library of the Ministry of Finance and Public Administration, Madrid, 2064

Central Library of the Ministry of Labour and Social Security, Caracas, 3049

Central Library of the Ministry of Popular Power for Foreign Affairs, Caracas, 3049

Central Library of the National Autonomous University of Mexico, 1497

Central Library of the National Autonomous University of Nicaragua, León, 1615

Central Library of the National University of Cuyo, 123

Central Library of the National University of Engineering, 1716

Central Library of the National University of Tucumán, 123

Central Library of the Navy, 122

Central Library of the Palace of Justice, Vienna, 195

Central Library of the Slovak Academy of Sciences, 2006

Central Library of the Technical University 'Federico Santa Maria', Valparaiso, 469

Central Library of the University of Carabobo, 3050

Central Library of the University of Oriente, 636

Central Library of the University of Paraná, 313

Central Library of the University of San Carlos of Guatemala, 985

Central Library of the VSB-Technical University of Ostrava, 657

Central Library 'Pedro Zulen', 1716

Central Library, University of Brasilia, 312

Central Library, University of Caldas, 594

Central Library, Vadodara, 1049

Central Library—Chapingo Autonomous University, 1497

Central Library—University of Peshawar, 1679

Central Luzon State University, 1738

Central Marine Research and Design Institute Ltd (CNIIMF), St Petersburg, 1900

Central Mechanical Engineering Research Institute, Durgapur, 1040

Central Medical Library, Bowshar, 1670

Central Medical Library, Faculty of Medicine, Ljubljana, 2019

Central Medical Library, Lagos, 1627

Central Medical Library, Warsaw, 1771

Central Medical Library—MU Sofia, Sofia, 361

Central Medical Veterinary Research Institute, Sofia, 356

Central Metallurgical Research and Development Institute, Cairo, 713

Central Methodist University, Fayette, 2787

Central Michigan University, 2744

Central Military Library, Bandung, 1113

Central Military Library, Madrid, 2064

Central Mindanao University, 1739

Central Mining Institute, Katowice, 1767

Central Mining Museum, Sopron, 1011

Central Mississippi Regional Library System, 2494

Central Municipal Library Gabriela Mistral, 313

Central Municipal Library, Lisbon, 1822

Central Museum, Nagpur, 1050

Central Museum of Armed Forces of the Russian Federation, 1909

Central Museum of Railway Transport of Russia, 1912

Central Museum of Textiles in Łodz, 1773

Central Museum of the Armed Forces, Luanda, 113

Central Museum of the City of Prague, 659

Central National Library of Montenegro 'Đurđe Crnojević', 1536

Central Naval Library, Madrid, 2064

Central Naval Museum, St Petersburg, 1912

Central Office of Statistics and Informatics, Caracas, 3048

Central Paper Research Institute, Pravdinsky, 1900

Central Pedagogical Library 'Mtro. Sebastián Morey Otero', 3026

Central Penn College, 2902

Central Philippine University, 1739

Central Public Library Dhaka, 225

Central Public Library State Cultural Centre Jaime Sabines, 1498

Central Research and Design Institute for the Silicate Industry, 1005

Central Research and Design Institute of Dwellings, Moscow, 1885

Central Research and Design Institute of Fuel Apparatus and Vehicle and Tractor Engines and Stationary Engines, St Petersburg, 1900

Central Research and Design Institute of Town Planning, Moscow, 1885

Central Research and Technical Library at the National Centre for Information and Documentation, Sofia, 362

Central Research Institute for Animal Sciences Research and Development, Bogor, 1111

Central Research Institute for Machine Building, Korolev, 1900

Central Research Institute for the Evaluation of Working Capacity and Vocational Assistance to Disabled Persons, Moscow, 1888

Central Research Institute of Coating Materials and Artificial Leathers, Moscow, 1900

Central Research Institute of Dermatology and Venereal Diseases, Moscow, 1888

Central Research Institute of Engineering Technology, Moscow, 1900

Central Research Institute of Epidemiology, Moscow, 1888

Central Research Institute of Gastroenterology, Moscow, 1888

Central Research Institute of Geological Prospecting for Base and Precious Metals, Moscow, 1900

Central Research Institute of Telecommunications, Moscow, 1900

Central Research Institute of the Ministry of Defence, Bolshevo, 1900

Central Research Institute, Solan, 1044

Central Research Laboratory for the Introduction of Personal Computers, Moscow, 1900

Central Research Library of the National Academy of Sciences of the Kyrgyz Republic, 1419

Central Research Station for Plant Cultivation on Sand, Dolj, 1838

Central Research Station for Tobacco Growing and Industrialization, Bucharest, 1839

Central Rice Research Institute, Cuttack, 1041

Central Road Research Institute, New Delhi, 1040

Central Roman-German Museum–Research Museum for Prehistory and Early History, 879

Central Saint Martins College of Art and Design, London, 2406

Central Salt and Marine Chemicals Research Institute, Bhavnagar, 1040

Central School of Ballet, London, 2413

Central Scientific Agricultural Library of the Russian Academy of Agricultural Sciences, 1905

Central Scientific Archive of the National Academy of Sciences of Belarus, Minsk, 250

Central Scientific Instruments Organization, Chandigarh, 1040

Central Scientific Library, 213

Central Scientific Library 'Andrei Lupan' of the Academy of Sciences of Moldova, 1525

Central Scientific Library, Ashgabat, 2240

Central Scientific Library of Scientific Committee of the Ministry of Education and Science of the Republic of Kazakhstan, 1365

Central Scientific Library of the National Academy of Sciences of Belarus 'Ya. Kolas', Minsk, 250

Central Scientific Medical Library, 1906

Central Scientific Research and Design Institute of the Wood Chemical Industry, Nizhny Novgorod, 1900

Central Secretariat Library, New Delhi, 1048

Central Seismological Observatory, Obninsk, 1895

Central Siberian Botanical Garden, 1911

Central Slovakia Museum Banská Bystrica, 2006

Central Society of Architects, Buenos Aires, 117

Central South University, Chang Sha, 501

Central Sports Research Institute, Moscow, 1887

Central State Archive and Museum of Literature and Art of Ukraine, 2254

Central State Archive, Koblenz, 868

Central State Archive of Public Organizations of Ukraine, Kyiv, 2254

Central State Archive of Supreme Bodies of Power and Government of Ukraine, 2254

Central State Archive of Thuringia in Weimar, 871

Central State Archive, Tashkent, 3032

Central State Archives, Moscow, 1905

Central State Archives of the Nation's Documentary Films and Photographs, Vladimir, 1908

Central State Archives of the Republic of Kazakhstan, 1365

Central State Archives, Sofia, 362

Central State CinePhotoFono Archive of Ukraine 'H. S. Pshenychniy', Lviv, 2254

Central State Historical Archive of Ukraine in Kyiv, 2254

Central State Museum of Kazakhstan, 1365

Central State Public Library, 1498

Central State University, Wilberforce, 2879

Central Statistical Library, Warsaw, 1771

Central Technical Library of the University of Ljubljana, 2019

Central Texas Library System, Inc., 2505

Central Tobacco Research Institute, Rajahmundry, 1041

Central Tuberculosis Research Institute, Moscow, 1888

Central University, Bogotá, 596

Central University for Nationalities, Beijing, 504

Central University, Guatemala City, 986

Central University Institute for the Study and Diagnosis of Malocclusions, 3028

Central University Library 'Carol I', 1845

Central University Library 'Eugen Todoran', 1847

Central University Library 'José Antonio Arze', Cochabamba, 291

Central University Library, Potosí, 292

Central University 'Marta Abreu' of Las Villa, 641

Central University of Bayamón, 3018

Central University of Ecuador, 703

Central University of Ecuador Library, 702

Central University of Finance and Economics, 504

Central University of Nicaragua, 1616

Central University of Paraguay, 1711

Central University of Technology, Free State, 2035

Central University of Technology, Guacara, 3057

Central University of the Caribbean, 3018

Central University of Venezuela, 3052

Central University, San José, 615

Central University, Santiago, 476

Central Veterinary Laboratory, Harare, 3078

Central Veterinary Laboratory, Lilongwe, 1468

Central Veterinary Research Station, Mazabuka, 3075

Central Washington University, Ellensburg, 2987

Central Water and Power Research Station, Pune, 1047

Central Zionist Archives, Jerusalem, 1173

Centralna Biblioteka Rolnicza im. Michała Oczapowskiego, Warsaw, 1771

Centralna Biblioteka Statystyczna, Warsaw, 1771

Centralna Biblioteka Wojskowa im. Marszałka Józefa Piłsudskiego, 1771

Centralna ekonomska knjižnica, Ljubljana, 2019

Centralna Komisja do Spraw Stopni i Tytułów, Warsaw, 1751

Centralna medicinska knjižnica, Medicinska fakulteta, Ljubljana, 2019

Centralna narodna biblioteka Crne Gore 'Đurđe Crnojević', 1536

Centralna tehniška knjižnica Univerze v Ljubljani, 2019

Centralne Muzeum Morskie w Gdańsku, 1772

Centralne Muzeum Włókiennictwa w Łodzi, 1773

Centralny Instytut Ochrony Pracy–Państwowy Instytut Badawczy (CIOP-PIB), Warsaw, 1767

Central-Western University 'Lisandro Alvarado', 3052

Centre Africain de Formation et de Recherche Administratives pour le Développement (CAFRAD), 57

Centre Canadien d'Architecture, 397

Centre Canadien des Eaux Intérieures, 392

Centre CEA de Cadarache (France-Bouches-du-Rhone), 775

Centre CEA de Fontenay-aux-Roses (Hauts-de-Seine), 775

Centre CEA de Grenoble (Isère), 775

Centre CEA de la Marcoule (Gard), 775

Centre CEA de Saclay (Essonne), 775

Centre CEA de Valduc, 775

Centre CEA/Cesta (Gironde), 775

Centre CEA/DAM Ile de France (Essonne), 775

Centre College, Danville, 2688

Centre Culturel Calouste Gulbenkian, Paris, 768

Centre Culturel Français, Bamako, 1483

Centre Culturel International d'Hammamet, 2209

Centre d'Archives et de Documentation Politiques et Sociales, Paris, 767

Centre d'Art, Port-au-Prince, 993

Centre d'Etude de l'Expression, Paris, 770

Centre d'étude et de Recherches Vétérinaires et Agrochimiques, Brussels, 262

Centre d'études, de Documentation et de Recherches Historiques 'Ahmed Baba' (CEDRAB), Timbuktu, 1483

Centre d'Etudes de l'Emploi, Noisy-le-Grand, 773

Centre d'études Economiques et Sociales d'Afrique Occidentale (CESAO), Bobo-Dioulasso, 374

Centre d'Etudes et de Documentation Economique, Juridique et Sociale, Cairo, 712

Centre d'études et de Recherches Multimédia et Études Euro-Méditerranéennes et Orientales (CERM-EMO), Mons, 265

Centre d'Etudes Linguistiques et Historiques par Tradition Orale, Niamey, 1621

Centre d'études Maghrébines à Tunis, 2207

Centre d'études Nord-Américaines de l'ULB, 262

Centre d'Etudes Prospectives et d'Informations Internationales, Paris, 773

Centre d'études Supérieures de la Renaissance, Tours, 774

Centre d'Etudes sur les Resources Végétales (CERVE), Brazzaville, 610

Centre d'Imagerie BioMedicale, Lausanne, 2144

Centre d'Information des Nations Unies, Brazzaville, 611

Centre d'Information et de Documentation Economique et Sociale (CIDES), Niamey, 1621

Centre d'Information et de Documentation sur les Droits de l'Enfant et de la Femme (CIDDEF), Algiers, 102

Centre de Co-opération Internationale en Recherche Agronomique pour le Développement (CIRAD), Cote d'Ivoire, 620

Centre de Coopération Internationale en Recherche Agronomique pour le Développement (CIRAD), Ouagadougou, 373

Centre de Co-opération Internationale en Recherche Agronomique pour le Développement (CIRAD), Paris, 773

Centre de Développement des Energies Renouvelables (CDER), Algiers, 102

Centre de Développement des Technologies Avancées, 102

Centre de Documentation Economique de la Chambre de Commerce et d'Industrie de Paris, 780

Centre de Documentation et d'Information Scientifique pour le Développement (CEDID), Paris, 780

Centre de Documentation Nationale, Tunis-Belvédère, 2207

Centre de documentation pédagogique de Nouvelle-Calédonie, 830

Centre de Formation des Musiciens Intervenants (CFMI), 789

Centre de Formation Pédagogique Emmanuel Mounier, 819

Centre de Formation Professionnelle Arts Appliqués, Geneva, 2167

Centre de Musique Canadienne, 388

Centre de Musique Hindemith, 2138

Centre de Recherche Agronomique de Djibélor, 1969

Centre de Recherche Agronomique de Foulaya, Kindia, 988

Centre de Recherche Agronomique de Kaolack, 1969

Centre de Recherche Agronomique de la Savane Humide, 2200

Centre de Recherche Agronomique de Saint-Louis, 1969

Centre de Recherche, des Archives et de Documentation, Commission Nationale pour l'UNESCO, N'Djamena, 462

Centre de Recherche en Astronomie, Astrophysique et Géophysique CRAAG, Algiers, 102

Centre de Recherche en Biotechnologie, Constantine, 102

Centre de Recherche en Economie Appliquée pour le Développement (CREAD), Algiers, 101

Centre de Recherche en Sciences Humaines (CRSH), Kinshasa, 607

Centre de Recherche en Technologie des Semi-Conducteurs pour l'Energétique (CRTSE), Algiers, 102

Centre de Recherche et d'Action pour la Paix (CERAP), Abidjan, 620

Centre de Recherche et d'Initiation des Projets de Technologie (CRIPT), Brazzaville, 611

Centre de Recherche Forestière du Littoral, Pointe-Noire, 610

Centre de Recherche Géographique et de Production Cartographique, Brazzaville, 611

Centre de Recherche Public de la Santé, Luxembourg, 1457

Centre de Recherche Public Henri Tudor, 1457

Centre de Recherche Scientifique et Technique sur les Régions Aride, 102

Centre de Recherche sur l'Information Scientifique et Technique, Algiers, 101

Centre de Recherches Atmosphériques, Campistrous, 775

Centre de Recherches Economiques, Sociologiques et de Gestion (CRESGE), Lille, 820

Centre de Recherches Géologiques et Minières, Kinshasa, 608

Centre de Recherches Historiques, Paris, 774

Centre de Recherches Océanographiques, Abidjan, 620

Centre de Recherches Océanographiques de Dakar-Thiaroye (CRODT), 1969

Centre de Recherches Zootechniques de Dahra-Djoloff, 1969

Centre de Recherches Zootechniques de Kolda, 1969

Centre de Sélection Bovine de Songa, 1954

Centre de Trobada de les Cultures Pirenenques, Andorra la Vella, 111

Centre d'Enseignement et de Recherche en Informatique (CERI), 791

Centre des Archives Contemporaines, Fontainebleau, 779

Centre des Archives d'Outre-Mer, Aix-en-Provence, 779

Centre des Monuments Nationaux (Monum), Paris, 784

Centre des Technologies Agronomiques, 262

Centre d'Estudis del Patrimoni Arqueològic de la Prehistòria, 2060

Centre d'Études et de Documentation Guerre et Société Contemporaines (CEGES), 267

Centre d'Interpretació de la Natura de les Valls d'Ordino, 112

Centre Européen d'Education Permanente (CEDEP), Fontainebleau, 821

Centre Européen de Recherches sur les Congrégations et les Ordres Religieux (CERCOR), Saint-Etienne, 776

Centre Européen pour l'Enseignement Supérieur (CEPES), 66

Centre for Adult Education (CAE), Melbourne, 142

Centre for Advanced Research in English, Birmingham, 2303

Centre for Advanced Research in International Agricultural Development, Bangor, 2307

Centre for Advanced Studies in Mathematics, Lahore, 1674

Centre for Advanced Studies in Physics (CASP), Lahore, 1676

Centre for Advanced Studies of Puerto Rico and the Caribbean, 3021

Centre for Advanced Welsh Music Studies, 2302

Centre for Agricultural Economic Research, Rehovot, 1169

Centre for Agricultural Research in Suriname, 2103

Centre for Agro-Based Industry, Bogor, 1111

Centre for Alcohol and Drug Studies, Paisley, 2297

Centre for Analysis of Social Exclusion, London, 2309

Centre for Animal and Veterinary Sciences (CECAV), Vila Real, 1818

Centre for Anthropology, Havana, 636

Centre for Applied Marine Sciences, Bangor, 2299

Centre for Applied Research and Study in Perceptual Psychoeducation, Porto, 1817

Centre for Applied Research in Educational Technologies (CARET), Cambridge, 2301

Centre for Arab Unity Studies, Beirut, 1433

Centre for Archaeological Research of Montenegro, 1536

Centre for Architectural Studies, Sofia, 357

Centre for Art Studies, 96

Centre for ASEAN Studies, 263

Centre for Asia Minor Studies, Athens, 970

Centre for Asian and African Studies, México, 1495

Centre for Asian Documentation, Kolkata, 1049

Centre for Astronomy of Heidelberg University, 942

Centre for Atmospheric Chemistry, Toronto, 457

Centre for Automotive Management, Loughborough, 2310

Centre for Aviation and Aerospace, Hsinchu, 2173

Centre for Basic Research, Kampala, 2243

Centre for Bhutan Studies, 287

Centre for Biblical Studies, Exeter, 2309

Centre for Biomedical Imaging, 2144

Centre for Brain Ageing and Vitality, 2304

Centre for Business Research, Cambridge, 2297

Centre for Cellular and Molecular Biology, Hyderabad, 1040

Centre for Chemical and Biological Analysis, 1700

Centre for Child and Family Research, Loughborough, 2304

Centre for City and Regional Studies, Hull, 2302

Centre for Climate Change, Environment, Energy and Sustainable Development (CEESD), 738

Centre for Cognitive Ageing and Cognitive Epidemiology, 2304

Centre for Comparative Criminology and Criminal Justice, Bangor, 2300

Centre for Conflict and Peace Studies, Kabul, 92

Centre for Conservation Studies, Guatemala City, 985

Centre for Construction Materials, State Material-Testing Foundation-Faculty and Institute of Material Science, 863

Centre for Creative Education, Plumstead, 2046

Centre for Crime and Justice Studies, London, 2309

Centre for Dance Research, London, 2302

Centre for Defence Studies, London, 2377

Centre for Democracy and Development, 57

Centre for Demographics, Urban and Environmental Studies, México, 1495

Centre for Development in Primary Health Care, 1700

Centre for Development Information, Colombo, 2093

Centre for Development Innovation, Wageningen, 1566

Centre for Development Studies—Central University of Venezuela, 3048

Centre for Diabetes Research, Jerusalem, 1170

Centre Universitaire de Mila, Mila, 108

Centre Universitaire de Naama, Naama, 108

Centre Universitaire de Rélizane, Rélizane, 108

Centre Universitaire de Tamanrasset, Tamanrasset, 108

Centre Universitaire de Tindouf, Tindouf, 108

Centre Universitaire de Tipaza, Tipaza, 108

Centre Universitaire d'El Bayadh, El Bayadh, 108

Centre Wallon de Recherches Agronomiques, 262

Centria Ammattikorkeakoulun Koulutustarjonta, 761

Centria University of Applied Sciences, 761

Centro Agronómico Tropical de Investigación y Enseñanza (CATIE), Turrialba, 613

Centro Amazónico de Antropología y Aplicación Práctica (CAAAP), 1715

Centro Aquícola do Rio Ave, 1821

Centro Argentino de Espeleología, 119

Centro Argentino de Información Científica y Tecnológica (CAICYT), 122

Centro Argentino de Ingenieros, 120

Centro Brasileiro de Pesquisas Físicas, 311

Centro Camuno di Studi Preistorici, 1198

Centro Ciência Viva de Amadora, 1823

Centro Científico Tropical, 613

Centro Co-ordinador y Difusor de Estudios Latinoamericanos, México, 1496

Centro Cultural Hispano-Guineano, Malabo, 726

Centro de Ambiente e Ciências da Terra do Instituto de Investigação Científica Tropical, 1817

Centro de Antropobiologia do Instituto de Investigação Científica Tropical, 1817

Centro de Antropología, 636

Centro de Antropologia Cultural e Social do Instituto de Investigação Científica Tropical, 1817

Centro de Arte la Estancia, 3050

Centro de Arte Moderna—Fundação Calouste Gulbenkian, 1824

Centro de Astronomia e Astrofísica da Universidade de Lisboa, 1820

Centro de Biotecnología Marina, Las Palmas de Gran Canaria, 2061

Centro de Botânica do Instituto de Investigação Científica Tropical, 1817

Centro de Cartografia do Instituto de Investigação Científica Tropical, 1817

Centro de Ciência Animal e Veterinária (CECAV), 1818

Centro de Ciências, Letras e Artes, 310

Centro de Cooperación Regional para la Educación de Adultos en América Latina y el Caribe (CREFAL), Pátzcuaro, 1492

Centro de Cristalografia e Mineralogia do Instituto de Investigação Científica Tropical, 1817

Centro de Dados Geológico-Mineiro Alfragide, 1821

Centro de Desarrollo Científico de Montañas, Guantanamo, 636

Centro de Desarrollo de Equipos e Instrumentos Científicos (CEDEIC), Havana, 636

Centro de Desenvolvimento da Tecnologia Nuclear, 311

Centro de Desenvolvimento Global do Instituto de Investigação Científica Tropical, 1817

Centro de Detecção Remota para o Desenvolvimento do Instituto de Investigação Científica Tropical, 1817

Centro de Diseño de Sistemas Automatizados de Computación (CEDISAC), Havana, 636

Centro de Documentação e Informação da Câmara dos Deputados do Brasil, 312

Centro de Documentación Bibliotecológica, 120

Centro de Documentación de la Secretaría de Economía y Sector Coordinado (CEDOCS), 1497

Centro de Documentación e Información Internacional, Buenos Aires, 122

Centro de Documentación Regional 'Juan Bautista Vázquez' de la Universidad de Cuenca, 701

Centro de Documentación y Archivo/ Fundación la Salle de Ciencias Naturales, 3049

Centro de Documentación y Estudios para la Historia de Madrid, 2060

Centro de Ecofisiologia, Bioquímica e Biotecnologia Vegetal do Instituto de Investigação Científica Tropical, 1817

Centro de Energia Nuclear na Agricultura, Piracicaba, 308

Centro de Estadísticas Nacionales y Comercio Internacional del Uruguay (CENCI Uruguay), 3025

Centro de Estudios Ambientales del Mediterráneo, 2061

Centro de Estudios Antropológicos de la Universidad Católica, 1710

Centro de Estudios Avanzados de Puerto Rico y El Caribe, 3021

Centro de Estudios Avanzados en Ciencias Sociales, 2055

Centro de Estudios Conservacionistas, Guatemala City, 985

Centro de Estudios de Asia y África, México, 1495

Centro de Estudios de Poblacion, 291

Centro de Estudios de Población y Desarrollo (CEPDE), Havana, 635

Centro de Estudios del Desarrollo— Universidad Central de Venezuela, 3048

Centro de Estudios Demográficos, Urbanos y Ambientales, México, 1495

Centro de Estudios e Investigaciones Técnicas de Gipuzkoa, 2062

Centro de Estudios Económicos, 1495

Centro de Estudios Educativos, AC, México, 1495

Centro de Estudios Histórico-Militares del Perú, 1715

Centro de Estudios Históricos, México, 1495

Centro de Estudios Internacionales, México, 1495

Centro de Estudios Lingüísticos y Literarios, México, 1495

Centro de Estudios Políticos y Constitucionales, 2052

Centro de Estudios Sociológicos, México, 1496

Centro de Estudios Superiores Universitarios, 290

Centro de Estudos Africanos e Asiáticos do Instituto de Investigação Científica Tropical, 1817

Centro de Estudos da Guiné-Bissau, 990

Centro de Estudos de Fitossanidade do Armazenamento do Instituto de Investigação Científica Tropical, 1817

Centro de Estudos de História e Cartografia Antiga do Instituto de Investigação Científica Tropical, 1817

Centro de Estudos de Pedologia do Instituto de Investigação Científica Tropical, 1817

Centro de Estudos de Produção e Tecnologia Agrícolas do Instituto de Investigação Científica Tropical, 1817

Centro de Estudos de Vectores e Doenças Infecciosas Doutor Francisco Cambournac, 1819

Centro de Estudos do Baixo Alentejo, 1818

Centro de Estudos do Território, Cultura e Desenvolvimento, 1817

Centro de Estudos em Letras, 1819

Centro de Estudos Geográficos da Universidade de Lisboa, 1818

Centro de Estudos Geológicos e Mineiros de Beja, 1821

Centro de Estudos Históricos e Etnológicos, 1818

Centro de Estudos Sociais da Faculdade de Economia da Universidade de Coimbra, 1818

Centro de Estudos Transdisciplinares para o Desenvolvimento (CETRAD), 1817

Centro de Etnologia Ultramarina do Instituto de Investigação Científica Tropical, 1817

Centro de Formación y Estudios (CENFORES), 3028

Centro de Fotogrametria do Instituto de Investigação Científica Tropical, 1817

Centro de Genómica e Biotecnologia (CGB), 1820

Centro de Geodesia do Instituto de Investigação Científica Tropical, 1817

Centro de Geografia do Instituto de Investigação Científica Tropical, 1817

Centro de Geologia da Universidade do Porto, 1818

Centro de Geologia do Instituto de Investigação Científica Tropical, 1817

Centro de Historia Larense, 3046

Centro de Informação e Biblioteca em Educação, Brasília, 313

Centro de Información 'Alvaro Castro Jenkins', 614

Centro de Información Bancaria y Económica, Banco Central de Cuba, 636

Centro de Información Bioagropecuaria y Forestal (CIBAGRO), Resistencia, 123

Centro de Información de la Comisión Nacional de Energía Atómica, San Martín, 123

Centro de Información de Recursos Naturales (CIREN), 468

Centro de Información Documental de Archivos, Madrid, 2064

Centro de Información y Documentación Agropecuario, Havana, 636

Centro de Información y Documentación Institucional, Panamá, 1703

Centro de Información y Estadística Industrial, Buenos Aires, 123

Centro de Innovación Para la Sociedad de la Información, 2062

Centro de Investigação das Ferrugens do Cafeeiro do Instituto de Investigação Científica Tropical, 1817

Centro de Investigação do Instituto de Estudos Políticos, 1818

Centro de Investigação e de Tecnologias Agro-Ambientais e Biológicas, 1818

Centro de Investigação em Antropologia e Saude, 1820

Centro de Investigação em Ciência e Engenharia Geológica, 1818

Centro de Investigação em Desporto, Saúde e Desenvolvimento Humano, 1819

Centro de Investigação Marinha e Ambiental, 1818

Centro de Investigación Ecológica y Aplicaciones Forestales, 2059

Centro de Investigación en Computación, México, 1497

Centro de Investigación en Contabilidad Social y Medioambiental, 2062

Centro de Investigación Operativa, 2061

Centro de Investigación para el Desarrollo Cultural y la Educación Artística, México, 1498

Centro de Investigación y de Estudios Avanzados del Instituto Politécnico Nacional, México, 1496

Centro de Investigación y Desarrollo de la Educación (CIDE), Santiago, 467

Centro de Investigación y Educación Popular, 593

Centro de Investigaciones Apícolas, Havana, 635

Centro de Investigaciones de Energía Solar, 636

Centro de Investigaciones Económicas, Buenos Aires, 120

Centro de Investigaciones Económicas Nacionales, Guatemala City, 984

Centro de Investigaciones Energéticas, Medioambientales y Tecnológicas, 2062

Centro de Investigaciones Lingüísticas, 2061

Centro de Investigaciones Neurobiológicas 'Prof. Dr Christfried Jakob', Buenos Aires, 121

Centro de Investigaciónes para el Mejoramiento Animal, 635

Centro de Investigaciones para la Industria Minero Metalúrgica, Havana, 636

Centro de Investigaciones para la Industria Minero-Metalúrgica, 636

Centro de Investigaciones Pesqueras, Havana, 635

Centro de Investigaciones Pesqueras y Piscicultura, 3025

Centro de Investigaciones Psicológicas y Sociológicas (CIPS), 636

Centro de Investigaciones Psiquiatricas, Psicológicas y Sexológicas de Venezuela, 3060

Centro de Investigaciones Sociológicas, 2059

Centro de Levantamientos Aeroespaciales y Aplicaciones de Sistemas de Información Geográfica para el Desarrollo Sostenible de los Recursos Naturales, 291

Centro de Matemática (CM), 1820

Centro de Navegación, 3028

Centro de Neurociências e Biologia Celular, 1819

Centro de Pesquisa e Gestão de Recursos Pesqueiros Continentais (CEPTA), 311

Centro de Pesquisas e Desenvolvimento (CEPED), 311

Centro de Petrologia e Geoquímica, 1819

Centro de Pré-História e Arqueologia do Instituto de Investigação Científica Tropical, 1817

Centro de Química—Vila Real (CQVR), 1820

Centro de Recursos Naturais e Ambiente, 1820

Centro de Recursos Naturales Renovables de la Zona Semiárida (CERZOS), Bahía Blanca, 121

Centro de Relaciones Internacionales, México, 1495

Centro de Sociedades e Culturas Tropicais do Instituto de Investigação Científica Tropical, 1818

Centro de Sócio-Economia do Instituto de Investigação Científica Tropical, 1818

Centro de Veterinária e Zootecnia do Instituto de Investigação Científica Tropical, 1818

Centro de Vulcanologia e Avaliação de Riscos Geológicos, 1819

Centro de Zoologia do Instituto de Investigação Científica Tropical, 1818

Centro di Documentazione per la Storia, l'Arte, l'Immagine di Genova, 1208

Centro di Informazione sulla Mobilità e le Equivalenze Accademiche, 1187

Centro di Responsabilità Scientifica IDAIC, 1193

Centro di Responsabilità Scientifica INFM, 1195

Centro di Ricerche Economiche e Sociali (CERES), 1197

Centro Educativo en Artes Diversificadas, 1705

Centro Escolar University, 1739

Centro Ingeniería Genética y Biotecnología de Cuba, 635

City Planning Institute of Japan, 1242
City University, Dhaka, 229
City University London, 2340
City University of Hong Kong, 581
City University of New York, 2820
City University of São Paulo, 343
City University of Science & Information Technology, Peshawar, 1681
City University of Seattle, 2987
CityVarsity, 2046
Civic Voice, London, 2279
Civica Biblioteca 'Angelo Mai', Bergamo, 1201
Civiche Raccolte Storiche di Milano, Biblioteca e Archivio, Milan, 1203
Civici Musei di Storia ed Arte, Trieste, 1213
Civici Musei e Gallerie di Storia ed Arte, 1213
Civici Musei—Castello Visconteo, Pavia, 1211
Civico Aquario Marino, Trieste, 1213
Civico Museo d'Arte Orientale, Trieste, 1213
Civico Museo del Mare, Trieste, 1213
Civico Museo di Guerra per la Pace 'Diego de Henriquez', Trieste, 1213
Civico Museo di Storia e Cultura Contadina Genovese e Ligure, 1208
Civico Museo di Storia ed Arte e Orto Lapidario, Trieste, 1213
Civico Museo di Storia Naturale, Trieste, 1213
Civico Museo di Storia Patria—Civico Museo Morpurgo de Nilma, Trieste, 1213
Civico Museo Sartorio, Trieste, 1213
Civico Museo Teatrale 'Carlo Schmidl', Trieste, 1213
Civico Orto Botanico, Trieste, 1213
Civil Defence Historical Museum, Copenhagen, 680
Civil Engineering Research Institute of Hokkaido, Sapporo, 1251
Civil Engineering Society, Moscow, 1882
Claflin University, 2927
Clare College, Cambridge, 2358
Clare College Library, 2313
Clare Hall, Cambridge, 2358
Claremont Graduate University, 2570
Claremont McKenna College, 2570
Claremont School of Theology, 2571
Clarence Fitzroy Bryant College, Basseterre, 1956
Clarion University, 2910
Clark Atlanta University, 2638
Clark College, 2987
Clark County Public Library, 2488
Clark University, 2714
Clarke University, 2679
Clarkson College, Omaha, 2798
Clarkson University, 2822
Clarksville Montgomery County Public Library, 2504
Classic Aircraft Aviation Museum, Inc., 2539
Classical Association, Cambridge, 2287
Classical Association of South Africa, 2028
Classical Museum, Konya, 2214
Classical Period Foundation Weimar, 881
Classical Philological Society of Innsbruck, 186
Classical Society of Japan, 1244
Classical Studies Institute, Coimbra, 1819
Claude Monet Foundation, Giverny, 783
Clausen Museum, 2510
Clausthal Institute of Environmental Technology, 862
Clausthaler Umwelttechnik-Institut GmbH, 862
Clay Center for the Arts and Sciences of West Virginia, 2545
Clayton County Library System, 2484
Clayton State University, 2638
Clear Creek Baptist Bible College, 2688
Clear Creek County District Library, 2480
Clearwater Christian College, 2626
Clearwater Historical Museum, 2519

Clearwater Public Library System, 2483
Cleary University, 2744
Clemson University, 2927
Clermont County Law Library Association, 2501
Cleveland Chiropractic College, Kansas City, 2787
Cleveland Chiropractic College, Los Angeles, 2571
Cleveland College of Art & Design, 2412
Cleveland Institute of Art, 2880
Cleveland Institute of Music, 2880
Cleveland Law Library, 2501
Cleveland Museum of Art, 2537
Cleveland Museum of Natural History, 2537
Cleveland Public Library, 2501
Cleveland State University, 2880
Cliff College, 2415
Clinical and Health Psychology Research Centre, London, 2309
Clinton Essex Franklin Library System, Plattsburgh, 2498
Clique College, 1481
Clock Tower, 1214
Clovis-Carver Public Library, 2497
Cluster Library, Vienna, 195
Clusterbibliothek, Vienna, 195
Clyfford Still Museum, 2513
Coady International Institute, 411
Coastal Carolina University, 2927
Coastal Galleries of Piran, 2020
Coastal Institute, Narragansett, 2471
Coastal Polytechnic School, Guayaquil, 709
Cobb County Public Library System, 2484
Cobra Museum of Modern Art, Amstelveen, 1579
Cobra Museum voor Moderne Kunst, Amstelveen, 1579
Cochin University of Science & Technology, 1057
Cocoa Research Institute of Ghana, 962
Cocoa Research Institute of Nigeria, 1625
Coconut Research Institute Library, Lunuwila, 2094
Coconut Research Institute, Lunuwila, 2092
Çocuk Sağlığı Enstitüsü, Hacettepe Üniversitesi İhsan Doğramacı Çocuk Hastanesi, Ankara, 2212
CODA Museum, Apeldoorn, 1580
Codarts, Hogeschool voor de Kunsten, 1596
Codarts University for the Arts, 1596
Codrington Library (All Souls College), Oxford, 2325
Coe College, 2679
Coeur d'Alene Public Library, 2485
Coffee Research Foundation, Ruiru, 1376
Coffee Research Institute, Harare, 3078
Coffee Rusts Research Centre, Oeiras, 1817
Cogswell Polytechnical College, 2571
Cohn-Haddow Center for Judaic Studies, 2467
Coimbra Branch, 1821
Coimbra Public Library, 1821
Coimbra Univ. Astronomical Observatory, 1820
Coimbra University School of Arts, 1832
Coin Cabinet, 875
Coin Cabinet, Gotha, 877
Coin Collection, Mainz, 879
Coker College, 2928
Colby College, 2698
Colby College Museum of Art, 2524
Colby-Sawyer College, 2802
Colchester Institute, 2410
Cold and Arid Regions Environmental and Engineering Research Institute, Lanzhou, 485
Cold Spring Harbor Laboratory, 2471
Colección Ornitológica Phelps, 3050
Colectia de arta plastica Alexandru Balintescu, 1850
Coleg Brenhinol Cerdd a Drama Cymru, 2433
Coleg Caerdydd a'r Fro, 2433
Coleg Cambria, 2433

Coleg Gwent, 2433
Coleg Gŵyr Abertawe, 2433
Coleg Llandrillo Cymru, 2433
Coleg Menai, 2433
Coleg Sir Gâr, 2433
Coleg y Cymoedd, 2433
Colegio Colombiano de Bibliotecología ASCOLBI, 591
Colegio de Abogados de la Ciudad de Buenos Aires, 117
Colegio de Abogados del Distrito Capital, 3046
Colegio de Arquitectos de Bolivia, 290
Colegio de Arquitectos de Chile, 465
Colegio de Arquitectos de Honduras, 995
Colegio de Arquitectos de Venezuela, 3045
Colegio de Arquitectos del Perú, 1714
Colegio de Bibliotecarios de Chile, A.G., 465
Colegio de Bibliotecólogos del Perú, 1714
Colegio de Bibliotecólogos y Archivólogos de Venezuela, 3046
Colegio de Farmacéuticos del Distrito Federal y Estado Miranda, 3046
Colegio de Géologos de Bolivia, 290
Colegio de Ingenieros de Chile, AG, 467
Colegio de Ingenieros de Guatemala, 984
Colegio de Ingenieros de Venezuela, 3047
Colegio de Ingenieros Forestales de Chile, 465
Colegio de Médicos del Distrito Metropolitano de Caracas, Caracas, 3046
Colegio de Médicos del Estado Miranda, 3046
Colegio de Médicos y Cirujanos de Costa Rica, 612
Colegio de Químico-Farmacéuticos y Bioquímicos de Chile, 465
Colegio Mayor de Nuestra Señora del Rosario, 599
Colegio Médico de El Salvador, 720
Colegio Nacional, México, 1493
Colegio Universitario de Administración y Mercadeo, 3059
Colegio Universitario de Caracas, 3059
Colegio Universitario de Cartago (CUC), 619
Colegio Universitario de Enfermería Centro Médico de Caracas, 3059
Colegio Universitario de Enfermería de la Alcaldía Metropolitana de Caracas, 3059
Colegio Universitario de Enfermería de la Cruz Roja de Venezuela, 3059
Colegio Universitario de Psicopedagogía, 3059
Colegio Universitario de Rehabilitación 'May Hamilton', 3060
Colegio Universitario de San Juan, 3021
Colegio Universitario 'Dr Rafael Belloso Chacín', 3060
Colegio Universitario 'Fermín Toro', 3060
Colegio Universitario 'Francisco de Miranda', 3060
Colegio Universitario 'Monseñor de Talavera', 3060
Colegio Universitario 'Profesor José Lorenzo Pérez', 3060
Coleman University, 2571
Colgate Rochester Crozer Divinity School, 2822
Colgate University, 2822
Collaborative Antwerp Psychiatric Research Institute, 263
Collection of Classical Antiquities at the Pergamon Museum and the Old Museum, 873
Collection of Modern Religious Art, Vatican City, 2857
Collection of Prints and Drawings of ETH Zurich, 2150
Collections Artistiques de l'Université de Liège, 271
College Art Association, New York, 2451
College Board, New York, 2444
Collège d'Enseignement Technique Agricole, Sibiti, 611

Collège de France, 815
Collège d'Europe, Bruges, 278
College for Creative Studies, Detroit, 2744
College for Financial Planning, 2596
College for Inspection and Human Resource Management in Maritime Sciences, Split, 632
College for Music and Theatre Munchen, 958
College for Music Nurnberg, 958
College in Sládkovičovo, 2016
Collège International de Chirurgiens, 73
Collège International pour la Recherche en Productique, 68
College Library of the Transtibiscan Church District and Library of Theology, 1007
Collège Libre des Sciences Sociales et Economiques, Paris, 822
Collège Médical, Luxembourg, 1456
College of African Wildlife Management, Mweka, 2186
College of Agora, 632
College of Agricultural and Environmental Education Vienna, 210
College of Agriculture at Križevci, 632
College of Agriculture, Darkhan, 1534
College of Agriculture, Food and Rural Enterprise, Antrim, 2418
College of Agriculture, Science and Education, Port Antonio, 1239
College of Architects of Bolivia, 290
College of Architects of Peru, 1714
College of Architects of Venezuela, 3045
College of Arms, London, 2319
College of Banking and Financial Studies, 1670
College of Basic Education, Adailiya, 1416
College of Business Administration, 1967
College of Business Education, Dar es Salaam, 2186
College of Business Studies, Hawalli, 1416
College of Central Florida, 2627
College of Charleston, 2928
College of Coastal Georgia, 2638
College of Commerce, Hanoi, 3071
College of Computer Training, 1164
College of Dunaújváros, 1025
College of Economics, 3071
College of Economics and Administration—Plovdiv, 372
College of Economics and Business Administration, 3069
College of Economics and Business, La Libertad, 724
College of Estate Management, Reading, 2412
College of Europe, Bruges, 278
College of Fine Arts 'Ernesto de la Cárcova', 135
College of Forestry Engineers of Chile, 465
College of Geologists of Bolivia, 290
College of Health Sciences, Bahrain, 220
College of Health Sciences, Faiha, 1416
College of Honduran Architects, 995
College of Idaho, 2649
College of Industrial Technology, 3069
College of Information Technology, Zagreb, 632
College of Integrated Chinese Medicine, 2413
College of Islamic Studies, Malé, 1481
College of Journalism, Zagreb, 631
College of Law, Guildford, 2409
College of Law, St Leonards, 178
College of Law, Thuong Tin, 3071
College of Librarianship of Peru, 1714
College of Management in Trenčín/City University of Seattle, 2016
College of Medical and Dental Sciences, Birmingham, 2413
College of Medicine and Allied Health Sciences, Freetown, 1993
College of Medicine and Pharmacy, 3069
College of Medicine, Blantyre, 1468
College of Menominee Nation, 2999

Deccan College Postgraduate and Research Institute, 1101
DECHEMA Gesellschaft für Chemische Technik und Biotechnologie eV, 852
DeCordova Sculpture Park and Museum, 2526
Deen Dayal Upadhyay Gorakhpur University, 1057
Deeside College, 2433
Defence Academy, Ulan Bator, 1533
Defence Institute of Advanced Technology, Pune, 1101
Defence Research and Development Institute, 2211
Defence Science and Technology Laboratory (DSTL), Salisbury, 2310
Defence Science and Technology Organisation, Canberra, 149
Defence Science and Technology Organisation, Fishermens Bend, 149
Defence Services Academy, Mandalay, 1550
Defence Services Technological Academy, Mandalay, 1549
Defiance College, 2880
Deichmanske Bibliotek, 1651
Deir ez-Zor Museum, 2169
DeKalb County Public Library, 2484
Delaware Agricultural Museum & Village, Dover, 2515
Delaware Art Museum, Wilmington, 2515
Delaware County Library System, Media, 2502
Delaware Division of Libraries, 2481
Delaware History Museum, Wilmington, 2515
Delaware Museum of Natural History, 2515
Delaware Public Archives, 2481
Delaware State Police Museum, Dover, 2515
Delaware State University, 2612
Delaware Valley College, 2903
Delft Centre for Aviation, 1574
Delft Centre for Engineering Design, 1574
Delft Institute for Earth-Oriented Space Research, 1574
Delft Institute for Information Technology in Service Engineering, 1575
Delft Institute of Microsystems and Nanoelectronics (Dimes), 1575
Delft University of Technology, 1585
Delft University Research Centre of Intelligent Sensor Microsystems, 1575
Delft University Wind Energy Research Institute, 1575
Delhi Public Library, 1048
Delmon University for Science and Technology, Manama, 219
Delphi Public Library, 2486
Delray Beach Public Library, 2483
Delta Community Library, 2477
Delta State University, 2784
Dementia Services Development Centre, Stirling, 2304
Demeure Historique, Paris, 768
Democracy for Development, Prishtina, 1411
Democritus University of Thrace, 975
Demokraci për Zhvillim, 1411
Demonstrative Library Maria da Conceição Moreira Salles/National Library Foundation, 312
Demopolis Public Library, 2477
Den Frie Lærerskole, 686
Den Grønlandske Forfatterforening, 690
Den Norske Forfatterforening, 1648
Den Norske Historiske Forening, 1648
Denbighshire Libraries and Archives, 2327
Denison University, 2880
Denki Gakkai, 1248
Denmark-America Foundation, 673
Denmark's Accreditation Institution, 671
Dennis Gabor College, 1026
Dennos Museum Center, 2527
Denshi Joho Tsushin Gakkai, 1248

Dental Association of Bosnia and Herzegovina, 297
Dental Council, Dublin, 1158
Dentistry Canada Fund, 391
Denver Art Museum, 2513
Denver Museum of Nature and Science, 2513
Denver Public Library, 2480
Denver Seminary, 2597
Departamento Administrativo de Ciencia, Tecnología e Innovación (COLCIENCIAS), 592
Departamento Administrativo Nacional de Estadística, 593
Departamento de Estudios Etnográficos y Coloniales, Santa Fé, 122
Departamento de Estudios Históricos Navales, Buenos Aires, 120
Departamento de Filosofía del Instituto de Teología para Religiosos, Caracas, 3042
Departamento de Servicios Bibliotecarios, Documentación e Información de la Asamblea Legislativa, 614
Departamento Nacional da Produção Mineral, 311
Département d'Amélioration des Méthodes pour l'Innovation Scientifique (CIRAD-AMIS), Montpellier, 773
Département d'élevage et de Médecine Vétérinaire (CIRAD-EMVT), Montpellier, 773
Département de la Guadeloupe Archives Départementales, 827
Département de Philosophie de l'Institut Catholique de l'Afrique Centrale, 3042
Département de Recherches Agronomiques de la République Malgache, 1465
Département des Cultures Annuelles (CIRAD-CA), Montpellier, 773
Département des Cultures Pérennes (CIRAD-CP), Montpellier, 773
Département des Études de Population à l'Union Douanière et Économique de l'Afrique Centrale, Bangui, 460
Département des Territoires, Environnement et Acteurs (CIRAD-TERA), Montpellier, 773
Département Environnement Technologie et Société (DENTES), 789
Département Forestier (CIRAD-Forêt), Montpellier, 773
Département Métiers de l'Image et du Son (SATIS), 789
Department and Collections for the History of Medicine, 197
Department for Business, Innovation and Skills, London, 2276
Department for Children, Schools and Family Library, London, 2319
Department for Cooperation with Africa, Asia and Eastern Europe, Madrid, 2051
Department for Culture, Media and Sport, London, 2276
Department for Education and Culture, Mariehamn, 763
Department for Education and Skills, Cardiff, 2276
Department for Education, Manchester, 2276
Department for Education, Sport and Culture, St Helier, 2440
Department for Employment and Learning, Belfast, 2276
Department for Higher Education and Science Policy, Helsinki, 740
Department for Innovation and Curricular Development, Lisbon, 1814
Department für Botanik und Biodiversitätsforschung, 190
Department of Administration of Science, Technology and Innovation, Bogotá, 592
Department of Agricultural Research, Maseru, 1437

Department of Agricultural Sciences of the National Academy of Sciences of Belarus, 247
Department of Agriculture, Kuala Lumpur, 1471
Department of Alternative Energy Development and Efficiency, Bangkok, 2188
Department of Antiquities and Museums, Safat, 1415
Department of Antiquities, Shahat (Cyrene), 1442
Department of Antiquities, Tripoli, 1442
Department of Archaeology and Museums, Islamabad, 1673
Department of Archives, Nassau, 217
Department of Archives, St James, 245
Department of Art Research and Inventory of the Federal Office for the Protection of Monuments, Vienna, 190
Department of Arts and Culture, Pretoria, 2026
Department of Arts, Heritage and the Gaeltacht, 1156
Department of Atomic Energy, Yangon, 1545
Department of Biogenic Amines of Polish Academy of Sciences, 1764
Department of Biological Sciences of the National Academy of Sciences of Belarus, 248
Department of Bitola, 1460
Department of Botany and Biodiversity Research, Vienna, 190
Department of Chamorro Affairs, Hagatna, 3012
Department of Chemistry and Earth Sciences of the National Academy of Sciences of Belarus, 248
Department of Culture and Tourism, Malabo, 726
Department of Culture, Arts and Leisure, Belfast, 2276
Department of Culture, Women Affairs and Citizenship, Nouméa, 829
Department of Earth and Atmospheric Sciences Museum, University of Alberta, 395
Department of Education, 1597
Department of Education and Children, Douglas, 2438
Department of Education and Skills, Dublin, 1156
Department of Education, Bangor, 2276
Department of Education, Canberra, 141
Department of Education, Culture and Sports, Oranjestad, 1597
Department of Education, Palikir, 1522
Department of Education, Pasig City, 1732
Department of Education, St Thomas, 3022
Department of Education, San Juan, 3014
Department of Education, Waigani, 1706
Department of Education, Washington, 2442
Department of Embryology, Baltimore, 2470
Department of Environmental Protection, Bermuda, 2434
Department of Ethnographical and Colonial Studies, 122
Department of Ethnography and Folk Art Orăştie, 1850
Department of Geological Survey, Lusaka, 3075
Department of Geology of the Ministry for Popular Power of Petroleum and Mining, Caracas, 3048
Department of Global Ecology, Stanford, 2470
Department of Health Library, London, 2319
Department of Higher Education and Recognition of Diplomas, Tiranë, 95
Department of Higher Education and Training, 2026
Department of Higher Education Institution Accreditation, 1523

Department of Higher Education, New Delhi, 1033
Department of Higher Education, Research, Science and Technology, 1706
Department of Humanitarian Sciences and Arts of the National Academy of Sciences of Belarus, 247
Department of International Development, London, 2300
Department of Kumanovo, 1460
Department of Libraries, Archives and Documentation Services, Kingstown, 1958
Department of Library, Documentation and Information of the Legislative Assembly, 614
Department of Medical Research (Lower Myanmar), Yangon, 1545
Department of Medical Sciences of the National Academy of Sciences of Belarus, 248
Department of Metallurgy, Harare, 3079
Department of Meteorology, Colombo, 2093
Department of Methodology, London, 2309
Department of Mineral Resources, Bangkok, 2188
Department of National Archives, Colombo, 2094
Department of Naval History Studies, Buenos Aires, 120
Department of Occupational Standards, Thimphu, 287
Department of Ohrid, 1460
Department of Physical and Engineering Sciences of the National Academy of Sciences of Belarus, 248
Department of Physics, Mathematics and Informatics of the National Academy of Sciences of Belarus, 248
Department of Planning & Infrastructure, Sydney, 147
Department of Planning & Natural Resources, St Thomas, 3022
Department of Plant Biology, Stanford, 2470
Department of Plant Protection, Karachi, 1676
Department of Prilep, 1460
Department of Prints and Drawings, Zagreb, 627
Department of Public Libraries, Dhaka, 225
Department of Quality Control in Education of the Ministry of Education, 247
Department of Records and Information Services, New York, 2498
Department of Religious Affairs, Yangon, 1545
Department of Research and Specialist Services, Harare, 3078
Department of Science and Technology, Taguig City, 1732
Department of Science Service, Bangkok, 2188
Department of Skopje, 1460
Department of Sports, Parks & Recreation, St Thomas, 3022
Department of Statistics, 1361
Department of Statistics and Censuses, San Salvador, 720
Department of Stip, 1460
Department of Strumica, 1461
Department of Terrestrial Magnetism, Washington, 2470
Department of Tetovo, 1461
Department of the Art and Museum Book Collections of the State Russian Museum, 1907
Department of the Treasury Library, Washington, 2482
Department of Tourism, Arts and Culture, 1706
Department of Veles, 1461
Department of Veterans Affairs, Headquarters Library, Washington, 2482

Don Bosco Catholic University, Campo Grande, 322
Don Bosco University, San Salvador, 722
Don Juan Institute of Valencia, 2066
Don Mariano Marcos Memorial State University, Bacnotan, 1739
Don State Agrarian University, 1914
Don State Technical University, Rostov-on-Don, 1937
Don Zonal Research and Development Institute of Agriculture, 1884
Donald F. and Mildred Topp Othmer Library of Chemical History, Philadelphia, 2502
Donald W. Reynolds Library, 2478
Doñana Biological Station, 2057
Donau Rektoren Konferenz, 62
Donbass State Academy of Civil Engineering and Architecture, 2267
Donbass State Engineering Academy, 2267
Donbass State Technical University, Alchevsk, 2263
Doncaster College, 2410
Doncaster Museum and Art Gallery, 2330
Donders Institute for Brain, Cognition and Behaviour, 1571
Donetsk Art Museum, 2254
Donetsk Botanical Gardens, 2255
Donetsk Institute for Physics and Engineering 'O. O. Galkin', 2252
Donetsk Musical-Pedagogical Institute, 2268
Donetsk National Technical University, 2264
Donetsk National University, 2257
Donetsk National University of Economics and Trade 'M. Tuhan-Baranovskiy', Donetsk, 2257
Donetsk Scientific Research Institute of Traumatology and Orthopaedics, 2250
Dong Nai College of Decorative Arts, Hanoi, 3071
Dong Yang University, 1398
Dong-a University, 1397
Dongbei University of Finance and Economics, 513
Dongbu Library, 1388
Dongduk Women's University, 1398
Dong-Eui University, 1398
Dong-Eui University Central Library, 1388
Dongguk University, 1398
Dongguk University Library, 1389
Donghua University, 513
Dongseo University, 1398
Dongshin University, 1398
Donnelly College, 2684
Donner Institute for Research in Religious and Cultural History, 747
Door County Maritime Museum, 2546
Dordrechts Museum, 1581
Dordt College, 2680
Dorodnicyn Computing Centre of the Russian Academy of Sciences (CC RAS), 1900
Dorset College, 1164
Dorset County Libraries, 2316
Dorset County Museum, 2330
Dorset Historical Society, 2544
Dortmund Museum of Art and Cultural History, 875
Doshisha University, 1334
Doshisha Women's College of Liberal Arts, 1334
Dostoevsky, F. M., Museum, Moscow, 1909
Dostoevsky Memorial Museum, St Petersburg, 1912
Douglas County Libraries, 2480
Dove Cottage and the Wordsworth Museum, 2331
Dover Public Library, Dover, 2481, 2495
Dow University of Health Sciences, 1682
Dowling College, 2834
Downing College, Cambridge, 2358
Downing College: the Maitland Robinson Library, 2313
Dozenal Society of America, 2460
Dr Andrés Bello University, 722

Dr B. R. Ambedkar Centre for Biomedical Research (ACBR), 1091
Dr B. R. Ambedkar National Institute of Technology, 1101
Dr B. R. Ambedkar Open University, 1058
Dr B. R. Ambedkar University, 1059
Dr Babasaheb Ambedkar Marathwada University, 1058
Dr Babasaheb Ambedkar Open University, 1058
Dr Babasaheb Ambedkar Technological University, 1058
Dr Balasaheb Sawant Konkan Agricultural University, 1058
Dr Balasaheb Sawant Konkan Krishi Vidyapeeth, 1058
Dr Bhau Daji Lad Mumbai City Museum, Mumbai, 1050
Dr Cecil Cyrus Museum, Kingstown, 1958
Dr Dimitrie Nanu Medical Documentation Library, 1845
Dr Enrique P. Fidanza Library of Leprosy, 122
Dr Francisco Cambournac Centre for the Study of Vectors and Infectious Diseases, 1819
Dr Francisco P. Moreno Museum of Patagonia, 124
Dr Gaspar Rodríguez Museum of France, 1710
Dr Harisingh Gour University, 1059
Dr Harisingh Gour Vishwavidyalaya, 1059
Dr Joaquín Menéndez Municipal Public Library, 123
'Dr José Evaristo Uriburu' Numismatics Museum, 124
Dr José Gustavo Guerrero Library, 720
'Dr José Matías Delgado' University, 722
Dr Juan Alvarez Argentine Library of the Municipality of Rosario, 123
Dr Julio Marc Provincial History Museum of Rosario, 124
Dr Karl Kummer Institut für Sozialreform, Sozial- und Wirtschaftspolitik, 189
Dr Luis Alonso Aparicio Pedagogical University of El Salvador, 723
'Dr Luis E. Betetta' Allergy Research Institute, 1716
Dr M. G. R. University, 1101
Dr Mahmud Husain Library, 1678
'Dr Manuel Antonio Sánchez Carvajal' Library, 3049
Dr Martin Luther King, Jr, Library, 2479
Dr N. T. R. University of Health Sciences, Andhra Pradesh, 1059
Dr Panjabrao Deshmukh Agricultural University, 1059
Dr Panjabrao Deshmukh Krishi Vidyapeeth, 1059
Dr Pilar Barbosa Bayamón Municipal Library, 3015
Dr Ram Manohar Lohia Avadh University, 1059
Dr Raziuddin Siddiqi Memorial Library, 1678
Dr Remeis-Sternwarte Bamberg, 861
Dr Sarvepalli Radhakrishnan Rajasthan Ayurveda University, 1060
Dr Soliman Fakeeh College for Nursing and Medical Science, 1967
Dr Sun Yat-Sen Library, Taipei, 2174
Dr Sun Yat-Sen Museum, 580
Dr Williams's Library, London, 2319
Dr Yahia Farès de Médéa University, 105
Dr Yashwant Singh Parmar University of Horticulture & Forestry, 1060
Dragan European University of Lugoj, 1863
Drake University, 2680
Drama School attached to the E. B. Vakhtangov State Theatre 'B. V. Shchukin', 1953
Drama School attached to the Maly Theatre 'M. S. Shchepkin', 1953
Drammen Library, 1651

Drammens Museum–Fylkesmuseum for Buskerud, 1652
Drammensbiblioteket, 1651
Dravidian University, Kuppam, 1058
Drenthe Archive, 1577
Drents Archief, 1577
Drents Museum, Assen, 1580
Dresden City Museum, 875
Dresden Museum of Zoology, 875
Dresden Public Libraries, 866
Drew University, Madison, 2808
Drexel University, 2903
Driestar Hogeschool, 1591
Dronning Mauds Minne Høgskolen, 1664
Druk Gyyelzin Tshula Lopdhey, 288
Drum Barracks Civil War Museum, 2512
Drury University, 2788
Drustva sudija Srbije, 1971
Društvo Arhivskih Radnika Bosne i Hercegovine, 297
Društvo Bibliotekara BiH, 297
Društvo Fizičara u BiH, 297
Društvo Istoričara BiH, 297
Društvo Ljekara BiH, 297
Društvo Matematičara Republike Srpske, 297
Društvo matematikov, fizikov in astronomov Slovenije, 2018
Društvo na Fizičarite na Republika Makedonija, 1459
Društvo na Likovnite Umetnici na Makedonija, 1459
Društvo na Literaturnite Preveduvači na Makedonija, 1459
Društvo na Muzejskite Rabotnici na Makedonija, 1459
Društvo na Pisatelite na Makedonija, 1459
Društvo Pisaca BiH, 297
Društvo Psihologa BiH, 297
Društvo Psihologa Republike Srpske, 297
Društvo slovenskih skladateljev, 2017
Društvo Urbanista Bosne i Hercegovine, 297
Društvo za Proučavanje i Unapredenje Pomorstva, 623
Društvo za Srpski Jezik i Književnost, 1972
Družbenomedicinski inštitut ZRC SAZU, 2019
Dryden Flight Research Center, Edwards, 2476
Državen Arhiv na Republika Makedonija, 1460
Državni arhiv Crne Gore, 1536
Državni hidrometeorološki zavod, 625
Državni univerzitet u Novom Pazaru, 1975
Državni zavod za zaštitu prirode, 625
Državniot Univerzitet vo Tetovo, 1461
DTU Aqua–National Institute of Aquatic Resources, Charlottenlund, 677
DTU Fødevareinstituttet, 675
DTU Veterinærinstituttet, 676
Dubai Aerospace Enterprise Flight Academy, 2273
Dubai Medical College for Girls, 2273
Dubai Municipality Public Libraries, 2271
Dubai Pharmacy College, 2273
Dubai Police Academy, 2273
Dubai School of Government, 2273
Dublin Business School, 1164
Dublin City Gallery the Hugh Lane, 1160
Dublin City Public Libraries and Archive, 1159
Dublin City University, 1161
Dublin Institute for Advanced Studies, 1164
Dublin Institute of Technology, 1163
Dublin University Biological Association, 1158
Dublin Writers Museum, 1160
Dublin Zoo, 1158
Dubnica Technology Institute in Dubnica nad Váhom, 2016
Dubnický Technologický Inštitút v Dubnici nad Váhom, 2016
Dubrovacki muzeji, 626

Dubrovnik International University, 628
Dubrovnik Museums, 626
Dubuque Museum of Art, 2522
Duchesne College, 179
Duke University, 2856
Duke University Library, 2499
Duksung Women's University, 1398
Duluth Public Library, 2493
Dulwich Picture Gallery, 2333
Dumbarton Oaks Research Library and Collection, Washington, 2482
Dumfries Museums, 2330
Dumlupınar Üniversitesi, 2220
Dun Laoghaire Institute of Art, Design and Technology, 1164
Duna Múzeum, 1009
Dunaújvárosi Főiskola, 1025
Duncan Public Library, 2501
Dundalk Institute of Technology, 1164
Dundee Libraries, 2316
Dundo Museum, 113
Dundurn Castle, Hamilton, 396
Dunedin Public Art Gallery, 1607
Dunedin Public Libraries, 1606
Dunkers Kulturhus, 2116
Dunklin County Library, 2494
Dunn-Seiler Geology Museum, 2529
Dunwoody College of Technology, 2768
Duquesne University, 2904
Durban Botanic Gardens, 2030
Durban Natural Science Museum, 2032
Durban University of Technology, 2035
Durham County Libraries, 2316
Durham Public Library, 2496
Durham University Library, 2316
Durmishidze Institute of Plant Biochemistry, 838
Durrës Public Library, 97
Duryu Public Library, 1388
Dutch Association for Aesthetics, 1563
Dutch Culture Historical Institute, 2027
Dutch Heritage Museum, 992
Dutch House of Representatives; Library Department and Documentation Department, 1579
Dutch Institute of Agricultural History, 1566
Dutch Museum, 2094
Dutch Mycological Society, 1563
Dutch National Research School Combination Catalysis Controlled by Chemical Design (NRSC-Catalysis), 1575
Dutch Naval Museum, 1581
Dutch Ornithological Union, 1563
Dutch Society for Philosophy of Science, 1563
Dutch Society of Educational Psychologists, 1560
Dutch Tile Museum, 1582
Duy Tan University, 3065
'Dvir Bialik' Municipal Central Public Library, 1174
Dwight D. Eisenhower Presidential Library and Museum, 2487
Dwight Foster Public Library, 2508
Dyal Singh Trust Library, 1679
Dzanelidze, A. I., Geological Institute, 839
Džemal Bijedić University of Mostar, 300
Dzhambul University, 1368

E

Eafit University, 601
'Eagle' Heraldry and Genealogy Society, 185
Eagle Public Library, 2485
Ealing Libraries, 2319
Earlham College, 2670
Early Childhood Research Centre, London, 2298
Early Christian Art Museum—Christian and Jewish Lapidaries, Vatican City, 3038
Early English Text Society, Oxford, 2287
Earth and Mineral Sciences Museum and Art Gallery, University Park, 2539

Ekaterinburg Region Institute of Dermatology and Venereal Diseases, 1889

Ekaterinburg State Theatrical Institute, 1953

Ekaterinburg Viral Infections Research Institute, 1889

Ekonomická Univerzita v Bratislave, 2007

Ekonomický Ústav SAV, Bratislava, 2003

Ekonomikas un Kulturas Augstskola, Riga, 1430

Ekonomiska Forskningsinstitutet, 2111

Ekonomiska Samfundet i Finland, 742

Ekonomisk-Historiska föreningen i Finland, Helsinki, 742

Ekonomski Institut Sarajevo, 298

Ekonomski Institut Tuzla, 298

Ekonomski Institut—Skopje Univerzitet Sv. Kiril i Metodij, 1459

El Colegio de México, 1503

El Domínico–Americano, 699

El Greco Museum, 2068

El Hassan Library and Media Centre, Princess Sumaya University for Technology, Amman, 1358

El Museo del Barrio, 2534

El Oued University, 104

El Paso Museum of Art, 2543

El Rito Library, 2497

El Tarf University, 104

Elam School of Fine Arts, Auckland, 1614

Elbasan Public Library, 97

Elda Vaccari Collection of Multicultural Studies, 147

El-Dalang University, 2100

El-Djazairia el-Mossilia, Algiers, 101

Eldoret Polytechnic, 1380

Eleanor D. Wilson Museum, 2544

Electoral Reform Society, 2281

Electric Power Research Centre, Tehran, 1134

Electricity and Renewable Energy Museum, Jakarta, 1114

Electricity and Water Institute, Daiyah, 1416

Electricity Museum, Encamp, 112

Electrochemical Society of India, 1038

Electrochemical Society, Pennington, 2461

Electronic Control Machines Research Institute, Moscow, 1900

Electronic Equipment and Machine Studies Science, Technology and Production Corporation, Ulan Bator, 1531

Electronics and Telecommunications Research Institute (ETRI), Daejeon, 1388

Electronics Research and Service Organization, Hsinchu, 2173

Electrotechnical Institute, Warsaw, 1768

Elektronikas un Datorzinātņu Institūts, Riga, 1428

Elektrotechnický Ústav SAV, 2005

Elektroteknisk Forening, Odense, 675

Elets State University 'I. A. Bunin', 1919

El-Gadarif University, 2100

Eliashvili Institute of Control Systems, Tbilisi, 839

Eliezer Ben-Yehudah Research Centre for History of Hebrew, 1170

Eliisa Vainikka, 741

El-Imam El-Mahdi University, 2101

Elinkeinoelämän Tutkimuslaitos (ETLA), Helsinki, 747

Elintarviketieteiden Seura ry, 741

Elintarviketurvallisuusvirsato—Evira, 746

Eliyava Institute of Bacteriophage, Microbiology and Virology, Tbilisi, 838

Elizabeth City State University, 2863

Elizabeth Sturm Library, 2495

Elizabeth University of Music, Hiroshima, 1356

Elizabethan House Museum, Great Yarmouth, 2336

Elizabethtown College, 2904

Elko-Lander-Eureka County Library System, 2495

Ella Sharp Museum of Art and History, 2528

Ellen Noël Art Museum of the Permian Basin, 2543

Elliniki Epitropi Atomikis Energhias, 969

Elliniki Mathimatiki Eteria, 968

Elliniko Anoikto Panepistimio, 975

Elmer E. Rasmuson and BioSciences Libraries, 2477

Elmhurst College, 2652

Elmira College, 2834

Elms College, 2714

Elon University, 2859

Els Esquirols Cultural and Arts Association, 111

'Elvira Cape' Provincial Library, 637

Emakeele Selts, 729

Emanuel Ringelblum Jewish Historical Institute, 1767

Emanuel University of Oradea, 1863

Embrapa Acre, 308

Embrapa Agrobiologia, 308

Embrapa Agroindústria de Alimentos, 308

Embrapa Agroindústria Tropical, 308

Embrapa Agropecuária do Oeste, 308

Embrapa Algodão, 308

Embrapa Amapá, 308

Embrapa Amazônia Ocidental, 308

Embrapa Amazônia Oriental, 309

Embrapa Arroz e Feijão, 309

Embrapa Caprinos e Ovinos, 309

Embrapa Cerrados, 309

Embrapa Clima Temperado, 309

Embrapa Florestas, 309

Embrapa Gado de Corte, 309

Embrapa Gado de Leite, 309

Embrapa Hortaliças, 309

Embrapa Informática Agropecuária, 309

Embrapa Instrumentação, 309

Embrapa Mandioca e Fruticultura, 309

Embrapa Meio Ambiente, 309

Embrapa Meio-Norte, 309

Embrapa Milho e Sorgo, 309

Embrapa Monitoramento por Satélite, Campinas, 309

Embrapa Pantanal, 309

Embrapa Pecuária Sudeste, 309

Embrapa Pecuária Sul, 309

Embrapa Recursos Genéticos e Biotecnologia, 309

Embrapa Rondônia, 309

Embrapa Roraima, 309

Embrapa Semi-Árido, 309

Embrapa Soja, 309

Embrapa Solos, 309

Embrapa Suínos e Aves, 309

Embrapa Tabuleiros Costeiros, 309

Embrapa Trigo, 309

Embrapa Uva e Vinho, 309

Embry-Riddle Aeronautical University, 2627

Embry-Riddle Aeronautical University—Worldwide, 2627

Emerson College, 2714

EMGO+ Institute for Health and Care Research, 1570

'Emil Racoviţă' Institute of Speleology of Romanian Academy, 1842

Emiliano Zapata Technological University of Estado de Morelos, 1512

Emilio A. Caraffa Provincial Museum of Fine Arts, 124

Emilio Cardenas University, 1508

Emily Dickinson Museum, 2526

Emirates Academy of Hospitality Management, 2273

Emirates Aviation College—Aerospace and Academic Studies, 2273

Emirates College for Management and Information Technology, 2273

Emirates College of Advanced Education, 2273

Emirates College of Technology, 2273

Emirates Institute for Banking and Financial Studies, 2273

EMLYON Business School, 821

Emmanuel Christian Seminary, 2935

Emmanuel College, Boston, 2715

Emmanuel College, Cambridge, 2358

Emmanuel College, Franklin Springs, 2639

Emmanuel College Library, Cambridge, 2313

Emmanuel College, Toronto, 449

Emmaus Bible College, 2680

Emory & Henry College, 2976

Emory University, 2639

Emporia State University, 2684

Empresa Brasileira de Pesquisa Agropecuária (EMBRAPA), 308

Enam Medical College, 243

Encamp Community Library, 112

Encarnación Valdés Library, 3015

Endeavour College of Natural Health, Brisbane, 179

Endicott College, 2715

Endocrinology Research Centre, Moscow, 1889

Energiagazdálkodási Tudományos Egyesület, Budapest, 1001

Energieonderzoek Centrum Nederland (ECN), 1575

Energiewirtschaftliches Institut an der Universität zu Köln, 857

Energy and Resources Laboratories, Hsinchu, 2173

Energy Institute, London, 2295

Energy Research Centre of the Netherlands (ECN), 1575

Energy Systems Institute, Irkutsk, 1900

Enfield Libraries, 2319

Engei Gakkai, 1241

Engelhardt Institute of Molecular Biology, Moscow, 1893

Engineering and Physical Sciences Research Council, Swindon, 2306

Engineering Council UK, London, 2295

Engineering Innovation Institute, Hull, 2310

Engineering Institute of Canada, 390

Engineering Institution of Zambia, 3074

Engineering Research Institute, Tokyo, 1251

Engineering Society in Finland, 746

Engineers' Association of Venezuela, 3047

Engineers Ireland, 1158

English Academy of Southern Africa, 2028

English Association, Leicester, 2287

English Association Sydney Inc., 144

English Centre of International PEN, 2287

English Folk Dance and Song Society, 2283

English Language and Applied Linguistics Postgraduate Centre, Birmingham, 2303

English Language Teaching Institute, Riyadh, 1967

English Place-Name Society, 2285

English Speaking Board, 2287

English Speaking Union of Sri Lanka, 2092

English-Speaking Union (of the Commonwealth), London, 2278

English-Speaking Union of the United States, 2446

Eni Corporate University—Scuola Enrico Mattei, 1231

ENIC Russia, Moscow, 1879

ENIC/NARIC Albania, 95

ENIC/NARIC Andorra, 111

ENIC/NARIC Armenia, 136

ENIC-NARIC Austria, 183

ENIC/NARIC Azerbaijan, Baku, 211

ENIC/NARIC Belarus, 247

ENIC/NARIC Bosnia and Herzegovina, Sarajevo, 296

ENIC/NARIC Bulgaria, 354

ENIC/NARIC Croatia, 623

ENIC/NARIC Czech Republic, 651

ENIC/NARIC Estonia, 728

ENIC/NARIC Finland, 740

ENIC/NARIC France, 766

ENIC/NARIC Georgia, 837

ENIC/NARIC Germany, 844

ENIC/NARIC Holy See, 3037

ENIC/NARIC Hungary, 998

ENIC/NARIC Iceland, 1028

ENIC/NARIC Ireland, 1156

ENIC/NARIC Israel, 1166

ENIC/NARIC Liechtenstein, 1444

ENIC/NARIC Luxembourg, 1456

ENIC/NARIC Macedonia, 1458

ENIC/NARIC Malta, 1484

ENIC/NARIC Moldova, 1523

ENIC/NARIC Monaco, 1528

ENIC/NARIC Montenegro, 1535

ENIC/NARIC Netherlands, 1559

ENIC/NARIC New Zealand, 1602

ENIC/NARIC Norway, Oslo, 1647

ENIC-NARIC of the Federation Wallonia-Brussels (Belgium), 258

ENIC/NARIC Poland, 1751

ENIC/NARIC Portugal, 1814

ENIC/NARIC Romania, 1835

ENIC/NARIC San Marino, 1960

ENIC/NARIC Serbia, 1971

ENIC/NARIC Slovakia, 2000

ENIC–NARIC Slovenia, 2017

ENIC/NARIC Sweden, 2107

ENIC/NARIC Turkey, 2210

ENIC/NARIC Ukraine, 2247

ENIC/NARIC United Kingdom, 2276

ENIC/NARIC United States of America, 2443

ENILIA-ENSMIC, Lycée de l'Alimentation, Paris, 818

Enoch Pratt Free Library, Baltimore, 2490

Enosi Ellinon Vivliothikonomon kai Epistimon Pliroforisis (EEBEP), Athens, 968

Enosis Ellinon Chimikon, 968

Enosis Hellinon Mousourgon, 968

Enrique Larreta Museum of Spanish Art, 123

Enrique Udaondo Museographic Complex, 124

Ente Nazionale Italiano di Unificazione (UNI), 1193

Entebbe Botanical Gardens, 2243

Enterprise Public Library, 2477

Entomological Society of America, 2459

Entomological Society of Canada, 389

Entomological Society of China, 482

Entomological Society of Finland, 744

Entomological Society of Israel, 1168

Entomological Society of Japan, 1246

Entomological Society of Moldova, 1524

Entomological Society of New South Wales Inc., 145

Entomological Society of New Zealand, 1604

Entomological Society of Nigeria, 1624

Entomological Society of Peru, 1715

Entomological Society of Queensland, 145

Entomology Museum of León, 1616

Entrepreneurship and Small Business Research Institute, 2111

Enugu State Library Board, Enugu, 1626

Enugu State University of Science and Technology, 1641

Enumclaw Public Library, 2507

Environment Agency Austria, Vienna, 191

Environment and Earth Sciences Centre, Lisbon, 1817

Environment Unit, Port Vila, 3036

Environmental Mutagen Society, Reston, 2459

Environmental Protection UK, 2295

Environmental Research Institute, 283

Environmental Sciences Research Institute, Coleraine, 2308

Eötvös József College, 1025

Eötvös József Főiskola, 1025

Eötvös Loránd Fizikai Társulat, 1000

Eötvös Loránd Tudományegyetem, 1015

Eötvös Loránd Tudományegyetem Egyetemi Könyvtár, 1005

Eötvös Loránd University, 1015

EPA National Library Network, Washington, 2482

EPF—Ecole d'Ingénieurs, Sceaux, 823

Epifânio Dória Public Library, 312

Epimelitirion Ikastikon Technon Ellados, 968

Episcopal Divinity School, 2715

Episcopal Museum of Vic, 2069

Episcopal Theological College of Pécs, 1026

Épitéstudományi Egyesület, Budapest, 999

Eppley Institute for Research in Cancer and Allied Diseases, 2468

Eranos Vindobonensis, 185

ERASMUS (European Community Action Scheme for the Mobility of University Students), 63

Erasmus Universiteit Rotterdam, 1584

Erasmus University, 1584

Erasmus University College, Brussels, 279

Erasmushogeschool-Brussel, 279

Erciyes Üniversitesi, 2220

Eretz-Israel Museum, Tel-Aviv, 1175

Erfgoed Delft en Omstreken, 1577

Erfgoedbibliotheek Hendrik Conscience, 266

Erfgoedvereniging Heemschut, Amsterdam, 1560

Erhvervsakademi Arhus, 686

Erhvervsakademi Dania, 686

Erhvervsakademi Kolding, 686

Erhvervsakademiet Lillebælt, 686

Erhvervsarkivet Statens Erhvervshistoriske Arkiv, 677

Erich Schmid Institute of Solid Material Sciences, Leoben, 192

Erich-Schmid-Institut für Materialwissenschaft, Leoben, 192

Erindale College, Mississauga, 449

Erkel Ferenc Múzeum, 1009

Ernest Hemingway Museum, 637

Ernesto Peltzer Library of Central Bank of Venezuela, 3049

Ernst-Moritz-Arndt-Universität Greifswald, 890

Ershov, A. P., Institute of Informatics Systems, Novosibirsk, 1900

Erskine College, 2928

Ersman Hygiene Research Institute, 1889

Ersta Sköndal Högskola, 2133

Ersta Sköndal University College, 2133

Erzbischöfliche Diözesan- und Dombibliothek mit Bibliothek St Albertus Magnus, 865

Erzbischöfliches Dom- und Diözesanmuseum, Vienna, 197

ESADE (Escuela Superior de Administración y Dirección de Empresas), Barcelona, 2089

Esbjerg Kommunes Biblioteker, 678

Esbjerg Public Library, 678

ESC Bordeaux, 821

ESC Bretagne Brest, 821

ESC Pau—Groupe Ecole Supérieure de Commerce de Pau, 821

Escaldes-Engordany Arts Centre, 112

Escaldes-Engordany Community Library, 112

ESCEM—Groupe Ecole Supérieure de Commerce et de Management, 821

Escher in Het Paleis, 1583

Escher in the Palace, the Hague, 1583

Escola Náutica Infante D. Henrique, 1830

Escola Superior Agrária de Elvas (ESAE), 1831

Escola Superior Artística do Porto, 1832

Escola Superior de Actividades Imobiliárias, 1830

Escola Superior de Belas-Artes, Oporto, 1832

Escola Superior de Communicação Social, Lisbon, 1831

Escola Superior de Dança, Lisbon, 1831

Escola Superior de Educação (ESE), Portalegre, 1831

Escola Superior de Educação, Lisbon, 1831

Escola Superior de Enfermagem da Cruz Vermelha Portuguesa de Oliveira de Azeméis, 1830

Escola Superior de Enfermagem de Coimbra, 1830

Escola Superior de Enfermagem de Lisboa, 1830

Escola Superior de Hotelaria e Turismo do Estoril, 1830

Escola Superior de Música, Lisbon, 1831

Escola Superior de Saúde de Portalegre, Portalegre, 1831

Escola Superior de Saúde Egas Moniz, 1830

Escola Superior de Teatro e Cinema, Lisbon, 1831

Escola Superior de Tecnologia da Saúde de Coimbra, 1830

Escola Superior de Tecnologia da Saúde de Lisboa (ESTeSL), 1831

Escola Superior de Tecnologia da Saúde do Porto, 1830

Escola Superior de Tecnologia e Gestão (ESTG), Portalegre, 1831

Escola Superior Enfermagem S. José de Cluny, 1830

Escola Superior Gallaecia, 1830

Escola Universitária das Artes de Coimbra, 1832

Escola Universitária Vasco da Gama, 1830

ESCP Europe Business School Berlin, 956

ESCP Europe Wirtschaftshochschule Berlin, 956

ESCP-EAP European School of Management, 821

Escuela Agrícola Panamericana Zamorano, 997

Escuela Andaluza de Salud Pública, 2089

Escuela de Artes Plásticas de Puerto Rico, 3021

Escuela de Aviación Militar, Maracay, 3058

Escuela de Comunicación Mónica Herrera, 724

Escuela de Danzas 'aída V. Mastrazzi', Buenos Aires, 135

Escuela de Folklore de San Miguelito, 1705

Escuela de Guerra del Ejército, 2090

Escuela de Guerra Naval, Montevideo, 3028

Escuela de Optometría, Bayamon, 3021

Escuela de Sanidad 'Dr José Scosería', 3028

Escuela Española de Historia y Arqueología, CSIC Roma, 1198

Escuela Especializada en Ingeniería ITCA-FEPADE, 724

Escuela Internacional de Agricultura y Ganadería, 1620

Escuela Libre de Derecho Universidad, 617

Escuela Militar de Aeronáutica, 3028

Escuela Multidisciplinaria de Arte Dramático 'Margarita Xirgú' (EMAD), 3028

Escuela Nacional de Agricultura 'Roberto Quiñónez', 724

Escuela Nacional de Arte Dramático, Buenos Aires, 135

Escuela Nacional de Arte Lírico, 3028

Escuela Nacional de Artes Plásticas 'Rafael Rodríguez Padilla', 987

Escuela Nacional de Bellas Artes 'Prilidiano Pueyrredón', Buenos Aires, 135

Escuela Nacional de Ciencias Forestales (ESNACIFOR), 997

Escuela Nacional de Danza, Montevideo, 3028

Escuela Nacional de Danzas, Panamá, 1705

Escuela Nacional de Medicina del Trabajo, 2061

Escuela Nacional de Policía, Montevideo, 3028

Escuela Nacional de Teatro, Panamá, 1705

Escuela Nacional Superior Autónoma de Bellas Artes del Perú, 1730

Escuela Nacional Superior de Folklore 'José María Arguedas', 1730

Escuela Naval, Montevideo, 3028

Escuela Politécnica del Ejercito, 709

Escuela Politécnica Nacional, Quito, 709

Escuela Superior Autónoma de Bellas Artes 'Diego Quispe Tito' de Cusco, 1730

Escuela Superior de Arte Dramático de Murcia, 2090

Escuela Superior de Arte 'Neptali Rincón', 3060

Escuela Superior de Bellas Artes de San Carlos, 2090

Escuela Superior de Bellas Artes 'Ernesto de la Cárcova', Buenos Aires, 135

Escuela Superior de Bellas Artes 'Hernando Siles', 295

Escuela Superior de Economía y Negocios—ESEN, 724

Escuela Superior de Formación Artística 'Gudelia Alarco de Vargas', 1730

Escuela Superior de Formación Artística Pública 'Condorcunca', 1731

Escuela Superior de Formación Artística Pública 'José Maria Valle Riestra', 1731

Escuela Superior de Gestión Comercial y Marketing (ESIC), 2059

Escuela Superior de Música Reina Sofía, 2090

Escuela Superior Politécnica Agropecuaria de Manabí, 709

Escuela Superior Politécnica de Chimborazo, 709

Escuela Superior Politécnica del Litoral, 709

Escuela Superior Pública de Arte Carlos Baca Flor, 1731

Escuela Universitaria Centro de Diseño Industrial, 3028

Escuelas Católicas, 2055

ESEADE University Institute, 135

ESIDEC—Ecole Supérieure Internationale de Commerce de Metz, 821

Esie Museum, 1627

ESIEE Paris, Noisy-le-Grand, 823

Esigodini Agricultural Institute, 3081

Esitpa—Ecole d'Ingénieurs en Agriculture, Val de Reuil, 821

Eskilstuna Municipal Library, 2113

Eskilstuna stads bibliotek, 2113

Eskişehir Arkeoloji Müzesi, 2214

Eskitis Institute for Cell and Molecular Therapies, 147

ESME Sudria, 823

Espace Maritime et Portuaire du Havre, 783

Española Public Library, 2497

Espeland Marine Biological Station, 1650

ESPEME Nice, 820

Espéranto-Jeunes (JEFO), 769

Espoo City Library/Regional Central Library, 748

ESS Jean Piaget, 1831

ESSEC Business School, 1999

Essener Kolleg für Geschlechterforschung, 937

Essex Biomedical Sciences Institute, 2304

Essex County Council Libraries, 2315

Estação Agronómica Nacional, 1818

Estación Biológica de los Llanos, 3048

Estación de Investigaciones Marinas (EDIMAR), Isla de Margarita, 3048

Estación Experimental Agro-Industrial 'Obispo Colombres', 120

Estación Experimental Táchira, Rubio, 3048

Estación Experimental Vista Florida, 1715

Estación Hidrobiológica de Puerto Quequén, 121

Estanislao S. Zeballos Public Library, 123

Esterházy Castle Museum—Fertőd, 1009

Esterházy-Kastély Fertőd, 1009

Estonian Academy of Arts, 731

Estonian Academy of Music and Theatre, 731

Estonian Academy of Sciences, 728

Estonian Academy of Security Sciences, 734

Estonian Aviation Academy, 734

Estonian Biocentre, 730

Estonian Business School, 731

Estonian Chemical Society, 729

Estonian Energy Research Institute, 730

Estonian Entrepreneurship University of Applied Sciences, 733

Estonian Geographical Society, 729

Estonian History Museum, 731

Estonian Information Technology College, 734

Estonian Institute for Futures Studies, 729

Estonian Institute of Economic Research, 729

Estonian Interuniversity Population Research Centre, 730

Estonian Literary Museum, 731

Estonian Literary Society, 729

Estonian Marine Institute, 730

Estonian Maritime Academy, 734

Estonian Meteorological and Hydrological Institute, 730

Estonian Mother Tongue Society, 729

Estonian Musicological Society, 728

Estonian National Defence College, 734

Estonian National Museum, 731

Estonian Naturalists' Society, 729

Estonian Open Air Museum, 731

Estonian Rectors' Conference, 728

Estonian Research Institute of Agriculture, 729

Estonian Semiotics Association, 729

Estonian Society for the Study of Religions, 729

Estonian Society of Human Genetics, 729

Estonian Theatre and Music Museum, 731

Estonian Union of the History and Philosophy of Science, 729

Estonian University of Life Sciences, 731

Estonian University of Life Sciences, Institute of Forestry and Rural Engineering, 730

Estonian–American Business Academy, 733

Estorick Collection of Modern Italian Art, London, 2333

Estyn, Cardiff, 2278

Esztergomi Hittudományi Főiskola, 1026

Eszterházy Károly College, 1026

Eszterházy Károly Főiskola, 1026

Etablissement Communal d'Enseignement Supérieur Artistique 'Le 75', 282

Etaireia Kypriakon Spoudon, 644

Etairia Ellinon Logotechnon, 968

Etairia Ellinon Theatricon Syngrapheon, 968

ETEA Loyola—Facultad de Ciencias Económicas y Empresariales, 2090

EThames Graduate School, 2410

ETH-Bibliothek, Zürich, 2147

eThekwini Municipal Library, 2031

Ethiopia National Archives and Library Agency, 736

Ethiopian Institute of Agricultural Research, Addis Ababa, 736

Ethiopian Library and Information Association, 735

Ethiopian Mapping Agency, 736

Ethiopian Medical Association, 736

Ethiopian Public Health Association, 736

Ethniko Idryma Erevnon, 969

Ethniko Metsovio Polytechneio, 975

Ethnikon Kai Kapodistriakon Panepistimion Athinon, 976

Ethnographic and Folk Culture Society, Lucknow, 1046

Ethnographic Collection, Lübeck, 878

Ethnographic Institute of the Serbian Academy of Sciences and Arts, 1972

Ethnographic Museum, 97

Ethnographic Museum 'Andrés Barbero', 1710

Ethnographic Museum of Veliko Tărnovo, Veliko Tărnovo, 364

Ethnographic Museum, Vlorë, 98

Ethnographic Museum Zagreb, 627

Ethnographic Museum—the 'Rupe' Museum, 626

Ethnographic Open Air Museum of Latvia, 1429

Ethnographical and Archaeological Museum, Tzintzuntzan, 1500

Ethnographical Museum, Ankara, 2214

Ethnographical Museum, Arkhangai, 1531

Ethnographical Museum Brasov, 1848

Ethnographical Museum Dresden, 878

Ethnographical Museum Herrnhut, 878

Ethnographical Museum in Leipzig, 878

Ethnographical Museum in Toruń, 1773

Ethnographical Museum, Khartoum, 2100

Ethnographical Museum, Khentii, 1531

Ethnographical Museum of Belgrade, 1974

Ethnographical Museum of Split, 627

Ethnological Missionary Museum, Vatican City, 3038

Ethnological Museum, Barcelona, 2065

Ethnological Museum, Berlin, 873

Ethnological Museum, Nicosia, 646

Ethnological Museum of Geographical Society of Lisbon, Lisbon, 1824

Ethnological Museum of Porto, 1825

Ethnologisches Museum, Berlin, 873

Ethnology Society of Romania, 1838

Ethnomusicology Research and Studies Centre, 1700

Ethnos—Suomen Kansatieteilijöiden Yhdistys, 743

Ethnos—The Association of Finnish Ethnologists, 743

Etnografisch Museum, 269

Etnografiska Museet, 2118

Etnografski muzej Split, 627

Etnografski Muzej u Beogradu, 1974

Etnografski Muzej Zagreb, 627

Etnologický ústav AV ČR, v.v.i., 656

Eton College Library, 2316

Etpison Museum, 1697

Etruscan Academy, 1188

Eugene Public Library, 2502

Eugenides Foundation Library, 972

Eugenio Maria de Hostos Faculty of Law, 3021

Eugeniusz Geppert Academy of Art and Design in Wrocław, 1813

Euler Institute for Discrete Mathematics and its Applications, 1572

Euler International Institute of Mathematics, 1895

Eunice Kennedy Shriver National Institute of Child Health and Human Development, Bethesda, 2469

Euphrates University, 2222

Eurandom, 1572

Eureka College, 2653

Euroacademy, Tallinn, 734

Euroakadeemia, Tallinn, 734

EuroArab Management School (EAMS), Granada, 2089

EuroAsian Universities Association, 63

Euro-Mediterranean University, Portorož, 2020

Europa Nostra, 53

Europacentrum Jean Monnet, 262

Europäische Bibliotheken für Theologie, 55

Europäische Gesellschaft für Ingenieur-Ausbildung, 68

Europäischer Verband für Erwachsenenbildung, 63

Europa-Universität Viadrina, 890

European Academy of Sciences and Arts, 50

European Association for Health Information and Libraries, 55

European Association for International Education, 63

European Association for Population Studies, 57

European Association for Quality Assurance in Higher Education (ENQA), 67

European Association of Distance Teaching Universities, 63

European Association of Institutions in Higher Education (EURASHE), 63

European Atomic Energy Community (Euratom), 82

European Banking Centre, Tilburg, 1564

European Business School London, 2412

European Centre for Advanced Research in Economics and Statistics, 262

European Centre for Executive Development, Fontainebleau, 821

European Centre for Medium-Range Weather Forecasts, 82

European Centre for Social Welfare Policy and Research, 57

European College Dukagjini, 1413

European College of Business and Management, London, 2412

European College of Economics and Management, 372

European Consortium for Accreditation, 67

European Construction Institute, Loughborough, 2298

European Cooperation in Science and Technology (COST), 266

European Cultural Centre, Bucharest, 1836

European Cultural Foundation, 53

European Distance and E-Learning Network (EDEN), 63

European Economic Association, 57

European Federation of Internal Medicine, 75

European Festivals Association, 80

European Forum at the Hebrew University, 1168

European Foundation for Management Development (EFMD), 57

European Geosciences Union, 82

European Humanities University, 1450

European Institute, London, 2298

European Institute of Education and Social Policy, 63

European Institute of Environmental Medicine, 82

European Institute of Public Administration, Maastricht, 1595

European Institute of Retailing and Services Studies (EIRASS), Eindhoven, 1564

European Institute of Technology, Paris, 823

European Journalism Observatory, Lugano, 2143

European Molecular Biology Laboratory, 82

European Molecular Biology Organization (EMBO), 82

European Movement, London, 2281

European Muslim Research Centre, 2309

European Organization for Civil Aviation Equipment (EUROCAE), 68

European Organization for Nuclear Research (CERN), 83

European Physical Society, 83

European Policies Research Centre, Glasgow, 2300

European Research Council, 83

European Research Institute, Birmingham, 2298

European Research Institute in Service Science (ERISS), Tilburg, 1565

European School of Economics, 2412

European School of Osteopathy, 2413

European Science Foundation, 83

European Society of Anaesthesiology (ESA), 75

European Society of Cardiology, 75

European Southern Observatory, 83

European Southern Observatory (ESO), Santiago, 468

European Space Agency (ESA), 83

European University Association, 63

European University College Brussels, 2273

European University Institute, Florence, 1231

European University of Cyprus, 646

European University of Lefke, 648

European Values Study (EVS), Tilburg, 1565

EuroPort Business School, 1591

Europos Humanitarinis Universitetas, 1450

Euskal Herriko Unibertsitatea, 2076

Euskaltzaindia, Bilbao, 766

Eustis Memorial Library, 2483

Evaluation Agency Baden-Württemberg, 844

Evaluation and Accreditation Commission, Khartoum, 2099

Evaluation Committee of Private Universities (ECPU), Nicosia, 644

Evaluationsagentur Baden-Württemberg (evalag), 844

Evanđeoski teološki fakultet, 631

Evandro Chagas Institute, 310

Evangel University, Springfield, 2788

Evangelical Academy in Vienna, 188

Evangelical Press Society of Bavaria, 869

Evangelical Seminary, Myerstown, 2904

Evangelical Seminary of Puerto Rico, 3021

Evangelical Theological Seminary, Osijek, 631

Evangelical University of El Salvador, 723

Evangelical University of Paraguay, 1712

Evangelical University of the Americas, 617

Evangelical-Lutheran Theological University, Budapest, 1025

Evangélikus Hittudományi Egyetem, Budapest, 1025

Evangelische Akademie Wien, 188

Evangelischer Presseverband für Bayern eV, Munich, 869

Evansville Museum of Arts, History & Science, 2521

Evelyn Hone College of Applied Arts and Commerce, Lusaka, 3076

Everest College Phoenix, 2553

Everest University, 2628

Everett Public Library, 2507

Evergreen Museum & Library, 2525

Evergreen State College, Olympia, 2987

Everhart Museum of Natural History, Science and Art, 2539

Everson Museum of Art, 2534

Evolução Litosférica e Meio Ambiente Superficial, 1819

Evolutionsmuseet, Uppsala, 2120

Évora Public Library, 1821

Ewell Sale Stewart Library and Archives of the Academy of Natural Sciences, Philadelphia, 2503

Ewha Womans University Library, 1389

Ewha Women's University, 1398

Ewing Memorial Library, 1679

Excelsior College, 2834

Executive Committee of the Bolivian University, 290

Exeter Cathedral Library and Archives, 2317

Exeter Centre for Ethno-Political Studies (EXCEPS), 2300

Exeter Centre for the Study of Esotericism (EXESESO), 2309

Exeter College, 2410

Exeter College Library, Oxford, 2325

Exeter College, Oxford, 2399

Exeter Historical Society, 2531

Exeter MR Research Centre, 2304

Exeter Turkish Studies, 2309

Experimental and Research Centre for Leather, Ulan Bator, 1531

Experimental and Research Centre for Wool, Ulan Bator, 1531

Experimental Factory for Analytical Instrumentation, St Petersburg, 1901

Experimental Factory for Scientific Instrumentation, Chernogolovka, 1901

Experimental Institute of Agricultural Zoology, Florence, 1197

Experimental Natural Philosophy Society, Rotterdam, 1564

Experimental Psychology Society, Bristol, 2293

Experimental Research Institute of Metal-Cutting Machine Tools, Moscow, 1901

Experimental Station of Táchira, 3048

Experimental Station of the Research Institute for Arable Farming, Korçë, 96

Experimental Station Vista Florida, 1715

Experimental University Institute of Technology 'Andrés Eloy Blanco', 3059

Expertise Centrum Hoger Onderwijs, 263

Exposition Permanente du Débarquement, Arromanches, 782

EXPres, 1565

Externado University of Colombia, 601

Ezequiel Dias Foundation, 311

F

F. Brooke Whiting House & Museum, 2525

Faaborg Museum, 680

Fabian Society, London, 2281

Fachbereichsbibliothek Rechtswissenschaften, Vienna, 195

Fachgebiet Wasserwirtschaft und Hydrosystemmodellierung, 853

Fachhochschule IMC Krems, 209

Fachhochschule Nordwestschweiz, 2166

Fachhochschule Technikum Kärnten, 209

Fachhochschule Technikum Wien, 209

Fachhochschule Vorarlberg, 209

Fachhochschule Westschweiz, 2166

Fachhochschul-Studiengang Bauingenieurwesen-Baumanagement, 208

Fachhochschul-Studiengang Burgenland GmbH, Eisenstadt, 208

Fachhochschul-Studiengang Oberösterreich, Graz, 208

Fachhochschul-Studiengang Salzburg, 209

Fachhochschul-Studiengang bfi Wien, 209

Fachhochschul-Studiengänge Campus Wien, 209

Fachhochschul-Studiengänge der Wiener Neustadt, 209

Fachhochschul-Studiengänge Kufstein, 209

Fachhochschul-Studiengänge St Pölten, 209

Fachhochschul-Studiengänge Technikum Joanneum, Graz, 209

Fachhochschul-Studiengänge WIFI Steiermark, Graz, 209

Facoltà di Teologia di Lugano, 2166

Faculdade de Direito da Guiné-Bissau, 990

Facultad de Arquitectura y Estudios Ambientales, Heredia, 616

Facultad de Derecho Eugenio María de Hostos, 3021

Facultad de Derecho, San Juan, 3021

Facultad de Teología de Granada (Institución Universitaria de la Compañía de Jesús), 2083

Facultad de Teología del Uruguay 'Monseñor Mariano Soler', 3028

Facultad de Teología Pontificia y Civil de Lima, 1718

Facultad Latinoamericana de Ciencias Sociales—FLACSO, 709

Faculté de Droit et Science Politique, 793

Faculté de Langues, Littératures et Civilisations Étrangères, 814

Faculté de Médecine, de Pharmacie et d'Odonto-Stomatologie, Bamako, 1483

Faculté de Psychologie, 814

Faculté d'Économie, Gestion et AES, 793

Faculté des Lettres et Sciences Sociales, Brest, 822

Faculté des Sciences, Espaces, Sociétés, 814

Faculté d'Histoire, Arts et Archéologie, 814

Faculté Libre de Théologie Protestante de Paris, 822

Faculté Polytechnique de Mons, 276

Faculteit Katholieke Theologie te Utrecht, 1592

Faculteit voor Vergelijkende Godsdienstwetenschappen, Antwerp, 279

Fukui University of Technology, Fukui, 1328
Fukuoka Institute of Technology, Fukuoka, 1328
Fukuoka University, 1334
Fukushima Medical University, 1328
Fukushima University, 1261
Fukuyama University, Hiroshima, 1261
Fulda Theology Faculty, 959
Fuller Theological Seminary, Pasadena, 2572
Fulton County Public Library, 2486
Fund Assistance to Private Education (FAPE), Makati City, 1732
Fundação Bunge, 306
Fundação Carlos Chagas, 307
Fundação Casa de Rui Barbosa, 314
Fundação Ezequiel Dias, 311
Fundação Getúlio Vargas, 307
Fundação Instituto Brasileiro de Geografia e Estatística, 314
Fundação Joaquim Nabuco, 311
Fundação Macau, 587
Fundação 'Oswaldo Cruz', 310
Fundação para a Ciência e a Tecnologia, 1817
Fundação Universidade Federal de Rondônia, 337
Fundació Catalana per a la Recerca i la Innovació (FCRI), 2059
Fundación Galileo Galilei, 2061
Fundación Hondureña de Investigación Agrícola (FHIA), 995
Fundación Instituto Botánico de Venezuela 'Dr Tobías Lasser', 3048
Fundación Instituto d'Estudis Nord-Americans, Barcelona, 2051
Fundación Juan March, 2051
Fundación la Salle de Ciencias Naturales, Caracas, 3047
Fundación Miguel Lillo, 121
Fundación Museo del Aire de Honduras, 996
Fundación Nacional para la Cultura Popular, San Juan, 3014
Fundación Omar Dengo, 613
Fundación para el Fomento de la Lectura (FUNDALECTURA), 591
Fundación para el Museo del Hombre Hondureño, 996
Fundación Puertorriqueña de las Humanidades, 3014
Fundación Teresa Carreño, 3060
Fundamental Scientific Library of the National Academy of Sciences of Armenia, 138
Fundepos Alma Mater University, 617
Funen Art Academy, 687
Funen Art Museum, 681
Funen Village, 681
Furman University, 2929
Furness College, 2410
Futuribles International, 57
Fuwai Hospital, Beijing, 484
Fuzhou University, 515
Fylkingen, 2108
Fyns Kunstmuseum, 681
Fynske Kunstakademi, 687
Fynske Landsby, 681
Fyzikální ústav AV ČR, 655
Fyzikálny Ústav SAV, 2005
Fyziologicky Ústav AV CR, v.v.i., 654

G

G. A. Krestov Institute of Solution Chemistry, 1896
G. Călinescu Institute of Literary History and Theory, 1841
G. E. Pukhov Institute for Modelling in Energy Engineering, Kyiv, 2253
G. G. Devyatykh Institute of the Chemistry of High-Purity Substances, 1896
G. Mavlynov Institute of Seismology, 3031
G. Oprescu Institute of the Art History, 1840
G. S. Pisarenko Institute for Problems of Strength, Kyiv, 2253
G. S. Rakovski National Defence Academy, 372
G. Tsulukidze Mining Institute, 839

G. V. Kurdyumov Institute for Metal Physics, Kyiv, 2251
G. W. Leibnitz Minerva Centre for Research in Computer Sciences, 1172
Gabinet Numismàtic, 2066
Gabinete de Apoio ao Ensino Superior, 587
Gabinetto Disegni e Stampe degli Uffizi, Florence, 1207
Gabonakutató Nonprofit Közhasznú Kft., 1002
Gábor Dénes Főiskola, 1026
Gabriel René Moreno Autonomous University, 292
Gabriela Mistral Museum of Education, 470
Gabriela Mistral Museum of Vicuña, 470
Gabriela Mistral University, 477
Gad & Birgit Rausing Library, 1679
Gadsden Museum of Art, 2509
Gaeddu College of Business Studies, 288
Gaelic League, Dublin, 1158
Gagarin State Technical University, Saratov (SSTU), 1938
Gaigab Museum, 1442
Gainesville State College, 2641
Gainsborough Old Hall, 2332
Gakujutsu Bunken Fukyu-Kai, 1242
Gakushuin University, 1334
Gál Ferenc Főiskola Szeged, 1026
Galata Museo del Mare, Genoa, 1208
Galatasaray Üniversitesi, 2222
Galati Museum of History, 1849
Galaţi 'V. A. Urechia' County Library, 1846
Galen University, 284
Galería de Arte Nacional, Caracas, 3050
Galería Nacional de Bellas Artes, Santo Domingo, 695
Galería Nacional, San José, 614
Galeria del Mar, St John, 3023
Galeria e Arteve e Kosovës, 1411
Galeria Kombetare e Arteve, Tiranë, 98
Galerie David d'Angers, 782
Galerie de la Marine, Nice, 784
Galerie des Ponchettes, Nice, 784
Galerie hlavního města Prahy, 659
Galerie Nationale du Jeu de Paume, 784
Galerie umění Karlovy Vary, 658
Galeries Nationales du Panthéon Bouddhique, Paris, 784
Galerija Matica Srpska, Novi Sad, 1974
Galerija umjetnina Split, 627
Galileo Galilei Foundation, 2061
Galileo University, 986
Gallaudet Research Institute, 2468
Gallaudet University, Washington, 2616
Galle National Museum, 2094
Gallen-Kallela Museum, 749
Gallen-Kallelan Museo, Espoo, 749
Galleri Kontrast, 2118
Galleri Tapper-Popermajer, 2120
Galleria Borghese, Rome, 1211
Galleria Civica d'Arte Moderna e Contemporanea, Turin, 1213
Galleria d'Arte Moderna, Florence, 1207
Galleria d'Arte Moderna, Milan, 1213
Galleria d'Arte Moderna Palazzo Forti, 1214
Galleria degli Uffizi, Florence, 1207
Galleria del Costume, Florence, 1208
Galleria dell' Accademia, Florence, 1207
Galleria di Palazzo Bianco, Genoa, 1208
Galleria di Palazzo Rosso, Genoa, 1209
Galleria Giorgio Franchetti alla Ca' d'Oro, Venice, 1214
Galleria Internazionale d'Arte Moderna di Ca' Pesaro, Venice, 1214
Galleria, Museo e Medagliere Estense, Modena, 1210
Galleria Nazionale d'Arte Antica di Palazzo Barberini, 1211
Galleria Nazionale d'Arte Moderna e Contemporanea, 1212
Galleria Nazionale delle Marche—Palazzo Ducale, Urbino, 1213
Galleria Nazionale dell'Umbria, Perugia, 1211
Galleria Nazionale di Palazzo Spinola, Genoa, 1209

Galleria Nazionale, Parma, 1211
Galleria Palatina e Appartamenti Reali, Florence, 1208
Galleria Rinaldo Carnielo, 1207
Galleria Sabauda, Turin, 1213
Gallerie d'Arte Moderna e Contemporanea, Ferrara, 1207
Gallerie dell'Accademia, Venice, 1214
Gallery of Costume, Manchester, 2335
Gallery of Modern Art (GOMA), Glasgow, 2331
Gallery of Modern Art, Zagreb, 627
Gallery of Modern Hungarian Art, 1011
Galton Institute, London, 2294
Galway Arts Centre, 1160
Galway City Centre Library, Galway, 1160
Galway City Museum, 1160
Galway County Libraries, 1160
Galway-Mayo Institute of Technology, 1164
Gamalei, N. F., Institute of Epidemiology and Microbiology, Moscow, 1889
Gambia College, 836
Gambia National Library, 835
Gambia National Museum, 835
Game and Fisheries Museum, Aquarium and Library, Entebbe, 2243
Gamgol Library, 1388
Gampaha Wickramarachchi Ayurveda Institute, 2098
Gamtos Tyrimų Centras, Vilnius, 1448
Gamtos Tyrimų Centro Botanikos Institutas, Vilnius, 1448
Gandan Library, Ulan Bator, 1531
Gandhara University, 1683
Gandhi Memorial Museum, 1050
Gandhigram Rural Institute, 1101
Gandhi-Tappoo Centre for Writing, Ethics and Peace Studies, 738
Gang Seo Public Library, 1388
Gangam Calligraphy Museum, 1390
Gangneung Yeongdong College, 1409
Gangneung–Wonju National University, 1391
Ganja State University, 215
Gannon University, 2904
Gansu Agricultural University, 516
Gansu Provincial Library, 489
GAP Institute, 1411
Gapar Aitiev Kyrgyz National Museum of Fine Arts, 1419
Gara-Kala Experimental Station for Plant Genetic Resources, 2239
Garda College, 1164
Garden and Museum of Tropical Agriculture, Lisbon, 1824
Garden Organic, Coventry, 2299
Gardendale Martha Moore Public Library, 2477
Gardiner Public Library, 2490
Gardner-Webb University, 2859
Garfield County Libraries, 2480
Gari Melchers Home and Studio, 2544
Garni Geophysical Observatory, 137
Garni Space Astronomy Institute, 137
Garrett-Evangelical Theological Seminary, 2653
Gas Institute, Kyiv, 2251
Gáspár Károli University of the Reformed Church in Hungary, 1025
Gaston Berger University, 1970
Gaston County Museum, 2536
Gaston-Lincoln Regional Library, 2500
Gateshead College, 2410
Gauguin Art Centre and Museum, 828
Gauhati University, 1061
Gauteng Library and Archive Services, 2031
Gavar State University, 139
Gävle City Library, 2113
Gävle stadsbibliotek, 2113
Gävle University College, 2134
Gävleborg County Museum, 2116
Gayer-Anderson Museum, Cairo, 714
Gazi Husrav-Bey Library, 299
Gazi Husrev-Begova biblioteka, 299
Gazi Üniversitesi, 2223
Gaziantep Üniversitesi, 2223
Gaziosmanpaşa Üniversitesi, 2223
GC University, Lahore, 1683
Gdańsk History Museum, 1772

Gdańsk Scientific Society, 1752
Gdańsk University of Technology, 1800
Gdański Uniwersytet Medyczny, 1775
Gdańskie Towarzystwo Naukowe, 1752
Gdynia Maritime University, 1810
Gebze Yüksek Teknoloji Enstitüsü, 2223
Gedik Ahmed Paşa Library, 2213
Geffrye Museum, 2333
Geheimes Staatsarchiv Preussischer Kulturbesitz, 864
Geld Museum, 1583
Gelders Archief, 1577
Gelders Archives, 1577
Gemäldegalerie Alte Meister, Dresden, 875
Gemäldegalerie, Berlin, 873
Gemäldegalerie der Akademie der Bildenden Künste Wien, 197
Gemäldegalerie Neue Meister, Dresden, 875
Gemeentearchief Kampen, 1578
Gemeentemusea Deventer, 1581
Gemeentemuseum Den Haag, 1583
Gemeentemuseum Helmond, 1581
Gemeinsame Wissenschaftskonferenz, 843
Gemmological Association Great Britain, 2295
Gems Museum, 1546
Genealogical Association of Nova Scotia, 388
Genealogical Institute of the Maritimes, 388
Genealogical Institute, São Paulo, 307
Genealogical Society of Finland, 743
Genealogical Society of South Africa, 2027
Genealogiska Samfundet i Finland, 743
Geneeskundige Stichting Koningin Elisabeth, 264
General Archive of Puerto Rico, 3015
General Archive of the Nation, San Salvador, 720
General Archives of Central America, Guatemala City, 985
General Archives of the City of Tel-Aviv-Yafo, 1174
General Archives of the Nation, Caracas, 3049
General Archives of the Nation, México, 1497
General Association of Engineers of Romania, 1838
General Bureau of Statistics in Suriname, 2103
General Council of Spanish Pharmacists, 2054
General Council of the Bar, London, 2281
General Council on Music, Sitges, 2053
General Directorate of Disaster Affairs Earthquake Research Department, 2212
General Directorate of Geology and Mines, 375
General Directorate of Mineral Research and Exploration Library, Ankara, 2213
General Directorate of Municipal Libraries, 123
General Division of Art Education and Research, México, 1498
General Jonas Zemaitis Military Academy of Lithuania, 1455
General Library of University of the East, 3049
General Library University Campus of Mayagüez, 3015
General Library University of Coimbra, 1821
General Netherlands Philosophical Society, 1563
General Physics Institute, Moscow, 1896
General San Martín Public Library, 123
General Sciences Library of Ho Chi Minh City, 3065
General Sir John Kotelawala Defence University, 2095
General Society of Authors and Publishers, Madrid, 2054
Generaldirektion Statistik, 264

Generolo Jono Žemaičio Lietuvos Karo Akademija, 1455
Genetic Resources Institute, Harare, 3078
Genetics Society, London, 2291
Genetics Society of America, 2459
Genetics Society of Canada, 389
Genetics Society of Chile, 466
Genetics Society of China, 482
Genetics Society of Nigeria, 1624
Genetika, Moscow, 1894
Genetikai Intézet, Szeged, 1004
Geneva Association, 58
Geneva College, Beaver Falls, 2905
Geneva University of Art and Design, 2167
Genghis Khan World Academy, 1530
Génie Industriel, Grenoble, 788
Gennadius Library, 972
Genomics Research Centre, 148
Genootschap Architectura et Amicitia, 1560
Genootschap ter bevordering van Natuur-, Genees- en Heelkunde, 1562
Gentofte Bibliotekerne, 678
Geochemical Society, St Louis, 2461
Geodesy Centre, Lisbon, 1817
Geodetic and Research Branch, Survey of India, 1045
Geodetic Institute of Bosnia and Herzegovina, 298
Geodetic Section, Army Topographic Service, Bandung, 1112
Geodetic Society of Japan, 1247
Geodetical and Geophysical Research Institute of the Hungarian Academy of Sciences, 1004
Geodetski Institutet, Masala, 747
Geodetski Zavod Bosne i Hercegovine, 298
Geodezijos Institutas, Vilnius, 1448
Geofysiska Sällskapet, Helsinki, 745
Geofyzikální ústav AV ČR, v.v.i., 655
Geofyzikálny Ústav SAV, 2005
Geografiska Sällskapet i Finland, 743
Geografski inštitut Antona Melika ZRC SAZU, 2018
Geografsko Društvo na R. Makedonija, 1459
Geografsko Društvo Republike Srpske, 297
Geografsko Društvo u Federaciji BiH, 297
Geographical and Historical Academy of Guatemala, 984
Geographical and Historical Society, Santa Cruz, 290
Geographical Association, Sheffield, 2285
Geographical Institute 'Jovan Cvijić', 1973
Geographical Institute, Research Centre for Astronomy and Earth Sciences of the Hungarian Academy of Sciences, 1003
Geographical Museum of the Anton Melik Geographical Institute at ZRC SAZU, 2020
Geographical Society Bern, 2139
Geographical Society of Berlin, 847
Geographical Society of China, 480
Geographical Society of Federation of Bosnia and Herzegovina, 297
Geographical Society of Finland, 743
Geographical Society of India, 1036
Geographical Society of Ireland, 1157
Geographical Society of Lima, 1715
Geographical Society of Macedonia, 1459
Geographical Society of Moldova, 1524
Geographical Society of New South Wales Inc., 143
Geographical Society of Republic of Srpska, 297
Geographický Ústav SAV, 2003
Geographische Gesellschaft Bern, 2139
Geographisch-Ethnographische Gesellschaft Zürich, 2139
Geographisch-Ethnologische Gesellschaft Basel, 2139
Geography Centre, Lisbon, 1817
Geologica Belgica, Brussels, 261

Geological and Mining Data Centre, Alfragide, 1821
Geological and Mining Studies Centre, Beja, 1821
Geological and Palaeontological Institute and Museum, Hamburg, 861
Geological Association, Mendig, 851
Geological Association of Canada, 390
Geological Institute of Kola Science Centre, 1896
Geological Institute of Romania, 1843
Geological Institute of Slovak Academy of Sciences, 2005
Geological Institute, São Paulo, 307
Geological Institute 'Strashimir Dimitrov', Sofia, 359
Geological Institute, Ulan-Ude, 1896
Geological, Mining and Metallurgical Society of India, 1039
Geological, Mining and Metallurgical Society of Liberia, 1439
Geological Mining Service, Paramaribo, 2103
Geological Museum, Copenhagen, 679
Geological Museum, Helsinki, 749
Geological Museum of China, Beijing, 489
Geological Museum of Portugal, Lisbon, 1824
Geological Museum of the Institute of Geology, Yerevan, 138
Geological Museum of the Seminary of Barcelona, 2065
Geological Museum, Oslo, 1653
Geological Museum, Seoul, 1389
Geological Research Authority, Khartoum, 2100
Geological Research Authority of the Sudan Library, Khartoum, 2100
Geological Research Institute, Tiranë, 97
Geological Society for Greece, 969
Geological Society of America, 2461
Geological Society of Australia, 146
Geological Society of Belgium, 261
Geological Society of Chile, 467
Geological Society of China, 482
Geological Society of Denmark, 675
Geological Society of Finland, 745
Geological Society of Japan, 1247
Geological Society of London, 2292
Geological Society of London, Library and Information Services, 2320
Geological Society of Norway, 1649
Geological Society of Romania, 1838
Geological Society of South Africa, 2029
Geological Society of Spain, 2055
Geological Society of Sweden, 2110
Geological Society of Trinidad and Tobago, 2204
Geological Society of Viet Nam, 3062
Geological Society of Zimbabwe, 3078
Geological Survey and Mines Bureau, Dehiwala, 2093
Geological Survey and Mines Department, Entebbe, 2243
Geological Survey and Mines Department, Mbabane, 2105
Geological Survey Department, Accra, 962
Geological Survey Department, Maseru, 1437
Geological Survey Department, Mogadishu, 2024
Geological Survey Division, Freetown, 1992
Geological Survey of Austria, Vienna, 191
Geological Survey of Bangladesh, 224
Geological Survey of Botswana, 303
Geological Survey of Canada, 392
Geological Survey of Denmark and Greenland, 677
Geological Survey of Estonia, 730
Geological Survey of Ethiopia, 736
Geological Survey of Finland, 747
Geological Survey of India, 1045
Geological Survey of Israel, 1171
Geological Survey of Malawi, 1468
Geological Survey of New South Wales, 148
Geological Survey of Norway, 1650
Geological Survey of Slovenia, 2019

Geological Survey of Sweden, 2112
Geological Survey of Tanzania, Dodoma, 2183
Geological Survey of Western Australia, 149
Geological Survey of Zimbabwe, 3079
Geologický ústav AV ČR, v.v.i., 655
Geologický Ústav SAV, 2005
Geologijos ir Geografijos Institutas, Vilnius, 1448
Geologisch Mijnbouwkundige Dienst, 2103
Geologische Bundesanstalt, Vienna, 191
Geologische Vereinigung eV, Mendig, 851
Geologisch-Paläontologisches Institut und Museum, Universität Hamburg, 861
Geologisk Museum, 679
Geologisk museum, Oslo, 1653
Geologiska Föreningen, Stockholm, 2110
Geologiska Forskningscentralen, 747
Geologiska Museet, Helsinki, 749
Geologiska Sällskapet i Finland, 745
Geologists' Association, London, 2292
Geologists' Association of Albania, 96
Geology Centre, Lisbon, 1817
Geology Centre of the University of Porto, Porto, 1818
Geology Institute, Skopje, 1460
Geološki Zavod, Skopje, 1460
Geološki Zavod Slovenije, 2019
Geomedical Research Office of the Heidelberg Academy of Sciences, 859
Geomedizinische Forschungsstelle der Heidelberger Akademie der Wissenschaften, 859
Geophysical Institute AS CR, 655
Geophysical Institute, Coimbra, 1819
Geophysical Institute of Israel, Holon, 1171
Geophysical Institute of Peru, 1716
Geophysical Institute of Slovak Academy of Sciences, 2005
Geophysical Laboratory, Washington, 2470
Geophysical Observatory, Addis Ababa, 736
Geophysical Society of Finland, 745
Geoponiko Panepistimio Athinon, 976
Georg-Agricola Gesellschaft zur Förderung der Geschichte der Naturwissenschaften und der Technik eV, 849
Georg-August-Universität Göttingen, 891
George A. Smathers Libraries, 2483
George Bacovia University of Bacău, 1863
'George Barițiu' County Library Brașov, 1844
George C. Marshall Space Flight Center, Alabama, 2476
George Fox University, 2893
George H. W. Bush Presidential Library and Museum, 2505
George Hail Free Library, 2503
George Herdman Library, 2439
George Mason University, 2977
George Padmore Research Library on African Affairs, Accra, 963
George R. Gardiner Museum of Ceramic Art, 397
George Washington University, 2616
George Washington University Libraries, 2482
George Whitefield College, 2046
Georgetown College, 2689
Georgetown University, 2622
Georgetown University Library, 2482
Georgi Dimitrov National Museum, 363
Georgi Nadjakov Institute of Solid State Physics, 359
Georgia College and State University, 2641
Georgia Health Sciences University, 2642
Georgia Institute of Technology, 2642
Georgia Museum of Art, 2518
Georgia O'Keeffe Museum, 2533
Georgia Southern University, 2642

Georgia Southwestern State University, 2642
Georgia State University, 2642
Georgian Academy of Physical Education, Tbilisi, 840
Georgian Botanical Society, 838
Georgian Court University, Lakewood, 2809
Georgian Geographical Society, 837
Georgian Geological Society, 838
Georgian National Academy of Sciences, 837
Georgian National Museum, 839
Georgian National Museum—National Gallery, 840
Georgian National Speleological Society, 838
Georgian Neuroscience Association, Tbilisi, 837
Georgian Philosophy Society, 838
Georgian 'S. Rustaveli' State Institute of Theatre and Cinematography, 842
Georgian Society of Geneticists and Selectioners, 838
Georgian Society of Parasitologists, 838
Georgian State Academy of Animal Husbandry and Veterinary Medicine, Tbilisi, 840
Georgian State Agrarian University, 842
Georgian State Art Museum, 840
Georgian State Institute of Subtropical Agriculture, 842
Georgian State Museum of Oriental Art, 840
Georgian Technical University, 840
Georg-Speyer-Haus, Institut für Tumorbiologie und experimentelle Therapie, 859
Georg-Speyer-Haus, Institute for Tumor Biology and Experimental Therapy, 859
Geoscience Australia (GA), Canberra, 149
Geoscience Society of New Zealand, 1604
GeoScience Victoria, 149
Geosciences Institute, Madrid, 2057
Geospatial Information Authority of Japan, Ibaraki, 1250
Gépipari Tudományos Egyesület (GTE), Budapest, 1001
Gerald R. Ford Presidential Library & Museum, 2493
Gereformeerde Hogeschool, 1592
Germa Museum, 1442
German Academic Exchange Service, 844
German Academy for Regional Geography, 847
German Academy for Urban and Regional Spatial Planning, 856
German Academy of Sciences Leopoldina, 845
German Adult Education Association, 844
German Aerospace Centre, 862
German Agricultural Society, 845
German Archaeological Institute, 859
German Archaeological Institute at Athens, 970
German Archaeological Institute, Cairo, 713
German Archaeological Institute, Madrid, 2053
German Archaeological Institute Rome, 1198
German Architecture Museum, 876
German Association for Asian Studies, 851
German Association for East European Studies, 846
German Association for Materials Research and Testing, 852
German Association for Psychiatry, Psychotherapy and Psychosomatics (DGPPN), 848
German Association for Research on Sexuality, 859
German Association of Mining Surveyors, 852
German Association of University Professors and Lecturers, 844
German Bible Archive, 867

Greenlandic Authors' Society, 690
Greenlandic National Library, 690
Greenlandic Society, 675
Greenlands Teacher-Training College, Nuuk, 691
Greensboro College, 2859
Greensboro Historical Museum, 2536
Greenside Design Center College of Design, 2046
Greenville College, 2653
Greenville County Library System, 2504
Greenville County Museum of Art, 2541
Greenwich Libraries, 2320
Greenwich Library, 2481
Greenwich School of Management, 2409
Greenwich University, Karachi, 1683
Gregg Museum of Art & Design, 2536
Gregor Mendel Institute of Molecular Plant Biology GmbH, 191
Gregorian Egyptian Museum, Vatican City, 3038
Gregorian Etruscan Museum, Vatican City, 3038
Gregorian Institute of Lisbon, 1815
Gregorian Museum of Profane Art, Vatican City, 3038
Gremial Uruguaya de Médicos Radiólogos, 3025
Grenada National Museum, 983
Grenada National Trust, 983
Grenada Public Library, 983
Gressenhall Farm and Workhouse, 2336
Gretsa University, Thika, 1378
Greve Bibliotek, 678
Greve Library, 678
Grey Art Gallery, 2534
Grey College, Durham, 2360
Grieg Academy, 1668
Griegakademiet, 1668
Griffith College, 1164
Griffith Observatory, 2512
Griffith University, 162
'Grigore Antipa' National Natural History Museum, 1848
Grigoriev Institute of Medical Radiology, 2250
Grimsby Institute, 2410
Grinnell College, 2680
Grodno State Agrarian University, 254
Grodno State Historical and Archaeological Museum, 251
Grodno State Medical University, 254
Grodno Zonal Planting Institute, 248
Groei & Bloei, 1560
Groeningemuseum, Bruges, 269
Groenlandica, 690
Groep T—Internationale Hogeschool Leuven, 279
Gróf Esterházy Károly Kastély- és Tájmúzeum, 1010
Groningen Biomolecular Science and Biotechnology Institute, 1571
Groningen Centre for Law and Governance, 1567
Groningen Centre of Energy Law, 1568
Groningen Institute for Educational Research, 1569
Groningen Institute of Archaeology, 1569
Groningen Research Institute for the Study of Culture (ICOG), 1565
Groningen Research Institute of Pharmacy (GRIP), 1571
Groninger Museum, 1581
Grønlands Handelsskole, Nuuk, 691
Grønlands Nationalmuseum og Arkiv, 690
Grønlands Seminarium, 691
Grønlands Socialpædagogiske Seminarium, 691
Grønlands Universitet, 691
Grønlandske Landsbibliotek, 690
Grønlandske Selskab, 675
Grossherzoglich-Hessische Porzellansammlung, 874
Group for Research on Ethnic Relations, Migration and Equality (GERME), 262
Group T—International University College Leuven, 279
Groupe CPA—Centre de Perfectionnement aux Affaires, Paris, 821

Groupe de Recherche en Histoire Océanienne Contemporaine (GRHOC), 829
Groupe de Recherche sur les Relations Ethniques, les Migrations et l'Egalité (GERME), 262
Groupe des Ecoles des Mines, 818
Groupe EAC—Ecole Supérieure d'Economie, d'Art et de Communication, Paris, 821
Groupe ENI (Ecoles Nationales d'Ingénieurs), 818
Groupe ESA—Ecole Supérieure d'Agriculture d'Angers, Angers, 821
Groupe ESC Clermont, Clermont-Ferrand, 816
Groupe ESC Lille—Ecole Supérieure de Commerce de Lille, 821
Groupe ESCEM Campus Poitiers, 821
Groupe IPAC, 820
Grove City College, 2905
Grove Museum of Victorian Life, 2439
Growth and Bloom, Zoetermeer, 1560
Grozny State Oil Institute, 1952
Grünes Gewölbe, Dresden, 875
Grupo Argentino del Color, 119
Grupo de Florestas e Produtos Florestais do Instituto de Investigação Científica Tropical, 1818
Grupo Universitario Latinoamericano de Estudio para la Reforma y el Perfeccionamiento de la Educación (GULERPE), Caracas, 3046
Grŵp Llandrillo Menai, 2433
Grŵp NPTC Group, 2433
GSI Helmholtz Centre for Heavy Ion Research GmbH, 862
GSI Helmholtzzentrum für Schwerionenforschung GmbH, Darmstadt, 862
Guadalajara Lamar University, 1511
Guadalajara Regional Museum, 1498
Guam Chamber of Commerce, Hagåtña, 3012
Guam Council on the Arts and Humanities, 3012
Guam Department of Education, 3012
Guam Gallery of Arts, 3013
Guam Historic Resources Division, 3012
Guam Law Library, 3013
Guam Library Association, 3012
Guam Medical Association, 3012
Guam Museum Foundation, Inc, Hagatna, 3012
Guam Museum of Culture, Art and History, 3013
Guam Preservation Trust, 3012
Guam Public Library System, 3013
Guam Symphony Society, 3012
Guanabacoa Muncipal Museum, 637
Guanajuato Campus, 1509
Guangdong Pharmaceutical University, 516
Guangxi Normal University, 516
Guangxi Traditional Chinese Medical University, 517
Guangxi University, 517
Guangzhou Institute of Chemistry, 486
Guangzhou Institute of Geochemistry, 486
Guangzhou University, 517
Guangzhou University of Traditional Chinese Medicine, 517
Guardian News and Media Archive, 2320
Guarulhos University, 349
Guatemala Academy of Letters, 984
Guatemala Bank Library, 985
Guatemala Engineers Association, 984
Guatemalan Association of Natural History, 984
Guayama Campus, 3020
Gubkin, Acad. I. M., Petroleum and Gas Society, Moscow, 1882
Gubkin Russian State University of Oil and Gas, 1901, 1938
Guernsey Museums & Galleries, 2438
Guggenheim Bilbao Museo, 2066
Guggenheim Museum Bilbao, 2066
Gugushvili, P. V., Institute of Economics, 838
GUIDE—Research Institute for Chronic Diseases and Drug Innovation, 1570

Guild of Church Musicians, Blechingley, 2283
Guildford College, 2410
Guildford School of Acting, 2414
Guildhall Library, City of London, 2320
Guildhall School of Music and Drama, 2414
GuildHE, London, 2277
Guilford College, 2859
Guilin Library of Guangxi Zhuang Autonomous Region, 488
Guille Allès Library, 2438
Guizhou Provincial Library, 488
Guizhou University, 517
Gujarat Ayurved University, 1061
Gujarat Research Society, 1043
Gujarat University, 1061
Gujarat Vidyapeeth Granthalaya, 1049
Gujarat Vidyapeeth Library, 1049
Gujarat Vidyapith, 1101
Gukje Digital University, 1409
Gulbarga University, 1061
Gulbenkian Library, Jerusalem, 1173
Gulbenkian Science Institute, 1819
Gulf Arab States Educational Research Centre, Shamia, 1414
Gulf Coast State College, 2630
Gulf College of Hospitality and Tourism, Muharraq, 220
Gulf Cooperation Council Folklore Centre, Doha, 1833
Gulf Medical University, 2272
Gulf University, 1519
Gulf University for Science and Technology, 1415
Gulf University, Sanad, 220
Gulisashvili, V. Z., Institute of Mountain Forestry, Tbilisi, 838
Gulistan Davlat Universiteti, 3033
Gulistan State University, 3033
Guliyev, A.M., Institute of Additive Chemistry, Baku, 213
Gulu University, 2244
Gunma University, 1262
Gurakuqi, Luigi, House-Museum, Shkodër, 98
Gurkha Memorial Museum, Pokhara, 1558
Guru Ghasidas University, 1062
Guru Ghasidas Vishwavidyalaya, 1062
Guru Gobind Singh Indraprastha University, 1062
Guru Jambeshwar University of Science & Technology, 1062
Guru Nanak Dev University, 1062
Gurukul Kangri University, 1101
Gurukul Kangri Vishwavidyalaya, 1101
Gustav III's Antikmuseum, 2118
Gustav III's Museum of Antiquities, 2118
Gustavo Lopes Pinto Municipal Library, 1823
Gustavus Adolphus College, 2768
Gutenberg-Museum, Mainz, 879
Guyana Geology and Mines Commission, 992
Guyana Marine Turtle Conservation Society, 991
Guyana National Museum, 992
Guyana Zoological Park, National Parks Commission, 992
Gwacheon Provincial Library of Gyeonggi, 1388
Gwangju Museum of Art, 1389
Gwangju National Museum, 1389
Gwebi College of Agriculture, 3081
Gweru Polytechnic, 3081
Gwynedd Libraries, 2313
Gwynedd Museum and Art Gallery, 2328
Gwynedd-Mercy College, 2905
Gyeonggi Museum of Modern Art, 1389
Gyeonggi Provincial Museum, 1389
Gyeongju National Museum, 1390
Gyeongsang National University, 1391
Gyeongsangbuk-Do Forest Science Museum, 1390
Gymnastik- och Idrottshögskolan, 2134
Gyógyszerészeti és Egészségügyi, Minőség- és Szervezetfejlesztési Intézet Egészségpolitikai Szakkönyvtár, Budapest, 1005
Györffy István Nagykun Múzeum, 1010
Györi Hittudománti Föiskola, 1026

Győr-Moson-Sopron Megyei Múzeumok Igazgatósága Soproni Múzeum, 1011
Gyumri M. Nalbandian State Pedagogical Institute, 139

H

H. C. Andersens Barndomshjem i Munkemøllestræde, 681
H. E. J. Research Institute of Chemistry, 1676
H. G. Wells Society, Durham, 2287
H. H. Meeter Center for Calvin Studies, 2468
H. R. MacMillan Space Centre, Vancouver, 395
'H. S. Skovoroda' Institute of Philosophy, Kyiv, 2252
Ha Noi Institute of Stage and Cinematography, Hanoi, 3062
HAAGA-HELIA Ammattikorkeakoulu, 761
HAAGA-HELIA University of Applied Sciences, 761
Hacettepe Üniversitesi, 2223
Hachinohe Institute of Technology, 1328
Hackney Libraries, 2320
Hadassah College, 1186
Hadhramout University of Science and Technology, Mukalla, 3073
Hadlow College, 2411
Hadtörténeti Könyvtár és Térképtár, Budapest, 1005
Hadtörténeti Múzeum, Budapest, 1008
Haegang Ceramics Museum, 1389
Haeju Historical Museum, 1385
Haematological Research Centre, Moscow, 1889
Haematology Oncology Research Center, 1145
HafenCity University Hamburg— University of the Built Environment and Metropolitan Development, 894
Haffenreffer Museum of Anthropology, 2540
Haffkine Institute for Training, Research and Testing, 1044
Hafnarfjörður Public Library, 1030
Hafrannsóknastofnunin, 1030
Hagedorn Research Institute, 676
Hagfrœðistofnun, Reykjavík, 1029
Haggerty Museum of Art, 2546
Hagley Museum and Library, Wilmington, 2515
Hagstofa Íslands, 1029
Hague Academy of International Law, 71
Hague Conference on Private International Law, 71
Hahoe Mask Museum, 1390
Haifa AMLI Library of Music, 1173
Haifa Museum of Art, 1174
Haigazian University, Beirut, 1434
Haines Borough Public Library, 2477
Haiphong Museum, 3065
Haiphong University of Medicine, 3066
Hajdúsági Múzeum, 1009
Hajee Mohammad Danesh University of Science and Technology, Dinajpur, 230
Hajvery University, 1683
Hakluyt Society, London, 2285
Hakodate City Library, 1252
Hakodate City Museum, 1254
Hakodate University, 1335
Hakone Museum of Art, 1254
Hakuoh University, 1329
Hakutsuru Bijitsukan, 1254
Halbert Centre for Canadian Studies, Jerusalem, 1168
Haliç Üniversitesi, 2226
Haliç University, 2226
Halifax Regional Library, 393
Halil Hamit Paşa Library, 2213
Hall County Library System, 2484
Hall of State, Dallas, 2543
Hallands Kulturhistoriska Museum, 2120
Halle Institute for Economic Research, 857
Hallepoort, 270

Hallwylska Museet, 2119
Hallym University, 1399
Halmstad City Library, 2113
Halmstad University, 2134
Halmstads Stadsbibliotek, 2113
Halton Libraries, 2327
Hama Museum, 2169
Hamamatsu University School of
    Medicine, 1329
Hamburg Arts Centre, 877
Hamburg Institute of International
    Economics (HWWI), 857
Hamburg Museum of Art and Industry,
    877
Hamburg Observatory, 861
Hamburg University of Music and
    Theatre, 958
Hamburg University of Technology, 925
Hamburger Bahnhof—Museum für
    Gegenwart—Berlin, 873
Hamburger Kunsthalle, 877
Hamburger Sternwarte, 861
Hamburgisches
    WeltWirtschaftsInstitut
    gemeinnützige GmbH (HWWI), 857
Hamdan Bin Mohammed e-University,
    2272
Hamdard Foundation Pakistan,
    Karachi, 1674
Hamdard University, Karachi, 1683
Hamden Public Library, 2481
Häme Museum, 750
Hämeen Ammattikorkeakoulu,
    Hämeenlinna, 761
Hämeen Museo, Tampere, 750
Hamhung Historical Museum, 1385
Hamilton and Sinclair Libraries, 2485
Hamilton College, 2835
Hamilton County Law Library, 2501
Hamilton Public Library, 394
Hamilton-Wenham Public Library, 2492
HAMK University of Applied Sciences,
    761
Hamline University, 2768
Hammarskjöld Memorial Library,
    Kitwe, 3075
Hammer Museum, Haines, 2510
Hammer Museum, Los Angeles, 2512
Hammersmith & Fulham Libraries,
    2320
Hammonds House Museum, 2518
Hampden-Sydney College, 2977
Hampshire College, 2716
Hampshire County Public Library, 2507
Hampshire Libraries and Information
    Service, 2328
Hampton Court Palace, 2333
Hampton Public Library, 2506
Hampton University, 2977
Hampton University Museum, 2544
Hamptonne Country Life Museum,
    2440
Han Nam University, 1399
Hanbat Library, 1388
Hancock County Library System, 2494
Hancock County Public Library, 2486
Handelshochschule Leipzig (HHL), 957
Handelshögskolan i Stockholm, 2134
Handelshögskolans i Stockholm—
    Bibliotek, 2114
Handelshøjskolen i København, 684
Handelshøjskolens Bibliotek, 678
Handelshøyskolen BI, 1666
Hango Agricultural College, 2202
Hanken School of Economics, 758
Hanken Svenska Handelshögskolans
    Bibliotek, Helsinki, 748
Hankuk Aviation University, 1408
Hankuk University of Foreign Studies,
    1399
Hankyong National University, 1407
Hanlyo University, 1408
Hannan University, 1329
Hannibal-LaGrange University, 2789
Hanoi Agricultural University, 3066
Hanoi Architectural University, 3066
Hanoi College of Fine Arts, 3071
Hanoi College of Pharmacy, 3071
Hanoi Cultural College, 3071
Hanoi Law University, 3066
Hanoi Medical University, 3066
Hanoi National Conservatory of Music,
    3071

Hanoi National Economics University,
    3066
Hanoi National University of
    Education, 3066
Hanoi Open University, 3066
Hanoi University of Civil Engineering,
    3066
Hanoi University of Culture, 3066
Hanoi University of Drama and
    Cinematography, 3071
Hanoi University of Fine Arts, 3066
Hanoi University of Foreign Studies,
    3066
Hanoi University of Foreign Trade,
    3067
Hanoi University of Industrial Fine
    Arts, 3067
Hanoi University of Mining and
    Geology, 3067
Hanoi University of Technology, 3067
Hanoi Water Resources University,
    3067
Hanover College, 2671
Hanover Medical School, 907
Hanover Society of Natural History, 850
Hanover State Museum, 877
Hans Christian Andersen Museum, 681
Hans Christian Andersens Hus, 681
Hans Christian Anderson's Childhood
    Home in Munkemøllestræde, 681
Hans Raj College, 1107
Hansági Múzeum, 1010
Hansard Society, 2281
Hanseo University, 1399
Hanshin University, 1399
Hansung University, 1399
Hanyang University, 1399
Hanze University Groningen,
    University of Applied Sciences, 1592
Hanzehogeschool Groningen,
    University of Applied Sciences, 1592
Haramaya University, Dire Dawa, 737
Harare City Library, 3079
Harare Institute of Technology, 3080
Harare Polytechnic, 3081
Harbin Engineering University, 518
Harbin Institute of Technology, 518
Harbin Medical University, 518
Harbin Normal University, 519
Harbin University of Science and
    Technology, 519
Harbor Defense Museum, 2535
Harding School of Theology, 2935
Harding University, 2561
Hardin-Simmons University, 2950
Haringey Libraries, 2320
Harleian Society, London, 2285
Harlow College, 2410
Harn Museum of Art, 2517
Harokopio Panepistimion, 977
Harokopio University, 977
Harper Adams University College,
    Newport, 2433
Harpers Ferry National Historical Park,
    2545
Harran Üniversitesi, 2227
Harriet Irving Library, Fredericton, 393
Harrington College of Design, 2653
Harris County Public Library, 2505
Harris Manchester College, Oxford,
    2399
Harris Museum and Art Gallery, 2337
Harrison County Public Library, 2486
Harris-Stowe State University, 2789
Harrow Libraries, 2320
Harry and Michael Sacher Institute for
    Legislative Research and
    Comparative Law, 1169
Harry Fischel Institute for Research in
    Talmud and Jewish Law, 1172
Harry Ransom Center, the University of
    Texas at Austin, 2468
Harry S. Truman Library and Museum,
    2494
Harry S. Truman Research Institute for
    the Advancement of Peace, 1168
Harstad University College, 1665
Hartebeesthoek Radio Astronomy
    Observatory, Krugersdorp, 2030
Hartford Seminary, 2601
Hartwick College, 2835
Harvard Art Museums, 2527
Harvard University, 2716
Harvard University Library, 2492

Harvard–Smithsonian Center for
    Astrophysics (CfA), Cambridge,
    2472
Harveian Society of London, 2289
Harvest Bible College, Robina Town
    Centre, 179
Harvest West Bible College Inc.,
    Belmont, 181
Harvey M. Krueger Family Centre for
    Nanoscience and Nanotechnology,
    1172
Harvey Mudd College, 2572
Harwinton Public Library, 2481
Harwood Museum of Art, 2533
Hasanuddin University Library, 1113
Haskell Indian Nations University,
    2685
Háskóli Íslands, 1031
Háskólinn í Reykjavík, 1031
Háskólinn á Akureyri, 1031
Háskólinn á Bifröst, 1031
Háskólinn á Hólum, 1031
Hassan Usman Katsina Polytechnic,
    1645
Hasselblad Centre for High Resolution
    Digital Imaging, Rochester, 2310
Hasselt Universiteit, 272
Hastings College, 2800
Hastings Museum of Natural and
    Cultural History, 2530
Hatay Museum, 2214
Hatfield College, Durham, 2360
Hatta Foundation Library, 1113
Hauptstaatsarchiv Stuttgart, 871
Haus der Wannsee-Konferenz, Gedenk-
    und Bildungsstätte, 873
Haute École Albert Jacquard, 279
Haute École Blaise Pascal, 279
Haute École Catholique Charleroi-
    Europe, 279
Haute École Charlemagne, 279
Haute École d'Art et de Design,
    Lausanne, 2167
Haute École d'Art et de Design-Genève,
    Geneva, 2167
Haute École de Bruxelles, 279
Haute École de la Communauté
    Française du Hainaut, 279
Haute École de la Communauté
    Française du Luxembourg
    Schuman, 279
Haute École de la Communauté
    Française Paul-Henri Spaak, 279
Haute École de la Province de Liège, 279
Haute École de la Province de Namur,
    279
Haute École de la Ville de Liège, 279
Haute École de Namur, 279
Haute École Francisco Ferrer de la Ville
    de Bruxelles, 279
Haute École Galilée, 280
Haute École Léonard de Vinci, 280
Haute École Libre de Bruxelles—Ilya
    Prigogine, 280
Haute École Libre du Hainaut
    Occidental, 280
Haute École Libre Mosane, 280
Haute École Lucia de Brouckère, 280
Haute École Pédagogique des Cantons
    de Berne, du Jura et de Neuchâtel—
    BEJUNE, 2166
Haute École Provinciale de Hainaut
    Condorcet, 280
Haute École Spécialisée Bernoise, 2166
Haute École Spécialisée de la Suisse
    Orientale, 2166
Havana Athenaeum, 634
Havana Museum of Colonial Art, 637
Haverford College, 2905
Havering College of Further and Higher
    Education, 2411
Havering Libraries, 2320
Havforskningsinstituttet, Bergen, 1650
Havstovan, 688
Haw Kham Royal Palace Museum, 1424
Hawaii Legislative Reference Bureau,
    2485
Hawaii Pacific University, 2648
Hawai'i State Art Museum, 2519
Hawaii State Law Library System, 2485
Hawaiian Historical Society Library,
    2485
Hawassa University, Awassa, 737
Hawke's Bay Cultural Trust, 1608

Hawke's Bay Medical Research
    Foundation (Inc.), 1605
Hawke's Bay Museum and Art Gallery,
    1608
Hays Public Library, 2487
Hayward Gallery, London, 2333
Haywood County Public Library, 2500
Hazara University, 1684
HBO Nederland, 1592
Hbo-Opleidingen Hogeschool Inholland
    Bibliotheek, 1578
HBO-Raad, the Hague, 1560
Head Office of State Archives, Warsaw,
    1771
Headley-Whitney Museum, 2523
Heads of Universities Committee,
    Kowloon, 578
Health and Life Sciences University,
    203
Health Design and Technology
    Institute, 2310
Health, Development, Information and
    Policy Institute, 1699
Health Economics Bergen, 1649
Health Institute Library, 314
Health Protection Agency, Salisbury,
    2304
Health Research Board, Dublin, 1159
Health Research Council of New
    Zealand, 1605
Health Sciences University of
    Hokkaido, 1329
Health Services and Technology
    Research and Development Centre,
    Surabaya, 1112
HealthONE Denver Medical Library,
    2480
Heard Museum, 2510
Heart and Diabetes Center NRW, 859
Heat Physics Department of the Uzbek
    Academy of Sciences, 3031
Heat Technology and Industrial Ecology
    Institute, Ulan Bator, 1531
Hebei Medical University, 520
Hebei Normal University, 520
Hebei University, 521
Hebei University Library, 488
Hebei University of Economics and
    Business, 522
Hebrew College, Brookline, 2727
Hebrew Theological College, 2653
Hebrew Union College—Jewish
    Institute of Religion, 1186
Hebrew Union College—Jewish
    Institute of Religion, New York,
    2835
Hebrew University, 1505
Hebrew University Center of Excellence
    in Agriculture and Environmental
    Health, 1169
Hebrew University of Jerusalem, 1177
Hebrew University of Jerusalem, the
    Library of Agriculture, Food and
    Environment, 1174
Hebrew Writers Association in Israel,
    1167
Hebron Theological College, 2046
Hebron University, 1701
HEC School of Management, Jouy-en-
    Josas, 822
Hechtingsinstituut, 1575
Hector Kobbekaduwa Agrarian
    Research and Training Institute,
    2092
Hector Kobbekaduwa Agrarian
    Research and Training Institute
    Library, 2094
Hector Pieterson Museum,
    Johannesburg, 2033
Hedeselskabet, 676
Hedmark University College, 1665
Hedmarksmuseet, Hamar, 1652
Heeresgeschichtliches Museum,
    Vienna, 197
Hefei University of Technology, 522
Heidelberg Academy of Sciences and
    Humanities, 845
Heidelberg University Biochemistry
    Centre, Heidelberg, 942
Heidelberg University of Education, 910
Heidelberg University, Tiffin, 2881
Heidelberger Akademie der
    Wissenschaften, 845
Heilongjiang Provincial Library, 488

Hollins University, 2977
Hollis Social Library, 2496
Hollywood Heritage Museum, 2512
Hollywood Museum, 2512
Holmes Institute, Melbourne, 181
Holmesglen Institute, 181
Holocaust Memorial Centre, Budapest, 1008
Holokauszt Emlékközpont, 1008
Holter Museum of Art, 2530
Holy Apostles College & Seminary, 2601
Holy Cross College, 2411
Holy Cross College, Notre Dame, 2671
Holy Family Red Crescent Medical College, 243
Holy Family University, Philadelphia, 2905
Holy Names University, Oakland, 2573
Holzforschung Austria, 192
Holztechnikum Kuchl, 209
Home Office Information Services Centre, London, 2320
Homer Public Library, 2477
Homerton College, Cambridge, 2358
Homewood Museum, 2525
Homs Museum, 2169
Honam University, 1399
Honam University Library, 1388
Honduran Coffee Institute, 995
Honduran Foundation for Agricultural Research, 995
Honduran Institute of Anthropology and History, 995
Honduran Institute of Inter-American Culture, 995
Hong Duc University, Thanh Hoa City, 3068
Hong Kong Academy for Performing Arts, 586
Hong Kong Baptist University, 581
Hong Kong Central Library, 579
Hong Kong Chinese Speaking PEN Centre, 579
Hong Kong Council for Accreditation of Academic & Vocational Qualifications, 578
Hong Kong Design Institute, 586
Hong Kong Examinations and Assessment Authority, 578
Hong Kong Film Archive, 579
Hong Kong Heritage Museum, 580
Hong Kong Institute of Certified Public Accountants, 578
Hong Kong Institute of Education, 586
Hong Kong Library Association, 578
Hong Kong Management Association, 578
Hong Kong Maritime Museum, 580
Hong Kong Medical Association, 579
Hong Kong Museum of Art, 580
Hong Kong Museum of History, 580
Hong Kong Observatory, 580
Hong Kong Polytechnic University, 582
Hong Kong Public Libraries, 579
Hong Kong Science Museum, 580
Hong Kong Space Museum, 580
Hong Kong University of Science and Technology, 582
Hong Kong Visual Arts Centre, 580
Hong-Ik University, 1399
Honolulu Academy of Arts, 2519
Honolulu Community College Library, 2485
Honorable Society of Kings Inn, 1165
Honorable Society of King's Inns, Dublin, 1157
Honourable Society of Cymmrodorion, 2285
Hood College, Frederick, 2700
Hood Museum of Art, 2531
Hoofdstedelijke Openbare Bibliotheek, 267
Hooksett Public Library, 2496
Hoover Institution on War, Revolution and Peace, 2479
Hoover Public Library, 2477
Hope Africa University, 376
Hope College, 2746
Hope International University, Fullerton, 2573
Hopp Ferenc Kelet-Ázsiai Művészeti Múzeum, 1008

Horia Hulubei National Institute of Physics and Nuclear Engineering, 1843
Horniman Museum and Gardens, 2334
Horry County Memorial Library, 2504
Horsens Art Museum, 681
Horsens Kunstmuseum, 681
Horseshoe Bend Regional Library, 2477
Horta Museum, Brussels, 270
Horticultural Research and Development Institute, Peradeniya, 2092
Horticultural Research Institute, Giza, 712
Horticultural Research Institute, Harare, 3078
Hortus Botanicus Amsterdam, 1580
Hortus Botanicus, Leiden, 1571
Hortus Haren Holland, 1571
Hōryūji, 1254
Hōryūji Temple, 1254
Hosei University, 1336
Hosei-Shi Gakkai, 1242
Hoseo University, 1400
Hoshi University, 1329
Hosokai, 1242
Hospitaalmuseum, Bruges, 269
Hotchkiss Library of Sharon, 2481
Hotelschool the Hague—International University of Hospitality Management, 1584
Houari Boumediene University of Science and Technology, 105
Houghton College, 2836
Hounslow Library Network, 2320
House and Studio of José Clemente Orozco, 1498
House Museum named after D. Kunayev, 1365
House Museum of José Martí, 637
House of Alijn, Ghent, 270
House of Cane, Trois-Ilets, 828
House of Commons Library, 2320
House of Ecuadorian Culture 'Benjamin Carrión', 700
House of Literature, 266
House of Lords Library, 2320
House of Murillo Museum, 292
House of Representatives Library, Washington, 2482
House of the Americas, Havana, 634
House of the Wannsee Conference, Memorial and Educational Site, 873
Houses of the Oireachtas (Parliament) Library and Research Service, 1159
Housing and Building National Research Centre, Cairo, 712
Housing Policy and Practice Unit, Stirling, 2300
Houston Area Library System, 2505
Houston Baptist University, 2950
Houston Public Library, 2505
Howard and Alba Leahy Library, Vermont, 2506
Howard Payne University, 2950
Howard University, 2624
Howard University Library System, Washington, 2482
Howe Library, 2496
Howest: Hogeschool West-Vlaanderen, 280
Howon University, 1408
Høyskolen Campus Kristiania, 1666
Høyskolen Diakonova, 1666
Høyskolen for Ledelse og Teologi, 1666
Hoyt Institute of Fine Arts, 2540
Hristo Botev National Museum, 362
Hrvatska Akademija Znanosti i Umjetnosti, 623
Hrvatska akademska i istraživačka mreža (CARNet), 623
Hrvatski državni arhiv, 626
Hrvatski muzej naivne umjetnosti, 627
Hrvatski pedagoško-Književni zbor, 624
Hrvatski povijesni muzej, 627
Hrvatski prirodoslovni muzej, 627
Hrvatski restauratorski zavod, Zagreb, 625
Hrvatski Savez Građevinskih Inženjera, 624
Hrvatski školski Muzej, 627
Hrvatsko Farmaceutsko Društvo, 624
Hrvatsko geografsko društvo, 624
Hrvatsko Knjižničarsko Društvo, 623

Hrvatsko Kulturno Društvo 'Napredak', Sarajevo, 296
Hrvatsko Muzejsko Društvo, 624
Hrvatsko Numizmatičko Društvo, 624
Hrvatsko Prirodoslovno Društvo, 624
'Hrvatsko zagorje' Polytechnic, Krapina, 632
Hrvatskog katoličkog sveučilišta, 628
Hrvatskog Liječničkog Zbor, 624
Huachiew Chalermprakiet University, 2191
Hualpén Museum, 469
Huanuco University, 1720
Huaqiao University, 524
Huazhong Agricultural University, 524
Huazhong University of Science and Technology, 524
Hubei Provincial Library, 489
Hubei University, 524
Hubert H. Humphrey Center for Experimental Medicine and Cancer Research, 1171
Hubert Kariuki Memorial University, Dar es Salaam, 2183
Hubrecht Institute, 1571
Hudson Museum, 2525
Hue Royal Antiquities Museum, 3065
Hue University of Agriculture and Forestry, Huê, 3068
Hue University, Thua Thien Huê, 3068
Hughes Hall, Cambridge, 2358
Hugo Sinzheimer Institute, 1568
Hugo Sinzheimer Instituut (HSUIK), 1568
Huguenot Memorial Museum, 2033
Huguenot Society of Great Britain and Ireland, 2285
Hui No'eau Visual Arts Center, 2519
Huíla Regional Museum, 114
Hulett Museum and Art Gallery, 2547
Hull College, 2411
Hull Environment Research Institute (HERI), 2308
Hull Institute for Mathematical Science and Applications, 2307
Hull International Fisheries Institute, Hull, 2299
Hull York Medical School, 2413
Hult International Business School, 2728
Humacao Community College, 3021
HUMAK Humanistinen Ammattikorkeakoulu, Kiviranta, 761
HUMAK University of Applied Sciences, Helsinki, 761
Human Resources University, Phnom Penh, 380
Human Rights Centre, Sarajevo, 298
Human Sciences Research Council (HSRC), Pretoria, 2030
Humanistica University College, 1413
Humboldt Gesellschaft für Wissenschaft, Kunst und Bildung eV, 847
Humboldt Society for Science, Art and Education, 847
Humboldt State University, Arcata, 2573
Humboldt-Universität zu Berlin, 896
Humid Forest Ecoregional Centre, Yaoundé, 383
Hunan Agricultural University, 525
Hunan Normal University, 526
Hunan Provincial Library, 488
Hunan University, 526
Hunedoara-Deva 'Ovid Densusianu' District Library, 1846
Hungarian Academy of Sciences, Budapest, 998
Hungarian Accreditation Committee, 998
Hungarian Association for Geo-Information (HUNAGI), 1000
Hungarian Association for the Protection of Industrial Property and Copyright, 1001
Hungarian Association of Agricultural Sciences, 999
Hungarian Astronautical Society, 1000
Hungarian Biochemical Society, 1000
Hungarian Biological Society, 1000
Hungarian Biomass Association, 1000
Hungarian Biophysical Society, 1000

Hungarian Central Statistical Office Library, 1006
Hungarian Chemical Society, 1001
Hungarian Chemistry Museum, 1012
Hungarian Dairy Research Institute, 1002
Hungarian Dance Academy Budapest, 1027
Hungarian Electrotechnical Association, 1001
Hungarian Entomological Society, 1000
Hungarian Environmental and Water Management Museum, 1009
Hungarian Ethnographical Society, 1001
Hungarian Forestry Association, 999
Hungarian Geological and Geophysical Institute, 1004
Hungarian Geological Society, 1000
Hungarian Historical Society, 1000
Hungarian Hydrological Society, 1000
Hungarian Institute for Higher Educational Research, 1003
Hungarian Jewish Archives, 1006
Hungarian Library Institute, 1002
Hungarian Meteorological Society, 1001
Hungarian Mining and Metallurgical Society, 1001
Hungarian Museum of Architecture, 1008
Hungarian Museum of Science, Technology and Transport, 1008
Hungarian Museum of Sport, 1008
Hungarian Museum of Trade and Tourism, 1008
Hungarian Music Council, 999
Hungarian Music Society, 999
Hungarian National Gallery, 1008
Hungarian National Museum, 1008
Hungarian Natural History Museum, 1008
Hungarian Oil and Gas Museum, 1012
Hungarian Open Air Museum, 1011
Hungarian PEN Centre, 1000
Hungarian Philosophical Association, 1001
Hungarian Psychological Association, 1001
Hungarian Rectors' Conference, 998
Hungarian Scientific Association for Transport, 1001
Hungarian Scientific Society for Food Industry, 999
Hungarian Society for Pharmaceutical Sciences, 1000
Hungarian Society for Surveying, Mapping and Remote Sensing, 999
Hungarian Society of Textile Technology and Science, 1002
Hungarian Sociological Association, 1001
Hungarian Speleological Society, 1001
Hungarian Theatre Museum and Institute, 999
Hungarian University of Fine Arts, 1017
Hungarian Writers' Association, 1000
Hunter College, 2821
Hunter Museum of American Art, 2542
Hunterdon Art Museum, 2532
Hunterian Art Gallery, Glasgow, 2331
Hunterian Museum, Glasgow, 2331
Hunterian Museum, London, 2334
Huntingdon College, 2549
Huntington Library, Art Collections and Botanical Gardens, 2512
Huntington Library, Art Collections and Botanical Gardens, Library, 2479
Huntington Medical Research Institutes, Pasadena, 2468
Huntington Museum of Art, 2545
Huntington University, 2671
Huntington University, Sudbury, 403
Huntley Project Museum of Irrigated Agriculture, 2530
Huntsman Marine Science Centre, 391
Huntsville Museum of Art, 2509
Huria Kristen Batak Protestan Nommensen University, 1126
Huron University College, London, Ont., 455
Húsavík Whale Museum, 1030
Huseyn Javid Memorial Flat—Museum, 213

Institute for History, Madrid, 2056

Institute for History of Art, Florence, 1190

Institute for Humanities and Cultural Studies (IHCS), Tehran, 1134

Institute for Hydraulic Engineering and Calibration of Hydrometrical Current-Meters, Vienna, 192

Institute for Hydrochemistry and Chemical Balneology at the Technical University of Munich, 859

Institute for Ibero-American Cooperation, Madrid, 2051

Institute for Informatics and Telematics, Pisa, 1195

Institute for Information Law, Amsterdam, 1568

Institute for Innovation and Governance Studies (IGS), Enschede, 1568

Institute for Integrated Sensor Systems, 193

Institute for Interdisciplinary Mountain Research, Innsbruck, 190

Institute for International and Intercultural Studies, Bellaterra, 2059

Institute for International Economic and Political Studies, Moscow, 1886

Institute for International Economic Studies, 2111

Institute for International Legal Studies, Rome, 1194

Institute for International Relations, Hanoi, 3062

Institute for International Studies, Leiden, 1569

Institute for Land Reclamation, 248

Institute for Language and Folklore, Uppsala, 2112

Institute for Legal Studies of the Hungarian Academy of Sciences, 1002

Institute for Legal Studies, Sofia, 358

Institute for Legislation and Comparative Law, Moscow, 1886

Institute for Lexicography of Austrian Dialects and Names, Vienna, 190

Institute for Linguistic Studies, St Petersburg, 1888

Institute for Literary Studies of the Hungarian Academy of Sciences, 1003

Institute for Logic, Language and Computation, 1575

Institute for Macromolecular Studies of CNR, 1196

Institute for Management of Architectural and Archaeological Heritage, Lisbon, 1815

Institute for Management Research, Nijmegen, 1568

Institute for Market Analysis and Agricultural Trade Policy, Brunswick, 857

Institute for Market, Consumption and Business Cycles Research, 1761

Institute for Materials Research, 932

Institute for Materials Research and Testing, Santiago, 468

Institute for Mathematics, Astrophysics and Particle Physics, 1572

Institute for Mechanized Construction and Rock Mining, Warsaw, 1768

Institute for Media and Journalism, Lugano, 2143

Institute for Medical Research and Occupational Health, Zagreb, 625

Institute for Medical Research (IMR), Kuala Lumpur, 1472

Institute for Medical Research, Jerusalem, 1171

Institute for Medical Technology Assessment (iMTA), 1575

Institute for Medieval and Early Modern Material Culture, 192

Institute for Medieval and Early Modern Material Culture, Krems an der Donau, 190

Institute for Mediterranean Affairs, Inc., Washington, 2451

Institute for Mediterranean Agriculture and Forest Systems, Ercolano, 1193

Institute for Mediterranean Studies, Rethymnon, 971

Institute for Membrane Technology, Rende, 1196

Institute for Metals Superplasticity Problems of RAS, Ufa, 1896

Institute for Microelectronics and Microsystems, Catania, 1196

Institute for Microtechnology, Mainz, 899

Institute for Migration and Ethnic Studies, Amsterdam, 1573

Institute for Molecules and Materials (IMM), Nijmegen, 1572

Institute for Multidisciplinary Research in Quantitative Modelling and Analysis, Louvain-la-Neuve, 262

Institute for Musicology, Research Centre for the Humanities, Hungarian Academy of Sciences, 1003

Institute for Natural Resources and Agrobiology, Seville, 2057

Institute for Natural Sciences, Nukus, 3031

Institute for Nature Conservation and Biodiversity, Lisboa, 1820

Institute for Nature Management, Minsk, 249

Institute for Nuclear Research, Hungarian Academy of Sciences, 1004

Institute for Occupational Health, Kyiv, 2250

Institute for Operations Research and the Management Sciences, Hanover, 2451

Institute for Organic Syntheses and Photoreactivity, Bologna, 1196

Institute for Petroleum Research, Clausthal-Zellerfeld, 863

Institute for Photonics and Nanotechnologies, Rome, 1195

Institute for Plant Genetic Resources 'K. Malkov', Sadovo, 356

Institute for Plant Protection and the Environment, Belgrade, 1972

Institute for Plasma and Nuclear Fusion, Lisboa, 1820

Institute for Plasma Physics, 1195

Institute for Plasma Research, Gandhinagar, 1046

Institute for Plastics Technology, Aachen, 916

Institute for Policy Research and Development, Kathmandu, 1557

Institute for Political and International Studies (IPIS), Tehran, 1134

Institute for Political and International Studies Library and Documentation Centre, Tehran, 1135

Institute for Political Science, Centre for Social Sciences, Hungarian Academy of Sciences, 1003

Institute for Prevention and Occupational Medicine of the German Social Accident Insurance, 859

Institute for Problems of Cryobiology and Cryomedicine, Kharkiv, 2250

Institute for Process and Application Technology in Ceramics, Aachen, 916

Institute for Programming Research and Algorithmics, 1572

Institute for Psychosocial Intervention and Communication Research, 210

Institute for Public Policy, Bishkek, 1418

Institute for Quantum Optics and Quantum Information, 192

Institute for Reference Materials and Measurements, 266

Institute for Relations between Italy and the Countries of Africa, Latin America and the Middle and Far East, 1197

Institute for Research and Development of Chemical Processes, 291

Institute for Research in Fundamental Sciences, 1134

Institute for Research in Humanities Library, Kyoto, 1252

Institute for Research in Mathematics Education, Cayenne, 824

Institute for Research in Rationalization, Aachen, 916

Institute for Research in Social Communication of Slovak Academy of Sciences, 2005

Institute for Research into Dangerous Substances, 861

Institute for Research of Crimes Against Humanity and International Law, 298

Institute for Research of Eretz Israel, Jerusalem, 1172

Institute for Research on Combustion, Naples, 1195

Institute for Research on Grapes, 3052

Institute for Research on Judicial Systems, Bologna, 1194

Institute for Research on Population and Social Policies, Rome, 1194

Institute for Retail Studies, Stirling, 2298

Institute for Ritual and Liturgical Studies, Tilburg, 1574

Institute for Roses, Essential and Medical Cultures, Kazanlak, 357

Institute for School Development in Siberia, the Far East and the North, Tomsk, 1887

Institute for Science and Art, Vienna, 190

Institute for Science, Innovation and Society (ISIS), 1575

Institute for Science of Labour, 1249

Institute for Scientific and Artistic Work in Split, 624

Institute for Scientific and Technological Research, Butare, 1954

Institute for Security and Development Policy, Nacka, 2111

Institute for Security Policy at Kiel University (ISPK), 888

Institute for Security, Technology, and Society, Hanover, 2475

Institute for Serbian Language SASA, 1973

Institute for Service Industry Research, Naples, 1194

Institute for Social & Economic Research, Colchester, 2301

Institute for Social and Economic Change, Bengaluru, 1042

Institute for Social and Environmental Research—Nepal, 1557

Institute for Social Reform and Social Politics, Vienna, 189

Institute for Social Research in Zagreb, 625

Institute for Social Research, Vilnius, 1447

Institute for Socio-Economic Problems of the Aral Sea Region, Nukus, 3032

Institute for Socio-Economic Studies of Population, St Petersburg, 1886

Institute for Sociology, Centre for Social Sciences, Hungarian Academy of Sciences, 1005

Institute for Sociology of Slovak Academy of Sciences, 2005

Institute for Soil, Climate and Water, Pretoria, 2029

Institute for Soil Sciences and Agricultural Chemistry, Centre for Agricultural Research, Hungarian Academy of Sciences, 1002

Institute for Solar Physics of Stockholm University, 2112

Institute for Spatial Design, 189

Institute for Sport & Leisure, Enschede, 1565

Institute for Standardization of Bosnia and Herzegovina, 298

Institute for State and Law, Minsk, 249

Institute for Steel Structures and Shell Structures, Graz, 192

Institute for Structural Analysis, 192

Institute for Studies and Design of Oil and Gas Technology, Tiranë, 97

Institute for Studies and Technology of Minerals, Tiranë, 97

Institute for Superconductors, Innovative Materials and Devices, Genoa, 1196

Institute for Surface and Coating Analysis, Kaiserslautern, 927

Institute for Sustainable Agriculture, Córdoba, 2058

Institute for Sustainable Development, Msida, 1485

Institute for Sustainable Plant Protection, Turin, 1193

Institute for Systems Analysis and Computer Science, Rome, 1195

Institute for Systems Analysis, Moscow, 1901

Institute for Systems based on Optoelectronics and Microtechnology, Madrid, 2063

Institute for Technical Physics and Materials Science, Research Centre for Natural Sciences, Hungarian Academy of Sciences, 1004

Institute for Technological Research, São Paulo, 312

Institute for Technologies Applied to Cultural Heritage, Monterotondo Stazione, 1194

Institute for Technology and the Storage of Agricultural Products, Bet-Dagan, 1169

Institute for Technology of Nuclear and Other Mineral Raw Materials, 1973

Institute for Textile Technology and Process Engineering Denkendorf, 863

Institute for the Arts and Humanities, University Park, 2466

Institute for the Bulgarian Language, Sofia, 358

Institute for the Coastal Marine Environment, Naples, 1195

Institute for the Conservation and Valorization of Cultural Heritage, Sesto Fiorentino, 1194

Institute for the Contemporary Urban Project, Mendrisio, 2143

Institute for the Control of Foot and Mouth Disease and Dangerous Infections, Sliven, 357

Institute for the Cultural and Intellectual History of Asia, Vienna, 191

Institute for the Danube Region and Central Europe, 63

Institute for the Dynamics of Environmental Processes, Venice, 1194

Institute for the Encouragement of Scientific Research and Innovation of Brussels, 258

Institute for the European Intellectual Lexicon and the History of Ideas, Rome, 1194

Institute for the History and Philosophy of Science in Zagreb, 624

Institute for the History of Philosophical and Scientific Thought in the Modern Age, Naples, 1194

Institute for the History of Science and Technology—St Petersburg Branch, 1893

Institute for the History of the Italian Revival, 1190

Institute for the Integration of Latin America and the Caribbean, 120

Institute for the Occupational Training of Youth, Moscow, 1887

Institute for the Philosophy of Science, Salzburg, 190

Institute for the Protection of Cultural Monuments of Serbia, 1972

Institute for the Protection of the Cultural, Historical and Natural Heritage of Bosnia and Herzegovina, 298

Institute for the Protection of the Cultural, Historical and Natural Heritage of the Canton of Sarajevo, 298

Institute for the Protection of the Mother and Newborn Child, Hanoi, 3063

Institute for the Psychological Sciences, 2977

Institute for the Structure of Matter, Rome, 1195

Institute for the Study of Ancient Culture, 190

Institute for the Study of International Aspects of Competition, Kingston, 2467

Institute for the Study of International Politics, Milan, 1197

Institute for the study of Judaism, Brussels, 265

Institute for the Study of Labour, 857

Institute for the Study of Mankind in Africa, Johannesburg, 2030

Institute for the Study of Regionalism, Federalism and Self-Government, Rome, 1194

Institute for the Study of Societies and Knowledge, Sofia, 360

Institute for the Study of the Americas, London, 2385

Institute for the Study on Ancient Mediterranean, National Research Council (CNR-ISMA), Monterotondo, 1194

Institute for the Training and Development of Human Resources, Panamá, 1702

Institute for Theological and Leadership Philosophy Jaffray, 1131

Institute for Theoretical Physics, Amsterdam, 1572

Institute for Tourism Studies, Macao, 589

Institute for Trade Studies and Research, Tehran, 1134

Institute for Training and Development of Human Resources, Panamá, 1703

Institute for Transport and Maritime Management Antwerp, 266

Institute for Tropical Ecosystem Studies, San Juan, 3015

Institute for Tropical Technology, Hanoi, 3064

Institute for University Co-operation, 1187

Institute for Urban and Regional Research, Vienna, 192

Institute for Urban History (City Archives), Frankfurt, 866

Institute for Urbanism, 189

Institute for Veterinary Medical Research, Centre for Agricultural Research, Hungarian Academy of Sciences, 1002

Institute for Veterinary Research, Lubango, 113

Institute for Water and Environmental Problems, Barnaul, 1894

Institute for Western Affairs, Poznań, 1762

Institute for Wetland and Water Research (IWWR), 1572

Institute for World Economics, Research Centre for Economic and Regional Studies of the Hungarian Academy of Sciences, 1002

Institute for World Economy, Bucharest, 1840

Institute of Acoustics and Sensors, Rome, 1196

Institute of Acoustics, Beijing, 486

Institute of Acoustics, St Albans, 2292

Institute of Advanced Chemistry of Catalonia, 2059

Institute of Advanced Legal Studies Library, London, 2320

Institute of Advanced Legal Studies, London, 2384

Institute of Advanced Studies in Education Deemed University, 1102

Institute of Advanced Study, Basel, 2144

Institute of African Studies, Freetown, 1992

Institute of Agricultural and Environmental Engineering, Wageningen, 1575

Institute of Agricultural and Environmental Sciences, Tartu, 729

Institute of Agricultural and Food Biotechnology, 1760

Institute of Agricultural and Food Economics, 1760

Institute of Agricultural and Food Information, Prague, 657

Institute of Agricultural Biology and Biotechnology, Milan, 1193

Institute of Agricultural Economics, Kyiv, 2249

Institute of Agricultural Economics, Minsk, 248

Institute of Agricultural Economics, Sofia, 357

Institute of Agricultural Engineering, Bet-Dagan, 1169

Institute of Agricultural Information (with Central Agricultural Library), Sofia, 362

Institute of Agricultural Research and Training (IART), Ibadan, 1625

Institute of Agricultural Science of South Viet Nam, 3062

Institute of Agriculture, Chabani, 2249

Institute of Agriculture, Lithuanian Research Centre for Agriculture and Forestry, 1447

Institute of Agriculture 'Obraztsov Chiflik', 357

Institute of Agriculture, Skopje, 1459

Institute of Agriculture—Karnobat, 357

Institute of Agriculture—Kyustendil, 357

Institute of Agro-Environmental and Forest Biology, Porano, 1194

Institute of American Indian and Alaska Native Culture and Arts Development, 2815

Institute of American Studies, Beijing, 484

Institute of Analytical Chemistry AS CR, 655

Institute of Analytical Chemistry, Hamhung, 1384

Institute of Analytical Instrumentation, St Petersburg, 1901

Institute of Andean Biology, Lima, 1716

Institute of Andorran Studies, 111

Institute of Animal Biochemistry and Genetics of Slovak Academy of Sciences, 2004

Institute of Animal Husbandry Research, Tiranë, 96

Institute of Animal Physiology and Genetics AS CR, 655

Institute of Animal Physiology of Slovak Academy of Sciences, 2004

Institute of Animal Production, 248

Institute of Animal Science and Pastures, Nova Odessa, 310

Institute of Animal Science, Bet-Dagan, 1169

Institute of Animal Science, Kostinbrod, 357

Institute of Anthropological and Spatial Studies ZRC SAZU, 2018

Institute of Anthropology and History, Guatemala City, 985

Institute of Applied and Computational Mathematics, Heraklion, 970

Institute of Applied Astronomy, St Petersburg, 1896

Institute of Applied Botany at Hamburg University, 860

Institute of Applied Ecology, Shenyang, 485

Institute of Applied Geosciences, Graz, 190

Institute of Applied Linguistics, Rīga, 1427

Institute of Applied Manpower Research, Delhi, 1047

Institute of Applied Mathematics and Information Technology, Pavia, 1195

Institute of Applied Mathematics and Mechanics, Donetsk, 2253

Institute of Applied Mathematics, Beijing, 485

Institute of Applied Mathematics, Vladivostok, 1901

Institute of Applied Mechanics, 188

Institute of Applied Mechanics and Structures, 122

Institute of Applied Mechanics, Izhevsk, 1901

Institute of Applied Mechanics, Moscow, 1901

Institute of Applied Optics, Mogilev, 249

Institute of Applied Physics, Chişinău, 1525

Institute of Applied Physics, Minsk, 250

Institute of Applied Physics, Nizhnii Novgorod, 1896

Institute of Applied Physics, Sesto Fiorentino, 1195

Institute of Applied Problems of Physics, Ashtarak, 138

Institute of Applied Social Studies, Birmingham, 2309

Institute of Appropriate Technology, Dhaka, 224

Institute of Aquaculture, 969

Institute of Arab and Islamic Studies, Exeter, 2309

Institute of Arab Music, Cairo, 711

Institute of Arab Research and Studies, Cairo, 712

Institute of Archaeological Heritage—Monuments and Sites, Lecce, 1194

Institute of Archaeology, 1700

Institute of Archaeology and Ancient History, Chişinău, 1524

Institute of Archaeology and Ethnography, Baku, 212

Institute of Archaeology and Ethnography, Yerevan, 137

Institute of Archaeology and Ethnology of the Polish Academy of Sciences, 1763

Institute of Archaeology and History of Art of the Romanian Academy, 1840

Institute of Archaeology and Museum Studies, Jos, 1626

Institute of Archaeology at ZRC SAZU, 2018

Institute of Archaeology, Beijing, 484

Institute of Archaeology, Delhi, 1043

Institute of Archaeology, Hanoi, 3062

Institute of Archaeology, Iceland, 1029

Institute of Archaeology in Iasi, 1840

Institute of Archaeology, Kyiv, 2249

Institute of Archaeology, Moscow, 1887

Institute of Archaeology of Slovak Academy of Sciences, 2003

Institute of Archaeology, Pyongyang, 1384

Institute of Archaeology, Samarqand, 3031

Institute of Archaeology, Tiranë, 96

Institute of Archaeology, Ulan Bator, 1530

Institute of Architectural Theory, History of Art and Cultural Studies, Graz, 188

Institute of Architectural Typologies, Graz, 189

Institute of Architecture and Art, Baku, 212

Institute of Architecture and Building Engineering, Pyongyang, 1384

Institute of Architecture and Landscape, Graz, 188

Institute of Architecture and Media, Graz, 188

Institute of Architecture and Town Planning, Ulan Bator, 1530

Institute of Architecture Technology, Graz, 188

Institute of Architecture, Vilnius, 1447

Institute of Arctic Studies, Hanover, 2471

Institute of Area Studies, 1700

Institute of Argumentation, Linguistics and Semiotics, Lugano, 2144

Institute of Art, Folklore Studies and Ethnography 'M. T. Rylsky', Kyiv, 2252

Institute of Art History AS CR, v.v.i., 654

Institute of Art History, Bratislava, 2003

Institute of Art of the Polish Academy of Sciences, 1763

Institute of Art Studies, Sofia, 358

Institute of Arts, Ethnography and Folklore, Minsk, 250

Institute of Astro- and Particle Physics, University of Innsbruck, Innsbruck, 191

Institute of Astronomy and Astrophysics, 264

Institute of Astronomy, Cambridge, 2308

Institute of Astronomy, México, 1496

Institute of Astronomy, Moscow, 1896

Institute of Astronomy University of Latvia, 1428

Institute of Astrophysics, Dushanbe, 2179

Institute of Astrophysics, Göttingen, 861

Institute of Asturian Studies, Oviedo, 2055

Institute of Atmospheric Optics, Tomsk, 1896

Institute of Atmospheric Physics AS CR, v.v.i., 656

Institute of Atmospheric Physics, Moscow, 1896

Institute of Atmospheric Sciences and Climate, Bologna, 1194

Institute of Atmospheric Sounding, Beijing, 486

Institute of Atomic and Molecular Sciences, Taipei, 2173

Institute of Atomic Physics and Spectroscopy, Riga, 1428

Institute of Automatics and Information Technology, Bishkek, 1419

Institute of Automation and Control Processes, Vladivostok, 1901

Institute of Automation and Electrometry, Novosibirsk, 1901

Institute of Automation, Beijing, 487

Institute of Avian Research 'Vogelwarte Helgoland', 860

Institute of Aviation, Warsaw, 1768

Institute of Bangladesh Studies, Rajshahi, 224

Institute of Bankers in South Africa, 2027

Institute of Banking Studies, Safat, 1416

Institute of Basic Medical Sciences, Beijing, 484

Institute of Beekeeping, P. I. Prokopovych, Kyiv, 2249

Institute of Bibliographical Research, México, 1495

Institute of Biochemistry and Biophysics of the Polish Academy of Sciences, 1765

Institute of Biochemistry, Bucharest, 1842

Institute of Biochemistry, Grodno, 249

Institute of Biochemistry, Molecular Biology and Biotechnology, Colombo, 2098

Institute of Biochemistry, Szeged, 1004

Institute of Biochemistry, Tashkent, 3031

Institute of Biocomputation and Physics of Complex Systems, 2062

Institute of Biodiversity and Ecosystem Research, Sofia, 359

Institute of Biodiversity Conservation and Research, Addis Ababa, 736

Institute of Bioecology, Nukus, 3031

Institute of Bioelectronic and Molecular Microsystems, Bangor, 2311

Institute of Bioenergy Crops and Sugar Beet, Kyiv, 2249

Institute of Bioengineering, Elche, 2061

Institute of Biological Chemistry, Taipei, 2173

Institute of Biological, Environmental and Rural Sciences, Aberystwyth, 2433

Institute of Biological, Environmental and Rural Sciences—ibers—Aberystwyth University, Aberystwyth, 2299

Institute of Biological Instrumentation, Moscow, 1901

Institute of Biological Problems of the North, Magadan, 1893

Institute of Biological Research Cluj-Napoca, 1842

Institute of Biological Research Iasi, 1842

Institute of Biological Sciences, Rajshahi, 223

Institute of Biology and Experimental Medicine, 121

Institute of Ecology and Geography, Chişinău, 1524

Institute of Ecology, Tallinn, 730

Institute of Ecology, Technology and Innovation GmbH, Vienna, 193

Institute of Ecology, Xalapa, 1496

Institute of Eco-Museal Research Tulcea, 1842

Institute of Economic Affairs, London, 2281

Institute of Economic Analysis, Barcelona, 2056

Institute of Economic and International Problems of the Assimilation of the Ocean, Vladivostok, 1893

Institute of Economic and Social Development, Buenos Aires, 120

Institute of Economic and Social Problems of the North, Syktyvkar, 1886

Institute of Economic Growth, Delhi, 1047

Institute of Economic Research, Khabarovsk, 1886

Institute of Economic Research of Slovak Academy of Sciences, 2003

Institute of Economic Studies, Reykjavík, 1029

Institute of Economics, Almaty, 1363

Institute of Economics and Business Administration, La Libertad, 725

Institute of Economics and Business, Almaty, 1363

Institute of Economics and Demographics, Dushanbe, 2179

Institute of Economics and Foreign Economic Relations, 1930

Institute of Economics and Management, Tallinn, 734

Institute of Economics and Social Sciences of Estonian University of Life Sciences, 729

Institute of Economics, Baku, 212

Institute of Economics, Beijing, 484

Institute of Economics, Ekaterinburg, 1886

Institute of Economics, Hanoi, 3062

Institute of Economics, Kyiv, 2249

Institute of Economics, Latvian Academy of Sciences, 1427

Institute of Economics, Lugano, 2143

Institute of Economics, Minsk, 250

Institute of Economics, Moscow, 1886

Institute of Economics named after Alyshbaev J., 1418

Institute of Economics of the Lithuanian Academy of Sciences, 1448

Institute of Economics of the Polish Academy of Sciences, 1762

Institute of Economics, Research Centre for Economic and Regional Studies, Hungarian Academy of Sciences, 1002

Institute of Economics, Sarajevo, 298

Institute of Economics, Taipei, 2172

Institute of Economics, Tashkent, 3031

Institute of Economics, Ulan Bator, 1530

Institute of Economics, Yerevan, 137

Institute of Economics—Sts Cyril and Methodius University in Skopje, 1459

Institute of Economy and Demography, Dushanbe, 2179

Institute of Ecosystem Study, Pallanza Verbania, 1195

Institute of Education and Research, Dhaka, 223

Institute of Education Development, Tiranë, 96

Institute of Education Library, Yangon, 1546

Institute of Education, London, 2375

Institute of Education Sciences, Bellaterra, 2060

Institute of Education Sciences (IES), Washington, 2467

Institute of Education Sciences, Salamanca, 2060

Institute of Education Sciences, Tarragona, 2060

Institute of Education, Yangon, 1549

Institute of Electrical and Electronics Engineers, New York, 2464

Institute of Electrical Engineering of Slovak Academy of Sciences, 2005

Institute of Electrical Engineers of Japan (IEEJ), 1248

Institute of Electrical Research, Cuernavaca, 1497

Institute of Electricity, Pyongsong, 1385

Institute of Electrodynamics, Kyiv, 2253

Institute of Electron Technology, Warsaw, 1769

Institute of Electronic Materials Technology, Warsaw, 1769

Institute of Electronic Measurement Kvarz, Nizhny Novgorod, 1901

Institute of Electronic Structure and Laser, Heraklion, 972

Institute of Electronics and Computer Science, Riga, 1428

Institute of Electronics, Beijing, 487

Institute of Electronics, Computer and Telecommunications Engineering, Turin, 1195

Institute of Electronics, Informatics and Automation, Hanoi, 3064

Institute of Electronics, Information and Communication Engineers, Tokyo, 1248

Institute of Electronics, Minsk, 250

Institute of Electronics named after U. A. Arifov, 3032

Institute of Electrophysics, Ekaterinburg, 1896

Institute of Energetics Problems, Minsk, 250

Institute of Energetics, Tiranë, 97

Institute of Energy Economics, Japan, 1251

Institute of Energy, Hanoi, 3064

Institute of Energy Problems of Chemical Physics, Moscow, 1896

Institute of Energy Research, Moscow, 1901

Institute of Energy Resources and Geoecology, Jalal-Abad, 1418

Institute of Energy Technology, Chittagong, 224

Institute of Engineering Cybernetics, Minsk, 250

Institute of Engineering Geodesy and Measurement Systems, Graz, 189

Institute of Engineering Mechanics 'A. M. Pidhorny', Kharkiv, 2253

Institute of Engineering Mechanics, China Earthquake Administration, Harbin, 487

Institute of Engineering Science, Ekaterinburg, 1901

Institute of Engineering Thermophysics, Beijing, 487

Institute of Engineering Thermophysics, Kyiv, 2253

Institute of Engineers of Chile, 467

Institute of English Studies, London, 2385

Institute of Enterprise, Warsaw, 1762

Institute of Entrepreneurship and Service of Tajikistan, 2180

Institute of Environment and Sustainable Development, 265

Institute of Environmental and Water Studies, Birzeit, 1699

Institute of Environmental Engineering of the Polish Academy of Sciences, 1759

Institute of Environmental Geology and Geoengineering, Monterotondo Stazione, 1194

Institute of Environmental Health Science, Detroit, 2471

Institute of Environmental Hygiene and Toxicology, Gelsenkirchen, 859

Institute of Environmental Protection, Pyongyang, 1384

Institute of Environmental Research and Sustainable Development, Athens, 971

Institute of Environmental Science and Research Ltd (ESR), 1606

Institute of Environmental Science, Rajshahi, 224

Institute of Environmental Studies, Karachi, 1676

Institute of Epidemiological Diagnosis and Reference, México, 1496

Institute of Epidemiology and Infectious Diseases 'L. V. Gromashevsky', Kyiv, 2250

Institute of Epidemiology and Microbiology, Irkutsk, 1889

Institute of Epidemiology and Microbiology, Vladivostok, 1889

Institute of Epidemiology, Disease Control and Research and National Influenza Centre (IEDCR), Dhaka, 223

Institute of Ergonomics and Human Factors, Loughborough, 2295

Institute of Estuarine and Coastal Studies, Hull, 2308

Institute of Ethiopian Studies, Addis Ababa, 736

Institute of Ethiopian Studies Library, Addis Ababa, 736

Institute of Ethnic Classics, Pyongyang, 1384

Institute of Ethnic Literature, Beijing, 484

Institute of Ethnological Studies, Lima, 1715

Institute of Ethnology and Folklore Research, Zagreb, 625

Institute of Ethnology and Folklore Studies with Ethnographic Museum, Sofia, 360

Institute of Ethnology AS CR, v.v.i., 656

Institute of Ethnology, Hanoi, 3064

Institute of Ethnology of Slovak Academy of Sciences, 2005

Institute of Ethnology of the Hungarian Academy of Sciences, 1005

Institute of Ethnology, Taipei, 2173

Institute of Ethnomusicology ZRC SAZU, 2018

Institute of Europe, Moscow, 1886

Institute of European and American Studies, Taipei, 2173

Institute of European Law, Birmingham, 2301

Institute of European Public Law, Hull, 2301

Institute of European Studies and Human Rights, Salamanca, 2060

Institute of European Studies, Beijing, 484

Institute of European Tort Law, Vienna, 189

Institute of Experimental and Clinical Medicine, Rīga, 1427

Institute of Experimental Biology, Almaty, 1364

Institute of Experimental Botany AS CR, 655

Institute of Experimental Cardiology, Moscow, 1891

Institute of Experimental Endocrinology, Moscow, 1889

Institute of Experimental Endocrinology of Slovak Academy of Sciences, 2004

Institute of Experimental Medicine AS CR v.v.i, 654

Institute of Experimental Medicine, Caracas, 3048

Institute of Experimental Medicine of the Hungarian Academy of Sciences, 1003

Institute of Experimental Medicine of the National Health Service, Santiago, 467

Institute of Experimental Medicine, St Petersburg, 1889

Institute of Experimental Meteorology, Obninsk, 1896

Institute of Experimental Mineralogy, Moscow, 1896

Institute of Experimental Morphology, Pathology and Anthropology with Museum, Sofia, 359

Institute of Experimental Pharmacology and Toxicology, Bratislava, 2004

Institute of Experimental Physics of Slovak Academy of Sciences, 2005

Institute of Experimental Phytopathology and Entomology of Slovak Academy of Sciences, 2004

Institute of Experimental Psychology of Slovak Academy of Sciences, 2005

Institute of Experimental Veterinary Medicine 'S. N. Wyshelesski', 248

Institute of Family Sciences, Salamanca, 2062

Institute of Far Eastern Studies, Moscow, 1886

Institute of Ferrous Metals, Nampo, 1384

Institute of Finance, Hanoi, 3062

Institute of Finance, Lugano, 2143

Institute of Finance Management, Dar es Salaam, 2186

Institute of Fine Organic Chemistry, Yerevan, 137

Institute of Fiscal Studies, Madrid, 2060

Institute of Fisheries and Aquaculture, Varna, 357

Institute of Fisheries and Maritime Research, Lisbon, 1820

Institute of Fisheries Ecology, 856

Institute of Fisheries, Kyiv, 2249

Institute of Folk Culture, Tiranë, 97

Institute of Folk Medicine, Tiranë, 97

Institute of Food Production Sciences, Bari, 1193

Institute of Food Research, Norwich, 2299

Institute of Food Science and Technology, Dhaka, 223

Institute of Food Science and Technology, London, 2295

Institute of Food Science, Avellino, 1193

Institute of Food Substances, Moscow, 1893

Institute of Food Technologists, Chicago, 2465

Institute of Forage Crops—Pleven, 357

Institute of Foreign Economic Research, Moscow, 1886

Institute of Foreign Languages, Podgorica, 1535

Institute of Forensic Research, Cracow, 1762

Institute of Forest and Walnut Studies named after Gan, P. A., 1418

Institute of Forest Ecology of the Slovak Academy of Sciences, 2004

Institute of Forest Research, Uspenskoe, 1884

Institute of Forestry, Ekaterinburg, 1884

Institute of Forestry, Lithuanian Research Centre for Agriculture and Forestry, 1447

Institute of Forestry Research, Havana, 635

Institute of French Language and Civilization, Neuchâtel, 2144

Institute of Fruit Growing and Vineyard Research, 96

Institute of Fuel Research and Development, Dhaka, 223

Institute of Fuel, Songrim, 1385

Institute of Fundamental Technological Research of the Polish Academy of Sciences, 1769

Institute of Gastroenterology, Dushanbe, 2179

Institute of Gene Biology (IGB), Moscow, 1894

Institute of General and Experimental Biology, Siberian Branch, Russian Academy of Sciences, Ulan-Ude, 1893

Institute of General and Inorganic Chemistry, Minsk, 249

Institute of General and Inorganic Chemistry, Sofia, 360

Institute of General and Inorganic Chemistry, Tashkent, 3032

Institute of General and Inorganic Chemistry 'V. I. Vernadsky', Kyiv, 2251

Institute of General and Inorganic Chemistry, Yerevan, 138

Institute of General Genetics and Cytology, Almaty, 1364

Institute of General Organic Chemistry, Madrid, 2059

Institute of General Pathology and Pathophysiology, Moscow, 1889

Institute of Genetic Resources, Baku, 212

Institute of Genetics 'Acad. Doncho Kostoff', 359

Institute of Genetics and Animal Breeding of the Polish Academy of Sciences, 1760

Institute of Genetics and Biophysics, Naples, 1195

Institute of Genetics and Cytology, Minsk, 249

Institute of Genetics and Developmental Biology, Beijing, 485

Institute of Genetics and Plant Experimental Biology, Tashkent, 3031

Institute of Genetics and Plant Physiology, Chişinău, 1524

Institute of Genetics, Pyongyang, 1384

Institute of Genetics, Szeged, 1004

Institute of Geochemistry, Guiyang, 486

Institute of Geochemistry, Irkutsk, 1896

Institute of Geochemistry, Mineralogy and Ore Formation, Kyiv, 2252

Institute of Geodesy and Cartography, Warsaw, 1763

Institute of Geodesy and Geoinformatics, Riga, 1427

Institute of Geodynamics, Athens, 971

Institute of Geodynamics Sabba S. Ştefănescu of Romanian Academy, 1842

Institute of Geoecology, Ulan Bator, 1531

Institute of Geography, Almaty, 1363

Institute of Geography and Conservation of Natural Resources, Mérida, 3048

Institute of Geography, Baku, 212

Institute of Geography, Moscow, 1887

Institute of Geography of Slovak Academy of Sciences, 2003

Institute of Geography, Pyongyang, 1384

Institute of Geography, Ulan Bator, 1530

Institute of Geography—Romanian Academy, 1840

Institute of Geological and Nuclear Sciences Ltd, Lower Hutt, 1606

Institute of Geological Sciences, Hanoi, 3063

Institute of Geological Sciences, Kyiv, 2252

Institute of Geological Sciences of the Polish Academy of Sciences, 1766

Institute of Geological Sciences, Yerevan, 138

Institute of Geology & Mineral Exploration, Athens, 970

Institute of Geology and Geochemistry of Combustible Minerals, Lviv, 2252

Institute of Geology and Geography, Vilnius, 1448

Institute of Geology and Geophysics, Beijing, 486

Institute of Geology and Mineral Enrichment, Ulan Bator, 1531

Institute of Geology and Seismology, Chişinău, 1525

Institute of Geology AS CR, v.v.i., 655

Institute of Geology at Tallinn University of Technology, 730

Institute of Geology, Baku, 213

Institute of Geology, Beijing, 486

Institute of Geology, Dushanbe, 2179

Institute of Geology, Earthquake Engineering and Seismology, Dushanbe, 2178

Institute of Geology, Makhachkala, 1896

Institute of Geology, Mining and Metallurgy, 1716

Institute of Geology, Moscow, 1896

Institute of Geology named after M. M. Adyshev, 1418

Institute of Geology of Karelian Research Centre, 1896

Institute of Geology, Pyongsong, 1384

Institute of Geology, Sarajevo, 298

Institute of Geology, Syktyvkar, 1896

Institute of Geology, Ufa, 1896

Institute of Geomechanics and Subsoil Development, Bishkek, 1418

Institute of Geomechanics, Beijing, 486

Institute of Geomechanics, Moscow, 1896

Institute of Geonics AS CR, 654

Institute of Geophysics and Astronomy, Havana, 636

Institute of Geophysics and Engineering Seismology, Gjumry, 138

Institute of Geophysics, Ekaterinburg, 1896

Institute of Geophysics, Kyiv, 2252

Institute of Geophysics of the Polish Academy of Sciences, 1766

Institute of Geosciences and Earth Resources, Pisa, 1194

Institute of Geotechnical Mechanics, Dnipropetrovsk, 2253

Institute of Geotechnics of Slovak Academy of Sciences, 2005

Institute of Germanic and Romance Studies, London, 2385

Institute of Gerontology, Detroit, 2468

Institute of Gerontology, Kyiv, 2250

Institute of Glass and Ceramic Research and Testing, 223

Institute of Global Climate and Ecology, Moscow, 1893

Institute of Grains and Feed Industry, Sofia, 357

Institute of Haematology and Blood Diseases Hospital, Tianjing, 484

Institute of Haematology and Blood Transfusion, Tashkent, 3031

Institute of Haematology and Blood Transfusion, Warsaw, 1764

Institute of Health Economics, Dhaka, 223

Institute of Health Policy & Management, Rotterdam, 1570

Institute of Health, São Paulo, 310

Institute of Health Science of Royal Cambodian Armed Forces, 378

Institute of Health Sciences, Ruwi, 1670

Institute of Health Sciences-North, 1831

Institute of Heraldic and Genealogical Studies, Canterbury, 2285

Institute of High Current Electronics, Tomsk, 1901

Institute of High Energy Physics, Beijing, 486

Institute of High Energy Physics, Vienna, 191

Institute of High Pressure Physics of the Polish Academy of Sciences, 1767

Institute of Higher Education, Jowzjan, 94

Institute of Higher Education, Moscow, 1887

Institute of Higher Education of French Guiana, 825

Institute of Higher Military Education, Buenos Aires, 135

Institute of Higher Nervous Activity and Neurophysiology of RAS, Moscow, 1893

Institute of High-Pressure Physics, Troitsk, 1896

Institute of High-Temperature Electrochemistry, Ekaterinburg, 1896

Institute of High-Temperature Physics, Moscow, 1897

Institute of Highway Engineering and Transport Planning, Graz, 189

Institute of Himalayan Bioresource Technology, 1040

Institute of Historical Research, Athens, 969

Institute of Historical Research Library, London, 2320

Institute of Historical Research, London, 2385

Institute of Historical Science, Research Centre for Humanities of the Hungarian Academy of Sciences, 1003

Institute of Historical Studies, Sofia, 358

Institute of History and Archaeology, Ekaterinburg, 1887

Institute of History and Cultural Heritage, Bishkek, 1418

Institute of History and Philology, Taipei, 2172

Institute of History, Archaeology and Ethnography named after A. Donish, Dushanbe, 2179

Institute of History, Archaeology and Ethnography, Nukus, 3031

Institute of History, Archaeology and Ethnography of the Peoples of the Far East, Vladivostok, 1887

Institute of History AS CR, 654

Institute of History, Ashgabat, 2239

Institute of History, Baku, 212

Institute of History, Chişinău, 1524

Institute of History, Hanoi, 3063

Institute of History, Language and Literature, Ufa, 1887

Institute of History, Minsk, 249

Institute of History of Nicaragua and Central America, 1615

Institute of History of Slovak Academy of Sciences, 2003

Institute of History, Philology and Philosophy, Novosibirsk, 1887

Institute of History, Pyongyang, 1384

Institute of History, Sarajevo, 298

Institute of History, Tallinn, 729

Institute of History, Tashkent, 3031

Institute of History, Tiranë, 96

Institute of History, Ulan Bator, 1530

Institute of History, Yerevan, 137

Institute of Horticulture, Lithuanian Research Centre for Agriculture and Forestry, 1447

Institute of Housing, Real Estate, Urban and Regional Development Ltd, Bochum, 856

Institute of Human and Animal Physiology, Almaty, 1364

Institute of Human Genetics, Moscow, 1890

Institute of Human Genetics of the Polish Academy of Sciences, 1764

Institute of Human Morphology, Moscow, 1889

Institute of Human Resource Advancement, Colombo, 2098

Institute of Humanities and Social Sciences, 379

Institute of Humanities, Khorog, 2179

Institute of Hydraulic Engineering and Water Resources Management, Graz, 189

Institute of Hydraulic Engineering, Pyongyang, 1385

Institute of Hydraulic Studies and Design, Tiranë, 97

Institute of Hydraulics and Hydrology, Chingleput, 1047

Institute of Hydrobiology, Kyiv, 2251

Institute of Hydrobiology, Wuhan, 485

Institute of Hydrodynamics AS CR, v.v.i., 656

Institute of Hydrodynamics, Novosibirsk, 1897

Institute of Hydroengineering of the Polish Academy of Sciences, 1767

Institute of Hydrogeology and Engineering Geology, Tashkent, 3032

Institute of Hydrogeology and Engineering Geology, Tbilisi, 839

Institute of Hydrogeology and Environmental Geology, Zhengding, 487

Institute of Hydrology of Slovak Academy of Sciences, 2005

Institute of Hydromechanics, Kyiv, 2253

Institute of Hydrometeorology, Tbilisi, 839

Institute of Hydrometeorology, Tiranë, 97

Institute of Hydroponics Problems, Yerevan, 137

Institute of Hygiene, Epidemiology and Microbiology, Ulan Bator, 1530

Institute of Hygiene, Vilnius, 1448

Institute of Iberoamerican Thought, Salamanca, 2062

Institute of Immunology, Moscow, 1889

Institute of Immunology, Tashkent, 3031

Institute of Indigenous Medicine, 2093

Institute of Industrial and Financial Analysis, Madrid, 2060

Institute of Industrial Biology, Pyongsong, 1385

Institute of Industrial Biotechnology, Lahore, 1676

Institute of Industrial Chemistry, Hanoi, 3064

Institute of Industrial Economics, Beijing, 484

Institute of Industrial Economics, Donetsk, 2249

Institute of Industrial Electronics Engineering, Karachi, 1677

Institute of Industrial Engineers, Norcross, 2465

Institute of Industrial Medicine and Human Ecology, Angarsk, 1889

Institute of Industrial Organic Chemistry, Warsaw, 1769

Institute of Industrial Science, 1248

Institute of Industrial Technologies and Automation, Milan, 1196

Institute of Influenza, St Petersburg, 1889

Institute of Informatics and Applied Mathematics, Tiranë, 97

Institute of Informatics and Control Problems, Almaty, 1365

Institute of Informatics and Mathematical Modelling of Technological Processes, Apatity, 1901

Institute of Informatics of Slovak Academy of Sciences, 2005

Institute of Informatics Problems of the Russian Academy of Sciences (IPIRAN), 1901

Institute of Information and Communication Technologies, Sofia, 361

Institute of Information and Communication Technology, Dhaka, 224

Institute of Information and Prognoses of Education, Bratislava, 2003

Institute of Information Recording, Kyiv, 2253

Institute of Information Science and Automation, St Petersburg, 1901

Institute of Information Science and Technology 'Alessandro Faedo', 1195

Institute of Information Science, Taipei, 2173

Institute of Information Technology, Baku, 213

Institute of Information Technology, Dhaka, 224

Institute of Information Technology, Hanoi, 3064

Institute of Information Theory and Automation AS CR, 656

Institute of Information Transmission Problems (Kharkevich Institute), Moscow, 1901

Institute of Inland Waters, 969

Institute of Inorganic and Surface Chemistry, Padua, 1196

Institute of Inorganic Chemistry and Electrochemistry, Tbilisi, 839

Institute of Inorganic Chemistry AS CR, v.v.i., 655

Institute of Inorganic Chemistry, Hamhung, 1384

Institute of Inorganic Chemistry of Slovak Academy of Sciences, 2005

Institute of Inorganic Methodologies and Plasmas, Monterotondo Scalo, 1195

Institute of Integrated Development Studies, Kathmandu, 1557

Institute of Intelligent Systems for Automation, Bari, 1196

Institute of Internal Medicine, Novosibirsk, 1889

Institute of International Affairs, Pyongyang, 1384

Institute of International Affairs, Reykjavík, 1029

Institute of International and Comparative Agricultural Law, Florence, 1193

Institute of International and Social Studies, Tallinn, 730

Institute of International Business, Atlanta, 2467

Institute of International Education, New York, 2445

Institute of International Law, 71

Institute of International Politics and Economics, Belgrade, 1972

Institute of International Public Law and International Relations, Thessaloniki, 970

Institute of International Relations, 96

Institute of International Studies, 472

Institute of International Studies, Ulan Bator, 1530

Institute of Ionized Gas, Padua, 1195

Institute of Ionosphere, Almaty, 1364

Institute of Ionosphere, Kharkiv, 2252

Institute of Irrigation and Drainage Studies and Designs, Tiranë, 96

Institute of Islamic Culture, Lahore, 1673

Institute of Ismaili Studies, London, 2309

Institute of IT Professionals New Zealand, 1605

Institute of Jamaica, Kingston, 1237

Institute of Jewish Studies, Antwerp, 263

Institute of Juche Literature, Pyongyang, 1384

Institute of Judicial Administration, Birmingham, 2301

Institute of Justice, Warsaw, 1762

Institute of Karst Geology, Guilin, 486

Institute of Kiswahili Research, Dar es Salaam, 2183

Institute of Kyrgyz Language and Literature named after Ch. Aitmatov, 1418

Institute of Laboratory Animal Sciences, Beijing, 484

Institute of Labour and Social Studies, Warsaw, 1762

Institute of Labour Science and Social Affairs, Hanoi, 3062

Institute of Landscape Ecology of Slovak Academy of Sciences, 2004

Institute of Language and Literature named after Alisher Navoi, 3031

Institute of Language and Literature named after Alisher Navoi, Nukus, 3031

Institute of Language, Literature and Arts, Makhachkala, 1887

Institute of Language, Literature and History, Syktyvkar, 1887

Institute of Language, Literature, Oriental Studies and Written Heritage named after Rudaki, 2178

Institute of Language, Literature, Oriental Studies and Written Heritage named after Rudaki, Dushanbe, 2179

Institute of Language, Sarajevo, 298

Institute of Laser and Information Technology, Shatura, 1901

Institute of Laser Research, 1928

Institute of Laser Technology, Sofia, 361

Institute of Latin American Studies, Beijing, 484

Institute of Latin American Studies, Berlin, 891

Institute of Latvian History at University of Latvia, 1427

Institute of Law, Ahmedabad, 1107

Institute of Law, Beijing, 484

Institute of Law, Birzeit, 1699

Institute of Law, Lugano, 2143

Institute of Law, Pyongyang, 1384

Institute of Law Studies of the Polish Academy of Sciences, 1762

Institute of Law, University of Iceland, 1029

Institute of Legal Information Theory and Techniques, Florence, 1194

Institute of Legal Practice and Development, 1955

Institute of Lexicology and Lexicography of the Portuguese Language, 1819

Institute of Library Economics and Documentation, 101

Institute of Limnology, St Petersburg, 1893

Institute of Linguistics and Literature, 97

Institute of Linguistics, Beijing, 484

Institute of Linguistics, Bishkek, 1418

Institute of Linguistics, Chişinău, 1524

Institute of Linguistics, Hanoi, 3063

Institute of Linguistics, Literature and History, Petrozavodsk, 1888

Institute of Linguistics, Moscow, 1888

Institute of Linguistics, Msida, 1485

Institute of Linguistics 'O. O. Potebni', Kyiv, 2250

Institute of Linguistics, Pyongyang, 1384

Institute of Linguistics 'Ya. Kolas', Minsk, 249

Institute of Literary Research of the Polish Academy of Sciences, 1763

Institute of Literature and Folklore, Chişinău, 1524

Institute of Literature, Folklore and Art of the University of Latvia, 1427

Institute of Literature, Minsk, 249

Institute of Literature 'Shevchenko, T. G.', Kyiv, 2250

Institute of Literature, Sofia, 358

Institute of Lithuanian Literature and Folklore, 1448

Institute of Lithuanian Scientific Society, 1447

Institute of Macedonian Literature, 1460

Institute of Machine Mechanics and Reliability, Minsk, 250

Institute of Machine Mechanics, Tbilisi, 839

Institute of Machinery and Industrial Instruments, Hanoi, 3064

Institute of Machinery Sciences, Bishkek, 1419

Institute of Macromolecular Chemistry AS CR, 656

Institute of Macromolecular Chemistry, Hamhung, 1384

Institute of Macro-Molecular Compounds, St Petersburg, 1897

Institute of Malariology, Parasitology and Entomology, Hanoi, 3063

Institute of Management, Ahmedabad, 1107

Institute of Management and Development, Pursat, 381

Institute of Management and Technology, Enugu, 1645

Institute of Management, Lugano, 2143

Institute of Management Science, Kompong Cham, 381

Institute of Management Sciences, 1684

Institute of Management Sciences, Peshawar, 1684

Institute of Management Services, Lichfield, 2295

Institute of Management Technology, 2273

Institute of Marine Biological Resources, 969

Institute of Marine Biology and Genetics, 969

Institute of Marine Biology and Oceanography, Freetown, 1992

Institute of Marine Biology, Kotor, 1536

Institute of Marine Biology, Vladivostok, 1894

Institute of Marine Engineering, Science and Technology (IMarEST), London, 2295

Institute of Marine Geology and Geophysics, Yuzhno-Sakhalinsk, 1897

Institute of Marine Research, Bergen, 1650

Institute of Marine Science, Karachi, 1677

Institute of Marine Sciences, Barcelona, 2057

Institute of Marine Sciences, Venice, 1194

Institute of Marine Technology, 1549

Institute of Marine Technology, Boca del Río, 1496

Institute of Maritime and Tropical Medicine, Gdynia, 1764

Institute of Marketing and Communication Management, Lugano, 2143

Institute of Materia Medica, Beijing, 484

Institute of Materials and Machine Mechanics of Slovak Academy of Sciences, 2006

Institute of Materials for Electronics and Magnetism, Parma, 1196

Institute of Materials, Minerals and Mining, London, 2295

Institute of Materials Research of Slovak Academy of Sciences, 2005

Institute of Materials Science, Tashkent, 3032

Institute of Materials Workshop, Trieste, 1195

Institute of Mathematical Machines, Warsaw, 1768

Institute of Mathematical Sciences, Chennai, 1045

Institute of Mathematical Statistics, Beachwood, 83

Institute of Mathematics and Computer Science, Chişinău, 1524

Institute of Mathematics and Computer Science, University of Latvia, 1428

Institute of Mathematics and Informatics, Sofia, 359

Institute of Mathematics and its Applications, Southend-on-Sea, 2292

Institute of Mathematics and Mathematical Modeling, Almaty, 1364

Institute of Mathematics and Mechanics, Ashgabat, 2240

Institute of Mathematics and Mechanics, Baku, 212

Institute of Mathematics and Mechanics, Ekaterinburg, 1901

Institute of Mathematics AS CR, 655

Institute of Mathematics, Beijing, 485

Institute of Mathematics, Dushanbe, 2179

Institute of Mathematics, Hanoi, 3063

Institute of Mathematics, Kyiv, 2251

Institute of Mathematics, México, 1496

Institute of Mathematics, Minsk, 249

Institute of Mathematics of Bahía Blanca, 120

Institute of Mathematics of the Polish Academy of Sciences, 1765

Institute of Mathematics, Physics and Mechanics, Ljubljana, 2019

Institute of Mathematics, Pyongsong, 1384

Institute of Mathematics, Taipei, 2173

Institute of Mathematics, Tashkent, 3031

Institute of Mathematics, Ulan Bator, 1531

Institute of Mathematics with Computer Center, Ufa, 1895

Institute of Mathematics, Yerevan, 137

Institute of Measurement and Control, London, 2296

Institute of Measurement Science of Slovak Academy of Sciences, 2005

Institute of Mechanical Engineering, Pyongsong, 1385

Institute of Mechanical Technology Studies and Design, Tiranë, 97

Institute of Mechanics and Seismic Stability of Structures, Tashkent, 3032

Institute of Mechanics, Beijing, 487

Institute of Mechanics, Hanoi, 3064

Institute of Mechanics, Sofia, 360

Institute of Mechanics, Yerevan, 138

Institute of Mechanization of Animal Husbandry, Zaporizhzhya, 2249

Institute of Medical and Biological Cybernetics, Novosibirsk, 1889

Institute of Medical and Social Care Research, London, 2304

Institute of Medical Biotechnology, Tbilisi, 838

Institute of Medical Climatology and Rehabilitation, Vladivostok, 1889

Institute of Medical Genetics, Tomsk, 1892

Institute of Medical Information, Beijing, 488

Institute of Medical Instrument Making, Moscow, 1901

Institute of Medical Problems of the North, Krasnoyarsk, 1889

Institute of Medical Problems, Osh, 1418

Institute of Medicine, Washington, 2446

Institute of Mediterranean and Oriental Cultures, Polish Academy of Sciences, 1759

Institute of Mediterranean European History, Cagliari, 1194

Institute of Metal Physics, Ekaterinburg, 1897

Institute of Metal Research, Shenyang, 486

Institute of Metal Science, Equipment and Technologies 'Acad. A. Balevski' with Hydroaerodynamics Centre, Sofia, 361

Institute of Metallo-Organic Chemistry, Nizhnii Novgorod, 1897

Institute of Metallurgy and Materials Science of the Polish Academy of Sciences, 1768

Institute of Metallurgy and Ore Enrichment, Almaty, 1365

Institute of Metallurgy, Ekaterinburg, 1897

Institute of Meteorology and Hydrology, Hanoi, 3063

Institute of Meteorology and Hydrology, Ulan Bator, 1531

Institute of Meteorology and Water Management—National Research Institute, 1760

Institute of Meteorology, Havana, 636

Institute of Meteorology, Lisbon, 1820

Institute of Meteorology, Sarajevo, 298

Institute of Methodologies for Environmental Analysis, Tito Scalo, 1194

Institute of Metrology named after D. I. Mendeleyev (VNIIM), St Petersburg, 1897

Institute of Microbial Technology, Chandigarh, 1040

Institute of Microbiology, Abovian, 137

Institute of Microbiology and Biotechnology, Chişinău, 1524

Institute of Microbiology and Biotechnology, Riga, 1428

Institute of Microbiology and Virology, Almaty, 1364

Institute of Microbiology, Baku, 212

Institute of Microbiology, Beijing, 485

Institute of Microbiology, Epidemiology and Infectious Diseases, Almaty, 1364

Institute of Microbiology, Minsk, 249

Institute of Microbiology, Tashkent, 3031

Institute of Microcirculation, Beijing, 484

Institute of Microelectronics Technology and High-Purity Materials, Moscow, 1903

Institute of Microgravity 'Ignacio da Riva', 2063

Institute of Military History, Moscow, 1888

Institute of Mineral Resources, Beijing, 486

Institute of Mineral Resources, Tashkent, 3032

Institute of Mineralogy and Crystallography 'Acad. Ivan Kostov', 361

Institute of Mineralogy, Miass, 1897

Institute of Minerals and Materials Technology, Bhubaneswar, 1040

Institute of Mining and the Chemical Industry, Lviv, 2253

Institute of Mining Engineers of Chile, 467

Institute of Mining, Khabarovsk, 1901

Institute of Mining, Novosibirsk, 1901

Institute of Mining of the North, Yakutsk, 1902

Institute of Mining, Perm, 1902

Institute of Mining Science and Technology, Hanoi, 3064

Institutet för Näringslivsforskning, 2111
Institutet för rymdfysik, 2112
Institutet för Social Forskning, 2112
Institutet för Språk och Folkminnen, 2112
Instituti GAP, 1411
Instituti i Arkeologjisë, 96
Instituti i Duhanit, Cërrik, 96
Instituti i Energjetikës, 97
Instituti i Fizikës Bërthamore, 97
Instituti i Gjuhësisë dhe i Letërsisë, Tiranë, 97
Instituti i Hidrometeorologjisë, 97
Instituti i Historisë, Tiranë, 96
Instituti i Informatikës dhe i Matematikës së Aplikuar, 97
Instituti i Kërkimeve Biologjike, Tiranë, 97
Instituti i Kërkimeve Bujqësore Lushnje, 96
Instituti i Kërkimeve Pyjore dhe Kullotave, 96
Instituti i Kërkimeve të Foragjere, 96
Instituti i Kërkimeve të Pemëve Frutore dhe Vreshtave, Tiranë, 96
Instituti i Kërkimeve të Ushqimit, 97
Instituti i Kërkimeve të Zooteknisë, 96
Instituti i Kërkimeve Veterinare, 96
Instituti i Kerkimit te Bimeve te Arave, Stacioni Eksperimental, 96
Instituti i Kosovës për Drejtësi, 1411
Instituti i Kulturës Popullore, 97
Instituti i Mbrojtjes Bimeve, 96
Instituti i Mjekësisë Popullore, 97
Instituti i Monumenteve të Kulturës, 96
Instituti i Perimeve dhe i Patates, 96
Instituti i Shëndetit Publik, 97
Instituti i Sizmologjise, 97
Instituti i Studimeve dhe i Projektimeve të Hidrocentraleve, 97
Instituti i Studimeve dhe i Projektimeve të Minierave, 97
Instituti i Studimeve dhe i Projektimeve të Teknologjisë Kimike, 97
Instituti i Studimeve dhe i Projektimeve të Teknologjisë Mekanike, 97
Instituti i Studimeve dhe i Projektimeve të Veprave të Kullimit dhe Ujitjes, 96
Instituti i Studimeve dhe i Projektimeve Teknologjike të Mineraleve, 97
Instituti i Studimeve dhe i Projektimeve Teknologjike të Naftës e të Gazit, 97
Instituti i Studimeve dhe i Teknologjisë Ndërtimit, 97
Instituti i Studimeve dhe Projektimeve Mekanike, 97
Instituti i Studimeve dhe Projektimeve të Gjeologjisë, 97
Instituti i Studimeve e Projektimeve Urbanistikë, 96
Instituti i Studimeve të Marrëdhënieve Ndërkombëtare, Tiranë, 96
Instituti i Studimit të Tokave, 96
Instituti i Ullirit dhe i Agrumeve, 96
Instituti i Zhvillimit të Arsimit, 96
Instituti Kombëtar i Shëndetësisë Publike te Kosovës, 1411
Instituti Kosovar për Kërkime dhe Zhvillime të Politikave, 1411
Institution for Research of Materials and Development of New Technologies, 1460
Institution för Spanska, Portugisiska och Latinamerikastudier, 2111
Institution of Agricultural Engineers (IAgrE), Bedford, 2279
Institution of Certificated Mechanical and Electrical Engineers, South Africa, 2029
Institution of Chemical Engineers, Rugby, 2296
Institution of Civil Engineers, London, 2296
Institution of Civil Engineers (Republic of Ireland Division), 1158
Institution of Electrical and Electronics Engineers Pakistan (IEEEP), 1675
Institution of Electronics and Telecommunication Engineers (IETE), New Delhi, 1039
Institution of Electronics, Higher Bebington, 2296

Institution of Engineering and Technology Library and Archives, London, 2320
Institution of Engineering and Technology, Stevenage, 2296
Institution of Engineering Designers, Westbury, 2296
Institution of Engineers and Shipbuilders in Scotland, 2296
Institution of Engineers, Australia trading as Engineers Australia, 147
Institution of Engineers, Bangladesh, 222
Institution of Engineers (India), 1039
Institution of Engineers of Kenya, 1376
Institution of Engineers (Pakistan), 1675
Institution of Engineers, Sri Lanka, 2092
Institution of Environmental Sciences, London, 2290
Institution of Ferdinando the Catholic, 2055
Institution of Fire Engineers, Stratford-upon-Avon, 2296
Institution of Gas Engineers and Managers, Kegworth, 2296
Institution of Highways and Transportation, London, 2296
Institution of Lighting Professionals, Rugby, 2296
Institution of Marine Research, Coimbra, 1820
Institution of Mechanical Engineers, London, 2296
Institution of Professional Engineers New Zealand, 1605
Institution of Russian Academy of Education Ushinsky State Pedagogical Library, 1907
Institution of Structural Engineers, London, 2296
Institution Saint Jude, Lille, 820
Instituto Açoriano de Cultura, 1815
Instituto 'Adolfo Lutz', 310
Instituto Agronômico, Campinas, 309
Instituto Americano de Educación Superior, San Salvador, 724
Instituto Andaluz de Geofísica y Prevención de Desastres Sísmicos, 2062
Instituto Andaluz Interuniversitario de Criminología, 2060
Instituto Antártico Argentino, 121
Instituto Antártico Chileno, 468
Instituto Argentino de Normalización y Certificación (IRAM), 122
Instituto Argentino de Oceanografía, 121
Instituto Arqueológico, Histórico e Geográfico Pernambucano, 307
Instituto Azucarero Dominicano, 694
Instituto 'Benjamin Constant', 310
Instituto Biológico, São Paulo, 311
Instituto Boliviano de Ciencia y Tecnología Nuclear, 291
Instituto Bonaerense de Numismática y Antigüedades, 118
Instituto Botânico 'Dr Júlio Henriques', 1820
Instituto Brasileiro de Economia, 306
Instituto Brasileiro de Educação, Ciência e Cultura (IBECC), 306
Instituto Brasileiro de Estudos e Pesquisas de Gastroenterologia (IBEPEGE), 310
Instituto Brasileiro de Geografia e Estatística, 310
Instituto Brasileiro de Informação em Ciência e Tecnologia (IBICT), 313
Instituto Brasileiro de Petróleo, Gás e Biocombustíveis, 312
Instituto Brasileiro do Meio Ambiente e dos Recursos Naturais Renováveis (IBAMA), 309
Instituto Butantan, 310
Instituto Caribe de Antropología y Sociología, Caracas, 3048
Instituto Caro y Cuervo, 591
Instituto Cartográfico Militar de las Fuerzas Armadas, Santo Domingo, 694

Instituto Centroamericano de Administración Pública (ICAP), 619
Instituto Cervantes, Algiers, 101
Instituto Cervantes, Amman, 1358
Instituto Cervantes, Athens, 968
Instituto Cervantes, Beirut, 1432
Instituto Cervantes, Berlin, 848
Instituto Cervantes, Brussels, 260
Instituto Cervantes, Budapest, 1000
Instituto Cervantes, Cairo, 711
Instituto Cervantes, Damascus, 2168
Instituto Cervantes de Lisboa, 1816
Instituto Cervantes din Bucuresti, 1837
Instituto Cervantes, Dublin, 1158
Instituto Cervantes, Istanbul, 2211
Instituto Cervantes, London, 2287
Instituto Cervantes, Madrid, 2051
Instituto Cervantes, Manila, 1733
Instituto Cervantes, Moscow, 1881
Instituto Cervantes, New York, 2454
Instituto Cervantes, Paris, 769
Instituto Cervantes, Rabat, 1539
Instituto Cervantes, Rio de Janeiro, 307
Instituto Cervantes, Rome, 1191
Instituto Cervantes, Stockholm, 2109
Instituto Cervantes, Tel Aviv, 1167
Instituto Cervantes, Tunis, 2207
Instituto Cervantes, Utrecht, 1562
Instituto Cervantes, Vienna, 186
Instituto Cervantes, Warsaw, 1754
Instituto CEU de Humanidades Ángel Ayala, 2059
Instituto Científico y Tecnológico de Navarra, 2062
Instituto Colombiano Agropecuario, 592
Instituto Colombiano de Antropología e Historia, 593
Instituto Colombiano de Crédito Educativo y Estudios Técnicos en el Exterior (ICETEX), 590
Instituto Colombiano de Normas Técnicas y Certificación (ICONTEC), 593
Instituto Colombiano del Petróleo, 593
Instituto Colombiano para el Fomento de la Educación Superior (ICFES), 591
Instituto Colombiano para la Evaluación de la Educación, 593
Instituto Complutense de Análisis Económico, 2060
Instituto Complutense de Ciencia de la Administración, 2051
Instituto Conmemorativo Gorgas de Estudios de la Salud, 1702
Instituto Costarricense de Investigación y Enseñanza en Nutrición y Salud, 613
Instituto Cubano de Investigaciones de los Derivados de la Caña de Azúcar (ICIDCA), 635
Instituto Cultural do Governo da R. A. E. de Macau, 587
Instituto da Conservação da Natureza e da Biodiversidade, 1820
Instituto de Algodão de Moçambique, 1543
Instituto de Altos Estudios de la Defensa Nacional, 3060
Instituto de Altos Estudios Diplomáticos 'Pedro Gual', 3060
Instituto de Altos Estudios en Salud Publica 'Dr Arnoldo Gabaldon', 3060
Instituto de Altos Estudios Estratégicos, Asunción, 1713
Instituto de Altos Estudios Nacionales, 709
Instituto de Altos Estudos, 1817
Instituto de Análisis Industrial y Financiero, 2060
Instituto de Antropología e Historia, Guatemala City, 985
Instituto de Arte Peruano 'José Sabogal', 1714
Instituto de Astrofísica de Canarias (IAC), 2062
Instituto de Astronomía, México, 1496
Instituto de Bibliografía del Ministerio de Educación de la Provincia de Buenos Aires, 120
Instituto de Biocomputación y Física de Sistemas Complejos, 2062
Instituto de Bioingeniería, 2061

Instituto de Biología Andina, Lima, 1716
Instituto de Biología Molecular y Celular, 2061
Instituto de Biología y Medicina Experimental, 121
Instituto de Biologia Molecular e Celular, Porto, 1819
Instituto de Botánica 'Carlos Spegazzini', La Plata, 121
Instituto de Botánica 'Darwinion', 121
Instituto de Botânica, São Paulo, 311
Instituto de Cancerología 'Cupertino Arteaga', 291
Instituto de Chile, 465
Instituto de Cibernética, Matemática y Física (ICIMAF), Havana, 636
Instituto de Ciencias Biomédicas de Abel Salazar, 1819
Instituto de Ciencias de la Educación, 2060
Instituto de Ciencias de la Familia, 2062
Instituto de Ciencias Naturales Alexander von Humboldt, 468
Instituto de Ciencias Naturales, Bogotá, 593
Instituto de Ciências Sociais, 1821
Instituto de Cooperación Iberoamericana, Madrid, 2051
Instituto de Cultura Alimentaria Bircher-Benner, 1716
Instituto de Cultura Dominicana, 694
Instituto de Cultura Puertorriqueña, 3014
Instituto de Derecho Público, 2060
Instituto de Desarrollo Económico y Social, Buenos Aires, 120
Instituto de Diagnóstico y Referencia Epidemiológicos, México, 1496
Instituto de Ecología, AC, Xalapa, 1496
Instituto de Economia Agrícola, São Paulo, 309
Instituto de Energía Solar, 2061
Instituto de Engenharia Nuclear, 311
Instituto de Enseñanza Superior del Ejército, 135
Instituto de España, Madrid, 2051
Instituto de Estudios de la Democracia, 2060
Instituto de Estudios del Caribe, San Juan, 3015
Instituto de Estudios Etnológicos, 1715
Instituto de Estudios Europeos y Derechos Humanos, 2060
Instituto de Estudios Fiscales, 2060
Instituto de Estudios Para El Desarrollo, 1565
Instituto de Estudios Superiores de Administración, Caracas, 3060
Instituto de Estudios Superiores de Medicina Oriental Japón-Nicaragua, 1620
Instituto de Estudos Clássicos, 1819
Instituto de Filosofía, Havana, 636
Instituto de Fomento Pesquero, Valparaíso, 467
Instituto de Formação Turística, 589
Instituto de Geofísica y Astronomía, 636
Instituto de Geografía Tropical, Havana, 635
Instituto de Geografía y Conservación de Recursos Naturales, Mérida, 3048
Instituto de Gestão do Património Arquitectónico e Arqueológico, 1815
Instituto de Historia de Nicaragua y Centroamérica, 1615
Instituto de Historia y Cultura Naval, Madrid, 2053
Instituto de Información, 3028
Instituto de Información Científica y Tecnológica (IDICT), 636
Instituto de Ingeniería Sanitaria y Ambiental, 291
Instituto de Ingenieros de Chile, 467
Instituto de Ingenieros de Minas de Chile, 467
Instituto de Investigação Agronómica, Huambo, 113
Instituto de Investigação Científica 'Bento da Rocha Cabral', 1820
Instituto de Investigação Científica Tropical, 1817

Instituto de Investigação das Pescas e do Mar (INRB), 1820

Instituto de Investigação Veterinária, Lubango, 113

Instituto de Investigación Agropecuaria de Panamá, Panama, 1702

Instituto de Investigación de Drogodependencias, 2062

Instituto de Investigación y Desarrollo de Procesos Químicos, 291

Instituto de Investigaciones Agropecuarias 'Jorge Dimitrov', 635

Instituto de Investigaciones Agropecuarias, Santiago, 467

Instituto de Investigaciones Alérgicas 'Dr Luis E. Betetta', San Miguel, 1716

Instituto de Investigaciones Antropológicas, 468

Instituto de Investigaciones Arqueológicas y Museo 'R. P. Gustavo le Paige', 467

Instituto de Investigaciones Avícolas, Havana, 635

Instituto de Investigaciones Bibliográficas, México, 1495

Instituto de Investigaciones Biológicas Clemente Estable, 3026

Instituto de Investigaciones Bioquímicas (INIBIBB), Bahía Blanca, 121

Instituto de Investigaciones de Sanidad Vegetal, Havana, 635

Instituto de Investigaciones Eléctricas, Cuernavaca, 1497

Instituto de Investigaciones en Viandas Tropicales, Santo Domingo, 635

Instituto de Investigaciones Forestales, Havana, 635

Instituto de Investigaciones Fundamentales en Agricultura Tropical 'Alejandro de Humboldt', 635

Instituto de Investigaciones Industriales, 291

Instituto de Investigaciones Marinas y Costeras 'José Benito Vives de Andreis' (INVEMAR), 593

Instituto de Investigaciones Médicas 'Alfredo Lanari', Buenos Aires, 121

Instituto de Investigaciones Porcinas, Bauta, 635

Instituto de Investigaciones Veterinarias, Maracay, 3048

Instituto de Investigaciones y Ensayes de Materiales (IDIEM), 468

Instituto de la Ingeniería de España, 2055

Instituto de la Patagonia, 468

Instituto de las Naciones Unidas para Formación Profesional e Investigaciones, 60

Instituto de Lexicología e Lexicografia da Língua Portuguesa, 1819

Instituto de Literatura y Lingüística 'José Antonio Portuondo Valdor', Havana, 635

Instituto de Matemática de Bahía Blanca (INMABB), 120

Instituto de Matemáticas, México, 1496

Instituto de Mecánica Aplicada y Estructuras, 122

Instituto de Medicina Experimental, Caracas, 3048

Instituto de Medicina Experimental del Servicio Nacional de Salud, Santiago, 467

Instituto de Medicina Molecular, 1819

Instituto de Meteorología (INSMET), 636

Instituto de Meteorologia, 1820

Instituto de Neurociencias, 2061

Instituto de Neurociencias 'Federico Olóriz', 2061

Instituto de Nutrición de Centro América y Panamá (INCAP), Guatemala City, 985

Instituto de Nutrición y Tecnología de los Alimentos 'José Mataix Verdú', 2062

Instituto de Oceanología, Havana, 635

Instituto de Orientação Profissional da Faculdade de Psicologia da Universidade de Lisboa, 1818

Instituto de Patalogia e Imunologia da Universidade do Porto, 1819

Instituto de Pensamento Iberoamericano, 2062

Instituto de Pesquisas do Jardim Botânico do Rio de Janeiro, 311

Instituto de Pesquisas Energéticas e Nucleares, 311

Instituto de Pesquisas Tecnológicas, São Paulo, 312

Instituto de Pesquisas Veterinárias 'Desidério Finamor', 309

Instituto de Planeamiento Regional y Urbano (IPRU), Buenos Aires, 120

Instituto de Plasmas e Fusão Nuclear, 1820

Instituto de Radioproteção e Dosimetria, Rio de Janeiro, 311

Instituto de Relaciones Europeo-Latinoamericanas (IRELA), Madrid, 2059

Instituto de Robótica, 2062

Instituto de Salud Pública de Chile, 467

Instituto de Saúde, São Paulo, 310

Instituto de Sistemas Optoelectrónicos y Microtecnología, 2063

Instituto de Tecnológia de Pernambuco (ITEP), 312

Instituto de Tecnológia do Paraná, 312

Instituto de Teología para Religiosos–ITER, Caracas, 3042

Instituto de Valencia de Don Juan, 2066

Instituto de Zootecnia, Nova Odessa, 310

Instituto del Mar del Perú (IMARPE), 1716

Instituto del Patrimonio Cultural de España, 2060

Instituto do Ceará, 307

Instituto dos Advogados Brasileiros (IAB), 306

Instituto Egipcio de Estudios Islámicos, 2052

Instituto Español Bíblico y Arqueológico. Casa de Santiago, 2062

Instituto Español de Enseñanza Secundaria 'Severo Ochoa', 1542

Instituto Español de Oceanografía, 2061

Instituto Especializado de Educacion Superior de Profesionales de la Salud de El Salvador, 724

Instituto Especializado de Educación Superior 'El Espíritu Santo', 724

Instituto Especializado de Educación Superior para la Formación Diplomática, 724

Instituto Especializado de Nivel Superior Centro Cultural Salvadoreño Americano, 725

Instituto Especializado de Nivel Superior Escuela Militar 'Capitán General Gerardo Barrios', 725

Instituto Estadual do Ambiente (INEA), 311

Instituto Evandro Chagas, 310

Instituto Feijoo del Siglo XVIII, 2061

Instituto Florestal (Estado de São Paulo), 310

Instituto Forestal, Concepción, 467

Instituto García Oviedo, 2060

Instituto Genealógico Brasileiro, 307

Instituto Geofísico, 1819

Instituto Geofísico del Perú, 1716

Instituto Geográfico 'Agustín Codazzi', 593

Instituto Geográfico Militar, Asunción, 1710

Instituto Geográfico Militar, La Paz, 291

Instituto Geográfico Militar, Quito, 701

Instituto Geográfico Militar, Santiago, 465

Instituto Geográfico Nacional, 2053

Instituto Geográfico Nacional, Buenos Aires, 121

Instituto Geográfico Nacional 'Ing. Alfredo Obiols Gómez', 985

Instituto Geográfico Nacional, Lima, 1715

Instituto Geográfico Português, 1815

Instituto Geológico, Minero y Metalúrgico, Lima, 1716

Instituto Geológico, São Paulo, 307

Instituto Geológico y Minero de España, 2063

Instituto Gregoriano de Lisboa, 1815

Instituto Gulbenkian de Ciência, 1819

Instituto Hidrográfico, 1821

Instituto Histórico da Ilha Terceira (IHIT), 1815

Instituto Histórico e Geográfico Brasileiro, 307

Instituto Histórico y Geográfico del Uruguay, 3024

Instituto Hondureño de Antropología e Historia, 995

Instituto Hondureño de Cultura Interamericana (IHCI), 995

Instituto Hondureño del Café, 995

Instituto Iberoamericano de Derecho Agrario, Reforma Agraria y Cooperativismo (IIDARA), Mérida, 3048

Instituto Indigenista Interamericano, México, 1496

Instituto Interamericano de Cooperación para la Agricultura, 51

Instituto Interamericano de Estadística, 57

Instituto Interamericano del Niño, Montevideo, 3026

Instituto Internacional de la UNESCO para la Educación en América Latina y el Caribe, 66

Instituto Internacional para la Educación Superior en América Latina y el Caribe (IESALC), 63, 66

Instituto Interuniversitario de Estudios de Iberoamérica y Portugal, 2059

Instituto Isaac Newton, Santiago, 468

Instituto Latinoamericano de Computación, Managua, 1620

Instituto Latinoamericano de las Naciones Unidas para la Prevención del Delito y Tratamiento del Delincuente (ILANUD), 613

Instituto Latinoamericano y del Caribe de Planificación Económica y Social (ILPES), Santiago, 467

Instituto Médico Sucre, 291

Instituto Médio Industrial de Luanda, 114

Instituto Meteorológico Nacional, San José, 613

Instituto Metodista Universitario Crandon, 3028

Instituto Mexicano del Petróleo, 1497

Instituto Militar de Estudios Superiores, 3029

Instituto Municipal de Botánica, Jardín Botánico 'Carlos Thays', 121

Instituto Nacional Agrario, Tegucigalpa, 995

Instituto Nacional Autónomo de Investigaciones Agropecuarias, 701

Instituto Nacional de Administração, 1830

Instituto Nacional de Administración Pública, Madrid, 2052

Instituto Nacional de Antropología e Historia, México, 1497

Instituto Nacional de Antropología y Pensamiento Latinoamericano, Buenos Aires, 122

Instituto Nacional de Astrofísica, Optica y Electrónica, Tonanzintla, 1496

Instituto Nacional de Bellas Artes y Literature, 1493

Instituto Nacional de Cancer, Rio de Janeiro, 310

Instituto Nacional de Cancerología, Bogotá, 593

Instituto Nacional de Cardiología 'Ignacio Chávez', 1496

Instituto Nacional de Estadística, Guatemala City, 984

Instituto Nacional de Estadística, La Paz, 291

Instituto Nacional de Estadística, Lima, 1715

Instituto Nacional de Estadística, Madrid, 2052

Instituto Nacional de Estadística, Montevideo, 3025

Instituto Nacional de Estadística y Censos, Buenos Aires, 120

Instituto Nacional de Estadística y Censos, Quito, 701

Instituto Nacional de Estadística y Censos, San José, 613

Instituto Nacional de Estadística y Geografía, Aguascalientes, 1493

Instituto Nacional de Estadísticas, Santiago, 467

Instituto Nacional de Estatistica de Cabo Verde, 459

Instituto Nacional de Estatística, 1816

Instituto Nacional de Estudios de Teatro, 120

Instituto Nacional de Estudios Históricos de las Revoluciones de México (INEHRM), México, 1495

Instituto Nacional de Estudios Lingüísticos (INEL), La Paz, 291

Instituto Nacional de Estudos e Pesquisa (INEP), 990

Instituto Nacional de Estudos e Pesquisas Educacionais 'Anísio Teixeira', 310

Instituto Nacional de Estudos e Pesquisas Educacionais Anísio Teixeira (INEP), 306

Instituto Nacional de Higiene, Epidemiología y Microbiología, Havana, 635

Instituto Nacional de Higiene 'Rafael Rangel', 3060

Instituto Nacional de Higiene y Medicina Tropical 'Leopoldo Izquieta Pérez', 701

Instituto Nacional de Investigação Agronómica, Maputo, 1543

Instituto Nacional de Investigación Agropecuaria, 3025

Instituto Nacional de Investigación y Desarrollo Pesquero, Mar del Plata, 120

Instituto Nacional de Investigación y Tecnología Agraria y Alimentaria (INIA), 2059

Instituto Nacional de Investigaciones Agrícolas de Venezuela, 3048

Instituto Nacional de Investigaciones Forestales, Agrícolas y Pecuarias, México, 1495

Instituto Nacional de Investigaciones Nucleares, Ocoyoacac, 1496

Instituto Nacional de la Pesca, México, 1496

Instituto Nacional de Limnología, Santa Fe, 121

Instituto Nacional de Linguística, Dili, 2199

Instituto Nacional de Medicina Legal, Coimbra, 1819

Instituto Nacional de Medicina Legal y Ciencias Forenses, 592

Instituto Nacional de Medicina Nuclear, La Paz, 291

Instituto Nacional de Meteorología e Hidrología, Quito, 701

Instituto Nacional de Meteorologia, 311

Instituto Nacional de Meteorologia, Maputo, 1543

Instituto Nacional de Música, Panama, 1705

Instituto Nacional de Neurología y Neurocirugía, México, 1496

Instituto Nacional de Normalización, 468

Instituto Nacional de Nutrición, Caracas, 3048

Instituto Nacional de Oncología y Radiobiología de La Habana, 635

Instituto Nacional de Parasitología, Asunción, 1710

Instituto Nacional de Pesca, Guayaquil, 701

Instituto Nacional de Pesquisas da Amazônia, 310

Instituto Nacional de Pesquisas Espaciais (INPE), São José dos Campos, 312

Instituto Nacional de Recursos Biológicos IP, 1818

Instituto Nacional de Salud, Asunción, 1713

Instituto Nacional de Salud, Bogotá, 593

Instituto Nacional de Salud, Lima, 1716

Sfeclei de Zahăr şi Substanţelor Dulci, 1838

Institutul de Cercetare—Dezvoltare pentru Ecologie Acvatica, Pescuit si Acvacultura, 1838

Institutul de Cercetare—Dezvoltare pentru Pajisti Brasov, 1838

Institutul de Cercetare—Dezvoltare pentru Pomicultura Piteşti-Mărăcineni, 1838

Institutul de Cercetare—Dezvoltare pentru Protecţia Plantelor, 1838

Institutul de Cercetări Biologice Cluj-Napoca, 1842

Institutul de Cercetări Biologice Iaşi, 1842

Institutul de Cercetări Chimice, 1842

Institutul de Cercetări Dezvoltare pentru Legumicultură şi Floricultură, 1839

Institutul de Cercetări Eco-Muzeale Tulcea, 1842

Institutul de Cercetări Juridice 'Acad. Andrei Rădulescu', 1840

Institutul de Cercetări pentru Cereale şi Plante Tehnice, 1839

Institutul de Cercetări pentru Inteligenţă Artificială 'Mihai Drăgănescu' Academia Romana, 1840

Institutul de Cercetări pentru Viticultură şi Vinificaţie Valea Calugareasca, 1839

Institutul de Cercetări şi Amenajări Silvice, 1839

Institutul de Cercetări Socio-Umane 'C. S. Nicolaescu-Plopsor', 1843

Institutul de Cercetări Socio-Umane din Sibiu, 1843

Institutul de Cercetări Socio-Umane 'Gheorghe Şincai' al Academiei Române, 1843

Institutul de Chimie Alimentară Research and Development, 1839

Institutul de Chimie Fizică 'Ilie Murgulescu' al Academiei Române, 1842

Institutul de Chimie Macromoleculară 'Petru Poni' al Academiei Romane, 1842

Institutul de Chimie Organică 'Costin D. Neniţescu' al Academiei Române, 1842

Institutul de Chimie Timişoara al Academiei Romane, 1842

Institutul de Economie Mondială, Bucharest, 1840

Institutul de Economie Naţională, Bucharest, 1840

Institutul de Endocrinologie 'C.I. Parhon', 1841

Institutul de Etnografie şi Folclor 'Constantin Brăiloiu', 1843

Institutul de Filologie Română 'Al. Philippide', 1841

Institutul de Filosofie si Psihologie 'Constantin Rădulescu-Motru', 1843

Institutul de Fiziologie Normală şi Patologică 'D. Danielopolu', 1841

Institutul de Fonoaudiologie şi Chirurgie Funcţională ORL 'Prof. Dr. D. Hociotă', 1841

Institutul de Geodinamică Sabba S. Ştefănescu al Academiei Romane, 1842

Institutul de Geografie, 1840

Institutul de Informatică Teoretică, 1844

Institutul de Istoria Artei 'G. Oprescu', 1840

Institutul de Istorie 'A. D. Xenopol' Iaşi, 1841

Institutul de Istorie 'Nicolae Iorga', 1841

Institutul de Istorie şi Teorie Literară 'G. Călinescu', 1841

Institutul de Lingvistica 'Iorgu Iordan–Al. Rosetti', 1841

Institutul de Matematică 'Octav Mayer', 1842

Institutul de Matematică 'Simion Stoilow' al Academiei Romane, 1842

Institutul de Mecanica Solidelor al Academiei Române, 1844

Institutul de Medicină Internă 'Nicolae Gh. Lupu', 1841

Institutul de Neurologie şi Psihiatrie, 1841

Institutul de Patologie şi Genetică Medicală 'V. Babeş', 1841

Institutul de Prognoză Economică, Bucharest, 1840

Institutul de Sănătate Publică 'Prof. Dr Iuliu Moldovan', 1841

Institutul de Sănătate Publică 'Prof. Dr Leonida Georgescu', Timişoara, 1841

Institutul de Sociologie 'Dimitrie Gusti', 1843

Institutul de Speologie 'Emil Racoviţă' al Academiei Romane, 1842

Institutul de Stat de Relaţii Internaţionale din Moldova, 1527

Institutul de Statistică Matematică şi Matematică Aplicată 'Gheorghe Mihoc-Caius Iacob' al Academiei Romana, 1842

Institutul de Ştiinţe Politice şi Relaţii Internaţionale, 1844

Institutul de Ştiinţe Socio-Umane, 1844

Institutul de Studii Banatice 'Titu Maiorescu', 1844

Institutul de Virusologie Stefan S. Nicolau, 1841

Institutul Geologic al României, 1843

Institutul 'Gheorghe Zane' de Cercetări Economice şi Sociale, 1840

Institutul Naţional de Cercetare Dezvoltare pentru Chimie si Petrochimie, 1843

Institutul National de Cercetare Dezvoltare pentru Metale Neferoase Şi Rare, 1844

Institutul Naţional de Cercetare-Dezvoltare 'Delta Dunarii', 1843

Institutul Naţional de Cercetare—Dezvoltare Marină 'Grigore Antipa', 1839

Institutul Naţional de Cercetare—Dezvoltare în Construcţii, Urbanism şi Dezvoltare Teritorială Durabilă URBAN-INCERC, 1839

Institutul Naţional de Cercetare—Dezvoltare pentru Biologie si Nutriţie Animala, 1839

Institutul Naţional de Cercetare-Dezvoltare pentru Cartof si Sfeclă de Zahar Brasov, 1839

Institutul Naţional de Cercetare—Dezvoltare pentru Fizică Tehnică—IFT Iaşi, 1843

Institutul Naţional de Cercetare—Dezvoltare pentru Pedologie, Agrochimie şi Protecţia Mediului—ICPA Bucureşti, 1839

Institutul Naţional de Cercetare—Dezvoltare pentru Protecţia Mediului, 1844

Institutul Naţional de Cercetare—Dezvoltare pentru Ştiinţe Biologice, 1842

Institutul Naţional de Cercetări Economice 'Costin C. Kiritescu', 1840

Institutul Naţional de Educaţie Fizică şi Sport, Chişinău, 1527

Institutul Naţional de Informare şi Documentare, 1844

Institutul Naţional de Medicină Legală 'Mina Minovici', 1841

Institutul Naţional de Meteorologie şi Hidrologie, 1843

Institutul National de Metrologie, 1843

Institutul Naţional de Sănătate Publică, Bucureşti, 1841

Institutul Naţional pentru Fizică şi Inginerie Nucleară 'Horia Hulubei', 1843

Institutul Oncologic 'Prof. Dr Al. Trestioreanu' Bucuresti, 1842

Institutul pentru Controlul de Stat al Medicamentului şi Cercetări Farmaceutice 'Petre Ionescu-Stoian', 1842

Institutul Teologic Baptist din Bucureşti, 1878

Institutul Teologic Protestant Cluj, 1878

Institutul Teologic Romano-Catolic 'Sf. Iosif' Iaşi, 1878

Institutum Romanum Finlandiae, Rome, 1198

Instituut Beleid & Management Gezondheidszorg (iBMG), 1570

Instituut ter Bevordering van het Wetenschappelijk Onderzoek en de Innovatie van Brussel, 258

Instituut voor Bedrijfs- en Industriële Statistiek (IBIS), 1565

Instituut voor Biodiversiteit en Ecosysteem Dynamica, 1572

Instituut voor de Studie van de Letterkunde in de Nederlanden, 263

Instituut voor Fundamentele en Klinische Bewegingswetenschappen, 1570

Instituut voor Hoge Energie Fysica (IHEF), 1572

Instituut voor Hoger Beroepsonderwijs in Suriname, 2104

Instituut voor Informatierecht, 1568

Instituut voor Internationale Studien, 1569

Instituut voor Joodse Studies, 263

Instituut voor Milieu & Duurzame Ontwikkeling, 265

Instituut voor Milieu en Agritechniek (IMAG-DLO), 1575

Instituut voor Milieuvraagstukken (IVM), 1569

Instituut voor Mobiliteit, 266

Instituut voor Natuur- en Bosonderzoek, 265

Instituut voor Onderwijs- en Informatiewetenschappen, 263

Instituut voor Ontwikkelingsbeleid en-Beheer, 262

Instituut voor Plantenziektenkundig Onderzoek (IPO–DLO), Wageningen, 1571

Instituut voor Programmatuurkunde en Algoritmiek, Eindhoven, 1572

Instituut voor Psychosynthese, 1593

Instituut voor Rituele en Liturgische Studies (IRiLiS), 1574

Instituut voor Samenwerking tussen Universiteit en Arbeidersbeweging, 262

Instituut voor Theoretische Fysica, 1572

Instytut Agrofizyki im. Bohdana Dobrzańskiego PAN, 1760

Instytut Archeologii i Etnologii PAN, 1763

Instytut Automatyki Systemów Energetycznych, Wrocław, 1767

Instytut Badań Edukacyjnych, 1762

Instytut Badań Literackich PAN, 1763

Instytut Badań Rynku, Konsumpcji i Koniunktur, Warsaw, 1761

Instytut Badań Systemowych PAN, 1767

Instytut Badawczy Dróg i Mostów, Warsaw, 1767

Instytut Badawczy Leśnictwa, Warsaw, 1760

Instytut Biochemii i Biofizyki PAN, 1765

Instytut Biocybernetyki i Inżynierii Biomedycznej im. Macieja Nałęcza PAN, 1763

Instytut Biologii Doświadczalnej im M. Nenckiego PAN, 1765

Instytut Biologii Ssaków PAN, 1765

Instytut Biopolimerów i Włókien Chemicznych, Łódź, 1767

Instytut Biotechnologii Przemysłu Rolno–Spożywczego, Warsaw, 1760

Instytut Botaniki im. Władysława Szafera PAN, 1765

Instytut Budownictwa, Mechanizacji i Elektryfikacji Rolnictwa, Warsaw, 1760

Instytut Budownictwa Wodnego PAN, 1767

Instytut Ceramiki i Materiałów Budowlanych, Gliwice, 1767

Instytut Chemii Bioorganicznej PAN, 1765

Instytut Chemii Fizycznej PAN, 1766

Instytut Chemii i Techniki Jądrowej, Warsaw, 1768

Instytut Chemii Organicznej PAN, 1766

Instytut Chemii Przemysłowej im. Prof. Ignacego Mościckiego, 1768

Instytut Dendrologii PAN, 1765

Instytut Ekonomiki Rolnictwa i Gospodarki Żywnościowej—Państwowy Instytut Badawczy, Warsaw, 1760

Instytut Ekspertyz Sądowych im. Prof. dra Jana Sehna, 1762

Instytut Elektrotechniki, Warsaw, 1768

Instytut Energetyki, Warsaw, 1768

Instytut Farmaceutyczny, 1763

Instytut Farmakologii PAN, 1764

Instytut Filozofii i Socjologii PAN, 1767

Instytut Fizjologii i Żywienia Zwierząt im. Jana Kielanowskiego PAN, 1760

Instytut Fizjologii Roślin im. Franciszka Górskiego PAN, 1760

Instytut Fizyki Jądrowej im. Henryka Niewodniczańskiego PAN, 1766

Instytut Fizyki Molekularnej PAN, 1766

Instytut Fizyki PAN, 1766

Instytut Fizyki Plazmy i Laserowej Mikrosyntezy, 1766

Instytut Genetyki Człowieka PAN w Poznaniu, 1764

Instytut Genetyki i Hodowli Zwierząt PAN, 1760

Instytut Genetyki Roślin PAN, 1760

Instytut Geodezji i Kartografii, 1763

Instytut Geofizyki PAN, 1766

Instytut Geografii i Przestrzennego Zagospodarowania im. S. Leszczyckiego PAN, 1763

Instytut Gospodarki Przestrzennej i Mieszkalictwa, 1761

Instytut Hematologii i Transfuzjologii, 1764

Instytut Historii im. Tadeusza Manteuffla Polskiej Akademii Nauk, 1763

Instytut Historii Nauki im. Ludwika i Aleksandra Birkenmajerów PAN, 1765

Instytut Immunologii i Terapii Doświadczalnej im. Ludwika Hirszfelda PAN, 1764

Instytut Informatyki Teoretycznej i Stosowanej PAN, 1768

Instytut Inżynierii Chemicznej PAN, 1768

Instytut Języka Polskiego PAN, 1763

Instytut Kardiologii im. Prymasa Tysiąclecia Stefana Kardynała Wyszyńskiego, 1764

Instytut Katalizy i Fizykochemii Powierzchni im. Jerzego Habera PAN, 1766

Instytut Kształcenia Zawodowego, Kędzierzyn-Koźle, 1763

Instytut Kultur Śródziemnomorskich i Orientalnych PAN, 1759

Instytut Kultury, Warsaw, 1759

Instytut Łączności Państwowy Instytut Badawczy, Warsaw, 1768

Instytut Lotnictwa, Warsaw, 1768

Instytut Maszyn Matematycznych, Warsaw, 1768

Instytut Maszyn Przepływowych im. Roberta Szewalskiego PAN, 1768

Instytut Matematyczny PAN, 1765

Instytut Matki i Dziecka, 1764

Instytut Medycyny Doświadczalnej i Klinicznej im. M. J. Mossakowskiego PAN, 1764

Instytut Medycyny Pracy i Zdrowia Środowiskowego, 1764

Instytut Medycyny Pracy im. prof. J. Nofera, 1764

Instytut Medycyny Wsi im. Witolda Chodźki, 1764

Instytut Mechaniki Górotworu PAN, 1766

Instytut Mechanizacji Budownictwa i Górnictwa Skalnego, Warsaw, 1768

Instytut Medycyny Morskiej i Tropikalnej, 1764

Instytut Metali Nieżelaznych Gliwice, 1768

Instytut Metalurgii i Inżynierii Materiałowej im. Aleksandra Krupkowskiego PAN, 1768

Ionio Panepistimio, 978
Iorgu Iordan–Al. Rosetti Institute of
   Linguistics, 1841
Iowa City Public Library, 2487
Iowa Museum Association, West des
   Moines, 2522
Iowa State University, 2680
Iowa State University Library, 2487
Iowa State University Museums, 2522
Iowa Wesleyan College, 2681
IP Australia Library, 149
Iparművészeti Múzeum, 1008
Iparművészeti Múzeum Könyvtára,
   1006
IPIT Instituut voor Maatschappelijke
   Veiligheidsvraagstukken, 1565
Iqaluit Centennial Library, 393
Iqbal Academy, Lahore, 1674
Iqbal Institute, Srinagar, 1041
Iqra University, 1685
Iquique Regional Museum, 469
Iran Animal Science Research Institute,
   1134
Iran Banking Institute, 1148
Iran Bastan Museum, 1135
Iran Bastan Museum Library, 1135
Iran Management Association, 1133
Iran University of Medical Sciences and
   Health Services Central Library
   and Documentation Centre, 1135
Iran University of Science and
   Technology, 1137
Iranian Cultural Heritage Organization
   Documentation Centre, 1135
Iranian Information and
   Documentation Centre (IRANDOC),
   1135
Iranian Mathematical Society, 1134
Iranian Society of Microbiology, 1134
Irapuato-Salamanca Campus, 1509
Iraq Military Museum, 1150
Iraq National Museum, 1150
Iraq Natural History Research Centre
   and Museum, 1151
Iraqi Academy Library, 1150
Iraqi Academy of Science, 1150
Iraqi Medical Association, 1150
Iraqi Museum Library, 1150
Iraqi National Library and Archives,
   Baghdad, 1150
Irish Astronomical Society, 1158
Irish Baptist College, 2418
Irish Management Institute, 1165
Irish Manuscripts Commission, 1159
Irish Medical Organisation, 1158
Irish Museum of Modern Art, 1160
Irish PEN, 1158
Irish Recorded Music Association, 1157
Irish Texts Society, London, 1158
Irish Theatre Archive, 1159
Irish Universities Association, 1157
Irkutsk Antiplague Research Institute
   of Siberia and the Far East, 1890
Irkutsk Institute of Orthopaedics and
   Traumatology, 1890
Irkutsk Institute of Railway Engineers,
   1952
Irkutsk Research Institute of
   Epidemiology and Microbiology,
   1890
Irkutsk State Academy of Economics,
   1949
Irkutsk State Agricultural Academy,
   1948
Irkutsk State Linguistic University,
   1935
Irkutsk State Medical University, 1934
Irkutsk State University, 1921
Irkutsk State University Library, 1905
Iron and Steel Institute of Japan, 1248
Iron and Steel Institute 'Z. I. Nekrasov',
   Dnipropetrovsk, 2253
'Iron Gates' Regional Museum, 1849
Ironbridge Gorge Museums, 2332
Ironwork Museum, 881
Irrigation and Power Research
   Institute, Amritsar, 1048
Irrigation Research Institute, Lahore,
   1677
Isaac Fernández Blanco Museum of
   Spanish-American Art, 123
Isaac Newton Institute for
   Mathematical Sciences, Cambridge,
   2307

Isaac Newton Institute, Santiago, 468
Isaacs Art Center Museum and Gallery,
   Kamuela, 2519
Isabela State University, 1740
Isabella Stewart Gardner Museum,
   2527
Ísafjarðar Public Library, 1030
ISEC University of Business, 1505
Isfahan University of Medical Sciences
   and Health Services, 1138
Isfahan University of Technology, 1138
ISGF–Schweizer Institut für Sucht- und
   Gesundheits- forschung Zürich,
   2144
Ishinomaki Senshu University, 1337
Işık Üniversitesi, 2227
ISL InfoCentre/Library, 864
Isla Center for the Arts, 3013
Islâm Araþtýrmalarý Merkezi, Istanbul,
   2212
Islamabad Medical and Dental College,
   1696
Islamabad Public Library, 1678
Islami Bank Medical College, 243
Islamia College Library, Lahore, 1679
Islamia College, Peshawar, 1685
Islamia University of Bahawalpur, 1685
Islamic and Arabic Studies College,
   2273
Islamic Arts and Crafts School, Tripoli,
   1443
Islamic Arts Museum Malaysia, Kuala
   Lumpur, 1473
Islamic Association, Manama, 219
Islamic Azad University, Tehran, 1138
Islamic College, London, 2415
Islamic Documentation and Information
   Centre (IDIC), Karachi, 1678
Islamic Educational, Scientific and
   Cultural Organization (ISESCO), 65
Islamic Library, Malé, 1481
Islamic Library, Yogyakarta, 1113
Islamic Museum, Tripoli, 1442
Islamic Research and Training
   Institute, Jeddah, 1963
Islamic Research Centre, 1700
Islamic Research Foundation, Astan
   Quds Razavi, 1134
Islamic Research Institute, Islamabad,
   1677
Islamic University in Medina, 1964
Islamic University in Niger, 1622
Islamic University in Uganda, 2244
Islamic University, Kushtia, 231
Islamic University Library, Medina,
   1963
Islamic University of Gaza, 1701
Islamic University of Indonesia, 1127
Islamic University of North Sumatra,
   1127
Islamic University of Riau, 1127
Islamic University of Technology,
   Gazipur, 231
Islamic World Academy of Sciences
   (IAS), 87
Island Resources Foundation, St
   Thomas, 3022
Isle of Anglesey County Libraries, 2318
Isle of Man College of Further & Higher
   Education, 2439
Isle of Man Family History Society,
   2438
Isle of Man Natural History and
   Antiquarian Society, 2438
Isle of Wight Council Library Services,
   2324
Íslenzka frædafélag, Hillerød, 674
Islington Library and Heritage Services,
   2320
ISM Chicago Gallery, 2520
ISM University of Management and
   Economics, Kaunas, 1455
'Ismail Qemal' Technological University
   of Vlorë, 99
Ismail Rahimtulla Trust Library, 1377
ISPE University College, 1413
Isra University, Hyderabad, 1685
Israel Academy of Sciences and
   Humanities, 1166
Israel Antiquities Authority, 1167
Israel Antiquities Authority Archives
   Branch, 1173
Israel Atomic Energy Commission, Tel-
   Aviv, 1172

Israel Bar, 1167
Israel Bible Museum, Safad, 1175
Israel Ceramic and Silicate Institute,
   1172
Israel Chemical Society, 1168
Israel Exploration Society, 1170
Israel Fiber Institute, Jerusalem, 1172
Israel Geographical Association, 1167
Israel Geological Society, 1168
Israel Gerontological Data Center
   (IGDC), 1171
Israel Gerontological Society, 1167
Israel Institute for Biological Research,
   1171
Israel Institute of Metals, 1172
Israel Institute of Plastics, 1172
Israel Mathematical Union, 1168
Israel Matz Institute for Research in
   Jewish Law, 1169
Israel Medical Association, 1167
Israel Meteorological Service, 1171
Israel Museum, 1174
Israel Music Institute, 1167
Israel Oceanographic and Limnological
   Research, 1171
Israel Oriental Society, 1168
Israel Painters and Sculptors
   Association, 1167
Israel Physical Society, 1168
Israel Political Science Association,
   1167
Israel Prehistoric Society, 1167
Israel Psychological Association, 1168
Israel Science Foundation, 1171
Israel Society for Neuroscience, 1167
Israel Society of Aeronautics and
   Astronautics, 1168
Israel Society of Biochemistry and
   Molecular Biology, 1168
Israel Society of Internal Medicine, 1167
Israel Society of Libraries and
   Information Professionals (ASMI),
   1167
Israel Society of Plant Sciences, 1168
Israel State Archives, 1173
Israel University, 706
Israel Wine Institute, Rehovot, 1172
Israeli Center for Libraries, Jerusalem,
   1167
Issam Sartawi Centre, 1700
Issyk-Kul State University named after
   K. Tynystanov, 1420
Istanbul Arkeoloji Müzeleri, 2214
İstanbul Bİlgi Üniversitesi, 2227
Istanbul Bilgi University, 2227
Istanbul Commerce University, Izmir,
   2228
İstanbul Deniz Müzesi, 2214
İstanbul Kültür Üniversitesi, 2227
Istanbul Naval Museum, 2214
Istanbul Resim ve Heykel Müzesi, 2214
İstanbul Teknik Üniversitesi, 2227
Istanbul Teknik Üniversitesi
   Kütüphane ve Dokümantasyon
   Daire, 2213
İstanbul Tİcaret ÜniversiteSİ, 2228
İstanbul Üniversitesi, 2227
Istanbul University Library and
   Documentation Centre, 2213
Istituti Culturali ed Artistici, Forlì,
   1208
Istituto Affari Internazionali, Rome,
   1197
Istituto Agronomico per l'Oltremare,
   Florence, 1189
'Istituto Carlo Cattaneo' Research
   Foundation, 1200
Istituto Centrale per i Beni Sonori ed
   Audiovisivi, Rome, 1205
Istituto Centrale per il Catalogo Unico
   delle Biblioteche Italiane e per le
   Informazioni Bibliografiche, Rome,
   1205
Istituto Centrale per il Restauro e la
   Conservazione del Patrimonio
   Archivistico e Librario, Rome, 1189
Istituto Centrale per la
   Demoetnoantropologia Museo
   Nazionale delle Arti e Tradizioni
   Popolari, Rome, 1211
Istituto dei Materiali per l'Elettronica
   ed il Magnetismo, 1196
Istituto dei Sistemi Complessi, 1195

Istituto di Acustica e Sensoristica 'Orso
   Mario Corbino', 1196
Istituto di Analisi dei Sistemi ed
   Informatica 'Antonio Ruberti', 1195
Istituto di Argomentazione, Linguistica
   e Semiotica, Lugano, 2144
Istituto di Biochimica delle Proteine,
   1195
Istituto di Biofisica, 1195
Istituto di Bioimmagini e Fisiologia
   Molecolare, 1196
Istituto di Biologia Agro-Ambientale e
   Forestale, 1194
Istituto di Biologia Cellulare, 1196
Istituto di Biologia e Biotecnologia
   Agraria, 1193
Istituto di Biologia e Patologia
   Molecolari, 1195
Istituto di Biomedicina e di
   Immunologia Molecolare 'Alberto
   Monroy', 1196
Istituto di Biomembrane e
   Bioenergetica, 1195
Istituto di Biometeorologia, 1193
Istituto di Biostrutture e Bioimmagini,
   1196
Istituto di Calcolo e Reti ad Alte
   Prestazioni, 1195
Istituto di Chimica Biomolecolare, 1196
Istituto di Chimica dei Composti Organo
   Metallici, 1196
Istituto di Chimica del Riconoscimento
   Molecolare, 1196
Istituto di Chimica e Tecnologia dei
   Polimeri, 1196
Istituto di Chimica Inorganica e delle
   Superfici, 1196
Istituto di Cibernetica 'Edoardo
   Caianiello', 1195
Istituto di Cristallografia, 1196
Istituto di Diritto, Lugano, 2143
Istituto di Diritto Romano e dei Diritti
   dell'Oriente Mediterraneo, Rome,
   1189
Istituto di Elettronica e di Ingegneria
   dell'Informazione e delle
   Telecomunicazioni, 1195
Istituto di Filosofia 'Aloisianum', 3040
Istituto di Fisica Applicata 'Nello
   Carrara', 1195
Istituto di Fisica del Plasma 'Piero
   Caldirola', 1195
Istituto di Fisiologia Clinica, 1196
Istituto di Fotonica e Nanotecnologie,
   1195
Istituto di Genetica delle Popolazioni,
   1195
Istituto di Genetica e Biofisica 'Adriano
   Buzzati Traverso', 1195
Istituto di Genetica Molecolare, 1196
Istituto di Genetica Vegetale, 1193
Istituto di Geologia Ambientale e
   Geoingegneria, 1194
Istituto di Geoscienze e Georisorse, 1194
Istituto di Informatica e Telematica,
   1195
Istituto di Ingegneria Biomedica, 1196
Istituto di Linguistica Computazionale
   'Antonio Zampolli', 1194
Istituto di Marketing e Comunicazione
   Aziendale, Lugano, 2143
Istituto di Matematica Applicata e
   Tecnologie Informatiche, 1195
Istituto di Metodologie Chimiche, 1196
Istituto di Metodologie Inorganiche e dei
   Plasmi, 1195
Istituto di Metodologie per l'Analisi
   Ambientale, 1194
Istituto di Neurobiologia e Medicina
   Molecolare, 1196
Istituto di Neurogenetica e
   Neurofarmacologia, 1196
Istituto di Neuroscienze, 1196
Istituto di Norvegia in Roma, 1198
Istituto di Ricerca per il Progetto
   Urbano Contemporaneo, Mendrisio,
   2143
Istituto di Ricerca per la Protezione
   Idrogeologica, 1194
Istituto di Ricerca sui Sistemi
   Giudiziari, 1194
Istituto di Ricerca sulle Acque, 1194
Istituto di Ricerca sull'Impresa e lo
   Sviluppo, 1194

Japanese Society for the Study of Pain, 1244

Japanese Society for Tuberculosis, 1245

Japanese Society of Applied Entomology and Zoology, 1246

Japanese Society of Applied Glycoscience, 1241

Japanese Society of Cultural Anthropology, 1247

Japanese Society of Developmental Biologists, 1245

Japanese Society of Fisheries Science, 1241

Japanese Society of Gastroenterology, 1244

Japanese Society of German Literature, 1243

Japanese Society of Haematology, 1245

Japanese Society of Internal Medicine, 1244

Japanese Society of Irrigation, Drainage and Reclamation Engineering, 1248

Japanese Society of Medical Entomology and Zoology, 1246

Japanese Society of Microscopy, 1246

Japanese Society of Naval Architects and Ocean Engineers, 1241

Japanese Society of Neurology, 1245

Japanese Society of Nuclear Medicine, 1244

Japanese Society of Oral and Maxillofacial Surgeons, 1244

Japanese Society of Parasitology, 1245

Japanese Society of Pathology, 1244

Japanese Society of Pharmacognosy, 1244

Japanese Society of Plant Physiologists, 1246

Japanese Society of Psychiatry and Neurology, 1244

Japanese Society of Sericultural Science, 1241

Japanese Society of Snow and Ice, 1247

Japanese Society of Social Psychology, 1247

Japanese Society of Soil Science and Plant Nutrition, 1241

Japanese Society of Tribologists, 1248

Japanese Society of Veterinary Science, 1241

Japanese Society of Western History, 1243

Japanese Sociological Society, 1248

Japanese Stomatological Society, 1244

Japanese Studies Institute, Beijing, 484

Jardim Botânico, 1820

Jardim e Museu Agrícola Tropical do Instituto de Investigação Científica Tropical, 1824

Jardin Botanique de Montréal, 391

Jardín Botánico de Bogotá 'José Celestino Mutis', 594

Jardín Botánico Nacional de Cuba, Havana, 637

Jardín Botánico y Museo de Historia Natural, 1710

Jarvis Christian College, 2950

Jász Múzeum, 1010

Jatiya Kabi Kazi Nazrul Islam University, 232

Jaume Morera Art Museum, 2066

Javanese Culture and Art Museum, 1115

Javna Biblioteka Unsko-Sanskog Kantona, 299

Jawaharlal Institute of Postgraduate Medical Education and Research, 1108

Jawaharlal Nehru Agricultural University, Jabalpur, 1065

Jawaharlal Nehru Centre for Advanced Scientific Research, 1102

Jawaharlal Nehru Krishi Vishwavidyalaya, Jabalpur, 1065

Jawaharlal Nehru Technological University, 1065

Jawaharlal Nehru Tropical Botanic Garden and Research Institute, Thiruvananthapuram, 1045

Jawaharlal Nehru University, 1065

Jay C. Byers Memorial Library, 2502

Jaypee University of Information Technology, 1065

Jazan Museum, 1963

Jazan University, 1964

Jāzepa Vītola Latvijas Mūzikas Akadēmija, 1430

Jāzeps Vītols Latvian Academy of Music, 1430

Jazykovedný Ústav Ľudovit Štúra SAV, 2003

Jazz Music Institute, Brisbane, 179

Jean and Alexander Heard Library, 2504

Jean Jacques Rousseau University, 1618

Jean Piaget University of Angola, 114

Jeddah College of Technology, 1967

Jeddah Health Institute, 1967

Jednota českých matematiků a fyziků, 653

Jednota Slovenských Matematikov a Fyzikov, 2002

Jefferson College of Health Sciences, 2978

Jefferson County Library, 2494, 2502

Jefferson Davis Parish Library, 2489

Jefferson Patterson Park and Museum, State Museum of Archaeology, 2525

Jefferson-Madison Regional Library, 2506

Jeff's Seaside Museum, 3013

Jefri Bolkiah College of Engineering, Kuala Belait, 353

Jeju National University, 1391

Jenkins Law Library, Philadelphia, 2503

Jeonju National Museum, 1390

Jeonju University, 1400

Jerez Archaeological Museum Town Library, 2063

Jericho Local Urban Observatory Centre, 1700

Jersey Archive, 2440

Jersey Heritage, 2440

Jersey Library, 2440

Jersey Museum and Art Gallery, St Helier, 2440

Jersey War Tunnels, 2440

Jerusalem Academy of Jewish Studies, 1186

Jerusalem Academy of Music and Dance, 1186

Jerusalem Artists' House, 1174

Jerusalem City (Public) Library, 1173

Jerusalem College of Technology, 1186

Jerusalem Institute for Israel Studies, 1169

Jerusalem University College, 1186

Jerusalemer Institut der Görres-Gesellschaft, Jerusalem, 1167

Jerzy Haber Institute of Catalysis and Surface Chemistry of the Polish Academy of Sciences, 1766

Jessamine County Public Library, 2488

Jesuit School of Philosophy and Theology 'Arrupe College', 3040

Jesus College, Cambridge, 2358

Jesus College Library, Oxford, 2325

Jesus College Old Library, Cambridge, 2314

Jesus College, Oxford, 2399

Jet Propulsion Laboratory, Pasadena, 2476

Jeunesses Musicales de France, 768

Jeunesses Musicales International (JMI), 81

Jeunesses Musicales of Sarajevo, 297

Jewish Historical Cultural Museum, 1600

Jewish Historical Museum, Amsterdam, 1580

Jewish Historical Society of Delaware Archives, 2481

Jewish Historical Society of England, 2285

Jewish History Museum, Tucson, 2510

Jewish Museum, 881

Jewish Museum in Prague, 659

Jewish Museum, New York, 2535

Jewish Museum of Bosnia and Herzegovina, 300

Jewish Museum, Stockholm, 2118

Jewish Music Research Centre, 1170

Jewish Oral Traditions Research Centre, 1172

Jewish Theological Seminary Library, New York, 2498

Jewish Theological Seminary, New York, 2836

Jewish Theological Seminary–University of Jewish Studies, 1025

Jiangnan University, 528

Jiangsu University, 529

Jiangxi Agricultural University, 529

Jiangxi Provincial Library, 489

Jigme Namgyel Polytechnic, 288

Jihočeská Univerzita v Českých Budějovicích, 660

Jihočeské muzeum v Českých Budějovicích, 658

Jikei University, 1337

Jilin Provincial Library, 488

Jilin University, 529

Jilin University Library, 488

Jill Dando Institute of Security and Crime Science, 2301

Jim Gatchell Memorial Museum, 2547

Jimma University, 737

Jimmy Carter Library & Museum, 2484

Jinan University, 530

Jingu Bunko, 1252

Jingu Chokokan, 1254

Jingu Historical Museum, 1254

Jingu Nogyokan, 1254

Jinju National University, 1408

Jinnah Postgraduate Medical Centre, 1696

Jinnah University for Women, 1685

Jishoji (Ginkakuji), 1255

Jiwaji University, 1065

JMC Academy, Surry Hills, 178

Joaquim Nabuco Foundation, 311

Jôchi Daigaku, 1353

Jodrell Bank Observatory, 2308

Joe Alon Centre for Regional and Folklore Studies, D N Negel, 1170

Joensau Regional Library—Central Library of North Karelia, 748

Joensuun seutukirjasto—Pohjois-Karjalan maakuntakirjasto, 748

Jõgeva Plant Breeding Institute, 729

Jõgeva Sordiaretuse Instituut, 729

Johann Bernoulli Institute for Mathematics and Computing Science (JBI), 1572

Johänn Heinrich von Thünen Institute, Hamburg, 856

Johann Radon Institute for Computational and Applied Mathematics, 193

Johann Strauss Society of Vienna, 184

Johann Strauss-Gesellschaft Wien, 184

Johanna Museet, 2118

Johannes Gutenberg University Mainz, 897

Johannes Kepler Universität Linz, 198

Johannes Kepler University, Linz, 198

Johannesburg Art Gallery, 2033

John A. Hartford Foundation, New York, 2457

John and Mable Ringling Museum of Art, 2517

John Brown University, 2561

John Cabot University, Rome, 1232

John Carroll University, 2881

John Carter Brown Library, 2503

John Crerar Library of the University of Chicago, 2486

John Eugene Derrickson Memorial Library, Wilmington, 2481

John F. Kennedy Presidential Library and Museum, 2492

John F. Kennedy Space Center, Cape Canaveral, 2476

John F. Kennedy University, 2573

John F. Kennedy University of Argentina, 125

John G. McCullough Free Library, 2506

John G. Shedd Aquarium, 2520

John Innes Centre, Norwich, 2299

John Jay College of Criminal Justice, 2821

John Mackintosh Hall Library, 2437

John Marshall Law School, 2654

John Paul II Catholic University of Lublin, 1775

John Paul II Institute for Marriage & Family, East Melbourne, 181

John Paul II University, Managua, 1618

John Paul II University, San José, 618

John Snow College, Stockton, 2360

John von Neumann Computer Society, 1001

John W. Graham Library, University of Trinity College, 394

John Wesley Theological College, 1026

John Young Museum of Art, 2519

Johns Hopkins Archaeological Museum, Baltimore, 2525

Johns Hopkins University, Baltimore, 2701

Johns Hopkins University Libraries, Baltimore, 2490

Johns Hopkins University—School of Advanced International Studies Europe at Bologna, 1232

Johnson & Wales University, 2925

Johnson C. Smith University, 2860

Johnson City Public Library, 2504

Johnson County Kansas Law Library, 2487

Johnson County Library System, 2509

Johnson State College, 2973

Johnson University, 2936

Joho Kagaku Gijutsu Kyokai, 1242

Joho-Jigyo, Kagaku-Gijutsu Shinko Kiko, 1242

Joint Art Library of the Nationalmuseum and the Museum of Modern Art, Stockholm, 2114

Joint Institute for Nuclear Research, Dubna, 1898

Joint Laboratory of Solid State Chemistry of the Institute of Macromolecular Chemistry AS CR and Pardubice University, 655

Joint Library of the Hellenic and Roman Societies, London, 2320

Joint Research Unit Ecology of Guiana Forests, 824

Joint Russian-Vietnamese Tropical Research and Technological Centre, Leninsky, 1902

Joint Science Conference, Bonn, 843

Jöklarannsóknafélag Íslands, 1029

Jolo Branch Museum, 1735

Pjóðminjasafn Íslands, 1030

Jomo Kenyatta University of Agriculture and Technology, 1378

Jones College, 2631

Jones International University, 2598

Jones Memorial Library, 2506

Jönköping International Business School, 2135

Jönköping Public Library, 2114

Jönköping University, 2134

Joods Historisch Museum, Amsterdam, 1580

Jordan Archaeological Museum, 1358

Jordan Historical Museum of the Twenty, 396

Jordan Library and Information Association, 1358

Jordan Schnitzer Museum of Art, 2539

Jordan University of Science and Technology (JUST), 1359

Jordbrugsakademikernes (JA), Klampenborg, 672

Jorge Amado University Centre, 318

Jorge B. Vargas Museum and Filipiniana Research Centre, 1736

Jorge Dimitrov Livestock Research Institute, 635

Jorge Eliécer Gaitán Memorial Museum, 594

Jorge Garcés Borrero Departmental Library, 594

Jorge Palacios Preciado Central Library, Pedagogical and Technological University of Colombia, 594

Jorge Tadeo Lozano University of Bogotá, 596

Jorvik Viking Centre, 2337

Jósa András Múzeum, 1010

José A. Negri Library of the College of Notaries, 122

'José Antonio Echeverría' Library, 636

José Antonio Portuondo Valdor Institute of Literature and Linguistics, 635

José Benito Vives de Andreis Institute of Marine and Coastal Research, 593

José Carlos Mariátegui University, 1721

José Cecilio del Valle University, 996
José Celestino Mutis Botanical Gardens of Bogotá, 594
José do Rosario Vellano University, 325
'José Limón' National Centre for Research, Information and Documentation on Dance, 1498
José Luis Bello y González Museum of Art, 1499
'José Ma. Lafragua' Library, 1497
'José María Vargas' University, 3054
José Martí National Library, 636
José Sabogal Institute of Peruvian Art, 1714
José Sinues Ibercaja Library, 2065
Josep Pallach Institute of Education Sciences, Girona, 2060
Joseph Conrad Society, 2287
Joseph Haydn Conservatory of Burgenland, 210
Joseph Haydn Konservatorium des Landes Burgenland, 210
Joseph P. Horner Memorial Library, Philadelphia, 2503
Josephine Butler College, Stockton, 2360
Joshua Mqabuko Nkomo Polytechnic, 3081
Josip Bepo Benković, 1536
Josip Jurja Strossmayer University of Osijek, 628
Þjóðskjalasafn Íslands, 1030
Joslyn Art Museum, 2530
Journalism Institute, Beijing, 484
Journey Museum, Rapid City, 2541
Jovan Hadži Institute of Biology at ZRC SAZU, 2019
Jowzjan Provincial Library, 92
Joyce K. Carver Soldotna Public Library, 2477
Jozef Pilsudski Regional and Municipal Public Library in Lodz, 1770
József Egry Memorial Museum, 1007
József Katona Memorial House, 1010
JSC Bekturov Institute of Chemical Sciences, 1364
JSC International Research and Production Holding 'Phytochemistry', Karaganda, 1364
JTI—Institutet för jordbruks- och miljöteknik, 2111
JTI—Swedish Institute of Agricultural and Environmental Engineering, 2111
Juan B. Ambrosetti Ethnographical Museum, 123
Juan B. Castagnino Municipal Museum of Fine Arts, 124
Juan Bautista Vázquez Regional Documentation Centre, 701
Juan Cornelio Moyano Museum of Anthropology and Natural Sciences, 124
Juan de Vargas Customs Museum, 292
Juan Misael Saracho Autonomous University, 293
Juan Pablo Pérez Alfonzo Library, Caracas, 3049
Juan Ramón Molina National Library of Honduras, 995
Juárez Autonomous University of Tabasco, 1518
Juárez University of the State of Durango, 1507
Jubail Industrial College, 1967
Judges' Association of Serbia, 1971
Judiciary Library, Guatemala City, 985
Jüdisches Museum Rendsburg, Schleswig, 881
Judiska Museet, Stockholm, 2118
Judson College, 2549
Judson University, 2654
Juilliard School, 2837
Jule Collins Smith Museum of Fine Art, 2509
Jülich Research Centre, 861
Julius-Maximilians-Universität Würzburg, Mainz, 899
Junagadh Agricultural University, 1066
Juneau Public Libraries, 2477
Jungang Library, 1388
Juniata College, 2906
Junta de Historia Eclesiástica Argentina, 118

Junta Nacional Protectora y Conservadora del Patrimonio Histórico y Artístico de la Nación, Caracas, 3046
Juraj Dobrila University of Pula, 629
Jura-Museum, 880
Jurby Transport Museum, 2439
Justice System Training & Research Institute, Bristol, 2474
Justus-Liebig-Universität Giessen, 900
Jutland Archaeological Society, North Jutland, 673
Jutland Art Academy, 687
Jutland Historical Society, 674
Jysk Arkaeologisk Selskab Nordjylland, 673
Jysk Selskab for Historie, 674
Jyske Kunstakademi, 687
Jyske Musikkonservatorium, 687
Jyväskylä University Library, 748
Jyväskylä University Museum, 750
Jyväskylän Ammattikorkeakoulu, 761
Jyväskylän Yliopisto, 756
Jyväskylän Yliopiston Kirjasto, 748
Jyväskylän Yliopiston Museo, 750

K

K. I. Satpaev Institute of Geological Sciences, Almaty, 1364
K. I. Skryabin All-Russia Research and Development Institute of Helminthology, 1885
K Mart Center for Retail and International Marketing, 1169
K. N. Toosi University of Technology, 1139
K. R. Cama Oriental Institute, 1043
K. Stanislavsky's Memorial House, 1910
K. U. Leuven Universiteitsbibliotheek, 268
Kabale University, 2244
Kabarak University, 1378
Kabarda-Balkar Art Museum, 1911
Kabardino-Balkar Land Improvement Institute, 1951
Kabardino-Balkar State University Library, 1907
Kabardino-Balkarian State University, 1921
Kabayan Branch, 1735
Kabinet Grafike, 627
Kabinet pro klasická studia FLÚ AV ČR, v.v.i., 654
Kabinet za Arhitekturu i Urbanizam, Arhiv za Likovne Umjetnosti Hrvatske Akademije Znanosti i Umjetnosti, 624
Kaboora Institute of Higher Education, 94
Kabul Art School, 94
Kabul Educational University, 93
Kabul Health Sciences Institute, 94
Kabul Medical University, 93
Kabul Public Library, 92
Kabul University, 93
Kabul University Library, 92
Kabushikikaisha Mitsubishi Sogo Kenkyusho, 1249
Kadir Has Üniversitesi, 2228
Kaduna Polytechnic, 1645
Kaduna State Library Board, 1627
Kaesong City Library, 1385
Kaesong Historical Library, 1385
Kafkas Üniversitesi, 2228
Kagawa University, 1274
Kagoshima Prefectural Library, 1252
Kagoshima University, 1275
Kahan i Kutturan Guahan, 3012
Kahan i Kutturan Guahan—The Gallery, 3013
Kahramanmaraş Sütçü Imam Üniversitesi, 2228
Kailali Public Library, 1557
'Kairos' College for Public Relations and Media Studies, 632
Kaiser Library, 1557
Kaiserliche Hofburg, Innsbruck, 196
Kaitseväe Ühendatud Õppeasutused, 734
Kajaani University of Applied Sciences, 761

Kajaanin Ammattikorkeakoulu, Kajaani, 761
Kakatiya University, 1066
Kalaidos Fachhochschule, 2166
Kalakshetra Foundation, 1109
Kalamazoo College, 2746
Kalamazoo Institute of Arts, 2528
Kalashnikov Izhevsk State Technical University, 1938
Kalinga Institute of Industrial Technology, 1102
Kaliningrad State Technical University, 1938
Kalmar Public Library, 2114
Kalmar Stadsbibliotek, 2114
Kalmyk State University, 1921
Kalmyk State University Library, 1905
Kaluga Regional Art Museum, 1908
Kamakura Kokuhokan, 1254
Kamarupa Anusandhana Samiti, 1043
Kamchatka State Fishing Fleet Academy, 1951
Kameshwar Singh Darbhanga Sanskrit University, 1066
Kampala International University, 2244
Kampala University, 2244
Kampong Cham National School of Agriculture, 378
Kamra tal-Periti Malta, Gzira, 1484
Kamuzu College of Nursing, 1468
Kamyanets-Podilsky State Historical Museum-Preserve, 2255
Kanagawa Prefectural Kanazawa Bunko Museum, 1256
Kanagawa Prefectural Library, 1254
Kanagawa University, Yokohama, 1275
Kanawha County Public Library, 2507
Kanazawa City Libraries, 1252
Kanazawa College of Art, 1356
Kanazawa Municipal Izumino Library, 1252
Kanazawa University, 1275
Kandahar Museum, 93
Kandahar Provincial Library, 93
Kandahar University, 94
Kandy National Museum, 2094
Kangnam University, 1400
Kangwon National University, 1391
Kangwon Provincial Library, 1385
Kanizsan Dorottya Múzeum, 1010
Kannada University, Hampi, 1066
Kannur University, 1066
Kano State Library Board, 1627
Kano State Polytechnic, 1645
Kano State University of Technology, Wudil, 1642
Kansai University, 1337
Kansai University Library, 1253
Kansallisarkisto, 748
Kansalliskirjasto, 748
Kansalliskirjasto, Slaavilainen Kirjasto, 748
Kansas African American Museum, 2523
Kansas Aviation Museum, 2523
Kansas City Art Institute, 2789
Kansas City Museum, 2529
Kansas City Public Library, 2494
Kansas City University of Medicine and Biosciences, 2789
Kansas Historical Society, 2453
Kansas Museum of History, 2523
Kansas State University, 2685
Kansas Supreme Court Law Library, 2487
Kansas Wesleyan University, 2685
Kantonalni Zavod za Zaštitu Kulturno-Historisjkog i Prirodnog Naslijedja Sarajevo, 298
Kantonalni-Županijski Arhiv Travnik, 299
Kantonsbibliothek Vadiana St Gallen, 2147
Kantons-und Universitätsbibliothek Freiburg, 2146
Kanzelhöhe Solar Observatory of the University of Graz, Treffen, 191
Kaohsiung Medical University, 2177
Kaohsiung Museum of Fine Arts, 2174
KaosPilots, 687
Kapisa Provincial Library, 93
Kapitza, P. L., Institute of Physical Problems, Moscow, 1898
Kaplan Holborn College, 2411

Kaplan Professional, Sydney, 178
Kaplan University, 2681
Kaposvár University, 1016
Kaposvári Egyetem, 1016
Kapteyn Astronomical Institute, 1571
Karachi Institute of Economics and Technology, 1685
Karachi Theosophical Society, 1675
Karadeniz Technical University, 2228
Karadeniz Teknik Üniversitesi, 2228
Karaganda 'Bolashak' University, 1368
Karaganda Economical University of Kazpotrebsoyuz, 1368
Karaganda Metallurgical Institute, 1374
Karaganda Regional History and Local Lore Museum, 1366
Karaganda Regional Museum of Fine Arts, 1366
Karaganda Regional Universal Research Library named after N. V. Gogol, 1365
Karaganda State Medical University, 1368
Karaganda State Technical University, 1368
Karaganda State University Library, 1365
Karaganda State University named after academician E. A. Buketov, 1368
Karakalpak Branch of the Uzbek Academy of Sciences, 3030
Karakalpak Historical Museum, 3032
Karakalpak State Museum of Art named after I. V. Savitsky, 3032
Karakalpak State University, 3033
Karakol branch of Moscow Institute of Business and Law, 1423
Karakoram International University, 1685
Karel de Grote-Hogeschool, 281
Karelia Ammattikorkeakoulu, 761
Karelia University of Applied Sciences, 761
Karelian Museum of Fine Arts, 1911
Karelian State Regional Museum, 1912
Karen Blixen Museet, 682
Karen Blixen Museum, 682
Kargin, V. A., Polymer Research Institute, 1902
Karkaraly History Museum, 1366
Karkonoska Państwowa Szkoła Wyższa w Jeleniej Górze, 1811
Karkonosze College in Jelenia Góra, 1811
Karl C. Harrison Museum of George Washington, 2509
Karl-Franzens-Universität Graz, 199
Karlovac University of Applied Sciences, 632
Karlovarské muzeum, 658
Karlovy Vary Art Gallery, 658
Karlovy Vary Museum, 658
Karlsruhe Institute of Technology, 861
Karlsruhe University of Education, 910
Karlsruher Instituts für Technologie, 902
Karlstad University, 2123
Karlstads Universitet, 2123
Karnatak Historical Research Society, 1043
Karnatak University, 1067
Karnataka Government Secretariat Library, 1049
Karnataka State Open University, 1067
Karnataka State Women's University, 1067
Kärntner Landesarchiv, 193
Kärntner Landeskonservatorium, 210
Karol Lipinski Academy of Music in Wrocław, 1812
Karol Szymanowski Academy of Music in Katowice, 1813
Károli Gáspár Református Egyetem, Budapest, 1025
Karolinska Förbundet, 2109
Karolinska Institute University Library, 2114
Karolinska Institutet, 2135
Karolinska Institutet, Universitetsbiblioteket, 2114
Károly Róbert College, 1026
Károly Róbert Főiskola, 1026

Krylov Shipbuilding Research Institute, St Petersburg, 1902
Krypiakevych, I., Institute of Ukrainian Studies, Lviv, 2249
Krzhizhanovsky, G. M., State Energy Research Institute, 1902
Książnica Pomorska im. Stanisława Staszica w Szczecinie, 1771
K-State Libraries, 2487
KU Leuven Campus Brussels, 272
KU Libraries University of Kansas, 2488
Kuala Lumpur Public Library, 1472
Kuban State Agrarian University, 1915
Kuban State Medical Academy, 1950
Kuban State Technical University, 1939
Kuban State University, 1923
Kuban State University Library, 1905
Kubinyi Ferenc Múzeum, 1011
Kucherenko, V. A., State Central Research and Experimental Design Institute for Complex Problems of Civil Engineering and Building Structures, Moscow, 1885
Kuffner Observatory, Vienna, 191
Kuffner-Sternwarte, 191
Kügelgenhaus–Museum der Dresdner Romantik, Dresden, 875
Kühne Logistics University, 904
Kuki-Chowa Eisei Kogakkai, 1248
Kulturen in Lund, 2117
Kulturhistorisches Museum der Hansestadt Stralsund, 881
Kulturhistorisk Museum, Oslo, 1652
Kulturhuset, 2118
Kulturparken Småland AB, 2120
Kulturrådet, 2108
Kulturstyrelsen, Copenhagen, 672
Kuluttajatutkimuskeskus, Helsinki, 746
Kulyab State University, 2180
Kumamoto Arts and Crafts Museum, 1254
Kumamoto Prefectural University, 1329
Kumamoto University, 1281
Kumaun University, 1068
Kumi University, 2244
Kumoh National University of Technology, 1408
Kunar Provincial Library, 93
Kunayev Institute of Mining, 1365
Kunduz Higher Education Institution, 94
Kunduz Provincial Library, 93
Kungl. Fysiografiska Sällskapet i Lund, 2110
Kungl. Gustav Adolfs Akademien för svensk folkkultur, 2110
Kungl. Humanistiska Vetenskaps-Samfundet i Uppsala, 2108
Kungl. Ingenjörsvetenskapsakademien—IVA, 2110
Kungl Krigsvetenskapsakademien, 2108
Kungl. Musikaliska Akademien, 2109
Kungl. Musikhögskolan i Stockholm, 2135
Kungl. Myntkabinettet—Sveriges Ekonomiska Museum, 2118
Kungl. Örlogsmannasällskapet, 2110
Kungl. Skogs- och Lantbruksakademien, 2108
Kungl. Skogs- och Lantbruksakademiens Bibliotek, 2114
Kungl. Skytteanska Samfundet, 2110
Kungl. Vetenskaps- och Vitterhets-Samhället i Göteborg (KVVS), 2108
Kungl. Vetenskapsakademien, 2108
Kungl. Vetenskaps-Societeten i Uppsala, 2108
Kungl. Vitterhets Historie och Antikvitets Akademien, 2108
Kungliga Akademien för de fria Konsterna (Konstakademien), 2109
Kungliga biblioteket—Sveriges nationalbibliotek, 2114
Kungliga Konsthögskolan, 2135
Kungliga Tekniska Högskolan, 2135
Kungliga Tekniska Högskolans Bibliotek, 2115
Kunitachi College of Music, 1356
Kunming Institute of Zoology, 485

Kunming Medical University, 531
Kunming University of Science and Technology, 531
Kunsan National University, 1392
Kunsill Malti għall Kwalifiki, 1484
Kunst Museum Bayreuth, 872
Kunst- og designhøgskolen i Bergen, 1668
Kunst- und Museumsbibliothek mit Rheinischem Bildarchiv, 865
Kunstakademie Düsseldorf, 957
Kunstakademiet i Trondheim, Norges Teknisk-Naturvitenskaplige Universitet, 1668
Kunstbibliothek Staatliche Museen zu Berlin, 864
KunstCentret Silkeborg Bad, 682
Kunsten Museum of Modern Art Aalborg, 679
Kunstforeningen GL STRAND, 673
Kunstgewerbemuseum, Berlin, 873
Kunstgewerbemuseum, Dresden, 875
Kunsthal Rotterdam, 1583
Kunsthalle Bremen—Der Kunstverein in Bremen, 874
Kunsthalle Düsseldorf, 876
Kunsthalle Mannheim, 879
Kunsthalle Nürnberg im KunstKulturQuartier, 880
Kunsthallen Brandts, 681
Kunsthaus Glarus, 2148
Kunsthaus Zürich, 2150
Kunsthistorische Gesellschaft, Vienna, 184
Kunsthistorisches Institut in Florenz—Max-Planck-Institut, Florence, 853
Kunsthistorisches Museum Sammlungen Schloss Ambras, 196
Kunsthistorisches Museum, Vienna, 197
Kunsthochschule Berlin-Weissensee, Hochschule für Gestaltung, 957
Kunsthøgskolen i Oslo (KHiO), 1668
Künstlerhaus (Gesellschaft Bildender Künstler Österreichs), 184
Kunstmuseum Basel, 2147
Kunstmuseum, Bern, 2148
Kunstmuseum Bonn, 874
Kunstmuseum Liechtenstein, 1444
Kunstmuseum Luzern, 2149
Kunstmuseum Olten, 2149
Kunstmuseum, St Gallen, 2149
Kunstmuseum Solothurn, 2149
Kunstmuseum Stuttgart, 881
Kunstmuseum Winterthur, 2150
Kunstnerforeningen af 18. November, Copenhagen, 673
Kunstsammlung Nordrhein-Westfalen, Düsseldorf, 876
Kunstskolen, 691
Kunstverein St Gallen, 2139
Kuopio Art Museum, 750
Kuopio City Library, 749
Kuopion kaupunginkirjasto, 749
Kuopion Taidemuseo, 750
Kupferstichkabinett der Akademie der Bildenden Künste, Vienna, 197
Kupferstich-Kabinett, Dresden, 875
Kupferstichkabinett–Sammlung der Zeichnungen und Druckgraphik, Berlin, 873
Kuppuswami Sastri Research Institute, 1043
Kurchatov, I. V., Institute of Atomic Energy, Moscow, 1898
Kurdish Institute, 776
Kurdish Library, 2115
Kurdiska Biblioteket, 2115
Kurgan Agricultural Institute, 1951
Kurgan State University, 1923
Kurnakov Institute of General and Inorganic Chemistry, Moscow, 1898
Kurpfälzisches Museum der Stadt Heidelberg, 877
Kursk Deineka Picture Gallery, 1909
Kursk Research and Development Institute of the Agro-Industrial Complex, 1884
Kursk State Agricultural Academy 'I. I. Ivanov', 1948
Kursk State Medical University, 1934
Kursk State Technical University, 1939
Kursk State University, 1923
Kurt Bösch University Institute, 2165

Kurtuluş Savaşı ve Cumhuriyet Müzeleri, 2214
Kurukshetra University, 1068
Kurume University, 1342
Kushinga Phikelela Polytechnic, 3081
Kushinga-Phikelela National Farmer Training Centre, 3081
Kushiro City Museum, 1254
Kushiro-Shiritsu Hakubutsukan, 1254
Kutaisi 'N. I. Muskhelishvili' Technical University, 842
Kutaisi Scientific Centre, 838
Kutztown University, 2911
Kuvempu University, 1068
Kuwait Foundation for the Advancement of Science, 1415
Kuwait Institute for Medical Specialization, 1415
Kuwait Institute for Scientific Research, 1415
Kuwait Medical Association, 1414
Kuwait Medical Genetics Centre, 1414
Kuwait National Museum, 1415
Kuwait University, 1415
Kuwait University Libraries, 1415
Kuwait–Maastricht Business School, 1416
Kuyper College, 2746
Kuzbass State Technical University named after T.F. Gorbachev, 1939
KVI, Groningen, 1573
Kvibergs Museum, 2116
Kwa Muhle Museum, Durban, 2033
Kwame Nkrumah University of Science and Technology, 963
Kwame Nkrumah University of Science and Technology Library, Kumasi, 963
Kwandong University, 1401
Kwangju University, 1392
Kwangwoon University, 1402
Kwansei Gakuin University, 1342
Kwansei Gakuin University Library, 1252
Kwara State Library Board, 1627
Kwara State Polytechnic, 1645
KwaZulu-Natal Museum, 2034
KwaZulu-Natal Provincial Library Service, 2031
Kwekwe Polytechnic, 3081
Kyambogo University, 2244
Kyiv Museum of Russian Art, 2255
Kyiv 'N. D. Strazhesko' Research Institute of Cardiology, 2250
Kyiv National Economic University named after Vadym Hetman, 2258
Kyiv National Linguistic University, 2258
Kyiv National University of Construction and Architecture, 2265
Kyiv National University of Trade and Economics, 2258
Kyiv National University 'Taras Shevchenko' Library, 2254
'Kyiv Polytechnic Institute' National Technical University of Ukraine, 2265
Kyiv Research Institute of Oncology, 2250
Kyiv State Institute of Culture, 2268
Kyiv State Literary Museum 'Lessya Ukrainka', 2255
Kykkos Monastery Museum, 646
Kymenlaakson Ammattikorkeakoulu, Kotka, 762
Kymenlaakson University of Applied Sciences, 762
Kyonggi University, 1402
Kyoto City University of Arts, 1356
Kyoto Institute of Technology, 1283
Kyoto Kokuritsu Hakubutsukan, 1255
Kyoto National Museum, 1255
Kyoto Notre Dame University, Kyoto, 1342
Kyoto Pharmaceutical University, 1342
Kyoto Prefectural Library and Archives, 1252
Kyoto Prefectural University of Medicine, 1329
Kyoto Sangyo University, 1329
Kyoto University, 1283
Kyoto University Library, 1252
Kyoto-Shi Bijutsukan, 1255

Kypriake Enose Bivbiothikonomon-Epistemonon Pleroforeses (KEBEP), 644
Kyrgyz Adult Education Association, 1417
Kyrgyz Geographical Society, 1417
Kyrgyz National Agrarian University named after K. I. Skriabin, 1421
Kyrgyz National Conservatory, 1421
Kyrgyz National University 'Zhusup Balasagyn', 1421
Kyrgyz Research Institute of Mineral Raw Materials, 1418
Kyrgyz Scientific Research Institute of Obstetrics and Paediatrics, 1418
Kyrgyz State Academy of Law, 1421
Kyrgyz State Institute of Arts named after B. Beishenalieva, 1421
Kyrgyz State Institute of Physical Training, 1421
Kyrgyz State Medical Academy, 1423
Kyrgyz State Technical University named after I. Razzakov, 1422
Kyrgyz State University of Construction, Transport and Architecture named after N. Isanov, 1422
Kyrgyz-Russian Academy of Education, 1421
Kyrgyz-Russian Slavic University, 1421
Kyrgyzstan Library Information Consortium, 1417
Kyrgyzstan-Turkey Manas University, 1421
Kyrgyz-Uzbek University, 1422
Kyung Hee Cyber University, 1409
Kyung Hee University, 1402
Kyungil University, 1402
Kyungnam University, 1402
Kyungpook National University, 1392
Kyungpook National University Library, 1388
Kyungsung University, 1402
Kyungwon University, 1402
Kyushu Institute of Design, 1289
Kyushu Institute of Technology, 1289
Kyushu Sangyo University, 1329
Kyushu University, 1289
Kyzylorda Humanitarian University named after Korkyt Ata, 1370
Kyzylorda Regional Library named after A. Tazhibayev, 1365
Kyzylorda State University named after Korkyt Ata, 1371

L

L. and A. Birkenmajer Institute for the History of Science of the Polish Academy of Sciences, 1765
L. D. Landau Institute of Theoretical Physics, Moscow, 1898
L. I. Medved's Institute of Ecohygiene and Toxicology, Kyiv, 2250
L. M. Isaev Research Institute of Medical Parasitology, 3031
L. N. Gumilyov Eurasian National University, 1371
L. R. Klein—Centro Stone, 2060
L. V. Pisarzhevsky Institute of Physical Chemistry, Kyiv, 2252
La Colombaria Tuscan Academy of Science and Literature, 1188
La Escuela Nacional de Administración y Hacienda Pública–Instituto Universitario de Tecnología (ENAHP-IUT), 3060
La Estancia Art Centre, 3050
La Fondation du Roi Abdul Aziz pour les Études Islamiques et les Sciences Humaines, 1539
La France Latine—Revue d'études d'Oc, Paris, 769
La Gran Colombia University, 602
La Hougue Bie Museum, 2440
LA Law Library (Los Angeles County Law Library), 2479
La Massana Community Library, 112
La Paz Geographical Society, 290
La Plata Museum, 124
La Roche College, 2906
La Salle Bajio University, 1509

La Salle Foundation of Natural Sciences, Caracas, 3047
La Salle Laguna University, 1507
'La Salle' Society of Natural Sciences, 3047
La Salle University, 2906
La Salle University, Bogotá, 597
La Salle University, Cancún, 1517
La Salle University, Mexico City, 1506
La Salle University of Morelia, 1512
La Salle University of Pachuca, 1510
La Salle University of the Northwest, 1518
La Salle University of Victoria, 1520
La Savane des Esclaves, 828
La Serena Archaeological Museum, 469
La Sierra University, 2573
La Société Bibliographique de Canada, 387
La Société Guernesiaise, 2438
La Trobe University, 170
La Trobe University Library, 151
La UICN, la Unión Internacional para la Conservacion de la Naturaleza, 87
Lääketieteellinen Radioisotooppiyhdistys, 744
Lääketieteellisen Fysiikan ja Tekniikan Yhdistys ry, 744
Labor für konstruktiven Ingenieurbau, 193
Labor Studies Center—Labor@Wayne, Detroit, 2474
Laboratoire Central de Recherches Vétérinaires, Maisons-Alfort, 773
Laboratoire d'Astronomie de Lille 1, 776
Laboratoire d'Investigation et de Recherche Clinique, 264
Laboratoire de Biotechnologie de l'Environnement, Narbonne, 777
Laboratoire de Recherches Vétérinaires et Zootechniques de Farcha, N'Djamena, 462
Laboratoire Départemental d'Analyses, 828
Laboratoire Public d'Essais et d'études, Casablanca, 1539
Laboratoř anorganických materiálů, Prague, 656
Laboratorio Arte Alameda, 1498
Laboratório de Análises, Rio de Janeiro, 311
Laboratorio di Storia delle Alpi, 2143
Laboratório Nacional de Energia e Geologia (LNEG), 1821
Laboratório Nacional de Engenharia Civil, 1821
Laboratorium Kesehatan Daerah, 1112
Laboratory Animal Centre, 746
Laboratory for Molecular Infection Medicine Sweden, 2112
Laboratory for Research in Fluid Dynamics and Combustion Technologies, Zaragoza, 2059
Laboratory for Structural Engineering, 193
Laboratory of Experimental Biological Models, Moscow, 1890
Laboratory of Experimental Biomedical Models, Tomsk, 1892
Laboratory of History of the Alps, 2143
Laboratory of Inorganic Materials, 656
Laboratory of Polar Medicine, Norilsk, 1890
Labour Law Society, Woerden, 1561
Labour Lawyers Association of Japan, 1242
Labouré College, 2728
l'Académie des Sciences du Monde Islamique, 87
LACMA–Los Angeles County Museum of Art, 2512
Laconia Historical & Museum Society, 2532
Lacquerware Technological College, 1550
Laczkó Dezső Múzeum, 1012
Ladha Meghji Indian Public Library, Mwanza, 2183
Ladoke Akintola University of Technology, 1642
Lady Hardinge Medical College, New Delhi, 1108
Lady Lever Art Gallery, 2333

Lady Margaret Hall, Oxford, 2399
Lady Shri Ram College for Women, 1107
Lafayette College, 2906
Lafayette Public Library System, 2489
Lafer Centre for Women and Gender Studies, 1168
Lagastofnun Háskóla Íslands, 1029
Lagos City Libraries, 1627
Lagos State Polytechnic, 1645
Lagos State University, 1642
LaGrange College, 2643
Lahden Ammattikorkeakoulu, 762
Lahore College for Women University, 1686
Lahore Fort Museum, 1679
Lahore Museum, 1679
Lahore School of Economics, 1686
Lahore University of Management Sciences, 1686
Lahore Zoo, 1679
Lahti University of Applied Sciences, 762
Laing Art Gallery, Newcastle upon Tyne, 2336
Lake Agassiz Regional Library, 2493
Lake Chad Research Institute (LCRI), Maiduguri, 1625
Lake Champlain Maritime Museum, 2544
Lake Constance Natural History Museum, 878
Lake County Law Library, 2501
Lake Erie College, 2882
Lake Erie College of Osteopathic Medicine, 2906
Lake Forest College, 2655
Lake Forest Graduate School of Management, 2655
Lake Geneva Public Library, 2508
Lake Region Public Library, 2500
Lake Superior State University, 2746
Lake Worth Public Library, 2484
Lakehead University, 402
Lakeland College, 3000
Lakeview Museum of Arts & Sciences, 2520
Lakshmibai National University of Physical Education, Gwalior, 1102
Lalit Kala Akademi, 1035
Lalit Narayan Mithila University, 1069
Lalit Narayan Mithila Vishvidyalaya, 1069
Lambeth Libraries and Archives, 2321
Lambeth Palace Library, 2321
Lamont-Doherty Earth Observatory, Palisades, 2472
Lampeter Campus Learning Resource Centre, 2318
Lamu Museum, 1377
Lancashire Libraries, 2326
Lancaster Bible College, 2906
Lancaster General College of Nursing & Health Sciences, 2907
Lancaster Theological Seminary, 2907
Lancaster University Library, 2318
Land Use Research Institute, Kyiv, 2249
Landbunaðarháskóli Íslands, 1031
Landcare Research, Lincoln, 1606
Landelijk Expertisecentrum Sociale Interventie, 1593
Lander University, 2929
Landesamt für Archäologie mit Landesmuseum für Vorgeschichte, Dresden, 875
Landesamt für Denkmalpflege und Archäologie Sachsen-Anhalt (Landesmuseum für Vorgeschichte), 877
Landesamt für Natur, Umwelt und Verbraucherschutz Nordrhein-Westfalen, 863
Landesarchiv Baden-Württemberg–Abteilung Staatsarchiv Sigmaringen, 870
Landesarchiv Baden-Württemberg—Generallandesarchiv Karlsruhe, 868
Landesarchiv Baden-Württemberg—Staatsarchiv Ludwigsburg, Ludwigsburg, 868
Landesarchiv Berlin, 864
Landesarchiv Nordrhein-Westfalen, 866

Landesarchiv Nordrhein-Westfalen Abteilung Westfalen, 869
Landesarchiv Nordrhein-Westfalen-Staats- und Personenstandarchiv Detmold, 865
Landesarchiv Saarbrücken, 870
Landesarchiv Schleswig-Holstein, 870
Landesarchiv, Speyer, 870
Landesbibliothek, Coburg, 865
Landesbibliothek Mecklenburg-Vorpommern, Schwerin, 870
Landesbibliothek, Oldenburg, 870
Landesbibliothekszentrum Rheinland-Pfalz, 868
Landesbibliothekszentrum, Zweibrücken, 872
Landesbibliothekszentrum/Pfälzische Landesbibliothek, 868
Landeshauptarchiv Koblenz, 868
Landeshauptarchiv Sachsen-Anhalt, Magdeburg, 868
Landeskirchliches Archiv der Evangelisch-Lutherischen Kirche in Bayern, 870
Landesmuseum für Kärnten, 196
Landesmuseum für Kärnten, Kärntner Botanikzentrum, 196
Landesmuseum für Kunst und Kulturgeschichte, Münster, 880
Landesmuseum für Kunst und Kulturgeschichte, Schleswig, 881
Landesmuseum Mainz, 879
Landesmuseum Württemberg, 881
Landessternwarte Königstuhl, 861
Landsarkivet for Fyn, 679
Landsarkivet for Nørrejylland, 679
Landsarkivet i Lund, 2114
Landsbókasafn Íslands-Háskólabókasafn, 1030
Landscape Institute, London, 2279
Landslaget for Lokalhistorie, 1648
Landsskjalasavnið, 689
Lane Memorial Library, 2496
Langley Research Center, Hampton, Virginia, 2476
Langston University, 2888
Language and Literature Bureau Library, Bandar Seri Begawan, 352
Language Centre of the Ministry of National Education, Jakarta, 1112
Language Council of Sweden, 2109
Language Institute, Sarajevo, 298
Language Resource Centre, 1700
Language Teaching Institute, Doha, 1834
Lankaran State University, 216
Länsmuseet Gävleborgs, 2116
Lanzhou Institute of Physics, 486
Lanzhou University, 531
Lao Buddhist Fellowship Organization, 1424
Lao National Museum, 1424
Lao-American College, 1425
Lapin Yliopisto, 757
Lappeenrannan Teknillinen Korkeakoulu, 757
Lappeenranta University of Technology, 757
Laramie County Library, 2509
Larco Museum, 1717
Larense Historical Centre, 3046
Large Binocular Telescope Observatory (LBTO), 2473
Larimar Museum, 695
Larnaca District Archaeological Museum, 645
Larnaca Municipal Library, 645
Larnaca Municipal Museum of Natural History, 645
Lars Bohman Gallery, 2118
Las Vegas-Clark County Library District, 2495
LASALLE College of the Arts, 1999
LaSalle Parish Library, 2489
Lasbela University of Agriculture, Water and Marine Sciences, 1686
Lasell College, 2728
Laser Centre of Technical University of Madrid, 2062
L'Association Internationale des Bibliothèques, Archives et Centres de Documentation Musicaux, 80

L'Association Suisse de Politique Extérieure, 2138
László Teleki Foundation, 1003
L'Atelier, Alexandria, 711
Latin America Institute, Moscow, 1886
Latin American and Caribbean Centre on Health Sciences Information, 314
Latin American and Caribbean Institute for Economic and Social Planning, Santiago, 467
Latin American Association of Analysis, Modification and Cognitive Behavioural Therapy, 75
Latin American Association of Linguistics and Philology, 53
Latin American Autonomous University, Medellín, 595
Latin American Biblical University, 615
Latin American Faculty of Social Sciences—FLACSO, 709
Latin American Information and Documentation Network for Education, 467
Latin American Information and Documentation Network for Education, Santiago, 467
Latin American Institute for Educational Communication, 65
Latin American Institute of Computing, Managua, 1620
Latin American Institute of Social Research, Quito, 701
Latin American Private Open University, 294
Latin American Technical University, 724
Latin American University Group for Reform and Improvement in Education, 3046
Latin American University of Foreign Trade, 1705
Latin American University of Science and Technology, 1705
Latin American University of Science and Technology, Managua, 1618
Latin American University of Science and Technology, San José, 618
Latin University of America, 1512
Latin University of Costa Rica, 618
Latin University of Panama, 1705
Latvia State Institute of Fruit-Growing, 1428
Latvia University of Agriculture, 1429
Latvian Academy of Culture, 1430
Latvian Academy of Sciences, 1426
Latvian Academy of Sport Education, 1431
Latvian Biomedical Research and Study Centre, 1427
Latvian Christian Academy, 1430
Latvian Institute of Aquatic Ecology, 1427
Latvian Institute of Organic Synthesis, 1428
Latvian Language Institute of the University of Latvia, 1427
Latvian Maritime Academy, 1430
Latvian National Museum of Art, 1429
Latvian Rectors' Council, 1426
Latvian State Forest Research Institute 'Silava', 1428
Latvian State Institute of Agrarian Economics, 1427
Latvian State Institute of Wood Chemistry, 1428
Latvijas Biomedicīnas Pētījumu un Studiju Centrs, 1427
Latvijas Dabas Muzejs, 1429
Latvijas Etnogrāfiskais Brīvdabas Muzejs, 1429
Latvijas Hidroekologijas Institūts, 1427
Latvijas Juras Akademija, 1430
Latvijas Kulturas Akademija, 1430
Latvijas Lauksaimniecības Universitāte, 1429
Latvijas Mākslas Akadēmija, 1430
Latvijas Nacionālā Aizsardzības Akadēmija, 1430
Latvijas Nacionala Biblioteka, 1428
Latvijas Nacionālā Vēstures Muzeja, 1429
Latvijas Nacionālais Mākslas Muzejs, 1429

M

Ministry of Education and Higher Education, Beirut, 1432

Ministry of Education and Higher Education, Doha, 1833

Ministry of Education and Higher Education, Ramallah, 1698

Ministry of Education and Human Resource Development, Roseau, 693

Ministry of Education and Human Resource Development, St George's, 983

Ministry of Education and Human Resources Development, Honiara, 2023

Ministry of Education and Human Resources, Phoenix, 1489

Ministry of Education and Information, Basseterre, 1956

Ministry of Education and Religious Affairs, Athens, 967

Ministry of Education and Research, Oslo, 1647

Ministry of Education and Research, Stockholm, 2107

Ministry of Education and Research, Tartu, 728

Ministry of Education and Science, Astana, 1362

Ministry of Education and Science, Bishkek, 1417

Ministry of Education and Science, Dushanbe, 2178

Ministry of Education and Science, Kyiv, 2247

Ministry of Education and Science, Lisbon, 1814

Ministry of Education and Science, Malabo, 726

Ministry of Education and Science, Moscow, 1879

Ministry of Education and Science, Riga, 1426

Ministry of Education and Science, Skopje, 1458

Ministry of Education and Science, Sofia, 354

Ministry of Education and Science, Tbilisi, 837

Ministry of Education and Science, Tiranë, 95

Ministry of Education and Science, Ulan Bator, 1529

Ministry of Education and Science, Vilnius, 1446

Ministry of Education and Science, Yerevan, 136

Ministry of Education and Skills Development, Gaborone, 303

Ministry of Education and Sport, Praia, 459

Ministry of Education and Sports, Kampala, 2242

Ministry of Education and Sports, Vientiane, 1424

Ministry of Education and Training, Hanoi, 3061

Ministry of Education and Training, Maseru, 1437

Ministry of Education and Training, Mbabane, 2105

Ministry of Education and Vocational Training, Dar es Salaam, 2182

Ministry of Education and Youth, Belmopan, 283

Ministry of Education and Youth, Sant Julià de Lòria, 111

Ministry of Education, Ashgabat, 2239

Ministry of Education, Asmara, 727

Ministry of Education, Baghdad, 1149

Ministry of Education, Baku, 211

Ministry of Education, Bandar Seri Begawan, 352

Ministry of Education, Bangkok, 2187

Ministry of Education, Beijing, 479

Ministry of Education, Bikenibeu, 1382

Ministry of Education, Brasilia, 306

Ministry of Education, Buenos Aires, 117

Ministry of Education, Cairo, 710

Ministry of Education, Chişinău, 1523

Ministry of Education, Church, Culture and Gender Equality, 690

Ministry of Education, Colombo, 2091

Ministry of Education, Culture and Higher Education, 2024

Ministry of Education, Culture and Science, the Hague, 1559

Ministry of Education, Culture and Sport, Madrid, 2050

Ministry of Education, Culture and Vocational Training, São Tomé, 1961

Ministry of Education, Culture, Sports, Science and Technology, Tokyo, 1240

Ministry of Education, Culture, Youth and Sports Affairs, Philipsburg, 1601

Ministry of Education, Damascus, 2168

Ministry of Education, Dhaka, 221

Ministry of Education, Dili, 2199

Ministry of Education, Employment and Gender Affairs, George Town, 2435

Ministry of Education, Financial Services, Gaming, Telecommunications and Justice, Gibraltar, 2437

Ministry of Education, Georgetown, 991

Ministry of Education, Guatemala City, 984

Ministry of Education, Hamilton, 2434

Ministry of Education, Havana, 634

Ministry of Education, Higher Education, Youth and Sports, Papeete, 825

Ministry of Education, Human Resource Development and Labour, Castries, 1957

Ministry of Education, Jerusalem, 1166

Ministry of Education, Kabul, 91

Ministry of Education, Kathmandu, 1556

Ministry of Education, Kigali, 1954

Ministry of Education, Kingston, 1237

Ministry of Education, Kingstown, 1958

Ministry of Education, Koror, 1697

Ministry of Education, La Paz, 290

Ministry of Education, Lima, 1714

Ministry of Education, Luanda, 113

Ministry of Education, Majuro, 1486

Ministry of Education, Malé, 1480

Ministry of Education, Managua, 1615

Ministry of Education, Manama, 218

Ministry of Education, Maputo, 1543

Ministry of Education, Minsk, 247

Ministry of Education, Monrovia, 1439

Ministry of Education, Mont Fleuri, 1991

Ministry of Education, Muscat, 1669

Ministry of Education, Nairobi, 1375

Ministry of Education, Nassau, 217

Ministry of Education, National Heritage, Culture and Arts, Suva, 738

Ministry of Education, Nay Pyi Taw, 1545

Ministry of Education, Panamák, 1028

Ministry of Education, Science and Sport, Ljubljana, 2017

Ministry of Education, Science and Technological Development, Belgrade, 1971

Ministry of Education, Science and Technology, Freetown, 1992

Ministry of Education, Science and Technology, Juba, 2049

Ministry of Education, Science and Technology, Lilongwe, 1467

Ministry of Education, Science and Technology, Prishtina, 1410

Ministry of Education, Science, Culture and Sports, Willemstad, 1599

Ministry of Education, Science, Research and Sport, Bratislava, 2000

Ministry of Education, Science, Technology and Innovation, St Michael, 245

Ministry of Education, Science, Vocational Training and Early Education, Lusaka, 3074

Ministry of Education, Seoul, 1387

Ministry of Education, Singapore, 1994

Ministry of Education, Sports and Culture, Apia, 1959

Ministry of Education, Sports and Culture, Vaiaku, 2241

Ministry of Education, Sports, Youth and Gender Affairs, St Johns, 115

Ministry of Education, Taipei, 2171

Ministry of Education, Tegucigalpa, 995

Ministry of Education, Tehran, 1133

Ministry of Education, Thimphu, 287

Ministry of Education, Trainings & Standards in Higher Education, Islamabad, 1672

Ministry of Education, Tripoli, 1441

Ministry of Education, Tunis, 2206

Ministry of Education, Universities and Research, Rome, 1187

Ministry of Education, Wellington, 1602

Ministry of Education, Windhoek, 1553

Ministry of Education, Women Affairs and Culture Library, Nukualofa, 2202

Ministry of Education, Women's Affairs and Culture, Nuku'alofa, 2202

Ministry of Education, Yaren, 1555

Ministry of Education, Youth and Sport, Phnom-Penh, 377

Ministry of Education, Youth and Sports, Prague, 651

Ministry of Employment and Professional Training, Bamako, 1482

Ministry of Employment and Professional Training, Yaoundé, 383

Ministry of Employment, Technical Education and Vocational Training, Conakry, 988

Ministry of Endowments and Religious Affairs Central Library, 1150

Ministry of External Affairs, Education and Culture, Vaduz, 1444

Ministry of Foreign Affairs Library, Tokyo, 1253

Ministry of Health and Medical Education, Tehran, 1133

Ministry of Health, Sports, Youth & Culture, George Town, 2435

Ministry of Heritage and Culture, Muscat, 1669

Ministry of Higher and Specialized Secondary Education, Tashkent, 3030

Ministry of Higher and Tertiary Education, Science and Technology Development, Harare, 3077

Ministry of Higher and University Education and Scientific Research, Kinshasa, 607

Ministry of Higher Education & Scientific Research, Abu Dhabi, 2270

Ministry of Higher Education and Research, Djibouti, 692

Ministry of Higher Education and Research, Lomé, 2200

Ministry of Higher Education and Research, Luxembourg, 1456

Ministry of Higher Education and Research, Paris, 766

Ministry of Higher Education and Science, Copenhagen, 671

Ministry of Higher Education and Scientific Research, 1464, 3072

Ministry of Higher Education and Scientific Research, Abidjan, 620

Ministry of Higher Education and Scientific Research, Algiers, 100

Ministry of Higher Education and Scientific Research, Amman, 1357

Ministry of Higher Education and Scientific Research, Baghdad, 1149

Ministry of Higher Education and Scientific Research, Bamako, 1482

Ministry of Higher Education and Scientific Research, Bujumbura, 375

Ministry of Higher Education and Scientific Research, Conakry, 988

Ministry of Higher Education and Scientific Research, Cotonou, 285

Ministry of Higher Education and Scientific Research, Khartoum, 2099

Ministry of Higher Education and Scientific Research (MESRS), Tunis, 2206

Ministry of Higher Education and Scientific Research, N'Djamena, 462

Ministry of Higher Education and Scientific Research, Niamey, 1621

Ministry of Higher Education and Scientific Research, Tripoli, 1441

Ministry of Higher Education, Brazzaville, 610

Ministry of Higher Education, Cairo, 710

Ministry of Higher Education, Colombo, 2091

Ministry of Higher Education, Damascus, 2168

Ministry of Higher Education, Havana, 634

Ministry of Higher Education, Kabul, 91

Ministry of Higher Education, Pyongyang, 1383

Ministry of Higher Education, Research, Science and Technology, Banjul, 835

Ministry of Higher Education, Riyadh, 1962

Ministry of Higher Education, Ruwi, 1669

Ministry of Higher Education, Safat, 1414

Ministry of Higher Education, Science and Innovation, Praia, 459

Ministry of Higher Education, Science and Technology, Santo Domingo, 694

Ministry of Higher Education, Scientific Research and Management Training, Rabat, 1538

Ministry of Higher Education, Universities, Regional Academic Centres and Scientific Research, Dakar, 1968

Ministry of Higher Education, Yaoundé, 383

Ministry of Home and Cultural Affairs, Thimphu, 287

Ministry of Human Resource Development, New Delhi, 1033

Ministry of Human Resources, Budapest, 998

Ministry of Information & Culture, Kabul, 91

Ministry of Information, Culture and Tourism, Monrovia, 1439

Ministry of Information, Culture and Tourism, Vientiane, 1424

Ministry of Information, Youth, Culture and Sports, Dar es Salaam, 2182

Ministry of Islamic Affairs, Culture and Endowments, Djibouti, 692

Ministry of Justice and Education, Oranjestad, 1598

Ministry of Justice Library, Tokyo, 1253

Ministry of Livestock Development, Department of Veterinary Services, Nairobi, 1376

Ministry of Manpower, 1994

Ministry of National and Technical Education, Abidjan, 620

Ministry of National Education, 1482, 1968

Ministry of National Education, Algiers, 100

Ministry of National Education and Literacy, Ouagadougou, 373

Ministry of National Education and Professional Training, Djibouti, 692

Ministry of National Education and Vocational Training, 1538

Ministry of National Education and Vocational Training, Luxembourg, 1456

Ministry of National Education and Vocational Training, Port-au-Prince, 993

Ministry of National Education, Ankara, 2210

Ministry of National Education, Antananarivo, 1464

Ministry of National Education, Bogotá, 590

Ministry of National Education, Bucharest, 1835

Ministry of National Education, Higher and Technical Education,

Professional Training, Culture, Youth and Sports, Libreville, 833

Ministry of National Education, Higher Education and Research, Bangui, 460

Ministry of National Education, Literacy and the Promotion of National Languages, 1621

Ministry of National Education, Nouakchott, 1487

Ministry of National Education, Paris, 766

Ministry of National Education, Research, Culture and the Arts, Moroni, 606

Ministry of National Education, Warsaw, 1751

Ministry of National Education, Youth and Sport, 644

Ministry of National Education, Youth, Culture and Sport, Bissau, 990

Ministry of Popular Power for Culture, Caracas, 3045

Ministry of Popular Power for Education, Caracas, 3045

Ministry of Popular Power for Science, Technology and Innovation, Caracas, 3045

Ministry of Popular Power for University Education, Caracas, 3045

Ministry of Pre-University Education and Literacy, Conakry, 988

Ministry of Primary and Secondary Education and Literacy, Lomé, 2200

Ministry of Primary and Secondary Education and Professional Training, Kinshasa-Gombe, 607

Ministry of Primary and Secondary Education, Professional and Vocational Training and Literacy, Bujumbura, 375

Ministry of Professional Training and Employment, 1621

Ministry of Professional Training, Apprenticeships and Handicrafts, 1968

Ministry of Public Education, 2099

Ministry of Public Education, San José, 612

Ministry of Public Education, Tashkent, 3030

Ministry of Public Service, Sustainable Development, Energy, Science and Technology, 1957

Ministry of Science and Communications, 2099

Ministry of Science and Higher Education, Warsaw, 1751

Ministry of Science and Technology, 2203

Ministry of Science and Technology, Addis Ababa, 735

Ministry of Science and Technology, Baghdad, 1149

Ministry of Science and Technology, Bangkok, 2187

Ministry of Science and Technology, Beijing, 479

Ministry of Science and Technology, Dhaka, 221

Ministry of Science and Technology, Hanoi, 3061

Ministry of Science and Technology, Islamabad, 1672

Ministry of Science and Technology, Luanda, 113

Ministry of Science and Technology, Maputo, 1543

Ministry of Science and Technology, Nay Pyi Taw, 1545

Ministry of Science and Technology, New Delhi, 1033

Ministry of Science and Technology, San José, 612

Ministry of Science and Technology, Vientiane, 1424

Ministry of Science, Education and Sports, Zagreb, 623

Ministry of Science, ICT and Future Planning, 1387

Ministry of Science, Podgorica, 1535

Ministry of Science, Research and Technology, Tehran, 1133

Ministry of Science, Technology and Innovation, Brasilia, 306

Ministry of Science, Technology and Innovation, Putrajaya, 1470

Ministry of Science, Technology and Productive Innovation, Buenos Aires, 117

Ministry of Science, Technology and Space, Jerusalem, 1166

Ministry of Science, Technology and the Environment, Havana, 634

Ministry of Science, Technology, Energy and Mining, Kingston, 1237

Ministry of Scientific Research and Innovation, Ouagadougou, 373

Ministry of Scientific Research and Innovation, Yaoundé, 383

Ministry of Scientific Research and Technological Innovation, Brazzaville, 610

Ministry of Secondary and Higher Education, Ouagadougou, 373

Ministry of Secondary Education, Technical and Professional Training, the Conversion and Integration of Youths, Cotonou, 285

Ministry of Social and Community Development, Culture and Gender Affairs, Basseterre, 1956

Ministry of Sports and Culture, Kigali, 1954

Ministry of Sports, Arts and Culture, Harare, 3077

Ministry of Sports, Culture and the Arts, Nairobi, 1375

Ministry of Sports, Culture and Youth Affairs, 2105

Ministry of Sports, Culture, Heritage and Youth, Gibraltar, 2437

Ministry of Technical Education and Professional Training, 1464

Ministry of Technical Education and Professional Training, Lomé, 2200

Ministry of Technical Education and Vocational Training, San'a, 3072

Ministry of Technical Education, Vocational Training and Employment, Brazzaville, 610

Ministry of Technology and Research, Colombo, 2091

Ministry of Tertiary Education and Skills Training, St James, 2203

Ministry of Tertiary Education, Science, Research and Technology, Ebene, 1489

Ministry of the Arts and Multiculturalism, Port-of-Spain, 2203

Ministry of the French-Speaking Community, Office for Compulsory Education, 258

Ministry of the French-Speaking Community, Office for Higher Education, Brussels, 258

Ministry of the German-Speaking Community, Eupen, 258

Ministry of the Interior Academy, 372

Ministry of the Promotion of Arts and Culture, Bangui, 460

Ministry of Tourism and Culture, 1991

Ministry of Tourism and Culture, Banjul, 835

Ministry of Tourism and Culture, Belize City, 283

Ministry of Tourism and Culture, Freetown, 1992

Ministry of Tourism and Culture, Kuala Lumpur, 1470

Ministry of Tourism, Civil Aviation and Culture, St George's, 983

Ministry of Tourism, Civil Aviation and Culture, St Johns, 115

Ministry of Tourism, Environment and Culture, Maseru, 1437

Ministry of Tourism, Malé, 1480

Ministry of Tourism (MTE), Ecology, Culture and Air Transport, Papeete, 825

Ministry of Tourism, Sports and Culture, Kingstown, 1958

Ministry of Tourism, Wildlife and Culture, 1467

Ministry of Training and Vocational Education, Algiers, 100

Ministry of Youth and Culture, Kingston, 1237

Ministry of Youth, National Service, Sport and Culture, Windhoek, 1553

Ministry of Youth, Sport and Culture, Gaborone, 303

Ministry of Youth, Sport, Culture and the Arts, Konshasa, 607

Ministry of Youth, Sports and Culture, Bujumbura, 375

Ministry of Youth, Sports and Culture, Nassau, 217

Ministry of Youth, Sports and Culture, Niamey, 1621

Minneapolis College of Art and Design, 2769

Minneapolis Institute of Arts, 2528

Minnesota Historical Society, 2453

Minnesota Historical Society Library, 2493

Minnesota Lakes Maritime Museum, 2528

Minnesota Museum of American Art, 2528

Minnesota State Archives, 2493

Minnesota State Colleges and Universities, 2769

Minnesota State Law Library, 2493

Minnesota State Library Services, 2449

Minnesota State University Library, 2493

Minnesota State University, Mankato, 2769

Minnesota State University Moorhead, 2769

Minno-Geološki Universitet 'Sv. Ivan Rilski', 366

Minobusan Homotsukan, 1255

Minot State University, 2873

Minsk Institute of Management, 256

Minsk State Higher Education College of Civil Aviation, 256

Minsk State Linguistic University, 254

Mint Museum, 2536

MINTEK, Randburg, 2030

Mints, Acad. A. L., Institute of Radio Technology JSC, 1902

Minufiya University, 717

Mio, V., House-Museum, Korçë, 98

Miramichi Natural History Museum, 396

'Miran Jarc' Regional Public Library, 2020

Miras University, 1371

Miroslav Krleza Institute of Lexicography, 625

Mirpur University of Science & Technology, 1687

Miryang National University, 1408

Misericordia University, 2903

Misgav Yerushalaim Centre for the Study of Sephardi and Oriental Jewry, 1172

Misjonshøgskolen (MHS), Stavanger, 1667

Miškų institutas Lietuvos Agrarinių ir Miškų Mokslų Centras, 1447

Miskolci Egyetem, 1017

Miskolci Egyetem Könyvtár, Levéltár, Múzeum, 1007

Misr University for Science and Technology (MUST), 718

Mission Sociologique du Haut-Oubangui, 460

Missionary Museum, King William's Town, 2034

Mississippi Armed Forces Museum, 2529

Mississippi College, 2784

Mississippi Museum of Art, 2529

Mississippi Museum of Natural Science, 2529

Mississippi Office of Geology, 2467

Mississippi State University, 2784

Mississippi University for Women, 2785

Mississippi Valley State University, 2785

Missoula Public Library, 2495

Missouri Baptist University, 2790

Missouri Botanical Garden, 2471

Missouri Southern State University, 2790

Missouri State Archives, 2494

Missouri State Library, 2494

Missouri State University, 2790

Missouri University of Science and Technology, 2795

Missouri Valley College, 2791

Missouri Western State University, 2791

Mitchell College, 2602

Mitchell Library, 2317

Mitre Museum, 124

Mittag-Leffler Institute, 2112

Mittatekniikan Keskus, 747

Mittuniversitetet, 2127

Mittweida College—University of Applied Sciences, 959

Miyagi Gakuin Women's College, 1343

Miyake Medical Institute, Takamatsu City, 1250

Mizoram University, 1074

Mlezu Institute of Agriculture, 3081

MLibrary University of Michigan, 2493

MMKM Elektrotechnikai Múzeuma, 1008

M-Museum Leuven, 271

MOA Museum of Art, Atami, 1254

Mobile VINN Excellence Centre, 2113

Model University, 1521

Modern Art Museum of Fort Worth, 2543

Modern Art Oxford, 2336

Modern Church, Liverpool, 2294

Modern College of Business and Science, 1671

Modern History Museum, Dubrovnik, 626

Modern History Research Association, 859

Modern Humanitarian University, Khujand, 2180

Modern Humanities Research Association, Bath, 2303

Modern Language Association, New York, 2454

Modern Language Association of Poland, 1754

Modern Language Society, Helsinki, 744

Modern Magyar Képtár, 1011

Moderna galerija, Ljubljana, 2020

Moderna Galerija, Zagreb, 627

Moderna Museet, 2119

MODUL University Vienna, 201

Modular Open University, 723

Mody Institute of Technology & Science, 1103

Moesgaard Museum, 681

Moesgård Museum, 681

Mogilev Oblast Library 'V. I. Lenin', 251

Mogilev State Foodstuffs University, 254

Mogilev State University 'A. A. Kuleshov', 254

Mogoşoaia National Cultural Centre, 1850

Mohamed Boudiaf of Oran University of Science and Technology, 105

Mohamed Chérif Messaadia University of Souk Ahras, 107

Mohamed El Bachir El Ibrahimi University of Bordj Bou Arréridj, 107

Mohammad Ali Jinnah University, 1687

Mohan Lal Sukhadia University, 1074

Mohand Akli Ouelhadj University Bouira, 107

Mohi-ud-Din Islamic University, Nerian Sharif, 1687

Moholy-Nagy Müvészeti Egyetem, 1018

Moholy-Nagy University of Art and Design Budapest, 1018

Mohyla míru, Prace u Brna, 659

Moi University, 1379

Mokpo National Maritime University, 1395

Mokpo National University, 1395

Mokpo Natural History Museum, 1390

Mokslininkų Sąjungos Institutas, 1447

Mokslo, Inovacijų ir Technologijų Agentūra, 1447

Mokwon University, 1402

Molde University College—Specialized University in Logistics, 1666

'Moldova' Iaşi National Museum Complex, 1850

Moldova State University, 1526

Moldova State University Library, 1525
Moldovan Sociological Association, 1524
Moldovan State Agrarian University, 1525
Molecular Biology Institute of Barcelona, 2057
Molecular Medicine Ireland, 1159
Molloy College, Rockville Centre, 2839
Mombasa Polytechnic University College, 1381
Mommsen Society eV, 848
Mommsen-Gesellschaft eV, 848
Momoyama Gakuin University, Osaka, 1343
Mon State Museum, Mon, 1546
Monash South Africa, 2047
Monash University, 170
Monash University Library, 151
Monasterio de las Descalzas Reales, 2067
Monasterio de Santa Maria la Real de las Huelgas, 2067
Monasterio de Yuste, 2067
Mondragon Unibertsitatea, 2069
Mondriaanhuis, 1584
Money Museum, Utrecht, 1583
Money Museum Yotin Kòrtá, 1600
Mong Ha Library, 588
Mongol Higher School, 1534
Mongolian Academy of Sciences, 1529
Mongolian Business Institute, 1534
Mongolian Civil Engineers' Association, 1530
Mongolian Development Research Centre, 1530
Mongolian Muslims' Society, Ulan Bator, 1530
Mongolian National Council for Education Accreditation, 1529
Mongolian National Gallery of Modern Art, Ulan Bator, 1531
Mongolian National Higher School, Ulan Bator, 1534
Mongolian National Mining Association, Ulan Bator, 1530
Mongolian National Water Association, 1530
Mongolian State Education University, 1532
Mongolian State University of Agriculture, 1532
Mongolian State University of Arts and Culture, Ulan Bator, 1532
Mongolian University of Science and Technology, 1532
Mongui Maduro Library, 1600
Monica Herrera School of Communications, 724
Monmouth College, 2657
Monmouth County Historical Association Museum & Library, 2532
Monmouth University, West Long Branch, 2809
Monmouthshire Libraries & Information Service, 2315
Monos Higher School of Medicine, Ulan Bator, 1534
Monroe College, 2839
Monroe County Library System, 2493
Monroe County Library System, Rochester, 2498
Monroe County Public Library, 2507
Mons. Fremiot Torres Oliver Library, 3015
Monseñor Oscar Arnulfo Romero University, 723
Montana Cowboy Hall of Fame, 2530
Montana Historical Society Museum, 2530
Montana State Library, 2495
Montana State University, 2797
Montana State University—Billings, 2797
Montana State University—Great Falls College of Technology, 2797
Montana State University—Northern, 2797
Montana Tech, Butte, 2797
Montané Anthropological Museum, 637
Montanuniversität Leoben, 201
Montclair Art Museum, 2532
Montclair State University, 2809

Montclair State University Art Gallery, 2532
Monteávila University, 3054
Montenegrin Academy of Sciences and Arts, 1535
Montenegrin PEN Centre, 1535
Monterey Institute of International Studies: a Graduate School of Middlebury College, 2575
Monterrey Metropolitan University, 1514
Montevideo Astronomical Observatory, 3026
Montgomery City-County Public Library, 2477
Montgomery County Law Library, 2501
Montgomery Museum of Fine Arts, 2509
Montpellier SupAgro, 816
Montréal Biodôme, 397
Montreal Diocesan Theological College, Montréal, 403
Montréal Museum of Fine Arts, 397
Montreat College, 2861
Montserrat College of Art, 2735
Monumen Perjuangan Rakyat (MONPERA) Sumatera Bagian Selatan, 1114
Monumenta Germaniae Historica, 847
Monumental Brass Society, Whitchurch, 2285
Monywa University, 1547
Moody Bible Institute, 2657
Moominvalley of the Tampere Art Museum, 750
Moore College, Newtown, 178
Moore College of Art and Design, 2909
Moorepark-Animal and Grassland Research and Innovation Centre, 1159
Moorland-Spingarn Research Center, Washington, 2482
Móra Ferenc Múzeum, 1011
Moralogy Kenkyusho, 1247
Moravian College, 2909
Moravian Gallery in Brno, 658
Moravian Library, 656
Moravian Provincial Museum, 658
Moravian Society of History and Literature, 652
Moravian-Silesian Research Library in Ostrava, 657
Moravská galerie v Brně, 658
Moravská zemská knihovna, Brno, 656
Moravské zemské muzeum, 658
Moravskoslezská Vědecká Knihovna v Ostravě, 657
Mordechai Zagagi Centre for Finance and Accounting, 1169
Mordovian N. P. Ogarev State University Library, 1907
Mordovian Republic S. D. Erzi Museum of Fine Arts, 1913
Morehead Planetarium and Science Center, 2536
Morehead State University, 2690
Morehouse College, 2644
Morehouse School of Medicine, 2644
Morgan Library & Museum, New York, 2498
Morgan State University, Baltimore, 2705
Mori Art Museum, 1256
Morling College, Macquarie Park, 178
Morris College, 2929
Morris Museum, 2532
Morris Museum of Art, 2518
Morrison University, Reno, 2801
Morski Instytut Rybacki—Państwowy Instytut Badawczy, Gdynia, 1761
Morton-James Public Library, Nebraska City, 2495
Mosad Harav Kook, 1186
Moscow Agricultural Academy 'K. A. Timiryazev', 1948
Moscow Architectural Institute, 1951
Moscow Art Theatre Museum, 1910
Moscow Aviation Institute (State Technical University), 1939
Moscow Choreographic Institute, 1953
Moscow Engineering Physics Institute (State University), 1939

Moscow G. N. Gabrichevskii Institute of Epidemiology and Microbiology, 1890
Moscow Helmholtz Research Institute of Eye Diseases, 1890
Moscow Higher School of Industrial Art, 1953
Moscow House of Scientists, 1882
Moscow Institute of Economics, Statistics and Informatics, 1951
Moscow Institute of Municipal Economy and Construction, 1951
Moscow Institute of Physics and Technology (State University), 1939
Moscow Institute of Printing, 1952
Moscow Kremlin Museums, 1910
Moscow Literary Institute of the Union of Writers 'M. Gorky', 1953
Moscow Municipal Research First Aid Institute, 1890
Moscow Radiotechnical Institute, 1898
Moscow Research Institute of Psychiatry, 1890
Moscow Scientific-Industrial Association 'Spektr', 1902
Moscow Society of Naturalists, 1882
Moscow State Academy of Applied Biotechnology, 1950
Moscow State Academy of Fine Chemical Technology 'M. V. Lomonosov', 1939
Moscow State Academy of Food Industry, 1950
Moscow State Academy of Instrumentation and Informatics, 1950
Moscow State Academy of Light Industry, 1949
Moscow State Academy of Veterinary Medicine and Biotechnology 'K. I. Skryabin', 1948
Moscow State Academy of Water Transport, 1951
Moscow State Agro-Engineering University, V. P. Goryachkin, 1915
Moscow State Art Institute 'V. I. Surikov', 1953
Moscow State Automobile and Road Technical University, 1939
Moscow State Conservatoire 'P. I. Tchaikovsky', 1952
Moscow State Food Institute, 1952
Moscow State Forestry University, 1940
Moscow State Geological Prospecting Academy, 1950
Moscow State Industrial University, 1940
Moscow State Institute of Culture, 1953
Moscow State Institute of Electronics and Mathematics (Technical University), 1940
Moscow State Institute of International Relations, 1952
Moscow State Institute of Radio Engineering, Electronics and Automation (Technical University), 1940
Moscow State Linguistic University, 1936
Moscow State Mining University, 1940
Moscow State Regional University, Moscow, 1924
Moscow State Technical University 'mami', 1940
Moscow State Technical University 'N. E. Bauman', 1940
Moscow State Technical University of Civil Aviation, 1940
Moscow State Technological University, Stankin, 1940
Moscow State Textile University, 1940
Moscow State University 'M. V. Lomonosov', 1924
Moscow State University Museum of Zoology, 1910
Moscow State University of Civil Engineering, 1940
Moscow State University of Engineering Ecology, 1940
Moscow State University of Environmental Engineering, 1941
Moscow State University of Geodesy and Cartography, 1941

Moscow State University of Land Management, 1915
Moscow State University of Medicine and Dentistry named after A. I. Evdokimov, 1934
Moscow State University of Railway Engineering, 1941
Moscow Technical University of Communication and Informatics, 1941
Moscow Technological Institute, 1952
Moscow University of Consumer Cooperatives, 1924
Moshe Shilo Centre for Marine Biogeochemistry, Jerusalem, 1171
Moshi University College of Cooperative and Business Studies, Moshi, 2186
Moshood Abiola Polytechnic, Abeokuta, 1645
Moss Landing Marine Laboratories, 2471
Mossakowski Medical Research Centre of the Polish Academy of Sciences, 1764
Mostar Public Library, 299
Mosul Museum, 1151
Mote Marine Laboratory, 2471
Mother and Child Care Institute, Khabarovsk, 1890
Mother and Child Research Institute, Warsaw, 1764
Mother Teresa Women's University, 1075
Motilal Nehru Institute of Research & Business Administration (MONIRBA), 1041
Motilal Nehru National Institute of Technology, 1103
Moto Moto Museum, Mbala, 3075
Motor Transport Institute, Warsaw, 1769
Motors Institute, Naples, 1195
Moudjahid Museum, 103
Moulton College, 2412
Mount Allison University, 407
Mount Allison University Libraries and Archives, Sackville, 393
Mount Aloysius College, Cresson, 2909
Mount Carmel College of Nursing, Columbus, 2883
Mount Graham International Observatory, 2560
Mount Graham International Observatory (MGIO), Safford, 2473
Mount Holyoke College, 2735
Mount Ida College, 2735
Mount John University Observatory, 1606
Mount Kenya University, Thika, 1379
Mount Makulu Agricultural Research Station, 3075
Mount Marty College, 2932
Mount Mary College, 3001
Mount Mercy University, 2682
Mount Olive College, 2861
Mount Saint Mary College, 2839
Mount St Mary's College, Los Angeles, 2575
Mount St Mary's University, Emmitsburg, 2706
Mount Saint Vincent University, 407
Mount Vernon Nazarene University, 2883
Mountain Home Public Library, 2485
Mountain Museum Flensburg, 876
Mountain Regional Library System, 2484
Mountain Taiga Station, Gornotaezhnoe, 1893
Mountains of the Moon University, 2245
Mountview Academy of Theatre Arts, 2414
Mozart Residence, 196
Mozarteum, Salzburg, 196
Mozarteum University Salzburg, 205
Mozarts Wohnhaus, 196
Mozgássérültek Pető András Nevelőképző és Nevelőintézete, 1003
Mpisi Cattle Breeding Experimental Station, 2105
Mrauk U Archaeological Museum, 1546
MRC Anatomical Neuropharmacology Unit, Oxford, 2304

MRC Asthma UK Centre in Allergic Mechanisms of Asthma, 2304
MRC Biomedical Nuclear Magnetic Resonance Centre, London, 2305
MRC Biostatistics Unit, Cambridge, 2305
MRC Cancer Unit, 838
MRC Centre for Behavioural and Clinical Neuroscience Institute (BCNI), 2305
MRC Centre for Developmental and Biomedical Genetics, 2305
MRC Centre for Developmental Neurobiology, 2305
MRC Centre for Drug Safety Science, 2305
MRC Centre for Genomics and Global Health, 2305
MRC Centre for Neuromuscular Diseases, 2305
MRC Centre for Neuropsychiatric Genetics and Genomics, 2305
MRC Centre for Outbreak Analysis and Modelling, 2305
MRC Centre for Regenerative Medicine, 2305
MRC Centre for Reproductive Health, Edinburgh, 2305
MRC Centre for Transplantation, 2305
MRC Centre for Virus Research, Glasgow, 2305
MRC Clinical Sciences Centre, London, 2305
MRC Clinical Trials Units, London, 2305
MRC Cognition and Brain Sciences Unit, Cambridge, 2305
MRC Epidemiology Unit, 2305
MRC Functional Genomics Unit, 2305
MRC Human Genetics Unit, Edinburgh, 2305
MRC Human Immunology Unit, Oxford, 2305
MRC Human Nutrition Research, Cambridge, 2305
MRC Institute of Hearing Research, Nottingham, 2305
MRC Integrative Epidemiology Unit, 2305
MRC International Nutrition Group, 2305
MRC Laboratories, the Gambia, 2305
MRC Laboratory for Molecular Cell Biology, London, 2305
MRC Laboratory of Molecular Biology (LMB), 2305
MRC Lifecourse Epidemiology Unit, Southampton, 2305
MRC Metabolic Diseases Unit, 2305
MRC Mitochondrial Biology Unit, Cambridge, 2305
MRC Molecular Haematology Unit, Oxford, 2305
MRC National Institute for Medical Research, London, 2306
MRC Prion Unit, London, 2305
MRC Protein Phosphorylation and Ubiquitylation Unit, Dundee, 2305
MRC Social and Public Health Sciences Unit, Glasgow, 2305
MRC Social, Genetic and Developmental Psychiatry Centre, London, 2306
MRC Technology, London, 2306
MRC Toxicology Unit, Leicester, 2306
MRC Unit for Lifelong Health and Ageing, 2306
MRC/Cancer Research UK/BHF Clinical Trial Service Unit & Epidemiological Studies Unit (CTSU), 2305
MRC/UCL Centre for Medical Molecular Virology, 2306
MRC/University of Birmingham Centre for Immune Regulation, 2306
MRC/University of Edinburgh Centre for Inflammation Research, 2306
MRC/University of Sussex Centre in Genome Damage and Stability, 2306
MRC/UVRI Uganda Research Unit on AIDS, 2306
MRI Global, Kansas City, 2470
MS ActionAid Denmark, 673

M/S Museet for Søfart, 680
Msunduzi Municipal Library Services, 2031
Mt Myohyang-San Museum, 1385
Mt Sterling—Montgomery County Library, 2488
Mtskheta Institute of Archaeology, 838
MTT Agrifood Research Finland, 746
MTT Agrifood Research Finland Library, 748
MTT (Maa ja elintarviketalouden tutkimuskeskus) kirjasto, 748
MU Libraries University of Missouri, 2494
Muğla Üniversitesi, 2231
Muhammadiyah University of Malang, 1129
MUHBA Park Güell, 2065
MUHBA Plaça del Rei, 2065
MUHBA Santa Caterina, 2065
Muhlenberg College, 2910
Muiderslot, 1582
Mukhanyo Theological College, 2047
Multidimensional Tourism Institute, Rovaniemi, 746
Multidisciplinary School of Dramatic Arts 'Margarita Xirgú', 3028
Multimedia University, 1474
Multiple Sclerosis International Federation, 79
Multnomah County Library, 2502
Multnomah University, 2894
Mulvane Art Museum, 2523
Mumbai Marathi Granth Sangrahalaya, 1043
Muminov, I., Institute of Philosophy and Law, 3031
Munch Museum, Oslo, 1652
München Bavarian Natural History Collections, 879
Münchner Entomologische Gesellschaft eV, 850
Münchner Stadtbibliothek, 869
Mundo Maya University, 1518
Munich Entomological Society, 850
Munich School of Philosophy, 959
Municipal and County Library, Bergen, 1651
Municipal and Provincial Archives of Vienna, 195
Municipal Archive in the Raschi House, 872
Municipal Archives, Leipzig, 868
Municipal Archives of Lisbon, 1822
Municipal Archives of Rotterdam, 1579
Municipal Art Gallery of Fine Arts, Bruges, 269
Municipal Cultural Museum, Escaldes-Engordany, 112
Municipal Economy and Services Society, Moscow, 1880
Municipal Folk Art Museum, 645
Municipal Gallery and Art Collection Dresden, 875
Municipal Historical Archives, Porto, 1822
Municipal Institute of Botany, Botanical Garden Carlos Thays, 121
Municipal Library, Constantine, 102
Municipal Library Adelpho Poli Monjardim, 314
Municipal Library and Archives of Trier, 871
Municipal Library and Historical Archive of Lima, 1718
Municipal Library 'Dr Francisco Albero Schinca', 3026
Municipal Library, Esch-sur-Alzette, 1457
Municipal Library, Florida, 3026
Municipal Library, Funchal, 1821
Municipal Library, Guimarães, 1822
Municipal Library, Isfahan, 1134
Municipal Library 'Joaquín de Salterain', 3026
Municipal Library, La Paz, 291
Municipal Library, Limassol, 645
Municipal Library, Luanda, 113
Municipal Library, Maastricht, 1578
Municipal Library of Akureyri, 1030
Municipal Library of Bratislava, 2006
Municipal Library of Prague, 657
Municipal Library of Santarém, 1822

Municipal Library of Santo Domingo, 695
Municipal Library, Porto, 1822
Municipal Library, Quito, 702
Municipal Library, Vila Nova de Gaia, 1823
Municipal Museum and Historical Archive, 3027
Municipal Museum Coruche, 1823
Municipal Museum, Göttingen, 877
Municipal Museum 'Hipólito Cabaço', 1823
Municipal Museum, Kőszeg, 1010
Municipal Museum of Art and History 'Alberto Mena Caamano', 702
Municipal Museum of Guayaquil, 702
Municipal Museum of Subotica, 1974
Municipal Museum 'Santos Rocha', 1824
Municipal Museums of Deventer, 1581
Municipal Piloto Public Library, 1716
Municipal Public Library, Manizales, 594
Municipal Public Library of Arequipa, 1716
Municipal Reference Center, 2485
Munkácsy Mihály Múzeum, 1007
Munroe-Meyer Institute, 2469
Münzkabinett der Staatlichen Museen zu Berlin, Stiftung Preussischer Kulturbesitz, Berlin, 873
Münzkabinett, Dresden, 875
Münzkabinett, Gotha, 877
Münzsammlung, Mainz, 879
Murdoch University, 175
Murdoch University International Study Center, 2274
Mureş County Library, 1847
Mureş County Museum, 1851
Muriel and Philip Berman Medical Library, Hebrew University of Jerusalem, 1173
Murmansk Marine Biological Institute, 1894
Murmansk State Technical University, 1941
Muroran Institute of Technology, 1289
Murray Edwards College, Cambridge, 2358
Murray State University, 2690
Musa Heritage Gallery (Mus'Art), 384
Musashino Academia Musicae, 1356
Muscarelle Museum of Art, 2545
Muscat College, 1671
Musculoskeletal Therapy Foundation Training, Amersfoort, 1594
Musea Brugge, 269
Musée & Jardins van Buuren, 270
Musée Antoine Wiertz, 270
Musée Archéologique d'El Jem, 2207
Musée Archéologique de Makthar, 2207
Musée Archéologique de Namur, 271
Musée Archéologique de Sfax, 2207
Musée Archéologique de Sousse (Kasbah), 2208
Musée Archéologique, Larache, 1540
Musée Archéologique, Nîmes, 784
Musée Archéologique, Rabat, 1540
Musée Archéologique, Strasbourg, 787
Musée Archéologique, Tétouan, 1540
Musée Archéologique Théo Desplans, 787
Musée Ariana, 2148
Musée Arsenal, 787
Musée Astronomique de l'Observatoire de Paris, 785
Musée Atger, Montpellier, 784
Musée Automobile de la Sarthe, 783
Musée Basque et de l'histoire Bayonne, 782
Musée Batha, 1540
Musée Bernadotte, 786
Musée Calvet, Avignon, 782
Musée Cantini, 783
Musée Cantonal des Beaux-Arts, Lausanne, 2148
Musée Carnavalet—Histoire de Paris, Paris, 785
Musée Cernuschi, Paris, 785
Musée Cognacq-Jay, Paris, 785
Musée Constantin Meunier, 270
Musée Curtius, 271
Musée d'Ansembourg, Liège, 271
Musée d'Anthropologie Préhistorique de Monaco, 1528

Musée d'Aquitaine, 782
Musée d'Archéologie et de Folklore, Verviers, 271
Musée d'Archéologie Méditerranéenne, Marseilles, 783
Musée d'Archéologie, Nice, 784
Musée d'Archéologie, Tournai, 271
Musée d'Armes du Borj-Nord, Fès, 1540
Musée d'Armes et d'Histoire Militaire, Tournai, 271
Musée d'Armes, Liège, 271
Musée d'Art Africain, Dakar, 1969
Musée d'Art Ancien, Brussels, 270
Musée d'art Contemporain de Montréal, 397
Musée d'Art et d'Histoire, Fribourg, 2148
Musée d'art et d'histoire, Geneva, 2148
Musée d'Art et d'Histoire, Neuchâtel, 2149
Musée d'art et d'Histoire, Nice, 784
Musée d'art et d'histoire, St-Denis, 787
Musée d'Art et d'Industrie, St-Etienne, 787
Musée d'Art Islamique du Ribat, 2207
Musée d'Art Moderne, Brussels, 270
Musée d'Art Moderne de la Ville de Paris, 785
Musée d'Art Moderne de Saint-Etienne Métropole, St-Etienne, 787
Musée d'Art Moderne et Contemporain, Geneva, 2148
Musée d'Art Moderne et d'Art Contemporain de la Ville de Liège, 271
Musée d'Art Moderne et d'Art Contemporain, Nice, 784
Musée d'Art Religieux et d'Art Mosan, Liège, 271
Musée d'Ennery, Paris, 785
Musée d'ethnographie de Genève, 2148
Musée d'Ethnographie, Neuchâtel, 2149
Musée d'Extrême-Orient, Brussels, 270
Musée d'Histoire Contemporaine, Paris, 785
Musée d'Histoire des Sciences, Geneva, 2148
Musée d'Histoire et des Arts Décoratifs, Tournai, 271
Musée d'Histoire Naturelle, Nîmes, 784
Musée d'Orsay, 785
Musée Dar El Jamaï, 1540
Musée Dar Si Saïd, 1540
Musée d'Art Contemporain, 1540
Musée de Bretagne, 786
Musée de Cluny, 786
Musée de Folklore, Tournai, 271
Musée de Grenoble, 783
Musée de Groesbeeck-de Croix, 271
Musée de la Céramique, Rouen, 786
Musée de la Ferronnerie, Rouen, 786
Musée de la Kasbah, Tangier, 1540
Musée de la Marine et de l'Economie de Marseille, 784
Musée de la Marine, Paris, 785
Musée de la Mer, Gorée, 1969
Musée de la Mine, St-Etienne, 787
Musée de la Mode et du Textile, Paris, 785
Musée de la Monnaie, Paris, 785
Musée de la Photographie, Charleroi, 270
Musée de la Poste, Paris, 785
Musée de la Publicité, Paris, 785
Musée de la Reine Bérengère, le Mans, 783
Musée de la Révolution Française, Vizille, 788
Musée de la Société Archéologique de Touraine, 787
Musée de la Vie Wallonne, 271
Musée de la Ville de Nouméa, 830
Musée de l'Air et de l'Espace, le Bourget, 785
Musée de l'Amérique Française, 397
Musée de l'Armée, Paris, 785
Musée de l'Histoire de France, Paris, 785
Musée de l'Histoire Maritime, 830
Musée de l'Homme, Paris, 785
Musée de l'Hôtel de Ville, Amboise, 782
Musée de l'Hôtel Dubocage de Bléville, 783

National Institute of Advanced Industrial Science and Technology, Tokyo, 1252

National Institute of Advanced Studies, Quito, 709

National Institute of Agricultural Botany, Cambridge, 2299

National Institute of Agrobiological Sciences (NIAS), Tsukuba, 1249

National Institute of Allergy and Infectious Diseases, Bethesda, 2469

National Institute of Animal Health, Ibaraki, 1249

National Institute of Animal Husbandry, Hanoi, 3062

National Institute of Anthropology and History, México, 1497

National Institute of Anthropology and Latin American Thought, 122

National Institute of Applied Optics, Florence, 1195

National Institute of Archaeology and History of Art, Rome, 1190

National Institute of Archaeology with Museum Bulgarian Academy of Sciences, Sofia, 363

National Institute of Archaeology with Museum, Sofia, 358

National Institute of Art, 135

National Institute of Arthritis and Musculoskeletal and Skin Diseases, Bethesda, 2469

National Institute of Astrophysics, Optics and Electronics, Tonantzintla, 1496

National Institute of Aviation Technology, Moscow, 1902

National Institute of Biological Resources IP, 1818

National Institute of Business, Phnom Penh, 378

National Institute of Cartography and Remote Detection, 101

National Institute of Chemical Physics and Biophysics, Tallinn, 730

National Institute of Crop Science, Ibaraki, 1249

National Institute of Dental and Craniofacial Research, Bethesda, 2469

National Institute of Deserts, Flora and Fauna, Ashgabat, 2239

National Institute of Design, Ahmedabad, 1043

National Institute of Development Administration, Bangkok, 2194

National Institute of Diabetes and Digestive and Kidney Diseases, Bethesda, 2469

National Institute of Dramatic Art, Sydney, 178

National Institute of Drug Quality Control, Hanoi, 3063

National Institute of Economic and Social Research, London, 2301

National Institute of Economic Research 'Costin C. Kiritescu', 1840

National Institute of Education, Maharagama, 2093

National Institute of Education, Minsk, 249

National Institute of Education, Phnom Penh, 378

National Institute of Educational Planning and Administration, New Delhi, 1103

National Institute of Environmental Health Sciences, Bethesda, 2469

National Institute of Fashion Technology, New Delhi, 1108

National Institute of Fine Arts and Literature, México, 1493

National Institute of Folk and Traditional Heritage, 1673

National Institute of Forestry, Agriculture and Livestock Research, México, 1495

National Institute of Forestry Research, Algiers, 101

National Institute of General Medical Sciences, Bethesda, 2469

National Institute of Genetics, Mishima City, 1250

National Institute of Geophysics and Volcanology, 1200

National Institute of Geophysics, Geodesy and Geography, Sofia, 358

National Institute of Haematology and Immunology, Budapest, 1003

National Institute of Health and Family Welfare (NIHFW), New Delhi, 1108

National Institute of Health and Nutrition, Tokyo, 1250

National Institute of Health, Asunción, 1713

National Institute of Health, Bogotá, 593

National Institute of Health Dr Ricardo Jorge, 1819

National Institute of Health, Lima, 1716

National Institute of Health Sciences, Tokyo, 1250

National Institute of Historical and Cultural Research, Islamabad, 1676

National Institute of Hydrology, Roorkee, 1048

National Institute of Hygiene and Epidemiology, Hanoi, 3063

National Institute of Hygiene and Safety, 101

National Institute of Hygiene and Topical Medicine, Guayaquil, 701

National Institute of Hygiene, Epidemiology and Microbiology, 635

National Institute of Industrial Technology, Buenos Aires, 122

National Institute of Infectious Diseases, Tokyo, 1250

National Institute of Japanese Literature, 1250

National Institute of Japanese Literature Library, Tokyo, 1253

National Institute of Legal Medicine and Forensic Sciences, Bogotá, 592

National Institute of Legal Medicine, Coimbra, 1819

National Institute of Library and Information Science, Colombo, 2098

National Institute of Limnology, 121

National Institute of Linguistic Studies (INEL), La Paz, 291

National Institute of Livestock and Grassland Science, Tsukuba, 1249

National Institute of Medical Herbalists, Exeter, 2413

National Institute of Medicinal Materials, Hanoi, 3063

National Institute of Medicine, Ulan Bator, 1530

National Institute of Mental Health and Neurosciences, Bengaluru, 1103

National Institute of Mental Health, National Center of Neurology and Psychiatry, Ichikawa, 1250

National Institute of Mental Health (NIMH), 2470

National Institute of Meteorology and Hydrology, Bucharest, 1843

National Institute of Meteorology and Hydrology, Quito, 701

National Institute of Meteorology and Hydrology, Sofia, 360

National Institute of Meteorology, Brasilia, 311

National Institute of Metrology, Bucharest, 1843

National Institute of Music, Panama, 1705

National Institute of Naval Architecture Studies and Experiments, Rome, 1200

National Institute of Neurological Disorders and Stroke, Bethesda, 2470

National Institute of Neurology and Neurosurgery, México, 1496

National Institute of Nuclear Medicine, La Paz, 291

National Institute of Nuclear Research, Ocoyoacac, 1496

National Institute of Nuclear Science and Technology, 777

National Institute of Nursing Research, Bethesda, 2470

National Institute of Nutrition, Caracas, 3048

National Institute of Nutrition, Hanoi, 3063

National Institute of Nutrition, Hyderabad, 1044

National Institute of Occupational and Environmental Health Research, Hanoi, 3063

National Institute of Occupational Safety and Health, Kawasaki City, 1250

National Institute of Oceanography, Panaji, 1041

National Institute of Oncology and Radiobiology in Havana, 635

National Institute of Oncology, Budapest, 1004

National Institute of Otolaryngology, Hanoi, 3063

National Institute of Paediatrics, Hanoi, 3063

National Institute of Parasitology, Asunción, 1710

National Institute of Pharmaceutical Education and Research, Mohali, 1099

National Institute of Pharmaceutical Research and Development (NIPRD), Idu, 1626

National Institute of Polar Research, 1250

National Institute of Population and Social Security Research, Tokyo, 1249

National Institute of Public Administration, Jakarta, 1112

National Institute of Public Administration, Lahore, 1675

National Institute of Public Administration, Lusaka, 3076

National Institute of Public Administration, Madrid, 2052

National Institute of Public Health, Bucharest, 1841

National Institute of Public Health, Cuernavaca, 1496

National Institute of Public Health of Kosovo, 1411

National Institute of Public Health, Phnom-Penh, 378

National Institute of Public Health, Tokyo, 1250

National Institute of Public Health— National Institute of Hygiene, Warsaw, 1764

National Institute of Renaissance Studies, Florence, 1198

National Institute of Research and Development for Biological Sciences, Bucharest, 1842

National Institute of Research and Development for Chemistry and Petrochemistry, Bucharest, 1843

National Institute of Research and Development for Non-Ferrous and Rare Metals, Pantaleon, 1844

National Institute of Research and Development for Potato and Sugar Beet Brasov, 1839

National Institute of Research and Development for Technical Physics, Iaşi, 1843

National Institute of Rock Mechanics, Kolar Gold Fields, 1046

National Institute of Roman Studies, 1198

National Institute of Rural Development, Rajendranagar, 1047

National Institute of Science Communication and Information Resources, 1048

National Institute of Science, Technology and Development Studies, New Delhi, 1041

National Institute of Scientific and Technical Research, Hammam-Lif, 2207

National Institute of Seismology, Vulcanology, Meteorology and Hydrology, Guatemala City, 985

National Institute of Social Sciences, New York, 2463

National Institute of Standardization, Santiago, 468

National Institute of Standards and Technology, Gaithersburg, 2476

National Institute of Standards and Technology Research Library, Gaithersburg, 2491

National Institute of Statistics and Censuses, Buenos Aires, 120

National Institute of Statistics and Censuses, San José, 613

National Institute of Statistics and Economic Studies–Regional Directorate of Réunion, 831

National Institute of Statistics and Geography, Aguascalientes, 1493

National Institute of Statistics, La Paz, 291

National Institute of Statistics, Lima, 1715

National Institute of Statistics, Montevideo, 3025

National Institute of Statistics, Rome', 1197

National Institute of Studies and Research, Bissau, 990

National Institute of Technology, Agartala, 1103

National Institute of Technology, Bandung, 1132

National Institute of Technology, Calicut, 1103

National Institute of Technology, Durgapur, 1103

National Institute of Technology, Hamirpur, 1103

National Institute of Technology, Jamshedpur, 1103

National Institute of Technology, Karnataka, 1104

National Institute of Technology, Kurukshetra, 1104

National Institute of Technology, Patna, 1104

National Institute of Technology, Raipur, 1104

National Institute of Technology, Rourkela, 1104

National Institute of Technology, Silchar, 1104

National Institute of Technology, Srinagar, 1104

National Institute of Technology, Standardization and Metrology, 1710

National Institute of Technology, Tiruchirapalli, 1104

National Institute of Technology, Warangal, 1104

National Institute of Telecommunications, Warsaw, 1768

National Institute of Town Planning, 1189

National Institute of Traditional Medicine, 288

National Institute of Traditional Medicine, Hanoi, 3063

National Institute of Training, Amman, 1361

National Institute of Tuberculosis and Respiratory Diseases, Hanoi, 3063

National Institute of Vegetable and Tea Science, Shizuoka, 1249

National Institute of Verdi Studies, 1190

National Institute of Veterinary Research, Hanoi, 3062

National Institute of Water and Atmospheric Research Ltd (NIWA), Auckland, 1606

National Institute on Aging, Bethesda, 2470

National Institute on Alcohol Abuse and Alcoholism (NIAAA), 2470

National Institute on Deafness and Other Communication Disorders, Bethesda, 2470

National Institute on Drug Abuse (NIDA), 2470

National Institute on Minority Health and Health Disparities, Bethasda, 2470

National Institutes of Health, Bethesda, 2469

National Institutes of Health Library, Bethesda, 2491

O

P

P. G. Demidov Yaroslavl State University Library, 1908

P. J. Vejvanovského Conservatory, Kromeriz, 669

P. O. Sukhoi State Technical University of Gomel, 254

P. P. Lukianenko Krasnodar Research and Development Institute of Agriculture, 1884

P. P. Shirshov Institute of Oceanology of the Russian Academy of Sciences, Moscow, 1898

PA College, Larnaca, 650

Paccioli University of Córdoba, 1520

Pace University, 2847

Pacific Adventist University, Boroko, 1707

Pacific Fisheries Research Centre (TINRO), Vladivostok, 1885

Pacific Forestry Centre, Victoria, 391

Pacific Institute of Bio-Organic Chemistry, Vladivostok, 1894

Pacific Institute of Geography, Vladivostok, 1888

Pacific Islands Museums Association (PIMA), Port Vila, 3036

Pacific Islands University, 3013

Pacific Lutheran Theological Seminary, Berkeley, 2576

Pacific Lutheran University, 2988

Pacific National University, Khabarovsk, 1926

Pacific Northwest College of Art, 2894

Pacific Oaks College, 2576

Pacific Regional Centre, 616

Pacific School of Religion, Berkeley, 2576

Pacific Science Association, 87

Pacific Sociological Association, San Diego, 2463

Pacific State University of Economics, Vladivostok, 1926

Pacific Union College, Angwin, 2576

Pacific University - School of Business, 705

Pacific University, Portland, 2894

Pacific War Museum, 3013

Pacifica Graduate Institute, Carpinteria, 2576

Paço dos Duques de Bragança, 1824

Pädagogische Hochschule, 2166

Pädagogische Hochschule Bern, 2166

Pädagogische Hochschule des Cantons St Gallen, 2167

Pädagogische Hochschule Freiburg, 910

Pädagogische Hochschule Heidelberg, 910

Pädagogische Hochschule Karlsruhe, 910

Pädagogische Hochschule Ludwigsburg, 910

Pädagogische Hochschule Schwäbisch Gmünd, 910

Pädagogische Hochschule Weingarten, 911

Padiglione delle Carrozze, Vatican City, 3038

Padmashree Dr D. Y. Patil University, 1105

Padmashree Dr D. Y. Patil Vidyapeeth, 1105

Paediatric Society in Bosnia and Herzegovina, 297

Paediatrics Society, Conchabamba, 290

Paediatrics Society of Ecuador, 701

Paediatrics Society of Madrid and Castilla la Mancha, 2054

Paediatrics Society of Uruguay, 3025

Pahrump Community Library, 2495

Paichai University, 1403

Paier College of Art, Inc., 2602

Paine College, 2644

Paisii Hilendarski University of Plovdiv, 367

Paisley Campus Library, University of West of Scotland, 2326

Paisley Enterprise Research Centre, 2298

Pakistan Academy of Letters, 1674

Pakistan Academy of Medical Sciences, 1674

Pakistan Academy of Sciences, 1674

Pakistan Agricultural Research Council, 1675

Pakistan American Cultural Centre, 1674

Pakistan Association for the Advancement of Science, 1674

Pakistan Atomic Energy Commission (PAEC), Islamabad, 1677

Pakistan Council for Science and Technology, 1676

Pakistan Council of Architects and Town Planners, 1673

Pakistan Council of Research in Water Resources, 1677

Pakistan Council of Scientific and Industrial Research (PCSIR), 1676

Pakistan Engineering Council, 1672

Pakistan Forest Institute, 1675

Pakistan Historical Society, 1673

Pakistan Institute of Cotton Research and Technology, 1677

Pakistan Institute of Development Economics, 1688

Pakistan Institute of Human Rights, 1675

Pakistan Institute of International Affairs, 1673

Pakistan Institute of International Affairs Library, 1679

Pakistan Institute of Management, 1677

Pakistan Library Association, 1673

Pakistan Medical Association, 1674

Pakistan Medical Research Council, 1676

Pakistan Meteorological Department, 1677

Pakistan National Central Library and Culture Centre, 1678

Pakistan National Council of the Arts, 1673

Pakistan Philosophical Congress, 1674

Pakistan Scientific and Technological Information Centre (PASTIC), 1678

Pakistan Standards and Quality Control Authority, 1677

Pakistan Study Centre, Karachi, 1675

Pakistan Writers Guild, 1674

Pakistani Swedish Institute of Technology, 1696

Paktia University, 94

Palace Het Loo, 1580

Palace Museum, Beijing, 489

Palace Museum Darmstadt, 875

Palace Museum of the Government, 1498

Palace of Peralada Library, 2064

Palace of the Dukes of Braganza, 1824

Palace of the Governors, 2533

Palacio del Mar—Aquarium, San Sebastián, 2068

Palacio Real de Aranjuez, 2067

Palacio Real de la Almudaina, 2067

Palacio Real de la Granja de San Ildefonso, 2067

Palacio Real de Madrid, 2068

Palacio Real de Riofrío, 2068

Palacio Sitio de El Pardo, 2068

Palacký University, 665

Palaentological Society, 851

Palaeontographical Society, London, 2293

Palaeontological Society, Boulder, 2462

Palaeontological Society of China, 482

Palaeontological Society of Japan, 1247

Palaeontological Society, St Petersburg, 1882

Palaeontology Centre, Ulan Bator, 1531

Palais de la Découverte, Paris, 786

Palais des Beaux-Arts de Lille, 783

Palais du Cinéma, Paris, 786

Palais Galliera Musée de la Mode de la Ville de Paris, 786

Palais Lascaris, 784

Palais Rohan, 787

Paläontologische Gesellschaft, Munich, 851

Paläontologisches Institut und Museum der Universität, Zürich, 2150

Palau Association of Libraries (PAL), 1697

Palau Community College, 1697

Palau Congress Library, 1697

Palau Conservation Society, 1697

Palau International Coral Reef Center, 1697

Palau National Archives, 1697

Palau National Scholarship Board, 1697

Palau Public Library, 1697

Palawan State University, Puerto Princesa City, 1742

Palazzo Altemps, 1212

Palazzo dei Diamanti, Ferrara, 1207

Palazzo della Ragione 'Il Salone', Padua, 1210

Palazzo Ducale e Castello di San Giorgio, Mantua, 1209

Palazzo Ducale, Venice, 1214

Palazzo Madama—Museo Civico d'Arte Antica, Turin, 1213

Palazzo Massari, Ferrara, 1207

Palazzo Massimo, 1212

Palazzo Mocenigo, Venice, 1214

Paleis Het Loo Nationaal Museum, 1580

Paleontological Research Institution, Ithaca, 2467

Paleontološki inštitut Ivana Rakovca ZRC SAZU, 2019

Palestine Exploration Fund, London, 2285

Palestine Polytechnic University, Hebron, 1701

Palestine Technical College, Deir al-Balah, 1701

Palestinian Academic Society for the Study of International Affairs, 1699

Palestinian PEN Centre, 1167

Paley Center for Media, New York, 2535

Palladin Institute of Biochemistry, Kyiv, 2251

Palm Beach Atlantic University, 2632

Palm Beach County Library System, 2484

Palm Beach State College, 2632

Palm Harbor Library, 2484

Palmer College of Chiropractic, 2682

Palmer Museum of History & Art, 2510

Palmerston North City Library and Community Services, 1607

Palmerston North Medical Research Foundation, 1606

Palmyra National Museum, 2169

Palo Alto University, 2576

Palóc Múzeum, 1007

Palompon Institute of Technology, 1750

Pamantasan Ng Lungsod Ng Maynila, 1742

Památník Leoše Janáčka, Brno, 658

Památník Lidice, 658

Památník národního písemnictví, Prague, 659

Památník Terezín, 660

Pamir Biological Institute, Khorog, 2179

Pamukkale Üniversitesi, 2235

Pan African Institute for Development, 59

Pan American Health Organization/ World Health Organization, Guyana, 991

Pan American University, Aguascalientes, 1500

Pan American University, Guatemala City, 987

Pan American University, Jalisco, 1512

Pan American University, Mexico City, 1507

Pan American University of El Salvador, 723

Pan American University, Panamá, 1705

Pan-African Institute for Development, East and Southern Africa, 3075

Pan-African Union of Science and Technology, 610

Pan-African University, Lagos, 1644

Panama Rectors' Council, 1702

Panama University, 1704

Panamanian Academy of Language, 1702

Pan-American Institute of Geography and History, 87

Pan-American Library, Cuenca, 701

Panamerican University of Puerto, 3056

Pandit Ravishankar Shukla University, Raipur, 1077

Panepistimio Kritis, 979

Panepistimio Peloponnesou, 980

Panepistimio Thesalias, 981

Panepistimion Aegaeou, 978

Panepistimion Ioanninon, 978

Panepistimion Makedonias, 979

Panepistimion Patron, 979

Panepistimion Pireos, 980

Pan-European University, 2007

Paneurópska Vysoká Škola, 2007

Panevėžio Kolegija, 1455

Panevėžys College, 1455

Panfilov, K. D., Academy of Municipal Economics, Moscow, 1885

Pangasinan State University, 1742

Panhellenic Association of Life Sciences, 969

Panjab University, 1077

Panjab University Extension Library, 1049

Pañññāsāstra University of Cambodia, 381

Pannon Egyetem, 1019

Pannon Egyetem, Egyetemi Könyvtár és Levéltár, 1007

Pannon Egyetem, Georgikon Kar, Kari Könyvtár és Levéltár, 1007

Pannon Egyetem Műszaki Kémiai Kutatóintézet, 1005

Pannonhalmi Főapátság Gyűjteménye, 1010

Pansasarimuseo, 750

Państwowa Wyższa Szkoła Filmowa Telewizyjna i Teatralna im. Leona Schillera w Łodzi, 1813

Państwowa Wyższa Szkoła Informatyki i Przedsiębiorczości w Łomży, 1811

Państwowa Wyższa Szkoła Teatralna im. Ludwika Solskiego w Krakowie, 1813

Państwowa Wyższa Szkoła Techniczno-Ekonomiczna im. ks. Bronisława Markiewicza w Jarosławiu, 1811

Państwowa Wyższa Szkoła Zawodowa im. Jana Grodka w Sanoku, 1811

Państwowa Wyższa Szkoła Zawodowa im. Papieża Jana Pawła II w Białej Podlaskiej, 1811

Państwowa Wyższa Szkoła Zawodowa im. Prezydenta Stanisława Wojciechowskiego w Kaliszu, 1811

Państwowa Wyższa Szkoła Zawodowa im. Rotmistrza Wiltoda Pileckiego w Oświęcimiu, 1811

Państwowa Wyższa Szkoła Zawodowa im. Stanisława Pigonia w Krośnie, 1811

Państwowa Wyższa Szkoła Zawodowa im. Stanisława Staszica w Pile, 1811

Państwowa Wyższa Szkoła Zawodowa im. Szymona Szymonowica w Zamościu, 1811

Państwowa Wyższa Szkoła Zawodowa im. Witelona w Legnicy, 1811

Państwowa Wyższa Szkoła Zawodowa w Chełmie, 1811

Państwowa Wyższa Szkoła Zawodowa w Ciechanowie, 1811

Państwowa Wyższa Szkoła Zawodowa w Elblągu, 1811

Państwowa Wyższa Szkoła Zawodowa w Głogowie, 1811

Państwowa Wyższa Szkoła Zawodowa w Gnieźnie, 1812

Państwowa Wyższa Szkoła Zawodowa w Gorzowie Wielkopolskim, 1812

Państwowa Wyższa Szkoła Zawodowa w Koninie, 1812

Państwowa Wyższa Szkoła Zawodowa w Nowym Sączu, 1812

Państwowa Wyższa Szkoła Zawodowa w Nysie, 1812

Państwowa Wyższa Szkoła Zawodowa w Płocku, 1812

Państwowa Wyższa Szkoła Zawodowa w Raciborzu, 1812

Państwowa Wyższa Szkoła Zawodowa w Sulechowie, 1812

Państwowa Wyższa Szkoła Zawodowa w Tarnowie, 1812

Państwowa Wyższa Szkoła Zawodowa w Wałczu, 1812

Państwowa Wyższa Szkoła Zawodowa we Włocławku, 1811

Państwowe Muzeum Archeologiczne w Warszawie, Warsaw, 1774

Perm State Technical University, 1942
Perm State University, 1927
Perm State University Scientific Library, 1907
Permanent Exhibition of Musical Instruments, St Petersburg, 1913
Permanent Exhibition of the Landings, 782
Permanent International Committee of Linguists, 48
Permanent Tchaikovsky Exhibition in the Tchaikovsky Concert Hall, Moscow, 1910
Pernambuco State Public Library, 313
Perpustakaan Dewan Perwakilan Rakyat Republik Indonesia, 1113
Perpustakaan Islam, 1113
Perpustakaan Jajasan Hatta, 1113
Perpustakaan Kuala Lumpur, 1472
Perpustakaan Nasional, 1113
Perpustakaan Negara Malaysia, 1472
Perpustakaan Negeri Sabah, 1472
Perpustakaan Pusat Institut Teknologi Bandung, 1113
Perpustakaan Pusat Penelitian dan Pengembangan Geologi, 1113
Perpustakaan (Pusat) Universitas Indonesia, 1113
Perpustakaan Sejarah Politik dan Sosial, Jakarta, 1113
Perpustakaan Sultan Abdul Samad, 1473
Perpustakaan Sultan Ismail, 1472
Perpustakaan Sultanah Bahiyah, Universiti Utara Malaysia, 1473
Perpustakaan Sultanah Zanariah, 1472
Perpustakaan Umum Makassar, 1113
Perpustakaan Universiti Sains Malaysia, 1473
Persatuan Insinyur Indonesia, 1111
Persmuseum, Amsterdam, 1580
Perth Bible College, 182
Perth Observatory, 149
Peru State College, Nebraska, 2800
Perusahaan Negara Bio-Farma, Bandung, 1112
Peruvian Academy of Language, 1714
Peruvian Academy of Stomatology, 1715
Peruvian Academy of Surgery, 1715
Peruvian Association of Astronomy, 1715
Peruvian Electrotechnical Association, 1715
Peruvian Gastronomy House, 1717
Peruvian Geological Society, 1715
Peruvian Institute of Hispanic Culture, 1715
Peruvian Marine Institute, 1716
Peruvian Medical Association, 1715
Peruvian Medical Federation, 1715
Peruvian Nuclear Energy Institute, 1716
Peruvian Society of Pneumology, 1715
Peruvian Speleological and Karstological Society, 1715
Peruvian Union University, 1728
Peruvian University Cayetano Heredia, 1728
Peruvian University of Applied Sciences, 1728
Peruvian University of Science and Informatics, 1728
Peshawar Museum, 1679
Pest Megyei Múzeumok Igazgatósága Ferenczy Múzeum Szentendre, 1011
Petalouda Art Gallery, 974
Peter Harrison Centre for Disability Sport, 2298
Peter the Great Museum of Anthropology and Ethnography (Kunstkamera), 1913
Peterborough Cathedral Archives & Library, 2326
Peterborough Libraries and Archives, 2326
Peterhof State Museum Reserve, 1911
Peterhouse, Cambridge, 2358
Peterhouse (Perne) Library, 2314
Petersburg Public Library, 2478
Petersburg State Transport University, 1942
Petőfi Birthplace and Memorial Museum, 1010

Petőfi Irodalmi Múzeum, Budapest, 1009
Petőfi Literary Museum, 1009
Petőfi Szülőház és Emlékmúzeum, 1010
Petra Christian University, 1125
Petrarch Academy of Literature, Arts and Science, 1188
Petre Andrei University of Iaşi, 1865
Petre Ionescu-Stoian State Institute for Drug Control and Pharmaceutical Research, 1842
Petrochemical Technology Research Centre, Ulan Bator, 1531
Petrographic Museum, Moscow, 1910
Petroleum Institute, Abu Dhabi, 2274
Petroleum Training Institute, Effurun, 1645
Petroleum University of Technology, Tehran, 1139
Petroleum—Gas University of Ploieşti, 1865
Petrozavodsk State University, 1927
Petru Maior University of Târgu Mureş, 1865
'Petru Poni' Institute of Macromolecular Chemistry of Romanian Academy, 1842
Pettaquamscutt Historical Society Museum, 2540
Pevsner Public Library, Haifa, 1173
Pewaukee Public Library, 2508
Pfeiffer University, 2861
Pha That Luang, Vientiane, 1424
Phansi Museum, 2033
Pharma Denmark, 674
Pharmaceutical College of Federal District and Miranda State, 3046
Pharmaceutical Museum of the Central Drug Research Institute, Moscow, 1910
Pharmaceutical Research Institute, Warsaw, 1763
Pharmaceutical Sciences Library, University of Copenhagen, 678
Pharmaceutical Society of Ghana, 962
Pharmaceutical Society of Ireland (PSI), 1158
Pharmaceutical Society of Japan, 1245
Pharmaceutical Society of Republika Srpske, 297
Pharmaceutical Society of Zimbabwe, 3078
Pharmacological Society of Canada, 389
Pharmacological Society of Macedonia, 1459
Pharmacy Board of Trinidad and Tobago, 2203
Pharmacy Council of India, 1037
Pharmacy Museum, Cluj-Napoca, 1849
Pharmacy Research Institute, Moscow, 1890
Pharmadanmark, 674
Pharmakon, 686
Phelps Ornithological Collection, 3050
Philadelphia Biblical University, 2915
Philadelphia College of Osteopathic Medicine, 2915
Philadelphia History Museum, 2540
Philadelphia Museum of Art, 2540
Philadelphia University, 2915
Philadelphia University, Amman, 1359
Philander Smith College, 2562
Philatelic Collections, Library and Archives Canada, 395
Philatelic Museum of the Bank of the Republic, Medellín, 594
Philbrook Museum of Art, 2538
Philip and Muriel Berman Centre for Biblical Archaeology, 1170
Philippine Accrediting Association of Schools, Colleges and Universities (PAASCU), Quezon City, 1732
Philippine Association of Colleges and Universities, Commission on Accreditation (PACUCOA), Quezon City, 1732
Philippine Association of Colleges and Universities (PACU), 1732
Philippine Association of Private Schools, Colleges and Universities (PAPSCU), Manila, 1732
Philippine Association of State Universities and Colleges, 1733
Philippine Historical Association, 1733

Philippine Institute of Civil Engineers, 1733
Philippine Institute of Mining, Metallurgical and Geological Engineers, 1733
Philippine Institute of Volcanology and Seismology, Quezon City, 1734
Philippine Medical Association, 1733
Philippine Normal University, Manila, 1742
Philippine Nuclear Research Institute, 1734
Philippine Paediatric Society, Inc., 1733
Philippine Pharmacists Association, 1733
Philippine Rice Research Institute, Muñoz, 1734
Philippine Science Centrum, 1736
Philippine Society of Agricultural Engineers, Quezon City, 1733
Philippine Society of Mechanical Engineers, Quezon City, 1733
Philippine Textile Research Institute, 1734
Philippine Veterinary Medical Association, 1733
Philippine Women's University, 1742
Philippine Women's University Library, 1735
Philipps-Universität Marburg, 911
Philips College, Nicosia, 650
Philipsburg Jubilee Library, 1601
Phillips Collection, Washington, 2517
Phillips Theological Seminary, 2890
Philological Society, London, 2287
Philosophical Society of England, 2293
Philosophical Society of Finland, 745
Philosophical Society of Great Britain, Rickmansworth, 2293
Philosophical Society of Turkey, 2211
Philosophical-Theological College—Faculty of Theology SVD St Augustin, 913
Philosophische Gesellschaft Wien, 188
Philosophische-Theologische Hochschule der Salesianer, Benediktbeuern, 3042
Philosophisch-Theologische Hochschule der Salesianer Don Boscos Benediktbeuern, 913
Philosophisch-Theologische Hochschule Sankt Georgen, 959
Philosophisch-Theologische Hochschule Vallendar GmbH, 913
Philosophisch-Theologische Hochschule—Theologische Fakultät SVD St Augustin, 913
Philosophy Institute, Beijing, 487
Philosophy of Education Society, Champaign, 2451
Philosophy of Science Association, Bloomsburg, 2462
Phippen Museum, 2511
Phnom Penh International University, 381
Phoenix Art Museum, 2511
Phoenix Institute of Australia, 181
Phoenix Public Library, 2478
Photogrammetry Centre, Lisbon, 1817
Phthisiology and Pulmonology Research Institute, Kyiv, 2250
Phuket Marine Biological Center, Bangkok, 2188
Phuthadikobo Museum, 304
Physical Research Laboratory, Ahmedabad, 1046
Physical Science Laboratory, Las Cruces, 2473
Physical Society in Bosnia and Herzegovina, 297
Physical Society of Japan, 1247
Physical Society of Moldova, 1524
Physical Society of Republic of China, Taipei, 2172
Physical Technical Institute, Almaty, 1364
Physical Technological Institute, Moscow, 1903
Physical-Technical Institute for Research on Heat and Noise Technology at the Technological Industrial Museum, Vienna, 193
Physical-Technical Institute, Izhevsk, 1903

Physical-Technical Institute, Minsk, 250
Physical–Technical Institute, Tashkent, 3032
Physicians' Society of Bosnia and Herzegovina, 297
Physikalisch-Technische Bundesanstalt, 863
Physikalisch-Technische Versuchsanstalt für Wärme- und Schalltechnik am Technologischen Gewerbemuseum, Vienna, 193
Physiological Society, London, 2291
Physiological Society of Japan, 1245
Physiological Society of New Zealand, 1604
Phytopathological Society of Japan, 1241
PIANC—World Association for Waterborne Transport Infrastructure, 71
Piauí Museum, 316
Picasso Museum, Barcelona, 2066
Pidstryhach Institute of Applied Problems of Mechanics and Mathematics, Lviv, 2253
Piedmont College, 2645
Pierce County Library System, 2507
Pierides Museum, 645
Pierson Library, 2506
Piet Zwart Institute, 1569
Pietro Micca and 1706 Siege of Turin Civic Museum, 1213
Pig Breeding Institute 'O. V. Kvasnitsky', 2249
Pig Research Institute, Havana, 635
Pikes Peak Library District, 2480
Pilgrim Society, Plymouth, 2453
Pilgrimage Museum of Santiago, 2068
Pilot Plant and Process Development Centre, 223
Pima Air & Space Museum, 2511
Pima County Public Library, 2478
PIMSAT University, 1688
Pinacoteca Ambrosiana, Milan, 1210
Pinacoteca Casa Rusca, Locarno, 2149
Pinacoteca Civica 'Melozzo degli Ambrogi', 1208
Pinacoteca dell'Accademia dei Concordi e del Seminario Vescovile, Rovigo, 1212
Pinacoteca dell'Accademia dei Concordi, Rovigo, 1205
Pinacoteca di Brera, Milan, 1210
Pinacoteca do Estado de São Paulo, 316
Pinacoteca e Musei del Comune, Forlì, 1208
Pinacoteca Manfrediniana, Venice, 1214
Pinacoteca Nazionale, Bologna, 1207
Pinacoteca Nazionale, Siena, 1207
Pinacoteca Provinciale, Bari, 1206
Pinacoteca Tosio Martinengo, 1207
Pinacoteca Vaticana, 3038
Pine Manor College, 2737
Pine Mountain Regional Library System, 2485
Pinetown Museum, Durban, 2033
Ping Shan Tang Clan Gallery and Heritage Trail Visitors Centre, 580
Pinngortitaleriffik, 690
Pioneer Dental College, 244
Pioneer Heritage Townsite Center, Frederick, 2538
Pioneer Museum, 2034, 2542
Pioneer Trails Regional Museum, 2536
Pioneer Woman Museum, Ponca City, 2538
Pir Mehr Ali Shah Arid Agriculture Rawalpindi, 1688
Pirbright Institute, Newbury, 2299
Pitt Rivers Museum, 2336
Pittsburg State University, 2686
Pittsburgh Theological Seminary, 2916
Pitzer College, 2577
Pjeter Budi University College, 1413
PK Anokhin Research Institute of Normal Physiology, Moscow, 1890
Placer County Library, 2479
Plague Prevention Research Institute for the Caucasus and Transcaucasia, 1890
Plains Art Museum, 2536
Plainsong and Medieval Music Society, Westhumble, 2283

School of Agriculture of the Tropical Humid Region, 614
School of Applied Construction Engineering and Management, 208
School of Applied Science bfi Vienna, 209
School of Applied Science Carinthia, 209
School of Applied Science Vienna, 209
School of Applied Sciences Burgenland, 208
School of Applied Sciences Kufstein, 209
School of Applied Sciences of Upper Austria, 208
School of Applied Sciences St Pölten, 209
School of Applied Sciences Salzburg, 209
School of Applied Sciences Technikum Joanneum, 209
School of Applied Sciences Vienna Campus, 209
School of Applied Sciences Vorarlberg, 209
School of Applied Sciences Wiener Neustadt, 209
School of Applied Sciences WIFI Styria, 209
School of Arabic Studies, Granada, 2056
School of Architecture and Urban Design, Tilburg, 1596
School of Architecture, Architectural Association, London, 2412
School of Art 'Neptali Rincón', 3060
School of Arts Carlos Baca Flor, 1731
School of Arts, Nuuk, 691
School of Catholic Theology, Tilburg University, 1592
School of Commerce Studies, 108
School of Design and Crafts, Gothenburg, 2134
School of Divinity, Edinburgh, 2425
School of Economics and Management in Public Administration in Bratislava, 2016
School of Education, University of Iceland, 1030
School of Finance and Banking, 1955
School of Fine Arts, Christchurch, 1614
School of Folklore of San Miguelito, 1705
School of Foreign Service in Qatar, 1834
School of French Language and Culture, Geneva, 2161
School of Health and Human Sciences, Colchester, 2306
School of Health 'Dr José Scosería', 3028
School of Health Technology of Coimbra, 1830
School of Health Technology Porto, 1830
School of Higher Vocational Education in Nysa, 1812
School of Hispanic-American Studies, Seville, 2056
School of Hospitality and Tourism, Estoril, 1830
School of Nursing of the Portuguese Red Cross Oliveira de Azemeis, 1830
School of Optometry, 3021
School of Oriental and African Studies Library, London, 2322
School of Oriental and African Studies, London, 2381
School of Philosophy Driyarkara, 1132
School of Physical Education and Sport, Geneva, 2161
School of Planning and Architecture, New Delhi, 1105
School of Professional Psychology at Forest Institute, Springfield, 2794
School of Psychotherapy and Counselling Psychology, London, 2413
School of Real Estate, Lisbon, 1830
School of Social Work, Harare, 3081
School of the Art Institute of Chicago, 2660
School of the Museum of Fine Arts, Boston, 2737
School of Theology and Ministry Studies, Lincoln, 2310
School of Visual Arts, New York, 2850
School of Visual Arts of Puerto Rico, 3021
Schotten Abbey Archives, Vienna, 194
Schreiner University, 2953

Schulamt, Vaduz, 1444
Schwäbisch Gmünd University of Education, 910
Schweizer Heimatschutz, 2137
Schweizerische Akademie der Medizinischen Wissenschaften, 2141
Schweizerische Botanische Gesellschaft, 2141
Schweizerische Entomologische Gesellschaft, Neuchâtel, 2141
Schweizerische Gesellschaft für Afrikastudien, 2142
Schweizerische Gesellschaft für Aussenpolitik, 2138
Schweizerische Gesellschaft für Chirurgie, 2141
Schweizerische Gesellschaft für Geschichte, 2140
Schweizerische Gesellschaft für Mikrotechnik, 2142
Schweizerische Gesellschaft für Orthopädie und Traumatologie, 2141
Schweizerische Gesellschaft für Psychologie, 2142
Schweizerische Musikforschende Gesellschaft, 2139
Schweizerische Philosophische Gesellschaft, 2142
Schweizerische Sprachwissenschaftliche Gesellschaft, 2141
Schweizerische Theologische Gesellschaft, 2142
Schweizerische Vereinigung für Altertumswissenschaft, 2140
Schweizerische Vereinigung für Internationales Recht, 2138
Schweizerischer Apothekerverband, 2141
Schweizerischer Berufsverband für Angewandte Psychologie, 2142
Schweizerischer Ingenieur- und Architektenverein, 2137
Schweizerischer Notarenverband, 2138
Schweizerischer Tonkünstlerverein, 2139
Schweizerischer Verband der Ingenieur-Agronomen und der Lebensmittel-Ingenieure, Zollikofen, 2142
Schweizerischer Werkbund, 2139
Schweizerisches Bundesarchiv, 2145
Schweizerisches Institut für Allergie- und Asthmaforschung, 2144
Schweizerisches Institut für Rechtsvergleichung, 2143
Schweizerisches Landesmuseum, 2150
Schweizerisches Sozialarchiv, 2147
SCI, Ascot, 2297
SCI (Society of Chemical Industry), London, 2293
Science & Technology Australia, 145
Science and Advice for Scottish Agriculture (SASA), 2299
Science and Technology Centre, 1700
Science and Technology Facilities Council, Swindon, 2308
Science and Technology Foundation, Lisbon, 1817
Science and Technology Foundation, Ulan Bator, 1530
Science and Technology Information Institute, Department of Science and Technology, Metro Manila, 1735
Science and Technology Museum of the School of Mines, 315
Science and Technology Policy Research Institute, Accra, 962
Science Centre and Technology Museum 'noesis', 974
Science Council of Japan, 1241
Science Council of Japan Library, 1253
Science Discovery Centre, 1700
Science Education Institute, Manila, 1734
Science for Life Laboratory, 2112
Science Foundation Ireland, 1156
Science, Letters and Arts Centre, Campinas, 310
Science Museum Library, London, 2322
Science Museum, London, 2335

Science Museum of Minnesota, 2528
Science Museum Oklahoma, 2538
Science Policy Research Centre, Dublin, 1158
Science Production Association 'Orgstankinprom', Moscow, 1904
Science Society of Thailand, 2188
Science University of Islamiques Emir Abdelkader of Constantine, 105
Science University of Peru, 1720
Science+Innovation Group, 1602
Scienceworks Museum, Melbourne, 153
Scientific Agricultural Society of Finland, 741
Scientific and Engineering Centre 'sniip', Moscow, 1904
Scientific and Practical Center for Foodstuffs, Minsk, 250
Scientific and Practical Institute of Biotechnologies in Animal Husbandry and Veterinary Medicine, Maximovca, 1524
Scientific and Production Association 'Akadempribor', Tashkent, 3032
Scientific and Production Centre for Preventive Medicine, Bishkek, 1418
Scientific and Production Enterprise with Sugar Beet Research Institute 'Prof. Ivan Ivanov', Shumen District, 357
Scientific and Production Institute for Veterinary Preparations 'Vetbiopharm', Vratsa, 357
Scientific and Research Institute for Architecture and Town Planning Theory, Moscow, 1886
Scientific and Research Institute for Chemical and Technical Problems, Bishkek, 1419
Scientific and Research Institute for Energy and Communications, Bishkek, 1419
Scientific and Research Institute for Physical and Technical Problems, Bishkek, 1419
Scientific and Research Institute for Standardization and Certification in the Engineering Industry, Moscow, 1904
Scientific and Research Institute of Motor Transport, Moscow, 1904
Scientific and Technical Complex 'Progress', Moscow, 1904
Scientific and Technical Information Service, Brussels, 267
Scientific and Technical Library of Kazakhstan, 1365
Scientific and Technical Library of Kyrgyzstan, 1419
Scientific and Technical Library of Moldova, 1525
Scientific and Technical Research Centre for Arid Regions, 102
Scientific and Technical Research Council of Turkey, 2211
Scientific and Technical Union of Civil Engineering, Sofia, 356
Scientific and Technical Union of Forestry, Sofia, 356
Scientific and Technical Union of Mining, Geology and Metallurgy, Sofia, 356
Scientific and Technical Union of Power Engineers, Sofia, 356
Scientific and Technical Union of Specialists in Agriculture, Sofia, 354
Scientific and Technical Union of Textiles, Clothing and Leather, Sofia, 356
Scientific and Technical Union of the Food Industry, Sofia, 356
Scientific and Technical Union of Transport, Sofia, 356
Scientific and Technical Union of Water Affairs in Bulgaria, 356
Scientific and Technological Centre of Machinery Construction, Almaty, 1365
Scientific and Technological Institute for Communications and Transport, Hanoi, 3064
Scientific and Technological Institute, Navarre, 2062

Scientific Archives of the Bulgarian Academy of Sciences, Sofia, 362
Scientific Association for Infocommunication, Budapest, 1001
Scientific Centre of Agriculture and Plant Protection, Echmiadzin, 137
Scientific Centre of Clinical and Experimental Medicine, Novosibirsk, 1892
Scientific Centre of Complex Transportation Problems, Moscow, 1904
Scientific Centre, Salmiya, 1415
Scientific Clinical Center of Eye Disease named after S. Karanov, Ashgabat, 2239
Scientific Clinical Centre of Cardiology, Ashgabat, 2239
Scientific Committee on Antarctic Research, 47
Scientific Committee on Frequency Allocations for Radio Astronomy and Space Science, 47
Scientific Committee on Oceanic Research, 47
Scientific Committee on Problems of the Environment, 47
Scientific Committee on Solar-Terrestrial Physics, 47
Scientific Documentation Centre, Baghdad, 1150
Scientific Information Centre, Karachi, 1679
Scientific Institute of Public Health, 264
Scientific Institute of Thermal Insulation, Vilnius, 1449
Scientific Institute attached to the Russian Institute for the History of Arts, 1907
Scientific Library of Al-Farabi Kazakh National University, 1365
Scientific Library of Baku State University, 213
Scientific Library of Donetsk National University, 2254
Scientific Library of Dubrovnik, 625
Scientific Library of Moscow M. V. Lomonosov State University, 1906
Scientific Library of North-Eastern Federal University, 1908
Scientific Library of Petrozavodsk State University, 1907
Scientific Library of Polish Academy of Arts and Sciences and Polish Academy of Sciences in Cracow, 1770
Scientific Library of the Geographical Research Institute of the Hungarian Academy of Sciences, 1006
Scientific Library of the KNU Balasagina, 1419
Scientific Library of the National Bank of Belgium, 267
Scientific Library of the Odessa National I. I. Mechnikov University, 2254
Scientific Library of the Russian Academy of Arts, 1907
Scientific Library of the State Tretyakov Gallery, Moscow, 1906
Scientific Library of Ural State University 'M. Gorky', 1905
Scientific Library of Voronezh State University, 1908
Scientific Library, Tiranë, 97
Scientific Library Yuriy Fedkovych Chernivtsi National University, 2253
Scientific, Literary and Artistic Athenaeum in Madrid, 2053
Scientific Medical Society of Anatomists-Pathologists, Moscow, 1882
Scientific Museum Javier Cabrera, 1717
Scientific Practical Centre 'Cardiology', Minsk, 249
Scientific Production Centre 'Modern Information Technologies', Tashkent, 3032
Scientific Research Centre for Radiobiology and Radiation Ecology, Tbilisi, 838

Société Mathématique du Canada, 390
Société Mathématique Suisse, 2141
Société Médicale des Hôpitaux de Paris, 771
Société Médico-Psychologique, Boulogne, 771
Société Mycologique de France, 771
Société Nationale d'Horticulture de France (SNHF), 767
Société Nationale de Protection de la Nature, Paris, 771
Société Nationale des Antiquaires de France, 769
Société Nationale des Beaux-Arts, Paris, 768
Société Nationale Française de Gastro-Entérologie, 771
Société Odontologique de Paris, 771
Société Paléontologique Suisse, 2142
Société Philosophique de Louvain, 261
Société pour la Protection des Paysages et de l'Esthétique de la France, 767
Société pour le Développement Minier de la Côte d'Ivoire (SODEMI), 621
Société Royale Belge d'Astronomie, de Météorologie et de Physique du Globe, 261
Société Royale Belge de Géographie, 259
Société Royale Belge des Electriciens, 262
Société Royale Belge des Ingénieurs et des Industriels, 262
Société Royale d'Archéologie de Bruxelles, 259
Société Royale d'Astronomie d'Anvers, 261
Société Royale d'Economie Politique de Belgique, 259
Société Royale de Chimie, Brussels, 261
Société Royale des Sciences de Liège, 260
Société Scientifique d'Hygiène Alimentaire, Paris, 771
Société Scientifique de Bruxelles, 260
Société Suisse d'Economie et de Statistique, 2138
Société Suisse d'Etudes Africaines, 2142
Société Suisse d'Histoire, 2140
Société Suisse d'Histoire de la Médecine et des Sciences Naturelles, 2141
Société Suisse d'Orthopédie et de Traumatologie, 2141
Société Suisse d'Astrophysique et d'Astronomie, 2145
Société Suisse de Cartographie, 2140
Societe Suisse de Chimie, 2142
Société Suisse de Chirurgie, 2141
Société Suisse de Droit International, 2138
Société Suisse de Linguistique, 2141
Société Suisse de Médecine Interne, 2141
Société Suisse de Musicologie, 2139
Société Suisse de Numismatique, 2140
Société Suisse de Philosophie, 2142
Société Suisse de Physique, 2142
Société Suisse de Psychologie, 2142
Société Suisse de Sociologie, 2142
Société Suisse de Théologie, 2142
Société Suisse des Beaux-Arts, 2139
Société Suisse des Bibliophiles, 2138
Société Suisse des Ingénieurs et des Architectes, 2137
Société Suisse des Pharmaciens, 2141
Société Suisse des Traditions Populaires, 2142
Société Vaudoise d'Histoire et d'Archéologie, 2140
Société Vaudoise des Sciences Naturelles, 2141
Société Vétérinaire Pratique de France, 767
Société Zoologique de France, 771
Societies and Tropical Cultures Centre, Lisbon, 1818
Society for Aesthetics, 652
Society for Ancient Philosophy eV, 851
Society for Anthropology, Potsdam, 851
Society for Applied Anthropology, Oklahoma City, 2463
Society for Army Historical Research, London, 2286
Society for Art History in Finland, 743

Society for Biochemistry and Molecular Biology, 849
Society for Biochemistry and Molecular Biology of Chile, 467
Society for Biotechnology, Japan, 1241
Society for Chemical Engineering and Biotechnology, 852
Society for Classical Philology, Helsinki, 743
Society for Coptic Archaeology, Cairo, 711
Society for Danish Language and Literature, 674
Society for Developmental Biology, Bethesda, 2459
Society for Economic Botany, St Louis, 2460
Society for Endocrinology, Bristol, 2290
Society for Ethnomusicology, Bloomington, 2452
Society for Experimental Biology and Medicine, Maywood, 2460
Society for Forensic Science and Right Pyschology, Munich, 851
Society for General Microbiology, Reading, 2292
Society for Geographical Studies, 1190
Society for History of Protestantism in Austria, 188
Society for Industrial and Applied Mathematics Society, Philadelphia, 2460
Society for International Development, 59
Society for Manyo Studies, 1243
Society for Medicine and Law in Israel, 1167
Society for Medieval Archaeology, Shrewsbury, 2286
Society for Mining, Metallurgy and Exploration, Englewood, 2465
Society for Nature and Environment, Utrecht, 1562
Society for Nautical Research, London, 2286
Society for Near Eastern Studies in Japan, 1243
Society for Oceanian Studies, 825
Society for Organization and Management Science, Budapest, 1001
Society for Post-Medieval Archaeology Ltd, London, 2286
Society for Psychiatry and Neurology, 187
Society for Public Economy, 846
Society for Renaissance Studies, London, 2286
Society for Research and Promotion of Maritime Science and Sport, Rijeka, 623
Society for Research in Asiatic Music, 1250
Society for Research into Higher Education, London, 2302
Society for Research on Germany, 858
Society for Slavic Studies, 186
Society for Social and Economic History, Bonn, 846
Society for Social Medicine in Finland, 744
Society for the Advancement of Music, Amsterdam, 1561
Society for the Advancement of Science, Søreidgrend, 1649
Society for the Dissemination of Scientific Knowledge, Budapest, 1000
Society for the German Language, Wiesbaden, 847
Society for the History of Danish Culture, 674
Society for the History of Ideas, 851
Society for the History of Technology, Charlottesville, 2465
Society for the Preservation of Norwegian Ancient Monuments, 1648
Society for the Promotion of Educational Research, Frankfurt, 858
Society for the Promotion of Greek Education, Athens, 968
Society for the Promotion of Hellenic Studies, London, 2287

Society for the Promotion of Natural Science, Copenhagen, 674
Society for the Promotion of Roman Studies, London, 2287
Society for the Protection of Ancient Buildings, London, 2280
Society for the Protection of Nature in Israel, 1168
Society for the Scientific Study of Religion, Indianapolis, 2463
Society for the Study of Evolution, Waterville, 2463
Society for the Study of Finnish, 743
Society for the Study of Japanese Language, 1243
Society for the Study of Medieval Languages and Literature, Oxford, 2287
Society for Theatre Research, London, 2284
Society for Underwater Technology, London, 2297
Society for Walloon Language and Literature, 260
Society for Water, Soil and Air Purity, 860
Society of Actuaries, Schaumburg, 2451
Society of Agricultural Meteorology of Japan, 1246
Society of American Archivists, 2449
Society of American Foresters, 2448
Society of American Historians, 2453
Society of Antiquaries Library & Collections, London, 2323
Society of Antiquaries of London, 2286
Society of Antiquaries of Scotland, 2286
Society of Architects, 652
Society of Architectural Historians, Chicago, 2448
Society of Architectural Illustration, Stroud, 2284
Society of Arts, Literature and Welfare, Chittagong, 222
Society of Australian Genealogists, 144
Society of Authors, London, 2287
Society of Authors, Rio de Janeiro, 307
Society of Automotive Engineers of China, 483
Society of Automotive Engineers, Warrendale, 2465
Society of Biblical Literature, Atlanta, 2454
Society of Biological Chemists (India), 1038
Society of Biological Sciences of Romania, 1837
Society of Biology, 2292
Society of Bollandistes, 261
Society of Botanists of Moldova, 1524
Society of British Neurological Surgeons, 2290
Society of Chartered Surveyors Ireland, 1157
Society of Chemical Industry (Canadian Section), 390
Society of Childcare and Paediatrics, Caracas, 3047
Society of Christian Scholars in the Netherlands, 1562
Society of College, National and University Libraries (SCONUL), London, 2280
Society of Comparative Art Research, Vienna, 190
Society of Comparative Law, Freiburg, 846
Society of Composers, Authors and Music Publishers of Canada (SOCAN), 388
Society of Consulting Marine Engineers and Ship Surveyors, London, 2297
Society of Contemporary Music and Intermedia Art, Stockholm, 2108
Society of Cypriot Studies, Nicosia, 644
Society of Czech Writers, 652
Society of Dairy Technology, Launceston, 2279
Society of Danish Electrotechnicians, 675
Society of Dentistry of Chile, 466
Society of Designer Craftsmen, London, 2284
Society of Digestive Diseases, Madrid, 2054

Society of Dyers and Colourists, Bradford, 2297
Society of Economic Geologists, Littleton, 2462
Society of Economics, Tokyo, 1243
Society of Electrical and Electronics Engineers of Israel, 1168
Society of Engineers and Architects of Antioquia, 592
Society of Estonian Areal Studies, 728
Society of Ethnography and Popular Culture, Vienna, 188
Society of Fibre Science and Technology, Japan, 1247
Society of Finnish Composers, 743
Society of French-Speaking Neurosurgeons, 79
Society of Friends of Music in Vienna, 184
Society of Friends of the History and Monuments of Cracow, 1754
Society of Friends of the Württemberg State Library, 846
Society of Genealogists, London, 2286
Society of Geneticists of Moldova, 1524
Society of Geographical Sciences of Romania, 1837
Society of Geomagnetism and Earth, Planetary and Space Science, 1246
Society of Glass Technology, Sheffield, 2297
Society of Greek Playwrights, Athens, 968
Society of Heating, Air-Conditioning and Sanitary Engineers of Japan, 1248
Society of Helminthologists, Moscow, 1882
Society of Historical Sciences of Romania, 1837
Society of Hops Research, Wolnzach, 856
Society of Hungarian Linguistic, 1000
Society of Hungarian Literary History, 999
Society of Hydrobiologists and Ichthyologists, 1524
Society of Icelandic Composers, 1029
Society of Instrument and Control Engineers, 1248
Society of Irish Foresters, 1157
Society of Japanese Virologists, 1245
Society of Liberian Authors, 1439
Society of Librarians of Puerto Rico, 3014
Society of Light Industry, Moscow, 1883
Society of Literary Translators of Macedonia, 1459
Society of Malawi, 1467
Society of Manufacturing Engineers, Dearborn, 2465
Society of Mathematicians of Macedonia, 1459
Society of Mathematicians of Republika Srpska, 297
Society of Mathematicians of Serbia, 1972
Society of Mathematicians, Physicists and Astronomers of Slovenia, 2018
Society of Medical Jurisprudence, New York, 2458
Society of Medical Psychology, Psychoanalysis and Psychosomatic Medicine, Buenos Aires, 119
Society of Medicine and Surgery, Bologna, 1192
Society of Microbiology of Chile, 466
Society of Miniaturists, Ilkley, 2283
Society of Mongolian Surgeons, 1529
Society of Naturalists Luxembourg, 1456
Society of Naval Architects & Marine Engineers, Jersey City, 2465
Society of Netherlands Literature, 1562
Society of Non-Ferrous Metallurgy, Moscow, 1882
Society of Obstetrics and Gynaecology, Caracas, 3046
Society of Occupational Medicine, London, 2290
Society of Operations Engineers, London, 2297
Society of Oriental Researches, Kyoto, 1243

Society of Ornithologists, Moscow, 1882
Society of Peruvian Engineers, 1715
Society of Petroleum Engineers, Richardson, 2465
Society of Pharmacology of Chile, 466
Society of Physicians and Naturalists in Iaşi, 1837
Society of Physicists of Macedonia, 1459
Society of Plant Physiology and Biochemistry of Moldova, 1524
Society of Polish Surgeons, 1757
Society of Polish Town Planners, 1753
Society of Polymer Science, Japan, 1246
Society of Protozoologists, St Petersburg, 1882
Society of Psychologists, Moscow, 1882
Society of Radiology and Diagnostic Imaging, Caracas, 3047
Society of Rheology, Madison, 2465
Society of Science and Letters of Przemyśl, 1753
Society of Scribes & Illuminators, London, 2284
Society of Sea Water Science, Japan, 1247
Society of Serbian Language and Literature, Belgrade, 1972
Society of Slovak Archivists, 2001
Society of Slovene Composers, 2017
Society of South African Geographers, 2027
Society of Swedish Authors in Finland, 743
Society of Swedish Composers, 2108
Society of Swedish Literature in Finland, 744
Society of the Food Industry, Moscow, 1883
Society of the Friends of History, Helsinki, 743
Society of the History of Sciences and Technology, 653
Society of the Instrument Manufacturing Industry and Metrologists, Moscow, 1883
Society of the Polish Free University, 1753
Society of the Timber and Forestry Industry, Moscow, 1880
Society of Town Planning of Bosnia and Herzegovina, 297
Society of Vertebrate Paleontology, Bethesda, 2460
Society of Wildlife Artists, London, 2283
Socio-Economic Research Institute, Kolkata, 1042
Socio-Economics Centre, Lisbon, 1818
Sociological Association of Ukraine, 2248
Sociologický ústav AV ČR, 656
Sociologický Ústav SAV, 2005
Sociomedical Institute at ZRC SAZU, 2019
Sodertorn University, 2134
Södertörns Högskola, 2134
SOD-Opleidingen, Woerden, 1594
Sofia Imber Museum of Contemporary Art in Caracas, 3050
Sofia Art Gallery, 364
Sofia City Library, 362
Sofia Museum of History, 364
Sofia University 'St Kliment Ohridski', 367
Sofiiski Universitet 'Sveti Kliment Ohridski', 367
Sogang University, 1404
Sogn og Fjordane University College, 1665
Sogo Kenkyu Kaihatsu Kiko, 1248
Sögufélag, 1029
Sohar University, 1670
Soil Research Institute, Bogor, 1111
Soil Research Institute, Kumasi, 962
Soil Resources Agency, Sofia, 355
Soil Science Research Institute, Pyongyang, 1384
Soil Science Society, Moscow, 1880
Soil Science Society of America, 2448
Soil Science Society of China, 480
Soil, Water and Environment Research Institute, Giza, 712
Sojourner-Douglass College, 2706
Sojuz na društvata na arhivskite rabotnici na Makedonija, 1459

Sojuz na Društvata na Veterinarnite Lekari i Tehničari na Makedonija, 1458
Sojuz na Ekonomistite na Makedonija, 1459
Sojuz na Istoricarite na Republika Makedonija, 1459
Sojuz na Kompozitorite na Makedonija, 1459
Sojuz na Matematičari na Makedonija, 1459
Soka University, 1353
Sokhumi Botanical Garden, 839
Sokhumi State University, 841
Sokoine National Agricultural Library, Morogoro, 2183
Sokoine University of Agriculture, 2184
Sol Plaatje University, 2037
Sola Scriptura Ministers Training and Theological College, 1026
Sola Scriptura Teológiai Főiskola, 1026
Solar Energy Development Unit, 102
Solar Energy Institute, Madrid, 2061
Solar Museum Monjardim, 316
Solar Observatory Ticinese, Locarno, 2145
Solar-Terrestrial Influences Laboratory, Sofia, 360
Solomon Islands College of Higher Education, 2023
Solomon Islands National Archives, 2023
Solomon Islands National Library, 2023
Solomon Islands National Museum and Cultural Centre, 2023
Solomon Islands National University Library, 2023
Solomon R. Guggenheim Museum, 2534
Solusi University, 3081
SOM Research Institute, 1568
Somali National Museum, 2024
Somerset College, 2412
Somerset County Council Library Service, 2313
Somerset County Library System, Princess Anne, 2491
Somerville College, Oxford, 2399
Somogyi Károly Városi és Megyei Könyvtár, 1007
Söngskólinn í Reykjavík, 1031
Sonnenobservatorium Kanzelhöhe der Universität Graz, 191
Sonoma State University, 2580
Soochow University, 559
Soochow University, Taipei, 2176
Sookmyung Women's University, 1405
Soongsil University, 1405
Sophia (Jôchi) University Library, 1253
Sophia University, 1353
Sophiahemmet Högskola, 2134
Sophiahemmet University, 2134
Soprintendenza alla Galleria Nazionale d'Arte Moderna e Contemporanea, Rome, 1212
Soprintendenza per i Beni Archeologici della Liguria, Genoa, 1209
Soprintendenza Speciale per i Beni Archeologici di Roma, 1212
Soreq Nuclear Research Centre, 1172
SORIN Biomedica SpA, Saluggia, 1200
Sorolla Museum, Madrid, 2067
Sorprintendza Speciale per i Beni Archeologici di Napoli e Pompei, 1210
Sør-Trøndelag University College, 1665
Sosiaalilääketieteen Yhdistys ry, 744
Sotamuseo, 749
Sotheby's Institute of Art, 2412
Sourasky Central Library, Tel-Aviv University, 1174
Sous Directeur des Agréments, du Contrôle et des Equivalences, Algiers, 100
Sous Directeur des Sciences Exactes, des Technologies et des Sciences de la Nature et de la Vie, Algiers, 100
Sous Directeur des Sciences Sociales et Humaines, des Lettres et des Langues, Algiers, 100
Sous Directeur du Suivi Pédagogique et de l'Evaluation, Algiers, 100
Sous-Direction de l'Archéologie, Paris, 774

South Africa House, Amsterdam, 1560
South African Academy for Science and Arts, 2027
South African Archaeological Society, 2027
South African Astronomical Observatory, 2030
South African Bureau of Standards, Pretoria, 2030
South African Chemical Institute, 2029
South African College of Applied Psychology, 2047
South African Institute of Architects, 2027
South African Institute of Electrical Engineers, 2029
South African Institute of International Affairs, 2027
South African Institute of Physics, 2029
South African Institute of Race Relations, 2029
South African Institution of Civil Engineering (SAICE), 2029
South African Institution of Mechanical Engineering (SAIMechE), 2029
South African Medical Association, 2028
South African Medical Research Council, Tygerberg, 2030
South African Museums Association, 2027
South African National Association for the Visual Arts (SANAVA), 2027
South African National Biodiversity Institute (SANBI), 2028
South African PEN Centre, 2028
South African Qualifications Authority (SAQA), 2027
South African Society for Animal Science, 2027
South African Society for Biochemistry and Molecular Biology, 2028
South African Society for Microbiology, 2028
South African Society of Basic and Clinical Pharmacology, 2028
South African Society of Dairy Technology, 2027
South African Society of Obstetricians and Gynaecologists, 2028
South African Theological Seminary, 2047
South Asia Institute, Heidelberg, 942
South Asian Institute of Technology and Medicine, 2098
South Australian Museum, 152
South Berwick Public Library, 2490
South Bohemian Museum in České Budějovice, 658
South Carolina College of Pharmacy, 2930
South Carolina Confederate Relic Room & Military Museum, 2541
South Carolina State Library, 2504
South Carolina State Museum, 2541
South Carolina State University, 2930
South Cheshire College, 2411
South China Agricultural University, 559
South China Botanical Garden, 485
South China Normal University, 560
South China Sea Institute of Oceanology, Guangzhou, 485
South China University of Technology, 561
South College, Knoxville, 2938
South Colombian University, 604
South Cross University, 343
South Dakota Agricultural Heritage Museum, 2542
South Dakota Art Museum, 2542
South Dakota School of Mines and Technology, 2933
South Dakota State Archives, 2504
South Dakota State Library, 2504
South Dakota State University, 2933
South Dakota State University Library, 2504
South East European University, 1462
South Eastern Education and Library Board, 2312
South Eastern Regional College, Lisburn, 2418
South Eastern University of Sri Lanka, 2095

South Essex College, 2411
South Gloucestershire and Stroud College, 2411
South Hamgyong Provincial Library, 1385
South Hwanghae Provincial Library, 1385
South Kazakhstan Scientific and Research Institute of Agriculture, 1363
South Kazakhstan Technical University, 1374
South London Gallery, 2335
South Pyongan Provincial Library, 1385
South Russia State Technical University (Novocherkassk Polytechnic Institute), 1945
South St Landry Community Library, 2489
South Shields Museum and Art Gallery, 2336
South Texas College, 2953
South Texas College of Law, 2953
South Thames College, 2411
South University, Savannah, 2646
South Ural Research and Development Institute of Fruit, Vegetable and Potato Growing, 1885
South Ural State University, 1929
South Valley University, Kena, 718
South Wales Institute of Engineers Educational Trust, 2297
South West College, Enniskillen, 2418
South Western University of Finance and Economics, 561
Southampton City Art Gallery, 2337
Southampton City Libraries, 2327
Southampton Solent University, 2346
Southbank Institute of Technology, South Brisbane, 180
South-East Asia University, 2196
Southeast Asian Ministers of Education Organization Regional Center for Educational Innovation and Technology (SEAMEO INNOTECH), Quezon City, 1734
Southeast Asian Ministers of Education Organization (SEAMEO), 66
Southeast Missouri State University, 2794
Southeast Regional University, Oaxaca, 1514
Southeast University, Dhaka, 234
Southeast University, Nanjing, 561
Southeastern Baptist College, 2785
Southeastern Baptist Theological Seminary, Wake Forest, 2862
Southeastern Bible College, 2550
Southeastern Louisiana University, 2696
Southeastern Oklahoma State University, 2891
Southeastern University, Lakeland, 2634
Southend-on-Sea Libraries, 2327
Southern Academy of Music and Dramatic Arts (SMKS), 687
Southern Adventist University, 2938
Southern Africa Association for the Advancement of Science, 2028
Southern Africa Bible College, 2047
Southern African Institute of Forestry, 2027
Southern African Institute of Mining and Metallurgy, 2029
Southern African Society of Aquatic Scientists, 2028
Southern African Wildlife Management Association, 2028
Southern Arkansas University, 2562
Southern Association of Colleges and Schools: Commission on Colleges, Decatur, 2443
Southern Baptist Theological Seminary, 2691
Southern Business School, Helderkruin, 2047
Southern California Academy of Sciences, 2458
Southern California College of Optometry, 2580
Southern California University of Health Sciences, Whittier, 2580

State Priekuli Plant Breeding Institute, 1427
State Public Historical Library of Russia, 1907
State Public Scientific and Technical Library of the Siberian Department of the Russian Academy of Sciences, 1907
State Pushkin Museum, Moscow, 1911
State Pushkin Museum of Fine Arts, Moscow, 1911
State Records Authority of New South Wales, 150
State Research and Design Institute of Chemical Engineering 'Khimtekhnologiya', Severodonetsk, 2253
State Research and Project Development Institute of Maritime Transport, Moscow, 1905
State Research Centre for Maternal and Child Health, Ulan Bator, 1530
State Research Centre of Virology and Biotechnology (Vector), Koltsovo, 1895
State Research Institute Centre for Innovative Medicine, Vilnius, 1448
State Research Institute for the Nitrogen Industry and the Products of Organic Synthesis, Moscow, 1905
State Research Institute for the Operation and Repair of Civil Aviation Equipment, Moscow, 1905
State Research Institute for the Standardization and Control of Drugs, Moscow, 1892
State Research Institute of Building Constructions, Kyiv, 2249
State Research Institute of Civil Aviation, Moscow, 1905
State Research Institute of Eye Diseases, Moscow, 1892
State Research Institute of Highly Pure Biopreparations (IHPB), 1895
State Research Institute of Non-Ferrous Metals, Moscow, 1899
State Research Institute of Soil Science and Agrochemistry, Tashkent, 3031
State Research Institute of the Rare Metals Industry, Moscow, 1905
State Russian Museum, 1913
State School of Fine Arts, Mandalay, 1550
State School of Fine Arts, Yangon, 1550
State School of Higher Education in Chełm, 1811
State School of Higher Education in Oświęcim, 1811
State School of Higher Professional Education in Elbląg, 1811
State School of Higher Professional Education in Konin, 1812
State School of Music and Drama, Mandalay, 1550
State School of Music and Drama, Yangon, 1550
State Scientific Agricultural Library of Ukrainian Academy of Agricultural Sciences, 2254
State Scientific and Technical Library of Ukraine, 2254
State Scientific Centre of Drugs, Kharkiv, 2250
State Scientific Institution Voronezh Scientific Research Institute of Agriculture, 1885
State Scientific Library in Banska Bystrica, 2006
State Scientific Library in Košiče, 2006
State Scientific Library in Prešov, 2006
State Scientific Research Institute of Medical Polymers, Moscow, 1892
State Scientific Research Institute on Medical Problems of the Far North, Nadym, 1892
State Secretariat for Education and Research SER, 2144
State Secretariat for Education, Research and Innovation, Bern, 2136
State Serum Institute, Copenhagen, 677
State Students Admission Commission, Baku, 211
State Studies Foundation, Vilnius, 1447

State Technological University of Madhya Pradesh, 1080
State Titanium Research and Design Institute, Zaporizhzhya, 2253
State Tretyakov Gallery, 1911
State University College at Buffalo, 2851
State University College at Cortland, 2851
State University College at Fredonia, 2851
State University College at Geneseo, 2851
State University College at New Paltz, 2851
State University College at Old Westbury, 2851
State University College at Oneonta, 2851
State University College at Oswego, 2851
State University College at Plattsburgh, 2851
State University College at Purchase, 2851
State University Empire State College, 2851
State University for the Humanities, Moscow, 1930
State University in Novi Pazar, 1975
State University Institute of Technology at Utica/Rome, 2852
State University of Amazonas, 317
State University of Bangladesh, 235
State University of Campinas, 347
State University of Ceará, 319
State University of Central West, 328
State University of Goiás, 321
State University of Health Sciences of Alagoas, 317
State University of Jakarta, 1121
State University of Londrina, 328
State University of Makassar, 1121
State University of Malang, 1121
State University of Manado, 1121
State University of Management, 1930
State University of Maranhão, 321
State University of Maringá, 328
State University of Mato Grosso, 322
State University of Mato Grosso do Sul, 322
State University of Medan, 1121
State University of Montes Claros, 323
State University of New York, 2850
State University of New York at Potsdam, 2851
State University of New York College of Agriculture and Technology at Cobleskill, 2852
State University of New York College of Agriculture and Technology at Morrisville, 2852
State University of New York College of Environmental Science and Forestry, 2852
State University of New York College of Optometry at New York City, 2852
State University of New York College of Technology at Canton, 2852
State University of New York College of Technology at Delhi, 2852
State University of New York College of Technology at Farmingdale, 2852
State University of New York Maritime College, 2852
State University of New York—Alfred State, 2851
State University of New York—College at Brockport, 2851
State University of Pará, 326
State University of Paraíba, 326
State University of Piauí, 330
State University of Ponta Grossa, 328
State University of Rio de Janeiro, 331
State University of Rio Grande do Norte, 333
State University of Rio Grande do Sul, 335
State University of Roraima, 337
State University of Santa Catarina, 341
State University of Santa Elena Peninsula, 705
State University of Santana Feira, 318
State University of Semarang, 1121

State University of Southern Manabi, 705
State University of Surabaya, 1121
State University of Tetova, 1461
State University of the Valley of Ecatepec, 1508
State University of West Parana, 328
State V. V. Mayakovsky Museum, Moscow, 1911
Statens Arkiver, 678
Statens Folkhälsoinstitut, 2112
Statens försvarshistoriska museer, 2119
Statens Forsvarshistoriske Museum, 680
Statens Geotekniska Institut, 2113
Statens Konstmuseum, 750
Statens Maritima Museer, 2119
Statens Museum for Kunst, 680
Statens Scenekunstskole, 687
Statens Serum Institut, Copenhagen, 677
Statens Veterinärmedicinska Anstalt, 2111
Statesboro Regional Public Libraries, 2485
Station Biologique de Roscoff, 775
Station de Radioastronomie de Nançay, 776
Station de Recherches sur le Cocotier de Semé-Podji, 285
Station de Recherches sur le Palmier à Huile de Pobe, 285
Station Fruitière du Congo, Loudima, 611
Station Géophysique de Lamto, 621
Station ISAR/PNAP, 1954
Station Karama, 1954
Station Rubona, 1954
Station Rwerere, 1954
Station Tamira, 1954
Statistical and Social Inquiry Society of Ireland, 1157
Statistical Institute for Asia and the Pacific, 60
Statistical Library, Statistics Bureau, Management and Coordination Agency, Tokyo, 1253
Statistical Society of Australia, Inc., 146
Statistics Austria, 189
Statistics Denmark, 676
Statistics Denmark's Information Service and Library, 678
Statistics Finland, 747
Statistics Iceland, 1029
Statistics Norway, 1649
Statistics Norway, Library and Information Centre, 1651
Statistics Sweden, 2111
Statistics Sweden Library, 2115
Statistik Austria, 189
Statistisches Bundesamt, Wiesbaden, 858
Statistisk Sentralbyrå, Oslo, 1649
Statistisk Sentralbyrås Bibliotek og Informasjonssenter, Oslo, 1651
Statistiska Centralbyrån, 2111
Statistiska Centralbyråns Bibliotek, 2115
Statistiska Samfundet i Finland, 742
Staţiunea Centrală de Cercetări pentru Cultura şi Industrializarea Tutunului, 1839
Staţiunea de Cercetare—Dezvoltare Agricola Brăila, 1839
Státní technická knihovna, Prague, 657
Státní úřad pro jadernou bezpečnost, Prague, 655
Státní vědecká knihovna, České Budějovice, 656
Štátna Vedecká Knižnica v Banskej Bystrici, 2006
Štátna Vedecká Knižnica v Košiciach, 2006
Štátna Vedecká Knižnica v Prešove, 2006
Statsarkivet i Hamar, 1651
Statsbiblioteket, Århus, 678
Statsøkonomisk Forening, Oslo, 1648
Stavanger Bibliotek, 1652
Stavanger Library, 1652
Stavanger Museum, 1653
Stavropol Museum of Fine Arts, 1913
Stavropol Research and Development Institute of Agriculture, 1885

Stavropol State Agrarian University, 1915
Stavropol State Medical Academy, 1950
Stavropol State University, 1930
Stavros Niarchos Foundation, 968
Stazione Zoologica 'Anton Dohrn', 1199
Stedelijk Museum Alkmaar, 1579
Stedelijk Museum, Amsterdam, 1580
Stedelijk Museum de Lakenhal Leiden, 1582
Stedelijk Museum Schiedam, 1583
Stedelijk Museum voor Actuele Kunst, 271
Stedelijke Musea Mechelen, 271
Stedelijke Openbare Bibliotheek, 269
Steel Construction Institute, Ascot, 2297
Steering Committee for Culture, Heritage and Landscape (CDCPP), 66
Steering Committee for Higher Education and Research (CDESR), 66
Stefan Banach International Mathematical Centre, 1766
Ştefan Cel Mare University, 1866
Stefan Meyer Institut für Mittelenergiephysik, Vienna, 191
Stefan Meyer Institute of Medium Energy Physics, Vienna, 191
Stefan S. Nicolau Institute of Virology, 1841
Steiermärkische Landesbibliothek, 193
Steiermärkisches Landesarchiv, 193
Stein Rokkan Centre for Social Studies, 1649
Stein Rokkan Senter for Flerfaglige Samfunnsstudier, 1649
Steinbeis University Berlin, 920
Steinbeis-Hochschule Berlin, 920
Steinerbiblioteket, 747
Steinsburgmuseum, Weimar, 881
Steklov Mathematical Institute, Moscow, 1895
Stellenbosch Academy of Design and Photography, 2047
Stellenbosch Museum, 2034
Stellenbosch University, 2037
Stellenbosch University Library and Information Service, 2032
Stenden Hogeschool, 1594
Stenden South Africa, Port Alfred, 2047
Stenden University Qatar, 1834
Stennis Space Center, Mississippi, 2476
Stepanakert Museum of the History of Nagornyi-Karabakh, 213
Stephan Angeloff Institute of Microbiology, 359
Stephen B. Luce Library, Throgs Neck, 2499
Stephen F. Austin State University, 2955
Stephen J. Betze Library, Georgetown, 2482
Stephens College, 2794
Stephenson College, Stockton, 2360
Stephenson Railway Museum, 2336
Sterling and Francine Clark Art Institute, 2527
Sterling College, Common, 2975
Sterling College, Sterling, 2686
Sternwarte Kremsmünster, 196
Sterrenkundig Instituut Anton Pannekoek, 1572
Stetson University, 2634
Steunpunt Gelijkekansenbeleid, 262
Stevens Institute of Technology, 2814
Stevenson University, 2708
Stichting Arnhemse Openbare en Gelderse Wetenschappelijke Bibliotheek, 1577
Stichting Nationale Parken Bonaire (STINAPA Bonaire), 1597
Stichting Natuur en Milieu, 1562
Stichting Opleidingen Musculoskeletale Therapie, 1594
Stichting Surinaams Museum, 2103
Stichting voor Christelijke Filosofie, Amersfoort, 1563
Stichting voor Fundamenteel Onderzoek der Materie (FOM), 1573
Stichting voor Wetenschappelijk Onderzoek van de Tropen (WOTRO), 1571

Tomsk State University of Control Systems and Radioelectronics, 1946
Tonga Institute of Science and Technology, 2202
Tonga Library Association, 2202
Tonga National Qualifications and Accreditation Board (TNQAB), 2202
Tonga Wildlife Centre, 2202
Tongass Historical Museum, 2510
Tongji Medical College, 566
Tongji University, 566
Tónlistarfélagið, 1029
Tónlistarskólinn í Reykjavík, 1032
Tønsberg and Nøtterøy Public Library, 1652
Tønsberg og Nøtterøy Bibliotek, 1652
Tónskáldafélag Íslands, 1029
Top Education Institute, Sydney, 179
Top Institute for Evidence Based Education Research (TIER), Amsterdam, 1569
Topchiev, A. V., Institute of Petro-Chemical Synthesis, Moscow, 1905
Topeka and Shawnee County Public Library, 2488
Topkapı Palace Museum, 2214
Toraigyrov Oblast Universal Scientific Library, 1365
Torbay Libraries, 2328
Torcuato di Tella Institute, 120
Torcuato di Tella University, 135
Torfaen Libraries, 2326
Tornaritis-Pierides Municipal Museum of Marine Life, 645
Tornquist Library, 122
Tornyai János Múzeum és Közművelődési Központ, 1009
Toronto Biomedical NMR Centre, 392
Toronto Public Library, 394
Torre Civica di Mestre, Venice, 1214
Torre dell'Orologio, Venice, 1214
Tórshavn Public Library, 688
Toshkent Avtomobil-Yo'llar Instituti, 3035
Toshkent Davlat Iqtisodiyot Universiteti, 3034
Toshkent Davlat Yuridik Instituti, 3035
Toshkent Islom Universiteti, 3034
Toshkent Moliya Instituti, 3035
Totem Heritage Center, 2510
Tottori University, 1314
Tougaloo College, 2785
Tourism University, San José, 616
Touro College, 2852
Towarzystwo Chirurgów Polskich, 1757
Towarzystwo im. Fryderyka Chopina, Warsaw, 1754
Towarzystwo Internistów Polskich, 1757
Towarzystwo Literackie im. Adama Mickiewicza, 1754
Towarzystwo Miłośników Historii i Zabytków Krakowa, 1754
Towarzystwo Naukowe Organizacji i Kierownictwa, 1759
Towarzystwo Naukowe Płockie, 1752
Towarzystwo Naukowe w Toruniu, 1752
Towarzystwo Naukowe Warszawskie, 1752
Towarzystwo Przyjaciół Nauk w Przemyślu, 1753
Towarzystwo Urbanistów Polskich, 1753
Towarzystwo Wiedzy Powszechnej, 1753
Towarzystwo Wolnej Wszechnicy Polskiej, 1753
Tower Hamlets Idea Stores, 2323
Town and Country Planning Association, London, 2280
Town Hall Library of the State Capital of Stuttgart, 871
Town Hall Museum Vierschaar, 1584
Town Museum, Bayan-Ölgii, 1531
Town of Chapel Hill Public Library, 2500
Towneley Hall Art Gallery and Museums, 2329
Towson University, 2707
Toy Museum and Workshop, Kecskemet, 1010
Toyama University, 1314
Toyo Bunko, Tokyo, 1253
Tōyō Ongaku Gakkai, 1250
Toyo University, 1355

Toyohashi University of Technology, 1314
Toyokuni Jinja Hómotsuden, 1255
Toyoshi-Kenkyu-Kai, 1243
Traditional Medicine Association of Viet Nam, Hanoi, 3061
Traditional Medicine Science, Technology and Production Corporation, Ulan Bator, 1531
Trafford Centre for Medical Research, Brighton, 2306
Tragor Ignác Múzeum, 1011
Training School of Public Art 'José Maria Valle Riestra', 1731
Trakai Historical Museum, 1449
Trakia University, 369
Trakiyski Universitet, 369
Trakya Üniversitesi, 2236
Tram Museum, Porto, 1825
Trammell & Margaret Crow Collection of Asian Art, 2543
Transcaucasian Hydrometeorological Research Institute, 839
Transdisciplinary Studies Centre for Development, Vila Real, 1817
Transfer Group Rotterdam, 1594
Transfergroep Rotterdam, 1594
Transitional Justice Institute, Newtownabbey, 2301
Transnationale Universiteit Limburg, 1595
Transport and Telecommunication Institute, Rīga, 1431
Transport Infrastructure and Logistics (TRAIL) Research School, 1566
Transport Library, Seoul, 1389
Transport Museum, Budapest, 1008
Transport Museum Dresden, 876
Transport Research and Production Corporation, Ulan Bator, 1531
Transport Research Institute, Inc., Žilina, 2006
Transport Research Institute, Vilnius, 1449
Transporto Institutas, Vilnius, 1449
Transportøkonomisk Institutt, Oslo, 1651
Transylvania County Library, 2500
Transylvania University, 2691
Transylvania University of Brașov Central Library, 1844
Transylvanian Museum of Ethnography, 1849
Tranzo—Scientific Centre for Care and Welfare, 1566
Trapholt, Kolding, 681
Treasure Hall of the Oyamazumi Shrine, 1255
Treasury and Cabinet Office Library, London, 2323
Tree and Timber Institute, Sesto Fiorentino, 1195
Trenčianska Univerzita Alexandra Dubčeka v Trenčíne, 2011
Trent University, 414
Trenton City Museum, 2533
Tresham College of Further and Higher Education, Corby, 2411
TRESOAR Fries Historisch en Letterkundig Centrum, 1578
TRESOAR Frisian Historical and Literary Centre, 1578
Trevecca Nazarene University, 2939
Trevelyan College, Durham, 2360
TRI Princeton, 2476
Tribhuvan University, 1558
Tribhuvan University Central Library, 1557
Trine University, 2675
Trinidad and Tobago Institute of Architects, 2203
Trinidad Music Association, 2203
Trinity Bible College, 2874
Trinity Christian College, 2661
Trinity College, Cambridge, 2358
Trinity College Dublin, the University of Dublin, 1162
Trinity College, Hartford, 2603
Trinity College Library, Cambridge, 2314
Trinity College Library, Dublin, 1160
Trinity College Library, Oxford, 2326
Trinity College of Nursing & Health Sciences, 2661

Trinity College, Oxford, 2399
Trinity Evangelical Divinity School, Deerfield, 2662
Trinity Graduate School, Deerfield, 2662
Trinity Hall, Cambridge, 2358
Trinity Hall Library, 2314
Trinity International University, Deerfield, 2661
Trinity Laban Conservatoire of Music and Dance, London, 2414
Trinity Lutheran College, 2989
Trinity Lutheran Seminary, 2885
Trinity School for Ministry, 2918
Trinity University, San Antonio, 2961
Trinity Washington University, Washington, 2625
Trinity Western University, 414
Tripura University, 1086
TRL Ltd, Wokingham, 2311
Trnava University in Trnava, 2011
Troitsk Research Centre, 1899
Tromsø Museum (Universitetetsmuseet), 1653
Tromso University Museum, 1653
Trondheim Academy of Fine Art, Norwegian University of Science and Technology, 1668
Tropenmuseum, 1580
Tropical Agriculture Research Station, Mayaguez, 3015
Tropical Agronomic Centre for Research and Education (CATIE), Turrialba, 613
Tropical Diseases Research Centre, Ndola, 3075
Tropical Forestry Research Institute, Guangzhou, 483
Tropical Pesticides Research Institute, Arusha, 2183
Tropical Science Centre, San José, 613
Tropical Science Research Institute, Lisbon, 1817
Trout Museum of Art, 2546
Troy University, 2550
Troy University ITS Sharjah Campus, 2274
Troy University, Montgomery, 2550
Troy University, Phenix City, 2550
Truett McConnell College, 2646
Truman State University, 2794
Truva Müzesi, 2214
Tsarskoe Selo State Museum, 1912
Tselinny Scientific and Research Institute of Mechanization and Electrification in Agriculture, 1363
Tsereteli, G. V., Institute of Oriental Studies, 838
Tsereteli Institute of Philosophy, Tbilisi, 839
Tshwane University of Technology, 2038
Tsinghua University, 566
Tsinghua University Library, 488
Tsiolkovsky, K. E., State Museum of the History of Cosmonautics, 1908
Tskhinvali Pedagogical Institute–Georgian Sector, Gori, 841
Tsubouchi Memorial Theatre Museum, Waseda University, 1256
Tsuda College, 1355
Tsuru University, 1355
Tswaing Meteorite Crater Museum, 2034
TTÜ Geoloogia Instituut, 730
TTÜ Küberneetika Instituut, 730
TU Delft Library, 1577
Tuberculosis and Lung Disease Center, 1145
TÜbiTAK Marmara Araştırma Merkezi Gen Mühendisliği ve Biyoteknoloji Araştırma Enstitüsü, 2212
TÜbiTAK Marmara Research Centre Genetic Engineering and Biotechnology Institute, 2212
TUBITAK Space Technologies Research Institute, 2212
TÜbiTAK Uzay Teknolojileri Araştırma Enstitüsü, 2212
Tubman Centre of African Cultures, 1439
Tucker House Museum, 2435
Tucson Museum of Art and Historic Block, 2511

Tudományos Ismeretterjesztő Társulat, Budapest, 1000
Tufts University, 2738
Tuguegarao Branch, 1736
Tula Art Museum, 1914
Tula Museum of Regional Studies, 1914
Tula Research and Development Institute of Agriculture, 1885
Tula State University, 1946
Tulane University, 2695
Tulane University Libraries, 2489
Tulcea County Library 'Panait Cerna', 1847
Tulkarm Community College, 1701
Tulsa City-County Library, 2502
Tumaini University, Arusha, 2185
Tumba College of Technology, 1955
Tun Abdul Razak Library, Selangor, 1473
Tun Abdul Razak Research Centre, Hertford, 2311
Tun Razak Library, Ipoh, 1472
Tunghai University, Taichung, 2177
Tunku Abdul Rahman University College, 1479
Tuol Sleng Genocide Museum, 378
Tupou College Museum, 2202
Turan University, 1373
'Turan-Astana' University, 1372
Turgenev, I. S., State Literary Museum, 1911
Turgenev Library No. 13, 1907
Türk Bilim Tarihi Kurumu, 2212
Türk Cerrahi Derneği, 2211
Türk Dil Kurumu, 2211
Türk Hukuk Kurumu, 2210
Türk Kültürünü Araştırma Enstitüsü, 2211
Türk Kütüphaneciler Derneği, 2210
Türk Mikrobiyoloji Cemiyeti, 2211
Türk Nöropsikiyatri Derneği, 2211
Türk Ortopedi ve Travmatoloji Birliği Derneği, Ankara, 2211
Türk Oto-Rino-Larengoloji Cemiyeti, 2211
Türk Tabipleri Birliği, 2211
Türk Tarih Kurumu, 2211
Türk Tibbi Elektro Radyografi Cemiyeti, 2211
Türk Tıp Tarihi Kurumu, 2211
Türk Tüberküloz ve Toraks Derneği, 2211
Türk Üniversite Rektörleri Komitesi, 2210
Türk Üroloji Derneği, 2211
Türk ve Islam Eserleri Müzesi, Istanbul, 2214
Türk Veteriner Hekimleri Birliği, 2210
Turkish Association of Tuberculosis and Thorax, 2211
Turkish Ceramics Museum, Konya, 2215
Turkish Cultural Research Institute, 2211
Turkish Grand National Assembly Library and Archives Services Department, 2213
Turkish Language Institute, Ankara, 2211
Turkish Law Association, 2210
Turkish Marine Research Foundation, 2212
Turkish Medical Association, 2211
Turkish Microbiological Society, 2211
Turkish Neuropsychiatric Society, 2211
Turkish Veterinary Medical Association, 2210
Türkiye Bilimsel ve Teknik Araştırma Kurumu, 2211
Türkiye Büyük Millet Meclisi Kütüphane ve Arşiv Hizmetleri Başkanlığı, Ankara, 2213
Türkiye Deniz Araştırmaları Vakfı (TUDAV), 2212
Türkiye Felsefe Kurumu, 2211
Türkiye Kimya Derneği, 2211
Türkiye Matematik Derneği, 2211
Turkmen Agricultural University named after S. A. Niyazov, 2240
Turkmen History Museum, 2240
Turkmen Institute of National Economy, 2240
Turkmen Medical Institute, 2240

U

University of Guadalajara Library Services, 1497
University of Guam, 3013
University of Guam, Robert F. Kennedy Memorial Library, 3013
University of Guanajuato, 1509
University of Guayaquil, 704
University of Guelph, 432
University of Gujrat, 1693
University of Guyana, 992
University of Guyana Library, 992
University of Habana, 640
University of Haifa, 1184
University of Haifa Library, 1173
University of Hargeisa, Hargeisa, 2025
University of Hartford, 2607
University of Hawai'i at Manoa, 2648
University of Hawaii Maui College Library, 2485
University of Hawai'i System, 2648
University of Hawai'i—West O'ahu, 2648
University of Health Sciences Antigua, 115
University of Health Sciences, Lahore, 1693
University of Health Sciences, Phnom-Penh, 380
University of Health Sciences, Ulan Bator, 1533
University of Helsinki, 753
University of Hertfordshire, 2363
University of Holguin 'Oscar Lucero Moya', 641
University of Holy Qu'ran and Islamic Sciences, Omdurman, 2102
University of Hong Kong, 584
University of Hong Kong Libraries, 579
University of Hong Kong Museum Society, 578
University of Houston System, 2961
University of Houston–Clear Lake, 2961
University of Houston–Downtown, 2961
University of Houston—Victoria, 2962
University of Hradec Králové, 662
University of Huddersfield, 2363
University of Huddersfield Library, 2317
University of Huelva, 2075
University of Hull, 2363
University of Hull, Library and Learning Innovation, 2318
University of Hyderabad, 1091
University of Ibadan, 1634
University of Ibero-America, San José, 616
University of Iceland, 1031
University of Idaho, 2649
University of Illinois, 2662
University of Illinois at Springfield, 2662
University of Illinois at Urbana-Champaign, 2663
University of Illinois (Urbana-Champaign) Library, 2486
University of Ilorin, 1635
University of Incheon, 1408
University of Indianapolis, 2675
University of Information Technology and Sciences, Dhaka, 240
University of International Business, Almaty, 1373
University of International Business and Economics, Beijing, 567
University of International Relations, Beijing, 567
University of Ioannina, 978
University of Iowa, 2682
University of Iowa Libraries, 2487
University of Iowa Museum of Art, 2522
University of Iowa Museum of Natural History, 2522
University of Isfahan, 1146
University of Isfahan Library, 1134
University of Istmo, 1704
University of Itaúna, 323
University of J. Selyeho in Komárno, 2012
University of Jaén, 2075
University of Jaffna, 2095
University of Jammu, 1091
University of Johannesburg, 2039
University of Jordan, 1360

University of Jordan Library, 1358
University of Jos, 1636
University of Juba, 2049
University of Juba Library, 2049
University of Jyväskylä, 756
University of Kalyani, 1091
University of Kansas, 2686
University of Karachi, 1693
University of Karbala, 1153
University of Kashmir, 1092
University of Keele, 2364
University of Keele Library, 2317
University of Kelaniya, 2096
University of Kent, 2366
University of Kentucky, 2692
University of Kentucky Libraries, 2488
University of Kerala, 1092
University of Khartoum, 2102
University of Khartoum Library, 2100
University of Khemis Miliana, 104
University of King's College, Halifax, 432
University of Klagenfurt, 198
University of Konstanz, 944
University of Konstanz Library, 868
University of Kordofan, 2102
University of Kragujevac, 1982
University of Kufa, 1153
University of KwaZulu-Natal, 2040
University of KwaZulu-Natal Libraries, 2031
University of la Salle, San José, 616
University of la Serena, 473
University of la Verne, 2592
University of Lagos, 1636
University of Lagos Library, 1627
University of Lahore, 1694
University of Lake Tanganyika, 376
University of Lampung, 1120
University of Lancaster, 2367
University of Lapland, 757
University of Latvia, 1429
University of Latvia Institute of Chemical Physics, 1428
University of Latvia Institute of Philosophy and Sociology, 1428
University of Leeds, 2367
University of Leicester, 2370
University of Leicester Library, 2318
University of Leoben, 201
University of Lethbridge, 432
University of Liberal Arts Bangladesh, 240
University of Liberia, 1440
University of Liberia Libraries, 1439
University of Liechtenstein, 1445
University of Liège, 273
University of Life Sciences in Lublin, 1790
University of Lima, 1720
University of Limerick, 1163
University of Limpopo, 2040
University of Limpopo Libraries and Information Services, 2032
University of Lincoln, 2370
University of Lisbon, 1828
University of Liverpool, 2370
University of Liverpool Library, 2318
University of Ljubljana, 2021
University of Lleida, 2087
University of Łódź, 1784
University of London, 2371
University of London Observatory, 2309
University of Los Andes, Merida, 3053
University of Los Lagos, 473
University of Los Llanos, 599
University of Louisiana at Lafayette, 2697
University of Louisiana at Monroe, 2697
University of Louisiana System, 2695
University of Louisville, 2692
University of Lübeck, 956
University of Lucerne, 2155
University of Lucknow, 1093
University of Lugano, 2154
University of Maastricht, 1586
University of Macao, 588
University of Macedonia, 979
University of Macedonia Library & Information Centre, 973
University of Madeira, 1827
University of Madras, 1093
University of Magallanes, 473
University of Magdalena, 598

University of Maiduguri, 1637
University of Maine at Augusta, 2699
University of Maine at Machias, 2699
University of Maine at Presque Isle, 2700
University of Maine, Farmington, 2700
University of Maine, Fort Kent, 2700
University of Maine System, 2699
University of Malaga, 2076
University of Malakand, 1694
University of Malawi, 1468
University of Malawi Chancellor College Library, 1468
University of Malaya, 1475
University of Malaya Library, 1473
University of Malta, 1485
University of Malta Library, 1485
University of Management and Economics, Battambang, 382
University of Management and Technology, Lahore, 1694
University of Managua, 1617
University of Manchester, 2385
University of Manchester Library, 2324
University of Mandalay, 1548
University of Mandalay Library, 1546
University of Manila, 1745
University of Manila Central Library, 1735
University of Manitoba, 433
University of Manitoba Libraries, 393
University of Mannheim, 947
University of Margarita, 3053
University of Maribor, 2021
University of Maribor Library, 2020
University of Marilia, 343
University of Mary, Bismarck, 2874
University of Mary Hardin-Baylor, 2962
University of Mary Washington, 2981
University of Maryland, Baltimore, 2708
University of Maryland, Baltimore County, 2708
University of Maryland Center for Environmental Science, 2472
University of Maryland, College Park, 2708
University of Maryland, Eastern Shore, 2708
University of Maryland Libraries, 2491
University of Maryland System, 2707
University of Maryland, University College, 2708
University of Mascara, 104
University of Massachusetts, 2741
University of Massachusetts, Boston, 2741
University of Massachusetts, Dartmouth, 2741
University of Massachusetts, Lowell, 2741
University of Massachusetts Medical School, 2742
University of Matanzas 'Camilo Cienfuegos', 641
University of Mauritius, 1490
University of Mauritius Library, 1490
University of Medellín, 600
University of Medical Sciences, San José, 615
University of Medical Technology, 1548
University of Medicine & Dentistry of New Jersey, 2814
University of Medicine 1, 1548
University of Medicine 1 Library, Yangon, 1546
University of Medicine 2, 1548
University of Medicine 2 Library, Yangon, 1546
University of Medicine and Pharmacy 'Carol Davila' from Bucharest, 1869
University of Medicine and Pharmacy 'Gr. T. Popa', 1870
University of Medicine and Pharmacy 'Victor Babeş' Timisoara, 1871
University of Medicine and Pharmacy—Craiova, 1869
University of Medicine Library, Mandalay, 1546
University of Medicine, Magway, 1549
University of Medicine, Mandalay, 1549
University of Mekelle, 737
University of Melbourne, 173
University of Melbourne Library, 151

University of Memphis, 2940
University of Mendoza, 127
University of Miami, 2635
University of Michigan, 2754
University of Michigan Museum of Art, 2528
University of Michigan—Flint, 2763
University of Midwifery Education and Studies Maastricht, 1591
University of Mindanao, 1745
University of Mining and Geology 'St Ivan Rilski', 366
University of Minnesota, 2771
University of Minnesota, Duluth, 2782
University of Minnesota Libraries, 2493
University of Minnesota, Morris, 2782
University of Minnesota, Rochester, 2783
University of Miskolc, 1017
University of Miskolc Library, Archives, Museum, 1007
University of Mississippi, 2785
University of Mississippi Medical Center, 2786
University of Mississippi Museum, 2529
University of Missouri System, 2795
University of Missouri—Kansas City, 2795
University of Missouri—St Louis, 2795
University of Miyazaki, 1314
University of Mobile, 2551
University of Mogi das Cruzes, 343
University of Mons, 274
University of Montana, 2798
University of Montana Western, Dillon, 2798
University of Montemorelos, 1513
University of Montenegro, 1536
University of Monterrey, 1513
University of Montevallo, 2551
University of Montevideo, 3027
University of Moratuwa, 2096
University of Morón, 128
University of Mostar, 300
University of Mosul, 1153
University of Mosul Central Library, 1150
University of Mount Union, 2886
University of Mpumalanga, 2041
University of M'sila, 104
University of Mumbai, 1093
University of Music, 958
University of Music and Performing Arts, Graz, 204
University of Music and Performing Arts Mannheim, 958
University of Music and Performing Arts Stuttgart, 959
University of Music and Performing Arts Vienna, 204
University of Music and Theatre 'Felix Mendelssohn Bartholdy' Leipzig, 958
University of Music Detmold, 958
University of Music, Drama and Media Hanover, 958
University of Music Karlsruhe, 958
University of Music Lübeck, 959
University of Music Saar, 958
University of Music Wuerzburg, 958
University of Mysore, 1093
University of Nairobi, 1380
University of Nairobi Libraries, 1377
University of Namibia, 1554
University of Nariño, 600
University of National and World Economy, Sofia, 370
University of Natural Resources and Applied Life Sciences, Vienna, 204
University of Navarra, 2077
University of Navojoa, 1518
University of Nebraska, 2800
University of Nebraska at Lincoln, 2801
University of Nebraska at Omaha, 2801
University of Nebraska Libraries, 2495
University of Nebraska Medical Center, 2801
University of Nebraska State Museum, 2531
University of Negros Occidental-Recoletos, 1745
University of Nevada, Las Vegas, 2802
University of Nevada, Reno, 2802
University of New Brunswick, 436